SCOTT®

1990 Standard Postage Stamp Catalogue

ONE HUNDRED AND FORTY-SIXTH EDITION IN FOUR VOLUMES

VOLUME 4

EUROPEAN COUNTRIES and COLONIES
INDEPENDENT NATIONS of
AFRICA, ASIA, LATIN AMERICA
P - Z

PRESIDENT/PUBLISHER	**Wayne Lawrence**
EDITORIAL DIRECTOR	**Richard L. Sine**
EDITOR	**William W. Cummings**
ASSISTANT EDITOR	**William H. Hatton**
VALUING EDITOR	**Martin J. Frankevicz**
NEW ISSUES EDITOR	**Robin A. Denaro**
COMPUTER CONTROL COORDINATOR	**Elaine Cottrel**
VALUING ANALYSTS	**David C. Akin**
	Roger L. Listwan
EDITORIAL ASSISTANTS	**Joyce A. Cecil**
	Beth Brown
ART/PRODUCTION DIRECTOR	**Edward Heys**
PRODUCTION COORDINATOR	**Nancy S. Martin**
DIRECTOR OF MARKETING & SALES	**Stuart J. Morrissey**
SALES DIRECTOR	**Jeff Lawrence**
ADVERTISING MANAGER	**David Lodge**

Scott Publishing Co.

911 Vandemark Road, Sidney, Ohio 45365

A division of AMOS PRESS INC., publishers of *Linn's Stamp News, Coin World, Cars & Parts* magazine and *The Sidney Daily News.*

Table of Contents

See Volumes 2 and 3 for nations of Africa, Asia, Europe, Latin America and their affiliated territories, A-F and G-O.

See Volume 1 for United States and Affiliated Territories, United Nations and British Commonwealth of Nations.

Copyright Notice

Trademark Notice

ISBN 0-89487-123-4 Soft cover
ISBN 0-89487-128-5 Hard cover

Library of Congress Card No. 2-3301

Scott Publishing Co.

911 VANDEMARK ROAD, SIDNEY, OHIO 45365 513-498-0802

SCOTT®

Welcome to our 1990 Volume 4

As with the earlier volumes of Scott's 1990 edition, very quickly as you look through the pages of this volume, you will find that this truly is a new Catalogue built onto an old chassis... 126 years old, to be sure. We have been listening to you since Scott Publishing Co. arrived at its home in Sidney, Ohio, and we are continuing to adjust our Catalogue presentation to meet your needs.

Although written and said many times until now, the 1990 edition of the Scott Catalogue cannot have the catalogue value of stamps within its pages compared to the values of the preceding year. Catalogue values of all stamps listed this year reflect *actual retail values* as we have found them in the marketplace.

Also, we have adjusted the grading level at which stamps are valued. Scott now values stamps at a grade of Fine-Very Fine, with an illustrated description of what we mean by that grade on the pages which follow.

The practice of purchasing stamps at a fraction of "Scott" no longer is valid. You now can expect to pay approximately the listed catalogue value when you purchase from dealer price lists, approval selections, or at stamp shows. Deep discounts will now be the exception rather than the rule.

If you purchase stamps at auction, you may need to adjust your bidding habits. Bidding at large discounts from catalogue value will decrease your chances of acquiring a lot. For best results, compare the catalogue values in this volume with recent auction realizations and place your own bids with that information in mind.

Bargains may still occur at auction sales, particularly when a specific lot is not in demand at the time of the sale. Also, when reviewing auction catalogues, be aware of the terms and conditions of that sale. Be certain of which stamp catalogue is being used as reference, and which catalogue values are being used in the text of the auction catalogue.

To determine the catalogue values used this year, we have consulted literally hundreds of dealer price lists, carefully reviewed the results of scores of public auctions, scoured the philatelic media for ads with prices, and listened to the advice of more outside experts than Scott has ever used in the past.

As an example, nearly 450 dealers — known to produce price lists — were queried for a copy. In addition, nearly 250 dealers, collectors and specialty societies were invited to provide more explicit information on stamps within their areas of expertise. Response has been tremendous, with the accompanying Acknowledgments section a testament. We continue to hear from additional persons invited to assist, so the list shown in this volume is not yet complete. Other important information that we use comes from you the user of this Catalogue. We receive hundreds of letters with questions which lead to corrections and amplifications within our pages. Our thanks go out to everyone who helps in that way.

You have given us direction in more areas than only that of catalogue values. The introduction to this Volume is very different than in the past. A "mini-introduction" is designed to quickly acclimate everyone to what can be an awesome bulk of information. The pages which follow the "mini-introduction" are a completely revised approach to both our Catalogue and the basics of stamp collecting in general.

By the time you complete the introduction, you should not be surprised by terms and concepts you find in the individual country listings within the text of this volume.

For the first time, some unused stamps are valued in a never-hinged state on a country-by-country basis. Previously, there were two cut-off dates used: one for British Commonwealth and the other for the remainder of the countries of the world. Where "never-hinged" is a factor in the valuing, a note appears both at the beginning of the country itself as well as just before the point in the listings where the change begins.

This Catalogue continues to evolve in response to what we hear you telling us. Some years the evolution process appears to be moving more rapidly than in others, but the process continues nevertheless. That evolution is much easier with all of the support we receive from those who use the Catalogue.

Sincerely,

Richard L. Sine

Richard L. Sine
Editorial Director

Catalogue Information

Catalogue Value

The Scott Catalogue value is a retail price, what you could expect to pay for the stamp in a grade of Fine-Very Fine. The value listed is a reference which reflects recent actual dealer selling prices.

Dealer retail price lists, public auction results, published prices in advertising, and individual solicitation of retail prices from dealers, collectors, and specialty organizations have been used in establishing the values found in this catalogue.

Use this catalogue as a guide in your own buying and selling. The actual price you pay for a stamp may be higher or lower than the catalogue value because of one or more of the following: the amount of personal service a dealer offers, increased interest in the country or topic represented by the stamp or set, whether an item is a "loss leader," part of a special sale, or otherwise is being sold for a short period of time at a lower price, or if at a public auction you are able to obtain an item inexpensively because of little interest in the item at that time.

For unused stamps, more recent issues are valued as never hinged, with the beginning point determined on a country-by-country basis. Notes to show the beginning points are prominently noted in the text.

Grade

A stamp's grade and condition are crucial to its value. Values quoted in this catalogue are for stamps graded at Fine-Very Fine and with no faults. A very few stamps are listed in other conditions, and so marked when that is the predominant way they are known. The accompanying illustrations show an example of a Fine-Very Fine grade between the grades immediately below and above it: Fine and Very Fine.

FINE stamps have the design noticeably off-center on two sides. Imperforate stamps may have small margins and earlier issues may show the design touching one edge of the stamp. Used stamps may have heavier than usual cancellations.

FINE-VERY FINE stamps may be somewhat off-center on one side, or only slightly off-center on two sides. Imperforate stamps will have two margins at least normal size and the design will not touch the edge. *Early issues of a country may be printed in such a way that the design naturally is very close to the edges.* Used stamps will not have a cancellation that detracts from the design. This is the grade used to establish Scott Catalogue values.

VERY FINE stamps may be slightly off-center on one side, with the design well clear of the edge. Imperforate stamps will have three margins at least normal size. Used stamps will have light or otherwise neat cancellations.

Condition

The above definitions describe *grade,* which is centering and (for used stamps) cancellation. *Condition* refers to the soundness of the stamp, i.e., faults, repairs, and other factors influencing price.

Copies of a stamp which are of a lesser grade and/or condition trade at lower prices. Those of exceptional quality often command higher prices.

Factors that increase the value of a stamp include exceptionally wide margins, particularly fresh color, and the presence of selvage.

Factors other than faults that decrease the value of a stamp include missing gum or regumming, hinge remnant, foreign object adhering to gum, natural inclusion, or a straight edge.

Faults include a missing piece, tear, clipped perforation, pin or other hole, surface scuff, thin spot, crease, toning, oxidation or other form of color changeling, short or pulled perforation, stains or such man-made changes as reperforation or the chemical removal or lightening of a cancellation.

Scott Publishing Co. recognizes that there is no formal, enforced grading scheme for postage stamps, and that the final price you pay for a stamp or obtain for a stamp you are selling will be determined by individual agreement at the time of the transaction.

Fine→

SCOTT CATALOGUES VALUE STAMPS IN THIS GRADE

Fine-Very Fine→

Very Fine→

Acknowledgments

Our appreciation and gratitude go to the following individuals and organizations who have assisted us in preparing information included in the 1990 Scott Catalogues. This list is not complete, for those who provide information for later volumes may not yet be included. Also, some helpers prefer anonymity. These individuals have generously shared their stamp knowledge with others through the medium of the Scott Catalogue.

Those who follow, provided information that is in addition to the hundreds of dealer price lists and advertisements and scores of auction catalogues and realizations which were used in producing the Catalogue Values used herein. It is from those noted here that we have been able to obtain information on items not normally seen in published lists and advertisements. Support from these people of course goes beyond data leading to Catalogue Values, for they also are key to editorial changes.

Joseph F. Albert
Simon Andrews
B.J. Ammel
Mike Armus
Joseph J. Atallah
Frank Bachenheimer
M.S. Batchelor
Frederick Bean
Jules K. Beck
C.A. Beckwith
David Bein
Russ Bell
Ernest L. Bergman
Hank Bieniecki
Brian M. Bleckwenn
John R. Boker
Mike Bryne
Frank Buono
Roman Burkiewicz
Joseph Bush
E.J. Chamberlin
Henry Chlanda
Dr. Leonard Cohen
Howard G. DeVoe
P.J. Drossos
Bob Dumaine
Donald W. East
Victor E. Engstrom
Norman Epstein
Stephen I. Esrati
Henry O. Feldman
Richard Frajola
Stephen I. Frater
Marvin Frey
Richard Friedberg
Earl H. Galitz
Frank Geiger
Peter Georgiadis
Brian M. Green
Horacio E. Groio
Rudolf Hamar
Ray Hanser
Leo John Harris
John B. Head
Bruce Hecht
Clifford O. Herrick
William Herzig
Jayson Hyun
Eric Jackson
Vincent E. Jay
Jack M. Jonza
H. Karen
Stanford M. Katz
Lewis S. Kaufman
Patricia Kaufmann
Jim Kerr
Herman Kerst
W. Kolakowski
Stanley Kronenberg
Warren Lauzon
Steve Levine
Rosario LoGuidice
Bob Lovell
Gary J. Lyon
David MacDonnell
Donald L. MacPeek
Nick Macris
Sam Malamud
Nick Markov
Clyde E. Maxwell
Max Mayo
Mike McKillip
Hector Mena
Richard H. Muller
Victor Ostolaza
Souilen V. Panirian
Frank E. Patterson
Stanley Piller
Daniel N. Pinchot
Gilbert N. Plass
Richard Pyznar
Patrick Riggs
Peter A. Robertson
Michael Rogers
P.J. Ronay
Jacques A. Schiff, Jr.
Richard Schwartz
Michael Shamilzadeh
William E. Shelton
J. Randall Shoemaker
Richard Simchak
James W. Smith
Jay Smith
Sherwood Springer
Linda Stanfield
Joanna Taylor
Scott Trepel
Gary A. Van Cott
Carlos Vieiro
Jerome S. Wagshal
Daniel C. Warren
Richard A. Washburn
William R. Weiss
Robert Zeigler

American Philatelic Society
P.O. Box 8000, State College, PA 16803

American Revenue Association
Bruce Miller, Suite 332, 701 S. First Ave., Arcadia, CA 91006

American Society of Netherlands Philately
Harold F. MacDonald, 2354 Roan Lane, Walnut Creek, CA 94596

Booklet Collectors Club
Larry Rosenblum, 1016 East El Camino Real, P.O. Box 107, Sunnyvale, CA 94087

Bureau Issues Association
William S. Dunn, 750 Jersey St., Denver, CO 80220

Canal Zone Study Group
Richard H. Salz, 60 27th Ave., San Francisco, CA 94121

China Stamp Society
Paul H. Gault, 140 W. 18th Ave., Columbus, OH 43210

Confederate Stamp Alliance
Brian Green, P.O. Box 1816, Kernersville, NC 27285

Costa Rica Collectors, Society of
T.C. Willoughby, 7600 Ridgemont Dr., Newburgh, IN 47630

Eire Philatelic Association
Robert C. Jones, 8 Beach St., Brockton, MA 02402

Estonian Philatelic Society
Rudolf Hamar, 243 34th St., New York, NY 10016

Ethiopian Philatelic Society
Miss Hugette Gagnon, P.O. Box F110-45, Blaine, WA 98230

Great Britain Collectors Club
Larry Rosenblum, 1016 East El Camino Real, P.O. Box 107, Sunnyvale, CA 94087

Haiti Philatelic Society
Carroll L. Lloyd, 2117 Oak Lodge Road, Baltimore, MD 21228

Hellenic Philatelic Society of America
Nicholas Asimakopulos, MD, 541 Cedar Hill Ave., Wyckoff NJ 07481

International Philippine Philatelic Society
Mrs. E.C. Stanfield, P.O. Box 1936, Manila, PHILIPPINES

Korea Stamp Society
Harold L. Klein, P.O. Box 750, Lebanon, PA 17042

Latin American Philatelic Society
Piet Steen, P.O. Box 820, Hinton, AB, CANADA T0E 1B0

Mexico-Elmhurst Philatelic Society International
Robert Jones, 2350 Bunker Hill Way, Costa Mesa, CA 92626

Nepal and Tibet Philatelic Study Group
Roger D. Skinner, 1020 Covington Road, Los Altos, CA 94022

Philatelic Foundation
21 E. 40th St., New York, NY 10016

Rhodesian Study Circle
William R. Wallace, P.O. Box 16381, San Francisco, CA 94116

Rossica, Society of Russian Philately
Norman Epstein, 33 Crooke Ave., Brooklyn, NY 11226

Sarawak Specialists Society
C. Jackson Selsor, 2300 Front St., San Diego, CA 92102

Society for Hungarian Philately
P.O. Box 1162, Fairfield, CT 06432

St. Helena, Ascension & Tristan da Cunha Philatelic Society
R.V. Skavaril, 222 East Torrence Road, Columbus, OH 43214

The Spanish Main Society
Brian Moorhouse, P.O. Box 105, Peterborough, PE3 8TQ, ENGLAND

Ukrainian Philatelic/Numismatic Society
I. Kuzyck, P.O. Box 8363, Alexandria, VA 22360

Understanding the Listings

On the opposite page is an enlarged "typical" listing from this catalogue. Following are detailed explanations of each of the highlighted parts of the listing.

1 **Scott number** — Stamp collectors use Scott numbers to identify specific stamps when buying, selling, or trading stamps, and for ease in organizing their collections. Each stamp issued by a country has a unique number. Therefore, Germany Scott 99 can only refer to a single stamp. Although the Scott Catalogue usually lists stamps in chronological order by date of issue, when a country issues a set of stamps over a period of time the stamps within that set are kept together without regard of date of issue. This follows the normal collecting approach of keeping stamps in their natural sets.

When a country is known to be issuing a set of stamps over a period of time, a group of consecutive catalogue numbers is reserved for the stamps in that set, as issued. If that group of numbers proves to be too few, capital-letter suffixes are added to numbers to create enough catalogue numbers to cover all items in the set. Scott uses a suffix letter, i.e., "A," "b," etc., only once. If there is a Scott 16A in a set, there will not be a Scott 16a also.

There are times when the block of numbers is too large for the set, leaving some numbers unused. Such gaps in the sequence also occur when the editors move an item elsewhere in the catalogue or it is removed from the listings entirely. Scott does not attempt to account for every possible number, but rather it does attempt to assure that each stamp is assigned its own number.

Scott numbers designating regular postage normally are only numerals. Scott numbers for other types of stamps, i.e., air post, semi-postal, and so on, will have a prefix of either a capital letter or a combination of numerals and capital letters.

2 **Illustration number** — used to identify each illustration. For most sets, the lowest face-value stamp is shown. It then serves as an example of the basic design approach for the set. Where more than one stamp in a set uses the same illustration number, that number needs to be used with the design paragraph or description line (noted below) to be certain of the exact design on each stamp within the set. Where there are both vertical and horizontal designs in a set, a single illustration may be used, with the exceptions noted in the design paragraph or description line. Illustrations normally are 75 percent of the original size of the stamp. An effort has been made to note all illustrations not at that percentage. Overprints are shown at 100 percent of the original, unless otherwise noted.

3 **Paper color** — the color of the paper is noted in italic type when the paper used is not white.

4 **Listing styles** — There are two principal types of catalogue listings: major and minor.

Majors normally are in a larger type style than minor listings. They also may be distinguished by having as their catalogue number a numeral with or without a capital-letter suffix and with or without a prefix.

Minors are in a smaller type style and have a small-letter suffix (or, only have the small letter itself shown if the listing is immediately beneath its major listing). These listings show a variety of the "normal," or major item. Examples include color variation or a different watermark used for that stamp only.

Examples of major numbers are 16, 28A, B97, C13A, 10N5, and 10N6A. Examples of minor numbers are 16a and C13b.

5 **Basic information on stamp or set** — introducing each stamp issue, this section normally includes the date of issue, method of printing, perforation, watermark, and sometimes some additional information. New information on method of printing, watermark or perforation measurement appears only when that information changes. Dates of issues are as precise as Scott is able to confirm, either year only; month and year; or month, day, and year.

6 **Denomination** — normally the face value of the stamp, i.e., the cost of the stamp at the post office at the time of issue.

7 **Color or other description** — this line provides information to solidify identification of the stamp. Historically, when stamps normally were printed in a single color, only the color appeared here. With modern printing techniques, which include multicolor presses which mix inks on the paper, earlier methods of color identification are no longer applicable. When space permits, a description of the stamp design replaces the terms "multi" or "multicolored."

8 **Year of issue** — in stamp sets issued over more than one year, the number in parentheses signifies the year the single stamp appeared. Stamps without a date appeared during the first year of the span. Dates are not always given for minor varieties.

9 **Value unused and value used** — the catalogue values are based on stamps which are in a grade of Fine-Very Fine. Unused values refer to items which have not seen postal or other duty for which they were intended. For pre-1900 issue, unused stamps must have at least most of their original gum; for later issues, complete gum is expected. Stamps issued without gum are noted. Unused values are for never-hinged stamps beginning at the point immediately following a prominent notice in the actual listing. The same information also appears at the beginning of the country's information. See the section "Catalogue Values" for an explanation of the meaning of these values.

10 **Changes in basic set information** — bold type is used to show any change in the basic data on within a set of stamps, i.e., perforation from one stamp to the next or a different paper or printing method or watermark.

11 **Total value of set** — the total value of sets of five or more stamps, issued after 1900, are shown on a separate line. The line also notes the range of Scott numbers and total number of stamps included in the total.

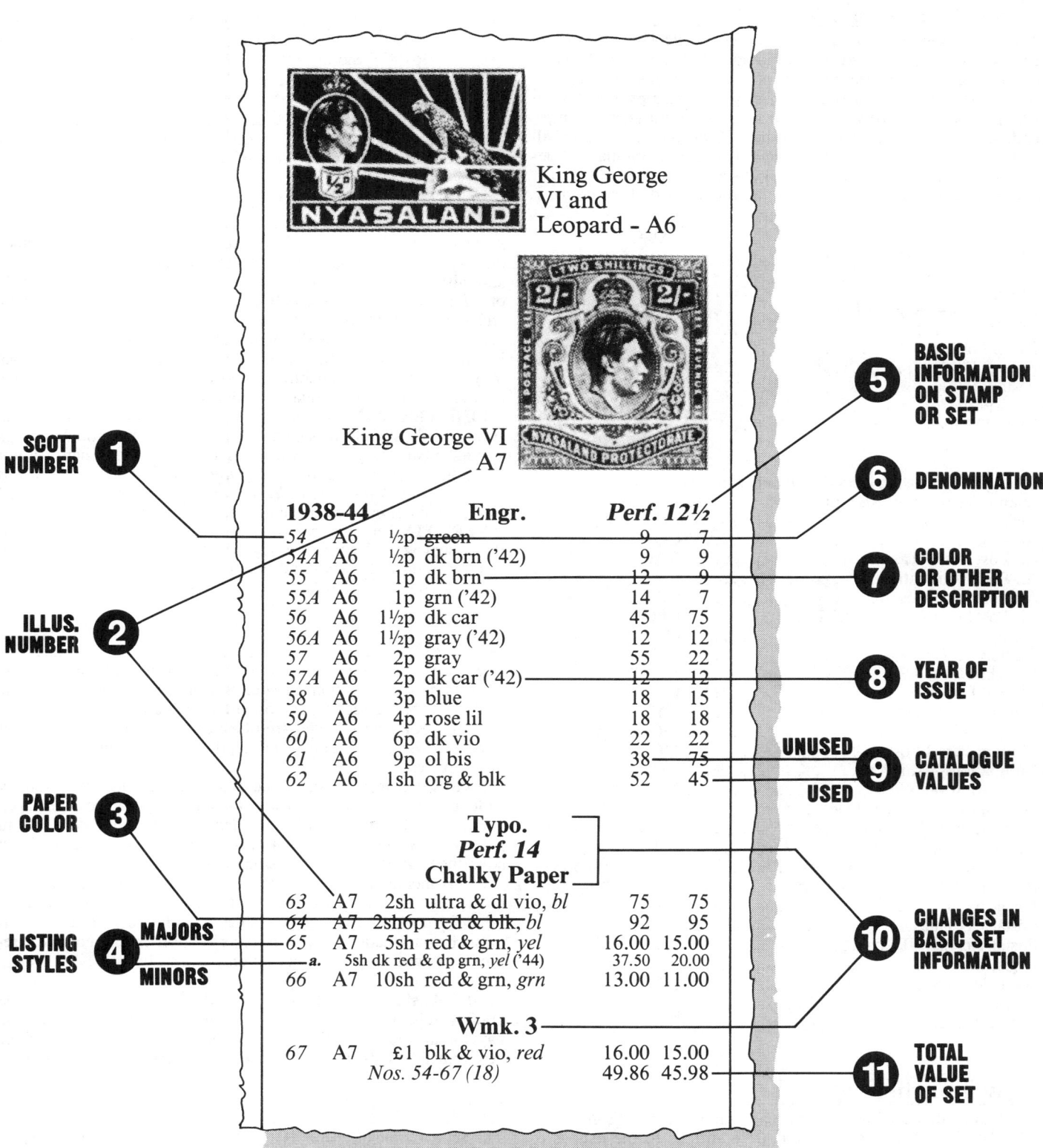

King George VI and Leopard - A6

King George VI
A7

1938-44 **Engr.** ***Perf. 12½***

54	A6	½p	green	9	7
54A	A6	½p	dk brn ('42)	9	9
55	A6	1p	dk brn	12	9
55A	A6	1p	grn ('42)	14	7
56	A6	1½p	dk car	45	75
56A	A6	1½p	gray ('42)	12	12
57	A6	2p	gray	55	22
57A	A6	2p	dk car ('42)	12	12
58	A6	3p	blue	18	15
59	A6	4p	rose lil	18	18
60	A6	6p	dk vio	22	22
61	A6	9p	ol bis	38	75
62	A6	1sh	org & blk	52	45

Typo.
Perf. 14
Chalky Paper

63	A7	2sh	ultra & dl vio, *bl*	75	75
64	A7	2sh6p	red & blk, *bl*	92	95
65	A7	5sh	red & grn, *yel*	16.00	15.00
a.		5sh	dk red & dp grn, *yel* ('44)	37.50	20.00
66	A7	10sh	red & grn, *grn*	13.00	11.00

Wmk. 3

67	A7	£1	blk & vio, *red*	16.00	15.00
			Nos. 54-67 (18)	49.86	45.98

1. **SCOTT NUMBER**
2. **ILLUS. NUMBER**
3. **PAPER COLOR**
4. **LISTING STYLES** — **MAJORS** / **MINORS**
5. **BASIC INFORMATION ON STAMP OR SET**
6. **DENOMINATION**
7. **COLOR OR OTHER DESCRIPTION**
8. **YEAR OF ISSUE**
9. **CATALOGUE VALUES** — **UNUSED** / **USED**
10. **CHANGES IN BASIC SET INFORMATION**
11. **TOTAL VALUE OF SET**

Special Notices

Classification of stamps

The *Scott Standard Postage Stamp Catalogue* lists stamps by country of issue. The next level is a listing by section on the basis of the function of the stamps. The principal sections cover regular postage stamps; air post stamps; postage due stamps, registration stamps, special delivery and express stamps, semi-postal stamps, and, so on. Except for regular postage, Catalogue numbers for all sections include a prefix letter (or number-letter combination) denoting the class to which the stamp belongs.

Following is a listing of the most commonly used of the prefixes.

Category	Prefix
Air Post	C
Military	M
Newspaper	P
Occupation — Regular Issues	N
Official	O
Parcel Post	Q
Postage Due	J
Postal Tax	RA
Semi-Postal	B
Special Delivery	E
War Tax	MR

Other prefixes used by more than one country are:

Acknowledgment of Receipt	H
Air Post Official	CO
Air Post Parcel Post	CQ
Air Post Postal Tax	RAC
Air Post Registration	CF
Air Post Semi-Postal	CB
Air Post Semi-Postal Official	CBO
Air Post Special Delivery	CE
Authorized Delivery	EY
Franchise	S
Insured Letter	G
Marine Insurance	GY
Military Air Post	MC
Military Parcel Post	MQ
Occupation — Air Post	NC
Occupation — Official	NO
Occupation — Postage Due	NJ
Occupation — Postal Tax	NRA
Occupation — Semi-Postal	NB
Occupation — Special Delivery	NE
Parcel Post Authorized Delivery	QY
Postal-fiscal	AR
Postal Tax Due	RAJ
Postal Tax Semi-Postal	RAB
Registration	F
Semi-Postal Special Delivery	EB
Special Delivery Official	EO
Special Handling	QE

New issue listings

Updates to this catalogue appear each month in the *Scott Stamp Monthly*. Included in this update are additions to the listings of countries found in *Scott Standard Postage Stamp Catalogue* and the *Specialized Catalogue of United States Stamps*, new issues of countries not listed in the catalogues, and corrections and updates to current editions of this catalogue.

From time to time there will be changes in the listings from the *Scott Stamp Monthly* to the next edition of the catalogue, as additional information becomes available.

The catalogue update section of the *Scott Stamp Monthly* is the most timely presentation of this material available. Annual subscription to the *Scott Stamp Monthly* is $18 from Scott Publishing Co., P.O. Box 828, Sidney, OH 45365.

Number changes

A list of catalogue number changes from the previous edition of the catalogue appears at the back of each volume.

Grade

A stamp's grade and condition are crucial to its value. Values quoted in this catalogue are for stamps graded at Fine-Very Fine and with no faults. The illustrations on page vi show an example of a Fine-Very Fine grade between the grades immediately below and above it: Fine and Very Fine.

FINE stamps have the design noticeably off-center on two sides. Imperforate stamps may have small margins and earlier issues may show the design touching one edge of the stamp. Used stamps may have heavier than usual cancellations.

FINE-VERY FINE stamps may be somewhat off-center on one side, or only slightly off-center on two sides. Imperforate stamps will have two margins at least normal size and the design will not touch the edge. *Early issues of a country may be printed in such a way that the design naturally is very close to the edges.* Used stamps will not have a cancellation that detracts from the design.

VERY FINE stamps may be slightly off-center on one side, with the design well clear of the edge. Imperforate stamps will have three margins at least normal size. Used stamps will have light or otherwise neat cancellations.

Condition

The above definitions describe *grade*, which is centering and (for used stamps) cancellation. *Condition* refers to the soundness of the stamp, i.e., faults, repairs, and other factors influencing price.

Copies of a stamp which are of a lesser grade and/or condition trade at lower prices. Those of exceptional quality often command higher prices.

Factors that increase the value of a stamp include exceptionally wide margins, particularly fresh color, and the presence of selvage.

Factors other than faults that decrease the value of a stamp include missing gum or regumming, hinge remnant, foreign object adhering to gum, natural inclusion, or a straight edge.

Faults include a missing piece, tear, clipped perforation, pin or other hole, surface scuff, thin spot, crease, toning, oxidation or other form of color changeling, short or pulled perforation, stains or such man-made changes as reperforation or the chemical removal or lightening of a cancellation.

Scott Publishing Co. recognizes that there is no formal, enforced grading scheme for postage stamps, and that the final price you pay for a stamp or obtain for a stamp you are selling will be determined by individual agreement at the time of the transaction.

Catalogue Value

The Scott Catalogue value is a retail price, what you could expect to pay for the stamp in a grade of Fine-Very Fine. The value listed is a reference which reflects recent actual dealer selling prices.

Dealer retail price lists, public auction results, published prices in advertising, and individual solicitation of retail prices from dealers, collectors, and specialty organizations have been used in establishing the values found in this catalogue.

Use this catalogue as a guide in your own buying and selling. The actual price you pay for a stamp may be higher or lower than the catalogue value because of one or more of the following: the amount of personal service a dealer offers, increased interest in the country or topic represented by the stamp or set, whether an item is a "loss leader," part of a special sale, or otherwise is being sold for a short period of time at a lower price, or if at a public auction you are able to obtain an item inexpensively because of little interest in the item at that time.

For unused stamps, more recent issues are valued as never-hinged, with the beginning point determined on a country-by-country basis. Notes in the text prominently show the beginning points of these designations.

As a point of philatelic-economic fact, the lower the value shown for an item in this catalogue, the greater the percentage of that value which is attributed to dealer mark-up and profit margin. Thus, a packet of 1,000 different items — each of which has a catalogue value of five cents — normally sells for considerably less than 50 dollars!

Persons wishing to establish the specific value of a stamp or other philatelic item may wish to consult with recognized stamp experts (collectors or dealers) and review current information or recent developments which would affect stamp prices.

Scott Publishing Co. assumes no obligation to revise the values during the distribution period of this catalogue or to advise users of other facts, such as stamp availability, political and economic conditions, or collecting preferences, any of which may have an immediate positive or negative impact on values.

Understanding valuing notations

The *absence of a value* does not necessarily suggest that a stamp is scarce or rare. In the U.S. listings, a dash in the value column means that the stamp is known in a stated form or variety, but information is lacking or insufficient for purposes of establishing a usable catalogue value.

Stamp values in *italics* generally refer to items which are difficult to value accurately. For expensive items, i.e., value at $1,000 or more, a value in italics represents an item which trades very seldom, such as a unique item. For inexpensive items, a value in italics represents a warning. One example is a "blocked" issue where the issuing postal administration controlled one stamp in a set in an attempt to make the whole set more valuable. Another example is a single item with a very low face value which sells in the marketplace, at the time of issue, at an extreme multiple of face value. Some countries have released back issues of stamps in a canceled-to-order form, sometimes covering as much as 10 years.

The Scott Catalogue values for used stamps reflect canceled-to-order material when such are found to predominate in the marketplace for the issue involved. Frequently notes appear in the stamp listings to specify items which are valued as canceled-to-order or if there is a premium for postally used examples.

Another example of a warning to collectors is a stamp that used has a value considerably higher than the unused version. Here, the collector is cautioned to be certain the used version has a readable, contemporary cancellation.

The *minimum catalogue value* of a stamp is five cents, to cover a dealer's costs and then preparing it for resale. As noted, the sum of these values does not properly represent the "value" of a packet of unsorted or unmounted stamps sold in bulk. Such large mixtures or packets generally consist of only the lower-valued stamps.

Values in the "unused" column are for stamps that have been hinged, unless there is a specific note in a listing after which unused stamps are valued as never-hinged. A similar note will appear at the beginning of the country's listings, noting exactly where the dividing point between hinged and never-hinged is for each section of the listings. Where a value for a used stamp is considerably higher than for the unused stamp, the value applies to a stamp showing a distinct contemporary postmark of origin.

Many countries sell canceled-to-order stamps at a marked reduction of face value. Countries which sell or have sold canceled-to-order stamps at *full* face value include Australia, Netherlands, France, and Switzerland. It is almost impossible to identify such stamps, if the gum has been removed, because official government canceling devices are used. Postally used copies on cover, of these items, are usually worth more than the canceled-to-order stamps with original gum.

Abbreviations

Scott Publishing Co. uses a consistent set of abbreviations throughout this catalogue to conserve space while still providing necessary information. The first block shown here refers to color names only:

COLOR ABBREVIATIONS

amb	amber	ind	indigo
anil	aniline	int	intense
ap	apple	lav	lavender
aqua	aquamarine	lem	lemon
az	azure	lil	lilac
bis	bister	lt	light
bl	blue	mag	magenta
bld	blood	man	manila
blk	black	mar	maroon
bril	brilliant	mv	mauve
brn	brown	multi	multicolored
brnsh	brownish	mlky	milky
brnz	bronze	myr	myrtle
brt	bright	ol	olive
brnt	burnt	olvn	olvine
car	carmine	org	orange
cer	cerise	pck	peacock
chlky	chalky	pnksh	pinkish
cham	chamois	Prus	Prussian
chnt	chestnut	pur	purple
choc	chocolate	redsh	reddish
chr	chrome	res	reseda
cit	citron	ros	rosine
cl	claret	ryl	royal
cob	cobalt	sal	salmon
cop	copper	saph	sapphire
crim	crimson	scar	scarlet
cr	cream	sep	sepia
dk	dark	sien	sienna
dl	dull	sil	silver
dp	deep	sl	slate
db	drab	stl	steel
emer	emerald	turq	turquoise
gldn	golden	ultra	ultramarine
grysh	grayish	ven	venetian
grn	green	ver	vermilion
grnsh	greenish	vio	violet
hel	heliotrope	yel	yellow
hn	henna	yelsh	yellowish

When no color is given for an overprint or surcharge, black is the color used. Abbreviations for colors used for overprints and surcharges are: "(B)", "(Bk)" or "(Blk)," black; "(Bl)," blue; "(R)," red; "(G)," green; etc.

Additional abbreviations in this catalogue are shown below:

Adm. . . . . Administration
AFL. . . . . American Federation of Labor

Anniv. . . . . . . Anniversary
APU . . . . Arab Postal Union
APS. . . . . American Philatelic Society
ASEAN. . . . . Association of South East Asian Nations
ASPCA . . . . . American Society for the Prevention of Cruelty to Animals
Assoc. . . . . . . Association

b. . . . . Born
BEP. . . . . Bureau of Engraving and Printing
Bicent. . . . . . . Bicentennial
Bklt. . . . . Booklet
Brit. . . . . British
btwn. . . . . Between
Bur. . . . . Bureau

c. or ca. . . . . . Circa
CAR . . . . Central African Republic
Cat. . . . . Catalogue
Cent. . . . . Centennial, century, centenary
CEPT . . . . . . Conference Europeenne des Administrations des Postes et des Telecommunications
CIO. . . . . Congress of Industrial Organizations
Conf. . . . . Conference
Cong.. . . . . . . Congress
Cpl. . . . . Corporal
CTO . . . . Canceled to order

d. . . . . Died
Dbl. . . . . Double
DDR. . . . . . . German Democratic Republic (East Germany)

ECU . . . . European currency unit
EEC. . . . . European Economic Community
EKU . . . . Earliest known use
Engr. . . . . Engraved
Exhib. . . . . . . Exhibition
Expo. . . . . Exposition

FAO . . . . Food and Agricultural Organization of the United Nations
Fed. . . . . Federation
FIP . . . . Federation International de Philatelie

GB. . . . . Great Britain
Gen. . . . . General
GPO . . . . General post office

Horiz. . . . . . . Horizontal

ICAO . . . . . . International Civil Aviation Organization
ICY. . . . . International Cooperation Year
IEY . . . . International Education Year
ILO . . . . International Labor Organization
Imperf. . . . . . Imperforate
Impt. . . . . Imprint
Intl. . . . . International
Invtd. . . . . . . Inverted
IQSY. . . . . . . International Quiet Sun Year
ITU. . . . . International Telecommunications Union
ITY. . . . . International Tourism Year
IWY . . . . International Women's Year
IYC. . . . . International Year of the Child
IYD. . . . . International Year of the Disabled
IYP . . . . International Year of Peace
IYSH. . . . . . . International Year of Shelter for the Homeless
IYY. . . . . International Youth Year

L . . . . Left
Lieut.. . . . . . . Lieutenant
Litho. . . . . . . Lithographed
LL . . . . Lower left
LR. . . . . Lower right

mm . . . . Millimeter
Ms. . . . . Manuscript

NASA . . . . . . National Aeronautics and Space Administration
Natl. . . . . National
NATO. . . . . . North Atlantic Treaty Organization
No. . . . . Number
NY . . . . New York
NYC . . . . New York City

OAU . . . . Organization of African Unity
OPEC . . . . . . Organization of Petroleum Exporting Countries
Ovpt.. . . . . . . Overprint
Ovptd.. . . . . . Overprinted

P# . . . . Plate number
Perf.. . . . . Perforated, perforation
Phil.. . . . . Philatelic
Photo. . . . . . . Photogravure
PO. . . . . Post office
Pr. . . . . Pair
P.R. . . . . Puerto Rico
PRC . . . . People's Republic of China (Mainland China)
Prec. . . . . Precancel, precanceled
Pres. . . . . President

Rio . . . . Rio de Janeiro
ROC . . . . Republic of China (Taiwan)

SEATO . . . . . South East Asia Treaty Organization
Sgt. . . . . Sergeant
Soc. . . . . Society
Souv. . . . . Souvenir
SSR . . . . Soviet Socialist Republic
St. . . . . Saint, street
Surch. . . . . . . Surcharge

Typo.. . . . . . . Typographed

UAE . . . . United Arab Emirates
UAMPT . . . . Union of African and Malagasy Posts and Telecommunications
UL. . . . . Upper left
UN . . . . United Nations
UNCTAD. . . United Nations Conference on Trade and Development
UNESCO . . . United Nations Educational, Scientific and Cultural Organization
UNICEF. . . . United Nations Children's Fund
UNPA. . . . . . United Nations Postal Administration
Unwmkd. . . . Unwatermarked
UPU . . . . Universal Postal Union
UR . . . . Upper Right
US. . . . . United States
USPO . . . . . . United States Post Office Department
USPS. . . . . . . United States Postal Service
USSR . . . . . . Union of Soviet Socialist Republics

Vert. . . . . Vertical
VP. . . . . Vice president

WCY....... World Communications Year
WFUNA.... World Federation of United Nations Associations
WHO ...... World Health Organization
Wmk. ...... Watermark
Wmkd. ..... Watermarked
WMO ...... World Meteorological Organization
WRY....... World Refugee Year
WWF ...... World Wildlife Fund
WWI....... World War I
WWII ...... World War II

YAR .... Yemen Arab Republic
Yemen PDR Yemen People's Democratic Republic

Examination

Scott Publishing Co. will not pass upon the genuiness, grade or condition of stamps, because of the time and responsibility involved. Rather, there are several expertizing groups which undertake this work for both collectors and dealers. Neither can Scott Publishing Co. appraise or identify philatelic material. The Company cannot take responsibility for unsolicited stamps or covers.

How to order from your dealer

It is not necessary to write the full description of a stamp as listed in this catalogue. All that you need is the name of the country, the Scott Catalogue number and whether the item is unused or used. For example, "Japan Scott 422 unused" is sufficient to identify the stamp of Japan listed as "422 A206 5y brown."

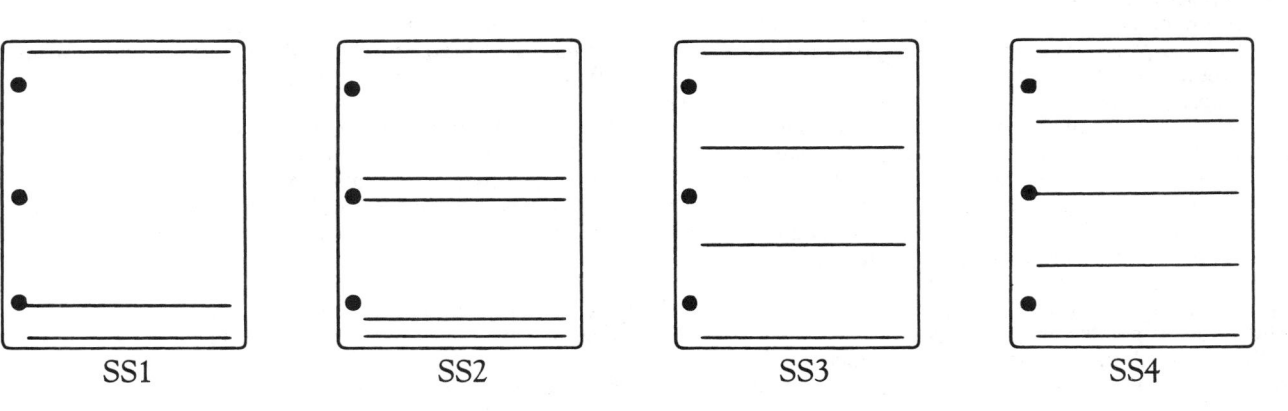

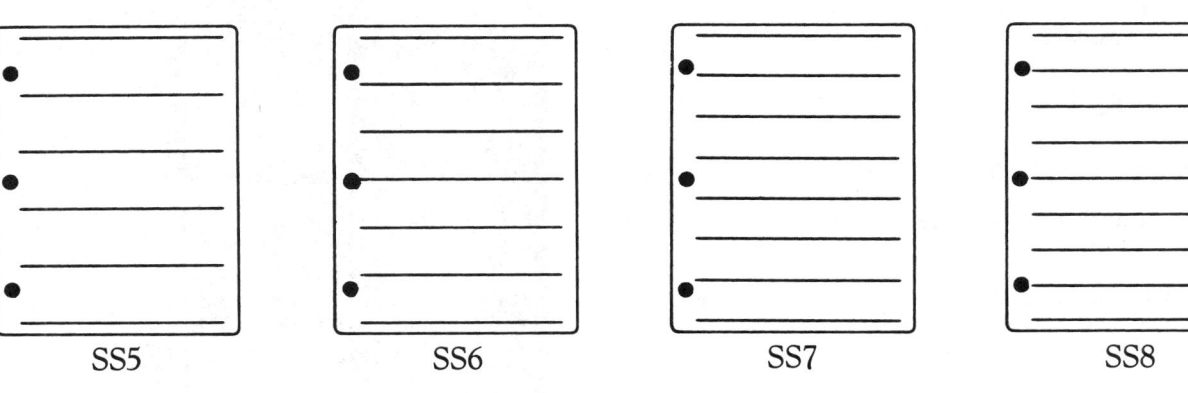

Basic Stamp Information

A stamp collector's knowledge of the combined elements that make a given issue of a stamp unique determines his or her ability to identify stamps. These elements include paper, watermark, method of separation, printing, design and gum. On the following pages each of these important areas is described.

PAPER

Paper is a material composed of a compacted web of cellulose fibers formed into sheets. Paper may be manufactured in sheets, or may have been part of a roll before being cut to size. The fibers most often used for the paper on which stamps are printed are bark, wood, straw and certain grasses with linen or cotton rags added for greater strength. Grinding and bleaching these fibers reduces them to a slushy pulp. Sizing and sometimes coloring matter are added to the pulp. Thin coatings of pulp are poured onto sieve-like frames, which allow the water to run off while retaining the matted pulp. Mechanical processes convert the pulp, when it is almost dry, by passing it through smooth or engraved rollers — dandy rolls — or placed between cloth in a press then flattens and dries the product under pressure.

Stamp paper falls broadly into two types: wove and laid. The nature of the surface of the frame onto which the pulp is first fed causes the differences in appearance between the two. If the surface is smooth and even the paper will be of uniform texture throughout, showing no light and dark areas when held to a light. This is known as *wove paper.* Early paper-making machines poured the pulp onto continuously circulating web of felt, but modern machines feed the pulp onto a cloth-like screen made of closely interwoven fine wires. This paper, when held to a light, will show little dots or points very close together. The proper name for this is "wire wove," but the type is still consider wove. Any U.S. or British stamp printed after 1880 will serve as an example of wire wove paper.

Closed spaced parallel wires, with cross wires at wider intervals, make up the frames used for *laid paper.* A greater thickness of the pulp will settle between the wires. The paper, when held to a light, will show alternate light and dark lines. The spacing and the thickness of the lines may vary, but on any one sheet of paper they are all alike. See Russia Scott 31-38 for an example of laid paper.

Batonne, from the French word meaning "a staff," is used if the lines are spaced quite far apart, like the ruling on a writing tablet. Batonne paper may be either wove or laid. If laid, fine laid lines can be seen between the batons. The laid lines, which are a form of watermark, may be geometrical figures such as squares, diamonds, rectangles, or wavy lines.

Quadrille is the term used when the lines form little squares. *Oblong quadrille* is the term used when rectangles rather than squares are formed. See Mexico-Guadalajara Scott 35-37.

Paper also is classified as thick or thin, hard or soft, and by color if dye is added during manufacture. Such colors may be yellowish, greenish, bluish and reddish. Following are brief explanations of other types of paper used for stamps:

Pelure — A very thin, hard and often brittle paper, it is sometimes bluish or grayish. See Serbia Scott 169-170.

Native — A term applied to handmade papers used to produce some of the early stamps of the Indian states. Japanese paper, originally made of mulberry fibers and rice flour, is part of this group. See Japan Scott 1-18.

Manila — Often used to make stamped envelopes and wrappers, it is a coarse textured stock, usually smooth on one side and rough on the other. A variety of colors are known.

Silk — Introduced by the British in 1847 as a safeguard against counterfeiting, bits of colored silk thread are scattered throughout it. Silk-thread paper has uninterrupted threads of colored silk arranged so that one or more threads run through the stamp or postal stationery. See Great Britain Scott 5-6.

Granite — Filled with minute fibers of various colors and lengths, this should not be confused with either type of silk paper. See Austria Scott 172-175.

Chalky — A chalk-like substance coats the surface to discourage the cleaning and reuse of canceled stamps. Because the design is imprinted on the water-soluble coating of the stamp, any attempt to remove a cancellation will destroy the stamp. *Do not soak these stamps in any fluid.* To remove a stamp printed on chalky paper from an envelope, wet the paper from underneath the stamp until the gum dissolves enough to release the stamp from the paper. See St. Kitts-Nevis Scott 89-90.

India — Another name for this paper, originally introduced from China about 1750, is "China Paper." It is a thin, opaque paper often used for plate and die proofs by many countries.

Double — In philately, this has two distinct meanings. The first, used experimentally as a means to discourage reuse, is two-ply paper, usually a combination of a thick and a thin sheet, joined during manufacture. The design is printed on the thin paper. Any attempt to remove a cancellation would destroy the design. The second occurs on the rotary press, when the end of one paper roll is glued to the next roll to save time feeding the paper through the press. Stamp designs are printed over the joined paper and, if overlooked by inspectors, may get into post office stocks.

Goldbeater's Skin — Used for the 1866 issue of Prussia, it was made of a tough translucent paper. The design was printed in reverse on the back of the stamp, and the gum applied over the printing. It is impossible to remove stamps printed on this type of paper from the paper to which they are affixed without destroying the design.

Ribbed — An uneven, corrugated surface made by passing the paper through ridged roller. This type exists on some copies of U.S. Scott 163.

Various other substances have been used for stamp manufacture, including wood, aluminum, copper, silver and gold foil; plastic; and silk and cotton fabrics. Stamp collectors and dealers consider most of these as novelties designed for sale to collectors.

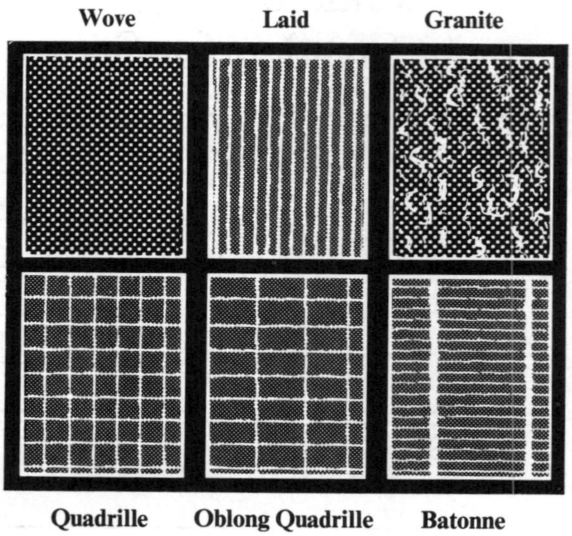

WATERMARKS

Watermarks are an integral part of the paper, for they are formed in the process of paper manufacture. They consist of small designs formed of wire or cut from metal and soldered to the surface of the dandy roll or mold. The designs may be in the form of crowns, stars, anchors, letters, etc. These pieces of metal — known in the paper-making industry as "bits" — impress a design into the paper. The design may be seen by holding the stamp to the light. Some are more easily seen with a watermark detector. This important tool is a small black tray into which the stamp is placed face down and dampened with a watermark detection fluid that brings up the watermark in the form of dark lines against a lighter background.

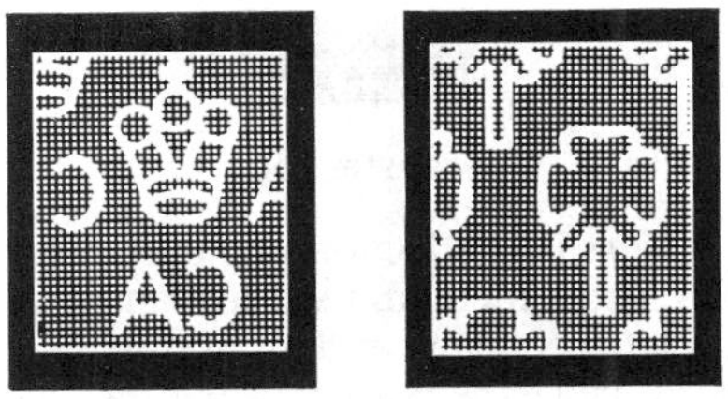

Multiple watermarks of Crown Agents and Burma

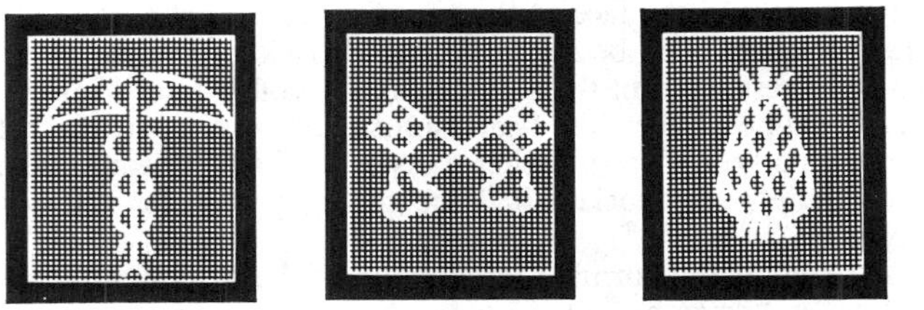

Watermarks of Uruguay, Vatican and Jamaica

WARNING: Some inks used in the photogravure process dissolve in watermark fluids. (See section below on Soluble Printing Inks.) There also are electric watermark detectors, which come with plastic filter disks of various colors. The disks neutralize the color of the stamp, permitting the watermark to be seen more easily.

Watermarks may be found reversed, inverted, sideways or diagonal, as seen from the back of the stamp. The relationship of watermark to stamp design depends on the position of the printing plates or how paper is fed through the press. On machine-made paper, watermarks normally are read from right to left. The design is repeated closely throughout the sheet in a "multiple-watermark design." In a "sheet watermark," the design appears only once on the sheet, but extends over many stamps. Individual stamps may carry only a small fraction or none of the watermark.

"Marginal watermarks" occur in the margins of sheets or panes of stamps. They occur outside the border of paper (ostensibly outside the area where stamps are to be printed) a large row of letters may spell the name of the country or the manufacturer of the paper. Careless press feeding may cause parts of these letters to show on stamps of the outer row of a pane.

For easier reference, Scott Publishing Co. identifies and assigns a number to watermarks. See the numerical index of watermarks at the back of this volume.

Soluble Printing Inks

WARNING: Most stamp colors are permanent. That is, they are not seriously affected by light or water. Some colors may fade from excessive exposure to light. There are stamps printed with inks which dissolve easily in water or fluids used to detect watermarks. Use of these inks is intentional to prevent the removal of cancellations. Water affects all aniline prints, those on safety paper, and some photogravure printings — known as *fugitive colors.*

Separation

"Separation" is the general term used to describe methods of separating stamps. The earliest issues, such as the 1840 Penny Black of Great Britain (Scott 1), did not have any means provided for separating. It was expected they would be cut apart with scissors. These are imperforate stamps. Many stamps first issued imperforate were later issued perforated. Care therefore must be observed in buying imperforate stamps to be certain they were issued imperforate and are not perforated copies that have been altered by having the perforations trimmed away. Imperforate stamps sometimes are valued as singles, as within this catalogue. But, imperforate varieties of normally perforated stamps should be collected in pairs or larger pieces as indisputable evidence of their imperforate character.

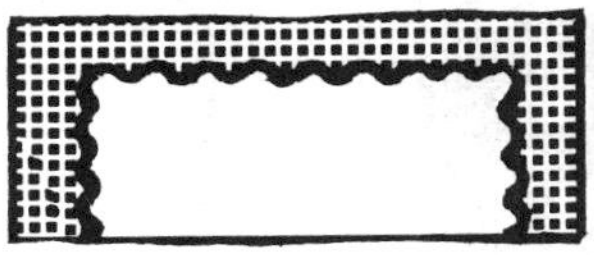

perce en arc

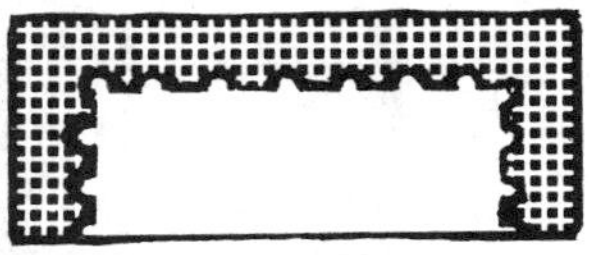

perce en lignes

perce en points

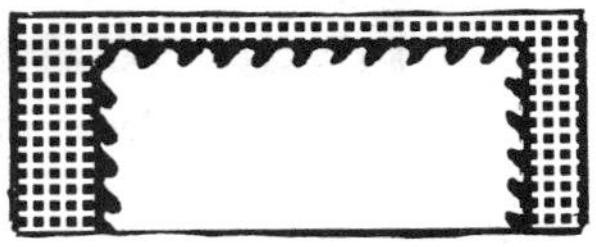

oblique roulette

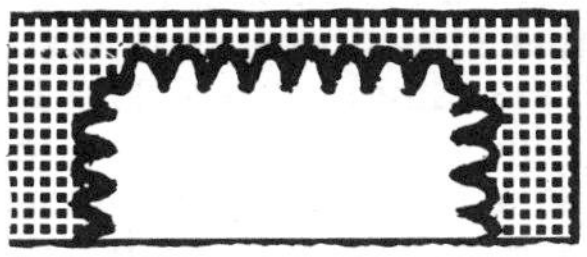

perce en scie

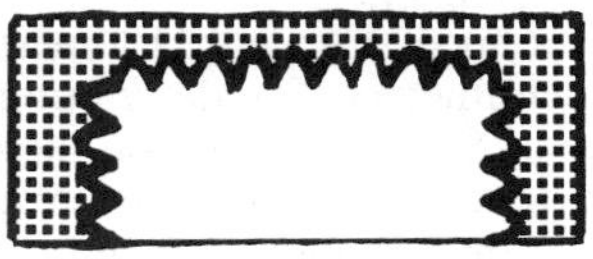

perce serpentin

ROULETTING

Separation is brought about by two general methods during stamp production, rouletting and perforating. In rouletting, the paper is cut partly or wholly through, with no paper removed. In perforating, a part of the paper is removed. Rouletting derives its name from the French roulette, a spur-like wheel. As the wheel is rolled over the paper, each point makes a small cut. The number of cuts made in two centimeters determines the gauge of the roulette, just as the number of perforations in two centimeters determines the gauge of the perforation (see below).

The shape and arrangement of the teeth on the wheels varies. Various roulette types generally carry French names:

Perce en lignes — rouletted in lines. The paper receives short, straight cuts in lines. See Mexico Scott 500.

Perce en points — pin-perforated. This differs from a small perforation because no paper is removed, although round, equidistant holes are pricked through the paper. See Mexico Scott 242-256.

Perce en arc and *perce en scie* — pierced in an arc or sawtoothed designs, forming half circles or small triangles. See Hanover (German States) Scott 25-29.

Perce en serpentin — serpentine roulettes. The cuts form a serpentine or wavy line. See Brunswick (German States) Scott 13-18.

PERFORATION

The other chief style of separation of stamps, and the one which is in universal use today, is perforating. By this process, paper between the stamps is cut away in a line of holes, usually round, leaving little bridges of paper between the stamps to hold them together. These little bridges, which project from the stamp when it is torn from the pane are called the teeth of the perforation. As the size of the perforation is sometimes the only way to differentiate between two otherwise identical stamps, it is necessary to be able to measure and describe them. This is done with a perforation gauge, a ruler-like device that has dots to show how many perforations may be counted in the space of two centimeters. Two centimeters is the space universally adopted in which to measure perforations.

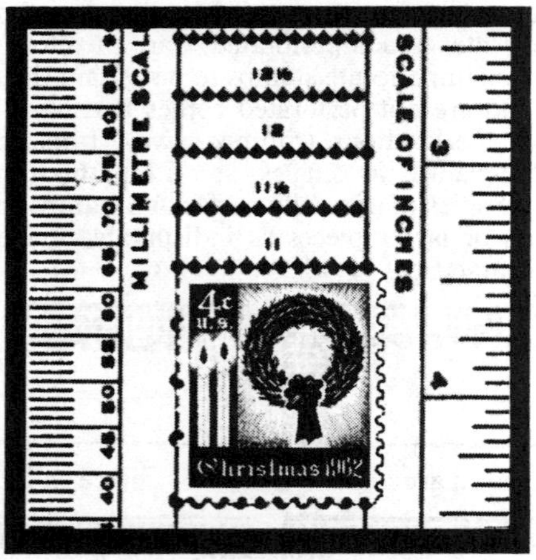

Perforation gauge

To measure the stamp, run it along the gauge until the dots on it fit exactly into the perforations of the stamp. The number to the side of the line of dots which fit the stamp's perforation is the measurement, i.e., an "11" means that 11 perforations fit between two centimeters. The description of the stamp is "perf. 11." If the gauge of the perforations on the top and bottom of a stamp differs from that on the sides, the result is a *compound perforation.* In measuring compound perforations, the gauge at top and bottom is always given first, then the sides. Thus, a stamp that measures 10 1/2 at top and bottom and 11 at the sides is "perf. 10 1/2 x 11." See U.S. Scott 1526.

There are stamps known with perforations different on three or all four sides. Descriptions of such items are in clockwise order, beginning with the top of the stamp.

A perforation with small holes and teeth close together is a "fine perforation." One with large holes and teeth far apart is a "coarse perforation." Holes jagged rather than clean cut, are "rough perforations." *Blind perforations* are the slight impressions left by the perforating pins if they fail to puncture the paper. Multiples of stamps showing blind perforations may command a slight premium over normally perforated stamps.

Printing Processes

ENGRAVING (Intaglio)

Master die — The initial operation in the engraving process is making of the master die. The die is a small flat block of soft steel on which the stamp design is recess engraved in reverse.

Master die

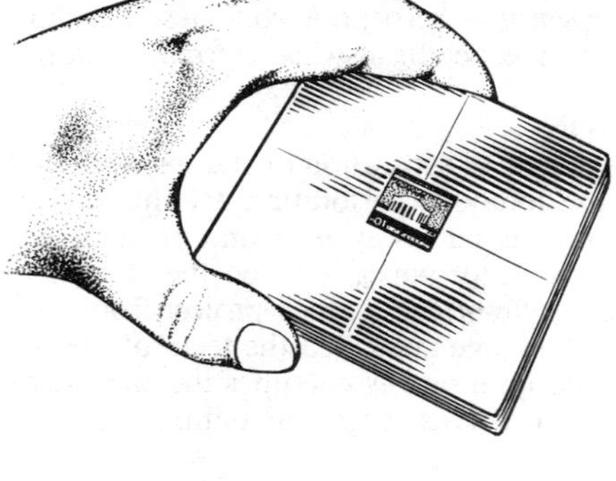

Photographic reduction of the original art is made to the appropriate size, and it serves as a tracing guide for the initial outline of the design. After completion of the engraving, the die is hardened to withstand the stress and pressures of later transfer operations.

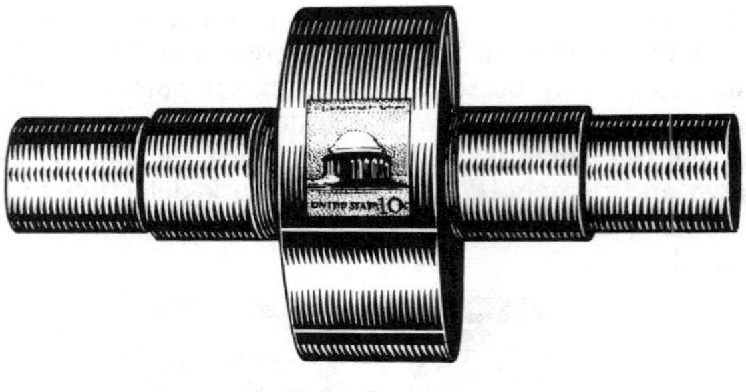

Transfer roll

Transfer roll — Next is production of the transfer roll which, as the name implies, is the medium used to transfer the subject from the die to the plate. A blank roll of soft steel, mounted on a mandrel, is placed under the bearers of the transfer press to allow it to roll freely on its axis. The hardened die is placed on the bed of the press and the face of the transfer roll is applied on the die, under pressure. The bed is then rocked back and forth under increasing pressure until the soft steel of the roll is forced into every engraved line of the die. The resulting impression on the roll is known as a "relief" or a "relief transfer." After the required number of reliefs are "rocked in," the soft steel transfer roll is also hardened.

A "relief" is the normal reproduction of the design on the die in reverse. A "defective relief" may occur during the "rocking in" process because of a minute piece of foreign material lodging on the die, or some other cause. Imperfections in the steel of the transfer roll may result in a breaking away of parts of the design. A damaged relief continued in use will transfer a repeating defect to the plate. Deliberate alterations of reliefs sometimes occur. "Broken reliefs" and "altered reliefs" designate these changed conditions.

Plate — The final step in the procedure is the making of the printing plate. A flat piece of soft steel replaces the die on the bed of the transfer press. One of the reliefs on the transfer roll is applied on this soft steel. "Position dots" determine the position on the plate. The dots have been lightly marked in advance. After the correct position of the relief is determined, pressure is applied. By following the same method used in making the transfer roll, a transfer is entered. This transfer reproduces the design of the relief in reverse and in detail. There are as many transfers entered on the plate as there are subjects printed on the sheet of stamps.

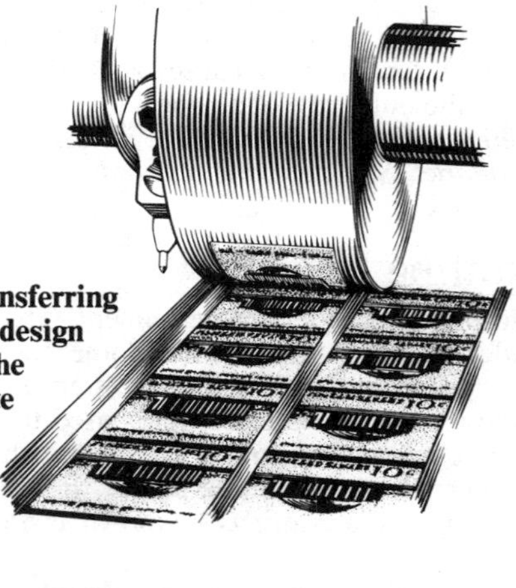

Transferring the design to the plate

Following the entering of the required transfers, the position dots, layout dots and lines, scratches, etc., generally are burnished out. Added at this time are any required *guide lines, plate numbers* or other *marginal markings.* A proof impression is then taken and, if approved, the plate machined for fitting to the press, hardened and sent to the plate vault ready for use.

On press, the plate is inked and the surface automatically wiped clean, leaving the ink in the depressed lines only. Paper under pressure is forced down into the engraved depressed lines, thereby receiving the ink. Thus, the ink lines on engraved stamps are slightly raised; and, conversely, slight depressions occur on the back of the stamp. Historically, paper had been dampened before inking. Newer processes do not require this procedure. Thus, there are both *wet* and *dry printings* of some stamps.

Rotary Press — Until 1915, only flat plates were used to print engraved stamps. Rotary press printing was introduced in 1915. After approval, *rotary press plates* require additional machining. They are curved to fit the press cylinder. "Gripper slots" are cut into the back of each plate to receive the "grippers," which hold the plate securely on the press. The plate is then hardened. Stamps printed from rotary press plates are usually longer or wider than the same stamps printed from flat press plates. The stretching of the plate during the curving process causes this enlargement.

Re-entry — In order to execute a re-entry, the transfer roll is reapplied to the plate, usually at some time after its first use on the press. Worn-out designs can be resharpened by carefully re-entering the transfer roll. If the transfer roll is not precisely in line with the impression of the plate, the registration will not be true and a double transfer will result. After a plate has been curved for the rotary press, it is impossible to make a re-entry.

Double Transfer — This is a description of the condition of a transfer on a plate that shows evidence of a duplication of all, or a portion of the design. It is usually the result of the changing of the registration between the transfer roll and the plate during the rocking-in of the original entry.

It is sometimes necessary to remove the original transfer from a plate and repeat the process a second time. If the finished re-transfer shows indications of the original impression attributable to incomplete erasure, the result is a double transfer.

Re-engraved — Either the die that has been used to make a plate or the plate itself may have its "temper" drawn (softened) and be re-cut. The resulting impressions from such a re-engraved die or plate may differ slightly from the original issue, and are known as "re-engraved."

Short Transfer — Sometimes the transfer roll is not rocked its entire length in entering a transfer onto a plate, so that the finished transfer fails to show the complete design. This is known as a "short transfer." See U.S. Scott 8.

TYPOGRAPHY (Letterpress, Surface Printing)
As it relates to the printing of postage stamps, typography is the reverse of engraving. Typography includes all printing where the design is above the surface area, whether it is wood, metal, or in some instances hard rubber.

The master die and the engraved die are made in much the same manner. In this instance, however, the area not used as a printing surface is cut away, leaving the surface area raised. The original die is then reproduced by stereotyping or electrotyping. The resulting electrotypes are assembled in the required number and format of the desired sheet of stamps. The plate used in printing the stamps is an electroplate of these assembled electrotypes.

Ink is applied to the raised surface and the pressure of the press transfers the ink impression to the paper. In contrast with engraving, the fine lines of typography are impressed on the surface of the stamp. When viewed from the back (as on a typewritten page), the corresponding line work will be raised slightly above the surface.

PHOTOGRAVURE (Rotogravure, Heliogravure)
In this process, the basic principles of photography are applied to a sensitized metal plate, as opposed to photographic paper. The design is transferred photographically to the plate through a halftone screen, breaking the reproduction into tiny dots. The plate is treated chemically and the dots form depressions of varying depths, depending on the degrees of shade in the design. Ink is lifted out of the depressions in the plate when the paper is pressed against the plate in a manner similar to that of engraved printing.

LITHOGRAPHY
The principle that oil and water will not mix is the basis for lithography. The stamp design is drawn by hand or transferred from engraving to the surface of a lithographic stone or metal plate in a greasy (oily) ink. The stone (or plate) is wet with an acid fluid, causing it to repel the printing ink in all areas not covered by the greasy ink.

Transfer paper is used to transfer the design from the original stone of plate. A series of duplicate transfers are grouped and, in turn, transferred to the final printing plate.

Photolithography — The application of photographic processes to lithography. This process allows greater flexibility of design, related to use of halftone screens combined with linework.

Offset — A development of the lithographic process. A rubber-covered blanket cylinder takes up the impression from the inked lithographic plate. From the "blanket" the impression is *offset* or transferred to the paper. Offset printing systems have largely displaced lithography because of its greater flexibility and speed. The term "lithography" covers both processes, and results are almost identical.

Sometimes two or even three printing methods are combined in producing stamps.

EMBOSSED (Relief) Printing
Embossing is a method in which the design first is sunk into the metal of the die. Printing is done against a yielding platen, such as leather or linoleum. The platen is forced into the depression of the die, thus forming the design on the paper in relief.

Embossing may be done without color (see Sardinia Scott 4-6); with color printed around the embossed area (see Great Britain Scott 5 and most U.S. envelopes); and with color in exact registration with the embossed subject (see Canada Scott 656-657).

INK COLORS
Inks or colored papers used in stamp printing usually are of mineral origin. The tone of any given color may be affected by many aspects: heavier pressure will cause a more intense color, slight interruptions in the ink feed will cause a lighter tint.

Hand-mixed ink formulas produced under different conditions (humidity and temperature) at different times account for notable color variations in early printings, mostly 19th century, of the same stamp (see U.S. Scott 248-250, 279B, etc.).

Papers of different quality and consistency used for the same stamp printing may affect color shade. Most pelure papers, for example, show a richer color when compared with wove or laid papers. See Russia Scott 181a.

The very nature of the printing processes can cause a variety of differences in shades or hues of the same stamp. Some of these shades are scarcer than others and are of particular interest to the advanced collector.

Tagged Stamps

Tagging also is known as *luminescence, fluorescence,* and *phosphorescence.* Some tagged stamps have bars (Great Britain and Canada), frames (South Africa), or an overall coating of luminescent material applied after the stamps have been printed (United States). Another tagging method is to incorporate the luminescent material into some or all colors of the printing ink. See Australia Scott 366 and Netherlands Scott 478. A third is to mix the luminescent material with the pulp during the paper manufacturing process or apply it as a surface coating afterwards: "fluorescent" papers. See Switzerland Scott 510-514 and Germany Scott 848.

The treated stamps show up in specific colors when exposed to ultraviolet light. The wave length of light radiated by the luminescent material determines the colors and activates the triggering mechanism of the electronic machinery for sorting, facing or canceling letters.

Various fluorescent substances have been used as paper whiteners, but the resulting "hi-brite papers" show up differently under ultraviolet light and do not trigger the machines. The Scott Catalogue does not recognize these papers.

Many countries now use tagging in its various forms to expedite mail handling, following introduction by Great Britain, on an experimental basis, in 1959. Among these countries, and dates of their dates of introduction, are Germany, 1961; Canada and Denmark, 1962; United States, Australia, Netherlands and Switzerland, 1963; Belgium and Japan, 1966; Sweden and Norway, 1967; Italy, 1968; and Russia, 1969.

Certain stamps were issued with and without the luminescent feature. In those instances, Scott lists the "tagged" variety in the United States, Canada, Great Britain and Switzerland listings and notes the situation in some of the other countries.

Gum

The gum on the back of a stamp may be smooth, rough, dark, white, colored or tinted. It may be either obvious or virtually invisible as on Canada Scott 453 or Rwanda Scott 287-294. Most stamp gumming adhesives use gum arabic or dextrine as a base. Certain polymers such as polyvinyl alcohol (PVA) have been used extensively since World War II.The PVA gum which the security printers Harrison & Sons of Great Britain introduced in 1968 is dull, slightly yellowish and almost invisible.

The *Scott Standard Postage Stamp Catalogue* does not list items by types of gum. The Scott *Specialized Catalogue of United States Stamps* does differentiate among some types of gum for certain issues.

Stamps having full *original gum* sell for more than those from which the gum has been removed. Reprints of stamps may have gum differing from the original issues.

Many stamps have been issued without gum and the catalogue will note this fact. See China Scott 1438-1440. Sometimes, gum may have been removed to preserve the stamp. Germany Scott B68 is valued in the catalogue with gum removed.

Reprints and Reissues

These are impressions of stamps (usually obsolete) made from the original plates or stones. If valid for postage and from obsolete issues, they are *reissues.* If they are from current issues, they are *second, third,* etc., *printings.* If designated for a particular purpose, they are *special printings.*

Scott normally lists those reissues and reprints that are valid for postage.

When reprints are not valid for postage, but made from original dies and plates by authorized persons, they are *official reprints. Private reprints* are made from original plates and dies by private hands. *Official reproductions* or imitations are made from new dies and plates by government authorization.

For the United States' 1876 Centennial, the U.S. government made official imitations of its first postage stamps. Produced were copies of the first two stamps (listed as Scott 3-4), reprints of the demonetized pre-1861 issues and reissues of the 1861 stamps, the 1869 stamps and the then-current 1875 denominations. An example of the private reprint is that of the New Haven, Connecticut, postmaster's provisional.

Most reprints differ slightly from the original stamp in some characteristic, such as gum, paper, perforation, color or watermark. Sometimes the details are followed so meticulously that only a student of that specific stamp is able to distinguish the reprint from the original.

Remainders and Canceled to Order

Some countries sell their stock of old stamps when a new issue replaces them. To avoid postal use, the *remainders* usually are canceled with a punch hole, a heavy line or bar, or a more-or-less regular cancellation. The most famous merchant of remainders was Nicholas F. Seebeck. In the 1880's and 1890's, he arranged printing contracts between the Hamilton Bank Note Co., of which he was a director, and several Central and South American countries. The contracts provided that the plates and all remainders of the yearly issues became the property of Hamilton. Seebeck saw to it that ample stock remained. The "Seebecks," both remainders and reprints, were standard packet fillers for decades.

Some countries also issue stamps *canceled to order (CTO),* either in sheets with original gum or stuck onto pieces of paper or envelopes and canceled. Such CTO items generally are worth less than postally used stamps. Most can be detected by the presence of gum. However, as the CTO practice goes back at least to 1885, the gum inevitably has been washed off some stamps so they could pass for postally used. The normally applied postmarks usually differ slightly and specialists are able to tell the difference. When applied individually to envelopes by philatelically minded persons, CTO material is known as *favor canceled* and generally sells at large discounts.

Cinderellas and Facsimiles

Cinderella is a catchall term used by stamp collectors to describe phantoms, fantasies, bogus items, municipal issues, exhibition seals, local revenues, transportation stamps, labels, poster stamps, and so on. Some cinderella collectors include in their collections local postage issues, telegraph stamps, essays and proofs, forgeries and counterfeits.

A *fantasy* is an adhesive created for a nonexistent stamp-issuing authority. Fantasy items range from imaginary countries (Kingdom of Sedang, Principality of Trinidad, or Occusi-Ambeno), to nonexistent locals (Winans City Post), or nonexistent transportation lines (McRobish & Co.'s Acapulco-San Francisco Line).

On the other hand, if the entity exists and might have issued stamps or did issue other stamps, the items are *bogus* stamps. These would include the Mormon postage stamps of Utah, S. Allan Taylor's Guatemala and Paraguay inventions, the propaganda issues for the South Moluccas and the adhesives of the Page & Keyes local post of Boston.

Phantoms is another term for both fantasy and bogus issues.

Facsimiles are copies or imitations made to represent original stamps, but which do not pretend to be originals. A catalogue illustration is such a facsimile. Illustrations from the Moens catalogue of the last century were occasionally colored and passed off as stamps. Since the beginning of stamp collecting, facsimiles have been made for collectors as space fillers or for reference. They often carry the word "facsimile," "falsch" (German), "sanko" or "mozo" (Japanese), or "faux" (French) overprinted on the face or stamped on the back.

Counterfeits or Forgeries

Unauthorized imitations of stamps, intended to deprive the post office of revenue, are *postal counterfeits* or *postal forgeries.* These items often command higher prices in the philatelic marketplace than the genuine stamps they imitate. Sales are illegal. Governments can, and do, prosecute those who trade in them.

The first postal forgery was of Spain's 4-cuarto carmine of 1854 (the real one is Scott 25). The forgers lithographed it, though the original was typographed. Apparently they were not satisfied and soon made an engraved forgery, which is common, unlike the scarce lithographed counterfeit. Postal forgeries quickly followed in Spain, Austria, Naples, Sardinia and the Roman States.

An infamous counterfeit to defraud is the 1-shilling Great Britain "Stock Exchange" forgery of 1872, used on telegraphs at the exchange that year. It escaped detection until a stamp dealer noticed it in 1898. Many postal counterfeits are known of U.S. stamps.

Wartime propaganda stamps of World War I and World War II may be classed as postal counterfeits. They were distributed by enemy governments or resistance groups.

Philatelic forgeries or *counterfeits* are unauthorized imitations of stamps designed to deceive and defraud stamp collectors. Such spurious items first appeared on the market around 1860 and most old-time collections contain one or more. Many are crude and easily spotted, even by the non-specialist, but some can deceive the experts.

An important supplier of these early philatelic forgeries was the Hamburg printer Gebruder Spiro. Many others with reputations in this craft were S. Allan Taylor, George Hussey, James Chute, George Forune, Benjamin & Sarpy, Julius Goldner, E. Oneglia and L.H. Mercier. Among the noted 20th century forgers were Francois Fournier, Jean Sperati, and the prolific Raoul DeThuin.

Fraudulently produced copies are known of most classic rarities, many medium-priced stamps and, in this century, cheap stamps destined for beginners' packets. Few new philatelic forgeries have appeared in recent decades, however, and virtually no new frauds of valuable classics. Successful imitation of engraved work is virtually impossible.

It has proven far easier to produce a fake by altering a genuine stamp than to duplicate a stamp completely.

Repairs, Restoration and Fakes

Scott Publishing Co. bases its catalogue values on stamps which are free of defects and otherwise meet the standards set forth earlier in this introduction. Stamp collectors desire to have the finest copy of an item possible. Even within given grading categories there are variances. This leads to practice that is not universally defined, nor accepted, that of stamp *restoration.*

There are differences of opinion about what is "permissible" when it comes to restoration. Applying a soft erasure carefully to a stamp to remove dirt marks is one form of restoration, as is the washing of the stamp in mild soap and water. More severe forms of restoration are the pressing out of creases, or the removal of stains caused by tape. To what degree each of the above is "acceptable" is dependent on the individual situation. Further along the spectrum is the freshening of a stamp's color by removing oxide build-up or removing toning or the effects of wax paper left next to stamps shipped to the tropics.

At some point along this spectrum the concept of *repair* replaces that of "restoration." Repairs include filling in thin spots, mending tears by reweaving, adding a missing perforation tooth. Regumming stamps may have been acceptable as a restoration technique decades ago, but today it is considered a form of fakery.

Restored stamps may not sell at a discount, and it is possible that the value of individual restored items may be enhanced over that of their pre-restoration state. Specific situations will dictate the resultant value of such an item. Repaired stamps sell at substantial discounts.

When the purchaser of an item has any reason to suspect an item has been repaired, and the detection of such a repair is beyond his own ability, he should seek expert advice. There are services that specialize in such advice.

Fakes are genuine stamps altered in some way to make them more desirable. One student of this part of stamp collecting has estimated that by the 1950's more than 30,000 varieties of fakes were known. That number has grown. The widespread existence of fakes makes it important for stamp collectors to study their philatelic holdings and use relevant literature. Likewise, they should buy from reputable dealers who will guarantee their stamps and make full and prompt refund should a purchase be declared not genuine by some mutually agreed-upon authority. Because fakes always have some genuine characteristics, it is not always possible to obtain unanimous agreement among experts regarding specific items. These students may change their opinions as philatelic knowledge increases. More than 80 percent of all fakes on the philatelic market today are regummed, reperforated (or, perforated for the first time), or bear altered overprints, surcharges or cancellations.

Stamps can be chemically treated to alter or eliminate colors. For example, a pale rose stamp can be recolored into a blue of high market value, or a "missing color" variety can be created. Designs may be changed by "painting," or a stroke or a dot added or bleached out to turn an ordinary variety into a seemingly scarcer stamp. Part of a stamp can be bleached and reprinted in a different version, achieving an inverted center or frame. Margins can be added or repairs done so deceptively that the stamps move from the "repaired" into the "fake" category.

The fakers have not left the backs of the stamps untouched. They may create false watermarks, add fake grills or press out genuine grills. A thin India paper proof may be glued onto a thicker backing to "create" an issued stamp, or a proof printed on cardboard maybe shaved down. Silk threads are impressed into paper and stamps have been split so that a rare paper variety is "added" to an otherwise inexpensive stamp. The most common treatment to the back of a stamp, however, is regumming.

Some in the business of faking stamps openly advertise "foolproof" application of "original gum" to stamps that lack it. This is faking, not counterfeiting. It is believed that few early stamps have survived without being hinged. The large number of never-hinged examples of such earlier material offered for sale thus suggests the widespread extent of regumming activity. Regumming also may be used to hide repairs or thin spots. Dipping the stamp into watermark fluid often will reveal these flaws.

Fakers also tamper with separations. Ingenious ways to add margins are known. Perforated wide-margin stamps may be falsely represented as imperforate when trimmed. Reperforating is commonly done to create scarce coil or perforation varieties and to eliminate the straight-edge stamps found in sheet margin positions of many earlier issues. Custom has made straight edges less desirable. Fakers have obliged by perforating straight-edged stamps so that many are now uncommon, if not rare.

Another fertile field of the faker is that of the overprint, surcharge and cancellation. The forging of rare surcharges or overprints began in the 1880's or 1890's. These forgeries are sometimes difficult to detect, but the experts have identified almost all. Only occasionally are overprints or cancellations removed to create unoverprinted stamps or seemingly unused items. "SPECIMEN" overprints may be removed — scraping and repainting is one way — to create unoverprinted varieties. Fakers use inexpensive revenues or pen-canceled stamps to generate "unused" stamps for further faking by adding other markings. The quartz lamp and a high-powered magnifying glass help in detecting cancellation removal.

The bigger problem, however, is the addition of overprints, surcharges or cancellations — many with such precision that they are very difficult to ascertain. Plating of the stamps or the overprint can be an important method of detection.

Fake postmarks may range from many spurious fancy cancellations, to the host of markings applied to transatlantic covers, to adding "normal" postmarks to World War II-vintage definitives of some countries whose stamps are valued at far more used than unused. With the advance of cover collecting and the widespread interest in postal history, a fertile new field for fakers has come about. Some have tried to create entire covers. Others specialize in adding stamps, tied by fake cancellations, to genuine stampless covers, or replacing less expensive or damaged stamps with more valuable ones. Detailed study of postal rates in effect at the time of the cover in question, including the analysis of each handstamp in the period, ink analysis and similar techniques, usually will unmask the fraud.

Terminology

Booklets — Many countries have issued stamps in small booklets for the convenience of users. This idea is becoming increasingly more popular today in many countries. Booklets have been issued in all sizes and forms, often with advertising on the covers, on the panes of stamps or on the interleaving.

The panes may be printed from special plates or made from regular sheets. All panes from booklets issued by the United States and many from those of other countries contain stamps that are straight edged on the bottom and both sides, but perforated between. Any stamp-like unit in the pane, either printed or blank, which is not a postage stamp, is considered a *label* in the catalogue listings.

Scott lists and values panes only. Complete booklets are listed only in a very few cases. See Grenada Scott 1055. Panes are listed only when they are not fashioned from existing sheet stamps and, therefore, are identifiable from their sheet-stamp counterparts.

Panes usually do not have a "used" value because there is little market activity in used panes, even though many exist used.

Cancellations — the marks or obliterations put on a stamp by the postal authorities to show that the stamp has done service and is no longer valid for postage. If made with a pen, the marking is a "pen cancellation." When the location of the post office appears in the cancellation, it is a "town cancellation." When calling attention to a cause or celebration, it is a "slogan cancellation." Many other types and styles of cancellations exist, such as duplex, numerals, targets, etc.

Coil Stamps — stamps issued in rolls for use in dispensers, affixing and vending machines. Those of the United States, Canada, Sweden and some other countries are perforated horizontally or vertically only, with the outer edges imperforate. Coil stamps of some countries, such as Great Britain, are perforated on all four sides.

Covers — envelopes, with or without adhesive postage stamps, which have passed through the mail and bear postal or other markings of philatelic interest. Before the introduction of envelopes in about 1840, people folded letters and wrote the address on the outside. Many people covered their letters with an extra sheet of paper on the outside for the address, producing the term "cover." Used air letter sheets, stamped envelopes, and other items of postal stationery also are considered covers.

Errors — stamps having some unintentional deviation from the normal. Errors include, but are not limited to, mistakes in color, paper, or watermark; inverted centers or frames on multicolor printing, surcharges or overprints, and double impressions. Factually wrong or misspelled information, if it appears on all examples of a stamp, even if corrected later, is not classified as a philatelic error.

Overprinted and Surcharged Stamps — Overprinting is a wording or design placed on stamps to alter the place of use (i.e., "Canal Zone" on U.S. stamps), to adapt them for a special purpose ("Porto" on Denmark's 1913-20 regular issues for use as postage due stamps, Scott J1-J7), or for a special occasion (Guatemala Scott 374-378).

A *surcharge* is an overprint which changes or restates the face value of the item.

Surcharges and overprints may be handstamped, typeset or, occasionally, lithographed or engraved. A few hand-written overprints and surcharges are known.

Precancels — stamps canceled before they are placed in the mail. Precanceling is done to expedite the handling of large mailings.

In the United States, precancellations generally identified the point of origin. That is, the city and state names or initials appeared, usually centered between parallel lines. More recently, bureau precancels retained the parallel lines, but the city and state designation was dropped. Recent coils have a "service inscription" to show the mail service paid for by the stamp. Since these stamps do not receive any further cancellation when used as intended, they fall under the general precancel umbrella.

Such items may not have parallel lines as part of the precancellation.

In France, the abbreviation *Affranchts* in a semicircle together with the word *Postes* is the general form. Belgian precancellations are usually a box in which the name of the city appears. Netherlands' precancellations have the name of the city enclosed between a large and small circle, sometimes called a "life-saver."

Precancellations of other countries usually follow these patterns, but may be any arrangement of bars, boxes and city names.

Precancels are listed in the catalogue only if the precancel changes the denomination (Belgium Scott 477-478); the precanceled stamp is different from the non-precancel version (untagged U.S. stamps); or, if the stamp only exists precanceled (France Scott 1096-1099, U.S. Scott 2265).

Proofs and Essays — Proofs are impressions taken from an approved die, plate or stone in which the design and color are the same as the stamp issued to the public. Trial color proofs are impressions taken from approved dies, plates or stones in varying colors. An essay is the impression of a design that differs in some way from the stamp as issued.

Provisionals — stamps issued on short notice and intended for temporary use pending the arrival of regular issues. They usually are issued to meet such contingencies as changes in government or currency, shortage of necessary postage values, or military occupation.

In the 1840's, postmasters in certain American cities issued stamps that were valid only at specific post offices. In 1861, postmasters of the Confederate States also issued stamps with limited validity. Both of these examples are known as "postmaster's provisionals."

Se-Tenant — joined, referring to an unsevered pair, strip or block of stamps differing in design, denomination or overprint. See U.S. Scott 2158a.

Tete Beche — A pair of stamps in which one is upside down in relation to the other. Some of these are the result of intentional sheet arrangements, i.e. Morocco Scott B10-B11. Others occurred when one or more electrotypes accidentally were placed upside down on the plate. See Colombia Scott 57a. Separation of the stamps, of course, destroys the tete beche variety.

Specimens — One of the regulations of the Universal Postal Union requires member nations to send samples of all stamps they put into service to the International Bureau in Switzerland. Member nations of the UPU receive these specimens as samples of what stamps are valid for postage. Many are overprinted, handstamped or initial-perforated "Specimen," "Canceled" or "Muestra." Some are marked with bars across the denominations (China-Taiwan), punched holes (Czechoslovakia) or back inscriptions (Mongolia).

Stamps distributed to government officials or for publicity purposes, and stamps submitted by private security printers for official approval, also may receive such defacements.

These markings prevent postal use, and all such items generally are known as "specimens."

Colonies, Former Colonies, Offices, Territories Controlled by Parent States

Belgium

Belgian Congo
Ruanda-Urundi

Denmark

Danish West Indies
Faroe Islands
Greenland
Iceland

Finland

Aland Islands

France

COLONIES PAST AND PRESENT, CONTROLLED TERRITORIES

Afars & Issas, Territory of
Alaouites
Alexandretta
Algeria
Alsace & Lorraine
Ajouan
Annam & Tonkin
Benin
Cambodia (Khmer)
Cameroun
Castellorizo
Chad
Cilicia
Cochin China
Comoro Islands
Dahomey
Diego Suarez
Djibouti (Somali Coast)
Fezzan
French Congo
French Equatorial Africa
French Guiana
French Guinea
French India
French Morocco
French Polynesia (Oceania)
French Southern & Antarctic Territories
French Sudan
French West Africa
Gabon
Germany
Ghadames
Grand Comoro
Guadeloupe
Indo-China
Inini
Ivory Coast
Laos
Latakia
Lebanon
Madagascar
Martinique
Mauritania
Mayotte
Memel
Middle Congo
Moheli
New Caledonia
New Hebrides
Niger Territory
Nossi-Be
Obock
Reunion
Rouad, Ile
Ste.-Marie de Madagascar
St. Pierre & Miquelon
Senegal
Senegambia & Niger
Somali Coast
Syria
Tahiti
Togo
Tunisia
Ubangi-Shari
Upper Senegal & Niger
Upper Volta
Viet Nam
Wallis & Futuna Islands

POST OFFICES IN FOREIGN COUNTRIES

China
Crete
Egypt
Turkish Empire
Zanzibar

Germany

EARLY STATES

Baden
Bavaria
Bergedorf
Bremen
Brunswick
Hamburg
Hanover
Lubeck
Mecklenburg-Schwerin
Mecklenburg-Strelitz
Oldenburg
Prussia
Saxony
Schleswig-Holstein
Wurttemberg

FORMER COLONIES

Cameroun (Kamerun)
Caroline Islands
German East Africa
German New Guinea
German South-West Africa
Kiauchau
Mariana Islands
Marshall Islands
Samoa
Togo

Italy

EARLY STATES

Modena
Parma
Romagna
Roman States
Sardinia
Tuscany
Two Sicilies
    Naples
    Neapolitan Provinces
    Sicily

FORMER COLONIES, CONTROLLED TERRITORIES, OCCUPATION AREAS

Aegean Islands
    Calimno (Calino)
    Caso
    Cos (Coo)
    Karki (Carchi)
    Leros (Lero)
    Lipso
    Nisiros (Nisiro)
    Patmos (Patmo)
    Piscopi
    Rodi (Rhodes)
    Scarpanto
    Simi
    Stampalia
Castellorizo
Corfu
Cyrenaica
Eritrea
Ethiopia (Abyssinia)
Fiume
Ionian Islands
    Cephalonia
    Ithaca
    Paxos
Italian East Africa
Libya
Oltre Giuba
Saseno
Somalia (Italian Somaliland)
Tripolitania

POST OFFICES IN FOREIGN COUNTRIES

"ESTERO"*
Austria
China
    Peking
    Tientsin
Crete
Tripoli
Turkish Empire
    Constantinople
    Durazzo
    Janina
Jerusalem
Salonika
Scutari
Smyrna
Valona

*Stamps overprinted "ESTERO" were used in various parts of the world.

Netherlands

Aruba
Netherlands Antilles (Curacao)
Netherlands Indies
Netherlands New Guinea
Surinam (Dutch Guiana)

Portugal

COLONIES PAST AND PRESENT, CONTROLLED TERRITORIES

Angola
Angra
Azores
Cape Verde
Funchal
Horta
Inhambane
Kionga
Lourenco Marques
Macao
Madeira
Mozambique
Mozambique Co.
Nyassa
Ponta Delgada
Portuguese Africa
Portuguese Congo
Portuguese Guinea
Portuguese India
Quelimane
St. Thomas & Prince Islands
Tete
Timor
Zambezia

Russia

ALLIED TERRITORIES AND REPUBLICS, OCCUPATION AREAS

Armenia
Aunus (Olonets)
Azerbaijan
Batum
Estonia
Far Eastern Republic
Georgia
Karelia
Latvia
Lithuania
North Ingermanland
Ostland
Russian Turkestan
Siberia
South Russia
Tannu Tuva
Transcaucasian Fed. Republics
Ukraine
Wenden (Livonia)
Western Ukraine

Spain

COLONIES PAST AND PRESENT, CONTROLLED TERRITORIES

Aguera, La
Cape Juby
Cuba
Elobey, Annobon & Corisco
Fernando Po
Ifni
Mariana Islands
Philippines
Puerto Rico
Rio de Oro
Rio Muni
Spanish Guinea
Spanish Morocco
Spanish Sahara
Spanish West Africa

POST OFFICES IN FOREIGN COUNTRIES

Morocco
Tangier
Tetuan

Common Design Types

Pictured in this section are issues where one illustration has been used for a number of countries in the Catalogue. Not included in this section are overprinted stamps or those issues which are illustrated in each country.

EUROPA

Europa Issue, 1956

The design symbolizing the cooperation among the six countries comprising the Coal and Steel Community is illustrated in each country.

Belgium	496-497
France	805-806
Germany	748-749
Italy	715-716
Luxembourg	318-320
Netherlands	368-369

Europa Issue, 1958

"E" and Dove
CD1

European Postal Union at the service of European integration.

1958, Sept. 13

Belgium	527-528
France	889-890
Germany	790-791
Italy	750-751
Luxembourg	341-343
Netherlands	375-376
Saar	317-318

Europa Issue, 1959

6-Link Endless Chain
CD2

1959, Sept. 19

Belgium	536-537
France	929-930
Germany	805-806
Italy	791-792
Luxembourg	354-355
Netherlands	379-380

Europa Issue, 1960

19-Spoke Wheel
CD3

First anniversary of the establishment of C.E.P.T. (Conference Europeenne des Administrations des Postes et des Telecommunications.)

The spokes symbolize the 19 founding members of the Conference.

1960, Sept.

Belgium	553-554
Denmark	379
Finland	376-377
France	970-971
Germany	818-820
Great Britain	377-378
Greece	688
Iceland	327-328
Ireland	175-176
Italy	809-810
Luxembourg	374-375
Netherlands	385-386
Norway	387
Portugal	866-867
Spain	941-942
Sweden	562-563
Switzerland	400-401
Turkey	1493-1494

Europa Issue, 1961

19 Doves Flying as One
CD4

The 19 doves represent the 19 members of the Conference of European Postal and Telecommunications Administrations C.E.P.T.

1961-62

Belgium	572-573
Cyprus	201-203
France	1005-1006
Germany	844-845
Great Britain	383-384
Greece	718-719
Iceland	340-341
Italy	845-846
Luxembourg	382-383
Netherlands	387-388
Spain	1010-1011
Switzerland	410-411
Turkey	1518-1520

Europa Issue 1962

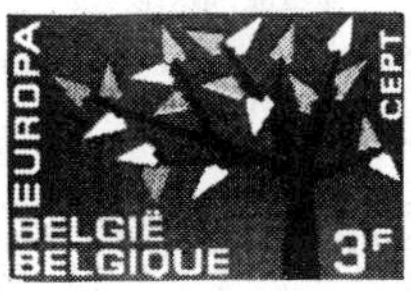

Young Tree with 19 Leaves
CD5

The 19 leaves represent the 19 original members of C.E.P.T.

1962-63

Belgium	582-583
Cyprus	219-221
France	1045-1046
Germany	852-853
Greece	739-740
Iceland	348-349
Ireland	184-185
Italy	860-861
Luxembourg	386-387
Netherlands	394-395
Norway	414-415
Switzerland	416-417
Turkey	1553-1555

Europa Issue, 1963

Stylized Links, Symbolizing Unity
CD6

1963, Sept.

Belgium	598-599
Cyprus	229-231
Finland	419
France	1074-1075
Germany	867-868
Greece	768-769
Iceland	357-358
Ireland	188-189
Italy	880-881
Luxembourg	403-404
Netherlands	416-417
Norway	441-442
Switzerland	429
Turkey	1602-1603

Europa Issue, 1964

Symbolic Daisy
CD7

5th anniversary of the establishment of C.E.P.T. The 22 petals of the flower symbolize the 22 members of the Conference.

1964, Sept.

Austria	738
Belgium	614-615
Cyprus	244-246
France	1109-1110
Germany	897-898
Greece	801-802
Iceland	367-368
Ireland	196-197
Italy	894-895
Luxembourg	411-412
Monaco	590-591
Netherlands	428-429
Norway	458
Portugal	931-933
Spain	1262-1263
Switzerland	438-439
Turkey	1628-1629

Europa Issue, 1965

Leaves and "Fruit"
CD8

1965

Belgium	636-637
Cyprus	262-264
Finland	437
France	1131-1132
Germany	934-935
Greece	833-834
Iceland	375-376
Ireland	204-205
Italy	915-916
Luxembourg	432-433
Monaco	616-617
Netherlands	438-439
Norway	475-476
Portugal	958-960
Switzerland	469
Turkey	1665-1666

Europa Issue, 1966

Symbolic Sailboat
CD9

1966, Sept.

Andorra, French	172
Belgium	675-676
Cyprus	275-277
France	1163-1164
Germany	963-964
Greece	862-863
Iceland	384-385
Ireland	216-217
Italy	942-943
Liechtenstein	415
Luxembourg	440-441
Monaco	639-640
Netherlands	441-442
Norway	496-497
Portugal	980-982
Switzerland	477-478
Turkey	1718-1719

Europa Issue, 1967

Cogwheels
CD10

1967

Andorra, French	174-175
Belgium	688-689
Cyprus	297-299
France	1178-1179
Greece	891-892
Germany	969-970
Iceland	389-390
Ireland	232-233
Italy	951-952
Liechtenstein	420
Luxembourg	449-450
Monaco	669-670
Netherlands	444-447
Norway	504-505
Portugal	994-996
Spain	1465-1466
Switzerland	482
Turkey	B120-B121

Europa Issue, 1968

Golden Key with C.E.P.T. Emblem
CD11

1968

Andorra, French	182-183
Belgium	705-706
Cyprus	314-316
France	1209-1210
Germany	983-984
Greece	916-917
Iceland	395-396
Ireland	242-243
Italy	979-980
Liechtenstein	442
Luxembourg	466-467
Monaco	689-691
Netherlands	452-453
Portugal	1019-1021
San Marino	687
Spain	1526
Turkey	1775-1776

Europa Issue, 1969

"EUROPA" and "CEPT"
CD12

Tenth anniversary of C.E.P.T.

1969

Andorra, French	188-189
Austria	837
Belgium	718-719
Cyprus	326-328
Denmark	458
Finland	483
France	1245-1246
Germany	996-997
Great Britain	585
Greece	947-948

Iceland	406-407
Ireland	270-271
Italy	1000-1001
Jugoslavia	1003-1004
Liechtenstein	453
Luxembourg	474-475
Monaco	722-724
Netherlands	475-476
Norway	533-534
Portugal	1038-1040
San Marino	701-702
Spain	1567
Sweden	814-816
Switzerland	500-501
Turkey	1799-1800
Vatican	470-472

Europa Issue, 1970

Interwoven Threads CD13

1970

Andorra, French	196-197
Belgium	741-742
Cyprus	340-342
France	1271-1272
Germany	1018-1019
Greece	985, 987
Iceland	420-421
Ireland	279-281
Italy	1013-1014
Jugoslavia	1024-1025
Liechtenstein	470
Luxembourg	489-490
Monaco	768-770
Netherlands	483-484
Portugal	1060-1062
San Marino	729-730
Spain	1607
Switzerland	515-516
Turkey	1848-1849

Europa Issue, 1971

"Fraternity, Cooperation, Common Effort"—CD14

1971

Andorra, French	205-206
Belgium	803-804
Cyprus	365-367
Finland	504
France	1304
Germany	1064-1065
Greece	1029-1030
Iceland	429-430
Ireland	305-306
Italy	1038-1039
Jugoslavia	1052-1053
Liechtenstein	485
Luxembourg	500-501
Malta	425-427
Monaco	797-799
Netherlands	488-489
Portugal	1094-1096
San Marino	749-750
Spain	1675-1676
Switzerland	531-532
Turkey	1876-1877

Europa Issue, 1972

Sparkles, Symbolic of Communications CD15

1972

Andorra, French	210-211
Andorra, Spanish	62
Belgium	825-826
Cyprus	380-382
Finland	512-513
France	1341
Germany	1089-1090
Greece	1049-1050
Iceland	439-440
Ireland	316-317
Italy	1065-1066
Jugoslavia	1100-1101
Liechtenstein	504
Luxembourg	512-513
Malta	450-453
Monaco	831-832
Netherlands	494-495
Portugal	1141-1143
San Marino	771-772
Spain	1718
Switzerland	544-545
Turkey	1907-1908

Europa Issue, 1973

Post Horn and Arrows CD16

1973

Andorra, French	319-320
Andorra, Spanish	76
Belgium	839-840
Cyprus	396-398
Finland	526
France	1367
Germany	1114-1115
Greece	1090-1092
Iceland	447-448
Ireland	329-330
Italy	1108-1109
Jugoslavia	1138-1139
Liechtenstein	528-529
Luxembourg	523-524
Malta	469-471
Monaco	866-867
Netherlands	504-505
Norway	604-605
Portugal	1170-1172
San Marino	802-803
Spain	1753
Switzerland	580-581
Turkey	1935-1936

PORTUGAL & COLONIES

Vasco da Gama Issue

Fleet Departing—CD20

Fleet Arriving at Calicut CD21

Embarking at Rastello—CD22

Muse of History CD23

Flagship San Gabriel, da Gama and Camoens CD24

Archangel Gabriel, the Patron Saint CD25

Flagship San Gabriel CD26

Vasco da Gama CD27

Fourth centenary of Vasco da Gama's discovery of the route to India.

1898

Azores	93-100
Macao	67-74
Madeira	37-44
Portugal	147-154
Port. Africa	1-8
Port. india	189-196
Timor	45-52

Pombal Issue
POSTAL TAX

Marquis de Pombal CD28

Planning Reconstruction of Lisbon, 1755 CD29

Pombal Monument, Lisbon CD30

Sebastiao Jose' de Carvalho e Mello, Marquis de Pombal (1699-1782), statesman, rebuilt Lisbon after earthquake of 1755. Tax was for the erection of Pombal monument. Obligatory on all mail on certain days throughout the year.

1925

Angola	RA1-RA3
Azores	RA9-RA11
Cape Verde	RA1-RA3
Macao	RA1-RA3
Madeira	RA1-RA3
Mozambique	RA1-RA3
Portugal	RA11-RA13
Port. Guinea	RA1-RA3
Port. India	RA1-RA3
St. Thomas & Prince Islands	RA1-RA3
Timor	RA1-RA3

Pombal Issue
POSTAL TAX DUES

Marquis de Pombal CD31

Planning Reconstruction of Lisbon, 1755 CD32

Pombal Monument, Lisbon CD33

1925

Angola	RAJ1-RAJ3
Azores	RAJ2-RAJ4
Cape Verde	RAJ1-RAJ3
Macao	RAJ1-RAJ3
Madeira	RAJ1-RAJ3
Mozambique	RAJ1-RAJ3
Portugal	RAJ2-RAJ4
Port. Guinea	RAJ1-RAJ3
Port. India	RAJ1-RAJ3
St. Thomas & Prince Islands	RAJ1-RAJ3
Timor	RAJ1-RAJ3

Vasco da Gama CD34

Mousinho de Albuquerque CD35

Dam CD36

Prince Henry the Navigator CD37

Affonso de Albuquerque CD38

1938-39

Angola	274-291
Cape Verde	234-251
Macao	289-305
Mozambique	270-287
Port. Guinea	233-250
Port. India	439-453
St. Thomas & Prince Islands	302-319, 323-340
Timor	223-239

Plane over Globe CD39

1938-39

Angola	C1-C9
Cape Verde	C1-C9
Macao	C7-C15
Mozambique	C1-C9
Port. Guinea	C1-C9
Port. India	C1-C8
St. Thomas & Prince Islands	C1-C18
Timor	C1-C9

Lady of Fatima Issue

Our Lady of the Rosary, Fatima, Portugal
CD40

1948-49

Angola	315-318
Cape Verde	266
Macao	336
Mozambique	325-328
Port. Guinea	271
Port. India	480
St. Thomas & Prince Islands	351
Timor	254

A souvenir sheet of 9 stamps was issued in 1951 to mark the extension of the 1950 Holy Year. The sheet contains: Angola No. 316, Cape Verde No. 266, Macao No. 336, Mozambique No. 325, Portuguese Guinea No. 271, Portugese India Nos. 480, 485, St. Thomas & Prince Islands No. 351, Timor No. 254.

The sheet also contains a portrait of Pope Pius XII and is inscribed "Encerramento do Ano Santo, Fatima 1951." It was sold for 11 escudos.

Holy Year Issue

Church Bells and Dove
CD41

Angel Holding Candelabra
CD42

Holy Year, 1950.

1950-51

Angola	331-332
Cape Verde	268-269
Macao	339-340
Mozambique	330-331
Port. Guinea	273-274
Port. India	490-491, 496-503
St. Thomas & Prince Islands	353-354
Timor	258-259

A souvenir sheet of 8 stamps was issued in 1951 to mark the extension of the Holy Year. The sheet contains: Angola No. 331, Cape Verde No. 269, Macao No. 340, Mozambique No. 331, Portuguese Guinea No. 275, Portuguese India No. 490, St. Thomas & Prince Islands No. 354, Timor No. 258, some with colors changed. The sheet contains doves and is inscribed "Encerramento do Ano Santo, Fatima 1951." It was sold for 17 escudos.

Holy Year Conclusion Issue

Our Lady of Fatima
CD43

Conclusion of Holy Year. Sheets contain alternate vertical rows of stamps and labels bearing quotation from Pope Pius XII, different for each colony.

1951

Angola	357
Cape Verde	270
Macao	352
Mozambique	356
Port. Guinea	275
Port. India	506
St. Thomas & Prince Islands	355
Timor	270

Medical Congress Issue

Medical Examination
CD44

First National Congress of Tropical Medicine, Lisbon, 1952.
Each stamp has a different design.

1952

Angola	358
Cape Verde	287
Macao	364
Mozambique	359
Port. Guinea	276
Port. India	516
St. Thomas & Prince Islands	356
Timor	271

POSTAGE DUE STAMPS

CD45

1952

Angola	J37-J42
Cape Verde	J31-J36
Macao	J53-J58
Mozambique	J51-J56
Port. Guinea	J40-J45
Port. India	J47-J52
St. Thomas & Prince Islands	J52-J57
Timor	J31-J36

Sao Paulo Issue

Father Manuel de Nobrega and View of Sao Paulo
CD46

400th anniversary of the founding of Sao Paulo, Brazil.

1954

Angola	385
Cape Verde	297
Macao	382
Mozambique	395
Port. Guinea	291
Port. India	530
St. Thomas & Prince Islands	369
Timor	279

Tropical Medicine Congress Issue

Securidaca Longipedunculata
CD47

Sixth International Congress for Tropical Medicine and Malaria, Lisbon, Sept. 1958.
Each stamp shows a different plant.

1958

Angola	409
Cape Verde	303
Macao	392
Mozambique	404
Port. Guinea	295
Port. India	569
St. Thomas & Prince Islands	371
Timor	289

Sports Issue

Flying
CD48

Each stamp shows a different sport.

1962

Angola	433-438
Cape Verde	320-325
Macao	394-399
Mozambique	424-429
Port. Guinea	299-304
St. Thomas & Prince Islands	374-379
Timor	313-318

Anti-Malaria Issue

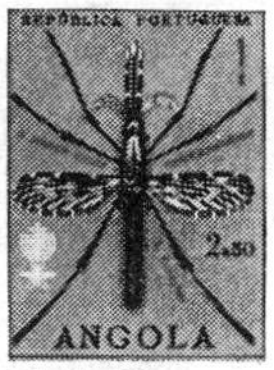

Anopheles Funestus and Malaria Eradication Symbol
CD49

World Health Organization drive to eradicate malaria.

1962

Angola	439
Cape Verde	326
Macao	400
Mozambique	430
Port. Guinea	305
St. Thomas & Prince Islands	380
Timor	319

Airline Anniversary Issue

Map of Africa, Super Constellation and Jet Liner
CD50

Tenth anniversary of Transportes Aereos Portugueses (TAP).

1963

Angola	490
Cape Verde	327
Mozambique	434
Port. Guinea	318
St. Thomas & Prince Islands	381

National Overseas Bank Issue

Antonio Teixeira de Sousa
CD51

Centenary of the National Overseas Bank of Portugal.

1964, May 16

Angola	509
Cape Verde	328
Port. Guinea	319
St. Thomas & Prince Islands	382
Timor	320

ITU Issue

ITU Emblem and St. Gabriel
CD52

Centenary of the International Communications Union.

1965, May 17

Angola	511
Cape Verde	329
Macao	402
Mozambique	464
Port. Guinea	320
St. Thomas & Prince Islands	383
Timor	321

National Revolution Issue

St. Paul's Hospital, and Commercial and Industrial School
CD53

40th anniversary of the National Revolution.
Different buildings on each stamp.

1966, May 28

Angola	525
Cape Verde	338
Macao	403
Mozambique	465
Port. Guinea	329
St. Thomas & Prince Islands	392
Timor	322

Navy Club Issue

Mendes Barata and Cruiser Dom Carlos I
CD54

Centenary of Portugal's Navy Club.
Each stamp has a different design.

1967, Jan. 31

Angola	527-528
Cape Verde	339-340
Macao	412-413
Mozambique	478-479
Port. Guinea	330-331
St. Thomas & Prince Islands	393-394
Timor	323-324

Admiral Coutinho Issue

Admiral Gago Coutinho and his First Ship
CD55

Centenary of the birth of Admiral Carlos Viegas Gago Coutinho (1869-1959), explorer and aviation pioneer.
Each stamp has a different design.

1969, Feb. 17

Angola	547
Cape Verde	355
Macao	417
Mozambique	484
Port. Guinea	335
St. Thomas & Prince Islands	397
Timor	335

Administration Reform Issue

Luiz Augusto Rebello da Silva
CD56

Centenary of the administration reforms of the overseas territories.

1969, Sept. 25

Angola	549
Cape Verde	357
Macao	419
Mozambique	491
Port. Guinea	337
St. Thomas & Prince Islands	399
Timor	338

Marshal Carmona Issue

Marshal A.O. Carmona
CD57

Birth centenary of Marshal Antonio Oscar Carmona de Fragoso (1869-1951), President of Portugal.
Each stamp has a different design.

1970, Nov. 15

Angola	563
Cape Verde	359
Macao	422
Mozambique	493
Port. Guinea	340
St. Thomas & Prince Islands	403
Timor	341

Olympic Games Issue

Racing Yachts and Olympic Emblem
CD59

20th Olympic Games, Munich, Aug. 26-Sept. 11.
Each stamp shows a different sport.

1972, June 20

Angola	569
Cape Verde	361
Macao	426
Mozambique	504
Port. Guinea	342
St. Thomas & Prince Islands	408
Timor	343

Lisbon-Rio de Janeiro Flight Issue

"Santa Cruz" over
Fernando de Noronha
CD60

50th anniversary of the Lisbon to Rio de Janeiro flight by Arturo de Sacadura and Coutinho, March 30-June 5, 1922.
Each stamp shows a different stage of the flight.

1972, Sept. 20

Angola	570
Cape Verde	362
Macao	427
Mozambique	505
Port. Guinea	343
St. Thomas & Prince Islands	409
Timor	344

WMO Centenary Issue

WMO Emblem
CD61

Centenary of international meterological cooperation.

1973, Dec. 15

Angola	571
Cape Verde	363
Macao	429
Mozambique	509
Port. Guinea	344
St. Thomas & Prince Islands	410
Timor	345

FRENCH COMMUNITY

Colonial Exposition Issue

People of French Empire
CD70

Women's Heads
CD71

France Showing Way to Civilization
CD72

"Colonial Commerce"
CD73

International Colonial Exposition, Paris 1931.

1931

Cameroun	213-216
Chad	60-63
Dahomey	97-100
Fr. Guiana	152-155
Fr. Guinea	116-119
Fr. India	100-103
Fr. Polynesia	76-79
Fr. Sudan	102-105
Gabon	120-123
Guadeloupe	138-141
Indo-China	140-142
Ivory Coast	92-95
Madagascar	169-172
Martinique	129-132
Mauritania	65-68
Middle Congo	61-64
New Caledonia	176-179
Niger	73-76
Reunion	122-125
St. Pierre & Miquelon	132-135
Senegal	138-141
Somali Coast	135-138
Togo	254-257
Ubangi-Shari	82-85
Upper Volta	66-69
Wallis & Futuna Isls.	85-88

Paris International Exposition Issue

Colonial Arts Exposition Issue

"Colonial Resources"
CD74 CD77

Overseas Commerce
CD75

Exposition Building and Women
CD76

"France and the Empire"
CD78

Cultural Treasures of the Colonies
CD79

Souvenir sheets contain one imperf. stamp.

1937

Cameroun	217-222A
Dahomey	101-107
Fr. Equatorial Africa	27-32, 73
Fr. Guiana	162-168
Fr. Guinea	120-126
Fr. India	104-110
Fr. Polynesia	117-123
Fr. Sudan	106-112
Guadeloupe	148-154
Indo-China	193-199
Inini	41
Ivory Coast	152-158
Kwangchowan	132
Madagascar	191-197
Martinique	179-185
Mauritania	69-75
New Caledonia	208-214
Niger	72-83
Reunion	167-173
St. Pierre & Miquelon	165-171
Senegal	172-178
Somali Coast	139-145
Togo	258-264
Wallis & Futuna Isls.	89

Curie Issue

Pierre and Marie Curie
CD80

40th anniversary of the discovery of radium. The surtax was for the benefit of the International Union for the Control of Cancer.

1938

Cameroun	B1
Dahomey	B2
France	B76
Fr. Equatorial Africa	B1
Fr. Guiana	B3
Fr. Guinea	B2
Fr. India	B6
Fr. Polynesia	B5
Fr. Sudan	B1
Guadeloupe	B3
Indo-China	B14
Ivory Coast	B2
Madagascar	B2
Martinique	B2
Mauritania	B3
New Caledonia	B4
Niger	B1
Reunion	B4
St. Pierre & Miquelon	B3
Senegal	B3
Somali Coast	B2
Togo	B1

Caillie Issue

Rene Caille and Map of
Northwestern Africa
CD81

Death centenary of Rene Caillie (1799-1838), French explorer.
All three denominations exist with colony name omitted.

1939

Dahomey	108-110
Fr. Guinea	161-163
Fr. Sudan	113-115
Ivory Coast	160-162
Mauritania	109-111
Niger	84-86
Senegal	188-190
Togo	265-267

New York World's Fair Issue

Natives and New York Skyline
CD82

1939

Cameroun	223-224
Dahomey	111-112
Fr. Equatorial Africa	78-79
Fr. Guiana	169-170
Fr. Guinea	164-165
Fr. India	111-112
Fr. Polynesia	124-125
Fr. Sudan	116-117
Guadeloupe	155-156
Indo-China	203-204
Inini	42-43
Ivory Coast	163-164
Kwangchowan	121-122
Madagascar	209-210
Martinique	186-187
Mauritania	112-113
New Caledonia	215-216
Niger	87-88
Reunion	174-175
St. Pierre & Miquelon	205-206
Senegal	191-192
Somali Coast	179-180
Togo	268-269
Wallis & Futuna Isls.	90-91

French Revolution Issue

Storming of the Bastille
CD83

150th anniversary of the French Revolution. The surtax was for the defense of the colonies.

1939

Cameroun	B2-B6
Dahomey	B3-B7
Fr. Equatorial Africa	B4-B8, CB1
Fr. Guiana	B4-B8, CB1
Fr. Guinea	B3-B7
Fr. India	B7-B11
Fr. Polynesia	B6-B10, CB1
Fr. Sudan	B2-B6
Guadeloupe	B4-B8
Indo-China	B15-B19, CB1
Inini	B1-B5
Ivory Coast	B3-B7
Kwangchowan	B1-B5
Madagascar	B3-B7, CB1
Martinique	B3-B7
Mauritania	B4-B8
New Caledonia	B5-B9, CB1
Niger	B2-B6
Reunion	B5-B9, CB1
St. Pierre & Miquelon	B4-B8
Senegal	B4-B8, CB1
Somali Coast	B3-B7
Togo	B2-B6
Wallis & Futuna Isls.	B1-B5

Plane over Coastal Area
CD85

All five denominations exist with colony name omitted.

1940

Dahomey	C1-C5
Fr. Guinea	C1-C5
Fr. Sudan	C1-C5
Ivory Coast	C1-C5
Mauritania	C1-C5
Niger	C1-C5
Senegal	C12-C16
Togo	C1-C5

Colonial Infantryman
CD86

1941

Cameroun	B13B
Dahomey	B13
Fr. Equatorial Africa	B8B
Fr. Guiana	B10
Fr. Guinea	B13
Fr. India	B13
Fr. Polynesia	B12
Fr. Sudan	B12
Guadeloupe	B10
Indo-China	B19B
Inini	B7
Ivory Coast	B13
Kwangchowan	B7
Madagascar	B9
Martinique	B9
Mauritania	B14
New Caledonia	B11
Niger	B12
Reunion	B11
St. Pierre & Miquelon	B8B
Senegal	B14
Somali Coast	B9
Togo	B10B
Wallis & Futuna Isls.	B7

Cross of Lorraine and Four-motor Plane
CD87

1941-5

Cameroun	C1-C7
Fr. Equatorial Africa	C17-C23
Fr. Guiana	C9-C10
Fr. India	C1-C6
Fr. Polynesia	C3-C9
Fr. West Africa	C1-C3
Guadeloupe	C1-C2
Madagascar	C37-C43
Martinique	C1-C2
New Caledonia	C7-C13
Reunion	C18-C24
St. Pierre & Miquelon	C1-C7
Somali Coast	C1-C7

Transport Plane
CD88

Caravan and Plane—CD89

1942

Dahomey	C6-C13
Fr. Guinea	C6-C13
Fr. Sudan	C6-C13
Ivory Coast	C6-C13
Mauritania	C6-C13
Niger	C6-C13
Senegal	C17-C25
Togo	C6-C13

Red Cross Issue

Marianne
CD90

The surtax was for the French Red Cross and national relief.

1944

Cameroun	B28
Fr. Equatorial Africa	B38
Fr. Guiana	B12
Fr. India	B14
Fr. Polynesia	B13
Fr. West Africa	B1
Guadeloupe	B12
Madagascar	B15
Martinique	B11
New Caledonia	B13
Reunion	B15
St. Pierre & Miquelon	B13
Somali Coast	B13
Wallis & Futuna Isls.	B9

Eboue Issue

Felix Eboue
CD91

Felix Eboue, first French colonial administrator to proclaim resistance to Germany after French surrender in World War II.

1945

Cameroun	296-297
Fr. Equatorial Africa	156-157
Fr. Guiana	171-172
Fr. India	210-211
Fr. Polynesia	150-151
Fr. West Africa	15-16
Guadeloupe	187-188
Madagascar	259-260
Martinique	196-197
New Caledonia	274-275
Reunion	238-239
St. Pierre & Miquelon	322-323
Somali Coast	238-239

Victory Issue

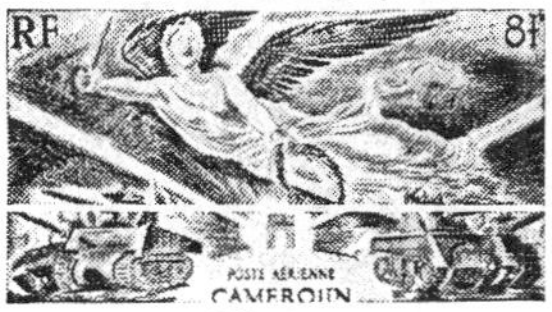

Victory
CD92

European victory of the Allied Nations in World War II.

1946, May 8

Cameroun	C8
Fr. Equatorial Africa	C24
Fr. Guiana	C11
Fr. India	C7
Fr. Polynesia	C10
Fr. West Africa	C4
Guadeloupe	C3
Indo-China	C19
Madagascar	C44
Martinique	C3
New Caledonia	C14
Reunion	C25
St. Pierre & Miquelon	C8
Somali Coast	C8
Wallis & Futuna Isls.	C1

Chad to Rhine Issue

Leclerc's Departure from Chad
CD93

Battle at Cufra Oasis
CD94

Tanks in Action, Mareth
CD95

Normandy Invasion
CD96

Entering Paris
CD97

Liberation of Strasbourg
CD98

"Chad to the Rhine" march, 1942-44, by Gen. Jacques Leclerc's column, later French 2nd Armored Division.

1946, June 6

Cameroun	C9-C14
Fr. Equatorial Africa	C25-C30
Fr. Guiana	C12-C17
Fr. India	C8-C13
Fr. Polynesia	C11-C16
Fr. West Africa	C5-C10
Guadeloupe	C4-C9
Indo-China	C20-C25
Madagascar	C45-C50
Martinique	C4-C9
New Caledonia	C15-C20
Reunion	C26-C31
St. Pierre & Miquelon	C9-C14
Somali Coast	C9-C14
Wallis & Futuna Isls.	C2-C7

UPU Issue

French Colonials, Globe and Plane
CD99

75th anniversary of the Universal Postal Union.

1949, July 4

Cameroun	C29
Fr. Equatorial Africa	C34
Fr. India	C17
Fr. Polynesia	C20
Fr. West Africa	C15
Indo-China	C26
Madagascar	C55
New Caledonia	C24
St. Pierre & Miquelon	C18
Somali Coast	C18
Togo	C18
Wallis & Futuna Isls.	C10

Tropical Medicine Issue

Doctor Treating Infant
CD100

The surtax was for charitable work.

1950

Cameroun	B29
Fr. Equatorial Africa	B39
Fr. India	B15
Fr. Polynesia	B14
Fr. West Africa	B3
Madagascar	B17
New Caledonia	B14
St. Pierre & Miquelon	B14
Somali Coast	B14
Togo	B11

Military Medal Issue

Medal, Early Marine and Colonial Soldier
CD101

Centenary of the creation of the French Military Medal.

1952

Cameroun	332
Comoro Isls.	39
Fr. Equatorial Africa	186
Fr. India	233
Fr. Polynesia	179
Fr. West Africa	57
Madagascar	286
New Caledonia	295
St. Pierre & Miquelon	345
Somali Coast	267
Togo	327
Wallis & Futuna Isls.	149

Liberation Issue

Allied Landing, Victory Sign and Cross of Lorraine
CD102

10th anniversary of the liberation of France.

1954, June 6

Cameroun	C32
Comoro Isls.	C4
Fr. Equatorial Africa	C38
Fr. India	C18
Fr. Polynesia	C23
Fr. West Africa	C17
Madagascar	C57
New Caledonia	C25
St. Pierre & Miquelon	C19
Somali Coast	C19
Togo	C19
Wallis & Futuna Isls.	C11

FIDES Issue

Plowmen
CD103

Efforts of FIDES, the Economic and Social Development Fund for Overseas Possessions (Fonds d' Investissement pour le Developpement Economique et Social).

Each stamp has a different design.

1956

Cameroun	326-329
Comoro Isls.	43
Fr. Polynesia	181
Madagascar	292-295
New Caledonia	303
Somali Coast	268
Togo	331

Flower Issue

Euadania
CD104

Each stamp shows a different flower.

1958-9

Cameroun	333
Comoro Isls.	45
Fr. Equatorial Africa	200-201
Fr. Polynesia	192
Fr. So. & Antarctic Terr.	11
Fr. West Africa	79-83
Madagascar	301-302
New Caledonia	304-305
St. Pierre & Miquelon	357
Somali Coast	270
Togo	348-349
Wallis & Futuna Isls.	152

Human Rights Issue

Sun, Dove and U.N. Emblem
CD105

10th anniversary of the signing of the Universal Declaration of Human Rights.

1958

Comoro Isls.	44
Fr. Equatorial Africa	202
Fr. Polynesia	191
Fr. West Africa	85
Madagascar	300
New Caledonia	306
St. Pierre & Miquelon	356
Somali Coast	274
Wallis & Futuna Isls.	153

C.C.T.A. Issue

Map of Africa and Cogwheels
CD106

10th anniversary of the Commission for Technical Cooperation in Africa south of the Sahara.

1960

Cameroun	335
Cent. African Rep.	3
Chad	66
Congo, P.R.	90
Dahomey	138
Gabon	150
Ivory Coast	180
Madagascar	317
Mali	9
Mauritania	117
Niger	104
Upper Volta	89

Air Afrique Issue, 1961

Modern and Ancient Africa, Map and Planes
CD107

Founding of Air Afrique (African Airlines).

1961-62

Cameroun	C37
Cent. African Rep.	C5
Chad	C7
Congo, P.R.	C5
Dahomey	C17
Gabon	C5
Ivory Coast	C18
Mauritania	C17
Niger	C22
Senegal	C31
Upper Volta	C4

Anti-Malaria Issue

Malaria Eradication Emblem
CD108

World Heatlh Organization drive to eradicate malaria.

1962, Apr. 7

Cameroun	B36
Cent. African Rep.	B1
Chad	B1
Comoro Isls.	B1
Congo, P.R.	B3
Dahomey	B15
Gabon	B4
Ivory Coast	B15
Madagascar	B19
Mali	B1
Mauritania	B16
Niger	B14
Senegal	B16
Somali Coast	B15
Upper Volta	B1

Abidjan Games Issue

Relay Race
CD109

Abidjan Games, Ivory Coast, Dec. 24-31, 1961.
Each stamp shows a different sport.

1962

Chad	83-84
Cent. African Rep.	19-20
Congo, P.R.	103-104
Gabon	163-164
Niger	109-111
Upper Volta	103-105

African and Malagasy Union Issue

Flag of African and Malagasy Union
CD110

First anniversary of the Union.

1962, Sept. 8

Cameroun	373
Cent. African Rep.	21
Chad	85
Congo, P.R.	105
Dahomey	155
Gabon	165
Ivory Coast	198
Madagascar	332
Mauritania	170
Niger	112
Senegal	211
Upper Volta	106

Telstar Issue

Telstar and Globe Showing Andover and Pleumeur-Bodou
CD111

First television connection of the United States and Europe through the Telstar satellite, July 11-12, 1962.

1962-63

Andorra, French	154
Comoro Isls.	C7
Fr. Polynesia	C29
Fr. So. & Antarctic Terr.	C5
New Caledonia	C33
Somali Coast	C31
St. Pierre & Miquelon	C26
Wallis & Futuna Isls.	C17

Freedom From Hunger Issue

World Map and Wheat Emblem
CD112

United Nations Food and Agriculture Organization's "Freedom from Hunger" campaign.

1963, Mar. 21

Cameroun	B37-B38
Cent. African Rep.	B2
Chad	B2
Congo, P.R.	B4
Dahomey	B16
Gabon	B5
Ivory Coast	B16
Madagascar	B21
Mauritania	B17
Niger	B15
Senegal	B17
Upper Volta	B2

Red Cross Centenary Issue

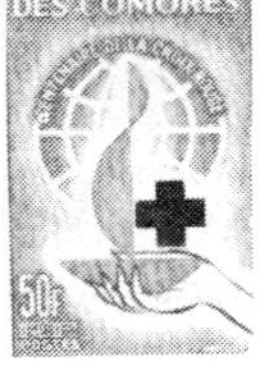

Centenary Emblem
CD113

Centenary of the International Red Cross.

1963, Sept. 2

Comoro Isls.	55
Fr. Polynesia	205
New Caledonia	328
St. Pierre & Miquelon	367
Somali Coast	297
Wallis & Futuna Isls.	165

African Postal Union Issue

UAMPT Emblem, Radio Masts, Plane and Mali
CD114

Establishment of the African and Malagasy Posts and Telecommunications Union, UAMPT.

1963, Sept. 8

Cameroun	C47
Cent. African Rep.	C10
Chad	C9
Congo, P.R.	C13
Dahomey	C19
Gabon	C13
Ivory Coast	C25
Madagascar	C75
Mauritania	C22
Niger	C27
Rwanda	36
Senegal	C32
Upper Volta	C9

Air Afrique Issue, 1963

Symbols of Flight
CD115

First anniversary of Air Afrique and inauguration of DC-8 service.

1963, Nov. 19

Cameroun	C48
Chad	C10
Congo, P.R.	C14
Gabon	C18
Ivory Coast	C26
Mauritania	C26
Niger	C35
Senegal	C33

Europafrica Issue

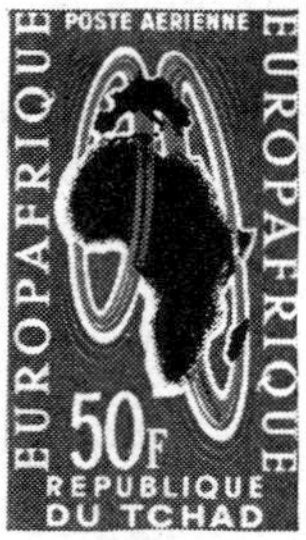

Europe and Africa Linked Together
CD116

Signing of an economic agreement between the European Economic Community and the African and Malagasy Union, Yaounde, Cameroun, July 20, 1963.

1963-64

Cameroun	402
Chad	C11
Cent. African Rep.	C12
Congo, P.R.	C16
Gabon	C19
Ivory Coast	217
Niger	C43
Upper Volta	C11

Human Rights Issue

Scales of Justice and Globe
CD117

15th anniversary of the Universal Declaration of Human Rights.

1963, Dec. 10

Comoro Isls.	58
Fr. Polynesia	206
New Caledonia	329
St. Pierre & Miquelon	368
Somali Coast	300
Wallis & Futuna Isls.	166

PHILATEC Issue

Stamp Album, Champs Elysees Palace and Horses of Marly
CD118

"PHILATEC," International Philatelic and Postal Techniques Exhibition, Paris, June 5-21, 1964.

1963-64

Comoro Isls.	60
France	1078
Fr. Polynesia	207
New Caledonia	341
St. Pierre & Miquelon	369
Somali Coast	301
Wallis & Futuna Isls.	167

Cooperation Issue

Maps of France and Africa and Clasped Hands
CD119

Cooperation between France and the French-speaking countries of Africa and Madagascar.

1964

Cameroun	409-410
Cent. African Rep.	39
Chad	103
Congo, P.R.	121
Dahomey	193
France	1111
Gabon	175
Ivory Coast	221
Madagascar	360
Mauritania	181
Niger	143
Senegal	236
Togo	495

ITU Issue

Telegraph, Syncom Satellite and ITU Emblem
CD120

Centenary of the International Telecommunication Union.

1965, May 17

Comoro Isls.	C14
Fr. Polynesia	C33
Fr. So. & Antarctic Terr.	C8
New Caledonia	C40
New Hebrides	124-125

St. Pierre & Miquelon	C29
Somali Coast	C36
Wallis & Futuna Isls.	C20

French Satellite A-1 Issue

Diamant Rocket and Launching Installation
CD121

Launching of France's first satellite, Nov. 26, 1965.

1965-66

Comoro Isls.	C15-C16
France	1137-1138
Fr. Polynesia	C40-C41
Fr. So. & Antarctic Terr.	C9-C10
New Caledonia	C44-C45
St. Pierre & Miquelon	C30-C31
Somali Coast	C39-C40
Wallis & Futuna Isls.	C22-C23

French Satellite D-1 Issue

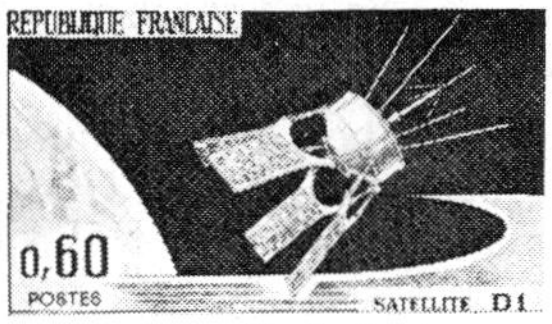

D-1 Satellite in Orbit
CD122

Launching of the D-1 satellite at Hammaguir, Algeria, Feb. 17, 1966.

1966

Comoro Isls.	C17
France	1148
Fr. Polynesia	C42
Fr. So. & Antarctic Terr.	C11
New Caledonia	C46
St. Pierre & Miquelon	C32
Somali Coast	C49
Wallis & Futuna Isls.	C24

Air Afrique Issue, 1966

Planes and Air Afrique Emblem
CD123

Introduction of DC-8F planes by Air Afrique.

1966

Cameroun	C79
Cent. African Rep.	C35
Chad	C26
Congo, P.R.	C42
Dahomey	C42
Gabon	C47
Ivory Coast	C32
Mauritania	C57
Niger	C63
Senegal	C47
Togo	C54
Upper Volta	C31

African Postal Union, 1967

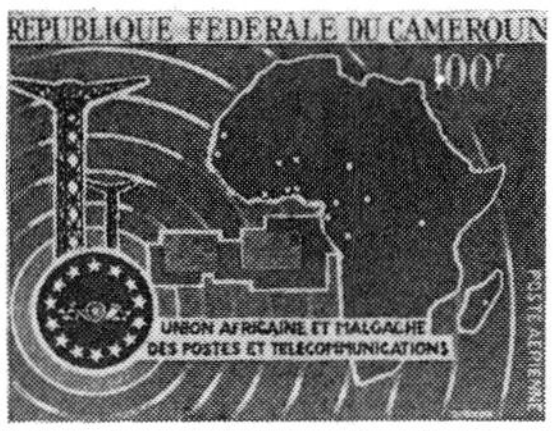

Telecommunications Symbols and Map of Africa
CD124

Fifth anniversary of the establishment of the African and Malagasy Union of Posts and Telecommunications, UAMPT.

1967

Cameroun	C90
Cent. African Rep.	C46
Chad	C37
Congo, P.R.	C57
Dahomey	C61
Gabon	C58
Ivory Coast	C34
Madagascar	C85
Mauritania	C65
Niger	C75
Rwanda	C1-C3
Senegal	C60
Togo	C81
Upper Volta	C50

Monetary Union Issue

Gold Token of the Ashantis, 17-18th Centuries
CD125

Fifth anniversary of the West African Monetary Union.

1967, Nov. 4

Dahomey	244
Ivory Coast	259
Mauritania	238
Niger	204
Senegal	294
Togo	623
Upper Volta	181

WHO Anniversary Issue

Sun, Flowers and WHO Emblem
CD126

20th anniversary of the World Health Organization.

1968, May 4

Afars & Issas	317
Comoro Isls.	73
Fr. Polynesia	241-242
Fr. So. & Antarctic Terr.	31
New Caledonia	367
St. Pierre & Miquelon	377
Wallis & Futuna Isls.	169

Human Rights Year Issue

Human Rights Flame
CD127

International Human Rights Year.

1968, Aug. 10

Afars & Issas	322-323
Comoro Isls.	76
Fr. Polynesia	243-244
Fr. So. & Antarctic Terr.	32
New Caledonia	369
St. Pierre & Miquelon	382
Wallis & Futuna Isls.	170

2nd PHILEXAFRIQUE Issue

Gabon No. 131 and Industrial Plant
CD128

Opening of PHILEXAFRIQUE, Abidjan, Feb. 14.

Each stamp shows a local scene and stamp.

1969, Feb. 14

Cameroun	C118
Cent. African Rep.	C65
Chad	C48
Congo, P.R.	C77
Dahomey	C94
Gabon	C82
Ivory Coast	C38-C40
Madagascar	C92
Mali	C65
Mauritania	C80
Niger	C104
Senegal	C68
Togo	C104
Upper Volta	C62

Concorde Issue

Concorde in Flight
CD129

First flight of the prototpye Concorde super-sonic plane at Toulouse, Mar. 1, 1969.

1969

Afars & Issas	C56
Comoro Isls.	C29
France	C42
Fr. Polynesia	C50
Fr. So. & Antarctic Terr.	C18
New Caledonia	C63
St. Pierre & Miquelon	C40
Wallis & Futuna Isls.	C30

Development Bank Issue

Bank Emblem—CD130

Fifth anniversary of the African Development Bank.

1969

Cameroun	499
Chad	217
Congo, P.R.	181-182
Ivory Coast	281
Mali	127-128
Mauritania	267
Niger	220
Senegal	317-318
Upper Volta	201

ILO Issue

ILO Headquarters, Geneva, and Emblem
CD131

50th anniversary of the International Labor Organization.

1969-70

Afars & Issas	337
Comoro Isls.	83
Fr. Polynesia	251-252
Fr. So. & Antarctic Terr.	35
New Caledonia	379
St. Pierre & Miquelon	396
Wallis & Futuna Isls.	172

ASECNA Issue

Map of Africa, Plane and Airport
CD132

10th anniversary of the Agency for the Security of Aerial Navigation in Africa and Madagascar (ASECNA, Agence pour la Securite de la Navigation Aerienne en Afrique et a Madagascar).

1969-70

Cameroun	500
Cent. African Rep.	119
Chad	222
Congo, P.R.	197
Dahomey	269
Gabon	260
Ivory Coast	287
Mali	130
Niger	221
Senegal	321
Upper Volta	204

U.P.U. Headquarters Issue

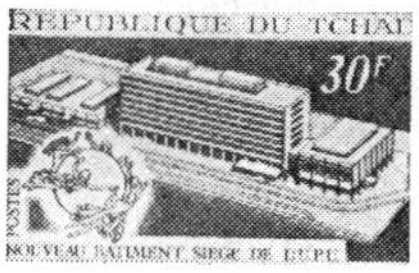

U.P.U. Headquarters and Emblem
CD133

New Universal Postal Union headquarters, Bern, Switzerland.

1970

Afars & Issas	342
Algeria	443
Cameroun	503-504
Cent. African Rep.	125
Chad	225
Comoro Isls.	84
Congo, P.R.	216
Fr. Polynesia	261-262
Fr. So. & Antarctic Terr.	36
Gabon	258
Ivory Coast	295
Madagascar	444
Mali	134-135
Mauritania	283
New Caledonia	382
Niger	231-232
St. Pierre & Miquelon	397-398
Senegal	328-329
Tunisia	535
Wallis & Futuna Isls.	173

De Gaulle Issue

General de Gaulle 1940
CD134

First anniversay of the death of Charles de Gaulle, (1890-1970), President of France.

1971-72

Afars & Issas	356-357
Comoro Isls.	104-105
France	1322-1325
Fr. Polynesia	270-271
Fr. So. & Antarctic Terr.	52-53
New Caledonia	393-394
Reunion	377, 380
St. Pierre & Miquelon	417-418
Wallis & Futuna Isls.	177-178

African Postal Union Issue, 1971

Carved Stool, UAMPT Building, Brazzaville, Congo
CD135

10th anniversary of the establishment of the African and Malagasy Posts and Telecommunications Union, UAMPT.

Each stamp has a different native design.

1971, Nov. 13

Cameroun	C177
Cent. African Rep.	C89
Chad	C94
Congo, P.R.	C136
Dahomey	C146
Gabon	C120
Ivory Coast	C47
Mauritania	C113
Niger	C164
Rwanda	C8
Senegal	C105
Togo	C166
Upper Volta	C97

West African Monetary Union Issue

African Couple, City, Village and Commemorative Coin
CD136

10th anniversary of the West African Monetary Union.

1972, Nov. 2

Dahomey	300
Ivory Coast	331
Mauritania	299
Niger	258
Senegal	374
Togo	825
Upper Volta	280

African Postal Union Issue, 1973

Telecommunications Symbols and Map of Africa
CD137

11th anniversary of the African and Malagasy Posts and Telecommunications Union (UAMPT).

1973, Sept. 12

Cameroun	574
Cent. African Rep.	194
Chad	272
Congo, P.R.	289
Dahomey	311
Gabon	320
Ivory Coast	361
Madagascar	500
Mauritania	304
Niger	287
Rwanda	540
Senegal	393
Togo	849
Upper Volta	285

Philexafrique II—Essen Issue

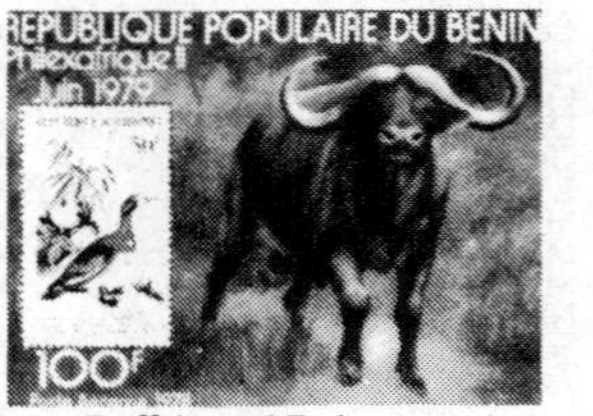

Buffalo and Dahomey
No. C33
CD138

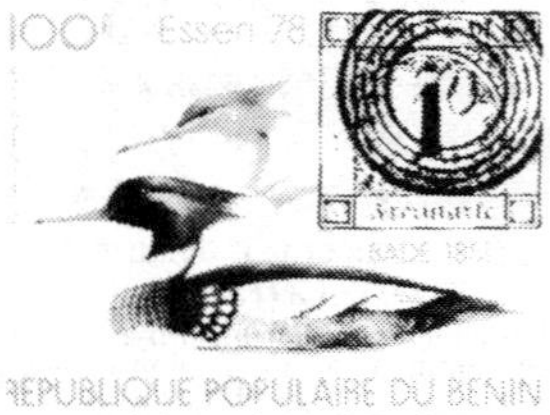

Wild Ducks and Baden
No. 1
CD139

Designs: Indigenous fauna, local and German stamps.

Types CD138-CD139 printed horizontally and vertically se-tenant in sheets of 10 (2x5). Label between horizontal pairs alternately commemoratives Philexafrique II, Libreville, Gabon, June 1978, and 2nd International Stamp Fair, Essen, Germany, Nov. 1-5.

1978-1979

Benin	C285-C286
Central Africa	C200-C201
Chad	C238-C239
Congo Republic	C245-C246
Djibouti	C121-C122
Gabon	C215-C216
Ivory Coast	C64-C65
Mali	C356-C357
Mauritania	C185-C186
Niger	C291-C292
Rwanda	C12-C13
Senegal	C146-C147
Togo	C363-C364
Upper Volta	C253-C254

Historical Footnotes

Scouting Year: 75th anniversary of scouting and 125th birth anniversary of its founder, Lord Baden-Powell (1857-1941).

Robert Koch: Centenary of tuberculosis bacillus discovery by Robert Koch (1843-1910), German physician. Awarded 1905 Nobel Prize for physiology and medicine; also discovered cholera bacillus, 1883.

George Washington: 250th birth anniversary of George Washington (1732-1799), first U.S. president.

Charles Darwin: Death centenary of Charles Darwin (1809-1882), British naturalist. Traveled through South America and Australasia, 1831-1836, aboard the Beagle developing his theory of evolution. Published findings in *On the Origin of Species,* 1859.

Norman Rockwell (1894-1978): American illustrator who is best known for his paintings of people in everyday situations. Many of his works have been on the covers of *The Saturday Evening Post, Boy's Life, American Boy* and *St. Nicholas.*

Lewis B. Carroll (1832-1898): English author of the childhood classics *Alice in Wonderland* and *Through the Looking Glass.* He also wrote many works on mathematics under his real name, Charles Lutwidge Dodgson.

World Cup Soccer: The 12th World Cup Soccer Championship was held in Spain from June 13th to July 11th. The series, held every 4 years, opened in Barcelona with Belgium over Argentina before a crowd of 95,000. The 52 games were held in 17 stadiums in 14 cities with 24 participating teams. The final game was played in Madrid with Italy defeating Germany by a score of 3 to 1.

Olympic Games: The 14th Winter Olympic Games were held in Sarajevo, Jugoslavia, Feb. 7-18, 1984. Russia captured 25 medals, though East Germany won the most gold, with 9. The United States Received 4 gold and 4 silver medals, primarily on the surprisingly strong showing of the ski team.

The 23rd Olympic Games were held in Los Angeles, July 28-August 12, 1984, marred by a boycott by Russia and other eastern bloc nations. The boycott was viewed as a retaliatory action against the U.S. led boycott of the 1980 Moscow Olympics. The U.S. gathered 174 medals, 83 of them gold, to lead all participants.

Universal Postal Union Congress: The 19th Universal Postal Union Congress was held in Hamburg, Germany, July 18-July 27, 1984. It was attended by approximately 750 delegates from 166 member countries.

International Stamp Exhibition:
AUSIPEX '84 Melbourne, Australia, Sept. 21-30, 1984.
PHILATELIA '84 Stuttgart, Germany, Oct. 5-7, 1984.
FILACENTO '84 The Hague, Netherlands, Sept. 6-9, 1984.
ITALIA '85 Rome, Italy, Oct. 25-Nov. 3, 1985.

PANAMA

LOCATION — Central America between Costa Rica and Colombia
GOVT. — Republic
AREA — 30,134 sq. mi.
POP. — 1,970,000 (est. 1983)
CAPITAL — Panama

Formerly a department of the Republic ofColombia, Panama gained its independence in 1903. Dividing the country at its center is the Panama Canal.

100 Centavos = 1 Peso
100 Centesimos = 1 Balboa (1906)

Catalogue values for unused stamps in this country are for Never Hinged items, beginning with Scott 350 in the regular postage section, Scott C82 in the airpost section, Scott CB1 in the airpost semi-postal section, and Scott RA21 in the postal tax section.

Issued under Colombian Dominion

Coat of Arms
A1 A2

1878 Unwmk. Litho. *Imperf.*
Thin Wove Paper.

1	A1	5c gray grn	25.00	22.50
a		5c yel grn	25.00	22.50
2	A1	10c blue	65.00	60.00
3	A1	20c rose red	40.00	35.00
4	A2	50c buff	*1,500.*	

All values of this issue are known rouletted unofficially.

Medium Thick Paper.

5	A1	5c bl grn	25.00	22.50
6	A1	10c blue	65.00	
7	A2	50c orange	16.50	

Nos. 5-7 were printed before Nos. 1-4, according to Panamanian archives.

Values for used Nos. 1-5 are for handstamped postal cancellations.

These stamps have been reprinted in a number of shades, on thin to moderately thick, white or yellowish paper. They are without gum or with white, crackly gum. Some of the 50c stamps appear to have been reprinted from the original stone; they are all in a golden yellow shade, less brownish than the orange originals. All values have been reprinted from new stones made from retouched dies. The marks of retouching are plainly to be seen in the sea and clouds. On the original 10c the shield in the upper left corner has two blank sections; on the reprints the design of this shield is completed. The impression of these reprints is frequently blurred.

Map of Panama
A3 A4

1887-88 *Perf. 13½*

8	A3	1c blk, *green*	1.00	1.00
9	A3	2c blk, *pink* ('88)	1.00	1.20
a		2c blk, *sal*	1.00	1.20
10	A3	5c blk, *blue*	1.00	40
11	A3	10c blk, *yellow*	1.00	45
a		Imperf., pair		
12	A3	20c blk, *lilac*	1.10	65
13	A3	50c brn ('88)	1.50	80
a		Imperf.		
		Nos. 8-13 (6)	6.60	4.50

1892 Pelure Paper

14	A3	50c brown	1.60	1.00

The stamps of this issue have been reprinted on papers of slightly different colors from those of the originals. These are: 1c yellow green, 2c deep rose, 5c bright blue, 10c straw, 20c violet. The 50c is printed from a very worn stone, in a lighter brown than the originals. The series includes a 10c on lilac paper. All these stamps are to be found perforated, imperforate, imperforate horizontally or imperforate vertically. At the same time that they were made, impressions were struck upon a variety of glazed and surface-colored papers.

Wove Paper

1892-96 Engr. *Perf. 12*

15	A4	1c green	25	22
16	A4	2c rose	40	25
17	A4	5c blue	60	50
18	A4	10c orange	35	25
19	A4	20c vio ('95)	50	35
20	A4	50c bis brn ('96)	50	35
21	A4	1p lake ('96)	6.00	4.00
		Nos. 15-21 (7)	8.60	5.92

Preceding Issues Surcharged:

HABILITADO. 1894 1 CENTAVO. — a

HABILITADO. 1894 1 CENTAVO. — b

HABILITADO. 1894 5 CENTAVOS. — c

HABILITADO. 1894 5 CENTAVOS. — d

HABILITADO. 1894 5 CENTAVOS. — e

HABILITADO. 1894 10 CENTAVOS. — f

HABILITADO. 1894 10 CENTAVOS, — g

1894 Black Surcharge

22	(a)	1c on 2c rose	50	42
a		Inverted surcharge	2.50	2.50
b		Double surcharge		
23	(b)	1c on 2c rose	40	35
a		"CCNTAVO"	2.50	2.50
b		Inverted surcharge	2.50	2.50
c		Double surcharge	5.50	5.50

Red Surcharge

24	(c)	5c on 20c blk, *lil*	1.40	1.20
a		Inverted surcharge	9.00	9.00
b		Double surcharge		
c		Without "HABILITADO"		
25	(d)	5c on 20c blk, *lil*	2.00	1.90
a		"CCNTAVOS"	7.50	7.50
b		Inverted surcharge	9.00	9.00
c		Double surcharge		
d		Without "HABILITADO"		
26	(e)	5c on 20c blk, *lil*	3.50	3.00
a		Inverted surcharge	9.00	9.00
b		Double surcharge		
27	(f)	10c on 50c brn	1.50	1.50
a		"1894" omitted		
b		Inverted surcharge		
c		"CCNTAVOS"	12.00	
28	(g)	10c on 50c brn	8.00	8.00
a		"CCNTAVOS"	25.00	
b		Inverted surcharge		

Pelure Paper.

29	(f)	10c on 50c brn	1.90	1.60
a		"1894" omitted	4.00	
b		Inverted surcharge	9.00	9.00
30	(g)	10c on 50c brn	6.50	6.00
a		"CCNTAVOS"		
b		Without "HABILITADO"		
c		Inverted surcharge	16.00	16.00
d		Double surcharge		
		Nos. 22-30 (9)	25.70	23.97

There are several settings of these surcharges. Usually the surcharge is about 15½ mm. high, but in one setting, it is only 13 mm. All the types are to be found with a comma after "CENTAVOS". Nos. 24, 25, 26, 29 and 30 exist with the surcharge printed sideways. Nos. 23, 24 and 29 may be found with an inverted "A" instead of "V" in "CENTAVOS". There are also varieties caused by dropped or broken letters.

Issues of the Republic.
Issued in the City of Panama.
Stamps of 1892-96 Overprinted:

REPUBLICA DE
PANAMA

1903, Nov. 16
Rose Handstamp.

51	A4	1c green	1.00	65
52	A4	2c rose	2.50	1.90
53	A4	5c blue	65	55
54	A4	10c yellow	1.10	1.00
55	A4	20c violet	2.00	1.50
56	A4	50c bis brn	5.50	4.00
57	A4	1p lake	30.00	25.00
		Nos. 51-57 (7)	42.75	34.60

Blue Black Handstamp.

58	A4	1c green	1.00	55
59	A4	2c rose	65	55
60	A4	5c blue	4.00	3.50
61	A4	10c yellow	2.25	1.90
62	A4	20c violet	6.00	4.50
63	A4	50c bis brn	6.00	4.50
64	A4	1p lake	30.00	25.00
		Nos. 58-64 (7)	49.90	40.50

The stamps of this issue are to be found with the handstamp placed horizontally, vertically or diagonally; inverted; double; double, one inverted; double, both inverted; in pairs, one without handstamp; etc.

This handstamp has been reprinted in brown rose on the 1, 5, 20 and 50c, in purple on the 1, 2, 50c and 1p, and in magenta on the 5, 10, 20 and 50c. Reprints were also made in rose and black when the handstamp was nearly worn out, so that the "R" of "REPUBLICA" appears to be shorter than usual, and the bottom part of "LI" has been broken off. The "P" of "PANAMA" leans to the left and the tops of "NA" are broken. Many of these varieties are found inverted, double, etc.

Overprinted

PANAMA PANAMA

1903, Dec. 3
Bar in Similar Color to Stamp.
Black Overprint.

65	A4	2c rose	1.20	1.00
a		"PANAMA" 15mm long	1.60	
b		Violet bar	4.50	
66	A4	5c blue	80.00	
a		"PANAMA" 15mm long	80.00	
67	A4	10c yellow	1.20	1.20
a		"PANAMA" 15mm long	3.00	
b		Horizontal ovpt.	11.00	

Gray Black Overprint.

68	A4	2c rose	1.00	80
a		"PANAMA" 15mm long	1.20	

Carmine Overprint.

69	A4	5c blue	1.20	1.20
a		"PANAMA" 15mm long	1.90	
b		Bar only	20.00	18.00
c		Double overprint		
70	A4	20c violet	4.00	3.50
a		"PANAMA" 15mm long	4.50	
b		Double overprint, one in blk	22.50	
		Nos. 65,67-70 (5)	8.60	7.70

This overprint was set up to cover fifty stamps. "PANAMA" is normally 13mm. long and 1¾mm. high but, in two rows in each sheet, it measures 15 to 16mm. This word may be found with one or more of the letters taller than usual; with one, two or three inverted "V"s" instead of "A"s"; with an inverted "Y" instead of "A"; an inverted "N"; an "A" with accent; and a fancy "P". Owing to misplaced impressions, stamps exist with "PANAMA" once only, twice on one side, or three times.

Overprinted in Red

PANAMA PANAMA

1903, Dec.

71	A4	1c green	40	35
a		"PANAMA" 15mm long	60	
b		"PANAMA" reading down	2.25	
c		"PANAMA" reading up and down	2.25	
d		Double overprint	5.50	
72	A4	2c rose	25	22
a		"PANAMA" 15mm long	60	
b		"PANAMA" reading down		
c		"PANAMA" reading up and down	2.50	
d		Double overprint	5.50	
73	A4	20c violet	1.00	80
a		"PANAMA" 15mm long	1.50	
b		"PANAMA" reading down		
c		"PANAMA" reading up and down	5.50	5.50
d		Double overprint	12.00	12.00
74	A4	50c bis brn	2.00	1.60
a		"PANAMA" 15mm long	3.50	
b		"PANAMA" reading up and down	8.00	8.00
c		Double overprint	4.00	4.00
75	A4	1p lake	4.50	4.50
a		"PANAMA" 15mm long	4.00	
b		"PANAMA" reading up and down	11.00	11.00
c		Double ovpt.	10.00	
d		Inverted ovpt.		16.00
		Nos. 71-75 (5)	8.15	7.47

This setting appears to be a re-arrangement (or two very similar re-arrangements) of the previous "b". The overprint covers fifty stamps. "PANAMA" usually reads upward but sheets of the 1, 2 and 20c exist with the word reading upward on one half the sheet and downward on the other half.

In one re-arrangement one stamp in fifty has the word reading in both directions. Nearly all the varieties of setting "b" are repeated in setting "c" excepting the inverted "Y" and fancy "P". There are also additional varieties of large letters and "PANAMA" occasionally has an "A" missing or inverted. There are misplaced impressions, as the previous setting.

Overprinted in Red

PANAMA PANAMA

1904-05

76	A4	1c green	25	22
a		Both words reading up	1.20	
b		Both words reading down	2.25	
c		Double overprint		
d		Pair, one without overprint	6.00	
e		"PANAAM"	16.00	
f		Inverted "M" in "PANAMA"	60	
77	A4	2c rose	25	22
a		Both words reading up	2.00	
b		Both words reading down	2.00	
c		Double overprint	8.00	
d		Double overprint, one inverted	11.00	
e		Inverted "M" in "PANAMA"	60	
78	A4	5c blue	35	25
a		Both words reading up	2.50	
b		Both words reading down	3.50	
c		Inverted overprint	10.00	
d		"PANAAM"	20.00	
e		"PANANA"	6.50	
f		"PAMANA"	4.00	
g		Inverted "M" in "PANAMA"	1.40	
h		Double overprint	16.00	
79	A4	10c yellow	35	25
a		Both words reading up	4.00	
b		Both words reading down	4.00	
c		Double overprint	12.00	
d		Inverted overprint	5.50	
e		"PANANA"	8.00	
f		Inverted "M" in "PANAMA"	2.00	
g		Red brown overprint	6.00	3.50
80	A4	20c violet	1.60	1.00
a		Both words reading up	4.00	
b		Both words reading down	8.00	
81	A4	50c bis brn	2.50	2.00
a		Both words reading up	8.25	
b		Both words reading down	8.00	
c		Double overprint		
82	A4	1p lake	4.00	3.50
a		Both words reading up	10.00	
b		Both words reading down	10.00	
c		Double overprint		
d		Double overprint, one inverted	16.00	
		Nos. 76-82 (7)	9.30	7.44

This overprint is also set up to cover fifty stamps. One stamp in each fifty has "PANAMA" reading upward at both sides. Another has the word reading downward at both sides, a third has an inverted "V" in place of the last "A" and a fourth has a small thick "N". In a resetting all these varieties are corrected except the inverted "V". There are misplaced overprints as before.

Later printings show other varieties and have the bar 2½ instead of 2mm wide. The colors of the various printings of Nos. 76 to 82 range from carmine to almost pink.

Experts consider the black overprint on the 50c to be bogus.

The 20c violet and 50c bister brown exist with bar 2½mm wide, including the error "PAMANA", but are not known to have been issued. Some copies have been canceled "to oblige".

Issued in Colon.

Handstamped in Magenta or Violet — REPUBLICA DE PANAMA

On Stamps of 1892-96.

1903-04

101 A4 1c green 45 40
102 A4 2c rose 55 50
103 A4 5c blue 65 55
104 A4 10c yellow 2.00 1.60
105 A4 20c violet 4.00 3.50
106 A4 1p lake 80.00 70.00

On Stamps of 1887-92.

Ordinary Wove Paper.

107 A3 50c brown 20.00 15.00
Nos. 101-107 (7) 107.65 91.55

Pelure Paper.

108 A3 50c brown 70.00

Handstamped in Magenta, Violet or Red — PANAMA

On Stamps of 1892-96.

109 A4 1c green 5.50 4.00
110 A4 2c rose 5.50 4.00
111 A4 5c blue 5.50 4.00
112 A4 10c yellow 8.25 6.00
113 A4 20c violet 12.00 9.00
114 A4 1p lake 70.00 60.00

On Stamps of 1887-92.

Ordinary Wove Paper.

115 A3 5c brown 35.00 25.00
Nos. 109-115 (7) 141.75 112.00

Pelure Paper.

116 A3 50c brown 50.00 37.50

The first note after No. 64 applies also to Nos. 101-116.

The handstamps on Nos. 109-116 have been counterfeited.

REPUBLICA DE PANAMA

Stamps with this overprint were a private speculation. They exist on cover.

Overprinted g — *República de Panamá.*

On Stamps of 1892-96.

Carmine Overprint.

129 A4 1c green 40 35
a Inverted overprint 6.00
b Double overprint 2.25
c Double overprint, one inverted 6.00
130 A4 5c blue 50 40

Brown Overprint.

131 A4 1c green 12.00
a Double overprint, one inverted

Black Overprint.

132 A4 1c green 40.00 30.00
a Vertical overprint 42.50
b Inverted overprint 42.50
c Double overprint, one inverted 42.50
133 A4 2c rose 50 40
a Inverted overprint
134 A4 10c yellow 50 40
a Inverted overprint 4.00
b Double overprint 16.00
c Double overprint, one inverted 6.00
135 A4 20c violet 50 40
a Inverted overprint 4.00
b Double overprint 5.50
136 A4 1p lake 16.00 14.00

On Stamps of 1887-88.

Blue Overprint.

Ordinary Wove Paper.

137 A3 50c brown 3.00 2.50

Pelure Paper.

138 A3 50c brown 3.00 2.50
a Double overprint 14.00

This overprint is set up to cover fifty stamps. In each fifty there are four stamps without accent on the last "a" of "Panama", one with accent on the "a" of "Republica" and one with a thick, upright "i".

Overprinted in Carmine — REPUBLICA DE PANAMA.

On Stamp of 1892-96.

139 A4 20c violet 70.00 55.00
a Double overprint

Issued in Bocas del Toro.

Stamps of 1892-96 Overprinted.

Handstamped in Violet — R DE PANAMA

1903-04

151 A4 1c green 20.00 14.00
152 A4 2c rose 20.00 14.00
153 A4 5c blue 25.00 16.00
154 A4 10c yellow 15.00 8.25
155 A4 20c violet 50.00 30.00
156 A4 50c bis brn 100.00 55.00
157 A4 1p lake 140.00 110.00
Nos. 151-157 (7) 370.00 247.25

The handstamp is known double and inverted. Counterfeits exist.

Handstamped in Violet — Panama

158 A4 1c green 70.00
159 A4 2c rose 70.00
160 A4 5c blue 80.00
161 A4 10c yellow 100.00
162 A4 1p lake 225.00

This handstamp was applied to these 5 stamps only by favor, experts state. Counterfeits are numerous.

General Issues

A5

1905, Feb. 4 Engr. *Perf. 12*

179 A5 1c green 60 40
180 A5 2c rose 80 50

Panama's Declaration of Independence from the Colombian Republic, Nov. 3, 1903.

Surcharged in Vermilion on Stamps of 1892-96 Issue:

Panamá 1 ct. Panamá

1906

181 A4 1c on 20c vio 25 22
a "Panrma" 2.25 2.25
b "Pnnama" 2.25 2.25
c "Pauama" 2.25 2.25
d Inverted surcharge 4.00 4.00
e Double surcharge 3.50 3.50
f Double surcharge, one inverted

PANAMÁ 2 cts. PANAMÁ

182 A4 2c on 50c bis brn 25 22
a 3rd "A" of "PANAMA" inverted 2.25 2.25
b Both "PANAMA" reading down 4.00 4.00
c Double surcharge
d Inverted surcharge 2.50

The 2c on 20c violet was never issued to the public.

Carmine Surcharge.

183 A4 5c on 1p lake 60 40
a Both "PANAMA" reading down 6.00 6.00
b "5" omitted
c Double surcharge
d Inverted surcharge
e 3rd "A" of "PANAMA" inverted 5.50 5.50

On Stamp of 1903-04, No. 75.

184 A4 5c on 1p lake 60 40
a "PANAMA" 15mm long
b "PANAMA" reading up and down
c Both "PANAMA" reading down
d Inverted surcharge
e Double surcharge
f 3rd "A" of "PANAMA" inverted

National Flag — A6

Vasco Nuñez de Balboa — A7

Hernández de Córdoba A8

Coat of Arms A9

Justo Arosemena A10

Manuel J. Hurtado A11

José de Obaldía A12

Tomás Herrera A13

José de Fábrega — A14

1906-07 Engr. *Perf. 11½*

185 A6 ½c org & multi 45 35
186 A7 1c dk grn & blk 45 35
187 A8 2c scar & blk 60 35
188 A9 2½c red org 60 35
189 A10 5c bl & blk 80 35
a 5c ultra & blk 1.00 50
190 A11 8c pur & blk 1.00 65
191 A12 10c vio & blk 1.20 50
192 A13 25c brn & blk 2.50 1.00
193 A14 50c black 6.50 3.50
Nos. 185-193 (9) 14.10 7.40

Inverted centers exist of Nos. 185-187, 189, 189a, 190-193, Value, each $25. Nos. 185-193 exist imperf.

Map — A17

Balboa — A18

Córdoba A19

Arms A20

Arosemena A21

Obaldía A23

1909-15 *Perf. 12*

195 A17 ½c org ('11) 65 40
a Booklet pane of 6
196 A17 ½c rose ('15) 65 45
197 A18 1c dk grn & blk 65 45
a Inverted center
b Bklt. pane of 6 65.00
198 A19 2c red & blk 65 25
a Bklt. pane of 6 65.00
199 A20 2½c red org 1.00 25
a Booklet pane of 6
200 A21 5c bl & blk 1.20 25
a Bklt. pane of 6 65.00
201 A23 10c vio & blk 3.50 1.00
a Booklet pane of 6
Nos. 195-201 (7) 8.30 3.05

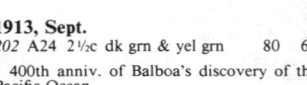

Balboa Sighting Pacific Ocean, His Dog at His Feet — A24

1913, Sept.

202 A24 2½c dk grn & yel grn 80 65

400th anniv. of Balboa's discovery of the Pacific Ocean.

Panama Exposition Issue.

Chorrera Falls — A25

Map of Panama Canal — A26

Balboa Taking Possession of the Pacific A27

Ruins of Cathedral of Old Panama A28

Palace of Arts — A29

Gatun Locks — A30

Culebra Cut — A31

Santo Domingo Monastery's Flat Arch — A32

1915-16 *Perf. 12*

204 A25	½c ol grn & blk	60	35
205 A26	1c dk grn & blk	65	35
206 A27	2c car & blk	80	35
a	2c ver & blk ('16)	80	35
208 A28	2½c scar & blk	1.00	40
209 A29	3c vio & blk	1.20	50
210 A30	5c bl & blk	1.50	40
a	Center inverted	650.00	550.00
211 A31	10c org & blk	2.50	80
212 A32	20c brn & blk	12.50	4.00
a	Center inverted	300.00	
	Nos. 204-212 (8)	20.75	7.15

Manuel J. Hurtado — A33

1916

213 A33	8c vio & blk	5.50	2.25

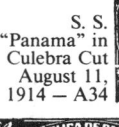

S. S. "Panama" in Culebra Cut August 11, 1914 — A34

S. S. "Panama" in Culebra Cut August 11, 1914 — A35

S. S. "Cristobal" in Gatun Lock — A36

1918

214 A34	12c pur & blk	18.00	5.00
215 A35	15c brt bl & blk	12.00	2.50
216 A36	24c yel brn & blk	18.00	2.50

No. 208 Surcharged in Dark Blue

1519 1919

2 CENTESIMOS 2

1919, Aug. 15

217 A28	2c on 2½c scar & blk	30	30
a	Inverted surcharge	10.00	8.25
b	Double surcharge	12.00	10.00

City of Panama, 400th anniversary.

Dry Dock at Balboa — A38

Ship in Pedro Miguel Lock — A39

1920 **Engr.**

218 A38	50c org & blk	20.00	10.00
219 A39	1b dk vio & blk	30.00	15.00

Centenary of Independence Issue.

Arms of Panama City A40

José Vallarino A41

"Land Gate" A42

Simon Bolivar A43

Statue of Cervantes A44

Bolivar's Tribute A45

Carlos de Ycaza — A46

Municipal Building in 1821 and 1921 — A47

Statue of Balboa A48

Spanish Church A49

Herrera A50

Fábrega A51

1921, Nov.

220 A40	½c orange	60	25
221 A41	1c green	60	20
222 A42	2c carmine	70	25
223 A43	2½c red	1.60	1.00
224 A44	3c dl vio	1.60	1.00
225 A45	5c blue	1.20	40
226 A46	8c ol grn	6.00	2.50
227 A47	10c violet	3.50	1.40
228 A48	15c lt bl	4.50	1.60
229 A49	20c ol brn	8.25	4.00
230 A50	24c blk brn	8.25	4.50
231 A51	50c black	15.00	6.50
	Nos. 220-231 (12)	51.80	23.60

Centenary of independence.

Hurtado A52

Arms A53

1921, Nov. 28

232 A52	2c dk grn	50	35

Issued to commemorate the birth centenary of Manuel José Hurtado (1821-1887), president and folklore writer.

No. 208 Surcharged in Black

1923

2 CENTESIMOS 2

1923

233 A28	2c on 2½c scar & blk	35	35

Surcharge varieties include wrong or omitted date, double surcharge and pair, one without surcharge. Value $2.50 each.

Two stamps in each sheet have a bar above "CENTESIMOS."

1924, May **Engr.**

234 A53	½c orange	15	6
235 A53	1c dk grn	15	6
236 A53	2c carmine	20	6
237 A53	5c dk bl	40	12
238 A53	10c dk vio	55	18
239 A53	12c ol grn	70	35
240 A53	15c ultra	90	35
241 A53	24c yel brn	1.90	50
242 A53	50c orange	4.25	90
243 A53	1b black	6.50	2.25
	Nos. 234-243 (10)	15.70	4.83

Bolivar Congress Issue.

Bolivar A54

Statue of Bolivar A55

Bolivar Hall — A56

1926, June 10 *Perf. 12½*

244 A54	½c orange	25	10
245 A54	1c dk grn	25	10
246 A54	2c scarlet	30	18
247 A54	4c gray	38	18
248 A54	5c dk bl	50	30
249 A55	8c lilac	1.00	45
250 A55	10c dl vio	90	42
251 A55	12c ol grn	1.25	65
252 A55	15c ultra	1.75	75
253 A55	20c brown	3.75	1.20
254 A56	24c blk vio	4.50	90
255 A56	50c black	7.50	3.00
	Nos. 244-255 (12)	22.33	8.23

Lindbergh's Airplane, "The Spirit of St. Louis" — A57

Lindbergh's Airplane and Map of Panama A58

1928, Jan. 9 **Typo.** ***Rouletted 7***

256 A57	2c dk red & blk, *sal*	30	25
257 A58	5c dk bl, *grn*	45	38

Commemorating the visit of Colonel Charles A. Lindbergh to Central America by airplane.

No. 232 Overprinted in Red

1903
NOV 3 BRE
1928

1928, Nov. 1 *Perf. 12*

258 A52	2c dk grn	25	16

25th anniversary of the Republic.

No. 247 Surcharged in Black

1830 - 1930
17 DE DICIEMBRE
UN CENTESIMO

1930, Dec. 17 *Perf. 12½, 13*

259 A54	1c on 4c gray	22	20

Issued in commemoration of the centenary of the death of Simon Bolivar, the Liberator.

Nos. 244-246 Overprinted in Red or Blue. **HABILITADA**

1932 *Perf. 12½.*

260 A54	½c org (R)	20	20
261 A54	1c dk grn (R)	22	16
a	Double overprint	18.00	
262 A54	2c scar (Bl)	16	16

No. 252 Surcharged in Red

HABILITADA
10 c.

263 A55	10c on 15c ultra	65	35
a	Double surcharge	55.00	

No. 220 Overprinted as in 1932 in Black.

1933 *Perf. 12*

Overprint 19mm. Long

264 A40	½c orange	35	20
a	Overprint 17mm. Long		

Dr. Manuel Amador Guerrero — A60

1933, July 3 Engr. *Perf. 12½*

265	A60	2c dk red	40	20

Commemorative of the centenary of the birth of Dr. Manuel Amador Guerrero, founder of the Republic of Panama and its first President.

No. 251 Surcharged in Red

HABILITADA
10 c.

1933

266	A55	10c on 12c ol grn	1.00	65

No. 253 Overprinted in Red HABILITADA

267	A55	20c brown	1.40	1.00

José Domingo de Obaldia — A61

Quotation from Emerson — A63

National Institute — A64

Designs: 2c, Eusebio A. Morales. 12c, Justo A. Facio. 15c, Pablo Arosemena.

1934, July Engr. *Perf. 14*

268	A61	1c dk grn	80	50
269	A61	2c scarlet	80	50
270	A63	5c dk bl	1.25	80
271	A64	10c brown	3.50	1.40
272	A61	12c yel grn	6.00	2.00
273	A61	15c Prus bl	8.25	2.25
		Nos. 268-273 (6)	20.60	7.45

Issued in commemoration of the 25th anniversary of the First National Institute.

Nos. 248, 227 Overprinted in Black or Red HABILITADA

1935-36 *Perf. 12½, 12*

274	A54	5c dk bl	40	25
275	A47	10c vio (R) ('36)	65	35

No. 225 Surcharged in Red

HABILITADA
B. 0.01

1936 *Perf. 11½*

276	A45	1c on 5c bl	40	35
a.		Lines of surcharge 1½mm between	6.50	

No. 241 Surcharged in Blue

1836 1936

PABLO AROSEMENA
2 CENTESIMOS

1936, Sept. 24 *Perf. 12*

277	A53	2c on 24c yel brn	50	40
a.		Double surch.	20.00	

Issued to commemorate the centenary of the birth of Pablo Arosemena, president of Panama in 1910-12. See Nos. C19-C20.

Ruins of Custom House, Portobelo A67

Designs: 1c, Panama Tree. 2c, "La Pollera." 5c, Simon Bolivar. 10c, Cathedral Tower Ruins, Old Panama. 15c, Francisco Garcia y Santos, 20c, Madden Dam, Panama Canal. 25c, Columbus. 50c, Gaillard Cut. 1b, Panama Cathedral.

1936, Dec. Engr. *Perf. 11½*

278	A67	½c yel org	40	20
279	A67	1c bl grn	40	20
280	A67	2c car rose	40	20
281	A67	5c blue	65	25
282	A67	10c dk vio	1.00	40
283	A67	15c turq bl	1.00	55
284	A67	20c red	1.60	1.00
285	A67	25c blk brn	2.00	1.40
286	A67	50c orange	6.50	3.50
287	A67	1b black	15.00	10.00
		Nos. 278-287 (10)	28.95	17.70

Issued to commemorate the 4th Postal Congress of the Americas and Spain. See Nos. C21-C26.

Stamps of 1936 Overprinted in Red or Blue

U
P
U

1937

288	A67	½c yel org (R)	35	20
a.		Inverted overprint	18.00	
289	A67	1c bl grn (R)	40	20
290	A67	2c car rose (Bl)	40	20
291	A67	5c bl (R)	40	25
292	A67	10c dk vio (R)	1.00	40
293	A67	15c turq bl (R)	5.50	3.00
294	A67	20c red (Bl)	1.60	1.00
295	A67	25c blk brn (R)	2.50	1.40
296	A67	50c org (Bl)	8.25	5.00
297	A67	1b blk (R)	15.00	10.00
		Nos. 288-297 (10)	35.40	21.65

See Nos. C27-C32.

Stamps of 1921-26 Overprinted in Red or Blue 1937-38

1937, July *Perf. 12, 12½*

298	A54	½c org (R)	80	65
a.		Inverted overprint	30.00	
299	A41	1c grn (R)	25	22
a.		Inverted overprint	30.00	
300	A54	1c dk grn (R)	25	22
301	A52	2c dk grn (R)	35	20
302	A54	2c scar (Bl)	35	25

Stamps of 1921-26 Surcharged in Red

1937-38
2¢

303	A54	2c on 4c gray	40	25
304	A46	2c on 8c ol grn	40	25
305	A55	2c on 8c lil	40	25
306	A55	2c on 10c dl vio	40	25
307	A55	2c on 12c ol grn	40	25
308	A48	2c on 15c lt bl	40	25
309	A50	2c on 24c blk brn	40	25
310	A51	2c on 50c blk	40	25
		Nos. 298-310 (13)	5.20	3.54

Footnotes often refer you to other stamps of the same design.

Ricardo Arango A77

Juan A. Guizado A78

Fire Fighting A79

Modern Fire Fighting Equipment A80

Firemen's Monument A81

David H. Brandon A82

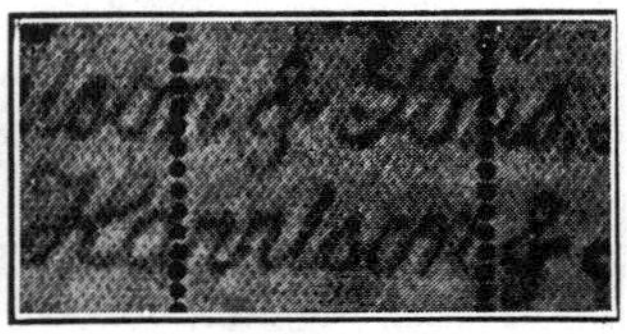

Wmk. 233

Wmk. "Harrison & Sons, London" in Script Letters. (233)
Perf. 14x14½, 14½x14

1937, Nov. 25 Photo.

311	A77	½c org red	40	20
312	A78	1c green	40	20
313	A79	2c red	40	25
314	A80	5c brt bl	60	25
315	A81	10c purple	1.00	60
316	A82	12c yel grn	1.60	1.00
		Nos. 311-316,C40-C42 (9)	6.75	4.25

50th anniversary of the Fire Department.

Cathedral Tower and Statue of Liberty, Flags of Panama and United States — A83

Engr. & Litho.
1938, Dec. 7 Unwmk. *Perf. 12½*
Center in Black; Flags in Red and Ultramarine.

317	A83	1c dp grn	30	15
318	A83	2c carmine	38	18
319	A83	5c blue	65	30
320	A83	12c olive	1.25	45
321	A83	15c brt ultra	1.50	75
		Nos. 317-321 (5)	4.08	1.83

150th anniv. of the Constitution of the United States of America. See Nos. C49-C53.

No. 236 Overprinted in Black

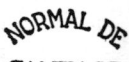

NORMAL DE
SANTIAGO
JUNIO 5 1938

1938, June 5 *Perf. 12*

321A	A53	2c carmine	25	22
b.		Inverted overprint	22.50	

Opening of the Normal School at Santiago, Veraguas Province, June 5, 1938. See Nos. C53A-C53B.

Gatun Lake — A84

Designs: 1c, Pedro Miguel Locks. 2c, Allegory. 5c, Culebra Cut. 10c, Ferryboat. 12c, Aerial View of Canal. 15c, Gen. William C. Gorgas. 50c, Dr. Manuel A. Guerrero. 1b, Woodrow Wilson.

1939, Aug. 15 Engr. *Perf. 12½*

322	A84	½c yellow	25	5
323	A84	1c dp bl grn	30	8
324	A84	2c dl rose	38	10
325	A84	5c dl bl	65	12
326	A84	10c dk vio	75	30
327	A84	12c ol grn	75	38
328	A84	15c ultra	75	50
329	A84	50c orange	2.00	1.25
330	A84	1b dk brn	3.75	2.50
		Nos. 322-330 (9)	9.58	5.28

Issued to commemorate the 25th anniversary of the opening of the Panama Canal. See Nos. C54-C61.

Stamps of 1924 Overprinted in Black or Red

CONSTITUCION
1941

1941, Jan. 2 *Perf. 12*

331	A53	½c orange	30	20
332	A53	1c dk grn (R)	35	20
333	A53	2c carmine	35	22
334	A53	5c dk bl (R)	40	20
335	A53	10c dk vio (R)	60	40
336	A53	15c ultra (R)	1.25	60
337	A53	50c dp org	6.50	3.50
338	A53	1b blk (R)	15.00	6.00
		Nos. 331-338 (8)	24.75	11.32

Issued to commemorate the new constitution of Panama which became effective Jan. 2, 1941. See Nos. C67-C71.

Liberty — A93

Black Overprint

1942, Feb. 19 Engr.

339	A93	10c purple	80	65

Surcharged with New Value.

340	A93	2c on 5c dk bl	65	50

See No. C72.

Flags of Panama and Costa Rica A94

1942 Engraved and Lithographed

341 A94 2c rose red, dk bl & dp rose	30	22

Issued to commemorate the first anniversary of the settlement of the Costa Rica-Panama border dispute. See No. C73.

National Emblem A95

Farm Girl A96

Cart Laden with Sugar Cane (Inscribed "ACARRERO DE CAÑA") — A97

Balboa Taking Possession of the Pacific A98

Golden Altar of San Josė — A99

San Blas Indian Woman and Child — A101

Santo Tomas Hospital A100

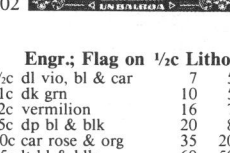

Modern Highway A102

1942 Engr.; Flag on ½c Litho.

342 A95 ½c dl vio, bl & car	7	5
343 A96 1c dk grn	10	5
344 A97 2c vermilion	16	7
345 A98 5c dp bl & blk	20	8
346 A99 10c car rose & org	35	20
347 A100 15c lt bl & blk	60	50
348 A101 50c org red & ol blk	1.40	1.00
349 A102 1b black	2.00	65
Nos. 342-349 (8)	4.88	2.60

See Nos. 357, 365, 376, 377, 380, 395, 409.

Catalogue values for unused stamps in this section, from this point to the end of the section, are for Never Hinged items.

Flag of Panama A103

Arms of Panama A104

Engraved; Flag on 2c Lithographed

1947, Apr. Unwmk. *Perf. 12½*

350 A103 2c car, bl & red	14	10
351 A104 5c dp bl	16	16

Issued to commemorate the second anniversary of the National Constitutional Assembly of 1945.

No. 241 Surcharged in Black

Habilitada
CORREOS
B/. 0.50

1947 *Perf. 12*

352 A53 50c on 24c yel brn	1.00	1.00
a "Habiiltada"	2.00	2.00

Nos. C6C, C75, C74 and C87 Surcharged in Black or Carmine

HABILITADA
CORREOS
B/. 0.0½

353 AP5 ½c on 8c gray blk	8	8
a "B/.0.0½ CORREOS" (transposed)	2.50	2.50
354 AP34 ½c on 8c dk ol brn & blk (C)	8	8
355 AP34 1c on 7c rose car	12	12
356 AP42 2c on 8c vio	16	12
Nos. 352-356 (5)	1.44	1.40

Flag Type of 1942.

1948 Engr. and Litho.

357 A95 ½c car, org, bl & dp car	14	10

Monument to Firemen of Colon — A105

American-La France Fire Engine — A106

Designs: 20c, Firemen and hose cart. 25c, New Central Fire Station, Colon. 50c, Maximino Walker. 1b, J. J. A. Ducruet.

1948 Engr.

Center in Black.

358 A105 5c dp car	20	14
359 A106 10c orange	35	20
360 A106 20c gray bl	65	38
361 A106 25c chocolate	65	50
362 A105 50c purple	1.10	50
363 A105 1b dp grn	1.75	1.00
Nos. 358-363 (6)	4.70	2.72

Issued to commemorate the 50th anniversary of the founding of the Colon Fire Department.

Cervantes — A107

1948 Unwmk. *Perf. 12½*

364 A107 2c car & blk	25	14

Issued to commemorate the 400th anniversary of the birth of Miguel de Cervantes Saavedra, novelist, playwright and poet. See Nos. C105-C106.

Oxcart Type of 1942 Redrawn. Inscribed: "ACARREO DE CAÑA".

1948 *Perf. 12*

365 A97 2c vermilion	40	10

No. 365 Surcharged or Overprinted in Black

1949, May 23

366 A97 1c on 2c ver	16	10
367 A97 2c vermilion	16	10
a Inverted overprint	2.00	2.00
Nos. 366-367,C108-C111 (6)	3.63	3.51

Issued to commemorate the centenary of the incorporation of Chiriqui Province.

Stamps and Types of 1942-48 Issues Overprinted in Black or Red

1874 ~ 1949
U.P.U.

1949, Sept. Engr.

368 A96 1c dk grn	12	8
369 A97 2c ver (#365)	20	10
370 A98 5c bl (R)	30	18
Nos. 368-370,C114-C118 (8)	3.75	2.78

75th anniv. of the UPU.

Overprint on No. 368 is slightly different and smaller, 15½x12mm.

Francisco Javier de Luna — A108

Dr. Carlos J. Finlay — A109

1949, Dec. 7 *Perf. 12½*

371 A108 2c car & blk	22	14

Issued to commemorate the 200th anniversary of the founding of the University of San Javier. See No. C119.

1950, Jan. 12 Unwmk. *Perf. 12*

372 A109 2c car & gray blk	35	14

Issued to honor Dr. Carlos J. Finlay (1833-1915), Cuban physician and biologist who found that a mosquito transmitted yellow fever. See No. C120.

Nos. 343, 357 and 345, Overprinted or Surcharged in Carmine or Black

CENTENARIO
del Gral. José
de San Martín
17 de Agosto
de 1950

1950, Aug. 17

373 A96 1c dk grn	14	8
374 A95 2c on ½c car, org, bl & dp car (Bk)	16	10
375 A98 5c dp bl & blk	22	16
Nos. 373-375,C121-C125 (8)	4.12	3.09

Issued to commemorate the centenary of the death of Gen. Jose de San Martin.

The overprint is in four lines on No. 375.

Types of 1942.

1950 Engr.

376 A97 2c ver & blk	14	5
377 A98 5c blue	25	10

No. 376 is inscribed "ACARREO DE CAÑA".

Nos. 376 and 377 Overprinted in Green or Carmine

Tercer Centenario del
Natalicio de San Juan
Bautista de La Salle.
1651-1951

1951, Sept. 26

378 A97 2c ver & blk (G)	14	10
379 A98 5c bl (C)	22	14

Issued to commemorate the 500th anniversary of the birth of St. Jean-Baptiste de la Salle.

The overprint exists (a) inverted on both stamps, (b) with top line omitted and second line repeated in its place. Value, each $12.50.

Altar Type of 1942.

1952 Engr. *Perf. 12*

380 A99 10c pur & org	35	16

No. 357 Surcharged "1952" and New Value in Black.

1952

381 A95 1c on ½c multi	14	5

Queen Isabella I and Arms — A110

1952, Oct. 20 Engr. *Perf. 12½*

Center in Black

382 A110 1c green	8	7
383 A110 2c carmine	12	8
384 A110 5c dk bl	16	10
385 A110 10c purple	22	20
Nos. 382-385,C131-C136 (10)	6.16	5.09

Issued to commemorate the 500th anniversary of the birth of Queen Isabella I of Spain.

No. 380 and Type of 1942 Surcharged "B/ .0.01 1953" in Black or Carmine.

1953 *Perf. 12.*

387 A99 1c on 10c pur & org	7	5
388 A100 1c on 15c blk (C)	14	5

A similar surcharge on No. 346 was privately applied.

Baptism of the Flag — A111

Manuel Amador Guerrero and Senora de Amador A112

Designs: 12c, Santos Jorge A. and Jeronimo de la Ossa. 20c, Revolutionary Junta. 50c, Old city hall. 1b, National coinage.

1953, Nov. 3 Engr. *Perf. 12*

389 A111	2c purple	14	7
390 A112	5c red org	16	5
391 A112	12c dp red vio	35	14
392 A112	20c sl gray	50	22
393 A111	50c org yel	1.00	60
394 A112	1b blue	2.25	1.25
	Nos. 389-394 (6)	4.40	2.33

Issued to commemorate the 50th anniversary of the founding of the Republic of Panama. See Nos. C140-C145.

Farm Girl Type of 1942.

1954 Unwmk. *Perf. 12.*

395 A96 1c dp car rose 5 5

Surcharged with New Value in Black.

396 A96 3c on 1c dp car rose 8 5

Monument to Gen. Tomas Herrera — A113

1954 Litho. *Perf. 12½*

397 A113 3c purple 16 7

Centenary of the death of Gen. Tomas Herrera. See Nos. C148-C149.

Tocumen International Airport A114

1955

398 A114 ½c org brn 5 5

Pres. J. A. Remon Cantera — A115

1955, June 1

399 A115 3c lil rose & blk 10 7

Issued in tribute to Pres. JoséAntonio Remon Cantera, 1908-1955. See No. C153.

Victor de la Guardia y Ayala and Miguel Chiari A116

1955, Sept. 13

400 A116 5c violet 16 7

Centenary of province of Coclé.

Ferdinand de Lesseps — A117

First Excavation of Panama Canal A118

Design: 50c, Theodore Roosevelt.

1955, Nov. 16

401 A117	3c rose brn, *rose*	30	8
402 A118	25c vio bl, *lt bl*	65	50
403 A117	50c vio, *lt vio*	1.50	1.00
	Nos. 401-403,C155-C156 (5)	4.61	3.25

Issued to commemorate the 150th anniversary of the birth of Ferdinand de Lesseps, French promoter connected with building of Panama Canal. Imperforates exist, but were not sold at any post office.

Arms of Panama City A119

Carlos A. Mendoza A120

Perf. 12½

1956, Aug. 17 Litho. Unwmk.

404 A119 3c green 12 5

Issued to commemorate the sixth Inter-American Congress of Municipalities, Panama City, Aug. 14-19, 1956.

For souvenir sheet see C182a.

Wmk. 311- Star and RP Multiple

1956, Sept. 13 Wmk. 311

405 A120 10c rose red & dp grn 20 12

Issued to commemorate the centenary of the birth of Pres. Carlos A. Mendoza.

National Archives A121

Design: 25c, Pres. Belisario Porras.

1956, Nov. 27

406 A121	15c gray	40	20
407 A121	25c dk car rose & bluish blk	60	40

Issued to commemorate the centenary of the birth of Pres. Belisario Porras. See Nos. C183-C184.

Pan-American Highway, Panama — A122

1957, Aug. 1

408 A122 3c gray grn 10 5

Issued to publicize the 7th Pan-American Highway Congress. See Nos. C185-C187.

Hospital Type of 1942.

1957 Unwmk. Engr. *Perf. 12*

409 A100 15c black 35 16

Manuel Espinosa Batista A123

Flags of 21 American Nations A124

Wmk. 311

1957, Sept. 20 Litho. *Perf. 12½*

410 A123 5c grn & ultra 14 7

Issued to commemorate the centenary of the birth of Manuel Espinosa B., independence leader.

No. 398 Surcharged "1957" and New Value in Violet or Black.

1957 Unwmk.

411 A114	1c on ½c org brn (V)	5	5
412 A114	3c on ½c org brn	10	5

No. 391 Surcharged "1958," New Value and Dots.

1958 Engr. *Perf. 12*

413 A112 3c on 12c dp red vio 10 5

Perf. 12½

1958, July 10 Litho. Unwmk.

Center yellow & black; flags in national colors.

414 A124	1c lt gray	7	5
415 A124	2c brt yel grn	10	5
416 A124	3c red org	14	5
417 A124	7c vio bl	22	8
	Nos. 414-417,C203-C206 (8)	3.29	2.63

Issued to commemorate the 10th anniversary of the Organization of American States.

Brazilian Pavilion, Brussels Fair — A125

Pavilions: 3c, Argentina. 5c, Venezuela. 10c, Great Britain.

1958, Sept. 8 Wmk. 311

418 A125	1c org yel & emer	5	5
419 A125	3c lt bl & ol	10	5
420 A125	5c lt brn & sl	14	7
421 A125	10c aqua & redsh brn	20	16
	Nos. 418-421,C207-C209 (7)	2.79	2.58

World's Fair, Brussels, Apr. 17-Oct. 19.

A souvenir sheet containing Nos. 418-421 and C207-C209 is listed as No. C209a.

Pope Pius XII as Young Man A126

U. N. Headquarters Building A127

Wmk. 311

1959, Jan. Litho. *Perf. 12½*

422 A126 3c org brn 14 7

Issued in memory of Pope Pius XII, 1876-1958. See Nos. C210-C212a.

Human Rights Issue

Design: 15c, Humanity looking into sun.

1959, Apr. 14 Wmk. 311

423 A127	3c mar & ol	7	5
424 A127	15c org & emer	35	22
	Nos. 423-424,C213-C217 (7)	3.11	2.70

Issued to commemorate the 10th anniversary (in 1958) of the signing of the Universal Declaration of Human Rights.

Nos. 423-424 Overprinted in Dark Blue

8A REUNION
C.E.P.A.L.
MAYO 1959

1959, May 16

425 A127	3c mar & ol	10	8
426 A127	15c org & emer	35	20
	Nos. 425-426,C218-C221 (6)	2.96	2.25

Issued to commemorate the 8th Reunion of the Economic Commission for Latin America.

Eusebio A. Morales A128

National Institute A129

Portrait: 13c, Abel Bravo.

Wmk. 311

1959, July 27 Litho. *Perf. 12½*

427 A128	3c car rose	8	5
428 A128	13c brt grn	25	14
429 A129	21c lt bl	40	25
	Nos. 427-429,C222-C223 (5)	97	59

50th anniversary, National Institute.

Soccer — A130

Fencing — A131

Designs: 3c, Swimming. 20c, Hurdling.

1959, Oct. 26

430 A130	1c gray & emer	5	5
431 A130	3c brt bl & red brn	10	5
432 A130	20c emer & red brn	45	40
	Nos. 430-432,C224-C226 (6)	1.70	1.37

Issued to commemorate the 3rd Pan American Games, Chicago, Aug. 27-Sept. 7, 1959.

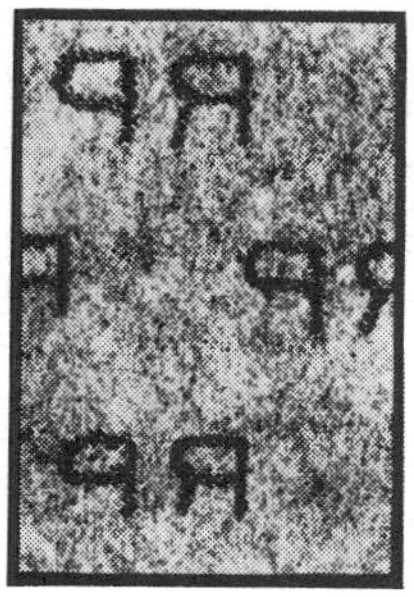

Wmk. 343-
RP Multiple

Design: 5c, Soccer.

Wmk. 343

1960, Sept. 22 Litho. *Perf. 12½*
433 A131 3c lt vio & mag 10 5
434 A131 5c bl grn & emer 16 7
Nos. 433-434,C234-C237 (6) 1.59 1.33

Issued to commemorate the 17th Olympic Games, Rome, Aug. 25-Sept. 11.

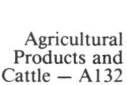

Agricultural Products and Cattle — A132

1961, Mar. 3 Wmk. 311 *Perf. 12½*
435 A132 3c bl grn 10 5

Issued to publicize the second agricultural and livestock census, Apr. 16, 1961.

Children's Hospital A133

1961, May 2
436 A133 3c grnsh bl 8 5

Issued to commemorate the 25th anniversary of the Lions Club of Panama.

Flags of Panama and Costa Rica A134

1961, Oct. 2 Wmk. 343 *Perf. 12½*
437 A134 3c car & bl 12 7

Issued to commemorate the meeting of Presidents Mario Echandi of Costa Rica and Roberto F. Chiari of Panama at Paso Canoa, Apr. 21, 1961. See No. C251.

Arms of Colon A135

Mercury and Cogwheel A136

1962, Feb. 28 Litho. Wmk. 311
438 A135 3c car, yel & vio bl 8 5

Issued to publicize the third Central American Municipal Assembly, Colon, May 13-17. See No. C255.

1962, Mar. 16 Wmk. 343
439 A136 3c red org 7 5

First industrial and commercial census.

Social Security Hospital A137

1962, June 1 *Perf. 12½*
440 A137 3c ver & gray 7 5

Opening of the Social Security Hospital.

Church of San Francisco de Veraguas A138

Ruins of Cathedral of Panama — A139

Designs: 3c, David Cathedral. 5c, Natá Church. 10c, Don Bosco Church. 15c, Church of the Virgin of Carmen. 20c, Colon Cathedral. 25c, Greek Orthodox Temple. 50c, Cathedral of Panama. 1b, Protestant Church of Colon.

1962-64 Litho. Wmk. 343
Buildings in Black

441 A138 1c red & bl 5 5
442 A139 2c red & yel 5 5
443 A138 3c vio & yel 7 5
444 A139 5c rose & lt grn 10 7
445 A139 10c grn & yel 20 12
445A A139 10c red & bl ('64) 20 12
446 A139 15c ultra & lt grn 25 16
447 A139 20c red & pink 30 20
448 A138 25c grn & pink 35 22
449 A139 50c ultra & pink 65 42
450 A138 1b lil & yel 1.75 1.50
Nos. 441-450 (11) 3.97 2.96

Issued to publicize freedom of religion in Panama. Issue dates: No. 445A, June 4, 1964; others, July 20, 1962.
See Nos. C256-C265; souvenir sheet No. C264a.

Panama Canal Bridge during Construction A140

1962, Oct. 12 *Perf. 12½*
451 A140 3c car & gray 8 5

Issued to commemorate the opening of the Panama Canal Bridge (Thatcher Ferry Bridge), Oct. 12, 1962. See No. C273.

Fire Brigade Exercises, Inauguration of Aqueduct, 1906 — A141

Portraits of Fire Brigade Officials: 3c, Lt. Col. Luis Carlos Endara P., Col. Raul Arango N. and Major Ernesto Arosemena A. 5c, Guillermo Patterson Jr., David F. de Castro, Pres. T. Gabriel Duque, Telmo Rugliancich and Tomas Leblanc.

1963 Wmk. 311 *Perf. 12½*
452 A141 1c emer & blk 5 5
453 A141 3c vio bl & blk 7 5
454 A141 5c mag & blk 10 7
Nos. 452-454,C279-C281 (6) 1.03 89

Issued to commemorate the 75th anniversary (in 1962) of the Panamanian Fire Brigade.

Nos. 440, 443, 451, 453 and 407 Surcharged "VALE" and New Value in Black or Red.

1963 Wmk. 343 *Perf. 12½*
455 A137 4c on 3c ver & gray 14 5
456 A138 4c on 3c vio & yel 14 5
457 A140 4c on 3c car & gray 14 5

Wmk. 311

458 A141 4c on 3c vio bl & blk 14 5
459 A121 10c on 25c dk car rose & bluish blk (R) 35 10
Nos. 455-459 (5) 91 30

Pres. Francisco J. Orlich, Costa Rica A142

Vasco Nuñez de Balboa A143

Flags and Presidents: 2c, Luis A. Somoza, Nicaragua. 3c, Dr. Ramon Villeda M., Honduras. 4c, Roberto F. Chiari, Panama.

Perf. 12½x12
1963, Dec. 18 Litho. Unwmk.
Portrait in Slate Green

460 A142 1c lt grn, red & ultra 10 10
461 A142 2c lt bl, red & ultra 12 12
462 A142 3c pale pink, red & ultra 16 12
463 A142 4c rose, red & ultra 20 16

Issued to commemorate the meeting of Central American Presidents with Pres. John F. Kennedy, San José, March 18-20, 1963. See also Nos. C292-C294.

1964, Jan. 22 Photo. *Perf. 13*
464 A143 4c grn, *pale rose* 10 5

450th anniv. of Balboa's discovery of the Pacific Ocean. See No. C295.

No. C231 Surcharged in Red: "Correos B/.0.10"

1964 Wmk. 311 Litho. *Perf. 12½*
465 AP74 10c on 21c lt bl 16 14

Type of 1962 Overprinted in Red: "HABILITADA"

1964 Wmk. 343
466 A138 1b red, bl & blk 1.60 1.50

Eleanor Roosevelt A147

Keel-billed Toucan A148

Perf. 12x12½
1964, Oct. 9 Litho. Unwmk.
478 A147 4c car & blk, *grnsh* 12 8

Issued to honor Eleanor Roosevelt (1884-1962). See Nos. C345-C345a.

Canceled to Order
Canceled sets of new issues have been sold by the government. Postally used copies are worth more.

1965, Oct. 27 Unwmk. *Perf. 14*

Song Birds: 2c, Scarlet macaw. 3c, Red-crowned woodpecker. 4c, Blue-gray tanager (horiz.).

479 A148 1c brt pink & multi 5 5
480 A148 2c multi 5 5
481 A148 3c brt vio & multi 5 5
482 A148 4c org yel & multi 7 5
Nos. 479-482,C346-C347 (6) 46 39

Snapper — A149

Design: 2c, Dolphin.

1965, Dec. 7 Litho.
483 A149 1c multi 5 5
484 A149 2c multi 8 5
Nos. 483-484,C348-C351 (6) 1.29 1.04

No. 448 Surcharged

1966, June 27 Wmk. 343 *Perf. 12½*
485 A138 13c on 25c grn & pink 30 16

The "25c" has not been obliterated.

Hen and Chicks A150

Domestic Animals: 3c Rooster. 5c, Pig (horiz.). 8c, Cow (horiz.).

1967, Feb. 3 Unwmk. *Perf. 14*
486 A150 1c multi 5 5
487 A150 3c multi 5 5
488 A150 5c multi 9 5
489 A150 8c multi 15 8
Nos. 486-489,C360-C363 (8) 2.04 1.59

New World Anhinga A151

Birds: 1c, Quetzals. 3c, Turquoise-browed motmot. 4c, Double-collared aracari (horiz.). 5c, Macaw. 13c, Belted kingfisher.

1967, July 20
490 A151 ½c lt bl & multi 5 5
491 A151 1c lt gray & multi 5 5
492 A151 3c pink & multi 7 5
493 A151 4c lt grn & multi 8 5

494	A151	5c buff & multi	10	5
495	A151	13c yel & multi	30	16
		Nos. 490-495 (6)	65	41

Red Deer, by Franz Marc A152

Animal Paintings by Franz Marc: 3c, Tiger (vert.). 5c, Monkeys. 8c, Blue Fox.

1967, Sept. 1 ***Perf. 14***

496	A152	1c multi	5	5
497	A152	3c multi	7	5
498	A152	5c multi	10	5
499	A152	8c multi	20	8
		Nos. 496-499,C364-C367 (8)	1.87	1.15

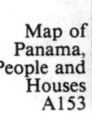

Map of Panama, People and Houses A153

Design: 10c, Map of Americas and people (vert.).

Wmk. MEX and Eagle in Circle, Multiple. (350)

1969, Aug. **Photo.**

500	A153	5c vio bl	10	7
501	A153	10c brt rose lil	20	14

Issued to publicize the 1970 census.

Cogwheel A154

1969, Aug.

502	A154	13c yel & dk bl gray	20	16

Issued to commemorate the 50th anniversary of Rotary International of Panama.

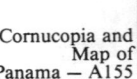

Cornucopia and Map of Panama — A155

Perf. 14½x15

1969, Oct. 10 **Litho.** **Unwmk.**

503	A155	10c lt bl & multi	16	10

Issued to commemorate the first anniversary of the October 11 Revolution.

Map of Panama and Ruins A156

Natá Church A157

Designs: 5c, Farmer, wife and mule. 13c, Hotel Continental. 20c, Church of the Virgin of Carmen. 21c, Gold altar, San Jose Church. 25c, Del Rey bridge. 30c, Dr. Justo Arosemena monument. 34c, Cathedral of Panama. 38c, Municipal Palace. 40c, French Plaza. 50c, Thatcher Ferry Bridge (Bridge of the Americas). 59c, National Theater.

Perf. 14½x15, 15x14½

1969-70 **Litho.** **Unwmk.**

504	A156	3c org & blk	7	5
505	A156	5c lt bl grn ('70)	10	5
506	A157	8c dl brn ('70)	16	14
507	A156	13c emer & blk	22	12
508	A157	20c vio brn ('70)	30	22
509	A157	21c yel ('70)	30	22
510	A156	25c lt bl grn ('70)	40	25
511	A157	30c blk ('70)	45	40
512	A156	34c org brn ('70)	55	40
513	A156	38c brt bl ('70)	55	40
514	A156	40c org yel ('70)	60	40
515	A156	50c brt rose lil & blk	80	60
516	A156	59c brt rose lil ('70)	90	55
		Nos. 504-516 (13)	5.40	3.80

Stadium and Discus Thrower A158

Flor del Espiritu Santo — A159

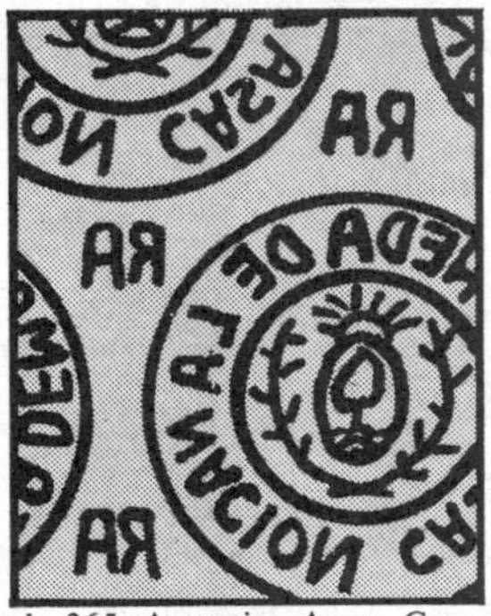
Wmk. 365- Argentine Arms, Casa de Moneda de la Nacion & RA Mult

Wmk. 365

1970, Jan. 6 **Litho.** ***Perf. 13½***

517	A158	1c ultra & multi	5	5
518	A158	2c ultra & multi	5	5
519	A158	3c ultra & multi	5	5
520	A158	5c ultra & multi	9	5
521	A158	10c ultra & multi	18	10
522	A158	13c ultra & multi	22	14
523	A159	13c pink & multi	22	14
524	A158	25c ultra & multi	42	35
525	A158	30c ultra & multi	55	42
		Nos. 517-525,C368-C369 (11)	2.63	1.93

Issued to publicize the 11th Central American and Caribbean Games, Feb. 28-Mar. 14.

Office of Comptroller General, 1970 — A160

Designs: 5c, Alejandro Tapia and Martin Sosa, first Comptrollers, 1931-34 (horiz.). 8c, Comptroller's emblem. 13c, Office of Comptroller General, 1955-70 (horiz.).

1971, Feb. 25 **Litho.** **Wmk. 365**

526	A160	3c yel & multi	6	5
527	A160	5c brn, buff & gold	10	5
528	A160	8c gold & multi	16	8
529	A160	13c blk & multi	25	15

Comptroller General's Office, 40th anniv.

Indian Alligator Design — A161

1971, Aug. 18 **Wmk. 343** ***Perf. 13½***

530	A161	8c multi	16	14

Fifth anniversary of SENAPI (Servicio Nacional de Artesania y Pequenas Industrias).

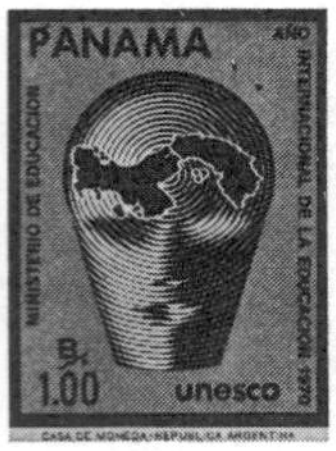

Education Year Emblem, Map of Panama — A162

1971, Aug. 19 **Litho.**

531	A162	1b multi	1.60	1.20

International Education Year, 1970.

Congress Emblem A163

1972, Aug. 25

532	A163	25c multi	55	35

9th Inter-American Conference of Saving and Loan Associations, Panama City, Jan. 23-29, 1971.

UPU Headquarters, Bern — A164

Design: 30c, Universal Postal Union Monument, Bern (vert.).

1971, Dec. 14 **Wmk. 343**

533	A164	8c multi	16	8
534	A164	30c multi	55	35

Inauguration of Universal Postal Union Headquarters, Bern, Switzerland.

Cow, Pig and Produce A165

1971, Dec. 15

535	A165	3c yel, brn & blk	6	5

3rd agricultural census.

Map of Panama and "4-S" Emblem A166

1971, Dec. 16

536	A166	2c multi	5	5

Rural youth 4-S program.

UNICEF Emblem, Children A167

Wmk. 365

1972, Sept. 12 **Litho.** ***Perf. 13½***

537	A167	1c yel & multi	5	5

25th anniv. (in 1971) of UNICEF. See Nos. C390-C392a.

Tropical Fruits A168

1972, Sept. 13

538	A168	1c *shown*	5	5
539	A168	2c *Isla de Noche*	5	5
540	A168	3c *Carnival float*, vert.	6	5
		Nos. 538-540,C393-C395 (6)	92	55

Tourist publicity.

VALE 10¢
ONU
CONSEJO DE SEGURIDAD
15 · 21 Marzo 1973

Nos. 516, 531 and 511 Surcharged in Red

Perf. 14½x15, 15x14½, 13½

Wmk. 343, Unwmkd.

1973, Mar. 16

541	A156	8c on 59c brt rose lil	10	8
542	A162	10c on 1b multi	14	12
543	A157	13c on 30c blk	20	14

U.N. Security Council Meeting, Panama City, Mar. 15-21. Surcharges differ in size and are adjusted to fit shape of stamp. See No. C402.

José Daniel Crespo, Educator — A169

Wmk. 365

1973, June 20 **Litho.** ***Perf. 13½***

544	A169	3c lt bl & multi	7	5
		Nos. 544,C403-C413 (12)	5.18	2.55

Nos. 511-512 and 509 Surcharged in Red **VALE 13¢**

Perf. 15x14½, 14½x15

1974, Nov. 11 **Unwmk.**

545 A157 5c on 30c blk 7 5
546 A156 10c on 34c org brn 14 10
547 A157 13c on 21c yel 18 14
Nos. 545-547,C417-C421 (8) 91 70

Surcharge vertical on No. 546.

Bolivar, Thatcher Ferry Bridge, Men with Flags — A170

Perf. 12½

1976, Mar. 30 **Litho.** **Unwmk.**

548 A170 6c multi 8 5

150th anniversary of Congress of Panama. See Nos. C426-C428.

Evibacus Princeps A171

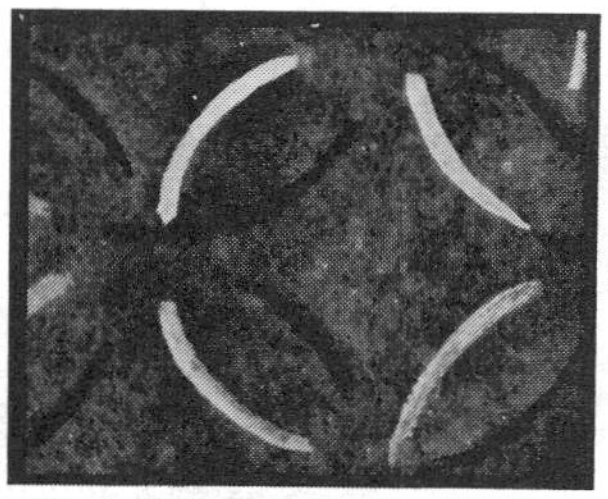

Wmk. 377- Interlocking Circles

Marine life: 3c, Ptitosarcus sinuosus (vert.). 4c, Acanthaster planci. 7c, Starfish. 1b, Mithrax spinossimus.

Perf. 12½x13, 13x12½

1976, May 6 **Litho.** **Wmk. 377**

549 A171 2c multi 5 5
550 A171 3c multi 5 5
551 A171 4c multi 5 5
552 A171 7c multi 10 7
Nos. 549-552,C429-C430 (6) 88 58

Souvenir Sheet

Imperf

553 A171 1b multi 3.00

Flag Bearer from Bolivar Monument A172

Bolivar and Argentine Flag A173

Designs: Stamps of type A172 show details of Bolivar Monument, Panama City; type A173 shows head of Bolivar and flags of Latin American countries.

Perf. 13½

1976, June 22 **Unwmk.** **Litho.**

554 A172 20c *shown* 25 20
555 A173 20c *shown* 25 20
556 A173 20c *Bolivia* 25 20
557 A173 20c *Brazil* 25 20
558 A173 20c *Chile* 25 20
559 A172 20c *Battle scene* 25 20
560 A173 20c *Colombia* 25 20
561 A173 20c *Costa Rica* 25 20
562 A173 20c *Cuba* 25 20
563 A173 20c *Ecuador* 25 20
564 A173 20c *El Salvador* 25 20
565 A173 20c *Guatemala* 25 20
566 A173 20c *Guyana* 25 20
567 A173 20c *Haiti* 25 20
568 A172 20c *Assembly* 25 20
569 A172 20c *Liberated people* 25 20
570 A173 20c *Honduras* 25 20
571 A173 20c *Jamaica* 25 20
572 A173 20c *Mexico* 25 20
573 A173 20c *Nicaragua* 25 20
574 A173 20c *Panama* 25 20
575 A173 20c *Paraguay* 25 20
576 A173 20c *Peru* 25 20
577 A173 20c *Dominican Rep.* 25 20
578 A172 20c *Bolivar and flag bearer* 25 20
579 A173 20c *Surinam* 25 20
580 A173 20c *Trinidad-Tobago* 25 20
581 A173 20c *Uruguay* 25 20
582 A173 20c *Venezuela* 25 20
583 A172 20c *Indian delegation* 25 20
Nos. 554-583 (30) 7.50 6.00

Souvenir Sheet

584 Sheet of 3 2.25
a A172 30c, *Bolivar and flag bearer* 50
b A172 30c, *Monument, top* 50
c A172 40c, *Inscription tablet* 65

Amphictyonic Congress of Panama, sesquicentennial. Nos. 554-583 printed se-tenant in sheets of 30 (6x5) with black marginal inscription and control number. No. 584 perf. and imperf., has green marginal inscription.

Nicanor Villalaz, Designer of Coat of Arms — A174

National Lottery Building, Panama City — A175

1976, Nov. 12 **Litho.** ***Perf. 12½***

585 A174 5c dk bl 7 5
586 A175 6c multi 8 5

Contadora Island A176

1976, Dec. 29 ***Perf. 12½***

587 A176 3c multi 10 5

Presidents Carter and Omar Torrijos Signing Panama Canal Treaties — A177

Design: 23c, like No. 588. Design includes Alejandro Orfila, Secretary General of OAS.

1978, Jan. **Litho.** ***Perf. 12***

Size: 90x40mm.

588 A177 Strip of 3 1.40
a 3c multi 5
b 40c multi 55
c 50c multi 65

Perf. 14

Size: 36x26mm.

589 A177 23c multi 30 22

Signing of Panama Canal Treaties, Washington, D.C., Sept. 7, 1977.

Presidents Carter and Torrijos Signing Treaties — A178

Design: 3c, Treaty signing.

1978, Nov. 13 **Litho.** ***Perf. 12***

590 A178 Strip of 3 1.20
a 5c multi (30x40mm) 7
b 35c multi (30x40mm) 45
c 41c multi (45x40mm) 55

Size: 36x26mm.

591 A178 3c multi 5 5

Signing of Panama Canal Treaties, Panama City, Panama, June 6, 1978.

World Trade Center, Colon A179

1978 **Litho.** ***Perf. 12***

592 A179 6c multi 8 5

Free Zone of Colon, 30th anniversary.

Melvin Jones, Lions Emblem A180

1978, Dec. 5

593 A180 50c multi 65 55

Birth centenary of Melvin Jones, founder of Lions International.

Soldier with Children, Ship, Flag A181

"75," Coat of Arms A182

Rotary Emblem, "75" A183

Pres. Torrijos and Carter, Flags, Ship — A184

UPU Emblem, Globe — A185

Boy and Girl Inside Heart — A186

1979, Oct. 1 **Litho.** ***Perf. 14***

594 A181 3c multi 5 5
595 A182 6c multi 8 5
596 A183 17c multi 22 16
597 A184 23c multi 30 20
598 A185 35c multi 45 30
599 A186 50c multi 65 42
Nos. 594-599 (6) 1.75 *1.18*

Return of Canal Zone to Panama, October 1 (3c, 23c); National Bank, 75th anniversary; Rotary International, 75th anniversary; 18th Universal Postal Union Congress, Rio de Janeiro, Sept.-Oct., 1979; International Year of the Child.

Colon Station, St. Charles Hotel, Engraving — A187

Postal Headquarters, Balboa, Inauguration — A188

Return of Canal Zone to Panama, Oct. 1, 1979 — A189

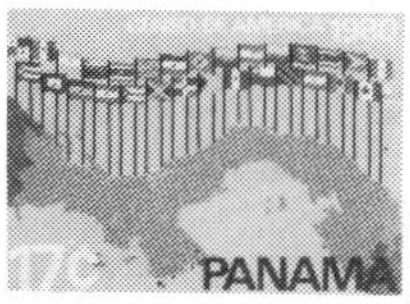

Census of the Americas A190

Panamanian Tourist and Convention Center Opening A191

Inter-American Development Bank, 25th Anniversary — A192

Canal Zone Centenary A193

Olympic Stadium, Moscow '80 Emblem A194

1980, June 17 Litho. *Perf. 12*

600	A187	1c rose vio	5	5
601	A188	3c multi	5	5
602	A189	6c multi	8	5
603	A190	17c multi	22	16
604	A191	23c multi	30	20
605	A192	35c multi	45	30
606	A193	41c pale rose & blk	55	38
607	A194	50c multi	65	42
		Nos. 600-607 (8)	2.35	1.61

Transpanamanian Railroad centenary (1c); 22nd Summer Olympic Games, Moscow, July 19-Aug. 3 (50c).

La Salle Congregation, 75th Anniv. (1979) — A195

Louis Braille — A196

1981, May 15 Litho. *Perf. 12*

608	A195	17c multi	22	16

1981, May 15

609	A196	23c multi	30	20

Intl. Year of the Disabled.

Bull's Blood — A197

1981, June 26 Litho. *Perf. 12*

610	A197	3c shown	5	5
611	A197	6c Lory, vert.	8	5
612	A197	41c Hummingbird, vert.	55	38
613	A197	50c Toucan	65	42

Apparition of the Virgin to St. Catherine Laboure, 150th Anniv. — A198

1981, June 26 Litho. *Perf. 12*

614	A198	35c multi	45	35

Pres. Torrijos and Bayano Dam A199

Wmk. 343

1982, Mar. Litho. *Perf. 10½*

615	A199	17c multi	22	16

National Solidarity — A200

1981, Nov. 30 Litho. *Perf. 10½*

616	A200	3c multi	5	5

First Death Anniv. of Pres. Omar Torrijos Herrera A201

Wmk. 381: "Panama" and Design

1982, May 14 Litho. *Perf. 10½*

617	A201	5c Aerial view	7	5
618	A201	6c Army camp	8	5
619	A201	50c Felipillo Engineering Works	65	40
		Nos. 617-619,C433-C434 (5)	1.80	1.10

Ricardo J. Alfaro (1882-1977), Statesman A202

Designs: Photos by Luiz Gutierrez Cruz.

1982, Aug. 18 Wmk. 381

620	A202	3c multi	5	5

See Nos. C436-C437.

1983 World Cup — A203

Wmk. 381 "Panama" and Design

1982, Dec. 27 Litho. *Perf. 10½*

621	A203	50c Italian team	65	48

See Nos. C438-C440.

Chamber of Commerce Expo Comer '83, Jan. 12-16 A204

1983 Litho. Wmk. 381 *Perf. 10½*

622	A204	17c multi	22	14

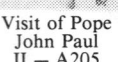

Visit of Pope John Paul II — A205

Bank Emblem — A206

Various portraits of the Pope. 35c airmail.

Wmk. 382 (Stars)

1983, Mar. 1 Litho. *Perf. 12x11*

623	A205	6c multi	8	5
624	A205	17c multi	22	14
625	A205	35c multi	45	25

1983, Mar. 18

626	A206	50c multi	65	40

24th Council Meeting of Inter-American Development Bank, Mar. 21-23.

Simon Bolivar (1783-1830) A207

1983, July 25 Litho. *Perf. 12*

627	A207	50c multi	65	40

Souvenir Sheet

Imperf

628	A207	1b like 50c	1.40	80

World Communications Year — A208

1983, Oct. 9 Litho. *Perf. 14*

629	A208	30c UPAE emblem	40	22
630	A208	40c WCY emblem	55	32
631	A208	50c UPU emblem	65	40
632	A208	60c Dove in flight	80	50

Souvenir Sheet

Imperf

633	A208	1b multi	1.40	80

No. 633 contains designs of Nos. 629-632 without denominations. Margin shows coat of arms; black marginal inscription. Size: 151x150mm.

Freedom of Worship A209

1983, Oct. 21 Litho. *Perf. 11½*

634	A209	3c Panama Mosque	5	5
635	A209	5c Bahai Temple	7	5
636	A209	6c St. Francis Church	8	5
637	A209	17c Shevet Ahim Synagogue	22	14

Ricardo Miro (1883-1940), Poet — A210

The Prophet, by Alfredo Sinclair — A211

Famous Men: 3c, Richard Newman (1883-1946), educator. 5c, Cristobal Rodriguez (1883-1943), politician. 6c, Alcibiades Arosemena (1883-1958), industrialist and financier. 35c, Cirilo Martinez (1883-1924), linguist.

1983, Nov. 8 Litho. *Perf. 14*

638	A210	1c multi	5	5
639	A210	3c multi	5	5
640	A210	5c multi	7	5
641	A210	6c multi	8	5
642	A210	35c multi	45	28
		Nos. 638-642 (5)	70	48

1983, Dec. 12 *Perf. 12*

Paintings: No. 643, Village House, by Juan Manuel Cedeno. No. 644, Large Nude, by Manuel Chong Neto. 3c, On Another Occasion, by Spiros Vamvas. 6c, Punta Chame Landscape, by Guillermo Trujillo. 28c, Neon Light, by Alfredo Sinclair. 41c, Highland Girls, by Al Sprague. 1b, Bright Morning, by Ignacio Mallol Pibernat. Nos. 643-647, 650 horiz.

643	A211	1c multi	5	5
644	A211	1c multi	5	5
645	A211	3c multi	5	5
646	A211	6c multi	8	5
647	A211	28c multi	38	22
648	A211	35c multi	45	28
649	A211	41c multi	55	35
650	A211	1b multi	1.40	80
		Nos. 643-650 (8)	3.01	1.85

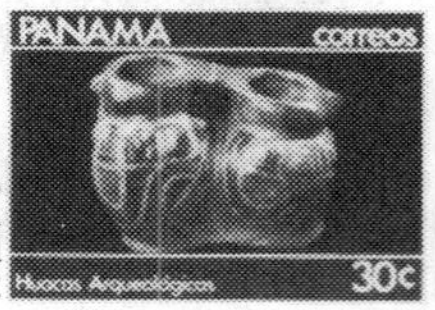

Double Cup, Indian Period A212

Pottery: 40c, Raised dish, Tonosi period. 50c, Jug with face, Canazas period (vert.). 60c, Bowl, Conte (vert.).

1984, Jan. 16 Litho. *Perf. 12*

651	A212	30c multi	40	20
652	A212	40c multi	55	30
653	A212	50c multi	65	40
654	A212	60c multi	80	55

Souvenir Sheet

Imperf

655	A212	1b like 30c	1.40	80

Pre-Olympics — A213

1984, June Litho. *Perf. 14*

656	A213	19c Baseball	25	14
657	A213	19c Basketball, vert.	25	14
658	A213	19c Boxing	25	14
659	A213	19c Swimming, vert.	25	14

For unused stamps, more recent issues are valued as never hinged, with the beginning point determined on a country-by-country basis. Notes to show the beginning points are prominently placed in the text.

Roberto Duran — A214

Paintings — A215

1984 Olympic Games — A214a

1984, June 14 Litho. *Perf. 14*
660 A214 26c multi 35 18

1984 Litho. *Perf. 14*
660A A214a 6c Shooting 8 5
660B A214a 30c Weight lifting 40 20
660C A214a 37c Wrestling 50 25
660D A214a 1b Long jump 1.40 80

Souvenir Sheet

660E A214a 1b Running 1.40 80

Nos. 660B-660D are airmail. No. 660E contains one stamp (size: 45x45x64mm); multicolored inscribed margin pictures natl. coat of arms and black control number. Size: 75x85mm.

1984, Sept. 17 Litho. *Perf. 14*

Paintings by Panamanian artists: 1c, Woman Thinking, by Manuel Chong Neto. 3c, The Child, by Alfredo Sinclair. 6c, A Day in the Life of Rumalda, by Brooke Alfaro. 30c, Highlands People, by Al Sprague. 37c, Intermission during the Dance, by Roberto Sprague. 44c, Punta Chame Forest, by Guillermo Trujillo. 50c, The Blue Plaza, by Juan Manuel Cedeno. 1b, Ira, by Spiros Vamvas.

661 A215 1c multi 5 5
662 A215 3c multi, horiz. 5 5
663 A215 6c multi, horiz. 8 5
664 A215 30c multi 40 20
665 A215 37c multi, horiz. 50 25
666 A215 44c multi, horiz. 60 35
667 A215 50c multi, horiz. 65 40
668 A215 1b multi, horiz. 1.40 80
Nos. 661-668 (8) 3.73 2.15

Postal Sovereignty A216

1984, Oct. 1 Litho. *Perf. 12*
669 A216 19c Pres. Torrijos, canal 25 14

Fauna A217

1984, Dec. 5 Engr. *Perf. 14*
670 A217 3c Manatee 5 5
671 A217 30c Gato negro 40 22
672 A217 44c Tigrillo congo 60 38
673 A217 50c Puerco de monte 65 40

Souvenir Sheet

674 A217 1b Perezoso de tres dedos, vert. 1.40 80

Nos. 671-673 are airmail.

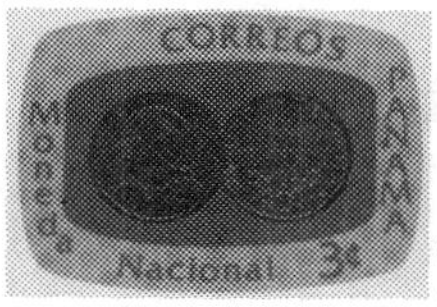

Coins A218

1985, Jan. 17 Litho. *Perf. 11x12*
675 A218 3c 1935 1c 5 5
676 A218 3c 1904 10c 5 5
677 A218 6c 1916 5c 8 5
678 A218 30c 1904 50c 40 22
679 A218 37c 1962 half-balboa 50 30
680 A218 44c 1953 balboa 55 36
Nos. 675-680 (6) 1.63 1.03

Nos. 678-680 are airmail.

Contadora Type of 1985
Souvenir Sheet

1985, Oct. 1 Litho. *Perf. 13½x13*
680A AP108 1b Dove, flags, map 1.40 80

Cargo Ship in Lock A219

1985, Oct. 16 *Perf. 14*
681 A219 19c multi 25 15

Panama Canal, 70th anniv. (1984).

UN 40th Anniv. A220

1986, Jan. 17 Litho. *Perf. 14*
682 A220 23c multi 45 28

Intl. Youth Year A221

1986, Jan. 17
683 A221 30c multi 60 35

Waiting Her Turn, by Al Sprague (b.1938) — A222

Oil paintings: 5c, Aerobics, by Guillermo Trujillo (b.1927). 19c, Cardboard House, by Eduardo Augustine (b.1954). 30c, Door to the Homeland, by Juan Manuel Cedeno (b.1914). 36c, Supper for Three, by Brooke Alfaro (b.1949). 42c, Tenderness, by Alfredo Sinclair (b.1915). 50c, Woman and Character, by Manuel Chong Neto (b.1927). 60c, Cella lillies, by Maigualida de Diaz (b.1950).

1986, Jan. 21
684 A222 3c multi 6 5
685 A222 5c multi 10 6
686 A222 19c multi 38 24
687 A222 30c multi 60 35
688 A222 36c multi 72 45
689 A222 42c multi 85 52
690 A222 50c multi 1.00 60
691 A222 60c multi 1.20 72
Nos. 684-691 (8) 4.91 2.99

Miss Universe Pageant A223

1986, July 7 Litho. *Perf. 12*
692 A223 23c Atlapa Center 45 28
693 A223 60c Emblem, vert. 1.20 72

Halley's Comet A224

Designs: 30c, Panama la Vieja Cathedral tower, vert.

1986, Oct. 30 Litho. *Perf. 13½*
694 A224 23c multi 46 28
695 A224 30c multi 60 35

Size: 75x86mm.
Imperf

695A A224 1b multi 2.00

1986 World Cup Soccer Championships, Mexico — A225

Illustrations from Soccer History, by Sandoval and Meron.

1986, Oct. 30
696 A225 23c Argentina, winner 46 28
697 A225 30c Fed. Rep. of Germany, second 60 35
698 A225 37c Argentina, Germany 74 45

Souvenir Sheet

698A A225 1b Argentina, diff. 2.00

15th Central American and Caribbean Games, Dominican Republic — A226

1986, Nov. 21
699 A226 20c shown 40 24
700 A226 23c Montage of events 46 28

Christmas A227

1986, Dec. 18 Litho.
701 A227 23c multi 46 30
702 A227 36c multi 72 48
703 A227 42c multi 84 55

Intl. Peace Year A228

Tropical Carnival, Feb.-Mar. A229

1986, Dec. 30 *Perf. 13½*
704 A228 8c multi 16 12
705 A228 19c multi 38 25

1987, Jan. 27 Litho. *Perf. 13½*
706 A229 20c Dragon 40 30
707 A229 35c Sun 70 52

Size: 74x84mm.
Imperf

708 A229 1b like 35c 2.00 1.50

Panama Lions Club, 50th Anniv. (in 1985) A230

1987, Feb. 17 Litho. *Perf. 14*
709 A230 37c multi 75 58

Dated 1986.

Flowering Plants — A231

Birds A232

1987, Mar. 5
710 A231 3c Brownea macrophylla 6 5
711 A232 5c Thraupis episcopus 10 8
712 A231 8c Solandra grandiflora 16 12
713 A232 15c Tyrannus melancholicus 30 22
714 A231 19c Barleria micans 38 28
715 A232 23c Pelecanus occidentalis 45 35
716 A231 30c Cordia dentata 60 45
717 A232 36c Columba cayennensis 72 55
Nos. 710-717 (8) 2.77 2.10

Dated 1986.

Monument and Octavio Mendez Pereira, Founder A233

1987, Mar. 26 Litho. *Perf. 14*
718 A233 19c multi 38 28

University of Panama, 50th anniv. (in 1985). Stamp dated "1986."

UNFAO, 40th Anniv. (in 1985)
A234

1987, Apr. 9 *Perf. 13½*
719 A234 10c blk, pale ol & yel org 20 15
720 A234 45c blk, dk grn & yel grn 90 70

Natl. Theater, 75th Anniv.
A235

Baroque composers: 19c, Schutz (1585-1672). 37c, Bach. 60c, Handel. Nos. 721, 723-724 vert.

1987, Apr. 28 *Perf. 14*
721 A235 19c multi 38 28
722 A235 30c shown 60 45
723 A235 37c multi 75 60
724 A235 60c multi 1.20 90

Inter-American Development Bank, 25th Anniv. — A236

1987, May 13 **Litho.** *Perf. 14*
725 A236 23c multi 50 38

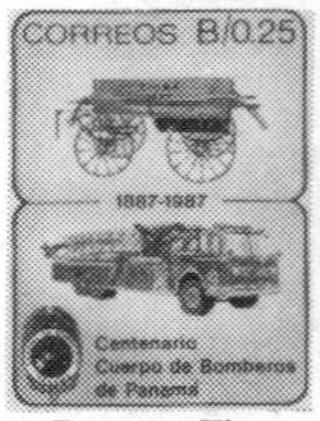

Panama Fire Brigade, Cent.
A237

10th Pan American Games, Indianapolis
A238

1987, Nov. 28 **Litho.** *Perf. 14*
726 A237 25c Fire wagon, 1887, and modern ladder truck 55 42
727 A237 35c Fireman carrying victim 78 58

1987, Dec. 11
728 A238 15c Wrestling, horiz. 35 26
729 A238 23c Tennis 50 38
730 A238 30c Swimming, horiz. 65 48
731 A238 41c Basketball 90 68
732 A238 60c Cycling 1.30 1.00
Nos. 728-732 (5) 3.70 2.80

Souvenir Sheet

733 A238 1b Weight lifting 2.25 1.75

Christmas
A239

Religious paintings: 22c, Adoration of the Magi, by Albrecht Nentz (d. 1479). 35c, Virgin Adored by Angels, by Matthias Grunewald (d. 1528). 37c, The Virgin and Child, by Konrad Witz (c. 1400-1445).

1987, Dec. 17
734 A239 22c multi 48 35
735 A239 35c multi 78 58
736 A239 37c multi 80 60

Intl. Year of Shelter for the Homeless
A240

1987, Dec. 29 *Perf. 14*
737 A240 45c shown 1.00 75
738 A240 50c Woman, boy, girl, shack, housing in perspective 1.10 82

Reforestation Campaign
A241

Say No to Drugs
A242

1988, Jan. 14 **Litho.** *Perf. 14½x14*
739 A241 35c dull grn & yel grn 78 58
740 A241 40c red & pink 90 68
741 A241 45c brn & lem 1.00 75

Dated 1987.

1988, Jan. 14
742 A242 10c org lil rose 22 16
743 A242 17c yel grn & lil rose 38 28
744 A242 25c pink & sky blue 55 42

Child Survival Campaign
A243

1988, Feb. 29 **Litho.** *Perf. 14*
745 A243 20c Breast-feeding 45 35
746 A243 31c Universal immunization 70 52
747 A243 45c Growth and development, vert. 1.00 75

Fish — A244

1988, Mar. 14
748 A244 7c Myripristis jacobus 16 12
749 A244 35c Pomacanthus paru 80 60
750 A244 60c Holocanthus tricolor 1.35 1.00
751 A244 1b Equetus punctatus 2.25 1.70

Girl Guides, 75th Anniv. — A245

1988, Apr. 14
752 A245 35c multi 80 60

Christmas
A246

St. John Bosco (1815-1888)
A247

Paintings: 17c, *Virgin and Gift-givers.* 45c, *Virgin of the Rosary and St. Dominic.*

1988, Dec. 29 **Litho.** *Perf. 12*
753 A246 17c multi 40 30
754 A246 45c multi 1.00 75

See No. C446.

1989, Jan. 31
755 A247 10c Portrait 22 16
756 A247 20c Basilica 48 35

1988 Summer Olympics, Seoul
A248

Athletes and medals.

1989, Mar. 17 **Litho.** *Perf. 12*
757 A248 17c Running 38 30
758 A248 25c Wrestling 55 42
759 A248 60c Weight lifting 1.30 98

Souvenir Sheet

760 A248 1b Swimming, vert. 2.20 1.65

See No. C447.

AIR POST STAMPS

Special Delivery Stamp No. E3 Surcharged in Dark Blue

CORREO AEREO
25  25
VEINTICINCO CENTESIMOS

1929, Feb. 8 **Unwmk.** *Perf. 12½*
C1 SD1 25c on 10c org 1.00 80
a. Inverted surcharge 22.50 22.50

Nos. E3-E4 Overprinted in Blue

CORREO AEREO

1929
C2 SD1 10c orange 50 50
a. Inverted overprint 16.00 14.00
b. Double overprint 16.00 14.00

Some specialists claim the red overprint is a proof impression.

With Additional Surcharge of New Value

C3 SD1 15c on 10c org 50 50
C4 SD1 25c on 20c dk brn 1.10 1.00
a. Double surcharge 14.00 14.00

No. E3 Surcharged in Blue

CORREO AEREO
5
CENTESIMOS

1930, Jan. 25
C5 SD1 5c on 10c org 50 50

No. 219 Overprinted in Red

CORREO
AEREO

1930, Feb. 28 *Perf. 12*
C6 A39 1b dk vio & blk 16.00 12.00

Airplane over Map of Panama
AP5 AP6

1930-41 **Engr.** *Perf. 12*
C6A AP5 5c bl ('41) 14 5
C6B AP5 7c rose car ('41) 22 7
C6C AP5 8c gray blk ('41) 22 7
C7 AP5 15c dp grn 30 5
C8 AP5 20c rose 35 5
C9 AP5 25c dp bl 65 65
Nos. C6A-C9 (6) 1.88 94

See No. C112.

1930, Aug. 4 *Perf. 12½*
C10 AP6 5c ultra 14 5
C11 AP6 10c orange 22 20
C12 AP6 30c dp vio 5.50 4.00
C13 AP6 50c dp red 1.40 50
C14 AP6 1b black 5.50 3.50
Nos. C10-C14 (5) 12.76 8.25

Amphibian
AP7

1931, Nov. **Typo.**

Without Gum

C15 AP7 5c dp bl 80 1.00
a. 5c gray bl 80 80
b. Horiz. pair, imperf. btwn. 50.00

Issued Nov. 24 to commemorate the start of regular airmail service between Panama City and the western provinces, but valid only on Nov. 28-29 on mail carried by aquaplane "3 Noviembre."

Many sheets have a papermaker's watermark "DOLPHIN BOND" in double-lined capitals.

No. C9 Surcharged in Red 19mm long

HABILITADA
20 c.

1932, Dec. 14 *Perf. 12*
C16 AP5 20c on 25c dp bl 3.50 50

Surcharge 17mm long

C16A AP5 20c on 25c dp bl 200.00 2.50

Special Delivery Stamp No. E4 Overprinted in Red or Black

CORREO AEREO

1934 *Perf. 12½.*
C17 SD1 20c dk brn 80 50
C17A SD1 20c dk brn (Bk) 65.00 55.00

Surcharged In Black

CORREO AEREO
10
CENTESIMOS

1935, June
C18 SD1 10c on 20c dk brn 80 50

Same Surcharge with Small "10"
C18A SD1 10c on 20c dk brn 40.00 5.00
b. Horiz. pair, imperf. vert. 80.00

Nos. 234 and 242 Surcharged in Blue

1836-1936
CORREO AEREO
PABLO AROSEMENA
5 CENTESIMOS

1936, Sept. 24
C19 A53 5c on ½c org 250.00 275.00
C20 A53 5c on 50c org 1.00 80
a. Double surcharge 60.00 60.00

Issued in commemoration of the centenary of the birth of President Pablo Arosemena.
It is claimed that No. C19 was not regularly issued.

Urraca Monument — AP8

Human Genius Uniting the Oceans AP9

Designs: 20c, Panama City. 30c, Balboa Monument. 50c, Pedro Miguel Locks. 1b, Palace of Justice.

1936, Dec. 1 Engr. *Perf. 12*
C21 AP8 5c blue 65 35
C22 AP9 10c yel org 80 60
C23 AP9 20c red 2.00 1.40
C24 AP8 30c dk vio 3.50 2.50
C25 AP9 50c car rose 8.25 6.00
C26 AP9 1b black 10.00 6.50
Nos. C21-C26 (6) 25.20 17.35

Issued to commemorate the 4th Postal Congress of the Americas and Spain.

Nos. C21-C26 Overprinted in Red or Blue

U
P
U

1937, Mar. 29
C27 AP8 5c bl (R) 40 40
a. Invert. ovpt. 35.00
C28 AP9 10c yel org (Bl) 65 50
C29 AP9 20c red (Bl) 1.60 1.25
a. Double ovpt. 35.00
C30 AP8 30c dk vio (R) 4.00 3.50
C31 AP8 50c car rose (Bl) 16.00 16.00
a. Double ovpt. 120.00
C32 AP9 1b blk (R) 20.00 16.00
Nos. C27-C32 (6) 42.65 37.65

Regular Stamps of 1921-26 Surcharged in Red

CORREO
AEREO
5¢

1937, June 30 *Perf. 12, 12½*
C33 A55 5c on 15c ultra 65 65
C34 A55 5c on 20c brn 65 65
C35 A47 10c on 10c vio 1.50 1.40

Regular Stamps of 1920-26 Surcharged in Red

CORREO AEREO
5¢

C36 A56 5c on 24c blk vio 65 65
C37 A39 5c on 1b dk vio & blk 50 50
C38 A56 10c on 50c blk 2.00 1.60
a. Inverted surcharge 18.00

No. 248 Overprinted in Red

CORREO
AEREO

Perf. 12½.
C39 A54 5c dk bl 65 65
a. Double overprint 18.00
Nos. C33-C39 (7) 6.60 6.10

Fire Dept. Badge AP14

Florencio Arosemena AP15

José Gabriel Duque — AP16

Perf. 14x14½
1937, Nov. 25 Photo. Wmk. 233
C40 AP14 5c blue 50 35
C41 AP15 10c orange 65 90
C42 AP16 20c crimson 1.20 50

50th anniversary of the Fire Department.

Basketball — AP17

Baseball AP18

Designs: 7c, Swimming. 8c, Boxing. 15c, Soccer.

1938, Feb. 2 *Perf. 14x14½, 14½x14*
C43 AP17 1c rose red 90 22
C44 AP18 2c green 90 10
C45 AP18 7c gray blk 1.25 25
C46 AP18 8c red brn 1.25 25
C47 AP17 15c ultra 3.00 1.25
a. Souv. sheet of 5 10.00 10.00
b. As "a", No. C43 omitted 2,500.
Nos. C43-C47 (5) 7.30 2.07

4th Central American Caribbean Games.

No. C47a measures 140x140mm. and contains one each of Nos. C43-C47 plus arms and inscriptions.

Cathedral Tower and Statue of Liberty, Flags of Panama and U.S. — AP22

Engraved and Lithographed
1938, Dec. 7 Unwmk. *Perf. 12½*
Center in Black, Flags in Red and Ultra.
C49 AP22 7c gray 28 22
C50 AP22 8c brt ultra 40 22
C51 AP22 15c red brn 50 50
C52 AP22 50c orange 6.26 6.25
C53 AP22 1b black 6.25 6.25
Nos. C49-C53 (5) 13.69 13.44

Issued in commemoration of the 150th anniversary of the Constitution of the United States of America.

Nos. C12 and C7 Surcharged in Red

7¢ 7¢
NORMAL DE
SANTIAGO
JUNIO 5 1938

1938, June 5 *Perf. 12½, 12*
C53A AP6 7c on 30c dp vio 40 40
c. Double surch. 18.00
d. Invtd. surch. 27.50
C53B AP5 8c on 15c dp grn 40 40
e. Invtd. surch. 22.50

Opening of the Normal School at Santiago, Veraguas Province, June 5, 1938. The 8c surcharge has no bars.

Belisario Porras — AP23

Designs: 2c, William Howard Taft. 5c, Pedro J. Sosa. 10c, Lucien Bonaparte Wise. 15c, Armando Reclus. 20c, Gen. George W. Goethals. 50c, Ferdinand de Lesseps. 1b, Theodore Roosevelt.

1939, Aug. 15 Engr.
C54 AP23 1c dl rose 35 10
C55 AP23 2c dp bl grn 35 12
C56 AP23 5c indigo 50 20
C57 AP23 10c dk vio 65 22
C58 AP23 15c ultra 1.25 35
C59 AP23 20c rose pink 3.50 1.60
C60 AP23 50c dk brn 4.00 80
C61 AP23 1b black 6.50 4.50
Nos. C54-C61 (8) 17.10 7.89

Opening of Panama Canal, 25th anniv.

Flags of the 21 American Republics AP31

1940, Apr. 15 Unwmk.
C62 AP31 15c blue 42 35

Pan American Union, 50th anniversary.

Stamps of 1939-40 Surcharged in Black:

a 5 5
b AEREO SIETE
c SIETE
d 8— 8

1940, Aug. 12
C63 AP23 (a) 5c on 15c lt ultra 22 22
a. "7 AEREO 7" on 15c lt ultra (#C58) 40.00 40.00
C64 A84 (b) 7c on 15c ultra 40 25
C65 AP23 (c) 7c on 20c rose pink 40 25
C66 AP31 (d) 8c on 15c bl 40 25

Stamps of 1924-30 Overprinted in Black or Red:

e 7 CONSTITUCION 7 CENTESIMOS 1941 CENTESIMOS AEREO
CONSTITUCION 1941 AEREO 15
f
CONSTITUCION 1941
g

1941, Jan. 2 *Perf. 12½, 12*
C67 SD1 (e) 7c on 10c org 80 80
C68 A53 (f) 15c on 24c yel brn (R) 2.50 2.00
C69 AP5 (g) 20c rose 2.50 2.00
C70 AP6 (g) 50c dp red 6.00 4.00
C71 AP6 (g) 1b blk (R) 13.50 8.25
Nos. C67-C71 (5) 25.30 17.05

Issued in commemoration of the new constitution of Panama which became effective January 2, 1941.

Liberty — AP32

Black Overprint.
1942, Feb. 19 Engr. *Perf. 12*
C72 AP32 20c chnt brn 2.00 1.60

Flags of Panama and Costa Rica AP33

Engr. & Litho.
1942, Apr. 25 Unwmk.
C73 AP33 15c dp grn, dk bl & dp rose 55 14

Issued to commemorate the first anniversary of the settlement of the Costa Rica-Panama border dispute.

Foreign postal stationery (stamped envelopes, postal cards and air letter sheets) lies beyond the scope of this Catalogue, which is limited to adhesive postage stamps.

Swordfish
AP34

J. D. Arosemena Normal School
AP35

Alejandro Melendez G.
AP40

Designs: 8c, Gate of Glory, Portobelo. 15c, Taboga Island, Balboa Harbor. 50c, Firehouse. 1b, Gold animal figure.

1942, June 4 **Engr.** ***Perf. 12***

C74 AP34 7c rose car	50	16
C75 AP34 8c dk ol brn & blk	16	7
C76 AP34 15c dk vio	25	7
C77 AP35 20c red brn	35	7
C78 AP34 50c ol grn	65	35
C79 AP34 1b blk & org yel	1.60	80
Nos. C74-C79 (6)	3.51	1.52

See Nos. C96-C99, C113 and C126.

1943, Dec. 16

Design: 5b, Ernesto T. Lefevre.

C80 AP40 3b dk ol gray	4.50	4.50
C81 AP40 5b dk bl	7.00	6.00

Catalogue values for unused stamps in this section, from this point to the end of the section, are for Never Hinged items.

Nos. C6C and C7 Surcharged in Carmine

AEREO
B/. 0.10
1947

1947, Mar. 8 ***Perf. 12***

C82 AP5 5c on 8c gray blk	14	10
a. Double overprint	25.00	
C83 AP5 10c on 15c dp grn	50	35

Nos. C74 to C76 Surcharged in Black or Carmine

AEREO
B/. 0.10
1947

C84 AP34 5c on 7c rose car (Bk)	16	16
a. Double surch.		375.00
C85 AP34 5c on 8c dk ol brn & blk	16	16
C86 AP34 10c on 15c dk vio	25	22
a. Double surch.	10.00	10.00

National Theater — AP42

1947, Apr. 7 **Engr.** **Unwmk.**

C87 AP42 8c violet	40	25

Issued to commemorate the second anniversary of the National Constitutional Assembly of 1945.

Manuel Amador Guerrero
AP43

Manuel Espinosa B. — AP44

Designs: 5c, José Agustin Arango. 10c, Federico Boyd. 15c, Ricardo Arias. 50c, Carlos Constantino Arosemena. 1b, Nicanor de Obarrio. 2b, Tomas Arias.

1948, Feb. 11 ***Perf. 12½***

Center in Black.

C88 AP43 3c blue	35	22
C89 AP43 5c brown	35	22
C90 AP43 10c orange	35	22
C91 AP43 15c dp cl	35	22
C92 AP44 20c dp car	65	50
C93 AP44 50c dk gray	1.20	65
C94 AP44 1b green	3.50	2.50
C95 AP44 2b yellow	8.00	6.00
Nos. C88-C95 (8)	14.75	10.53

Issued to honor members of the Revolutionary Junta of 1903.

Types of 1942.

1948, June 14 ***Perf. 12***

C96 AP34 2c carmine	75	8
C97 AP34 15c ol gray	25	10
C98 AP35 20c green	25	12
C99 AP34 50c rose car	3.50	2.00

Franklin D. Roosevelt and Juan D. Arosemena
AP45

Four Freedoms
AP46

Monument to F. D. Roosevelt
AP47

Map showing Boyd-Roosevelt Trans-Isthmian Highway
AP48

Franklin D. Roosevelt
AP49

1948, Sept. 15 ***Perf. 12½***

C100 AP45 5c dp car & blk	16	14
C101 AP46 10c yel org	30	25
C102 AP47 20c dl grn	35	35
C103 AP48 50c dp ultra & blk	65	60
C104 AP49 1b gray blk	1.50	1.20
Nos. C100-C104 (5)	2.96	2.54

Issued in tribute to Franklin Delano Roosevelt (1882-1945).

Monument to Cervantes
AP50

Design: 10c, Don Quixote attacking windmill.

1948, Nov. 15

C105 AP50 5c dk bl & blk	16	10
C106 AP50 10c pur & blk	35	25

Issued to commemorate the 400th anniversary of the birth of Miguel de Cervantes Saavedra, novelist, playwright and poet.

No. C106 Overprinted in Carmine

"CENTENARIO DE
JOSE GABRIEL DUQUE"

"18 de Enero de 1949"

1949, Jan.

C107 AP50 10c pur & blk	40	38
a. Inverted ovpt.	8.00	

Issued to commemorate the centenary of the birth of José Gabriel Duque (1849-1918), newspaper publisher and philanthropist.

Nos. C96, C6A, C97 and C99 Overprinted in Black or Red

h

i

1949, May

C108 AP34(h) 2c carmine	16	16
a. Double ovpt.	5.00	
C109 AP5(i) 5c bl (R)	25	25
C110 AP34(h) 15c ol gray (R)	65	65
C111 AP34(h) 50c rose car	2.25	2.25

Issued to commemorate the centenary of the incorporation of Chiriqui Province.

Types of 1930-42.

Design: 10c, Gate of Glory, Portobelo.

1949, Aug. 4 ***Perf. 12***

C112 AP5 5c orange	16	8
C113 AP34 10c dk bl & blk	20	14

Stamps of 1943-49 Overprinted or Surcharged in Black, Green or Red

1949, Sept. 9

C114 AP34 2c carmine	12	12
a. Inverted ovpt.	14.00	
b. Double ovpt.	14.00	
C115 AP5 5c org (G)	38	25
a. Inverted ovpt.	8.00	
b. Double ovpt.	20.00	
c. Double ovpt., one inverted	20.00	
C116 AP34 10c dk bl & blk (R)	38	30
C117 AP40 25c on 3b dk ol gray (R)	50	50
C118 AP34 50c rose car	1.75	1.25
Nos. C114-C118 (5)	3.13	2.42

Issued to commemorate the 75th anniversary of the formation of the Universal Postal Union.

No. C115 has small overprint, 15½x12mm., like No. 368. Overprint on Nos. C114, C116 and C118 as illustrated. Surcharge on No. C117 is arranged vertically, 29x18mm.

University of San Javier
AP51

1949, Dec. 7 **Engr.** ***Perf. 12½***

C119 AP51 5c dk bl & blk	35	14

See note after No. 371.

Mosquito — AP52

1950, Jan. 12 ***Perf. 12***

C120 AP52 5c dp ultra & gray blk	1.40	65

Issued to honor Dr. Carlos J. Finlay. See note after No. 372.

Nos. C96, C112, C113 and C9 Overprinted in Black or Carmine (5 or 4 lines)

CENTENARIO
del Gral. José
de San Martín
17 de Agosto
de 1950

1950, Aug. 17 **Unwmk.**

C121 AP34 2c carmine	35	25
C122 AP5 5c orange	35	35
C123 AP34 10c dk bl & blk (C)	50	40
C124 AP5 25c dp bl (C)	80	65

Same on No. 362, Overprinted "AEREO"

C125 A105 50c pur & blk (C)	1.60	1.10
Nos. C121-C125 (5)	3.60	2.75

Issued to commemorate the centenary of the death of Gen. José de San Martin.

Firehouse Type of 1942.

1950, Oct. 30 **Engr.**

C126 AP34 50c dp bl	2.00	1.00

Nos. C113 and C81 Surcharged in Carmine or Orange

AEREO
B/. 0.02
X 1952 X

1952, Feb. 20

C127 AP34 2c on 10c	16	10
a. Pair, one without surcharge	250.00	
C128 AP34 5c on 10c (O)	20	8
b. Pair, one without surcharge	250.00	
C128A AP40 1b on 5b	25.00	25.00

The surcharge on No. C128A is arranged to fit stamp, with four bars covering value panel at bottom, instead of crosses.

Nos. 376 and 380 Surcharged "AEREO 1952" and New Value in Carmine or Black.

1952, Aug. 1

C129 A97 5c on 2c ver & blk (C)	14	8
a. Inverted surcharge	22.50	
C130 A99 25c on 10c pur & org	65	60

Isabella Type of Regular Issue

Perf. 12½

1952, Oct. 20 Unwmk. Engr.

Center in Black

C131	A110	4c red org	8	7
C132	A110	5c ol grn	10	7
C133	A110	10c orange	35	30
C134	A110	25c gray bl	55	35
C135	A110	50c chocolate	1.00	60
C136	A110	1b black	3.50	3.25
		Nos. C131-C136 (6)	5.58	4.64

Issued to commemorate the 500th anniversary of the birth of Queen Isabella I of Spain.

No. C113 Surcharged "5 1953" in Carmine.

1953, Apr. 22 *Perf. 12*

C137 AP34 5c on 10c dk bl & blk 35 10

Masthead of La Estrella — AP54

1953, July

C138	AP54	5c rose car	16	14
C139	AP54	10c blue	22	20

Centenary of Panama's first newspaper, La Estrella.

Act of Independence — AP55

Senora de Remon and Pres. José A. Remon Cantera AP56

Designs: 7c, Pollera. 25c, National flower. 50c, Marcos A. Salazar, Esteban Huertas and Domingo Diaz A. 1b, Dancers.

1953, Nov.

C140	AP55	2c dp ultra	9	7
C141	AP56	5c dp grn	14	7
C142	AP56	7c gray	20	14
C143	AP56	25c black	1.50	65
C144	AP56	50c dk brn	80	65
C145	AP56	1b red org	2.25	1.00
		Nos. C140-C145 (6)	4.98	2.58

Founding of republic, 50th anniversary.

Nos. C138-C139 Surcharged with New Value in Black or Red

1953-54

C146	AP54	1c on 5c rose car ('54)	7	5
C147	AP54	1c on 10c bl (R)	7	5

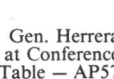

Gen. Herrera at Conference Table — AP57

Design: 1b, Gen. Herrera leading troops.

1954, Dec. 4 Litho. *Perf. 12½*

C148	AP57	6c dp grn	14	7
C149	AP57	1b scar & blk	2.50	2.25

Issued to commemorate the centenary of the death of Gen. Tomas Herrera.

Rotary Emblem and Map — AP58

1955, Feb. 23

C150	AP58	6c rose vio	14	7
C151	AP58	21c red	50	35
C152	AP58	1b black	4.00	2.25
a.		1b vio blk	4.50	4.00

Issued to commemorate the 50th anniversary of the founding of Rotary International.

Pres. J. A. Remon Cantera — AP59

1955, June 1

C153 AP59 6c rose vio & blk 16 7

Issued in tribute to Pres. José Antonio Remon Cantera, 1908-1955.

No. C151 Surcharged

B/.xxxxxxxx0.15

1955, Dec. 7

C154 AP58 15c on 21c red 40 35

Pedro J. Sosa — AP60

First Barge Going through Canal and de Lesseps AP61

Perf. 12½

1955, Nov. 22 Unwmk. Litho.

C155	AP60	5c grn, *lt grn*	16	7
C156	AP61	1b red lil & blk	2.00	1.60

Issued to commemorate the 150th anniversary of the birth of Ferdinand de Lesseps. Imperforates exist.

Pres. Dwight D. Eisenhower AP62

Statue of Bolivar AP63

Bolivar Hall AP64

Portraits-Presidents: C158, Pedro Aramburu, Argentina. C159, Dr. Victor Paz Estenssoro, Bolivia. C160, Dr. Juscelino Kubitschek O., Brazil. C161, Gen. Carlos Ibanez del Campo, Chile. C162, Gen. Gustavo Rojas Pinilla, Colombia. C163, Jose Figueres, Costa Rica. C164, Gen. Fulgencio Batista y Zaldivar, Cuba. C165, Gen. Hector B. Trujillo Molina, Dominican Rep. C166, José Maria Velasco Ibarra, Ecuador. C167, Col. Carlos Castillo Armas, Guatemala. C168, Gen. Paul E. Magloire, Haiti. C169, Julio Lozano Diaz, Honduras. C170, Adolfo Ruiz Cortines, Mexico. C171, Gen. Anastasio Somoza, Nicaragua. C172, Ricardo Arias Espinosa, Panama. C173, Gen. Alfredo Stroessner, Paraguay. C174, Gen. Manuel Odria, Peru. C175, Col. Oscar Osorio, El Salvador. C176, Dr. Alberto F. Zubiria, Uruguay. C177, Gen. Marcos Perez Jimenez, Venezuela. 1b, Simon Bolivar.

1956, July 18

C157	AP62	6c rose car & vio bl	65	35
C158	AP62	6c brt grnsh bl & blk	25	20
C159	AP62	6c bis & blk	25	20
C160	AP62	6c emer & blk	25	20
C161	AP62	6c lt grn & brn	25	20
C162	AP62	6c yel & grn	25	20
C163	AP62	6c brt vio & grn	25	20
C164	AP62	6c dl pur & vio bl	25	20
C165	AP62	6c red lil & sl grn	25	20
C166	AP62	6c cit & vio bl	25	20
C167	AP62	6c ap grn & brn	25	20
C168	AP62	6c brn & vio bl	25	20
C169	AP62	6c brt car & grn	25	20
C170	AP62	6c red & brn	40	25
C171	AP62	6c lt bl & grn	25	20
C172	AP62	6c vio bl & grn	25	20
C173	AP62	6c org & blk	25	20
C174	AP62	6c bluish gray & brn	25	20
C175	AP62	6c sal rose & blk	25	20
C176	AP62	6c dk grn & vio bl	25	20
C177	AP62	6c dk org brn & dk grn	25	20
C178	AP63	20c dk bluish gray	65	50
C179	AP64	50c green	1.00	1.00
C180	AP63	1b brown	2.50	1.60
		Nos. C157-C180 (24)	9.95	7.50

Issued to commemorate the Pan-American Conference, Panama City, July 21-22, 1956, and the 130th anniversary of the first Pan-American Conference. Imperforates exist.

Ruins of First Town Council Building — AP65

Design: 50c, City Hall, Panama City.

1956, Aug. 14

C181	AP65	25c red	50	35
C182	AP65	50c black	1.00	90
a.		Souvenir sheet of 3	2.25	2.25

Issued to commemorate the sixth Inter-American Congress of Municipalities, Panama City, Aug. 14-19, 1956.

No. C182a contains one each of Nos. 404, C181-C182, imperf., with inscription in gold border. The sheet sold for 85c.

Monument AP66

St. Thomas Hospital AP67

1956, Nov. 27 Wmk. 311

C183	AP66	5c green	10	5
C184	AP67	15c dk car	25	20

Issued to commemorate the centenary of the birth of Pres. Belisario Porras.

Highway Construction — AP68

Designs: 20c, Road through jungle, Darien project. 1b, Map of Americas showing Pan-American Highway.

Wmk. 311

1957, Aug. 1 Litho. *Perf. 12½*

C185	AP68	10c black	15	9
C186	AP68	20c lt bl & blk	50	25
C187	AP68	1b green	2.25	1.90
a.		AP65 Souvenir sheet of 3, unwmkd.	5.00	5.00

Nos. C185-C187a were issued to publicize the 7th Pan-American Highway Congress.

No. C187a is No. C182a overprinted in black: "VII degree CONGRESSO INTER-AMERICANO DE CARRETERAS 1957."

No. C153 Surcharged "1957" and New Value.

1957, Aug. 13 Unwmk.

C188 AP59 10c on 6c rose vio & blk 20 16

Remon Polyclinic — AP69

Customs House, Portobelo AP70

Buildings: C191, Portobelo Castle. C192, San Jeronimo Castle. C193, Remon Hippodrome. C194, Legislature. C195, Interior and Treasury Department. C196, El Panama Hotel. C197, San Lorenzo Castle.

Wmk. 311

1957, Oct. Litho. *Perf. 12½*

Design in Black.

C189	AP69	10c lt bl	22	12
C190	AP70	10c lilac	22	12
C191	AP70	10c gray	22	12
C192	AP70	10c lil rose	22	12
C193	AP70	10c ultra	22	12
C194	AP70	10c brn ol	22	12
C195	AP70	10c org yel	22	12
C196	AP70	10c yel grn	22	12
C197	AP70	1b red	2.25	1.60
		Nos. C189-C197 (9)	4.01	2.56

No. C148 Surcharged with New Value and "1958" in Red

1958, Feb. 11 Unwmk.

C198 AP57 5c on 6c dp grn 20 7

United Nations Emblem — AP71

Flags of Panama and U.N. AP72

1958, March 5 Litho. Wmk. 311
C199 AP71 10c brt grn 16 10
C200 AP71 21c lt ultra 35 25
C201 AP71 50c orange 70 60
C202 AP72 1b gray, ultra & car 2.00 1.60
a. Souvenir sheet of 4 5.50 5.50

Issued to commemorate the tenth anniversary of the United Nations (in 1955).

No. C202a measures 127x102mm. and contains one each of Nos. C199-C202, imperf. Marginal inscription in carmine and ultramarine. The sheet also exists with the 10c and 50c omitted.

OAS Type of Regular Issue, 1958.

Designs: 10c, 1b, Flags of 21 American Nations. 50c, Headquarters in Washington.

1958, July 10 Unwmk. *Perf. 12½*
Center yellow and black; flags in national colors.
C203 A124 5c lt bl 10 8
C204 A124 10c car rose 16 12
C205 A124 50c gray 60 60
C206 A124 1b black 1.90 1.60

Issued to commemorate the 10th anniversary of the Organization of American States.

Type of Regular Issue.

Pavilions: 15c, Vatican City. 50c, United States. 1b, Belgium.

1958, Sept. 8 Wmk. 311 *Perf. 12½*
C207 A125 15c gray & lt vio 25 20
C208 A125 50c dk gray & org brn 65 65
C209 A125 1b brt vio & bluish grn 1.40 1.40
a. Souv. sheet of 7 3.50 3.50

World's Fair, Brussels, Apr. 17-Oct. 19. No. C209a contains one each of Nos. 418-421 and C207-C209 with marginal inscription and fair emblem in slate and light brown. Size: 128½x102mm. Sold for 2b.

Pope Type of Regular Issue

Portraits of Pius XII: 5c, As cardinal. 30c, Wearing papal tiara. 50c, Enthroned.

1959, Jan. 21 Litho. Wmk. 311
C210 A126 5c violet 10 10
C211 A126 30c lil rose 50 40
C212 A126 50c bl gray 80 65
a. Souvenir sheet of 4 1.90 1.90

Issued in memory of Pope Pius XII, 1876-1958.

No. C212a measures 127x85½mm. and contains one each of Nos. C210-C212 and No. 422, imperf. and watermarked sideways. Marginal inscriptions and ornaments in colors of stamps. Sold for 1b. The sheet also exists with 30c omitted. No. C212a with C.E.P.A.L. overprint is listed as No. C221a.

Human Rights Issue
Type of Regular Issue, 1959

Designs: 5c, Humanity looking into sun. 10c, 20c, Torch and U. N. emblem. 50c, U. N. Flag. 1b, U. N. Headquarters building.

1959, Apr. 14 *Perf. 12½*
C213 A127 5c emer & bl 10 8
C214 A127 10c gray & org brn 14 10
C215 A127 20c brn & gray 25 20
C216 A127 50c grn & ultra 70 65
C217 A127 1b red & bl 1.50 1.40
Nos. C213-C217 (5) 2.69 2.43

Nos. C213-C215, C212a Overprinted and C216 Surcharged in Red or Dark Blue

8A REUNION
C.E.P.A.L.
MAYO 1959

1959, May 16
C218 A127 5c emer & bl (R) 10 8
C219 A127 10c gray & org brn (Bl) 16 14
C220 A127 20c brn & gray (R) 35 25
C221 A127 1b on 50c grn & ultra (R) 1.90 1.50
a. Souvenir sheet of 4 4.00 4.00

Issued to commemorate the 8th Reunion of the Economic Commission for Latin America.

This overprint also exists on Nos. C216-C217. These have been disavowed by Panama's postmaster general.

No. C221a is No. C212a with two-line black overprint at top of sheet: "8a. REUNION DE LA C.E.P.A.L. MAYO 1959."

Type of Regular Issue, 1959.

Portraits: 5c, Justo A. Facio, Rector. 10c, Ernesto de la Guardia, Jr., Pres. of Panama.

Wmk. 311
1959, July 27 Litho. *Perf. 12½*
C222 A128 5c black 8 7
C223 A128 10c black 16 8

Type of Regular Issue, 1959.

Designs: 5c, Boxing. 10c, Baseball. 50c, Basketball.

1959, Oct. 26 Wmk. 311 *Perf. 12½*
C224 A130 5c blk & red brn 10 8
C225 A130 10c gray & red brn 20 14
C226 A130 50c lt ultra & org 80 65

Nos. C143-C145 Overprinted in Vermilion, Red or Black

NACIONES UNIDAS
AÑO MUNDIAL.
REFUGIADOS.
1959–1960

Unwmk.
1960, Feb. 6 Engr. *Perf. 12*
C227 AP56 25c blk (V) 25 20
C228 AP56 50c dk brn (R) 65 40
C229 AP56 1b red org 1.50 1.25

Issued to publicize World Refugee Year, July 1, 1959-June 30, 1960.

The revenues from the sale of Nos. C227-C229 went to the United Nations Refugee Fund.

Administration Building, National University — AP74

Designs: 21c, Humanities building. 25c, Medical school. 30c, Dr. Octavio Mendez Pereria first rector of University.

Wmk. 311
1960, Mar. 23 Litho. *Perf. 12½*
C230 AP74 10c brt grn 14 10
C231 AP74 21c lt bl 30 20
C232 AP74 25c ultra 40 25
C233 AP74 30c black 42 35

Issued to commemorate the 25th anniversary of the founding of the National University.

Olympic Games Issue
Type of Regular Issue, 1960

Designs: 5c, Basketball. 10c, Bicycling (horiz.). 25c, Javelin thrower. 50c, Athlete with Olympic torch.

Wmk. RP Multiple (343).
1960, Sept. 22 *Perf. 12½*
C234 A131 5c org & red 7 7
C235 A131 10c ocher & blk 16 14
C236 A131 25c lt bl & dk bl 40 35
C237 A131 50c brn & blk 70 65
a. Souv. sheet of 2, #C236-C237 2.25 2.25

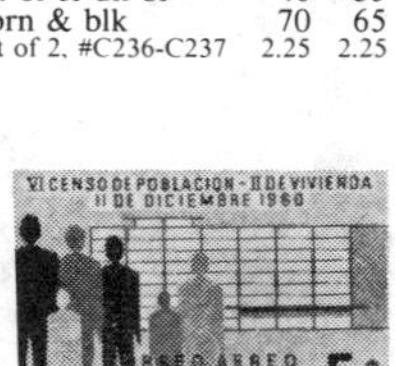

Citizens' Silhouettes AP75

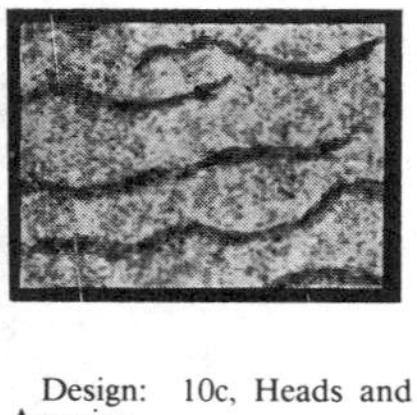
Wmk. 229-Wavy Lines

Design: 10c, Heads and map of Central America.

1960 Litho. Wmk. 229
C238 AP75 5c black 7 7
C239 AP75 10c brown 16 14

Issued to publicize the 6th census of population and the 2nd census of dwellings (No. C238), Dec. 11, 1960, and the All America Census, 1960 (No. C239).

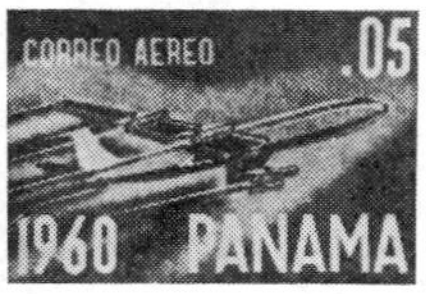

Boeing 707 Jet Liner AP76

1960, Dec. 1 Wmk. 343 *Perf. 12½*
C240 AP76 5c lt grnsh bl 10 7
C241 AP76 10c emerald 16 14
C242 AP76 20c red brn 35 25

Souvenir Sheet

U.N. Emblem — AP77

Wmk. 311
1961, March 7 Litho. *Imperf.*
C243 AP77 80c blk & car rose 1.40 1.40

15th anniv. (in 1960) of the UN.

No. C243 Overprinted in Blue with Large Uprooted Oak Emblem and "Ano de los Refugiados."

1961, June 2
C244 AP77 80c blk & car rose 2.50 2.50

Issued to commemorate World Refugee Year, July 1, 1959-June 30, 1960.

Lions International Issue
Type of Regular Issue, 1961.

Designs: 5c, Helen Keller School for the Blind. 10c, Children's summer camp. 21c, Arms of Panama and Lions emblem.

1961, May 2 Wmk. 311 *Perf. 12½*
C245 A133 5c black 8 7
C246 A133 10c emerald 20 8
C247 A133 21c ultra, yel & red 38 25

Nos. C230 and C236 Surcharged in Black or Red

HABILITADA
en
B/. 0.01

1961 Wmk. 311 (1c); Wmk. 343
C248 AP74 1c on 10c brt grn 10 7
C249 A131 1b on 25c lt bl & dk bl (Bk) 1.50 1.40
C250 A131 1b on 25c lt bl & dk bl (R) 1.50 1.40

Pres. Roberto F. Chiari and Pres. Mario Echandi AP78

Wmk. 343
1961, Oct. 2 Litho. *Perf. 12½*
C251 AP78 1b blk & gold 1.50 1.25

Issued to commemorate the meeting of the Presidents of Panama and Costa Rica at Paso Canoa, Apr. 21, 1961.

Dag Hammarskjold AP79

1961, Dec. 27 *Perf. 12½*
C252 AP79 10c black 16 14

Issued in memory of Dag Hammarskjold, Secretary General of the United Nations, 1953-61.

No. C230 Surcharged

Vale B/. 0.15

1962, Feb. 21 Wmk. 311
C253 AP74 15c on 10c brt grn 25 20

XX

No. C236 Surcharged

VALE
B/. 1.00

Wmk. 343
C254 A131 1b on 25c lt bl & dk bl 1.50 1.25

City Hall, Colon AP80

1962, Feb. 28 Litho. Wmk. 311
C255 AP80 5c vio bl & blk 16 10

Issued to publicize the third Central American Municipal Assembly, Colon, May 13-17.

Church Type of Regular Issue, 1962.

Designs: 5c, Church of Christ the King. 7c, Church of San Miguel. 8c, Church of the Sanctuary. 10c, Saints Church. 15c, Church of St. Ann. 21c, Canal Zone Synagogue (Now used as USO Center). 25c, Panama Synagogue. 30c, Church of St. Francis. 50c, Protestant Church, Canal Zone. 1b, Catholic Church, Canal Zone.

Wmk. 343
1962-64 Litho. *Perf. 12½*
Buildings in Black
C256 A138 5c pur & buff 7 7
C257 A138 7c lil rose & brt pink 12 10
C258 A139 8c pur & bl 14 10
C259 A139 10c lil & sal 16 10
C259A A139 10c grn & dl red brn ('64) 20 20
C260 A139 15c red & buff 22 20
C261 A138 21c brn & bl 35 30
C262 A138 25c bl & pink 40 35
C263 A139 30c lil rose & bl 45 42
C264 A138 50c lil & lt grn 70 65
a. Souvenir sheet of 4 2.00 2.00
C265 A139 1b bl & sal 1.50 1.40
Nos. C256-C265 (11) 4.31 3.89

Issued to publicize freedom of religion in Panama. Issue dates: No. C259A, June 4, 1964; others, July 20, 1962.

No. C264a contains one each of Nos. 448-449 and C262 and C264 imperf. with black marginal inscription. Size: 133x107mm.

Nos. C234 and C236 Overprinted and Surcharged "IX JUEGOS C.A. Y DEL CARIBE KINGSTON-1962" and Games Emblem in Black, Green, Orange or Red.

1962 Wmk. 343 *Perf. 12½*

C266 A131	5c org & red	10	9
C267 A131	10c on 25c lt bl & dk bl (G)	18	15
C268 A131	15c on 25c lt bl & dk bl (O)	28	25
C269 A131	20c on 25c lt bl & dk bl (R)	32	30
C270 A131	25c lt bl & dk bl	40	35
	Nos. C266-C270 (5)	1.28	1.14

Issued to commemorate the Ninth Central American and Caribbean Games, Kingston, Jamaica, Aug. 11-25.

Nos. CB1-CB2 Surcharged

V
A
L
E
.20
¢
XX

1962, May 3 Wmk. 311

C271 SPAP1	10c on 5c + 5c car rose	1.20	80
C272 SPAP1	20c on 10c + 10c vio bl	1.90	80

Type of Regular Issue, 1962.

Design: 10c, Canal bridge completed.

Wmk. 343

1962, Oct. 12 Litho. *Perf. 12½*

C273 A140	10c bl & blk	16	14

John H. Glenn, "Friendship 7" Capsule AP81

UPAE Emblem AP82

Designs: 10c, "Friendship 7" capsule and globe (horiz.). 31c, Capsule in space (horiz.). 50c, Glenn with space helmet.

1962, Oct. 19 Wmk. 311 *Perf. 12½*

C274 AP81	5c rose red	10	10
C275 AP81	10c yellow	20	16
C276 AP81	31c blue	80	60
C277 AP81	50c emerald	1.00	80
a.	Souvenir sheet of 4	2.25	2.25

Issued to commemorate the first orbital flight of U.S. astronaut Lt. Col. John H. Glenn, Jr., Feb. 20, 1962. No. C277a contains one each of No. C274-C277, imperf. Green background with rose red inscription and black control number. Sold for 1b. Size: 76x100mm.

1963, Jan. 8 Litho. Wmk. 343

C278 AP82	10c multi	16	10

Issued to commemorate the 50th anniversary of the founding of the Postal Union of the Americas and Spain, UPAE.

Type of Regular Issue

Designs: 10c, Fire Engine "China", Plaza de Santa Ana. 15c, 14th Street team. 21c, Fire Brigade emblem.

1963, Jan. 22 Wmk. 311 *Perf. 12½*

C279 A141	10c org & blk	16	14
C280 A141	15c lil & blk	20	16
C281 A141	21c gold, red & ultra	45	42

"FAO" and Wheat Emblem — AP83

1963, Mar. 21 Litho.

C282 AP83	10c grn & red	20	16
C283 AP83	15c ultra & red	25	22

FAO "Freedom from Hunger" campaign.

No. C245 Overprinted in Yellow, Orange or Green: "XXII Convención / Leonistica / Centroamericana / Panama, 18-21 / Abril 1963"

1963, Apr. 18 Wmk. 311 *Perf. 12½*

C284 A133	5c blk (Y)	10	8
C285 A133	5c blk (O)	10	8
C286 A133	5c blk (G)	10	8

22nd Central American Lions Congress, Panama, Apr. 18-21.

No. C230 Surcharged:

HABILITADO

Vale B/. 0.04

1963, June 11

C287 AP74	4c on 10c brt grn	8	5

Nos. 445 and 432 Overprinted "AEREO" Vertically

1963 Wmk. 343 *Perf. 12½*

C288 A139	10c grn, yel & blk	16	14

Wmk. 311

C289 A130	20c emer & red brn	30	22

No. C234 Overprinted: "LIBERTAD DE PRENSA 20-VIII-63"

1963, Aug. 20 Wmk. 343

C290 A131	5c org & red	10	8

Freedom of Press Day, Aug. 20, 1963.

No. C232 Surcharged in Red: "VALE 10¢"

1963, Oct. 9 Wmk. 311 *Perf. 12½*

C291 AP74	10c on 25c ultra	16	14

Type of Regular Issue, 1963

Flags and Presidents: 5c, Julio A. Rivera, El Salvador. 10c, Miguel Ydigoras F., Guatemala. 21c, John F. Kennedy, USA.

Perf. 12½x12

1963, Dec. 18 Litho. Unwmk.

Portrait in Slate Green.

C292 A142	5c yel, red & ultra	30	30
C293 A142	10c bl, red & ultra	50	40
C294 A142	21c org yel, red & ultra	1.50	1.40

Balboa Type of Regular Issue, 1964

1964, Jan. 22 Photo. *Perf. 13*

C295 A143	10c dk vio, *pale pink*	20	16

No. C261 Surcharged in Red: "VALE B/.0.50"

1964 Wmk. 343 Litho. *Perf. 12½*

C296 A138	50c on 21c brn, bl & blk	1.00	70

Type of 1962 Overprinted: "HABILITADA"

C297 A139	1b emer, yel & blk	1.90	1.60

Nos. 434 and 444 Surcharged: "Aéreo B/.0.10"

1964 Wmk. 343 *Perf. 12½*

C298 A131	10c on 5c bl grn & emer	20	14
C299 A139	10c on 5c rose, lt grn & blk	20	14

St. Patrick's Cathedral, New York — AP84

Cathedrals: No. C301, St. Stephen's, Vienna. No. C302, St. Sofia's, Sofia. C303, Notre Dame, Paris. No. C304, Cologne. C305, St. Paul's, London. C306, Metropolitan, Athens. C307, St. Elizabeth's, Kosice, Czechoslovakia (inscr. Kassa, Hungary). No. C308, New Delhi. C309, Milan. C310, Guadalupe Basilica. C311, New Church, Delft, Netherlands. C312, Lima. C313, St. John's Poland. C314, Lisbon. C315, St. Basil's, Moscow. C316, Toledo. C317, Stockholm. C318, Basel. C319, St. George's Patriarchal Church, Istanbul. 1b, Panama City. 2b, St. Peter's Basilica, Rome.

Unwmk.

1964, Feb. 17 Engr. *Perf. 12*

Center in Black

C300 AP84	21c olive	40	25
C301 AP84	21c chocolate	40	25
C302 AP84	21c aqua	40	25
C303 AP84	21c red brn	40	25
C304 AP84	21c magenta	40	25
C305 AP84	21c red	40	25
C306 AP84	21c org red	40	25
C307 AP84	21c blue	40	25
C308 AP84	21c brown	40	25
C309 AP84	21c green	40	25
C310 AP84	21c vio bl	40	25
C311 AP84	21c dk sl grn	40	25
C312 AP84	21c violet	40	25
C313 AP84	21c black	40	25
C314 AP84	21c emerald	40	25
C315 AP84	21c dp vio	40	25
C316 AP84	21c ol grn	40	25
C317 AP84	21c car rose	40	25
C318 AP84	21c Prus grn	40	25
C319 AP84	21c dk brn	40	25
C320 AP84	1b dk bl	1.50	75
C321 AP84	2b yel grn	3.00	1.50
a.	Souv. sheet of 6	6.50	6.50
	Nos. C300-C321 (22)	12.50	7.25

Issued to commemorate Vatican II, the 21st Ecumenical Council of the Roman Catholic Church.

No. C321a contains 6 imperf. stamps similar to Nos. C300, C303, C305, C315, C320 and C321. Black marginal inscription and red control number. Size: 198x138mm. Sold for 3.85b.

Six stamps of this set (Nos. C300, C305, C309, C319, C321a) were overprinted "1964." The overprint is olive bister on the stamps, yellow on the souvenir sheet. The overprint is reported to exist also in yellow gold on the same six stamps and in olive bister on the souvenir sheet.

Roosevelt Type of Regular Issue

Perf. 12x12½

1964, Oct. 9 Litho. Unwmk.

C345 A147	20c grn & blk, *buff*	35	30
a.	Souv. sheet of 2	55	55

Issued to honor Eleanor Roosevelt (1884-1962). No. C345a contains two imperf. stamps similar to Nos. 478 and C345. Lilac margin with white inscription and red control number. Size: 87x76mm.

Bird Type of Regular Issue, 1965.

Song Birds: 5c, Common troupial (horiz.). 10c, Crimson-backed tanager (horiz.).

1965, Oct. 27 Unwmk. *Perf. 14*

C346 A148	5c dp org & multi	8	7
C347 A148	10c brt bl & multi	16	12

Fish Type of Regular Issue

Designs: 8c, Shrimp. 12c, Hammerhead. 13c, Atlantic sailfish. 25c, Seahorse (vert.).

1965, Dec. 7 Litho.

C348 A149	8c multi	16	12
C349 A149	12c multi	25	20
C350 A149	13c multi	25	22
C351 A149	25c multi	50	40

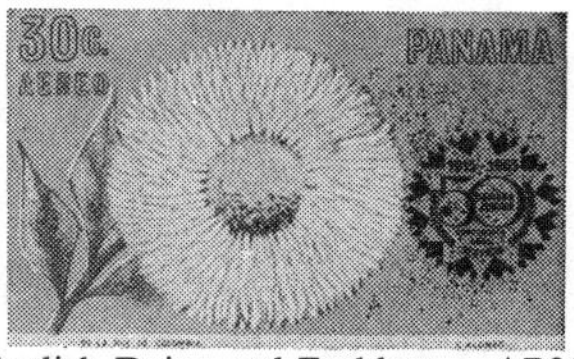

English Daisy and Emblem — AP85

Designs (Junior Chamber of Commerce Emblem and): No. C353, Hibiscus. No. C354, Orchid. No. C355, Water lily. No. C356, Gladiolus. No. C357, Flor del Espiritu Santo.

1966, Mar. 16

C352 AP85	30c brt pink & multi	50	40
C353 AP85	30c sal & multi	50	40
C354 AP85	30c pale yel & multi	50	40
C355 AP85	40c lt grn & multi	80	50
C356 AP85	40c bl & multi	80	50
C357 AP85	40c pink & multi	80	50
	Nos. C352-C357 (6)	3.90	2.70

Issued to commemorate the 50th anniversary of the Junior Chamber of Commerce.

Nos. C224 and C236 Surcharged

1966, June 27 Wmk. 311 *Perf. 12½*

C358 A130	3c on 5c blk & red brn	8	7

Wmk. 343

C359 A131	13c on 25c lt & dk bl	30	22

The old denominations are not obliterated on Nos. C358-C359.

Animal Type of Regular Issue, 1967

Domestic Animals: 10c, Pekingese dog. 13c, Zebu (horiz.). 30c, Cat. 40c, Horse (horiz.).

1967, Feb. 3 Unwmk. *Perf. 14*

C360 A150	10c multi	20	16
C361 A150	13c multi	25	20
C362 A150	30c multi	55	45
C363 A150	40c multi	70	55

Young Hare, by Durer AP86

Designs: 10c, St. Jerome and the Lion, by Albrecht Durer. 20c, Lady with the Ermine, by Leonardo Da Vinci. 30c, The Hunt, by Delacroix (horiz.).

1967, Sept. 1

C364 AP86	10c blk, buff & car	20	14
C365 AP86	13c lt yel & multi	25	16
C366 AP86	20c multi	40	22
C367 AP86	30c multi	60	40

Games Type of Regular Issue and

San Blas Indian Girl — AP87

Design: 13c, Thatcher Ferry bridge.

1970, Jan. 6 Litho. *Perf. 13½*

C368 A158	13c multi	25	16
C369 AP87	30c multi	55	42
a.	"AEREO" omitted	*50.00*	*50.00*

See notes after No. 525.

Juan D. Arosemena and Arosemena Stadium — AP88

Designs: 2c, 3c, 5c, like 1c. No. C374, Basketball. No. C375, New Panama Gymnasium. No. C376, Revolution Stadium. No. C377, Panamanian man and woman in Stadium. 30c, Stadium, eternal flame, arms of Mexico, Puerto Rico and Cuba.

Wmk. Argentine Arms & "RA" (365)

1970, Oct. 7 ***Perf. 13½***

C370	AP88	1c pink & multi	5	5
C371	AP88	2c pink & multi	5	5
C372	AP88	3c pink & multi	5	5
C373	AP88	5c pink & multi	7	5
C374	AP88	13c lt bl & multi	18	14
C375	AP88	13c lil & multi	18	14
C376	AP88	13c yel & multi	18	14
C377	AP88	13c pink & multi	18	14
C378	AP88	30c yel & multi	40	30
a.		Souvenir sheet	50	50
		Nos. C370-C378 (9)	1.34	1.06

Issued to commemorate the 11th Central American and Caribbean Games, Feb. 28-Mar. 14. No. C378a contains one imperf. stamp similar to No. C378. Bright pink margin with black commemorative inscription and control number. Size: 85x75mm.

Astronaut on Moon — AP89

EXPO '70 Emblem and Pavilion — AP90

Design: No. C380, U.S. astronauts Charles Conrad, Jr., Richard F. Gordon, Jr. and Alan L. Bean.

1971 **Wmk. 343** ***Perf. 13½***

C379	AP89	13c gold & multi	35	20
C380	AP89	13c lt grn & multi	35	20

Man's first landing on the moon, Apollo 11, July 20, 1969 (No. C379) and Apollo 12 moon mission, Nov. 14-24, 1969.

Issue dates: No. C379, Aug. 20; No. C380, Aug. 23.

1971, Aug. 24 **Litho.**

C381	AP90	10c pink & multi	14	14

EXPO '70 International Exposition, Osaka, Japan, Mar. 15-Sept. 13.

Flag of Panama AP91

Design: 13c, Map of Panama superimposed on Western Hemisphere, and tourist year emblem.

1971, Dec. 11 **Wmk. 343**

C382	AP91	5c multi	10	7
C383	AP91	13c multi	25	16

Proclamation of 1972 as Tourist Year of the Americas.

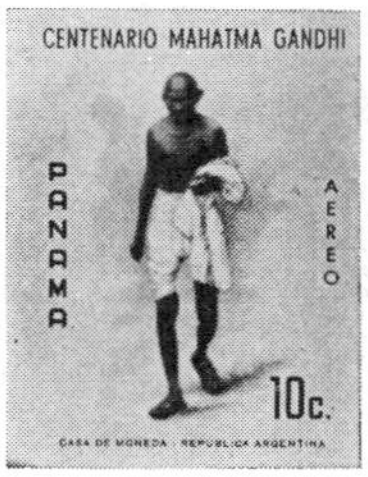

Mahatma Gandhi AP92

1971, Dec. 17

C384	AP92	10c blk & multi	20	14

Centenary of the birth of Mohandas K. Gandhi (1869-1948), leader in India's fight for independence.

Central American Independence Issue

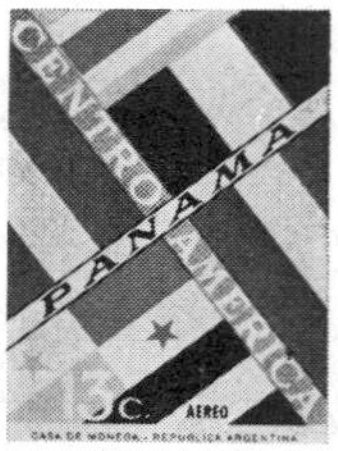

Flags of Central American States — AP92a

1971, Dec. 20

C385	AP92a	13c multi	25	16

Panama No. 4 — AP93

1971, Dec. 21

C386	AP93	8c red, dk bl & blk	16	8

2nd National Philatelic and Numismatic Exposition, 1970.

Natá Church — AP94

1972, Sept. 7 **Wmk. 365**

C387	AP94	40c lt bl & multi	70	40

450th anniversary of the founding of Natá.

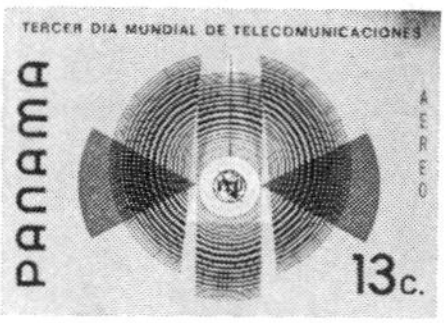

Telecommunications Emblem — AP95

1972, Sept. 8

C388	AP95	13c lt bl, dp bl & blk	18	14

3rd World Telecommunications Day (in 1971).

Apollo 14 AP96

1972, Sept. 11

C389	AP96	13c tan & multi	55	22

Apollo 14 U.S. moon mission, Jan. 1-Feb. 9, 1971.

Shoeshine Boy Counting Coins — AP97

1972, Sept. 12

C390	AP97	5c *shown*	7	5
C391	AP97	8c *Mother & Child*	10	7
C392	AP97	50c *UNICEF emblem*	65	40
a.		Souv. sheet of 1, imperf.	1.20	1.20

25th anniv. (in 1971) of the UNICEF.

San Blas Cloth, Cuna Indians AP98

1972, Sept. 13

C393	AP98	5c *shown*	10	7
C394	AP98	8c *Beaded necklace, Guaymi Indians*	16	8
C395	AP98	25c *View of Portobelo*	50	25
a.		Souv. sheet of 2	80	80

Tourist publicity. No. C395a contains 2 imperf. stamps similar to Nos. C393 and C395. Black marginal inscription and control number. Size: 96x128mm.

Baseball and Games' Emblem AP99

Designs (Games' Emblem and): 10c, Basketball (vert.). 13c, Torch (vert.). 25c, Boxing. 50c, Map and flag of Panama, Bolivar. 1b, Medals.

Perf. 12½

1973, Feb. 9 **Litho.** **Unwmk.**

C396	AP99	8c rose red & yel	14	8
C397	AP99	10c blk & ultra	16	10
C398	AP99	13c bl & multi	25	16
C399	AP99	25c blk, yel grn & red	50	25
C400	AP99	50c grn & multi	1.20	50
C401	AP99	1b multi	2.25	1.00
		Nos. C396-401 (6)	4.50	2.09

7th Bolivar Games, Panama City, Feb. 17-March 3.

No. C387 Surcharged in Red Similar to No. 542.

1973, Mar. 16 **Wmk. 365** ***Perf. 13½***

C402	AP94	13c on 40c multi	22	14

U.N. Security Council Meeting, Panama City, Mar. 15-21.

Portrait Type of Regular Issue 1973

Designs: 5c, Isabel Herrera Obaldia, educator. 8c, Nicolas Victoria Jaén, educator. 10c, Forest Scene, by Roberto Lewis. No. C406, Portrait of a Lady, by Manuel E. Amador. No. C407, Ricardo Miró, poet. 20c, Portrait, by Isaac Benitez. 21c, Manuel Amador Guerrero, statesman. 25c, Belisario Porras, statesman. 30c, Juan Demostenes Arosemena, statesman. 34c, Octavio Mendez Pereira, writer. 38c, Ricardo J. Alfaro, writer.

1973, June 20 **Litho.** ***Perf. 13½***

C403	A169	5c pink & multi	10	7
C404	A169	8c pink & multi	16	10
C405	A169	10c gray & multi	20	14
C406	A169	13c pink & multi	35	16
C407	A169	13c pink & multi	35	16
C408	A169	20c bl & multi	50	20
C409	A169	21c yel & multi	50	22
C410	A169	25c pink & multi	50	25
C411	A169	30c gray & multi	65	35
C412	A169	34c lt bl & multi	80	40
C413	A169	38c lt bl & multi	1.00	45
		Nos. C403-C413 (11)	5.11	2.50

Famous Panamanians.

Nos. C403, C410, and C412 Overprinted in Black or Red

FP
1923
1973
Bodas de Oro
Escuela Profesional
Isabel Herrera Obaldía

1973, Sept. 14 **Litho.** ***Perf. 13½***

C414	A169	5c pink & multi	14	7
C415	A169	25c pink & multi	50	25
C416	A169	34c bl & multi (R)	80	50

50th anniversary of the Isabel Herrera Obaldia Professional School.

Nos. C395, C408, C413, C412 and C409 Surcharged in Red

VALE 8¢

1974, Nov. 11 **Litho.** ***Perf. 13½***

C417	AP98	1c on 25c multi	5	5
C418	A169	3c on 20c multi	5	5
C419	A169	8c on 38c multi	10	7
C420	A169	10c on 34c multi	14	10
C421	A169	13c on 21c multi	18	14
		Nos. C417-C421 (5)	52	41

Women's Hands, Panama Map, UN and IWY Emblems AP100

Victoria Sugar Plant, Sugar Cane, Map of Veraguas Province AP101

Perf. 12½

1975, May 6 **Litho.** **Unwmk.**

C422	AP100	17c bl & multi	40	16
a.		Souvenir sheet	65	65

International Women's Year 1975. No. C422a contains one typographed imperf. stamp similar to No. C422; black marginal inscription with IWY emblem. Without gum. Size: 88x76mm.

1975, Oct. 9 **Litho.** ***Perf. 12½***

Designs: 17c, Bayano electrification project and map of Panama (horiz.). 33c, Tocumen International Airport and map (horiz.).

C423	AP101	17c bl, buff & blk	35	14
C424	AP101	27c ultra & yel grn	50	22
C425	AP101	33c bl & multi	65	25

7th anniversary of the Oct. 11, 1968, Revolution.

Bolivar Statue and Flags — AP102

Bolivar Hall, Panama City AP103

Design: 41c, Bolivar with flag of Panama, ruins of Old Panama City.

1976, Mar.

C426 AP102 23c multi	30	20
C427 AP103 35c multi	45	28
C428 AP102 41c multi	55	38

150th anniversary of Congress of Panama. Issue dates: 23c, Mar. 15; others Mar. 30.

Marine Life Type of 1976

Marine life: 17c, Diodon hystrix (vert.). 27c, Pocillopora damicornis.

Perf. 13x12½, 12½x13

1976, May 6 Litho. Wmk. 377

C429 A171 17c multi	25	14
C430 A171 27c multi	38	22

Cerro Colorado AP104

1976, Nov. 12 Litho. *Perf. 12½*

C431 AP104 23c multi 30 20

Cerro Colorado copper mines, Chiriqui Province.

Genl. Omar Torrijos Herrera (1929-1981) AP105

1982, Feb. Litho. *Perf. 10½*

C432 AP105 23c multi 35 20

Herrera Type of 1982

Wmk. 311

1982, May 14 Litho. *Perf. 10½*

C433 A201 35c Security Council reunion, 1973	45	28
C434 A201 41c Torrijos Airport	55	32

Souvenir Sheet

Imperf

C435 A201 23c like # C432 1.40 1.00

No. C435 has blue margin; black control number. Size: 86x75mm. Sold for 1b.

Alfaro Type of 1982

Photos by Luiz Gutierrez Cruz.

1982, Aug. 18 Wmk. 381

C436 A202 17c multi	25	14
C437 A202 23c multi	30	18

World Cup Type of 1982

Wmk. 381 "Panama" and Design

1982, Dec. 27 Litho. *Perf. 10½*

C438 A203 23c Map	30	18
C439 A203 35c Pele, vert.	45	28
C440 A203 41c Cup, vert.	55	30

1b imperf. souvenir sheet exists in design of 23c; black control number. Size; 85x75mm.

Nicolas A. Solano (1882-1943), Tuberculosis Researcher AP106

Wmk. 382 (Stars)

1983, Feb. 8 Litho. *Perf. 10½*

C441 AP106 23c brown 35 20

World Food Day — AP107

Contadora Group for Peace — AP108

1984, Oct. 16 Litho. *Perf. 12*

C442 AP107 30c Hand grasping fork 40 20

1985, Oct. 1 Litho. *Perf. 14*

C443 AP108 10c multi	14	8
C444 AP108 20c multi	25	16
C445 AP108 30c multi	40	22

Christmas Type of 1988

1988, Dec. 29 Litho. *Perf. 12*

C446 A246 35c *St. Joseph and the Infant* 80 60

Olympics Type of 1989

1989, Mar. 17 Litho. *Perf. 12*

C447 A248 35c Boxing 78 58

AIR POST SEMI-POSTAL STAMPS

Catalogue values for unused stamps in this section, from this point to the end of the section, are for Never Hinged items.

"The World Against Malaria" — SPAP1

Wmk. 311

1961, Dec. 20 Litho. *Perf. 12½*

CB1 SPAP1 5c + 5c car rose	65	50
CB2 SPAP1 10c + 10c vio bl	65	50
CB3 SPAP1 15c + 15c dk grn	65	50

Issued to support the World Health Organization's drive to eradicate malaria.

SPECIAL DELIVERY STAMPS

Nos. 211-212 Overprinted in Red **EXPRESO**

1926 Unwmk. *Perf. 12*

E1 A31 10c org & blk	6.50	2.50
a. "EXRPESO"	40.00	
E2 A32 20c brn & blk	8.00	2.50
a. "EXRPESO"	40.00	
b. Double overprint	35.00	35.00

Bicycle Messenger SD1

1929 Engr. *Perf. 12½*

E3 SD1 10c orange	1.20	65
E4 SD1 20c dk brn	2.25	1.00

REGISTRATION STAMPS

Issued under Colombian Dominion

R1

1888 Unwmk. Engr. *Perf. 13½*

F1 R1 10c blk, *gray* 10.00 6.50

Imperforate and part-perforate copies without gum and those on surface-colored paper are reprints.

R2

Magenta, Violet or Blue Black Handstamped Overprint

1898 *Perf. 12*

F2 R2 10c yellow 7.00 6.50

The handstamp on No. F2 was also used as a postmark.

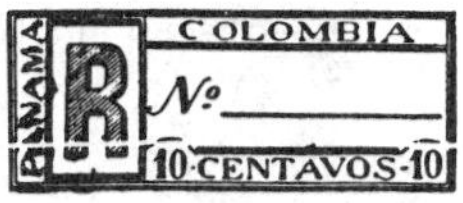
R3

1900 Litho. *Perf. 11*

F3 R3 10c blk, *lt bl* 4.00 3.50

1901

F4 R3 10c brn red 30.00 25.00

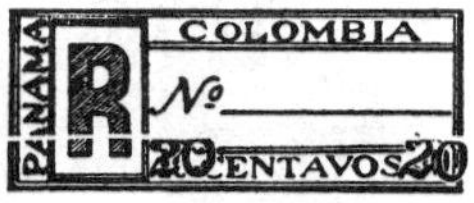
R4

Blue Black Surcharge

1902

F5 R4 20c on 10c brn red 25.00 20.00

Issues of the Republic
Issued in the City of Panama
Registration Stamps of Colombia Handstamped

R9

Handstamped in Blue Black or Rose REPUBLICA DE PANAMA

1903-04 *Imperf.*

F6 R9 20c red brn, *bl*	45.00	42.50
F7 R9 20c bl, *bl* (R)	45.00	42.50

Reprints exist of Nos. F6 and F7; see note after No. 64.

With Additional Surcharge in Rose **10.**

F8 R9 10c on 20c red brn, *bl*	60.00	55.00
b. "10" in bl blk	60.00	55.00
F9 R9 10c on 20c bl, *bl*	60.00	55.00

Handstamped in Rose

Panamá

.10

F10 R9 10c on 20c red brn, *bl*	60.00	55.00
F11 R9 10c on 20c bl, *bl*	45.00	42.50

Issued in Colon

Regular Issues Handstamped "R/COLON" in Circle (as on F2) Together with Other Overprints and Surcharges.

Handstamped **REPUBLICA DE PANAMA**

1903-04 *Perf. 12*

F12 A4 10c yellow 2.50 2.00

Handstamped **PANAMA**

F13 A4 10c yellow 22.50

Overprinted in Red

PANAMA PANAMA

F14 A4 10c yellow 2.50 2.00

Overprinted in Black *República de Panamá*

F15 A4 10c yellow 6.00 4.50

The handstamps on Nos. F12 to F15 are in magenta, violet or red; various combinations of these colors are to be found. They are struck in various positions, including double, inverted, one handstamp omitted, etc.

Colombia No. F13 Handstamped Like No. F12 in Violet

Imperf

F16 R9 20c red brn, *bl* 60.00 55.00

Overprinted Like No. F15 in Black

F17 R9 20c red brn, *bl* 6.50 6.00

No. F17 Surcharged in Manuscript

F18 R9 10c on 20c red brn, *bl* 60.00 55.00

No. F17 Surcharged in Purple **10**

F19 R9 10c on 20c red brn, *bl* 82.50 80.00

No. F17 Surcharged in Violet **10**

F20 R9 10c on 20c red brn, *bl* 82.50 80.00

The varieties of the overprint which are described after No. 138 are also to be found on the Registration and Acknowledgment of Receipt stamps. It is probable that Nos. F17 to F20 inclusive owe their existence more to speculation than to postal necessity.

Issued in Bocas del Toro.
Colombia Nos. F17 and F13 Handstamped in Violet

R DE PANAMA

1903-04

F21 R9 20c bl, *bl* 125.00 120.00
F22 R9 20c red brn, *bl* 125.00 120.00

No. F21 Surcharged in Manuscript in Violet or Red

F23 R9 10c on 20c bl, *bl* 150.00 140.00

Colombia Nos. F13, F17 Handstamped in Violet **Panama**

Surcharged in Manuscript (a) "10" (b) "10cs" in Red

F25 R9 10 on 20c red brn, *bl* 70.00 65.00
F26 R9 10cs on 20c bl, *bl* 55.00 50.00

No. F25 without surcharge is bogus, according to leading experts.

General Issue.

R5

1904	**Engr.**	***Perf. 12***
F27 R5 10c green		1.00 50

Nos. 190 and 213 Surcharged in Red **R 5 cts.**

1916-17

F29 A11 5c on 8c pur & blk 2.50 2.00
a. "5" inverted 55.00
b. Large, round "5" 7.00
c. Inverted surcharge 11.00 11.00
d. Tete beche surcharge
F30 A33 5c on 8c vio & blk ('17) 3.00 80
a. Inverted surcharge 8.25 8.25
b. Tete beche surcharge
c. Double surcharge 40.00

Stamps similar to No. F30, overprinted in green were unauthorized.

INSURED LETTER STAMPS

Stamps of 1939 Surcharged in Black

0 05 0 05
SEGURO POSTAL
HABILITADO

1942	**Unwmk.**	***Perf. 12½***
G1 AP23 5c on 1b blk		50 35
G2 A84 10c on 1b dk brn		80 50
G3 AP23 25c on 50c dk brn		2.00 80

ACKNOWLEDGMENT OF RECEIPT STAMPS

Issued under Colombian Dominion.

Experts consider this handstamp-"A.R. / COLON / COLOMBIA"-to be a cancellation or a marking intended for a letter to receive special handling. It was applied at Colon to various stamps in 1897-1904 in different colored inks for philatelic sale. It exists on cover, usually with the bottom line removed by masking the handstamp.

Nos. 17-18 Handstamped in Rose **AR**

1902

H4 A4 5c blue 5.00 5.00
H5 A4 10c yellow 10.00 10.00

This handstamp was also used as a postmark.

Issues of the Republic.
Issued in the City of Panama.
Colombia No. H3 Handstamped.

AR2

Handstamped in Rose REPUBLICA DE PANAMA

1903-04	**Unwmk.**	***Imperf.***
H9 AR2 10c bl, *bl*		9.00 8.25

Reprints exist of No. H9, see note after No. 64.

No. H9 Surcharged with New Value.

H10 AR2 5c on 10c bl, *bl* 3.50 3.50

Colombia No. H3 Handstamped in Rose **Panamá**

H11 AR2 10c bl, *bl* 16.00 14.00

Issued in Colon.

Handstamped in Magenta or Violet REPUBLICA DE PANAMA

Imperf.

H17 AR2 10c bl, *bl* 14.00 12.00

Handstamped PANAMA

H18 AR2 10c bl, *bl* 82.50 70.00

Overprinted in Black

República de Panamá.

H19 AR2 10c bl, *bl* 10.00 7.00

No. H19 Surcharged in Manuscript

H20 AR2 10c on 5c on 10c bl, *bl* 100.00 82.50

Issued in Bocas del Toro.
Colombia No. H3 Handstamped in Violet and Surcharged in Manuscript in Red

Panama

1904

H21 AR2 5c on 10c bl, *bl*

No. H21 without surcharge is bogus.

General Issue

AR3

1904	**Engr.**	***Perf. 12.***
H22 AR3 5c blue		1.00 80

No. 199 Overprinted in Violet **A. R.**

1916

H23 A20 2½c red org 1.00 80
a. "R.A." for "A.R." 50.00
b. Double ovpt. 8.00
c. Inverted ovpt. 8.00

LATE FEE STAMPS

Issues of the Republic
Issued in the City of Panama

LF3

Colombia No. I4 Handstamped in Rose or Blue Black REPUBLICA DE PANAMA

1903-04	**Unwmk.**	***Imperf.***
I1 LF3 5c pur, *rose*		10.00 9.00
I2 LF3 5c pur, *rose* (Bl Blk)		14.00 12.50

Reprints exist of Nos. I1 and I2; see note after No. 64.

General Issue.

LF4

1904	**Engr.**	***Perf. 12.***
I3 LF4 2½c lake		80 65

No. 199 Overprinted with Typewriter Retardo

1910, Aug. 12

I4 A20 2½c red org 120.00 100.00

Used only on Aug. 12-13.

Handstamped **RETARDO**

1910

I5 A20 2½c red org 60.00 50.00

No. 195 Surcharged in Green *RETARDO* UN CENTÉSIMO

1917

I6 A17 1c on ½c org 80 65
a. "UN CENTESIMO" inverted 50.00
b. Double surcharge 10.00
c. Inverted surcharge 6.50 6.50

Same Surcharge on No. 196.

1921

I7 A17 1c on ½c rose 25.00 20.00

POSTAGE DUE STAMPS

San Geronimo Castle Gate, Portobelo
D1

Statue of Columbus
D2

Pedro J. Sosa — D4

D5

Design: 4c, Capitol, Panama City.

1915	**Unwmk.**	**Engr.**	***Perf. 12***
J1 D1 1c ol brn			2.25 25
J2 D2 2c ol brn			3.00 22
J3 D1 4c ol brn			4.50 50
J4 D4 10c ol brn			3.00 65

Type D1 was intended to show a gate of San Lorenzo Castle, Chagres, and is so inscribed.

1930	***Perf. 12½***
J5 D5 1c emerald	80 22
J6 D5 2c dk red	80 20
J7 D5 4c dk bl	1.20 25
J8 D5 10c violet	1.20 40

POSTAL TAX STAMPS

Pierre and Marie Curie — PT1

1939	**Unwmk.**	**Engr.**	***Perf. 12.***
RA1 PT1 1c rose car			50 14
RA2 PT1 1c green			50 14
RA3 PT1 1c orange			50 14
RA4 PT1 1c blue			50 14

See Nos. RA6-RA18, RA24-RA27, RA30.

Stamp of 1924 Overprinted in Black LUCHA CONTRA EL CANCER

1940
RA5 A53 1c dk grn 1.40 1.00

Inscribed 1940

1941
RA6 PT1 1c rose car 40 10
RA7 PT1 1c green 40 10
RA8 PT1 1c orange 40 10
RA9 PT1 1c blue 40 10

Inscribed 1942

1942
RA10 PT1 1c violet 40 14

Inscribed 1943

1943
RA11 PT1 1c rose car 40 14
RA12 PT1 1c green 40 14
RA13 PT1 1c orange 40 14
RA14 PT1 1c blue 40 14

Inscribed 1945

1945
RA15 PT1 1c rose car 40 16
RA16 PT1 1c green 40 16
RA17 PT1 1c orange 40 16
RA18 PT1 1c blue 40 16

Nos. 234 and 235 Surcharged in Black or Red

CANCER
B/. 0.01
1947

1946 Unwmk. *Perf. 12*
RA19 A53 1c on ½c org 50 14
RA20 A53 1c on 1c dk grn (R) 50 14

Catalogue values for unused stamps in this section, from this point to the end of the section, are for Never Hinged items.

Same Surcharged in Black on Nos. 239 and 241.

1947
RA21 A53 1c on 12c ol grn 40 14
RA22 A53 1c on 24c yel brn 40 14

Surcharged in Red on No. 342.

RA23 A95 1c on ½c dl vio, bl & car 40 10

Type of 1939.
Inscribed: 1947.

1947
RA24 PT1 1c rose car 40 7
RA25 PT1 1c green 40 7
RA26 PT1 1c orange 40 7
RA27 PT1 1c blue 40 7

Nos. C100 and C101 Surcharged in Black

a
LUCHA CONTRA EL CANCER
1 CENTESIMO 1

b
LUCHA CONTRA EL CANCER
1 CENTESIMO 1

1949 Unwmk. *Perf. 12½*
RA28 AP45 (a) 1c on 5c dp car & blk 35 8
a. Inverted surcharge 10.00
RA29 AP46 (b) 1c on 10c yel org 35 8

Type of 1939
Inscribed 1949

1949 *Perf. 12*
RA30 PT1 1c brown 40 7

The tax from the sale of Nos. RA1-RA30 was used for the control of cancer.

Stadium
PT2

Torch Emblem
PT3

Discobolus
PT4

Design: No. RA33, Stadium, different view.

1951 Unwmk. Engr. *Perf. 12½.*
RA31 PT2 1c car & blk 65 16
RA32 PT3 1c dk bl & blk 65 16
RA33 PT2 1c grn & blk 65 16

1952

Design: No. RA34, Turners' emblem.

RA34 PT3 1c org & blk 65 16
RA35 PT4 1c pur & blk 1.60 16

The tax from the sale of Nos. RA31-RA35 was used to promote physical education.

Boys Doing Farm Work — PT5

1958 Wmk. 311 Litho. *Perf. 12½*
Size: 35x24mm.
RA36 PT5 1c rose red & gray 14 5

Type of 1958
Inscribed 1959

1959 Size: 35x24mm
RA37 PT5 1c gray & emer 8 5
RA38 PT5 1c vio bl & gray 8 5

Type of 1958
Inscribed 1960

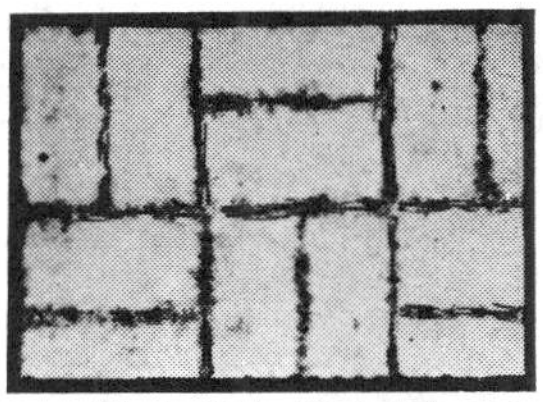
Wmk. 334- Rectangles

1960 Litho. Wmk. 334 *Perf. 13½*
Size: 32x23mm
RA39 PT5 1c car & gray 8 7

Nos. C235 and C241 Surcharged in Black or Red

XX

1¢

"Rehabilitación de Menores"

1961 Wmk. 343 *Perf. 12½*
RA40 A131 1c on 10c ocher & blk 10 7
RA41 AP76 1c on 10c emer (R) 10 7
a. Invtd. surch.

Girl at Sewing Machine
PT6

Wmk. RP Multiple (343).
1961, Nov. 24 Litho. *Perf. 12½*
RA42 PT6 1c brt vio 7 5
RA43 PT6 1c rose lil 7 5
RA44 PT6 1c yellow 7 5
RA45 PT6 1c blue 7 5
RA46 PT6 1c emerald 7 5
Nos. RA42-RA46 (5) 35 25

1961, Dec. 1

Design: Boy with hand saw.

RA47 PT6 1c red lil 7 5
RA48 PT6 1c rose 7 5
RA49 PT6 1c orange 7 5
RA50 PT6 1c blue 7 5
RA51 PT6 1c gray 7 5
Nos. RA47-RA51 (5) 35 25

Boy Scout
PT7

Map of Panama, Flags
PT8

Designs: Nos. RA57-RA61, Girl Scout.

Wmk. 343
1964, Feb. 7 Litho. *Perf. 12½*
RA52 PT7 1c olive 7 5
RA53 PT7 1c gray 7 5
RA54 PT7 1c lilac 7 5
RA55 PT7 1c car rose 7 5
RA56 PT7 1c blue 7 5
RA57 PT7 1c bluish grn 7 5
RA58 PT7 1c violet 7 5
RA59 PT7 1c orange 7 5
RA60 PT7 1c yellow 7 5
RA61 PT7 1c brn org 7 5
Nos. RA52-RA61 (10) 70 50

The tax from Nos. RA36-RA61 was for youth rehabilitation.

Perf. 12½
1973, Jan. 22 Litho. Unwmk.
RA62 PT8 1c black 5 5

7th Bolivar Sports Games, Feb. 17-Mar. 3, 1973. The tax was for a new post office in Panama City.

Farm Cooperative — PT9

Designs: No. RA64, 5b silver coin. No. RA65, Victoriano Lorenzo. No. RA66, RA69, Cacique Urraca. No. RA67-RA68, RA70, Post Office.

1973-75
RA63 PT9 1c brt yel grn & ver 7 5
RA64 PT9 1c gray & red 7 5
RA65 PT9 1c ocher & red 7 5
RA66 PT9 1c org & red 7 5
RA67 PT9 1c bl & red 7 5
RA68 PT9 1c bl ('74) 7 5
RA69 PT9 1c org ('74) 7 5
RA70 PT9 1c ver ('75) 10 5
Nos. RA63-RA70 (8) 59 40

The tax was for a new post office in Panama City.

Stamps of 1969-1973 Surcharged in Violet Blue, Yellow, Black or Carmine

VALE 1¢
PRO EDIFICIO

1975
RA75 A168 1c on 1c (#538; VB) 7 5
RA76 A168 1c on 2c (#539; Y) 7 5
RA77 A164 1c on 30c (#534; B) 7 5
RA78 A157 1c on 30c (#511; B) 7 5
RA79 A156 1c on 40c (#514; B) 7 5
RA80 A156 1c on 50c (#515; B) 7 5
RA81 A169 1c on 20c (#C408; C) 7 5
RA82 A169 1c on 25c (#C410; B) 7 5
RA83 AP98 1c on 25c (#C395; B) 7 5
RA84 A169 1c on 30c (#C411; B) 7 5
RA85 AP94 1c on 40c (#C387; C) 7 5
Nos. RA75-RA85 (11) 77 55

The tax was for a new post office in Panama City. Surcharge vertical, reading down on No. RA75 and up on Nos. RA76, RA78 and RA83. Nos. RA75-RA85 were obligatory on all mail.

PT10

PT11

1980, Dec. 3 Litho. *Perf. 12*
RA86 PT10 2c *Boys* 5 5
RA87 PT10 2c *Boy and chicks* 5 5
RA88 PT10 2c *Working in fields* 5 5
RA89 PT10 2c *Boys feeding piglet* 5 5
a. Souvenir sheet of 4 1.40

Tax was for Children's Village (Christmas 1980). Nos. RA86-RA89 se-tenant and were obligatory on all mail. No. RA89a contains Nos. RA86-RA89; black marginal inscription and control number. Size: 155x170mm. Sold for 1b.

1981, Nov. 1 Litho. *Perf. 12*
RA90 PT11 2c Boy, pony 5 5
RA91 PT11 2c Nativity 5 5
RA92 PT11 2c Tree 5 5
RA93 PT11 2c Church 5 5

Souvenir Sheet

RA94 Sheet of 4 *6.50*
a.-d. PT11 2c, Children's drawings

Tax was for Children's Village. Nos. RA90-RA93 se-tenant and were obligatory on all mail. No. RA94 has black marginal inscription and control number. Size: 131x140mm. Sold for 5b.

PT12

1982, Nov. 1 Litho. *Perf. 13½x12½*
RA95 PT12 2c Carpentry 5 5
RA96 PT12 2c Beekeeping 5 5
RA97 PT12 2c Pig farming, vert. 5 5
RA98 PT12 2c Gardening, vert. 5 5

Tax was for Children's Village (Christmas 1982). Nos. RA95-RA96 and RA97-RA98 se-tenant and were obligatory on all mail.

Children's Drawings — PT13

1983, Nov. 1 Litho. *Perf. 14½*
RA99 TP13 2c Annunciation 5 5
RA100 PT13 2c Bethlehem and Star 5 5
RA101 PT13 2c Church and Houses 5 5
RA102 PT13 2c Flight into Egypt 5 5

Souvenir sheets exist showing undenominated designs of Nos. RA99, RA101 and Nos. RA100, RA102 respectively. They sold for 2b each.

Boy — PT14

1984, Nov. 1 Litho. *Perf. 12x12½*

RA103 PT14 2c White-collared shirt 5 5
RA104 PT14 2c T-shirt 5 5
RA105 PT14 2c Checked shirt 5 5
RA106 PT14 2c Scout uniform 5 5

Tax was for Children's Village. Obligatory on all mail. Issued se-tenant. An imperf. souvenir sheet sold for 2b, with designs similar to Nos. RA103-RA106, exists.

Christmas
1985 — PT15

Inscriptions: No. RA107, "Ciudad del Nino es . . . mi vida." No. RA108, "Feliz Navidad." No. RA109, "Feliz Ano Nuevo." No. RA110, "Gracias."

1985, Dec. 10 Litho. *Perf.*

RA107 PT15 2c multi 5 5
RA108 PT15 2c multi 5 5
RA109 PT15 2c multi 5 5
RA110 PT15 2c multi 5 5

Nos. RA107-RA110 obligatory on all mail: tax for Children's Village. A souvenir sheet, perf. and imperf., sold for 2b, with designs of Nos. RA107-RA110.

Children's Village, 20th Anniv. — PT16

Inscriptions and Choco, Cuna, Embera and Guaymies tribal folk figures: No. RA111, "1966-1986." No. RA112, "Ciudad del Nino es . . . mi vida." No. RA113, "20 anos de fundacion." No. RA114, "Gracias."

1986, Nov. 1 Litho. *Perf. 13½*

RA111 PT16 2c multi 5 5
RA112 PT16 2c multi 5 5
RA113 PT16 2c multi 5 5
RA114 PT16 2c multi 5 5

Nos. RA111-RA114 obligatory on all mail through Nov., Dec. and Jan.; tax for Children's Village. Printed se-tenant. Sheets of 4 exist perf. and imperf. Sold for 2b.

PARAGUAY

LOCATION — South America, bounded by Bolivia, Brazil and Argentina.
GOVT. — Republic
AREA — 157,042 sq. mi.
POP. — 3,477,000 (1983)
CAPITAL — Asuncion

10 Reales = 100 Centavos = 1 Peso
100 Centimos = 1 Guarani (1944)

Values of early Paraguay stamps vary according to condition. Quotations for Nos. 1-9 are for fine copies. Very fine to superb specimens sell at much higher prices, and inferior or poor copies sell at reduced prices, depending on the condition of the individual specimen.

Catalogue values for unused stamps in this country are for Never Hinged items, beginning with Scott 430 in the regular postage section, Scott B11 in the semi-postal section, and Scott C154 in the airpost section.

Vigilant Lion Supporting Liberty Cap
A1 A2

A3

Unwmk.

1870, Aug. 1 Litho. *Imperf.*

1 A1 1r rose 3.00 3.00
2 A2 2r blue 35.00 35.00
3 A3 3r black 85.00 85.00

Unofficial reprints of 2r in blue and other colors are on thicker paper than originals. They show a colored dot in upper part of "S" of "DOS" in upper right corner.

Handstamp Surcharged

1878 Black Surcharge

4 A1 5c on 1r rose 32.50 32.50
5 A2 5c on 2r blue 150.00 140.00
5E A3 5c on 3r black 250.00 200.00

Blue Surcharge

5F A1 5c on 1r rose 32.50 32.50
5H A2 5c on 2r blue *500.00 500.00*
6 A3 5c on 3r black 150.00 150.00

The surcharge may be found inverted, double, sideways and omitted.

The originals are surcharged in dull black or dull blue. The reprints are in intense black and bright blue. The reprint surcharges are overinked and show numerous breaks in the handstamp.

Handstamp Surcharged

Black Surcharge

7 A2 5c on 2r blue 250.00 190.00
8 A3 5c on 3r black 200.00 160.00

Blue Surcharge

9 A3 5c on 3r black 110.00 110.00
a. Double surcharge, large and small "5" *650.00 650.00*

The surcharge on Nos. 7, 8 and 9 is usually placed sideways. It may be found double or inverted on Nos. 8 and 9.

Nos. 4 to 9 have been extensively counterfeited.

A4

A4a

1879 Litho. *Perf. 12½*
Thin Paper

10 A4 5r orange 38
11 A4 10r red brown 45
a. Imperf.
b. Imperf. vertically, pair 11.25

Nos. 10 and 11 were never placed in use.

1879-81 Thin Paper

12 A4a 5c org brown 90 90
13 A4a 10c blue grn ('81) 1.25 1.25

Reprints of Nos. 10-13 are imperf., perf. 11½, 12, 12½ or 14. They have yellowish gum and the 10c is deep green.

A5

A6

A7

1881, Aug. Litho. *Perf. 11½-13½*

14 A5 1c blue 45 38
a. Imperf., pair 1.75 1.75
15 A6 2c rose red 45 38
a. 2c dull orange red 45 38
b. Imperf., pair 1.75 1.75
c. Horiz. or vert. pair, imperf. btwn. 1.50 1.50
16 A7 4c brown 45 38
a. Imperf., pair 1.75 1.75
b. Horiz. or vert. pair, imperf. btwn. 1.50 1.50

A8

A9

Handstamped in Black or Gray

1881, July *Perf. 12½*

17 A8 1c on 10c bl grn 5.75 5.75
18 A9 2c on 10c bl grn 5.75 5.75

A10

1884, May 8 Handstamped *Imperf.*

19 A10 1c on 1r rose 2.00 1.75

The surcharges on Nos. 17-19 exist double, inverted and in pairs with one omitted. Counterfeits exist.

Seal of the Treasury
A11 A12

1884, Aug. 3 Litho. *Perf. 11½, 12½*

20 A11 1c green 25 18
a. Imperf., pair 1.00
21 A11 2c rose red 25 18
a. Imperf., pair 1.75
22 A11 5c blue 25 18
a. Imperf., pair 3.75

Shades exist.

Perf. 11½, 11½x12, 12½x11½

1887 Typo.

23 A12 1c green 12 6
24 A12 2c rose 12 8
25 A12 5c blue 20 12
26 A12 7c brown 42 30
27 A12 10c lilac 30 18
28 A12 15c orange 30 18
29 A12 20c pink 30 18
Nos. 23-29 (7) 1.76 1.10

See Nos. 42-45.

Symbols of Liberty from Coat of Arms
A13

Pres. Candido Bareiro
A14

1889, Feb. Litho. *Perf. 11½*

30 A13 15c red violet 1.25 1.25
a. Imperf., pair 5.00 5.00

Oval Overprint Handstamped in Violet

1892, Oct. 12 *Perf. 12x12½*

31 A14 10c vio blue 4.50 2.00

Discovery of America by Columbus, 400th anniversary. Overprint reads: "1492 / 12 DE OCTUBRE / 1892." Sold only on day of issue.

Cirilo A. Rivarola
A15

Salvador Jovellanos
A16

Juan B. Gil — A17

Higinio Uriarte — A18

Candido Bareiro — A19

Gen. Bernardino Caballero — A20

Gen. Patricio Escobar — A21

Juan G. González — A22

1892-96 Litho. *Perf. 12x12½*

32 A15 1c gray (centavos) 10 5
33 A15 1c gray (centavo) ('96) 10 6
34 A16 2c green 10 5
a. Chalky paper ('96) 10 6
35 A17 4c carmine 10 5
a. Chalky paper ('96) 12 8
36 A18 5c vio ('93) 12 5
a. Chalky paper ('96) 10 8
37 A19 10c vio bl (punched) ('93) 18 15
Unpunched ('96) 4.00 1.50
38 A19 10c dull bl ('96) 15 12
39 A20 14c yel brn 42 38
40 A21 20c red ('93) 65 38
41 A22 30c light grn 1.00 65
Nos. 32-41 (10) 2.92 1.94

The 10c violet blue (No. 37) was, until 1896, issued punched with a circular hole in order to prevent it being fraudulently overprinted as No. 31.

Nos. 33 and 38 are on chalky paper.

Seal Type of 1887

1892 Typo.

42 A12 40c slate bl 1.75 90
43 A12 60c yellow 75 38
44 A12 80c light bl 65 38
45 A12 1p olive grn 65 38

A23

A24

1895, Aug. 1 *Perf. 11 ½x12*
46 A23 5c on 7c brown 25 15

Telegraph Stamps Surcharged

1896, Apr. **Engr.** *Perf. 11 ½*
Denomination in Black
47 A24 5c on 2c brn & gray 38 25
a. Inverted surcharge 10.00 10.00
48 A24 5c on 4c yel & gray 38 25
a. Inverted surcharge 7.50 7.50

Nos. 28, 42 Surcharged

Provisorio
10
Centavos

1898-99 **Typo.**
49 A12 10c on 15c org ('99) 45 35
a. Inverted surcharge 14.00 14.00
b. Double surcharge 9.00 9.00
50 A12 10c on 40c sl bl 20 15

Surcharge on No. 49 has small "c."

Telegraph Stamps Surcharged

1900, May 14 **Engr.** *Perf. 11 ½*
50A A24 5c on 30c grn, gray & blk 1.25 90
50B A24 10c on 50c dl vio, gray & blk 3.00 2.00

The basic telegraph stamps are like those used for Nos. 47-48, but the surcharges on Nos. 50A-50B consist of "5 5" and "10 10" above a blackout rectangle covering the engraved denominations.

A 40c red, bluish gray and black telegraph stamp (basic type of A24) was used provisionally in August, 1900, for postage. Value, postally used, $5.

Seal of the Treasury — A25

1900, Sept. **Engr.** *Perf. 11 ½, 12*
51 A25 2c gray 10 8
52 A25 3c org brn 12 9
53 A25 5c dark grn 12 9
54 A25 8c dark brn 15 10
55 A25 10c car rose 15 10
56 A25 24c deep blue 30 15
Nos. 51-56 (6) 94 61

1901, Apr. **Litho.** *Perf. 11 ½*
Small Figures
57 A25 2c rose 15 9
58 A25 5c vio brown 15 10
59 A25 40c blue 65 22

1901-02
Larger Figures
60 A25 1c gray grn ('02) 10 6
61 A25 2c gray 10 8
a. Half used as 1c on cover 38
62 A25 4c pale blue 10 8
63 A25 5c violet 15 9
64 A25 8c gray brn ('02) 12 10
65 A25 10c rose red ('02) 18 10
66 A25 28c orange ('02) 30 18
67 A25 40c blue 30 15
Nos. 60-67 (8) 1.35 84

J. B. Egusquiza — A26

A27

Perf. 12x12 ½
1901, Sept. 24 **Typo.**
Chalky Paper
68 A26 1p slate 30 20

1902, Aug.
Red Surcharge
69 A27 20c on 24c dp bl 25 15
a. Inverted surcharge 6.25

A27a

A28

Black Surcharge
1902, Dec. 22 *Perf. 12x12 ½*
70 A27a 1c on 14c yel brn 18 10
a. No period after "cent" 90 75
b. Comma after "cent" 65 50
c. Accent over "Un" 65 50

1903 *Perf. 11 ½*
71 A28 5c on 60c yel 25 15
72 A28 5c on 80c lt bl 18 10

A29

A30

A31

1902-03 *Perf. 12*
73 A29 1c on 1p slate ('03) 12 9
a. No period after "cent" 1.65 1.50
Perf. 11 ½
74 A30 5c on 8c gray brn 25 15
a. No period after "cent" 90 75
b. Double surcharge 3.50 3.00
76 A31 5c on 28c org 25 18
a. No period after "cent" 90 75
b. Comma after "cent" 38 30

The surcharge on Nos. 73 and 74 is found reading both upward and downward.

Sentinel Lion with Right Paw Ready to Strike for "Peace and Justice"
A32 A33

Perf. 11 ½
1903, Feb. 28 **Litho.** **Unwmk.**
77 A32 1c gray 15 10
78 A32 2c blue green 18 12
79 A32 5c blue 25 10
80 A32 10c orange brn 30 12
81 A32 20c carmine 30 15
82 A32 30c deep blue 38 15
83 A32 60c purple 1.00 65
Nos. 77-83 (7) 2.56 1.39

1903, Sept.
84 A33 1c yel grn 12 8
85 A33 2c red org 12 8
86 A33 5c dark blue 15 10
87 A33 10c purple 20 12
88 A33 20c dark green 65 30
89 A33 30c ultramarine 75 20
90 A33 60c ocher 75 50
Nos. 84-90 (7) 2.74 1.38

Nos. 84-90 exist imperf. Value for pairs, $3 each for 1c-20c, $4 for 30c, $5 for 60c.

The three-line overprint "Gobierno provisorio Ago. 1904" is fraudulent.

Sentinel Lion at Rest
A35 A36

Perf. 11 ½, 12, 11 ½x12
1905-10 **Engr.**
Dated "1904"
91 A35 1c orange 12 5
92 A35 1c ver ('07) 12 5
93 A35 1c grnsh bl ('07) 12 8
94 A35 2c ver ('06) 12 8
95 A35 2c ol grn ('07) 30.00
96 A35 2c car rose ('08) 12 8
97 A35 5c dark blue 12 8
98 A35 5c slate bl ('06) 12 8
99 A35 5c yellow ('06) 12 8
100 A35 10c bister ('06) 12 8
101 A35 10c emerald ('07) 12 8
102 A35 10c dp ultra ('08) 12 8
103 A35 20c violet ('06) 30 20
104 A35 20c bister ('07) 30 20
105 A35 20c ap grn ('07) 25 12
106 A35 30c turq bl ('06) 30 12
107 A35 30c bl gray ('07) 30 10
108 A35 30c dl lil ('08) 38 18
109 A35 60c choc ('07) 25 15
110 A35 60c org brn ('07) 3.50 1.25
111 A35 60c sal pink ('10) 3.50 1.25
Nos. 91-94,96-111 (20) 10.40 4.39

All but Nos. 92 and 104 exist imperf. Value for pair, $3 each, except No. 95 at $17.50 and Nos. 109-111 at $7.50 each pair.

1904, Aug. **Litho.** *Perf. 11 ½*
112 A36 10c blue 25 15
a. Imperf., pair 3.00

No. 112 Surcharged in Black

PAZ
12 Dic. 1904
30
centavos

1904, Dec.
113 A36 30c on 10c blue 38 25

Peace between a successful revolutionary party and the government previously in power.

Governmental Palace, Asunción — A37

Dated "1904"
1906-10 **Engr.** *Perf. 11 ½, 12*
Center in Black
114 A37 1p brt rose 1.25 75
115 A37 1p brn org ('07) 50 25
116 A37 1p ol gray ('07) 50 25
117 A37 2p turq ('07) 25 18
118 A37 2p lake ('09) 25 20
119 A37 2p brn org ('10) 30 20
120 A37 5p red ('07) 75 50
121 A37 5p ol grn ('10) 75 50
122 A37 5p dull bl ('10) 75 50
123 A37 10p brn org ('07) 70 50
124 A37 10p deep bl ('10) 70 50
125 A37 10p choc ('10) 75 50
126 A37 20p ol grn ('07) 1.75 1.65
127 A37 20p violet ('10) 1.75 1.65
128 A37 20p yellow ('10) 1.75 1.65
Nos. 114-128 (15) 12.70 9.78

Nos. 94 and 95 Surcharged

Habilitado
en
5
CENTAVOS

1907
129 A35 5c on 2c ver 20 15
a. "5" omitted 1.00 1.00
b. Inverted surcharge 1.25 1.25
c. Double surcharge
d. Double surcharge, one inverted 1.00 1.00
e. Double surcharge, both invtd. 6.00 6.00
130 A35 5c on 2c ol grn 25 15
a. "5" omitted 1.00 1.00
b. Inverted surcharge 1.00 1.00
c. Double surcharge 2.00 2.00
d. Bar omitted 2.00 2.00

Official Stamps of 1906-08 Surcharged

Habilitado
en
5
CENTAVOS

1908
131 O17 5c on 10c bister 18 12
a. Double surcharge 3.00 3.00
132 O17 5c on 10c vio 18 12
a. Inverted surcharge 1.50 1.50
133 O17 5c on 20c emer 18 12
134 O17 5c on 20c vio 18 12
a. Inverted surcharge 1.50 1.50
135 O17 5c on 30c sl bl 65 65
136 O17 5c on 30c turq bl 65 65
a. Inverted surcharge
b. Double surcharge 3.00 3.00
137 O17 5c on 60c choc 12 10
a. Double surcharge 6.00 6.00
138 O17 5c on 60c red brn 20 12
a. Inverted surcharge 38 38
Nos. 131-138 (8) 2.34 2.00

Same Surcharge on Official Stamps of 1903
139 A32 5c on 30c dp bl 1.25 1.10
140 A32 5c on 60c purple 50 30
a. Double surcharge 2.50 2.50

Official Stamps of 1906-08 Overprinted

Habilitado

141 O17 5c deep bl 20 12
a. Inverted overprint 1.50 1.50
b. Bar omitted 4.50 4.50
c. Double overprint 2.00 2.00
142 O17 5c slate bl 25 20
a. Inverted overprint 1.25 1.25
b. Double overprint 1.75 1.75
c. Bar omitted 4.50 4.50
143 O17 5c greenish bl 15 10
a. Inverted overprint 1.25 1.25
b. Bar omitted 3.75 3.75
144 O18 1p brn org & blk 25 22
a. Double overprint 1.00 1.00
b. Double overprint, one inverted 1.25 1.25
c. Triple overprint, two inverted 2.25 2.25
145 O18 1p brt rose & blk 42 35
a. Bar omitted
Nos. 141-145 (5) 1.27 99

Regular Issues of 1906-08 Surcharged

Habilitado en
5
CENTAVOS

1908
146 A35 5c on 1c grnsh bl 8 8
a. Inverted surcharge 50 50
b. Double surcharge 75 75
c. "5" omitted 1.50 1.50
147 A35 5c on 2c car rose 8 5
a. Inverted surcharge 50 50
b. "5" omitted 1.25 1.25
c. Double surcharge 75 75
d. Double surcharge, one invtd.
148 A35 5c on 60c org brn 12 8
a. Inverted surcharge 75 75
b. "5" omitted 1.00 1.00
149 A35 5c on 60c sal pink 12 10
a. Double surcharge 50 50
b. Double surcharge, one invtd. 3.50 3.50
150 A35 5c on 60c choc 10 8
a. Inverted surcharge 1.25 1.25
151 A35 20c on 1c grnsh bl 12 10
a. Inverted surcharge 1.50 1.50
152 A35 20c on 2c ver 6.00 5.00
153 A35 20c on 2c car rose 3.50 3.00
a. Inverted surcharge 12.50

154 A35 20c on 30c dl lil 20 18
a. Inverted surcharge 1.50 1.50
b. Double surcharge
155 A35 20c on 30c turq bl 1.50 1.50
Nos. 146-155 (10) 11.82 10.17

Same Surcharge on Regular Issue of 1901-02

156 A25 5c on 28c org 1.25 1.10
157 A25 5c on 40c dk bl 38 30
a. Inverted surcharge 1.50 1.50

Same Surcharge on Official Stamps of 1908

158 O17 5c on 10c emer 18 12
a. Double surcharge
159 O17 5c on 10c red lil 18 12
a. Double surcharge 2.00 2.00
b. "5" omitted 1.50 1.50
160 O17 5c on 20c bis 38 30
a. Double surcharge 1.25 1.25
161 O17 5c on 20c sal pink 38 30
a. "5" omitted 1.75 1.75
162 O17 5c on 30c bl gray 12 10
163 O17 5c on 30c yel 8 5
a. "5" omitted 1.50 1.50
b. Inverted surcharge 1.25 1.25
164 O17 5c on 60c org brn 20 15
a. Double surcharge 5.00 5.00
165 O17 5c on 60c dp ultra 12 8
a. Inverted surcharge 2.50 2.50
b. "5" omitted 1.50
Nos. 158-165 (8) 1.64 1.22

Same Surcharge on No. O52

166 A32 20c on 5c blue 1.25 1.00
a. Inverted surcharge 3.00 3.75

Surcharged

Habilitado en
20
CENTAVOS

1908

On Stamp of 1887

167 A12 20c on 2c car 2.50 2.00
a. Inverted surcharge 7.50

On Official Stamps of 1892

168 A12 5c on 15c org 2.50 1.75
169 A12 5c on 20c pink 40.00 32.50
170 A12 5c on 50c gray 17.50 12.50
170A A12 20c on 5c blue 1.50 1.25
b. Inverted surcharge 8.75 8.75

Nos. 151, 152, 153, 155, 167, 170A, while duly authorized, all appear to have been sold to a single individual, and although they paid postage, it is doubtful whether they can be considered as ever having been placed on sale to the public.

Nos. O82-O84 Surcharged (Date in Red)

Habilitado
1908
UN CENTAVO

1908-09

171 O18 1c on 1p brt rose & blk 20 15
172 O18 1c on 1p lake & blk 18 12
173 O18 1c on 1p brn org & blk ('09) 90 65

Varieties of surcharge on Nos. 171-173 include: "CETTAVO"; date omitted, double or inverted; third line double or omitted.

Types of 1905-1910 Overprinted

1908

1908, Mar. 5 *Perf. 11 ½*

174 A35 1c emerald 8 5
175 A35 5c yellow 8 6
176 A35 10c lilac brn 10 8
177 A35 20c yel orange 8 5
178 A35 30c red 25 20
179 A35 60c magenta 20 18
180 A37 1p light bl 12 10
Nos. 174-180 (7) 91 72

Overprinted

1909

1909, Sept.

181 A35 1c blue gray 8 5
182 A35 1c scarlet 8 6
183 A35 5c dark grn 8 6
184 A35 5c deep org 8 6
185 A35 10c rose 12 10
186 A35 10c bis brn 12 10
187 A35 20c yellow 8 6
188 A35 20c violet 10 8
189 A35 30c org brn 30 20
190 A35 30c dull bl 30 20
Nos. 181-190 (10) 1.34 97

Coat of Arms above Numeral of Value — A38

"The Republic" — A39

1910-21 **Litho.** *Perf. 11 ½*

191 A38 1c gray blk 6 5
192 A38 5c brt vio 8 5
a. Pair, imperf. between 1.00 1.00
193 A38 5c bl grn ('19) 8 5
194 A38 5c lt bl ('21) 8 5
195 A38 10c yel grn 8 5
196 A38 10c dp vio ('19) 10 5
197 A38 10c red ('21) 8 5
198 A38 20c red 8 5
199 A38 50c car rose 30 15
200 A38 75c dp bl 12 5
a. Diag. half perforated ('11) 12 10
Nos. 191-200 (10) 1.06 60

Nos. 191-200 exist imperforate.
No. 200a was authorized for use as 20c.

1911 **Engr.**

201 A39 1c ol grn & blk 8 5
202 A39 2c dk bl & blk 10 8
203 A39 5c car & indigo 15 10
204 A39 10c dp bl & brn 18 10
205 A39 20c ol grn & ind 18 10
206 A39 50c lilac & indigo 30 15
207 A39 75c ol grn & red lil 30 15
Nos. 201-207 (7) 1.29 73

Centenary of National Independence.
The 1c, 2c, 10c and 50c exist imperf. Value for pairs, $1.50 each.

No. 199 Surcharged

Habilitada
en
VEINTE

1912

208 A38 20c on 50c car rose 10 5
a. Inverted surcharge 1.00 1.00
b. Double surcharge 1.00 1.00
c. Bar omitted 1.75 1.75

National Coat of Arms — A40

1913 **Engr.** *Perf. 11 ½*

209 A40 1c gray 5 5
210 A40 2c orange 5 5
211 A40 5c lilac 5 5
212 A40 10c green 5 5
213 A40 20c dull red 5 5
214 A40 40c rose 5 5
215 A40 75c deep blue 8 5
216 A40 80c yellow 8 5
217 A40 1p light blue 8 5
218 A40 1.25p pale blue 15 10
219 A40 3p greenish bl 18 8
Nos. 209-219 (11) 87 63

Nos. J7-J10 Overprinted

HABILITADO
1918

1918

220 D2 5c yellow brn 5 5
221 D2 10c yellow brn 5 5
222 D2 20c yellow brn 8 8
223 D2 40c yellow brn 10 8

The lack of a value for a listed item does not necessarily indicate rarity.

Nos. J10 and 214 Surcharged

HABILITADO
EN 0.05
1918

224 D2 5c on 40c yel brn 8 8
225 A40 30c on 40c rose 8 5
Nos. 220-225 (6) 44 39

Nos. 220-225 exist with surcharge inverted, double and double with one inverted.
The surcharge "Habilitado-1918-5 cents 5" on the 1c gray official stamps of 1914, is bogus.

No. J11 Overprinted

HABILITADO
1920

1920

229 D2 1p yel brn 10 5
a. Inverted overprint 65 65
b. Double overprint
c. Double overprint, one inverted
d. Double overprint inverted
e. "AABILITADO" 75 75
f. "1929" for "1920" 75 75
g. Overprint lines 8mm apart 20 10

Nos. 216 and 219 Surcharged

HABILITADO
en *0.50*
1920

230 A40 50c on 80c yel 12 6
231 A40 1.75p on 3p grnsh bl 75 65

Same Surcharge on No. J12

232 D2 1p on 1.50p yel brn 22 9

Nos. 230-232 exist with various surcharge errors, including inverted, double, double inverted and double with one inverted.

Parliament Building A41

1920 **Litho.** *Perf. 11 ½*

233 A41 50c red & blk 22 12
a. "CORRLOS" 1.50 1.50
234 A41 1p lt bl & blk 65 30
235 A41 1.75p dk bl & blk 12 10
236 A41 3p org & blk 1.00 15

50th anniv. of the Constitution.
All values exist imperforate and Nos. 233, 235 and 236 with center inverted. It is doubtful that any of these varieties were regularly issued.

No. 215 Surcharged

50

1920

237 A40 50c on 75c deep bl 30 8

Nos. 200, 215 Surcharged

50

1921

241 A38 50c on 75c deep bl 10 5
242 A40 50c on 75c deep bl 15 8

A42

1922, Feb. 8 **Litho.** *Perf. 11 ½*

243 A42 50c car & dk bl 10 8
a. Imperf. pair 50
b. Center inverted 10.00 10.00
244 A42 1p dk bl & brn 10 8
a. Imperf. pair 50
b. Center inverted 12.50 12.50

"C" overprints, listed under Nos. L1-L37, were applied to Nos. 243-244 and various stamps of types A40, A44-A52, A54, A57-A60 and D2.

Rendezvous of Conspirators A43

1922-23

245 A43 1p deep blue 10 8
246 A43 1p scar & dk bl ('23) 12 8
247 A43 1p red vio & gray ('23) 12 8
248 A43 1p org & gray ('23) 15 8
249 A43 5p dark violet 38 18
250 A43 5p dk bl & org brn ('23) 38 18
251 A43 5p dl red & lt bl ('23) 38 18
252 A43 5p emer & blk ('23) 38 18
Nos. 245-252 (8) 2.01 1.04

National Independence.

No. 218 Surcharged "Habilitado en $1:-1924" in Red

1924

253 A40 1p on 1.25p pale bl 8 8

This stamp was for use in Asuncion. Nos. L3 to L5 were for use in the interior, as is indicated by the "C" in the surcharge.

Map of Paraguay — A44

1924 **Litho.** *Perf. 11 ½*

254 A44 1p dark blue 8 5
255 A44 2p car rose 12 6
256 A44 4p light blue 18 9
a. Perf. 12 38 9

Nos. 254-256 exist imperf. Value $3 each pair.

Gen. José E. Diaz A45

Columbus A46

1925-26 *Perf. 11 ½, 12*

257 A45 50c red 8 5
258 A45 1p dark blue 10 8
259 A45 1p emer ('26) 8 5

Nos. 257-258 exist imperf. Value $1 each pair.

1925 *Perf. 11 ½*

260 A46 1p blue 20 10
a. Imperf., pair 2.00

Nos. 194, 214-215, J12 Surcharged in Black or Red

Habilitado
en
1 centavo

1926

261	A38	1c on 5c lt bl	5	5
262	A40	7c on 40c rose	10	6
263	A40	15c on 75c dp bl (R)	5	5
264	D2	1.50p on 1.50p yel brn	12	8

Nos. 194, 179 and 256 Surcharged "Habilitado" and New Values

1927

265	A38	2c on 5c lt bl	5	5
266	A35	50c on 60c mag	10	10
a.		Invtd. surcharge	2.00	
267	A44	1.50p on 4p lt bl	8	5

Official Stamp of 1914 Surcharged "Habilitado" and New Value

268	O19	50c on 75c dp bl	5	5

National Emblem A47

Pedro Juan Caballero A48

Map of Paraguay A49

Fulgencio Yegros A50

Ignacio Iturbe A51

Oratory of the Virgin, Asuncion A52

Perf. 12, 11, 11½, 11x12

1927-38 **Typo.**

269	A47	1c lt red ('31)	5	5
270	A47	2c org red ('30)	5	5
271	A47	7c lilac	5	5
272	A47	7c emerald ('29)	5	5
273	A47	10c gray grn ('28)	5	5
a.		10c light green ('31)	5	5
274	A47	10c lil rose ('30)	5	5
275	A47	10c light bl ('35)	5	5
276	A47	20c dull bl ('28)	5	5
277	A47	20c lil brn ('30)	5	5
278	A47	20c lt vio ('31)	5	5
279	A47	20c rose ('35)	5	5
280	A47	50c ultramarine	5	5
281	A47	50c dl red ('28)	5	5
282	A47	50c orange ('30)	8	8
283	A47	50c gray ('31)	5	5
284	A47	50c brn vio ('34)	5	5
285	A47	50c rose ('36)	5	5
286	A47	70c ultra ('28)	8	8
287	A48	1p emerald	5	5
288	A48	1p org red ('30)	5	5
289	A48	1p brn org ('34)	5	5
290	A49	1.50p brown	8	5
291	A49	1.50p lilac ('28)	15	5
292	A49	1.50p rose red ('32)	8	5
293	A50	2.50p bister	5	5
294	A51	3p gray	20	15
295	A51	3p rose red ('36)	8	5
296	A51	3p brt vio ('36)	5	5
297	A52	5p chocolate	20	18
298	A52	5p violet ('36)	10	5
299	A52	5p pale org ('38)	8	5
300	A49	20p red ('29)	1.40	1.10
301	A49	20p emerald ('29)	1.40	1.10
302	A49	20p vio brn ('29)	1.40	1.10
		Nos. 269-302 (34)	6.38	5.14

No. 281 is also known perf. 10½x11½.

Papermaker's watermarks are sometimes found on No. 271 ("GLORIA BOND" in double-lined circle) and No. 280 ("Extra Vencedor Bond").

Arms of Juan de Salazar de Espinosa A53

Columbus A54

1928, Aug. 15 ***Perf. 12***

303	A53	10p vio brn	1.25	90

Issued in commemoration of Juan de Salazar de Espinosa, founder of Asuncion.

A papermaker's watermark ("INDIAN BOND EXTRA STRONG S.&C") is sometimes found on Nos 303, 305-307.

1928 **Litho.**

304	A54	10p ultra	50	25
305	A54	10p vermilion	50	25
306	A54	10p dp red	50	25

President Rutherford B. Hayes of USA and Villa Occidental — A55

1928, Nov. 20 ***Perf. 12***

307	A55	10p gray brn	4.00	2.00
308	A55	10p red brn	4.00	2.00

50th anniv. of the Hayes' Chaco decision.

Portraits of Archbishop Bogarin — A56

1930, Aug. 15

309	A56	1.50p lake	1.00	75
310	A56	1.50p turq bl	1.00	75
311	A56	1.50p dl vio	1.00	75

Archbishop Juan Sinforiano Bogarin, first archbishop of Paraguay.

No. 272 Surcharged

Habilitado
en
CINCO

1930

312	A47	5c on 7c emer	5	5

A57

1930-39 **Typo.** ***Perf. 11½, 12***

313	A57	10p brown	50	20
314	A57	10p brn red, *bl* ('31)	50	20
315	A57	10p dk bl, *pink* ('32)	50	20
316	A57	10p gray brn ('36)	38	18
317	A57	10p gray ('37)	38	18
318	A57	10p blue ('39)	15	12
		Nos. 313-318 (6)	2.41	1.08

1st Paraguayan postage stamp, 60th anniv.

Gunboat "Humaitá" — A58

1931 ***Perf. 12***

319	A58	1.50p purple	38	22

60th anniv. of the Constitution. See Nos. C39-C53.

View of San Bernardino — A59

1931, Aug.

320	A59	1p lt grn	25	15

Founding of San Bernardino, 50th anniv.

Nos. 309-310 Overprinted in Blue or Red

FELIZ
AÑO NUEVO
1932

1931, Dec. 31

321	A56	1.50p lake (Bl)	75	75
322	A56	1.50p turq blue (R)	75	75

Map of the Gran Chaco — A60

1932-35 **Typo.** ***Perf. 12***

323	A60	1.50p deep vio	15	10
324	A60	1.50p rose ('35)	10	8

Nos. C74-C78 Surcharged

CORREOS
1 PESO
FELIZ AÑO NUEVO
1933

1933 **Litho.**

325	AP18	50c on 4p ultra	25	20
326	AP18	1p on 8p red	50	38
327	AP18	1.50p on 12p bl grn	50	38
328	AP18	2p on 16p dk vio	50	38
329	AP18	5p on 20p org brn	1.25	1.00
		Nos. 325-329 (5)	3.00	2.34

Flag of the Race Issue

Flag with Three Crosses: Caravels of Columbus — A61

1933, Oct. 10 **Litho.** ***Perf. 11***

330	A61	10c red brn, ol grn & violet	8	6
331	A61	20c dl red, pale bl & violet	8	6
332	A61	50c bl grn, ver & vio	10	6
333	A61	1p sl gray, yel brn & violet	10	9
334	A61	1.50p dk bl, yel grn & violet	10	9
335	A61	2p blk brn, bl grn & violet	25	25
336	A61	5p ol grn, org brn & violet	50	50
337	A61	10p pale bl, blk brn & violet	50	50
		Nos. 330-337 (8)	1.71	1.61

441st anniv. of the sailing of Christopher Columbus from the port of Palos, Aug. 3, 1492, on his first voyage to the New World.

Monstrance A62

Arms of Asuncion A63

1937, Aug. **Unwmk.** ***Perf. 11½***

338	A62	1p dk bl, yel & red	5	5
339	A62	3p dk bl, yel & red	6	5
340	A62	10p dk bl, yel & red	12	10

1st Natl. Eucharistic Congress, Asuncion.

1937, Aug.

341	A63	50c vio & buff	5	5
342	A63	1p bis & lt grn	5	5
343	A63	3p red & lt bl	5	5
344	A63	10p car rose & buff	12	9
345	A63	20p blue & drab	15	15
		Nos. 341-345 (5)	42	39

Founding of Asuncion, 400th anniv.

Oratory of the Virgin, Asuncion — A64

Carlos Antonio Lopez — A65

José Eduvigis Diaz — A66

1938-39 **Typo.** ***Perf. 11, 12***

346	A64	5p olive grn	18	8
347	A64	5p pale rose ('39)	25	10
348	A64	11p vio brown	18	10

Founding of Asuncion, 400th anniv.

1939 ***Perf. 12***

349	A65	2p lt ultra & pale brn	18	12
350	A66	2p lt ultra & brn	20	15

Reburial of ashes of Pres. Carlos Antonio Lopez (1790-1862) and Gen. José Eduvigis Diaz in the National Pantheon, Asuncion.

Pres. Patricio Escobar and Ramon Zubizarreta A67

Pres. Bernardino Caballero and Senator Jose S. Decoud A68

1939-40 Litho. *Perf. 11½*

Heads in Black

351	A67	50c dl org ('40)		6	5
352	A67	1p lt vio ('40)		12	8
353	A67	2p red brn ('40)		18	10
354	A67	5p lt ultra		25	15
		Nos. 351-354,C122-C123 (6)		7.86	7.63

Founding of the University of Asuncion, 50th anniv.

Varieties of this issue include inverted heads (50c, 1p, 2p); doubled heads; Caballero and Decoud heads in 50c frame: imperforates and part-perforates. Copies with inverted heads were not officially issued.

Coats of Arms — A69

Pres. Baldomir of Uruguay, Flags of Paraguay, Uruguay A70

Designs: 2p, Pres. Benavides, Peru. 3p, US Eagle and Shield. 5p, Pres. Alessandri, Chile. 6p, Pres. Vargas, Brazil. 10p, Pres. Ortiz, Argentina.

1939 Engr.; Flags Litho. *Perf. 12*

Flags in National Colors

355	A69	50c vio blue	12	10
356	A70	1p olive	10	6
357	A70	2p blue grn	12	9
358	A70	3p sepia	25	18
359	A70	5p orange	20	15
360	A70	6p dull vio	50	40
361	A70	10p bister brn	38	25
		Nos. 355-361 (7)	1.67	1.23

First Buenos Aires Peace Conference. See Nos. C113-121.

Coats of Arms of New York and Asuncion A76

1939, Nov. 30

362	A76	5p scarlet	12	10
363	A76	10p deep blue	25	18
364	A76	11p dk blue grn	35	30
365	A76	22p olive blk	45	38

New York World's Fair. See Nos. C124-C126.

Paraguayan Soldier — A77

Paraguayan Woman — A78

Cowboys — A79

Plowing — A80

View of Paraguay River — A81

Oxcart A82

Pasture A83

Pirareta Falls — A84

1940, Jan. 1 Photo. *Perf. 12½*

366	A77	50c deep org	8	8
367	A78	1p brt red vio	10	10
368	A79	3p bright grn	15	12
369	A80	5p chestnut	20	12
370	A81	10p magenta	25	15
371	A82	20p violet	45	32
372	A83	50p cobalt bl	1.10	45
373	A84	100p black	2.25	1.40
		Nos. 366-373 (8)	4.58	2.74

Second Buenos Aires Peace Conference.

Map of the Americas — A85

1940, May Engr. *Perf. 12*

374	A85	50c red org	5	5
375	A85	1p green	8	6
376	A85	5p dark blue	12	10
377	A85	10p brown	38	38
		Nos. 374-377,C127-C130 (8)	4.01	3.17

Pan American Union, 50th anniversary.

Reproduction of Type A1 — A86

Sir Rowland Hill — A87

The Scott Catalogue value is a retail price, what you could expect to pay for the stamp in a grade of Fine-Very Fine. The value listed is a reference which reflects recent actual dealer selling price.

Reproductions of Types A2 and A3

A88 A89

1940, Aug. 15 Photo. *Perf. 13½*

378	A86	1p aqua & brt red vio	50	25
379	A87	5p dp yel grn & red brn	65	32
380	A88	6p org brn & ultra	1.50	65
381	A89	10p ver & black	1.50	1.00

Postage stamp centenary.

Dr. José Francia

A90 A91

1940, Sept. 20 Engr. *Perf. 12*

382	A90	50c car rose	12	10
383	A91	50c plum	12	10
384	A90	1p bright grn	12	10
385	A91	5p deep blue	12	10

Centenary of the death of Dr. Jose Francia (1766-1840), dictator of Paraguay, 1814-1840.

No. 366 Surcharged in Black

7-IX-40

DUELO NACIONAL

5 PESOS

1940, Sept. 7 *Perf. 12½*

386	A77	5p on 50c dp org	20	20

In honor of Pres. Jose F. Estigarribia who died in a plane crash Sept. 7, 1940.

No. 360 Overprinted in Black

Visita al Paraguay
Agosto de 1941

1941, Aug. *Perf. 12*

387	A70	6p multi	20	20

Visit to Paraguay of Pres. Vargas of Brazil.

Nos. C113-C115 Overprinted "HABILITADO" and Bars in Blue or Red

1942, Jan. 17 *Perf. 12½*

388	AP25	1p multi (Bl)	12	10
389	AP26	3p multi (R)	15	10
390	AP27	5p multi (R)	18	10

Coat of Arms — A92

1942-43 Litho. *Perf. 11, 12, 11x12*

391	A92	1p light green	6	5
392	A92	1p orange ('43)	5	5
393	A92	7p light blue	8	5
394	A92	7p yel brn ('43)	5	5

The Indian Francisco — A93

Arms of Irala — A95

Domingo Martinez de Irala and His Vision A94

1942, Aug. 15 Engr. *Perf. 12*

395	A93	2p green	65	30
396	A94	5p rose	65	30
397	A95	7p sapphire	65	25
		Nos. 395-397,C131-C133 (6)	9.50	7.35

400th anniversary of Asuncion.

Pres. Higinio Morinigo, Scenes of Industry & Agriculture A96

Christopher Columbus A97

1943, Aug. 15 Unwmk.

398	A96	7p blue	9	8

1943, Aug. 15

399	A97	50c violet	18	15
400	A97	1p gray brn	15	10
401	A97	5p dark grn	45	12
402	A97	7p brt ultra	25	10

Discovery of America, 450th anniv.

No. 296 Surcharged in Black

Habilitado
en
un céntimo

1944 *Perf. 12, 11, 11½, 11x12*

403	A51	1c on 3p brt vio	5	5

Nos. 398 and 402 Surcharged "1944 / 5 Centimos 5" in Red

1944 *Perf. 12*

404	A96	5c on 7p blue	10	5
405	A97	5c on 7p brt ultra	10	5

Imperforates

Starting with No. 406, many Paraguayan stamps exist imperforate.

Primitive Postal Service among Indians — A98

Ruins of Humaita Church — A99

Locomotive of early Paraguayan Railroad — A100

Early Merchant Ship — A102

Marshal Francisco S. Lopez — A101

Port of Asunción A103

Birthplace of Paraguay's Liberation A104

Monument to Heroes of Itororo — A105

1944-45 Unwmk. Engr. *Perf. 12½*

406	A98	1c black	8	5
407	A99	2c cop brn ('45)	10	10
408	A100	5c light olive	25	15
409	A101	7c lt blue ('45)	12	8
410	A102	10c grn ('45)	25	20
411	A103	15c dark bl ('45)	25	20
412	A104	50c black brn	45	45
413	A105	1g dk rose car ('45)	90	50
		Nos. 406-413 (8)	2.40	1.73

See Nos. 435, 437, 439, 441, C134-C146, C158-C162.

No. 409 Surcharged in Red

1945

414	A101	5c on 7c lt bl	8	8

Handshake, Map and Flags of Paraguay and Panama — A106

Designs: 3c, Venezuela Flag. 5c, Colombia Flag. 2g, Peru Flag.

Engr.; Flags Litho. in Natl. Colors

1945, Aug. 15 Unwmk. *Perf. 12½*

415	A106	1c dark green	5	5
416	A106	3c lake	8	6
417	A106	5c blue blk	10	6
418	A106	2g brown	1.10	75

Goodwill visits of Pres. Higinio Morinigo during 1943. See Nos. C147-C153.

Nos. B6 to B9 Surcharged "1945" and New Value in Black

1945 Engr. *Perf. 12*

419	SP4	2c on 7p + 3p red brn	8	6
420	SP4	2c on 7p + 3p purple	10	8
421	SP4	2c on 7p + 3p car rose	8	6
422	SP4	2c on 7p + 3p saph	10	8
423	SP4	5c on 7p + 3p red brn	12	8
424	SP4	5c on 7p + 3p purple	12	8
425	SP4	5c on 7p + 3p car rose	12	8
426	SP4	5c on 7p + 3p saph	12	8
		Nos. 419-426 (8)	84	60

Similar Surcharge in Red on Nos. 409, 398 and 402

Perf. 12½, 12

427	A101	5c on 7c lt blue	12	9
428	A96	5c on 7p blue	15	10
429	A97	5c on 7p brt ultra	15	12

Nos. 427-429 exist with black surcharge.

Catalogue values for unused stamps in this section, from this point to the end of the section, are for Never Hinged items.

Coat of Arms ("U.P.U." at bottom) — A110

1946 Litho. *Perf. 11, 12, 11x12*

430	A110	5c gray	5	5

See Nos. 459-463, 478-480, 498-506, 525-536, 633-646.

Nos. B6 to B9 Surcharged "1946" and New Value in Black

1946 *Perf. 12*

431	SP4	5c on 7p + 3p red brn	32	25
432	SP4	5c on 7p + 3p purple	32	25
433	SP4	5c on 7p + 3p car rose	32	25
434	SP4	5c on 7p + 3p saph	32	25

First Telegraph in South America — A111

Colonial Jesuit Altar — A113

Monument to Antequera A112

1946, Sept. 21 Engr. *Perf. 12½*

435	A102	1c rose car	5	5
436	A111	2c purple	5	5
437	A98	5c ultra	8	5
438	A112	10c org yel	10	9
439	A105	15c brn olive	12	12
440	A113	50c deep grn	30	20
441	A104	1g brt ultra	65	38
		Nos. 435-441 (7)	1.35	94

See Nos. C135-C138, C143.

Marshal Francisco Solano Lopez — A114

1947, May 15 *Perf. 12*

442	A114	1c purple	5	5
443	A114	2c org red	5	5
444	A114	5c green	6	6
445	A114	15c ultra	8	8
446	A114	50c dark grn	25	25
		Nos. 442-446 (5)	49	49

See Nos. C163-C167.

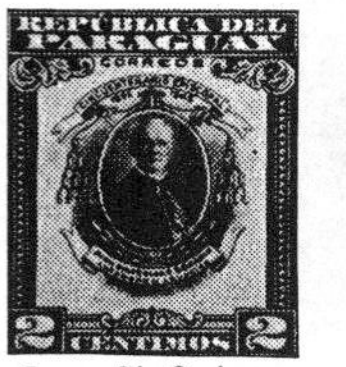
Juan Sinforiano Bogarin, Archbishop of Asuncion A115

Archbishopric Coat of Arms A116

Projected Monument of the Sacred Heart of Jesus A117

Vision of Projected Monument A118

1948, Jan. 6 Engr. *Perf. 12½*

447	A115	2c dark blue	6	6
448	A116	5c deep car	5	5
449	A117	10c gray blk	10	8
450	A118	15c green	20	12

Establishment of the Archbishopric of Asuncion, 50th anniv.
See Nos. C168-C175.

"Political Enlightenment" A119

1948, Sept. 11 Engr. & Litho.

451	A119	5c car red & bl	5	5
452	A119	15c red org, red & bl	10	9

Issued to honor the Barefeet, a political group. See Nos. C176-C177.

C. A. Lopez, J. N. Gonzalez and Freighter Paraguari A120

1949 Litho.

Centers in Carmine, Black, Ultramarine and Blue

453	A120	2c orange	5	5
454	A120	5c blue vio	5	5
455	A120	10c black	6	5
456	A120	15c violet	10	6
457	A120	50c blue grn	12	9
458	A120	1g dull vio brn	20	15
		Nos. 453-458 (6)	58	45

Paraguay's merchant fleet centenary.

Type of 1946

1950 Unwmk. *Perf. 10½*

459	A110	5c red	5	5
460	A110	10c blue	5	5
461	A110	50c rose lilac	5	5
462	A110	1g pale violet	9	6

1951

Coarse Impression

463	A110	30c green	5	5

Blocks of Four of Nos. 459, 460 and 463 Overprinted in Various Colors

(Illustration Reduced One-Half)

1951, Apr. 18

464	A110	5c red (Bk), block	15	12
465	A110	10c bl (R), block	25	18
466	A110	30c grn (V), block	38	30

1st Economic Cong. of Paraguay, Apr. 18, 1951.

Columbus Lighthouse A121

1952, Feb. 11 *Perf. 10*

467	A121	2c org brn	5	5
468	A121	5c light ultra	5	5
469	A121	10c rose	5	5
470	A121	15c light blue	5	5
471	A121	20c lilac	5	5
472	A121	50c orange	10	10
473	A121	1g bluish grn	18	18
		Nos. 467-473 (7)	53	53

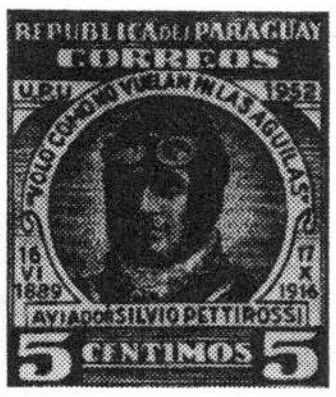
Silvio Pettirossi, Aviator — A122

1954, Mar. Litho. *Perf. 10*

474	A122	5c blue	5	5
475	A122	20c rose pink	5	5
476	A122	50c vio brn	5	5
477	A122	60c lt vio	10	8
		Nos. 474-477, C201-C204 (8)	64	62

Arms Type of 1946

1954 *Perf. 11*

478	A110	10c vermilion	5	5

Perf. 10

478A	A110	10c ver, redrawn	5	5
479	A110	10g orange	25	20
480	A110	50g vio brn	1.25	1.00

No. 478A measures 20½x24mm, has 5 frame lines at left and 6 at right. No. 478 measures 20x24½mm, has 6 frame lines at left and 5 at right.

Three National Heroes — A123

1954, Aug. 15 Litho. *Perf. 10*

481	A123	5c light vio	5	5
482	A123	20c light blue	5	5
483	A123	50c rose pink	5	5
484	A123	1g org brn	5	5
485	A123	2g blue grn	10	10
		Nos. 481-485 (5)	30	30

Marshal Francisco S. Lopez, Pres. Carlos A. Lopez and Gen. Bernardino Caballero.
See Nos. C216-C220.

Pres. Alfredo Stroessner and Pres. Juan D. Peron — A124

Photo. & Litho.

1955, Apr. Wmk. 90 *Perf. 13x13½*

Frames and Flags in Blue and Carmine

486	A124	5c	brn, yel brn & sal pink	5	5
487	A124	10c	lil rose, dp cl & cream	5	5
488	A124	50c	gray, blk & cr	5	5
489	A124	1.30g	rose lil, rose vio & cream	6	5
490	A124	2.20g	ultra, dk bl & cr	12	9
	Nos. 486-490,C221-C224 (9)			76	67

Visit of Pres. Juan D. Peron of Argentina.

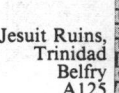

Jesuit Ruins, Trinidad Belfry A125

Santa Maria Cornice — A126

Jesuit Ruins: 20c, Corridor at Trinidad. 2.50g, Tower of Santa Rosa. 5g, San Cosme gate. 15g, Church of Jesus. 25g, Niche at Trinidad.

Perf. 12½x12, 12x12½

1955, June 19 Engr. Unwmk.

491	A125	5c	org yel	5	5
492	A125	20c	olive bis	5	5
493	A126	50c	lt red brn	5	5
494	A126	2.50g	olive	5	5
495	A125	5g	yel brn	6	5
496	A125	15g	blue grn	22	15
497	A126	25g	deep grn	45	25
	Nos. 491-497 (7)			93	65

25th anniv. of the priesthood of Monsignor Rodriguez. See Nos. C225-C232.

Arms Type of 1946

Perf. 10, 11 (No. 500)

1956-58 Litho. Unwmk.

498	A110	5c	brn ('57)	5	5
499	A110	30c	red brn ('57)	5	5
500	A110	45c	gray olive	5	5
500A	A110	90c	lt vio bl	5	5
501	A110	2g	ocher	5	5
502	A110	2.20g	lil rose	5	5
503	A110	3g	ol bis ('58)	5	5
503A	A110	4.20g	emer ('57)	5	5
504	A110	5g	ver ('57)	8	5
505	A110	10g	lt grn ('57)	15	10
506	A110	20g	blue ('57)	30	22
	Nos. 498-506 (11)			93	77

No. 500A exists with four-line, carmine overprint: "DIA N. UNIDAS 24 Octubre 1945-1956". It was not regularly issued and no decree authorizing it is known.

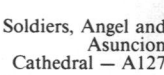

Soldiers, Angel and Asuncion Cathedral — A127

Design: Nos. 513-519, Soldier and nurse in medallion and flags.

Perf. 13½

1957, June 12 Photo. Unwmk.

Granite Paper

Flags in Red and Blue

508	A127	5c	bl grn	5	5
509	A127	10c	carmine	5	5
510	A127	15c	ultra	5	5
511	A127	20c	dp claret	5	5
512	A127	25c	gray blk	5	5
513	A127	30c	lt blue	5	5
514	A127	40c	gray blk	5	5
515	A127	50c	dark car	5	5
516	A127	1g	bluish grn	5	5
517	A127	1.30g	ultra	5	5
518	A127	1.50g	dp claret	5	5
519	A127	2g	brt grn	8	5
	Nos. 508-519 (12)			63	60

Heroes of the Chaco war. See Nos. C233-C245.

Statue of St. Ignatius (Guarani Carving) — A128

Blessed Roque Gonzales and St. Ignatius A129

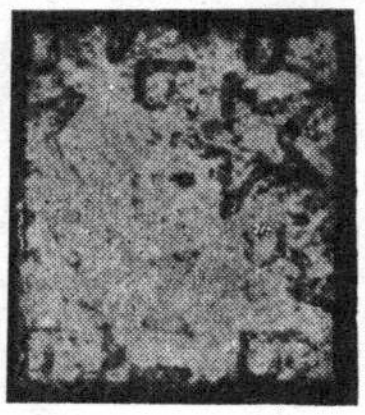

Wmk. 319 - Stars and R P Multiple

Design: 1.50g, St. Ignatius and San Ignacio Monastery.

Wmk. 319

1958, Mar. 15 Litho. *Perf. 11*

520	A128	50c	dk red brn	5	5
521	A129	50c	lt bl grn	5	5
522	AP91	1.50g	brt vio	5	5
523	A128	3g	light bl	8	5
524	A129	6.25g	rose car	12	9
	Nos. 520-524 (5)			35	29

St. Ignatius of Loyola (1491-1556). See Nos. 704-707.

Arms Type of 1946

1958-64 Litho. *Perf. 10, 11*

525	A110	45c	gray olive	5	5
526	A110	50c	rose vio	5	5
527	A110	70c	lt brn ('59)	5	5
527A	A110	90c	vio blue	5	5
528	A110	1g	violet	5	5
529	A110	1.50g	lilac ('59)	5	5
529A	A110	2g	bister ('64)	5	5
530	A110	3g	ol bis ('59)	5	5
531	A110	4.50g	lt ultra ('59)	5	5
531A	A110	5g	rose red ('59)	6	5
531B	A110	10g	bl grn ('59)	15	10
532	A110	12.45g	yel green	12	10
533	A110	15g	dl orange	15	12
534	A110	30g	citron	28	20
535	A110	50g	brown red	42	30
536	A110	100g	gray vio	85	65
	Nos. 525-536 (16)			2.48	1.97

Pres. Alfredo Stroessner A130

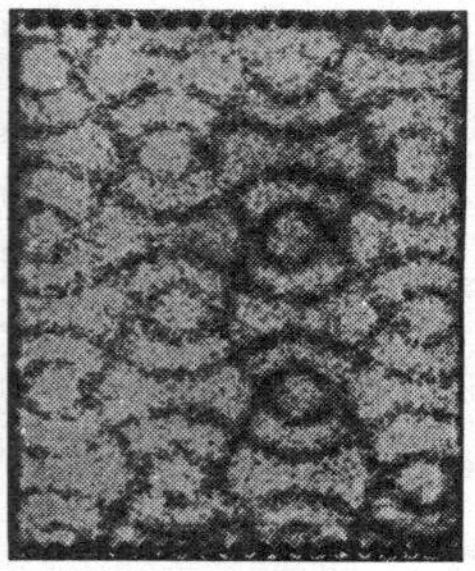

Wmk. 320 - Interlacing Lines

Wmk. 320

1958, Aug. 15 Litho. *Perf. 13½*

Center in Slate

537	A130	10c	sal pink	5	5
538	A130	15c	violet	5	5
539	A130	25c	yel grn	5	5
540	A130	30c	light fawn	5	5
541	A130	50c	rose car	6	5
542	A130	75c	light ultra	6	5
543	A130	5g	lt bl grn	10	8
544	A130	10g	brown	10	8
	Nos. 537-544 (8)			52	46

Re-election of President General Alfredo Stroessner. See Nos. C246-C251.

Nos. 491-497 Surcharged in Red

Perf. 12½x12, 12x12½

1959, May 14 Engr. Unwmk.

545	A125	1.50g	on	5c org yel		5	5
546	A125	1.50g	on	20c ol bis		5	5
547	A126	1.50g	on	50c lt red brn		5	5
548	A126	3g	on	2.50g ol		5	5
549	A125	6.25g	on	5g yel brn		8	8
550	A125	20g	on	15g bl grn		25	25
551	A126	30g	on	25g dp grn		38	38
	Nos. 545-551 (7)					91	91

The surcharge is made to fit the stamps. See Nos. C252-C259.

Counterfeits of surcharge exist.

Goalkeeper Catching Soccer Ball A131

WRY Emblem A132

1960, Mar. 18 Photo. *Perf. 12½*

556	A131	30c	brt red & bl grn	5	5
557	A131	50c	plum & dk bl	5	5
558	A131	75c	ol grn & org	5	5
559	A131	1.50g	dk vio & bl grn	5	5
	Nos. 556-559,C262-C264 (7)			95	95

Olympic Games of 1960.

1960, Apr. 7 Litho. *Perf. 11*

560	A132	25c	sal & yel grn	8	5
561	A132	50c	lt yel grn & red org	10	8
562	A132	70c	lt brn & lil rose	25	20
563	A132	1.50g	lt bl & ultra	25	20
564	A132	3g	gray & bis brn	50	45
	Nos. 560-564,C265-C268 (9)			5.03	4.26

World Refugee Year, July 1, 1959-June 30, 1960 (1st issue).

UN Emblem and Dove — A133

Flags of UN and Paraguay and UN Emblem — A134

Designs: 3g, Hand holding seales. 6g, Hands breaking chains. 20g, Flame.

1960, Apr. 21 *Perf. 12½x13*

565	A133	1g	dk car & bl	5	5
566	A133	3g	blue & org	5	5
567	A133	6g	gray grn & sal	5	5
568	A133	20g	ver & yel	12	12
	Nos. 565-568,C269-C271 (7)			1.47	1.47

Miniature sheets exist, perf. and imperf., containing one each of Nos. 565-568, all printed in purple and orange.

Perf. 13x13½

1960, Oct. 24 Photo. Unwmk.

569	A134	30c	lt bl, red & bl	5	5
570	A134	75c	yel, red & bl	5	5
571	A134	90c	pale lil, red & bl	5	5
	Nos. 569-571,C272-C273 (5)			26	26

15th anniversary of the United Nations.

International Bridge, Arms of Brazil, Paraguay A135

Truck Carrying Logs A136

1961, Jan. 26 Litho. *Perf. 14*

572	A135	15c	green	5	5
573	A135	30c	dull blue	5	5
574	A135	50c	orange	5	5
575	A135	75c	vio blue	5	5
576	A135	1g	violet	5	5
	Nos. 572-576,C274-C277 (9)			1.09	99

Inauguration of the International Bridge between Paraguay and Brazil.

Unwmk.

1961, Apr. 10 Photo. *Perf. 13*

Designs: 90c, 2g, Logs on river barge. 1g, 5g, Radio tower.

577	A136	25c	yel grn & rose car	5	5
578	A136	90c	blue & yel	5	5
579	A136	1g	car rose & org	5	5
580	A136	2g	ol grn & sal	8	5
581	A136	5g	lilac & emer	10	8
	Nos. 577-581,C278-C281 (9)			1.66	1.41

Paraguay's progress, "Paraguay en Marcha."

P. J. Caballero, José G. R. Francia, F. Yegros, Revolutionary Leaders — A137

1961, May 16 Litho. *Perf. 14½*

582	A137	30c	green	5	5
583	A137	50c	lil rose	5	5
584	A137	90c	violet	5	5
585	A137	1.50g	Prus bl	5	5
586	A137	3g	olive bis	5	5
587	A137	4g	ultra	5	5
588	A137	5g	brown	6	5
	Nos. 582-588 (7)			36	35

150th anniv. of Independence (1st issue). See Nos. C282-C287.

"Chaco Peace" A138

Puma A139

1961, June 12 ***Perf. 14x14½***

589 A138 25c vermilion 5 5
590 A138 30c green 5 5
591 A138 50c red brn 5 5
592 A138 1g bright vio 5 5
593 A138 2g dk bl gray 5 5
Nos. 589-593,C288-C290 (8) 1.45 1.35

Chaco Peace; 150th anniv. of Independence (2nd issue).

1961, Aug. 16 **Unwmk.** ***Perf. 14***

594 A139 75c dull vio 5 5
595 A139 1.50g brown 5 5
596 A139 4.50g green 6 6
597 A139 10g Prus blue 12 12
Nos. 594-597,C291-C293 (7) 2.83 2.68

150th anniv. of Independence (3rd issue).

University Seal — A140

Hotel Guarani — A141

1961, Sept. 18 ***Perf. 14x14½***

598 A140 15c ultra 5 5
599 A140 25c dk red 5 5
600 A140 75c bl grn 5 5
601 A140 1g orange 5 5
Nos. 598-601,C294-C296 (7) 88 88

Founding of the Catholic University in Asuncion; 150th anniv. of Independence (4th issue).

1961, Oct. 14 **Litho.** ***Perf. 15***

602 A141 50c slate bl 5 5
603 A141 1g green 5 5
604 A141 4.50g lilac 5 5
Nos. 602-604,C297-C300 (7) 91 86

Opening of the Hotel Guarani; 150th anniv. of Independence (5th issue).

Tennis Racket and Balls in Flag Colors — A142

1961, Oct. 16 **Litho.** ***Perf. 11***

605 A142 35c multi 5
606 A142 75c multi 5
607 A142 1.50g multi 5
608 A142 2.25g multi 5
609 A142 4g multi 8
Nos. 605-609 (5) 28

28th South American Tennis Championships, Asuncion, Oct. 15-23 (1st issue). Some specialists question the status of this issue. See Nos. C301-C303.

Imperforates exist in changed colors as well as two imperf. souvenir sheets with stamps in changed colors.

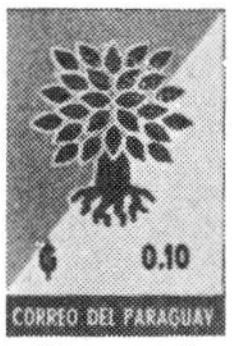

Uprooted Oak Emblem A145

Tennis Player A146

1961, Dec. 30 **Unwmk.** ***Perf. 11***

619 A145 10c ultra & lt bl 5
620 A145 25c maroon & org 5
621 A145 50c car rose & pink 5
622 A145 75c dk bl & yel grn 5

World Refugee Year, 1959-60 (2nd issue). Imperforates in changed colors and souvenir sheets exist. Some specialists question the status of this issue.
See Nos. C307-C309.

1962, Jan. 5 ***Perf. 15x14½***

623 A146 35c Prussian bl 5 5
624 A146 75c dark vio 5 5
625 A146 1.50g red brn 5 5
626 A146 2.25g emerald 5 5
Nos. 623-626,C310-C313 (8) 1.38 1.38

28th South American Tennis Championships, 1961 (2nd issue) and the 150th anniv. of Independence (6th issue).

Scout Bugler — A147

1962, Feb. 6 ***Perf. 11***
Olive Green Center

627 A147 10c dp magenta 5
628 A147 20c red orange 5
629 A147 25c dk brown 5
630 A147 30c emerald 5
631 A147 50c indigo 5
Nos. 627-631 (5) 25

Issued to honor the Boy Scouts. Imperfs. in changed colors exist. Some specialists question the status of this issue.
See Nos. C314-C316.

Arms Type of 1946

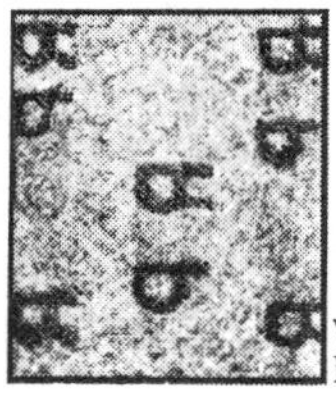
Wmk. 347 - RP Multiple

1962-68 **Litho.** **Wmk. 347**

634 A110 50c steel bl ('63) 5 5
635 A110 70c dull lil ('63) 5 5
636 A110 1.50g violet ('63) 5 5
637 A110 3g dp bl ('68) 5 5
638 A110 4.50g redsh brn ('67) 5 5
639 A110 5g lilac ('64) 5 5
640 A110 10g car rose ('63) 7 5
641 A110 12.45g ultra 8 8
642 A110 15.45g org ver 12 9
643 A110 18.15g lilac 14 10
644 A110 20g lt brn ('63) 14 10
645 A110 50g dl red brn ('67) 35 18
646 A110 100g bl gray ('63) 70 42
Nos. 634-646 (13) 1.90 1.32

Map and Laurel Branch A148

UN Emblem A149

Perf. 14x14½
1962, Apr. 14 **Unwmk.**

647 A148 50c ocher 5 5
648 A148 75c vio blue 5 5
649 A148 1g purple 5 5
650 A148 1.50g brt grn 5 5
651 A148 4.50g vermilion 5 5
Nos. 647-651,C320-C321 (7) 81 81

Day of the Americas; 150th anniv. of Independence (7th issue).

1962, Apr. 23 ***Perf. 15***

652 A149 50c bister brn 5 5
653 A149 75c dp claret 5 5
654 A149 1g Prussian bl 5 5
655 A149 2g orange brn 5 5
Nos. 652-655,C322-C325 (8) 1.65 1.65

United Nations; 150th anniv. of Independence (8th issue).

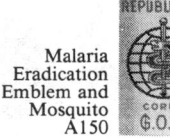

Malaria Eradication Emblem and Mosquito A150

Design: 75c, 1g, 1.50g, Microscope, anopheles mosquito and eggs.

Perf. 14x13½
1962, May 23 **Wmk. 346**

656 A150 30c pink, ultra & blk 5
657 A150 50c bis, grn & blk 5
658 A150 75c rose red, blk & bis 5
659 A150 1g brt grn, blk & bis 5
660 A150 1.50g dl red brn, blk & bis 5
Nos. 656-660 (5) 25

WHO drive to eradicate malaria. Imperforates exist in changed colors. Some specialists question the status of this issue.
See Nos. C326-C330.

Stadium — A151

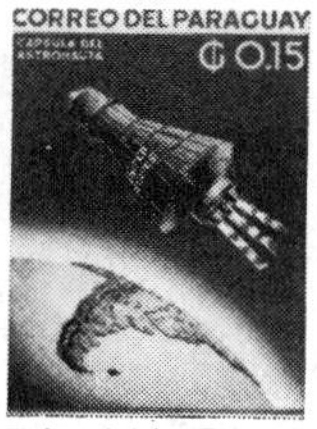

Friendship 7 over South America — A153

Freighter A152

Perf. 13½x14
1962, July 28 **Litho.** **Wmk. 346**

661 A151 15c yel & dk brn 5
662 A151 25c brt grn & dk brn 5
663 A151 30c lt vio & dk brn 5
664 A151 40c dl org & dk brn 5
665 A151 50c brt yel grn & dk brn 5
Nos. 661-665 (5) 25

World Soccer Championships, Chile, May 30-June 17. Some specialists question the status of this issue. Imperfs. exist. See Nos. C331-C333.

Perf. 14½x15
1962, July 31 **Unwmk.**

Designs: Various merchantmen.

666 A152 30c bister brn 5 5
667 A152 90c slate bl 5 5
668 A152 1.50g brown red 5 5
669 A152 2g green 5 5
670 A152 4.20g vio blue 8 8
Nos. 666-670,C334-C335 (7) 78 70

Issued to honor the merchant marine.

Perf. 13½x14
1962, Sept. 4 **Litho.** **Wmk. 346**

671 A153 15c dk bl & bis 5
672 A153 25c vio brn & bis 5
673 A153 30c dk sl grn & bis 5
674 A153 40c dk gray & bis 5
675 A153 50c dk vio & bis 5
Nos. 671-675 (5) 25

US manned space flights. Imperfs. in changed colors exist. Some specialists question the status of this issue.
See Nos. C336-C338.

Discus Thrower A154

Pres. Alfredo Stroessner A156

Peace Dove and Cross A155

1962, Oct. 1 **Litho.**

676 A154 15c blk & yel 5
677 A154 25c blk & lt grn 5
678 A154 30c blk & pink 5
679 A154 40c blk & pale vio 5
680 A154 50c blk & lt bl 5
Nos. 676-680 (5) 25

Olympic Games from Amsterdam 1928 to Tokyo 1964. Each stamp is inscribed with date and place of various Olympic Games. Imperfs. in changed colors exist. Some specialists question the status of this issue. See Nos. C339-C341.

Perf. 14½
1962, Oct. 11 **Litho.** **Unwmk.**

681 A155 50c olive 5 5
682 A155 70c dark blue 5 5
683 A155 1.50g bister 5 5
684 A155 2g violet 5 5
685 A155 3g brick red 5 5
Nos. 681-685,C342-C347 (11) 1.65 1.30

Vatican II, the 21st Ecumenical Council of the Roman Catholic Church, which opened Oct. 11, 1962.

1963, Aug. 6 **Wmk. 347** ***Perf. 11***

686 A156 50c ol gray & sep 5 5
687 A156 75c buff & sepia 5 5
688 A156 1.50g lt lil & sep 6 6
689 A156 3g emer & sepia 12 6
Nos. 686-689,C348-C350 (7) 1.46 1.09

3rd presidential term of Alfredo Stroessner.

Popes Paul VI, John XXIII and St. Peter's, Rome — A157

1964, May 23

690 A157 1.50g claret & org 5 5
691 A157 3g cl & dk grn 5 5
692 A157 4g cl & bister 5 5
Nos. 690-692,C351-C353 (6) 1.58 1.32

National holiday of St. Maria Auxiliadora (Our Lady of Perpetual Help).

Coats of Arms of Paraguay and France
A158

Design: 3g, Presidents Stroessner and de Gaulle.

1964, Oct. 6

693 A158 1.50g brown 5 5
694 A158 3g ultramarine 5 5
695 A158 4g gray 5 5
Nos. 693-695,C354-C356 (6) 1.58 1.32

Visit of Pres. Charles de Gaulle of France.

Map of Americas A159 — Cattleya Warscewiczii A160

Overprint: "Centenario de la Epopeya Nacional 1.864-1.870"

1965, Apr. 26 Wmk. 347 *Perf. 11*

696 A159 1.50g dull grn 5 5
697 A159 3g car red 5 5
698 A159 4g dark blue 5 5
Nos. 696-698,C357-C358 (5) 79 62

Centenary of National Epic. Not issued without overprint.

1965, June 28 Unwmk. *Perf. 14½*

699 A160 20c purple 5 5
700 A160 30c blue 5 5
701 A160 90c bright mag 5 5
702 A160 1.50g green 5 5
703 A160 4.50g orange 6 6
Nos. 699-703,C359-C361 (8) 1.11 86

150th anniv. of Independence (1811-1961).

St. Ignatius Type of 1958

1966, Apr. 20 Wmk. 347 *Perf. 11*

704 A129 15c ultramarine 5 5
705 A129 25c ultramarine 5 5
706 A129 75c ultramarine 5 5
707 A129 90c ultramarine 5 5
Nos. 704-707,C362-C365 (8) 75 63

350th anniv. of the founding of San Ignacio Guazu Monastery.

Rubén Dario — A161 — Globe and Lions Emblem — A162

1966, July 16

708 A161 50c ultramarine 5 5
709 A161 70c bister brn 5 5
710 A161 1.50g rose car 5 5
711 A161 3g violet 5 5
712 A161 4g greenish bl 5 5
713 A161 5g black 5 5
Nos. 708-713,C366-C370 (11) 1.53 93

50th death anniv. of Ruben Dario (pen name of Felix Rubén Garcia Sarmiento, 1867-1916), Nicaraguan poet, newspaper correspondent and diplomat.

1967, May 9 Litho.

Designs: 1.50g, 3g, Melvin Jones. 4g, 5g, Lions' Headquarters, Chicago.

714 A162 50c light vio 5 5
715 A162 70c blue 5 5
716 A162 1.50g ultra 5 5
717 A162 3g brown 5 5
718 A162 4g Prussian grn 5 5
719 A162 5g ol gray 5 5
Nos. 714-719,C371-C375 (11) 1.25 93

50th anniversary of Lions International.

WHO Emblem A163

1968, Aug. 12 Wmk. 347 *Perf. 11*

720 A163 3g bluish grn 5 5
721 A163 4g brt pink 5 5
722 A163 5g bister brn 5 5
723 A163 10g violet 5 5
Nos. 720-723,C376-C378 (7) 1.60 1.05

WHO, 20th anniv.; cent. of the national epic.

"World United in Peace" — A164

1969, June 28 Wmk. 347 *Perf. 11*

724 A164 50c rose 5 5
725 A164 70c ultra 5 5
726 A164 1.50g light brn 5 5
727 A164 3g lil rose 5 5
728 A164 4g emerald 5 5
729 A164 5g violet 7 7
730 A164 10g brt lilac 14 14
Nos. 724-730 (7) 46 46

Peace Week.

Francisco Solano — A165 — Paraguay No. 2 — A166

1970, Mar. 1 Wmk. 347 *Perf. 11*

731 A165 1g bis brn 5 5
732 A165 2g violet 5 5
733 A165 3g brt pink 5 5
734 A165 4g rose claret 5 5
735 A165 5g blue 5 5
736 A165 10g bright grn 7 5
Nos. 731-736,C382-C385 (10) 1.06 83

Marshal Francisco Solano Lopez (1827-1870), President of Paraguay.

1970, Aug. 15 Litho.

Designs (First Issue of Paraguay): 2g, 10g, No. 1. 3g, No. 3. 5g, No. 2.

737 A166 1g car rose 5 5
738 A166 2g ultra 5 5
739 A166 3g org brn 5 5
740 A166 5g violet 6 5
741 A166 10g lilac 12 9
Nos. 737-741,C386-C388 (8) 1.50 1.27

Centenary of stamps of Paraguay.

UNESCO and Paraguay Emblems, Globe, Teacher and Pupil — A167

1971, May 18

742 A167 3g ultra 5 5
743 A167 5g lilac 5 5
744 A167 10g emerald 7 5
Nos. 742-744,C389-C392 (7) 1.04 77

International Education Year.

UNICEF, 25th Anniv. (in 1971) — A168 — OAS Emblem — A170

Acaray Dam A169

1972, Jan. 24

Granite Paper

745 A168 1g red brn 5 5
746 A168 2g ultra 5 5
747 A168 3g lil rose 5 5
748 A168 4g violet 5 5
749 A168 5g emerald 5 5
750 A168 10g claret 7 5
Nos. 745-750,C393-C395 (9) 84 67

1972, Nov. 16 *Perf. 13½x13*

Granite Paper

Designs: 2g, Francisco Solano Lopez monument. 3g, Friendship Bridge. 5g, Tebicuary River Bridge. 10g, Hotel Guarani.

751 A169 1g sepia 5 5
752 A169 2g brown 5 5
753 A169 3g brt ultra 5 5
754 A169 5g brt pink 5 5
755 A169 10g dl grn 7 5
Nos. 751-755,C396-C399 (9) 1.64 1.22

Tourism Year of the Americas.

1973 Litho. *Perf. 13x13½*

Granite Paper

756 A170 1g multi 5 5
757 A170 2g multi 5 5
758 A170 3g multi 5 5
759 A170 4g multi 5 5
760 A170 5g multi 6 5
761 A170 10g multi 7 5
Nos. 756-761,C400-C403 (10) 1.70 1.27

Org. of American States, 25th anniv.

Hand Holding Letter — A171 — EXPOPAR 73, Paraguayan Industrial Exhib. — A172

Wmk. 347

1973, July 10 Litho. *Perf. 11*

762 A171 2g lil rose & blk 5 5

No. 762 was issued originally as a nonobligatory stamp to benefit mailmen, but its status was changed to regular postage.

1973, Aug. 11 *Perf. 13x13½*

Granite Paper

763 A172 1g org brn 5 5
764 A172 2g vermilion 5 5
765 A172 3g blue 5 5
766 A172 4g emerald 5 5
767 A172 5g lilac 5 5
Nos. 763-767,C404-C405 (7) 57 47

"U.P.U.," Pantheon, Carrier Pigeon, Globe A173

1975, Feb. Wmk. 347 *Perf. 13½x13*

768 A173 1g blk & lilac 5 5
769 A173 2g blk & rose red 5 5
770 A173 3g blk & ultra 5 5
771 A173 5g blk & blue 5 5
772 A173 10g blk & lil rose 7 6
Nos. 768-772,C406-C407 (7) 59 53

Centenary of Universal Postal Union.

Institute of Higher Education A174

Perf. 13½x13

1976, Mar. 16 Litho. Wmk. 347

773 A174 5g vio, blk & red 5 5
774 A174 10g ultra, blk & red 7 6

Inauguration of Institute of Higher Education, Sept. 23, 1974. See No. C408.

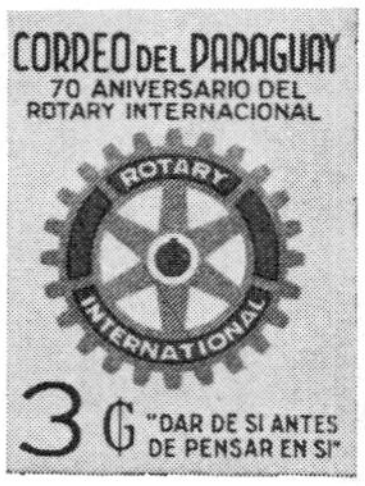

Rotary Intl., 70th Anniv. — A175

1976, Mar. 16 *Perf. 13x13½*

775 A175 3g blk, bl & cit 5 5
776 A175 4g car, bl & cit 5 5

See No. C409.

IWY Emblem, Woman's Head — A176

1976, Mar. 16

777 A176 1g ultra & brn 5 5
778 A176 2g car & brn 5 5

Intl Women's Year (1975). See No. C410.

Mburucuya Flowers — A177

Weaver with Ostrich Feather Panel — A178

Designs: 1g, Ostrich feather panel. 2g, Black palms.

1977 Litho. Wmk. 347

779 A178	1g multi	5	5
780 A177	2g multi	5	5
781 A177	3g multi	5	5
782 A178	5g multi	8	5
	Nos. 779-782,C411-C412 (6)	78	58

Issue dates: 2g, 3g, Apr. 25; 1g, 5g, June 27.

Francisco Solano Lopez — A179

1977, July 24 Litho. *Perf. 13x13½*

783 A179	10g brown	12	8

Marshal Francisco Solano Lopez (1827-1870), President of Paraguay. See Nos. C413-C414.

National College A180

1978 Litho. *Perf. 13½x13*

784 A180	3g claret	5	5
785 A180	4g vio blue	5	5
786 A180	5g lilac	5	5
	Nos. 784-786,C415-C417 (6)	76	60

Centenary of National College in Asuncion.

José Estigarribia, Bugler, Flag of Paraguay A181

1978 Litho. *Perf. 13x13½*

787 A181	3g multi	5	5
788 A181	5g multi	5	5
789 A181	10g multi	8	6
	Nos. 787-789,C418-C420 (6)	79	61

Induction of Jose Felix Estigarribia (1888-1940), general and president of Paraguay, into Salon de Bronce (National Heroes' Hall of Fame).

Congress Emblem A182

1979, Aug. Litho. *Perf. 13x13½*

790 A182	10g red, bl & blk	8	6

22nd Latin-American Tourism Congress, Asuncion. See No. C421.

Pilar City Bicentennial — A183

Perf. 13½x13

1980, July 17 Wmk. 347

791 A183	5g multi	5	5

See No. C422.

Paraguay Airlines Boeing 707 Service Inauguration — A183a

1980, Sept. 17 Litho. *Perf. 13½x13*

791A A183a	20g multi	16	12

See No. C422A.

UPU Membership Centenary — A184

1981, Aug. 18 Litho. *Perf. 13½x13*

792 A184	5g rose lake & blk	5	5
793 A184	10g lil & blk	8	6
	Nos. 792-793,C427-C429 (5)	89	68

Itaipua Dam, Pres. Stroessner — A185

1983, Jan. 22 Litho. Wmk. 347

794 A185	3g multi	5	5
795 A185	5g multi	5	5
796 A185	10g multi	8	6
797 A185	20g multi	16	12
798 A185	25g multi	20	15
799 A185	50g multi	40	30
	Nos. 794-799 (6)	94	73

25th anniv. of Stroessner City. Nos. 797-799 airmail.

Paraguay Official Stamps, Cent. — A187

Designs: Nos. 806-808, No. O1. Nos. 809-811, No. O4.

1986, Aug. 28 Litho. *Perf. 13x13½*

806 A187	5g multi	5	5
807 A187	15g multi	5	5
808 A187	40g multi	10	8
809 A187	65g multi	18	14
810 A187	100g multi	25	18
811 A187	150g multi	38	28
	Nos. 806-811 (6)	1.01	78

Nos. 809-811 are airmail.

Colorado Party, Cent. A188

Bernardino Caballero (founder), President Stroessner and: 5g, 10g, 25g, Three-lane highway. 150g, 170g, 200g, Power lines.

Perf. 13½x13

1987, Sept. 11 Wmk. 347

812 A188	5g multi	5	5
813 A188	10g multi	5	5
814 A188	25g multi	6	5
815 A188	150g multi	35	26
816 A188	170g multi	38	28
817 A188	200g multi	45	35
	Nos. 812-817 (6)	1.34	1.04

Nos. 815-817 are airmail.

Visit of Pope John Paul II — A189

Rosette window and crucifix.

1988, May 5 Litho. *Perf. 13x13½*

818 A189	10g blue & blk	5	5
819 A189	20g blue & blk	10	8
820 A189	50g blue & blk	22	16

> Recent issues are recorded in the Scott Chronicle of New issues beginning with Vol. 1, No. 2.
> Previous issues are recorded in For the Record at the back of this volume.

SEMI-POSTAL STAMPS

Red Cross Nurse — SP1

Unwmk.

1930, July 22 Typo. *Perf. 12*

B1	SP1	1.50p + 50c gray vio	1.00	65
B2	SP1	1.50p + 50c dp rose	1.00	65
B3	SP1	1.50p + 50c dark bl	1.00	65

The surtax was for the benefit of the Red Cross Society of Paraguay.

College of Agriculture — SP2

1930

B4	SP2	1.50p + 50c bl, *pink*	25	25

Surtax for the Agricultural Institute.

The sheet of No. B4 has a papermaker's watermark: "Vencedor Bond".

A 1.50p+50c red on yellow was prepared but not regularly issued. Value 20 cents.

Red Cross Headquarters SP3

Our Lady of Asuncion SP4

1932

B5	SP3	50c + 50c rose	25	20

1941 Engr.

B6	SP4	7p + 3p red brn	30	25
B7	SP4	7p + 3p purple	30	25
B8	SP4	7p + 3p car rose	30	25
B9	SP4	7p + 3p sapphire	30	25

No. 361 Surcharged in Black

1944

B10	A70	10c on 10p multi	35	25

The surtax was for the victims of the San Juan earthquake in Argentina.

> **Catalogue values for unused stamps in this section, from this point to the end of the section, are for Never Hinged items.**

No. C169 Surcharged in Carmine "AYUDA AL ECUADOR 5 + 5"

1949 Unwmk. *Perf. 12½*

B11	AP62	5c + 5c on 30c dk bl	8	8

Surtax for the victims of the Ecuador earthquake.

AIR POST STAMPS

Official Stamps of 1913 Surcharged — Correo Aéreo Habilitado en $ 2:85

1929, Jan. 1 Unwmk. *Perf. 11½*

No.	Type	Description	Unused	Used
C1	O19	2.85p on 5c lilac	75	65
C2	O19	5.65p on 10c grn	50	38
C3	O19	11.30p on 50c rose	75	50

Counterfeits of surcharge exist.

Regular Issues of 1924-27 Surcharged as in 1929

1929, Feb. 26 *Perf. 12*

No.	Type	Description	Unused	Used
C4	A51	3.40p on 3p gray	1.75	1.10
a.		Surch. "Correo / en $3.40 / Habilitado / Aereo"	8.75	
b.		Double surcharge	8.75	
c.		"Aero" instead of "Aéreo"		
C5	A44	6.80p on 4p lt bl	1.75	1.10
a.		Surch. "Correo / Aereo / en $6.80 / Habilitado"	8.75	
C6	A52	17p on 5p choc	1.75	1.10
a.		Surch. "Correo / Habilitado / Habilitado / en 17p"	4.50	
b.		Double surcharge	8.75	

Wings AP1

Pigeon with Letter AP2

Airplanes AP3

1929-31 Typo. *Perf. 12*

No.	Type	Description	Unused	Used
C7	AP1	2.85p gray grn	50	45
a.		Imperf., pair	37.50	
C8	AP1	2.85p turq grn ('31)	25	20
C9	AP2	5.65p brown	75	38
C10	AP2	5.65p scar ('31)	38	25
C11	AP3	11.30p chocolate	50	38
a.		Imperf., pair	37.50	
C12	AP3	11.30p deep bl ('31)	25	25
		Nos. C7-C12 (6)	2.63	1.91

Sheets of these stamps sometimes show portions of a papermaker's watermark "Indian Bond C. Extra Strong."

Excellent counterfeits are plentiful.

Regular Issues of 1924-28 Surcharged in Black or Red — Correo Aéreo Habilitado en $ 3.40

1929 *Perf. 11½, 12*

No.	Type	Description	Unused	Used
C13	A47	95c on 7c lilac	20	15
C14	A47	1.90p on 20c dl bl	20	15
C15	A44	3.40p on 4p lt bl (R)	25	20
a.		Double surcharge	2.00	
C16	A44	4.75p on 4p lt bl (R)	45	38
a.		Double surcharge	2.00	
C17	A51	6.80p on 3p gray	50	50
a.		Double surcharge	3.00	
C18	A52	17p on 5p choc	1.50	1.50
a.		Horiz. pair, imperf. between	25.00	
		Nos. C13-C18 (6)	3.10	2.88

Six stamps in the sheet of No. C17 have the "$" and numerals thinner and narrower than the normal type.

The Catalogue editors cannot undertake to appraise, identify or judge the genuineness or condition of stamps.

Airplane and Arms — AP4

Cathedral of Asuncion — AP5

Airplane and Globe — AP6

1930 *Perf. 12*

No.	Type	Description	Unused	Used
C19	AP4	95c dp red, *pink*	25	25
C20	AP4	95c dk bl, *blue*	25	25
C21	AP5	1.90p lt red, *pink*	25	25
C22	AP5	1.90p violet, *blue*	25	25
C23	AP6	6.80p blk, *lt bl*	25	25
C24	AP6	6.80p green, *pink*	25	30
		Nos. C19-C24 (6)	1.50	1.55

Sheets of Nos. C19-C24 have a papermaker's watermark: "Extra Vencedor Bond."

Counterfeits exist.

Stamps and Types of 1927-28 Overprinted in Red — CORREO AEREO

1930

No.	Type	Description	Unused	Used
C25	A47	10c ol grn	10	8
a.		Double overprint	2.50	
C26	A47	20c dl bl	12	8
a.		"CORREO CORREO" instead of "CORREO AEREO"	2.50	
b.		"AEREO AEREO" instead of "CORREO AEREO"	2.50	
C27	A48	1p emerald	50	50
C28	A51	3p gray	50	50

AP7

AP8

AP9

AP10

1930

Red or Black Surcharge

No.	Type	Description	Unused	Used
C29	AP7	5c on 10c gray grn (R)	5	5
a.		"AEREO" omitted	15.00	
C30	AP7	5c on 70c ultra (R)	5	5
a.		Vert. pair, imperf. between	20.00	
C31	AP10	20c on 1p org red	18	18
a.		"CORREO" double	3.00	3.00
b.		"AEREO" double	3.00	3.00
C32	AP7	40c on 50c org (R)	12	10
a.		"AEREO" omitted	4.50	4.50
b.		"CORREO" double	3.00	3.00
c.		"AEREO" double	3.00	3.00
C33	AP8	6p on 10p red	90	75
C34	AP9	10p on 20p red	4.00	3.75
C35	AP9	10p on 20p vio brn	4.00	3.75
		Nos. C29-C35 (7)	9.30	8.63

Declaration of Independence AP11

1930, May 14 Typo.

No.	Type	Description	Unused	Used
C36	AP11	2.85p dark blue	25	25
C37	AP11	3.40p dark grn	25	20
C38	AP11	4.75p deep lake	25	20

Natl. Independence Day, May 14, 1811.

Gunboat "Paraguay" — AP12

1931-39 *Perf. 11½, 12*

No.	Type	Description	Unused	Used
C39	AP12	1p claret	12	12
C40	AP12	1p dk bl ('36)	12	12
C41	AP12	2p orange	15	15
C42	AP12	2p dk brn ('36)	15	15
C43	AP12	3p turq green	30	28
C44	AP12	3p lt ultra ('36)	30	30
C45	AP12	3p brt rose ('39)	25	25
C46	AP12	6p dark grn	38	38
C47	AP12	6p violet ('36)	45	40
C48	AP12	6p dl bl ('39)	35	35
C49	AP12	10p vermilion	90	80
C50	AP12	10p bluish grn ('35)	1.25	1.25
C51	AP12	10p yel brn ('36)	1.00	1.00
C52	AP12	10p dk blue ('36)	65	65
C53	AP12	10p lt pink ('39)	85	85
		Nos. C39-C53 (15)	7.22	7.05

1st constitution of Paraguay as a Republic and the arrival of the "Paraguay" and "Humaita."

Counterfeits of Nos. C39 to C53 are plentiful.

Regular Issue of 1924 Surcharged

3 3
Correo Aéreo

"Graf Zeppelin"

1931, Aug. 22

No.	Type	Description	Unused	Used
C54	A44	3p on 4p lt bl	6.00	5.00

Overprinted — Correo Aêreo

"Graf Zeppelin"

No.	Type	Description	Unused	Used
C55	A44	4p lt bl	6.00	5.00

On Nos. C54-C55 the Zeppelin is handstamped. The rest of the surcharge or overprint is typographed.

War Memorial AP13

Orange Tree and Yerba Mate AP14

Yerba Mate — AP15

Palms — AP16

Eagle — AP17

1931-36 Litho.

No.	Type	Description	Unused	Used
C56	AP13	5c lt bl	8	5
a.		Horiz. pair, imperf. btwn.	6.25	
C57	AP13	5c dp grn ('33)	6	6
C58	AP13	5c lt red ('33)	12	6
C59	AP13	5c vio ('35)	5	5
C60	AP14	10c dp vio	8	8
C61	AP14	10c brn lake ('33)	8	8
C62	AP14	10c yel brn ('33)	8	5
C63	AP14	10c ultra ('35)	5	5
a.		Imperf., pair	5.50	
C64	AP15	20c red	8	6
C65	AP15	20c dl blue ('33)	12	12
C66	AP15	20c emer ('33)	10	5
C67	AP15	20c yel brn ('35)	5	5
a.		Imperf., pair	3.75	
C68	AP16	40c dp grn	10	9
C69	AP16	40c slate bl ('35)	9	5
C70	AP16	40c red ('36)	12	10
C71	AP17	80c dull blue	10	9
C72	AP17	80c dl grn ('33)	15	12
C73	AP17	80c scar ('33)	12	9
		Nos. C56-C73 (18)	1.63	1.30

Airship "Graf Zeppelin" — AP18

1932, April Litho.

No.	Type	Description	Unused	Used
C74	AP18	4p ultra	1.10	1.00
a.		Imperf., pair	5.00	
C75	AP18	8p red	1.75	1.25
C76	AP18	12p blue grn	1.40	1.10
C77	AP18	16p dark vio	3.00	2.00
C78	AP18	20p orange brn	3.00	2.75
		Nos. C74-C78 (5)	10.25	8.10

"Graf Zeppelin" over Brazilian Terrain AP19

"Graf Zeppelin" over Atlantic — AP20

1933, May 5

No.	Type	Description	Unused	Used
C79	AP19	4.50p dp bl	1.25	1.00
C80	AP19	9p dp rose	2.50	2.00
a.		Horiz. pair, imperf. btwn.	150.00	
C81	AP19	13.50p blue grn	2.50	2.00
C82	AP20	22.50p bis brn	6.25	5.00
C83	AP20	45p dull vio	8.75	8.75
		Nos. C79-C83 (5)	21.25	18.75

Excellent counterfeits are plentiful.

Posts and Telegraph Building, Asuncion AP21

1934-37 *Perf. 11½*

No.	Type	Description	Unused	Used
C84	AP21	33.75p ultra	1.50	1.25
C85	AP21	33.75p car ('35)	1.50	1.25
a.		33.75p rose ('37)	1.25	1.25
C86	AP21	33.75p emer ('36)	2.00	1.50
C87	AP21	33.75p bis brn ('36)	50	50

Nos. C79-C83 Overprinted in Black — 1 9 3 4

1934, May 26

No.	Type	Description	Unused	Used
C88	AP19	4.50p deep bl	1.50	1.25
C89	AP19	9p dp rose	1.75	1.50
C90	AP19	13.50p blue grn	5.00	4.50
C91	AP20	22.50p bis brn	4.00	3.50
C92	AP20	45p dull vio	8.75	8.00
		Nos. C88-C92 (5)	21.00	18.75

Types of 1933 Issue Overprinted in Black **1935**

1935

C93	AP19	4.50p rose red	2.00	1.50
C94	AP19	9p lt grn	2.50	2.00
C95	AP19	13.50p brown	7.50	6.00
C96	AP20	22.50p violet	6.25	5.50
C97	AP20	45p blue	17.50	15.00
		Nos. C93-C97 (5)	35.75	30.00

Tobacco Plant — AP22

1935-39 **Typo.**

C98	AP22	17p light brn	2.00	2.00
C99	AP22	17p carmine	3.75	3.75
C100	AP22	17p dark blue	2.50	2.50
C101	AP22	17p pale yel grn ('39)	1.50	1.50

Excellent counterfeits are plentiful.

Church of Incarnation AP23

1935-38

C102	AP23	102p carmine	3.75	3.00
C103	AP23	102p blue	3.75	3.00
C103A	AP23	102p ind ('36)	2.50	2.50
C104	AP23	102p yel brn	2.75	2.75
a.		Imperf., pair	15.00	
C105	AP23	102p vio ('37)	1.25	1.25
C106	AP23	102p brn org ('38)	1.10	1.10
		Nos. C102-C106 (6)	15.10	13.60

Excellent counterfeits are plentiful.

Types of 1934-35 Surcharged in Red

Habilitado en $ 24.—

1937, Aug. 1

C107	AP21	24p on 33.75p sl bl	50	38
C108	AP23	65p on 102p ol bis	1.25	90
C109	AP23	84p on 102p bl grn	1.25	75

Plane over Asuncion AP24

1939, Aug. 3 Typo. *Perf. 10½, 11½*

C110	AP24	3.40p yel green	50	50
C111	AP24	3.40p orange brn	30	25
C112	AP24	3.40p indigo	30	25

Buenos Aires Peace Conference Issue

Flags of Paraguay and Bolivia — AP25

Coats of Arms — AP26

President Ortiz of Argentina, Flags of Paraguay, Argentina AP27

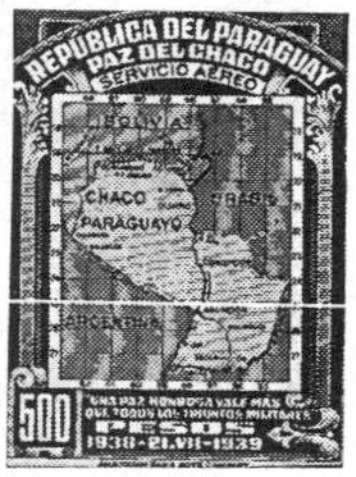

Map of Paraguay with New Chaco Boundary AP28

Designs: 10p, Pres. Vargas, Brazil. 30p, Pres. Alessandri, Chile. 50p, US Eagle and Shield. 100p, Pres. Benavides, Peru. 200p, Pres. Baldomir, Uruguay.

Engr.; Flags Litho.

1939, Nov. ***Perf. 12½***

Flags in National Colors

C113	AP25	1p red brn	8	6
C114	AP26	3p dark bl	10	8
C115	AP27	5p olive blk	10	9
C116	AP27	10p violet	12	10
C117	AP27	30p orange	25	12
C118	AP27	50p blk brn	30	20
C119	AP27	100p brt grn	45	40
C120	AP27	200p green	2.50	1.75
C121	AP28	500p black	6.25	6.25
		Nos. C113-C121 (9)	10.15	9.05

Pres. Bernardino Caballero and Senator Jose S. Decond AP34

1939, Sept. **Litho.** ***Perf. 12***

C122	AP34	28p rose & blk	3.25	3.25
C123	AP34	90p yel grn & blk	4.00	4.00

Founding of the University of Asunción, 50th anniv.

Map with Asuncion to New York Air Route AP35

Map of the Americas AP36

1939, Nov. 30 **Engr.**

C124	AP35	30p brown	2.50	2.00
C125	AP35	80p orange	3.00	3.00
C126	AP35	90p purple	5.00	5.00

New York World's Fair.

1940, May ***Perf. 12***

C127	AP36	20p rose car	18	15
C128	AP36	70p vio bl	45	18
C129	AP36	100p Prus grn	50	50
C130	AP36	500p dk vio	2.25	1.75

Founding of the Pan American Union, 50th anniv.

The Indian Francisco AP37

Arms of Irala AP39

Domingo Martinez de Irala and His Vision AP38

1942, Aug. 15

C131	AP37	20p dp plum	65	50
C132	AP38	70p fawn	1.90	1.50
C133	AP39	500p ol gray	5.00	4.50

400th anniversary of Asunción.

Imperforates

Starting with No. C134, many Paraguayan air mail stamps exist imperforate.

Port of Asunción AP40

First Telegraph in South America AP41

Early Merchant Ship — AP42

Birthplace of Paraguay's Liberation AP43

Monument to Antequera AP44

Locomotive of First Paraguayan Railroad AP45

Values quoted in this catalogue are for stamps graded at Fine-Very Fine and with no faults. An illustrated guide to grade is provided in introductory material, beginning on Page V.

Monument to Heroes of Itororó — AP46

Primitive Postal Service among Indians — AP48

Government House AP47

Colonial Jesuit Altar — AP49

Ruins of Humaitá Church — AP50

Oratory of the Virgin — AP51

Marshal Francisco S. Lopez — AP52

1944-45 **Unwmk.** ***Perf. 12½***

C134	AP40	1c blue	5	5
C135	AP41	2c green	5	5
C136	AP42	3c brn vio	8	8
C137	AP43	5c brt bl grn	8	8
C138	AP44	10c dk vio	12	10
C139	AP45	20c dk brn	25	12
C140	AP46	30c light bl	20	20
C141	AP47	40c olive	25	25
C142	AP48	70c brn red	38	32
C143	AP49	1g org yel	90	65
C144	AP50	2g cop brn	1.10	90
C145	AP51	5g blk brn	2.50	2.50
C146	AP52	10g indigo	6.00	6.00
		Nos. C134-C146 (13)	11.96	11.30

See Nos. C158-C162.

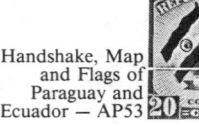

Handshake, Map and Flags of Paraguay and Ecuador — AP53

Flags: 40c, Bolivia. 70c, Mexico. 1g, Chile. 2g, Brazil. 5g, Argentina. 10g, US.

Engr.; Flags Litho. in Natl. Colors

1945, Aug. 15

C147	AP53	20c orange	20	18
C148	AP53	40c olive	20	18
C149	AP53	70c lake	22	20
C150	AP53	1g slate bl	38	38
C151	AP53	2g blue vio	50	50
C152	AP53	5g green	75	75
C153	AP53	10g brown	3.75	3.75
		Nos. C147-C153 (7)	6.00	5.94

Goodwill visits of Pres. Higinio Morinigo during 1943.

Sizes: Nos. C147-C151, 30x26mm.; 5g, 32x28mm.; 10g, 33x30mm.

Catalogue values for unused stamps in this section, from this point to the end of the section, are for Never Hinged items.

Nos. C139-C142 Surcharged "1946" and New Value in Black

1946 Engr. *Perf. 12½*

C154	AP45	5c on 20c dk brn	40	40
C155	AP46	5c on 30c lt bl	40	40
C156	AP47	5c on 40c olive	40	40
C157	AP48	5c on 70c brn red	40	40

Types of 1944-45

1946, Sept. 21 Engr.

C158	AP50	10c dp car	5	5
C159	AP40	20c emerald	8	8
C160	AP47	1g brn org	30	30
C161	AP52	5g purple	90	90
C162	AP51	10g rose car	2.50	2.50
		Nos. C158-C162 (5)	3.83	3.83

Marshal Francisco Solano Lopez — AP60

1947, May. 15 *Perf. 12*

C163	AP60	32c car lake	10	10
C164	AP60	64c org brn	18	18
C165	AP60	1g Prus grn	25	25
C166	AP60	5g Prus grn & brn vio	75	75
C167	AP60	10g dk car rose & dk yel grn	1.25	1.25
		Nos. C163-C167 (5)	2.53	2.53

Archbishopric Coat of Arms — AP61

Projected Monument of the Sacred Heart of Jesus — AP62

Vision of Projected Monument AP63

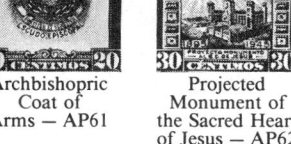

Juan Sinforiano Bogarin, Archbishop of Asuncion AP64

1948, Jan. 6 Unwmk. *Perf. 12½*

Size: 25½x31mm

C168	AP61	20c gray blk	5	5
C169	AP62	30c dark blue	8	8
C170	AP63	40c lilac	10	8
C171	AP64	70c org red	12	12
C172	AP62	1g brn red	18	18
C173	AP63	2g red	50	50

Size: 25½x34mm

C174	AP64	5g brt car & dk bl	90	90
C175	AP61	10g dk grn & brn	1.25	1.25
		Nos. C168-C175 (8)	3.18	3.16

Establishment of the Archbishopric of Asuncion, 50th anniv.

Type of Regular Issue of 1948 Inscribed "AEREO"

1948, Sept. 11 Engr. & Litho.

C176	A119	69c dk grn, red & bl	50	50
C177	A119	5g dk bl, red & bl	2.00	1.75

The Barefeet, a political group.

No. C171 Surcharged in Black

DUELO NACIONAL
5 CENTIMOS 5

1949, June 29

C178	AP64	5c on 70c org red	10	10

Archbishop Juan Sinforiano Bogarin (1863-1949).

Symbols of UPU AP65

Franklin D. Roosevelt AP66

1950, Sept. 4 Engr. *Perf. 13½x13*

C179	AP65	20c grn & vio	10	10
C180	AP65	30c rose vio & brn	12	12
C181	AP65	50c gray & grn	12	12
C182	AP65	1g bl & brn	15	15
C183	AP65	5g rose & blk	38	38
		Nos. C179-C183 (5)	87	87

UPU, 75th anniv. (in 1949).

Engr.; Flags Litho.

1950, Oct. 2 *Perf. 12½*

Flags in Carmine & Violet Blue.

C184	AP66	20c red	8	8
C185	AP66	30c black	8	8
C186	AP66	50c claret	10	10
C187	AP66	1g dk gray grn	15	15
C188	AP66	5g dp bl	38	38
		Nos. C184-C188 (5)	79	79

Franklin D. Roosevelt (1882-1945).

Urn Containing Remains of Columbus AP67

1952, Feb. 11 Litho. *Perf. 10*

C189	AP67	10c ultra	5	5
C190	AP67	20c green	5	5
C191	AP67	30c lilac	5	5
C192	AP67	40c rose	5	5
C193	AP67	50c bister brn	6	6
C194	AP67	1g blue	8	8
C195	AP67	2g orange	15	15
C196	AP67	5g red brn	30	30
		Nos. C189-C196 (8)	79	79

Queen Isabella I — AP68

1952, Oct. 12

C197	AP68	1g vio blue	8	8
C198	AP68	2g chocolate	12	12
C199	AP68	5g dull grn	25	25
C200	AP68	10g lil rose	55	55

500th birth anniv. of Queen Isabella I of Spain (in 1951).

Silvio Pettirossi, Aviator — AP69

1954, Mar.

C201	AP69	40c brown	5	5
C202	AP69	55c green	6	6
C203	AP69	80c ultra	6	6
C204	AP69	1.30g gray bl	22	22

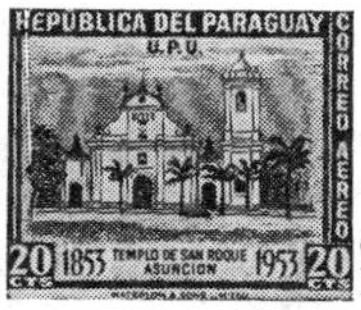

Church of San Roque — AP70

1954, June 20 Engr. *Perf. 12x13*

C205	AP70	20c carmine	5	5
C206	AP70	30c brn vio	5	5
C207	AP70	50c ultra	5	5
C208	AP70	1g red brn & bl grn	8	8
C209	AP70	1g red brn & lil rose	8	8
C210	AP70	1g red brn & blk	8	8
C211	AP70	1g red brn & org	8	8
a.		Miniature sheet of 4	30	30
C212	AP70	5g dk red brn & vio	12	12
C213	AP70	5g dk red brn & ol grn	12	12
C214	AP70	5g dk red brn & org yel	12	12
C215	AP70	5g dk red brn & yel org	12	12
a.		Miniature sheet of 4	65	65
		Nos. C205-C215 (11)	95	95

Centenary (in 1953) of the establishment of the Church of San Roque, Asuncion.

Nos. C211a and C215a contain typographed reproductions respectively of Nos. C208-C211 and C212-C215 perf. 12x12½. Issued without gum.

Three National Heroes — AP71

Unwmk.

1954, Aug. 15 Litho. *Perf. 10*

C216	AP71	5g violet	12	12
C217	AP71	10g ol grn	25	25
C218	AP71	20g gray brn	45	38
C219	AP71	50g vermilion	1.00	1.00
C220	AP71	100g blue	3.25	3.25
		Nos. C216-C220 (5)	5.07	5.00

Issued to honor Marshal Francisco S. Lopez, Pres. Carlos A. Lopez and Gen. Bernardino Caballero.

Pres. Alfredo Stroessner and Pres. Juan D. Peron AP72

Photo. & Litho.

1955, Apr. Wmk. 90 *Perf. 13x13½*

Frames & Flags in Blue & Carmine

C221	AP72	60c ol grn & cream	5	5
C222	AP72	2g bl grn & cream	8	8
C223	AP72	3g brn org & cream	12	10
C224	AP72	4.10g brt rose pink & cr	18	15

Visit of Pres. Juan D. Peron of Argentina.

Jesuit Ruins, Trinidad Belfry AP73

Santa Maria Cornice — AP74

Jesuit Ruins: 3g, Corridor at Trinidad. 6g, Tower of Santa Rosa. 10g, San Cosme gate. 20g, Church of Jesus. 30g, Niche at Trinidad. 50g, Sacristy at Trinidad.

Perf. 12½x12, 12x12½

1955, June 19 Engr. Unwmk.

C225	AP73	2g aqua	5	5
C226	AP73	3g ol grn	5	5
C227	AP74	4g lt bl grn	5	5
C228	AP74	6g brown	5	5
C229	AP73	10g rose	6	6
C230	AP73	20g brn ol	10	10
C231	AP74	30g dk grn	30	25
C232	AP74	50g dp aqua	35	30
		Nos. C225-C232 (8)	1.01	91

25th anniv. of the priesthood of Monsignor Rodriguez.

Soldier and Flags AP75

"Republic" and Soldier AP76

1957, June 12 Photo. *Perf. 13½*

Granite Paper

Flags in Red and Blue

C233	AP75	10c ultra	5	5
C234	AP75	15c dp claret	5	5
C235	AP75	20c red	5	5
C236	AP75	25c light bl	5	5
C237	AP75	50c bluish grn	5	5
C238	AP75	1g rose car	5	5
C239	AP76	1.30g dp claret	5	5
C240	AP76	1.50p light bl	5	5
C241	AP76	2g emerald	5	5
C242	AP76	4.10g red	5	5
C243	AP76	5g gray blk	8	5
C244	AP76	10g bluish grn	10	8
C245	AP76	25g ultra	25	20
		Nos. C233-C245 (13)	93	83

Heroes of the Chaco war.

Type of Stroessner Regular Issue, 1958

1958, Aug. 16 Litho. Wmk. 320

Center in Slate

C246	A130	12g rose lilac	25	25
C247	A130	18g orange	30	30
C248	A130	23g org brn	50	50
C249	A130	36g emerald	50	50
C250	A130	50g citron	65	65
C251	A130	65g gray	1.00	1.00
		Nos. C246-C251 (6)	3.20	3.20

Re-election of Pres. General Alfredo Stroessner.

Nos. C225-C232 Surcharged in Red

1,50

Perf. 12½x12, 12x12½

1959, May 26 Engr. Unwmk.

C252	AP73	4g	on 2g aqua	10	8
C253	AP73	12.45g	on 3g ol grn	18	15
C254	AP74	18.15g	on 6g brown	25	22
C255	AP73	23.40g	on 10g rose	35	28
C256	AP73	34.80g	on 20g brn ol	50	38
C257	AP74	36g	on 4g lt bl grn	55	40
C258	AP74	43.95g	on 30g dk grn	65	45
C259	AP74	100g	on 50g dp aqua	1.50	1.00
			Nos. C252-C259 (8)	4.08	2.96

The surcharge is made to fit the stamps. Counterfeits of surcharge exist.

UN Emblem — AP77

Unwmk.

1959, Aug. 27 Typo. *Perf. 11*

C260	AP77	5g	ocher & ultra	50	40

Visit of Dag Hammarskjold, Secretary General of the UN, Aug. 27-29.

Map and UN Emblem AP78

Uprooted Oak Emblem AP79

1959, Oct. 24 Litho. *Perf. 10*

C261	AP78	12.45g	bl & sal	20	15

United Nations Day, Oct. 24, 1959.

Olympic Games Type of Regular Issue

Design: Basketball.

1960, Mar. 18 Photo. *Perf. 12½*

C262	A131	12.45g	red & dk bl	15	15
C263	A131	18.15g	lil & gray ol	20	20
C264	A131	36g	bl grn & rose car	40	40

The Paraguayan Philatelic Agency reported as spurious the imperf. souvenir sheet reproducing one of No. C264.

1960, Apr. 7 Litho. *Perf. 11*

C265	AP79	4g	grn & pink	45	38
C266	AP79	12.45g	bl & yel grn	90	65
C267	AP79	18.15g	car & ocher	1.25	75
C268	AP79	23.40g	red org & bl	1.25	1.50

World Refugee Year, July 1, 1959-June 30, 1960 (1st issue).

Human Rights Type of Regular Issue, 1960

Designs: 40g, UN Emblem. 60g, Hands holding scales. 100g, Flame.

1960, Apr. 21 *Perf. 12½x13*

C269	A133	40g	dk ultra & red	25	25
C270	A133	60g	grnsh bl & org	30	30
C271	A133	100g	dk ultra & red	65	65

UN Declaration of Human Rights.

An imperf. miniature sheet exists, containing one each of Nos. C269-C271, all printed in green and vermilion.

UN Type of Regular Issue

Perf. 13x13½

1960, Oct. 24 Photo. Unwmk.

C272	A134	3g	org, red & bl	5	5
C273	A134	4g	pale grn, red & bl	6	6

15th anniversary of the United Nations.

International Bridge, Paraguay-Brazil AP80

1961, Jan. 26 Litho. *Perf. 14*

C274	AP80	3g	carmine	8	6
C275	AP80	12.45g	brn lake	18	15
C276	AP80	18.15g	Prus grn	20	18
C277	AP80	36g	dk bl	38	35
a.			Souvenir sheet of 4	75	75

Inauguration of the International Bridge between Paraguay and Brazil. No. C277a contains one each of Nos. C274-C277, imperf.

"Paraguay en Marcha" Type of 1961

Designs: 12.45g, Truck carrying logs. 18.15g, Logs on river barge. 22g, Radio tower. 36g, Jet plane.

1961, Apr. 10 Photo. *Perf. 13*

C278	A136	12.45g	yel & vio bl	25	20
C279	A136	18.15g	pur & ocher	30	25
C280	A136	22g	ultra & ocher	38	30
C281	A136	36g	brt grn & yel	40	38

Issued to publicize Paraguay's progress.

Declaration of Independence — AP81

1961, May 16 Litho. *Perf. 14½*

C282	AP81	12.45g	dl red brn	12	12
C283	AP81	18.15g	dk bl	20	18
C284	AP81	23.40g	green	25	22
C285	AP81	30g	lilac	30	28
C286	AP81	36g	rose	40	38
C287	AP81	44g	olive	50	45
			Nos. C282-C287 (6)	1.77	1.63

150th anniv. of Independence (1st issue).

"Paraguay" and Clasped Hands AP82

South American Tapir AP83

1961, June 12 *Perf. 14x14½*

C288	AP82	3g	vio bl	15	15
C289	AP82	4g	rose claret	15	15
C290	AP82	100g	gray grn	90	80

Chaco Peace; 150th anniv. of Independence (2nd issue).

1961, Aug. 16 Unwmk. *Perf. 14*

C291	AP83	12.45g	claret	65	50
C292	AP83	18.15g	ultra	65	65
C293	AP83	34.80g	red brn	1.25	1.25

150th anniv. of Independence (3rd issue).

Catholic University Type of Regular Issue, 1961

1961, Sept. 18 *Perf. 14x14½*

C294	A140	3g	bis brn	8	8
C295	A140	12.45g	lil rose	20	20
C296	A140	36g	blue	40	40

Hotel Guarani Type of Regular Issue, 1961

Design: Hotel Guarani, different view.

1961, Oct. 14 Litho. *Perf. 15*

C297	A141	3g	dl red brn	5	5
C298	A141	4g	ultra	6	6
C299	A141	18.15g	orange	25	22
C300	A141	36g	rose car	40	38

Tennis Type of Regular Issue, 1961

1961, Oct. 16 Unwmk. *Perf. 11*

C301	A142	12.45g	multi	25	
C302	A142	20g	multi	45	
C303	A142	50g	multi	1.00	

Some specialists question the status of this issue.

Two imperf. souvenir sheets exist containing four 12.45s stamps each in a different color with simulated perforations and black marginal inscription.

WRY Type of Regular Issue, 1961

Design: Oak emblem rooted in ground, wavy-lined frame.

1961, Dec. 30

C307	A145	18.15g	brn & red	20	
C308	A145	36g	car & emer	45	
C309	A145	50g	emer & org	65	

Imperforates in changed colors and souvenir sheets exist. Some specialists question the status of this issue.

Tennis Type of Regular Issue, 1962

Design: Map of South America and tennis player using backhand stroke.

1962, Jan. 5 *Perf. 15x14½*

C310	A146	4g	carmine	8	8
C311	A146	12.45g	red lil	20	20
C312	A146	20g	bl grn	35	35
C313	A146	50g	org brn	55	55

Lord Baden-Powell AP84

1962, Feb. 6 *Perf. 11*

C314	AP84	12.45g	car rose & bl	25	
C315	AP84	36g	car rose & emer	75	
C316	AP84	50g	car rose & org yel	1.00	

Issued to honor the Boy Scouts. Imperfs. in changed colors and perf. and imperf. souvenir sheets exist. Some specialists question the status of this issue.

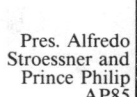

Pres. Alfredo Stroessner and Prince Philip AP85

1962, Mar. 9 Litho.

Portraits in Ultramarine

C317	AP85	12.45g	grn & buff	12	12
C318	AP85	18.15g	red & pink	18	18
C319	AP85	36g	brn & yel	32	32

Visit of Prince Philip, Duke of Edinburgh. perf. and imperf. souvenir sheets exist.

Day of the Ameriocas Type of Regular Issue, 1962

Design: 20g, 50g, Hands holding globe.

Perf. 14x14½

1962, Apr. 14 Unwmk.

C320	A148	20g	lil rose	18	18
C321	A148	50g	orange	38	38

UN Type of Regular Issue, 1962

Design: UN Headquarters, New York.

1962, Apr. 23 *Perf. 15*

C322	A149	12.45g	dl vio	20	20
C323	A149	18.15g	ol grn	30	30
C324	A149	23.40g	brn red	45	45
C325	A149	30g	carmine	50	50

Malaria Type of Regular Issue, 1962

Designs: 3g, 4g, Malaria eradication emblem. 12.45g, 18.15g, 36g, Mosquito, UN emblem and microscope.

Perf. 14x13½

1962, May 23 Wmk. 346

C326	A150	3g	bl, red & blk	5	
C327	A150	4g	grn, red & blk	5	
C328	A150	12.45g	ol bis, grn & blk	18	
C329	A150	18.15g	rose lil, red & blk	38	
C330	A150	36g	rose red, vio bl & blk	1.00	

Imperforates exist in changed colors. Two souvenir sheets exist, one containing one copy of No. C330, the other an imperf. 36g in blue, red & black. Some specialists question the status of this issue.

Soccer Players and Globe AP86

1962, July 28 Litho.

C331	AP86	12.45g	brt rose, blk & vio	38	
C332	AP86	18.15g	lt red brn, blk & vio	55	
C333	AP86	36g	gray grn, blk & brn	1.10	

World Soccer Championships, Chile, May 30-June 17, 1962. A souvenir sheet contains one No. C333 with dull orange marginal inscription and emblem. Some specialists question the status of this issue.

Ship's Wheel AP87

Lt. Col. John H. Glenn, Jr. and Lt. Cmdr. Scott Carpenter AP88

Design: 44g, Like 12.45g with diagonal colorless band in background.

Perf. 15x14½

1962, July 31 Unwmk.

C334	AP87	12.45g	dk red	12	10
C335	AP87	44g	blue	38	32

Issued to honor the Merchant Marine.

Perf. 13½x14

1962, Sept. 4 Litho. Wmk. 346

C336	AP88	12.45g	car lake & gray	12	
C337	AP88	18.15g	red lil & gray	20	
C338	AP88	36g	dl cl & gray	40	

US manned space flights. Imperfs. in changed colors and two souvenir sheets exist. Some specialists question the status of this issue.

Olympic Games Type of Regular Issue, 1962

Olympic flame and: 12.45g, Melbourne, 1956. 18.15g, Rome, 1960. 36g, Tokyo, 1964.

1962, Oct. 1

C339	A154	12.45g	brt grn, lt grn & choc	12	
C340	A154	18.15g	ol brn, yel & choc	20	
C341	A154	36g	rose red, pink & choc	40	

Imperfs. in changed colors and two souvenir sheets exist. Some specialists question the status of this issue.

The indexes in each volume of the Scott Catalogue contain many listings which help to identify stamps.

Dove Symbolizing Holy Ghost AP89

Perf. 14½

1962, Oct. 11 Litho. Unwmk.

C342 AP89	5g	vio bl	7	6
C343 AP89	10g	brt grn	14	10
C344 AP89	12.45g	lake	14	12
C345 AP89	18.15g	orange	25	20
C346 AP89	23.40g	violet	30	22
C347 AP89	36g	rose red	50	35
Nos. C342-C347 (6)			1.40	1.05

Vatican II. See note after No. 685.

Stroessner Type of 1963

1963, Aug. 6 Litho. Wmk. 347

C348 A156	12.45g	pink & cl	18	15
C349 A156	18.15g	pink & grn	25	22
C350 A156	36g	pink & vio	75	50

Third presidential term of Alfredo Stroessner. A 36g imperf. souvenir sheet exists.

National Holiday Type of 1964

Design: Asuncion Cathedral, Popes Paul VI and John XXIII.

1964, May 23

C351 A157	12.45g	sl grn & lem	18	15
C352 A157	18.15g	pur & lem	25	22
C353 A157	36g	vio bl & lem	1.00	80

De Gaulle Visit Type of 1964

Designs: 12.45g, 36g, Presidents Stroessner and de Gaulle. 18.15g, Coats of Arms of Paraguay and France.

1964, Oct. 6

C354 A158	12.45g	lilac	18	15
C355 A158	18.15g	bl grn	25	22
C356 A158	36g	magenta	1.00	80

National Epic Type of 1965

1965, Apr. 26 Wmk. 347 *Perf. 11*

C357 A159	12.45g	brn & blk	14	12
C358 A159	36g	brt lil & blk	50	35

Not issued without overprint.

Ceibo Tree — AP90

1965, June 28 Unwmk. *Perf. 14½*

C359 AP90	3g	brn red	5	5
C360 AP90	4g	green	5	5
C361 AP90	66g	brn org	75	50

150th anniv. of Independence.

St. Ignatius and San Ignacio Monastery AP91

1966, Apr. 20 Wmk. 347 *Perf. 11*

C362 AP91	3g	brown	5	5
C363 AP91	12.45g	sepia	10	8
C364 AP91	18.15g	sepia	15	10
C365 AP91	23.40g	sepia	25	20

Founding of San Ignacio Guazu Monastery, 350th anniv.

"Paraguay de Fuego" by Dario — AP92

Medical Laboratory "Health" — AP93

1966, July 16 Litho.

C366 AP92	12.45g	blue	8	6
C367 AP92	18.15g	red lil	10	9
C368 AP92	23.40g	org brn	25	10
C369 AP92	36g	brt grn	38	18
C370 AP92	50g	rose car	42	20
Nos. C366-C370 (5)			1.23	63

See note after No. 713.

1967, May 9 Wmk. 347

Designs: 12.45g, 18.15g, Library "Education."

C371 AP93	12.45g	dk brn	8	6
C372 AP93	18.15g	violet	10	9
C373 AP93	23.40g	rose cl	12	10
C374 AP93	36g	Prus blue	30	18
C375 AP93	50g	rose car	35	20
Nos. C371-C375 (5)			95	63

50th anniversary of Lions International.

WHO Emblem AP94

Torch, Book, Houses AP95

1968, Aug. 12 Litho. *Perf. 11*

C376 AP94	36g	blk brn	30	18
C377 AP94	50g	rose cl	35	22
C378 AP94	100g	brt bl	75	45

WHO, 20th anniv.; cent. of the national epic.

1969, June 28 Wmk. 347 *Perf. 11*

C379 AP95	36g	blue	50
C380 AP95	50g	bister brn	65
C381 AP95	100g	rose car	1.25

National drive for teachers' homes.

Solano Lopez Type of Regular Issue

1970, March 1 Wmk. 347 *Perf. 11*

C382 A165	15g	lt Prus bl	10	8
C383 A165	20g	org brn	14	10
C384 A165	30g	gray grn	22	15
C385 A165	40g	gray brn	28	20

Centenary Type of Regular Issue

1970, Aug. 15 Litho.

Designs (First Issue of Paraguay): 15g, No. 3. 30g, No. 2. 36g, No. 1.

C386 A166	15g	vio brn	22	18
C387 A166	30g	dp grn	45	38
C388 A166	36g	brt pink	50	42

UNESCO Type of Regular Issue

1971, May 18 Litho. *Perf. 11*

C389 A167	20g	claret	14	10
C390 A167	25g	brt pink	18	12
C391 A167	30g	brown	20	15
C392 A167	50g	gray olive	35	25

UNICEF Type of Regular Issue

1972, Jan. 24

Granite Paper

C393 A168	20g	brt bl	14	10
C394 A168	25g	lt ol	18	12
C395 A168	30g	dk brn	20	15

Tourism Year Type of Regular Issue

Designs: 20g, Bus and car on highway. 25g, Hospital of Institute for Social Service. 50g, "Presidente Stroessner" of state merchant marine. 100g, "Electra C" of Paraguayan airlines.

1972, Nov. 16 *Perf. 13½x13*

Granite Paper

C396 A169	20g	rose car	14	10
C397 A169	25g	gray	18	12
C398 A169	50g	violet	35	25
C399 A169	100g	brt lil	70	50

OAS Type of Regular Issue

1973 Litho. *Perf. 13x13½*

Granite Paper

C400 A170	20g	multi	14	10
C401 A170	25g	multi	18	12
C402 A170	50g	multi	35	25
C403 A170	100g	multi	70	50

EXPOPAR 73 Type of Regular Issue

1973, Aug. 11 Litho. *Perf. 13x13½*

Granite Paper

C404 A172	20g	lilac rose	14	10
C405 A172	25g	rose claret	18	12

UPU Type of 1974

1975, Feb. Wmk. 347 *Perf. 13½x13*

C406 A173	20g	blk & brn	14	12
C407 A173	25g	blk & emer	18	15

Institute Type of 1976

1976, Mar. 16 Litho. Wmk. 347

C408 A174	30g	brn, blk & red	22	18

Rotary Type of 1976

1976, Mar. 16 *Perf. 13x13½*

C409 A175	25g	emer, bl & lem	18	12

IWY Type of 1976

1976, Mar. 16 Wmk. 347

C410 A176	20g	grn & brn	14	10

Types of 1977

Designs: 20g, Rose tabebuia. 25g, Woman holding ceramic pot.

1977 Litho. *Perf. 13x13½*

C411 A177	20g	multi	25	18
C412 A178	25g	multi	30	20

Issue dates: 20g, Apr. 25; 25g, June 27.

Marshal Type of 1977

1977, July 24 Litho. Wmk. 347

C413 A179	50g	dk vio	50	38
C414 A179	100g	green	1.00	75

National College Type 1978

1978 Litho. *Perf. 13½x13*

C415 A180	20g	brown	16	12
C416 A180	25g	vio blk	20	15
C417 A180	30g	brt grn	25	18

Estigarribia Type of 1978

1978 Litho. *Perf. 13x13½*

C418 A181	20g	multi	16	12
C419 A181	25g	multi	20	15
C420 A181	30g	multi	25	18

Tourism Type of 1979

1979, Aug. Wmk. 347 Litho.

C421 A182	50g	red, bl & blk	40	30

Pilar Type of 1980

1980, July 17 Litho. *Perf. 13½x13*

C422 A183	25g	multi	20	15

Jet Type of 1980

1980, Sept. 17 Litho. Wmk. 347

C422A A183a	100g	multi	80	65

Metropolitan Seminary Centenary — AP96

1981, Mar. 26 Litho. Wmk. 347

C423 AP96	5g	ultra	5	5
C424 AP96	10g	red brn	8	6
C425 AP96	25g	green	20	15
C426 AP96	50g	gray	40	30

UPU Issue of 1981

1981, Aug. 18 Litho. *Perf. 13½x13*

C427 A184	20g	grn & blk	16	12
C428 A184	25g	lt red brn & blk	20	15
C429 A184	50g	bl & blk	40	30

Mother Maria Mazzarello (1837-1881), Co-Founder of Daughters of Mary — AP97

1981, Dec. 30 Litho. *Perf. 13x13½*

C430 AP97	20g	blk & grn	16	14
C431 AP97	25g	blk & red brn	20	15
C432 AP97	50g	blk & gray vio	40	30

Inter-American Development Bank, 25th Anniv. AP98

1985, Apr. 25 Litho. Wmk. 347

C433 AP98	3g	dl red brn, org & yel	5	5
C434 AP98	5g	vio, org & yel	5	5
C435 AP98	10g	rose vio, org & yel	5	5
C436 AP98	50g	sep, org & yel	7	6
C437 AP98	65g	bl, org & yel	9	7
C438 AP98	95g	pale bl grn, org & yel	12	9
Nos. C433-C438 (6)			43	37

UN, 40th Anniv. — AP99

1986, Feb. 27 Wmk. 392

C439 AP99	5g	bl & sepia	5	5
C440 AP99	10g	bl & gray	5	5
C441 AP99	50g	bl & grysh brn	14	12

Japanese Emigrants in Paraguay, 50th Anniv. — AP100

1986, Nov. 6 *Perf. 13½x13, 13x13½*

C442 AP100	5g	La Colemna Vineyard	5	5
C443 AP100	10g	Cherry, lapacho flowers	5	5
C444 AP100	20g	Integration monument, vert.	5	5

Caacupe Basilica and Pope John Paul II
AP101

Perf. 13½x13

1988, May 5 **Litho.** **Wmk. 347**

C445	AP101	100g multi	45	35
C446	AP101	120g multi	55	42
C447	AP101	150g multi	68	52

Visit of Pope John Paul II.

*** 75º ANIVERSARIO DE FUNDACION CENTRO FILATELICO DEL PARAGUAY 15 JUNIO-1913 - 1988**

No. C440 Overprinted

Perf. 13x13½

1988, June 15 **Wmk. 392**

C448	AP99	10g blue & sil	5	5

Paraguay Philatelic Center 75th Anniv.

Founding of "New Germany" and 1st Cultivation of Herbal Tea, Cent. — AP100

Perf. 13x13½, 13½x13

1988, June 18 **Litho.** **Wmk. 347**

C449	AP100	90g Cauldron, vert.	42	32
C450	AP100	105g Farm workers carrying crop	48	35
C451	AP100	120g like 105g	55	42

Government Palace and Pres. Stroessner — AP101

Wmk. 347

1988, Aug. 5 **Litho.** ***Perf. 13½***

C452	AP101	200g multi	40	30
C453	AP101	500g multi	1.00	1.00
C454	AP101	1000g multi	2.00	2.00

Pres. Stroessner's new term in office, 1988-1993. Size of letters in watermark on 200g, 1000g: 5mm. On 500g, 10mm.

POSTAGE DUE STAMPS

D1

D2

1904 **Unwmk.** **Litho.** ***Perf. 11½***

J1	D1	2c green	20	18
J2	D1	4c green	20	18
J3	D1	10c green	20	18
J4	D1	20c green	20	18

1913 **Engr.**

J5	D2	1c yellow brown	5	5
J6	D2	2c yellow brown	5	5
J7	D2	5c yellow brown	5	5
J8	D2	10c yellow brown	8	5
J9	D2	20c yellow brown	8	5
J10	D2	40c yellow brown	8	5
J11	D2	1p yellow brown	8	5
J12	D2	1.50p yellow brown	10	8
		Nos. J5-J12 (8)	57	43

INTERIOR OFFICE ISSUES

The "C" signifies "Campaña" (rural). These stamps were sold by Postal Agents in country districts, who received a commission on their sales. These stamps were available for postage in the interior but not in Asuncion or abroad.

Nos. 243-244 Overprinted in Red **C**

1922

L1	A42	50c car & dk bl	10	5
L2	A42	1p dk bl & brn	12	8

The overprint on Nos. L1-L2 exists double or inverted. Counterfeits exist.

Nos. 215, 218, J12 Surcharged **C Habilitado en $ 1:— 1924**

1924

L3	A40	50c on 75c deep bl	8	5
L4	A40	1p on 1.25p pale bl	8	5
L5	D2	1p on 1.50p yel brn	8	6

Nos. L3-L4 exist imperf.

Nos. 254, 257-260 Overprinted in Black or Red **C**

1924-26

L6	A45	50c red ('25)	5	5
L7	A44	1p dk blue (R)	5	5
L8	A45	1p dk bl (R) ('25)	5	5
L9	A46	1p blue (R) ('25)	6	5
L10	A45	1p emerald ('26)	5	5
		Nos. L6-L10 (5)	26	25

Nos. L6, L8-L9 exist imperf. Value $2.50 each pair.

Same Overprint on Stamps and Type of 1927-36 in Red or Black

1927-39

L11	A47	50c ultra (R)	5	5
L12	A47	50c dl red ('28)	5	5
L13	A47	50c orange ('29)	5	5
L14	A47	50c lt bl ('30)	5	5
L15	A47	50c gray (R) ('31)	5	5
L16	A47	50c bluish grn (R) ('33)	5	5
L17	A47	50c vio (R) ('34)	5	5
L18	A48	1p emerald	5	5
L19	A48	1p org red ('29)	5	5
L20	A48	1p lil brn ('31)	5	5
L21	A48	1p dk bl (R) ('33)	5	5
L22	A48	1p brt vio (R) ('35)	5	5
L23	A49	1.50p brown	5	5
a.		Double overprint	1.50	
L24	A49	1.50p lilac ('28)	5	5
L25	A49	1.50p dull bl (R)	5	5
L26	A50	2.50p bister ('28)	15	6
L27	A50	2.50p vio (R) ('36)	5	5
L28	A51	3p gray (R)	8	5
L29	A51	3p rose red ('39)	9	5
L30	A52	5p vio (R) ('36)	6	5
L31	A57	10p gray brn (R) ('36)	30	25
		Nos. L11-L31 (21)	1.48	1.26

Types of 1931-35 and No. 305 Overprinted in Black or Red **C**

1931-36

L32	A59	1p light red	5	5
L33	A58	1.50p dp bl (R)	5	5
L34	A60	1.50p bis brn ('32)	6	5
L35	A60	1.50p grn (R) ('34)	6	5
L36	A60	1.50p bl (R) ('36)	6	5
L37	A54	10p vermilion	1.25	1.25
		Nos. L32-L37 (6)	1.53	1.50

OFFICIAL STAMPS

O1

O2

O3

O4

O5

O6

O7

Unwmk.

1886, Aug. 20 **Litho.** ***Imperf.***

O1	O1	1c orange	3.00	3.00
O2	O2	2c violet	3.00	3.00
O3	O3	5c red	3.00	3.00
O4	O4	7c green	3.00	3.00
O5	O5	10c brown	3.00	3.00
O6	O6	15c sl bl	3.00	3.00
a.		Wavy lines on face of stamp		
b.		"OFICIAL" omitted	1.25	
O7	O7	20c claret	3.00	3.00
		Nos. O1-O7 (7)	21.00	21.00

Nos. O1 to O7 have the date and various control marks and letters printed on the back of each stamp in blue and black.

The overprints exist inverted on all values.

Nos. O1 to O7 have been reprinted from new stones made from slightly retouched dies.

O8

O9

O10

O11

O12

O13

O14

1886 ***Perf. 11½***

O8	O8	1c dark green	50	50
O9	O9	2c scarlet	50	50
O10	O10	5c dull blue	50	50
O11	O11	7c orange	50	50
O12	O12	10c lake	50	50
O13	O13	15c brown	50	50
O14	O14	20c blue	50	50
		Nos. O8-O14 (7)	3.50	3.50

The overprint exists inverted on all values. Value $1.50.

No. 20 Overprinted **OFICIAL**

1886, Sept. 1

O15	A11	1c dark green	1.50	1.50

O15

Handstamped Surcharge in Black

1889 ***Imperf.***

O16	O15	3c on 15c violet	1.50	1.00
O17	O15	5c on 15c red brn	1.50	1.00

Perf. 11½

O18	O15	1c on 15c maroon	1.50	1.00
O19	O15	2c on 15c maroon	1.50	1.00

Counterfeits of Nos. O16-O19 abound.

Regular Issue of 1887 Handstamp Overprinted in Violet ***OFICIAL***

Perf. 11½-12½ & Compounds

1890 **Typo.**

O20	A12	1c green	12	10
O21	A12	2c rose red	12	10
O22	A12	5c blue	12	10
O23	A12	7c brown	3.75	2.50
O24	A12	10c lilac	15	12
O25	A12	15c orange	45	25
O26	A12	20c pink	38	30
		Nos. O20-O26 (7)	5.09	3.47

Nos. O20-O26 exist with double overprint and all but the 20c with inverted overprint.

Nos. O20-O22, O24-O26 exist with blue overprint. The status is questioned. Value, set $15.

Stamps and Type of 1887 Regular Issue Overprinted in Black **OFICIAL**

1892

O33	A12	1c green	9	6
O34	A12	2c rose red	9	6
O35	A12	5c blue	9	6
O36	A12	7c brown	1.75	1.00
O37	A12	10c lilac	65	22
O38	A12	15c orange	18	9
O39	A12	20c pink	22	10
O40	A12	50c gray	12	12
		Nos. O33-O40 (8)	3.19	1.71

No. 26 Overprinted *Oficial*

1893

O41	A12	7c brown	10.00	5.00

Counterfeits of No. O41 exist.

O16

1901, Feb. Engr. *Perf. 11½, 12½*

O42	O16	1c dull blue	20	20
O43	O16	2c rose red	8	6
O44	O16	4c dark brown	8	6
O45	O16	5c dark green	8	6
O46	O16	8c orange brn	8	8
O47	O16	10c car rose	10	10
O48	O16	20c deep blue	15	12
		Nos. O42-O48 (7)	77	68

A 12c deep green, type O16, was prepared but not issued.

No. 45 Overprinted **Oficial**

1902 *Perf. 12x12½*

O49	A12	1p olive grn	9	9
a.		Inverted overprint	10.00	

Counterfeits of No. O49a exist.

Regular Issue of 1903 Overprinted *OFICIAL*

1903 *Perf. 11½*

O50	A32	1c gray	8	5
O51	A32	2c blue green	8	5
O52	A32	5c blue	9	6
O53	A32	10c orange brn	8	5
O54	A32	20c carmine	8	5
O55	A32	30c deep blue	8	5
O56	A32	60c purple	12	10
		Nos. O50-O56 (7)	61	41

O17

O18

1905-08 Engr. *Perf. 11½, 12*

O57	O17	1c gray grn	15	8
O58	O17	1c ol grn ('05)	20	8
O59	O17	1c brn org ('06)	45	10
O60	O17	1c ver ('08)	25	12
O61	O17	2c brown org	15	8
O62	O17	2c gray grn ('05)	15	8
O63	O17	2c red ('06)	75	25
O64	O17	2c gray ('08)	38	20
O65	O17	5c deep bl ('06)	20	12
O66	O17	5c gray bl ('08)	1.50	1.00
O67	O17	5c grnsh bl ('08)	75	65
O68	O17	10c violet ('06)	12	8
O69	O17	20c violet ('08)	65	38
		Nos. O57-O69 (13)	5.70	3.22

1908

O70	O17	10c bister	3.50
O71	O17	10c emerald	3.50
O72	O17	10c red lilac	4.50
O73	O17	20c bister	3.00
O74	O17	20c salmon pink	3.50
O75	O17	20c green	3.50
O76	O17	30c turquoise bl	3.35
O77	O17	30c blue gray	3.50
O78	O17	30c yellow	1.50
O79	O17	60c chocolate	3.50
O80	O17	60c orange brn	4.00
O81	O17	60c deep ultra	3.00
O82	O18	1p brt rose & blk	22.50
O83	O18	1p lake & blk	22.50
O84	O18	1p brn org & blk	22.50
		Nos. O70-O84 (15)	107.85

Nos. O70-O84 were not issued, but were surcharged or overprinted for use as regular postage stamps. See Nos. 131, 133, 135-138, 144-145, 158-165, 171-173.

O19

1913 *Perf. 11½*

O85	O19	1c gray	5	5
O86	O19	2c orange	5	5
O87	O19	5c lilac	5	5
O88	O19	10c green	5	5
O89	O19	20c dull red	5	5
O90	O19	50c rose	5	5
O91	O19	75c deep blue	5	5
O92	O19	1p dull blue	5	5
O93	O19	2p yellow	12	12
		Nos. O85-O93 (9)	52	52

Type of Regular Issue of 1927-38 Overprinted in Red **OFICIAL**

1935

O94	A47	10c light ultra	5	5
O95	A47	50c violet	5	5
O96	A48	1p orange	5	5
O97	A60	1.50p green	8	5
O98	A50	2.50p violet	8	6
		Nos. O94-O98 (5)	31	26

Overprint is diagonal on 1.50p.

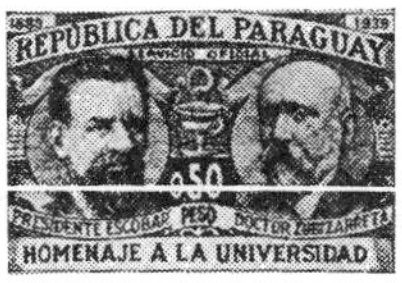
President Escobar and Ramon Zubizarreta
O20

1940 Litho. *Perf. 12.*

O99	O20	50c red brn & blk	5	5
O100	O20	1p rose pink & blk	5	5
O101	O20	2p lt bl grn & blk	5	5
O102	O20	5p ultra & blk	5	5
O103	O20	10p lt vio & blk	8	5
O104	O20	50p dp org & blk	30	25
		Nos. O99-O104 (6)	58	50

Founding of the University of Asunción, 50th anniv.

PERU

LOCATION — West coast of South America
GOVT. — Republic
AREA — 496,093 sq. mi.
POP. — 18,300,000 (est. 1982)
CAPITAL — Lima

8 Reales = 1 Peso (1857)
100 Centimos = 8 Dineros =
4 Pesetas = 1 Peso (1858)
100 Centavos = 1 Sol (1874)
100 Centimos = 1 Inti (1985)

Catalogue values for unused stamps in this country are for Never Hinged items, beginning with Scott 426 in the regular postage section, Scott B1 in the semi-postal section, Scott C78 in the airpost section, Scott CB1 in the airpost semi-postal section, and Scott RA31 in the postal tax section.

Values of early Peru stamps vary according to condition. Quotations for Nos. 1-15 are for fine copies. Very fine to superb specimens sell at much higher prices, and inferior or poor copies sell at reduced prices, depending on the condition of the individual specimen.

Sail and Steamship — A1

Design: 2r, Ship sails eastward.

1857, Dec. 1 Unwmk. Engr. *Imperf.*

1	A1	1r blue, *bl*	1,350.	1,500.
2	A1	2r brn red, *bl*	1,500.	1,650.

The Pacific Steam Navigation Co. gave a quantity of these stamps to the Peruvian government so that a trial of prepayment of postage by stamps might be made.

Stamps of 1 and 2 reales, printed in various colors on white paper, laid and wove, were prepared for the Pacific Steam Navigation Co. but never put in use. Value $50 each on wove paper, $400 each on laid paper.

Coat of Arms
A2 A3

A4

Wavy Lines in Spandrels

1858, Mar. 1 Litho.

3	A2	1d deep bl	190.00	25.00
4	A3	1p rose red	800.00	120.00
5	A4	½peso rose red	*3,500.*	*3,500.*
6	A4	½peso buff	*1,500.*	550.00
a		½peso orange yellow	*1,500.*	550.00

A5

A6

Large Letters

1858, Dec.

Double-lined Frame

7	A5	1d slate bl	225.00	25.00
8	A6	1p red	225.00	45.00

A7

A8

1860-61

Zigzag Lines in Spandrels

9	A7	1d blue	90.00	7.50
a		Prussian blue	90.00	14.00
b		Cornucopia on white ground	200.00	42.50
c		Zigzag lines broken at angles	140.00	16.50
10	A8	1p rose	225.00	20.00
a		1p brick red	225.00	20.00
b		Cornucopia on white ground	225.00	20.00

Retouched, 10 lines instead of 9 in left label

11	A8	1p rose	120.00	22.50
a		Pelure paper	180.00	22.50

A9

A10

1862-63 Embossed

12	A9	1d red	14.00	2.50
a		Arms embossed sideways	400.00	82.50
b		Thick paper	25.00	8.25
c		Diag. half used on cover		140.00
13	A10	1p brn ('63)	82.50	25.00
a		Diag. half used on cover		1,000.

Counterfeits of Nos. 13 and 15 exist.

A11

1868-72

14	A11	1d green	10.00	2.00
a		Arms embossed inverted	*1,125.*	*700.00*
b		Diagonal half used on cover		350.00
15	A10	1p org ('72)	82.50	25.00
a		Diagonal half used on cover		

Nos. 12-15, 19 and 20 were printed in horizontal strips. Stamps may be found printed on two strips of paper where the strips were joined by overlapping.

Llamas — A12

A13

A14

1866-67 Engr. *Perf. 12*

16	A12	5c green	5.00	65
17	A13	10c vermilion	5.00	1.40
18	A14	20c brown	20.00	3.50
a		Diagonal half used on cover		375.00

See Nos. 109, 111, 113.

Locomotive and Arms
A15

Llama
A16

1871, Apr. Embossed *Imperf.*

19	A15	5c scarlet	75.00	25.00
a		5c pale red	75.00	25.00

20th anniv. of the first railway in South America, linking Lima and Callao.

The so-called varieties "ALLAO" and "CALLA" are due to over-inking.

1873, Mar. *Rouletted Horiz.*

20	A16	2c dk ultra	35.00	*250.00*

Counterfeits are plentiful.

Sun God of the Incas — A17

Coat of Arms
A18 A19

A20

A21

A22

A23

Embossed with Grill

1874-84 Engr. *Perf. 12*

21	A17	1c org ('79)	50	40
22	A18	2c dk vio	65	50
23	A19	5c blue ('77)	85	25
24	A19	5c ultra ('79)	10.00	1.65
25	A20	10c grn ('76)	25	22
a		Imperf., pair	25.00	
26	A20	10c slate ('84)	2.00	22
a		Diag. half used as 5c on cover		
27	A21	20c brn red	1.40	65
28	A22	50c green	9.00	2.25
29	A23	1s rose	1.40	1.20
		Nos. 21-29 (9)	26.05	7.34

No. 25a lacks the grill.

No. 26 with overprint "DE OFICIO" is said to have been used to frank mail of Gen. A. A. Caceres during the civil war against Gen. Miguel Iglesias, provisional president. Experts question its status.

1880

30	A17	1c green	1.40
31	A18	2c rose	1.40

Nos. 30 and 31 were prepared for use but not issued without overprint.

See Nos. 104-108, 110, 112, 114-115.

Stamps of 1874-80 Overprinted in Red, Blue or Black

Reduced illustration

1880, Jan. 5

32	A17	1c green (R)	50	40
a		Inverted overprint	10.00	10.00
b		Double overprint	13.50	13.50
33	A18	2c rose (Bl)	80	65
a		Inverted overprint	10.00	10.00
b		Double overprint	14.00	12.00
34	A18	2c rose (Bk)	45.00	35.00
a		Inverted overprint		
b		Double overprint		
35	A19	5c ultra (R)	1.40	1.00
a		Inverted overprint	10.00	10.00
b		Double overprint	14.00	14.00
36	A22	50c green (R)	27.50	17.50
a		Inverted overprint	45.00	45.00
b		Double overprint	55.00	55.00
37	A23	1s rose (Bl)	70.00	45.00
a		Inverted overprint	110.00	110.00
b		Double overprint	110.00	110.00

Stamps of 1874-80 Overprinted in Red or Blue

Reduced illustration

1881, Jan. 28

38	A17	1c green (R)	65	50
a		Inverted overprint	8.25	8.25
b		Double overprint	14.00	14.00
39	A18	2c rose (Bl)	14.00	9.00
a		Inverted overprint	17.50	15.00
b		Double overprint	25.00	20.00
40	A19	5c ultra (R)	1.00	65
a		Inverted overprint	14.00	14.00
b		Double overprint	20.00	20.00
41	A22	50c grn (R)	450.00	250.00
a		Inverted overprint	600.00	
42	A23	1s rose (Bl)	82.50	65.00
a		Inverted overprint	150.00	

Reprints of Nos. 38 to 42 were made in 1884. In the overprint the word "PLATA" is 3mm high instead of 2½mm. The cross bars of the letters "A" of that word are set higher than on the original stamps. The 5c is printed in blue instead of ultramarine.

For stamps of 1874-80 overprinted with Chilean arms or small UPU "horseshoe," see Nos. N11-N23.

Stamps of 1874-79 Handstamped in Black or Blue

1883

65	A17	1c org (Bk)	85	65
66	A17	1c org (Bl)	45.00	
68	A19	5c ultra (Bk)	6.50	4.00
69	A20	10c grn (Bk)	55	50
70	A20	10c grn (Bl)	4.00	3.50
71	A22	50c grn (Bk)	6.00	2.50
73	A23	1s rose (Bk)	10.00	5.00

This overprint is found in 11 types.

The 1c green, 2c dark violet and 20c brown red, overprinted with triangle, are fancy varieties made for sale to collectors and never placed in regular use.

Overprinted Triangle and "Union Postal Universal Peru" in Oval

1883

77	A22	50c grn (R & Bk)	120.00	60.00
78	A23	1s rose (Bl & Bk)	140.00	90.00

The 1c green, 2c rose and 5c ultramarine, over printed with triangle and "U. P. U. Peru" oval, were never placed in regular use.

Overprinted Triangle and "Union Postal Universal Lima" in Oval

1883

79	A17	1c grn (R & Bl)	50.00	37.50
80	A17	1c grn (R & Bk)	4.00	3.50
a		Oval overprint inverted		
b		Double overprint of oval		
81	A18	2c rose (Bl & Bk)	4.00	3.50
82	A19	5c ultra (R & Bk)	6.50	5.00
83	A19	5c ultra (R & Bl)	6.50	5.00
84	A22	50c grn (R & Bk)	140.00	90.00
85	A23	1s rose (Bl & Bk)	190.00	125.00

Some authorities question the status of No. 79.

Nos. 80, 81, 84, and 85 were reprinted in 1884. They have the second type of oval overprint with "PLATA" 3mm high.

Overprinted Triangle and

86	A17	1c grn (Bk & Bk)	60	50
a		Horseshoe inverted	10.00	
87	A17	1c grn (Bl & Bk)	3.50	2.50
88	A18	2c ver (Bk & Bk)	65	50
89	A19	5c bl (Bk & Bk)	80	65
90	A19	5c bl (Bl & Bk)	7.00	6.50
91	A19	5c bl (R & Bk)	1,500.	1,100.

Overprinted Horseshoe Alone

1883, Oct. 23

95	A17	1c green	1.20	80
96	A18	2c vermilion	1.20	4.00
a		Double overprint		
97	A19	5c blue	1.65	1.50
98	A19	5c ultra	20.00	15.00
99	A22	50c rose	57.50	57.50
100	A23	1s ultra	30.00	22.50

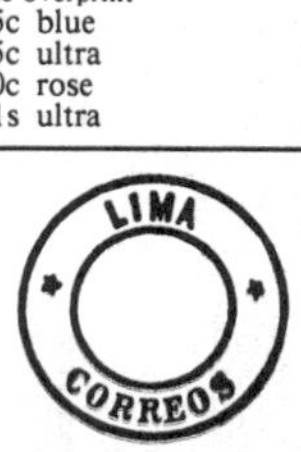

The 2c violet overprinted with the above design in red and triangle in black also the 1c green overprinted with the same combination plus the horseshoe in black, are fancy varieties made for sale to collectors.

No. 23 Overprinted in Black

1884, Apr. 28

103	A19	5c blue	65	40
a		Double overprint	5.00	5.00

Stamps of 1c and 2c with the above overprint, also with the above and "U. P. U. LIMA" oval in blue or "CORREOS LIMA" in a double-lined circle in red, were made to sell to collectors and were never placed in use.

Without Overprint or Grill

1886-95

104	A17	1c dl vio	35	16
105	A17	1c vermilion ('95)	40	22
106	A18	2c green	50	16
107	A18	2c dp ultra ('95)	35	22
108	A19	5c orange	50	20
109	A12	5c claret ('95)	1.00	50
110	A20	10c slate	25	14
111	A13	10c org ('95)	80	35
112	A21	20c blue	4.00	65
113	A14	20c dp ultra ('95)	6.50	1.40
114	A22	50c red	1.40	65
115	A23	1s brown	1.20	50
		Nos. 104-115 (12)	17.25	5.15

Overprinted Horseshoe in Black and Triangle in Rose Red

1889

116	A17	1c green	50	42
a		Horseshoe inverted	5.00	

Nos. 30 and 25 Overprinted "Union Postal Universal Lima" in Oval in Red

1889, Sept. 1

117	A17	1c green	80	65
117A	A20	10c green	1.50	1.00

The overprint on Nos. 117 and 117A is of the second type with "PLATA" 3mm high.

Stamps of 1874-80 Overprinted in Black

Pres. Remigio Morales Bermudez

1894, Oct. 23

118	A17	1c orange	50	42
a		Inverted overprint	7.00	7.00
b		Double overprint	7.00	7.00
119	A17	1c green	40	35
a		Inverted overprint	3.50	3.50
b		Dbl. inverted ovpt.	5.00	5.00
120	A18	2c violet	40	35
a		Diagonal half used as 1c		
b		Inverted overprint	7.00	7.00
c		Double overprint	7.00	
121	A18	2c rose	40	35
a		Double overprint	7.00	7.00
b		Inverted overprint	7.00	7.00
122	A19	5c blue	2.00	1.40
122A	A19	5c ultra	3.50	1.40
b		Inverted overprint	10.00	10.00
123	A20	10c green	40	35
a		Inverted overprint	7.00	7.00
124	A22	50c green	1.40	1.20
a		Inverted overprint	10.00	10.00
		Nos. 118-124 (8)	9.00	5.82

Same, with Additional Overprint of Horseshoe

125	A18	2c vermilion	35	25
a		Head inverted	2.50	2.50
b		Head double	5.00	5.00
126	A19	5c blue	80	50
a		Head inverted	7.00	7.00
127	A22	50c rose	42.50	30.00
a		Head double	55.00	45.00
b		Head inverted		
128	A23	1s ultra	100.00	90.00
a		Both overprints inverted	125.00	110.00
b		Head double	125.00	110.00

A23a

1895 *Perf. 11½*

Vermilion Surcharge

129	A23a	5c on 5c grn	8.00	5.00
130	A23a	10c on 10c ver	6.50	4.00
131	A23a	20c on 20c brn	7.00	4.50
132	A23a	50c on 50c ultra	8.00	5.00
133	A23a	1s on 1s red brn	8.25	6.50
		Nos. 129-133 (5)	37.75	25.00

Nos 129-133 were used only in Tumbes. The basic stamps were prepared by revolutionaries in northern Peru.

"Liberty"
A23b A23c

1895, Sept. 8 Engr.

134	A23b	1c gray vio	1.50	80
135	A23b	2c green	1.50	80
136	A23b	5c yellow	1.50	80
137	A23b	10c ultra	1.50	80
138	A23c	20c orange	1.50	1.20
139	A23c	50c dark bl	9.00	5.50
140	A23c	1s car lake	45.00	30.00
		Nos. 134-140 (7)	61.50	39.90

Success of the revolution against the government of General Caceres and of the election of President Pierola.

Manco Capac, Founder of Inca Dynasty A24

Francisco Pizarro Conqueror of the Inca Empire A25

General José de La Mar — A26

1896-1900

141	A24	1c ultra	35	14
a		1c blue (error)	45.00	40.00
142	A24	1c yel grn ('98)	35	7
143	A24	2c blue	35	14
144	A24	2c scar ('99)	35	8
145	A25	5c indigo	50	16
146	A25	5c grn ('97)	50	7
147	A25	5c grnsh bl ('99)	35	5
148	A25	10c yellow	80	22
149	A25	10c gray blk ('00)	80	10
150	A25	20c orange	1.65	22
151	A26	50c car rose	3.50	80
152	A26	1s org red	5.50	1.00
153	A26	2s claret	2.25	80
		Nos. 141-153 (13)	17.25	3.85

The 5c in black is a chemical changeling.

Paucartambo Bridge A27

Post and Telegraph Building, Lima — A28

Pres. Nicolás de Piérola — A29

1897, Dec. 31

154 A27 1c dp ultra	65	35
155 A28 2c brown	65	22
156 A29 5c brt rose	1.00	25

Opening of new P.O. in Lima.

A30

A31

1897, Nov. 8

157 A30 1c bister	40	35
a Inverted overprint	2.50	2.50
b Double overprint	10.00	10.00

1899

158 A31 5s org red	1.65	1.40
159 A31 10s blue grn	500.00	425.00

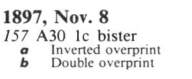

Pres. Eduardo de Romaña A32

Admiral Miguel L. Grau A33

Col. Francisco Bolognesi A33a

Pres. Romaña A33b

1900 Frame Litho., Center Engr.

160 A32 22c yel grn & blk	8.00	85

1901, Jan.

161 A33 1c green & blk	65	22
162 A33a 2c red & black	65	22
163 A33b 5c dl vio & blk	1.00	22

Advent of 20th century.

A34

Municipal Hygiene Institute Lima — A35

1902 Engr.

164 A34 22c green	35	20

1905

165 A35 12c dp bl & blk	65	22

Same Surcharged in Red or Violet

UN CENTAVO

1907

166 A35 1c on 12c dp bl & blk (R)	25	20
a Inverted surcharge	8.00	8.00
b Double surcharge	8.00	8.00
167 A35 2c on 12c dp bl & blk (V)	50	35
a Double surcharge	8.00	8.00
b Inverted surcharge	8.00	8.00

Monument of Bolognesi A36

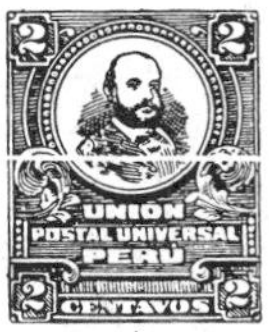

Admiral Grau A37

Llama — A38

Statue of Bolivar — A39

City Hall, Lima, formerly an Exhibition Building — A40

School of Medicine, Lima — A41

Post and Telegraph Building, Lima — A42

Grandstand at Santa Beatrix Race Track — A43

Columbus Monument — A44

1907

168 A36 1c yel grn & blk	22	14
169 A37 2c red & vio	22	14
170 A38 4c olive grn	5.50	65
171 A39 5c bl & blk	40	10
172 A40 10c red brn & blk	1.00	22
173 A41 20c dk grn & blk	22.50	50
174 A42 50c black	22.50	65
175 A43 1s pur & grn	125.00	1.65
176 A44 2s dp bl & blk	120.00	120.00
Nos. 168-176 (9)	297.34	124.05

A particular stamp may be scarce, but if few collectors want it, its market value may remain relatively low.

Manco Capac A45

Columbus A46

Pizarro — A47

San Martin — A48

Bolívar — A49

La Mar — A50

Ramón Castilla — A51

Grau — A52

Bolognesi — A53

1909

177 A45 1c gray	14	7
178 A46 2c green	14	7
179 A47 4c vermilion	22	10
180 A48 5c violet	14	7
181 A49 10c deep blue	35	10
182 A50 12c pale blue	80	14
183 A51 20c brn red	1.00	22
184 A52 50c yellow	4.00	35
185 A53 1s brn red & blk	9.00	35
Nos. 177-185 (9)	15.79	1.47

No. 165 Surcharged in Red

UNION POSTAL 8 Cts. Sud Americana

1913, Jan.

186 A35 8c on 12c dp bl & blk	65	22

Stamps of 1899-1908 Surcharged in Magenta

UN CENTAVO 1915 — a

UN CENTAVO 1915 — b

2 CENTAVOS 1915 — c

1915

On Issues of 1898-1900

187 A24(a) 1c on 1c yel grn	16.50	12.00
a Inverted surcharge	22.50	18.00
188 A25(a) 1c on 10c gray blk	80	55

On Issue of 1905

189 A35(c) 2c on 12c dp bl & blk	22	16
a Inverted surcharge		

On Issue of 1907

190 A36(a) 1c on 1c yel grn & blk	65	50
191 A37(a) 1c on 2c red & vio	1.00	80
192 A38(b) 1c on 4c ol grn	1.65	1.40
a Inverted surcharge	4.00	4.00
193 A40(b) 1c on 10c red brn & blk	35	20
a Inverted surcharge	2.50	2.50
193C A40(c) 2c on 10c red brn & blk	100.00	100.00
194 A41(c) 2c on 20c dk grn & blk	14.00	12.00
195 A42(c) 2c on 50c blk	1.65	1.65

Stamps of 1909 Surcharged in Red, Green or Violet

Vale 1 Centavo 1916 — d

VALE 2 CENTAVOS 1916 — e

VALE 10 CENTAVOS 1916 — f

1916

196 A50(d) 1c on 12c pale bl (R)	16	14
a Double surcharge	2.00	2.00
b Green surcharge	4.50	4.50
197 A51(d) 1c on 20c brn red (G)	16	14
198 A52(d) 1c on 50c yel (G)	16	14
a Inverted surcharge	2.00	2.00
199 A47(e) 2c on 4c ver (V)	16	14
200 A53(f) 10c on 1s red & blk (G)	40	25
a "VALF"	3.50	3.50
Nos. 196-200 (5)	1.04	81

Official Stamps of 1909-14 Overprinted or Surcharged in Green or Red:

FRANQUEO 1916 — g

FRANQUEO VALE 2 Cts 1916 — h

1916

201 O1 1c red (G)	14	14
202 O1 2c on 50c ol grn (R)	16	16
203 O1 10c bis brn (G)	20	14

Postage Due Stamps of 1909 Surcharged in Violet-Black

204 D7 2c on 1c brn	40	40
205 D7 2c on 5c brn	14	14
206 D7 2c on 10c brn	14	14
207 D7 2c on 50c brn	14	14
Nos. 201-207 (7)	1.32	1.26

Many copies of Nos. 187 to 207 have a number of pin holes. It is stated that these holes were made at the time the surcharges were printed.

The varieties which we list of the 1915 and 1916 issues were sold to the public at post offices. Many other varieties which were previously listed are now known to have been delivered to one speculator or to have been privately printed by him from the surcharging plates which he had acquired.

No. 179 Surcharged in Black

Un Centavo

1917

208	A47	1c on 4c ver	22	16
a		Double surcharge	4.00	4.00
b		Inverted surcharge	4.00	4.00

San Martin
A54

Columbus at
Salamanca
A62

Funeral of
Atahualpa
A63

Battle of Arica,
"Arica, the Last
Cartridge"
A64

Designs: 2c, Bolivar. 4c, José Gálvez. 5c, Manuel Pardo. 8c, Grau. 10c, Bolognesi. 12c, Castilla. 20c, General Cáceres.

1918 **Engr.**

Centers in Black

209	A54	1c orange	10	7
210	A54	2c green	14	7
211	A54	4c lake	22	7
212	A54	5c dp ultra	22	5
213	A54	8c red brn	60	25
214	A54	10c grnsh bl	35	7
215	A54	12c dl vio	80	16
216	A54	20c ol grn	1.00	16
217	A62	50c vio brn	4.50	35
218	A63	1s greenish bl	12.00	50
219	A64	2s dp ultra	21.00	65
		Nos. 209-219 (11)	40.93	2.40

Augusto B.
Leguia — A65

1919, Dec. **Litho.**

220	A65	5c bl & blk	16	16
a		Imperf.	35	35
b		Center inverted	11.00	11.00
221	A65	5c brn & blk	15	16
a		Imperf.	35	35
b		Center inverted	11.00	11.00

Constitution of 1919.

San Martin
A66

Thomas
Cochrane
A70

Oath of Independence — A69

Designs: 2c, Field Marshal Arenales. 4c, Field Marshal Las Heras. 10c, Martin Jean Guisse. 12c, Vidal. 20c, Leguia. 50c, San Martin monument. 1s, San Martin and Leguia.

1921, July 28 **Engr.; 7c Litho.**

222	A66	1c ol brn & red brn	35	14
a		Center inverted	450.00	425.00
223	A66	2c green	35	16
224	A66	4c car rose	1.00	50
225	A69	5c ol brn	40	14
226	A70	7c violet	80	35
227	A66	10c ultra	80	35
228	A66	12c blk & slate	2.50	40
229	A66	20c car & gray blk	2.50	65
230	A66	50c vio brn & dl vio	9.00	2.25
231	A69	1s car rose & yel grn	14.00	4.50
		Nos. 222-231 (10)	31.70	9.44

Centenary of Independence.

A76

A77

1923

232	A76	5c on 8c red brn & blk	40	20

Red Brown Surcharge

1924

233	A77	4c on 5c ultra & blk	25	16
a		Inverted surcharge	3.50	3.50
b		Double surcharge, one inverted	4.50	4.50

Simón Bolívar
A78 A79 A80

Perf. 14, 14x14½, 14½, 13½

1924 **Engr.; Photo. (4c, 5c)**

234	A78	2c olive grn	35	7
235	A79	4c yel grn	50	10
236	A79	5c black	1.20	10
237	A80	10c carmine	50	7
238	A78	20c ultra	1.20	14
239	A78	50c dl vio	3.75	65
240	A78	1s yel brn	9.00	2.00
241	A78	2s dull blue	25.00	11.00
		Nos. 234-241 (8)	41.50	14.13

Centenary of the Battle of Ayacucho which ended Spanish power in South America.

No. 237 exists imperf.

José Tejada
Rivadeneyra
A81

Mariano
Melgar
A82

Iturregui
A83

Leguia
A84

José de La
Mar
A85

Monument
of José
Olaya
A86

Statue of
Maria
Bellido
A87

De Saco
A88

José Leguia — A89

1924-29 **Engr.** ***Perf. 12***

Size: 18½x23mm

242	A81	2c olive gray	10	5
243	A82	4c dk grn	10	7
244	A83	8c black	1.65	80
245	A84	10c org red	16	7
245A	A85	15c dp bl ('28)	50	16
246	A86	20c blue	65	14
247	A86	20c yel ('29)	1.00	16
248	A87	50c violet	6.00	35
249	A88	1s bis brn	8.25	80
250	A89	2s ultra	22.50	3.50
		Nos. 242-250 (10)	40.91	6.10

See Nos. 258, 260, 276-282.

No. 246 Surcharged in Red:

DOS Centavos 1925 a

DOS Centavos 1925 b

1925

251	A86(a)	2c on 20c bl	*350.00*	
252	A86(b)	2c on 20c bl	80	50
a		Inverted surcharge	35.00	35.00
b		Double surch., one inverted	50.00	50.00

No. 245 Overprinted **Plebiscito**

1925

253	A84	10c org red	65	65
a		Inverted overprint	14.00	14.00

This stamp was for exclusive use on letters from the plebiscite provinces of Tacna and Arica, and posted on the Peruvian transport "Ucayali" anchored in the port of Africa.

No. 213 Surcharged

Habilitada 2 Cts. 1929 a

Habilitada 2 centavos 1929 b

1929

255	A54(a)	2c on 8c red brn & blk	50	50
256	A54(b)	2c on 8c red brn & blk	65	65

No. 247 Surcharged **Habilitada 15 cts. 1929**

257	A86	15c on 20c yel	65	65
a		Inverted surcharge	6.50	6.50

Coil Stamps

Stamps of 1924 Issue

1929 ***Perf. 14 Horizontally***

258	A81	2c ol gray	40.00	17.50
260	A84	10c org red	45.00	15.00

Postal Tax Stamp of 1928 Overprinted **Habilitada Franqueo**

1930 ***Perf. 12***

261	PT6	2c dk vio	35	35
a		Inverted overprint	2.50	2.50

No. 247 Surcharged **Habilitada 2 Cts. 1930**

262	A86	2c on 20c yel	22	22

Air Post Stamp of 1928 Surcharged **Habilitada Franqueo 2 Cts. 1930**

263	AP1	2c on 50c dk grn	20	14
a		"Habitada"	1.00	1.00

Coat of
Arms — A91

Lima
Cathedral — A92

Designs: 10c, Children's Hospital. 50c, Madonna and Child.

Perf. 12x11½, 11½x12

1930, July 5 **Litho.**

264	A91	2c green	85	55
265	A92	5c scarlet	2.00	1.20
266	A92	10c dark blue	1.40	80
267	A91	50c bis brn	22.50	12.00

6th Pan American Congress for Child Welfare. By error the stamps are inscribed "Seventh Congress."

Type of 1924 Overprinted in Black, Green or Blue

1930, Dec. 22 **Photo.** ***Perf. 15x14***

Size: 18¼x22mm

268	A84	10c org red (Bk)	16	5
a		Inverted overprint	10.00	10.00
b		Without overprint	6.50	6.50
c		Double surcharge	5.00	5.00

Same with Additional Surcharge of Numerals in Each Corner

269	A84	2c on 10c org red (G)	7	5
a		Inverted surcharge	12.00	
270	A84	4c on 10c org red (G)	16	14
a		Double surcharge	8.25	8.25

Engr.

Perf. 12

Size: 19x23½mm

271	A84	15c on 10c org red (Bl)	20	14
a		Inverted surcharge	10.00	10.00
b		Double surcharge	10.00	10.00

Bolivar — A95

1930, Dec. 16 **Litho.**

272	A95	2c buff	35	35
273	A95	4c red	65	30
274	A95	10c blue grn	35	22
275	A95	15c slate gray	65	50

Death cent. of General Simón Bolívar.

Types of 1924-29 Issues
Size: 18x22mm

1931 Photo. *Perf. 15x14*

276	A81	2c olive grn		16	7
277	A82	4c dark grn		16	7
279	A85	15c deep blue		50	10
280	A86	20c yellow		1.00	20
281	A87	50c violet		1.00	25
282	A88	1s ol brn		1.65	35
		Nos. 276-282 (6)		4.47	1.04

Pizarro — A96

Old Stone Bridge, Lima — A97

1931, July 28 Litho. *Perf. 11*

283	A96	2c slate bl	2.00	1.40
284	A96	4c deep brn	2.00	1.40
285	A96	15c dark grn	2.00	1.40
286	A97	10c rose red	2.00	1.40
287	A97	10c mag & lt grn	2.00	1.40
288	A97	15c yel & bl gray	2.00	1.40
289	A97	15c dk sl & red	2.00	1.40
		Nos. 283-289 (7)	14.00	9.80

1st Peruvian Phil. Exhib., Lima, July, 1931.

Manco Capac A99

Sugar Cane Field A102

Oil Refinery A100

Guano Deposits A104

Picking Cotton A103

Mining A105

Llamas — A106

1931-32 *Perf. 11, 11x11½*

292	A99	2c ol blk	22	7
293	A100	4c dk grn	50	16
295	A102	10c red org	80	8
a		Vertical pair, imperf. between	30.00	
296	A103	15c turq bl	1.40	16
297	A104	20c yellow	4.00	25
298	A105	50c gray lil	4.50	25
299	A106	1s brn ol	12.00	65
		Nos. 292-299 (7)	23.42	1.62

Arms of Piura — A107

1932, July 28 *Perf. 11½x12*

300	A107	10c dk bl	6.00	5.50
301	A107	15c dp vio	6.00	5.50

400th anniv. of the founding of the city of Piura. On sale one day. Counterfeits exist. See No. C3.

Parakas A108

Chimu A109

Inca — A110

Perf. 11½, 12, 11½x12

1932, Oct. 15

302	A108	10c dk vio	16	5
303	A109	15c brn red	35	10
304	A110	50c dk brn	50	16

4th centenary of the Spanish conquest of Peru.

Arequipa and El Misti A111

President Luis M. Sanchez Cerro A112

Monument to Simón Bolivar at Lima A115

Statue of Liberty A116

1932-34 Photo. *Perf. 13½*

305	A111	2c black	16	5
306	A111	2c blue blk	16	5
307	A111	2c grn ('34)	16	5
308	A111	4c dk brn	16	5
309	A111	4c org ('34)	16	5
310	A112	10c vermilion	16.50	8.25
311	A115	15c ultra	35	5
312	A115	15c mag ('34)	35	8
313	A115	20c red brn	50	10
314	A115	20c vio ('34)	50	14
315	A115	50c dk grn ('33)	65	12
316	A115	1s dp org	4.50	22
317	A115	1s org brn	6.00	35
		Nos. 305-317 (13)	30.15	9.56

1934

318	A116	10c rose	50	5

Pizarro A117

The Inca A119

Coronation of Huascar — A118

1934-35 *Perf. 13.*

319	A117	10c crimson	16	5
320	A117	15c ultra	50	5
321	A118	20c deep bl ('35)	1.00	7
322	A118	50c dp red brn	1.00	14
323	A119	1s dark vio	2.25	35
		Nos. 319-323 (5)	4.91	66

Pizarro and the Thirteen A120

Belle of Lima — A122

Francisco Pizarro — A123

Designs: 4c, Lima Cathedral. 1s, Veiled woman of Lima.

1935, Jan. 18 *Perf. 13½*

324	A120	2c brown	35	20
325	A120	4c violet	50	38
326	A122	10c rose red	50	20
327	A123	15c ultra	80	40
328	A120	20c slate gray	1.40	50
329	A122	50c olive grn	2.00	1.00
330	A122	1s Prus bl	4.50	2.25
331	A123	2s org brn	12.00	8.25
		Nos. 324-331 (8)	22.05	13.18

4th centenary of the founding of Lima. See Nos. C6-C12.

View of Ica — A125

Lake Huacachina, Health Resort — A126

An enhanced introduction to the Scott Catalogue begins on Page V. A thorough understanding of the material presented there will greatly aid your use of the catalogue itself.

Grapes — A127

Cotton Boll — A128

Zuniga y Velazco and Philip IV — A129

Supreme God of the Nazcas — A130

Engr.; Photo. (10c)

1935, Jan. 17 *Perf. 12½*

332	A125	4c gray bl	1.00	1.00
333	A126	5c dark car	35	1.00
334	A127	10c magenta	4.00	1.65
335	A126	20c green	1.65	1.20
336	A128	35c dark car	8.00	4.00
337	A129	50c org & brn	5.50	4.00
338	A130	1s pur & red	16.50	10.00
		Nos. 332-338 (7)	37.00	22.85

Founding of the City of Ica, 300th anniv.

Pizarro and the Thirteen — A131

1935-36 Photo. *Perf. 13½*

339	A131	2c dp claret	10	7
340	A131	4c bl grn ('36)	14	8

"San Cristobal," First Peruvian Warship — A132

Grand Marshal Josede La Mar — A138

Naval College at Punta A133

Independence Square, Callao — A134

Aerial View of Callao
A135

Plan of Walls of Callao in 1746
A137

Packetboat "Sacramento" — A139

Viceroy José Antonio Manso de Velasco — A140

Fort Maipú — A141

Plan of Fort Real Felipe
A142

Design: 15c, Docks and Custom House.

1936, Aug. 27 Photo. *Perf. 12½*

341	A132	2c black	65	20
342	A133	4c bl grn	65	16
343	A134	5c yel brn	65	14
344	A135	10c bl gray	65	20
345	A135	15c green	65	22
346	A137	20c dk brn	65	22
347	A138	50c purple	1.40	45
348	A139	1s ol grn	12.00	1.65

Engr.

349	A140	2s violet	16.50	6.50
350	A141	5s carmine	22.50	14.00
351	A142	10s red org & brn	55.00	40.00
		Nos. 341-351 (11)	111.30	63.74

Founding of the Province of Callao, cent. See No. C13.

Nos. 340, 321 and 323 Surcharged in Black

Habilitado

S. 0.10 Cts.

1936 *Perf. 13½, 13*

353	A131	2c on 4c bl grn	7	5
a		"0.20" for "0.02"	3.50	3.50
354	A118	10c on 20c dp bl	14	14
a		Double surcharge	3.50	
b		Inverted surcharge	3.50	
355	A119	10c on 1s dk vio	20	20

Many varieties of the surcharge are found on these stamps: no period after "S", no period after "Cts", period after "2", "S" omitted, various broken letters, etc.

The surcharge on No. 355 is horizontal.

Peruvian Cormorants (Guano Deposits)
A143

Oil Well at Talara
A144

Avenue of the Republic, Lima
A146

San Marcos University at Lima
A148

Post Office, Lima — A149

Viceroy Manuel de Amat y Junyent — A150

Designs: 10c, "El Chasqui" (Inca Courier). 20c, Municipal Palace and Museum of Natural History. 5s, Joseph A. de Pando y Riva. 10s, Dr. José Davila Condemarin.

1936-37 Photo. *Perf. 12½*

356	A143	2c lt brn	50	14
357	A143	2c grn ('37)	65	10
358	A144	4c blk brn	50	22
359	A144	4c int blk ('37)	25	14
360	A143	10c crimson	35	7
361	A143	10c ver ('37)	10	5
362	A146	15c ultra	65	14
363	A146	15c brt bl ('37)	20	7
364	A146	20c black	65	16
365	A146	20c blk brn ('37)	22	10
366	A148	50c org yel	2.50	50
367	A148	50c dk gray vio ('37)	65	16
368	A149	1s brn vio	5.00	65
369	A149	1s ultra ('37)	1.40	20

Engr.

370	A150	2s ultra	11.00	2.00
371	A150	2s dk vio ('37)	3.50	35
372	A150	5s slate bl	11.00	2.00
373	A150	10s dk vio & brn	60.00	22.50
		Nos. 356-373 (18)	99.12	29.55

No. 370 Surcharged in Black

Habilit.

Un Sol

1937

374	A150	1s on 2s ultra	2.50	2.25

Children's Holiday Center, Ancon
A153

Chavin Pottery
A154

Highway Map of Peru — A155

Archaeological Museum, Lima — A156

Industrial Bank of Peru — A157

Worker's Houses, Lima — A158

Toribio de Luzuriaga
A159

Historic Fig Tree
A160

Idol from Temple of Chavin
A161

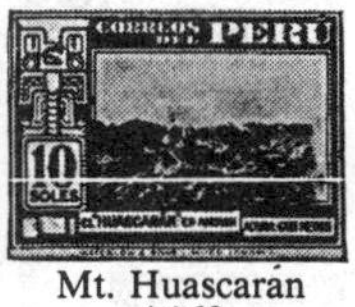
Mt. Huascaran
A162

Imprint: "Waterlow & Sons Limited, Londres"

1938, July 1 Photo. *Perf. 12½, 13*

375	A153	2c emerald	7	5
376	A154	4c org brn	10	5
377	A155	10c scarlet	20	5
378	A156	15c ultra	25	5
379	A157	20c magenta	14	5
380	A158	50c greenish bl	40	5
381	A159	1s dp claret	1.00	7
382	A160	2s green	3.50	20

Engr.

383	A161	5s dl vio & brn	8.25	50
384	A162	10s blk & ultra	14.00	65
		Nos. 375-384 (10)	27.91	1.72

See Nos. 410-418, 426-433, 438-441.

Palace Square
A163

Lima Coat of Arms
A164

Government Palace — A165

1938, Dec. 9 Photo. *Perf. 12½*

385	A163	10c sl grn	50	20

Engraved and Lithographed

386	A164	15c blk, gold, red & bl	80	25

Photo.

387	A165	1s olive	2.00	80

8th Pan-American Conference at Lima, Dec. 1938. See Nos. C62-C64.

No. 377 Surcharged in Black

Habilitada
5
cts.

1940 *Perf. 13*

388	A155	5c on 10c scar	10	5
a		Inverted surcharge		

National Radio Station — A166

Overprint: "FRANQUEO POSTAL"

1941 Litho. *Perf. 12*

389	A166	50c dl yel	2.00	16
390	A166	1s violet	2.00	20
391	A166	2s dl gray grn	5.00	50
392	A166	5s fawn	27.50	8.25
393	A166	10s rose vio	42.50	6.50
		Nos. 389-393 (5)	79.00	15.61

Gonzalo Pizarro and Orellana
A167

Francisco de Orellana
A168

Francisco Pizarro
A169

Map of South America with Amazon as Spaniards Knew It in 1542
A170

Gonzalo Pizarro A171

Discovery of the Amazon River A172

1943, Feb. *Perf. 12½*

394 A167 2c crimson 10 7
395 A168 4c slate 14 7
396 A169 10c yel brn 20 10
397 A170 15c vio blue 50 20
398 A171 20c yel olive 20 14
399 A172 25c dull org 2.00 35
400 A168 30c dp magenta 35 20
401 A170 50c blue grn 65 40
402 A167 70c violet 2.50 65
403 A171 80c lt bl 2.50 65
404 A172 1s cocoa brn 4.50 65
405 A169 5s intense blk 9.00 4.00
Nos. 394-405 (12) 22.64 7.48

400th anniv. of the discovery of the Amazon River by Francisco de Orellana in 1542.

No. 377 Surcharged in Black

1943 *Perf. 13*

406 A155 10c on 10c scar 10 5

Samuel Finley Breese Morse — A173

1944 *Perf. 12½*

407 A173 15c light bl 16 12
408 A173 30c olive gray 50 16

Centenary of invention of the telegraph.

Types of 1938
Imprint: "Columbian Bank Note Co."

1945-47 Litho. *Perf. 12½*

410 A153 2c green 5 5
411 A154 4c org brn ('46) 5 5
412 A156 15c ultra 8 5
413 A157 20c magenta 1.65 5
414 A158 50c grnsh bl 16 5
415 A159 1s vio brn 25 7
416 A160 2s dl grn 65 8
417 A161 5s dl vio & brn 4.00 35
418 A162 10s blk & ultra ('47) 5.00 50
Nos. 410-418 (9) 11.89 1.25

No. 415 Surcharged in Black

Habilitada S|o. 0.20

1946

419 A159 20c on 1s vio brn 22 8
a Surcharge reading down 8.25 8.25

Demand, as well as supply, determines a stamp's market value. One is as important as the other.

A174

A175

A176

A177

A178

Overprint: "Habilitada I Congreso Nac. de Turismo Lima-1947"

Perf. 12½

1947, Apr. 15 Litho. Unwmk.

420 A174 15c blk & car 25 14
421 A175 1s olive brn 38 20
422 A176 1.35s yel grn 38 25
423 A177 3s Prus blue 80 50
424 A178 5s dull grn 1.90 90
Nos. 420-424 (5) 3.71 1.99

1st National Tourism Congress, Lima. The basic stamps were prepared, but not issued, for the 5th Pan American Highway Congress of 1944.

Catalogue values for unused stamps in this section, from this point to the end of the section, are for Never Hinged items.

Types of 1938
Imprint: "Waterlow & Sons Limited, Londres."

Perf. 13x13½, 13½x13

1949-51 Photo.

426 A154 4c chocolate 5 5
427 A156 15c aquamarine 6 5
428 A157 20c blue vio 9 5
429 A158 50c red brn 18 5
430 A159 1s blk brn 35 6
431 A160 2s ultra 75 12

Engr.
Perf. 12½

432 A161 5s ultra & red brn ('50) 90 38
433 A162 10s dk bl grn & blk ('51) 2.25 75
Nos. 426-433 (8) 4.63 1.51

Monument to Admiral Miguel L. Grau — A179

1949, June 6 *Perf. 12½*

434 A179 10c ultra & bl grn 12 5

Types of 1938
Imprint: "Inst. de Grav. Paris."

1951 *Perf. 12½x12, 12x12½*

438 A156 15c peacock grn 6 5
439 A157 20c violet 8 5
440 A158 50c org brn 12 5
441 A159 1s dark brn 22 8

Nos. 375 and 438 Surcharged in Black

HABILITADA
S|. 0.01

1951-52 *Perf. 12½, 12½x12*

445 A153 1c on 2c emer 5 5
446 A156 10c on 15c pck grn 6 5
446A A156 10c on 15c pck grn (small surcharge)('52) 6 5

On No. 446A "Sl. 0.10" is in smaller type measuring 11½mm See No. 456.

Nos. 445-446A exist with surcharge double.

Water Promenade — A180

Post Boy — A181

Designs: 4c, 50c, 1s, 2s, Various buildings, Lima. 20c, Post Office Street, Lima. 5s, Lake Llangamuco, Ancachs. 10s, Ruins of Machu-Picchu.

Overprint: "V Congreso Panamericano de Carreteras 1951"

1951, Oct. 13 Unwmk. *Perf. 12*

Black Overprint

447 A180 2c dk grn 5 5
448 A180 4c brt red 6 5
449 A181 15c gray 9 5
450 A181 20c ol brn 12 5
451 A180 50c dp plum 14 6
452 A180 1s blue 22 8
453 A180 2s dp bl 35 12
454 A180 5s brn lake 1.10 1.10
455 A181 10s chocolate 1.90 90
Nos. 447-455 (9) 4.03 2.46

5th Pan-American Congress of Highways, 1951.

No. 438 Surcharged in Black

HABILITADA
S|o. 0.05

1952 Unwmk. *Perf. 12½x12*

456 A156 5c on 15c pck grn 8 5

Tourist Hotel, Tacna A182

Vicuna A183

Contour Farming, Cuzco A184

Gen. Marcos Perez Jimenez A185

Designs: 5c, Fishing boat and principal fish. 10c, Matarani. 15c, Locomotive No. 80 and coaches. 25c, Engineering school. 30c, Ministry of Public Health and Social Assistance. 1s, Paramonga fortress. 2s, Monument to Native Farmer.

Imprint: "Thomas De La Rue & Co. Ltd."

Perf. 13, 12 (A184)

1952-53 Litho. Unwmk.

457 A182 2c red lil ('53) 6 5
458 A182 5c green 6 5
459 A182 10c yel grn ('53) 14 5
460 A182 15c gray ('53) 6 5
461 A183 20c red brn ('53) 38 12
462 A182 25c rose red 14 5
463 A182 30c indigo ('53) 9 5
464 A184 50c green ('53) 45 8
465 A184 1s brown 30 6
466 A184 2s Prus grn ('53) 35 9
Nos. 457-466 (10) 2.03 65

See Nos. 468-478, 483-488, 497-501, C184-C185, C209.

1956, July 25 Engr. *Perf. 13½x13*

467 A185 25c brown 6 5

Visit of Gen. Marcos Perez Jimenez, Pres. of Venezuela, June 1955.

Types of 1952-53
Designs as before
Imprint: "Thomas De La Rue & Co. Ltd."

1957-59 Litho. *Perf. 13, 12*

468 A182 15c brown ('59) 25 5
469 A182 25c green ('59) 25 5
470 A182 30c rose red 14 6
471 A184 50c dull pur 22 6
472 A184 1s lt vio bl 30 8
473 A184 2s gray ('58) 42 12
Nos. 468-473 (6) 1.58 42

Types of 1952-53
Designs as Before
Imprint: "Joh. Enschedé en Zonen-Holland"

Perf. 12½x13½, 13½x12½, 13x14.

1960 Litho. Unwmk.

474 A183 20c lt red brn 18 5
475 A182 30c lil rose 12 5
476 A184 50c rose vio 14 5
477 A184 1s lt vio bl 20 6
478 A184 2s gray 42 9
Nos. 474-478 (5) 1.06 30

No. 475 measures 33x22mm. No. 470 measures 32x22½mm.

Symbols of the Eucharist A186

Trumpeting Angels A187

Design: 50c, Cross and "JHS".

1960, Aug. 10 Photo. *Perf. 11½*

479 A186 50c ultra, blk & dk red 12 8
480 A186 1s multi 25 12

Nos. 479-480 were intended for voluntary use to help finance the 6th National Eucharistic Congress at Piura, Aug. 25-28, 1960. Authorized for payment of postage on day of issue only, Aug. 10, but through misunderstanding within the Peruvian postal service they were accepted for payment of postage by some post offices until late in December. Reauthorized for postal use, they were again sold and used, starting in July, 1962. See Nos. RA37-RA38.

1961, Dec. 20 Litho. *Perf. 10½*

481 A187 20c brt bl 28 7

Christmas. Valid for postage for one day, Dec. 20. Used thereafter as a voluntary seal to benefit a fund for postal employees.

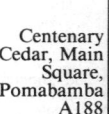

Centenary Cedar, Main Square, Pomabamba A188

Unwmk.

1962, Sept. 7 Engr. *Perf. 13*

482 A188 1s red & grn 40 14

Cent. (in 1961) of Pomabamba province.

Types of 1952-53

Designs: 20c, Vicuña. 30c, Port of Matarani. 40c, Gunboat. 50c, Contour farming. 60c, Tourist hotel, Tacna. 1s, Paramonga, Inca fortress.

Imprint: "Thomas De La Rue & Co. Ltd."

Perf. 13x13½, 13½x13, 12 (A184)

1962, Nov. 19 Litho. Wmk. 346

483 A183 20c rose claret 14 7
484 A182 30c dark blue 10 5
485 AP49 40c orange 14 5
486 A184 50c lt bluish grn 14 5
487 A182 60c grnsh blk 16 7
488 A184 1s rose 22 10
Nos. 483-488 (6) 90 39

Wheat Emblem and Symbol of Agriculture, Industry — A189

1963, July 23 Unwmk. *Perf. 12½*

489 A189 1s red org & ocher 12 7

FAO "Freedom from Hunger" campaign. See No. C190.

Alliance for Progress Emblem A190

Pacific Fair Emblem A191

1964, June 22 Litho. *Perf. 12x12½*

490 A190 40c multi 5 5

Alliance for Progress. See note after US No. 1234. See Nos. C192-C193.

1965, Oct. 30 Litho. *Perf. 12x12½*

491 A191 1.50s multi 10 7
492 A191 2.50s multi 20 10
493 A191 3.50s multi 25 16

4th Intl. Pacific Fair, Lima, Oct. 30-Nov. 14.

Santa Claus and Letter A192

1965, Nov. 2 *Perf. 11*

494 A192 20c red & blk 10 5
495 A192 50c grn & blk 16 5
496 A192 1s bl & blk 35 7

Christmas. Valid for postage for one day, Nov. 2. Used Nov. 3, 1965-Jan. 31, 1966, as voluntary seals for the benefit of a fund for postal employees. See Nos. 522-524.

Types of 1952-62

Designs: 20c, Vicuña. 30c, Port of Matarani. 40c, Gunboat. 50c, Contour farming. 1s, Paramonga, Inca fortress.

Imprint: "I.N.A."

Perf. 12, 13½x14 (A184)

1966, Aug. 8 Litho. Unwmk.

497 A183 20c brn red 5 5
498 A182 30c dk bl 5 5
499 AP49 40c orange 5 5
500 A184 50c gray grn 7 5
501 A184 1s rose 10 5
Nos. 497-501 (5) 32 25

Postal Tax Stamps Nos. RA40, RA43 Surcharged

XHabilitadoX

XX
Habilitado

S.0.10
a

S/. 0.10
b

Perf. 14x14½, 12½x12

1966, May 9 Litho.

501A PT11 (a) 10c on 2c lt brn 5 5
501B PT14 (b) 10c on 3c lt car 5 5

Map of Peru, Cordillera Central and Pelton Wheel A193

1966, Nov. 24 Photo. *Perf. 13½x14*

502 A193 70c bl, blk & vio bl 8 7

Opening of the Huinco Hydroelectric Center. See No. C205.

Inca Wind Vane and Sun A194

Perf. 13½x14

1967, Apr. 18 Photo. Unwmk.

503 A194 90c dp lil rose, blk & gold 8 5

6-year building program. See No. C212.

Pacific Fair Emblem A195

Indian and Wheat A197

Gold Alligator, Mochica Culture A196

1967, Oct. 9 Photo. *Perf. 12*

504 A195 1s gold, dk grn & blk 8 5

5th Intl. Pacific Fair, Lima, Oct. 27-Nov. 12. See No. C216.

1968, Aug. 16 Photo. *Perf. 12*
Sculptures in Gold Yellow and Brown

Designs (gold sculptures of the pre-Inca Yunca tribes): 2.60s, Bird (vert.). 3.60s, Lizard. 4.60s, Bird (vert.). 5.60s, Jaguar.

505 A196 1.90s dp magenta 14 8
506 A196 2.60s black 16 10
507 A196 3.60s dp magenta 25 14
508 A196 4.60s black 30 14
509 A196 5.60s dp magenta 35 16
Nos. 505-509 (5) 1.20 62

See Nos. B1-B5.

1969, Mar. 3 Litho. *Perf. 11*
Black Surcharge

Designs: 3s, 4s, Farmer digging in field.

510 A197 2.50s on 90c brn & yel 14 10
511 A197 3s on 90c lil & brn 16 14
512 A197 4s on 90c rose & grn 22 16
Nos. 510-512,C232-C233 (5) 1.12 76

Agrarian Reform Law.

Nos. 510-512 were not issued without surcharge.

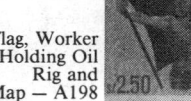

Flag, Worker Holding Oil Rig and Map — A198

1969, Apr. 9 Litho. *Perf. 12*

513 A198 2.50s multi 14 10
514 A198 3s gray & multi 16 14
515 A198 4s lil & multi 20 16
516 A198 5.50s lt bl & multi 25 20

Nationalization of the Brea Parinas oilfields, Oct. 9, 1968.

Kon Tiki Raft, Globe and Jet — A199

1969, June 17 Litho. *Perf. 11*

517 A199 2.50s dp bl & multi 14 7
Nos. 517,C238-C241 (5) 76 55

1st Peruvian Airlines (APSA) flight to Europe.

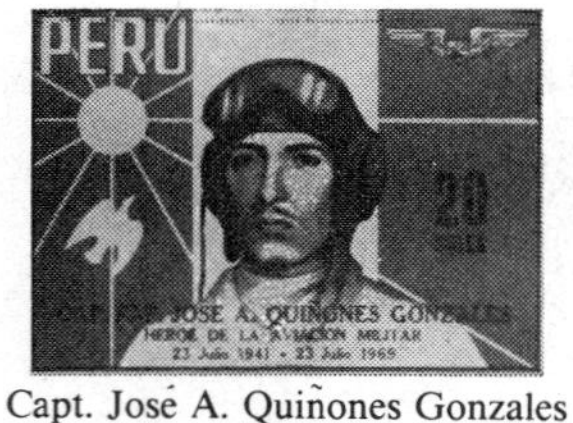

Capt. José A. Quiñones Gonzales (1914-41), Military Aviator — A200

1969, July 23 Litho. *Perf. 11*

518 A200 20s red & multi 1.20 60

See No. C243.

Freed Andean Farmer A201

1969, Aug. 28 Litho. *Perf. 11*

519 A201 2.50s dk bl, lt bl & red 14 8

Enactment of the Agrarian Reform Law of June 24, 1969. See Nos. C246-C247.

Adm. Miguel Grau A202

1969, Oct. 8 Litho. *Perf. 11*

520 A202 50s dk bl & multi 2.25 1.65

Issued for Navy Day.

Flags and "6" — A203

1969, Nov. 14

521 A203 2.50s gray & multi 12 8

6th Intl. Pacific Trade Fair, Lima, Nov. 14-30. See Nos. C251-C252.

Santa Claus Type of 1965

Design: Santa Claus and letter inscribed "FELIZ NAVIDAD Y PROSPERO AÑO NUEVO."

1969, Dec. 1 Litho. *Perf. 11*

522 A192 20c red & blk 5 5
523 A192 20c org & blk 5 5
524 A192 20c brn & blk 5 5

Christmas. Valid for postage for one day, Dec. 1, 1969. Used after that date as postal tax stamps.

Gen. Francisco Bolognesi and Soldier — A204

Puma-shaped Jug, Vicus Culture — A205

1969, Dec. 9

525 A204 1.20s lt ultra, blk & gold 10 5

Army Day, Dec. 9. See No. C253.

1970, Feb. 23 Litho. *Perf. 11*

526 A205 2.50s buff, blk & brn 14 8
Nos. 526,C281-C284 (5) 1.20 85

Ministry of Transport and Communications A206

1970, Apr. 1 Litho. *Perf. 11*

527 A206 40c org & gray 5 5
528 A206 40c gray & lt gray 5 5
529 A206 40c brick red & gray 5 5
530 A206 40c brt pink & gray 5 5
531 A206 40c org brn & gray 5 5
Nos. 527-531 (5) 25 25

Ministry of Transport and Communications, 1st anniv.

Anchovy A207

Fish: No. 533, Pacific hake.

1970, Apr. 30 Litho. *Perf. 11*

532 A207 2.50s vio bl & multi 14 7
533 A207 2.50s vio bl & multi 14 7
Nos. 532-533,C285-C287 (5) 85 40

Nos. 532-533 are printed se-tenant in sheet with Nos. C285-C287, arranged in horizontal strips of five.

Composite Head; Soldier and Farmer — A208

1970, June 24 Litho. *Perf. 11*

534 A208 2.50s gold & multi 16 7

"United people and army building a new Peru." See Nos. C290-C291.

Cadets, Chorrillos College, and Arms A209

Coat of Arms and: No. 536, Cadets of La Punta Naval College. No. 537, Cadets of Las Palmas Air Force College.

1970, July 27 Litho. *Perf. 11*

535 A209 2.50s blk & multi 42 16
536 A209 2.50s blk & multi 42 16
537 A209 2.50s blk & multi 42 16

Peru's military colleges. Nos. 535-537 printed se-tenant.

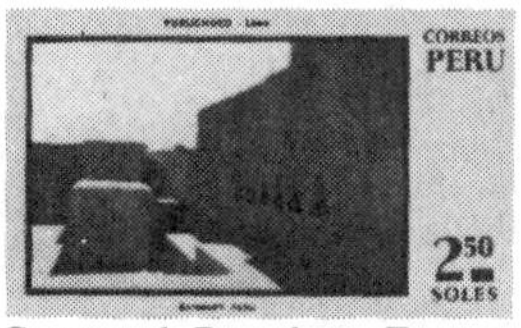

Courtyard, Puruchuco Fortress, Lima — A210

1970, Aug. 6

538 A210 2.50s multi 14 7
Nos. 538,C294-C297 (5) 1.27 58

Issued for tourist publicity.

Nativity, Cuzco School A211

Christmas paintings: 1.50s, Adoration of the Kings, Cuzco School. 1.80s, Adoration of the Shepherds, Peruvian School.

1970, Dec. 23 Litho. *Perf. 11*

539 A211 1.20s multi 5 5
540 A211 1.50s multi 7 5
541 A211 1.80s multi 10 5

St. Rosa of Lima — A212

1971, Apr. 12 Litho. *Perf. 11*

542 A212 2.50s multi 14 7

300th anniv. of the canonization of St. Rosa of Lima (1586-1617), first saint born in the Americas.

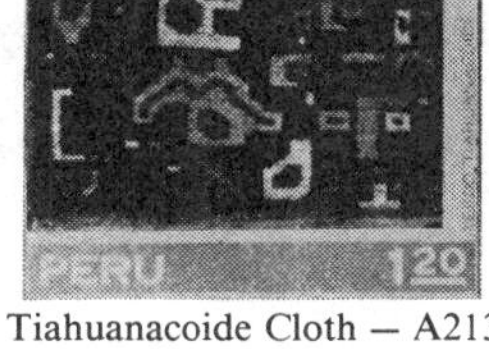

Tiahuanacoide Cloth — A213

Design: 2.50s, Chancay cloth.

1971, Apr. 19

543 A213 1.20s bl & multi 10 5
544 A213 2.50s yel & multi 20 7
Nos. 543-544,C306-C308 (5) 1.32 43

The only foreign revenue stamps listed in this Catalogue are those authorized for prepayment of postage.

Nazca Sculpture, 5th Century, and Seriolella — A214

1971, June 7 Litho. *Perf. 11*

545 A214 1.50s multi 14 5
Nos. 545,C309-C312 (5) 2.02 57

Publicity for 200-mile zone of sovereignty of the high seas.

Mateo Garcia Pumacahua A215

Portraits: No. 547, Mariano Melgar. No. 548, Micaela Bastidas. No. 549, Jose Faustino Sanchez Carrion. No. 550, Francisco Antonia de Zela. No. 551, Jose Baquijano y Carrillo. No. 552, Martin Jorge Guise.

1971

546 A215 1.20s ver & blk 7 5
547 A215 1.20s gray & multi 7 5
548 A215 1.50s dk bl & multi 8 5
549 A215 2s dk bl & multi 10 5
550 A215 2.50s ultra & multi 14 7
551 A215 2.50s gray & multi 14 7
552 A215 2.50s dk bl & multi 14 7
Nos. 546-552 (7) 74 41

150th anniv. of independence, and to honor the heroes of the struggle for independence.

Issue dates: Nos. 546, 550, May 10; Nos. 547, 551, July 5; Nos. 548-549, 552, July 27.

See Nos. C313-C325.

Gongora Portentosa — A216

Designs: Various Peruvian orchids.

1971, Sept. 27 *Perf. 13½x13*

553 A216 1.50s pink & multi 12 5
554 A216 2s pink & multi 16 5
555 A216 2.50s pink & multi 18 7
556 A216 3s pink & multi 22 8
557 A216 3.50s pink & multi 35 8
Nos. 553-557 (5) 1.03 33

"Progress of Liberation," by Teodoro Nunez Ureta A217

Design: 3.50s, Detail from painting by Teodoro Nunez Ureta.

1971, Nov. 4 *Perf. 13x13½*

558 A217 1.20s multi 7 5
559 A217 3.50s multi 20 10

2nd Ministerial meeting of the "Group of 77." See No. C331.

Plaza de Armas, Lima, 1843 — A218

Design: 3.50s, Plaza de Armas, Lima, 1971.

1971, Nov. 6

560 A218 3s pale grn & blk 25 8
561 A218 3.50s lt brick red & blk 35 10

3rd Annual Intl. Stamp Exhibition, EXFILIMA '71, Lima, Nov. 6-14.

Army Coat of Arms — A219

1971, Dec. 9 Litho. *Perf. 13½x13*

562 A219 8.50s multi 55 20

Sesquicentennial of Peruvian Army.

Flight into Egypt A220

Old Stone Sculptures of Huamanga: 2.50s, Three Kings. 3s, Nativity.

1971, Dec. 18 *Perf. 13x13½*

563 A220 1.80s multi 18 5
564 A220 2.50s multi 25 7
565 A220 3s gray & multi 35 8

Christmas. See Nos. 597-599.

Fisherman, by J. M. Ugarte Elespuru A221

Gold Statuette, Chimu, c. 1500 A222

Paintings by Peruvian Workers: 4s, Threshing Grain in Cajamarca, by Camilo Blas. 6s, Huanca Highlanders, by JoseSabogal.

1971, Dec. 30 *Perf. 13½x13*

566 A221 3.50s blk & multi 35 10
567 A221 4s blk & multi 42 10
568 A221 6s blk & multi 60 14

To publicize the revolution and change of order.

1972, Jan. 31 Litho. *Perf. 13½x13*

Ancient Jewelry: 4s, Gold drummer, Chimu. 4.50s, Quartz figurine, Lambayeque culture, 5th century. 5.40s, Gold necklace and pendant, Mochiqua, 4th century. 6s, Gold insect, Lambayeque culture, 14th century.

569 A222 3.90s red, blk & ocher 30 10
570 A222 4s red, blk & ocher 30 10
571 A222 4.50s brt bl, blk & ocher 38 10

572	A222	5.40s red, blk & ocher	42	12
573	A222	6s red, blk & ocher	50	14
		Nos. 569-573 (5)	1.90	56

Popeye Catalufa A223

Fish: 1.50s, Guadara. 2.50s, Jack mackerel.

1972, Mar. 20 *Perf. 13x13½*

574	A223	1.20s lt bl & multi	8	5
575	A223	1.50s lt bl & multi	10	5
576	A223	2.50s lt bl & multi	16	7
		Nos. 574-576,C333-C334 (5)	89	39

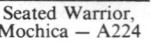

Seated Warrior, Mochica — A224

"Bringing in the Harvest" (July) — A225

Painted pottery jugs of Mochica culture, 5th century: 1.50s, Helmeted head. 2s, Kneeling deer. 2.50s, Helmeted head. 3s, Kneeling warrior.

1972, May 8 *Perf. 13½x13*

Emerald Background

577	A224	1.20s multi	12	5
578	A224	1.50s multi	15	5
579	A224	2s multi	22	5
580	A224	2.50s multi	28	7
581	A224	3s multi	38	7
		Nos. 577-581 (5)	1.15	29

1972-73 **Litho.** *Perf. 13½x13*

Designs: Monthly woodcuts from Calendario Incaico.

Black Vignette & Inscriptions

582	A225	2.50s red brn, *July*	35	7
583	A225	3s grn, *Aug.*	60	7
584	A225	2.50s rose, *Sept.*	35	7
585	A225	3s lt bl, *Oct.*	50	7
586	A225	2.50s org, *Nov.*	50	7
587	A225	3s lil, *Dec.*	50	7
588	A225	2.50s brn, *Jan.* ('73)	35	7
589	A225	3s pale grn, *Feb.* ('73)	50	7
590	A225	2.50s bl, *Mar.* ('73)	35	7
591	A225	3s org, *Apr.* ('73)	50	7
592	A225	2.50s lil rose, *May* ('73)	35	7
593	A225	3s yel & blk *June* ('73)	50	7
		Nos. 582-593 (12)	5.35	84

400th anniversary of publication of the Calendario Incaico by Felipe Guaman Poma de Ayala.

Family Tilling Field — A226

Oil Derricks — A228

Sovereignty of the Sea (Inca Frieze) A227

Perf. 13½x13, 13x13½

1972, Oct. 31 **Litho.**

594	A226	2s multi	10	5
595	A227	2.50s multi	14	7
596	A228	3s gray & multi	16	7

4th anniversaries of land reforms and the nationalization of the oil industry and 15th anniversary of the claim to a 200-mile zone of sovereignty of the sea.

Christmas Type of 1971

Sculptures from Huamanga, 17-18th cent.: 1.50s, Holy Family, wood (vert.). 2s, Holy Family with lambs, stone. 2.50s, Holy Family in stable, stone (vert.).

1972, Nov. 30

597	A220	1.50s buff & multi	10	5
598	A220	2s buff & multi	14	5
599	A220	2.50s buff & multi	16	7

Morning Glory — A228a

Mayor on Horseback, by Fierro — A229

1972, Dec. 29 **Litho.** *Perf. 13*

600	A228a	1.50s shown	10	5
601	A228a	2.50s Amaryllis	16	7
602	A228a	3s Liabum excelsum	20	7
603	A228a	3.50s Bletia (orchid)	22	8
604	A228a	5s Cantua buxifolia	28	14
		Nos. 600-604 (5)	96	41

1973, Aug. 13 **Litho.** *Perf. 13*

Paintings by Francisco Pancho Fierro (1803-1879): 2s, Man and Woman, 1830. 2.50s, Padre Abregu Riding Mule. 3.50s, Dancing Couple. 4.50s, Bullfighter Estevan Arredondo on Horseback.

605	A229	1.50s sal & multi	10	5
606	A229	2s sal & multi	14	5
607	A229	2.50s sal & multi	16	9
608	A229	3.50s sal & multi	22	10
609	A229	4.50s sal & multi	40	16
		Nos. 605-609 (5)	1.02	45

Presentation in the Temple A230

Christmas Paintings of the Cuzqueña School: 2s, Holy Family (vert.). 2.50s, Adoration of the Kings.

1973, Nov. 30 **Litho.** *Perf. 13x13½*

610	A230	1.50s multi	8	5
611	A230	2s multi	10	5
612	A230	2.50s multi	14	7

Peru No. 20 — A231

1974, Mar. 1 **Litho.** *Perf. 13*

613	A231	6s gray & dk bl	40	16

Peruvian Philatelic Assoc., 25th anniv.

Non-ferrous Smelting Plant, La Oroya A232

Colombia Bridge, San Martin A233

Designs: 8s, 10s, Different views, Santiago Antunez Dam, Tayacaja.

1974 **Litho.** *Perf. 13x13½*

614	A232	1.50s blue	5	5
615	A233	2s multi	7	5
616	A232	3s rose claret	12	7
617	A232	4.50s green	16	12
618	A233	8s multi	30	16
619	A233	10s multi	38	20
		Nos. 614-619 (6)	1.08	65

"Peru Determines its Destiny."
Issue Dates: 2s, 8s, 10s, July 1. 1.50s, 3s, 4.50s, Dec. 6.

Battle of Junin, by Felix Yanez A234

Design: 2s, 3s, Battle of Ayacucho, by Felix Yanez.

1974 **Litho.** *Perf. 13x13½*

620	A234	1.50s multi	10	5
621	A234	2s multi	10	5
622	A234	2.50s multi	14	10
623	A234	3s multi	16	10

Sesquicentennial of the Battles of Junin and Ayacucho.
Issue dates: 1.50s, 2.50s, Aug. 6. 2s, 3s, Oct. 9.
See Nos. C400-C404.

Indian Madonna — A235

1974, Dec. 20 **Litho.** *Perf. 13½x13*

624	A235	1.50s multi	8	5

Christmas. See No. C417.

Maria Parado de Bellido A236

International Women's Year Emblem — A237

IWY Emblem, Peruvian Colors and: 2s, Micaela Bastidas. 2.50s, Juana Alarco de Dammert.

Perf. 13x13½, 13½x13

1975, Sept. 8 **Litho.**

625	A236	1.50s bl grn, red & blk	7	5
626	A237	2s blk & red	8	5
627	A236	2.50s pink, blk & red	10	5
628	A237	3s red, blk & ultra	16	5

International Women's Year.

St. Juan Macias — A238

1975, Nov. 14 *Perf. 13½x13*

629	A238	5s blk & multi	25	10

Canonization of Juan Macias in 1975.

Louis Braille A239

1976, Mar. 2 **Litho.** *Perf. 13x13½*

630	A239	4.50s gray, red & blk	16	10

Sesquicentennial of the invention of Braille system of writing for the blind by Louis Braille (1809-1852).

Peruvian Flag — A240

1976, Aug. 29 **Litho.** *Perf. 13x13½*

631	A240	5s gray, blk & red	16	10

Revolutionary Government, Phase II, 1st anniversary.

St. Francis, by El Greco — A241

Indian Mother — A242

1976, Dec. 9 **Litho.** *Perf. 13½x13*

632	A241	5s gold, buff & brn	25	10

St. Francis of Assisi, 750th death anniv.

1976, Dec. 23

633	A242	4s multi	25	8

Christmas.

Chasqui Messenger A243

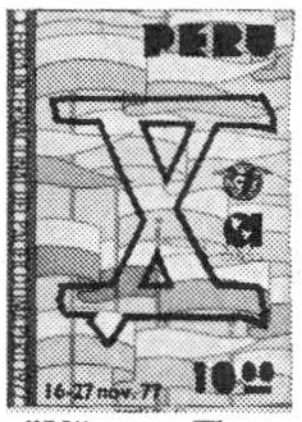

"X" over Flags A244

1977 Litho. *Perf. 13½x13*

634	A243	6s grnsh bl & blk	25	14
635	A243	8s red & blk	25	14
636	A243	10s ultra & blk	50	25
637	A243	12s lt grn & blk	50	35

See Nos. C465-C467.

1977, Nov. 25 Litho. *Perf. 13½x13*

638	A244	10s multi	20	10

10th Intl. Pacific Fair, Lima, Nov. 16-27.

Republican Guard Badge — A245

Indian Nativity — A246

1977, Dec. 1

639	A245	12s multi	22	14

58th anniversary of Republican Guard.

1977, Dec. 23

640	A246	8s multi	14	7

Christmas. See No. C484.

Nos. 495, 494, 496 Surcharged with New Value and Bar in Red, Dark Blue or Black: "FRANQUEO / 10.00 / RD-0161-77"

1977, Dec. *Perf. 11*

641	A192	10s on 50c grn & blk (R)	25	10
642	A192	20s on 20c red & blk (DB)	50	20
643	A192	30s on 1s bl & blk (B)	65	35

Inca Head — A247

1978 Litho. *Perf. 13½x13*

644	A247	6s brt grn	8	5
645	A247	10s red	14	10
646	A247	16s red brn	20	20
		Nos. 644-646,C486-C489 (7)	3.29	2.52

Flags of Germany, Argentina, Austria, Brazil A248

Argentina '78 Emblem and Flags of Participants: No. 648, 652, Hungary, Iran, Italy, Mexico. No. 649, 653, Scotland, Spain, France, Netherlands. No. 650, 654, Peru, Poland, Sweden and Tunisia. No. 651, like No. 647.

1978 Litho. *Perf. 13x13½*

647	A248	10s bl & multi	20	10
648	A248	10s bl & multi	20	10
649	A248	10s bl & multi	20	10
650	A248	10s bl & multi	20	10
651	A248	16s bl & multi	20	7
652	A248	16s bl & multi	20	7
653	A248	16s bl & multi	20	7
654	A248	16s bl & multi	20	7
		Nos. 647-654 (8)	1.60	68

11th World Soccer Cup Championship, Argentina, June 1-25. Nos. 647-650 and 651-654 printed se-tenant in blocks of 4.

Issue dates: Nos. 647-650, June 28. Nos. 651-654, Dec. 4.

Thomas Faucett, Planes of 1928, 1978 A249

1978, Oct. 19 Litho. *Perf. 13*

655	A249	40s multi	40	25

Faucett Aviation, 50th anniversary.

Nazca Bowl, Huaco A250

1978-79 Litho. *Perf. 13x13½*

656	A250	16s vio bl ('79)	14	7
657	A250	20s green ('79)	16	10
658	A250	25s lt grn ('79)	20	14
659	A250	35s rose red ('79)	35	16
660	A250	45s dk brown	40	22
661	A250	50s black	50	25
662	A250	55s car rose ('79)	50	25
663	A250	70s lil rose ('79)	60	38
664	A250	75s blue	65	40
665	A250	80s salmon ('79)	65	40
667	A250	200s brt vio ('79)	1.65	1.00
		Nos. 656-667 (11)	5.80	3.37

Peruvian Nativity — A252

Ministry of Education, Lima — A253

1978, Dec. 28 Litho. *Perf. 13½x13*

672	A252	16s multi	14	7

1979, Jan. 4

673	A253	16s multi	14	7

National Education Program.

Nos. RA40, B1-B5 and 509 Surcharged in Various Colors. No. RA40 Overprinted also:

Habilitado
Dif.-Porte
S/. 2.00
a

SOBRE TASA OFICIAL
S/. 3.00
b

Habilitado
R.D. Nº 0118
S/. 35.00
c

1978, July-Aug.

674	PT11(a)	2s on 2c (O)	5	5
675	PT11(b)	3s on 2c (Bk)	5	5
676	PT11(a)	4s on 2c (G)	5	5
677	PT11(a)	5s on 2c (V)	5	5
678	PT11(b)	6s on 2c (DBl)	5	5
679	SP1	20s on 1.90s + 90c (G)	65	10
680	SP1	30s on 2.60s + 1.30s (Bl)	65	16
681	PT11(c)	35s on 2c (C)	22	20
682	PT11(c)	50s on 2c (LtBl)	1.65	25
683	SP1	55s on 3.60s + 1.80s (VBl)	80	30
684	SP1	65s on 4.60s + 2.30s (Go)	80	35
685	A196	80s on 5.60s (VBl)	55	40
686	SP1	85s on 20s + 10s (Bk)	1.20	40
		Nos. 674-686 (13)	6.77	2.41

Surcharge on Nos. 679-680, 683-684, 686 includes heavy bar over old denomination.

Battle of Iquique A254

Heroes' Crypt A255

Col. Francisco Bolognesi A256

War of the Pacific: No. 688, Col. Jose J. Inclan. No. 689, Corvette Union running Arica blockade. No. 690, Battle of Angamos, Aguirre, Miguel Grau (1838-1879), Perre. No. 690A, Lt. Col. Pedro Ruiz Gallo. 85s, Marshal Andres A. Caceres. No. 692, Naval Battle of Angamos. No. 697, Col. Bolognesi's Reply, by Angeles de la Cruz. No. 698, Col. Alfonso Ugarte on horseback.

Perf. 13½x13, 13x13½

1979-80 Litho.

687	A254	14s multi	8	5
688	A256	25s multi	35	12
689	A254	25s multi	16	12
690	A254	25s multi	22	12
690A	A256	25s multi ('80)	16	12
691	A256	85s multi	55	40
692	A254	100s multi	65	42
693	A254	100s multi	65	42
694	A256	115s multi	1.20	45
695	A255	200s multi	4.00	80
696	A256	200s multi	1.20	80
697	A254	200s multi	1.20	80
698	A254	200s multi	1.20	80
		Nos. 687-698 (13)	11.62	5.42

Peruvian Red Cross, Cent. A257

1979, May 4 *Perf. 13x13½*

699	A257	16s multi	10	10

Billiard Balls — A258

Arms of Cuzco — A259

1979, June 4 *Perf. 13½x13*

700	A258	34s multi	25	14

1979, June 24

701	A259	50s multi	35	20

Inca Sun Festival, Cuzco.

Peru Colors, Tacna Monument A260

Telecom 79 A261

1979, Aug. 28 Litho. *Perf. 13½x13*

702	A260	16s multi	14	7

Return of Tacna Province to Peru, 50th anniv.

1979, Sept. 20

703	A261	15s multi	10	7

3rd World Telecommunications Exhibition, Geneva, Sept. 20-26.

Caduceus — A262

Gold Jewelry — A264

World Map, "11," Fair Emblem A263

1979, Nov. 13

704	A262	25s multi	20	12

Stomatology Academy of Peru, 50th anniv.; 4th Intl. Congress.

1979, Nov. 24

705	A263	55s multi	38	25

11th Pacific Intl. Trade Fair, Lima, Nov. 14-25.

1979, Dec. 19 *Perf. 13½x13*

706	A264	85s multi	55	40

Larco Herrera Archaeological Museum.

Christmas A265

1979, Dec. 27 Litho. *Perf. 13x13½*

707	A265	25s multi	20	12

Queen Sofia and King Juan Carlos I, Visit to Peru — A266

1979 **Litho.** ***Perf. 13x13½***
708 A266 75s multi 55 15

No. RA40 Surcharged in Black, Green or Blue

1979, Oct. 8
709 PT11 7s on 2c brn 5 5
710 PT11 9s on 2c brn (G) 7 5
711 PT11 15s on 2c brn (B) 10 7

Nos. 702, 687, 700, 663 Surcharged
Perf. 13½x13, 13x13½
1980, Apr. 14 **Litho.**
712 A260 20s on 16s multi 14 10
713 A254 25s on 14s multi 16 12
714 A258 65s on 34s multi 42 35
715 A250 80s on 70s lil rose 55 40
Nos. 712-715,C501-C502 (6) 1.79 1.32

Liberty Holding Arms of Peru — A267

Chimu Cult Cup — A268

Civic duties: 15s, Respect the Constitution. 20s, Honor country. 25s, Vote. 30s, Military service. 35s, Pay taxes. 45s, Contribute to national progress. 50s, Respect rights.

1980 **Litho.**
716 A267 15s grnsh bl 10 7
717 A267 20s sal pink 14 10
718 A267 25s ultra 16 12
719 A267 30s lil rose 20 15
720 A267 35s black 22 16
721 A267 45s lt bl grn 30 22
722 A267 50s brown 50 22
Nos. 716-722 (7) 1.62 1.04

1980, July 9 **Litho.**
723 A268 35s multi 22 16

Map of Peru and Liberty — A269

Return to Civilian Government — A270

Perf. 13½x13, 13x13½
1980, Sept. 9 **Litho.**
724 A269 25s multi 16 12
725 A270 35s multi 22 16

Scott's International Album provides spaces for an extensive representative collection of the world's postage stamps.

Machu Picchu A271

1980, Nov. 10 **Litho.** ***Perf. 13x13½***
726 A271 25s multi 16 12

World Tourism Conf., Manila, Sept. 27.

Tupac Amaru Rebellion Bicent. — A272

150th Death Anniv. of Simon Bolivar (in 1980) — A274

Christmas A273

1980, Dec. 22 **Litho.** ***Perf. 13½x13***
727 A272 25s multi 16 12

1980, Dec. 31 **Litho.** ***Perf. 13***
728 A273 15s multi 10 7

1981, Jan. 28 **Litho.** ***Perf. 13½x13***
729 A274 40s multi 30 22

Nos. 725, 667, 694 Surcharged
1981 **Litho.** ***Perf. 13x13½***
730 A270 25s on 35s multi 18 12
731 A250 85s on 200s brt vio 65 50
732 A256 100s on 115s multi 75 60

Return to Constitutional Government, July 28, 1980 — A275

1981, Mar. 26 **Litho.** ***Perf. 13½x13***
733 A275 25s multi 18 14

Tupac Amaru and Micaela Bastidas, Bronze Sculptures, by Miguel Baca-Rossi A276

1981, May 18 **Litho.** ***Perf. 13x13½***
734 A276 60s multi 45 35

Rebellion of Tupac Amaru and Micaela Bastidas, bicentenary.

Nos. 733, RA41 and Voluntary Postal Tax Stamps of 1965 Surcharged in Black, Dull Brown or Lake

Cross, Unleavened Bread, Wheat A276a

Chalice, Host A276b

Perf. 13½x13, Rouletted 11 (#735, 737B), 11½ (#737A)
1981 **Litho., Photo. (#737A-737B)**
735 PT17 40s on 10c No. RA41 9 6
736 A275 40s on 25s No. 733 9 6
737 A275 130s on 25s No. 733 (Dull Brn) 30 20
737A A276a 140s on 50c brn, yel & red 32 20
737B A276b 140s on 1s multi 32 20
737C A275 140s on 25s No. 733 (Lake) 32 20
Nos. 735-737C (6) 1.44 92

Issue dates: No. 735, Apr. 12. Nos. 736, 737, 737C, Apr. 6. No. 737A, Apr. 15. No. 737B, Apr. 28.

Carved Stone Head, Huamachuco Tribe — A277

Designs: Nos. 739, 742, 749 Pottery vase, Inca (vert.). No. 740, Head (diff. vert.). Nos. 743, 749A-749B, Huaco idol (fish), Nazca. 100s, Pallasca (vert.). 140s, Puma.

Perf. 13½x13, 13x13½
1981-82 **Litho.**
738 A277 30s dp rose lil 22 15
739 A277 40s org ('82) 30 18
740 A277 40s ultra 30 18
742 A277 80s brn ('82) 60 38
743 A277 80s red ('82) 60 38
745 A277 100s lil rose 75 50
748 A277 140s lt bl grn 1.00 70
749 A277 180s grn ('82) 1.40 90
749A A277 240s grnsh bl ('82) 90 70
749B A277 280s vio ('82) 1.00 75
Nos. 738-749B (10) 7.07 4.82

Postal and Philatelic Miseum, 50th Anniv. — A278

1981, May 31 ***Perf. 13½x13***
750 A278 130s multi 60 52

1979 Constitution Assembly President Victor Raul Haya de la Torre — A279

1981, Oct. 7 **Litho.** ***Perf. 13½x13***
751 A279 30s pur & gray 22 15

Inca Messenger, by Guaman Poma (1526-1613) A280

Intl. Year of the Disabled A280a

1981 **Litho.** ***Perf. 12***
752 A280 30s lilac & blk 22 15
753 A280 40s ver & blk 18 38
754 A280 130s brt yel grn & blk 50 38
755 A280 140s brt bl & blk 50 38
756 A280 200s yel brn & blk 75 58
Nos. 752-756 (5) 2.15 1.87

Christmas. Issue dates: 30s, 40s, 200s, Dec. 21; others, Dec. 31.

1981 **Litho.** ***Perf. 13½x13***
756A A280a 100s multi 60 38

Nos. 377, C130, C143, J56, O33, RA36, RA39, RA40, RA42, RA43 Surcharged in Brown, Black, Orange, Red, Green or Blue

1982
757 PT11 10s on 2c (#RA40, Br) 18 12
758 A155 10s on 10c (#377, Bk) 5 5
758A AP60 40s on 1.25s (#C143, Bk) 9 6
758B PT15 70s on 5c (#RA36, R) 16 12
759 D7 80s on 10c (#J56, Bk) 15 9
760 O1 80s on 10c (#O33, Bk) 15 9
761 PT14 80s on 3c (#RA43, O) 15 9
762 PT17 100s on 10c (#RA42, R) 18 12
763 AP57 100s on 2.20s (#C130, R) 18 12
764 PT14 150s on 3c (#RA39, G) 28 18
765 PT14 180s on 3c (#RA43, R) 35 22
766 PT14 200s on 3c (#RA43, Bl) 38 25
767 AP60 240s on 1.25s (#C143, R) 45 30
768 PT15 280s on 5c (#RA36, Bk) 52 35
Nos. 757-768 (14) 3.27 2.16

Nos. 758A, 763, 767 airmail. Nos. 759 and 760 surcharged "Habilitado / Franq. Postal / 80 Soles".

Jorge Basadre (1903-1908), Historian — A281

Julio C. Tello (1882-1947), Archaeologist A282

Perf. 13½x13, 13x13½
1982, Oct. 13 **Litho.**
769 A281 100s pale grn & blk 18 12
770 A282 200s lt grn & dk bl 35 25

9th Women's World Volleyball Championship, Sept. 12-26 — A283

Rights of the Disabled — A284

1982, Oct. 18 *Perf. 12*
771 A283 80s blk & red 15 9

1982, Oct. 22
772 A284 200s bl & red 35 25

Brena Campaign Centenary A285

1982, Oct. 26 *Perf. 13x13½*
773 A285 70s Andres Caceres medallion 12 7

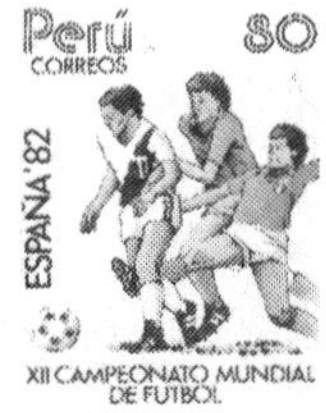

1982 World Cup — A286

16th Intl. Congress of Latin Notaries, Lima, June — A287

1982, Nov. 2 *Perf. 12*
774 A286 80s multi 15 9

1982, Nov. 6
775 A287 500s Emblem 90 60

Handicrafts Year — A288

1982, Nov. 24 *Perf. 13x13½*
776 A288 200s Clay bull figurine 35 25

Christmas A289

Pedro Vilcapaza A290

1982 *Perf. 13½x13*
777 A289 280s Holy Family 52 35

1982, Dec. 2 *Perf. 13½x13*
778 A290 240s blk & lt brn 45 30

Death centenary of Indian leader against Spanish during Andes Rebellion.

Jose Davila Condemarin (1799-1882), Minister of Posts (1849-76) A291

1982, Dec. 10 *Perf. 13x13½*
779 A291 150s bl & blk 28 18

10th Anniv. of Intl. Potato Study Center, Lima A292

1982, Dec. 27 *Perf. 13x13½*
780 A292 240s multi 45 30

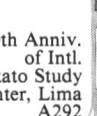

450th Anniv. of City of San Miguel de Piura A293

1982, Dec. 31 *Perf. 13x13½*
781 A293 280s Arms 52 35

TB Bacillus Centenary A294

1983, Jan. 18 *Perf. 12*
782 A294 240s Microscope, slide 45 30

St. Teresa of Jesus of Avila (1515-1582), by Jose Espinoza de los Monteros, 1682 — A295

1983, Mar. 1
783 A295 100s multi 18 12

10th Anniv. of State Security Service A296

1983, Mar. 8
784 A296 100s bl & org 18 12

Horseman's Ornamental Silver Shoe, 19th Cent. A297

1983, Mar. 18
785 A297 250s multi 45 30

30th Anniv. of Santiago Declaration A298

75th Anniv. of Lima and Callao State Lotteries A300

25th Anniv. of Lima-Bogota Airmail Service — A299

1983, Mar. 25
786 A298 280s Map 50 32

1983, Apr. 8
787 A299 150s Jet 28 18

1983, Apr. 26
788 A300 100s multi 18 12

Nos. 739, 773, 771, 778, 780, 782, 781, 786, 777, 749, 774 Surcharged in Black or Green

1983			**Litho.**	
789	A277	100s on 40s org	18	12
790	A285	100s on 70s multi	18	12
791	A283	100s on 80s blk & red	18	12
792	A290	100s on 240s multi	18	12
793	A292	100s on 240s multi	18	12
794	A294	100s on 240s ol grn	18	12
795	A293	150s on 280s multi (G)	25	18
796	A298	150s on 280s multi	25	18
797	A289	200s on 280s multi	38	25
798	A277	300s on 180s grn	58	38
799	A277	400s on 180s grn	75	50
800	A286	500s on 80s multi	90	60
		Nos. 789-800 (12)	4.19	2.81

Military Ships A301

1983, May 2 *Perf. 12*
801 A301 150s Cruiser Almirante Grau, 1907 25 18
802 A301 350s Submarine Ferre, 1913 65 40

Simon Bolivar Birth Bicentenary A302

Christmas A303

1983, Dec. 13 **Litho.** *Perf. 14*
803 A302 100s blk & lt bl 18 12

1983, Dec. 16
804 A303 100s Virgin and Child 18 12

25th Anniv. of Intl. Pacific Fair — A304

Col. Leoncio Prado (1853-83) — A306

World Communications Year (in 1983) — A305

1983
805 A304 350s multi 65 40

1984, Jan. 27 **Litho.** *Perf. 14*
806 A305 700s multi 1.25 90

1984, Feb. 3 **Litho.** *Perf. 14*
807 A306 150s ol & ol brn 10 6

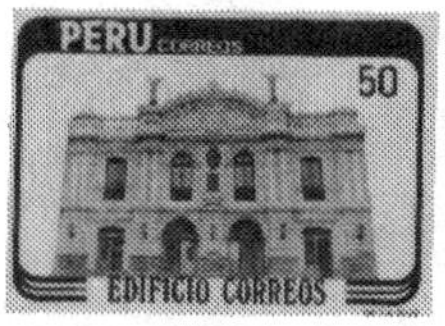

Postal Building A307

Pottery — A308

Arms of City of Callao — A310

Shipbuilding and Repair — A309

Peruvian Flora — A311

Peruvian Fauna — A312

1984		**Litho.**	*Perf. 14*	
808	A307	50s Ministry of Posts, Lima	5	5
809	A308	100s Water jar	6	5
810	A308	150s Llama	10	6
811	A308	200s Painted vase	14	8
812	A309	250s shown	16	12
813	A309	300s Mixed cargo ship	20	12
814	A310	350s shown	22	15
815	A310	400s Arms of Cajamarca	22	15
816	A310	500s Arms of Ayacucho	30	18
817	A311	700s Canna edulis ker	40	28

818 A312 1000s Lagothrix flavicauda 55 38
Nos. 808-818 (11) 2.40 1.62

Issue dates: 400s, June 21; 500s, June 22.
See Nos. 844-855, 884.

Hipolito Unanue (1758-1833) A313

Ricardo Palma (1833-1919), Writer A314

1984, Nov. 14 Litho. *Perf. 14*
819 A313 50s dl grn 5 5

1984, Mar. 20
820 A314 200s purple 14 8

1984 Summer Olympics — A315

1984, Mar. 30
821 A315 500s Shooting 35 22
822 A315 750s Hurdles 50 35

Independence Declaration Act — A316

1984, July 18 Litho. *Perf. 14*
823 A316 350s Signing document 20 15

Admiral Grau — A317

Naval Battle — A318

1984, Oct. 8 Litho. *Perf. 12½*
824 Block of 4 1.10 75
a A317 600s Knight of the Seas, by Pablo Muniz 28 18
b A318 600s Battle of Angamos 28 18
c A317 600s Congressional seat 28 18
d A318 600s Battle of Iquique 28 18

150th Anniv. of the birth of Admiral Miguel Grau.

Peruvian Naval Vessels A319

1984, Dec. Litho. *Perf. 14*
825 A319 250s Destroyer Almirante Guise, 1934 12 6
826 A319 400s Gunboat America, 1905 18 9

Christmas A320

1984, Dec. 11 Litho. *Perf. 13x13½*
827 A320 1000s multi 45 30

Victor Andres Belaunde (1883-1967), President of UN General Assembly, 1959-60 — A321

1984, Dec. 14 Litho. *Perf. 14*
828 A321 100s brn lake 22 12

450th Anniv., Founding of Cuzco — A322

1984, Dec. 20 Litho. *Perf. 13½x13*
829 A322 1000s Street scene 42 28

15th Pacific Intl. Fair, Lima A323

1984, Dec. 28 Litho. *Perf. 13x13½*
830 A323 1000s Llama 42 28

450th Anniv., Lima — A324

Visit of Pope John Paul II — A325

1985, Jan. 17 Litho. *Perf. 13½x13*
831 A324 1500s The Foundation of Lima, by Francisco Gamarra 50 35

1985, Jan. 31 Litho. *Perf. 13½x13*
832 A325 2000s Portrait 52 35

Microwave Tower — A326

Jose Carlos Mariategui (1894-1924), Author — A327

1985, Feb. 28 Litho. *Perf. 13½x13*
833 A326 1100s multi 20 14

ENTEL Peru, Natl. Telecommunications Org., 15th anniv.

1985-86 Photo. *Perf. 13½x13*

Designs: 500s, Francisco Garcia Calderon (1832-1905), president. No. 837, Mariategui. No. 838, Oscar Miro Quesada (1884-1981), jurist. No. 839, Cesar Vallejo (1892-1938), author. No. 840, Jose Santos Chocano (1875-1934), poet.

836 A327 500s lt ol grn 9 6
837 A327 800s dl red 18 12
838 A327 800s dk ol grn 18 12
839 A327 800s Prus bl ('86) 8 5
840 A327 800s dk red brn ('86) 8 5
Nos. 836-840 (5) 61 40

See Nos. 901-905.

American Air Forces Cooperation System, 25th Anniv. — A328

1985, Apr. 16
842 A328 400s Member flags, emblem 14 9

Jose A. Quinones Gonzales (1914-1941), Air Force Captain A329

1985, Apr. 22 *Perf. 13x13½*
843 A329 1000s Portrait, bomber 22 15

Types of 1984

Design: 200s, Entrance arch and arcade, Central PO admin. building, vert. No. 845, Spotted Robles Moqo bisque vase, Pacheco, Ica. No. 846, Huaura bisque cat. No. 847, Robles Moqo bisque llama head. No. 848, Huancavelica city arms. No. 849, Huanuco city arms. No. 850, Puno city arms. No. 851, Llama wool industry. No. 852, Hymenocallis amancaes. No. 853, Penguins, Antarctic landscape.

1985-86 Litho. *Perf. 13½x13*
844 A307 200s sl bl 6 5
845 A308 500s bis brn 9 5
846 A308 500s dl yel brn 9 5
847 A308 500s blk brn 9 5
848 A310 700s brt org yel 18 12
849 A310 700s brt bl ('86) 8 5
850 A310 900s brn ('86) 9 6
851 A309 1100s multi 12 8
852 A311 1100s multi 12 8
853 A312 1500s multi 15 10
Nos. 844-853 (10) 1.07 69

Natl. Aerospace Institute Emblem, Globe A330

1985, May 24 *Perf. 13x13½*
858 A330 900s ultra 20 14

14th Inter-American Air Defense Day.

Founding of Constitution City — A333

1985, July Litho. *Perf. 13½x13*
859 A333 300s Map, flag, crucifix 6 5

Natl. Radio Society, 55th Anniv. A334

1985, July 24 *Perf. 13x13½*
860 A334 1300s bl & brt org 16 12

San Francisco Convent Church — A335

Doctrina Christiana Frontispiece, 1585, Lima — A336

1985, Oct. 12 *Perf. 13½x13*
861 A335 1300s multi 16 12

1985, Oct. 23
862 A336 300s pale buff & blk 8 5

1st printed book in South America, 400th anniv.

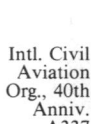

Intl. Civil Aviation Org., 40th Anniv. A337

1985, Oct. 31 *Perf. 13x13½*
863 A337 1100s 1920 Curtis Jenny 14 9

Christmas A338

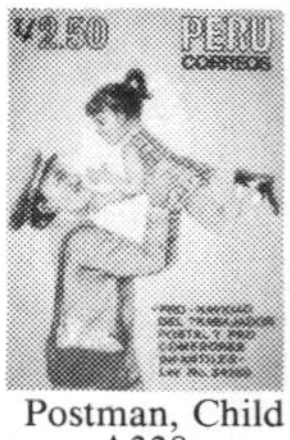

Postman, Child A338a

1985, Dec. 30 Litho. ***Perf. 13½x13***
864 A338 2.50i Virgin and child, 17th cent. 22 15

1985, Dec. 30 Litho. ***Perf. 13½x13***
864A A338a 2.50i multi 28 22

Christmas charity for children's and postal workers' funds.

Founding of Trujillo, 450th Anniv. — A339

1986, Mar. 5 Litho. ***Perf. 13½x13***
865 A339 3i City arms 40 25

Restoration of Chan Chan Ruins, Trujillo Province A340

1986, Apr. 5 Litho. ***Perf. 13x13½***
866 A340 50c Bas-relief 8 6

Santa Rosa de Lima, Birth Quadricent. A341

16th Intl. Pacific Fair A342

1986, Apr. 30 Litho. ***Perf. 13½x13***
867 A341 7i multi 90 60

1986, May 20
868 A342 1i Natl. products symbols, 16 12 8

Intl. Youth Year A343

1986, May 23 ***Perf. 13x13½***
869 A343 3.50i multi 42 28

Pedro Vilcapaza (1740-1781), Independence Hero — A344

1986, June 27 Litho. ***Perf. 13½x13***
870 A344 50c brown 8 6

UN, 40th Anniv. A345

1986, Aug. 8 Litho. ***Perf. 13x13½***
871 A345 3.50i multi 40 30

Fernando and Justo Albujar Fayaque, Manuel Guarniz Lopez, Natl. Heroes — A346

1986, Aug. 11 ***Perf. 13½x13***
872 A346 50c grysh brn 6 5

Peruvian Navy A347

1986, Aug. 19 ***Perf. 13x13½***
873 A347 1.50i R-1, 1926 18 14
874 A347 2.50i Abtao, 1954 30 22

Flora Type of 1984

1986 Litho. ***Perf. 13½x13***
880 A311 80c Tropaeolum majus 10 8
881 A311 80c Datura candida 10 8
884 A312 2i Canis nudus 30 22
885 A312 2i Penelope albipennis 35 28

Canchis Province Folk Costumes — A348

1986, Aug. 26 Litho. ***Perf. 13½x13***
890 A348 3i multi 35 25

Tourism Day — A349

1986, Aug. 29 ***Perf. 13x13½***
891 A349 4i Sacsayhuaman 48 35

1986, Oct. 12 Litho. ***Perf. 13x13½***
891A A349 4i Intihuatana, Cuzco 50 38

Interamerican Development Bank, 25th Anniv. — A350

1986, Sept. 4
892 A350 1i multi 12 10

Beatification of Sr. Ana de Los Angeles A351

1986, Sept. 15
893 A351 6i Sr. Ana, Pope John Paul II 72 55

Jorge Chavez (1887-1910), Aviator, and Bleriot XI 1M — A352

VAN '86 — A353

1986, Sept. 23 ***Perf. 13½x13***
894 A352 5i multi 60 45

Chavez's flight over the Alps, 75th anniv.

1986, Sept. 26
895 A353 50c lt bl 6 5

Ministry of Health vaccination campaign, Sept. 27-28, Oct. 25-26, Nov. 22-23.

Natl. Journalism Day — A354

1986, Oct. 1
896 A354 1.50i multi 18 14

Peruvian Navy A355

1986, Oct. 7 Litho. ***Perf. 13x13½***
897 A355 1i Brigantine Gamarra, 1848 15 12
898 A355 1i Monitor Manco Capac, 1880 15 12

Institute of Higher Military Studies, Caem, 35th Anniv. A356

1986, Oct. 31 Litho. ***Perf. 13x13½***
899 A356 1i multi 18 14

Boy, Girl — A357

1986, Nov. 3 ***Perf. 13½x13***
900 A357 2.50i red, brn & blk 38 30

Christmas charity for children and postal workers' funds.

Famous Peruvians Type of 1985

1986-87
901 A327 50c Carrion 6 5
902 A327 50c Barrenechea 10 8
904 A327 80c Jose de la Riva Aguero ('87) 6 5
905 A327 80c Barrenechea ('87) 6 5

Issue dates: No. 904, Oct. 22. No. 905, Nov. 9.

Christmas A358

SENATI, 25th Anniv. A359

1986, Dec. 3
908 A358 5i St. Joseph and Child 75 58

1986, Dec. 19 ***Perf. 13½x13***
909 A359 4i multi 60 45

Shipibo Tribal Costumes A360

World Food Day A361

1987, Apr. 24 Litho. ***Perf. 13½x13***
910 A360 3i multi 45 35

1987, May 26
911 A361 50c multi 8 6

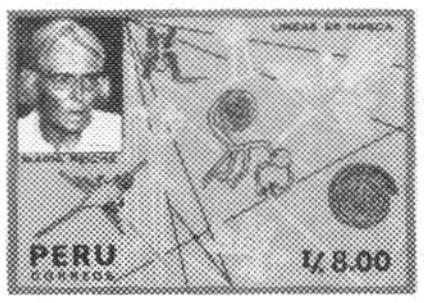

Preservation of the Nasca Lines A362

Design: Nasca Lines and Dr. Maria Reiche (b. 1903), archaeologist.

1987, June 13 Litho. ***Perf. 13x13½***
912 A362 8i multi 1.20 90

A little time given to the study of the arrangement of the Scott Catalogue can make it easier to use effectively.

Mariano Santos (1850-1900), "The Hero of Tarapaca," 1879, Chilean War — A363

1987, July 15 Litho. ***Perf. 13½x13***
913 A363 50c vio 12 8

Dated 1986.

Natl. Horse Club, 50th Anniv. A364

1987, July 19 ***Perf. 13x13½***
914 A364 3i multi 45 35

Dated 1986.

Gen. Felipe Santiago Salaverry (1806-1836), Revolution Leader — A365

1987, Aug 13 ***Perf. 13½x13***
915 A365 2i multi 30 22

Dated 1986.

Colca's Canyon — A366

AMIFIL '87 — A367

1987, Sept. 8 Litho. ***Perf. 13½x13***
916 A366 6i multi 52 38

10th Natl. Philatelic Exposition, Arequipa. Dated 1986.

1987, Sept. 10
917 A367 1i Nos. 1-2 12 8

Dated 1986.

Jose Maria Arguedas (b. 1911), Anthropologist, Author — A368

1987, Sept. 19
918 A368 50c brown 6 5

Arequipa Chamber of Commerce & Industry A369

1987, Sept. 23 ***Perf. 13x13½***
919 A369 2i multi 22 16

Vaccinate Every Child Campaign A370

1987, Sept. 30 Litho. ***Perf. 13x13½***
920 A370 50c org brn 6 5

Argentina, Winner of the 1986 World Cup Soccer Championships — A371

1987, Nov. 18
921 A371 4i multi 32 22

Restoration of Chan Chan Ruins, Trujillo Province A372

Design: Chimu culture (11th-15th cent.) bas-relief.

1987, Nov. 27
922 A372 50c multi 5 5

See No. 936.

Halley's Comet A373

1987, Dec. 7
923 A373 4i Comet, Giotto satellite 32 22

Jorge Chavez Dartnell (1887-1910), Aviator — A374

Founding of Lima, 450th Anniv. (in 1985) — A375

1987, Dec. 15 ***Perf. 13½x13***
924 A374 2i yel bis, cl brn & gold 16 12

1987, Dec. 18 Litho. ***Perf. 13½x13***
925 A375 2.50i Osambela Palace 20 15

Dated 1985.

Discovery of the Ruins at Machu Picchu, 75th Anniv. (in 1986) A376

1987, Dec. ***Perf. 13x13½***
926 A376 9i multi 65 48

Dated 1986.

St. Francis's Church, Cajamarca A377

1988, Jan. 23 Litho. ***Perf. 13x13½***
927 A377 2i multi 16 12

Cultural Heritage. Dated 1986.

Participation of Peruvian Athletes in the Olympics, 50th Anniv. — A378

Design: Athletes on parade, poster publicizing the 1936 Berlin Games.

1988, Mar. 1 Litho. ***Perf. 13½x13***
928 A378 1.50i multi 12 10

Dated 1986.

Ministry of Education, 150th Anniv. A379

1988, Mar. 10 ***Perf. 13x13½***
929 A379 1i multi 8 6

Coronation of the Virgin of the Evangelization by Pope John Paul II — A380

1988, Mar. 14 Litho. ***Perf. 13x13½***
930 A380 10i multi 48 24

Dated 1986.

Rotary Intl. Involvement in Anti-Polio Campaign A381

1988, Mar. 16
931 A381 2i org, gold & dark blue 15 8

Postman, Cathedral A382

St. John Bosco (1815-1888), Educator A384

Meeting of 8 Latin-American Presidents, Acapulco, 1st Anniv. — A383

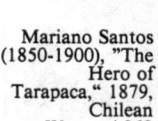

1988, Apr. 29 Litho. *Perf. 13½x13*
932 A382 9i brt blue 28 14

Christmas charity for children and postal workers' funds.

1988, May 4 *Perf. 13x13½*
933 A383 9i multi 28 14

1988, June 1 *Perf. 13½x13*
934 A384 5i multi 12 6

1st Peruvian Scientific Expedition to the Antarctic A385

1988, June 2 *Perf. 13x13½*
935 A385 7i Ship Humboldt, globe 16 8

Restoration of Chan-Chan Ruins, Trujillo Province A386

1988, June 7
936 A386 4i Bas-relief 10 5

Cesar Vallejo (1892-1938), Poet — A387

Journalists' Fund — A388

1988, June 15 *Perf. 13½x13*
937 A387 25i buff, blk & brn 58 30

1988, July 12 Litho. *Perf. 13½x13*
938 A388 4i buff & deep ultra 10 5

Type A44 — A389

1988, Sept. 1 Litho. *Perf. 13½x13*
939 A389 20i blk, lt pink & ultra 16 8

EXFILIMA '88, discovery of America 500th anniv.

17th Intl. Pacific Fair A390

1988, Sept. 6 *Perf. 13x13½*
940 A390 4i multi 5 5

Painting by Jose Sabogal (1888-1956) A391

1988, Sept. 7
941 A391 12i multi 10 5

Peru Kennel Club Emblem, Dogs — A392

1988, Sept. 9 *Perf. 13½x13*
942 A392 20i multi 16 8

CANINE '88 Intl. Dog Show, Lima.

Alfonso de Silva (1902-1934), Composer, and Score to Esplendido de Flores — A393

1988, Sept. 27 Litho. *Perf. 13x13½*
943 A393 20i multi 16 8

2nd State Visit of Pope John Paul II — A394

1988 Summer Olympics, Seoul — A395

1988, Oct. 10 *Perf. 13½x13*
944 A394 50i multi 40 20

1988, Nov. 10 Litho. *Perf. 13½x13*
945 A395 25i Women's volleyball 20 10

Women's Volleyball Championships (1982) — A396

Chavin Culture Ceramic Vase — A397

1988, Nov. 16 *Perf. 12*
Surcharged in Red
946 A396 95i on 300s multi 78 40

No. 946 not issued without overprint.
Christmas charity for children's and postal workers' funds.

1988 Litho. *Perf. 12*
Surcharged in Henna or Black
947 A397 40i on 100s red brn 16 8
948 A397 80i on 10s blk 32 16

Nos. 947-948 not issued without overprint. Issue dates: 40i, Dec. 15. 80i, Dec. 22.

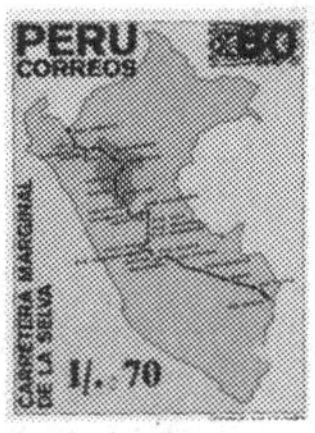

Rain Forest Border Highway — A398

Codex of the Indian Kings, 1681 — A399

1989, Jan. 27 Litho. *Perf. 12*
Surcharged in Black
949 A398 70i on 80s multi 20 10

Not issued without surcharge.

1989, Feb. 10
Surcharged in Olive Brown
950 A399 230i on 300s multi 50 25

Not issued without surcharge.

SEMI-POSTAL STAMPS

Catalogue values for unused stamps in this section, from this point to the end of the section, are for Never Hinged items.

Gold Funerary Mask SP1

Designs: 2.60s+1.30s, Ceremonial knife (vert.). 3.60s+1.80s, Ceremonial vessel. 4.60s+2.30s, Goblet with precious stones (vert.). 20s+10s, Earplug.

Perf. 12x12½, 12½x12
1966, Aug. 16 Photo. Unwmk.
B1 SP1 1.90s + 90c multi 35 35
B2 SP1 2.60s + 1.30s multi 40 40
B3 SP1 3.60s + 1.80s multi 60 60
B4 SP1 4.60s + 2.30s multi 80 80
B5 SP1 20s + 10s multi 3.50 3.50
Nos. B1-B5 (5) 5.65 5.65

The designs show gold objects of the 12th-13th centuries Chimu culture. The surtax was for tourist publicity.

AIR POST STAMPS

No. 248 Overprinted in Black

Servicio Aéreo

1927, Dec. 10 Unwmk. *Perf. 12*
C1 A87 50c violet 37.50 25.00

Two types of overprint. Counterfeits exist.

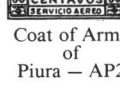

President Augusto Bernardino Leguia — AP1

Coat of Arms of Piura — AP2

1928, Jan. 12 **Engr.**
C2 AP1 50c dk grn 65 35

1932, July 28 **Litho.**
C3 AP2 50c scarlet 20.00 19.00

400th anniv. of the city of Piura. On sale one day. Counterfeits exist.

Airplane in Flight — AP3

1934, Feb. Engr. *Perf. 12½*
C4 AP3 2s blue 3.50 35
C5 AP3 5s brown 8.00 65

Funeral of Atahualpa AP4

Palace of Torre-Tagle — AP7

Designs: 35c, Mt. San Cristobal. 50c, Avenue of Barefoot Friars. 10s, Pizarro and the Thirteen.

1935, Jan. 18 Photo. *Perf. 13½*
C6 AP4 5c emerald 25 12
C7 AP4 35c brown 38 25
C8 AP4 50c org yel 65 50
C9 AP4 1s plum 1.25 75
C10 AP7 2s red org 2.00 1.50
C11 AP4 5s dp claret 8.25 4.50
C12 AP4 10s dk blue 32.50 25.00
Nos. C6-C12 (7) 45.28 32.62

4th centenary of founding of Lima.
Nos. C6-C12 overprinted "Radio Nacional" are revenue stamps.

"La Callao," First Locomotive in South America AP9

1936, Aug. 27 *Perf. 12½*
C13 AP9 35c gray blk 2.50 1.40

Founding of the Province of Callao, cent.

Nos. C4-C5 Surcharged "Habilitado" and New Value, like Nos. 353-355

1936, Nov. 4

C14	AP3 5c on 2s bl	35	7
C15	AP3 25c on 5s brn	65	25
a.	Double surcharge	13.50	13.50
b.	No period between "O" and "25 Cts"	1.40	1.40
c.	Inverted surcharge	16.50	

There are many broken letters in this setting.

La Mar Park, Lima AP10

Jorge Chávez AP14

Aerial View of Peruvian Coast AP16

View of the "Sierra" — AP17

St. Rosa of Lima — AP22

Designs: 15c, Mail Steamer "Inca" on Lake Titicaca. 20c, Native Quena (flute) Player and Llama. 30c, Ram at Model Farm, Puno. 50c, Mines of Peru. 1s, Train in Mountains. 1.50s, Jorge Chavez Aviation School. 2s, Transport Plane. 5s, Aerial View of Virgin Forests.

1936-37 Photo. *Perf. 12½*

C16	AP10	5c brt grn	15	5
C17	AP10	5c emer ('37)	18	8
C18	AP10	15c lt ultra	38	8
C19	AP10	15c blue ('37)	25	10
C20	AP10	20c gray blk	1.00	10
C21	AP10	20c pale ol grn ('37)	65	12
C22	AP14	25c mag ('37)	30	8
C23	AP10	30c hn brn	3.00	65
C24	AP10	30c dk ol brn ('37)	90	12
C25	AP14	35c brown	2.00	1.75
C26	AP10	50c yellow	30	25
C27	AP10	50c brn vio ('37)	45	12
C28	AP16	70c Prus grn	4.00	3.00
C29	AP16	70c pck grn ('37)	65	38
C30	AP17	80c brn blk	4.50	3.50
C31	AP17	80c ol blk ('37)	90	38
C32	AP10	1s ultra	3.00	30
C33	AP10	1s red brn ('37)	1.75	18
C34	AP14	1.50s red brn	5.00	4.00
C35	AP14	1.50s org yel ('37)	3.00	30
		Engr.		
C36	AP10	2s dp bl	10.00	5.00
C37	AP10	2s yel grn ('37)	6.25	50
C38	AP16	5s green	12.50	2.50
C39	AP22	10s car & brn	100.00	75.00
		Nos. C16-C39 (24)	161.11	98.54

Air Post Stamps of 1936 Surcharged in Black or Red

Habilit.
Un Sol

1936, June 26

C40	AP10 15c on 30c hn brn	65	38
C41	AP14 15c on 35c brn	65	22
C42	AP16 15c on 70c Prus grn	4.00	2.50
C43	AP17 25c on 80c brn blk (R)	4.00	2.50
C44	AP10 1s on 2s dp bl	6.50	3.50
	Nos. C40-C44 (5)	15.80	9.10

Surcharge on No. C43 is vertical, reading down.

First Flight in Peru, 1911 AP23

Jorge Chávez AP24

Airport of Limatambo at Lima — AP25

Map of Aviation Lines from Peru — AP26

Designs: 10c, Juan Bielovucic (1889-?) flying over Lima race course, Jan. 14, 1911. 15c, Jorge Chavez-Dartnell (1887-1910), French-born Peruvian aviator who flew from Brixen to Domodossola in the Alps and died of plane-crash injuries.

1937, Sept. 15 Engr. *Perf. 12*

C45	AP23 10c violet	35	10
C46	AP24 15c dk grn	50	10
C47	AP25 25c gray brn	35	10
C48	AP26 1s black	1.65	1.20

Inter-American Technical Conference of Aviation, Sept. 1937.

Government Restaurant at Callao — AP27

Monument on the Plains of Junin — AP28

Rear Admiral Manuel Villar — AP29

View of Tarma — AP30

Dam, Ica River — AP31

View of Iquitos — AP32

Highway and Railroad Passing AP33

Mountain Road AP34

Plaza San Martín, Lima — AP35

National Radio of Peru AP36

Stele from Chavin Temple AP37

Ministry of Public Works, Lima — AP38

Crypt of the Heroes, Lima — AP39

Imprint: "Waterlow & Sons Limited, Londres."

1938, July 1 Photo. *Perf. 12½, 13*

C49	AP27	5c vio brn	6	5
C50	AP28	15c dk brn	6	5
C51	AP29	20c dp mag	30	10
C52	AP30	25c dp grn	10	5
C53	AP31	30c orange	9	5
C54	AP32	50c green	25	22
C55	AP33	70c sl bl	50	5
C56	AP34	80c olive	75	8
C57	AP35	1s sl grn	6.25	3.00
C58	AP36	1.50s purple	1.50	6
		Engr.		
C59	AP37	2s ind & org brn	2.00	38
C60	AP38	5s brown	12.50	50
C61	AP39	10s ol grn & ind	50.00	25.00
		Nos. C49-C61 (13)	74.36	29.59

See Nos. C73-C75, C89-C93, C103.

Torre-Tagle Palace — AP40

National Congress Building AP41

Manuel Ferreyros, José Gregorio Paz Soldán and Antonio Arenas — AP42

1938, Dec. 9 Photo. *Perf. 12½*

C62	AP40 25c brt ultra	65	38
C63	AP41 1.50s brn vio	1.75	1.25
C64	AP42 2s black	1.10	75

8th Pan-American Conference at Lima.

No. C52 Surcharged in Black

Habilit.
0.15

1942 *Perf. 13*

C65	AP30 15c on 25c dp grn	1.00	8

Types of 1938

Imprint: "Columbian Bank Note Co."

1945-46 Unwmk. Litho. *Perf. 12½*

C73	AP27 5c vio brn	10	5
C74	AP31 30c orange	20	5
C75	AP36 1.50s pur ('46)	32	25

Nos. C73 and C54 Overprinted in Black

PRIMER VUELO
PIA
LIMA - NUEVA YORK

1947, Sept. 25 *Perf. 12½, 13*

C76	AP27 5c vio brn	5	5
C77	AP32 50c green	10	8

1st Peru Intl. Airways flight from Lima to New York City, Sept. 27-28, 1947.

Catalogue values for unused stamps in this section, from this point to the end of the section, are for Never Hinged items.

Peru-Great Britain Air Route — AP43

Basketball Players — AP44

Designs: 5s, Discus thrower. 10s, Rifleman.

1948, July 29 Photo. *Perf. 12½*

C78	AP43 1s blue	1.75	1.75
	Carmine Overprint, "AEREO"		
C79	AP44 2s red brn	2.50	2.50
C80	AP44 5s yel grn	4.00	4.00
C81	AP44 10s yellow	5.00	5.00
a.	Souvenir sheet, #C78-C81, perf. 13	16.25	16.25

Peru's participation in the 1948 Olympic Games held at Wembley, England, during July and August. Postally valid for four days, July 29-Aug. 1, 1948. Proceeds went to the Olympic Committee.

A surtax of 2 soles on No. C81a was for the Children's Hospital.

Remainders of Nos. C78-C81 and C81a were overprinted "Melbourne 1956" and placed on sale Nov. 19, 1956, at all post offices as "voluntary stamps" with no postal validity. Clerks were permitted to postmark them to please collectors, and proceeds were to help pay the cost of sending Peruvian athletes to Australia. On April 14, 1957, postal authorities declared these stamps valid for one day, April 15, 1957. The overprint was applied to 10,000 sets and 21,000 souvenir sheets. Value, set, $10; sheet, $10.

No. C55 Surcharged in Red

Habilitada.
S/. 0.10

1948, Dec. ***Perf. 13***

C82	AP33	10c on 70c slate bl	8	5
C83	AP33	20c on 70c slate bl	8	5
C84	AP33	55c on 70c slate bl	12	5

Nos. C52, C55 and C56 Surcharged in Black

Habilitada
S/. 0.10

1949, Mar. 25

C85	AP30	5c on 25c dp grn	8	5
C86	AP30	10c on 25c dp grn	8	5
C87	AP33	15c on 70c sl bl	10	5
C88	AP34	30c on 80c olive	65	10

The surcharge is vertical, reading up, on No. C87.

Types of 1938
Imprint: "Waterlow & Sons Limited, Londres."
Perf. 13x13½, 13½x13

1949-50 **Photo.**

C89	AP27	5c ol bis	5	5
C90	AP31	30c red	8	5
C91	AP33	70c blue	12	5
C92	AP34	80c cerise	30	10
C93	AP36	1.50s vio brn ('50)	35	20
		Nos. C89-C93 (5)	90	45

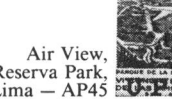

Air View, Reserva Park, Lima — AP45

Flags of the Americas and Spain AP46

Designs: 30c, National flag. 55c, Huancayo Hotel. 95c, Blanca-Ancash Cordillera. 1.50s, Arequipa Hotel. 2s, Coal chute and dock, Chimbote. 5s, Town hall, Miraflores. 10s, Hall of National Congress, Lima.

Overprinted "U. P. U. 1874-1949" in Red or Black

1951, Apr. 2 **Engr.** ***Perf. 12***

C94	AP45	5c bl grn	5	5
C95	AP45	30c blk & car	10	8
a.		Inverted overprint		
C96	AP45	55c yel grn (Bk)	10	8
C97	AP45	95c dk grn	15	12
C98	AP45	1.50s dp car (Bk)	20	18
C99	AP45	2s dp bl	25	22
C100	AP45	5s rose car (Bk)	3.00	3.00
C101	AP45	10s purple	4.00	4.50
C102	AP46	20s dk brn & ultra	7.00	7.00
		Nos. C94-C102 (9)	14.85	15.23

UPU, 75th anniv. (in 1949).
Nos. C94-C102 exist without overprint, but were not regularly issued. Value, set, $200.

Type of 1938
Imprint: "Inst. de Grav. Paris."

1951, May **Engr.** ***Perf. 12½x12***

C103	AP27	5c ol bis	6	5

Type of 1938 Surcharged in Black

HABILITADA
S|o. 0.25

1951

C108	AP31	25c on 30c rose red	10	5

Thomas de San Martin y Contreras and Jeronimo de Aliaga y Ramirez — AP47

San Marcos University — AP48

Designs: 50c, Church and convent of Santo Domingo. 1.20s, P. de Peralta Barnuevo, T. de San Martin y Contreras and J. Baquijano y Carrillo de Cordova. 2s, T. Rodriguez de Mendoza, J. Hipolito Unanue y Pavon and J. Cayetano Heredia y Garcia. 5s, Arms of the University, 1571 and 1735.

Perf. 11½x12½

1951, Dec. 10 **Litho.**

C109	AP47	30c gray	8	5
C110	AP48	40c ultra	8	5
C111	AP48	50c car rose	10	8
C112	AP47	1.20s emerald	15	12
C113	AP47	2s slate	25	10
C114	AP47	5s multi	1.10	15
		Nos. C109-C114 (6)	1.76	55

400th anniversary of the founding of San Marcos University.

River Gunboat Marañon AP49

Peruvian Cormorants AP50

National Airport, Lima AP51

Tobacco Plant AP52

Manco Capac Monument AP54

Garcilaso de la Vega AP53

Designs: 1.50s, Housing Unit No. 3. 2.20s, Inca Solar Observatory.

Imprint: "Thomas De La Rue & Co. Ltd."

1953-60 **Unwmk.** ***Perf. 13, 12***

C115	AP49	40c yel grn	7	5
a.		40c blue green ('57)	8	5
C116	AP50	75c dk brn	60	14
C116A	AP50	80c pale brn red ('60)	25	5
C117	AP51	1.25s blue	14	7
C118	AP49	1.50s cerise	16	10
C119	AP51	2.20s dk bl	80	16
C120	AP52	3s brown	70	22
C121	AP53	5s bister	60	14
C122	AP54	10s dl vio brn	1.50	35
		Nos. C115-C122 (9)	4.82	1.28

See Nos. C158-C162, C182-C183, C186-C189, C210-C211.

Queen Isabella I — AP55

Fleet of Columbus — AP56

Perf. 12½x11½, 11½x12½

1953, June 18 **Engr.** **Unwmk.**

C123	AP55	40c dp car	14	10
C124	AP56	1.25s emerald	20	16
C125	AP55	2.15s dp plum	42	30
C126	AP56	2.20s black	65	30

500th birth anniv. (in 1951) of Queen Isabella I of Spain.

Arms of Lima and Bordeaux AP57

Designs: 50c, Eiffel Tower and Cathedral of Lima. 1.25s, Admiral Dupetit-Thouars and frigate "La Victorieuse." 2.20s, Presidents Coty and Prado and exposition hall.

1957, Sept. 16 ***Perf. 13***

C127	AP57	40c cl, grn & ultra	7	7
C128	AP57	50c grn, blk & hn brn	7	5
C129	AP57	1.25s bl, ind & dk grn	16	14
C130	AP57	2.20s bluish blk, bl & red brn	35	25

French Exposition, Lima, Sept. 15-Oct. 1.

Pre-Stamp Postal Markings — AP58

Designs: 10c, 1r Stamp of 1857. 15c, 2r Stamp of 1857. 25c, 1d Stamp of 1860. 30c, 1p Stamp of 1858. 40c, ½p Stamp of 1858. 1.25s, José Davila Condemarin. 2.20s, Ramon Castilla. 5s, Pres. Manuel Prado. 10s, Shield of Lima containing stamps.

Perf. 12½x13

1957, Dec. 1 **Engr.** **Unwmk.**

C131	AP58	5c sil & blk	5	5
C132	AP58	10c lil rose & bl	5	5
C133	AP58	15c grn & red brn	5	5
C134	AP58	25c org yel & bl	5	5
C135	AP58	30c vio brn & org brn	5	5
C136	AP58	40c blk & bis	7	5
C137	AP58	1.25s dk bl & dk brn	22	16
C138	AP58	2.20s red & sl bl	40	35
C139	AP58	5s lil rose & mar	1.00	80
C140	AP58	10s ol grn & lil	1.65	1.40
		Nos. C131-C140 (10)	3.59	3.01

Centenary of Peruvian postage stamps. No. C140 issued to publicize the Peruvian Centenary Phil. Exhib. (PEREX).

Carlos Paz Soldan — AP59

Port of Callao and Pres. Manuel Prado AP60

Design: 1s, Ramon Castilla.

Perf. 14x13½, 13½x14

1958, Apr. 7 **Litho.** **Wmk. 116**

C141	AP59	40c brn & pale rose	10	5
C142	AP59	1s grn & lt grn	14	8
C143	AP60	1.25s dl pur & ind	20	14

Centenary of the telegraph connection between Lima and Callao and the centenary of the political province of Callao.

Flags of France and Peru — AP61

Cathedral of Lima and Lady AP62

Designs: 1.50s, Horseback rider and mall in Lima. 2.50s, Map of Peru showing national products.

Perf. 12½x13, 13x12½

1958, May 20 **Engr.** **Unwmk.**

C144	AP61	50c dl vio, bl & car	7	5
C145	AP62	65c multi	10	7
C146	AP62	1.50s bl, brn vio & ol	20	12
C147	AP61	2.50s sl grn, grnsh bl & cl	25	16

Peruvian Exhibition in Paris, May 20-July 10.

Bro. Martin de Porres Velasquez AP63

First Royal School of Medicine (Now Ministry of Government and Police) — AP64

Designs: 1.20s, Daniel Alcides Carrion Garcia. 1.50s, Jose Hipolito Unanue Pavon.

Perf. 13x13½, 13½x13

1958, July 24 Litho. Unwmk.

C148 AP63	60c	multi	10	5
C149 AP63	1.20s	multi	14	8
C150 AP63	1.50s	multi	14	10
C151 AP64	2.20s	black	20	16

Daniel A. Carrion (1857-1885), medical martyr.

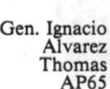

Gen. Ignacio Alvarez Thomas AP65

1958, Nov. 13 *Perf. 13x12½*

C152 AP65	1.10s	brn lake, bis & ver	16	14
C153 AP65	1.20s	blk, bis & ver	20	16

General Thomas (1787-1857), fighter for South American independence.

"Justice" and Emblem — AP66

1958, Nov. 13

Star in Blue and Olive Bister

C154 AP66	80c	emerald	7	7
C155 AP66	1.10s	red org	10	10
C156 AP66	1.20s	ultra	14	10
C157 AP66	1.50s	lil rose	16	10

Lima Bar Assoc., 150th anniv.

Types of 1953-57

Designs: 80c, Peruvian cormorants. 3.80s, Inca Solar Observatory.

Imprint: "Joh. Enschedé en Zonen-Holland"

Perf. 12½x14, 14x13, 13x14

1959, Dec. 9 Unwmk.

C158 AP50	80c	brn red	14	5
C159 AP52	3s	lt grn	60	22
C160 AP51	3.80s	orange	1.00	25
C161 AP53	5s	brown	60	25
C162 AP54	10s	org ver	1.20	40
	Nos. C158-C162 (5)		3.54	1.17

WRY Emblem, Dove, Rainbow and Farmer — AP67

Peruvian Cormorant Over Ocean — AP68

1960, Apr. 7 Litho. *Perf. 14x13*

C163 AP67	80c	multi	25	22
C164 AP67	4.30s	multi	55	40
a.	Souvenir sheet of 2		7.00	7.00

World Refugee Year, July 1, 1959-June 30, 1960.

No. C164a contains one each of Nos. C163-C164, imperf. Sold for 15 sol.

1960, May 30 *Perf. 14x13½*

C165 AP68	1s	multi	35	10

Intl. Pacific Fair, Lima, 1959.

Lima Coin of 1659 AP69

1961, Jan. 19 Unwmk. *Perf. 13x14*

C166 AP69	1s	org brn & gray	14	8
C167 AP69	2s	Prus bl & gray	20	16

1st National Numismatic Exposition, Lima, 1959; 300th anniv. of the first dated coin (1659) minted at Lima.

The Earth AP70

1961, Mar. 8 Litho. *Perf. 13½x14*

C168 AP70	1s	multi	15	14

International Geophysical Year.

Frigate Amazonas AP71

1961, Mar. 8 Engr. *Perf. 13½*

C169 AP71	50c	brn & grn	7	7
C170 AP71	80c	dl vio & red org	10	8
C171 AP71	1s	grn & sep	20	12

Centenary (in 1958) of the trip around the world by the Peruvian frigate Amazonas.

Machu Picchu Sheet

A souvenir sheet was issued Sept. 11, 1961, to commemorate the 50th anniversary of the discovery of the ruins of Machu Picchu, ancient Inca city in the Andes, by Hiram Bingham. It contains two bicolored imperf. airmail stamps, 5s and 10s, lithographed in a single design picturing the mountaintop ruins. The sheet was valid for one day and was sold in a restricted manner. Value $7.50.

Olympic Torch, Laurel and Globe — AP72

Fair Emblem and Llama — AP73

1961, Dec. 13 Unwmk. *Perf. 13*

C172 AP72	5s	gray & ultra	40	35
C173 AP72	10s	gray & car	80	60
a.	Souvenir sheet		2.25	2.25

17th Olympic Games, Rome, Aug. 25-Sept. 11, 1960.

No. C173a contains one each of Nos. C172-C173, imperf.

1962, Jan. Litho. *Perf. 10½x11*

C174 AP73	1s	multi	16	14

2nd International Pacific Fair, Lima, 1961.

Map Showing Disputed Border, Peru-Ecuador AP74

1962, May 25 *Perf. 10½*

Gray Background

C175 AP74	1.30s	blk, red & car rose	16	16
C176 AP74	1.50s	blk, red & emer	20	20
C177 AP74	2.50s	blk, red & dk bl	25	25

20th anniversary of the settlement of the border dispute with Ecuador by the Protocol of Rio de Janeiro.

Cahuide and Cuauhtemoc AP75

Designs: 2s, Tupac Amaru (Jose G. Condorcanqui) and Miguel Hidalgo. 3s, Pres. Manuel Prado and Pres. Adolfo Lopez Mateos of Mexico.

1962, May 25 Engr. *Perf. 13*

C178 AP75	1s	dk car rose, red & brt grn	10	8
C179 AP75	2s	grn, red & brt grn	20	14
C180 AP75	3s	brn, red & brt grn	25	16

Exhibition of Peruvian art treasures in Mexico.

Agriculture, Industry and Archaeology AP76

1962, Sept. 7 Litho. *Perf. 14x13½*

C181 AP76	1s	blk & gray	7	7

Cent. (in 1961) of Pallasca Ancash province.

Types of 1953-60

Designs: 1.30s, Guanayes. 1.50s, Housing Unit No. 3. 1.80s, Locomotive No. 80 (like No. 460). 2s, Monument to Native Farmer. 3s, Tobacco plant. 4.30s, Inca Solar Observatory. 5s, Garcilaso de la Vega. 10s, Inca Monument.

Imprint: "Thomas De La Rue & Co. Ltd."

1962-63 Wmk. 346 Litho. *Perf. 13*

C182 AP50	1.30s	pale yel	20	14
C183 AP49	1.50s	claret	22	10
C184 A182	1.80s	dark bl	25	10

Perf. 12

C185 A184	2s	emer ('63)	25	14
C186 AP52	3s	lil rose	35	16
C187 AP51	4.30s	orange	65	25
C188 AP53	5s	citron	65	35

Perf. 13½x14

C189 AP54	10s	vio bl ('63)	1.20	50
	Nos. C182-C189 (8)		3.77	1.74

Freedom from Hunger Issue

Type of Regular Issue

1963, July 23 Unwmk. *Perf. 12½*

C190 A189	4.30s	lt grn & ocher	50	40

For unused stamps, more recent issues are valued as never hinged, with the beginning point determined on a country-by-country basis. Notes to show the beginning points are prominently placed in the text.

Jorge Chávez and Wing AP77

Fair Poster AP78

1964, Feb. 20 Engr. *Perf. 13*

C191 AP77	5s	org brn, dk brn & bl	65	35

50th anniversary of the first crossing of the Alps by air (Sept. 23, 1910) by the Peruvian aviator Jorge Chávez.

Alliance for Progress Type of Regular Issue

Design: 1.30s, Same, horizontal.

Perf. 12½x12, 12x12½

1964, June 22 Litho.

C192 A190	1.30s	multi	14	12
C193 A190	3s	multi	25	22

1965, Jan. 15 Unwmk. *Perf. 14½*

C194 AP78	1s	multi	10	8

3rd International Pacific Fair, Lima 1963.

Basket, Globe, Pennant AP79

St. Martin de Porres AP80

1965, Apr. 19 *Perf. 12x12½*

C195 AP79	1.30s	vio & red	22	12
C196 AP79	4.30s	bis brn & red	55	30

4th Women's Intl. Basketball Championship.

1965, Oct. 29 Litho. *Perf. 11*

Designs: 1.80s, St. Martin's miracle: dog, cat and mouse feeding from same dish. 4.30s, St. Martin with cherubim in Heaven.

C197 AP80	1.30s	gray & multi	14	8
C198 AP80	1.80s	gray & multi	20	10
C199 AP80	4.30s	gray & multi	42	25

Canonization of St. Martin de Porres Velasquez (1579-1639), on May 6, 1962.

Victory Monument, Lima, and Battle Scene — AP81

Designs: 3.60s, Monument and Callao Fortress. 4.60s, Monument and José Galvez.

1966, May 2 Photo. *Perf. 14x13½*

C200 AP81	1.90s	multi	25	20
C201 AP81	3.60s	brn, yel & bis	40	25
C202 AP81	4.60s	multi	60	40

Centenary of Peru's naval victory over the Spanish Armada at Callao, May, 1866.

Civil Guard Emblem AP82

Design: 1.90s, Emblem and various activities of Civil Guard.

1966, Aug. 30 Photo. *Perf. 13½x14*

C203 AP82 90c multi 8 8
C204 AP82 1.90s dp lil rose, gold & blk 16 14

Centenary of the Civil Guard.

Hydroelectric Center Type of Regular Issue

1966, Nov. 24 Photo. *Perf. 13½x14*

C205 A193 1.90s lil, blk & vio bl 16 14

Sun Symbol, Ancient Carving — AP83

Designs: 3.60s, Map of Peru and spiral (horiz.). 4.60s, Globe with map of Peru.

Perf. 14x13½, 13½x14

1967, Feb. 16 Litho.

C206 AP83 2.60s red org & blk 22 16
C207 AP83 3.60s dp bl & blk 35 22
C208 AP83 4.60s tan & multi 40 30

Photography exhibition "Peru Before the World" which opened simultaneously in Lima, Madrid, Santiago de Chile and Washington, Sept. 27, 1966.

Types of 1953-60

Designs: 2.60s, Monument to Native Farmer. 3.60s, Tobacco plant. 4.60s, Inca Solar Observatory.

Imprint: "I.N.A."

1967, Jan. *Perf. 13½x14, 14x13½*

C209 A184 2.60s brt grn 22 16
C210 AP52 3.60s lil rose 35 20
C211 AP51 4.60s orange 40 25

Wind Vane and Sun Type of Regular Issue

1967, Apr. 18 Photo. *Perf. 13½x14*

C212 A194 1.90s yel brn, blk & gold 16 14

St. Rosa of Lima by Angelino Medoro AP84

Lions Emblem AP85

St. Rosa Painted by: 2.60s, Carlo Maratta. 3.60s, Cuzquena School, 17th century.

1967, Aug. 30 Photo. *Perf. 13½*

C213 AP84 1.90s blk, gold & multi 25 14
C214 AP84 2.60s blk, gold & multi 42 16
C215 AP84 3.60s blk, gold & multi 60 22

350th death anniv. of St. Rosa of Lima.

Fair Type of Regular Issue

1967, Oct. 27 Photo. *Perf. 12*

C216 A195 1s gold, brt red lil & blk 10 7

1967, Dec. 29 Litho. *Perf. 14x13½*

C217 AP85 1.60s brt bl & vio bl, *grysh* 14 10

50th anniversary of Lions International.

Decorated Jug, Nazca Culture AP86

Antarqui, Inca Messenger AP87

Painted pottery jugs of pre-Inca Nazca culture: 2.60s, Falcon. 3.60s, Round jug decorated with grain-eating bird. 4.60s, Two-headed snake. 5.60s, Marine bird.

1968, June 4 Photo. *Perf. 12*

C218 AP86 1.90s multi 14 12
C219 AP86 2.60s multi 16 14
C220 AP86 3.60s blk & multi 22 20
C221 AP86 4.60s brn & multi 30 25
C222 AP86 5.60s gray & multi 38 35
Nos. C218-C222 (5) 1.20 1.06

1968, Sept. 2 Litho. *Perf. 12*

Design: 5.60s, Alpaca and jet liner.

C223 AP87 3.60s multi 30 12
C224 AP87 5.60s red, blk & brn 42 16

12th anniv. of Peruvian Airlines (APSA).

Human Rights Flame — AP88

1968, Sept. 5 Photo. *Perf. 14x13½*

C225 AP88 6.50s brn, red & grn 22 20

International Human Rights Year.

Discobolus and Mexico Olympics Emblem AP89

1968, Oct. 19 Photo. *Perf. 13½*

C226 AP89 2.30s yel, brn & dk bl 14 8
C227 AP89 3.50s yel grn, sl bl & red 18 12
C228 AP89 5s brt pink, blk & ultra 25 16
C229 AP89 6.50s lt bl, mag & brn 38 22
C230 AP89 8s lil, ultra & car 40 25
C231 AP89 9s org, vio & grn 42 30
Nos. C226-C231 (6) 1.77 1.13

19th Olympic Games, Mexico City, Oct. 12-27.

Hand, Corn and Field AP90

1969, Mar. 3 Litho. *Perf. 11*

C232 AP90 5.50s on 1.90s grn & yel 25 16
C233 AP90 6.50s on 1.90s bl, grn & yel 35 20

Agrarian Reform Law. Nos. C232-C233 were not issued without surcharge.

Peruvian Silver 8-reales Coin, 1568 AP91

1969, Mar. 17 Litho. *Perf. 12*

C234 AP91 5s yel, gray & blk 20 14
C235 AP91 5s bl grn, gray & blk 20 14

400th anniv. of the first Peruvian coinage.

Ramon Castilla Monument AP92

Design: 10s, Pres. Ramon Castilla.

1969, May 30 Photo. *Perf. 13½*

Size: 27x40mm

C236 AP92 5s emer & ind 35 14

Perf. 12

Size: 21x37mm

C237 AP92 10s plum & brn 65 30

Ramon Castilla (1797-1867), president of Peru (1845-1851 and 1855-1862), on the occasion of the unveiling of the monument in Lima.

Airline Type of Regular Issue

1969, June 17 Litho. *Perf. 11*

C238 A199 3s org & multi 10 8
C239 A199 4s multi 14 10
C240 A199 5.50s ver & multi 18 14
C241 A199 6.50s vio & multi 20 16

First Peruvian Airlines (APSA) flight to Europe.

Radar Antenna, Satellite and Earth — AP93

1969, July 14 Litho. *Perf. 11*

C242 AP93 20s multi 1.00 55
a. Souv. sheet 1.20 1.20

Opening of the Lurin satellite earth station near Lima.

No. C242a contains one imperf. stamp with simulated perforations similar to No. C242.

Gonzales Type of Regular Issue

1969, July 23 Litho. *Perf. 11*

C243 A200 20s red & multi 1.20 55

WHO Emblem AP94

1969, Aug. 14 Photo. *Perf. 12*

C244 AP94 5s gray, red brn, gold & blk 16 14
C245 AP94 6.50s dl org, gray bl, gold & blk 20 16

WHO, 20th anniv.

Agrarian Reform Type of Regular Issue

1969, Aug. 28 Litho. *Perf. 11*

C246 A201 3s lil & blk 10 8
C247 A201 4s brn & buff 14 12

Garcilaso de la Vega — AP95

Designs: 2.40s, De la Vega's coat of arms. 3.50s, Title page of "Commemtarios Reales que tratan del origen de los Yncas," Lisbon, 1609.

1969, Sept. 18 Litho. *Perf. 12x12½*

C248 AP95 2.40s emer, sil & blk 10 7
C249 AP95 3.50s ultra, buff & blk 14 10
C250 AP95 5s sil, yel, blk & brn 20 14
a. Souv. sheet of 3 90 90

Garcilaso de la Vega, called "Inca" (1539-1616), historian of Peru.

No. C250a contains 3 imperf. stamps similar to Nos. C248-C250.

Fair Type of Regular Issue, 1969

1969, Nov. 14 Litho. *Perf. 11*

C251 A203 3s bis & multi 10 8
C252 A203 4s multi 14 10

Bolognesi Type of Regular Issue

1969, Dec. 9 Litho. *Perf. 11*

C253 A204 50s lt brn, blk & gold 3.00 1.40

Arms of Amazonas — AP96

1970, Jan. 6 Litho. *Perf. 11*

C254 AP96 10s multi 35 30

ILO Emblem AP97

1970, Jan. 16

C278 AP97 3s dk vio bl & lt ultra 16 8

ILO, 50th anniv.

Motherhood and UNICEF Emblem AP98

1970, Jan. 16 Photo. *Perf. 13½x14*

C279	AP98	5s	yel, gray & blk	22	14
C280	AP98	6.50s	brt pink, gray & blk	35	20

Vicus Culture Type of Regular Issue, 1970

Ceramics of Vicus Culture, 6th-8th Centuries: 3s, Squatting warrior. 4s, Jug. 5.50s, Twin jugs. 6.50s, Woman and jug.

1970, Feb. 23 Litho. *Perf. 11*

C281	A205	3s	buff, blk & brn	16	14
C282	A205	4s	buff, blk & brn	20	16
C283	A205	5.50s	buff, blk & brn	30	22
C284	A205	6.50s	buff, blk & brn	40	25

Fish Type of Regular Issue

Fish: No. C285, Swordfish. No. C286, Yellowfin tuna. 5.50s, Wolf fish.

1970, Apr. 30 Litho. *Perf. 11*

C285	A207	3s	vio bl & multi	14	5
C286	A207	3s	vio bl & multi	15	7
C287	A207	5.50s	vio bl & multi	28	14

Nos. C285-C287 are printed se-tenant in sheet with Nos. 532-533, arranged in horizontal strips of five.

Telephone AP99

UN Headquarters, N.Y. AP100

1970, June 12 Litho. *Perf. 11*

C288	AP99	5s	multi	25	10
C289	AP99	10s	multi	55	22

Nationalization of the Peruvian telephone system, Mar. 25, 1970.

Soldier-Farmer Type of Regular Issue

1970, June 24 Litho. *Perf. 11*

C290	A208	3s	gold & multi	20	7
C291	A208	5.50s	gold & multi	35	14

1970 June 26

C292	AP100	3s	vio bl & lt bl	10	7

25th anniversary of United Nations.

Rotary Club Emblem AP101

1970, July 18

C293	AP101	10s	blk, red & gold	70	20

Rotary Club of Lima, 50th anniversary.

Tourist Type of Regular Issue

Designs: 3s, Ruins of Sun Fortress, Trujillo. 4s, Sacsayhuaman Arch, Cuzco (vert.). 5.50s, Arch and Lake Titicaca, Puno (vert.). 10s, Machu Picchu, Cuzco (vert.)

1970, Aug. 6 Litho. *Perf. 11*

C294	A210	3s	multi	15	7
C295	A210	4s	multi	20	10
C296	A210	5.50s	multi	28	14
C297	A210	10s	multi	50	20
a.			Souvenir sheet of 5	1.65	1.65

No. C297a contains 5 imperf. stamps similar to Nos. 538, C294-C297 with simulated perforations.

The first value column gives the catalogue value of an unused stamp, the second that of a used stamp.

Procession, Lord of Miracles — AP102

Designs: 4s, Cockfight, by T. Nuñez Ureta. 5.50s, Altar of Church of the Nazarene (vert.). 6.50s, Procession, by J. Vinatea Reinoso. 8s, Procession, by Jose Sabogal (vert.).

1970, Nov. 30 Litho. *Perf. 11*

C298	AP102	3s	blk & multi	15	7
C299	AP102	4s	blk & multi	20	10
C300	AP102	5.50s	blk & multi	25	14
C301	AP102	6.50s	blk & multi	35	16
C302	AP102	8s	blk & multi	40	20
			Nos. C298-C302 (5)	1.35	67

October Festival in Lima.

"Tight Embrace" (from ancient monolith) AP103

1971, Feb. 8 Litho. *Perf. 11*

C303	AP103	4s	ol gray, yel & red	22	10
C304	AP103	5.50s	dk bl, pink & red	30	14
C305	AP103	6.50s	sl, buff & red	35	16

Issued to express Peru's gratitude to the world for aid after the Ancash earthquake, May 31, 1970.

Textile Type of Regular Issue

Designs: 3s, Chancay tapestry (vert.). 4s, Chancay lace. 5.50s, Paracas cloth (vert.).

1971, Apr. 19 Litho. *Perf. 11*

C306	A213	3s	multi	25	7
C307	A213	4s	grn & multi	35	10
C308	A213	5.50s	multi	42	14

Fish Type of Regular Issue

Fish Sculptures and Fish: 3.50s, Chimu Inca culture, 14th century and Chilean sardine. 4s, Mochica culture, 5th century, and engraulis ringens. 5.50s, Chimu culture, 13th century, and merluccios peruanos. 8.50s, Nazca culture, 3rd century, and brevoortis maculatachilcae.

1971, June 7 Litho. *Perf. 11*

C309	A214	3.50s	multi	30	8
C310	A214	4s	multi	38	10
C311	A214	5.50s	multi	50	14
C312	A214	8.50s	multi	70	20

Independence Type of 1971

Paintings: No. C313, Toribio Rodriguez de Mendoza. No. C314, José de la Riva Agüero. No. C315, Francisco Vidal. 3.50s, José de San Martin. No. C317, Juan P. Viscardo y Guzman. No. C318, Hipolito Unanue. 4.50s, Liberation Monument, Paracas. No. C320, José G. Condorcanqui-Tupac Amaru. No. C321, Francisco J. de Luna Pizarro. 6s, March of the Numancia Battalion (horiz.). 7.50s, Peace Tower, monument for Alvarez de Arenales (horiz.). 9s, Liberators' Monument, Lima (horiz.). 10s, Independence Proclamation in Lima (horiz.).

1971 Litho. *Perf. 11*

C313	A215	3s	brt mag & blk	12	7
C314	A215	3s	gray & multi	12	7
C315	A215	3s	dk bl & multi	12	7
C316	A215	3.50s	dk bl & multi	15	9
C317	A215	4s	emer & blk	16	10
C318	A215	4s	gray & multi	16	10
C319	A215	4.50s	dk bl & multi	18	12
C320	A215	5.50s	brn & blk	22	14
C321	A215	5.50s	gray & multi	22	14
C322	A215	6s	dk bl & multi	22	15
C323	A215	7.50s	dk bl & multi	30	18
C324	A215	9s	dk bl & multi	38	20
C325	A215	10s	dk bl & multi	40	20
			Nos. C313-C325 (13)	2.75	1.63

150th anniversary of independence, and to honor the heroes of the struggle for independence. Sizes: 6s, 10s, 45x35mm., 7.50s, 9s, 41x39mm. Others 31x49mm.

Issue dates: Nos. C313, C317, C320, May 10; Nos. C314, C318, C321, July 5; others July 27.

Ricardo Palma — AP104

Weight Lifter — AP105

1971, Aug. 27 *Perf. 13*

C326	AP104	7.50s	ol bis & blk	60	18

Sesquicentennial of National Library. Ricardo Palma (1884-1912) was a writer and director of the library.

1971, Sept. 15

C327	AP105	7.50s	brt bl & blk	50	18

25th World Weight Lifting Championships, Lima.

Flag, Family, Soldier's Head — AP106

1971, Oct. 4

C328	AP106	7.50s	blk, lt bl & red	50	18
a.			Souvenir sheet	1.00	1.00

3rd anniversary of the revolution of the armed forces. No. C328a contains one imperf. stamp similar to No. C328.

"Sacramento" — AP107

1971, Oct. 8

C329	AP107	7.50s	lt bl & dk bl	38	18

Sesquicentennial of Peruvian Navy.

Peruvian Order of the Sun AP108

1971, Oct. 8

C330	AP108	7.50s	multi	38	20

Sequicentennial of the Peruvian Order of the Sun.

Liberation Type of Regular Issue

Design: 50s, Detail from painting "Progress of Liberation," by Teodoro Nunez Ureta.

1971, Nov. 4 Litho. *Perf. 13x13½*

C331	A217	50s	multi	3.00	1.00

2nd Ministerial meeting of the "Group of 77."

Fair Emblem — AP109

1971, Nov. 12 *Perf. 13*

C332	AP109	4.50s	multi	20	14

7th Pacific International Trade Fair.

Fish Type of Regular Issue

Fish: 3s, Pontinus furcirhinus dubius. 5.50s, Hogfish.

1972, Mar. 20 Litho. *Perf. 13x13½*

C333	A223	3s	lt bl & multi	20	8
C334	A223	5.50s	lt bl & multi	35	14

Teacher and Children, by Teodoro Nunez Ureta AP110

1972, Apr. 10 Litho. *Perf. 13x13½*

C335	AP110	6.50s	multi	35	16

Enactment of Education Reform Law.

White-tailed Trogon — AP111

1972, June 19 Litho. *Perf. 13½x13*

C336	AP111	2s	shown	15	5
C337	AP111	2.50s	Amazonian umbrella bird	18	7
C338	AP111	3s	Peruvian cock-of-the-rock	22	8
C339	AP111	6.50s	Cuvier's toucan	45	15
C340	AP111	8.50s	Blue-crowned motmot	65	22
			Nos. C336-C340 (5)	1.65	57

Quipu and Map of Americas AP112

Inca Runner, Olympic Rings AP113

1972, Aug. 21

C341	AP112	5s	blk & multi	22	14

4th Interamerican Philatelic Exhibition, EXFILBRA, Rio de Janeiro, Aug. 26-Sept. 2.

1972, Aug. 28

C342	AP113	8s	buff & multi	55	15

20th Olympic Games, Munich, Aug. 26-Sept. 11.

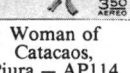

Woman of Catacaos, Piura — AP114

Funerary Tower, Sillustani, Puno — AP115

Regional Costumes: 2s, Tupe (Yauyos) woman of Lima. 4s, Indian with bow and arrow, from Conibo, Loreto. 4.50s, Man with calabash, Cajamarca. 5s, Moche woman, Trujillo. 6.50s, Man and woman of Ocongate, Cuzco. 8s, Chucupana woman, Ayacucho. 8.50s, Cotuncha woman, Junin. 10s, Woman of Puno dancing "Pandilla."

1972-73

C343	AP114	2s blk & multi	10	5
C344	AP114	3.50s blk & multi	20	10
C345	AP114	4s blk & multi	22	10
C346	AP114	4.50s blk & multi	25	10
C346A	AP114	5s blk & multi	25	10
C347	AP114	6.50s blk & multi	38	15
C347A	AP114	8s blk & multi	40	18
C347B	AP114	8.50s blk & multi	42	20
C348	AP114	10s blk & multi	55	20
		Nos. C343-C348 (9)	2.77	1.18

Issue dates: 3.50s, 4s and 6.50s, Sept. 29, 1972. 2s, 4.50s and 10s, Apr. 30, 1973. 5s, 8s and 8.50s, Oct. 15, 1973.

Perf. 13½x13, 13x13½

1972, Oct. 16 **Litho.**

Archaeological Monuments: 1.50s, Stone of the 12 angles, Cuzco. 3.50s, Ruins of Chavin, Ancash (horiz.). 5s, Wall and gate, Chavin, Ancash (horiz.). 8s, Ruins of Machu Picchu (horiz.).

C349	AP115	1.50s multi	14	5
C350	AP115	3.50s multi	22	8
C351	AP115	4s multi	25	8
C352	AP115	5s multi	35	10
C353	AP115	8s multi	65	20
		Nos. C349-C353 (5)	1.61	51

Inca Poncho — AP116

Designs: Inca ponchos, various textile designs.

1973, Jan. 29 **Litho.** ***Perf. 13½x13***

C354	AP116	2s multi	10	5
C355	AP116	3.50s multi	20	7
C356	AP116	4s multi	20	8
C357	AP116	5s multi	25	10
C358	AP116	8s multi	50	16
		Nos. C354-C358 (5)	1.25	46

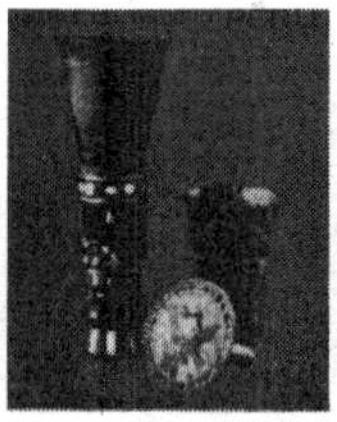

Goblets and Ring, Mochica, 10th Century — AP117

Antique Jewelry: 2.50s, Golden hands and arms, Lambayeque, 12th century. 4s, Gold male statuette, Mochica, 8th century. 5s, Two gold brooches, Nazca, 8th century. 8s, Flayed puma, Mochica, 8th century.

1973, Mar. 19 **Litho.** ***Perf. 13½x13***

C359	AP117	1.50s multi	10	5
C360	AP117	2.50s multi	14	5
C361	AP117	4s multi	20	8
C362	AP117	5s multi	25	10
C363	AP117	8s multi	50	16
		Nos. C359-C363 (5)	1.19	44

Andean Condor — AP118

Indian Guide, by José Sabogal — AP119

Protected Animals: 5s, Vicuña. 8s, Spectacled bear.

1973, Apr. 16 **Litho.** ***Perf. 13½x13***

C364	AP118	4s blk & multi	20	8
C365	AP118	5s blk & multi	25	10
C366	AP118	8s blk & multi	42	16

See Nos. C372-C376, C411-C412.

1973, May 7 **Litho.** ***Perf. 13½x13***

Peruvian Paintings: 8.50s, Portrait of a Lady, by Daniel Hernandez. 20s, Man Holding Figurine, by Francisco Laso.

C367	AP119	1.50s multi	7	5
C368	AP119	8.50s multi	38	16
C369	AP119	20s multi	90	40

Basket and World Map AP120

1973, May 26 ***Perf. 13x13½***

C370	AP120	5s green	25	10
C371	AP120	20s lil rose	1.10	40

1st International Basketball Festival.

Darwin's Rhea — AP121

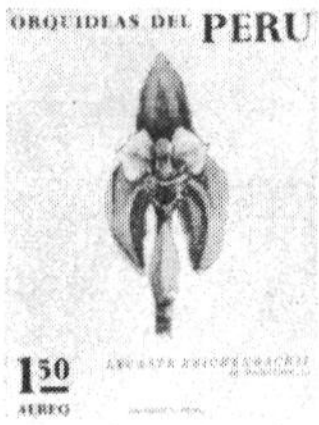

Orchid — AP122

1973, Sept. 3 **Litho.** ***Perf. 13½x13***

C372	AP121	2.50s shown	14	5
C373	AP121	3.50s Giant otter	18	7
C374	AP121	6s Greater flamingo	30	12
C375	AP121	8.50s Bush dog, horiz.	42	16
C376	AP121	10s Chinchilla, horiz.	50	20
		Nos. C372-C376 (5)	1.54	60

Protected animals.

1973, Sept. 27

Designs: Various orchids.

C377	AP122	1.50s blk & multi	10	5
C378	AP122	2.50s blk & multi	16	5
C379	AP122	3s blk & multi	20	7
C380	AP122	3.50s blk & multi	22	7
C381	AP122	8s blk & multi	55	16
		Nos. C377-C381 (5)	1.23	40

Pacific Fair Emblem — AP123

1973, Nov. 14 **Litho.** ***Perf. 13½x13***

C382	AP123	8s blk, red & gray	50	20

8th International Pacific Fair, Lima.

Cargo Ship ILO AP124

Designs: 2.50s, Boats of Pescaperu fishing organization. 8s, Jet and seagull.

1973, Dec. 14 **Litho.** ***Perf. 13***

C383	AP124	1.50s multi	8	5
C384	AP124	2.50s multi	14	5
C385	AP124	8s multi	42	16

Issued to promote government enterprises.

Lima Monument AP125

1973, Nov. 27 ***Perf. 13***

C386	AP125	8.50s red & multi	42	16

50th anniversary of Air Force Academy. Monument honors Jorge Chavez, Peruvian aviator.

Bridge at Yananacu, by Enrique Camino Brant AP126

Paintings: 10c, Peruvian Birds, by Teodoro Nunez Ureta (vert.). 50s, Boats of Totora, by Jorge Vinatea Reinoso.

Perf. 13x13½, 13½x13

1973, Dec. 28

C387	AP126	8s multi	40	16
C388	AP126	10s multi	50	18
C389	AP126	50s multi	2.25	1.00

Moral House, Arequipa AP127

Landscapes: 2.50s, El Misti Mountain, Arequipa. 5s, Puya Raymondi (cacti), (vert.). 6s, Huascaran Mountain. 8s, Lake Querococha. Views on 5s, 6s, 8s are views in White Cordilleras Range, Ancash Province.

1974, Feb. 11

C390	AP127	1.50s multi	10	5
C391	AP127	2.50s multi	14	5
C392	AP127	5s multi	22	10
C393	AP127	6s multi	30	14
C394	AP127	8s multi	50	16
		Nos. C390-C394 (5)	1.26	50

San Jeronimo's, Cuzco — AP128

Churches of Peru: 3.50s, Cajamarca Cathedral. 5s, San Pedro's, Zepita-Puno (horiz.). 6s, Cuzco Cathedral. 8.50s, Santo Domingo, Cuzco.

1974, May 6

C395	AP128	1.50s multi	7	5
C396	AP128	3.50s multi	16	7
C397	AP128	5s multi	22	8
C398	AP128	6s multi	25	12
C399	AP128	8.50s multi	50	16
		Nos. C395-C399 (5)	1.20	48

Surrender at Ayacucho, by Daniel Hernandez AP129

Designs: 6s, Battle of Junin, by Felix Yañex. 7.50s, Battle of Ayachucho, by Felix Yanez.

1974 **Litho.** ***Perf. 13x13½***

C400	AP129	3.50s multi	16	8
C401	AP129	6s multi	35	12
C402	AP129	7.50s multi	40	14
C403	AP129	8.50s multi	50	18
C404	AP129	10s multi	65	20
		Nos. C400-C404 (5)	2.06	72

Sesquicentennial of the Battles of Junin and Ayacucho and of the surrender at Ayacucho.
Issue dates: 7.50s, Aug. 6. 6s, Oct. 9. Others, Dec. 9.

Chavin Stone, Ancash — AP130

Machu Picchu, Cuzco AP131

Designs: Nos. C407, C409, Different bas-reliefs from Chavin Stone. No. C408, Baths of Tampumacchay, Cuzco. No. C410, Ruins of Kencco, Cuzco.

Perf. 13½x13, 13x13½

1974, Mar. 25

C405	AP130	3s multi	14	7
C406	AP131	3s multi	14	7
C407	AP130	5s multi	20	8
C408	AP131	5s multi	20	8
C409	AP130	10s multi	40	20
C410	AP131	10s multi	40	20
		Nos. C405-C410 (6)	1.48	70

Cacajao Rubicundus AP132

1974, Oct. 21 ***Perf. 13½x13***

C411 AP132 8s multi 40 16
C412 AP132 20s multi 1.00 40

Protected animals.

Inca Gold Mask AP133

1974, Nov. 8 ***Perf. 13x13½***

C413 AP133 8s yel & multi 40 16

8th World Mining Congress, Lima.

Chalan, Horseman's Cloak — AP134

1974, Nov. 11 Litho. ***Perf. 13½x13***

C414 AP134 5s multi 25 10
C415 AP134 8.50s multi 50 16

Pedro Paulet and Aerial Torpedo AP135

1974, Nov. 28 Litho. ***Perf. 13x13½***

C416 AP135 8s bl & vio 40 16

UPU, cent. Pedro Paulet, inventor of the mail-carrying aerial torpedo.

Christmas Type of 1974

Design: 6.50s, Indian Nativity scene.

1974, Dec. 20 ***Perf. 13½x13***

C417 A235 6.50s multi 25 14

Andean Village, Map of South American West Coast AP136

1974, Dec. 30

C418 AP136 6.50s multi 35 14

Meeting of Communications Ministers of Andean Pact countries.

Map of Peru, Modern Buildings, UN Emblem — AP137

1975, Mar. 12 Litho. ***Perf. 13x13***

C419 AP137 6s blk, gray & red 16 14

2nd United Nations Industrial Development Organization Conference, Lima.

Nos. C187, C211 and C160 Surcharged with New Value and Heavy Bar in Dark Blue

Wmk. 346

1975, April Litho. ***Perf. 12***

C420 AP51 2s on 4.30s org 14 5

Perf. 13½x14, 13x14

Unwmk.

C421 AP51 2.50s on 4.60s org 16 8
C422 AP51 5s on 3.80s org 16 10

World Map and Peruvian Colors AP138

1975, Aug. 25 Litho. ***Perf. 13x13½***

C423 AP138 6.50s lt bl, vio bl & red 25 16

Conference of Foreign Ministers of Nonaligned Countries.

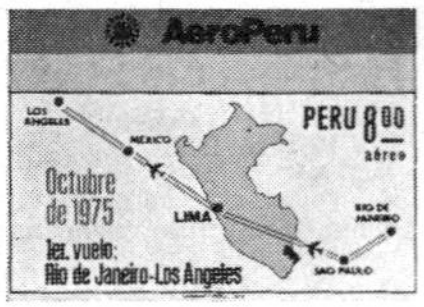

Map of Peru and Flight Route AP139

1975, Oct. 23 Litho. ***Perf. 13x13½***

C424 AP139 8s red, pink & blk 35 16

AeroPeru's first flights: Lima-Rio de Janeiro, Lima-Los Angeles.

Fair Poster AP140

Col. Francisco Bolognesi AP141

1975, Nov. 21 Litho. ***Perf. 13½x13***

C425 AP140 6s blk, bis & red 50 14

9th International Pacific Fair, Lima, 1975.

1975, Dec. 23 Litho. ***Perf. 13½x13***

C426 AP141 20s multi 80 35

160th birth anniv. of Col. Francisco Bolognesi.

Indian Mother and Child AP142

Inca Messenger, UPAE Emblem AP143

1976, Feb. 23 Litho. ***Perf. 13½x13***

C427 AP142 6s gray & multi 35 14

Christmas 1975.

1976, Mar. 19 Litho. ***Perf. 13½x13***

C428 AP143 5s red, blk & tan 40 10

11th Congress of the Postal Union of the Americas and Spain, UPAE.

Nos. C187, C211, C160, C209, C210 Surcharged in Dark Blue or Violet Blue (No Bar)

Perf. 12, 13x14, 13½x14, 14x13½

1976 Wmk. 346, Unwmkd.

C429 AP51 2s on 4.30s org 10 5
C430 AP51 3.50s on 4.60s org 16 7
C431 AP51 4.50s on 3.80s org 20 10
C432 AP51 5s on 4.30s org 25 10
C433 AP51 6s on 4.60s org 35 12
C434 A184 10s on 2.60s brt grn 50 20
C435 AP52 50s on 3.60s lil rose (VB) 2.00 1.40
Nos. C429-C435 (7) 3.56 2.04

Stamps of 1962-67 Surcharged with New Value and Heavy Bar in Black, Red, Green, Dark Blue or Orange

Perf. 14x13½, 11, 13½x14, 12

1976-77 Wmk. 346, Unwmkd.

C436 AP52 1.50s on 3.60s (Bk) #C210 10 5
C437 A184 2s on 2.60s (R) #C209 ('77) 10 5
C438 AP52 2s on 3.60s (G) #C210 16 5
C439 AP80 2s on 4.30s (Bk) #C199 16 5
C440 A184 3s on 2.60s (Bk) #C209 ('77) 10 6
C441 A184 4s on 2.60s (DBl) #C209 16 8
C442 AP52 4s on 3.60s (DBl) #C210 ('77) 16 8
C443 AP51 5s on 4.30s (R) #C187 22 10
C444 AP83 6s on 4.60s (Bk) #C208 ('77) 35 12
C445 AP51 6s on 4.60s (DBl) #C211 ('77) 35 12
C446 AP51 7s on 4.30s (Bk) #C187 ('77) 20 14
C447 AP52 7.50s on 3.60s (DBl) #C210 40 15
C448 AP52 8s on 3.60s (O) #C210 40 16
C449 AP51 10s on 4.30s (Bk) #C187 ('77) 20 14
C450 AP51 10s on 4.60s (DBl) #C211 50 20
C451 AP86 24s on 3.60s (Bk) #C220 ('77) 1.40 45
C452 AP86 28s on 4.60s (Bk) #C221 ('77) 80 42
C453 AP86 32s on 5.60s (Bk) #C222 ('77) 80 50
C454 A184 50s on 2.60s (O) #C209 ('77) 2.50 1.00
C455 AP52 50s on 3.60s (G) #C210 2.00 1.00
Nos. C436-C455 (20) 11.06 4.92

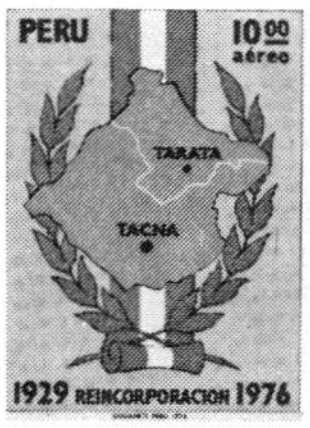

Map of Tacna and Tarata Provinces — AP144

1976, Aug. 28 Litho. ***Perf. 13½x13***

C456 AP144 10s multi 35 14

Re-incorporation of Tacna Province into Peru, 47th anniversary.

Investigative Police Badge AP145

"Declaration of Bogota" AP146

1976, Sept. 15 Litho. ***Perf. 13½x13***

C457 AP145 20s multi 65 35

Investigative Police of Peru, 54th anniv.

1976, Sept. 22

C458 AP146 10s multi 35 16

Declaration of Bogota for cooperation and world peace, 10th anniversary.

Pal Losonczi and Map of Hungary — AP147

1976, Nov. 2 Litho. ***Perf. 13½x13***

C459 AP147 7s ultra & blk 35 14

Visit of Pres. Pal Losonczi of Hungary, Oct. 1976.

Map of Amazon Basin, Colors of Peru and Brazil AP148

1976, Dec. 16 Litho. ***Perf. 13***

C460 AP148 10s bl & multi 35 16

Visit of Gen. Ernesto Geisel, president of Brazil, Nov. 5, 1976.

Liberation Monument, Lima AP149

1977, Mar. 9 Litho. ***Perf. 13x13½***

C461 AP149 20s red buff & blk 50 40

Army Day.

Map of Peru and Venezuela, South America AP150

1977, Mar. 14

C462 AP150 12s buff & multi 50 22

Meeting of Pres. Francisco Morales Bermudez Cerrutti of Peru and Pres. Carlos Andres Perez of Venezuela, Dec. 1976.

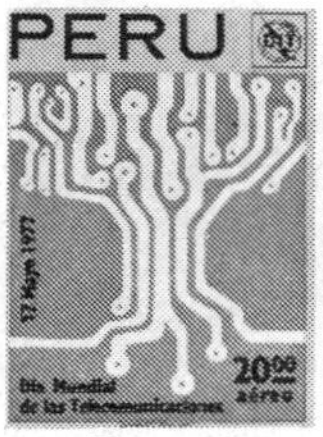

Electronic Tree — AP151

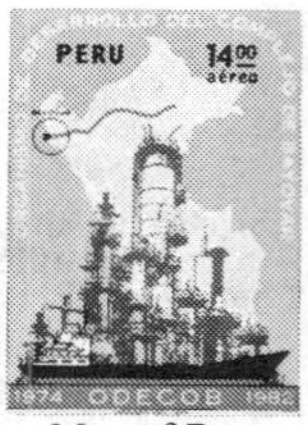

Map of Peru, Refinery, Tanker — AP152

1977, May 30 Litho. ***Perf. 13½x13***

C463 AP151 20s gray, red & blk 65 35

World Telecommunications Day.

1977, July 13 Litho. *Perf. 13½x13*
C464 AP152 14s multi 42 20

Development of Bayovar oil complex.

Messenger Type of 1977

1977 Litho. *Perf. 13½x13*
C465 A243 24s mag & blk 65 40
C466 A243 28s bl & blk 1.40 50
C467 A243 32s rose brn & blk 80 50

Arms of Arequipa AP153

Gen. Jorge Rafael Videla AP154

1977, Sept. 3 Litho. *Perf. 13½x13*
C468 AP153 10s multi 20 10

Gold of Peru Exhibition, Arequipa 1977.

1977, Oct. 8 Litho. *Perf. 13½x13*
C469 AP154 36s multi 65 25

Visit of Jorge Rafael Videla, president of Argentina.

Stamps of 1953-67 Surcharged with New Value and Heavy Bar in Black, Dark Blue or Green

Perf. 13½x14, 14x13½, 12, 12½x11½, 13½, 13x14

1977 Unwmk. Wmk. 346
C470 AP83 2s on 3.60s (Bk) #C207 7 5
C471 AP51 2s on 4.60s (DB) #C211 7 5
C472 AP51 4s on 4.60s (DB) #C211 7 5
C473 AP51 5s on 4.30s (Bk) #C187 35 10
C474 AP52 5s on 3.60s (Bk) #C210 10 5
C475 AP55 10s on 2.15s (Bk) #C125 35 7
C476 AP52 10s on 3.60s (DB) #C210 65 7
C477 AP84 10s on 3.60s (Bk) #C215 50 16
C478 AP52 20s on 3.60s (DB) #C210 35 14
C479 AP51 100s on 3.80s (G) #C160 2.00 1.40
Nos. C470-C479 (10) 4.51 2.14

Nos. C223-C224 Surcharged with New Value, Heavy Bars and: "FRANQUEO"

1977 Litho. *Perf. 12*
C480 AP87 6s on 3.60s multi 40 14
C481 AP87 8s on 3.60s multi 50 16
C482 AP87 10s on 5.60s multi 50 22

Adm. Miguel Grau — AP155

1977, Dec. 15 Litho. *Perf. 13½x13*
C483 AP155 28s multi 38 25

Navy Day. Miguel Grau (1838-1879), Peruvian naval commander.

Christmas Type of 1977

Design: 20s, Indian Nativity.

1977, Dec. 23
C484 A246 20s multi 50 20

Andrés Bello, Flag and Map of Participants AP156

1978, Jan. 12 Litho. *Perf. 13*
C485 AP156 30s multi 40 25

8th Meeting of Education Ministers honoring Andrés Bello, Lima.

Inca Type of 1978

1978 Litho. *Perf. 13½x13*
C486 A247 24s dp rose lil 32 22
C487 A247 30s salmon 40 30
C488 A247 65s brt bl 90 65
C489 A247 95s dk bl 1.25 1.00

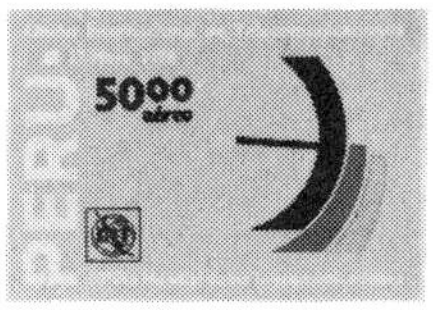

Antenna, ITU Emblem AP157

1978, July 3 Litho. *Perf. 13x13½*
C490 AP157 50s gray & multi 65 45

10th World Telecommunications Day.

San Martin, Flag Colors of Peru and Argentina AP158

1978, Sept. 4 Litho. *Perf. 13½x13*
C491 AP158 30s multi 40 30

Gen. José de San Martin (1778-1850), soldier and statesman, protector of Peru.

Stamps of 1965-67 Surcharged "Habilitado / R.D. No. O118" and New Value in Red, Green, Violet Blue or Black

1978 Litho.
C492 AP83 34s on 4.60s multi (R) #C208 22 16
C493 AP79 40s on 4.30s multi (G) #C196 25 20
C494 A184 70s on 2.60s brt grn (VB) #C209 45 40
C495 AP52 110s on 3.60s lil rose (Bk) #C210 70 65
C496 AP80 265s on 4.30s gray & multi (Bk) #C199 1.75 1.50
Nos. C492-C496 (5) 3.37 2.91

Stamps and Type of 1968-78 Surcharged in Violet Blue, Black or Red

1978 Litho.
C497 AP86 25s on 4.60s brn & multi (VB) #C221 16 14
C498 A247 45s on 28s dk grn (Bk) 30 22
C499 A247 75s on 28s dk grn (R) 50 40
C500 AP86 105s on 5.60s gray & multi (R) #C222 80 65

Nos. C498-C499 not issued without surcharge.

Nos. C486, C467 Surcharged

1980, Apr. 14 Litho. *Perf. 13½x13*
C501 A247 35s on 24s dp rose lil 22 15
C502 A243 45s on 32s rose brn & blk 30 20

No. C130 Surcharged in Black.

1981, Nov. Engr. *Perf. 13*
C503 AP57 30s on 2.20s multi 22 15
C504 AP57 40s on 2.20s multi 30 18

No. C130 Surcharged and Overprinted in Green: "12 Feria / Internacional / del / Pacifico 1981"

1981, Nov. 30
C505 AP57 140s on 2.20s multi 1.10 75

12th Intl. Pacific Fair.

AIR POST SEMI-POSTAL STAMPS

Catalogue values for unused stamps in this section, from this point to the end of the section, are for Never Hinged items.

Chavin Griffin SPAP1

Designs: 1.50s+1s, Bird. 3s+2.50s, Cat. 4.30s+3s, Mythological figure (vert.). 6s+ 4s, Chavin god (vert.).

Perf. 12½x12, 12x12½

1963, Apr. 18 Litho. Wmk. 346
Design in Gray and Brown
CB1 SPAP1 1s + 50c sal pink 16 16
CB2 SPAP1 1.50s + 1s bl 16 16
CB3 SPAP1 3s + 2.50s lt grn 50 50
CB4 SPAP1 4.30s + 3s grn 65 65
CB5 SPAP1 6s + 4s cit 80 80
Nos. CB1-CB5 (5) 2.27 2.27

The designs are from ceramics found by archaeological excavations of the 14th century Chavin culture. The surtax was for the excavations fund.

Henri Dunant and Centenary Emblem SPAP2

Perf. 12½x12

1964, Jan. 29 Unwmk.
Emblem in Gray & Red
CB6 SPAP2 1.30s + 70c pale rose & sl grn 16 16
CB7 SPAP2 4.30s + 1.70s lt bl & sl grn 42 24

Centenary of International Red Cross.

SPECIAL DELIVERY STAMPS

Regular Issue of 1900 Overprinted in Black

1908 Unwmk. *Perf. 12.*
E1 A25 10c gray blk 20.00 15.00

Regular Issue of 1907 Overprinted in Violet

1909
E2 A40 10c red brn & blk 25.00 16.00

Regular Issue of 1909 Handstamped in Violet

1910
E3 A49 10c dp bl 18.00 15.00

Two handstamps were used to make No. E2. Impressions from them measure 22½x6½mm. and 24x6½mm.

Counterfeits exist of Nos. E1-3.

POSTAGE DUE STAMPS

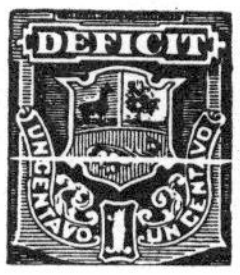

Coat of Arms — D1

Steamship and Llama
D2 D3

D4

D5

1874-86 Unwmk. Engr. *Perf. 12*
With Grill.
J1 D1 1c bis ('79) 16 14
 a. Without grill ('86) 10
J2 D2 5c vermilion 22 16
 a. Without grill ('86) 14
J3 D3 10c orange 35 25
 a. Without grill ('86) 20
J4 D4 20c blue 50 35
 a. Without grill ('86) 35
J5 D5 50c brown 9.00 3.50
 a. Without grill ('86) 3.50

A 2c green exists, but was not regularly issued.

Overprinted in Blue or Red

1881
"PLATA" 2½mm. High.
J6 D1 1c bis (Bl) 3.50 2.50
J7 D2 5c ver (Bl) 6.50 6.00
 a. Double overprint
 b. Inverted ovpt. 16.50 16.50
J8 D3 10c org (Bl) 6.50 6.00
 a. Inverted overprint 16.50 16.50
J9 D4 20c bl (R) 25.00 20.00
J10 D5 50c brn (Bl) 55.00 50.00

In the reprints of this overprint "PLATA" is 3 mm. high instead of 2½ mm. Besides being struck in the regular colors it was also applied to the 1, 5, 10 and 50c in red and the 20c in blue.

Overprinted in Red

1881

J11	D1 1c bister	5.00	5.00
J12	D2 5c vermilion	6.50	6.00
J13	D3 10c orange	8.00	6.50
J14	D4 20c blue	25.00	20.00
J15	D5 50c brown	80.00	65.00

Originals of Nos. J11 to J15 are overprinted in brick-red, oily ink; reprints in thicker, bright red ink. The 5c exists with reprinted overprint in blue.

Overprinted "Union Postal Universal Lima Plata", in Oval in first named color and Triangle in second named color.

1883

J16	D1 1c bis (Bl & Bk)	4.00	2.50
J17	D1 1c bis (Bk & Bl)	6.50	6.00
J18	D2 5c ver (Bl & Bk)	6.50	6.00
J19	D3 10c org (Bl & Bk)	6.50	5.00
J20	D4 20c bl (R & Bk)	450.00	450.00
J21	D5 50c brn (Bl & Bk)	55.00	50.00

Reprints of Nos. J16 to J21 have the oval overprint with "PLATA" 3mm. high. The 1c also exists with the oval overprint in red.

Overprinted in Black

1884

J22	D1 1c bister	35	35
J23	D2 5c vermilion	40	40
J24	D3 10c orange	50	40
J25	D4 20c blue	80	50
J26	D5 50c brown	2.50	90
	Nos. J22-J26 (5)	4.55	2.55

The triangular overprint is found in 11 types.

Overprinted "Lima Correos" in Circle in Red and Triangle in Black.

1884

J27	D1 1c bister	12.50	11.00

Reprints of No. J27 have the overprint in bright red. At the time they were made the overprint was also printed on the 5, 10, 20 and 50c Postage Due stamps.

Postage Due stamps overprinted with Sun and "CORREOS LIMA" (as shown above No. 103), alone or in combination with the "U. P. U. LIMA" oval or "LIMA CORREOS" in double-lined circle, are fancy varieties made to sell to collectors and never placed in use.

Overprinted **DEFICIT**

1896-97

J28	D1 1c bister	25	22
a.	Double overprint		
J29	D2 5c vermilion	25	22
a.	Double overprint		
b.	Inverted overprint		
J30	D3 10c orange	35	35
a.	Inverted overprint		
J31	D4 20c blue	50	40
a.	Double overprint		
J32	A22 50c red ('97)	55	50
J33	A23 1s brn ('97)	80	65
a.	Double overprint		
b.	Inverted ovpt.		
	Nos. J28-J33 (6)	2.70	2.34

The Scott Catalogue value is a retail price, what you could expect to pay for the stamp in a grade of Fine-Very Fine. The value listed is a reference which reflects recent actual dealer selling price.

Liberty — D6

1899 **Engr.**

J34	D6 5s yel grn	1.00	*5.00*
J35	D6 10s dl vio	900.00	900.00

No. 159 Surcharged in Black **DEFICIT CINCO CENTAVOS**

1902

J36	A31 5c on 10s bl grn	1.00	80
a.	Double surcharge	12.00	12.00

No. J4 Surcharged in Black **DÉFICIT UN CENTAVO**

J37	D4 1c on 20c bl	50	40
a.	"DEFICIT" omitted	6.50	2.00
b.	"DEFICIT" double	6.50	2.00
c.	"UN CENTAVO" double	6.00	2.00
d.	"UN CENTAVO" omitted	8.15	6.00

Surcharged Vertically like No. J36.

J38	D4 5c on 20c bl	1.00	1.00

Similar Surcharge on No. J35.

J39	D6 1c on 10s dl vio	50	50

D7

1909 **Engr.** ***Perf. 12.***

J40	D7 1c red brn	35	14
J41	D7 5c red brn	35	14
J42	D7 10c red brn	40	16
J43	D7 50c red brn	60	20

1921

Size: 18 1/4x22mm.

J44	D7 1c vio brn	16	16
J45	D7 2c vio brn	16	16
J46	D7 5c vio brn	25	20
J47	D7 10c vio brn	40	16
J48	D7 50c vio brn	1.40	50
J49	D7 1s vio brn	6.00	2.00
J50	D7 2s vio brn	9.00	2.50
	Nos. J44-J50 (7)	17.37	5.68

Nos. J49 and J50 have the circle at the center replaced by a shield containing "S/.", in addition to the numeral.

In 1929 during a shortage of regular postage stamps, some of the Postage Due stamps of 1921 were used instead.

Type of 1909-22.

Size: 18 3/4x23mm.

J50A	D7 2c vio brn	40	16
J50B	D7 10c vio brn	65	16

Type of 1909-22 Issues.

1932 **Photo.** ***Perf. 14 1/2x14***

J51	D7 2c vio brn	40	16
J52	D7 10c vio brn	65	16

Regular Stamps of 1934-35 Overprinted in Black **"Deficit"**

1935 ***Perf. 13.***

J53	A131 2c dp cl	40	16
J54	A117 10c crimson	50	40

Type of 1909-32.
Size: 19x23mm.
Imprint: "Waterlow & Sons, Limited, Londres."

1936 **Engr.** ***Perf. 12 1/2.***

J55	D7 2c lt brn	16	14
J56	D7 10c gray grn	40	16

OFFICIAL STAMPS

Regular Issue of 1886 Overprinted in Red

a 

1890, Feb. 2

O2	A17 1c dl vio	1.40	1.40
a.	Double overprint	8.25	8.25
O3	A18 2c green	1.40	1.40
a.	Double overprint		
b.	Inverted overprint	8.25	8.25
O4	A19 5c orange	1.65	1.65
a.	Inverted overprint	8.25	8.25
b.	Double overprint	8.25	8.25
O5	A20 10c slate	80	65
a.	Double overprint	8.25	8.25
b.	Inverted overprint	8.25	8.25
O6	A21 20c blue	2.50	2.00
a.	Double overprint	8.25	8.25
b.	Inverted overprint	8.25	8.25
O7	A22 50c red	4.00	2.00
a.	Inverted overprint	12.00	
b.	Double overprint		
O8	A23 1s brown	5.00	3.50
a.	Double overprint	16.50	16.50
b.	Inverted overprint	16.50	16.50

Nos. 118-124 (Bermudez Ovpt.) Overprinted Type "a" in Red

1894, Oct.

O9	A17 1c green	1.40	1.20
a.	"Gobierno" and head inverted	6.50	5.50
b.	Double overprint of "Gobierno"		
O10	A17 1c orange	22.50	20.00
O11	A18 2c rose	1.40	1.20
a.	Overprinted head inverted	10.00	10.00
b.	Both overprints inverted		
O12	A18 2c violet	1.40	1.20
a.	"Gobierno" double		
O13	A19 5c ultra	22.50	20.00
a.	Both overprints inverted		
O14	A19 5c blue	10.00	9.00
O15	A20 10c green	3.50	2.50
O16	A22 50c green	5.00	4.50

Nos. 125-126 ("Horseshoe" Ovpt.) Overprinted Type "a" in Red

O17	A18 2c vermilion	1.65	1.50
O18	A19 5c blue	1.65	1.50

Nos. 105, 107, 109, 113 Overprinted Type "a" in Red

1895, May

O19	A17 1c vermilion	8.25	8.25
O20	A18 2c dp ultra	8.25	8.25
O21	A12 5c claret	6.50	6.00
O22	A14 20c dp ultra	6.50	6.00

Nos. O2-O22 have been extensively counterfeited.

Nos. 141, 148, 149, 151 Overprinted in Black **GOBIERNO**

1896-1901

O23	A24 1c ultra	14	10
O24	A25 10c yellow	1.00	50
a.	Double overprint		
O25	A25 10c gray blk ('01)	14	10
O26	A26 50c brt rose	40	25

O1

1909-14 **Engr.** ***Perf. 12***

Size: 18 1/2x22mm

O27	O1 1c red	10	7
a.	1c brown red	10	7
O28	O1 1c org ('14)	22	16
O29	O1 10c bis brn ('14)	14	7
a.	10c violet brown	16	7
O30	O1 50c ol grn ('14)	65	35
a.	50c blue green	1.00	35

Size: 18 3/4x23 1/2mm

O30B	O1 10c vio brn	35	16
	Nos. O27-O30B (5)	1.46	81

1933 **Photo.** ***Perf. 15x14***

O31	O1 10c vio brn	35	14

No. 319 Overprinted in Black **"Servicio Oficial"**

1935 **Unwmk.** ***Perf. 13***

O32	A117 10c crimson	10	7

Type of 1909-33
Imprint: "Waterlow & Sons, Limited, Londres."

1936 **Engr.** ***Perf. 12 1/2***

Size: 19x23mm

O33	O1 10c lt brn	10	17
O34	O1 50c gray grn	35	20

PARCEL POST STAMPS

PP1

PP2

PP3

1897 **Typeset** **Unwmk.** ***Perf. 12***

Q1	PP1 1c dl lil	2.25	1.90
Q2	PP2 2c bister	2.50	2.25
a.	2c olive	2.50	2.25
b.	2c yellow	2.50	2.25
c.	Laid paper	65.00	65.00
Q3	PP2 5c dk bl	10.00	6.50
a.	Tete beche pair	*375.00*	
Q4	PP3 10c vio brn	14.00	10.00
Q5	PP3 20c rose red	16.50	14.00
Q6	PP3 50c bl grn	45.00	37.50
	Nos. Q1-Q6 (6)	90.25	72.15

Surcharged in Black **UN CENTAVO**

1903-04

Q7	PP3 1c on 20c rose red	11.50	10.00
Q8	PP3 1c on 50c bl grn	11.50	10.00
Q9	PP3 5c on 10c vio brn	80.00	65.00
a.	Inverted surcharge	120.00	110.00
b.	Double surcharge		

POSTAL TAX STAMPS

Plebiscite Issues

These stamps were not used in Tacna and Arica (which were under Chilean occupation) but were used in Peru to pay a supplementary tax on letters, etc.

It was intended that the money derived from the sale of these stamps should be used to help defray the expenses of the plebiscite.

Morro Arica — PT1

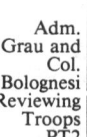

Adm. Grau and Col. Bolognesi Reviewing Troops PT2

Bolognesi Monument — PT3

1925-26 Unwmk. Litho. *Perf. 12*

RA1 PT1	5c dp bl	1.20	35
RA2 PT1	5c rose red	80	22
RA3 PT1	5c yel grn	65	22
RA4 PT2	10c brown	2.25	80
RA5 PT3	50c bl grn	18.00	9.00
	Nos. RA1-RA5 (5)	22.90	10.59

PT4

1926

RA6 PT4	2c orange	22	14

PT5

1927-28

RA7 PT5	2c dp org	50	10
RA8 PT5	2c red brn	50	14
RA9 PT5	2c dk bl	50	14
RA10 PT5	2c gray vio	35	10
RA11 PT5	2c bl grn ('28)	35	10
RA12 PT5	20c red	2.00	80
	Nos. RA7-RA12 (6)	4.20	1.38

PT6

1928 Engr.

RA13 PT6	2c dk vio	20	10

The use of the Plebiscite stamps was discontinued July 26, 1929, after the settlement of the Tacna-Arica controversy with Chile.

Unemployment Fund Issues

These stamps were required in addition to the ordinary postage, on every letter or piece of postal matter. The money obtained by their sale was to assist the unemployed.

Nos. 273-275 Surcharged

Habilitada
Pro
Desocupados
2 Cts.

1931

RA14 A95	2c on 4c red	65	35
a.	Inverted surcharge	3.50	3.50
RA15 A95	2c on 10c bl grn	50	35
a.	Inverted surcharge	3.50	3.50
RA16 A95	2c on 15c sl gray	50	35
a.	Inverted surcharge	3.50	3.50

"Labor" PT7

Blacksmith PT8

Two types of Nos. RA17-RA18:
I - Imprint 15mm.
II - Imprint 13¾mm.

Perf. 12x11½, 11½x12

1931-32 Litho.

RA17 PT7	2c emer (I)	7	7
a.	Type II	7	
RA18 PT7	2c rose car (I) ('32)	7	7
a.	Type II	7	

1932-34

RA19 PT8	2c dp gray	7	7
RA20 PT8	2c pur ('34)	7	7

Monument of 2nd of May — PT9

Perf. 13, 13½, 13x13½

1933-35 Photo.

RA21 PT9	2c bl vio	14	7
RA22 PT9	2c org ('34)	14	7
RA23 PT9	2c brn vio ('35)	14	5

No. 307 Overprinted in Black

a **Pro-Desocupados**

1934 *Perf. 13½*

RA24 A111	2c green	10	5
a.	Inverted overprint	1.40	1.20

No. 339 Overprinted in Black

Pro
Desocupados

1935

RA25 A131	2c dp cl	7	5

No. 339 Overprinted Type "a" in Black

1936 Unwmk. *Perf. 13½*

RA26 A131	2c dp cl	7	5

No. RA23 Overprinted in Black

"Ley 8310"

1936 *Perf. 13x13½*

RA27 PT9	2c brn vio	10	7
a.	Double overprint	1.40	
b.	Overprint reading down	1.40	
c.	Overprint double, reading down	1.40	

St. Rosa of Lima PT10

"Protection" by John Q. A. Ward PT11

1937 Engr. *Perf. 12*

RA28 PT10	2c car rose	14	5

Nos. RA27 and RA28 represented a tax to help erect a church.

Imprint: "American Bank Note Company"

1938 Litho.

RA29 PT11	2c brown	14	5

The tax was to help the unemployed.

Type of 1938 Redrawn
Imprint: "Columbian Bank Note Company."

1943 *Perf. 12½*

RA30 PT11	2c dl cl brn	10	5

See note above No. RA14. See Nos. RA34, RA40.

Catalogue values for unused stamps in this section, from this point to the end of the section, are for Never Hinged items.

PT12

PT13

1949 *Perf. 12½, 12*
Black Surcharge

RA31 PT12	3c on 4c vio bl	55	6
RA32 PT13	3c on 10c bl	55	6

The tax was for an education fund.

Symbolical of Education PT14

Emblem of Congress PT15

1950 Typo. *Perf. 14*
Size: 16½x21mm

RA33 PT14	3c dp car	15	6

See Nos. RA35, RA39, RA43

Type of 1938
Imprint: "Thomas De La Rue & Co. Ltd."

1951 Litho.

RA34 PT11	2c lt redsh brn	15	6

Type of 1950
Imprint: "Thomas De La Rue & Company, Limited."

1952 Unwmk. *Perf. 14, 13*
Size: 16½x21½mm

RA35 PT14	3c brn car	15	6

1954 *Rouletted 13*

RA36 PT15	5c bl & red	22	6

The tax was to help finance the National Marian Eucharistic Congress.

Piura Arms and Congress Emblem — PT16

1960 Litho. *Perf. 10½*

RA37 PT16	10c ultra, red, grn & yel	18	6
a.	Green ribbon inverted		
RA38 PT16	10c ultra & red	18	9

Nos. RA37-RA38 were used to help finance the 6th National Eucharistic Congress, Piura, Aug. 25-28. Obligatory on all domestic mail until Dec. 31, 1960. Both stamps exist imperf.

Type of 1950
Imprint: "Bundesdruckerei Berlin"

1961 *Perf. 14*
Size: 17½x22½mm

RA39 PT14	3c dp car	8	7

Type of 1938
Imprint: "Harrison and Sons Ltd"

1962, Apr. Litho. *Perf. 14x14½*

RA40 PT11	2c lt brn	10	8

Symbol of Eucharist — PT17

1962, May 8 *Rouletted 11*

RA41 PT17	10c bl & org	8	7

Issued to raise funds for the Seventh National Eucharistic Congress, Huancayo, 1964. Obligatory on all domestic mail.

1962
Imprint: "Iberia"

RA42 PT17	10c bl & org	8	7

Type of 1950

1965, Apr. Litho. *Perf. 12½x12*
Imprint: "Thomas de La Rue"
Size: 18x22mm

RA43 PT14	3c lt car	16	10

Type of 1962 Overprinted in Red with three "X," Bars and: "Periodista / Peruano / LEY / 16078"

1966, July 2 Litho. *Pin Perf.*
Imprint: "Iberia"

RA44 PT17	10c vio & org	8	7

No. RA43 Surcharged in Green or Black

HABILITADO
"Fondo del Periodista Peruano"
Ley 16078
S/o. 0.10
b

Habilitado
«Fondo del Periodista Peruano»
Ley 16078
S/. 0.10
c

HABILITADO
"Fondo del Periodista Peruano"
Ley 16078
S/o. 0.10
d

1966-67 *Perf. 12x12½*

RA45 PT14 (b)	10c on 3c lt car (G)	80	10
RA46 PT14 (c)	10c on 3c lt car (Bk)	65	7
RA47 PT14 (c)	10c on 3c lt car (G)	14	8
RA48 PT14 (d)	10c on 3c lt car (G)	22	7

The surtax of Nos. RA44-RA48 was for the Peruvian Journalists' Fund.

Pen Made of Newspaper
PT18

Temple at Chan-Chan
PT19

1967, Dec. Litho. *Perf. 11*

RA49 PT18 10c dk red & blk 7 7

The surtax was for the Peruvian Journalists' fund.

1967, Dec. 27

Designs: No. RA51, Side view of temple. Nos. RA52-RA55, Various stone bas-reliefs from Chan-Chan.

RA50 PT19 20c bl & grn 7 5
RA51 PT19 20c multi 7 5
RA52 PT19 20c brt bl & blk 7 5
RA53 PT19 20c emer & blk 7 5
RA54 PT19 20c sep & blk 7 5
RA55 PT19 20c lil rose & blk 7 5
Nos. RA50-RA55 (6) 42 30

The surtax was for the excavations at Chan-Chan, northern coast of Peru. (Mochica-Chimu pre-Inca period).

Type of 1967 Surcharged in Red: "VEINTE / CENTAVOS / R.S. 16-8-68"

Designs: No. RA56, Handshake. No. RA57, Globe and pen.

1968, Oct. Litho. *Perf. 11*

RA56 PT18 20c on 50c multi 10 10
RA57 PT18 20c on 1s multi 7 7

Nos. RA56-RA57 without surcharge were not obligatory tax stamps.

No. C199 surcharged "PRO NAVIDAD/ Veinte Centavos/R.S. 5-11-68" was not a compulsory postal tax stamp.

No. RA43 Surcharged Similar to Type "c"

1968, Oct. *Perf. 12½x12*

RA58 PT14 20c on 3c lt car 7 7

Surcharge lacks quotation marks and 4th line reads: Ley 17050.

OCCUPATION STAMPS

Issued under Chilean Occupation.

Stamps formerly listed as Nos. N1-N10 are regular issues of Chile canceled in Peru.

Stamps of Peru, 1874-80, Overprinted in Red, Blue or Black

1881-82 *Perf. 12*

N11 A17 1c org (Bl) 50 1.00
a. Inverted overprint
N12 A18 2c dk vio (Bk) 50 4.00
a. Inverted overprint 16.50
b. Double overprint 22.50
N13 A18 2c rose (Bk) 1.65 *22.50*
a. Inverted overprint
N14 A19 5c bl (R) 55.00 82.50
a. Inverted overprint
N15 A19 5c ultra (R) 90.00 100.00
N16 A20 10c grn (R) 50 *1.65*
a. Inverted overprint 6.50 6.50
b. Double overprint 12.00 12.00
N17 A21 20c brn red (Bl) 100.00 120.00

Reprints of No. N17 have the overprint in bright blue; on the originals it is in dull ultramarine. Nos. N11 and N12 exist with reprinted overprint in red or yellow. There are numerous counterfeits with the overprint in both correct and fancy colors.

Same, with Additional Overprint in Black

1882

N19 A17 1c grn (R) 65 1.00
a. Arms inverted 8.25 10.00
b. Arms double 5.50 6.50
c. Horseshoe inverted 12.00 13.50
N20 A19 5c bl (R) 1.00 1.00
a. Arms inverted 13.50 15.00
b. Arms double 13.50 15.00
N21 A22 50c rose (Bk) 2.00 2.50
a. Arms inverted 10.00
N22 A22 50c rose (Bl) 2.00 3.50
N23 A23 1s ultra (R) 4.00 5.50
a. Arms inverted 13.50
b. Horseshoe inverted 16.50
c. Arms and horseshoe inverted 20.00
d. Arms double 13.50
Nos. N19-N23 (5) 9.65 13.50

PROVISIONAL ISSUES

Stamps Issued in Various Cities of Peru during the Chilean Occupation of Lima and Callao

During the Chilean-Peruvian War which took place in 1879 to 1882, the Chilean forces occupied Lima and Callao, the two largest cities in Peru. As these cities were the source of supply of postage stamps, Peruvians in other sections of the country were left without stamps and were forced to the expedient of making provisional issues from whatever material was at hand. Many of these were former canceling devices made over for this purpose. Counterfeits exist of many of the overprinted stamps.

ANCACHS

(See Note under "Provisional Issues")

Regular Issue of Peru, Overprinted in Manuscript in Black

1884 Unwmk. *Perf. 12*

1N1 A19 5c blue 57.50 55.00

Regular Issues of Peru, Overprinted in Black

Overprinted **FRANCA**

1N2 A19 5c blue 18.00 16.50

Overprinted

1N3 A19 5c blue 90.00 82.50
1N4 A20 10c green 55.00 40.00
1N5 A20 10c slate 55.00 35.00

Same, with Additional Overprint "FRANCA"

1N6 A20 10c green 82.50 42.50

Overprinted

1N7 A19 5c blue 30.00 25.00
1N8 A20 10c green 30.00 25.00

Same, with Additional Overprint "FRANCA"

1N9 A20 10c green

A1

Revenue Stamp of Peru, 1878-79, Overprinted in Black "CORREO Y FISCAL" and "FRANCA"

1N10 A1 10c yellow 37.50 37.50

APURIMAC

(See Note under "Provisional Issues")

Provisional Issue of Arequipa Overprinted in Black

Overprint Covers Two Stamps

1885 Unwmk. *Imperf.*

2N1 A6 10c gray 100.00 90.00

Some experts question the status of No. 2N1.

AREQUIPA

(See Note under "Provisional Issues")

Coat of Arms
A1 A2

Overprint ("PROVISIONAL 1881-1882") in Black

1881, Jan. Unwmk. *Imperf.*

3N1 A1 10c blue 2.50 3.50
a. 10c ultramarine 2.50 4.00
b. Double overprint 12.00 13.50
c. Overprinted on back of stamp 8.25 10.00
3N2 A2 25c rose 2.50 6.00
a. "2" in upper left corner inverted 8.25
b. "Cevtavos" 8.25 10.00
c. Double overprint 12.00 13.50

The overprint also exists on 5s yellow.

The overprints "1883" in large figures or "Habilitado 1883" are fraudulent.

With Additional Overprint Handstamped in Red

1881, Feb.

3N3 A1 10c blue 3.50 3.50
a. 10c ultramarine 13.50 8.25

A4

1883 Litho.

3N7 A4 10c dl rose 3.50 5.00
a. 10c vermilion 3.50 5.00

Overprinted in Blue like No. 3N3.

3N9 A4 10c vermilion 5.00 4.00
a. 10c dull rose 5.00 4.00

Reprints of No. 3N9 are in different colors from the originals, orange, bright red, etc. They are printed in sheets of 20 instead of 25.

Redrawn

3N10 A4 10c brick red (Bl) 165.00

The redrawn stamp has small triangles without arabesques in the lower spandrels. The palm branch at left of the shield and other parts of the design have been redrawn.

Same Overprint in Black, Violet or Magenta On Regular Issues of Peru

1884 Embossed with Grill *Perf. 12*

3N11 A17 1c org (Bk, V or M) 6.50 6.50
3N12 A18 2c dk vio (Bk) 6.50 6.50
3N13 A19 5c bl (Bk, V or M) 2.00 1.35
a. 5c ultramarine (Bk or M) 8.25 6.50
3N15 A20 10c sl (Bk) 3.50 2.50
3N16 A21 20c brn red (Bk, V or M) 25.00 25.00
3N18 A22 50c grn (Bk or V) 25.00 25.00
3N20 A23 1s rose (Bk or V) 35.00 35.00

A5

A6

Rear Admiral M. L. Grau
A7

Col. Francisco Bolognesi
A8

Same Overprint as on Previous Issues

1885 *Imperf.*

3N22 A5 5c ol (Bk) 6.50 6.50
a. Without overprint 6.50 6.50
3N23 A6 10c gray (Bk) 6.50 6.00
a. Without overprint 5.50 4.00
3N25 A7 5c bl (Bk) 6.50 6.00
a. Without overprint 5.50 4.00
3N26 A8 10c ol (Bk) 6.50 4.00
a. Without overprint 5.50 4.00

These stamps have been reprinted without overprint; they exist however with forged overprint. Originals are on thicker paper with distinct mesh, reprints on paper without mesh.

AYACUCHO

(See Note under "Provisional Issues")

Provisional Issue of Arequipa Overprinted in Black

1881 Unwmk. *Imperf.*

4N1 A1 10c blue 82.50 70.00
a. 10c ultramarine 82.50 70.00

CHACHAPOYAS

(See Note under "Provisional Issues")

Regular Issue of Peru Overprinted in Black

1884 Unwmk. *Perf. 12.*

5N1 A19 5c ultra 100.00 90.00

CHALA

(See Note under "Provisional Issues")

Regular Issues of Peru Overprinted in Black

1884 **Unwmk.** ***Perf. 12***
6N1 A19 5c blue 8.25 6.50
6N2 A20 10c slate 10.00 8.25

CHICLAYO

(See Note under "Provisional Issues")

Regular Issue of Peru Overprinted in Black

1884 **Unwmk.** ***Perf. 12***
7N1 A19 5c blue 16.50 10.00

Same, Overprinted

7N2 A19 5c blue 35.00 22.50

CUZCO

(See Note under "Provisional Issues")

Provisional Issues of Arequipa Overprinted in Black

1881-85 **Unwmk.** ***Imperf.***
8N1 A1 10c blue 70.00 60.00
8N2 A4 10c red 70.00 60.00

Overprinted "CUZCO" in an oval of dots

8N5 A5 5c olive 110.00 100.00
8N6 A6 10c gray 80.00 75.00

Regular Issue of Peru Overprinted in Black "CUZCO" in a Circle

Perf. 12
8N7 A19 5c blue 50.00 50.00

Provisional Issues of Arequipa Overprinted in Black

1883 ***Imperf.***
8N9 A4 10c red 10.00 10.00

Same Overprint in Black on Regular Issues of Peru

1884 ***Perf. 12***
8N10 A19 5c blue 16.50 10.00
8N11 A20 10c slate 16.50 10.00

Same Overprint in Black on Provisional Issues of Arequipa

Imperf.
8N12 A5 5c olive 35.00 35.00
8N13 A6 10c gray 10.00 10.00

Postage Due Stamps of Peru Surcharged in Black

Perf. 12
8N14 D1 10c on 1c bis 110.00 100.00
8N15 D3 10c on 10c org 110.00 100.00

HUACHO

(See Note under "Provisional Issues")

Regular Issues of Peru Overprinted in Black

1884 **Unwmk.** ***Perf. 12***
9N1 A19 5c blue 10.00 10.00
9N2 A20 10c green 6.00 6.00
9N3 A20 10c slate 16.50 16.50

MOQUEGUA

(See Note under "Provisional Issues")

Provisional Issues of Arequipa Overprinted in Violet

Overprint 27mm. wide (illustration reduced).

1881-83 **Unwmk.** ***Imperf.***
10N1 A1 10c blue 42.50 40.00
10N2 A4 10c red ('83) 42.50 40.00

Same Overprint on Regular Issues of Peru in Violet

1884 ***Perf. 12***
10N3 A17 1c orange 42.50 40.00
10N4 A19 5c blue 37.50 30.00

Red Overprint

10N5 A19 5c blue 30.00 25.00

Same Overprint in Violet on Provisional Issues of Peru of 1880

Perf. 12
10N6 A17 1c grn (R) 8.25 6.50
10N7 A18 2c rose (Bl) 10.00 10.00
10N8 A19 5c bl (R) 20.00 20.00

Same Overprint in Violet on Provisional Issue of Arequipa

1885 ***Imperf.***
10N9 A6 10c gray 57.50 50.00

Regular Issues of Peru Overprinted in Violet

Perf. 12
10N10 A19 5c blue 110.00 65.00
10N11 A20 10c slate 45.00 25.00

Same Overprint in Violet on Provisional Issue of Arequipa

Imperf.
10N12 A6 10c gray 70.00 65.00

PAITA

(See Note under "Provisional Issues")

Regular Issues of Peru Overprinted

Black Overprint

1884 **Unwmk.** ***Perf. 12***
11N1 A19 5c blue 22.50 22.50
a. 5c ultramarine
11N2 A20 10c green 15.00 15.00
11N3 A20 10c slate 22.50 22.50

Red Overprint

11N4 A19 5c blue 22.50 22.50

Overprint lacks ornaments on Nos. 11N4-11N5.

Violet Overprint. Letters 5½mm High

11N5 A19 5c ultra 22.50 22.50
a. 5c blue

PASCO

(See Note under "Provisional Issues")

Regular Issues of Peru Overprinted in Magenta or Black

1884 **Unwmk.** ***Perf. 12***
12N1 A19 5c bl (M) 16.50 14.00
a. 5c ultramarine (M) 22.50 22.50
12N2 A20 10c grn (Bk) 35.00 30.00
12N3 A20 10c sl (Bk) 65.00 57.50

PISCO

(See Note under "Provisional Issues")

Regular Issue of Peru Overprinted in Black

1884 **Unwmk.** ***Perf. 12***
13N1 A19 5c blue 190.00 165.00

PIURA

(See Note under "Provisional Issues")

Regular Issues of Peru Overprinted in Black

1884 **Unwmk.** ***Perf. 12***
14N1 A19 5c blue 20.00 10.00
a. 5c ultramarine 25.00 13.50
14N2 A21 20c brn red 82.50 82.50
14N3 A22 50c green 200.00 200.00

Same Overprint in Black on Provisional Issues of Peru of 1881

14N4 A17 1c grn (R) 22.50 22.50
14N5 A18 2c rose (Bl) 40.00 40.00
14N6 A19 5c ultra (R) 50.00 50.00

Regular Issues of Peru Overprinted in Violet, Black or Blue

14N7 A19 5c bl (V) 16.50 10.00
a. 5c ultramarine (V) 16.50 10.00
b. 5c ultramarine (Bk) 16.50 10.00
14N8 A21 20c brn red (Bk) 82.50 82.50
14N9 A21 20c brn red (Bl) 82.50 82.50

Same Overprint in Black on Provisional Issues of Peru of 1881

14N10 A17 1c grn (R) 20.00 20.00
14N11 A19 5c bl (R) 22.50 22.50
a. 5c ultramarine (R) 40.00 40.00

Regular Issues of Peru Overprinted in Black

14N13 A19 5c blue 4.00 3.50
14N14 A21 20c brn red 82.50 82.50

Regular Issues of Peru Overprinted in Black

14N15 A19 5c ultra 70.00 65.00
14N16 A21 20c brn red 135.00 120.00

Same Overprint on Postage Due Stamp of Peru

14N18 D3 10c orange 100.00 82.50

PUNO

(See Note under "Provisional Issues")

Provisional Issue of Arequipa Overprinted in Violet or Blue

Diameter of outer circle 20½mm., PUNO 11½mm wide, M 3½mm wide.
Other types of this overprint are fraudulent.

1882-83 **Unwmk.** ***Imperf.***
15N1 A1 10c bl (V) 16.50 16.50
a. 10c ultramarine (V) 20.00 20.00
15N3 A2 25c red (V) 25.00 20.00
15N4 A4 10c dl rose (Bl) 25.00 25.00
a. 10c vermilion (Bl) 25.00 25.00

The overprint also exists on 5s yellow of Arequipa.

Same Overprint in Magenta on Regular Issues of Peru

1884 ***Perf. 12***
15N5 A17 1c orange 12.00 12.00
15N6 A18 2c violet 42.50 42.50
15N7 A19 5c blue 8.25 8.25

Violet Overprint

15N8 A19 5c blue 8.25 8.25
a. 5c ultramarine 12.00 12.00

Same Overprint in Black on Provisional Issues of Arequipa

1885 ***Imperf.***
15N10 A5 5c olive 16.50 13.50
15N11 A6 10c gray 5.50 5.50
15N12 A8 10c olive 10.00 10.00

Regular Issues of Peru Overprinted in Magenta

1884 ***Perf. 12***
15N13 A17 1c orange 10.00 8.25
15N14 A18 2c violet 13.50 12.00
15N15 A19 5c blue 5.50 5.50
a. 5c ultramarine 11.00 11.00
15N16 A20 10c green
15N17 A21 20c brn red 82.50 82.50
15N18 A22 50c green

YCA

(See Note under "Provisional Issues")

Regular Issues of Peru Overprinted in Violet

1884 **Unwmk.** ***Perf. 12***
16N1 A17 1c orange 40.00 40.00
16N3 A19 5c blue 12.00 8.25

Black Overprint

16N5 A19 5c blue 10.00 6.50

Magenta Overprint

16N6 A19 5c blue 10.00 6.50
16N7 A20 10c slate 30.00 30.00

Regular Issues of Peru Overprinted in Black

16N12 A19 5c blue 150.00 135.00
16N13 A21 20c brown 190.00 165.00

Regular Issues of Peru Overprinted in Carmine

16N14	A19	5c blue	150.00	135.00
16N15	A20	10c slate	190.00	165.00

Same, with Additional Overprint

16N21	A19	5c blue	165.00	150.00
16N22	A21	20c brn red	250.00	225.00

Various other stamps exist with the overprints "YCA" and "YCA VAPOR" but they are not known to have been issued. Some of them were made to fill a dealer's order and others are reprints or merely cancellations.

PHILIPPINES

LOCATION — Group of about 7,100 islands and islets in the Malay Archipelago, north of Borneo, in the North Pacific Ocean.
GOVT. — Republic
AREA — 115,830 sq. mi.
POP. — 53,350,000 (est. 1984)
CAPITAL — Manila

The islands were ceded to the United States by Spain in 1898. On November 15, 1935, they were given their independence, subject to a transition period which ended July 4, 1946. On that date the Commonwealth became the Republic of the Philippines.

8 Cuartos = 1 Real
100 Centavos de Peso = 1 Peso (1864)
100 Centimos de Escudo = 1 Escudo (1871)
100 Centimos de Peseta = 1 Peseta (1872)
1000 Milesimas de Peso = 100 Centimos or Centavos = 1 Peso (1878)
100 Cents = 1 Dollar (1899)
100 Centavos = 1 Peso (1906)
100 Centavos (Sentimos) = 1 Peso (Piso) (1946)

Catalogue values for unused stamps in this country are for Never Hinged items, beginning with Scott 497 in the regular postage section, Scott B1 in the semi-postal section, Scott C64 in the airpost section, Scott E11 in the special delivery section, Scott J63 in the postage due section, and Scott O44 in the officials section.

Values of early Philippine stamps vary according to condition. Quotations for Nos. 1-32 are for fine copies. Very fine to superb specimens sell at much higher prices, and inferior or poor copies sell at reduced prices, depending on the condition of the individual specimen.

Issued under Spanish Dominion.

The stamps of Philippine Islands punched with a round hole had been withdrawn from use and punched to indicate that they were no longer available for postage. In this condition they sell for only a trifle, as compared to postally used copies.

Queen Isabella II
A1 A2

1854 Unwmk. Engr. *Imperf.*

1	A1	5c orange	1,000.	140.00
a		5c brn org	1,100.	165.00
2	A1	10c carmine	300.00	100.00
a		10c pale rose	450.00	165.00
4	A2	1r sl bl	300.00	125.00
a		1r bl	375.00	175.00
b		1r ultra	375.00	175.00
c		"CORROS"	*2,500.*	*800.00*
5	A2	2r green	400.00	110.00
a		2r yel grn	400.00	140.00

Forty varieties of each value.

A3

1855 Litho.

6	A3	5c pale ver	1,000.	250.00

Four varieties.

Redrawn

7	A3	5c vermilion	*8,000.*	*800.00*

In the redrawn stamp the inner circle is smaller and is not broken by the labels at top and bottom. Only one variety.

Queen Isabella II
A4 A5

Wmk. 104- Loops

1856 Wmk. 104 Typo.

8	A4	1r grn, *bl*	80.00
9	A4	2r car, *bl*	75.00

Nos. 8 and 9 can be distinguished from the Cuban stamps of 1855 only by the cancellations.

1859, Jan. 1 Litho. Unwmk.

10	A5	5c vermilion	10.00	5.50
a		5c scar	14.00	6.50
b		5c org	20.00	10.00
11	A5	10c rose	10.00	5.50

Four varieties of each value.

Dot after CORREOS
A6 A7

1861-62

12	A6	5c vermilion	15.00	7.00
13	A7	5c dull red ('62)	20.00	8.00

Colon after CORREOS — A8

A8a

A9

A10

1863

14	A8	5c vermilion	12.00	6.00
15	A8	10c carmine	22.50	14.00
16	A8	1r violet	350.00	175.00
17	A8	2r blue	300.00	150.00
18	A8a	1r gray grn	125.00	65.00
20	A9	1r green	70.00	25.00
a		1r emer	50.00	25.00

No. 18 has "CORREOS" 10½mm. long, the point of the bust is rounded and is about 1mm. from the circle which contains 94 pearls.

No. 20 has "CORREOS" 11mm. long, and the bust ends in a sharp point which nearly touches the circle of 76 pearls.

1864 Typo.

21	A10	3⅛c blk, *buff*	2.00	1.25
22	A10	6⅞c grn, *rose*	2.00	75
23	A10	12⅜c bl, *sal*	4.50	75
24	A10	25c red, *buff*	4.50	2.50

Preceding Issues Handstamped

HABILITADO POR LA NACION

1868-74

25	A2	1r sl bl ('74)	*1,900.*	*800.00*
25A	A2	2r grn ('74)	*3,500.*	*775.00*
26	A4	1r grn, *bl* ('73)	120.00	55.00
27	A4	2r car, *bl* ('73)	140.00	50.00
28	A5	10c rose ('74)	50.00	35.00
29	A7	5c red ('73)	60.00	30.00
30	A8	5c ver ('72)	45.00	25.00
31	A8	1r vio ('72)	450.00	250.00
32	A8	2r bl ('72)	400.00	225.00
33	A8a	1r gray grn ('71)	42.50	15.00
34	A9	1r emer ('71)	7.50	3.00
35	A10	3⅛c blk, *buff*	6.50	3.00
36	A10	6⅞c grn, *rose*	6.50	3.00
37	A10	12⅜c bl, *sal*	25.00	12.00
38	A10	25c ver, *buff*	13.50	7.00

"Spain"
A11

King Amadeo
A12

1871 Typo. *Perf. 14*

39	A11	5c blue	20.00	2.00
40	A11	10c dp grn	5.00	2.00
41	A11	20c brown	25.00	10.00
42	A11	40c rose	35.00	6.50

1872

43	A12	12c rose	6.50	2.00
a		Imperf.	40.00	
44	A12	16c blue	45.00	12.00
a		16c ultra	65.00	40.00
45	A12	25c gray lil	6.50	1.50
a		25c lilac	11.00	6.50
46	A12	62c violet	15.00	3.00
47	A12	1p25c yel brn	35.00	8.00

"Peace"
A13

King Alfonso XII
A14

1874

48	A13	12c gray lil	7.00	2.00
49	A13	25c ultra	2.50	75
50	A13	62c rose	22.50	2.00
51	A13	1p25c brown	85.00	15.00
a		Imperf.	200.00	

1875-77

52	A14	2c rose	1.50	40
53	A14	2c dk bl ('77)	80.00	42.50
54	A14	6c org ('77)	6.00	1.50
55	A14	10c bl ('77)	2.50	50
56	A14	12c lilac	2.50	50
57	A14	20c vio brn	7.00	2.00
58	A14	25c dp grn	6.00	50

Imperforates of type A14 probably are from proof or trial sheets.

Nos. 52, 63 Handstamp Surcharged in Black or Blue

HABILITADO 12 CS PTA

1877-79

59	A14	12c on 2c rose (Bk)	25.00	7.50
60	A16	12c on 25m blk (Bk) ('79)	32.50	10.00
61	A16	12c on 25m blk (Bl) ('79)	100.00	70.00

Surcharge exists inverted and double.

A16

1878-79 Typo.

62	A16	0.0625 (62½m) gray	25.00	5.00
62A	A16	0.0625 (62½m) lil	25.00	5.00
63	A16	25m black	2.00	25
64	A16	25m grn ('79)	32.50	10.00
65	A16	50m dl lil	12.00	4.00
66	A16	100m carmine	40.00	15.00
67	A16	100m yel grn ('79)	4.50	1.50
68	A16	125m blue	3.00	35
69	A16	200m rose ('79)	12.00	3.50
70	A16	200m vio rose ('79)	120.00	60.00
71	A16	250m bis ('79)	5.00	1.00

Imperforates of type A16 probably are from proof or trial sheets.

Stamps of 1878-79 Surcharged:

UNIVERSAL DE
CONVENIO CORREOS
HABILITADO
2 cént de peso
a

UNIVERSAL DE
CONVENIO CORREOS
HABILITADO
2 cént de peso
b

1879

72	A16 (a)	2c on 25c grn	25.00	5.00
a		Double surcharge		
73	A16 (a)	8c on 100m car	25.00	5.00
a		"COREROS"	60.00	30.00
74	A16 (b)	2c on 25m grn	60.00	17.50
75	A16 (b)	8c on 100m car	60.00	17.50

A19

Original state: The medallion is surrounded by a heavy line of color of nearly even thickness, touching the line below "Filipinas"; the opening in the hair above the temple is narrow and pointed.

1st retouch: The line around the medallion is thin, except at the upper right, and does not touch the horizontal line above it; the opening in the hair is slightly wider and rounded; the lock of hair above the forehead is shaped like a broad "V" and ends in a point; there is a faint white line below it, which is not found on the original. The shape of the hair and the width of the white line vary.

2nd retouch: The lock of hair is less pointed; the white line is much broader.

1880-86 Typo.

76	A19	2c rose	38	18
77	A19	2½c brown	2.25	18
78	A19	2⁴⁄₈c ultra ('82)	32	18
79	A19	2⁴⁄₈c ultra, 1st retouch ('83)	28	18
80	A19	2⁴⁄₈c ultra, 2nd retouch ('86)	3.75	38
81	A19	5c gray ('82)	28	18
a		5c gray bl	38	20
82	A19	6⅞c dp grn ('82)	1.75	90
83	A19	8c yel brn	7.00	1.40
84	A19	10c green	175.00	100.00
85	A19	10c brn lil ('82)	1.25	22
a		10c brn vio	2.00	1.00
86	A19	12⁴⁄₈c brt rose ('82)	65	22
87	A19	20c bis brn ('82)	1.25	22
88	A19	25c dk brn ('82)	1.90	22

See also Nos. 137-139.

Stamps and Type of 1880-86 Handstamp Surcharged in Black, Green or Red:

c

d

e

f

1881-88

Black Surcharge.

89	A19 (c)	2c on 2½c brn	2.50	1.00
91	A19 (f)	10c on 2⁴⁄₈c ultra (#80) ('87)	4.00	1.00
92	A19 (d)	20c on 8c brn ('83)	6.00	1.75
93	A19 (d)	1r on 2c car ('83)	30.00	16.50
94	A19 (d)	2r on 2⁴⁄₈c ultra ('83)	4.00	1.00

Green Surcharge

95	A19 (e)	8c on 2c car ('83)	4.00	1.50
96	A19 (d)	10c on 2c car ('83)	3.00	1.50
97	A19 (d)	1r on 2c car ('83)	60.00	20.00
98	A19 (d)	1r on 5c gray bl ('83)	4.00	1.50
99	A19 (d)	1r on 8c brn ('83)	5.00	1.50

Red Surcharge.

100	A19 (f)	1c on 2⁴⁄₈c ultra (#79) ('87)	60	40
101	A19 (f)	1c on 2⁴⁄₈c ultra (#80) ('87)	1.90	90
102	A19 (d)	16c on 2⁴⁄₈c ultra ('83)	5.00	1.50
103	A19 (d)	1r on 2c car ('83)	4.00	1.50
104	A19 (d)	1r on 5c bl gray ('83)	8.00	3.25

Surcharges exist double or inverted on many of Nos. 89-104.

Handstamp Surcharged in Magenta

g

h

1887

105	A19 (g)	8c on 2⁴⁄₈c (#79)	60	30
106	A19 (g)	8c on 2⁴⁄₈c (#80)	65	65

1888

107	A19 (h)	2⁴⁄₈c on 1c gray grn	80	55
108	A19 (h)	2⁴⁄₈c on 5c bl gray	1.00	40
109	N1 (h)	2⁴⁄₈c on ⅛c grn	35	15
110	A19 (h)	2⁴⁄₈c on 50m bis	1.40	65
111	A19 (h)	2⁴⁄₈c on 10c grn	1.00	40

No. 109 is surcharged on a newspaper stamp of 1886-89 and has the inscriptions shown on cut N1.

On Revenue Stamps

R1

R2

R3

Handstamp Surcharged in Black, Yellow, Green, Red or Magenta:

j

k

HABILITADO
PARA
CORREOS
m

1881-88

Black Surcharge

112	R1 (c)	2c on 10c bis	14.00	9.00
113	R1 (j)	2⁴⁄₈c on 10c bis	1.50	60
114	R1 (j)	2⁴⁄₈c on 2r bl	140.00	60.00
115	R1 (j)	8c on 10c bis	140.00	65.00
116	R1 (j)	8c on 2r bl	5.50	1.50
118	R1 (d)	1r on 12⁴⁄₈c gray bl ('83)	4.50	2.50
119	R1 (d)	1r on 10c bis ('82)	5.00	2.50

Yellow Surcharge

120	R2 (e)	2c on 200m grn ('82)	3.75	1.50
121	R1 (d)	16c on 2r bl ('83)	3.00	1.90

Green Surcharge

122	R1 (d)	1r on 10c bis ('83)	8.00	2.00

Red Surcharge

123	R1(d+j)	2r on 8c on 2r bl ('82)	25.00	10.00
124	R1(d)	1r on 12⁴⁄₈c gray bl ('83)	3.50	2.00
125	R1(k)	6²⁄₈c on 12⁴⁄₈c gray bl ('85)	3.50	1.65
126	R3(d)	1r on 10p bis ('83)	30.00	19.00
127	R1(m)	1r green	65.00	50.00
127A	R1(m)	2r blue	140.00	80.00
128	R2(d)	1r on 1p grn ('83)	17.50	12.00
129	R2(d)	1r on 200m grn ('83)	55.00	30.00

Magenta Surcharge

130	R2(h)	2⁴⁄₈c on 200m grn ('88)	2.00	1.00
131	R2(h)	2⁴⁄₈c on 20c brn ('88)	8.00	4.00

On Telegraph Stamps.

T1

T2

Surcharged in Red, or Black

1883-88

132	T1 (d)	2r on 250m ultra (R)	5.00	2.50
133	T1 (d)	20c on 250m ultra	25.00	20.00
134	T1 (d)	2r on 250m ultra	7.00	3.75
135	T1 (d)	1r on 20c on 250m ultra (R & Bk)	5.00	2.50

Magenta Surcharge

136	T2 (h)	2⁴⁄₈c on 1c bis ('88)	60	40

Type of 1880-86 Redrawn.

1887-88

137	A19	50m bister	50	25
138	A19	1c yel grn ('88)	50	20
139	A19	6c yel brn ('88)	8.00	1.50

King Alfonso XIII — A36

1890-97 Typo.

140	A36	1c vio ('92)	50	20
141	A36	1c rose ('94)	3.00	1.25
142	A36	1c bl grn ('96)	1.50	40
143	A36	1c cl ('97)	6.25	2.50
144	A36	2c claret	15	10
145	A36	2c vio ('92)	20	15
146	A36	2c dk brn ('94)	15	7
147	A36	2c ultra ('96)	25	25
148	A36	2c gray brn ('96)	7	7
149	A36	2⁴⁄₈c dl bl	30	10
150	A36	2⁴⁄₈c ol gray ('92)	20	15
151	A36	5c dk bl	30	10
152	A36	5c dk ol gray	60	20
153	A36	5c grn ('92)	25	20
154	A36	5c lil ('92)	225.00	90.00
155	A36	5c vio brn ('96)	5.00	1.90
156	A36	5c bl grn ('96)	3.00	1.00
157	A36	6c brn vio ('92)	20	15
158	A36	6c red org ('94)	50	25
159	A36	6c car rose ('96)	3.00	1.50
160	A36	8c yel grn	15	10
161	A36	8c ultra ('92)	50	20
162	A36	8c red brn ('94)	25	7
163	A36	10c bl grn	1.00	15
164	A36	10c pale cl ('91)	60	15
165	A36	10c cl ('92)	25	5
166	A36	10c yel brn ('96)	25	5
167	A36	12⁴⁄₈c yel grn	20	10
168	A36	12⁴⁄₈c org ('94)	60	15
169	A36	15c red brn ('92)	60	20
170	A36	15c rose ('94)	60	25
171	A36	15c bl grn ('96)	1.50	1.00
172	A36	20c rose	30.00	12.00
173	A36	20c sal ('91)	8.00	2.50
174	A36	20c gray brn ('92)	1.50	25
175	A36	20c dk vio ('94)	3.00	1.20
176	A36	20c org ('96)	2.50	1.00
177	A36	25c brown	3.75	1.00
178	A36	25c dl bl ('91)	1.50	20
179	A36	40c dk vio ('97)	9.00	2.50
180	A36	80c cl ('97)	16.50	5.50

Many of Nos. 140-180 exist imperf.

Stamps of Previous Issues Handstamp Surcharged in Blue, Red, Black or Violet

1897

Blue Surcharge.

181	A36	5c on 5c grn	1.25	75
182	A36	15c on 15c red brn	1.50	70
183	A36	20c on 20c gray brn	4.50	3.00

Red Surcharge.

185	A36	5c on 5c grn	1.50	90

Black Surcharge.

187	A36	5c on 5c grn	15.00	8.25
188	A36	15c on 15c rose	2.00	1.25
189	A36	20c on 20c dk vio	12.00	7.00
190	A36	20c on 25c brn	7.00	5.50

Violet Surcharge.

191	A36	15c on 15c rose	3.00	2.00

Inverted, double and other variations of this surcharge exist.

The 5c on 5c blue gray was released during U.S. Administration. The surcharge is a mixture of red and black inks.

Impressions in violet black are believed to be reprints. The following varieties are known: 5c on 5c blue green, 15c on 15c rose, 15c on 15c red brown, 20c on 20c gray brown, 20c on 20c dark violet, 20c on 25c brown. These surcharges are to be found double, inverted, etc.

King Alfonso XIII — A39

1898 Typo.

192	A39	1m org brn	6	6
193	A39	2m org brn	6	6
194	A39	3m org brn	9	6
195	A39	4m org brn	1.75	65
196	A39	5m org brn	6	6
197	A39	1c blk vio	6	6
198	A39	2c dk bl grn	6	6
199	A39	3c dk brn	6	6
200	A39	4c orange	3.75	2.00
201	A39	5c car rose	9	6
202	A39	6c dk bl	40	25
203	A39	8c gray brn	20	12
204	A39	10c vermilion	60	40
205	A39	15c dl ol grn	60	35
206	A39	20c maroon	60	40
207	A39	40c violet	40	35
208	A39	60c black	1.75	90
209	A39	80c red brn	1.75	90
210	A39	1p yel grn	4.00	2.75
211	A39	2p sl bl	8.00	3.00

Nos. 192-211 exist imperf. Value $1,000.

Issued under U.S. Administration

Regular Issues of the United States Overprinted in Black

On US No. 260

1899-1900 Unwmk. *Perf. 12*

212 A96 50c orange 425.00 250.00

On US Nos. 279, 279d, 267, 268, 281, 282C, 283, 284, 275 and 275a.

Wmk. 191

213 A87 1c yel grn 2.50 60
214 A88 2c org red, III 1.20 40
a 2c car, type III 1.65 65
b Booklet pane of 6 ('00) 225.00 *120.00*
215 A89 3c purple 4.25 1.20
216 A91 5c blue 4.25 1.00
a Inverted overprint *3,000.*
217 A94 10c brn, I 13.50 3.50
217A A94 10c org brn, II 165.00 35.00
218 A95 15c ol grn 22.50 5.50
a 15c lt ol grn 30.00 8.25
219 A96 50c orange 85.00 25.00
a 50c red org *165.00*
Nos. 213-219 (8) 298.20 72.20

On US Nos. 280b, 282 and 272.

1901

220 A90 4c org brn 13.50 4.00
221 A92 6c lake 13.75 5.50
222 A93 8c vio brn 18.00 5.50

On US Nos. 276, 276A, 277a and 278.

Red Overprint.

223 A97 $1 blk, type I 325.00 175.00
223A A97 $1 blk, type II 2,000. 1,000.
224 A98 $2 dk bl 450.00 225.00
225 A99 $5 dk grn 1,100. 700.00

On US Nos. 300-313 and shades.

1903-04

226 A115 1c bl grn 2.25 25
227 A116 2c carmine 3.75 90
228 A117 3c brt vio 42.50 10.00
229 A118 4c brn ('04) 45.00 15.00
a 4c org brn 45.00 12.50
230 A119 5c blue 6.00 65
231 A120 6c brnsh lake ('04) 47.50 12.50
232 A121 8c vio blk ('04) 20.00 7.50
233 A122 10c pale red brn ('04) 11.25 1.75
a 10c red brn 14.00 2.50
b Pair, one without overprint 700.00
234 A123 13c pur blk 17.50 8.75
a 13c brn vio 17.50 8.75
235 A124 15c ol grn 30.00 6.50
236 A125 50c orange 87.50 25.00
Nos. 226-236 (11) 313.25 *88.80*

Red Overprint

237 A126 $1 black 325.00 150.00
238 A127 $2 dk bl ('04) 1,000. 600.00
239 A128 $5 dk grn ('04) 1,200. 700.00

On US Nos. 319, 319c in Black

1904

240 A129 2c carmine 5.50 2.50
a Bklt. pane of 6 *1,200.*
b 2c scar 6.50 2.75

José Rizal A40

Arms of Manila A41

Wmk. 191PI- Double-lined PIPS

Designs: 4c, McKinley. 6c, Magellan. 8c, Miguel Lopez de Legaspi. 10c, Gen. Henry W. Lawton. 12c, Lincoln. 16c, Adm. William T. Sampson. 20c, Washington. 26c, Francisco Carriedo. 30c, Franklin.

Each Inscribed "Philippine Islands / United States of America".

Wmk. 191PI

1906, Sept. 8 Engr. *Perf. 12*

241 A40 2c dp grn 30 6
a 2c yellow green ('10) 50 6
b Booklet pane of 6 225.00
242 A40 4c carmine 40 6
a 4c carmine lake ('10) 75 6
b Booklet pane of 6 225.00
243 A40 6c violet 1.25 15
244 A40 8c brown 2.25 75
245 A40 10c blue 1.65 10
246 A40 12c brn lake 5.00 2.25
247 A40 16c vio blk 3.25 25
248 A40 20c org brn 3.75 40
249 A40 26c vio brn 6.00 2.50
250 A40 30c ol grn 4.50 1.60
251 A41 1p orange 25.00 11.00
252 A41 2p black 35.00 1.50
253 A41 4p dk bl 100.00 17.50
254 A41 10p dk grn 200.00 85.00
Nos. 241-254 (14) 388.35 123.12

Change of Colors

1909-13 *Perf. 12*

255 A40 12c red org 8.00 3.00
256 A40 16c ol grn 2.00 50
257 A40 20c yellow 7.50 1.50
258 A40 26c bl grn 1.50 80
259 A40 30c ultra 10.00 4.00
260 A41 1p pale vio 30.00 6.00
260A A41 2p vio brn ('13) 80.00 3.00
Nos. 255-260A (7) 139.00 18.80

Wmk. 190PI- Single-lined PIPS

1911 Wmk. 190PI *Perf. 12*

261 A40 2c green 60 10
a Booklet pane of 6 200.00
262 A40 4c car lake 3.00 12
a 4c car
b Booklet pane of 6 200.00
263 A40 6c dp vio 1.75 10
264 A40 8c brown 8.00 50
265 A40 10c blue 3.00 10
266 A40 12c orange 2.00 50
267 A40 16c ol grn 2.25 20
268 A40 20c yellow 2.00 15
a 20c org 2.00 15
269 A40 26c bl grn 2.75 30
270 A40 30c ultra 3.25 50
271 A41 1p pale vio 20.00 50
272 A41 2p vio brn 25.00 1.00
273 A41 4p dp bl 650.00 60.00
274 A41 10p dp grn 200.00 22.50
Nos. 261-274 (14) 923.60 86.57

1914

275 A40 30c gray 10.00 65

1914-23 *Perf. 10.*

276 A40 2c green 1.50 12
a Booklet pane of 6 200.00
277 A40 4c carmine 1.50 15
a Booklet pane of 6 200.00
278 A40 6c lt vio 35.00 15.00
a 6c dp vio 37.50 7.00
279 A40 8c brown 35.00 12.50
280 A40 10c dk bl 22.50 25
281 A40 16c ol grn 70.00 5.00
282 A40 20c orange 20.00 1.00
283 A40 30c gray 50.00 3.50
284 A41 1p pale vio 110.00 4.00
Nos. 276-284 (9) 345.50 41.52

1918-26 *Perf. 11*

285 A40 2c green 20.00 5.00
a Bklt. pane of 6 *600.00*
286 A40 4c carmine 27.50 3.00
a Bklt. pane of 6 *600.00*
287 A40 6c dp vio 37.50 2.00
287A A40 8c lt brn 225.00 40.00
288 A40 10c dk bl 50.00 1.75
289 A40 16c ol grn 100.00 8.00
289A A40 20c orange 55.00 10.00
289C A40 30c gray 50.00 17.50
289D A41 1p pale vio 60.00 15.00
Nos. 285-289D (9) 625.00 102.25

1917-25 Unwmk. *Perf. 11*

290 A40 2c yel grn 7 5
a 2c dk grn 8 5
b Vert. pair, imperf. horiz.
c Horiz. pair, imperf. btwn. *1,000.*
d Vertical pair, imperf. between *1,200.*
e Booklet pane of 6 *16.50*
291 A40 4c carmine 7 5
a 4c lt rose 16 5
b Booklet pane of 6 12.00
292 A40 6c dp vio 20 5
a 6c lil 25 5
b 6c red vio 25 7
c Booklet pane of 6 250.00
293 A40 8c yel brn 14 8
a 8c org brn 14 8
294 A40 10c dp bl 14 5
295 A40 12c red org 25 10
296 A40 16c lt ol grn 35.00 16
a 16c ol bis 35.00 35
297 A40 20c org yel 22 7
298 A40 26c green 38 42
a 26c bl grn 45 25
299 A40 30c gray 35 7
300 A41 1p pale vio 21.00 80
a 1p red lil 21.00 80
b 1p pale rose lil 21.00 1.00
301 A41 2p vio brn 20.00 50
302 A41 4p blue 14.00 35
a 4p dk bl 14.00 35
Nos. 290-302 (13) 91.82 2.75

1923-26

Design: 16c, Adm. George Dewey.

303 A40 16c ol bis 50 14
a 16c ol grn 1.00 14
304 A41 10p dp grn ('26) 30.00 5.50

Legislative Palace — A42

1926, Dec. 20 Unwmk. *Perf. 12*

319 A42 2c grn & blk 35 20
a Horiz. pair, imperf. between *190.00*
b Vert. pair, imperf. between *300.00*
320 A42 4c car & blk 35 25
a Horiz. pair, imperf. between *190.00*
b Vert. pair, imperf. between *225.00*
321 A42 16c ol grn & blk 65 55
a Horiz. pair, imperf. between *225.00*
b Vert. pair, imperf. between *300.00*
c Double impression of center *375.00*
322 A42 18c lt brn & blk 80 50
a Double impression of center *375.00*
b Vert. pair, imperf. between *300.00*
323 A42 20c org & blk 1.20 80
a 20c org & brn *250.00*
b Imperf., pair *300.00 300.00*
c As "a", imperf., pair *250.00*
d Vert. pair, imperf. between *300.00*
324 A42 24c gray & blk 1.00 65
a Vert. pair, imperf. between *300.00*
325 A42 1p rose lil & blk 45.00 22.50
a Vert. pair, imperf. between *325.00*
Nos. 319-325 (7) 49.35 25.45

Opening of the Legislative Palace.

Coil Stamp
Rizal Type of 1906

1928 *Perf. 11 Vertically*

326 A40 2c green 4.25 5.00

Types of 1906-23

1925 Unwmk. *Imperf.*

340 A40 2c yel grn ('31) 12 12
341 A40 4c car rose ('31) 20 20
342 A40 6c vio ('31) 2.00 2.00
343 A40 8c brn ('31) 1.75 1.75
344 A40 10c bl ('31) 2.00 2.00
345 A40 12c dp org ('31) 3.00 3.00
346 A40 16c ol grn *(Dewey)* ('31) 2.25 2.25
347 A40 20c org yel ('31) 2.25 2.25
348 A40 26c grn ('31) 2.25 2.25
349 A40 30c lt gray ('31) 2.50 2.50
350 A41 1p lt vio ('31) 8.00 8.00
351 A41 2p brn vio ('31) 20.00 20.00
352 A41 4p bl ('31) 60.00 60.00
353 A41 10p grn ('31) 175.00 175.00
Nos. 340-353 (14) 281.32 281.32

Two imperforate issues were made, in 1925 and 1931. They differ in shade.

Mount Mayon, Luzon — A43

Post Office, Manila — A44

Canceled-to-order stamps are often from remainders. Most collectors of canceled stamps prefer postally used specimens.

Pier No. 7, Manila Bay A45

(See footnote) A46

Rice Planting A47

Rice Terraces A48

Baguio Zigzag — A49

1932, May 3 *Perf. 11*

354 A43 2c yel grn 75 35
355 A44 4c rose car 50 35
356 A45 12c orange 75 75
357 A46 18c red org 25.00 12.50
358 A47 20c yellow 1.00 80
359 A48 24c dp vio 1.50 1.00
360 A49 32c ol brn 1.50 1.15
Nos. 354-360 (7) 31.00 16.90

The 18c vignette was intended to show Pagsanjan Falls in Laguna, central Luzon, and is so labeled. Through error the stamp pictures Vernal Falls in Yosemite National Park, California.

Nos. 302, 302a Surcharged in Orange or Red

1932

368 A41 1p on 4p bl (O) 2.50 50
a 1p on 4p dk bl (O) 3.50 1.50
369 A41 2p on 4p dk bl (R) 4.50 1.00
a 2p on 4p bl (R) 4.50 1.00

Baseball Players — A50

Tennis Player — A51

Basketball Players — A52

1934, Apr. 14 Typo. *Perf. 11½*

380 A50 2c yel brn 15 15
381 A51 6c ultra 30 25
a Vert. pair, imperf. btwn. *900.00*
382 A52 16c vio brn 70 70
a Imperf. horizontally (pair) *900.00*

Tenth Far Eastern Championship Games.

José Rizal
A53

Woman and Carabao
A54

La Filipina
A55

Pearl Fishing
A56

Fort Santiago — A57

Salt Spring — A58

Magellan's Landing, 1521
A59

"Juan de la Cruz"
A60

Rice Terraces — A61

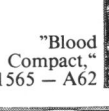

"Blood Compact," 1565 — A62

Barasoain Church, Malolos
A63

Battle of Manila Bay, 1898 — A64

Montalban Gorge — A65

George Washington — A66

1935, Feb. 15 **Engr.** ***Perf. 11***

383	A53 2c rose	5	5
384	A54 4c yel grn	5	5
385	A55 6c dk brn	9	6
386	A56 8c violet	12	12
387	A57 10c rose car	25	20
388	A58 12c black	18	15
389	A59 16c dk bl	18	12
390	A60 20c lt ol grn	25	6
391	A61 26c indigo	35	35
392	A62 30c org red	35	35
393	A63 1p red org & blk	2.50	1.85
394	A64 2p bis brn & blk	5.00	1.75
395	A65 4p bl & blk	5.00	3.75
396	A66 5p grn & blk	10.00	2.25
	Nos. 383-396 (14)	24.37	11.11

Commonwealth Issues

The Temples of Human Progress — A67

1935, Nov. 15

397	A67 2c car rose	15	10
398	A67 6c dp vio	20	15
399	A67 16c blue	30	20
400	A67 36c yel grn	50	45
401	A67 50c brown	80	80
	Nos. 397-401 (5)	1.95	1.70

Issued in commemoration of the inauguration of the Philippine Commonwealth on Nov. 15th, 1935.

Jose Rizal — A68

President Manuel L. Quezon — A69

1936, June 19 ***Perf. 12***

402	A68 2c yel brn	10	10
403	A68 6c sl bl	15	10
a	Imperf. vertically, pair	*800.00*	
404	A68 36c red brn	75	70

Issued to commemorate the 75th anniversary of the birth of José Rizal.

1936, Nov. 15 ***Perf. 11***

408	A69 2c org brn	6	6
409	A69 6c yel grn	12	10
410	A69 12c ultra	18	15

Issued in commemoration of the first anniversary of the Commonwealth.

Stamps of 1935 Overprinted in Black

COMMON-
WEALTH
a

COMMONWEALTH
b

1936-37 ***Perf. 11***

411	A53 (a) 2c rose	6	5
a	Booklet pane of 6	5.00	*1.00*
412	A54 (b) 4c yel grn ('37)	75	40
413	A55 (a) 6c dk brn	25	10
414	A56 (b) 8c vio ('37)	35	30
415	A57 (b) 10c rose car	20	6
a	"Commonwealt"		
416	A58 (b) 12c blk ('37)	20	8
417	A59 (b) 16c dk bl	25	20
418	A60 (a) 20c lt ol grn ('37)	75	50
419	A61 (b) 26c ind ('37)	65	45
420	A62 (b) 30c org red	30	15
421	A63 (b) 1p red org & blk	1.00	30
422	A64 (b) 2p bis brn & blk ('37)	7.00	3.00
423	A65 (b) 4p bl & blk ('37)	25.00	4.00
424	A66 (b) 5p grn & blk ('37)	2.50	1.65
	Nos. 411-424 (14)	39.26	11.24

Map of Philippines
A70

Arms of Manila
A71

1937, Feb. 3

425	A70 2c yel grn	10	6
426	A70 6c lt brn	18	10
427	A70 12c sapphire	20	10
428	A70 20c dp org	35	5
429	A70 36c dp vio	60	50
430	A70 50c carmine	70	35
	Nos. 425-430 (6)	2.13	1.16

33rd Eucharistic Congress.

1937, Aug. 27 ***Perf. 11***

431	A71 10p gray	6.50	3.00
432	A71 20p hn brn	3.50	2.00

Stamps of 1935 Overprinted in Black

COMMON-
WEALTH
a

COMMONWEALTH
b

1938-40 ***Perf. 11.***

433	A53 (a) 2c rose ('39)	5	5
a	Booklet pane of 6	2.50	*50*
b	"WEALTH COMMON-"	*2,000.*	
c	Hyphen omitted		
434	A54 (b) 4c yel grn ('40)	30	25
435	A55 (a) 6c dk brn ('39)	5	5
a	6c gldn brn	8	5
436	A56 (b) 8c vio ('39)	5	5
a	"Commonwealt"	50.00	
437	A57 (b) 10c rose car ('39)	5	5
438	A58 (b) 12c blk ('40)	5	5
439	A59 (b) 16c dk bl	9	5
440	A60 (a) 20c lt ol grn ('39)	10	5
441	A61 (b) 26c ind ('40)	15	15
442	A62 (b) 30c org red ('39)	80	45
443	A63 (b) 1p red org & blk	30	12
444	A64 (b) 2p bis brn & blk	2.00	50
445	A65 (b) 4p bl & blk ('40)	32.50	32.50
446	A66 (b) 5p grn & blk ('40)	3.50	2.00
	Nos. 433-446 (14)	39.99	36.32

Overprint "b" measures 18½x1¾mm. No. 433b occurs in booklet pane, No. 433a, position 5; all copies are straight-edged, left and bottom.

Stamps of 1917-37 Surcharged in Red, Violet or Black

FIRST
FOREIGN
TRADE
WEEK
2
CENTAVOS
MAY 21-27,1939
a

FIRST FOREIGN
TRADE WEEK
50CENTAVOS50
MAY21-27, 1939
6CENTAVOS6
b

FIRST FOREIGN
TRADE WEEK
MAY 21-27,1939
c

1939, July 5

449	A54 2c on 4c yel grn (R)	10	8
450	A40 6c on 26c bl grn (V)	20	20
a	6c on 26c grn	1.00	45
451	A71 50c on 20p hn brn (Bk)	1.25	1.25

Foreign Trade Week.

Triumphal Arch — A72

Malacanan Palace — A73

1939, Nov. 15 ***Perf. 11***

452	A72 2c yel grn	10	8
453	A72 6c carmine	15	10
454	A72 12c brt bl	25	10

1939, Nov. 15

455	A73 2c green	10	6
456	A73 6c orange	15	10
457	A73 12c carmine	25	8

Nos. 452-457 commemorate the 4th anniversary of the Commonwealth.

President Quezon Taking Oath of Office
A74

José Rizal
A75

1940, Feb. 8

458	A74 2c dk org	10	8
459	A74 6c dk grn	15	12
460	A74 12c purple	30	15

4th anniversary of Commonwealth.

Rotary Press Printing

1941, Apr. 14 ***Perf. 11x10½***
Size: 19x22½mm

461	A75 2c apple green	5	5

Flat Plate Printing

1941-43 Size: 18¾x22mm ***Perf. 11***

462	A75 2c apple grn ('43)	12	6
a	2c pale apple green	25	6
b	Booklet pane of 6 (ap grn) ('43)	1.50	*1.50*
c	Booklet pane of 6 (pale ap grn)	4.00	*3.50*

No. 462 was issued only in booklet panes and all copies have straight edges.

Further printings were made in 1942 and 1943 in different shades from the first supply of stamps sent to the islands.

Philippine Stamps of 1935-41, Handstamped in Violet

VICTORY

1944 ***Perf. 11, 11x10½***

463	A53 2c rose (#411)	*225.00*	*125.00*
a	Booklet pane of 6	*1,850.*	
463B	A53 2c rose (#433)	*1,450.*	*1,450.*
464	A75 2c ap grn (#461)	2.50	2.50
465	A54 4c yel grn (#384)	*25.00*	*25.00*
466	A55 6c dk brn (#385)	*1,350.*	*750.00*
467	A69 6c yel grn (#409)	*100.00*	*85.00*
468	A55 6c dk brn (#413)	*550.00*	*300.00*
469	A72 6c car (#453)	*125.00*	*100.00*
470	A73 6c org (#456)	*500.00*	*300.00*
471	A74 6c dk grn (#459)	*150.00*	*90.00*
472	A56 8c vio (#436)	12.50	15.00
473	A57 10c rose car (#415)	*100.00*	*60.00*
474	A57 10c rose car (#437)	*125.00*	*80.00*
475	A69 12c ultra (#410)	*300.00*	*110.00*
476	A72 12c brt bl (#454)	*3,500.*	*1,400.*
477	A74 12c pur (#460)	*175.00*	*100.00*
478	A59 16c dk bl (#389)	*700.00*	
479	A59 16c dk bl (#417)	*350.00*	*120.00*
480	A59 16c dk bl (#439)	*130.00*	*100.00*
481	A60 20c lt ol grn (#440)	27.50	27.50
482	A62 30c org red (#420)	*200.00*	*125.00*
483	A62 30c org red (#442)	*275.00*	*135.00*
484	A63 1p red org & blk (#443)	*7,000.*	*4,500.*

Types of 1935-37 Overprinted

VICTORY
COMMON-
WEALTH
a

VICTORY
COMMONWEALTH
b

1945 ***Perf. 11.***

485	A53 (a) 2c rose	10	6
486	A54 (b) 4c yel grn	12	8
487	A55 (a) 6c gldn brn	15	10
488	A56 (b) 8c violet	20	18
489	A57 (b) 10c rose car	20	15
490	A58 (b) 12c black	30	18
491	A59 (b) 16c dk bl	40	15
492	A60 (a) 20c lt ol grn	45	12
493	A62 (b) 30c org red	60	50
494	A63 (b) 1p red org & blk	1.75	40
	Nos. 485-494 (10)	4.27	1.92

Nos. 431-432 Overprinted in Black **VICTORY**

No.	Type	Description	Unused	Used
495	A71	10p gray	40.00	13.50
496	A71	20p hn brn	35.00	15.00

Catalogue values for unused stamps in this section, from this point to the end of the section, are for Never Hinged items.

José Rizal — A76

Rotary Press Printing.

1946, May 28 *Perf. 11x10½*

No.	Type	Description	Unused	Used
497	A76	2c sepia	10	6

Republic

Philippine Girl Holding Flag of the Republic — A77

Unwmk.

1946, July 4 **Engr.** *Perf. 11*

No.	Type	Description	Unused	Used
500	A77	2c carmine	20	20
501	A77	6c green	35	20
502	A77	12c blue	50	35

Issued to commemorate the independence of the Philippines, July 4, 1946.

No. 497 Overprinted in Brown

PHILIPPINES
50TH ANNIVERSARY MARTYRDOM OF RIZAL
1896 ~ 1946

1946, Dec. 30 *Perf. 11x10½*

No.	Type	Description	Unused	Used
503	A76	2c sepia	20	15

Issued to commemorate the 50th anniversary of the execution of José Rizal.

Rizal Monument A78

Bonifacio Monument A79

Jones Bridge — A80

Santa Lucia Gate — A81

Mayon Volcano A82

Avenue of Palms A83

1947 **Engr.** *Perf. 12*

No.	Type	Description	Unused	Used
504	A78	4c blk brn	14	5
505	A79	10c red org	16	5
506	A80	12c dp bl	22	8
507	A81	16c sl gray	1.35	80
508	A82	20c red brn	40	10
509	A83	50c dl grn	1.00	65
510	A83	1p violet	2.00	50
		Nos. 504-510 (7)	5.27	2.23

Manuel L. Quezon — A84

1947, May 1 **Typo.**

No.	Type	Description	Unused	Used
511	A84	1c green	12	8

See No. 515.

Pres. Manuel A. Roxas Taking Oath of Office A85

1947, July 4 **Unwmk.** *Perf. 12½*

No.	Type	Description	Unused	Used
512	A85	4c car rose	20	15
513	A85	6c dk grn	45	45
514	A85	16c purple	1.00	65

First anniversary of republic.

Quezon Type
Souvenir Sheet

1947, Nov. 28 *Imperf.*

No.	Type	Description	Unused	Used
515	A84	Sheet of four	65	65
a		1c brt grn	12	12

Marginal inscription in carmine. Size: 63½x84½mm.

United Nations Emblem A87

1947, Nov. 24 *Perf. 12½*

No.	Type	Description	Unused	Used
516	A87	4c dk car & pink	1.40	1.20
a		Imperf.	2.00	2.00
517	A87	6c pur & pale vio	2.00	2.00
a		Imperf.	2.00	2.00
518	A87	12c dp bl & pale bl	2.25	2.25
a		Imperf.	2.00	2.00

Issued to honor the conference of the Economic Commission in Asia and the Far East, held at Baguio.

Gen. Douglas MacArthur — A88

1948, Feb. 3 **Engr.** *Perf. 12*

No.	Type	Description	Unused	Used
519	A88	4c purple	30	14
520	A88	6c rose car	55	40
521	A88	16c brt ultra	90	40

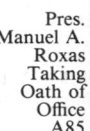

Threshing Rice — A89

1948, Feb. 23 **Typo.** *Perf. 12½*

No.	Type	Description	Unused	Used
522	A89	2c grn & pale yel grn	75	50
523	A89	6c brn & cr	90	65
524	A89	18c dp bl & pale bl	2.50	2.00

Conf. of the FAO held at Baguio. No. 524 exists imperf. See No. C67.

Manuel A. Roxas A90

José Rizal A91

1948, July 15 **Engr.** *Perf. 12*

No.	Type	Description	Unused	Used
525	A90	2c black	20	12
526	A90	4c black	25	20

Issued in tribute to President Manuel A. Roxas who died April 15, 1948.

1948, June 19 **Unwmk.**

No.	Type	Description	Unused	Used
527	A91	2c brt grn	6	5
a		Booklet pane of 6	1.25	

Scout Saluting A92

Sampaguita, National Flower A93

1948, Oct. 31 **Typo.** *Imperf.*

No.	Type	Description	Unused	Used
528	A92	2c choc & grn	35	15
a		Perf. 11½	1.00	50
529	A92	4c choc & pink	40	25
a		Perf. 11½	1.20	70

Issued to commemorate the 25th anniversary of the foundation of the Boy Scouts of the Philippines.
No. 528 exists part perforate.

1948, Dec. 8 *Perf. 12½*

No.	Type	Description	Unused	Used
530	A93	3c blk, pale bl & grn	32	25

U.P.U. Monument, Bern — A94

Unwmk.

1949, Oct. 9 **Engr.** *Perf. 12*

No.	Type	Description	Unused	Used
531	A94	4c green	14	7
532	A94	6c dl vio	15	7
533	A94	18c bl gray	60	20

Souvenir Sheet.

Imperf

No.	Type	Description	Unused	Used
534		Sheet of three	55	45
a		A94 4c grn	14	10
b		A94 6c dl vio	16	14
c		A94 18c bl	20	20

75th anniv. of the UPU.
In 1960 an unofficial, 3-line overprint ("President D. D. Eisenhower /Visit to the Philippines/June 14-16, 1960") was privately applied to No. 534.
See No. 901.

Gen. Gregorio del Pilar at Tirad Pass — A95

1949, Dec. 2 *Perf. 12*

No.	Type	Description	Unused	Used
535	A95	2c red brn	12	10
536	A95	4c green	25	22

Issued to mark the 50th anniversary of the death of Gen. Gregorio P. del Pilar and fifty-two of his men at Tirad Pass.

Globe — A96

Red Lauan Tree — A97

1950, Mar. 1

No.	Type	Description	Unused	Used
537	A96	2c purple	15	7
538	A96	6c dk grn	22	7
539	A96	18c dp bl	50	15
		Nos. 537-539,C68-C69 (5)	1.90	59

Issued to publicize the 5th World Congress of the Junior Chamber of Commerce, Manila, March 1-8, 1950.

1950, Apr. 14

No.	Type	Description	Unused	Used
540	A97	2c green	12	7
541	A97	4c purple	35	20

Issued on the occasion of the 50th anniversary of the Bureau of Foresty.

F. D. Roosevelt with his Stamps A98

Lions Club Emblem A99

1950, May 22

No.	Type	Description	Unused	Used
542	A98	4c dk brn	22	18
543	A98	6c car rose	38	35
544	A98	18c blue	90	70

Issued to honor Franklin D. Roosevelt and to commemorate the 25th anniversary of the formation of the Philatelic Association of the Philippines. See No. C70.

1950, June 4 **Engr.**

No.	Type	Description	Unused	Used
545	A99	2c orange	42	42
546	A99	4c violet	55	55

Issued to commemorate the convention of the Lions Club, Manila, June 1950. See Nos. C71-C72.

Pres. Elpidio Quirino Taking Oath — A100

1950, July 4 **Unwmk.** *Perf. 12*

No.	Type	Description	Unused	Used
547	A100	2c car rose	7	10
548	A100	4c magenta	12	10
549	A100	6c bl grn	20	15

Issued on the occasion of the 4th anniversary of the Republic of the Philippines.

No. 527 Surcharged in Black.

1950, Sept. 20

No.	Type	Description	Unused	Used
550	A91	1c on 2c brt grn	8	5

Dove over Globe — A101

1950, Oct. 23

No.	Type	Description	Unused	Used
551	A101	5c green	25	20
552	A101	6c rose car	25	20
553	A101	18c ultra	55	42

Baguio Conference of 1950.

Headman of Barangay Inspecting Harvest A102

1951, Mar. 31 Litho. *Perf. 12½*

554 A102 5c dl grn		16	7
a	Imperf.	16	16
555 A102 6c red brn		25	25
a	Imperf.	25	25
556 A102 18c vio bl		65	65
a	Imperf.	65	65

The government's Peace Fund campaign.

Arms of Manila A103

Arms of Cebu A104

Arms of Zamboanga A105

Arms of Iloilo A106

1951 Engr. *Perf. 12*

Various Frames.

557 A103 5c purple	40	35
558 A103 6c gray	25	22
559 A103 18c brt ultra	40	35

Various Frames.

560 A104 5c crim rose	40	35
561 A104 6c bis brn	25	22
562 A104 18c violet	40	35

Various Frames.

563 A105 5c bl grn	45	38
564 A105 6c red brn	30	22
565 A105 18c lt bl	45	38

Various Frames.

566 A106 5c brt grn	55	42
567 A106 6c violet	38	25
568 A106 18c dp bl	55	42
Nos. 557-568 (12)	4.78	3.91

Issue dates: A103, Feb. 3. A104, Apr. 27. A105, June 19. A106, Aug. 26.

U. N. Emblem and Girl Holding Flag — A107

Liberty Holding Declaration of Human Rights — A108

1951, Oct. 24 Unwmk. *Perf. 11½*

569 A107 5c red	55	25
570 A107 6c bl grn	45	25
571 A107 18c vio bl	1.10	70

United Nations Day, Oct. 24, 1951.

1951, Dec. 10 *Perf. 12*

572 A108 5c green	40	22
573 A108 6c red org	55	40
574 A108 18c ultra	1.00	60

Universal Declaration of Human Rights.

Students and Department Seal — A109

1952, Jan. 31

575 A109 5c org red	40	32

Issued to commemorate the 50th anniversary (in 1951) of the Philippine Educational System.

Milkfish and Map A111

1952, Oct. 27 *Perf. 12½*

578 A111 5c org brn	90	55
579 A111 6c dp bl	55	45

Issued to publicize the 4th Indo-Pacific Fisheries Council Meeting, Quezon City, Oct. 23-Nov. 7, 1952.

Maria Clara — A112

1952, Nov. 16

580 A112 5c dp bl	40	8
581 A112 6c brown	40	12

Issued to publicize the first Pan-Asian Philatelic Exhibition, PANAPEX, Manila, Nov. 16-22, 1952. See also No. C73.

Wright Park, Baguio City — A113

Francisco Baltazar, Poet — A114

1952, Dec. 15 *Perf. 12*

582 A113 5c red org	60	60
583 A113 6c dp bl grn	90	75

Issued to publicize the third Lions District Convention, Baguio City.

1953, Mar. 27

584 A114 5c citron	35	30

National Language Week.

Values quoted in this catalogue are for stamps graded at Fine-Very Fine and with no faults. An illustrated guide to grade is provided in introductory material, beginning on Page V.

"Gateway to the East" — A115

Presidents Quirino and Sukarno — A116

1953, Apr. 30

585 A115 5c turq grn	25	8
586 A115 6c vermilion	32	12

Philippines International Fair.

1953, Oct. 5 Engr. & Litho.

587 A116 5c multi	15	8
588 A116 6c multi	20	20

Second anniversary of the visit of Indonesia's President Sukarno.

Marcelo H. del Pilar — A117

Portraits: 1c, Manuel L. Quezon. 2c, José Abad Santos (different frame). 3c, Apolinario Mabini (different frame). 10c, Father José Burgos. 20c, Lapu-Lapu. 25c, Gen. Antonio Luna. 50c, Cayetano Arellano. 60c, Andres Bonifacio. 2p, Graciano L. Jaena.

Perf. 12, 12½, 13, 14x13½

1952-60 Engr.

589 A117 1c red brn ('53)	5	5
590 A117 2c gray ('60)	5	5
591 A117 3c brick red ('59)	5	5
592 A117 5c crim rose	7	5
595 A117 10c ultra ('55)	14	5
597 A117 20c car lake ('55)	25	5
598 A117 25c yel grn ('58)	35	16
599 A117 50c org ver ('59)	65	22
600 A117 60c car rose ('58)	80	35
601 A117 2p violet	2.50	80
Nos. 589-601 (10)	4.91	1.83

Doctor Examining Boy — A118

1953, Dec. 16

603 A118 5c lil rose	25	22
604 A118 6c ultra	32	30

Issued to commemorate the 50th anniversary of the founding of the Philippine Medical Association.

First Philippine Stamps, Magellan's Landing and Manila Scene A119

1954, Apr. 25 *Perf. 13*

Stamp of 1854 in Orange

605 A119 5c purple	50	32
606 A119 18c dp bl	1.00	85
607 A119 30c green	2.25	2.00
Nos. 605-607,C74-C76 (6)	9.90	8.37

Centenary of Philippine postage stamps.

Nos. 592 and 509 Overprinted or Surcharged in Black

FIRST NATIONAL BOY SCOUTS
JAMBOREE
APRIL 23-30, 1954

1954, Apr. 23 *Perf. 12*

608 A117 5c crim rose	1.00	85
609 A83 18c on 50c dl grn	1.75	1.25

Issued to publicize the first National Boy Scout Jamboree, Quezon City, April 23-30, 1954.

The surcharge on No. 609 is reduced to fit the size of the stamp.

Discus Thrower and Games Emblem A120

Designs: 18c, Swimmer. 30c, Boxers.

1954, May 31 *Perf. 13*

610 A120 5c dk bl, *bl*	70	50
611 A120 18c dk grn, *grn*	1.10	85
612 A120 30c dp cl, *rose*	1.75	1.50

2nd Asian Games, Manila, May 1-9.

Nos. 505 and 508 Surcharged in Blue

5
MANILA CONFERENCE
OF
5 1954

1954, Sept. 6 *Perf. 12*

613 A79 5c on 10c red org	15	10
614 A82 18c on 20c red brn	55	52

Issued to publicize the Manila Conference, 1954.

The surcharge is arranged to obliterate the original denomination.

Allegory of Independence A121

"Immaculate Conception," by Murillo A122

1954, Nov. 30 *Perf. 13*

615 A121 5c dk car	22	16
616 A121 18c dp bl	65	40

Issued to commemorate the 56th anniversary of the declaration of the first Philippine Independence.

1954, Dec. 30 *Perf. 12*

617 A122 5c blue	38	25

Issued to mark the end of the Marian Year.

Mayon Volcano, Moro Vinta and Rotary Emblem A123

1955, Feb. 23 Engr. *Perf. 13*
618 A123 5c dl bl 20 10
619 A123 18c dk car rose 65 50

Rotary International, 50th anniversary. See No. C77.

Allegory of Labor A124

Pres. Ramon Magsaysay A125

1955, May 26 *Perf. 13x12½*
620 A124 5c brown 35 25

Issued in connection with the Labor-Management Congress, Manila, May 26-28, 1955.

1955, July 4 *Perf. 12½*
621 A125 5c blue 16 14
622 A125 20c red 50 50
623 A125 30c green 80 80

9th anniversary of the Republic.

Village Well A126

1956, Mar. 16 *Perf. 12½x13½*
624 A126 5c violet 25 25
625 A126 20c dl grn 60 55

Issued to publicize the drive for improved health conditions in rural areas.

No. 592 Overprinted

WCOTP CONFERENCE
MANILA

1956, Aug. 1 Unwmk. *Perf. 12*
626 A117 5c crim rose 32 30

Issued to commemorate the fifth Annual Conference of the World Confederation of Organizations of the Teaching Profession, Manila, Aug. 1-8, 1956.

Nurse and Disaster Victims A127

Engraved; Cross Lithographed in Red
1956, Aug. 30
627 A127 5c violet 42 40
628 A127 20c gray brn 55 45

Issued to commemorate 50 years of Red Cross Service in the Philippines.

Monument to U. S. Landing, Leyte — A128

1956-57 Litho. *Perf. 12½*
629 A128 5c car rose 10 10
a Imperf. ('57) 42 42

Issued to commemorate the landing of the U.S. forces under Gen. Douglas MacArthur on Leyte, Oct. 20, 1944.

Santo Tomas University A129

1956, Nov. 13 Photo. *Perf. 11½*
630 A129 5c brn car & choc 32 22
631 A129 60c lil & red brn 1.25 1.10

Issued in honor of the University of Santo Tomas.

Statue of Christ by Rizal — A130

1956, Nov. 28 Engr. *Perf. 12*
632 A130 5c gray ol 25 20
633 A130 20c rose car 55 52

Issued in connection with the Second National Eucharistic Congress, Manila, Nov. 28-Dec. 2, and to commemorate the centenary of the Feast of the Sacred Heart.

Nos. 561, 564 and 567 Surcharged with New Value in Blue or Black.

1956 Unwmk. *Perf. 12*
634 A104 5c on 6c bis brn (Bl) 12 12
635 A105 5c on 6c red brn (Bl) 12 12
636 A106 5c on 6c vio (Bk) 12 12

Girl Scout, Emblem and Tents A131

1957, Jan. 19 Litho. *Perf. 12½*
637 A131 5c dk bl 32 32
a Imperf. 42 42

Issued to commemorate the centenary of the Scout movement and for the Girl Scout World Jamboree, Quezon City, Jan. 19-Feb. 2, 1957.

Copies of Nos. 637 and 637a (No. 48 in sheet) exist with heavy black rectangular handstamps obliterating erroneous date at left, denomination and cloverleaf emblem.

Pres. Ramon Magsaysay — A132

1957, Aug. 31 Engr. *Perf. 12*
638 A132 5c black 10 7

Issued to commemorate Pres. Ramon Magsaysay, (1907-1957).

"Spoliarium" by Juan Luna — A133

1957, Oct. 23 *Perf. 14x14½*
639 A133 5c rose car 12 8

Issued to commemorate the centenary of the birth of Juan Luna, painter.

Sergio Osmena and First National Assembly — A134

1957, Oct. 16 *Perf. 12½x13½*
640 A134 5c bl grn 12 10

Issued to commemorate the 50th anniversary of the First Philippine Assembly and to honor Sergio Osmena, Speaker of the Assembly.

Nos. 595 and 597 Surcharged in Carmine or Black

GARCIA-MACAPAGAL
DEC.30.1957
INAUGURATION
5 5

1957, Dec. 30 *Perf. 14x13½*
641 A117 5c on 10c ultra (C) 15 15
642 A117 10c on 20c car lake 22 22

Issued to commemorate the inauguration of Carlos P. Garcia as president and Diosdado Macapagal as vice-president, Dec. 30.

University of the Philippines — A135

1958 Engr. *Perf. 13½x13*
643 A135 5c dk car rose 30 12

Issued to commemorate the 50th anniversary of the founding of the University of the Philippines.

Pres. Carlos P. Garcia — A136

1958 Photo. *Perf. 11½*
Granite Paper
644 A136 5c multi 10 8
645 A136 20c multi 40 30

12th anniversary of Philippine Republic.

Manila Cathedral A137

Perf. 13x13½, 12
1958, Dec. 8 Engr.
646 A137 5c multi 20 12

Issued to commemorate the inauguration of the rebuilt Manila Cathedral, Dec. 8, 1958.

No. 592 Surcharged **OneCentavo**

1959 *Perf. 12*
647 A117 1c on 5c crim rose 12 5

Nos. B4-B5 Surcharged with New Values and Bars

1959 *Perf. 13*
648 SP4 1c on 2c + 2c red 5 5
649 SP5 6c on 4c + 4c vio 8 8

Issued on Feb. 3, 1959, the 14th anniversary of the liberation of Manila from the Japanese forces.

Philippine Flag — A138

1959, Feb. 8 Unwmk. *Perf. 13*
650 A138 6c dp ultra, yel & dp car 7 7
651 A138 20c dp car, yel & dp ultra 15 15

Seal of Bulacan Province — A139

Seal of Bacolod City — A140

1959 Engr. *Perf. 13*
652 A139 6c lt yel grn 10 8
653 A139 20c rose red 22 15

Issued in conjunction with the 60th anniversary of the Malolos constitution.

1959

Design: 6c, 25c, Seal of Capiz Province and portrait of Pres. Roxas.

654 A139 6c lt brn 7 7
655 A139 25c purple 22 20

Issued on the 11th anniversary of the death of Pres. Manuel A. Roxas.

1959
656 A140 6c bl grn 10 7
657 A140 10c rose lil 15 10

Nos. 658-803 were reserved for the rest of a projected series showing seals and coats of arms of provinces and cities.

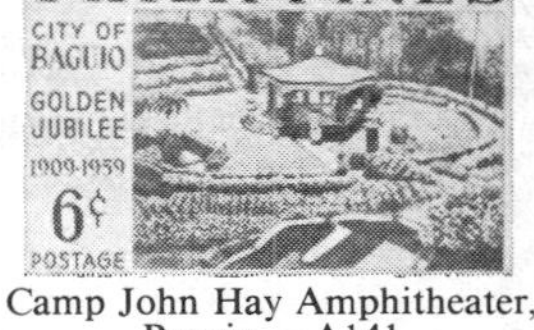

Camp John Hay Amphitheater, Baguio — A141

Perf. 13½ (6c, 25c), 12 (6c)

1959, Sept. 1

804 A141 6c brt grn 12 10
805 A141 25c rose red 25 20

Issued to commemorate the 50th anniversary of the city of Baguio.

No. 533 Surcharged in Red

6¢ UNITED NATIONS DAY

1959, Oct. 24 *Perf. 12*

806 A94 6c on 18c bl 10 7

Issued for United Nations Day, Oct. 24.

Maria Cristina Falls — A142

1959, Nov. 18 Photo. *Perf. 13½, 12*

807 A142 6c vio & dp yel grn 12 7
808 A142 30c grn & brn 35 25

No. 504 Surcharged with New Value and Bars

1959 Engr. *Perf. 12*

809 A78 1c on 4c blk brn 8 5

Manila Atheneum Emblem — A143

1959, Dec. 10 *Perf. 13½, 12*

810 A143 6c ultra 7 7
811 A143 30c rose red 35 25

Issued to commemorate the centenary of the Manila Atheneum (Ateneo de Manila), a school, and to mark a century of progress in education.

Manuel Quezon A144

José Rizal A145

1959-60 Engr. *Perf. 13*

812 A144 1c ol gray ('60) 7 5

Perf. 14x12

813 A145 6c gray bl 10 5

A146

Perf. 12½x13½

1960 Unwmk. Photo.

814 A146 6c brn & gold 12 10

Issued to commemorate the 25th anniversary of the Philippine Constitution. See No. C82.

Site of Manila Pact A147

1960 Engr. *Perf. 12½*

815 A147 6c emerald 7 7
816 A147 25c orange 30 22

Issued to commemorate the 5th anniversary (in 1959) of the Congress of the Philippines establishing the South-East Asia Treaty Organization (SEATO).

Sunset at Manila Bay and Uprooted Oak Emblem A148

1960, Apr. 7 Photo. *Perf. 13½*

817 A148 6c multi 7 7
818 A148 25c multi 30 22

Issued to publicize World Refugee Year, July 1, 1959-June 30, 1960.

A149

1960, July 29 *Perf. 13½*

819 A149 5c lt grn, red & gold 10 8
820 A149 6c bl, red & gold 12 8

Issued to commemorate the 50th anniversary of the founding of the Philippine Tuberculosis Society.

Basketball A150

Design: 10c, Runner.

1960, Nov. 30 *Perf. 13x13½*

821 A150 6c lt grn & brn 12 7
822 A150 10c rose lil & brn 15 10

Issued to commemorate the 17th Olympic Games, Rome, Aug. 25-Sept. 11. See Nos. C85-C86.

Footnotes often refer you to other stamps of the same design.

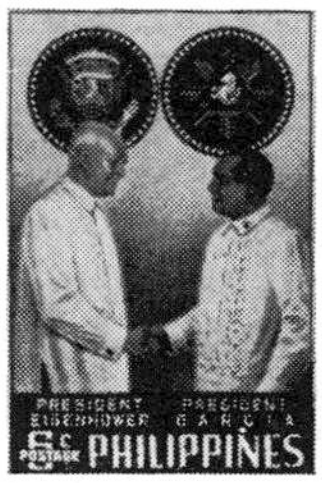

Presidents Eisenhower and Garcia and Presidential Seals — A151

1960, Dec. 30 *Perf. 13½*

823 A151 6c multi 15 12
824 A151 20c ultra, red & yel 40 20

Issued to commemorate the visit of Pres. Dwight D. Eisenhower to the Philippines, June 14, 1960.

Nos. 539, 616, 619, 553, 606 and 598 Surcharged with New Values and Bars in Red or Black.

1960-61 Engr. *Perf. 12, 13, 12½*

825 A96 1c on 18c dp bl (R) 5 5
826 A121 5c on 18c dp bl (R) 10 7
827 A123 5c on 18c dp car rose 20 15
828 A101 10c on 18c ultra (R) 15 12
829 A119 10c on 18c dp bl & org (R) 20 15
830 A117 20c on 25c yel grn ('61) 20 12
Nos. 825-830 (6) 90 66

On No. 830, no bars are overprinted, the surcharge "20 20" serving to cancel the old denomination.

Mercury and Globe — A152

1961, Jan. 23 Photo. *Perf. 13½*

831 A152 6c red brn, bl, blk & gold 8 7

Issued to commemorate the Manila Postal Conference, Jan. 10-23. See also No. C87.

Nos. B10, B11 and B11a Surcharged "2nd National Boy Scout Jamboree Pasonanca Park" and New Value in Black or Red

1961, May 2 Engr. *Perf. 13*

Yellow Paper

832 SP8 10c on 6c + 4c car 10 10
833 SP8 30c on 25c + 5c bl (R) 32 32
a Tete beche, *wht* (10c on 6c + 4c & 30c on 25c + 5c) (Bk) 50 50

Issued to publicize the Second National Boy Scout Jamboree, Pasonanca Park, Zamboanga City.

De la Salle College, Manila A153

1961, June 16 Photo. *Perf. 11½*

834 A153 6c multi 8 8
835 A153 10c multi 15 8

Issued to commemorate the 50th anniversary of the founding of De la Salle College, Manila.

José Rizal as Student A154

Designs: 6c, Rizal and birthplace at Calamba, Laguna. 10c, Rizal and parents. 20c, Rizal with Juan Luna and F. R. Hidalgo in Madrid. 30c, Rizal's execution.

1961 Unwmk. *Perf. 13½*

836 A154 5c multi 7 7
837 A154 6c multi 8 8
838 A154 10c grn & red brn 15 12
839 A154 20c brn red & grnsh bl 22 20
840 A154 30c vio, lil & org brn 32 25
Nos. 836-840 (5) 84 72

Centenary of the birth of JoséRizal.

Nos. 815-816 Overprinted

I K A

15 KAARAWAN Republika ng Pilipinas Hulyo 4, 1961

1961, July 4 Engr. *Perf. 12½*

841 A147 6c emerald 20 20
842 A147 25c orange 32 32

15th anniversary of the Republic.

Colombo Plan Emblem and Globe Showing Member Countries — A155

1961, Oct. 8 Photo. *Perf. 13x11½*

843 A155 5c multi 7 7
844 A155 6c multi 8 7

Issued to commemorate the 7th anniversary of the admission of the Philippines to the Colombo Plan.

Government Clerk — A156

1961, Dec. 9 Unwmk. *Perf. 12½*

845 A156 6c vio, bl & red 12 7
846 A156 10c gray bl & red 30 15

Issued to honor the Philippine government employees.

No. C83 Surcharged

1961, Nov. 30 Engr. *Perf. 14x14½*

847 AP11 6c on 10c car 12 12

Issued to commemorate the 50th anniversary of the Philippine Amateur Athletic Federation.

No. 655 Surcharged with New Value and: "MACAPAGAL-PELAEZ INAUGURATION DEC. 30, 1961"

1961, Dec. 30 *Perf. 12½*

848 A139 6c on 25c pur 14 7

Issued to commemorate the inauguration of President Diosdado Macapagal and Vice-President Emanuel Pelaez.

No. B8 Surcharged

1962, Jan. 23 Photo. *Perf. 13½x13*

849 SP7 6c on 5c grn & red 10 8

Vanda Orchids A157

Apolinario Mabini A158

Orchids: 6c, White mariposa. 10c, Sander's dendrobe. 20c, Sanggumay.

1962, Mar. 9 Photo. *Perf. 13½x14*

Dark Blue Background

850	A157	5c rose, grn & yel	9	9
851	A157	6c grn & yel	14	14
852	A157	10c grn, car & brn	15	15
853	A157	20c lil, brn & grn	25	25
a		Se-tenant block of 4, #850-853	65	65
b		As "a," imperf.	90	90

Printed in sheets of 40, containing 10 blocks of Nos. 850-853 se-tenant.

Perf. 13½; 14 (1s); 13x12 (#857, 10s).

1962-69 Engr. Unwmk.

Portraits: 1s, Manuel L. Quezon. 5s, Marcelo H. del Pilar. 6s, Jose Rizal. No. 857A Rizal (wearing shirt). 10s, Father Jose Burgos. 20s, Lapu-Lapu. 30s, Rajah Soliman. 50s, Cayetano Arellano. 70s, Sergio Osmena. 1p (No. 863), Emilio Jacinto. 1p (No. 864), JoseM. Panganiban.

854	A158	1s org brn ('63)	5	5
855	A158	3s rose red	5	5
856	A158	5s car rose ('63)	5	5
857	A158	6s dk red brn	7	5
857A	A158	6s pck bl ('64)	7	5
858	A158	10s brt pur ('63)	8	5
859	A158	20s Prus bl ('63)	12	5
860	A158	30s vermilion	24	7
861	A158	50s vio ('63)	40	8
862	A158	70s brt bl ('63)	50	22
863	A158	1p grn ('63)	1.00	20
864	A158	1p dp org ('69)	60	25
		Nos. 854-864 (12)	3.23	1.17

Pres. Macapagal Taking Oath of Office — A159

1962 Photo. *Perf. 13½*

Vignette Multicolored

865	A159	6s blue	7	5
866	A159	10s green	10	7
867	A159	30s violet	30	10

Issued to commemorate the swearing in of President Diosdado Macapagal, Dec. 30, 1961.

Volcano in Lake Taal and Malaria Eradication Emblem A160

1962, Oct. 24 Unwmk. *Perf. 11½*

Granite Paper

868	A160	6s multi	7	7
869	A160	10s multi	10	7
870	A160	70s multi	70	50

Issued on United Nations Day for the World Health Organization drive to eradicate malaria.

No. 598 Surcharged in Red

1762 1962
BICENTENNIAL
Diego Silang
Revolt
20

1962, Nov. 15 Engr. *Perf. 12*

871 A117 20s on 25c yel grn 20 15

Issued to commemorate the bicentennial of the Diego Silang revolt in Ilocos Province.

No. B6 Overprinted with Sideways Chevron Obliterating Surtax.

1962, Dec. 23 *Perf. 12*

872 SP6 5c on 5c + 1c dp bl 10 8

Nos. 855, 857 Surcharged with New Value and Old Value Obliterated.

1963 *Perf. 13½*

873 A158 1s on 3s rose red 6 5

Perf. 13x12

874 A158 5s on 6s dk red brn 7 6

No. 601 Surcharged

1763 1963
DIEGO SILANG BICENTENNIAL
ARPHEX
20 CENTAVOS

1963, June 12 *Perf. 12*

875	A117	6s on 2p vio	10	7
876	A117	20s on 2p vio	22	22
877	A117	70s on 2p vio	65	55

Issued to publicize the Diego Silang Bicentennial Art and Philatelic Exhibition, ARPHEX, Manila, May 28-June 30.

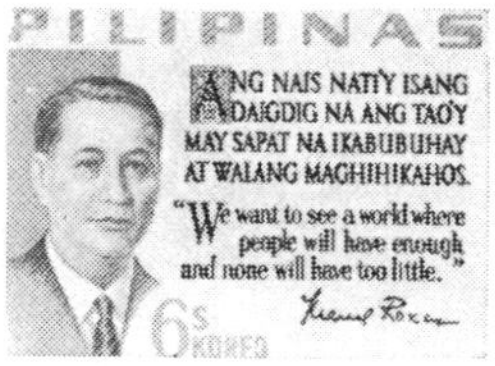

Pres. Manuel Roxas A161

1963-73 Engr. *Perf. 13½*

878	A161	6s brt bl & blk, *bluish*	7	5
879	A161	30s brn & blk	35	10

Pres. Ramon Magsaysay

880	A161	6s lil & blk	7	5
881	A161	30s yel grn & blk	30	8

Pres. Elpidio Quirino

882	A161	6s grn & blk ('65)	7	5
883	A161	30s rose lil & blk ('65)	30	8

Gen. (Pres.) Emilio Aguinaldo

883A	A161	6s dp cl & blk ('66)	7	5
883B	A161	30s bl & blk ('66)	30	8

Pres. José P. Laurel

883C	A161	6s lt red brn & blk ('66)	7	5
883D	A161	30s bl & blk ('66)	30	8

Pres. Manuel L. Quezon

883E	A161	10s bl gray & blk ('67)	7	5
883F	A161	30s lt vio & blk ('67)	30	8

Pres. Sergio Osmeña

883G	A161	10s rose lil & blk ('70)	7	5
883H	A161	40s grn & blk ('70)	30	7

Pres. Carlos P. Garcia

883I	A161	10s multi ('73)	7	5
883J	A161	30s multi ('73)	30	8
		Nos. 878-883J (16)	3.01	1.05

Nos. 878-883J honor former presidents.

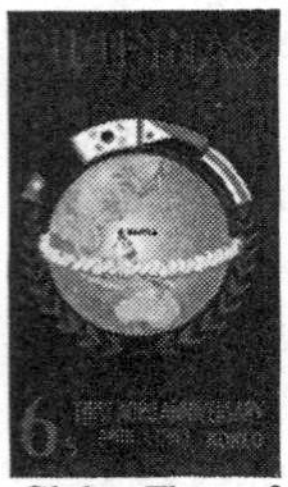

Globe, Flags of Thailand, Korea, China, Philippines A162

Red Cross Centenary Emblem A163

1963, Aug. 26 Photo. *Perf. 13½x13*

884	A162	6s dk grn & multi	8	6
885	A162	20s dk grn & multi	18	10

Issued to commemorate the first anniversary of the Asian-Oceanic Postal Union.

1963, Sept. 1 *Perf. 11½*

886	A163	5s lt vio, gray & red	7	5
887	A163	6s ultra, gray & red	7	5
888	A163	20s grn, gray & red	20	12

Centenary of the International Red Cross.

Bamboo Dance — A164

Folk Dances: 6s, Dance with oil lamps. 10s, Duck dance. 20s, Princess Gandingan's rock dance.

1963, Sept. 15 Unwmk. *Perf. 14*

889	A164	5s multi	7	7
890	A164	6s multi	8	8
891	A164	10s multi	12	12
892	A164	20s multi	22	22

Printed in sheets of 40, containing 10 blocks of Nos. 889-892 se-tenant.

Pres. Macapagal and Filipino Family — A165

1963, Sept. 28 *Perf. 14*

893	A165	5s bl & multi	8	5
894	A165	6s yel & multi	7	6
895	A165	20s lil & multi	15	12

Issued to publicize Pres. Macapagal's 5-year Socioeconomic Program.

Presidents Lopez Mateos and Macapagal — A166

1963, Sept. 28 Photo. *Perf. 13½*

896	A166	6s multi	8	8
897	A166	30s multi	20	12

Issued to commemorate the visit of Pres. Adolfo Lopez Mateos of Mexico to the Philippines.

Andres Bonifacio — A167

1963, Nov. 30 Unwmk. *Perf. 12*

898	A167	5s gold, brn, gray & red	6	5
899	A167	6s sil, brn, gray & red	8	5
900	A167	25s brnz, brn, gray & red	24	22

Issued to commemorate the centenary of the birth of Andres Bonifacio, national hero and poet.

Souvenir Sheet

No. 534 Overprinted: "UN ADOPTION/DECLARATION OF HUMAN RIGHTS/15TH ANNIVERSARY DEC. 10, 1963"

1963, Dec. 10 Engr. *Imperf.*

901 A94 Sheet of three 55 55

Issued to commemorate the 15th anniversary of the Universal Declaration of Human Rights.

Woman holding Sheaf of Rice — A168

1963, Dec. 20 Photo. *Perf. 13½x13*

902 A168 6s brn & multi 7 5

FAO "Freedom from Hunger" campaign. See Nos. C88-C89.

Bamboo Organ A169

Apolinario Mabini A170

1964, May 4 *Perf. 13½*

903	A169	5s multi	7	5
904	A169	6s multi	7	5
905	A169	20s multi	20	12

The bamboo organ in the Church of Las Pinas, Rizal, was built by Father Diego Cera, 1816-1822.

Wmk. 233-"Harrison & Sons, London." in Script

Wmk. 233

1964, July 23 Photo. *Perf. 14½*

906	A170	6s pur & gold	7	5
907	A170	10s red brn & gold	10	7
908	A170	30s brt grn & gold	22	15

Issued to commemorate the centenary of the birth of Apolinario Mabini (1864-1903), national hero and a leader of the 1898 revolution.

Flags Surrounding SEATO Emblem A171

Pres. Macapagal Signing Agricultural Land Reform Code A172

Unwmk.

1964, Sept. 8 Photo. *Perf. 13*

Flags and Emblem Multicolored

909	A171	6s dk bl & yel	8	5
910	A171	10s dp grn & yel	10	7
911	A171	25s dk brn & yel	20	15

Issued to commemorate the 10th anniversary of the South-East Asia Treaty Organization (SEATO).

1964, Dec. 21 Wmk. 233 *Perf. 14½*

912	A172	3s multi	7	5
913	A172	6s multi	8	5

Issued to commemorate the signing of the Agricultural Land Reform Code. See No. C90.

Basketball — A173

Sport: 10s, Women's relay race. 20s, Hurdling. 30s, Soccer.

1964, Dec. 28 *Perf. 14½x14*

915	A173	6s lt bl, dk brn & gold	8	8
a		Imperf.	10	10
916	A173	10s gold, pink & dk brn	12	8
a		Imperf.	15	15
b		Gold omitted		
917	A173	20s gold, dk brn & yel	22	12
a		Imperf.	32	32
918	A173	30s emer, dk brn & gold	30	22
a		Imperf.	40	40

18th Olympic Games, Tokyo, Oct. 10-25.

Presidents Lubke and Macapagal and Coats of Arms A174

1965, Apr. 19 Unwmk. *Perf. 13½*

919	A174	6s ol grn & multi	8	5
920	A174	10s multi	10	5
921	A174	25s dp bl & multi	18	15

Issued to commemorate the visit of Pres. Heinrich Lubke of Germany, Nov. 18-23, 1964.

Emblems of Manila Observatory and Weather Bureau A175

1965, May 22 Photo. *Perf. 13½*

922	A175	6s lt ultra & multi	8	5
923	A175	20s lt vio & multi	12	8
924	A175	50s bl grn & multi	40	25

Issued to commemorate the centenary of the Meteorological Service in the Philippines.

Pres. John F. Kennedy — A176

Perf. 14½x14

1965, May 29 Wmk. 233

Center Multicolored

925	A176	6s gray	10	5
926	A176	10s brt vio	14	7
927	A176	30s ultra	35	20

Issued in memory of President John F. Kennedy (1917-63).

Nos. 925-927 exist with ultramarine of tie omitted.

The 6s and 30s exist imperf. Value, each $30.

King and Queen of Thailand, Pres. and Mrs. Macapagal — A177

Perf. 12½x13

1965, June 12 Unwmk.

928	A177	2s brt bl & multi	5	5
929	A177	6s bis & multi	7	5
930	A177	30s red & multi	22	12

Issued to commemorate the visit of King Phumiphon Aduldet and Queen Sirikit of Thailand, July 1963.

Princess Beatrix and Evangelina Macapagal A178

Perf. 13x12½

1965, July 4 Photo. Unwmk.

931	A178	2s bl & multi	5	5
932	A178	6s blk & multi	7	5
933	A178	10s multi	10	7

Issued to commemorate the visit of Princess Beatrix of the Netherlands, Nov. 21-23, 1962.

Cross and Rosary Held Before Map of Philippines — A179

Design: 6s, Map of Philippines, cross and Legaspi-Urdaneta monument.

1965, Oct. 4 Unwmk. *Perf. 13*

934	A179	3s multi	7	5
935	A179	6s multi	10	5

Issued to commemorate the 400th anniversary of the Christianization of the Philippines. See Nos. C91-C92 and souvenir sheet No. C92a.

Presidents Sukarno and Macapagal and Prime Minister Tunku Abdul Rahman A180

1965, Nov. 25 *Perf. 13*

Flags of Indonesia, Philippines and Malaysia in Red, Yellow and Dark Blue

936	A180	6s dk bl	7	5
937	A180	10s chocolate	7	7
938	A180	25s green	20	12

Signing of the Manila Accord (Mapilindo) by Malaya, Philippines and Indonesia.

Bicyclists and Globe A181

1965, Dec. 5 *Perf. 13½*

939	A181	6s multi	5	5
940	A181	10s multi	10	7
941	A181	25s multi	20	12

Issued to commemorate the Second Asian Cycling Championship, Philippines, Nov. 28-Dec. 5.

Nos. B21-B22 Surcharged

10s

MARCOS-LOPEZ
INAUGURATION
DEC. 30, 1965

1965, Dec. 30 Engr. *Perf. 13*

942	SP12	10s on 6s + 4s grn & rose lil	10	10
943	SP12	30s on 30s + 5s brt bl & cl	24	24

Issued to commemorate the inauguration of President Ferdinand Marcos and Vice-President Fernando Lopez.

Antonio Regidor — A182

1966, Jan. 21 *Perf. 12x11*

944	A182	6s blue	7	5
945	A182	30s brown	22	20

Issued to honor Dr. Antonio Regidor, Secretary of the High Court of Manila and President of Public Instruction.

No. 857A Overprinted in Red: "HELP ME STOP / SMUGGLING / Pres. MARCOS"

1966, May 1 Engr. *Perf. 13½*

946	A158	6s pck bl	10	6

Issued to publicize the anti-smuggling drive of the government.

Exists with overprint inverted, double, double inverted and double with one inverted.

See No. 1209 for No. 946 with black 5s surcharge.

Girl Scout Giving Scout Sign A183

1966, May 26 Litho. *Perf. 13x12½*

947	A183	3s ultra & multi	5	5
948	A183	6s emer & multi	8	5
949	A183	20s brn & multi	20	12

Philippine Girl Scouts, 25th anniversary.

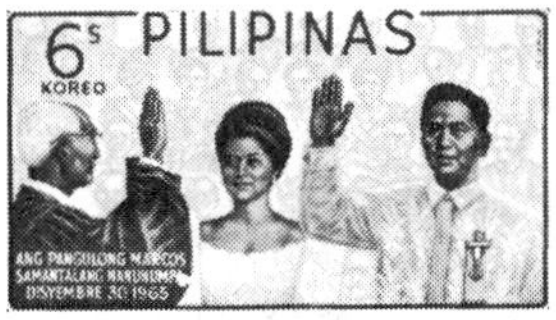

Pres. Marcos Taking Oath of Office — A184

1966, June 12 *Perf. 12½*

950	A184	6s bl & multi	7	5
951	A184	20s emer & multi	10	7
952	A184	30s yel & multi	22	20

Issued to commemorate the inauguration of President Ferdinand E. Marcos, Dec. 30, 1965.

Seal of Manila and Historical Scenes — A185

1966, June 24

953	A185	6s multi	7	7
954	A185	30s multi	20	15

Adoption of the new seal of Manila.

Old and New Philippine National Bank Buildings — A186

Designs: 6s, Entrance to old bank building and 1p silver coin.

1966, July 22 Photo. *Perf. 14x13½*
955 A186 6s gold, ultra, sil & blk 8 5
956 A186 10s multi 15 7

Issued to commemorate the 50th anniversary of the Philippine National Bank. See No. C93.

Post Office, Annex Three A187

1966, Oct. 1 Wmk. 233 *Perf. 14½*
957 A187 6s lt vio, yel & grn 8 5
958 A187 10s rose cl, yel & grn 8 7
959 A187 20s ultra, yel & grn 20 10

60th anniversary of Postal Savings Bank.

Nos. 950 and 952 Overprinted in Emerald or Black

Perf. 12½
1966, Oct. 24 Litho. Unwmk.
960 A184 6s multi (E) 7 7
961 A184 30s multi 25 22

Manila Summit Conference, Oct. 23-27.

Nos. 915a-918a Overprinted

50th ANNIVERSARY
LIONS INTERNATIONAL
1967

Wmk. 233
1967, Jan. 14 Photo. *Imperf.*
962 A173 6s lt bl, dk brn & gold 8 6
963 A173 10s gold, dk brn & pink 10 8
964 A173 20s gold, dk brn & yel 20 12
965 A173 30s emer, dk brn & gold 30 30

Issued to commemorate the 50th anniversary of Lions International. The Lions emblem is in the lower left corner on the 6s, in the upper left corner on the 10s and in the upper right corner on the 30s.

"Succor" by Fernando Amorsolo — A188

Unwmk.
1967, May 15 Litho. *Perf. 14*
966 A188 5s sep & multi 10 5
967 A188 20s bl & multi 20 10
968 A188 2p grn & multi 1.75 1.00

25th anniversary of the Battle of Bataan.

Nos. 857A and 913 Surcharged
1967, Aug. Engr. *Perf. 13½*
969 A158 4s on 6s pck bl 8 5

Wmk. 233
Photo. *Perf. 14½*
970 A172 5s on 6s multi 8 5

Issue dates: 4s, Aug. 10; 5s, Aug. 7.

Gen. Douglas MacArthur and Paratroopers Landing on Corregidor — A189

Unwmk.
1967, Aug. 31 Litho. *Perf. 14*
971 A189 6s multi 10 10
972 A189 5p multi 2.50 2.25

25th anniversary, Battle of Corregidor.

Bureau of Posts, Manila, Jones Bridge over Pasig River — A190

1967, Sept. 15 Litho. *Perf. 14x13½*
973 A190 4s multi & blk 12 12
974 A190 20s multi & red 12 7
975 A190 50s multi & vio 32 25

65th anniversary of the Bureau of Posts.

Philippine Nativity Scene — A191

1967, Dec. 1 Photo. *Perf. 13½*
976 A191 10s multi 10 10
977 A191 40s multi 30 22

Christmas 1967.

Chinese Garden, Rizal Park, Presidents Marcos and Chiang Kai-shek — A192

Designs (Presidents' heads and scenes in Chinese Garden, Rizal Park, Manila): 10s, Gate. 20s, Landing pier.

1967-68 Photo. *Perf. 13½*
978 A192 5s multi 5 5
979 A192 10s multi ('68) 8 8
980 A192 20s multi 12 8

Sino-Philippine Friendship Year 1966-67.

Makati Center Post Office, Mrs. Marcos and Rotary Emblem — A193

1968, Jan. 9 Litho. *Perf. 14*
981 A193 10s bl & multi 8 8
982 A193 20s grn & multi 15 15
983 A193 40s multi 30 30

Issued to commemorate the first anniversary of the Makati Center Post Office.

Nos. 882, 883C and B27 Surcharged with New Value and Two Bars.
1968
984 A161 5s on 6s grn & blk 7 5
985 A161 5s on 6s lt red brn & blk 7 5
986 SP14 10s on 6s + 5s ultra & red 7 5

Felipe G. Calderon, Barasoain Church and Malolos Constitution — A194

1968, Apr. 4 Litho. *Perf. 14*
987 A194 10s lt ultra & multi 8 6
988 A194 40s grn & multi 35 25
989 A194 75s multi 65 60

Issued to commemorate the centenary of the birth of Felipe G. Calderon (1868-1909), lawyer and author of the Malolos Constitution.

Earth and Transmission from Philippine Station to Satellite — A195

1968, Oct. 21 Photo. *Perf. 13½*
990 A195 10s blk & multi 15 12
991 A195 40s multi 45 35
992 A195 75s multi 75 60

Issued to commemorate the inauguration of the Philcomsat Station in Tany, Luzon, May 2, 1968.

Tobacco Industry and Tobacco Board's Emblem — A196

1968, Nov. 15 Photo. *Perf. 13½*
993 A196 10s blk & multi 10 8
994 A196 40s bl & multi 35 30
995 A196 70s crim & multi 60 50

Philippine tobacco industry.

Kudyapi A197

Philippine Musical Instruments: 20s, Ludag (drum). 30s, Kulintangan. 50s, Subing (bamboo flute).

1968, Nov. 22 Photo. *Perf. 13½*
996 A197 10s multi 8 6
997 A197 20s multi 15 12
998 A197 30s multi 28 25
999 A197 50s multi 45 40

Concordia College A198

1968, Dec. 8 *Perf. 13x13½*
1000 A198 10s multi 8 8
1001 A198 20s multi 12 10
1002 A198 70s multi 40 32

Issued to commemorate the centenary of the Colegio de la Concordia, Manila, a Catholic women's school. Issued Dec. 8 (Sunday), but entered the mail Dec. 9.

Singing Children — A199

1968, Dec. 16 *Perf. 13½*
1003 A199 10s multi 10 8
1004 A199 40s multi 40 35
1005 A199 75s multi 75 60

Christmas 1968.

Tarsier A200

Animals: 10s, Tamarau. 20s, Carabao. 75s, Mouse deer.

1969, Jan. 8 Photo. *Perf. 13½*
1006 A200 2s blk & multi 5 5
1007 A200 10s multi 7 5
1008 A200 20s org & multi 10 8
1009 A200 75s grn & multi 50 40

Opening of the hunting season.

Emilio Aguinaldo and Historical Building, Cavite — A201

1969, Jan. 23 Litho. *Perf. 14*
1010 A201 10s yel & multi 15 10
1011 A201 40s bl & multi 45 28
1012 A201 70s multi 75 60

Issued to commemorate the centenary of the birth of Emilio Aguinaldo (1869-1964), commander of Filipino forces in rebellion against Spain.

Guard Turret, San Andres Bastion, Manila, and Rotary Emblem — A202

1969, Jan. 29 Photo. *Perf. 12½*
1013 A202 10s ultra & multi 8 8

Issued to commemorate the 50th anniversary of the Manila Rotary Club. See Nos. C96-C97.

Claro M. Recto — A203

1969, Feb. 10 Engr. *Perf. 13*
1014 A203 10s brt rose lil 8 5

Issued to honor Senator Claro M. Recto (1890-1960), lawyer and Supreme Court judge.

No. 973 Overprinted

PHILATELIC WEEK
NOV. 24-30, 1968

1969, Feb. 14 Litho. *Perf. 14x13½*
1015 A190 4s multi & blk 15 6

Issued to commemorate Philatelic Week, Nov. 24-30, 1968.

José Rizal College, Mandaluyong — A204

1969, Feb. 19 Photo. *Perf. 13*
1016 A204 10s multi 10 8
1017 A204 40s multi 35 25
1018 A204 50s multi 45 38

Issued to commemorate the 50th anniversary of the founding of Rizal College.

No. 948 Surcharged in Red with New Value, 2 Bars and: "4th NATIONAL BOY / SCOUT JAMBOREE / PALAYAN CITY-MAY, 1969"

1969, May 12 Litho. *Perf. 13x12½*
1019 A183 5s on 6s multi 12 8

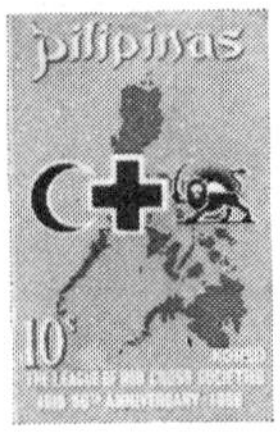

Map of Philippines, Red Crescent, Cross, Lion and Sun Emblems — A205

1969, May 26 Photo. *Perf. 12½*
1020 A205 10s gray, ultra & red 10 6
1021 A205 40s lt ultra, dk bl & red 40 25
1022 A205 75s bis, brn & red 60 55

Issued to commemorate the 50th anniversary of the League of Red Cross Societies.

Pres. and Mrs. Marcos Harvesting Miracle Rice — A206

1969, June 13 Photo. *Perf. 14*
1023 A206 10s multi 10 6
1024 A206 40s multi 40 30
1025 A206 75s multi 60 55

Issued to publicize the introduction of IR8 (miracle) rice, produced by the International Rice Research Institute.

Holy Child of Leyte and Map of Leyte
A207

1969, June 30 *Perf. 13½*
1026 A207 5s emer & multi 6 5
1027 A207 10s crim & multi 10 8

Issued to commemorate the 80th anniversary of the return of the image of the Holy Child of Leyte to Tacloban. See No. C98.

Philippine Development Bank — A208

1969, Sept. 12 Photo. *Perf. 13½*
1028 A208 10s dk bl, blk & grn 10 7
1029 A208 40s rose car, blk & grn 50 25
1030 A208 75s brn, blk & grn 75 55

Issued to commemorate the inauguration of the new building of the Philippine Development Bank in Makati, Rizal.

Common Birdwing
A209

Butterflies: 20s, Tailed jay. 30s, Red Helen. 40s, Birdwing.

1969, Sept. 15 Photo. *Perf. 13½*
1031 A209 10s multi 7 6
1032 A209 20s multi 12 7
1033 A209 30s multi 20 12
1034 A209 40s multi 30 18

World's Children and UNICEF Emblem
A210

1969, Oct. 6
1035 A210 10s bl & multi 8 6
1036 A210 20s multi 10 8
1037 A210 30s multi 15 12

Issued for the 15th anniversary of Universal Children's Day.

An enhanced introduction to the Scott Catalogue begins on Page V. A thorough understanding of the material presented there will greatly aid your use of the catalogue itself.

Monument and Leyte Landing — A211

1969, Oct. 20 *Perf. 13½x14*
1038 A211 5s lt grn & multi 8 5
1039 A211 10s yel & multi 10 8
1040 A211 40s pink & multi 30 18

Issued to commemorate the 25th anniversary of the landing of the U.S. forces under Gen. Douglas MacArthur on Leyte, Oct. 20, 1944.

Philippine Cultural Center, Manila — A212

1969, Nov. 4 Photo. *Perf. 13½*
1041 A212 10s ultra 8 8
1042 A212 30s brt rose lil 20 15

Issued to publicize the Cultural Center of the Philippines, containing theaters, a museum and libraries.

Nos. 889-892 Surcharged or Overprinted: "1969 PHILATELIC WEEK"

1969, Nov. 24 Photo. *Perf. 14*
1043 A164 5s multi 5 5
1044 A164 5s on 6s multi 5 5
1045 A164 10s multi 12 10
1046 A164 10s on 20s multi 12 10

Philatelic Week, Nov. 23-29.

Melchora Aquino — A213

1969, Nov. 30 *Perf. 12½*
1047 A213 10s multi 8 6
1048 A213 20s multi 15 10
1049 A213 30s dk bl & multi 25 15

Issued to commemorate the 50th anniversary of the death of Melchora Aquino (Tandang Sora; 1812-1919), the Grand Old Woman of the Revolution.

No. 950 Surcharged with New Value, 2 Bars and: "PASINAYA, IKA -2 PANUNUNGKULAN / PANGULONG FERDINAND E. MARCOS / DISYEMBRE 30, 1969"

1969, Dec. 30 Litho. *Perf. 12½*
1050 A184 5s on 6s multi 20 6

Issued to commemorate the inauguration of Pres. Ferdinand E. Marcos and Vice Pres. Fernando Lopez for a second term, Dec. 30.

Pouring Ladle and Iligan Steel Mills — A214

1970, Jan. 20 Photo. *Perf. 13½*
1051 A214 10s ver & multi 8 6
1052 A214 20s multi 15 12
1053 A214 30s ultra & multi 25 18

Issued to publicize the Iligan Integrated Steel Mills, Northern Mindanao, the first Philippine steel mills.

Nos. 857A, 904 and 906 Surcharged with New Value and Two Bars

Perf. 13½

1970, Apr. 30 Unwmk. Engr.
1054 A158 4s on 6s pck bl 5 5

Photo.

1055 A169 5s on 6s multi 5 5

Perf. 14½

Wmk. 233

1056 A170 5s on 6s pur & gold 5 5

New U.P.U. Headquarters and Monument, Bern — A215

Perf. 13½

1970, May 20 Unwmk. Photo.
1057 A215 10s bl, dk bl & yel 10 6
1058 A215 30s lt grn, dk bl & yel 32 18

Opening of the new UPU Headquarters in Bern.

Emblem, Mayon Volcano and Filipina — A216

1970, Sept. 6 Photo. *Perf. 13½x14*
1059 A216 10s brt bl & multi 8 10
1060 A216 20s multi 18 12
1061 A216 30s multi 30 15

Issued to publicize the 15th International Conference on Social Welfare, Manila, Sept. 6-12.

Crab, by Alexander Calder, and Map of Philippines
A217

1970, Oct. 5 *Perf. 13x13½*
1062 A217 10s emer & multi 12 10
1063 A217 40s multi 35 20
1064 A217 50s ultra & multi 50 30

Campaign against cancer.

Scaled Tridacna
A218

Sea Shells: 10s, Royal spiny oyster. 20s, Venus comb. 40s, Glory of the sea.

1970, Oct. 19 Photo. *Perf. 13½*

1065 A218 5s blk & multi 5 5
1066 A218 10s dk grn & multi 8 6
1067 A218 20s multi 15 8
1068 A218 40s dk bl & multi 32 20

Nos. 922, 953 and 955 Surcharged **4S FOUR**

Photogravure; Lithographed

1970, Oct. 26 *Perf. 13½, 12½*

1069 A175 4s on 6s multi 5 5
1070 A185 4s on 6s multi 5 5
1071 A186 4s on 6s multi 5 5

One line surcharge on No. 1071.

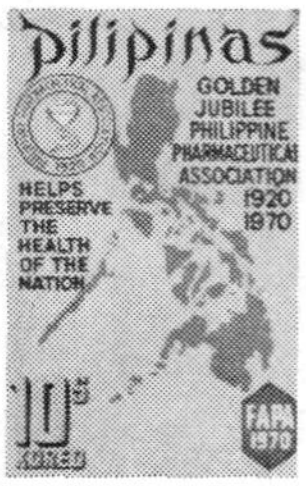

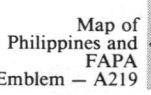

Map of Philippines and FAPA Emblem — A219

1970, Nov. 16 Photo. *Perf. 13½*

1072 A219 10s dp org & multi 8 6
1073 A219 50s lt vio & multi 40 20

Issued to commemorate the opening of the 4th General Assembly of the Federation of Asian Pharmaceutical Associations (FAPA) and the 3rd Asian Congress of Pharmaceutical Sciences.

Hundred Islands of Pangasinan, Peddler's Cart — A220

Designs: 20s, Tree house in Pasonanca Park, Zamboanga City. 30s, Sugar industry, Negros Island, Mt. Kanlaon, Woman and Carabao statue, symbolizing agriculture. 2p, Miagao Church, Iloilo, and horse-drawn calesa.

1970, Nov. 12 *Perf. 12½x13½*

1074 A220 10s multi 8 8
1075 A220 20s multi 12 10
1076 A220 30s multi 18 16
1077 A220 2p multi 1.10 65

Tourist publicity. See Nos. 1086-1097.

No. 884 Surcharged: "UPU-AOPU / Regional Seminar / Nov. 23-Dec. 5, 1970 / TEN 10s"

1970, Nov. 22 Photo. *Perf. 13½x13*

1078 A162 10s on 6s multi 10 10

Universal Postal Union and Asian-Oceanic Postal Union Regional Seminar, Nov. 23-Dec. 5.

No. 915 Surcharged Vertically: "1970 PHILATELIC WEEK"

Perf. 14½x14

1970, Nov. 22 Wmk. 233

1079 A173 10s on 6s multi 10 5

Philatelic Week, Nov. 22-28.

Scott's editorial staff cannot undertake to identify, authenticate or appraise stamps and postal markings.

Pope Paul VI, Map of Far East and Australia — A221

Perf. 13½x14

1970, Nov. 27 Photo. Unwmk.

1080 A221 10s ultra & multi 8 7
1081 A221 30s multi 18 12

Visit of Pope Paul VI, Nov. 27-29, 1970. See No. C99.

Mariano Ponce — A222

1970, Dec. 30 Engr. *Perf. 14½*

1082 A222 10s rose car 8 5

Mariano Ponce (1863-1918), editor and legislator. See Nos. 1136-1137.

PATA Emblem — A223

1971, Jan. 21 Photo. *Perf. 14½*

1083 A223 5s brt grn & multi 7 5
1084 A223 10s bl & multi 10 8
1085 A223 70s brn & multi 30 22

Pacific Travel Association (PATA), 20th annual conference, Manila, Jan. 21-29.

Tourist Type of 1970

Designs: 10s, Filipina and Ang Nayong (7 village replicas around man-made lagoon). 20s, Woman and fisherman, Estancia. 30s, Pagsanjan Falls. 5p, Watch Tower, Punta Cruz, Boho.

Perf. 12½x13½

1971, Feb. 15 Photo.

1086 A220 10s multi 6 6
1087 A220 20s multi 8 7
1088 A220 30s multi 15 15
1089 A220 5p multi 1.25 1.25

1971, Apr. 19

Designs: 10s, Cultured pearl farm, Davao. 20s, Coral divers, Davao, Mindanao. 40s, Moslem Mosque, Zamboanga. 1p, Rice terraces, Banaue.

1090 A220 10s multi 8 6
1091 A220 20s multi 10 8
1092 A220 40s multi 15 12
1093 A220 1p multi 35 30

1971, May 3

Designs: 10s, Spanish cannon, Zamboanga. 30s, Magellan's cross, Cebu City. 50s, Big Jar monument in Calamba, Laguna. 70s, Mayon Volcano, Legaspi.

1094 A220 10s multi 8 6
1095 A220 30s multi 10 8
1096 A220 50s multi 15 15
1097 A220 70s multi 32 20

Family and Emblem A224

1971, March 21 Photo. *Perf. 13½*

1098 A224 20s lt grn & multi 8 7
1099 A224 40s pink & multi 15 12

Regional Conference of the International Planned Parenthood Federation for Southeast Asia and Oceania, Baguio City, March 21-27.

No. 955 Surcharged **FIVE 5S**

1971, June 10 Photo. *Perf. 14x13½*

1100 A186 5s on 6s multi 10 5

Allegory of Law A225

1971, June 15 Photo. *Perf. 13*

1101 A225 15s org & multi 8 8

60th anniversary of the University of the Philippines Law College. See No. C100.

Manila Anniversary Emblem — A226

1971, June 24

1102 A226 10s multi 8 8

400th anniversary of the founding of Manila. See No. C101.

Santo Tomas University, Arms of Schools of Medicine and Pharmacology — A227

1971, July 8 Photo. *Perf. 13½*

1103 A227 5s yel & multi 8 5

Centenary of the founding of the Schools of Medicine and Surgery, and Pharmacology at the University of Santo Tomas, Manila. See No. C102.

No. 957 Surcharged

1971, July 11 Wmk. 233 *Perf. 14½*

1104 A187 5s on 6s multi 7 7

World Congress of University Presidents, Manila.

Our Lady of Guia Appearing to Filipinos and Spanish Soldiers — A228

1971, July 8 Photo. *Perf. 13½*

1105 A228 10s multi 8 8
1106 A228 75s multi 32 30

4th centenary of appearance of the statue of Our Lady of Guia, Ermita, Manila.

Bank Building, Plane, Car and Workers — A229

1971, Sept. 14 *Perf. 12½*

1107 A229 10s bl & multi 8 6
1108 A229 30s lt grn & multi 18 15
1109 A229 1p multi 40 32

70th anniversary of the First National City Bank in the Philippines.

No. 944 Surcharged **FOUR 4S**

Perf. 12x11

1971, Nov. 24 Engr. Unwmk.

1110 A182 4s on 6s bl 7 5
1111 A182 5s on 6s bl 8 5

No. 957 Surcharged **5S FIVE** **1971-PHILATELIC-WEEK**

Wmk. 233

1971, Nov. 24 Photo. *Perf. 14½*

1112 A187 5s on 6s multi 8 6

Philatelic Week, 1971.

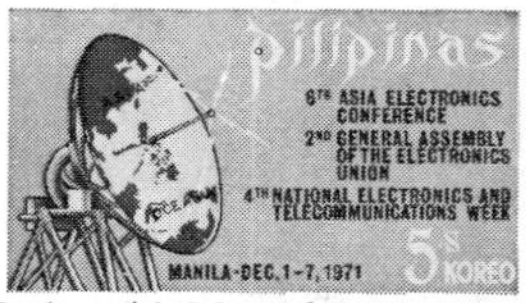

Radar with Map of Far East and Oceania — A230

1972, Feb. 29 Photo. *Perf. 14x14½*

1113 A230 5s org yel & multi 8 5
1114 A230 40s red org & multi 32 20

Electronics Conferences, Manila, Dec. 1-7, 1971.

Fathers Gomez, Burgos and Zamora — A231

1972, Apr. 3 *Perf. 13x12½*
1115 A231 5s gold & multi 5 5
1116 A231 60s gold & multi 25 25

Centenary of the deaths of Fathers Mariano Gomez, José Burgos and Jacinto Zamora, martyrs for Philippine independence from Spain.

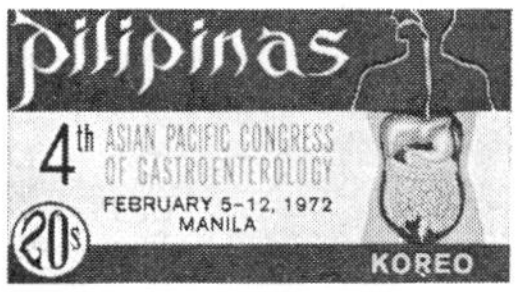

Digestive Tract — A232

1972, Apr. 11 Photo. *Perf. 12½x13*
1117 A232 20s ultra & multi 12 8

4th Asian Pacific Congress of Gastroenterology, Manila, Feb. 5-12. See No. C103.

No. 953 Surcharged

≡ 5s FIVE

1972, Apr. 20 *Perf. 12½*
1118 A185 5s on 6s multi 5 5

No. O69 with Two Bars over "G." and "O."

1972, May 16 Engr. *Perf. 13½*
1119 A158 50s violet 25 15

Nos. 883A, 909 and 929 Surcharged with New Value and 2 Bars

1972, May 29 Engr. *Perf. 13½*
1120 A161 10s on 6s dp cl & blk 7 5

Photo.

Perf. 13
1121 A171 10s on 6s multi 7 5

Perf. 12½x13
1122 A177 10s on 6s multi 7 5

Independence Monument, Manila — A233

1972, May 31 Photo. *Perf. 13x12½*
1123 A233 5s brt bl & multi 10 5
1124 A233 50s red & multi 50 14
1125 A233 60s emer & multi 65 20

Visit ASEAN countries (Association of South East Asian Nations).

"K," Skull and Crossbones — A234

Development of Philippine Flag: No. 1126, 3 "K's" in a row ("K" stands for Katipunan). No. 1127, 3 "K's" as triangle. No. 1128, One "K." No. 1130, 3 "K's," sun over mountain on white triangle. No. 1131, Sun over 3 "K's." No. 1132, Tagalog "K" in sun. No. 1133, Sun with human face. No. 1134, Tricolor flag, forerunner of present flag. No. 1135, Present flag. Nos. 1126, 1128, 1130-1131, 1133, 1135 inscribed in Tagalog.

1972, June 12 Photo. *Perf. 13*
1126 A234 30s ultra & red 18 14
1127 A234 30s ultra & red 18 14
1128 A234 30s ultra & red 18 14
1129 A234 30s ultra & blk 18 14
1130 A234 30s ultra & red 18 14
1131 A234 30s ultra & red 18 14
1132 A234 30s ultra & red 18 14
1133 A234 30s ultra & red 18 14
1134 A234 30s ultra, red & blk 18 14
1135 A234 30s ultra, yel & red 18 14
Block of 10 1.90 1.50

Nos. 1126-1135 printed se-tenant in sheets of 50 (5x10).

Portrait Type of 1970

Portraits: 40s, Gen. Miguel Malvar. 1p, Julian Felipe.

1972 Engr. *Perf. 14*
1136 A222 40s rose red 20 5
1137 A222 1p dp bl 55 20

Honoring Gen. Miguel Malvar (1865-1911), revolutionary leader, and Julian Felipe (1861-1944), composer of Philippine national anthem.
Issue dates: 40s, July 10; 1p, June 26.

Parrotfish A235

1972, Aug. 14 Photo. *Perf. 13*
1138 A235 5s *shown* 5 5
1139 A235 10s *Sunburst butterflyfish* 8 6
1140 A235 20s *Moorish idol* 15 8

Tropical fish. See No. C104.

Development Bank of the Philippines A236

1972, Sept. 12
1141 A236 10s gray bl & multi 8 6
1142 A236 20s lil & multi 10 7
1143 A236 60s tan & multi 32 20

25th anniversary of the Development Bank of the Philippines.

Pope Paul VI A237

1972, Sept. 26 Unwmk. *Perf. 14*
1144 A237 10s lt grn & multi 6 6
1145 A237 50s lt vio & multi 25 20

First anniversary (in 1971) of the visit of Pope Paul VI to the Philippines, and for his 75th birthday. See No. C105.

Nos. 880, 899 and 925 Surcharged with New Value and 2 Bars

1972, Sept. 29 Engr. *Perf. 13½*
1146 A161 10s on 6s lil & blk 8 5

Photo. *Perf. 12*
1147 A167 10s on 6s multi 8 5

Perf. 14½x14
Wmk. 233
1148 A176 10s on 6s multi 8 5

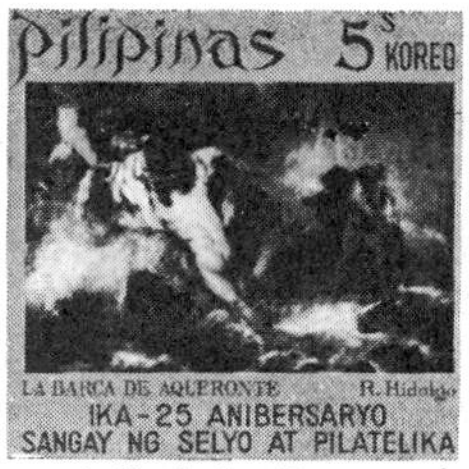

Charon's Bark, by Resurreccion Hidalgo — A238

Paintings: 10s, Rice Workers' Meal, by F. Amorsolo. 30s, "Spain and the Philippines," by Juan Luna (vert.). 70s, Song of Maria Clara, by F. Amorsolo.

Perf. 14x13
1972, Oct. 16 Unwmk. Photo.

Size: 38x40mm.
1149 A238 5s sil & multi 5 5
1150 A238 10s sil & multi 7 6

Size: 24x56mm.
1151 A238 30s sil & multi 15 15

Size: 38x40mm.
1152 A238 70s sil & multi 32 32

25th anniversary of the organization of the Stamp and Philatelic Division.

Lamp, Nurse, Emblem — A239

1972, Oct. 22 *Perf. 12½x13½*
1153 A239 5s vio & multi 5 5
1154 A239 10s bl & multi 6 5
1155 A239 70s org & multi 25 22

50th anniversary of the Philippine Nursing Association.

Heart, Map of Philippines A240

1972, Oct. 24 *Perf. 13*
1156 A240 5s pur, emer & red 5 5
1157 A240 10s bl, emer & red 7 6
1158 A240 30s emer, bl & red 15 12

"Your heart is your health," World Health Month.

First Mass on Limasawa, by Carlos V. Francisco — A241

1972, Oct. 31 *Perf. 14*
1159 A241 10s brn & multi 10 8

450th anniversary of the first mass in the Philippines, celebrated by Father Valderama on Limasawa, Mar. 31, 1521. See No. C106.

Nos. 878, 882, 899 Surcharged: "ASIA PACIFIC SCOUT CONFERENCE NOV. 1972"

1972, Nov. 13 Engr. *Perf. 13½*
1160 A161 10s on 6s bl & blk 10 7
1161 A161 10s on 6s grn & blk 10 7

Photo. *Perf. 12*
1162 A167 10s on 6s multi 10 7

Asia Pacific Scout Conference, Nov. 1972.

Torch, Olympic Emblems — A242

Perf. 12½x13½
1972, Nov. 15 Photo.
1163 A242 5s bl & multi 5 5
1164 A242 10s multi 7 6
1165 A242 70s org & multi 32 25

20th Olympic Games, Munich, Aug. 26-Sept. 11.

Nos. 896 and 919 Surcharged with New Value, Two Bars and: "1972 PHILATELIC WEEK"

1972, Nov. 23 Photo. *Perf. 13½*
1166 A166 10s on 6s multi 7 7
1167 A174 10s on 6s multi 7 7

Philatelic Week 1972.

Manunggul Burial Jar, 890-710 B.C. — A243

Designs: No. 1169, Ngipet Duldug Cave ritual earthenware vessel, 155 B.C. No. 1170, Metal age chalice, 200-600 A.D. No. 1171, Earthenware vessel, 15th century.

1972, Nov. 29

1168 A243 10s grn & multi		8	5
1169 A243 10s lil & multi		8	5
1170 A243 10s bl & multi		8	5
1171 A243 10s yel & multi		8	5

College of Pharmacy and Univ. of the Philippines Emblems — A244

1972, Dec. 11 *Perf. 12½x13½*

1172 A244 5s lt vio & multi	7	5
1173 A244 10s yel grn & multi	8	5
1174 A244 30s ultra & multi	20	12

60th anniversary of the College of Pharmacy of the University of the Philippines.

Christmas Lantern Makers, by Jorge Pineda A245

1972, Dec. 14 Photo. *Perf. 12½*

1175 A245 10s dk bl & multi	7	5
1176 A245 30s brn & multi	15	10
1177 A245 50s grn & multi	25	22

Christmas 1972.

Red Cross Flags, Pres. Roxas and Mrs. Aurora Quezon A246

1972, Dec. 21

1178 A246 5s ultra & multi	5	5
1179 A246 20s multi	10	8
1180 A246 30s brn & multi	15	12

25th anniv. of the Philippine Red Cross.

Nos. 894 and 936 Surcharged with New Value and 2 Bars

1973, Jan. 22 Photo. *Perf. 14, 13*

1181 A165 10s on 6s multi	8	5
1182 A180 10s on 6s multi	8	5

San Luis University, Luzon — A247

1973, Mar. 1 Photo. *Perf. 13½x14*

1183 A247 5s multi	5	5
1184 A247 10s yel & multi	6	5
1185 A247 75s multi	30	25

60th anniversary of San Luis University, Baguio City, Luzon.

Jesus Villamor and Fighter Planes — A248

1973, Apr. 9 Photo. *Perf. 13½x14*

1186 A248 10s multi	8	5
1187 A248 2p multi	70	70

Col. Jesus Villamor (1914-1971), World War II aviator who fought for liberation of the Philippines.

Nos. 932, 957, 070 Surcharged with New Values and 2 Bars

1973, Apr. 23 Photo. *Perf. 13x13½*

1188 A178 5s on 6s multi	7	5

Perf. 14½
Wmk. 233

1189 A187 5s on 6s multi	7	5

Engr. Unwmk.

1190 A222 15s on 10s rose car	10	5

Two additional bars through "G.O." on No. 1190.

ITI Emblem, Performance and Actor Vic Silayan — A249

1973, May 15 Photo. *Perf. 13x12½*

1191 A249 5s bl & multi	5	5
1192 A249 10s yel grn & multi	7	6
1193 A249 50s org & multi	20	12
1194 A249 70s rose & multi	30	18

1st Third World Theater Festival, sponsored by the UNESCO affiliated International Theater Institute, Manila, Nov. 19-30, 1971.

Josefa Llanes Escoda — A250

Designs: No. 1196, Gabriela Silang. No. 1197, Rafael Palma. 30s, Jose Rizal. 60s, Marcela Agoncillo. 90s, Teodoro R. Yangco. 1.10p, Dr. Pio Venezuela. 1.20p, Gregoria de Jesus. No. 1204, Pedro A. Paterno. No. 1205, Teodora Alonso. 1.80p, Edilberto Evangelista. 5p, Fernando M. Guerrero.

1973-78 Engr. *Perf. 14½*

1195 A250 15s sepia	8	5

Litho. *Perf. 12½*

1196 A250 15s vio ('74)	5	5
1197 A273 15s emer ('74)	5	5
1198 A250 30s vio bl ('78)	7	5
1199 A250 60s dl red brn	22	22
1200 A273 90s brt bl ('74)	30	15
1202 A273 1.10p brt bl ('74)	38	18
1203 A250 1.20p dl red ('78)	25	14
1204 A250 1.50p lil rose	50	42
1205 A273 1.50p brn ('74)	50	20
1206 A250 1.80p green	60	55
1208 A250 5p blue	1.65	1.65
Nos. 1195-1208 (12)	4.65	3.71

1973-74 *Imperf.*

1196a A250 15s vio ('74)	10	10
1197a A273 15s emer ('74)	10	10
1199a A250 60s dl red brn	36	36
1200a A273 90s brt bl ('74)	55	50
1202a A273 1.10p brt bl ('74)	65	65
1204a A250 1.50p lil rose	75	65
1205a A273 1.50p brn ('74)	90	90
1206a A250 1.80p green	90	90
1208a A250 5p blue	2.50	2.50
Nos. 1196a-1208a (9)	6.81	6.66

Honoring: Escoda (1898-194?), leader of Girl Scouts and Federation of Women's Clubs. Silang (1731-63), "the Ilocana Joan of Arc". Palma (1874-1939), journalist, statesman, educator. Rizal (1861-96), natl. hero. Agoncillo (1859-1946), designer of 1st Philippine flag, 1898. Yangco (1861-1939), patriot and philanthropist. Valenzuela (1869-1956), physician and newspaperman.

Gregoria de Jesus, independence leader. Paterno (1857-1911), lawyer, writer, patriot. Alonso (1827-1911), mother of Rizal. Evangelista (1862-97), army engineer, patriot. Guerrero (1873-1929), journalist, political leader.

No. 946 surcharged with New Value

1973, June 4 Engr. *Perf. 13½*

1209 A158 5s on 6s pck bl	5	5

Anti-smuggling campaign.

No. 925 Surcharged

1973, June 4 Wmk. 233

1210 A176 5s on 6s multi	5	5

10th anniversary of death of John F. Kennedy (1917-1963).

Pres. Marcos, Farm Family, Unfurling of Philippine Flag — A251

Perf. 12½x13½

1973, Sept. 24 Photo. Unwmk.

1211 A251 15s ultra & multi	7	7
1212 A251 45s red & multi	15	15
1213 A251 90s multi	32	32

75th anniversary of Philippine independence and 1st anniversary of proclamation of martial law.

Imelda Romualdez Marcos A252

1973, Oct. 31 Photo. *Perf. 13*

1214 A252 15s dl bl & multi	7	7
1215 A252 50s multi	18	18
1216 A252 60s lil & multi	22	22

Imelda Romualdez Marcos, First Lady of the Philippines.

Presidential Palace, Manila, Pres. and Mrs. Marcos — A253

1973, Nov. 15 Litho. *Perf. 14*

1217 A253 15s rose & multi	7	7
1218 A253 50s ultra & multi	15	15

See No. C107.

INTERPOL Emblem — A254

1973, Dec. 18 Photo. *Perf. 13*

1219 A254 15s ultra & multi	10	7
1220 A254 65s lt grn & multi	30	15

50th anniversary of International Criminal Police Organization.

Cub and Boy Scouts — A255

Design: 15s, Various Scout activities; inscribed in Tagalog.

1973-74 Litho. *Perf. 12½*

1221 A255 15s bis & emer	8	7
a Imperf. ('74)	10	10
1222 A255 65s bis & brt bl	28	22
a Imperf. ('74)	40	40

50th anniversary of Philippine Boy Scouts.

Issue dates: Nos. 1221-1222, Dec. 28, 1973. Nos. 1221a-1222a, Feb. 4, 1974, although first day covers are dated Dec. 28, 1973.

Manila, Bank Emblem and Farmers — A256

Designs: 60s, Old bank building. 1.50p, Modern bank building.

1974, Jan. 3 Photo. *Perf. 12½x13½*

1223 A256 15s sil & multi	8	6
1224 A256 60s sil & multi	20	12
1225 A256 1.50p sil & multi	50	30

25th anniversary of the Central Bank of the Philippines.

UPU Emblem, Maria Clara Costume — A257

Filipino Costumes: 60s, Balintawak and UPU emblem. 80s, Malong costume and UPU emblem.

1974, Jan. 15 *Perf. 12½*
1226 A257 15s multi 8 6
1227 A257 60s multi 20 12
1228 A257 80s multi 30 18

Centenary of Universal Postal Union.

No. 1192 Surcharged in Red with New Value, 2 Bars and: "1973 / PHILATELIC WEEK"

1974, Feb. 4 Photo. *Perf. 13x12½*
1229 A249 15s on 10s multi 8 6

Philatelic Week, 1973. First day covers exist dated Nov. 26, 1973.

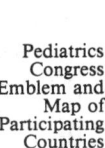

Nos. 1186 and 1136 Overprinted and Surcharged

1974, Mar. 25 Photo. *Perf. 13½x14*
1230 A248 15s on 10s multi 8 6

Engr. *Perf. 14*
1231 A222 45s on 40s rose red 14 12

25th anniversary of Lions International of the Philippines. The overprint on No. 1230 arranged to fit shape of stamp.

Pediatrics Congress Emblem and Map of Participating Countries A258

1974, Apr. 30 Litho. *Perf. 12½*
1232 A258 30s brt bl & red 10 9
a Imperf. 12 8
1233 A258 1p dl grn & red 32 20
a Imperf. 42 32

Asian Congress of Pediatrics, Manila, Apr. 30-May 4.

Nos. 912, 954-955 Surcharged with New Value and Two Bars

Wmk. 233

1974, Aug. 1 Photo. *Perf. 14½*
1234 A172 5s on 3s multi 5 5

Perf. 12½

Litho. Unwmk.
1235 A185 5s on 6s multi 5 5

Photo. *Perf. 14x13½*
1236 A186 5s on 6s multi 5 5

WPY Emblem A259

1974, Aug. 15 Litho. *Perf. 12½*
1237 A259 5s org & bl blk 5 5
a Imperf. 5 5
1238 A259 2p lt grn & dk bl 60 32
a Imperf. 65 50

World Population Year, 1974.

Red Feather Community Chest Emblem A260

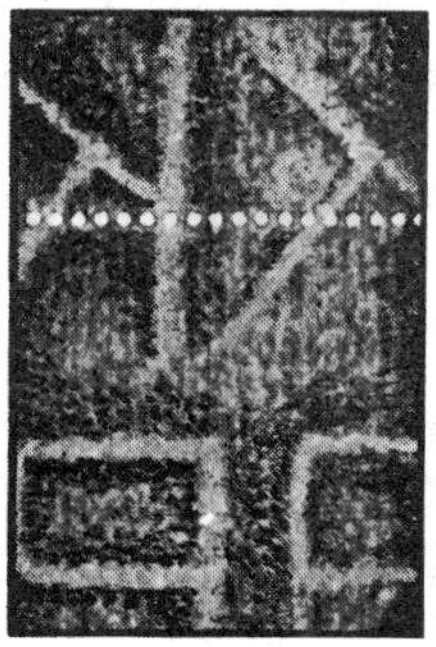

Wmk. 372-"K" and "P" Multiple

Wmk. 372

1974, Sept. 5 Litho. *Perf. 12½*
1239 A260 15s brt bl & red 7 5
a Imperf. 10 10
1240 A260 40s emer & red 15 10
a Imperf. 20 20
1241 A260 45s red brn & red 20 10
a Imperf. 20 20

25th anniversary of the Philippine Community Chest.

Sultan Kudarat, Flag, Order and Map of Philippines — A261

Perf. 13½x14

1975, Jan. 13 Photo. Unwmk.
1242 A261 15s multi 8 5

Sultan Mohammad Dipatuan Kudarat, 16th-17th century ruler.

Mental Health Association Emblem — A262

Wmk. 372

1975, Jan. 20 Litho. *Perf. 12½*
1243 A262 45s emer & org 12 10
a Imperf. 20 20
1244 A262 1p emer & pur 25 20
a Imperf. 32 32

Philippine Mental Health Association, 25th anniversary.

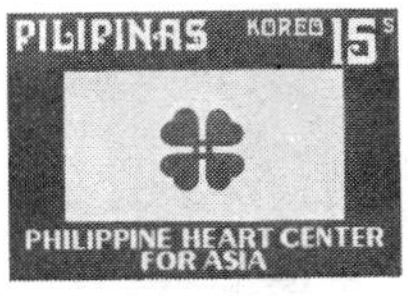

4-Leaf Clover A263

1975, Feb. 14
1245 A263 15s vio bl & red 8 5
a Imperf. 9 9
1246 A263 50s emer & red 12 12
a Imperf. 18 18

Philippine Heart Center for Asia, inauguration.

Military Academy, Cadet and Emblem — A264

Perf. 13½x14

1975, Feb. 17 Unwmk.
1247 A264 15s grn & multi 10 7
1248 A264 45s plum & multi 24 15

Philippine Military Academy, 70th anniversary.

Helping the Disabled — A265

Perf. 12½, Imperf.

1975, Mar. 17 Wmk. 372
1249 A265 Block of 10 1.65 1.25
a.-j. 45s grn, any single 12 8

25th anniversary (in 1974) of Philippine Orthopedic Association.

Nos. B43, B50-B51 Surcharged with New Value and Two Bars

1975, Apr. 15 Unwmk.
1250 SP18 5s on 15s + 5s 5 5
1251 SP16 60s on 70s + 5s 22 20
1252 SP18 1p on 1.10p + 5s 25 22

"Grow and Preserve Forests"
A266 A267

1975, May 19 Litho. *Perf. 14½*
1253 A266 45s blk, brn & grn 14 10
1254 A267 45s blk, brn & grn 14 10

Forest conservation. Nos. 1253-1254 printed se-tenant in sheets of 100.

Jade Vine — A268

1975, June 9 Photo. *Perf. 14½*
1255 A268 15s multi 10 5

Imelda R. Marcos, IWY Emblem — A269

Civil Service Emblem — A270

Wmk. 372

1975, July 2 Litho. *Perf. 12½*
1256 A269 15s bl & blk 8 8
a Imperf. 10 10
1257 A269 80s pink, bl & grn 32 25
a Imperf. 32 32

International Women's Year 1975.

1975, Sept. 19 Litho. *Perf. 12½*
1258 A270 15s multi 8 8
a Imperf. 8 8
1259 A270 50s multi 20 10
a Imperf. 20 20

Dam and Emblem A271

1975, Sept. 30
1260 A271 40s org & vio bl 10 10
a Imperf. 15 15
1261 A271 1.50p brt rose & vio bl 42 32
a Imperf. 52 52

Manila Harbor, 1875 A272

1975, Nov. 4 Unwmk. *Perf. 13x13½*
1262 A272 1.50p red & multi 42 25

Hong Kong and Shanghai Banking Corporation, centenary of Philippines service.

Norberto Romualdez (1875-1941), Scholar and Legislator — A273

Jose Rizal Monument, Luneta Park — A273a

Noted Filipinos: No. 1264, Rafael Palma (1874-1939), journalist, statesman, educator. No. 1265, Rajah Kalantiaw, chief of Panay, author of ethical-penal code (1443). 65s, Emilio Jacinto (1875-1899), patriot. No. 1269, Gen. Gregorio del Pilar (1875-1899), military hero. No. 1270, Lope K. Santos (1879-1963), grammarian, writer. 1.60p, Felipe Agoncillo (1859-1941), lawyer, cabinet member.

Wmk. 372

1975-81 Litho. *Perf. 12½*
1264 A273 30s brn ('77) 8 5
1265 A273 30s dp rose ('78) 8 5
1266 A273a 40s yel & blk ('81) 14 7
1267 A273 60s violet 14 7
a Imperf. 22 22
1268 A273 65s lil rose 15 7
a Imperf. 24 24
1269 A273 90s lil rose 20 8
a Imperf. 32 32

1270 A273 90s grn ('78) 14 7
1272 A273 1.60p blk ('76) 50 15
Nos. 1264-1272 (8) 1.43 61

See Nos. 1195-1208.

A274

1975, Nov. 22 Litho. *Perf. 12½*
1275 A274 60s multi 15 12
1276 A274 1.50p multi 40 32

40th anniversary of 1st landing of the Pan American World Airways China Clipper in the Philippines.

Nos. 1199 and 1205 Overprinted

1975, Nov. 22 Unwmk.
1277 A250 60s dl red brn 15 15
1278 A273 1.50p brown 32 32

Airmail Exhibition, Nov. 22-Dec. 9.

APO Emblem — A275

1975, Nov. 24 Wmk. 372
1279 A275 5s ultra & multi 8 5
a Imperf. 7 7
1280 A275 1p bl & multi 35 25
a Imperf. 40 40

Amateur Philatelists' Organization, 25th anniversary.

San Agustin Church — A276

Philippine Churches: 30s, Morong Church (horiz.). 45s, Basilica of Taal (horiz.). 60s, San Sebastian Church.

1975, Dec. 23 Litho. *Perf. 12½*
1281 A276 20s bluish grn 8 8
a Imperf. 12 12
1282 A276 30s yel org & blk 10 8
a Imperf. 15 15
1283 A276 45s rose, brn & blk 15 10
a Imperf. 20 20
1284 A276 60s yel, bis & blk 20 15
a Imperf. 32 32

Holy Year 1975.

Foreign postal stationery (stamped envelopes, postal cards and air letter sheets) lies beyond the scope of this Catalogue, which is limited to adhesive postage stamps.

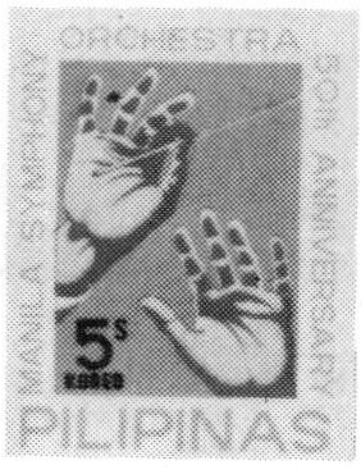

Conductor's Hands — A277

1976, Jan. 27
1285 A277 5s org & multi 5 5
1286 A277 50s multi 20 15

Manila Symphony Orchestra, 50th anniversary.

PAL Planes of 1946 and 1976 A278

1976, Feb. 14
1287 A278 60s bl & multi 15 10
1288 A278 1.50p red & multi 42 32

Philippine Airlines, 30th anniversary.

National University — A279

1976, Mar. 30
1289 A279 45s bl, vio bl & yel 12 10
1290 A279 60s lt bl, vio bl & pink 20 12

National University, 75th anniversary.

Eye Examination A280

1976, Apr. 7 Litho. *Perf. 12½*
1291 A280 15s multi 8 5

World Health Day: "Foresight prevents blindness."

Book and Emblem — A281

1976, May 24 Unwmk.
1292 A281 1.50p grn & multi 45 40

National Archives, 75th anniversary.

Santo Tomas University, Emblems A282

1976, June 7 Wmk. 372
1293 A282 15s yel & multi 8 5
1294 A282 50s multi 15 12

Colleges of Education and Science, Santo Tomas University, 50th anniversary.

Maryknoll College — A283

Wmk. 372
1976, July 26 Litho. *Perf. 12½*
1295 A283 15s lt bl & multi 8 5
1296 A283 1.50p bis & multi 42 32

Maryknoll College, Quezon City, 50th anniversary.

No. 1164 Surcharged in Dark Violet

Perf. 12½x13½
1976, July 30 Photo.
1297 A242 15s on 10s multi 10 7

21st Olympic Games, Montreal, Canada, July 17-Aug. 1.

Police College, Manila — A284

1976, Aug. 8 Litho. *Perf. 12½*
1298 A284 15s multi 8 8
a Imperf. 10 10
1299 A284 60s multi 20 12
a Imperf. 32 32

Philippine Constabulary, 75th anniversary.

Surveyors — A285

1976, Sept. 2 Wmk. 372
1300 A285 80s multi 22 20

Bureau of Lands, 75th anniversary.

Monetary Fund and World Bank Emblems A286

Virgin of Antipollo A287

1976, Oct. 4 Litho. *Perf. 12½*
1301 A286 60s multi 15 12
1302 A286 1.50p multi 42 32

Joint Annual Meeting of the Board of Governors of the International Monetary Fund and the World Bank, Manila, Oct. 4-8.

1976, Nov. 26 *Perf. 12½*
1303 A287 30s multi 8 8
1304 A287 90s multi 20 14

Virgin of Antipolo, Our Lady of Peace and Good Voyage, 350th anniversary of arrival of statue in the Philippines and 50th anniversary of the canonical coronation.

No. 1184 Surcharged with New Value and 2 Bars and Overprinted: "1976 PHILATELIC WEEK"

Perf. 13½x14
1976, Nov. 26 Photo. Unwmk.
1305 A247 30s on 10s multi 8 8

Philatelic Week 1976.

People Going to Church A288

Wmk. 372
1976, Dec. 1 Litho. *Perf. 12½*
1306 A288 15s bl & multi 5 5
1307 A288 30s bl & multi 12 7

Christmas 1976.

Symbolic Diamond and Book A289

Galicano Apacible A290

1976, Dec. 13
1308 A289 30s grn & multi 10 7
1309 A289 75s grn & multi 22 15

Philippine Educational System, 75th anniversary.

No. 1202 and 1208 Surcharged with New Value and 2 Bars

1977, Jan. 17 Unwmk.
1310 A273 1.20p on 1.10p bl 32 20
1311 A250 3p on 5p bl 65 60

1977 Litho. Wmk. 372 *Perf. 12½*

Design: 30s, José Rizal.

1313 A290 30s multi 8 5
1318 A290 2.30p multi 52 35

Dr. José Rizal (1861-1896) physician, poet and national hero (30s). Dr. Galicano

Apacible (1864-1949), physician, statesman (2.30p).
Issue dates: 30s, Feb. 16; 2.30p, Jan. 24.

Emblem, Flags, Map of AOPU
A291

1977, Apr. 1 **Wmk. 372**

1322	A291	50s multi	10	7
1323	A291	1.50p multi	32	25

Asian-Oceanic Postal Union (AOPU), 15th anniversary.

Cogwheels and Worker — A292

1977, Apr. 21 **Perf. 12½**

1324	A292	90s blk & multi	25	22
1325	A292	2.30p blk & multi	50	42

Asian Development Bank, 10th anniversary.

Farmer at Work and Receiving Money — A293

1977, May 14 **Litho.** **Wmk. 372**

1326	A293	30s org red & multi	8	5

National Commission on Countryside Credit and Collection, campaign to strengthen the rural credit system.

Solicitor General's Emblem
A294

1977, June 30 **Litho.** **Perf. 12½**

1327	A294	1.65p multi	32	20

Office of the Solicitor General, 75th anniversary.

Conference Emblem
A295

1977, July 29 **Litho.** **Perf. 12½**

1328	A295	2.20p bl & multi	45	25

8th World Conference of the World Peace through Law Center, Manila, Aug. 21-26.

ASEAN Emblem
A296

1977, Aug. 8

1329	A296	1.50p grn & multi	35	20

Association of South East Asian Nations (ASEAN), 10th anniversary.

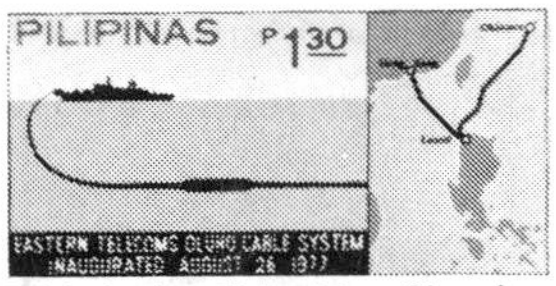

Cable-laying Ship, Map Showing Cable Route — A297

1977, Aug. 26 **Litho.** **Perf. 12½**

1330	A297	1.30p multi	30	20

Inauguration of underwater telephone cable linking Okinawa, Luzon and Hong Kong.

President Marcos — A298

1977, Sept. 11 **Wmk. 372**

1331	A298	30s multi	8	5
1332	A298	2.30p multi	55	35

Ferdinand E. Marcos, president of the Philippines, 60th birthday.

People Raising Flag — A299

1977, Sept. 21 **Litho.** **Perf. 12½**

1333	A299	30s multi	8	5
1334	A299	2.30p multi	55	35

5th anniversary of "New Society."

Bishop Gregorio Aglipay — A300

1977, Oct. 1 **Litho.** **Perf. 12½**

1335	A300	30s multi	7	5
1336	A300	90s multi	22	12

Philippine Independent Aglipayan Church, 75th anniversary.

Fairchild FC-2 over World Map — A301

1977, Oct. 28 **Wmk. 372**

1337	A301	2.30p multi	52	32

First scheduled Pan American airmail service, Key West to Havana, 50th anniversary.

No. 1280 Surcharged with New Value, 2 Bars and Overprinted in Red: "1977 / PHILATELIC / WEEK"

1977, Nov. 22 **Litho.** **Perf. 12½**

1338	A275	90s on 1p multi	20	12

Philatelic Week.

Children Celebrating and Star from Lantern — A302

1977, Dec. 1 **Unwmk.**

1339	A302	30s multi	8	5
1340	A302	45s multi	14	8

Christmas 1977.

Scouts and Map showing Jamboree Locations — A303

1977, Dec. 27

1341	A303	30s multi	8	5

National Boy Scout Jamboree, Tumauini, Isabela; Capitol Hills, Cebu City; Mariano Marcos, Davao, Dec. 27, 1977-Jan. 5, 1978.

Far Eastern University Arms — A304

1978, Jan. 26 **Litho.** **Wmk. 372**

1342	A304	30s gold & multi	8	5

Far Eastern University, 50th anniversary.

Sipa
A305

Designs: Various positions of Sipa ballgame.

1978, Feb. 28 **Perf. 12½**

1343	A305	5s bl & multi	5	5
1344	A305	10s bl & multi	5	5
1345	A305	40s bl & multi	12	7
1346	A305	75s bl & multi	24	10

Nos. 1343-1346 printed se-tenant with continuous design.

Arms of Meycauayan
A306

1978, Apr. 21 **Litho.** **Perf. 12½**

1347	A306	1.05p multi	22	12

400th anniversary of Meycauayan, founded 1578-1579.

Moro Vinta and UPU Emblem — A307

Designs (UPU Emblem and): 2.50p, No. 1350b, Horse-drawn mail cart. No. 1350a, like 5p. No. 1350c, Steam locomotive. No. 1350d, Three-master.

1978, June 9 **Litho.** **Perf. 13½**

1348	A307	2.50p multi	60	40
1349	A307	5p multi	1.10	80

Souvenir Sheet

Perf. 12½x13

1350		Sheet of 4	10.00	
a	A307	7.50p multi	2.00	2.00
b	A307	7.50p multi	2.00	2.00
c	A307	7.50p multi	2.00	2.00
d	A307	7.50p multi	2.00	2.00

CAPEX International Philatelic Exhibition, Toronto, Ont., June 9-18. No. 1350 has red marginal inscription. Size of stamps: 36½x25mm; sheet; 90x73mm.
No. 1350 exists imperf. in changed colors.

Andres Bonifacio Monument, by Guillermo Tolentino — A308

Wmk. 372

1978, July 10 **Litho.** **Perf. 12½**

1351	A308	30s multi	8	5

Rook, Knight and Globe
A309

1978, July 17

1352 A309 30s vio bl & red 7 5
1353 A309 2p vio bl & red 42 30

World Chess Championship, Anatoly Karpov and Viktor Korchnoi, Baguio City, 1978.

Miners A310

1978, Aug. 12 Litho. ***Perf. 12½***

1354 A310 2.30p multi 45 25

75th anniversary of Benguet gold mining industry.

Manuel Quezon and Quezon Memorial — A311

1978, Aug. 19

1355 A311 30s multi 8 5
1356 A311 1p multi 22 10

Manuel Quezon (1878-1944), first president of Commonwealth of the Philippines.

Law Association Emblem, Philippine Flag — A312

1978, Aug. 27 Litho. ***Perf. 12½***

1357 A312 2.30p multi 45 32

58th International Law Conference, Manila, Aug. 27-Sept. 2.

Pres. Sergio Osmena (1878-1961) A313

1978, Sept. 8

1358 A313 30s multi 8 5
1359 A313 1p multi 22 10

Map Showing Cable Route, Cablelaying Ship — A314

1978, Sept. 30

1360 A314 1.40p multi 30 18

ASEAN Submarine Cable Network, Philippines-Singapore cable system, inauguration.

Basketball, Games' Emblem A315

1978, Oct. 1

1361 A315 30s multi 8 5
1362 A315 2.30p multi 45 32

8th Men's World Basketball Championship, Manila, Oct. 1-15.

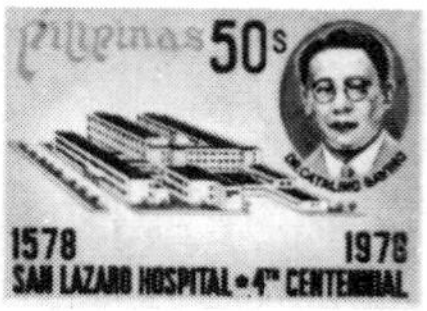

San Lazaro Hospital and Dr. Catalino Gavino A316

1978, Oct. 13 Litho. ***Perf. 12½***

1363 A316 50s multi 12 6
1364 A316 90s multi 20 10

San Lazaro Hospital, 400th anniversary.

Nurse Vaccinating Child — A317

1978, Oct. 24

1365 A317 30s multi 7 5
1366 A317 1.50p multi 35 20

Eradication of smallpox.

No. 1268 Surcharged

1978 PHILATELIC WEEK

60s

1978, Nov. 23

1367 A273 60s on 65s lil rose 14 7

Philatelic Week.

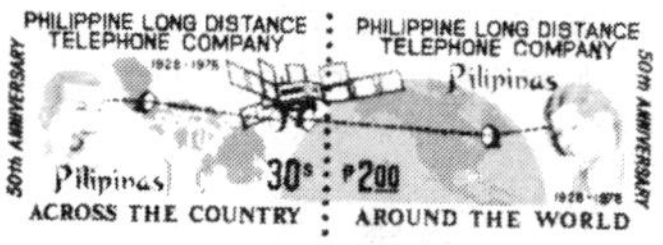

"The Telephone Across Country and World"
A318 A319

Wmk. 372

1978, Nov. 28 Litho. ***Perf. 12½***

1368 A318 30s multi 7 5
1369 A319 2p multi 42 30

Philippine Long Distance Telephone Company, 50th anniversary. Nos. 1368-1369 printed se-tenant in sheets of 30.

Traveling Family — A320

1978, Nov. 28

1370 A320 30s multi 7 5
1371 A320 1.35p multi 32 12

Decade of Philippine children.

Church and Arms of Agoo A321

1978, Dec. 7 Litho. ***Perf. 12½***

1372 A321 30s multi 8 5
1373 A321 45s multi 12 8

400th anniversary of the founding of Agoo.

Church and Arms of Balayan A322

1978, Dec. 8

1374 A322 30s multi 7 5
1375 A322 90s multi 22 10

400th anniversary of the founding of Balayan.

Dr. Honoria Acosta Sison (1888-1970), 1st Philippine Woman Physician — A323

1978, Dec. 15

1376 A323 30s multi 8 5

Family, Houses, U.N. Emblem A324

1978, Dec. Litho. ***Perf. 12½***

1377 A324 30s multi 7 5
1378 A324 3p multi 65 40

30th anniversary of Universal Declaration of Human Rights.

Chaetodon Trifasciatus — A325

Fish: 1.20p, Balistoides niger. 2.20p, Rhinecanthus aculeatus. 2.30p, Chelmon rostratus. No. 1383, Chaetodon mertensi. No. 1384, Euxiphipops xanthometapon.

1978, Dec. 29 ***Perf. 14***

1379 A325 30s multi 7 5
1380 A325 1.20p multi 25 10
1381 A325 2.20p multi 42 22
1382 A325 2.30p multi 45 25
1383 A325 5p multi 1.00 55
1384 A325 5p multi 1.00 55
Nos. 1379-1384 (6) 3.19 1.72

Carlos P. Romulo, U.N. Emblem A326

1979, Jan. 14 Litho. ***Perf. 12½***

1385 A326 30s multi 7 5
1386 A326 2p multi 50 25

Carlos P. Romulo (1899-1985), pres. of UN General Assembly and Security Council.

Rotary Emblem and "60" A327

Rosa Sevilla de Alvero A328

1979, Jan. 26 **Wmk. 372**

1387 A327 30s multi 8 5
1388 A327 2.30p multi 55 22

Rotary Club of Manila, 60th anniversary.

1979, Mar. 4 Litho. ***Perf. 12½***

1389 A328 30 rose 7 5

Rosa Sevilla de Alvero, educator and writer, birth centenary.

Oil Well and Map of Palawan A329

Wmk. 372

1979, Mar. 21 Litho. ***Perf. 12½***

1390 A329 30s multi 8 5
1391 A329 45s multi 12 8

First Philippine oil production, Nido Oil Reef Complex, Palawan.

Merrill's Fruit Doves A330

Birds: 1.20p, Brown tit babbler. 2.20p, Mindoro imperial pigeons. 2.30p, Steere's pittas. No. 1396, Koch's and red-breasted pittas. No. 1397, Philippine eared nightjar.

Perf. 14x13½

1979, Apr. 16 **Unwmk.**

1392 A330 30s multi 7 5
1393 A330 1.20p multi 25 10
1394 A330 2.20p multi 42 22
1395 A330 2.30p multi 45 25
1396 A330 5p multi 1.00 55
1397 A330 5p multi 1.00 55
Nos. 1392-1397 (6) 3.19 1.72

Association Emblem and Reader
A331

Wmk. 372

1979, Apr. 3 Litho. *Perf. 12½*

1398	A311	30s multi	7	5
1399	A311	75s multi	15	7
1400	A311	1p multi	22	8

Association of Special Libraries of the Philippines, 25th anniversary.

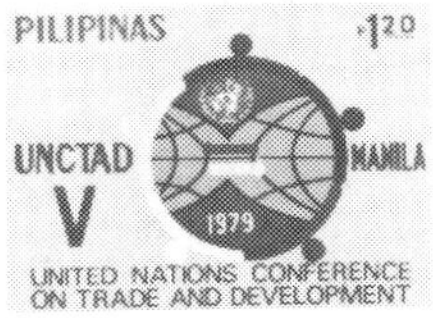

UNCTAD Emblem
A332

Wmk. 372

1979, May 3 Litho. *Perf. 12½*

1401	A332	1.20p multi	22	10
1402	A332	2.30p multi	50	20

5th Session of United Nations Conference on Trade and Development, Manila, May 3-June 1.

Civet Cat
A333

Philippine Animals: 1.20p, Macaque. 2.20p, Wild boar. 2.30p, Dwarf leopard. No. 1407, Asiatic dwarf otter. No. 1408, Anteater.

1979, May 14 *Perf. 14*

1403	A333	30s multi	7	5
1404	A333	1.20p multi	25	12
1405	A333	2.20p multi	42	22
1406	A333	2.30p multi	45	25
1407	A333	5p multi	1.00	55
1408	A333	5p multi	1.00	55
		Nos. 1403-1408 (6)	3.19	1.74

Dish Antenna — A334

Design: 1.30p, World map.

1979, May 17 *Perf. 12½*

1409	A334	90s multi	18	7
1410	A334	1.30p multi	24	10

11th World Telecommunications Day, May 17.

Mussaenda Donna Evangelina — A335

Philippine Mussaendas: 1.20p, Dona Esperanza. 2.20p, Dona Hilaria. 2.30p, Dona Aurora. No. 1415, Gining Imelda. No. 1416, Dona Trining.

1979, June 11 Litho. *Perf. 14*

1411	A335	30s multi	7	5
1412	A335	1.20p multi	7	5
1413	A335	2.20p multi	42	22
1414	A335	2.30p multi	45	25
1415	A335	5p multi	1.00	55
1416	A335	5p multi	1.00	55
		Nos. 1411-1416 (6)	3.01	1.67

Manila Cathedral, Coat of Arms — A336

1979, June 25 *Perf. 12½*

1417	A336	30s multi	7	5
1418	A336	75s multi	15	7
1419	A336	90s multi	20	10

Archdiocese of Manila, 400th anniversary.

Patrol Boat, Naval Arms
A337

1979, June 26

1420	A337	30s multi	8	5
1421	A337	45s multi	8	8

Philippine Navy Day.

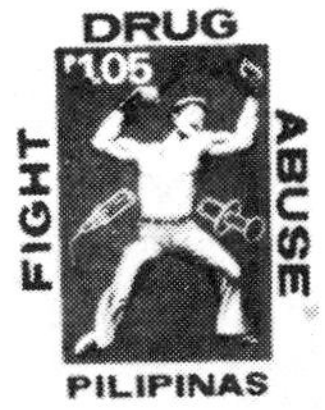

Man Breaking Chains, Broken Syringe — A338

1979, July 23 Litho. *Perf. 12½*

1422	A338	30s multi	7	5
1423	A338	90s multi	20	10
1424	A338	1.05p multi	24	12

Fight drug abuse.

Afghan Hound
A339

Designs: 90s, Striped tabbies. 1.20p, Dobermann pinscher. 2.20p, Siamese cats. 2.30p, German shepherd. 5p, Chinchilla cats.

1979, Aug. 6 *Perf. 14*

1425	A339	30s multi	7	5
1426	A339	90s multi	20	10
1427	A339	1.20p multi	24	12
1428	A339	2.20p multi	45	15
1429	A339	2.30p multi	50	42
1430	A339	5p multi	1.00	50
		Nos. 1425-1430 (6)	2.46	1.34

The lack of a value for a listed item does not necessarily indicate rarity.

Children Playing IYC Emblem
A340

Designs: Children playing and IYC emblem (diff.).

1979, Aug. 31 Litho. *Perf. 12½*

1431	A340	15s multi	5	5
1432	A340	20s multi	8	5
1433	A340	25s multi	8	5
1434	A340	1.20p multi	20	10

International Year of the Child.

Hands Holding Emblem — A341

1979, Sept. 27 Litho. *Perf. 12½*

1435	A341	30s multi	8	5
1436	A341	1.35p multi	25	10

Methodism in the Philippines, 80th anniversary.

Emblem and Coins
A342

Wmk. 372

1979, Nov. 15 Litho. *Perf. 12½*

1437	A342	30s multi	8	5

Philippine Numismatic and Antiquarian Society, 50th anniversary.

Concorde over Manila and Paris
A343

Design: 2.20p, Concorde over Manila.

1979, Nov. 22

1438	A343	1.05p multi	20	15
1439	A343	2.20p multi	45	32

Air France service to Manila, 25th anniversary.

No. 1272 Surcharged in Red

1979, Nov. 23

1440	A273	90s on 1.60 blk	20	10

Philatelic Week. Surcharge similar to No. 1367.

Transport Association Emblem
A344

1979, Nov. 27

1441	A344	75s multi	18	8
1442	A344	2.30p multi	48	35

International Air Transport Association, 35th annual general meeting, Manila.

Local Government Year
A345

Mother and Children, Ornament
A346

1979, Dec. 14 Litho. *Perf. 12½*

1443	A345	30s multi	8	5
1444	A345	45s multi	12	8

Christmas 1979: 90s, Stars.

1979, Dec. 17

1445	A346	30s multi	8	5
1446	A346	90s multi	24	15

Rheumatic Pain Spots and Congress Emblem
A347

Wmk. 372

1980, Jan. 20 Litho. *Perf. 12½*

1447	A347	30s multi	12	5
1448	A347	90s multi	32	15

Southeast Asia and Pacific Area League Against Rheumatism, 4th Congress, Manila, Jan. 19-24.

Gen. Douglas MacArthur
A348

Designs: 30s, MacArthur's birthplace (Little Rock, Ark) and burial place (Norfolk, Va.). 2.30p, MacArthur's cap, Sunglasses and pipe. 5p, MacArthur and troops wading ashore at Leyte, Oct. 20, 1944.

1980, Jan. 26 Wmk. 372 *Perf. 12½*

1449	A348	30s multi	12	5
1450	A348	75s multi	22	12
1451	A348	2.30p multi	70	50

Souvenir Sheet

1452	A348	5p multi	1.90	1.00

Gen. Douglas MacArthur (1880-1964). Margin of No. 1452 contains signature and quote.

Knights of Columbus of Philippines, 75th Anniversary
A349

1980, Feb. 14

1453	A349	30s multi	12	5
1454	A349	1.35p multi	48	28

Philippine Military Academy, 75th Anniversary — A350

Wmk. 372

1980, Feb. 17 Litho. *Perf. 12½*

1455	A350	30s multi	12	5
1456	A350	1.20p multi	42	20

Philippines Women's University, 75th Anniversary — A351

1980, Feb. 21

1457	A351	30s multi	12	5
1458	A351	1.05p multi	38	18

Disaster Relief A352

Rotary International, 75th Anniversary (Paintings by Carlos Botong Francisco): Nos. 1459 and 1460 each in continuous design.

1980, Feb. 23 *Perf. 12½*

1459		Strip of 5	60	28
a	A352	30s single stamp	12	5
1460		Strip of 5	4.00	1.90
a	A352	2.30p single stamp	80	38

6th Centenary of Islam in Philippines — A353

Wmk. 372

1980, Mar. 28 Litho. *Perf. 12½*

1461	A353	30s multi	12	5
1462	A353	1.30p multi	45	20

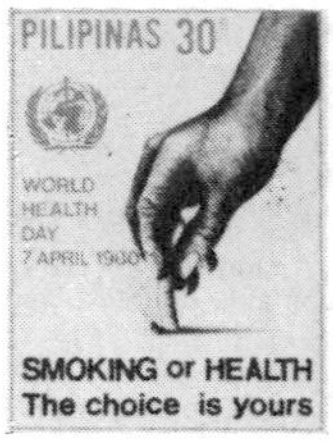

Hand Crushing Cigarette, WHO Emblem — A354

1980, Apr. 14

1463	A354	30s multi	12	5
1464	A354	75s multi	24	14

World Health Day (Apr. 17); anti-smoking campaign.

Philippine Girl Scouts, 40th Anniversary — A355

Wmk. 372

1980, May 26 Litho. *Perf. 12½*

1465	A355	30s multi	12	5
1466	A355	2p multi	38	18

Jeepney (Public Jeep) A356

1980, June 24 Litho. *Perf. 12½*

1467	A356	30s *Jeepney* (diff.)	12	5
1468	A356	1.20p *shown*	40	20

Nos. 1272, 1206 Surcharged in Red

Wmk. 372 (1.35p)

1980, Aug. 1 Litho. *Perf. 12½*

1469	A273	1.35p on 1.60p blk	52	26
1470	A250	1.50p on 1.80p grn	60	30

Independence, 82nd Anniversary.

Association Emblem — A357

1980, Aug. 1 Wmk. 372

1471	A357	30s multi	12	5
1472	A357	2.30p multi	80	75

International Association of Universities, 7th General Conference, Manila, Aug. 25-30.

Congress Emblem, Map of Philippines A358

Wmk. 372

1980, Aug. 18 Litho. *Perf. 12½*

1473	A358	30s lt grn & blk	14	6
1474	A358	75s lt bl & blk	28	16
1475	A358	2.30p sal & blk	90	48

International Federation of Library Associations and Institutions, 46th Congress, Manila, Aug. 18-23.

Kabataang Barangay (New Society), 5th Anniversary — A359

1980, Sept. 19 Litho. *Perf. 12½*

1476	A359	30s multi	14	6
1477	A359	40s multi	15	7
1478	A359	1p multi	38	20

Nos. 1389, 1422, 1443, 1445, 1327 Surcharged in Blue, Black or Red

Wmk. 372

1980, Sept. 26 Litho. *Perf. 12½*

1479	A328	40s on 30s rose (Bl)	16	7
1480	A338	40s on 30s multi	16	7
1481	A345	40s on 30s multi	16	7
1482	A346	40s on 30s multi (R)	16	7
1483	A294	2p on 1.65p multi (R)	80	40
		Nos. 1479-1483 (5)	1.44	68

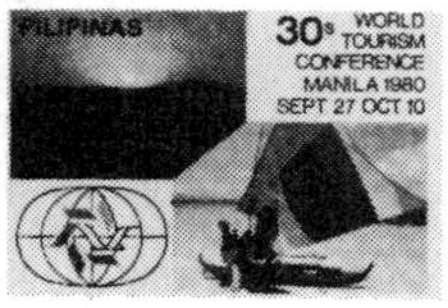

Catamaran, Conference Emblem A360

1980, Sept. 27

1484	A360	30s multi	14	6
1485	A360	2.30p multi	85	52

World Tourism Conference, Manila, Sept. 27.

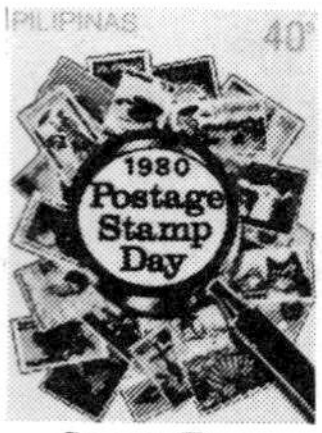

Stamp Day A361

UN, 35th Anniv. A362

1980, Oct. 9

1486	A361	40s multi	16	7
1487	A361	1p multi	40	20
1488	A361	2p multi	80	40

1980, Oct. 20

Designs: 40s, UN Headquarters and Emblem, Flag of Philippines. 3.20p, UN and Philippine flags, UN headquarters.

1489	A362	40s multi	16	7
1490	A362	3.20p multi	1.25	85

Murex Alabaster A363

1980, Nov. 2

1491	A363	40s *shown*	16	7
1492	A363	60s *Bursa bubo*	22	14
1493	A363	1.20p *Homalocantha zamboi*	42	20
1494	A363	2p *Xenophora pallidula*	80	38

INTERPOL Emblem on Globe — A364

1980, Nov. 5 Litho. Wmk. 372

1495	A364	40s multi	16	7
1496	A364	1p multi	40	18
1497	A364	3.20p multi	1.25	85

49th General Assembly Session of INTERPOL (International Police Organization), Manila, Nov. 13-21.

Central Philippine University, 75th Anniversary A365

1980, Nov. 17 Unwmk.

1498	A365	40s multi	15	7
1499	A365	3.20p multi	1.25	80

No. 1257 Surcharged

Wmk. 372

1980, Nov. 21 Litho. *Perf. 12½*

1500	A269	1.20p on 80s multi	42	20

Philatelic Week 1980. Surcharge similar to No. 1367.

No. 1358 Surcharged

1980, Nov. 30

1501	A313	40s on 30s multi	16	7

APO Philatelic Society, 30th anniversary.

Christmas Tree, Present and Candy Cane — A366

Perf. 12½

1980, Dec. 15 Litho. Unwmk.

1502	A366	40s multi	16	7

Christmas 1980.

No. 1467 Surcharged

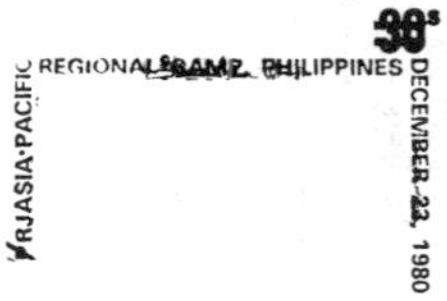

1981, Jan. 2

1503	A356	40c on 30s multi	16	7

Nos. 1370, 1257 Surcharged in Red or Black

1981

1504	A320	10s on 30s (R) multi	5	5
1505	A269	85s on 80s multi	32	16

Issue dates: 10s, Jan. 12; 85s, Jan. 2.

Heinrich Von Stephan, UPU Emblem A367

1981, Jan. 30

1506	A367	3.20p multi	1.25	60

Heinrich von Stephan (1831-1897), founder of Universal Postal Union, birth sesquicentennial.

For unused stamps, more recent issues are valued as never hinged, with the beginning point determined on a country-by-country basis. Notes to show the beginning points are prominently placed in the text.

Pope John Paul II Greeting Crowd — A368

Designs: 90s, Pope, signature (vert.). 1.20p, Pope, cardinals (vert.). 3p, Pope giving blessing, Vatican arms, Manila Cathedral. 7.50p, Pope, light on map of Philippines (vert.).

Perf. 13½x14

1981, Feb. 17				**Unwmk.**	
1507	A368	90s	multi	35	16
1508	A368	1.20p	multi	45	22
1509	A368	2.30p	multi	90	42
1510	A368	3p	multi	1.10	55

Souvenir Sheet

1511	A368	7.50p	multi	3.00	1.40

Visit of Pope John Paul, Feb. 17-22. No. 1511 has multicolored margin showing Vatican arms. Size: 76x92mm.

Nos. 1364, 1423, 1268, 1446, 1261, 1206, 1327 Surcharged

1981		**Litho.**		***Perf. 12½***	
1512	A316	40s	on 90s multi	16	7
1513	A338	40s	on 90s multi	16	7
1514	A273	40s	on 65s lil rose	16	7
1515	A346	40s	on 90s multi	16	7
1517	A271	1p	on 1.50p brt rose & vio bl	42	18
1518	A250	1.20p	on 1.80p grn	45	22
1519	A294	1.20p	on 1.65p multi	45	22
1520	A271	2p	on 1.50p brt rose & vio bl	85	35
			Nos. 1512-1520 (8)	2.81	1.25

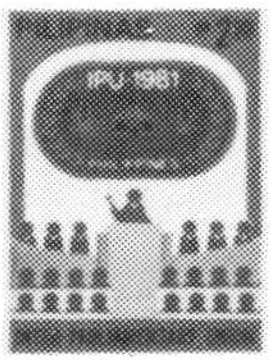

Inter-Parliamentary Session — A369

1981, Apr. 20				**Wmk. 372**	
1521	A369	2p	multi	80	38
1522	A369	3.20p	multi	1.25	65

68th Spring Meeting of the Inter-Parliamentary Union, Manila, Apr. 20-25.

Unless otherwise stated, all issues on granite paper.

Bubble Coral — A370

Wmk. 372

1981, May 22		**Litho.**		***Perf. 12½***	
1523	A370	40s	shown	16	7
1524	A370	40s	Branching coral	16	7
1525	A370	40s	Brain coral	16	7
1526	A370	40s	Table coral	16	7

Nos. 1523-1526 se-tenant.

Philippine Motor Assoc., 50th Anniv. — A371

Designs: Vintage cars. Nos. 1527-1530 se-tenant.

1981, May 25					
1527	A371	40s	Presidents car	16	7
1528	A371	40s	1930	16	7
1529	A371	40s	1937	16	7
1530	A371	40s	shown	16	7

Re-inauguration of Pres. Ferdinand E. Marcos — A372

1981, June 30					
1531	A372	40s	multi	16	7

Souvenir Sheet

Imperf

1532	A372	5p	multi	1.90	90

No. 1531 exists imperf.

St. Ignatius Loyola, Founder of Jesuit Order A373

400th Anniv. of Jesuits in Philippines: No. 1534, Jose, Rizal, Ateneo University. No. 1535, Father Federico Faura, Manila Observatory. No. 1536, Father Saturnino Urios, map of Philippines. Nos. 1533-1536 se-tenant.

1981, July 31					
1533	A373	40s	multi	16	7
1534	A373	40s	multi	16	7
1535	A373	40s	multi	16	7
1536	A373	40s	multi	16	7

Souvenir Sheet

Imperf

1537	A373	2p	multi	90	35

No. 1537 contains vignettes of Nos. 1533-1536. Size: 89x88mm.

Gen. Gregorio del Pilar (1875-1899) — A374

Design: 40s, Isabelo de los Reyes (1867-1938), labor union founder. No. 1540, Magsaysay. No. 1541, Francisco Dagohoy. No. 1543, Ambrosia R. Bautista, signer of Declaration of Independence, 1898, No. 1544, Juan Sumulong (1875-1942), statesman. 2.30p, Nicanor Abelardo (1893-1934), composer. 3.20p, Gen. Vicente Lim (1888-1945), first Philippine graduate of West Point.

Wmk. 372

1981-82		**Litho.**		***Perf. 12½***	
1538	A374	40c	grnsh bl ('82)	16	7
1539	A374	1p	blk & red brn	42	18
1540	A374	1.20p	blk & lt red brn	45	22
1541	A374	1.20p	brown ('82)	45	22
1543	A374	2p	blk & red brn	85	35
1544	A374	2p	rose lil ('82)	85	35
1545	A374	2.30p	lt red brn ('82)	90	38
1546	A374	3.20p	gray bl ('82)	1.25	65
			Nos. 1538-1546 (8)	5.33	2.42

See Nos. 1672-1680, 1682-1683, 1685.

Chief Justice Fred Ruiz Castro 67th Birth Anniv. — A375

Intl. Year of the Disabled — A376

1981, Sept. 2					
1551	A375	40s	multi	16	7

Wmk. 372

1981, Oct. 24		**Litho.**		***Perf. 12½***	
1552	A376	40s	multi	16	7
1553	A376	3.20p	multi	1.25	65

24th Intl. Red Cross Conference, Manila, Nov. 7-14 — A376a

1981, Nov. 7					
1554	A376a	40s	multi	15	7
1555	A376a	2p	multi	80	35
1556	A376a	3.20p	multi	1.20	60

Intramuros Gate, Manila — A377

1981, Nov. 13					
1557	A377	40s	black	16	7

Manila Park Zoo Concert Series, Nov. 20-30 A378

1981, Nov. 20					
1558	A378	40s	multi	16	7

No. 1329 Overprinted "1981 Philatelic Week" and Surcharged.

Wmk. 372

1981, Nov. 23		**Litho.**		***Perf. 12½***	
1559	A296	1.20p	on 1.50p multi	45	22

Nos. 1205, 1347, 1371 Surcharged.

1981, Nov. 25		**Litho.**		***Perf. 12½***	
1560	A306	40s	on 1.05p multi	16	7
1561	A320	40s	on 1.35p multi	16	7
1562	A273	1.20p	on 1.50p brn	45	22

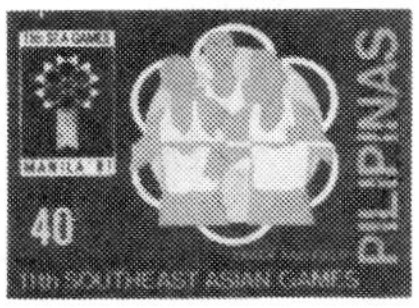

11th Southeast Asian Games, Manila, Dec. 6-15 — A379

1981, Dec. 3					
1563	A379	40s	Running	16	7
1564	A379	1p	Bicycling	45	18
1565	A379	2p	Pres. Marcos, Intl. Olympic Pres. Samaranch	90	35
1566	A379	2.30p	Soccer	90	42
1567	A379	2.80p	Shooting	1.10	50
1568	A379	3.20p	Bowling	1.25	65
			Nos. 1563-1568 (6)	4.76	2.17

Manila Intl. Film Festival, Jan. 18-29 A380

Wmk. 372

1982, Jan. 18		**Litho.**		***Perf. 12½***	
1569	A380	40s	Film Center	16	7
1570	A380	2p	Golden trophy, vert.	90	35
1571	A380	3.20p	Trophy, diff., vert.	1.25	65

Manila Metropolitan Waterworks and Sewerage System Centenary — A381

1982, Jan. 22					
1572	A381	40s	blue	16	7
1573	A381	1.20p	brown	45	22

Nos. 1268, 1302, 1328 Surcharged in Black.

1982, Jan. 28					
1574	A273	1p	on 65s lil rose	45	20
1575	A286	1p	on 1.50p multi	45	20
1576	A295	3.20p	on 2.20p multi	1.25	65

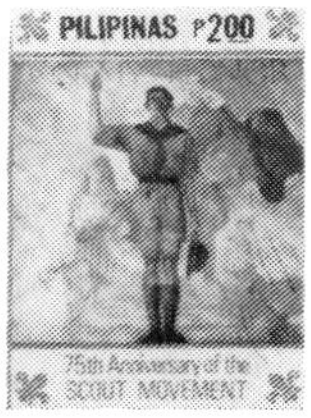

Scouting Year — A382

1982, Feb. 22					
1577	A382	40s	Portrait	16	7
1578	A382	2p	Scout giving salute	90	35

25th Anniv. of Children's Museum and Library Foundation A383

1982, Feb. 25					
1579	A383	40s	Mural	16	7
1580	A383	1.20p	Children playing	45	22

77th Anniv. of Philippine Military Academy A384

Wmk. 372

1982, Mar. 25		**Litho.**		***Perf. 12½***	
1581	A384	40s	multi	16	7
1582	A384	1p	multi	45	20

40th Bataan Day A385

1982, Apr. 9
1583 A385 40s Soldier 16 7
1584 A385 2p "Reunion for Peace" 90 35

Souvenir Sheet
Imperf
1585 A385 3.20p Cannon, flag 1.25 70

No. 1585 contains one stamp, 38x28mm.

No. B27 Surcharged.

1982 Photo. *Perf. 13½*
1586 SP14 10s on 6 + 5s multi 5 5

Aurora Aragon Quezon (1888-1949), Former First Lady — A386

1982, Apr. 28 Litho. *Perf. 12½*
1587 A386 1p rose pink 45 20

See No. 1684.

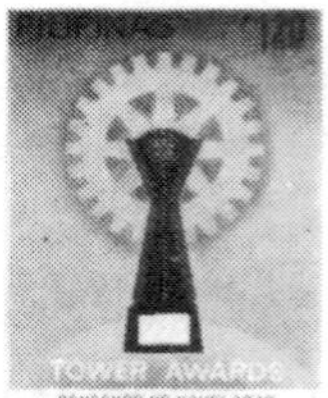

7th Towers Awards — A387

1982, May 1
1588 A387 40s Man holding award 16 7
1589 A387 1.20p Award 45 22

United Nations Conference on Human Environment, 10th Anniv. — A388

1982, June 5
1590 A388 40s Turtle 16 7
1591 A388 3.20p Philippine eagle 1.25 65

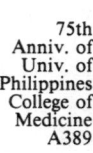

75th Anniv. of Univ. of Philippines College of Medicine A389

1982, June 10
1592 A389 40s multi 16 7
1593 A389 3.20p multi 1.25 65

Natl. Livelihood Movement A390

1982, June 12
1594 A390 40s multi 16 7

See No. 1681.

Adamson Univ., 50th Anniv. — A391

1982, June 21
1595 A391 40s bl & multi 16 7
1596 A391 1.20p lt vio & multi 45 22

Social Security, 25th Anniv. — A392

Pres. Marcos, 65th Birthday — A393

1982, Sept. 1 *Perf. 13½x13*
1597 A392 40s multi 16 7
1598 A392 1.20p multi 45 22

1982, Sept. 11 *Perf. 13½x13*
1599 A393 40s sil & multi 16 7
1600 A393 3.20p sil & multi 1.25 65
a Souv. sheet of 2, #1599-1600, imperf. 1.40 70

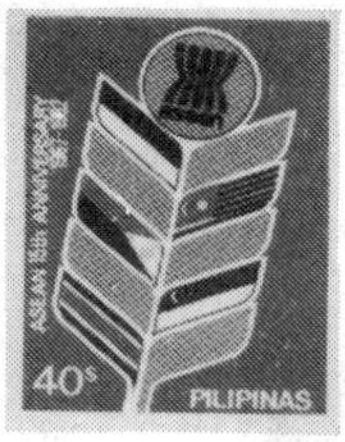

15th Anniv. of Assoc. of Southeast Asian Nations (ASEAN) A394

1982, Sept. 22 Litho. *Perf. 12½*
1601 A394 40s Flags 16 7

St. Teresa of Avila (1515-1582) A395

1982, Oct. 15 *Perf. 13x13½*
1602 A395 40s Text 16 7
1603 A395 1.20p Map 45 22
1604 A395 2p Map 90 35

10th Anniv. of Tenant Farmers' Emancipation Decree — A396

Perf. 13x13½
1982, Oct. 21 Litho. Wmk. 372
1605 A396 40s Pres. Marcos signing law 16 7

See No. 1654.

350th Anniv. of St. Isabel College A397

1982, Oct. 22
1606 A397 40s multi 16 7
1607 A397 1p multi 45 20

Reading Campaign A398

1982, Nov. 4
1608 A398 40s yel & multi 16 7
1609 A398 2.30p grn & multi 90 38

42nd Skal Club World Congress, Manila, Nov. 7-12 A399

1982, Nov. 7
1610 A399 40s Heads 16 7
1611 A399 2p Chief 90 35

25th Anniv. of Bayanihan Folk Arts Center A400

Designs: Various folk dances.

1982, Nov. 10 Litho. *Perf. 13x13½*
1612 A400 40s multi 16 7
1613 A400 2.80p multi 1.10 50

TB Bacillus Centenary A401

1982, Dec. 7 Wmk. 372
1614 A401 40s multi 16 7
1615 A401 2.80p multi 1.10 50

Christmas 1982 A402

1982, Dec. 10
1616 A402 40s multi 16 7
1617 A402 1p multi 45 20

Philatelic Week, Nov. 22-28 A403

Perf. 13x13½
1982, Nov. 28 Litho. Wmk. 372
1618 A403 40s yel & multi 16 7
1619 A403 1p sil & multi 45 20

Visit of Pres. Marcos to the US, Sept. A404

1982, Dec. 18
1620 A404 40s multi 16 7
1621 A404 3.20p multi 1.25 60
a Souv. sheet of 2, #1620-1621 1.50 70

UN World Assembly on Aging, July 26-Aug. 6 A405

Senate Pres. Eulogio Rodreiguez, Sr. (1883-1964) A406

1982, Dec. 24
1622 A405 1.20p Woman 45 22
1623 A405 2p Man 90 35

1983, Jan. 21
1624 A406 40s grn & multi 16 7
1625 A406 1.20p org & multi 45 22

1983 Manila Intl. Film Festival, Jan. 24-Feb. 4 — A407

1983, Jan. 24
1626 A407 40s blk & multi 16 7
1627 A407 3.20p pink & multi 1.25 60

Beatification of Lorenzo Ruiz (1981) — A408

Perf. 13x13½
1983, Feb. 18 Litho. Wmk. 372
1628 A408 40s multi 16 7
1629 A408 1.20p multi 45 22

400th Anniv. of Local Printing Press A409

1983, Mar. 14

1630	A409	40s blk & grn	16	7

Safety at Sea — A410

1983, Mar. 17 *Perf. 13½x13*

1631	A410	40s multi	16	7

25th anniv. of Inter-Governmental Maritime Consultation Org. Convention.

Intl. Org. of Supreme Audit Institutions, 11th Congress, Manila, Apr. 19-27 — A411

Perf. 13x13½

1983, Apr. 8 Litho. Wmk. 372

1632	A411	40s Symbols	16	7
1633	A411	2.80p Emblem	1.10	50
a		Souv. sheet of 2, 1632-1633, imperf.	1.40	65

Type of 1982 Overprinted in Red: "7th BSP NATIONAL JAMBOREE 1983"

1983, Apr. 13 *Perf. 12½*

1634	A390	40s multi	16	7

Boy Scouts of Philippines jamboree.

No. 1249 Surcharged.

1983, Apr. 15

1635		Block of 10	1.65	70
a.-j.	A265	40s on 45s, any single	16	7

75th Anniv. of Dental Assoc. — A412

Perf. 13½x13

1983, May 9 Litho. Wmk. 372

1636	A412	40s multi	16	7

75th Anniv. of University of the Philippines — A413

Perf. 13½x13

1983, June 17 Litho. Wmk. 372

1637	A413	40s Statue	16	7
1638	A413	1.20p Statue, diff., diamond	45	22

Visit of Japanese Prime Minister Yasuhiro Nakasone, May 6-8 — A414

Perf. 13x13½

1983, June 20 Litho. Wmk. 372

1639	A414	40s multi	16	7

25th Anniv. of Natl. Science and Technology Authority A415

1983, July 11

1640	A415	40s Animals, produce	16	7
1641	A415	40s Heart, food, pill	16	7
1642	A415	40s Factories, windmill, car	16	7
1643	A415	40s Chemicals, house, book	16	7

Science Week. Nos. 1640-1643 se-tenant.

World Communications Year — A416

Wmk. 372

1983, Oct. 24 Litho. *Perf. 12½*

1644	A416	3.20p multi	1.25	60

Philippine Postal System Bicentennial A417

1983, Oct. 31

1645	A417	40s multi	16	7

Christmas — A418

Star of the East and Festival Scene in continuous design.

1983, Nov. 15 Litho. *Perf. 12½*

1646		Strip of 5	80	35
a-e	A418	40s single stamp	16	7
f		Souvenir sheet	80	

Xavier University, 50th Anniv. A419

1983, Dec. 1 Litho. *Perf. 14*

1647	A419	40s multi	16	7
1648	A419	60s multi	24	10

Ministry of Labor and Employment, Golden Jubilee — A420

1983, Dec. 8 Litho. *Perf. 12½*

1649	A420	40s brt ultra & multi	16	7
1650	A420	60s gold & multi	24	10

50th Anniv. of Women's Suffrage Movement A421

1983, Dec. 7

1651	A421	40s multi	16	7
1652	A421	60s multi	24	10

Philatelic Week A422

Stamp Collecting: a. Cutting. b. Sorting. c. Soaking. d. Affixing hinges. e. Mounting stamp.

1983, Dec. 20

1653		Strip of 5	1.00	40
a.-e	A422	50s, any single	20	8

Emancipation Type of 1982

1983 Litho. *Perf. 13*

Size: 32x22mm

1654	A396	40s multi	5	5

Philippine Cockatoo A423

Princess Tarhata Kiram A424

1984, Jan. 9 *Perf. 14*

1655	A423	40s shown	5	5
1656	A423	2.30p Guaiabero	24	10
1657	A423	2.80p Crimson-spotted racket-tailed parrots	28	12
1658	A423	3.20p Large-billed parrot	32	12
1659	A423	3.60p Tanygnathus sumatranus	35	14
1660	A423	5p Hanging parakeets	50	20
		Nos. 1655-1660 (6)	1.74	73

1984, Jan. 16 *Perf. 13*

1661	A424	3p grn & red	30	12

Order of Virgin Mary, 300th Anniv. A425

Dona Concha Felix de Calderon A426

1984, Jan. 23 *Perf. 13½x13*

1662	A425	40s blk & multi	5	5
1663	A425	60s red & multi	5	5

1984, Feb. 9 *Perf. 13*

1664	A426	60s blk & bl grn	5	5
1665	A426	3.60p red & bl grn	35	14

Nos. 1546, 1599, 1618 Surcharged

1984, Feb. 20

1666	A393	60s on 40s multi (R)	6	5
1667	A403	60s on 40s multi	6	5
1668	A374	3.60p on 3.20p gray bl (R)	35	14

No. 1685 Surcharged

1985, Oct. 21 Litho. *Perf. 12½*

1669	A374	3.60p on 4.20p rose lil	28	14

Portrait Type of 1981

Designs: No. 1672, Gen. Artemio Ricarte. No. 1673, Teodoro M. Kalaw. No. 1674, Pres. Carlos P. Garcia. No. 1675, Senator Quintin Paredes. No. 1676, Dr. Deogracias V. Villadolid (1896-1976), 1st director, Bureau of Fisheries. No. 1677, Santiago Fonacier (1885-1940), archbishop. No. 1678, 2p, Vicente Orestes Romualdez (1885-1970), lawyer. 3p, Francisco Dagohoy.

Perf. 13, 12½x13 (3p), 12½ (2p)

1984-85 Litho.

1672	A374	60s blk & lt brn	6	5
1673	A374	60s blk & pur	6	5
1674	A374	60s black	6	5
1675	A374	60s dl bl	9	5
1676	A374	60s brn blk ('85)	9	5
1677	A374	60s dk red ('85)	9	5
1678	A374	60s cob bl ('85)	9	5
1679	A374	2p brt rose ('85)	16	9
1680	A374	3p pale brn	25	12

Issue dates: No. 1672, Mar. 22; No. 1673, Mar. 31; No. 1674, June 14. No. 1675, Sept. 12. No. 1676, Mar. 22. No. 1677, May 21. No. 1678, 2p, July 3. 3p, Sept. 7.

Types of 1982

1984

1681	A390	60s #1594	6	5
1682	A374	1.80p #1546	18	7
1683	A374	2.40p #1545	25	10
1684	A386	3.60p Quezon	35	14
1685	A374	4.20p #1544	40	18
		Nos. 1681-1685 (5)	1.24	54

Issue dates: No. 1685, Mar. 26; others May 5.

Ayala Corp. Sesquicentenary — A427

Night Views of Manila.

1984, Apr. 25 Litho. *Perf. 13x13½*

1686	A427	70s multi	8	5
1687	A427	3.60p multi	35	14

ESPANA '84 — A428

Designs: 2.50p, No. 1690d, Our Lady of the Most Holy Rosary with St. Dominic, by C. Francisco. 5p, No. 1690a, Spoliarium, by Juan Luna. No. 1690b, Blessed Virgin of Manila as Patroness of Voyages, Galleon showing map of Panama-Manila. No. 1690c. Illustrations from The Monkey and the Turtle, by Rizal (first children's book published in Philippines, 1885.)

1984, Apr. 27 ***Perf. 14***
1688 A428 2.50p multi 28 12
1689 A428 5p multi 55 25

Size: 94x60mm
Perf. 14½x15, Imperf.

1690 Sheet of 4 3.50 1.55
a A428 7.50p multi 85 38
b A428 7.50p multi 85 38
c A428 7.50p multi 85 38
d A428 7.50p multi 85 38

Nos. 1688-1689 se-tenant.

Maria Pax Mendoza Guazon — A429

1984, May 26 ***Perf. 13***
1691 A429 60s brt bl & red 6 5
1692 A429 65s brt bl, red & blk 7 5

Butterflies — A430

1984, Aug. 2 **Litho.** ***Perf. 14***
1693 A430 60s Adolias amlana 6 5
1694 A430 2.40p Papilio daedalus 20 10
1695 A430 3p Prothoe frankii semperi 25 12
1696 A430 3.60p Troides magellanus 28 14
1697 A430 4.20p Yoma sabina vasuki 35 18
1698 A430 5p Chilasa idaeoides 40 20
Nos. 1693-1698 (6) 1.54 79

Baguio City, 75th Anniv. A432

1984, Aug. 24 **Litho.** ***Perf. 12½***
1706 A432 1.20p The Mansion 10 6

Light Rail Transit A433

1984, Sept. 10 ***Perf. 13x13½***
1707 A433 1.20p multi 10 6

No. 1, Australia No. 59 and Koalas A434

1984, Sept. 21 ***Perf. 14½x15***
1708 A434 3p multi 25 12
1709 A434 3.60p multi 28 14

Souvenir Sheet

1710 Sheet of 3 5.00 2.50
a A434 20p multi 1.65 80

AUSIPEX '84. No. 1710 contains 3 No. 1710a, multicolored margin with AUSIPEX emblems. Size: 75x90mm. Exists imperf.

No. 1609 Surcharged with 2 Black Bars and Ovptd. "14-17 NOV. 84 / R.I. ASIA REGIONAL CONFERENCE."

1984, Nov. 11 **Litho.** ***Perf. 13x13½***
1713 A398 1.20p on 2.30p multi 10 5

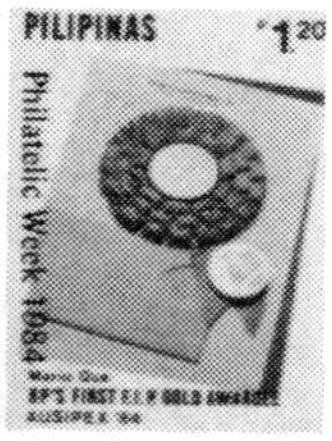

Philatelic Week — A435

1984, Nov. 22 ***Perf. 13½x13***
1714 A435 1.20p Gold medal 10 5
1715 A435 3p Winning stamp exhibit 25 12

Se-tenant. SUIPEX '84 and Mario Que, 1st Philippine exhibitor to win FIP Gold Award.

Ships A436

1984, Nov. **Litho.** ***Perf. 13½x13***
1718 A436 60s Caracao canoes 6 5
1719 A436 1.20p Chinese junk 10 5
1720 A436 6p Spanish galleon 50 25
1721 A436 7.20p Casco 60 30
1722 A436 8.40p Steamboat 70 35
1723 A436 20p Cruise liner 1.65 80
Nos. 1718-1723 (6) 3.61 1.80

Ateneo de Manila University, 125th Anniv. A438

1984, Dec. 7 **Litho.** ***Perf. 13x13½***
1730 A438 60s ultra & gold 6 5
1731 A438 1.20p dk ultra & sil 10 5

Christmas A439

Jaycees, Youth Development A440

1984, Dec. 8 ***Perf. 13½x13***
1732 A439 60s Madonna and Child 6 5
1733 A439 1.20p Holy family 10 5

Printed se-tenant.

1984, Dec. 19

Abstract painting by Raoul G. Isidro.

1734 Strip of 10 1.65 85
a.-e. A440 60s, any single 6 5
f.-j. A440 3p, any single 25 12

Natl. Jaycees Awards, 25th anniv.

Dried Tobacco Leaf and Plant A441

1985, Jan. 14 ***Perf. 13x13½***
1735 A441 60s multi 6 5
1736 A441 3p multi 25 12

Philippine-Virginia Tobacco Admin., 25th anniv.

No. 1537 Surcharged.

1985, Jan. **Litho.** ***Imperf.***
1737 A373 3p on 2p multi 35 14

Comes with missing period ("p300").

Natl. Research Council Emblem A442

1985, Feb. 3 **Litho.** ***Perf. 13x13½***
1738 A442 60s bl, dk bl & blk 7 5
1739 A442 1.20p org, dk bl & blk 18 8

Pacific Science Assoc., 5th intl. congress, Manila, Feb. 3-7.

Medicinal Plants A443

1985, Mar. 15 ***Perf. 12½***
1740 A443 60s Carmona retusa 6 5
1741 A443 1.20p Orthosiphon aristatus 10 5
1742 A443 2.40p Vitex negundo 20 10
1743 A443 3p Aloe barbadensis 25 12
1744 A443 3.60p Quisqualis indica 28 14
1745 A443 4.20p Blumea balsamifera 35 18
Nos. 1740-1745 (6) 1.24 64

INTELSAT, 20th Anniv. — A444

1985, Apr. 6 ***Perf. 13x13½***
1746 A444 60s multi 6 5
1747 A444 3p multi 25 12

Tax Research Institute, 25th Anniv. — A445

1985, Apr. 22 ***Perf. 13½x13***
1748 A445 60s multi 8 5

Intl. Rice Research Institute, 25th Anniv. A446

1985, May 27 ***Perf. 13x13½***
1749 A446 60s Planting 6 5
1750 A446 3p Paddies 10 5

1st Spain-Philippines Peace Treaty, 420th Anniv. — A447

Designs: 1.20p, Blessed Infant of Cebu, statue, shrine and basilica. 3.60p, King Tupas of Cebu and Miguel Lopez de Legaspi signing treaty, 1565.

1985, June 4 ***Perf. 12½***
1751 A447 1.20p multi 10 5
1752 A447 3.60p multi 28 14

One label picturing the seal of Cebu City printed between se-tenant pairs of Nos. 1751-1752.

No. 1532 Ovptd. "10th Anniversary Philippines and People's Republic of China Diplomatic Relations 1975-1985."

1985, June 8 ***Imperf.***
1753 A372 5p multi 40 20

Arbor Week, June 9-15 — A448

1985, June 9 ***Perf. 13½x13***
1754 A448 1.20p multi 10 6

Battle of Bessang Pass, 40th Anniv. A449

1985, June 14 ***Perf. 13x13½***
1755 A449 1.20p multi 10 6

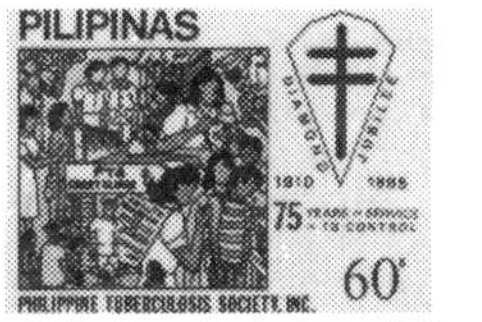

Natl. Tuberculosis Soc., 75th Anniv. — A450

1985, July 29
1756 A450 60s Immunization, research 7 5
1757 A450 1.20p Charity seal 12 7

Nos. 1756-1757 printed se-tenant.

No. 1297 Surcharged with Bars, New Value and Scout Emblem in Gold, Ovptd. "GSP" and "45th Anniversary Girl Scout Charter" in Black.

Perf. 12½x13½

1985, Aug. 19 **Photo.**
1758 A242 2.40p on 15s on 10s 20 10
1759 A242 4.20p on 15s on 10s 35 18
1760 A242 7.20p on 15s on 10s 60 30

Virgin Mary Birth Bimillennium A451

Statues and paintings.

1985, Sept. 8 **Litho.** ***Perf. 13½x13***
1761 A451 1.20p Fatima 10 5
1762 A451 2.40p Beaterio 20 10
1763 A451 3p Penafrancia 25 12
1764 A451 3.60p Guadalupe 30 14

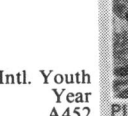

Intl. Youth Year A452

Prize-winning children's drawings.

1985, Sept. 23 ***Perf. 13x13½***
1765 A452 2.40p Agriculture 20 10
1766 A452 3.60p Education 30 14

Girl and Rice Terraces A453

1985, Sept. 26
1767 A453 2.40p multi 20 10

World Tourism Organization, 6th general assembly, Sofia, Bulgaria, Sept. 17-26.

Export Year — A454

UN, 40th Anniv. — A455

1985, Oct. 8 ***Perf. 13½x13***
1768 A454 1.20p multi 10 5

1985, Oct. 24
1769 A455 3.60p multi 30 14

1st Transpacific Airmail Service, 50th Anniv. A456

1985, Nov. 22 ***Perf. 13x13½***
1770 A456 3p China Clipper on water 25 12
1771 A456 3.60p China Clipper, map 30 14

Natl. Bible Week A457

1985, Dec. 3 ***Perf. 12½***
1774 A457 60s multi 6 5
1775 A457 3p multi 25 12

Christmas 1985 A458

1985, Dec. 8 ***Perf. 13x13½***
1776 A458 60s Panuluyan 6 5
1777 A458 3p Pagdalaw 25 12

Scales of Justice A459

1986, Jan. 12
1778 A459 60s lil rose & blk 6 5
1779 A459 3p brt grn, lil rose & blk 25 12

University of the Philippines, College of Law, 75th anniv.
See No. 1838.

Flores de Heidelberg, by Jose Rizal — A460

Design: 60s, Noli Me Tangere.

1986 **Litho.** **Wmk.** ***Perf. 13***
1780 A460 60s violet 5 5
1781 A460 1.20p bluish grn 10 5
1782 A460 3.60p redsh brn 28 14

Issue dates: 60s, 1.20p, Feb. 21. 3.60p, July 10.

Philippine Airlines, 45th Anniv. A461

Aircraft: No. 1783a, Douglas DC3, 1946. No. 1783b, Douglas DC4 Skymaster, 1946. No. 1783c, Douglas DC6, 1948. No. 1783d, Vickers Viscount 784, 1957. No. 1784a, Fokker Friendship F27 Mark 100, 1960. No. 1784b, Douglas DC8 Series 50, 1962. No. 1784c, Bac One Eleven Series 500, 1964. No. 1784d, McDonnell Douglas DC10 Series 30, 1974. No. 1785a, Beech Model 18, 1941. No. 1785b, Boeing 747, 1980.

1986, Mar. 15 **Wmk.**
1783 Block of 4 25 20
a.-d A461 60s, any single 6 5
1784 Block of 4 80 40
a.-d A461 2.40p, any single 20 10
1785 Pair 60 28
a.-b A461 3.60p, any single 30 14
Nos. 1783-1785 (3) 1.65 88

See No. 1842.

Bataan Oil Refining Corp., 25th Anniv. A462

Perf. 13½x13, 13x13½

1986, Apr. 12 **Wmk.**
1786 A462 60s Refinery, vert. 6 5
1787 A462 3p shown 25 12

EXPO '86, Vancouver A463

1986, May 2 **Wmk.** ***Perf. 13x13½***
1788 A463 60s multi 6 5
1789 A463 3p multi 25 12

Asian Productivity Organization, 25th Anniv. — A464

1986 **Wmk.**
1790 A464 60s ap grn, sage grn & org 6 5
1791 A464 3p ap grn, sage grn & org 25 12

Wmk. ***Perf. 13***
Size: 30x22mm.
1792 A464 3p pale brn 25 12

Issue dates: Nos. 1790-1791, May 15. No. 1792, July 10.

AMERIPEX '86 — A465

Election of Corazon Aquino, 7th Pres. — A466

1986, May 22 **Wmk.** ***Perf. 13½x13***
1793 A465 60s No. 241 6 5
1794 A465 3p No. 390 25 12

See No. 1835.

1986, May 25 **Wmk.**

Portrait of Aquino and: 60s, Salvador Laurel, vice-president, and hands in symbolic gestures of peace and freedom. 1.20p, Symbols of communication and transportation. 2.40p, Parade. 3p, Military. 7.20p, Vice-president, parade, horiz.

1795 A466 60s multi 6 5
1796 A466 1.20p multi 10 5
1797 A466 2.40p multi 20 10
1798 A466 3p multi 25 12

Souvenir Sheet

Imperf

1799 A466 7.20p multi 55 28

De La Salle University, 75th Anniv. A467

Designs: 60s, Statue of St. John the Baptist de la Salle, Paco buildings, 1911, and university, 1986. 2.40p, St. Miguel Febres Cordero, buildings, 1911. 3p, St. Benilde, buildings, 1986. 7.20p, Founding fathers.

1986, June 16 **Wmk.** ***Perf. 13x13½***
1800 A467 60s grn, blk & pink 6 5
1801 A467 2.40p grn, blk & bl 20 10
1802 A467 3p grn, blk & yel 25 12

Souvenir Sheet

Imperf

1803 A467 7.20p grn & blk 55 28

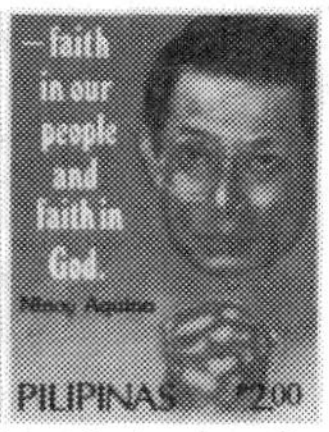

Memorial to Benigno S. Aquino, Jr. (1932-83)

A468 A469

Perf. 13½x13, 13x13½

1986, Aug. 21 **Wmk.**
1804 A468 60s dl bluish grn 6 5
1805 A469 2p shown 16 8
1806 A469 3.60p The Filipino is worth dying for, horiz. 30 14

Souvenir Sheet

Imperf

1807 A469 10p Hindi ka nag-iisa, horiz. 80 40

See No. 1836.

Indigenous Orchids — A470

Quiapo District, 400th Anniv. — A471

1986, Aug. 28 **Wmk.** ***Perf. 13½x13***
1808 A470 60s Vanda sanderiana 6 5
1809 A470 1.20p Epigeneium lyonii 10 5
1810 A470 2.40p Paphiopedilum philippinense 20 10
1811 A470 3p Amesiella philippinensis 25 12

Perf. 13½x13, 13x13½

1986, Aug. 29 **Wmk.**

Designs: 60s, Our Lord Jesus the Nazarene, statue, Quiapo church. 3.60p, Quiapo church, 1930, horiz.

1812 A471 60s pink, blk & lake 6 5
1813 A471 3.60p pale grn, blk & dk ultra 30 14

General Hospital, 75th Anniv. — A472

1986, Sept. 1 **Wmk.** ***Perf. 13½x13***

1814 A472 60s bl & multi 6 5
1815 A472 3p grn & multi 25 12

See No. 1841.

Halley's Comet A473

1986, Sept. 25 **Wmk.** ***Perf. 13x13½***

1816 A473 60s Comet, Earth 6 5
1817 A473 2.40p Comet, Earth, Moon 20 10

74th FDI World Dental Congress, Manila A474

Perf. 13x13½

1986, Nov. 10 **Litho.** **Wmk.**

1818 A474 60s Handshake 7 5
1819 A474 3p Jeepney bus 35 18

See Nos. 1837, 1840.

Insects A475

Intl. Peace Year — A476

Manila YMCA, 75th Anniv. — A477

Perf. 13x13½, 13½x13

1986, Nov. 21 **Wmk.**

1820 A475 60s Butterfly, beetles 7 5
1821 A476 1p bl & blk 12 6
1822 A475 3p Dragonflies 35 18

Philately Week.

1986, Nov. 28 **Wmk.** ***Perf. 13x13½***

1823 A477 2p blue 25 12
1824 A477 3.60p red 42 20

See No. 1839.

Philippine Normal College, 85th Anniv. A478

Various arrangements of college crest and buildings, 1901-1986.

1986, Dec. 12 **Wmk.**

1825 A478 60s multi 7 5
1826 A478 3.60p buff, ultra & gldn brn 42 20

Christmas A479

Perf. 13½x13, 13x13½

1986, Dec. 15 **Wmk.**

1827 A479 60s Holy family 7 5
1828 A479 60s Mother and child, doves 7 5
1829 A479 60s Child touching mother's face 7 5
1830 A479 1p Adoration of the shepherds 12 6
1831 A479 1p Mother, child signaling peace 12 6
1832 A479 1p Holy family, lamb 12 6
1833 A479 1p Mother, child blessing food 12 6
Nos. 1827-1833 (7) 69 39

Nos. 1827-1829, vert.

No. 1780 Surcharged

1987, Jan. 6 **Litho.** **Wmk.** ***Perf. 13***

1834 A460 1p on 60s vio 8 5

Types of 1986

Designs: 75s, No. 390, AMERIPEX '86. 1p, Benigno S. Aquino, Jr. 3.25p, Handshake, 74th World Dental Congress. 3.50p, Scales of Justice. 4p, Manila YMCA emblem. 4.75p, Jeepney bus. 5p, General Hospital. 5.50p, Boeing 747, 1980.

1987, Jan. 16 **Wmk.** **Litho.** ***Perf. 13***
Size: 22x31mm, 31x22mm

1835 A465 75s brt yel grn 8 5
1836 A468 1p blue 12 6
1837 A474 3.25p dull grn 40 20
1838 A459 3.50p dark car 42 20
1839 A477 4p blue 45 22
1840 A474 4.75p dl yel grn 55 28
1841 A472 5p olive bister 65 32
1842 A461 5.50p dk bl gray 65 32
Nos. 1835-1842 (8) 3.32 1.65

All but 75s dated "1-1-87."

Manila Hotel, 75th Anniv. A480

1987, Jan. 30 **Wmk.** ***Perf. 13x13½***

1843 A480 1p Hotel, c. 1912 12 6
1844 A480 4p Hotel, 1987 45 22
1845 A480 4.75p Lobby 55 28
1846 A480 5.50p Foyer 65 32

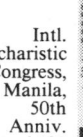

Intl. Eucharistic Congress, Manila, 50th Anniv. A481

Perf. 13½x13, 13x13½

1987, Feb. 7 **Wmk.**

1847 A481 75s Emblem, vert. 8 5
1848 A481 1p shown 12 6

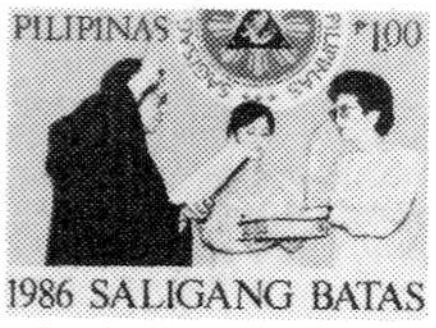

Swearing-in Pres. Aquino — A482

Text — A483

Perf. 13½x13, 13x13½

1987, Mar. 4 **Wmk.**

1849 A482 1p multi 12 6
1850 A483 5.50p blue & deep bister 70 35

Ratification of the new constitution.

See No. 1905.

Lyceum College and Founder, Jose P. Laurel A484

Perf. 13x13½

1987, May 7 **Litho.** **Wmk.**

1851 A484 1p multi 8 5
1852 A484 2p multi 16 8

Lyceum of the Philippines, 35th anniv.

Government Service Insurance System — A485

1987, June 1 ***Perf. 13½x13***

1853 A485 1p Salary and policy loans 12 6
1854 A485 1.25p Disability, medicare 16 7
1855 A485 2p Retirement benefits 25 12
1856 A485 3.50p Life insurance 42 20

Davao City, 50th Anniv. A486

Perf. 13x13½

1987, Mar. 16 **Litho.** **Wmk.**

1857 A486 1p Falconer, woman planting, city seal 10 6

Salvation Army in the Philippines, 50th Anniv. — A487

Natl. League of Women Voters, 50th Anniv. — A488

Perf. 13½x13

1987, June 5 **Photo.** **Wmk.**

1858 A487 1p multi 10 6

1987, July 15 **Wmk.**

1859 A488 1p pink & blue 10 6

Gen. Vicente Lukban (1860-1916) — A489

Design: No. 1862, Wenceslao Q. Vinzons (1910-1942). No. 1863, Brig.-gen. Mateo M. Capinpin (1887-1958).

No. 1864, Jesus Balmori (1882-1948).

Perf. 13x13½, 12½(#1862)

1987 **Litho.** **Wmk.**

1861 A489 1p olive grn 10 6
1862 A489 1p dull greenish blue 10 6
1863 A489 1p dull red brn 8 5
1864 A489 1p rose red & rose claret 8 5

Issue dates: No. 1861, July 31. No. 1862, Sept. 9. No. 1863, Oct. 15. No. 1864, Dec. 17.

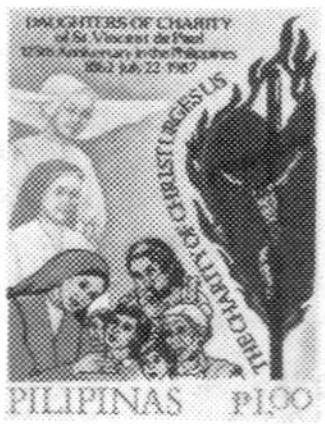

Nuns (1862-1987), Children, Crucifix, Sacred Heart — A490

Perf. 13½x13

1987, July 22 **Litho.** **Wmk.**

1881 A490 1p multi 10 6

Daughters of Charity of St. Vincent de Paul in the Philippines, 125th anniv.

Map of Southeast Asia, Flags of ASEAN Members A491

1987, Aug. 7 **Wmk.** ***Perf. 13x13½***

1882 A491 1p multi 10 6

ASEAN, 20th anniv.

Exports Campaign A492

1987, Aug. 11 Wmk. *Perf. 13*

1883 A492 1p shown 8 5
1884 A492 2p Worker, gearwheel 16 8

Inscribed "Bumili Ng / Gawang Pilipino."

Wmk. 389

Canonization of Lorenzo Ruiz by Pope John Paul II, Oct. 18 — A493

First Filipino saint: 1p, Ruiz, stained glass window showing Crucifixion. 5.50p, Ruiz at prayer, execution in 1637.

Perf. 13½x13

1987, Oct. 10 Litho. Wmk. 389

1885 A493 1p multi 8 5
1886 A493 5.50p multi 48 25

Size: 57x57mm.

Imperf

1887 A493 8p like 5.50p 70 35

No. 1887 has denomination at LL.

No. 1841 Surcharged.

1987, Oct. 12 Wmk. *Perf. 13*

1888 A472 4.75p on 5p olive bis 40 20

Order of the Good Shepherd Sisters in Philippines, 65th Anniv. A494

Perf. 13x13½

1987, Oct. 27 Wmk. 389

1889 A494 1p multi 8 5

Natl. Boy Scout Movement, 50th Anniv. A495

Founders: J. Vargas, M. Camus, J.E.H. Stevenot, A.N. Luz, V. Lim, C. Romulo and G.A. Daza.

Perf. 13x13½

1987, Oct. 28 Litho. Wmk. 389

1890 A495 1p multi 8 5

Philippine Philatelic Club, 50th Anniv. A496

1987, Nov. 7 *Perf. 13x13½*

1891 A496 1p multi 8 5

Order of the Dominicans in the Philippines, 400th Anniv. A497

Designs: 1p, First missionaries shipwrecked, church and image of the Virgin, vert. 4.75p, J.A. Jeronimo Guerrero, Br., Diego de St. Maria and Letran Dominican College. 5.50p, Pope with Dominican representatives.

Perf. 13½x13, 13x13½

1987, Nov. 11

1892 A497 1p multi 8 5
1893 A497 4.75p multi 40 20
1894 A497 5.50p multi 48 25

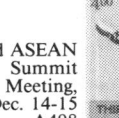

3rd ASEAN Summit Meeting, Dec. 14-15 A498

Perf. 13x13½

1987, Dec. 5 Wmk. 389

1895 A498 4p multi 32 16

Christmas 1987 — A499

1987, Dec. 8 *Perf. 13½x13*

1896 A499 1p Postal service 8 5
1897 A499 1p 5-Pointed stars 8 5
1898 A499 4p Procession, church 32 16
1899 A499 4.75p Gift exchange 38 18
1900 A499 5.50p Bamboo cannons 42 20
1901 A499 8p Pig, holiday foods 60 32
1902 A499 9.50p Traditional foods 75 38
1903 A499 11p Serving meal 85 42
Nos. 1896-1903 (8) 3.48 1.76

Wmk. 391- Natl. Crest, Rising Sun and Eagle

Exports Type of 1987

Design: Worker, gearwheel.

Wmk. 391

1987, Dec. 16 Litho. *Perf. 13*

1904 A492 4.75p lt blue & blk 38 20

Constitution Ratification Type of 1987

1987, Dec. 16 Wmk. *Perf. 13*

1905 A483 5.50p brt yel grn & brt org 42 20

Grand Masonic Lodge of the Philippines, 75th Anniv. A500

Perf. 13x13½

1987, Dec. 19 Wmk. 389

1906 A500 1p multi 8 5

United Nations Projects A501

Designs: a, Intl. Fund for Agricultural Development (IFAD). b, Transport and Communications Decade for Asia and the Pacific. c, Intl. Year of Shelter for the Homeless (IYSH). d, World Health Day, 1987.

Perf. 13x13½

1987, Dec. 22 Litho. Wmk. 389

1907 Strip of 4+label 32 20
a.-d. A501 1p any single 8 5

Label pictures U.N. emblem.

7th Opening of Congress A502

Designs: 1p, Official seals of the Senate and Quezon City House of Representatives, gavel, vert. 5.50p, Congress in session.

Perf. 13½x13, 13x13½

1988, Jan. 25 Wmk. 389

1908 A502 1p multi 12 6
1909 A502 5.50p multi 58 30

St. John Bosco (1815-1888), Educator — A503

1988, Jan. 31 *Perf. 13x13½*

1910 A503 1p multi 12 6
1911 A503 5.50p multi 58 30

Buy Philippine Goods — A504

Perf. 13½x13

1988, Feb. 1 Litho. Wmk. 389

1912 A504 1p buff, ultra, blk & scar 12 6

Nos. 1782, 1806, 1813, 1824, 1826 Surcharged

Wmk. (#1913, 1916) 389 (#1914, 1917), 391 (#1915)

Perf. 13 (#1782), 13x13½

1988, Feb. 14

1913 A460 3p on 3.60p redsh brn 32 16
1914 A469 3p on 3.60p multi 32 16
1915 A471 3p on 3.60p pale grn, blk & dark ultra 32 16
1916 A477 3p on 3.60p red 32 16
1917 A478 3p on 3.60p buff, ultra & golden brn 32 16
Nos. 1913-1917 (5) 1.60 80

Use Zip Codes — A505

1988, Feb. 25 Wmk. *Perf. 13*

1918 A505 60s multi 8 5
1919 A505 1p multi 12 6

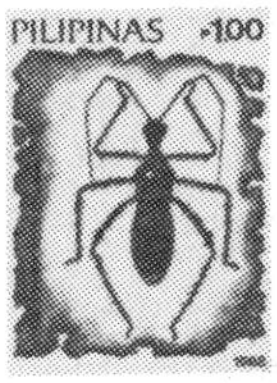

Insects That Prey on Other Insects — A506

1988, Mar. 11 Wmk. 390 *Perf. 13*

1920 A506 1p Vesbius purpureus 12 6
1921 A506 5.50p Campsomeris aurulenta 58 30

Solar Eclipse 1988 A507

Perf. 13x13½

1988, Mar. 18 Unwmk.

1922 A507 1p multi 12 6
1923 A507 5.50p multi 58 30

Toribio M. Teodoro (1887-1965), Shoe Manufacturer A508

Perf. 13

1988, Apr. 27 Litho. Wmk.

1924 A508 1p buff, dark olive bister & brt rose 12 6
1925 A508 1.20p pale blue grn, blk & scar 15 8

College of the Holy Spirit, 75th Anniv. — A509

Designs: 1p, Emblem and motto "Truth in Love." 4p, Arnold Janssen, founder, and Sr. Edelwina, director from 1920 to 1947.

Perf. 13½x13

1988, May 22 **Unwmk.**

1926 A509 1p blk, maroon & gold 12 6
1927 A509 4p blk, olive grn & maroon 48 24

Intl. Conference of Newly Restored Democracies A510

Perf. 13½x13

1988, June 4 **Litho.** **Unwmk.**

1928 A510 4p dark ultra, brt blue & blk 42 20

Juan Luna and Felix Hidalgo — A511

1988, June 15 **Wmk.** ***Perf. 13***

1929 A511 1p dark olive bister, pale yel & blk 8 5
1930 A511 5.50p dark olive bister, buff & blk 45 22

First Natl. Juan Luna and Felix Resurreccion Hidalgo Commemorative Exhibition, June 15-Aug. 15. Artists Luna and Hidalgo won medals at the 1884 Madrid Fine Arts Exhibition.

Natl. Irrigation Administration, 25th Anniv. — A512

Perf. 13½x13

1988, June 22 **Litho.** **Wmk. 372**

1931 A512 1p multi 10 5
1932 A512 5.50p multi 55 28

Natl. Olympic Committee Emblem and Sporting Events A513

Designs: 1p, Scuba diving, Siquijor Is. 1.20p, Big game fishing, Aparri, Cagayan Province. 4p, Yachting, Manila Central. 5.50p, Climbing Mt. Apo. 8p, Golf, Cebu, Cebu Is. 11p, Cycling through Marawi, Mindanao Is.

1988, July 11 ***Perf. 13x13½***

1933 A513 1p multi 10 5
1934 A513 1.20p multi 12 6
1935 A513 4p multi 40 20
1936 A513 5.50p multi 55 28
1937 A513 8p multi 80 40
1938 A513 11p multi 1.10 55
Nos. 1933-1938 (6) 3.07 1.54

4p, 8p, 1p and 5.50p also exist in strips of 4 plus center label picturing torch and inscribed "Philippine Olympic Week, May 1-7, 1988."

Nos. 1797, 1801, 1810 and 1817 Surcharged with 2 Bars and New Value in Black or Gold

Perf. 13½x13, 13x13½

1988, Aug. 1 **Wmk. as Before**

1939 A466 1.90p on 2.40p #1797 20 10
1940 A467 1.90p on 2.40p #1801 20 10
1941 A470 1.90p on 2.40p #1810 20 10
1942 A473 1.90p on 2.40p #1817 (G) 20 10

Land Bank of the Philippines, 25th Anniv. — A514

Philippine Intl. Commercial Bank, 50th Anniv. — A515

Perf. 13x13½

1988, Aug. 8 **Litho.** **Wmk. 372**

1943 A514 1p shown 10 5
1944 A515 1p shown 10 5
1945 A514 5.50p like No. 1943 55 28
1946 A515 5.50p like No. 1944 55 28

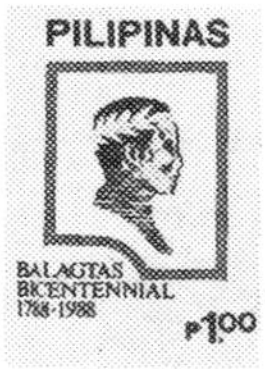

Profile of Francisco Balagtas Baltasar (b. 1788), Tagalog Language Poet, Author — A516

1988, Aug. 8 **Litho.** **Wmk.** ***Perf. 13***

1947 A516 1p Facing right 10 5
1948 A516 1p Facing left 10 5

Quezon Institute, 50th Anniv. A517

Perf. 13x13½

1988, Aug. 18 **Litho.** **Wmk. 372**

1949 A517 1p multi 10 5
1950 A517 5.50p multi 55 28

Philippine Tuberculosis Soc.

Mushrooms A518

1988 Summer Olympics, Seoul A519

1988, Sept. 13 **Wmk. 391** ***Perf. 13***

1951 A518 60s Brown 6 5
1952 A518 1p Rat's ear fungus 10 5
1953 A518 2p Abalone 20 10
1954 A518 4p Straw 40 20

1988, Sept. 19 ***Perf. 13½x13***

1955 A519 1p Women's archery 10 5
1956 A519 1.20p Women's tennis 12 6
1957 A519 4p Boxing 40 20
1958 A519 5.50p Women's running 55 28
1959 A519 8p Swimming 80 40
1960 A519 11p Cycling 1.10 55
Nos. 1955-1960 (6) 3.07 1.54

Souvenir Sheet

Imperf

1961 Sheet of 4 2.25 1.15
a. A519 5.50p Weight lifting 55 28
b. A519 5.50p Basketball, horiz. 55 28
c. A519 5.50p Judo 55 28
d. A519 5.50p Shooting, horiz. 55 28

Department of Justice, Cent. A520

1988, Sept. 26 ***Perf. 13x13½***

1962 A520 1p multi 10 5

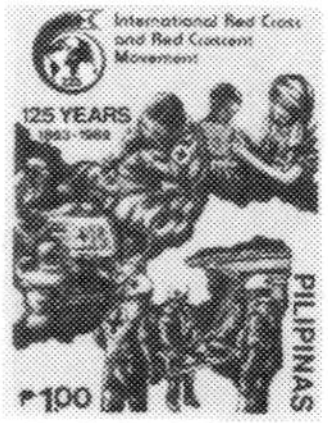

Intl. Red Cross and Red Crescent Organizations, 125th Annivs. — A521

Christian Children's Fund, 50th Anniv. — A522

1988, Sept. 30 ***Perf. 13½x13***

1963 A521 1p multi 10 5
1964 A521 5.50p multi 55 28

1988, Oct. 6

1965 A522 1p multi 10 5

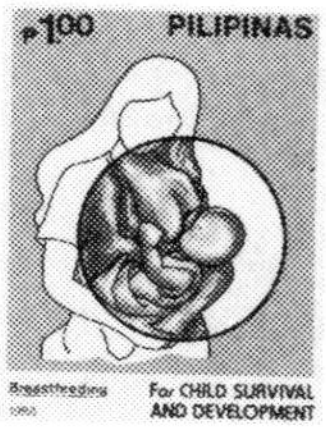

U.N. Campaigns A523

Designs: a, Breast-feeding. b, Growth monitoring. c, Immunization. d, Oral rehydration. e, Oral rehydration therapy. f, Youth on crutches.

Perf. 13½x13

1988 **Litho.** **Wmk. 392**

1966 Strip of 5 50 25
a.-e. A523 1p any single 10 5

Child Survival Campaign (Nos. 1966a-1966d); Decade for Disabled Persons (No. 1966e).

Bacolod City Charter, 50th Anniv. A524

1988, Oct. 19 **Litho.** ***Perf. 13x13½***

1967 A524 1p multi 12 6

UST Graduate School, 50th Anniv. — A525

Dona Aurora Aragon Quezon (b. 1888) — A526

1988 **Litho.** **Unwmk.** ***Perf. 13½x13***

1968 A525 1p multi 12 6

1988 **Wmk. 391** ***Perf. 13***

1969 A526 1p multi 10 5
1970 A526 5.50p multi 58 30

Malate Church, 400th Anniv. A527

Designs: a. Church, 1776. b. Statue and anniv. emblem. c. Church, 1880. d. Church, 1988. Printed se-tenant in a continuous design.

1988

1971 Block of 4 45 20
a.-d. A527 1p any single 11 5

U.N. Declaration of Human Rights, 40th Anniv. A528

1988 **Wmk.** ***Perf. 13½x13***

1972 A528 1p shown 12 6
1973 A528 1p Commission on human rights 12 6

Long Distance Telephone Company A529

Philatelic Week, Nov. 24-30 A530

1988 **Wmk.**

1974 A529 1p Communications tower 12 6

1988 **Wmk. 391** ***Perf. 13***

Emblem and: a. Post Office, "1938." b. Stamp counter. c. Framed stamp exhibits, four people. d. Exhibits, eight people. Printed se-tenant in a continuous design.

1975 Block of 4 45 20
a.-d. A530 1p any single 11 5

Christmas A531

Designs: 75s, Handshake, peave dove, vert. 1p, Children making ornaments. 2p, Boy carrying decoration. 3.50p, Tree, vert. 4.75p, Candle, vert. 5.50p, Man, star, heart.

1988, Dec. **Wmk. 391**

1976	A531	75s multi	8	5
1977	A531	1p shown	10	5
1978	A531	2p multi	20	10
1979	A531	3.50p multi	35	18
1980	A531	4.75p multi	50	25
1981	A531	5.50p multi	58	30
		Nos. 1976-1981 (6)	1.81	93

Gen. Santos City, 50th Anniv. A532

1989 Litho. Wmk. ***Perf. 13x13½***

1982	A532	1p multi	12	6

Guerrilla Fighters A533

Oblates of Mary Immaculate, 50th Anniv. A534

Emblem and: No. 1983, Miguel Z. Ver (1918-1942). No. 1984, Eleuterio L. Adevoso (1922-1975). Printed se-tenant in a continuous design.

1989 **Wmk. 391**

1983	A533	1p multi	12	6
1984	A533	1p multi	12	6

1989 Wmk. ***Perf. 13½x13***

1985	A534	1p multi	12	6

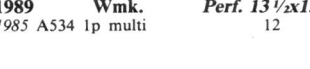

Fiesta Islands '89 — A535

1989 Litho. Wmk. 391 ***Perf. 13***

1986	A535	4.75p Sinulog	52	25
1987	A535	5.50p Lenten festival	60	30
1988	A535	6.25p Iloilo Paraw regatta	68	35

SEMI-POSTAL STAMPS

Catalogue values for unused stamps in this section are for Never Hinged items.

Republic

Epifanio de los Santos, Trinidad H. Pardo and Teodoro M. Kalaw — SP1

Doctrina Christiana, Cover Page — SP2

"Noli Me Tangere," Cover Page — SP3

Unwmk.

1949, Apr. 1 Engr. ***Perf. 12***

B1	SP1	4c + 2c sep	65	50
B2	SP2	6c + 4c vio	2.00	1.35
B3	SP3	18c + 7c bl	2.50	2.25

The surtax was for restoration of war-damaged public libraries.

War Widow and Children — SP4

Disabled Veteran — SP5

1950, Nov. 30

B4	SP4	2c + 2c red	7	8
B5	SP5	4c + 4c vio	28	28

The surtax was for war widows and children and disabled veterans of World War II.

Mrs. Manuel L. Quezon SP6

1952, Aug. 19 ***Perf. 12***

B6	SP6	5c + 1c dp bl	10	10
B7	SP6	6c + 2c car rose	28	28

The surtax was used to encourage planting and care of fruit trees among Philippine children. See No. 872.

Quezon Institute SP7

1958, Aug. 19 Photo. ***Perf. 13½, 12***

Cross in Red

B8	SP7	5c + 5c grn	10	10
B9	SP7	10c + 5c dp vio	32	32

These stamps were obligatory on all mail from Aug. 19-Sept. 30.

The surtax on all semi-postals from Nos. B8-B9 onward was for the Philippine Tuberculosis Society unless otherwise stated.

Scout Cooking — SP8

Design: 25c+5c, Archery.

1959 Engr. ***Perf. 13***

Yellow Paper.

B10	SP8	6c + 4c car	12	12
B11	SP8	25c + 5c bl	42	42
a.		Nos. B10-B11 tete bèche, *white*	85	85
		Nos. B10-B11,CB1-CB3 (5)	2.39	2.39

Issued to publicize the 10th Boy Scout World Jamboree, Makiling National Park, July 17-26. The surtax was to finance the Jamboree.

For souvenir sheet see No. CB3a.

Nos. B8-B9 Surcharged in Red

HELP
FIGHT
3+5 T B

1959 Photo. ***Perf. 13½, 12***

Cross in Red.

B12	SP7	3c + 5c on 5c + 5c grn	10	10
a.		"3 + 5" and bars omitted		
B13	SP7	6c + 5c on 10c + 5c dp vio	14	10

Bohol Sanatorium — SP9

1959, Aug. 19 Engr. ***Perf. 12***

Cross in Red.

B14	SP9	6c + 5c yel grn	10	10
B15	SP9	25c + 5c vio bl	35	28

No. B8 Surcharged "Help Prevent TB" and New Value.

1960, Aug. 19 Photo. ***Perf. 13½, 12***

B16	SP7	6c + 5c on 5c + 5c grn & red	18	14

Roxas Memorial T.B. Pavilion SP10

Perf. 11½

1961, Aug. 19 Unwmk. Photo.

B17	SP10	6c + 5c brn & red	18	14

Emiliano J. Valdes T.B. Pavilion SP11

1962, Aug. 19

Cross in Red

B18	SP11	6s + 5s dk vio	14	10
B19	SP11	30s + 5s ultra	35	25
B20	SP11	70s + 5s brt bl	80	65

José Rizal Playing Chess SP12

Design: 30s+5s, Rizal fencing.

1962, Dec. 30 Engr. ***Perf. 13***

B21	SP12	6s + 4s grn & rose lil	20	20
B22	SP12	30s + 5s brt bl & cl	42	42

Surtax for Rizal Foundation.

Map of Philippines and Cross — SP13

1963, Aug. 19 Unwmk. ***Perf. 13***

B23	SP13	6s + 5s vio & red	8	5
B24	SP13	10s + 5s grn & red	14	10
B25	SP13	50s + 5s brn & red	52	35

Negros Oriental T.B. Pavilion SP14

1964, Aug. 19 Photo. ***Perf. 13½***

Cross in Red

B26	SP14	5s + 5s brt pur	7	5
B27	SP14	6s + 5s ultra	10	5
B28	SP14	30s + 5s brn	35	25
B29	SP14	70s + 5s grn	65	60

No. B27 Surcharged in Red with New Value and Two Bars

1965, Aug. 19

Cross in Red

B30	SP14	1s + 5s on 6s + 5s ultra	12	5
B31	SP14	3s + 5s on 6s + 5s ultra	18	10

Stork-billed Kingfisher — SP15

Birds: 5s+5s, Rufous hornbill. 10s+5s, Monkey-eating eagle. 30s+5s, Great-billed parrot.

1967, Aug. 19 Photo. ***Perf. 13½***

B32	SP15	1s + 5s multi	7	7
B33	SP15	5s + 5s multi	7	7
B34	SP15	10s + 5s multi	10	10
B35	SP15	30s + 5s multi	35	35

1969, Aug. 15 Litho. ***Perf. 13½***

Birds: 1s+5s, Three-toed woodpecker. 5s+5s, Philippine trogon. 10s+5s, Mt. Apo lorikeet. 40s+5s, Scarlet minivet.

B36	SP15	1s + 5s multi	7	7
B37	SP15	5s + 5s multi	10	10
B38	SP15	10s + 5s multi	18	14
B39	SP15	40s + 5s multi	35	25

The Catalogue editors cannot undertake to appraise, identify or judge the genuineness or condition of stamps.

Julia V. de Ortigas and Tuberculosis Society Building — SP16

1970, Aug. 3 Photo. *Perf. 13½*

B40 SP16 1s + 5s multi 7 5
B41 SP16 5s + 5s multi 10 10
B42 SP16 30s + 5s multi 35 35
B43 SP16 70s + 5s multi 45 45

Mrs. Julia V. de Ortigas was president of the Philippine Tuberculosis Society, 1932-1969.

Mabolo, Santol, Chico, Papaya SP17

Philippine Fruits: 10s+5s, Balimbing, atis, mangosteen, macupa, bananas. 40s+5s, Susong-kalabao, avocado, duhat, watermelon, guava, mango. 1p+5s, Lanzones, oranges, sirhuelas, pineapple.

1972, Aug. 1 Litho. *Perf. 13*

B44 SP17 1s + 5s multi 5 5
B45 SP17 10s + 5s multi 7 7
B46 SP17 40s + 5s multi 25 25
B47 SP17 1p + 5s multi 50 50

Nos. B45-B46 Surcharged with New Value and 2 Bars.

1973, June 15

B48 SP17 15s + 5s on 10s + 5s multi 10 10
B49 SP17 60s + 5s on 40s + 5s multi 32 32

Dr. Basilio J. Valdes and Veterans Memorial Hospital — SP18

1974, July 8 Litho. *Perf. 12½*

Cross in Red

B50 SP18 15s + 5s bl grn 7 7
a. Imperf. 10 10
B51 SP18 1.10p + 5s vio bl 40 35
a. Imperf. 50 50

Dr. Valdes (1892-1970) was president of Philippine Tuberculosis Society.

AIR POST STAMPS

Madrid-Manila Flight Issue

Regular Issue of 1917-26 Overprinted in Red or Violet

1926, May 13 Unwmk. *Perf. 11*

C1 A40 2c grn (R) 5.00 4.00
C2 A40 4c car 6.50 4.50
a. Inverted overprint 1,200.
C3 A40 6c lil (R) 35.00 12.00
C4 A40 8c org brn 35.00 12.00
C5 A40 10c dp bl (R) 35.00 12.00
C6 A40 12c red org 40.00 17.50
C7 A40 16c lt ol grn *(Sampson)* 1,350. 1,000.
C8 A40 16c ol bis *(Sampson)* (R) 2,000. 1,650.
C9 A40 16c ol grn *(Dewey)* 40.00 17.50
C10 A40 20c org yel 40.00 17.50
C11 A40 26c bl grn 40.00 17.50
C12 A40 30c gray 40.00 17.50
C13 A41 2p vio brn (R) 350.00 250.00
C14 A41 4p dk bl (R) 600.00 350.00
C15 A41 10p dp grn 900.00 600.00

Same Overprint on No. 269
Perf. 12
Wmk. 190PI

C16 A40 26c bl grn 2,000.

Same Overprint on No. 284
Perf. 10

C17 A41 1p pale vio 120.00 85.00

Issued to commemorate the flight of Spanish aviators Gallarza and Loriga from Madrid to Manila.

London-Orient Flight Issue.

Regular Issue of 1917-25 Overprinted in Red

1928, Nov. 9 Unwmk. *Perf. 11*

C18 A40 2c green 60 40
C19 A40 4c carmine 60 50
C20 A40 6c violet 2.25 1.75
C21 A40 8c org brn 2.50 2.25
C22 A40 10c dp bl 2.50 2.25
C23 A40 12c red org 3.50 3.00
C24 A40 16c ol grn *(Dewey)* 2.75 2.25
C25 A40 20c org yel 3.50 3.00
C26 A40 26c bl grn 10.00 7.50
C27 A40 30c gray 10.00 7.50

Same Overprint on No. 271
Perf. 12
Wmk. 190PI

C28 A41 1p pale vio 35.00 35.00
Nos. C18-C28 (11) 73.20 65.40

Commemorating an airplane flight from London to Manila.

Nos. 354-360 Overprinted

1932, Sept. 27 Unwmk. *Perf. 11*

C29 A43 2c yel grn 45 45
C30 A44 4c rose car 50 50
C31 A45 12c orange 80 80
C32 A46 18c red org 4.00 4.00
C33 A47 20c yellow 2.25 2.25
C34 A48 24c dp vio 2.25 2.25
C35 A49 32c ol brn 2.25 2.25
Nos. C29-C35 (7) 12.50 12.50

Visit of Capt. Wolfgang von Gronan on his round-the-world flight.

Regular Issue of 1917-25 Overprinted

1933, Apr. 11

C36 A40 2c green 45 45
C37 A40 4c carmine 50 50
C38 A40 6c dp vio 80 80
C39 A40 8c org brn 1.75 1.65
C40 A40 10c dk bl 1.50 1.25
C41 A40 12c orange 1.25 1.25
C42 A40 16c ol grn *(Dewey)* 1.25 1.25
C43 A40 20c yellow 1.25 1.25
C44 A40 26c green 1.50 1.50
a. 26c bl grn 2.50 2.50
C45 A40 30c gray 2.00 1.85
Nos. C36-C45 (10) 12.25 11.75

Commemorating the flight from Madrid to Manila of aviator Fernando Rein y Loring.

No. 290b Overprinted

1933, May 26 Unwmk. *Perf. 11*

C46 A40 2c green 65 50

Regular Issue of 1932 Overprinted

C47 A44 4c rose car 7 5
C48 A45 12c orange 35 12
C49 A47 20c yellow 35 20
C50 A48 24c dp vio 35 22
C51 A49 32c ol brn 50 30
Nos. C46-C51 (6) 2.27 1.39

Nos. 387, 392 Overprinted in Gold

1935, Dec. 2

C52 A57 10c rose car 25 25
C53 A62 30c org red 50 50

Issued to commemorate the China Clipper flight from Manila to San Francisco, December 2-5, 1935.

Regular Issue of 1917-25 Surcharged in Various Colors

1936, Sept. 6 *Perf. 11.*

C54 A40 2c on 4c car (Bl) 8 6
C55 A40 6c on 12c red org (V) 15 12
C56 A40 16c on 26c bl grn (Bk) 30 30
a. 16c on 26c grn 1.50 1.00

Issued to commemorate the Manila-Madrid flight by aviators Antonio Arnaiz and Juan Calvo.

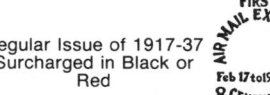

Regular Issue of 1917-37 Surcharged in Black or Red

1939, Feb. 17

C57 A40 8c on 26c bl grn (Bk) 1.00 55
a. 8c on 26c grn (Bk) 2.00 75
C58 A71 1p on 10p gray (R) 3.00 2.50

Issued to commemorate the first Air Mail Exhibition, held Feb. 17-19, 1939.

Moro Vinta and Clipper — AP1

1941, June 30

C59 AP1 8c carmine 1.10 70
C60 AP1 20c ultra 1.40 55
C61 AP1 60c bl grn 2.00 1.00
C62 AP1 1p sepia 1.00 65

No. C47 Handstamped in Violet

VICTORY

1944, Dec. 3 Unwmk. *Perf. 11.*

C63 A44 4c rose car 1,650. 1,000.

Catalogue values for unused stamps in this section, from this point to the end of the section, are for Never Hinged items.

Republic.

Manuel L. Quezon and Franklin D. Roosevelt AP2

Unwmk.

1947, Aug. 19 Engr. *Perf. 12*

C64 AP2 6c dk grn 40 40
C65 AP2 40c red org 75 75
C66 AP2 80c dp bl 2.00 2.00

Threshing Rice — AP3

1948, Feb. 23 Typo. *Perf. 12½*

C67 AP3 40c dk car & pink 9.00 5.50

FAO conf. held at Baguio.

Globe — AP4

1950, Mar. 1 Engr. *Perf. 12.*

C68 AP4 30c dp org 38 15
C69 AP4 50c car rose 65 15

Issued to publicize the 5th World Congress of the Junior Chamber of Commerce, Manila, March 1-8, 1950.

F. D. Roosevelt Type of 1950
Souvenir Sheet

1950, May 22 *Imperf.*

C70 A98 80c dp grn 1.25 1.25

Lions Club Emblem AP6

Maria Clara in 19th Century Costume AP7

1950, June 2 *Perf. 12*

C71 AP6 30c emerald 60 45
C72 AP6 50c ultra 70 60
a. Souv. sheet of 2, #C71-C72 1.40 1.40

Issued to commemorate the convention of the Lions Club, Manila, June 1950.

1952, Nov. 16 *Perf. 12½*

C73 AP7 30c rose car 85 70

Issued to publicize the first Pan-Asian Philatelic Exhibition, PANAPEX, Manila, Nov. 16-22, 1952.

First Philippine Stamp, Magellan's Landing and Manila Scene
AP8

1954, Apr. 25 ***Perf. 13***

1854 Stamp in Orange.

C74 AP8 10c dk brn	1.00	85
C75 AP8 20c dk grn	1.65	1.35
C76 AP8 50c carmine	3.50	3.00

Centenary of Philippine postage stamps.

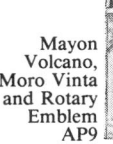

Mayon Volcano, Moro Vinta and Rotary Emblem
AP9

1955, Feb. 23

C77 AP9 50c bl grn	1.25	85

Issued to commemorate the 50th anniversary of the founding of Rotary International.

Lt. José Gozar
AP10

Portraits: 20c, 50c, Lt. Gozar. 30c, 70c, Lt. Basa.

1955 **Engr.** ***Perf. 13***

C78 AP10 20c dp vio	45	14
C79 AP10 30c red	52	14
C80 AP10 50c bluish grn	70	20
C81 AP10 70c blue	1.10	88

Issued in honor of Lt. José Gozar and Lt. Cesar Fernando Basa, Filipino aviators in World War II.

Constitution Type of Regular Issue.

1960, Feb. 8 **Photo.** ***Perf. 12½x13½***

C82 A146 30c brt bl & sil	32	25

Air Force Plane of 1935 and Saber Jet
AP11

1960, May 2 **Engr.** ***Perf. 14x14½***

C83 AP11 10c carmine	18	10
C84 AP11 20c ultra	35	25

25th anniversary of Philippine Air Force.

Olympic Type of Regular Issue

Designs: 30c, Sharpshooter. 70c, Woman swimmer.

1960, Nov. 30 **Photo.** ***Perf. 13x13½***

C85 A150 30c org & brn	42	35
C86 A150 70c grnsh bl & vio brn	85	70

Postal Conference
Type of Regular Issue, 1961

1961, Feb. 23 ***Perf. 13½x13***

C87 A152 30c multi	28	22

Freedom from Hunger
Type of Regular Issue

1963, Dec. 20 **Photo.**

C88 A168 30s lt grn & multi	28	20
C89 A168 50s multi	45	35

Land Reform
Type of Regular Issue

1964, Dec. 21 **Wmk. 233** ***Perf. 14½***

C90 A172 30s multi	25	20

Mass Baptism by Father Andres de Urdaneta, Cebu — AP12

Design: 70s, World map showing route of the Cross from Spain to Mexico to Cebu, and two galleons.

Unwmk.

1965, Oct. 4 **Photo.** ***Perf. 13***

C91 AP12 30s multi	25	14
C92 AP12 70s multi	55	32
a. Souvenir sheet of 4	1.40	1.40

400th anniv. of the Christianization of the Philippines. No. C92a contains four imperf. stamps similar to Nos. 934-935 and C91-C92 with simulated perforation.

Souvenir Sheet

Family and Progress Symbols — AP13

1966, July 22 **Photo.** ***Imperf.***

C93 AP13 70s multi	65	65

Issued to commemorate the 50th anniversary of the Philippine National Bank. No. C93 contains one stamp with simulated perforation superimposed on a facsimile of a 50p banknote of 1916. Size of stamp: 55x27mm.; sheet, 156x69mm.

Eruption of Taal Volcano and Refugees — AP14

1967, Oct. 1 **Photo.** ***Perf. 13½x13***

C94 AP14 70s multi	52	45

Eruption of Taal Volcano, Sept. 28, 1965.

Eruption of Taal Volcano — AP15

1968, Oct. 1 **Litho.** ***Perf. 13½***

C95 AP15 70s multi	52	52

Eruption of Taal Volcano, Sept. 28, 1965.

Rotary Type of 1969

1969, Jan. 29 **Photo.** ***Perf. 12½***

C96 A202 40s grn & multi	25	18
C97 A202 75s red & multi	52	42

Holy Child Type of Regular Issue

1969, June 30 **Photo.** ***Perf. 13½***

C98 A207 40s ultra & multi	28	20

Pope Type of Regular Issue

1970, Nov. 27 **Photo.** ***Perf. 13½x14***

C99 A221 40s vio & multi	28	20

Law College Type of Regular Issue

1971, June 15 ***Perf. 13***

C100 A225 1p grn & multi	45	42

Manila Type of Regular Issue

1971, June 24

C101 A226 1p multi & bl	65	45

Santo Tomas Type of Regular Issue

1971, July 8 **Photo.** ***Perf. 13½***

C102 A227 2p lt bl & multi	90	80

Congress Type of Regular Issue

1972, Apr. 11 **Photo.** ***Perf. 13½x13***

C103 A232 40s grn & multi	25	20

Tropical Fish Type of Regular Issue

1972, Aug. 14 **Photo.** ***Perf. 13***

C104 A235 50s *Dusky angelfish*	42	20

Pope Paul VI Type of Regular Issue

1972, Sept. 26 **Photo.** ***Perf. 14***

C105 A237 60s lt bl & multi	32	32

First Mass Type of Regular Issue

1972, Oct. 31 **Photo.** ***Perf. 14***

C106 A241 60s multi	28	25

Presidential Palace Type of Regular Issue

1973, Nov. 15 **Litho.** ***Perf. 14***

C107 A253 60s multi	20	20

No. C92a Surcharged and Overprinted with U.S. Bicentennial Emblems and: "U.S.A. BICENTENNIAL / 1776-1976" in Black

Unwmk.

1976, Sept. 23 **Photo.** ***Imperf.***

C108 Sheet of 4	45	45
a. A179 5s on 3s multi	5	5
b. A179 5s on 6s multi	5	5
c. AP12 15s on 30s multi	8	8
d. AP12 50s on 70s multi	25	25

American Bicentennial. Nos. C108a-C108d are overprinted with Bicentennial emblem and 2 bars over old denomination. Inscription and 2 Bicentennial emblems overprinted in margin. Overprint and surcharges exist in red.

Souvenir Sheet

Netherlands No. 1 and Philippines No. 1 and Windmill
AP16

1977, May 26 **Litho.** ***Perf. 14½***

C109 Sheet of 3	6.50	6.50
a. AP16 7.50p multi	1.90	1.90

AMPHILEX '77, International Stamp Exhibition, Amsterdam, May 26-June 5.

Exists imperf. Value $12.50.

Souvenir Sheet

Philippines and Spain Nos. 1, Bull and Matador
AP17

1977, Oct. 7 **Litho.** ***Perf. 12½x13***

C110 Sheet of 3	8.00	8.00
a. AP17 7.50p multi	2.00	2.00

ESPAMER '77 (Exposicion Filatelica de America y Europa), Barcelona, Spain, Oct. 7-13.

Exists imperf. Value $12.50.

Nos. B10 and CB3a Surcharged

1979, July 5 **Engr.** ***Perf. 13***

C111 SP8 90s on 6c + 4c car, *yel*	18	18

Souvenir Sheet

White Paper

C112 Sheet of 5	70	70
a. SP8 50s on 6c + 4c car	10	
b. SP8 50s on 25c + 5c bl	10	
c. SP8 50s on 30c + 10c grn	10	
d. SP8 50s on 70c + 20c red brn	10	
e. SP8 50s on 80c + 20c vio	10	

First Scout Philatelic Exhibition, Quezon City, July 4-14, commemorating 25th anniversary of First National Jamboree.

Surcharge on No. C111 includes "AIR-MAIL." Violet marginal inscriptions on No. C112 overprinted with heavy bars; new commemorative inscriptions and Scout emblem added. Size: 171x89mm.

AIR POST SEMI-POSTAL STAMPS

Catalogue values for unused stamps in this section, from this point to the end of the section, are for Never Hinged items.

Type of Semi-Postal Issue, 1959.

Designs: 30c+10c, Bicycling. 70c+20c, Scout with plane model. 80c+20c, Pres. Carlos P. Garcia and scout shaking hands.

Perf. 13.

1959, July 17 **Unwmk.** **Engr.**

CB1 SP8 30c + 10c grn	30	30
CB2 SP8 70c + 20c red brn	65	65
CB3 SP8 80c + 20c vio	90	90
a. Souvenir sheet of five	2.00	2.00

Issued to publicize the 10th Boy Scout World Jamboree, Makiling National Park, July 17-26. The surtax was to finance the Jamboree.

No. CB3a measures 171x89mm. and contains one each of Nos. CB1-CB3 and types of Nos. B10-B11 on white paper. Marginal inscription in violet. Sold for 4p.

SPECIAL DELIVERY STAMPS

United States No. E5 Overprinted in Red **PHILIPPINES**

1901, Oct. 15 **Wmk. 191** ***Perf. 12***

E1 SD3 10c dk bl	70.00	80.00

Special Delivery Messenger
SD2

1906 **Engr.** **Wmk. 191PI**

E2 SD2 20c ultra	30.00	8.00
b. 20c pale ultra	30.00	10.00

See Nos. E3-E6.

Special Printing

Overprinted in Red as No. E1 on United States No. E6

1907

E2A SD4 10c ultra	*1,600.*	

1911 **Wmk. 190PI**

E3 SD2 20c dp ultra	20.00	2.00

1916 *Perf. 10*
E4 SD2 20c dp ultra 125.00 30.00

1919 Unwmk. *Perf. 11*
E5 SD2 20c ultra 60 25
a. 20c pale bl 1.00 25
b. 20c dl vio 60 25

1925-31 *Imperf.*
E6 SD2 20c dl vio ('31) 20.00 *25.00*

Type of 1919 Overprinted in Black — COMMONWEALTH

1939 *Perf. 11*
E7 SD2 20c bl vio 30 30

Nos. E5b and E7, Handstamped in Violet — VICTORY

1944 *Perf. 11*
E8 SD2 20c dl vio (#E5b) *400.00 300.00*
E9 SD2 20c bl vio (#E7) *200.00 165.00*

Type SD2 Overprinted "VICTORY" As No. 486

1945
E10 SD2 20c bl vio 85 85
a. "IC" close together 3.50 3.50

Catalogue values for unused stamps in this section, from this point to the end of the section, are for Never Hinged items.

Republic

Manila Post Office and Messenger SD3

Unwmk.
1947, Dec. 22 Engr. *Perf. 12*
E11 SD3 20c rose lil 52 38

Post Office Building, Manila, and Hands with Letter — SD4

1962, Jan. 23 *Perf. 13½x13*
E12 SD4 20c lil rose 25 20

SPECIAL DELIVERY OFFICIAL STAMP

Type of 1906 Issue Overprinted — O.B.

1931 Unwmk. *Perf. 11.*
EO1 SD2 20c dl vio 85 65
a. No period after "B" 25.00 20.00
b. Double ovpt.

POSTAGE DUE STAMPS

Postage Due Stamps of the United States Nos. J38 to J44 Overprinted in Black — PHILIPPINES

1899, Aug. 16 Wmk. 191 *Perf. 12*
J1 D2 1c dp cl 2.50 1.00
J2 D2 2c dp cl 2.50 90
J3 D2 5c dp cl 5.50 1.90
J4 D2 10c dp cl 7.50 3.75
J5 D2 50c dp cl 82.50 50.00

1901, Aug. 31
J6 D2 3c dp cl 7.50 5.00
J7 D2 30c dp cl 110.00 50.00
Nos. J1-J7 (7) 218.00 112.55

No. J1 was used to pay regular postage September 5-19, 1902.

Post Office Clerk — D3

Unwmk.
1928, Aug. 21 Engr. *Perf. 11*
J8 D3 4c brn red 15 15
J9 D3 6c brn red 15 15
J10 D3 8c brn red 15 15
J11 D3 10c brn red 20 20
J12 D3 12c brn red 20 20
J13 D3 16c brn red 25 25
J14 D3 20c brn red 20 20
Nos. J8-J14 (7) 1.30 1.30

No. J8 Surcharged in Blue — 3 CVOS. 3

1937
J15 D3 3c on 4c brn red 25 15

Nos. J8 to J14 Handstamped in Violet — VICTORY

1944
J16 D3 4c brn red *130.00*
J17 D3 6c brn red *90.00*
J18 D3 8c brn red *100.00*
J19 D3 10c brn red *90.00*
J20 D3 12c brn red *90.00*
J21 D3 16c brn red *100.00*
J22 D3 20c brn red *100.00*
Nos. J16-J22 (7) *700.00*

Catalogue values for unused stamps in this section, from this point to the end of the section, are for Never Hinged items.

Republic

D4

Unwmk.
1947, Oct. 20 Engr. *Perf. 12*
J23 D4 3c rose car 12 12
J24 D4 4c brt vio bl 30 25
J25 D4 6c ol grn 38 38
J26 D4 10c orange 50 50

OFFICIAL STAMPS

Official Handstamped Overprints.

"Officers purchasing stamps for government business may, if they so desire, overprint them with the letters 'O.B.' either in writing with black ink or by rubber stamps but in such a manner as not to obliterate the stamp that postmasters will be unable to determine whether the stamps have been previously used". C. M. Cotterman, Director of Posts, Dec. 26, 1905. Beginning with Jan. 1, 1906, all branches of the Insular Government used postage stamps to prepay postage instead of franking them as before. Some officials used manuscript, some utilized typewriters, some made press-printed overprints, but by far the larger number used rubber stamps. The majority of these read "O.B." but other forms were: "OFFICIAL BUSINESS" or "OFFICIAL MAIL" in two lines, with variations on many of these. These "O.B." overprints are known on US 1899-1901 stamps; on 1903-06 stamps in red and blue; on 1906 stamps in red, blue, black, yellow and green. "O.B." overprints were also made on the centavo and peso stamps of the Philippines, per order of May 25, 1907. Beginning in 1926 the stamps were overprinted and issued by the Government, but some post offices continued to handstamp "O.B."

Regular Issue of 1926 Overprinted in Red — OFFICIAL

1926, Dec. 20 Unwmk. *Perf. 12*
O1 A42 2c grn & blk 2.50 1.75
O2 A42 4c car & blk 2.50 1.60
a. Vert. pair, imperf. btwn. *375.00*
O3 A42 18c lt brn & blk 7.00 6.00
O4 A42 20c org & blk 6.00 2.00

Issued to commemorate the opening of the Legislative Palace.

Regular Issue of 1917-26 Overprinted — O. B.

1931 *Perf. 11.*
O5 A40 2c green 6 5
a. No period after "B" 10.00 5.00
b. No period after "O"
O6 A40 4c carmine 8 5
a. No period after "B" 10.00 5.00
O7 A40 6c dp vio 10 8
O8 A40 8c yel brn 10 8
O9 A40 10c dp bl 40 12
O10 A40 12c red org 25 15
a. No period after "B" 30.00
O11 A40 16c lt ol grn *(Dewey)* 25 10
a. 16c ol bis 1.50 30
O12 A40 20c org yel 30 10
a. No period after "B" 15.00 15.00
O13 A40 26c green 45 45
a. 26c bl grn 1.25 1.00
O14 A40 30c gray 40 35
Nos. O5-O14 (10) 2.39 1.53

Same Overprint on Regular Issue of 1935.

1935
O15 A53 2c rose 6 5
a. No period after "B" 10.00 5.00
O16 A54 4c yel grn 6 5
a. No period after "B" 10.00 7.50
O17 A55 6c dk brn 10 6
a. No period after "B" 17.50 17.50
O18 A56 8c violet 12 12
O19 A57 10c rose car 15 6
O20 A58 12c black 20 15
O21 A59 16c dk bl 20 15
O22 A60 20c lt ol grn 20 15
O23 A61 26c indigo 40 35
O24 A62 30c org red 45 40
Nos. O15-O24 (10) 1.94 1.54

Same Overprint on Overprinted Issue of 1936-37.

1937-38 *Perf. 11*
O25 A53 2c rose 8 5
a. No period after "B" 6.50 3.50
O26 A60 20c lt ol grn ('38) 1.00 75

Regular Issue of 1935, Overprinted in Black:

O. B. COMMON-WEALTH — a
O. B. COMMONWEALTH — b

1938-40 *Perf. 11*
O27 A53(a) 2c rose 8 5
a. Hyphen omitted 17.50 15.00
b. No period after "B" 20.00 15.00
O28 A54(b) 4c yel grn 10 8
O29 A55(a) 6c dk brn 15 6
O30 A56(b) 8c violet 15 10
O31 A57(b) 10c rose car 18 10
a. No period after "O" 25.00 25.00
O32 A58(b) 12c black 18 18
O33 A59(b) 16c dk bl 25 12
O34 A60(a) 20c lt ol grn ('40) 35 35
O35 A61(b) 26c indigo 45 45
O36 A62(b) 30c org red 40 40
Nos. O27-O36 (10) 2.29 1.89

No. 461 Overprinted in Black — c — O. B.

Perf. 11x10½
1941, Apr. 14 Unwmk.
O37 A75 2c ap grn 6 6

Official Stamps Handstamped in Violet — VICTORY

1944 *Perf. 11, 11x10½*
O38 A53 2c (#O27) *130.00 85.00*
O39 A75 2c (#O37) 5.00 3.00
O40 A54 4c (#O16) *25.00 20.00*
O40A A55 6c (#O29) *3,000.*
O41 A57 10c (#O31) *100.00*
O42 A60 20c (#O22) *3,500.*
O43 A60 20c (#O26) *1,400.*

Catalogue values for unused stamps in this section, from this point to the end of the section, are for Never Hinged items.

No. 497 Overprinted Type "c" in Black

Perf. 11x10½
1946, June 19 Unwmk.
O44 A76 2c sepia 5 5

Republic

Nos. 504, 505 and 507 Overprinted in Black — d — O. B.

1948 Unwmk. *Perf. 12*
O50 A78 4c blk brn 10 5
a. Invtd. ovpt. 25.00
b. Dbl. ovpt. 25.00
O51 A79 10c red org 20 5
O52 A81 16c sl gray 1.40 52

The overprint on No. O51 comes in two sizes: 13mm., applied in Manila, and 12½mm., applied in New York.

Nos. 527, 508 and 509 Overprinted in Black — e — O. B.

Overprint Measures 14mm
O53 A91 2c brt grn 38 5

1949
O54 A82 20c red brn 52 10

Overprint Measures 12mm
O55 A83 50c dl grn 90 52

No. 550 Overprinted Type "e" in Black

Overprint Measures 14mm

1950
O56 A91 1c on 2c brt grn 7 5

Nos. 589, 592, 595 and 597 Overprinted in Black — f — O. B.

Overprint Measures 15mm

1952-55
O57 A117 1c red brn ('53) 6 5
O58 A117 5c crim rose 10 5
O59 A117 10c ultra ('55) 18 5
O60 A117 20c car lake ('55) 42 6

No. 647 Overprinted — g — O B

1959 Engr. *Perf. 12*
O61 A117 1c on 5c crim rose 6 5

No. 813 Overprinted Type "f" Overprint measures 16½mm

1959
O62 A145 6c gray bl 14 8

Nos. 856-861 Overprinted

G. O. — h
G. O. — j
G. O. — k
G.O. — l

1962-64 *Perf. 13½*
O63 A158(j) 5s car rose ('63) 5 5

Perf. 13x12

O64	A158(h)	6s dk red brn	5	5

Perf. 13½

O65	A158(k)	6s pck bl ('64)	6	5
O66	A158(j)	10s brt pur ('63)	8	5
O67	A158(j)	20s Prus bl ('63)	14	5
O68	A158(j)	30s vermilion	28	10
O69	A158(k)	50s vio ('63)	42	10
		Nos. O63-O69 (7)	1.08	45

"G.O." stands for "Gawaing Opisyal," Tagalog for "Official Business."
On 6s overprint "k" is 10mm. wide.

No. 1082 Overprinted Type "l"

1970, Dec. 30 Engr. Perf. 14

O70	A222	10s rose car	7	5

NEWSPAPER STAMPS

N1

N2

1886-89 Unwmk. Typo. Perf. 14

P1	N1	⅛c yel grn	25	10
P2	N1	1m rose	25	10
P3	N1	2m blue	25	10
P4	N1	5m dk brn	25	10

1890-96

P5	N2	⅛c dk vio	8	8
P6	N2	⅛c grn ('92)	80	20
P7	N2	⅛c org brn ('94)	12	5
P8	N2	⅛c dl bl ('96)	60	35
P9	N2	1m dk vio	8	8
P10	N2	1m grn ('92)	1.65	40
P11	N2	1m ol gray ('94)	12	5
P12	N2	1m ultra ('96)	20	5
P13	N2	2m dk vio	8	8
P14	N2	2m grn ('92)	1.65	40
P15	N2	2m ol gray ('94)	12	5
P16	N2	2m brn ('96)	20	5
P17	N2	5m dk vio	8	8
P18	N2	5m grn ('92)	65.00	17.50
P19	N2	5m ol gray ('94)	12	5
P20	N2	5m dp bl grn ('96)	1.40	60

Imperfs. exist of Nos. P8, P9, P11, P12, P16, P17 and P20.

OCCUPATION STAMPS

Issued under Japanese Occupation.
Nos. 461, 438 and 439 Overprinted with Bars in Black.

1942-43 Unwmk. Perf. 11x10½, 11.

N1	A75	2c ap grn	5	5
a.		Pair, one without overprint		
N2	A58	12c blk ('43)	10	10
N3	A59	16c dk bl	3.00	2.25

Nos. 435, 442, 443 and 423 Surcharged in Black

a

b

c

d

Perf. 11

N4	A55	5c on 6c gldn brn	10	10
a.		Top bar shorter, thinner	20	20
b.		5(c) on 6c dk brn	20	20
c.		As "b", top bar shorter and thinner	20	20
N5	A62	16c on 30c org red ('43)	20	20
N6	A63	50c on 1p red org & blk ('43)	60	60
a.		Dbl. surch.		*250.00*
N7	A65	1p on 4p bl & blk ('43)	67.50	52.50

On Nos. N4 and N4b, the top bar measures 1½x22½mm. On Nos. N4a and N4c, the top bar measures 1x21mm and the "5" is smaller and thinner.

No. 384 Surcharged in Black

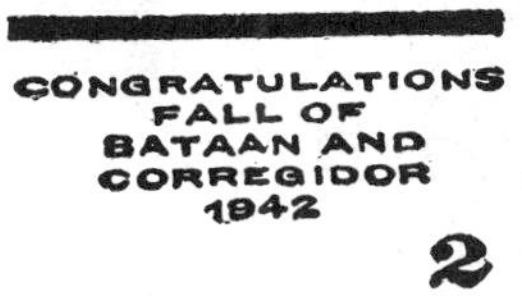

1942, May 18

N8	A54	2c on 4c yel grn	1.25	1.00

Issued to commemorate Japan's capture of Bataan and Corregidor. The American-Filipino forces finally surrendered May 7, 1942.

No. 384 Surcharged in Black

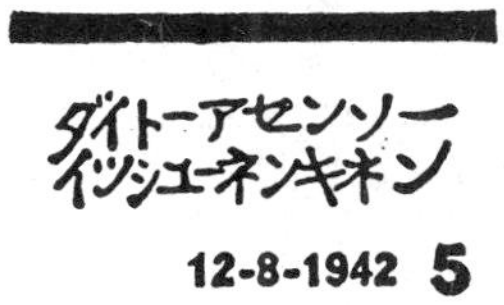

1942, Dec. 8

N9	A54	5c on 4c yel grn	45	30

Issued to commemorate the first anniversary of the "Greater East Asia War".

Nos. C59 and C62 Surcharged in Black

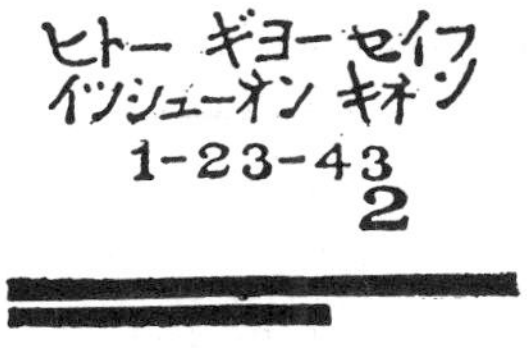

1943, Jan. 23

N10	AP1	2c on 8c car	20	20
N11	AP1	5c on 1p sep	40	40

Issued to commemorate the first anniversary of the Philippine Executive Commission.

Nipa Hut
OS1

Rice
Planting
OS2

Mt. Mayon
and Mt. Fuji
OS3

Moro Vinta
OS4

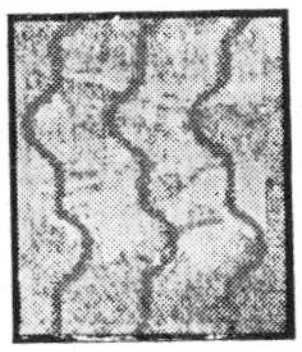
Wmk. 257- Curved
Wavy Lines

Engr., Typo. (2c, 6c, 25c)
1943-44 Wmk. 257 Perf. 13

N12	OS1	1c dp org	5	5
N13	OS2	2c brt grn	5	5
N14	OS1	4c sl grn	5	5
N15	OS3	5c org brn	5	5
N16	OS2	6c red	5	5
N17	OS3	10c bl grn	5	5
N18	OS4	12c stl bl	50	50
N19	OS4	16c dk brn	5	5
N20	OS1	20c rose vio	55	55
N21	OS3	21c violet	10	10
N22	OS2	25c pale brn	5	5
N23	OS3	1p dp car	12	10
N24	OS4	2p dl vio	1.20	1.00
N25	OS4	5p dk ol	4.00	3.50
		Nos. N12-N25 (14)	6.87	6.15

Map of Manila
Bay Showing
Bataan and
Corregidor
OS5

1943, May 7 Photo. Unwmk.

N26	OS5	2c car red	12	12
N27	OS5	5c brt grn	18	18

Issued to commemorate the first anniversary of the fall of Bataan and Corregidor.

No. 440 Surcharged in Black

1943, June 20 Engr. Perf. 11

N28	A60	12c on 20c lt ol grn	25	20
a.		Double surcharge		

Issued to commemorate the 350th anniversary of the printing press in the Philippines. "Limbagan" is Tagalog for "printing press."

Rizal
Monument,
Filipina and
Philippine
Flag — OS6

1943, Oct. 14 Photo. Perf. 12

N29	OS6	5c lt bl	10	10
a.		Imperf.	12	12
N30	OS6	12c orange	14	14
a.		Imperf.	16	16
N31	OS6	17c rose pink	16	16
a.		Imperf.	22	22

Issued to commemorate the "Independence of the Philippines." Japan granted "independence" Oct. 14, 1943, when the puppet republic was founded.

The imperforate stamps were issued without gum. See No. NB4.

José Rizal
OS7

Rev. José
Burgos
OS8

Apolinario
Mabini — OS9

1944, Feb. 17 Litho. Perf. 12

N32	OS7	5c blue	22	22
a.		Imperf.	22	22
N33	OS8	12c carmine	12	12
a.		Imperf.	12	12
N34	OS9	17c dp org	16	16
a.		Imperf.	16	16

See No. NB8.

Nos. C60 and C61 Surcharged in Black

1944, May 7 Perf. 11

N35	AP1	5c on 20c ultra	50	50
N36	AP1	12c on 60c bl grn	1.00	1.00

Issued to commemorate the second anniversary of the fall of Bataan and Corregidor.

José P.
Laurel — OS10

1945, Jan. 12 Litho. Imperf.
Without Gum.

N37	OS10	5c dl vio brn	7	6
N38	OS10	7c bl grn	10	8
N39	OS10	20c chlky bl	15	12

Issued belatedly on Jan. 12, 1945, to commemorate the first anniversary of the puppet Philippine Republic, Oct. 14, 1944. "S" stands for "sentimos".

OCCUPATION SEMI-POSTAL STAMPS

Woman, Farming
and
Cannery — OSP1

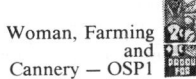

Unwmk.

1942, Nov. 12 Litho. *Perf. 12*

NB1 OSP1 2c + 1c pale vio 15 15
NB2 OSP1 5c + 1c brt grn 10 10
NB3 OSP1 16c + 2c org 13.00 10.00

Issued to promote the campaign to produce and conserve food. The surtax aided the Red Cross.

"Independence of the Philippines" Type
Souvenir Sheet

1943, Oct. 14 *Imperf.*
Without Gum

NB4 OS6 Sheet of three 35.00 *2.00*

Issued to commemorate the "Independence of the Philippines."
No. NB4 contains one each of Nos. N29a-N31a. Lower inscription from Rizal's "Last Farewell." Size: 127x177mm. Sold for 2.50p.

Nos. N18, N20 and N21 Surcharged in Black

BAHA
1943
+21

1943, Dec. 8 Wmk. 257 *Perf. 13*

NB5 OS4 12c + 21c stl bl 15 15
NB6 OS1 20c + 36c rose vio 12 12
NB7 OS3 21c + 40c vio 15 15

The surtax was for the benefit of victims of a Luzon flood. "Baha" is Tagalog for "flood."

Type of 1944
Souvenir Sheet
Unwmk.

1944, Feb. 9 Litho. *Imperf.*
Without Gum

NB8 OSP3 Sheet of three 2.00 *2.50*

No. NB8 contains one each of Nos. N32a-N34a.
Sheet sold for 1p, surtax going to a fund for the care of heroes' monuments.

OCCUPATION POSTAGE DUE STAMP

No. J15 Overprinted with Bar in Blue.

1942, Oct. 14 Unwmk. *Perf. 11*

NJ1 D3 3c on 4c brn red 20.00 9.00

On copies of No. J15, two lines were drawn in India ink with a ruling pen across "United States of America" by employees of the Short Paid Section of the Manila Post Office to make a provisional 3c postage due stamp which was used from Sept. 1, 1942, (when the letter rate was raised from 2c to 5c) until Oct. 14 when No. NJ1 went on sale.

OCCUPATION OFFICIAL STAMPS

Nos. 461, 413, 435, 435a and 442 Overprinted or Surcharged in Black with Bars and

公用
(K.P.)

1943-44 Unwmk. *Perf. 11x10½, 11.*

NO1 A75 2c ap grn 8 8
a. Double ovpt.
NO2 A55 5(c) on 6c dk brn (#413) ('44) 20.00 20.00
NO3 A55 5(c) on 6c gldn brn (#435a) 15 15
a. Narrower spacing between bars 20 20
b. 5(c) on 6c dk brn (#435) 15 12
c. As "b", narrower spacing between bars 20 20
NO4 A62 16c on 30c org red 45 45
a. Wider spacing between bars 45 45

On Nos. NO3 and NO3b, the bar deleting "United States of America" is 9¾ to 10mm. above the bar deleting "Common-". On Nos. NO3a and NO3c, the spacing is 8 to 8½mm.
On No. NO4 the center bar is 19 mm. long, 3½ mm. below the top bar and 6 mm. above the Japanese characters. On No. NO4a, the center bar is 20½ mm. long, 9 mm below the top bar and 1 mm. above the Japanese characters.

"K. P." stands for Kagamitang Pampamahalaan, "Official Business" in Tagalog.

Nos. 435 and 435a Surcharged in Black

5
REPUBLIKA NG PILIPINAS (K. P.)

1944 *Perf. 11.*

NO5 A55 5c on 6c gldn brn 10 10
a. 5c on 6c dk brn 10 10

Nos. O34 and C62 Overprinted in Black

Pilipinas
REPUBLIKA
a

K.P.
REPUBLIKA NG PILIPINAS
b (K. P.)

NO6 A60(a) 20c lt ol grn 35 35
NO7 AP1(b) 1p sepia 1.00 1.00

POLAND

LOCATION — Europe between Russia and Germany.
GOVT. — Republic
AREA — 120,628 sq. mi.
POP. — 36,399,000 (est. 1983)
CAPITAL — Warsaw

100 Kopecks = 1 Ruble
100 Fenigi = 1 Marka (1918)
100 Halerzy = 1 Korona (1918)
100 Groszy = 1 Zloty (1924)

Catalogue values for unused stamps in this country are for Never Hinged items, beginning with Scott 566 in the regular postage section, Scott B63 in the semi-postal section, Scott C28 in the airpost section, and Scott J146 in the postage due section.

Values for No. 1 are for fine copies. Very fine to superb specimens sell at much higher prices, and inferior or poor copies sell at reduced prices, depending on the condition of the individual specimen.

Issued under Russian Dominion

Coat of Arms — A1

Perf. 11½ to 12½
1860 Typo. Unwmk.

1 A1 10k bl & rose 525.00 200.00
a 10k blue & carmine 650.00 250.00
b 10k dark blue & rose 650.00 250.00
c Added blue frame for inner oval 975.00 425.00
d Imperf.

Used for letters within the Polish territory and to Russia. Postage on all foreign letters was paid in cash.
These stamps were superseded by those of Russia in 1865.

Issues of the Republic

Local issues were made in various Polish cities during the German occupation. In the early months of the Republic many issues were made by overprinting the German occupation stamps with the words "Poczta Polska" and an eagle or bars often with the name of the city. These issues were not authorized by the Government but were made by the local authorities and restricted to local use. In 1916 a series of stamps was issued for the Polish Legion and in 1917-18 the Polish Expeditionary Force used surcharged Russian stamps. The regularity of these issues is questioned.

Warsaw Issues

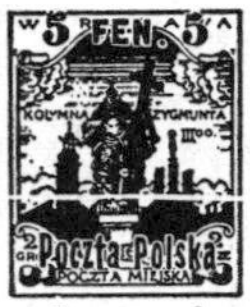
Statue of Sigismund III — A2

Coat of Arms of Warsaw — A3

Polish Eagle — A4

Sobieski Monument — A5

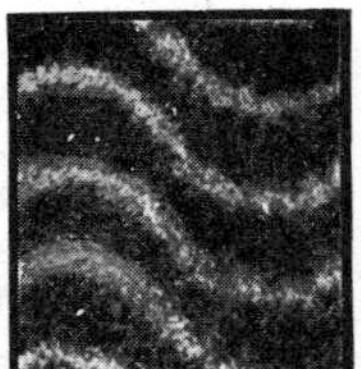
Wmk. 145 - Wavy Lines

Stamps of the Warsaw Local Post Surcharged

1918, Nov. 17 Wmk. 145 *Perf. 11½*

11 A2 5f on 2gr brn & buff 70 55
a Inverted surcharge 37.50 32.50
12 A3 10f on 6gr grn & buff 65 50
a Inverted surcharge 4.50 4.00
13 A4 25f on 10gr rose & buff 1.50 1.10
a Inverted surcharge 9.00 8.00
14 A5 50f on 20gr bl & buff 4.00 3.25
a Inverted surcharge 130.00 100.00

Nos. 11-14 exist imperforate.

Occupation Stamps Nos. N6 to N16 Overprinted or Surcharged:

5
Poczta Polska — a
Poczta Polska — b

Wmk. Lozenges (125)

1918-19 *Perf. 14, 14½*

15 A16 3pf brn ('19) 15.00 10.50
16 A22 5pf on 2½pf gray 25 25
17 A16 5pf on 3pf brn 2.75 1.90
18 A16 5pf green 52 45
19 A16 10pf carmine 10 10
20 A22 15pf dk vio 10 10
21 A16 20pf blue 16 18
a 20pf ultramarine *350.00 350.00*
23 A22 25pf on 7½pf org 25 15
24 A16 30pf org & blk, *buff* 10 10
25 A16 40pf lake & blk 35 38
26 A16 60pf magenta 52 55
Nos. 15-26 (11) 20.10 14.66

There are two settings of this overprint. The first printing, issued Dec. 5, 1918, has space of 3½mm. between the middle two bars. The second printing, issued Jan. 15, 1919, has space of 4½mm. No. 15 comes only in the second setting; all others in both. The overprint on No. 21a is very glossy.
Varieties of this overprint and surcharge are numerous: double; inverted; misspellings (Pocata, Poczto, Pelska); letters omitted, inverted or wrong font; 3 bars instead of 4, etc.
Counterfeits exist.

Lublin Issue

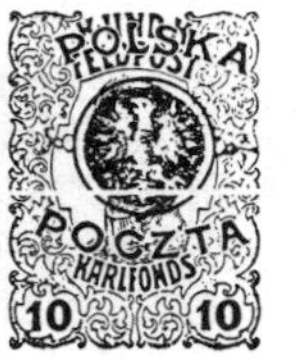
A6

A7

Austrian Military Semi-Postal Stamps of 1918 Overprinted

1918, Dec. 5 Unwmk. *Perf. 12½x13*

27 A6 10h gray grn 7.50 6.50
a Inverted overprint 17.50 17.50
28 A7 20h magenta 7.50 6.50
a Inverted overprint 17.50 17.50
29 A6 45h blue 7.50 6.50
a Inverted overprint 17.50 17.50

Austrian Military Stamps of 1917 Surcharged

1918-19 *Perf. 12½*

30 M3 3hal on 3h ol gray 24.00 21.00
a Inverted surcharge 225.00 225.00
b Perf. 11½ 30.00 21.00
c Perf. 11½x12½ 40.00 40.00
31 M3 3hal on 15h brt rose 3.00 2.25
a Inverted surcharge 20.00 20.00

Surcharged in Black

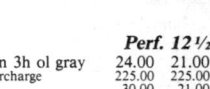

32 M3 10hal on 30h sl grn 3.00 2.00
a Inverted surcharge 20.00 20.00
b Brown surcharge (error) 60.00 50.00
34 M3 25hal on 40h ol bis 4.75 3.00
a Inverted surcharge 30.00 30.00
b Perf. 11½ 15.00 9.00
35 M3 45hal on 60h rose 3.25 2.50
a Inverted surcharge 20.00 20.00
36 M3 45hal on 80h dl bl 5.50 4.75
a Inverted surcharge 30.00 30.00
37 M3 50hal on 60h rose 3.25 2.75
a Inverted surcharge 20.00 20.00

Similar surcharge with bars instead of stars over original value

38 M3 45hal on 80h dl bl 6.25 5.25
a Inverted surcharge 20.00 20.00

Overprinted

39 M3 50h dp grn 27.50 19.00
a Inverted overprint 80.00 80.00
40 M3 90h dk vio 4.00 3.00
a Inverted overprint 20.00 20.00
Nos. 30-40 (10) 84.50 65.50

Cracow Issues

Austrian Stamps of 1916-18 Overprinted

POCZTA
◇
POLSKA

1919, Jan. 17 **Typo.**

41	A37	3h brt vio	175.00	150.00
42	A37	5h lt grn	175.00	150.00
43	A37	6h dp org	21.00	14.00
a		Inverted overprint	1,000.	
44	A37	10h magenta	185.00	160.00
45	A37	12h lt bl	17.50	13.00
46	A39	40h ol grn	14.00	13.00
a		Inverted overprint	100.00	100.00
b		Double overprint	400.00	
47	A39	50h bl grn	4.75	4.00
a		Inverted overprint		1,750.
48	A39	60h dp bl	3.75	3.50
a		Inverted overprint	100.00	75.00
49	A39	80h org brn	3.75	3.50
a		Inverted overprint.	100.00	100.00
b		Double overprint	125.00	125.00
50	A39	90h red vio	625.00	550.00
51	A39	1k car, *yel*	6.75	4.75

Engr.

52	A40	2k blue	4.00	3.75
53	A40	3k car rose	45.00	37.50
54	A40	4k yel grn	67.50	57.50
55	A40	10k dp vio	3,150.	3,600.

The 3k is on granite paper.
The overprint on Nos. 52 to 55 is slightly larger than illustration and different ornament between lines of type.

Same Overprint on Nos. 168-171

1919 **Typo.**

56	A42	15h dl red	5.00	4.75
57	A42	20h dk grn	60.00	65.00
58	A42	25h blue	650.00	600.00
59	A42	30h dl vio	125.00	100.00

Austria No. 157 Surcharged

POLSKA
POCZTA
25

1919, Jan. 24

60	A39	25h on 80h org brn	2.50	2.50
a		Inverted surcharge	60.00	60.00

Excellent counterfeits of Nos. 27 to 60 exist.

Polish Eagle — A9

1919, Feb. 25 **Litho.** ***Imperf.***

Without gum

Yellowish Paper

61	A9	2h gray	24	24
62	A9	3h dl vio	24	24
63	A9	5h green	6	6
64	A9	6h orange	10.50	10.50
65	A9	10h lake	6	6
66	A9	15h brown	6	6
67	A9	20h ol grn	24	24

Bluish Paper

68	A9	25h car	6	6
69	A9	50h indigo	6	6
70	A9	70h dp bl	24	24
71	A9	1k ol gray & car	45	65
		Nos. 61-71 (11)	12.21	12.41

Nos. 61-71 exist with privately applied perforations.
Counterfeits exist.

Posen (Poznan) Issue

A9a

A9b

German Stamps of 1906-20 Overprinted in Black

Perf. 14, 14½

1919, Aug. 5 **Wmk. 125**

72	A9a	5pf on 2pf gray	18.00	13.00
73	A9a	5pf on 7½pf org	1.90	1.10
a		Inverted surch.	100.00	
74	A9a	5pf on 20pf bl vio	1.50	95
75	A9b	10pf on 25pf org & blk, *yel*	3.75	2.50
76	A9b	10pf on 40pf lake & blk	2.00	1.10
		Nos. 72-76 (5)	27.15	18.65

Counterfeits exist.

Germany Nos. 96 and 98 Surcharged in Red or Green

5 10

1919, Sept. 15

77	A22	5pf on 2pf gray (R)	150.00	115.00
a		Inverted surcharge	3,000.	
78	A22	10pf on 7½pf org (G)	125.00	85.00

Nos. 77-78 are a provisional issue for use in Gniezno.
Counterfeit surcharges abound.

For Northern Poland

Eagle and Fasces, Symbolical of United Poland
A10 A11

"Agriculture" A12

"Peace" A13

Polish Cavalryman A14

1919, Jan. 27 ***Imperf.***

Wove or Ribbed Paper

81	A10	3f bis brn	10	7
82	A10	5f green	10	7
83	A10	10f red vio	10	7
84	A10	15f dp rose	10	7
85	A11	20f deep bl	10	7
86	A11	25f ol grn	15	10
87	A11	50f bl grn	15	10
88	A12	1m violet	1.40	1.00
89	A12	1.50m dp grn	2.50	1.40
90	A12	2m dk brn	2.25	1.40
91	A13	2.50m org brn	9.00	6.25
92	A14	5m red vio	12.00	6.25
		Nos. 81-92 (12)	27.95	16.85

Perf. 10, 11, 11½, 10x11½, 11½x10

1919-20

93	A10	3f bis brn	8	6
94	A10	5f green	8	6
95	A10	10f red vio	8	6
96	A10	10f brn ('20)	8	6
97	A10	15f dp rose	8	6
98	A10	15f ver ('20)	8	6
99	A11	20f dp bl	8	6
100	A11	25f ol grn	8	6
101	A11	40f brt vio ('20)	8	6
102	A11	50f bl grn	8	6
103	A12	1m violet	40	20
105	A12	1.50m dp grn	80	40
106	A12	2m dk brn	80	40
107	A13	2.50m org brn	1.25	1.25
108	A14	5m red vio	2.00	1.25
		Nos. 93-108 (15)	6.05	4.10

Several denominations among Nos. 81-132 are found with double impression or in pairs imperf. between.
See Nos. 140-152C, 170-175.

For Southern Poland

A15

A16

A17

A18

A19

1919, Jan. 27 ***Imperf.***

109	A15	3h red brn	7	7
110	A15	5h emerald	7	7
111	A15	10h orange	7	7
112	A15	15h vermilion	7	7
113	A16	20h gray brn	7	7
114	A16	25h light bl	7	7
115	A16	50h org brn	10	7
116	A17	1k dk grn	10	10
117	A17	1.50k red brn	3.75	2.75
118	A17	2k dark bl	1.90	1.65
119	A18	2.50k dk vio	8.75	4.50
120	A19	5k slate bl	9.75	5.75
		Nos. 109-120 (12)	24.77	15.24

Perf. 10, 11½, 10x11½, 11½x10

121	A15	3h red brn	5	5
122	A15	5h emerald	5	5
123	A15	10h orange	5	5
124	A15	15h vermilion	5	5
125	A16	20h gray brn	5	5
126	A16	25h light bl	5	5
127	A16	50h org brn	5	5
128	A17	1k dk grn	40	30
129	A17	1.50k red brn	1.10	40
130	A17	2k dark bl	1.10	40
131	A18	2.50k dk vio	1.25	55
132	A19	5k slate bl	2.00	1.00
		Nos. 121-132 (12)	6.20	3.00

National Assembly Issue

A20

Ignacy Jan Paderewski — A21

Adalbert Trampczynski — A22

Eagle Watching Ship — A24

Designs: 25f, Gen. Josef Pilsudski. 1m, Griffin.

1919-20 ***Perf. 11½***

Wove or Ribbed Paper

133	A20	10f red vio	12	8
134	A21	15f brn red	32	20
a		Imperf., pair	25.00	
135	A22	20f dp brn (21x25mm)	25	24
136	A22	20f dp brn (17x20mm) ('20)	50	75
137	A21	25f ol grn	15	15
138	A24	50f Prus bl	20	15
139	A24	1m purple	25	24
		Nos. 133-139 (7)	1.79	1.81

First National Assembly of Poland.

General Issue

1919 ***Perf. 9 to 14½ and Compound***

Thin Laid Paper

140	A11	25f ol grn	8	5
141	A11	50f bl grn	8	5
142	A12	1m dk gray	22	8
143	A12	2m bis brn	65	15
144	A13	3m red brn	32	15
a		Pair, imperf. vert.	5.00	5.75
145	A14	5m red vio	15	15
146	A14	6m dp rose	15	15
a		Pair, imperf. vert.	6.50	6.50
147	A14	10m brn red	22	20
a		Horizontal pair, imperf.	6.50	6.50
148	A14	20m gray grn	40	38
		Nos. 140-148 (9)	2.27	1.36

Type of 1919 Redrawn

Perf. 9 to 14½ and Compound

1920-22

Thin Laid or Wove Paper

149	A10	1m red	7	6
150	A10	2m gray grn	10	6
151	A10	3m light bl	10	6
152	A10	4m rose red	10	6
152A	A10	5m dk vio	10	6
b		Pair, imperf. vert.	5.25	5.25
152C	A10	8m gray brn ('22)	24	22
		Nos. 149-152C (6)	71	52

The word "POCZTA" is in smaller letters and the numerals have been enlarged.
The color of No. 152A varies from dark violet to red brown.

No. 101 Surcharged

3 Mk.

Perf. 10, 11½, 10x11½, 11½x10

1921, Jan. 25

Thick Wove Paper

153	A11	3m on 40f brt vio	15	10
a		Double surcharge	20.00	20.00
b		Inverted surcharge	20.00	20.00

Sower and Rainbow of Hope — A27

Perf. 9 to 14½ and Compound

1921 **Litho.**

Thin Laid or Wove Paper

Size: 28x22mm

154	A27	10m slate blue	15	10
155	A27	15m light brn	20	10
155A	A27	20m red	15	15

Signing of peace treaty with Russia.
See No. 191.

Sun (Peace) Breaking into Darkness (Despair) A28

"Peace" and "Agriculture" A29

"Peace" — A30

Perf. 11, 11½, 12, 12½, 13 and Compound

1921, May 2

156 A28 2m green 1.10 42
157 A28 3m blue 1.10 42
158 A28 4m red 75 42
a 4m carmine rose (error) *200.00*
159 A29 6m car rose 1.10 45
160 A29 10m slate bl 80 55
161 A30 25m dk vio 2.00 1.10
162 A30 50m sl bl & buff 1.25 75
Nos. 156-162 (7) 8.10 4.11

Issued to commemorate the Constitution.

Polish Eagle — A31

Perf. 9 to 14½ and Compound

1921-23

163 A31 25m vio & buff 8 8
164 A31 50m car & buff 8 8
a Imperf. horizontally
165 A31 100m blk brn & org 8 8
166 A31 200m blk & rose ('23) 22 12
167 A31 300m ol grn ('23) 22 12
168 A31 400m brn ('23) 22 12
169 A31 500m brn vio ('23) 22 12
169A A31 1000m org ('23) 22 12
169B A31 2000m dull bl ('23) 22 8
Nos. 163-169B (9) 1.56 92

Type of 1919 and

Miner — A32

Perf. 9 to 14½ and Compound

1922-23

170 A10 5f blue 8 12
171 A10 10f lt vio 8 12
172 A11 20f pale red 8 12
173 A11 40f vio brn 8 12
174 A11 50f orange 8 12
175 A11 75f bl grn 8 12
176 A32 1m black 12 15
177 A32 1.25m dk grn 12 18
178 A32 2m dp rose 12 18
179 A32 3m emerald 12 18
180 A32 4m dp ultra 12 18
181 A32 5m yel brn 12 18
182 A32 6m red org 15 18
183 A32 10m lil brn 15 18
184 A32 20m dp vio 15 22
185 A32 50m olive grn 18 25
187 A32 80m ver ('23) 38 75
188 A32 100m vio ('23) 38 75
189 A32 200m org ('23) 1.40 2.25
190 A32 300m pale bl ('23) 4.00 3.75
Nos. 170-190 (20) 7.99 10.10

This issue was to commemorate the union of Upper Silesia with Poland.

There were two printings of Nos. 176 to 190, the first being from flat plates, the second from rotary press on thin paper with perforations 12½.

Nos. 173 and 175 are printed from new plates showing larger value numerals and a single "f".

Sower Type Redrawn

Size: 25x21mm

1922 Thick or Thin Wove Paper

191 A27 20m carmine 28 12

In this stamp the design has been strengthened and made more distinct, especially the ground and the numerals in the upper corners.

Nicolaus Copernicus A33

Father Stanislaus Konarski A34

1923 ***Perf. 10 to 12½***

192 A33 1000m indigo 80 30
193 A34 3000m brown 45 30
a "Konapski" 6.75 5.25
194 A33 5000m rose 80 30

Nicolaus Copernicus (1473-1543), astronomer (Nos. 192, 194); Stanislaus Konarski (1700-1773), educator, and the creation by the Polish Parliament of the Commission of Public Instruction (No. 193).

No. 163 Surcharged

10 TYSIECY

1923 ***Perf. 9 to 14½ and Compound***

195 A31 10000m on 25m vio & buff 18 8
a Double surcharge 5.00
b Inverted surcharge 7.50

Stamps of 1921 Surcharged

MK MK 25,000

196 A27 25000m on 20m red 38 12
a Double surcharge 5.00 5.00
b Inverted surcharge 10.00
197 A27 50000m on 10m grnsh bl 18 9
a Double surcharge 5.00 5.00
b Inverted surcharge 7.50 7.50

No. 191 Surcharged

MK MK 25,000

198 A27 25000m on 20m car 28 9
a Double surcharge 5.00 5.00
b Inverted surcharge 7.50

No. 150 Surcharged with New Value

1924

199 A10 20000m on 2m gray grn 45 15
a Inverted surcharge 7.50 7.50
b Double surcharge 5.00 5.00

Type of 1919 Issue Surcharged with New Value

200 A10 100000m on 5m red brn 18 8
a Double surcharge 5.00 5.00
b Inverted surcharge 7.50 7.50

Arms of Poland — A35

Perf. 10 to 14½ and Compound

1924 Litho.

Thin Paper

205 A35 10,000m lil brn 30 24
206 A35 20,000m ol grn 30 16
207 A35 30,000m scarlet 1.00 32
208 A35 50,000m ap grn 2.00 32
209 A35 100,000m brn org 60 28
210 A35 200,000m lt bl 30 12
211 A35 300,000m red vio 60 32
212 A35 500,000m brn 60 65
213 A35 1,000,000m pale rose 60 *2.75*
214 A35 2,000,000m dk grn 1.00 *6.50*
Nos. 205-214 (10) 7.30 *11.66*

Arms of Poland A36

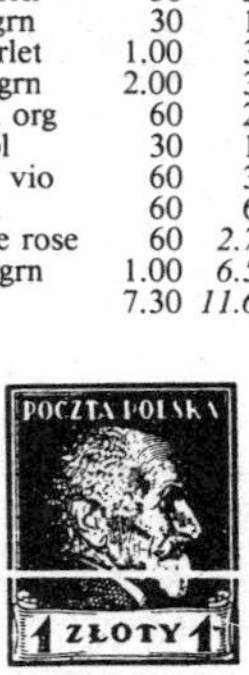

President Stanislaus Wojciechowski A37

1924 ***Perf. 10 to 13½ and Compound***

215 A36 1g org brn 25 8
216 A36 2g dk brn 25 8
217 A36 3g orange 32 8
218 A36 5g ol grn 65 8
219 A36 10g bl grn 85 8
220 A36 15g red 85 8
221 A36 20g blue 1.65 16
222 A36 25g red brn 2.25 32
a 25g indigo *3,000.* *4,250.*
223 A36 30g dp vio 16.00 24
a 30g gray blue *250.00*
224 A36 40g indigo 3.00 32
225 A36 50g magenta 2.75 28

Perf. 11½, 12

226 A37 1z scarlet 18.00 1.00
Nos. 215-226 (12) 46.82 2.80

Holy Gate of Wilno (Vilnius) A38

Poznan Town Hall A39

Sigismund Monument, Warsaw A40

Wawel Castle at Cracow A41

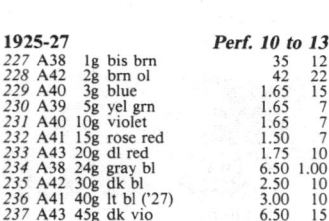

Sobieski Statue at Lwow — A42

Ship of State — A43

1925-27 ***Perf. 10 to 13***

227 A38 1g bis brn 35 12
228 A42 2g brn ol 42 22
229 A40 3g blue 1.65 15
230 A39 5g yel grn 1.65 7
231 A40 10g violet 1.65 7
232 A41 15g rose red 1.50 7
233 A43 20g dl red 1.75 10
234 A38 24g gray bl 6.50 1.00
235 A42 30g dk bl 2.50 10
236 A41 40g lt bl ('27) 3.00 10
237 A43 45g dk vio 6.50 15
Nos. 227-237 (11) 27.47 2.15

1926-27 Redrawn

238 A40 3g blue 2.50 42
239 A39 5g yel grn 3.00 18
240 A40 10g violet 4.50 18
241 A41 15g rose red 4.50 18

On Nos. 229 to 232 inclusive the lines representing clouds touch the numerals. On the redrawn stamps the numerals have white outlines, separating them from the cloud lines.

Marshal Pilsudski A44

Frederic Chopin A45

1927 Typo. ***Perf. 12½, 11½***

242 A44 20g red brn 2.25 15
243 A45 40g dp ultra 14.50 1.00

See No. 250.

President Ignacy Moscicki — A46

1927, May 4 ***Perf. 11½***

245 A46 20g red 4.00 38

Dr. Karol Kaczkowski A47

Julius Slowacki A48

1927, May 27 ***Perf. 11½, 12½***

246 A47 10g gray grn 2.50 1.50
247 A47 25g carmine 6.00 2.00
248 A47 40g dk blue 8.00 2.00

4th Intl. Congress of Millitary Medicine and Pharmacy, Warsaw, May 30-June 4.

1927, June 28 ***Perf. 12½***

249 A48 20g rose 4.50 25

Transfer from Paris to Cracow of the remains of Julius Slowacki, poet.

Pilsudski Type of 1927

Design Redrawn

1928 ***Perf. 11½, 12x11½, 12½x13***

250 A44 25g yel brn 2.25 15

Souvenir Sheet

A49

1928, May 3 Engr. ***Perf. 12½***

251 A49 Sheet of two 225.00 275.00
a 50g blk brn 90.00 100.00
b 1z blk brn 90.00 100.00

1st Natl. Phil. Exhib., Warsaw, May 3-13.

Sold to each purchaser of a ticket to the Warsaw Philatelic Exhibition, which cost 1.50 zloty.

Counterfeits exist.

Marshal Pilsudski A49a

Pres. Moscicki A50

Perf. 10½ to 14 and Compound

1928-31

Wove Paper

253 A49a 50g bluish slate 3.75 10
254 A49a 50g bl grn ('31) 10.50 15

See No. 315.

Perf. 12 x 12½, 11½ to 13½ and Compound

1928

Laid Paper

255 A50 1z blk, *cr* 9.00 25
a Horizontally laid paper ('30) 60.00 2.50

See Nos. 305, 316.

General Josef Bem A51

Henryk Sienkiewicz A52

1928, May Typo. *Perf. 12½*
Wove Paper

256 A51 25g rose red 3.25 25

Return from Syria to Poland of the ashes of General Josef Bem.

1928, Oct.

257 A52 15g ultra 2.00 10

Eagle Arms — A53

"Swiatowid," Ancient Slav God — A54

1928-29 *Perf. 12 x 12½*

258 A53 5g dk vio 30 5
259 A53 10g green 90 15
260 A53 25g red brn 50 10

1928, Dec. 15 *Perf. 12½x12*

261 A54 25g brown 2.00 15

Poznan Agricultural Exhibition.

King John III Sobieski A55

Stylized Soldiers A56

1930, July *Perf. 12x12½*

262 A55 75g claret 3.75 18

1930, Nov. 1 *Perf. 12½*

263 A56 5g vio brn 32 10
264 A56 15g dk bl 2.00 22
265 A56 25g red brn 1.10 7
266 A56 30g dl red 6.00 2.50

Centenary of insurrection of 1830.

Kosciuszko, Washington, Pulaski — A57

1932, May 3 *Perf. 11½*
Laid Paper

267 A57 30g brown 1.40 25

200th birth anniv. of George Washington.

Coat of Arms — A58

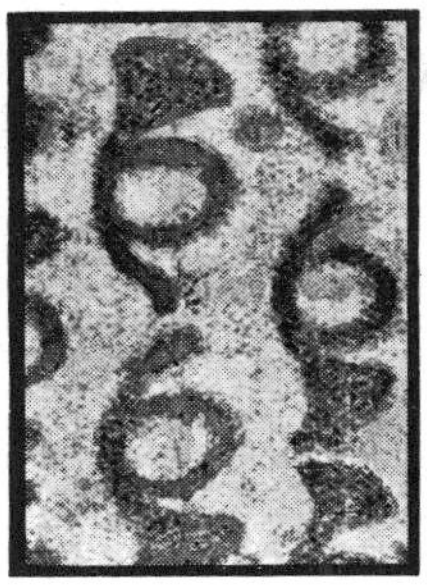

Wmk. 234 - Multiple Post Horns

Perf. 12x12½
1932-33 Typo. Wmk. 234

268 A58 5g dl vio ('33) 32 5
269 A58 10g green 32 5
270 A58 15g red brn ('33) 32 5
271 A58 20g gray 65 6
272 A58 25g buff 85 6
273 A58 30g dp rose 2.75 6
274 A58 60g blue 18.00 45
Nos. 268-274 (7) 23.21 78

City Hall of Torun — A59

1933, Jan. 2 Engr. *Perf. 11½*

275 A59 60g dark bl 30.00 70

700th anniversary of the founding of the City of Torun by the Grand Master of the Knights of the Teutonic Order.
See No. B28.

Altar Panel of St. Mary's Church, Cracow — A60

Perf. 11½-12½ & Compound
1933, July 10 Unwmk.
Laid Paper

277 A60 80g red brn 13.00 1.00

400th death anniv. of Veit Stoss, sculptor and woodcarver.

John III Sobieski and Allies before Vienna, painted by Jan Matejko — A61

1933, Sept. 12 Laid Paper

278 A61 1.20z indigo 27.50 4.50

250th anniv. of the deliverance of Vienna by the Polish and allied forces under command of John III Sobieski, King of Poland, when besieged by the Turks in 1683.

The indexes in each volume of the Scott Catalogue contain many listings which help to identify stamps.

Cross of Independence A62

Josef Pilsudski A63

Wmk. 234
1933, Nov. 11 Typo. *Perf. 12½*

279 A62 30g scarlet 5.75 32

15th anniversary of independence.

Type of 1932 Overprinted in Red or Black

Wyst. Filat.
1934
Katowice

1934, May 5 *Perf. 12*

280 A58 20g gray (R) 30.00 22.50
281 A58 30g dp rose 30.00 22.50

Katowice Philatelic Exhibition. Counterfeits exist.

Perf. 11½ to 12½ and Compound
1934, Aug. 6 Engr. Unwmk.

282 A63 25g gray bl 90 22
283 A63 30g blk brn 2.50 32

Polish Legion, 20th anniversary.

Nos. 274, 277-278 Surcharged in Black or Red

1934 Wmk. 234 *Perf. 12x12½*

284 A58 55g on 60g bl 4.00 48

Perf. 11½-12½ & Compound
Unwmk.

285 A60 25g on 80g red brn 5.00 48
286 A61 1z on 1.20z ind (R) 12.50 1.90
a Figure "1" in surcharge 5mm high instead of 4½mm 12.50 1.90

Surcharge of No. 286 includes bars.

Pilsudski Mourning Issue

Marshal Pilsudski — A64

1935 *Perf. 11 to 13 and Compound*

287 A64 5g black 70 14
288 A64 15g black 70 22
289 A64 25g black 1.40 18
290 A64 45g black 3.50 1.25
291 A64 1z black 6.75 4.00
Nos. 287-291 (5) 13.05 5.79

Nos. 287 and 288 are typographed, Nos. 290 and 291 lithographed. No. 289 exists both typographed and lithographed.
See No. B35b.

Nos. 270, 282 Overprinted in Blue or Red

Kopiec
Marszalka
Pilsudskiego

1935 Wmk. 234 *Perf. 12x12½*

292 A58 15g red brn 85 38

Perf. 11½, 11½x12½
Unwmk.

293 A63 25g gray bl (R) 2.75 1.25

Issued in connection with the proposed memorial to Marshal Pilsudski, the stamps were sold at Cracow exclusively.

"The Dog Cliff" A65

President Ignacy Moscicki A75

Designs: 10g, "Eye of the Sea." 15g, M. S. "Pilsudski." 20g, View of Pieniny. 25g, Belvedere Palace. 30g, Castle in Mira. 45g, Castle at Podhorce. 50g, Cloth Hall, Cracow. 55g, Raczynski Library, Poznan. 1z, Cathedral, Wilno.

1935-36 Typo. *Perf. 12½x13*

294 A65 5g vio bl 65 8
295 A65 10g yel grn 65 8
296 A65 15g Prus grn 2.00 8
297 A65 20g vio blk 1.00 8

Engr.

298 A65 25g myr grn 85 8
299 A65 30g rose red 2.25 20
300 A65 45g plum ('36) 1.10 20
301 A65 50g blk ('36) 1.10 20
302 A65 55g bl ('36) 10.00 40
303 A65 1z brn ('36) 4.00 1.10
304 A75 3z blk brn 2.50 2.25
Nos. 294-304 (11) 26.10 4.75

See Nos. 308-311.

Type of 1928 inscribed "1926. 3. VI. 1936" on Bottom Margin

1936, June 3

305 A50 1z ultra 6.25 3.50

Presidency of Ignacy Moscicki, 10th anniv.

Nos. 299, 302 Overprinted in Blue or Red

GORDON-BENNETT 30.VIII.
1936

1936, Aug. 15

306 A65 30g rose red 10.00 5.75
307 A65 55g bl (R) 10.00 5.75

Gordon-Bennett Intl. Balloon Race. Counterfeits exist.

Scenic Type of 1935-36

Designs: 5g, Church at Czestochowa. 10g, Maritime Terminal, Gdynia. 15g, University, Lwow. 20g, Municipal Building, Katowice.

1937 Engr. *Perf. 12½*

308 A65 5g vio bl 14 8
309 A65 10g green 42 8
310 A65 15g red brn 28 8
311 A65 20g org brn 42 12

Marshal Smigly-Rydz A80

President Moscicki A81

1937 *Perf. 12½x13*

312 A80 25g slate grn 18 10
313 A80 55g blue 45 15

Souvenir Sheets
Types of 1928-37

1937

314 A80 25g dk brn, sheet of four 16.00 22.50
a Single stamp 2.50 2.50
315 A49a 50g dp bl, sheet of four 16.00 22.50
a Single stamp 2.50 2.50
316 A50 1z gray blk, sheet of four 16.00 22.50
a Single stamp 2.50 2.50

Each of the above stamps is printed in a block of four on a sheet of paper measuring 111x125 mm. Inscribed in red at top; "26VI-

I.VII-1937" with the Romanian coat of arms at the left and the Polish at the right.
Visit of King Carol of Romania to Poland, June 26-July 1.
See No. B35c.

1938, Feb. 1 *Perf. 12½*
317 A81 15g sl grn 15 7
318 A81 30g rose vio 60 15

71st birthday of President Moscicki.

Kosciuszko, Paine and Washington and View of New York City — A82

1938, Mar. 17 *Perf. 12x12½*
319 A82 1z gray bl 1.00 1.75

150th anniv. of the US Constitution.

Boleslaus I and Emperor Otto III at Gnesen — A83

Marshal Pilsudski — A95

Designs: 10g, King Casimir III. 15g, King Ladislas II Jagello and Queen Hedwig. 20g, King Casimir IV. 25g, Treaty of Lublin. 30g, King Stephen Bathory commending Wielock, the peasant. 45g, Stanislas Zolkiewski and Jan Chodkiewicz. 50g, John III Sobieski entering Vienna. 55g, Union of nobles, commoners and peasants. 75g, Dabrowski, Kosciuszko and Poniatowski. 1z, Polish soldiers. 2z, Romuald Traugutt.

1938, Nov. 11 **Engr.** *Perf. 12½*
320 A83 5g red org 7 7
321 A83 10g green 7 7
322 A83 15g fawn 20 12
323 A83 20g pck bl 32 15
324 A83 25g dl vio 10 10
325 A83 30g rose red 50 12
326 A83 45g black 32 15
327 A83 50g brt red vio 2.00 12
328 A83 55g ultra 65 10
329 A83 75g dl grn 1.65 1.25
330 A83 1z orange 1.25 1.10
331 A83 2z car rose 8.00 6.50
332 A95 3z gray blk 6.50 11.00
Nos. 320-332 (13) 21.63 20.85

20th anniv. of Poland's independence. See No. 339.

Souvenir Sheet

Marshal Pilsudski, Gabriel Narutowicz, President Moscicki, Marshal Smigly-Rydz — A96

1938, Nov. 11 *Perf. 12½*
333 A96 Sheet of four 14.00 16.00
a 25g dl vio *(Pilsudski)* 1.65 1.75
b 25g dl vio *(Narutowicz)* 1.65 1.75
c 25g dl vio *(Moscicki)* 1.65 1.75
d 25g dl vio *(Smigly-Rydz)* 1.65 1.75

20th anniv. of Poland's independence.

Poland Welcoming Teschen People — A97

Skier — A98

1938, Nov. 11
334 A97 25g dl vio 1.75 38

Restoration of the Teschen territory ceded by Czechoslovakia.

1939, Feb. 6
335 A98 15g org brn 90 1.10
336 A98 25g dl vio 1.10 50
337 A98 30g rose red 1.75 1.10
338 A98 55g brt ultra 5.00 4.00

Intl. Ski Meet, Zakopane, Feb. 11-19.

Type of 1938

Design: 15g, King Ladislas II Jagello and Queen Hedwig.

Re-engraved

1939, Mar. 2 *Perf. 12½*
339 A83 15g redsh brn 22 10

No. 322 with crossed swords and helmet at lower left. No. 339, swords and helmet have been removed.

Marshal Pilsudski Reviewing Troops — A99

1939, Aug. 1 **Engr.**
340 A99 25g dl rose vio 38 65

Polish Legion, 25th anniv. See No. B35a.

Polish Peoples Republic

Romuald Traugutt A100

Tadeusz Kosciuszko A101

Design: 1z, Jan Henryk Dabrowski.

Perf. 11½
1944, Sept. 7 **Litho.** **Unwmk.**
Without Gum
341 A100 25g crim rose 35.00 35.00
342 A101 50g dp grn 42.50 47.50
343 A101 1z dp ultra 37.50 47.50

Counterfeits exist.

Polish Eagle A103

Grunwald Monument, Cracow A104

1944, Sept. 13 **Photo.** *Perf. 12½*
344 A103 25g dp red 45 35
a 25g dull red, typo. 60
345 A104 50g dk sl grn 35 15

No. 344a was not put on sale without surcharge. See Nos. 346, 349a, C20.

No. 344 Surcharged in Black

— 1 zł —
31.XII.1943
K. R. N.
31.XII.1944
a

— 2 zł —
P. K. W. N.
31.XII.1944
b

— 3 zł —
31.XII.1944
R. T. R. P.
c

1944-45
345A A103 1z on 25g 1.25 1.40
345B A103 2z on 25g ('45) 1.25 1.40
345C A103 3z on 25g ('45) 1.25 1.40

Issued to honor Polish government agencies. K. R. N. - Krajowa Rada Narodowa (Polish National Council), P. K. W. N. - Polski Komitet Wyzwolenia Narodu (Polish National Liberation Committee) and R. T. R. P. - Rzad Tymczasowy Rzeczypospolitej Polskiej (Temporary Administration of the Polish Republic).
Counterfeits exist.

No. 344a Surcharged in Brown

1'50
ZL

1945, Sept. 1
346 A103 1.50z on 25g dl red 42 15
a 1.50z on 25g dp red, #344 350.00 250.00

No. 344 Surcharged in Blue

— 3 zł —
Kielce
15. I. 1945

1945, Feb. 12
347 A103 3z on 25g red 3.00 4.75
348 A103 3z on 25g red *(Radom, 16. I. 1945)* 2.25 2.75
349 A103 3z on 25g red *(Warszawa, 17. I. 1945)* 4.50 5.25
a 3z on 25g dl red, #344a 110.00 125.00
350 A103 3z on 25g red *(Czestochowa, 17. I. 1945)* 2.25 2.75
351 A103 3z on 25g red *(Krakow, 19. I. 1945)* 2.25 2.75
352 A103 3z on 25g red *(Lodz, 19. I. 1945)* 2.25 2.75
353 A103 3z on 25g red *(Gniezno, 22. I. 1945)* 2.25 2.75
354 A103 3z on 25g red *(Bydgoszcz, 23. I. 1945)* 2.25 2.75
355 A103 3z on 25g red *(Kalisz, 24. I. 1945)* 2.25 2.75
356 A103 3z on 25g red *(Zakopane, 29. I. 1945)* 2.25 2.75
Nos. 347-356 (10) 25.50 32.00

Dates overprinted are those of liberation for each city.
Counterfeits exist.

Grunwald Monument, Cracow A105

Kosciuszko Statue, Cracow A106

Cloth Hall, Cracow A107

Copernicus Memorial A108

Wawel Castle — A109

1945, Apr. 10 **Photo.** *Perf. 10½, 11*
357 A105 50g dk vio brn 15 12
a 50g dark brown 42 35
358 A106 1z henna brn 28 24
359 A107 2z sapphire 42 35
360 A108 3z dp red vio 1.10 48
361 A109 5z bl grn 2.50 3.25
Nos. 357-361 (5) 4.45 4.44

Liberation of Cracow Jan. 19, 1945.
Nos. 357 to 361 exist imperforate.
No. 357a is a coarser printing from a new plate showing designer's name (J. Wilczyk) in lower left margin. No. 357 does not show his name.

Nos. 341 and 342 Surcharged in Black or Red:

5 zł
22.I.1863.
d

5 zł.
24. III. 1794
e

1945 *Perf. 11½*
362 A100(d) 5z on 25g crim rose 22.50 25.00
363 A101(e) 5z on 50g dp grn (R) 5.75 6.75

No. 362 was issued without gum.

No. 345 Surcharged in Brown

1 Zł

1945, Sept. 10 *Perf. 12½*

364	A104 1z on 50g dk sl grn	25	15

Lodz Skyline — A110

Kosciuszko Monument, Lodz — A111

Flag Bearer Carrying Wounded Comrade — A112

1945 **Litho.** *Perf. 11; 9 (3z)*

365	A110 1z dp ultra	40	15
366	A111 3z dl red vio	45	35
367	A112 5z dp car	1.50	1.50

Nos. 365 and 367 commemorate the liberation of Lodz and Warsaw.

Grunwald Battle Scene A113

Eagle Breaking Fetters and Manifesto of Freedom A114

1945, July 16

368	A113 5z dp bl	7.00	7.75

Battle of Grunwald (Tannenberg), July 15, 1410.

1945, July 22

369	A114 3z rose car	11.00	12.00

1st anniv. of the liberation of Poland.

Crane Tower, Gdansk A115

Stock Tower, Gdansk A116

Ancient High Gate, Gdansk — A117

1945, Sept. 15 **Photo.** **Unwmk.**

370	A115 1z olive	9	10
371	A116 2z sapphire	15	10
372	A117 3c dk vio	45	22

Recovery of Poland's access to the sea at Gdansk (Danzig).

Exist imperf. Value, set $25.

Civilian and Soldiers in Rebellion — A118

1945, Nov. 29

373	A118 10z black	6.50	6.00

115th anniv. of the "November Uprising" against the Russians, Nov. 29, 1830.

Warsaw Castle, 1939 and 1945 — A119

Views of Warsaw, 1939 and 1945: 3z, Cathedral of St. John. 3.50z, City Hall. 6z, Post Office. 8z, Army General Staff Headquarters. 10z, Holy Cross Church.

1945-46 **Unwmk.** ***Imperf.***

374	A119 1.50z crimson	16	10
375	A119 3z dk bl	28	10
376	A119 3.50z lt bl grn	70	42
377	A119 6z gray blk ('46)	28	22
378	A119 8z brn ('46)	1.40	42
379	A119 10z dk vio ('46)	60	22
	Nos. 374-379 (6)	3.42	1.48

Nos. 374 to 379 Overprinted in Black

WARSZAWA WOLNA 17 Styczeń 1945—1946

1946, Jan. 17

383	A119 1.50z crimson	90	1.25
384	A119 3z dk bl	90	1.25
385	A119 3.50z lt bl grn	90	1.25
386	A119 6z gray blk	90	1.25
387	A119 8z brown	90	1.25
388	A119 10z dk vio	90	1.25
	Nos. 383-388 (6)	5.40	7.50

1st anniv. of the liberation of Warsaw, Jan. 17, 1945.
Counterfeits exist.

Polish Revolutionist A125

Infantry Advancing A126

1946, Jan. 22 *Perf. 11*

389	A125 6z slate bl	5.50	5.00

Revolt of Jan. 22, 1863.

1946, May 9

390	A126 3z brown	20	10

Polish freedom, first anniversary.

Premier Edward Osubka-Morawski Pres. Boleslaw Bierut and Marshal Michael Rola-Zymierski — A127

Perf. 11x10½

1946, July 22 **Unwmk.**

391	A127 3z purple	1.90	2.00

Bedzin Castle A128

Duke Henry IV of Silesia, from Tomb at Wroclaw A129

Lanckrona Castle A130

1946, Sept. 1 **Photo.** ***Imperf.***

392	A128 5z ol gray	15	8
393	A128 5z brown	15	8

Perf. 10½

394	A129 6z gray blk	30	15

Imperf

395	A130 10z deep bl	65	20

Perforated copies of Nos. 392, 393 and 395 are said to have been privately made.

Jan Matejko, Jacek Malczewski, Josef Chelmonski A131

Adam Chmielowski (Brother Albert) — A132

Designs: 3z, Chopin. 5z, Wojciech Boguslawski, Helena Modjeska and Stefan Jaracz. 6z, Alexander Swietockowski, Stephen Zeromski and Boleslaw Prus. 10z, Marie Sklodowska Curie. 15z, Stanislaw Wyspianski, Juliusz Slowacki and Jan Kasprowicz. 20z, Adam Mickiewicz.

1947 ***Perf. 11, Imperf.***

396	A131 1z blue	20	12
397	A132 2z brown	32	18
398	A132 3z Prus grn	50	18
399	A131 5z ol grn	65	18
400	A131 6z gray grn	1.25	70
401	A132 10z gray brn	1.00	18
402	A131 15z sepia	1.50	55
403	A132 20z gray blk	1.50	75
	Nos. 396-403 (8)	6.92	2.84

No. 394 Surcharged in Red

5 * ZŁ *

1947, Feb. 25 *Perf. 10½*

404	A129 5z on 6z gray blk	25	15

Types of 1947

1947 **Photo.** ***Perf. 11, Imperf.***

405	A131 1z sl gray	14	14
406	A132 2z orange	14	10
407	A132 3z ol grn	1.10	35
408	A131 5z ol brn	24	10
409	A131 6z car rose	40	20
410	A132 10z blue	70	18
411	A131 15z chnt brn	55	32
412	A132 20z dk vio	40	50
a	Souvenir sheet of 8	140.00	165.00
	Nos. 405-412 (8)	3.67	1.89

No. 412a contains one each of Nos. 405 to 412, perf. 11½. The sheet has a face value of 62z and a surtax of 438z.

Laborer A139

Farmer A140

Fisherman A141

Miner A142

1947, Aug. 20 **Engr.** ***Perf. 13***

413	A139 5z rose brn	65	12
414	A140 10z brt bl grn	14	8
415	A141 15z dk bl	70	12
416	A142 20z brn blk	45	8

Allegory of the Revolution A143

Insurgents A144

1948, Mar. 15 **Photo.** ***Perf. 11***

417	A143 15z brown	25	10

Centenary of the Revolution of 1848. See Nos. 430-432.

1948, Apr. 19

418	A144 15z gray blk	1.10	1.25

5th anniv. of the ghetto uprising, Warsaw, Apr. 19, 1943.

Decorated Bicycle Wheel A145

1948, May 1

419	A145 15z brt rose & bl	2.25	80

1st Intl. Bicycle Peace Race, Warsaw-Prague-Warsaw.

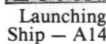

Launching Ship — A146

Loading Freighter — A147

Design: 35z, Racing yacht "Gen. Mariusz Zaruski."

1948, June 22

420 A146 6z violet	1.10	1.25
421 A147 15z brn car	1.25	1.25
422 A147 35z sl gray	2.25	2.00

Polish Merchant Marine.

Cyclists — A148

A149

1948, June 22

423 A148 3z gray	1.65	1.10
424 A148 6z brown	1.65	1.90
425 A148 15z green	1.65	2.50

7th Circuit of Poland Bicycle Race, June 22-July 4.

1948, July 15

426 A149 6z blue	28	25
427 A149 15z red	65	25
428 A149 18z rose brn	55	12
429 A149 35z dk brn	55	25

Exhibition to commemorate the recovery of Polish territories, Wroclaw, 1948.

Gen. Henryk Dembinski and Gen. Josef Bem — A150

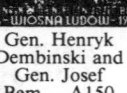

Symbolical of United Youth — A151

Designs: 35z, S. Worcell, P. Sciegienny and E. Dembowski. 60z, Friedrich Engels and Karl Marx.

1948, July 15

430 A150 30z dk brn	42	30
431 A150 35z ol grn	2.00	30
432 A150 60z brt rose	60	45

Revolution of 1848, cent. See No. 417.

1948, Aug. 8

433 A151 15z blue	42	25

Intl. Congress of Democratic Youth, Warsaw, Aug.

Stagecoach Leaving Torun Gate — A152

1948, Sept. 4

434 A152 15z brown	48	28

Philatelic Exhibition, Torun, Sept.

Clock Dial and Locomotive A153

Pres. Boleslaw Bierut A154

1948, Oct. 6 *Perf. 11½*

435 A153 18z blue	4.00	4.75

European Railroad Schedule Conference, Cracow.

1948-49 Unwmk. *Perf. 11, 11½*

436 A154 2z org ('49)	5	5
437 A154 3z bl grn ('49)	7	7
438 A154 5z brown	5	5
439 A154 6z slate	30	15
440 A154 10z vio ('49)	9	5
441 A154 15z dp car	15	8
442 A154 18z gray grn	35	20
443 A154 30z blue	55	15
444 A154 35z vio brn	1.65	30
Nos. 436-444 (9)	3.26	1.10

Workers Carrying Flag — A155

Designs: 15z, Marx, Engels, Lenin and Stalin. 25z, Ludwig Warynski.

Inscribed: "Kongres Jednosci Klasy Robotniczej 8. XII. 1948."

1948, Dec. 8 *Perf. 11*

445 A155 5z crimson	50	15
446 A155 15z dl vio	50	45
447 A155 25z brown	1.10	38

Redrawn

Dated: "XII. 1948."

Designs as before.

1948, Dec. 15 *Perf. 11½*

448 A155 5z brn car	1.75	90
449 A155 15z brt bl	1.75	90
450 A155 25z dk grn	2.50	1.75

Congress of the Union of the Working Class, Warsaw, Dec. 1948.

"Socialism" A156

Designs: 5z, "Labor." 15z, "Peace."

Perf. 11½

1949, May 31 Unwmk. Photo.

451 A156 3z car rose	90	90
452 A156 5z dp bl	90	90
453 A156 15z dp grn	1.25	1.25

8th Trade Union Congress, June 5, 1949.

Warsaw Scene A157

Pres. Boleslaw Bierut A158

Radio Station — A159

Perf. 13x12½, 12½x13

1949, July 22 Litho.

454 A157 10z gray blk	2.00	1.10
455 A158 15z lil rose	1.25	1.25
456 A159 35z gray bl	1.25	1.10

5th anniv. of "People's Poland."

Stagecoach and World Map — A160

Designs: 30z, Ship and map. 80z, Plane and map.

1949, Oct. 10 Engr. *Perf. 13x12½*

457 A160 6z gray pur	80	1.25
458 A160 30z blue	2.00	1.25
459 A160 80z dl grn	4.25	2.75

UPU, 75th anniv.

Symbolical of United Poland — A161

1949 *Perf. 13½x13*

460 A161 5z brn red	75	15
461 A161 10z rose red	18	7
462 A161 15z green	18	7
463 A161 35z dk brn	60	32

Congress of the People's Movement for Unity.

Adam Mickiewicz A162

Frederic Chopin A163

Design: 35z, Juliusz Slowacki.

1949, Dec. 5 *Perf. 12½*

464 A162 10z brn vio	2.25	1.10
465 A162 15z brn rose	3.50	1.75
466 A162 35z dp bl	2.25	1.10

Mail Delivery A164

Adam Mickiewicz and Pushkin A165

1950, Jan. 21

467 A164 15z red vio	2.25	1.25

3rd Congress of PTT Trade Unions, Jan. 21-23, 1950.

1949, Dec. 15

468 A165 15z lilac	2.50	1.25

Polish-Soviet friendship.

Pres. Boleslaw Bierut A166

Julian Marchlewski A167

1950, Feb. 25 Engr. *Perf. 12x12½*

469 A166 15z red	28	15

See Nos. 478-484, 490-496.

1950, Mar. 23 Photo. *Perf. 11x10½*

470 A167 15z gray blk	55	30

25th death anniv. of Julian Marchlewski, author and political leader.

Reconstruction, Warsaw — A168

Perf. 11, 12 and Compounds of 13

1950, Apr. 15

471 A168 5z dark brn	12	8

See No. 497.

Worker Holding Hammer, Flag and Olive Branch — A169

Workers of Three Races with Flag — A170

1950, Apr. 26 *Perf. 11½*

472 A169 10z dp lil rose	90	20
473 A170 15z brn ol	90	15

60th anniversary of Labor Day.

Freedom Monument, Poznan A171

Dove on Globe A172

1950, Apr. 27

474 A171 15z chocolate	22	10

Poznan Fair, Apr. 29-May 14, 1950.

1950, May 15 Unwmk.

475 A172 10z dk grn	60	14
476 A172 15z dk brn	30	8

Day of Intl. Action for World Peace.

Polish Workers A173

Hibner, Kniewski and Rutkowski A174

1950, July 20 *Perf. 12½x13*

477	A173	15z	vio bl	12	8

Poland's 6-year plan. See Nos. 507A-510, 539.

Bierut Type of 1950, No Frame

1950 **Engr.** *Perf. 12x12½*

478	A166	5z	dl grn	5	5
479	A166	10z	dl red	8	5
480	A166	15z	dp bl	55	12
481	A166	20z	vio brn	15	6
482	A166	25z	yel brn	24	6
482A	A166	30z	rose brn	28	12
483	A166	40z	brown	20	6
484	A166	50z	olive	90	24
			Nos. 478-484 (8)	2.45	76

1950, Aug. 18 **Photo.** *Perf. 11*

485	A174	15z	gray blk	1.40	50

25th anniv. of the execution of three Polish revolutionists, Wladyslaw Hibner, Wladyslaw Kniewski and Henryk Rutkowski.

Worker and Dove A175

Dove by Picasso A176

1950, Aug. 31 **Engr.** *Perf. 12½*

486	A175	15z	gray grn	28	10

Polish Peace Congress, Warsaw, 1950.

"GROSZY"

To provide denominations needed as a result of the currency revaluation of Oct. 28, 1950, each post office was authorized to surcharge stamps of its current stock with the word "Groszy." Many types and sizes of this surcharge exist. The surcharge was applied to most of Poland's 1946-1950 issues. All stamps of that period could receive the surcharge upon request of anyone. Counterfeits exist.

1950, Nov. 13

487	A176	40g	blue	90	30
488	A176	45g	brn red	30	10

2nd World Peace Congress.

Josef Bem and Battle Scene — A177

1950, Dec. 10

489	A177	45g	blue	1.50	1.00

Death centenary of Gen. Josef Bem.

Type of 1950 with Frame Omitted

Perf. 12x12½

1950, Dec. 16 **Engr.** **Unwmk.**

490	A166	5g	brn vio	7	8
491	A166	10g	bluish grn	10	8
492	A166	15g	dp yel grn	7	6
493	A166	25g	dk red	7	6
493A	A166	30g	red	20	8
494	A166	40g	vermilion	10	8
495	A166	45g	dp bl	85	18
496	A166	75g	brown	55	15
			Nos. 490-496 (8)	2.01	77

Reconstruction Type of 1950

Perf. 11, 11x11½, 13x11

1950 **Photo.**

497	A168	15g	green	12	8

Woman and Doves — A178

1951, Mar. 2 **Engr.** *Perf. 12½*

498	A178	45g	dk red	22	15

Congress of Women, March 3-4, 1951.

Gen. Jaroslaw Dabrowski A179

1951, Mar. 24 *Perf. 12x12½*

499	A179	45g	dk grn	18	14

80th anniv. of the Insurrection of Paris and the death of Gen. Jaroslaw Dabrowski.

Dove Type of 1950 Surcharged

1951, Apr. 20 *Perf. 12½*

500	A176	45g	on 15z brn red	38	15

Worker and Flag — A180

Steel Mill, Nowa Huta — A181

1951, Apr. 25 **Photo.** *Perf. 14x11*

501	A180	45g	scarlet	35	12

Labor Day, May 1.

1951 **Engr.** *Perf. 12½*

502	A181	40g	dk bl	7	5
503	A181	45g	black	10	5
504	A181	60g	brown	15	8
505	A181	90g	dk car	30	10

Pioneer Saluting A182

Boy and Girl Pioneers A183

1951, Apr. 1 **Photo.**

506	A182	30g	ol brn	75	50
507	A183	45g	brt grnsh bl	6.25	70

Issued to publicize Children's Day, June 1, 1951.

Workers Type of 1950

1951 **Unwmk.** **Engr.** *Perf. 12½x13*

507A	A173	45g	vio bl	10	7
508	A173	75g	blk brn	15	7
509	A173	1.15z	dk grn	40	20
510	A173	1.20z	dk red	25	20

Issued to publicize Poland's 6-year plan.

Stanislaw Staszyk — A184

Congress Emblem — A186

Z. F. von Wroblewski and Karol S. Olszewski A185

Portraits: 40g, Marie Sklodowska Curie. 60g, Marceli Nencki. 1.15z, Nicolaus Copernicus.

Perf. 12½, 14x11

1951, Apr. 25 **Photo.**

511	A184	25g	car rose	1.75	1.25
512	A184	40g	ultra	22	15
513	A185	45g	purple	6.50	1.25
514	A184	60g	green	50	15
515	A184	1.15z	claret	1.65	60
516	A186	1.20z	gray	1.25	45
			Nos. 511-516 (6)	11.87	3.85

1st Congress of Polish Science.

Feliks E. Dzerzhinski — A187

1951, July 5 **Engr.** *Perf. 12x12½*

517	A187	45g	chnt brn	20	8

25th death anniv. of Feliks E. Dzerzhinski, Polish revolutionary, organizer of Russian secret police.

Pres. Boleslaw Bierut — A188

1951, July 22 *Perf. 12½*

518	A188	45g	dk car	50	15
519	A188	60g	dp grn	11.50	6.00
520	A188	90g	dp bl	1.00	32

7th anniv. of the formation of the Polish People's Republic.

Flag and Sports Emblem A189

Youths Encircling Globe A190

Perf. 12½, 14x11

1951, Sept. 8 **Photo.**

521	A189	45g	green	85	38

National Sports Festival, 1951.

Type of 1950 with Frame Omitted Surcharged with New Value in Black

1951, Sept. 1 **Engr.** *Perf. 12½x11½*

522	A166	45g	on 35z org red	20	10

1951, Aug. 5 **Photo.** *Perf. 12½x11*

523	A190	40g	dp ultra	40	20

3rd World Youth Festival, Berlin, Aug. 5-19.

Joseph V. Stalin A191

Frederic Chopin and Stanislaw Moniuszko A192

1951, Oct. 30 **Engr.** *Perf. 12½*

524	A191	45g	lake	15	7
525	A191	90g	gray blk	30	14

Month of Polish-Soviet friendship, Nov. 1951.

1951, Nov. 15 **Unwmk.**

526	A192	45g	gray	20	6
527	A192	90g	brnsh red	90	24

Festival of Polish Music, 1951.

Apartment House Construction A193

Coal Mining A194

Design: Nos. 529-530, Electrical installation.

1951-52

Inscribed: "Plan 6," etc.

528	A193	30g	dl grn	12	6
529	A193	30g	gray blk ('52)	12	8
530	A193	45g	red ('52)	22	12
531	A194	90g	chocolate	38	12
532	A193	1.15z	vio brn ('52)	42	12
533	A194	1.20z	dp bl ('52)	42	18
			Nos. 528-533,B68-B69A (9)	2.93	1.38

Poland's 6-year plan.

Pawel Finder — A195

Flag, Workman, Mother and Child — A196

Portrait: 1.15z, Malgorzata Fornalska.

1952, Jan. 18

534	A195	90g	chocolate	18	9
535	A195	1.15z	red org	24	18

Polish Workers Party, 10th anniv.

1952, Mar. 8 *Perf. 12½x12*

536	A196	1.20z	dp car	28	15

Intl. Women's Day, Mar. 8, 1952. See No. B64.

The Scott Catalogue value is a retail price, what you could expect to pay for the stamp in a grade of Fine-Very Fine. The value listed is a reference which reflects recent actual dealer selling price.

Gen. Karol Swierczewski-Walter
A197

Pres. Boleslaw Bierut
A198

1952, Mar. 28 *Perf. 12½*
537 A197 90g bl gray 28 20

Gen. Karol Swierczewski-Walter (1896-1947). See No. B65.

1952, Apr. 18
538 A198 90g dl grn 55 45

60th birth anniv. of Pres. Boleslaw Bierut. See Nos. B66-B67.

Souvenir Sheet

A199

1951, Nov. 15
539 A199 Sheet of four 17.50 11.50
a 45g red brn (A173) 1.25 1.00
b 75g red brn (A173) 1.25 1.00
c 1.15z red brn (A173) 1.25 1.00
d 1.20z red brn (A173) 1.25 1.00

Polish Philatelic Association Congress, Warsaw, 1951. Sold for 5 zloty.

Workers with Flag
A200

J. I. Kraszewski
A201

1952, May 1 Unwmk. *Perf. 12½*
540 A200 75g dp grn 25 15

Labor Day, May 1, 1952. See No. B70.

1952, May

Portraits: 1z, Hugo Kollontaj. 1.15z, Maria Konopnicka.

Various Frames

541 A201 25g brn vio 28 15
542 A201 1z yel grn 30 9
543 A201 1.15z red brn 60 35
Nos. 541-543,B71-B72 (5) 1.80 83

Nikolai Gogol
A202

Gymnast
A203

1952, June 5
544 A202 25g dp grn 60 38

100th death anniv. of Nikolai V. Gogol, writer.

1952, June 21 Photo. *Perf. 13*
545 A203 1.15z Runners 1.40 90
546 A203 1.20z shown 60 52

See Nos. B75-B76.

Racing Cyclists
A204

Shipyard Worker and Collier
A205

1952, Apr. 25 *Perf. 13½*
547 A204 40g blue 90 42

5th Intl. Peace Bicycle Race, Warsaw-Berlin-Prague.

1952, June 28 Engr. *Perf. 12½*
548 A205 90g vio brn 60 32

Shipbuilders' Day, 1952. See Nos. B77-B78.

Concrete Works, Wierzbica
A206

Bugler
A207

1952, June 17
549 A206 3z gray 75 38
550 A206 10z brn red 1.25 25

1952, July 17 *Perf. 12½x12*
551 A207 90g brown 40 15

Youth Festival, 1952. See Nos. B79-B80.

Celebrating New Constitution
A208

Power Plant, Jaworzno
A209

1952, July 22 Photo. *Perf. 12½*
552 A208 3z vio & dk brn 30 24

Proclamation of a new constitution. See No. B81.

1952, Aug. 7 **Engr.**
553 A209 1z black 45 25
554 A209 1.50z dp grn 45 15

See No. B82.

A particular stamp may be scarce, but if few collectors want it, its market value may remain relatively low.

Grywald
A210

Parachute Descent
A211

Design: 1z, Niedzica.

1952, Aug. 18
555 A210 60g dk grn 35 40
556 A210 1z red ("Niedzica") 60 10
a 1z red ("Niedziga") 2.25 75

See No. B85.

1952, Aug. 23
557 A211 90g dp bl 55 45

Aviation Day, Aug. 23. See Nos. B86-B87.

Avicenna
A212

Shipbuilding
A213

Portrait: 90g, Victor Hugo.

1952, Sept. 1
558 A212 75g red brn 28 12
559 A212 90g sepia 20 8

Anniversaries of the births of Avicenna (1000th) and Victor Hugo (150th).

1952, Sept. 10
560 A213 5g dp grn 8 5
561 A213 15g red brn 12 8

Reconstruction of Gdansk shipyards.

Assault on the Winter Palace, 1917
A214

1952, Nov. 7 *Perf. 12x12½*
562 A214 60g dk brn 50 32

35th anniv. of the Russian Revolution. See No. B92.
Exists imperf. Value $24.

Auto Assembly Plant, Zeran — A215

Dove — A216

1952, Dec. 12 *Perf. 12½*
563 A215 1.15z brown 35 14

See No. B99.

1952, Dec. 12 **Photo.**
564 A216 30g green 50 20
565 A216 60g ultra 1.10 52

Congress of Nations for Peace, Vienna, Dec. 12-19, 1952.

Catalogue values for unused stamps in this section, from this point to the end of the section, are for Never Hinged items.

Soldier with Flag — A217

Karl Marx — A218

1953, Feb. 2 Unwmk. *Perf. 11*
Flag in Carmine
566 A217 60g ol gray 3.25 85
567 A217 80g bl gray 70 40

10th anniv. of the Battle of Stalingrad.

1953, Mar. 14 *Perf. 12½*
568 A218 60g dl bl 15.00 8.25
569 A218 80g dk brn 70 32

70th death anniv. of Karl Marx.

Cyclists and Arms of Warsaw
A219

Flag and Globe
A220

Arms: No. 571, Berlin. No. 572, Prague.

1953, Apr. 30
570 A219 80g dk brn 1.00 35
571 A219 80g dk grn 1.00 35
572 A219 80g red 12.00 8.75

6th Intl. Peace Bicycle Race, Warsaw-Berlin-Prague.

1953, Apr. 28
573 A220 60g vermilion 3.00 1.25
574 A220 80g carmine 50 12

Labor Day, May 1, 1953.

Boxer — A221

Design: 95g, Boxing match.

1953, May 17
575 A221 40g red brn 1.10 42
576 A221 80g orange 11.00 5.25
577 A221 95g vio brn 1.65 1.50

European Championship Boxing Matches, Warsaw, May 17-24, 1953.

Copernicus Watching Heavens, by Jan Matejko
A222

Nicolaus Copernicus — A223

Perf. 12x12½, 12½x12

1953, May 22 **Engr.**

578 A222	20g	brown	1.10	35
579 A223	80g	dp bl	9.25	4.50

480th birth anniv. of Nicolaus Copernicus, astronomer.

Fishing Boat A224

Old Part of Warsaw A225

Design: 1.35z, Freighter "Czech."

1953, July 15 ***Perf. 12½***

580 A224	80g	dk grn	1.10	25
581 A224	1.35z	dp bl	2.00	90

Issued for Merchant Marine Day.

1953, July 15 **Photo.**

582 A225	20g	red brn	18	6
583 A225	2.35z	blue	1.75	90

36th anniv. of the proclamation of "People's Poland."

Students of Two Races — A226

Schoolgirl and Dove — A227

Design: 1.35z, Congress badge (similar to AP7).

1953, Aug. 24

584 A226	40g	dk brn	25	12
585 A227	1.35z	green	60	8
586 A227	1.50z	blue	1.40	1.25
	Nos. 584-586,C32-C33 (5)		4.35	2.65

3rd World Congress of Students, Warsaw, 1953.

Nurse Feeding Baby — A228

Design: 1.75z, Nurse instructing mother.

1953, Nov. 21

587 A228	80g	rose car	6.25	3.00
588 A228	1.75z	dp grn	35	15

Poland's Social Health Service.

Mieczyslaw Kalinowski A229

Battle Scene, Polish and Soviet Flags A230

Portrait: 1.75z, Roman Pazinski.

1953, Oct. 10

589 A229	45g	brown	3.00	2.00
590 A230	80g	brn lake	48	10
591 A229	1.75z	ol gray	48	16

10th anniv. of Poland's People's Army.

Jan Kochanowski A231

Courtyard, Wawel Castle A232

Portrait: 1.35z, Mikolaj Rej.

1953, Nov. 10 **Engr.**

592 A231	20g	red brn	15	6
593 A232	80g	dp plum	30	6
594 A231	1.35z	gray blk	1.25	60

Issued for the "Renaissance Year."

Palace of Culture, Warsaw A233

Designs: 1.75z, Constitution Square. 2z, Old Section, Warsaw.

1953, Nov. 30 ***Perf. 12x12½***

595 A233	80g	vermilion	6.75	1.10
596 A233	1.75z	dp bl	48	38
597 A233	2z	vio brn	4.00	2.25

Issued for the reconstruction of Warsaw.

Ice Dancer A236

Skier A237

Design: 2.85z, Ice hockey player.

1953, Dec. 31 **Litho.** ***Perf. 12½***

602 A236	80g	blue	1.25	30
603 A237	95g	bl grn	1.75	50
604 A236	2.85z	dk red	4.75	2.00

Canceled to Order

The government stamp agency began late in 1951 to sell canceled sets of new issues. Values in the second ("used") column are for these canceled-to-order stamps. Postally used copies are worth more.

Children at Play — A238

Designs: 80g, Girls on the way to school. 1.50z, Two students in class.

1953, Dec. 31 **Photo.**

605 A238	10g	violet	15	6
606 A238	80g	red brn	60	25
607 A238	1.50z	dk grn	4.00	1.65

Krynica Spa A239

Dunajec Canyon, Pieniny Mountains A240

Designs: 80g, Morskie Oko, Tatra Mts. 2z, Windmill and framework, Ciechocinek.

1953, Dec. 16

608 A239	20g	bl & rose brn	15	10
609 A240	80g	bl grn & dk vio	1.65	90
610 A240	1.75z	ol bis & dk grn	65	10
611 A239	2z	brick red & blk	95	15

Electric Passenger Train A241

Spinning Mill, Worker A242

1954, Jan. 26 **Engr.**

Design: 80g, Electric locomotive and cars.

612 A241	60g	deep bl	6.00	4.00
613 A241	80g	red brn	52	18

1954, Mar. 24 **Photo.**

Designs: 40g, Woman letter carrier. 80g, Woman tractor driver.

614 A242	20g	dp grn	1.25	45
615 A242	40g	dp bl	52	12
616 A242	80g	dk brn	35	12

Flags and May Flowers A243

"Peace" Uniting Three Capitals A244

1954, Apr. 28

617 A243	40g	chocolate	60	22
618 A243	60g	dp bl	60	12
619 A243	80g	car rose	60	20

Labor Day, May 1, 1954.

1954, Apr. 29 ***Perf. 12½x12***

Design: No. 621, Dove, olive branch and wheel.

620 A244	80g	red brn	50	12
621 A244	80g	dp bl	52	12

7th Intl. Bicycle Tour, May 2-17, 1954.

Demand, as well as supply, determines a stamp's market value. One is as important as the other.

A245

Glider and Framed Clouds — A246

1954, Apr. 30 **Engr.** ***Perf. 11½***

622 A245	25g	gray	55	20
623 A245	80g	brn car	20	7

3rd Trade Union Congress, Warsaw 1954.

1954, May 31 **Photo.** ***Perf. 12½***

Designs: 60g, Glider and flags. 1.35z, Glider and large cloud.

624 A246	45g	dk grn	55	6
625 A246	60g	purple	2.00	80
626 A246	60g	brown	1.10	14
627 A246	1.35z	blue	1.40	28

Intl. Glider Championships, Leszno.

Fencing — A247

Handstand on Horizontal Bars — A248

Design: 1z, Relay racers.

1954, July 17

628 A247	25g	vio brn	1.40	30
629 A248	60g	Prus bl	1.40	15
630 A247	1z	vio bl	2.75	45

Javelin Throwers A249

Studzianki Battle Scene A250

1954, July 17 ***Perf. 12***

631 A249	60g	rose brn & dk red brn	1.25	22
632 A249	1.55z	gray & blk	1.10	35

Nos. 628-632 were issued to publicize the second Summer Spartacist Games, 1954.

1954, Aug. 24 ***Perf. 12½***

Design: 1z, Soldier and flag bearer.

633 A250	60g	dk grn	1.50	40
634 A250	1z	vio bl	6.50	1.25

10th anniversary, Battle of Studzianki.

Railway Signal A251

Farmer Picking Fruit A252

Design: 60g, Modern train.

1954, Sept. 9

635 A251	40g	dl bl	2.00	70
636 A251	60g	black	1.90	32

Issued to publicize Railwaymen's Day.

1954, Sept. 15

637	A252	40g violet	1.25	52
638	A252	60g black	55	15

Month of Polish-Soviet friendship.

View of Elblag
A253

Chopin and Piano
A254

Cities: 45g, Gdansk. 60g, Torun. 1.40z, Malbork. 1.55z, Olsztyn.

1954, Oct. 16 Engr. *Perf. 12x12½*

639	A253	20g dk car, *bl*	1.75	70
640	A253	45g brn, *yel*	16	7
641	A253	60g dk grn, *cit*	20	7
642	A253	1.40z dk bl, *pink*	45	7
643	A253	1.55z dk vio brn, *cr*	65	15
		Nos. 639-643 (5)	3.21	1.06

Pomerania's return to Poland, 500th anniv.

1954, Nov. 8 Photo. *Perf. 12½*

644	A254	45g dk brn	50	8
645	A254	60g dk grn	95	12
646	A254	1z dk bl	2.25	55

5th Intl. Competition of Chopin's Music.

Coal Mine — A255

Designs: 20g, Soldier, flag and map. 25g, Steel mill. 40g, Relaxing worker in deck chair. 45g, Building construction. 60g, Tractor in field. 1.15z, Lublin Castle. 1.40z, Books and publications. 1.55z, Loading ship. 2.10z, Attacking tank.

Photo.; Center Engr.

1954-55 *Perf. 12½x12*

647	A255	10g red brn & choc	95	15
648	A255	20g rose & grnsh blk	55	45
649	A255	25g bis & blk ('55)	1.25	25
650	A255	40g yel org & choc	38	25
651	A255	45g cl & vio brn	75	25
652	A255	60g emer & red brn ('55)	75	35
653	A255	1.15z brt bl grn & sep	75	75
654	A255	1.40z org & choc	7.50	3.50
655	A255	1.55z bl & ind	1.50	1.00
656	A255	2.10z ultra & ind	2.50	2.00
		Nos. 647-656 (10)	16.88	8.95

10th anniversary of "People's Poland."
Issue dates: 25g, 60g, 1955. Others, Dec. 23, 1954.

Photo.; Center Litho.

1954, Oct. 30

656A	A255	25g bis & blk	2.00	1.40
656B	A255	60g emer & red brn	1.10	90

Insurgents Attacking Russians — A256

Designs: 60g, Gen. Tadeusz Kosciuszko and insurgents. 1.40z, Kosciuszko leading attack in Cracow.

1954, Nov. 30 Engr. *Perf. 12½*

657	A256	40g grnsh blk	35	14
658	A256	60g vio brn	52	16
659	A256	1.40z dk gray	1.40	70

160th anniv. of the Insurrection of 1794.

Bison — A257

Animals: 60g, European elk. 1.90z, Chamois. 3z, Beaver.

Engr.; Background Photo.

1954, Dec. 22

660	A257	45g yel grn & blk brn	35	14
661	A257	60g emer & dk brn	35	14
662	A257	1.90z bl & blk brn	50	14
663	A257	3z bl grn & dk brn	1.50	42

Exist imperf. Value, set $3.50.

Liberators Entering Warsaw
A258

Frederic Chopin
A259

Design: 60g, Allegory of freedom (Warsaw Mermaid).

1955, Jan. 17 Photo.

664	A258	40g red brn	48	32
665	A258	60g dull bl	1.25	65

Liberation of Warsaw, 10th anniversary.

1955, Feb. 22 Engr.

666	A259	40g dk brn	35	7
667	A259	60g indigo	65	20

5th Intl. Competition of Chopin's Music, Feb. 22-Mar. 21.

Brothers in Arms Monument
A260

Sigismund III
A261

Warsaw monuments: 5g, Mermaid. 10g, Feliks E. Dzerzhinski. 40g, Nicolaus Copernicus. 45g, Marie Sklodowska Curie. 60g, Adam Mickiewicz. 1.55z, Jan Kilinski.

1955, May 3 Unwmk. *Perf. 12½*

668	A260	5g dk grn, *grnsh*	5	5
669	A260	10g vio brn, *yel*	5	5
670	A261	15g blk brn, *bluish*	5	5
671	A260	20g dk bl, *pink*	5	5
672	A260	40g vio, *vio*	35	10
673	A261	45g vio brn, *cr*	48	22
674	A260	60g dk bl, *gray*	35	10
675	A261	1.55z sl bl, *grysh*	95	32
		Nos. 668-675 (8)	2.33	94

See Nos. 737-739.

Palace of Culture and Flags of Poland and USSR — A262

Design: 60g, Monument.

Perf. 12½x12, 11

1955, Apr. 21 Photo.

676	A262	40g rose red	15	7
677	A262	40g lt brn	45	28
678	A262	60g Prus bl	20	7
679	A262	60g dk ol brn	20	7

10th anniv. of the Polish-USSR treaty of friendship.

Arms and Bicycle Wheels
A263

Poznan Town Hall and Fair Emblem
A264

Design: 60g, Three doves above road.

1955, Apr. 25 *Perf. 12*

680	A263	40g chocolate	35	14
681	A263	60g ultra	22	6

8th Intl. Peace Bicycle Race, Prague-Berlin-Warsaw.

1955, June 10 Photo. *Perf. 12½*

682	A264	40g brt ultra	30	14
683	A264	60g dl red	15	6

24th Intl. Fair at Poznan, July 3-24, 1955.

"Laikonik" Carnival Costume — A265

A265a

1955, June 16 Typo. *Perf. 12*

Multicolored Centers

684	A265	20g emer & hn	30	22
685	A265a	40g brt org & lil	42	8
686	A265	60g bl & car	1.25	30

Cracow Celebration Days.

Pansies — A266

Designs: 40g, 60g, (No. 690), Dove and Tower of Palace of Science and Culture. 45g, Pansies. 60g, (No. 691), 1z, "Peace" (POKOJ) and Warsaw Mermaid.

1955, July 13 Litho. *Perf. 12*

687	A266	25g vio brn, org & car	15	7
688	A266	40g gray bl & gray blk	15	7
689	A266	45g brn lake, yel & car	30	10
690	A266	60g sep & org	24	15
691	A266	60g ultra & lt bl	24	15
692	A266	1z pur & lt bl	75	50
		Nos. 687-692 (6)	1.83	1.04

5h World Festival of Youth, Warsaw, July 31-Aug. 14, 1955.
Exist imperf. Value, set $3.

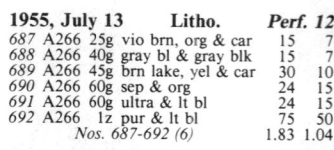

Motorcyclists
A267

Stalin Palace of Culture and Science, Warsaw
A268

1955, July 20 Photo. *Perf. 12½*

693	A267	40g chocolate	30	20
694	A267	60g dk grn	24	7

13th Intl. Motorcycle Race in the Tatra Mountains, Aug. 7-9, 1955.

1955, July 21

695	A268	60g ultra	15	7
696	A268	60g gray	15	7
697	A268	75g bl grn	35	15
698	A268	75g brown	35	15

Polish National Day, July 22, 1955. Sheets contain alternating copies of the 60g values or the 75g values respectively.

Athletes
A269

Stadium
A270

Designs: 40g, Hammer throwing. 1z, Basketball. 1.35z, Sculling. 1.55z, Swimming.

1955, July 27 Unwmk. *Perf. 12½*

699	A269	20g chocolate	7	5
700	A269	40g plum	14	7
701	A270	60g dl bl	24	7
702	A269	1z org ver	45	14
703	A269	1.35z dl vio	60	14
704	A269	1.55z pck grn	1.00	50
		Nos. 699-704 (6)	2.50	97

2nd International Youth Games, 1955.
Exist imperf. Value, set $3.50.

Town Hall, Szczecin (Stettin) — A271

Revolutionaries with Flag — A272

Designs: 40g, Cathedral, Wroclaw (Breslau) 60g, Town Hall, Zielona Gora (Grunberg). 95g, Town Hall, Opole (Oppeln).

1955, Sept. 22 Engr. *Perf. 11½*

705	A271	25g dl grn	12	10
706	A271	40g red brn	16	8
707	A271	60g vio bl	40	8
708	A271	95g dk gray	60	24

10th anniv. of the acquisition of Western Polish Territories.

1955, Sept. 30 Photo. *Perf. 12x12½*

709	A272	40g dk brn	25	20
710	A272	60g dk car rose	22	10

Revolution of 1905, 50th anniversary.

Adam Mickiewicz A273

Mickiewicz Monument, Paris — A274

Designs: 60g, Death mask. 95g, Statue, Warsaw.

1955, Oct. 10 *Perf. 12x12½, 12½*

711	A273	20g dk brn	15	8
712	A274	40g brn org & dk brn	18	8
713	A274	60g grn & brn	25	8
714	A274	95g brn red & blk	1.50	50

Death centenary of Adam Mickiewicz, poet, and to publicize the celebration of Mickiewicz year.

Teacher and Child A275

Rook and Hands A276

Design: 60g, Flame and open book.

Perf. 12½x13

1955, Oct. 21 Unwmk.

715	A275	40g brown	1.50	25
716	A275	60g ultra	2.50	85

50th anniv. of the Polish Teachers' Trade Union.

1956, Feb. 9 *Perf. 12½*

Design: 60g, Chess knight and hands.

717	A276	40g dk red	1.90	85
718	A276	60g blue	1.50	15

First World Chess Championship of the Deaf and Dumb, Feb. 9-23.

Captain and S. S. Kilinski A277

Designs: 10g, Sailor and barges. 20g, Dock worker and S. S. Pokoj. 45g, Shipyard and worker. 60g, Fisherman, S. S. Chopin and trawlers.

1956, Mar. 16 Engr. *Perf. 12x12½*

719	A277	5g green	5	5
720	A277	10g car lake	5	5
721	A277	20g dp ultra	10	5
722	A277	45g rose brn	55	20
723	A277	60g vio bl	45	5
		Nos. 719-723 (5)	1.20	40

Snowflake and Ice Skates A278

Cyclist A279

Designs: 40g, Snowflake and Ice Hockey sticks. 60g, Snowflake and Skis.

1956, Mar. 7 Photo. *Perf. 12½*

724	A278	20g brt ultra & blk	3.50	1.50
725	A278	40g brt grn & vio bl	52	8
726	A278	60g lil & lake	52	12

XI World Students Winter Sport Championship, Mar. 7-13.

1956, Apr. 25

727	A279	40g dk bl	1.25	40
728	A279	60g dk grn	20	8

9th Intl. Peace Bicycle Race, Warsaw-Berlin-Prague, May 1-15.

Zakopane Mountains and Shelter — A280

Designs: 40g, Map, compass and knapsack. 60g, Map of Poland and canoe. 1.15z, Skis and mountains.

1956, May 25

729	A280	30g dk grn	25	7
730	A280	40g lt red brn	25	7
731	A280	60g blue	95	50
732	A280	1.15z dl pur	45	12

Polish Tourist industry.

No. 593 Surcharged with New Values

1956, July 6 Engr. *Perf. 12½*

733	A232	10g on 80g dp plum	18	8
734	A232	40g on 80g dp plum	14	8
735	A232	60g on 80g dp plum	28	8
736	A232	1.35z on 80g dp plum	70	32

The size and type of surcharge and obliteration of old value differ for each denomination.

Type of 1955

1956, July 10

Warsaw Monuments: 30g, Ghetto Monument. 40g, John III Sobieski. 1.55z, Prince Joseph Poniatowski.

737	A260	30g black	14	5
738	A260	40g red brn, *grnsh*	30	16
739	A260	1.55z vio brn, *pnksh*	42	16

No. 737 measures 22½x28mm., instead of 21x27mm.

Polish and Russian Dancers A281

Design: 60g, Open book and cogwheels.

1956, Sept. 14 Litho. *Perf. 12*

740	A281	40g brn red & brn	30	20
741	A281	60g bis & red	15	8

Polish-Soviet Friendship month.

Ludwiga Warzynska and Children A282

Bee on Clover and Beehive A283

1956, Sept. 17 Photo. *Perf. 12½*

742	A282	40g dl red brn	70	20
743	A282	60g blue	32	7

Issued in honor of a heroic school teacher who saved three children from a burning house.

1956, Oct. 30 Litho. Unwmk.

Design: 60g, Father Jan Dzierzon.

744	A283	40g org yel & brn	75	25
745	A283	60g yel & brn	22	7

50th death anniv. of Father Jan Dzierzon, the inventor of the modernized beehive.

"Lady with the Ermine" by Leonardo da Vinci A284

Designs: 40g, Niobe. 60g, Madonna by Veit Stoss.

1956 Engr. *Perf. 11½x11*

746	A284	40g dk grn	2.50	75
747	A284	60g dk vio	80	24
748	A284	1.55z chocolate	1.65	24

Intl. Museum Week (UNESCO), Oct. 8-14.

Fencer A285

Designs: 20g, Boxer. 25g, Sculling. 40g, Steeplechase racer. 60g, Javelin thrower. No. 755, Woman gymnast. No. 756, Woman broad jumper.

1956 Engr. *Perf. 11½*

750	A285	10g sl & chnt	14	7
751	A285	20g lt brn & dl vio	24	7
752	A285	25g lt bl & blk	35	15
753	A285	40g brt bl grn & redsh brn	28	7
754	A285	60g rose car & ol brn	35	14
755	A285	1.55z lt vio & sep	1.40	1.00
756	A285	1.55z org & chnt	90	22
		Nos. 750-756 (7)	3.66	1.72

16th Olympic Games, Melbourne, Nov. 22-Dec. 8.

15th Century Mailman — A286

Lithographed and Engraved

1956, Nov. 30 Unwmk. *Perf. 12½*

757	A286	60g lt bl & blk	1.10	70

Reopening of the Postal Museum in Wroclaw.

Skier and Snowflake A287

Ski Jumper and Snowflake A288

Design: 1z, Skier in right corner.

1957, Jan. 18 Photo. *Perf. 12½*

758	A287	40g blue	30	7
759	A288	60g dk grn	30	10
760	A287	1z purple	55	30

50 years of skiing in Poland.

Globe and Tree — A289

UN Emblem — A290

UN Building, NY — A291

1957, Feb. 26 Photo. *Perf. 12*

761	A289	5g mag & brt grnsh bl	30	20
762	A290	15g bl & gray	38	20
763	A291	40g brt bl grn & gray	70	45

Issued in honor of the United Nations. Exist imperf. Value, set $4.25.

An imperf. souvenir sheet exists, containing a 1.50z stamp in a redrawn design similar to A291. The stamp is blue and bright bluish green Value, $25 unused, $14 canceled.

Skier — A292

Sword, Foil and Saber on World Map — A293

1957, Mar. 22 *Perf. 12½*

764	A292	60g blue	48	22
765	A292	60g brown	65	28

12th anniv. of the death of the skiers Bronislaw Czech and Hanna Marusarzowna.

1957, Apr. 20 Unwmk. *Perf. 12½*

Designs: No. 767, Fencer facing right. No. 768, Fencer facing left.

766	A293	40g dp plum	55	32
767	A293	60g carmine	38	7
768	A293	60g ultra	38	7
a		Nos. 767-768 se-tenant	1.25	50

World Youth Fencing Championships, Warsaw.

Nos. 767-768 are printed se-tenant in the sheet, the fencers facing each other with swords crossed on No. 768.

Values quoted in this catalogue are for stamps graded at Fine-Very Fine and with no faults. An illustrated guide to grade is provided in introductory material, beginning on Page V.

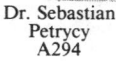

Dr. Sebastian Petrycy
A294

Bicycle Wheel and Carnation
A295

Doctors' Portraits: 20g Wojciech Oczko. 40g, Jedrzej Sniadecki. 60g, Tytus Chalubinski. 1z, Wladyslaw Bieganski. 1.35z, Jozef Dietl. 2.50z, Benedykt Dybowski. 3z, Henryk Jordan.

Portraits Engr., Inscriptions Typo.

1957 *Perf. 11½*

769 A294 10g sep & ultra 5 5
770 A294 20g emer & cl 5 5
771 A294 40g gray & org red 7 5
772 A294 60g bl & pale brn 35 16
773 A294 1z org & dk bl 15 6
774 A294 1.35z gray brn & grn 20 6
775 A294 2.50z dl vio & lil rose 42 6
776 A294 3z vio & ol brn 50 8
Nos. 769-776 (8) 1.79 57

1957, May 4 Photo. *Perf. 12½*

Design: 1.50z, Cyclist.

777 A295 60g ultra 55 20
778 A295 1.50z brt car rose 18 14

10th Intl. Peace Bicycle Race, Warsaw-Berlin-Prague.

Poznan Fair Emblem
A296

Turk's Cap
A297

1957, June 8 Litho. Unwmk.

779 A296 60g ultra 22 10
780 A296 2.50z lt bl grn 30 10

Issued to publicize the 26th Fair at Poznan.

1957, Aug. 12 Photo. *Perf. 12*

Flowers: No. 782, Carline Thistle. No. 783, Sea Holly. No. 784, Edelweiss. No. 785, Lady's-slipper.

781 A297 60g bl grn & cl 18 7
782 A297 60g gray, grn & yel 18 7
783 A297 60g lt bl & grn 18 7
784 A297 60g gray & yel grn 18 7
785 A297 60g lt grn, mar & yel 75 25
Nos. 781-785 (5) 1.47 53

Fire Fighter
A298

Town Hall, Leipzig and Congress Emblem
A299

Designs: 60g, Child and flames. 2.50z, Grain and flames.

1957, Sept. 11 ***Perf. 12***

786 A298 40g blk & red 7 5
787 A298 60g dk grn & org red 7 5
788 A298 2.50z vio & red 42 20

Intl. Fire Brigade Conf., Warsaw.

1957, Sept. 25 Photo. *Perf. 12½*

789 A299 60g violet 15 10

4th Intl. Trade Union Congress, Leipzig, Oct. 4-15.

"Girl Writing Letter" by Fragonard
A300

Karol Libelt
A301

1957, Oct. 9 ***Perf. 12***

790 A300 2.50z dk bl grn 45 10

Issued for Stamp Day, Oct. 9.

1957, Nov. 15 Photo. *Perf. 12½*

791 A301 60g car lake 16 10

Centenary of the Poznan Scientific Society and to honor Karol Libelt, politician and philosopher.

Broken Chain and Revolutionary Flag — A302

Jan A. Komensky (Comenius) — A303

Design: 2.50z, Lenin Statue, Poronin.

1957, Nov. 7

792 A302 60g brt bl & red 10 8
793 A302 2.50z blk & red brn 25 12

40th anniv. of the Russian Revolution.

1957, Dec. 11 ***Perf. 12***

794 A303 2.50z brt car 25 10

300th anniv. of the publication of "Didactica Opera Omnia."

Henri Wieniawski
A304

Andrzej Strug
A305

1957, Dec. 2 ***Perf. 12½***

795 A304 2.50z blue 25 10

3rd Wieniawski Violin Competition in Poznan.

1957, Dec. 16 Unwmk. *Perf. 12½*

796 A305 2.50z brown 18 10

20th death anniv. of Andrzej Strug, novelist.

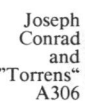

Joseph Conrad and "Torrens"
A306

1957, Dec. 30 Engr. *Perf. 12x12½*

797 A306 60g brn, *grnsh* 14 8
798 A306 2.50z dk bl, *pink* 42 18

Birth cent. of Joseph Conrad, Polish-born English writer.

Postilion and Stylized Plane
A307

Town Hall at Biecz
A308

Designs: 40g, Tomb of Prosper Prowano, globe with plane and satellite. 60g, St. Mary's Church, Cracow, mail coach and plane. 95g, Mail coach and postal bus. 2.10z, Medieval postman and train. 3.40z, Medieval galleon and modern ships.

1958 Litho. *Perf. 12½*

799 A307 40g lt bl & vio brn 5 5
800 A307 60g pale vio & blk 6 5
801 A307 95g lem & vio 6 5
802 A307 2.10z gray & ultra 42 32
803 A307 2.50z brt bl & blk 30 9
804 A307 3.40z aqua & mar 30 9
Nos. 799-804 (6) 1.19 65

400th anniversary of the Polish posts. Imperfs. exist of all but No. 803.

1958, Mar. 29 Engr. *Perf. 12½*

Town Halls: 40g, Wroclaw. 60g, Tarnow (horiz.). 2.10z, Danzig. 2.50z, Zamosc.

805 A308 20g green 5 5
806 A308 40g brown 6 5
807 A308 60g dk bl 6 5
808 A308 2.10z rose lake 24 7
809 A308 2.50z violet 35 14
Nos. 805-809 (5) 76 36

Giant Pike Perch — A309

Fishes: 60g, Salmon (vert.). 2.10z, Pike (vert.). 2.50z, Trout (vert.). 6.40z, Grayling (horiz.).

1958, Apr. 22 Photo. *Perf. 12*

810 A309 40g bl, blk, grn & yel 9 6
811 A309 60g yel grn, dk grn & bl 9 6
812 A309 2.10z dk bl, grn & yel 28 12
813 A309 2.50z pur, blk & yel grn 1.10 24
814 A309 6.40z bl grn, brn & red 65 30
Nos. 810-814 (5) 2.21 78

Casimir Palace, Warsaw University
A310

Stylized Glider and Cloud
A311

1958, May 14 Unwmk. *Perf. 12½*

815 A310 2.50z vio bl 20 12

140th anniv. of the University of Warsaw.

1958, June 14 Litho.

Design: 2.50z, Design reversed.

816 A311 60g gray bl & blk 14 6
817 A311 2.50z gray & blk 35 14

7th Intl. Glider Competitions.

Fair Emblem
A312

Armed Postman and Mail Box
A313

1958, June 9

818 A312 2.50z blk & rose 20 10

27th Fair at Poznan.

1958, Sept. 1 Engr. *Perf. 11*

819 A313 60g dk bl 15 10

19th anniversary of the defense of the Polish post office at Danzig (Gdansk). Inscribed: "You were the first."

Letter, Quill and Postmark
A314

Polar Bear
A315

1958, Oct. 9 Litho.

820 A314 60g blk, bl grn & ver 42 25

Issued for Stamp Day. Exists imperf.

1958 Sept. 30 Photo. *Perf. 12½x12*

Design: 2.50z, Rocket and Sputnik.

821 A315 60g black 18 7
822 A315 2.50z dk bl 55 14

Intl. Geophysical Year.

Partisan's Cross — A316

Designs: 60g, Virtuti Militari Cross. 2.50z, Grunwald Cross.

1958, Oct. 10 ***Perf. 11***

823 A316 40g blk, grn & ocher 15 7
824 A316 60g blk, bl & yel 15 7
825 A316 2.50z multi 60 20

Polish People's Army, 15th anniv.

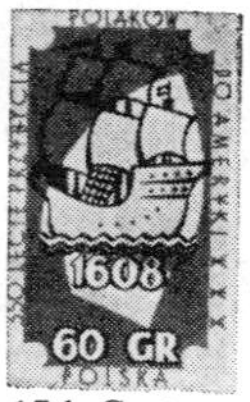

17th Century Ship — A317

UNESCO Building, Paris — A318

Design: 2.50z, Polish immigrants.

1958, Oct. 29 *Perf. 11*
826 A317 60g dk sl grn 10 7
827 A317 2.50z dk car rose 25 12

350th anniversary of the arrival of the first Polish immigrants in America.

1958, Nov. 3 **Unwmk.**
828 A318 2.50z yel grn & blk 32 10

Opening of UNESCO Headquarters in Paris, Nov. 3.

Stagecoach — A319

Wmk. 326 - Post Horn Multiple

Wmk. 326
1958, Oct. 26 **Engr.** *Perf. 12½*
829 A319 2.50z slate, *buff* 80 48
a Souvenir sheet of 6 6.75 6.75

Philatelic exhibition in honor of the 400th anniv. of the Polish post, Warsaw, Oct. 25-Nov. 10.

Souvenir Sheet
1958, Dec. 12 **Unwmk.** *Imperf.*
Printed on Silk
830 A319 50z dk bl 8.75 8.75

400th anniversary of the Polish posts.

Stanislaw Wyspianski A320

Kneeling Figure A321

Portrait: 2.50z, Stanislaw Moniuszko.

1958, Nov. 25 **Engr.** *Perf. 12½*
831 A320 60g dk vio 10 7
832 A320 2.50z dk sl grn 30 14

Stanislaw Wyspianski, painter and poet, and Stanislaw Moniuszko, composer.

1958, Dec. 10 **Litho.**
833 A321 2.50z lt brn & red brn 28 10

Signing of the Universal Declaration of Human Rights, 10th anniv.

Red Flag A322

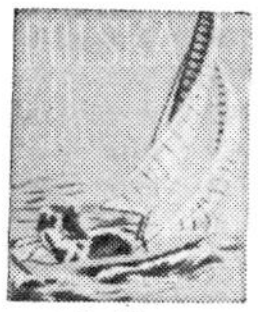
Sailing A323

1958, Dec. 16 **Photo.**
834 A322 60g plum & red 10 8

40th anniv. of the Communist Party of Poland.

1959, Jan. 3

Sports: 60g, Girl archer. 95g, Soccer. 2z, Horsemanship.

835 A323 40g lt bl & vio bl 20 12
836 A323 60g sal & brn vio 18 9
837 A323 95g grn & brn vio 30 20
838 A323 2z dp bl & lt grn 28 20

Hand at Wheel A324

Wheat, Hammer and Flag A325

Design: 1.55z, Factory.

1959, Mar. 10 **Wmk. 326** *Perf. 12½*
839 A324 40gr red, bis & blk 8 5
840 A325 60gr multi 8 7
841 A324 1.55z gray, ver & blk 35 12

3rd Workers Congress.

Amanita Phalloides — A326

Designs: Various mushrooms.

1959, May 8 **Photo.** *Perf. 11½*
842 A326 20g yel, grn & brn 1.10 52
843 A326 30g multi 15 7
844 A326 40g multi 50 7
845 A326 60g yel grn, brn & ocher 50 7
846 A326 1z multi 32 10
847 A326 2.50z bl, grn & brn 65 15
848 A326 3.40z multi 85 35
849 A326 5.60z dl yel, brn & grn 2.50 1.40
Nos. 842-849 (8) 6.57 2.73

"Storks," by Jozef Chelmonski A327

Paintings by Polish Artists: 60g, Mother and Child, Stanislaw Wyspianski (vert.). 1z, Mme. de Romanet, Henryk Rodakowski (vert.). 1.50z, Old Man and Death, Jacek Malczewski (vert.). 6.40z, River Scene, Aleksander Gierymski.

1959 **Engr.** *Perf. 12, 12½x12*
850 A327 40g gray grn 15 10
851 A327 60g dl pur 20 10
852 A327 1z int blk 25 10
853 A327 1.50z brown 40 22
854 A327 6.40z blue 1.65 55
Nos. 850-854 (5) 2.65 1.07

Nos. 850 and 854 measure 36x28mm; Nos. 851 and 853, 28x36mm; No. 852, 28x37mm.

The only foreign revenue stamps listed in this Catalogue are those authorized for prepayment of postage.

Miner and Globe A328

Map of Poland and Symbol of Agriculture A329

1959, July 1 **Litho.**
855 A328 2.50z multi 30 10

3rd Miners' Conference, Katowice, July 1959.

Perf. 12x12½
1959, July 21 **Wmk. 326**

Map of Poland and: 60g, Symbol of industry. 1.50z, Symbol of art and science.

856 A329 40g blk, bl & grn 8 5
857 A329 60g blk & ver 9 5
858 A329 1.50z blk & bl 15 10

15 years of the Peoples' Republic of Poland.

Lazarus Ludwig Zamenhof A330

Map of Austria and Flower A331

Design: 1.50z, Star, globe and flag.

1959, July 24 *Perf. 12½*
859 A330 60g blk & grn, *ol* 8 7
860 A330 1.50z ultra, grn & red, *gray* 42 14

Centenary of the birth of Lazarus Ludwig Zamenhof, author of Esperanto, and in conjunction with the Esperanto Congress in Warsaw.

1959, July 27 **Litho.**
861 A331 60g sep, red & grn, *yel* 7 7
862 A331 2.50z bl, red, & grn, *gray* 45 20

7th World Youth Festival, Vienna, July 26-Aug. 14.

Symbolic Plane — A332

1959, Aug. 24 **Wmk. 326** *Perf. 12½*
863 A332 60g vio bl, grnsh bl & blk 15 8

30th anniv. of LOT, the Polish airline.

Sejm (Parliament) Building — A333

1959, Aug. 27 **Photo.** *Perf. 12x12½*
864 A333 60g lt grn, blk & red 7 7
865 A333 2.50z vio gray, blk & red 35 15

48th Interparliamentary Conference, Warsaw.

No. 640 Overprinted in Blue:
"BALPEX I - GDANSK 1959"

1959, Aug. 30 **Engr.** **Unwmk.**
866 A253 45g brn, *yel* 50 28

Intl. Phil. Exhib. of Baltic States at Gdansk.

Stylized Dove and Globe — A334

Wmk. 326
1959, Sept. 1 **Photo.** *Perf. 12½*
867 A334 60g bl & gray 10 8

World Peace Movement, 10th anniv.

Red Cross Nurse — A335

Designs: 60g, Nurse. 2.50z, Henri Dunant.

1959, Sept. 21 **Litho.** *Perf. 12½*
Size: 21x26mm
868 A335 40g red, lt grn & blk 9 8
869 A335 60g bis brn, brn & red 9 8

Perf. 11
Size: 23x23mm
870 A335 2.50z red, pink & blk 45 32

40th anniversary of the Polish Red Cross and the centenary of the Red Cross.

Polish-Chinese Friendship Society Emblem A336

Flower Made of Stamps A337

Wmk. 326
1959, Sept. 28 **Litho.** *Perf. 11*
871 A336 60g multi 30 16
872 A336 2.50z multi 20 14

Polish-Chinese friendship.

1959, Oct. 9 *Perf. 12½*
873 A337 60g lt grnsh bl, grn & red 10 8
874 A337 2.50z red, grn & vio 28 16

Issued for Stamp Day, 1959.

Sputnik 3 — A338

Designs: 60g, Rocket. 2.50z, Earth, moon and Sputnik 2.

1959, Nov. 7 **Photo.** **Wmk. 326**
875 A338 40g Prus bl & gray 22 9
876 A338 60g mar & blk 32 20
877 A338 2.50z grn & dk bl 90 48

Issued on the 42nd anniversary of the Russian Revolution to commemorate the landing of the Soviet moon rocket.
Exist imperf. Value, set $2.50.

Child Doing Homework A339

Charles Darwin A340

Design: 60g, Three children leaving school.

Lithographed and Engraved

1959, Nov. 14 *Perf. 11½*

878	A339	40g grn & dk brn	10	8
879	A339	60g bl & red	15	8

"1,000 Schools" campaign for the 1,000th anniversary of Poland.

1959, Dec. 10 Engr. *Perf. 11*

Scientists: 10g, Dmitri I. Mendeleev. 60g, Albert Einstein. 1.50z, Louis Pasteur. 1.55z, Isaac Newton. 2.50z, Nicolaus Copernicus.

880	A340	20g	dk bl	8	5
881	A340	40g	ol gray	8	5
882	A340	60g	claret	8	5
883	A340	1.50g	dk vio brn	12	6
884	A340	1.55z	dk grn	40	12
885	A340	2.50z	violet	90	48
	Nos. 880-885 (6)			1.66	81

Man from Rzeszow — A341

Woman from Rzeszow — A342

Regional Costumes: 40g, Cracow. 60g, Kurpiow. 1z, Silesia. 2z, Lowicz. 2.50z, Mountain people. 3.10z, Kujawy. 3.40z, Lublin. 5.60z, Szamotuli. 6.50z, Lubuski.

Engraved and Photogravure

1959-60 Wmk. 326 *Perf. 12, Imperf.*

886	A341	20g	sl grn & blk	6	6
887	A342	20g	sl grn & blk	6	6
888	A341	40g	lt bl & rose car ('60)	6	6
889	A342	40g	rose car & bl ('60)	6	6
890	A341	60g	blk & pink	6	6
891	A342	60g	blk & pink	6	6
892	A341	1z	grnsh red & dk red	9	6
893	A342	1z	grnsh bl & dk red	9	6
894	A341	2z	yel & ultra ('60)	16	15
895	A342	2z	yel & ultra ('60)	16	15
896	A341	2.50z	grn & rose lil	24	22
897	A342	2.50z	grn & rose lil	24	22
898	A341	3.10z	yel grn & sl grn ('60)	30	30
899	A342	3.10z	yel grn & sl grn ('60)	30	30
900	A341	3.40z	gray grn & brn ('60)	35	35
901	A342	3.40z	gray grn & brn ('60)	35	35
902	A341	5.60z	yel grn & gray bl	85	65
903	A342	5.60z	yel grn & gray bl	85	65
904	A341	6.50z	vio & gray grn ('60)	85	65
905	A342	6.50z	vio & gray grn ('60)	85	65
	Nos. 886-905 (20)			6.04	5.12

The male and female costume stamps of each denomination were printed se-tenant in sheets of 56.

An enhanced introduction to the Scott Catalogue begins on Page V. A thorough understanding of the material presented there will greatly aid your use of the catalogue itself.

Piano — A343

Frederic Chopin — A344

Design: 1.50z, Musical note and manuscript.

1960, Feb. 22 Litho. *Perf. 12*

906	A343	60g	brt vio & blk	35	32
907	A343	1.50z	blk, gray & red	55	22

Perf. 12½x12

Engr.

908	A344	2.50z	black	2.00	90

150th anniversary of the birth of Frederic Chopin and to publicize the Chopin music competition.

Stamp of 1860 — A345

Designs: 60g, Ski meet stamp of 1939. 1.35z, Design from 1860 issue. 1.55z, 1945 liberation stamp. 2.50z, 1957 stamp day stamp.

Litho. (40g, 1.35z); Litho. and Photo.

Perf. 11½x11

1960, Mar. 21 Wmk. 326

909	A345	40g	multi	15	7
910	A345	60g	vio, ultra & blk	28	15
911	A345	1.35z	gray, red & bl	65	35
912	A345	1.55z	grn, car & blk	65	20
913	A345	2.50z	ap grn, dk grn & blk	85	35
	Nos. 909-913 (5)			2.58	1.12

Centenary of Polish stamps. Nos. 909-913 were also issued in sheets of four. Value, $275.

Discus Thrower, Amsterdam 1928 — A346

Polish Olympic Victories: No. 915, Runner. No. 916, Bicyclist. No. 917, Steeplechase. No. 918, Trumpeters. No. 919, Boxers. No. 920, Olympic flame. No. 921 Woman jumper.

Lithographed and Embossed

Perf. 12x12½

1960, June 15 Unwmk.

914	A346	60g	bl & blk	14	10
915	A346	60g	car rose & blk	14	10
916	A346	60g	vio & blk	14	10
917	A346	60g	bl grn & blk	14	10
918	A346	2.50z	ultra & blk	45	25
919	A346	2.50z	chnt & blk	45	25
920	A346	2.50z	red & blk	45	25
921	A346	2.50z	emer & blk	45	25
	Nos. 914-921 (8)			2.36	1.40

17th Olympic Games, Rome, Aug. 25-Sept. 11.

Nos. 914-917 and Nos. 918-921 are printed se-tenant in the sheets. The oval lines of each set of 4 stamps form the stadium oval.

Nos. 914-921 exist imperf. Value, set $3.50.

Tomb of King Wladyslaw II Jagiello — A347

Battle of Grunwald by Jan Matejko — A348

Design: 90g, Detail from Grunwald monument.

Perf. 11x11½

1960 Wmk. 326 Engr.

922	A347	60g	vio brn	30	12
923	A347	90g	ol gray	60	30

Size: 78x37mm

924	A348	2.50z	dk gray	1.75	1.00

550th anniversary, Battle of Grunwald.

The Annunciation — A349

Carvings by Veit Stoss, St. Mary's Church, Cracow: 30g, Nativity. 40g, Adoration of the Kings. 60g, The Resurrection. 2.50z, The Ascension. 5.60z, Descent of the Holy Ghost. 10z, The Assumption of the Virgin (vert.).

1960 Wmk. 326 Engr. *Perf. 12*

925	A349	20g	Prus bl	18	7
926	A349	30g	lt red brn	9	7
927	A349	40g	violet	20	10
928	A349	60g	dl grn	20	10
929	A349	2.50z	rose lake	65	22
930	A349	5.60z	dk brn	4.00	2.75
	Nos. 925-930 (6)			5.32	3.31

Miniature Sheet

Imperf

931	A349	10z	black	4.50	4.00

No. 931 contains one vertical stamp which measures 72x95mm.

Ignacy Jan Paderewski A350

1960, Sept. 26 *Perf. 12½*

932	A350	2.50z	black	25	10

Birth cent. of Ignacy Jan Paderewski, statesman and musician.

Lukasiewicz and Kerosene Lamp — A351

Engr. & Photo.

1960, Sept. 14 *Perf. 11*

933	A351	60g	cit & blk	15	8

5th Pharmaceutical Congress; Ignacy Lukasiewicz, chemist-pharmacist.

No. 909 Overprinted: "DZIEN ZNACZKA 1960"

1960 Litho. *Perf. 11½x11*

934	A345	40g	multi	75	55

Issued for Stamp Day, 1960.

Great Bustard A352

Birds: 20g, Raven. 30g, Great cormorant. 40g, Black stork. 50g, Eagle owl. 60g, White-tailed sea eagle. 75g, Golden eagle. 90g, Short-toed eagle. 2.50z, Rock thrush. 4z, European kingfisher. 5.60z, Wall creeper. 6.50z, European roller.

1960 Unwmk. Photo. *Perf. 11½*

Birds in Natural Colors

935	A352	10g	gray & blk	10	8
936	A352	20g	gray & blk	10	12
937	A352	30g	gray & blk	10	12
938	A352	40g	gray & blk	14	15
939	A352	50g	pale grn & blk	20	12
940	A352	60g	pale grn & blk	28	12
941	A352	75g	pale grn & blk	28	12
942	A352	90g	pale grn & blk	40	16
943	A352	2.50z	pale ol gray & blk	2.50	1.65
944	A352	4z	pale ol gray & blk	1.65	60
945	A352	5.60z	pale ol gray & blk	2.75	65
946	A352	6.50z	pale ol gray & blk	4.50	2.00
	Nos. 935-946 (12)			13.00	5.89

Gniezno A353

Front Page of "Merkuriusz" A354

Historic Towns: 10g, Cracow. 20g, Warsaw. 40g, Poznan. 50g, Plock. 60g, Kalisz. No. 952A, Tczew. 80g, Frombork. 90g, Torun, 95g, Puck (ships). 1z, Slupsk. 1.15z, Gdansk (Danzig). 1.35z, Wroclaw. 1.50z, Szczecin. 1.55z, Opole. 2z, Kolobrzeg. 2.10z, Legnica. 2.50z, Katowice. 3.10z, Lodz. 5.60z, Walbrzych.

1960-61 Engr. *Perf. 11½, 13x12½*

947	A353	5g	red brn	8	5
948	A353	10g	green	8	5
949	A353	20g	dk brn	8	5
950	A353	40g	vermilion	8	5
951	A353	50g	violet	8	5
952	A353	60g	rose cl	8	5
952A	A353	60g	lt ultra ('61)	15	8
953	A353	80g	blue	10	5
954	A353	90g	brn ('61)	15	8
955	A353	95g	ol gray	10	5

Engraved and Lithographed

956	A353	1z	org & gray	10	5
957	A353	1.15z	sl grn & sal	10	8
958	A353	1.35z	lil rose & lt grn	10	8
959	A353	1.50z	sep & pale grn	10	8
960	A353	1.55z	car lake & buff	10	8
961	A353	2z	dk bl & pink	15	8
962	A353	2.10z	sep & yel	12	8
963	A353	2.50z	dl vio & pale grn	20	12
964	A353	3.10z	ver & gray	22	12
965	A353	5.60z	sl grn & lt grn	55	15
	Nos. 947-965 (20)			2.72	1.48

Lithographed and Embossed

1961 Wmk. 326 *Perf. 12*

Newspapers: 60g, "Proletaryat," first issue, Sept. 15, 1883. 2.50z, "Rzeczpospolita," first issue, July 23, 1944.

966	A354	40g	blk, ultra & emer	45	20
967	A354	60g	blk, org brn & yel	45	20
968	A354	2.50z	blk, vio & bl	2.75	2.25

300th anniv. of the Polish newspaper Merkuriusz.

Ice Hockey A355

Part of Cogwheel A356

Sports: 60g, Ski jump. 1z, Soldiers on skis. 1.50z, Slalom.

1961, Feb. 1 Litho. Wmk. 326

969	A355	40g	lt vio, blk & yel	30	15
970	A355	60g	lt ultra, blk & car	90	50
971	A355	1z	lt bl, ol & red	4.00	2.00
972	A355	1.50z	grnsh bl, blk & yel	75	32

1st Winter Spartacist Games of Friendly Armies.

1961, Feb. 11 *Perf. 12½*

973	A356	60g	red & blk	15	10

Fourth Congress of Polish Engineers.

Maj. Yuri A. Gagarin A357

Design: 60g, Globe and path of rocket.

1961, Apr. 27 Photo. *Perf. 12*

974	A357	40g	dk red & blk	75	32
975	A357	60g	ultra, blk & car	45	20

1st man in space, Yuri A. Gagarin, Apr. 12, 1961.

Emblem of Poznan Fair A358

1961, May 25 Litho. *Perf. 12½x12*

977	A358	40g	brt bl, blk & red org	9	7
978	A358	1.50z	red org, blk & brt bl	18	10
a			Souv. sheet of 2	2.00	1.90

30th Intl. Fair at Poznan.
No. 978a contains two of No. 978 with simulated perforation and blue marginal inscriptions. Sold for 4.50z. Issued July 29, 1961.

Tadeusz Kosciuszko — A359

Famous Poles: No. 979, Mieszko I. No. 980, Casimir Wielki. No. 981, Casimir Jagiello. No. 982, Nicolaus Copernicus. No. 983, Andrzej Frycz-Modrzewski.

Photogravure and Engraved

1961, June 15 *Perf. 11x11½*

Black Inscriptions and Designs

979	A359	60g	chalky bl	10	6
980	A359	60g	dp rose	10	6
981	A359	60g	slate	10	6
982	A359	60g	dl vio	65	20
983	A359	60g	lt brn	12	8
984	A359	60g	ol gray	12	8
			Nos. 979-984 (6)	1.19	54

See Nos. 1059-1064, 1152-1155.

Trawler — A360

Designs: Various Polish Cargo Ships.

Unwmk.

1961, June 24 Litho. *Perf. 11*

985	A360	60g	multi	30	10
986	A360	1.55z	multi	35	10
987	A360	2.50z	multi	60	30
988	A360	3.40z	multi	70	50
989	A360	4z	multi	1.10	90
990	A360	5.60z	multi	2.75	1.65
			Nos. 985-990 (6)	5.80	3.55

Issued to honor the Polish ship industry. Sizes (width): 60g, 2.50z, 54mm.; 1.55z, 3.40z, 4z, 80mm.; 5.60z, 108mm.

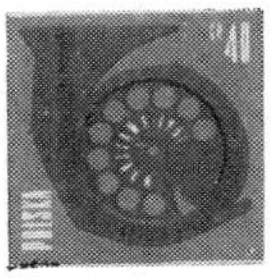
Post Horn and Telephone Dial — A361

Post horn and: 60g, Radar screen. 2.50z, Conference emblem, globe.

1961, June 26

991	A361	40g	sl, gray & red org	12	8
992	A361	60g	gray, yel & vio	12	8
993	A361	2.50z	ol bis, brt bl & vio bl	35	25
a			Souv. sheet of 3, #991-993	2.25	1.50

Conference of Communications Ministers of Communist Countries, Warsaw.
No. 993a sold for 5z.

Seal of Opole, 13th Century A362

Cement Works, Opole A363

Designs: No. 996, Tombstone of Henry IV and seal, Wroclaw. No. 997, Apartment houses, Wroclaw. No. 998, Seal of Conrad II and Silesian eagle. No. 999, Steel works, Gorzow. No. 1000, Seal of Prince Barnim I. No. 1001, Seaport, Szczecin. No. 1002, Seal of Princess Elizabeth. No. 1003, Factory, Szczecinek. No. 1004, Seal of Unislaw. No. 1005, Shipyard, Gdansk. No. 1005A, Tower, Frombork Cathedral. No. 1005B, Chemical Laboratory, Kortowo.

1961-62 Wmk. 326 Engr. *Perf. 11*

Western Territories

994	A362	40g	brn, *grysh*	7	5
995	A363	40g	brn, *grysh*	7	5
996	A362	60g	vio, *pink*	10	7
997	A363	60g	vio, *pink*	10	7
998	A362	95g	grn, *bluish* ('62)	15	10
999	A363	95g	grn, *bluish* ('62)	15	10
1000	A362	2.50z	ol grn, *grnsh*	32	15
1001	A363	2.50z	ol grn, *grnsh*	32	15

Northern Territories

1002	A362	60g	vio bl, *bluish* ('62)	10	7
1003	A363	60g	vio bl, *bluish* ('62)	10	7
1004	A362	1.55z	brn, *buff* ('62)	15	7
1005	A363	1.55z	brn, *buff* ('62)	15	7
1005A	A362	2.50z	sl bl, *grysh* ('62)	32	15
1005B	A363	2.50z	sl bl, *grysh* ('62)	32	15
			Nos. 994-1005B (14)	2.42	1.32

Sheets of 56 with alternating rows of horizontal and vertical stamps. The horizontal stamps also alternate with a label with commemorative inscription. Each sheet contains 28 se-tenant pairs of types A362-A363 with label.

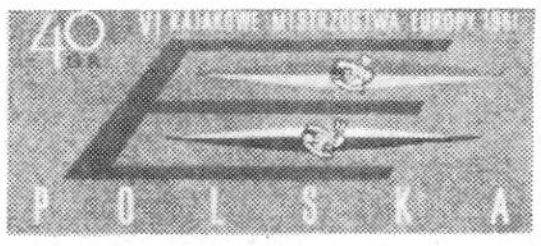
Kayak Race Start and "E" — A364

Designs: 60g, Four-man canoes and "E". 2.50z, Paddle, Polish flag and "E" (vert.).

Wmk. 326

1961, Aug. 18 Litho. *Perf. 12½*

1006	A364	40g	bl grn, yel & red	15	6
1007	A364	60g	multi	15	6
1008	A364	2.50z	multi	90	35

6th European Canoe Championships, Poznan, Aug. 18-20. Exist imperf. Value, set $1.75

Maj. Gherman Titov, Star, Globe, Orbit A365

Dove and Earth A366

Perf. 12x12½

1961, Aug. 24 Photo. Unwmk.

1009	A365	40g	pink, blk & red	25	10
1010	A366	60g	bl & blk	25	10

Manned space flight of Vostok 2, Aug. 6-7, in which Russian Maj. Gherman Titov orbited the earth 17 times.

Insurgents' Monument, St. Ann's Mountain — A367

Design: 1.55z, Cross of Silesian Insurgents.

Wmk. 326

1961, Sept. 15 Litho. *Perf. 12*

1011	A367	60g	gray & emer	9	8
1012	A367	1.55z	gray & bl	18	12

40th anniv. of the third Silesian uprising.

"PKO," Initials of Polish Savings Bank A368

Designs (Initials and): No. 1014, Bee and clover. No. 1015, Ant. No. 1016, Squirrel. 2.50z, Savings bankbook.

1961, Oct. 2 Wmk. 326 *Perf. 12*

1013	A368	40g	ver, blk & org	15	10
1014	A368	60g	bl, blk & brt pink	15	10
1015	A368	60g	bis brn, blk & ocher	15	7
1016	A368	60g	brt grn, blk & dl red	15	7
1017	A368	2.50z	car rose, gray & blk	1.75	1.40
			Nos. 1013-1017 (5)	2.35	1.74

Issued to publicize Savings Month.

Mail Cart, by Jan Chelminski — A369

1961, Oct. 9 Engr. *Perf. 12x12½*

1018	A369	60g	dp grn	25	9
1019	A369	60g	vio brn	25	9

40th anniv. of the Polish Postal Museum; Stamp Day.

Congress Emblem A370

1961, Nov. 20 Wmk. 326 *Perf. 12*

1020	A370	60g	black	10	8

Issued to publicize the Fifth World Congress of Trade Unions, Moscow, Dec. 4-16.

Seal of Kopasyni Family, 1284 A371

Child and Syringe A372

Designs: 60g, Seal of Bytom, 14th century. 2.50z, Emblem of International Miners Congress, 1958.

1961, Dec. 4 Litho. *Perf. 11x11½*

1021	A371	40g	multi	15	7
1022	A371	60g	bl, gray bl & vio bl	15	7
1023	A371	2.50z	yel grn, grn & blk	45	24

1,000 years of the Polish mining industry.

Perf. 12½x12, 12x12½

1961, Dec. 11

Designs: 60g, Children of three races (horiz.). 2.50z, Mother, child and milk bottle.

1024	A372	40g	lt bl & blk	12	7
1025	A372	60g	org & blk	12	7
1026	A372	2.50z	brt bl grn & blk	50	24

15th anniversary of UNICEF.

Emblem A373

Design: 60g, Map with oil pipe line from Siberia to Central Europe.

1961, Dec. 12 Wmk. 326 *Perf. 12*

1027 A373 40g dk red, yel & vio bl 15 10
1028 A373 60g vio bl, bl & red 12 8

15th session of the Council of Mutual Economic Assistance of the Communist States.

Ground Beetle — A374

Black Apollo Butterfly A375

Insects: 30g, Violet runner. 40g, Alpine longicorn beetle. 50g, Great oak capricorn beetle. 60g, Gold runner. 80g, Stag-horned beetle. 1.35z, Death's-head moth. 1.50z, Tiger-striped swallowtail butterfly. 1.55z, Apollo butterfly. 2.50z, Red ant. 5.60z, Bumble bee.

Perf. 12½x12

1961, Dec. 30 Photo. Unwmk.

Insects in Natural Colors

1029 A374 20g bis brn 15 10
1030 A374 30g pale gray grn 15 7
1031 A374 40g pale yel grn 15 7
1032 A374 50g bl grn 15 7
1033 A374 60g dl rose lil 15 10
1034 A374 80g pale grn 22 10

Perf. 11½

1035 A375 1.15z ultra 30 12
1036 A375 1.35z sapphire 30 12
1037 A375 1.50z bluish grn 50 15
1038 A375 1.55z brt pur 42 15
1039 A375 2.50z brt grn 1.65 40
1040 A375 5.60z org brn 8.00 3.25
Nos. 1029-1040 (12) 12.14 4.70

Worker with Gun A376

Women Skiers A377

Designs: No. 1042, Worker with trowel and gun. No. 1043, Worker with hammer. No. 1044, Worker at helm. No. 1045, Worker with dove and banner.

Perf. 12½x12

1962, Jan. 5 Litho. Unwmk.

1041 A376 60g red, blk & grn 8 8
1042 A376 60g red, blk & sl 8 8
1043 A376 60g blk & vio bl, *red* 8 8
1044 A376 60g blk & bis, *red* 14 8
1045 A376 60g blk & gray, *red* 14 15
Nos. 1041-1045 (5) 52 47

Polish Workers' Party, 20th anniversary.

Lithographed and Embossed

1962, Feb. 14 *Perf. 12*

Designs: 60g, Long distance skier. 1.50z, Ski jump (vert.). 10z, FIS emblem (vert.).

1046 A377 40g gray, red & gray bl 8 6
a 40g sep, red & dl bl 40 12
1047 A377 60g gray, red & gray bl 15 8
a 60g sep, red & dl bl 50 28
1048 A377 1.50z gray, red & gray bl 25 18
a 1.50z gray, lil & red 1.50 80

Souvenir Sheet

Imperf

1049 A377 10z gray, red & gray bl 2.25 2.00

World Ski Championships at Zakopane (FIS).

No. 1049 contains one stamp with simulated perforation and gray blue inscription. The sheet sold for 15z.

Each of Nos. 1046-1048 exists in a souvenir sheet of four. Value, set of 3, $57.50.

Broken Flower and Prison Cloth (Auschwitz) — A378

Majdanek Concentration Camp — A379

Design: 1.50z, Proposed memorial, Treblinka concentration camp.

Wmk. 326

1962, Apr. 3 Engr. *Perf. 11½*

1050 A378 40g sl bl 15 7
1051 A379 60g dk gray 24 10
1052 A378 1.50z dk vio 52 22

Issued during International Resistance Movement Month to commemorate the millions who died in concentration camps, 1940-45.

Bicyclist A380

Designs: 2.50z, Cyclists in race. 3.40z, Wheel and arms of Berlin, Prague and Warsaw.

Unwmk.

1962, Apr. 27 Litho. *Perf. 12*

1053 A380 60g bl & blk 14 6
1054 A380 2.50z yel & blk 35 12
1055 A380 3.40z lil & blk 52 18

15th Intl. Peace Bicycle Race, Warsaw-Berlin-Prague.

Size of Nos. 1053 and 1055: 36x22mm. No. 1054: 74x22mm.

Lenin in Bialy Dunajec A381

Karol Swierczewski-Walter A382

Designs: 60g, Lenin. 2.50z, Lenin and Cracow fortifications.

Engraved and Photogravure

Perf. 11x11½

1962, May 25 Wmk. 326

1056 A381 40g pale grn & Prus grn 50 14
1057 A381 60g pink & dp cl 15 8
1058 A381 2.50z yel & dk brn 32 14

50th anniv. of Lenin's arrival in Poland.

Famous Poles Type of 1961

Famous Poles: No. 1059, Adam Mickiewicz. No. 1060, Juliusz Slowacki. No. 1061, Frederic Chopin. No. 1062, Romuald Traugutt. No. 1063, Jaroslaw Dabrowski. No. 1064, Maria Konopnicka.

1962, June 20 Engr. & Photo.

Black Inscriptions and Designs

1059 A359 60g dl grn 20 12
1060 A359 60g brn org 12 8

Perf. 12x12½

Litho.

1061 A359 60g dl bl 12 8
1062 A359 60g brn ol 12 8
1063 A359 60g rose lil 12 8
1064 A359 60g bl grn 12 8
Nos. 1059-1064 (6) 80 52

Perf. 11x11½

1962, July 14 Engr. Unwmk.

1065 A382 60g black 10 8

15th death anniv. of General Karol Swierczewski-Walter, organizer of the new Polish army.

Crocus A383

The Poisoned Well by Jacek Malczewski A384

Flowers: No. 1067, Orchid. No. 1068, Monkshood. No. 1069, Gas plant. No. 1070, Water lily. No. 1071, Gentian. No. 1072, Daphne mezereum. No. 1073, Cowbell. No. 1074, Anemone. No. 1075, Globeflower. No. 1076, Snowdrop. No. 1077, Adonis vernalis.

Unwmk.

1962, Aug. 8 Photo. *Perf. 12*

Flowers in Natural Colors

1066 A383 60g dl yel & red 15 12
1067 A383 60g redsh brn & vio 65 32
1068 A383 60g pink & lil 10 7
1069 A383 90g ol & grn 15 7
1070 A383 90g yel grn & red 15 10
1071 A383 90g lt ol grn & red 15 10
1072 A383 1.50z gray bl & bl 25 12
1073 A383 1.50z yel grn & dk grn 40 15
1074 A383 1.50z Prus grn & dk bl 25 12
1075 A383 2.50z gray grn & dk bl 52 35
1076 A383 2.50z dk bl grn & dk bl 52 35
1077 A383 2.50z gray bl & grn 85 40
Nos. 1066-1077 (12) 4.14 2.27

1962, Aug. 15 Engr. Wmk. 326

1078 A384 60g black, *buff* 30 15

Issued in sheets of 40 with alternating label for FIP Day (Federation Internationale de Philatelie), Sept. 1. Also issued in miniature sheet of four. Value, $26

Pole Vault — A385

Designs: 60g, Relay race. 90g, Javelin. 1z, Hurdles. 1.50z, High jump. 1.55z, Discus. 2.50z, 100m. dash. 3.40z, Hammer throw.

Unwmk.

1962, Sept. 12 Litho. *Perf. 11*

1079 A385 40g multi 6 5
1080 A385 60g multi 6 5
1081 A385 90g multi 9 6
1082 A385 1z multi 12 6
1083 A385 1.50z multi 15 9
1084 A385 1.55z multi 18 9
1085 A385 2.50z multi 30 15
1086 A385 3.40z multi 75 24
Nos. 1079-1086 (8) 1.71 79

7th European Athletic Championships, Belgrade, Sept. 12-16.

Exist imperf. Value, set $3.

Anopheles Mosquito A386

Pavel R. Popovich and Andrian G. Nikolayev A387

Designs: 1.50z, Malaria blood cells. 2.50z, Cinchona flowers. 3z, Anopheles mosquito.

1962, Oct. 1 Wmk. 326 *Perf. 13x12*

1087 A386 60g ol blk, dk brn & bl grn 8 5
1088 A386 1.50z red, gray & brt vio 16 7
1089 A386 2.50z multi 38 16

Miniature Sheet

Imperf

1090 A386 3z multi 90 60

WHO drive to eradicate malaria.

1962, Oct. 6 *Perf. 12½x12*

Design: 2.50z, Two stars in orbit around earth. 10z, Two stars in orbit.

1091 A387 60g vio, blk & cit 12 8
1092 A387 2.50z Prus bl, blk & red 24 15

Souvenir Sheet

Perf. 12x11

1093 A387 10z sl bl, blk & red 1.65 1.50

1st Russian group space flight, Vostoks III and IV, Aug. 11-15, 1962.

Woman Mailing Letter — A388

Mazovian Princes' Mansion, Warsaw — A389

1962, Oct. 9 Engr. *Perf. 12½x12*

1094 A388 60g black 8 8
1095 A388 2.50z red brn 32 12

Issued for Stamp Day, 1962. The design is from the painting "A Moment of Decision," by Anthony Kamienski.

1962, Oct. 13 Litho.

1096 A389 60g red & blk 15 8

25th anniversary of the founding of the Polish Democratic Party.

Cruiser "Aurora" — A390

Photo. & Engr.

1962, Nov. 3 *Perf. 11*

1097	A390	60g	red & dk bl	15	8

45th anniv. of the Russian October revolution.

Janusz Korczak by K. Dunikowski A391

King on Horseback A392

Illustrations from King Matthew books: 90g, King giving fruit to Island girl. 1z, King handcuffed and soldier with sword. 2.50z, King with dead bird. 5.60z, King ice skating in moonlight.

Perf. 13x12

1962, Nov. 12 Unwmk. Litho.

1098	A391	40g	brn, bis & sep	12	8
1099	A392	60g	multi	12	8
1100	A392	90g	multi	25	12
1101	A392	1z	multi	25	8
1102	A392	2.50z	brn, yel & brt grn	50	32
1103	A392	5.60z	brn, dk bl & grn	1.75	80
			Nos. 1098-1103 (6)	2.99	1.48

20th anniversary of the death of Dr. Janusz Korczak (Henryk Goldszmit), physician, pedagogue and writer, in the Treblinka concentration camp, Aug. 5, 1942.

View of Old Warsaw — A393

1962, Nov. 26 Wmk. 326 *Perf. 11*

1104	A393	3.40z	multi	38	22
a			Sheet of 4	3.00	2.50

5th Trade Union Congress, Warsaw, Nov. 26-Dec. 1.

Orphan Mary and the Dwarf — A394

Various Scenes from "Orphan Mary and the Dwarfs" by Maria Konopnicka.

Perf. 13x12

1962, Dec. 31 Unwmk. Litho.

1105	A394	40g	multi	25	12
1106	A394	60g	multi	1.65	1.00
1107	A394	1.50z	multi	42	10
1108	A394	1.55z	multi	42	12
1109	A394	2.50z	multi	50	32
1110	A394	3.40z	multi	1.65	1.25
			Nos. 1105-1110 (6)	4.89	2.91

120th anniversary of the birth of Maria Konopnicka, poet and fairy tale writer.

Romuald Traugutt A395

Perf. 11½x11

1963, Jan. 31 Wmk. 326

1111	A395	60g	aqua, blk & pale pink	15	8

Centenary of the 1863 insurrection and to honor its leader, Romuald Traugutt.

Tractor and Wheat A396

Designs: 60g, Man reaping and millet. 2.50z, Combine and rice.

Perf. 12x12½

1963, Feb. 25 Litho. Wmk. 326

1112	A396	40g	gray, bl, blk & ocher	15	5
1113	A396	60g	brn red, blk, brn & grn	52	22
1114	A396	2.50z	yel, buff, blk & grn	42	15

FAO "Freedom from Hunger" campaign.

Cocker Spaniel — A397

Dogs: 30g, Polish sheep dog. 40g, Boxer. 50g, Airedale terrier (vert.). 60g, French bulldog (vert.). 1z, Poodle (vert.). 2.50z, Hunting dog. 3.40z, Sheep dog (vert.). 6.50z, Great Dane.

1963, Mar. 25 Unwmk. *Perf. 12½*

1115	A397	20g	lil, blk & org brn	12	8
1116	A397	30g	rose car & blk	15	8
1117	A397	40g	lil, blk & yel grn	20	8
1118	A397	50g	multi	25	8
1119	A397	60g	lt bl & blk	32	12
1120	A397	1z	yel grn & blk	60	55
1121	A397	2.50z	org, blk & brn	1.10	52
1122	A397	3.40z	red org & blk	2.25	1.10
1123	A397	6.50z	brt yel & blk	4.00	3.00
			Nos. 1115-1123 (9)	8.99	5.61

Egyptian Ship — A398

Fighter and Ruins of Warsaw Ghetto — A399

Ancient Ships: 10g, Phoenician merchant ship. 20g, Greek trireme. 30g, 3rd century merchantman. 40g, Scandinavian "Gokstad." 60g, Frisian "Kogge." 1z. 14th century "Holk." 1.15z, 15th century "Caraca."

Photo. (Background) & Engr.

1963, Apr. 5 *Perf. 11½*

1124	A398	5g	brn, *tan*	5	5
1125	A398	10g	grn, *gray grn*	5	5
1126	A398	20g	ultra, *gray*	5	5
1127	A398	30g	blk, *gray ol*	7	5
1128	A398	40g	lt bl, *bluish*	7	5
1129	A398	60g	cl, *gray*	10	8
1130	A398	1z	blk, *bl*	12	8
1131	A398	1.15z	grn, *pale rose*	35	12
			Nos. 1124-1131 (8)	86	53

See Nos. 1206-1213, 1299-1306.

Perf. 11½x11

1963, Apr. 19 Wmk. 326

1132	A399	2.50z	gray brn & gray	32	15

Warsaw Ghetto Uprising, 20th anniv.

Centenary Emblem — A400

Perf. 12½x12

1963, May 8 Litho. Unwmk.

1133	A400	2.50z	bl, yel & red	40	15

Intl. Red Cross, cent. Every other stamp in sheet inverted.

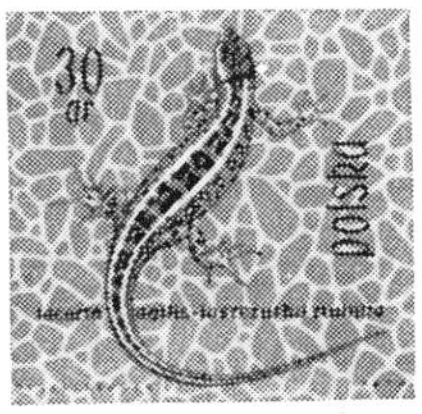
Sand Lizard A401

Designs: 40g, Smooth snake. 50g, European pond turtle. 60g, Grass snake. 90g, Slow worm. 1.15z, European tree frog. 1.35z, Alpine newt. 1.50z, Crested newt. 1.55z, Green toad. 2.50z, Firebellied toad. 3z, Fire salamander. 3.40z, Natterjack.

Perf. 11½

1963, June 1 Unwmk. Photo.

Reptiles and Amphibians in Natural Colors

1134	A401	30g	grnsh gray & blk	9	5
1135	A401	40g	gray ol & blk	9	5
1136	A401	50g	bis brn & blk	15	6
1137	A401	60g	tan & blk	15	6
1138	A401	90g	gray grn & blk	15	6
1139	A401	1.15z	gray & blk	15	6
1140	A401	1.35z	gray bl & dk bl	28	15
1141	A401	1.50z	bluish grn & blk	35	20
1142	A401	1.55z	bluish gray & blk	28	15
1143	A401	2.50z	gray vio & blk	28	15
1144	A401	3z	gray grn & blk	60	28
1145	A401	3.40z	gray & blk	1.65	1.25
			Nos. 1134-1145 (12)	4.22	2.52

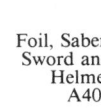

Foil, Saber, Sword and Helmet A402

Designs: 40g, Fencers and knights in armor. 60g, Fencers and dragoons. 1.15z, Contemporary and 18th cent. fencers. 1.55z, Fencers and old houses, Gdansk. 6.50z, Arms of Gdansk (vert.).

Perf. 12x12½, 12½x12

1963, June 29 Litho. Unwmk.

1146	A402	20g	brn & org	7	5
1147	A402	40g	dk bl & bl	10	8
1148	A402	60g	red & dp org	10	8
1149	A402	1.15z	grn & emer	15	8
1150	A402	1.55z	vio & lil	32	15
1151	A402	6.50z	yel brn, mar & yel	1.10	45
			Nos. 1146-1151 (6)	1.84	89

28th World Fencing Championships, Gdansk, July 15-28. A souvenir sheet exists containing one each of Nos. 1147-1150. Value, $30.

Famous Poles Type of 1961

Famous Poles: No. 1152, Ludwik Warynski. No. 1153, Ludwik Krzywicki. No. 1154, Marie Sklodowska Curie. No. 1155, Karol Swierczewski-Walter.

Perf. 12x12½

1963, July 20 Wmk. 326

Black Inscriptions and Designs

1152	A359	60g	red brn	6	8
1153	A359	60g	gray brn	6	8
1154	A359	60g	blue	30	15
1155	A359	60g	green	9	8

Valeri Bykovski — A403

Designs: 60g, Valentina Tereshkova. 6.50z, Rockets "Falcon" and "Mew" and globe.

Unwmk.

1963, Aug. 26 Litho. *Perf. 11*

1156	A403	40g	ultra, emer & blk	10	5
1157	A403	60g	grn, ultra & blk	10	8
1158	A403	6.50z	multi	75	30

Space flights of Valeri Bykovski June 14-19, and Valentina Tereshkova, first woman cosmonaut, June 16-19, 1963.

Basketball A404

Designs: Various positions of ball, hands and players. 10z, Town Hall, People's Hall and Arms of Wroclaw.

1963, Sept. 16 Unwmk. *Perf. 11½*

1159	A404	40g	multi	5	5
1160	A404	50g	fawn, grn & blk	6	6
1161	A404	60g	red, lt grn & blk	6	8
1162	A404	90g	multi	9	8
1163	A404	2.50z	multi	18	12
1164	A404	5.60z	multi	85	30
			Nos. 1159-1164 (6)	1.29	69

Souvenir Sheet

Imperf

1165	A404	10z	multi	1.65	1.00

13th European Men's Basketball Championship, Wroclaw, Oct. 4-13. No. 1165 contains one stamp; inscription on margin also commemorates the simultaneous European Sports Stamp Exhibition. Sheet sold for 15z.

Eagle and Ground-to-Air Missile — A405

Eagle and: 40g, Destroyer. 60g, Jet fighter plane. 1.15z, Radar. 1.35z, Tank. 1.55z, Self-propelled rocket launcher. 2.50z, Amphibious troop carrier. 3z, Swords and medieval and modern soldiers.

1963, Oct. 1 *Perf. 12x12½*

1166	A405	20g	multi	7	5
1167	A405	40g	vio, grn & red	7	5
1168	A405	60g	multi	10	5
1169	A405	1.15z	multi	12	7
1170	A405	1.35z	multi	12	7
1171	A405	1.55z	multi	12	8

1172	A405	2.50z multi	18	8
1173	A405	3z multi	40	18
		Nos. 1166-1173 (8)	1.18	63

Polish People's Army, 20th anniversary.

"Love Letter" by Wladyslaw Czachorski — A406

Perf. 11½

1963, Oct. 9 Unwmk. Engr.

1174	A406	60g dk red brn	20	10

Issued for Stamp Day.

Nos. 1156-1158 Overprinted: "23-28 X. 1963" and name of astronaut

1963 Litho. *Perf. 11*

1175	A403	40g ultra, emer & blk	20	8
1176	A403	60g grn, ultra & blk	28	10
1177	A403	6.50z multi	1.25	65

Visit of Valentina Tereshkova and Valeri Bykovski to Poland, Oct. 23-28. The overprints are: 40g, W. F. Bykowski / w Polsce; 60g, W. W. Tierieszkowa / w Polsce; 6.50z, W. F. BYKOWSKI I W. W. TIERIESZKOWA W POLSCE.

Konstantin E. Tsiolkovsky's Rocket and Rocket Speed Formula — A407

American and Russian Spacecrafts: 40g, Sputnik 1. 50g, Explorer 1. 60g, Lunik 2. 1z, Lunik 3. 1.50z, Vostok 1. 1.55z, Friendship 7. 2.50z, Vostoks 3 & 4. 5.60z, Mariner 2. 6.50z, Mars 1.

Perf. 12½x12

1963, Nov. 11 Litho. Unwmk.

Black Inscriptions

1178	A407	30g dl bl grn & gray	5	5
1179	A407	40g lt ol grn & gray	5	5
1180	A407	50g vio bl & gray	6	5
1181	A407	60g brn org & gray	6	5
1182	A407	1z brt grn & gray	6	8
1183	A407	1.50z org red & gray	9	8
1184	A407	1.55z bl & gray	9	8
1185	A407	2.50z lil & gray	15	8
1186	A407	5.60z brt yel grn & gray	50	24
1187	A407	6.50z grnsh bl & gray	85	30
		Nos. 1178-1187 (10)	1.96	1.06

Conquest of space. A souvenir sheet contains 2 each of Nos. 1186-1187. Value $35.

Arab Stallion "Comet" — A408

Horses from Mazury Region — A409

Horses: 30g, Tarpans (wild horses). 40g, Horse from Sokolka. 50g, Arab mares and foals (horiz.). 90g, Steeplechasers (horiz.). 1.55z, Arab stallion "Witez II." 2.50z, Head of Arab horse, facing right. 4z, Mixed breeds (horiz.). 6.50z, Head of Arab horse, facing left.

Perf. 11½x11 (A408); 12½x12, 12

1963, Dec. 30 Photo.

1188	A408	20g blk, yel & car	8	8
1189	A408	30g multi	16	8
1190	A408	40g multi	16	8

Sizes: 75x26mm (50g, 90g, 4z); 28x38mm (60g, 1.55z, 2.50z, 6.50z)

1191	A409	50g multi	20	12
1192	A409	60g yel, dp rose & blk	20	12
1193	A409	90g multi	28	12
1194	A409	1.55z multi	48	18
1195	A409	2.50z multi	60	18
1196	A409	4z multi	1.40	48
1197	A409	6.50z yel, dl bl & blk	2.50	1.50
		Nos. 1188-1197 (10)	6.06	2.94

Issued to publicize Polish horse breeding.

Ice Hockey A410

Sports: 30g, Slalom. 40g, Skiing. 60g, Speed skating. 1z, Ski jump. 2.50z, Tobogganing. 5.60z, Cross-country skiing. 6.50z, Figure skating pair.

1964, Jan. 25 Litho. *Perf. 12x12½*

1198	A410	20g multi	5	5
1199	A410	30g multi	8	5
1200	A410	40g multi	8	5
1201	A410	60g multi	8	5
1202	A410	1z multi	18	7
1203	A410	2.50z multi	30	14
1204	A410	5.60z multi	48	28
1205	A410	6.50z multi	85	55
		Nos. 1198-1205 (8)	2.10	1.24

9th Winter Olympic Games, Innsbruck, Jan. 29-Feb. 9. A souvenir sheet contains 2 each of Nos. 1203, 1205. Value $27.50.

Ship Type of 1963

Sailing Ships: 1.35z, Caravel of Columbus (vert.). 1.50z, Galleon. 1.55z, Polish warship. 1627 (vert.). 2z, Dutch merchant ship (vert.). 2.10z, Line ship. 2.50z, Frigate. 3z, 19th century merchantman. 3.40z, "Dar Pomorza," 20th century school ship (vert.).

1964, Mar. 19 Engr. *Perf. 12½*

1206	A398	1.35z ultra	8	8
1207	A398	1.50z claret	8	8
1208	A398	1.55z black	12	8
1209	A398	2z violet	12	8
1210	A398	2.10z green	14	8
1211	A398	2.50z car rose	18	8
1212	A398	3z ol grn	30	8
1213	A398	3.40z brown	42	12
		Nos. 1206-1213 (8)	1.44	68

European Cat — A411

Designs: 40g, 60g, 1.55z, 2.50z, 6.50z, Various European cats. 50g, Siamese cat. 90g, 1.35z, 3.40z, Various Persian cats. 60g, 90g, 1.35z, 1.55z horizontal.

1964, Apr. 30 Litho. *Perf. 12½*

Cats in Natural Colors; Black Inscriptions

1216	A411	30g yellow	16	9
1217	A411	40g orange	16	9
1218	A411	50g yellow	14	9
1219	A411	60g brt grn	32	9
1220	A411	90g lt brn	16	9
1221	A411	1.35z emerald	16	9
1222	A411	1.55z vio bl	48	18
1223	A411	2.50z lilac	1.40	55
1224	A411	3.40z rose	1.65	90
1225	A411	6.50z violet	3.25	1.50
		Nos. 1216-1225 (10)	7.88	3.67

King Casimir III, the Great — A412

1964, May 5 Engr. *Perf. 11x11½*

Designs: No. 1227, Hugo Kollataj. No. 1228, Jan Dlugosz. No. 1229, Nicolaus Copernicus. 2.50z, King Wladyslaw II Jagiello and Queen Jadwiga.

Size: 22x35mm

1226	A412	40g dl claret	8	5
1227	A412	40g green	8	5
1228	A412	60g violet	12	5
1229	A412	60g dk bl	15	5

Size: 35½x37mm

1230	A412	2.50z gray brn	35	15
		Nos. 1226-1230 (5)	78	35

Jagiellonian University, Cracow, 600th anniv.

Lapwing A413

Waterfowl: 40g, White-spotted bluethroat. 50g, Black-tailed godwit. 60g, Osprey. 90g, Gray heron. 1.35z, Little gull. 1.55z, Shoveler. 5.60z, Arctic loon. 6.50z, Great crested grebe.

Perf. 11½

1964, June 5 Unwmk. Photo.

Birds in Natural Colors; Black Inscriptions

Size: 34x34mm

1231	A413	30g chalky bl	8	5
1232	A413	40g bister	8	5
1233	A413	50g brt yel grn	8	5

Perf. 11½x11

Size: 34x48mm

1234	A413	60g blue	8	5
1235	A413	90g lemon	9	7
1236	A413	1.35z green	22	7

Perf. 11½

Size: 34x34mm

1237	A413	1.55z olive	22	14
1238	A413	5.60z bl grn	65	35
1239	A413	6.50z brt grn	1.00	55
		Nos. 1231-1239 (9)	2.50	1.38

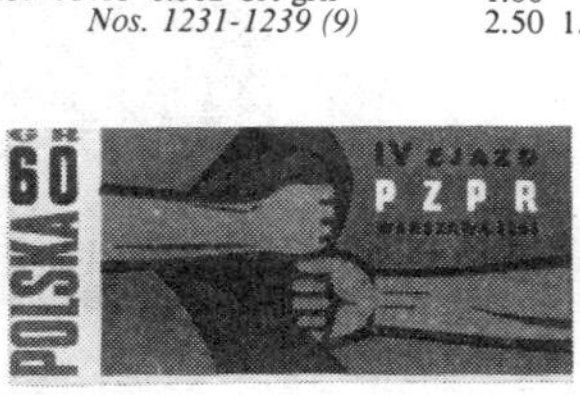

Hands Holding Red Flag — A414

Designs: No. 1241, Red and white ribbon around hammer. No. 1242, Hammer and rye. No. 1243, Brick wall under construction and red flag.

1964, June 15 Litho. *Perf. 11*

1240	A414	60g ol bis, red, blk & pink	9	8
1241	A414	60g red, gray & blk	9	8
1242	A414	60g mag, blk & yel	9	8
1243	A414	60g gray, red, sal & blk	9	8

4th congress of the Polish United Workers Party.

Symbols of Peasant-Worker Alliance — A415

Atom Symbol and Book — A416

Shipyard, Gdansk — A417

Designs: No. 1245, Stylized oak. No. 1247, Factory and cogwheel. No. 1248, Tractor and grain. No. 1249, Pen, brush, mask and ornament. No. 1251, Lenin Metal Works, Nowa Huta. No. 1252, Cement factory, Chelm. No. 1253, Power Station, Turoszow. No. 1254, Oil refinery, Plock. No. 1255, Sulphur mine, Tarnobrzeg.

1964 Litho. *Perf. 12x12½*

1244	A415	60g red, org & blk	9	5
1245	A415	60g grn, red, ocher, bl & blk	9	5

Photo.

Perf. 11

1246	A416	60g gray & dp vio bl	7	6
1247	A416	60g brt bl & blk	7	6
1248	A416	60g emer & blk	7	6
1249	A416	60g org & red	7	6

Photogravure and Engraved

1250	A417	60g dl bl grn & ultra	7	6
1251	A417	60g brt pink & pur	7	6
1252	A417	60g gray & gray brn	7	6
1253	A417	60g grn & sl grn	7	6
1254	A417	60g sal & cl	7	6
1255	A417	60g cit & sep	7	6
		Nos. 1244-1255 (12)	88	70

20th anniversary of the Polish People's Republic.

Warsaw Fighters, 1944 — A418

1964, Aug. 1 Litho. *Perf. 12½x12*

1256	A418	60g multi	15	10

20th anniv. of the Warsaw insurrection against German occupation.

Running — A419

Women's High Jump — A420

Olympic Sports — A421

Sport: 40g, Rowing (single). 60g, Weight lifting. 90g, Relay race (square). 1z, Boxing (square). 2.50z, Soccer (square). 6.50z, Diving.

Unwmk.

1964, Aug. 17 Litho. *Perf. 11*

1257 A419 20g multi 10 5
1258 A419 40g grnsh bl, bl & yel 10 5
1259 A419 60g vio bl, red & rose lil 12 8
1260 A419 90g dk brn, red & yel 18 8
1261 A419 1z dk vio, lil & gray 18 8
1262 A419 2.50z multi 38 20
1263 A420 5.60z multi 95 48
1264 A420 6.50z multi 1.50 80
Nos. 1257-1264 (8) 3.51 1.82

Souvenir Sheet

Imperf

1265 A421 Sheet of 4, multi 2.50 1.65
a 2.50z Sharpshooting 32 22
b 2.50z Canoeing 32 22
c 5z Fencing 32 22
d 5z Basketball 32 22

18th Olympic Games, Tokyo, Oct. 10-25. Size of stamps in No. 1265: 24x24mm. A souvenir sheet containing 2 each of Nos. 1263-1264 with black marginal inscription exists. Value $26.

For unused stamps, more recent issues are valued as never hinged, with the beginning point determined on a country-by-country basis. Notes to show the beginning points are prominently placed in the text.

Warsaw Mermaid and Stars A422

Stefan Zeromski by Monika Zeromska A423

1964, Sept. 7 *Perf. 12½x12*

1266 A422 2.50z vio & blk 28 10

Issued to commemorate the 15th Astronautical Congress, Warsaw, Sept. 7-12.

1964, Sept. 21 Photo. *Perf. 12½*

1267 A423 60g ol gray 18 8

Stefan Zeromski (1864-1925), writer.

Gun and Hand Holding Hammer A424

Globe and Red Flag A425

1964, Sept. 21 Litho. *Perf. 11*

1268 A424 60g brt grn, blk & red 15 8

Issued to commemorate the Third Miners' Militia Congress, Warsaw, Sept. 24-26.

1964, Sept. 28 Photo. *Perf. 12½*

1269 A425 60g blk & red org 15 8

First Socialist International, centenary.

Stagecoach by Jozef Brodowski — A426

1964, Oct. 9 Engr. *Perf. 11½*

1270 A426 60g green 14 8
1271 A426 60g lt brn 14 8

Issued for Stamp Day.

Eleanor Roosevelt (1884-1962) — A427

1964, Oct. 10 *Perf. 12½*

1272 A427 2.50z black 20 10

Proposed Monument for Defenders of Westerplatte, 1939 — A428

Polish Soldiers Crossing Oder River, 1945 A429

Designs: No. 1274, Virtuti Military Cross. No. 1275, Nike, proposed monument for the martyrs of Bydgoszcz (woman with sword and torch). No. 1277, Battle of Studzianki, 1944.

Perf. 12x11, 11x12

1964, Nov. 16 Engr. Unwmk.

1273 A428 40g bl vio 9 6
1274 A428 40g slate 9 6
1275 A428 60g dk bl 9 6
1276 A429 60g dk bl grn 9 6
1277 A429 60g grnsh blk 9 6
Nos. 1273-1277 (5) 45 30

Struggle and martyrdom of the Polish people, 1939-45. The vertical stamps are printed in sheets of 56 stamps (8x7) with 7 labels in each outside vertical row. The horizontal stamps are printed in sheets of 50 stamps (5x10) with 10 labels in each outside vertical row. See Nos. 1366-1368.

Souvenir Sheet

Col. Vladimir M. Komarov, Boris B. Yegorov and Dr. Konstantin Feoktistov — A430

1964, Nov. 21 Litho. *Perf. 11½x11*

1278 A430 Souv. sheet of 3 85 65
a 60g red & blk *(Komarov)* 25 12
b 60g brt grn & blk *(Feoktistov)* 25 12
c 60g ultra & blk *(Yegorov)* 25 12

Russian three-manned space flight in space ship Voskhod, Oct. 12-13, 1964. Size of stamps: 27x36mm.

Cyclamen A431

Garden Flowers: 30g, Freesia. 40g, Monique rose. 50g, Peony. 60g, Royal lily. 90g, Oriental poppy. 1.35z, Tulip. 1.50z, Narcissus. 1.55z, Begonia. 2.50z, Carnation. 3.40z, Iris. 5.60z, Camellia.

1964, Nov. 30 Photo. *Perf. 11*

Size: 35½x35½mm

Flowers in Natural Colors

1279 A431 20g violet 6 5
1280 A431 30g dp lil 6 5
1281 A431 40g blue 6 5
1282 A431 50g vio bl 6 5
1283 A431 60g lilac 8 5
1284 A431 90g dp grn 10 8

Size: 26x37½mm

1285 A431 1.35z dk bl 15 8
1286 A431 1.50z dp car 35 24
1287 A431 1.55z green 15 7
1288 A431 2.50z ultra 30 10
1289 A431 3.40z redsh brn 60 24
1290 A431 5.60z ol gray 1.10 60
Nos. 1279-1290 (12) 3.07 1.66

Future Interplanetary Spacecraft — A432

Designs: 30g, Launching of Russian rocket. 40g, Dog Laika and launching tower. 60g, Lunik 3 photographing far side of the Moon. 1.55z, Satellite exploring the ionosphere. 2.50z, Satellite "Elektron 2" exploring radiation belt. 5.60z, "Mars 1" between Mars and Earth.

Perf. 12½x12

1964, Dec. 30 Litho. Unwmk.

1291 A432 20g multi 8 5
1292 A432 30g multi 8 5
1293 A432 40g ol grn, blk & bl 8 5
1294 A432 60g dk bl, blk & dk red 10 5
1295 A432 1.55z gray & multi 25 7
1296 A432 2.50z multi 52 15
1297 A432 5.60z multi 90 40
Nos. 1291-1297,B108 (8) 3.51 1.47

Issued to publicize space research.

Warsaw Mermaid, Ruins and New Buildings A433

1965, Jan. 15 Engr. *Perf. 11x11½*

1298 A433 60g sl grn 10 8

Liberation of Warsaw, 20th anniversary.

Ship Type of 1963

Designs as before.

1965, Jan. 25 Engr. *Perf. 12½*

1299 A398 5g dk brn 5 5
1300 A398 10g sl grn 5 5
1301 A398 20g sl bl 5 5
1302 A398 30g gray ol 5 5
1303 A398 40g dk bl 5 5
1304 A398 60g claret 8 8
1305 A398 1z red brn 10 8
1306 A398 1.15z dk red brn 15 8
Nos. 1299-1306 (8) 58 49

Edaphosaurus — A434

Dinosaurs: 30g, Cryptocleidus (vert.). 40g, Brontosaurus. 60g, Mesosaurus (vert.). 90g, Stegosaurus. 1.15z, Brachiosaurus (vert.). 1.35z, Styracosaurus. 3.40z, Corythosaurus (vert.). 5.60z, Rhamphorhynchus (vert.). 6.50z, Tyrannosaurus.

1965, Mar. 5 Litho. *Perf. 12½*

1307 A434 20g multi 8 8
1308 A434 30g multi 8 8
1309 A434 40g multi 8 8
1310 A434 60g multi 8 8
1311 A434 90g multi 28 10
1312 A434 1.15z multi 14 10
1313 A434 1.35z multi 16 10
1314 A434 3.40z multi 42 16
1315 A434 5.60z multi 90 35
1316 A434 6.50z multi 1.40 90
Nos. 1307-1316 (10) 3.62 2.03

See Nos. 1395-1403.

Symbolic Wax Seal — A435

Russian and Polish Flags, Oil Refinery-Chemical Plant, Plock — A436

1965, Apr. 21 ***Perf. 12½x12, 12½***

1317	A435	60g multi		9	8
1318	A436	60g multi		9	8

20th anniversary of the signing of the Polish-Soviet treaty of friendship, mutual assistance and postwar cooperation.

Polish Eagle and Town Coats of Arms — A437

1965, May 8 **Engr.** ***Perf. 11½***

1319	A437	60g car rose	14	8

20th anniversary of regaining the Western and Northern Territories.

Dove A438

1965, May 8 **Litho.** ***Perf. 12x12½***

1320	A438	60g red & blk	14	8

Victory over Fascism, 20th anniversary.

ITU Emblem — A439

"The People's Friend" and Clover — A440

Factory and Rye A441

Perf. 12½x12

1965, May 17 **Litho.** **Unwmk.**

1321	A439	2.50z brt bl, lil, yel & blk	28	10

ITU, cent.

1965, June 5 ***Perf. 11***

1322	A440	40g multi	10	5
1323	A441	60g multi	10	8

Issued to commemorate the 70th anniversary of the "Popular Movement" in Poland.

Finn Class Yachts A442

Yachts: 30g, Dragon class. 40g, 5.5-m. class. 50g, Group of Finn class. 60g, V-class. 1.35z, Group of Cadet class. 4z, Group of Star class. 5.60z, Two Flying Dutchmen. 6.50z, Two Amethyst class. 15z, Finn class race. (30g, 40g, 60g, 5.60z vertical)

1965, June 14 **Litho.** ***Perf. 12½***

1324	A442	30g multi	8	8
1325	A442	40g multi	8	8
1326	A442	50g multi	10	8
1327	A442	60g multi	10	8
1328	A442	1.35z multi	14	10
1329	A442	4z multi	50	22
1330	A442	5.60z multi	90	42
1331	A442	6.50z multi	1.40	70
		Nos. 1324-1331 (8)	3.30	1.76

Miniature Sheet

Perf. 11

1332	A442	15z multi	1.65	1.25

World Championships of Finn Class Yachts, Gdynia, July 22-29. No. 1332 contains one stamp 48x22mm.

Marx and Lenin — A443

Photogravure and Engraved

1965, June 14 ***Perf. 11½x11***

1333	A443	60g blk, *ver*	10	8

6th Conference of Ministers of Post of Communist Countries, Peking, June 21-July 15.

Warsaw's Coat of Arms, 17th Century A444

Old Town Hall, 18th Century A445

Designs: 10g, Artifacts, 13th century. 20g, Tombstone of last Duke of Mazovia. 60g, Barbican, Gothic-Renaissance castle. 1.50z, Arsenal, 19th century. 1.55z, National Theater. 2.50z, Staszic Palace. 3.40z, Woman with sword from Heroes' Memorial and Warsaw Mermaid seal.

Perf. 11x11½, 11½x11, 12x12½, 12½x12

1965, July 21 **Engr.** **Unwmk.**

1334	A444	5g car rose	5	5
1335	A444	10g green	5	5
1336	A445	20g vio bl	5	5
1337	A445	40g brown	5	5
1338	A445	60g orange	6	5
1339	A445	1.50z black	8	8
1340	A445	1.55z gray bl	12	8
1341	A445	2.50z lilac	22	10

Perf. 11½

Photogravure and Engraved

1342	A444	3.40z cit & blk	70	60
		Nos. 1334-1342 (9)	1.38	1.11

700th anniversary of Warsaw.

No. 1342 is perforated all around, with lower right quarter perforated to form a 21x26mm stamp within a stamp. It was issued in sheets of 25 (5x5).

IQSY Emblem A446

Designs: 2.50z, Radar screen, Torun. 3.40z, Solar system.

1965, Aug. 9 **Litho.**

1343	A446	60g vio, ver, brt grn & blk		8	5
a		60g ultra, org, yel, bl & blk		8	5
1344	A446	2.50z red, yel, pur & blk		25	8
a		2.50z red brn, yel, gray & blk		25	8
1345	A446	3.40z org & multi		32	14
a		3.40z ol gray & multi		32	14

International Quiet Sun Year, 1964-65.

Odontoglossum Grande — A447

Weight Lifting — A448

Orchids: 30g, Cypripedium hibridum. 40g, Lycaste skinneri. 50g, Cattleya. 60g, Vanda sanderiana. 1.35z, Cypripedium hibridum. 4z, Sobralia. 5.60z, Disa grandiflora. 6.50z, Cattleya labiata.

1965, Sept. 6 **Photo.** ***Perf. 12½x12***

1346	A447	20g multi	8	8
1347	A447	30g multi	8	8
1348	A447	40g multi	8	8
1349	A447	50g multi	10	8
1350	A447	60g multi	10	8
1351	A447	1.35z multi	18	10
1352	A447	4z multi	42	30
1353	A447	5.60z multi	90	42
1354	A447	6.50z multi	1.40	75
		Nos. 1346-1354 (9)	3.34	1.97

1965, Oct. 8 **Photo.** **Unwmk.**

Sport: 40g, Boxing. 50g, Relay race, men. 60g, Fencing. 90g, Women's 80-meter hurdles. 3.40z, Relay race, women. 6.50z, Hop, step and jump. 7.10z, Volleyball, women.

1355	A448	30g gold & multi	10	7
1356	A448	40g gold & multi	10	7
1357	A448	50g sil & multi	10	7
1358	A448	60g gold & multi	10	7
1359	A448	90g sil & multi	15	7
1360	A448	3.40z gold & multi	50	14
1361	A448	6.50z gold & multi	85	42
1362	A448	7.10z brnz & multi	1.00	60
		Nos. 1355-1362 (8)	2.90	1.51

Victories won by the Polish team in 1964 Olympic Games. Each denomination printed in sheets of eight stamps and two center labels showing medals.

Mail Coach, by Piotr Michalowski — A449

Design: 2.50z, Departure of Coach, by Piotr Michalowski.

1965, Oct. 9 **Engr.** ***Perf. 11x11½***

1363	A449	60g brown	14	7
1364	A449	2.50z sl grn	22	10

Issued for Stamp Day, 1965. Sheets of 50 with labels se-tenant inscribed "Dzien Znaczka 1965 R."

UN Emblem A450

Memorial, Plaszow A451

1965, Oct. 24 **Litho.** ***Perf. 12½x12***

1365	A450	2.50z ultra	25	10

20th anniversary of United Nations.

Perf. 12x11, 11x12

1965, Nov. 29 **Engr.**

Designs: No. 1367, Kielce Memorial. No. 1368, Chelm Memorial (horiz.).

1366	A451	60g grnsh gray	14	6
1367	A451	60g chocolate	14	6
1368	A451	60g black	14	6

Note after No. 1277 applies also to Nos. 1366-1368.

Wolf A452

Animals: 30g, Lynx. 40g, Red fox. 50g, Badger. 60g, Brown bear. 1.50z, Wild boar. 2.50z, Red deer. 5.60z, European bison. 7.10z, Moose.

1965, Nov. 30 **Photo.** ***Perf. 11½***

1369	A452	20g multi	8	8
1370	A452	30g multi	8	8
1371	A452	40g multi	8	8
1372	A452	50g multi	8	8
1373	A452	60g multi	10	8
1374	A452	1.50z multi	45	15
1375	A452	2.50z multi	45	15
1376	A452	5.60z multi	1.00	45
1377	A452	7.10z multi	1.25	90
		Nos. 1369-1377 (9)	3.57	2.05

Gig — A453

Horse-drawn carriages, Lancut Museum: 40g, Coupe. 50g, Lady's basket. 60g, Vis-a-vis. 90g, Cab. 1.15z, Berlinka. 2.50z, Hunting break. 6.50z, Caleche ala Daumont. 7.10z, English break.

1965, Dec. 30 **Litho.** ***Perf. 11***

Size: 50x23mm

1378	A453	20g multi	8	5
1379	A453	40g lil & multi	8	5
1380	A453	50g org & multi	8	6
1381	A453	60g fawn & multi	8	6
1382	A453	90g yel & multi	12	6

Size: 76x23mm

1383	A453	1.15z multi	12	9
1384	A453	2.50z ol & multi	35	20
1385	A453	6.50z multi	90	45

Size: 103x23mm

1386	A453	7.10z bl & multi	1.65	90
		Nos. 1378-1386 (9)	3.46	1.92

Cargo Ship (No. 1389) — A454

Designs: No. 1387, Supervising Technical Organization (NOT) emblem, symbols of industry. No. 1388, Pit head and miners' badge (vert.). No. 1390, Chemical plant, Plock. No. 1391, Combine. No. 1392, Railroad train. No. 1393, Building crane (vert.). No. 1394, Pavilion and emblem of 35th International Poznan Fair.

1966 Litho. *Perf. 11*

1387	A454	60g multi	9	8
1388	A454	60g multi	9	8
1389	A454	60g multi	9	8
1390	A454	60g multi	9	8
1391	A454	60g multi	9	8
1392	A454	60g multi	9	8
1393	A454	60g multi	9	8
1394	A454	60g multi	9	8
		Nos. 1387-1394 (8)	72	64

20th anniversary of the nationalization of Polish industry. No. 1394 also commemorates the 35th International Poznan Fair. Nos. 1387-1388 issued in connection with the 5th Congress of Polish Technicians, Katowice. Printed in sheets of 20 stamps and 20 labels with commemorative inscription within cogwheel on each label.

Dates of issue: Nos. 1387-1388, Feb. 10; others, May 21.

Dinosaur Type of 1965

1966, March 5 Litho. *Perf. 12½*

Prehistoric Vertebrates: 20g, Dinichthys. 30g, Eusthenopteron. 40g, Ichthyostega. 50g, Mastodonsaurus. 60g, Cynognathus. 2.50z, Archaeopteryx (vert.). 3.40z, Brontotherium. 6.50z, Machairodus. 7.10z, Mammoth.

1395	A434	20g multi	7	5
1396	A434	30g multi	7	5
1397	A434	40g multi	7	5
1398	A434	50g multi	7	5
1399	A434	60g multi	20	6
1400	A434	2.50z multi	25	15
1401	A434	3.40z multi	40	20
1402	A434	6.50z multi	85	45
1403	A434	7.10z multi	1.50	90
		Nos. 1395-1403 (9)	3.48	1.96

Henryk Sienkiewicz A455

Photogravure and Engraved

1966, Mar. 30 *Perf. 11½*

1404	A455	60g black, *dl yel*	15	8

Henryk Sienkiewicz (1846-1916), author and winner of 1905 Nobel Prize.

Soccer Game A456

Peace Dove and War Memorial A457

Designs: Various phases of soccer. Each stamp inscribed with the place and the result of final game in various preceding soccer championships.

1966, May 6 *Perf. 13x12*

1405	A456	20g multi	5	5
1406	A456	40g multi	5	5
1407	A456	60g multi	8	8
1408	A456	90g multi	12	8
1409	A456	1.50z multi	25	12
1410	A456	3.40z multi	40	15
1411	A456	6.50z multi	85	38
1412	A456	7.10z multi	1.10	60
		Nos. 1405-1412 (8)	2.90	1.51

World Cup Soccer Championship, Wembley, England, July 11-30. Each denomination printed in sheets of 10 (5x2).

See No. B109.

Typo. & Engr.

1966, May 9 *Perf. 11½*

1413	A457	60g sil & multi	10	8

21st anniversary of victory over Fascism.

Women's Relay Race — A458

Designs: 20g, Start of men's short distance race (vert.). 60g, Javelin (vert.). 90g, Women's 80-meter hurdles. 1.35z, Discus (vert.). 3.40z, Finish of men's medium distance race. 6.50z, Hammer throw (vert.) 7.10z, High jump.

Perf. 11½x11, 11x11½

1966, June 18 Litho.

1414	A458	20g multi	5	5
1415	A458	40g multi	5	5
1416	A458	60g multi	8	8
1417	A458	90g multi	8	8
1418	A458	1.35z multi	12	8
1419	A458	3.40z multi	35	15
1420	A458	6.50z multi	48	32
1421	A458	7.10z multi	60	50
		Nos. 1414-1421 (8)	1.81	1.31

Souvenir Sheet

Design: 5z, Long distance race.

Imperf

1422	A458	5z multi	1.00	55

European Athletic Championships, Budapest, August, 1966. No. 1422 contains one stamp 57x27mm.

Polish Eagle A459

Flowers and Farm Produce A460

Designs: Nos. 1424, 1426, Flag of Poland. No. 1425, Polish Eagle.

Photogravure and Embossed

Perf. 12½x12

1966, July 21 Unwmk.

1423	A459	60g gold, red & blk	9	8
1424	A459	60g gold, red & blk	9	8
1425	A459	2.50z gold, red & blk	25	12
1426	A459	2.50z gold, red & blk	25	12

1000th anniversary of Poland. Nos. 1423-1424 and 1425-1426 printed in 2 sheets of 10 (5x2); top row in each sheet in eagle design, bottom row in flag design.

1966, Aug. 15 Photo. *Perf. 11*

Designs: 60g, Woman holding loaf of bread. 3.40z, Farm girls holding harvest wreath.

Size: 22x50mm

1427	A460	40g gold & multi	22	8
1428	A460	60g gold & multi	22	8

Size: 48x50mm

1429	A460	3.40z vio bl & multi	55	35

Issued to publicize the harvest festival.

Chrysanthemum — A461

Flowers: 20g, Poinsettia. 30g, Centaury. 40g, Rose. 60g, Zinnias. 90g, Nasturtium. 5.60z, Dahlia. 6.50z, Sunflower. 7.10z, Magnolia.

1966, Sept. 1 *Perf. 11½*

Flowers in Natural Colors

1430	A461	10g gold & blk	8	5
1431	A461	20g gold & blk	8	5
1432	A461	30g gold & blk	8	5
1433	A461	40g gold & blk	8	5
1434	A461	60g gold & blk	8	8
1435	A461	90g gold & blk	60	25
1436	A461	5.60z gold & blk	75	25
1437	A461	6.50z gold & blk	1.10	52
1438	A461	7.10z gold & blk	85	65
		Nos. 1430-1438 (9)	3.70	1.95

Map Showing Tourist Attractions — A462

Designs: 20g, Lighthouse, Hel. 40g, Amethyst yacht on Masurian Lake. No. 1442, Poniatowski Bridge, Warsaw, and sailboat. No. 1443, Mining Academy, Kielce. 1.15z, Dunajec Gorge. 1.35z, Old oaks, Rogalin. 1.55z, Planetarium, Katowice. 2z, M.S. Batory and globe.

Perf. 12½x12, 11½x12

1966, Sept. 15 Engr.

1439	A462	10g car rose	5	5
1440	A462	20g ol gray	5	5
1441	A462	40g grysh bl	5	5
1442	A462	60g redsh brn	7	5
1443	A462	60g black	7	5
1444	A462	1.15z green	8	8
1445	A462	1.35z vermilion	10	8
1446	A462	1.55z violet	12	8
1447	A462	2z dk gray	15	10
		Nos. 1439-1447 (9)	74	59

Stableman with Percherons, by Piotr Michalowski — A463

Design: 2.50z, "Horses and Dogs" by Michalowski.

1966, Sept. 8 *Perf. 11x11½*

1448	A463	60g gray brn	10	8
1449	A463	2.50z green	18	10

Issued for Stamp Day, 1966.

Capital of Romanesque Column from Tyniec and Polish Flag — A464

Engraved and Photogravure

1966, Oct. 7 *Perf. 11½*

1450	A464	60g dk brn & rose	10	8

Polish Cultural Congress.

Soldier A465

1966, Oct. 20 Litho. *Perf. 11x11½*

1451	A465	60g blk, ol grn, & dl red	15	8

Participation of the Polish Jaroslaw Dabrowski Brigade in the Spanish Civil War.

Green Woodpecker A466

Forest Birds: 10g, The eight birds of the set combined. 30g, Eurasian jay. 40g, European golden oriole. 60g, Hoopoe. 2.50z, European redstart. 4z, Siskin (finch). 6.50z, Chaffinch. 7.10z, Great tit.

1966, Nov. 17 Photo. *Perf. 11½*

Birds in Natural Colors; Black Inscription

1452	A466	10g lt grn	8	8
1453	A466	20g dl vio bl	8	8
1454	A466	30g dl grn	8	8
1455	A466	40g gray	8	8
1456	A466	60g gray grn	8	8
1457	A466	2.50z lt ol grn	25	15
1458	A466	4z dl vio	90	35
1459	A466	6.50z green	65	42
1460	A466	7.10z gray bl	1.25	70
		Nos. 1452-1460 (9)	3.45	2.02

Ceramic Ram, c. 4000 B.C. — A467

Designs: No. 1462, Bronze weapons and ornaments, c. 3500 B.C. (horiz.). No. 1463, Biskupin, settlement plan, 2500 B.C.

1966, Dec. 10 Engr. *Perf. 11x11½*

1461	A467	60g dl vio bl	10	8
1462	A467	60g brown	10	8
1463	A467	60g green	10	8

Polish Eagle, Hammer and Grain — A468

Designs: 60g, Eagle and map of Poland.

1966, Dec. 20 Litho. *Perf. 11*

1464	A468	40g brn, red & bluish lil	6	5
1465	A468	60g brn, red & ol grn	10	8

Millenium of Poland.

Gemini, American Spacecraft — A469

Spacecraft: 20g, Vostok (USSR). 60g, Ariel 2 (Great Britain). 1.35z, Proton 1 (USSR). 1.50z, FR 1 (France). 3.40z, Alouette (Canada). 6.50z, San Marco 1 (Italy). 7.10z, Luna 9 (USSR).

1966, Dec. 20 ***Perf. 11½x11***

1466	A469	20g	tan & multi	5	5
1467	A469	40g	brn & multi	5	5
1468	A469	60g	gray & multi	8	5
1469	A469	1.35z	multi	12	8
1470	A469	1.50z	multi	12	8
1471	A469	3.40z	multi	32	16
1472	A469	6.50z	multi	65	22
1473	A469	7.10z	multi	85	48
			Nos. 1466-1473 (8)	2.24	1.17

Dressage — A470

Horses: 20g, Horse race. 40g, Jump. 60g, Steeplechase. 90g, Trotting. 5.90z, Polo. 6.60z, Stallion "Ofir." 7z, Stallion "Skowronek."

1967, Feb. 25 Photo. ***Perf. 12½***

1474	A470	10g	ultra & multi	8	5
1475	A470	20g	org & multi	8	5
1476	A470	40g	ver & multi	8	6
1477	A470	60g	multi	10	8
1478	A470	90g	grn & multi	18	8
1479	A470	5.90z	multi	70	18
1480	A470	6.60z	multi	90	40
1481	A470	7z	vio & multi	1.75	90
			Nos. 1474-1481 (8)	3.87	1.80

Janov Podlaski stud farm, 150th anniv.

Memorial at Auschwitz (Oswiecim) A471

Emblem of Memorials Administration A472

Memorials at: No. 1484, Oswiecim-Monowice. No. 1485, Westerplatte (Walcz). No. 1486, Lodz-Radugoszcz. No. 1487, Stutthof. No. 1488, Lambinowice-Jencom. No. 1489, Zagan.

1967 Engr. ***Perf. 11½x11, 11x11½***

1482	A471	40g	brn ol	8	5
1483	A472	40g	dl vio	8	5
1484	A472	40g	black	8	5
1485	A472	40g	green	8	5
1486	A472	40g	black	8	5
1487	A471	40g	ultra	8	5
1488	A471	40g	brown	8	5
1489	A472	40g	dp plum	8	5
			Nos. 1482-1489 (8)	64	40

Issued to commemorate the martyrdom and fight of the Polish people, 1939-45.

Issue dates: Nos. 1482-1484, Apr. 10. Nos. 1485-1487, Oct. 9. Nos. 1488-1489, Dec. 28.

See Nos. 1620-1624.

Striped Butterflyfish — A473

Tropical fish: 10g, Imperial angelfish. 40g, Barred butterflyfish. 60g, Spotted triggerfish. 90g, Undulate triggerfish. 1.50z, Striped triggerfish. 4.50z, Black-eye butterflyfish. 6.60z, Blue angelfish. 7z, Saddleback butterflyfish.

1967, Apr. 1 Litho. ***Perf. 11x11½***

1492	A473	5g	multi	7	5
1493	A473	10g	multi	7	5
1494	A473	40g	multi	10	8
1495	A473	60g	multi	12	8
1496	A473	90g	multi	12	8
1497	A473	1.50z	multi	15	10
1498	A473	4.50z	multi	50	28
1499	A473	6.60z	multi	65	42
1500	A473	7z	multi	1.10	70
			Nos. 1492-1500 (9)	2.88	1.84

Bicyclists — A474

1967, May 5 Litho. ***Perf. 11***

1501	A474	60g	multi	14	8

20th Warsaw-Berlin-Prague Bicycle Race.

Men's 100-meter Race A475

Sports and Olympic Rings: 40g, Steeplechase. 60g, Women's relay race. 90g, Weight lifter. 1.35z, Hurdler. 3.40z, Gymnast on vaulting horse. 6.60z, High jump. 7z, Boxing.

1967, May 24 Litho. ***Perf. 11***

1502	A475	20g	multi	7	5
1503	A475	40g	multi	7	5
1504	A475	60g	multi	7	5
1505	A475	90g	multi	10	8
1506	A475	1.35z	multi	15	8
1507	A475	3.40z	multi	38	14
1508	A475	6.60z	multi	75	24
1509	A475	7z	multi	90	52
			Nos. 1502-1509 (8)	2.49	1.21

19th Olympic Games, Mexico City, 1968. Nos. 1502-1509 printed in sheets of 8, (2x4) with label showing emblem of Polish Olympic Committee between each two horizontal stamps. See No. B110.

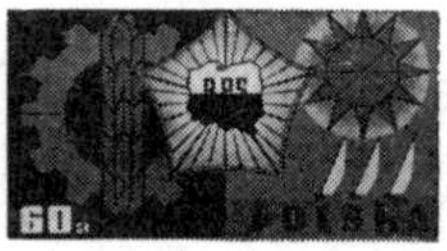

Badge of Socialist Working Brigade A476

1967, June 2

1510	A476	60g	multi	10	8

6th Congress of Polish Trade Unions. Printed in sheets of 20 stamps and 20 labels and in miniature sheets of 4 stamps and 4 labels.

Mountain Arnica — A477

Medicinal Plants: 60g, Columbine. 3.40z, Gentian. 4.50z, Ground pine. 5z, Iris sibirica. 10z, Azalea pontica.

1967, June 14 ***Perf. 11½x11***
Flowers in Natural Colors

1511	A477	40g	blk & brn org	5	5
1512	A477	60g	blk & lt bl	5	8
1513	A477	3.40z	blk & dp org	30	10
1514	A477	4.50z	blk & lt vio	32	14
1515	A477	5z	blk & mar	35	14
1516	A477	10z	blk & bis	85	42
			Nos. 1511-1516 (6)	1.92	93

Monument for Silesian Insurgents A478

1967, July 21 Litho. ***Perf. 11½***

1517	A478	60g	multi	10	8

Unveiling of the monument for the Silesian Insurgents of 1919-21 at Katowice, July, 1967.

Marie Curie — A479

Designs: No. 1519, Curie statue, Warsaw. No. 1520, Nobel Prize diploma.

1967, Aug. 1 Engr. ***Perf. 11½x11***

1518	A479	60g	dk car rose	18	8
1519	A479	60g	violet	12	8
1520	A479	60g	sepia	18	8

Marie Sklodowska Curie (1867-1934), discoverer of radium and polonium.

Sign Language and Emblem A480

1967, Aug. 1 Litho. ***Perf. 11x11½***

1521	A480	60g	brt bl & blk	10	8

5th Congress of the World Federation of the Deaf, Warsaw, Aug. 10-17.

Flowers of the Meadows A481

Flowers: 40g, Poppy. 60g, Morning glory. 90g, Pansy. 1.15z, Common pansy. 2.50z, Corn cockle. 3.40z, Wild aster. 4.50z, Common pimpernel. 7.90z, Chicory.

1967, Sept. 5 Photo. ***Perf. 11½***

1522	A481	20g	multi	8	5
1523	A481	40g	multi	8	5
1524	A481	60g	multi	8	8
1525	A481	90g	multi	8	8
1526	A481	1.15z	multi	12	8
1527	A481	2.50z	multi	25	16
1528	A481	3.40z	multi	38	16
1529	A481	4.50z	multi	75	48
1530	A481	7.90z	multi	95	48
			Nos. 1522-1530 (9)	2.77	1.62

Wilanow Palace, by Wincenty Kasprzycki — A482

Engraved and Photogravure
1967, Oct. 9 ***Perf. 11½***

1531	A482	60g	ol blk & lt bl	10	8

Issued for Stamp Day, 1967.

Cruiser Aurora — A483

Designs: No. 1533, Lenin and library. No. 1534, Luna 10, earth and moon.

1967, Oct. 9 Litho. ***Perf. 11***

1532	A483	60g	gray, red & blk	12	8
1533	A483	60g	gray, dl red & blk	12	8
1534	A483	60g	gray, red & blk	15	10

Russian Revolution, 50th anniv.

Tadeusz Kosciusko — A485

Engraved and Photogravure
1967, Oct. 14 ***Perf. 12x11***

1540	A485	60g	choc & ocher	8	8
1541	A485	2.50z	sl grn & rose car	15	15

Tadeusz Kosciusko (1746-1817), Polish patriot and general in the American Revolution.

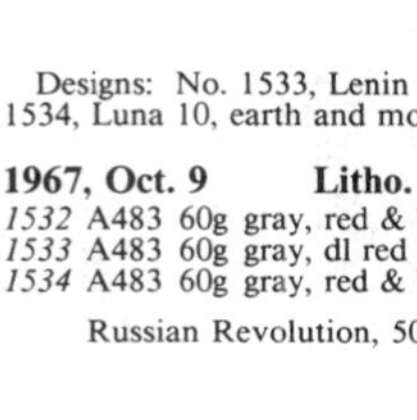

Vanessa Butterfly A486

Designs: Various Butterflies.

1967, Oct. 14 Litho. ***Perf. 11½***
Butterflies in Natural Colors

1542	A486	10g	green	6	6
1543	A486	20g	lt vio bl	6	6
1544	A486	40g	yel grn	6	6
1545	A486	60g	gray	9	6
1546	A486	2z	lemon	15	10
1547	A486	2.50z	Prus grn	18	10

1548	A486	3.40z blue	30	12
1549	A486	4.50z rose lil	1.00	40
1550	A486	7.90z bister	1.65	90
		Nos. 1542-1550 (9)	3.55	1.86

Polish Woman, by Antoine Watteau
A487

Paintings from Polish Museums: 20g, Lady with the Ermine, by Leonardo da Vinci. 60g, Dog Fighting Heron, by Abraham Hondius. 2z, Guitarist after the Hunt, by J. Baptiste Greuze. 2.50z, Tax Collectors, by Marinus van Reymerswaele. 3.40z, Portrait of Daria Flodorowna, by Fiodor St. Rokotov. 4.50z, Still Life with Lobster, by Jean de Heem (horiz.). 6.60z, Landscape (from the Good Samaritan), by Rembrandt (horiz.).

Perf. 11½x11, 11x11½

1967, Nov. 15 **Photo.**

1551	A487	20g gold & multi	12	8
1552	A487	40g gold & multi	9	8
1553	A487	60g gold & multi	9	8
1554	A487	2z gold & multi	18	10
1555	A487	2.50z gold & multi	25	14
1556	A487	3.40z gold & multi	35	14
1557	A487	4.50z gold & multi	85	42
1558	A487	6.60z gold & multi	1.00	70
		Nos. 1551-1558 (8)	2.93	1.74

Ossolinski Medal, Book and Flags — A488

1967, Dec. 12 **Litho.** ***Perf. 11***

1559	A488	60g lt bl, red & lt brn	15	8

150th anniversary of the founding of the Ossolineum, a center for scientific and cultural activities, by Count Josef Maximilian Ossolinski.

Wladyslaw S. Reymont (1867-1924), Writer, Nobel Prize Winner — A489

1967, Dec. 12

1560	A489	60g dk brn, ocher & red	15	8

Ice Hockey
A490

Designs: 60g, Skiing. 90g, Slalom. 1.35z, Speed skating. 1.55z, Long-distance skiing. 2z, Sledding. 7z, Biathlon. 7.90z, Ski jump.

1968, Jan. 10

1561	A490	40g multi	8	5
1562	A490	60g multi	8	8
1563	A490	90g multi	10	8
1564	A490	1.35z multi	15	7
1565	A490	1.55z multi	15	7
1566	A490	2z multi	20	10
1567	A490	7z multi	52	35
1568	A490	7.90z multi	85	52
		Nos. 1561-1568 (8)	2.13	1.32

10th Winter Olympic Games, Grenoble, France, Feb. 6-18, 1968.

Puss in Boots — A491

Fairy Tales: 40g, The Fox and the Raven. 60g, Mr. Twardowski (man flying on a cock). 2z, The Fisherman and the Fish. 2.50z, Little Red Riding Hood. 3.40z, Cinderella. 5.50z, Thumbelina. 7z, Snow White.

1968, Mar. 15 **Litho.** ***Perf. 12½***

1569	A491	20g multi	5	5
1570	A491	40g lt vio & multi	5	5
1571	A491	60g multi	8	5
1572	A491	2z ol & multi	20	14
1573	A491	2.50z ver & multi	25	14
1574	A491	3.40z multi	45	16
1575	A491	5.50z multi	65	42
1576	A491	7z multi	1.10	70
		Nos. 1569-1576 (8)	2.83	1.71

Bird-of-Paradise Flower — A492

Exotic Flowers: 10g, Clianthus dampieri. 20g, Passiflora quadrangularis. 40g, Coryphanta vivipara. 60g, Odontonia. 90g, Protea cynaroides.

1968, May 15 **Litho.** ***Perf. 11½***

1577	A492	10g sep & multi	6	6
1578	A492	20g multi	6	6
1579	A492	30g brn & multi	6	6
1580	A492	40g ultra & multi	6	6
1581	A492	60g multi	9	8
1582	A492	90g multi	15	10
		Nos. 1577-1582,B111-B112 (8)	2.33	1.37

"Peace" by Henryk Tomaszewski
A493

Design: 2.50z, Poster for Gounod's Faust, by Jan Lenica.

1968, May 29 **Litho.** ***Perf. 11½x11***

1583	A493	60g gray & multi	10	8
1584	A493	2.50z gray & multi	18	10

2nd Intl. Poster Biennial Exhibition, Warsaw.

A little time given to the study of the arrangement of the Scott Catalogue can make it easier to use effectively.

Zephyr Glider — A494

Polish Gliders: 90g, Storks. 1.50z, Swallow. 3.40z, Flies. 4z, Seal. 5.50z, Pirate.

1968, May 29 ***Perf. 12½***

1585	A494	60g multi	8	5
1586	A494	90g multi	8	8
1587	A494	1.50z multi	12	8
1588	A494	3.40z multi	40	16
1589	A494	4z multi	52	28
1590	A494	5.50z multi	65	42
		Nos. 1585-1590 (6)	1.85	1.07

11th Intl. Glider Championships, Leszno.

Child Holding Symbolic Stamp
A495

Sosnowiec Memorial
A496

Design: No. 1592, Balloon over Poznan Town Hall.

1968, July 2 **Litho.** ***Perf. 11½x11***

1591	A495	60g multi	12	6
1592	A495	60g multi	12	6

75 years of Polish philately; "Tematica 1968" stamp exhibition in Poznan. Printed in sheets of 12 (4x3) se-tenant, arranged checkerwise.

Photogravure and Engraved

1968, July 20 ***Perf. 11x11½***

1593	A496	60g brt rose lil & blk	12	8

The monument by Helena and Roman Husarski and Witold Ceckiewicz was unveiled Sept. 16, 1967, to honor the revolutionary deeds of Silesian workers and miners.

Relay Race and Sculptured Head
A497

Sports and Sculptures: 40g, Boxing. 60g. Basketball. 90g, Long jump. 2.50z, Women's javelin. 3.40z, Athlete on parallel bars. 4z, Bicycling. 7.90z, Fencing.

1968, Sept. 2 **Litho.** ***Perf. 11x11½***
Size: 35x26mm

1594	A497	30g sep & multi	5	5
1595	A497	40g brn org, brn & blk	5	5
1596	A497	60g gray & multi	8	5
1597	A497	90g vio & multi	8	8
1598	A497	2.50z multi	20	8
1599	A497	3.40z brt grn, blk & lt ultra	30	12
1600	A497	4z multi	32	18
1601	A497	7.90z multi	65	35
		Nos. 1594-1601,B113 (9)	3.23	1.81

19th Olympic Games, Mexico City, Oct. 12-27.

Jewish Woman with Lemons, by Aleksander Gierymski
A498

Polish Paintings: 40g, Knight on Bay Horse, by Piotr Michalowski. 60g, Fisherman, by Leon Wyczolkowski. 1.35z, Eliza Parenska, by Stanislaw Wyspianski. 1.50z, "Manifest," by Wojciech Weiss. 4.50z, Stancyk (Jester), by Jan Matejko (horiz.). 5z, Children's Band, by Tadeusz Makowski (horiz.). 7z, Feast II, by Zygmunt Waliszewski (horiz.).

Perf. 11½x11, 11x11½

1968, Oct. 10 **Litho.**

1602	A498	40g gray & multi	6	5
1603	A498	60g gray & multi	6	5
1604	A498	1.15z gray & multi	9	8
1605	A498	1.35z gray & multi	15	8
1606	A498	1.50z gray & multi	30	16
1607	A498	4.50z gray & multi	40	22
1608	A498	5z gray & multi	65	30
1609	A498	7z gray & multi	75	48
		Nos. 1602-1609 (8)	2.46	1.42

Issued in sheets of 4 stamps and 2 labels inscribed with painter's name.

"September, 1939" by M. Bylina — A499

Paintings: No. 1611, Partisans, by L. Maciag. No. 1612, Tank in Battle, by M. Bylina. No. 1613, Monte Cassino, by A. Boratynski. No. 1614, Tanks Approaching Warsaw, by S. Garwatowski. No. 1615, Battle on the Neisse, by M. Bylina. No. 1616, On the Oder, by K. Mackiewicz. No. 1617, "In Berlin," by M. Bylina. No. 1618, Warship "Blyskawica" by M. Mokwa. No. 1619, "Pursuit" (fighter planes), by T. Kulisiewicz.

Litho., Typo. & Engr.

1968, Oct. 12 ***Perf. 11½***

1610	A499	40g pale yel, ol & vio	8	5
1611	A499	40g lil, red lil & ind	8	5
1612	A499	40g gray, dk bl & ol	8	5
1613	A499	40g pale sal, org brn & blk	8	5
1614	A499	40g pale grn, dk grn & plum	8	5
1615	A499	60g gray, vio bl & blk	12	8
1616	A499	60g pale grn, ol grn & vio brn	12	8
1617	A499	60g pink, car & grnsh blk	12	8
1618	A499	60g pink, brn & grn	12	8
1619	A499	60g lt bl, grnsh bl & blk	12	8
		Nos. 1610-1619 (10)	1.00	65

Polish People's Army, 25th anniversary.

Memorial Types of 1967

Designs: No. 1620, Tomb of the Unknown Soldier, Warsaw. No. 1621, Nazi War Crimes Memorial, Zamosc. No. 1622, Guerrilla Memorial, Plichno. No. 1623, Guerrilla Memorial, Kartuzy. No. 1624, Polish Insurgents' Memorial, Poznan.

Perf. 11½x11, 11x11½

1968, Nov. 15 **Engr.**

1620	A471	40g slate	8	5
1621	A472	40g dl red	8	5
1622	A472	40g dk bl	8	5
1623	A471	40g sepia	8	5
1624	A472	40g sepia	8	5
		Nos. 1620-1624 (5)	40	25

Issued to commemorate the martyrdom and fight of the Polish people, 1939-45.

Strikers, S. Lentz
A500

Paintings: No. 1626, "Manifesto," by Wojciech Weiss. No. 1627, Party members, by F. Kowarski (horiz.).

Perf. 11½x11, 11x11½

1968, Nov. 11 **Litho.**

1625	A500	60g dk red & multi	9	6
1626	A500	60g dk red & multi	9	6
1627	A500	60g dk red & multi	9	6

5th Congress of the Polish United Workers' Party.

Departure for the Hunt, by Wojciech Kossak — A501

Hunt Paintings: 40g, Hunting with Falcon, by Juliusz Kossak. 60g, Wolves' Raid, by A. Wierusz-Kowalski. 1.50z, Bear Hunt, by Julian Falat. 2.50z, Fox Hunt, by T. Sutherland. 3.40z, Boar Hunt, by Frans Snyders. 4.50z, Hunters' Rest, by W. G. Pierow. 8.50z, Lion Hunt in Morocco, by Delacroix.

1968, Nov. 20 ***Perf. 11***

1628	A501	20g multi	8	5
1629	A501	40g multi	8	5
1630	A501	60g multi	8	5
1631	A501	1.50z multi	18	8
1632	A501	2.50z multi	16	10
1633	A501	3.40z multi	35	12
1634	A501	4.50z multi	70	40
1635	A501	8.50z multi	1.25	80
		Nos. 1628-1635 (8)	2.88	1.65

Afghan Greyhound
A502

Dogs: 20g, Maltese. 40g, Rough-haired fox terrier (vert.). 1.50z, Schnauzer. 2.50z, English setter. 3.40z, Pekinese. 4.50z, German shepherd. 8.50z, Pointer.

1969, Feb. 2 ***Perf. 11x11½, 11½x11***

Dogs in Natural Colors

1636	A502	20g gray & brt grn	15	10
1637	A502	40g gray & org	24	12
1638	A502	60g gray & lil	24	12
1639	A502	1.50z gray & blk	24	15
1640	A502	2.50z gray & brt pink	40	22
1641	A502	3.40z gray & dk grn	65	30
1642	A502	4.50z gray & ver	1.25	55
1643	A502	8.50z gray & vio	2.50	1.25
		Nos. 1636-1643 (8)	5.67	2.81

General Assembly of the Intl. Kennel Federation, Warsaw, May 1969.

Eagle-on-Shield House Sign — A503

1969, Feb. 23 **Litho.** ***Perf. 11½x11***

1644	A503	60g gray, red & blk	10	8

9th Congress of Democratic Movement.

Sheaf of Wheat
A504

1969, Mar. 29 **Litho.** ***Perf. 11½x11***

1645	A504	60g multi	10	8

5th Congress of the United Peasant Party, Warsaw, March 29-31.

Runner — A505

Olympic Rings and: 20g, Woman gymnast. 40g, Weight lifting. 60g, Women's javelin.

1969, Apr. 25 **Litho.** ***Perf. 11½x11***

1646	A505	10g org & multi	5	5
1647	A505	20g ultra & multi	5	5
1648	A505	40g yel & multi	8	5
1649	A505	60g red & multi	10	8
		Nos. 1646-1649,B114-B117 (8)	2.20	1.07

50th anniv. of the Polish Olympic Committee, and the 75th anniv. of the Intl. Olympic Committee.

Sailboat and Lighthouse, Kolobrzeg Harbor — A506

Designs: 40g, Tourist map of Swietokrzyski National Park. 60g, Ruins of 16th century castle, Niedzica (vert.). 1.50z, Castle of the Dukes of Pomerania and ship, Szczecin. 2.50z, View of Torun and Vistula. 3.40z, View of Klodzko (vert.). 4z, View of Sulejow. 4.50z, Market Place, Kazimierz Dolny (vert.).

1969, May 20 **Litho.** ***Perf. 11***

1650	A506	40g multi	5	5
1651	A506	60g multi	8	5
1652	A506	1.35z multi	8	6
1653	A506	1.50z multi	10	7
1654	A506	2.50z multi	12	8
1655	A506	3.40z multi	18	10
1656	A506	4z multi	25	14
1657	A506	4.50z multi	42	18
		Nos. 1650-1657 (8)	1.28	73

Issued for tourist publicity. Printed in sheets of 15 stamps and 15 labels. Domestic plants on labels of 40g, 60g and 1.35z, coats of arms on others.

See Nos. 1731-1735.

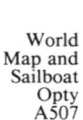

World Map and Sailboat Opty
A507

1969, June 21 **Litho.** ***Perf. 11x11½***

1658	A507	60g multi	15	10

Leonid Teliga's one-man voyage around the world, Casablanca, Jan. 21, 1967, to Las Palmas, Apr. 16, 1969.

Nicolaus Copernicus, Woodcut by Tobias Stimer — A508

Designs: 60g, Copernicus, by Jeremias Falck, 15th century globe and map of constellations. 2.50z, Copernicus, painting by Jan Matejko and map of heliocentric system.

Photo., Engr. & Litho.

1969, June 26 ***Perf. 11½***

1659	A508	40g dl yel, sep & dp car	14	7
1660	A508	60g grnsh gray, blk & dp car	14	7
1661	A508	2.50z lt vio brn, ol & dp car	42	16

Nicolaus Copernicus (1473-1543), astronomer.

"Memory" Pathfinders' Cross and Protectors' Badge
A509

Frontier Guard and Embossed Arms of Poland
A510

Coal Miner — A511

Designs: No. 1663, "Defense," military eagle and Pathfinders' cross. No. 1664, "Labor," map of Poland and Pathfinders' cross.

Photo., Engr. & Litho.

1969, July 19 ***Perf. 11x11½***

1662	A509	60g ultra, blk & red	10	8
1663	A509	60g grn, blk & red	10	8
1664	A509	60g car, blk & grn	10	8

5th National Alert of Polish Pathfinders' Union.

1969, July 21 **Litho. & Embossed**

Designs: No. 1666, Oil refinery-chemical plant, Plock. No. 1667, Combine harvester. No. 1668, Rebuilt Grand Theater, Warsaw. No. 1669, Marie Sklodowska-Curie Monument and University, Lublin. No. 1671, Chemical industry (sulphur) worker. No. 1672, Steelworker. No. 1673, Ship builder and ship.

1665	A510	60g red & multi	8	5
1666	A510	60g red & multi	8	5
1667	A510	60g red & multi	8	5
1668	A510	60g red & multi	8	5
1669	A510	60g red & multi	8	5

Perf. 11½x11

Litho.

1670	A511	60g gray & multi	8	5
1671	A511	60g gray & multi	8	5
1672	A511	60g gray & multi	8	5
1673	A511	60g gray & multi	8	5
		Nos. 1665-1673 (9)	72	45

25th anniversary of the Polish People's Republic. Nos. 1665-1669 are printed se-tenant in sheets of 20 (5x4); Nos. 1670-1673 are se-tenant in sheets of 20 (4x5).

Landing Module on Moon, and Earth — A512

1969, Aug. 21 **Litho.** ***Perf. 12x12½***

1674	A512	2.50z multi	80	42

Man's first landing on the moon, July 20, 1969. US astronauts Neil A. Armstrong and Col. Edwin E. Aldrin, Jr., with Lieut. Col. Michael Collins piloting Apollo 11. Issued in sheets of 8 stamps and 2 tabs with decorative border. One tab shows Apollo 11 with lunar landing module, the other shows module's take-off from moon. Value, sheet. $22.50.

Motherhood, by Stanislaw Wyspianski — A513

Polish Paintings: 40g, "Hamlet," by Jacek Malczewski. 60g, Indian Summer (sleeping woman), by Jozef Chelmonski. 2z, Two Girls, by Olga Boznanska (vert.). 2.50z, "The Sun of May" (Breakfast on the Terrace), by Jozef Mehoffer (vert.). 3.40z, Woman Combing her Hair, by Wladyslaw Slewinski. 5.50z, Still Life, by Jozef Pankiewicz. 7z, The Abduction of the King's Daughter, by Witold Wojtkiewicz.

Perf. 11x11½, 11½x11

1969, Sept. 4 **Photo.**

1675	A513	20g gold & multi	5	5
1676	A513	40g gold & multi	5	5
1677	A513	60g gold & multi	10	8
1678	A513	2z gold & multi	20	10
1679	A513	2.50z gold & multi	20	10
1680	A513	3.40z gold & multi	32	15
1681	A513	5.50z gold & multi	80	32
1682	A513	7z gold & multi	1.25	52
		Nos. 1675-1682 (8)	2.97	1.37

Issued in sheets of 4 stamps and 2 labels inscribed with painter's name.

Nike — A514

1969, Sept. 19 **Litho.** ***Perf. 11½x11***

1683	A514	60g gray, red & bis	10	8

4th Congress of the Union of Fighters for Freedom and Democracy.

Details from Memorial, Majdanek Concentration Camp — A515

1969, Sept. 20 *Perf. 11*

1684 A515 40g brt lil, gray & blk	10	8

Unveiling of a monument to the victims of the Majdanek concentration camp. The monument was designed by the sculptor Wiktor Tolkin.

Costumes from Krczonow, Lublin — A516

Regional Costumes: 60g, Lowicz, Lodz. 1.15z, Rozbark, Katowice. 1.35z, Lower Silesia, Wroclaw. 1.50z, Opoczno, Lodz. 4.50z, Sacz, Cracow. 5z, Highlanders, Cracow. 7z, Kurpiow, Warsaw.

1969, Sept. 30 Litho. ***Perf. 11½x11***

1685 A516	40g multi	5	5
1686 A516	60g multi	8	5
1687 A516	1.15z multi	8	8
1688 A516	1.35z multi	10	8
1689 A516	1.50z multi	12	9
1690 A516	4.50z multi	40	24
1691 A516	5z multi	60	42
1692 A516	7z multi	48	30
	Nos. 1685-1692 (8)	1.91	1.31

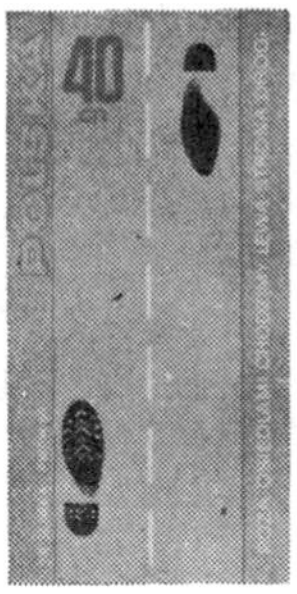

"Walk at Left" — A517

Traffic safety: 60g, "Drive Carefully" (horses on road). 2.50z, "Lower your Lights" (automobile on road).

1969, Oct. 4 *Perf. 11*

1693 A517	40g multi	5	5
1694 A517	60g multi	8	6
1695 A517	2.50z multi	18	6

ILO Emblem and Welder's Mask — A518

1969, Oct. 20 ***Perf. 11x11½***

1696 A518 2.50z vio bl & ol	15	10

ILO, 50th anniversary.

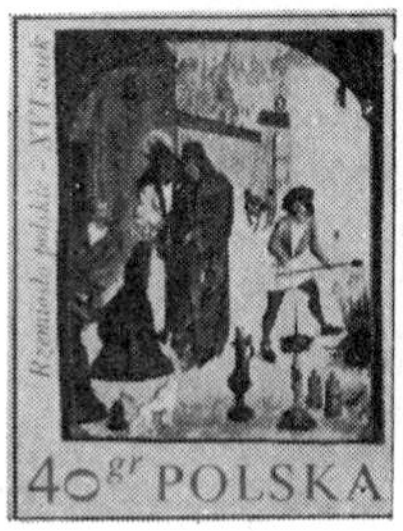

Bell Foundry A519

Miniatures from Behem's Code, completed 1505: 60g, Painter's studio. 1.35z, Wood carvers. 1.55z, Shoemaker. 2.50z, Cooper. 3.40z, Bakery. 4.50z, Tailor. 7z, Bowyer's shop.

1969, Nov. 12 Litho. ***Perf. 12½***

1697 A519	40g gray & multi	5	5
1698 A519	60g gray & multi	8	5
1699 A519	1.35z gray & multi	9	8
1700 A519	1.55z gray & multi	12	8
1701 A519	2.50z gray & multi	18	10
1702 A519	3.40z gray & multi	24	15
1703 A519	4.50z gray & multi	35	22
1704 A519	7z gray & multi	75	40
	Nos. 1697-1704 (8)	1.86	1.13

Angel — A520

Folk Art (Sculptures): 40g, Sorrowful Christ (head). 60g, Sorrowful Christ (seated figure). 2z, Crying woman. 2.50z, Adam and Eve. 3.40z, Woman with birds.

1969, Dec. 19 Litho. ***Perf. 12½***
Size: 21x36mm

1705 A520	20g lt bl & multi	6	5
1706 A520	40g lil & multi	8	5
1707 A520	60g multi	9	6
1708 A520	2z multi	18	10
1709 A520	2.50z multi	20	12
1710 A520	3.40z multi	28	18
	Nos. 1705-1710,B118-B119 (8)	2.11	1.10

Leopold Staff (1878-1957) A521

Polish Writers: 60g, Wladyslaw Broniewski (1897-1962). 1.35z, Leon Kruczkowski (1900-1962). 1.50z, Julian Tuwim (1894-1953). 1.55z, Konstanty Ildefons Galczynski (1905-1953). 2.50z, Maria Dabrowska (1889-1965). 3.40z, Zofia Nalkowska (1885-1954).

Litho., Typo. & Engr.

1969, Dec. 30 ***Perf. 11x11½***

1711 A521	40g ol grn & blk, *grnsh*	6	5
1712 A521	60g dp car & blk, *pink*	8	5
1713 A521	1.35z vio bl & blk, *grysh*	12	6
1714 A521	1.50z pur & blk, *pink*	15	6
1715 A521	1.55z dp grn & blk, *grnsh*	15	8
1716 A521	2.50z ultra & blk, *gray*	20	10
1717 A521	3.40z red brn & blk, *pink*	28	15
	Nos. 1711-1717 (7)	1.04	55

The first value column gives the catalogue value of an unused stamp, the second that of a used stamp.

Statue of Nike and Polish Colors A522

1970, Jan. 17 Photo. ***Perf. 11½***

1718 A522 60g sil, gold, red & blk	15	8

Warsaw liberation, 25th anniversary.

Medieval Print Shop and Modern Color Proofs — A523

1970, Jan. 20 Litho. ***Perf. 11½x11***

1719 A523 60g multi	10	8

Centenary of Polish printers' trade union.

Ringnecked Pheasant A524

Game Birds: 40g, Mallard drake. 1.15z, Woodcock. 1.35z, Ruffs (males). 1.50z, Wood pigeon. 3.40z, Black grouse. 7z, Gray partridges (cock and hen). 8.50z, Capercaillie cock giving mating call.

1970, Feb. 28 Litho. ***Perf. 11½***

1720 A524	40g multi	8	8
1721 A524	60g multi	85	12
1722 A524	1.15z multi	8	8
1723 A524	1.35z multi	10	8
1724 A524	1.50z multi	24	12
1725 A524	3.40z multi	25	12
1726 A524	7z multi	1.10	65
1727 A524	8.50z multi	1.25	85
	Nos. 1720-1727 (8)	3.95	2.10

Lenin in his Kremlin Study, Oct. 1918, and Polish Lenin Steel Mill — A525

Designs: 60g, Lenin addressing 3rd International Congress in Leningrad, 1920, and Luna 13. 2.50z, Lenin with delegates to 10th Russian Communist Party Congress, Moscow, 1921, dove and globe.

Engr. & Typo.

1970, Apr. 22 ***Perf. 11***

1728 A525	40g grnsh blk & dl red	6	5
1729 A525	60g sep & dp lil rose	8	6
a	Souvenir sheet of 4	85	48
1730 A525	2.50z bluish blk & ver	18	8

Lenin (1870-1924), Russian communist leader.

No. 1729a commemorates the Cracow Intl. Phil. Exhib.

Tourist Type of 1969

Designs: No. 1731, Townhall, Wroclaw (vert.). No. 1732, Cathedral, Piast Castle tower and church towers, Opole. No. 1733, Castle, Legnica. No. 1734, Castle Tower, Bolkow. No. 1735, Town Hall, Brzeg.

1970, May 9 Litho. ***Perf. 11***

1731 A506	60g Wroclaw	14	8
1732 A506	60g Opole	14	8
1733 A506	60g Legnica	14	8
1734 A506	60g Bolkow	14	8
1735 A506	60g Brzeg	14	8
	Nos. 1731-1735 (5)	70	40

Issued for tourist publicity. Printed in sheets of 15 stamps and 15 labels, showing coats of arms.

Polish and Russian Soldiers before Brandenburg Gate — A526

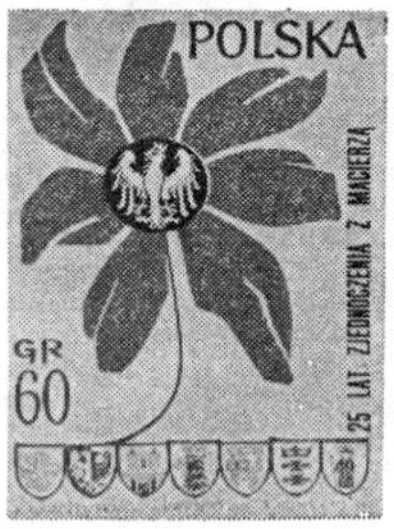

Flower, Eagle and Arms of 7 Cities — A527

Lithographed and Engraved

1970, May 9 ***Perf. 11***

1736 A526 60g tan & multi	9	8

Perf. 11½

1737 A527 60g sil, red & sl grn	9	8

25th anniversary of victory over Germany and of Polish administration of the Oder-Neisse border area.

Peasant Movement Flag A528

1970, May 15 Litho. ***Perf. 11½***

1738 A528 60g ol & multi	15	8

Polish peasant movement, 75th anniv.

Inauguration of New UPU Headquarters, Bern — A529

1970, May 20

1739 A529 2.50z bl & vio bl	15	10

Soccer — A530

1970, May 30 *Perf. 11½x11*

1740	A530	60g multi	20	10

European Soccer Cup Finals. Printed in sheets of 15 stamps and 15 se-tenant labels inscribed with the scores of the games.

Lamp of Learning — A531

1970, June 3 *Perf. 11½*

1741	A531	60g blk, bis & red	10	8

Plock Scientific Society, 150th anniversary.

Cross-country Race — A532

Designs: No. 1743, Runners from ancient Greek vase. No. 1744, Archer, drawing by W. Skoczylas.

1970, June 16 Photo. *Perf. 11x11½*

1742	A532	60g yel & multi	15	7
1743	A532	60g blk & multi	15	7
1744	A532	60g dk bl & multi	15	7

10th session of the Intl. Olympic Academy. See No. B120.

Copernicus, by Bacciarelli and View of Bologna — A533

Designs: 60g, Copernicus, by W. Lesseur and view of Padua. 2.50z, Copernicus, by Zinck Nora and view of Ferrara.

Photo., Engr. & Typo.

1970, June 26 *Perf. 11½*

1745	A533	40g org & multi	8	8
1746	A533	60g ol & multi	8	8
1747	A533	2.50z multi	38	12

Nicolaus Copernicus (1473-1543), Polish astronomer.

Aleksander Orlowski (1777-1832), Self-portrait — A534

Miniatures: 40g, Jan Matejko (1838-1893), self-portrait. 60g, King Stefan Batory (1533-1586), anonymous painter. 2z, Maria Leszczynska (1703-1768), anonymous French painter. 2.50z, Maria Walewska (1789-1817), by Jacquotot Marie-Victoire. 3.40z, Tadeusz Kosciuszko (1746-1817), by Jan Rustem. 5.50z, Samuel Bogumil Linde (1771-1847), by G. Landolfi. 7z, Michal Oginski (1728-1800), by Windisch Nanette.

Litho. & Photo.

1970, Aug. 27 *Perf. 11½*

1748	A534	20g gold & multi	8	8
1749	A534	40g gold & multi	8	8
1750	A534	60g gold & multi	8	8
1751	A534	2z gold & multi	12	10
1752	A534	2.50z gold & multi	24	15
1753	A534	3.40z gold & multi	35	24
1754	A534	5.50z gold & multi	60	35
1755	A534	7z gold & multi	1.00	52
		Nos. 1748-1755 (8)	2.55	1.60

Nos. 1748-1755 printed in sheets of 4 stamps and 2 labels. The miniatures show famous Poles and are from collections in the National Museums in Warsaw and Cracow.

Poster for Chopin Competition A535

Photogravure and Engraved

1970, Sept. 8 *Perf. 11x11½*

1756	A535	2.50z blk & vio	18	10

8th Intl. Chopin Piano Competition, Warsaw, Oct. 7-25.

UN Emblem A536

1970, Sept. 8 Photo. *Perf. 11½*

1757	A536	2.50z multi	20	10

United Nations, 25th anniversary.

Poles — A537

Design: 60g, Family, home and Polish flag.

1970, Sept. 15 Litho. *Perf. 11½x11*

1758	A537	40g gray & multi	9	8
1759	A537	60g multi	12	8

National Census, Dec. 8, 1970.

Grunwald Cross and Warship Piorun (Thunderbolt) — A538

Grunwald Cross and Warship: 60g, Orzel (Eagle). 2.50z, Garland.

1970, Sept. 25 Engr. *Perf. 11½x11*

1760	A538	40g sepia	12	8
1761	A538	60g black	15	8
1762	A538	2.50z dp brn	45	12

Polish Navy during World War II.

Cellist, by Jerzy Nowosielski A539

Paintings: 40g, View of Lodz, by Benon Liberski. 60g, Studio Concert, by Waclaw Taranczewski. 1.50z, Still Life, by Zbigniew Pronaszko. 2z, Woman Hanging up Laundry, by Andrzej Wroblewski. 3.40z, "Expressions," by Maria Jarema (horiz.). 4z, Canal in the Forest, by Piotr Potworowski (horiz.). 8.50z, "The Sun," by Wladyslaw Strzeminski (horiz.).

1970, Oct. 9 Photo. *Perf. 11½*

1763	A539	20g multi	5	5
1764	A539	40g multi	5	5
1765	A539	60g multi	8	5
1766	A539	1.50z multi	14	10
1767	A539	2z multi	16	12
1768	A539	3.40z multi	24	12
1769	A539	4z multi	42	22
1770	A539	8.50z multi	90	48
		Nos. 1763-1770 (8)	2.04	1.19

Issued for Stamp Day.

Luna 16 Landing on Moon — A540

Stag — A541

1970, Nov. 20 Litho. *Perf. 11½x11*

1771	A540	2.50z multi	28	12

Luna 16 Russian unmanned, automatic moon mission, Sept. 12-24. Issued in sheets of 8 stamps and 2 tabs with bluish black commemorative inscription. One tab shows rocket launching; the other, parachute landing of capsule. Value, sheet $18.

1970, Dec. 23 Photo. *Perf. 11½x12*

Designs from 16th Century Tapestries in Wawel Castle: 1.15z, Stork. 1.35z, Leopard fighting dragon. 2z, Man's head. 2.50z, Child holding bird. 4z, God, Adam and Eve. 4.50z, Panel with monogram of King Sigismund Augustus. 5.50z, Poland's coat of arms.

1772	A541	60g multi	8	5
1773	A541	1.15z pur & multi	10	8
1774	A541	1.35z multi	12	8
1775	A541	2z sep & multi	18	10
1776	A541	2.50z dk bl & multi	22	12
1777	A541	4z grn & multi	52	22
1778	A541	4.50z multi	65	32
		Nos. 1772-1778 (7)	1.87	97

Souvenir Sheet

Imperf

1779	A541	5.50z blk & multi	1.00	50

See No. B121. No. 1779 contains one stamp 48x57mm.

Transatlantic Liner Stefan Batory — A542

Polish Ships: 40g, School sailing ship Dar Pomorza. 1.15z, Ice breaker Perkun. 1.35z, Rescue ship R-1. 1.50z, Freighter Ziemia Szczecinska. 2.50z, Tanker Beskidy. 5z, Express freighter Hel. 8.50z, Ferry Gryf.

1971, Jan. 30 Photo. *Perf. 11*

1780	A542	40g ver & multi	5	5
1781	A542	60g multi	7	5
1782	A542	1.15z bl & multi	10	8
1783	A542	1.35z yel & multi	12	8
1784	A542	1.50z multi	18	8
1785	A542	2.50z vio & multi	24	12
1786	A542	5z multi	52	24
1787	A542	8.50z bl & multi	85	42
		Nos. 1780-1787 (8)	2.13	1.12

Checiny Castle A543

Polish Castles: 40g, Wisnicz. 60g, Bedzin. 2z, Ogrodzieniec. 2.50z, Niedzica. 3.40z, Kwidzyn. 4z, Pieskowa Skala. 8.50z, Lidzbark Warminski.

1971, Mar. 5 Litho. *Perf. 11*

1788	A543	20g multi	5	5
1789	A543	40g multi	5	5
1790	A543	60g multi	8	6
1791	A543	2z multi	14	8
1792	A543	2.50z multi	15	8
1793	A543	3.40z multi	25	14
1794	A543	4z multi	30	18
1795	A543	8.50z multi	65	42
		Nos. 1788-1795 (8)	1.67	1.06

Fighting in Pouilly Castle, Jaroslaw Dabrowski and Walery Wroblewski — A544

1971, Mar. 3 *Perf. 12½x12½*

1796	A544	60g vio bl, brn & red	10	8

Centenary of the Paris Commune.

Seedlings — A545

Bishop Marianos — A546

Designs: 60g, Forest. 1.50z, Clearing.

1971, Mar. 30 Photo. *Perf. 11½x11*

Sizes: 26x34mm (40g, 1.50z); 26x47mm (60g)

1797	A545	40g grn & multi	8	5
1798	A545	60g grn & multi	12	8
1799	A545	1.50z grn & multi	25	12

Proper forest management.

1971, Apr. 20

Frescoes from Faras Cathedral, Nubia, 8th-12th centuries: 60g, St. Anne. 1.15z, 1.50z, 7z, Archangel Michael (diff. frescoes). 1.35z, Hermit Anamon of Tuna el Gabel. 4.50z,

Cross with symbols of four Evangelists. 5z, Christ protecting Nubian dignitary.

1800	A546	40g	gold & multi	5	5
1801	A546	60g	gold & multi	8	8
1802	A546	1.15z	gold & multi	10	8
1803	A546	1.35z	gold & multi	12	8
1804	A546	1.50z	gold & multi	15	10
1805	A546	4.50z	gold & multi	50	20
1806	A546	5z	gold & multi	52	22
1807	A546	7z	gold & multi	65	32
	Nos. 1800-1807 (8)			2.17	1.13

Polish archaeological excavations in Nubia.

Silesian Insurrectionists — A547

1971, May 3 Photo. *Perf. 11*

1808	A547 60g dk red brn & gold		12	8
a	Souv. sheet of 3+3 labels		90	45

50th anniversary of the 3rd Silesian uprising. Printed in sheets of 15 stamps and 15 labels showing Silesian Insurrectionists monument in Katowice.

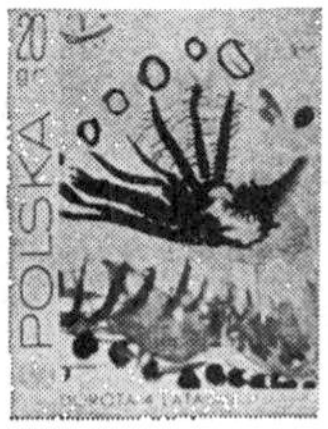

Peacock on the Lawn, by Dorota, 4 years old — A548

Children's Drawings and UNICEF Emblem: 40g, Our Army (horiz.). 60g, Spring. 2z, Cat with Ball (horiz.). 2.50z, Flowers in Vase. 3.40z, Friendship (horiz.). 5.50z, Clown. 7z, The Unknown Planet (horiz.).

Perf. 11½x11, 11x11½

1971, May 20

1809	A548	20g	multi	5	5
1810	A548	40g	multi	5	5
1811	A548	60g	multi	7	6
1812	A548	2z	multi	15	8
1813	A548	2.50z	multi	15	10
1814	A548	3.40z	multi	25	14
1815	A548	5.50z	multi	40	22
1816	A548	7z	multi	65	35
	Nos. 1809-1816 (8)			1.77	1.05

25th anniversary of UNICEF.

Fair Emblem — A549

1971, June 1 Photo. *Perf. 11½x11*

1817 A549 60g ultra, blk & dk car 10 8

40th International Poznan Fair, June 13-22.

Collegium Maius, Cracow — A550

Designs: 40g, Copernicus House, Torun (vert.). 2.50z, Olsztyn Castle. 4z, Frombork Cathedral (vert.).

1971, June Litho. *Perf. 11*

1818	A550	40g	multi	9	6
1819	A550	60g	blk, red brn & sep	12	8
1820	A550	2.50z	multi	25	10
1821	A550	4z	multi	45	18

Nicolaus Copernicus (1473-1543), astronomer. Printed in sheets of 15 with labels showing portrait of Copernicus, page from "Euclid's Geometry," astrolabe or drawing of heliocentric system, respectively.

Paper Cut-out A551

Worker, by Xawery Dunikowski A552

Designs: Various paper cut-outs (folk art).

Photo., Engr. & Typo.

1971, July 12 *Perf. 12x11½*

1822	A551	20g	blk & brt grn, *bluish*	5	5
1823	A551	40g	sl grn & dk ol, *lt gray*	5	5
1824	A551	60g	brn & bl, *gray*	8	6
1825	A551	1.15z	plum & brn, *buff*	8	8
1826	A551	1.35z	dk grn & ver, *yel grn*	12	10
	Nos. 1822-1826 (5)			38	34

1971, July 21 Photo. *Perf. 11½x12*

Sculptures: No. 1828, Founder, by Xawery Dunikowski. No. 1829, Miners, by Magdalena Wiecek. No. 1830, Woman harvester, by Stanislaw Horno-Poplawski.

1827	A552	40g	sil & multi	8	6
1828	A552	40g	sil & multi	8	6
1829	A552	60g	sil & multi	12	8
1830	A552	60g	sil & multi	12	8
a	Souvenir sheet of 4, #1827-1830			1.00	60

Punched Tape and Cogwheel A553

1971, Sept. 2 Litho. *Perf. 11x11½*

1831 A553 60g pur & red 10 8

6th Congress of Polish Technicians, held at Poznan, February, 1971.

Angel, by Jozef Mehoffer, 1901 A554

Water Lilies, by Wyspianski A555

Stained Glass Windows: 60g, Detail from "The Elements" by Stanislaw Wyspianski. 1.35z, Apollo, by Wyspianski, 1904. 1.55z, Two Kings, 14th century. 3.40z, Flight into Egypt, 14th century. 5.50z, St. Jacob the Elder, 14th century.

1971, Sept. 15 Photo. *Perf. 11½x11*

1832	A554	20g	gold & multi	5	5
1833	A555	40g	gold & multi	5	5
1834	A555	60g	gold & multi	8	6
1835	A555	1.35z	gold & multi	12	8
1836	A554	1.55z	gold & multi	15	8
1837	A554	3.40z	gold & multi	24	10
1838	A554	5.50z	gold & multi	35	18
	Nos. 1832-1838,B122 (8)			1.79	1.05

Mrs. Fedorowicz, by Witold Pruszkowski (1846-1896) — A556

Paintings of Women: 50g, Woman with Book, by Tytus Czyzewski (1885-1945). 60g, Girl with Chrysanthemums, by Olga Boznanska (1865-1940). 2.50z, Girl in Red Dress, by Jozef Pankiewicz (1866-1940; horiz.). 3.40z, Nude, by Leon Chwistek (1884-1944; horiz.). 4.50z, Strange Garden (woman), by Jozef Mehoffer (1869-1946). 5z, Artist's Wife with White Hat, by Zbigniew Pronaszko (1885-1958).

Perf. 11½x11, 11x11½

1971, Oct. 9 Litho.

1839	A556	40g	gray & multi	5	5
1840	A556	50g	gray & multi	5	5
1841	A556	60g	gray & multi	7	8
1842	A556	2.50z	gray & multi	20	10
1843	A556	3.40z	gray & multi	28	12
1844	A556	4.50z	gray & multi	42	22
1845	A556	5z	gray & multi	55	32
	Nos. 1839-1845,B123 (8)			2.32	1.29

Stamp Day, 1971. Printed in sheets of 4 stamps and 2 labels inscribed "Women in Polish Paintings."

Royal Castle, Warsaw A557

1971, Oct. 14 Photo. *Perf. 11x11½*

1846 A557 60g gold, blk & brt red 10 8

P-11C Dive Bombers A558

Planes and Polish Air Force Emblem: 1.50z, PZL 23-A Karas fighters. 3.40z, PZL Los bomber.

1971, Oct. 14

1847	A558	90g	multi	10	8
1848	A558	1.50z	bl, red & blk	14	8
1849	A558	3.40z	multi	30	12

Martyrs of the Polish Air Force, 1939.

Lunar Rover and Astronauts A559

Design: No. 1851, Lunokhod 1 on moon (vert.).

Perf. 11x11½, 11½x11

1971, Nov. 17

1850	A559	2.50z	multi	24	12
1851	A559	2.50z	multi	24	12

Apollo 15 U.S. moon exploration mission, July 26-Aug. 7 (No. 1850); Luna 17 unmanned automated U.S.S.R. moon mission, Nov. 10-17 (No. 1851). Printed in sheets of 6 stamps and 2 labels, with marginal inscriptions.

Worker at Helm — A560

Shipbuilding — A561

Designs: No. 1853, Worker. No. 1855, Apartment houses under construction. No. 1856, "Bison" combine harvester. No. 1857, Polish Fiat 125. No. 1858, Mining tower. No. 1859, Chemical plant.

1971, Dec. 8 *Perf. 11½x11*

1852	A560	60g	gray, ultra & red		10	8
1853	A560	60g	red & gray		10	8
	Strip of 2 + label				20	16

Perf. 11x11½

1854	A561	60g	red, gold & blk	10	8
1855	A561	60g	red, gold & blk	10	8
1856	A561	60g	red, gold & blk	10	8
1857	A561	60g	red, gold & blk	10	8
1858	A561	60g	red, gold & blk	10	8
1859	A561	60g	red, gold & blk	10	8
	Block of 6			60	50
a	Souvenir sheet of 6, #1854-1859			75	50
	Nos. 1852-1859 (8)			80	64

6th Congress of the Polish United Worker's Party. Nos. 1852-1853 printed setenant in sheets of 30 with 15 labels showing congress emblem. Nos. 1854-1859 printed se-tenant in sheets of 36 with outline of map of Poland extending over block of 6 stamps.

Cherry Blossoms — A562

Blossoms: 20g, Niedzwiecki's apple. 40g, Pear. 60g, Peach. 1.15z, Japanese magnolia. 1.35z, Red hawthorne. 2.50z, Apple. 3.40z, Red chestnut. 5z, Acacia robinia. 8.50z, Cherry.

1971, Dec. 28 Litho. *Perf. 12½*

Blossoms in Natural Colors

1860	A562	10g	dl bl & blk	6	5
1861	A562	20g	grnsh bl & blk	6	5
1862	A562	40g	lt vio & blk	8	5
1863	A562	60g	grn & blk	8	8
1864	A562	1.15z	Prus bl & blk	12	8
1865	A562	1.35z	ocher & blk	15	10
1866	A562	2.50z	grn & blk	18	12
1867	A562	3.40z	ocher & blk	35	20
1868	A562	5z	tan & blk	48	25
1869	A562	8.50z	bis & blk	1.00	52
	Nos. 1860-1869 (10)			2.56	1.50

Fighting Worker, by J. Jarnuszkiewicz — A563

Photogravure and Engraved

1972, Jan. 5 *Perf. 11½*
1870 A563 60g red & blk 10 8

Polish Workers' Party, 30th anniversary.

Luge and Sapporo '72 Emblem — A564

Sapporo '72 Emblem and: 60g, Women's slalom (vert.). 1.65z, Biathlon (vert.). 2.50z, Ski jump.

1972, Jan. 12 Photo. *Perf. 11*

1871	A564	40g sil & multi	8	6
1872	A564	60g sil & multi	10	8
1873	A564	1.65z sil & multi	22	12
1874	A564	2.50z sil & multi	42	22

11th Winter Olympic Games, Sapporo, Japan, Feb. 3-13. See No. B124.

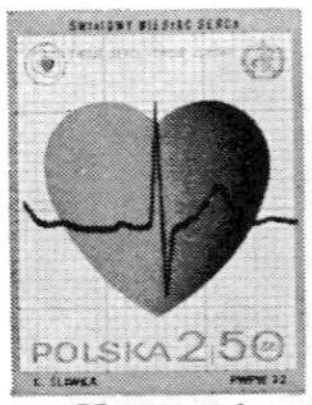
Heart and Electrocardiogram A565

Bicyclists Racing A566

1972, Mar. 28 Photo. *Perf. 11½x11*
1875 A565 2.50z bl, red & blk 18 10

"Your heart is your health," World Health Day.

1972, May 2 *Perf. 11*
1876 A566 60g sil & multi 10 8

25th Warsaw-Berlin-Prague Bicycle Race.

Berlin Monument A567

Olympic Runner A568

1972, May 9 Engr. *Perf. 11½x11*
1877 A567 60g grnsh blk 10 8

Unveiling of monument for Polish soldiers and German anti-Fascists in Berlin, May 14.

1972, May 20 *Perf. 11½x11*

Olympic Rings and "Motion" Symbol and: 30g, Archery. 40g, Boxing. 60g, Fencing. 2.50z, Wrestling. 3.40z, Weight lifting. 5z, Bicycling. 8.50z, Sharpshooting.

1878	A568	20g multi	8	5
1879	A568	30g multi	8	5
1880	A568	40g multi	8	5
1881	A568	60g gray & multi	8	8
1882	A568	2.50z multi	22	8
1883	A568	3.40z multi	40	18
1884	A568	5z bl & multi	52	24
1885	A568	8.50z multi	90	50
		Nos. 1878-1885 (8)	2.36	1.23

20th Olympic Games, Munich, Aug. 26-Sept. 10. See No. B125.

Vistula and Cracow — A569

1972, May 28 Photo. *Perf. 11½x11*
1886 A569 60g red, grn & ocher 10 8

50th anniversary of Polish Immigrants Society in Germany (Rodlo).

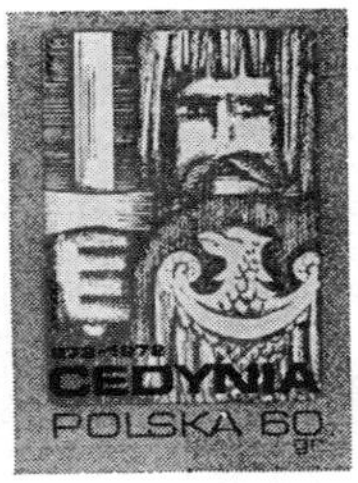
Knight of King Mieszko I — A570

1972, June 12
1887 A570 60g gold, red brn, yel & blk 10 8

Millennium of the Battle of Cedynia (Cidyny).

Zoo Animals — A571

1972, Aug. 20 Litho. *Perf. 12½*
Buff & Multicolored

1888	A571	20g	Cheetah	10	7
1889	A571	40g	Giraffe (vert.)	10	7
1890	A571	60g	Toco toucan	10	7
1891	A571	1.35z	Chimpanzee	18	10
1892	A571	1.65z	Gibbon	20	15
1893	A571	3.40z	Crocodile	28	18
1894	A571	4z	Kangaroo	85	45
1895	A571	4.50z	Tiger (vert.)	1.65	1.00
1896	A571	7z	Zebra	1.90	1.25
			Nos. 1888-1896 (9)	5.36	3.34

Ludwik Warynski — A572

1972, Sept. 1 Photo. *Perf. 11*
1897 A572 60g multi 10 8

90th anniversary of Proletariat Party, founded by Ludwik Warynski. Printed in sheets of 25 stamps each se-tenant with label showing masthead of party newspaper "Proletariat."

Feliks Dzerzhinski A573

1972, Sept. 11 Litho. *Perf. 11x11½*
1898 A573 60g red & blk 10 8

Feliks Dzerzhinski (1877-1926), Russian politician of Polish descent.

Congress Emblem — A574

1972, Sept. 15 Photo. *Perf. 11½x11*
1899 A574 60g multi 10 8

25th Congress of the International Cooperative Union, Warsaw, Sept. 1972.

"In the Barracks," by Moniuszko A575

Scenes from Operas or Ballets by Moniuszko: 20g, The Countess. 40g, The Frightful Castle. 60g, Halka. 1.15z, A New Don Quixote. 1.35z, Verbum Nobile. 1.55z, Ideal. 2.50z, Paria.

Photogravure and Engraved

1972, Sept. 15 *Perf. 11½*

1900	A575	10g gold & vio	5	5
1901	A575	20g gold & dk brn	5	5
1902	A575	40g gold & sl grn	5	5
1903	A575	60g gold & ind	6	5
1904	A575	1.15z gold & dk bl	10	8
1905	A575	1.35z gold & dk bl	15	8
1906	A575	1.55z gold & grnsh blk	15	8
1907	A575	2.50z gold & dk brn	32	18
		Nos. 1900-1907 (8)	93	62

Stanislaw Moniuszko (1819-1872), composer.

"Amazon," by Piotr Michalowski A576

Paintings: 40g, Ostafi Daszkiewicz, by Jan Matejko. 60g, "Summer Rain" (dancing woman), by Wojciech Gerson. 2z, Woman from Naples, by Aleksander Kotsis. 2.50z, Girl Taking Bath, by Pantaleon Szyndler. 3.40z, Count of Thun (child), by Artur Grottger. 4z, Rhapsodist (old man), by Stanislaw Wyspianski. 60g and 2.50z inscribed "DZIEN ZNACZKA 1972."

1972, Sept. 28 Photo. *Perf. 10½x11*

1908	A576	30g gold & multi	8	5
1909	A576	40g gold & multi	8	5
1910	A576	60g gold & multi	8	8
1911	A576	2z gold & multi	15	10
1912	A576	2.50z gold & multi	15	12
1913	A576	3.40z gold & multi	30	15
1914	A576	4z gold & multi	65	40
		Nos. 1908-1914,B126 (8)	2.74	1.60

Stamp Day.

Copernicus, by Jacob van Meurs, 1654, Heliocentric System A577

Portraits of Copernicus: 60g, 16th century etching and Prussian coin, 1530. 2.50z, by Jeremiah Falck, 1645, and coat of arms of King of Prussia, 1520. 3.40z, Copernicus with lily of the valley, and page from Theophilactus Simocatta's "Letters on Customs."

1972, Sept. 28 Litho. *Perf. 11x11½*

1915	A577	40g brt bl & blk	5	5
1916	A577	60g ocher & blk	7	5
1917	A577	2.50z red & blk	16	9
1918	A577	3.40z yel grn & blk	35	20

Nicolaus Copernicus (1473-1543), astronomer. See No. B127.

Nos. 1337-1338 Surcharged in Red or Black

50 GR X a

= 1^{50} ZŁ b

1972 Engr. *Perf. 11½x11*

1919	A445(a)	50g on 40g brn (R)	5	5
1920	A445(a)	90g on 40g brn (R)	8	5
1921	A445(a)	1z on 40g brn (R)	8	5
1922	A445(b)	1.50z on 60g org	9	5
1923	A445(a)	2.70z on 40g brn (R)	16	9
1924	A445(b)	4z on 60g org	24	10
1925	A445(b)	4.50z on 60g org	25	14
1926	A445(b)	4.90z on 60g org	30	15
		Nos. 1919-1926 (8)	1.25	68

Issue dates: Nos. 1919-1920, Nov. 17; others Oct. 2.

The Little Soldier, by E. Piwowarski A578

1972, Oct. 16 Litho. *Perf. 11½*
1927 A578 60g rose & blk 9 8

Children's health center "Centrum Zdrowia Dziecka," to be built as memorial to children killed during Nazi regime.

Warsaw Royal Castle, 1656, by Erik J. Dahlbergh A579

1972, Oct. 16 Photo. *Perf. 11x11½*
1928 A579 60g vio, bl & blk 9 8

Rebuilding of Warsaw Castle, destroyed during World War II.

Canceled-to-order stamps are often from remainders. Most collectors of canceled stamps prefer postally used specimens.

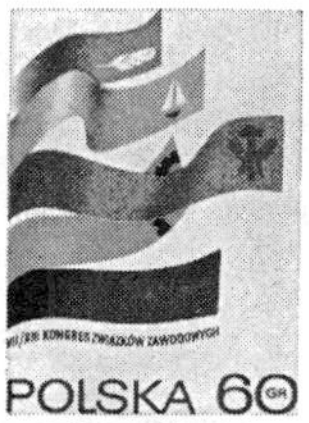

Ribbons with Symbols of Trade Union Activities
A580

Mountain Lodge, Chocholowska Valley
A581

1972, Nov. 13 ***Perf. 11½x11***

1929 A580 60g multi		9	8

7th and 13th Polish Trade Union congresses, Nov. 13-15.

1972, Nov. 13 ***Perf. 11***

Mountain Lodges in Tatra National Park: 60g, Hala Ornak, West Tatra (horiz.). 1.55z, Hala Gasienicowa. 1.65z, Pieciu Stawow Valley (horiz.). 2.50z, Morskie Oko, Rybiego Potoku Valley

1930 A581	40g multi	6	5
1931 A581	60g multi	10	6
1932 A581	1.55z multi	14	8
1933 A581	1.65z multi	14	8
1934 A581	2.50z multi	28	14
Nos. 1930-1934 (5)		72	41

Japanese Azalea — A582

Flowering Shrubs: 50g, Alpine rose. 60g, Pomeranian honeysuckle. 1.65z, Chinese quince. 2.50z, Viburnum. 3.40z, Rhododendron. 4z, Mock orange. 8.50z, Lilac.

1972, Dec. 15 **Litho.** ***Perf. 12½***

1935 A582	40g gray & multi	5	5
1936 A582	50g bl & multi	8	5
1937 A582	60g multi	8	5
1938 A582	1.65z ultra & multi	16	10
1939 A582	2.50z ocher & multi	24	12
1940 A582	3.40z multi	30	20
1941 A582	4z multi	55	22
1942 A582	8.50z multi	1.10	52
Nos. 1935-1942 (8)		2.56	1.31

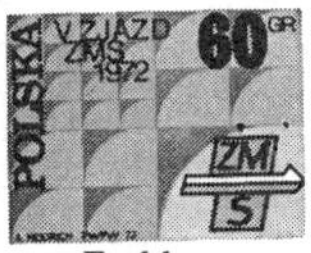

Emblem
A583

Copernicus
A584

1972, Dec. 15 **Photo.** ***Perf. 11½***

1943 A583 60g red & multi		10	8

5th Congress of Socialist Youth Union.

Coil Stamps

1972, Dec. 28 **Photo.** ***Perf. 14***

1944 A584	1z dp cl	10	7
1945 A584	1.50z yel brn	18	10

Nicolaus Copernicus (1473-1543), astronomer. Black control number on back of every 5th stamp.

Piast Knight, 10th Century
A585

Polish Cavalry: 40g, Knight, 13th century. 60g, Knight of Ladislas Jagello, 15th century (horiz.). 1.35z, Hussar, 17th century. 4z, National Guard Uhlan, 18th century. 4.50z, Congress Kingdom Period, 1831. 5z, Light cavalry, 1939 (horiz.). 7z, Light cavalry, People's Army, 1945.

1972, Dec. 28 ***Perf. 11***

1946 A585	20g vio & multi	5	5
1947 A585	40g multi	8	5
1948 A585	60g org & multi	8	8
1949 A585	1.35z org & multi	12	8
1950 A585	4z org & multi	32	15
1951 A585	4.50z org & multi	40	22
1952 A585	5z brn & multi	65	32
1953 A585	7z multi	90	50
Nos. 1946-1953 (8)		2.60	1.45

Man and Woman, Sculpture by Wiera Muchina — A586

Design: 60g, Globe with Red Star.

1972, Dec. 30

1954 A586	40g gray & multi	7	5
1955 A586	60g blk, red & vio bl	10	8

50th anniversary of the Soviet Union.

Copernicus, by M. Bacciarelli
A587

Portraits of Copernicus: 1.50z, painted in Torun, 16th century. 2.70z, by Zinck Nor. 4z, from Strasbourg clock. 4.90z, Copernicus in his Observatory, by Jan Matejko (horiz.).

Perf. 11½x11, 11x11½

1973, Feb. 18 **Photo.**

1956 A587	1z brn & multi	8	6
1957 A587	1.50z multi	12	8
1958 A587	2.70z multi	20	14
1959 A587	4z multi	35	20
1960 A587	4.90z multi	50	28
Nos. 1956-1960 (5)		1.25	76

Nicolaus Copernicus (1473-1543), astronomer.

Footnotes often refer you to other stamps of the same design.

Piast Coronation Sword, 12th Century — A588

Lenin Monument, Nowa Huta — A589

Polish Art: No. 1962, Kruzlowa Madonna, c. 1410. No. 1963, Hussar's armor, 17th century. No. 1964, Wawel head, wood, 16th century. No. 1965, Cock, sign of Rifle Fraternity, 16th century. 2.70z, Cover of Queen Anna Jagiellonka's prayer book (eagle), 1582. 4.90z, Skarbimierz Madonna, wood, c. 1340. 8.50z, The Nobleman Tenczynski, portrait by unknown artist, 17th century.

1973, Mar. 28 **Photo.** ***Perf. 11½x11***

1961 A588	50g vio & multi	5	5
1962 A588	1z lt bl & multi	8	6
1963 A588	1z ultra & multi	8	6
1964 A588	1.50z bl & multi	10	8
1965 A588	1.50z grn & multi	10	8
1966 A588	2.70z multi	18	10
1967 A588	4.90z multi	35	15
1968 A588	8.50z blk & multi	1.00	42
Nos. 1961-1968 (8)		1.94	1.00

1973, Apr. 28 **Litho.** ***Perf. 11x11½***

1969 A589 1z multi		10	8

Unveiling of Lenin Monument at Nowa Huta.

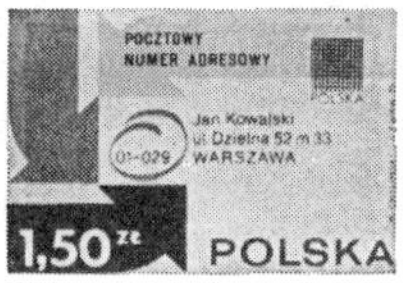

Envelope Showing Postal Code — A590

1973, May 5 ***Perf. 11x11½***

1970 A590 1.50z multi		12	8

Introduction of postal code system in Poland.

Wolf — A591

1973, May 21 **Photo.** ***Perf. 11***

1971 A591	50g shown	7	5
1972 A591	1z Mouflon	10	7
1973 A591	1.50z Moose	12	7
1974 A591	2.70z Capercaillie	25	8
1975 A591	3z Deer	30	10
1976 A591	4.50z Lynx	42	20
1977 A591	4.90z European hart	1.10	42
1978 A591	5z Wild boar	1.25	70
Nos. 1971-1978 (8)		3.61	1.69

Intl. Hunting Committee Congress and 50th anniv. of Polish Hunting Assoc.

US Satellite "Copernicus" over Earth
A592

Design: No. 1980, USSR satellite Salyut over earth.

1973, June 20

1979 A592	4.90z multi	42	25
1980 A592	4.90z multi	42	25

American and Russian astronomical observatories in space. No. 1979 issued in sheets of 6 stamps and 2 labels showing constellations and Nicolaus Copernicus. No. 1980 issued in sheets of 6 stamps and 2 labels showing astronauts and Soyuz 11.

Flame Rising from Book — A593

1973, June 26 **Litho.**

1981 A593 1.50z bl & multi		12	8

2nd Polish Science Congress, Warsaw, June 26-29.

Arms of Poznan on 14th Century Seal
A594

Marceli Nowotko
A595

Polska '73 Emblem and: 1.50z, Tombstone of Nicolas Tomicki, 1524. 2.70z, Kalisz paten, 12th century. 4z, Lion knocker from bronze gate, Gniezno, 12th century (horiz.).

Perf. 11½x11, 11x11½

1973, June 30

1982 A594	1z pink & multi	8	8
1983 A594	1.50z org & multi	10	8
1984 A594	2.70z buff & multi	18	10
1985 A594	4z yel & multi	32	12

POLSKA '73 Intl. Phil. Exhib., Poznan, Aug. 19-Sept. 2. See No. B128.

1973, Aug. 8 **Litho.** ***Perf. 11½x11***

1986 A595 1.50z red & blk		12	8

Marceli Nowotko (1893-1942), labor leader, member of Central Committee of Communist Party of Poland.

Emblem and Orchard — A596

Human Environment Emblem and: 90g, Grazing cows. 1z, Stork's nest. 1.50z, Pond with fish and water lilies. 2.70z, Flowers on meadow. 4.90z, Underwater fauna and flora. 5z, Forest scene. 6.50z, Still life.

1973, Aug. 30 **Photo.** ***Perf. 11***

1987 A596	50g blk & multi	6	5
1988 A596	90g blk & multi	8	5
1989 A596	1z blk & multi	8	5
1990 A596	1.50z blk & multi	10	8
1991 A596	2.70z blk & multi	15	12
1992 A596	4.90z blk & multi	45	20
1993 A596	5z blk & multi	65	25
1994 A596	6.50z blk & multi	1.10	40
Nos. 1987-1994 (8)		2.67	1.20

Protection of the environment.

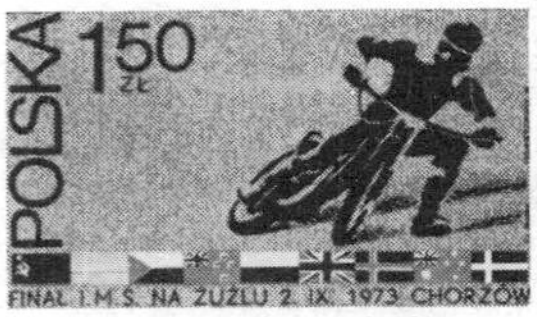

Motorcyclist — A597

1973, Sept. 2 *Perf. 11½*
1995 A597 1.50z sil & multi 12 8

Finals in individual world championship motorcycle race on cinder track, Chorzow, Sept. 2.

Tank A598

1973, Oct. 12 Litho. *Perf. 12½*
1996 A598 1z shown 8 6
1997 A598 1z Fighter plane 8 6
1998 A598 1.50z Missile 16 8
1999 A598 1.50z Warship 16 8

Polish People's Army, 30th anniversary.

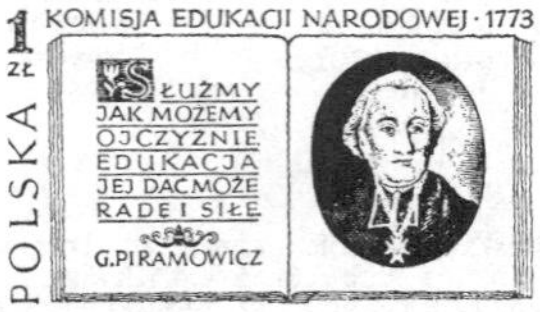

Grzegorz Piramowicz — A599

Design: 1.50z, J. Sniadecki, Hugo Kollataj and Julian Ursyn Niemcewicz.

Photogravure and Engraved

1973, Oct. 13 *Perf. 11½x11*
2000 A599 1z buff & dk brn 8 8
2001 A599 1.50z gray & sl grn 14 8

Bicentenary of the National Education Commission.

Henryk Arctowski, and Penguins A600

Polish Scientists: No. 2003, Pawel Edmund Strzelecki and Kangaroo. No. 2004, Benedykt Tadeusz Dybowski and Lake Baikal. No. 2005, Stefan Rogozinski, sailing ship "Lucja-Malgorzata." 2z, Bronislaw Malinowski, Trobriand Island drummers. 2.70z, Stefan Drzewiecki and submarine. 3z, Edward Adolf Strasburger and plants. 8z, Ignacy Domeyko, geological strata.

1973, Nov. 30 Photo. *Perf. 10½x11*
2002 A600 1z gold & multi 8 5
2003 A600 1z gold & multi 8 5
2004 A600 1.50z gold & multi 8 6
2005 A600 1.50z gold & multi 8 6
2006 A600 2z gold & multi 12 7
2007 A600 2.70z gold & multi 18 8
2008 A600 3z gold & multi 25 14
2009 A600 8z gold & multi 85 42
Nos. 2002-2009 (8) 1.72 93

Polish Flag — A601

1973, Dec. 15 Photo. *Perf. 11½x11*
2010 A601 1.50z dp ultra, red & gold 12 8

Polish United Workers' Party, 25th anniv.

Jelcz-Berliet Bus — A602

Designs: Polish automotives.

1973, Dec. 28 Photo. *Perf. 11x11½*
2011 A602 50g shown 5 5
2012 A602 90g Jelcz 316 7 5
2013 A602 1z Polski Fiat 126p 8 8
2014 A602 1.50z Polski Fiat 125p 10 8
2015 A602 4z Nysa M-521 bus 35 18
2016 A602 4.50z Star 660 truck 45 22
Nos. 2011-2016 (6) 1.10 66

Iris — A603

Flowers: 1z, Dandelion. 1.50z, Rose. 3z, Thistle. 4z, Cornflowers. 4.50z, Clover. (Paintings by Stanislaw Wyspianski.)

1974, Jan. 22 Engr. *Perf. 12x11½*
2017 A603 50g lilac 6 5
2018 A603 1z green 7 5
2019 A603 1.50z red org 10 6
2020 A603 3z dp vio 28 10
2021 A603 4z vio bl 42 14
2022 A603 4.50z emerald 50 18
Nos. 2017-2022 (6) 1.43 58

Cottage, Kurpie A604

Designs: 1.50z, Church, Sekowa. 4z, Town Hall, Sulmierzyce. 4.50z, Church, Lachowice. 4.90z, Windmill, Sobienie-Jeziory. 5z, Orthodox Church, Ulucz.

1974, Mar. 5 Photo. *Perf. 11x11½*
2023 A604 1z multi 8 6
2024 A604 1.50z yel & multi 12 8
2025 A604 4z pink & multi 28 12
2026 A604 4.50z lt bl & multi 30 15
2027 A604 4.90z multi 35 15
2028 A604 5z pink & multi 45 18
Nos. 2023-2028 (6) 1.58 74

Mail Coach and UPU Emblem — A605

Embroidery from Cracow — A606

1974, Mar. 30 *Perf. 11½x12*
2029 A605 1.50z multi 15 10

Centenary of Universal Postal Union.

1974, May 7 Photo. *Perf. 11½x11*

Embroideries from: 1.50z, Lowicz. 4z, Slask.

2030 A606 50g multi 6 5
2031 A606 1.50z multi 12 8
2032 A606 4z multi 38 18
a Souv. sheet of 3, imperf. 1.75 1.25
b Souv. sheet of 3, perf. 11½x11 3.25 2.50

SOCPHILEX IV International Philatelic Exhibition, Katowice, May 18-June 2.

No. 2032a contains 3 imperf. stamps similar to No. 2032. Violet margin with silver inscription and white lace pattern from Koniakow. Sold for 17z.

No. 2032b is similar to No. 2032a, with white margin, blue inscription, silver lace and perf. 11½x11. Sold for 17z plus 15z for 4 envelopes.

Association Emblem A607

Soldier and Dove A608

1974, May 8 Litho. *Perf. 12x11½*
2033 A607 1.50z gray & red 12 8

5th Congress of the Assoc. of Combatants for Liberty and Democracy, Warsaw, May 8-9.

1974, May 9 *Perf. 11½x11*
2034 A608 1.50z org, lt bl & blk 12 8

29th anniversary of victory over Fascism.

Comecon Building, Moscow A609

1974, May 15 *Perf. 11x11½*
2035 A609 1.50z gray bl, bis & red 12 8

25th anniv. of the Council of Mutual Economic Assistance.

Soccer Ball and Games' Emblem A610

Design: No. 2037, Soccer players, Olympic rings and 1972 medal.

1974, June 15 Photo. *Perf. 11x11½*
2036 A610 4.90z ol & multi 42 20
a Souvenir sheet of 4 + 2 labels 2.25 1.10
2037 A610 4.90z ol & multi 42 20
a Souvenir sheet of 4, #2036-2037 14.00 5.00

World Cup Soccer Championship, Munich, June 13-July 7.

No. 2036a issued to commemorate Poland's silver medal in 1974 Championship.

Sailing Ship, 16th Century A611

Chess, by Jan Kochanowski A612

Polish Sailing Ships: 1.50z, "Dal," 1934. 2.70z, "Opty," sailed around the world, 1969. 4z, "Dar Pomorza," winner "Operation Sail," 1972. 4.90z, "Polonez," sailed around the world, 1973.

1974, June 29 Litho. *Perf. 11½x11*
2038 A611 1z multi 7 6
2039 A611 1.50z multi 10 8
2040 A611 2.70z multi 20 10
2041 A611 4z grn & multi 42 22
2042 A611 4.90z dp bl & multi 60 28
Nos. 2038-2042 (5) 1.39 74

1974, July 15 Litho. *Perf. 11½x11*

Design: 1.50z, "Education," etching by Daniel Chodowiecki.

2043 A612 1z multi 10 8
2044 A612 1.50z multi 22 12

10th International Chess Festival, Lublin.

Man and Map of Poland — A613

Polish Eagle — A614

1974, July 21 Photo. *Perf. 11½x11*
2045 A613 1.50z blk, gold & red 12 8
2046 A614 1.50z sil & multi 12 8
2047 A614 1.50z red & multi 12 8

People's Republic of Poland, 30th anniv.

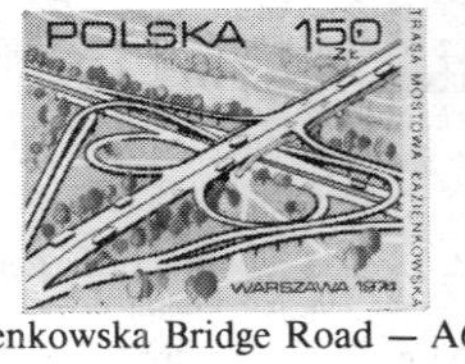

Lazienkowska Bridge Road — A615

1974, July 21 *Perf. 11x11½*
2048 A615 1.50z multi 12 10

Opening of Lazienkowska Bridge over Vistula south of Warsaw.

Strawberries and Congress Emblem — A616

1974, Sept. 10 Photo. *Perf. 11½*

2049 A616	50g	shown	5	5
2050 A616	90g	Black currants	7	5
2051 A616	1z	Apples	8	6
2052 A616	1.50z	Cucumbers	12	8
2053 A616	2.70z	Tomatoes	15	10
2054 A616	4.50z	Peas	28	18
2055 A616	4.90z	Pansies	42	22
2056 A616	5z	Nasturtiums	90	40
		Nos. 2049-2056 (8)	2.07	1.14

19th Intl. Horticultural Congress, Warsaw, Sept.

Civic Militia and Security Service Badge — A617

Polish Child, by Lukasz Orlowski — A618

1974, Oct. 3 Photo. *Perf. 11½x11*

2057 A617	1.50g	multi	10	8

30th anniv. of the Civic Militia and the Security Service.

1974, Oct. 9

Polish paintings of Children: 90g, Girl with Pigeon, Anonymous artist, 19th century. 1z, Girl, by Stanislaw Wyspianski. 1.50z, The Orphan from Poronin, by Wladyslaw Slewinski. 3z, Peasant Boy, by Kazimierz Sichulski. 4.50z, Florentine Page, by Aleksander Gierymski. 4.90z, The Artist's Son Tadeusz, by Piotr Michalowski. 6.50z, Boy with Doe, by Aleksander Kotsis.

2058 A618	50g	multi	5	5
2059 A618	90g	multi	7	5
2060 A618	1z	multi	8	6
2061 A618	1.50z	multi	10	8
2062 A618	3z	multi	24	10
2063 A618	4.50z	multi	35	15
2064 A618	4.90z	multi	42	22
2065 A618	6.50z	multi	55	28
		Nos. 2058-2065 (8)	1.86	99

Children's Day. The 1z and 1.50z are inscribed "Dzien Znaczka (Stamp Day) 1974."

Cracow Manger — A619

King Sigismund Vasa — A620

Masterpieces of Polish art: 1.50z, Flight into Egypt, 1465. 4z, King Jan Olbracht.

1974, Dec. 2 Litho. *Perf. 11½x11*

2066 A619	1z	multi	9	6
2067 A619	1.50z	multi	12	8
2068 A620	2z	multi	18	10
2069 A620	4z	multi	45	20

Angler — A621

Designs: 1.50z, Hunter with bow and arrow. 4z, Boy snaring geese. 4.50z, Beekeeper. Designs from 16th century woodcuts.

1974-77 Engr. *Perf. 11½x11*

2070 A621	1z	black	8	8
2071 A621	1.50z	indigo	12	8
2071A A621	4z	sl grn	22	10
2071B A621	4.50z	dk brn	25	12

Issue dates: 1z, 1.50z, Dec. 30, 1974. 4z, 4.50z, Dec. 12, 1977.

Pablo Neruda, by Osvaldo Guayasamin A622

1974, Dec. 31 Litho. *Perf. 11½x11*

2072 A622	1.50z	multi	10	8

Pablo Neruda (1904-1973), Chilean poet.

Nike Monument and Opera House, Warsaw — A623

1975, Jan. 17 Photo. *Perf. 11*

2073 A623	1.50z	multi	10	8

30th anniversary of the liberation of Warsaw.

Hobby Falcon A624

"Auschwitz" A625

1975, Jan. 23 *Perf. 11½x12*

2074 A624	1z	Lesser kestrel, male	12	8
2075 A624	1z	same, female	12	8
2076 A624	1.50z	Red-footed falcon, male	18	8
2077 A624	1.50z	same, female	18	8
2078 A624	2z	shown	30	10
2079 A624	3z	Kestrel	45	22
2080 A624	4z	Merlin	1.40	45
2081 A624	8z	Peregrine	2.00	90
		Nos. 2074-2081 (8)	4.75	1.99

Falcons. Stamps of same denominations printed se-tenant in sheets of 50.

Photogravure and Engraved

1975, Jan. 27 *Perf. 11½x11*

2082 A625	1.50z	red & blk	18	10

30th anniversary of the liberation of Auschwitz (Oswiecim) concentration camp.

Women's Hurdle Race A626

Designs: 1.50z, Pole vault. 4z, Hop, step and jump. 4.90z, Sprinting.

1975, Mar. 8 Litho. *Perf. 11x11½*

2083 A626	1z	multi	10	6
2084 A626	1.50z	ol & multi	12	8
2085 A626	4z	multi	35	12
2086 A626	4.90z	grn & multi	42	22

6th European Indoor Athletic Championships, Katowice, Mar. 1975.

St. Anne, by Veit Stoss, Arphila Emblem A627

1975, Apr. 15 Photo. *Perf. 11x11½*

2087 A627	1.50z	multi	12	8

ARPHILA 75, International Philatelic Exhibition, Paris, June 6-10.

Amateur Radio Union Emblem, Globe A628

1975, Apr. 15 Litho. *Perf. 11½*

2088 A628	1.50z	multi	12	8

International Amateur Radio Union Conference, Warsaw, Apr. 1975.

Mountain Guides' Badge and Sudetic Mountains — A629

Designs: No. 2089, Pine, badge and Tatra Mountains (vert.). No. 2090, Gentian and Tatra Mountains (vert.). No. 2092, Yew branch with berries, and Sudetic Mountains. No. 2093, River, Beskids Mountains and badge (vert.). No. 2094, Arnica and Beskids Mountains (vert.).

1975, Apr. 30 Photo. *Perf. 11*

2089 A629	1z	multi	8	6
2090 A629	1z	multi	8	6
2091 A629	1.50z	multi	8	6
2092 A629	1.50z	multi	8	6
2093 A629	4z	multi	40	18
2094 A629	4z	multi	40	18
		Nos. 2089-2094 (6)	1.12	60

Centenary of Polish Mountain Guides Organizations. Stamps of same denomination printed se-tenant in sheets of 50, showing continuous design.

Hands Holding Tulips and Rifle — A630

Warsaw Treaty Members' Flags — A631

1975, May 9 *Perf. 11½x11*

2095 A630	1.50z	bl & multi	12	8

End of WWII, 30th anniv.; victory over Fascism.

1975, May 14

2096 A631	1.50z	bl & multi	12	8

20th anniversary of the signing of the Warsaw Treaty (Bulgaria, Czechoslovakia, German Democratic Rep., Hungary, Poland, Romania, USSR).

Cock and Hen, Congress Emblem — A632

1975, June 23 Photo. *Perf. 12x11½*

2097 A632	50g	shown	8	5
2098 A632	1z	Geese	8	6
2099 A632	1.50z	Cattle	14	8
2100 A632	2z	Cow	22	8
2101 A632	3z	Arabian stallion	35	10
2102 A632	4z	Wielkopolska horses	42	14
2103 A632	4.50z	Pigs	70	35
2104 A632	5z	Sheep	1.40	52
		Nos. 2097-2104 (8)	3.39	1.38

20th Congress of the European Zootechnical Federation, Warsaw.

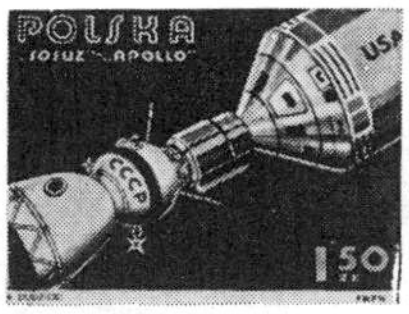

Apollo and Soyuz Linked in Space A633

Designs: No. 2106, Apollo. No. 2107, Soyuz.

1975, July 15 *Perf. 11x11½*

2105 A633	1.50z	dp ultra & multi	12	7
2106 A633	4.90z	dp ultra & multi	30	22
2107 A633	4.90z	dp ultra & multi	30	22
a		Souvenir sheet of 6+2 labels	6.50	4.00

Apollo Soyuz space test project (Russo-American cooperation), launching July 15; link-up, July 17. Nos. 2106-2107 printed se-tenant. No. 2107a contains 2 each of Nos. 2105-2107.

Health Fund Emblem — A634

1975, July 12 *Perf. 11½x11*

2108 A634	1.50z	sil, blk & bl	12	8

National Fund for Health Protection.

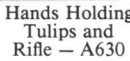

"E" and Polish Flag
A635

1975, July 30 Litho. ***Perf. 11x11½***

2109	A635	4z lt bl, red & blk	32	15

European Security and Cooperation Conference, Helsinki, July 30-Aug. 1.

UN Emblem and Sunburst
A636

1975, July 25

2110	A636	4z bl & multi	32	15

30th anniversary of the United Nations.

Bolek and Lolek
A637

Cartoon Characters and Children's Health Center Emblem: 1z, Jacek and Agatka. 1.50z, Reksio, the dog. 4z, Telesfor, the dragon.

1975, Aug. 30 Photo. ***Perf. 11x11½***

2111	A637	50g	vio bl & multi	5	5
2112	A637	1z	multi	9	6
2113	A637	1.50z	multi	12	12
2114	A637	4z	multi	45	18

Children's television programs.

Circular Bar Graph and Institute's Emblem
A638

IWY Emblem, White, Yellow and Brown Women
A639

1975, Sept. 1 Litho. ***Perf. 11½x11***

2115	A638	1.50z multi	12	8

International Institute of Statistics, 40th session, Warsaw, Sept. 1975.

1975, Sept. 8 Photo.

2116	A639	1.50z multi	12	8

International Women's Year.

First Poles Arriving on "Mary and Margaret" 1608
A640

George Washington
A641

Designs: 1.50z, Polish glass blower and glass works, Jamestown, 1608. 2.70z, Helena Modrzejewska (1840-1909), Polish actress, came to US in 1877. 4z, Casimir Pulaski (1747-1779), and 6.40z, Tadeusz Kosciusko (1748-1817), heroes of American War of Independence.

1975, Sept. 24 Litho. ***Perf. 11x11½***

2117	A640	1z	blk & multi	9	6
2118	A640	1.50z	blk & multi	14	8
2119	A640	2.70z	blk & multi	20	8
2120	A640	4z	blk & multi	32	15
2121	A640	6.40z	blk & multi	48	22
			Nos. 2117-2121 (5)	1.23	59

Souvenir Sheet

Perf. 12

2122	A641	Sheet of 3+3 labels	1.75	1.50
a		4.90z shown	55	30
b		4.90z Kosciusko	55	30
c		4.90z Pulaski	55	30

American Revolution, bicentenary. No. 2122 contains 3 stamps and 3 labels showing respectively: American flag and Polish inscription; Polish flag and English inscription; raising the flag at Yorktown.

Albatross Biplane, 1918-1925
A642

Design: 4.90z, IL 62 jet, 1975.

1975, Sept. 25 ***Perf. 11x11½***

2123	A642	2.40z buff & multi	14	7
2124	A642	4.90z gray & multi	42	20

50th anniversary of Polish air post stamps.

Frederic Chopin
A643

Dunikowski, Self-portrait
A644

1975, Oct. 7 Photo.

2125	A643	1.50z gold, lt vio & blk	12	8

9th International Chopin Piano Competition, Warsaw, Oct. 7-28.
Printed in sheets of 50 stamps with alternating labels with commemorative inscription.

1975, Oct. 9 ***Perf. 11½x11***

Sculptures: 1z, "Breath." 1.50z "Maternity."

2126	A644	50g	sil & multi	5	5
2127	A644	1z	sil & multi	10	8
2128	A644	1.50z	sil & multi	12	8

Stamp Day; Xawery Dunikowski (1875-1964), sculptor. See No. B131.

Town Hall, Zamosc
A645

Lodz, by Wladyslaw Strzeminski
A646

Design: 1z, Arcades, Kazimierz Dolny (horiz.).

Coil Stamps

1975, Nov. 11 Photo. ***Perf. 14***

2129	A645	1z ol grn	8	5
2130	A645	1.50z rose brn	12	5

European Architectural Heritage Year. Black control number on back of every fifth stamp of Nos. 2129-2130.

1975, Nov. 22 Litho. ***Perf. 12½***

2131	A646	4.50z multi	45	18
a		Souvenir sheet	90	50

Lodz 75, 12th Polish Philatelic Exhibition, commemorating 25th anniversary of Polish Philatelists Union.

Piast Family Eagle
A647

Designs: 1.50z, Seal of Prince Boleslaw of Legnica. 4z, Coin of Prince Jerzy Wilhelm (1660-1675).

1975, Nov. 29 Engr. ***Perf. 11x11½***

2132	A647	1z green	8	6
2133	A647	1.50z brown	10	8
2134	A647	4z dl vio	28	12

Piast dynasty's influence on the development of Silesia.

"7" Inscribed "ZJAZD" and "PZPR" — A648

"VII ZJAZD PZPR" — A649

1975, Dec. 8 Photo. ***Perf. 11½x11***

2135	A648	1z lt bl & multi	8	5
2136	A649	1.50z sil, red & ultra	10	8

7th Congress of Polish United Workers' Party.

Ski Jump — A650

Designs (Winter Olympic Games Emblem and): 1z, Ice hockey. 1.50z, Slalom. 2z, Speed skating. 4z, Luge. 6.40z, Biathlon.

1976, Jan. 10 ***Perf. 11x11½***

2137	A650	50g	sil & multi	5	5
2138	A650	1z	sil & multi	9	6
2139	A650	1.50z	sil & multi	12	8
2140	A650	2z	sil & multi	18	8
2141	A650	4z	sil & multi	38	12
2142	A650	6.40z	sil & multi	65	25
			Nos. 2137-2142 (6)	1.47	64

12th Winter Olympic Games, Innsbruck, Austria, Feb. 4-15.

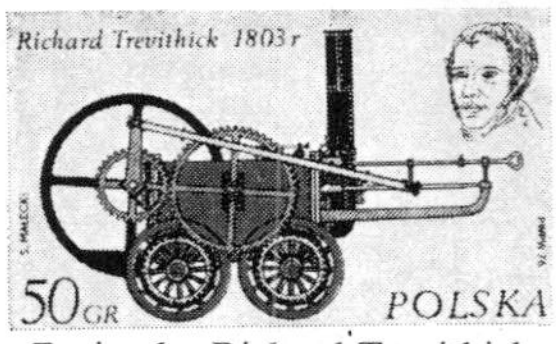

Engine by Richard Trevithick, 1803 — A651

Locomotives by: 1z, M. Murray and J. Blenkinsop, 1810. No. 2145, George Stephenson's Rocket, 1829. No. 2146, Polish electric locomotive, 1969. 2.70z, Stephenson, 1837. 3z, Joseph Harrison, 1840. 4.50z, Thomas Rogers, 1855. 4.90z, Chrzanow (Polish), 1922.

1976, Feb. 13 Photo. ***Perf. 11½x12***

2143	A651	50g	multi	5	5
2144	A651	1z	multi	8	6
2145	A651	1.50z	multi	10	8
2146	A651	1.50z	multi	10	8
2147	A651	2.70z	multi	22	12
2148	A651	3z	multi	22	12
2149	A651	4.50z	multi	85	48
2150	A651	4.90z	multi	90	55
			Nos. 2143-2150 (8)	2.52	1.54

History of the locomotive.

Telephone, Radar and Satellites, ITU Emblem — A652

1976, Mar. 10 ***Perf. 11***

2151	A652	1.50z multi	12	8

Centenary of first telephone call by Alexander Graham Bell, Mar. 10, 1876.

Atom Symbol and Flags of Communist Countries
A653

1976, Mar. 10 Litho. ***Perf. 11½***

2152	A653	1.50z multi	12	8

Joint Institute of Nuclear Research, Dubna, USSR, 20th anniversary.

Ice Hockey — A654

Design: 1.50z, Like 1z, reversed.

1976, Apr. 8 Photo. *Perf. 11½x11*

2153 A654	1z	multi	8	6
2154 A654	1.50z	multi	14	7

Ice Hockey World Championship 1976, Katowice.

Soldier and Map of Sinai A655

1976, Apr. 30 Photo. *Perf. 11x11½*

2155 A655	1.50z	multi	14	10

Polish specialist troops serving with UN Forces in Sinai Peninsula.

No. 2155 printed se-tenant with label with commemorative inscription.

Sappers' Monument, by Stanislaw Kulow, Warsaw A656

Interphil 76, Philadelphia A657

Design: No. 2157, First Polish Army Monument, by Bronislaw Koniuszy, Warsaw.

1976, May 8 *Perf. 11½*

2156 A656	1z	gold & multi	7	6
2157 A656	1z	sil & multi	7	6

Memorials unveiled on 30th anniv. of WWII victory.

1976, May 20 Litho. *Perf. 11½x11*

2158 A657	8.40z	gray & multi	52	32

Interphil 76, Intl. Phil. Exhib., Philadelphia, May 29-June 6.

Wielkopolski Park and Owl — A658

National Parks: 1z, Wolinski Park and eagle. 1.50z, Slowinski Park and sea gull. 4.50z, Bieszczadzki Park and lynx. 5z, Ojcowski Park and bat. 6z, Kampinoski Park and elk.

1976, May 22 Photo. *Perf. 12x11½*

2159 A658	90g	multi	8	6
2160 A658	1z	multi	8	6
2161 A658	1.50z	multi	9	8
2162 A658	4.50z	multi	35	15
2163 A658	5z	multi	38	18
2164 A658	6z	multi	48	22
		Nos. 2159-2164 (6)	1.46	75

UN Headquarters, Dove-shaped Globe — A659

1976, June 29 Litho. *Perf. 11x11½*

2165 A659	8.40z	multi	52	32

UN postage stamps, 25th anniversary.

Fencing and Olympic Rings A660

1976, June 30 Photo.

2166 A660	50g	shown	6	5
2167 A660	1z	Bicycling	8	6
2168 A660	1.50z	Soccer	12	8
2169 A660	4.20z	Boxing	32	15
2170 A660	6.90z	Weight lifting	52	28
2171 A660	8.40z	Running	60	35
		Nos. 2166-2171 (6)	1.70	97

21st Olympic Games, Montreal, Canada, July 17-Aug. 1. See No. B132.

Polish Theater, Poznan — A662

1976, July 12 Litho. *Perf. 11x11½*

2173 A662	1.50z	gray ol & org	12	8

Polish Theater in Poznan, centenary.

Czekanowski, Lake Baikal A663

1976, Sept. 3 Photo. *Perf. 11x11½*

2174 A663	1.50z	sil & multi	12	8

Aleksander Czekanowski (1833-1876), geologist, death centenary.

Siren A664

Designs: 1z, Sphinx (vert.). 2z, Lion. 4.20z, Bull. 4.50z, Goat. Designs from Corinthian vases, 7th century B.C.

Perf. 11x11½, 11½x11

1976, Oct. 30 Photo.

2175 A664	1z	gold & multi	6	6
2176 A664	1.50z	gold & multi	9	8
2177 A664	2z	gold & multi	12	8
2178 A664	4.20z	gold & multi	28	16
2179 A664	4.50z	gold & multi	30	18
		Nos. 2175-2179,B133 (6)	1.95	1.06

Stamp Day.

Warszawa M20 — A665

Automobiles: 1.50z, Warszawa 223. 2z, Syrena 104. 4.90z, Polski Fiat 125.

1976, Nov. 6 Photo. *Perf. 11*

2180 A665	1z	multi	7	6
2181 A665	1.50z	multi	10	6
2182 A665	2z	multi	12	9
2183 A665	4.90z	multi	32	16
a		Souvenir sheet of 4 + 2 labels, #2180-2183	1.16	55

Zeran Automobile Factory, Warsaw, 25th anniv.

Pouring Ladle — A666

Virgin and Child, Epitaph, 1425 — A667

1976, Nov. 26 Litho. *Perf. 11*

2184 A666	1.50z	multi	12	8

First steel production at Katowice Foundry.

1976, Dec. 15

Design: 6z, The Beautiful Madonna, sculpture, c. 1410.

2185 A667	1z	multi	8	6
2186 A667	6z	multi	40	20

Polish Trade Union Emblem — A668

1976, Dec. 29

2187 A668	1.50z	multi	12	8

8th Polish Trade Union Congress.

Tanker Zawrat Unloading, Gdansk — A669

Designs: No. 2189, Ferry "Gryf" and cars at pier, Gdansk. No. 2190, Loading containers, Gdynia. No. 2191, "Stefan Batory" and "People of the Sea" monument, Gdynia. 2z, Barge and cargoship "Ziemia Szczecinska", Szczecin. 4.20z, Coal loading installations, Swinoujscie. 6.90z, Liner, hydrofoil and lighthouse, Kolobrzeg. 8.40z, Map of Polish Coast with ports, ships and emblem of Union of Polish Ports.

1976, Dec. 29 Photo. *Perf. 11*

2188 A669	1z	multi	7	6
2189 A669	1z	multi	7	6
2190 A669	1.50z	multi	10	8
2191 A669	1.50z	multi	10	8
2192 A669	2z	multi	7	8
2193 A669	4.20z	multi	24	14
2194 A669	6.90z	multi	45	24
2195 A669	8.40z	multi	50	28
		Nos. 2188-2195 (8)	1.60	1.02

Polish ports.

Nurse Helping Old Woman — A670

Civilian Defense Medal — A671

1977, Jan. 24 Litho. *Perf. 11½x11*

2196 A670	1.50z	multi	12	8

Polish Red Cross.

1977, Feb. 26 Litho. *Perf. 11*

2197 A671	1.50z	multi	12	8

Civilian Defense.

Ball on the Road — A672

1977, Mar. 12 Photo.

2198 A672	1.50z	ol & multi	12	8

Social Action Committee (founded 1966), "Stop, Child on the Road!"

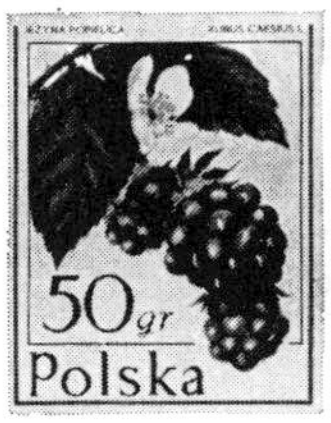

Dewberry — A673

Designs: Forest fruits.

1977, Mar. 17 *Perf. 11½x11*

2199 A673	50g	shown	5	5
2200 A673	90g	Cranberry	8	5
2201 A673	1z	Wild strawberry	8	6
2202 A673	1.50z	Bilberry	10	8
2203 A673	2z	Raspberry	12	6
2204 A673	4.50z	Blueberry	30	15
2205 A673	6z	Dog rose	35	20
2206 A673	6.90z	Hazelnut	45	24
		Nos. 2199-2206 (8)	1.53	89

Flags of USSR and Poland as Computer Tape — A674

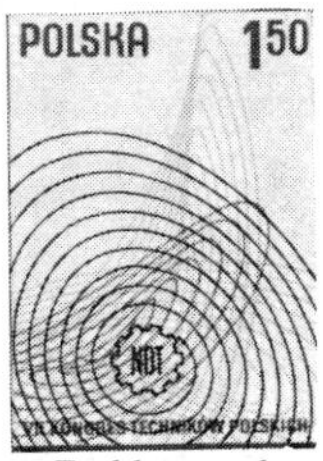

Emblem and Graph — A675

1977, Apr. 4 Litho. *Perf. 11½x11*

2207 A674	1.50z	red & multi	12	8

Scientific and technical cooperation between Poland and USSR, 30th anniversary.

1977, Apr. 22

2208 A675	1.50z	red & multi	12	8

7th Congress of Polish Engineers.

Venus, by Rubens A676

Paintings by Flemish painter Peter Paul Rubens (1577-1640): 1.50z, Bathsheba. 5z, Helene Fourment. 6z, Self-portrait.

1977, Apr. 30 ***Perf. 11½***

Frame in Gray Brown

2209	A676	1z	multi	8	6
2210	A676	1.50z	multi	12	8
2211	A676	5z	multi	38	18
2212	A676	6z	multi	40	22

See No. B134.

Peace Dove A677

1977, May 6 ***Perf. 11x11½***

2213	A677	1.50z	blk, ultra & yel	12	8

Congress of World Council of Peace, Warsaw, May 6-11.

Bicyclist A678

1977, May 6 **Photo.**

2214	A678	1.50z	gray & multi	12	8

30th International Peace Bicycling Race, Warsaw-Berlin-Prague.

Wolf A679

Violinist, by Jacob Toorenvliet A680

Wildlife Fund Emblem and: No. 2216, Great bustard. No. 2217, Kestrel. 6z, Otter.

1977, May 12 **Photo.** ***Perf. 11½x11***

2215	A679	1z	sil & multi	8	6
2216	A679	1.50z	sil & multi	12	8
2217	A679	1.50z	sil & multi	12	8
2218	A679	6z	sil & multi	40	20

Wildlife protection.

1977, May 16

2219	A680	6z	gold & multi	42	25

AMPHILEX '77 Intl. Phil. Exhib., Amsterdam, May 26-June 5. No. 2219 issued in sheets of 6.

Midsummer Bonfire — A681

Folk Customs: 1z, Easter cock. 1.50z, Dousing the women on Easter Monday. 3z, Harvest festival. 6z, Christmas procession with creche. 8.40z, Wedding dance. 1z, 1.50z, 3z, 6z vertical.

Perf. 11x11½, 11½x11

1977, June 13 **Photo.**

2220	A681	90g	multi	8	5
2221	A681	1z	multi	7	5
2222	A681	1.50z	multi	10	6
2223	A681	3z	multi	18	8
2224	A681	6z	multi	38	18
2225	A681	8.40z	multi	55	24
	Nos. 2220-2225 (6)			1.36	66

Henryk Wieniawski and Musical Symbol — A682

1977, June 30 **Litho.** ***Perf. 11½x11***

2226	A682	1.50z	gold, blk & red	12	8

Wieniawski Music Festivals, Poznan: 5th Intl. Lute Competition, June 30-July 10, and 7th Intl. Violin Competition, Nov. 13-27.

Parnassius Apollo — A683

Butterflies: No. 2228, Nymphalis polychloros. No. 2229, Papilio machaon. No. 2230, Nymphalis antiopa. 5z, Fabriciana adippe. 6.90z, Argynnis paphia.

1977, Aug. 22 **Photo.** ***Perf. 11***

2227	A683	1z	multi	7	5
2228	A683	1z	multi	7	5
2229	A683	1.50z	multi	10	6
2230	A683	1.50z	multi	10	6
2231	A683	5z	multi	50	15
2232	A683	6.90z	multi	85	40
	Nos. 2227-2232 (6)			1.69	77

Arms of Slupsk, Keyboard A684

Feliks Dzerzhinski A685

1977, Sept. 3 ***Perf. 11½***

2233	A684	1.50z	multi	12	8

Slupsk Piano Festival.

1977, Sept. 10 **Litho.** ***Perf. 11½x11***

2234	A685	1.50z	ol bis & sep	12	8

Feliks E. Dzerzhinski (1877-1926), organizer and head of Russian Secret Police (Cheka).

Earth and Sputnik A686

1977, Oct. 1 **Litho.** ***Perf. 11x11½***

2235	A686	1.50z	ultra & car	12	8
a.			Souvenir sheet of 3+3 labels	55	50

60th anniv. of the Russian Revolution and 20th anniv. of Sputnik space flight. Printed in sheets of 15 stamps and 15 carmine labels showing Winter Palace, Leningrad.

Boleslaw Chrobry's Denarius, 11th Century — A687

Silver Coins: 1z, King Kazimierz Wielki's Cracow groszy, 14th century. 1.50z, Legniza-Brzeg-Wolow thaler, 17th century. 4.20z, King Augustus III guilder, Gdansk, 18th century. 4.50z, 5z (ship), 1936. 6z, 100z, Poland's millenium, 1966.

1977, Oct. 9 **Photo.** ***Perf. 11½x11***

2236	A687	50g	sil & multi	5	5
2237	A687	1z	sil & multi	7	6
2238	A687	1.50z	sil & multi	10	8
2239	A687	4.20z	sil & multi	32	14
2240	A687	4.50z	sil & multi	40	20
2241	A687	6z	sil & multi	65	25
	Nos. 2236-2241 (6)			1.59	78

Stamp Day.

Monastery, Przasnysz A688

Architectural landmarks: No. 2242, Wolin Gate (vert.). No. 2243, Church, Debno (vert.). No. 2245, Cathedral, Plock. 6z, Castle, Kornik. 6.90z, Palace and Garden, Wilanow.

Perf. 11½x11, 11x11½

1977, Nov. 21 **Photo.**

2242	A688	1z	multi	7	6
2243	A688	1z	multi	7	6
2244	A688	1.50z	multi	10	8
2245	A688	1.50z	multi	10	8
2246	A688	6z	multi	35	15
2247	A688	6.90z	multi	45	22
	Nos. 2242-2247 (6)			1.14	65

Vostok (USSR) and Mercury (USA) A689

1977, Dec. 28 **Photo.** ***Perf. 11x11½***

2248	A689	6.90z	ultra & multi	48	28
a.			Souvenir sheet of 6	4.50	3.50

20 years of space conquest. No. 2248a contains 6 No. 2248 (2 tete-beche pairs) and 2 labels, one showing Sputnik 1 and "4.X.1957," the other Explorer 1 and "31.1.1958."

DN Class Iceboats — A690

Design: No. 2250, One iceboat.

1978, Feb. 6 **Litho.** ***Perf. 11***

2249	A690	1.50z	lt ultra & blk	12	8
2250	A690	1.50z	lt ultra & blk	12	8

6th World Iceboating Championships, Feb. 6-11. Nos. 2249-2250 printed se-tenant with label in between, sheets of 16 stamps and 8 labels showing Championship emblem.

Electric Locomotive, Katowice Station, 1957 — A691

Locomotives in Poland: No. 2252, Narrow-gauge engine and Gothic Tower, Znin. No. 2253, Pm36 and Cegielski factory, Poznan, 1936. No. 2254, Electric train and Otwock Station, 1936. No. 2255, Marki Train and Warsaw Stalow Station, 1907. 4.50z, Ty51 coal train and Gdynia Station, 1933. 5z, Tr21 and Chrzanow factory, 1920. 6z, "Cockerill" and Vienna Station, 1848.

1978, Feb. 28 **Photo.** ***Perf. 12x11½***

2251	A691	50g	multi	5	5
2252	A691	1z	multi	7	5
2253	A691	1z	multi	7	5
2254	A691	1.50z	multi	10	8
2255	A691	1.50z	multi	10	8
2256	A691	4.50z	multi	30	12
2257	A691	5z	multi	32	15
2258	A691	6z	multi	40	22
	Nos. 2251-2258 (8)			1.41	80

Pierwsze Wzloty, 1896, and Czeslaw Tanski A692

Polish Sport Planes: 1z, Zwyciezcy-Challenge, 1932, F. Zwirko and S. Wigura (vert.). 1.50z, RWD-5 bis over South Atlantic, 1933, and S. Skarzynski (vert.). 4.20z, MI-2 helicopter over mountains, Pezetel emblem (vert.). 6.90z, PZL-104 Wilga 35, Pezetel emblem. 8.40z, Motoszybowiec SZD-45 Ogar.

Perf. 11x11½, 11½x11

1978, Apr. 15

2259	A692	50g	multi	5	5
2260	A692	1z	multi	7	6
2261	A692	1.50z	multi	10	8
2262	A692	4.20z	multi	28	10
2263	A692	6.90z	multi	45	22
2264	A692	8.40z	multi	55	24
	Nos. 2259-2264 (6)			1.50	75

Soccer A693

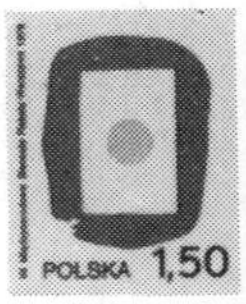

Poster A694

Design: 6.90z, Soccer ball (horiz.).

Perf. 11½x11, 11x11½

1978, May 12 **Litho.**

2265	A693	1.50z multi		10	7
2266	A693	6.90z multi		50	25

11th World Cup Soccer Championships, Argentina, June 1-25.

1978, June 1 ***Perf. 12x11½***

2267	A694	1.50z multi	12	8

7th International Poster Biennale, Warsaw.

Fair Emblem — A695

1978, June 10 ***Perf. 11***

2268	A695	1.50z multi	12	8

50th International Poznan Fair.

Polonez Passenger Car — A696

1978, June 10 **Photo.** ***Perf. 11***

2269	A696	1.50z multi	12	8

Maj. Miroslaw Hermaszewski A697

Design: 6.90z, Hermaszewski, globe and trajectory (horiz.).

Perf. 11½x11, 11x11½

1978, June 27 **Photo.**

2270	A697	1.50z multi	14	6
2271	A697	6.90z multi	50	24

1st Polish cosmonaut on Russian space mission. Printed in sheets of 6 stamps and 2 labels.

Youth Festival Emblem A698

1978, July 12 **Litho.** ***Perf. 11½***

2272	A698	1.50z multi	12	8

11th Youth Festival, Havana, July 28-Aug. 5.

Foreign postal stationery (stamped envelopes, postal cards and air letter sheets) lies beyond the scope of this Catalogue, which is limited to adhesive postage stamps.

Souvenir Sheet

Flowers — A699

1978, July 20 ***Perf. 11½x11***

2273	A699	1.50z gold & multi	25	15

30th anniv. of Polish Youth Movement.

Anopheles Mosquito and Blood Cells — A700

Design: 6z, Tsetse fly and blood cells.

1978, Aug. 19 **Litho.** ***Perf. 11½x11***

2274	A700	1.50z multi	10	8
2275	A700	6z multi	45	20

4th International Parasitological Congress.

Norway Maple, Environment Emblem — A701

Jan Zizka, Battle of Grunwald, by Jan Matejko — A702

Human Environment Emblem and: 1z, English oak. 1.50z, White poplar. 4.20z, Scotch pine. 4.50z, White willow. 6z, Birch.

1978, Sept. 6 **Photo.** ***Perf. 14***

2276	A701	50g gold & multi	5	5
2277	A701	1z gold & multi	8	5
2278	A701	1.50z gold & multi	12	6
2279	A701	4.20z gold & multi	30	10
2280	A701	4.50z gold & multi	32	14
2281	A701	6z gold & multi	42	18
		Nos. 2276-2281 (6)	1.29	58

Protection of the environment.

Souvenir Sheet

1978, Sept. 8 ***Perf. 11½x11***

2282	A702	6z gold & multi	48	35

PRAGA '78 Intl. Phil. Exhib., Prague, Sept. 8-17.

Letter, Telephone and Satellite — A703

1978, Sept. 20 **Litho.** ***Perf. 11***

2283	A703	1.50z multi	12	8

20th anniversary of the Organization of Ministers of Posts and Telecommunications of Warsaw Pact countries.

Peace, by Andre le Brun — A704

1978-79 **Litho.** ***Perf. 11½ (1z), 12½***

2284	A704	1z violet	12	5
2285	A704	1.50z steel bl ('79)	18	10
2286	A704	2z brn ('79)	15	10
2287	A704	2.50z ultra ('79)	20	12

Polish Unit, UN Middle East Emergency Force — A706

Designs: No. 2289, Color Guard, Kosziusko Division (4 soldiers). No. 2290, Color Guard, field training (3 soldiers).

1978, Oct. 6 **Photo.** ***Perf. 12x11½***

2289	A706	1.50z multi	12	8
2290	A706	1.50z multi	12	8
2291	A706	1.50z multi	12	8

35th anniversary of People's Army.

Young Man, by Raphael A707

1978, Oct. 9 ***Perf. 11***

2292	A707	6z multi	42	15

Stamp Day.

Dr. Korczak and Children — A708

1978, Oct. 11 **Litho.** ***Perf. 11½x11***

2293	A708	1.50z multi	12	8

Dr. Janusz Korczak, physician, educator, writer, birth centenary.

Wojciech Boguslawski (1757-1829) A709

Polish dramatists: 1z, Aleksander Fredro (1793-1878). 1.50z, Juliusz Slowacki (1809-1849). 2z, Adam Mickiewicz (1798-1855). 4.50z, Stanislaw Wyspianski (1869-1907). 6z, Gabriela Zapolska (1857-1921).

1978, Nov. 11 **Litho.** ***Perf. 11½***

2294	A709	50g multi	5	5
2295	A709	1z multi	7	5
2296	A709	1.50z multi	10	8
2297	A709	2z multi	14	8
2298	A709	4.50z multi	30	10
2299	A709	6z multi	42	18
		Nos. 2294-2299 (6)	1.08	54

Polish Combatants Monument, and Eiffel Tower, Paris — A710

1978, Nov. 2 **Photo.** ***Perf. 11x11½***

2300	A710	1.50z brn, red & bl	12	8

Przewalski Mare and Colt A711

Animals: 1z, Polar bears. 1.50z, Indian elephants. 2z, Jaguars. 4.20z, Gray seals. 4.50z, Hartebeests. 6z, Mandrills.

1978, Nov. 10

2301	A711	50g multi	5	5
2302	A711	1z multi	7	5
2303	A711	1.50z multi	10	6
2304	A711	2z multi	14	8
2305	A711	4.20z multi	24	8
2306	A711	4.50z multi	30	10
2307	A711	6z multi	42	15
		Nos. 2301-2307 (7)	1.32	57

Warsaw Zoological Gardens, 50th anniv.

Adolf Warski (1868-1937) A712

Party Emblem A713

Portraits: No. 2309, Julian Lenski (1889-1937). No. 2310, Aleksander Zawadzki (1899-1964). No. 2311, Stanislaw Dubois (1901-1942).

Perf. 11½x11, 11x11½

1978, Dec. 15 **Photo.**

2308	A712	1.50z red & brn	10	6
2309	A712	1.50z red & blk	10	6
2310	A712	1.50z red & dk vio	10	6
2311	A712	1.50z red & dk bl	10	6
2312	A713	1.50z blk, red & gold	10	6
		Nos. 2308-2312 (5)	50	30

Polish United Workers' Party, 30th anniv.

LOT Planes, 1929 and 1979 A714

1979, Jan. 2 Photo. ***Perf. 11x11½***
2313 A714 6.90z gold & multi 42 18

LOT, Polish airline, 50th anniversary.

Train and IYC Emblem — A715

Children's Paintings: 1z, Children with toys. 1.50z, Children in meadow. 6z, Family.

1979, Jan. 13 ***Perf. 11***
2314 A715 50g multi 5 5
2315 A715 1z multi 7 5
2316 A715 1.50z multi 10 8
2317 A715 6z multi 42 18

International Year of the Child.

Artist's Wife, by Karol Mondral — A716

Modern Polish Graphic Arts: 50g, "Lightning," by Edmund Bartlomiejcyk (horiz.). 1.50z, Musicians, by Tadeusz Kulisiewicz. 4.50z, Portrait of a Brave Man, by Wladyslaw Skoczylas.

Perf. 11½x12, 12x11½
1979, Mar. 5 Engr.
2318 A716 50g brt vio 5 5
2319 A716 1z sl grn 7 5
2320 A716 1.50z bl gray 10 6
2321 A716 4.50z vio bl 30 12

Andrzej Frycz-Modrzewski, Stefan Batory, Jan Zamoyski — A717

Photogravure and Engraved
1979, Mar. 12 ***Perf. 12x11½***
2322 A717 1.50z cr & sep 10 8

Royal Tribunal in Piotrkow Trybunalski. 400th anniversary.

Pole Vault and Olympic Emblem — A718

Olympic Emblem and: 1.50z, High jump. 6z, Cross-country skiing. 8.40z, Equestrian.

1979, Mar. 26 Photo. ***Perf. 12x11½***
2323 A718 1z multi 8 5
2324 A718 1.50z multi 8 6
2325 A718 6z multi 35 15
2326 A718 8.40z multi 50 20

1980 Olympic Games.

The lack of a value for a listed item does not necessarily indicate rarity.

Flounder — A720

Fish and Environmental Protection Emblem: 90g, Perch. 1z, Grayling. 1.50z, Salmon. 2z, Trout. 4.50z, Pike. 5z, Carp. 6z, Catfish and frog.

1979, Apr. 26 Photo. ***Perf. 11½x11***
2327 A720 50g multi 5 5
2328 A720 90g multi 7 5
2329 A720 1z multi 7 5
2330 A720 1.50z multi 10 6
2331 A720 2z multi 12 8
2332 A720 4.50z multi 30 12
2333 A720 5z multi 32 12
2334 A720 6z multi 40 18
Nos. 2327-2334 (8) 1.43 71

Polish angling, centenary, and protection of the environment.

A721

1979, Apr. 30 Litho. ***Perf. 11x11½***
2335 A721 1.50z multi 12 8

Council for Mutual Economic Aid of Socialist Countries, 30th anniversary.

Faces and Emblem — A722

1979, May 7 ***Perf. 11***
2336 A722 1.50z red & blk 12 8

6th Congress of Association of Fighters for Liberty and Democracy, Warsaw, May 7-8.

St. George's Church, Sofia A722a

1979, May 15 Photo. ***Perf. 11x11½***
2337 A722a 1.50z multi 12 8

Philaserdica '79 Phil. Exhib., Sofia, Bulgaria, May 18-27.

Pope John Paul II, Cracow Cathedral A723

Designs: 8.40z, Pope John Paul II, Auschwitz-Birkenau Memorial. 50z, Pope John Paul II.

1979, June 2 Photo. ***Perf. 11x11½***
2338 A723 1.50z multi 14 6
2339 A723 8.40z multi 60 30

Souvenir Sheet
Perf. 11½x11
2340 A723 50z multi 2.75 2.50

Visit of Pope John Paul II to Poland, June 2-11. No. 2340 contains one stamp 26x35mm.
A variety of No. 2340 with silver margin exists.

Paddle Steamer Prince Ksawery and Old Warsaw — A724

Designs: 1.50z, Steamer Gen. Swierczewski and Gdansk, 1914. 4.50z, Tug Aurochs and Plock, 1960. 6z, Motor ship Mermaid and modern Warsaw, 1959.

1979, June 15 Litho. ***Perf. 11***
2341 A724 1z multi 7 6
2342 A724 1.50z multi 10 6
2343 A724 4.50z multi 30 12
2344 A724 6z multi 42 18

Vistula River navigation, 150th anniversary.

Kosciuszko Monument, Philadelphia A725

1979, July 1 Photo. ***Perf. 11½***
2345 A725 8.40z multi 48 25

Gen. Tadeusz Kosziuszko (1746-1807), Polish soldier and statesman who served in American Revolution.

Mining Machinery A726

Eagle and People A727

Design: 1.50z, Salt crystals.

1979, July 14 Photo. ***Perf. 14***
2346 A726 1z lt brn & blk 8 5
2347 A726 1.50z bl grn & blk 10 8

Wieliczka ancient rock-salt mines.

1979, July 21 ***Perf. 11½x11***

Design: No. 2349, Man with raised hand and flag.

2348 A727 1.50z red, bl & gray 10 8
2349 A727 1.50z sil, red & blk 10 8

35 years of Polish People's Republic.

Souvenir Sheet
1979, Sept. 2 Photo. ***Perf. 11½x11***
2350 A727 Sheet of 2, #2348-2349, plus label 48 35

13th National Philatelic Exhibition.

Poland No. 1, Rowland Hill (1795-1879), Originator of Penny Postage A728

1979, Aug. 16 Litho. ***Perf. 11½x11***
2351 A728 6z multi 40 18

Souvenir Sheet

The Rape of Europa, by Bernardo Strozzi A729

1979, Aug. 20 Photo. ***Perf. 11x11½***
2352 A729 10z multi 70 48

Europhil '79, Intl. Phil. Exhib.

Wojciech Jastrzebowski A730

1979, Aug. 27 ***Perf. 11½x11***
2353 A730 1.50z multi 12 8

Economic Congress.

Postal Workers' Monument A731

1979, Sept. 1 ***Perf. 11x11½***
2354 A731 1.50z multi 12 8

40th anniversary of Polish postal workers' resistance to Nazi invaders. See No. B137.

ITU Emblem, Radio Antenna A732

1979, Sept. 24 ***Perf. 11x11½***
2355 A732 1.50z multi 12 8

Intl. Radio Consultative Committee (CCIR) of the ITU, 50th anniv.

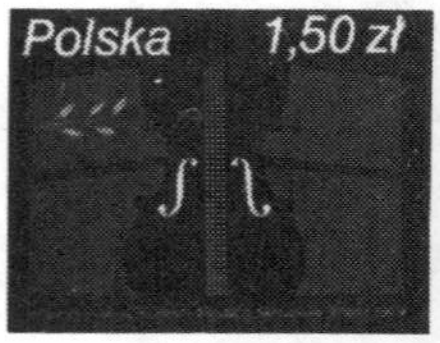

Violin A733

1979, Sept. 25 Litho.
2356 A733 1.50z dk bl, org, grn 12 8

Henryk Wieniawski Young Violinists' Competition, Lublin.

Pulaski Monument, Buffalo — A734

Gen. Franciszek Jozwiak — A735

1979, Oct. 1 Photo. *Perf. 11½x12*

2357	A734	8.40z	multi	48	22

Gen. Casimir Pulaski (1748-1779), Polish nobleman who served in American Revolutionary War.

1979, Oct. 3 *Perf. 11½x11*

2358	A735	1.50z	bl, gold	12	8

35th anniv. of Civil and Military Security Service, founded by Gen. Franciszek Jozwiak (1895-1966).

Drive-in Post Office — A736

Designs: 1.50z, Parcel sorting. 4.50z, Loading mail train. 6z, Mobile post office.

1979, Oct. 9 *Perf. 11½*

2359	A736	1z	multi	7	6
2360	A736	1.50z	multi	10	8
2361	A736	4.50z	multi	30	12
2362	A736	6z	multi	42	18

Stamp Day.

Holy Family — A737

Design: 6.90z, Nativity (horiz.).

Perf. 11½x11, 11x11½

1979, Dec. 4 Photo.

2363	A737	2z	multi	15	8
2364	A737	6.90z	multi	45	20

Soyuz 30 and Salyut 6 — A738

Space Achievements: 1.50z, Kopernik 500 and Copernicus satellite. 2z, Lunik 2 and Ranger 7. 4.50z, Yuri Gagarin and Vostok. 6.90z, Neil Armstrong and Apollo 11.

1979, Dec. 28 Photo. *Perf. 11½x11*

2365	A738	1z	multi	7	5
2366	A738	1.50z	multi	10	8
2367	A738	2z	multi	12	8
2368	A738	4.50z	multi	30	12
2369	A738	6.90z	multi	40	18
a			Souvenir sheet of 5	1.40	1.00
			Nos. 2365-2369 (5)	99	51

No. 2369a contains Nos. 2365-2369, tete beche plus label.

Trotters — A739

Designs: Horse Paintings.

1980, Jan. 31 Photo. *Perf. 11½x12*

2370	A739	1z	Stagecoach	8	5
2371	A739	2z	Horse, trainer	9	8
2372	A739	2.50z	shown	12	8
2373	A739	3z	Fox hunt	15	8
2374	A739	4z	Sled	18	10
2375	A739	6z	Hay cart	30	16
2376	A739	6.50z	Pairs	32	16
2377	A739	6.90z	Hurdles	32	18
			Nos. 2370-2377 (8)	1.56	89

Sierakov horse stud farm, 150th anniv.

Party Slogan on Map of Poland — A740

Worker, by Janusz Stanny — A741

1980, Feb. 11 Photo. *Perf. 11½x11*

2378	A740	2.50z	multi	16	9
2379	A741	2.50z	multi	16	9

Polish United Workers' Party, 8th Congress.

Equestrian, Olympic Rings — A742

1980, Mar. 31 *Perf. 12x11½*

2380	A742	2z	shown	14	8
2381	A742	2.50z	Archery	16	10
2382	A742	6.50z	Biathlon	42	20
2383	A742	8.40z	Volleyball	50	25

13th Winter Olympic Games, Lake Placid, N.Y., Feb. 12-24 (6.50z); 22nd Summer Olympic Games, Moscow, July 19-Aug. 3. See No. B138.

Map and Old Town Hall, 1591, Zamosc A743

1980, Apr. 3 Litho. *Perf. 11½*

2384	A743	2.50z	multi	18	10

Zamosc, 400th anniversary.

Arms of Poland and Russia A744

1980, Apr. 21 Litho. *Perf. 11½*

2385	A744	2.50z	multi	18	10

Treaty of Friendship, Cooperation and Mutual Assistance between Poland and USSR, 35th anniversary.

Lenin, 110th Birth Anniversary — A745

1980, Apr. 22 Photo. *Perf. 11*

2386	A745	2.50z	multi	18	10

Workers Marching — A746

Dove Over Liberation Date — A747

1980, May 1 *Perf. 11½x11*

2387	A746	2.50z	multi	18	10

Revolution of 1905, 75th anniversary.

1980, May 9 *Perf. 11½x12*

2388	A747	2.50z	multi	18	10

Victory over fascism, 35th anniversary.

Arms of Treaty-signing Countries A748

1980, May 14 Litho. *Perf. 11½x11*

2389	A748	2z	red & blk	18	10

Signing of Warsaw Pact (Bulgaria, Czechoslovakia, German Democratic Rep., Hungary, Poland, Romania, USSR), 25th anniversary.

Caverns, (1961 Expedition) Map of Cuba — A749

1980, May 22 Photo. *Perf. 14*

2390	A749	2z	shown	12	8
2391	A749	2z	Seals, Antarctica, 1959	12	8
2392	A749	2.50z	Ethnology, Mongolia, 1963	15	8
2393	A749	2.50z	Archaeology, Syria, 1959	15	8
2394	A749	6.50z	Mountain climbing, Nepal, 1978	35	18
2395	A749	8.40z	Paleontology, Mongolia, 1963	42	22
			Nos. 2390-2395 (6)	1.31	72

Malachowski Lyceum, Arms of Polish Order of Labor A750

Xerocomus Parasiticus A751

1980, June 7 Photo. *Perf. 11x12*

2396	A750	2z	blk & dl grn	15	10

Malachowski Lyceum (oldest school in Plock), 800th anniversary.

1980, June 30 *Perf. 11½x11*

2397	A751	2z	shown	12	8
2398	A751	2z	Clathrus ruber	12	8
2399	A751	2.50z	Phallus hadriani	15	8
2400	A751	2.50z	Strobilomyces floccopus	15	8
2401	A751	8z	Sparassis crispa	42	22
2402	A751	10.50z	Langermannia gigantea	55	28
			Nos. 2397-2402 (6)	1.51	82

Sandomierz Millenium — A752

1980, July 12 Photo. *Perf. 11x11½*

2403	A752	2.50z	dk brn	22	12

"Lwow," T. Ziolkowski — A753

Ships and Teachers: 2.50z, Antoni Garnuszewski, A. Garnuszewski. 6z, Zenit, A. Ledochowski. 6.50z, Jan Turlejski, K. Porebski. 6.90z, Horyzon, G. Kanski. 8.40z, Dar Pomorza, K. Maciejewicz.

1980, July 21 Litho. *Perf. 11*

2404	A753	2z	multi	15	8
2405	A753	2.50z	multi	18	10
2406	A753	6z	multi	38	20
2407	A753	6.50z	multi	45	22

2408 A753 6.90z multi 45 24
2409 A753 8.40z multi 52 30
Nos. 2404-2409 (6) 2.13 1.14

Marize Maritime High School.

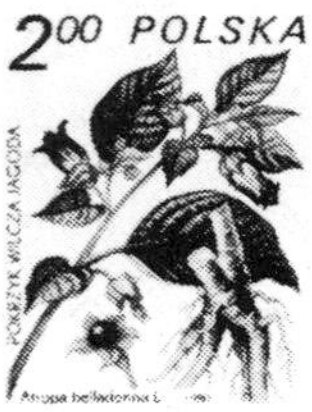

Atropa Belladonna A754

Designs: Medicinal plants.

1980, Aug. 15 Litho. *Perf. 11½x11*
2410 A754 2z shown 16 8
2411 A754 2.50z Datura innoxia 20 10
2412 A754 3.40z Valeriana 22 12
2413 A754 5z Mentha piperita 40 18
2414 A754 6.50z Calendula 48 25
2415 A754 8z Salvia officinalis 52 28
Nos. 2410-2415 (6) 1.98 1.01

Jan Kochanowski (1530-1584), Poet — A755

1980, Aug. 20 *Perf. 11*
2416 A755 2.50z multi 22 12

United Nations, 35th Anniversary A756

1980, Sept. 19 Photo. *Perf. 11x11½*
2417 A756 8.40z multi 60 32

Chopin Piano Competition — A757

1980, Oct. 2 Litho. *Perf. 11½*
2418 A757 6.90z blk & tan 60 32

Mail Pick-up — A758

1980, Oct. 9 Photo. *Perf. 12x11½*
2419 A758 2z shown 15 8
2420 A758 2.50z Letter sorting 18 10
2421 A758 6z Loading mail plane 45 22
2422 A758 6.50z Mail boxes 45 24
a Souvenir sheet of 4, #2419-2422 4.25 3.00

Stamp Day.

Girl Embracing Dove, UN Emblem A759

1980, Nov. 21 Litho. *Perf. 11x11½*
2423 A759 8.40z multi 70 35

UN Declaration on the Preparation of Societies for Life in Peace.

Battle of Olzynska Grochowska, by W. Kossak — A760

1980, Nov. 29 Photo. *Perf. 11*
2424 A760 2.50z multi 25 12

Battle of Olzynska Grochowska, 1830.

Horse-drawn Fire Engine — A761

Designs: Horse-drawn vehicles.

1980, Dec. 16
2425 A761 2z shown 18 10
2426 A761 2.50z Passenger coach 22 12
2427 A761 3z Beer wagon 24 12
2428 A761 5z Sled 45 18
2429 A761 6z Bus 50 25
2430 A761 6.50z Two-seater 55 25
Nos. 2425-2430 (6) 2.14 1.02

Honor to the Silesian Rebels, by Jan Borowczak A762

Pablo Picasso A763

1981, Jan. 22 Engr. *Perf. 11½*
2431 A762 2.50z gray grn 18 12

Silesian uprising, 60th anniversary.

1981, Mar. 10 Photo. *Perf. 11½x11*
2432 A763 8.40z multi 55 32
a Miniature sheet of 2 + 2 labels 1.65 85

Pablo Picasso (1881-1973), artist, birth centenary. No. 2432 se-tenant with label showing A Crying Woman. Sold for 20.80z.

Balloon Flown by Pilatre de Rozier, 1783 — A764

Gordon Bennett Cup (Balloons): No. 2434, J. Blanchard, J. Jeffries, 1875. 2.50z, F. Godard, 1850. 3z, F. Hynek, Z. Burzynski, 1933. 6z, Z. Burzynski, N. Wysocki, 1935. 6.50z, B. Abruzzo, M. Anderson, P. Newman, 1978. 10.50z, Winners' names, 1933-1935, 1938.

1981, Mar. 25 Photo. *Perf. 11½x12*
2433 A764 2z multi 16 8
2434 A764 2z multi 16 8
2435 A764 2.50z multi 20 10
2436 A764 3z multi 22 10
2437 A764 6z multi 45 24
2438 A764 6.50z multi 48 25
Nos. 2433-2438 (6) 1.67 85

Souvenir Sheet

Imperf

2439 A764 10.50z multi 95 70

Iphegenia, by Franz Anton Maulbertsch (1724-1796), WIPA '81 Emblem — A765

1981, May 11 Litho. *Perf. 11½*
2440 A765 10.50z multi 85 48

WIPA '81 Intl. Phil. Exhib., Vienna, May 22-31.

Wroclaw, 1493 A766

Gen. Wladyslaw Sikorski (1881-1943) A767

1981, May 15 Photo. *Perf. 14*
2441 A766 6.50z brown 50 22

See Nos. 2456-2459.

1981, May 20 *Perf. 11½x11*
2442 A767 6.50z multi 42 22

Kwan Vase, 18th Cent. — A768

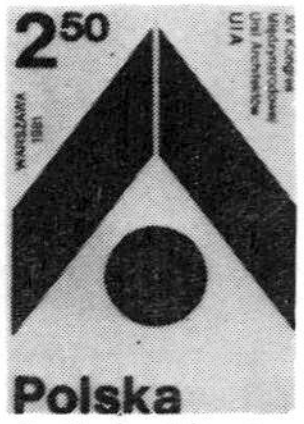

Intl. Architects Union, 14th Congress, Warsaw — A769

1981, June 15
2443 A768 1z shown 8 5
2444 A768 2z Cup, saucer, 1820 15 8
2445 A768 2.50z Jug, 1820 18 9
2446 A768 5z Portrait plate, 1880 38 15
2447 A768 6.50z Vase, 1900 45 20
2448 A768 8.40z Basket, 1840 52 24
Nos. 2443-2448 (6) 1.76 81

1981, July 15 Litho.
2449 A769 2.50z multi 18 10

Moose, Rifle and Pouch — A770

1981, July 30
2450 A770 2z shown 12 8
2451 A770 2z Boar 12 8
2452 A770 2.50z Fox 18 8
2453 A770 2.50z Elk 18 8
2454 A770 6.50z Greylag goose 45 20
2455 A770 6.50z Fen duck, horiz. 45 20
Nos. 2450-2455 (6) 1.50 72

City Type of 1981

1981, July 28 Photo. *Perf. 11x11½*
2456 A766 4z Gdansk, 1652, vert. 30 12
2457 A766 5z Krakow, 1493, vert. 40 18
2458 A766 6z Legnica, 1744 50 22
2459 A766 8z Warsaw, 1618 65 28

A770a

1982, Nov. 2 Photo. *Perf. 11½*
2461 A770a 12z Vistula River 22 10
2463 A770a 17z Kasimierz Dolny 32 12
2466 A770a 25z Gdansk 45 22

Wild Bison — A771

1981, Aug. 27 *Perf. 11½x11*
2471 Strip of 5 2.25 1.10
a.-e. A771 6.50z, any single 42 20

60th Anniv. of Polish Tennis Federation A772

1981, Sept. 17 Photo. *Perf. 11x11½*
2472 A772 6.50z multi 50 22

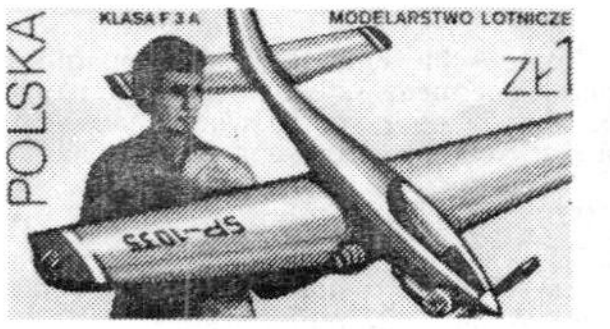

Model Airplane — A773

1981, Sept. 24 *Perf. 14*

2473	A773	1z	shown	8	5
2474	A773	2z	Boats	15	8
2475	A773	2.50z	Racing cars	18	10
2476	A773	4.20z	Gliders	30	14
2477	A773	6.50z	Radio-controlled racing cars	45	18
2478	A773	8z	Yachts	48	22
			Nos. 2473-2478 (6)	1.64	77

Intl. Year of the Disabled — A774

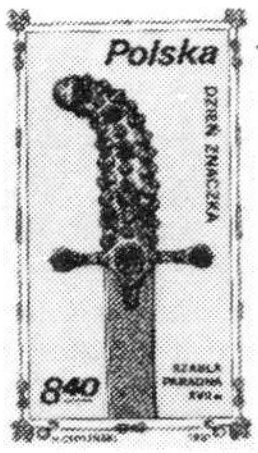

Stamp Day — A775

1981, Sept. 25 Litho. *Perf. 11½x11*

2479	A774	8.40z	multi	52	28

1981, Oct. 9 Photo. *Perf. 14*

2480	A775	2.50z	Pistol, 18th cent., horiz.	16	8
2481	A775	8.40z	Sword, 18th cent.	50	24

Henryk Wieniawski (1835-1880), Violinist and Composer A776

Bronislaw Wesolowski (1870-1919) A777

1981, Oct. 10 *Perf. 11½x12*

2482	A776	2.50z	multi	18	10

1981, Oct. 15 **Litho.**

Working Movement Leaders: 2z, Malgorzata Fornalska (1902-1944). 2.50z, Maria Koszutska (1876-1939). 6.50z, Marcin Kasprzak (1860-1905).

2483	A777	50g	grn & blk	5	5
2484	A777	2z	bl & blk	16	8
2485	A777	2.50z	brn & blk	18	8
2486	A777	6.50z	lil rose & blk	45	18

World Food Day — A778

1981, Oct. 16 *Perf. 11½x11*

2487	A778	6.90z	multi	48	22

Old Theater, Cracow, 200th Anniv. — A779

Theater Emblem and: 2z, Helena Modrzejewska (1840-1909), actress. 2.50z, Stanislaw Kozmian (1836-1922), theater director, 1865-1885, founder of Cracow School. 6.50z, Konrad Swinarski (1929-1975), stage manager.

Photo. & Engr.

1981, Oct. 17 *Perf. 12x11½*

2488	A779	2z	multi	16	14
2489	A779	2.50z	multi	20	9
2490	A779	6.50z	multi	40	20
2491	A779	8z	multi	50	24

Souvenir Sheet

Vistula River Project — A780

1981, Dec. 20 Litho. *Perf. 11½x12*

2492	A780	10.50z	multi	80	65

Flowering Succulent Plants A781

1981, Dec. 22 Photo. *Perf. 13*

2493	A781	90g	Epiphyllopsis gaertneri	6	5
2494	A781	1z	Cereus tonduzii	8	5
2495	A781	2z	Cylindropuntia leptocaulis	16	8
2496	A781	2.50z	Cylindroppuntia fulgida	22	9
2497	A781	2.50z	Caralluma lugardi	22	9
2498	A781	6.50z	Nopalea cochenillifera	42	20
2499	A781	6.50z	Lithopsps helmutii	42	20
2500	A781	10.50z	Cylindropuntia spinosior	85	35
			Nos. 2493-2500 (8)	2.43	1.11

Polish Workers' Party, 40th Anniv. — A782

Stoneware Plate, 1890 — A783

1982, Jan. 5 Photo. *Perf. 11½x11*

2501	A782	2.50z	multi	22	12

1982, Jan. 20

Porcelain or Stoneware: 2z, Plate, mug, 1790. 2.50z, Soup tureen, gravy dish, 1830. 6z, Salt and pepper dish, 1844. 8z, Stoneware jug, 1840. 10.50z, Stoneware figurine, 1740.

2502	A783	1z	multi	8	5
2503	A783	2z	multi	12	8
2504	A783	2.50z	multi	16	10
2505	A783	6z	multi	42	25
2506	A783	8z	multi	55	32
2507	A783	10.50z	multi	70	42
			Nos. 2502-2507 (6)	2.03	1.22

Ignacy Lukasiewicz (1822-1882), Oil Lamp Inventor — A784

Designs: Various oil lamps.

1982, Mar. 22 Photo. *Perf. 11½x11*

2508	A784	1z	multi	8	5
2509	A784	2z	multi	12	8
2510	A784	2.50z	multi	18	10
2511	A784	3.50z	multi	25	15
2512	A784	9z	multi	65	35
2513	A784	10z	multi	70	40
			Nos. 2508-2513 (6)	1.98	1.13

Karol Szymanowski (1882-1937), Composer A785

1982, Apr. 8

2514	A785	2.50z	dk brn & gold	15	12

Victory in Challenge Trophy Flights A786

1982, May 5 Photo. *Perf. 11x11½*

2515	A786	27z	RWD-6 monoplane	95	55
2516	A786	31z	RWD-9	1.40	70
a			Souvenir sheet of 2, #2515-2516	2.75	1.25

Henryk Sienkiewicz (1846-1916), Writer — A787

1982 World Cup — A788

Polish Nobel Prize Winners: 15z, Wladyslaw Reymont (1867-1925), writer, 1924. 25z, Marie Curie (1867-1934), physicist 1903, 1911. 31z, Czeslaw Milosz (b. 1911), poet, 1980.

1982, May 10 Litho. *Perf. 11½x11*

2517	A787	3z	blk & dk grn	12	8
2518	A787	15z	blk & brn	55	24
2519	A787	25z	black	90	40
2520	A787	31z	blk & gray	1.00	52

Perf. 11½x11, 11x11½

1982, May 28 **Photo.**

2521	A788	25z	Ball	80	50
2522	A788	27z	Bull, ball, horiz.	1.00	55

Souvenir Sheet

Maria Kaziera Sobieska — A789

1982, June 11 Photo. *Perf. 11½x11*

2523	A789	65z	multi	2.50	1.25

PHILEXFRANCE '82 Intl. Stamp Exhibition, Paris, June 11-21.

Assoc. Presidents Stanislaw Sierakowski and Boleslaw Domanski — A790

1982, July 20 **Litho.**

2524	A790	4.50z	multi	25	15

Assoc. of Poles in Germany, 60th anniv.

2nd UN Conference on Peaceful Uses of Outer Space, Vienna, Aug. 9-21 — A791

1982, Aug. 9 **Photo.**

2525	A791	31z	Globe	1.25	65

No. 2441 Surcharged

1982, Aug. 20

2526	A766	10z	on 6.50z brn	40	22

Black Madonna of Jasna Gora, 600th Anniv. A792

Designs: 2.50z, Father Augustin Kordecki (1603-1673). 25z, Siege of Jasna Gora by Swedes, 1655 (horiz.).

1982, Aug. 26 *Perf. 11*

2527	A792	2.50z	multi	8	6
2528	A792	25z	multi	80	28
2529	A792	65z	multi	2.50	1.10

A souvenir sheet of 2 No. 2529 exists.

Workers' Movement A793

1982, Sept. 3 *Perf. 11½x11*

2530	A793	6z multi	25	12

Norbert Barlicki (1880-1941) A794

Carved Head, Wawel Castle A795

Workers' Activists: 6z, Pawel Finder (1904-1944). 15z, Marian Buczek (1896-1939). 20z, Cezaryna Wojnarowska (1861-1911). 29z, Ignacy Daszynski (1866-1936).

1982, Sept. 10 *Perf. 12x11½*

2531	A794	5z multi	28	10
2532	A794	6z multi	30	12
2533	A794	15z multi	75	28
2534	A794	20z multi	95	32
2535	A794	29z multi	1.10	40
		Nos. 2531-2535 (5)	3.38	1.22

1982, Sept. 25

2536	A795	60z Woman's head	2.75	1.00
2537	A795	100z Man's head	3.75	1.75

TB Bacillus Centenary A796

St. Maximilian Kolbe (1894-1941) A797

1982, Sept. 22 *Perf. 11½x11*

2538	A796	10z Koch	32	15
2539	A796	25z Oko Bujwid (1857-1942), bacteriologist	80	40

1982, Oct.

2540	A797	27z multi	85	40

50th Anniv. of Polar Research A798

1982, Oct. 25 **Litho.** *Perf. 11½*

2541	A798	27z multi	85	40

The Catalogue editors cannot undertake to appraise, identify or judge the genuineness or condition of stamps.

Stanislaw Zaremba (1863-1942), Mathematician — A799

Mathematicians: 6z, Waclaw Sierpinski (1882-1969). 12z, Zygmunt Janiszewski (1888-1920). 15z, Stefan Banach (1892-1945).

1982, Nov. 23 **Photo.** *Perf. 11x11½*

2542	A799	5z multi	15	12
2543	A799	6z multi	20	10
2544	A799	12z multi	40	28
2545	A799	15z multi	50	25

First Anniv. of Military Rule — A800

1982, Dec. 13 *Perf. 12x11½*

2546	A800	2.50z Medal obverse and reverse	12	10

Cracow Monuments Restoration A801

1982, Dec. 20 **Litho.** *Perf. 11½x11*

2547	A801	15z Deanery portal	50	25
2548	A801	25z Law College portal	80	40

Souvenir Sheet

Lithographed and Engraved

Imperf

2549	A801	65z City map	2.00	1.25

No. 2549 contains one stamp 22x27mm.

See Nos. 2593-2594, 2656-2657, 2717-2718, 2809, 2847.

Map of Poland, by Bernard Wapowski, 1526 A802

Maps: 6z, Warsaw, Polish Kingdom Quartermaster, 1839. 8z, Poland, Romer's Atlas, 1908. 25z, Krakow, by A. Buchowiecki, 1703, astrolabe, 17th cent.

1982, Dec. 28 **Litho.** *Perf. 11½*

2550	A802	5z multi	18	8
2551	A802	6z multi	24	10
2552	A802	8z multi	35	15
2553	A802	25z multi	1.00	40

120th Anniv. of 1863 Uprising — A803

1983, Jan. 22 **Photo.** *Perf. 12x11½*

2554	A803	6z The Battle, by Arthur Grottger (1837-67)	25	12

Warsaw Theater Sesquicentennial — A804

1983, Feb. 24 **Photo.** *Perf. 11*

2555	A804	6z multi	25	12

10th Anniv. of UN Conference on Human Environment, Stockholm — A805

1983, Mar. 24 **Litho.** *Perf. 11½*

2556	A805	5z Wild flowers	16	10
2557	A805	6z Swan, carp, eel	20	12
2558	A805	17z Hoopoe	52	32
2559	A805	30z Fish	90	50
2560	A805	31z Deer, fawn, buffalo	90	50
2561	A805	38z Fruit	1.00	60
		Nos. 2556-2561 (6)	3.68	2.14

Karol Kurpinski (1785-1857), Composer A806

Famous People: 6z, Maria Jasnorzewska Pawlikowska (1891-1945), poet. 17z, Stanislaw Szober (1879-1938), linguist. 25z, Tadeusz Banachiewicz (1882-1954), astronomer. 27z, Jaroslaw Iwaszkiewicz (1894-1980), writer. 31z, Wladyslaw Tatarkiewicz (1886-1980), philosopher, art historian.

1983, Mar. 25 **Photo.** *Perf. 11½x11*

2562	A806	5z tan & brn	20	10
2563	A806	6z pink & vio	25	12
2564	A806	17z dk grn & lt grn	55	28
2565	A806	25z bis & brn	85	42
2566	A806	27z lt bl & dk bl	95	45
2567	A806	31z vio & pur	1.10	55
		Nos. 2562-2567 (6)	3.90	1.92

Polish Medalists in 22nd Olympic Games, 1980 A807

1983, Apr. 5 *Perf. 11x11½*

2568	A807	5z Steeplechase	15	8
2569	A807	6z Equestrian	20	10
2570	A807	15z Soccer, 1982 World Cup	50	25
2571	A807	27z + 5z Pole vault	1.00	50

Warsaw Ghetto Uprising, 40th Anniv. — A808

Customs Cooperation Council, 30th Anniv. — A809

1983, Apr. 19 **Photo.** *Perf. 11½x11*

2572	A808	6z Heroes' Monument, by Natan Rappaport	25	12

Se-tenant with label showing anniversary medal.

1983, Apr. 28

2573	A809	5z multi	15	10

Second Visit of Pope John Paul II — A810

Portraits of Pope. 31z vert.

1983, June 16 **Photo.** *Perf. 11*

2574	A810	31z multi	1.10	50
2575	A810	65z multi	2.25	1.10
	a	Souvenir sheet	3.00	1.50

Army of King John III Sobieski — A811

1983, July 5 *Perf. 11½x11*

2576	A811	5z Dragoons	15	8
2577	A811	5z Knight in armor	15	8
2578	A811	6z Non-commissioned infantry officers	20	10
2579	A811	15z Light cavalryman	50	25
2580	A811	27z Hussars	90	45
		Nos. 2576-2580 (5)	1.90	96

750th Anniv. of Torun Municipality — A812

1983, Aug. 25 **Photo.** *Perf. 11*

2581	A812	6z multi	25	12
	a	Souv. sheet of 4	4.00	4.00

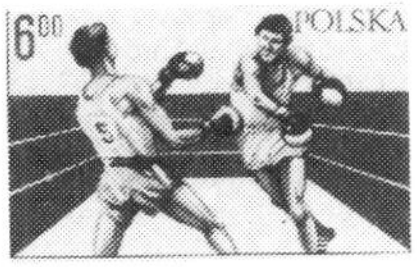
60th Anniv. of Polish Boxing Union
A813

1983, Nov. 4 Litho. *Perf. 11½x11*
2582 A813 6z multi 25 12

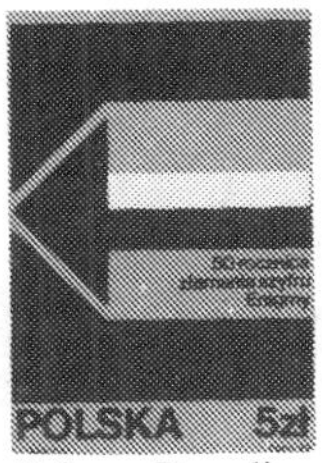
Enigma Decoding Machine, 50th Anniv. — A813a

Girl Near House — A813b

1983, Aug. 16 Litho. *Perf. 11½x11*
2582A A813a 5z multi 15 10

1983 Photo. *Perf. 11½x12*
2582B A813b 6z multi 25 12

Portrait of King John III Sobieski
A814

300th Anniv. of Victory over the Turks in Vienna (King's Portraits by): No. 2584, Unknown court painter. No. 2585, Sobieski on Horseback, by Francesco Trevisani (1656-1746). 25z, Jerzy Eleuter Szymonowicz-Siemiginowski (1660-1711). 65z+10z, Sobieski at Vienna, by Jan Matejko (1838-1893).

1983, Sept. 12 *Perf. 11*
2583 A814 5z multi 15 8
2584 A814 6z multi 20 10
2585 A814 6z multi 20 10
2586 A814 25z multi 80 40

Souvenir Sheet
Imperf
2587 A814 65z + 10z multi 2.25 1.50

Polish Peoples' Army, 40th Anniv. — A815

Designs: No. 2588, General Zygmunt Berling (1896-1980). No. 2589, Wanda Wasilewska (1905-1964). No. 2591, Troop formation.

1983, Oct. 12 Photo. *Perf. 11*
2588 A815 5z multi 15 8
2589 A815 5z multi 15 8
2590 A815 6z multi 20 10
2591 A815 6z multi, horiz. 20 10

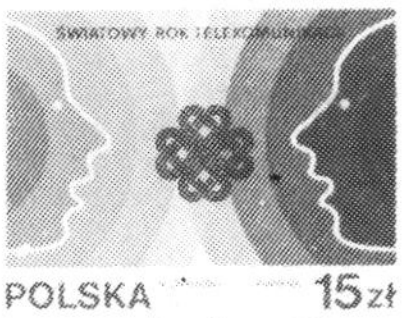
World Communications Year — A816

1983, Oct. 18 Photo. *Perf. 11*
2592 A816 15z multi 50 25

Cracow Restoration Type of 1982

1983, Nov. 25 Litho. *Perf. 11*
2593 A801 5z Cloth Hall, horiz. 18 10
2594 A801 6z Town Hall Tower 28 12

Traditional Hats — A818

Natl. People's Council, 40th Anniv. — A819

1983, Dec. 16 Photo. *Perf. 11½x11*
2595 A818 5z Biskupianski 14 8
2596 A818 5z Rozbarski 14 8
2597 A818 6z Warminsko-Mazurski 16 9
2598 A818 6z Cieszynski 16 9
2599 A818 25z Kurpiowski 65 38
2600 A818 38z Lubuski 1.00 55
Nos. 2595-2600 (6) 2.25 1.27

1983, Dec. 31
2601 A819 6z Hand holding sword (poster) 25 12

People's Army, 40th Anniv.
A820

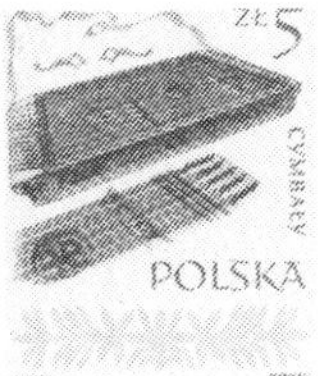
Musical Instruments
A821

1984, Jan. 1 Litho. *Perf. 11½x11*
2602 A820 5z Gen. Bem Brigade badge 20 10

1984, Feb. 10 Photo.
2603 A821 5z Dulcimer 12 7
2604 A821 6z Drum, tambourine 15 8
2605 A821 10z Accordion 25 14
2606 A821 15z Double bass 30 20
2607 A821 17z Bagpipes 45 24
2608 A821 29z Figurines by Tadeusz Zak 85 38
Nos. 2603-2608 (6) 2.12 1.11

Wincenty Witos (1874-1945), Prime Minister — A822

1984, Mar. 2 Litho. *Perf. 11½x11*
2609 A822 6z grn & sepia 18 10

Local Flowers (Clematis Varieties)
A823

1984, Mar. 26 Photo. *Perf. 11x11½*
2610 A823 5z Lanuginosa 16 7
2611 A823 6z Tangutica 20 8
2612 A823 10z Texensis 24 14
2613 A823 17z Alpina 52 24
2614 A823 25z Vitalba 70 35
2615 A823 27z Montana 80 38
Nos. 2610-2615 (6) 2.62 1.26

The Ecstasy of St. Francis, by El Greco
A824

1984, Apr. 21 *Perf. 11*
2616 A824 27z multi 75 32

1984 Summer Olympics
A825

1984, Apr. 25 Litho. *Perf. 11x11½*
2617 A825 5z Handball 15 7
2618 A825 6z Fencing 18 8
2619 A825 15z Bicycling 45 20
2620 A825 16z Running 48 22
2621 A825 17z Running, diff. 52 24
a Souvenir sheet of 2, #2620-2621 1.10 75
2622 A825 31z Skiing (winter games) 80 45
Nos. 2617-2622 (6) 2.58 1.26

No. 2621a sold for 43z.

Battle of Monte Cassino, 40th Anniv. — A826

1984, May 18 Photo. *Perf. 11½x11*
2623 A826 15z Memorial Cross 42 20

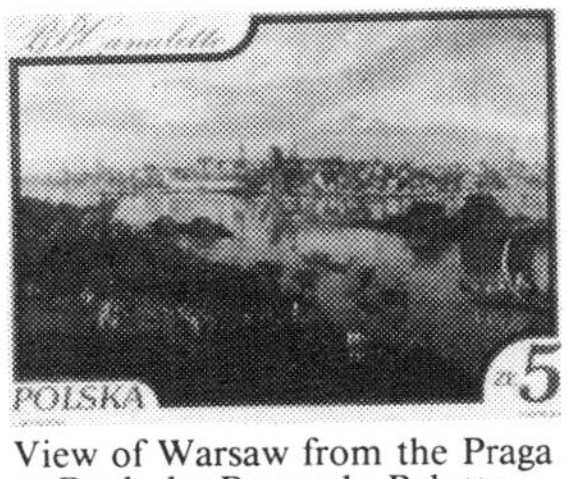
View of Warsaw from the Praga Bank, by Bernardo Belotto Canaletto — A827

Paintings of Vistula River views: 6z, Trumpet Festivity, by Aleksander Gierymski. 25z, The Vistula near the Bielany District, by Jozef Rapacki. 27z, Steamship Harbor in the Powisle District, by Franciszek Kostrzewski.

1984, June 20 Photo. *Perf. 11*
2624 A827 5z multi 15 8
2625 A827 6z multi 18 9
2626 A827 25z multi 75 35
2627 A827 27z multi 75 40

Warrior's Head, Wawel Castle — A828

Sculptures: 3.50z, Eastern ruler. No. 2628A, Woman wearing wreath. 10z, Man wearing hat.

1984-85 Photo. *Perf. 11½x12*
2628 A828 3.50z brown ('85) 10 8
2628A A828 5z dk cl ('85) 10 8
2628B A828 10z brt ultra ('85) 20 12

Coil Stamp
Perf. 13½x14
2629 A828 5z dk bl grn 20 12

Issue dates: No. 2628, Jan. 24, 1985. Nos. 2628A, 2628B, July 8, 1985. No. 2629, July 10, 1984. No. 2629 has black control number on back of every fifth stamp.
See Nos. 2738-2744.

Order of Grunwald Cross — A829

Designs: 6z, Order of Revival of Poland. 10z, Order of the Banner of Labor, First Class. 16z, Order of Builders of People's Poland.

1984, July 21 Photo. *Perf. 11½*
2630 A829 5z multi 15 8
2631 A829 6z multi 20 9
2632 A829 10z multi 32 15
2633 A829 16z multi 52 24
a Sheet of 4, #2630-2633, perf. 11½x12 3.25 3.00

40th anniversary of July Manifesto (Origin of Polish People's Republic).

Warsaw Uprising, 40th Anniv.
A830

1984, Aug. 1
2634 A830 4z multi 12 6
2635 A830 5z multi 15 6
2636 A830 6z multi 18 9
2637 A830 25z multi 75 35

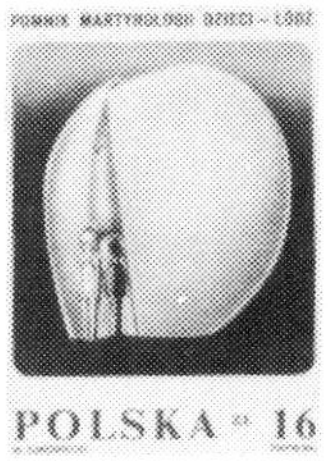
Broken Heart Monument, Lodz — A831

1984, Aug. 31
2638 A831 16z multi 48 22

Defense of Oksywie Holm, Col. S. Dabek — A832

1984, Sept. 1

2639 A832 5z shown 15 8
2640 A832 6z Bzura River battle, Gen. T. Kutrzeba 18 10

Invasion of Poland, 45th anniversary.
See Nos. 2692-2693, 2757, 2824-2826, 2864-2866.

Polish Militia, 40th Anniv. A833

1984, Sept. 29 Photo. *Perf. 11½*

2641 A833 5z shown 15 8
2642 A833 6z Militiaman at Control Center 18 10

Polish Aviation A834

1984, Nov. 6 Photo. *Perf. 11x11½*

2643 A834 5z Balloon ascent, 1784 12 9
2644 A834 5z Powered flight, 1911 12 9
2645 A834 6z Balloon Polonez, 1983 14 14
2646 A834 10z Modern gliders 22 16
2647 A834 16z Wilga, 1983 35 30
2648 A834 27z Farman, 1914 60 48
2649 A834 31z Los and PZL P-7 65 48
Nos. 2643-2649 (7) 2.20 1.74

Protected Animals A835

Perf. 11x11½, 11½x11

1984, Dec. 4 Photo.

2650 A835 4z Mustela nivalis 10 6
2651 A835 5z Martes foina 12 8
2652 A835 5z Mustela erminea vert. 12 8
2653 A835 10z Castor fiber 22 12
2654 A835 10z Lutra lutra, vert. 22 12
2655 A835 65z Marmota marmota, vert. 1.25 65
Nos. 2650-2655 (6) 2.03 1.11

Cracow Restoration Type of 1982

Perf. 11½x11, 11x11½

1984, Dec. 10 Litho.

2656 A801 5z Royal Cathedral, Wawel 12 8
2657 A801 15z Royal Castle, Wawel, horiz. 32 14

Religious Buildings — A837

Perf. 11½x12, 12x11½

1984, Dec. 28 Photo.

2658 A837 5z Protestant Church, Warsaw 12 7
2659 A837 10z Saint Andrew Church, Cracow 22 12
2660 A837 15z Greek Orthodox Church, Rychwald 35 16
2661 A837 20z Orthodox Church, Warsaw 45 20
2662 A837 25z Tykocin Synagogue, horiz. 55 25
2663 A837 31z Tartar Mosque, Kruszyniany, horiz. 65 30
Nos. 2658-2663 (6) 2.34 1.10

Classic and Contemporary Fire Engines — A838

Designs: 4z, Horse-drawn fire pump, 19th cent. 10z, Polski Fiat, c. 1930. 12z, Jelcz 315, 1970s. 15z, Horse-drawn hand pump, 1899. 20z, Jelcz engine, Magirus power ladder, 1970s. 30z, Hand pump, 18th cent.

1985, Feb. 25 Photo. *Perf. 11x11½*

2664 A838 4z multi 10 6
2665 A838 10z multi 24 10
2666 A838 12z multi 28 12
2667 A838 15z multi 35 18
2668 A838 20z multi 48 22
2669 A838 30z multi 70 35
Nos. 2664-2669 (6) 2.15 1.03

Battle of Raclawice, April, 1794, by Jan Styka, 1894 — A839

1985, Apr. 4 *Perf. 11*

2670 A839 27z multi 55 30

Kosciuszko Insurrection cent.

Wincenty Rzymowski (1883-1950), Democratic Party Founder — A840

1985, Apr. 11 Litho. *Perf. 11½*

2671 A840 10z sal rose & dk vio bl 22 12

Intl. Youth Year — A841

1985, Apr. 25 Photo. *Perf. 11½x11*

2672 A841 15z Blue jeans, badge 32 15

Prince Boleslaw Krzywousty (1085-1138) — A842

Regional maps and: 5z, Shown. 10z, Wladyslaw Gomulka (1905-1982), sec.-gen. of the Polish Workers Party, prime minister 1945-49. 20z, Piotr Zaremba (b. 1910), president of Gdansk Province 1945-50.

1985, May 8 Litho. *Perf. 11½*

2673 A842 5z multi 12 8
2674 A842 10z multi 22 10
2675 A842 20z multi 45 20

Restoration of the Western & Northern Territories to Polish control, 40th anniv.

Victory Berlin 1945, by Jozef Mlynarski (b. 1925) — A843

Painting: Polish and Soviet soldiers at Brandenburg Gate, May 9, 1945.

1985, May 9 Photo. *Perf. 12x11½*

2676 A843 5z multi 14 10

Liberation from German occupation, 40th anniv.

Warsaw Treaty Org., 30th Anniv. — A844

1985, May 14 Litho. *Perf. 11½x11*

2677 A844 5z Emblem, member flags 1410

World Wildlife Fund A845

Endangered Wildlife: Canis lupus.

1985, May 25 Photo. *Perf. 11x11½*

2678 A845 5z Wolves, winter landscape 12 8
2679 A845 10z Female, cubs 22 10
2680 A845 10z Wolf 22 10
2681 A845 20z Wolves, summer landscape 45 20

Folk Instruments A846

1985, June 25 *Perf. 11½x11*

2682 A846 5z Wooden rattle 12 8
2683 A846 10z Jingle 22 12
2684 A846 12z Clay whistles 24 12
2685 A846 20z Wooden fiddles 45 22
2686 A846 25z Tuned bells 52 24
2687 A846 31z Shepherd's flutes, ram's horn, ocarina 65 35
Nos. 2682-2687 (6) 2.20 1.13

O.R.P. Iskra and Emblem — A847

Photogravure and Engraved

1985, June 29

2688 A847 5z bluish blk & yel 14 10

Polish Navy, 40th anniv.

Tomasz Nocznicki (1862-1944) A848

Polish Labor Movement founders: 20z, Maciej Rataj (1884-1940).

1985, July 26 Engr. *Perf. 11x11½*

2689 A848 10z grnsh blk 24 12
2690 A848 20z brn blk 48 24

Natl. labor movement, 90th anniv.

Polish Field Hockey Assn., 50th Anniv. A849

1985, Aug. 22 Litho. *Perf. 11½x11*

2691 A849 5z multi 22 12

World War II Battles Type of 1984

Designs: 5z, Defense of Wizny, Capt. Wladyslaw Raginis. 10z, Attack on Mlawa, Col. Wilhelm Andrzej Liszka-Lawicz.

1985, Sept. 1 Photo. *Perf. 12x11½*

2692 A832 5z multi 12 8
2693 A832 10z multi 24 12

Pafawag Railway Rolling Stock Co. A850

1985, Sept. 18 Litho. ***Perf. 11½***

2694 A850 5z Box car 12 8
2695 A850 10z 201 E locomotive 24 15
2696 A850 17z Two-axle coal car 42 24
2697 A850 20z Passenger car 52 28

Wild Ducks A851

1985, Oct. 21 Photo. ***Perf. 11x11½***

2698 A851 5z Anas crecca 12 6
2699 A851 5z Anas querquedula 12 6
2700 A851 10z Aythya fuligula 24 12
2701 A851 15z Bucephala clangula 35 18
2702 A851 25z Somateria mollissima 60 30
2703 A851 29z Netta rufina 70 35
Nos. 2698-2703 (6) 2.13 1.07

UN, 40th Anniv. A852

1985, Oct. 24 Litho. ***Perf. 11½x11***

2704 A852 27z multi 55 28

Polish Ballet, 200th Anniv. — A853

1985, Dec. 4

2705 A853 5z Prima ballerina 12 6
2706 A853 15z Male dancer 35 18

Paintings by Stanislaw Ignacy Witkiewicz (1885-1939) — A854

Designs: 5z, Marysia and Burek in Ceylon. No. 2708, Woman with a Fox. No. 2709, Self-portrait, 1931. 20z, Compositions, 1917. 25z, Portrait of Nena Stachurska, 1929. Nos. 2707, 2709-2711 vert.

Perf. 11½x11, 11x11½

1985, Dec. 6 Photo.

2707 A854 5z multi 12 6
2708 A854 10z multi 24 12
2709 A854 10z multi 24 12
2710 A854 20z multi 48 24
2711 A854 25z multi 60 30
Nos. 2707-2711 (5) 1.68 84

Values quoted in this catalogue are for stamps graded at Fine-Very Fine and with no faults. An illustrated guide to grade is provided in introductory material, beginning on Page V.

Souvenir Sheet

Johann Sebastian Bach — A855

1985, Dec. 30 ***Perf. 11½x11***

2712 A855 65z multi 1.50 1.50
a. With inscription 1.50 1.50

No. 2712a inscribed "300 Rocznica Urodzin Jana Sebastiana Bacha."

Profile, Emblem, Sigismond III Column, Royal Castle Tower — A856

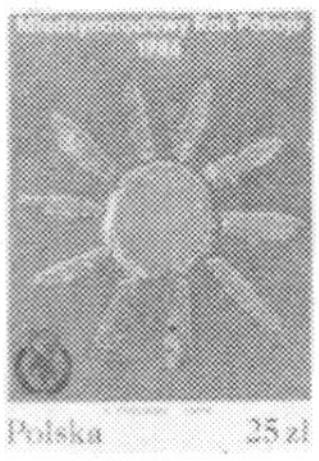

Intl. Peace Year — A858

Halley's Comet A857

1986, Jan. 16 ***Perf. 11½x11***

2713 A856 10z lt ultra, brt ultra & ultra 25 12

Congress of Intellectuals for World Peace, Warsaw.

1986, Feb. 7 Photo. ***Perf. 11½***

Designs: No. 2714, Michal Kamienski (1879-1973), astronomer, orbit diagram. No. 2715, Comet, Vega, Giotto, Planet-A, ICE-3 space probes.

2714 A857 25z multi 50 30
2715 A857 25z multi 50 30

1986, Mar. 20 Photo. ***Perf. 11½x11***

2716 A858 25z turq bl, yel & ultra 60 38

Cracow Restoration Type of 1982

Designs: 5z, Collegium Maius, Jagiellonian Museum. 10z, Town Hall, Kazimierz.

1986, Mar. 20 Litho. ***Perf. 11½***

2717 A801 5z multi 12 10
2718 A801 10z multi 25 15

Wildlife A859

1986, Apr. 15 Photo. ***Perf. 11½x11***

2719 A859 5z Perdix perdix 12 6
2720 A859 5z Oryctolagus cuniculus 12 6
2721 A859 10z Dama dama 20 10
2722 A859 10z Phasianus colchicus 20 10
2723 A859 20z Lepus europaeus 42 20
2724 A859 40z Ovis ammon 80 35
Nos. 2719-2724 (6) 1.86 87

Nos. 2719-2720, 2723-2724 vert.

Stanislaw Kulczynski (1895-1975), Scientist, Party Leader — A860

Photogravure and Engraved

1986, May 3 ***Perf. 11½x11***

2725 A860 10z buff & choc 22 12

Warsaw Fire Brigade, 150th Anniv. — A861

Painting detail: The Fire Brigade on the Cracow Outskirts on Their Way to a Fire, 1871, by Josef Brodowski (1828-1900).

1986, May 16 ***Perf. 11***

2726 A861 10z dl brn & dk brn 22 12

Paderewski A862

1986, May 22 ***Perf. 11½x11***

2727 A862 65z multi 1.25 70

AMERIPEX'86.

1986 World Cup Soccer Championships, Mexico — A863

1986, May 26 ***Perf. 11½***

2728 A863 25z multi 48 22

Ferryboats — A864

1986, June 18 Photo. ***Perf. 11***

2729 A864 10z Wilanow 20 12
2730 A864 10z Wawel 20 12
a. Souvenir sheet of 2, #2729-2730 1.40 1.00
2731 A864 15z Pomerania 30 15
2732 A864 25z Rogalin 55 25
a. Souvenir sheet of 2, #2731-2732 2.75 1.90

Nos. 2729-2732 printed se-tenant with labels picturing historic sites from the names of cities serviced. No. 2730a sold for 30z; No. 2732a for 55z. Surtax for the Natl. Assoc. of Philatelists.

Antarctic Agreement, 25th Anniv. A865

Map of Antarctica and: 5z, A. B. Dobrowolski, Kopernik research ship. 40z, H. Arctowski, Professor Siedlecki research ship.

1986, June 23 Litho. ***Perf. 11½x11***

2733 A865 5z ver, pale grn & blk 10 5
2734 A865 40z org, pale vio & dk vio 80 40

Polish United Workers' Party, 10th Congress A866

1986, July 29 Photo. ***Perf. 11x11½***

2735 A866 10z red & dk gray bl 20 10

Wawel Heads Type of 1984-85

Designs: 15z, Woman wearing a wreath (like No. 2628A). No. 2739, Thinker. No. 2740, Eastern ruler. 40z, Youth wearing beret. 200z, Man's head.

Perf. 11½x12, 14 (No. 2740)

1986-89 Engr.

2738 A828 15z rose brn ('88) 18 8
2739 A828 20z green 38 18
2740 A828 20z pck blue ('89) 40 20
2742 A828 40z gray 75 35
2744 A828 200z dk gray 3.75 1.75

Issue dates: Nos. 2739, 2742, July 30, 1986. No. 2740, Mar. 31, 1989. No. 2744, Nov. 11, 1986.

No. 2740 is a coil stamp, has black control number on back of every fifth stamp.

Jasna Gora Monastery Collection A867

Designs: No. 2746, The Paulinite Church on Skalka in Cracow, oil painting detail, circa 1627. No. 2747, Jesse's Tree, oil on wood, 17th cent. No. 2748, Gilded chalice, 18th cent. No. 2749, Virgin Mary embroidery, 15th cent.

1986, Aug. 15 Photo. ***Perf. 11½x11***

2746 A867 5z multi 10 6
2747 A867 5z multi 10 6
2748 A867 20z multi 40 20
2749 A867 40z multi 80 40

Victories of Polish Athletes at 1985 World Championships — A868

Designs: No. 2750, Precision Flying, Kissimmee, Florida, won by Waclaw Nycz. No. 2751, Wind Sailing, Tallinn, USSR, won by Malgorzata Palasz-Piasecka. No. 2752, Glider Acrobatics, Vienna, won by Jerzy Makula. No. 2753, Greco-Roman Wrestling (82kg), Kolboten, Norway, won by Bogdan Daras. No. 2754, Road Cycling, Giavera del Montello, Italy, won by Lech Piasecki. No. 2755, Women's Modern Pentathlon, Montreal, won by Barbara Kotowska.

1986, Aug. 21 *Perf. 11 1/2*

2750	A868	5z multi	10	6
2751	A868	10z multi	20	10
2752	A868	10z multi	20	10
2753	A868	15z multi	30	14
2754	A868	20z multi	48	20
2755	A868	30z multi	60	28
		Nos. 2750-2755 (6)	1.88	88

STOCKHOLMIA '86 — A869

1986, Aug. 28 *Perf. 11x11 1/2*

2756	A869	65z multi	1.40	70
a		Souvenir sheet	1.40	70

World War II Battles Type of 1984

Design: Battle of Jordanow, Col. Stanislaw Maczek, motorized cavalry 10th brigade commander-in-chief.

1986, Sept. 1 *Perf. 12x11 1/2*

2757	A832	10z multi	20	10

Albert Schweitzer A870

World Post Day A871

Photogravure and Engraved

1986, Sept. 26 *Perf. 12x11 1/2*

2758	A870	5z pale bl vio, sep & buff	12	8

1986, Oct. 9 Litho. *Perf. 11x11 1/2*

2759	A871	40z org, ultra & sep	75	35
a		Souv. sheet of 2	8.00	4.00

No. 2759a sold for 120z.

Folk and Fairy Tale Legends A872

Designs: No. 2760, Basilisk. No. 2761, Duke Popiel, vert. No. 2762, Golden Duck. No. 2763, Boruta, the Devil, vert. No. 2764, Janosik the Thief, vert. No. 2765, Lajkonik, conqueror of the Tartars, 13th cent., vert.

1986, Oct. 28 Photo. *Perf. 11 1/2x11*

2760	A872	5z multi	10	5
2761	A872	5z multi	10	5
2762	A872	10z multi	20	9
2763	A872	10z multi	20	9
2764	A872	20z multi	35	18
2765	A872	50z multi	95	42
		Nos. 2760-2765 (6)	1.90	88

Prof. Tadeusz Kotarbinski (1886-1981) — A873

1986, Nov. 19 Litho. *Perf. 11 1/2*

2766	A873	10z sep, buff & brn blk	28	10

17th-20th Cent. Architecture — A874

Designs: No. 2767, Church, Baczal Dolny. No. 2768, Windmill, Zygmuntow. 10z, Oravian cottage, Zubrzyca Gorna. 15z, Kashubian Arcade cottage, Wazydze. 25z, Barn, Grzawa. 30z, Water mill, Molkowice Stare.

Perf. 11x11 1/2, 11 1/2x11

1986, Nov. 26 **Photo.**

2767	A874	5z multi	10	5
2768	A874	5z multi, vert.	10	5
2769	A874	10z multi	20	9
2770	A874	15z multi	28	12
2771	A874	25z multi	50	22
2772	A874	30z multi	55	28
		Nos. 2767-2772 (6)	1.73	81

Royalty A875

Photogravure and Engraved

1986, Dec. 4 *Perf. 11*

2773	A875	10z Mieszko I	20	10
2774	A875	25z Dobrava	50	25

See Nos. 2838-2839, 2884-2885.

New Year 1987 A876

1986, Dec. 12 Photo. *Perf. 11x11 1/2*

2775	A876	25z multi	48	22

Warsaw Cyclists Soc., Cent. A877

Designs: No. 2776, First trip to Bielany, uniformed escort, 1887. No. 2777, Jan Stanislaw Skrodzki (1867-1957), 1895 record-holder. No. 2778, Dynasy Society building, 1892-1937. No. 2779, Mieczyslaw Baranski, champion, 1896. No. 2780, Karolina Kociecka (b. 1875), female competitor. No. 2781, Henryk Weiss (d. 1912), Dynasy champion, 1904-1908.

Perf. 13x12 1/2, 12 1/2x13

1986, Dec. 19 **Litho.**

2776	A877	5z multi	10	5
2777	A877	5z multi	10	5
2778	A877	10z multi	20	8
2779	A877	10z multi	20	9
2780	A877	30z multi	55	28
2781	A877	50z multi	95	45
		Nos. 2776-2781 (6)	2.10	1.00

Nos. 2777-2781 vert.

Henryk Arctowski Antarctic Station, King George Island, 10th Anniv. A878

Wildlife and ships: No. 2782, Euphausia superba, training freighter Antoni Garnuszewski. No. 2783, Notothenia rossi, Dissostichus mawsoni, Zulawy transoceanic ship. No. 2784, Fulmarus glacialoides, yacht Pogoria. No. 2785, Pigoscelis adeliae, yacht Gedania. 30z, Arctocephalus, research boat Dziunia. 40z, Hydrurga leptonyx, ship Kapitan Ledochowski.

1987, Feb. 13 Litho. *Perf. 11 1/2*

2782	A878	5z multi	10	6
2783	A878	5z multi	10	6
2784	A878	10z multi	20	10
2785	A878	10z multi	20	10
2786	A878	30z multi	60	28
2787	A878	40z multi	85	38
		Nos. 2782-2787 (6)	2.05	98

Paintings by Leon Wyczolkowski (1852-1936) — A879

1987, Mar. 20 Photo. *Perf. 11*

2788	A879	5z Cineraria Flowers, 1924	10	5
2789	A879	10z Portrait of a Woman, 1883	20	10
2790	A879	10z Wood Church, 1910	20	10
2791	A879	25z Harvesting Beetroot, 1910	50	25
2792	A879	30z Wading Fishermen, 1891	60	30
2793	A879	40z Self-portrait, 1912	80	40
		Nos. 2788-2793 (6)	2.40	1.20

Nos. 2789 and 2791 vert.

The Ravage, 1866, by Artur Grottger (1837-1867) — A880

1987, Mar. 26 Photo. *Perf. 11*

2794	A880	15z dark brn & buff	22	12

Gen. Karol Swierczewski-Walter (1897-1947) — A881

1987, Mar. 27 Engr. *Perf. 11 1/2x12*

2795	A881	15z olive grn	22	12

Pawel Edmund Strzelecki (1797-1873), Explorer — A882

1987, Apr. 23 Photo. *Perf. 11 1/2x11*

2796	A882	65z olive blk	1.10	65

Colonization of Australia, bicentennial.

2nd PRON Congress A883

1987, May 8 Litho. *Perf. 11 1/2*

2797	A882	10z pale gray, brn, red & brt ultra	20	10

Patriotic Movement of the National Renaissance Congress.

Motor Vehicles — A884

1987, May 19 Photo. *Perf. 12x11 1/2*

2798	A884	10z 1936 Saurer-Zawrat	20	10
2799	A884	10z 1928 CWS T-1	20	10
2800	A884	15z 1928 Ursus-A	30	15
2801	A884	15z 1936 Lux-Sport	30	15
2802	A884	25z 1939 Podkowa 100	50	25
2803	A884	45z 1935 Sokol 600 RT	90	45
		Nos. 2798-2803 (6)	2.40	1.20

Royal Castle, Warsaw — A885

1987, June 5

2804	A885	50z multi	90	50

A886

State Visit of Pope John Paul II — A887

1987, June 8 *Perf. 11*

2805 A886	15z	shown	30	15
2806 A886	45z	Portrait, diff.	90	45

Souvenir Sheet

Perf. 12x11½

2807 A887	50z	shown	1.00	1.00

Nos. 2805-2806 printed se-tenant in a continuous design.

Cracow Restoration Type of 1982

1987, July 6 **Litho.** *Perf. 11½*

2809 A801	10z	Barbican Gate, Wawel, horiz.	20	10

Esperanto Language, Cent. A890

1987, July 25 **Litho.** *Perf. 11½*

2811 A890	45z	Ludwig L. Zamenhof	80	38

Poznan and Town Hall, by Stanislaw Wyspianski A891

1987, Aug. 3

2812 A891	15z	blk & pale sal	22	12

POZNAN '87, Aug. 8-16.

31st World Apiculture Congress, Warsaw — A892

1987, Aug. 20 **Photo.** *Perf. 11½x11*

2813 A892	10z	Queen	16	10
2814 A892	10z	Worker	16	10
2815 A892	15z	Drone	25	15
2816 A892	15z	Box hive, orchard	25	15
2817 A892	40z	Bee collecting pollen	70	40
2818 A892	50z	Beekeeper collecting honey	85	50
		Nos. 2813-2818 (6)	2.37	1.40

Success of Polish Athletes at World Championship Events — A894

1987, Sept. 24 **Litho.** *Perf. 14*

2820 A894	10z	Acrobatics, France	16	8
2821 A894	15z	Kayak, Canada	24	12
2822 A894	20z	Marksmanship, E. Germany	32	16
2823 A894	25z	Wrestling, Hungary	40	20

World War II Battles Type of 1984

Designs: No. 2824, Battle of Mokra, Julian Filipowicz. No. 2825, Battle scene near Oleszycami, Brig.-Gen. Josef Rudolf Kustron. 15z, Air battles over Warsaw, pilot Stefan Pawlikowski.

1987, Sept. 1 **Photo.** *Perf. 12x11½*

2824 A832	10z	multi	20	10
2825 A832	10z	multi	20	10
2826 A832	15z	multi	30	15

Jan Hevelius (1611-1687), Astronomer, and Constellations — A895

1987, Sept. 15 **Litho.** *Perf. 11½*

2827 A895	15z	Hevelius, sextant, vert.	24	12
2828 A895	40z	shown	65	35

Souvenir Sheet

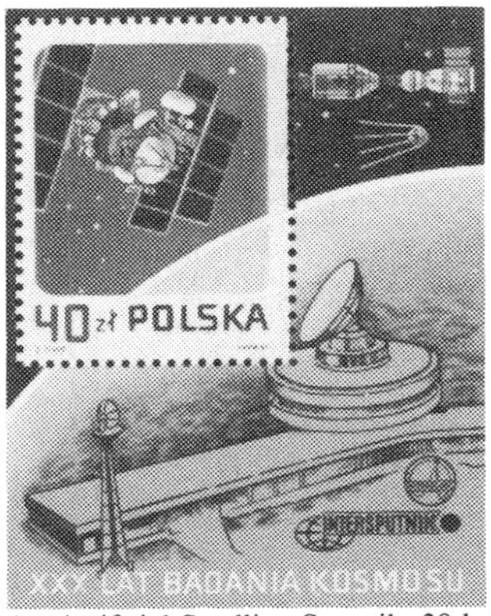

1st Artificial Satellite, Sputnik, 30th Anniv. — A896

1987, Oct. 2 **Photo.** *Perf. 11½x11*

2829 A896	40z	Stacionar 4 satellite	1.00	1.00

World Post Day — A897

Design: Ignacy Franciszek Przebendowski (1730-1791), postmaster general, and post office building, 19th cent., Krakowskie Przedmiescie, Warsaw.

1987, Oct. 9 **Litho.**

2830 A897	15z	lt olive grn & rose claret	22	12

Col. Stanislaw Wieckowski — A898

Photo. & Engr.

1987, Oct. 16 *Perf. 12x11½*

2831 A898	15z	deep blue & blk	22	12

Col. Wieckowski (1884-1942), physician and social reformer executed by the Nazis at Auschwitz.

HAFNIA '87 — A899

Fairy tales by Hans Christian Andersen (1805-1875): No. 2832, The Little Mermaid. No. 2833, The Nightingale. No. 2834, The Wild Swan. No. 2835, The Match Girl. 30z, The Snow Queen. 40z, The Brave Toy Soldier.

1987, Oct. 16 **Photo.** *Perf. 11x11½*

2832 A899	10z	multi	20	10
2833 A899	10z	multi	20	10
2834 A899	20z	multi	40	20
2835 A899	20z	multi	40	20
2836 A899	30z	multi	60	30
2837 A899	40z	multi	80	40
		Nos. 2832-2837 (6)	2.60	1.30

Royalty Type of 1986

Photo. & Engr.

1987, Dec. 4 *Perf. 11*

2838 A875	10z	Boleslaw I Chrobry	20	10
2839 A875	15z	Mieszko II	30	15

New Year 1988 A900

1987, Dec. 14 **Photo.** *Perf. 11x11½*

2840 A900	15z	multi	30	15

Dragonflies A901

Perf. 11x11½, 11½x11

1988, Feb. 23 **Photo.**

2841 A901	10z	Anax imperator	20	10
2842 A901	15z	Libellula quadrimaculata, vert.	30	15
2843 A901	15z	Calopteryx splendens	30	15
2844 A901	20z	Cordulegaster annulatus, vert.	40	20
2845 A901	30z	Sympetrum pedemontanum	60	30
2846 A901	50z	Aeschna viridis, vert.	1.00	50
		Nos. 2841-2846 (6)	2.80	1.40

Cracow Restoration Type of 1982

1988, Mar. 8 **Litho.** *Perf. 11½x11*

2847 A801	15z	Florianska Gate, 1300	30	15

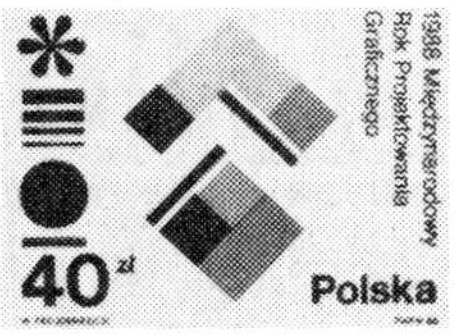

Intl. Year of Graphic Design A903

1988, Apr. 28 **Photo.** *Perf. 11x11½*

2848 A903	40z	multi	80	40

Antique Clocks — A904

Clocks in the Museum of Artistic and Precision Handicrafts, Warsaw, and clockworks: No. 2849, Frisian wall clock, 17th cent., vert. No. 2850, Anniversary clock and rotary pendulum, 20th cent. No. 2851, Carriage clock, 18th cent., vert. No. 2852, Louis XV rococo bracket clock, 18th cent., vert. 20z, Pocket watch, 19th cent. 40z, Gdansk six-sided clock signed by Benjamin Zoll, 17th cent.

Perf. 11½x12, 12x11½

1988, May 19 **Photo.**

2849 A904	10z	lt grn & multi	20	10
2850 A904	10z	pur & multi	20	10
2851 A904	15z	dl org & multi	30	15
2852 A904	15z	brn & multi	30	15
2853 A904	20z	multi	40	20
2854 A904	40z	multi	80	40
		Nos. 2849-2854 (6)	2.20	1.10

1988 Summer Olympics, Seoul — A905

1988, June 27 **Photo.** *Perf. 11x11½*

2855 A905	15z	Triple jump	30	15
2856 A905	20z	Wrestling	40	20
2857 A905	20z	Two-man kayak	40	20
2858 A905	25z	Judo	50	25
2859 A905	40z	Shooting	80	40
2860 A905	55z	Swimming	1.10	55
		Nos. 2855-2860 (6)	3.50	1.75

See No. B148.

Natl. Industry A906

1988, Aug. 23 **Photo.** *Perf. 11x11½*

Size: 35x27mm

2861 A906	45z	Los "Elk" aircraft	90	45

State Aircraft Works, 60th anniv.

See Nos. 2867, 2871, 2881-2883.

16th European Regional FAO Conference, Krakow — A907

Designs: 15z, Computers and agricultural growth. 40z, Balance between industry and nature.

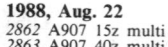

1988, Aug. 22 *Perf. 11½x11*

2862	A907	15z multi	30	15
2863	A907	40z multi	80	40

World War II Battles Type of 1984

Battle scenes and commanders: 15z, Modlin, Brig.-Gen. Wiktor Thommee. No. 2865, Warsaw, Brig.-Gen. Walerian Czuma. No. 2866, Tomaszow Lubelski, Brig.-Gen. Antoni Szylling.

1988, Sept. 1 Photo. *Perf. 12x11½*

2864	A832	15z multi	30	15
2865	A832	20z multi	40	20
2866	A832	20z multi	40	20

Natl. Industries Type of 1988

Design: Stalowa Wola Ironworks, 50th anniv.

1988, Sept. 5 *Perf. 11x11½*
Size: 35x27mm

2867	A906	15z multi	30	15

World Post Day — A909

Design: Postmaster Tomasz Arciszewski (1877-1955), Post and Telegraph Administration emblem used from 1919 to 1927.

1988, Oct. 9 Litho. *Perf. 11½x11*

2868	A909	20z multi	40	20

World War II Combat Medals — A910

1988, Oct. 12 **Photo.**

2869	A910	20z Battle of Lenino Cross	40	20
2870	A910	20z shown	40	20

Natl. Industries Type of 1988

Design: Air Force Medical Institute, 60th anniv.

1988, Oct. 12 *Perf. 11x11½*
Size: 38x27mm

2871	A906	20z multi	40	20

Stanislaw Malachowski, Kazimierz Nestor Sapieha — A912

1988, Oct. 16 *Perf. 11*

2872	A912	20z multi	40	20

Bicentennial of the Sejm (Parliament).

National Leaders — A913

1988, Nov. 11 *Perf. 12x11½*

2873	A913	15z Wincenty Witos	30	15
2874	A913	15z Ignacy Daszynski	30	15
2875	A913	20z Wojciech Korfanty	40	20
2876	A913	20z Stanislaw Wojciechowski	40	20
2877	A913	20z Julian Marchlewski	40	20
2878	A913	200z Ignacy Paderewski	4.00	2.00
2879	A913	200z Jozef Pilsudski	4.00	2.00
2880	A913	200z Gabriel Narutowicz	4.00	2.00
a.		Souv. sheet of 3, #2878-2880	12.00	12.00
		Nos. 2873-2880 (8)	13.80	6.90

Natl. independence, 70th anniv.

Natl. Industry Types of 1988

Designs: 15z, Wharf, Gdynia. 20z, Industrialist Hipolit Cegielski, 1883 steam locomotive. 40z, Poznan fair grounds, Upper Silesia Tower.

1988 Photo. *Perf. 11x11½*
Size: 39x27mm

2881	A906	15z multi	30	15
2882	A906	20z multi	40	20

Size: 35x27mm

2883	A906	40z multi	80	40

70th anniv. of Polish independence. Gdynia Port, 65th anniv (15z); Metal Works in Poznan, 142nd anniv. (20z); and Poznan Intl. Fair 60th anniv. (40z).

Issue dates: 15z, Dec. 12; 20z, Nov. 28; 40z, Dec. 21.

Royalty Type of 1986
Photo. & Engr.

1988, Dec. 4 *Perf. 11*

2884	A875	10z Rycheza	20	10
2885	A875	15z Kazimierz I Odnowiciel	30	15

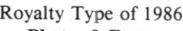

New Year 1989 A914

1988, Dec. 9 Photo. *Perf. 11x11½*

2886	A914	20z multi	40	20

Unification of Polish Workers' Unions, 40th Anniv. — A915

1988, Dec. 15 *Perf. 11½x12*

2887	A915	20z blk & ver	40	20

Fire Boats — A916

1988, Dec. 29 Litho. *Perf. 14*

2888	A916	10z Blysk	20	10
2889	A916	15z Zar	30	15
2890	A916	15z Plomien	30	15
2891	A916	20z Strazak 4	40	20
2892	A916	20z Strazak 11	40	20
2893	A916	45z Strazak 25	90	45
		Nos. 2888-2893 (6)	2.50	1.25

Horses — A917

1989, Mar. 6 Photo. *Perf. 11*

2894	A917	15z Lippizaner	30	15
2895	A917	15z Arden, vert.	30	15
2896	A917	20z English	40	20
2897	A917	20z Arabian, vert.	40	20
2898	A917	30z Wielkopolski	60	30
2899	A917	70z Polish, vert.	1.40	70
		Nos. 2894-2899 (6)	3.40	1.70

SEMI-POSTAL STAMPS

Regular Issue of 1919 Surcharged in Violet

a

b

1919, May 3 Unwmk. *Imperf.*

B1	A10(a)	5f + 5f grn	16	20
B2	A10(a)	10f + 5f red vio	1.90	1.40
B3	A10(a)	15f + 5f dp red	35	20
B4	A11(b)	25f + 5f ol grn	35	20
B5	A11(b)	50f + 5f bl grn	55	32

Perf. 11½

B6	A10(a)	5f + 5f grn	22	16
B7	A10(a)	10f + 5f red vio	45	16
B8	A10(a)	15f + 5f dp red	22	16
B9	A11(b)	25f + 5f ol grn	28	16
B10	A11(b)	50f + 5f bl grn	90	42
		Nos. B1-B10 (10)	5.38	3.38

Commemorative of the First Polish Philatelic Exhibition. The surtax benefited the Polish White Cross Society.

Regular Issue of 1920 Surcharged in Carmine

1921, Mar. 5 *Perf. 9*

Thin Laid Paper

B11	A14	5m + 30m red vio	4.00	6.50
B12	A14	6m + 30m dp rose	4.00	6.50
B13	A14	10m + 30m lt red	10.00	10.50
B14	A14	20m + 30m gray grn	32.50	32.50

Counterfeits, differently perforated, exist of Nos. B11-14.

SP1

Light of Knowledge — SP2

1925, Jan. 1 **Typo.** *Perf. 12½*

B15	SP1	1g org brn	10.00	13.00
B16	SP1	2g dk brn	10.00	13.00
B17	SP1	3g orange	10.00	13.00
B18	SP1	5g ol grn	10.00	13.00
B19	SP1	10g bl grn	10.00	13.00
B20	SP1	15g red	10.00	13.00
B21	SP1	20g blue	10.00	13.00
B22	SP1	25g red brn	10.00	13.00
B23	SP1	30g dp vio	10.00	13.00
B24	SP1	40g indigo	30.00	13.00
B25	SP1	50g magenta	10.00	13.00
		Nos. B15-B25 (11)	130.00	143.00

"Na Skarb" means "National Funds". These stamps were sold at a premium of 50 groszy each, for charity.

1927, May 3 *Perf. 11½*

B26	SP2	10g + 5g choc & grn	8.75	3.50
B27	SP2	20g + 5g dk bl & buff	8.75	3.50

"NA OSWIATE" means "For Public Instruction". The surtax aided an Association of Educational Societies.

Torun Type of 1933

1933, May 21 **Engr.**

B28 A59 60g (+40g) red brn, *buff* 18.00 12.00

Issued in connection with the Philatelic Exhibition at Torun, May 21 to 28, 1933, and sold at a premium of 40g to aid the exhibition funds.

Souvenir Sheet

Stagecoach and Wayside Inn — SP3

1938, May 3 **Engr.** *Perf. 12, Imperf.*

B29	SP3	Sheet of four	67.50	62.50
a.		45g green	7.50	7.50
b.		55g blue	7.50	7.50

5th Phil. Exhib., Warsaw, May 3-8. The sheet contains two 45g and two 55g stamps. Sold for 3z, a surtax of 1z.

Souvenir Sheet

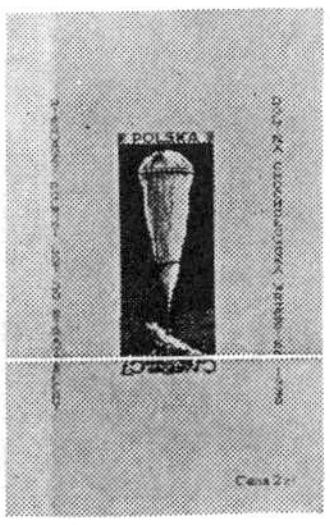

Stratosphere Balloon over Mountains — SP4

1938, Sept. 15 *Perf. 12½*

B31 SP4 75g dp vio, sheet 57.50 55.00

Issued in advance of a proposed Polish stratosphere flight. Sold for 2z, a surtax of 1.25z.

Winterhelp Issue

SP5

1938-39

B32	SP5	5g + 5g red org	50	85
B33	SP5	25g + 10g dk vio ('39)	80	1.25
B34	SP5	55g + 15g brt ultra ('39)	1.65	2.00

Souvenir Sheet

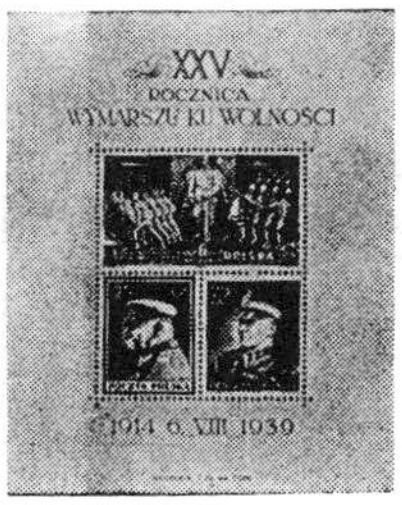

SP6

1939, Aug. 1

B35	SP6	Sheet of three	18.00	20.00
a.		25g dk bl gray *(Marshal Pilsudski Reviewing Troops)*	3.50	3.50
b.		25g dk bl gray *(Marshal Pilsudski)*	3.50	3.50
c.		25g dk bl gray *(Marshal Smigly-Rydz)*	3.50	3.50

25th anniv. of the founding of the Polish Legion. The sheets sold for 1.75z, the 1z surtax going to the National Defense fund.

Polish People's Republic

Polish Warship SP7

Sailing Vessel — SP8

Polish Naval Ensign and Merchant Flag — SP9

Crane and Crane Tower, Gdansk SP10

1945, Apr. 24 **Typo.** *Perf. 11*

B36	SP7	50g + 2z red	2.25	2.25
B37	SP8	1z + 3z dp bl	2.25	2.25
B38	SP9	2z + 4z dk car	2.25	2.25
B39	SP10	3z + 5z ol grn	2.25	2.25

Polish Maritime League, 25th anniv.

City Hall, Poznan — SP11

1945, June 16 **Photo.**

B40 SP11 1z + 5z grn 15.00 15.00

Postal Workers' Convention, Poznan, June 16, 1945. Exists imperf.

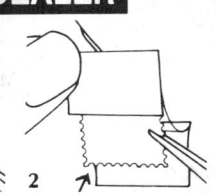

Last Stand at Westerplatte — SP12

1945, Sept. 1
B41 SP12 1z + 9z stl bl 11.50 11.50

Polish army's last stand at Westerplatte, Sept. 1, 1939. Exists imperf.

"United Industry" — SP13

1945, Nov. 18 Unwmk. *Perf. 11*
B42 SP13 1.50z + 8.50z sl blk 4.75 5.00

Trade Unions Congress, Warsaw, Nov. 18.

Polish Volunteers in Spain — SP14

1946, Mar. 10
B43 SP14 3z + 5z red 3.00 3.00

Participation of the Jaroslaw Dabrowski Brigade in the Spanish Civil War.

14th Century Piast Eagle and Soldiers SP15

"Death" Spreading Poison Gas over Majdanek Prison Camp SP16

1946, May 2
B44 SP15 3z + 7z brn 60 42

Silesian uprisings of 1919-21, 1939-45.

1946, Apr. 29
B45 SP16 3z + 5z Prus grn 2.25 2.50

Issued to recall Majdanek, a concentration camp of World War II near Lublin.

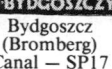

Bydgoszcz (Bromberg) Canal — SP17

Map of Polish Coast and Baltic Sea — SP18

1946, Apr. 19 Unwmk. *Perf. 11*
B46 SP17 3z + 2z ol blk 2.25 3.00

600th anniv. of Bydgoszcz (Bromberg).

1946, July 21
B47 SP18 3z + 7z dp bl 1.10 90

Maritime Holiday of 1946. The surtax was for the Polish Maritime League.

Salute to P.T.T. Casualty and Views of Gdansk — SP19

1946, Sept. 14
B48 SP19 3z + 12z sl 1.25 90

Issued in honor of Polish postal employees killed in the German attack on Danzig (Gdansk), Sept. 1939.

School Children — SP20

Designs: 6z+24z, Courtyard of Jagiellon University, Cracow. 11z+19z, Gregor Piramowicz (1735-1801), founder of Education Commission.

1946, Oct. 10 Unwmk. *Perf. 11½*

B49 SP20	3z + 22z dk red	27.50	35.00
B49A SP20	6z + 24z dk bl	27.50	35.00
B49B SP20	11z + 19z dk grn	27.50	35.00
c.	Souvenir sheet of 3, #B49-B49B	315.00	375.00

Polish educational work. Surtax was for International Bureau of Education.
No. B49c sold for 100z.

Stanislaw Stojalowski, Jakob Bojko, Jan Stapinski and Wincenty Witos — SP21

1946, Dec. 1

B50 SP21	5z + 10z bl grn	1.00	90
B51 SP21	5z + 10z dl bl	1.00	90
B52 SP21	5z + 10z dk ol	1.00	90

50th anniv. of the Peasant Movement. The surtax was for education and cultural improvement among the Polish peasantry.

No. 391 Surcharged in Red

+7 SEJM USTAWODAWCZY 19.I 1947

1947, Feb. 4 *Perf. 11x10½*
B53 A127 3z + 7z pur 5.75 5.00

Opening of the Polish Parliament, Jan. 19, 1947.

No. 344 Surcharged in Blue

5+15zł XXII MISTRZOSTWA NARCIARSKIE POLSKI 1947

1947, Feb. 21 *Perf. 12½*
B54 A103 5z + 15z on 25g dp red 1.40 2.00

Ski Championship Meet, Zakopane. Counterfeits exist.

Emil Zegadlowicz SP22

1947, Mar. 1 Photo. *Perf. 11*
B55 SP22 5z + 15z dl gray grn 1.00 70

Nurse and War Victims SP23

Adam Chmielowski SP24

1947, June 1 *Perf. 10½*
B56 SP23 5z + 5z ol blk & red 2.25 1.90

The surtax was for the Red Cross.

1947, Dec. 21 *Perf. 11*
B57 SP24 2z + 18z dk vio 1.00 70

Zamkowy Square and Proposed Highway — SP25

1948, Nov. 1
B58 SP25 15z + 5z grn 30 20

The surtax was to aid in the reconstruction of Warsaw.

Infant and TB Crosses SP26

Marceli Nowotko SP27

1948, Dec. 16 *Perf. 11½*
Various Portraits of Children

B59 SP26	3z + 2z dl grn	2.00	1.50
B60 SP26	5z + 5z brn	2.00	1.50
B61 SP26	6z + 4z vio	1.65	1.50
B62 SP26	15z + 10z car lake	1.65	1.50

Alternate vertical rows of stamps was ten different labels. The surtax was for anti-tuberculosis work among children.

Catalogue values for unused stamps in this section, from this point to the end of the section, are for Never Hinged items.

Perf. 12½
1952, Jan. 18 Engr. Unwmk.
B63 SP27 45g + 15g dk car 18 15

Polish Workers Party, 10th anniv.

Women's Day Type of Regular Issues of 1952

1952, Mar. 8 *Perf. 12½x12*
B64 A196 45g + 15g choc 22 10

Swierczewski-Walter Type of 1952

1952, Mar. 28 *Perf. 12½*
B65 A197 45g + 15g choc 28 8

Bierut Type of 1952

1952, Apr. 18

B66 A198	45g + 15g red	40	20
B67 A198	1.20z + 15g ultra	40	18

Type of Regular Issue of 1951-52 Inscribed "Plan 6," etc.

Design: 45g+15g, Electrical installation.

1952

B68 A193	30g + 15g brn red	35	18
B69 A193	45g + 15g choc	60	30
B69A A194	1.20z + 15g red org	30	22

Labor Day Type of Regular Issue of 1952

1952, May 1
B70 A200 45g + 15g car rose 12 7

Similar to Regular Issue of 1952

Portraits: 30g+15g, Maria Konopnicka. 45g+15g, Hugo Kollataj.

1952, May
Different Frames

B71 A201	30g + 15g bl grn	42	12
B72 A201	45g + 15g brn	20	12

Issue dates: No. B71, May 10. No. B72, May 20.

Leonardo da Vinci SP28

Swimmers SP30

Pres. Bierut and Children — SP29

1952, June 1
B73 SP28 30g + 15g ultra 85 42

500th birth anniv. of Leonardo da Vinci.

1952, June 1 Photo. *Perf. 13½x14*
B74 SP29 45g + 15g bl 1.65 48

Intl. Children's Day, June 1.

1952, June 21 *Perf. 13*

Design: 45g+15g, Soccer players and trophy.

B75 SP30	30g + 15g bl	3.75	1.40
B76 SP30	45g + 15g pur	1.75	35

Yachts SP31

"Dar Pomorza" SP32

1952, June 28 Engr. *Perf. 12½*

B77 SP31	30g + 15g dp bl grn	1.75	60
B78 SP32	45g + 15g dp ultra	45	22

Shipbuilders' Day, 1952.

Workers on Holiday — SP33

Students SP34

Perf. 12½x12, 12x12½

1952, July 17

B79	SP33 30g + 15g dp grn	28	20
B80	SP34 45g + 15g red	60	15

Issued to publicize the Youth Festival, 1952.

Constitution Type of Regular Issue

1952, July 22 **Photo.** ***Perf. 11***

B81	A208 45g + 15g lt bl grn & dk brn	75	24

Power Plant Type of Regular Issue

1952, Aug. 7 **Engr.** ***Perf. 12½***

B82	A209 45g + 15g red	45	7

Ludwik Warynski SP36

Church of Frydman SP37

1952, July 31

B83	SP36 30g + 15g dk red	30	12
B84	SP36 45g + 15g blk brn	28	20

70th birth anniv. of Ludwik Warynski, political organizer.

1952, Aug. 18

B85	SP37 45g + 15g vio brn	70	25

Aviator Watching Glider SP38

Henryk Sienkiewicz SP39

Design: 45g+15g, Pilot entering plane.

1952, Aug. 23

B86	SP38 30g + 15g grn	45	30
B87	SP38 45g + 15g brn red	1.75	90

Aviation Day, Aug. 23.

1952, Oct. 25

B88	SP39 45g + 15g vio brn	35	22

Henryk Sienkiewicz (1846-1916), author of "Quo Vadis" and other novels, Nobel prizewinner (literature, 1905).

Revolution Type of Regular Issue

1952, Nov. 7 ***Perf. 12x12½***

B92	A214 45g + 15g red brn	65	15

Exists imperforate.

Lenin SP42

Miner SP43

1952, Nov. 7 ***Perf. 12½***

B93	SP42 30g + 15g vio brn	22	12
B94	SP42 45g + 15g brn	55	28
a.	"LENIN" omitted		20.00

Month of Polish-Soviet friendship, Nov. 1952.

1952, Dec. 4

B95	SP43 45g + 15g blk brn	18	10
B96	SP43 1.20z + 15g brn	52	20

Miners' Day, Dec. 4.

Henryk Wieniawski and Violin SP44

Truck Factory, Lublin SP45

1952, Dec. 5 **Photo.**

B97	SP44 30g + 15g dk grn	45	28
B98	SP44 45g + 15g pur	2.25	55

Henryk Wieniawski; 2nd Intl. Violin Competition.

Type of Regular Issue of 1952

1952, Dec. 12 **Engr.**

B99	A215 45g + 15g dp grn	20	8

1953, Feb. 20

B100	SP45 30g + 15g dp bl	20	16
B101	SP45 60g + 20g vio brn	40	8

Souvenir Sheets

Town Hall in Poznan — SP46

Photo. & Litho.

1955, July 7 ***Imperf.***

B102	SP46 2z pck grn & ol grn	2.75	1.75
B103	SP46 3z car rose & ol blk	15.00	10.00

6th Polish Philatelic Exhibition in Poznan. Sheets sold for 3z and 4.50z respectively.

The indexes in each volume of the Scott Catalogue contain many listings which help to identify stamps.

"Peace" (POKOJ) and Warsaw Mermaid — SP47

Design: 1z, Pansies (A266) and inscription on map of Europe, Africa and Asia.

1955, Aug. 3

B104	SP47 1z bis, rose vio & yel	2.25	1.50
B105	SP47 2z ol gray, ultra & lt bl	11.00	7.50

Intl. Phil. Exhib., Warsaw, Aug. 1-14, 1955. Sheets sold for 2z and 3z respectively.

Souvenir Sheet

Chopin and Liszt — SP48

1956, Oct. 25 **Photo.** ***Imperf.***

B106	SP48 4z dk bl grn	27.50	13.00

Day of the Stamp; Polish-Hungarian friendship. The sheet sold for 6z.

Souvenir Sheet

Stamp of 1860 — SP49

Wmk. 326

1960, Sept. 4 **Litho.** ***Perf. 11***

B107	SP49 Sheet of four	37.50	30.00
a.	10z + 10z bl, red & blk	6.50	6.50

Intl. Phil. Exhib. "POLSKA 60" Warsaw, Sept. 3-11.

No. B107 sold only with 5z ticket to exhibition.

Type of Space Issue, 1964

Design: 6.50z+2z, Yuri A. Gagarin in space capsule.

Perf. 12½x12

1964, Dec. 30 **Unwmk.**

B108	A432 6.50z + 2z Prus grn & multi	1.50	65

Miniature Sheet

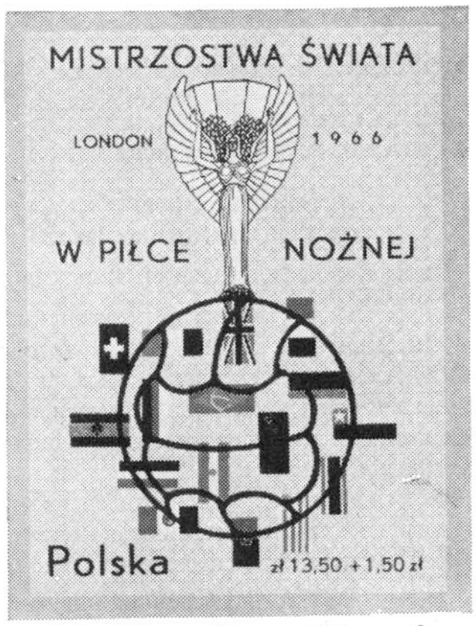

Jules Rimet Cup and Flags of Participating Countries — SP50

1966, May 9 **Litho.** ***Imperf.***

B109	SP50 13.50z + 1.50z gray & multi	1.90	1.00

World Cup Soccer Championship, Wembley, England, July 11-30.

Souvenir Sheet

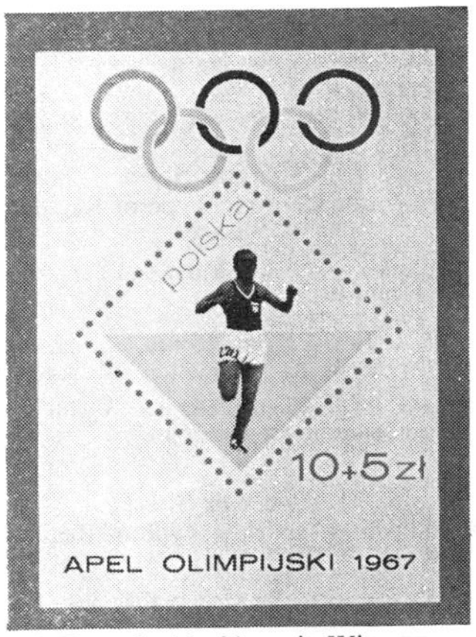

J. Kusocinski, Olympic Winner 10,000-Meter Race, 1932 — SP51

1967, May 24 **Litho.** ***Imperf.***

B110	SP51 10z + 5z multi	1.40	1.00

19th Olympic Games, Mexico City, 1968. Simulated perforations.

Flower Type of Regular Issue

Flowers: 4z+2z, Abutilon. 8z+4z, Rosa polyantha hybr.

1968, May 15 **Litho.** ***Perf. 11½***

B111	A492 4z + 2z vio & multi	60	30
B112	A492 8z + 4z lt vio & multi	1.25	65

Olympic Type of Regular Issue, 1968

Design: 10z+5z, Runner with Olympic torch and Chin cultic carved stone disc showing Mayan ball player and game's scoreboard.

1968, Sept. 2 Litho. *Perf. 11½*
Size: 56x45mm
B113 A497 10z + 5z multi 1.50 85

19th Olympic Games, Mexico City, Oct. 12-27. The surtax was for the Polish Olympic Committee.

Olympic Type of Regular Issue, 1969

Olympic Rings and: 2.50z+50g, Women's discus. 3.40z+1z, Running. 4z+1.50z, Boxing. 7z+2z, Fencing.

1969, Apr. 25 Litho. *Perf. 11½x11*
B114 A505 2.50z + 50g multi 25 9
B115 A505 3.40z + 1z multi 32 15
B116 A505 4z + 1.50z multi 50 20
B117 A505 7z + 2z multi 85 40

Folk Art Type of Regular Issue

Designs: 5.50z+1.50z, Choir. 7z+1.50z, Organ grinder.

1969, Dec. 19 Litho. *Perf. 11½x11*
Size: 24x36mm
B118 A520 5.50z + 1.50z multi 52 24
B119 A520 7z + 1.50z multi 70 30

Souvenir Sheet
Sports Type of Regular Issue

Design: 10z+5z, "Horse of Glory," by Z. Kaminski.

1970, June 16 Photo. *Imperf.*
B120 A532 10z + 5z multi 1.50 90

The surtax was for the Polish Olympic Committee. No. B120 contains one imperf. stamp with simulated perforations.

Souvenir Sheet
Tapestry Type of Regular Issue

Design: 7z+3z, Satyrs holding monogram of King Sigismund Augustus.

1970, Dec. 23 Photo. *Imperf.*
B121 A541 7z + 3c multi 1.75 1.00

Type of Regular Issue

Design: 8.50z+4z, Virgin Mary, 15th century stained glass window.

1971, Sept. 15 *Perf. 11½x11*
B122 A555 8.50z + 4z multi 75 45

Painting Type of Regular Issue

Design: 7z+1z, Nude, by Wojciech Weiss (1875-1950).

1971, Oct. 9 Litho.
B123 A556 7z + 1z multi 70 35

Souvenir Sheet
Winter Olympic Type of Regular Issue

Design: 10z+5z, Slalom and Sapporo '72 emblem (vert.).

1972, Jan. 12 Photo. *Imperf.*
B124 A564 10z + 5z multi 1.40 90

No. B124 contains one stamp with simulated perforations, 27x52mm.

Souvenir Sheet
Summer Olympic Type of Regular Issue

Design: 10z+5z, Archery (like 30g).

1972, May 20 Photo. *Perf. 11½x11*
B125 A568 10z + 5z multi 1.65 1.00

Painting Type of Regular Issue, 1972

Design: 8.50z+4z, Portrait of a Young Lady, by Jacek Malczewski (horiz.).

1972, Sept. 28 Photo. *Perf. 11x10½*
B126 A576 8.50z + 4z multi 1.25 65

Souvenir Sheet

Copernicus SP52

Engraved and Phogogravure
1972, Sept. 28 *Perf. 11½*
B127 SP52 10z + 5z vio bl, gray & car 1.50 85

Nicolaus Copernicus (1473-1543), astronomer. No. B127 shows the Ptolemaic and Copernican concepts of solar system from L'Harmonica Microcosmica, by Cellarius, 1660.

Souvenir Sheet

Poznan, 1740, by F. B. Werner — SP53

1973, Aug. 19 *Imperf.*
B128 SP53 10z + 5z ol & dk brn 1.50 90
a. 10z + 5z pale lil & dk brn 4.25 4.00

POLSKA 73 Intl. Phil. Exhib., Poznan, Aug. 19-Sept. 2. No. B128 contains one stamp with simulated perforations.
No. B128a was sold only in combination with an entrance ticket.

Copernicus, by Marcello Baciarelli — SP54

1973, Sept. 27 Photo. *Perf. 11x11½*
B129 SP54 4z + 2z multi 50 28

Stamp Day. The surtax was for the reconstruction of the Royal Castle in Warsaw.

Souvenir Sheet

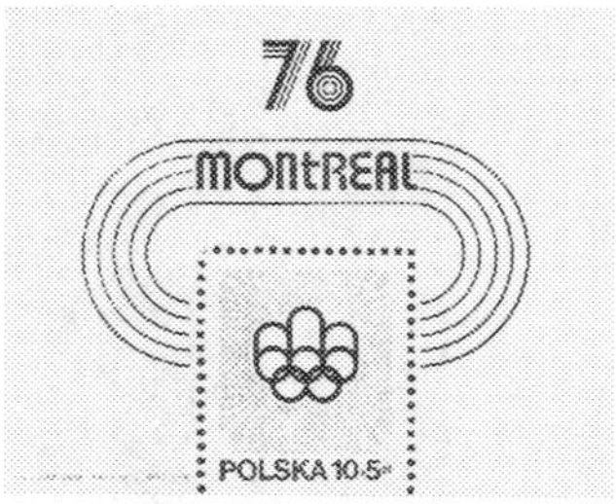

Montreal Olympic Games Emblem — SP55

Photo. & Engr.
1975, Mar. 8 *Perf. 12*
B130 SP55 10z + 5z sil & grn 1.50 1.00

21st Olympic Games, Montreal, July 17-Aug. 8, 1976.

Dunikowski Type of 1975

Design: 8z+4z, Mother and Child, from Silesian Insurrectionist Monument, by Dunikowski.

1975, Oct. 9 Photo. *Perf. 11½x11*
B131 A644 8z + 4z multi 1.00 45

Souvenir Sheet

Volleyball — SP56

Engraved and Photogravure
1976, June 30 *Perf. 11½*
B132 SP56 10z + 5z blk & car 1.25 70

21st Olympic Games, Montreal, Canada, July 17-Aug. 1. No. B132 contains one perf. 11½ stamp and is perf. 11½ all around.

Corinthian Art Type 1976

Design: 8z+4z, Winged Sphinx (vert.).

1976, Oct. 30 Photo. *Perf. 11½x11*
B133 A664 8z + 4z multi 1.10 50

Souvenir Sheet

Stoning of St. Stephen, by Rubens — SP57

1977, Apr. 30 Engr. *Perf. 12x11½*
B134 SP57 8z + 4z sep 1.10 65

Peter Paul Rubens (1577-1640), Flemish painter. No. B134 is arranged similar to type SP55 but with sheet margins perforated all around and stamp on top.

Souvenir Sheet

Kazimierz Gzowski — SP58

1978, June 6 Photo. *Perf. 11½x11*
B135 SP58 8.40z + 4z multi 1.10 55

CAPEX, '78 Canadian Intl. Phil. Exhib., Toronto, June 9-18.
K. S. Gzowski (1813-1898), Polish engineer and lawyer living in Canada, built International Bridge over Niagara River.

Souvenir Sheet

Olympic Rings — SP59

1979, May 19 Engr. *Imperf.*
B136 SP59 10z + 5z blk 1.00 75

1980 Olympic Games.

Monument Type of 1979
Souvenir Sheet
1979, Sept. 1 Photo. *Imperf.*
B137 A731 10z + 5z multi 1.25 75

Surtax was for monument.

Summer Olympic Type of 1980
Souvenir Sheet
1980, Mar. 31 Photo. *Perf. 11x11½*
B138 A742 10.50z + 5z Kayak 1.00 75

No. B138 contains one stamp 42x30mm.

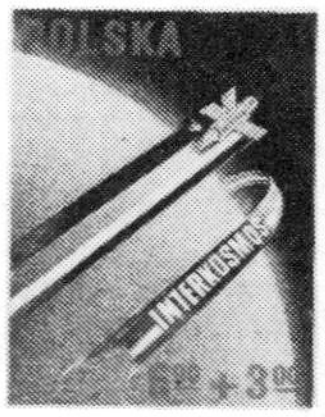

Intercosmos Cooperative Space Program — SP60

1980, Apr. 12 *Perf. 11½x11*
B139 SP60 6.90z + 3z multi 85 75

1970 Uprising Memorial — SP61

Designs: 2.50z + 1z, Triple Crucifix, Gdansk (27x46mm.). 6.50z + 1z, Monument, Gdynia.

1981, Dec. 16 Photo. *Perf. 11½x12*
B140 SP61 2.50 + 1z blk & red 70 32
B141 SP61 6.50 + 1z blk & lil 1.00 70

Portrait of a German Princess, by Lucas Cranach — SP62

1984, May 15 Photo. *Perf. 11½x12*
B142 SP62 27z + 10z multi 1.50 80

1984 UPU Congress, Hamburg. No. B142 issued se-tenant with multicolored label showing UPU emblem and text.

An enhanced introduction to the Scott Catalogue begins on Page V. A thorough understanding of the material presented there will greatly aid your use of the catalogue itself.

Souvenir Sheet

Madonna with Child, St. John and the Angel, by Sandro Botticelli (1445-1510), Natl. Museum, Warsaw — SP63

1985, Sept. 25 Photo. *Perf. 11*

B143 SP63 65z + 15z multi 2.50 1.75
a. Inscribed: 35 LAT POL-SKIEGO . . . 4.75 4.75

ITALIA '85. Surtax for Polish Association of Philatelists.

No. B143a was for the 35th anniv. of the Polish Philatelic Union.

Joachim Lelewel (1786-1861), Historian — SP64

1986, Dec. 22 Photo. *Perf. 11½x12*

B144 SP64 10z + 5z multi 30 18

Surtax for the Natl. Committee for School Aid.

Polish Immigrant Settling in Kasubia, Ontario — SP65

1987, June 13 Photo. *Perf. 12x11½*

B145 SP65 50z + 20z multi 1.40 70

CAPEX '87, Toronto, Canada. Surtaxed for the Polish Philatelists' Union.

Souvenir Sheet

OLYMPHILEX '87, Rome — SP66

1987, Aug. 28 Litho. *Perf. 14*

B146 SP66 45z + 10z like No. 2617 1.10 1.10

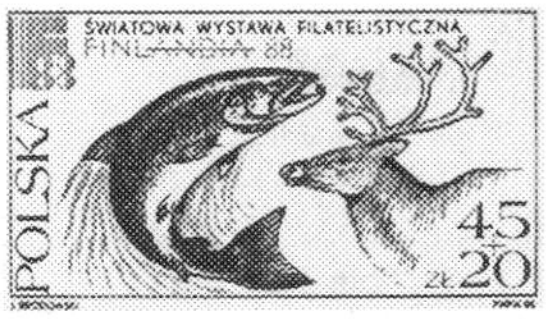

FINLANDIA '88 — SP67

1988, June 1 Photo. *Perf. 12x11½*

B147 SP67 45z +20z Salmon, reindeer 1.30 65

Souvenir Sheet

Jerzy Kukuczka, Mountain Climber Awarded Medal by the Intl. Olympic Committee for Climbing the Himalayas — SP68

1988, Aug. 17 Photo. *Perf. 11x11½*

B148 SP68 70z +10z multi 1.60 80

Surtax for the Polish Olympic Fund.

AIR POST STAMPS

Biplane — AP1

Perf. 12½

1925, Sept. 10 Typo. Unwmk.

C1	AP1	1g lt bl	52	1.75
C2	AP1	2g orange	52	1.75
C3	AP1	3g yel brn	52	1.75
C4	AP1	5g dk brn	52	70
C5	AP1	10g dk grn	1.40	60
C6	AP1	15g red vio	2.00	70
C7	AP1	20g ol grn	8.75	3.50
C8	AP1	30g dl rose	5.50	1.25
C9	AP1	45g dk vio	7.00	3.50
		Nos. C1-C9 (9)	26.73	15.50

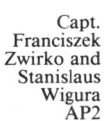

Counterfeits exist.

Capt. Franciszek Zwirko and Stanislaus Wigura AP2

Perf. 11½ to 12½ and Compound

1933, Apr. 15 Engr. Wmk. 234

C10 AP2 30g gray grn 12.50 90

Winning of the circuit of Europe flight by two Polish aviators in 1932. The stamp was available for both air mail and ordinary postage.

Nos. C7 and C10 Overprinted in Red

Challenge 1934

1934, Aug. 28 Unwmk. *Perf. 12½*

C11 AP1 20g ol grn 12.50 6.00

Wmk. 234

Perf. 11½

C12 AP2 30g gray grn 7.00 1.75

Polish People's Republic

Douglas Plane over Ruins of Warsaw — AP3

Unwmk.

1946, Mar. 5 Photo. *Perf. 11*

C13	AP3	5z grnsh blk	32	12
a.		Without control number	4.00	40
C14	AP3	10z dk vio	32	12
C15	AP3	15z blue	1.00	25
C16	AP3	20z rose brn	65	12
C17	AP3	25z dk bl grn	1.25	38
C18	AP3	30z red	2.00	55
		Nos. C13-C18 (6)	5.54	1.54

The 10z, 20z and 30z were issued only with control number in lower right stamp margin. The 15z and 25z exist only without number. The 5z comes both ways.

Nos. C13-C18 exist imperforate.

Nos. 345, 344 and 344a Surcharged in Red or Black

a
ZŁ 40 ZŁ
LOTNICZA

b
LOTNICZA
ZŁ 50 ZŁ

1947, Sept. 10 *Perf. 12½*

C19 A104(a) 40z on 50g dk sl grn (R) 1.50 90
C20 A103(b) 50z on 25g dl red 1.75 1.75
a. 50z on 25g deep red 2.50 1.75

Counterfeits exist.

Centaur — AP4

1948 *Perf. 11*

C21	AP4	15z dk vio	1.25	22
C22	AP4	25z dp bl	65	15
C23	AP4	30z brown	50	35
C24	AP4	50z dk grn	1.10	35
C25	AP4	75z gray blk	1.25	45
C26	AP4	100z red org	1.25	35
		Nos. C21-C26 (6)	6.00	1.87

Pres. F. D. Roosevelt AP5

Airplane Mechanic and Propeller AP5a

Designs: 100z, Casimir Pulaski. 120z, Tadeusz Kosciusko.

1948, Dec. 30 Photo. *Perf. 11½*

Granite Paper

C26A	AP5	80z bl blk	15.00	22.50
C26B	AP5	100z purple	16.00	18.00
C26C	AP5	120z dp bl	16.00	18.00
d.		Souvenir sheet of 3	165.00	225.00

No. C26d contains stamps similar to Nos. C26A-C26C with colors changed: 80z ultramarine, 100z carmine rose, 120z dark green. Sold for 500z.

1950, Feb. 6 Engr. *Perf. 12½*

C27 AP5a 500z rose lake 3.00 2.50

Catalogue values for unused stamps in this section, from this point to the end of the section, are for Never Hinged items.

Seaport AP6

Designs: 90g, Mechanized farm. 1.40z, Warsaw. 5z, Steel mill.

1952, Apr. 10 *Perf. 12x12½*

C28	AP6	55g int bl	9	8
C29	AP6	90g dl grn	20	8
C30	AP6	1.40z vio brn	30	12
C31	AP6	5z gray blk	1.10	40

Nos. C28-C31 exist imperf. Value $10.

Congress Badge — AP7

1953, Aug. 23 Photo. *Imperf.*

C32 AP7 55g brn lil 85 30
C33 AP7 75g brn org 1.25 90

3rd World Congress of Students, Warsaw 1953.

Souvenir Sheet

AP8

1954, May 23 Engr. *Perf. 12x12½*

C34 AP8 5z gray grn, sheet 27.50 17.50

3rd congress of the Polish Phil. Assoc., Warsaw, 1954. Sold for 7.50 zlotys. A similar sheet, imperf. and in dark blue, was issued but had no postal validity.

A particular stamp may be scarce, but if few collectors want it, its market value may remain relatively low.

Paczkow Castle, Luban
AP9

Plane over "Peace" Steelworks
AP10

Designs: 80g, Kazimierz Dolny. 1.15z, Wawel castle, Cracow. 1.50z, City Hall, Wroclaw. 1.55z, Laziersky Square, Warsaw. 1.95z, Cracow gate, Lublin.

1954, July 9 *Perf. 12½*

C35	AP9	60g dk gray grn	12	12
C36	AP9	80g red	10	8
C37	AP9	1.15z black	90	38
C38	AP9	1.50z rose lake	35	18
C39	AP9	1.55z dp gray bl	35	12
C40	AP9	1.95z chocolate	70	30
		Nos. C35-C40 (6)	2.52	1.18

Wmk. 326 ('58 Values); Unwmkd.
1957-58 Engr. & Photo. *Perf. 12½*

Plane over: 1.50z, Castle Square, Warsaw. 3.40z, Old Market, Cracow. 3.90z, King Boleslaw Chrobry Wall, Szczecin. 4z, Karkonosze mountains. 5z, Gdansk. 10z, Ruins of Liwa Castle. 15z, Old City, Lublin. 20z, Kasprowy Wierch Peak and cable car. 30z, Porabka dam. 50z, M. S. Batory and Gdynia harbor.

C41	AP10	90g blk & pink	10	8
C42	AP10	1.50z brn & sal	12	6
C43	AP10	3.40z sep & buff	28	10
C44	AP10	3.90z dk brn & cit	48	42
C45	AP10	4z ind & lt grn	22	8
C46	AP10	5z mar & gray ('58)	40	12
C47	AP10	10z sep & grn ('58)	80	22
C48	AP10	15z vio bl & pale bl	1.00	45
C49	AP10	20z vio blk & lem ('58)	2.00	60
C50	AP10	30z ol gray & bis ('58)	2.75	1.25
C51	AP10	50z dk bl & gray ('58)	4.50	1.65
		Nos. C41-C51 (11)	12.65	5.03

1959, May 23 Litho. Wmk. 326

C52	AP10	10z sepia	1.75	1.50
a.		With 5z label	2.25	2.25

65th anniv. of the Polish Philatelic Society. Sheet of 6 stamps and 2 each of 3 different labels. Each label carries an added charge of 5z for a fund to build a Society clubhouse in Warsaw.

Jantar Glider — AP11

Contemporary aviation: 10z, Mi6 transport helicopter. 20z, PZL-106 Kruk, crop spraying plane. 50z, Plane over Warsaw Castle.

1976-78 Unwmk. Engr. *Perf. 11½*

C53	AP11	5z dk bl grn	40	25
C54	AP11	10z dk brn	80	50
C55	AP11	20z grnsh blk	1.50	75
C56	AP11	50z claret	3.00	1.90

Issue dates: 5z, 10z, Mar. 27, 1976. 20z, Feb. 15, 1977. 50z, Feb. 2, 1978.

AIR POST SEMI-POSTAL STAMP

Polish People's Republic

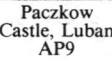

Wing of Jet Plane and Letter — SPAP1

Perf. 11½
1957, Mar. 28 Unwmk. Photo.

CB1	SPAP1	4z + 2z bl	2.75	3.50
a.		Souv. sheet	8.50	4.50

7th Polish National Philatelic Exhibition, Warsaw. Sheet of 12 with 4 diagonally arranged gray labels.

No. CB1a contains one 4z+2z ultramarine, type SPAP1, imperf., with marginal inscriptions in bright pink. Size: 56x75mm.

POSTAGE DUE STAMPS

Cracow Issues

Postage Due Stamps of Austria, 1916, Overprinted in Black or Red

POCZTA
◇
POLSKA

1919, Jan. 10 Unwmk. *Perf. 12½*

J1	D4	5h rose red	6.50	5.75
J2	D4	10h rose red	*2,250.*	*2,250.*
J3	D4	15h rose red	3.25	2.75
a.		Inverted overprint	150.00	
J4	D4	20h rose red	350.00	350.00
J5	D4	25h rose red	15.00	12.00
J6	D4	30h rose red	*800.00*	*750.00*
J7	D4	40h rose red	250.00	200.00
J8	D5	1k ultra (R)	*2,400.*	*2,400.*
J9	D5	5k ultra (R)	*2,400.*	*2,400.*
J10	D5	10k ultra (R)	*10,000.*	*9,000.*
a.		Black overprint	*14,000.*	*16,000.*

The overprint on Nos. J8 to J10 is slightly larger than illustration and has different ornament between lines of type.

D6

Type of Austria, 1916-18, Surcharged in Black

1919, Jan. 10

J11	D6	15h on 36h vio	300.00	225.00
J12	D6	50h on 42h choc	30.00	30.00
a.		Double surcharge	275.00	275.00

Counterfeits exist of Nos. J1 to J12.

Regular Issues

Numerals of Value
D7 D8

1919 Typo. *Perf. 11½*

J13	D7	2(f) red org	35	32
J14	D7	4(f) red org	16	18
J15	D7	5(f) red org	8	8
J16	D7	10(f) red org	8	8
J17	D7	20(f) red org	8	8
J18	D7	30(f) red org	8	8
J19	D7	50(f) red org	8	8
J20	D7	100(f) red org	75	45
J21	D7	500(f) red org	1.65	1.25
J22	D7	2(h) dk bl	12	8
J23	D7	4(h) dk bl	12	8
J24	D7	5(h) dk bl	12	8
J25	D7	10(h) dk bl	12	8
J26	D7	20(h) dk bl	12	8
J27	D7	30(h) dk bl	12	8
J28	D7	50(h) dk bl	12	8
J29	D7	100(h) dk bl	30	22
J30	D7	500(h) dk bl	1.25	1.10
		Nos. J13-J30 (18)	5.70	4.48

Counterfeits exist.

1920 *Perf. 9, 10, 11½*
Thin Laid Paper

J31	D7	20(f) dk bl	60	48
J32	D7	100(f) dk bl	30	24
J33	D7	200(f) dk bl	52	48
J34	D7	500(f) dk bl	30	24

Regular Issue of 1919 Surcharged

6 Mk.
dopłata

1921, Jan. 25 *Imperf.*
Wove Paper

J35	A9	6m on 15h brn	40	42
J36	A9	6m on 25h car	40	42
J37	A9	20m on 10h lake	1.10	1.10
J38	A9	20m on 50h ind	1.25	1.40
J39	A9	35m on 70h dp bl	11.00	12.00
		Nos. J35-J39 (5)	14.15	15.34

Counterfeits exist.

Perf. 9 to 14½ and Compound
1921-22 Typo.
Thin Laid or Wove Paper
Size: 17x22mm

J40	D8	1m indigo	28	12
J41	D8	2m indigo	28	12
J42	D8	4m indigo	28	12
J43	D8	6m indigo	28	12
J44	D8	8m indigo	28	12
J45	D8	20m indigo	28	12
J46	D8	50m indigo	28	12
J47	D8	100m indigo	50	18
		Nos. J40-J47 (8)	2.46	1.02

Nos. J44-J45, J41 Surcharged

Perf. 9 to 14½ and Compound
1923, Nov.

J48	D8	10,000(m) on 8m ind	28	8
J49	D8	20,000(m) on 20m ind	28	15
J50	D8	50,000(m) on 2m ind	1.90	70

Type of 1921-22 Issue

1923 Typo. *Perf. 12½*
Size: 19x24mm

J51	D8	50m indigo	12	10
J52	D8	100m indigo	12	10
J53	D8	200m indigo	12	10
J54	D8	500m indigo	12	10
J55	D8	1000m indigo	12	10
J56	D8	2000m indigo	12	10
J57	D8	10,000m indigo	8	10
J58	D8	20,000m indigo	8	10
J59	D8	30,000m indigo	15	10
J60	D8	50,000m indigo	35	15
J61	D8	100,000m indigo	35	10
J62	D8	200,000m indigo	40	10
J63	D8	300,000m indigo	40	25
J64	D8	500,000m indigo	60	15
J65	D8	1,000,000m indigo	1.40	45
J66	D8	2,000,000m indigo	2.50	45
J67	D8	3,000,000m indigo	2.75	65
		Nos. J51-J67 (17)	9.78	3.20

D9

D10

1924 *Perf. 10 to 13½ and Compound*
Size: 20x25½mm

J68	D9	1g brown	28	22
J69	D9	2g brown	28	22
J70	D9	4g brown	28	22
J71	D9	6g brown	55	22
J72	D9	10g brown	3.25	22
J73	D9	15g brown	2.50	40
J74	D9	20g brown	6.00	40
J75	D9	25g brown	5.00	40
J76	D9	30g brown	1.10	40
J77	D9	40g brown	1.10	40
J78	D9	50g brown	1.10	40
J79	D9	1z brown	1.00	55
J80	D9	2z brown	1.00	55
J81	D9	3z brown	1.90	2.25
J82	D9	5z brown	1.90	85
		Nos. J68-J82 (15)	27.24	7.70

Nos. J68-J69 and J72-J75 exist measuring 19½x24½mm.

1930, July *Perf. 12½*

J83	D10	5g ol brn	70	20

Postage Due Stamps of 1924 Surcharged

50
groszy

Perf. 10 to 13½ and Compound
1934-38

J84	D9	10g on 2z brn ('38)	45	35
J85	D9	15g on 2z brn	45	35
J86	D9	20g on 1z brn	45	35
J87	D9	20g on 5z brn	2.25	70
J88	D9	25g on 40g brn	1.40	70
J89	D9	30g on 40g brn	95	70
J90	D9	50g on 40g brn	95	85
J91	D9	50g on 3z brn ('35)	1.90	1.25
		Nos. J84-J91 (8)	8.80	5.25

No. 255a Surcharged in Red or Indigo

DOPŁATA 25 GR

1934-36 **Laid Paper**

J92	A50	10g on 1z blk, *cr* (R) ('36)	80	15
a.		Vertically laid paper (No. 255)	25.00	18.00
J93	A50	20g on 1z blk, *cr* (R) ('36)	2.50	65
J94	A50	25g on 1z blk, *cr* (I)	80	24
a.		Vertically laid paper (No. 255)	30.00	18.00

D11

1939, Nov. 25 Typo. *Perf. 12½x12*

J95	D11	5g dk bl grn	10	8
J96	D11	10g dk bl grn	10	8
J97	D11	15g dk bl grn	10	8
J98	D11	20g dk bl grn	52	20
J99	D11	25g dk bl grn	15	16
J100	D11	30g dk bl grn	35	20
J101	D11	50g dk bl grn	70	1.25
J102	D11	1z dk bl grn	2.00	1.65
		Nos. J95-J102 (8)	4.02	3.70

Polish People's Republic

Post Horn with Thunderbolts
D12

Polish Eagle
D13

Perf. 11x10½
1945, May 20 Litho. Unwmk.
Size: 25½x19mm

J103	D12	1z org brn	15	10
J104	D12	2z org brn	20	15
J105	D12	3z org brn	25	20
J106	D12	5z org brn	35	30

Type of 1945
Perf. 11, 11½ (P) or Imperf. (I)
1946-49 **Photo.**
Size: 29x21½mm

J106A	D12	1z org brn (P) ('49)	20	15
J107	D12	2z org brn (P,I)	20	15
J108	D12	3z org brn (P,I)	20	15
J109	D12	5z org brn (I)	20	15
J110	D12	6z org brn (I)	20	15
J111	D12	10z org brn (I)	25	20
J112	D12	15z org brn (P,I)	35	30
J113	D12	25z org brn (P,I)	50	45
J114	D12	100z brn (P) ('49)	1.00	50
J115	D12	150z brn (P) ('49)	1.75	50
		Nos. J106A-J115 (10)	4.85	2.70

1950 Engr. *Perf. 12x12½*

J116	D13	5z red brn	8	8
J117	D13	10z red brn	8	8
J118	D13	15z red brn	12	8
J119	D13	20z red brn	28	12
J120	D13	25z red brn	32	18
J121	D13	50z red brn	48	35
J122	D13	100z red brn	1.00	70
		Nos. J116-J122 (7)	2.36	1.59

1951-52

J123	D13	5g red brn	8	5
J124	D13	10g red brn	8	5
J125	D13	15g red brn	8	5
J126	D13	20g red brn	12	10
J127	D13	25g red brn	16	10
J128	D13	30g red brn	22	15
J129	D13	50g red brn	25	20
J130	D13	60g red brn	30	20
J131	D13	90g red brn	38	25
J132	D13	1z red brn	60	45
J133	D13	2z red brn	95	75
J134	D13	5z brn vio	2.00	1.75
		Nos. J123-J134 (12)	5.22	4.10

1953, Apr. Photo. Without imprint

J135	D13	5g red brn	12	8
J136	D13	10g red brn	12	8
J137	D13	15g red brn	12	8
J138	D13	20g red brn	12	8
J139	D13	25g red brn	16	10
J140	D13	30g red brn	25	15
J141	D13	50g red brn	42	25
J142	D13	60g red brn	50	30
J143	D13	90g red brn	60	50
J144	D13	1z red brn	80	50
J145	D13	2z red brn	1.50	1.25
		Nos. J135-J145 (11)	4.71	3.37

Catalogue values for unused stamps in this section, from this point to the end of the section, are for Never Hinged items.

1980, Sept. 2 Litho. *Perf. 12½*

J146	D13	1z lt red brn	8	5
J147	D13	2z gray ol	18	10
J148	D13	3z dl vio	28	12
J149	D13	5z brown	45	20

OFFICIAL STAMPS

O1

Perf. 10, 11½, 10x11½, 11½x10

1920, Feb. 1 Litho. Unwmk.

O1	O1	3(f) vermilion	14	12
O2	O1	5(f) vermilion	14	18
O3	O1	10(f) vermilion	14	18
O4	O1	15(f) vermilion	14	18
O5	O1	25(f) vermilion	14	18
O6	O1	50(f) vermilion	14	18
O7	O1	100(f) vermilion	28	25
O8	O1	150(f) vermilion	28	38
O9	O1	200(f) vermilion	52	38
O10	O1	300(f) vermilion	28	38
O11	O1	600(f) vermilion	52	38
		Nos. O1-O11 (11)	2.72	2.79

Numerals Larger
Stars inclined outward

1920, Nov. 20 *Perf. 11½*
Thin Laid Paper

O12	O1	5(f) red	12	15
O13	O1	10(f) red	50	45
O14	O1	15(f) red	35	35
O15	O1	25(f) red	1.10	1.10
O16	O1	50(f) red	65	65
		Nos. O12-O16 (5)	2.72	2.70

Polish Eagle
O3 O4

Perf. 12x12½

1933, Aug. 1 Typo. Wmk. 234

O17	O3	(30g) vio *(Zwyczajna)*	95	12
O18	O3	(80g) red *(Polecona)*	2.25	30

1935, Apr. 1

O19	O4	(25g) bl vio *(Zwyczajna)*	15	10
O20	O4	(55g) car *(Polecona)*	30	15

Stamps inscribed "Zwyczajna" or "Zwykla" were for ordinary official mail. Those with "Polecona" were for registered official mail.

Polish People's Republic

Polish Eagle — O5

Perf. 11, 14

1945, July 1 Photo. Unwmk.

O21	O5	(5z) bl vio *(Zwykla)*	40	8
	a.	Imperf.	1.00	1.00
O22	O5	(10z) red *(Polecona)*	80	20
	a.	Imperf.	1.65	1.25

Control number at bottom right: M-01705 on No. O21; M-01706 on No. O22.

Type of 1945 Redrawn

1946, July 31

O23	O5	(5z) dl bl vio *(Zwykla)*	30	15
O24	O5	(10z) dl rose red *(Polecona)*	50	22

The redrawn stamps appear blurred and the eagle contains fewer lines of shading.
Control number at bottom right: M-01709 on Nos. O23-O26.

Redrawn Type of 1946

1946, July 31 *Imperf.*

O25	O5	(60g) dl bl vio *(Zwykla)*	35	12
O26	O5	(1.55z) dl rose red *(Polecona)*	35	20

Type of 1945, 2nd Redrawing
No Control Number at Lower Right

Perf. 11, 11½, 11x12½

1952 Unwmk.

O27	O5	(60g) bl *(Zwykla)*	22	12
O28	O5	(1.55z) red *(Polecona)*	38	20

Redrawn Type of 1952

1954 *Perf. 13x11, 11½, 14*

O29	O5	(60g) sl gray *(Zwykla)*	1.40	60

O6

Perf. 11x11½, 12x12½

1954, Aug. 15 Engr.

O30	O6	(60g) dk bl *(Zwykla)*	25	12
O31	O6	(1.55z) red *(Polecona)*	45	24

Polish People's Republic, 10th anniversary.

NEWSPAPER STAMPS

Austrian Newspaper Stamps of 1916 Overprinted

POCZTA
◇
POLSKA

1919, Jan. 10 Unwmk. *Imperf.*

P1	N9	2h brown	7.25	6.00
P2	N9	4h green	2.75	2.00
P3	N9	6h dk bl	2.75	2.00
P4	N9	10h orange	32.50	32.50
P5	N9	30h claret	4.00	3.50
		Nos. P1-P5 (5)	49.25	46.00

OCCUPATION STAMPS

Issued under German Occupation

German Stamps of 1905 Overprinted

Russisch-
Polen

Perf. 14, 14½

1915, May 12 Wmk. 125

N1	A16	3pf brown	35	45
N2	A16	5pf green	45	55
N3	A16	10pf carmine	45	55
N4	A16	20pf ultra	65	80
N5	A16	40pf lake & blk	3.50	4.25
		Nos. N1-N5 (5)	5.40	6.60

German Stamps of 1905-17 Overprinted

Gen.-Gouv.
Warschau

1916-17

N6	A22	2½pf gray	28	24
N7	A16	3pf brown	1.10	435
N8	A16	5pf green	1.10	80
N9	A22	7½pf orange	90	14
N10	A16	10pf carmine	1.10	24
N11	A22	15pf yel brn	5.25	1.65
N12	A22	15pf dk vio ('17)	70	24
N13	A16	20pf ultra	1.75	52
N14	A16	30pf org & blk, *buff*	7.50	2.75
N15	A16	40pf lake & blk	2.75	14
N16	A16	60pf magenta	3.75	1.10
		Nos. N6-N16 (11)	26.18	12.17

6 Groschen 6

German Stamps of 1934 Surcharged in Black

Deutsche Post
OSTEN

1939, Dec. 1 Wmk. 237 *Perf. 14*

N17	A64	6g on 3(pf) bis	30	30
N18	A64	8g on 4(pf) dl bl	30	32
N19	A64	12g on 6(pf) dk grn	30	30
N20	A64	16g on 8(pf) ver	75	90
N21	A64	20g on 10(pf) choc	30	30
N22	A64	24g on 12(pf) dp car	30	30
N23	A64	30g on 15(pf) mar	90	85
N24	A64	40g on 20(pf) brt bl	75	40
N25	A64	50g on 25(pf) ultra	75	70
N26	A64	60g on 30(pf) ol grn	75	40
N27	A64	80g on 40(pf) red vio	90	85
N28	A64	1z on 50(pf) dk grn & blk	2.25	1.25
N29	A64	2z on 100(pf) org & blk	4.25	2.75
		Nos. N17-N29 (13)	12.80	9.62

Stamps of Poland 1937, Surcharged in Black or Brown

1940 Unwmk. *Perf. 12½, 12½x13*

N30	A80	24g on 25g sl grn	1.10	1.75
N31	A81	40g on 30g rose vio	40	65
N32	A80	50g on 55g bl	35	52

Similar Surcharge on Stamps of 1938-39

N33	A83	2g on 5g red org	22	35
N34	A83	4(g) on 5g red org	22	35
N35	A83	6(g) on 10g grn	22	35
N36	A83	8(g) on 10g grn (Br)	28	45
N37	A83	10(g) on 10g grn	22	35
N38	A83	12(g) on 15g redsh brn (On No. 339)	22	35
N39	A83	16(g) on 15g redsh brn (On No. 339)	28	45
N40	A83	24g on 25g dl vio	22	35
N41	A83	30(g) on 30g rose red	28	45
N42	A83	50(g) on 50g brt red vio	35	55
N43	A83	60(g) on 55g ultra	7.50	9.25
N44	A83	80(g) on 75g dl grn	7.50	9.25
N45	A83	1z on 1z org	7.50	9.25
N46	A83	2z on 2z car rose	5.00	5.50
N47	A95	3z on 3z gray blk	5.00	5.50

Poland German Occupation stamps can be mounted in Scott's Germany Part II Album.

Similar Surcharge on Semi-Postal Stamps of 1939

N48	SP5	30g on 5g+5g red org	35	55
N49	SP5	40g on 25g+10g dk vio	35	55
N50	SP5	1z on 55g+15g brt ultra	7.25	6.50

Similar Surcharge on Postage Due Stamps of 1939

Perf. 12½x12

N51	D11	50(g) on 20g dk bl grn	65	1.10
N52	D11	50(g) on 25g dk bl grn	13.00	13.00
N53	D11	50(g) on 30g dk bl grn	40.00	35.00
N54	D11	50(g) on 50g dk bl grn	65	90
N55	D11	50(g) on 1z dk bl grn	1.10	90
		Nos. N30-N55 (26)	100.21	104.17

The surcharge on Nos. N30 to N55 is arranged to fit the shape of the stamp and obliterate the original denomination. On some values, "General Gouvernement" appears at the bottom. Counterfeits exist.

St. Florian's Gate, Cracow
OS1

Palace, Warsaw
OS13

Designs: 8g, Watch Tower, Cracow. 10g, Cracow Gate, Lublin. 12g, Courtyard and statue of Copernicus. 20g, Dominican Church, Cracow. 24g, Wawel Castle, Cracow. 30g, Church, Lublin. 40g, Arcade, Cloth Hall, Cracow. 48g, City Hall, Sandomierz. 50g, Court House, Cracow. 60g, Courtyard, Cracow. 80g, St. Mary's Church, Cracow.

1940-41 Unwmk. Photo. *Perf. 14*

N56	OS1	6(g) brown	25	50
N57	OS1	8(g) brn org	25	50
N58	OS1	8(g) bl blk ('41)	25	35
N59	OS1	10(g) emerald	15	22
N60	OS1	12(g) dk grn	2.75	28
N61	OS1	12(g) dp vio ('41)	25	15
N62	OS1	20(g) dk ol brn	8	8
N63	OS1	24(g) hn brn	8	8
N64	OS1	30(g) purple	8	15
N65	OS1	30(g) vio brn ('41)	10	30
N66	OS1	40(g) sl blk	10	15
N67	OS1	48(g) chnt brn ('41)	55	75
N68	OS1	50(g) brt bl	10	15
N69	OS1	60(g) sl grn	12	22
N70	OS1	80(g) dl pur	25	28
N71	OS13	1z rose lake	1.90	1.00
N72	OS13	1z Prus grn ('41)	52	50
		Nos. N56-N72 (17)	7.78	5.66

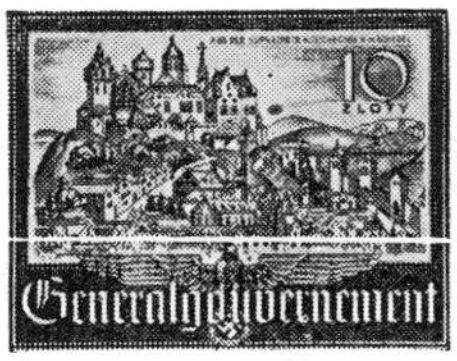

Cracow Castle and City, 15th Century
OS14

1941, Apr. 20 Engr. *Perf. 14½*

N73	OS14	10z red & ol blk	2.00	2.25

Printed in sheets of 8.

Rondel and Florian's Gate, Cracow
OS15

Design: 4z, Tyniec Monastery, Vistula River.

1941 *Perf. 13½x14*

N74	OS15	2z dk ultra	35	45
N75	OS15	4z sl grn	48	60

Adolf Hitler — OS17

1941-43 Unwmk. Photo. Perf. 14

N76	OS17	2(g) gray blk	10	16
N77	OS17	6(g) gldn brn	10	16
N78	OS17	8(g) sl bl	10	16
N79	OS17	10(g) green	10	12
N80	OS17	12(g) purple	10	12
N81	OS17	16(g) org red	35	40
N82	OS17	20(g) blk brn	10	16
N83	OS17	24(g) henna	10	12
N84	OS17	30(g) rose vio	32	16
N85	OS17	32(g) dk bl grn	35	32
N86	OS17	40(g) brt bl	12	16
N87	OS17	48(g) chestnut	40	35
N88	OS17	50(g) vio bl ('43)	12	16
N89	OS17	60(g) dk ol ('43)	12	16
N90	OS17	80(g) dk vio ('43)	12	16
		Nos. N76-N90 (15)	2.60	2.87

A 20g black brown exists with head of Hans Frank substituted for that of Hitler. It was printed and used by Resistance movements.
Nos. N76-N80, N82-N90 exist imperf.

1942-44 Engr. Perf. 12½

N91	OS17	50(g) vio bl	40	48
N92	OS17	60(g) dk ol	40	48
N93	OS17	80(g) dk red vio	40	48
N94	OS17	1(z) sl grn	40	48
a.		Perf. 14 ('44)	52	60
N95	OS17	1.20(z) dk brn	45	55
a.		Perf. 14 ('44)	60	80
N96	OS17	1.60(z) bl vio	50	60
a.		Perf. 14 ('44)	75	1.10
		Nos. N91-N96 (6)	2.55	3.07

Exist imperf.

Rondel and Florian's Gate, Cracow
OS18

Designs: 4z, Tyniec Monastery, Vistula River. 6z, View of Lwow. 10z, Cracow Castle and City, 15th Century.

1943-44 Perf. 13½x14

N100	OS18	2z sl grn	15	15
N101	OS18	4z dk gray vio	28	35
N102	OS18	6z sepia ('44)	48	50
N103	OS18	10z org brn & gray blk	52	60

OCCUPATION SEMI-POSTAL STAMPS

Issued under German Occupation

Types of 1940 Occupation Postage Stamps Surcharged in Red

Unwmk.

1940, Aug. 17 Photo. Perf. 14

NB1	OS1	12(g) + 8(g) ol gray	3.25	4.00
NB2	OS1	24(g) + 16(g) ol gray	3.25	4.00
NB3	OS1	50(g) + 50(g) ol gray	4.00	4.50
NB4	OS1	80(g) + 80(g) ol gray	4.00	4.50

German Peasant Girl in Poland — OSP1

Designs: 24g+26g, Woman wearing scarf. 30g+20g, Similar to type OSP4.

Poland Offices in Danzig stamps can be mounted in Scott's Germany Part II Album.

1940, Oct. 26 Engr. Perf. 14½
Thick Paper

NB5	OSP1	12(g) + 38(g) dk sl grn	2.75	3.25
NB6	OSP1	24(g) + 26(g) cop red	2.75	3.25
NB7	OSP1	30(g) + 20(g) dk pur	3.50	4.50

Issued to commemorate the first anniversary of the General Government.

German Peasant — OSP4

1940, Dec. 1 Perf. 12

NB8	OSP4	12(g) + 8(g) dk grn	1.00	1.10
NB9	OSP4	24(g) + 16(g) rose red	1.65	1.90
NB10	OSP4	30(g) + 30(g) vio brn	2.00	2.50
NB11	OSP4	50(g) + 50(g) ultra	2.75	3.00

The surtax was for war relief.

Adolf Hitler — OSP5

Unwmk.
1942, Apr. 20 Engr. Perf. 11
Thick Cream Paper

NB12	OSP5	30(g) + 1z brn car	25	35
NB13	OSP5	50(g) + 1z dk ultra	25	35
NB14	OSP5	1.20(z) + 1z brn	25	35

To commemorate Hitler's 53rd birthday.
Printed in sheets of 25, with marginal inscription: 20. April 1942.

Ancient Lublin — OSP6

Designs: 24g+6g, 1z+1z, Modern Lublin.

1942, Aug. 15 Photo. Perf. 12½

NB15	OSP6	12(g) + 8(g) rose vio	9	12
NB16	OSP6	24(g) + 6(g) hn	9	12
NB17	OSP6	50(g) + 50(g) dp bl	16	22
NB18	OSP6	1z + 1z dp grn	35	50

600th anniversary of Lublin.

Veit Stoss — OSP8

Adolf Hitler — OSP13

Designs: 24g+26g, Hans Durer. 30g+30g, Johann Schuch. 50g+50g, Joseph Elsner. 1z+1z, Nicolaus Copernicus.

1942, Nov. 20 Engr. Perf. 13½x14

NB19	OSP8	12(g) + 18g dl pur	12	20
NB20	OSP8	24(g) + 26g dl hn	12	20
NB21	OSP8	30(g) + 30g dl rose vio	12	20
NB22	OSP8	50(g) + 50g dl bl vio	15	25
NB23	OSP8	1(z) + 1z dl myr grn	35	45
		Nos. NB19-NB23 (5)	86	1.30

1943, Apr. 20

NB24	OSP13	12(g) + 1z pur	10	18
NB25	OSP13	24(g) + 1z rose car	10	18
NB26	OSP13	84(g) + 1z myr grn	35	35

To commemorate Hitler's 54th birthday.

Type of 1942 Overprinted in Black

24. MAI 1543
24. MAI 1943

1943, May 24

NB27	OSP8	1(z) + 1z rose lake	80	1.10

To commemorate the 400th anniversary of the death of the astronomer, Nicolaus Copernicus (1473-1543).
Printed in sheets of 10, with marginal inscription in rose lake.

Cracow Gate, Lublin
OSP14

Adolf Hitler
OSP19

Designs: 24g+76g, Cloth Hall, Cracow. 30g+70g, New Government Building, Radom. 50g+1z, Bruhl Palace, Warsaw. 1z+2z, Town Hall, Lwow.
The center of the designs is embossed with the emblem of the National Socialist Party.

1943 Photogravure, Embossed

NB28	OSP14	12(g) + 38(g) dk grn	12	14
NB29	OSP14	24(g) + 76(g) red	12	14
NB30	OSP14	30(g) + 70(g) rose vio	12	14
NB31	OSP14	50(g) + 1z brt bl	12	14
NB32	OSP14	1z + 2z bl blk	22	35
		Nos. NB28-NB32 (5)	70	91

3rd anniversary of the National Socialist Party in Poland.

1944, Apr. 20 Photo. Perf. 14x13½

NB33	OSP19	12(g) + 1z grn	10	18
NB34	OSP19	24(g) + 1z brn red	10	18
NB35	OSP19	84(g) + 1z dk vio	15	18

To commemorate Hitler's 55th birthday.
Printed in sheets of 25 with decorative border.

Conrad Celtis — OSP20

Designs: 24g+26g, Andreas Schluter. 30g+30g, Hans Boner. 50g+50g, Augustus II. 1z+1z, Georg Gottlieb Pusch.

1944, July 15 Engr. Perf. 13½x14

NB36	OSP20	12(g) + 18g dk grn	8	8
NB37	OSP20	24(g) + 26g dk red	8	8
NB38	OSP20	30(g) + 30g rose vio	8	8
NB39	OSP20	50(g) + 50g ultra	15	32
NB40	OSP20	1(z) + 1z dl red brn	15	32
		Nos. NB36-NB40 (5)	54	88

Cracow Castle
OSP25

1944, Oct. 26 Perf. 14½

NB41	OSP25	10z + 10z red & blk	9.00	11.50
a.		Imperf.	10.00	
b.		10z + 10z car & grnsh blk	16.00	18.00

To commemorate the fifth anniversary of the General Government, October 26, 1944.

Printed in sheets of 8, with marginal inscription in black.

OCCUPATION RURAL DELIVERY STAMPS

Issued under German Occupation

OSD1

Perf. 13½
1940, Dec. 1 Photo. Unwmk.

NL1	OSD1	10g red org	50	*60*
NL2	OSD1	20g red org	50	*90*
NL3	OSD1	30g red org	50	*90*
NL4	OSD1	50g red org	1.25	*1.90*

OCCUPATION OFFICIAL STAMPS

Issued under German Occupation

Eagle and Swastika
OOS1

Perf. 12, 13½x14
1940, Apr. Photo. Unwmk.
Size: 31x23 mm.

NO1	OOS1	6g lt brn	1.10	1.50
NO2	OOS1	8g gray	1.10	1.50
NO3	OOS1	10g green	1.10	1.50
NO4	OOS1	12g dk grn	1.25	1.90
NO5	OOS1	20g dk brn	1.25	3.25
NO6	OOS1	24g hn brn	20.00	50
NO7	OOS1	30g rose lake	1.75	2.75
NO8	OOS1	40g dl vio	1.75	4.50
NO9	OOS1	48g dl ol	7.25	4.75
NO10	OOS1	50g ryl bl	1.50	2.75
NO11	OOS1	60g dk ol grn	1.10	1.90
NO12	OOS1	80g rose vio	1.10	1.90

Size: 35x26 mm.

NO13	OOS1	1z gray blk & brn vio	3.50	4.75
NO14	OOS1	3z gray blk & chnt	3.50	4.50
NO15	OOS1	5z gray blk & org brn	4.75	6.25
		Nos. NO1-NO15 (15)	52.00	44.20

1940 Perf. 12
Size: 21¼x16¼ mm.

NO16	OOS1	6g brown	65	1.10
NO17	OOS1	8g slate	1.10	1.75
NO18	OOS1	10g dp grn	1.75	2.00
NO19	OOS1	12g sl grn	1.75	2.00
NO20	OOS1	20g blk brn	90	1.10
NO21	OOS1	24g cop brn	65	1.10
NO22	OOS1	30g rose lake	1.10	1.75
NO23	OOS1	40g dl pur	1.75	2.00
NO24	OOS1	50g ryl bl	1.75	2.00
		Nos. NO16-NO24 (9)	11.40	14.80

Nazi Emblem and Cracow Castle — OOS2

1943 Photo. Perf. 14

NO25	OOS2	6(g) brown	10	15
NO26	OOS2	8(g) sl bl	10	15
NO27	OOS2	10(g) green	10	15
NO28	OOS2	12(g) dk vio	35	24
NO29	OOS2	16(g) red org	10	15
NO30	OOS2	20(g) dk brn	18	15
NO31	OOS2	24(g) dk red	35	15
NO32	OOS2	30(g) rose vio	18	15
NO33	OOS2	40(g) blue	18	15
NO34	OOS2	60(g) ol grn	18	15
NO35	OOS2	80(g) dl cl	28	15
NO36	OOS2	100(g) sl blk	35	60
		Nos. NO25-NO36 (12)	2.45	2.34

POLISH OFFICES ABROAD

OFFICES IN DANZIG

Poland Nos. 215-225 Overprinted **PORT GDAŃSK**

1925, Jan. 5 Unwmk. *Perf. 11½x12*

1K1	A36	1g org brn	45	95
1K2	A36	2g dk brn	60	2.50
1K3	A36	3g orange	60	95
1K4	A36	5g ol grn	15.00	6.00
1K5	A36	10g bl grn	5.00	1.90
1K6	A36	15g red	30.00	4.50
1K7	A36	20g blue	1.75	95
1K8	A36	25g red brn	1.75	95
1K9	A36	30g dp vio	2.00	95
1K10	A36	40g indigo	2.00	95
1K11	A36	50g magenta	5.50	1.25
		Nos. 1K1-1K11 (11)	64.65	21.85

Same Overprint on Poland Nos. 230-231

1926 *Perf. 11½, 12*

1K11A	A39	5g yel grn	52.50	37.50
1K12	A40	10g violet	12.50	15.00

No. 232 Overprinted **PORT GDAŃSK**

1926-27

1K13	A41	15g rose red	42.50	40.00

Same Overprint on Redrawn Stamps of 1926-27

Perf. 13

1K14	A39	5g yel grn	1.65	1.75
1K15	A40	10g violet	1.65	1.75
1K16	A41	15g rose red	3.25	3.75
1K17	A43	20g dl red	2.75	2.25
		Nos. 1K13-1K17 (5)	51.80	49.50

Same Overprint on Poland Nos. 250, 255

1928-30 *Perf. 12½*

1K18	A44	25g yel brn	4.00	1.50

Laid Paper

Perf. 11½x12, 12½x11½

1K19	A50	1z blk, *cr* ('30)	24.00	24.00

Poland Nos. 258-260 Overprinted **PORT GDAŃSK**

1929-30 *Perf. 12x12½*

1K20	A53	5g dk vio	1.65	2.00
1K21	A53	10g grn ('30)	1.65	2.00
1K22	A53	25g red brn	2.75	2.00

Same Overprint on Poland No. 257

1931, Jan. 5 *Perf. 12½*

1K23	A52	15g ultra	2.75	4.00

Poland No. 255 Overprinted in Dark Blue **PORT GDAŃSK**

1933, July 1 *Perf. 11½*

Laid Paper

1K24	A50	1z blk, *cream*	82.50	105.00

Counterfeits exist of No. 1K24.

Poland Nos. 268-270 Overprinted in Black **PORT GDAŃSK**

1934-36 Wmk. 234 *Perf. 12 x 12½*

1K25	A58	5g dl vio	3.25	3.75
1K26	A58	10g grn ('36)	35.00	*72.50*
1K27	A58	15g red brn	3.25	3.75

Poland Nos. 294, 296, 298 Overprinted in Black in one or two lines **PORT GDAŃSK**

1935-36 Unwmk. *Perf. 12½ x 13*

1K28	A65	5g vio bl	3.50	3.00
1K29	A65	15g Prus grn	3.50	4.75
1K30	A65	25g myr grn	3.50	2.00

Same Overprint in Black on Poland Nos. 308, 310

1937, June 5

1K31	A65	5g vio bl	1.10	1.65
1K32	A65	15g red brn	1.10	1.65

Counterfeit overprints are known on Nos. 1K1-1K32.

Polish Merchants Selling Wheat in Danzig, 16th Century — A2

1938, Nov. 11 Engr. *Perf. 12½*

1K33	A2	5g red org	60	95
1K34	A2	15g red brn	60	95
1K35	A2	25g dl vio	60	1.65
1K36	A2	55g brt ultra	1.40	3.00

OFFICES IN THE TURKISH EMPIRE

Stamps of Poland 1919, Overprinted in Carmine

LEVANT

1919, May Unwmk. *Perf. 11½*

Wove Paper

2K1	A10	3f bis brn	27.50	65.00
2K2	A10	5f green	27.50	65.00
2K3	A10	10f red vio	27.50	65.00
2K4	A10	15f red	27.50	65.00
2K5	A11	20f dp bl	27.50	65.00
2K6	A11	25f ol grn	27.50	65.00
2K7	A11	50f bl grn	27.50	65.00

Overprinted **L E V A N T**

2K8	A12	1m violet	27.50	65.00
2K9	A12	1.50m dp grn	27.50	65.00
2K10	A12	2m dk brn	27.50	65.00
2K11	A13	2.50m org brn	27.50	65.00
2K12	A14	5m red vio	27.50	65.00
		Nos. 2K1-2K12 (12)	330.00	

Counterfeit cancellations are plentiful.

Reprints are lighter, shiny red. Value set $22.50

Polish stamps with "P.P.C." overprint (Poste Polonaise Constantinople) were used on consular mail for a time.

Stamps of 1919-20 Overprinted in Red:

a

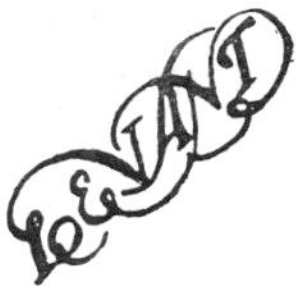
b

1921, May 25 Thin Laid Paper

2K13	A10(a)	1m red	1.25
2K14	A10(a)	2m gray grn	1.65
2K15	A10(a)	3m lt bl	1.50
2K16	A10(a)	4m rose red	2.00
2K17	A14(b)	6m dp rose	2.50
2K18	A14(b)	10m brn red	5.25
2K19	A14(b)	20m gray grn	7.75
		Nos. 2K13-2K19 (7)	21.90

Nos. 2K13-2K19 were not issued.
Counterfeits exist of Nos. 2K1-2K19.

EXILE GOVERNMENT IN GREAT BRITAIN

These stamps were issued by the Polish government in exile for letters posted from Polish merchant ships and warships.

United States Embassy Ruins, Warsaw — A1

Polish Ministry of Finance Ruins, Warsaw — A2

Destruction of Mickiewicz Monument, Cracow — A3

Polish Submarine "Orzel" — A8

Ruins of Warsaw A4

Polish Machine Gunners A5

Armored Tank A6

Polish Planes in Great Britain A7

Perf. 12½, 11½x12

1941, Dec. 15 Engr. Unwmk.

3K1	A1	5g rose vio	30	52
3K2	A2	10g dk bl grn	60	70
3K3	A3	25g black	95	1.25
3K4	A4	55g dk bl	1.25	1.50
3K5	A5	75g ol grn	3.00	3.75
3K6	A6	80g dk car rose	3.00	3.75
3K7	A7	1z slate bl	3.00	3.75
3K8	A8	1.50z cop brn	3.00	4.25
		Nos. 3K1-3K8 (8)	15.10	19.47

These stamps were used for correspondence carried on Polish ships and, on certain days, in Polish Military camps in Great Britain.

Polish Air Force in Battle of the Atlantic — A9

Polish Army in France, 1939-40 — A11

Polish Merchant Navy A10

Polish Army in Narvik, Norway, 1940 — A12

The Homeland Fights On — A15

Polish Army in Libya, 1941-42 A13

General Sikorsky and Polish Soldiers in the Middle East, 1943 A14

The Secret Press in Poland A16

1943, Nov. 1

3K9	A9	5g rose lake	30	65
3K10	A10	10g dk bl grn	60	1.00
3K11	A11	25g dk vio	60	1.00
3K12	A12	55g sapphire	90	1.65
3K13	A13	75g brn car	1.50	2.25
3K14	A14	80g rose car	2.00	2.75
3K15	A15	1z ol blk	2.00	2.75
3K16	A16	1.50z black	2.75	3.25
		Nos. 3K9-3K16 (8)	10.65	15.30

Nos. 3K5 to 3K8 Surcharged in Blue

MONTE CASSINO
18. V. 1944

Gr55

Perf. 12½, 11½x12

1944, June 27 Unwmk.

3K17	A5	45g on 75g ol grn	6.00	6.00
3K18	A6	55g on 80g dk car rose	6.00	6.00
3K19	A7	80g on 1z sl bl	6.00	6.00
3K20	A8	1.20z on 1.50z cop brn	6.00	6.00

Capture of Monte Cassino by the Poles, May 18, 1944.

EXILE GOVERNMENT IN GREAT BRITAIN SEMI-POSTAL STAMP

Heroic Defenders of Warsaw — SP1

Perf. 11½

1945, Feb. 3 Unwmk. Engr.

3KB1	SP1	1z + 2z sl grn	3.75	5.00

Warsaw uprising, Aug. 1-Oct. 3, 1944.

PONTA DELGADA

LOCATION — An administrative district of the Azores comprising the islands of Sao Miguel and Santa Maria.
GOVT. — A district of Portugal
AREA — 342 sq. mi.
POP. — 124,000 (approx.)
CAPITAL — Ponta Delgada

1000 Reis = 1 Milreis

King Carlos
A1 A2

Perf. 11½, 12½, 13½

1892-93 Typo. Unwmk.

1	A1	5r yellow	50	50
a.		Diagonal half used as 2½r on piece		2.50
b.		Perf. 11½	5.00	4.25
2	A1	10r redsh vio	1.40	85
3	A1	15r chocolate	1.65	1.25
4	A1	20r lavender	2.00	1.25
a.		Perf. 13½	3.75	2.25
5	A1	25r dp grn	1.50	50
6	A1	50r ultra	3.50	1.25
7	A1	75r carmine	7.75	6.00
8	A1	80r yel grn	10.50	8.50
9	A1	100r brn, *yel*	6.25	4.50
10	A1	150r car, *rose*	35.00	30.00
11	A1	200r dk bl, *bl*	30.00	27.50
12	A1	300r dk bl, *sal*	42.50	35.00

The reprints are on paper slightly thinner that that of the originals, and unsurfaced. They have white gum and clean-cut perf. 13½ or 11½. Lowest valued, Nos. 1-9, $4 each, Nos. 10-12, $20 each.

1897-1905 *Perf. 11½*

Name and Value in Black except Nos. 25 and 34.

13	A2	2½r gray	22	16
14	A2	5r orange	25	16
15	A2	10r lt grn	25	16
16	A2	15r brown	5.00	3.50
17	A2	15r gray grn ('99)	85	60
18	A2	20r dl vio	95	70
19	A2	25r sea grn	1.65	60
20	A2	25r rose red ('99)	60	22
21	A2	50r blue	1.50	1.10
22	A2	50r ultra ('05)	12.50	10.50
23	A2	65r sl bl ('98)	42	38
a.		Imperf.		
24	A2	75r rose	3.50	2.25
25	A2	75r brn & car, *yel* ('05)	10.50	7.75
26	A2	80r violet	1.65	85
27	A2	100r dk bl, *bl*	1.65	1.25
28	A2	115r org brn, *rose* ('98)	1.50	1.10
29	A2	130r gray brn, *buff* ('98)	1.50	1.10
30	A2	150r lt brn, *buff*	1.50	1.25
31	A2	180r sl, *pnksh* ('98)	1.50	1.10
32	A2	200r red vio, *pnksh*	6.00	4.25
33	A2	300r bl, *rose*	6.00	4.25
a.		Perf. 12½	35.00	27.50
34	A2	500r blk & red, *bl*	12.00	8.50
a.		Perf. 12½	16.00	10.50
		Nos. 13-34 (22)	71.49	51.73

The stamps of Ponta Delgada were superseded by those of the Azores, which in 1931 were replaced by those of Portugal.

PORTUGAL

LOCATION — Southern Europe, on the western coast of the Iberian Peninsula.
GOVT. — Republic
AREA — 35,516 sq. mi.
POP. — 9,930,000 (est. 1983)
CAPITAL — Lisbon

Figures for area and population include the Azores and Madeira, which are integral parts of the republic. The republic was established in 1910. See Azores, Funchal, Madeira.

1000 Reis = 1 Milreis
10 Reis = 1 Centimo
100 Centavos = 1 Escudo (1912)

Catalogue values for unused stamps in this country are for Never Hinged items, beginning with Scott 662 in the regular postage section, Scott C11 in the airpost section, Scott J65 in the postage due section, and Scott O2 in the officials section.

Values of early Portugal stamps vary according to condition. Quotations for Nos. 1-51 are for fine copies. Very fine to superb specimens sell at much higher prices, and inferior or poor copies sell at reduced prices, depending on the condition of the individual specimen.

Queen Maria II
A1 A2

A3 A4

Typo. & Embossed

1853 Unwmk. *Imperf.*

1	A1	5r org brn	1,350.	100.00
2	A2	25r blue	500.00	5.00
3	A3	50r dp yel grn	1,800.	100.00
a		50r bl grn	2,200.	300.00
4	A4	100r lilac	6,000.	500.00

The stamps of the 1853 issue were reprinted in 1864, 1885, 1905 and 1953. Many stamps of subsequent issues were reprinted in 1885 and 1905. The reprints of 1864 are on thin white paper with white gum. The originals have brownish gum which often stains the paper. The reprints of 1885 are on a stout, very white paper. They are usually ungummed, but occasionally have a white gum with yellowish spots. The reprints of 1905 are on creamy white paper of ordinary quality with shiny white gum.

When perforated the reprints of 1885 have a rather rough perforation 13½with small holes; those of 1905 have a clean-cut perforation 13½ with large holes making sharp pointed teeth.

The colors of the reprints usually differ from those of the originals, but actual comparison is necessary.

The reprints are often from new dies which differ slightly from those used for the originals.

5 reis: There is a defect in the neck which makes the Adam's apple appear very large in the first reprint. The later ones can be distinguished by the paper and the shades and by the absence of the pendant curl.

25 reis: The burelage of the ground work in the original is sharp and clear, while in the 1864 reprints it is blurred in several places; the upper and lower right hand corners are very thick and blurred. The central oval is less than ½ mm. from the frame at the sides in the originals and fully ¾ mm. in the 1885 and 1905 reprints.

50 reis: In the reprints of 1864 and 1885 there is a small break in the upper right hand diagonal line of the frame, and the initials of the engraver (F. B. F.), which in the originals are plainly discernible in the lower part of the bust, do not show. The reprints of 1905 have not the break in the frame and the initials are distinct.

100 reis: The small vertical lines at top and bottom at each side of the frame are heavier in the reprints of 1864 than in the originals. The reprints of 1885 and 1905 can be distinguished only by the paper, gum and shades.

Reprints of 1953 have thick paper, no gum and dates "1853/1953" on back.

Values of lowest-cost reprints (1885) of Nos. 1-3, $50 each; of No. 4, $100.

King Pedro V
A5 A6

A7 A8

1855 With Straight Hair

TWENTY-FIVE REIS:
Type I. Pearls mostly touch each other and oval outer line.
Type II. Pearls are separate from each other and oval outer line.

5	A5	5r red brn	1,800.	300.00
6	A6	25r bl, type II	425.00	7.00
a		25r bl, type I	600.00	10.00
7	A7	50r green	200.00	20.00
8	A8	100r lilac	400.00	25.00

Several types of No. 5 exist, differing in number of pearls encircling head (74 to 89) and other details.

All values were reprinted in 1885 and 1905. Value for lowest-cost, $15 each.

1856 With Curled Hair

TWENTY-FIVE REIS:
Type I. The network is fine (single lines).
Type II. The network is coarse (double lines).

9	A5	5r brn (shades)	140.00	12.00
10	A6	25r bl, type II	140.00	5.00
a		25r bl, type I	*1,650.*	13.00

1858

11	A6	25r rose, type II	100.00	1.25

The 5r dark brown, formerly listed and sold at about $1, is now believed by the best authorities to be a reprint made before 1866. It is printed on thin yellowish white paper with yellowish white gum and is known only unused. The same remarks will apply to a 25r blue which is common unused but not known used. It is printed from a die which was not used for the issued stamps but the differences are slight and can only be told by expert comparison.

Nos. 9 and 10, also 10a in rose, were reprinted in 1885 and Nos. 9, 10, 10a and 11 in 1905. Value of lowest-cost reprints, $15 each.

King Luiz
A9 A10

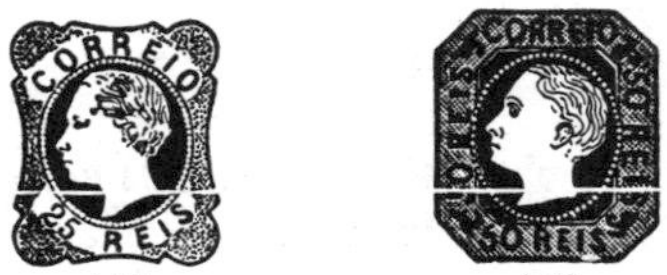

A11 A12

A13

1862-64

FIVE REIS.
Type I. The distance between "5" and "reis" is 3 mm.
Type II. The distance between "5" and "reis" is 2 mm.

12	A9	5r brn, type I	30.00	2.75
a		5r brn, type II	55.00	8.25
13	A10	10r orange	52.50	18.00
14	A11	25r rose	37.50	1.65
15	A12	50r yel grn	265.00	32.50
16	A13	100r lil ('64)	315.00	32.50

All values were reprinted in 1885 and all except the 25r in 1905. Value of lowest-cost reprints, $10 each.

King Luiz
A14 A15

1866-67 *Imperf.*

17	A14	5r black	45.00	3.75
18	A14	10r yellow	82.50	37.50
19	A14	20r bister	62.50	27.50
20	A14	25r rose ('67)	90.00	2.00
21	A14	50r green	110.00	27.50
22	A14	80r orange	110.00	30.00
23	A14	100r dk lil ('67)	120.00	37.50
24	A14	120r blue	130.00	27.50

Some values with unofficial percéen croix (diamond) perforation were used in Madeira.

All values were reprinted in 1885 and 1905. Value $10 each.

Typographed & Embossed

1867-70 *Perf. 12½*

25	A14	5r black	57.50	16.00
26	A14	10r yellow	110.00	42.50
27	A14	20r bis ('69)	135.00	42.50
28	A14	25r rose	27.50	1.90
29	A14	50r grn ('68)	135.00	42.50
30	A14	80r org ('69)	160.00	47.50
31	A14	100r lil ('69)	135.00	47.50
32	A14	120r blue	145.00	27.50
33	A14	240r pale vio ('70)	390.00	195.00

Two types each of 5r and 100r differ in the position of the "5" at upper right and the "100" at lower right in relation to the end of the label.

Nos. 25-33 were reprinted in 1885 and 1905. Some of the 1885 reprints were perforated 12½ as well as 13½. Value of the lowest-cost reprints, $10 each.

1870-84 *Perf. 12½, 13½*

34	A15	5r black	21.00	21.00
a		Imperf.	*350.00*	
b		Perf. 11		150.00
c		Perf. 14	65.00	24.00
35	A15	10r yel ('71)	27.50	8.50
a		Imperf.	*350.00*	
b		Perf. 11		150.00
c		Perf. 14	120.00	65.00
36	A15	10r bl grn ('79)	95.00	47.50
37	A15	10r yel grn ('80)	40.00	7.25
38	A15	15r lil brn ('75)	32.50	6.00
39	A15	20r bister	24.00	3.50
a		Imperf.	*350.00*	
b		Perf. 11		150.00
40	A15	20r rose ('84)	90.00	12.00
41	A15	25r rose	9.50	75
a		Imperf.	350.00	
b		Perf. 11		150.00
c		Perf. 14	120.00	3.50
42	A15	50r pale grn	47.50	3.50
b		Perf. 11		175.00
43	A15	50r bl ('79)	95.00	9.00
44	A15	80r orange	35.00	1.75
a		Perf. 14	165.00	110.00
b		Perf. 11		175.00
45	A15	100r pale lil ('71)	22.50	1.50
a		Perf. 14	210.00	110.00
46	A15	120r bl, perf. 12½ ('71)	115.00	27.50
a		Perf. 13½		
47	A15	150r pale bl ('76)	135.00	42.50
b		Perf. 13½	275.00	70.00
48	A15	150r yel ('80)	47.50	3.00
49	A15	240r pale vio ('73)	600.00	350.00
b		Perf. 11		
50	A15	300r dl vio ('76)	47.50	9.50
51	A15	1000r blk ('84)	90.00	20.00

Two types each of 15r, 20r and 80r differ in the distance between the figures of value.

All values of the issues of 1870-84 were reprinted in 1885 and 1905. Value of the lowest-cost reprints, $10 each.

King Luiz
A16 A17

A18 A19

1880-81 Typo. *Perf. 12½, 13½*

52	A16	5r black	9.00	90
53	A17	25r bluish gray	100.00	6.00
54	A18	25r gray	9.00	85
55	A18	25r brn vio ('81)	9.00	85
56	A19	50r bl ('81)	100.00	4.00

All values were reprinted in 1885 and 1905. Value of the lowest-cost reprints, $5 each.

A20 A21

King Luiz
A22 A23

A24 A24a

1882-87 *Perf. 11½, 12½, 13½.*

57	A20	2r blk ('84)	4.00	3.25
58	A21	5r blk ('83)	4.25	45
59	A22	10r grn ('84)	10.50	85
60	A23	25r brown	7.25	55
61	A24	50r blue	11.00	45
62	A24a	500r blk ('84)	175.00	100.00
63	A24a	500r vio p. 12½ ('87)	100.00	15.00
a		Perf. 13½	150.00	50.00

The stamps of the 1882-87 issues were reprinted in 1885, 1893 and 1905. Value of the lowest-cost reprints, $5 each.

A25 A26

1887

64	A25	20r rose	18.00	4.00
65	A26	25r violet	10.50	35
66	A26	25r lil rose	10.50	35

Nos. 64-66 were reprinted in 1905. Value $5 each.

King Carlos — A27

1892-93 *Perf. 11½, 12½, 13½*

67	A27	5r orange	4.00	50
68	A27	10r redsh vio	9.25	50
69	A27	15r chocolate	4.75	1.40
70	A27	20r lavender	8.00	1.90
71	A27	25r dk grn	9.25	50
72	A27	50r blue	12.00	1.25
73	A27	75r car ('93)	25.00	1.65
a		Perf. 11½	80.00	3.50
74	A27	80r yel grn	27.50	12.50
75	A27	100r brn, *buff* ('93)	21.00	1.10
a		Perf. 11½	100.00	3.50
76	A27	150r car, *rose* ('93)	47.50	11.00
77	A27	200r dk bl, *bl* ('93)	47.50	12.50
78	A27	300r dk bl, *sal* ('93)	52.50	14.00

Nos. 76-78 were reprinted in 1900 (perf. 11½), and all values in 1905 (perf. 13½). Values of the lowest-cost reprints of Nos. 67-75, $6 each; of Nos. 76-78, $12 each.

Stamps and Types of Previous Issues Overprinted in Black or Red:

PROVISORIO
a

PROVISORIO
b

PROVISORIO
c

1892

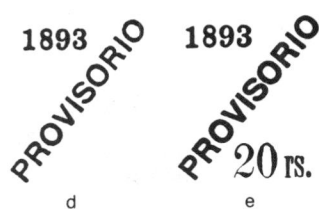

79	A21 (a)	5r gray blk	7.00	2.00
a		Double ovpt.	240.00	90.00
80	A22 (b)	10r green	7.00	2.75
a		Invtd. ovpt.		
b		Double ovpt.	240.00	100.00

1892-93

81	A21 (c)	5r gray blk (R)	4.75	3.00
82	A22 (c)	10r grn (R)	5.75	3.25
a		Inverted overprint	60.00	60.00
83	A25 (c)	20r rose	10.50	4.75
84	A26 (c)	25r rose lil	5.25	2.00
85	A24 (c)	50r bl (R) ('93)	25.00	20.00

1893

86	A15 (c)	15r bis brn (R)	4.00	3.00
87	A15 (c)	80r yellow	35.00	30.00

Nos. 86-87 are found in two types each. See note below No. 51.

Some of Nos. 79-87 were reprinted in 1900 and all values in 1905. Value of lowest-cost reprint, $10.

Stamps and Types of Previous Issues Overprinted or Surcharged in Black or Red:

1893
PROVISORIO
d

1893
PROVISORIO
20 rs.
e

1893 *Perf. 11½, 12½.*

88	A21 (d)	5r gray blk (R)	7.50	5.25
89	A22 (d)	10r grn (R)	9.00	7.00
a		"1938"	70.00	62.50
b		"1863"	70.00	62.50
90	A25 (d)	20r rose	20.00	10.00
a		Invtd. ovpt.		
91	A26 (e)	20r on 25r lil rose	16.00	14.00
92	A26 (d)	25r lil rose	45.00	30.00
a		Invtd. ovpt.	100.00	100.00
93	A24 (d)	50r bl (R)	40.00	25.00

Perf. 12½

94	A15 (e)	50r on 80r yel	50.00	40.00
95	A15 (e)	75r on 80r yel	30.00	25.00
96	A15 (d)	80r yellow	35.00	27.50

Nos. 94-96 are found in two types each. See note below No. 51.

Some of Nos. 88-96 were reprinted in 1900 and all values in 1905. Value of lowest-cost reprint, $10 each.

Prince Henry the Navigator Issue.

Prince Henry on his Ship — A46

Prince Henry Directing Fleet Maneuvers A47

Symbolic of Prince Henry's Studies — A48

1894 Litho. *Perf. 14*

97	A46	5r orange	2.00	60
98	A46	10r magenta	2.50	60
99	A46	15r red brn	3.75	1.40
100	A46	20r dl vio	4.75	2.00
101	A47	25r gray grn	3.75	80
102	A47	50r blue	8.00	2.00
103	A47	75r car rose	15.00	4.75
104	A47	80r yel grn	18.00	6.50
105	A47	100r lt brn, *pale buff*	13.00	4.75
		Engr.		
106	A48	150r lt car, *pale rose*	35.00	8.00
107	A48	300r dk bl, *sal buff*	45.00	12.00
108	A48	500r dp vio, *pale lil*	100.00	30.00
109	A48	1000r gray blk, *grysh*	125.00	37.50
		Nos. 97-109 (13)	375.75	110.90

Commemorating the fifth centenary of the birth of Prince Henry the Navigator.

King Carlos — A49

1895-1905 Typo. *Perf. 11½*
Value in Black or Red (#122, 131, 131a)

110	A49	2½r gray	15	8
a		Imperf.		
111	A49	5r orange	15	8
112	A49	10r lt grn	20	9
113	A49	15r brown	32.50	1.10
114	A49	15r gray grn ('99)	16.00	95
115	A49	20r gray vio	22	18
116	A49	25r sea grn	25.00	16
117	A49	25r car rose ('99)	15	9
118	A49	50r blue	32.50	25
119	A49	50r ultra ('05)	20	14
120	A49	65r sl bl ('98)	20	14
121	A49	75r rose	35.00	1.50
122	A49	75r brn, *yel* ('05)	45	38
123	A49	80r violet	75	55
124	A49	100r dk bl, *bl*	32	18
125	A49	115r org brn, *pink*('98)	1.65	1.25
126	A49	130r gray brn, *straw*('98)	1.10	55
127	A49	150r lt brn, *straw*	37.50	7.50
128	A49	180r sl, *pnksh*('98)	4.75	4.50
129	A49	200r red lil, *pnksh*	1.10	40
130	A49	300r bl, *rose*	1.25	40
131	A49	500r blk, *bl* ('96)	2.75	1.90
a		Perf. 12½	47.50	14.00
		Nos. 110-131 (22)	193.89	22.37

Several values of the above type exist without figures of value, also with figures inverted or otherwise misplaced but they were not regularly issued.

St. Anthony and his Vision
A50

St. Anthony Ascends to Heaven
A52

St. Anthony Preaching to Fishes
A51

St. Anthony, from Portrait
A53

Perf. 11½, 12½ and Compound
1895 Typo.

132	A50	2½r black	3.75	75
		Litho.		
133	A51	5r brn org	4.25	95
134	A51	10r red lil	7.75	3.50
135	A51	15r chocolate	10.50	4.00
136	A51	20r gray vio	10.50	4.00
137	A51	25r grn & vio	7.75	75
138	A52	50r bl & brn	19.00	7.50
139	A52	75r rose & brn	30.00	18.00
140	A52	80r lt grn & brn	35.00	22.50
141	A52	100r choc & blk	32.50	13.00
142	A53	150r car & bis	85.00	47.50
143	A53	200r bl & bis	75.00	45.00
144	A53	300r sl & bis	92.50	55.00
145	A53	500r vio brn & grn	200.00	130.00
146	A53	1000r vio & grn	300.00	165.00
		Nos. 132-146 (15)	913.50	517.45

Commemorating the seventh centenary of the birth of Saint Anthony of Padua. Stamps have eulogy in Latin printed on the back.

Vasco da Gama Issue
Common Design Types

1898 Engr. *Perf. 12½ to 16.*

147	CD20	2½r bl grn	50	20
148	CD21	5r red	50	20
149	CD22	10r red vio	3.00	65
150	CD23	25r yel grn	2.25	22
151	CD24	50r dk bl	3.75	1.65
152	CD25	75r vio brn	14.00	4.75
153	CD26	100r bis brn	12.00	4.00
154	CD27	150r bister	20.00	12.00
		Nos. 147-154 (8)	56.00	23.67

King Manuel II
A62 A63

1910 Typo. *Perf. 14½x15.*

156	A62	2½r violet	20	9
157	A62	5r black	20	9
158	A62	10r gray grn	28	9
159	A62	15r lil brn	1.25	80
160	A62	20r carmine	60	45
161	A62	25r vio brn	28	9
162	A62	50r dk bl	65	30
163	A62	75r bis brn	3.75	2.25
164	A62	80r slate	1.25	1.10
165	A62	100r brn, *lt grn*	5.25	1.65
166	A62	200r dk grn, *sal*	2.75	1.90
167	A62	300r blk, *azure*	3.50	2.75
168	A63	500r ol grn & vio brn	6.75	5.75
169	A63	1000r dk bl & blk	16.00	14.00
		Nos. 156-169 (14)	42.71	31.31

Preceding Issue Overprinted in Carmine or Green

REPUBLICA

1910

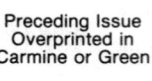

170	A62	2½r violet	25	8
171	A62	5r black	24	8
172	A62	10r gray grn	1.40	38
173	A62	15r lil brn	35	30
174	A62	20r car (G)	1.75	90
175	A62	25r vio brn	42	15
176	A62	50r dk bl	3.25	1.00
177	A62	75r bis brn	4.50	2.00
178	A62	80r slate	1.40	1.00
179	A62	100r brn, *lt grn*	75	35
180	A62	200r dk grn, *sal*	1.25	90
181	A62	300r blk, *azure*	1.90	1.75
182	A63	500r ol grn & vio brn	4.50	4.25
183	A63	1000r dk bl & blk	9.75	8.50
		Nos. 170-183 (14)	31.71	21.64

The numerous inverted and double overprints on this issue were unofficially and fraudulently made.

The 50r with blue overprint is a fraud.

Vasco da Gama Issue Overprinted or Surcharged:

REPUBLICA
a

REPUBLICA REPUBLICA

REIS 15 REIS
b

1$000
c

1911 *Perf. 12½ to 16*

185	CD20(a)	2½r bl grn	20	12
a		Inverted overprint	8.00	8.00
186	CD21(b)	15r on 5r red	28	15
a		Inverted surcharge	7.25	7.25
187	CD23(a)	25r yel grn	28	15
188	CD24(a)	50r dk bl	1.50	55
a		Inverted overprint	10.00	10.00
189	CD25(a)	75r vio brn	18.00	13.00
190	CD27(b)	80r on 150r bis	2.50	1.65
191	CD26(a)	100r bis brn	2.50	1.00
a		Inverted overprint	10.00	10.00
192	CD22(c)	1000r on 10r red vio	20.00	14.00
		Nos. 185-192 (8)	45.26	30.62

Common Design Types pictured in section at front of book.

Postage Due Stamps of 1898 Overprinted or Surcharged for Regular Postage:

REPUBLICA

REPUBLICA
d

Rs 300 Rs
e

1911 *Perf. 12*

193	D1(d)	5r black	24	15
a		Double overprint, one inverted	7.00	7.00
194	D1(d)	10r magenta	35	22
195	D1(d)	20r orange	1.50	90
196	D1(d)	200r brn, *buff*	21.00	14.00
197	D1(e)	300r on 50r sl	15.00	10.50
198	D1(e)	500r on 100r car, *pink*	7.75	5.25
a		Invtd. surch.	22.50	21.00
		Nos. 193-198 (6)	45.84	31.02

Vasco da Gama Issue of Madeira Overprinted or Surcharged Types "a", "b" and "c".

1911 *Perf. 12½ to 16*

199	CD20(a)	2½r bl grn	1.10	85
a		Dbl. ovpt.		
200	CD21(b)	15r on 5r red	1.00	85
a		Inverted surcharge	5.00	4.50
201	CD23(a)	25r yel grn	2.50	2.00
202	CD24(a)	50r dk bl	4.25	3.00
a		Inverted overprint	12.00	11.50
203	CD25(a)	75r vio brn	3.25	2.25
a		Inverted overprint	9.00	8.50
204	CD27(b)	80r on 150r bis	4.25	2.50
a		Inverted surcharge	12.00	11.50
205	CD26(a)	100r bis brn	9.00	3.00
a		Inverted overprint	12.00	11.50
206	CD22(c)	1000r on 10r red vio	9.00	8.50
		Nos. 199-206 (8)	34.35	22.95

Ceres — A64

With Imprint

1912-31 Typo. *Perf. 15x14, 12x11½*

207	A64	¼c dk ol	10	8
208	A64	½c black	10	8
209	A64	1c dp grn	52	15
210	A64	1c choc ('18)	8	6
211	A64	1½c chocolate	2.00	70
212	A64	1½c dp grn ('18)	8	8
213	A64	2c carmine	2.25	65
214	A64	2c org ('18)	8	6
215	A64	2c yel ('24)	12	15
216	A64	2c choc ('26)	16	20
217	A64	2½c violet	12	6
218	A64	3c car rose ('17)	8	8
219	A64	3c ultra ('21)	8	6
220	A64	3½c lt grn ('18)	8	8
221	A64	4c lt grn ('19)	8	8
222	A64	4c org ('26)	16	20
223	A64	5c dp bl	1.50	20
224	A64	5c yel brn ('18)	42	12
225	A64	5c ol brn ('23)	8	8
226	A64	5c blk brn ('31)	10	8
227	A64	6c pale rose ('20)	8	6
228	A64	6c brn ('24)	12	14
229	A64	6c red brn ('30)	10	8
230	A64	7½c yel brn	2.50	50
231	A64	7½c dp bl ('18)	12	12
232	A64	8c slate	20	8
233	A64	8c bl grn ('22)	12	15
234	A64	8c org ('24)	12	15
235	A64	10c org brn	8	6
236	A64	10c red ('31)	10	8
237	A64	12c bl gray ('20)	75	32
238	A64	12c dp grn ('21)	16	15
239	A64	13½c chlky bl ('20)	35	22
240	A64	14c dk bl, *yel*('20)	52	40
241	A64	14c brt vio ('21)	16	15
242	A64	15c plum	90	35
243	A64	15c blk ('23)	12	8
244	A64	16c brt ultra ('24)	24	30
245	A64	20c vio brn, *grn*	6.00	85
246	A64	20c brn, *buff*('20)	6.00	1.00
247	A64	20c dk brn ('21)	20	12
248	A64	20c dp grn ('23)	15	15
249	A64	20c gray ('24)	15	12
250	A64	24c grnsh bl ('21)	20	15
251	A64	25c sal pink ('23)	7	6
252	A64	25c lt gray ('26)	35	15
253	A64	25c bl grn ('30)	35	15
254	A64	30c brn, *pink*	47.50	4.00
255	A64	30c lt brn, *yel*('17)	2.50	85
256	A64	30c gray brn ('21)	20	12
257	A64	30c dk brn ('24)	4.25	1.50
258	A64	32c dp grn ('24)	24	15
259	A64	36c red ('21)	24	15
260	A64	40c dk bl ('23)	22	22
261	A64	40c choc ('24)	14	25
262	A64	40c grn ('26)	20	8
263	A64	48c rose ('24)	90	60
264	A64	50c org, *sal*	5.00	65
265	A64	50c yel ('21)	35	15
266	A64	50c bis ('30)	90	40
267	A64	50c red brn ('30)	90	25
268	A64	60c bl ('21)	42	22
269	A64	64c pale ultra ('24)	1.10	1.25
270	A64	75c dl rose ('23)	2.50	1.65
271	A64	75c car rose ('30)	90	32
272	A64	80c brn rose ('21)	70	32
273	A64	80c vio ('24)	22	20
274	A64	80c dk grn ('30)	90	32
275	A64	90c chlky bl ('21)	60	22
276	A64	96c dp rose ('26)	8.50	10.00
277	A64	1e dp grn, *bl*	6.00	85
278	A64	1e vio ('21)	1.40	52
a		Perf. 15x14	52.50	16.00
279	A64	1e dk bl ('23)	1.25	85
280	A64	1e gray vio ('24)	38	22
281	A64	1e brn lake ('30)	3.25	50
282	A64	1.10e yel brn ('21)	1.40	52
283	A64	1.20e yel grn ('21)	75	32
284	A64	1.20e buff ('24)	15.00	13.00
285	A64	1.20e pur brn ('31)	1.25	50
286	A64	1.25e dk bl ('31)	1.10	50
287	A64	1.50e blk vio ('23)	2.50	1.10
288	A64	1.50e lil ('24)	3.50	1.65
289	A64	1.60e dp bl ('24)	2.50	65
290	A64	2e sl grn ('21)	21.00	1.00
291	A64	2e red vio ('31)	11.00	3.50
292	A64	2.40e ap grn ('26)	52.50	47.50
293	A64	3e pink ('26)	50.00	47.50
294	A64	3.20e gray grn ('24)	5.50	4.75
295	A64	4.50e org ('31)	30.00	17.00
296	A64	5e emer ('24)	5.00	2.00
297	A64	10e pink ('24)	37.50	14.00
298	A64	20e pale turq ('24)	90.00	62.50
		Nos. 207-298 (92)	450.59	254.19

Presidents of Portugal and Brazil and Aviators Cabral and Coutinho
A65

1923 Litho. *Perf. 14.*

299	A65	1c brown	7	10
300	A65	2c orange	10	10
301	A65	3c ultra	10	10
302	A65	4c yel grn	7	10
303	A65	5c bis brn	7	10
304	A65	10c brn org	7	10
305	A65	15c black	7	10
306	A65	20c bl grn	7	10
307	A65	25c rose	7	10
308	A65	30c ol brn	42	40
309	A65	40c chocolate	7	7
310	A65	50c yellow	8	12
311	A65	75c violet	15	15
312	A65	1e dp bl	25	18
313	A65	1.50e ol grn	42	40
314	A65	2e myr grn	70	65
		Nos. 299-314 (16)	2.78	2.87

Issued to commemorate the flight of Sacadura Cabral and Gago Coutinho from Portugal to Brazil.

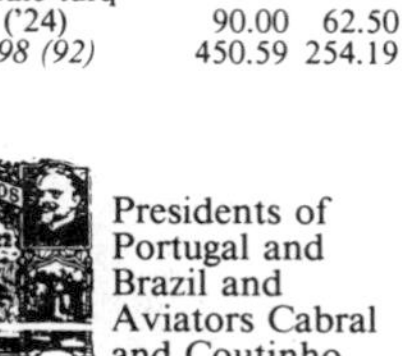

Camoens at Ceuta — A66

Camoens Saving the Lusiads — A67

Luis de Camoens — A68

First Edition of the Lusiads — A69

Monument to Camoens — A72

Camoens Dying — A70

Tomb of Camoens
A71

Engr.; Values Typo. in Black

1924, Nov. 11 *Perf. 14, 14½*

315	A66	2c lt bl	10	10
316	A66	3c orange	10	10
317	A66	4c dk gray	10	10
318	A66	5c yel grn	10	10
319	A66	6c lake	10	10
320	A67	8c org brn	10	10
321	A67	10c gray vio	10	10
322	A67	15c ol grn	10	10
323	A67	16c vio brn	12	12
324	A67	20c dp org	12	12
325	A68	25c lilac	12	12
326	A68	30c dk brn	12	12
327	A68	32c dk grn	22	22
328	A68	40c ultra	7	7
329	A68	48c red brn	50	70
330	A69	50c red org	60	65
331	A69	64c green	60	65
332	A69	75c dk vio	60	65
333	A69	80c bister	50	60
334	A69	96c lake	50	60
335	A70	1e slate	40	45
336	A70	1.20e lt brn	90	65
337	A70	1.50e red	55	60
338	A70	1.60e dk bl	55	65
339	A70	2e ap grn	1.00	70
340	A71	2.40e grn, *grn*	1.50	90
341	A71	3e dk bl, *bl*	60	65
a		Value double	60.00	
b		Value omitted		
342	A71	3.20e blk, *green*	60	65
343	A71	4.50e blk, *orange*	1.50	1.25
344	A71	10e dk brn, *pnksh*	2.75	2.75
345	A72	20e dk vio, *lil*	3.50	2.75
		Nos. 315-345 (31)	18.72	17.42

Issued to commemorate the 400th anniversary of the birth of Luis de Camoens, poet.

Castello-Branco's House at Sao Miguel de Seide — A73

Castello-Branco's Study — A74

Demand, as well as supply, determines a stamp's market value. One is as important as the other.

Camillo Castello-Branco
A75

Teresa de Albuquerque
A76

Mariana and Joao de Cruz — A77

Simao de Botelho — A78

1925, Mar. 26 *Perf. 12½.*

346	A73	2c	orange	12	12
347	A73	3c	green	12	12
348	A73	4c	ultra	12	12
349	A73	5c	scarlet	12	12
350	A73	6c	brn vio	12	12
a			"6" and "C" omitted		
351	A73	8c	blk brn	12	12
352	A74	10c	pale bl	12	12
353	A75	15c	ol grn	12	12
354	A74	16c	red org	18	12
355	A74	20c	dk vio	15	12
356	A75	25c	car rose	18	12
357	A74	30c	bis brn	18	12
358	A74	32c	green	40	55
359	A75	40c	grn & blk	18	12
360	A74	48c	red brn	70	1.10
361	A76	50c	bl grn	30	30
362	A76	64c	org brn	1.10	1.65
363	A76	75c	gray blk	40	55
364	A75	80c	brown	40	55
365	A76	96c	car rose	60	85
366	A76	1e	gray vio	40	40
367	A76	1.20e	yel grn	60	65
368	A77	1.50e	dk bl, *bl*	5.25	5.25
369	A75	1.60e	indigo	1.75	1.10
370	A77	2e	dk grn, *grn*	2.25	1.10
371	A77	2.40e	red, *org*	16.00	13.00
372	A77	3e	lake, *bl*	22.50	21.00
373	A77	3.20e	*green*	10.50	10.00
374	A75	4.50e	red & blk	5.25	1.75
375	A77	10e	brn, *yel*	5.25	1.00
376	A78	20e	*orange*	5.75	32
			Nos. 346-376 (31)	81.23	62.68

Issued to commemorate the centenary of the birth of Camillo Castello-Branco, novelist.

First Independence Issue.

Alfonso the Conqueror, First King of Portugal — A79

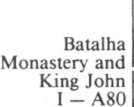

Batalha Monastery and King John I — A80

Battle of Aljubarrota — A81

Filipa de Vilhena Arming her Sons — A82

King John IV (The Duke of Braganza) A83

Independence Monument, Lisbon A84

1926, Aug. 13 *Perf. 14, 14½.*

Center in Black.

377	A79	2c	orange	12	12
378	A80	3c	ultra	12	12
379	A79	4c	yel grn	12	12
380	A80	5c	blk brn	12	12
381	A79	6c	ocher	12	12
382	A80	15c	dk grn	12	12
383	A79	16c	dp bl	28	45
384	A81	20c	dl vio	30	45
385	A82	25c	scarlet	30	45
386	A81	32c	dp grn	38	55
387	A82	40c	yel brn	12	12
388	A80	46c	carmine	70	1.10
389	A82	50c	ol bis	70	1.10
390	A83	64c	bl grn	1.10	1.25
391	A82	75c	red brn	1.10	1.25
392	A84	96c	dl red	1.50	2.25
393	A83	1e	blk vio	1.75	3.00
394	A81	1.60e	myr grn	2.50	3.50
395	A84	3e	plum	8.00	10.00
396	A84	4.50e	ol grn	9.00	12.00
397	A81	10e	carmine	10.00	15.00
			Nos. 377-397 (21)	38.45	53.19

The use of these stamps instead of the regular issue was obligatory on Aug. 13th and 14th, Nov. 30th and Dec. 1st, 1926.

Surcharged with Bars and

2 C.

1926

Center in Black

397A	A80	2c on 5c blk brn	50	75
397B	A80	2c on 46c car	60	75
397C	A83	2c on 64c bl grn	50	55
397D	A82	3c on 75c red brn	50	55
397E	A84	3c on 96c dl red	75	80
397F	A83	3c on 1e blk vio	55	60
397G	A81	4c on 1.60e myr grn	3.50	3.75
397H	A84	4c on 3e plum	1.65	2.50
397J	A84	6c on 4.50e ol grn	1.65	2.50
397K	A81	6c on 10e car	1.65	2.50
		Nos. 397A-397K (10)	11.85	15.25

There are two styles of the ornaments in these surcharges.

Ceres — A85

Without Imprint

1926, Dec. 2 **Typo.** *Perf. 13½x14*

398	A85	2c	chocolate	5	5
399	A85	3c	brt bl	5	5
400	A85	4c	dp org	5	5
401	A85	5c	dp brn	5	5
402	A85	6c	org brn	5	5
403	A85	10c	org red	5	5
404	A85	15c	black	8	8
405	A85	16c	ultra	8	8
406	A85	25c	gray	8	8
407	A85	32c	dp grn	14	18
408	A85	40c	bl grn	8	5
409	A85	48c	rose	32	45
410	A85	50c	ocher	24	32
411	A85	64c	dp bl	35	50
412	A85	80c	violet	85	22
413	A85	96c	car rose	50	55
414	A85	1e	red brn	2.75	22
415	A85	1.20e	yel brn	3.00	22
416	A85	1.60e	dk bl	38	14
417	A85	2e	green	4.75	32
418	A85	3.20e	ol grn	1.40	55
419	A85	4.50e	yellow	1.25	22
420	A85	5e	brn ol	30.00	35
421	A85	10e	red	1.75	28
			Nos. 398-421 (24)	48.30	5.11

Second Independence Issue.

Gonçalo Mendes da Maia — A86

Dr. Joao das Regras — A88

Guimaraes Castle — A87

Battle of Montijo A89

Brites de Almeida A90

Joao Pinto Ribeiro A91

1927, Nov. 29 **Engr.** *Perf. 14*

Center in Black

422	A86	2c	brown	8	8
423	A87	3c	ultra	8	8
424	A86	4c	orange	8	8
425	A88	5c	ol brn	8	8
426	A89	6c	org brn	8	8
427	A87	15c	blk brn	10	10
428	A88	16c	dp bl	24	30
429	A86	25c	gray	24	30
430	A89	32c	bl grn	60	60
431	A90	40c	yel grn	18	22
432	A86	48c	brn red	2.75	2.50
433	A87	80c	dk vio	2.25	2.75
434	A90	96c	dl red	3.25	4.50
435	A88	1.60e	myr grn	4.00	5.00
436	A91	4.50e	bister	5.00	6.00
			Nos. 422-436 (15)	19.01	22.67

The use of these stamps instead of the regular issue was compulsory on Nov. 29th, 30th, Dec. 1st, 2nd, 1927. The money derived from their sale was used for the purchase of a palace for a war museum, the organization of an international exposition in Lisbon, in 1940, and for fetes to be held in that year in commemoration of the eighth centenary of the founding of Portugal and the third centenary of its restoration.

Third Independence Issue.

Gualdim Paes A93

The Siege of Santarem A94

Battle of Rolica — A95

Battle of Atoleiros A96

Joana de Gouveia A97

Matias de Albuquerque — A98

1928, Nov. 28

Center in Black

437	A93	2c	lt bl	10	10
438	A94	3c	lt grn	10	10
439	A95	4c	lake	10	10
440	A96	5c	ol grn	10	10
441	A97	6c	org brn	10	10
442	A94	15c	slate	20	30
443	A95	16c	dk vio	20	30
444	A93	25c	ultra	24	38
445	A97	32c	dk grn	1.00	1.75
446	A96	40c	ol brn	16	16
447	A95	50c	red org	3.00	2.50
448	A94	80c	lt gray	2.50	3.75
449	A97	96c	carmine	5.25	8.50
450	A96	1e	claret	8.50	11.00
451	A93	1.60e	dk bl	3.25	5.00
452	A98	4.50e	yellow	3.25	5.00
			Nos. 437-452 (16)	28.05	39.14

Obligatory Nov. 27-30. See note after No. 436.

A99

Surcharged in Black.

1928-29 *Perf. 12x11½, 15x14.*

453	A99	4c on 8c org	10	15
454	A99	4c on 30c dk brn	10	15
455	A99	10c on ¼c dk ol	12	15
a		Inverted surch.	1.65	
456	A99	10c on ½c blk (R)	20	15
a		Perf. 15x14	22	30
457	A99	10c on 1c choc	15	15
a		Perf. 15x14	16.00	22.80
458	A99	10c on 4c grn	10	15
a		Perf. 15x14	20.00	27.50
459	A99	10c on 4c org	10	15
460	A99	10c on 5c ol brn	10	15
461	A99	15c on 16c bl	10	20
462	A99	15c on 16c ultra	50	50
463	A99	15c on 20c brn	11.50	12.00
464	A99	15c on 20c gray	10	20
465	A99	15c on 24c grnsh bl	65	32
466	A99	15c on 25c gray	10	15
467	A99	15c on 25c sal pink	10	12
468	A99	16c on 32c dp grn	25	40
469	A99	40c on 2c org	10	12
470	A99	40c on 2c yel	1.25	1.65
471	A99	40c on 2c choc	10	15
472	A99	40c on 3c ultra	10	15
473	A99	40c on 50c yel	10	15
474	A99	40c on 60c dl bl	25	22
a		Perf. 15x14	4.00	3.25
475	A99	40c on 64c pale ultra	25	25
476	A99	40c on 75c dl rose	25	25
477	A99	40c on 80c vio	22	22
478	A99	40c on 90c chlky bl	2.00	1.50
a		Perf. 15x14	3.25	3.00
479	A99	40c on 1e gray vio	22	32
480	A99	40c on 1.10e yel brn	22	32
481	A99	80c on 6c pale rose	22	32
482	A99	80c on 6c choc	22	25
483	A99	80c on 48c rose	32	42
484	A99	80c on 1.50e lil	50	42
485	A99	96c on 1.20e yel grn	1.25	1.10
486	A99	96c on 1.20e buff	1.65	1.50
487	A99	1.60e on 2e sl grn	8.00	8.00
488	A99	1.60e on 3.20e gray grn	3.50	3.25
489	A99	1.60e on 20e pale turq	4.50	4.00
		Nos. 453-489 (37)	39.49	39.65

Stamps of 1912-26 Overprinted in Black or Red

Revalidado

1929 *Perf. 12x11½*

490	A64	10c org brn	10	15
a		Perf. 15x14	35.00	35.00
491	A64	15c blk (R)	10	15
492	A64	40c lt grn	10	15
493	A64	40c chocolate	10	15
494	A64	96c dp rose	1.65	1.25
495	A64	1.60e brt bl	4.00	4.00
a		Double ovpt.		
		Nos. 490-495 (6)	6.05	5.85

Liberty A100

"Portugal" Holding Volume of "Lusiads" A101

1929, May *Perf. 12x11½.*

496	A100	1.60e on 5c red brn	2.25	2.50

1931-38 **Typo.** *Perf. 14.*

497	A101	4c bis brn	8	8
498	A101	5c ol gray	8	8
499	A101	6c lt gray	8	8
500	A101	10c dk vio	8	8
501	A101	15c gray blk	8	8
502	A101	16c brt bl	35	18
503	A101	25c dp grn	1.25	15
a		Imperf.		
504	A101	25c brt bl ('33)	1.25	18
505	A101	30c dk grn ('33)	52	18
506	A101	40c org red	3.00	6
507	A101	48c fawn	32	25
508	A101	50c lt brn	8	6
509	A101	75c car rose	1.50	55
510	A101	80c emerald	8	12
511	A101	95c car rose ('33)	4.50	2.50
512	A101	1e claret	13.00	8
513	A101	1.20e ol grn	85	55
514	A101	1.25e dk bl	65	15
515	A101	1.60e dk bl ('33)	9.25	1.50
516	A101	1.75e dk bl ('38)	12	15
517	A101	2e dl vio	22	15
518	A101	4.50e orange	52	15
519	A101	5e yel grn	52	15
		Nos. 497-519 (23)	38.38	7.51

Birthplace of St. Anthony A102

Font where St. Anthony was Baptized A103

Lisbon Cathedral A104

St. Anthony with Infant Jesus A105

Santa Cruz Cathedral A106

The only foreign revenue stamps listed in this Catalogue are those authorized for prepayment of postage.

St. Anthony's Tomb at Padua A107

1931, June **Typo.** *Perf. 12*

528	A102	15c plum	15	8

Litho.

529	A103	25c gray & pale grn	30	18
530	A104	40c gray brn & buff	18	15
531	A105	75c dl rose & pale rose	7.25	5.25
532	A106	1.25e gray & pale bl	14.00	7.50
533	A107	4.50e gray vio & lil	7.25	1.25
		Nos. 528-533 (6)	29.13	14.41

Commemorating the seventh centenary of the death of St. Anthony of Padua and Lisbon.

Nuno Alvares Pereira (1360-1431), Portuguese Warrior and Statesman — A108

1931, Nov. 1 **Typo.** *Perf. 12x11½*

534	A108	15c black	35	42
535	A108	25c gray grn & blk	35	32
536	A108	40c orange	75	32
a		Value omitted	15.00	15.00
537	A108	75c car rose	4.50	5.50
538	A108	1.25e dk bl & pale bl	7.75	6.00
539	A108	4.50e choc & lt grn	35.00	24.00
a		Value omitted	105.00	105.00
		Nos. 534-539 (6)	48.70	36.56

Nos. 528-533 Surcharged

40 C.

1933 *Perf. 12.*

543	A104	15c on 40c gray brn & buff	25	20
544	A102	40c on 15c plum	70	55
545	A103	40c on 25c gray & pale grn	45	25
546	A105	40c on 75c dl rose & pale rose	2.75	2.00
547	A106	40c on 1.25e gray & pale bl	2.75	2.00
548	A107	40c on 4.50e gray vio & lil	2.75	2.00
		Nos. 543-548 (6)	9.65	7.00

Nos. 534-539 Surcharged

15 C.

1933 *Perf. 12x11½*

549	A108	15c on 40c org	22	18
550	A108	40c on 15c blk	1.10	1.00
551	A108	40c on 25c gray grn	32	22
552	A108	40c on 75c car rose	2.75	1.75
553	A108	40c on 1.25e dk bl	2.75	1.75
554	A108	40c on 4.50e choc & lt grn	2.75	1.75
		Nos. 549-554 (6)	9.89	6.65

President Carmona A109

Head of a Colonial A110

1934, May 28 **Typo.** *Perf. 11½.*

556	A109	40c brt vio	5.00	10

1934, July *Perf. 11½x12.*

558	A110	25c dk brn	65	22
559	A110	40c scarlet	3.75	12
560	A110	1.60e dk bl	9.25	5.00

Colonial Exposition.

Roman Temple, Evora A111

Prince Henry the Navigator A112

"All for the Nation" A113

Coimbra Cathedral A114

1935-41 *Perf. 11½x12*

561	A111	4c black	7	7
562	A111	5c blue	7	7
563	A111	6c choc ('36)	10	8

Perf. 11½, 12x11½ (1.75e)

564	A112	10c turq grn	24	8
565	A112	15c red brn	7	8
a		Booklet pane of 4		
566	A113	25c dp bl	2.75	14
a		Booklet pane of 4		
567	A113	40c brown	55	6
a		Booklet pane of 4		
568	A113	1e rose red	2.75	20
568A	A114	1.75e blue	21.00	52
568B	A113	10e gray blk ('41)	3.80	75
569	A113	20e turq grn ('41)	4.75	60
		Nos. 561-569 (11)	36.15	2.65

Queen Maria A115

Rod and Bowl of Aesculapius A116

Typographed, Head Embossed

1935, June 1 *Perf. 11½*

570	A115	40c scarlet	50	14

First Portuguese Philatelic Exhibition.

1937, July 24 **Typo.** *Perf. 11½x12*

571	A116	25c blue	2.50	50

Issued in commemoration of the centenary of the establishment of the School of Medicine in Lisbon and Oporto.

Gil Vicente A117

Grapes A118

1937

572	A117	40c dk brn	4.00	10
573	A117	1e rose red	55	10

Issued to commemorate the 400th anniversary of the death of Gil Vicente (1465-1536), Portuguese playwright. Design shows him in cowherd role in his play, "Auto do Vaqueiro."

1938 *Perf. 11½*

575	A118	15c brt pur	35	30
576	A118	25c brown	50	70
577	A118	40c dp red lil	3.25	20
578	A118	1.75e dp bl	5.25	6.00

Issued in connection with the International Vineyard and Wine Congress.

Emblem of Portuguese Legion — A119

1940, Jan. 27 **Unwmk.** *Perf. 11½*

579	A119	5c dl yel	8	8
580	A119	10c violet	8	8
581	A119	15c brt bl	8	8
582	A119	25c brown	3.00	20
583	A119	40c dk grn	6.25	8
584	A119	80c yel grn	25	12
585	A119	1e brt red	8.25	60
586	A119	1.75e dk bl	1.40	60
a		Souvenir sheet of 8	100.00	125.00
		Nos. 579-586 (8)	19.39	1.84

Issued in honor of the Portuguese Legion.

No. 586a measures 157x171mm and contains one each of Nos. 579-586 with marginal date "1939." The sheet sold for 5.50e, the proceeds going to various charities.

Portuguese World Exhibition A120

King John IV — A121

Discoveries Monument, Belém — A122

King Alfonso I — A123

Perf. 12x11½, 11½x12

1940-41 **Engr.**

587	A120	10c brn vio	8	8
588	A121	15c dk grnsh bl	8	8
589	A122	25c dk sl grn	30	12
590	A121	35c yel grn	25	16
591	A123	40c ol bis	60	5
592	A120	80c dk vio	1.50	12
593	A122	1e dk red	3.00	48
594	A123	1.75e ultra	1.65	60
a		Souvenir sheet of 8 ('41)	16.00	22.50
		Nos. 587-594 (8)	7.46	1.69

The 10c and 80c commemorate the Portuguese International Exhibition, Lisbon; 15c and 35c, 300th anniversary of the restoration of the monarchy; 40c and 1.75e, 800th anniversary of Portuguese independence.

No. 594a contains one each of Nos. 587-594; ornamental border. Sold for 10e. Size: 159x223mm.

Sir Rowland Hill — A124

1940-41 Typo. *Perf. 11 ½x12*

595	A124	15c	dk vio brn	14	7
596	A124	25c	dp org brn	12	7
597	A124	35c	green	14	8
598	A124	40c	brn vio	24	7
599	A124	50c	turq grn	5.00	90
600	A124	80c	lt bl	40	42
601	A124	1e	crimson	5.25	85
602	A124	1.75e	dk bl	2.00	90
a			Souvenir sheet of 8 ('41)	11.00	25.00
			Nos. 595-602 (8)	13.29	3.36

Postage stamp centenary.

No. 602a contains one each of Nos. 595-602 and marginal date "1940." Sold for 10e. Size: 161x153mm.

Fisherwoman of Nazare A126

Native of Coimbra A127

Native of Saloio A128

Fisherwoman of Lisbon A129

Native of Olhao A130

Native of Aveiro A131

Native of Madeira A132

Native of Viana do Castelo A133

Rancher of Ribatejo A134

Peasant of Alentejo A135

1941, Apr. 4 Typo. *Perf. 11 ½.*

605	A126	4c	sage grn	7	5
606	A127	5c	org brn	7	5
607	A128	10c	red vio	70	35
608	A129	15c	lt yel grn	7	7
609	A130	25c	rose vio	50	20
610	A131	40c	yel grn	7	5
611	A132	80c	lt bl	90	60
612	A133	1e	rose red	2.25	65
613	A134	1.75e	dl bl	2.75	1.50
614	A135	2e	red org	10.50	10.50
a			Sheet of ten	32.50	87.50
			Nos. 605-614 (10)	17.88	14.02

No. 614a measures 163x146mm. and contains one each of Nos. 605-614, with monogram and "1941" in margins. The sheet sold for 10e.

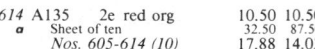

Ancient Sailing Vessel — A136

1943 *Perf. 14.*

615	A136	5c	black	5	5
616	A136	10c	fawn	5	5
617	A136	15c	lil gray	6	5
618	A136	20c	dl vio	6	5
619	A136	30c	brn vio	6	5
620	A136	35c	dk bl grn	6	5
621	A136	50c	plum	10	5
622	A136	1e	dp rose	1.90	5
623	A136	1.75e	indigo	8.00	25
624	A136	2e	dl cl	60	5
625	A136	2.50e	crim rose	85	5
626	A136	3.50e	grnsh bl	4.00	35
627	A136	5e	dp org	50	5
628	A136	10e	bl gray	60	5
629	A136	15e	bl grn	10.00	35
630	A136	20e	ol gray	27.50	20
631	A136	50e	salmon	85.00	30
			Nos. 615-631 (17)	139.39	2.05

See also Nos. 702-710.

Farmer A137

Postrider A138

1943, Oct. *Perf. 11 ½.*

632	A137	10c	dl bl	22	20
633	A137	50c	red	25	20

Congress of Agricultural Science.

1944, May Unwmk.

634	A138	10c	dk vio brn	8	8
635	A138	50c	purple	8	8
636	A138	1e	cerise	50	28
637	A138	1.75e	brt bl	42	60
a			Sheet of four	8.00	19.00

3rd Philatelic Exhibition, Lisbon.

No. 637a contains one each of Nos. 634-637; marginal decorations. Sold for 7.50e. Size: 82x122mm.

Portrait of Avellar Brotero — A139

Statue of Brotero — A140

1944-45 Typo. *Perf. 11 ½x12*

638	A139	10c	chocolate	7	7
639	A140	50c	dl grn	32	8
640	A140	1e	carmine	1.10	32
641	A139	1.75e	dk bl	1.00	65
a			Sheet of four ('45)	10.00	20.00

Issued to commemorate the 200th anniversary of the birth of Avellar Brotero, botanist.

No. 641a measures 145x195mm. and contains one each of Nos. 638-641 and marginal decorations. The sheet sold for 7.50e.

Gil Eannes — A141

Designs: 30c, Joao Goncalves Zarco. 35c, Bartolomeu Dias. 50c, Vasco da Gama. 1e, Pedro Alvares Cabral. 1.75e, Fernando Magellan. 2e, Goncalo Velho. 3.50e, Diogo Cao.

1945, July 29 Engr. *Perf. 13 ½.*

642	A141	10c	vio brn	5	5
643	A141	30c	yel brn	7	8
644	A141	35c	bl grn	12	10
645	A141	50c	dk ol grn	20	10
646	A141	1e	vermilion	90	20
647	A141	1.75e	sl bl	1.00	70
648	A141	2e	black	1.25	50
649	A141	3.50e	car rose	2.50	1.10
a			Sheet of eight	12.50	18.00
			Nos. 642-649 (8)	6.09	2.83

Portuguese navigators of 15th and 16th centuries.

No. 649a contains one each of Nos. 642-649; marginal decorations. Sold for 15e. Size: 167x172mm.

Pres. Antonio Oscar de Fragoso Carmona A149

Astrolabe A150

Perf. 11 ½

1945, Nov. 12 Photo. Unwmk.

650	A149	10c	brt vio	8	7
651	A149	30c	cop brn	8	7
652	A149	35c	dk grn	8	7
653	A149	50c	dk ol	20	10
654	A149	1e	dk red	2.75	60
655	A149	1.75e	dk bl	2.50	1.00
656	A149	2e	dp cl	13.00	1.90
657	A149	3.50e	sl blk	6.25	2.75
a			Sheet of eight	67.50	85.00
			Nos. 650-657 (8)	24.94	6.56

No. 657a measures 135½x98mm. and contains one each of Nos. 650-657 and decorative border. The sheet sold for 15e.

1945-46 Litho.

658	A150	10c	lt brn	8	8
659	A150	50c	gray grn	12	9
660	A150	1e	brn red	1.10	25
661	A150	1.75e	dl chlky bl	85	1.10
a			Sheet of four ('46)	15.00	22.50

Issued to commemorate the centenary of the Portuguese Naval School.

No. 661a measures 114½x135mm. and contains one each of Nos. 658-661, marginal decorations and "1945." The sheet sold for 7.50e.

Catalogue values for unused stamps in this section, from this point to the end of the section, are for Never Hinged items.

Silves Castle A151

Almourol Castle A152

Designs-Castles: 30c, Leiria. 35c, Feira. 50c, Guimaraes. 1.75e, Lisbon. 2e, Braganca. 3.50e, Ourem.

1946, June 1 Engr.

662	A151	10c	brn vio	5	5
663	A151	30c	brn red	10	8
664	A151	35c	ol grn	10	8
665	A151	50c	gray blk	25	8
666	A152	1e	brt car	7.50	40
667	A152	1.75e	dk bl	6.00	1.00
a			Sheet of four	75.00	100.00
668	A152	2e	dk gray grn	16.00	1.25
669	A152	3.50e	org brn	10.00	1.40
			Nos. 662-669 (8)	40.00	4.34

No. 667a is printed on buff granite paper. The sheet measures 135 x 102 mm., and sold for 12.50e.

Figure with Tablet and Arms — A153

Madonna and Child — A154

1946, Nov. 19 *Perf. 12x11 ½*

670	A153	50c	dk bl	32	12
a			Sheet of four	52.50	70.00

Issued to commemorate the centenary of the establishment of the Bank of Portugal.

No. 670a measures 155x143½mm. and has a border and marginal inscriptions. The sheet sold for 7.50e.

1946, Dec. 8 Unwmk. *Perf. 13 ½*

671	A154	30c	gray blk	15	7
672	A154	50c	dp grn	15	7
673	A154	1e	rose car	1.10	32
674	A154	1.75e	brt bl	1.75	65
a			Sheet of four ('47)	30.00	42.50

Issued to commemorate the 300th anniversary of the proclamation making the Virgin Mary patroness of Portugal.

No. 674a measures 108½x159mm. and contains one each of Nos. 671-674, and marginal decorations and inscriptions. The sheet sold for 7.50e.

Shepherdess, Caramullo A155

Surrender of the Moors, 1147 A163

Designs: 30c, Timbrel player, Malpique. 35c, Flute player, Monsanto. 50c, Woman of Avintes. 1e, Field laborer, Maia. 1.75e, Woman of Algarve. 2e, Bastonet player, Miranda. 3.50e, Woman of the Azores.

1947, Mar. 1 Photo. *Perf. 11 ½*

675	A155	10c	rose vio	10	8
676	A155	30c	dk red	10	8
677	A155	35c	dk ol grn	10	8
678	A155	50c	dk brn	20	8
679	A155	1e	red	3.50	25
680	A155	1.75e	sl bl	4.00	1.75
681	A155	2e	pck bl	19.00	1.25
682	A155	3.50e	sl blk	9.25	2.00
a			Sheet of eight	145.00	160.00
			Nos. 675-682 (8)	36.25	5.57

No. 682a measures 135x98mm. and contains one each of Nos. 675-682, and decorative border. The sheet sold for 15e.

1947, Oct. 13 Engr. *Perf. 12 ½*

683	A163	5c	bl grn	5	5
684	A163	20c	dk car	12	7
685	A163	50c	violet	20	10
686	A163	1.75e	dk bl	2.25	2.25
687	A163	2.50e	chocolate	3.25	4.00
688	A163	3.50e	sl blk	5.50	6.50
			Nos. 683-688 (6)	11.37	12.97

Issued to commemorate the 800th anniversary of the conquest of Lisbon from the Moors.

St. John de Britto
A164 A165

1948, May 28 *Perf. 11½x12*

689	A164	30c	green	10	8
690	A165	50c	dk brn	10	8
691	A164	1e	rose car	3.75	60
692	A165	1.75e	blue	4.50	70

Issued to commemorate the 300th anniversary of the birth of St. John de Britto.

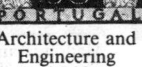

Architecture and Engineering A166 — King John I A167

1948, May 28 *Perf. 13x12½*

693	A166	50c	vio brn	15	12

Issued to publicize the Exposition of public Works and the National Congress of Engineering and Architecture, 1948.

Perf. 11½

1949, May 6 Unwmk. Photo.

Designs: 30c, Philippa of Lancaster. 35c, Prince Ferdinand. 50c, Prince Henry the Navigator. 1e, Nuno Alvarez Pereira. 1.75e, John das Regras. 2e, Fernao Lopes. 3.50e, Affonso Domingues.

694	A167	10c	brn vio & cr	10	10
695	A167	30c	dk bl grn & cr	10	10
696	A167	35c	dk ol grn & cr	10	10
697	A167	50c	dp bl & cr	38	10
698	A167	1e	dk red & cr	38	10
699	A167	1.75e	dk gray & cr	7.50	4.00
700	A167	2e	dk gray bl & cr	4.00	55
701	A167	3.50e	dk brn & gray	12.50	10.00
a			Sheet of 8	20.00	25.00
			Nos. 694-701 (8)	25.06	15.05

No. 701a contains one each of Nos. 694-701 and ornamental border. Sold for 15e.

Ship Type of 1942.

1948-49 Typo. Perf. 14

702	A136	80c	dp grn	3.25	15
703	A136	1e	dp cl ('48)	2.00	5
704	A136	1.20e	dp car	3.25	15
705	A136	1.50e	olive	21.00	15
706	A136	1.80e	yel org	21.00	90
707	A136	2e	dp bl	4.00	20
708	A136	4e	orange	27.50	60
709	A136	6e	yel grn	47.50	65
710	A136	7.50e	grnsh gray	21.00	90
			Nos. 702-710 (9)	150.50	3.75

Angel, Coimbra Museum A168 — Symbols of the U.P.U. A169

1949, Dec. 20 Engr. *Perf. 13x14*

711	A168	1e	red brn	4.50	15
712	A168	5e	ol brn	60	15

Issued to publicize the 16th International Congress of History and Art.

1949, Dec. 29

713	A169	1e	brn vio	9	8
714	A169	2e	dp bl	25	15
715	A169	2.50e	dp grn	1.40	32
716	A169	4e	brn red	4.25	2.00

75th anniv. of the UPU.

Madonna of Fatima A170 — St. John of God Helping Ill Man A171

1950, May 13 *Perf. 11½x12*

717	A170	50c	dk grn	22	10
718	A170	1e	dk brn	95	10
719	A170	2e	blue	1.90	85
720	A170	5e	lilac	27.50	10.00

Issued to commemorate the Holy Year, 1950, and to honor "Our Lady of the Rosary" at Fatima.

1950, Oct. 30 Engr. Unwmk.

721	A171	20c	gray vio	10	8
722	A171	50c	cerise	18	12
723	A171	1e	ol grn	30	15
724	A171	1.50e	dp org	3.75	1.10
725	A171	2e	blue	2.75	32
726	A171	4e	chocolate	12.50	2.00
			Nos. 721-726 (6)	19.58	3.77

Issued to commemorate the 400th anniversary of the death of St. John of God.

Guerra Junqueiro A172 — Fisherman and Catch A173

1951, Mar. 2 Litho. *Perf. 13½*

727	A172	50c	dk brn	1.50	30
728	A172	1e	dk sl gray	38	20

Birth centenary of Guerra Junqueiro, poet.

1951, Mar. 9

729	A173	50c	gray grn, *buff*	1.50	30
730	A173	1e	rose lake, *buff*	38	10

3rd National Congress of Fisheries.

Dove — A174

Pope Pius XII — A175

1951, Oct. 11

731	A174	20c	dk brn & buff	8	5
732	A174	90c	dk ol grn & cr	1.90	50
733	A175	1e	dp cl & pink	1.65	9
734	A175	2.30e	dk bl grn & bl	2.25	45

End of the Holy Year.

15th Century Colonists, Terceira A176

1951, Oct. 24 *Perf. 13x13½*

735	A176	50c	dk bl, *sal*	1.00	25
736	A176	1e	dk brn, *cr*	45	25

Issued to commemorate the 500th anniversary (in 1950) of the colonizing of the island of Terceira.

Student, Soldiers and Workers A177

1951, Nov. 22 *Perf. 13½x13*

737	A177	1e	vio brn	1.25	8
738	A177	2.30e	dk bl	1.00	28

Issued to commemorate the 25th anniversary of the national revolution.

16th Century Coach — A178

Designs: Various coaches.

Perf. 13x13½

1952, Jan. 8 Engr. Unwmk.

739	A178	10c	purple	10	10
740	A178	20c	ol gray	10	10
741	A178	50c	stl bl	25	12
742	A178	90c	green	80	90
743	A178	1e	red org	40	12
744	A178	1.40e	rose pink	2.00	2.50
745	A178	1.50e	rose brn	2.50	1.50
746	A178	2.30e	dp ultra	80	85
			Nos. 739-746 (8)	6.95	6.19

Issued to honor the National Museum of Coaches.

Symbolical of NATO — A179

1952, Apr. 4 Litho. *Perf. 12½*

747	A179	1e	grn & blk	8.25	32
748	A179	3.50e	gray & vio bl	125.00	18.00

3rd anniv. of the signing of the North Atlantic Treaty.
Value of set hinged, $55.

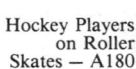

Hockey Players on Roller Skates — A180

1952, June 28 *Perf. 13x13½*

749	A180	1e	dk bl & gray	2.25	15
750	A180	3.50e	dk red brn	3.25	1.75

Issued to publicize the 8th World Championship Hockey-on-Skates matches.

Francisco Gomes Teixeira A181 — St. Francis and Two Boys A182

1952, Nov. 25 *Perf. 14x14½*

751	A181	1e	cerise	38	7
752	A181	2.30e	dp bl	2.50	1.75

Issued to commemorate the centenary of the birth of Francisco Gomes Teixeira (1851-1932), mathematician.

1952, Dec. 23 *Perf. 13½*

753	A182	1e	dk grn	30	12
754	A182	2e	dp cl	55	25
755	A182	3.50e	chlky bl	8.75	5.00
756	A182	5e	dk pur	16.00	1.10

Issued to commemorate the 400th anniversary of the death of St. Francis Xavier.

Marshal Carmona Bridge A183

Designs: 1.40e, "28th of May" Stadium. 2e, University City, Coimbra. 3.50e, Salazar Dam.

1952, Dec. 10 Unwmk. *Perf. 12½*
Buff Paper

757	A183	1e	red brn	25	20
758	A183	1.40e	dl pur	3.75	3.00
759	A183	2e	dk grn	2.75	1.00
760	A183	3.50e	dk bl	4.50	2.50

Issued to commemorate the centenary of the foundation of the Ministry of Public Works.

Equestrian Seal of King Diniz — A184

1953-56 Litho.

761	A184	5c	grn, *cit*	10	5
762	A184	10c	ind, *sal*	10	5
763	A184	20c	org red, *cit*	10	5
763A	A184	30c	rose lil, *cr* ('56)	8	5
764	A184	50c	gray	10	5
765	A184	90c	dk grn, *cit*	4.75	20
766	A184	1e	vio brn, *rose*	18	5
767	A184	1.40e	rose red	4.75	35
768	A184	1.50e	red, *cr*	18	5
769	A184	2e	gray	18	5
770	A184	2.30e	blue	7.75	25
771	A184	2.50e	gray blk, *sal*	25	5
772	A184	5e	rose vio, *cr*	25	5
773	A184	10e	bl, *cit*	80	5
774	A184	20e	bis brn, *cit*	1.75	5
775	A184	50e	rose vio	2.25	12
			Nos. 761-775 (16)	23.57	1.52

St. Martin of Braga A185 — Guilherme Gomes Fernandes A186

Perf. 13x13½

1953, Feb. 26 **Unwmk.**

776	A185	1e	gray blk & gray	45	12
777	A185	3.50e	dk brn & yel	4.00	3.50

Issued to commemorate the 14th centenary of the arrival of St. Martin of Dume on the Iberian peninsula.

1953, Mar. 28 ***Perf. 13***

778	A186	1e	red vio	38	9
779	A186	2.30e	dp bl	3.75	3.00

Issued to commemorate the birth of Guilherme Gomes Fernandes, General Inspector of the Firemen of Porto.

Emblems of Automobile Club A187

1953, Apr. 15 ***Perf. 12½***

780	A187	1e	dk grn & yel grn	45	10
781	A187	3.50e	dk brn & buff	4.75	2.75

Issued to commemorate the 50th anniversary of the Portuguese Automobile Club.

Princess St. Joanna A188

Queen Maria II A189

Perf. 14½x14

1953, May 14 **Litho.** **Unwmk.**

782	A188	1e	blk & gray grn	65	8
783	A188	3.50e	dk bl & bl	4.50	3.75

Issued to commemorate the 500th anniversary of the birth of Princess St. Joanna.

1953, Oct. 3 **Photo.** ***Perf. 13½***

Background of Lower Panel in Gold.

784	A189	50c	red brn	10	5
785	A189	1e	cl brn	10	5
786	A189	1.40e	dk vio	70	45
787	A189	2.30e	dp bl	1.50	1.25
788	A189	3.50e	vio bl	1.50	1.25
789	A189	4.50e	dk bl grn	1.40	55
790	A189	5e	dk ol grn	2.50	45
791	A189	20e	red vio	25.00	6.25
			Nos. 784-791 (8)	32.80	10.30

Issued to commemorate the centenary of Portugal's first postage stamp.

Allegory A190

1954, Sept. 22 ***Perf. 13***

792	A190	1e	bl & dk grnsh bl	52	9
793	A190	1.50e	buff & dk brn	1.00	30

Issued to commemorate the 150th anniversary of the founding of the State Secretariat for Financial Affairs.

Open Textbook — A191

Cadet and College Arms — A192

1954, Oct. 15 **Litho.**

794	A191	50c	blue	8	5
795	A191	1e	red	8	5
796	A191	2e	dk grn	7.50	25
797	A191	2.50e	org brn	6.50	48

National literacy campaign.

1954, Nov. 17

798	A192	1e	choc & lt grn	60	6
799	A192	3.50e	dk bl & gray grn	2.00	1.25

150th anniversary of the Military College.

Manuel da Nobrega and Crucifix A193

King Alfonso I A194

1954, Dec. 17 **Engr.** ***Perf. 14x13***

800	A193	1e	brown	28	7
801	A193	2.30e	dp bl	12.00	6.50
802	A193	3.50e	gray grn	4.75	1.00
803	A193	5e	green	11.00	1.50

Issued to commemorate the 400th anniversary of the founding of Sao Paulo, Brazil.

1955, Mar. 17 ***Perf. 13½x13***

Kings: 20c, Sancho I. 50c, Alfonso II. 90c, Sancho II. 1e, Alfonso III. 1.40e, Diniz. 1.50e, Alfonso IV. 2e, Pedro I. 2.30e, Ferdinand I.

804	A194	10c	rose vio	10	6
805	A194	20c	dk ol grn	10	6
806	A194	50c	dk bl grn	10	6
807	A194	90c	green	60	60
808	A194	1e	red brn	24	12
809	A194	1.40e	car rose	1.65	1.50
810	A194	1.50e	ol brn	70	50
811	A194	2e	dp org	2.00	1.40
812	A194	2.30e	vio bl	2.00	1.25
			Nos. 804-812 (9)	7.49	5.55

Telegraph Pole — A195

A. J. Ferreira da Silva — A196

1955, Sept. 16 **Litho.** ***Perf. 13½***

813	A195	1e	ocher & hn brn	25	10
814	A195	2.30e	gray grn & Prus bl	4.25	1.40
815	A195	3.50e	lem & dp grn	4.25	75

Issued to commemorate the centenary of the telegraph system in Portugal.

1956, May 8 **Photo.** **Unwmk.**

816	A196	1e	bl & dk bl	28	10
817	A196	2.30e	grn & dk grn	3.00	1.75

Issued to commemorate the centenary of the birth of Prof. Antonio Joaquim Ferreira da Silva, chemist.

Steam Locomotive, 1856 A197

Madonna, 15th Century A198

Design: 1.50e, 2e, Electric train, 1956.

1956, Oct. 28 **Litho.** ***Perf. 13***

818	A197	1e	lt & dk ol grn	20	6
819	A197	1.50e	Prus bl & lt grnsh bl	80	15
820	A197	2e	dk org brn & bis	6.00	45
821	A197	2.50e	choc & brn	7.00	60

Centenary of the Portuguese railways.

1956, Dec. 8 **Photo.**

822	A198	1e	dp grn & lt ol grn	22	8
823	A198	1.50e	dk red brn & ol bis	42	25

Mothers' Day, Dec. 8.

J. B. Almeida Garrett A199

1957, Mar. 7 **Engr.** ***Perf. 13½x14***

824	A199	1e	sepia	20	10
825	A199	2.30e	lt pur	6.50	3.00
826	A199	3.50e	dl grn	1.25	48
827	A199	5e	rose car	10.50	4.00

Issued in honor of Joao Baptista da Silva Leitao de Almeida Garrett, poet.

Cesario Verde A200

Exhibition Emblems A201

1957, Dec. 12 **Litho.** ***Perf. 13½***

828	A200	1e	cit & brn	35	8
829	A200	3.30e	gray grn, yel grn & dk ol	95	60

Issued in honor of Jose Joaquim de Cesario Verde (1855-1886), poet.

1958, Apr. 7

830	A201	1e	multi	20	6
831	A201	3.30e	multi	75	55

Issued for the Universal and International Exposition at Brussels.

Queen St. Isabel — A202

Institute for Tropical Medicine — A203

Design: 2e, 5e, St. Teotonio.

Perf. 14½x14

1958, July 10 **Photo.** **Unwmk.**

832	A202	1e	rose brn & buff	10	8
833	A202	2e	dk grn & buff	15	12
834	A202	2.50e	pur & buff	65	18
835	A202	5e	brn & buff	1.00	20

1958, Sept. 4 **Litho.** ***Perf. 13***

836	A203	1e	dk grn & lt gray	55	6
837	A203	2.50e	bl & pale bl	1.75	35

Issued to publicize the 6th International Congress for Tropical Medicine and Malaria, Lisbon, Sept. 1958, and the opening of the new Tropical Medicine Institute.

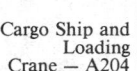

Cargo Ship and Loading Crane — A204

1958, Nov. 27 **Unwmk.** ***Perf. 13***

838	A204	1e	brn & dk brn	1.25	6
839	A204	4.50e	vio bl & dk bl	1.00	55

Issued to commemorate the 2nd National Congress of the Merchant Marine, Porto.

Queen Leonor — A205

1958, Dec. 17

840	A205	1e	multi	12	6
841	A205	1.50e	bis, blk, bl & dk bis brn	1.10	9
a			Dark bis brn omitted		
842	A205	2.30e	multi	90	20
843	A205	4.10e	multi	85	24

Issued to commemorate the 500th anniversary of the birth of Queen Leonor.

Arms of Aveiro — A206

Symbols of Hope and Peace — A207

1959, Aug. 30 **Litho.** ***Perf. 13***

844	A206	1e	ol bis, brn, gold & sil	25	6
845	A206	5e	grnsh gray, gold & sil	1.90	35

Millennium of Aveiro.

1960, Mar. 2 ***Perf. 12½***

846	A207	1e	lt vio & blk	40	15
847	A207	3.50e	gray & dk grn	1.75	1.75

Issued to commemorate the 10th anniversary (in 1959) of the North Atlantic Treaty Organization.

Open Door to "Peace" and WRY Emblem A208

Glider A209

1960, Apr. 7 **Unwmk.** ***Perf. 13***

848	A208	20c	multi	8	8
849	A208	1e	multi	32	9
850	A208	1.80e	yel grn, org & blk	35	42

Issued to publicize World Refugee Year, July 1, 1959-June 30, 1960.

1960, May 2

Designs: 1.50e, Plane. 2e, Plane and parachutes. 2.50e, Model plane.

851	A209	1e	yel, gray & bl	8	8
852	A209	1.50e	multi	52	22
853	A209	2e	bl grn, yel & blk	75	35
854	A209	2.50e	grnsh bl, ocher & red	1.40	45

Issued to commemorate the 50th anniversary (in 1959) of the Aero Club of Portugal.

Father Cruz — A210

University of Evora Seal — A211

1960, July 18 Unwmk. Perf. 13
855 A210 1e dp brn 14 9
856 A210 4.30e Prus bl & blk 2.50 2.50

Issued to honor Father Cruz, "father of the poor."

1960, July 18 Litho.
857 A211 50c vio bl 6 5
858 A211 1e red brn & yel 12 8
859 A211 1.40e rose cl & rose 85 50

Issued to commemorate the 400th anniversary of the founding of the University of Evora.

Arms of Prince Henry — A212

Arms of Lisbon and Symbolic Ship — A213

Designs: 2.50e, Caravel. 3.50e, Prince Henry. 5e, Prince Henry's motto. 8e, Prince Henry's sloop. 10e, Old chart of Sagres region of Portugal.

1960, Aug. 4 Photo. Perf. 12x12½
860 A212 1e gold & multi 10 10
861 A212 2.50e gold & multi 85 30
862 A212 3.50e gold & multi 1.00 1.00
863 A212 5e gold & multi 1.75 38
864 A212 8e gold & multi 40 38
865 A212 10e gold & multi 2.75 1.50
Nos. 860-865 (6) 6.85 3.66

Issued to commemorate the 500th anniversary of the death of Prince Henry the Navigator.

Europa Issue, 1960
Common Design Type
1960, Sept. 16 Litho. Perf. 13
Size: 31x21mm.
866 CD3 1e ultra & gray bl 16 14
867 CD3 3.50e brn red & rose red 1.65 1.65

1960, Nov. 17 Perf. 13
868 A213 1e gray ol, blk & vio bl 28 10
869 A213 3.30e bl, blk & ultra 2.50 2.50

Issued to commemorate the Fifth National Philatelic Exhibition, Lisbon, part of the Prince Henry the Navigator festivities. (The ship in the design is in honor of Prince Henry).

Flag and Laurel — A214

1960, Dec. 20 Litho. Perf. 13
870 A214 1e multi 22 20

50th anniversary of the Republic.

King Pedro V A215

1961, Aug. 3 Engr. Perf. 13
871 A215 1e gray brn & dk grn 22 8
872 A215 6.50e dk bl & blk 95 45

Issued to commemorate the centenary of the founding of the Faculty of Letters, Lisbon University.

Setubal Sea Gate and Ships A216

1961, Aug. 24 Litho. Perf. 12x11½
873 A216 1e gold & multi 20 6
874 A216 4.30e gold & multi 4.25 3.00

Centenary of the city of Setubal.

Clasped Hands and CEPT Emblem — A217

Tomar Castle and River Nabao — A218

Europa Issue, 1961
1961, Sept. 18 Perf. 13½x13
875 A217 1e bl & lt bl 10 10
876 A217 1.50e grn & brt grn 60 60
877 A217 3.50e brn, pink & red 90 90

1962, Jan. 26 Perf. 11½x12
878 A218 1e gold & multi 15 8
879 A218 3.50e gold & multi 95 90

800th anniversary of the city of Tomar.

National Guardsman A219

Archangel Gabriel A220

1962, Feb. 20 Unwmk. Perf. 13½
880 A219 1e multi 10 6
881 A219 2e multi 1.10 30
882 A219 2.50e multi 90 25

Issued to commemorate the 50th anniversary of the Republican National Guard.

1962, Mar. 24 Litho. Perf. 13
883 A220 1e ol, pink & red brn 50 7
884 A220 3.50e ol, pink & dk grn 30 30

Issued for St. Gabriel's Day. St. Gabriel is patron of telecommunications.

Tents and Scout Emblem A221

1962, June 11 Unwmk. Perf. 13
885 A221 20c gray, bis, yel & blk 8 8
a Double impression of gray frame lettering
886 A221 50c multi 8 8
887 A221 1e multi 32 8
888 A221 2.50e multi 1.50 25
889 A221 3.50e multi 35 30
890 A221 6.50e multi 35 30
Nos. 885-890 (6) 2.68 1.09

Issued to commemorate the 50th anniversary of the Portuguese Boy Scouts and the 18th Boy Scout World Conference, Sept. 19-24, 1961.

Children Reading A222

Designs: 1e, Vaccination. 2.80e, Children playing ball. 3.50e, Guarding sleeping infant.

1962, Sept. 10 Litho. Perf. 13½
891 A222 50c bluish grn, yel & blk 8 6
892 A222 1e pale bl, yel & blk 42 6
893 A222 2.80e dp org yel & blk 85 50
894 A222 3.50e dl rose, yel & blk 1.25 85

Issued to commemorate the Tenth International Congress of Pediatrics, Lisbon, Sept. 9-15.

Europa Issue, 1962

19-Cell Honeycomb A223

1962, Sept. 17
895 A223 1e bl, dk bl & gold 10 8
896 A223 1.50e lt & dk grn & gold 52 40
897 A223 3.50e dp rose, mar & gold 50 65

The 19 cells represent the 19 original members of the Conference of European Postal and Telecommunications Administrations, C.E.P.T.

St. Zenon, the Courier A224

European Soccer Cup and Emblem A225

1962, Dec. 1 Unwmk. Perf. 13½
898 A224 1e multi 12 6
899 A224 2e multi 52 50
900 A224 2.80e multi 1.00 1.00

Issued for Stamp Day.

1963, Feb. 5 Perf. 13½
901 A225 1e multi 38 12
902 A225 4.30e multi 75 75

Issued to commemorate the victories of the Benfica Club of Lisbon in the 1961 and 1962 European Soccer Championships.

Wheat Emblem A226

1963, Mar. 21 Litho.
903 A226 1e multi 10 6
904 A226 3.30e multi 60 70
905 A226 3.50e multi 70 50

FAO "Freedom from Hunger" campaign.

Stagecoach A227

1963, May 7 Perf. 12x11½
906 A227 1e gray, lt & dk bl 15 8
907 A227 1.50e bis, dk brn & lil rose 80 25
908 A227 5e org brn, dk brn & rose lil 18 22

Issued to commemorate the centenary of the first International Postal Conference, Paris, 1863.

St. Vincent de Paul by Monsaraz — A228

1963, July 10 Photo. Perf. 13½x14
Gold Inscription
909 A228 20c lt bl & ultra 6 6
a Gold inscription omitted 55.00
910 A228 1e gray & sl 16 6
911 A228 2.80e grn & sl 80 80
a Gold inscription omitted 65.00
912 A228 5e dp rose car & sl 80 38

Issued to commemorate the tercentenary of the death of St. Vincent de Paul.

Emblem of Order and Knight A229

1963, Aug. 13 Litho. Perf. 11½
913 A229 1e multi 15 6
914 A229 1.50e multi 18 8
915 A229 2.50e multi 1.25 32

Issued to commemorate the 800th anniversary of the Military Order of Avis.

Europa Issue, 1963

Stylized Bird — A230

1963, Sept. 16 Perf. 13½
916 A230 1e lt bl, gray & blk 16 6
917 A230 1.50e grn, gray & blk 1.10 48
918 A230 3.50e red, gray & blk 1.40 1.10

Jet Plane — A231

Apothecary Jar — A232

1963, Dec. 1 Unwmk. Perf. 13½
919 A231 1e dk bl & lt bl 12 8
920 A231 2.50e dk grn & yel grn 65 28
921 A231 3.50e org brn & org 85 55

Issued to commemorate the 10th anniversary of Transportes Aereos Portugueses, TAP.

1964, Apr. 9 Litho.
922 A232 50c brn ol, dk brn & blk 12 12
923 A232 1e rose brn, dp cl & blk 15 8
924 A232 4.30e dk gray, sl & blk 3.25 3.25

Issued to commemorate the 4th centenary of the publication (in Goa, Apr. 10, 1563) of "Coloquios Dos Simples e Drogas" (Herbs and Drugs in India) by Garcia D'Orta.

Emblem of National Overseas Bank — A233

Mt. Sameiro Church — A234

1964, May 19 Unwmk. *Perf. 13½*
925 A233 1e bis, yel & dk bl 8 6
926 A233 2.50e ocher, yel & grn 1.00 38
927 A233 3.50e bis, yel & brn 70 50

Centenary of National Overseas Bank.

1964, June 5 Litho.
928 A234 1e red brn, bis & dl brn 8 6
929 A234 2e brn, bis & dl brn 52 30
930 A234 5e dk vio bl, bis & gray 75 48

Issued to commemorate the centenary of the Shrine of Our Lady of Mt. Sameiro, Braga.

Europa Issue, 1964
Common Design Type
1964, Sept. 14 Unwmk. *Perf. 13½*
Size: 19x32mm.
931 CD7 1e bl, lt bl & dk bl 20 10
932 CD7 3.50e rose brn, buff & dk brn 90 55
933 CD7 4.30e grn, yel grn & dk grn 1.40 2.00

Partial Eclipse of Sun — A235

Olympic Rings, Emblems of Portugal and Japan — A236

1964
934 A235 1e multi 18 6
935 A235 8e multi 70 45

International Quiet Sun Year, 1964-65.

1964, Dec. 1 Unwmk. *Perf. 13½*
Black Inscriptions; Olympic Rings in Pale Yellow
936 A236 20c tan, red & vio bl 8 8
937 A236 1e ultra, red & vio bl 14 8
938 A236 1.50e yel grn, red & vio bl 90 45
939 A236 6.50e rose lil, red & vio bl 1.00 1.00

18th Olympic Games, Tokyo, Oct. 10-25.

Eduardo Coelho A237

Traffic Signs and Signals A238

1964, Dec. 28 Litho. *Perf. 13½*
940 A237 1e multi 14 10
941 A237 5e multi 85 65

Issued to commemorate the centenary of the founding of Portugal's first newspaper, "Diario de Noticias," and to honor the founder, Eduardo Coelho, journalist.

1965, Feb. 15 Litho.
942 A238 1e yel, red & emer 15 8
943 A238 3.30e multi 1.75 2.00
944 A238 3.50e red, yel & emer 85 45

Issued to publicize the First National Traffic Congress, Lisbon, Feb. 15-19.

Ferdinand I, Duke of Braganza A239

Coimbra Gate, Angel with Censer and Sword A240

1965, Mar. 16 Unwmk. *Perf. 13½*
945 A239 1e rose brn & blk 10 8
946 A239 10e Prus grn & blk 90 65

Issued to commemorate the 500th anniversary of the city of Braganza (in 1964).

1965, Apr. 27 *Perf. 11½x12*
947 A240 1e bl & multi 8 6
948 A240 2.50e multi 90 40
949 A240 5e multi 1.00 65

Issued to commemorate the 9th centenary (in 1964) of the capture of the city of Coimbra from the Moors.

ITU Emblem — A241

1965, May 17 *Perf. 13½*
950 A241 1e bis brn, ol grn & ol 9 6
951 A241 3.50e ol, rose cl & dp cl 80 40
952 A241 6.50e yel grn, dl bl & sl bl 45 35

Issued to commemorate the centenary of the International Telecommunication Union.

Calouste Gulbenkian A242

1965, July 20 Litho. *Perf. 13½*
953 A242 1e multi 35 7
954 A242 8e multi 35 30

Issued to honor Calouste Gulbenkian (1869-1955), oil industry pioneer and sponsor of the Gulbenkian Foundation.

Red Cross — A243

1965, Aug. 17 Unwmk. *Perf. 13½*
955 A243 1e grn, red & blk 12 8
956 A243 4e ol, red & blk 75 60
957 A243 4.30e lt rose brn, red & blk 4.50 4.50

Centenary of the Portuguese Red Cross.

Europa Issue, 1965
Common Design Type
1965, Sept. 27 Litho. *Perf. 13*
Size: 31x24mm.
958 CD8 1e saph, grnsh bl & dk bl 12 12
959 CD8 3.50e rose brn, sal & brn 1.00 1.00
960 CD8 4.30e grn, yel grn & dk grn 2.75 2.00

Military Plane — A244

1965, Oct. 20 *Perf. 13½*
961 A244 1e ol grn, red & dk grn 10 8
962 A244 2e sep, red & dk grn 65 30
963 A244 5e chlky bl, red & dk grn 1.10 60

Issued to commemorate the 50th anniversary of the founding of the Portuguese Air Force.

Woman A245

Chrismon with Alpha and Omega A246

Designs: Characters from Gil Vicente Plays.

1965, Dec. 1 Litho. *Perf. 13½*
964 A245 20c ol, pale yel & blk 6 6
965 A245 1e brn, pale yel & blk 9 8
966 A245 2.50e dk red, buff & blk 1.25 22
967 A245 6.50e bl, gray & blk 25 22

Issued to commemorate the 500th anniversary of the birth of Gil Vicente (1465?-1536?).

1966, Mar. 28 Litho. *Perf. 13½*
968 A246 1e ol bis, gold & blk 18 6
969 A246 3.30e gray, gold & blk 1.75 1.50
970 A246 5e rose cl, gold & blk 1.00 45

Issued to commemorate the Congress of the International Committee for the Defense of Christian Civilization, Lisbon.

Symbols of Peace and Labor — A247

1966, May 28 Litho. *Perf. 13½*
971 A247 1e dk bl, sl bl & lt sl bl 7 6
972 A247 3.50e ol, ol brn, & lt ol 75 42
973 A247 4e dk brn, brn car & dl rose 60 35

40th anniversary of National Revolution.

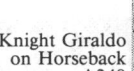

Knight Giraldo on Horseback A248

1966, June 8
974 A248 1e multi 30 7
975 A248 8e multi 35 35

Issued to commemorate the 800th anniversary of the conquest of Evora from the Moors.

Salazar Bridge — A249

Designs: 2.80e, 4.30e, View of bridge (vert.).

1966, Aug. 6 Litho. *Perf. 13½*
976 A249 1e gold & red 16 8
977 A249 2.50e gold & ultra 1.00 35
978 A249 2.80e sil & dp ultra 1.10 90
979 A249 4.30e sil & dk grn 1.10 90

Issued to commemorate the opening of the Salazar Bridge over the Tejo River. Lisbon.

Europa Issue, 1966
Common Design Type
1966, Sept. 26 Litho. *Perf. 11½x12*
Size: 26x32mm.
980 CD9 1e bl & blk 15 15
981 CD9 3.50e red brn & blk 1.65 1.65
982 CD9 4.30e yel grn & blk 1.65 1.65

Pestana A250

Bocage A251

Portraits: 20c, Camara Pestana (1863-1899), bacteriologist. 50c, Egas Moniz (1874-1955), neurologist. 1e, Antonio Pereira Coutinho (1851-1939), botanist. 1.50e, José Correa da Serra (1750-1823), botanist. 2e, Ricardo Jorge (1858-1938), hygienist and anthropologist. 2.50e, J. Liete de Vasconcelos (1858-1941), ethnologist. 2.80e, Maximiano Lemos (1860-1923), medical historian. 4.30e, JoséAntonio Serrano, anatomist.

1966, Dec. 1 Litho. *Perf. 13½*
Portrait and Inscription in Dark Brown and Bister
983 A250 20c gray grn 6 6
984 A250 50c orange 6 6
985 A250 1e lemon 8 8
986 A250 1.50e bis brn 12 8
987 A250 2e brn org 85 8
988 A250 2.50e pale grn 1.10 12
989 A250 2.80e salmon 1.25 1.25
990 A250 4.30e Prus bl 1.65 1.40
Nos. 983-990 (8) 5.17 3.13

Issued to honor Portuguese scientists.

1966, Dec. 28 Litho. *Perf. 11½x12*
991 A251 1e bis, grnsh gray & blk 8 6
992 A251 2e brn org, grnsh gray & blk 35 20
993 A251 6e gray, grnsh gray & blk 60 48

Issued to commemorate the 200th anniversary of the birth of Manuel Maria Barbosa du Bocage (1765-1805), poet.

Europa Issue, 1967
Common Design Type
1967, May 2 Litho. *Perf. 13*
Size: 21½x31mm.
994 CD10 1e lt bl, Prus bl & blk 15 15
995 CD10 3.50e sal, brn red & blk 1.10 1.10

996	CD10	4.30e yel grn, ol grn & blk	1.65	1.65

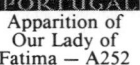

Apparition of Our Lady of Fatima — A252

Statues of Roman Senators — A253

Designs: 2.80e, Church and Golden Rose. 3.50e, Statue of the Pilgrim Virgin, with lilies and doves. 4e, Doves holding crown over Chapel of the Apparition.

1967, May 13 ***Perf. 11½x12***

997	A252	1e multi	8	8
998	A252	2.80e multi	48	80
999	A252	3.50e multi	20	20
1000	A252	4e multi	26	25

Issued to commemorate the 50th anniversary of the apparition of the Virgin Mary to 3 shepherd children at Fatima.

1967, June 1 **Litho.** ***Perf. 13***

1001	A253	1e gold & rose cl	8	8
1002	A253	2.50e gold & dl bl	90	42
1003	A253	4.30e gold & gray grn	52	52

Introduction of a new civil law code.

Shipyard, Margueira, Lisbon — A254

Design: 2.80e, 4.30e, Ship's hull and map showing location of harbor.

1967, June 23

1004	A254	1e aqua & multi	8	6
1005	A254	2.80e multi	40	45
1006	A254	3.50e multi	40	24
1007	A254	4.30e multi	50	48

Issued to commemorate the inauguration of the Lisnave Shipyard at Margueira, Lisbon.

Symbols of Healing A255

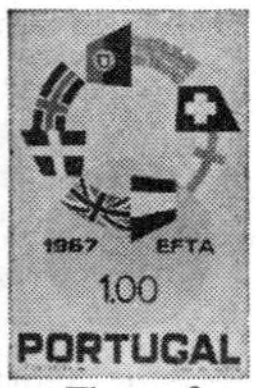

Flags of EFTA Nations A256

1967, Oct. 8 **Litho.** ***Perf. 13½***

1008	A255	1e multi	8	6
1009	A255	2e multi	52	20
1010	A255	5e multi	85	60

Issued to publicize the 6th European Congress of Rheumatology, Lisbon, Oct. 8-13.

1967, Oct. 24 **Litho.** ***Perf. 13½***

1011	A256	1e bis & multi	8	6
1012	A256	3.50e buff & multi	50	50
1013	A256	4.30e gray & multi	1.50	1.50

Issued to publicize the European Free Trade Association. See note after Norway No. 501.

A little time given to the study of the arrangement of the Scott Catalogue can make it easier to use effectively.

Tables of the Law — A257

1967, Dec. 27 **Litho.** ***Perf. 13½***

1014	A257	1e olive	8	6
1015	A257	2e red brn	45	20
1016	A257	5e green	75	55

Centenary of abolition of death penalty.

Bento de Goes — A258

1968, Feb. 14 **Engr.** ***Perf. 12x11½***

1017	A258	1e ol, ind & dk brn	40	8
1018	A258	8e org brn, dl pur & ol grn	65	48

Issued to commemorate the 360th anniversary (in 1967) of the death of Bento de Goes (1562-1607), Jesuit explorer of the route to China.

Europa Issue, 1968
Common Design Type

1968, Apr. 29 **Litho.** ***Perf. 13***
Size: 31x21mm.

1019	CD11	1e multi	12	12
1020	CD11	3.50e multi	1.25	1.25
1021	CD11	4.30e multi	2.75	2.75

Mother's and Child's Hands — A259

1968, May 26 **Litho.** ***Perf. 13½***

1022	A259	1e lt gray, blk & red	8	6
1023	A259	2e sal, blk & red	60	25
1024	A259	5e lt bl, blk & red	85	65

Issued to commemorate the 30th anniversary of the Mothers' Organization for National Education.

"Victory over Disease" and WHO Emblem A260

1968, July 10 **Litho.** ***Perf. 12½***

1025	A260	1e multi	8	6
1026	A260	3.50e multi	40	28
1027	A260	4.30e tan & multi	3.00	3.00

Issued for the 20th anniversary of the World Health Organization.

Madeira Grapes and Wine A261

Joao Fernandes Vieira — A262

Designs: 1e, Fireworks on New Year's Eve. 1.50e, Mountains and valley. 3.50e, Woman doing Madeira embroidery. 4.30e, Joao Gonçalves Zarco. 20e, Muschia aurea (flower.)

Perf. 12x11½, 11½x12
1968, Aug. 17 **Litho.**

1028	A261	50c multi	8	8
1029	A261	1e multi	12	8
1030	A261	1.50e multi	18	10
1031	A262	2.80e multi	1.40	1.40
1032	A262	3.50e multi	95	50
1033	A262	4.30e multi	4.00	4.00
1034	A262	20e multi	2.25	70
		Nos. 1028-1034 (7)	8.98	6.86

Issued to publicize Madeira and the Lubrapex 1968 stamp exhibition.

Design descriptions in Portuguese, French and English printed on back of stamps.

Pedro Alvares Cabral A263

Cabral's Fleet A264

Design: 3.50e, Cabral's coat of arms (vert.).

Perf. 12x12½, 12½x12
1969, Jan. 30 **Engr.**

1035	A263	1e vio bl, bl & gray bl	12	8
1036	A263	3.50e dp cl	1.50	1.00
		Litho.		
1037	A264	6.50e grn & multi	1.10	1.10

Issued to commemorate the 5th centenary of the birth of Pedro Alvarez Cabral (1468-1520), navigator, discoverer of Brazil. Nos. 1035-1037 have description of the designs printed on the back in Portuguese, French and English.

Europa Issue, 1969
Common Design Type

1969, Apr. 28 **Litho.** ***Perf. 13***
Size: 31x22½mm.

1038	CD12	1e dp bl & multi	12	10
1039	CD12	3.50e multi	1.25	1.00
1040	CD12	4.30e grn & multi	2.00	1.50

King José I and Arms of National Press — A265

1969, May 14 **Litho.** ***Perf. 11½x12***

1041	A265	1e multi	8	6
1042	A265	2e multi	55	20
1043	A265	8e multi	42	42

Bicentenary of the National Press.

ILO Emblem — A266

1969, May 28 ***Perf. 13***

1044	A266	1e bluish grn, blk & sil	10	7
1045	A266	3.50e red, blk & sil	60	30
1046	A266	4.30e brt bl, blk & sil	1.00	85

Issued to commemorate the 50th anniversary of the International Labor Organization.

Juan Cabrillo Rodriguez A267

Vianna da Motta, by Columbano Bordalo Pinheiro A268

1969, July 16 **Litho.** ***Perf. 11½x12***

1047	A267	1e multi	8	8
1048	A267	2.50e multi	75	25
1049	A267	6.50e multi	55	55

Bicentenary of San Diego, Calif., and honoring Juan Cabrillo Rodriguez, explorer of California coast.

Backs inscribed. See note below No. 1034.

1969, Sept. 24 **Litho.** ***Perf. 12***

1050	A268	1e multi	40	8
1051	A268	9e gray & multi	42	55

Issued to commemorate the centenary of the birth of Vianna da Motta (1868-1948), pianist and composer.

Gago Coutinho and 1922 Seaplane A269

Design: 2.80e, 4.30e, Adm. Coutinho and Coutinho sextant.

1969, Oct. 22

1052	A269	1e grnsh gray, dk & lt brn	9	8
1053	A269	2.80e yel bis, dk & lt brn	65	65
1054	A269	3.30e gray bl, dk & lt brn	1.00	1.00
1055	A269	4.30e lt rose brn, dk & lt brn	1.40	1.25

Issued to commemorate the centenary of the birth of Admiral Carlos Viegas Gago Coutinho (1869-1959), explorer and aviation pioneer.

Vasco da Gama — A270

Designs: 2.80e, Da Gama's coat of arms. 3.50e, Map showing route to India and compass rose (horiz.). 4e, Da Gama's fleet (horiz.).

Perf. 12x11½, 11½x12

1969, Dec. 30 **Litho.**

1056	A270	1e	multi	14	10
1057	A270	2.80e	multi	1.65	1.65
1058	A270	3.50e	multi	1.25	70
1059	A270	4e	multi	1.00	42

500th anniversary of the birth of Vasco da Gama (1469-1525), navigator who found sea route to India.

Design descriptions in Portuguese, French and English printed on back of stamps.

Europa Issue, 1970

Common Design Type

1970, May 4 **Litho.** ***Perf. 13½***

Size: 31x22mm.

1060	CD13	1e	dk bl & pale yel	25	25
1061	CD13	3.50e	red brn & pale yel	1.65	1.65
1062	CD13	4.30e	ol & pale yel	2.50	2.25

Distillation Plant — A271

Design: 2.80e, 6e, Catalytic cracking tower.

1970, June 5 **Litho.** ***Perf. 13***

1063	A271	1e	dk bl & dl bl	8	6
1064	A271	2.80e	sl grn & pale grn	75	75
1065	A271	3.30e	dk ol grn & ol	60	55
1066	A271	6e	dk brn & dl ocher	50	35

Opening of the Oporto Oil Refinery.

Marshal Carmona and Oak Leaves A272

Designs: 2.50e, Carmona, Portuguese coat of arms and laurel. 7e, Carmona and ferns.

Litho. & Engr.

1970, July 1 ***Perf. 12x12½***

1067	A272	1e	ol grn & blk	8	8
1068	A272	2.50e	red, ultra & blk	60	30
1069	A272	7e	sl bl & blk	55	55

Issued to commemorate the centenary of the birth of Marshal Antonio Oscar de Fragoso Carmona (1869-1951), President of Portugal, 1926-1951.

Emblem of Plant Research Station A273

1970, July 29 **Litho.**

1070	A273	1e	multi	8	8
1071	A273	2.50e	multi	60	22
1072	A273	5e	multi	85	45

Issued to commemorate the 25th anniversary of the Plant Research Station at Elvas.

Compass Rose and EXPO Emblem — A274

Designs: 5e, Monogram of Christ (IHS) and EXPO emblem. 6.50e, "Portugal and Japan" as written in old manuscripts, and EXPO emblem.

1970, Sept. 16 **Litho.** ***Perf. 13***

1073	A274	1e	gold & multi	8	6
1074	A274	5e	sil & multi	65	22
1075	A274	6.50e	multi	1.25	1.25

Issued to commemorate EXPO '70 International Exhibition, Osaka, Japan, March 15-Sept. 13. See No. C11.

Castle (from Arms of Santarem) A275

Designs: No. 1077, Star and wheel, from Covilha coat of arms. 2.80e, Ram and Covilha coat of arms. 4e, Knights on horseback and Santarem coat of arms.

1970, Oct. 7 **Litho.** ***Perf. 12x11½***

1076	A275	1e	multi	8	6
1077	A275	1e	ultra & multi	8	6
1078	A275	2.80e	red & multi	1.10	1.10
1079	A275	4e	gray & multi	45	35

Nos. 1076 and 1079 commemorate the centenary of the City of Santarem; Nos. 1077-1078 commemorate the centenary of the City of Covilha.

Paddlesteamer Great Eastern Laying Cable — A276

Designs: 2.80e, 4e, Cross section of cable.

1970, Nov. 21 **Litho.** ***Perf. 14***

1080	A276	1e	multi	10	8
1081	A276	2.50e	multi	90	35
1082	A276	2.80e	multi	1.25	1.25
1083	A276	4e	multi	90	65

Centenary of the Portugal-Great Britain submarine telegraph cable.

Grapes and Woman Filling Baskets A277

Designs: 1e, Worker carrying basket of grapes, and jug. 3.50e, Glass of wine, and barge with barrels on River Douro. 7e, Wine bottle and barrels.

1970, Dec. 20 **Litho.** ***Perf. 12x11½***

1084	A277	50c	multi	8	8
1085	A277	1e	multi	8	8
1086	A277	3.50e	multi	50	8
1087	A277	7e	multi	50	45

Publicity for port wine export.

Mountain Windmill, Bussaco Hills — A278

Francisco Franco (1885-1955) — A279

Windmills: 50c, Beira Litoral Province. 1e, Estremadura Province. 2e, St. Miguel, Azores. 3.30e, Porto Santo, Madeira. 5e, Pico, Azores.

1971, Feb. 24 **Litho.** ***Perf. 13***

1088	A278	20c	multi	6	5
1089	A278	50c	lt bl & multi	8	5
1090	A278	1e	gray & multi	8	6
1091	A278	2e	multi	40	8
1092	A278	3.30e	ocher & multi	1.10	1.10
1093	A278	5e	multi	90	30
			Nos. 1088-1093 (6)	2.62	1.64

Backs inscribed. See note below No. 1034.

Europa Issue, 1971

Common Design Type

1971, May 3 **Photo.** ***Perf. 14***

Size: 32x22mm.

1094	CD14	1e	dk bl, lt grn & blk	18	18
1095	CD14	3.50e	red brn, yel & blk	1.25	1.10
1096	CD14	7.50e	ol, yel & blk	1.90	1.90

Perf. 11½x12½; 13½ (2.50e, 4e)

1971, July 7 **Engr.**

Designs: 1e, Antonio Teixeira Lopes (1866-1942). 1.50e, Antonio Augusto da Costa Mota (1862-1930). 2.50e, Rui Roque Gameiro (1906-1935). 3.50e, JoseSimoes de Almedia (nephew; 1880-1950). 4e, Francisco dos Santos (1878-1930).

1097	A279	20c	black	8	6
a			Perf. 13½	1.10	22
1098	A279	1e	claret	8	6
1099	A279	1.50e	sepia	20	14
1100	A279	2.50e	dk bl	45	14
1101	A279	3.50e	car rose	48	18
1102	A279	4e	gray grn	95	80
			Nos. 1097-1102 (6)	2.24	1.38

Portuguese sculptors.

Pres. Antonio Salazar — A280

1971, July 27 **Engr.** ***Perf. 13½***

1103	A280	1e	multi	12	6
a			Perf. 12½x12	*35.00*	1.10
1104	A280	5e	multi	52	20
1105	A280	10e	multi	85	40
a			Perf. 12½x12	*18.00*	65

Wolframite Crystals A281

Minerals: 2.50e, Arsenopyrite (gold). 3.50e, Beryllium. 6.50e, Chalcopyrite (copper).

1971, Sept. 24 **Litho.** ***Perf. 12***

1106	A281	1e	multi	8	6
1107	A281	2.50e	car & multi	75	28
1108	A281	3.50e	grn & multi	30	15
1109	A281	6.50e	bl & multi	45	30

Spanish-Portuguese-American Economic Geology Congress.

Town Gate, Castelo Branco A282

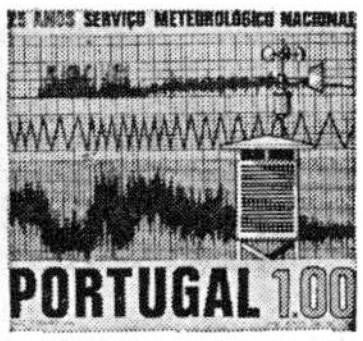

Weather Recording Station and Barograph Charts A283

Designs: 3e, Memorial column. 12.50e, Arms of Castelo Branco (horiz.).

1971, Oct. 7 ***Perf. 14***

1110	A282	1e	multi	14	6
1111	A282	3e	multi	75	32
1112	A282	12.50e	multi	60	30

Bicentenary of Castelo Branco as a town.

1971, Oct. 29 ***Perf. 13½***

Designs: 4e, Stratospheric weather balloon and weather map of southwest Europe and North Africa. 6.50e, Satellite and aerial map of Atlantic Ocean off Portugal.

1113	A283	1e	buff & multi	9	6
1114	A283	4e	multi	1.10	52
1115	A283	6.50e	blk, dl red brn & org	48	30

25 years of Portuguese meteorological service.

Missionaries and Ship — A284

1971, Nov. 24

1116	A284	1e	gray, ultra & blk	10	10
1117	A284	3.30e	dp bis, lil & blk	75	75
1118	A284	4.80e	ol, grn & blk	75	75

400th anniversary of the martyrdom of a group of Portuguese missionaries on the way to Brazil.

"Man" A285

Designs: 3.30e, "Earth" (animal, vegetable, mineral). 3.50e, "Air" (birds). 4.50e, "Water" (fish).

1971, Dec. 22 **Litho.** ***Perf. 12***

1119	A285	1e	brn & multi	8	8
1120	A285	3.30e	lt bl, yel & grn	28	20
1121	A285	3.50e	lt bl, rose & vio	30	9
1122	A285	4.50e	lt bl, grn & ultra	1.10	75

Nature conservation.

City Hall, Sintra — A286

Designs: 5c, Aqueduct, Lisbon. 50c, University, Coimbra. 1e, Torre dos Clerigos, Porto. 1.50e, Belem Tower, Lisbon. 2.50e, Castle, Vila da Feira. 3e, Misericordia House, Viana do Castelo. 3.50e, Window, Tomar Convent. 8e, Ducal Palace, Guimaraes. 10e, Cape Girao, Madeira. 20e, Episcopal Garden, Castelo Branco. 100e, Lakes of Seven Cities, Azores.

1972-73 **Litho.** ***Perf. 12½***

Size: 22x17½mm

1123	A286	5c	gray, grn & blk	32	32
1124	A286	50c	gray bl, blk & org	16	5
1125	A286	1e	grn, blk & brn	10	5
1126	A286	1.50e	bl, bis & blk	10	8
1127	A286	2.50e	brn, dk brn & gray	32	8
1128	A286	3e	yel, blk & brn	48	10
1129	A286	3.50e	dp org, sl & brn	32	10
1130	A286	8e	blk, ol & grn	3.25	28

Perf. 13½

Size: 31x22mm

1131	A286	10e	gray & multi	1.00	25
1132	A286	20e	grn & multi	6.50	35
1133	A286	50e	gray bl, ocher & blk	2.00	35
1134	A286	100e	grn & multi	4.50	1.10
			Nos. 1123-1134 (12)	19.05	3.11

"CTT" and year date printed in minute gray multiple rows on back of stamps.

Issue dates: 1e, 1.50e, 50e, 100e, Mar. 1; 50c, 3e, 10e, 20e, Dec. 6, 1972; 5c, 2.50e, 3.50e, 8e, Sept. 5, 1973.

See Nos. 1207-1214.

Tagging

Starting in 1975, phosphor (bar or L-shape) was applied to the face of most definitives and commemoratives.

Stamps issued both with and without tagging include Nos. 1124-1125, 1128, 1130-1131, 1209, 1213-1214, 1250, 1253, 1257, 1260, 1263.

Window, Pinhel Church A287

Heart and Pendulum A288

Designs: 1e, Arms of Pinhel (horiz.). 7.50e, Stone lantern.

1972, Mar. 29 **Perf. 13½**

1135	A287	1e	bl & multi	8	8
a			Perf. 11½x12½	16.00	45
1136	A287	2.50e	multi	60	20
1137	A287	7.50e	bl & multi	50	40

Bicentenary of Pinhel as a town.

1972, Apr. 24

Designs: 4e, Heart and spiral pattern. 9e, Heart and continuing coil pattern.

1138	A288	1e	vio & red	9	8
1139	A288	4e	grn & red	1.25	80
1140	A288	9e	brn & red	52	48

"Your heart is your health," World Health Day.

Europa Issue 1972

Common Design Type

1972, May 1 **Perf. 13½**

Size: 21x31mm.

1141	CD15	1e	gray & multi	15	15
1142	CD15	3.50e	sal & multi	65	65
1143	CD15	6e	grn & multi	1.25	1.25

Trucks — A289

1972, May 17 **Litho.** **Perf. 13½**

1144	A289	1e	*shown*	8	6
1145	A289	4.50e	*Taxi*	75	45
1146	A289	8e	*Autobus*	60	40

13th Congress of International Union of Road Transport (I.R.U.), Estoril, May 15-18.

Soccer, Olympic Rings A290

1972, July 26 **Litho.** **Perf. 14**

1147	A290	50c	*shown*	6	6
1148	A290	1e	*Running*	8	8
1149	A290	1.50e	*Equestrian*	14	8
1150	A290	3.50e	*Swimming, women's*	38	18
1151	A290	4.50e	*Yachting*	52	50
1152	A290	5e	*Gymnastics, women's*	90	38
			Nos. 1147-1152 (6)	2.08	1.28

20th Olympic Games, Munich, Aug. 26-Sept. 11.

Marquis of Pombal — A291

Tomé de Sousa — A292

1972, Aug. 28 **Perf. 13½**

1153	A291	1e	*shown*	9	6
1154	A291	2.50e	*Scientific apparatus*	75	28
1155	A291	8e	*Seal of Univ. of Coimbra*	60	45

Bicentenary of the Pombaline reforms of University of Coimbra.

1972, Oct. 5 **Litho.** **Perf. 13½**

Designs: 2.50e, José Bonifacio. 3.50e, Dom Pedro IV. 6e, Allegory of Portuguese-Brazilian Community.

1156	A292	1e	gray & multi	8	6
1157	A292	2.50e	grn & multi	32	15
1158	A292	3.50e	multi	32	18
1159	A292	6e	bl & multi	60	30

150th anniversary of Brazilian independence.

Sacadura Cabral, Gago Coutinho and Plane — A293

Designs: 2.50e, 3.80e, Map of flight from Lisbon to Rio de Janeiro. 2.80e, Like 1e.

1972, Nov. 15 **Perf. 11½x12½**

1160	A293	1e	bl & multi	10	8
a			Perf. 13½	10.50	1.25
1161	A293	2.50e	multi	52	15
1162	A293	2.80e	multi	60	60
1163	A293	3.80e	multi	70	70
a			Perf. 13½	*25.00*	*16.00*

50th anniversary of the Lisbon to Rio de Janeiro flight by Commander Arturo de Sacadura Cabral and Adm. Carlos Viegas Gago Coutinho, Mar. 30-June 5, 1922.

Luiz Camoens A294

Designs: 3e, Hand saving manuscript from sea. 10e, Symbolic of man's questioning and discovering the unknown.

1972, Dec. 27 **Litho.** **Perf. 13**

1164	A294	1e	org brn, buff & blk	8	6
1165	A294	3e	dl bl, lt grn & blk	65	24
1166	A294	10e	red brn, buff & yel	90	42

4th centenary of the publication of The Lusiads by Luiz Camoens (1524-1580).

Graphs and Sequence Count — A295

Designs: 4e, Odometer. 9e, Graphs.

1973, Apr. 11 **Litho.** **Perf. 14½**

1167	A295	1e	gray & multi	9	8
1168	A295	4e	gray & multi	65	28
1169	A295	9e	gray & multi	48	25

Productivity Conference '72, Jan. 17-22, 1972.

Europa Issue 1973

Common Design Type

1973, Apr. 30 **Perf. 13**

Size: 31x29mm.

1170	CD16	1e	multi	14	14
1171	CD16	4e	brn red & multi	1.50	1.90
1172	CD16	6e	grn & multi	2.50	2.50

Gen. Medici, Arms of Brazil and Portugal A296

Designs: 2.80e, 4.80e, Gen. Medici and world map.

Lithographed and Engraved

1973, May 16 **Perf. 12x11½**

1173	A296	1e	dk grn, blk & sep	8	8
1174	A296	2.80e	ol & multi	40	35
1175	A296	3.50e	dk bl, blk & buff	40	30
1176	A296	4.80e	multi	32	25

Visit of Gen. Emilio Garrastazu Medici, President of Brazil, to Portugal.

Child and Birds — A297

Designs: 4e, Child and flowers. 7.50e, Child.

1973, May 28 **Litho.** **Perf. 13**

1177	A297	1e	ultra & multi	9	6
1178	A297	4e	multi	60	20
1179	A297	7.50e	bis & multi	75	45

To pay renewed attention to children.

Transportation, Weather Map — A298

Designs: 3.80e, Communications: telegraph, telephone, radio, satellite. 6e, Postal service: mailbox, truck, mail distribution diagram.

1973, June 25

1180	A298	1e	multi	6	5
1181	A298	3.80e	multi	22	18
1182	A298	6e	multi	52	40

Ministry of Communications, 25th anniv.

Pupil and Writing Exercise — A299

Designs: 4.50e, Illustrations from 18th century primer. 5.30e, School and children, by 9-year-old Marie de Luz (horiz.). 8e, Symbolic chart of teacher-pupil link (horiz.).

1973, Oct. 24 **Litho.** **Perf. 13**

1183	A299	1e	bl & multi	8	8
1184	A299	4.50e	brn & multi	55	20
1185	A299	5.30e	lt bl & multi	48	35
1186	A299	8e	grn & multi	90	55

Bicentenary of primary state school education.

Oporto Streetcar, 1910 A300

Designs: 1e, Horse-drawn streetcar, 1872. 3.50e, Double-decker Leyland bus, 1972.

1973, Nov. 7

Size: 31½x34mm.

1187	A300	1e	brn, yel & blk	8	8
1188	A300	3.50e	choc & multi	1.00	60

Size: 37½x27mm.

Perf. 12½

1189	A300	7.50e	buff & multi	90	55

Cent. of public transportation in Oporto.

Servicemen's League Emblem A301

Death of Nuno Gonzalves A302

Designs: 2.50e, Sailor, soldier and aviator. 11e, Military medals.

1973, Nov. 28 **Litho.** **Perf. 13**

1190	A301	1e	multi	9	9
1191	A301	2.50e	multi	95	45
1192	A301	11e	dk bl & multi	65	52

50th anniv. of the Servicemen's League.

1973, Dec. 19

1193	A302	1e	sl bl & org	8	8
1194	A302	10e	vio brn & org	55	42

600th anniversary of the heroism of Nuno Gonzalves, alcaide of Faria Castle.

Damiao de Gois, by Dürer (?) — A303

"The Exile," by Soares dos Reis — A304

Designs: 4.50e, Title page of Cronica de Principe D. Joao. 7.50e, Lute and score of Dodecachordon.

1974, Apr. 5 Litho. *Perf. 12*

1195	A303	1e multi	14	8
1196	A303	4.50e multi	80	30
1197	A303	7.50e multi	90	35

400th anniversary of the death of Damiao de Gois (1502-1574), humanist, writer, composer.

Europa Issue 1974

1974, Apr. 29 Litho. *Perf. 13*

1198	A304	1e multi	35	35
1199	A304	4e dk red & multi	5.50	2.25
1200	A304	6e dk grn & multi	6.25	4.50

Pattern of Light Emission A305

Designs: 4.50e, Spiral wave radiation pattern. 5.30e, Satellite and earth.

1974, June 26 Litho. *Perf. 14*

1201	A305	1.50e gray ol	8	6
1202	A305	4.50e dk bl	1.00	45
1203	A305	5.30e brt rose lil	32	30

Establishment of satellite communications network via Intelsat among Portugal, Angola and Mozambique.

Diffusion of Hertzian Waves A306

Designs (Symbolic): 3.30e, Messages through space. 10e, Navigation help.

1974, Sept. 4 Litho. *Perf. 12*

1204	A306	1.50e multi	8	6
1205	A306	3.30e multi	50	45
1206	A306	10e multi	1.10	60

Centenary of the birth of Guglielmo Marconi (1874-1937), Italian electrical engineer and inventor.

Buildings Type of 1972-73

Designs: 10c, Ponte do Lima (Roman bridge). 30c, Alcobaça Monastery, interior. 2e, City Hall, Bragança. 4e, New Gate, Braga. 4.50e, Dolmen of Carrazeda. 5e, Roman Temple, Evora. 6e, Leca do Balio Monastery. 7.50e, Almourol Castle.

1974, Sept. 18 Litho. *Perf. 12½*
Size: 22x17½mm.

1207	A286	10c multi	10	10
1208	A286	30c multi	10	8
1209	A286	2e multi	10	5
1210	A286	4e multi	35	8
1211	A286	4.50e multi	60	8
1212	A286	5e multi	6.25	8
1213	A286	6e multi	1.75	18
1214	A286	7.50e multi	90	10
		Nos. 1207-1214 (8)	10.15	75

"CTT" and year date printed in minute gray multiple rows on back of stamps.

Postilion, Truck and Letter A307

Designs: 2e, Hand holding letter. 3.30e, Packet and steamship. 4.50e, Pigeon and letters. 5.30e, Hand holding sealed letter. 20e, Old and new locomotives.

1974, Oct. 9 Litho. *Perf. 13*

1220	A307	1.50e brn & multi	8	8
1221	A307	2e multi	45	10
1222	A307	3.30e ol & multi	14	15
1223	A307	4.50e multi	45	42
1224	A307	5.30e multi	35	30
1225	A307	20e multi	1.25	1.00
a		Souvenir sheet of 6	4.50	4.50
		Nos. 1220-1225 (6)	2.72	2.05

Centenary of Universal Postal Union. No. 1225a contains one each of Nos. 1220-1225, arranged to show a continuous design with a globe in center. Blue and indigo marginal design and inscription. Size: 106x146mm. Sold for 50e.

Luisa Todi, Singer (1753-1833) A308

Marcos Portugal, Composer (1762-1838) A309

Portuguese Musicians: 2e, Joao Domingos Bomtempo (1775-1842). 2.50e, Carlos Seixas (1704-1742). 3e, Duarte Lobo (1565-1646). 5.30e, Joao de Sousa Carvalho (1745-1798).

1974, Oct. 30 Litho. *Perf. 12*

1226	A308	1.50e brt pink	8	8
1227	A308	2e vermilion	60	22
1228	A308	2.50e brown	50	8
1229	A308	3e bluish blk	35	22
1230	A308	5.30e sl grn	38	35
1231	A309	11e rose lake	38	35
		Nos. 1226-1231 (6)	2.29	1.30

Coat of Arms of Beja — A310

Designs: 3.50e, Men of Beja in costumes from Roman times to date. 7e, Moorish Arches and view across plains.

1974, Nov. 13

1232	A310	1.50e multi	8	8
1233	A310	3.50e multi	60	50
1234	A310	7e multi	1.00	50

2,000th anniversary of Beja.

Annunciation A311

Rainbow and Dove A312

Designs: 4.50e, Adoration of the Shepherds. 10e, Flight into Egypt. Designs show Portuguese costumes from Nazare township.

1974, Dec. 4 Litho. *Perf. 13*

1235	A311	1.50e red & multi	8	6
1236	A311	4.50e multi	1.25	30
1237	A311	10e bl & multi	85	42

Christmas 1974.

1974, Dec. 18 *Perf. 12*

1238	A312	1.50e multi	6	6
1239	A312	3.50e multi	1.50	42
1240	A312	5e multi	1.00	25

Armed Forces Movement of Apr. 25, 1974.

Egas Moniz — A313

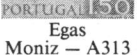

Soldier as Farmer, Farmer as Soldier — A314

Designs: 3.30e, Lobotomy probe and Nobel Prize medal, 1949. 10e, Cerebral angiograph, 1927.

1974, Dec. 27 Engr. *Perf. 11½x12*

1241	A313	1.50e yel & multi	8	8
1242	A313	3.30e brn & ocher	22	35
1243	A313	10e gray & ultra	1.00	35

Egas Moniz (1874-1955), brain surgeon, birth centenary.

1975, Mar. 21 Litho. *Perf. 12*

1244	A314	1.50e grn & multi	12	8
1245	A314	3e gray & multi	1.25	20
1246	A314	4.50e multi	1.65	40

Cultural progress and citizens' guidance campaign.

Hands and Dove — A315

Designs: 4.50e, Brown hands reaching for dove. 10e, Dove with olive branch and arms of Portugal.

1975, Apr. 23 Litho. *Perf. 13½*

1247	A315	1.50e red & multi	9	8
1248	A315	4.50e brn & multi	1.10	35
1249	A315	10e grn & multi	1.25	48

Movement of April 25th, first anniversary. Slogans in Portuguese, French and English printed on back of stamps.

God's Hand Reaching Down — A316

Designs: 4.50e, Jesus' hand holding up cross. 10e, Dove (Holy Spirit) descending.

1975, May 13 Litho. *Perf. 13½*

1250	A316	1.50e multi	8	8
1251	A316	4.50e plum & multi	1.50	42
1252	A316	10e bl & multi	1.50	55

Holy Year 1975.

Europa Issue 1975

Horseman of the Apocalypse, 12th Century — A317

Design: 10e, The Poet Fernando Pessoa, by Almada Negreiros (1893-1970).

1975, May 26

1253	A317	1.50e multi	25	12
1254	A317	10e multi	4.50	3.50

Assembly Building A318

1975, June 2 Litho. *Perf. 13½*

1255	A318	2e red, blk & yel	8	8
1256	A318	20e emer, blk & yel	1.75	1.00

Opening of Constituent Assembly.

Hikers — A319

Designs: 4.50e, Campsite on lake. 5.30e, Mobile homes on the road.

1975, Aug. 4 Litho. *Perf. 13½*

1257	A319	2e multi	50	8
1258	A319	4.50e multi	90	35
1259	A319	5.30e multi	35	45

36th Rally of the International Federation of Camping and Caravanning, Santo Andre Lake.

People and Sapling — A320

Designs (UN Emblem and): 4.50e, People and dove. 20e, People and grain.

1975, Sept. 17 Litho. *Perf. 13½*

1260	A320	2e grn & multi	20	8
1261	A320	4.50e vio & multi	90	20
1262	A320	20e multi	2.00	55

United Nations, 30th anniversary.

Icarus and Rocket — A321

Designs: 4.50e, Apollo and Soyuz in space. 5.30e, Robert H. Goddard, Robert Esnault-Pelterie, Hermann Oberth and Konstantin Tsiolkovski. 10e, Sputnik, man in space, moon landing module.

1975, Sept. 26 Litho. *Perf. 13½*
Size: 30½x26½mm.

1263	A321	2e grn & multi	20	8
1264	A321	4.50e brn & multi	90	30
1265	A321	5.30e lil & multi	30	30

Size: 65x28mm.

1266	A321	10e bl & multi	2.00	52

26th Congress of International Astronautical Federation, Lisbon, Sept. 1975.

Land Survey A322

Designs: 8e, Ocean survey. 10e, People of many races and globe.

1975, Nov. 19 Litho. *Perf. 12x12½*

1267 A322 2e ocher & multi 20 8
1268 A322 8e bl & multi 60 52
1269 A322 10e dk vio & multi 1.40 55

Centenary of Lisbon Geographical Society.

Arch and Trees — A323

Designs: 8e, Plan, pencil and ruler. 10e, Hand, old building and brick tower.

1975, Nov. 28 *Perf. 13½*

1270 A323 2e dk bl & gray 18 12
1271 A323 8e dk car & gray 1.50 1.40
1272 A323 10e ocher & multi 1.65 1.50

European Architectural Heritage Year 1975.

Nurse and Hospital Ward — A324

Designs (IWY Emblem and): 2e, Farm workers. 3.50e, Secretary. 8e, Factory worker.

1975, Dec. 30 Litho. *Perf. 13½*

1273 A324 50c multi 8 8
1274 A324 2e multi 55 10
1275 A324 3.50e multi 55 28
1276 A324 8e multi 60 55
a Souvenir sheet of 4 2.50 2.50

International Women's Year 1975. No. 1276a contains 4 stamps similar to Nos. 1273-1276 in slightly changed colors; blue and gray marginal inscription and IWY emblem. Size: 102x115mm. Sold for 25e.

Pen Nib as Plowshare A325

1976, Feb. 6 Litho. *Perf. 12*

1277 A325 3e dk bl & red org 22 8
1278 A325 20e org, ultra & red 2.00 95

Portuguese Society of Writers, 50th anniversary.

Telephones, 1876, 1976 — A326

Design: 10.50e, Alexander Graham Bell and telephone.

1976, Mar. 10 Litho. *Perf. 12x12½*

1279 A326 3e yel grn, grn & blk 60 8
1280 A326 10.50e rose, red & blk 1.65 52

Centenary of first telephone call by Alexander Graham Bell, March 10, 1876.

Industry and Shipping — A327

Design: 1e, Garment, food and wine industries.

1976, Apr. 7 Litho. *Perf. 12½*

1281 A327 50c red brn 20 12
1282 A327 1e slate 30 12

Support of national production.

Europa Issue 1976

Carved Spoons, Olive Wood — A328

Design: 20e, Gold filigree pendant, silver box and CEPT emblem.

1976, May 3 Litho. *Perf. 12x12½*

1283 A328 3e ol & multi 35 15
1284 A328 20e tan & multi 6.75 5.25

Stamp Collectors A329

Designs: 7.50e, Stamp exhibition and hand canceler. 10e, Printing and designing stamps.

1976, May 29 Litho. *Perf. 14½*

1285 A329 3e multi 8 8
1286 A329 7.50e multi 42 30
1287 A329 10e multi 1.10 30

Interphil 76, International Philatelic Exhibition, Philadelphia, Pa., May 29-June 6.

King Ferdinand I — A330

Designs: 5e, Plowshare, farmers chasing off hunters. 10e, Harvest.

1976, July 2 Litho. *Perf. 12*

1288 A330 3e lt bl & multi 12 12
1289 A330 5e yel grn & multi 75 52
1290 A330 10e multi 80 75
a Souvenir sheet of 3 2.50 2.50

Agricultural reform law (compulsory cultivation of uncultivated lands), 600th anniversary. No. 1290a contains one each of Nos. 1288-1290, black marginal inscription with text of law of May 28, 1375. Size: 230x148mm. Sold for 30e.

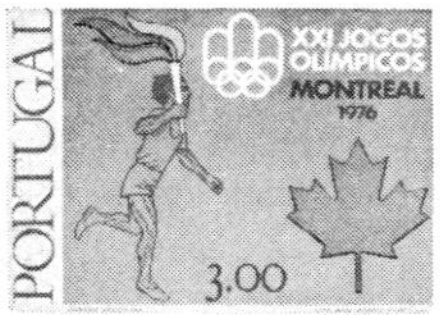

Torch Bearer A331

Designs (Montreal Games' Emblem, Maple Leaf and): 7e, Women's relay race. 10.50e, Olympic flame.

1976, July 16 *Perf. 13½*

1291 A331 3e red & multi 15 8
1292 A331 7e red & multi 95 52
1293 A331 10.50e red & multi 1.25 48

21st Olympic Games, Montreal, Canada, July 17-Aug. 1.

Farm A332

1976, Sept. 15 Litho. *Perf. 12*

1294 A332 3e *shown* 48 15
a Perf. 13½ 30.00 15.00
1295 A332 3e *Ship* 48 15
a Perf. 13½ 1.50 1.10
1296 A332 3e *City* 48 15
a Perf. 13½ 35.00 18.00
1297 A332 3e *Factory* 80 15
a Perf. 13½ 60 45
b Souv. sheet of 4, #1294-1297 6.75 6.75

Fight against illiteracy. No. 1297b sold for 25e.

Azure-winged Magpie — A333

Designs: 5e, Lynx. 7e, Portuguese laurel cherry. 10.50e, Little wild carnations.

1976, Sept. 30 Litho. *Perf. 12*

1298 A333 3e multi 24 8
1299 A333 5e multi 70 15
1300 A333 7e multi 70 52
1301 A333 10.50e multi 90 70

Portucale 77, 2nd International Thematic Exhibition, Oporto, Oct. 29-Nov. 6, 1977.

Exhibition Hall — A334

Design: 20e, Symbolic stamp and emblem.

1976, Oct. 9 Litho. *Perf. 13½*

1302 A334 3e bl & multi 18 8
1303 A334 20e ocher & multi 2.25 1.10
a Souv. sheet of 2, #1302-1303 2.50 2.50

6th Luso-Brazilian Philatelic Exhibition, LUBRAPEX 76, Oporto, Oct. 9. No. 1303a sold for 30e.

Bank Emblem and Family A335

Designs: 7e, Emblem and grain. 15e, Emblem and cog wheels.

1976, Oct. 29 *Perf. 12*

1304 A335 3e org & multi 9 8
1305 A335 7e grn & multi 95 45
1306 A335 15e bl & multi 1.10 55

Trust Fund Bank centenary.

Sheep Grazing on Marsh A336

Designs: 3e, Drainage ditches. 5e, Fish in water. 10e, Ducks flying over marsh.

1976, Nov. 24 Litho. *Perf. 14*

1307 A336 1e multi 18 12
1308 A336 3e multi 45 18
1309 A336 5e multi 95 30
1310 A336 10e multi 1.25 45

Protection of wetlands.

"Liberty" — A337

1976, Nov. 30 Litho. *Perf. 13½*

1311 A337 3e gray, grn & ver 45 15

Constitution of 1976.

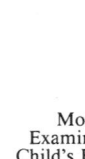

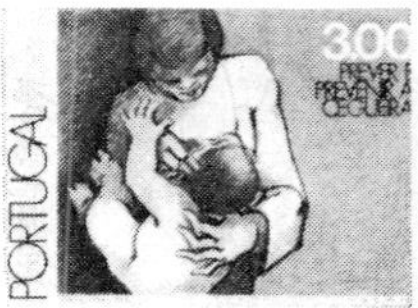

Mother Examining Child's Eyes A338

Designs: 5e, Welder with goggles. 10.50e, Blind woman reading Braille.

1976, Dec. 13

1312 A338 3e multi 15 8
1313 A338 5e multi 65 15
1314 A338 10.50e multi 95 65

World Health Day and campaign against blindness.

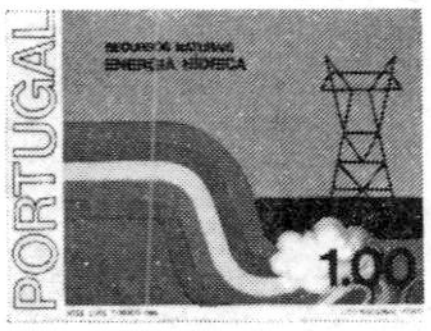

Hydroelectric Energy — A339

Abstract Designs: 4e, Fossil fuels. 5e, Geothermal energy. 10e, Wind power. 15e, Solar energy.

1976, Dec. 30

1315 A339 1e multi 16 8
1316 A339 4e multi 32 12
1317 A339 5e multi 35 12
1318 A339 10e multi 65 40
1319 A339 15e multi 1.25 70
Nos. 1315-1319 (5) 2.73 1.42

Sources of energy.

Map of Council of Europe Members A340

1977, Jan. 28 Litho. *Perf. 12*

1320 A340 8.50e multi 55 55
1321 A340 10e multi 55 55

Portugal's joining Council of Europe.

Alcoholic and Bottle — A341

Designs (Bottle and): 5e, Symbolic figure of broken life. 15e, Bars blotting out the sun.

1977, Feb. 4 *Perf. 13*

1322 A341 3e multi 10 10
1323 A341 5e ocher & multi 38 20
1324 A341 15e org & multi 90 70

Anti-alcoholism Day and 10th anniversary of Portuguese Anti-alcoholism Society.

Trees Tapped for Resin — A342

Designs: 4e, Trees stripped for cork. 7e, Trees and logs. 15e, Trees at seashore as windbreakers.

1977, Mar. 21 Litho. *Perf. 13½*

1325	A342	1e multi	10	8
1326	A342	4e multi	24	12
1327	A342	7e multi	90	35
1328	A342	15e multi	1.00	65

Forests, a natural resource.

"Suffering" A343

Designs: 6e, Man exercising. 10e, Group exercising. All designs include emblems of World Health Organization and Portuguese Institute for Rheumatology.

1977, Apr. 13 Litho. *Perf. 12x12½*

1329	A343	4e blk, brn & ocher	15	8
1330	A343	6e blk, bl & vio	60	52
1331	A343	10e blk, pur & red	52	24

International Rheumatism Year.

Europa 1977

Southern Plains Landscape A344

Design: 8.50e, Northern mountain valley.

1977, May 2

1332	A344	4e multi	38	25
1333	A344	8.50e multi	1.65	1.10
a		Min. sheet, 2 each #1332-1333	12.50	12.50

Pope John XXI Enthroned A345

Petrus Hispanus, the Physician A346

1977, May 20 Litho. *Perf. 13½*

1334	A345	4e multi	25	15
1335	A346	15e multi	60	60

Pope John XXI (Petrus Hispanus), only Pope of Portuguese descent, 7th death centenary.

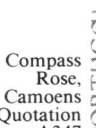

Compass Rose, Camoens Quotation A347

1977, June 8 *Perf. 12*

1336	A347	4e multi	18	8
1337	A347	8.50e multi	55	52

Camoens Day and to honor Portuguese overseas communities.

Student, Computer and Book — A348

Designs (Book and): No. 1339, Folk dancers, flutist and boat. No. 1340, Tractor drivers. No. 1341, Atom and people.

1977, July 20 Litho. *Perf. 12x12½*

1338	A348	4e multi	22	18
1339	A348	4e multi	22	18
1340	A348	4e multi	22	18
1341	A348	4e multi	22	18
a		Souvenir sheet of 4	3.50	3.50

Continual education. No. 1341a contains one each of Nos. 1338-1341; brown and ultramarine inscription and emblem in margin. Size: 148x96mm. Sold for 20e.

Pyrites, Copper, Chemical Industry A349

Designs: 5e, Marble, statue, public buildings. 10e, Iron ore, girders, crane. 20e, Uranium ore, atomic diagram.

1977, Oct. 4 Litho. *Perf. 12x11½*

1342	A349	4e multi	14	8
1343	A349	5e multi	42	16
1344	A349	10e multi	45	22
1345	A349	20e multi	1.25	55

Natural resources from the subsoil.

Alexandre Herculano A350

1977, Oct. 19 Engr. *Perf. 12x11½*

1346	A350	4e multi	14	10
1347	A350	15e multi	55	50

Alexandre Herculano de Carvalho Araujo (1810-1877), historian, novelist, death centenary.

Maria Pia Bridge A351

Design: 4e, Arrival of first train, ceramic panel by Jorge Colaco, St. Bento railroad station.

1977, Nov. 4 Litho. *Perf. 12x11½*

1348	A351	4e multi	16	8
1349	A351	10e multi	80	80

Centenary of extension of railroad across Douro River.

Poveiro Bark A352

Coastal Fishing Boats: 3e, Do Mar bark. 4e, Nazaré bark. 7e, Algarve skiff. 10e, Xavega bark. 15e, Bateira de Buarcos.

1977, Nov. 19 *Perf. 12*

1350	A352	2e multi	32	8
1351	A352	3e multi	16	8
1352	A352	4e multi	16	16
1353	A352	7e multi	24	16
1354	A352	10e multi	40	40
1355	A352	15e multi	90	65
a		Souvenir sheet of 6	3.00	3.00
		Nos. 1350-1355 (6)	2.18	1.53

PORTUCALE 77, 2nd International Topical Exhibition. Oporto, Nov. 19-20. No. 1355a contains one each of Nos. 1350-1355; gray margin with black inscription. Size: 148x105mm. Sold for 60e.

Nativity A353

Children's Drawings: 7e, Nativity. 10e, Holy Family (vert.). 20e, Star and Christ Child (vert.).

Perf. 12x11½, 11½x12

1977, Dec. 12 Litho.

1356	A353	4e multi	10	10
1357	A353	7e multi	45	32
1358	A353	10e multi	45	35
1359	A353	20e multi	1.65	75

Christmas 1977.

Old Desk and Computer — A354

Designs: Work tools, old and new.

1978-83 Litho. *Perf. 12½*

Size: 22x17mm

1360	A354	50c	Medical	6	5
1361	A354	1e	Household	6	5
1362	A354	2e	Communications	6	5
1363	A354	3e	Garment making	8	5
1364	A354	4e	Office	10	10
1365	A354	5e	Fishing craft	12	10
1366	A354	5.50e	Weaving	12	8
1367	A354	6e	Plows	16	10
1368	A354	6.50e	Aviation	14	14
1369	A354	7e	Printing	20	10
1370	A354	8e	Carpentry	18	10
1371	A354	8.50e	Potter's wheel	20	5
1372	A354	9e	Photography	20	10
1373	A354	10e	Saws	20	12
1373A	A354	12.50e	Compasses ('83)	18	12
1373B	A354	16e	Mail processing ('83)	18	12

Perf. 13½

Size: 31x22mm

1374	A354	20e Construction	55	35
1375	A354	30e Steel industry	65	32
a		Incomplete arch	65	32
1376	A354	40e Transportation	75	70
1377	A354	50e Chemistry	1.10	55
1378	A354	100e Shipbuilding	2.00	90
1379	A354	250e Telescopes	4.75	2.75
		Nos. 1360-1379 (22)	12.04	7.00

Red Mediterranean Soil — A355

Designs: 5e, Stone formation. 10e, Alluvial soil. 20e, Black soil.

1978, Mar. 6 Litho. *Perf. 12*

1380	A355	4e multi	16	8
1381	A355	5e multi	20	8
1382	A355	10e multi	32	32
1383	A355	20e multi	1.25	55

Soil, a natural resource.

Street Crossing A356

Designs: 2e, Motorcyclist. 2.50e, Children in back seat of car. 5e, Hands holding steering wheel. 9e, Driving on country road. 12.50e, "Avoid drinking and driving."

1978, Apr. 19 Litho. *Perf. 12*

1384	A356	1e multi	8	6
1385	A356	2e multi	9	8
1386	A356	2.50e multi	22	8
1387	A356	5e multi	38	8
1388	A356	9e multi	55	30
1389	A356	12.50e multi	65	60
		Nos. 1384-1389 (6)	1.97	1.20

Road safety campaign.

Europa Issue 1978

Roman Tower, Belmonte A357

Design: 40e, Belem Monastery of Hieronymite monks (inside).

1978, May 2

1390	A357	10e multi	40	40
1391	A357	40e multi	1.65	1.65
a		Souvenir sheet of 4	10.00	10.00

No. 1391a contains 2 each of Nos. 1390-1391, imperf.; gray marginal inscription. Size: 11x95mm. Sold for 120e.

Trajan's Bridge — A358

Roman Tablet from Bridge — A359

1978, June 14 Litho. *Perf. 13½*

1392	A358	5e multi	16	10
1393	A359	20e multi	95	95

1900th anniv. of Chaves (Aquae Flaviae).

Running A360

Designs: 10e, Bicycling. 12.50e, Watersport. 15e, Soccer.

1978, July 24 Litho. *Perf. 12*

1394	A360	5e multi	15	8
1395	A360	10e multi	30	18
1396	A360	12.50e multi	45	45
1397	A360	15e multi	45	30

Sport for all the people.

Pedro Nunes A361

Design: 20e, "Nonio" navigational instrument and diagram from "Tratado da Rumaçao do Globo."

1978, Aug. 9 Litho. *Perf. 12x11½*

1398	A361	5e multi	14	10
1399	A361	20e multi	75	50

Pedro Nunes (1502-1578), navigator and cosmographer.

Trawler, Frozen Fish Processing, Can of Sardines A362

Fishing Industry: 9e, Deep-sea trawler, loading and unloading at dock. 12.50e, Trawler with radar and instruction in use of radar. 15e, Trawler with echo-sounding equipment, microscope and test tubes.

1978, Sept. 16 Litho. *Perf. 12x11½*

1400	A362	5e multi	15	8
1401	A362	9e multi	18	12
1402	A362	12.50e multi	45	40
1403	A362	15e multi	55	30

Natural resources.

Postrider A363

Designs: No. 1405, Carrier pigeon. No. 1406, Envelopes. No. 1407, Pen.

1978, Oct. 30 Litho. *Perf. 12*

1404	A363	5e yel & multi	24	18
1405	A363	5e bl gray & multi	24	18
1406	A363	5e grn & multi	24	18
1407	A363	5e red & multi	24	18

Introduction of Postal Code.

Human Figure, Flame Emblem A364

Design: 40e, Human figure pointing the way and flame emblem.

1978, Dec. 7 Litho. *Perf. 12*

1408	A364	14e multi	25	25
1409	A364	40e multi	1.10	1.10
a		Souvenir sheet of 4	3.75	4.75

Universal Declaration of Human Rights, 30th anniversary and 25th anniversary of European Declaration. No. 1409a contains 2 each Nos. 1408-1409; gray marginal inscription. Size: 120x100mm.

Sebastiao Magalhaes Lima A365

1978, Dec. 7

1410	A365	5e multi	20	8

Sebastiao Magalhaes Lima (1850-1928), lawyer, journalist, statesman.

The first value column gives the catalogue value of an unused stamp, the second that of a used stamp.

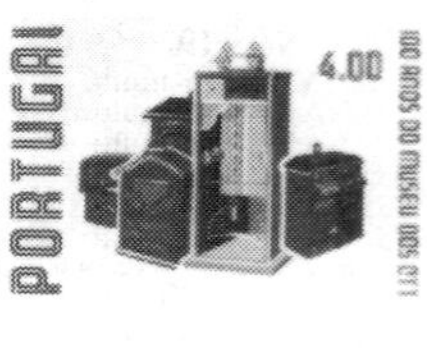

Mail Boxes and Scale A366

Designs: 5e, Telegraph and condenser lens. 10e, Portugal Nos. 2-3 and postal card printing press, 1879. 14e, Book and bookcases, 1879, 1979.

1978, Dec. 20

1411	A366	4e multi	16	10
1412	A366	5e multi	20	8
1413	A366	10e multi	32	16
1414	A366	14e multi	75	65
a		Souvenir sheet of 4	1.65	1.65

Centenary of Postal Museum and Postal Library; 125th anniversary of Portuguese stamps (10e). No. 1414a contains Nos. 1411-1414; gray marginal inscription. Size: 120x99mm. Sold for 40e.

Emigrant at Railroad Station A367

Designs: 14e, Farewell at airport. 17e, Emigrant greeting child at railroad station.

1979, Feb. 21 Litho. *Perf. 12*

1415	A367	5e multi	9	8
1416	A367	14e multi	30	30
1417	A367	17e multi	75	65

Portuguese emigration.

Automobile Traffic — A368

Designs: 5e, Pneumatic drill. 14e, Man with bull horn.

1979, Mar. 14 *Perf. 13½*

1418	A368	4e multi	15	15
1419	A368	5e multi	9	9
1420	A368	14e multi	35	35

Combat noise pollution.

NATO Emblem A369

1979, Apr. 4 Litho. *Perf. 12*

1421	A369	5e multi	14	7
1422	A369	50e multi	1.40	1.25
a		Souv. sheet, 2 each #1421-1422	3.25	3.25

NATO, 30th anniv.

Europa Issue 1979

Mail Delivery, 16th Century A370

Design: 40e, Mail delivery, 19th century.

1979, Apr. 30 Litho. *Perf. 12*

1423	A370	14e multi	32	32
1424	A370	40e multi	80	80
a		Souv. sheet, 2 each #1423-1424	6.25	6.25

Mother, Infant, Dove — A371

Designs (IYC Emblem and): 5.50e, Children playing ball. 10e, Child in nursery school. 14e, Black and white boys.

1979, June 1 Litho. *Perf. 12x12½*

1425	A371	5.50e multi	15	10
1426	A371	6.50e multi	18	10
1427	A371	10e multi	25	18
1428	A371	14e multi	45	35
a		Souvenir sheet of 4	1.50	1.50

International Year of the Child. No. 1428a contains Nos. 1425-1428. Gray marginal inscription. Size: 111x104mm. Sold for 40e.

Salute to the Flag — A372

1979, June 8

1429	A372	6.50e multi	22	18
a		Souvenir sheet of 9	2.25	2.25

Portuguese Day.

Pregnant Woman A373

Designs: 17e, Boy sitting in a cage. 20e, Face, and hands using hammer.

1979, June 6 Litho. *Perf. 12x12½*

1430	A373	6.50e multi	20	20
1431	A373	17e multi	48	48
1432	A373	20e multi	52	52

Help for the mentally retarded.

Children Reading Book, UNESCO Emblem A374

Design: 17e, Teaching deaf child, and UNESCO emblem.

1979, June 25

1433	A374	6.50e multi	20	12
1434	A374	17e multi	48	48

International Bureau of Education, 50th anniversary.

Water Cart, Brasiliana '79 Emblem A375

Brasiliana '79 Philatelic Exhibition: 5.50e, Wine sledge. 6.50e, Wine cart. 16e, Covered cart. 19e, Mogadouro cart. 20e, Sand cart.

1979, Sept. 15 Litho. *Perf. 12*

1435	A375	2.50e multi	12	8
1436	A375	5.50e multi	15	12
1437	A375	6.50e multi	18	18
1438	A375	16e multi	35	35
1439	A375	19e multi	40	35
1440	A375	20e multi	45	30
		Nos. 1435-1440 (6)	1.65	1.38

Antonio Jose de Almeida (1866-1929) A376

Republican Leaders: 6.50e, Afonso Costa (1871-1937). 10e, Teofilo Braga (1843-1924). 16e, Bernardino Machado (1851-1944). 19.50e, Joao Chagas (1863-1925). 20e, Elias Garcia (1830-1891).

1979, Oct. 4 *Perf. 12½x12*

1441	A376	5.50e multi	12	8
1442	A376	6.50e multi	15	8
1443	A376	10e multi	20	10
1444	A376	16e multi	30	30
1445	A376	19.50e multi	35	60
1446	A376	20e multi	35	30
		Nos. 1441-1446 (6)	1.47	1.46

See Nos. 1454-1459.

Red Cross and Family A377

Red Cross and: 20e, Doctor examining elderly man.

1979, Oct. 26 *Perf. 12x12½*

1447	A377	6.50e multi	15	15
1448	A377	20e multi	55	55

National Health Service Campaign.

Holy Family, 17th Century Mosaic A378

Mosaics, Lisbon Tile Museum: 6.50e, Nativity, 16th century. 16e, Flight into Egypt, 18th century.

1979, Dec. 5 Litho. *Perf. 12x12½*

1449	A378	5.50e multi	12	12
1450	A378	6.50e multi	18	18
1451	A378	16e multi	45	45

Christmas 1979.

Rotary International, 75th Anniversary A379

1980, Feb. 22 *Perf. 12x11½*

1452	A379	16e *shown*	42	42
1453	A379	50e *Emblem, torch*	1.10	1.10

Portrait Type of 1979

Leaders of the Republican Movement: 3.50e, Alvaro de Castro (1878-1928). 5.50e, Antonio Sergio (1883-1969). 6.50e, Norton de Matos (1867-1955). 11e, Jaime Cortesao (1884-1960). 16e, Teixeira Gomes (1860-1941). 20e, Jose Domingues dos Santos (1885-1958). Nos. 1454-1459 horizontal.

1980, Mar. 19

1454	A376	3.50e	multi	12	10
1455	A376	5.50e	multi	18	15
1456	A376	6.50e	multi	18	15
1457	A376	11e	multi	35	35
1458	A376	16e	multi	48	38
1459	A376	20e	multi	48	32
			Nos. 1454-1459 (6)	1.79	1.45

Europa Issue

Serpa Pinto (1864-1900), Explorer of Africa — A380

1980, Apr. 14

1460	A380	16e	*shown*	20	20
1461	A380	60e	*Vasco da Gama (1468-1524)*	85	85
a			Souvenir sheet of 4	3.50	3.50

No. 1461a contains 2 each Nos. 1460-1461. Silver margin shows Europa emblem. Size: 108x110mm.

Barn Owl A381

1980, May 6 Litho. *Perf. 12x11½*

1462	A381	6.50e	*shown*	25	18
1463	A381	16e	*Red fox*	52	52
1464	A381	19.50e	*Timber wolf*	60	50
1465	A381	20e	*Golden eagle*	60	52
a			Souvenir sheet of 4	2.25	2.25

European Campaign for the Protection of Species and their Habitat (Lisbon Zoo animals); London 1980 International Stamp Exhibition, May 6-14. No. 1465a contains Nos. 1462-1465; blue margin shows London 1980 emblem. Size: 110½x108mm.

Luiz Camoens A382

Lithographed & Engraved

1980, June 9 *Perf. 11½x12*

1446	A382	6.50e	multi	15	15
1467	A382	20e	multi	50	50

Luiz Camoens (1524-1580), 400th death anniversary. Nos. 1466-1467 each se-tenant with label showing poetry text.

Mendes Pinto and Chinese Men A383

1980, June 30 Litho. *Perf. 12x11½*

1468	A383	6.50e	*shown*	20	18
1469	A383	10e	*Battle at sea*	28	28

A Peregrinacao (The Peregrination,) by Fernao Mendes Pinto (1509-1583), written in 1580, published in 1614.

St. Vincent and Old Lisbon A384

Designs: 8e, Lantern Tower, Evora Cathedral. 11e, Jesus with top hat, Miranda do Douro Cathedral, and mountain. 16e, Our Lady of the Milk, Braga Cathedral, and Canicada Dam. 19.50e, Pulpit, Santa Cruz Monastery, Coimbra, and Aveiro River. 20e, Algarve chimney, and Rocha Beach.

1980, Sept. 17 Litho. *Perf. 12x12½*

1470	A384	6.50e	multi	16	12
1471	A384	8e	multi	20	16
1472	A384	11e	multi	25	20
1473	A384	16e	multi	35	35
1474	A384	19.50e	multi	42	42
1475	A384	20e	multi	42	32
			Nos. 1470-1475 (6)	1.80	1.57

World Tourism Conf., Manila, Sept. 27.

Caravel, Lubrapex '80 Emblem A385

1980, Oct. 18 Litho. *Perf. 12x11½*

1476	A385	6.50e	*shown*	18	12
1477	A385	8e	*Three-master Nau*	22	16
1478	A385	16e	*Galleon*	42	42
1479	A385	19.50e	*Paddle steamer*	48	32
a			Souvenir sheet of 4	3.00	3.00

Lubrapex '80 Stamp Exhibition, Lisbon, Oct. 18-26. No. 1479a contains Nos. 1476-1479; light green marginal inscription. Size: 132x88mm.

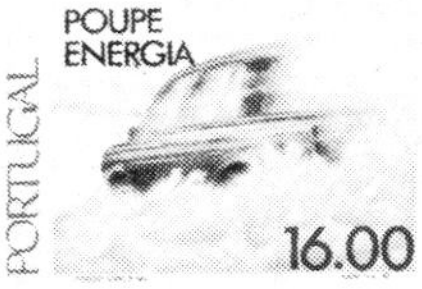

Car Emitting Gas Fumes A386

1980, Oct. 31

1480	A386	6.50e	*Light bulbs*	20	15
1481	A386	16e	*shown*	40	40

Energy conservation.

Student, School and Sextant A387

1980, Dec. 19 Litho. *Perf. 12x11½*

1482	A387	6.50e	*Founder, book, emblem*	16	12
1483	A387	19.50e	*shown*	42	40

Lisbon Academy of Science bicentennial.

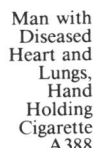

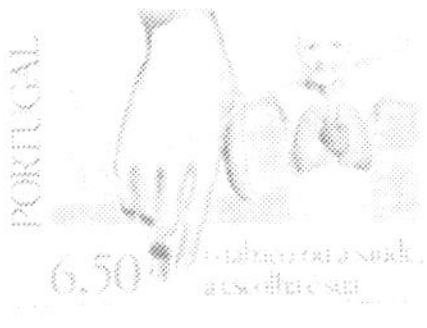

Man with Diseased Heart and Lungs, Hand Holding Cigarette A388

1980, Dec. 19 *Perf. 13½*

1484	A388	6.50e	*shown*	18	15
1485	A388	19.50e	*Healthy man rejecting cigarette*	48	48

Anti-smoking campaign.

Census Form and Houses A389

1981, Jan. 1 Litho. *Perf. 13½*

1486	A389	6.50e	*Form, head*	20	10
1487	A389	16e	*shown*	40	40

Fragata on Tejo River A390

1981, Feb. 23 Litho. *Perf. 12x12½*

1488	A390	8e	shown	20	10
1489	A390	8.50e	Rabelo, Douro River	20	10
1490	A390	10e	Moliceiro, Aveiro River	20	12
1491	A390	16e	Barco, Lima River	32	28
1492	A390	19.50e	Carocho, Minho River	35	32
1493	A390	20e	Varino, Tejo River	35	24
			Nos. 1488-1493 (6)	1.62	1.16

Rajola Tile, Valencia, 15th Century A391

1981, Mar. 16 Litho. *Perf. 11½x12*

1494	A391	8.50e	multi	22	15
a			Miniature sheet of 6	2.50	2.50

1981, June 13

Design: Moresque tile, Coimbra 16th cent.

1495	A391	8.50e	multi	22	15
a			Miniature sheet of 6	2.50	2.50

1981, Aug. 28

Design: No. 1496, Arms of Duke of Braganza, 1510.

1496	A391	8.50e	multi	22	15
a			Miniature sheet of 6	2.50	2.50

1981, Dec. 16

Design: No. 1497, Pisanos design, 1595.

1497	A391	8.50e	multi	22	15
a			Miniature sheet of 6	2.50	2.50
b			Souv. sheet of 4, #1494-1497	2.00	2.00

See Nos. 1528-1531, 1563-1566. 1593-1596, 1617-1620.

Perdigueiro A392

1981, Mar. 16 *Perf. 12*

1498	A392	7e	Cao de agua	16	10
1499	A392	8.50e	Serra de aires	24	12
1500	A392	15e	shown	35	18
1501	A392	22e	Podengo	50	35
1502	A392	25.50e	Castro laboreiro	55	35
1503	A392	33.50e	Serra da estrela	75	35
			Nos. 1498-1503 (6)	2.55	1.45

Portuguese Kennel Club, 50th anniversary.

Workers and Rainbow A393

1981, Apr. 30 Litho. *Perf. 12x12½*

1504	A393	8.50e	shown	22	22
1505	A393	25.50e	Rainbow, demonstration	50	50

International Workers' Day.

Europa Issue

Dancer in National Costume — A394

1981, May 11 *Perf. 13½*

1506	A394	22e	shown	38	38
1507	A394	48e	Painted boat, horiz.	95	95
a			Souv. sheet, 2 each #1506-1507	2.75	2.75

St. Anthony Writing A395

St. Anthony of Lisbon, 750th Anniversary of Death: 70e, Blessing people.

1981, June 13 *Perf. 12x11½*

1508	A395	8.50e	multi	20	20
1509	A395	70e	multi	1.40	1.40

500th Anniv. of King Joao II — A396

1981, Aug. 28 *Perf. 12x11½*

1510	A396	8.50e	shown	30	30
1511	A396	27e	Joao II leading army	95	95

125th Anniv. of Portuguese Railroads — A397

Designs: Locomotives.

1981, Oct. 28 Litho. *Perf. 12x11½*

1512	A397	8.50e	Dom Luis, 1862	22	15
1513	A397	19e	Pacific 500, 1925	38	35
1514	A397	27e	ALCO 1500, 1948	55	45
1515	A397	33.50e	BB 2600 ALSTHOM, '74	75	38

Pearier Pump Fire Engine, 1856 — A398

1981, Nov. 18 Litho. ***Perf. 12x12½***

1516 A398 7e shown 16 10
1517 A398 8.50e Ford, 1927 22 10
1518 A398 27e Renault, 1914 55 40
1519 A398 33.50e Snorkel, Ford 1978 70 50

Christmas 1981 — A399

Designs: Clay creches.

1981, Dec. 16 ***Perf. 12½x12***

1520 A399 7e multi 20 8
1521 A399 8.50e multi 22 10
1522 A399 27e multi 70 48

800th Birth Anniv. of St. Francis of Assisi — A400

1982, Jan. 20 Litho. ***Perf. 12½x12***

1523 A400 8.50e With animals 22 10
1524 A400 27e Building church 60 45

Centenary of Figueira da Foz — A401

1982, Feb. 24 Litho. ***Perf. 13½***

1525 A401 10e St. Catherine Fort 22 8
1526 A401 19e Tagus Bridge, ships 40 30

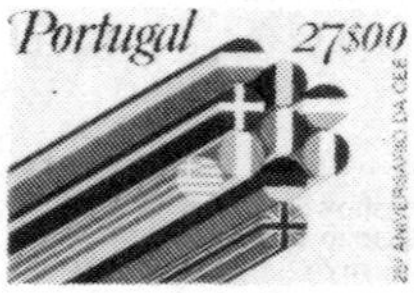
25th Anniv. of European Economic Community A402

1982, Feb. 24 ***Perf. 12x11½***

1527 A402 27e multi 65 42
a Souvenir sheet of 4 2.75 2.75

Tile Type of 1981

Design: Italo-Flemish pattern, 17th cent.

1982, Mar. 24 Litho. ***Perf. 11½x12***

1528 A391 10e multi 22 15
a Miniature sheet of 6 2.25 2.25

1982, June 11 ***Perf. 12x11½***

Design: 10e, Oriental fabric pattern altar frontal, 17th cent.

1529 A391 10e multi 20 15
a Miniature sheet of 6 2.25 2.25

1982, Sept. 22 ***Perf. 12***

Design: No. 1530, Greek cross, 1630-1640.

1530 A391 10e multi 18 15
a Miniature sheet of 6 2.25 2.25

1982, Dec. 15 ***Perf. 11½x12***

Design: No. 1531, Blue and white design, Mother of God Convent, Lisbon, 1670.

1531 A391 10e red & bl 18 15
a Miniature sheet of 6 2.25 2.25
b Souv. sheet of 4, #1528-1531 1.65 1.65

Major Sporting Events of 1982 — A403

Designs: 27e, Lisbon Sail. 33.50e, 25th Roller-hockey Championships, Lisbon and Barcelos, May 1-16. 50e, Intl. 470 Class World Championships, Cascais Bay. 75e, Espana '82 World Cup Soccer.

1982, Mar. 24 ***Perf. 12x12½***

1532 A403 27e multi 60 35
1533 A403 33.50e multi 70 45
1534 A403 50e multi 1.10 65
1535 A403 75e multi 1.65 1.00

Telephone Centenary — A404

1982, Apr. 14 Litho. ***Perf. 11½x12***

1536 A404 10e Phone, 1882 20 8
1537 A404 27e 1887 55 42

Europa 1982 — A405

Design: Embassy of King Manuel to Pope Leo X, 1514.

1982, May 3 ***Perf. 12x11½***

1538 A405 33.50e multi 65 42
a Miniature sheet of 4 3.00 3.00

Visit of Pope John Paul II — A406

Designs: Pope John Paul and cathedrals.

1982, May 13 ***Perf. 14***

1539 A406 10e Fatima 32 20
1540 A406 27e Sameiro 85 52
1541 A406 33.50e Lisbon 1.00 65
a Min. sheet, 2 each #1539-1541 4.75 4.75

Tejo Estuary Nature Reserve Birds — A407

1982, June 11 ***Perf. 11½x12***

1542 A407 10e Dunlin 22 10
1543 A407 19e Red-crested pochard 45 28
1544 A407 27e Greater flamingo 65 40
1545 A407 33.50e Black-winged stilt 85 48

PHILEXFRANCE '82 Stamp Exhibition, Paris, June 11-21.

TB Bacillus Centenary — A408

1982, July 27 ***Perf. 12x11½***

1546 A408 27e Koch 55 32
1547 A408 33.50e Virus, lungs 70 25

Don't Drink and Drive! — A409

1982, Sept. 22 ***Perf. 12***

1548 A409 10e multi 22 12

Boeing 747 A410

Lubrapex '82 Stamp Exhibition (Historic Flights): 10e, South Atlantic crossing, 1922. 19e, South Atlantic night crossing, 1927. 33.50e, Lisbon-Rio de Janeiro discount fare flights, 1960-1967. 50e, Portugal-Brazil service, 10th anniv.

1982, Oct. 15 ***Perf. 12x11½***

1549 A410 10e Fairey III D MK2 22 10
1550 A410 19e Dornier DO 40 22
1551 A410 33.50e DC-7C 65 40
1552 A410 50e shown 1.00 60
a Souvenir sheet of 4 2.75 2.75

No. 1552a contains Nos. 1549-1552; blue margin shows balloonist. Size: 156x98mm.

Marques de Pombal, Statesman, 200th Anniv. of Death — A411

1982, Nov. 24 Litho. ***Perf. 12x11½***

1553 A411 10e multi 22 12

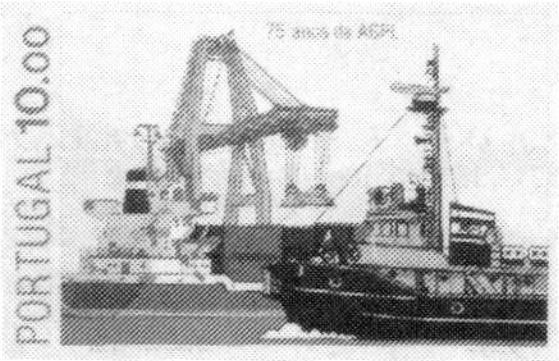
75th Anniv. of Port Authority of Lisbon — A412

1983, Jan. 5 ***Perf. 12½***

1554 A412 10e Ships 22 14

French Alliance Centenary A413

1983, Jan. 5 ***Perf. 12x11½***

1555 A413 27e multi 55 35

Export Effort A414

1983, Jan. 28

1556 A414 10e multi 20 12

World Communications Year — A415

1982, Feb. 23 Litho. ***Perf. 11½x12***

1557 A415 10e bl & multi 20 12
1558 A415 33.50e lt brn & multi 65 40

Naval Uniforms and Ships — A416

1983, Feb. 23 ***Perf. 13½***

1559 A416 12.50e Midshipman, 1782, Vasco da Gama 24 15
1560 A416 25e Sailor, 1845, Estefania 45 30
1561 A416 30e Sargent, 1900, Adamastor 60 35
1562 A416 37.50e Midshipman, 1892, Comandante Joao Belo 75 45
a Bklt. pane, #1559-1562 3.00

Tile Type of 1981

Design: No. 1563, Hunting scene, 1680.

1983, Mar. 16 ***Perf. 12x11½***

1563 A391 12.50e multi 25 15
a Miniature sheet of 6 1.75 1.75

1983, June 16

Design: No. 1564, Birds, 18th cent.

1564 A391 12.50e multi 28 18
a Miniature sheet of 6 1.75 1.75

1983, Oct. 19

Design: No. 1565, Flowers and Birds, 18th cent.

1565 A391 12.50e multi 22 14
a Miniature sheet of 6 1.75 1.75

1983, Nov. 23 ***Perf. 12x11½***

Design: 12.50e, Figurative tile, 18th cent.

1566 A391 12.50e multi 22 14
a Miniature sheet of 6 1.75 1.75
b Souv. sheet of 4, #1563-1566 1.25 1.25

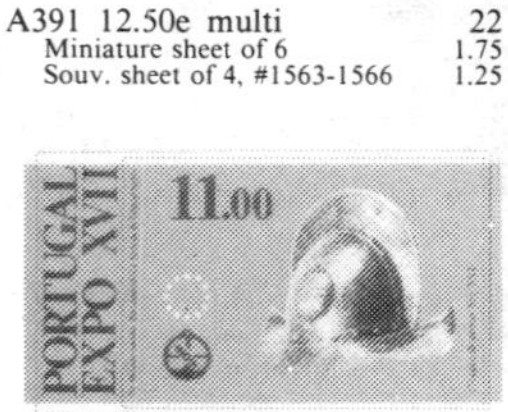
17th European Arts and Sciences Exhibition, Lisbon — A417

Portuguese Discoveries and Renaissance Europe: 11e, Helmet, 16th cent. 12.50e, Astrolabe. 25e, Ships, Flemish tapestry. 30e, Column capital, 12th cent. 37.50e, Hour glass. 40e, Chinese panel painting.

1983, Apr. 6
1567 A417 11e multi 25 16
1568 A417 12.50e multi 28 18
1569 A417 25e multi 55 32
1570 A417 30e multi 65 40
1571 A417 37.50e multi 85 50
1572 A417 40e multi 90 52
a Souvenir sheet of 6 3.75 3.75
Nos. 1567-1572 (6) 3.48 2.08

No. 1572a contains Nos. 1567-1572. Size: 115x118mm.

Europa Issue

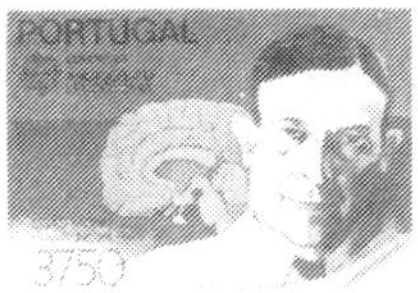

Egas Moniz (1874-1955), Cerebral Angiography and Pre-frontal Leucotomy Pioneer — A418

1983, May 5 Litho. *Perf. 12½*
1573 A418 37.50e multi 60 60
a Souvenir sheet of 4 2.50 2.50

European Conference of Ministers of Transport — A419

1983, May 16
1574 A419 30e multi 85 38

Endangered Sea Mammals A420

1983, July 29 Litho. *Perf. 12x11½*
1575 A420 12.50e Sea wolf 18 12
1576 A420 30e Dolphin 45 28
1577 A420 37.50e Killer whale 55 35
1578 A420 80e Humpback whale 1.25 75
a Souvenir sheet of 4 3.25 3.25

BRASILIANA '83 Intl. Stamp Exhibition, Rio de Janeiro, July 29-Aug. 7. No. 1578a contains Nos. 1575-1578. Size: 134x82mm.

600th Anniv. of Revolution of 1383 — A421

1983, Sept. 14 *Perf. 13½*
1579 A421 12.50e Death of Joao Fernandes Andeiro 25 14
1580 A421 30e Rebellion 60 32

First Manned Balloon Flight A422

Designs: 16e, Bartolomeu Lourenco de Gusmao, Passarola flying machine. 51e, Montgolfier Balloon, first flight.

1983, Nov. 9 Litho. *Perf. 12x11½*
1581 A422 16e multi 28 18
1582 A422 51e multi 85 52

Christmas 1983 — A423

Stained Glass Windows, Monastery at Batalha: 12.50e, Adoration of the Magi. 30e, Flight to Egypt.

1983, Nov. 23 *Perf. 12½*
1583 A423 12.50e multi 22 14
1584 A423 30e multi 52 32

Lisbon Zoo Centenary A424

1984, Jan. 18 Litho. *Perf. 12x11½*
1585 A424 16e Siberian tigers 50 30
1586 A424 16e White rhinoceros 50 30
1587 A424 16e Damalisco Albifronte 50 30
1588 A424 16e Cheetahs 50 30

Nos. 1585-1588 se-tenant.

Military Type of 1983

Air Force Dress Uniforms and Planes: 16e, 1954; Hawker Hurricane II, 1943. 35e, 1960; Republic F-84G Thunderjet. 40e, Paratrooper, 1966; 2502 Nord Noratlas, 1960. 51e, 1966; Corsair II, 1982.

1984, Feb. 5 Litho. *Perf. 13½*
1589 A416 16e multi 25 15
1590 A416 35e multi 55 35
1591 A416 40e multi 65 40
1592 A416 51e multi 80 48
a Bklt. pane of 4, #1589-1592 2.90

Tile Type of 1981

Design: 16e, Royal arms, 19th cent.

1984, Mar. 8 Litho. *Perf. 12x11½*
1593 A391 16e multi 25 15
a Miniature sheet of 6 1.65 1.65

1984, July 18

Design: 16e, Pombal Palace wall tile, 19th cent.

1594 A391 16e multi 25 15
a Miniature sheet of 6 1.65 1.65

1984, Aug. 3 *Perf. 11½x12*

Design: No. 1595, Facade covering, 19th cent.

1595 A391 16e multi 25 15
a Miniature sheet of 6 1.65 1.65

1984, Oct. 17

Design: Grasshoppers, by Rafael Bordaro Pinhiero, 19th cent.

1596 A391 16e multi 24 12
a Miniature sheet of 6 1.50 1.50
b Souv. sheet of 4, #1593-1596 1.00 1.00

25th Lisbon Intl. Fair, May 9-13 A425

Events: 40e, World Food Day. 51e, 15th Rehabilitation Intl. World Congress, Lisbon, June 4-8 (vert.).

1984, Apr. 3
1597 A425 35e multi 75 35
1598 A425 40e multi 90 40
1599 A425 51e multi 1.10 48

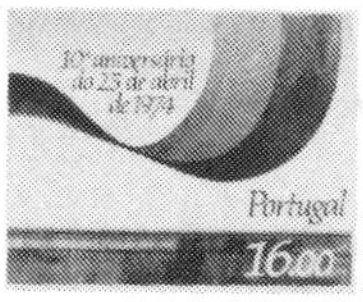

April 25th Revolution, 10th Anniv. — A426

1984, Apr. 25 *Perf. 13½*
1600 A426 16e multi 40 18

Europa (1959-84) A427

1984, May 2 *Perf. 12x11½*
1601 A427 51e multi 80 48
a Souvenir sheet of 4 4.75 4.75

LUBRAPEX '84 and Natl. Early Art Museum Centenary A428

Paintings: 16e, Nun, 15th cent. 40e, St. John, by Master of the Retable of Santiago, 16th cent. 51e, View of Lisbon, 17th cent. 66e, Cabeca de Jovem, by Domingos Sesqueira, 19th cent.

1984, May 9 Litho. *Perf. 12x11½*
1602 A428 16e multi 30 18
1603 A428 40e multi 70 40
1604 A428 51e multi 95 52
1605 A428 66e multi 1.10 60
a Souvenir sheet of 4 3.75 2.75

No. 1605a contains Nos. 1602-1605; tan and black margin. Size: 110x110mm.

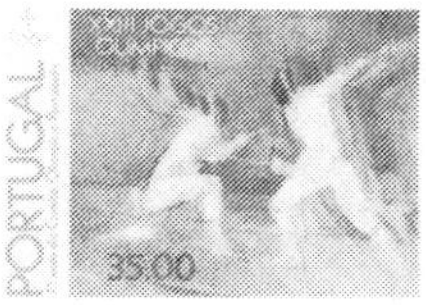

1984 Summer Olympics A429

1984, June 5
1606 A429 35e Fencing 52 32
1607 A429 40e Gymnastics 60 38
1608 A429 51e Running 75 45
1609 A429 80e Pole vault 1.25 75

Souvenir Sheet

1610 A429 100e Hurdles 2.25 1.50

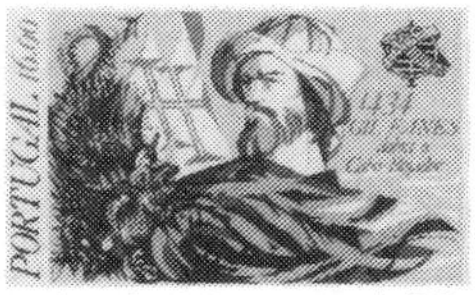

Historical Events — A430

Designs: 16e, Gil Eanes, explorer who reached west coast of Africa, 1434. 51e, King Peter I of Brazil and IV of Portugal.

1984, Sept. 24 *Perf. 12x11½*
1611 A430 16e multi 32 18
1612 A430 51e multi 85 45

See Brazil No. 1954.

Canceled-to-order stamps are often from remainders. Most collectors of canceled stamps prefer postally used specimens.

Infantry Grenadier, 1740 — A431

1985, Jan. 23 Litho. *Perf. 13½*
1613 A431 20e shown 30 15
1614 A431 46e 5th Cavalry Regiment Officer, 1810 70 35
1615 A431 60e Artillery Corporal, 1892 90 45
1616 A431 100e Engineering Soldier, 1985 1.50 75
a Bklt. pane of 4, #1613-1616 3.50

Tile Type of 1981

Design: Tile from entrance hall of Lisbon's Faculdade de Letras, by Jorge Barradas, 20th cent.

1985, Feb. 13 Litho. *Perf. 12*
1617 A391 20e multi 30 15
a Miniature sheet of 6 1.80 1.80

1985, June 11 *Perf. 12x11½*

Design: Explorer and sailing ship, detail from tile panel by Maria Keil, Avenida Infante Santo, Lisbon.

1618 A391 20e multi 25 12
a Miniature sheet of 6 1.50 1.50

1985, Aug. 20

Profile and key, detail from a 20th century tile mural by Querubim Lapa.

1619 A391 20e multi 28 14
a Miniature sheet of 6 1.75 1.75

1985, Nov. 15 *Perf. 12*

Design: Geometric designs and flowers, by Manuel Cargaleiro.

1620 A391 20e multi 25 12
a Miniature sheet of 6 1.50 1.50
b Souv. sheet of 4, #1617-1620 1.00 1.00

Kiosks — A432

1985, Mar. 19 Litho. *Perf. 11½x12*
1621 A432 20e Green kiosk 50 14
1622 A432 20e Red kiosk 50 14
1623 A432 20e Gray kiosk 50 14
1624 A432 20e Blue kiosk 50 14
a Strip of 4, #1621-1624 2.00

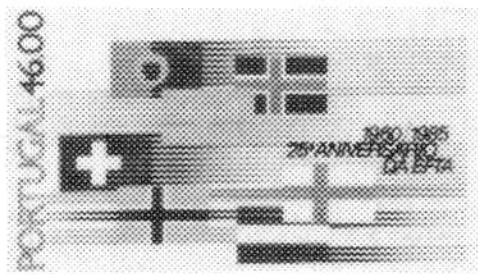

25th Anniv., European Free Trade Association — A433

1985, Apr. 10 Litho. *Perf. 12x11½*
1625 A433 46e Flags of members 80 30

Intl. Youth Year A434

1985, Apr. 10 **Litho.**

1626 A434 60e Heads of boy and girl 1.10 40

Europa 1985-Music A435

1985, May 6 Litho. ***Perf. 11½x12***

1627 A435 60e Woman playing tambourine 80 40
a Souvenir sheet of 4 3.25 3.25

Historic Anniversaries — A436

Designs: 20e, King John I at the Battle of Aljubarrota, 1385. 46e, Queen Leonor (1458-1525) founding the Caldas da Rainha Hospital. 60e, Cartographer Pedro Reinel, earliest Portuguese map, c. 1483.

1985, July 5 Litho. ***Perf. 12x11½***

1628 A436 20e multi 28 14
1629 A436 46e multi 60 30
1630 A436 60e multi 80 40

See Nos. 1678-1680.

Traditional Architecture A437

1985-89 **Litho.** ***Perf. 12***

1631 A437 50c Saloia, Estremadura 5 5
1632 A437 1e Beira interior 5 5
1633 A437 1.50e Ribatejo 5 5
1634 A437 2.50e Transmontanas 5 5
1635 A437 10e Minho and Douro Litoral 15 8
1636 A437 20e Farm house, Minho 28 14
1637 A437 22.50e Alentejo 32 16
1638 A437 25e African Sitio, Algarve 35 18
1639 A437 27e Beira Interior 45 22
1640 A437 29e Hill country 45 22
1641 A437 30e Algarve 50 25
1642 A437 40e Beira Interior 62 30
1643 A437 50e Private home, Beira Litoral 70 35
1644 A437 55e Tras-os-Montes 90 45
1645 A437 60e Beira Litoral 95 48
1646 A437 70e Estremadura Sul and Alentejo 1.10 55
1647 A437 80e Estremadura 1.10 55
1648 A437 90e Minho 1.25 62
1649 A437 100e Adobe Monte, Alentejo 1.30 65
1650 A437 500e Algarve 7.40 3.70
Nos. 1631-1650 (20) 18.02 9.10

Issue dates: 20e, 25e, 50e, 100e, Aug. 20, 1985. 2.50e, 22.50e, 80e, 90e, Mar. 10, 1986. 10e, 40e, 60e, 70e, Mar. 6, 1987. 1.50e, 27e, 30e, 55e, Mar. 15, 1988. 50c, 1e, 29e, 500e, Mar. 8, 1989.

Aquilino Ribeiro (1885-1963), Author — A438

Writers: 46c, Fernando Pessoa (1888-1935), poet.

1985, Oct. 2 **Litho.** ***Perf. 12***

1651 A438 20e multi 25 12
1652 A438 46e multi 60 30

Natl. Parks and Reserves A439

1985, Oct. 25

1653 A439 20e Berlenga Island 25 12
1654 A439 40e Estrela Mountain Chain 52 25
1655 A439 46e Boquilobo Marsh 60 30
1656 A439 80e Formosa Lagoon 1.00 50

Souvenir Sheet

1657 A439 100e St. Jacinto Dunes 1.25 1.25

ITALIA '85.

Christmas 1985 — A440

Illuminated codices from The Prayer Times Book, Book of King Manuel, 1517-1538.

1985, Nov. 15 ***Perf. 11½x12***

1658 A440 20e The Nativity 25 12
1659 A440 46e Adoration of the Magi 60 30

Postrider A441

1985, Dec. 13 Litho. ***Perf. 13½***

1660 A441 A(22.50e) lt yel grn & dp yel grn 32 16

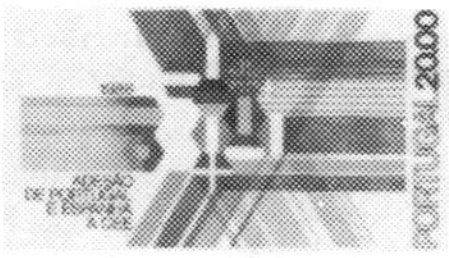

Flags of EEC Member Nations A442

Design: 57.50e, Map of EEC, flags.

1986, Jan. 7 **Litho.** ***Perf. 12***

1661 A442 20e multi 25 12
1662 A442 57.50e multi 75 38
a Souv. sheet of 4 2.25 2.25

Admission of Portugal and Spain to the European Economic Community, Jan. 1. See Spain Nos. 2463-2466.

No. 1662a contains 2 alternating pairs of Nos. 1661-1662 inscribed with EUROPEX '86 exhibition emblem and text; multicolored margin pictures sea view of Lisbon, from old print. Size: 127x90mm.

Castles A443

1986, Feb. 18 **Litho.** ***Perf. 12***

1663 A443 22.50e Beja 32 16
a Bklt. pane of 4 1.30
1664 A443 22.50e Feira 32 16
a Bklt. pane of 4 1.30

1986, Apr. 10

1665 A443 22.50e Guimaraes 32 16
a Bklt. pane of 4 1.30
1666 A443 22.50e Braganca 32 16
a Bklt. pane of 4 1.30

1986, Sept. 18

1667 A443 22.50e Montemor-o-Velho 32 16
a Bklt. pane of 4 1.30
1668 A443 22.50e Belmonte 32 16
a Bklt. pane of 4 1.30

See Nos. 1688-1695, 1723-1726.

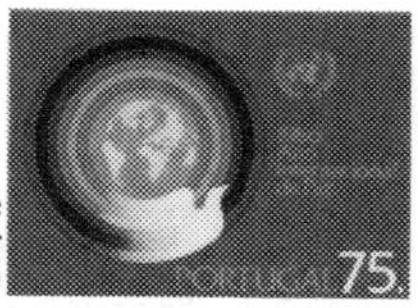

Intl. Peace Year A445

1986, Feb. 18 **Litho.** ***Perf. 12***

1669 A445 75e multi 1.00 50

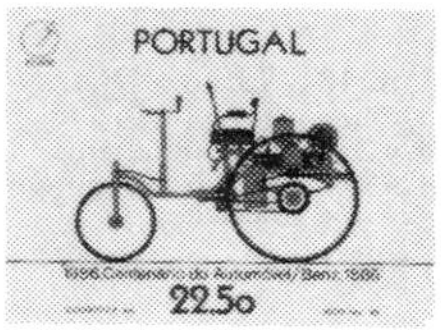

Automobile Centenary — A446

1986, Apr. 10 **Litho.** ***Perf. 12***

1670 A446 22.50e 1886 Benz 32 16
1671 A446 22.50e 1886 Daimler 32 16

Nos. 1670-1671 printed se-tenant in sheets of 16.

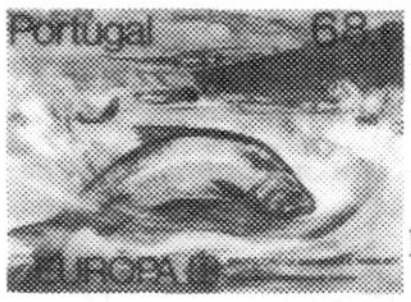

Europa 1986 — A447

1986, May 5 **Litho.**

1672 A447 68.50e Shad 1.05 52
a Souvenir sheet of 4 4.25 4.25

Horse Breeds A448

1986, May 22 **Litho.** ***Perf. 12***

1673 A448 22.50e Alter 32 16
1674 A448 47.50e Lusitano 68 35
1675 A448 52.50e Garrano 75 38
1676 A448 68.50e Sorraia 1.00 50

Souvenir Sheet

Halley's Comet A449

1986, June 24

1677 A449 100e multi 1.50 1.50

Anniversaries Type of 1985

Designs: 22.50e, Diogo Cao, explorer, heraldic pillar erected at Cape Lobo, 1484, 1st expedition. No. 1679, Manuel Passos, Corinthian column. No. 1680, Joao Baptista Ribeiro, painter, Oporto Academy director, c. 1836, and musicians.

1986, Aug. 28 **Litho.**

1678 A436 22.50e multi 32 16
1679 A436 52.50e multi 75 38
1680 A436 52.50e multi 75 38

Diogo Cao's voyages, 500th anniv. Academies of Fine Art, 150th anniv.

Stamp Day — A450

Natl. Guard, 75th Anniv. — A451

Order of Engineers, 50th Anniv. — A452

Anniversaries and events: No. 1681, Postal card, 100th anniv.

1986, Oct. 24 **Litho.**

1681 A450 22.50e multi 32 16
1682 A450 47.50e multi 68 35
1683 A450 52.50e multi 75 38

Watermills A453

1986, Nov. 7

1684 A453 22.50e Duoro 32 15
1685 A453 47.50e Coimbra 68 35
1686 A453 52.50e Gerez 75 38
1687 A453 90e Braga 1.25 62
a Souv. sheet of 4, #1684-1687 3.00 3.00

LUBRAPEX '86. No. 1687a issued Nov. 21. Size: 140x114mm.

Castle Type of 1986

1987, Jan. 16 **Litho.**

1688 A443 25e Silves 35 18
a Bklt. pane of 4 1.40
1689 A443 25e Evora Monte 35 18
a Bklt. pane of 4 1.40

1987, Apr. 10

1690 A443 25e Leiria 38 20
a Bklt. pane of 4 + label 1.55
1691 A443 25e Trancoso 38 20
a Bklt. pane of 4 + label 1.55

Bklt. labels picture the Leiria and Guarda coat of arms, respectively.

1987, Sept. 15

1692 A443 25e St. George 38 20
a Bklt. pane of 4 + label 1.55
1693 A443 25e Marvao 38 20
a Bklt. pane of 4 + label 1.55

Bklt. labels picture the Lisbon and Portalegre coats of arms, respectively.

1988, Jan. 19

1694 A443 27e Fernando's Walls of Oporto 45 22
a Bklt. pane of 4 + label 1.80
1695 A443 27e Almourol 45 22
a. Bklt. pane of 4 + label 1.80
Nos. 1688-1695 (8) 3.12 1.60

Bklt. labels picture the Oporto and Santarem coasts of arms, respectively.

Natl. Tourism Organization, 75th Anniv. — A454

1987, Feb. 10 Litho. *Perf. 12*

1696 A454 25e Beach houses, Tocha 40 20
1697 A454 57e Boats, Espinho 90 45
1698 A454 98e Chafariz Fountain, Arraioles 1.50 75

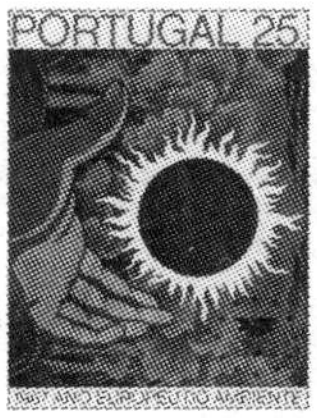

European Nature Conservation Year — A455

1987, Mar. 20 *Perf. 12x12½*

1699 A455 25e shown 40 20
1700 A455 57e Hands, flower, map 90 45
1701 A455 74.50e Hands, star, rainbow 1.15 58

Europa 1987 — A456

Modern architecture: Bank Borges and Irmao Agency, 1986, Vila do Conde.

1987, May 5 Litho. *Perf. 12*

1702 A456 74.50e multi 1.25 62
a Souv. sheet of 4 5.00 5.00

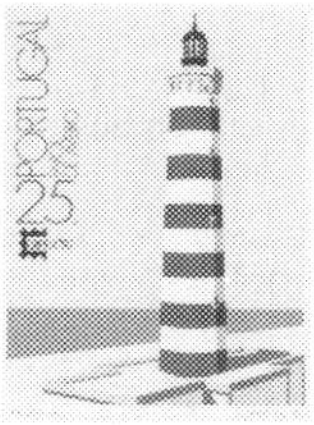

Lighthouses A457

1987, June 12 *Perf. 11½x12*

1703 A457 25e Aveiro 40 20
1704 A457 25e Berlenga 40 20
1705 A457 25e Cape Mondego 40 20
1706 A457 25e Cape St. Vincente 40 20
a Strip of 4, #1703-1706 1.60 80

Printed in sheet of 16 in strips of 4.

Amadeo de Souza-Cardoso (1887-1919), Painter — A458

1987, Aug. 27 Litho. *Perf. 12*

1707 A458 74.50e multi 1.10 55

Portguese Royal Library, Rio de Janeiro, 150th anniv. A459

1987, Aug. 27 *Perf. 12x11½*

1708 A459 12.50e multi 20 10

Paper Currency of Portugal, 300th Anniv. A460

1987, Aug. 27 *Perf. 12x11½*

1709 A460 100e multi 1.50 75

Voyages of Bartolomeu Dias (d. 1499), 500th Anniv. A461

1987, Aug. 27 *Perf. 12x11½*

1710 A461 25e Departing from Lisbon, 1487 38 20
1711 A461 25e Discovering the African Coast, 1488 38 20

Nos. 1710-1711 printed se-tenant in a continuous design.
See Nos. 1721-1722.

Souvenir Sheet

Phonograph Record, 100th Anniv. — A462

1987, Oct. 9 Litho. *Perf. 12*

1712 Sheet of 2 3.00 3.00
a A462 75e Compact-disc player 1.10 1.10
b A462 125e Gramophone 1.90 1.90

Christmas A463

Various children's drawings, Intl. Year of the Child emblem.

1987, Nov. 6

1713 A463 25e Angels, magi, tree 38 20
1714 A463 27e Friendship circle 88 45
1715 A463 74.50e Santa riding dove 1.10 58
a Souv. sheet of 3 2.40 2.40

World Wildlife Fund A464

Lynx, *Lynx pardina.*

1988, Feb. 3 Litho. *Perf. 12*

1716 A464 27e Stalking 45 22
1717 A464 27e Carrying prey 45 22
1718 A464 27e Two adults 45 22
1719 A464 27e Adult, young 45 22
a Strip of 4, Nos. 1716-1719 1.80 1.80

Printed in a continuous design, 4 strips of 4 in sheets of 16.

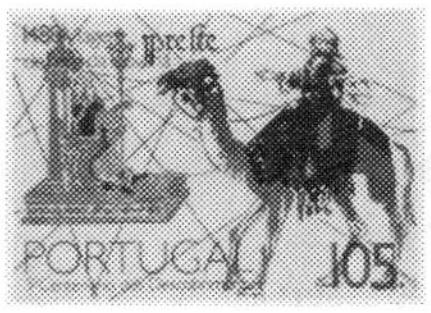

Journey of Pero da Covilha to the East, 500th Anniv. A465

1988, Feb. 3

1720 A465 105e multi 1.65 82

Bartolomeu Dias Type of 1987

Discovery of the link between the Atlantic and Indian Oceans by Dias, 500th Anniv.: No. 1721, Tidal wave, ship. No. 1722, Henricus Martelus Germanus's map (1489), picturing the African coast and linking the two oceans.

1988, Feb. 3

1721 A461 27e multi 45 22
1722 A461 27e multi 45 22
a Bklt. pane of 4, Nos. 1710-1711, 1721-1722 1.70

Nos. 1721-1722 printed se-tenant in a continuous design.

Castle Type of 1986

1988, Mar. 15 Litho. *Perf. 12*

1723 A443 27e Vila Nova de Cerveira 45 22
a Bklt. pane of 4 + label 1.80
1724 A443 27e Palmela 45 22
a Bklt. pane of 4 + label 1.80

Booklet labels picture the Viana do Castelo and Setubal coats of arms, respectively.

1988, July 1

1725 A443 27e Chaves 45 22
a. Bklt. pane of 4 + label 1.80
1726 A443 27e Penedono 45 22
a. Bklt. pane of 4 + label 1.80

Booklet labels picture the Vila Real and Viseu coats of arms, respectively.

Europa 1988 A466

Transportation: Mail coach, Lisbon-Oporto route, 1855-1864.

1988, Apr. 21 Litho. *Perf. 12*

1735 A466 80e multi 1.35 68
a Souv. sheet of 4 5.40 5.40

Jean Monnet (1888-1979), Economist A467

1988, May 9 Litho.

1736 A467 60e multi 98 50

For unused stamps, more recent issues are valued as never hinged, with the beginning point determined on a country-by-country basis. Notes to show the beginning points are prominently placed in the text.

Souvenir Sheet

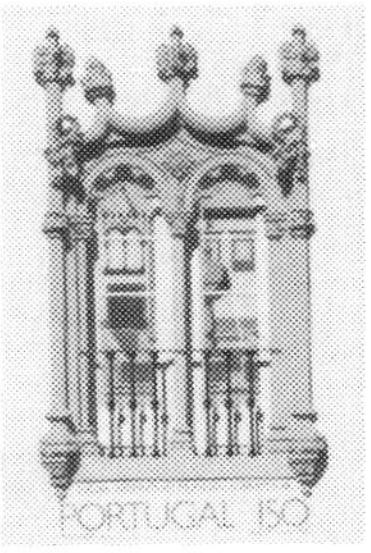

National Heritage (Patrimony) A468

Design: 150e, Belvedere of Cordovil House and Fountain of Porta de Moura reflected in the Garcia de Resende balcony window, Evora, 16th cent.

1988, May 13 *Perf. 13½x12½*

1737 A468 150e multi 2.50 2.50

No. 1737 has inscribed margin picturing LUBRAPEX '88 and UNESCO emblems.

20th Cent. Paintings by Portuguese Artists — A469

Designs: 27e, *Viola,* c. 1916, by Amadeo de Souza-Cardoso (1887-1918). 60e, *Jugglers and Tumblers Do Not Fall,* 1949, by Jose de Almada Negreiros (1893-1970). 80e, *Still-life with Guitar,* c. 1940, by Eduardo Viana (1881-1967).

1988, Aug. 23 Litho. *Perf. 11½x12*

1738 A469 27e multi 42 20
1739 A469 60e multi 90 45
1740 A469 80e multi 1.20 60
a. Miniature sheet of 3, Nos. 1738-1740 2.55 2.55

See Nos. 1748-1750, 1754-1756.

1988 Summer Olympics, Seoul A470

1988, Sept. 16 Litho. *Perf. 12x11½*

1741 A470 27e Archery 40 20
1742 A470 55e Weight lifting 82 40
1743 A470 60e Judo 90 45
1744 A470 80e Tennis 1.20 60

Souvenir Sheet

1745 A470 200e Yachting 3.00 3.00

Remains of the Roman Civilization in Portugal A471

Mozaics: 27e, "Winter Image," detail of *Mosaic of the Four Seasons,* limestone and glass, 3rd cent., House of the Waterworks, Coimbra. 80e, *Fish in Marine Water,* limestone, 3rd-4th cent., cover of a tank wall, public baths, Faro.

1988, Oct. 18 Litho. *Perf. 12*

1746 A471 27e multi 40 20
1747 A471 80e multi 1.15 58

20th Cent. Art Type of 1988

Paintings by Portuguese artists: 27e, *Burial,* 1938, by Mario Eloy. 60e, *Lisbon Roofs,* c. 1936, by Carlos Botelho. 80e, *Avejao Lirico,* 1939, by Antonio Pedro.

1988, Nov. 18 Litho. *Perf. 11½x12*

1748 A469 27e multi 42 20
1749 A469 60e multi 92 45
1750 A469 80e multi 1.25 62
a. Souv. sheet of 3, #1748-1750 2.60 2.60
b. Souv. sheet of 6, #1738-1740, 1748-1750 5.25 5.25

Braga Cathedral, 900th Anniv. A472

1989, Jan. 20 *Perf. 12*

1751 A472 30e multi 45 22

INDIA '89 — A473

Designs: 55e, Caravel, Sao Jorge da Mina Fort, 1482. 60e, Navigator using astrolabe, 16th cent.

1989, Jan. 20

1752 A473 55e multi 85 42
1753 A473 60e multi 92 45

20th Cent. Art Type of 1988

Paintings by Portuguese artists: 29e, *Antithesis of Calm,* 1940, by Antonio Dacosta. 60c, *Lunch of the Unskilled Mason,* c. 1926, by Julio Pomar. 87e, *Simums,* 1949, by Vespeira.

1989, Feb. 15 Litho. *Perf. 11½x12*

1754 A469 29e multi 40 20
1755 A469 60e multi 82 40
1756 A469 87e multi 1.20 60
a. Souv. sheet of 3, #1754-1756 2.50 2.50

Special Occasions — A474

1989, Feb. 15 Litho. *Perf. 12*

1772 A474 29e multi 40 20
a. Bklt. pane of 8 3.25
1773 A474 60e With love 80 40
a. Bklt. pane of 8 6.40

European Parliament Elections — A475

1989, Mar. 8 Litho. *Perf. 11½x12*

1774 A475 60e multi 90 45

Europa 1989 A476

Children's toys.

1989, Apr. 26 Litho. *Perf. 12*

1775 A476 80e Top 1.20 60

Souvenir Sheet

1776 Sheet of 4 4.80 4.80
a. A476 80e Tops 1.20 1.20

No. 1776 contains 2 each of Nos. 1775, 1776a.

Surface Transportation, Lisbon — A477

Designs: 29e, Carris Co. elevated railway, Bica Street. 65e, Carris electric tram. 87e, Carmo Elevator, Santa Justa Street. 100e, Carris doubledecker bus. 250e, Transtejo Co. riverboat *Cacilheiro.*

1989, May 22 Litho. *Perf.*

1777 A477 29e multi 45 22
1778 A477 65e multi 98 50
1779 A477 87e multi 1.30 65
1780 A477 100e multi 1.50 75

Souvenir Sheet

1781 A477 250e multi 3.75 3.75

AZORES

Starting in 1980, stamps inscribed Azores and Madeira were valid and sold in Portugal.

Azores No. 2 — A33

Design: 19.50e, Azores No. 6.

1980, Jan. 2 Litho. *Perf. 12*

314 A33 6.50e multi 15 5
315 A33 19.50e multi 50 20
a. Souv. sheet of 2, #314-315 90 90

Map of Azores A34

1980, Sept. 17 Litho. *Perf. 12x11½*

316 A34 50c shown 5 5
317 A34 1e Cathedral 5 5
318 A34 5e Windmill 12 6
319 A34 6.50e Local women 15 8
320 A34 8e Coastline 20 12
321 A34 30e Ponta Delgada 60 32
Nos. 316-321 (6) 1.17 68

World Tourism Conf., Manila, Sept. 27.

Europa Issue 1981

St. Peter's Cavalcade, St. Miguel Island — A35

1981, May 11 Litho. *Perf. 12*

322 A35 22e multi 52 25
a. Souvenir sheet of 2 1.10 1.10

Bulls Attacking Spanish Soldiers A36

Battle of Salga Valley, 400th Anniv.: 33.50e, Friar Don Pedro leading citizens.

1981, July 24 Litho. *Perf. 12x11½*

323 A36 8.50e multi 18 12
324 A36 33.50e multi 80 45

Tolpis Azorica — A37

Designs: Local flora.

1981, Sept. 21 Litho. *Perf. 12½x12*

325 A37 7e shown 16 8
326 A37 8.50e Ranunculus azoricus 20 12
327 A37 20e Platanthera Micranta 38 12
328 A37 50e Laurus azorica 1.00 32
a. Bklt. pane of 4 (#325-328) 1.90

1982, Jan. 29

329 A37 4e Myosotis azorica 10 6
330 A37 10e Lactuca Watsoniana 24 16
331 A37 27e Vicia dennesiana 60 22
332 A37 33.50e Azorina vidalii 75 25
a. Bklt. pane of 4 1.90

See Nos. 338-341.

Europa 1982 — A38

1982, May 3 Litho. *Perf. 12x11½*

333 A38 33.50e Heros of Mindelo embarkation, 1832 65 32
a. Souvenir sheet of 3 2.00 2.00

Chapel of the Holy Ghost — A39

Designs: Various Chapels of the Holy Ghost.

1982, Nov. 24 Litho. *Perf. 12½x12*

334 A39 27e multi 75 25
335 A39 33.50e multi 95 40

Eruopa 1983 — A40

1983, May 5 Litho. *Perf. 12½*

336 A40 37.50e Geothermal energy 70 35
a. Souvenir sheet of 3 2.50 2.50

Flag of the Autonomous Region A41

1983, May 23 Litho. *Perf. 12x11½*

337 A41 12.50e multi 30 15

Flower Type of 1981

1983, June 16 *Perf. 12½x12*

338 A37 12.50e St. John's wort 25 12
339 A37 30e Prickless bramble 60 30
340 A37 37.50e Romania bush 75 38
341 A37 100e Common juniper 1.90 1.00
a. Bklt. pane of 4 (#338-341) 3.50

Woman Wearing Terceira Cloaks — A42

1984, Mar. 8 Litho. *Perf. 13½*

342 A42 16e Jesters costumes, 18th cent. 30 15
343 A42 51e shown 90 45

Europa (1959-84) A43

1984, May 2 *Perf. 12x11½*

344 A43 51e multi 90 40
a. Souvenir sheet of 3 2.75 2.75

Megabombus Ruderatus — A44

1984, Sept. 3 Litho. *Perf. 12x11½*

345 A44 16e shown 24 12
a. Perf. 12 vert. 24 12
346 A44 35e Pieris brassicae azorensis 52 26
a. Perf. 12 vert. 52 26
347 A44 40e Chrysomela banksi 60 30
a. Perf. 12 vert. 60 30
348 A44 51e Phlogophora interrupta 75 38
a. Perf. 12 vert. 75 38
b. Booklet pane of 4 (#345a-348a) 2.50

1985, Feb. 13

349 A44 20e Polyspilla polyspilla 30 15
a. Perf. 12 vert. 30 15
350 A44 40e Sphaerophoria nigra 65 32
a. Perf. 12 vert. 65 32
351 A44 46e Colias croceus 75 38
a. Perf. 12 vert. 75 38
352 A44 60e Hipparchia azorina 1.00 50
a. Perf. 12 vert. 1.00 50
b. Bklt. pane of 4 (#349a-352a) 3.00

Europa 1985-Music A45

1985, May 6 Litho. *Perf. 11½x12*

353 A45 60e man playing folia drum 1.00 40
a. Souvenir sheet of 3 3.00 3.00

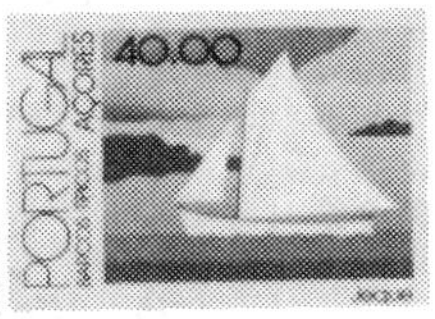

Native Boats A46

1985, June 19 Litho. *Perf. 12x12½*

354 A46 40e Jeque 60 25
355 A46 60e Bote 90 38

Europa 1986 — A47

1986, May Litho.

356 A47 68.50e Pyrrhula murina 1.05 52
a. Souvenir sheet of 3 3.25 3.25

Regional Architecture A48

19th Century fountains: 22.50e, Alto das Covas, Angra do Heroismo. 52.50e, Faja de Baixo, San Miguel. 68.50e, Gates of St. Peter, Terceira. 100e, Agua d'Alto, San Miguel.

1986, Sept. 18 Litho. *Perf. 12*

357 A48 22.50e multi 35 18
358 A48 52.50e multi 80 40
359 A48 68.50e multi 1.05 52
360 A48 100e multi 1.50 75
a. Bklt. pane of 4, #357-360, perf. 12 vert. 3.75

Traditional Modes of Transportation — A49

1986, Nov. 7 Litho.

361 A49 25e Isle of Santa Maria ox cart 35 18
362 A49 75e Ram cart 1.05 52

Europa 1987 — A50

Modern architecutre: Regional Assembly, Horta, designed by Manuel Correia Fernandes and Luis Miranda.

1987, May 5 Litho. *Perf. 12*

363 A50 74.50e multi 1.20 60
a. Souvenir sheet of 4 5.00 5.00

Portugal Regional Issues of Azores can be mounted in Scott's annual Portugal Supplement.

Windows and Balconies A51

1987, July 1 *Perf. 12*

364 A51 51e Santa Cruz, Graciosa 80 40
365 A51 74.50e Ribiera Grande, San Miguel 1.15 58

Aviation History A52

Seaplanes.

1987, Oct. 9 *Perf. 12x11½*

366 A52 25e NC-4 Curtiss Flyer, 1919 38 20
367 A52 57e Dornier DO-X, 1932 88 45
368 A52 74.50e Savoia-Marchetti S 55-X, 1933 1.15 58
369 A52 125e Lockheed Sirius, 1933 1.90 95
a. Bklt. pane of 4, #366-369 4.25

Europa 1988 — A53

1988, Apr. 21 Litho. *Perf. 12*

370 A53 80e multi 1.35 68
a. Souvenir sheet of 4 5.40 5.40

Birds — A54

1988, Oct. 18 Litho.

371 A54 27e Columba palambus azorica 40 20
372 A54 60e Scolopax rusticola 88 45
373 A54 80e Sterna dougallii 1.15 58
374 A54 100e Buteo buteo 1.45 72
a. Bklt. pane of 4, #371-374 3.90

Coats of Arms A55

1988, Nov. 18 Litho.

375 A55 55e Dominion of Azores 85 42
376 A55 80e Bettencourt family 1.20 60

Portugal Regional Issues of Madeira can be mounted in Scott's annual Portugal Supplement.

Wildlife Conservation A56

Various kinglets, *Regulus regulus.*

1989, Jan. 20 Litho.

377 A56 30e Adult on branch 45 22
378 A56 30e Two adults 45 22
379 A56 30e Adult, nest 45 22
380 A56 30e Bird in flight 45 22
a. Block of 4, Nos. 377-380 1.80 88

Europa 1989 — A57

Children's toys.

1989, Apr. 26 Litho.

381 A57 80e Tin boat 1.20 60

Souvenir Sheet

382 Sheet of 4 (2 each Nos. 381, 382a) 4.80 4.80
a. A57 80e Tin boat, diff. 1.20 1.20

MADEIRA

Type of Azores, 1980

Designs: 6.50e, Madeira No. 2. 19.50e, Madeira No. 5.

1980, Jan. 2 Litho. *Perf. 12*

66 A33 6.50e multi 15 5
67 A33 19.50e multi 50 20
a. Souv. sheet of 2, #66-67 90 90

Grapes and Wine — A7

1980, Sept. 17 Litho. *Perf. 12x11½*

68 A7 50c Bullock cart 5 5
69 A7 1e shown 5 5
70 A7 5e Produce map of Madeira 12 8
71 A7 6.50e Basket and lace 16 5
72 A7 8e Orchid 20 12
73 A7 30e Madeira boat 55 35
Nos. 68-73 (6) 1.13 70

World Tourism Conf., Manila, Sept. 27.

Europa Issue 1981

O Bailinho Folk Dance A8

1981, May 11 Litho. *Perf. 12*

74 A8 22e multi 42 22
a. Souvenier sheet of 2 1.50 1.10

Explorer Ship — A9

1981, July 1 Litho. *Perf. 12x11½*

75 A9 8.50e shown 12 7
76 A9 33.50e Map 60 20

Discovery of Madeira anniv.

Dactylorhiza Foliosa — A10

Designs: Local flora.

1981, Oct. 6 Litho. *Perf. 12½x12*

77 A10 7e shown 15 12
78 A10 8.50e Echium candicans 18 12
79 A10 20e Geranium maderense 40 12
80 A10 50e Isoplexis sceptrum 95 35
a. Bklt. pane of 4 (#77-80) 1.90

See Nos. 82-85, 90-93.

Europa 1982 — A11

1982, May 3 Litho. *Perf. 12x11½*

81 A11 33.50e Sugar mills, 15th cent. 60 30
a. Souvenir sheet of 3 2.00 2.00

1982, Aug. 31 Litho. *Perf. 12½x12*

82 A10 9e Goodyera macrophylla 12 8
83 A10 10e Armeria maderensis 18 8
84 A10 27e Viola paradoxa 35 20
85 A10 33.50e Scilla maderensis 90 45
a. Bklt. pane of 4 (#82-85) 1.65

Brinco Dancing Dolls — A12

1982, Dec. 15 Litho. *Perf. 13½*

86 A12 27e shown 65 40
87 A12 33.50e Dancers 85 50

Europa 1983 — A13

1983, May 5 Litho. *Perf. 12½*

88 A13 37.50e Levadas irrigation system 70 32
a. Souvenir sheet of 3 2.25 2.25

Flag of the Autonomous Region A14

1983, July 1 Litho. *Perf. 12x11½*

89 A14 12.50e multi 30 30

Flower Type of 1981

1983, Oct. 19 Litho. *Perf. 12½x12*

90 A10 12.50e Matthiola maderensis 30 30
91 A10 30e Erica maderensis 65 30

92 A10 37.50e Cirsium latifolium 75 30
93 A10 100e Clethra arborea 2.00 1.00

Europa (1959-84) A15

1984, May 2 Litho. *Perf. 12x11½*
94 A15 51e multi 80 40
a. Souvenir sheet of 3 3.00 3.00

Madeira Rally (Auto Race), 25th Anniv. — A16

Various cars.

1984, Aug. 3 Litho. *Perf. 11½x12*
95 A16 16e multi 40 20
96 A16 51e multi 1.00 50

Traditional Means of Transportation — A17

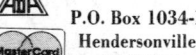

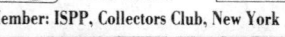

1984, Nov. 22 *Perf. 12*
97 A17 16e Mountain sledge 25 12
98 A17 35e Hammock 52 25
99 A17 40e Winebag carriers' procession 60 30
100 A17 51e Carreira Boat 75 38
a. Bklt. pane of 4, Nos. 97-100 2.15

See Nos. 104-107.

Europa 1985-Music — A18

1985, May 6 Litho. *Perf. 11½x12*
101 A18 60e Man playing guitar 1.00 40
a. Souvenir sheet of 3 4.00 4.00

Marine Life — A19

1985, July 5 Litho. *Perf. 12*
102 A19 40e Aphanopus carbo 52 28
103 A19 60e Lampris guttatus 80 40

See Nos. 108-109.

Transportation type of 1984

1985, Sept. 11 Litho. *Perf. 12x11½*
104 A17 20e Ox-drawn sledge 35 16
105 A17 40e Mountrain train 65 32
106 A17 46e Fish vendors 75 38
107 A17 60e Coastal steamer 1.00 50
a. Bklt. pane of 4, Nos. 104-107 2.20

Marine Life Type of 1985

1986, Jan. 7 Litho.
108 A19 20e Thunnus obesus 25 12
109 A19 75e Beryx decadactylus 1.00 50

Europa 1986 — A20

1986, May 5 Litho.
110 A20 68.50e Great Shearwater 1.05 52
a. Souvenir sheet of 3 3.25 3.25

forts in Funchal and Machico A21

1986, July 1 Litho. *Perf. 12*
111 A21 22.50e Sao Lourenco, 1583 32 16
112 A21 52.50e Sao Joao do Pico, 1611 75 38
113 A21 68.50e Sao Tiago, 1614 1.00 50
114 A21 100e Sao do Amparo, 1706 1.45 75
a. Bklt. pane of 4, #111-114 3.75

Indigenous Birds — A22

1987, Mar. 6 Litho.
115 A22 25e Regulus ignicapillus madeirensis 40 20
116 A22 57e Columba trocaz 90 45
117 A22 74.50e Tyto alba schmitzi 1.15 58
118 A22 125e Pterodroma madeira 1.95 1.00
a. Bklt. pane of 4 #115-#118 4.50

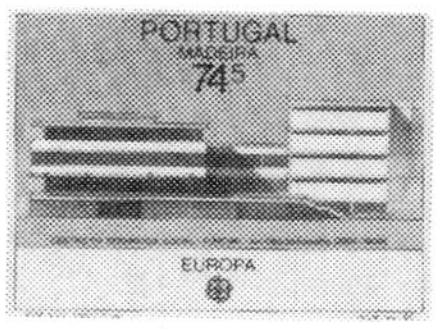

Europa 1987 — A23

Modern Architecture: Social Services Center, Funchal, designed by Raul Chorao Ramalho.

1987, May 5 Litho. *Perf. 12*
119 A23 74.50e multi 1.20 60
a. Souvenir sheet of 4 5.00 5.00

Natl. Monuments A24

1987, July 1 *Perf. 12x12½*
120 A24 51e Funchal Castle, 15th cent. 80 40
121 A24 74.50e Old Town Hall, Santa Cruz, 16th cent. 1.15 58

Europa 1988 — A25

Transportation Modern mail boat PS 13 TL.

1988, Apr. 21 Litho. *Perf. 12*
122 A25 80e multi 1.35 68
a. Souvenir sheet of 4 5.40 5.40

Indigenous Birds — A26

1988, June 15 Litho.
123 A26 27e Redbreast 45 22
124 A26 60e Rock sparrow 98 50
125 A26 80e Chaffinch 1.30 65
126 A26 100e Sparrow-hawk 1.65 82
a. Bklt. pane of 4, Nos. 123-126 4.40

Portraits of Christopher Columbus and Purported Residences on Madeira A27

1988, July 1 Litho.
127 A27 55e Funchal, 1480-1481, vert. 88 45
128 A27 80e Porto Santo 1.30 65

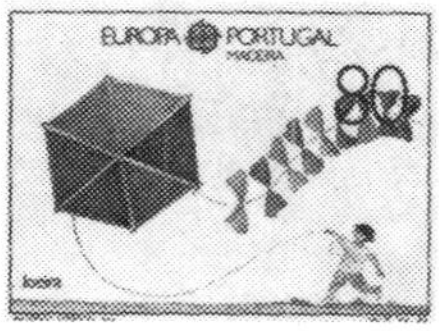

Europa 1989 — A28

Children's toys.

1989, Apr. 26 Litho.
129 A28 80e Kite 1.20 60

Souvenir Sheet
130 Sheet of 4 (2 each Nos. 129, 130a) 4.80 4.80
a. A28 80e Kite, diff. 1.20 1.20

AIR POST STAMPS

Symbol of Aviation AP1

Perf. 12x11½
1936-41 Unwmk. Typo.
C1 AP1 1.50e dk bl 35 35
C2 AP1 1.75e red org 55 35
C3 AP1 2.50e rose red 70 35
C4 AP1 3e brt bl ('41) 4.00 5.00
C5 AP1 4e dp yel grn ('41) 6.25 7.25
C6 AP1 5e car lake 90 35
C7 AP1 10e brn lake 1.40 30
C8 AP1 15e org ('41) 4.00 4.50

C9 AP1 20e blk brn 4.25 1.25
C10 AP1 50e brn vio ('41) 60.00 30.00
Nos. C1-C10 (10) 82.40 49.70

Nos. C1-C10 exist imperf.

Catalogue values for unused stamps in this section, from this point to the end of the section, are for Never Hinged items.

EXPO Type of Regular Issue

1970, Sept. 16 Litho. *Perf. 13*
C11 A274 3.50e sil & multi 35 20

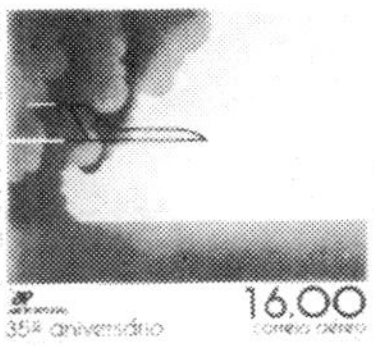

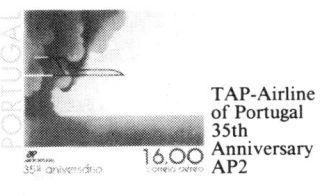

TAP-Airline of Portugal 35th Anniversary AP2

Design: 19e, Jet flying past sun.

1979, Sept. 21 Litho. *Perf. 12x11½*
C12 AP2 16e multi 35 35
C13 AP2 19e multi 45 45

POSTAGE DUE STAMPS

Vasco da Gama Issue.

The Zamorin of Calicut Receiving Vasco da Gama — D1

Unwmk.
1898, May 1 Typo. *Perf. 12*
Denomination in Black.
J1 D1 5r black 2.25 1.65
a. Value and "Continente" omitted 3.75 2.25
J2 D1 10r lil & blk 3.75 2.25
J3 D1 20r org & blk 5.50 3.00
J4 D1 50r sl & blk 15.00 6.00
J5 D1 100r car & blk, *pink* 45.00 22.50
J6 D1 200r brn & blk, *buff* 55.00 27.50

D2

D3

1904 *Perf. 11½x12*
J7 D2 5r brown 50 40
J8 D2 10r orange 1.50 50
a. Imperf.
J9 D2 20r lilac 6.00 3.00
J10 D2 30r gray grn 2.50 1.65
J11 D2 40r gray vio 2.50 1.65
J12 D2 50r carmine 20.00 4.25
a. Imperf.
J13 D2 100r dl bl 5.00 2.50
a. Imperf.
Nos. J7-J13 (7) 38.00 13.95

Preceding Issue Overprinted in Carmine or Green **REPUBLICA**

1910
J14 D2 5r brown 40 30
J15 D2 10r orange 40 30
J16 D2 20r lilac 80 30
J17 D2 30r gray grn 55 30
J18 D2 40r gray vio 55 30
J19 D2 50r car (G) 2.75 1.40
J20 D2 100r dl bl 2.75 1.40
Nos. J14-J20 (7) 8.20 4.30

See note after No. 183.

1915, Mar. 18 Typo.
J21 D3 ½c brown 30 30
J22 D3 1c orange 30 30
J23 D3 2c claret 30 30
J24 D3 3c green 30 30
J25 D3 4c gray vio 30 30
J26 D3 5c carmine 30 30
J27 D3 10c dk bl 30 30
Nos. J21-J27 (7) 2.10 2.10

1921-27
J28 D3 ½c gray grn ('22) 10 12
J29 D3 4c gray grn ('27) 10 12
J30 D3 8c gray grn ('23) 10 12
J31 D3 10c gray grn ('22) 20 22
J32 D3 12c gray grn 12 22
J33 D3 16c gray grn ('23) 12 12
J34 D3 20c gray grn 12 22
J35 D3 24c gray grn 20 22
J36 D3 32c gray brn ('23) 20 22
J37 D3 36c gray grn 50 45
J38 D3 40c gray grn ('23) 50 45
J39 D3 48c gray grn ('23) 20 30
J40 D3 50c gray grn 20 30
J41 D3 60c gray grn 20 30
J42 D3 72c gray grn 20 30
J43 D3 80c gray grn ('23) 2.50 90
J44 D3 1.20e gray grn 85 90
Nos. J28-J44 (17) 6.41 5.48

D4

D5

1932-33
J45 D4 5c buff 32 25
J46 D4 10c lt bl 15 25
J47 D4 20c pink 35 40
J48 D4 30c bl grn 45 50
J49 D4 40c lt grn 45 50
J50 D4 50c gray 45 50
J51 D4 60c rose 70 80
J52 D4 80c vio brn 4.50 80
J53 D4 1.20e gray ol ('33) 3.25 4.00
Nos. J45-J53 (9) 10.62 8.00

1940, Feb. 1 Unwmk. *Perf. 12½*
J54 D5 5c bis, perf. 14 12 22
J55 D5 10c rose lil 12 22
J56 D5 20c dk car rose 12 22
J57 D5 30c purple 12 22
J58 D5 40c cerise 12 22
J59 D5 50c brt bl 12 22
J60 D5 60c yel grn 12 22
J61 D5 80c scarlet 18 15
J62 D5 1e brown 35 15
J63 D5 2e dk rose vio 50 12
J64 D5 5e org yel, perf. 14 1.40 1.40
a. Perf. 12½
Nos. J54-J64 (11) 3.27 3.36

Nos. J54-J64 were first issued perf. 14. In 1955 all but the 5c were reissued in perf. 12½.

Catalogue values for unused stamps in this section, from this point to the end of the section, are for Never Hinged items.

D6

1967-84 Litho. *Perf. 11½*
J65 D6 10c dp org, red brn & yel 5 5
J66 D6 20c bis, dk brn & yel 5 5
J67 D6 30c org, red brn & yel 5 5
J68 D6 40c ol bis, dk brn & yel 5 5
J69 D6 50c ultra, dk bl & bl 5 5
J70 D6 60c grnsh bl, dk grn & lt bl 5 5
J71 D6 80c bl, dk bl & lt bl 5 5
J72 D6 1e vio bl, dk bl & lt bl 5 5
J73 D6 2e grn, dk grn & lt grn 8 8
J74 D6 3e lt grn, grn & yel ('75) 15 15
J75 D6 4e bl grn, dk grn & yel ('75) 15 15
J76 D6 5e cl, dp cl & pink 15 15
J77 D6 9e vio, dk vio & pink ('75) 28 28
J78 D6 10e lil, pur & pale vio ('75) 28 28
J79 D6 20e red, brn & pale vio ('75) 52 52
J80 D6 40e dp red lil, rose vio & bluish lil ('84) 1.05 1.05
J81 D6 50e lil, brn & pale gray ('84) 1.35 1.35
Nos. J65-J81 (17) 4.41 4.41

OFFICIAL STAMPS

No. 567 Overprinted in Black **OFICIAL**

1938 Unwmk. *Perf. 11½.*
O1 A113 40c brown 18 6

Catalogue values for unused stamps in this section, from this point to the end of the section, are for Never Hinged items.

O1

1952, Sept. Litho. *Perf. 12½*
O2 O1 blk & cr 10 5

1975, June
O3 O1 blk & yel 55 40

NEWSPAPER STAMPS

N1

Perf. 11½, 12½, 13½
1876 Typo. Unwmk.
P1 N1 2½r bister 5.75 65
a. 2½r olive green 5.75 65

Various shades.

PARCEL POST STAMPS

Mercury and Commerce PP1

1920-22 Unwmk. Typo. *Perf. 12*
Q1 PP1 1c lil brn 8 12
Q2 PP1 2c orange 8 12
Q3 PP1 5c lt brn 8 12
Q4 PP1 10c red brn 8 12
Q5 PP1 20c gray bl 25 12
Q6 PP1 40c car rose 25 22
Q7 PP1 50c black 35 30
Q8 PP1 60c dk bl ('21) 35 30
Q9 PP1 70c gray brn ('21) 1.25 1.25
Q10 PP1 80c ultra ('21) 1.65 1.40
Q11 PP1 90c lt vio ('21) 1.50 1.40
Q12 PP1 1e lt grn 1.50 60
Q13 PP1 2e pale lil ('22) 4.25 1.50
Q14 PP1 3e ol ('22) 5.00 2.00
Q15 PP1 4e ultra ('22) 14.00 3.75
Q16 PP1 5e gray ('22) 15.00 2.50
Q17 PP1 10e choc ('22) 30.00 4.00
Nos. Q1-Q17 (17) 75.67 19.82

Parcel Post Package PP2

1936 *Perf. 11½*
Q18 PP2 50c ol brn 10 16
Q19 PP2 1e bis brn 10 16
Q20 PP2 1.50e purple 10 16
Q21 PP2 2e car lake 1.10 16
Q22 PP2 2.50e ol grn 1.10 16
Q23 PP2 4.50e brn lake 1.40 16
Q24 PP2 5e violet 3.25 24
Q25 PP2 10e orange 4.25 70
Nos. Q18-Q25 (8) 11.40 1.90

POSTAL TAX STAMPS

These stamps represent a special fee for the delivery of postal matter on certain days in each year. The money derived from their sale is applied to works of public charity.

Regular Issues Overprinted in Carmine **ASSISTENCIA**

1911, Oct. 4 Unwmk. *Perf. 14½x15*
RA1 A62 10r gray grn 2.00 85

The 20r carmine of this type was for use on telegrams.

1912, Oct. 4 *Perf. 15x14½*
RA2 A64 1c dp grn 1.65 75

The 2c carmine of this type was for use on telegrams.

"Lisbon" PT1

"Charity" PT2

1913, June 8 Litho. *Perf. 12x11½*
RA3 PT1 1c dk grn 45 32

The 2c dark brown of this type was for use on telegrams.

1915, Oct. 4 Typo.
RA4 PT2 1c carmine 25 21

The 2c plum of this type was for use on telegrams.
See No. RA6.

No. RA4 Surcharged **15 ctvs.**

1924, Oct. 4
RA5 PT2 15c on 1c dl red 50 25

The 30c on 2c claret of this type was for use on telegrams.

Charity Type of 1915 Issue.

1925, Oct. 4 *Perf. 12½.*
RA6 PT2 15c carmine 25 20

The 30c brown violet of this type was for use on telegrams.

Comrades of the Great War Issue.

Muse of History with Tablet — PT3

1925, Apr. 8 Litho. *Perf. 11.*

RA7 PT3 10c brown 45 40
RA8 PT3 10c green 45 40
RA9 PT3 10c rose 45 40
RA10 PT3 10c ultra 45 40

The use of these stamps, in addition to the regular postage, was obligatory on certain days of the year. If the tax represented by these stamps was not prepaid, it was collected by means of Postal Tax Due Stamp No. RAJ1.

Pombal Issue
Common Design Types
Engraved; Value and "Continente" Typographed in Black.

1925, May 8 *Perf. 12 1/2.*

RA11 CD28 15c ultra 15 12
RA12 CD29 15c ultra 35 45
RA13 CD30 15c ultra 35 45

Olympic Games Issue.

Hurdler — PT7

1928 Litho. *Perf. 12*

RA14 PT7 15c dl red & blk 3.75 4.00

The use of this stamp, in addition to the regular postage, was obligatory on May 22nd, 23rd and 24th, 1928. Ten per cent. of the money thus obtained was retained by the Postal Administration; the balance was given to a Committee in charge of Portuguese participation in the Olympic games at Amsterdam.

POSTAL TAX DUE STAMPS

PTD1

PTD2

Comrades of the Great War Issue.

1925 Unwmk. Typo. *Perf. 11x11 1/2.*

RAJ1 PTD1 20c brn org 90 1.00

See Note after No. RA10.

Pombal Issue.
Common Design Types

1925 *Perf. 12 1/2.*

RAJ2 CD31 30c ultra 50 60
RAJ3 CD32 30c ultra 50 60
RAJ4 CD33 30c ultra 50 60

When the compulsory tax was not paid by the use of stamps Nos. RA11 to RA13, double the amount was collected by means of Nos. RAJ2 to RAJ4.

Olympic Games Issue.

1928 Litho. *Perf. 11 1/2.*

RAJ5 PTD2 30c lt red & blk 1.65 1.40

FRANCHISE STAMPS

These stamps are supplied by the Government to various charitable, scientific and military organizations for franking their correspondence. This franking privilege was withdrawn in 1938.

Footnotes often refer you to other stamps of the same design.

FOR THE RED CROSS SOCIETY

F1

Perf. 11 1/2

1889-1915 Unwmk. Typo.

1S1 F1 rose & blk ('15) 45 32
a. ver & blk ('08) 2.50 1.00
b. red & blk, perf. 12 1/2 15.00 3.00

No. 151 Overprinted in Green

COMISSAO PORTUGUESA DOS PRISIONEIROS DE GUERRA

1917

1S3 F1 rose & blk 45.00 35.00
a. Inverted overprint 67.50 67.50

"Charity" Extending Hope to Invalid — F1a

1926 Litho. *Perf. 14.*
Inscribed "LISBOA".

1S4 F1a blk & red 2.50 3.50

Inscribed "DELEGACOES".

1S5 F1a blk & red 2.50 3.50

No. 1S4 was for use in Lisbon. No. 1S5 was for the Red Cross chapters outside Lisbon.

Camoens Issue of 1924 Overprinted in Black or Red

CRUZ VERMELHA
Porte franco
1927

1927

1S6 A68 40c ultra 50 75
1S7 A68 48c red brn 50 75
1S8 A69 64c green 50 75
1S9 A69 75c dk vio 50 75
1S10 A71 4.50e blk, *org* (R) 50 75
1S11 A71 10e dk brn, *pnksh* 50 75
Nos. 1S6-1S11 (6) 3.00 4.50

Camoens Issue of 1924 Overprinted in Red

Porte franco
1928

1928

1S12 A67 15c ol grn 75 1.00
1S13 A67 16c vio brn 75 1.00
1S14 A68 25c lilac 75 1.00
1S15 A68 40c ultra 75 1.00
1S16 A70 1.20e lt brn 75 1.00
1S17 A70 2e ap grn 75 1.00
Nos. 1S12-1S17 (6) 4.50 6.00

Camoens Issue of 1924 Overprinted in Red

Porte franco
1929

1929

1S18 A68 30c dk brn 60 75
1S19 A68 40c ultra 60 75
1S20 A69 80c bister 60 75
1S21 A70 1.50e red 60 75
1S22 A70 1.60e dk bl 60 75
1S23 A71 2.40e grn, *grn* 60 75
Nos. 1S18-1S23 (6) 3.60 4.50

Same Overprint Dated "1930"

1930

1S24 A68 40c ultra 60 75
1S25 A69 50c red org 60 75
1S26 A69 96c lake 60 75
1S27 A70 1.60e dk bl 60 75
1S28 A71 3e dk bl, *bl* 60 75
1S29 A72 20e dk vio, *lil* 60 75
Nos. 1S24-1S29 (6) 3.60 4.50

Camoens Issue of 1924 Overprinted in Red

Porte franco
1931

1931

1S30 A68 25c lilac 65 75
1S31 A68 32c dk grn 65 75
1S32 A68 40c ultra 65 75
1S33 A69 96c lake 65 75
1S34 A70 1.60e dk bl 65 75
1S35 A71 3.20e blk, *green* 65 75
Nos. 1S30-1S35 (6) 3.90 4.50

Same Overprint Dated "1932"

1931

1S36 A67 20c dp org 65 1.10
1S37 A68 40c ultra 65 1.10
1S38 A68 48c red brn 65 1.10
1S39 A69 64c green 65 1.10
1S40 A70 1.60e dk bl 65 1.10
1S41 A71 10e dk brn, *pnksh* 65 1.10
Nos. 1S36-1S41 (6) 3.90 6.60

Nos. 1S6-1S11 Overprinted in Red

1933

1932

1S42 A68 40c ultra 80 1.40
1S43 A68 48c red brn 80 1.40
1S44 A69 64c green 80 1.40
1S45 A69 75c dk vio 80 1.40
1S46 A71 4.50e blk, *orange* 80 1.40
1S47 A71 10e dk brn, *pnksh* 80 1.40
Nos. 1S42-1S47 (6) 4.80 8.40

Dated "1934"

1933

1S48 A68 40c ultra 80 1.40
1S49 A68 48c red brn 80 1.40
1S50 A69 64c green 80 1.40
1S51 A69 75c dk vio 80 1.40
1S52 A71 4.50e blk, *orange* 80 1.40
1S53 A71 10e dk brn, *pnksh* 80 1.40
Nos. 1S48-1S53 (6) 4.80 8.40

Dated "1935"

1935

1S54 A68 40c ultra 1.10 1.90
1S55 A68 48c red brn 1.10 1.90
1S56 A69 64c green 1.10 1.90
1S57 A69 75c dk vio 1.10 1.90
1S58 A71 4.50e blk, *orange* 1.10 1.90
1S59 A71 10e dk brn, *pnksh* 1.10 1.90
Nos. 1S54-1S59 (6) 6.60 11.40

Camoens Issue of 1924 Overprinted in Black or Red

Cruz
Vermelha
Porte
Franco
1936

1935

1S60 A68 25c lilac 50 75
1S61 A68 40c ultra (R) 50 75
1S62 A69 50c red org 50 75
1S63 A70 1e slate 50 75
1S64 A70 2e ap grn 50 75
1S65 A72 20e dk vio, *lil* 50 75
Nos. 1S60-1S65 (6) 3.00 4.50

Camoens Issue of 1924 Overprinted in Red

CRUZ VERMELHA PORTUGUESA
19 36
Porte Franco

1936

1S66 A68 30c dk brn 50 75
1S67 A68 32c dk grn 50 75
1S68 A69 80c bister 50 75
1S69 A70 1.20e lt brn 50 75
1S70 A71 3e dk bl, *bl* 50 75
1S71 A71 4.50e blk, *yel* 50 75
Nos. 1S66-1S71 (6) 3.00 4.50

No. 1S4 Overprinted "1935".

1936 Unwmk. *Perf. 14*

1S72 F1a blk & red 2.75 5.00

Same Stamp with Additional Overprint "Delegacoes"

1S73 F1a blk & red 2.75 5.00

After the government withdrew the franking privilege in 1938, the Portuguese Red Cross Society distributed charity labels which lacked postal validity.

FOR CIVILIAN RIFLE CLUBS

Rifle Club Emblem — F2

Perf. 11 1/2x12

1899-1910 Typo. Unwmk.

2S1 F2 bl grn & car ('99) 10.00 9.00
2S2 F2 brn & yel grn ('00) 10.00 9.00
2S3 F2 car & buff ('01) 1.50 1.50
2S4 F2 bl & org ('02) 1.50 1.50
2S5 F2 grn & org ('03) 1.50 1.50
2S6 F2 lt brn & car ('04) 1.50 1.50
2S7 F2 mar & ultra ('05) 1.50 1.50
2S8 F2 ultra & buff ('06) 1.50 1.50
2S9 F2 choc & yel ('07) 1.50 1.50
2S10 F2 car & ultra ('08) 1.50 1.50
2S11 F2 bl & yel grn ('09) 1.50 1.50
2S12 F2 bl grn & brn, *pink* ('10) 1.50 1.50
Nos. 2S1-2S12 (12) 35.00 33.00

FOR THE GEOGRAPHICAL SOCIETY OF LISBON

Coat of Arms
F3 F4

1903-34 Unwmk. Litho. *Perf. 11 1/2*

3S1 F3 blk, rose, bl & red 5.50 2.25
3S2 F3 bl, yel, red & grn ('09) 6.25 3.25
3S3 F4 blk, org, bl & red ('11) 1.10 75
3S4 F4 blk & brn org ('22) 3.00 2.75
3S5 F4 blk & bl ('24) 7.25 4.50
3S6 F4 blk & rose ('26) 2.50 2.25
3S7 F4 blk & grn ('27) 2.50 2.25
3S8 F4 bl, yel & red ('29) 2.00 1.50
3S9 F4 bl, red & vio ('30) 2.00 1.50
3S10 F4 dp bl, lil & red ('31) 2.00 1.50
3S11 F4 bis brn & red ('32) 2.00 1.50
3S12 F4 lt grn & red ('33) 2.00 1.50
3S13 F4 bl & red ('34) 2.00 1.50
Nos. 3S1-3S13 (13) 40.10 27.00

No. 3S12 with three-line overprint, "C.I.C.I. Portugal 1933," was not valid for postage and was sold only to collectors.

No. 3S2 was reprinted in 1933. Green vertical lines behind "Porte Franco" omitted. Value $7.50.

F5

1934 Litho. *Perf. 11 1/2.*

3S15 F5 bl & red 90 1.00

1935-38 *Perf. 11.*

3S16 F5 blue 4.50 6.00
3S17 F5 dk bl & red ('36) 1.50 1.75
3S18 F5 lil & red ('37) 1.40 80
3S19 F5 blk, grn & car ('38) 1.40 80

The inscription in the inner circle is omitted on No. 3S16.

FOR THE NATIONAL AID SOCIETY FOR CONSUMPTIVES

F10

Perf. 11½x12

1904, July **Typo.** **Unwmk.**

4S1 F10 brn & grn 3.00 3.00
4S2 F10 car & yel 3.00 3.00

PORTUGUESE AFRICA

For use in any of the Portuguese possessions in Africa.

1000 Reis = 1 Milreis
100 Centavos = 1 Escudo

Vasco da Gama Issue
Common Design Types
Perf. 13½ to 15½

1898, Apr. 1 **Engr.** **Unwmk.**

1 CD20 2½r bl grn 1.00 1.00
2 CD21 5r red 1.00 1.00
3 CD22 10r red vio 1.00 1.00
4 CD23 25r yel grn 1.00 1.00
5 CD24 50r dk bl 1.25 1.25
6 CD25 75r vio brn 6.75 6.75
7 CD26 100r bis brn 5.00 5.00
8 CD27 150r bister 7.25 6.75
Nos. 1-8 (8) 24.25 23.75

Commemorating Vasco da Gama's voyage to India.

POSTAGE DUE STAMPS

D1

1945 Unwmk. Typo. *Perf. 11½x12*
Denomination in Black.

J1 D1 10c claret 25 35
J2 D1 20c purple 25 35
J3 D1 30c dp bl 25 35
J4 D1 40c chocolate 25 35
J5 D1 50c red vio 40 60
J6 D1 1e org brn 1.10 1.40
J7 D1 2e yel grn 2.25 2.75
J8 D1 3e brt car 5.50 5.50
J9 D1 5e org yel 10.00 10.00
Nos. J1-J9 (9) 20.25 21.65

Common Design Types pictured in section at front of book.

WAR TAX STAMPS

Liberty
WT1

Perf. 12x11½, 15x14.

1919 **Typo.** **Unwmk.**
Overprinted in Black, Orange or Carmine.

MR1 WT1 1c grn (Bk) 50 50
MR2 WT1 4c grn (O) 50 50
MR3 WT1 5c grn (C) 50 50

Some authorities consider No. MR2 a revenue stamp.

PORTUGUESE CONGO

LOCATION — The northernmost district of the Portuguese Angola Colony on the southwest coast of Africa.
CAPITAL — Cabinda.

Stamps of Angola replaced those of Portuguese Congo.

1000 Reis = 1 Milreis
100 Centavos = 1 Escudo (1913)

King Carlos
A1 A2

Perf. 11½, 12½, 13½

1894, Aug. 5 **Typo.** **Unwmk.**

1 A1 5r yellow 75 60
a. Perf. 13½ 15.00 12.50
2 A1 10r redsh vio 1.40 80
a. Perf. 13½ 17.50 14.00
3 A1 15r chocolate 2.50 2.00
4 A1 20r lavender 2.00 1.75
5 A1 25r green 1.25 80
6 A1 50r lt bl 2.75 2.00
7 A1 75r rose 4.00 3.00
a. Perf. 12½ 17.50 15.00
8 A1 80r yel grn 7.00 6.00
a. Perf. 12½ 17.50 12.50
9 A1 100r brn, *yel* 5.25 3.25
a. Perf. 13½ 22.50 15.00
10 A1 150r car, *rose* 10.00 9.00
11 A1 200r dk bl, *bl* 10.00 9.00
12 A1 300r dk bl, *sal* 12.50 11.00
Nos. 1-12 (12) 59.40 49.20

1898-1903 ***Perf. 11½***
Name & Value in Black except 500r

13 A2 2½r gray 25 20
14 A2 5r orange 25 20
15 A2 10r lt grn 40 35
16 A2 15r brown 1.65 1.25
17 A2 15r gray grn ('03) 75 60
18 A2 20r gray vio 75 65
19 A2 25r sea grn 1.10 75
20 A2 25r car rose ('03) 80 45
21 A2 50r dp bl 1.65 1.25
22 A2 50r brn ('03) 2.50 1.50
23 A2 65r dl bl ('03) 8.25 7.25
24 A2 75r rose 2.75 2.50
25 A2 75r red lil ('03) 2.75 2.50
26 A2 80r violet 3.00 2.50
27 A2 100r dk bl, *bl* 2.25 2.00
28 A2 115r org brn, *pink* ('03) 6.00 5.50
29 A2 130r brn, *straw* ('03) 10.00 10.00
30 A2 150r brn, *buff* 3.25 2.75
31 A2 200r red lil, *pnksh* 4.25 3.00
32 A2 300r dk bl, *rose* 3.25 2.75
33 A2 400r dl bl, *straw* ('03) 9.00 9.00
34 A2 500r blk & red, *bl* ('01) 16.00 10.00
35 A2 700r vio, *yelsh* ('01) 25.00 17.50
Nos. 13-35 (23) 105.85 84.45

Surcharged in Black — 65 RÉIS

1902 ***Perf. 11½, 12½, 13½***
On Issue of 1894

36 A1 65r on 15r choc 3.50 3.00
a. Perf. 11½ 13.00 7.50
37 A1 65r on 20r lav 4.00 3.00
38 A1 65r on 25r grn 4.00 3.00
a. Perf. 11½ 15.00 9.00
39 A1 65r on 300r bl, *sal* 4.50 4.50
40 A1 115r on 10r red vio 4.00 3.00
41 A1 115r on 50r lt bl 3.00 2.50
42 A1 130r on 5r yel 3.50 2.75
a. Inverted surch. 12.00 12.00
43 A1 130r on 75r rose 3.50 3.00
a. Perf. 12½ 7.00 6.00
44 A1 130r on 100r brn, *yel* 4.00 3.00
a. Inverted surch. 20.00 17.50
b. Perf. 11½ 16.00 12.50
45 A1 400r on 80r yel grn 1.75 1.00
46 A1 400r on 150r car, *rose* 1.25 1.10
47 A1 400r on 200r bl, *bl* 1.25 1.10

On Newspaper Stamp of 1894

48 N1 115r on 2½r brn 3.75 2.75
a. Inverted surch. 12.50 12.50
Nos. 36-48 (13) 42.00 33.70

Nos. 16, 19, 21 and 24 Overprinted in Black — PROVISORIO

1902 ***Perf. 11½***

49 A2 15r brown 2.00 1.40
50 A2 25r sea green 2.00 1.40
51 A2 50r blue 2.00 1.40
52 A2 75r rose 4.00 2.75

No. 23 Surcharged — 50 RÉIS

1905

53 A2 50r on 65r dull blue 3.50 2.25

Angola Stamps of 1898-1903 (Port. Congo type A2) Overprinted or Surcharged:

CONGO REPUBLICA — a
CONGO REPUBLICA 25 — b

1911

54 (a) 2½r gray 1.00 90
55 (a) 5r orange 1.40 1.25
56 (a) 10r lt grn 1.40 1.25
a. "REPUBLICA" inverted 10.00 10.00
57 (a) 15r gray grn 1.40 1.25
a. "REPUBLICA" inverted 10.00 10.00
58 (b) 25r on 200r red vio, *pnksh* 2.25 2.00
a. "REPUBLICA" inverted 10.00 10.00
b. "CONGO" double 10.00 10.00

Thin Bar and "CONGO" as Type "b"

59 (a) 2½r gray 1.10 90
Nos. 54-59 (6) 8.55 7.55

Issue of 1898-1903 Overprinted in Carmine or Green — c — REPUBLICA

1911

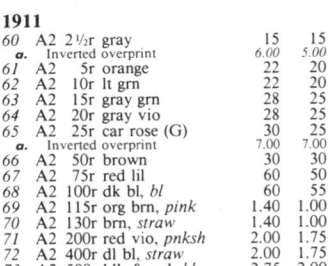

60 A2 2½r gray 15 15
a. Inverted overprint 6.00 5.00
61 A2 5r orange 22 20
62 A2 10r lt grn 22 20
63 A2 15r gray grn 28 25
64 A2 20r gray vio 28 25
65 A2 25r car rose (G) 30 25
a. Inverted overprint 7.00 7.00
66 A2 50r brown 30 30
67 A2 75r red lil 60 50
68 A2 100r dk bl, *bl* 60 55
69 A2 115r org brn, *pink* 1.40 1.00
70 A2 130r brn, *straw* 1.40 1.00
71 A2 200r red vio, *pnksh* 2.00 1.75
72 A2 400r dl bl, *straw* 2.00 1.75
73 A2 500r blk & red, *bl* 2.75 2.00
74 A2 700r vio, *yelsh* 2.75 2.00
Nos. 60-74 (15) 15.25 12.15

Vasco da Gama Issue of Various Portuguese Colonies Surcharged — REPUBLICA CONGO ¼ C.

1913

On Stamps of Macao

75 CD20 ¼c on ½a bl grn 1.40 1.40
76 CD21 ½c on 1a red 1.40 1.40
77 CD22 1c on 2a red vio 1.40 1.40
78 CD23 2½c on 4a yel grn 1.40 1.40
79 CD24 5c on 8a dk bl 1.40 1.40
80 CD25 7½c on 12a vio brn 2.75 2.75
81 CD26 10c on 16a bis brn 2.00 2.00
82 CD27 15c on 24a bis 2.00 2.00
Nos. 75-82 (8) 13.75 13.75

On Stamps of Portuguese Africa

83 CD20 ¼c on 2½r bl grn 90 90
84 CD21 ½c on 5r red 90 90
85 CD22 1c on 10r red vio 90 90
86 CD23 2½c on 25r yel grn 90 90
87 CD24 5c on 50r dk bl 1.25 1.25
88 CD25 7½c on 75r vio brn 2.25 2.25
89 CD26 10c on 100r bis brn 1.40 1.40
a. Inverted surch. 11.00 11.00
90 CD27 15c on 150r bis 1.75 1.50
Nos. 83-90 (8) 10.25 10.00

On Stamps of Timor

91 CD20 ¼c on ½a bl grn 1.40 1.40
92 CD21 ½c on 1a red 1.40 1.40
93 CD22 1c on 2a red vio 1.40 1.40
94 CD23 2½c on 4a yel grn 1.40 1.40
95 CD24 5c on 8a dk bl 1.40 1.40
a. Double surch. 11.00 11.00
96 CD25 7½c on 12a vio brn 2.75 2.75
97 CD26 10c on 16a bis brn 2.50 2.50
98 CD27 15c on 24a bis 2.50 2.50
Nos. 91-98 (8) 14.75 14.75
Nos. 75-98 (24) 38.75 38.50

Ceres — A3

1914 **Typo.** ***Perf. 15x14***
Name and Value in Black

99 A3 ¼c ol brn 30 25
a. Inscriptions inverted
100 A3 ½c black 55 40
101 A3 1c bl grn 2.75 1.75
102 A3 1½c lil brn 1.10 75
103 A3 2c carmine 1.10 85
104 A3 2½c lt vio 35 30
105 A3 5c dp bl 65 60
106 A3 7½c yel brn 90 85
107 A3 8c slate 1.50 1.00
108 A3 10c org brn 1.50 1.00
109 A3 15c plum 1.75 1.00
110 A3 20c yel grn 2.00 1.50
111 A3 30c brn, *grn* 2.50 1.65
112 A3 40c brn, *pink* 3.50 2.50
113 A3 50c org, *sal* 3.50 2.50
114 A3 1e grn, *bl* 5.00 3.00
Nos. 99-114 (16) 28.95 19.90

Issue of 1898-1903 Overprinted Locally in Green or Red — REPUBLICA

1914-18 ***Perf. 11½***

117 A2 50r brn (G) 65 60
118 A2 75r rose (G) 125.00 110.00
119 A2 75r red lil (G) 70 65
120 A2 100r bl, *bl* (R) 70 65
121 A2 200r red vio, *pink* (G) 1.10 1.00
122 A2 400r dl bl, *straw* (R) ('18) 55.00 40.00
123 A2 500r blk & red, *bl* (R) 37.50 30.00

Same on Nos. 51-52

124 A2 50r bl (R) 75 65
125 A2 75r rose (G) 1.40 1.00

Same on No. 53

126 A2 50r on 65r dl bl (R) 1.10 1.00
Nos. 117,119-126 (9) 98.90 75.55

No. 118 was not regularly issued.

Provisional Issue of 1902 Overprinted Type "c" in Red

1915 ***Perf. 11½, 13½***

127 A1 115r on 10r red vio 25 20
a. Perf. 13½ 15.00 12.50
128 A1 115r on 50r lt bl 25 20
a. Perf. 11½ 1.75 60
129 A1 130r on 5r yel 30 25
130 A1 130r on 75r rose 1.40 60
131 A1 130r on 100r brn, *buff* 40 35
135 N1 115r on 2½r brn 40 35

Nos. 49, 51 Overprinted Type "c"

136 A2 15r brown 40 35
137 A2 50r blue 40 35

No. 53 Overprinted Type "c"

138 A2 50r on 65r dl bl 50 35
Nos. 127-138 (9) 4.30 3.00

NEWSPAPER STAMP

N1

Perf. 12½, 13½

1894, Aug. 5 Typo. Unwmk.

P1 N1 2½r brown 60 40

PORTUGUESE GUINEA

LOCATION — On the west coast of Africa between Senegal and Guinea.
GOVT. — Former Portuguese Overseas Territory.
AREA — 13,944 sq. mi.
POP. — 560,000 (est. 1970).
CAPITAL — Bissau.

The territory, including the Bissagos Islands, became an independent republic on Sept. 10, 1974. See Guinea-Bissau in Vol. III.

1000 Reis = 1 Milreis
100 Centavos = 1 Escudo (1913)

Catalogue values for unused stamps in this country are for Never Hinged items, beginning with Scott 273 in the regular postage section, Scott J40 in the postage due section, and Scott RA17 in the postal tax section.

Values of early Portuguese Guinea stamps vary according to condition. Quotations for Nos. 1-7 are for fine copies. Very fine to superb specimens sell at much higher prices, and inferior or poor copies sell at reduced prices, depending on the condition of the individual specimen.

Stamps of Cape Verde, 1877-85 Overprinted in Black — GUINÉ

1881 Unwmk. *Perf. 12½.*
Without Gum (Nos. 1-7)

1 A1 5r black *1,000. 800.00*
1A A1 10r yel *1,100. 800.00*
2 A1 20r bister *450.00 225.00*
3 A1 25r rose *1,100. 700.00*
4 A1 40r blue *1,000. 800.00*
a. Cliche of Mozambique in Cape Verde plate *5,500. 5,500.*
4B A1 50r green *1,100. 800.00*
5 A1 100r lilac *275.00 150.00*
6 A1 200r orange *475.00 425.00*
7 A1 300r brown *475.00 425.00*

Overprinted in Red or Black — GUINÉ

1881-85 *Perf. 12½, 13½*

8 A1 5r blk (R) 2.50 2.00
9 A1 10r yellow 125.00 100.00
10 A1 10r grn ('85) 6.00 5.50
11 A1 20r bister 2.00 1.75
12 A1 20r rose ('85) 6.00 5.50
a. Double overprint
13 A1 25r carmine 1.40 1.25
a. Perf. 13½ 62.50 30.00
14 A1 25r vio ('85) 2.00 1.75
a. Double overprint
15 A1 40r blue 125.00 75.00
a. Cliche of Mozambique in Cape Verde plate *1,000. 800.00*
16 A1 40r yel ('85) 1.10 1.25
a. Cliche of Mozambique in Cape Verde plate 30.00 27.50
b. Imperf.
c. As "a," imperf.
d. Double ovpt.
17 A1 50r green 150.00 75.00
18 A1 50r bl ('85) 4.50 2.25
a. Imperf.
b. Double overprint
19 A1 100r lilac 5.00 4.00
a. Inverted overprint
20 A1 200r orange 9.50 6.50
21 A1 300r yel brn 13.00 10.00
a. 300r lake brn 13.00 10.00

Varieties of this overprint may be found without accent on "E" of "GUINE", or with grave instead of acute accent.

Stamps of the 1879-85 issues were reprinted on a smooth white chalky paper, ungummed, and on thin white paper with shiny white gum and clean-cut perforation 13½. Value of lowest selling reprints, $4 each.

King Luiz — A3

1886 Typo. *Perf. 12½, 13½*

22 A3 5r gray blk 2.50 2.00
a. Imperf.
23 A3 10r green 5.00 3.25
a. Perf. 13½ 5.00 4.50
b. Imperf.
24 A3 20r carmine 5.50 4.25
25 A3 25r red lil 6.75 4.25
a. Imperf.
26 A3 40r chocolate 6.00 5.00
a. Perf. 12½ 70.00 45.00
27 A3 50r blue 8.50 3.00
a. Imperf.
28 A3 80r gray 11.00 11.00
a. Perf. 12½ 62.50 50.00
29 A3 100r brown 12.00 12.00
a. Perf. 12½ 30.00 20.00
30 A3 200r gray lil 30.00 20.00
31 A3 300r orange 37.50 30.00
a. Perf. 13½ 165.00 165.00

Reprinted in 1905 on thin white paper with shiny white gum and clean-cut perforation 13½. Nos. 22, 27-29, value $2 each. Nos. 23, 25-26, 30-31, value $20 each.

King Carlos
A4 A5

1893-94 *Perf. 11½*

32 A4 5r yellow 1.50 90
a. Perf. 12½ 2.00 1.25
33 A4 10r red vio 1.50 90
34 A4 15r chocolate 1.75 1.25
35 A4 20r lavender 1.75 1.25
36 A4 25r bl grn 1.75 1.25
37 A4 50r lt bl 3.25 2.00
a. Perf. 12½ 7.50 4.50
38 A4 75r rose 10.00 7.50
39 A4 80r lt grn 10.00 7.50
40 A4 100r brn, *buff* 10.00 7.50
41 A4 150r car, *rose* 10.00 8.00
42 A4 200r dk bl, *bl* 11.00 8.00
43 A4 300r dk bl, *sal* 15.00 12.00
Nos. 32-43 (12) 77.50 58.05

Almost all of Nos. 32-43 were issued without gum.

1898-1903 *Perf. 11½*
Name & Value in Black except 500r

44 A5 2½r gray 35 30
45 A5 5r orange 35 30
46 A5 10r lt grn 35 30
47 A5 15r brown 2.75 1.75
48 A5 15r gray grn ('03) 1.25 1.10
49 A5 20r gray vio 1.10 1.00
50 A5 25r sea grn 1.65 1.00
51 A5 25r car ('03) 65 60
52 A5 50r dk bl 2.50 1.25
53 A5 50r brn ('03) 2.00 1.40
54 A5 65r dl bl ('03) 7.00 6.00
55 A5 75r rose 15.00 8.00
56 A5 75r lil ('03) 3.00 2.00
57 A5 80r brt vio 2.50 1.75
58 A5 100r dk bl, *bl* 2.25 1.75
a. Perf. 12½ 45.00 20.00
59 A5 115r org brn, *pink* ('03) 7.00 5.50
60 A5 130r brn, *straw* ('03) 8.00 5.50
61 A5 150r lt brn, *buff* 8.00 3.00
62 A5 200r red lil, *pnksh* 8.00 3.00
63 A5 300r bl, *rose* 7.00 3.75
64 A5 400r dl bl, *straw* ('03) 8.00 6.00
65 A5 500r blk & red, *bl* ('01) 10.00 7.00
66 A5 700r vio, *yelsh* ('01) 15.00 9.00
Nos. 44-66 (23) 113.70 71.25

Stamps issued in 1903 were without gum.

Issue of 1886 Surcharged in Black or Red — 65 RÉIS

1902, Oct. 20 *Perf. 12½, 13½*

67 A3 65r on 10r grn 5.00 4.00
68 A3 65r on 20r car 5.00 4.00
69 A3 65r on 25r red lil 5.00 4.00
70 A3 115r on 40r choc 4.50 4.00
a. Perf. 13½ 10.00 7.50
71 A3 115r on 50r bl 4.50 4.00
72 A3 115r on 300r org 6.00 5.25
73 A3 130r on 80r gray 6.00 5.25
74 A3 130r on 100r brn 6.00 5.25
a. Perf. 13½ 14.00 12.00
75 A3 400r on 200r gray lil 11.00 10.00
76 A3 400r on 5r gray blk (R) 22.00 20.50
Nos. 67-76 (10) 75.00 66.25

Reprints of No. 76 are in black and have clean-cut perforation 13½. Value $4 each.

Same Surcharge on Issue of 1893-94.
Perf. 11½, 12½, 13½

77 A4 65r on 10r red vio 4.00 3.25
78 A4 65r on 15r choc 4.00 3.25
79 A4 65r on 20r lav 4.00 3.25
80 A4 65r on 50r lt bl 2.50 2.25
81 A4 115r on 5r yel 3.25 2.75
a. Inverted surcharge 25.00 25.00
b. Perf. 12½ 22.50 18.00
82 A4 115r on 25r bl grn 3.50 3.00
83 A4 130r on 150r car, *rose* 4.50 4.00
84 A4 130r on 200r dk bl, *bl* 4.50 4.00
85 A4 130r on 300r dk bl, *sal* 4.50 4.00
86 A4 400r on 75r rose 2.00 1.50
87 A4 400r on 80r lt grn 2.00 1.50
88 A4 400r on 100r brn, *buff* 2.00 1.50

Same Surcharge on No. P1

89 N1 115r on 2½r brn 4.00 3.50
Nos. 77-89 (13) 44.75 37.75

Issue of 1898 Overprinted in Black — PROVISORIO

1902, Oct. 20 *Perf. 11½*

90 A5 15r brown 1.40 1.10
91 A5 25r sea grn 2.00 1.25
92 A5 50r dk bl 2.00 1.25
93 A5 75r rose 4.00 3.50

No. 54 Surcharged in Black — 50 RÉIS

1905

94 A5 50r on 65r dl bl 4.00 2.25

Issue of 1898-1903 Overprinted in Carmine or Green — REPUBLICA

1911 *Perf. 11½*

95 A5 2½r gray 35 30
a. Inverted overprint 4.00 4.00
96 A5 5r orange 35 30
97 A5 10r lt grn 65 45
98 A5 15r gray grn 65 45
99 A5 20r gray vio 65 45
100 A5 25r car (G) 65 45
a. Double overprint 6.50 6.50
101 A5 50r brown 40 35
102 A5 75c lilac 40 35
103 A5 100r dk bl, *bl* 1.40 70
104 A5 115r org brn, *pink* 1.40 70
105 A5 130r brn, *straw* 1.40 70
106 A5 200r red lil, *pink* 6.00 3.00
107 A5 400r dl bl, *straw* 2.25 1.35
108 A5 500r blk & red, *bl* 2.50 1.35
109 A5 700r vio, *yelsh* 3.75 2.00
Nos. 95-109 (15) 22.80 12.90

Issued without gum: Nos. 101-102, 104-105, 107.

Issue of 1898-1903 Overprinted in Red — REPUBLICA

1913 *Perf. 11½*
Without Gum (Nos. 110-115)

110 A5 15r gray grn 6.75 6.00
111 A5 75r lilac 6.75 6.00
a. Inverted ovpt.
112 A5 100r bl, *bl* 5.00 4.00
a. Inverted ovpt.
113 A5 200r red lil, *pnksh* 22.50 22.50
a. Inverted ovpt.

Same Overprint on Nos. 90 and 93 in Red.

114 A5 15r brown 8.00 6.50
a. "REPUBLICA" double
b. "REPUBLICA" inverted *14.00 14.00*
115 A5 75r rose 8.00 6.00
a. "REPUBLICA" inverted
Nos. 110-115 (6) 57.00 51.00

Vasco da Gama Issue of Various Portuguese Colonies Surcharged — REPUBLICA GUINE ¼ C.

1913

On Stamps of Macao

116 CD20 ¼c on ½a bl grn 1.50 1.50
117 CD21 ½c on 1a red 1.50 1.50
118 CD22 1c on 2a red vio 1.50 1.50
119 CD23 2½c on 4a yel grn 1.50 1.50
120 CD24 5c on 8a dk bl 1.50 1.50
121 CD25 7½c on 12a vio brn 3.00 3.00
122 CD26 10c on 16a bis brn 1.50 1.50
a. Invtd. surch. 18.00 18.00
123 CD27 15c on 24a bis 2.50 2.50
Nos. 116-123 (8) 14.50 14.50

On Stamps of Portuguese Africa

124 CD20 ¼c on 2½c bl grn 1.25 1.25
125 CD21 ½c on 5r red 1.25 1.25
126 CD22 1c on 10r red vio 1.25 1.25
127 CD23 2½c on 25r yel grn 1.25 1.25
128 CD24 5c on 50r dk bl 1.25 1.25
129 CD25 7½c on 75r vio brn 3.25 3.25
130 CD26 10c on 100r bis brn 1.25 1.25
131 CD27 15c on 150r bis 3.50 3.50
Nos. 124-131 (8) 14.25 14.25

On Stamps of Timor

132 CD20 ¼c on ½a bl grn 1.50 1.50
133 CD21 ½c on 1a red 1.50 1.50
134 CD22 1c on 2a red vio 1.50 1.50
135 CD23 2½c on 4a yel grn 1.50 1.50
136 CD24 5c on 8a dk bl 1.50 1.50
137 CD25 7½c on 12a vio brn 2.75 2.75
138 CD26 10c on 16a bis brn 1.50 1.50
139 CD27 15c on 24a bis 2.75 2.75
Nos. 132-139 (8) 14.50 14.50
Nos. 116-139 (24) 43.25 43.25

Ceres — A6

1914-26 *Perf. 15x14, 12x11½*
Name and Value in Black

140 A6 ¼c ol brn 20 10
141 A6 ½c black 20 10
142 A6 1c bl grn 1.25 1.10
143 A6 1c yel grn ('22) 10 10
144 A6 1½c lil brn 20 10
145 A6 2c carmine 20 10
146 A6 2c gray ('25) 20 75
147 A6 2½c lt vio 15 5
148 A6 3c org ('22) 20 75
149 A6 4c dp red ('22) 20 75
150 A6 4½c gray ('22) 20 75
151 A6 5c dp bl 60 50
152 A6 5c brt bl ('22) 20 10
153 A6 6c lil ('22) 20 75
154 A6 7c ultra ('22) 30 75
155 A6 7½c yel brn 20 10
156 A6 8c slate 20 10
157 A6 10c org brn 15 10
158 A6 12c bl grn ('22) 60 35
159 A6 15c plum 7.50 5.50
160 A6 15c brn rose ('22) 45 30
161 A6 20c yel grn 20 10
162 A6 24c ultra ('25) 1.75 1.50
163 A6 25c brn ('25) 2.25 2.00
164 A6 30c brn, *grn* 6.25 5.50
165 A6 30c gray grn ('22) 80 25
166 A6 40c brn, *pink* 3.25 3.00
167 A6 40c turq bl ('22) 60 35
168 A6 50c org, *sal* 3.25 3.00

169 A6 50c vio ('25) 1.50 70
170 A6 60c dk bl ('22) 1.50 70
171 A6 60c dp rose ('26) 2.25 1.40
172 A6 80c brt rose ('22) 1.50 90
173 A6 1e grn, *bl* 3.50 3.25
174 A6 1e pale rose ('22) 2.25 1.10
175 A6 1e ind ('26) 2.75 2.25
176 A6 2e dk vio ('22) 2.75 1.10
177 A6 5e buff ('25) 10.50 7.25
178 A6 10e pink ('25) 22.50 13.00
179 A6 20e pale turq ('25) 52.50 27.50
Nos. 140-179 (40) 135.35 88.05

Provisional Issue of 1902 Overprinted in Carmine

REPUBLICA

1915 ***Perf. 11½, 12½, 13½***
180 A3 115r on 40r choc 65 60
a. Perf. 13½ 8.25 5.75
181 A3 115r on 50r bl 80 70
182 A3 130r on 80r gray 2.75 1.75
a. Perf. 12½ 25.00 20.00
183 A3 130r on 100r brn 2.25 1.75
a. Perf. 13½ 11.00 8.50
184 A4 115r on 5r yel 75 60
a. Perf. 11½ 4.50 4.00
185 A4 115r on 25r bl grn 70 60
186 A4 130r on 150r car, *rose* 1.10 75
187 A4 130r on 200r bl, *bl* 75 65
188 A4 130r on 300r dk bl, *sal* 1.00 75
189 N1 115r on 2½r brn 1.10 80
a. Perf. 13½ 12.50 12.00
b. Inverted ovpt. 12.50 12.00

On Nos. 90, 92, 94

Perf. 11½
190 A5 15r brown 75 65
191 A5 50r dk bl 75 65
192 A5 50r on 65r dl bl 75 65
Nos. 180-192 (13) 14.10 10.90

Nos. 64, 66 Overprinted REPUBLICA

1919 **Without Gum** ***Perf. 11½***
193 A5 400r dl bl, *straw* 16.00 13.00
194 A5 700r vio, *yelsh* 7.50 5.50

Nos. 140, 141 and 59 Surcharged:

$04 centavos
a

$12 CENTAVOS
b

1920, Sept. ***Perf. 15x14, 11½***
Without Gum
195 A6(a) 4c on ¼c ol brn 3.50 2.50
196 A6(a) 6c on ½c blk 3.50 2.50
197 A5(b) 12c on 115r org brn, *pink* 5.00 4.00

Nos. 86-88 Surcharged

República

40 C.

1925 ***Perf. 11½***
203 A4 40c on 400r on 75r 1.00 70
204 A4 40c on 400r on 80r 65 50
205 A4 40c on 400r on 100r 65 50

Nos. 171-172, 176 Surcharged

70 C.

1931 ***Perf. 12x11½***
211 A6 50c on 60c dp rose 2.00 1.50
212 A6 70c on 80c pink 2.25 1.75
213 A6 1.40e on 2e dk vio 4.50 3.50

Ceres — A7

1933 **Wmk. 232** ***Perf. 12 x 11½***
214 A7 1c bister 10 10
215 A7 5c ol brn 10 10
216 A7 10c violet 10 10
217 A7 15c black 15 10
218 A7 20c gray 15 10
219 A7 30c dk grn 15 10
220 A7 40c red org 35 20
221 A7 45c lt bl 75 50
222 A7 50c lt brn 75 50
223 A7 60c ol grn 75 50
224 A7 70c org brn 75 60
225 A7 80c emerald 1.10 75
226 A7 85c dp rose 2.25 1.25
227 A7 1e red brn 1.10 80
228 A7 1.40e dk bl 3.50 2.00
229 A7 2e red vio 2.25 1.75
230 A7 5e ap grn 7.50 4.50
231 A7 10e ol bis 15.00 7.50
232 A7 20e orange 50.00 20.00
Nos. 214-232 (19) 86.80 41.45

Common Design Types

Engr.; Name & Value Typo. in Black

1938 **Unwmk.** ***Perf. 13½x13***
233 CD34 1c gray grn 10 10
234 CD34 5c org brn 10 10
235 CD34 10c dk car 10 10
236 CD34 15c dk vio brn 15 15
237 CD34 20c slate 35 20
238 CD35 30c rose vio 40 25
239 CD35 35c brt grn 50 30
240 CD35 40c brown 50 30
241 CD35 50c brt red vio 50 30
242 CD36 60c gray blk 50 30
243 CD36 70c brn vio 50 30
244 CD36 80c orange 1.10 65
245 CD36 1e red 1.15 45
246 CD37 1.75e blue 1.40 90
247 CD37 2e brn car 4.25 1.25
248 CD37 5e ol grn 5.00 2.00
249 CD38 10e bl vio 6.25 2.50
250 CD38 20e red brn 22.50 4.00
Nos. 233-250 (18) 45.35 14.15

Fort of Cacheu
A8

Nuno Tristam — A9

Ulysses S. Grant — A10

Designs: 3.50e, Teixeira Pinto. 5e, Honorio Barreto. 20e, Bissau Church.

Unwmk.

1946, Jan. 12 **Litho.** ***Perf. 11***
251 A8 30c gray & lt gray 60 50
252 A9 50c blk & pink 50 30
253 A9 50c gray grn & lt grn 50 30
254 A10 1.75e bl & lt bl 2.00 1.25
255 A10 3.50e red & pink 3.50 2.00
256 A10 5e lt brn & buff 7.75 4.25
257 A8 20e vio & lt vio 11.00 5.50
a. Sheet of seven ('47) 60.00 60.00
Nos. 251-257 (7) 25.85 14.10

Discovery of Guinea, 500th anniversary.
No. 257a contains one each of Nos. 251-257. Size: 175½x221mm. Sold for 40 escudos.

Scott's editorial staff cannot undertake to identify, authenticate or appraise stamps and postal markings.

Guinea Village
A11

U.P.U. Symbols
A12

Designs: 10c, Crowned crane. 20c, 3.50e, Tribesman 35c, 5e, Woman in ceremonial dress. 50c, Musician. 70c, Man. 80c, 20e, Girl. 1e, 2e, Drummer. 1.75e, Antelope.

1948, Apr. **Photo.** ***Perf. 11½.***
258 A11 5c chocolate 10 10
259 A11 10c lt vio 85 75
260 A11 20c dl rose 30 25
261 A11 35c green 30 25
262 A11 50c dp org 20 15
263 A11 70c dp gray bl 25 25
264 A11 80c dk ol grn 35 30
265 A11 1e rose red 55 40
266 A11 1.75e ultra 3.25 1.50
267 A11 2e blue 8.50 1.00
268 A11 3.50e org brn 1.10 80
269 A11 5e slate 1.75 1.25
270 A11 20e violet 5.00 3.00
a. Sheet of 13 60.00 60.00
Nos. 258-270 (13) 22.50 10.00

No. 270a measures 176x158mm, and contains Nos. 258-270 plus two labels. Sheet sold for 40 escudos.

Lady of Fatima Issue.

Common Design Type

1948, Oct. **Litho.** ***Perf. 14½.***
271 CD40 50c dp grn 2.75 2.25

1949, Oct. ***Perf. 14.***
272 A12 2e dp org & cr 2.75 2.25

Universal Postal Union, 75th anniversary.

Catalogue values for unused stamps in this section, from this point to the end of the section, are for Never Hinged items.

Holy Year Issue.

Common Design Types

1950, May ***Perf. 13x13½.***
273 CD41 1e brn lake 1.25 1.00
274 CD42 3e bl grn 1.90 1.40

Holy Year Extension Issue.

Common Design Type

1951, Oct. ***Perf. 14.***
275 CD43 1e choc & pale brn 90 60

Medical Congress Issue.

Common Design Type

Design: Physical examination.

1952 ***Perf. 13½***
276 CD44 50c pur & choc 40 30

Exhibition Entrance
A13

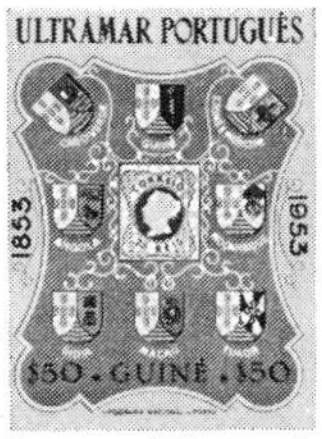

Stamp of Portugal and Arms of Colonies
A14

1953, Jan. **Litho.** ***Perf. 13***
277 A13 10c brn lake & ol 9 8
278 A13 50c dk bl & bis 48 22
279 A13 3e blk, dk brn & sal 1.50 75

Issued to commemorate the Exhibition of Sacred Missionary Art held at Lisbon in 1951.

1953 **Photo.** **Unwmk.**

Stamp and Arms Multicolored.
280 A14 50c lem & gray bl 60 50

Centenary of Portugal's first postage stamps.

Analeptes Trifasciata — A15

1953 ***Perf. 11½.***

Various Beetles in Natural Colors.
281 A15 5c yellow 10 10
282 A15 10c blue 10 10
283 A15 30c org ver 10 10
284 A15 50c yel grn 12 12
285 A15 70c gray brn 28 22
286 A15 1e orange 35 22
287 A15 2e pale ol grn 80 22
288 A15 3e lil rose 1.10 60
289 A15 5e lt bl grn 2.00 65
290 A15 10e lilac 2.75 90
Nos. 281-290 (10) 7.70 3.23

Sao Paulo Issue

Common Design Type

1954 **Litho.** ***Perf. 13½***
291 CD46 1e lil rose, bl gray & blk 30 15

Belem Tower, Lisbon, and Colonial Arms — A16

1955, Apr. 14
292 A16 1e bl & multi 25 10
293 A16 2.50e gray & multi 55 20

Issued to publicize the visit of Pres. Francisco H. C. Lopes.

Fair Emblem, Globe and Arms — A17

1958 **Unwmk.** ***Perf. 12x11½***
294 A17 2.50e multi 60 50

World's Fair at Brussels.

Tropical Medicine Congress Issue

Common Design Type

Design: Maytenus senegalensis.

1958 ***Perf. 13½***
295 CD47 5e multi 1.90 1.00

Honorio Barreto
A18

Nautical Astrolabe
A19

1959, Apr. 29 **Litho.** ***Perf. 13½***
296 A18 2.50e multi 25 20

Issued to commemorate the centenary of the death of Honorio Barreto, governor of Portuguese Guinea.

1960, June 25 *Perf. 13½*
297 A19 2.50e multi 25 20

Issued to commemorate the 500th anniversary of the death of Prince Henry the Navigator.

Traveling Medical Unit — A20

1960 **Unwmk.** *Perf. 14½*
298 A20 1.50e multi 25 20

Issued to commemorate the 10th anniversary of the Commission for Technical Cooperation in Africa South of the Sahara (C.C.T.A.).

Sports Issue
Common Design Type

1962, Jan. 18 **Litho.** *Perf. 13½*

299	CD48	50c	Automobile race	8	8
300	CD48	1e	Tennis	60	22
301	CD48	1.50e	Shot put	22	15
302	CD48	2.50e	Wrestling	45	15
303	CD48	3.50e	Trapshooting	45	18
304	CD48	15e	Volleyball	1.40	80
			Nos. 299-304 (6)	3.20	1.58

Anti-Malaria Issue
Common Design Type

Design: Anopheles gambiae.

1962 **Unwmk.** *Perf. 13½*
305 CD49 2.50e multi 60 30

African Spitting Cobra — A21

Snakes: 35c, African rock python. 70c, Boomslang. 80c, West African mamba. 1.50e, Smythe's water snake. 2e, Common night adder (horiz.). 2.50e, Green swamp snake. 3.50e, Brown house snake. 4e, Spotted wolf snake. 5e, Common puff adder. 15e, Striped beauty snake. 20e, African egg-eating snake (horiz.).

1963, Jan. 17 **Litho.** *Perf. 13½*

306	A21	20c	multi	15	10
307	A21	35c	multi	15	10
308	A21	70c	multi	35	25
309	A21	80c	multi	35	25
310	A21	1.50e	multi	55	25
311	A21	2e	multi	40	15
312	A21	2.50e	multi	1.25	25
313	A21	3.50e	multi	45	20
314	A21	4e	multi	45	25
315	A21	5e	multi	45	25
316	A21	15e	multi	80	50
317	A21	20e	multi	1.25	60
			Nos. 306-317 (12)	6.60	3.15

Airline Anniversary Issue
Common Design Type

1963 **Litho.** *Perf. 14½*
318 CD50 2.50e lt brn & multi 60 30

National Overseas Bank Issue
Common Design Type

Design: 2.50e, Joao de Andrade Córvo.

1964, May 16 *Perf. 13½*
319 CD51 2.50e multi 60 35

ITU Issue
Common Design Type

1965, May 17 **Unwmk.** *Perf. 14½*
320 CD52 2.50e lt bl & multi 1.75 70

Soldier, 1548 — A22

Designs: 40c, Rifleman, 1578. 60c, Rifleman, 1640. 1e, Grenadier, 1721. 2.50e, Fusiliers captain, 1740. 4.50e, Infantryman, 1740. 7.50e, Sergeant major, 1762. 10e, Engineers' officer, 1806.

1966, Jan. 8 **Litho.** *Perf. 13½*

321	A22	25c	multi	18	12
322	A22	40c	multi	20	12
323	A22	60c	multi	28	15
324	A22	1e	multi	35	18
325	A22	2.50e	multi	1.00	35
326	A22	4.50e	multi	1.75	1.00
327	A22	7.50e	multi	1.75	1.25
328	A22	10e	multi	2.25	1.50
			Nos. 321-328 (8)	7.76	4.67

National Revolution Issue
Common Design Type

Design: 2.50e, Berta Craveiro Lopes School and Central Pavilion of Bissau Hospital.

1966, May 28 **Litho.** *Perf. 11½*
329 CD53 2.50e multi 50 30

Navy Club Issue
Common Design Type

Designs: 50c, Capt. Oliveira Muzanty and cruiser Republica. 1e, Capt. Afonso de Cerqueira and torpedo boat Guadiana.

1967, Jan. 31 **Litho.** *Perf. 13*
330 CD54 50c multi 30 15
331 CD54 1e multi 70 50

Sacred Heart of Jesus Monument and Chapel of the Apparition A23

Pres. Rodrigues Thomas A24

1967, May 13 *Perf. 12½x13*
332 A23 50c multi 20 15

Issued to commemorate the 50th anniversary of the appearance of the Virgin Mary to three shepherd children at Fatima.

1968, Feb. 2 **Litho.** *Perf. 13½*
333 A24 1e multi 20 15

Issued to commemorate the 1968 visit of Pres. Americo de Deus Rodrigues Thomaz.

Cabral's Coat of Arms — A25

1968, Apr. 22 **Litho.** *Perf. 14*
334 A25 2.50e multi 50 20

500th anniversary, birth of Pedro Alvares Cabral, navigator who took possession of Brazil for Portugal.

Admiral Coutinho Issue
Common Design Type

Design: 1e, Adm. Coutinho and astrolabe.

1969, Feb. 17 **Litho.** *Perf. 14*
335 CD55 1e multi 30 20

Da Gama Coat of Arms — A26

Arms of King Manuel I — A27

Vasco da Gama Issue

1969, Aug. 29 **Litho.** *Perf. 14*
336 A26 2.50e multi 30 15

Issued to commemorate the 500th anniversary of the birth of Vasco da Gama (1469-1524), navigator.

Administration Reform Issue
Common Design Type

1969, Sept. 25 **Litho.** *Perf. 14*
337 CD56 50c multi 20 10

King Manuel I Issue

1969, Dec. 1 **Litho.** *Perf. 14*
338 A27 2e multi 30 20

Pres. Ulysses S. Grant and View of Bolama — A28

1970, Oct. 25 **Litho.** *Perf. 13½*
339 A28 2.50e multi 40 20

Centenary of Pres. Grant's arbitration in 1868 of Portuguese-English dispute concerning Bolama.

Marshal Carmona Issue
Common Design Type

Design: 1.50e, Antonio Oscar Carmona in general's uniform.

1970, Nov. 15 **Litho.** *Perf. 14*
340 CD57 1.50e multi 30 20

Luiz Camoens — A29

1972, May 25 **Litho.** *Perf. 13*
341 A29 50c brn org & multi 20 15

4th centenary of publication of The Lusiads by Luiz Camoens (1524-1580).

Olympic Games Issue
Common Design Type

Design: 2.50e, Weight lifting, hammer throw and Olympic emblem.

1972, June 20 *Perf. 14x13½*
342 CD59 2.50e multi 40 20

Lisbon-Rio de Janeiro Flight Issue
Common Design Type

Design: 1e, "Lusitania" taking off from Lisbon.

1972, Sept. 20 **Litho.** *Perf. 13½*
343 CD60 1e multi 20 15

WMO Centenary Issue
Common Design Type

1973, Dec. 15 **Litho.** *Perf. 13*
344 CD61 2e lt brn & multi 30 20

AIR POST STAMPS

Common Design Type
Perf. 13½x13

1938, Sept. 19 **Engr.** **Unwmk.**
Name and Value in Black

C1	CD39	10c	scarlet	38	30
C2	CD39	20c	purple	38	30
C3	CD39	50c	orange	45	30
C4	CD39	1e	ultra	55	38
C5	CD39	2e	lil brn	4.75	3.25
C6	CD39	3e	dk grn	1.25	85
C7	CD39	5e	red brn	3.00	95
C8	CD39	9e	rose car	3.50	2.00
C9	CD39	10e	magenta	8.50	2.75
			Nos. C1-C9 (9)	22.76	11.08

No. C7 exists with overprint "Exposicao Internacional de Nova York, 1939-1940" and Trylon and Perisphere.

POSTAGE DUE STAMPS

D1

D2

1904 **Unwmk.** **Typo.** *Perf. 12*
Without Gum

J1	D1	5r	yel grn	40	32
J2	D1	10r	slate	40	32
J3	D1	20r	yel brn	40	32
J4	D1	30r	red org	1.25	1.00
J5	D1	50r	gray brn	1.25	1.00
J6	D1	60r	red brn	2.50	1.75
J7	D1	100r	lilac	2.50	1.65
J8	D1	130r	dl bl	2.50	1.65
J9	D1	200r	carmine	4.00	3.25
J10	D1	500r	violet	8.75	4.00
			Nos. J1-J10 (10)	23.95	15.26

Same Overprinted in Carmine or Green **REPUBLICA**

1911
Without Gum

J11	D1	5r	yel grn	22	18
J12	D1	10r	slate	22	18
J13	D1	20r	yel brn	32	28
J14	D1	30r	red org	32	28
J15	D1	50r	gray brn	32	28
J16	D1	60r	red brn	90	65
J17	D1	100r	lilac	1.75	90
J18	D1	130r	dl bl	1.75	90
J19	D1	200r	car (G)	1.75	1.40
J20	D1	500r	violet	1.00	90
			Nos. J10-J20 (11)	17.30	9.95

Nos. J2-J10 Overprinted **REPUBLICA**

1919
Without Gum

J21	D1	10r	slate	5.00	5.00
J22	D1	20r	yel brn	5.50	5.50
J23	D1	30r	red org	4.00	3.50
J24	D1	50r	gray brn	1.50	1.25
J25	D1	60r	red brn	200.00	150.00
J26	D1	100r	lilac	1.50	1.25
J27	D1	130r	dl bl	20.00	17.50
J28	D1	200r	carmine	2.25	2.00
J29	D1	500r	violet	17.00	15.00
			Nos. J21-J24,J26-J29 (8)	56.75	51.00

No. J25 was not regularly issued but exists on genuine covers.

1921

J30	D2	½c yel grn	15	10
J31	D2	1c slate	15	10
J32	D2	2c org brn	15	10
J33	D2	3c orange	15	10
J34	D2	5c gray brn	15	10
J35	D2	6c lt brn	15	10
J36	D2	10c red vio	25	25
J37	D2	13c dl bl	25	25
J38	D2	20c carmine	30	30
J39	D2	50c gray	30	30
		Nos. J30-J39 (10)	2.00	1.70

Catalogue values for unused stamps in this section, from this point to the end of the section, are for Never Hinged items.

Common Design Type

Photogravure and Typographed

1952 Unwmk. *Perf. 14*

Numeral in Red, Frame Multicolored.

J40	CD45	10c ol grn	5	5
J41	CD45	30c purple	5	5
J42	CD45	50c dk grn	5	5
J43	CD45	1e vio bl	20	20
J44	CD45	2e ol blk	30	30
J45	CD45	5e brn red	65	65
		Nos. J40-J45 (6)	1.30	1.30

WAR TAX STAMPS

WT1

Perf. 11½x12

1919, May 20 Typo. Unwmk.

MR1	WT1	10r brn, buff & blk	35.00	20.00
MR2	WT1	40r brn, buff & blk	30.00	17.50
MR3	WT1	50r brn, buff & blk	30.00	17.50

The 40r is not overprinted "REPUBLICA".

Some authorities consider Nos. MR2-MR3 to be revenue stamps.

NEWSPAPER STAMP

N1

Perf. 12½, 13½

1893 Typo. Unwmk.

P1	N1	2½r brown	65	60

POSTAL TAX STAMPS

Pombal Issue

Common Design Types

1925 Unwmk. Engr. *Perf. 12½*

RA1	CD28	15c red & blk	65	60
RA2	CD29	15c red & blk	65	60
RA3	CD30	15c red & blk	65	60

Coat of Arms PT7

1934, Apr. 1 Typo. *Perf. 11½*

Without Gum

RA4	PT7	50c red brn & grn	9.00	5.00

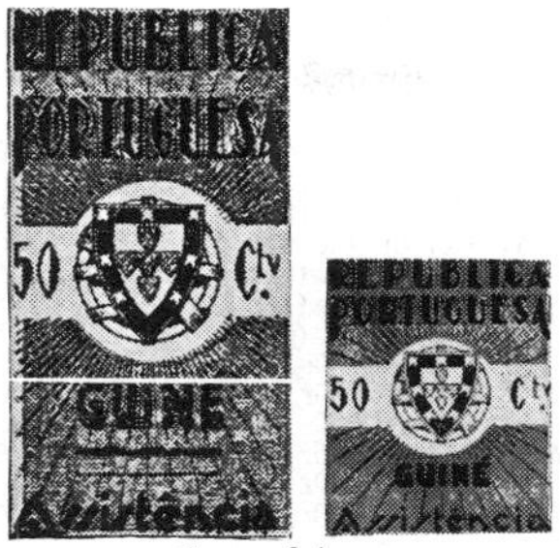

Coat of Arms
PT8 PT9

1938-40

Without Gum

RA5	PT8	50c ol bis & cit	7.50	5.25
RA6	PT8	50c lt grn & ol brn ('40)	7.50	5.25

1942 *Perf. 11*

Without Gum

RA7	PT9	50c blk & yel	2.00	80

1959, July Unwmk.

Without Gum

RA8	PT9	30c dk ocher & blk	20	20

See Nos. RA24-RA26.

Lusignian Cross
PT10 PT11

1967 Typo. *Perf. 11x11½*

Without Gum

RA9	PT10	50c pink, red & blk	1.25	1.25
RA10	PT10	1e grn, red & blk	1.25	1.25
RA11	PT10	5e gray, red & blk	2.00	2.00
RA12	PT10	10e lt bl, red & blk	4.00	4.00

The tax was for national defense.

A 50e was used for revenue only.

1967, Aug. Typo. *Perf. 11*

Without Gum

RA13	PT11	50c pink, blk & red	95	95
RA14	PT11	1e pale grn, blk & red	95	95
RA15	PT11	5e gray, blk & red	1.65	1.65
RA16	PT11	10e lt bl, blk & red	2.50	2.50

The tax was for national defense.

Catalogue values for unused stamps in this section, from this point to the end of the section, are for Never Hinged items.

Carved Figurine — PT12

Art from Bissau Museum: 1e, Tree of Life, with 2 birds (horiz.). No. RA19, Man wearing horned headgear ("Vaca Bruto"). No. RA20, As RA19, inscribed "Tocador de Bombolon." 2.50e, The Magistrate. 5e, Man bearing burden on head. 10e, Stylized pelican.

1968 Litho. *Perf. 13½*

RA17	PT12	50c gray & multi	8	8
a.		Yellow paper	50	
RA18	PT12	1e multi	14	8
RA19	PT12	2e lt bl & multi *(Vaca Bruto)*	16	14
RA20	PT12	2e *(Tocador de Bombolon)*	*10.00*	
RA21	PT12	2.50e multi	28	20
RA22	PT12	5e multi	42	35
RA23	PT12	10e multi	90	70
		Nos. RA17-RA19,RA21-RA23 (6)	1.98	1.55

Obligatory on all inland mail Mar. 15-Apr. 15 and Dec. 15-Jan. 15, and all year on parcels.

A souvenir sheet embracing Nos. RA17-RA19 and RA21-RA23 exists. The stamps have simulated perforations. Value $3.50.

Arms Type of 1942

1968 Typo. *Perf. 11*

Without Gum

RA24	PT9	2.50e lt bl & blk	40	40
RA25	PT9	5e grn & blk	75	75
RA26	PT9	10e dp bl & blk	1.50	1.50

No. RA20 Surcharged

1968 Litho. *Perf. 13½*

RA27	PT12	50c on 2e multi	45	45
RA28	PT12	1e on 2e multi	45	45

Black and White Hands Holding Sword
PT13

Mother and Children
PT14

1968 Litho. *Perf. 13½*

RA29	PT13	50c pink & multi	5	5
RA30	PT13	1e multi	10	10
RA31	PT13	2e yel & multi	30	30
RA32	PT13	2.50e buff & multi	45	45
RA33	PT13	3e multi	50	50
RA34	PT13	4e gray & multi	55	55
RA35	PT13	5e multi	75	75
RA36	PT13	10e multi	1.75	1.75
		Nos. RA29-RA36 (8)	4.45	4.45

The surtax was for national defense. Other denominations exist: 8e, 9e, 15e.

1971, June Litho. *Perf. 13½*

RA37	PT14	50c multi	15	15
RA38	PT14	1e multi	15	15
RA39	PT14	2e multi	20	20
RA40	PT14	3e multi	30	30
RA41	PT14	4e multi	35	35
RA42	PT14	5e multi	60	60
RA43	PT14	10e multi	1.10	1.10
		Nos. RA37-RA43 (7)	2.85	2.85

A 20e exists.

POSTAL TAX DUE STAMPS

Pombal Issue

Common Design Types

1925 Unwmk. *Perf. 12½*

RAJ1	CD31	30c red & blk	60	50
RAJ2	CD32	30c red & blk	60	50
RAJ3	CD33	30c red & blk	60	50

PORTUGUESE INDIA

LOCATION — West coast of the Indian peninsula.

GOVT. — Former Portuguese colony.

AREA — 1,537 sq. mi.

POP. — 649,000 (1958).

CAPITAL — Panjim (Nova-Goa).

The colony was seized by India on Dec. 18, 1961, and annexed by that republic.

1000 Reis = 1 Milreis
12 Reis = 1 Tanga (1881-82)
(Real = singular of Reis)
16 Tangas = 1 Rupia
100 Centavos = 1 Escudo (1959)

Catalogue values for unused stamps in this country are for Never Hinged items, beginning with Scott 490 in the regular postage section, Scott J43 in the postage due section, and Scott RA6 in the postal tax section.

Values of early Portuguese India stamps vary according to condition. Quotations for Nos. 1-55 are for fine copies. Very fine to superb specimens sell at much higher prices, and inferior or poor copies sell at reduced prices, depending on the condition of the individual specimen.

Numeral of Value
A1 A2

A1: Large figures of value. "REIS" in Roman capitals. "S" and "R" of "SERVICO" smaller and "E" larger than the other letters. 33 lines in background. Side ornaments of four dashes.

A2: Large figures of value. "REIS" in block capitals. "S," "E" and "R" same size as other letters of "SERVICO". 44 lines in background. Side ornaments of five dots.

Handstamped from a Single Die.

Perf. 13 to 18 & Compound

1871, Oct. 1 Unwmk.

Thin Transparent Brittle Paper.

1	A1	10r black	600.00	400.00
2	A1	20r dk car	1,500.	350.00
3	A1	40r Prus bl	450.00	350.00
4	A1	100r yel grn	500.00	400.00
5	A1	200r ocher yel	600.00	450.00

1872

Thick Soft Wove Paper.

5A	A1	10r black	*1,400.*	300.00
6	A1	20r dk car	*1,500.*	250.00
7	A1	20r org ver	*1,500.*	250.00
8	A1	200r ocher yel	*1,400.*	700.00
9	A1	300r dp red vio		*1,600.*

The 600r and 900r of type A1 are bogus.

1872 *Perf. 12½ to 14½ & Compound*

10	A2	10r black	190.00	100.00
11	A2	20r vermilion	250.00	90.00
a.		"20" omitted		*1,100.*
12	A2	40r blue	90.00	70.00
a.		Tete beche pr.	*6,000.*	
13	A2	100r dp grn	90.00	70.00
14	A2	200r yellow	300.00	275.00
15	A2	300r red vio	300.00	225.00
a.		Imperf.		
16	A2	600r red vio	175.00	150.00
a.		"600" double	*600.00*	
17	A2	900r red vio	190.00	200.00

An unused 100r blue green exists with watermark of lozenges and gray burelage on back. Experts believe it to be a proof.

White Laid Paper.

18	A2	10r black	30.00	25.00
a.		Tete beche pair		*7,000.*
19	A2	20r vermilion	35.00	30.00
20	A2	40r blue	50.00	40.00
a.		"40" double	*350.00*	
b.		Tete beche pair	*1,600.*	*1,600.*
21	A2	100r green	60.00	50.00
a.		"100" double	*400.00*	
22	A2	200r yellow	200.00	185.00

1873

Re-issues.

Thin Bluish Toned Paper

23 A2 20r vermilion 200.00 175.00
24 A1 10r black 10.00 7.00
a. "1" inverted 150.00 125.00
b. "10" double 450.00
25 A1 20r vermilion 8.00 6.00
a. "20" double 450.00
b. "20" inverted
26 A1 300r dp vio 75.00 70.00
a. "300" double 500.00
27 A1 600r dp vio 100.00 90.00
a. "600" double 550.00
b. "600" inverted 700.00
28 A1 900r dp vio 100.00 90.00
a. "900" double 550.00
b. "900" triple 1,100.

Nos. 23 to 26 are re-issues of Nos. 11, 5A, 7, and 9. The paper is thinner and harder than that of the 1871-72 stamps and slightly transparent. It was originally bluish white but is frequently stained yellow by the gum.

A3

A4

A3: Same as A1 with small figures.
A4: Same as A2 with small figures.

1874

Thin Bluish Toned Paper

29 A3 10r black 37.50 30.00
30 A3 20r vermilion 500.00 350.00
a. "20" double 700.00

1875

31 A4 10r black 35.00 25.00
32 A4 15r rose 11.00 10.00
a. "15" inverted 500.00
b. "15" double
33 A4 20r vermilion 50.00 30.00
a. "0" missing 750.00
b. "20" sideways 750.00
c. "20" double

A5

A6

A5: Re-cutting of A1.
Small figures. "REIS" in Roman capitals. Letters larger. "V" of "SERVICO" barred. 33 lines in background. Side ornaments of five dots.
A6: First re-cutting of A2.
Small figures. "REIS" in block capitals. Letters re-cut. "V" of "SERVICO" barred. 41 lines above and 43 below "REIS". Side ornaments of five dots.

1876 ***Perf. 12½ to 13½ & Compound***

34 A5 10r black 18.00 14.00
35 A5 20r vermilion 15.00 12.00
a. "20" double
36 A6 10r black 5.50 3.50
a. Double impression
b. "10" double 500.00
37 A6 15r rose 375.00 340.00
a. "15" omitted 1,100.
38 A6 20r vermilion 18.00 15.00
39 A6 40r blue 105.00 95.00
40 A6 100r green 190.00 150.00
a. Imperf.
41 A6 200r yellow 900.00 700.00
42 A6 300r violet 600.00 500.00
a. "300" omitted
43 A6 600r violet 800.00 750.00
44 A6 900r violet 1,000. 850.00

A7

A8

A9

A7: Same as A5 with addition of a star above and a bar below the value.
A8: Second re-cutting of A2. Same as A6 but 41 lines both above and below "REIS". Star above and bar below value.
A9: Third re-cutting of A2. 41 lines above and 38 below "REIS". Star above and bar below value. White line around central oval.

1877

45 A7 10r black 30.00 21.00
46 A8 10r black 37.50 30.00
47 A9 10r black 30.00 21.00
a. "10" omitted
48 A9 15r rose 35.00 30.00
49 A9 20r vermilion 8.00 6.00
50 A9 40r blue 17.50 15.00
a. "40" omitted
51 A9 100r green 62.50 55.00
a. "100" omitted
52 A9 200r yellow 92.50 77.50
53 A9 300r violet 115.00 105.00
54 A9 600r violet 115.00 105.00
55 A9 900r violet 115.00 105.00

No. 47, 20r, 40r and 200r exist imperf.

Portuguese Crown — A10

Perf. 12½, 13½

1877, July 15 **Typo.**

56 A10 5r black 3.50 2.75
57 A10 10r yellow 9.00 7.75
a. Imperf.
58 A10 20r bister 9.00 6.75
59 A10 25r rose 10.00 9.00
60 A10 40r blue 15.00 12.50
a. Perf. 12½ 175.00 135.00
61 A10 50r yel grn 32.50 22.50
62 A10 100r lilac 15.00 13.00
63 A10 200r orange 20.00 15.00
64 A10 300r yel brn 32.50 27.50

1880-81

65 A10 10r green 7.50 6.75
66 A10 25r slate 42.50 30.00
a. Perf. 12½ 85.00 60.00
67 A10 25r violet 27.50 19.00
68 A10 40r yellow 35.00 27.50
69 A10 50r dk bl 21.00 17.00

The stamps of the 1877-81 issues were reprinted in 1885, on stout very white paper, ungummed and with rough perforation 13½. They were again reprinted in 1905 on thin white paper with shiny white gum and clean-cut perforation 13½ with large holes. Value of the lowest-cost reprint, $1 each.

Stamps of 1871-77 Surcharged with New Values.
Black Surcharge.

1881

70 A1 1½r on 20r (#2) 450.00
71 A1 1½r on 20r (#7) 375.00
72 A2 1½r on 20r (#11) 350.00
73 A1 1½r on 20r (#25) 225.00 200.00
74 A4 1½r on 20r (#33) 135.00 125.00
a. Inverted surcharge
75 A5 1½r on 20r (#35) 110.00 80.00
76 A6 1½r on 20r (#38) 125.00 110.00
77 A9 1½r on 20r (#49) 200.00 140.00
78 A4 5r on 15r (#32) 2.50 2.50
a. Double surcharge
b. Inverted surcharge
78C A6 5r on 15r (#37) 160.00 160.00
79 A5 5r on 20r (#35) 2.75 2.75
a. Double surcharge
b. Inverted surcharge
80 A6 5r on 20r (#38) 2.00 2.00
a. Double surcharge
b. Inverted surcharge
81 A9 5r on 20r (#49) 5.00 4.00
a. Double surcharge
b. Invtd. surcharge

Red Surcharge.

82 A2 5r on 10r (#18) 250.00 250.00
83 A1 5r on 10r (#24) 325.00 275.00
84 A3 5r on 10r (#29) 1,300.
85 A4 5r on 10r (#31) 110.00 110.00
86 A5 5r on 10r (#34) 5.50 5.50
a. Double surcharge
87 A6 5r on 10r (#36) 7.50 6.25
a. Inverted surcharge
88 A7 5r on 10r (#45) 85.00 50.00
a. Inverted surcharge
89 A8 5r on 10r (#46) 70.00 50.00
90 A9 5r on 10r (#47) 30.00 25.00
a. Inverted surcharge
b. Double surcharge

Similar Surcharge, Handstamped.
Black Surcharge.

1883

91 A5 1½r on 10r (#34) 450.00
92 A6 1½r on 10r (#36) 450.00
93 A9 1½r on 10r (#47) 375.00 325.00
94 A1 4½r on 40r (#3) 400.00
95 A2 4½r on 40r (#12) 27.50 27.50
96 A2 4½r on 40r (#20) 27.50 27.50
98 A6 4½r on 40r (#39) 27.50 27.50
99 A1 4½r on 100r (#4) 400.00
100 A2 4½r on 100r (#13) 35.00 35.00
101 A2 4½r on 100r (#21) 35.00 35.00
102 A6 4½r on 100r (#40) 35.00 35.00
104 A1 6r on 100r (#4) 650.00
105 A2 6r on 100r (#13) 250.00
106 A2 6r on 100r (#21) 200.00 150.00
107 A6 6r on 100r (#40) 275.00 200.00
108 A1 6r on 200r (#5) 450.00 325.00
109 A2 6r on 200r (#14) 200.00
110 A2 6r on 200r (#22) 200.00 200.00
111 A6 6r on 200r (#41) 400.00
112 A9 6r on 200r (#52) 375.00 375.00

Stamps of 1877-81 Surcharged in Black **1 1/2**

1881-82

113 A10 1½r on 5r blk 1.00 85
a. With additional surcharge "4½" in bl 50.00 40.00
114 A10 1½r on 10r grn 1.00 90
a. With additional surcharge "6" 70.00 60.00
115 A10 1½r on 20r bis 8.50 6.75
a. Inverted surcharge
b. Double surcharge
c. Pair, one without surcharge
116 A10 1½r on 25r sl 35.00 27.50
117 A10 1½r on 100r lil 55.00 37.50
118 A10 4½r on 10r grn 165.00 150.00
119 A10 4½r on 20r bis 3.50 2.50
a. Inverted surcharge
120 A10 4½r on 25r vio 10.50 8.50
121 A10 4½r on 100r lil 105.00 85.00
122 A10 6r on 10r yel 42.50 35.00
123 A10 6r on 10r grn 9.25 6.75
124 A10 6r on 20r bis 15.00 11.00
125 A10 6r on 25r sl 30.00 21.00
126 A10 6r on 25r vio 2.00 1.65
127 A10 6r on 40r bl 75.00 62.50
128 A10 6r on 40r yel 37.50 30.00
129 A10 6r on 50r grn 42.50 32.50
130 A10 6r on 50r bl 60.00 50.00

Surcharged in Black **1 T**

131 A10 1t on 10r grn 105.00 95.00
a. With additional surcharge "6"
132 A10 1t on 20r bis 42.50 37.50
133 A10 1t on 25r sl 32.50 22.50
134 A10 1t on 25r vio 12.00 7.75
135 A10 1t on 40r bl 17.00 12.00
136 A10 1t on 50r grn 50.00 37.50
137 A10 1t on 50r bl 22.50 17.00
138 A10 1t on 100r lil 21.00 12.00
139 A10 1t on 200r org 42.50 37.50
140 A10 2t on 25r sl 32.50 30.00
a. Small "T" 50.00 35.00
141 A10 2t on 25r vio 12.50 10.50
142 A10 2t on 40r bl 37.50 30.00
143 A10 2t on 40r yel 47.50 37.50
144 A10 2t on 50r grn 14.00 12.00
a. Inverted surcharge
145 A10 2t on 50r bl 80.00 67.50
146 A10 2t on 100r lil 10.50 8.50
147 A10 2t on 200r org 35.00 30.00
148 A10 2t on 300r brn 30.00 27.50
149 A10 4t on 10r grn 12.50 10.50
a. Inverted surcharge
150 A10 4t on 50r grn 12.00 9.25
a. With additional surcharge "2" 105.00 77.50
151 A10 4t on 200r org 35.00 30.00
152 A10 8t on 20r bis 30.00 21.00
153 A10 8t on 25r rose 165.00 150.00
154 A10 8t on 40r bl 42.50 35.00
155 A10 8t on 100r lil 35.00 30.00
156 A10 8t on 200r org 30.00 27.50
157 A10 8t on 300r brn 42.50 35.00

1882

Blue Surcharge.

158 A10 4½r on 5r blk 7.75 6.75

Similar Surcharge, Handstamped.

1883

159 A10 1½r on 5r blk 14.00 10.00
160 A10 1½r on 10r grn 14.00 7.00
161 A10 4½r on 100r lil 190.00 165.00

The "2" in "½" is 3mm. high, instead of 2mm. as on Nos. 113, 114 and 121.

The handstamp is known double on Nos. 159-161.

A12

1882-83 **Typo.**

With or Without Accent on "E" of "REIS".

162 A12 1½r black 45 40
a. "½" for "1½"
163 A12 4½r ol bis 45 40
164 A12 6r green 60 40
165 A12 1t rose 60 40
166 A12 2t blue 60 40
167 A12 4t lilac 2.75 2.50
168 A12 8t orange 2.75 2.50

There were three printings of the 1882-83 issue. The first had "REIS" in thick letters with acute accent on the "E." The second had "REIS" in thin letters with accent on the "E." The third had the "E" without accent. In the first printing the "E" sometimes had a grave or circumflex accent.

The third printing may be divided into two sets, with or without a small circle in the cross of the crown.

Stamps doubly printed or with value omitted, double, inverted or misplaced are printer's waste.

Nos. 162-168 were reprinted on thin white paper, with shiny white gum and clean-cut perforation 13½. Value of lowest-cost reprint, $1 each.

"REIS" no serifs. A13

"REIS" with serifs. A14

1883 **Litho.** ***Imperf.***

169 A13 1½r black 1.25 1.00
a. Tete beche pair
b. "1½" double 375.00 300.00
170 A13 4½r ol grn 12.50 11.00
a. "4½" omitted 375.00 300.00
171 A13 6r green 12.50 11.00
a. Tete beche pair 1,500.
b. "6" omitted 400.00 325.00
172 A14 1½r black 65.00 16.00
a. "1½" omitted 375.00 325.00
173 A14 6r green 57.50 40.00
a. "6" omitted 425.00 375.00

Nos. 169-171 exist with unofficial perf. 12.

King Luiz — A15

King Carlos — A16

Perf. 12½, 13½

1886, Apr. 29 **Embossed**

174 A15 1½r black 1.65 85
a. Perf. 13½ 105.00 62.50
175 A15 4½r bister 1.90 95
a. Perf. 13½ 27.50 12.50
176 A15 6r dp grn 1.90 1.25
a. Perf. 13½ 30.00 14.00
177 A15 1t brt rose 3.75 1.65
178 A15 2t dp bl 6.00 2.75
179 A15 4t gray vio 6.00 3.75
180 A15 8t orange 6.00 3.75
Nos. 174-180 (7) 27.20 14.95

Nos. 178-179 were reprinted. Originals have yellow gum. Reprints have white gum and clean-cut perforation 13½. Value, $4 each.

Perf. 11½, 12½, 13½.

1895-96 **Typo.**

181 A16 1½r black 90 40
182 A16 4½r pale org 90 40
a. Perf. 13½ 6.00 1.50
183 A16 6r green 90 40
a. Perf. 12½ 2.75 1.00
184 A16 9r gray lil 3.50 2.75
185 A16 1t lt bl 1.25 50
a. Perf. 12½ 4.00 1.65
186 A16 2t rose 90 50
a. Perf. 12½ 3.75 2.00

187 A16 4t dk bl 1.50 75
a. Perf. 12½ 3.75 2.00
188 A16 8t brt vio 3.00 2.00
Nos. 181-188 (8) 12.85 7.70

No. 184 was reprinted. Reprints have white gum, and clean-cut perforation 13½. Value $10.

Vasco da Gama Issue.
Common Design Types

1898, May 1 Engr. *Perf. 14 to 15*

189 CD20 1½r bl grn 90 80
190 CD21 4½r red 90 80
191 CD22 6r red vio 90 70
192 CD23 9r yel grn 90 90
193 CD24 1t dk bl 1.50 1.50
194 CD25 2t vio brn 2.00 1.75
195 CD26 4t bis brn 2.00 1.75
196 CD27 8t bister 4.00 3.50
Nos. 189-196 (8) 13.10 11.70

King Carlos — A17

1898-1903 Typo. *Perf. 11½*
Name and Value in Black except No. 219.

197 A17 1r gray ('02) 30 15
198 A17 1½r orange 25 15
199 A17 1½r sl ('02) 25 20
200 A17 2r org ('02) 25 20
201 A17 2½r yel brn ('02) 30 25
202 A17 3r dp bl ('02) 25 15
203 A17 4½r lt grn 60 40
204 A17 6r brown 60 45
205 A17 6r gray grn ('02) 25 15
206 A17 9r dl vio 75 45
a. 9r gray lil 1.25 1.25
208 A17 1t sea grn 75 45
209 A17 1t car rose ('02) 40 20
210 A17 2t blue 1.00 40
a. Perf. 13½ 25.00 7.00
211 A17 2t brn ('02) 2.00 1.25
212 A17 2½t dl bl ('02) 6.50 5.00
213 A17 4t bl, *bl* 2.00 1.25
214 A17 5t brn, *straw* ('02) 2.00 1.25
215 A17 8t red lil, *pnksh* 2.00 1.25
216 A17 8t red vio, *pink* ('02) 4.50 2.25
217 A17 12t bl, *pink* 3.00 1.50
218 A17 12t grn, *pink* ('02) 4.50 2.50
219 A17 1rp blk & red, *bl* 7.00 4.00
220 A17 1rp dl bl, *straw* ('02) 9.00 5.00
221 A17 2rp vio, *yelsh* 10.00 6.00
222 A17 2rp gray blk, *straw* ('03) 15.00 10.00
Nos. 197-222 (25) 73.45 44.85

Several stamps of this issue exist without value or with value inverted but they are not known to have been issued in this condition. The 1r and 6r in carmine rose are believed to be color trials.

No. 210 Surcharged in Black — **1½ Reis**

1900

223 A17 1½r on 2t blue 2.75 60
a. Inverted surcharge
b. Perf. 13½ 25.00 20.00

Stamps of 1885-96 Surcharged in Black or Red — **1 REAL**

On Stamps of 1886.

1902 *Perf. 12½, 13½*

224 A15 1r on 2t bl 85 45
225 A15 2r on 4½r bis 30 25
a. Inverted surcharge *8.00 8.00*
b. Double surcharge
226 A15 2½r on 6r grn 30 25
227 A15 3r on 1t rose 30 25
228 A15 2½t on 1½r blk (R) 1.65 1.25
229 A15 2½t on 4t gray vio 2.00 1.25
230 A15 5t on 8t org 1.00 60
a. Perf. 12½ 25.00 15.00

On Stamps of 1895-96.
Perf. 11½, 12½, 13½

231 A16 1r on 6r grn 30 25
232 A16 2r on 8t brt vio 30 25
233 A16 2½r on 9r gray vio 30 30
234 A16 3r on 4½r yel 1.25 90
a. Inverted surcharge 9.00 9.00
235 A16 3r on 1t lt bl 1.25 80
236 A16 2½t on 1½r blk (R) 2.00 75
237 A16 5t on 2t rose 2.00 75
a. Perf. 12½ 32.50 20.00
238 A16 5t on 4t dk bl 2.00 75
a. Perf. 12½ 32.50 20.00
Nos. 224-238 (15) 15.80 9.05

Nos. 224, 229, 231, 233, 234, 235 and 238 were reprinted in 1905. They have whiter gum than the originals and very clean-cut perf. 13½. Value $2.50 each.

Nos. 204, 208, 210 Overprinted — **PROVISORIO**

1902 *Perf. 11½*

239 A17 6r brown 1.10 90
a. Inverted overprint
240 A17 1t sea grn 1.50 90
241 A17 2t blue 1.50 90
a. Perf. 13½ 135.00 90.00

No. 212 Surcharged in Black — **2 TANGAS**

1905

243 A17 2t on 2½t dl bl 1.75 1.50

Stamps of 1898-1903 Overprinted in Lisbon in Carmine or Green — **REPUBLICA**

1911

244 A17 1r gray 15 12
a. Inverted overprint 2.00 2.00
245 A17 1½r slate 15 12
a. Double overprint 2.00 2.00
246 A17 2r orange 25 20
a. Double overprint
b. Inverted overprint 3.00 3.00
247 A17 2½r yel brn 25 15
248 A17 3r dp bl 25 15
249 A17 4½r lt grn 30 20
250 A17 6r gray grn 20 15
251 A17 9r gray lil 30 20
252 A17 1t car rose (G) 30 20
253 A17 2t brown 30 20
254 A17 4t bl, *bl* 1.10 95
255 A17 5t brn, *straw* 1.10 95
256 A17 8t vio, *pink* 3.50 2.00
257 A17 12t grn, *pink* 3.50 2.00
258 A17 1rp dl bl, *straw* 4.75 3.75
259 A17 2rp gray blk, *straw* 7.25 5.50
Nos. 244-259 (16) 23.65 16.84

A18

Values are for pairs, both halves.

1911 Perforated Diagonally.

260 A18 1r on 2r org 75 65
a. Without diagonal perf. 2.00 1.50
b. Cut diagonally instead of perf. 2.50 2.00

Stamps of Preceding Issues Perforated Vertically through the Middle and Each Half Surcharged with New Value:

3 Reis

3 Reis **6 Reis** **6 Reis**
a b

Values are for pairs, both halves of the stamp

1912-13

On Issue of 1898-1903.

260C A17(a) 1r on 2r org 25 20
261 A17(a) 1r on 1t car 25 20
262 A17(a) 1r on 5t brn, *straw* 27.50 12.50
263 A17(b) 1r on 5t brn, *straw* 3.50 2.75
264 A17(a) 1½r on 2½r yel brn 70 60
264C A17(a) 1½r on 4½r lt grn 8.00 4.00
265 A17(a) 1½r on 9r gray lil 50 40
266 A17(a) 1½r on 4t bl, *bl* 50 40
267 A17(a) 2r on 2½r yel brn 65 40
268 A17(a) 2r on 4t bl, *bl* 90 65
269 A17(a) 3r on 2½r yel brn 65 40
270 A17(a) 3r on 2t brn 65 45
271 A17(a) 6r on 4½r lt grn 65 55
272 A17(a) 6r on 9r gray lil 65 50
273 A17(b) 6r on 9r dl vio 4.00 3.25
274 A17(b) 6r on 8t red vio, *pink* 1.50 90

On Provisional Issue of 1902.

275 A16(b) 1r on 5t on 2t rose 11.50 9.00
276 A16(b) 1r on 5t on 4t bl 6.00 5.75
277 A15(b) 1r on 5t on 8t org 2.25 1.50
278 A15(a) 2r on 2½r on 6r grn 2.50 2.00
279 A16(a) 2r on 2½r on 9r gray vio 16.00 16.50
280 A16(b) 3r on 5t on 2t rose 7.00 5.75
281 A16(b) 3r on 5t on 4t bl 7.00 5.75
282 A15(b) 3r on 5t on 8t org 2.25 1.50

On Issue of 1911.

283 A17(a) 1r on 1r gray 25 25
283B A17(a) 1r on 2r org 25 25
284 A17(a) 1r on 1t car 30 25
285 A17(a) 1r on 5t brn, *straw* 30 25
285A A17(b) 1r on 5t brn, *straw*
285B A17(a) 1½r on 4½r lt grn 40 30
286 A17(a) 3r on 2t brn 9.00 6.75
289 A17(a) 6r on 9r gray lil 50 40

There are several settings of these surcharges and many minor varieties of the letters and figures, notably a small "6". Nos. 260-289 were issued mostly without gum.

More than half of Nos. 260C-289 exist with inverted or double surcharge, or with bisecting perforation omitted. The legitimacy of these varieties is questioned. Price of inverted surcharges, $3-$15; double surcharges, $1-$4; perf. omitted, $1.50-$15.

Similar surcharges made without official authorization on stamps of type A17 are: 2r on 2½r, 3r on 2½r, 3r on 5t, and 6r on 4½r.

Vasco da Gama Issue Overprinted — **REPUBLICA**

1913

290 CD20 1½r bl grn 30 25
291 CD21 4½r red 30 25
a. Double overprint
292 CD22 6r red vio 40 35
a. Double overprint
293 CD23 9r yel grn 40 35
294 CD24 1t dk bl 90 50
295 CD25 2t vio brn 2.00 1.10
296 CD26 4t org brn 1.10 90
297 CD27 8t bister 2.00 1.25
Nos. 290-297 (8) 7.40 4.95

Issues of 1898-1913 Overprinted Locally in Red — **REPÚBLICA**

1913-15

On Issues of 1898-1903.

300 A17 2r orange 4.50 4.00
301 A17 2½r yel brn 50 45
302 A17 3r dp bl 6.00 5.00
303 A17 4½r lt grn 1.75 1.50
304 A17 6r gray grn 13.00 12.00
305 A17 9r gray lil 1.75 1.25
306 A17 1t sea grn 12.50 11.00
307 A17 2t blue 20.00 12.00
309 A17 4t bl, *bl* 11.00 9.00
310 A17 5t brn, *straw* 17.50 12.00
311 A17 8t red vio, *pink* 25.00 20.00
312 A17 12t grn, *pink* 3.50 2.50
313 A17 1rp blk & red, *bl* 20.00 15.00
314 A17 1rp dl bl, *straw* 6.50 5.50
315 A17 2rp gray blk, *straw* 10.00 8.00
316 A17 2rp vio, *yelsh* 8.00 6.00
Nos. 300-316 (16) 161.50 125.20

Inverted or double overprints exist on 2½r, 4½r, 9r, 1rp and 2rp.

Nos. 300-316 were issued without gum except 4½r and 9r.

Nos. 302, 304, 306, 307, 310, 311 and 313 were not regularly issued. Nor were the 1½r, 2t brown and 12t blue on pink with preceding overprint.

Same Overprint in Red or Green
On Provisional Issue of 1902

317 A15 1r on 2t bl 6.00 5.00
a. "REPUBLICA" inverted
318 A15 2r on 4½r bis 6.00 5.00
a. "REPUBLICA" inverted
319 A15 2½r on 6r grn 70 60
a. "REPUBLICA" inverted 6.00 6.00
320 A15 2½t on 4t gray vio 20.00 12.00
321 A15 3r on 1t rose (R) 4.50 4.00
323 A15 5t on 8t org (G) 4.50 4.50
a. Red overprint 4.50 4.50
324 A16 1r on 6r grn 6.00 5.00
325 A16 2r on 8t vio 6.00 5.00
a. Inverted surcharge
327 A16 3r on 4½r yel 16.00 11.00
328 A16 3r on 1t lt bl 16.00 11.00
329 A16 5t on 2t rose (G) 3.25 2.75
330 A16 5t on 4t bl (G) 3.25 2.75
331 A16 5t on 4t bl (R) 3.75 3.75
a. "REPUBLICA" inverted
b. "REPUBLICA" double
Nos. 317-331 (13) 95.95 72.35

The 2½r on 1½r of types A15 and A16, the 3r on 1t (A15) and 2½r on 9r (A16) were clandestinely printed.

Some authorities question the status of No. 317-318, 320-321, 324, 327-328.

Same Overprint on Nos. 240-241

1913-15

334 A17 1t sea grn 7.00 5.00
335 A17 2t blue 6.50 6.00

This overprint was applied to No. 239 without official authorization.

On Issue of 1912-13 Perforated through the Middle.

Values are for pairs, both halves of the stamp.

336 A17(a) 1r on 2r org 3.50 3.00
340 A17(a) 1½r on 4½r lt grn 3.50 3.00
341 A17(a) 1½r on 9r gray lil 3.25 2.75
342 A17(a) 1½r on 4t bl, *bl* 5.00 4.50
343 A17(a) 2r on 2½r yel brn 3.00 2.50
344 A17(a) 2r on 4t bl, *bl* 5.00 4.00
345 A17(a) 3r on 2½r yel brn 3.25 2.75
346 A17(a) 3r on 2t brn 2.75 2.50
347 A17(a) 6r on 4½r lt grn 1.00 80
348 A17(a) 6r on 9r gray lil 1.50 1.50
350 A17(b) 6r on 8t red vio, *pink* 1.50 1.50
352 A16(b) 1r on 5t on 4t bl 20.00 17.50
354 A15(a) 2r on 2½r on 6r grn 3.25 2.75
Nos. 334-354 (15) 70.00 60.05

The 1r on 5t (A15), 1r on 1t (A17), 1½r on 2½r (A17), 3r on 5t on 8t (A15), and 6r on 9r (A17) were clandestinely printed.

Nos. 336, 347 exist with inverted surcharge.

Some authorities question the status of Nos. 341-345, 352 and 354.

Ceres — A21

Perf. 12 x 11½, 15 x 14.
1913-21 Typo.
Name and Value in Black

357 A21 1r ol brn 30 25
358 A21 1½r yel grn 30 25
a. Imperf.
359 A21 2r black 35 30
360 A21 2½r ol grn 35 40
361 A21 3r lilac 35 20
362 A21 4½r org brn 35 20
363 A21 5r bl grn 65 45
364 A21 6r lil brn 35 20
365 A21 9r ultra 55 25
366 A21 10r carmine 85 50
367 A21 1t lt vio 40 25
368 A21 2t dp bl 75 30
369 A21 3t yel brn 1.75 60
370 A21 4t slate 2.00 90

371 A21 8t plum 4.00 3.50
372 A21 12t brn, *grn* 3.50 3.00
373 A21 1rp brn, *pink* 21.00 14.00
374 A21 2rp org, *sal* 14.00 10.00
375 A21 3rp grn, *bl* 19.00 12.50
Nos. 357-375 (19) 70.80 48.05

The 1, 2, 2½, 3, 4½r, 1, 2, and 4t exist with the black inscriptions inverted and the 2½r with them double, one inverted, but it is not known that any of these were regularly issued.
See Nos. 401-410.

Nos. 249, 251-253, 256-259 Surcharged in Black — **1½ REIS**

1914
376 A17 1½r on 4½r grn 30 25
377 A17 1½r on 9r gray lil 40 30
378 A17 1½r on 12t grn, *pink* 50 45
379 A17 3r on 1t car rose 40 35
380 A17 3r on 2t brn 3.00 2.50
381 A17 3r on 8t red vio, *pink* 2.25 2.00
382 A17 3r on 1rp dl bl, *straw* 65 40
383 A17 3r on 2rp gray blk, *straw* 75 60

There are three varieties of the "2" in "1½".
Nos. 376-377 exist with inverted surcharge.

Vasco da Gama Issue Surcharged in Black — **REPUBLICA 1½ REIS**

384 CD21 1½r on 4½r red 35 28
385 CD23 1½r on 9r yel grn 45 30
386 CD24 3r on 1t dk bl 35 28
387 CD25 3r on 2t vio brn 55 45
388 CD26 3r on 4t org brn 28 22
389 CD27 3r on 8t bis 1.20 1.10
Nos. 376-389 (14) 11.43 9.48

Double, inverted and other surcharge varieties exist on Nos. 384-386, 389.

Stamps of 1898-1903 Surcharged in Red — **REPUBLICA 1½ REIS**

1915
390 A17 1½r on 4½r grn 27.50 20.00
a. "REPUBLICA" omitted *35.00 35.00*
b. "REPUBLICA" inverted
391 A17 1½r on 9r gray lil 10.00 7.50
a. "REPUBLICA" omitted
392 A17 1½r on 12t grn, *pink* 80 60
394 A17 3r on 2t brn 5.00 3.50
395 A17 3r on 1rp dl bl, *straw* 15.00
396 A17 3r on 2rp gray blk, *straw* 5.00 4.00

Nos. 390, 390a, 390b, 391, 391a and 395 were not regularly issued. The 3r on 2½r (A17) was surcharged without official authorization.

Preceding Issues Overprinted in Carmine — **REPUBLICA**

1915
On No. 230
397 A15 5t on 8t org 1.50 1.40
On Nos. 241, 243
398 A17 2t blue 90 90
399 A17 2t on 2½t dl bl 1.50 90

No. 359 Surcharged in Carmine — **1½ REAL**

1922
400 A21 1½r on 2r blk 50 42

Ceres Type of 1913-21.
1922-25 Typo. *Perf. 12x11½*
Name and Value in Black.
401 A21 4r blue 1.25 1.10
402 A21 1½t gray grn 1.25 85
403 A21 2½t turq bl 1.25 90
404 A21 3t4r yel brn 5.00 3.50
405 A21 4t gray ('25) 1.75 75
406 A21 8t dl rose 7.00 5.00
407 A21 1rp gray brn 16.50 15.00
408 A21 2rp yellow 20.00 15.00
409 A21 3rp bluish grn 30.00 22.50
410 A21 5rp car rose 35.00 25.00
Nos. 401-410 (10) 119.00 89.60

Vasco da Gama and Flagship A22

1925, Jan. 30 Litho.
Without Gum
411 A22 6r brown 3.50 2.50
412 A22 1t red vio 5.00 3.00

Issued to commemorate the 400th anniversary of the death of Vasco da Gama (1469?-1524), Portuguese navigator.

Monument to St. Francis — A23

Image of St. Francis — A25

Autograph of St. Francis A24

Image of St. Francis — A26

Tomb of St. Francis — A28

Church of Bom Jesus at Goa — A27

1931, Dec. 3 *Perf. 14*
414 A23 1r gray grn 50 45
415 A24 2r brown 50 45
416 A25 6r red vio 95 50
417 A26 1½t yel brn 4.25 2.50
418 A27 2t dp bl 5.50 3.75
419 A28 2½t lt red 9.25 3.75
Nos. 414-419 (6) 20.95 11.40

Issued in commemoration of the Exposition of St. Francis Xavier at Goa, in December, 1931.

Nos. 371 and 404 Surcharged — **2½ T.**

1931-32 *Perf. 15x14, 12x11½*
420 A21 1½r on 8t plum ('32) 1.40 1.00
423 A21 2½t on 3t4r yel brn 17.50 15.00

"Portugal" and Vasco da Gama's Flagship "San Gabriel" — A29

Wmk. Maltese Cross. (232)
1933 Typo. *Perf. 11½x12*
424 A29 1r bister 15 5
425 A29 2r ol brn 15 5
426 A29 4r violet 15 5
427 A29 6r dk grn 15 5
428 A29 8r black 20 10
429 A29 1t gray 25 15
430 A29 1½t dp rose 30 15
431 A29 2t brown 35 20
432 A29 2½t dk bl 1.50 40
433 A29 3t brt bl 1.50 40
434 A29 5t red org 1.50 40
435 A29 1rp ol grn 5.50 2.50
436 A29 2rp maroon 11.00 5.00
437 A29 3rp orange 12.50 6.00
438 A29 5rp ap grn 30.00 25.00
Nos. 424-438 (15) 65.20 40.50

Common Design Types
Perf. 13½x13
1938, Sept. 1 Engr. Unwmk.
Name and Value in Black.
439 CD34 1r gray grn 10 10
440 CD34 2r org brn 10 10
441 CD34 3r dk vio brn 10 10
442 CD34 6r brt grn 10 10
443 CD35 10r dk car 35 22
444 CD35 1t brt red vio 35 22
445 CD35 1½t red 40 22
446 CD37 2t orange 40 22
447 CD37 2½t blue 40 22
448 CD37 3t slate 80 28
449 CD36 5t rose vio 1.40 45
450 CD36 1rp brn car 4.00 80
451 CD36 2rp ol grn 6.25 2.50
452 CD38 3rp bl vio 10.00 6.00
453 CD38 5rp red brn 22.50 3.25
Nos. 439-453 (15) 47.25 14.78

Stamps of 1933 Surcharged in Black — **1 tanga**

1941, June Wmk. 232 *Perf. 11½x12*
454 A29 1t on 1½t dp rose 2.00 1.40
455 A29 1t on 1rp ol grn 2.00 1.40
456 A29 1t on 2rp mar 2.00 1.40
457 A29 1t on 5rp ap grn 2.00 1.40

Nos. 430-431 Surcharged — **3 RÉIS**

1943
458 A29 3r on 1½t dp rose 1.00 75
459 A29 1t on 2t brn 2.50 2.00

Nos. 434, 428, 437 and 432 Surcharged in Dark Blue or Carmine

1 REAL — a **6 Réis** — b

1945-46 Wmk. 232 *Perf. 11½x12*
460 A29(a) 1r on 5t red org (DB) 65 45
461 A29(b) 2r on 8r blk (C) 50 40
462 A29(b) 3r on 3rp org (Bl) ('46) 1.75 1.50
463 A29(b) 6r on 2½t dk bl (C) 1.75 1.75

St. Francis Xavier A30

Luis de Camoens A31

Garcia de Orta — A32

St. John de Britto — A33

Arch of the Viceroy A34

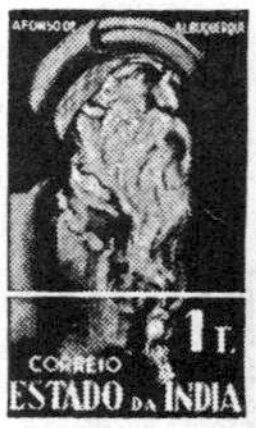
Affonso de Albuquerque A35

Vasco da Gama A36

Francisco de Almeida A37

Perf. 11½
1946, May 28 Litho. Unwmk.
464 A30 1r blk & gray blk 45 25
465 A31 2r rose brn & pale rose brn 45 25
466 A32 6r ocher & dl yel 45 25
467 A33 7r vio & pale vio 2.00 50
468 A34 9r sep & buff 2.00 50
469 A35 1t dk sl grn & sl grn 2.00 50
470 A36 3½t ultra & pale ultra 2.25 1.10
471 A37 1rp choc & bis brn 5.50 1.40
a. Min. sheet of 8 17.50 17.50
Nos. 464-471 (8) 15.10 4.75

No. 471a measures 166x229mm. and contains one each of Nos. 464-471, and decorative border. The sheet sold for 1½ rupias.
See No. 476.

No. 428, 431 and 433 Surcharged in Carmine or Black — **1 Real**

1946 Wmk. 232 *Perf. 11½x12*
472 A29 (c) 1r on 8r blk (C) 60 50
473 A29 (b) 3r on 2t brn 60 55
474 A29 (b) 6r on 3t brt bl 2.00 1.75

Type of 1946 and

Joao de Castro — A38

José Vaz — A39

The Scott Catalogue value is a retail price, what you could expect to pay for the stamp in a grade of Fine-Very Fine. The value listed is a reference which reflects recent actual dealer selling price.

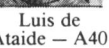

Luis de Ataide — A40

Duarte Pacheco Pereira — A41

1948 Unwmk. Litho. *Perf. 11½*

475 A38	3r brt ultra & lt bl	90	50
476 A30	1t dk grn & yel grn	1.25	60
477 A39	1½t dk pur & dl vio	2.00	1.10
478 A40	2½t brt ver	2.25	1.65
479 A41	7½t dk brn & org brn	4.00	2.25
a.	Min. sheet of 5	16.00	16.00
	Nos. 475-479 (5)	10.40	6.10

No. 476 measures 21x31mm.

No. 479a measures 106x146mm. and contains one each of Nos. 475-479. Marginal inscriptions in gray. The sheet sold for 1 rupia.

Lady of Fatima Issue

Common Design Type

1948 *Perf. 14½*

480 CD40 1t dk bl grn 2.25 1.90

Our Lady of Fatima — A42

1949 Litho. *Perf. 14*

481 A42	1r blue	60	50
482 A42	3r org yel	60	50
483 A42	9r dk car rose	1.10	70
484 A42	2t green	2.75	1.10
485 A42	9t org red	3.00	1.25
486 A42	2rp dk vio brn	5.75	2.75
487 A42	5rp ol grn	12.00	3.00
488 A42	8rp vio bl	27.50	9.25
	Nos. 481-488 (8)	53.30	19.05

Issued to honor Our Lady of the Rosary at Fatima, Portugal.

U.P.U. Symbols — A42a

1949, Oct.

489 A42a 2½t scar & pink 2.25 1.50

U.P.U., 75th anniversary.

Catalogue values for unused stamps in this section, from this point to the end of the section, are for Never Hinged items.

Holy Year Issue.

Common Design Types

1950, May *Perf. 13x13½*

490 CD41	1r ol bis	75	70
491 CD42	2t dk gray grn	1.25	70

See Nos. 496-503.

No. 443 Surcharged in Black

1 Real

1950 *Perf. 13½x13*

492 CD35	1r on 10r dk car	25	25
493 CD35	2r on 10r dk car	25	25

Similar Surcharge on No. 447 in Black or Red.

494 CD37	1r on 2½t bl	25	25
495 CD37	3r on 2½t bl (R)	25	25

Letters with serifs, small (lower case) "r" in "real" and "reis".

Holy Year Issue

Common Design Types

1951 Litho. *Perf. 13½.*

496 CD41	1r dp car rose	22	22
497 CD41	2r emerald	30	25
498 CD42	3r red brn	30	25
499 CD41	6r gray	35	35
500 CD42	9r brt pink	75	55
501 CD41	1t bl vio	50	45
502 CD42	2t yellow	85	55
503 CD41	4t vio brn	85	55
	Nos. 496-503 (8)	4.12	3.17

Holy Year (1950).

No. 447 with Surcharge Similar to Nos. 492-493 in Red.

1951 *Perf. 13½x13*

504 CD37	6r on 2½t bl	30	30
505 CD37	1t on 2½t bl	25	25

Letters with serifs, small (lower case) "r" in "reis."

Holy Year Extension Issue

Common Design Type

1951 Litho. *Perf. 14*

506 CD43 1rp bl vio & pale vio 1.50 1.00

José Vaz A43

Ruins of Sancoale Church A44

Design: 12t, Altar.

1951 Litho. *Perf. 14½*

Dated: "1651-1951."

507 A43	1r Prus bl & pale bl	10	10
508 A44	2r ver & red brn	10	10
509 A43	3r gray blk & gray	40	25
510 A44	1t vio bl & ind	10	5
511 A43	2t dp cl & cl	25	15
512 A44	3t ol grn & blk	40	20
513 A43	9t ind & ultra	50	40
514 A44	10t lil & vio	85	50
515 A44	12t blk brn & brn	1.25	75
	Nos. 507-515 (9)	3.95	2.50

Issued to commemorate the 300th anniversary of the birth of José Vaz.

Medical Congress Issue.

Common Design Type

Design: Medical School, Goa.

1952 Unwmk. *Perf. 13½.*

516 CD44 4½t blk & lt bl 3.00 1.65

Foreign postal stationery (stamped envelopes, postal cards and air letter sheets) lies beyond the scope of this Catalogue, which is limited to adhesive postage stamps.

St. Francis Xavier Issue

Statue of Saint Francis Xavier — A44a

1952, Oct. 25 Litho. *Perf. 14*

517 A44a	6r aqua & multi	25	20
518 A44a	2t cr & multi	2.00	55
519 A44a	5t pink & sil	3.50	1.25

Souvenir Sheets

A45

St. Francis Xavier and his Tomb, Goa — A46

Perf. 13.

520 A45	9t brn & dk brn	8.50	8.50
a.	Single stamp	5.00	5.00
521 A46	Sheet of two	8.50	8.50
a.	4t org buff & blk	2.50	2.50
b.	8t sl & blk	2.50	2.50

Nos. 517 to 521 were issued to commemorate the 400th anniversary of the death of St. Francis Xavier.

Numeral A47

St. Francis Xavier A48

1952, Dec. 4 Litho. *Perf. 13½*

522 A47	3t black	6.00	6.00
523 A48	5t dk vio & blk	6.00	6.00
a.	Strip of 2 + label	16.00	16.00

Issued to publicize Portuguese India's first stamp exhibition, Goa, 1952.

No. 523a consists of a tete bêche pair of Nos. 522-523 separated by a label publicizing the exhibition.

Statue of Virgin Mary — A49

Stamp of Portugal and Arms of Colonies — A49a

1953, Jan.

524 A49	6r dk & lt bl	15	15
525 A49	1t brn & buff	75	50
526 A49	3t dk pur & pale ol	2.50	1.25

Exhibition of Sacred Missionary Art held at Lisbon in 1951.

Stamp Centenary Issue.

1953 Typo.

Stamp and Arms Multicolored.

527 A49a 1t pale grn & bl grn 60 50

Centenary of Portugal's first postage stamps.

C. A. da Gama Pinto — A50

1954, Apr. 10 Litho. *Perf. 11½*

528 A50	3r gray & ol grn	25	20
529 A50	2t blk & gray blk	15	10

Issued to commemorate the centenary of the birth of C. A. da Gama Pinto, ophthalmologist and author.

Sao Paulo Issue

Common Design Type

1954, Oct. 2 Unwmk. *Perf. 13½*

530 CD46 2t dk Prus bl, bl & blk 25 25

Affonso de Albuquerque School A51

Msgr. Sebastiao Rodolfo Dalgado A52

1955, Feb. 26

531 A51 9t multi 85 60

Issued to commemorate the centenary (in 1954) of the founding of the Affonso de Albuquerque National School.

1955, Nov. 15 Unwmk. *Perf. 13½*

532 A52	1r multi	20	20
533 A52	1t multi	50	25

Issued to commemorate the centenary of the birth of Msgr. Sebastiao Rodolfo Dalgado.

Francisco de Almeida A53

Manuel Antonio de Susa A54

Map of Bassein by Pedro Barreto de Resendo, 1635 — A55

Portraits: 9r, Affonso de Albuquerque. 1t, Vasco da Gama. 1½t, Filipe Nery Xavier. 3t, Nuno da Cunha. 4t, Agostino Vicente Lourenco. 8t, Jose Vaz. 9t, Manuel Godinho de Heredia. 10t, Joao de Castro. 2rp, Antonio Caetano Pacheco. 3rp, Constantino de Braganca.
Maps of ancient forts, drawn in 1635: 2½t, Mombaim (Bombay). 3½t, Damao (Daman). 5t, Diu. 12t, Cochin. 1rp, Goa.

Inscribed:
"450 Aniversario da Fundacao do Estado da India 1505-1955."

Perf. 11½x12 (A53), 14½ (A54), 12½ (A55)

1956, Mar. 24 **Unwmk.**

534 A53 3r multi 15 15
535 A54 6r multi 15 15
536 A53 9r multi 30 25
537 A53 1t multi 30 25
538 A54 1½t multi 15 15
539 A55 2t multi 2.00 1.25
540 A55 2½t multi 1.25 75
541 A53 3t multi 30 15
542 A55 3½t multi 1.25 75
543 A54 4t multi 15 15
544 A55 5t multi 55 30
545 A54 8t multi 45 30
546 A54 9t multi 45 30
547 A53 10t multi 40 25
548 A55 12t multi 1.00 60
549 A55 1rp multi 1.75 1.00
550 A54 2rp multi 1.25 60
551 A53 3rp multi 1.75 1.00
Nos. 534-551 (18) 13.60 8.35

Issued to commemorate the 450th anniversary of the Portuguese settlements in India.

Map of Damao and Nagar Aveli — A56

Arms of Vasco da Gama — A57

1957 **Litho.** ***Perf. 11½***
Map and Inscriptions in Black, Red, Ocher and Blue

552 A56 3r gray & buff 10 10
553 A56 6r bl grn & pale lem 10 10
554 A56 3t pink & lt gray 12 10
555 A56 6t blue 18 18
556 A56 11t ol bis & lt vio gray 45 40
557 A56 2rp lt vio & pale gray 1.25 75
558 A56 3rp cit & pink 1.50 1.00
559 A56 5rp mag & pink 2.25 1.75
Nos. 552-559 (8) 5.95 4.38

1958, Apr. 3 **Unwmk.** ***Perf. 13x13½***

Arms of: 6r, Lopo Soares de Albergaria. 9r, Francisco de Almeida. 1t, Garcia de Noronha. 4t, Alfonso de Albuquerque. 5t, Joao de Castro. 11t, Luis de Ataide. 1r, Nuno da Cunha.

Arms in Original Colors
Inscriptions in Black and Red

560 A57 2r buff & ocher 10 10
561 A57 6r gray & ocher 10 10
562 A57 9r pale bl & emer 10 10
563 A57 1t pale cit & brn 20 10
564 A57 4t pale bl grn & lil 25 15
565 A57 5t buff & bl 30 20
566 A57 11t pink & lt brn 50 40
567 A57 1rp pale grn & mar 80 60
Nos. 560-567 (8) 2.35 1.75

Brussels Fair Issue

Exhibition Emblem and View — A58

1958, Dec. 15 **Litho.** ***Perf. 14½***

568 A58 1rp multi 50 40

World's Fair, Brussels, Apr. 17-Oct. 19.

Tropical Medicine Congress Issue
Common Design Type

Design: Holarrhena antidysenterica.

1958, Dec. 15 ***Perf. 13½***

569 CD47 5t gray, brn, grn & red 1.00 40

Stamps of 1955-58 Surcharged with New Values and Bars.

1959, Jan. 1 **Litho.** **Unwmk.**

570 A57 5c on 2r (#560) 12 10
571 A56 10c on 3r (#552) 10 10
572 A57 15c on 6r (#561) 10 10
573 A57 20c on 9r (#562) 10 10
574 A57 30c on 1t (#563) 12 10
575 A55 40c on 2t (#539) 15 12
576 A55 40c on 2½t (#540) 30 25
577 A55 40c on 3½t (#542) 15 10
578 A56 50c on 3t (#554) 12 10
579 A53 80c on 3t (#541) 12 10
580 A53 80c on 10t (#547) 65 55
581 A53 80c on 3rp (#551) 75 65
582 A57 1e on 4t (#564) 12 10
583 A57 1.50e on 5t (#565) 15 15
584 A56 2e on 6t (#555) 25 25
585 A56 2.50e on 11t (#556) 30 30
586 A57 4e on 11t (#566) 40 40
587 A57 4.50e on 1rp (#567) 45 40
588 A56 5e on 2rp (#557) 45 40
589 A56 10e on 3rp (#558) 1.40 1.10
590 A56 30e on 5rp (#559) 3.00 1.25
Nos. 570-590 (21) 9.30 6.72

Types of 1946-1958 Surcharged with New Values: Old Values Obliterated.

1959 **Litho.** **Unwmk.**

591 A39 40c on 1½t dl pur 25 10
592 A54 40c on 1½t multi 25 12
593 CD46 40c on 2t bl & gray 70 50
594 A49 80c on 3t blk & pale cit 25 10
595 A36 80c on 3½t dk bl 35 15
596 CD47 80c on 5t gray, brn, grn & red 35 30
597 A58 80c on 1rp multi 70 40
Nos. 591-597 (7) 2.85 1.67

Coin, Manuel I — A59

Arms of Prince Henry — A60

Various Coins from the Reign of Manuel I (1495-1521) to the Republic.

Perf. 13½x13

1959, Dec. 1 **Litho.** **Unwmk.**
Inscriptions in Black and Red.

598 A59 5c lt bl & gold 6 6
599 A59 10c pale brn & gold 6 6
600 A59 15c pale grn & gray 5 5
601 A59 30c sal & gray 5 5
602 A59 40c pale yel & gray 6 5
603 A59 50c lil & gray 6 5
604 A59 60c pale yel grn & gray 8 5
605 A59 80c lt bl & gray 8 8
606 A59 1e ocher & gray 10 8
607 A59 1.50e bl & gray 12 10
608 A59 2e pale bl & gold 15 12
609 A59 2.50e pale gray & gold 20 15
610 A59 3e cit & gray 22 18
611 A59 4e pink & gray 30 20
612 A59 4.40e pale bis & vio brn 35 30
613 A59 5e pale dl vio & gray 45 40
614 A59 10e brt yel & gray 90 75
615 A59 20e beige & gray 1.75 1.50
616 A59 30e brt yel grn & lt cop brn 2.75 2.25
617 A59 50e lt gray & gray 4.50 4.00
Nos. 598-617 (20) 12.29 10.48

1960, June 25 ***Perf. 13½***

618 A60 3e multi 50 40

Issued to commemorate the 500th anniversary of the death of Prince Henry the Navigator.
Portugal continued to print special-issue stamps for its lost colony after its annexation by India Dec. 18, 1961. Stamps of India were first used on Dec. 29. Stamps of Portuguese India remained valid until Jan. 5, 1962.

AIR POST STAMPS

Common Design Type
Perf. 13½x13

1938, Sept. 1 **Engr.** **Unwmk.**
Name and Value in Black.

C1 CD39 1t scarlet 50 25
C2 CD39 2½t purple 60 25
C3 CD39 3½t orange 60 25
C4 CD39 4½t ultra 1.50 42
C5 CD39 7t lil brn 1.65 50
C6 CD39 7½t dk grn 2.25 75
C7 CD39 9t red brn 4.00 1.10
C8 CD39 11t magenta 4.50 1.10
Nos. C1-C8 (8) 15.60 4.62

No. C4 exists with overprint "Exposicao Internacional de Nova York, 1939-1940" and Trylon and Perisphere.

POSTAGE DUE STAMPS

D1

1904 **Unwmk.** **Typo.** ***Perf. 11½***
Name and Value in Black

J1 D1 2r gray grn 30 30
J2 D1 3r yel grn 30 30
J3 D1 4r orange 30 30
J4 D1 5r slate 30 30
J5 D1 6r gray 30 30
J6 D1 9r yel brn 40 40
J7 D1 1t red org 70 50
J8 D1 2t gray brn 1.50 1.00
J9 D1 5t dl bl 2.25 2.00
J10 D1 10t carmine 3.00 2.75
J11 D1 1rp dl vio 9.00 5.00
Nos. J1-J11 (11) 18.35 13.15

Nos. J1-J11 Overprinted in Carmine or Green

REPUBLICA

1911

J12 D1 2r gray grn 10 10
J13 D1 3r yel grn 10 10
J14 D1 4r orange 15 10
J15 D1 5r slate 15 10
J16 D1 6r gray 20 20
J17 D1 9r yel brn 30 20
J18 D1 1t red org 35 30
J19 D1 2t gray brn 60 50
J20 D1 5t dl bl 1.25 1.10
J21 D1 10t car (G) 2.00 1.50
J22 D1 1rp dl vio 3.00 2.00
Nos. J12-J22 (11) 8.20 6.20

Nos. J1-J11 Overprinted

REPÚBLICA

1914

J23 D1 2r gray grn 25 25
J24 D1 3r yel grn 25 25
J25 D1 4r orange 25 25
J26 D1 5r slate 25 25
J27 D1 6r gray 50 40
J28 D1 9r yel brn 50 50
J29 D1 1t red org 75 50
J30 D1 2t gray brn 2.50 1.50
J31 D1 5t dl bl 2.50 2.00
J32 D1 10t carmine 3.75 2.50
J33 D1 1rp dl vio 6.25 4.25
Nos. J23-J33 (11) 17.75 12.65

Nos. 432, 433 and 434 Surcharged In Red or Black

3
RÉIS
Porteado

1943 **Wmk. 232** ***Perf. 11½x12.***

J34 A29 3r on 2½t dk bl (R) 60 40
J35 A29 6r on 3t brt bl (R) 80 80
J36 A29 1t on 5t red org (Bk) 1.75 1.50

D2

1945 **Typo.** **Unwmk.**
Country Name and Denomination in Black.

J37 D2 2r brt car 65 65
J38 D2 3r blue 65 65
J39 D2 4r org yel 65 65
J40 D2 6r yel grn 65 65
J41 D2 1t bis brn 65 65
J42 D2 2t chocolate 65 65
Nos. J37-J42 (6) 3.90 3.90

Catalogue values for unused stamps in this section, from this point to the end of the section, are for Never Hinged items.

Nos. 467 and 471 Surcharged in Carmine or Black

Porteado
2 Réis

1951, Jan. 1 ***Perf. 11½***

J43 A33 2r on 7r vio & pale vio (C) 55 45
J44 A33 3r on 7r vio & pale vio (C) 55 45
J45 A37 1t on 1rp choc & bis brn 55 45
J46 A37 2t on 1rp choc & bis brn 55 45

Common Design Type
Photogravure and Typographed

1952 ***Perf. 14***
Numeral in Red; Frame Multicolored.

J47 CD45 2r olive 15 12
J48 CD45 3r black 15 12
J49 CD45 6r dk bl 15 12
J50 CD45 1t dk car 30 20
J51 CD45 2t orange 50 50
J52 CD45 10t vio bl 2.00 2.00
Nos. J47-J52 (6) 3.25 3.06

Nos. J47-J49 and J51-52 Surcharged with New Value and Bars.

1959, Jan.
Numeral in Red; Frame Multicolored

J53 CD45 5c on 2r ol 15 12
J54 CD45 10c on 3r blk 15 12
J55 CD45 15c on 6r dk bl 25 20
J56 CD45 60c on 2t org 90 90
J57 CD45 60c on 10t vio bl 1.75 1.75
Nos. J53-J57 (5) 3.20 3.09

WAR TAX STAMPS

WT1

The lack of a value for a listed item does not necessarily indicate rarity.

Overprinted in Black or Carmine

Perf. 15x14

1919, Apr. 15 Typo. Unwmk.

Denomination in Black

MR1	WT1	0:00:05,48rp grn	1.40	1.10
MR2	WT1	0:01:09,94rp grn	4.00	2.25
MR3	WT1	0:02:03,43rp grn (C)	4.00	2.25

Some authorities consider No. MR2 a revenue stamp.

POSTAL TAX STAMPS

Pombal Issue.

Common Design Types

1925 Unwmk. *Perf. 12½.*

RA1	CD28	6r rose & blk	45	45
RA2	CD29	6r rose & blk	45	45
RA3	CD30	6r rose & blk	45	45

Mother and Child — PT1

1948 Litho. *Perf. 11.*

RA4	PT1	6r yel grn	2.75	2.50
RA5	PT1	1t carmine	2.75	2.50

See Nos. RA7-RA7A, RA9, RA12.

Catalogue values for unused stamps in this section, from this point to the end of the section, are for Never Hinged items.

Type of 1948 Surcharged with New Value and Bar in Black.

1951

RA6	PT1	1t on 6r car	2.50	2.00

Type of 1948

1952-53

RA7	PT1	1t gray	2.25	1.65
RA7A	PT1	1t red org ('53)	2.25	1.50

No. RA5 Overprinted in Black

«Revalidado»
P. A. P.

1953

RA8	PT1	1t carmine	6.25	5.50

Type of 1948

1954 Typo.

RA9	PT1	6r pale bis	3.50	3.00

Mother and Child
PT2 PT3

Surcharged in Black.

1956 Typo. *Perf. 11*

RA10	PT2	1t on 4t lt bl	11.00	10.00

Litho. *Perf. 13*

RA11	PT3	1t blk, pale grn & red	1.25	60

See No. RA14.

Type of 1948 Redrawn

1956 *Perf. 11*

Without Gum

RA12	PT1	1t bluish grn	3.25	3.00

Denomination in white oval at left.

No. RA11 Surcharged with New Value and Bars in Red

1957 *Perf. 13½*

RA13	PT3	6r on 1t blk, pale grn & red	90	60

Type of 1956

1958 Unwmk. *Perf. 13*

RA14	PT3	1t dk bl, sal & grn	90	60

No. RA14 Surcharged with New Values and Four Bars

1959, Jan. Litho. *Perf. 13*

RA15	PT3	20c on 1t	55	55
RA16	PT3	40c on 1t	55	55

Arms and People Seeking Help — PT4

1960 *Perf. 13½*

RA17	PT4	20c brn & red	25	25

POSTAL TAX DUE STAMPS

Pombal Issue.

Common Design Types

1925 Unwmk. *Perf. 12½.*

RAJ1	CD31	1t rose & blk	60	60
RAJ2	CD32	1t rose & blk	60	60
RAJ3	CD33	1t rose & blk	60	60

See note after Portugal No. RAJ4.

PUERTO RICO

(Porto Rico)

LOCATION — A large island in the West Indies, east of Hispaniola.
GOVT. — Former Spanish Colony.
AREA — 3,435 sq. mi.
POP. — 953,243 (1899).
CAPITAL — San Juan.

The island was ceded to the United States by the Treaty of 1898.

100 Centimes = 1 Peseta
1000 Milesimas = 100 Centavos = 1 Peso (1881)
100 Cents = 1 Dollar (1898)

Issued under Spanish Dominion.

Puerto Rican stamps of 1855-73, a part of the Spanish colonial period, were also used in Cuba. They are listed as Cuba Nos. 1-4, 9-14, 18-21, 32-34, 35A-37, 39-41, 43-45, 47-49, 51-53, 55-57.

Stamps of Cuba Overprinted in Black:

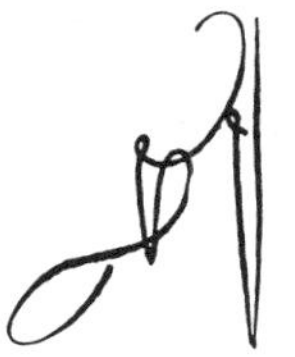
a
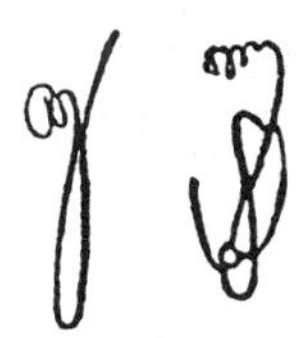
b

c

d

1873 Unwmk. *Perf. 14.*

1	A10 (a)	25c gray	22.50	1.50
2	A10 (a)	50c brown	60.00	4.50
3	A10 (a)	1p red brn	125.00	12.50

1874

4	A11 (b)	25c ultra	15.00	2.00

1875

5	A12 (b)	25c ultra	13.00	2.00
6	A12 (b)	50c green	24.00	2.00
a.		Invtd. ovpt.	135.00	67.50
7	A12 (b)	1p brown	67.50	11.00

1876

8	A13 (c)	25c bl gray	3.25	1.50
9	A13 (c)	50c ultra	7.50	2.00
10	A13 (c)	1p black	30.00	6.75
11	A13 (d)	25c bl gray	13.00	1.00
12	A13 (d)	1p black	37.50	6.75

Varieties of overprint on Nos. 8-11 include: inverted, double, partly omitted.

King Alfonso XII
A5 A6

1877 Typo.

13	A5	5c yel brn	3.75	1.00
a.		5c car (error)	150.00	120.00
14	A5	10c carmine	10.00	1.65
a.		10c brn (error)	150.00	120.00
15	A5	15c dp grn	18.00	5.50
16	A5	25c ultra	7.75	1.00
17	A5	50c bister	10.00	2.75

Same, Dated "1878".

1878

18	A5	5c ol bis	9.50	9.50
19	A5	10c red brn	110.00	60.00
20	A5	25c dp grn	1.40	85
21	A5	50c ultra	5.50	1.40
22	A5	1p bister	8.00	3.50

Same, Dated "1879".

1879

23	A5	5c lake	6.75	2.00
24	A5	10c dk brn	6.75	2.00
25	A5	15c dk ol grn	6.75	2.00
26	A5	25c blue	2.00	85
27	A5	50c dk grn	6.75	2.00
28	A5	1p gray	25.00	8.00

Imperforates of type A5 are from proof or trial sheets.

1880

29	A6	¼c dp grn	22.50	8.00
30	A6	½c brt rose	4.00	1.50
31	A6	1c brn lil	8.50	4.00
32	A6	2c gray lil	3.25	2.00
33	A6	3c buff	3.25	2.00
34	A6	4c black	3.25	2.75
35	A6	5c gray grn	2.00	1.25
36	A6	10c rose	3.00	1.25
37	A6	15c yel brn	4.00	1.50
38	A6	25c gray bl	2.00	1.00
39	A6	40c gray	7.50	1.00
40	A6	50c dk brn	15.00	4.00
41	A6	1p ol bis	37.50	6.75

Same, Dated "1881".

1881

42	A6	½m lake	24	10
43	A6	1m violet	25	14
44	A6	2m pale rose	35	25
45	A6	4m brt grn	50	20
46	A6	6m brn lil	50	38
47	A6	8m ultra	1.25	85
48	A6	1c gray grn	2.25	85
49	A6	2c lake	3.00	1.90
50	A6	3c dk brn	5.00	2.75
51	A6	5c gray bl	1.50	25
52	A6	8c brown	1.50	85
53	A6	10c slate	12.00	4.75
54	A6	20c ol bis	19.00	6.75

Alfonso XII Alfonso XIII
A7 A8

1882-86

55	A7	½m rose	25	10
a.		½m sal rose	30	24
56	A7	½m lake ('84)	50	40
57	A7	1m pale lake	50	40
58	A7	1m brt rose ('84)	25	10
59	A7	2m violet	25	10
60	A7	4m brn lil	25	10
61	A7	6m brown	40	10
62	A7	8m yel grn	40	10
63	A7	1c gray grn	25	10
64	A7	2c rose	1.00	10
65	A7	3c yellow	3.00	1.25
a.		Cliche of 8c in plate of 3c	110.00	
66	A7	3c yel brn ('84)	3.00	50
a.		Cliche of 8c in plate of 3c	22.50	
67	A7	5c gray bl	11.00	60
68	A7	5c gray bl, 1st retouch ('84)	11.00	2.50
69	A7	5c gray bl, 2nd retouch ('86)	95.00	4.00
70	A7	8c gray brn	3.00	10
71	A7	10c dk grn	3.00	25
72	A7	20c gray lil	4.00	25
a.		20c ol brn (error)	50.00	
73	A7	40c blue	27.50	7.50
74	A7	80c ol bis	27.50	8.75

For differences between the original and the retouched stamps see note on the 1883-86 issue of Cuba.

1890-97

75	A8	½m black	24	6
76	A8	½m ol gray ('92)	6	6
77	A8	½m red brn ('94)	6	6
78	A8	½m dl vio ('96)	6	6
79	A8	1m emerald	28	6
80	A8	1m dk vio ('92)	6	6
81	A8	1m ultra ('94)	6	6
82	A8	1m dp brn ('96)	6	6
83	A8	2m lil rose	24	6
84	A8	2m vio brn ('92)	6	6
85	A8	2m red org ('94)	6	6
86	A8	2m yel grn ('96)	6	6
87	A8	4m dk ol grn	9.00	4.50
88	A8	4m ultra ('92)	6	6
89	A8	4m yel brn ('94)	6	6
90	A8	4m bl grn ('96)	45	24
91	A8	6m dk brn	27.50	9.00
92	A8	6m pale rose ('92)	12	6
93	A8	8m ol bis	27.50	18.00
94	A8	8m yel grn ('92)	12	6
95	A8	1c yel brn	24	6
96	A8	1c bl grn ('91)	45	9
97	A8	1c vio brn ('94)	2.75	14
98	A8	1c cl ('96)	28	6
99	A8	2c dk vio	90	70
100	A8	2c red brn ('92)	70	9
101	A8	2c lil ('94)	1.10	14
102	A8	2c org brn ('96)	28	6
103	A8	3c sl bl	6.00	70
104	A8	3c org ('92)	55	9
105	A8	3c ol gray ('94)	1.90	14
106	A8	3c bl ('96)	9.00	24
107	A8	3c cl brn ('97)	18	6
108	A8	4c sl bl ('94)	45	14
109	A8	4c gray brn ('96)	38	6
110	A8	5c brn vio	9.00	38
111	A8	5c yel grn ('94)	1.90	28
112	A8	5c bl grn ('92)	55	6
113	A8	5c bl ('96)	18	6
114	A8	6c org ('94)	28	6
115	A8	6c vio ('96)	18	6
116	A8	8c ultra	8.50	1.40
117	A8	8c gray brn ('92)	14	6
118	A8	8c dl vio ('94)	5.25	90
119	A8	8c car rose ('96)	90	60
120	A8	10c rose	3.75	60
a.		10c sal rose	6.75	2.10
121	A8	10c lil rose ('92)	70	14
122	A8	20c red org	3.50	3.00
123	A8	20c lil ('92)	85	24
124	A8	20c car rose ('94)	60	14
125	A8	20c ol gray ('96)	2.50	70
126	A8	40c orange	72.50	24.00
127	A8	40c sl bl ('92)	2.25	1.40
128	A8	40c cl ('94)	2.75	2.10
129	A8	40c sal ('96)	2.50	1.40
130	A8	80c yel grn	210.00	90.00
131	A8	80c org ('92)	6.00	3.75
132	A8	80c blk ('97)	20.00	7.25

Imperforates of type A8 were not issued and are variously considered to be proofs or printer's waste.

Landing of Columbus on Puerto Rico
A9

Alfonso XIII
A10

1893 **Litho.** ***Perf. 12***

133	A9	3c dk grn	95.00	27.50

400th anniversary, landing of Columbus on Puerto Rico. Counterfeits exist.

1898 **Typo.**

135	A10	1m org brn	7	7
136	A10	2m org brn	7	7
137	A10	3m org brn	7	7
138	A10	4m org brn	85	38
139	A10	5m org brn	7	7
140	A10	1c blk vio	7	7
a.		Tete beche pair	*900.00*	
141	A10	2c dk bl grn	7	7
142	A10	3c dk brn	7	7
143	A10	4c orange	1.00	55
144	A10	5c brt rose	7	7
145	A10	6c dk bl	52	7
146	A10	8c gray brn	15	7
147	A10	10c vermilion	15	7
148	A10	15c dl ol grn	15	7
149	A10	20c maroon	1.25	38
150	A10	40c violet	70	60
151	A10	60c black	70	60
152	A10	80c red brn	2.50	2.25
153	A10	1p yel grn	5.00	4.75
154	A10	2p sl bl	14.00	6.00
		Nos. 135-154 (20)	*27.53*	16.35

Nos. 135-154 exist imperf. Value, set $1,200.

Stamps of 1890-97 Handstamped in Rose or Purple

Habilitado
PARA
1898 y 99.

1898

154A	A8	½m dl vio	8.00	4.00
155	A8	1m dp brn	1.25	1.25
156	A8	2m yel grn	28	28
157	A8	4m bl grn	28	28
158	A8	1c claret	50	70
159	A8	2c org brn	50	70
160	A8	3c blue	14.00	6.75
161	A8	3c cl brn	35	35
162	A8	4c gray brn	35	35
163	A8	4c sl bl	8.50	5.75
164	A8	5c yel grn	5.00	5.00
165	A8	5c blue	30	30
166	A8	6c violet	30	28
167	A8	8c car rose (P)	50	30
a.		Rose overprint	4.75	4.75
168	A8	20c ol gray	85	85
169	A8	40c salmon	2.50	2.50
170	A8	80c black	12.00	10.00

As usual with handstamps there are many inverted, double and similar varieties. Counterfeits of Nos. 154A-170 abound.

Issued under U.S. Administration

A11

A12

Ponce Issue

1898 **Unwmk.** ***Imperf.***

200	A11	5c vio, *yelsh*	*5,000.*	

Counterfeits exist of Nos. 200-201.

Coamo Issue

1898 **Unwmk.** ***Imperf.***

201	A12	5c black	300.00	300.00

There are ten varieties in the setting. The stamps bear the control mark "F. Santiago" in violet.

United States Nos. 279, 267, 281, 272 and 282C Overprinted in Black at 36 degree angle

PORTO RICO

1899 **Wmk. 191** ***Perf. 12***

210	A87	1c yel grn	4.50	1.25
a.		Ovpt. at 25 degree angle	6.00	1.75
211	A88	2c car, type III	4.00	1.00
a.		Ovpt. at 25 degree angle	5.00	1.40
212	A91	5c blue	6.00	1.50
213	A93	8c vio brn	20.00	12.50
a.		Ovpt. at 25 degree angle	25.00	13.50
c.		"PORTO RIC"	85.00	85.00
214	A94	10c brn, type I	14.00	4.00
		Nos. 210-214 (5)	*48.50*	20.25

Misspellings of the overprint, actually broken letters (PORTO RICU, PORTU RICO, FORTO RICO), are found on 1c, 2c, 8c and 10c.

United States Nos. 279 and 267 Overprinted Diagonally in Black

PUERTO RICO

1900

215	A87	1c yel grn	4.50	1.25
216	A88	2c carmine	4.00	85
a.		2c org red	4.50	85
b.		Inverted ovpt.		*3,250.*

POSTAGE DUE STAMPS

United States Nos. J38, J39 and J42 Overprinted in Black at 36 degree angle

PORTO RICO

1899 **Wmk. 191** ***Perf. 12***

J1	D2	1c dp cl	15.00	5.50
a.		Ovpt. at 25 degree angle	18.00	6.75
J2	D2	2c dp cl	10.00	5.00
a.		Ovpt. at 25 degree angle	13.50	5.75
J3	D2	10c dp cl	100.00	37.50
a.		Ovpt. at 25 degree angle	125.00	45.00

Stamps of Puerto Rico were replaced by those of the United States.

WAR TAX STAMPS

Stamps of 1890-94 Overprinted or Surcharged by Handstamp

IMPUESTO
DE GUERRA

1898 **Unwmk.** ***Perf. 14***

Purple Overprint or Surcharge.

MR1	A8	1c yel brn	5.50	4.00
MR2	A8	2c on 2m org	2.00	1.90
MR3	A8	2c on 5c bl grn	3.00	2.50
MR4	A8	2c dk vio	30	20
MR5	A8	2c lilac	60	60
MR6	A8	2c red brn	30	20
MR7	A8	5c bl grn	30	20
MR8	A8	5c on 5c bl grn	3.50	2.50

Rose Surcharge.

MR9	A8	2c on 2m org	1.25	1.25
MR10	A8	5c on 1m dk vio	20	20
MR11	A8	5c on 1m dl bl	30	30

Magenta Surcharge.

MR12	A8	5c on 1m dk vio	20	20
MR13	A8	5c on 1m dl bl	1.75	1.75

Nos. MR2 to MR13 were issued as War Tax Stamps (2c on letters or sealed mail; 5c on telegrams) but, during the early days of the American occupation, they were accepted for ordinary postage.

Double, inverted and similar varieties of overprints are numerous in this issue.

QUELIMANE

LOCATION — A district of the Mozambique Province in Portuguese East Africa.
GOVT. — Part of the Portuguese East Africa Colony.
AREA — 39,800 sq. mi.
POP. — 877,000 (approx.).
CAPITAL — Quelimane.

This district was formerly a part of Zambezia. Quelimane stamps were replaced by those of Mozambique.

100 Centavos = 1 Escudo

Vasco da Gama Issue of Various Portuguese Colonies Surcharged as

REPUBLICA
QUELIMANE
¼ C.

1913 **Unwmk.** ***Perf. 12½ to 16***

On Stamps of Macao

1	CD20	¼c on ½a bl grn	1.75	2.00
2	CD21	½c on 1a red	1.75	2.00
3	CD22	1c on 2a red vio	1.75	2.00
4	CD23	2½c on 4a yel grn	1.75	2.00
5	CD24	5c on 8a dk bl	1.75	2.00
6	CD25	7½c on 12a vio brn	2.50	3.00
7	CD26	10c on 16a bis brn	1.75	2.00
a.		Inverted surcharge	10.00	
8	CD27	15c on 24a bis	1.75	2.00
		Nos. 1-8 (8)	14.75	17.00

On Stamps of Portuguese Africa

9	CD20	¼c on 2½r bl grn	1.75	2.00
10	CD21	½c on 5r red	1.75	2.00
11	CD22	1c on 10r red vio	1.75	2.00
12	CD23	2½c on 25r yel grn	1.75	2.00
13	CD24	5c on 50r dk bl	2.00	2.25
14	CD25	7½c on 75r vio brn	2.50	3.00
15	CD26	10c on 100r bis	1.75	2.00
16	CD27	15c on 150r bis	1.75	2.00
		Nos. 9-16 (8)	15.00	17.25

On Stamps of Timor

17	CD20	¼c on ½a bl grn	1.75	2.00
18	CD21	½c on 1a red	1.75	2.00
19	CD22	1c on 2a red vio	1.75	2.00
20	CD23	2½c on 4a yel grn	1.75	2.00
21	CD24	5c on 8a dk bl	1.75	2.00
22	CD25	7½c on 12a vio brn	2.50	3.00
23	CD26	10c on 16a bis brn	1.75	2.00
24	CD27	15c on 24a bis	1.75	2.00
		Nos. 17-24 (8)	14.75	17.00
		Nos. 1-24 (24)	44.50	51.25

Ceres — A1

1914 **Typo.** ***Perf. 15x14***

Name and Value in Black

25	A1	¼c ol brn	80	1.25
26	A1	½c black	1.25	1.25
27	A1	1c bl grn	1.10	1.00
a.		Imperf.		
28	A1	1½c lil brn	1.65	1.40
29	A1	2c carmine	1.75	1.40
30	A1	2½c lt vio	50	45
31	A1	5c dp bl	1.25	1.25
32	A1	7½c yel brn	1.25	1.00
33	A1	8c slate	1.35	1.25
34	A1	10c org brn	1.25	1.00
35	A1	15c plum	3.00	2.50
36	A1	20c yel grn	1.50	1.00
37	A1	30c brn, *grn*	4.00	3.00
38	A1	40c brn, *pink*	4.00	3.00
39	A1	50c org, *sal*	4.00	3.00
40	A1	1e grn, *bl*	5.00	5.00
		Nos. 25-40 (16)	33.65	28.75

REUNION

LOCATION — An island in the Indian Ocean about 400 miles east of Madagascar.
GOVT. — Former French colony.
AREA — 970 sq. mi.
POP. — 490,000 (est. 1974).
CAPITAL — St. Denis.

The colony of Reunion became an integral part of the Republic, acquiring the same status as the departments in metropolitan France, under a law effective Jan. 1, 1947.

On Jan. 1, 1975, stamps of France replaced those inscribed or overprinted "CFA."

100 Centimes = 1 Franc

Catalogue values for unused stamps in this country are for Never Hinged items, beginning with Scott 224 in the regular postage section, Scott B15 in the semi-postal section, Scott C18 in the airpost section, and Scott J26 in the postage due section.

Values of early Reunion stamps vary according to condition. Quotations for Nos. 1-2 are for fine copies. Very fine to superb specimens sell at much higher prices, and inferior or poor copies sell at reduced prices, depending on the condition of the individual specimen.

A1

A2

1852 **Unwmk.** **Typo.** ***Imperf.***

1	A1	15c blk, *blue*	*20,000.*	*10,000.*
2	A2	30c blk, *blue*	*20,000.*	*10,000.*

Four varieties of each value.

The reprints are printed on a more bluish paper than the originals. They have a frame of a thick and a thin line, instead of one thick and two thin lines. Value, $24 each.

Stamps of French Colonies Surcharged or Overprinted in Black:

5 c.
R
a

RÉUNION
b

1885

3	A1(a)	5c on 40c org, *yelsh*	150.00	150.00
a.		Inverted surcharge	500.00	500.00
4	A1(a)	25c on 40c org, *yelsh*	20.00	18.00
a.		Inverted surcharge	180.00	180.00
b.		Double surcharge	180.00	180.00
5	A5(a)	5c on 30c brn, *yelsh*	20.00	18.00
a.		"5" inverted	650.00	650.00
b.		Double surcharge	180.00	180.00
6	A4(a)	5c on 40c org, *yelsh* (I)	16.00	15.00
a.		5c on 40c org, *yelsh* (II)	700.00	700.00
b.		Inverted surcharge		
c.		Double surcharge		
7	A8(a)	5c on 30c brn, *yelsh*	3.00	3.00
8	A8(a)	5c on 40c ver, *straw*	40.00	30.00
a.		Inverted surcharge		
b.		Double surcharge		
9	A8(a)	10c on 40c ver, *straw*	4.00	3.50
10	A8(a)	20c on 30c brn, *yelsh*	25.00	20.00

Overprint Type "b"
With or Without Accent on "E"

1891

11	A4	40c org, *yelsh* (I)	225.00	175.00
a.		40c org, *yelsh* (II)	*1,600.*	*1,600.*
12	A7	80c car, *pnksh*	25.00	20.00
13	A8	30c brn, *yelsh*	14.00	14.00
14	A8	40c ver, *straw*	10.00	10.00
15	A8	75c car, *rose*	140.00	140.00
16	A8	1fr brnz grn, *straw*	18.00	16.00

Perf. 14x13½

17	A9	1c blk, *lil bl*	1.40	1.20
a.		Inverted overprint	8.00	8.00
b.		Double overprint	12.50	12.50
18	A9	2c brn, *buff*	1.80	1.50
a.		Inverted overprint	8.00	8.00
19	A9	4c claret, *lav*	3.25	2.50
a.		Inverted overprint	25.00	25.00

20 A9 5c grn, *grnsh* 3.25 2.00
a. Inverted overprint 12.00 12.00
b. Double overprint 15.00 15.00
21 A9 10c blk, *lav* 12.00 2.00
a. Inverted overprint 20.00 20.00
b. Double overprint 20.00 17.50
22 A9 15c blue 16.00 2.00
a. Inverted overprint 35.00 35.00
23 A9 20c red, *grn* 12.00 9.00
a. Inverted overprint 42.50 42.50
b. Double surcharge 35.00 32.50
24 A9 25c blk, *rose* 12.00 2.50
a. Inverted overprint 42.50 42.50
25 A9 35c dp vio, *yel* 9.00 9.00
b. Inverted overprint 50.00 50.00
26 A9 40c red, *straw* 25.00 21.00
a. Inverted overprint 65.00 65.00
27 A9 75c car, *rose* 225.00 200.00
a. Inverted overprint 450.00 450.00
28 A9 1fr brnz grn, *straw* 200.00 180.00
a. Inverted overprint 450.00 450.00

The varieties "RUNION", "RUENION", "REUNIONR", "REUNIOU" and "REUNOIN" are found on most stamps of this group. There are also many broken letters.

No. 23 with Additional Surcharge in Black:

02c 2 2 2
c d e f

1891

29 A9(c) 02c on 20c red, *grn* 3.50 3.50
30 A9(c) 15c on 20c red, *grn* 5.00 5.00
31 A9(d) 2c on 20c red, *grn* 1.10 1.10
32 A9(e) 2c on 20c red, *grn* 90 90
33 A9(f) 2c on 20c red, *grn* 1.60 1.60

Navigation and Commerce — A14

1892-1905 **Typo.**
Name of Colony in Blue or Carmine

34 A14 1c blk, *lil bl* 42 35
35 A14 2c brn, *buff* 42 35
36 A14 4c claret, *lav* 70 60
37 A14 5c grn, *grnsh* 2.00 80
38 A14 5c yel grn ('00) 42 42
39 A14 10c blk, *lav* 2.50 80
40 A14 10c red ('00) 55 55
41 A14 15c bl, quadrille paper 7.00 90
42 A14 15c gray ('00) 1.60 42
43 A14 20c red, *grn* 5.50 3.50
44 A14 25c blk, *rose* 5.25 80
a. "Reunion" double 110.00 110.00
45 A14 25c bl ('00) 6.25 6.25
46 A14 30c brn, *bis* 5.75 3.50
47 A14 40c red, *straw* 7.00 6.00
48 A14 50c car, *rose* 22.50 12.50
a. "Reunion" in red and blue 110.00 110.00
49 A14 50c brn, *az* ("Reunion" in car) ('00) 15.00 14.00
50 A14 50c brn, *az* ("Reunion" in bl) ('05) 18.00 15.00
51 A14 75c dp vio, *org* 20.00 15.00
a. "Reunion" double 110.00 110.00
52 A14 1fr brnz grn, *straw* 15.00 9.00
a. "Reunion" double 110.00 110.00
Nos. 34-52 (19) 135.86 90.74

French Colonies No. 52 Surcharged in Black:

2 c. 2 c. 2 c.
g h j

1893

53 A9(g) 2c on 20c red, *grn* 65 65
54 A9(h) 2c on 20c red, *grn* 1.40 1.40
55 A9(j) 2c on 20c red, *grn* 6.25 6.25

Reunion Nos. 47-48, 51-52 Surcharged in Black

5 c.

1901

56 A14 5c on 40c red, *straw* 1.50 1.50
a. Inverted surcharge 11.00 11.00
b. No bar 55.00 55.00
c. Thin "5"
d. "5" inverted 375.00 375.00
57 A14 5c on 50c car, *rose* 1.60 1.60
a. Inverted surcharge 11.00 11.00
b. No bar 55.00 55.00
c. Thin "5"

58 A14 15c on 75c vio, *org* 5.50 5.50
a. Inverted surcharge 11.00 11.00
b. No bar 55.00 55.00
c. Thin "5" and small "1" 11.00 10.00
d. As "c," inverted
59 A14 15c on 1fr brnz grn, *straw* 5.50 5.50
a. Inverted surcharge 11.00 11.00
b. No bar 55.00 55.00
c. Thin "5" and small "1" 11.00 10.00
d. As "c," inverted

Map of Reunion A19

Coat of Arms and View of St. Denis — A20

View of St. Pierre — A21

1907-30 **Typo.**

60 A19 1c vio & car rose 5 5
61 A19 2c brn & ultra 5 5
62 A19 4c ol grn & red 5 5
63 A19 5c grn & red 5 5
64 A19 5c org & vio ('22) 5 5
65 A19 10c car & grn 60 8
66 A19 10c grn ('22) 5 5
67 A19 10c brn red & org red, *bluish* ('26) 5 5
68 A19 15c blk & ultra 5 5
69 A19 15c gray grn & bl grn ('26) 12 12
70 A19 15c bl & lt red ('28) 12 12
71 A20 20c gray grn & bl grn 5 5
72 A20 25c dp bl & vio brn 90 65
73 A20 25c lt brn & bl ('22) 10 10
74 A20 30c yel brn & grn 16 16
75 A20 30c rose & pale rose ('22) 12 12
76 A20 30c gray & car rose ('26) 10 10
77 A20 30c dp grn & yel grn ('28) 35 35
78 A20 35c ol grn & bl 40 16
79 A20 40c gray grn & brn ('25) 7 7
80 A20 45c vio & car rose 40 16
81 A20 45c red brn & ver ('26) 16 16
82 A20 45c vio & red org ('28) 80 80
83 A20 50c red brn & ultra 90 30
84 A20 50c bl & ultra ('22) 7 7
85 A20 50c yel & vio ('26) 7 7
86 A20 60c dk bl & yel brn ('26) 7 7
87 A20 65c vio & lt bl ('28) 35 30
88 A20 75c red & car rose 16 12
89 A20 75c ol brn & red vio ('28) 70 60
90 A20 90c brn red & brt red ('30) 2.50 2.25
91 A21 1fr ol grn & bl 30 20
92 A21 1fr blue ('26) 20 20
93 A21 1fr yel brn & lav ('28) 30 16
94 A21 1.10fr org brn & rose lil ('28) 40 30
95 A21 1.50fr dk bl & ultra ('30) 4.00 3.00
96 A21 2fr red & grn 1.50 1.00
97 A21 3fr red vio ('30) 4.25 3.00
98 A21 5fr car & vio brn 3.00 1.60
Nos. 60-98 (39) 23.62 16.84

Stamps of 1892-1900 Surcharged in Black or Carmine

05 10

1912

99 A14 5c on 2c brn, *buff* 35 35
100 A14 5c on 15c gray (C) 35 35
a. Inverted surcharge 60.00 60.00
101 A14 5c on 20c red, *grn* 50 50
102 A14 5c on 25c blk, *rose* (C) 35 35
103 A14 5c on 30c brn, *bis* (C) 35 35
104 A14 10c on 40c red, *straw* 35 35
105 A14 10c on 50c brn, *az* (C) 1.25 1.25
106 A14 10c on 75c dp vio, *org* 3.50 3.50
Nos. 99-106 (8) 7.00 7.00

Two spacings between the surcharged numerals are found on Nos. 99 to 106.

No. 62 Surcharged 0,01

1917

107 A19 1c on 4c ol grn & red 50 50
a. Inverted surcharge 15.00 15.00
b. Double surcharge 25.00 25.00

Stamps and Types of 1907-30 Surcharged in Black or Red

40

1922-33

108 A20 40c on 20c grn & yel ('22) 25 25
109 A20 50c on 45c red brn & ver ('33) 35 28
109A A20 50c on 45c vio & red org ('33) 110.00 100.00
b. Double surcharge 550.00
110 A20 50c on 65c vio & lt bl ('33) 35 28
111 A20 60c on 75c red & rose ('22) 16 16
112 A19 65c on 15c blk & ultra (R) ('25) 45 45
113 A19 85c on 15c blk & ultra (R) ('25) 45 45
114 A20 85c on 75c red & cer ('25) 45 45
115 A20 90c on 75 brn red & rose red ('27) 60 60
Nos. 108-109,110-115 (8) 3.06 2.92

Stamps and Type of 1907-30 Surcharged with New Value and Bars in Black or Red

1924-27

116 A21 25c on 5fr car & brn 25 25
a. Double surcharge 27.50
117 A21 1.25fr on 1fr bl (R) ('26) 15 15
a. Double surcharge 32.50 32.50
118 A21 1.50fr on 1fr ind & ultra, *bluish* ('27) 25 25
a. Double surcharge 40.00 40.00
119 A21 3fr on 5fr dl red & lt bl ('27) 80 80
120 A21 10fr on 5fr bl grn & brn red ('27) 5.50 5.00
121 A21 20fr on 5fr blk brn & rose ('27) 7.00 6.00
Nos. 116-121 (6) 13.95 12.45

Colonial Exposition Issue
Common Design Types

1931 **Engr.** ***Perf. 12½***
Name of Country Typo. in Black

122 CD70 40c dp grn 1.10 1.10
123 CD71 50c violet 1.25 1.25
124 CD72 90c red org 1.25 1.25
125 CD73 1.50fr dull blue 1.25 1.25

Cascade of Salazie — A22

Waterfowl Lake and Anchain Peak — A23

Leon Dierx Museum, St. Denis — A24

Perf. 12, 12½ and Compound

1933-40 **Engr.**

126 A22 1c violet 5 5
127 A22 2c dark brown 5 5
128 A22 3c rose vio ('40) 5 5
129 A22 4c olive green 5 5
130 A22 5c red orange 5 5
131 A22 10c ultramarine 5 5
132 A22 15c black 5 5
133 A22 20c indigo 5 5
134 A22 25c red brown 7 7
135 A22 30c dark green 10 10
136 A23 35c green ('38) 16 16
137 A23 40c ultramarine 10 7
138 A23 40c brn blk ('40) 12 12
139 A23 45c red violet 30 20
140 A23 45c green ('40) 12 12
141 A23 50c red 5 5
142 A23 55c brn org ('38) 16 15
143 A23 60c dull bl ('40) 12 12
144 A23 65c olive green 45 30
145 A23 70c ol grn ('40) 12 12
146 A23 75c dark brown 1.50 1.25
147 A23 80c black ('38) 16 16
148 A23 90c carmine 70 60
149 A23 90c dl rose vio ('39) 16 16
150 A23 1fr green 65 12
151 A23 1fr dk car ('38) 40 16
152 A23 1fr black ('40) 5 5
153 A24 1.25fr orange brown 16 12
154 A24 1.25fr brt car rose ('39) 32 32
155 A22 1.40fr pck bl ('40) 16 16
156 A24 1.50fr ultramarine 5 5
157 A22 1.60fr dk car rose ('40) 32 32
158 A24 1.75fr olive green 20 16
159 A22 1.75fr dk bl ('38) 20 16
160 A24 2fr vermilion 12 12
161 A22 2.25fr brt ultra ('39) 55 55
162 A22 2.50fr chnt ('40) 32 32
163 A24 3fr purple 12 12
164 A24 5fr magenta 35 16
165 A24 10fr dark blue 30 20
166 A24 20fr red brown 50 45
Nos. 126-166 (41) 9.56 7.69

Paris International Exposition Issue
Common Design Types

1937 ***Perf. 13***

167 CD74 20c dp vio 60 50
168 CD75 30c dk grn 65 65
169 CD76 40c car rose 65 65
170 CD77 50c dk brn & blk 70 70
171 CD78 90c red 70 70
172 CD79 1.50fr ultra 70 70
Nos. 167-172 (6) 4.00 3.90

Colonial Arts Exhibition Issue
Souvenir Sheet
Common Design Type

1937 ***Imperf.***

173 CD74 3fr ultra 2.00 2.00

New York World's Fair Issue
Common Design Type

1939 **Engr.** ***Perf. 12½x12***

174 CD82 1.25fr car lake 35 35
175 CD82 2.25fr ultra 35 35

St. Denis Roadstead and Marshal Petain A25

1941 **Unwmk.** ***Perf. 11½x12***

176 A25 1fr brown 20
177 A25 2.50fr blue 20

Nos. 176-177 were issued by the Vichy goverment, and were not placed on sale in Reunion.

No. 144 Surcharged in Carmine 1f

1943

177A A23 1fr on 65c ol grn 35 5

V1

Stamps of the above design and stamps of type A26, without "RF", were issued in 1943 and 1944 by the Vichy Government, but were not placed on sale in Reunion.

Stamps of 1907 Overprinted in Blue Violet

France Libre

q

1943 Unwmk. *Perf. 14x13½*

178	A19(q)	4c ol gray & pale red	1.20	1.20
179	A20(q)	75c red & lil rose	35	35
180	A21(q)	5fr car & vio brn	18.00	18.00

Stamps of 1933-40 Overprinted in Carmine, Black or Blue Violet

France

Libre

r

Perf. 12½

181	A22(r)	1c rose vio (C)	25	25
182	A22(r)	2c blk brn (C)	25	25
183	A22(r)	3c rose vio (C)	25	25
184	A22(r)	4c ol yel (C)	25	25
185	A22(r)	5c red org	25	25
186	A22(r)	10c ultra (C)	25	25
187	A22(r)	15c blk (C)	25	25
188	A22(r)	20c ind (C)	25	25
189	A22(r)	25c red brn (BlV)	25	25
190	A22(r)	30c dk grn (C)	25	25
191	A23(q)	35c green	25	25
192	A23(q)	40c dl ultra (C)	25	25
193	A23(q)	40c brn blk (C)	25	25
194	A23(q)	45c red vio	25	25
195	A23(q)	45c green	25	25
196	A23(q)	50c org red	25	25
197	A23(q)	55c brn org	25	25
198	A23(q)	60c dl bl (C)	90	90
199	A23(q)	65c ol grn	25	25
200	A23(q)	70c ol grn (C)	55	55
201	A23(q)	75c dk brn (C)	1.00	1.00
202	A23(q)	80c blk (C)	25	25
203	A23(q)	90c dl rose vio	25	25
204	A23(q)	1fr green	25	25
205	A23(q)	1fr dk car	25	25
206	A23(q)	1fr blk (C)	60	60
207	A24(q)	1.25fr org brn (BlV)	25	25
208	A24(q)	1.25fr brt car rose	55	55
209	A22(r)	1.40fr pck bl (C)	55	55
210	A24(q)	1.50fr ultra (C)	25	25
211	A22(r)	1.60fr dk car rose	60	60
212	A24(q)	1.75fr ol grn (C)	30	30
213	A22(r)	1.75fr dk bl (C)	1.20	1.20
214	A24(q)	2fr vermilion	25	25
215	A22(r)	2.25fr brt ultra (C)	55	55
216	A22(r)	2.50fr chnt (BlV)	1.90	1.90
217	A24(q)	3fr pur (C)	25	25
218	A24(q)	5fr brn lake (BlV)	55	55
219	A24(q)	10fr dk bl (C)	2.00	2.00
220	A24(q)	20fr red brn (BlV)	3.75	3.75

New York World's Fair Issue Overprinted in Black or Carmine

221	CD82(q)	1.25fr car lake	65	65
222	CD82(q)	2.25fr ultra (C)	65	65
		Nos. 178-222 (45)	42.35	42.35

No. 177A Overprinted Type "q"

1943 Unwmk. *Perf. 12½*

223	A23	1fr on 65c ol grn	25	25

Catalogue values for unused stamps in this section, from this point to the end of the section, are for Never Hinged items.

Produce of Reunion
A26

1943 Photo. *Perf. 14½x14*

224	A26	5c dull brn	5	5
225	A26	10c dark bl	5	5
226	A26	25c emerald	5	5
227	A26	30c deep org	5	5
228	A26	40c dk sl grn	12	12
229	A26	80c rose vio	16	16
230	A26	1fr red brn	15	15
231	A26	1.50fr crimson	16	16
232	A26	2fr black	16	16
233	A26	2.50fr ultra	16	16
234	A26	4fr dark vio	20	20
235	A26	5fr bister	25	25
236	A26	10fr dark brn	50	50
237	A26	20fr dk green	60	60
		Nos. 224-237 (14)	2.66	2.66

Eboue Issue

Common Design Type

1945 Engr. *Perf. 13*

238	CD91	2fr black	25	25
239	CD91	25fr Prussian grn	35	35

Nos. 224, 226 and 233 Surcharged with New Values and Bars in Carmine or Black

1945 *Perf. 14½x14*

240	A26	50c on 5c dl brn (C)	5	5
241	A26	60c on 5c dl brn (C)	5	5
242	A26	70c on 5c dl brn (C)	5	5
243	A26	1.20fr on 5c dl brn (C)	12	12
244	A26	2.40fr on 25c emer	12	12
245	A26	3fr on 25c emer	20	20
246	A26	4.50fr on 25c emer	25	25
247	A26	15fr on 2.50fr ultra (C)	32	32
		Nos. 240-247 (8)	1.16	1.16

Cliff — A27

Cutting Sugar Cane — A28

Cascade
A29

Banana Tree
A30

Mountain Scene — A31

Ship Approaching Reunion
A32

1947 Unwmk. Photo. *Perf. 13½*

249	A27	10c org & grnsh blk	5	5
250	A27	30c org & brt bl	5	5
251	A27	40c org & brn	5	5
252	A28	50c bl grn & brn	10	10
253	A28	60c dk bl & brn	10	10
254	A28	80c brn & ol brn	16	16
255	A29	1fr dl bl & vio brn	10	10
256	A29	1.20fr bl grn & gray	16	16
257	A29	1.50fr org & vio brn	16	16
258	A30	2fr gray bl & bl grn	16	16
259	A30	3fr vio brn & bl grn	16	16
260	A30	3.60fr dl red & rose red	20	20
261	A30	4fr gray bl & buff	20	16
262	A31	5fr rose lil & brn	20	20
263	A31	6fr bl & brn	35	30
264	A31	10fr org & ultra	55	38
265	A32	15fr gray bl & vio brn	1.40	1.00
266	A32	20fr bl & org	1.60	1.40
267	A32	25fr rose lil & brn	2.00	1.50
		Nos. 249-267 (19)	7.75	6.39

Stamps of France, 1945-49, Surcharged in Black or Carmine

10c CFA a

2F-CFA b

1949 Unwmk. *Perf. 14x13½, 13*

268	A154(a)	10c on 30c blk, red org & yel	16	10
269	A155(a)	30c on 50c brn, yel & red	15	12
270	A146(a)	50c on 1fr rose red	20	20
271	A146(a)	60c on 2fr lt bl grn	3.25	60
272	A147(b)	1fr on 3fr dp rose	38	30
273	A147(b)	2fr on 4fr lt bl grn	1.90	50
274	A147(b)	2.50fr on 5fr bl	9.00	6.00
275	A147(b)	3fr on 6fr crim rose	80	30
276	A147(b)	4fr on 10fr brt vio	80	40
277	A162(a)	5fr on 20fr sl gray (C)	1.50	50
278	A147(b)	6fr on 12fr ultra	3.25	60
279	A160(a)	7fr on 12fr rose car	2.25	80
280	A165(a)	8fr on 25fr dk bl (C)	11.00	2.00
281	A165(a)	10fr on 25fr blk brn (C)	60	50
282	A174(a)	11fr on 18fr dk bl (C)	3.75	1.00
		Nos. 268-282 (15)	38.99	13.92

The letters "C. F. A." are the initials of "Colonies Francaises d'Afrique," referring to the currency which is expressed in French Africa francs.

The surcharge on Nos. 277, 279, 282 includes two bars.

1950 *Perf. 14x13½*

283	A182(a)	10c on 50c bl, red & yel	12	10
284	A182(a)	1fr on 2fr grn, yel & red (#619)	3.75	2.00
285	A147(b)	2fr on 5fr lt grn	5.00	2.00

Surcharged Type "a" and Bars

1950-51 *Perf. 13*

286	A188	5fr on 20fr dk red	3.50	45
287	A185	8fr on 25fr dp ultra ('51)	1.60	50

Stamps of France, 1951-52, Surcharged in Black or Red

1951-52 *Perf. 14x13½, 13*

288	A182(a)	50c on 1fr bl, red & yel	20	20
289	A182(a)	1fr on 2fr vio bl, red & yel (#662)	35	30
290	A147(b)	2fr on 5fr dl vio	55	40
291	A147(b)	3fr on 6fr grn	2.25	1.00
292	A220(a)	5fr on 20fr dk pur ('52)	55	50
293	A147(b)	6fr on 12fr red org ('52)	3.75	60
294	A215(a)	8fr on 40fr vio (R) ('52)	2.25	35
295	A147(b)	9fr on 18fr cer	4.00	1.90
296	A208(a)	15fr on 30fr ind (R)	1.50	60
		Nos. 288-296 (9)	15.40	5.85

The surcharge on Nos. 292, 294 and 296 include two bars.

France, No. 697 Surcharged Type "a" in Black

1953 *Perf. 14x13½*

297	A182	50c on 1fr blk, red & yel	20	20

France, No. 688 Surcharged in Black

=

c

3F CFA

Perf. 13

298	A230	3fr on 6fr dp plum & car	40	30

France Nos. 703 and 705 Surcharged Type "a" in Red or Blue

1954

299	A235	8fr on 40fr choc & ind (R)	12.00	3.50
300	A235	20fr on 75fr org & cl	45.00	21.00

France Nos. 698, 721, 713, and 715 Surcharged Type "a" in Black

Perf. 14x13½, 13

301	A182	1fr on 2fr brn, bl & yel	60	30
302	A241	4fr on 10fr aqua & org brn	80	38
303	A238	8fr on 40fr dk brn, vio brn & org brn	3.00	20
304	A238	20fr on 75fr dp car & mag	3.50	50

The surcharge on Nos. 303 and 304 includes two bars.

France Nos. 737, 719 and 722-724 Surcharged in Black or Red

305	A182(a)	1fr on 2fr blk, red & yel	30	30
306	A241(a)	2fr on 6fr ultra, ind & dk grn (R)	30	25
307	A242(a)	6fr on 12fr rose vio & dk vio	1.40	38
308	A241(b)	9fr on 18fr bl, dk grn & ind	3.50	2.50
309	A241(a)	10fr on 20fr blk brn, bl grn & red brn	1.50	50
		Nos. 299-309 (11)	71.90	29.81

The surcharge on Nos. 306-308 includes two bars; on No. 309 three bars.

France No. 720 Surcharged Type "c" in Red, Bars at Lower Left

1955 *Perf. 13*

310	A241	3fr on 8fr brt bl & dk grn	50	30

France Nos. 785, 774-779 Surcharged Type "a" in Black or Red

Perf. 14x13½, 13

1955-56 Typo., Engr.

311	A182	50c on 1fr bl, red & yel	10	10
312	A265	2fr on 6fr car lake ('56)	50	40
313	A265	3fr on 8fr ind	35	30
314	A265	4fr on 10fr dp ultra	35	30
315	A265	5fr on 12fr vio & brn (R)	60	30
316	A265	6fr on 18fr bluish grn & ind (R)	40	30
317	A265	10fr on 25fr org brn & red brn	65	20
		Nos. 311-317 (7)	2.95	1.90

The surcharge on Nos. 312-317 includes two bars.

France Nos. 801-804 Surcharged Type "a" or "b" in Black or Red

1956 Engr. *Perf. 13*

318	A280(a)	8fr on 30fr gray vio & blk (R)	2.00	20
319	A280(b)	9fr on 40fr brn & vio brn	2.50	80
320	A280(a)	15fr on 50fr rose vio & vio	2.50	65
321	A280(a)	20fr on 75fr ind, grn & bl (R)	3.50	90

The surcharge on Nos. 318, 319 and 321 includes two bars.

France Nos. 837 and 839 Surcharged Type "a" in Red

1957 ***Perf. 13***

322 A294 7fr on 15fr dk bl grn & sep 60 40
323 A265 17fr on 70fr blk & dl grn 3.00 1.20

The surcharge on Nos. 322-323 includes two bars.

No. 322 has three types of "7" in the sheet of 50. There are 34 of the "normal" 7; 10 of a slightly thinner 7, and 6 of a slightly thicker 7.

France Nos. 755-756, 833-834, 851-855, 908, 949 Surcharged in Black or Red Type "a", "b" or

d **50F CFA**

Typographed, Engraved

1957-60 ***Perf. 14x13½, 13***

324 A236(b) 2fr on 6fr org 20 15
325 A302(b) 3fr on 10fr dk ol bis & vio brn ('58) 20 20
326 A236(b) 4fr on 12fr red lil 1.60 40
327 A236(b) 5fr on 10fr brt grn 90 25
328 A303(b) 6fr on 18fr ind & dk brn 35 30
329 A302(a) 9fr on 25fr bl gray & vio brn (R) ('58) 50 32
330 A252(a) 10fr on 20fr ultra (R) 55 12
331 A252(a) 12fr on 25fr rose red 2.50 20
332 A303(a) 17fr on 35fr car rose & lake 1.60 80
333 A302(a) 20fr on 50fr ol grn & ol bis 80 42
334 A302(a) 25fr on 85fr dp cl 2.00 62
335 A339(d) 50fr on 1fr vio bl, bl & grn ('60) 1.50 45
Nos. 324-335 (12) 12.70 4.23

The surcharge includes two bars on Nos. 324, 326-327, 329-331, 333 and 335.

France Nos. 973, 939 and 968 Surcharged

2f CFA e **12f CFA** f

1961-63 **Typo.** ***Perf. 14x13½***

336 A318(e) 2fr on 5c multi 10 10
337 A336(e) 5fr on 10c brt grn 20 20
338 A336(b) 5fr on 10c brt grn ('63) 62 30
339 A349(f) 12fr on 25c lake & gray 16 10

The surcharge on No. 337 includes three bars. No. 338 has "b" surcharge and two bars.

France Nos. 943, 941 and 946 Surcharged "CFA" and New Value in Two Lines in Black or Red

Engraved, Typographed

1961 **Unwmk.** ***Perf. 13, 14x13½***

340 A338 7fr on 15c bl & ind 50 28
341 A337 10fr on 20c grnsh bl & car rose 10 10
342 A339 20fr on 50c sl grn & lt cl (R) 8.25 2.25

Surcharge on No. 342 includes 3 bars.

France Nos. 1047-1048 Surcharged with New Value, "CFA" and Two Bars

1963, Jan. 2 **Engr.** ***Perf. 13***

343 A394 12fr on 25c gray, yel & grn 50 50
344 A395 25fr on 50c dk bl, grn & ultra 50 50

1st television connection of the US and Europe through the Telstar satellite, July 11-12, 1962.

France Nos. 1040-1041, 1007 and 1009 Surcharged Similarly to Type "e"

Typographed, Engraved

1963 ***Perf. 14x13½, 13***

345 A318 2fr on 5c ver, ultra & yel 10 10
346 A318 5fr on 10c red, ultra & yel 10 10
347 A372 7fr on 15c bl & pur 20 20
348 A372 20fr on 45c vio bl, red brn & grn 50 20

Two-line surcharge on No. 345; No. 347 has currency expressed in capital "F" and two heavy bars through old value; two thin bars on No. 348.

France No. 1078 Surcharged Type "e" in Two Lines in Dark Blue.

1964, Feb. 8 **Engr.** ***Perf. 13***

349 CD118 12fr on 25c dk gray, sl grn & dk car 50 40

"PHILATEC," International Philatelic and Postal Techniques Exhib., Paris, June 5-21, 1964.

France Nos. 1092, 1094 and 1102 Surcharged with New Value and "CFA"

Typographed, Engraved

1964 ***Perf. 14x13½, 13***

350 A318 1fr on 2c emer, vio bl & yel 10 10
351 A318 6fr on 18c multi 20 20
352 A420 35fr on 70c sl, grn & car 60 50

Surcharge on No. 352 includes two bars.

France Nos. 1095, 1126, 1070 Surcharged with New Value and "CFA"

1965

353 A318 15fr on 30c vio bl & red 20 10
354 A440 25fr on 50c multi 45 38
355 A408 30fr on 60c ultra, dk grn & hn brn 60 50

Two bars obliterate old denomination on Nos. 354-355.

Etienne Regnault, "Le Taureau" and Coast of Reunion — A33

1965, Oct. 3 **Engr.** ***Perf. 13***

356 A33 15fr bluish blk & dk car 30 20

Tercentenary of settlement of Reunion.

France No. 985 Surcharged with New Value, Two Bars and "CFA"

1966, Feb. 13 **Engr.** ***Perf. 13***

357 A360 10fr on 20c bl & car 80 30

French Satellite A-1 Issue

France Nos. 1137-1138 Surcharged with New Value, Two Bars and "CFA" and Red

1966, Mar. 27 **Engr.** ***Perf. 13***

358 CD121 15fr on 30c Prus bl, brt bl & blk 45 40
359 CD121 30fr on 60c blk, Prus bl & brt bl 55 50
a. Strip of 2 + label 1.10 1.10

France Nos. 1142, 1143, 1101 and 1127 Surcharged with New Value, "CFA" and Two Bars

1967-69 **Typo.** ***Perf. 14x13***

360 A446 2fr on 5c bl & red 10 10

Photo. ***Perf. 13***

360A A446 10fr on 20c multi ('69) 12 10

Engr.

361 A421 20fr on 40c multi 28 25
362 A439 30fr on 60c bl & red brn 40 30

EXPO '67 Issue

France No. 1177 Surcharged with New Value, "CFA" and Two Bars

1967, June 12 **Engr.** ***Perf. 13***

363 A473 30fr on 60c dl bl & bl grn 50 45

EXPO '67, Montreal, Apr. 28-Oct. 27.

Lions Issue

France No. 1196 Surcharged in Violet Blue with New Value, "CFA" and Two Bars

1967, Oct. 29 **Engr.** ***Perf. 13***

364 A485 20fr on 40c dk car & vio bl 42 32

50th anniversary of Lions International.

France No. 1130 Surcharged in Violet Blue with New Value, "CFA" and Two Bars

1968, Feb. 26 **Engr.** ***Perf. 13***

365 A440 50fr on 1fr gray, grn & brn 65 50

France No. 1224 Surcharged with New Value, "CFA" and Two Bars

1968, Oct. 21 **Engr.** ***Perf. 13***

366 A508 20fr on 40c multi 40 35

20 years of French Polar expeditions.

France Nos. 1230-1231 Surcharged with New Value, "CFA" and Two Bars

1969, Apr. 13 **Engr.** ***Perf. 13***

367 A486 15fr on 30c grn 25 20
368 A486 20fr on 40c dp car 30 10

France No. 1255 Surcharged with New Value, "CFA" and Two Bars

1969, Aug. 18 **Engr.** ***Perf. 13***

370 A526 35fr on 70c multi 70 50

Napoleon Bonaparte (1769-1821).

France No. 1293 Surcharged with New Value and "CFA"

1971, Jan. 16 **Engr.** ***Perf. 13***

371 A555 25fr on 50c rose car 35 10

France No. 1301 Surcharged with New Value and "CFA"

1971, Apr. 13 **Engr.** ***Perf. 13***

372 A562 40fr on 80c multi 55 50

France No. 1309 Surcharged with New Value, "CFA" and 2 Bars

1971, June 5 **Engr.** ***Perf. 13***

373 A569 15fr on 40c multi 30 30

Aid for rural families.

France No. 1312 Surcharged with New Value and "CFA"

1971, Aug. 30 **Engr.** ***Perf. 13***

374 A571 45fr on 90c multi 45 40

France No. 1320 Surcharged with New Value and "CFA"

1971, Oct. 18

375 A573 45fr on 90c multi 60 50

40th anniversary of the first assembly of presidents of artisans' guilds.

Réunion Chameleon A34

1971, Nov. 8 **Photo.** ***Perf. 13***

376 A34 25fr multi 50 30

Nature protection.

Common Design Type and

De Gaulle in Brazzaville, 1944 — A35

Designs: No. 377, Gen. de Gaulle, 1940. No. 379, de Gaulle entering Paris, 1944. No. 380, Pres. de Gaulle, 1970.

1971, Nov. 9 **Engr.**

377 CD134 25fr black 45 40
378 A35 25fr ultra 45 40
379 A35 25fr rose red 45 40
380 CD134 25fr black 45 40
a. Strip of 4 + label 2.00 1.60

Charles de Gaulle (1890-1970), president of France. Nos. 377-380 printed se-tenant in sheets of 20 containing 5 strips of 4 plus labels with Cross of Lorraine and inscription.

France No. 1313 Surcharged with New Value and "CFA"

1972, Jan. 17 **Engr.** ***Perf. 13***

381 A570 50fr on 1.10fr multi 60 50

Map of South Indian Ocean, Penguin and Ships — A36

1972, Jan. 31 **Engr.** ***Perf. 13***

382 A36 45fr blk, bl & ocher 60 60

Bicentenary of the discovery of the Crozet and Kerguelen Islands.

France No. 1342 Surcharged with New New Value, "CFA" and 2 Bars in Red

1972, May. 8 **Engr.** ***Perf. 13***

383 A590 15fr on 40c red 30 30

20th anniv. of Blood Donors' Assoc. of Post and Telecommunications Employees.

France Nos. 1345-1346 Surcharged with New Value, "CFA" and 2 Bars

1972, June 5 **Typo.** ***Perf. 14x13***

384 A593 15fr on 30c multi 20 20
385 A593 25fr on 50c multi 25 20

Introduction of postal code system.

France No. 1377 Surcharged with New Value, "CFA" and 2 Bars in Ultramarine

1973, June 12 **Engr.** ***Perf. 13***

386 A620 45fr on 90c multi 50 40

France Nos. 1374, 1336 Surcharged with New Value and "CFA" in Ultramarine or Red

1973 **Engr.** ***Perf. 13***

387 A617 50fr on 1fr multi (U) 45 38
388 A586 100fr on 2fr multi (R) 1.10 55

Issue dates: 50fr, June 24; 100fr, Oct. 13. On No. 388, two bars cover "2.00".

France No. 1231C Surcharged with New Value, "CFA" and 2 Bars

1973, Nov. **Typo.** ***Perf. 14x13***

389 A486 15fr on 30c bl grn 28 20

France No. 1390 Surcharged with New Value, "CFA" and 2 Bars in Red

1974, Jan. 20 **Engr.** ***Perf. 13***

390 A633 25fr on 50c multi 30 20

ARPHILA 75 Phil. Exhib., Paris, June 1975.

France Nos. 1394-1397 Surcharged "100 FCFA" in Black, Ultramarine or Brown

Engr. (#391, 393), Photo. (#392, 394)

1974 ***Perf. 12x13, 13x12***

391 A637 100fr on 2fr (Bk) 90 75
392 A638 100fr on 2fr (U) 90 75
393 A639 100fr on 2fr (Br) 1.00 75
394 A640 100fr on 2fr (U) 90 75

Nos. 391-394 printed in sheets of 25 with alternating labels publicizing "ARPHILA 75," Paris June 6-16, 1975.

Two bars obliterate original denomination on Nos. 391-393.

France No. 1401 Surcharged "45 FCFA" and 2 Bars in Red

1974, Apr. 29 Engr. *Perf. 13*
395 A644 45fr on 90c multi 55 45

Reorganized sea rescue organization.

France No. 1415 Surcharged with New Value, 2 Bars and "FCFA" in Ultramarine

1974, Oct. 6 Engr. *Perf. 13*
396 A657 60fr on 1.20fr multi 65 60

Centenary of Universal Postal Union.

France Nos. 1292A and 1294B Surcharged with New Value and "FCFA" in Ultramarine

1974, Oct. 19 Typo. *Perf. 14x13*
397 A555 30fr on 60c grn 1.00 1.00

Engr.
Perf. 13
398 A555 40fr on 80c car rose 1.20 1.00

SEMI-POSTAL STAMPS

Regular Issue of 1907 Surcharged in Black or Red

1915 Unwmk. *Perf. 14x13½*
B1 A19 10c + 5c car & grn (Bk) 42.50 40.00
a. Inverted surcharge 100.00 80.00
B2 A19 10c + 5c car & grn (R) 50 50
a. Inverted surcharge 22.50 22.50

Regular Issue of 1907 Surcharged in Red

1916
B3 A19 10c + 5c car & grn 40 40

Curie Issue
Common Design Type

1938 *Perf. 13*
B4 CD80 1.75fr + 50c brt ultra 5.00 5.00

French Revolution Issue
Common Design Type

1939 Photo. Unwmk.
Name and Value Typo. in Black
B5 CD83 45(c) + 25(c) grn 3.00 3.00
B6 CD83 70(c) + 30(c) brn 3.00 3.00
B7 CD83 90(c) + 35(c) red org 3.00 3.00
B8 CD83 1.25fr + 1fr rose pink 3.00 3.00
B9 CD83 2.25fr + 2fr blue 3.00 3.00
Nos. B5-B9 (5) 15.00 15.00

Common Design Type and

Artillery Colonel
SP1

Colonial Infantry
SP2

1941 Unwmk. *Perf. 13½*
B10 SP1 1fr + 1fr red 40
B11 CD86 1.50fr + 3fr claret 40
B12 SP2 2.50fr + 1fr blue 40

Nos. B10-B12 were issued by the Vichy government and were not placed on sale in Reunion.

In 1944 the Vichy government surcharged Nos. 176-177 with "OEUVRES COLONIALES" and surtax, changing the denomination of the 2.50fr to 50c. These were not placed on sale in Reunion.

Catalogue values for unused stamps in this section, from this point to the end of the section, are for Never Hinged items.

Red Cross Issue
Common Design Type

1944 *Perf. 14½x14*
B15 CD90 5fr + 20fr blk 35 35

The surtax was for the French Red Cross and national relief.

France Nos. B365-B366 Surcharged with New Value, "CFA" and Two Bars

1962, Dec. 10 Engr. *Perf. 13*
Cross in Red
B16 SP219 10fr + 5fr on 20c + 10c redsh brn 1.20 1.20
B17 SP219 12fr + 5fr on 25c + 10c dl grn 1.20 1.20

The surtax was for the Red Cross.

France Nos. B374-B375 Surcharged with New Value, "CFA" and Two Bars in Red

1963, Dec. 9
Cross in Red
B18 SP223 10fr + 5fr on 20c + 10c blk 2.00 2.00
B19 SP223 12fr + 5fr on 25c + 10c sl grn 2.00 2.00

Centenary of the Intl. Red Cross. The surtax was for the Red Cross.

France Nos. B385-B386 Surcharged with New Value, "CFA" and Two Bars in Dark Blue

1964, Dec. 13 Unwmk. *Perf. 13*
Cross in Carmine
B20 SP230 10fr + 5fr on 20c + 10c blk 80 80
B21 SP230 12fr + 5fr on 25c + 10c blk 80 80

Jean Nicolas Corvisart (1755-1821) and Dominique Larrey (1766-1842), physicians. The surtax was for the Red Cross.

France Nos. B392-B393 Surcharged with New Value, "CFA" and Two Bars

1965, Dec. 12 Engr. *Perf. 13*
Cross in Carmine
B22 SP233 12fr + 5fr on 25c + 10c sl 80 80
B23 SP233 15fr + 5fr on 30c + 10c dl red brn 80 80

The surtax was for the Red Cross.

France Nos. B402-B403 Surcharged with New Value, "CFA" and Two Bars

1966, Dec. 11 Engr. *Perf. 13*
Cross in Carmine
B24 SP237 12fr + 5fr on 25c + 10c grn 65 60
B25 SP237 15fr + 5fr on 30c + 10c slate 65 60

The surtax was for the Red Cross.

France Nos. B409-B410 Surcharged with New Value, "CFA" and Two Bars

1967, Dec. 17 Engr. *Perf. 13*
Cross in Carmine
B26 SP240 12fr + 5fr on 25c + 10c dl vio & lt brn 1.25 1.25
B27 SP240 15fr + 5fr on 30c + 10c grn & lt brn 1.25 1.25

Surtax for the Red Cross.

France Nos. B421-B424 Surcharged with New Value, "CFA" and Two Bars

1968-69 Engr. *Perf. 13*
Cross in Carmine
B28 SP244 12fr + 5fr on 25c + 10c pur & sl bl 1.00 80
B29 SP244 15fr + 5fr on 30c + 10c 1.00 80
B30 SP244 20fr + 7fr on 40c + 15c dk brn & brn ('69) 70 70
B31 SP244 20fr + 7fr on 40c + 15c pur & Prus bl ('69) 70 70

The surtax was for the Red Cross.

France No. B425 Surcharged with New Value, "CFA" and Two Bars

1969, Mar. 17 Engr. *Perf. 13*
B32 SP245 15fr + 5fr on 30c + 10c multi 50 50

Stamp Day.

France No. B440 Surcharged with New Value, "CFA" and Two Bars

1970, Mar. 16 Engr. *Perf. 13*
B33 SP249 20fr + 5fr on 40c + 10c multi 50 40

Stamp day.

France Nos. B443-B444 Surcharged with New Value "CFA" and Two Bars

1970, Dec. 14 Engr. *Perf. 13*
Cross in Carmine
B34 SP252 20fr + 7fr on 40c + 15c grn 1.50 1.40
B35 SP252 20fr + 7fr on 40c + 15c cop red 1.50 1.40

The surtax was for the Red Cross.

France No. B451 Surcharged with New Value, "CFA" and Two Bars

1971, Mar. 29 Engr. *Perf. 13*
B36 SP254 25fr + 5fr on 50c + 10c multi 40 35

Stamp Day.

France Nos. B452-B453 Surcharged with New Value, "CFA" and Two Bars

1971, Dec. 13
Cross in Carmine
B37 SP255 15fr + 5fr on 30c + 10c vio bl 65 65
B38 SP255 25fr + 5fr on 50c + 10c dp car 65 65

The surtax was for the Red Cross.

France No. B460 Surcharged with New Value and "CFA"

1972, Mar. 20 Engr. *Perf. 13*
B39 SP257 25fr + 5fr on 50c + 10c multi 42 42

Stamp Day.

France Nos. B461-B462 Surcharged with New Value, "CFA" and Two Bars in Red or Green

1972, Dec. 16 Engr. *Perf. 13*
B40 SP258 15fr + 5fr on 30c + 10c sl grn & red (R) 60 60
B41 SP258 25fr + 5fr on 50c + 10c red (G) 65 65

Surtax was for the Red Cross.

France No. B470 Surcharged with New Value, "CFA" and Two Bars in Red

1973, Mar. 26 Engr. *Perf. 13*
B42 SP260 25fr + 5fr on 50c + 10c grnsh bl 65 60

Stamp Day.

The Catalogue editors cannot undertake to appraise, identify or judge the genuineness or condition of stamps.

France Nos. B471-B472 Surcharged with New Value, "CFA" and Two Bars in Red

1973, Dec. 3 Engr. *Perf. 13*
B43 SP261 15 + 5fr on 30c + 10c sl grn & red 65 65
B44 SP261 25 + 5fr on 50c + 10c 80 80

Surtax was for the Red Cross.

France No. B477 Surcharged "25 + 5 FCFA"

1974, Mar. 11 Engr. *Perf. 13*
B45 SP263 25fr + 5fr on 50c + 10c multi 30 30

Stamp Day.

France Nos. B479-B480 Surcharged with New Value, "FCFA" and Two Bars in Green or Red

1974, Nov. 30 Engr. *Perf. 13*
B46 SP265 30fr + 7fr on 60c + 15c (G) 65 65
B47 SP266 40fr + 7fr on 80c + 15c (R) 80 80

Surtax was for the Red Cross.

AIR POST STAMPS

No. 141 Overprinted in Blue

RÉUNION • FRANCE
par avion
« *ROLAND GARROS* »

1937, Jan. 23 Unwmk. *Perf. 12½*
C1 A23 50c red 110.00 100.00
a. Pair, one without ovpt. 600.00 600.00
b. Inverted overprint *1,500.*

Flight of the "Roland Garros" from Reunion to France by aviators Laurent, Lenier and Touge in Jan.-Feb., 1937.

Airplane and Landscape — AP2

1938, Mar. 1 Engr. *Perf. 12½*
C2 AP2 3.65(fr) sl bl & car 30 30
C3 AP2 6.65(fr) brn & org red 30 30
C4 AP2 9.65(fr) car & ultra 30 30
C5 AP2 12.65(fr) brn & grn 65 65

Plane and Bridge over East River
AP3

Plane and Landscape
AP4

1942, Oct. 19 *Perf. 12x12½*
C6 AP3 50c ol & pur 15
C7 AP3 1fr dk bl & scar 15
C8 AP3 2fr brn & blk 20
C9 AP3 3fr rose lil & grn 28
C10 AP3 5fr red org & red brn 28

Frame Engr., Center Photo.
C11 AP4 10fr dk grn, red org & vio 25
C12 AP4 20fr dk bl, brn vio & red 38

C13 AP4 50fr brn car, Prus grn & bl 42
Nos. C6-C13 (8) 2.11

There is doubt whether Nos. C6-C13 were officially placed in use.

V2

Stamps of the above design were issued in 1943 by the Vichy Government, but were not placed on sale in Reunion.

Nos. C2-C5 Overprinted in Black or Carmine

France
Libre

1943	Unwmk.	Perf. 12½	
C14 AP2	3.65fr sl bl & car	1.20	1.20
C15 AP2	6.65fr brn & org red	1.20	1.20
C16 AP2	9.65fr car & ultra (C)	1.20	1.20
C17 AP2	12.65fr brn & grn	1.20	1.20

Catalogue values for unused stamps in this section, from this point to the end of the section, are for Never Hinged items.

Common Design Type

1944	Photo.	Perf. 14½x14	
C18 CD87	1fr dk org	15	15
C19 CD87	1.50fr brt red	15	15
C20 CD87	5fr brn red	16	16
C21 CD87	10fr black	25	25
C22 CD87	25fr ultra	25	25
C23 CD87	50fr dk grn	25	25
C24 CD87	100fr plum	45	45
	Nos. C18-C24 (7)	1.66	1.66

Victory Issue

Common Design Type

1946, May 8	Engr.	Perf. 12½	
C25 CD92	8fr ol gray	35	35

European victory of the Allied Nations in WWII.

Chad to Rhine Issue

Common Design Types

1946, June 6			
C26 CD93	5fr orange	45	45
C27 CD94	10fr sepia	45	45
C28 CD95	15fr grnsh blk	45	45
C29 CD96	20fr lil rose	55	55
C30 CD97	25fr grnsh bl	60	60
C31 CD98	50fr green	60	60
	Nos. C26-C31 (6)	3.10	3.10

Shadow of Plane — AP5

Plane over Reunion — AP6

Air View of Reunion and Shadow of Plane — AP7

Perf. 13x12½

1947, Mar. 24	Photo.	Unwmk.	
C32 AP5	50fr ol grn & bl gray	3.25	2.50
C33 AP6	100fr dk brn & org	4.50	4.00
C34 AP7	200fr dk bl & org	5.75	5.50

France, Nos. C18 to C21 Surcharged and Bars, in Carmine or Black

20F
CFA
c

1949	Unwmk.	Perf. 13	
C35 AP7	20fr on 40fr dk grn (C)	1.00	55
C36 AP8	25fr on 50fr rose pink	1.20	55
C37 AP9	50fr on 100fr dk bl (C)	3.25	1.90
C38 AP10	100fr on 200fr red	15.00	11.00

France Nos. C24, C26 and C27 Surcharged Type "c" and Bars in Black

1949-51			
C39 AP12	100fr on 200fr dk bl grn ('51)	42.50	13.50
C40 AP12	200fr on 500fr brt red	20.00	12.00
C41 AP13	500fr on 1000fr sep, *bl* ('51)	100.00	90.00

France Nos. C29-C32 Surcharged "CFA," New Value and Bars in Blue or Red

1954, Feb. 10			
C42 AP15(c)	50fr on 100fr red brn & bl	1.40	65
C43 AP15	100fr on 200fr blk brn & vio bl (R)	3.00	55
C44 AP15(c)	200fr on 500fr car & org	14.00	9.00
C45 AP15	500fr on 1000fr vio brn, bl grn & ind	16.00	8.25

France Nos. C35-C36 Surcharged "CFA," New Values and Bars in Red or Black

1957-58	Engr.	Perf. 13	
C46 AP17	200fr on 500fr dp ultra & blk (R)	9.00	4.00
C47 AP17	500fr on 1000fr lil, ol blk & blk ('58)	14.00	8.00

France Nos. C37, C39-C40 Surcharged "CFA," New Value and Bars in Red or Black

1961-64			
C48 AP15	100fr on 2fr vio bl & ultra	2.00	75
C49 AP17	200fr on 5fr dp ultra & blk	3.00	1.25
C50 AP17	500fr on 10fr lil, ol & blk (B) ('64)	8.25	3.50

France No. C41 Surcharged "CFA," New Value and Two Bars in Red

1967, Jan. 27	Engr.	Perf. 13	
C51 AP17	100fr on 2fr sl bl & ind	1.00	40

France No. C45 Surcharged in Red with "CFA," New Value and Two Bars in Red

1972, May 14	Engr.	Perf. 13	
C52 AP21	200fr on 5fr multi	2.50	1.10

AIR POST SEMI-POSTAL STAMP

French Revolution Issue

Common Design Type

1939	Unwmk.	Perf. 13	
	Name and Value Typo. in Orange		
CB1 CD83	3.65fr + 4fr brn blk	7.00	7.00

V3

Stamps of the above design and type of Cameroun V10 inscribed "Reunion" were issued in 1942 by the Vichy Government, but were not placed on sale in Reunion.

POSTAGE DUE STAMPS

D1

D2

1889-92	Unwmk.	Type-set	Imperf.
	Yellowish or Bluish White Paper		
J1 D1	5c black	6.00	3.75
J2 D1	10c black	8.25	3.75
J3 D1	15c black ('92)	18.00	9.00
J4 D1	20c black	15.00	8.25
J5 D1	30c black	12.50	7.00

Ten varieties of each value.
Nos. J1-J5 exist with double impression. Values $12.50-$25.

1907	Typo.	Perf. 14x13½	
J6 D2	5c carmine, *yel*	22	22
J7 D2	10c blue, *bl*	22	22
J8 D2	15c blk, *bluish*	30	30
J9 D2	20c carmine	30	30
J10 D2	30c green, *grnsh*	45	45
J11 D2	50c red, *green*	55	55
J12 D2	60c carmine, *bl*	55	55
J13 D2	1fr violet	90	90
	Nos. J6-J13 (8)	3.49	3.49

Type of 1907 Issue Surcharged

= 2F. =

1927			
J14 D2	2fr on 1fr org red	3.50	3.50
J15 D2	3fr on 1fr org brn	3.50	3.50

Arms of Reunion
D3

Numeral
D4

1933	Engr.	Perf. 13x13½	
J16 D3	5c deep vio	5	5
J17 D3	10c dark grn	5	5
J18 D3	15c orange brn	5	5
J19 D3	20c light red	5	5
J20 D3	30c olive grn	10	10
J21 D3	50c ultra	20	20
J22 D3	60c black brn	20	20
J23 D3	1fr light vio	20	20
J24 D3	2fr deep bl	20	20
J25 D3	3fr carmine	20	20
	Nos. J16-J25 (10)	1.30	1.30

Catalogue values for unused stamps in this section, from this point to the end of the section, are for Never Hinged items.

1947	Unwmk. Photo.	Perf. 13	
J26 D4	10c dk vio	5	5
J27 D4	30c brown	5	5
J28 D4	50c bl grn	5	5
J29 D4	1fr orange	12	12
J30 D4	2fr red vio	15	15
J31 D4	3fr red brn	15	15
J32 D4	4fr blue	42	42
J33 D4	5fr henna brn	42	42
J34 D4	10fr slate grn	42	42
J35 D4	20fr vio blue	55	55
	Nos. J26-J35 (10)	2.38	2.38

France, Nos. J83 to J92 Surcharged in Black

50c
CFA

1949-53			
J36 D5	10c on 1fr brt ultra	10	10
J37 D5	50c on 2fr turq bl	10	10
J38 D5	1fr on 3fr brn org	20	20
J39 D5	2fr on 4fr dp vio	30	30
J40 D5	3fr on 5fr brt pink	1.90	1.50
J41 D5	5fr on 10fr red org	55	50
J42 D5	10fr on 20fr ol bis	1.40	1.25
J43 D5	20fr on 50fr dk grn ('50)	4.25	2.50
J44 D5	50fr on 100fr dp grn ('53)	12.50	8.25
	Nos. J36-J44 (9)	21.30	14.70

Same Surcharge on France Nos. J93, J95-J96

1962-63	Typo.	Perf. 14x13½	
J46 D6	1fr on 5c brt pink ('63)	70	70
J47 D6	10fr on 20c ol bis ('63)	1.25	1.25
J48 D6	20fr on 50c dk grn	11.00	8.00

France Nos. J98-J102, J104-J105 Surcharged with New Value and "CFA"

1964-71	Unwmk.	Perf. 14x13½	
J49 D7	1fr on 5c car rose, red & grn	10	10
J50 D7	5fr on 10c car rose, brt bl & grn	15	15
J51 D7	7fr on 15c brn, grn & red	20	20
J52 D7	10fr on 20c multi ('71)	70	50
J53 D7	15fr on 30c brn, ultra & grn	20	20
J54 D7	20fr on 50c vio bl, car & grn	30	30
J55 D7	50fr on 1fr vio bl, lil & grn	90	60
	Nos. J49-J55 (7)	2.55	2.05

PARCEL POST STAMP

No. 40 Overprinted

Colis Postaux

1906	Unwmk.	Perf. 14x13½	
Q1 A14	10c red	4.00	4.00

RIO DE ORO

LOCATION — On the northwest coast of Africa, bordering on the Atlantic Ocean.
GOVT. — Spanish Colony.
AREA — 71,600 sq. mi.
POP. — 24,000.
CAPITAL — Villa Cisneros.

Rio de Oro became part of Spanish Sahara.

100 Centimos = 1 Peseta

King Alfonso XIII
A1 A2

Control Numbers on Back in Blue

1905	Unwmk.	Typo.		Perf. 14
1	A1	1c blue green	1.75	1.10
2	A1	2c claret	1.75	1.10
3	A1	3c bronze grn	1.75	1.10
4	A1	4c dark brown	1.75	1.10
5	A1	5c orange red	1.75	1.10
6	A1	10c dk gray brn	1.75	1.10
7	A1	15c red brown	1.75	1.10
8	A1	25c dark blue	32.50	11.50
9	A1	50c dark green	16.00	5.25
10	A1	75c dark vio	16.00	7.50
11	A1	1p org brown	13.00	3.25
12	A1	2p buff	35.00	17.50
13	A1	3p dull vio	27.50	7.50
14	A1	4p blue grn	27.50	7.50
15	A1	5p dull blue	32.50	13.00
16	A1	10p pale red	85.00	32.50
		Nos. 1-16 (16)	297.25	113.20

No. 8 Handstamp Surcharged in Rose

a

1907				
17	A1	15c on 25c dk bl	125.00	32.50

The surcharge exists inverted, double and in violet, normally positioned.

Control Numbers on Back in Blue

1907				Typo.
18	A2	1c claret	2.00	1.40
19	A2	2c black	2.00	1.40
20	A2	3c dark brn	2.00	1.40
21	A2	4c red	2.00	1.40
22	A2	5c black brn	2.00	1.40
23	A2	10c chocolate	2.00	1.40
24	A2	15c dark blue	2.00	1.40
25	A2	25c deep green	4.75	1.40
26	A2	50c blk violet	4.75	1.40
27	A2	75c org brown	4.75	1.40
28	A2	1p orange	8.50	1.40
29	A2	2p dull vio	3.00	1.40
30	A2	3p blue grn	3.00	1.40
a.		Cliche of 4p in plate of 3p	175.00	110.00
31	A2	4p dark blue	4.75	2.50
32	A2	5p red	4.75	2.50
33	A2	10p deep grn	6.00	4.75
		Nos. 18-33 (16)	58.25	27.95

Nos. 9-10 Handstamp Surcharged in Red

1907
10
Cens

1907				
34	A1	10c on 50c dk grn	45.00	10.00
a.		"10" omitted	100.00	52.50
35	A1	10c on 75c dk vio	27.50	10.00

No. 12 Handstamp Surcharged in Violet

1908
2
Cens

1908				
36	A1	2c on 2p buff	27.50	10.50

No. 36 is found with "1908" measuring 11mm and 12mm.

Same Surcharge in Red on No. 26

38	A2	10c on 50c blk vio	20.00	4.50

A 5c on 10c (No. 23) was not officially issued.

Nos. 25, 27-28 Handstamp Surcharged Type "a" in Red, Violet or Green

1908				
39	A2	15c on 25c dp grn (R)	18.00	4.00
40	A2	15c on 75c org brn (V)	25.00	5.00
a.		Green surcharge	32.50	13.00
41	A2	15c on 1p org (V)	27.50	5.00
42	A2	15c on 1p org (R)	27.50	10.00
43	A2	15c on 1p org (G)	27.50	10.00
		Nos. 39-43 (5)	125.50	34.00

As this surcharge is handstamped, it exists in several varieties: double, inverted, in pairs with one surcharge omitted, etc.

A3

1908				Imperf.
44	A3	5c on 50c grn (C)	80.00	32.50
45	A3	5c on 50c grn (V)	115.00	55.00

The surcharge, which is handstamped, exists in many variations.

Nos. 44-45 are found with and without control numbers on back.

King Alfonso XIII — A4

Control Numbers on Back in Blue

1909		Typo.		Perf. 14½
46	A4	1c red	40	32
47	A4	2c orange	40	32
48	A4	5c dark green	40	32
49	A4	10c orange red	40	32
50	A4	15c blue green	40	32
51	A4	20c dark vio	1.00	48
52	A4	25c deep blue	1.00	48
53	A4	30c claret	1.00	48
54	A4	40c chocolate	1.00	48
55	A4	50c red violet	1.40	48
56	A4	1p dark brown	2.25	1.65
57	A4	4p car rose	2.75	2.00
58	A4	10p claret	5.50	4.00
		Nos. 46-58 (13)	17.90	11.65

Stamps of 1905 Handstamped in Black

1910
10
Céntimos

1910				
60	A1	10c on 5p dl bl	8.25	7.25
a.		Red surcharge	47.50	27.50
62	A1	10c on 10p pale red	8.25	6.50
a.		Violet surcharge	72.50	35.00
b.		Green surcharge	72.50	35.00
65	A1	15c on 3p dl vio	8.25	7.25
a.		Imperf.	72.50	
66	A1	15c on 4p bl grn	8.25	7.25
a.		10c on 4p bl grn	425.00	125.00

See note after No. 43.

Nos. 31 and 33 Surcharged in Red or Violet

2
Cents

1911-13				
67	A2	2c on 4p dk bl (R)	6.50	2.50
68	A2	5c on 10p dp grn (V)	17.00	2.50

Nos. 29-30 Surcharged in Black

10
Céntimos

69	A2	10c on 2p dull vio	9.00	2.50
69A	A2	10c on 3p bl grn ('13)	90.00	10.50

Nos. 30, 32 Handstamped Type "a"

69B	A2	15c on 3p bl grn ('13)	72.50	6.00
70	A2	15c on 5p red	6.50	2.75
		Nos. 67-70 (6)	201.50	26.75

King Alfonso XIII
A5 A6

Control Numbers on Back in Blue

1912		Typo.		Perf. 13½
71	A5	1c car rose	20	10
72	A5	2c lilac	20	10
73	A5	5c deep green	20	10
74	A5	10c red	20	10
75	A5	15c brown org	20	10
76	A5	20c brown	20	10
77	A5	25c dull blue	20	10
78	A5	30c dark violet	20	10
79	A5	40c blue green	20	10
80	A5	50c lake	20	10
81	A5	1p red	1.50	40
82	A5	4p claret	3.25	1.65
83	A5	10p dark brown	4.50	2.00
		Nos. 71-83 (13)	11.25	5.05

Control Numbers on Back in Blue

1914				Perf. 13
84	A6	1c olive black	20	10
85	A6	2c maroon	20	10
86	A6	5c deep green	20	10
87	A6	10c orange red	20	10
88	A6	15c orange red	20	10
89	A6	20c dp claret	20	10
90	A6	25c dark blue	20	10
91	A6	30c blue green	20	10
92	A6	40c brn orange	20	10
93	A6	50c dark brown	20	10
94	A6	1p dull lilac	1.50	1.25
95	A6	4p car rose	3.50	1.25
96	A6	10p dull vio	4.50	3.00
		Nos. 84-96 (13)	11.50	6.50

Nos. 71-83 Overprinted in Black

1917

1917				Perf. 13½
97	A5	1c car rose	5.25	50
98	A5	2c lilac	5.25	50
99	A5	5c deep grn	1.00	50
100	A5	10c red	1.00	50
101	A5	15c orange brn	1.00	50
102	A5	20c brown	1.50	50
103	A5	25c dull blue	1.50	50
104	A5	30c dark violet	1.50	50
105	A5	40c blue grn	1.65	50
106	A5	50c lake	1.65	50
107	A5	1p red	7.25	2.00
108	A5	4p claret	10.00	2.50
109	A5	10p dark brown	13.00	3.75
		Nos. 97-109 (13)	51.55	13.25

Nos. 97-109 exist with overprint inverted or double (value 50 percent over normal) and in dark blue (value twice normal).

King Alfonso XIII — A7

Control Numbers on Back in Blue

1919		Typo.		Perf. 13
114	A7	1c brown	55	35
115	A7	2c claret	55	35
116	A7	5c light green	55	35
117	A7	10c carmine	55	35
118	A7	15c orange	55	35
119	A7	20c orange	55	35
120	A7	25c blue	55	35
121	A7	30c green	55	35
122	A7	40c vermilion	55	35
123	A7	50c brown	55	35
124	A7	1p lilac	3.75	2.00
125	A7	4p rose	6.00	3.50
126	A7	10p violet	7.00	5.00
		Nos. 114-126 (13)	22.25	14.00

A8 A9

Control Numbers on Back in Blue

1920				Perf. 13
127	A8	1c gray lilac	55	35
128	A8	2c rose	55	35
129	A8	5c light red	55	35
130	A8	10c lilac	55	35
131	A8	15c light brn	55	35
132	A8	20c greenish bl	55	35
133	A8	25c yellow	55	35
134	A8	30c dull blue	3.25	2.25
135	A8	40c orange	1.90	90
136	A8	50c dull rose	1.90	90
137	A8	1p gray green	1.90	90
138	A8	4p lilac rose	3.75	2.00
139	A8	10p brown	8.50	5.00
		Nos. 127-139 (13)	25.05	14.40

Control Numbers on Back in Blue

1922				
140	A9	1c yellow	55	35
141	A9	2c red brown	55	35
142	A9	5c blue green	55	35
143	A9	10c pale red	55	35
144	A9	15c myrtle grn	55	35
145	A9	20c turq blue	55	35
146	A9	25c deep blue	55	35
147	A9	30c deep rose	1.00	90
148	A9	40c violet	1.00	90
149	A9	50c orange	1.00	90
150	A9	1p lilac	3.25	1.40
151	A9	4p claret	5.50	3.00
152	A9	10p dark brn	8.75	5.25
		Nos. 140-152 (13)	24.35	14.80

For subsequent issues see Spanish Sahara.

RIO MUNI

LOCATION — West Africa, bordering on Cameroun and Gabon Republics.
GOVT. — Province of Spain
AREA — 9,500 sq. mi.
POP. — 183,377 (1960).
CAPITAL — Bata.

Rio Muni and the island of Fernando Po are the two provinces that constitute Spanish Guinea. Separate stamp issues for the two provinces were decreed in 1960.

Spanish Guinea Nos. 1-84 were used only in the territory now called Rio Muni.

Rio Muni united with Fernando Po on Oct. 12, 1968, to form the Republic of Equatorial Guinea.

100 Centimos = 1 Peseta

Catalogue values for all unused stamps in this country are for Never Hinged items.

Boy Reading and Missionary
A1

Quina Plant
A2

1960	Unwmk.	Photo.		Perf. 13x12½
1	A1	25c dl vio bl	6	6
2	A1	50c ol brn	6	6
3	A1	75c dl grysh pur	6	6
4	A1	1p org ver	6	6
5	A1	1.50p brt bl grn	6	6
6	A1	2p red lil	15	6
7	A1	3p sapphire	30	6
8	A1	5p red brn	85	8
9	A1	10p lt ol grn	1.50	25
		Nos. 1-9 (9)	3.10	75

1960 *Perf. 13x12½*

Design: 80c, Croton plant.

10	A2	35c sl grn		5	5
11	A2	80c Prus grn		15	5

See Nos. B1-B2.

Map of Rio Muni A3

Designs: 50c, 1p, Gen. Franco. 70c, Government Palace.

1961, Oct. 1 *Perf. 12½x13*

12	A3	25c gray vio	6	5
13	A3	50c ol brn	6	5
14	A3	70c brt grn	6	5
15	A3	1p red org	15	5

25th anniversary of the nomination of Gen. Francisco Franco as Chief of State.

Rio Muni Headdress — A4

Design: 50c, Rio Muni idol.

1962, July 10 *Perf. 13x12½*

16	A4	25c violet	6	5
17	A4	50c green	8	5
18	A4	1p org brn	15	5

Issued for child welfare.

Cape Buffalo A5

Design: 35c, Gorilla (vert.).

Perf. 13x12½, 12½x13

1962, Nov. 23 **Photo.** **Unwmk.**

19	A5	15c dk ol grn	6	5
20	A5	35c magenta	6	5
21	A5	1p brn org	20	5

Issued for Stamp Day.

Mother and Child — A6

Father Joaquin Juanola — A7

1963, Jan. 29 *Perf. 13x12½*

22	A6	50c green	10	5
23	A6	1p brn org	10	5

Issued to help the victims of the Seville flood.

1963, July 6 *Perf. 13x12½*

Design: 50c, Blessing hand, cross and palms.

24	A7	25c dl vio	5	5
25	A7	50c brn ol	5	5
26	A7	1p org red	15	5

Issued for child welfare.

Praying Child and Arms — A8

Branch of Copal Tree — A9

1963, July 12

27	A8	50c dl grn	10	5
28	A8	1p redsh brn	10	5

Issued for Barcelona flood relief.

Perf. 13x12½, 12½x13

1964, Mar. 6 **Photo.**

Design: 50c, Flowering quina (horiz.).

29	A9	25c brt vio	5	5
30	A9	50c bl grn	5	5
31	A9	1p dk car rose	15	5

Issued for Stamp Day 1963.

Tree Pangolin A10

Design: 50c, Chamelon.

1964, June 1 *Perf. 13x12½*

32	A10	25c vio blk	5	5
33	A10	50c ol gray	6	5
34	A10	1p fawn	15	5

Issued for child welfare.

Dwarf Crocodile A11

Designs: 15c, 70c, 3p, Dwarf crocodile. 25c, 1p, 5p, Leopard. 50c, 1.50p, 10p, Black rhinoceros.

1964, July 1

35	A11	15c lt brn	5	5
36	A11	25c violet	5	5
37	A11	50c olive	5	5
38	A11	70c green	10	5
39	A11	1p brn car	38	5
40	A11	1.50p bl grn	38	5
41	A11	3p dk bl	60	6
42	A11	5p brown	1.50	60
43	A11	10p green	4.25	1.25
		Nos. 35-43 (9)	7.36	2.21

Greshoff's Tree Frog A12

Design: 1p, Helmet guinea fowl (vert.).

Perf. 13x12½, 12½x13

1964, Nov. 23 **Photo.** **Unwmk.**

44	A12	50c green	5	5
45	A12	1p dp cl	6	5
46	A12	1.50p bl grn	15	6

Issued for Stamp Day, 1964.

Woman's Head A13

Woman Chemist A14

Design: 1.50p, Logger.

1964 **Photo.** *Perf. 13x12½*

47	A13	50c dp grn	6	5
48	A14	1p red org	6	5
49	A14	1.50p bl grn	15	6

Issued to commemorate 25 years of peace.

Goliath Beetle A15

Beetle: 1p, Acridoxena hewaniana.

1965, June 1 **Photo.** *Perf. 12½x13*

50	A15	50c Prus grn	5	5
51	A15	1p sepia	6	5
52	A15	1.50p black	15	6

Issued for child welfare.

Ring-necked Pheasant — A16

Leopard and Arms of Rio Muni A17

Perf. 13x12½, 12½x13

1965, Nov. 23 **Photo.**

53	A16	50c grnsh gray	6	5
54	A17	1p sepia	30	6
55	A16	2.50p lilac	1.40	55

Issued for Stamp Day, 1965.

Elephant and Parrot A18

Design: 1.50p, Lion and boy.

Perf. 12½x13

1966, June 1 **Photo.** **Unwmk.**

56	A18	50c olive	6	5
57	A18	1p dk pur	6	5
58	A18	1.50p brt Prus bl	15	6

Issued for child welfare.

Water Chevrotain A19

Designs: 40c, 4p, Tree pangolin (vert.).

1966, Nov. 23 **Photo.** *Perf. 13*

59	A19	10c brn & yel brn	5	5
60	A19	40c brn & yel	5	5
61	A19	1.50p bl & rose lil	6	6
62	A19	4p dk bl & emer	25	15

Issued for Stamp Day, 1966.

A20

Designs: 40c, 4p, Vine creeper.

1967, June 1 **Photo.** *Perf. 13*

63	A20	10c grn & yel	5	5
64	A20	40c blk, rose car & grn	5	5
65	A20	1.50p bl & org	6	6
66	A20	4p blk & grn	25	15

Issued for child welfare.

Potto — A21

Designs: 1p, River hog (horiz.). 3.50p, African golden cat (horiz.).

1967, Nov. 23 **Photo.** *Perf. 13*

67	A21	1p blk & red brn	6	6
68	A21	1.50p brn & grn	6	6
69	A21	3.50p org brn & grn	30	20

Issued for Stamp Day 1967.

Zodiac Issue

Cancer — A22

Signs of the Zodiac: 1.50p, Taurus. 2.50p, Gemini.

1968, Apr. 25 **Photo.** *Perf. 13*

70	A22	1p brt mag, *lt yel*	6	6
71	A22	1.50p brn, *pink*	6	6
72	A22	2.50p dk vio, *yel*	25	15

Issued for child welfare.

SEMI-POSTAL STAMPS

Type of Regular Issue, 1960

Designs: 10c+5c, Croton plant. 15c+5c, Flower and leaves of croton.

1960 **Unwmk.** **Photo.** *Perf. 13x12½*

B1	A2	10c + 5c mar	6	6
B2	A2	15c + 5c bis brn	6	6

The surtax was for child welfare.

Bishop Juan de Ribera — SP1

Design: 20c+5c, The clown Pablo de Valladolid by Velazquez. 30c+10c, Juan de Ribera statue.

1961 *Perf. 13x12½*

B3 SP1 10c + 5c rose brn 6 6
B4 SP1 20c + 5c dk sl grn 6 6
B5 SP1 30c + 10c ol brn 6 6
B6 SP1 50c + 20c brn 15 6

Issued for Stamp Day, 1960.

Mandrill SP2

Design: 25c+10c, Elephant (vert.).

Perf. 12½x13, 13x12½

1961, June 21 **Unwmk.**

B7 SP2 10c + 5c rose brn 6 6
B8 SP2 25c + 10c gray vio 6 6
B9 SP2 80c + 20c dk grn 15 6

The surtax was for child welfare.

Statuette — SP3

Design: 25c+10c, 1p+10c, Male figure.

1961, Nov. 23 *Perf. 13x12½*

B10 SP3 10c + 5c rose brn 6 6
B11 SP3 25c + 10c dk pur 6 6
B12 SP3 30c + 10c ol blk 6 6
B13 SP3 1p + 10c red org 15 6

Issued for Stamp Day 1961.

ROMANIA

Rumania, Roumania

LOCATION — Southeastern Europe, bordering on the Black Sea.
GOVT. — Republic.
AREA — 91,699 sq. mi.
POP. — 22,600,000 (est. 1984).
CAPITAL — Bucharest.

Romania was formed in 1859 from a union of the principalities of Moldavia and Walachia. It became a kingdom in 1881. Following World War I, the original territory was considerably enlarged by the addition of Bessarabia, Bukovina, Transylvania, Crisana, Maramures and Banat. The republic was established in 1948.

40 Parale = 1 Piaster
100 Bani = 1 Leu (plural "Lei") (1868)

Catalogue values for unused stamps in this country are for Never Hinged items, beginning with Scott 475 in the regular postage section, Scott B82 in the semi-postal section, Scott C24 in the airpost section, Scott CB1 in the airpost semi-postal section, Scott J82 in the postage due section, Scott O1 in the official section, Scott RA16 in the postal tax section, and Scott RAJ1 in the postal tax postage due section.

Values of early Romanian stamps vary according to condition. Quotations for Nos. 1-14 are for fine copies. Very fine to superb specimens sell at much higher prices, and inferior or poor copies sell at reduced prices, depending on the condition of the individual specimen.

Moldavia

Coat of Arms
A1 A2

Handstamped

1858, July **Unwmk.** *Imperf.*

Laid Paper

1 A1 27pa blk, *rose* *19,000* *5,000.*
a Tete beche pair
2 A1 54pa bl, *grn* *4,200.* *2,000.*
3 A1 108pa bl, *rose* *14,000.* *4,500.*

Wove Paper

4 A1 81pa bl, *bl* *21,000.* *21,000.*

Cut to shape or octagonally, Nos. 1-4 sell for one-fourth to one-third of these prices.

1858

Bluish Wove Paper

5 A2 5pa black *11,500.* *4,250.*
a Tete beche pair
6 A2 40pa blue 125.00 85.00
a Tete beche pair *650.00* *1,750.*
7 A2 80pa red *6,750.* *500.00*
a Tete beche pair

1859

White Wove Paper

8 A2 5pa black *8,000.* *4,250.*
a Tete beche pair
b Frame broken at bottom 75.00
c As "b", tete beche pair 300.00
9 A2 40pa blue 75.00 55.00
b Tete beche pair 300.00 *1,000.*
10 A2 80pa red 185.00 110.00
b Tete beche pair *975.00* *3,000.*

No. 8b has a break in the frame at bottom below "A". It was never placed in use.

Moldavia-Walachia

Coat of Arms — A3

Printed by Hand from Single Dies

1862

White Laid Paper

11 A3 3pa orange 200.00 *2,250.*
a 3pa yellow 200.00 *2,250.*
b Tete beche pair
12 A3 6pa carmine 165.00 180.00
a Tete beche pair
13 A3 6pa red 165.00 180.00
14 A3 30pa blue 45.00 60.00
a Tete beche pair 135.00

White Wove Paper

15 A3 3pa org yel 30.00 *90.00*
a 3pa lemon 60.00 *90.00*
b Tete beche pair 120.00 *1,000.*
16 A3 6pa carmine 24.00 *90.00*
a Tete beche pair 95.00
17 A3 6pa vermilion 18.00 *55.00*
a Tete beche pair 72.50
18 A3 30pa blue 27.50 17.00
a Tete beche pair 105.00

Nos. 11 to 18 inclusive were printed with a hand press, one at a time, from single dies. The impressions were very irregularly placed and occasionally overlapped. Sheets contained thirty-two stamps in four rows of eight. The third and fourth rows were printed inverted, thus making the second and third rows tete beche, foot to foot. All values come in distinct shades, frequently even on the same sheet. The paper of this and the following issues through No. 52 often shows a bluish, grayish or yellowish tint.

1864 **Typographed from Plates**

White Wove Paper

19 A3 3pa yellow 22.50 *1,250.*
a Tete beche pair 95.00
b Pair, one sideways 60.00
20 A3 6pa dp rose 2.50
a Tete beche pair 14.00
b Pair, one sideways 6.75
21 A3 30pa dp bl 3.00 *30.00*
a Tete beche pair 15.00
b Pair, one sideways 7.50
c Bluish wove paper *75.00*

Stamps of 1862 and 1864 issues can usually be distinguished by colors. In the 1862 issue the 3pa and 6pa are often blurred and appear greasy; the 30pa is usually clearly printed. The 30pa of 1864 usually has a large dot at left of eagle's crown.

Plates for the 1864 issue contained 40 cliches in 5 rows of 8. The first and second rows were inverted. Cliches in the third row were placed sideways, 4 with head to right and 4 with head to left, making one tete beche pair. The fourth and fifth rows were normally placed.

No. 20 was never placed in use. All values exist in shades, light to dark.

Counterfeit cancellations exist on Nos. 11-21.

Three stamps in this design- 2pa, 5pa, 20pa- were printed on white wove paper in 1864, but never placed in use. Value, set $6.50.

Romania

Prince Alexandru Ioan Cuza — A4

TWENTY PARALES

Type I - The central oval does not touch the inner frame. The "I" of "DECI" extends above and below the other letters.

Type II - The central oval touches the frame at the bottom. The "I" of the "DECI" is the same height as the other letters.

1865, Jan. **Unwmk.** **Litho.** *Imperf.*

22 A4 2pa orange 15.00 *75.00*
a 2pa yellow 21.00 *90.00*
b 2pa ocher 75.00 *165.00*
23 A4 5pa blue 7.25 *90.00*
24 A4 20pa red, type I 3.00 5.50
a Bluish paper 120.00
25 A4 20pa red, type II 3.00 5.50
a Bluish paper 120.00

The 20pa types are found se-tenant.

White Laid Paper

26 A4 2pa orange 18.00 *60.00*
a 2pa ocher 45.00
27 A4 5pa blue 32.50 *225.00*

Prince Carol — A5

Type I — A6

Type II — A7

TWENTY PARALES

Type I - A6. The Greek border at the upper right goes from right to left.

Type II - A7. The Greek border at the upper right goes from left to right.

1866-67

Thin Wove Paper

29 A5 2pa blk, *yellow* 3.25 *21.00*
a Thick paper 27.50 *165.00*
30 A5 5pa blk, *dk bl* 17.00 *165.00*
a 5pa black, *indigo* 60.00 *300.00*
b Thick paper 24.00 *210.00*
31 A6 20pa blk, *rose*, (I) 4.00 5.00
a Dot in Greek border, thin paper 350.00 105.00
b Thick paper 75.00 32.50
c Dot in Greek border, thick paper 100.00 60.00
32 A7 20pa blk, *rose*, (II) 5.00 6.00
a Thick paper 75.00 35.00

The 20pa types are found se-tenant.

Faked cancellations are known on Nos. 22-27, 29-32.

The white dot of Nos. 31a and 31c occurs in extreme upper right border.

Thick paper was used in 1866, thin in 1867.

Prince Carol
A8 A9

1868-70

33 A8 2b orange 12.00 7.25
a 2b yellow 24.00 30.00
34 A8 3b vio ('70) 14.00 12.00
35 A8 4b dk blue 32.50 17.00
36 A8 18b scarlet 140.00 5.50
a 18b rose 140.00 5.50

1869

37 A9 5b org yel 35.00 15.00
a 5b deep orange 40.00 15.00
38 A9 10b blue 17.00 7.25
a 10b ultramarine 40.00 15.00
b 10b indigo 50.00 21.00
40 A9 15b vermilion 40.00 12.00
41 A9 25b org & bl 22.50 9.00
42 A9 50b bl & red 140.00 14.00
a 50b indigo & red 185.00 14.00

No. 40 on laid paper was not issued. All copies have a pale blue circular cancellation. Value $1,250.

Prince Carol
A10 A11

1871-72 *Imperf.*

43 A10 5b rose 27.50 7.25
a 5b vermilion 30.00 9.00
44 A10 10b org yel 40.00 12.00
a Laid paper *275.00* *250.00*
45 A10 10b blue 100.00 21.00
46 A10 15b red 100.00 60.00
47 A10 25b ol brn 20.00 14.00

Values quoted in this catalogue are for stamps graded at Fine-Very Fine and with no faults. An illustrated guide to grade is provided in introductory material, beginning on Page V.

1872

48	A10	10b ultra	14.00	14.00
a		Laid paper	67.50	90.00
b		10b greenish blue	95.00	105.00
49	A10	50b bl & red	130.00	135.00

No. 48 is a provisional issue printed from a new plate in which the head is placed further right.

Faked cancellations are found on No. 49.

1872 ***Perf. 12½***

Wove Paper

50	A10	5b rose	27.50	12.00
a		5b vermilion	*875.00*	*400.00*
51	A10	10b blue	40.00	10.50
a		10b ultramarine	42.50	14.00
52	A10	25b dk brn	14.00	12.00

No. 43a with faked perforation is frequently offered as No. 50a.

Paris Print, Fine Impression

1872 **Typo.** ***Perf. 14x13½***

Tinted Paper

53	A11	1½b brnz grn, *bluish*	2.75	30
54	A11	3b grn, *bluish*	8.50	60
55	A11	5b bis, *pale buff*	5.00	45
56	A11	10b blue	5.50	45
57	A11	15b red brn, *pale buff*	55.00	3.00
58	A11	25b org, *pale buff*	60.00	4.00
59	A11	50b rose, *pale rose*	67.50	6.00

Nos. 53-59 exist imperf.

Bucharest Print, Rough Impression

Perf. 11, 11½, 13½, and Compound

1876-79

60	A11	1½b brnz grn, *bluish*	4.00	30
61	A11	5b bis, *yelsh*	12.00	38
b		Printed on both sides		*75.00*
62	A11	10b bl, *yelsh* ('77)	14.00	45
a		10b pale bl, *yelsh*	12.00	45
b		10b dk bl, *yelsh*	17.00	60
d		Cliche of 5b in plate of 10b ('79)	185.00	80.00
63	A11	10b ultra, *yelsh* ('77)	20.00	60
64	A11	15b red brn, *yelsh*	40.00	75
65	A11	30b org red, *yelsh* ('78)	110.00	6.00
a		Printed on both sides		*210.00*

No. 62d has been reprinted in dark blue. The originals are in dull blue. Value of reprint, $20.

Perf. 11, 11½, 13½ and Compound

1879

66	A11	1½b blk, *yelsh*	1.75	12
b		Imperf.		12.00
67	A11	3b ol grn, *bluish*	5.75	52
a		Diagonal half used as 1½b on cover		
68	A11	5b grn, *bluish*	2.00	15
69	A11	10b rose, *yelsh*	6.75	18
b		Cliche of 5b in plate of 10b	100.00	*600.00*
70	A11	15b rose red, *yelsh*	30.00	3.00
71	A11	25b bl, *yelsh*	24.00	2.50
72	A11	50b bis, *yelsh*	47.50	2.50

There are two varieties of the numerals on the 15b and 50b.

No. 69b has been reprinted in dark rose. Originals are in pale rose. Value of reprint, $20.

King Carol I
A12 A13

1880

White Paper

73	A12	15b brown	6.75	30
74	A12	25b blue	12.00	45

No. 74 exists imperf.

Perf. 13½, 11½ & Compound

1885-89

75	A13	1½b black	1.25	22
a		Printed on both sides		
76	A13	3b violet	3.50	30
a		Half used as 1½b on cover		
77	A13	5b green	35.00	3.00
78	A13	15b red brn	6.75	45
79	A13	25b blue	6.75	45

Tinted Paper

80	A13	1½b blk, *bluish*	2.50	45
81	A13	3b vio, *bluish*	3.50	60
82	A13	3b ol grn, *bluish*	3.50	30
83	A13	5b bl grn, *bluish*	2.75	45
84	A13	10b rose, *pale buff*	5.00	45
85	A13	15b red brn, *pale buff*	12.00	45
86	A13	25b bl, *pale buff*	12.00	75
87	A13	50b bis, *pale buff*	40.00	3.00

Wmk. 163 - Coat of Arms

This is not a true watermark, having been impressed after the paper was manufactured.

1889 **Wmk. 163**

Thin Pale Yellowish Paper

88	A13	1½b black	22.50	1.40
89	A13	3b violet	15.00	1.40
90	A13	5b green	15.00	1.50
91	A13	10b rose	19.00	1.40
92	A13	15b red brn	45.00	2.75
93	A13	25b dk bl	25.00	2.25

King Carol I
A14 A15

1890 ***Perf. 13½, 11½ & Compound***

94	A14	1½b maroon	2.50	38
95	A14	3b violet	19.00	65
96	A14	5b emerald	5.50	55
97	A14	10b red	6.00	1.10
a		10b rose	14.00	2.10
98	A14	15b dk brn	15.00	1.10
99	A14	25b gray bl	11.00	1.10
100	A14	50b orange	47.50	9.50

1891 **Unwmk.**

101	A14	1½b lil rose	85	15
b		Printed on both sides		*45.00*
102	A14	3b lilac	1.00	15
a		3b violet	1.40	22
b		Printed on both sides		
c		Impressions of 5b on back	*85.00*	*75.00*
103	A14	5b emerald	1.40	24
104	A14	10b pale red	5.75	40
a		Printed on both sides	*100.00*	*85.00*
105	A14	15b gray brn	6.50	30
106	A14	25b gray bl	4.00	30
107	A14	50b orange	45.00	2.50

Nos. 101-107 exist imperf.

1891

108	A15	1½b claret	1.00	48
109	A15	3b lilac	1.00	48
110	A15	5b emerald	2.75	1.90
111	A15	10b red	3.00	1.90
112	A15	15b gray brn	1.00	60

25th year of the reign of King Carol I.

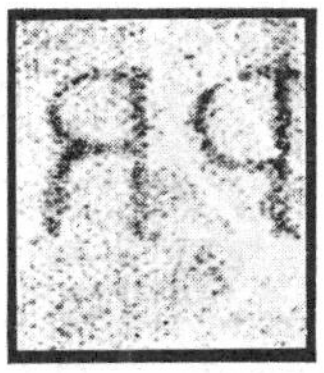

Wmk. 164 - PR

1894 **Wmk. 164**

113	A14	3b lilac	5.00	90
114	A14	5b pale grn	3.50	90
115	A14	25b gray bl	6.75	2.25
116	A14	50b orange	14.00	4.75

King Carol I
A17 A18

A19

A20

A21

A23

Wmk. 200 - PR

1893-98 **Wmk. 164 & 200**

117	A17	1b pale brn	50	5
118	A17	1½b black	40	6
119	A18	3b chocolate	50	5
120	A19	5b blue	60	5
a		Cliche of the 25b in the plate of 5b	47.50	*60.00*
121	A19	5b yel grn ('98)	2.50	5
a		5b emerald	3.00	15
122	A20	10b emerald	1.75	5
123	A20	10b rose ('98)	3.00	15
124	A21	15b rose	1.50	5
125	A21	15b blk ('98)	3.00	22
126	A19	25b violet	1.75	5
127	A19	25b ind ('98)	4.75	22
128	A19	40b gray grn	10.00	18
129	A19	50b orange	7.50	22
130	A23	1 l bis & rose	10.00	45
131	A23	2 l org & brn	17.50	90
		Nos. 117-131 (15)	*65.25*	*2.75*

This watermark may be found in two sizes, 12 and 15mm high. (Wmks. 164 and 200). The paper also varies in thickness.

A 3b orange of type A18; 10b brown, type A20; 15b rose, type A21, and 25b bright green with similar but different border, all watermarked "P R", were prepared but never issued.

Value, each $4.50.

See Nos. 132-157, 224-229.

King Carol I — A24

Perf. 11½, 13½ and Compound

1900-03 **Unwmk.**

Thin Paper, Tinted Rose on Back

132	A17	1b pale brn	50	6
133	A24	1b brn ('01)	50	6
134	A24	1b blk ('03)	50	6
135	A18	3b red brn	40	5
136	A19	5b emerald	1.25	5
137	A20	10b rose	1.25	5
a		10b orange (error)	27.50	27.50
138	A21	15b black	85	5
139	A21	15b lil gray ('01)	1.25	5
140	A21	15b dk vio ('03)	2.50	5
141	A19	25b blue	2.50	6
142	A19	40b gray grn	6.75	9
143	A19	50b orange	6.75	12
144	A23	1 l bis & rose ('01)	15.00	15
145	A23	1 l grn & blk ('03)	12.50	38
146	A23	2 l org & brn ('01)	14.00	75
147	A23	2 l red brn & blk ('03)	14.00	75
		Nos. 132-147 (16)	80.50	2.78

No. 132 inscribed BANI; Nos. 133-134 BAN.

Wmk. 167 - Coat of Arms Covering 25 Stamps

(Reduced illustration.)

1900, July **Wmk. 167**

148	A17	1b pale brn	1.75	1.40
149	A18	3b red brn	1.75	1.40
150	A19	5b emerald	3.50	1.50
151	A20	10b rose	3.50	1.50
152	A21	15b black	3.50	1.50
153	A19	25b blue	8.50	2.00
154	A19	40b gray grn	14.00	2.75
155	A19	50b orange	14.00	2.75
156	A23	1 l bis & rose	17.00	3.50
157	A23	2 l org & brn	20.00	4.00
		Nos. 148-157 (10)	87.50	22.30

Mail Coach Leaving PO — A25

1903 **Unwmk.** ***Perf. 14x13½***

Thin Paper, Tinted Rose on Face

158	A25	1b gray brn	1.00	40
159	A25	3b brn vio	1.90	55
160	A25	5b pale grn	3.50	95
161	A25	10b rose	2.75	95
162	A25	15b black	2.75	85
163	A25	25b blue	8.50	3.75
164	A25	40b dl grn	10.00	4.50
165	A25	50b orange	17.00	6.75
		Nos. 158-165 (8)	47.40	18.70

Counterfeits are plentiful. See note after No. 172. See No. 428.

King Carol I and Façade of New Post Office — A26

1903 **Engr.** ***Perf. 13½x14***

Thick Toned Paper

166	A26	15b black	1.75	1.40
167	A26	25b blue	4.25	2.25
168	A26	40b gray grn	4.50	3.00
169	A26	50b orange	4.50	3.00
170	A26	1 l dk brn	5.25	3.00
171	A26	2 l dl red	30.00	11.50
a		2 l orange (error)	50.00	22.50
172	A26	5 l dl vio	40.00	24.00
		Nos. 166-172 (7)	90.25	48.15

Opening of the new PO in Bucharest (Nos. 158-172).

Counterfeits exist.

A particular stamp may be scarce, but if few collectors want it, its market value may remain relatively low.

Prince Carol Taking Oath of Allegiance, 1866 — A27

Prince in Royal Carriage A28

Prince Carol at Calafat in 1877 — A29

Prince Carol Shaking Hands with His Captive, Osman Pasha — A30

Carol I as Prince in 1866 and King in 1906 — A31

Romanian Army Crossing Danube A32

Romanian Troops Return to Bucharest in 1878 — A33

Prince Carol at Head of His Command in 1877 — A34

King Carol I at the Cathedral in 1896 — A35

King Carol I at Shrine of St. Nicholas, 1904 — A36

1906 Engr. *Perf. 12*

176	A27	1b bis & blk	18	14
177	A28	3b red brn & blk	24	18
178	A29	5b dp grn & blk	50	18
179	A30	10b car & blk	20	14
180	A31	15b dl vio & blk	18	14
181	A32	25b ultra & blk	2.00	70
a		25b olive grn & blk	2.00	70
182	A33	40b dk brn & blk	50	35
183	A34	50b bis brn & blk	60	35
184	A35	1 l ver & blk	70	50
185	A36	2 l org & blk	70	60
		Nos. 176-185 (10)	5.80	3.28

40 years' rule of Carol I as Prince and King.
No. 181a was never placed in use. Cancellations were by favor.

King Carol I — A37

1906

186	A37	1b bis & blk	18	10
187	A37	3b red brn & blk	55	20
188	A37	5b dp grn & blk	20	10
189	A37	10b car & blk	20	10
190	A37	15b dl vio & blk	45	18
191	A37	25b ultra & blk	5.00	2.50
192	A37	40b dk brn & blk	60	28
193	A37	50b bis brn & blk	60	28
194	A37	1 l red & blk	70	28
195	A37	2 l org & blk	70	28
		Nos. 186-195 (10)	9.18	4.30

25th anniversary of the Kingdom.

Plowman and Angel — A38

Exposition Building — A39

Exposition Buildings
A40 A41

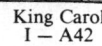

King Carol I — A42

Queen Elizabeth (Carmen Sylva) — A43

1906 Typo. *Perf. 11½, 13½*

196	A38	5b yel grn & blk	1.75	40
197	A38	10b car & blk	1.75	40
198	A39	15b vio & blk	2.50	70
199	A39	25b bl & blk	2.50	70
200	A40	30b red & blk brn	3.00	70
201	A40	40b grn & blk brn	3.00	85
202	A41	50b org & blk	3.00	1.25
203	A41	75b lt brn & dk brn	3.00	1.40
204	A42	1.50 l red lil & brn	12.00	6.00
a		Center inverted		
205	A42	2.50 l yel & brn	12.00	6.00
a		Center inverted		
206	A43	3 l brn org & brn	12.00	6.00
		Nos. 196-206 (11)	56.50	24.40

General Exposition. They were sold at post offices July 29-31, 1906, and were valid only for those three days. Those sold at the exposition are overprinted "S E" in black. Remainders were sold privately, both unused and canceled to order, by the Exposition promoters.

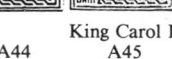

King Carol I
A44 A45 A46

Perf. 11½, 13½ & Compound

1908-18 Engr.

207	A44	5b pale yel grn	1.10	22
208	A44	10b carmine	95	8
209	A45	15b purple	9.50	1.50
210	A44	25b deep bl	95	8
211	A44	40b brt grn	60	8
212	A44	40b dk brn ('18)	2.75	75
213	A44	50b orange	75	8
214	A44	50b lt red ('18)	60	38
215	A44	1 l brown	95	20
216	A44	2 l red	4.25	1.50
		Nos. 207-216 (10)	22.40	4.87

Perf. 13½x14, 11½, 13½ & Compound

1909-18 Typo.

217	A46	1b black	9	6
218	A46	3b red brn	14	7
219	A46	5b yel grn	9	6
220	A46	10b rose	14	6
221	A46	15b dl vio	10.50	6.50
222	A46	15b ol grn	18	7
223	A46	15b red brn ('18)	48	35
		Nos. 217-223 (7)	11.62	7.17

Nos. 217-219, 222 exist imperf.
No. 219 in black is a chemical changeling.

Types of 1893-99

1911-19 White Paper Unwmk.

224	A17	1½b straw	70	45
225	A19	25b deep bl ('18)	35	14
226	A19	40b gray brn ('19)	70	60
227	A19	50b dl red ('19)	70	45
228	A23	1 l gray grn ('18)	1.25	35
229	A23	2 l org ('18)	1.40	45
		Nos. 224-229 (6)	5.10	2.44

Romania Holding Flag — A47

Romanian Crown and Old Fort on Danube — A48

Troops Crossing Danube — A49

View of Turtucaia — A50

Mircea the Great and Carol I — A51

View of Silistra — A52

Perf. 11½x13½, 13½x11½

1913, Dec. 25

230	A47	1b black	40	22
231	A48	3b ol gray & choc	90	40
232	A49	5b yel grn & blk brn	75	22
233	A50	10b org & gray	40	22
234	A51	15b bis & vio	90	40
235	A52	25b bl & choc	1.40	55
236	A49	40b bis & red vio	2.25	1.00
237	A48	50b yel & bl	2.50	2.00
238	A48	1 l bl & ol bis	7.50	4.50
239	A48	2 l org red & rose	9.00	6.00
		Nos. 230-239 (10)	26.00	15.51

Romania's annexation of Silistra.

No. 217 Handstamped in Red

25
BANI

Perf. 13½x14, 11½, 13½ & Compound

1918, May 1

240	A46	25b on 1b blk	28	18

This handstamp is found inverted.

No. 219 and 220 Overprinted in Black

1918

1918

241	A46	5b yel grn	35	24
a		Inverted overprint	5.00	2.75
b		Double overprint	5.00	
242	A46	10b rose	35	24
a		Inverted overprint	5.00	2.75
b		Double overprint	5.00	

Nos. 217, 219 and 220 Overprinted in Red or Black

1919, Nov. 8

245	A46	1b blk (R)	18	10
a		Inverted overprint	1.75	
b		Double overprint	3.50	2.00
246	A46	5b yel grn (Bk)	18	10
a		Double overprint	3.50	2.75
b		Inverted overprint	1.75	1.75
247	A46	10b rose (Bk)	18	10
a		Inverted overprint	1.75	1.75
b		Double overprint	3.50	2.50

Commemorating the recovery of Transylvania and the return of the King to Bucharest.

King Ferdinand — A53

1920-22 Typo.

248	A53	1b black	15	8
249	A53	5b yel grn	15	5
250	A53	10b rose	15	5
251	A53	15b red brn	45	12
252	A53	25b dp bl	95	14
253	A53	25b brown	45	8
254	A53	40b gray brn	75	12
255	A53	50b salmon	20	5
256	A53	1 l gray grn	75	6
257	A53	1 l rose	45	20
258	A53	2 l orange	75	20
259	A53	2 l dp bl	75	20
260	A53	2 l rose ('22)	1.90	1.25
		Nos. 248-260 (13)	7.85	2.60

Nos. 248-260 are printed on two papers: coarse, grayish paper with bits of colored fiber, and thinner white paper of better quality.
Nos. 248-251, 253 exist imperf.

King Ferdinand — A54

I II III

I II I II

TWO LEI

Type I - The "2" is thin, with tail 2½mm wide. Top of "2" forms a hook.

Type II - The "2" is thick, with tail 3mm wide. Top of "2" forms a ball.

Type III - The "2" is similar to type II. The "E" of "LEI" is larger and about 2mm wide.

THREE LEI

Type I - Top of "3" begins in a point. Top and middle bars of "E" of "LEI" are without serifs.

Type II - Top of "3" begins in a ball. Top and middle bars of "E" of "LEI" have serifs.

FIVE LEI

Type I - The "5" is 2½mm wide. The end of the final stroke of the "L" of "LEI" almost touches the vertical stroke.

Type II - The "5" is 3mm wide and the lines are broader than in type I. The end of the final stroke of the "L" of "LEI" is separated from the vertical by a narrow space.

Perf. 13½x14, 11½, 13½ & Compound

1920-26

261	A54	3b black	15	8
262	A54	5b black	8	5
263	A54	10b yel grn ('25)	8	5
a		10b olive green ('25)	35	
264	A54	25b bis brn	15	8
265	A54	25b salmon	15	8
266	A54	30b violet	20	8
267	A54	50b orange	12	5
268	A54	60b gray grn	60	30
269	A54	1 l violet	20	5
270	A54	2 l rose (I)	75	20
a		2 l claret (I)	19.00	
271	A54	2 l lt grn (II)	50	8
a		2 l light green (I)	75	12
b		2 l light green (III)	60	8
272	A54	3 l bl (I)	1.50	28
273	A54	3 l buff (II)	60	20
a		3 l buff (I)	3.00	45
274	A54	3 l sal (II)	24	5
a		3 l salmon (I)	1.25	75
275	A54	5 l car rose (II)	45	6
276	A54	5 l emer (I)	1.25	20
277	A54	5 l lt brn (II)	45	6
a		5 l light brown (I)	1.25	24
278	A54	6 l blue	1.75	60
279	A54	6 l carmine	2.75	95
280	A54	6 l ol grn ('26)	1.75	38
281	A54	7½ l pale bl	1.40	24
282	A54	10 l dp bl	1.40	20
		Nos. 261-282 (22)	16.52	4.32

Nos. 273 and 273a, also 274 and 274a, are found se-tenant. The 50b exists in three types.

Alba Iulia Cathedral A55

King Ferdinand A56

Coat of Arms A57

Queen Marie as Nurse A58

Michael the Brave and King Ferdinand A59

King Ferdinand A60

Queen Marie — A61

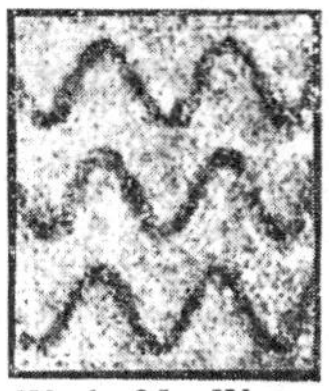

Wmk. 95 - Wavy Lines

Perf. 13½x14, 13½, 11½ & Compound

1922, Oct. 15 Photo. Wmk. 95

283	A55	5b black	7	7
a		Engraver's name omitted	2.50	1.40
284	A56	25b chocolate	24	18
285	A57	50b dp grn	50	24
286	A58	1 l ol grn	50	35
287	A59	2 l carmine	70	45
288	A60	3 l blue	1.40	70
289	A61	6 l violet	5.00	4.00
		Nos. 283-289 (7)	8.41	5.99

Coronation of King Ferdinand I and Queen Marie on Oct. 15, 1922, at Alba Iulia. All values exist imperforate.

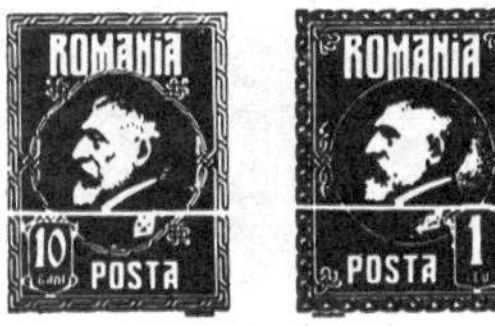

King Ferdinand A62 A63

1926, July 1 Unwmk. *Perf. 11*

291	A62	10b yel grn	18	18
292	A62	25b orange	18	18
293	A62	50b org brn	18	18
294	A63	1 l dk vio	18	18
295	A63	2 l dk grn	18	18
296	A63	3 l brn car	18	18
297	A63	5 l blk brn	18	18
298	A63	6 l dk ol	18	18
a		6 l bright blue (error)	70.00	70.00
300	A63	9 l slate	18	18
301	A63	10 l brt bl	18	18
b		10 l brown carmine (error)	70.00	70.00
		Nos. 291-301 (10)	1.80	1.80

60th birthday of King Ferdinand.
Exist imperf. Imperf. examples with watermark 95 are proofs.

King Carol I and King Ferdinand A69

King Ferdinand A70

A71

1927, Aug. 1 *Perf. 13½*

308	A69	25b brn vio	22	22
309	A70	30b gray blk	22	22
310	A71	50b dk grn	22	22
311	A69	1 l bluish sl	22	22
312	A70	2 l dp grn	25	25
313	A70	3 l violet	35	35
314	A71	4 l dk brn	42	42
315	A71	4.50 l hn brn	1.40	1.40
316	A70	5 l red brn	42	42
317	A71	6 l carmine	90	90
318	A69	7.50 l grnsh bl	65	65
319	A69	10 l brt bl	90	90
		Nos. 308-319 (12)	6.17	6.17

50th anniversary of Romania's independence from Turkish suzerainty.

Some values exist imperf. All exist imperf. and with value numerals omitted.

King Michael A72 A73

Perf. 13½x14 (25b, 50b); 13½

1928-29 Typo. Unwmk.

Size: 19x25mm

320	A72	25b black	12	8
321	A72	30b fawn ('29)	22	8
322	A72	50b ol grn	12	8

Photo.

Size: 18½x24½mm

323	A73	1 l violet	22	8
324	A73	2 l dp grn	25	8
325	A73	3 l brt rose	35	8
326	A73	5 l red brn	55	8
327	A73	7.50 l ultra	2.50	35
328	A73	10 l blue	2.00	18
		Nos. 320-328 (9)	6.33	1.09

See Nos. 343-345, 353-357.

Parliament House, Bessarabia A74

Designs: 1 l, 2 l, Parliament House, Bessarabia. 3 l, 5 l, 20 l, Hotin Fortress. 7.50 l, 10 l, Fortress Cetatea Alba.

1928, Apr. 29 Wmk. 95 *Perf. 13½*

329	A74	1 l dp grn	55	25
330	A74	2 l dp brn	55	25
331	A74	3 l blk brn	55	25
332	A74	5 l car lake	65	32
333	A74	7.50 l ultra	65	32
334	A74	10 l Prus bl	1.50	90
335	A74	20 l blk vio	1.90	1.10
		Nos. 329-335 (7)	6.35	3.39

Reunion of Bessarabia with Romania, 10th anniv.

King Carol I and King Michael A77

View of Constanta Harbor A78

Trajan's Monument at Adam Clisi A79

Cernavoda Bridge A80

1928, Oct. 25

336	A77	1 l bl grn	48	24
337	A78	2 l red brn	48	24
338	A77	3 l gray blk	60	24
339	A79	5 l dl lil	75	38
340	A79	7.50 l ultra	90	38
341	A80	10 l blue	1.25	60
342	A80	20 l car rose	1.90	75
		Nos. 336-342 (7)	6.36	2.83

50th anniv. of the union of Dobruja with Romania.

Michael Types of 1928-29

Perf. 13½x14

1928, Sept. 1 Typo. Wmk. 95

343	A72	25b black	35	10

Photo.

344	A73	7.50 l ultra	1.25	52
345	A73	10 l blue	2.50	35

Ferdinand I; Stephen the Great; Michael the Brave; Corvin and Constantine Brancoveanu A81

Union with Transylvania A82

Avram Jancu A83

Prince Michael the Brave — A84

Castle Bran — A85

King Ferdinand I — A86

1929, May 10 Photo. Wmk. 95

347	A81	1 l dk vio	1.25	60
348	A82	2 l ol grn	1.25	60
349	A83	3 l vio brn	1.50	75
350	A84	4 l cerise	1.50	90
351	A85	5 l orange	1.90	90
352	A86	10 l brt bl	2.25	1.50
		Nos. 347-352 (6)	9.65	5.25

Union of Transylvania and Romania.

Michael Type of 1928

1930 Unwmk. *Perf. 14½x14*

Size: 18x23mm

353	A73	1 l dp vio	40	8
354	A73	2 l dp grn	60	8
355	A73	3 l car rose	1.50	8
356	A73	7.50 l ultra	2.25	50
357	A73	10 l dp bl	7.50	3.75
		Nos. 353-357 (5)	12.25	4.49

Stamps of 1928-30 Overprinted **8 IUNIE 1930**

On Nos. 320-322, 326, 328

Perf. 13½x14, 13½

1930, June 8 Typo.

359	A72	25b black	18	6
360	A72	30b fawn	24	6
361	A72	50b ol grn	24	6

Photo.

Size: 18½x24½mm

362	A73	5 l red brn	45	6
362A	A73	10 l brt bl	2.50	75

On Nos. 353-357

Perf. 14½x14

Size: 18x23mm

363	A73	1 l dp vio	24	75
364	A73	2 l dp grn	24	6
365	A73	3 l car rose	38	6

366	A73	7.50 l	ultra	1.40	45
367	A73	10 l	dp bl	1.10	30

On Nos. 343-344

Perf. 13½x14, 13½

Typo. **Wmk. 95**

368	A72	25b	black	45	18

Photo.

Size: 18½x24½mm

368A	A73	7.50 l	ultra	1.90	60
	Nos. 359-368A (12)			9.32	3.39

Accession to the throne by King Carol II. This overprint exists on No. 345.

King Carol II
A87 A88 A89

Wmk. 225 - Crown over PTT, Multiple

Perf. 13½, 14, 14x13½

1930 **Wmk. 225**

369	A87	25b	black	8	5
370	A87	50b	chocolate	24	20
371	A87	1 l	dk vio	10	5
372	A87	2 l	gray grn	18	5
373	A88	3 l	car rose	35	5
374	A88	4 l	org red	35	5
375	A88	6 l	car brn	45	5
376	A88	7.50 l	ultra	50	10
377	A89	10 l	dp bl	1.25	6
378	A89	16 l	pck grn	3.00	10
379	A89	20 l	orange	3.50	28
	Nos. 369-379 (11)			10.00	1.04

Exist imperf. See Nos. 405-414.

A90

A91

1930, Dec. 24 **Unwmk.** ***Perf. 13½***

380	A90	1 l	dl vio	52	18
381	A91	2 l	green	52	18
382	A91	4 l	vermilion	75	18
383	A91	6 l	brn car	1.90	18

First census in Romania.

King Carol II — A92

King Carol I — A93

King Ferdinand — A96

King Carol II — A94

King Carol II, King Ferdinand and King Carol I — A95

1931, May 10 **Photo.** **Wmk. 225**

384	A92	1 l	gray vio	2.50	85
385	A93	2 l	green	3.00	85
386	A94	6 l	red brn	4.50	1.50
387	A95	10 l	blue	7.50	3.00
388	A96	20 l	orange	8.50	4.75
	Nos. 384-388 (5)			26.00	10.95

50th anniversary of Romanian Kingdom.

Using Bayonet — A97

Romanian Infantryman 1870 — A98

Romanian Infantry 1830 — A99

King Carol I
A100

Infantry Advance
A101

King Ferdinand
A102

King Carol II
A103

1931, May 10

389	A97	25b	gray blk	75	48
390	A98	50b	dk red brn	1.10	55
391	A99	1 l	gray vio	1.25	60
392	A100	2 l	dp grn	2.25	90
393	A101	3 l	car rose	4.50	2.75
394	A102	7.50 l	ultra	6.00	3.75
395	A103	16 l	bl grn	7.50	5.00
	Nos. 389-395 (7)			23.35	14.03

Centenary of the Romanian Army.

Naval Cadet Ship "Mircea" — A104

King Carol II — A108

Designs: 10 l, Ironclad. 16 l, Light cruiser. 20 l, Destroyer.

1931, May 10

396	A104	6 l	red brn	3.75	1.75
397	A104	10 l	blue	3.75	1.75
398	A104	16 l	bl grn	14.00	3.00
399	A104	20 l	orange	7.50	4.00

50th anniversary of the Romanian Navy.

1931 **Unwmk.** **Engr.** ***Perf. 12***

400	A108	30 l	ol bis & dk bl	38	18
401	A108	50 l	red & dk bl	1.40	38
402	A108	100 l	dk grn & dk bl	1.75	50

Exist imperf.

Carol II, Ferdinand, Carol I — A109

Wmk. 230 - Crowns and Monograms

Wmk. 230

1931, Nov. 1 **Photo.** ***Perf. 13½***

403	A109	16 l	Prus grn	6.25	32

Exists imperf.

Carol II Types of 1930-31

Perf. 13½, 14, 14½ and Compound

1932 **Wmk. 230**

405	A87	25b	black	30	9
406	A87	50b	dk brn	42	15
407	A87	1 l	dk vio	75	9
408	A87	2 l	gray grn	75	9
409	A88	3 l	car rose	1.25	9
410	A88	4 l	org red	2.25	9
411	A88	6 l	car brn	4.00	15
412	A88	7.50 l	ultra	6.00	38
413	A89	10 l	dp bl	60.00	45
414	A89	20 l	orange	60.00	5.00
	Nos. 405-414 (10)			135.72	6.58

Alexander the Good
A110

King Carol II
A111

1932, May ***Perf. 13½***

415	A110	6 l	car brn	7.50	5.75

500th death anniv. of Alexander the Good, Prince of Moldavia, 1400-1432.

1932, June

416	A111	10 l	brt bl	7.50	45

Exists imperf.

Cantacuzino and Gregory Ghika, Founders of Coltea and Pantelimon Hospitals
A112

Session of the Congress
A113

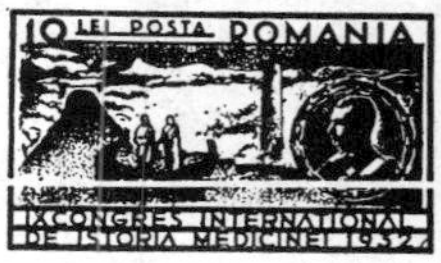

Aesculapius and Hygeia
A114

1932, Sept. ***Perf. 13½***

417	A112	1 l	car rose	4.75	3.50
418	A113	6 l	dp org	12.00	5.50
419	A114	10 l	brt bl	19.00	10.00

9th Intl. History of Medicine Congress, Bucharest.

Bull's Head and Post Horn
A116

Lion Rampant and Bridge
A117

Dolphins
A118

Eagle and Castles
A119

Coat of Arms
A120

Eagle and Post Horn
A121

Bull's Head and Post Horn — A122

1932, Nov. 20 **Typo.** ***Imperf.***

421	A116	25b	black	75	22
422	A117	1 l	violet	1.10	40
423	A118	2 l	green	1.40	45
424	A119	3 l	car rose	1.65	60
425	A120	6 l	red brn	2.25	75
426	A121	7.50 l	lt bl	2.25	75
427	A122	10 l	dk bl	3.00	1.10
	Nos. 421-427 (7)			12.40	4.27

75th anniv. of the first Moldavian stamps.

Mail Coach Type of 1903

1932, Nov. 20 ***Perf. 13½***

428	A25	16 l	bl grn	6.75	3.50

30th anniv. of the opening of the new post office, Bucharest, in 1903.

Arms of City of Turnu-Severin, Ruins of Tower of Emperor Severus — A123

Inauguration of Trajan's Bridge — A124

Prince Carol Landing at Turnu-Severin — A125

Bridge over the Danube A126

1933, June 2 Photo. *Perf. 14½x14*

429	A123	25b gray grn	25	15
430	A124	50b dl bl	50	20
431	A125	1 l blk brn	50	24
432	A126	2 l ol blk	1.25	35

Centenary of the incorporation in Walachia of the old Roman City of Turnu-Severin. Exist imperf.

Queen Elizabeth and King Carol I — A127

Profiles of Kings Carol I, Ferdinand and Carol II — A128

Castle Peles, Sinaia A129

1933, Aug.

433	A127	1 l dk vio	1.65	1.25
434	A128	3 l ol brn	1.65	1.25
435	A129	6 l vermilion	2.50	1.65

50th anniversary of the erection of Castle Peles, the royal summer residence at Sinaia. Exist imperf.

King Carol II
A130 A131

King Carol II — A132

1934, Aug. *Perf. 13½*

436	A130	50b brown	40	24
437	A131	2 l gray grn	70	30
438	A131	4 l red	1.10	38
439	A132	6 l dp claret	3.25	24

Nos. 436, 439 exist imperf.

The only foreign revenue stamps listed in this Catalogue are those authorized for prepayment of postage.

Child and Grapes A133

Woman and Fruit A134

1934, Sept. 14

440	A133	1 l dl grn	1.50	1.10
441	A134	2 l vio brn	1.50	1.10

National Fruit Week, Sept. 14-21. Exist imperf.

Crisan, Horia and Closca A135

Designs: 2 l, Crisan. 6 l, Closca. 10 l, Horia.

1935, Feb. 28

442	A135	1 l purple	38	25
443	A135	2 l green	50	38
444	A135	6 l brown	1.00	50
445	A135	10 l blue	2.00	1.00

150th anniversary of the death of three Romanian martyrs. Exist imperf.

King Carol II
A139 A140

A141 A142

A143

Wmk. 230

1935-40 Photo. *Perf. 13½*

446	A139	25b blk brn	5	5
447	A142	50b brown	6	5
448	A140	1 l purple	12	5
449	A141	2 l green	14	5
449A	A141	2 l dk bl grn ('40)	25	25
450	A142	3 l dp rose	14	6
450A	A142	3 l grnsh bl ('40)	30	30
451	A141	4 l vermilion	42	5
452	A140	5 l rose car ('40)	42	42
453	A143	6 l maroon	35	5
454	A140	7.50 l ultra	60	20
454A	A142	8 l mag ('40)	60	60
455	A141	9 l brt ultra ('40)	90	90
456	A142	10 l brt bl	30	18
456A	A143	12 l sl bl ('40)	52	52
457	A139	15 l dk brn ('40)	52	52
458	A143	16 l Prus bl	60	12
459	A143	20 l orange	42	24
460	A143	24 l dk car ('40)	85	85
		Nos. 446-460 (19)	7.56	5.46

Exist imperf.

Nos. 454, 456 Overprinted in Red

CEHOSLOVACIA YUGOSLAVIA

1920·1936

1936, Dec. 5

461	A140	7.50 l ultra	2.50	1.75
462	A142	10 l brt bl	2.50	1.75

16th anniversary of the Little Entente. Overprints in silver or gold are fraudulent.

Birthplace of Ion Creanga A144

Ion Creanga A145

1937, May 15

463	A144	2 l green	50	35
464	A145	3 l car rose	50	35
465	A144	4 l dp vio	75	50
466	A145	6 l red brn	75	65

Ion Creanga (1837-1889), writer. Exist imperf.

Cathedral at Curtea de Arges — A146

1937, July 1

467	A146	7.50 l ultra	1.25	48
468	A146	10 l blue	2.10	42

The Little Entente (Romania, Czechoslovakia, Jugoslavia). Exist imperf.

Souvenir Sheet

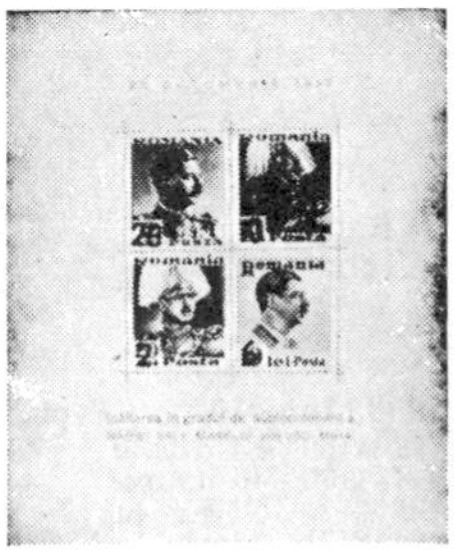

A146a

Surcharged in Black with New Values

1937, Oct. 25 Unwmk. *Perf. 13½*

469	A146a	Sheet of four	3.50	3.50
a		2 l on 20 l org	35	35
b		6 l on 10 l brt bl	35	35
c		10 l on 6 l mar	35	35
d		20 l on 2 l grn	35	35

Promotion of the Crown Prince Michael to the rank of Lieutenant on his 17th birthday.

Arms of Romania, Greece, Turkey and Jugoslavia A147

Perf. 13x13½

1938, Feb. 10 Wmk. 230

470	A147	7.50 l ultra	80	55
471	A147	10 l blue	1.40	55

The Balkan Entente.

A148

King Carol II
A149 A150

1938, May 10 *Perf. 13½*

472	A148	3 l dk car	35	20
473	A149	6 l vio brn	35	20
474	A150	10 l blue	50	28

New Constitution of Feb. 27, 1938.

Catalogue values for unused stamps in this section, from this point to the end of the section, are for Never Hinged items.

Prince Carol at Calatorie, 1866 A151

At Calafat A152

Examining Plans for a Monastery A153

Prince Carol and Carmen Sylva (Queen Elizabeth) A155

Sigmaringen and Peles Castles A154

Prince Carol, Age 6 — A156

1866 — A157

1877 — A158

Equestrian Statue — A159

Battle of Plevna A160

On Horseback A161

1914 — A162

Cathedral of Curtea de Arges — A164

King Carol I and Queen Elizabeth A163

Perf. 14, 14x13½, 13½

1939, Apr. 10 **Wmk. 230**

475	A151	25b ol blk	6	5
476	A152	50b vio brn	6	6
477	A153	1 l dk pur	15	8
478	A154	1.50 l green	8	5
479	A155	2 l myrtle grn	9	5
480	A156	3 l red org	9	5
481	A157	4 l rose lake	12	6
482	A158	5 l black	8	5
483	A159	7 l ol blk	9	5
484	A160	8 l dark bl	18	9
485	A161	10 l deep mag	22	12
486	A162	12 l dl blue	30	15
487	A163	15 l ultra	38	18
488	A164	16 l Prus grn	90	45
		Nos. 475-488 (14)	2.80	1.49

Centenary of the birth of King Carol I.

Souvenir Sheets

1939-40 ***Perf. 14x13½***

488A	Sheet of 3, #475, 476, 478	1.50	1.50
d	Imperf ('40)	2.25	2.25

Perf. 14x15½

488B	Sheet of 4, #480-482, 486	1.50	1.50
e	Imperf. ('40)	2.25	2.25
488C	Sheet of 4, 479, 483-485	1.50	1.50
f	Imperf. ('40)	2.25	2.25

No. 488A sold for 20 l, Nos. 488B-488C for 50 l, the surtax for national defense.

Nos. 488A-488C and 488d-488f were overprinted "PRO-PATRIA 1940" to aid the armament fund. Value, set of 6, $80.

Nos. 488A-488C exist with overprint of "ROMA BERLIN 1940" and bars, but these are not recognized as having been officially issued.

Romanian Pavilion A165

Romanian Pavilion A166

1939, May 8 ***Perf. 14x13½, 13½***

489	A165	6 l brn car	28	28
490	A166	12 l brt bl	28	28

New York World's Fair.

Mihail Eminescu
A167 A168

1939, May 22 ***Perf. 13½***

491	A167	5 l ol gray	35	35
492	A168	7 l brn car	35	35

Mihail Eminescu, poet, 50th death anniv.

Three Types of Locomotives — A169

Modern Train A170

Wood-burning Locomotive A171

Streamlined Locomotive A172

Railroad Terminal A173

1939, June 10 **Typo.** ***Perf. 14***

493	A169	1 l red vio	40	28
494	A170	4 l dp rose	55	28
495	A171	5 l gray lil	60	28
496	A171	7 l claret	70	35
497	A172	12 l blue	90	90
498	A173	15 l green	2.00	1.25
		Nos. 493-498 (6)	5.15	3.34

Romanian Railways, 70th anniversary.

Arms of Romania, Greece Turkey and Jugoslavia — A174

Wmk. 230

1940, May 27 **Photo.** ***Perf. 13½***

504	A174	12 l lt ultra	35	35
505	A174	16 l dl bl	35	35

The Balkan Entente.

King Michael A175

Prince Duca A176

1940-42 **Wmk. 230** ***Perf. 14***

506	A175	25b Prus grn	5	5
506A	A175	50b dk grn ('42)	5	5
507	A175	1 l purple	6	5
508	A175	2 l red org	8	5
508A	A175	4 l sl ('42)	5	5
509	A175	5 l rose pink	8	5
509A	A175	7 l dp bl ('42)	5	5
510	A175	10 l dp mag	24	5
511	A175	12 l dl bl	5	5
511A	A175	13 l dk vio ('42)	5	8
512	A175	16 l Prus bl	24	5
513	A175	20 l brown	1.25	5
514	A175	30 l yel grn	15	5
515	A175	50 l ol brn	20	8
516	A175	100 l rose brn	28	12
		Nos. 506-516 (15)	2.88	88

See Nos. 535A-553.

1941, Oct. 6 ***Perf. 13½***

517	A176	6 l lt brn	14	14
518	A176	12 l dk vio	18	18
519	A176	24 l brt bl	20	20

Crossing of the Dniester River by Romanian forces invading Russia.

Each of Nos. 517-519 exists in an imperf., ungummed souvenir sheet of four with marginal inscriptions including "1943." These were prepared by the civil government of Trans-Dniestria to be sold for 300 lei apiece to aid the Red Cross, but were not recognized by the national government at Bucharest. The sheets reached philatelic channels in 1946.

See Nos. 554-557.

Hotin Chapel, Bessarabia A177

Sucevita Monastery, Bucovina A179

Inscribed "Basarabia" or "Bucovina" at bottom

Designs: 50b, 9.50 l, Hotin Fortress, Bessarabia. 1.50 l, Soroca Fortress, Bessarabia. 2 l, 5.50 l, Tighina Fortress, Bessarabia. 3 l, Dragomirna Monastery, Bucovina. 6.50 l, Cetatea Alba Fortress, Bessarabia. 10 l, 130 l, Putna Monastery, Bucovina. 13 l, Milisauti Monastery, Bucovina. 26 l, St. Nicholas Monastery, Suceava, Bucovina. 39 l, Rughi Monastery, Bessarabia.

1941, Dec. 1 ***Perf. 13½***

520	A177	25b rose car	5	5
521	A179	50b red brn	5	5
522	A179	1 l dp vio	5	5
523	A179	1.50 l green	5	5
524	A179	2 l brn org	5	5
525	A177	3 l dk ol grn	12	6
526	A177	5 l ol blk	15	6
527	A179	5.50 l brown	15	9
528	A179	6.50 l magenta	28	22
529	A179	9.50 l gray blk	28	22
530	A179	10 l dk vio brn	18	6
531	A177	13 l slate bl	24	12
532	A179	17 l brn car	28	9
533	A179	26 l gray grn	35	24
534	A179	39 l bl grn	52	38
535	A179	130 l yel org	2.00	1.50
		Nos. 520-535 (16)	4.80	3.29

See Nos. B179-B187.

Wmk. 276 - Cross and Crown Multiple

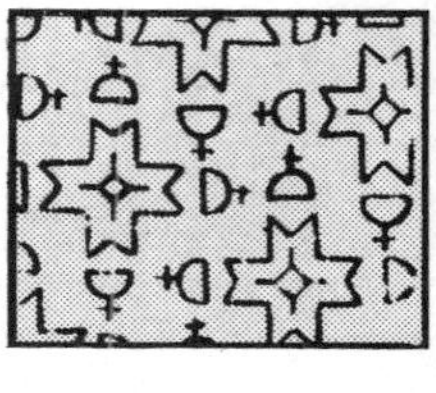

Type of 1940-42

1943-45 **Wmk. 276** ***Perf. 14***

535A	A175	25b Prus grn ('44)	5	5
536	A175	50b dk grn ('44)	5	5
537	A175	1 l dk vio ('43)	5	5
538	A175	2 l red org ('43)	5	5
539	A175	3 l red brn ('44)	5	5
540	A175	3.50 l brn ('43)	5	5
541	A175	4 l slate	5	5
542	A175	4.50 l dk brn ('43)	5	5
543	A175	5 l rose car	5	5
544	A175	6.50 l dl vio	5	5
545	A175	7 l dp bl	5	5
546	A175	10 l dp mag	5	5
547	A175	11 l brt ultra	5	5
548	A175	12 l dark bl	5	5
549	A175	15 l royal bl	5	5
550	A175	16 l dp blue	5	5
551	A175	20 l brn ('43)	5	5
551A	A175	29 l ultra ('45)	48	30
552	A175	30 l yel grn	15	5
553	A175	50 l ol blk	22	12
		Nos. 535A-553 (20)	1.70	1.32

Prince Duca Type of 1941

1943 ***Perf. 13½***

554	A176	3 l red org	6	6
555	A176	6 l dl brn	12	12
556	A176	12 l dl vio	15	15
557	A176	24 l brt bl	22	22

Andrei Saguna — A188

Andrei Muresanu A189

Designs: 4.50 l, Samuel Micu. 11 l, Gheorghe Sincai. 15 l, Michael the Brave. 31 l, Gheorghe Lazar. 35 l, Avram Jancu. 41 l, Simeon Barnutiu. 55 l, Three Heroes. 61 l, Petru Maior.

1945 **Inscribed "1944"** ***Perf. 14***

558	A188	25b rose red	28	28
559	A189	50b orange	20	20
560	A189	4.50 l brown	20	20
561	A188	11 l lt ultra	20	20
562	A188	15 l Prus grn	20	20
563	A189	31 l dl vio	20	20
564	A188	35 l bl blk	20	20
565	A188	41 l ol gray	20	20
566	A189	55 l red brn	20	20
567	A189	61 l dp mag	20	20
		Nos. 558-567,B251 (11)	2.56	2.56

Romania's liberation. The men pictured are Transylvanians.

King Michael
A198 A199

King Michael
A200 A201

1945			Photo.	
568 A198	50b gray bl		5	5
569 A199	1 l dl brn		5	5
570 A199	2 l violet		5	5
571 A198	2 l sepia		5	5
572 A199	4 l yel grn		5	5
573 A200	5 l dp mag		5	5
574 A198	10 l blue		5	5
575 A198	15 l magenta		5	5
576 A198	20 l dl blue		5	5
577 A200	25 l red org		5	5
578 A200	35 l brown		5	5
579 A200	40 l car rose		5	5
580 A199	50 l pale ultra		5	5
581 A199	55 l red		5	5
582 A200	75 l Prus grn		5	5
583 A201	80 l orange		5	5
584 A201	100 l dp red brn		5	5
585 A201	160 l yel grn		5	5
586 A201	200 l dk ol grn		22	5
587 A201	400 l dl vio		5	5
	Nos. 568-587 (20)		1.17	1.00

Nos. 571, 573, 580, 581, 585 and 587 are printed on toned paper, Nos. 576, 577, 583, 584 and 586 on both toned and white papers, others on white paper only.
See Nos. 610-624, 651-660.

Mail Carrier
A202

Telegraph Operator
A203

Lineman
A204

Post Office, Bucharest
A205

1945, July 20	Wmk. 276		*Perf. 13*	
588 A202	100 l dk brn		75	75
589 A202	100 l gray ol		75	75
590 A203	150 l brown		1.25	1.25
591 A203	150 l brt rose		1.25	1.25
592 A204	250 l lt gray ol		1.40	1.40
593 A204	250 l blue		1.40	1.40
594 A205	500 l dp mag		10.50	10.50
	Nos. 588-594 (7)		17.30	17.30

Issued in sheets of 4.

I. Ionescu, G. Titeica A. O. Idachimescu and V. Cristescu
A207

Allegory of Learning
A208

1945, Sept. 5		*Perf. 13½*	
596 A207	2 l sepia	8	8
597 A208	80 l bl blk	14	14

50th anniversary of "Gazeta Matematica," mathematics journal.

Cernavoda Bridge
A209

1945, Sept. 26		*Perf. 14*	
598 A209	80 l bl blk	18	12

50th anniversary of Cernavoda Bridge.

Blacksmith and Plowman — A210

1946, Mar. 6			
599 A210	80 l blue	18	15

Agrarian reform law of Mar. 23, 1945.

Atheneum, Bucharest A211 — Numeral in Wreath A212

Georges Enescu — A213

Wmk. 276

1946, Apr. 26	Photo.	*Perf. 13½*	
600 A211	10 l dk bl	9	6
601 A212	20 l red brn	9	6
602 A212	55 l pck bl	9	6
603 A213	80 l purple	18	15
a	Tete beche pair	60	60
604 A212	160 l red org	9	9
	Nos. 600-604,B330-B331 (7)	1.79	1.67

Philharmonic Society, 25th anniv.

Mechanic — A214

Designs: No. 606, Laborer. No. 607, Sower. No. 608, Reaper. 200 l, Students.

1946, May 1		*Perf. 13½x13*	
605 A214	10 l Prus grn	*38*	*38*
606 A214	10 l dk car rose	5	5
607 A214	20 l dl bl	*38*	*38*
608 A214	20 l dk red brn	5	5
609 A214	200 l brt red	9	9
	Nos. 605-609 (5)	*95*	*95*

Labor Day, May 1.

Michael Types of 1945

1946	Wmk. 276 Photo.	*Perf. 14*	
	Toned Paper		
610 A198	10 l brt red brn	5	5
611 A198	20 l vio brn	5	5
612 A201	80 l blue	5	5
613 A198	137 l yel grn	5	5
614 A201	160 l chalky bl	5	5
615 A201	200 l red org	5	5
616 A201	300 l sapphire	5	5
617 A201	360 l sepia	5	5
618 A199	400 l red org	5	5
619 A201	480 l brn red	5	6
620 A201	600 l dk ol grn	5	5
621 A201	1000 l Prus grn	5	5
622 A198	1500 l Prus grn	5	5
623 A201	2400 l magenta	7	5
624 A201	3700 l dull bl	7	5
	Nos. 610-624 (15)	79	76

Demetrius Cantemir A219 — Soccer A222

Designs: 100 l, "Cultural Ties." 300 l, "Economic Ties."

1946, Oct. 20		*Perf. 13½*	
625 A219	80 l dk brn	9	9
626 A219	100 l dp bl	9	9
627 A219	300 l bl blk	9	9

Romania-Soviet friendship. See Nos. B338-B339.

1946, Sept. 1		*Perf. 11½, Imperf.*	

Designs: 20 l, Diving. 50 l, Running. 80 l, Mountain climbing.

628 A222	10 l dp bl	35	35
629 A222	20 l brt red	35	35
630 A222	50 l dp vio	35	35
631 A222	80 l chocolate	35	35
	Nos. 628-631,B340,C26,CB6 (7)	3.15	3.15

Issued in sheets of 16.

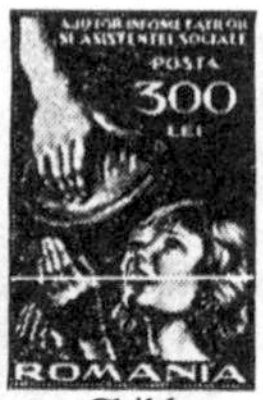

Weaving A226 — Child Receiving Bread A227

Transporting Relief Supplies A228 — CGM Congress Emblem A229

Wmk. 276

1946, Nov. 20	Photo.	*Perf. 14*	
636 A226	80 l dk ol brn	6	6
	Nos. 636,B342-B345 (5)	51	51

Democratic Women's Org. of Romania. See No. CB7.

Perf. 13½x14, 14x13½

1947, Jan. 15			
637 A227	300 l dk ol brn	15	12
638 A228	600 l magenta	15	12

Issued to publicize the social relief fund. See Nos. B346-B348.

1947, Feb. 10		*Perf. 13½*	
639 A229	200 l blue	14	8
640 A229	300 l orange	14	8
a	Se-tenant with No. 639	25	25
b	Se-tenant with No. 641	25	25
641 A229	600 l crimson	14	8

Congress of the United Labor Unions ("CGM").

Printed in sheets of 18 comprising 3 pairs of each denomination. Sheet yields 3 each of Nos. 640a and 640b.

Peace in Chariot
A230

Peace A231 — Flags of United States, Russia, Great Britain and Romania A232

Dove of Peace — A233

Perf. 14x13½, 13½x14

1947, Feb. 25			
642 A230	300 l dl vio	8	8
643 A231	600 l dk org brn	8	8
644 A232	3000 l blue	8	8
645 A233	7200 l sage grn	8	8

Signing of the peace treaty of February 10, 1947.

King Michael — A234

1947		*Perf. 13½*	
	Size: 25x30mm		
646 A234	3000 l blue	10	8
647 A234	7200 l dl vio	10	8
648 A234	15,000 l brt bl	15	8
649 A234	21,000 l magenta	15	10
650 A234	36,000 l violet	25	15
	Nos. 646-650 (5)	75	49

See Nos. 661-664.

Michael Types of 1945

1947	Wmk. 276 Photo.	*Perf. 14*	
651 A199	10 l red brn	8	5
652 A200	20 l magenta	8	5
653 A198	80 l blue	8	5
654 A199	200 l brt red	8	5
655 A198	500 l magenta	8	5
656 A200	860 l vio brn	10	5
657 A199	2500 l ultra	8	5
658 A198	5000 l sl gray	20	8
659 A198	8000 l Prus grn	35	15
660 A201	10,000 l dk brn	25	15
	Type of 1947		
	Size: 18x21½mm		
661 A234	1000 l gray bl	8	5
662 A234	5500 l yel grn	10	5
663 A234	20,000 l ol brn	15	6
664 A234	50,000 l red org	35	15
	Nos. 651-664 (14)	2.06	1.04

Harvesting Wheat
A235

Designs: 1 l, Log raft. 2 l, River steamer. 3 l, Resita. 5 l, Cathedral of Curtea de Arges. 10 l, View of Bucharest. 12 l, 36 l, Cernavoda Bridge. 15 l, 32 l, Port of Constantsa. 20 l, Petroleum field.

1947, Aug. 15 **Perf. 14½x14**

666 A235 50b red org 10 5
667 A235 1 l red brn 10 5
668 A235 2 l bl gray 10 5
669 A235 3 l rose crim 25 8
670 A235 5 l brt ultra 30 10
671 A235 10 l brt bl 35 10
672 A235 12 l violet 50 25
673 A235 15 l dp ultra 75 20
674 A235 20 l dk brn 1.50 50
675 A235 32 l vio brn 3.00 1.00
676 A235 36 l dk car rose 3.00 50
Nos. 666-676 (11) 9.95 2.88

Beehive, Savings Emblem — A236

1947, Oct. 31 **Perf. 13½**

677 A236 12 l dk car rose 28 20

World Savings Day, Oct. 31, 1947.

People's Republic

Map, Workers and Children A237

1948, Jan. 25 **Perf. 14½x14**

678 A237 12 l brt ultra 28 14

Issued to publicize the census of 1948.

Government Printing Plant and Press — A238

1948 **Perf. 14½x14**

679 A238 6 l magenta 90 50
680 A238 7.50 l dk Prus grn 50 14
b Tete beche pair 1.00 90

75th anniversary of Stamp Division of Romanian State Printing Works.
Issue dates: No. 680, Feb. 12. No. 679, May 20.

Romanian and Bulgarian Peasants Shaking Hands A239

1948, Mar. 25 **Wmk. 276**

680A A239 32 l red brn 35 18

Romanian-Bulgarian friendship.

Allegory of the People's Republic — A240

1948, Apr. 8 **Photo.** **Perf. 14x14½**

681 A240 1 l car rose 35 14
682 A240 2 l dl org 35 18
683 A240 12 l deep blue 50 30

New constitution.

Nos. 666 to 676 Overprinted in Black

1948, Mar. **Perf. 14½x14**

684 A235 50b red org 30 15
685 A235 1 l red brn 30 9
686 A235 2 l bl gray 55 15
687 A235 3 l rose crim 55 15
688 A235 5 l brt ultra 75 15
689 A235 10 l brt bl 1.10 20
690 A235 12 l violet 1.25 24
691 A235 15 l dp ultra 1.25 28
692 A235 20 l dk brn 1.50 45
693 A235 32 l vio brn 4.25 1.50
694 A235 36 l dk car rose 4.25 1.50
Nos. 684-694 (11) 16.05 4.86

Romanian Newspapers A241

1948, Sept. 12

695 A241 10 l red brn 28 12

Week of the Democratic Press, Sept. 12-19. See Nos. B396-B398.

No. 680A Surcharged with New Value in Black

1948, Aug. 17

696 A239 31 l on 32 l red brn 55 14

Monument to Soviet Soldier — A242

Proclamation of Islaz — A243

1948, Oct. 29 **Photo.** **Perf. 14x14½**

697 A242 10 l dk red 45 35

Sheets of 50 stamps and 50 labels. See Nos. B399-B400, CB16.

1948, June 1 **Perf. 14½x14**

698 A243 11 l car rose 35 18
Nos. 698,B409-B412 (5) 3.25 3.08

Centenary of Revolution of 1848.

Arms of Romanian People's Republic — A243a

1948, July 8 **Wmk. 276**

698A A243a 50b red ("Lei 0.50") 40 40
698B A243a 1 l red brn 25 5
698C A243a 2 l dk grn 25 5
698D A243a 3 l grnsh blk 35 6
698E A243a 4 l chocolate 35 6
698F A243a 5 l ultra 35 7
698G A243a 10 l dp bl 1.10 6

"Bani" instead of "Lei"

698H A243a 50b red ("Bani 0.50") 48 22
Nos. 698A-698H (8) 3.53 97

See Nos. 712-717.

Nicolae Balcescu (1819-1852), Writer — A244

Wmk. 289 - RPR Multiple

1948, Dec. 20 **Wmk. 289**

699 A244 20 l scarlet 35 12

Release from Bondage — A245

1948, Dec. 30 **Perf. 13½**

700 A245 5 l brt rose 28 16

First anniversary of the Republic.

Lenin, 25th Death Anniv. — A246

Folk Dance — A247

1949, Jan. 21

701 A246 20 l black 35 18

No. 701 exists imperf.

1949, Jan. 24 **Perf. 13½**

702 A247 10 l dp bl 35 18

90th anniv. of the union of the Danubian Principalities.

Ion C. Frimu and Revolutionary Scene — A248

1949, Mar. 22 **Perf. 14½x14**

703 A248 20 l red 35 18

No. 703 exists imperf.

Aleksander S. Pushkin, 150th Birth Anniv. — A249

1949, May 20 **Perf. 14x14½**

704 A249 11 l car rose 48 20
705 A249 30 l Prus grn 70 35

Globe and Post Horn — A250

Evolution of Mail Transportation — A251

Perf. 13½, 14½x14

1949, June 30 **Photo.** **Wmk. 289**

706 A250 20 l org brn 1.50 1.10
707 A251 30 l brt bl 1.10 75

UPU, 75th anniv.

Russian Army Entering Bucharest, August, 1944 A252

1949, Aug. 23 **Perf. 14½x14, Imperf.**

708 A252 50 l choc, *bl grn* 60 40

5th anniv. of the liberation of Romania by the Soviet army, Aug. 1944.

"Long Live Romanian-Soviet Amity" — A253

1949, Nov. 1 **Perf. 13½x14½**

709 A253 20 l dp red 35 28

National week of Romanian-Soviet friendship celebration, Nov. 1-7, 1949. Exists imperf.

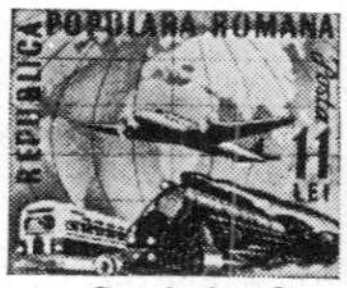

Symbols of Transportation A254

Joseph V. Stalin A256

1949, Dec. 10 **Perf. 13½**

710 A254 11 l blue 55 40
711 A254 20 l crimson 55 40

Intl. Conference of Transportation Unions, Dec. 10, 1949.
Alternate vertical rows of stamps and labels in sheet. Exist imperf.

Arms Type of 1948

1949-50 **Wmk. 289** **Perf. 14x13½**

712 A243a 50b red ("Lei 0.50") 35 30
713 A243a 1 l red brn 35 10
714 A243a 2 l dk grn 35 10
714A A243a 3 l grnsh blk 65 20
715 A243a 5 l ultra 50 25

716	A243a	5 l rose vio ('50)	70	10
717	A243a	10 l dp blue	90	25
		Nos. 712-717 (7)	3.80	1.25

1949, Dec. 21 ***Perf. 13½***

718	A256	31 l ol blk	48	22

Stalin's 70th birthday. Exists imperf.

Mihail Eminescu A257

Poem: "Life" A258

Designs: No. 721, "Third Letter." No. 722, "Angel and Demon." No. 723, "Emperor and Proletariat."

1950, Jan. 15 **Photo.** **Wmk. 289**

719	A257	11 l blue	45	18
720	A258	11 l purple	75	22
721	A258	11 l dk grn	45	45
722	A258	11 l red brn	45	18
723	A258	11 l rose pink	45	18
		Nos. 719-723 (5)	2.55	1.21

Birth cent. of Mihail Eminescu, poet.

Fair at Dragaica A259

Ion Andreescu (Self-portrait) — A260

Village Well A261

Perf. 14½x14, 14x14½

1950, Mar. 25

724	A259	5 l dk gray grn	45	22
725	A260	11 l ultra	75	22
726	A261	20 l brown	85	45

Birth cent. of Ion Andreescu, painter. No. 725 also exists imperf.

Graph and Factories A262

Design: 31 l, Tractor and Oil Derricks.

Inscribed: "Planul de Stat 1950."

Perf. 14½x14

1950, Apr. 23 **Wmk. 289**

727	A262	11 l red	60	24
728	A262	31 l violet	85	40

1950 plan for increased industrial production. No. 727 also exists imperf.

Young Man Holding Flag A263

Arms of Republic A264

1950, May 1 ***Perf. 14x14½***

729	A263	31 l org red	60	30

Labor Day, May 1. Exists imperf.

> Canceled to Order
> Canceled sets of new issues have long been sold by the government. Values in the second ("used") column are for these canceled-to-order stamps. Postally used copies are worth more.

1950 **Photo.** ***Perf. 12½***

730	A264	50b black	15	6
731	A264	1 l red	6	5
732	A264	2 l ol gray	5	5
733	A264	3 l violet	9	5
734	A264	4 l rose lil	6	5
735	A264	5 l red brn	9	5
736	A264	6 l dp grn	9	5
737	A264	7 l vio brn	15	5
738	A264	7.50 l blue	22	9
739	A264	10 l dk brn	48	5
740	A264	11 l rose car	48	5
741	A264	15 l dp bl	28	5
742	A264	20 l Prus grn	30	9
743	A264	31 l dl grn	45	6
744	A264	36 l dk org brn	75	28
		Nos. 730-744 (15)	3.70	1.08

See Nos. 947-961 which have similar design with white denomination figures.

Bugler and Drummer A265

Designs: 11 l, Three school children. 31 l, Drummer, flag-bearer and bugler.

1950, May 25 ***Perf. 14½x14***

745	A265	8 l blue	45	30
746	A265	11 l rose vio	75	45
747	A265	31 l org ver	1.50	90

Young Pioneers, 1st anniv.

Factory Worker — A266

Aurel Vlaicu and his First Plane — A267

1950, July 20 **Photo.** ***Perf. 14x14½***

748	A266	11 l red brn	30	18
749	A266	11 l red	30	18
750	A266	11 l blue	30	18
751	A266	11 l blk brn	30	18

Nationalization of industry, 2nd anniv.

1950, July 22 **Wmk. 289** ***Perf. 12½***

752	A267	3 l dk grn	35	18
753	A267	6 l dk bl	40	18
754	A267	8 l ultra	40	18

Aurel Vlaicu (1882-1913), pioneer of Romanian aviation.

Mother and Child A268

Lathe and Operator A269

1950, Sept. 9 ***Perf. 13½***

755	A268	11 l rose red	30	20
756	A269	20 l dk ol brn	30	20

Congress of the Committees for the Struggle for Peace.

Statue of Soviet Soldier — A270

1950, Oct. 6 ***Perf. 14x14½***

757	A270	30 l red brn	48	22

Celebration of Romanian-Soviet friendship, Oct. 7-Nov. 7, 1950.

No. 741 Overprinted in Carmine

TRĂIASCĂ
PRIETENIA
ROMÂNO-
MAGHIĂRAI

1950, Oct. 6 ***Perf. 12½***

758	A264	15 l dp bl	38	16

Romanian-Hungarian friendship.

"Agriculture," "Manufacturing" and Sports Badge — A271

Designs: 5 l, Student workers and Sports badge. 11 l, Track team and badge. 31 l, Calisthenics and badge.

1950, Oct. 30 ***Perf. 14½x14***

759	A271	3 l rose car	60	45
760	A271	5 l red brn	45	30
761	A271	5 l brt bl	45	30
762	A271	11 l green	45	30
763	A271	31 l brn ol	1.10	75
		Nos. 759-763 (5)	3.05	2.10

A272

"Industry" — A273

"Agriculture" — A274

1950, Nov. 2 ***Perf. 13½***

764	A272	11 l blue	28	15
765	A272	11 l red org	28	15

3rd Soviet-Romanian Friendship Congress.

Perf. 14x14½, 14½x14

1951, Feb. 9 **Photo.** **Wmk. 289**

766	A273	11 l red brn	12	9
767	A274	31 l deep bl	38	18

Industry and Agriculture Exposition. Exist imperf.

Ski Jump — A275

Ski Descent — A276

Designs: 5 l, Skating. 20 l, Hockey. 31 l, Bobsledding.

1951, Jan. 28 ***Perf. 13½***

768	A275	4 l blk brn	30	9
769	A275	5 l vermilion	45	18
770	A276	11 l dp bl	85	28
771	A275	20 l org brn	90	60
772	A275	31 l dk gray grn	1.90	1.10
		Nos. 768-772 (5)	4.40	2.25

9th World University Winter Games.

Medal for Work — A277

Orders: 4 l, Star of the Republic, Classes III, IV & V. 11 l, Work. 35 l, Star of the Republic, Classes I & II.

1951, May 1 ***Perf. 13½***

773	A277	2 l ol gray	30	18
774	A277	4 l blue	30	18
775	A277	11 l crimson	30	18
776	A277	35 l org brn	35	18

Labor Day. Exist imperf.

Camp of Young Pioneers A278

Pioneers Greeting Stalin — A279

Admitting New Pioneers
A280

1951, May 8 ***Perf. 14x14½, 14½x14***

777 A278 1 l gray grn 90 60
778 A279 11 l blue 90 22
779 A280 35 l red 75 28

Romanian Young Pioneers Organization.

Woman Orator and Flags
A281

Ion Negulici
A282

1951, Mar. 8 ***Perf. 14x14½***

780 A281 11 l org brn 35 18

Woman's Day, Mar. 8. Exists imperf.

1951, June 20 ***Perf. 14x14½***

781 A282 35 l rose red 75 55

Death cent. of Ion Negulici, painter.

Bicyclists
A283

1951, July 9 ***Perf. 14½x14***

782 A283 11 l chnt brn 1.65 65
a Tete beche pair 4.00 3.25

The 1951 Bicycle Tour of Romania.

Festival Badge — A284

Boy and Girl with Flag — A285

Youths Encircling Globe — A286

1951, Aug. 1 ***Perf. 13½***

783 A284 1 l scarlet 50 22
784 A285 5 l deep blue 50 22
785 A286 11 l deep plum 65 50

3rd World Youth Festival, Berlin.

Filimon Sarbu
A287

"Romania Raising the Masses"
A288

"Revolutionary Romania" — A289

1951, July 23 ***Perf. 14x14½***

786 A287 11 l dk brn 28 10

10th death anniv. of Filimon Sarbu, patriot.

Perf. 14x14½, 14½x14

1951, July 23

787 A288 11 l yel brn 85 35
788 A288 11 l rose vio 85 35
789 A289 11 l dk grn 85 35
790 A289 11 l org red 85 35

Death cent. of C. D. Rosenthal, painter.

Scanteia Building
A290

1951, Aug. 16 ***Perf. 14½x14***

791 A290 11 l blue 35 15

20th anniv. of the newspaper Scanteia.

Miner in Dress Uniform
A291

Order for National Defense
A293

Design: 11 l, Miner in work clothes.

1951, Aug. 12 ***Perf. 14x14½***

792 A291 5 l blue 24 16
793 A291 11 l plum 24 10

Issued to publicize Miner's Day.

1951, Aug. 12 ***Perf. 14x14½***

794 A293 10 l crimson 50 25

Choir
A294

Music Week Emblem
A295

An enhanced introduction to the Scott Catalogue begins on Page V. A thorough understanding of the material presented there will greatly aid your use of the catalogue itself.

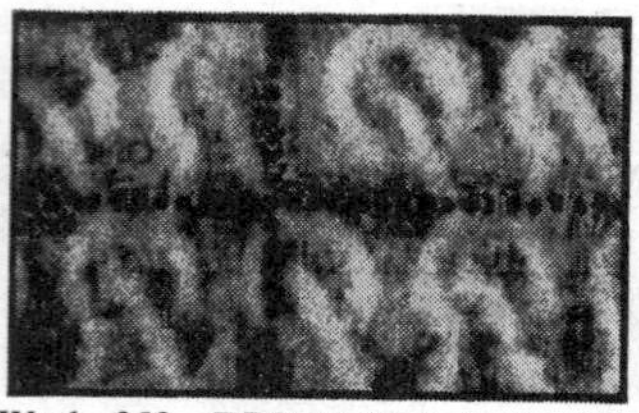

Wmk. 358 - RPR Multiple in Endless Rows

Design: No. 796, Orchestra and dancers.

Wmk. 358

1951, Sept. 22 **Photo.** ***Perf. 13½***

795 A294 11 l blue 35 20
796 A294 11 l red brn 50 40
797 A295 11 l purple 35 20

Music Week, Sept. 22-30, 1951.

Soldier — A296

Oil Field — A297

1951, Oct. 2

798 A296 11 l blue 32 14

Issued to publicize Army Day, Oct. 2, 1951.

1951-52

Designs: 2 l, Coal mining. 3 l, Romanian soldier. 4 l, Smelting ore. 5 l, Agricultural machinery. 6 l, Canal construction. 7 l, Agriculture. 8 l, Self-education. 11 l, Hydroelectric production. 35 l, Manufacturing.

799 A297 1 l blk brn 15 6
800 A297 2 l chocolate 15 6
801 A297 3 l scarlet 35 13
802 A297 4 l yel brn ('52) 20 15
803 A297 5 l green 35 10
804 A297 6 l brt bl ('52) 1.25 40
805 A297 7 l emerald 50 40
806 A297 8 l brn ('52) 50 40
807 A297 11 l blue 35 10
808 A297 35 l purple 1.35 80
Nos. 799-808,C35-C36 (12) 7.30 4.40

1951-55 Five Year Plan.

Arms of Soviet Union and Romania
A298

1951, Oct. 7 **Wmk. 358**

809 A298 4 l chnt brn, *cr* 35 15
810 A298 35 l org red 90 45

Month of Romanian-Soviet friendship, Oct. 7-Nov. 7.

Pavel Tcacenco
A299

Railroad Conductor
A300

1951, Dec. 15 ***Perf. 14x14½***

811 A299 10 l ol brn & dk brn 35 20

26th death anniv. of Pavel Tcacenco, revolutionary.

1952, Mar. 24 ***Perf. 13½***

812 A300 55b dk brn 1.50 70

Railroad Workers' Day, Feb. 16.

Ion L. Caragiale — A301

Announcing Caragiale Celebration — A302

Designs: No. 814, Book and painting "1907." No. 815, Bust and wreath.

1952, Apr. 1 ***Perf. 13½, 14½x14***

Inscribed: ". . . . I. L. Caragiale."

813 A301 55b chlky bl 95 35
814 A302 55b scarlet 95 35
815 A302 55b dp grn 95 35
816 A302 1 l brown 2.75 1.00

Birth cent. of Ion L. Caragiale, dramatist.

Types of 1952 Surcharged with New Value in Black or Carmine

1952-53

817 A302 20b on 11 l scar *(As No. 814)* 60 45
818 A302 55b on 11 l dp grn *(As No. 815)* (C) 75 60
819 A301 75b on 11 l chlky bl (C) 1.25 75

Various Issues Surcharged with New Values in Carmine or Black

On No. 678, Census

Perf. 14x13½

819A A240 50b on 12 l ultra 6.75 3.75

On No. 683, New Constitution

Perf. 14

820 A240 50b on 12 l dp bl 2.00 1.50

On No. 698, Revolution

820A A243 1.75 l on 11 l car rose (Bk) 25.00 12.00

On Nos. 704-705, Pushkin

1952 **Wmk. 358**

821 A249 10b on 11 l car rose (Bk) 2.50 1.75
822 A249 10b on 30 l Prus grn 2.50 1.75

On Nos. 719-723, Eminescu

Perf. 13½x13, 13x13½

823 A257 10b on 11 l bl 1.75 1.75
824 A258 10b on 11 l pur 1.75 1.75
825 A258 10b on 11 l dk grn 1.75 1.75
826 A258 10b on 11 l red brn (Bk) 1.75 1.75
827 A258 10b on 11 l rose pink (Bk) 1.75 1.75

On Nos. 724-725, Andreescu

Perf. 14

827A A259 55b on 5 l dk gray grn 5.00 2.75
827B A260 55b on 11 l ultra 5.00 2.75

On Nos. 727-728, Production Plan

Perf. 14½x14

827C A262 20b on 11 l red (Bk) 1.75 75
827D A262 20b on 31 l vio 1.75 75

On No. 729, Labor Day

Perf. 14

827E A263 55b on 31 l org red (Bk) 2.75 2.75

On Nos. 730-739 and 741-744, National Arms

Perf. 12½

828 A264 3b on 1 l red (Bk) 70 45
829 A264 3b on 2 l ol gray (Bk) 1.10 55
830 A264 3b on 4 l rose lil (Bk) 70 45

831 A264 3b on 5 l red brn (Bk) 1.10 55
832 A264 3b on 7.50 l bl (Bk) 3.25 1.40
833 A264 3b on 10 l dk brn (Bk) 1.10 55
834 A264 55b on 50b blk brn 3.25 70
835 A264 55b on 3 l vio 3.25 70
836 A264 55b on 6 l dp grn 3.25 70
837 A264 55b on 7 l vio brn 3.25 70
838 A264 55b on 15 l dp bl 5.00 70
839 A264 55b on 20 l Prus grn 3.25 70
840 A264 55b on 31 l dl grn 3.25 70
841 A264 55b on 36 l dk org brn 5.00 70

On Nos. 745-747, Young Pioneers
Perf. 14

841A A265 55b on 8 l bl 9.50 5.75
841B A265 55b on 11 l rose vio 9.50 5.75
841C A265 55b on 31 l org ver (Bk) 9.50 5.75

On Nos. 752-754, Vlaicu
Perf. 12½

842 A267 10b on 3 l dk grn 1.50 1.10
843 A267 10b on 6 l dk bl 1.50 1.10
844 A267 10b on 8 l ultra 1.50 1.10

Original denomination canceled with an "X."

On No. 756, Peace Congress
Perf. 13½

844A A269 20b on 20 l dk ol brn 2.25 1.90

On No. 759, Sports
Perf. 14½x14

845 A271 55b on 3 l rose car (Bk) 15.00 11.50

On No. 767, Exposition

846 A274 55b on 31 l dp bl 7.50 5.75

On Nos. 771-772, Winter Games
Perf. 13½

847 A275 55b on 20 l org brn (Bk) 19.00 7.50
848 A275 55b on 31 l dk gray grn 19.00 7.50

On Nos. 773-776, Labor Medals

849 A277 20b on 2 l ol gray 3.75 2.25
850 A277 20b on 4 l bl 3.75 2.25
851 A277 20b on 11 l crim (Bk) 3.75 2.25
852 A277 20b on 35 l org brn (Bk) 3.75 2.25

On Nov. 779, Young Pioneers
Perf. 14x14½

853 A280 55b on 35 l red (Bk) 13.00 9.50

On No. 792, Miners' Day

854 A291 55b on 5 l bl 11.00 7.50

On No. 794, Defense Order

855 A293 55b on 10 l crim (Bk) 5.75 3.75

On Nos. B409-B412, 1848 Revolution
1952 Wmk. 276 *Perf. 13x13½*

856 SP280 1.75 l on 2 l + 2 l car lake (Bk) 9.50 3.75
857 SP281 1.75 l on 5 l + 5 l dk vio 9.50 3.75
858 SP282 1.75 l on 10 l + 10 l dk ol brn 9.50 3.75
859 SP280 1.75 l on 36 l + 18 l dp bl 9.50 3.75

On Nos. 799-808, 5-Year Plan
Perf. 13½
Wmk. 358

860 A297 35b on 1 l blk brn 1.90 95
861 A297 35b on 2 l choc 6.00 1.10
862 A297 35b on 3 l scar (Bk) 3.00 1.90
863 A297 35b on 4 l yel brn (Bk) 3.50 2.25
a Red surcharge 15.00 12.00
864 A297 35b on 5 l grn 3.00 3.00
865 A297 1 l on 6 l brt bl 4.75 4.75
866 A297 1 l on 7 l emer 3.50 2.25
867 A297 1 l on 8 l brn 3.50 3.50
868 A297 1 l on 11 l bl 4.75 2.75
869 A297 1 l on 35 l pur 4.75 2.25

On Nos. 809-810, Romanian-Soviet Friendship

870 A298 10b on 4 l chnt brn, *cr* (Bk) 1.50 95
871 A298 10b on 35 l org red (Bk) 1.50 95

On No. 811, Tcacenco
Perf. 13½x14

872 A299 10b on 10 l ol brn & dk brn 1.90 1.40

Ivan P. Pavlov — A302a

Perf. 13½x13
1952, Apr. 14 Photo. Wmk. 358

873 A302a 1 l red brn 1.65 70

Meeting of Romanian-Soviet doctors in Bucharest.

Hammer and Sickle Medal — A303

1952, May 1

874 A303 55b org brn & chnt brn 75 10

Issued for Labor Day.

Medal for Motherhood A304

Leonardo da Vinci A305

Medals: 55b, Maternal glory. 1.75 l, Mother-Heroine.

1952, Apr. 7 *Perf. 13x13½*

875 A304 20b plum & sl gray 30 10
876 A304 55b hn brn 70 18
877 A304 1.75 l rose red & brn buff 1.75 40

International Women's Day.

1952, July 3

878 A305 55b purple 2.10 60

500th birth anniv. of Leonardo da Vinci.

Gogol and Scene from Taras Bulba A306

Nikolai V. Gogol — A307

1952, Apr. 1 *Perf. 13½x14, 14x13½*

879 A306 55b dp bl 95 22
880 A307 1.75 l ol gray 1.40 60

Death cent. of Nikolai V. Gogol, Russian writer.

Pioneers Saluting — A308

Labor Day Paraders Returning A309

Design: 55b, Pioneers studying nature.

1952, May 21 *Perf. 14*

881 A308 20b brown 45 14
882 A308 55b dp grn 1.25 22
883 A309 1.75 l blue 2.10 52

Third anniversary of Romanian Pioneers.

Infantry Attack, Painting by Grigorescu — A310

Miner — A311

Design: 1.10 l, Romanian and Russian soldiers.

1952, June 7 *Perf. 13x13½*

884 A310 50b rose brn 45 6
885 A310 1.10 l blue 75 30

Independence Proclamation of 1877, 75th anniv.

1952, Aug. 11 Wmk. 358

902 A311 20b rose red 1.25 25
903 A311 55b purple 1.25 15

Issued to publicize the Day of the Miner.

Book and Globe — A312

Chemistry Student A313

Students in Native Dress — A314

Design: 55b, Students playing soccer.

Perf. 13½x13, 13½x14, 13x13½.
1952, Sept. 5

904 A312 10b dp bl 15 8
905 A313 20b orange 70 40
906 A312 55b dp grn 2.00 50
907 A314 1.75 l rose red 3.00 1.00

Intl. Student Union Congress, Bucharest, Sept.

Soldier, Sailor and Aviator — A316

1952, Oct. 2 *Perf. 14*

909 A316 55b blue 48 22

Armed Forces Day, Oct. 2, 1952.

"Russia" Leading Peace Crusade — A317

Allegory: Romanian-Soviet Friendship — A318

1952, Oct. 7 *Perf. 13½x13, 13x13½.*

910 A317 55b vermilion 65 22
911 A318 1.75 l blk brn 1.65 75

Month of Romanian-Soviet friendship, Oct.

Rowing on Lake Snagov A319

Nicolae Balcescu A320

Design: 1.75 l, Athletes marching with flags.

1952, Oct. 20

912 A319 20b dp bl 2.75 52
913 A319 1.75 l rose red 5.00 1.10

1952, Nov. 29

914 A320 55b gray 1.90 75
915 A320 1.75 l lem bis 4.00 1.90

Death cent. of Nicolae Balcescu, poet.

Arms of Republic — A321

1952, Dec. 6 Wmk. 358

916 A321 55b dl grn 75 30

5th anniversary of socialist constitution.

Arms and Industrial Symbols A322

1953, Jan. 8 *Perf. 12½x13½*

917	A322	55b bl, yel & red	90	38

5th anniv. of the proclamation of the People's Republic.

Matei Millo, Costache Caragiale and Aristita Romanescu A323

1953, Feb. **Photo.** *Perf. 13x13½*

918	A323	55b brt ultra	1.50	38

National Theater of I. L. Caragiale, cent.

Iron Foundry Worker — A324

Worker — A325

Design: No. 921, Driving Tractor.

1953, Feb. *Perf. 13½x13, 13x13½*

919	A324	55b sl grn	32	12
920	A325	55b blk brn	32	12
921	A325	55b orange	65	32

3rd Congress of the Syndicate of the Romanian People's Republic.

"Strike at Grivita," Painted by G. Miclossy A326

Arms of Romanian People's Republic A327

1953, Feb. 16 *Perf. 13x13½*

922	A326	55b chestnut	1.25	50

20th anniv. of the oil industry strike of Feb. 16, 1933.

1953 *Perf. 12½*

923	A327	5b crimson	28	12
924	A327	55b purple	75	28

Flags of Romania and Russia, Farm Machinery A328

1953, Mar. 24 *Perf. 14*

925	A328	55b dk brn, *bl*	95	35

5th anniv. of the signing of a treaty of friendship and mutual assistance between Russia and Romania.

Map and Medal — A329

Rug — A330

Folk Dance A330a

1953, Mar. 24

926	A329	55b dk gray grn	1.75	52
927	A329	55b chestnut	2.25	52

20th World Championship Table Tennis Matches, Budapest, 1953.

1953

Designs: 10b, Ceramics. 20b, Costume of Campulung (Muscel). 55b, Apuseni Mts. costume.

Inscribed: "Arta Populara Romaneasca"

928	A330	10b dp grn	60	8
929	A330	20b red brn	1.25	12
929A	A330a	35b purple	1.75	20
930	A330	55b vio bl	2.75	20
931	A330	1 l brt red vio	4.00	40
		Nos. 928-931 (5)	10.35	1.00

Romanian Folk Arts.

Karl Marx — A331

Children Planting Tree — A332

Physics Class A333

1953, May 21 *Perf. 13½x13*

932	A331	1.55 l ol brn	1.40	70

70th death anniv. of Karl Marx.

1953, May 21 *Perf. 14*

Design: 55b, Flying model planes.

933	A332	35b dp grn	1.00	20
934	A332	55b dl bl	1.40	28
935	A333	1.75 l brown	3.25	70

Women and Flags A334

Discus Thrower A335

Students Offering Teacher Flowers A336

1953, June 18 *Perf. 13½x13*

936	A334	55b red brn	1.00	28

3rd World Congress of Women, Copenhagen, 1953.

1953, Aug. 2 **Wmk. 358** *Perf. 14*

Designs: 55b, Students reaching toward dove. 1.75 l, Dance in local costumes.

937	A335	20b orange	52	10
938	A335	55b dp bl	90	18
939	A336	65b scarlet	1.25	52
940	A336	1.75 l red vio	3.50	70

4th World Youth Festival, Bucharest, Aug. 2-16.

Waterfall A337

Wheat Field A338

Design: 55b, Forester holding seedling.

1953, July 29 **Photo.**

941	A337	20b vio bl	55	14
942	A338	38b dl grn	1.40	55
943	A337	55b lt brn	1.50	25

Issued to publicize the Month of the Forest.

Vladimir V. Mayakovsky A339

1953, Aug. 22

944	A339	55b brown	75	24

60th birth anniv. of V. V. Mayakovsky, poet.

Miner Using Drill A340

1953, Sept. 19

945	A340	1.55 l sl blk	1.40	50

Issued to publicize Miners' Day.

Arms of Republic — A342

1952-53 *Perf. 12½*

Size: 20x24mm

947	A342	3b dp org	60	20
948	A342	5b crimson	80	5
949	A342	7b dk bl grn	80	20
950	A342	10b chocolate	1.00	5
951	A342	20b dp bl	1.25	5
952	A342	35b blk brn	2.75	8
953	A342	50b dk gray grn	3.25	5
954	A342	55b purple	7.25	7

Size: 24x29mm

955	A342	1.10 l dk brn	6.50	28
956	A342	1.75 l violet	24.00	40
957	A342	2 l ol blk	6.50	48
958	A342	2.35 l org brn	7.75	32
959	A342	2.55 l dp org	9.75	40
960	A342	3 l dk gray grn	10.00	32
961	A342	5 l dp crim	12.00	60
		Nos. 947-961 (15)	94.20	3.55

Stamps of similar design with value figures in color are Nos. 730-744.

Postal Administration Building and Telephone Employees — A343

Designs: 55b, Postal Adm. Bldg. and Letter carrier. 1 l, Map and communications symbols. 1.55 l, Postal Adm. Bldg. and Telegraph employees.

1953, Oct. 20 **Wmk. 358** *Perf. 14*

964	A343	20b dk red brn	18	9
965	A343	55b ol grn	30	12
966	A343	1 l brt bl	75	18
967	A343	1.55 l rose brn	1.10	45

50th anniv. of the construction of the Postal Administration Building.

Liberation Medal — A344

Soldier and Flag — A345

1953, Oct. 20 *Perf. 14x13½*

968	A344	55b dk brn	70	18

9th anniv. of the liberation of Romania.

1953, Oct. 2 *Perf. 13½*

969	A345	55b ol grn	70	35

Army Day, Oct. 2.

Girl with Model Plane A346

Designs: 20b, Parachute landing. 55b, Glider and pilot. 1.75 l, Plane in flight.

1953, Oct. 20 *Perf. 14*

970	A346	10b org & dk gray grn	2.25	48
971	A346	20b org brn & dk ol grn	4.50	28
972	A346	55b dk scar & rose lil	7.25	80
973	A346	1.75 l dk rose vio & brn	9.50	1.25

Issued to popularize civil aviation.

Workers and Flags — A347

Design: 1.55 l, Spasski Tower and lock on Volga-Don Canal.

1953, Nov. 25 *Perf. 13x13½*

974	A347	55b brown	48	12
975	A347	1.55 l rose brn	70	30

Month of Romanian-Soviet friendship, Oct. 7-Nov. 7.

Hemispheres and Clasped Hands — A348

Workers, Flags and Globe — A349

1953, Nov. 25 *Perf. 14*

976	A348	55b dk ol	38	15
977	A349	1.25 l crimson	90	38

World Congress of Trade Unions.

Ciprian Porumbescu A350

Harvesting Machine A351

1953, Dec. 16

978	A350	55b purple	4.00	90

Ciprian Porumbescu (1853-1883), composer.

Perf. 13x13½

1953, Dec. 16 **Wmk. 358**

Designs: 35b, Tractor in field. 2.55 l, Cattle.

979	A351	10b sepia	28	12
980	A351	35b dk grn	38	20
981	A351	2.55 l org brn	3.50	1.10

Aurel Vlaicu — A352

Lenin — A353

1953, Dec. 26 *Perf. 14*

982	A352	50b vio bl	75	22

40th death anniv. of Aurel Vlaicu, aviation pioneer.

1954, Jan. 21 *Perf. 13½*

983	A353	55b dk red brn, *buff*	75	22

30th death anniv. of Lenin.

Red Deer — A354

Designs: 55b, Children planting trees. 1.75 l, Mountain scene.

1954, Apr. 1

Yellow Surface-colored Paper

984	A354	20b dk brn	1.50	22
985	A354	55b violet	1.50	22
986	A354	1.75 l dk bl	3.25	70

Month of the Forest, April, 1954.

Calimanesti Rest Home A355

Workers' Rest Homes: 1.55 l, Sinaia. 2 l, Predeal. 2.35 l, Tusnad. 2.55 l, Govora.

1954, Apr. 15 *Perf. 14*

987	A355	5b blk brn, *cr*	25	12
988	A355	1.55 l dk vio brn, *bl*	90	24
989	A355	2 l dk grn, *pink*	1.40	25
990	A355	2.35 l ol blk, *grnsh*	1.40	70
991	A355	2.55 l dk red brn, *cit*	2.00	90
		Nos. 987-991 (5)	5.95	2.21

Octav Bancila A356

Globe, Child, Dove and Flowers A357

1954, May 26 *Perf. 13½*

992	A356	55b red brn & dk grn	2.75	1.40

10th death anniv. of Octav Bancila, painter.

1954, June 1 *Perf. 13x13½*

993	A357	55b brown	1.25	38

Children's Day, June 1.

Girl Feeding Calf — A358

Designs: 55b, Girl holding sheaf of grain. 1.75 l, Young students.

1954, July 5 *Perf. 14*

994	A358	20b grnsh blk	25	18
995	A358	55b blue	60	25
996	A358	1.75 l car rose	1.75	45

Stephen the Great — A359

Loading Coal on Conveyor Belt — A360

1954, July 10

997	A359	55b vio brn	1.50	50

Stephen of Moldavia (1433?-1504).

1954, Aug. 8 *Perf. 13x13½*

998	A360	1.75 l black	1.50	50

Issued to publicize Miners' Day, 1954.

A little time given to the study of the arrangement of the Scott Catalogue can make it easier to use effectively.

Victor Babes A361

Applicant Requesting Loan A362

1954, Aug. 15 *Perf. 14*

999	A361	55b rose red	1.50	50

Birth cent. of Victor Babes, serologist.

1954, Aug. 20

Design: 55b, Mutual aid declaration.

1000	A362	20b dp vio	28	12
1001	A362	55b dk redsh brn	45	25

5th anniv. of the Mutual Aid Organization.

Sailor and Naval Scene — A363

Monument to Soviet Soldier — A364

1954, Aug. 19 *Perf. 13x13½*

1002	A363	55b dp bl	90	35

Issued to publicize Navy Day.

1954, Aug. 23 *Perf. 13½x13*

1003	A364	55b scar & pur	90	35

10th anniv. of Romania's liberation.

House of Culture A365

Academy of Music, Bucharest A366

Aviator A367

Designs: 55b, Scanteia building. 1.55 l, Radio station.

1954, Sept. 6 *Perf. 14, 13½x13*

1004	A365	20b vio bl	18	6
1005	A366	38b violet	40	22
1006	A365	55b vio brn	40	12
1007	A366	1.55 l red brn	75	24

Issued to publicize Romania's cultural progress during the decade following liberation.

Perf. 13½x13

1954, Sept. 13 **Wmk. 358**

1008	A367	55b blue	90	45

Issued to publicize Aviation Day.

Chemical Plant and Oil Derricks A368

Dragon Pillar, Peking A369

1954, Sept. 21 *Perf. 13x13½*

1009	A368	55b gray	1.25	30

Intl. Conference of chemical and petroleum workers, Bucharest, Sept. 1954.

1954, Oct. 7 *Perf. 14*

1010	A369	55b dk ol grn, *cr*	1.25	30

Week of Chinese Culture.

D. T. Neculuta A370

ARLUS Emblem A371

1954, Oct. 17 *Perf. 13½x13*

1011	A370	55b purple	1.10	30

50th death anniv. of Dumitru T. Neculuta, poet.

1954, Oct. 22 *Perf. 14*

Design: 65b, Romanian and Russian women embracing.

1012	A371	55b rose car	45	15
1013	A371	65b dk pur	65	22

Month of Romanian-Soviet Friendship.

Gheorghe Tattarescu A372

Barbu Iscovescu A373

1954, Oct. 24 *Perf. 13½x13*

1014	A372	55b cerise	1.40	50

Gheorghe Tattarescu (1820-1894), painter.

1954, Nov. 3 *Perf. 14*

1015	A373	1.75 l red brn	2.50	70

Death cent. of Barbu Iscovescu, painter.

Wild Boar — A374

Globe and Clasped Hands — A375

Designs: 65b, Couple planting tree. 1.20 l, Logging.

Perf. 13½x13

1955, Mar. 15 **Wmk. 358**

1016	A374	35b brown	52	22
1017	A374	65b turq bl	90	35
1018	A374	1.20 l dk red	1.75	1.10

Month of the Forest, 1955.

1955, Apr. 5 **Photo.**

1019	A375	25b car rose	35	18

Intl. Conference of Universal Trade Unions (Federation Syndicale Mondiale), Vienna, Apr. 1955.

Teletype A376

Lenin A377

1955, Dec. 20 *Perf. 13½x13*

1020	A376	50b lilac	45	18

Romanian telegraph system, cent.

1955, Apr. 22 *Perf. 13½x14*

Various Portraits of Lenin.

1021	A377	20b ol bis & brn	22	15
1022	A377	55b cop brn	40	22
1023	A377	1 l vermilion	60	28

85th anniversary of the birth of Lenin.

Chemist A378

Volleyball A379

Designs: 5b, Steelworker. 10b, Aviator. 20b, Miner. 30b, Tractor driver. 35b, Pioneer. 40b, Girl student. 55b, Mason. 1 l, Sailor. 1.55 l, Spinner. 2.35 l, Soldier. 2.55 l, Electrician.

1955-56 **Wmk. 358** *Perf. 14*

1024	A378	3b blue	15	6
1025	A378	5b violet	8	5
1026	A378	10b chocolate	15	5
1027	A378	20b lil rose	24	5
1027A	A378	30b vio bl ('56)	40	12
1028	A378	35b grnsh bl	28	8
1028A	A378	40b slate	70	15
1029	A378	55b ol gray	40	5
1030	A378	1 l purple	75	5
1031	A378	1.55 l brn lake	1.40	5
1032	A378	2.35 l bis brn	2.10	60
1033	A378	2.55 l slate	2.25	38
		Nos. 1024-1033 (12)	8.90	1.69

1955, June 17

Design: 1.75 l, Woman volleyball player.

1034	A379	55b red vio, *pink*	1.40	70
1035	A379	1.75 l lil rose, *cr*	3.50	70

European Volleyball Championships, Bucharest.

For unused stamps, more recent issues are valued as never hinged, with the beginning point determined on a country-by-country basis. Notes to show the beginning points are prominently placed in the text.

Globe, Flag and Dove — A379a

Girls with Dove and Flag — A380

1955, May 7 **Photo.** *Perf. 13½*

1035A	A379a	55b ultra	75	24

Peace Congress, Helsinki.

1955, June 1 *Perf. 13½x14*

1036	A380	55b dk red brn	70	28

International Children's Day, June 1.

Russian War Memorial, Berlin — A381

Theodor Aman Museum — A382

1955, May 9

1037	A381	55b dp bl	60	22

Victory over Germany, 10th anniversary.

1955, June 28 *Perf. 13½, 14*

Bucharest Museums: 55b, Lenin and Stalin Museum. 1.20 l, Popular Arts Museum. 1.75 l, Arts Museum. 2.55 l, Simu Museum.

1038	A382	20b rose lil	22	14
1039	A382	55b brown	28	14
1040	A382	1.20 l gray blk	45	45
1041	A382	1.75 l sl grn	80	45
1042	A382	2.55 l rose vio	1.40	52
		Nos. 1038-1042 (5)	3.15	1.70

Nos. 1038, 1040 and 1042 measure 29x24½mm. Nos. 1039 and 1041 measure 32½x23mm.

Sharpshooter A383

1955, Sept. 11 *Perf. 13½*

1043	A383	1 l pale brn & sep	3.25	65

European Sharpshooting Championship meeting, Bucharest, Sept. 11-18.

Fire Truck, Farm and Factory — A384

1955, Sept. 13 **Wmk. 358**

1044	A384	55b carmine	55	24

Firemen's Day, Sept. 13.

Bishop Dosoftei — A385

Mother and Child — A386

Romanian writers: No. 1046, Stolnicul Constantin Cantacuzino. No. 1047, Dimitrie Cantemir. No. 1048, Enachita Vacarescu. No. 1049, Anton Pann.

1955, Sept. 9 **Photo.**

1045	A385	55b bluish gray	55	30
1046	A385	55b dp vio	55	30
1047	A385	55b ultra	55	30
1048	A385	55b rose vio	55	30
1049	A385	55b ol gray	55	30
		Nos. 1045-1049 (5)	2.75	1.50

1955, July 7 *Perf. 13½x14*

1050	A386	55b ultra	60	22

World Congress of Mothers, Lausanne.

Pioneers and Train Set — A387

Rowing — A388

Designs: 20b, Pioneers studying nature. 55b, Home of the Pioneers.

1955 *Perf. 12½*

1051	A387	10b brt ultra	15	6
1052	A387	20b grnsh bl	45	9
1053	A387	55b dp plum	1.25	28

Fifth anniversary of the Pioneer headquarters, Bucharest.

1955, Aug. 22 *Perf. 13x13½*

1054	A388	55b shown	2.75	60
1055	A388	1 l Sculling	5.25	90

European Women's Rowing Championship on Lake Snagov, Aug. 4-7.

Insect Pest Control A389

I. V. Michurin A390

Designs: 20b, Orchard. 55b, Vineyard. 1 l, Truck garden.

1955, Oct. 15 *Perf. 14x13½*

1056	A389	10b brt grn	28	12
1057	A389	20b lil rose	28	22
1058	A389	55b vio bl	70	28
1059	A389	1 l dp claret	1.25	60

Quality products of Romanian agriculture. See Nos. 1068-1071.

1955, Oct. 25 *Perf. 13½x14*

1060	A390	55b Prus bl	75	22

Birth cent. of I. V. Michurin, Russian agricultural scientist.

Congress Emblem A391

Globes and Olive Branches A392

1955, Oct. 20 *Perf. 13x13½*

1061	A391	20b cr & ultra	28	15

4th Soviet-Romanian Congress, Bucharest, Oct.

1955, Oct. 1 *Perf. 13½x13*

Design: 1 l, Three workers holding FSM banner.

1062	A392	55b dk ol grn	28	15
1063	A392	1 l ultra	45	15

Intl. Trade Union Org. (Federation Syndicale Mondiale), 10th anniv.

Sugar Beets — A393

Sheep and Shepherd — A394

Designs: 20b, Cotton. 55b, Flax. 1.55l, Sun Flower.

1955, Nov. 10 *Perf. 13½*

1064	A393	10b plum	30	15
1065	A393	20b sl grn	42	20
1066	A393	55b brt ultra	1.25	38
1067	A393	1.55 l dk red brn	2.75	60

1955, Dec. 10 *Perf. 14x13½*

Stock Farming: 10b, Pigs. 35b, Cattle. 55b, Horses.

1068	A394	5b yel grn & brn	28	20
1069	A394	10b ol bis & dk vio	60	20
1070	A394	35b brick red & brn	1.25	28
1071	A394	55b dk ol bis & brn	2.50	60

Issued to publicize animal husbandry.

Hans Christian Andersen — A395

Portraits: 55b, Adam Mickiewicz. 1 l, Friedrich von Schiller. 1.55 l, Baron de Montesquieu. 1.75 l, Walt Whitman. 2 l, Miguel de Cervantes.

Perf. 13½x14

1955, Dec. 17 **Engr.** **Unwmk.**

1072	A395	20b sl bl	30	14
1073	A395	55b dp ultra	50	14
1074	A395	1 l grnsh blk	65	18
1075	A395	1.55 l vio brn	1.75	50
1076	A395	1.75 l dl vio	2.00	85
1077	A395	2 l rose lake	2.00	85
		Nos. 1072-1077 (6)	7.20	2.66

Anniversaries of famous writers.

Bank Book and Savings Bank — A396

Perf. 14x13½

1955, Dec. 29 Photo. Wmk. 358

1078	A396 55b dp vio	1.25	75
1079	A396 55b blue	60	12

Advantages of systematic saving in a bank.

Census Date — A397

Design: 1.75 l, Family group.

Inscribed: "Recensamintul Populatiei"

1956, Feb. 3 ***Perf. 13½***

1080	A397 55b dp org	30	18
1081	A397 1.75 l emer & red brn	85	35
a.	Center inverted	*175.00*	*175.00*

National Census, Feb. 21, 1956.

Ring-necked Pheasant A398

Great Bustard A399

Street Fighting, Paris, 1871 A400

Animals: No. 1082, Hare. No. 1083, Bustard. 35b, Trout. 50b, Boar. No. 1087, Brown bear. 1 l, Lynx. 1.55 l, Red squirrel. 2 l, Chamois. 3.25 l, Pintail (duck). 4.25 l, Fallow deer.

1956 Wmk. 358 ***Perf. 14***

1082	A398 20b grn & blk	1.40	70
1083	A399 20b cit & gray blk	1.40	70
1084	A399 35b brt bl & blk	1.40	70
1085	A398 50b dp ultra & brn blk	1.40	1.10
1086	A398 55b ol bis & ind	1.65	1.10
1087	A398 55b dk bl grn & dk red brn	1.65	1.10
1088	A398 1 l dk grn & red brn	3.00	1.90
1089	A399 1.55 l lt ultra & red brn	3.25	2.75
1090	A399 1.75 l sl grn & dk brn	3.75	3.75
1091	A398 2 l ultra & brn blk	14.00	14.00
1092	A398 3.25 l lt grn & blk brn	14.00	6.75
1093	A399 4.25 l brn org & dk brn	14.00	8.50
	Nos. 1082-1093 (12)	60.90	43.05

Exist imperf. in changed colors. Value, set $17.50.

1956, May 29 ***Perf. 13½***

1094	A400 55b vermilion	70	22

85th anniversary of Commune of Paris.

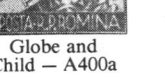

Globe and Child — A400a

Oak Tree — A401

1956, June 1 Photo. ***Perf. 13½x14***

1095	A400a 55b dp vio	90	22

Intl. Children's Day. The sheet of 100 contains 10 labels, each with "Peace" printed on it in one of 10 languages.

1956, June 11 Litho. Wmk. 358

Design: 55b, Logging train in timberland.

1096	A401 20b dk bl grn, *pale grn*	52	28
1097	A401 55b brn blk, *pale grn*	1.50	95

Month of the Forest, 1956.

Romanian Academy A402

1956, June 19 Photo. ***Perf. 14***

1098	A402 55b dk grn & dl yel	75	24

90th anniversary of Romanian Academy.

Red Cross Worker — A403

Woman Speaker and Globe — A404

1956, June 7

1099	A403 55b ol & red	1.25	60

Romanian Red Cross Congress, June 7-9.

1956, June 14

1100	A404 55b dk bl grn	70	25

Intl. Conference of Working Women, Budapest, June 14-17.

Traian Vuia and Planes — A405

1956, June 21 ***Perf. 13x13½***

1101	A405 55b grnsh blk & brn	70	22

50th anniversary of first flight by Traian Vuia, near Paris.

Ion Georgescu A406

1956, June 25 ***Perf. 14x13½***

1102	A406 55b dk red brn & dk grn	1.25	24

Ion Georgescu (1856-1898), sculptor.

White Cabbage Butterfly A407

June Bug — A408

Design: 55b, Colorado potato beetle.

Perf. 14x13½, 13½x14

1956, July 30

1103	A407 10b dp vio, pale yel & blk	2.50	28
1104	A407 55b ol blk & yel	3.75	38
1105	A408 1.75 l lt ol & dp plum	5.00	5.75
1106	A408 1.75 l gray ol & dk vio brn	5.00	70

Campaign against insect pests.

Girl Holding Sheaf of Wheat — A409

Dock Workers on Strike — A410

1956 ***Perf. 13½x14***

1107	A409 55b dl pur ("1949-1956")	1.40	30
a.	"1951-1956" (error)	2.75	2.00

7th anniversary of collective farming.

1956, Aug. 6

1108	A410 55b dk red brn	45	20

Dock workers' strike at Galati, 50th anniv.

Title Page and Printer A411

Maxim Gorki A412

1956, Aug. 13 ***Perf. 13½***

1109	A411 55b ultra	45	20

25th anniv. of the publication of "Scanteia" (The Spark).

1956, Aug. 29 ***Perf. 13½x14***

1110	A412 55b brown	45	20

Maxim Gorki (1868-1936), Russian writer.

Theodor Aman A413

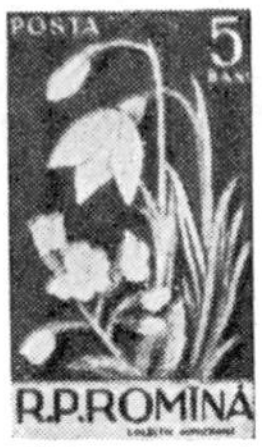

Primrose and Snowdrops A414

1956, Sept. 24 Engr.

1111	A413 55b gray blk	70	38

125th birth anniv. of Theodor Aman, painter.

1956, Sept. 26 Photo. ***Perf. 14x14½***

Flowers: 55b, Daffodil and violets. 1.75 l, Snapdragon and bellflowers. 3 l, Poppies and lilies of the valley.

Flowers in Natural Colors

1112	A414 5b bl, yel & red	42	24
1113	A414 55b blk, yel & red	95	42
1114	A414 1.75 l ind, pink & yel	2.75	60
1115	A414 3 l bl grn, dk bl grn & yel	3.50	85

Olympic Rings and Torch A415

Janos Hunyadi A416

Designs: 55b, Water polo. 1 l, Gymnastics. 1.55 l, Canoeing. 1.75 l, High jump.

1956, Oct. 25 ***Perf. 13½x14***

1116	A415 20b vermilion	28	15
1117	A415 55b ultra	50	15
1118	A415 1 l lil rose	75	22
1119	A415 1.55 l lt bl grn	1.25	22
1120	A415 1.75 l dp pur	1.50	60
	Nos. 1116-1120 (5)	4.28	1.34

16th Olympic Games, Melbourne, Nov. 22-Dec. 8.

1956, Oct. Wmk. 358

1121	A416 55b dp vio	60	20

Janos Hunyadi (1387-1456), national hero of Hungary. No. 1121 is found se-tenant with label showing Hunyadi Castle.

Benjamin Franklin A417

Georges Enescu as a Boy A418

Portraits: 35b, Sesshu (Toyo Oda). 40b, G. B. Shaw. 50b, Ivan Franco. 55b, Pierre Curie. 1 l, Henrik Ibsen. 1.55 l, Fedor Dostoevski. 1.75 l, Heinrich Heine. 2.55 l, Mozart. 3.25 l, Rembrandt.

1956 Unwmk.

1122	A417 20b vio bl	18	7
1123	A417 35b rose lake	24	12
1124	A417 40b chocolate	30	14
1125	A417 50b brn blk	35	10
1126	A417 55b dk ol	35	10
1127	A417 1 l dk bl grn	70	18
1128	A417 1.55 l dp pur	95	14
1129	A417 1.75 l brt bl	1.25	30
1130	A417 2.55 l rose vio	1.75	50
1131	A417 3.25 l dk bl	1.90	1.25
	Nos. 1122-1131 (10)	7.97	2.90

Great personalities of the world.

1956, Dec. 29 Engr.

Portrait: 1.75 l, Georges Enescu as an adult.

1132	A418 55b ultra	45	20
1133	A418 1.75 l dp cl	1.25	38

75th birth anniv. of Georges Enescu, musician and composer.

The first value column gives the catalogue value of an unused stamp, the second that of a used stamp.

Fighting Peasants, by Octav Bancila — A419

1957, Feb. 28 Photo. Wmk. 358
1134 A419 55b dk bl gray 75 22

50th anniversary of Peasant Uprising.

Stephen the Great — A420

1957, Apr. 24 ***Perf. 13½x14***
1147 A420 55b brown 45 24
1148 A420 55b ol blk 70 20

Enthronement of Stephen the Great, Prince of Moldavia, 500th anniv.

Dr. George Marinescu, Marinescu Institute and Congress Emblem A421

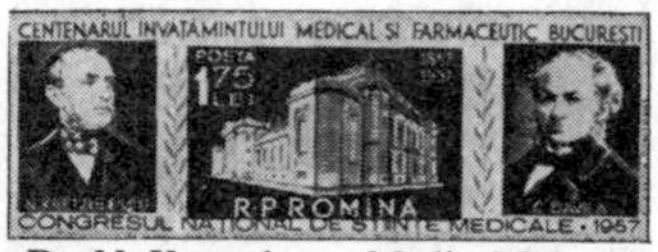

Dr. N. Kretzulescu, Medical School, Dr. C. Davila — A422

Designs: 35b, Dr. I. Cantacuzino and Cantacuzino Hospital. 55b, Dr. V. Babes and Babes Institute.

1957, May 5 ***Perf. 14x13½***
1149 A421 20b dp grn 22 5
1150 A421 35b dp red brn 28 18
1151 A421 55b red lil 48 32
1152 A422 1.75 l brt ultra & dk red 1.40 70

National Congress of Medical Science, Bucharest, May 5-6.
No. 1152 also commemorates the centenary of medical and pharmaceutical teaching in Bucharest. It measures 66x23mm.

Dove and Handle Bars — A423

Design: 55b, Cyclist.

1957, May 29 ***Perf. 13½x14***
1153 A423 20b brt ultra 18 14
1154 A423 55b dk brn 48 25

10th International Bicycle Peace Race.

Canceled-to-order stamps are often from remainders. Most collectors of canceled stamps prefer postally used specimens.

Woman Watching Gymnast A424

Woman Gymnast on Bar A425

Designs: 55b, Vaulting horse. 1.75 l, Acrobat.

1957, May 21 ***Perf. 13½***
1155 A424 20b emerald 18 12
1156 A425 35b brt red 32 18
1157 A425 55b brt bl 70 25
1158 A424 1.75 l red lil 1.75 52

European Women's Gymnastic meet, Bucharest.

Slide Rule, Caliper & Atomic Symbol A426

Rhododendron Hirsutum A427

Wmk. 358

1957, May 29 Photo. ***Perf. 14***
1159 A426 55b blue 60 18
1160 A426 55b brn red 1.00 32

2nd Congress of the Society of Engineers and Technicians, Bucharest, May 29-31.

1957, June 22 Litho. Unwmk.

Carpathian Mountain Flowers: 10b, Daphne Blagayana. 20b, Lilium Bulbiferum L. 35b, Leontopodium Alpinum. 55b, Gentiana Acaulis L. 1 l, Dianthus Callizonus. 1.55 l, Primula Carpatica Griseb. 1.75 l, Anemone Montana Hoppe.

Light Gray Background

1161 A427 5b brt rose 18 8
1162 A427 10b dk grn 28 12
1163 A427 20b red org 34 12
1164 A427 35b olive 50 15
1165 A427 55b ultra 60 20
1166 A427 1 l red 95 30
1167 A427 1.55 l yellow 1.75 35
1168 A427 1.75 l dk pur 3.00 60
Nos. 1161-1168 (8) 7.60 1.92

Nos. 1161-1168 also come se-tenant with a decorative label.

"Oxcart" by Grigorescu A428

Nicolae Grigorescu A429

Painting: 1.75 l, Battle scene.

1957, June 29 Photo. Wmk. 358
1169 A428 20b dk bl grn 40 12
1170 A429 55b dp brn 80 22
1171 A428 1.75 l chlky bl 2.10 90

50th death anniv. of Nicolae Grigorescu, painter.

Warship — A430

1957, Aug. 3 ***Perf. 13x13½***
1172 A430 1.75 l Prus bl 1.10 28

Issued for Navy Day, 1957.

Young Couple — A431

Festival Emblem — A432

Folk Dance — A433

Design: 55b, Girl with flags on hoop.

Perf. 14x14½, 14x14x12½ (A432), 13½x12½ (A433)

1957, July 28
1173 A431 20b red lil 18 6
1174 A431 55b emerald 28 9
1175 A432 1 l red org 70 30
1176 A433 1.75 l ultra 1.25 24

Moscow 1957 Youth Festival. No. 1173 measures 23x34mm. No. 1174 measures 22x38mm.

No. 1175 was printed in sheets of 50, alternating with 40 labels inscribed "Peace and Friendship" in 20 languages.

Bugler A434

Girl Holding Dove A435

1957, Aug. 30 Wmk. 358 ***Perf. 14***
1177 A434 20b brt pur 65 25

80th anniv. of the Russo-Turkish war.

1957, Sept. 3 ***Perf. 13½***
1178 A435 55b Prus grn & red 65 25

Issued in honor of the Red Cross.

Battle Scene — A436

1957, Aug. 31
1179 A436 1.75 l brown 65 32

Battle of Marasesti, 40th anniv.

Jumper and Dove — A437

Designs: 55b, Javelin thrower and bison. 1.75 l, Runner and stag.

1957, Sept. 14 Photo. ***Perf. 13½***
1180 A437 20b brt bl & blk 28 10
1181 A437 55b yel & blk 60 24
1182 A437 1.75 l brick red & blk 2.00 70

International Athletic Meet, Bucharest.

Statue of Ovid, Constanta A438

1957, Sept. 20 Photo. Wmk. 358
1183 A438 1.75 l vio bl 1.40 52

2000th anniv. of the birth of the Roman poet Publius Ovidius Naso.

Oil Field — A439

Design: 55b, Horse pulling drill, 1857.

1957, Oct. 5
1184 A439 20b dl red brn 20 7
1185 A439 20b indigo 20 7
1186 A439 55b vio blk 50 35

Centenary of Romanian oil industry.

Congress Emblem A440

1957, Sept. 28
1187 A440 55b ultra 42 24

4th International Trade Union Congress, Leipzig, Oct. 4-15.

Young Couple, Lenin Banner A441

Endre Ady A442

Designs: 35b, Lenin and Flags (horizontal). 55b, Lenin statue.

1957, Nov. 6 ***Perf. 14x14½, 14½x14***
1188 A441 10b crimson 14 5
1189 A441 35b plum 24 8
1190 A441 55b brown 35 24

Russian Revolution, 40th anniversary.

1957, Dec. 5 ***Perf. 14***
1191 A442 55b ol brn 55 22

80th birth anniv. of Endre Ady, Hungarian poet.

Oath of Bobilna A443

Bobilna Monument A444

Black-winged Stilt — A445

1957, Nov. 30
1192 A443 50b dp plum 30 7
1193 A444 55b sl bl 40 16

520th anniversary of the insurrection of the peasants of Bobilna in 1437.

Perf. 13½x14, 14x13½
1957, Dec. 27 **Photo.** **Wmk. 358**

Animals: 10b, Great white egret. 20b, White spoonbill. 50b, Sturgeon. 55b, Ermine (horiz.). 1.30 l, White pelican (horiz.).

1194 A445 5b red brn & gray 8 6
1195 A445 10b emer & ocher 15 6
1196 A445 20b brt red & ocher 20 8
1197 A445 50b bl grn & ocher 38 12
1198 A445 55b dp cl & gray 45 20
1199 A445 1.30 l pur & org 1.50 38
Nos. 1194-1199,C53-C54 (8) 6.91 1.75

Sputnik 2 and Laika A446

1957, Dec. 20 ***Perf. 14x13½***
1200 A446 1.20 l bl & dk brn 1.25 45
1201 A446 1.20 l grnsh bl & choc 1.25 45

Dog Laika, "first space traveler."

Romanian Arms, Flags — A447

Designs: 55b, Arms, "Industry and Agriculture." 1.20 l, Arms, "Art, Science and Sport (soccer)."

1957, Dec. 30 ***Perf. 13½***
1202 A447 25b ultra, red & ocher 18 9
1203 A447 55b dl yel 35 14
1204 A447 1.20 l crim rose 55 42

Proclamation of the Peoples' Republic, 10th anniv.

Flag and Wreath — A448

1958, Feb. 15 **Unwmk.** ***Perf. 13½***
1205 A448 1 l dk bl & red, *buff* 42 22
1206 A448 1 l brn & red, *buff* 42 22

Grivita Strike, 25th anniversary.

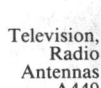

Television, Radio Antennas A449

Design: 1.75 l, Telegraph pole and wires.

1958, Mar. 21 ***Perf. 14x13½***
1207 A449 55b brt vio 30 18
1208 A449 1.75 l dp mag 80 35

Telecommunications Conference, Moscow, Dec. 3-17, 1957.

Nicolae Balcescu — A450

Romanian Writers: 10b, Ion Creanga. 35b, Alexandru Vlahuta. 55b, Mihail Eminescu. 1.75 l, Vasile Alecsandri. 2 l, Barbu S. Delavrancea.

1958 **Wmk. 358** ***Perf. 14x14½***
1209 A450 5b bluish blk 15 6
1210 A450 10b int blk 18 9
1211 A450 35b dk bl 22 9
1212 A450 55b dk red brn 35 15
1213 A450 1.75 l blk brn 70 22
1214 A450 2 l dk sl grn 1.25 28
Nos. 1209-1214 (6) 2.85 89

Fencer in Global Mask — A451

1958, Apr. 5 ***Perf. 14½x14***
1215 A451 1.75 l brt pink 1.10 38

Youth Fencing World Championships, Bucharest.

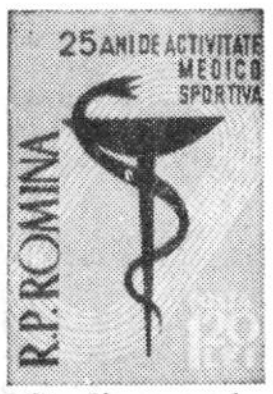

Stadium and Health Symbol A452

Globe and Dove A453

1958, Apr. 16 ***Perf. 14x14½***
1216 A452 1.20 l lt grn & red 85 24

25 years of sports medicine.

1958, May 15 **Photo.**
1217 A453 55b brt bl 48 16

4th Congress of the Intl. Democratic Women's Federation, June 1958.

Carl von Linne A454

Lepiota Procera A456

Portraits: 20b, Auguste Comte. 40b, William Blake. 55b, Mikhail I. Glinka. 1 l, Henry W. Longfellow. 1.75 l, Carlo Goldoni. 2 l, Jan A. Komensky.

Perf. 14x14½
1958, May 31 **Unwmk.**
1218 A454 10b Prus grn 12 6
1219 A454 20b brown 18 7
1220 A454 40b dp lil 28 14
1221 A454 55b dp bl 40 12
1222 A454 1 l dp mag 60 14
1223 A454 1.75 l dp vio bl 90 32
1224 A454 2 l olive 1.65 42
Nos. 1218-1224 (7) 4.13 1.27

Great personalities of the world.

1958, July **Litho.** **Unwmk.**

Mushrooms: 10b, Clavaria aurea. 20b, Amanita caesarea. 30b, Lactarius deliciosus. 35b, Armillaria mellea. 55b, Coprinus comatus. 1 l, Morchella conica. 1.55 l, Psalliota campestris. 1.75 l, Boletus edulis. 2 l, Cantharellus cibarius.

1225 A456 5b gray bl & brn 7 5
1226 A456 10b ol, ocher & brn 7 5
1227 A456 20b gray, red & yel 12 5
1228 A456 30b grn & dp org 18 14
1229 A456 35b lt bl & yel brn 20 7
1230 A456 55b pale grn, fawn & brn 35 10
1231 A456 1 l bl grn, ocher & brn 50 14
1232 A456 1.55 l gray, lt gray & pink 85 18
1233 A456 1.75 l emer, brn & buff 1.00 20
1234 A456 2 l dl bl & org yel 1.90 35
Nos. 1225-1234 (10) 5.24 1.33

Antarctic Map and Emil Racovita A457

Design: 1.20 l, Cave and Racovita.

1958, July 30 **Photo.** ***Perf. 14½x14***
1235 A457 55b ind & lt bl 52 18
1236 A457 1.20 l ol bis & dk vio 1.00 25

90th birth anniv. of Emil Racovita, explorer and naturalist.

Armed Forces Monument — A458

Designs: 75b, Soldier guarding industry. 1.75 l, Sailor raising flag and ship.

1958, Oct. 2 ***Perf. 13½x13***
1237 A458 55b org brn 18 7
1238 A458 75b dp mag 22 12
1239 A458 1.75 l brt bl 52 35

Day of the Armed Forces, Oct. 2. See No. C55.

Woman from Oltenia A459

Man from Oltenia A460

Regional Costumes: 40b, Tara Oasului. 50b, Transylvania. 55b, Muntenia. 1 l, Banat. 1.75 l, Moldavia.

1958 **Unwmk.** **Litho.** ***Perf. 13½x14***
1240 A459 35b blk & red, *dl yel* 16 12
1241 A460 35b blk & red, *dl yel* 16 12

Designs in Dark Brown and Deep Carmine

1242 A459 40b *pale brn* 20 16
1243 A460 40b *pale brn* 20 16
1244 A459 50b *lt lil* 24 12
1245 A460 50b *lt lil* 24 12
1246 A459 55b *gray* 38 15
1247 A460 55b *gray* 38 15
1248 A459 1 l *rose* 75 20
1249 A460 1 l *rose* 75 20
1250 A459 1.75 l *aqua* 1.00 28
1251 A460 1.75 l *aqua* 1.00 28
Nos. 1240-1251 (12) 5.46 2.06

Same denoms. se-tenant with label between. Exist imperf. Value, set $16.

Printer and Hand Press A461

Moldavia Stamp of 1858 A462

Designs: 55b, Scissors cutting strips of 1858 stamps. 1.20 l, Postilion and mail coach. 1.30 l, Postilion blowing horn and courier on horseback. 1.75 l, 2 l, 3.30 l, Various denominations of 1858 issue.

1958, Nov. 15 **Engr.** ***Perf. 14½x14***
1252 A461 35b vio bl 22 5
1253 A461 55b dk red brn 35 7
1254 A461 1.20 l dl bl 70 14
1255 A461 1.30 l brn vio 90 22
1256 A462 1.55 l gray brn 1.00 25
1257 A462 1.75 l rose cl 1.10 35
1258 A462 2 l dl vio 1.40 70
1259 A462 3.30 l dl red brn 2.10 80
Nos. 1252-1259 (8) 7.77 2.58

Centenary of Romanian stamps. See No. C57.
Exist imperf. Value, set $13.

Bugler A463

Runner A464

1958, Dec. 10 Photo. *Perf. 13½x13*

1260 A463 55b crim rose 48 22

Decade of teaching reforms.

Perf. 13½x14

1958, Dec. 9 Wmk. 358

1261 A464 1 l dp brn 90 28

Third Youth Spartacist Sports Meet.

Building and Flag — A465

Prince Alexandru Ioan Cuza — A466

1958, Dec. 16

1262 A465 55b dk car rose 30 15

Workers' Revolution, 40th anniversary.

Perf. 14x13½

1959, Jan. 27 Unwmk.

1263 A466 1.75 l dk bl 60 28

Centenary of the Romanian Union.

Friedrich Handel A467

Corn A468

Sheep — A469

Portraits: No. 1265, Robert Burns. No. 1266, Charles Darwin. No. 1267, Alexander Popov. No. 1268, Shalom Aleichem.

1959, Apr. 25 Photo. *Perf. 13½x14*

1264 A467 55b brown 32 10
1265 A467 55b indigo 32 18
1266 A467 55b slate 32 10
1267 A467 55b carmine 32 10
1268 A467 55b purple 32 10
Nos. 1264-1268 (5) 1.60 58

Various cultural anniversaries in 1959.

Perf. 13½x14, 14x13½

1959, June 1 Photo. Wmk. 358

Designs: No. 1270, Sunflower and bee. No. 1271, Sugar beet and refinery. No. 1273, Cattle. No. 1274, Rooster and hens. No. 1275, Tractor and grain. No. 1276, Loaded farm wagon. No. 1277, Farm couple and "10".

1269 A468 55b brt grn 25 7
1270 A468 55b red org 25 7
1271 A468 55b red lil 25 7
1272 A469 55b ol grn 25 7
1273 A469 55b red brn 25 7
1274 A469 55b yel brn 25 7
1275 A469 55b blue 25 7
1276 A469 55b brown 25 7

Unwmk.

1277 A469 5 l dp red lil 2.10 90
Nos. 1269-1277 (9) 4.10 1.46

10th anniv. of collective farming. Nos. 1272-1276 measure 33x23mm.; No. 1277 measures 38x27mm.

Young Couple A470

Steel Worker and Farm Woman A471

Design: 1.60 l, Dancer in folk costume.

Perf. 13½x14

1959, July 15 Unwmk.

1278 A470 1 l brt bl 35 14
1279 A470 1.60 l car rose 70 25

7th World Youth Festival, Vienna, July 26-Aug. 14.

1959, Aug. 23 Litho. *Perf. 13½x14*

1280 A471 55b multi 48 20
a Souv. sheet 70 48

15th anniv. of Romania's liberation from the Germans.

No. 1280a is ungummed and imperf. The blue, yellow and red vignette shows large "XV" and Romanian flag. Brown 1.20 l denomination and inscription in margin.

Prince Vlad Tepes and Document — A472

Designs: 40b, Nicolae Balcescu Street. No. 1283, Atheneum. No. 1284, Printing Combine. 1.55 l, Opera House. 1.75 l, Stadium.

1959, Sept. 20 Photo.

Centers in Gray

1281 A472 20b blue 55 18
1282 A472 40b brown 80 15
1283 A472 55b bis brn 90 32
1284 A472 55b rose lil 1.10 32
1285 A472 1.55 l pale vio 2.50 70
1286 A472 1.75 l bluish grn 2.75 1.10
Nos. 1281-1286 (6) 8.60 2.77

500th anniversary of the founding of Bucharest. See No. C71.

No. 1261 Overprinted with Shield in Silver, inscribed: "Jocurile Bucaresti Balcanice 1959"

1959, Sept. 12 Wmk. 358

1287 A464 1 l dp brn 3.25 3.25

Issued to commemorate the Balkan Games.

Soccer — A473

Motorcycle Race — A474

Sports: 40b, Ice hockey. 55b, Field ball. 1 l, Horse race. 1.50 l, Boxing. 1.55 l, Rugby. 1.60 l, Tennis.

1959 Unwmk. Litho. *Perf. 13½*

1288 A473 20b multi 18 5
1289 A474 35b multi 24 5
1290 A474 40b multi 28 5
1291 A473 55b multi 35 5
1292 A473 1 l multi 50 10
1293 A473 1.50 l multi 85 20
1294 A474 1.55 l multi 1.00 28
1295 A474 1.60 l multi 1.25 40
Nos. 1288-1295,C72 (9) 6.15 1.63

Russian Icebreaker "Lenin" A475

Perf. 14½x13½

1959, Oct. 25 Photo.

1296 A475 1.75 l bl vio 1.10 38

First atomic ice-breaker.

Stamp Album and Magnifying Glass A476

Purple Foxglove A477

1959, Nov. 15 Wmk. 358 *Perf. 14*

1297 A476 1.60 l vio bl + 40b label 1.10 55

Issued for Stamp Day.

Stamp and label were printed alternately in sheet. The 40b went to the Romanian Association of Philatelists.

1959, Dec. 15 Typo. Unwmk.

Medicinal Flowers in Natural Colors

1298 A477 20b shown 12 5
1299 A477 40b Peppermint 22 5
1300 A477 55b Cornflower 25 5
1301 A477 55b Daisies 32 5
1302 A477 1 l Autumn crocus 42 5
1303 A477 1.20 l Monkshood 48 5
1304 A477 1.55 l Poppies 70 28
1305 A477 1.60 l Linden 80 35
1306 A477 1.75 l Dog rose 95 35
1307 A477 3.20 l Buttercup 1.75 60
Nos. 1298-1307 (10) 6.01 1.88

Cuza University, Jassy, Centenary A478

1960, Nov. 26 Photo. Wmk. 358

1308 A478 55b brown 38 22

Gheorghe Cosbuc A479

Huchen (Salmon) A480

Romanian writers: 40b, Ion Luca Caragiale. 50b, Grigore Alexandrescu. 55b, Alexandru Donici. 1 l, Costache Negruzzi. 1.55 l, Dimitrie Bolintineanu.

1960, Jan. 20 *Perf. 14*

1309 A479 20b bluish blk 9 6
1310 A479 40b dp lil 22 15
1311 A479 50b brown 30 15
1312 A479 55b vio brn 35 15
1313 A479 1 l violet 60 22
1314 A479 1.55 l dk bl 1.10 38
Nos. 1309-1314 (6) 2.66 1.11

1960, Feb. 1 Engr. Unwmk.

Designs: 55b, Greek tortoise. 1.20 l, Shelduck.

1315 A480 20b blue 18 6
1316 A480 55b brown 30 9
1317 A480 1.20 l dk pur 75 18
Nos. 1315-1317,C76-C78 (6) 4.83 1.24

Woman, Dove and Globe — A481

Lenin — A482

1960, Mar. 1 Photo. *Perf. 14*

1318 A481 55b vio bl 48 22

50 years of Intl. Women's Day, Mar. 8.

1960, Apr. 22 Wmk. 358 *Perf. 13½*

Designs: 55b, Lenin statue, Bucharest. 1.55 l, Head of Lenin.

1319 A482 40b magenta 28 9
1320 A482 55b vio bl 35 15

Souvenir Sheet

1321 A482 1.55 l carmine 1.40 1.00

90th birth anniv. of Lenin.

Heroes Monument — A483

Design: 55b, Soviet war memorial.

1960, May 9 Wmk. 358 *Perf. 14*

1322 A483 40b vio bl 35 12
1323 A483 55b vio bl 35 22
a Strip of 2 (Nos. 1322-1323 and label) 1.65 80

15th anniversary of the liberation.

Nos. 1322-1323 exist imperf., printed in deep magenta. Value, set $3.25; label strip, $4.50.

Swimming A484

Sports: 55b, Women's gymnastics. 1.20 l, High jump. 1.60 l, Boxing. 2.45 l, Canoeing.

1960, June Unwmk. Typo. *Perf. 14*

Gray Background

1326 A484 40b bl & yel 35 35
1327 A484 55b blk, yel & emer 42 42
1328 A484 1.20 l emer & brick red 95 95
1329 A484 1.60 l bl, yel & blk 1.75 1.75
1330 A484 2.45 l blk, emer & brick red 1.75 1.75
Nos. 1326-1330 (5) 5.22 5.22

17th Olympic Games, Rome, Aug. 25-Sept. 11.

Nos. 1326-1330 were printed in one sheet, including se-tenant strips of two kinds in alternate rows: (a.) 40b, 55b and 1.20 l, (b.) 1.60 l, 2.45 l and two labels. When the two strips are placed together, the Olympic rings join. Gutters inscribed "Jocurile Olimpice-Roma-1960" separate the rows.

Exist imperf. (3.70 l replaced 2.45 l). Value, set $7.75.

Swimming — A485

Olympic Flame, Stadium — A486

Sports: 40b, Women's gymnastics. 55b, High jump. 1 l, Boxing. 1.60 l, Canoeing. 2 l, Soccer.

1960 Photo. Wmk. 358

1331	A485	20b chalky bl	15	6
1332	A485	40b dk brn red	30	6
1333	A485	55b blue	45	6
1334	A485	1 l rose red	60	9
1335	A485	1.60 l rose lil	75	22
1336	A485	2 l dl vio	1.40	40
		Nos. 1331-1336 (6)	3.65	89

Souvenir Sheets

Perf. 11½

1337	A486	5 l ultra	4.50	3.00

Imperf

1338	A486	6 l dl red	7.25	4.50

17th Olympic Games.

Badge, Worker and Factories A487

Perf. 13½

1960, June 20 Unwmk. Litho.

1339	A487	55b red org & dk car	38	22

Romanian Workers' Party, 3rd congress.

Leo Tolstoy — A488

Portraits: 20b, Mark Twain. 35b, Hokusai. 40b, Alfred de Musset. 55b, Daniel Defoe. 1 l, Janos Bolyai. 1.20 l, Anton Chekov. 1.55 l, Robert Koch. 1.75 l, Frederick Chopin.

1960 Wmk. 358 Photo. *Perf. 14*

1340	A488	10b dl pur	7	5
1341	A488	20b olive	12	6
1342	A488	35b blue	14	6
1343	A488	40b sl grn	18	12
1344	A488	55b dl brn vio	42	12
1345	A488	1 l Prus grn	70	25
1346	A488	1.20 l dk car rose	90	12
1347	A488	1.55 l gray bl	1.25	18
1348	A488	1.75 l brown	1.40	35
		Nos. 1340-1348 (9)	5.18	1.31

Various cultural anniversaries.

Students A489

Piano and Books A490

Designs: 5b, Diesel locomotive. 10b, Dam. 20b, Miner with drill. 30b, Ambulance and doctor. 35b, Textile worker. 50b, Nursery. 55b, Timber industry. 60b, Harvester. 75b, Feeding cattle. 1 l, Atomic reactor. 1.20 l, Oil derricks. 1.50 l, Coal mine. 1.55 l, Loading ship. 1.60 l, Athlete. 1.75 l, Bricklayer. 2 l, Steam roller. 2.40 l, Chemist. 3 l, Radio and television.

1960 Wmk. 358 Photo. *Perf. 14*

1349	A489	3b brt lil rose	8	5
1350	A489	5b ol bis	5	5
1351	A489	10b vio gray	7	5
1352	A489	20b bl vio	7	5
1353	A489	30b vermilion	10	5
1354	A489	35b crimson	10	5
1355	A490	40b ocher	12	5
1356	A489	50b bluish vio	16	5
1357	A489	55b blue	16	5
1358	A490	60b green	16	5
1359	A490	75b gray ol	28	5
1360	A489	1 l car rose	48	5
1361	A489	1.20 l black	38	5
1362	A489	1.50 l plum	48	5
1363	A490	1.55 l Prus grn	48	5
1364	A490	1.60 l dp bl	52	5
1365	A489	1.75 l red brn	60	5
1366	A489	2 l dk ol gray	75	8
1367	A489	2.40 l brt lil	80	12
1368	A489	3 l grysh bl	1.00	16
		Nos. 1349-1368,C86 (21)	7.94	1.36

Ovid Statue at Constanta A491

Black Sea Resorts: 35b, Constanta harbor. 40b, Vasile Rosita beach and vase. 55b, Ionian column and Mangalia beach. 1 l, Eforie at night. 1.60 l, Eforie and sailboat.

1960, Aug. 2 Litho. Unwmk.

1369	A491	20b multi	12	5
1370	A491	35b multi	16	5
1371	A491	40b multi	20	5
1372	A491	55b multi	24	5
1373	A491	1 l multi	60	12
1374	A491	1.60 l multi	90	20
		Nos. 1369-1374,C87 (7)	3.12	80

Emblem A492

Petrushka, Russian Puppet A493

Designs: Various Puppets.

1960, Aug. 20 Typo.

1375	A492	20b multi	6	5
1376	A493	40b multi	12	5
1377	A493	55b multi	18	5
1378	A493	1 l multi	38	6
1379	A493	1.20 l multi	38	12
1380	A493	1.75 l multi	60	22
		Nos. 1375-1380 (6)	1.72	55

International Puppet Theater Festival.

Footnotes often refer you to other stamps of the same design.

Children on Sled A494

Globe and Peace Banner A495

Children's Sports: 35b, Boys playing ball (horiz.). 55b, Ice skating (horiz.). 1 l, Running. 1.75 l, Swimming (horiz.).

Unwmk.

1960, Oct. 1 Litho. *Perf. 14*

1381	A494	20b multi	9	5
1382	A494	35b multi	15	6
1383	A494	55b multi	28	9
1384	A494	1 l multi	38	9
1385	A494	1.75 l multi	75	28
		Nos. 1381-1385 (5)	1.65	57

Perf. 13½x14

1960, Nov. 26 Photo. Wmk. 358

1386	A495	55b brt bl & yel	28	10

Intl. Youth Federation, 15th anniv.

Worker and Flags A496

Perf. 14x13

1960, Nov. 26 Litho. Unwmk.

1387	A496	55b dk car & red org	32	10

40th anniversary of the general strike.

Carp A497

Fish: 20b, Pikeperch. 40b, Black Sea turbot. 55b, Allis shad. 1 l, Wels (catfish.) 1.20 l, Sterlet. 1.60 l, Huchen (salmon).

1960, Dec. 5 Typo.

1388	A497	10b multi	6	5
1389	A497	20b multi	6	5
1390	A497	40b multi	24	9
1391	A497	55b multi	30	9
1392	A497	1 l multi	70	15
1393	A497	1.20 l multi	70	22
1394	A497	1.60 l multi	1.00	30
		Nos. 1388-1394 (7)	3.06	95

Kneeling Woman and Grapes A498

Steelworker by I. Irimescu A499

Designs: 30b, Farmers drinking (horiz.). 40b, Loading grapes into basket (horiz.). 55b, Woman cutting grapes. 75b, Vintner with basket. 1 l, Woman filling basket with grapes. 1.20 l, Vintner with jug. 5 l, Antique wine jug.

1960, Dec. 20 Litho. *Perf. 14*

1395	A498	20b brn & gray	9	5
1396	A498	30b red org & pale grn	15	5
1397	A498	40b dp ultra & gray ol	28	5
1398	A498	55b emer & buff	38	12
1399	A498	75b dk car rose & pale grn	38	12
1400	A498	1 l Prus grn & gray ol	45	22
1401	A498	1.20 l org brn & pale bl	75	35
		Nos. 1395-1401 (7)	2.48	96

Souvenir Sheet

Imperf

1402	A498	5 l dk car rose & bis	3.25	1.65

Each stamp represents a different wine-growing region: Dragasani, Dealul Mare, Odobesti, Cotnari, Tirnave, Minis, Murfatlar and Pietroasa.

Perf. 13½x14, 14x13½

1961, Feb. 16 Photo. Unwmk.

Modern Sculptures: 10b, G. Doja, I. Vlad. 20b, Meeting, B. Caragea. 40b, Georges Enescu, A. Angnel. 50b, Mihail Eminescu, C. Baraschi. 55b, Peasant Revolt, 1907, M. Constantinescu (horiz.). 1 l, "Peace," I. Jalea. 1.55 l, Building Socialism, C. Medrea. 1.75 l, Birth of an Idea, A. Szobotka.

1403	A499	5b car rose	12	6
1404	A499	10b violet	6	5
1405	A499	20b ol blk	9	6
1406	A499	40b ol bis	15	6
1407	A499	50b blk brn	18	9
1408	A499	55b org ver	18	9
1409	A499	1 l dp plum	40	15
1410	A499	1.55 l brt ultra	55	15
1411	A499	1.75 l green	85	30
		Nos. 1403-1411 (9)	2.58	1.01

Peter Poni, and Chemical Apparatus — A500

Romanian Scientists: 20b, A. Saligny and Danube bridge, Cernavoda. 55b, C. Budeanu and electrical formula. 1.55 l, Gh. Titeica and geometrical symbol.

1961, Apr. 11 Litho. *Perf. 13½x13*

Portraits in Brown Black

1412	A500	10b pink & vio bl	5	5
1413	A500	20b cit & mar	9	5
1414	A500	55b bl & red	22	6
1415	A500	1.55 l ocher & lil	75	22

Freighter "Galati" A501

Ships: 40b, Passenger ship "Oltenita." 55b, Motorboat "Tomis." 1 l, Freighter "Arad." 1.55 l, Tugboat. 1.75 l, Freighter "Dobrogea."

1961, Apr. 25 Typo. *Perf. 14x13*

1416	A501	20b multi	18	5
1417	A501	40b multi	18	5
1418	A501	55b multi	28	6
1419	A501	1 l multi	40	15
1420	A501	1.55 l multi	55	22
1421	A501	1.75 l multi	85	30
		Nos. 1416-1421 (6)	2.44	83

Marx, Lenin and Engels on Red Flag — A502

Designs: 55b, Workers. 1 l, "Industry and Agriculture" and Workers Party Emblem.

1961, Apr. 29 Litho.

1422	A502	35b red, bl & ocher	16	5
1423	A502	55b mar, red & gray	24	8

Souvenir Sheet
Imperf

1424 A502 1 l multi 1.25 70

40th anniv. of the Romanian Communist Party. Stamp of No. 1424 measures 55x33mm.

Roe Deer and Bronze Age Hunting Scene — A503

Lynx and Prehistoric Hunter — A504

Designs: 35b, Boar and Roman hunter. 40b, Brown bear and Roman tombstone. 55b, Red deer, 16th cent. hunter. 75b, Red fox and feudal hunter. 1 l, Black goat and modern hunter. 1.55 l, Rabbit and hunter with dog. 1.75 l, Badger and hunter. 2 l, Roebuck and hunter.

1961, July ***Perf. 13x14, 14x13***

1425	A503	10b	multi	9	5
1426	A504	20b	multi	18	5
1427	A504	35b	multi	24	5
1428	A504	40b	multi	30	5
1429	A503	55b	multi	40	5
1430	A504	75b	multi	60	15
1431	A503	1 l	multi	75	15
1432	A503	1.55 l	multi	90	18
1433	A503	1.75 l	multi	1.40	30
1434	A503	2 l	multi	1.65	40
			Nos. 1425-1434 (10)	6.51	1.43

Georges Enescu A505

1961, Sept. 7 **Litho.** ***Perf. 14x13***

1435 A505 3 l pale vio & vio brn 1.40 65

2nd Intl. Georges Enescu Festival, Bucharest.

Peasant Playing Panpipe A506

Heraclitus A507

Peasants playing musical instruments: 20b, Alpenhorn (horiz.). 40b, Flute. 55b, Guitar. 60b, Bagpipe. 1 l, Zither.

Perf. 13x14, 14x13
1961 **Unwmk.** **Typo.**
Tinted Paper

1436	A506	10b	multi	5	5
1437	A506	20b	multi	10	5
1438	A506	40b	multi	20	5
1439	A506	55b	multi	38	6
1440	A506	60b	multi	38	12
1441	A506	1 l	multi	55	18
			Nos. 1436-1441 (6)	1.66	51

Perf. 13½x13
1961, Oct. 25 **Photo.** **Wmk. 358**

Portraits: 20b, Francis Bacon. 40b, Rabindranath Tagore. 55b, Domingo F. Sarmiento. 1.35 l, Heinrich von Kleist. 1.75 l, Mikhail V. Lomonosov.

1442	A507	10b	maroon	9	6
1443	A507	20b	brown	9	6
1444	A507	40b	Prus grn	12	6
1445	A507	55b	cerise	18	6
1446	A507	1.35 l	brt bl	52	15
1447	A507	1.75 l	purple	70	18
			Nos. 1442-1447 (6)	1.70	57

Swimming — A508

Gold Medal, Boxing A509

Designs: No. 1449, Olympic torch. No. 1450, Water polo, Melbourne. No. 1451, Women's high jump, Rome.

Perf. 14x14½
1961, Oct. 30 **Photo.** **Unwmk.**

1448	A508	20b	bl gray	18	12
1449	A508	20b	vermilion	18	12
1450	A508	55b	ultra	48	28
1451	A508	55b	blue	48	28

Perf. 10½
Size: 33x33mm

Gold Medals: 35b, Pistol shooting, Melbourne. 40b, Sharpshooting, Rome. 55b, Wrestling. 1.35 l, Woman's high jump. 1.75 l, Three medals for canoeing.

Medals in Ocher

1452	A509	10b	Prus grn	18	8
1453	A509	35b	brown	35	12
1454	A509	40b	plum	38	12
1455	A509	55b	org red	48	18
1456	A509	1.35 l	dp ultra	80	28

Size: 46x32mm

1457	A509	1.75 l	dp car rose	1.50	55
			Nos. 1452-1457 (6)	3.69	1.33

Romania's gold medals in 1956, 1960 Olympics.

No. 1452-1457 exist imperf. Value set $3.50.

A souvenir sheet of one 4 l dark red & ocher was issued. Value unused $4.25, canceled $3.25.

Congress Emblem A510

Primrose A511

1961, Dec. **Litho.** ***Perf. 13½x14***

1458 A510 55b dk car rose 48 28

5th World Congress of Trade Unions, Moscow, Dec. 4-16.

Perf. 14x13½, 13½x14
1961, Sept. 15

Designs: 20b, Sweet William. 25b, Peony. 35b, Prickly pear. 40b, Iris. 55b, Buttercup. 1 l, Hepatica. 1.20 l, Poppy. 1.55 l, Gentian. 1.75 l, Carol Davilla and Dimitrie Brindza. 20b, 25b, 40b, 55b, 1.20 l, 1.55 l, are vertical.

1459	A511	10b	multi	5	5
1460	A511	20b	multi	6	5
1461	A511	25b	multi	9	5
1462	A511	35b	multi	18	5
1463	A511	40b	multi	22	5
1464	A511	55b	multi	28	9
1465	A511	1 l	multi	38	12
1466	A511	1.20 l	multi	45	15
1467	A511	1.55 l	multi	90	30
			Nos. 1459-1467 (9)	2.61	91

Souvenir Sheet
Imperf

1468 A511 1.75 l car, blk & grn 3.00 2.00

Centenary of the Bucharest Botanical Garden.

No. 1459-1467 exist imperf. Value, set $3.

United Nations Emblem A512

Cock and Savings Book A513

Designs: 20b, Map of Balkan peninsula and dove. 40b, Men of three races.

1961, Nov. 27 ***Perf. 13½x14***

1469	A512	20b	bl, yel & pink	24	7
1470	A512	40b	multi	50	14
1471	A512	55b	org, lil & yel	65	24

UN, 15th anniv. Nos. 1470-1471 are each printed with alternating yellow labels. Exist imperf. Value, set $2.75.

1962, Feb. 15 **Typo.** ***Perf. 13½***

Designs: 55b, Honeycomb, bee and savings book.

1472	A513	40b	multi	24	10
1473	A513	55b	multi	24	18

Issued to publicize Savings Day.

Soccer Player and Map of Europe A514

Wheat, Map and Tractor A515

1962, Apr. 20 **Litho.** ***Perf. 13x14***

1474 A514 55b emer & red brn 48 22

European Junior Soccer Championships, Bucharest.

1962, Apr. 27 ***Perf. 13½x14***

Designs: 55b, Medal honoring agriculture. 1.55 l, Sheaf of wheat, hammer & sickle.

1475	A515	40b	org & dk car	20	7
1476	A515	55b	yel, car & brn	24	7
1477	A515	1.55 l	multi	70	24

Collectivization of agriculture.

Canoe Race A516

Designs: 20b, Kayak. 40b, Eight-man shell. 55b, Two-man skiff. 1 l, Yachts. 1.20 l, Motorboats. 1.55 l, Sailboat. 3 l, Water slalom.

1962, May 15 **Photo.** ***Perf. 14x13***
Vignette in Bright Blue

1478	A516	10b	lil rose	5	5
1479	A516	20b	ol gray	9	5
1480	A516	40b	red brn	12	5
1481	A516	55b	ultra	22	5
1482	A516	1 l	red	28	5
1483	A516	1.20 l	dp plum	55	9
1484	A516	1.55 l	orange	75	15
1485	A516	3 l	violet	1.40	30
			Nos. 1478-1485 (8)	3.46	79

These stamps were also issued imperf. with color of denomination and inscription changed. Value, set unused $4.50, canceled $2.

Ion Luca Caragiale — A517

Portraits: 40b, Jean Jacques Rousseau. 1.75 l, Aleksander I. Herzen. 3.30 l, Ion Luca Caragiale (as a young man).

1962, June 9 ***Perf. 13½x14***

1486	A517	40b	dk sl grn	18	9
1487	A517	55b	magenta	22	9
1488	A517	1.75 l	dp bl	75	30

Souvenir Sheet
Perf. 11½

1489 A517 3.30 l brown 3.00 1.75

250th birth anniv. of J. J. Rousseau, French philosopher (No. 1486); 50th death anniversary of the death of I. L. Caragiale, Romanian author (Nos. 1487, 1489); and 150th birth anniv. of A. I. Herzen, Russian writer (No. 1489). No. 1489 contains one stamp 32x55mm.

Globes Surrounded with Flags — A518

1962, July 6 **Typo.** ***Perf. 11***

1490 A518 55b multi 40 14

8th Youth Festival for Peace and Friendship, Helsinki, July 28-Aug. 6.

Traian Vuia — A519

Fieldball Player and Globe — A520

Perf. 13½x14
1962, July 20 **Photo.** **Wmk. 358**

Portraits: 20b, Al. Davila. 35b, Vasile Pirvan. 40b, Ion Negulici. 55b, Grigore Cobilcescu. 1 l, Dr. Gheorghe Marinescu. 1.20 l, Ion Cantacuzino. 1.35 l, Victor Babes. 1.55 l, C. Levaditi.

1491	A519	15b	brown	9	6
1492	A519	20b	dl red brn	9	6
1493	A519	35b	brn mag	12	6
1494	A519	40b	bl vio	12	6
1495	A519	55b	brt bl	18	6
1496	A519	1 l	dp ultra	22	9
1497	A519	1.20 l	crimson	38	15
1498	A519	1.35 l	Prus grn	45	12
1499	A519	1.55 l	purple	90	12
			Nos. 1491-1499 (9)	2.55	78

Perf. 13x14

1962, May 12 Litho. Unwmk.

1500	A520	55b yel & vio	48	22

2nd Intl. Women's Fieldball Championships, Bucharest.

Same Surcharged in Violet Blue: "Campionana Mondiala 5 lei"

1962, July 31

1501	A520	5 l on 55b yel & vio	4.25	2.10

Romanian victory in the 2nd Intl. Women's Fieldball Championships.

Rod Fishing A521

Various Fishing Scenes.

1962, July 25 *Perf. 14x13*

1502	A521	10b multi	10	5
1503	A521	25b multi	10	10
1504	A521	40b bl & brick red	14	10
1505	A521	55b multi	20	10
1506	A521	75b sl, gray & bl	30	10
1507	A521	1 l multi	48	18
1508	A521	1.75 l multi	75	20
1509	A521	3.25 l multi	1.40	30
		Nos. 1502-1509 (8)	3.47	1.13

No. 1474 Surcharged in Dark Blue: "1962 Campioana Europeana 2 lei"

1962, July 31

1510	A514	2 l on 55b emer & red brn	1.65	1.25

Romania's victory in the European Junior Soccer Championships, Bucharest.

Child and Butterfly A522

Handicraft A523

Designs: 30b, Girl feeding bird. 40b, Boy and model sailboat. 55b, Children writing (horiz.). 1.20 l, Girl at piano, and boy playing violin. 1.55 l, Pioneers camping (horiz.).

Perf. 13x14, 14x13

1962, Aug. 25 Litho.

1511	A522	20b lt bl, red & brn	9	6
1512	A522	30b org, bl & red brn	14	6
1513	A522	40b chlky bl, dp org & Prus bl	15	8
1514	A522	55b cit, bl & red	24	5
1515	A522	1.20 l car, brn & dk vio	38	15
1516	A522	1.55 l bis, red & vio	70	15
		Nos. 1511-1516 (6)	1.70	55

1962, Oct. 12 *Perf. 13x14*

Designs: 10b, Food and drink. 20b, Chemical industry. 40b, Chinaware. 55b, Leather industry. 75b, Textiles. 1 l, Furniture. 1.20 l, Electrical appliances. 1.55 l, Household goods (sewing machine and pots).

1517	A523	5b multi	9	5
1518	A523	10b multi	6	5
1519	A523	20b multi	6	5
1520	A523	40b multi	18	6
1521	A523	55b multi	18	6
1522	A523	75b multi	22	9
1523	A523	1 l multi	30	15
1524	A523	1.20 l multi	55	18
1525	A523	1.55 l multi	90	30
		Nos. 1517-1525,C126 (10)	3.44	1.14

4th Sample Fair, Bucharest.

Lenin — A524

Bull — A525

1962, Nov. 7 *Perf. 10½*

1526	A524	55b vio bl, red & bis	35	22

Russian October Revolution, 45th anniv.

1962, Nov. 20 *Perf. 14x13, 13x14*

Designs: 20b, Sheep (horiz.). 40b, Merino ram (horiz.). 1 l, York pig. 1.35 l, Cow. 1.55 l, Heifer (horiz.). 1.75 l, Pigs (horiz.).

1527	A525	20b ultra & blk	9	6
1528	A525	40b bl, yel & sep	12	6
1529	A525	55b ocher, buff & sl grn	18	8
1530	A525	1 l gray, yel & brn	28	9
1531	A525	1.35 l dl grn, choc & blk	38	15
1532	A525	1.55 l org red, dk brn & blk	60	22
1533	A525	1.75 l dk vio bl, yel & org	75	40
		Nos. 1527-1533 (7)	2.40	1.06

Arms, Factory and Harvester A526

Perf. 14½x13½

1962, Dec. 30 Litho.

1534	A526	1.55 l multi	90	22

Romanian People's Republic, 15th anniv.

Strikers at Grivita, 1933 — A527

1963, Feb. 16 *Perf. 14x13½*

1535	A527	1.75 l red, vio & yel	70	22

30th anniv. of the strike of railroad and oil industry workers at Grivita.

Tractor Driver and "FAO" Emblem A528

Tomatoes A529

Designs: 55b, Farm woman, cornfield and combine. 1.55 l, Child drinking milk and milking machine. 1.75 l, Woman with basket of grapes and vineyard.

1963, Mar. 21 Photo. *Perf. 14½x13*

1536	A528	40b vio bl	9	6
1537	A528	55b bis brn	15	6
1538	A528	1.55 l rose red	45	15
1539	A528	1.75 l green	75	30

FAO "Freedom from Hunger" campaign.

Perf. 13½x14, 14x13½

1963, Apr. 25 Litho. Unwmk.

Designs: 40b, Hot peppers. 55b, Radishes. 75b, Eggplant. 1.20 l, Mild peppers. 3.25 l, Cucumbers (horiz.).

1540	A529	35b multi	10	6
1541	A529	40b multi	14	6
1542	A529	55b multi	16	6
1543	A529	75b multi	22	9
1544	A529	1.20 l multi	60	12
1545	A529	3.25 l multi	1.40	40
		Nos. 1540-1545 (6)	2.62	79

Woman Swimmer at Start — A530

Chicks — A531

Designs: 30b, Crawl (horiz.). 55b, Butterfly stroke (horiz.). 1 l, Backstroke (horiz.). 1.35 l, Breaststroke (horiz.). 1.55 l, Woman diver. 2 l, Water polo.

1963, June 15 *Perf. 13x14, 14x13*

1546	A530	25b yel brn, emer & gray	9	5
1547	A530	30b ol grn, gray & yel	12	5
1548	A530	55b bl, gray & red	18	6
1549	A530	1 l grn, gray & red	28	9
1550	A530	1.35 l ultra, car & gray	38	12
1551	A530	1.55 l pur, gray & org	70	15
1552	A530	2 l car rose, gray & org	75	45
		Nos. 1546-1552 (7)	2.50	97

1963, May 23 *Perf. 10½*

Domestic poultry: 30b, Hen. 40b, Goose. 55b, White cock. 70b, Duck. 1 l, Hen. 1.35 l, Tom turkey. 3.20 l, Hen.

Fowl in Natural Colors; Inscription in Dark Blue

1553	A531	20b ultra	9	5
1554	A531	30b tan	9	5
1555	A531	40b org brn	12	5
1556	A531	55b brt grn	14	5
1557	A531	70b lilac	28	6
1558	A531	1 l blue	38	9
1559	A531	1.35 l ocher	55	12
1560	A531	3.20 l yel grn	1.10	45
		Nos. 1553-1560 (8)	2.75	92

Women and Globe — A532

1963, June 15 Photo. *Perf. 14x13*

1561	A532	55b dk bl	28	9

Intl. Women's Congress, Moscow, June 24-29.

William M. Thackeray, Writer A533

Portraits: 50b, Eugene Delacroix, painter. 55b, Gheorghe Marinescu, physician. 1.55 l, Giuseppe Verdi, composer. 1.75 l, Stanislavski, actor and producer.

1963, July Unwmk. *Perf. 14x13*

Portrait in Black

1562	A533	40b pale vio	12	6
1563	A533	50b bis brn	18	9
1564	A533	55b olive	24	12
1565	A533	1.55 l rose brn	48	15
1566	A533	1.75 l pale vio bl	75	18
		Nos. 1562-1566 (5)	1.77	60

Walnuts A534

Designs: 20b, Plums. 40b, Peaches. 55b, Strawberries. 1 l, Grapes. 1.55 l, Apples. 1.60 l, Cherries. 1.75 l, Pears.

1963, Sept. 15 Litho. *Perf. 14x13½*

Fruits in Natural Colors

1567	A534	10b pale yel & brn ol	6	6
1568	A534	20b pale pink & red org	6	6
1569	A534	40b lt bl & bl	12	6
1570	A534	55b dl yel & rose car	15	6
1571	A534	1 l pale vio & vio	28	9
1572	A534	1.55 l yel grn & ultra	45	9
1573	A534	1.60 l yel & bis	75	12
1574	A534	1.75 l lt bl & grn	75	18
		Nos. 1567-1574 (8)	2.62	72

Women Playing Volleyball and Map of Europe — A535

Designs: 40b, Three men players. 55b, Three women players. 1.75 l, Two men players. 3.20 l, Europa Cup.

1963, Oct. 22 *Perf. 13½x14*

1575	A535	5b gray & lil rose	9	5
1576	A535	40b gray & vio bl	18	6
1577	A535	55b gray & grnsh bl	30	9
1578	A535	1.75 l gray & org brn	55	18
1579	A535	3.20 l gray & vio	1.10	45
		Nos. 1575-1579 (5)	2.22	83

European Volleyball Championships, Oct. 22-Nov. 4.

Pine Tree, Branch and Cone — A536

Design: 1.75 l, Beech forest and branch.

Perf. 13½

1963, Dec. 5 Unwmk. Photo.

1580	A536	55b dk grn	16	10
1581	A536	1.75 l dk bl	50	20

Reforestation program.

Silkworm Moth — A537

18th Century House, Ploesti — A538

Designs: 20b, Chrysalis, moth and worm. 40b, Silkworm on leaf. 55b, Bee over mountains (horiz.). 60b, 1.20 l, 1.35 l, 1.60 l, Bees pollinating various flowers (horiz.).

1963, Dec. 12 Litho. *Perf. 13x14*

1582	A537	10b multi	9	5
1583	A537	20b multi	9	6
1584	A537	40b multi	18	6
1585	A537	55b multi	28	9
1586	A537	60b multi	38	12
1587	A537	1.20 l multi	60	15

1588	A537	1.35 l	multi	75	28
1589	A537	1.60 l	multi	1.10	30
			Nos. 1582-1589 (8)	3.47	1.11

1963, Dec. 25 Engr. *Perf. 13*

Peasant Houses from Village Museum, Bucharest: 40b, Oltenia, 1875 (horiz.). 55b, Hunedoara, 19th Cent. (horiz.). 75b, Oltenia, 19th Cent. 1 l, Brasov, 1847. 1.20 l, Bacau, 19th Cent. 1.75 l, Arges, 19th Cent.

1590	A538	20b	claret	9	6
1591	A538	40b	blue	12	6
1592	A538	55b	dl vio	18	6
1593	A538	75b	green	22	8
1594	A538	1 l	brn & mar	38	9
1595	A538	1.20 l	gray ol	45	15
1596	A538	1.75 l	dk brn & ultra	85	22
			Nos. 1590-1596 (7)	2.29	72

Ski Jump
A539

Sports: 20b, Speed skating. 40b, Ice hockey. 55b, Women's figure skating. 60b, Slalom. 75b, Biathlon. 1 l, Bobsledding. 1.20 l, Cross-country skiing.

1963, Nov. 25 Litho. *Perf. 14*

1597	A539	10b	red & dk bl	10	5
1598	A539	20b	ultra & red brn	14	5
1599	A539	40b	emer & red brn	20	5
1600	A539	55b	vio & red brn	30	8
1601	A539	60b	org & vio bl	40	20
1602	A539	75b	lil rose & dk bl	50	20
1603	A539	1 l	bis & vio bl	85	32
1604	A539	1.20 l	grnsh bl & vio	90	45
			Nos. 1597-1604 (8)	3.39	1.40

9th Winter Olympic Games, Innsbruck, Jan. 29-Feb. 9, 1964.

Exist imperf. in changed colors. Value, set $5.50.

A souvenir sheet contains one imperf. stamp, a 1.50-lei ultramarine and red stamp showing the Olympic Ice Stadium at Innsbruck and the Winter Games emblem. Value $5.50.

Elena Teodorini as Carmen
A540

Munteanu Murgoci and Congress Emblem
A541

Designs: 10b, George Stephanescu, founder of Romanian opera. 35b, Ion Bajenaru as Petru Rares. 40b, D. Popovici as Alberich. 55b, Hariclea Darclee as Tosca. 75b, George Folescu as Boris Godunov. 1 l, Jean Athanasiu as Rigoletto. 1.35 l, Traian Grosavescu as Duke in Rigoletto. 1.55 l, N. Leonard as Hoffmann.

1964, Jan. 20 Photo. *Perf. 13*

Portrait in Dark Brown

1605	A540	10b	olive	5	5
1606	A540	20b	ultra	5	5
1607	A540	35b	green	9	5
1608	A540	40b	grnsh bl	12	5
1609	A540	55b	car rose	18	5
1610	A540	75b	lilac	18	5
1611	A540	1 l	blue	55	15
1612	A540	1.35 l	brt vio	75	18
1613	A540	1.55 l	red org	85	30
			Nos. 1605-1613 (9)	2.82	93

1964, Feb. 5 Unwmk. *Perf. 13*

1614	A541	1.60 l	brt bl, ind & bis	70	22

8th Intl. Soil Congress, Bucharest.

Asculaphid
A542

Insects: 10b, Thread-waisted wasp. 35b, Wasp. 40b, Rhyparioides metelkana moth. 55b, Tussock moth. 1.20 l, Kanetisa circe butterfly. 1.55 l, Beetle. 1.75 l, Horned beetle.

1964, Feb. 20 Litho. *Perf. 14x13*

Insects in Natural Colors

1615	A542	5b	pale lil	7	7
1616	A542	10b	lt bl & red	10	7
1617	A542	35b	pale grn	14	5
1618	A542	40b	ol grn	18	5
1619	A542	55b	ultra	20	14
1620	A542	1.20 l	pale grn & red	40	18
1621	A542	1.55 l	yel & brn	60	18
1622	A542	1.75 l	org & red	65	24
			Nos. 1615-1622 (8)	2.34	98

Tobacco Plant
A543

Jumping
A544

Garden flowers: 20b, Geranium. 40b, Fuchsia. 55b, Chrysanthemum. 75b, Dahlia. 1 l, Lily. 1.25 l, Day lily. 1.55 l, Marigold.

1964, Mar. 25 *Perf. 13x14*

1623	A543	10b	dk bl, grn & bis	12	5
1624	A543	20b	gray, grn & red	15	5
1625	A543	40b	pale grn, grn & red	18	12
1626	A543	55b	grn, lt grn & lil	22	6
1627	A543	75b	cit, red & grn	24	6
1628	A543	1 l	dp cl, rose cl, grn & org	40	9
1629	A543	1.25 l	sal, vio bl & grn	42	22
1630	A543	1.55 l	red brn, yel & grn	55	22
			Nos. 1623-1630 (8)	2.28	87

Unwmk.

1964, Apr. 25 Photo. *Perf. 13*

Horse Show Events: 40b, Dressage (horiz.). 1.35 l, Jumping. 1.55 l, Galloping (horiz.).

1631	A544	40b	lt bl, rose brn & blk	12	6
1632	A544	55b	lil, red & brn	18	9
1633	A544	1.35 l	brt grn, red & dk brn	55	18
1634	A544	1.55 l	pale yel, bl & dp cl	80	24

Hogfish
A545

Mihail Eminescu
A546

Fish (Constanta Aquarium): 10b, Peacock blenny. 20b, Mediterranean scad. 40b, Sturgeon. 50b, Sea horses. 55b, Yellow gurnard. 1 l, Beluga. 3.20 l, Stingray.

1964, May 10 Litho. *Perf. 14*

1635	A545	5b	multi	5	5
1636	A545	10b	multi	5	5
1637	A545	20b	multi	9	5
1638	A545	40b	multi	12	5
1639	A545	50b	multi	18	9
1640	A545	55b	multi	18	9
1641	A545	1 l	multi	45	15
1642	A545	3.20 l	multi	1.10	30
			Nos. 1635-1642 (8)	2.22	83

1964, June 20 Photo. *Perf. 13*

Portraits: 20b, Ion Creanga. 35b, Emil Girleanu. 55b, Michelangelo. 1.20 l, Galileo Galilei. 1.75 l, William Shakespeare.

Portraits in Dark Brown

1643	A546	5b	green	7	6
1644	A546	20b	magenta	14	6
1645	A546	35b	vermilion	25	7
1646	A546	55b	bister	28	12
1647	A546	1.20 l	ultra	52	25
1648	A546	1.75 l	violet	90	35
			Nos. 1643-1648 (6)	2.16	91

50th death anniv. of Emil Girleanu, writer; the 75th death anniversaries of Ion Creanga and Mihail Eminescu, writers; the 400th anniv. of the death of Michelangelo and the births of Galileo and Shakespeare.

Road through Gorge — A547

High Jump — A548

Designs: 55b, Lake Bilea and cottage. 1 l, Ski lift, Polana Brasov. 1.35 l, Ceahlaul peak and Lake Bicaz (horiz.). 1.75 l, Hotel Alpin.

1964, June 29 Engr.

1649	A547	40b	rose brn	12	6
1650	A547	55b	dk bl	18	6
1651	A547	1 l	dl pur	30	9
1652	A547	1.35 l	pale brn	45	15
1653	A547	1.75 l	green	55	28
			Nos. 1649-1653 (5)	1.60	64

Issued for tourist publicity.

1964, July 28 Photo.

Designs: 40b, Javelin throw. 55b, Running. 1 l, Discus throw. 1.20 l, Hurdling. 1.55 l, Map and flags of Balkan countries.

Size: 23x37½mm

1654	A548	30b	ver, yel & yel grn	12	5
1655	A548	40b	grn, yel, brn & vio	12	6
1656	A548	55b	gldn brn, yel & bl grn	22	8
1657	A548	1 l	brt bl, yel, brn & red	45	9
1658	A548	1.20 l	pur, yel, brn & grn	55	18

Litho.

Size: 23x45mm

1659	A548	1.55 l	multi	90	28
			Nos. 1654-1659 (6)	2.36	74

The 1964 Balkan Games.

Factory — A549

Designs: 55b, Flag and Coat of Arms (vert.). 75b, Combine. 1.20 l, Apartment buildings. 2 l, Flag, coat of arms, industrial and agricultural scenes. 55b, 2 l, Inscribed "A XX A aniversare a eliberarii patriei!"

1964, Aug. 23 Photo. *Perf. 13*

1660	A549	55b	multi	16	12
1661	A549	60b	multi	24	12
1662	A549	75b	multi	24	20
1663	A549	1.20 l	multi	48	20

Souvenir Sheet

Imperf

1664	A549	2 l	multi	1.25	75

20th anniv. of Romania's liberation. No. 1664 contains one stamp 110x70mm.

High Jump — A550

Sport: 30b, Wrestling. 35b, Volleyball. 40b, Canoeing. 55b, Fencing. 1.20 l, Women's gymnastics. 1.35 l, Soccer. 1.55 l, Sharpshooting.

1964, Sept. 1 Litho.

Olympic Rings in Blue, Yellow, Black, Green and Red

1665	A550	20b	yel & blk	20	5
1666	A550	30b	lil & blk	20	5
1667	A550	35b	grnsh bl & blk	20	5
1668	A550	40b	pink & blk	22	5
1669	A550	55b	lt yel grn & blk	32	5
1670	A550	1.20 l	org & blk	65	20
1671	A550	1.35 l	ocher & blk	80	30
1672	A550	1.55 l	bl & blk	90	48
			Nos. 1665-1672 (8)	3.49	1.23

18th Olympic Games, Tokyo, Oct. 10-25.

Nos. 1665-1669 exist imperf., in changed colors. Three other denominations exist, 1.60 l, 2 l and 2.40 l, imperf. Value, set of 8, unused $5.50, canceled $4.

An imperf. souvenir sheet contains a 3.25 l stamp showing a runner. Value unused $5.50 canceled $5.

Georges Enescu, Piano Keys and Neck of Violin — A551

Designs: 55b, Enescu at piano. 1.60 l, Enescu Festival medal. 1.75 l, Enescu bust by G. Anghel.

1964, Sept. 5 Engr.

1673	A551	10b	bl grn	6	5
1674	A551	55b	vio blk	18	9
1675	A551	1.60 l	dk red brn	48	25
1676	A551	1.75 l	dk bl	85	28

3rd Intl. Georges Enescu Festival, Bucharest, Sept., 1964.

Black Swans
A552

Designs: 5b, Indian python. 35b, Ostriches. 40b, Crowned cranes. 55b, Tigers. 1 l, Lions. 1.55 l, Grevy's zebras. 2 l, Bactrian camels.

Perf. 14x13

1964, Sept. 28 Litho. Unwmk.

1677	A552	5b	multi	5	5
1678	A552	10b	multi	8	5
1679	A552	35b	multi	12	5
1680	A552	40b	multi	18	5
1681	A552	55b	multi	22	6
1682	A552	1 l	multi	38	15
1683	A552	1.55 l	multi	75	22
1684	A552	2 l	multi	1.00	30
			Nos. 1677-1684 (8)	2.78	93

Issued to publicize the Bucharest Zoo. No. 1683 inscribed "BANI".

C. Brincoveanu, Stolnicul Cantacuzino, Gheorghe Lazar and Academy — A553

Designs: 40b, Alexandru Ioan Cuza, medal and University. 55b, Masks, curtain, harp, keyboard and palette (vert.). 75b, Women students in laboratory and auditorium. 1 l, Savings Bank building.

Perf. 13x13½, 13½x13

1964, Oct. 14 **Photo.**

1685	A553	20b multi	10	5
1686	A553	40b multi	14	7
1687	A553	55b multi	20	10
1688	A553	75b multi	24	14
1689	A553	1 l dk brn, yel & org	40	28
		Nos. 1685-1689 (5)	1.08	64

No. 1685 commemorates the 250th anniversary of the Royal Academy; Nos. 1686 and 1688 commemorate the centenary of the University of Bucharest; No. 1687 commemorates the centenary of the Academy of Art and No. 1689 commemorates the centenary of the Savings Bank.

Soldier's Head and Laurel — A554

1964, Oct. 25 **Litho.** ***Perf. 12x12½***

1690	A554	55b ultra & lt bl	28	12

Issued for Army Day.

Canadian Kayak Singles Gold Medal, Melbourne, 1956 A555

Romanian Olympic Gold Medals: 30b, Boxing, Melbourne, 1956. 35b, Rapid Silhouette Pistol, Melbourne, 1956. 40b, Women's High Jump, Rome, 1960. 55b, Wrestling, Rome, 1960. 1.20 l, Clay Pigeon Shooting, Rome, 1960. 1.35 l, High Jump, Tokyo, 1964. 1.55 l, Javelin, Tokyo, 1964.

1964, Nov. 30 **Photo.** ***Perf. 13½***

Medals in Gold and Brown

1691	A555	20b pink & ultra	14	5
1692	A555	30b yel grn & ultra	20	5
1693	A555	35b bluish grn & ultra	28	5
1694	A555	40b lil & ultra	40	7
1695	A555	55b org & ultra	48	10
1696	A555	1.20 l ol grn & ultra	70	24
1697	A555	1.35 l gldn brn & ultra	90	35
1698	A555	1.55 l rose lil & ultra	1.25	50
		Nos. 1691-1698 (8)	4.35	1.41

Romanian athletes who won gold medals in three Olympic Games.

Nos. 1691-1695 exist imperf., in changed colors. Three other denominations exist, 1.60 l, 2 l and 2.40 l, imperf. Value, set of 8, unused $5.75, canceled $4.

A 10 l souvenir sheet shows the 1964 Olympic gold medal and world map. Value unused $5.50, canceled $4.

Strawberries — A556

1964, Dec. 20 **Litho.** ***Perf. 13½x14***

Designs: 35b, Blackberries. 40b, Raspberries. 55b, Rose hips. 1.20 l, Blueberries. 1.35 l, Cornelian cherries. 1.55 l, Hazelnuts. 2.55 l, Cherries.

1703	A556	5b gray, red & grn	5	5
1704	A556	35b ocher, grn & dk vio bl	9	5
1705	A556	40b pale vio, car & grn	12	5
1706	A556	55b yel grn, grn & red	15	5
1707	A556	1.20 l sal pink, grn, brn & ind	38	12
1708	A556	1.35 l lt bl, grn & red	42	12
1709	A556	1.55 l gldn brn, grn & ocher	75	22
1710	A556	2.55 l ultra, grn & red	1.50	35
		Nos. 1703-1710 (8)	3.46	1.01

Syncom 3 — A557

UN Headquarters, N.Y. — A558

Space Satellites: 40b, Syncom 3 over TV antennas. 55b, Ranger 7 reaching moon (horiz.). 1 l, Ranger 7 and moon close-up (horiz.). 1.20 l, Voskhod. 5 l, Konstantin Feoktistov, Vladimir M. Komarov, Boris B. Yegorov and Voskhod.

Perf. 13x14, 14x13

1965, Jan. 5 **Litho.** **Unwmk.**

Size: 22x38mm, 38x22mm

1711	A557	30b multi	16	7
1712	A557	40b multi	35	7
1713	A557	55b multi	42	7
1714	A557	1 l multi	50	7
1715	A557	1.20 l multi, horiz.	85	14

Perf. 13½x13

Size: 52x30mm

1716	A557	5 l multi	2.00	65
		Nos. 1711-1716 (6)	4.28	1.07

1965, Jan. 25 ***Perf. 12x12½***

Design: 1.60 l, Arms and flag of Romania, and UN emblem.

1717	A558	55b ultra, red & gold	38	18
1718	A558	1.60 l ultra, red, gold & yel	75	25

20th anniv. of the UN and 10th anniv. of Romania's membership in the UN.

Greek Tortoise — A559

Reptiles: 10b, Bull lizard. 20b, Three-lined lizard. 40b, Sand lizard. 55b, Slow worm. 60b, Sand viper. 1 l, Desert lizard. 1.20 l, Orsini's viper. 1.35 l, Caspian whipsnake. 3.25 l, Four-lined snake.

1965, Feb. 25 **Photo.** ***Perf. 13½***

1719	A559	5b multi	6	5
1720	A559	10b multi	9	5
1721	A559	20b multi	12	5
1722	A559	40b multi	15	5
1723	A559	55b multi	18	6
1724	A559	60b multi	28	6
1725	A559	1 l multi	38	9
1726	A559	1.20 l multi	45	15
1727	A559	1.35 l multi	60	22
1728	A559	3.25 l multi	1.10	30
		Nos. 1719-1728 (10)	3.41	1.08

White Persian Cats — A560

Designs: 1.35 l, Siamese cat. Others, Various European cats. (5b, 10b, 3.25 l horizontal.)

1965, Mar. 20 **Litho.**

Size: 41x29mm, 29x41mm

Cats in Natural Colors

1729	A560	5b brn org & blk	6	5
1730	A560	10b brt bl & blk	6	5
1731	A560	40b yel grn, yel & blk	15	9
1732	A560	55b rose red & blk	24	9
1733	A560	60b yel & blk	40	9
1734	A560	75b lt vio & blk	48	9
1735	A560	1.35 l red org & blk	85	15

Perf. 13x13½

Size: 62x29mm

1736	A560	3.25 l blue	1.65	45
		Nos. 1729-1736 (8)	3.89	1.06

No. 1714 Surcharged in Violet

RANGER 9
24 - 3 - 1965

5 Lei

1965, Apr. 25 ***Perf. 14x13***

1737	A557	5 l on 1 l multi	12.50	12.50

Flight of the US rocket Ranger 9 to the moon, Mar. 24, 1965.

Dante Alighieri — A561

Portraits: 40b, Ion Bianu, philologist and historian. 55b, Anton Bacalbasa, writer. 60b, Vasile Conta, philosopher. 1 l, Jean Sibelius, Finnish composer. 1.35 l, Horace, Roman poet.

1965, May 10 **Photo.** ***Perf. 13½***

Portrait in Black

1738	A561	40b chalky bl	15	5
1739	A561	55b bister	18	6
1740	A561	60b lt lil	22	9
1741	A561	1 l dl red brn	45	15
1742	A561	1.35 l olive	60	22
1743	A561	1.75 l org red	1.10	30
		Nos. 1738-1743 (6)	2.70	87

ITU Emblem, Old and New Communication Equipment — A562

1965, May 15 **Engr.**

1744	A562	1.75 l ultra	90	45

ITU, centenary.

Iron Gate, Danube A562a

Arms of Jugoslavia and Romania and Djerdap Dam — A562b

Design: 55b (50d), Iron Gate hydroelectric plant and dam.

Perf. 12½x12

1965, May 20 **Litho.** **Unwmk.**

1745	A562a	30b (25d) lt bl & grn	5	5
1746	A562a	55b (50d) lt bl & dk red	24	5

Miniature Sheet

Perf. 13½x13

1747	A562b	Sheet of 4	2.75	2.75
a.		80b multi	22	14
b.		1.20 l multi	40	22

Issued simultaneously by Romania and Jugoslavia to commemorate the start of construction of the Iron Gate hydroelectric plant and dam. Valid for postage in both countries.

No. 1747 contains one each of Nos. 1747a, 1747b and Jugoslavia Nos. 771a and 771b. Only Nos. 1747a and 1747b were valid in Romania. Sold for 4 l. See Jugoslavia Nos. 769-771.

Small-bore Rifle Shooting, Kneeling — A563

Designs: 40b, Rifle shooting, prone. 55b, Rapid-fire pistol and map of Europe. 1 l, Free pistol and map of Europe. 1.60 l, Small-bore rifle, standing, and map of Europe. 2 l, 5 l, Marksmen in various shooting positions (all horizontal).

Perf. 12x12½, 12½x12

1965, May 30 **Litho.** **Unwmk.**

Size: 23x43mm, 43x23mm

1748	A563	20b multi	6	5
1749	A563	40b dl grn, pink & blk	9	6
1750	A563	55b multi	18	5
1751	A563	1 l pale grn, blk & ocher	38	9
1752	A563	1.60 l multi	60	12

Perf. 13½

Size: 51x28mm

1753	A563	2 l multi	75	28
		Nos. 1748-1753 (6)	2.06	65

European Shooting Championships, Bucharest.

Nos. 1749-1752 were issued imperf. in changed colors. Two other denominations exist, 3.25 l and 5 l, imperf. Value, set of 6, unused $4.25, canceled $1.75.

Fat-Frumos and the Giant A564

Fairy Tales: 40b, Fat-Frumos on horseback and Ileana Cosinzeana. 55b, Harap Alb and the Bear. 1 l, "The Moralist Wolf." 1.35 l, "The Ox and the Calif." 2 l, Wolf and bear pulling sled.

1965, June 25 Photo. *Perf. 13*

1756	A564	20b multi	18	5
1757	A564	40b multi	18	6
1758	A564	55b multi	22	6
1759	A564	1 l multi	40	9
1760	A564	1.35 l multi	60	12
1761	A564	2 l multi	85	28
		Nos. 1756-1761 (6)	2.43	66

Bee and Blossoms A565

Space Achievements A566

Design: 1.60 l, Exhibition Hall (horiz.).

Perf. 12x12½, 12½x12

1965, July 28 Litho. Unwmk.

1762	A565	55b org, bl & pink	28	14
1763	A565	1.60 l multi	50	24

20th Congress of the Intl Federation of Beekeeping Assocs. (Apimondia), Bucharest, Aug. 26-31.

1965, Aug. 25 Litho. *Perf. 12x12½*

Designs: 1.75 l, Col. Pavel Belyayev, Lt. Col. Alexei Leonov and Voskhod 2. 2.40 l, Early Bird over globe. 3.20 l, Lt. Col. Gordon Cooper and Lt. Com. Charles Conrad, Gemini 3 and globe.

1764	A566	1.75 l dk bl, bl & ver	80	14
1765	A566	2.40 l multi	1.10	25
1766	A566	3.20 l dk bl, lt bl & ver	2.25	52

European Quail — A567

Birds: 10b, Eurasian woodcock. 20b, Eurasian snipe. 40b, Turtle dove. 55b, Mallard. 60b, White-fronted goose. 1 l, Eurasian crane. 1.20 l, Glossy ibis. 1.35 l, Mute swan. 3.25 l, White pelican.

1965, Sept. 10 Photo. *Perf. 13½*

Size: 34x34mm

Birds in Natural Colors

1767	A567	5b red brn & rose lil	10	5
1768	A567	10b red brn & yel grn	10	5
1769	A567	20b brn & bl grn	18	5
1770	A567	40b lil & org brn	22	5
1771	A567	55b brt grn & lt brn	25	5
1772	A567	60b dl org & bl	32	5
1773	A567	1 l red & lil	42	10
1774	A567	1.20 l dk brn & grn	60	14
1775	A567	1.35 l org & ultra	80	14

Size: 32x73mm

1776	A567	3.25 l ultra & sep	2.10	45
		Nos. 1767-1776 (10)	5.09	1.13

Marx and Lenin A568

Vasile Alecsandri A569

1965, Sept. 6 Photo.

1777	A568	55b red, blk & yel	38	20

6th Conference of Postal Ministers of Communist Countries, Peking, June 21-July 15.

1965, Oct. 9 Unwmk. *Perf. 13½*

1778	A569	55b red brn, dk brn & gold	38	20

Alecsandri (1821-1890), statesman and poet.

Bird-of-Paradise Flower — A570

Flowers from Cluj Botanical Gardens: 10b, Stanhope orchid. 20b, Paphiopedilum insigne. 30b, Zanzibar water lily (horiz.). 40b, Ferocactus (horiz.). 55b, Cotton blossom (horiz.). 1 l, Hibiscus (horiz.). 1.35 l, Gloxinia. 1.75 l, Victoria water lily (horiz.). 2.30 l, Hibiscus, bird-of-paradise flower and greenhouse.

Perf. 12x12½, 12½x12

1965, Oct. 25 Litho.

Size: 23x43mm, 43x23mm

Flowers in Natural Colors

1779	A570	5b brown	5	5
1780	A570	10b green	5	5
1781	A570	20b dk bl	7	5
1782	A570	30b vio bl	10	5
1783	A570	40b red brn	10	5
1784	A570	55b dk red	14	5
1785	A570	1 l ol grn	30	5
1786	A570	1.35 l violet	48	10
1787	A570	1.75 l dk grn	80	14

Perf. 13½

Size: 52x30mm

1788	A570	2.30 l green	1.10	48
		Nos. 1779-1788 (10)	3.19	1.07

The orchid on No. 1780 is attached to the bottom of the limb.

Running A571

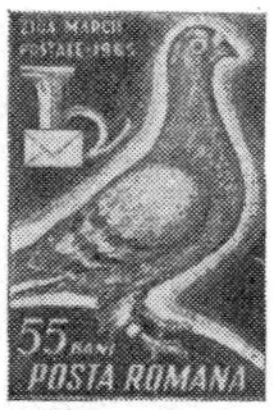

Pigeon and Post Horn A572

1965, Nov. 10 Photo. *Perf. 13½*

1789	A571	55b Soccer	14	5
1790	A571	1.55 l shown	48	10
1791	A571	1.75 l Woman diver	55	14
1792	A571	2 l Mountaineering	60	20
1793	A571	5 l Canoeing, horiz.	1.40	40
		Nos. 1789-1793 (5)	3.17	89

Spartacist Games. No. 1793 commemorates the Romanian victory in the European Kayak Championships.

1965, Nov. 15 Engr.

Designs: 1 l, Pigeon on television antenna and post horn (horiz.). 1.75 l, Flying pigeon and post horn (horiz.).

1794	A572	55b car & vio bl + 45b label	38	9
1795	A572	1 l grn & brn	38	15
1796	A572	1.75 l ol grn & sep	85	22

Issued for Stamp Day. No. 1794 is printed with alternating label showing post rider and emblem of Romanian Philatelists' Association and 45b additional charge. Stamp and label are imperf. between.

Chamois and Hunting Trophy A573

Hunting Trophy and: 1 l, Brown bear. 1.60 l, Red deer. 1.75 l, Wild boar. 3.20 l, Antlers of red beer.

1965, Dec. 10 Photo. *Perf. 13½*

Size: 37x22mm

1797	A573	55b rose lil, yel & brn	15	5
1798	A573	1 l brt grn, red & brn	28	5
1799	A573	1.60 l lt vio bl, org & brn	70	6
1800	A573	1.75 l rose, grn & blk	90	18

Size: 48x36½mm

1801	A573	3.20 l gray, gold, blk & org	1.40	38
		Nos. 1797-1801 (5)	3.43	72

Probe III Photographing Moon — A574

Designs: 5b, Proton I space station (vert.). 15b, Molniya I telecommunication satellite (vert.). 3.25 l, Mariner IV and Mars picture (vert.). 5 l, Gemini 5.

Perf. 12x12½, 12½x12

1965, Dec. 25 Litho.

1802	A574	5b multi	12	5
1803	A574	10b vio bl, red & gray	15	5
1804	A574	15b pur, gray & org	18	5
1805	A574	3.25 l vio bl, blk & red	2.25	28
1806	A574	5 l dk bl, gray & red org	3.50	60
		Nos. 1802-1806 (5)	6.20	1.03

Achievements in space research.

Cocker Spaniel — A575

Hunting Dogs: 5b, Dachshund (triangle). 40b, Retriever. 55b, Terrier. 60b, Red setter. 75b, White setter. 1.55 l, Pointers (rectangle). 3.25 l, Duck hunter with retriever (rectangle).

1965, Dec. 28 Photo. *Perf. 13½*

Size: 30x42mm

1807	A575	5b multi	7	6

Size: 33½x33½mm

1808	A575	10b multi	10	6
1809	A575	40b multi	24	6
1810	A575	55b multi	35	6
1811	A575	60b multi	50	10
1812	A575	75b multi	70	10

Size: 43x28mm

1813	A575	1.55 l multi	1.40	20
1814	A575	3.25 l multi	2.75	1.00
		Nos. 1807-1814 (8)	6.11	1.64

Chessboard, Queen and Jester — A576

Chessboard and: 20b, 1.60 l, Pawn and emblem. 55b, 1 l, Rook and knight on horseback.

1966, Feb. 25 Litho. *Perf. 13*

1815	A576	20b multi	10	5
1816	A576	40b multi	18	7
1817	A576	55b multi	28	7
1818	A576	1 l multi	55	10
1819	A576	1.60 l multi	1.00	14
1820	A576	3.25 l multi	2.50	65
		Nos. 1815-1820 (6)	4.61	1.08

Chess Olympics in Cuba.

Tractor, Grain and Sun — A577

1966, Mar. 5

1821	A577	55b lt grn & ocher	24	12

Founding congress of the National Union of Cooperative Farms.

Gheorghe Gheorghiu-Dej A578

Congress Emblem A579

1966, Mar. Photo. *Perf. 13½*

1822	A578	55b gold & blk	30	9
a		5 l souv. sheet	4.00	4.00

1st death anniv. of Pres. Gheorghe Gheorghiu-Dej (1901-65). No. 1822a contains design similar to No. 1822 with signature of Gheorghiu-Dej.

1966, Mar. 21 *Perf. 13x14½*

1823	A579	55b yel & red	30	9

1966 Congress of Communist Youth.

Folk Dancers of Moldavia — A580

Folk Dances: 40b, Oltenia. 55b, Maramaros. 1 l, Muntenia. 1.60 l, Banat. 2 l, Transylvania.

1966, Apr. 4 Engr. *Perf. 13½*
Center in Black

1824	A580	30b lilac	9	6
1825	A580	40b brick red	9	6
1826	A580	55b brt bl grn	18	6
1827	A580	1 l maroon	38	6
1828	A580	1.60 l dk bl	70	12
1829	A580	2 l yel grn	1.25	38
		Nos. 1824-1829 (6)	2.69	74

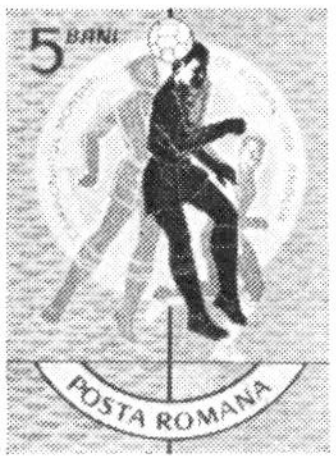
Soccer Game — A581

Designs: 10b, 15b, 55b, 1.75 l, Scenes of soccer play. 4 l, Jules Rimet Cup.

1966, Apr. 25 Litho. Unwmk.

1830	A581	5b multi	6	6
1831	A581	10b multi	9	6
1832	A581	15b multi	12	6
1833	A581	55b multi	45	6
1834	A581	1.75 l multi	1.10	15
1835	A581	4 l gold & multi	2.50	75
a		10 l souv. sheet	3.75	3.75
		Nos. 1830-1835 (6)	4.32	1.14

World Cup Soccer Championship, Wembley, England, July 11-30.
No. 1835a contains one 10 l multicolored stamp in design of 4 l, but larger (32x46 mm.) and imperf. No gum. Issued June 20.

Symbols of Industry — A582

1966, May 14 Photo.

1836	A582	55b multi	24	7

Romanian Trade Union Congress.

Red-breasted Flycatcher A583

Venus 3 (Russia) A584

Song Birds: 10b, Red crossbill. 15b, Great reed warbler. 20b, European redstart. 55b, European robin. 1.20 l, White-spotted bluethroat. 1.55 l, Yellow wagtail. 3.20 l, Common penduline tit.

1966, May 25 Photo. *Perf. 13½*

1837	A583	5b gold & multi	9	5
1838	A583	10b sil & multi	12	5
1839	A583	15b gold & multi	18	5
1840	A583	20b sil & multi	18	5
1841	A583	55b sil & multi	28	6
1842	A583	1.20 l gold & multi	38	6
1843	A583	1.55 l sil & multi	1.00	30
1844	A583	3.20 l gold & multi	1.65	45
		Nos. 1837-1844 (8)	3.88	1.07

1966, June 25

Designs: 20b, FR-1 (France). 1.60 l, Luna 9 (Russia). 5 l, Gemini 6 and 7 (US).

1845	A584	10b dp vio, gray & red	9	5
1846	A584	20b ultra, blk & red	15	5
1847	A584	1.60 l dk bl, blk & red	55	12
1848	A584	5 l bl, blk, brn & red	1.50	60

International achievements in space.

Urechia Nestor — A585

Portraits: 5b, George Cosbuc. 10b, Gheorghe Sincai. 40b, Aron Pumnul. 55b, Stefan Luchian. 1 l, Sun Yat-sen. 1.35 l, Gottfried Wilhelm Leibniz. 1.60 l, Romain Rolland. 1.75 l, Ion Ghica. 3.25 l, Constantin Cantacuzino.

1966, June 28

1849	A585	5b grn, blk & dk bl	6	5
1850	A585	10b rose car, grn & blk	6	5
1851	A585	20b grn, plum & blk	9	5
1852	A585	40b vio bl, brn & blk	9	5
1853	A585	55b brn org, bl grn & blk	20	5
1854	A585	1 l ocher, vio & blk	28	8
1855	A585	1.35 l bl & blk	35	14
1856	A585	1.60 l brt grn, dl vio & blk	55	14
1857	A585	1.75 l org, dl vio & blk	55	14
1858	A585	3.25 l bl, dk car & blk	1.00	30
		Nos. 1849-1858 (10)	3.23	1.05

Cultural anniversaries.

Country House, by Gheorghe Petrascu — A586

Paintings: 10b, Peasant Woman, by Nicolae Grigorescu (vert.). 20b, Reapers at Rest, by Camil Ressu. 55b, Man with the Blue Cap, by Van Eyck (vert.). 1.55 l, Train Compartment, by Daumier. 3.25 l, Betrothal of the Virgin, by El Greco (vert.).

1966, July 25 Unwmk.
Gold Frame

1859	A586	5b Prus grn & brn org	20	10
1860	A586	10b red brn & crim	20	10
1861	A586	20b brn & brt grn	20	14
1862	A586	55b vio bl & lil	30	20
1863	A586	1.55 l dk sl grn & org	1.40	50
1864	A586	3.25 l vio & ultra	3.00	1.40
		Nos. 1859-1864 (6)	5.30	2.44

See Nos. 1907-1912.

Hottonia Palustris — A587

Marine Flora: 10b, Ceratophyllum submersum. 20b, Aldrovanda vesiculosa. 40b, Callitriche verna. 55b, Vallisneria spiralis. 1 l, Elodea Canadensis rich. 1.55 l, Hippuris vulgaris. 3.25 l, Myriophyllum spicatum.

1966, Aug. 25 Litho. *Perf. 13½*
Size: 28x40mm

1865	A587	5b multi	5	5
1866	A587	10b multi	7	5
1867	A587	20b multi	7	5
1868	A587	40b multi	10	5
1869	A587	55b multi	18	6
1870	A587	1 l multi	45	7
1871	A587	1.55 l multi	70	24

Size: 28x50mm

1872	A587	3.25 l multi	1.40	38
		Nos. 1865-1872 (8)	3.02	95

Derivation of the Meter — A588

Design: 1 l, Metric system symbols.

1966, Sept. 10 Photo. *Perf. 13½*

1873	A588	55b sal & ultra	28	7
1874	A588	1 l lt grn & vio	45	18

Introduction of metric system in Romania, centenary.

Statue of Ovid and Medical School Emblem A589

Line Integral Denoting Work A590

I. H. Radulescu, M. Kogalniceanu and T. Savulescu — A591

Design: 1 l, Academy centenary medal.

1966, Sept. 30
Size: 22x27mm

1875	A589	40b lil gray, ultra, sep & gold	15	7
1876	A590	55b gray, brn, red & gold	15	7

Size: 22x34mm

1877	A589	1 l ultra, brn & gold	35	7

Size: 66x28mm

1878	A591	3 l org, dk brn & gold	95	40

Centenary of the Romanian Academy.

Crawfish A592

Molluscs and Crustaceans: 10b, Nassa reticulata (vert.). 20b, Stone crab. 40b, Campylaea trizona. 55b, Helix lucorum. 1.35 l, Mytilus galloprovincialis. 1.75 l, Lymnaea stagnalis. 3.25 l, Anodonta cygnaea. (10b, 40b, 55b, 1.75 l, are snails; 1.35 l, 3.25 l, are bivalves).

1966, Oct. 15
Animals in Natural Colors

1879	A592	5b dp org	5	5
1880	A592	10b lt bl	5	5
1881	A592	20b pale lil	5	5
1882	A592	40b yel grn	14	7
1883	A592	55b car rose	20	10
1884	A592	1.35 l brt grn	45	14
1885	A592	1.75 l ultra	55	20
1886	A592	3.25 l brt org	1.40	45
		Nos. 1879-1886 (8)	2.89	1.11

Cave Bear A593

Prehistoric Animals: 10b, Mammoth. 15b, Bison. 55b, Cave elephant. 1.55 l, Stags. 4 l, Dinotherium.

1966, Nov. 25
Size: 36x22mm

1887	A593	5b ultra, bl grn & red brn	7	5
1888	A593	10b vio, emer & brn	10	5
1889	A593	15b ol, grn & dk brn	18	5
1890	A593	55b lil, emer & brn	30	6
1891	A593	1.55 l ultra, grn & brn	95	18

Size: 43x27mm

1892	A593	4 l rose car, grn & brn	1.50	70
		Nos. 1887-1892 (6)	3.10	1.09

Putna Monastery, 500th Anniv. A594

1966 Photo. *Perf. 13½*

1893	A594	2 l multi	70	18

Yuri A. Gagarin and Vostok 1 — A595

Russian Achievements in Space: 10b, Trajectory of Sputnik 1 around globe (horiz.). 25b, Valentina Tereshkova and globe with trajectory of Vostok 6. 40b, Andrian G. Nikolayev, Pavel R. Popovich and globe with trajectory of Vostok 8. 55b, Alexei Leonov walking in space.

1967, Feb. 15 Photo. *Perf. 13½*

1894	A595	10b sil & multi	5	5
1895	A595	20b sil & multi	5	5
1896	A595	25b sil & multi	10	5
1897	A595	40b sil & multi	18	8
1898	A595	55b sil & multi	30	10
		Nos. 1894-1898,C163-C166 (9)	3.46	1.03

Ten years of space exploration.

Barn Owl — A596

Birds of Prey: 20b, Eagle owl. 40b, Saker falcon. 55b, Egyptian vulture. 75b, Osprey. 1 l, Griffon vulture. 1.20 l, Lammergeier. 1.75 l, Cinereous vulture.

1967, Mar. 20 Photo. Unwmk.
Birds in Natural Colors

1899	A596	10b	vio & ol	14	5
1900	A596	20b	bl & org	24	5
1901	A596	40b	emer & org	18	5
1902	A596	55b	yel grn & ocher	24	6
1903	A596	75b	rose lil & grn	24	7
1904	A596	1 l	yel org & blk	50	12
1905	A596	1.20 l	cl & yel	85	12
1906	A596	1.75 l	sal pink & gray	1.25	50
			Nos. 1899-1906 (8)	3.64	1.02

Painting Type of 1966

Paintings: 10b, Woman in Fancy Dress, by Ion Andreescu. 20b, Washwomen, by J. Al. Steriadi. 40b, Women weavers, by St. Dimitrescu (vert.). 1.55 l, Venus and Amor, by Lucas Cranach (vert.). 3.20 l, Hercules and the Lion of Numea, by Rubens. 5 l, Haman Asking Esther's Forgiveness, by Rembrandt (vert.).

1967, Mar. 30 *Perf. 13½*
Gold Frame

1907	A586	10b	dp bl & rose red	7	5
1908	A586	20b	dp grn & bis	10	5
1909	A586	40b	car & bl	18	5
1910	A586	1.55 l	dp plum & lt ultra	60	14
1911	A586	3.20 l	brn & grn	1.00	24
1912	A586	5 l	ol grn & org	2.25	70
			Nos. 1907-1912 (6)	4.20	1.23

Mlle. Pogany, by Brancusi A597

Sculptures: 5b, Girl's head. 10b, The Sleeping Muse (horiz.). 20b, The Infinite Column. 40b, The Kiss (horiz.). 55b, Earth Wisdom (seated woman). 3.25 l, Gate of the Kiss.

1967, Apr. 27 Photo. *Perf. 13½*

1913	A597	5b	dl yel, blk brn & ver	5	5
1914	A597	10b	bl grn, blk & lil	5	5
1915	A597	20b	lt bl, blk & rose red	10	5
1916	A597	40b	pink, sep & brt grn	18	7
1917	A597	55b	yel grn, blk & ultra	24	10
1918	A597	1.20 l	bluish lil, ol blk & org	40	18
1919	A597	3.25 l	emer, blk & cer	1.10	50
			Nos. 1913-1919 (7)	2.12	1.00

Constantin Brancusi (1876-1957), sculptor.

Coins of 1867 A598

Design: 1.20 l, Coins of 1966.

1967, May 4

1920	A598	55b	multi	24	10
1921	A598	1.20 l	multi	50	24

Centenary of Romanian monetary system.

Infantry Soldier, by Nicolae Grigorescu A599

1967, May 9

1922	A599	55b	multi	55	24

90th anniv. of Romanian independence.

Peasants Marching, by Stefan Luchian — A600

Painting: 40b, Fighting Peasants, by Octav Bancila (vert.).

1967, May 20 Unwmk. *Perf. 13½*

1923	A600	40b	multi	30	7
1924	A600	1.55 l	multi	1.25	70

60th anniversary of Peasant Uprising.

Centaury — A601

Carpathian Flora: 40b, Hedge mustard. 55b, Columbine. 1.20 l, Alpine violet. 1.75 l, Bell flower. 4 l, Dryas (horiz.).

1967, June 10 Photo.
Flowers in Natural Colors

1925	A601	20b	ocher	7	7
1926	A601	40b	violet	10	7
1927	A601	55b	bis & brn red	18	8
1928	A601	1.20 l	yel & red brn	35	14
1929	A601	1.75 l	bluish grn & car	50	20
1930	A601	4 l	lt ultra	1.40	35
			Nos. 1925-1930 (6)	2.60	91

Fortifications, Sibiu — A602

Map of Romania and ITY Emblem — A603

Designs: 40b, Cris Castle. 55b, Wooden Church, Plopis. 1.60 l, Ruins of Nuamtulua Fortress. 1.75 l, Mogosoaia Palace. 2.25 l, Voronet Church.

1967, June 29 Photo. *Perf. 13½*
Size: 33x33mm

1931	A602	20b	ultra & multi	7	5
1932	A602	40b	vio & multi	10	7
1933	A602	55b	multi	14	7
1934	A602	1.60 l	multi	38	10
1935	A602	1.75 l	multi	45	14

Size: 48x36mm

1936	A602	2.25 l	bl & multi	75	28
			Nos. 1931-1936 (6)	1.89	71

Souvenir Sheet
Imperf

1937	A603	5 l	lt bl, ultra & blk	2.50	1.40

International Tourist Year.

The Attack at Marasesti, by E. Stoica — A604

1967, July 24 Unwmk. *Perf. 13½*

1938	A604	55b	gray, Prus bl & brn	35	14

50th anniv. of the Battle of Marasesti and Oituz.

Dinu Lipatti, Pianist — A605

Designs: 20b, Al. Orascu, architect. 40b, Gr. Antipa, zoologist. 55b, M. Kogalniceanu, statesman. 1.20 l, Jonathan Swift, writer. 1.75 l, Marie Curie, scientist.

1967, July 29 Photo. *Perf. 13½*

1939	A605	10b	ultra, blk & pur	7	5
1940	A605	20b	org brn, blk & ultra	10	5
1941	A605	40b	bl grn, blk & org brn	14	7
1942	A605	55b	dp rose, blk & dk ol grn	20	7
1943	A605	1.20 l	ol, blk & brn	35	14
1944	A605	1.75 l	dl bl, blk & bl grn	70	35
			Nos. 1939-1944 (6)	1.56	73

Cultural anniversaries.

Wrestlers A606

Congress Emblem A607

Designs: 20b, 55b, 1.20 l, 2 l, Various fight scenes and world map (20b, 2 l horizontal); on 2 l maps are large and wrestlers small.

1967, Aug. 28

1945	A606	10b	ol & multi	7	6
1946	A606	20b	cit & multi	10	7
1947	A606	55b	bis & multi	14	7
1948	A606	1.20 l	multi	28	18
1949	A606	2 l	ultra, gold & dp car	1.00	40
			Nos. 1945-1949 (5)	1.59	78

World Greco-Roman Wrestling Championships, Bucharest.

1967, Aug. 28

1950	A607	1.60 l	lt bl, ultra & dp car	50	18

Intl. Linguists' Congress, Bucharest, Aug. 28-Sept. 2.

Ice Skating — A608

Designs: 40b, Biathlon. 55b, 5 l, Bobsledding. 1 l, Skiing. 1.55 l, Ice Hockey. 2 l, Emblem of 10th Winter Olympic Games. 2.30 l, Ski jump.

1967, Sept. 28 Photo. *Perf. 13½x13*

1951	A608	20b	lt bl & multi	7	5
1952	A608	40b	multi	10	7
1953	A608	55b	bl & multi	14	7
1954	A608	1 l	lil & multi	20	14
1955	A608	1.55 l	multi	30	14
1956	A608	2 l	gray & multi	50	18
1957	A608	2.30 l	multi	85	35
			Nos. 1951-1957 (7)	2.16	1.00

Souvenir Sheet
Imperf

1958	A608	5 l	lt bl & multi	3.50	3.00

10th Winter Olympic Games, Grenoble, France, Feb. 6-18, 1968.

Nos. 1951-1957 issued in sheets of 10 (5x2) and 5 labels.

Curtea de Arges Monastery, 450th Anniv. — A609

1967, Nov. 1 Unwmk. *Perf. 13½*

1959	A609	55b	multi	30	7

Romanian Academy Library, Bucharest, Cent. — A610

1967, Sept. 25 **Litho.**

1960	A610 55b ocher, gray & dk bl	30	7

Karl Marx and Title Page — A611

Lenin — A612

1967, Nov. 4 **Photo.**

1961	A611 40b rose cl, blk & yel	24	10

Centenary of the publication of "Das Kapital" by Karl Marx.

1967, Nov. 3

1962	A612 1.20 l red, blk & gold	35	10

Russian October Revolution, 50th anniv.

Monorail Leaving US EXPO Pavilion A613

Designs: 1 l, EXPO emblem and atom symbol. 1.60 l, Cup, world map and EXPO emblem. 2 l, EXPO emblem.

1967, Nov. 28 **Photo.**

1963	A613 55b grnsh bl, vio & blk	14	8
1964	A613 1 l red, blk & gray	28	12
1965	A613 1.60 l multi	40	24
1966	A613 2 l multi	60	28

EXPO '67 Intl. Exhib., Montreal, Apr. 28-Oct. 27. No. 1965 also commemorates Romania's victory in the World Fencing Championships in Montreal.

Truck A614

Arms of the Republic A615

Diesel Locomotive A616

Map Showing Telephone Network A617

Designs: 10b, Communications emblem (vert.). 20b, Train. 35b, Plane. 50b, Telephone (vert.). 60b, Small loading truck. 1.20 l, Autobus. 1.35 l, Helicopter. 1.50 l, Trolley bus. 1.55 l, Radio station and tower. 1.75 l, Highway. 2 l, Mail truck. 2.40 l, Television tower. 3.20 l, Jet plane. 3.25 l, Steamship. 4 l, Electric train. 5 l, World map and teletype.

Photo.; Engr. (type A615)

1967-68 ***Perf. 13½***

1967	A614	5b lt ol grn ('68)	5	5
1968	A614	10b hn brn ('68)	5	5
1969	A614	20b gray ('68)	5	5
1970	A614	35b bl blk ('68)	8	5
1971	A615	40b vio bl	10	5
1972	A614	50b org ('68)	12	5
1973	A615	55b dl org	14	5
1974	A614	60b org brn ('68)	14	5

Size: 22½x28mm, 28x22½mm

1975	A616	1 l emer ('68)	22	5
1976	A617	1.20 l red lil ('68)	28	5
1977	A617	1.35 l brt bl ('68)	30	5
1978	A616	1.50 l rose red ('68)	35	5
1979	A616	1.55 l dk brn ('68)	35	5
1980	A615	1.60 l rose red	38	5
1981	A617	1.75 l dp grn ('68)	40	5
1982	A617	2 l cit ('68)	60	5
1983	A616	2.40 l dk bl ('68)	75	5
1984	A617	3 l grnsh bl	75	5
1985	A617	3.20 l ocher ('68)	1.00	5
1986	A616	3.25 l ultra ('68)	1.00	5
1987	A617	4 l lil rose ('68)	1.25	5
1988	A617	5 l vio ('68)	1.40	5
		Nos. 1967-1988 (22)	9.76	1.10

40th anniv. of the first automatic telephone exchange; introduction of automatic telephone service (No. 1984).

See Nos. 2078-2079, 2269-2284.

Coat of Arms, Symbols of Agriculture and Industry — A618

Designs: 55b, Coat of arms. 1.60 l, Romanian flag. 1.75 l, Coat of arms and symbols of arts and education.

1967, Dec. 26 **Photo.** ***Perf. 13½***

Size: 27x48mm

1989	A618 40b multi	10	8
1990	A618 55b multi	14	8

Size: 33½x48mm

1991	A618 1.60 l multi	35	18

Size: 27x48mm

1992	A618 1.75 l multi	60	24

20th anniversary of the republic.

Souvenir Sheet

Anemones, by Stefan Luchian — A619

1968, Mar. 30 **Litho.** ***Imperf.***

1993	A619 10 l multi	4.75	4.75

Birth centenary of Stefan Luchian, Romanian painter.

Portrait of a Lady, by Misu Popp A620

Paintings: 10b, The Reveille of Romania, by Gheorghe Tattarescu. 20b, Composition, by Teodorescu Sionion (horiz.). 35b, The Judgment of Paris, by Hendrick van Balen (horiz.). 55b, Little Girl with Red Kerchief, by Nicolae Grigorescu. 60b, The Mystical Betrothal of St. Catherine, by Lamberto Sustris (horiz.). 1 l, Old Nicolas, the Zither Player, by Stefan Luchian. 1.60 l, Man with a Skull, by Dierick Bouts (?). 1.75 l, Madonna and Child with Fruit Basket, by Jan van Bylert. 2.40 l, Medor and Angelica, by Sebastiano Ricci (horiz.). 3 l, Summer, by Jacob Jordaens (horiz.). 3.20 l, 5 l, Ecce Homo, by Titian.

1968 **Photo.** ***Perf. 13½***

Gold Frame

Size: 28x49mm

1994	A620 10b multi	5	5

Size: 48½x36½mm, 36x48½mm

1995	A620 20b multi	5	5
1996	A620 35b multi	10	6
1997	A620 40b multi	14	6
1998	A620 55b multi	14	6
1999	A620 60b multi	20	7
2000	A620 1 l multi	30	8
2001	A620 1.60 l multi	45	14
2002	A620 1.75 l multi	45	18
2003	A620 2.40 l multi	85	30
2004	A620 3 l multi	95	50
2005	A620 3.20 l multi	1.50	70
	Nos. 1994-2005 (12)	5.18	2.25

Miniature Sheet

Imperf

2006	A620 5 l multi	4.50	4.50

Issue dates: 40b, 55b, 1, 1.60, 2.40, 3.20 and 5 lei, Mar. 28. Others, Sept. 9.

See Nos. 2088-2094, 2124-2130.

Human Rights Flame A621

WHO Emblem A622

1968, May 9 **Unwmk.** ***Perf. 13½***

2007	A621 1 l multi	45	18

Intl. Human Rights Year.

1968, May 14 **Photo.**

2008	A622 1.60 l multi	50	18

WHO, 20th anniversary.

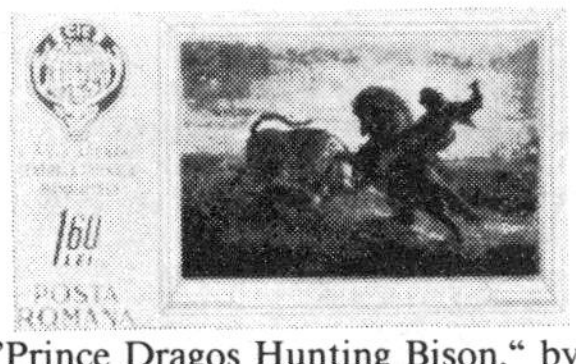

"Prince Dragos Hunting Bison," by Nicolae Grigorescu — A623

1968, May 17

2009	A623 1.60 l multi	60	24

15th Hunting Congress, Mamaia, May 23-29.

Pioneers and Liberation Monument — A624

Pioneers: 40b, receiving scarfs. 55b, building model planes and boat. 1 l, as radio amateurs. 1.60 l, folk dancing. 2.40 l, Girl Pioneers in camp.

1968, June 9 **Photo.** ***Perf. 13½***

2010	A624 5b multi	5	5
2011	A624 40b multi	10	6
2012	A624 55b multi	16	6
2013	A624 1 l multi	30	14
2014	A624 1.60 l multi	50	20
2015	A624 2.40 l multi	70	24
	Nos. 2010-2015 (6)	1.81	75

Ion Ionescu de la Brad — A625

Designs: 55b, Emil Racovita. 1.60 l, Prince Mircea of Walachia.

1968

Size: 28x43mm

2016	A625 40b multi	20	5
2017	A625 55b grn & multi	20	5

Size: 28x48mm

2018	A625 1.60 l gold & multi	45	18

Ion Ionescu de la Brad (1818-91); Emil Racovita (1868-1947), explorer and naturalist; 1.60 l, Prince Mircea (1386-1418). Dates of issue: 40b, 55b, June 24; 1.60 l, June 22.

Geranium A626

Designs: Various geraniums.

1968, July 20 **Photo.** ***Perf. 13½***

2019	A626 10b multi	5	5
2020	A626 20b multi	5	5
2021	A626 40b multi	10	6
2022	A626 55b multi	14	7
2023	A626 60b multi	14	10
2024	A626 1.20 l multi	30	14
2025	A626 1.35 l multi	40	20
2026	A626 1.60 l multi	85	24
	Nos. 2019-2026 (8)	2.03	91

The Scott Catalogue value is a retail price, what you could expect to pay for the stamp in a grade of Fine-Very Fine. The value listed is a reference which reflects recent actual dealer selling price.

Avram Iancu, by B. Iscovescu and Demonstrating Students — A627

Demonstrating Students and: 55b, Nicolae Balcescu, by Gheorghe Tattarescu. 1.60 l, Vasile Alecsandri, by N. Livaditti.

1968, July 25

2027	A627	55b	gold & multi	20	6
2028	A627	1.20 l	gold & multi	45	10
2029	A627	1.60 l	gold & multi	70	24

120th anniversary of 1848 revolution.

Boxing — A628

Atheneum and Harp — A629

Aztec Calendar Stone and: 10b, Javelin, Women's. 20b, Woman diver. 40b, Volleyball. 60b, Wrestling. 1.20 l, Fencing. 1.35 l, Canoeing. 1.60 l, Soccer. 5 l, Running.

1968, Aug. 28

2030	A628	10b	multi	5	5
2031	A628	20b	multi	6	5
2032	A628	40b	multi	10	7
2033	A628	55b	multi	12	7
2034	A628	60b	multi	14	10
2035	A628	1.20 l	multi	38	18
2036	A628	1.35 l	multi	45	24
2037	A628	1.60 l	multi	70	28
			Nos. 2030-2037 (8)	2.00	1.04

Souvenir Sheet

Imperf

2038	A628	5 l	multi	2.25	1.75

19th Olympic Games, Mexico City, Oct. 12-17.

1968, Aug. 20 Litho. *Perf. 12x12½*

2039	A629	55b	multi	24	10

Centenary of the Philharmonic Orchestra.

Globe and Emblem — A630

1968, Oct. 4 Litho. *Perf. 13½*

2040	A630	1.60 l	ultra & gold	50	18

Intl. Federation of Photograpic Art, 20th anniv.

Moldovita Monastery Church — A631

Historic Monuments: 10b, "The Triumph of Trajan," Roman metope (vert.). 55b, Cozia monastery church. 1.20 l, Court of Tirgoviste Palace. 1.55 l, Palace of Culture, Jassy. 1.75 l, Corvinus Castle, Hunedoara.

1968, Nov. 25 Engr. *Perf. 13½*

2041	A631	10b	dk bl, ol & brn	5	5
2042	A631	40b	rose car, bl & brn	10	5
2043	A631	55b	ol, brn & vio	14	5
2044	A631	1.20 l	yel, mar & gray	30	8
2045	A631	1.55 l	vio brn, dk bl & lt grn	50	18
2046	A631	1.75 l	org, blk & ol	1.00	28
			Nos. 2041-2046 (6)	2.09	69

Mute Swan — A632

Protected Birds and Animals: 20b, European stilts. 40b, Sheldrakes. 55b, Egret feeding young. 60b, Golden eagle. 1.20 l, Great bustards. 1.35 l, Chamois. 1.60 l, Bison.

1968, Dec. 20 Photo. *Perf. 13½*

2047	A632	10b	pink & multi	5	5
2048	A632	20b	multi	6	5
2049	A632	40b	lil & multi	10	5
2050	A632	55b	ol & multi	12	5
2051	A632	60b	multi	20	6
2052	A632	1.20 l	multi	45	10
2053	A632	1.35 l	bl & multi	50	14
2054	A632	1.60 l	multi	60	24
			Nos. 2047-2054 (8)	2.08	74

Michael the Brave's Entry into Alba Iulia, by D. Stoica — A633

Designs: 1 l, "The Round Dance of Union," by Theodor Aman. 1.75 l, Assembly of Alba Iulia.

1968, Dec. 1 Litho. *Perf. 13½*

2055	A633	55b	gold & multi	20	7
2056	A633	1 l	gold & multi	30	18
2057	A633	1.75 l	gold & multi	40	35
a			Souv. sheet of 3	1.50	1.50

50th anniv. of the union of Transylvania and Romania. No. 2057a contains 3 imperf. stamps similar to Nos. 2055-2057. Sold for 4 l.

Woman from Neamt — A634

Regional Costumes: 40b, Man from Neamt. 55b, Woman from Hunedoara. 1 l, Man from Hunedoara. 1.60 l, Woman from Brasov. 2.40 l, Man from Brasov.

1968, Dec. 28 *Perf. 12x12½*

2058	A634	5b	org & multi	5	5
2059	A634	40b	bl & multi	10	5
2060	A634	55b	multi	15	6
2061	A634	1 l	brn & multi	28	10
2062	A634	1.60 l	brn & multi	55	14
2063	A634	2.40 l	multi	1.00	35
			Nos. 2058-2063 (6)	2.13	75

1969, Feb. 15

Regional Costumes: 5b, Woman from Dolj. 40b, Man from Dolj. 55b, Woman from Arges. 1 l, Man from Arges. 1.60 l, Woman from Timisoara. 2.40 l, Man from Timisoara.

2064	A634	5b	multi	5	5
2065	A634	40b	multi	10	6
2066	A634	55b	lil & multi	15	7
2067	A634	1 l	rose & multi	28	12
2068	A634	1.60 l	multi	55	20
2069	A634	2.40 l	brn & multi	1.00	35
			Nos. 2064-2069 (6)	2.13	85

Fencing A635

Sports: 20b, Women's javelin. 40b, Canoeing. 55b, Boxing. 1 l, Volleyball. 1.20 l, Swimming. 1.60 l, Wrestling. 2.40 l, Soccer.

1969, Mar. 10 Photo. *Perf. 13½*

Denominations Black, Athletes in Gray

2070	A635	10b	pale brn	5	5
2071	A635	20b	violet	5	5
2072	A635	40b	blue	10	6
2073	A635	55b	red	15	7
2074	A635	1 l	green	24	10
2075	A635	1.20 l	brt bl	28	14
2076	A635	1.60 l	cerise	48	18
2077	A635	2.40 l	dp grn	85	28
			Nos. 2070-2077 (8)	2.20	93

Type of Regular Issue

Designs: 40b, Power lines. 55b, Dam.

1969, Jan. 10 Photo. *Perf. 13½*

2078	A614	40b	ultra	10	5
2079	A614	55b	rose red	18	7

Painting Type of 1968

Paintings (Nudes): 10b, Woman Carrying Jug, by Gheorghe Tattarescu. 20b, Reclining Woman, by Theodor Pallady (horiz.). 35b, Seated Woman, by Nicolae Tonitza. 60b, Venus and Amor, 17th century Flemish School. 1.75 l, 5 l, Diana and Endimion, by Marco Liberi. 3 l, The Three Graces, by Alessandro Varotari.

1969, Mar. 27 Photo. *Perf. 13½*

Gold Frame

Size: 37x49mm, 49x37mm

2088	A620	10b	multi	10	5
2089	A620	20b	multi	14	5
2090	A620	35b	multi	20	7
2091	A620	60b	multi	30	10
2092	A620	1.75 l	multi	70	35

Size: 27½x48½mm

2093	A620	3 l	multi	1.50	60
			Nos. 2088-2093 (6)	2.94	1.22

Miniature Sheet

Imperf

2094	A620	5 l	multi	3.00	3.00

No. 2094 contains one stamp 36½x48½mm. with simulated perforations.

No. 2093 is incorrectly inscribed Hans von Aachen.

ILO, 50th Anniv. — A636

Symbolic Head — A637

1969, Apr. 9 Photo. *Perf. 13½*

2095	A636	55b	multi	40	8

1969, Apr. 28

2096	A637	55b	ultra & multi	35	20
2097	A637	1.50 l	red & multi	90	50

Romania's cultural and economic cooperation with European countries.

Communications Symbol — A638

1969, May 12 Photo. *Perf. 13½*

2098	A638	55b	vio bl & bluish gray	35	10

7th Session of the Conference of Postal and Telecommunications Ministers, Bucharest.

Boxers, Referee and Map of Europe A639

Map of Europe and: 40b, Two boxers. 55b, Sparring. 1.75 l, Referee declaring winner.

1969, May 24

2099	A639	35b	multi	8	5
2100	A639	40b	multi	10	7
2101	A639	55b	multi	24	10
2102	A639	1.75 l	bl & multi	60	24

European Boxing Championships, Bucharest, May 31-June 8.

Apatura Ilia — A640

Designs: Various butterflies and moths.

1969, June 25 Photo. *Perf. 13½*

Insects in Natural Colors

2103	A640	5b	yel grn	5	5
2104	A640	10b	rose mag	5	5
2105	A640	20b	violet	5	5
2106	A640	40b	bl grn	10	5
2107	A640	55b	brt bl	12	5
2108	A640	1 l	blue	30	14
2109	A640	1.20 l	vio bl	40	20
2110	A640	2.40 l	yel bis	80	28
			Nos. 2103-2110 (8)	1.87	87

Communist Party Flag — A641

1969, Aug. 6 Photo. *Perf. 13½*

2111	A641	55b	multi	28	10

10th Romanian Communist Party Congress.

Torch, Atom Diagram and Book — A642

Broken Chain — A643

Designs: 40b, Symbols of agriculture, science and industry. 1.75 l, Pylon, smokestack and cogwheel.

1969, Aug. 10

2112 A642 35b multi 10 6
2113 A642 40b grn & multi 14 7
2114 A642 1.75 l multi 50 24

Exhibition showing the achievements of Romanian economy during the last 25 years.

1969, Aug. 23

Designs: 55b, Construction work. 60b, Flags.

2115 A643 10b multi 5 5
2116 A643 55b yel & multi 18 8
2117 A643 60b multi 24 10

25th anniversary of Romania's liberation from fascist rule.

Juggler on Unicycle A644

Branesti Mask A645

Circus Performers: 20b, Clown. 35b, Trapeze artists. 60b, Dressage and woman trainer. 1.75 l, Woman in high wire act. 3 l, Performing tiger and trainer.

1969, Sept. 29 Photo. *Perf. 13½*

2118 A644 10b lt bl & multi 5 5
2119 A644 20b lem & multi 5 5
2120 A644 35b lil & multi 10 5
2121 A644 60b multi 18 6
2122 A644 1.75 l multi 60 18
2123 A644 3 l ultra & multi 1.00 50
Nos. 2118-2123 (6) 1.98 89

Painting Type of 1968

Paintings: 10b, Venetian Senator, Tintoretto School. 20b, Sofia Kretzulescu, by Gheorghe Tattarescu. 35b, Phillip IV, by Velazquez. 60b, Man Reading and Child, by Hans Memling. 1.75 l, Doamnei d'Aguesseau, by Madame Vigée-Lebrun. 3 l, Portrait of a Woman, by Rembrandt. 5 l, The Return of the Prodigal Son, by Bernardino Licinio (horiz.).

1969

Gold Frame

Size: 36½x49mm

2124 A620 10b multi 5 5
2125 A620 20b multi 5 5
2126 A620 35b multi 10 5
2127 A620 60b multi 35 8
2128 A620 1.75 l multi 70 18
2129 A620 3 l multi 1.25 50
Nos. 2124-2129 (6) 2.50 91

Miniature Sheet

Imperf

2130 A620 5 l gold & multi 2.00 1.50

No. 2130 contains one stamp with simulated perforations.
Issue dates: 5 l, July 31. Others, Oct. 1.

1969, Nov. 24 Photo. *Perf. 13½*

Masks from: 55b, Tudora. 1.55 l, Birsesti. 1.75 l, Rudaria.

2131 A645 40b org & multi 10 5
2132 A645 55b multi 14 6
2133 A645 1.55 l red & multi 50 20
2134 A645 1.75 l multi 60 24

Armed Forces Memorial A646

1969, Oct. 25

2135 A646 55b red, blk & gold 20 10

25th anniversary of the People's Army.

Locomotives of 1869 and 1969 — A647

1969, Oct. 31

2136 A647 55b sil & multi 24 14

Bucharest-Filaret-Giurgevo railroad, cent.

Apollo 12 Landing Module — A648

1969, Nov. 24

2137 A648 1.50 l multi 55 50

2nd landing on the moon, Nov. 19, 1969, astronauts Captains Alan Bean, Charles Conrad, Jr. and Richard Gordon.
Printed in sheets of 4 with 4 labels (one label with names of astronauts, one with Apollo 12 emblem and 2 silver labels with picture of landing module, Intrepid).

Mother Goose in Goat Disguise — A649

Designs: 55b, Children singing and decorated tree, Sorcova. 1.50 l, Drummer and singer, Buhaiul. 2.40 l, Singer and bell ringer, Plugusurol.

1969, Dec. 25 Photo. *Perf. 13½*

2138 A649 40b bis & multi 10 7
2139 A649 55b lil & multi 14 8
2140 A649 1.50 l bl & multi 50 20
2141 A649 2.40 l multi 1.00 35

Issued for New Year 1970.

The Last Judgment (detail), Voronet Monastery — A650

North Moldavian Monastery Frescoes: 10b, Stephen the Great and family, Voronet. 20b, Three prophets, Sucevita. 60b, St. Nicholas (scene from his life), Sucevita (vert.). 1.75 l, Siege of Constantinople, 7th century, Moldovita. 3 l, Plowman, Voronet (vert.).

1969, Dec. 15

2142 A650 10b gold & multi 5 5
2143 A650 20b gold & multi 5 5
2144 A650 35b gold & multi 8 6
2145 A650 60b gold & multi 14 8
2146 A650 1.75 l gold & multi 35 20
2147 A650 3 l gold & multi 1.10 35
Nos. 2142-2147 (6) 1.77 79

Ice Hockey A651

Designs: 55b, Goalkeeper. 1.20 l, Two players with puck. 2.40 l, Player and goalkeeper.

1970, Jan. 20 *Perf. 13½*

2148 A651 20b yel & multi 5 5
2149 A651 55b multi 14 10
2150 A651 1.20 l pink & multi 38 24
2151 A651 2.40 l lt bl & multi 1.00 38

World Ice Hockey Championships, Bucharest and Galati, Feb. 24-Mar. 5.

Pasqueflower A652

Flowers: 10b, Adonis vernalis. 20b, Thistle. 40b, Almond tree blossoms. 55b, Iris. 1 l, Flax. 1.20 l, Sage. 2.40 l, Peony.

1970, Feb. 25 Photo. *Perf. 13½*

2152 A652 5b yel & multi 5 5
2153 A652 10b grn & multi 5 5
2154 A652 20b lt bl & multi 6 5
2155 A652 40b vio & multi 10 5
2156 A652 55b ultra & multi 12 6
2157 A652 1 l multi 22 14
2158 A652 1.20 l red & multi 38 18
2159 A652 2.40 l multi 75 28
Nos. 2152-2159 (8) 1.73 86

Japanese Print and EXPO '70 Emblem A653

Design: 1 l, Pagoda and EXPO '70 emblem.

1970, Mar. 23

Size: 34x50mm

2160 A653 20b gold & multi 10 5

Size: 29x92mm

2161 A653 1 l gold & multi 30 20

EXPO '70 Intl. Exhib., Osaka, Japan, Mar. 15-Sept. 13.
A souvenir sheet exists with perforated label in pagoda design of 1-lei. Issued Nov. 28, 1970. Value $1.65.

Camille, by Claude Monet (Maximum Card) — A654

1970, Apr. 19 Photo. *Perf. 13½*

2162 A654 1.50 l gold & multi 45 18

Franco-Romanian Maximafil Phil. Exhib.

Alexandru I. Cuza, by C. Popp de Szathmary A655

Lenin (1870-1924) A656

1970, Apr. 20 *Perf. 13½*

2163 A655 55b gold & multi 20 10

Alexandru Ioan Cuza (1820-1866), prince of Romania.

1970, Apr. 21 Photo. *Perf. 13½*

2164 A656 40b dk red & multi 14 10

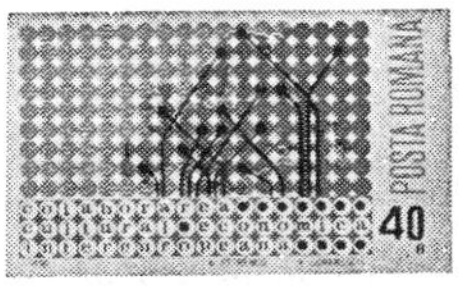

Map of Europe with Capital Cities A657

1970, Apr. 28

2165 A657 40b grn, brn org & blk 50 35
2166 A657 1.50 l ultra, yel brn & blk 1.00 70

Inter-European cultural and economic cooperation.

Victory Monument, Romanian and Russian Flags — A658

1970, May 9

2167 A658 55b red & multi 18 7

25th anniv. of victory over the Germans.

Greek Silver Drachm, 5th Century B.C. — A659

Coins: 20b, Getic-Dacian silver didrachm, 2nd-1st centuries B.C. 35b, Emperor Trajan's copper sestertius, 106 A.D. 60b, Mircea ducat, 1400. 1.75 l, Stephen the Great's silver groschen, 1460. 3 l, Brasov klippe-taler, 1601 (vert.).

1970, May 15

2168 A659 10b ultra, blk & sil 6 5
2169 A659 20b hn brn, blk & sil 8 6
2170 A659 35b grn, dk brn & gold 12 7
2171 A659 60b brn, blk & sil 16 10
2172 A659 1.75 l brt bl, blk & sil 50 24

2173 A659 3 l dk car, blk & sil 1.00 35
Nos. 2168-2173 (6) 1.92 87

Soccer Players and Ball — A660

Designs: Soccer ball and various scenes from soccer game.

1970, May 26 ***Perf. 13½***

2174	A660	40b multi	10	8
2175	A660	55b multi	12	10
2176	A660	1.75 l bl & multi	50	24
2177	A660	3.30 l multi	95	40

Souvenir Sheet

2178	A660	Souv. sheet of 4	2.00	1.50
a		1.20 l multi	28	14
b		1.50 l multi	35	18
c		1.55 l multi	38	20
d		1.75 l multi	38	20

9th World Soccer Championships for the Jules Rimet Cup, Mexico City, May 30-June 21. No. 2178 contains 4 stamps similar to Nos. 2174-2177, but with only one quarter of the soccer ball on each stamp, forming one large ball in the center of the block.

Moldovita Monastery A661

Designs: Frescoes from North Moldavian Monasteries.

1970, June 29 ***Perf. 13½***

Size: 36½x49mm

2179	A661	10b gold & multi	6	5

Size: 27½x49mm

2180	A661	20b gold & multi	8	6

Size: 36½x49mm, 48x37mm

2181	A661	40b gold & multi	14	10
2182	A661	55b gold & multi	20	14
2183	A661	1.75 l gold & multi	38	28
2184	A661	3 l gold & multi	1.00	48
		Nos. 2179-2184 (6)	1.86	1.11

Miniature Sheet

2185	A661	5 l gold & multi	1.75	1.75

Friedrich Engels (1820-1895), German Socialist — A662

1970, July 10 **Photo.** ***Perf. 13½***

2186 A662 1.50 l multi 45 18

Aerial View of Iron Gate Power Station A663

1970, July 13

2187 A663 35b bl & multi 18 7

Hydroelectric plant at the Iron Gate of the Danube.

Cargo Ship A664

1970, July 17

2188 A664 55b bl & multi 18 7

75th anniv. of the Romanian merchant marine.

Exhibition Hall and Oil Derrick A665

1970, July 20

2189 A665 1.50 l multi 45 18

International Bucharest Fair, Oct. 13-24.

Opening of UPU Headquarters, Bern — A666

1970, Aug. 17 **Photo.** ***Perf. 13½***

2190 A666 1.50 l ultra & sl grn 45 18

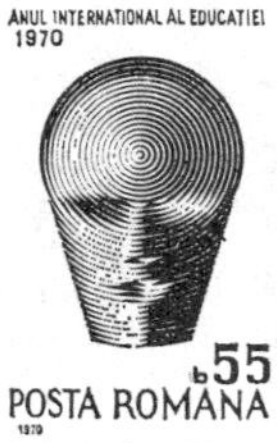

Education Year Emblem A667

Iceberg Rose A668

1970, Aug. 17

2191 A667 55b blk, pur & red 18 7

Issued for International Education Year.

1970, Aug. 21

Roses: 35b, Wiener charme. 55b, Pink luster. 1 l, Piccadilly. 1.50 l, Orange Delbard. 2.40 l, Sibelius.

2192	A668	20b dk red, grn & yel	6	5
2193	A668	35b vio, yel & grn	8	7
2194	A668	55b bl, rose & grn	12	10
2195	A668	1 l grn, car rose & yel	30	14
2196	A668	1.50 l dk bl, red & grn	45	24
2197	A668	2.40 l brt bl, dp red & grn	85	35
		Nos. 2192-2197 (6)	1.86	95

Spaniel and Pheasant, by Jean B. Oudry A669

Paintings: 10b, The Hunt, by Domenico Brandi. 35b, The Hunt, by Jan Fyt. 60b, After the Chase, by Jacob Jordaens. 1.75 l, 5 l, Game Merchant, by Frans Snyders (horiz.). 3 l, The Hunt, by Adriaen de Gryeff. Sizes: 37x49mm (10b, 35b); 35x33mm (20b, 60b, 3 l); 49x37mm (1.75 l, 3 l).

1970, Sept. 20 **Photo.** ***Perf. 13½***

2198	A669	10b gold & multi	5	5
2199	A669	20b gold & multi	8	6
2200	A669	35b gold & multi	10	7
2201	A669	60b gold & multi	20	12
2202	A669	1.75 l gold & multi	60	35
2203	A669	3 l gold & multi	1.25	50
		Nos. 2198-2203 (6)	2.28	1.15

Miniature Sheet

2204	A669	5 l gold & multi	2.00	2.00

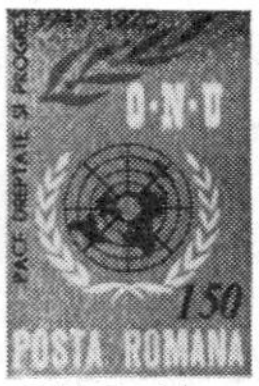

UN Emblem A670

Mother and Child A671

1970, Sept. 29

2205 A670 1.50 l lt bl, ultra & blk 45 18

25th anniversary of the United Nations.

1970, Sept. 25

Designs: 1.50 l, Red Cross relief trucks and tents. 1.75 l, Rebuilding houses.

2206	A671	55b bl gray, blk & ol	18	7
2207	A671	1.50 l ol, blk & car	45	18
		Strip of 3 (#2206-2207, C179)	1.40	70
2208	A671	1.75 l bl & multi	70	24

Issued to publicize the plight of the victims of the Danube flood. Nos. 2206-2207 and C179 are printed se-tenant.

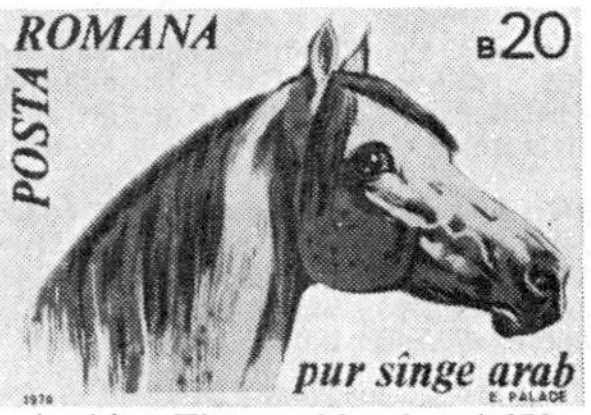

Arabian Thoroughbred — A672

Horses: 35b, American trotter. 55b, Ghidran (Anglo-American). 1 l, Northern Moravian. 1.50 l, Trotter thoroughbred. 2.40 l, Lippizaner.

1970, Oct. 10 **Photo.** ***Perf. 13½***

2209	A672	20b blk & multi	6	5
2210	A672	35b blk & multi	8	7
2211	A672	55b blk & multi	12	10
2212	A672	1 l blk & multi	28	18
2213	A672	1.50 l blk & multi	40	18
2214	A672	2.40 l blk & multi	95	35
		Nos. 2209-2214 (6)	1.89	93

Ludwig van Beethoven (1770-1827), Composer — A673

1970, Nov. 2

2215 A673 55b multi 24 7

Abstract, by Joan Miró — A674

1970, Dec. 10 **Photo.** ***Perf. 13½***

2216 A674 3 l ultra & multi 85 70

Souvenir Sheet

Imperf

2217 A674 5 l ultra & multi 1.90 1.90

Plight of the Danube flood victims. No. 2216 issued in sheets of 5 stamps and label with signature of Miro and date of flood. No. 2217 contains one stamp with simulated perforation.

The Sense of Sight, by Gonzales Coques A675

"The Senses," paintings by Gonzales Coques (1614-1684): 20b, Hearing. 35b, Smell. 60b, Taste. 1.75 l, Touch. 3 l, Bruckenthal Museum, Sibiu. 5 l, View of Sibiu, 1808 (horiz.).

1970, Dec. 15 **Photo.** ***Perf. 13½***

2218	A675	10b gold & multi	5	5
2219	A675	20b gold & multi	8	6
2220	A675	35b gold & multi	10	7
2221	A675	60b gold & multi	18	7
2222	A675	1.75 l gold & multi	60	35
2223	A675	3 l gold & multi	1.00	60
		Nos. 2218-2223 (6)	2.01	1.20

Miniature Sheet

Imperf

2224	A675	5 l gold & multi	2.00	2.00

Men of Three Races A676

1971, Feb. 23 **Photo.** ***Perf. 13½***

2225 A676 1.50 l multi 45 14

Intl. year against racial discrimination.

Tudor Vladimirescu, by Theodor Aman — A677

1971, Feb. 20

2226 A677 1.50 l gold & multi 45 14

Tudor Vladimirescu, patriot, 150th death anniv.

German Shepherd A677a

Dogs: 35b, Bulldog. 55b, Fox terrier. 1 l, Setter. 1.50 l, Cocker spaniel. 2.40 l, Poodle.

1971, Feb. 22

2227	A677a	20b	blk & multi	8	6
2228	A677a	35b	blk & multi	14	7
2229	A677a	55b	blk & multi	20	10
2230	A677a	1 l	blk & multi	28	18
2231	A677a	1.50 l	blk & multi	40	30
2232	A677a	2.40 l	blk & multi	85	55
			Nos. 2227-2232 (6)	1.95	1.26

Paris Commune A678

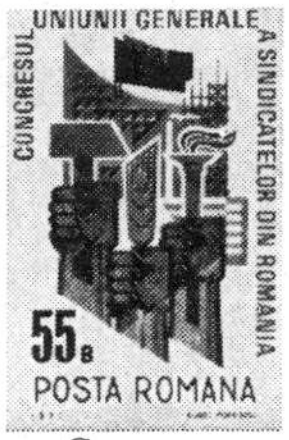

Congress Emblem A679

1971, Mar. 15 Photo. *Perf. 13½*

2233	A678	40b	multi	14	7

Centenary of the Paris Commune.

1971, March 23

2234	A679	55b	multi	18	7

Romanian Trade Unions Congress.

Rock Formation A680

Designs: 10b, Bicazului Gorge (vert.). 55b, Winter resort. 1 l, Danube Delta view. 1.50 l, Lakeside resort. 2.40 l, Venus, Jupiter, Neptune Hotels on Black Sea.

1971, Apr. 15
Size: 23x38mm, 38x23mm

2235	A680	10b	multi	6	5
2236	A680	40b	multi	10	7
2237	A680	55b	multi	18	10
2238	A680	1 l	multi	30	20
2239	A680	1.50 l	multi	50	28

Size: 76½x28mm

2240	A680	2.40 l	multi	1.00	45
			Nos. 2235-2240 (6)	2.14	1.15

Tourist publicity.

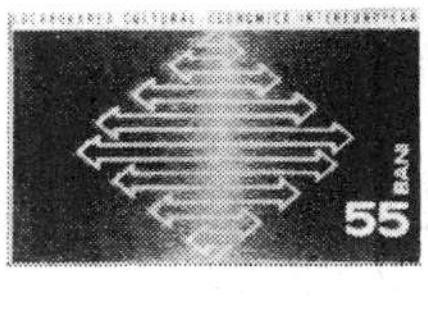

Arrow Pattern A681

Design: 1.75 l, Wave pattern.

1971, Apr. 28 Photo. *Perf. 13½*

2241	A681	55b	multi	75	60
2242	A681	1.75 l	multi	1.50	1.00

Inter-European Cultural and Economic Collaboration. Sheets of 10.

Historical Museum A682

Demonstration, by A. Anastasiu A684

Communist Party Emblem — A683

1971, May 7 Photo. *Perf. 13½*

2243	A682	55b	bl & multi	15	7

For Romania's Historical Museum.

1971, May 8

Design: 35b, Reading Proclamation, by Stefan Szonyi.

2244	A684	35b	multi	10	5
2245	A683	40b	multi	14	6
2246	A684	55b	multi	18	7

Romanian Communist Party, 50th anniv.

Souvenir Sheets

Motra Tone, by Kole Idromeno A685

Dancing the Hora, by Theodor Aman — A686

1971, May 25 Photo. *Perf. 13½*

2247	A685		Sheet of 6, multi	3.50	3.00
a		1.20 l	shown	50	38
b		1.20 l	Maid by V. Dimitrov-Maystora	50	38
c		1.20 l	Rosa Botzaris, by Joseph Stieler	50	38
d		1.20 l	Woman in Costume, by Katarina Ivanovic	50	38
e		1.20 l	Argeseanca, by Carol Popp de Szathmary	50	38
f		1.20 l	Woman in Modern Dress, by Calli Ibrahim	50	38
2248	A686	5 l	multi	2.25	2.25

Balkanphila III Stamp Exhibition, Bucharest, June 27-July 2.

No. 2247 contains 6 stamps in 3 rows and 6 labels showing exhibition emblem and "60b."

Pomegranate Flower — A687

Flowers: 35b, Slipperwort. 55b, Lily. 1 l, Mimulus. 1.50 l, Morning-glory. 2.40 l, Leaf cactus (horiz.).

1971, June 20

2249	A687	20b	ultra & multi	8	6
2250	A687	35b	red & multi	10	6
2251	A687	55b	ultra & multi	14	7
2252	A687	1 l	car & multi	35	14
2253	A687	1.50 l	car & multi	60	18
2254	A687	2.40 l	ultra & multi	95	35
			Nos. 2249-2254 (6)	2.22	86

Nude, by Iosif Iser A688

Paintings of Nudes: 20b, by Camil Ressu. 35b, by Nicolae Grigorescu. 60b, by Eugene Delacroix (odalisque). 1.75 l, by Auguste Renoir. 3 l, by Palma il Vecchio (Venus and Amor). 5 l, by Il Bronzino (Venus and Amor). 60b, 3 l, 5 l, horiz.

1971, July 25 Photo. *Perf. 13½*
Size: 38x50mm, 49x39mm, 29x50mm (20b)

2255	A688	10b	gold & multi	5	5
2256	A688	20b	gold & multi	6	6
2257	A688	35b	gold & multi	8	7
2258	A688	60b	gold & multi	14	8
2259	A688	1.75 l	gold & multi	38	24
2260	A688	3 l	gold & multi	1.40	50
			Nos. 2255-2260 (6)	2.11	1.00

Miniature Sheet
Imperf

2261	A688	5 l	gold & multi	2.00	2.00

Ships in Storm, by B. Peters — A689

Paintings of Ships by: 20b, Ludolf Backhuysen. 35b, Andries van Eertvelt. 60b, M. W. Arnold. 1.75 l, Ivan Konstantinovich Aivazovski. 3 l, Jean Steriadi. 5 l, N. Darascu (vert.).

1971, Sept. 15 Photo. *Perf. 13½*

2262	A689	10b	gold & multi	5	5
2263	A689	20b	gold & multi	6	5
2264	A689	35b	gold & multi	8	6
2265	A689	60b	gold & multi	14	8
2266	A689	1.75 l	gold & multi	45	28
2267	A689	3 l	gold & multi	1.00	48
			Nos. 2262-2267 (6)	1.78	1.00

Miniature Sheet

2268	A689	5 l	gold & multi	2.00	2.00

Types of Regular Issue

Designs as Before and: 3.60 l, Mail collector. 4.80 l, Mailman. 6 l, Ministry of Posts.

1971 Photo. *Perf. 13½*
Size: 16½x23mm, 23x16½mm

2269	A616	1 l	emerald	22	5
2270	A617	1.20 l	red lil	28	5
2271	A617	1.35 l	brt bl	30	5
2272	A616	1.50 l	org red	35	5
2273	A616	1.55 l	sepia	35	5
2274	A617	1.75 l	dp grn	38	5
2275	A617	2 l	citron	45	5
2276	A616	2.40 l	dk bl	55	5
2277	A617	3 l	grnsh bl	70	5
2278	A617	3.20 l	ocher	70	5
2279	A616	3.25 l	ultra	85	5
2280	A616	3.60 l	blue	1.00	5
2281	A617	4 l	lil rose	1.25	5
2282	A616	4.80 l	grnsh bl	1.40	6
2283	A617	5 l	violet	1.40	7
2284	A616	6 l	dp mag	1.50	10
			Nos. 2269-2284 (16)	11.68	88

Prince Neagoe Basarab A690

Theodor Pallady (Painter) A691

1971, Sept. 20 *Perf. 13½*

2288	A690	60b	gold & multi	20	10

450th anniversary of the death of Prince Neagoe Basarab of Walachia.

1971, Oct. 12 Photo. *Perf. 13½*

Portraits of: 55b, Benvenuto Cellini (1500-1571), sculptor. 1.50 l, Antoine Watteau (1684-1721), painter. 2.40 l, Albrecht Dürer (1471-1528), painter.

2289	A691	40b	gold & multi	10	7
2290	A691	55b	gold & multi	14	8
2291	A691	1.50 l	gold & multi	50	18
2292	A691	2.40 l	gold & multi	1.00	35

Anniversaries of famous artists.

Proclamation of Cyrus the Great — A692

Figure Skating — A693

1971, Oct. 12

2293	A692	55b	multi	18	7

2500th anniversary of the founding of the Persian empire by Cyrus the Great.

1971, Oct. 25

Designs: 20b, Ice hockey. 40b, Biathlon (skier). 55b, Bobsledding. 1.75 l, Skiing. 3 l, Sapporo '72 emblem. 5 l, Olympic flame and emblem.

2294	A693	10b	lt bl, blk & red	5	5
2295	A693	20b	multi	6	5
2296	A693	40b	multi	10	7
2297	A693	55b	lt bl, blk & red	14	8
2298	A693	1.75 l	lt bl, blk & red	55	24
2299	A693	3 l	lt bl, blk & red	90	40
			Nos. 2294-2299 (6)	1.80	89

Miniature Sheet
Imperf

2300	A693	5 l	multi	2.00	2.00

11th Winter Olympic Games, Sapporo, Japan, Feb. 3-13, 1972. Nos. 2294-2296 printed se-tenant in sheets of 15 (5x3); Nos. 2297-2298 printed se-tenant in sheets of 10 (5x2). No. 2300 contains one stamp 37x50mm.

St. George and the Dragon A694

Frescoes from North Moldavian Monasteries: 10b, 20b, 40b, Moldovita. 55b, 1.75 l, 5 l, Voronet. 3 l, Arborea (horiz.).

1971, Nov. 30 Photo. *Perf. 13½*

2301	A694	10b	gold & multi	5	5
2302	A694	20b	gold & multi	7	5
2303	A694	40b	gold & multi	12	7
2304	A694	55b	gold & multi	14	8
2305	A694	1.75 l	gold & multi	65	28
2306	A694	3 l	gold & multi	1.00	60
			Nos. 2301-2306 (6)	2.03	1.13

Miniature Sheet

Imperf

2307	A694	5 l	gold & multi	1.75	1.00

No. 2307 contains one stamp 44x56mm.

Ferdinand Magellan A695

Designs: 55b, Johannes Kepler and observation tower. 1 l, Yuri Gagarin and rocket orbiting earth. 1.50 l, Baron Ernest R. Rutherford, atom, nucleus and chemical apparatus.

1971, Dec. 20

2308	A695	40b	grn, brt rose & dk bl	12	5
2309	A695	55b	lil, bl & gray grn	14	6
2310	A695	1 l	vio & multi	30	18
2311	A695	1.50 l	red brn, grn & bl	50	24

450th anniversary of the death of Magellan (1480?-1521), navigator (40b); 400th anniv. of the birth of Kepler (1571-1630), astronomer; Gagarin, 1st man in space, 10th anniv.; centenary of birth of Ernest R. Rutherford (1871-1937), British physicist.

Matei Millo A696

Young Communists Union Emblem A697

Design: 1 l, Nicolae Iorga.

1971, Dec.

2312	A696	55b	bl & multi	14	6
2313	A696	1 l	pur & multi	28	14

75th anniv. of the death of Millo (1814-1896), playwright; centenary of the birth of Iorga (1871-1940), historian and politician.

1972, Feb.

2314	A697	55b	dk bl, red & gold	18	7

Young Communists Union, 50th anniv.

Young Animals — A698

1972, Mar. 10 Photo. *Perf. 13½*

2315	A698	20b	Lynx	7	5
2316	A698	35b	Foxes	10	6
2317	A698	55b	Roe fawns	15	8
2318	A698	1 l	Wild pigs	28	20
2319	A698	1.50 l	Wolves	40	28
2320	A698	2.40 l	Bears	85	35
			Nos. 2315-2320 (6)	1.85	1.02

Wrestling — A699

Olympic Rings and: 20b, Canoeing. 55b, Soccer. 1.55 l, Women's high jump. 2.90 l, Boxing. 6.70 l, Field ball.

1972, Apr. 25 Photo. *Perf. 13½*

2321	A699	10b	yel & multi	5	5
2322	A699	20b	multi	7	5
2323	A699	55b	gray & multi	15	8
2324	A699	1.55 l	grn & multi	40	18
2325	A699	2.90 l	multi	85	24
2326	A699	6.70 l	lil & multi	1.40	50
			Nos. 2321-2326 (6)	2.92	1.10

20th Olympic Games, Munich, Aug. 26-Sept. 10. See Nos. C186-C187.

Stylized Map of Europe and Links A700

Design: 2.90 l, Entwined arrows and links.

1972, Apr. 28

2327	A700	1.75 l	dp car, gold & blk	1.10	75
2328	A700	2.90 l	grn, gold & blk	1.50	1.00

Inter-European Cultural and Economic Collaboration. Nos. 2327-2328 printed se-tenant.

UIC Emblem and Trains A701

1972, May 20 Photo. *Perf. 13½*

2329	A701	55b	dp car rose, blk & gold	18	7

50th anniv., Intl. Railroad Union (UIC).

Souvenir Sheet

"Summer," by Peter Brueghel, the Younger — A702

1972, May 20 *Perf. 13x13½*

2330	A702	6 l	gold & multi	2.00	2.00

Belgica 72, Intl. Phil. Exhib., Brussels, June 24-July 9.

Peony — A703

Protected Flowers: 40b, Pink. 55b, Edelweiss. 60b, Nigritella rubra. 1.35 l, Narcissus. 2.90 l, Lady's slipper.

1972, June 5 Photo. *Perf. 13*

Flowers in Natural Colors

2331	A703	20b	dk vio bl	7	5
2332	A703	40b	chocolate	8	6
2333	A703	55b	dp bl	14	7
2334	A703	60b	dk grn	18	12
2335	A703	1.35 l	violet	50	18
2336	A703	2.90 l	dk Prus bl	90	40
			Nos. 2331-2336 (6)	1.87	88

Saligny Bridge, Cernavoda — A704

Danube Bridges: 1.75l, Giurgeni Bridge, Vadul. 2.75 l, Friendship Bridge, Giurgiu-Ruse.

1972, June 25 Photo. *Perf. 13½*

2337	A704	1.35 l	multi	35	15
2338	A704	1.75 l	multi	50	20
2339	A704	2.75 l	multi	85	28

North Railroad Station, Bucharest, Cent. A705

1972, July 4

2340	A705	55b	ultra & multi	24	10

Water Polo and Olympic Rings A706

Olympic Rings and: 20b, Pistol shoot. 55b, Discus. 1.55 l, Gymnastics, women's. 2.75 l, Canoeing. 6.40 l, Fencing.

1972, July 5 Photo. *Perf. 13½*

2341	A706	10b	ol, gold & lil	5	5
2342	A706	20b	red, gold & grn	5	5
2343	A706	55b	grn, gold & brn	12	8
2344	A706	1.55 l	vio, gold & ol	28	18
2345	A706	2.75 l	bl, gold & gray	50	24
2346	A706	6.40 l	pur, gold & gray	1.25	50
			Nos. 2341-2346 (6)	2.25	1.10

20th Olympic Games, Munich, Aug. 26-Sept. 11. See No. C187.

Stamp Printing Press — A707

1972, July 25

2347	A707	55b	multi	18	7

Centenary of the stamp printing office.

Stefan Popescu, Self-portrait — A708

1972, Aug. 10

2348	A708	55b	shown	10	5
2349	A708	1.75 l	Octav Bancila	28	20
2350	A708	2.90 l	Gheorghe Petrascu	50	22
2351	A708	6.50 l	Ion Andreescu	1.25	40

Self-portraits by Romanian painters.

Runner with Torch, Olympic Rings A709

City Hall Tower, Sibiu A710

1972, Aug. 13

2352	A709	55b	sil, bl & cl	18	10

Olympic torch relay from Olympia, Greece, to Munich, Germany, passing through Romania.

1972, Photo. *Perf. 13*

Designs: 1.85 l, St. Michael's Cathedral, Cluj. 2.75 l, Sphinx Rock, Mt. Bucegi (horiz.). 3.35 l, Heroes' Monument, Bucharest. 3.45 l, Sinaia Castle (horiz.). 5.15 l, Hydroelectric Works, Arges (horiz.). 5.60 l, Church of the Epiphany, Iasi. 6.20 l, Bran Castle. 6.40 l, Hunedoara Castle (horiz.). 6.80 l, Polytechnic Institute, Bucharest (horiz.). 7.05 l, Black Church, Brasov. 8.45 l, Atheneum, Bucharest. 9.05 l, Excavated Coliseum, Sarmizegetusa (horiz.). 9.10 l, Hydroelectric Station, Iron Gate (horiz.). 9.85 l, Monument, Cetatea. 11.90 l, Republic Palace (horiz.). 12.75 l, Television Station. 13.30 l, Arch, Alba Iulia (horiz.). 16.20 l, Clock Tower,.Sighisoara.

Size: 23x18mm, 17x24mm

2353	A710	1.85 l	brt pur	35	6
2354	A710	2.75 l	gray	50	6
2355	A710	3.35 l	magenta	60	6
2356	A710	3.45 l	green	55	6
2357	A710	5.15 l	brt bl	95	6
2358	A710	5.60 l	blue	1.00	5
2359	A710	6.20 l	cerise	1.10	6
2360	A710	6.40 l	sepia	1.25	6
2361	A710	6.80 l	rose red	1.25	6
2362	A710	7.05 l	black	1.40	6
2363	A710	8.45 l	rose red	1.50	6
2364	A710	9.05 l	dl grn	1.65	6
2365	A710	9.10 l	ultra	1.65	6
2366	A710	9.85 l	green	1.65	6

Size: 19½x29mm, 29x21mm

2367	A710	10 l	dp brn	1.90	18
2368	A710	11.90 l	bluish blk	2.25	20
2369	A710	12.75 l	dk vio	2.50	24
2370	A710	13.30 l	dl red	2.50	28
2371	A710	16.20 l	ol grn	3.00	35
	Nos. 2353-2371,C193 (20)			30.30	2.53

View of Satu-Mare — A711

1972, Oct. 5

2372	A711	55b	multi	20	7

Millennium of Satu-Mare.

Tennis Racket and Davis Cup A712

1972, Oct. 10 *Perf. 13½*

2373	A712	2.75 l	multi	85	35

Final tennis match for the Davis Cup between Romania and US, Bucharest, Oct. 13-15.

Venice, by Gheorge Petrascu — A713

Paintings of Venice by: 20b, N. Darascu. 55b, Petrascu. 1.55 l, Marius Bunescu. 2.75 l, N. Darascu (vert.). 6 l, Petrascu. 6.40 l, Marius Bunescu.

1972, Oct. 20

2374	A713	10b	gray & multi	5	5
2375	A713	20b	gray & multi	6	5
2376	A713	55b	gray & multi	10	7
2377	A713	1.55 l	gray & multi	28	18
2378	A713	2.75 l	gray & multi	55	24
2379	A713	6.40 l	gray & multi	1.40	50
	Nos. 2374-2379 (6)			2.44	1.09

Souvenir Sheet

2380	A713	6 l	gray & multi	2.00	2.00

Fencing, Bronze Medal — A714

Apollo 1, 2 and 3 — A715

Designs: 20b, Team handball, bronze medal. 35b, Boxing, silver medal. 1.45 l, Hurdles, women's, silver medal. 2.75 l, Pistol shoot, silver medal. 6.20 l, Wrestling, gold medal.

1972, Oct. 28

2381	A714	10b	red org & multi	5	5
2382	A714	20b	lt grn & multi	6	5
2383	A714	35b	multi	8	5
2384	A714	1.45 l	multi	28	18
2385	A714	2.75 l	ocher & multi	55	24
2386	A714	6.20 l	bl & multi	1.40	48
	Nos. 2381-2386 (6)			2.42	1.05

Romanian medalists at 20th Olympic Games. See No. C191.

1972, Dec. 27 **Photo.** *Perf. 13½*

2387	A715	10b	shown	5	5
2388	A715	35b	Grissom, Chaffee and White, 1967	7	5
2389	A715	40b	Apollo 4, 5, 6	10	5
2390	A715	55b	Apollo 7, 8	15	6
2391	A715	1 l	Apollo 9, 10	22	10
2392	A715	1.20 l	Apollo 11, 12	28	10
2393	A715	1.85 l	Apollo 13, 14	38	14
2394	A715	2.75 l	Apollo 15, 16	60	20
2395	A715	3.60 l	Apollo 17	1.10	40
	Nos. 2387-2395 (9)			2.95	1.15

Highlights of US Apollo space program. See No. C192.

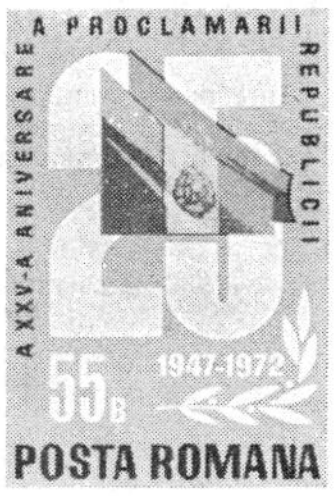

"25" and Flags — A716

Designs: 1.20 l, "25" and national emblem. 1.75 l, "25" and factory.

1972, Dec. 25

2396	A716	55b	bl & multi	18	7
2397	A716	1.20 l	yel & multi	35	18
2398	A716	1.75 l	ver & multi	60	24

25th anniversary of the Republic.

European Bee-eater A717

Globeflowers A718

Designs: No. 2400, Red-breasted goose. No. 2401, Penduline tit. No. 2403, Garden Turk's-cap. No. 2404, Gentian.

1973, Feb. 5 **Photo.** *Perf. 13*

2399	A717	1.40 l	gray & multi	24	10
2400	A717	1.85 l	multi	35	18
2401	A717	2.75 l	bl & multi	70	20
			Strip of 3	1.40	60
2402	A718	1.40 l	multi	24	10
2403	A718	1.85 l	yel & multi	35	14
2404	A718	2.75 l	multi	70	20
			Strip of 3	1.00	60

Nature protection. Nos. 2399-2401 and 2402-2404 printed se-tenant horizontally in 2 sheets of 15 (3x5).

Nicolaus Copernicus — A719

1973, Feb. 19 **Photo.** *Perf. 13x13½*

2405	A719	2.75 l	multi	70	35

Nicolaus Copernicus (1473-1543), Polish astronomer. Printed with alternating label publicizing Intl. Phil. Exhib., Poznan, Aug. 19-Sept. 2.

Suceava Woman A720

D. Paciurea (Sculptor) A721

Regional Costumes: 40b, Suceava man. 55b, Harghita woman. 1.75 l, Harghita man. 2.75 l, Gorj woman. 6.40 l, Gorj man.

1973, Mar. 15

2406	A720	10b	lt bl & multi	5	5
2407	A720	40b	multi	8	7
2408	A720	55b	bis & multi	10	7
2409	A720	1.75 l	lil & multi	30	10
2410	A720	2.75 l	multi	48	14
2411	A720	6.40 l	multi	1.25	45
	Nos. 2406-2411 (6)			2.26	88

1973, Mar. 26

Portraits: 40b, I. Slavici (1848-1925), writer. 55b, G. Lazar (1779-1823), writer. 6.40 l, A. Flechtenmacher (1823-1898), composer.

2412	A721	10b	multi	6	5
2413	A721	40b	multi	10	6
2414	A721	55b	multi	18	7
2415	A721	6.40 l	multi	1.25	50

Anniversaries of famous artists.

Map of Europe A722

Design: 3.60 l, Symbol of collaboration.

1973, Apr. 28 **Photo.** *Perf. 13½*

2416	A722	3.35 l	dp bl & gold	1.10	70
2417	A722	3.60 l	brt mag & gold	1.25	1.00

Inter-European cultural and economic cooperation. Nos. 2416-2417 printed se-tenant in sheets of 10 with blue marginal inscription.

Souvenir Sheet

The Rape of Proserpina, by Hans von Aachen — A723

1973, May 5

2418	A723	12 l	gold & multi	2.75	2.50

IBRA Munchen 1973, Intl. Stamp Exhib., Munich, May 11-20.

Foreign postal stationery (stamped envelopes, postal cards and air letter sheets) lies beyond the scope of this Catalogue, which is limited to adhesive postage stamps.

Prince Alexander I. Cuza — A724

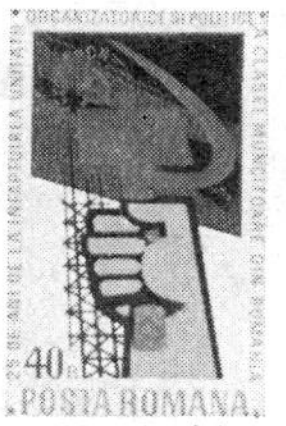

Hand with Hammer and Sickle — A725

1973, May 5 **Photo.** *Perf. 13½*

2419	A724	1.75 l	multi	50	18

Alexander Ioan Cuza (1820-1873), prince of Romania, Moldavia and Walachia.

1973, May 5

2420	A725	40b	gold & multi	18	7

Workers and Peasants Party, 25th anniv.

Romanian Flag, Bayonets Stabbing Swastika A726

WMO Emblem, Weather Satellite A727

1973, May 5

2421	A726	55b	multi	18	7

Anti-fascist Front, 40th anniversary.

1973, June 15

2422	A727	2 l	ultra & multi	50	20

Intl. meteorological cooperation, cent.

Dimitrie Ralet Holding Letter A728

Dimitrie Cantemir A729

Portraits with letters. 60b, Enachita Vacarescu, by A. Chladek. 1.55 l, Serdarul Dimitrie Aman, by C. Lecca.

1973, June 20

2423	A728	40b	multi	10	6
2424	A728	60b	multi	18	7
2425	A728	1.55 l	multi	50	24

"The Letter on Romanian Portraits." Socfilex III Philatelic Exhibition, Bucharest, July 20-29. See Nos. B432-B433.

1973, June 25

Design: 6 l, Portrait of Cantemir in oval frame.

2426	A729	1.75 l	multi	48	20

Souvenir Sheet

2427	A729	6 l	multi	2.00	1.40

300th anniversary of the birth of Dimitrie Cantemir (1673-1723), Prince of Moldavia, writer. No. 2427 contains one stamp 38x50mm.

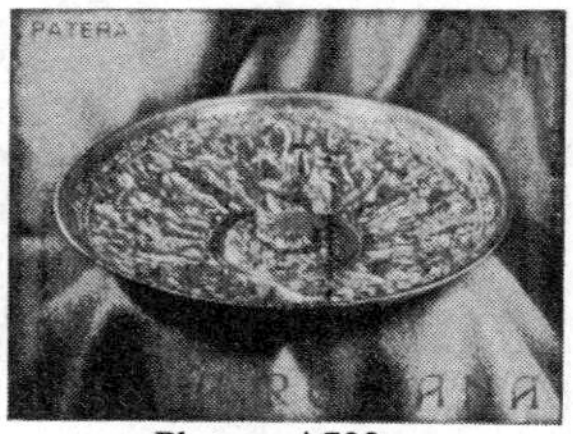

Plate — A730

Designs: 10b, Fibulae (vert.). 55b, Jug (vert.). 1.55 l, Necklaces and fibula. 2.75 l, Plate (vert.). 6.80 l, Octagonal bowl with animal handles. 12 l, Breastplate (vert.).

1973, July 25 Photo. *Perf. 13½*

2428	A730	10b vio bl & multi	5	5
2429	A730	20b grn & multi	6	5
2430	A730	55b red & multi	18	6
2431	A730	1.55 l multi	35	14
2432	A730	2.75 l plum & multi	60	20
2433	A730	6.80 l multi	1.50	48
		Nos. 2428-2433 (6)	2.74	98

Souvenir Sheet

2434	A730	12 l multi	2.75	2.50

Roman gold treasure of Pietroasa, 4th century.

Symbolic Flower, Map of Europe A731

Design: 5 l, Map of Europe, symbolic tree.

1973, Oct. 2 Photo. *Perf. 13½*

2435	A731	2.75 l multi	1.10	70
2436	A731	5 l multi	1.75	1.00
		Sheet of 4+2 labels	5.50	5.50

Conference for European Security and Cooperation, Helsinki, Finland, July 1973. Nos. 2435-2436 printed in sheets containing 2 each of Nos. 2435-2436 and 2 labels showing Conference Hall, Helsinki, and UN Building, Geneva.

Jug and Cloth, Oboga — A732

Designs: 20b, Plate and Pitcher, Vama. 55b, Bowl, Marginea. 1.55 l, Pitcher and plate, Sibiu-Saschiz. 2.75 l, Bowl and jug, Pisc. 6.80 l, Figurine (fowl), Oboga.

1973, Oct. 15 *Perf. 13*

2437	A732	10b multi	5	5
2438	A732	20b multi	6	5
2439	A732	55b multi	18	6
2440	A732	1.55 l multi	35	14
2441	A732	2.75 l multi	60	20
2442	A732	6.80 l multi	1.50	48
		Nos. 2437-2442 (6)	2.74	98

Pottery and cloths from various regions of Romania.

Women Workers, by G. Saru A733

Paintings of Workers: 20b, Construction Site, by M. Bunescu (horiz.). 55b, Shipyard Workers, by H. Catargi (horiz.). 1.55 l, Worker, by Catargi. 2.75 l, Miners, by A. Phoebus. 6.80 l, Spinner, by Nicolae Grigorescu. 12 l, Farmers at Rest, by Stefan Popescu (horiz.).

1973, Nov. 26 Photo. *Perf. 13½*

2443	A733	10b gold & multi	5	5
2444	A733	20b gold & multi	6	5
2445	A733	55b gold & multi	18	5
2446	A733	1.55 l gold & multi	35	14
2447	A733	2.75 l gold & multi	60	20
2448	A733	6.80 l gold & multi	1.50	48
		Nos. 2443-2448 (6)	2.74	97

Miniature Sheet

2449	A733	12 l gold & multi	2.50	2.25

City Hall, Craiova A734

Tugboat under Bridge A735

Designs: 10b, Infinite Column, by Constantin Brancusi (vert.). 20b, Heroes' Mausoleum, Marasesti. 35b, Risnov Citadel. 40b, Densus Church (vert.). 50b, Blaj Church (vert.). 55b, Maldaresti Fortress. 60b, National Theater, Iasi. 1 l, Curtea-de-Arges Monastery (vert.). 1.20 l, Tirgu-Mures Citadel. 1.45 l, Cargoship Dimbovita. 1.50 l, Muntenia passenger ship. 1.55 l, Three-master Mircea. 1.75 l, Motorship Transilvania. 2.20 l, Ore carrier Oltul. 3.65 l, Trawler Mures. 4.70 l, Tanker Arges.

1973-74 Photo. *Perf. 13*

2450	A734	5b lake	5	5
2451	A734	10b brt bl	5	5
2452	A734	20b orange	5	5
2453	A734	35b green	8	5
2454	A734	40b dk vio	10	5
2455	A734	50b ultra	12	5
2456	A734	55b org brn	15	5
2457	A734	60b carmine	15	5
2458	A734	1 l dp ultra	25	5
2459	A734	1.20 l ol grn	30	6
2460	A735	1.35 l gray	35	5
2461	A735	1.45 l dl bl	35	5
2462	A735	1.50 l car rose	38	5
2463	A735	1.55 l vio bl	38	5
2464	A735	1.75 l sl grn	45	5
2465	A735	2.20 l brt bl	60	5
2466	A735	3.65 l dl lil	95	7
2467	A735	4.70 l vio brn	1.40	10
		Nos. 2450-2467 (18)	6.16	98

Issue dates: Nos. 2450-2459, Dec. 15, 1973. Nos. 2460-2467, Jan. 28, 1974.

Boats at Montfleur, by Claude Monet — A736

Impressionistic paintings: 40b, Church of Moret, by Alfred Sisley (vert.). 55b, Orchard in Bloom, by Camille Pissarro. 1.75 l, Portrait of Jeanne, by Pissarro (vert.). 2.75 l, Landscape, by Auguste Renoir. 3.60 l, Portrait of a Girl, by Paul Cezanne (vert.). 10 l, Women Taking Bath, by Renoir (vert.).

1974, Mar. 15 Photo. *Perf. 13½*

2468	A736	20b bl & multi	5	5
2469	A736	40b bl & multi	8	6
2470	A736	55b bl & multi	14	6
2471	A736	1.75 l bl & multi	40	10
2472	A736	2.75 l bl & multi	60	20
2473	A736	3.60 l bl & multi	80	35
		Nos. 2468-2473 (6)	2.07	82

Souvenir Sheet

2474	A736	10 l bl & multi	2.25	1.90

Harness Racing A737

Designs: Various horse races.

1974, Apr. 5 Photo. *Perf. 13½*

2475	A737	40b ver & multi	8	6
2476	A737	55b bis & multi	10	6
2477	A737	60b multi	18	10
2478	A737	1.55 l multi	35	14
2479	A737	2.75 l multi	60	28
2480	A737	3.45 l multi	80	40
		Nos. 2475-2480 (6)	2.11	1.04

Centenary of horse racing in Romania.

Nicolae Titulescu — A738

1974, Apr. 16

2481	A738	1.75 l multi	50	20

Interparliamentary Session, Bucharest, Apr. 1974. Nicolae Titulescu (1883-1941) was the first Romanian delegate to the League of Nations.

Souvenir Sheet

Roman Memorial with First Reference to Napoca (Cluj) — A739

1974, Apr. 18 Photo. *Perf. 13*

2482	A739	10 l multi	2.25	1.90

1850th anniv. of the elevation of the Roman settlement of Napoca (Cluj) to a municipality.

Stylized Map of Europe A740

Design: 3.45 l, Satellite over earth.

1974, Apr. 25 Photo. *Perf. 13½x13*

2483	A740	2.20 l multi	1.25	70
2484	A740	3.45 l multi	1.50	1.00

Inter-European Cultural Economic Cooperation. Nos. 2483-2484 printed se-tenant in sheet of 10 with gold marginal inscription.

Young Pioneers with Banners, by Pepene Cornelia — A741

1974, Apr. 25 Photo. *Perf. 13½*

2485	A741	55b multi	20	7

25th anniv. of the Romanian Pioneers Org.

Mail Motorboat, UPU Emblem A742

UPU Emblem and: 40b, Mail train. 55b, Mailplane and truck. 1.75 l, Mail delivery by motorcycle. 2.75 l, Mailman delivering letter to little girl. 3.60 l, Young stamp collectors. 4 l, Mail collection. 6 l, Modern post office.

1974, May 11

2486	A742	20b gray & multi	5	5
2487	A742	40b multi	8	6
2488	A742	55b ultra & multi	18	6
2489	A742	1.75 l multi	40	20
2490	A742	2.75 l brn & multi	60	28
2491	A742	3.60 l org & multi	85	40
		Nos. 2486-2491 (6)	2.16	1.05

Souvenir Sheet

2492	A742	Sheet of 2	3.25	2.50
a		4 l multi	85	
b		6 l multi	1.40	

Centenary of Universal Postal Union.
Size of stamps of No. 2492, 28x24mm.
An imperf airmail UPU souvenir sheet of one (10 l) exists. The multicolored stamp is 49x38mm. This sheet is not known to have been sold to the public at post offices.

No. 2382 Surcharged with New Value and Overprinted: "ROMÂNIA / CAMPIOANA / MONDIALĂ / 1974"

1974, May 13

2493	A714	1.75 l on 20b multi	2.50	1.75

Romania's victory in World Handball Championship, 1974.

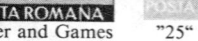

Soccer and Games Emblem — A743

"25" — A744

Designs: Games emblem and various scenes from soccer game.

1974, June 25 *Perf. 13½*

2494	A743	20b pur & multi	5	5
2495	A743	40b multi	8	6
2496	A743	55b ultra & multi	18	7
2497	A743	1.75 l brn & multi	40	20
2498	A743	2.75 l multi	60	28
2499	A743	3.60 l vio & multi	85	40
		Nos. 2494-2499 (6)	2.16	1.06

Souvenir Sheet

2500	A743	10 l multi	2.50	2.00

World Cup Soccer Championship, Munich, June 13-July 7. No. 2500 contains one horizontal stamp 50x38mm.
An imperf. 10 l airmail souvenir sheet exists showing a globe as soccer ball and satellite. Gray blue margin showing Soccer Cup, radio tower and stadium; black control number.

1974, June 10

2501	A744	55b bl & multi	20	7

25th anniv. of the Council for Mutual Economic Assistance (COMECON).

UN Emblem and People — A745

Hand Drawing Peace Dove — A746

1974, June 25 Photo. *Perf. 13½*
2502 A745 2 l multi 50 18

World Population Year.

1974, June 28
2503 A746 2 l ultra & multi 50 18

25 years of the National and Intl. Movement to Uphold the Cause of Peace.

Ioan, Prince of Wallachia A747

Soldier, Industry and Agriculture A748

Hunedoara Iron and Steel Works — A749

Designs: 1.10 l, Avram Iancu (1824-1872). 1.30 l, Dr. C. I. Parhon (1874-1969). 1.40 l, Bishop Dosoftei (1624-1693).

1974 Photo. *Perf. 13*
2504 A747 20b blue 6 5
2505 A748 55b car rose 18 5
2506 A749 1 l sl grn 28 7
2507 A747 1.10 l dk gray ol 28 7
2508 A747 1.30 l dp mag 30 8
2509 A747 1.40 l dk vio 38 10
Nos. 2504-2509 (6) 1.48 42

No. 2505 issued for Army Day, No. 2506 for 220th anniversary of Hunedoara Iron and Steel works; others for anniversaries of famous Romanians. Issue dates; 1l, June 17; others June 25.

Romanians and Flags — A750

Design: 40b, Romanian and Communist flags forming "XXX" (vert.).

1974, Aug. 20
2510 A750 40b gold, ultra & car 10 6
2511 A750 55b yel & multi 18 7

30th anniversary of Romania's liberation from Fascist rule.

Souvenir Sheet

View, Stockholm — A751

1974, Sept. 10 Photo. *Perf. 13*
2512 A751 10 l multi 2.25 2.00

Stockholmia 74 International Philatelic Exhibition, Stockholm, Sept. 21-29.

Thistle — A752

Designs: 40b, Checkered lily. 55b, Yew. 1.75 l, Azalea. 2.75 l, Forget-me-not. 3.60 l, Pinks.

1974, Sept. 15
2513 A752 20b plum & multi 5 5
2514 A752 40b multi 10 6
2515 A752 55b multi 18 7
2516 A752 1.75 l multi 40 20
2517 A752 2.75 l brn & multi 60 28
2518 A752 3.60 l multi 85 40
Nos. 2513-2518 (6) 2.18 1.06

Nature protection.

Isis, First Century A.D. A753

Archaeological art works excavated in Romania: 40b, Serpent, by Glycon. 55b, Emperor Trajan, bronze bust. 1.75 l, Roman woman, statue, 3rd century. 2.75 l, Mithraic bas-relief. 3.60 l, Roman man, statue, 3rd century.

1974, Oct. 20 Photo. *Perf. 13*
2519 A753 20b multi 5 5
2520 A753 40b ultra & multi 10 6
2521 A753 55b multi 18 7
2522 A753 1.75 l multi 40 20
2523 A753 2.75 l brn & multi 60 28
2524 A753 3.60 l multi 85 40
Nos. 2519-2524 (6) 2.18 1.06

Romanian Communist Party Emblem A754

Design: 1 l, similar to 55b.

1974, Nov. 20
2525 A754 55b blk, red & gold 18 7
2526 A754 1 l blk, red & gold 28 10

9th Romanian Communist Party Congress.

Discobolus and Olympic Rings A755

1974, Nov. 11
2527 A755 2 l ultra & multi 45 18

Romanian Olympic Committee, 60th anniv.

Skylab A756

1974, Dec. 14 Photo. *Perf. 13*
2528 A756 2.50 l multi 60 35

Skylab, manned U.S. space laboratory. No. 2528 printed in sheets of 4 stamps and 4 labels, showing Skylab, globe and black inscriptions. Black control number. A 10 l imperf. souvenir sheet exists showing Skylab.

Field Ball and Games' Emblem — A757

Designs: 1.75 l, 2.20 l, Various scenes from field ball; 1.75 l, vertical.

1975, Jan. 3
2529 A757 55b ultra & multi 18 7
2530 A757 1.75 l yel & multi 40 18
2531 A757 2.20 l multi 50 24

World University Field Ball Championship.

Values quoted in this catalogue are for stamps graded at Fine-Very Fine and with no faults. An illustrated guide to grade is provided in introductory material, beginning on Page V.

Rocks and Birches, by Andreescu A758

Paintings by Ion Andreescu (1850-1882): 40b, Farm Woman with Green Kerchief. 55b, Winter in the Woods. 1.75 l, Winter in Barbizon (horiz.). 2.75 l, Self-portrait. 3.60 l, Main Road (horiz.).

1975, Jan. 24
2532 A758 20b multi 5 5
2533 A758 40b multi 10 6
2534 A758 55b multi 18 7
2535 A758 1.75 l multi 40 20
2536 A758 2.75 l multi 60 28
2537 A758 3.60 l multi 85 40
Nos. 2532-2537 (6) 2.18 1.06

Torch with Flame in Flag Colors and Coat of Arms — A759

1975, Feb. 1
2538 A759 40b multi 14 6

Romanian Socialist Republic, 10th anniv.

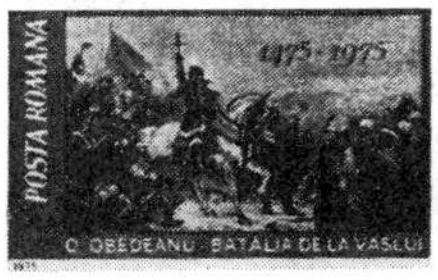

Vaslui Battle, by O. Obedeanu A760

1975, Feb. 8 Photo. *Perf. 13½*
2539 A760 55b gold & multi 18 7

500th anniv. of the battle at the High Bridge, Stephan the Great's victory over the Turks.

Woman Spinning, by Nicolae Grigorescu A761

Michelangelo, Self-portrait A762

1975, Mar. 1
2540 A761 55b gold & multi 18 6

International Women's Year.

1975, Mar. 10
2541 A762 5 l multi 85 38

Michelangelo Buonarroti (1475-1564), Italian sculptor, painter and architect.

Souvenir Sheet

Escorial Palace and España 75 Emblem — A763

1975, Mar. 15 Photo. *Perf. 13*
2542 A763 10 l multi 2.00 1.75

Espana 75 Intl. Phil. Exhib., Madrid, Apr. 4-13.

Letter with Postal Code, Pigeon A764

1975, Mar. 26 Photo. *Perf. 13½*
2543 A764 55b bl & multi 18 6

Introduction of postal code system.

Children's Science Pavilion — A765

1975, Apr. 10 Photo. *Perf. 13*
2544 A765 4 l multi 75 28

Oceanexpo 75, International Exhibition, Okinawa, July 20, 1975-Jan. 1976.

Peonies, by N. Tonitza A766

Design: 3.45 l, Chrysanthemums, by St. Luchian.

1975, Apr. 28
2545 A766 2.20 l gold & multi 85 50
2546 A766 3.45 l gold & multi 1.25 95

Inter-European Cultural and Economic Cooperation. Nos. 2544-2545 printed checkerwise in sheets of 10 (2x5).

1875 Meter Convention Emblem A767

1975, May 10 Photo. *Perf. 13*
2547 A767 1.85 l bl, blk & gold 50 18

Cent. of Intl. Meter Convention, Paris, 1875.

Mihail Eminescu and his Home — A768

1975, June 5
2548 A768 55b multi 18 10

Milhail Eminescu (1850-1889), poet.

Marble Plaque and Dacian Coins 1st-2nd Centuries — A769

1975, May 26
2549 A769 55b multi 18 10

2000th anniv. of the founding of Alba Iulia (Apulum).

Souvenir Sheet

"On the Bank of the Seine," by Th. Pallady — A770

1975, May 26
2550 A770 101 multi 2.25 1.90

ARPHILA 75, Paris, June 6-16.

Dr.Albert Schweitzer (1875-1965), Medical Missionary — A771

1974, Dec. 20 Photo. *Perf. 13½*
2551 A771 40b blk brn 10 5

Ana Ipatescu A772

Policeman with Walkie-talkie A773

1975, June 2 Photo. *Perf. 13½*
2552 A772 55b lil rose 18 6

Ana Ipatescu, fighter in 1848 revolution.

1975, Sept. 1
2553 A773 55b brt bl 20 6

Publicity for traffic rules.

Monument and Projected Reconstruction, Adam Clissi — A777

Roman Monuments: 55b, Emperor Trajan, bas-relief (vert.). 1.20 l, Trajan's column, Rome (vert.). 1.55 l, Governor Decibalus, bas-relief (vert.). 2 l, Excavated Roman city, Turnu-Severin. 2.25 l, Trajan's Bridge, ruin and projected reconstruction. No. 2569, Roman fortifications (vert.).

1975, June 26 Photo. *Perf. 13½*
2563 A777 55b red brn & blk 12 7
2564 A777 1.20 l vio bl & blk 24 14
2565 A777 1.55 l grn & blk 24 15
2566 A777 1.75 l dl rose & multi 35 20
2567 A777 2 l dl yel & blk 40 28
2568 A777 2.25 l brt bl & blk 50 35
Nos. 2563-2568 (6) 1.85 1.19

Souvenir Sheet

2569 A777 10 l multi 2.75 2.00

European Architectural Heritage Year.

An imperf. 10 l gold and dark brown souvenir sheet exists showing the Roman wolf suckling Romulus and Remus, with gray and gold margin.

A similar souvenir sheet exists with the Roman wolf 10 l, blue and multicolored margins, black inscriptions including "ESSEN 1978", red control number, imperf. It appeared in 1978, honoring the Intl. Stamp Fair, Essen, Germany.

Michael the Brave, by Sadeler A778

Michael the Brave Statue — A779

Designs: 1.20 l, Ottoman Messengers Offering Gifts to Michael the Brave, by Theodor Aman (horiz.). 2.75 l, Michael the Brave in Battle of Calugareni, by Aman.

1975, July 7
2571 A778 55b gold & blk 18 7
2572 A778 1.20 l gold & multi 28 14
2573 A778 2.75 l gold & multi 60 28

Souvenir Sheet

Imperf

2574 A779 10 l gold & multi 22.50 20.00

First political union of Romanian states under Michael the Brave, 375th anniv.

No. 2574 issued Sept. 20.

Larkspur — A780

1975, Aug. 15 Photo. *Perf. 13½*
2575 A780 20b shown 5 5
2576 A780 40b Field poppies 8 5
2577 A780 55b Xeranthemum annuum 18 7
2578 A780 1.75 l Rockrose 40 14
2579 A780 2.75 l Meadow sage 60 28
2580 A780 3.60 l Wild chicory 85 38
Nos. 2575-2580 (6) 2.16 97

No. 2541 Overprinted in Red:

Tîrg internaţional
de mărci poştale

Riccione — Italia
23–25 august 1975

1975, Aug. 23
2581 A762 5 l multi 1.75 85

Intl. Phil. Exhib., Riccione, Italy, Aug. 23-25.

Map Showing Location of Craiova, 1750 — A781

1975, Sept. 15 Photo. *Perf. 13½*
2582 A781 Strip of 3 55 28
a 20b ocher, yel, red & blk 7 6
b 55b ocher, yel, red & blk 14 10
c 1 l ocher, yel, red & blk 24 14

1750th anniv. of first documentation of Daco-Getian settlement of Pelendava and 500th anniversary of documentation of Craiova.

Size of Nos. 2582a, 2582c: 25x32mm.; of No. 2582b: 80x32mm.

Muntenian Rug — A782

Romanian Peasant Rugs: 40b, Banat. 55b, Oltenia. 1.75 l, Moldavia. 2.75 l, Oltenia. 3.60 l, Maramures.

1975, Oct. 5 Photo. *Perf. 13½*
2583 A782 20b dk bl & multi 5 5
2584 A782 40b blk & multi 8 6
2585 A782 55b multi 18 7
2586 A782 1.75 l blk & multi 40 14
2587 A782 2.75 l multi 60 28
2588 A782 3.60 l blk & multi 80 35
Nos. 2583-2588 (6) 2.11 95

Minibus
A783

1975, Nov. 5 Photo. *Perf. 13½*

2589	A783	20b	shown	5	5
2590	A783	40b	Gasoline truck	8	5
2591	A783	55b	Jeep	18	7
2592	A783	1.75 l	Flat-bed truck	40	14
2593	A783	2.75 l	Dacia automobile	60	28
2594	A783	3.60 l	Dump truck	85	35
			Nos. 2589-2594 (6)	2.16	94

Souvenir Sheet

Winter, by Peter Brueghel, the Younger — A784

1975, Nov. 25 Photo. *Perf. 13½*

2595 A784 10 l multi 2.50 2.00

THEMABELGA Intl. Topical Phil. Exhib., Brussels, Dec. 13-21.

Luge and Olympic Games' Emblem — A785

Innsbruck Olympic Games' Emblem and: 40b, Biathlon (vert.). 55b, Woman skier. 1.75 l, Ski jump. 2.75 l, Woman figure skater. 3.60 l, Ice hockey. 10 l, Two-man bobsled.

1976, Jan. 12 Photo. *Perf. 13½*

2596	A785	20b	bl & multi	6	5
2597	A785	40b	multi	7	6
2598	A785	55b	multi	18	8
2599	A785	1.75 l	ol & multi	40	14
2600	A785	2.75 l	multi	60	20
2601	A785	3.60 l	multi	80	38
			Nos. 2596-2601 (6)	2.11	91

Souvenir Sheet

2602 A785 10 l multi 2.50 2.00

12th Winter Olympic Games, Innsbruck, Austria, Feb. 4-15. An imperf. 10 l souvenir sheet exists showing slalom; Romanian flag, Games' emblem and red control number in margin.

Washington at Valley Forge, by W. T. Trego — A786

Paintings: 40b, Washington at Trenton, by John Trumbull (vert.). 55b, Washington Crossing the Delaware, by Emanuel Leutze. 1.75 l, The Capture of the Hessians, by Trumbull. 2.75 l, Jefferson, by Thomas Sully (vert.). 3.60 l, Surrender of Cornwallis at Yorktown, by Trumbull. 10 l, Signing of the Declaration of Independence, by Trumbull.

1976, Jan. 25 Photo. *Perf. 13½*

2603	A786	20b	gold & multi	5	5
2604	A786	40b	gold & multi	8	5
2605	A786	55b	gold & multi	18	7
2606	A786	1.75 l	gold & multi	40	14
2607	A786	2.75 l	gold & multi	60	28
2608	A786	3.60 l	gold & multi	75	35
			Nos. 2603-2608 (6)	2.06	94

Souvenir Sheet

2609 A786 10 l gold & multi 2.50 1.90

American Bicentennial. No. 2609 also commemorates Interphil 76 Intl. Phil. Exhib., Philadelphia, Pa., May 20-June 6. Printed in horizontal rows of 4 stamps with centered label showing Bicentennial emblem.

Prayer, by Brancusi
A787

Designs: 1.75 l, Architectural Assembly, by Brancusi. 3.60 l, Constantin Brancusi.

1976, Feb. 15 Photo. *Perf. 13½*

2610	A787	55b	pur & multi	18	7
2611	A787	1.75 l	bl & multi	40	18
2612	A787	3.60 l	multi	85	35

Constantin Brancusi (1876-1957), sculptor.

Anton Davidoglu
A788

Archives Museum
A789

Designs: 55b, Vlad Tepes. 1.20 l, Costache Negri.

1976, Feb. 25

2613	A788	40b	grn & multi	8	5
2614	A788	55b	grn & multi	18	10
2615	A788	1.20 l	grn & multi	28	14
2616	A789	1.75 l	grn & multi	40	18

Anniversaries: Anton Davidoglu (1876-1958), mathematician; Prince Vlad Tepes, commander in war against the Turks (d. 1476); Costache Negri (1812-1876), Moldavian freedom fighter; Romanian National Archives Museum, founded 1926.

The lack of a value for a listed item does not necessarily indicate rarity.

Dr. Carol Davila
A790

Vase with King Decebalus Portrait
A791

Designs: 1.75 l, Nurse with patient. 2.20 l, First aid.

1976, Apr. 20

2617	A790	55b	multi	18	7
2618	A790	1.75 l	multi	40	14
2619	A790	2.20 l	yel & multi	50	18

Romanian Red Cross cent. See No. C199.

1976, May 13

Design: 3.45 l, Vase with portrait of King Michael the Bold.

2620	A791	2.20 l	bl & multi	1.00	50
2621	A791	3.45 l	multi	2.50	1.25

Inter-European Cultural Economic Cooperation. Nos. 2620-2621 each printed in sheets of 4 with marginal inscriptions.

Coat of Arms — A792

Spiru Haret — A793

1976, June 12

2622 A792 1.75 l multi 40 18

1976, June 25

2628 A793 20b multi 14 6

Spiru Haret (1851-1912), mathematician.

Woman Athlete — A794

Romanian Olympic Emblem and: 40b, Boxing. 55b, Team handball. 1.75 l, 2-man scull (horiz.). 2.75 l, Gymnast on rings (horiz.). 3.60 l, 2-man canoe (horiz.). 10 l, Woman gymnast (horiz.).

1976, June 25 Photo. *Perf. 13½*

2629	A794	20b	org & multi	5	5
2630	A794	40b	multi	8	5
2631	A794	55b	multi	18	7
2632	A794	1.75 l	multi	40	14
2633	A794	2.75 l	vio & multi	60	28
2634	A794	3.60 l	bl & multi	85	46
			Nos. 2629-2634 (6)	2.16	1.05

Souvenir Sheet

2635 A794 10 l rose & multi 2.50 2.00

21st Olympic Games, Montreal, Canada, July 17-Aug. 1. No. 2635 contains one stamp 49x37mm.

An imperf. airmail 10 l souvenir sheet exists showing Olympic Stadium, Montreal.

Inscribed Stone Tablets, Banat — A795

Designs: 40b, Hekate, Bacchus, bas-relief. 55b, Ceramic fragment, bowl, coins. 1.75 l, Bowl, urn and cup. 2.75 l, Sword, lance and tombstone. 3.60 l, Lances, urn. 10 l, Clay vessel and silver coins.

1976, July 25

2636	A795	20b	multi	5	5
2637	A795	40b	multi	8	5
2638	A795	55b	org & multi	18	7
2639	A795	1.75 l	multi	40	14
2640	A795	2.75 l	fawn & multi	60	28
2641	A795	3.60 l	multi	85	35
			Nos. 2636-2641 (6)	2.16	94

Souvenir Sheet

2642 A795 10 l yel & multi 2.50 2.00

Daco-Roman archaeological treasures. No. 2642 issued Mar. 25. An imperf. 10 l souvenir sheet exists showing a silver and gold vase and silver coins; red control number.

Wolf Statue, 4th Century Map
A796

1976, Aug. 25

2643 A796 55b multi 18 7

Founding of Buzau, 1600th anniv.

Red Deer and Hunting Horn — A797

Game: 40b, Brown bear. 55b, Chamois. 1.75 l, Boar. 2.75 l, Red fox. 3.60 l, Lynx.

1976, Sept. 20

2644	A797	20b	buff & multi	5	5
2645	A797	40b	buff & multi	8	5
2646	A797	55b	buff & multi	18	5
2647	A797	1.75 l	buff & multi	40	14
2648	A797	2.75 l	buff & multi	60	28
2649	A797	3.60 l	buff & multi	85	35
			Nos. 2644-2649 (6)	2.16	92

Dan Grecu, Bronze Medal
A798

Nadia Comaneci — A799

Designs: 40b, Fencing, bronze medal. 55b Gheorge Megelea (Javelin), bronze medal. 1.75 l, Handball, silver medal. 2.75 l, Boxing, 1 bronze, 2 silver medals. 3.60 l, Wrestling, silver and bronze medals. 10 l, Vasile Daba (kayak), gold and silver medals (vert.).

1976, Oct. 20 Photo. *Perf. 13½*

2650	A798	20b	multi	5	5
2651	A798	40b	car & multi	8	5
2652	A798	55b	grn & multi	18	5
2653	A798	1.75 l	red & multi	40	15
2654	A798	2.75 l	bl & multi	60	28
2655	A798	3.60 l	multi	80	40
2656	A799	5.70 l	multi	1.40	48
			Nos. 2650-2656 (7)	3.51	1.46

Souvenir Sheet

2657	A798	10 l	multi	2.50	2.00

Romanian Olympic medalists. No. 2657 contains one stamp 37x50mm.

Milan Cathedral — A800

1976, Oct. 20 Photo. *Perf. 13½*

2658	A800	4.75 l	multi	1.10	50

ITALIA 76 Intl. Phil. Exhib., Milan, Oct. 14-24.

Oranges and Carnations, by Luchian — A801

Paintings by Stefan Luchian (1868-1916): 40b, Flower arrangement. 55b, Vase with flowers. 1.75 l, Roses. 2.75 l, Cornflowers. 3.60 l, Carnations in vase.

1976, Nov. 5

2659	A801	20b	multi	5	5
2660	A801	40b	multi	8	5
2661	A801	55b	multi	18	7
2662	A801	1.75 l	multi	40	14
2663	A801	2.75 l	multi	60	28
2664	A801	3.60 l	multi	85	35
			Nos. 2659-2664 (6)	2.16	94

Arms of Alba — A802

Designs: Arms of Romanian counties.

1976-77 Photo. *Perf. 13½*

2665	A802	55b	shown	25	10
2666	A802	55b	Arad	25	10
2667	A802	55b	Arges	25	10
2668	A802	55b	Bacau	25	10
2669	A802	55b	Bihor	25	10
2670	A802	55b	Bistrita-Nasaud	25	10
2671	A802	55b	Botosani	25	10
2672	A802	55b	Brasov	25	10
2673	A802	55b	Braila	25	10
2674	A802	55b	Buzau	25	10
2675	A802	55b	Caras-Severin	25	10
2676	A802	55b	Cluj	25	10
2677	A802	55b	Constanta	25	10
2678	A802	55b	Covasna	25	10
2679	A802	55b	Dimbovita	25	10
2680	A802	55b	Dolj	25	10
2681	A802	55b	Galati	25	10
2682	A802	55b	Gorj	25	10
2683	A802	55b	Harghita	25	10
2684	A802	55b	Hunedoara	25	10
2685	A802	55b	Ialomita	25	10
2686	A802	55b	Iasi	25	10
2687	A802	55b	Ilfov	25	10
2688	A802	55b	Maramures	25	10
2689	A802	55b	Mehedinti	25	10
2690	A802	55b	Mures	25	10
2691	A802	55b	Neamt	25	10
2692	A802	55b	Olt	25	10
2693	A802	55b	Prahova	25	10
2694	A802	55b	Salaj	25	10
2695	A802	55b	Satu-Mare	25	10
2696	A802	55b	Sibiu	25	10
2697	A802	55b	Suceava	25	10
2698	A802	55b	Teleorman	25	10
2699	A802	55b	Timis	25	10
2700	A802	55b	Tulcea	25	10
2701	A802	55b	Vaslui	25	10
2702	A802	55b	Vilcea	25	10
2703	A802	55b	Vrancea	25	10
2704	A802	55b	Postal emblem	25	10
			Nos. 2665-2704 (40)	10.00	4.00

Sheets of 50 (10x5) contain 5 designs: Nos. 2665-2669; 2670-2674; 2675-2679; 2680-2684; 2685-2689; 2690-2694; 2695-2699; 2700-2704. Each row of 10 contains 5 pairs of each design.

Issue dates: Nos. 2665-2679, Dec. 20, 1976. Nos. 2680-2704, Sept. 5, 1977.

Oxcart, by Grigorescu — A803

Paintings by Nicolae Grigorescu (1838-1907): 1 l, Self-portrait (vert.). 1.50 l, Shepherdess. 2.15 l, Woman Spinning with Distaff. 3.40 l, Shepherd (vert.). 4.80 l, Rest at Well.

1977, Jan. 20 Photo. *Perf. 13½*

2705	A803	55b	gray & multi	14	5
2706	A803	1 l	gray & multi	20	7
2707	A803	1.50 l	gray & multi	28	14
2708	A803	2.15 l	gray & multi	38	20
2709	A803	3.40 l	gray & multi	55	40
2710	A803	4.80 l	gray & multi	85	50
			Nos. 2705-2710 (6)	2.40	1.36

Cheia Telecommunications Station — A804

1977, Feb. 1

2711	A804	55b	multi	14	7

Red Deer A805

Protected Birds and Animals: 1 l, Mute swan. 1.50 l, Egyptian vulture. 2.15 l, Bison. 3.40 l, White-headed ruddy duck. 4.80 l, Kingfisher.

1977, Mar. 20 Photo. *Perf. 13½*

2712	A805	55b	multi	10	5
2713	A805	1 l	multi	14	7
2714	A805	1.50 l	multi	20	10
2715	A805	2.15 l	multi	35	14
2716	A805	3.40 l	multi	50	18
2717	A805	4.80 l	multi	75	30
			Nos. 2712-2717 (6)	2.04	84

Calafat Artillery Unit, by Sava Hentia — A806

Paintings: 55b, Attacking Infantryman, by Oscar Obedeanu (vert.). 1.50 l, Infantry Attack in Winter, by Stefan Luchian (vert.). 2.15 l, Battle of Plevna (after etching). 3.40 l, Artillery, by Nicolae Ion Grigorescu. 10 l, Battle of Grivita, 1877.

1977

2718	A806	55b	gold & multi	10	5
2719	A806	1 l	gold & multi	15	7
2720	A806	1.50 l	gold & multi	24	7
2721	A806	2.15 l	gold & multi	60	10
2722	A806	3.40 l	gold & multi	75	18
			Nos. 2718-2722,B442 (6)	3.09	92

Souvenir Sheet

2723	A806	10 l	gold & multi	2.75	2.00

Centenary of Romania's independence. A 10 l imperf. souvenir sheet exists showing victorious return of army, Dobruja, 1878.

Issue dates: Nos. 2718-2722, May 9; No. 2723, Apr. 25.

Sinaia, Carpathian Mountains A807

Design: 2.40 l, Hotels, Aurora, Black Sea.

1977, May 17

2724	A807	2 l	gold & multi	1.00	85
2725	A807	2.40 l	gold & multi	1.40	1.25

Inter-European Cultural and Economic Cooperation. Nos. 2724-2725 printed in sheets of 4 with marginal inscriptions.

Petru Rares A808

Ion Luca Caragiale A809

1977, June 10 Photo. *Perf. 13½*

2726	A808	40b	multi	10	6

450th anniversary of the elevation of Petru Rares to Duke of Moldavia.

1977, June 10

2727	A809	55b	multi	14	7

Ion Luca Caragiale (1852-1912), writer.

Red Cross Nurse, Children, Emblems A810

1977, June 10

2728	A810	1.50 l	multi	35	18

23rd Intl. Red Cross Conf., Bucharest.

Arch of Triumph, Bucharest A811

1977, June 10

2729	A811	2.15 l	multi	50	18

60th anniversary of the Battles of Marasesti and Oituz.

Peaks of San Marino, Exhibition Emblem — A812

1977, Aug. 28 Photo. *Perf. 13½*

2730	A812	4 l	brt bl & multi	1.00	35

Centenary of San Marino stamps, and San Marino '77 Phil. Exhib., San Marino, Aug. 28-Sept. 4.

Vaulting — A813

Gymnasts: 40b, Woman dancer. 55b, Man on parallel bars. 1 l, Woman on balance beam. 2.15 l, Man on rings. 4.80 l, Woman on double bars.

1977, Sept. 25 Photo. *Perf. 13½*

2731	A813	20b	multi	5	5
2732	A813	40b	multi	8	5
2733	A813	55b	multi	10	5
2734	A813	1 l	multi	20	7
2735	A813	2.15 l	multi	35	14
2736	A813	4.80 l	multi	1.25	30
	Nos. 2731-2736 (6)			2.03	66

"Carpati" near Cazane. Iron Gate — A814

Designs: 1 l, "Mircesti" at Orsova. 1.50 l, "Oltenita" at Calafat. 2.15 l, Water bus at Giurgiu. 3 l, "Herculane" at Tulcea. 3.40 l, "Muntenia" in Nature preserve, Sulina. 4.80 l, Map of Danube Delta with Sulina Canal. 10 l, Danubius, god of Danube, from Trajan's Column, Rome (vert.).

1977, Dec. 28

2737	A814	55b	multi	7	5
2738	A814	1 l	multi	14	7
2739	A814	1.50 l	multi	24	10
2740	A814	2.15 l	multi	40	14
2741	A814	3 l	multi	60	20
2742	A814	3.40 l	multi	65	20
2743	A814	4.80 l	multi	1.25	30
	Nos. 2737-2743 (7)			3.35	1.06

Souvenir Sheet

2744	A814	10 l	multi	2.75	2.00

European Danube Commission.

A 10 l imperf. souvenir sheet exists showing map of Danube from Regensburg to the Black Sea.

Flag and Arms of Romania A815

Designs: 1.20 l, Computer production in Romania. 1.75 l, National Theater, Craiova.

1977, Dec. 30

2745	A815	55b	multi	10	5
2746	A815	1.20 l	multi	18	8
2747	A815	1.75 l	multi	40	20

Proclamation of Republic, 30th anniversary.

Dancers A816

Designs: Romanian male folk dancers.

1977, Nov. 28 Photo. *Perf. 13½*

2748	A816	20b	multi	5	5
2749	A816	40b	multi	8	5
2750	A816	55b	multi	8	5
2751	A816	1 l	multi	14	7
2752	A816	2.15 l	multi	38	14
2753	A816	4.80 l	multi	1.25	30
	Nos. 2748-2753 (6)			1.98	66

Souvenir Sheet

2754	A816	10 l	multi	2.00	2.00

Firiza Dam A817

Hydroelectric Stations and Dams: 40b, Negovanu. 55b, Piatra Neamt. 1 l, Izvorul Muntelui-Bicaz. 2.15 l, Vidraru. 4.80 l, Iron Gate.

1978, Mar. 10 Photo. *Perf. 13½*

2755	A817	20b	multi	5	5
2756	A817	40b	multi	8	5
2757	A817	55b	multi	10	5
2758	A817	1 l	multi	14	7
2759	A817	2.15 l	multi	35	14
2760	A817	4.80 l	multi	1.00	30
	Nos. 2755-2760 (6)			1.72	66

Soccer and Argentina '78 Emblem — A818

Designs: Various soccer scenes and Argentina '78 emblem.

1978, Apr. 15

2761	A818	55b	bl & multi	7	5
2762	A818	1 l	org & multi	14	7
2763	A818	1.50 l	yel grn & multi	18	7
2764	A818	2.15 l	ver & multi	30	10
2765	A818	3.40 l	bl grn & multi	50	20
2766	A818	4.80 l	lil rose & multi	1.00	35
	Nos. 2761-2766 (6)			2.19	84

11th World Cup Soccer Championship, Argentina '78, June 1-25. See No. C222.

King Decebalus of Dacia Statue, Deva A819

Design: 3.40 l, King Mircea the Elder of Wallachia statue, Tulcea, and ship.

1978, May 22 Photo. *Perf. 13½*

2767	A819	1.30 l	gold & multi	1.00	70
2768	A819	3.40 l	gold & multi	1.75	1.25

Inter-European Cultural and Economic Cooperation. Nos. 2767-2768 printed in sheets of 4 with marginal inscriptions and control number.

Worker, Factory, Flag A821

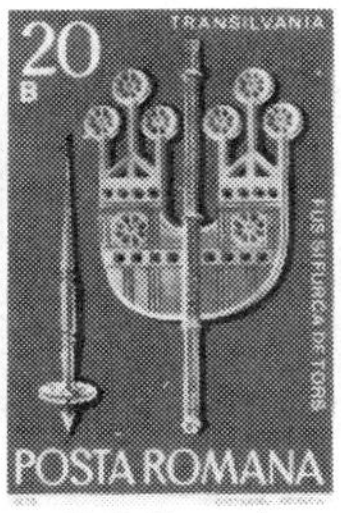

Spindle and Handle, Transylvania A822

1978, June 11 Photo. *Perf. 13½*

2770	A821	55b	multi	12	6

Nationalization of industry, 30th anniv.

1978, June 20

Wood Carvings: 40b, Cheese molds, Muntenia. 55b, Spoons, Oltenia. 1 l, Barrel, Moldavia. 2.15 l, Ladle and mug, Transylvania. 4.80 l, Water bucket, Oltenia.

2771	A822	20b	multi	5	5
2772	A822	40b	multi	8	5
2773	A822	55b	multi	8	5
2774	A822	1 l	multi	14	7
2775	A822	2.15 l	multi	30	14
2776	A822	4.80 l	multi	1.00	35
	Nos. 2771-2776 (6)			1.65	71

Danube Delta — A823

Designs: 1 l, Bran Castle (vert.). 1.50 l, Monastery, Suceava, Moldavia. 2.15 l, Caves, Oltenia. 3.40 l, Ski lift, Brasov. 4.80 l, Mangalia, Black Sea. 10 l, Strehaia Fortress (vert.).

1978, July 20 Photo. *Perf. 13½*

2777	A823	55b	multi	7	5
2778	A823	1 l	multi	14	7
2779	A823	1.50 l	multi	20	10
2780	A823	2.15 l	multi	30	10
2781	A823	3.40 l	multi	50	18
2782	A823	4.80 l	multi	1.00	35
	Nos. 2777-2782 (6)			2.21	85

Miniature Sheet

2783	A823	10 l	multi	2.50	2.00

Tourist publicity. No. 2783 contains one stamp 37x51mm. Issued July 30.

Electronic Microscope A824

Designs: 40b, Hydraulic excavator. 55b, Computer center. 1.50 l, Oil derricks. 3 l, Harvester combine (horiz.). 3.40 l, Petrochemical plant.

1978, Aug. 15 Photo. *Perf. 13½*

2784	A824	20b	multi	5	5
2785	A824	40b	multi	8	5
2786	A824	55b	multi	8	5
2787	A824	1.50 l	multi	24	7
2788	A824	3 l	multi	55	14
2789	A824	3.40 l	multi	70	24
	Nos. 2784-2789 (6)			1.70	60

Industrial development.

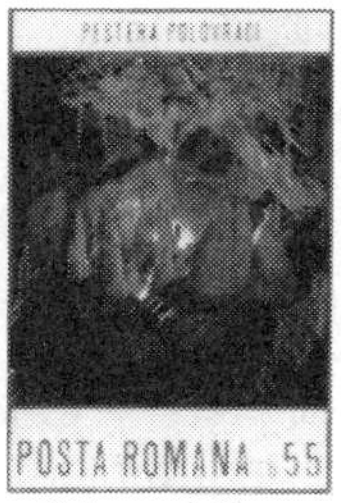

Polovraci Cave, Carpathians A825

"Racial Equality" A826

Caves: 1 l, Topolnita. 1.50 l, Ponoare. 2.15 l, Ratei, Mt. Bucegi. 3.40 l, Closani, Mt. Motrului. 4.80 l, Epuran. 1 l, 1.50 l, 4.80 l, Mt. Mehedinti.

1978, Aug. 25 Photo. *Perf. 13½*

2790	A825	55b	multi	7	5
2791	A825	1 l	multi	14	7
2792	A825	1.50 l	multi	20	7
2793	A825	2.15 l	multi	30	14
2794	A825	3.40 l	multi	50	18
2795	A825	4.80 l	multi	1.00	35
	Nos. 2790-2795 (6)			2.21	86

1978, Sept. 28

2796	A826	3.40 l	multi	50	20

Anti-Apartheid Year.

Gold Bas-relief — A827

Designs: 40b, Gold armband. 55b, Gold cameo ring. 1 l, Silver bowl. 2.15 l, Eagle from Roman standard (vert.). 4.80 l, Silver armband.

1978, Sept. 25

2797	A827	20b	multi	5	5
2798	A827	40b	multi	8	5
2799	A827	55b	multi	8	5
2800	A827	1 l	multi	14	7
2801	A827	2.15 l	multi	30	14
2802	A827	4.80 l	multi	1.00	35
	Nos. 2797-2802 (6)			1.65	71

Daco-Roman archaeological treasures. An imperf. 10 l souvenir sheet exists showing gold helmet (vert.); red control number.

Woman Gymnast, Games' Emblem — A828

Games' Emblem and: 1 l, Running. 1.50 l, Skiing. 2.15 l, Equestrian. 3.40 l, Soccer. 4.80 l, Handball.

1978, Sept. 15

2803	A828	55b	multi	7	5
2804	A828	1 l	multi	14	14
2805	A828	1.50 l	multi	20	10

2806	A828	2.15 l multi		30	14
2807	A828	3.40 l multi		50	20
2808	A828	4.80 l multi		1.00	35
		Nos. 2803-2808 (6)		2.21	98

Ptolemaic Map of Dacia
A829

Designs: 55b, Meeting House of Romanian National Council, Arad. 1.75 l, Pottery vases, 8th-9th centuries, found near Arad. Nos. 2809-2811 printed se-tenant.

1978, Oct. 21 Photo. *Perf. 13½*

2809	A829	40b multi	8	5
2810	A829	55b multi	8	5
2811	A829	1.75 l multi	35	18

2,000th anniversary of founding of Arad.

Assembly at Alba Iulia, 1919
A830

Warrior, Bas-relief
A831

Design: 1 l, Open book and Romanian flag.

1978, Dec. 1

2812	A830	55b gold & multi	10	5
2813	A830	1 l gold & multi	14	7

60th anniversary of national unity.

1979 Photo. *Perf. 13½*

Design: 1.50 l, Warrior on horseback, bas-relief.

2814	A831	55b multi	10	5
2815	A831	1.50 l multi	20	8

2,050 years since establishment of first centralized and independent Dacian state.

"Heroes of Vaslui"
A832

Ice Hockey, Globe, Emblem
A833

Children's Drawings: 1 l, Building houses. 1.50 l, Folk music of Tica. 2.15 l, Industrial landscape (horiz.). 3.40 l, winter customs (horiz.). 4.80 l, Pioneer festival (horiz.).

1979, Mar. 1

2816	A832	55b multi	7	5
2817	A832	1 l multi	14	7
2818	A832	1.50 l multi	20	7
2819	A832	2.15 l multi	30	10
2820	A832	3.40 l multi	50	18
2821	A832	4.80 l multi	1.00	35
		Nos. 2816-2821 (6)	2.21	82

International Year of the Child.

1979, Mar. 16 Photo. *Perf. 13½*

Design: 3.40 l, Ice hockey players, globe and emblem.

2822	A833	1.30 l multi	28	8
2823	A833	3.40 l multi	55	18

European Youth Ice Hockey Championship, Miercurea-Ciuc (1.30 l) and World Ice Hockey Championship, Galati (3.40 l). Printed se-tenant.

Dog's-tooth Violet — A834

Protected Flowers: 1 l, Alpine violet. 1.50 l, Linum borzaeanum. 2.15 l, Persian bindweed. 3.40 l, Primula auricula. 4.80 l, Transylvanian columbine.

1979, Apr. 25 Photo. *Perf. 13½*

2824	A834	55b multi	7	5
2825	A834	1 l multi	14	7
2826	A834	1.50 l multi	20	10
2827	A834	2.15 l multi	30	10
2828	A834	3.40 l multi	50	20
2829	A834	4.80 l multi	1.00	35
		Nos. 2824-2829 (6)	2.21	87

Mail Coach and Post Rider, 19th Century
A835

1979, May 3 Photo. *Perf. 13*

2830	A835	1.30 l multi	40	24

Inter-European Cultural and Economic Cooperation. Printed in sheets of 4 with marginal inscription and control number. See No. C231.

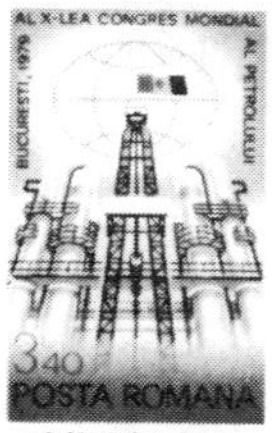

Oil Rig and Refinery
A836

Girl Pioneer
A837

1979, May 24 Photo. *Perf. 13*

2832	A836	3.40 l multi	50	18

10th World Petroleum Congress, Bucharest.

1979, June 20

2833	A837	55b multi	12	6

30th anniversary of Romanian Pioneers.

Children with Flowers, IYC Emblem
A838

IYC Emblem and: 1 l, Kindergarten. 2 l, Pioneers with rabbit. 4.60 l, Drummer, trumpeters, flags.

1979, July 18 Photo. *Perf. 13½*

2834	A838	40b multi	8	5
2835	A838	1 l multi	14	7
2836	A838	2 l multi	30	14
2837	A838	4.60 l multi	95	28

International Year of the Child.

Lady in a Garden, by Tattarescu
A839

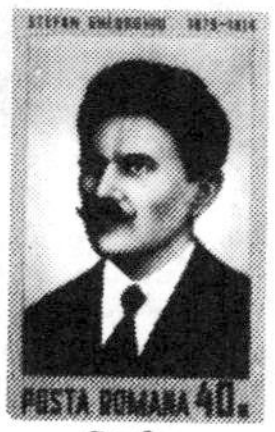

Stefan Gheorghiu
A840

Paintings by Gheorghe Tattarescu: 40b, Mountain woman. 55b, Mountain man. 1 l, Portrait of Gh. Magheru. 2.15 l, The artist's daughter. 4.80 l, Self-portrait.

1979, June 16

2838	A839	20b multi	5	5
2839	A839	40b multi	7	5
2840	A839	55b multi	7	5
2841	A839	1 l multi	14	7
2842	A839	2.15 l multi	30	14
2843	A839	4.80 l multi	1.00	35
		Nos. 2838-2843 (6)	1.63	71

1979, Aug.

Designs: 55b, Gheorghe Lazar monument. 2.15 l, Lupeni monument. 4.60 l, Women in front of Memorial Arch.

2844	A840	40b multi	7	5
2845	A840	55b multi	7	5
2846	A840	2.15 l multi	30	10
2847	A840	4.60 l multi	95	28

State Theater, Tirgu-Mures — A841

Modern Architecture: 40b, University, Brasov. 55b, Political Administration Buildings, Baia Mare. 1 l, Stefan Gheorghiu Academy, Bucharest. 2.15 l, Political Administration Building, Botosani. 4.80 l, House of Culture, Tirgoviste.

1979, June 25

2848	A841	20b multi	5	5
2849	A841	40b multi	7	5
2850	A841	55b multi	7	5
2851	A841	1 l multi	10	7
2852	A841	2.15 l multi	24	14
2853	A841	4.80 l multi	85	35
		Nos. 2848-2853 (6)	1.38	71

Flags of Russia and Romania — A842

Design: 1 l, Workers' Militia, by L. Suhar (horiz.).

1979, Aug. 20 Photo. *Perf. 13½*

2854	A842	55b multi	7	5
2855	A842	1 l multi	18	7

Liberation from Fascism, 35th anniversary.

Cargo Ship Galati
A843

Romanian Ships: 1 l, Cargo ship Bucuresti. 1.50 l, Ore carrier Resita. 2.15 l, Ore carrier Tomis. 3.40 l, Tanker Dacia. 4.80 l, Tanker Independenta.

1979, Aug. 27 Photo. *Perf. 13½*

2856	A843	55b multi	7	5
2857	A843	1 l multi	14	7
2858	A843	1.50 l multi	20	10
2859	A843	2.15 l multi	30	10
2860	A843	3.40 l multi	50	18
2861	A843	4.80 l multi	1.00	35
		Nos. 2856-2861 (6)	2.21	85

Olympic Stadium, Melbourne, 1956, Moscow '80 Emblem — A844

Moscow '80 Emblem and Olympic Stadiums: 1 l, Rome, 1960. 1.50 l, Tokyo, 1964. 2.15 l, Mexico City, 1968. 3.40 l, Munich, 1972. 4.80 l, Montreal, 1976. 10 l, Moscow, 1980.

1979, Oct. 23 Photo. *Perf. 13½*

2862	A844	55b multi	7	5
2863	A844	1 l multi	14	7
2864	A844	1.50 l multi	20	10
2865	A844	2.15 l multi	30	10
2866	A844	3.40 l multi	50	18
2867	A844	4.80 l multi	1.00	35
		Nos. 2862-2867 (6)	2.21	85

Souvenir Sheet

2868	A844	10 l multi	2.50	2.00

22nd Summer Olympic Games, Moscow, July 19-Aug. 3, 1980. No. 2868 contains one stamp 50x38mm.

No. 2868 airmail.

Arms of Alba Iulia — A845

Designs: Arms of Romanian cities.

1979, Oct. 25

2869	A845	1.20 l shown	28	8
2870	A845	1.20 l Arad	28	8
2871	A845	1.20 l Bacau	28	8
2872	A845	1.20 l Baia-Mare	28	8
2873	A845	1.20 l Birlad	28	8
2874	A845	1.20 l Botosani	28	8
2875	A845	1.20 l Braila	28	8
2876	A845	1.20 l Brasov	28	8
2877	A845	1.20 l Buzau	28	8
2878	A845	1.20 l Calarasi	28	8
2879	A845	1.20 l Cluj	28	8
2880	A845	1.20 l Constanta	28	8
2881	A845	1.20 l Craiova	28	8
2882	A845	1.20 l Dej	28	8
2883	A845	1.20 l Deva	28	8
2884	A845	1.20 l Turnu-Severin	28	8
2885	A845	1.20 l Focsani	28	8
2886	A845	1.20 l Galati	28	8
2887	A845	1.20 l Gheorghe Gheorghiu-Dej	28	8
2888	A845	1.20 l Giurgiu	28	8
2889	A845	1.20 l Hunedoara	28	8
2890	A845	1.20 l Iasi	28	8
2891	A845	1.20 l Lugoj	28	8
2892	A845	1.20 l Medias	28	8
2893	A845	1.20 l Odorheiu Seguiesc	28	8

1980, Jan. 5

2894	A845	1.20 l Oradea	28	8
2895	A845	1.20 l Petrosani	28	8
2896	A845	1.20 l Piatra-Neamt	28	8

2897 A845 1.20 l Pitesti 28 8
2898 A845 1.20 l Ploiesti 28 8
2899 A845 1.20 l Resita 28 8
2900 A845 1.20 l Rimnicu-Vilcea 28 8
2901 A845 1.20 l Roman 28 8
2902 A845 1.20 l Satu-Mare 28 8
2904 A845 1.20 l Siget-Marmatiei 28 8
2905 A845 1.20 l Sighisoara 28 8
2906 A845 1.20 l Suceava 28 8
2907 A845 1.20 l Tecuci 28 8
2908 A845 1.20 l Timisoara 28 8
2909 A845 1.20 l Tirgoviste 28 8
2910 A845 1.20 l Tirgu-Jiu 28 8
2911 A845 1.20 l Tirgu-Mures 28 8
2912 A845 1.20 l Tulcea 28 8
2913 A845 1.20 l Turda 28 8
2914 A845 1.20 l Turnu Magurele 28 8
2915 A845 1.20 l Bucharest 28 8
Nos. 2869-2915 (46) 12.88 3.68

Maramures Woman — A846

Regional Costumes: 40b, Maramures man. 55b, Vrancea woman. 1.50 l, Vrancea man. 3 l, Padureni woman. 3.40 l, Padureni man.

1979, Oct. 27

2916 A846 20b multi 6 5
2917 A846 40b multi 5 5
2918 A846 55b multi 7 5
2919 A846 1.50 l multi 24 10
2920 A846 3 l multi 48 18
2921 A846 3.40 l multi 55 20
Nos. 2916-2921 (6) 1.45 63

Snapdragons, by Stefan Luchian — A847

Flower Paintings by Luchian: 60b, Triple chrysanthemums. 1.55 l, Potted flowers on stairs.

1979, July 27

2922 A847 40b multi 7 5
2923 A847 60b multi 12 6
2924 A847 1.55 l multi 24 12

Socfilex, International Philatelic Exhibition, Bucharest. See. Nos. B445-B446.

Souvenir Sheet

Romanian Communist Party, 12th Congress — A848

1979, Oct.

2925 A848 5 l multi 1.25 50

Figure Skating, Lake Placid '80 Emblem, Olympic Rings — A849

1979, Dec. 27 Photo. *Perf. 13½*

2926 A849 55b shown 7 5
2927 A849 1 l Downhill skiing 14 7
2928 A849 1.50 l Biathlon 20 10
2929 A849 2.15 l Two-man bobsledding 28 14
2930 A849 3.40 l Speed skating 50 18
2931 A849 4.80 l Ice hockey 1.00 35
Nos. 2926-2931 (6) 2.19 89

Souvenir Sheet

2932 A849 10 l Ice hockey, diff. 2.50 1.75

13th Winter Olympic Games, Lake Placid, N.Y., Feb. 12-24, 1980. No. 2932 contains one stamp 38x50mm. An imperf. 10 l air post souvenir sheet exists showing four-man bobsledding; red control number.

"Calugareni", Expo Emblem — A850

1979, Dec. 29

2933 A850 55b shown 7 5
2934 A850 1 l "Orleans" 14 7
2935 A850 1.50 l No. 1059, type fawn 20 10
2936 A850 2.15 l No. 15021, type 1E 30 10
2937 A850 3.40 l "Pacific" 50 20
2938 A850 4.80 l Electric engine 060-EA 1.00 35
Nos. 2933-2938 (6) 2.21 87

Souvenir Sheet

2939 A850 10 l Diesel electric 2.50 2.00

Intl. Transport Exposition, Hamburg, June 8-July 1. No. 2939 contains one stamp 50x40mm.

Dacian Warrior, Trajan's Column, Rome — A851

Design: 1.50 l, Two warriors.

1980, Feb. 9 Photo. *Perf. 13½*

2940 A851 55b multi 10 6
2941 A851 1.50 l multi 30 10

2,050 years since establishment of first centralized and independent Dacian state.

Kingfisher — A852

1980, Mar. 25 Photo. *Perf. 13½*

2942 A852 55b shown 10 5
2943 A852 1 l Great white heron, vert. 14 7
2944 A852 1.50 l Red-breasted goose 20 10
2945 A852 2.15 l Red deer, vert. 30 14
2946 A852 3.40 l Roe deer 50 18
2947 A852 4.80 l European bison, vert. 1.00 35
Nos. 2942-2947 (6) 2.24 89

European Nature Protection Year. A 10 l imperf. souvenir sheet exists showing bears; red control number. See No. C232.

Souvenir Sheets

George Enescu Playing Violin A853

1980, May 6

2948 Sheet of 4 multi 2.25 2.25
a A853 1.30 l shown 35 18
b A853 1.30 l Conducting 35 18
c A853 1.30 l Playing piano 35 18
d A853 1.30 l Composing 35 18
2949 Sheet of 4 multi 4.75 4.75
a A853 3.40 l Beethoven in library 1.00 35
b A853 3.40 l Portrait 1.00 35
c A853 3.40 l At piano 1.00 35
d A853 3.40 l Composing 1.00 35

Inter-European Cultural and Economic Cooperation. Nos. 2948-2949 have gold marginal inscription, black control number.

Vallota Purpurea A854

Tudor Vladimirescu A855

1980, Apr. 10 Photo. *Perf. 13½*

2950 A854 55b shown 10 5
2951 A854 1 l Eichhornia crasipes 14 7
2952 A854 1.50 l Sprekelia formosissima 20 10
2953 A854 2.15 l Hypericum calycinum 30 14
2954 A854 3.40 l Camellia japonica 50 18
2955 A854 4.80 l Nelumbo nucifera 1.00 35
Nos. 2950-2955 (6) 2.24 89

1980, Apr. 24

Designs: 55b, Mihail Sadoveanu. 1.50 l, Battle against Hungarians. 2.15 l, Tudor Arghezi. 3 l, Horea.

2956 A855 40b multi 7 5
2957 A855 55b multi 7 5
2958 A855 1.50 l multi 20 10
2959 A855 2.15 l multi 30 14
2960 A855 3 l multi 40 18
Nos. 2956-2960 (5) 1.04 52

Anniversaries: 40b, Tudor Vladimirescu (1780-1821), leader of 1821 revolution, 200th birth anniversary; 55b, Mihail Sadoveanu (1880-1961), author, birth centenary; 1.50 l, Victory of Posada; 2.15 l, Tudor Arghezi (1880-1967), poet, birth centenary; 3 l, Horea (1730-1785), leader of 1784 uprising, 250th birth anniversary.

Dacian Fruit Bowl and Cup — A856

1980, May 8

2961 A856 1 l multi 18 7

Petrodava City, 2000th anniversary.

Javelin, Moscow '80 Emblem A857

1980, June 20 Photo. *Perf. 13½*

2962 A857 55b shown 10 5
2963 A857 1 l Fencing 14 7
2964 A857 1.50 l Shooting 20 10
2965 A857 2.15 l Kayak 30 14
2966 A857 3.40 l Wrestling 50 18
2967 A857 4.80 l Rowing 1.00 35
Nos. 2962-2967 (6) 2.24 89

Souvenir Sheet

2968 A857 10 l Handball 2.50 2.00

22nd Summer Olympic Games, Moscow, July 19-Aug. 3. No. 2968 contains one stamp 38x50mm. An imperf. 10 l air post souvenir sheet exists showing gymnast; red control number.

Congress Emblem A858

Fireman Rescuing Child A859

1980, Aug. 10 Photo. *Perf. 13½*

2969 A858 55b multi 14 6

15th Intl. Historical Sciences Congress, Bucharest.

1980, Aug. 25

2970 A859 55b multi 14 6

Firemen's Day, Sept. 13.

Chinese and Romanian Young Pioneers at Stamp Show — A860

1980, Sept. 18

2971 A860 1 l multi 20 7

Romanian-Chinese Phil. Exhib., Bucharest.

Souvenir Sheet

Parliament Building, Bucharest A861

1980, Sept. 30
2972 A861 10 l multi 2.50 2.00

European Security Conference, Madrid. An imperf. 10 l air post souvenir sheet exists showing Plaza Mayor, Madrid; red control number.

Knights and Chessboard — A862

1980, Oct. 1 Photo. *Perf. 13½*
2973 A862 55b shown 10 5
2974 A862 1 l Rooks 14 7
2975 A862 2.15 l Man 30 14
2976 A862 4.80 l Woman 1.00 35

Chess Olympiad, Valletta, Malta, Nov. 20-Dec. 8.

Dacian Warrior — A863

1980, Oct. 15
2977 A863 20b shown 5 5
2978 A863 40b Moldavian soldier, 15th cent. 8 5
2979 A863 55b Walachian horseman, 17th cent. 8 5
2980 A863 1 l Flag bearer, 19th cent. 14 7
2981 A863 1.50 l Infantryman, 19th cent. 20 10
2982 A863 2.15 l Lancer, 19th cent. 30 14
2983 A863 4.80 l Mounted Elite Corps Guard, 19th cent. 1.00 35
Nos. 2977-2983 (7) 1.85 81

Burebista Sculpture — A864

1980, Nov. 5 Photo. *Perf. 13½*
2984 A864 2 l multi 35 14

2050 years since establishment of first centralized and independent Dacian state.

George Oprescu (1881-1969), Art Critic — A865

National Dog Show — A866

Famous Men: 2.15 l, Marius Bunescu (1881-1971), painter. 3.40 l, Ion Georgescu (1856-1898), sculptor.

1981, Feb. 20 Photo. *Perf. 13½*
2985 A865 1.50 l multi 20 10
2986 A865 2.15 l multi 30 14
2987 A865 3.40 l multi 50 24

1981, Mar. 15

Designs: Dogs (40b, 1 l, 1.50 l, 3.40 l horiz.).

2988 A866 40b Mountain sheepdog 8 5
2989 A866 55b Saint Bernard 8 5
2990 A866 1 l Fox terrier 14 7
2991 A866 1.50 l German shepherd 20 10
2992 A866 2.15 l Boxer 30 14
2993 A866 3.40 l Dalmatian 50 24
2994 A866 4.80 l Poodle 1.00 35
Nos. 2988-2994 (7) 2.30 1.00

River Steamer Stefan cel Mare — A867

1981, Mar. 25
2995 A867 55b shown 7 5
2996 A867 1 l Vas de Supraveghere 14 7
2997 A867 1.50 l Tudor Vladimirescu 24 10
2998 A867 2.15 l Dredger Sulina 30 14
2999 A867 3.40 l Republica Populara Romana 50 24
3000 A867 4.80 l Sulina Canal 1.00 35
Nos. 2995-3000 (6) 2.25 95

Souvenir Sheet

3001 A867 10 l Galati 2.50 2.00

European Danube Commission, 125th anniv. An imperf. 10 l souvenir sheet exists showing map of Danube; red control number.

Carrier Pigeon A868

Designs: Various carrier pigeons and doves.

1981, Apr. 15 Photo. *Perf. 13½*
3002 A868 40b multi 7 5
3003 A868 55b multi 8 5
3004 A868 1 l multi 14 7
3005 A868 1.50 l multi 20 10
3006 A868 2.15 l multi 30 14
3007 A868 3.40 l multi 50 24
Nos. 3002-3007 (6) 1.29 65

Romanian Communist Party, 60th Anniv. — A869

Singing Romania Festival — A871

Folkdance, Moldavia A870

1981, Apr. 22 Photo. *Perf. 13½*
3008 A869 1 l multi 18 7

1981, May 4 Photo. *Perf. 13½*

Designs: Regional folkdances.

3009 Sheet of 4, multi 2.75 2.75
a A870 2.50 l shown 50 50
b A870 2.50 l Transylvania 50 50
c A870 2.50 l Banat 50 50
d A870 2.50 l Muntenia 50 50
3010 Sheet of 4, multi 2.75 2.75
a A870 2.50 l Maramures 50 50
b A870 2.50 l Dobruja 50 50
c A870 2.50 l Oltenia 50 50
d A870 2.50 l Crisana 50 50

Inter-European Cultural and Economic Cooperation. Nos. 3009-3010 have gold marginal inscription; black control number.

1981, July 15
3011 A871 55b Industry 10 5
3012 A871 1.50 l Electronics 24 10
3013 A871 2.15 l Agriculture 35 18
3014 A871 3.40 l Culture 50 30

University '81 Games, Bucharest A872

Theodor Aman, Artist, Birth Sesquicentennial A873

1981, July 17
3015 A872 1 l Book, flag 14 7
3016 A872 2.15 l Emblem 35 18
3017 A872 4.80 l Stadium, horiz. 1.00 35

1981, July 28

Aman Paintings: 40b, Self-portrait. 55b, Battle of Giurgiu. 1 l, The Family Picnic. 1.50 l, The Painter's Studio. 2.15 l, Woman in Interior. 3.40 l, Aman Museum, Bucharest. 55b, 1 l, 1.50 l, 3.40 l horiz.

3018 A873 40b multi 8 5
3019 A873 55b multi 10 5
3020 A873 1 l multi 14 7
3021 A873 1.50 l multi 28 10
3022 A873 2.15 l multi 35 18
3023 A873 3.40 l multi 60 24
Nos. 3018-3023 (6) 1.55 69

Thinker of Cernavoda, 3rd Cent. BC — A874

1981, July 30
3024 A874 3.40 l multi 50 24

16th Science History Congress.

Blood Donation Campaign A875

Romanian Musicians A877

Bucharest Central Military Hospital Sesquicentennial — A876

1981, Aug. 15 Photo. *Perf. 13½*
3025 A875 55b multi 14 6

1981, Sept. 1
3026 A876 55b multi 14 6

1981, Sept. 20

Designs : 40b, George Enescu (1881-1955). 55b, Paul Constantinescu (1909-1963). 1 l, Dinu Lipatti (1917-1950). 1.50 l, Ionel Periea (1900-1970). 2.15 l, Ciprian Porumbescu (1853-1883). 3.40 l, Mihail Jora (1891-1971).

3027 A877 40b multi 8 5
3028 A877 55b multi 10 5
3029 A877 1 l multi 14 7
3030 A877 1.50 l multi 28 14
3031 A877 2.15 l multi 35 18
3032 A877 3.40 l multi 50 24
Nos. 3027-3032 (6) 1.45 73

Stamp Day A879

1981, Nov. 5 Photo. *Perf. 13½*
3034 A879 2 l multi 35 14

Children's Games — A880

Illustrations by Eugen Palade (40b, 55b, 1 l) and Norman Rockwell.

1981, Nov. 25
3035 A880 40b Hopscotch 8 5
3036 A880 55b Soccer 10 5
3037 A880 1 l Riding stick horse 14 7
3038 A880 1.50 l Snagging the Big One 28 10
3039 A880 2.15 l A Patient Friend 35 18
3040 A880 3 l Doggone It 48 20
3041 A880 4 l Puppy Love 55 35
Nos. 3035-3041,C243 (8) 2.58 1.30

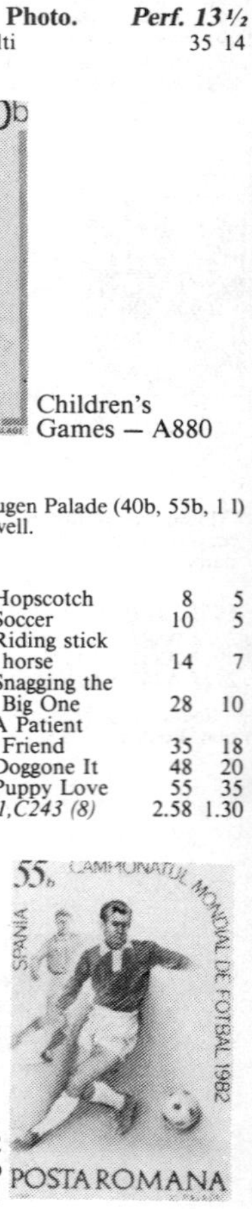

Espana '82 World Cup Soccer — A881

1981, Dec. 28
3042 A881 55b multi 10 5
3043 A881 1 l multi 18 7
3044 A881 1.50 l multi 28 10
3045 A881 2.15 l multi 35 18
3046 A881 3.40 l multi 50 24
3047 A881 4.80 l multi 1.00 38
Nos. 3042-3047 (6) 2.41 1.02

Souvenir Sheet

3048 A881 10 l multi 2.00 2.00

No. 3048 contains one stamp 38x50mm. An imperf. 10 l air post souvenir sheet exists showing game; red control number.

Prince Alexander the Good of Moldavia (ruled 1400-1432) — A882

Designs: 1.50 l, Bogdan Petriceicu Hasdeu (1838-1907), scholar. 2.15 l, Nicolae Titulescu (1882-1941), diplomat.

1982, Jan. 30 Photo. *Perf. 13½*

3049 A882 1 l multi 20 10
3050 A882 1.50 l multi 28 14
3051 A882 2.15 l multi 38 20

Bucharest Subway System A883

1982, Feb. 25

3052 A883 60b Union Square station entrance 14 8
3053 A883 2.40 l Heroes' Station platform 40 24

60th Anniv. of Communist Youth Union — A884

1982

3054 A884 1 l multi 20 7
3055 A884 1.20 l Construction worker 20 7
3056 A884 1.50 l Farm workers 28 10
3057 A884 2 l Research 35 18
3058 A884 2.50 l Workers 50 24
3059 A884 3 l Musicians, dancers 60 28
Nos. 3054-3059 (6) 2.13 94

Dog Sled A885

1982, Mar. 28 Photo. *Perf. 13½*

3060 A885 55b Dog rescuing child 10 5
3061 A885 1 l Shepherd, dog 18 7
3062 A885 3 l Hunting dog 55 35
3063 A885 3.40 l shown 60 35
3064 A885 4 l Spitz, woman 70 40
3065 A885 4.80 l Guide dog, woman 80 45
3066 A885 5 l Dalmatian, girl 95 48
3067 A885 6 l Saint Bernard 1.00 40
Nos. 3060-3067 (8) 4.88 2.55

1 l, 3 l, 4 l, 4.80 l, 5 l, vertical.

Bran Castle, Brasov, 1377 A886

1982, May 6

3068 Sheet of 4, multi 2.75 2.75
a. A886 2.50 l shown 60 60
b. A886 2.50 l Hunedoara, Corvinilor, 1409 60 60
c. A886 2.50 l Sinaia, 1873 60 60
d. A886 2.50 l Iasi, 1905 60 60
3069 Sheet of 4, multi 2.75 2.75
a. A886 2.50 l Neuschwanstein 60 60
b. A886 2.50 l Stolzenfels 60 60
c. A886 2.50 l Katz-Loreley 60 60
d. A886 2.50 l Linderhof 60 60

Inter-European Cultural and Economic Cooperation.

Souvenir Sheet

Constantin Brancusi in Paris Studio — A887

1982, June 5

3070 A887 10 l multi 2.50 2.00

PHILEXFRANCE '82 Intl. Stamp Exhibition, Paris, June 11-21.

Gloria C-16 Combine Harvester — A888

1982, June 29

3071 A888 50b shown 8 5
3072 A888 1 l Dairy farm 18 8
3073 A888 1.50 l Apple orchard 28 10
3074 A888 2.50 l Vineyard 40 20
3075 A888 3 l Irrigation 50 28
Nos. 3071-3075,C250 (6) 2.04 1.01

Souvenir Sheet

3076 A888 10 l Village 2.50 2.00

Agricultural modernization. No. 3076 contains one stamp 50x38mm.

Resort Hotels and Beaches — A890

1 l, 2.50 l, 3 l, 5 l horiz.

1982, Aug. 30 Photo. *Perf. 13½*

3078 A890 50b Baile Felix 8 5
3079 A890 1 l Predeal 20 8
3080 A890 1.50 l Baile Herculane 28 10
3081 A890 2.50 l Eforie Nord 40 20
3082 A890 3 l Olimp 60 24
3083 A890 5 l Neptun 95 40
Nos. 3078-3083 (6) 2.51 1.07

Genesis of Romanian People, by Sabin Balasa — A891

1982, Sept. 6

3084 A891 1 l Legend, horiz. 20 8
3085 A891 1.50 l Contrasts, horiz. 28 10
3086 A891 3.50 l Relay Runner, horiz. 60 28
3087 A891 4 l shown 75 40

Souvenir Sheet

Merry Peasant Girl, by Nicolae Grigorescu (d. 1907) A892

1982, Sept. 30 Photo. *Perf. 13½*

3088 A892 10 l multi 1.75 1.75

Bucharest Intl. Fair A893

1982, Oct. 2

3089 A893 2 l Exhibition Hall, flag 35 18

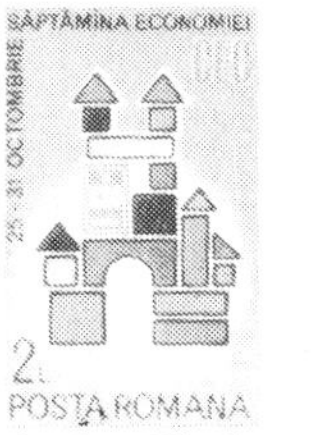

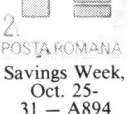

Savings Week, Oct. 25-31 — A894

Stamp Day — A895

1982, Oct. 25

3090 A894 1 l Girl holding bank book 18 8
3091 A894 2 l Poster 35 18

1982, Nov. 10

3092 A895 1 l Woman letter carrier 18 8
3093 A895 2 l Mailman 35 18

Scene from Ileana Sinziana, by Petre Ispirescu — A896

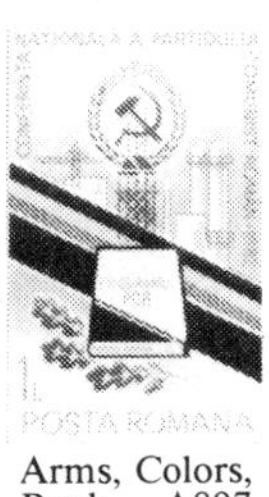
Arms, Colors, Book — A897

Fairytales: 50b, The Youngest Child and the Golden Apples, by Petre Ispirescu. 1 l, The Bear Hoaxed by the Fox, by Ion Creanga. 1.50 l, The Prince of Tear, by Mihai Eminescu. 2.50 l, The Little Bag with Two Coins Inside, by Ion Creanga. 5 l, Danila Prepeleac, by Ion Creanga.

1982, Nov. 30

3094 A896 50b multi 8 5
3095 A896 1 l multi 18 8
3096 A896 1.50 l multi 28 10
3097 A896 2.50 l multi 42 18
3098 A896 3 l multi 50 20
3099 A896 5 l multi 95 40
Nos. 3094-3099 (6) 2.41 1.01

1982, Dec. 16

3100 A897 1 l Closed book 18 8
3101 A897 2 l Open book 35 18

Natl. Communist Party Conference, Bucharest, Dec. 16-18.

A898

Designs: 50b, Wooden flask, Suceava. 1 l, Ceramic plate, Radauti. 1.50 l, Wooden scoop, Valea Mare, horiz. 2 l, Plate, jug, Vama. 3 l, Butter churn, wooden bucket, Moldavia. 3.50 l, Ceramic plates, Leheceni, horiz. 4 l, Wooden spoon, platter, Cluj. 5 l, Bowl, plate, Marginea. 6 l, Jug, flask, Bihor. 7 l, Spindle, shuttle, Transylvania. 7.50 l, Water buckets, Suceava. 8 l, Jug, Oboga; plate, Horezu. 10 l, Water buckets, Hunedoara, Suceava, horiz. 20 l, Wooden flask, beakers, Horezu. 30 l, Wooden spoons, Alba, horiz. 50 l, Ceramic dishes, Horezu.

1982, Dec. 22 Photo. *Perf. 13½*

3102 A898 50b red org 8 5
3103 A898 1 l dk blue 18 5
3104 A898 1.50 l org brn 28 5
3105 A898 2 l brt blue 35 5
3106 A898 3 l olive grn 50 5
3107 A898 3.50 l dk green 60 5
3108 A898 4 l lt brown 70 6
3109 A898 5 l gray blue 85 7

Size: 23x29mm, 29x23mm

3110 A898 6 l blue 1.00 8
3111 A898 7 l lake 1.25 9
3112 A898 7.50 l red vio 1.40 9
3113 A898 8 l brt grn 1.40 10
3114 A898 10 l red 1.75 12
3118 A898 20 l purple 3.50 25
3116 A898 30 l Prussian bl 5.00 38
3117 A898 50 l dk brown 8.50 65
Nos. 3102-3117 (16) 27.34 2.19

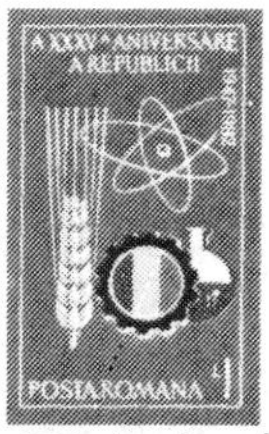

35th Anniv. of Republic A899

Grigore Manolescu (1857-92), as Hamlet A900

1982, Dec. 27

3118 A899 1 l Symbols of development 18 8
3119 A899 2 l Flag 35 18

1983, Feb. 28

Actors or Actresses in Famous Roles: 50b, Matei Millo (1814-1896) in The Discontented. 1 l, Mihail Pascaly (1829-1882) in Director Milo. 1.50 l, Aristizza Romanescu (1854-1918), in The Dogs. 2 l, C. I. Nottara (1859-1935) in Snowstorm. 3 l, Agatha Birsescu (1857-1939) in Medea. 4 l, Ion Brezeanu (1869-1940) in The Lost Letter. 5 l, Aristide Demetriad (1872-1930) in The Despotic Prince.

3120 A900 50b multi 8 5
3121 A900 1 l multi 18 8
3122 A900 1.50 l multi 28 10

3123	A900	2 l	multi	35	18
3124	A900	2.50 l	multi	42	18
3125	A900	3 l	multi	50	20
3126	A900	4 l	multi	70	35
3127	A900	5 l	multi	85	40
			Nos. 3120-3127 (8)	3.36	1.54

Hugo Grotius (1583-1645), Dutch Jurist — A901

1983, Apr. 30

3128	A901	2 l	brown	35	18

Romanian-Made Vehicles — A902

1983, May 3

3129	A902	50b	ARO-10	8	5
3130	A902	1 l	Dacia, 1300 station wagon	18	8
3131	A902	1.50 l	ARO-242 jeep	25	10
3132	A902	2.50 l	ARO-244	42	18
3133	A902	4 l	Dacia 1310	70	35
3134	A902	5 l	OLTCIT club passenger car	85	40
			Nos. 3129-3134 (6)	2.48	1.16

Johannes Kepler (1571-1630) — A903

Famous Men: No. 3135: b. Alexander von Humboldt (1769-1859), explorer. c. Goethe (1749-1832). d. Richard Wagner (1813-1883), composer. No. 3136: a. Ioan Andreescu (1850-1882), painter. b. George Constantinescu (1881-1965), engineer. c. Tudor Arghezi (1880-1967), poet. d. C.I. Parhon (1874-1969), endocrinologist.

1983, May 16

3135		Sheet of 4	2.50	2.50
a.-d.	A903	3 l, multi	55	55
3136		Sheet of 4	2.50	2.50
a.-d.	A903	3 l, multi	55	55

Inter-European Cultural and Economic Cooperation.

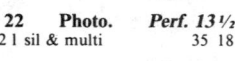

Workers' Struggle, 50th Anniv. — A904

1983, July 22 Photo. *Perf. 13½*

3137	A904	2 l	sil & multi	35	18

The indexes in each volume of the Scott Catalogue contain many listings which help to identify stamps.

Birds — A905

1983, Oct. 28 Photo. *Perf. 13½*

3138	A905	50b	Luscinia svecica	8	5
3139	A905	1 l	Sturnus roseus	18	8
3140	A905	1.50 l	Coracias garrulus	25	12
3141	A905	2.50 l	Merops apiaster	42	20
3142	A905	4 l	Emberiza schoeniclus	70	35
3143	A905	5 l	Lanius minor	85	42
			Nos. 3138-3143 (6)	2.48	1.22

Water Sports A906

1983, Sept. 16 Photo. *Perf. 13½*

3144	A906	50b	Kayak	8	5
3145	A906	1 l	Water polo	18	8
3146	A906	1.50 l	Canadian one-man canoes	25	12
3147	A906	2.50 l	Diving	42	20
3148	A906	4 l	Singles rowing	70	35
3149	A906	5 l	Swimming	85	42
			Nos. 3144-3149 (6)	2.48	1.22

Stamp Day A907

1983, Oct. 24

3150	A907	1 l	Mailman on bicycle	18	8
3151	A907	3.50 l	with 3 l label, flag	1.10	55

Souvenir Sheet

3152	A907	10 l	Unloading mail plane	1.75	1.75

No. 3152 is airmail, contains one stamp 38x51mm.

Geum Reptans A908

Flora (No. 3154): b. Papaver dubium. c. Carlina acaulis. d. Paeonia peregrina. e. Gentiana excisa. Fauna (No. 3155): a. Sciurus vulgaria. b. Grammia quenselii. c. Dendrocopos medius. d. Lynx. e. Tichodroma muraria.

1983, Oct. 28 Photo. *Perf. 13½*

3154		Strip of 5	1.40	1.40
a.-e.	A908	1 l multi	24	24
3155		Strip of 5	1.40	1.40
a.-e.	A908	1 l multi	24	24

Issued in sheets of 15.

Lady with Feather, by Cornelius Baba — A909

1983, Nov. 3

3156	A909	1 l	shown	18	8
3157	A909	2 l	Citizens	35	18
3158	A909	3 l	Farmers, horiz.	50	25
3159	A909	4 l	Resting in the Field, horiz.	70	35

Pact with Romania, 65th Anniv. — A910

1983, Nov. 30

3160	A910	1 l	Banner, emblem	18	8
3161	A910	2 l	Congress building, flags	35	18

Flags of Participating Countries, Post Office, Mailman — A911

1983, Dec. 17

3162	A911	1 l	shown	*18*	*8*
3163	A911	2 l	Congress building, woman letter carrier	*35*	*18*

Souvenir Sheet

3164	A911	10 l	Flags, Congress building	*1.75*	*1.75*

BALKANFILA '83 Stamp Exhibition, Bucharest. No. 3164 contains one stamp 38x50mm.

Souvenir Sheet

Orient Express Centenary (Paris-Istanbul) — A912

1983, Dec. 30

3165	A912	10 l	Leaving Gara de Nord, Bucharest, 1883	2.50	2.50

Black control number. Size: 91x79mm.

1984 Winter Olympics A913

1984, Jan. 14

3166	A913	50b	Cross-country skiing	8	5
3167	A913	1 l	Biathlon	18	8
3168	A913	1.50 l	Figure skating	25	12
3169	A913	2 l	Speed skating	35	18
3170	A913	3 l	Hockey	50	25
3171	A913	3.50 l	Bobsledding	60	30
3172	A913	4 l	Luge	70	35
3173	A913	5 l	Skiing	85	42
			Nos. 3166-3173 (8)	3.51	1.75

A 10 l imperf souvenir sheet exists showing ski jumping; red control number.

Souvenir Sheet

Prince Alexandru Ioan Cuza, Arms — A914

1984, Jan. 24 Photo. *Perf. 13½*

3174	A914	10 l	multi	1.75	1.75

Union of Moldavia and Walachia Provinces, 125th anniv.

Palace of Udriste Naturel (1596-1658), Chancery Official — A915

Famous Men: 1 l, Miron Costin (1633-91), poet. 1.50 l, Cisan (Marcu Giurgiu), (1733-85), peasant revolt leader. 2 l, Simion Barnutiu (1808-64), scientist. 3.50 l, Duiliu Zamfirescu (1858-1922), poet. 4 l, Nicolas Milescu (1636-1708), Court official.

1984, Feb. 8

3175	A915	50b	multi	6	5
3176	A915	1 l	multi	10	6
3177	A915	1.50 l	multi	16	8
3178	A915	2 l	multi	22	12
3179	A915	3.50 l	multi	38	20
3180	A915	4 l	multi	45	22
			Nos. 3175-3180 (6)	1.37	73

Souvenir Sheet

15th Balkan Chess Match, Herculane A916

Designs: Four successive moves culminating in checkmate.

1984, Feb. 20 Photo. *Perf. 13½*

3181		Sheet of 4	2.50	2.50
a.-d.	A916	3 l, Any single	60	60

Orsova Bridge A917

Bridges: No. 3182: b. Arges. c. Basarabi. d. Ohaba. No. 3183: a. Kohlbrand-Germany. b. Bosfor-Turcia. c. Europa-Austria. d. Turnului-Anglia.

1984, Apr. 24

3182		Sheet of 4	2.50	2.50
a.-d	A917	3 l multi	55	55
3183		Sheet of 4	2.50	2.50
a.-d	A917	3 l multi	55	55

Inter-European Cultural and Economic Cooperation.

Environmental Protection — A919

1984, Apr. 26 Photo. *Perf. 13½*

3190	A919	1 l Sunflower	22	12
3191	A919	2 l Stag	45	22
3192	A919	3 l Fish	70	35
3193	A919	4 l Bird	90	45

Danube Flowers A920

45th Anniv., Youth Anti-Fascist Committee A921

1984, Apr. 30 Photo. *Perf. 13½*

3194	A920	50b Sagittaria sagittifolia	12	6
3195	A920	1 l Iris pseudacorus	22	12
3196	A920	1.50 l Butomus umbellatus	32	16
3197	A920	3 l Nymphaea alba, horiz.	70	35
3198	A920	4 l Nymphoides peltata, horiz.	90	45
3199	A920	5 l Nuphar luteum, horiz.	1.10	60
		Nos. 3194-3199 (6)	3.36	1.74

1984, Apr. 30 Photo. *Perf. 13½*

3200	A921	2 l multi	45	22

25th Congress, Ear, Nose and Throat Medicine — A922

1984, May 30 Photo. *Perf. 13½*

3201	A922	2 l Congress seal	45	22

Souvenir Sheets

European Soccer Cup Championships — A922a

Soccer players and flags of: c, Romania. d, West Germany. e, Portugal. f, Spain. g, France. h, Belgium. i, Jugoslavia. j, Denmark.

1984, June 7 Photo. *Perf. 13½*

3201A		Sheet of 4	2.50	2.50
c.-f	A922a	3 l, Any single	60	60
3201B		Sheet of 4	2.50	2.50
g.-i	A922a	3 l, Any single	60	60

Summer Olympics — A923

1984, July 2 Photo. *Perf. 13½*

3202	A923	50b Boxing	10	6
3203	A923	1 l Rowing	20	10
3204	A923	1.50 l Team handball	30	15
3205	A923	2 l Judo	40	20
3206	A923	3 l Wrestling	60	30
3207	A923	3.50 l Fencing	75	38
3208	A923	4 l Kayak	80	40
3209	A923	5 l Swimming	1.00	50
		Nos. 3202-3209 (8)	4.15	2.09

Three imperf. 10 l souvenir sheets, one showing long jumping and two showing gymnastics, with red control numbers in margin exist.

Famous Romanians — A924

1984, July 28 Photo. *Perf. 13½*

3210	A924	1 l Micai Ciuca	20	10
3211	A924	2 l Petre Aurelian	40	20
3212	A924	3 l Alexandru Vlahuta	60	30
3213	A924	4 l Dimitrie Leonida	80	40

40th Anniv., Romanian Revolution A925

1984, Aug. 17 Photo. *Perf. 13½*

3214	A925	2 l multi	40	20

Romanian Horses — A926

1984, Aug. 30 Photo. *Perf. 13½*

3215	A926	50b Lippizaner	10	6
3216	A926	1 l Hutul	20	10
3217	A926	1.50 l Bucovina	30	15
3218	A926	2.50 l Nonius	50	28
3219	A926	4 l Arabian	80	40
3220	A926	5 l Romanian Mixed-breed	1.00	50
		Nos. 3215-3220 (6)	2.90	1.49

200th Anniv., 1784 Uprisings A927

1984, Nov. 1 Photo. *Perf. 13½*

3221	A927	2 l Monument	40	20

Children — A928

Paintings: 50b, Portrait of Child, by T. Aman. 1 l, Shepherd, by N. Grigorescu. 2 l, Girl with Orange, by S. Luchian. 3 l, Portrait of Child, by N. Tonitza. 4 l, Portrait of Boy, by S. Popp. 5 l, Portrait of Girl, by I. Tuculescu.

1984, Nov. 10 Photo. *Perf. 13½*

3222	A928	50b multi	10	6
3223	A928	1 l multi	20	10
3224	A928	2 l multi	40	20
3225	A928	3 l multi	60	30
3226	A928	4 l multi	80	40
3227	A928	5 l multi	1.00	50
		Nos. 3222-3227 (6)	3.10	1.56

Stamp Day A929

1984, Nov. 15 Photo. *Perf. 13½*

3228	A929	2 l Mail coach	60	30

No. 3228 se-tenant with 1 l Romanian Philatelic Association charity label.

Souvenir Sheet

13th Party Congress A930

1984, Nov. 17 Photo. *Perf. 13½*

3229	A930	10 l Party symbols	2.00	2.00

Souvenir Sheets

Romanian Medalists, 1984 Summer Olympic Games — A931

Designs, No. 3230: a., Ecaterina Szabo, gymnastic floor exercise. b., 500-meter four-women kayak. c., Anisoara Stanciu, long jump. d., Greco-Roman wrestling. e., Mircea Fratica, half middleweight judo. f., Corneliu Ion, rapid fire pistol. No. 3231: a., 1000-meter two-man scull. b., Weight lifting. c., Women's relays. d., Canoeing, pair oars without coxswain. e., Fencing, team foil. f., Ecaterina Szabo, all-around gymnastics.

1984, Oct. 29 Photo. *Perf. 13½*

3230		Sheet of 6	3.75	3.75
a.-f	A931	3 l, Any single	60	60
3231		Sheet of 6	3.75	3.75
a.-f	A931	3 l, Any single	60	60

Pelicans of the Danube Delta — A932

1984, Dec. 15

3232	A932	50b Flying	10	6
3233	A932	1 l On ground	20	10
3234	A932	1 l In water	20	10
3235	A932	2 l Nesting	40	20

Famous Men — A933

Designs: 50b, Dr. Petru Groza (1884-1958). 1 l, Alexandru Odobescu (1834-1895). 2 l, Dr. Carol Davila (1828-1884). 3 l, Dr. Nicolae G. Lupu (1884-1966). 4 l, Dr. Daniel Danielopolu (1884-1955). 5 l, Panait Istrati (1884-1935).

1984, Dec. 26

3236	A933	50b multi	10	6
3237	A933	1 l multi	20	10
3238	A933	2 l multi	40	20
3239	A933	3 l multi	60	30
3240	A933	4 l multi	80	40
3241	A933	5 l multi	1.00	50
		Nos. 3236-3241 (6)	3.10	1.56

Timisoara Power Station, Electric Street Lights, Cent. A934

1984, Dec. 29

3242	A934	1 l Generator, 1884	20	10
3243	A934	2 l Street arc lamp, Timisoara, 1884	40	20

Souvenir Sheets

European Music Year A935

Composers and opera houses, No. 3244: a., Moscow Theater, Tchaichovsky (1840-1893). b., Bucharest Theater, George Enescu (1881-1955). c., Dresden Opera, Wagner (1813-1883). d., Warsaw Opera, Stanislaw Moniuszko (1819-1872). No. 3245: a., Paris Opera, Gounod (1818-1893). b., Munich Opera, Strauss (1864-1949). c., Vienna Opera, Mozart (1756-1791). d., La Scala, Milan, Verdi (1813-1901).

1985, Mar. 28

3244	Sheet of 4	2.50	2.50
a.-d	A935 3 l, Any single	58	58
3245	Sheet of 4	2.50	2.50
a.-d	A935 3 l, Any single	58	58

August T. Laurian (1810-1881), Linguist and Historian A936

Intl. Youth Year A937

Famous men: 1 l, Grigore Alexandrescu (1810-1885), author. 1.50 l, Gheorghe Pop de Basesti (1835-1919), politician. 2 l, Mateiu Caragiale (1885-1936), author. 3 l, Gheorghe Ionescu-Sisesti (1885-1967), scientist. 4 l, Liviu Rebreanu (1885-1944), author.

1985, Mar. 29

3246	A936	50b	multi	10	6
3247	A936	1 l	multi	20	10
3248	A936	1.50 l	multi	30	16
3249	A936	2 l	multi	40	20
3250	A936	3 l	multi	60	30
3251	A936	4 l	multi	80	40
			Nos. 3246-3251 (6)	2.40	1.22

1985, Apr. 15

3252	A937	1 l	Scientific research	20	10
3253	A937	2 l	Construction	40	20

Souvenir Sheet

3254	A937	10 l	Intl. solidarity	2.00	2.00

No. 3254 contains one stamp 54x42mm.

Wildlife Conservation A938

End of World War II, 40th Anniv. A939

1985, May 6

3255	A938	50b	Nyctereutes procyonoides	10	6
3256	A938	1 l	Perdix perdix	20	10
3257	A938	1.50 l	Nyctea scandiaca	30	16
3258	A938	2 l	Martes martes	40	20
3259	A938	3 l	Meles meles	60	30
3260	A938	3.50 l	Lutra lutra	75	38
3261	A938	4 l	Tetrao urogallus	80	40
3262	A938	5 l	Otis tarda	1.00	50
			Nos. 3255-3262 (8)	4.15	2.10

1985, May 9

3263	A939	2 l	War monument, natl. and party flags	40	20

Union of Communist Youth, 12th Congress — A940

1985, May 14

3264	A940	2 l	Emblem	40	20

Danube-Black Sea Canal Opening, May 26, 1984 — A942

1985, June 7 *Perf. 13½*

3266	A942	1 l	Canal, map	20	10
3267	A942	2 l	Bridge over lock, Cernavoda	40	20
3268	A942	3 l	Bridge over canal, Medgidea	60	30
3269	A942	4 l	Agigea lock, bridge	80	40

Souvenir Sheet

3270	A942	10 l	Opening ceremony, Cernavoda, Ceaucescu	2.00	2.00

No. 3270 contains one stamp 54x42mm.

Audubon Birth Bicentenary — A943

North American bird species. Nos. 3271-3275 vert.

1985, June 26

3271	A943	50b	Turdus migratorius	10	6
3272	A943	1 l	Pelecanus occidentalis	20	10
3273	A943	1.50 l	Nyctanassa violarea	30	16
3274	A943	2 l	Icterus galbula	40	10
3275	A943	3 l	Podiceps grisegena	60	30
3276	A943	4 l	Anas platyrhynchos	80	40
			Nos. 3271-3276 (6)	2.40	1.12

20th Century Paintings by Ion Tuculescu — A944

1985, July 13

3277	A944	1 l	Fire, vert.	20	10
3278	A944	2 l	Circuit, vert.	40	20
3279	A944	3 l	Interior	60	30
3280	A944	4 l	Sunset	80	40

Butterflies A945

1985, July 15

3281	A945	50b	Inachis io	10	6
3282	A945	1 l	Papilio machaon	20	10
3283	A945	2 l	Vanessa atalanta	40	20
3284	A945	3 l	Saturnia pavonia	60	30
3285	A945	4 l	Ammobiota festiva	80	40
3286	A945	5 l	Smerinthus ocellatus	1.00	50
			Nos. 3281-3286 (6)	3.10	1.56

Natl. Communist Party Achievements — A946

Natl. and party flags, and: 1 l, Transfagarasan Mountain Road. 2 l, Danube-Black Sea Canal. 3 l, Bucharest Underground Railway. 4 l, Irrigation.

1985, July 29

3287	A946	1 l	multi	20	10
3288	A946	2 l	multi	40	20
3289	A946	3 l	multi	60	30
3290	A946	4 l	multi	80	40

Election of Gen.-Sec. Nicolae Ceausescu, 20th anniv.; Natl. Communist Congress, 20th anniv.

Romanian Socialist Constitution, 20th Anniv. — A947

1985, Aug. 5

3291	A947	1 l	Arms, wheat, dove	20	10
3292	A947	2 l	Arms, eternal flame	40	20

1986 World Cup Soccer Preliminaries — A948

Flags of participants; Great Britain, Northern Ireland, Romania, Finland, Turkey and: 50b, Sliding tackle. 1 l, Trapping the ball. 1.50 l, Heading the ball. 2 l, Dribble. 3 l, Tackle. 4 l, Scissor kick. 10 l, Dribble, diff.

1985, Oct. 15

3293	A948	50b	multi	10	6
3294	A948	1 l	multi	20	10
3295	A948	1.50 l	multi	30	16
3296	A948	2 l	multi	40	20
3297	A948	3 l	multi	60	30
3298	A948	4 l	multi	80	40
			Nos. 3293-3298 (6)	2.40	1.22

Souvenir Sheet

Motorcycle Centenary — A949

1985, Aug. 22 **Photo.** *Perf. 13½*

3300	A949	10 l	1885 Daimler Einspur	2.00	1.00

Retezat Natl. Park, 50th Anniv. — A950

1985, Aug. 29

3301	A950	50b	Senecio glaberrimus	10	6
3302	A950	1 l	Rupicapra rupicapra	20	10
3303	A950	2 l	Centaurea retezatensis	40	20
3304	A950	3 l	Viola dacica	60	30
3305	A950	4 l	Marmota marmota	80	40
3306	A950	5 l	Aquila chrysaetos	1.00	50
			Nos. 3301-3306 (6)	3.10	1.56

Souvenir Sheet

3307	A950	10 l	Lynx lynx	2.00	1.00

No. 3307 contains one stamp 42x54mm.

Tractors Manufactured by Universal — A951

1985, Sept. 10

3308	A951	50b	530 DTC	10	6
3309	A951	1 l	550 M HC	20	10
3310	A951	1.50 l	650 Super	30	15
3311	A951	2 l	850	40	20
3312	A951	3 l	S 1801 IF	60	30
3313	A951	4 l	A 3602 IF	80	40
			Nos. 3308-3313 (6)	2.40	1.21

Folk Costumes — A952

Women's and men's costumes from same region printed se-tenant, in continuous design.

1985, Sept. 28

3314	A952	50b	Muscel woman	10	6
3315	A952	50b	Muscel man	10	6
3316	A952	1.50 l	Bistrita-Nasaud woman	30	15
3317	A952	1.50 l	Bistrita-Nasaud man	30	15
3318	A952	2 l	Vrancea woman	40	20

3319 A952 2 l Vrancea man 40 20
3320 A952 3 l Vilcea woman 60 30
3321 A952 3 l Vilcea man 60 30
Nos. 3314-3321 (8) 2.80 1.42

Admission to UN, 30th Anniv. — A953

1985, Oct. 21
3322 A953 2 l multi 40 20

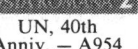

UN, 40th Anniv. — A954

Mineral Flowers — A955

1985, Oct. 21
3323 A954 2 l multi 40 20

1985, Oct. 28
3324 A955 50b Quartz and calcite, Herja 10 6
3325 A955 1 l Copper, Altin Tepe 20 10
3326 A955 2 l Gypsum, Cavnic 30 20
3327 A955 3 l Quartz, Ocna de Fier 60 30
3328 A955 4 l Stibium, Baiut 80 40
3329 A955 5 l Tetrahedrite, Cavnic 1.00 50
Nos. 3324-3329 (6) 3.00 1.56

Stamp Day A956

1985, Oct. 29
3330 A956 2 l multi 40 20

No. 3330 se-tenant with 1 l Romanian Philatelic Association charity label.

A Connecticut Yankee in King Arthur's Court, by Mark Twain — A957

The Three Brothers, by Jacob and Wilhelm Grimm — A958

Disney characters in classic fairy tales.

1985, Nov. 28
3331 A957 50b Hank Morgan awakes in Camelot 10 6
3332 A957 50b Predicts eclipse of sun 10 6
3333 A957 50b Mounting horse 10 6
3334 A957 50b Sir Sagramor 10 6
3335 A958 1 l Fencing with shadow 20 10
3336 A958 1 l Fencing, father 20 10
3337 A958 1 l Shoeing a horse 20 10
3338 A958 1 l Barber, rabbit 20 10
3339 A958 1 l Father, three sons 20 10
Nos. 3331-3339 (9) 1.40 74

Souvenir Sheets

3340 A957 5 l Tournament of knights 1.00 50
3341 A958 5 l Cottage 1.00 50

Miniature Sheets

Intereuropa 1986 — A959

Fauna and flora, No. 3343: a., Felis silvestris. b., Mustela erminea. c., Tetrao urogallus. d., Urso arctos. No. 3344: a., Dianthus callizonus. b., Pinus cembra. c., Salix sp. d., Rose pendulina.

1986, Mar. 25 Photo. *Perf. 13½*
3343 Sheet of 4 2.50 2.50
a.-d A959 3 l, any single 60 60
3344 Sheet of 4 2.50 2.50
a.-d A959 3 l, any single 60 60

Inventors and Adventurers — A960

Designs: 1 l, Orville and Wilbur Wright, Wright Flyer. 1.50 l, Jacques Cousteau, research vessel Calypso. 2 l, Amelia Earhart, Lockheed Electra. 3 l, Charles Lindbergh, Spirit of St. Louis. 3.50 l, Sir Edmund Hillary (1919-), first man to reach Mt. Everest summit. 4 l, Robert Edwin Peary, Arctic explorer. 5 l, Adm. Richard Byrd, explorer. 6 l, Neil Armstrong, first man on moon.

1985, Dec. 25 Photo. *Perf. 13½*
3345 A960 1 l multi 35 18
3346 A960 1.50 l multi 50 25
3347 A960 2 l multi 70 35
3348 A960 3 l multi 1.00 50
3349 A960 3.50 l multi 1.25 60
3350 A960 4 l multi 1.40 70
3351 A960 5 l multi 1.75 85
3352 A960 6 l multi 2.00 1.00
Nos. 3345-3352 (8) 8.95 4.43

Paintings by Nicolae Tonitza — A961

1986, Mar. 12 Photo. *Perf. 13½*
3353 A961 1 l Nina in Green 35 18
3354 A961 2 l Irina 70 35
3355 A961 3 l Woodman's Daughter 1.00 50
3356 A961 4 l Woman on the Verandah 1.40 70

Color Animated Films, 50th Anniv. — A962

Walt Disney characters in Concert Orchestra, 1935.

1986, Apr. 10 Photo. *Perf. 13½*
3357 A962 50b Clarabelle 18 8
3358 A962 50b Mickey Mouse 18 8
3359 A962 50b Paddy and Peter 18 8
3360 A962 50b Goofy 18 8
3361 A962 1 l Donald Duck 35 18
3362 A962 1 l Mickey Mouse, diff. 35 18
3363 A962 1 l Mickey and Donald 35 18
3364 A962 1 l Horace 35 18
3365 A962 1 l Donald and trombonist 35 18
Nos. 3357-3365 (9) 2.47 1.22

Souvenir Sheet

3366 A962 5 l Finale 1.75 85

1986 World Cup Soccer Championships, Mexico — A963

Various soccer plays and flags: 50b, Italy vs. Bulgaria. 1 l, Mexico vs. Belgium. 2 l, Canada vs. France. 3 l, Brazil vs. Spain. 4 l, Uruguay vs. Germany. 5 l, Morocco vs. Poland.

1986, May 9
3367 A963 50b multi 18 8
3368 A963 1 l multi 35 18
3369 A963 2 l multi 70 35
3370 A963 3 l multi 1.00 50
3371 A963 4 l multi 1.40 70
3372 A963 5 l multi 1.75 85
Nos. 3367-3372 (6) 5.38 2.66

An imperf. 10 l airmail souvenir sheet exists picturing stadium, flags of previous winners, satellite and map.

Hotels — A964

1986, Apr. 23 Photo. *Perf. 13½*
3373 A964 50b Diana, Herculane 18 8
3374 A964 1 l Termal, Felix 35 18
3375 A964 2 l Delfin, Meduza and Steaua de Mare, Eforie Nord 70 35
3376 A964 3 l Caciulata, Calimanesti Caciulata 1.00 50
3377 A964 4 l Palas, Slanic Moldova 1.40 70
3378 A964 5 l Bradet, Sovata 1.75 85
Nos. 3373-3378 (6) 5.38 2.66

Nicolae Ceausescu, Party Flag — A965

1986, May 8 Photo. *Perf. 13½*
3379 A965 2 l multi 70 35

Natl. Communist Party, 65th anniv.

Flowers — A966

1986, June 25 Photo. *Perf. 13½*
3380 A966 50b Tulipa gesneriana 18 18
3381 A966 1 l Iris hispanica 35 18
3382 A966 2 l Rosa hybrida 70 35
3383 A966 3 l Anemone coronaria 1.00 50
3384 A966 4 l Freesia refracta 1.40 70
3385 A966 5 l Chrysanthemum indicum 1.75 85
Nos. 3380-3385 (6) 5.38 2.76

Mircea the Great, Ruler of Wallachia, 1386-1418 — A967

1986, July 17 Photo. *Perf. 13½*
3386 A967 2 l multi 70 35

Ascent to the throne, 600th anniv.

Open Air Museum of Historic Dwellings, Bucharest, 50th Anniv. — A968

1986, July 21

3387	A968	50b Alba	18	8
3388	A968	1 l Arges	35	18
3389	A968	2 l Constantia	70	35
3390	A968	3 l Timis	1.00	50
3391	A968	4 l Neamt	1.40	70
3392	A968	5 l Gorj	1.75	85
		Nos. 3387-3392 (6)	5.38	2.66

Polar Research — A969

Exploration: 50b, Julius Popper, exploration of Tierra del Fuego (1886-93). 1 l, Bazil G. Assan, exploration of Spitzbergen (1896). 2 l, Emil Racovita, Antarctic expedition (1897-99). 3 l, Constantin Dumbrava, exploration of Greenland (1927-8). 4 l, Romanians with the 17th Soviet Antarctic expedition (1971-72). 5 l, Research on krill fishing (1977-80).

1986, July 23 Photo. *Perf. 13½*

3393	A969	50b multi	18	8
3394	A969	1 l multi	35	18
3395	A969	2 l multi	70	35
3396	A969	3 l multi	1.00	50
3397	A969	4 l multi	1.40	70
3398	A969	5 l multi	1.75	85
		Nos. 3393-3398 (6)	5.38	2.66

Natl. Cycling Championships A970

Various athletes.

1986, Aug. 29

3399	A970	1 l multi	35	18
3400	A970	2 l multi	70	35
3401	A970	3 l multi	1.00	50
3402	A970	4 l multi	1.40	70

Souvenir Sheet

3403	A970	10 l multi	3.50	1.75

No. 3403 contains one stamp 42x54mm.

Souvenir Sheet

Intl. Peace Year — A971

1986, July 25

3404	A971	5 l multi	1.75	85

Fungi — A972

1986, Aug. 15

3405	A972	50b Amanita rubescens	18	8
3406	A972	1 l Boletus luridus	35	18
3407	A972	2 l Lactarius piperatus	70	35
3408	A972	3 l Lepiota clypeolaria	1.00	50
3409	A972	4 l Russula cyanoxantha	1.40	70
3410	A972	5 l Tremiscus helvelloides	1.75	85
		Nos. 3405-3410 (6)	5.38	2.66

Famous Men — A973

Designs: 50b, Petru Maior (c. 1761-1821), historian. 1 l, George Topirceanu (1886-1937), doctor. 2 l, Henri Coanda (1886-1972), engineer. 3 l, Constantin Budeanu (1886-1959), engineer.

1986, Nov. 10 Photo. *Perf. 13½*

3411	A973	50b dl cl, gold & dk bl grn	18	8
3412	A973	1 l sl grn, gold & dk lil rose	35	18
3413	A973	2 l rose cl, gold & brt bl	70	35
3414	A973	3 l chlky bl, gold & choc	1.00	50

UNESCO, 40th Anniv. A974

1986, Nov. 10

3415	A974	4 l multi	1.40	70

Stamp Day — A975

1986, Nov. 15

3416	A975	2 l multi	1.00	50

No. 3416 printed se-tenant in a continuous design with 1 l Romanian Philatelic Association charity label.

Industry A976

1986, Nov. 28

3417	A976	50b F-300 oil rigs, vert.	18	8
3418	A976	1 l Promex excavator	35	18
3419	A976	2 l Pitesti refinery, vert.	70	35
3420	A976	3 l 110-ton dump truck	1.00	50
3421	A976	4 l Coral computer, vert.	1.40	70
3422	A976	5 l 350-megawatt turbine	1.75	85
		Nos. 3417-3422 (6)	5.38	2.66

Folk Costumes — A977

1986, Dec. 26

3423	A977	50b Capra	18	8
3424	A977	1 l Sorcova	35	18
3425	A977	2 l Plugusorul	70	35
3426	A977	3 l Buhaiul	1.00	50
3427	A977	4 l Caiutii	1.40	70
3428	A977	5 l Uratorii	1.75	85
		Nos. 3423-3428 (6)	5.38	2.66

Recycling Campaign — A978

1986, Dec. 30

3429	A978	1 l Metal	35	18
3430	A978	2 l Trees	70	35

Young Communists' League, 65th Anniv. — A979

1987, Mar. 18 Photo. *Perf. 13½*

3431	A979	1 l Flags, youth	35	18
3432	A979	2 l Emblem	70	35
3433	A979	3 l Flags, youth, diff.	1.00	50

Miniature Sheets

Intereuropa — A980

Modern architecture, No. 3434: a., Exposition Pavilion, Bucharest. b., Intercontinental Hotel, Bucharest. c., Europa Hotel, Black Sea coast. d., Polytechnic Institute, Bucharest. No. 3435: a., Administration Building, Satu Mare. b., House of Young Pioneers, Bucharest. c., Valahia Hotel, Tirgoviste. d., Caciulata Hotel, Caciulata.

1987, May 18 Photo. *Perf. 13½*

3434		Sheet of 4	3.00	3.00
a.-d.	A980	3 l, any single	75	75
3435		Sheet of 4	3.00	3.00
a.-d.	A980	3 l, any single	75	75

Collective Farming, 25th Anniv. — A981

1987, Apr. 25 Photo. *Perf. 13½*

3436	A981	2 l multi	50	25

Birch Trees by the Lakeside, by I. Andreescu — A982

Paintings in Romanian museums: 1 l, Young Peasant Girls Spinning, by N. Grigorescu. 2 l, Washerwoman, by S. Luchian. 3 l, Inside the Peasant's Cottage, by S. Dimitrescu. 4 l, Winter Landscape, by A. Ciucurencu. 5 l, Winter in Bucharest, by N. Tonitza, vert.

1987, Apr. 28

3437	A982	50b multi	14	7
3438	A982	1 l multi	25	14
3439	A982	2 l multi	50	25
3440	A982	3 l multi	75	38
3441	A982	4 l multi	1.00	50
3442	A982	5 l multi	1.40	70
		Nos. 3437-3442 (6)	4.04	2.04

Peasant Uprising of 1907, 80th Anniv. — A983

1987, May 30

3443	A983	2 l multi	50	25

Men's World Handball Championships — A984

Various plays.

1987, July 15

3444	A984	50b multi, vert.	14	7
3445	A984	1 l multi	25	14
3446	A984	2 l multi, vert.	50	25
3447	A984	3 l multi	75	38
3448	A984	4 l multi, vert.	1.00	50
3449	A984	5 l multi	1.40	70
		Nos. 3444-3449 (6)	4.04	2.04

A985

Natl. Currency — A986

1987, July 15

3450 A985 1 l multi 25 14

Souvenir Sheet

3451 A986 10 l multi 2.50 2.50

Landscapes A987

1987, July 31 Photo. *Perf. 13½*

3452 A987 50b Pelicans over the Danube Delta 14 7
3453 A987 1 l Transfagarasan Highway 25 14
3454 A987 2 l Hairpin curve, Bicazului 50 25
3455 A987 3 l Limestone peaks, Mt. Ceahlau 75 38
3456 A987 4 l Lake Capra, Mt. Fagaras 1.00 50
3457 A987 5 l Orchard, Borsa 1.25 70
Nos. 3452-3457 (6) 3.89 2.04

A988

Scenes from Fairy Tale by Peter Ispirescu (b. 1887) — A988a

1987, Sept. 25 Photo. *Perf. 13½*

3458 A988 50b shown 14 7
3459 A988 1 l multi, diff. 28 14
3460 A988 2 l multi, diff. 60 28
3461 A988 3 l multi, diff. 90 45
3462 A988 4 l multi, diff. 1.25 60
3463 A988 5 l multi, diff. 1.50 70
Nos. 3458-3463 (6) 4.67 2.24

Souvenir Sheet

3464 A988a 10 l shown 3.00 3.00

Miniature Sheets

Flora and Fauna A989

Designs, No. 3465: a., Aquilegia alpina. b., Pulsatilla vernalis. c., Aster alpinus. d., Soldanella pusilla baumg. e., Lilium bulbiferum. f., Arctostaphylos uva-ursi. g., Crocus vernus. h., Crepis aurea. i., Cypripedium calceolus. j., Centaurea nervosa. k., Dryas octopetala. l., Gentiana excisa.

No. 3466: a., Martes martes. b., Felis lynx. c., Ursus maritimus. d., Lutra lutra. e., Bison bonasus. f., Branta ruficollis. g., Phoenicopterus ruber. h., Otis tarda. i., Lyrurus tetrix. j., Gypaetus barbatus. k., Vormela peregusna. l., Oxyura leucocephala.

1987, Oct. 16

3465 Sheet of 12, flora
a.-l A989 1 l multi
3466 Sheet of 12, fauna
a.-l A989 1 l multi

Souvenir Sheet

PHILATELIA '87, Cologne — A990

1987, Oct. 19

3467 Sheet of 2 + 2 labels 1.50 1.50
a A990 3 l Bucharest city seal 75 75
b A990 3 l Cologne city arms 75 75

Locomotives — A991

1987, Oct. 15

3468 A991 50bL 45 H 14 7
3469 A991 1 l LDE 125 28 14
3470 A991 2 l LDH 70 60 28
3471 A991 3 l LDE 2100 90 45
3472 A991 4 l LDE 3000 1.25 60
3473 A991 5 l LE 5100 1.50 70
Nos. 3468-3473 (6) 4.67 2.24

Folk Costumes — A992

1987, Nov. 7

3474 A992 1 l Tirnave (woman) 28 14
3475 A992 1 l Tirnave (man) 28 14
3476 A992 2 l Buzau (woman) 60 28
3477 A992 2 l Buzau (man) 60 28
3478 A992 3 l Dobrogea (woman) 90 45
3479 A992 3 l Dobrogea (man) 90 45
3480 A992 4 l Ilfov (woman) 1.25 60
3481 A992 4 l Ilfov (man) 1.25 60
Nos. 3474-3481 (8) 6.06 2.94

Stamps of same denomination se-tenant.

Postwoman Delivering Mail — A993

1987, Nov. 15 Photo. *Perf. 13½*

3482 A993 2 l multi 90 45

Stamp Day. No. 3482 printed se-tenant in a continuous design with 1 l Romanian Philatelic Association charity label picturing postal van and cyclist.

Apiculture — A994

1987, Nov. 16 Photo. *Perf. 13½*

3483 A994 1 l Apis mellifica carpatica 28 14
3484 A994 2 l Bee pollinating sunflower 60 28
3485 A994 3 l Hives, Danube Delta 90 45
3486 A994 4 l Apiculture complex, Bucharest 1.25 60

1988 Winter Olympics, Calgary — A995

1987, Dec. 28 Photo. *Perf. 13½*

3487 A995 50b Biathlon 14 7
3488 A995 1 l Slalom 28 14
3489 A995 1.50 l Ice hockey 42 20
3490 A995 2 l Luge 60 28
3491 A995 3 l Speed skating 90 45
3492 A995 3.50 l Women's figure skating 1.00 50
3493 A995 4 l Downhill skiing 1.25 60
3494 A995 5 l Two-man bobsled 1.50 70
Nos. 3487-3494 (8) 6.09 2.94

An imperf. 10 l souvenir sheet picturing ski jumping also exists.

Traffic Safety A996

Designs: 50b, Be aware of children riding bicycles in the road. 1 l, Young Pioneer girl as crossing guard. 2 l, Do not open car doors in path of moving traffic. 3 l, Be aware of pedestrian crossings. 4 l, Observe the speed limit; do not attempt curves at high speed. 5 l, Protect small children.

1987, Dec. 10 Photo. *Perf. 13½*

3495 A996 50b multi 14 7
3496 A996 1 l multi 28 14
3497 A996 2 l multi 60 28
3498 A996 3 l multi 90 45
3499 A996 4 l multi 1.25 60
3500 A996 5 l multi 1.50 70
Nos. 3495-3500 (6) 4.67 2.24

October Revolution, Russia, 70th Anniv. — A997

1987, Dec. 26

3501 A997 2 l multi 60 28

40th Anniv. of the Romanian Republic — A998

1987, Dec. 30

3502 A998 2 l multi 60 28

70th Birthday of President Nicolae Ceausescu A999

1988, Jan. 26

3503 A999 2 l multi 60 28

Pottery A1000

1988, Feb. 26 Photo. *Perf. 13½*

3504 A1000 50b Marginea 14 7
3505 A1000 1 l Oboga 28 14
3506 A1000 2 l Horezu 60 28
3507 A1000 3 l Curtea De Arges 90 45
3508 A1000 4 l Birsa 1.25 60
3509 A1000 5 l Vama 1.50 70
Nos. 3504-3509 (6) 4.67 2.24

Miniature Sheets

Intereuropa A1001

Transportation and communication, No. 3510: a., Mail coach. b., ECS telecommunications satellite. c., Oltcit automobile. d., ICE high-speed electric train.

No. 3511: a., Santa Maria, 15th cent. b., Cheia Ground Station satellite dish receivers. c., Bucharest subway. d., Airbus-A320.

1988, Apr. 27 Photo. *Perf. 13½*

3510		Sheet of 4	5.25	5.25
a.-d	A1001 3 l any single		1.30	1.30
3511		Sheet of 4	5.25	5.25
a.-d	A1001 3 l any single		1.30	1.30

1988 Summer Olympics, Seoul — A1002

1988, June 28

3512	A1002	50b	Gymnastics	20	10
3513	A1002	1.50 l	Boxing	65	32
3514	A1002	2 l	Tennis	85	42
3515	A1002	3 l	Judo	1.30	65
3516	A1002	4 l	Running	1.70	85
3517	A1002	5 l	Rowing	2.15	1.05
			Nos. 3512-3517 (6)	6.85	3.39

An imperf. 10 l souvenir sheet exists.

19th-20th Cent. Clocks in the Ceasului Museum, Ploesti — A1003

1988, May 20 Photo. *Perf. 13½*

3518	A1003	50b	Arad Region porcelain	20	10
3519	A1003	1.50 l	French bronze	65	32
3520	A1003	2 l	French bronze, diff.	85	42
3521	A1003	3 l	Gothic bronze	1.30	65
3522	A1003	4 l	Saxony porcelain	1.70	85
3523	A1003	5 l	Bohemian porcelain	2.15	1.05
			Nos. 3518-3523 (6)	6.85	3.39

20th Cent. timepiece (50b); others 19th cent.

Accession of Constanin Brincoveanu as Prince Regent of Wallachia, 1688-1714, 300th Anniv. — A1004

1988, June 20

3524	A1004	2 l multi	85	42

1988 Summer Olympics, Seoul — A1005

1988, Sept. 1 Photo. *Perf. 13½*

3525	A1005	50b	Women's running	20	10
3526	A1005	1 l	Canoeing	42	20
3527	A1005	1.50 l	Women's gymnastics	65	32
3528	A1005	2 l	Kayaking	85	42
3529	A1005	3 l	Weight lifting	1.30	65
3530	A1005	3.50 l	Women's swimming	1.50	75
3531	A1005	4 l	Fencing	1.70	85
3532	A1005	5 l	Women's rowing (double)	2.15	1.05
			Nos. 3525-3532 (8)	8.77	4.34

An imperf. 10 l souvenir sheet exists picturing women's gymnastics.

Romania-China Philatelic Exhibition — A1006

1988, Aug. 5 Photo. *Perf. 13½*

3533	A1006	2 l multi	85	42

Souvenir Sheet

PRAGA '88 — A1007

1988, Aug. 26

3534	A1007	5 l Carnations, by Stefan Luchian	2.25	2.25

Miniature Sheets

Orchids A1008

Designs, No. 3535: a., Oncidium lanceanum. b., Cattleya trianae. c., Sophronitis cernua. d., Bulbophyllum lobbii. e., Lycaste cruenta. f., Mormolyce ringens. g., Phragmipedium schlimii. h., Angraecum sesquipedale. i., Laelia crispa. j., Encyclia atropurpurea. k., Dendrobium nobile. l., Oncidium splendidum.

No. 3536: a., Brassavola perrinii. b., Paphiopedilum maudiae. c., Sophronitis coccinea. d., Vandopsis lissochiloides. e., Phalaenopsis lueddemanniana. f., Chysis bractescens. g., Cochleanthes discolor. h., Phalaenopsis amabilis. i., Pleione pricei. j., Sobralia macrantha. k., Aspasia lunata. l., Cattleya citrina.

1988, Oct. 24

3535		Sheet of 12	5.25	5.25
a.-l.	A1008 1 l any single		42	42
3536		Sheet of 12	5.25	5.25
a.-l.	A1008 1 l any single		42	42

Miniature Sheets

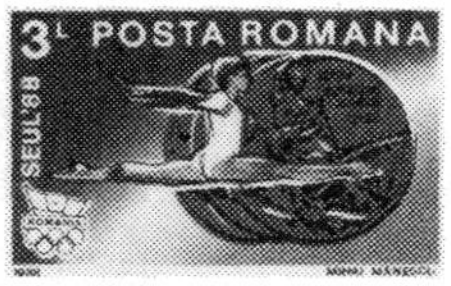

Events Won by Romanian Athletes at the 1988 Seoul Olympic Games A1009

Sporting event and medal, No. 3537: a., Women's gymnastics. b., Free pistol shooting. c., Weight lifting (220 pounds). d., Featherweight boxing.

No. 3538: a., Women's 1500 and 3000-meter relays. b., Women's 200 and 400-meter individual swimming medley. c., Wrestling (220 pounds). d., Rowing, coxless pairs and coxed fours.

1988, Dec. 7 Photo. *Perf. 13½*

3537		Sheet of 4	5.25	5.25
a.-d.	A1009 3 l any single		1.25	1.25
3538		Sheet of 4	5.25	5.25
a.-d.	A1009 3 l any single		1.25	1.25

Stamp Day A1010

1988, Nov. 13 Photo. *Perf. 13½*

3539	A1010	2 l multi	1.10	55

No. 3539 se-tenant in a continuous design with 1 l Romanian Philatelic Assoc. charity label picturing woman mail carrier, postal van and aircraft.

Unitary Natl. Romanian State, 70th Anniv. A1011

1988, Dec. 29

3540	A1011	2 l multi	85	42

Anniversaries — A1012

Designs: 50b, Athenaeum, Bucharest. 1.50 l, Trajan's Bridge, Drobeta, on a Roman bronze sestertius used in Romania from 103 to 105 A.D. 2 l, Ruins, Suceava. 3 l, Pitesti municipal coat of arms, scroll, architecture. 4 l, Trajan's Column (detail), 113 A.D. 5 l, Gold helmet discovered in Prahova County.

1988, Dec. 30

3541	A1012	50b	shown	18	10
3542	A1012	1.50 l	multi	55	28
3543	A1012	2 l	multi	72	35
3544	A1012	3 l	multi	1.10	55
3545	A1012	4 l	multi	1.45	72
3546	A1012	5 l	multi	1.80	90
			Nos. 3541-3546 (6)	5.80	2.90

Athenaeum, Bucharest, cent. (50b), Suceava, the capital of Moldavia from 1401 to 1565, 600th anniv. (2 l), and Pitesti municipal charter, 600th anniv. (3 l).

SEMI-POSTAL STAMPS

Queen Elizabeth Spinning — SP1

The Queen Weaving — SP2

Perf. 11½, 11½x13½

1906, Jan. 14 Typo. Unwmk.

B1	SP1	3b (+ 7b) brn		1.50	1.25
B2	SP1	5b (+ 10b) lt grn		1.50	1.25
B3	SP1	10b (+ 10b) rose red		5.00	2.75
B4	SP1	15b (+ 10b) vio		4.00	2.50

1906, Mar. 18

B5	SP2	3b (+ 7b) org brn	1.50	1.25
B6	SP2	5b (+ 10b) bl grn	1.50	1.25
B7	SP2	10b (+ 10b) car	5.00	2.75
B8	SP2	15b (+ 10b) red vio	4.00	2.50

Queen as War Nurse SP3

1906, Mar. 23 *Perf. 11½, 13½x11½*

B9	SP3	3b (+ 7b) org brn	1.50	1.25
B10	SP3	5b (+ 10b) bl grn	1.50	1.25
B11	SP3	10b (+ 10b) car	5.00	2.75
B12	SP3	15b (+ 10b) red vio	4.00	2.50

Booklet panes of 4 exist of Nos. B1-B3, B5-B7, B9-B12.

Counterfeits of Nos. B1-B12 are plentiful.

A particular stamp may be scarce, but if few collectors want it, its market value may remain relatively low.

SP4

1906, Aug. 4 *Perf. 12*

B13	SP4	3b (+ 7b) ol brn, buff & bl	75	60
B14	SP4	5b (+ 10b) grn, rose & buff	90	60
B15	SP4	10b (+ 10b) rose red, buff & bl	1.65	1.50
B16	SP4	15b (+ 10b) vio, buff & bl	4.50	2.25

Guardian Angel Bringing Poor to Crown Princess Marie
SP5

1907, Feb. Engr. *Perf. 11*
Center in Brown

B17	SP5	3b (+ 7b) org brn	1.50	1.25
B18	SP5	5b (+ 10b) dk grn	95	48
B19	SP5	10b (+ 10b) dk car	95	48
B20	SP5	15b (+ 10b) dl vio	75	55

Nos. B1-B20 were sold for more than face value. The surtax, shown in parenthesis, was for charitable purposes.

Map of Romania — SP9

Stephen the Great — SP10

Michael the Brave
SP11

Kings Carol I and Ferdinand
SP12

Adam Clisi Monument — SP13

1927, Mar. 15 Typo. *Perf. 13½*

B21	SP9	1 l + 9 l lt vio	70	45
B22	SP10	2 l + 8 l Prus grn	70	45
B23	SP11	3 l + 7 l dp rose	70	45
B24	SP12	5 l + 5 l dp bl	70	45
B25	SP13	6 l + 4 l ol grn	1.90	45
		Nos. B21-B25 (5)	4.70	2.25

50th anniv. of the Royal Geographical Society. The surtax was for the benefit of that society. The stamps were valid for postage only from Mar. 15-Apr. 14, 1927.

Boy Scouts in Camp
SP15

The Rescue
SP16

Prince Nicholas Chief Scout
SP18

King Carol II in Scout's Uniform
SP19

Design: 3 l+3 l, Swearing in a Tenderfoot.

1931, July 15 Photo. Wmk. 225

B26	SP15	1 l + 1 l car rose	95	70
B27	SP16	2 l + 2 l dp grn	1.25	95
B28	SP15	3 l + 3 l ultra	1.65	1.25
B29	SP18	4 l + 4 l ol gray	1.65	1.50
B30	SP19	6 l + 6 l red brn	3.50	1.75
		Nos. B26-B30 (5)	9.00	6.15

The surtax was for the benefit of the Boy Scout organization.

Boy Scout Jamboree Issue

Scouts in Camp
SP20

Semaphore Signaling
SP21

Trailing
SP22

Camp Fire
SP23

King Carol II
SP24

King Carol II and Prince Michael
SP25

1932, June 8 Wmk. 230

B31	SP20	25b + 25b pck grn	2.75	1.00
B32	SP21	50b + 50b brt bl	3.50	2.00
B33	SP22	1 l + 1 l ol grn	4.00	2.75
B34	SP23	2 l + 2 l org red	6.75	4.00
B35	SP24	3 l + 3 l Prus bl	12.00	8.00
B36	SP25	6 l + 6 l blk brn	14.00	10.00
		Nos. B31-B36 (6)	43.00	27.75

Tuberculosis Sanatorium — SP26

Memorial Tablet to Postal Employees Who Died in World War I — SP27

Carmen Sylva Convalescent Home — SP28

1932, Nov. 1

B37	SP26	4 l + 1 l dk grn	2.10	1.50
B38	SP27	6 l + 1 l choc	2.10	2.50
B39	SP28	10 l + 1 l dp bl	4.25	3.00

The surtax was given to a fund for the employees of the postal and telegraph services.

Philatelic Exhibition Issue
Souvenir Sheet

King Carol II
SP29

1932, Nov. 20 Unwmk. ***Imperf.***

B40	SP29	6 l + 5 l dk ol grn	10.50	10.50

Intl. Phil. Exhib. at Bucharest, Nov. 20-24, 1932. Each holder of a ticket of admission to the exhibition could buy a copy of the stamp. The ticket cost 20 lei.

Roadside Shrine
SP31

Woman Spinning
SP33

Woman Weaving
SP32

1934, Apr. 16 Wmk. 230 *Perf. 13½*

B41	SP31	1 l + 1 l dk brn	55	38
B42	SP32	2 l + 1 l blue	75	48
B43	SP33	3 l + 1 l sl grn	1.00	65

Weaving Exposition.

Boy Scout Mamaia Jamboree Issue

Semi-Postal Stamps of 1932 Overprinted in Black or Gold

1934, July 8

B44	SP20	25b + 25b pck grn	1.75	1.50
B45	SP21	50b + 50b brt bl (G)	2.75	1.50
B46	SP22	1 l + 1 l ol grn	3.50	2.75
B47	SP23	2 l + 2 l org red	4.00	3.50
B48	SP24	3 l + 3 l Prus bl (G)	7.75	6.75
B49	SP25	6 l + 6 l blk brn (G)	12.00	9.00
		Nos. B44-B49 (6)	31.75	25.00

Sea Scout Saluting
SP34

Scout Bugler
SP35

Sea and Land Scouts — SP36

King Carol II — SP37

Sea, Land and Girl Scouts — SP38

1935, June 8

B50	SP34	25b ol blk	90	70
B51	SP35	1 l violet	2.00	1.65
B52	SP36	2 l green	2.50	2.10
B53	SP37	6 l + 1 l red brn	3.75	2.25
B54	SP38	10 l + 2 l dk ultra	10.50	7.50
		Nos. B50-B54 (5)	19.65	14.20

Fifth anniversary of accession of King Carol II, and a national sports meeting held June 8. Surtax aided the Boy Scouts.
Nos. B50-B54 exist imperf.

King Carol II — SP39

1936, May

B55	SP39	6 l + 1 l rose car	50	35

Bucharest Exhibition and 70th anniversary of the dynasty. Exists imperf.

Girl of Oltenia — SP40

Girl of Saliste — SP42

Youth from Gorj — SP44

Designs: 1 l+1 l, Girl of Banat. 3 l+1 l, Girl of Hateg. 6 l+3 l, Girl of Neamt. 10 l+5 l, Youth and girl of Bucovina.

1936, June 8

B56	SP40	50b + 50b brn	38	25
B57	SP40	1 l + 1 l vio	38	25
B58	SP42	2 l + 1 l Prus grn	38	25
B59	SP42	3 l + 1 l car rose	38	25
B60	SP44	4 l + 2 l red org	70	52
B61	SP40	6 l + 3 l ol gray	70	60
B62	SP42	10 l + 5 l brt bl	1.40	1.10
		Nos. B56-B62 (7)	4.32	3.22

6th anniv. of accession of King Carol II. The surtax was for child welfare. Exist imperf.

Insignia of Boy Scouts
SP47 SP48

Jamboree Emblem SP49

Submarine "Delfinul" SP50

1936, Aug. 20

B63	SP47	1 l + 1 l brt bl	1.90	1.50
B64	SP48	3 l + 3 l ol gray	2.75	1.90
B65	SP49	6 l + 6 l car rose	3.50	2.75

Boy Scout Jamboree at Brasov (Kronstadt).

1936, Oct.

Designs: 3 l+2 l, Training ship "Mircea." 6 l+3 l, Steamship "S.M.R."

B66	SP50	1 l + 1 l pur	1.90	1.50
B67	SP50	3 l + 2 l ultra	1.75	1.50
B68	SP50	6 l + 3 l car rose	2.50	2.50

Marine Exhibition at Bucharest. Exist imperf.

Soccer SP53

Swimming SP54

Throwing the Javelin SP55

Skiing SP56

King Carol II Hunting SP57

Rowing SP58

Horsemanship SP59

Founding of the U.F.S.R. SP60

1937, June 8 Wmk. 230 *Perf. 13½*

B69	SP53	25b + 25b ol blk	35	24
B70	SP54	50b + 50b brn	35	24
B71	SP55	1 l + 50b vio	35	24
B72	SP56	2 l + 4 l sl grn	35	24
B73	SP57	3 l + 1 l rose lake	45	30
B74	SP58	4 l + 1 l red org	70	35
B75	SP59	6 l + 2 l dp cl	1.00	45
B76	SP60	10 l + 4 l brt bl	1.40	1.40
		Nos. B69-B76 (8)	4.95	3.46

25th anniversary of the Federation of Romanian Sports Clubs (U.F.S.R.); 7th anniversary of the accession of King Carol II. Exist imperf.

Start of Race — SP61

Javelin Thrower — SP62

Designs: 4 l+1 l, Hurdling. 6 l+1 l, Finish of race. 10 l+1 l, High jump.

1937, Sept. 1 Wmk. 230 *Perf. 13½*

B77	SP61	1 l + 1 l pur	35	35
B78	SP62	2 l + 1 l grn	45	38
B79	SP61	4 l + 1 l ver	55	55
B80	SP62	6 l + 1 l mar	85	85
B81	SP61	10 l + 1 l brt bl	2.25	1.75
		Nos. B77-B81 (5)	4.45	3.88

8th Balkan Games, Bucharest. Exist imperf.

Catalogue values for unused stamps in this section, from this point to the end of the section, are for Never Hinged items.

King Carol II — SP66

1938, May 24

B82	SP66	6 l + 1 l dp mag	42	24

Bucharest Exhibition (for local products), May 19-June 19, celebrating 20th anniversary of the union of Rumanian provinces. Exists imperf.

Dimitrie Cantemir SP67

Maria Doamna SP68

Mircea the Great SP69

Constantine Brancoveanu SP70

Stephen the Great — SP71

Prince Cuza — SP72

Michael the Brave SP73

Queen Elizabeth SP74

King Carol II — SP75

King Ferdinand I — SP76

King Carol I — SP77

1938, June 8 *Perf. 13½*

B83	SP67	25b + 25b ol blk	25	25
B84	SP68	50b + 50b brn	25	25
B85	SP69	1 l + 1 l blk vio	25	25
B86	SP70	2 l + 2 l dk yel grn	25	25
B87	SP71	3 l + 2 l dp mag	25	25
B88	SP72	4 l + 2 l scar	25	25
B89	SP73	6 l + 2 l vio brn	65	65
B90	SP74	7.50 l gray bl	65	65
B91	SP75	10 l brt bl	65	65
B92	SP76	16 l dk sl grn	1.10	1.10
B93	SP77	20 l vermilion	1.40	1.40
		Nos. B83-B93 (11)	5.95	5.95

8th anniv. of accession of King Carol II. Surtax was for Straja Tarii, a natl. org. for boys. Exist imperf.

"The Spring" — SP78

"Escorting Prisoners" SP79

"Rodica, the Water Carrier" SP81

Nicolae Grigorescu SP82

Design: 4 l+1 l, "Returning from Market."

1938, June 23 *Perf. 13½*

B94	SP78	1 l + 1 l brt bl	60	38
B95	SP79	2 l + 1 l yel grn	70	55
B96	SP79	4 l + 1 l ver	75	75
B97	SP81	6 l + 1 l lake	95	95
B98	SP82	10 l + 1 l brt bl	1.25	95
		Nos. B94-B98 (5)	4.25	3.58

Birth centenary of Nicolae Grigorescu, Romanian painter. Exist imperf.

St. George and the Dragon — SP83

1939, June 8 Photo.

B99	SP83	25b + 25b ol gray	38	38
B100	SP83	50b + 50b brn	38	38
B101	SP83	1 l + 1 l pale vio	38	38
B102	SP83	2 l + 2 l lt grn	38	38
B103	SP83	3 l + 2 l red vio	60	38
B104	SP83	4 l + 2 l red org	80	40
B105	SP83	6 l + 2 l car rose	90	40
B106	SP83	8 l gray vio	1.00	60
B107	SP83	10 l brt bl	1.10	75
B108	SP83	12 l brt ultra	1.40	1.25
B109	SP83	16 l bl grn	1.65	1.40
		Nos. B99-B109 (11)	8.97	6.70

9th anniv. of accession of King Carol II. Exist imperf.

King Carol II
SP87 SP88

An enhanced introduction to the Scott Catalogue begins on Page V. A thorough understanding of the material presented there will greatly aid your use of the catalogue itself.

SP89

SP90

SP91

Wmk. 230

1940, June 8 Photo. *Perf. 13½*

B113	SP87	1 l + 50b dl pur	25	14
B114	SP88	4 l + 1 l fawn	25	18
B115	SP89	6 l + 1 l bl	25	24
B116	SP90	8 l rose brn	38	30
B117	SP89	16 l ultra	50	38
B118	SP91	32 l dk vio brn	90	65
		Nos. B113-B118 (6)	2.53	1.89

10th anniversary of accession of King Carol II. Exist imperf.

King Carol II
SP92 SP93

1940, June 1

B119	SP92	1 l + 50b dk grn	12	9
B120	SP92	2.50 l + 50b Prus grn	18	12
B121	SP93	3 l + 1 l rose car	22	15
B122	SP92	3.50 l + 50b choc	28	18
B123	SP93	4 l + 1 l org brn	30	22
B124	SP93	6 l + 1 l saph	45	12
B125	SP93	9 l + 1 l brt bl	60	45
B126	SP93	14 l + 1 l dk bl grn	75	55
		Nos. B119-B126 (8)	2.90	1.88

Surtax was for Romania's air force. Exist imperf.

View of Danube SP94

Greco-Roman Ruins — SP95

Designs: 3 l+1 l, Hotin Castle. 4 l+1 l, Hurez Monastery. 5 l+1 l, Church in Bucovina. 8 l+1 l, Tower. 12 l+2 l, Village church, Transylvania. 16 l+2 l, Arch in Bucharest.

1940, June 8 *Perf. 14½x14, 14x14½*
Inscribed: "Straja Tarii 8 Junie 1940"

B127	SP94	1 l + 1 l dp vio	22	22
B128	SP95	2 l + 1 l red brn	28	28
B129	SP94	3 l + 1 l yel grn	28	28
B130	SP94	4 l + 1 l grnsh blk	35	35
B131	SP95	5 l + 1 l org ver	42	42
B132	SP95	8 l + 1 l brn car	55	55
B133	SP95	12 l + 2 l ultra	80	80
B134	SP95	16 l + 2 l dk bl gray	1.25	1.25
		Nos. B127-B134 (8)	4.15	4.15

Issued to honor Straja Tarii, a national organization for boys. Exist imperf.

King Michael SP102

Corneliu Codreanu SP103

1940-42 Photo. Wmk. 230

B138	SP102	1 l + 50b yel grn	5	5
B138A	SP102	2 l + 50b yel grn ('42)	5	5
B139	SP102	2.50 l + 50b dk bl grn	5	5
B140	SP102	3 l + 1 l pur	12	12
B141	SP102	3.50 l + 50b rose pink	14	14
B141A	SP102	4 l + 50b org ver ('42)	7	7
B142	SP102	4 l + 1 l brn	7	7
B142A	SP102	5 l + 1 l dp plum ('42)	42	42
B143	SP102	6 l + 1 l lt ultra	7	7
B143A	SP102	7 l + 1 l sl grn ('42)	12	12
B143B	SP102	8 l + 1 l dp vio ('42)	14	14
B143C	SP102	12 l + 1 l brn vio ('42)	14	14
B144	SP102	14 l + 1 l brt bl	28	28
B144A	SP102	19 l + 1 l lil rose ('42)	60	60
		Nos. B138-B144A (14)	2.32	2.32

1940, Nov. 8 Unwmk. *Perf. 13½*

B145	SP103	7 l + 30 l dk grn	2.50	2.00

13th anniv. of the founding of the Iron Guard by Corneliu Codreanu.

Vasile Marin — SP104

Design: 15 l+15 l, Ion Mota.

1941, Jan. 13

B146	SP104	7 l + 7 l rose brn	48	48
B147	SP104	15 l + 15 l sl bl	1.10	1.10

Souvenir Sheet
Imperf

B148		Sheet of two	22.50	22.50
a.	SP104	7 l + 7 l Prus grn	5.75	5.75
b.	SP104	15 l + 15 l Prus grn	5.75	5.75

Vasile Marin and Ion Mota, Iron Guardists who died in the Spanish Civil War.
No. B148 sold for 300 lei.

Crown, Leaves and Bible — SP107

Designs: 2 l+43 l, Library shelves. 7 l+38 l, Carol I Foundation, Bucharest. 10 l+35 l, King Carol I. 16 l+29 l, Kings Michael and Carol I.

Wmk. 230
1941, May 9 Photo. *Perf. 13½*
Inscribed: "1891 1941"

B149	SP107	1.50 l + 43.50 l pur	35	35
B150	SP107	2 l + 43 l rose brn	35	35
B151	SP107	7 l + 38 l rose	35	35
B152	SP107	10 l + 35 l ol blk	35	35
B153	SP107	16 l + 29 l brn	35	35
		Nos. B149-B153 (5)	1.75	1.75

50th anniv. of the Carol I Foundation, established to endow research and stimulate the arts.

Same Overprinted in Red or Black **CERNAUTI 5 Iulie 1941**

1941, Aug.

B154	SP107	1.50 l + 43.50 l pur (R)	1.10	1.10
B155	SP107	2 l + 43 l rose brn	1.10	1.10
B156	SP107	7 l + 38 l rose	1.10	1.10
B157	SP107	10 l + 35 l ol blk (R)	1.10	1.10
B158	SP107	16 l + 29 l brn	1.10	1.10

Occupation of Cernauti, Bucovina.

Same Overprinted in Red or Black **CHISINAU 16 Iulie 1941**

1941, Aug.

B159	SP107	1.50 l + 43.50 l pur (R)	1.10	1.10
B160	SP107	2 l + 43 l rose brn	1.10	1.10
B161	SP107	7 l + 38 l rose	1.10	1.10
B162	SP107	10 l + 35 l ol blk (R)	1.10	1.10
B163	SP107	16 l + 29 l brn	1.10	1.10
		Nos. B154-B163 (10)	11.00	11.00

Occupation of Chisinau, Bessarabia.

Romanian Red Cross — SP111

1941, Aug. *Perf. 13½*

B164	SP111	1.50 l + 38.50 l dl pur & car	45	45
B165	SP111	2 l + 38 l mag & red	45	45
B166	SP111	5 l + 35 l ol gray & car	45	45
B167	SP111	7 l + 33 l dl brn & car	45	45
B168	SP111	10 l + 30 l brt bl & car	45	45
		Nos. B164-B168 (5)	2.25	2.25

Souvenir Sheet
Imperf
Without Gum.

B169		Sheet of two	6.50	6.50
a.	SP111	7 l + 33 l brn & red	1.25	1.40
b.	SP111	10 l + 30 l brt bl & red	1.25	1.40

The surtax on Nos. B164-B169 was for the Romanian Red Cross.
No. B169 sold for 200 l.

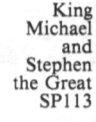

King Michael and Stephen the Great SP113

Hotin and Akkerman Castles SP114

Romanian and German Soldiers SP115

Soldiers SP116

1941, Oct. 11 *Perf. 14½x13½*

B170	SP113	10 l + 30 l ultra	50	50
B171	SP114	12 l + 28 l dl org red	50	50
B172	SP115	16 l + 24 l lt brn	50	50
B173	SP116	20 l + 20 l dk vio	50	50

Souvenir Sheet

SP118

Imperf.

B174	SP118	Sheet of two	4.25	4.25
a.		16 l bl gray	38	38
b.		20 l brn car	38	38

Sold for 200 l. The surtax aided the Anti-Bolshevism crusade.

Nos. B170-B174 Overprinted **ODESA 16 Oct.1941**

1941, Oct. *Perf. 14½x13½*

B175	SP113	10 l + 30 l ultra	60	60
B176	SP114	12 l + 28 l dl org red	60	60
B177	SP115	16 l + 24 l lt brn	60	60
B178	SP116	20 l + 20 l dk vio	60	60
a.		Sheet of 2 (No. B174)	4.25	4.25

Occupation of Odessa, Russia.

Types of Regular Issue, 1941

Designs: 3 l+50b, Sucevita Monastery, Bucovina. 5.50 l+50b, Rughi Monastery, Soroca, Bessarabia. 5.50 l+1 l, Tighina Fortress, Bessarabia. 6.50 l+1 l, Soroca Fortress, Bessarabia. 8 l+1 l, St. Nicholas Monastery, Suceava, Bucovina. 9.50 l+1 l, Milisauti Monastery, Bucovina. 10.50 l+1 l, Putna Monastery, Bucovina. 16 l+1 l, Cetatea Alba Fortress, Bessarabia. 25 l+1 l, Hotin Fortress, Bessarabia.

1941, Dec. 1 Wmk. 230 *Perf. 13½*

B179	A179	3 l + 50b rose brn	18	10
B180	A179	5.50 l + 50b red org	35	18
B181	A179	5.50 l + 1 l blk	35	18
B182	A179	6.50 l + 1 l dk brn	38	35
B183	A179	8 l + 1 l lt bl	35	18
B184	A177	9.50 l + 1 l gray bl	38	28
B185	A179	10.50 l + 1 l dk bl	38	14
B186	A179	16 l + 1 l vio	50	40
B187	A179	25 l + 1 l gray blk	60	45
		Nos. B179-B187 (9)	3.47	2.26

Titu Maiorescu SP128

Statue of Miron Costin at Jassy SP130

1942, Oct. 5

B188	SP128	9 l + 11 l dl vio	30	30
B189	SP128	20 l + 20 l yel brn	75	75
B190	SP128	20 l + 30 l bl	75	75

Souvenir Sheet
Imperf
Without Gum

B191	SP128	Sheet of three	3.75	3.75

The surtax aided war prisoners.
No. B191 contains one each of Nos. B188-B190, imperf. Sold for 200 l.

1942, Dec. *Perf. 13 ½*
B192 SP130 6 l + 44 l sep 1.00 1.50
B193 SP130 12 l + 38 l vio 1.00 1.50
B194 SP130 24 l + 26 l bl 1.00 1.50

Anniv. of the conquest of Transdniestria, and for use only in this territory which includes Odessa and land beyond the Duiester.

Michael, Antonescu, Hitler, Mussolini and Bessarabia Map
SP131

Michael, Antonescu and (inset) Stephen of Moldavia
SP132

Romanian Troops Crossing Pruth River to Retake Bessarabia
SP133

1942 Wmk. 230 Photo. *Perf. 13 ½*
B195 SP131 9 l + 41 l red brn 1.00 1.50
B196 SP132 18 l + 32 l ol gray 1.00 1.50
B197 SP133 20 l + 30 l brt ultra 1.00 1.50

First anniversary of liberation of Bessarabia.

Bucovina Coats of Arms
SP134 SP135

Design: 20 l+30 l, Bucovina arms with triple-barred cross.

1942, Nov. 1
B198 SP134 9 l + 41 l brt ver 1.00 1.50
B199 SP135 18 l + 32 l bl 1.00 1.50
B200 SP135 20 l + 30 l car rose 1.00 1.50

First anniversary of liberation of Bucovina.

Andrei Muresanu — SP137

1942, Dec. 30
B201 SP137 5 l + 5 l vio 38 38

80th death anniv. of Andrei Muresanu, writer.

Avram Jancu, National Hero — SP138

1943, Feb. 15
B202 SP138 16 l + 4 l brn 50 50

Nurse Aiding Wounded Soldier
SP139

1943, Mar. 1 *Perf. 14 ½x14*
B203 SP139 12 l + 88 l red brn & ultra 30 30
B204 SP139 16 l + 84 l brt ultra & red 30 30
B205 SP139 20 l + 80 l ol gray & red 30 30

Souvenir Sheet
Imperf

B206 Sheet of two 1.90 1.65
a. SP139 16 l + 84 l brt ultra & red 52 52
b. SP139 20 l + 80 l ol gray & red 52 52

Surtax on Nos. B203-B206 aided the Romanian Red Cross.
No. B206 sold for 500 l. Size: 100x60 mm.

Sword Hilt
SP141

Sword Severing Chain
SP142

Soldier and Family, Guardian Angel — SP143

Perf. 14x14 ½
1943, June 22 **Wmk. 276**
B207 SP141 36 l + 164 l brn 2.00 2.00
B208 SP142 62 l + 138 l brt bl 2.00 2.00
B209 SP143 76 l + 124 l ver 2.00 2.00

Souvenir Sheet
Imperf

B210 Sheet of two 8.50 8.50
a. SP143 62 l + 138 l dp bl 1.75 1.90
b. SP143 76 l + 124 l red org 1.75 1.90

2nd anniv. of Romania's entrance into WWII. No. B210 sold for 600 l.

Petru Maior — SP145

Horia, Closca and Crisan
SP148

Designs: 32 l+118 l, Gheorghe Sincai. 36 l+114 l, Timotei Cipariu. 91 l+109 l, Gheorghe Cosbuc.

Perf. 13 ½; 14 ½x14 (No. B214)
1943, Aug. 15 Photo. Wmk. 276
B211 SP145 16 l + 134 l red org 28 28
B212 SP145 32 l + 118 l lt bl 28 28
B213 SP145 36 l + 114 l vio 28 28
B214 SP148 62 l + 138 l car rose 28 28
B215 SP145 91 l + 109 l dk brn 28 28
Nos. B211-B215 (5) 1.40 1.40

See Nos. B219-B223.

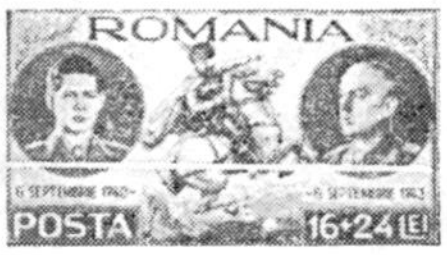

King Michael and Ion Antonescu
SP150

1943, Sept. 6
B216 SP150 16 l + 24 l bl 70 70

3rd anniv. of the government of King Michael and Marshal Ion Antonescu.

Symbols of Sports — SP151

1943, Sept. 26 *Perf. 13 ½*
B217 SP151 16 l + 24 l ultra 38 30
B218 SP151 16 l + 24 l red brn 38 30

The surtax was for the benefit of Romanian sports.

Portrait Type of 1943
1943, Oct. 1

Designs: 16 l+134 l, Samuel Micu. 51 l+99 l, George Lazar. 56 l+144 l, Octavian Goga. 76 l+ 124 l, Simeon Barnutiu. 77 l+123 l, Andrei Saguna.

B219 SP145 16 l + 134 l red vio 24 24
B220 SP145 51 l + 99 l org 24 24
B221 SP145 56 l + 144 l rose car 24 24
B222 SP145 76 l + 124 l sl bl 24 24
B223 SP145 77 l + 123 l brn 24 24
Nos. B219-B223 (5) 1.20 1.20

The surtax aided refugees.

Calafat, 1877 — SP157

Designs: 2 l +2 l, World War I scene. 3.50 l+3.50 l, Stalingrad, 1943. 4 l+4 l, Tisza, 1919. 5 l+5 l, Odessa, 1941. 6.50 l+6.50 l, Caucasus, 1942. 7 l+7 l, Sevastopol, 1942. 20 l+20 l, Prince Ribescu and King Michael.

1943, Nov. 10 Photo. *Perf. 13 ½*
B224 SP157 1 l + 1 l red brn 12 12
B225 SP157 2 l + 2 l dl vio 12 12
B226 SP157 3.50 l + 3.50 l lt ultra 12 12
B227 SP157 4 l + 4 l mag 12 12
B228 SP157 5 l + 5 l red org 25 25
B229 SP157 6.50 l + 6.50 l bl 25 25
B230 SP157 7 l + 7 l dp vio 35 35
B231 SP157 20 l + 20 l crim 45 45
Nos. B224-B231 (8) 1.78 1.78

Centenary of Romanian Artillery.

Emblem of Romanian Engineers' Association
SP165

1943, Dec. 19 *Perf. 14*
B232 SP165 21 l + 29 l sep 48 40

Society of Romanian Engineers, 25th anniv.

Motorcycle, Truck and Post Horn — SP166

Post Wagon
SP167

Roman Post Chariot
SP168

Post Rider — SP169

SP170

1944, Feb. 1 Wmk. 276 *Perf. 14*
B233 SP166 1 l + 49 l org red 1.10 1.10
B234 SP167 2 l + 48 l lil rose 1.10 1.10
B235 SP168 4 l + 46 l ultra 1.10 1.10
B236 SP169 10 l + 40 l dl vio 1.10 1.10

Souvenir Sheets
Perf. 14

B237 SP170 Sheet of three 2.75 4.00
a. SP166 1 l + 49 l org red 70 70
b. SP167 2 l + 48 l org red 70 70
c. SP168 4 l + 46 l org red 70 70

Imperf

B238 SP170 Sheet of three 2.75 4.00
a. SP166 1 l + 49 l dl vio 70 70
b. SP167 2 l + 48 l dl vio 70 70
c. SP168 4 l + 46 l dl vio 70 70

The surtax aided communications employees.
Nos. B237-B238 each sold for 200 l.

Nos. B233-B238 Overprinted **"1744 1944"**

1944, Feb. 28
B239 SP166 1 l + 49 l org red 1.75 1.75
B240 SP167 2 l + 48 l lil rose 1.75 1.75
B241 SP168 4 l + 46 l ultra 1.75 1.75
B242 SP169 10 l + 40 l dl vio 1.75 1.75

Souvenir Sheets
Perf. 14

B243 SP170 Sheet of three 4.75 5.25

Imperf

B244 SP170 Sheet of three 4.75 5.25

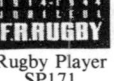

Rugby Player
SP171

Dr. N. Cretzulescu
SP172

1944, Mar. 16 *Perf. 15*

B245	SP171	16 l + 184 l crim	3.25	3.25

30th anniv. of the Romanian Rugby Assoc. The surtax was used to encourage the sport.

1944, Mar. 1 Photo. *Perf. 13½*

B246	SP172	35 l + 65 l brt ultra	48	48

Centenary of medical teaching in Romania.

Queen Mother Helen — SP173

1945, Feb. 10

B247	SP173	4.50 l + 5.50 l pur, sep & red	18	18
B248	SP173	10 l + 40 l brn, sep & red	18	18
B249	SP173	15 l + 75 l gray bl, sep & red	18	18
B250	SP173	20 l + 80 l hn brn, sep & red	18	18

The surtax aided the Romanian Red Cross.

Kings Ferdinand and Michael and Map SP174

1945, Feb. *Perf. 14*

B251	SP174	75 l + 75 l dk ol brn	48	48

Romania's liberation.

Stefan Tomsa Church, Radaseni SP175

Municipal Home SP176

Gathering Fruit — SP177

School SP178

1944 Wmk. 276 Photo. *Perf. 14*

B252	SP175	5 l + 145 l brt bl	40	30
B253	SP176	12 l + 138 l car rose	40	30
B254	SP177	15 l + 135 l red org	40	30
B255	SP178	32 l + 118 l dk brn	40	30

King Michael and Carol I Foundation, Bucharest — SP179

King Carol I and Foundation — SP180

1945, Feb. 10 *Perf. 13*

B256	SP179	20 l + 180 l dp org	14	8
B257	SP179	25 l + 175 l slate	14	8
B258	SP179	35 l + 165 l cl brn	14	8
B259	SP179	75 l + 125 l pale vio	14	8

Souvenir Sheet

Imperf

Without Gum

B260	SP180	200 l blue	3.00	3.75

The surtax on Nos. B256 to B260 was to aid in rebuilding the Public Library, Bucharest.

Nos. B256-B259 were printed in sheets of four.

No. B260 sold for 1200 lei.

Ion G. Duca SP181

Designs: 16 l+184 l, Virgil Madgearu. 20 l+180 l, Nikolai Jorga. 32 l+168 l, Ilie Pintilie. 35 l+165 l, Bernath Andrei. 36 l+164 l, Filimon Sarbu.

1945, Apr. 30 *Perf. 13*

B261	SP181	12 l + 188 l dk bl	24	24
B262	SP181	16 l + 184 l cl brn	24	24
B263	SP181	20 l + 180 l blk brn	24	24
B264	SP181	32 l + 168 l brt red	24	24
B265	SP181	35 l + 165 l Prus bl	24	24
B266	SP181	36 l + 164 l lt vio	24	24
		Nos. B261-B266 (6)	1.44	1.44

Souvenir Sheet

Imperf

B267		Sheet of two	10.00	11.50
a.	SP181	32 l + 168 l mag	2.00	2.25
b.	SP181	35 l + 165 l mag	2.00	2.25

Nos. B261-B267 were issued to honor six victims of Nazi terrorism.

No. B267 sold for 1,000 lei.

Books and Torch SP188

Flags of Russia and Romania SP189

Kremlin, Moscow SP190

Tudor Vladimirescu and Alexander Nevsky SP191

1945, May 20 *Perf. 14*

B268	SP188	20 l + 80 l ol grn	18	18
B269	SP189	35 l + 165 l brt rose	18	18
B270	SP190	75 l + 225 l bl	18	18
B271	SP191	80 l + 420 l cl brn	18	18

Souvenir Sheet

Imperf

Without Gum

B272		Sheet of two	5.25	6.00
a.	SP189	35 l + 165 l brt red	1.25	1.40
b.	SP190	75 l + 225 l brt red	1.25	1.40

1st Soviet-Romanian Congress, May 20, 1945.

No. B272 sold for 900 lei.

Karl Marx — SP193

Designs: 120 l+380 l, Friedrich Engels. 155 l+445 l, Lenin.

1945, June 30 *Perf. 13½*

B273	SP193	75 l + 425 l car rose	1.25	1.25
B274	SP193	120 l + 380 l bl	1.25	1.25
B275	SP193	155 l + 445 l dk vio brn	1.25	1.25

Imperf

B276	SP193	75 l + 425 l bl	3.75	3.75
B277	SP193	120 l + 380 l dk vio brn	3.75	3.75
B278	SP193	155 l + 445 l car rose	3.75	3.75
		Nos. B273-B278 (6)	15.00	15.00

Nos. B276-B278 were printed in sheets of 4.

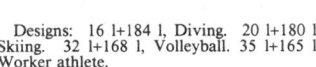

Woman Throwing Discus — SP196

Designs: 16 l+184 l, Diving. 20 l+180 l, Skiing. 32 l+168 l, Volleyball. 35 l+165 l, Worker athlete.

Wmk. 276

1945, Aug. 5 Photo. *Perf. 13*

B279	SP196	12 l + 188 l ol gray	90	90
B280	SP196	16 l + 184 l lt ultra	90	90
B281	SP196	20 l + 180 l dp grn	90	90
B282	SP196	32 l + 168 l mag	90	90
B283	SP196	35 l + 165 l brt bl	90	90

Imperf

B284	SP196	12 l + 188 l org red	90	90
B285	SP196	16 l + 184 l vio brn	90	90
B286	SP196	20 l + 180 l dp vio	90	90
B287	SP196	32 l + 168 l yel grn	90	90
B288	SP196	35 l + 165 l dk ol grn	90	90
		Nos. B279-B288 (10)	9.00	9.00

Nos. B279-B288 were printed in sheets of 9 inscribed in top margin.

Mail Plane and Bird Carrying Letter SP201

1945, Aug. 5 *Perf. 13½*

B289	SP201	200 l + 1000 l bl & dk bl	3.50	3.50
a.		With label	15.00	19.00

The surtax on Nos. B279-B289 was for the Office of Popular Sports.

Issued in sheets of 30 stamps and 10 labels, arranged 10x4 with second and fourth horizontal rows each having five alternating labels.

Agriculture and Industry United SP202

King Michael SP203

1945, Aug. 23 *Perf. 14*

B290	SP202	100 l + 400 l red	9	9
B291	SP203	200 l + 800 l bl	12	12

The surtax was for the Farmers' Front.

Political Amnesty SP204

Military Amnesty SP205

Agrarian Amnesty SP206

Tudor Vladimirescu SP207

Nicolae Horia SP208

Reconstruction — SP209

1945, Aug. *Perf. 13*

B292	SP204	20 l + 580 l choc	5.00	5.00
B293	SP204	20 l + 580 l mag	5.00	5.00
B294	SP205	40 l + 560 l bl	5.00	5.00
B295	SP205	40 l + 560 l sl grn	5.00	5.00
B296	SP206	55 l + 545 l red	5.00	5.00
B297	SP206	55 l + 545 l dk vio brn	5.00	5.00
B298	SP207	60 l + 540 l ultra	5.00	5.00
B299	SP207	60 l + 540 l choc	5.00	5.00
B300	SP208	80 l + 520 l red	5.00	5.00
B301	SP208	80 l + 520 l mag	5.00	5.00
B302	SP209	100 l + 500 l sl grn	5.00	5.00
B303	SP209	100 l + 500 l red brn	5.00	5.00
		Nos. B292-B303 (12)	60.00	60.00

1st anniv. of Romania's armistice with Russia. Issued in panes of four.

Nos. B292-B303 also exist on coarse grayish paper, ungummed (same value).

Electric Train SP210

Coats of Arms SP211

Truck on Mountain Road SP212

Oil Field SP213

"Agriculture" — SP214

1945, Oct. 1 ***Perf. 14***

B304 SP210 10 l + 490 l ol grn 18 18
B305 SP211 20 l + 480 l red brn 18 18
B306 SP212 25 l + 475 l brn vio 18 18
B307 SP213 55 l + 445 l ultra 18 18
B308 SP214 100 l + 400 l brn 18 18

Imperf

B309 SP210 10 l + 490 l bl 18 18
B310 SP211 20 l + 480 l vio 18 18
B311 SP212 25 l + 475 l bl grn 18 18
B312 SP213 55 l + 445 l gray 18 18
B313 SP214 100 l + 400 l dp mag 18 18
Nos. B304-B313 (10) 1.80 1.80

16th Congress of the General Assoc. of Romanian Engineers.

"Brotherhood" — SP215

Designs: 160 l+1840 l, "Peace." 320 l+1680 l, Hammer crushing Nazism. 440 l+2560 l, "World Unity."

1945, Dec. 5 ***Perf. 14***

B314 SP215 80 l + 920 l mag 9.25 9.25
B315 SP215 160 l + 1840 l org brn 9.25 9.25
B316 SP215 320 l + 1680 l vio 9.25 9.25
B317 SP215 440 l + 2560 l yel grn 9.25 9.25

World Trade Union Congress at Paris, Sept. 25-Oct. 10, 1945.

Nos. B290 and B291 Surcharged in Various Colors

1946, Jan. 20

B318 SP202 10 l + 90 l on 100 l+400 l red (Bk) 38 38
B319 SP203 10 l + 90 l on 200 l+800 l bl (R) 38 38
B320 SP202 20 l + 80 l on 100 l+400 l red (G) 38 38
B321 SP203 20 l + 80 l on 200 l+800 l bl (Bk) 38 38
B322 SP202 80 l + 120 l on 100 l+400 l red (Bl) 38 38
B323 SP203 80 l + 120 l on 200 l+800 l bl (Bk) 38 38
B324 SP202 100 l + 150 l on 100 l+400 l red (Bk) 38 38
B325 SP203 100 l + 150 l on 200 l+800 l bl (R) 38 38
Nos. B318-B325 (8) 3.04 3.04

Re-distribution of Land — SP219

Sower SP220

Ox Team Drawing Hay SP221

Old and New Plowing Methods SP222

1946, Mar. 6

B326 SP219 50 l + 450 l red 12 10
B327 SP220 100 l + 900 l red vio 12 12
B328 SP221 200 l + 800 l org 12 12
B329 SP222 400 l + 1600 l dk grn 12 12

Agrarian reform law of Mar. 23, 1945.

Philharmonic Types of Regular Issue

Perf. 13, 13½x13

1946, Apr. 26 **Photo.** **Wmk. 276**

B330 A211 200 l + 800 l brt red 60 60
a. Sheet of 12 14.00 17.50
B331 A213 350 l + 1650 l dk bl 65 65
a. Sheet of 12 14.00 17.50

Issued in sheets containing 12 stamps and 4 labels, with bars of music in the margins. Music and labels with No. B330 are slate gray, with No. B331 red orange.

Agriculture SP223

Dove SP228

Designs: 10 l+200 l, Hurdling. 80 l+200 l, Research. 80 l+300 l, Industry. 200 l+400 l, Workers and flag.

Wmk. 276

1946, July 28 **Photo.** ***Perf. 11½***

B332 SP223 10 l + 100 l dk org brn & red 18 18
B333 SP223 10 l + 200 l bl & red brn 18 18
B334 SP223 80 l + 200 l brn vio & brn 18 18
B335 SP223 80 l + 300 l dk org brn & rose lil 18 18
B336 SP223 200 l + 400 l Prus bl & red 18 28
Nos. B332-B336 (5) 90 1.00

Issued in panes of 4 stamps with marginal inscription.

1946, Oct. 20 ***Perf. 13½x13, Imperf.***

B338 SP228 300 l + 1200 l scar 48 22

Souvenir Sheet

Perf. 14x14½.

B339 SP228 1000 l scarlet 1.65 2.00

Romanian-Soviet friendship. No. B339 sold for 6000 lei.

Skiing — SP230

1946, Sept. 1 ***Perf. 11½, Imperf.***

B340 SP230 160 l + 1340 l dk grn 50 50

Surtax for Office of Popular Sports.

Spinning SP231

Reaping SP232

Riding SP233

Water Carrier SP234

1946, Nov. 20 ***Perf. 14***

B342 SP231 80 l + 320 l brt red 9 9
B343 SP232 140 l + 360 l dp org 9 9
B344 SP233 300 l + 450 l brn ol 12 12
B345 SP234 600 l + 900 l ultra 15 15

Democratic Women's Org. of Romania.

Angel with Food and Clothing SP235

Bread for Hungry Family SP236

Care for Needy SP237

1947, Jan. 15 ***Perf. 13½x14***

B346 SP235 1500 l + 3500 l red org 15 15
B347 SP236 3700 l + 5300 l dp vio 15 15

Miniature Sheet

Imperf

Without Gum

B348 SP237 5000 l + 5000 l ultra 1.10 1.65

The surtax on Nos. B346-B348 helped the social relief fund.

No. B348 is miniature sheet of one.

Student Reciting SP238

Allegory of Education — SP242

SP243

Designs: 300 l+300 l, Weaving class. 600 l+600 l, Young machinist. 1200 l+1200 l, Romanian school.

Perf. 14x13½

1947, Mar. 5 **Photo.** **Wmk. 276**

B349 SP238 200 l + 200 l vio bl 5 5
B350 SP238 300 l + 300 l red brn 5 5
B351 SP238 600 l + 600 l Prus grn 5 5
B352 SP238 1200 l + 1200 l ultra 5 5
B353 SP242 1500 l + 1500 l dp rose 5 5
Nos. B349-B353 (5) 25 25

Souvenir Sheet

Imperf

B354 SP243 3700 l + 3700 l dl brn & dl bl 75 90

50th anniv. of Romania's vocational schools.

Victor Babes — SP244

Designs: B356, Michael Eminescu. B357, Nicolae Grigorescu. B358, Peter Movila. B359, Aleksander S. Pushkin. B360, Mikhail V. Lomonosov. B361, Peter I. Tchaikovsky. B362, Ilya E. Repin.

1947, Apr. 18 ***Perf. 14***

B355 SP244 1500 l + 1500 l red org 12 12
B356 SP244 1500 l + 1500 l dk ol grn 12 12
B357 SP244 1500 l + 1500 l dk bl 12 12
B358 SP244 1500 l + 1500 l dp plum 12 12
B359 SP244 1500 l + 1500 l scar 12 12
B360 SP244 1500 l + 1500 l rose brn 12 12
B361 SP244 1500 l + 1500 l ultra 12 12
B362 SP244 1500 l + 1500 l choc 12 12
Nos. B355-B362 (8) 96 96

Transportation — SP252

Designs: No. B364, Farmer. No. B365, Farm woman. No. B366, Teacher and school. No. B367, Laborer and factory.

1947, May 1

B363 SP252 1000 l + 1000 l dk ol brn 10 10
B364 SP252 1500 l + 1500 l red brn 10 10
B365 SP252 2000 l + 2000 l bl 10 10
B366 SP252 2500 l + 2500 l red vio 10 10
B367 SP252 3000 l + 3000 l crim rose 10 10
Nos. B363-B367 (5) 50 50

Issued to publicize Labor Day, May 1, 1947.

No. 650 Surcharged in Carmine

2+3 LEI
C.B.A.
1947

1947, Sept. 6 *Perf. 13½*

B368 A234 2 l + 3 l on 36,000 l vio 48 48

Balkan Games of 1947, Bucharest.

Type of 1947 Surcharged in Carmine

ARLUS +5
1-7.XI.
1947

Design: Cathedral of Curtea de Arges.

1947, Oct. 30 *Imperf.*

B369 A235 5 l + 5 l brt ultra 35 35

Soviet-Romanian Congress, Nov. 1-7.

Plowing — SP257

Perf. 14x14½

1947, Oct. 5 **Photo.** **Wmk. 276**

B370 SP257 1 l + 1 l shown 9 9
B371 SP257 2 l + 2 l Sawmill 9 9
B372 SP257 3 l + 3 l Refinery 9 9
B373 SP257 4 l + 4 l Steel mill 12 12
Nos. B370-B373,CB12 (5) 91 63

17th Congress of the General Assoc. of Romanian Engineers.

Allegory of Industry, Science and Agriculture SP258

Winged Man Holding Hammer and Sickle SP259

1947, Nov. 10 *Perf. 14½x14*

B374 SP258 2 l + 10 l rose lake 14 14
B375 SP259 7 l + 10 l bluish blk 14 14

2nd Trade Union Conf., Nov. 10.

Convoy of Food for Moldavia SP260

"Three Years of Action" — SP264

Designs: 2 l+2 l, "Everything for the Front-Everything for Victory." 3 l+3 l, Woman, child and hospital. 4 l+4 l, "Help the Famine-stricken Regions."

1947, Nov. 7 *Perf. 14*

B376 SP260 1 l + 1 l dk gray bl 9 9
B377 SP260 2 l + 2 l dk brn 9 9
B378 SP260 3 l + 3 l rose lake 9 9
B379 SP260 4 l + 4 l brt ultra 15 15
B380 SP260 5 l + 5 l red 18 18
Nos. B376-B380 (5) 60 60

Issued in sheets of four.

Discus Thrower SP265

Labor SP266

Youths Following Filimon Sarbu Banner SP269

Designs: 2 l+2 l, Runner. 5 l+5 l, Boy and girl athletes.

Wmk. 276

1948, Feb. **Photo.** *Perf. 13½*

B381 SP265 1 l + 1 l dk brn 22 22
B382 SP265 2 l + 2 l car lake 30 30
B383 SP265 5 l + 5 l bl 45 45
Nos. B381-B383,CB13-CB14 (5) 2.87 2.15

Balkan Games of 1947.

1948, Mar. 15

Designs: 3 l+3 l, Agriculture. 5 l+5 l, Education.

B384 SP266 2 l + 2 l dk sl bl 25 25
B385 SP266 3 l + 3 l gray grn 30 20
B386 SP266 5 l + 5 l red brn 40 30

Imperf

B387 SP269 8 l + 8 l dk car rose 60 40
Nos. B384-B387,CB15 (5) 2.40 1.80

No. B387 issued in triangular sheets of 4.

Gliders — SP270

Sailboat Race SP271

Designs: No. B389, Early plane. No. B390, Plane over farm. No. B391, Transport plane. B393, Training ship, Mircea. B394, Danube ferry. B395, S.S. Transylvania.

1948, July 26 *Perf. 14x14½*

B388 SP270 2 l + 2 l bl 1.25 1.25
B389 SP270 5 l + 5 l pur 1.25 1.25
B390 SP270 8 l + 8 l dk car rose 1.25 1.25
B391 SP270 10 l + 10 l choc 1.25 1.25
B392 SP271 2 l + 2 l dk grn 1.00 1.00
B393 SP271 5 l + 5 l sl 1.00 1.00
B394 SP271 8 l + 8 l brt bl 1.00 1.00
B395 SP271 10 l + 10 l ver 1.00 1.00
Nos. B388-B395 (8) 9.00 9.00

Air and Sea Communications Day.

Type of Regular Issue and

Torch, Pen, Ink and Flag SP272

Alexandru Sahia SP273

Romanian-Soviet Association Emblem SP274

Perf. 14x13½, 13½x14, Imperf.

1948, Sept. 12

B396 A241 5 l + 5 l crim 90 90
B397 SP272 10 l + 10 l vio 1.10 1.10
B398 SP273 15 l + 15 l bl 1.10 1.10

Week of the Democratic Press, Sept. 12-19.

1948, Oct. 29 *Perf. 14*

Design: 15 l+15 l, Spasski Tower, Kremlin.

B399 SP274 10 l + 10 l gray grn 1.25 1.25
B400 SP274 15 l + 15 l dp ultra 1.50 1.50

No. B399 was issued in sheets of 50 stamps and 50 labels.

Symbols of United Labor SP275

Agriculture SP276

Industry SP277

Automatic Riflemen SP278

Soldiers Cutting Barbed Wire — SP279

1948, May 1 ***Perf. 14x13½, 13½x14.***

B401 SP275 8 l + 8 l red 2.00 2.00
B402 SP276 10 l + 10 l ol grn 2.00 2.00
B403 SP277 12 l + 12 l red brn 2.00 2.00

Labor Day, May 1. See No. CB17.

1948, May 9

Flags and Dates:
23 Aug 1944-9 Mai 1945

B404 SP278 1.50 l + 1.50l shown 95 95
B405 SP279 2 l + 2 l shown 95 95
B406 SP279 4 l + 4 l Field Artillery 95 95
B407 SP279 7.50 l + 7.50 l Tank 95 95
B408 SP279 8 l + 8 l War-ship 95 95
Nos. B404-B408,CB18-CB19 (7) 9.75 9.75

Issued to honor the Romanian Army.

Nicolae Balcescu SP280

Balcescu and Revolutionists SP281

Balcescu, Sandor Petőfi and Revolutionists — SP282

Design: No. B412, Balcescu and revolutionists.

1948, June 1 *Perf. 13x13½*

B409 SP280 2 l + 2 l car lake 60 60
B410 SP281 5 l + 5 l dk vio 60 60
B411 SP282 10 l + 10 l dk ol brn 60 60
B412 SP280 36 l + 18 l dp bl 1.10 1.10

Centenary of Revolution of 1848.

Loading Freighter SP283

Designs: 3 l+3 l, Lineman. 11 l+11 l, Transport plane. 15 l+15 l, Railroad train.

Wmk. 289

1948, Dec. 10 **Photo.** *Perf. 14*

Center in Black

B413 SP283 1 l + 1 l dk grn 30 30
B414 SP283 3 l + 3 l redsh brn 38 38
B415 SP283 11 l + 11 l dp bl 1.65 1.25
B416 SP283 15 l + 15 l red 2.10 1.90
a. Sheet of 4 5.75 6.75

No. B416a contains four imperf. stamps similar to Nos. B413-B416 in changed colors, center in brown. No gum.

Demand, as well as supply, determines a stamp's market value. One is as important as the other.

Runners — SP284

Parade of Athletes SP285

Perf. 13x13½, 13½x13

1948, Dec. 31

B421	SP284	5 l + 5 l grn		1.90	1.90
B422	SP285	10 l + 10 l brn vio		3.00	3.00

Imperf

B424	SP285	10 l + 10 l red		3.00	3.00
Nos. B421-B424,CB20-CB21 (5)				27.40	27.40

Nos. B421 to B424 were issued in sheets of four stamps, with ornamental border and "1948" in contrasting color.

Souvenir Sheet

SP286

1950, Jan. 27

B425	SP286	10 l carmine	1.10	42

Philatelic exhibition, Bucharest. Label and inscriptions in dark blue and blue. Sold for 50 lei.

Crossing the Buzau, by Denis Auguste Marie Raffet — SP287

1967, Nov. 15 Engr. *Perf. 13½*

B426	SP287	55b + 45b ocher & ind	40	20

Stamp Day.

Old Bucharest, 18th Century Painting — SP288

1968, Nov. 15 Photo. *Perf. 13½*

B427	SP288	55b + 45b multi	40	20

Stamp Day.

1969, Nov. 15

Design: 55b+45b, Courtyard, by M. Bouquet.

B428	SP288	55b + 45b multi	38	20

Stamp Day. Se-tenant label at right of stamp carries 45b surtax and initials A F R.

1970, Nov. 15

Design: Mail Coach in the Winter, by Emil Volkers.

B429	SP288	55b + 45b multi	40	16

Stamp Day. Se-tenant label at right of stamp (imperf. between) carries 45b surtax and initials A F R.

Lady with Letter, by Sava Hentia SP289

1971, Nov. 15 Photo. *Perf. 13½*

B430	SP289	1.10 l + 90b multi	48	38

Stamp Day. Se-tenant label below stamp carries 90b surtax and shows Romania No. 12.

Stamp Day Type of 1968

Design: 1.10 l+90b, Traveling Gypsies, by Emil Volkers.

1972, Nov. 15 Photo. *Perf. 13½*

B431	SP288	1.10 l + 90b multi	55	35

Stamp Day. Se-tenant label at left of stamp carries 90b surtax and A F R monogram.

Portrait Type of Regular Issue

Designs: 4 l+2 l, Barbat at his Desk, by B. Iscovescu. 6 l+2 l, The Poet Alecsandri with his Family, by N. Livaditti.

1973, June 20 Photo. *Perf. 13½*

B432	A728	4 l + 2 l multi	1.25	65

Souvenir Sheet

B433	A728	6 l + 2 l multi	1.90	1.90

No. B433 contains one stamp 38x50mm.

Postilion, by A. Verona — SP290

1973, Nov. 15 Photo. *Perf. 13½*

B434	SP290	1.10 l + 90b multi	38	20

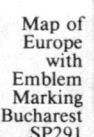

Stamp Day.

Map of Europe with Emblem Marking Bucharest SP291

1974, June 25 Photo. *Perf. 13½*

B435	SP291	4 l + 3 l multi	1.40	70

EUROMAX, European Exhibition of Maximaphily, Bucharest, Oct. 6-13.

Marketplace, Sibiu — SP292

1974, Nov. 15 Photo. *Perf. 13½*

B436	SP292	2.10 l + 1.90 l multi	90	45

Stamp Day.

No. B436 Overprinted in Red: "EXPOZITIA FILATELICA 'NATIONALA '74' / 15-24 noiembrie / Bucuresti"

1974, Nov. 15

B437	SP292	2.10 l + 1.90 l multi	2.50	90

NATIONALA '74 Philatelic Exhibition, Bucharest, Nov. 15-24.

Post Office, Bucharest SP293

Design: 2.10 l+1.90 l, like B438, side view.

1975, Nov. 15 Photo. *Perf. 13½*

B438	SP293	1.50 l + 1.50 l multi	60	30
B439	SP293	2.10 l + 1.90 l multi	1.10	45

Stamp Day.

No. 2612 Surcharged and Overprinted: "EXPOZITIA FILATELICA / BUCURESTI / 12-19.IX.1976"

1976, Sept. 12 Photo. *Perf. 13½*

B440	A787	3.60 l + 1.80 l	2.10	1.25

Philatelic Exhibition, Bucharest, Sept. 12-19.

Elena Cuza, by Theodor Aman SP294

Dispatch Rider Handing Letter to Officer SP295

1976, Nov. 15 Photo. *Perf. 13½*

B441	SP294	2.10 l + 1.90 l multi	90	45

Stamp Day.

Independence Type of 1977

Design: 4.80 l+2 l, Battle of Rahova, after etching.

1977, May 9 Photo. *Perf. 13½*

B442	A806	4.80 l + 2 l multi	1.25	45

1977, Nov. Photo. *Perf. 13½*

B443	SP295	2.10 l + 1.90 l multi	90	45

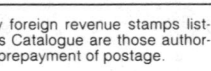

Stamp Day.

Dacian Warrior, from Trajan's Column, Rome — SP296

1978, Nov. 5 Photo. *Perf. 13x13½*

B444	SP296	6 l + 3 l multi	1.65	1.00

NATIONALA '78 Phil. Exhib., Bucharest.

Socfilex Type of 1979

Flower Paintings by Luchian: 4 l+2 l, Field flowers. 10 l+5 l, Roses.

1979, July 27 Photo. *Perf. 13½*

B445	A847	4 l + 2 l multi	1.10	38

Souvenir Sheet

B446	A847	10 l + 5 l multi	3.25	1.25

Socfilex, Oct. 26-Nov. 1, Intl. Phil. Exhib., Bucharest. No. B446 contains one stamp 50x38mm.

Stamp Day SP297

1979, Dec. 12 Photo. *Perf. 13½*

B447	SP297	2.10 l + 1.90 l multi	70	30

Souvenir Sheet

Stamp Day — SP298

1980, July 1 Photo. *Perf. 13½*

B448	SP298	5 l + 5 l multi	2.10	1.75

AIR POST STAMPS

Capt. C. G. Craiu's Airplane AP1

Wmk. 95 Vertical

1928 Photo. *Perf. 13½*

C1	AP1	1 l red brn	1.50	1.50
C2	AP1	2 l brt bl	1.50	1.50
C3	AP1	5 l car rose	1.50	1.50

Wmk. 95 Horizontal

C4	AP1	1 l red brn	1.50	1.50
C5	AP1	2 l brt bl	1.50	1.50
C6	AP1	5 l car rose	1.50	1.50

Nos. C4-C6 Overprinted **8 IUNIE 1930**

1930

C7 AP1 1 l red brn 4.50 4.50
C8 AP1 2 l brt bl 4.50 4.50
a. Vert. pair, imperf. btwn. *180.00*
C9 AP1 5 l car rose 4.50 4.50

Same Overprint on Nos. C1-C3
Wmk. 95 Vertical

C10 AP1 1 l red brn 30.00 30.00
C11 AP1 2 l brt bl 30.00 30.00
C12 AP1 5 l car rose 30.00 30.00

Nos. C7 to C12 commemorated the accession of King Carol II.
Excellent connterfeits are known of Nos. C10-C12.

King Carol II — AP2

1930, Oct. 4 **Unwmk.**
Bluish Paper

C13 AP2 1 l dk vio 70 35
C14 AP2 2 l gray grn 85 35
C15 AP2 5 l red brn 1.90 70
C16 AP2 10 l brt bl 3.50 85

Junkers Monoplane AP3

Monoplanes AP7

Designs: 3 l, Monoplane with biplane behind. 5 l, Biplane. 10 l, Monoplane flying leftward.

1931, Nov. 4 **Wmk. 230**

C17 AP3 2 l dl grn 40 15
C18 AP3 3 l carmine 50 20
C19 AP3 5 l red brn 70 20
C20 AP3 10 l blue 1.65 38
C21 AP7 20 l dk vio 3.25 90
Nos. C17-C21 (5) 6.50 1.83

Nos. C17 to C21 exist imperforate.

Souvenir Sheets

Plane over Resita AP8

Plane over Sinaia AP9

Wmk. 276
1945, Oct. 1 **Photo.** ***Perf. 13.***
Without Gum

C22 AP8 80 l sl grn 5.00 5.00

Imperf

C23 AP9 80 l magenta 3.50 3.50

16th Congress of the General Assoc. of Romanian Engineers.

Catalogue values for unused stamps in this section, from this point to the end of the section, are for Never Hinged items.

Plane AP10

Design: 500 l, Aviator and planes.

1946, Sept. 5 ***Perf. 13½x13***

C24 AP10 200 l yel grn & bl 1.00 75
C25 AP10 500 l org red & dl bl 1.00 75

Printed in sheets of four with marginal inscription.

Lockheed 12 Electra AP12

CGM Congress Emblem AP13

1946, Oct. ***Perf. 11½.***

C26 AP12 300 l crimson 40 40
a. Se-tenant with No. CB6 1.25 1.25

Sheet of 16 contains 8 each of Nos. C26 and CB6, arranged so se-tenant or normal pairs are available. Two sheet layouts exist, one with No. C26 in corners and one with No. CB6 in corners.

1947, Mar. **Wmk. 276** ***Perf. 13x14***

C27 AP13 1100 l blue 28 28

Congress of the United Labor Unions ("CGM"). Printed in sheets of 15.

"May 1" Supported by Parachutes AP14

Plane and Conference Banner AP17

Designs: No. C29, Air Force monument. No. C30, Plane over rural road.

1947, May 4 ***Perf. 11½***

C28 AP14 3000 l vermilion 14 14
C29 AP14 3000 l grnsh gray 14 14
C30 AP14 3000 l blk brn 14 14

Printed in sheets of four with marginal inscriptions.

1947, Nov. 10 ***Perf. 14***

C31 AP17 11 l bl & dp car 28 28

2nd Trade Union Conference, Nov. 10.

Emblem of the Republic and Factories AP18

Industry and Agriculture AP19

Transportation — AP20

Perf. 14x13½
1948-50 **Wmk. 289** **Photo.**

C32 AP18 30 l cerise 28 14
a. 30 l carmine ('50) 38 28
C33 AP19 50 l dk sl grn 38 20
C34 AP20 100 l ultra 1.10 55

Transportation AP21

Design: 30 l, Agriculture.

1951-52 **Wmk. 358** ***Perf. 13½***

C35 AP21 30 l dk grn ('52) 1.25 1.10
C36 AP21 50 l red brn 90 70

1951-55 Five Year Plan.

Nos. C32-C36 Surcharged with New Values in Blue or Carmine

1952 **Wmk. 289** ***Perf. 14x13½***

C37 AP18 3b on 30 l cer (Bl) 50 25
a. 3b on 30 l carmine (Bl) *7.25* *6.50*
C38 AP19 3b on 50 l dk sl grn 50 25
C39 AP20 3b on 100 l ultra 50 25

Perf. 13½
Wmk. 358

C40 AP21 1 l on 30 l dk grn *7.50* *2.25*
C41 AP21 1 l on 50 l red brn *7.50* *2.25*
Nos. C37-C41 (5) 16.50 5.25

Nos. 706 and 707 Surcharged in Blue or Carmine

1953 **Wmk. 289** ***Perf. 13½, 14***

C43 A250 3 l on 20 l org brn *7.50* *6.50*
C44 A251 5 l on 30 l brt bl (C) *9.75* *9.00*

Plane facing right and surcharge arranged to fit design on No. C44.

Plane over City — AP22

Sputnik 1 and Earth — AP23

Designs: 55b, Plane over Mountains. 1.75 l, over Harvest fields. 2.25 l, over Seashore.

Perf. 14½x14
1956, Dec. 15 **Photo.** **Wmk. 358**

C45 AP22 20b brt bl, org & grn 20 14
C46 AP22 55b brt bl, grn & ocher 35 10
C47 AP22 1.75 l brt bl & red org 1.25 15
C48 AP22 2.55 l brt bl & red org 1.50 38

1957, Nov. 6 ***Perf. 14***

Design: 3.75 l, Sputniks 1 and 2 circling globe.

C49 AP23 25b brt ultra 30 14
C50 AP23 25b dk bl grn 30 14
C51 AP23 3.75 l brt ultra 1.50 38
C52 AP23 3.75 l dk bl grn 1.50 38

Nos. C49 and C51 are printed se-tenant with gray label. Nos. C50 and C52 are printed se-tenant with brown label. Each sheet contains 27 triptychs with the center rows arranged tete-beche.
In 1958 Nos. C49-C52 were overprinted: 1.) "Expozitia Universal a Bruxelles 1958" and star. 2.) Large star. 3.) Small star.

Animal Type of Regular Issue, 1957

Birds: 3.30 l, Black-headed gull (horiz.). 5 l, Sea eagle (horiz.).

Perf. 14x13½
1957, Dec. 27 **Wmk. 358**

C53 A445 3.30 l ultra & gray 1.65 35
C54 A445 5 l car & org 2.50 50

Armed Forces Type of Regular Issue

Design: Flier and planes.

Perf. 13½x13
1958, Oct. 2 **Unwmk.** **Photo.**

C55 A458 3.30 l brt vio 90 55

Day of the Armed Forces, Oct. 2.

Earth and Sputnik 3 Orbit AP24

1958, Sept. 20 ***Perf. 14x13½***

C56 AP24 3.25 l ind & ocher 1.75 52

Launching of Sputnik 3, May 15, 1958.

Souvenir Sheet
Type of Regular Issue, 1958

Design: Tête bêche pair of 27pa of 1858.

Perf. 11½
1958, Nov. 15 **Unwmk.** **Engr.**

C57 A462 10 l blue 12.50 12.50

A similar sheet, printed in dull red and imperf., exists.
No. C57 was overprinted in 1959 in vermilion to commemorate the 10th anniv. of the State Philatelic Trade.
Values, $25 and $60.

Lunik I Leaving Earth AP25

Frederic Joliot-Curie AP26

1959, Feb. 4 **Photo.** ***Perf. 14***

C58 AP25 3.25 l vio bl, *pnksh* 4.50 90

Launching of the "first artificial planet of the solar system."

1959, Apr. 25 ***Perf. 13½x14***

C59 AP26 3.25 l ultra 2.50 70

Frederic Joliot-Curie; 10th anniv. of the World Peace Movement.

Rock Thrush
AP27

Birds: 20b, European golden oriole. 35b, Lapwing. 40b, Barn swallow. No. C64, Goldfinch. No. C65, Great spotted woodpecker. No. C66, Great tit. 1 l, Bullfinch. 1.55 l, Long-tailed tit. 5 l, Wall creeper. Nos. C62-C67 vertical.

1959, June 25 Litho. *Perf. 14*

Birds in Natural Colors

C60	AP27	10b gray, *cr*	9	5
C61	AP27	20b gray, *grysh*	9	5
C62	AP27	35b gray, *grysh*	12	5
C63	AP27	40b gray & red, *pnksh*	15	5
C64	AP27	55b gray, *buff*	22	6
C65	AP27	55b gray, *grnsh*	22	9
C66	AP27	55b gray & ol, *grysh*	22	9
C67	AP27	1 l gray and red, *cr*	75	12
C68	AP27	1.55 l gray & red, *pnksh*	90	12
C69	AP27	5 l gray, *grnsh*	3.75	90
		Nos. C60-C69 (10)	*6.51*	*1.58*

No. C58 Surcharged in Red

=
h. 00,02,24
14-IX-1959
PRIMA RACHETA COSMICA
IN LUNA
5 LEI

1959, Sept. 14 Photo. Unwmk.

C70	AP25	5 l on 3.25 l vio bl, *pnksh*	4.75	1.10

1st Russian rocket to reach the moon, Sept. 14, 1959.

Miniature Sheet

Prince Vlad Tepes and Document
AP28

1959, Sept. 15 Engr. *Perf. 11½x11*

C71	AP28	20 l vio brn	45.00	45.00

500th anniv. of the founding of Bucharest.

Sport Type of Regular Issue, 1959

Design: 2.80 l, Boating.

1959, Oct. 5 Litho. *Perf. 13½*

C72	A474	2.80 l multi	1.50	45

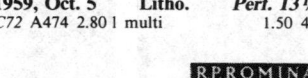

Soviet Rocket, Globe, Dog and Rabbit — AP29

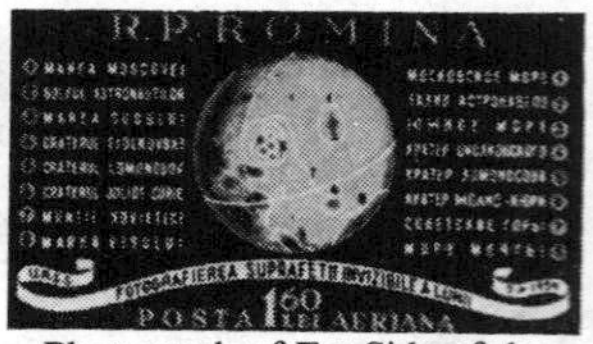

Photograph of Far Side of the Moon — AP30

Design: 1.75 l, Trajectory of Lunik 3, which hit the moon.

Perf. 14, 13½ (AP30)

1959, Dec. Photo. Wmk. 358

C73	AP29	1.55 l dk bl	2.25	30
C74	AP30	1.60 l dk vio bl, *buff*	3.00	38
C75	AP29	1.75 l dk bl	3.00	38

Soviet conquest of space.

Animal Type of Regular Issue, 1960.

Designs: 1.30 l, Golden eagle. 1.75 l, Black grouse. 2 l, Lammergeier.

Unwmk.

1960, Mar. 3 Engr. *Perf. 14*

C76	A480	1.30 l dk bl	85	28
C77	A480	1.75 l ol grn	1.25	28
C78	A480	2 l dk car	1.50	35

Aurel Vlaicu and Plane of 1910
AP31

Bucharest Airport and Turbo-Jet — AP32

Designs: 20b, Plane and Aurel Vlaicu. 35b, Amphibian ambulance plane. 40b, Plane spraying crops. 55b, Pilot and planes (vert.) 1.75 l, Parachutes at aviation sports meet.

Litho., Unwmk.: 10b, 20b, 1.60 l, 1.75 l. Photo., Wmk. 358: 35b, 40b, 55b.

1960, June 15 *Perf. 14*

C79	AP31	10b yel & brn	12	5
C80	AP31	20b red org & brn	14	5
C81	AP31	35b crimson	20	5
C82	AP31	40b violet	28	8
C83	AP31	55b blue	40	7
C84	AP32	1.60 l vio bl, yel & emer	95	22
C85	AP32	1.75 l bl, red, brn & pale grn	1.25	40
		Nos. C79-C85 (7)	3.34	92

50th anniv. of the first Romanian airplane flight by Aurel Vlaicu.

Bucharest Airport
AP33

Sputnik 4 Flying into Space
AP34

1960 Wmk. 358 Photo. *Perf. 14*

C86	AP33	3.20 l brt ultra	1.10	15

Type of Regular Issue, 1960

Black Sea Resort: 2 l, Beach at Mamaia.

1960, Aug. 2 Litho. Unwmk.

C87	A491	2 l grn, org & lt bl	90	28

1960, June 8 Photo. Wmk. 358

C88	AP34	55b dp bl	1.25	28

Launching of Sputnik 4, May 15, 1960.

Saturnia Pyri
AP35

Papilio Machaon
AP36

Limenitis Populi — AP37

Designs: 40b, Chrisophanus virgaureae. 1.60 l, Acherontia atropos. 1.75 l, Apatura iris (horiz.).

Perf. 13, 14x12½, 14

1960, Oct. 10 Typo. Unwmk.

C89	AP35	10b multi	7	5
C90	AP37	20b multi	8	5
C91	AP37	40b multi	14	5
C92	AP36	55b multi	28	8
C93	AP36	1.60 l multi	80	18
C94	AP36	1.75 l multi	90	18
		Nos. C89-C94 (6)	2.27	59

Compass Rose and Jet — AP38

Perf. 13½x14

1960, Nov. 1 Photo. Wmk. 358

C95	AP38	55b brt bl + 45b label	48	16

Stamp Day. In sheet, stamps alternate with olive bister label.

Skier
AP39

Slalom
AP40

Maj. Yuri A. Gagarin
AP41

Designs: 25b, Skiers going up. 40b, Bobsled. 55b, Ski jump. 1 l, Mountain climber. 1.55 l, Long-distance skier.

Perf. 14x13½, 13½x14

1961, Mar. 18 Litho. Unwmk.

C96	AP39	10b ol & gray	6	5
C97	AP40	20b gray & dk red	8	5
C98	AP40	25b gray & bl grn	8	6
C99	AP40	40b gray & pur	12	7
C100	AP39	55b gray & ultra	20	8
C101	AP40	1 l gray & brn lake	42	14
C102	AP39	1.55 l gray & brn	75	20
		Nos. C96-C102 (7)	1.71	65

Exist imperf. with changed colors. Value, set $3.75.

Perf. 14x14½, 14½x14

1961, Apr. 19 Photo. Unwmk.

Design: 3.20 l, Gagarin in space capsule and globe with orbit (horiz.).

C103	AP41	1.35 l brt bl	60	12
C104	AP41	3.20 l ultra	1.25	18

No. C104 exists imperf. in dk carmine rose. Value unused $3.75, canceled $2.

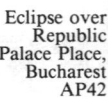

Eclipse over Republic Palace Place, Bucharest
AP42

Design: 1.75 l, Total Eclipse, Scinteia House and telescope.

Perf. 14x13½

1961, June 13 Wmk. 358

C106	AP42	1.60 l ultra	70	28
C107	AP42	1.75 l dk bl	70	28

Total solar eclipse of Feb. 15, 1961.

Maj. Gherman S. Titov
AP43

Globe and Stamps
AP44

Designs: 55b, "Peace" and Vostok 2 rocket. 1.75 l, Yuri A. Gagarin and Gherman S. Titov (horiz.).

Perf. 13½x14

1961, Sept. 11 Unwmk.

C108	AP43	55b dp bl	38	6
C109	AP43	1.35 l dp pur	55	15
C110	AP43	1.75 l dk car	90	20

Issued to honor the Russian space navigators Y. A. Gagarin and G. S. Titov.

1961, Nov. 15 Litho. *Perf. 13½x14*

C111	AP44	55b multi + 45b label	50	18

Stamp Day. In sheet, stamps alternate with red orange and blue label.

Railroad Station, Constanta
AP45

Buildings: 20b, Tower, RPR Palace place (vert.). 55b, Congress hall, Bucharest. 75b, Mill, Hunedoara. 1 l, Apartment houses, Bucharest. 1.20 l, Circus, Bucharest. 1.75 l, Worker's Club, Mangalia.

Perf. 13½x14, 14x13½

1961, Nov. 20 Typo.

C112	AP45	20b multi	9	5
C113	AP45	40b multi	16	5
C114	AP45	55b multi	16	5
C115	AP45	75b multi	25	7
C116	AP45	1 l multi	32	10
C117	AP45	1.20 l multi	65	32
C118	AP45	1.75 l multi	95	48
		Nos. C112-C118 (7)	2.58	1.12

Space Exploration Stamps and Dove
AP46

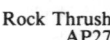

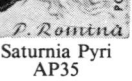

Design: Each stamp shows a different group of Romanian space exploration stamps.

1962, July 27 *Perf. 14x13½*

C119 AP46	35b	yel brn	14	6
C120 AP46	55b	green	22	8
C121 AP46	1.35 l	blue	40	16
C122 AP46	1.75 l	rose red	80	28
a.		Sheet of 4	2.25	90

Peaceful space exploration.

No. C122a contains four imperf. stamps similar to Nos. C119-C122 in changed colors and with one dove covering all four stamps. Stamps are printed together without space between.

Andrian G. Nikolayev — AP47

Designs: 1.60 l, Globe and trajectories of Vostoks 3 and 4. 1.75 l, Pavel R. Popovich.

Perf. 13½x14

1962, Aug. 20 **Photo.** **Unwmk.**

C123 AP47	55b	purple	35	16
C124 AP47	1.60 l	dk bl	1.00	35
C125 AP47	1.75 l	rose cl	1.25	40

1st Russian group space flight of Vostoks 3 and 4, Aug. 11-15, 1962.

Exhibition Hall AP48

The Coachmen by Szatmary AP49

1962, Oct. 12 **Litho.** *Perf. 14x13*

C126 AP48	1.60 l	bl, vio bl & org	90	15

4th Sample Fair, Bucharest.

1962, Nov. 15 *Perf. 13½x14*

C127 AP49	55b	Prus bl & blk + 45b label	75	28

Stamp Day. Alternating label shows No. 14 on cover.

No. C127 Overprinted in Violet

1963, Mar. 30

C128 AP49	55b	Prus bl & blk + 45b label	1.50	1.10

Romanian Philatelists' Assoc. meeting at Bucharest, Mar. 30. The overprint is centered on the stamp and label, about half of it on each.

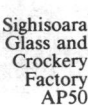

Sighisoara Glass and Crockery Factory AP50

Industrial Plants: 40b, Govora soda works. 55b, Tirgul-Jiu wood processing factory. 1 l, Savinesti chemical plant (synthetic fibers). 1.55 l, Hunedoara metal factory. 1.75 l, Brazi thermal power station.

Perf. 14x13

1963, Apr. 10 **Unwmk.** **Photo.**

C129 AP50	30b	dk bl & red	8	8
C130 AP50	40b	sl grn & pur	12	6
C131 AP50	55b	brn red & dp bl	14	8
C132 AP50	1 l	vio & brn	22	12
C133 AP50	1.55 l	ver & dk bl	50	9
C134 AP50	1.75 l	dk bl & mag	70	18
		Nos. C129-C134 (6)	1.76	61

Industrial achievements.

Lunik 4 Approaching Moon — AP51

1963, Apr. 29 *Perf. 13½x14*

C135 AP51	55b	dk ultra & red	45	18

Imperf

C136 AP51	1.75 l	vio & red	75	30

Moon flight of Lunik 4, Apr. 2, 1963.

Steam Locomotive AP52

Designs: 55b, Diesel locomotive. 75b, Trolley bus. 1.35 l, Passenger ship. 1.75 l, Plane.

1963, July 10 **Litho.** *Perf. 14½x13*

C137 AP52	40b	multi	18	9
C138 AP52	55b	multi	28	9
C139 AP52	75b	multi	38	15
C140 AP52	1.35 l	multi	70	18
C141 AP52	1.75 l	multi	1.10	24
		Nos. C137-C141 (5)	2.64	75

Valeri Bykovski AP53

Designs: 1.20 l, Bykovski (vert.). 1.60 l, Tereshkova (vert.). 1.75 l, Valentina Tereshkova.

1963 **Photo.**

C142 AP53	55b	blue	16	8
C143 AP53	1.75 l	rose red	60	18

Souvenir Sheet

Perf. 13

C144	Souv. sheet of 2	1.95	60
a. AP53	1.20 l ultra	50	28
b. AP53	1.60 l ultra	50	28

Space flights of Valeri Bykovski, June 14-19, and Valentina Tereshkova, first woman cosmonaut, June 16-19, 1963.

No. C79 Surcharged and Overprinted: "1913-1963 50 ani de la moarte"

Unwmk.

1963, Sept. 15 **Litho.** *Perf. 14*

C145 AP31	1.75 l	on 10b yel & brn	1.00	42

50th death anniv. of Aurel Vlaicu, aviation pioneer.

Centenary Stamp of 1958 — AP54

Stamps on Stamps: 40b, Sputnik 2 and Laika, No. 1200. 55b, Yuri A. Gagarin, No. C104a. 1.20 l, Nikolayev and Popovich, Nos. C123 & C125. 1.55 l, Postal Administration Bldg. and letter carrier, No. 965.

1963, Nov. 15 **Photo.** *Perf. 14x13½*

Size: 38x26mm

C146 AP54	20b	lt bl & dk brn	14	7
C147 AP54	40b	brt pink & dk bl	22	7
C148 AP54	55b	lt ultra & dk car rose	28	7
C149 AP54	1.20 l	ocher & pur	55	14
C150 AP54	1.55 l	sal pink & ol gray	65	18
		Nos. C146-C150,CB22 (6)	3.24	1.13

15th UPU Congress, Vienna.

Pavel R. Popovich AP55

Astronauts and flag: 5b, Yuri A. Gagarin. 10b, Gherman S. Titov. 20b, John H. Glenn, Jr. 35b, M. Scott Carpenter. 40b, Andrian G. Nikolayev. 60b, Walter M. Schirra. 75b, Gordon L. Cooper. 1 l, Valeri Bykovski. 1.40 l, Valentina Tereshkova. (5b, 10b, 20b, 35b, 60b and 75b are diamond shaped).

Perf. 13½

1964, Jan. 15 **Litho.** **Unwmk.**

Light Blue Background

C151 AP55	5b	red, yel & vio bl	9	5
C152 AP55	10b	red, yel & pur	9	5
C153 AP55	20b	red, ultra & ol gray	18	5
C154 AP55	35b	red, ultra & sl bl	22	6
C155 AP55	40b	red, yel & ultra	22	8
C156 AP55	55b	red, yel & ultra	38	9
C157 AP55	60b	ultra, red & sep	38	9
C158 AP55	75b	red, ultra & dk bl	45	12
C159 AP55	1 l	red, yel & mar	75	15
C160 AP55	1.40 l	red, yel & mar	90	18
		Nos. C151-C160 (10)	3.66	92

Nos. C151-C160 exist imperf. in changed colors. Value, set $6.50

A miniature sheet contains one imperf. horizontal 2 l ultramarine and yellow stamp. Size of stamp: 59½x43mm. Value unused $7.50, canceled $3.75

Modern and 19th Century Post Office Buildings AP56

Engr. & Typo.

1964, Nov. 15 *Perf. 13½*

C161 AP56	1.60 l	ultra + 40b label	75	30

Stamp Day. Stamp and label are imperf. between. Label is dark red. Inscription between stamp and label is yellow.

Plane Approaching Airport and Coach Leaving Gate — AP57

Engr. & Typo.

1966, Oct. 20 *Perf. 13½*

C162 AP57	55b	sep, ocher & grn + 45b label	48	20

Stamp Day. Label is ocher and sepia. Blue inscription between stamp and label.

Space Exploration Type of Regular Issue

US Achievements in Space: 1.20 l, Early Bird satellite and globe. 1.55 l, Mariner 4 transmitting pictures of the moon. 3.25 l, Gemini 6 & 7, rendezvous in space. 5 l, Gemini 8 meeting Agena rocket, and globe.

1967, Feb. 15 **Photo.** *Perf. 13½*

C163 A595	1.20 l	sil & multi	25	5
C164 A595	1.55 l	sil & multi	38	5
C165 A595	3.25 l	sil & multi	65	10
C166 A595	5 l	sil & multi	1.50	50

10 years of space exploration.

Plane Spraying Crops — AP58

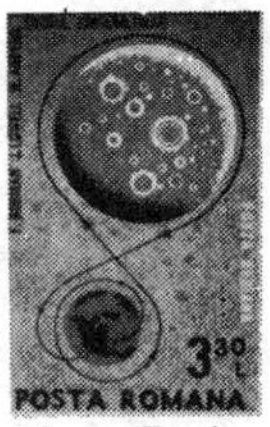

Moon, Earth and Path of Apollo 8 — AP59

Designs: 55b, Aerial ambulance over river (horiz.). 1 l, Red Cross and plane. 2.40 l, Biplane and Mircea Zorileanu, aviation pioneer.

Perf. 12x12½, 12½x12

1968, Feb. 28 **Litho.** **Unwmk.**

C167 AP58	40b	bl grn, blk & yel brn	12	5
C168 AP58	55b	multi	12	5
C169 AP58	1 l	ultra, pale grn & red org	28	8
C170 AP58	2.40 l	brt rose lil & multi	90	30

1969 **Photo.** *Perf. 13½*

Design: No. C172, Soyuz 4 and 5 over globe with map of Russia.

C171 AP59	3.30 l	multi	1.75	28
C172 AP59	3.30 l	multi	1.75	28

1st manned flight around the Moon, Dec. 21-27, 1968, and the first team flights of the Russian spacecrafts Soyuz 4 and 5, Jan. 16, 1969. See note after Hungary No. C284.

Issued in sheets of 4; decorative margin with silver panels and inscriptions in blue and black.

No. C171 was issued Jan. 17, No. C172, Mar. 28.

Apollo 9 and Lunar Landing Module over Earth AP60

Design: 2.40 l, Apollo 10 and lunar landing module over moon (vert.).

1969, June 15 Photo. *Perf. 13½*

C173 AP60 60b multi 15 6
C174 AP60 2.40 l multi 60 30

US space explorations, Apollo 9 and 10.

First Man on Moon — AP61

1969, July 24 Photo. *Perf. 13½*

C175 AP61 3.30 l multi 1.10 80

Man's first landing on the moon July 20, 1969, U.S. astronauts Neil A. Armstrong and Col. Edwin E. Aldrin, Jr., with Lieut. Col. Michael Collins piloting Apollo 11. Printed in sheets of 4.

1970, June 29

Design: 1.50 l, Apollo 13 capsule splashing down in Pacific.

C176 AP61 1.50 l multi 48 48

Flight and safe landing of Apollo 13, Apr. 11-17, 1970. Printed in sheets of 4.

BAC 1-11 Jet AP62

Design: 2 l, Fuselage BAC 1-11 and control tower, Bucharest airport.

1970, Apr. 6

C177 AP62 60b multi 18 9
C178 AP62 2 l multi 55 28

50th anniv. of Romanian civil aviation.

Flood Relief Type of Regular Issue

Design: 60b, Rescue by helicopter.

1970, Sept. 25 Photo. *Perf. 13½*

C179 A671 60b bl gray, blk & ol 30 15

Issued to publicize the plight of the victims of the Danube flood. No. C179 printed as a triptych with Nos. 2206-2207.

Henri Coanda's Model Plane AP63

1970, Dec. 1

C180 AP63 60b multi 25 14

Henri Coanda's first flight, 60th anniversary.

Luna 16 on Moon AP64

Design: No. C182, Lunokhod 1, unmanned vehicle on moon. No. C183, U.S. astronaut and vehicle on moon.

1971, Mar. 5 Photo. *Perf. 13½*

C181 AP64 3.30 l sil & multi 85 55
C182 AP64 3.30 l sil & multi 85 55
C183 AP64 3.30 l sil & multi 85 55

No. C181 commemorates Luna 16 Russian unmanned, automatic moon mission, Sept. 12-24, 1970 (labels are incorrectly inscribed Oct. 12-24). No. C182 commemorates Lunokhod 1 (Luna 17), Nov. 10-17, 1970. Nos. C181-C182 printed in sheets of 4 stamps, arranged checkerwise, and 4 labels. No. C183 commemorates Apollo 14 moon landing, Jan. 31-Feb. 9. Printed in sheets of 4 with 4 labels showing portraits of US astronauts Alan B. Shepard, Edgar D. Mitchell, Stuart A. Roosa, and Apollo 14 emblem.

Souvenir Sheet

Cosmonauts Patsayev, Dobrovolsky and Volkov — AP65

1971, July 26 Litho. *Perf. 13½*

C184 AP65 6 l blk & ultra 3.75 3.75

In memory of Russian cosmonauts Viktor I. Patsayev, Georgi T. Dobrovolsky and Vladislav N. Volkov, who died during Soyuz 11 space mission, June 6-30, 1971.

No. C184 exists imperf. in black & blue green; Size: 130x90mm.

Lunar Rover on Moon AP66

1971, Aug. 26 Photo.

C185 AP66 1.50 l bl & multi 75 60

US Apollo 15 moon mission, July 26-Aug. 7, 1971. No. C185 printed in sheets of 4 stamps and 4 labels showing astronauts David Scott, James Irwin, Alfred Worden and Apollo 15 emblem with dates.

No. C185 exists imperf. in green & multicolored. The sheet has a control number.

Olympic Souvenir Sheets

Designs: No. C186, Torchbearer and map of Romania. No. C187, Soccer.

1972 Photo. *Perf. 13½*

C186 A699 6 l pale grn & multi 3.75 3.75
C187 A699 6 l bl & multi 3.75 3.75

20th Olympic Games, Munich, Aug. 26-Sept. 11. No. C186 contains one stamp 50x38mm. No. C187 contains one stamp 48½x37mm.

Issue dates: No. C186, Apr. 25. No. C187, Sept. 29.

Two imperf. 6 l souvenir sheets exist, one showing equestrian, the other a satellite over globe.

Lunar Rover on Moon — AP67

1972, May 10 Photo. *Perf. 13½*

C188 AP67 3 l vio bl, rose & gray grn 90 45

Apollo 16 U.S. moon mission, Apr. 15-27, 1972. No. C188 printed in sheets of 4 stamps and 4 gray green and black labels showing Capt. John W. Young, Lt. Comdr. Thomas K. Mattingly 2nd, Col. Charles M. Duke, Jr., and Apollo 16 badge.

Aurel Vlaicu and Monoplane AP68

Design: 3 l, Traian Vuja and his flying machine.

1972, Aug. 15

C189 AP68 60b multi 20 10
C190 AP68 3 l multi 85 32

Romanian aviation pioneers.

Souvenir Sheet
Olympic Medals Type of Regular Issue

Design: 6 l, Olympic silver and gold medals (horiz.).

1972, Sept. 29 Litho. *Perf. 13½*

C191 A714 6 l multi 3.00 3.00

Romanian medalists at 20th Olympic Games. An imperf. 6 l souvenir sheet exists showing gold medal.

Souvenir Sheet
Apollo Type of Regular Issue

Design: 6 l, Lunar rover, landing module, rocket and astronauts on moon (horiz.).

1972, Dec. 27 Photo. *Perf. 13½*

C192 A715 6 l vio bl, bis & dl grn 3.00 3.00

No. C192 contains one stamp 48½x36mm.

An imperf. 6 l souvenir sheet exists showing surface of moon with landing sites of last 6 Apollo missions and landing capsule.

Type of Regular Issue, 1972

Design: Otopeni Airport (horiz.).

1972, Dec. 20 Photo. *Perf. 13*
Size: 29x21mm

C193 A710 14.60 l brt bl 2.75 45

Apollo and Soyuz Spacecraft AP69

Design: 3.25 l, Apollo and Soyuz after link-up.

1975, July 14 Photo. *Perf. 13½*

C196 AP69 1.75 l vio bl, red & ol 45 18
C197 AP69 3.25 l vio bl, red & ol 90 45

Apollo Soyuz space test project (Russo-American cooperation), launching July 15; link-up, July 17. Nos. C196-C197 printed in sheets of 4 stamps, arranged checkerwise, and 4 rose lilac labels showing Apollo-Soyuz emblem.

European Security and Cooperation Conference — AP70

1975, July 30 Photo. *Perf. 13½*

C198 AP70 Sheet of 4, multi 4.50 4.50
a. 2.75 l Map of Europe 55 55
b. 2.75 l Peace doves 55 55
c. 5 l Open book 1.00 1.00
d. 5 l Children playing 1.00 1.00

European Security and Cooperation Conference, Helsinki, July 30-Aug. 1. No. C198b inscribed "posta aeriana."

An imperf. 10 l souvenir sheet exists showing Helsinki on map of Europe.

Red Cross Type of 1976

Design: Blood donors, Red Cross plane.

1976, Apr. 20 Photo. *Perf. 13½*

C199 A790 3.35 l multi 70 45

De Havilland DH-9 — AP71

Airplanes: 40b, I.C.A.R. Comercial. 60b, Douglas DC-3. 1.75 l, AN-24. 2.75 l, IL-62. 3.60 l, Boeing 707.

1976, June 24 Photo. *Perf. 13½*

C200 AP71 20b bl & multi 7 5
C201 AP71 40b bl & multi 10 5
C202 AP71 60b multi 18 5
C203 AP71 1.75 l multi 50 14
C204 AP71 2.75 l bl & multi 70 20
C205 AP71 3.60 l multi 1.00 50
Nos. C200-C205 (6) 2.55 99

Romanian Airline, 50th anniversary.

Glider I.C.A.R.-1 — AP72

Gliders: 40b, I.S.-3d. 55b, R.G.-5. 1.50 l, I.S.-11. 3 l, I.S.-29D. 3.40 l, I.S.-28B.

1977, Feb. 20 Photo. *Perf. 13*

C206 AP72 20b multi 7 5
C207 AP72 40b multi 10 5
C208 AP72 55b multi 14 5
C209 AP72 1.50 l bl & multi 25 10
C210 AP72 3 l multi 60 18
C211 AP72 3.40 l multi 95 32
Nos. C206-C211 (6) 2.11 75

Souvenir Sheet

Boeing 707 over Bucharest Airport and Pioneers — AP73

1977, June 28 Photo. *Perf. 13½*

C212 AP73 10 l multi 2.50 2.50

European Security and Cooperation Conference, Belgrade.

An imperf. 10 l souvenir sheet exists showing Boeing 707, map of Europe and buildings.

Woman Letter Carrier, Mailbox AP74

Design: 30 l, Plane, newspapers, letters, packages.

1977 Photo. Perf. 13½

C213 AP74 20 l multi		3.50	1.75
C214 AP74 30 l multi		5.25	2.75

Issue dates: 20 l, July 25, 30 l, Sept. 10.

LZ-1 over Friedrichshafen, 1900 — AP75

Airships: 1 l, Santos Dumont's dirigible over Paris, 1901. 1.50 l, British R-34 over New York and Statue of Liberty, 1919. 2.15 l, Italia over North Pole, 1928. 3.40 l, Zeppelin LZ-127 over Brasov, 1929. 4.80 l, Zeppelin over Sibiu, 1929. 10 l, Zeppelin over Bucharest, 1929.

1978, Mar. 20 Photo. Perf. 13½

C215 AP75 60b multi	10	5
C216 AP75 1 l multi	14	7
C217 AP75 1.50 l multi	24	14
C218 AP75 2.15 l multi	32	14
C219 AP75 3.40 l multi	60	20
C220 AP75 4.80 l multi	1.25	32
Nos. C215-C220 (6)	2.65	92

Souvenir Sheet

C221 AP75 10 l multi	2.75	2.75

History of airships. No. C221 contains one stamp 50x37½mm.

Souvenir Sheet
Soccer Type of 1978

Design: 10 l, Two soccer players and Argentina '78 emblem.

1978, Apr. 15 Photo. Perf. 13½

C222 A818 10 l bl & multi	2.50	2.50

11th World Cup Soccer Championship, Argentina, June 1-25. No. C222 contains one stamp 37x50mm. A 10 l imperf. souvenir sheet exists showing goalkeeper.

Wilbur and Orville Wright, Flyer A AP76

Aviation History: 1 l, Louis Blériot and his plane over English Channel, 1909. 1.50 l, Anthony Fokker and Fokker F-VII trimotor, 1926. 2.15 l, Andrei N. Tupolev and ANT-25 monoplane, 1937. 3 l, Otto Lilienthal and glider, 1891-96. 3.40 l, Traian Vuia and his plane, Montesson, France, 1906. 4.80 l, Aurel Vlaicu and 1st Romanian plane, 1910. 10 l, Henri Coanda and his "jet," 1910.

1978, Dec. 18 Photo. Perf. 13½

C223 AP76 55b multi	8	5
C224 AP76 1 l multi	15	8
C225 AP76 1.50 l multi	22	12
C226 AP76 2.15 l multi	35	12
C227 AP76 3 l multi	50	15
C228 AP76 3.40 l multi	60	15
C229 AP76 4.80 l multi	75	28
Nos. C223-C229 (7)	2.65	95

Souvenir Sheet

C230 AP76 10 l multi	2.75	2.75

No. C230 contains one stamp 50x38mm.

Inter-Europa Type of 1979

Design: 3.40 l, Jet, mail truck and motorcycle.

1979, May 3 Photo. Perf. 13

C231 A835 3.40 l multi	60	18

Animal Type of 1980
Souvenir Sheet

1980, Mar. 25 Photo. Perf. 13½

C232 A852 10 l Pelicans	2.25	2.25

No. C232 contains one stamp 38x50mm.

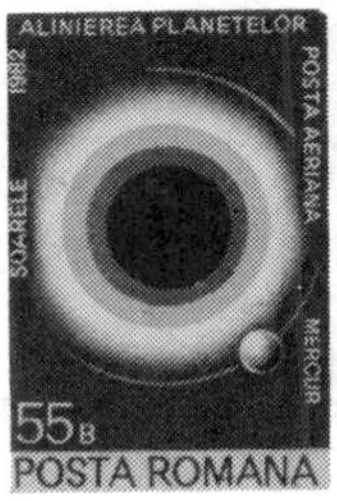

Mercury — AP77

1981, June 30 Photo. Perf. 13½

C233 AP77 55b shown	9	5
C234 AP77 1 l Venus, Earth, Mars	12	6
C235 AP77 1.50 l Jupiter	18	9
C236 AP77 2.15 l Saturn	28	12
C237 AP77 3.40 l Uranus	45	15
C238 AP77 4.80 l Neptune, Pluto	60	30
Nos. C233-C238 (6)	1.72	77

Souvenir Sheet

C239 AP77 10 l Earth	2.00	2.00

No. C239 contains one stamp 37x50mm. An imperf. 10 l souvenir sheet exists showing planets in orbit; red control number.

Romanian-Russian Space Cooperation — AP78

1981 Photo. Perf. 13½

C240 AP78 55b Soyuz 40	8	5
C241 AP78 3.40 l Salyut 6, Soyuz 40	40	22

Souvenir Sheet

C242 AP78 10 l Cosmonauts, spacecraft	2.00	2.00

No. C242 contains one stamp 50x39mm. Issue dates: 55b, 3.40 l, May 14; 10 l, June 30.

Children's Games Type of 1981

1981, Nov. 25

C243 A880 4.80 l Flying model planes	60	30

Standard Glider — AP79

1982, June 20 Photo. Perf. 13½

C244 AP79 50b shown	6	5
C245 AP79 1 l Excelsior D	14	6
C246 AP79 1.50 l Dedal I	22	8
C247 AP79 2.50 l Enthusiast	30	14
C248 AP79 4 l AK-22	50	24
C249 AP79 5 l Grifrom	70	30
Nos. C244-C249 (6)	1.92	87

Agriculture Type of 1982

1982, June 29

C250 A888 4 l Helicopter spraying insecticide	60	30

Vlaicu's Glider, 1909 — AP80

Aurel Vlaicu (1882-19), Aviator: 1 l, Memorial, Banesti-Prahova (vert.). 2.50 l, Hero Aviators Memorial, by Kotzebue and Fekete (vert.). 3 l, Vlaicu-1 glider, 1910.

1982, Sept. 27 Photo. Perf. 13½

C251 AP80 50b multi	8	5
C252 AP80 1 l multi	15	9
C253 AP80 2.50 l multi	38	15
C254 AP80 3 l multi	45	18

25th Anniv. of Space Flight AP81

Designs: 50b, H. Coanda, reaction motor, 1910. 1 l, H. Oberth, rocket, 1923. 1.50 l, Sputnik I, 1957. 2.50 l, Vostok I, 1961. 4 l, Apollo 11, 1969. 5 l, Columbia space shuttle, 1982. 10 l, Globe.

1983, Jan. 24

C255 AP81 50b multi	6	5
C256 AP81 1 l multi	14	6
C257 AP81 1.50 l multi	20	8
C258 AP81 2.50 l multi	32	14
C259 AP81 4 l multi	50	25
C260 AP81 5 l multi	65	30
Nos. C255-C260 (6)	1.87	88

Souvenir Sheet

C261 AP81 10 l multi	1.90	1.90

No. C261 contains one stamp 41x53mm.

First Romanian-built Jet Airliner AP82

1983, Jan. 25 Photo. Perf. 13½

C262 AP82 11 l Rombac 1-11	1.75	85

World Communications Year — AP83

1983, July 25 Photo. Perf. 13½

C263 AP83 2 l Boeing 707, Postal van	45	12

40th Anniv., Intl. Civil Aviation Organization — AP84

1984, Aug. 15 Photo. Perf. 13½

C265 AP84 50b Lockheed L-14	8	5
C266 AP84 1.50 l BN-2 Islander	24	12
C267 AP84 3 l Rombac	45	24
C268 AP84 6 l Boeing 707	90	45

Halley's Comet — AP85

1986, Jan. 27 Photo. Perf. 13½

C269 AP85 2 l shown	30	15
C270 AP85 4 l Space probes	60	30

An imperf. 10 l air post souvenir sheet exists showing comet and space probes, red control number.

Souvenir Sheet

Plane of Alexandru Papana, 1936 — AP86

1986, May 15 Photo. Perf. 13½

C271 AP86 10 l multi	2.75	2.75

AMERIPEX '86.

Aircraft AP87

1987, Aug. 10

C272 AP87 50b Henri Auguste glider, 1909	10	5
C273 AP87 1 l Sky diver, IS-28 B2 glider	20	10
C274 AP87 2 l IS-29 D-2 glider	38	20
C275 AP87 3 l IS-32 glider	60	30
C276 AP87 4 l IAR-35 glider	75	38
C277 AP87 5 l IS-28 M2, route	1.00	50
Nos. C272-C277 (6)	3.03	1.53

AIR POST SEMI-POSTAL STAMPS

Catalogue values for unused stamps in this section, from this point to the end of the section, are for Never Hinged items.

Corneliu Codreanu SPAP1

Unwmk.

1940, Dec. 1 Photo. Perf. 14

CB1 SPAP1 20 l + 5 l Prus grn	1.10	1.10

Propaganda for the Rome-Berlin Axis.

No. CB1 exists with overprint "1 Mai 1941 Jamboreea Nationala."

Plane over Sinaia — SPAP2

Designs: 200 l+800 l, Plane over Mountains.

1945, Oct. 1 Wmk. 276 *Imperf.*

CB2	SPAP2 80 l + 420 l gray	70	70
CB3	SPAP2 200 l + 800 l ultra	70	70

16th Congress of the General Assoc. of Romanian Engineers.

Souvenir Sheets

Re-distribution of Land — SPAP4

1946, May 4 Photo. *Perf. 14*

CB4	SPAP4 80 l blue	3.00	3.75

Agrarian reform law of Mar. 23, 1945. The sheet sold for 100 lei.

Plane Skywriting — SPAP5

1946, May 1 *Perf. 13*

CB5	SPAP5 200 l bl & brt red	3.75	4.50

Labor Day. The sheet sold for 10,000 lei.

Lockheed 12 Electra — SPAP6

1946, Sept. 1 *Perf. 11½*

CB6	SPAP6 300 l + 1200 l dp bl	85	85

No. CB6 exists se-tenant with No. C26. See note after No. C26.

The surtax was for the Office of Popular Sports.

Miniature Sheet

Women of Wallachia, Transylvania and Moldavia — SPAP7

1946, Dec. 20 Wmk. 276 *Imperf.*

CB7	SPAP7 500 l + 9500 l choc & red	1.90	2.25

Democratic Women's Org. of Romania.

SPAP8

1946, Oct. *Imperf.*

CB8	SPAP8 300 l (+ 1000 l) dp plum	5.00	5.25

The surtax was for the Office of Popular Sports. Sheets of four.

Laborer with Torch — SPAP9

1947, Mar. 1

CB9	SPAP9 3000 l + 7000 l choc	38	38

Sheets of four with marginal inscription.

Plane SPAP10

Plane above Shore Line SPAP11

1947, June 27 *Imperf.*

CB10	SPAP10 15,000 l + 15,000 l dk Prus grn	38	38

Sheets of four with marginal inscription.

1947, May 1 *Perf. 14x13*

CB11	SPAP11 3000 l + 12,000 l bl	28	28

Planes over Mountains SPAP12

Plane over Athletic Field SPAP13

1947, Oct. 5 *Perf. 14x14½*

CB12	SPAP12 5 l + 5 l bl	52	24

17th Congress of the General Assoc. of Romanian Engineers.

Wmk. 276

1948, Feb. 20 Photo. *Perf. 13½*

CB13	SPAP13 7 l + 7 l vio	80	48

Imperf

CB14	SPAP13 10 l + 10 l Prus grn	1.10	70

Balkan Games. Sheets of four with marginal inscription.

Swallow and Plane SPAP14

1948, Mar. 15 *Perf. 14x13½*

CB15	SPAP14 12 l + 12 l bl	85	65

Bucharest-Moscow Passenger Plane, Douglas DC-3 Dakota — SPAP15

1948, Oct. 29 *Perf. 14*

CB16	SPAP15 20 l + 20 l dp bl	6.50	6.50

Printed in sheets of 8 stamps and 16 small, red brown labels. Sheet yields 8 triptychs, each comprising 1 stamp flanked by label with Bucharest view and label with Moscow view.

Douglas DC-4 — SPAP16

1948, May 1 *Perf. 13½x14*

CB17	SPAP16 20 l + 20 l bl	6.50	5.75

Issued to publicize Labor Day, May 1, 1948.

Pursuit Plane and Victim SPAP17

Launching Model Plane SPAP18

1948, May 9 *Perf. 13*

CB18	SPAP17 3 l + 3 l shown	2.25	2.25
CB19	SPAP17 5 l + 5 l Bomber	2.75	2.75

Issued to honor the Romanian army.

1948, Dec. 31 *Perf. 13x13½*

CB20	SPAP18 20 l + 20 l dp ultra	9.75	9.75

Imperf

CB21	SPAP18 20 l + 20 l Prus bl	9.75	9.75

Nos. CB20 and CB21 were issued in sheets of four stamps, with ornamental border and "1948" in contrasting color.

UPU Type of Air Post Issue, 1963

Design: 1.60 l+50b, Globe, map of Romania, planes and UPU monument.

Perf. 14x13½

1963, Nov. 15 Litho. Unwmk.

Size: 75x27mm

CB22	AP54 1.60 l + 50b gray, brt grn & red org	1.40	60

Surtax for the Romanian Philatelic Federation.

POSTAGE DUE STAMPS

D1

Perf. 11, 11½, 13½ and Compound

1881 Typo. Unwmk.

J1	D1 2b brown	3.00	1.50
J2	D1 5b brown	15.00	2.50
a.	Tete beche pair	*190.00*	*75.00*
J3	D1 10b brown	19.00	1.50
J4	D1 30b brown	21.00	1.50
J5	D1 50b brown	12.00	1.50
J6	D1 60b brown	9.50	3.50

1885

J7	D1 10b pale red brn	6.00	60
J8	D1 30b pale red brn	6.00	60

1887-90

J9	D1 2b gray grn	3.00	75
J10	D1 5b gray grn	6.00	3.00
J11	D1 10b gray grn	6.00	3.00
J12	D1 30b gray grn	6.00	75

1888

J14	D1 2b grn, *yelsh*	75	75
J15	D1 5b grn, *yelsh*	2.25	2.25
J16	D1 10b grn, *yelsh*	19.00	2.75
J17	D1 30b grn, *yelsh*	11.50	1.10

1890-96 Wmk. 163

J18	D1 2b emerald	75	30
J19	D1 5b emerald	38	38
J20	D1 10b emerald	75	38
J21	D1 30b emerald	1.10	38
J22	D1 50b emerald	4.25	75
J23	D1 60b emerald	5.75	2.75

1898 Wmk. 200

J24	D1 2b bl grn	30	22
J25	D1 5b bl grn	60	20
J26	D1 10b bl grn	75	20
J27	D1 30b bl grn	75	20
J28	D1 50b bl grn	3.00	60
J29	D1 60b bl grn	3.75	1.40

1902-10 Unwmk.

Thin Paper, Tinted Rose on Back

J30	D1 2b green	38	15
J31	D1 5b green	20	12
J32	D1 10b green	20	12
J33	D1 30b green	35	12
J34	D1 50b green	1.75	38
J35	D1 60b green	3.75	1.90
	Nos. J30-J35 (6)	6.63	2.79

1908-11

White Paper

J36	D1 2b green	38	22
J37	D1 5b green	38	22
a.	Tete beche pair	11.50	11.50
J38	D1 10b green	20	12
a.	Tete beche pair	11.50	11.50
J39	D1 30b green	30	12
a.	Tete beche pair	11.50	11.50
J40	D1 50b green	1.50	75
	Nos. J36-J40 (5)	2.76	1.43

D2

Wmk. 165 - PR Interlaced

1911 Wmk. 165

J41	D2 2b dk bl, *grn*	12	8
J42	D2 5b dk bl, *grn*	12	8
J43	D2 10b dk bl, *grn*	12	6
J44	D2 15b dk bl, *grn*	12	9
J45	D2 20b dk bl, *grn*	12	9
J46	D2 30b dk bl, *grn*	24	9
J47	D2 50b dk bl, *grn*	30	12
J48	D2 60b dk bl, *grn*	38	18
J49	D2 2 l dk bl, *grn*	75	42
	Nos. J41-J49 (9)	2.27	1.21

The letters "P.R." appear to be embossed instead of watermarked. They are often faint or entirely invisible.

For unused stamps, more recent issues are valued as never hinged, with the beginning point determined on a country-by-country basis. Notes to show the beginning points are prominently placed in the text.

The 20b, type D2, has two types, differing in the width of the head of the "2." This affects Nos. J45, J54, J58, and J63.

Regular Issue of 1908 Overprinted TAXA DE PLATA

1918 **Unwmk.**

J50	A46	5b yel grn	75	30
a.		Inverted overprint	1.75	1.75
J51	A46	10b rose	75	30
a.		Inverted overprint	1.10	1.10

Postage Due Type of 1911
Wmk. 165

J52	D2	5b blk, *grn*	22	9
J53	D2	10b blk, *grn*	18	9
J54	D2	20b blk, *grn*	4.00	60
J55	D2	30b blk, *grn*	1.10	38
J55A	D2	50b blk, *grn*	3.00	90
		Nos. J52-J55A (5)	8.50	2.06

Perf. 11½, 13½ and Compound
1919 **Unwmk.**

J56	D2	5b blk, *grn*	15	6
J57	D2	10b blk, *grn*	15	6
J58	D2	20b blk, *grn*	55	15
J59	D2	30b blk, *grn*	45	9
J60	D2	50b blk, *grn*	1.10	38
		Nos. J56-J60 (5)	2.40	74

1920-26
White Paper

J61	D2	5b black	9	5
J62	D2	10b black	9	5
J63	D2	20b black	9	5
J64	D2	30b black	24	8
J65	D2	50b black	38	5
J66	D2	60b black	9	5
J67	D2	1 l black	30	5
J68	D2	2 l black	18	5
J69	D2	3 l blk ('26)	18	5
J70	D2	6 l blk ('26)	30	5
		Nos. J61-J70 (10)	1.94	53

1923-24

J74	D2	1 l blk, *pale grn*	24	12
J75	D2	2 l blk, *pale grn*	42	22
J76	D2	3 l blk, *pale grn* ('24)	1.10	55
J77	D2	6 l blk, *pale grn* ('24)	1.40	55

Postage Due Stamps of 1920-26 Overprinted 8 IUNIE 1930

1930 ***Perf. 13½***

J78	D2	1 l black	15	6
J79	D2	2 l black	18	12
J80	D2	3 l black	30	15
J81	D2	6 l black	45	24

Accession of King Carol II.

Catalogue values for unused stamps in this section, from this point to the end of the section, are for Never Hinged items.

Type of 1911 Issue

1931 **Wmk. 225**

J82	D2	2 l black	70	24

D3

1932-37 **Wmk. 230**

J83	D3	1 l black	6	5
J84	D3	2 l black	9	5
J85	D3	3 l black ('37)	12	5
J86	D3	6 l black ('37)	15	9

Type of 1911

1942 **Typo.** ***Perf. 13½***

J87	D2	50 l black	24	18
J88	D2	100 l black	38	24

Type of 1932

1946-47 **Unwmk.** ***Perf. 14***

J89	D3	20 l black	60	55
J90	D3	100 l black ('47)	45	24
J91	D3	200 l black	1.10	55

1946-47 **Wmk. 276**

J92	D3	20 l black	5	5
J93	D3	50 l black	6	6
J94	D3	80 l black	12	12
J95	D3	100 l black	18	18
J96	D3	200 l black	38	35
J97	D3	500 l black	48	48
J98	D3	5000 l black ('47)	1.25	1.25
		Nos. J92-J98 (7)	2.52	2.49

Crown and King Michael D3a

Perf. 14½x13½
1947 **Typo.** **Wmk. 276**

J98A	D3a	2 l carmine	30	15
J98B	D3a	4 l gray bl	60	30
J98C	D3a	5 l black	90	45
J98D	D3a	10 l vio brn	1.50	75

Same Overprinted R.P.R.

1948

J98E	D3a	2 l carmine	24	15
J98F	D3a	4 l gray bl	45	24
J98G	D3a	5 l black	60	30
J98H	D3a	10 l vio brn	1.10	52

In use, Nos. J98A-J106 and following issues were torn apart, one half being affixed to the postage due item and the other half being pasted into the postman's record book. Values are for unused and canceled-to-order pairs.

Communications Badge and Postwoman — D4

1950 **Unwmk.** **Photo.** ***Perf. 14½x14***

J99	D4	2 l org ver	45	45
J100	D4	4 l dp bl	45	45
J101	D4	5 l dk gray grn	60	60
J102	D4	10 l org brn	75	75

Wmk. 358

J103	D4	2 l org ver	60	45
J104	D4	4 l dp bl	60	45
J105	D4	5 l dk gray grn	85	60
J106	D4	10 l org brn	1.10	90
		Nos. J99-J106 (8)	5.40	4.65

Postage Due Stamps of 1950 Surcharged with New Values in Black or Carmine

1952 **Unwmk.**

J107	D4	4b on 2 l org ver	24	24
J108	D4	10b on 4 l dp bl (C)	24	24
J109	D4	20b on 5 l dk gray grn (C)	45	45
J110	D4	50b on 10 l org brn	75	75

Wmk. 358

J111	D4	4b on 2 l org ver	22	22
J112	D4	10b on 4 l dp bl (C)	22	22
J113	D4	20b on 5 l dk gray grn (C)	*2.50*	*1.25*
J114	D4	50b on 10 l org brn	*3.00*	*1.25*
		Nos. J107-J114 (8)	*7.62*	*4.62*

See note after No. J98H.

General Post Office and Post Horn — D5

1957 **Wmk. 358** ***Perf. 14***

J115	D5	3b black	5	5
J116	D5	5b red org	5	5
J117	D5	10b red lil	7	7
J118	D5	20b brt red	14	7
J119	D5	40b lt bl grn	35	14
J120	D5	1 l brt ultra	1.00	24
		Nos. J115-J120 (6)	1.66	62

See note after No. J98H.

General Post Office and Post Horn — D6

1967, Feb. 25 **Photo.** ***Perf. 13***

J121	D6	3b brt grn	5	5
J122	D6	5b brt bl	5	5
J123	D6	10b lil rose	5	5
J124	D6	20b vermilion	8	5
J125	D6	40b brown	20	8
J126	D6	1 l violet	55	16
		Nos. J121-J126 (6)	98	44

See note after No. J98H.

1970, Mar. 10 **Unwmk.**

J127	D6	3b brt grn	5	5
J128	D6	5b brt bl	5	5
J129	D6	10b lil rose	5	5
J130	D6	20b vermilion	6	5
J131	D6	40b brown	18	5
J132	D6	1 l violet	35	12
		Nos. J127-J132 (6)	74	37

See note after No. J98H.

Symbols of Communications — D7

Designs: 10b, Like 5b. 20b, 40b, Pigeons, head of Mercury and post horn. 50b, 1 l, General Post Office, post horn and truck.

1974, Jan. 1 **Photo.** ***Perf. 13***

J133	D7	5b brt bl	5	5
J134	D7	10b olive	5	5
J135	D7	20b lil rose	5	5
J136	D7	40b purple	9	5
J137	D7	50b brown	18	5
J138	D7	1 l orange	35	12
		Nos. J133-J138 (6)	77	37

See note after No. J98H.

Postal Symbols — D8

1982, Dec. 23 **Photo.** ***Perf. 13½***

J139	D8	25b Carrier pigeons	5	5
J140	D8	50b Mailbox	9	5
J141	D8	1 l like #J139	18	9
J142	D8	2 l Postal Headquarters	35	18
J143	D8	3 l like #J140	52	22
J144	D8	4 l like #J142	70	35
		Nos. J139-J144 (6)	1.89	94

See note after No. J98H.

OFFICIAL STAMPS

Catalogue values for unused stamps in this section, from this point to the end of the section, are for Never Hinged items.

Romania Austrian Occupation stamps can be mounted in Scott's Austria Album.

Romania German Occupation stamps can be mounted in Scott's Germany Part II Album.

Eagle Carrying National Emblem — O1

Coat of Arms — O2

1929 **Photo.** **Wmk. 95** ***Perf. 13½***

O1	O1	25b red org	18	5
O2	O1	50b dk brn	18	5
O3	O1	1 l dk vio	22	5
O4	O1	2 l ol grn	22	5
O5	O1	3 l rose car	35	5
O6	O1	4 l dk ol	35	5
O7	O1	6 l Prus bl	1.75	12
O8	O1	10 l dp bl	60	7
O9	O1	25 l car brn	1.25	1.25
O10	O1	50 l purple	3.50	3.50
		Nos. O1-O10 (10)	8.60	5.24

Type of Official Stamps of 1929 Overprinted 8 IUNIE 1930

1930 **Unwmk.**

O11	O1	25b red org	18	5
O12	O1	50b dk brn	18	7
O13	O1	1 l dk vio	35	7
O14	O1	3 l rose car	50	12

Nos. O11 to O14 were not placed in use without overprint.

Same Overprint on Official Stamps of 1929
Wmk. 95

O15	O1	25b red org	22	5
O16	O1	50b dk brn	22	5
O17	O1	1 l dk vio	22	5
O18	O1	2 l dp grn	22	5
O19	O1	3 l rose car	50	12
O20	O1	4 l ol blk	65	12
O21	O1	6 l Prus bl	1.75	5
O22	O1	10 l dp bl	70	14
O23	O1	25 l car brn	2.50	2.50
O24	O1	50 l purple	3.50	3.50
		Nos. O15-O24 (10)	10.48	6.63

Accession of King Carol II to the throne of Romania (Nos O11-O24).

Perf. 13½, 13½x14½
1931-32 **Typo.** **Wmk. 225**

O25	O2	25b black	22	14
O26	O2	1 l lilac	22	18
O27	O2	2 l emerald	35	35
O28	O2	3 l rose	60	60

1932 **Wmk. 230** ***Perf. 13½***

O29	O2	25b black	22	22
O30	O2	1 l violet	32	32
O31	O2	2 l emerald	48	48
O32	O2	3 l rose	60	60
O33	O2	6 l red brn	90	90
		Nos. O29-O33 (5)	2.52	2.52

PARCEL POST STAMPS

PP1

PP2

Perf. 11½, 13½ and Compound
1895 **Wmk. 163** **Typo.**

Q1	PP1	25b brn red	8.75	1.50

1896

Q2	PP1	25b vermilion	6.75	1.00

Perf. 13½ and 11½x13½
1898 **Wmk. 200**

Q3	PP1	25b brn red	6.00	1.00
a.		Tete beche pair		
Q4	PP1	25b vermilion	6.00	1.00

Thin Paper
Tinted Rose on Back

1905 **Unwmk.** ***Perf. 11½***

Q5	PP1	25b vermilion	4.50	85

1911 **White Paper**
Q6 PP1 25b pale red 4.50 85

Carmine Surcharge

1928 ***Perf. 13½***
Q7 PP2 5 l on 10b yel grn 85 20

POSTAL TAX STAMPS

Regular Issue of 1908 Overprinted **TIMBRU DE AJUTOR**

Perf. 11½, 13½, 11½x13½

1915 **Unwmk.**
RA1 A46 5b green 18 8
RA2 A46 10b rose 30 9

The "Timbru de Ajutor" stamps represent a tax on postal matter. The money obtained from their sale was turned into a fund for the assistance of soldiers' families.

Until 1923 the only "Timbru de Ajutor" stamps used for postal purposes were the 5b and 10b. Stamps of higher values with this inscription were used to pay the taxes on railway and theater tickets and other fiscal taxes. In 1923 the postal rate was advanced to 25b.

The Queen Weaving — PT1

1916-18 **Typo.**
RA3 PT1 5b gray blk 18 12
RA4 PT1 5b grn ('18) 45 12
RA5 PT1 10b brown 30 18
RA6 PT1 10b gray blk ('18) 45 12

Stamps of 1916 Overprinted in Red or Black **1918**

1918 ***Perf. 13½***
RA7 PT1 5b gray blk (R) 38 24
 a. Double overprint 3.00
 c. Black overprint 45
RA8 PT1 10b brn (Bk) 45 24
 a. Double overprint 4.50
 b. Double overprint, one inverted 4.50
 c. Inverted overprint 4.50

Same Overprint on RA1 and RA2

1919
RA11 A46 5b yel grn (R) *17.00 17.00*
RA12 A46 10b rose (Bk) *17.00 17.00*

Charity — PT3

Perf. 13½, 11½, 13½x11½

1921-24 **Typo.** **Unwmk.**
RA13 PT3 10b green 12 5
RA14 PT3 25b blk ('24) 9 5

Type of 1921-24 Issue

1928 **Wmk. 95**
RA15 PT3 25b black 75 30

Nos. RA13, RA14 and RA15 are the only stamps of type PT3 issued for postal purposes. Other denominations were used fiscally.

Catalogue values for unused stamps in this section, from this point to the end of the section, are for Never Hinged items.

Airplane PT4

Head of Aviator PT5

1931 **Photo.** **Unwmk.**
RA16 PT4 50b Prus bl 30 5
 a. Double impression 15.00
RA17 PT4 1 l dk red brn 30 5
RA18 PT4 2 l ultra 60 15

The use of these stamps, in addition to the regular postage, was obligatory on all postal matter for the interior of the country. The money thus obtained was to augment the National Fund for Aviation. When the stamps were not used to prepay the special tax, it was collected by means of Postal Tax Due stamps Nos. RAJ20 and RAJ21.

Nos. RA17 and RA18 were also used for other than postal tax.

1932 **Wmk. 230** ***Perf. 14 x 13½***
RA19 PT5 50b Prus bl 22 5
RA20 PT5 1 l red brn 35 5
RA21 PT5 2 l ultra 45 6

The notes after No. RA18 will apply also to Nos. RA19-RA21.

After 1937 use of Nos. RA20-RA21 was limited to other than postal matter.

Nos. RA19-RA21 exist imperf.

Two stamps similar to type PT5, but inscribed "Fondul Aviatiei," were issued in 1936: 10b sepia and 20b violet.

Aviator PT6

King Michael PT7

1937 ***Perf. 13½***
RA22 PT6 50b Prus grn 15 5
RA23 PT6 1 l red brn 22 5
RA24 PT6 2 l ultra 24 9

Stamps overprinted or inscribed "Fondul Aviatiei" other than Nos. RA22, RA23 or RA24 were used to pay taxes on other than postal matters.

1943 **Wmk. 276** **Photo.** ***Perf. 14***
RA25 PT7 50b org ver 6 6
RA26 PT7 1 l lil rose 6 6
RA27 PT7 2 l brown 6 6
RA28 PT7 4 l lt ultra 6 6
RA29 PT7 5 l dl lil 6 6
RA30 PT7 8 l yel grn 6 6
RA31 PT7 10 l blk brn 6 6
 Nos. RA25-RA31 (7) 42 42

The tax was obligatory on domestic mail.

Protection of Homeless Children — PT8

1945
RA32 PT8 40 l Prus bl 24 18

PT9

"Hope" — PT10

1947 **Unwmk.** **Typo.** ***Perf. 14x14½***

Black Surcharge

RA33 PT9 1 l on 2 l + 2 l pink 30 15
 a. Inverted surcharge
RA34 PT9 5 l on 1 l + 1 l gray grn *4.50 3.75*

1948 ***Perf. 14***
RA35 PT10 1 l rose *1.90* 6
RA36 PT10 1 l rose vio *2.10* 12

A 2 lei blue and 5 lei ocher in type PT10 were issued primarily for revenue purposes.

POSTAL TAX DUE STAMPS

Catalogue values for unused stamps in this section, from this point to the end of the section, are for Never Hinged items.

Postage Due Stamps of 1911 Overprinted **TIMBRU DE AJUTOR**

Perf. 11½, 13½, 11½x13½

1915 **Unwmk.**
RAJ1 D2 5b dk bl, *grn* 30 15
RAJ2 D2 10b dk bl, *grn* 30 15
 a. Wmk. 165 4.50 60

PTD1

PTD2

1916 **Typo.** **Unwmk.**
RAJ3 PTD1 5b brn, *grn* 15 12
RAJ4 PTD1 10b red, *grn* 15 12

1918
RAJ5 PTD1 5b red, *grn* 18 12
 a. Wmk. 165 30 22
RAJ6 PTD1 10b brn, *grn* 18 12
 a. Wmk. 165 30 22

Postal Tax Stamps of 1916, Overprinted in Red, Black or Blue **TAXA DE PLATA**

RAJ7 PT1 5b gray blk (R) 18 12
 a. Inverted overprint
RAJ8 PT1 10b brn (Bk) 24 15
 a. Inverted overprint
RAJ9 PT1 10b brn (Bl) *5.00 5.00*
 a. Vertical overprint *15.00 15.00*

Type of 1916

1921
RAJ10 PTD1 5b red 30 15
RAJ11 PTD1 10b brown 30 15

1922-25 **Typo.**

Greenish Paper

RAJ12 PTD2 10b brown 9 6
RAJ13 PTD2 20b brown 9 6
RAJ14 PTD2 25b brown 9 6
RAJ15 PTD2 50b brown 9 6

1923-26
RAJ16 PTD2 10b lt brn 9 6
RAJ17 PTD2 20b lt brn 9 6
RAJ18 PTD2 25b brown ('26) 9 6
RAJ19 PTD2 50b brown ('26) 9 6

J82 and Type of 1911 Postage Due Stamps Overprinted in Red **TIMBRUL AVIATIEI**

1931 **Wmk. 225** ***Perf. 13½***
RAJ20 D2 1 l black 8 5
RAJ21 D2 2 l black 8 5

When the Postal Tax stamps for the Aviation Fund issue (Nos. RA16 to RA18) were not used to prepay the obligatory tax on letters, etc., it was collected by affixing Nos. RAJ20 and RAJ21.

OCCUPATION STAMPS

ISSUED UNDER AUSTRIAN OCCUPATION

Emperor Karl of Austria
OS1 OS2

1917 **Unwmk.** **Engr.** ***Perf. 12½***
1N1 OS1 3b ol gray 95 80
1N2 OS1 5b ol grn 75 60
1N3 OS1 6b violet 75 60
1N4 OS1 10b org brn 14 7
1N5 OS1 12b dp bl 85 70
1N6 OS1 15b brt rose 75 60
1N7 OS1 20b red brn 14 7
1N8 OS1 25b ultra 18 14
1N9 OS1 30b slate 28 28
1N10 OS1 40b ol bis 28 28
 a. Perf. 11½ 40.00 19.00
 b. Perf. 11½x12½ 45.00 20.00
1N11 OS1 50b dp grn 28 28
1N12 OS1 60b rose 28 28
1N13 OS1 80b dl bl 14 7
1N14 OS1 90b dk vio 28 28
1N15 OS2 2 l rose, *straw* 40 28
1N16 OS2 3 l grn, *bl* 70 40
1N17 OS2 4 l rose, *grn* 70 40
 Nos. 1N1-1N17 (17) 7.85 6.13

Nos. 1N1-1N14 have "BANI" surcharged in red.

Nos. 1N1-1N17 also exist imperforate. Value, set $20.

OS3

OS4

1918
1N18 OS3 3b ol gray 14 14
1N19 OS3 5b ol grn 18 9
1N20 OS3 6b violet 22 22
1N21 OS3 10b org brn 25 25
1N22 OS3 12b dp bl 18 18
1N23 OS3 15b brt rose 14 14
1N24 OS3 20b red brn 14 14
1N25 OS3 25b ultra 14 14
1N26 OS3 30b slate 14 14
1N27 OS3 40b ol bis 18 18
1N28 OS3 50b dp grn 22 22
1N29 OS3 60b rose 22 22
1N30 OS3 80b dl bl 14 12
1N31 OS3 90b dk vio 18 20
1N32 OS4 2 l rose, *straw* 22 22
1N33 OS4 3 l grn, *bl* 28 28
1N34 OS4 4 l rose, *grn* 28 28
 Nos. 1N18-1N34 (17) 3.25 3.16

Exist. imperf. Value, set $17.50.

The complete series exists with "BANI" or "LEI" inverted, also with those words and the numerals of value inverted. Neither of these sets was regularly issued.

A set of 13 stamps similar to Austria Nos. M69-M81 was prepared for use in Romania in 1918, but not placed in use there. Denominations are in bani. It is reported that they were on sale after the armistice at the Vienna post office for a few days. Value $850.

ISSUED UNDER BULGARIAN OCCUPATION

Bulgarian Stamps of 1915-16 Overprinted in Red or Blue **Пощa въ Ромжния 1916—1917**

1916	Unwmk.	*Perf. 11 ½, 14.*	
2N1 A20	1s dk bl grn (R)	10	10
2N2 A23	5s grn & vio brn (R)	1.40	50
2N3 A24	10s brn & brnsh blk (Bl)	18	10
2N4 A26	25s ind & blk (Bl)	18	10

Nos. 2N1-2N4 were used in the Dobruja district.
Many varieties of overprint exist.

ISSUED UNDER GERMAN OCCUPATION

German Stamps of 1905-17 Surcharged

M.V.i.R. (Red or Black)
15 Bani (Black)

1917	Wmk. 125	*Perf. 14*	
3N1 A22	15b on 15pf dk vio (R)	70	70
3N2 A16	25b on 20pf ultra (Bk)	70	70
3N3 A16	40b on 30pf org & blk, *buff* (R)	17.00	17.00

"M.V.iR." are the initials of "Militär Verwaltung in Rumänien" (Military Administration of Romania).

German Stamps of 1905-17 Surcharged

M.V.i.R.
25 Bani

1917-18			
3N4 A16	10b on 10pf car	28	24
3N5 A22	15b on 15pf dk vio	2.25	2.25
3N6 A16	25b on 20pf ultra	40	40
3N7 A16	40b on 30pf org & blk, *buff*	50	50
a.	"40" omitted	50.00	67.50

German Stamps of 1905-17 Surcharged

Rumänien
25 Bani

1918			
3N8 A16	5b on 5pf grn	10	10
3N9 A16	10b on 10pf car	14	14
3N10 A22	15b on 15pf dk vio	10	10
3N11 A16	25b on 20pf bl vio	10	10
a.	25b on 20pf blue	18	18
3N12 A16	40b on 30pf org & blk, *buff*	18	18

German Stamps of 1905-17 Overprinted

Gültig
9. Armee

1918			
3N13 A16	10pf carmine	6.75	6.75
3N14 A22	15pf dk vio	10.00	10.00
3N15 A16	20pf blue	1.00	1.00
3N16 A16	30pf org & blk, *buff*	9.50	9.50

POSTAGE DUE STAMPS ISSUED UNDER GERMAN OCCUPATION

Postage Due Stamps and Type of Romania Overprinted in Red

M.V.i.R.

Perf. 11 ½, 13 ½ and Compound

1918		Wmk. 165	
3NJ1 D2	5b dk bl, *grn*	17.00	22.50
3NJ2 D2	10b dk bl, *grn*	22.50	27.50

The 20b, 30b and 50b with this overprint are fraudulent.

Unwmk.			
3NJ3 D2	5b dk bl, *grn*	2.00	2.00
3NJ4 D2	10b dk bl, *grn*	2.00	2.00
3NJ5 D2	20b dk bl, *grn*	2.00	2.00
3NJ6 D2	30b dk bl, *grn*	2.00	2.00
3NJ7 D2	50b dk bl, *grn*	2.00	2.00
	Nos. 3NJ1-3NJ7 (7)	49.50	60.00

OCCUPATION POSTAL TAX STAMPS ISSUED UNDER GERMAN OCCUPATION

Romanian Postal Tax Stamps and Type of 1916

Overprinted in Red or Black

M.V.i.R.

Perf. 11 ½, 13 ½ and Compound

1917		Unwmk.	
3NRA1 PT1	5b gray blk (R)	20	20
3NRA2 PT1	10b brn (Bk)	28	20

Same, Overprinted

M.V.i.R.

1917-18			
3NRA3 PT1	5b gray blk (R)	40	40
a.	Black overprint	5.00	5.00
3NRA4 PT1	10b brown (Bk)	40	40
3NRA5 PT1	10b violet (Bk)	35	35

Same, Overprinted in Red or Black

M.V.i.R.

1918			
3NRA6 PT1	5b gray blk (R)	*10.00*	
3NRA7 PT1	10b brown (Bk)	*10.00*	

Same, Overprinted

Gültig
9. Armee

1918			
3NRA8 PT1	10b violet (Bk)	18	18

OCCUPATION POSTAL TAX DUE STAMP ISSUED UNDER GERMAN OCCUPATION

Type of Romanian Postal Tax Due Stamp of 1916 Overprinted

M.V.i.R.

Perf. 11 ½, 13 ½, and Compound

1918		Wmk. 165	
3NRAJ1 PTD1	10b red, *grn*	2.75	3.50

ROMANIAN POST OFFICES IN THE TURKISH EMPIRE

40 Paras = 1 Piaster

King Carol I
A1 A2

Perf. 11 ½, 13 ½ and Compound

1896		Wmk. 200	
	Black Surcharge		
1 A1	10pa on 5b bl	19.00	19.00
2 A2	20pa on 10b emer	14.00	14.00
3 A1	1pia on 25b vio	14.00	14.00
	Violet Surcharge		
4 A1	10pa on 5b bl	10.00	10.00
5 A2	20pa on 10b emer	10.00	10.00
6 A1	1pia on 25b vio	10.00	10.00

Romanian Stamps of 1908-18 Overprinted in Black or Red

1919	Typo.	Unwmk.	
7 A46	5b yel grn	40	40
8 A46	10b rose	55	55
9 A46	15b red brn	55	55
10 A19	25b dp bl (R)	70	70
11 A19	40b gray brn (R)	1.40	1.40
	Nos. 7-11 (5)	3.60	3.60

All values exist with inverted overprint.

ROMANIAN POST OFFICES IN THE TURKISH EMPIRE POSTAL TAX STAMP

Romanian Postal Tax Stamp of 1918 Overprinted

Perf. 11 ½, 11 ½x13 ½

1919		Unwmk.
RA1 PT1	5b green	1.25 1.25

ROUAD, ILE

(Arwad)

LOCATION — An island in the Mediterranean, off the coast of Latakia, Syria.
GOVT. — French Mandate.

In 1916, while a French post office was maintained on Ile Rouad, stamps were issued by France.

25 Centimes = 1 Piaster

Stamps of French Offices in the Levant, 1902-06, Overprinted

ILE ROUAD

Perf. 14x13 ½

1916, Jan. 12		Unwmk.	
1 A2	5c green	250.00	125.00
2 A3	10c rose red	250.00	125.00
3 A5	1pi on 25c bl	250.00	125.00

Dangerous counterfeits exist.

Stamps of French Offices in the Levant, 1902-06, Overprinted Horizontally

ILE ROUAD

1916, Dec.			
4 A2	1c gray	45	45
5 A2	2c violet brn	45	45
6 A2	3c red orange	45	45
a.	Double overprint	40.00	40.00
7 A2	5c green	50	50
8 A3	10c rose	60	60
9 A3	15c pale red	65	65
10 A3	20c brn violet	1.00	1.00
11 A5	1pi on 25c blue	1.00	1.00
12 A3	30c violet	1.00	1.00
13 A4	40c red & pale bl	1.90	1.90
14 A6	2pi on 50c bis brn & lav	3.00	3.00
15 A6	4pi on 1fr cl & ol grn	4.50	4.50
16 A6	20pi on 5fr dk bl & buff	14.00	14.00
	Nos. 4-16 (13)	29.50	29.50

There is a wide space between the two words of the overprint on Nos. 13 to 16 inclusive. Nos. 4, 5 and 6 are on white and coarse, grayish (G. C.) papers.
(Note on G. C. paper follows France No. 184.)

RUANDA-URUNDI

(Belgian East Africa)

LOCATION — In central Africa, bounded by Congo, Uganda and Tanganyika.
GOVT. — Former United Nations trusteeship administered by Belgium.
AREA — 20,540 sq. mi.
POP. — 4,700,000 (est. 1958).
CAPITAL — Usumbura.

See German East Africa in Vol. III for stamps issued under Belgian occupation.
In 1962 the two parts of the trusteeship became independent states, the Republic of Rwanda and the Kingdom of Burundi.

100 Centimes = 1 Franc

Catalogue values for unused stamps in this country are for Never Hinged items, beginning with Scott 151 in the regular postage section, and Scott B26 in the semi-postal section.

Stamps of Belgian Congo, 1923-26, Overprinted

RUANDA
URUNDI

1924-26		*Perf. 12.*	
6 A32	5c org yel	10	10
7 A32	10c green	10	10
8 A32	15c ol brn	10	10
9 A32	20c ol grn	10	10
10 A44	20c grn ('26)	10	9
11 A44	25c red brn	18	10
12 A44	30c rose red	15	15
13 A44	30c ol grn ('25)	10	10
14 A32	40c vio ('25)	22	18
15 A44	50c gray bl	15	15
16 A44	50c buff ('25)	22	15
17 A44	75c red org	22	22
18 A44	75c gray bl ('25)	28	18
19 A44	1fr bis brn	30	28
20 A44	1fr dl bl ('26)	32	18
21 A44	3fr gray brn	2.25	1.50
22 A44	5fr gray	4.50	3.25
23 A44	10fr gray blk	11.00	7.25
	Nos. 6-23 (18)	20.39	14.18

Belgian Congo Nos. 112-113 Overprinted in Red or Black

RUANDA-URUNDI

1925-27		*Perf. 12 ½.*	
24 A44	45c dk vio (R) ('27)	22	22
25 A44	60c car rose (Bk)	30	28

Stamps of Belgian Congo, 1923-1927, Overprinted

RUANDA
URUNDI

1927-29			
26 A32	10c grn ('29)	15	15
27 A32	15c ol brn ('29)	60	50
28 A44	35c green	15	15
29 A44	75c sal red	20	20
30 A44	1fr rose red	32	25
31 A32	1.25fr dl bl	45	32
32 A32	1.50fr dl bl	38	30
33 A32	1.75fr dl bl	85	55

No. 32 Surcharged

175

34 A32	1.75fr on 1.50fr dl bl ('27)	38	32
	Nos. 26-34 (9)	3.48	2.74

Nos. 30 and 33 Surcharged

2

1931

35	A44	1.25fr	on 1fr rose red	2.00	95
36	A32	2fr	on 1.75fr dl bl	2.75	1.40

Porter — A1

Mountain Scene — A2

Designs: 5c, 60c, Porter. 15c, Warrior. 25c, Kraal. 40c, Cattle herders. 50c, Cape buffalo. 75c, Bahutu greeting. 1fr, Barundi women. 1.25fr, Bahutu mother. 1.50fr, 2fr, Making wooden vessel. 2.50fr, 3.25fr, Preparing hides. 4fr, Watuba potter. 5fr, Mututsi dancer. 10fr, Watusi warriors. 20fr, Urundi prince.

1931-38 Engr. *Perf. 11½.*

37	A1	5c	dp lil rose ('38)	8	8
38	A2	10c	gray	8	8
39	A2	15c	pale red	10	10
40	A2	25c	brn vio	8	8
41	A1	40c	green	22	22
42	A2	50c	gray lil	8	8
43	A1	60c	lil rose	8	8
44	A1	75c	gray blk	8	8
45	A2	1fr	rose red	10	10
46	A1	1.25fr	red brn	10	10
47	A2	1.50fr	brn vio ('37)	10	10
48	A2	2fr	dp bl	18	10
49	A2	2.50fr	dp bl ('37)	16	16
50	A2	3.25fr	brn vio	18	10
51	A2	4fr	rose	24	24
52	A1	5fr	gray	28	28
53	A1	10fr	brn vio	50	38
54	A1	20fr	brown	1.50	1.40
			Nos. 37-54 (18)	4.14	3.76

King Albert Memorial Issue.

King Albert — A16

1934 Photo.

55	A16	1.50fr	black	45	45

Stamps of 1931-38 Surcharged in Black

0F60 0F60

1941

56	A1	5c	on 40c grn	2.25	2.25
57	A2	60c	on 50c gray lil	1.50	1.50
58	A2	2.50fr	on 1.50fr brn vio	1.50	1.50
59	A2	3.25fr	on 2fr dp bl	6.00	6.00

Belgian Congo No. 173 Overprinted in Black

RUANDA URUNDI

Perf. 11.

60	A70	10c	lt gray	5.00	5.00

Belgian Congo Nos. 179, 181 Overprinted in Black

RUANDA URUNDI

1941

61	A70	1.75fr	orange	3.00	3.00
62	A70	2.75fr	vio bl	3.00	3.00

Belgian Congo No. 168 Surcharged in Black

RUANDA URUNDI

5 c.

1941 *Perf. 11½.*

63	A66	5c	on 1.50fr dp red brn & blk	12	12

Nos. 61-62 Surcharged with New Values and Bars in Black.

1942

64	A70	75c	on 1.75fr org	1.10	1.25
65	A70	2.50fr	on 2.75fr vio bl	3.00	3.00

Belgian Congo Nos. 167, 183 Surcharged in Black:

RUANDA URUNDI 75 c.

RUANDA URUNDI 2.50

1942 *Perf. 11, 11½.*

66	A65	75c	on 90c car & brn	70	65
a.			Inverted surcharge	8.00	8.00
67	A70	2.50fr	on 10fr rose red	1.10	85
a.			Inverted surcharge	6.50	6.50

Oil Palms — A17

Oil Palms — A18

Watusi Chief — A19

Askari — A21

Leopard A20

Zebra — A22

Askari — A23

Design: 100fr, Watusi chief.

1942-43 Engr. *Perf. 12½*

68	A17	5c	red	5	5
69	A18	10c	ol grn	8	8
70	A18	15c	brn car	8	8
71	A18	20c	dp ultra	8	8
72	A18	25c	brn vio	8	8
73	A18	30c	dl bl	8	8
74	A18	50c	dp grn	80	8
75	A18	60c	chestnut	8	8
76	A19	75c	dl lil & blk	12	8
77	A19	1fr	dk brn & blk	14	8
78	A19	1.25fr	rose red & blk	18	14
79	A20	1.75fr	dk gray brn	60	35
80	A20	2fr	ocher	60	28
81	A20	2.50fr	carmine	60	12
82	A21	3.50fr	dk ol grn	35	20
83	A21	5fr	orange	40	25
84	A21	6fr	brt ultra	40	25
85	A21	7fr	black	40	32
86	A21	10fr	dp brn	60	35
87	A21	20fr	org brn & blk	1.25	90
88	A21	50fr	red & blk ('43)	1.75	1.10
89	A21	100fr	grn & blk ('43)	3.50	2.75
			Nos. 68-89 (22)	12.22	7.78

Miniature sheets of Nos. 72, 76, 77 and 83 were printed in 1944 by the Belgian Government in London and given to the Belgian political review, "Message", which distributed them to its subscribers, one a month. Nos. 68-89 exist imperforate, but have no franking value. Value, set $100.

See note after Belgian Congo No. 225.

Baluba Carving of Former King — A25

Carved Figures and Masks of Baluba Tribe: 10c, 50c, 2fr, 10fr, "Ndoha," figure of tribal king. 15c, 70c, 2.50fr, "Tshimanyi," an idol. 20c, 75c, 3.50fr, "Buangakokoma," statue of a kneeling beggar. 25c, 1fr, 5fr, "Mbuta," sacred double cup carved with two faces, Man and Woman. 40c, 1.25fr, 6fr, "Ngadimuashi," female mask. 1.50fr, 50fr, "Buadi-Muadi," mask with squared features (full face). 20fr, 100fr, "Mbowa," executioner's mask with buffalo horns.

1948-50 Unwmk. *Perf. 12x12½*

90	A25	10c	dp org	6	5
91	A25	15c	ultra	6	5
92	A25	20c	brt bl	8	6
93	A25	25c	rose car	18	14
94	A25	40c	violet	6	6
95	A25	50c	ol brn	6	8
96	A25	70c	yel grn	6	6
97	A25	75c	magenta	12	12
98	A25	1fr	yel org & dk vio	12	8
99	A25	1.25fr	lt bl grn & mag	12	10
100	A25	1.50fr	ol & mag ('50)	48	35
101	A25	2fr	org & mag	14	8
102	A25	2.50fr	brn red & bl grn	14	6
103	A25	3.50fr	lt bl & blk	20	18
104	A25	5fr	bis & mag	32	18
105	A25	6fr	brn org & ind	40	12
106	A25	10fr	pale vio & red brn	55	20
107	A25	20fr	red org & vio brn	90	35
108	A25	50fr	dp org & blk	2.50	90
109	A25	100fr	crim & blk brn	4.25	2.25
			Nos. 90-109 (20)	10.80	5.47

Nos. 102 and 105 Surcharged with New Value and Bars in Black.

1949

110	A25	3fr	on 2.50fr	20	12
111	A25	4fr	on 6fr	15	12
112	A25	6.50fr	on 6fr	25	22

St. Francis Xavier — A26

Dissotis — A27

1953 *Perf. 12½x13.*

113	A26	1.50fr	ultra & gray blk	35	35

Issued to commemorate the 400th anniversary of the death of St. Francis Xavier.

1953 Unwmk. Photo. *Perf. 11½.*

Flowers: 15c, Protea. 20c, Vellozia. 25c, Littonia. 40c, Ipomoea. 50c, Angraecum. 60c, Euphorbia. 75c, Ochna. 1fr, Hibiscus. 1.25fr, Protea. 1.50fr, Schizoglossum. 2fr, Ansellia. 3fr, Costus. 4fr, Nymphaea. 5fr, Thunbergia. 7fr, Gerbera. 8fr, Gloriosa. 10fr, Silene. 20fr, Aristolochia.

Flowers in Natural Colors.

114	A27	10c	plum & ocher	5	5
115	A27	15c	red & yel grn	5	5
116	A27	20c	grn & gray	8	5
117	A27	25c	dk grn & dl org	8	8
118	A27	40c	grn & sal	8	8
119	A27	50c	dk car & aqua	10	8
120	A27	60c	bl grn & pink	12	8
121	A27	75c	dp plum & gray	12	8
122	A27	1fr	car & yel	18	8
123	A27	1.25fr	dk grn & bl	50	50
124	A27	1.50fr	vio & ap grn	18	8
125	A27	2fr	ol grn & buff	1.40	15
126	A27	3fr	ol grn & pink	38	8
127	A27	4fr	choc & lil	38	10
128	A27	5fr	dp plum & lt bl grn	65	10
129	A27	7fr	dk grn & fawn	75	28
130	A27	8fr	grn & lt yel	95	32
131	A27	10fr	dp plum & pale ol	1.50	25
132	A27	20fr	vio bl & dl sal	2.50	42
			Nos. 114-132 (19)	10.05	2.91

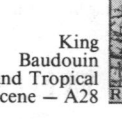

King Baudouin and Tropical Scene — A28

Designs: Various African Views.

Engr.; Portrait Photo. in Black

1955

133	A28	1.50fr	rose car	30	14
134	A28	3fr	green	25	10
135	A28	4.50fr	ultra	32	18
136	A28	6.50fr	deep claret	50	25

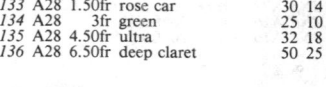

Mountain Gorilla — A29

Cape Buffaloes — A30

Animals: 40c, 2fr, Black-and-white colobus (monkey). 50c, 6.50fr, Impalas. 3fr, 8fr, Elephants. 5fr, 10fr, Eland and Zebras. 20fr, Leopard. 50fr, Lions.

1959-61 Unwmk. Photo. *Perf. 11½*

Granite Paper.

Size: 23x33mm., 33x23mm.

137	A29	10c	brn, crim, & blk brn	5	5
138	A30	20c	blk, gray & ap grn	5	5
139	A29	40c	mag, blk & gray grn	8	5
140	A30	50c	grn, org yel & brn	8	5
141	A29	1fr	brn, ultra & blk	8	8
142	A30	1.50fr	blk, gray & org	16	8
143	A29	2fr	grnsh bl, ind & brn	8	8
144	A30	3fr	brn, dp car & blk	14	8
145	A30	5fr	brn, dl yel, grn & blk	18	14
146	A30	6.50fr	red, org yel & brn	28	8
147	A30	8fr	bl, mag & blk	45	30
148	A30	10fr	multi	45	20

Size: 45x26½mm.

149	A30	20fr	multi ('61)	55	45
150	A30	50fr	red org, dp bl & brn ('61)	1.25	1.00
			Nos. 137-150 (14)	3.88	2.69

Catalogue values for unused stamps in this section, from this point to the end of the section, are for Never Hinged items.

Map of Africa and Symbolic Honeycomb A31

1960 **Unwmk.** ***Perf. 11½***

Inscription in French.

151 A31 3fr ultra & red 20 12

Inscription in Flemish.

152 A31 3fr ultra & red 20 14

Issued to commemorate the 10th anniversary of the Commission for Technical Co-operation in Africa South of the Sahara (C. C. T. A.)

No. 144 Surcharged with New Value and Bars.

1960

153 A30 3.50fr on 3fr 30 12

SEMI-POSTAL STAMPS

Belgian Congo Nos. B10-B11 Overprinted **RUANDA-URUNDI**

1925 **Unwmk.** ***Perf. 12½***

B1 SP1 25c + 25c car & blk 15 15
B2 SP1 25c + 25c car & blk 15 15

No. B2 inscribed "BELGISCH CONGO."
Commemorative of the Colonial Campaigns in 1914-1918. Nos. B1 and B2 alternate in the sheet.

Belgian Congo Nos. B12-B20 Overprinted in Blue or Red

RUANDA

URUNDI

1930 ***Perf. 11½***

B3 SP3 10c + 5c ver 35 35
B4 SP3 20c + 10c dk brn 70 70
B5 SP5 35c + 15c dp grn 1.40 1.40
B6 SP5 60c + 30c dl vio 1.65 1.65
B7 SP5 1fr + 50c dk car 2.50 2.50
B8 SP5 1.75fr + 75c dp bl (R) 2.75 2.75
B9 SP5 3.50fr + 1.50fr rose lake 5.75 5.75
B10 SP5 5fr + 2.50fr red brn 4.50 4.50
B11 SP5 10fr + 5fr gray blk 5.00 5.00
Nos. B3-B11 (9) 24.60 24.60

On Nos. B3, B4 and B7 there is a space of 26 mm. between the two words of the overprint. The surtax was for native welfare.

Queen Astrid with Native Children — SP1

Lion of Belgium and Inscription "Belgium Shall Rise Again" — SP2

1936 **Photo.**

B12 SP1 1.25fr + 5c dk brn 65 55
B13 SP1 1.50fr + 10c dl rose 65 55
B14 SP1 2.50fr + 25c dk bl 75 75

Issued in memory of Queen Astrid. The surtax was for the National League for Protection of Native Children.

1942 **Engr.** ***Perf. 12½***

B15 SP2 10fr + 40fr bl 2.00 2.00
B16 SP2 10fr + 40fr dk red 2.00 2.00

Nos. 74, 78, 79 and 82 Surcharged in Red

Au profit de la Croix Rouge + 50 Fr. Ten voordeele van het Roode Kruis
a

Ten voordeele van het Roode Kruis + 100 Fr. Au profit de la Croix Rouge
b

Au profit de la Croix Rouge + 100 Fr. Ten voordeele van het Roode Kruis
c

1945 **Unwmk.** ***Perf. 12½***

B17 A18 (a) 50c + 50fr dp grn 1.10 1.40
B18 A19 (b) 1.25fr + 100fr rose red & blk 1.50 1.65
B19 A20 (c) 1.75fr + 100fr dk gray brn 1.10 1.40
B20 A21 (b) 3.50fr + 100fr dk ol grn 1.50 1.65

Mozart at Age 7 — SP3

Queen Elizabeth and Mozart Sonata — SP4

1956 **Engr.** ***Perf. 11½***

B21 SP3 4.50fr + 1.50fr bluish vio 90 1.00
B22 SP4 6.50fr + 2.50fr cl 2.00 2.00

200th anniv. of the birth of Wolfgang Amadeus Mozart.
Surtax for the Pro-Mozart Committee.

Nurse and Children — SP5

Designs: 4.50fr+50c, Patient receiving injection. 6.50fr+50c, Patient being bandaged.

1957 **Photo.** ***Perf. 13x10½***

Cross in Carmine.

B23 SP5 3fr + 50c dk bl 55 55
B24 SP5 4.50fr + 50c dk grn 75 75
B25 SP5 6.50fr + 50c red brn 90 90

The surtax was for the Red Cross.

Catalogue values for unused stamps in this section, from this point to the end of the section, are for Never Hinged items.

Soccer SP6

Sports: 50c+25c, High Jumper. 1.50fr+50c, Hurdlers. 3fr+1.25fr, Javelin thrower. 6.50fr+3.50fr, Discus thrower.

1960 **Unwmk.** ***Perf. 13½***

B26 SP6 50c + 25c int bl & mar 8 8
B27 SP6 1.50fr + 50c dk car & blk 20 20
B28 SP6 2fr + 1fr blk & dk car 20 20
B29 SP6 3fr + 1.25fr org ver & grn 1.00 1.10
B30 SP6 6.50fr + 3.50fr ol grn & red 1.00 1.10
Nos. B26-B30 (5) 2.48 2.68

Issued to commemorate the 17th Olympic Games, Rome, Aug. 25-Sept. 11. The surtax was for the youth of Ruanda-Urundi.

Usumbura Cathedral — SP7

Designs: 1fr+50c, 5fr+2fr, Cathedral, sideview. 1.50fr+75c, 6.50fr+3fr, Stained glass window.

1961, Dec. 18 ***Perf. 11½***

B31 SP7 50c + 25c brn & buff 8 8
B32 SP7 1fr + 50c grn & pale grn 8 8
B33 SP7 1.50fr + 75c multi 8 8
B34 SP7 3.50fr + 1.50fr lt bl & brt bl 14 14
B35 SP7 5fr + 2fr car & sal 30 30
B36 SP7 6.50fr + 3fr multi 40 40
Nos. B31-B36 (6) 1.08 1.08

The surtax went for the construction and completion of the Cathedral at Usumbura.

POSTAGE DUE STAMPS

Belgian Congo Nos. J1-J7 Overprinted **RUANDA URUNDI**

1924-27 **Unwmk.** ***Perf. 14, 14½***

J1 D1 5c blk brn 12 12
J2 D1 10c dp rose 12 12
J3 D1 15c violet 18 18
J4 D1 30c green 25 25
J5 D1 50c ultra 32 30
J6 D1 50c brt bl ('27) 32 30
J7 D1 1fr gray 38 38
Nos. J1-J7 (7) 1.69 1.65

Belgian Congo Nos. J8-J12 Overprinted in Carmine **RUANDA URUNDI**

1943 ***Perf. 14x14½, 12½***

J8 D2 10c ol grn 6 6
J9 D2 20c dk ultra 8 8
J10 D2 50c green 12 12
J11 D2 1fr dk brn 18 18
J12 D2 2fr yel org 22 22
Nos. J8-J12 (5) 66 66

Nos. J8-J12 values are for stamps perf. 14x14½. Those perf. 12½ sell for about three times as much.

Belgian Congo Nos. J13-J19 Overprinted **RUANDA URUNDI**

1959 **Engr.** ***Perf. 11½***

J13 D3 10c ol brn 9 9
J14 D3 20c claret 9 9
J15 D3 50c green 9 9
J16 D3 1fr lt bl 14 14
J17 D3 2fr vermilion 18 18
J18 D3 4fr purple 35 35
J19 D3 6fr vio bl 45 45
Nos. J13-J19 (7) 1.39 1.39

Both capital and lower-case U's are found in this overprint.

RUSSIA

(Union of Soviet Socialist Republics)

LOCATION — Eastern Europe and Northern Asia.
GOVT. — Republic.
AREA — 8,650,000 sq. mi.
POP. — 276,300,000 (est. 1985).
CAPITAL — Moscow.

An empire until 1917, the government was overthrown in that year and a socialist union of republics was formed under the name of the Union of Soviet Socialist Republics. The USSR includes the following autonomous republics which have issued their own stamps: Armenia, Azerbaijan, Georgia and Ukraine.

100 Kopecks = 1 Ruble

Catalogue values for unused stamps in this country are for Never Hinged items, beginning with Scott 1021 in the regular postage section, Scott B58 in the semi-postal section, and Scott C82 in the airpost section.

Empire

Coat of Arms
A1 A2 A3

Wmk. 166

Wmk. Colorless Numerals (166)

1857, Dec. 10 **Typo.** ***Imperf.***

1 A1 10k brn & bl *3,500.* 300.00
Pen cancellation 75.00
Penmark & postmark 225.00

Genuine unused copies of No. 1 are exceedingly rare. Most of those offered are used with pen cancellation removed. The unused value is for a specimen without gum. The very few known stamps with original gum sell for much more.

1858, Jan. 10 ***Perf. 14½, 15***

2 A1 10k brn & bl 1,000. 100.00
3 A1 20k bl & org 2,500. 550.00
4 A1 30k car & grn 3,500. 2,000.

1858-64 **Unwmk.** ***Perf. 12½***

Wove Paper

5 A2 1k blk & yel ('64) 32.50 16.00
a 1k blk & org 32.50 16.00
6 A2 3k blk & grn ('64) 55.00 27.50
7 A2 5k blk & lil ('64) 60.00 35.00
8 A1 10k brn & bl 22.50 2.00
9 A1 20k bl & org 125.00 22.50
a Half used as 10k on cover *5,000.*
10 A1 30k car & grn 100.00 45.00

1863

11 A3 5k blk & bl 7.00 *200.00*

No. 11 was issued to pay local postage in St. Petersburg and Moscow. It is known to have been used in other cities. Copies canceled after July, 1864, are worth considerably less.

1865, June 2 ***Perf. 14½, 15***

12 A2 1k blk & yel 30.00 6.00
 a 1k blk & org 30.00 6.00
13 A2 3k blk & grn 35.00 4.25
14 A2 5k blk & lil 50.00 5.75
15 A1 10k brn & bl 60.00 1.75
 a Thick paper 115.00 6.00
17 A1 20k bl & org 125.00 12.50
18 A1 30k car & grn 175.00 22.50

Wmk. 168- Cyrillic EZGB & Wavy Lines

1866-70 **Wmk. 168**

Horizontally Laid Paper

19 A2 1k blk & yel 1.25 22
 a 1k blk & org 1.50 38
 b Imperf. *1,150.*
 c Vertically laid 125.00 20.00
 d Groundwork inverted *3,750.* *1,250.*
 e Thick paper 40.00 25.00
 f As "c," imperf. 2,750. 2,250.
 g As "b," "c" & "d" *5,000.* *5,000.*
20 A2 3k blk & dp grn 4.00 50
 a 3k blk & yel grn 4.00 50
 b Imperf. *1,500.*
 c Vertically laid 150.00 30.00
 d V's in groundwork (error) ('70) 550.00 35.00
22 A2 5k blk & lil 4.00 50
 a 5k blk & gray 60.00 10.00
 b Imperf. 1,500. 775.00
 c Vertically laid 650.00 100.00
 d As "c," imperf. *2,750.*
23 A1 10k brn & bl 12.00 85
 a Vertically laid 65.00 8.00
 b Center inverted *6,000.*
 c Imperf. *2,000.*
24 A1 20k bl & org 45.00 6.00
 a Vertically laid 675.00 50.00
25 A1 30k car & grn 55.00 17.00
 a Vertically laid 650.00 25.00

In Wmk. 168 the initials are those of the State Printing Plant.

Arms — A4

1875-79

26 A2 2k blk & red 2.50 45
 a Vertically laid 550.00 60.00
 b Groundwork inverted *7,500.*
27 A4 7k gray & rose ('79) 2.00 25
 a Imperf. *4,250.*
 b Vertically laid 500.00 60.00
 c Wmkd. hexagons ('79) *8,500.*
 d Center inverted *17,500.*
 e Center omitted 300.00 300.00
28 A4 8k gray & rose 3.25 75
 a Vertically laid 500.00 60.00
 b Imperf. *1,500.*
 c "C" instead of "B" in "Bocem" 25.00 25.00
29 A4 10k brn & bl 15.00 3.00
 a Center inverted *8,000.*
30 A4 20k bl & org 30.00 4.25
 a Cross-shaped "T" in bottom word 100.00 25.00
 b Center inverted *8,000.*

The hexagon watermark of No. 27c is that of revenue stamps. No. 27c exists with Perm postmark.

Imperial Eagle and Post Horns
A5 A6

Perf. 14 to 15 and Compound

1883-88 **Wmk. 168**

Horizontally Laid Paper

31 A5 1k orange 90 18
 a Imperf. 450.00 450.00
 b Groundwork inverted *4,000.* *4,000.*
 c 1k yel 90 25
32 A5 2k dk grn 1.25 25
 a 2k yel grn ('88) 1.25 25
 b Imperf. 450.00 410.00
 c Wove paper 450.00 325.00
 d Groundwork inverted *3,000.*
33 A5 3k carmine 1.25 18
 a Imperf. 500.00 500.00
 b Groundwork inverted *4,000.*
 c Wove paper 500.00 410.00
34 A5 5k red vio 1.10 18
 a Groundwork inverted *5,000.*
35 A5 7k blue 1.10 18
 a Imperf. 500.00 500.00
 b Groundwork inverted 675.00 600.00
36 A6 14k bl & rose 2.50 25
 a Imperf. 650.00 550.00
 b Center inverted *7,000.* *6,000.*
 c Diagonal half surchd. "7" in red, on cover ('84) *8,000.*
37 A6 35k vio & grn 14.00 2.10
38 A6 70k brn & org 18.00 2.10

Before 1882 the 1, 2, 3 and 5 kopecks had small numerals in the background; beginning with No. 31 these denominations have a background of network, like the higher values.

No. 36c is handstamped. It is known with cancellations of Tiflis and Kutais, both in Georgia. It is believed to be of philatelic origin.

A7

1884 ***Perf. 13½, 13½x11½***

Vertically Laid Paper

39 A7 3.50r blk & gray 650.00 400.00
 a Horiz. laid 7,000. 7,000.
40 A7 7r blk & org 650.00 400.00

Forgeries exist.

Imperial Eagle and Post Horns with Thunderbolts
A8 A9

With Thunderbolts Across Post Horns

Perf. 14 to 15 and Compound

1889, May 14

Horizontally Laid Paper

41 A8 4k rose 40 18
 a Groundwork invtd. 1,500.
42 A8 10k dk bl 40 12
43 A8 20k bl & car 1.40 20
44 A8 50k vio & grn 1.75 30

Perf. 13½

45 A9 1r lt brn, brn & org 10.50 1.00
 a Pair, imperf. between 425.00 425.00
 b Center omitted 250.00 250.00

See Nos. 57C, 60, 63, 66, 68, 82, 85, 87, 126, 129, 131.

Russia stamps through 1917 can be mounted in Scott's Soviet Republics Part I Album

A10 A11

A12 A13

1889-92 ***Perf. 14½x15***

Horizontally Laid Paper

46 A10 1k orange 18 10
 a Imperf. 450.00 450.00
47 A10 2k green 18 10
 a Imperf. 375.00 350.00
 b Groundwork inverted
48 A10 3k carmine 22 10
 a Imperf. 350.00 350.00
49 A10 5k red vio 35 10
 b Groundwork omitted 725.00 725.00
50 A10 7k dk bl 22 10
 a Imperf. 550.00 550.00
 b Groundwork inverted *2,750.*
 c Groundwork omitted 200.00 200.00
51 A11 14k bl & rose 1.10 15
 a Center inverted *4,000.* *4,000.*
52 A11 35k vio & grn 3.50 60

Perf. 13½

53 A12 3.50r blk & gray 17.50 4.00
54 A12 7r blk & yel 30.00 8.50
 a Dbl. impression of blk 275.00

Perf. 14 to 15 and Compound

1902-05

Vertically Laid Paper

55 A10 1k orange 12 8
 a Imperf. 600.00 600.00
 b Groundwork inverted 850.00 850.00
 c Groundwork omitted 200.00 200.00
56 A10 2k yel grn 12 8
 a 2k dp grn 7.50 70
 b Groundwork omitted 600.00 300.00
 c Groundwork inverted 850.00 850.00
 d Groundwork double 425.00 425.00
57 A10 3k rose red 14 8
 a Groundwork omitted 360.00 235.00
 b Dbl. impression 200.00 165.00
 d Imperf. 150.00 150.00
 e Groundwork inverted 210.00 210.00
57C A8 4k rose red ('04) 35 14
 f Dbl. impression 200.00 200.00
 g Groundwork inverted 1,500. 600.00
58 A10 5k red vio 35 14
 a 5k dl vio 4.25 2.00
 b Groundwork inverted *1,000.* *1,000.*
 c Imperf. 250.00 250.00
 d Groundwork omitted 250.00 165.00
59 A10 7k dk bl 28 10
 a Groundwork omitted 340.00 300.00
 b Imperf. 375.00 375.00
 c Groundwork inverted 340.00 340.00
60 A8 10k dk bl ('04) 28 10
 a Groundwork inverted 15.00 5.00
 b Groundwork omitted 165.00 35.00
 c Groundwork double 165.00 35.00
61 A11 14k bl & rose 80 14
 a Center invtd. 4,750. *3,250.*
 b Center omitted 1,100. 700.00
62 A11 15k brn vio & bl ('05) 95 14
 a Center omitted
 b Center inverted *4,000.* *3,500.*
63 A8 20k bl & car ('04) 80 10
64 A11 25k dl grn & lil ('05) 2.50 30
 a Center inverted *3,250.* *3,250.*
 b Center omitted 1,500. 1,500.
65 A11 35k dk vio & grn 2.75 30
 a Center inverted
 b Center omitted *1,500.*
66 A8 50k vio & grn ('05) 7.75 80
67 A11 70k brn & org 8.25 80

Perf. 13½

68 A9 1r lt brn, brn & org 7.75 48
 a Perf. 11½ 450.00 55.00
 b Perf. 13½x11½, 11½x13½ 675.00 625.00
 c Imperf. 250.00
 d Center invtd. 250.00 250.00
 e Center omitted 250.00 150.00
 f Horiz. pair, imperf. btwn. 340.00 165.00
69 A12 3.50r blk & gray 7.75 1.90
 a Center inverted *5,000.* *5,000.*
 b Imperf., pair 2,000. 2,000.
70 A12 7r blk & yel 7.75 1.90
 a Center inverted *5,000.* *5,000.*
 b Horizontal pair, imperf. between 2,000. 2,000.
 c Imperf., pair 2,000. 2,000.

1906 ***Perf. 13½***

71 A13 5r dk bl, grn & pale bl 22.50 2.75
 a Perf. 11½ 225.00 275.00
72 A13 10r car rose, yel & gray 40.00 5.50

The design of No. 72 differs in many details from the illustration. Nos. 71-72 were printed in sheets of 25.

See Nos. 80-81, 83-84, 86, 108-109, 125, 127-128, 130, 132-135, 137-138.

A14 A15

Vertical Lozenges of Varnish on Face.

1909-12 **Unwmk.** ***Perf. 14x14½***

Wove Paper

73 A14 1k dl org yel 7 14
 a 1k org yel ('09) 20 20
 c Dbl. impression 85.00 85.00
74 A14 2k dl grn 7 14
 a 2k grn ('09) 22 22
 b Double impression 25.00 25.00
75 A14 3k carmine 7 14
 a 3k rose red ('09) 22 22
76 A15 4k carmine 7 14
 a 4k car rose ('09) 22 22
77 A14 5k claret 7 14
 a 5k lil ('12) 65 65
 b Double impressions 22.50 22.50
78 A14 7k blue 7 14
 a 7k lt bl ('09) 1.50 65
 b Imperf. 225.00 225.00
79 A15 10k dk bl 7 14
 a 10k lt bl ('09) *500.00* *85.00*
 b 10k pale bl 6.00 1.00
80 A11 14k dk bl & car 14 14
 a 14k bl & rose ('09) 22 22
81 A11 15k red brn & dp bl 12 15
 a 15k dl vio & bl ('09) 85 40
 c Center omitted 115.00 85.00
 d Center double 50.00 50.00
82 A8 20k dl bl & dk car 14 14
 a 20k bl & car ('10) 85 55
 b Groundwork omitted 20.00 13.00
 c Center double 22.50 22.50
 d Center and value omitted 85.00 85.00
83 A11 25k dl grn & dk vio 16 16
 a 25k grn & vio ('09) 32 32
 b Center omitted 115.00 115.00
 c Center double 25.00 25.00
84 A11 35k red brn & grn 16 16
 a 35k brn vio & yel grn 52 42
 b 35k vio & grn ('09) 52 42
 c Center double 25.00 25.00
85 A8 50k red brn & grn 14 16
 a 50k vio & grn ('09) 50 40
 b Groundwork omitted 22.50 22.50
 c Center double 32.50 32.50
 d Center and value omitted 115.00 115.00
86 A11 70k brn & red org 14 16
 a 70k lt brn & org ('09) 32 25
 b Center double 40.00 40.00
 c Center omitted 115.00 115.00

Perf. 13½

87 A9 1r pale brn, dk brn & org 14 14
 a 1r pale brn, brn & org ('10) 25 22
 b Perf. 12½ 25 22
 c Groundwork inverted 20.00 20.00
 d Pair, imperf. between 22.50 22.50
 e Center inverted 25.00 25.00
 f Center double 16.00 16.00

See Nos. 119-124.

No. 87a was issued in sheets of 40 stamps, while Nos. 87 and 87b came in sheets of 50. Nos. 87g-87k are listed below No. 138a.

Nearly all values of this issue are known without the lines of varnish.

The 7k has two types: I. The scroll bearing the top inscription ends at left with three short lines of shading beside the first letter. Four pearls extend at lower left between the leaves and denomination panel. II. Inner lines of scroll at top left end in two curls; three pearls at lower left. Three clichés of type II (an essay) were included by mistake in the plate used for the first printing. Value of pair, type I with type II, unused $2,500.

SURCHARGES

Russian stamps of types A6-A15 with various surcharges may be found listed under Armenia, Batum, Far Eastern Republic, Georgia, Siberia, South Russia, Transcaucasian Federated Republics and Ukraine.

Peter I — A16

Alexander II — A17

Alexander III — A18

Peter I — A19

Nicholas II
A20 A21

Catherine II — A22

Nicholas I — A23

Alexander I — A24

Alexis Mikhailovich A25

Paul I A26

Elizabeth Petrovna A27

Michael Feodorovich A28

The Kremlin — A29

Winter Palace — A30

Romanov Castle — A31

Nicholas II — A32

Without Lozenges of Varnish

1913, Jan. 2 Typo. *Perf. 13½*

88	A16	1k brn org	25	10
a		Imperf., pair		
89	A17	2k yel grn	25	10
90	A18	3k rose red	25	10
a		Imperf., pair		
b		Double impression	550.00	
91	A19	4k dl red	20	10
92	A20	7k brown	20	10
a		Imperf., pair	850.00	
b		Double impression	400.00	400.00
93	A21	10k dp bl	40	18
a		Imperf., pair	850.00	
94	A22	14k bl grn	35	18
95	A23	15k yel brn	70	18
96	A24	20k ol grn	85	18
97	A25	25k red vio	85	32
98	A26	35k gray vio & dk grn	85	32
99	A27	50k brn & sl	1.00	42
100	A28	70k yel grn & brn	2.25	1.10

Engr.

101	A29	1r dp grn	8.00	4.00
102	A30	2r red brn	8.00	4.00
a		Imperf., pair	775.00	
103	A31	3r dk vio	20.00	11.00
a		Imperf., pair	775.00	
104	A32	5r blk brn	12.00	16.00
		Nos. 88-104 (17)	56.40	38.38

Issued in commemoration of the tercentenary of the founding of the Romanov dynasty. See Nos. 105-107, 112-116, 139-141.

Arms & 5-line Inscription on Black

1915, Oct. Typo. *Perf. 13½*

Thin Cardboard

Without Gum

105	A21	10k blue	38	*3.75*
a		Imperf.	50.00	
106	A23	15k brown	38	*3.75*
a		Imperf.	32.50	40.00
107	A24	20k ol grn	38	*3.75*
a		Imperf.	40.00	

Nos. 105-107, 112-116 and 139-141 were issued for use as paper money, but contrary to regulations were often used for postal purposes. Back inscription means: "Having circulation on par with silver subsidiary coins."

Types of 1906 Issue

Vertical Lozenges of Varnish on Face

1915 *Perf. 13½, 13½x13*

108	A13	5r ind, grn & lt bl	20	15
a		5r dk bl, grn & pale bl ('15)	2.50	65
b		Perf. 12½	3.25	1.00
c		Center double	40.00	
d		Pair, imperf. btwn.	200.00	
109	A13	10r car lake, yel & gray	25	20
a		10r car, yel & lt gray	40	25
b		10r rose red, yel & gray ('15)	85	50
c		10r car, yel & gray bl (error)	1,500.	
d		Groundwork inverted	500.00	
e		Center double	50.00	50.00

Nos. 108a and 109b were issued in sheets of 25. Nos. 108, 108b, 109 and 109a came in sheets of 50. Chemical forgeries of No. 109c exist. Genuine copies usually are centered to upper right.

Nos. 92, 94 Surcharged **10** **10**

1916

110	A20	10k on 7k brn	10	10
a		Invtd. surcharge	60.00	60.00
111	A22	20k on 14k bl grn	10	10
a		Invtd. surcharge	40.00	40.00

Types of 1913 Issue

Arms, Value & 4-line inscription on Back

Surcharged Large Numerals on Nos. 114-115

1916-17

Thin Cardboard

Without Gum

112	A16	1 on 1k brn org ('17)	28	*4.50*
113	A17	2 on 2k yel grn ('17)	28	*4.50*

Without Surcharge

114	A16	1k brn org	6.75	*32.50*
115	A17	2k yel grn	16.00	*55.00*
116	A18	3k rose red	32	*4.50*

See note after No. 107.

Nos. 78a, 80a Surcharged:

коп.10коп. a **к.20к.** b

1917 *Perf. 14x14½*

117	A14	10k on 7k lt bl	6	6
a		Inverted surcharge	60.00	60.00
b		Double surch.	60.00	
118	A11	20k on 14k bl & rose	6	6
a		Inverted surcharge	50.00	50.00

Provisional Government

Civil War

Type of 1889-1912 Issues

Vertical Lozenges of Varnish on Face

Two types of 7r:
Type I - Single outer frame line.
Type II - Double outer frame line.

1917 Typo. *Imperf.*

Wove Paper

119	A14	1k orange	7	7
120	A14	2k gray grn	7	7
121	A14	3k red	7	7
122	A15	4k carmine	14	20
123	A14	5k claret	7	7
124	A15	10k dk bl	6.00	8.00
125	A11	15k red brn & dp bl	7	7
a		Center omitted	55.00	
126	A8	20k bl & car	14	32
a		Groundwork omitted	16.00	16.00
127	A11	25k grn & gray vio	65	1.00
128	A11	35k red brn & grn	10	32
129	A8	50k brn vio & grn	16	25
a		Groundwork omitted	16.00	16.00
130	A11	70k brn & org	7	40
a		Center omitted	115.00	
131	A9	1r pale brn, brn & red org	7	10
a		Center inverted	20.00	20.00
b		Center omitted	20.00	20.00
c		Center double	16.00	16.00
d		Groundwork double	14.00	14.00
e		Groundwork inverted	10.00	10.00
f		Groundwork omitted	22.50	22.50
g		Frame double	16.00	16.00
132	A12	3.50r mar & lt grn	10	22
133	A13	5r dk bl, grn & pale bl	20	32
a		5r dk bl, grn & yel (error)	1,000.	
b		Groundwork inverted	500.00	
134	A12	7r dk grn & pink (I)	65	1.00
a		Center invtd.		
135	A13	10r scar, yel & gray	21.00	22.50
a		10r scar, grn & gray (error)	1,250.	

Vertical Lozenges of Varnish on Face

1917 *Perf. 13½, 13½x13*

137	A12	3.50r mar & lt grn	7	7
138	A12	7r dk grn & pink (II)	7	7
d		Type I	2.00	2.00

Perf. 12½

137a	A12	3.50r mar & lt grn	20	20
138a	A12	7r dk grn & pink (II)	1.00	1.00

Horizontal Lozenges of Varnish on Face

Perf. 13½x13

87g	A9	1r pale brn, brn & red org	10	10
h		Imperforate	10.00	
i		As "h," center omitted	22.50	
j		As "h," center inverted	22.50	
k		As "h," center double	22.50	
137b	A12	3.50r mar & lt grn	15	15
d		Imperforate	210.00	
138b	A12	7r dk grn & pink (II)	12	12
c		Imperforate	200.00	

Nos. 87g, 137b and 138b often show the eagle with little or no embossing.

Types of 1913 Issue

Surcharge & 4-line Inscription on Back

Surcharged Large Numerals

1917

Thin Cardboard, Without Gum

139	A16	1 on 1k brn org	40	*6.00*
a		Imperf.	22.50	22.50
140	A17	2 on 2k yel grn	65	*6.00*
a		Imperf.	22.50	22.50
b		Surch. omitted, imperf.	45.00	45.00

Without Surcharge

141	A18	3k rose red	40	*6.00*
a		Imperf.		

See note after No. 107.

Stamps overprinted with a Liberty Cap on Crossed Swords or with reduced facsimiles of pages of newspapers were a private speculation and without official sanction.

Russian Soviet Federated Socialist Republic

Severing Chain of Bondage — A33

1918 Typo. *Perf. 13½*

149	A33	35k blue	8	*1.25*
a		Imperf., pair	125.00	
150	A33	70k brown	8	*1.25*
a		Imperf., pair	350.00	

In 1918-1922 various revenue stamps were permitted to be used for postal duty, sometimes surcharged with new values, more often not.

Symbols of Agriculture A40

Symbols of Industry A41

Soviet Symbols of Agriculture and Industry A42

Science and Arts — A43

1921 Unwmk. Litho. *Imperf.*

177	A40	1r orange	32	*1.25*
178	A40	2r lt brn	32	*1.25*
179	A41	5r dl ultra	20	32
180	A42	20r blue	80	*3.00*
a		Pelure paper	3.25	2.75
b		Dbl. impression	20.00	
181	A40	100r orange	7	7
a		Pelure paper	7	14
182	A40	200r lt brn	10	24
a		200r ol brn	6.50	6.50
183	A43	250r dl vio	7	7
a		Pelure paper	7	7
b		Chalk surfaced paper	10	16
c		Tete beche pair	13.00	13.00
d		Double impression	20.00	
184	A40	300r green	10	24
a		Pelure paper	10.00	13.00
185	A41	500r blue	10	32
186	A41	1000r carmine	10	28
a		Chalk surfaced paper	10	16
b		Thick paper	10	16
c		Pelure paper	10	16
		Nos. 177-186 (10)	2.18	*7.04*

New Russia Triumphant — A44

Wmk. 169-Lozenges

1921, Aug. 10 Wmk. 169 Engr.

Type I - 37½mm by 23½mm.
Type II - 38½mm by 23¼mm.

187	A44	40r sl, type II	20	85
a		Type I	32	85

Initials Stand for Russian Soviet Federated Socialist Republic — A45

1921 Litho. Unwmk.

188 A45 100r orange 12 32
189 A45 250r violet 12 32
190 A45 1000r car rose 32 85

4th anniversary of Soviet Government. A 200r was not regularly issued. Value $20.

Nos. 177-179 Surcharged in Black

5000 руб.

1922

191 A40 5000r on 1r org 28 60
a Inverted surcharge 27.50 22.50
b Double surcharge, red & black 27.50 22.50
c Pair, one without surch. 40.00
192 A40 5000r on 2r lt brn 48 90
a Inverted surch. 20.00 15.00
b Double surcharge 24.00
193 A41 5000r on 5r ultra 28 45
a Invtd. surch. 40.00 30.00
b Dbl. surch. 40.00

No. 180 Surcharged

Р. С. Ф. С. Р.

5000 РУБЛЕЙ

194 A42 5000r on 20r bl 60 90
a Pelure paper 1.25 1.25
b Pair, one without surch. 40.00

Nos. 177-180, 187 Surcharged in Black or Red

РСФСР

10.000 Р.

Wmk. Lozenges (169)

195 A44 10,000r on 40r sl, type I 32 45
a Invtd. surch. 20.00 15.00
b Type II 1.75 1.75
c "1.0000" instead of "10.000" 60.00
d Dbl. surch. 40.00

Red Surcharge

Unwmk.

196 A40 5000r on 1r org 52 90
a Invtd. surch. 20.00 15.00
197 A40 5000r on 2r lt brn 60 1.25
a Invtd. surch. 40.00 30.00
198 A41 5000r on 5r ultra 60 1.25
199 A42 5000r on 20r bl 1.00 1.75
a Invtd. surch. 48.00 35.00

Wmk. Lozenges (169)

200 A44 10,000r on 40r sl, type I (R) 20 22
a Invtd. surch. 24.00 18.00
b Dbl. surch. 24.00 18.00
c With periods after Russian letters 48.00 35.00
d Type II 40 30
e As "a," type II 40.00 30.00
f As "c," type II 60.00 45.00

No. 183 Surcharged in Black or Blue Black

7500 руб.

1922, Mar. Unwmk.

201 A43 7500r on 250r dk vio (Bk) 8 9
a Pelure paper 8 9
b Chalk surfaced paper 16 24
c Blue black surch. 12 12
Nos. 191-201 (11) 4.96 8.76

Nos. 201, 201a and 201b exist with surcharge inverted (value about $15 each), and double (about $25 each).

Type of 1921 and

"Workers of the World Unite" A46

Wmk. 171

1922 Litho. Wmk. Diamonds (171)

202 A46 5000r dk vio 35 2.00
203 A42 7500r blue 16 22
204 A46 10,000r blue 1.50 2.00

Unwmk.

205 A42 7500r bl, *buff* 16 25
a Dbl. impression 17.50
206 A46 22,500r dk vio, *buff* 24 32
Nos. 202-206 (5) 2.41 4.79

No. 183 Surcharged Diagonally

100,000 РУБ.

1922 Unwmk. *Imperf.*

210 A43 100,000r on 250r 7 10
a Invtd. surch. 17.50 17.50
b Pelure paper 7 14
c Chalk surfaced paper 10 14
d As "b," invtd. surcharge 17.50 20.00

Marking 5th Anniversary of October Revolution — A48

1922 Typo.

211 A48 5r ocher & blk 12 12
212 A48 10r brn & blk 12 12
213 A48 25r vio & blk 35 50
a Pelure paper 16.00
214 A48 27r rose & blk 65 1.00
a Pelure paper 16.00
215 A48 45r bl & blk 45 65
a Pelure paper 20.00
Nos. 211-215 (5) 1.69 2.39

5th anniv. of the October Revolution. Sold in the currency of 1922 which was valued at 10,000 times that of the preceding years.

Stamps of 1909-18 Surcharged

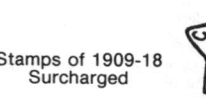

1922-23 *Perf. 14½x15*

216 A8 5r on 20k bl & car 15 40
a Invtd. surcharge 13.00 13.00
b Double surcharge 22.50 22.50
217 A11 20r on 15k red brn & bl 25 50
a Invtd. surch. 32.50 32.50
218 A11 20r on 70k brn & org 15 25
a Inverted surch 10.00 10.00
b Double surcharge 16.00 16.00
219 A8 30r on 50k brn red & grn 20 40
a Invtd. surcharge 13.00 13.00
c Groundwork omitted 16.00 16.00
d Double surch. 13.00 13.00
220 A11 40r on 15k red brn & bl 10 25
a Invtd. surch. 13.00 13.00
b Double surcharge 16.00 16.00
221 A11 100r on 15k red brn & bl 10 25
a Invtd. surch. 16.00 16.00
b Double surcharge 13.00 13.00
222 A11 200r on 15k red brn & bl 15 25
a Invtd. surch. 13.00 13.00
b Double surch. 10.00 10.00

Nos. 218-220, 222 exist in pairs, one without surcharge; Nos. 221-222 with triple surcharge; No. 221 with double surcharge, one inverted. Value, each $100.

Imperf

223 A8 5r on 20k bl & car 4.50 9.50
224 A11 20r on 15k red brn & bl *1,200.*
225 A11 20r on 70k brn & org 30 65
a Invtd. surch. 13.00 13.00
226 A8 30r on 50k brn vio & grn 2.25 4.00
227 A11 40r on 15k red brn & bl 10 25
a Invtd. surch. 22.50 22.50
b Double surch. 16.00 16.00
228 A11 100r on 15k red brn & bl 65 1.00
a Invtd. surch. 40.00 40.00
229 A11 200r on 15k red brn & bl 65 65
a Inverted surcharge 40.00 40.00
b Dbl. surcharge 27.50 27.50
Nos. 216-223,225-229 (13) 9.55 18.35

Worker A49

Soldier A50

1922-23 Typo. *Imperf.*

230 A49 10r blue 10 15
231 A50 50r brown 10 15
232 A50 70r brn vio 10 15
233 A50 100r red 20 25

1923 *Perf. 14x14½*

234 A49 10r dp bl, perf. 13½ 15 20
a Perf. 14 13.00 16.00
b Perf. 12½ 65 85
235 A50 50r brown 15 20
a Perf. 12½ 5.25 6.00
b Perf. 13½ 1.50 2.00
236 A50 70r brn vio 15 20
a Perf. 12½ 1.50 2.00
237 A50 100r red 20 30
a Cliche of 70r in plate of 100r 30.00 35.00

Soldier A51

Worker A52

Peasant — A53

1923 *Perf. 14½x15*

238 A51 3r rose 10 24
a Imperf. 10.00 20.00
239 A52 4r brown 10 24
a Imperf. 13.00 25.00
b As "a," dbl. impression 22.50
240 A53 5r lt bl 10 24
a Dbl. impression 8.00 10.00
b Imperf. 4.50 10.00
241 A51 10r gray 10 24
d Imperf. 4.50 10.00
e Dbl. impression 16.00
f As "d," dbl. impression 22.50
241A A51 20r brn vio 20 75
b Double impression 10.00 10.00
c Imperf. 40.00 47.50
Nos. 238-241A (5) 60 1.71

Stamps of 1r buff, type A52, and 2r green, type A53, perf. 12 and imperf. were prepared but not put in use. Value $1 each.

The imperfs of Nos. 238-241A were sold only by the philatelic bureau in Moscow.

Stamps of 20r, type A51, printed in gray black or dull violet are essays. Value $35 each.

The stamps of this and the following issues were sold for the currency of 1923, one ruble of which was equal to 100 rubles of 1922 and 1,000,000 rubles of 1921.

Union of Soviet Socialist Republics

Reaping — A54

Sowing — A55

Fordson Tractor A56

Symbolical of the Exhibition — A57

1923, Aug. 19 Litho. *Imperf.*

242 A54 1r brn & org 70 2.00
243 A55 2r dp grn & pale grn 70 2.00
244 A56 5r dp bl & pale bl 80 2.75
245 A57 7r rose & pink 85 3.50

Perf. 12½, 13½

246 A54 1r brn & org 1.75 3.50
a Perf. 12½ 15.00 25.00
247 A55 2r dp grn & pale grn, perf. 12½ 1.40 2.50
248 A56 5r dp bl & pale bl 1.65 4.25
a Perf. 13½ 6.00 12.00
249 A57 7r rose & pink 2.25 5.00
a Perf. 12½ 10.00 17.50
Nos. 242-249 (8) 10.10 25.50

Issued to commemorate the 1st Agriculture and Craftsmanship Exhibition, Moscow.

Worker A58

Soldier A59

Peasant — A60

1923 Unwmk. Litho. *Imperf.*

250 A58 1k orange 55 18
251 A60 2k green 70 28
252 A59 3k red brn 70 28
253 A58 4k dp rose 70 48
254 A58 5k lilac 70 48
255 A60 6k lt bl 55 22
256 A59 10k dk bl 55 22
257 A58 20k yel grn 2.25 40
258 A60 50k dk brn 3.25 1.40
259 A59 1r red & brn 3.75 1.65
Nos. 250-259 (10) 13.70 5.59

1924 *Perf. 14½x15*

261 A58 4k dp rose 100.00 30.00
262 A59 10k dk bl 100.00 30.00
263 A60 30k violet 25.00 9.50
264 A59 40k sl gray 25.00 9.50

See Nos. 273-290, 304-321.

Vladimir Ilyich Ulyanov (Lenin) A61

Worker A62

1924 *Imperf.*

265 A61 3k red & blk 70 1.00
266 A61 6k red & blk 70 1.00
267 A61 12k red & blk 70 1.00
268 A61 20k red & blk 1.40 1.10

Three printings of Nos. 265-268 differ in size of red frame.

Perf. 13½

269 A61	3k red & blk	1.10	1.25
270 A61	6k red & blk	1.10	1.25
271 A61	12k red & blk	1.40	1.65
272 A61	20k red & blk	2.25	1.90

Death of Lenin (1870-1924).
Forgeries of Nos. 265-272 exist.

Types of 1923

There are small differences between the lithographed stamps of 1923 and the typographed of 1924-25. On a few values this may be seen in the numerals.

Type A58: Lithographed. The two white lines forming the outline of the ear are continued across the cheek. Typographed. The outer lines of the ear are broken where they touch the cheek.

Type A59: Lithographed. At the top of the right shoulder a white line touches the frame at the left. Counting from the edge of the visor of the cap, lines 5, 6 and sometimes 7 touch at their upper ends. Typographed. The top line of the shoulder does not reach the frame. On the cap lines 5, 6 and 7 run together and form a white spot.

Type A60: In the angle above the first letter "C" there is a fan-shaped ornament enclosing four white dashes. On the lithographed stamps these dashes reach nearly to the point of the angle. On the typographed stamps the dashes are shorter and often only three are visible.

On unused copies of the typographed stamps the raised outlines of the designs can be seen on the backs of the stamps.

1924-25 Typo. *Imperf.*

273 A59	3k red brn	1.10	1.00
274 A58	4k dp rose	1.10	1.00
275 A59	10k dk bl	1.65	1.00
275A A60	50k brown	400.00	27.50

Other typographed and imperf. values include: 2k green, 5k lilac, 6k light blue, 20k green and 1r red and brown. Value, unused: $150, $100, $37.50, $150, and $175.

Nos. 273-275A were regularly issued. The 7k, 8k, 9k, 30k, 40k, 2r, 3r, and 5r also exist imperf. Value, set of 8, $75.

Perf. 14½x15
Typo.

276 A58	1k orange	65.00	5.50
277 A60	2k green	65	32
278 A59	3k red brn	85	40
279 A58	4k dp rose	85	40
280 A58	5k lilac	10.00	1.40
281 A60	6k lt bl	85	40
282 A59	7k chocolate	1.00	40
283 A58	8k brn ol	1.10	70
284 A60	9k org red	1.10	1.40
285 A59	10k dk bl	1.65	55
286 A58	14k sl bl	20.00	2.75
287 A60	15k yellow	*6,000.*	*125.00*
288 A58	20k gray grn	4.00	80
288A A60	30k violet	100.00	6.50
288B A59	40k sl gray	100.00	6.50
289 A60	50k brown	20.00	4.00
290 A59	1r red & brn	10.00	2.00
291 A62	2r grn & rose	20.00	3.25
	Nos. 276-286,288-291 (17)	357.05	37.27

See No. 323. Forgeries of No. 287 exist.

1925 *Perf. 12*

276a A58	1k orange	65	18
277a A60	2k green	8.00	95
278a A59	3k red brn	1.65	70
279a A58	4k dp rose	55.00	3.25
280a A58	5k lilac	4.50	80
282a A59	7k chocolate	2.25	20
283a A58	8k brn ol	80.00	4.00
284a A60	9k org red	13.00	5.50
285a A59	10k dk bl	2.75	40
286a A58	14k sl bl	2.75	40
287a A60	15k yellow	2.75	1.10
288c A58	20k gray grn	18.00	40
288d A60	30k violet	20.00	2.75
288e A59	40k sl gray	16.00	2.75
289a A60	50k brown	8.00	1.10
290a A59	1r red & brn	275.00	135.00
	Nos. 276a-290a (16)	510.30	159.48

Soldier — A63

Worker — A64

1924-25 *Perf. 13½*

292 A63	3r blk brn & grn	11.00	4.75
a	Perf. 10	285.00	50.00
b	Perf. 13½x10	250.00	315.00
293 A64	5r dk bl & gray brn	32.50	9.25
a	Perf. 10½	50.00	62.50

See Nos. 324-325.

Lenin Mausoleum, Moscow — A65

Wmk. 170

Wmk. Green Border and Rosettes (170)

1925, Jan. Photo. *Imperf.*

294 A65	7k dp bl	2.00	2.50
295 A65	14k dk grn	2.25	2.50
296 A65	20k car rose	2.25	2.50
297 A65	40k red brn	2.25	3.00

Perf. 13½x14

298 A65	7k dp bl	2.00	2.50
299 A65	14k dk grn	2.25	2.50
300 A65	20k car rose	2.25	2.50
301 A65	40k red brn	2.50	3.00

First anniversary of Lenin's death.

Nos. 294-301 are found on both ordinary and thick paper. Those on thick paper sell for twice as much, except for No. 301, which is scarcer on ordinary paper.

Lenin — A66

Wmk. 170

1925, July Engr. *Perf. 13½*

302 A66	5r red brn	18.00	4.50
a	Perf. 12½	32.50	10.00
b	Perf. 10½ ('26)	30.00	10.00
303 A66	10r indigo	18.00	8.50
a	Perf. 12½	150.00	82.50
b	Perf. 10½ ('26)	22.50	13.00

Imperfs. exist. Value, set $75.
See Nos. 407-408, 621-622

Types of 1923 Issue

1925-27 Wmk. 170 Typo. *Perf. 12*

304 A58	1k orange	45	35
305 A60	2k green	45	20
306 A59	3k red brn	45	35
307 A58	4k dp rose	35	24
308 A58	5k lilac	48	24
309 A60	6k lt bl	48	24
310 A59	7k chocolate	60	16
311 A58	8k brn ol	60	16
a	Perf. 14½x15	60.00	20.00
312 A60	9k red	90	40
313 A59	10k dk bl	90	28
a	10k pale bl ('27)	1.65	1.00
314 A58	14k sl bl	1.10	35
315 A60	15k yellow	1.75	1.00
316 A59	18k violet	1.40	24
317 A58	20k gray grn	1.65	24
318 A60	30k violet	2.00	24
319 A59	40k sl gray	2.75	35
320 A60	50k brown	4.25	35
321 A59	1r red & brn	4.25	35
a	Perf. 14½x15	125.00	15.00
322 A62	2r grn & rose red	21.00	3.75
a	Perf. 14½x15	9.00	2.00

Perf. 13½

324 A63	3r blk brn & grn	7.50	3.25
a	Perf. 12½	24.00	10.50
325 A64	5r dk bl & gray brn	15.00	3.25
	Nos. 304-325 (21)	68.31	15.99

Nos. 304-315, 317-325 exist imperf. Value, set $65.

Mikhail V. Lomonosov and Academy of Sciences — A67

1925, Sept. Photo. *Perf. 12½, 13½*

326 A67	3k org brn	4.75	2.25
a	Perf. 12½x12	10.50	6.50
b	Perf. 13½x12½	42.50	27.50
c	Perf. 13½	17.50	10.00
327 A67	15k dk ol grn	4.75	2.25
a	Perf. 12½	17.50	6.50

Issued to commemorate the bicentenary of the founding of the Russian Academy of Sciences. Exist unwatermarked, on thick paper with yellow gum, Perf. 13½. These are essays, later perforated and gummed.

Prof. Aleksandr S. Popov (1859-1905), Radio Pioneer — A68

1925, Oct. *Perf. 13½*

328 A68	7k dp bl	2.25	1.65
329 A68	14k green	3.50	2.00

Decembrist Exiles A69

Street Rioting in St. Petersburg A70

Revolutionist Leaders — A71

1925, Dec. 28 *Imperf.*

330 A69	3k ol grn	1.40	1.65
331 A70	7k brown	1.50	1.90
332 A71	14k car lake	2.00	2.50

Perf. 13½

333 A69	3k ol grn	1.75	1.40
a	Perf. 12½	50.00	30.00
334 A70	7k brown	1.75	1.40
335 A71	14k car lake	2.50	1.90
	Nos. 330-335 (6)	10.90	10.75

Centenary of Decembrist revolution.

Revolters Parading A72

Speaker Haranguing Mob A73

Street Barricade, Moscow A74

1925, Dec. 20 *Imperf.*

336 A72	3k ol grn	1.25	1.50
337 A73	7k brown	1.50	1.65
338 A74	14k car lake	2.00	2.00

Perf. 12½, 13½, 12x12½

339 A72	3k ol grn	1.25	1.25
a	Perf. 13½	4.50	4.25
340 A73	7k brown	3.25	3.00
a	Perf. 13½	13.00	10.50
b	Horizontal pair, imperf. between	55.00	50.00
341 A74	14k car lake	2.00	2.00
a	Perf. 13½	22.50	12.00
	Nos. 336-341 (6)	11.25	11.40

20th anniversary of Revolution of 1905.

Lenin — A75

Liberty Monument, Moscow — A76

1926 Wmk. 170 Engr. *Perf. 10½*

342 A75	1r dk brn	4.00	2.50
343 A75	2r blk vio	6.50	4.50
a	Perf. 12½	50.00	30.00
344 A75	3r dk grn	12.00	4.50

1926, July Litho. *Perf. 12x12½*

347 A76	7k bl grn & red	2.00	1.50
348 A76	14k bl grn & vio	2.50	1.50

Issued to commemorate the 6th International Esperanto Congress at Leningrad. Exist perf. 11½.

Nos. 282, 282a and 310 Surcharged in Black

8
КОП

1927, June Unwmk. *Perf. 14½x15*

349 A59	8k on 7k choc	1.25	1.00
a	Perf. 12	9.00	7.50
b	Invtd. surch.	125.00	105.00

Perf. 12
Wmk. 170

350 A59	8k on 7k choc	1.75	1.10
a	Invtd. surch.	45.00	35.00

The surcharge on Nos. 349-350 comes in two types: With space of 2mm. between lines, and with space of ¾mm. The latter is much scarcer.

Same Surcharge on Stamps of 1925-26 in Black or Red

Perf. 13½, 12½, 12 x 12½

353 A68	8k on 7k dp bl (R)	2.00	3.50
a	Inverted "8"	35.00	35.00
354 A70	8k on 7k brn	5.50	7.25
355 A73	8k on 7k brn	7.25	9.50
356 A76	8k on 7k bl grn & red	6.00	8.50

Imperf

357 A70	8k on 7k brn	2.50	4.00
358 A73	8k on 7k brn	2.50	4.00
	Nos. 349-350,353-358 (8)	28.75	38.85

Postage Due Stamps of 1925 Surcharged

ПОЧТОВАЯ
МАРКА
КОП. 8 КОП.

Lithographed or Typographed
Perf. 12, 14½x14

1927, June Unwmk.

359 D1	8k on 1k red, typo., perf. 12	1.10	1.10
a	Litho., perf. 12	20.00	20.00
b	Invtd. surch.	100.00	100.00

No.	Type	Description	Unused	Used
360	D1	8k on 2k vio	1.50	1.75
a		Invtd. surch.	100.00	100.00
361	D1	8k on 3k lt bl	1.40	1.65
a		Inverted surcharge	100.00	100.00
362	D1	8k on 7k org	1.50	1.75
a		Invtd. surch.	100.00	100.00
363	D1	8k on 8k grn	1.10	1.10
a		Invtd. surch.	100.00	100.00
364	D1	8k on 10k dk bl	1.40	1.65
a		Invtd. surch.	100.00	100.00
365	D1	8k on 14k brn	1.10	1.10
a		Inverted surcharge	100.00	100.00
		Nos. 359-365 (7)	9.10	10.10

Wmk. 170

1927, June **Typo.** ***Perf. 12***

No.	Type	Description	Unused	Used
366	D1	8k on 1k red	1.10	1.65
367	D1	8k on 2k vio	1.10	1.65
368	D1	8k on 3k lt bl	1.90	2.00
369	D1	8k on 7k org	1.90	2.00
370	D1	8k on 8k grn	1.10	1.65
371	D1	8k on 10k dk bl	1.10	1.65
372	D1	8k on 14k brn	1.10	1.65
		Nos. 366-372 (7)	9.30	12.25

Nos. 366, 368-372 exist with inverted surcharge. Value each, $100.

Dr. L. L. Zamenhof
A77

1927 **Photo.** ***Perf. 10½***

No.	Type	Description	Unused	Used
373	A77	14k yel grn & brn	2.00	1.90

Unwmk.

No.	Type	Description	Unused	Used
374	A77	14k yel grn & brn	2.00	1.90

40th anniversary of creation of Esperanto.

No. 374 exists perf. 10, 10x10½ and imperf. Value, imperf. pair $165.

Worker, Soldier, Peasant — A78

Worker and Sailor — A81

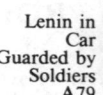

Lenin in Car Guarded by Soldiers
A79

Smolny Institute, Leningrad
A80

Map of the U.S.S.R.
A82

Men of Various Soviet Republics
A83

Workers of Different Races; Kremlin in Background — A84

Typo. (3k, 8k, 18k), Engr. (7k), Litho. (14k), Photo. (5k, 28k)
Perf. 13½, 12½x12, 11

1927, Oct. **Unwmk.**

No.	Type	Description	Unused	Used
375	A78	3k brt rose	90	80
a		Imperf. pair	215.00	
376	A79	5k dp brn	2.50	2.25
a		Imperf.	165.00	180.00
b		Perf. 12½	20.00	27.50
c		Perf. 12½x10½	22.50	16.00
377	A80	7k myr grn	2.75	2.75
a		Perf. 11½	32.50	20.00
b		Imperf. pair	500.00	
378	A81	8k brn & blk	1.50	95
a		Perf. 10½x12½	*32.50*	*27.50*
379	A82	14k dl bl & red	2.50	1.65
380	A83	18k blue	1.90	1.65
a		Imperf.	130.00	
381	A84	28k ol brn	7.25	5.75
a		Perf. 10	37.50	32.50
		Nos. 375-381 (7)	19.30	15.80

10th anniversary of October Revolution.

The paper of No. 375 has an overprint of pale yellow wavy lines.

No. 377b exists with watermark 170. Value, $1000.

Worker
A85

Peasant
A86

Lenin — A87

1927-28 **Typo.** ***Perf. 13½***

Chalk Surfaced Paper

No.	Type	Description	Unused	Used
382	A85	1k orange	25	20
383	A86	2k ap grn	25	15
385	A85	4k brt bl	25	15
386	A86	5k brown	25	15
388	A86	7k dk red ('28)	1.50	40
389	A85	8k green	75	15
391	A85	10k lt brn	75	15
392	A87	14k dk grn ('28)	1.00	25
393	A87	18k ol grn	1.00	25
394	A87	18k dk bl ('28)	1.50	38
395	A86	20k dk gray grn	1.00	25
396	A85	40k rose red	2.00	38
397	A86	50k brt bl	2.50	75
399	A85	70k gray grn	3.00	75
400	A86	80k orange	4.00	1.25
		Nos. 382-400 (15)	20.00	5.61

The 1k, 2k and 10k exist imperf. Value, each $175.

Soldier and Kremlin
A88

Sailor and Flag
A89

Cavalryman
A90

Aviator
A91

1928, Feb. 6

Chalk Surfaced Paper

No.	Type	Description	Unused	Used
402	A88	8k lt brn	70	28
a		Imperf.	100.00	70.00
403	A89	14k dp bl	1.50	75
404	A90	18k car rose	1.65	1.40
a		Imperf.	85.00	
405	A91	28k yel grn	2.00	1.75

10th anniversary of the Soviet Army.

Lenin Types of 1925-26

Wmk. Lozenges (169)

1928-29 **Engr.** ***Perf. 10, 10½***

No.	Type	Description	Unused	Used
406	A75	3r dk grn ('29)	5.75	2.50
407	A66	5r red brn	6.75	3.00
408	A66	10r indigo	11.50	4.75

Bugler Sounding Assembly
A92 A93

Perf. 12½x12

1929, Aug. 18 **Photo.** **Wmk. 170**

No.	Type	Description	Unused	Used
411	A92	10k ol brn	6.25	2.50
a		Perf. 10½	35.00	21.00
b		Perf. 12½x12x10½x12	50.00	21.00
412	A93	14k slate	3.00	1.90
a		Perf. 12½x12x10½x12	52.50	30.00

First All-Soviet Assembly of Pioneers.

Factory Worker — A95

Peasant — A96

Farm Worker — A97

Soldier — A98

Worker, Soldier, Peasant — A100

Worker — A103

Lenin — A104

Peasant — A107

Factory Worker — A109

Farm Worker — A111

Perf. 12x12½

1929-31 **Typo.** **Wmk. 170**

No.	Type	Description	Unused	Used
413	A103	1k orange	18	12
a		Perf. 10½	16.00	13.00
b		Perf. 14x14½	50.00	35.00
414	A95	2k yel grn	18	9
415	A96	3k blue	18	9
a		Perf. 14x14½	42.50	35.00
416	A97	4k claret	30	12
417	A98	5k org brn	30	12
a		Perf. 10½	32.50	30.00
418	A100	7k scarlet	1.10	55
419	A103	10k ol grn	50	9
a		Perf.10½	27.50	22.50

Unwmk.

No.	Type	Description	Unused	Used
420	A104	14k indigo	1.10	55
a		Perf. 10½	4.00	3.25

Wmk. 170

No.	Type	Description	Unused	Used
421	A100	15k dk ol grn ('30)	85	15
422	A107	20k green	85	15
a		Perf. 10½	50.00	27.50
423	A109	30k dk vio	1.40	45
424	A111	50k dp brn	1.90	1.00
425	A98	70k dk red ('30)	2.00	1.10
426	A107	80k red brn ('31)	1.90	1.10
		Nos. 413-426 (14)	12.74	5.68

Nos. 422, 423, 424 and 426 have a background of fine wavy lines in pale shades of the colors of the stamps.

See Nos. 456-466, 613A-619A, 743.

Symbolical of Industry
A112

Tractors Issuing from Assembly Line
A113

Iron Furnace (Inscription reads, "More Metal More Machines")
A114

Blast Furnace and Chart of Anticipated Iron Production — A115

1929-30 ***Perf. 12x12½***

No.	Type	Description	Unused	Used
427	A112	5k org brn	1.10	45
428	A113	10k ol grn	1.10	70

Perf. 12½x12

No.	Type	Description	Unused	Used
429	A114	20k dl grn	2.75	1.40
430	A115	28k vio blk	1.75	80

Publicity for greater industrial production. No. 429 exists perf. 10½. Value $200.

Red Cavalry in Polish Town after Battle
A116

Cavalry Charge
A117

Staff Officers of 1st Cavalry Army
A118

Plan of Action for 1st Cavalry Army
A119

1930, Feb. ***Perf. 12x12½***

No.	Type	Description	Unused	Used
431	A116	2k yel grn	1.25	90
432	A117	5k lt brn	1.25	90
433	A118	10k ol gray	2.75	1.25
434	A119	14k ind & red	1.00	90

1st Red Cavalry Army, 10th anniversary.

Students Preparing a Poster Newspaper
A120

1930, Aug. 15

435 A120 10k ol grn		90	50

Issued in connection with the Educational Exhibition at Leningrad, July 1 to August 15, 1930.

Telegraph Office, Moscow A121

Lenin Hydroelectric Power Station on Volkhov River A122

Wmk. Lozenges (169)

1930 Photo. *Perf. 10½*

436 A121 1r dp bl	4.00	3.50

Wmk. 170

437 A122 3r yel grn & blk brn	4.50	2.00

See Nos. 467, 469.

Battleship Potemkin A123

Inside Presnya Barricade — A124

Moscow Barricades in 1905 — A125

Perf. 12x12½, 12½x12

1930-31 Typo.

438 A123 3k red	1.40	55
439 A124 5k blue	1.40	70
440 A125 10k dk grn & red	2.50	1.00
Imperf		
452 A123 3k red ('31)	1.65	1.75
453 A124 5k dp bl ('31)	1.90	1.90
454 A125 10k dk grn & red ('31)	2.25	2.25
Nos. 438-454 (6)	11.10	8.15

Revolution of 1905, 25th anniversary.

Types of 1929-31 Regular Issue

1931-32 *Imperf.*

456 A103 1k orange	35	65
457 A95 2k yel grn	48	1.00
458 A96 3k blue	48	1.25
459 A97 4k claret	3.75	6.50
460 A98 5k org brn	1.40	2.75
462 A103 10k ol grn	11.00	20.00
464 A100 15k dk ol grn	13.00	22.50
466 A109 30k dl vio	16.00	35.00
467 A121 1r dk bl	30.00	47.50
Nos. 456-467 (9)	76.46	137.15

Nos. 459, 462-467 were sold only by the philatelic bureau.

Type of 1930 Issue

1931 Wmk. 170 *Perf. 12x12½*

469 A121 1r dk bl	1.75	75

Maxim Gorki — A133

1932-33 Photo.

470 A133 15k dk brn	4.00	3.50
a Imperf.	115.00	115.00
471 A133 35k dp ultra ('33)	10.50	8.75

40th anniversary of Gorki's literary activity.

Lenin Addressing the People A134

Revolution in Petrograd (Leningrad) A135

Dnieper Hydroelectric Power Station A136

Asiatics Saluting the Soviet Flag — A139

Breaking Prison Bars — A140

Designs (dated 1917 1932): 15k, Collective farm. 20k, Magnitogorsk metallurgical plant in Urals. 30k, Radio tower and heads of 4 men.

1932-33 *Perf. 12½x12; 12½ (30k)*

472 A134 3k dk vio	70	40
473 A135 5k dk brn	70	40
474 A136 10k ultra	1.40	95
475 A136 15k dk grn	80	60
476 A136 20k lake ('33)	1.10	90
477 A136 30k dk gray ('33)	3.50	1.10
478 A139 35k gray blk	70.00	27.50
Nos. 472-478 (7)	78.20	31.85

October Revolution, 15th anniversary.

1932, Nov. Litho. *Perf. 12½x12*

479 A140 50k dk red	5.25	3.75

Issued to commemorate the 10th anniversary of the International Revolutionaries' Aid Association.

Trier, Birthplace of Marx A141

Grave, Highgate Cemetery, London A142

Design: 35k, Portrait and signature of Karl Marx.

Perf. 12x12½, 12½x12

1933, Mar. Photo.

480 A141 3k dl grn	3.25	80
481 A142 10k blk brn	5.75	1.75
482 A142 35k brn vio	8.25	4.50

Issued to commemorate the 50th anniversary of the death of Karl Marx (1818-1883).

Fine Arts Museum, Moscow — A145

1932, Dec. *Perf. 12½*

485 A145 15k blk brn	15.00	13.00
486 A145 35k ultra	27.50	27.50
a Perf. 10½	37.50	27.50

Moscow Philatelic Exhibition, 1932.

Nos. 485 and 486 were also issued in imperf. sheets of 4 containing 2 of each value, on thick paper for presentation purposes.

Nos. 485 and 486a Surcharged

ЛЕНИНГРАД. 1933 г.
70
коп

1933, Mar. *Perf. 12½*

487 A145 30k on 15k blk brn	24.00	18.00
Perf. 10½		
488 A145 70k on 35k ultra	35.00	22.50

Leningrad Philatelic Exhibition, 1933.

Peoples of the Soviet Union

Kazaks A146

Lezghians A147

Tungus A150

Crimean Tartars — A148

Jews, Birobidzhan A149

Buryats A151

Yakuts A156

Chechens A152

Abkhas A153

Georgians A154

Nientzians A155

Great Russians — A157

Tadzhiks — A158

Transcaucasians — A159

Turkmen — A160

Ukrainians — A161

Uzbeks — A162

Byelorussians — A163

Koryaks A164

Bashkirs A165

Chuvashes A166

Perf. 12, 12x12½, 12½x12, 11x12, 12x11

1933, Apr. **Photo.**

489	A146	1k blk brn	1.00	55
490	A147	2k ultra	1.00	55
491	A148	3k gray grn	1.00	55
492	A149	4k gray blk	1.00	55
493	A150	5k brn vio	1.00	55
494	A151	6k indigo	1.00	35
495	A152	7k blk brn	1.00	35
496	A153	8k rose red	1.00	50
497	A154	9k ultra	1.75	65
498	A155	10k blk brn	2.00	1.65
499	A156	14k ol grn	1.75	65
500	A157	15k orange	2.00	65
501	A158	15k ultra	1.75	55
502	A159	15k dk brn	1.75	55
503	A160	15k rose red	2.75	1.50
504	A161	15k vio brn	2.00	65
505	A162	15k gray blk	2.00	65
506	A163	15k dl grn	2.00	65
507	A164	20k dl bl	6.25	1.50
508	A165	30k brn vio	6.25	1.25
509	A166	35k black	13.00	2.00
		Nos. 489-509 (21)	53.25	16.85

V. V. Vorovsky A169

Designs: 3k, V. M. Volodarsky. 5k, M. S. Uritzky.

1933, Oct. ***Perf. 12x12½***

514	A169	1k dl grn	75	55
515	A169	3k bl blk	1.10	75
516	A169	5k ol brn	2.25	90

No. 514 commemorates the 10th anniversary of the murder of Soviet Representative Vorovsky. No. 515 commemorates the 15th anniversary of the murder of the Revolutionist Volodarsky. No. 516 commemorates the 15th anniversary of the murder of the Revolutionist Uritzky.

See Nos. 531-532, 580-582.

Order of the Red Banner, 15th Anniv. — A173

1933, Nov. 17 **Unwmk.** ***Perf. 14***

518	A173	20k blk, red & yel	90	75
a.		Perf. 9½	175.00	125.00

No. 518a is a proof.

Commissar Schaumyan A174

Commissar Prokofii A. Dzhaparidze A175

Commissars Awaiting Execution — A176

Designs: 35k, Monument to the 26 Commissars. 40k, Worker, peasant and soldier dipping flags in salute.

1933, Dec. 1

519	A174	4k brown	7.25	1.50
520	A175	5k dk gray	7.25	1.50
521	A176	20k purple	4.75	1.50
522	A176	35k ultra	24.00	6.25
523	A176	40k carmine	14.00	7.50
		Nos. 519-523 (5)	57.25	18.25

Issued to commemorate the 15th anniversary of the execution of 26 commissars at Baku. No. 521 exists imperf.

Lenin's Mausoleum A179

1934, Feb. 7 **Engr.** ***Perf. 14***

524	A179	5k brown	2.00	48
a.		Imperf.	150.00	125.00
525	A179	10k sl bl	3.50	1.90
a.		Imperf.	150.00	125.00
526	A179	15k dk car	3.50	1.25
527	A179	20k green	3.50	1.25
528	A179	35k dk brn	6.25	2.00
		Nos. 524-528 (5)	18.75	6.88

10th anniversary of Lenin's death.

Ivan Fedorov A180

1934, Mar. 5

529	A180	20k car rose	3.50	2.50
a.		Imperf.	165.00	165.00
530	A180	40k indigo	8.50	3.50
a.		Imperf.	165.00	165.00

Issued to commemorate the 350th anniversary of the death of Ivan Fedorov, founder of printing in Russia.

Portrait Type of 1933

Designs: 10k, Yakov M. Sverdlov. 15k, Victor Pavlovich Nogin.

1934, Mar. **Photo.** **Wmk. 170**

531	A169	10k ultra	16.00	7.25
532	A169	15k red	19.00	12.00

15th anniversary of the death of Yakov M. Sverdlov, chairman of the All-Russian Central Executive Committee of the Soviets. 10th anniversary of the death of Victor Pavlovich Nogin, chairman Russian State Textile Syndicate.

Dmitri Ivanovich Mendeleev A184 A185

1934, Sept. 15 **Wmk. 170** ***Perf. 14***

536	A184	5k emerald	4.00	1.50
537	A185	10k blk brn	11.00	2.75
538	A185	15k vermilion	10.00	2.50
539	A184	20k ultra	5.75	2.50

Birth centenary of Prof. D. I. Mendeleev (1834-1907), chemist who discovered the Periodic Law of Classification of the Elements.

Imperfs. exist of 5k (value $100) and 15k (value $150).

Lenin as Child and Youth A186 A187

Demonstration before Lenin Mausoleum — A190

Designs: 5k, Lenin in middle age. 10k, Lenin the orator. 30k, Lenin and Stalin.

1934, Nov. 23 **Unwmk.** ***Perf. 14***

540	A186	1k ind & blk	1.65	80
541	A187	3k ind & blk	1.65	95
542	A187	5k ind & blk	3.25	1.40
543	A187	10k ind & blk	2.50	1.40
544	A190	20k brn org & ultra	5.00	2.50
545	A190	30k brn org & car	15.00	6.00
		Nos. 540-545 (6)	29.05	13.05

First decade without Lenin.

See Nos. 931-935, 937.

Bombs Falling on City A192

"Before War and Afterwards" A194

Designs: 10k, Refugees from burning town. 20k, "Plowing with the sword." 35k, "Comradeship."

1935, Jan. 1 **Wmk. 170** ***Perf. 14***

546	A192	5k vio blk	4.75	2.50
547	A192	10k ultra	9.75	4.50
548	A194	15k green	11.50	4.50
549	A194	20k dk brn	9.75	4.50
550	A194	35k carmine	35.00	8.75
		Nos. 546-550 (5)	70.75	24.75

Issued as anti-war propaganda, the designs symbolizing the horrors of modern warfare.

Subway Tunnel A197

Subway Station Cross Section A198

Subway Station A199

Train in Station — A200

1935, Feb. 25 **Wmk. 170** ***Perf. 14***

551	A197	5k orange	5.75	2.50
552	A198	10k dk ultra	7.25	4.00
553	A199	15k rose car	27.50	16.00
554	A200	20k emerald	12.00	6.50

Completion of Moscow subway.

Friedrich Engels — A201

1935, May **Wmk. 170** ***Perf. 14***

555	A201	5k carmine	5.00	95
556	A201	10k dk grn	2.50	1.50
557	A201	15k dk bl	5.00	1.90
558	A201	20k brn blk	3.50	2.50

Issued to commemorate the 40th anniversary of the death of Friedrich Engels (1820-1895), German socialist and collaborator of Marx.

Running — A202

Designs: 2k, Diving. 3k, Rowing. 4k, Soccer. 5k, Skiing. 10k, Bicycling. 15k, Tennis. 20k, Skating. 35k, Hurdling. 40k, Parade of athletes.

1935, Apr. 22 **Unwmk.** ***Perf. 14***

559	A202	1k org & ultra	1.10	55
560	A202	2k blk & ultra	1.40	55
561	A202	3k grn & blk brn	2.75	1.25
562	A202	4k rose red & ultra	1.75	85
563	A202	5k pur & blk brn	1.75	85
564	A202	10k rose red & vio	6.50	2.75
565	A202	15k blk & blk brn	13.00	5.75
566	A202	20k blk brn & ultra	11.00	4.00
567	A202	35k ultra & blk brn	16.00	8.25
568	A202	40k blk brn & car	13.00	5.75
		Nos. 559-568 (10)	68.25	30.55

Issued to commemorate the International Spartacist Games at Moscow.

A little time given to the study of the arrangement of the Scott Catalogue can make it easier to use effectively.

Silver Plate of Sassanian Dynasty — A212

1935, Sept. 10 — Wmk. 170

569	A212	5k org red	4.00	1.50
570	A212	10k dk yel grn	4.00	1.50
571	A212	15k dk vio	4.75	2.50
572	A212	35k blk brn	7.50	2.75

Issued to commemorate the Third International Exposition of Persian Art held in Leningrad, September 12-18, 1935.

Kalinin, the Worker A213

Mikhail Kalinin A216

Designs: 5k, Kalinin, the farmer. 10k, Kalinin, the orator.

1935, Nov. 20 — Unwmk. — *Perf. 14*

573	A213	3k rose lil	70	52
574	A213	5k green	70	52
575	A213	10k bl sl	80	80
576	A216	20k brn blk	1.40	1.00

Issued to commemorate the 60th birthday of Mikhail Kalinin, chairman of the Central Executive Committee of the U.S.S.R.
The 20k exists imperf. Value $90.

Leo Tolstoy
A217 A218

Design: 20k, Statue of Tolstoy.

1935, Dec. 4 — *Perf. 14*

577	A217	3k ol blk & vio	75	32
a		Perf. 11	2.50	65
578	A218	10k vio blk & blk brn	1.10	45
a		Perf. 11	4.50	1.65
579	A217	20k dk grn & blk brn	2.50	1.10
a		Perf. 11	7.00	2.00

Issued to commemorate the 25th anniversary of the death of Count Leo N. Tolstoy (1828-1910).

Portrait Type of 1933

Designs: 2k, Mikhail V. Frunze. 4k, N. E. Bauman. 40k, Sergei M. Kirov.

1935, Nov. — Wmk. 170 — *Perf. 11*

580	A169	2k purple	1.40	*2.75*
a		Perf. 14	7.25	55
581	A169	4k brn vio	2.25	*4.50*
a		Perf. 14	10.00	55
582	A169	40k blk brn	5.00	*6.50*
a		Perf. 14	24.00	1.65

Death of three revolutionary heroes.
Nos. 580-582 exist imperf. but were not regularly issued. Value, set $225.

Pioneers Preventing Theft from Mailbox A223

Designs: 3k, 5k, Pioneers preventing destruction of property. 10k, Helping recover kite. 15k, Girl Pioneer saluting.

1936, Apr. — Unwmk. — *Perf. 14*

583	A223	1k yel grn	60	35
a		Perf. 11	1.25	35
584	A223	2k cop red	1.75	35
a		Perf. 11	65	35
585	A223	3k sl bl	90	90
a		Perf. 11	3.50	45
586	A223	5k rose lake	75	35
a		Perf. 11	6.00	90
587	A223	10k gray bl	1.75	1.75
a		Perf. 11	15.00	1.10
588	A223	15k brn ol	9.00	6.00
a		Perf. 11	3.00	1.25
		Nos. 583-588 (6)	14.75	9.70
		Nos. 583a-588a (6)	29.40	4.40

N. A. Dobrolyubov A227

1936, Aug. 13 — Typo. — *Perf. 11½*

589	A227	10k rose lake	2.75	2.25
a		Perf. 14	5.00	2.50

Issued to commemorate the centenary of the birth of Nikolai A. Dobrolyubov, writer and critic.

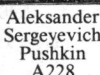

Aleksander Sergeyevich Pushkin A228

Statue of Pushkin, Moscow A229

Perf. 11 to 14 and Compound

1937, Feb. 1

Chalky or Ordinary Paper

590	A228	10k yel brn	28	20
591	A228	20k Prus grn	40	24
592	A228	40k rose lake	55	28
593	A229	50k blue	1.10	32
594	A229	80k car rose	1.50	45
595	A229	1r green	2.75	90
		Nos. 590-595 (6)	6.58	2.39

Souvenir Sheet

Imperf

596		Sheet of two	4.00	*17.00*
a		A228 10k brn	65	*2.25*
b		A229 50k brn	65	*2.25*

Death centenary of Aleksander Pushkin (1799-1837), writer and poet.

Tchaikovsky Concert Hall — A230

Designs: 5k, 15k, Telegraph Agency House. 10k, Tchaikovsky Concert Hall. 20k, 50k, Red Army Theater. 30k, Hotel Moscow. 40k, Palace of the Soviets.

1937, June — Photo. — Unwmk. — *Perf. 12*

597	A230	3k brn vio	65	32
598	A230	5k hn brn	65	32
599	A230	10k dk brn	1.10	32
600	A230	15k black	1.10	32
601	A230	20k ol grn	65	75
602	A230	30k gray blk	65	75
a		Perf. 11	50.00	32.50
603	A230	40k violet	1.25	1.00
a		Souv. sheet of 4, imperf.	6.75	*17.00*
604	A230	50k dk brn	1.25	1.00
		Nos. 597-604 (8)	7.30	4.78

First Congress of Soviet Architects. The 30k is watermarked Greek Border and Rosettes (170).
Nos. 597-601, 603-604 exist imperf. Value, each $250.

Feliks E. Dzerzhinski A235

Shota Rustaveli A236

1937, July 27 — Typo. — *Perf. 12*

606	A235	10k yel brn	28	15
607	A235	20k Prus grn	40	25
608	A235	40k rose lake	80	50
609	A235	80k carmine	95	60

Issued to commemorate the 10th anniversary of the death of F. E. Dzerzhinski, organizer of Soviet secret police. Exist imperf.

1938, Feb. — Unwmk. — Photo. — *Perf. 12*

610	A236	20k dp grn	95	25

Issued to commemorate the 750th anniversary of the publication of the poem "Knight in the Tiger Skin," by Shota Rustaveli, Georgian poet.
Exists imperf. Value $135.

Statue Surmounting Pavilion A237

Soviet Pavilion at Paris Exposition A238

1938 — Typo.

611	A237	5k red	32	15
a		Imperf.	40.00	
612	A238	20k rose	60	25
613	A237	50k dk bl	1.25	38

Issued to commemorate Russia's participation in the 1937 International Exposition at Paris.

Types of 1929-32 and Lenin Types of 1925-26

1937-52 — Unwmk. — *Perf. 11½x12, 12*

613A	A103	1k dl org ('40)	20.00	3.50
614	A95	2k yel grn ('39)	5.25	2.00
615	A97	4k cl ('40)	5.25	2.00
615A	A98	5k org brn ('46)	65.00	12.50
616	A109	10k bl ('38)	50	28
616A	A103	10k ol ('40)	90.00	12.50
616B	A109	10k blk ('52)	50	35
617	A97	20k dl grn	50	35
617A	A107	20k grn ('39)	65.00	12.50
618	A109	30k cl ('39)	11.50	3.50
619	A104	40k ind ('38)	2.00	90
619A	A111	50k dp brn ('40)	85	52

Engr.

620	A75	3r dk grn ('39)	1.10	90
621	A66	5r red brn ('39)	1.75	1.25
622	A66	10r ind ('39)	3.00	2.75

Nos. 615 to 619 exist imperforate but were not regularly issued.
No. 616B was re-issued in 1954-56 in slightly smaller format, 14½x21 mm., and in gray black. See note after No. 738.

Airplane Route from Moscow to North Pole — A239

Soviet Flag and Airplanes at North Pole — A240

1938, Feb. 25 — Litho. — *Perf. 12*

625	A239	10k db & blk	1.40	30
626	A239	20k bl gray & blk	1.75	60

Typo.

627	A240	40k dl grn & car	5.00	2.00
a		Imperf.	140.00	
628	A240	80k rose car & car	1.90	1.90
a		Imperf.	70.00	

Soviet flight to the North Pole.

Infantryman A241

Soldier A242

Stalin Reviewing Cavalry A246

Chapayev and Boy — A247

Designs: 30k, Sailor, 40k, Aviator. 50k, Antiaircraft soldier.

Unwmk.

1938, Mar. — Photo. — *Perf. 12*

629	A241	10k gray blk & dk red	28	12
630	A242	20k gray blk & dk red	38	18
631	A242	30k gray blk & dk red	70	24
632	A242	40k gray blk & dk red	1.00	45
633	A242	50k gray blk & dk red	1.25	60
634	A246	80k gray blk & dk red	2.00	60

Typo.

Perf. 12x12½

635	A247	1r blk & car	55	30
		Nos. 629-635 (7)	6.16	2.49

20th anniversary of Workers' and Peasants' Red Army.
No. 635 exists imperf. Value $125.

Aviators Chkalov, Baidukov, Beliakov and Flight Route — A248

Aviators Gromov, Danilin, Yumashev and Flight Route — A249

1938, Apr. 10 **Photo.**

636	A248	10k	blk & red	75	45
637	A248	20k	brn blk & red	1.00	45
638	A248	40k	brn & red	1.50	75
639	A248	50k	brn vio & red	2.50	75

Issued to commemorate the first Trans-Polar flight, June 18-20, 1937, from Moscow to Vancouver, Wash. Nos. 636-639 exist imperf. Value $125 each.

1938, Apr. 13

640	A249	10k	claret	1.25	30
641	A249	20k	brn blk	1.65	60
642	A249	50k	dl vio	1.75	75

Issued to commemorate the first Trans-Polar flight, July 12-14, 1937, from Moscow to San Jacinto, Calif. Nos. 640-642 exist imperf. Value, each $110.

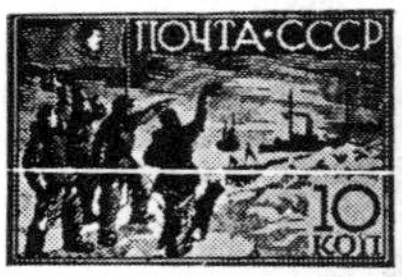
Arrival of the Rescuing Ice-breakers Taimyr and Murmansk A250

Ivan Papanin and His Men Aboard Ice-breaker Yermak — A251

1938, June 21 **Typo.** ***Perf. 12, 12½***

643	A250	10k	vio brn	2.75	55
644	A250	20k	dk bl	2.75	70

Photo.

645	A251	30k	ol brn	5.75	90
646	A251	50k	ultra	5.75	1.00
a			Imperf.	135.00	

Rescue of Papanin's North Pole Expedition.

Arms of Uzbek A252

Arms of U.S.S.R. A253

Designs: Different arms on each stamp.

Perf. 12, 12½

1937-38 **Unwmk.** **Typo.**

647	A252	20k	dp bl *(Armenia)*	1.10	38
648	A252	20k	dl vio *(Azerbaijan)*	1.10	38
649	A252	20k	brn org *(Byelorussia)*	*6.00*	*1.90*
650	A252	20k	car rose *(Georgia)*	1.10	38
651	A252	20k	bl grn *(Kazakh)*	1.10	38
652	A252	20k	emer *(Kirghiz)*	1.10	38
653	A252	20k	yel org *(Uzbek)*	1.10	38
654	A252	20k	bl *(R.S.F.S.R.)*	1.10	38
655	A252	20k	cl *(Tadzhik)*	1.10	38
656	A252	20k	car *(Turkmen)*	1.10	38
657	A252	20k	red *(Ukraine)*	1.10	38

Engr.

658	A253	40k	brn red	1.90	1.10
			Nos. 647-658 (12)	*18.90*	*6.80*

Constitution of U.S.S.R.
Issue dates: 40k, 1937. Others, 1938. See Nos. 841-842.

The Scott Catalogue value is a retail price, what you could expect to pay for the stamp in a grade of Fine-Very Fine. The value listed is a reference which reflects recent actual dealer selling price.

Nurse Weighing Child A264

Children at Lenin's Statue A265

Biology Lesson A266

Health Camp A267

Young Model Builders A268

1938, Sept. 15 **Unwmk.** ***Perf. 12***

659	A264	10k	dk bl grn	65	15
660	A265	15k	dk bl grn	65	22
661	A266	20k	vio brn	85	22
662	A267	30k	claret	1.10	40
663	A266	40k	lt brn	1.25	55
664	A268	50k	dp bl	1.75	70
665	A268	80k	lt grn	2.75	70
			Nos. 659-665 (7)	9.00	2.94

Child welfare.

View of Yalta A269

Crimean Shoreline — A272

Designs: No. 667, View along Crimean shore. No. 668, Georgian military highway. No, 670, View near Yalta. No. 671, "Swallows' Nest" Castle. 20k, Dzerzhinski Rest House for workers. 30k, Sunset in Crimea. 40k, Alupka. 50k, Gursuf. 80k, Crimean Gardens. 1r, "Swallows' Nest" Castle (horiz.).

Unwmk.

1938, Sept. 21 **Photo.** ***Perf. 12***

666	A269	5k	brown	42	30
667	A269	5k	blk brn	42	30
668	A269	10k	sl grn	55	30
669	A272	10k	brown	55	30
670	A269	15k	blk brn	55	30
671	A272	15k	dk brn	55	30
672	A269	20k	dk brn	90	30
673	A272	30k	blk brn	90	40
674	A269	40k	brown	1.40	40
675	A272	50k	dp sl grn	1.40	80
676	A269	80k	brown	2.00	80
677	A269	1r	sl grn	4.50	1.40
			Nos. 666-677 (12)	14.14	5.90

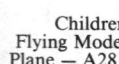

Children Flying Model Plane — A281

Glider A282

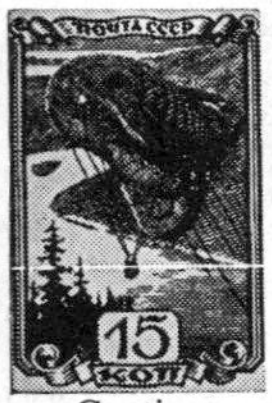
Captive Balloon A283

Dirigible over Kremlin A284

Parachute Jumpers — A285

Hydroplane A286

Balloon in Flight — A287

Balloon Ascent — A288

Four-motor Plane — A289

Unwmk.

1938, Oct. 7 **Typo.** ***Perf. 12***

678	A281	5k	vio brn	60	35
679	A282	10k	ol gray	60	35
680	A283	15k	pink	1.10	35
681	A284	20k	dp bl	1.10	35
682	A285	30k	claret	1.65	60
683	A286	40k	dp bl	2.00	60
684	A287	50k	bl grn	4.00	90
685	A288	80k	brown	3.50	1.50
686	A289	1r	bl grn	4.75	1.25
			Nos. 678-686 (9)	19.30	6.25

Mayakovsky Station, Moscow Subway — A290

Sokol Terminal A291

Kiev Station A292

Dynamo Station A293

Train in Tunnel A294

Revolution Square Station A295

Unwmk.

1938, Nov. 7 **Photo.** ***Perf. 12***

687	A290	10k	dp red vio	1.25	60
688	A291	15k	dk brn	1.15	60
689	A292	20k	blk brn	1.50	60
690	A293	30k	dk red vio	1.50	60
691	A294	40k	blk brn	1.50	90
692	A295	50k	dk brn	1.50	1.25
			Nos. 687-692 (6)	8.40	4.55

Issued in connection with the opening of the second line of the Moscow subway.

Girl with Parachute A296

Young Miner A297

Harvesting A298

Designs: 50k, Students returning from school. 80k, Aviator and sailor.

1938, Dec. 7 **Typo.** ***Perf. 12***

693	A296	20k	dp bl	60	24
694	A297	30k	dp cl	60	24
695	A298	40k	vio brn	75	24
696	A296	50k	dp rose	1.00	45
697	A298	80k	dp bl	3.00	65
			Nos. 693-697 (5)	5.95	1.82

Issued to commemorate the 20th anniversary of the Young Communist League (Komsomol).

Diving
A301

Discus Thrower
A302

Designs: 15k, Tennis. 20k, Acrobatic motorcyclists. 30k, Skier. 40k, Runners. 50k, Soccer. 80k, Physical culture.

Unwmk.

1938, Dec. 28 Photo. *Perf. 12*

698	A301	5k scarlet	1.65	55
699	A302	10k black	1.65	55
700	A302	15k brown	1.90	55
701	A302	20k green	1.90	90
702	A302	30k dl vio	4.75	1.00
703	A302	40k dp grn	5.75	1.40
704	A302	50k blue	4.75	1.00
705	A302	80k dp bl	4.75	1.75
		Nos. 698-705 (8)	27.10	7.70

Gorki Street, Moscow — A309

Dynamo Subway Station
A315

Foundryman
A316

Designs: 20k, Council House & Hotel Moscow. 30k, Lenin Library. 40k, Crimea Bridge. 50k, Bridge over Moscow River. 80k, Khimki Station.

Paper with network as in parenthesis

1939, Mar. Typo. *Perf. 12*

706	A309	10k brn *(red brn)*	80	32
707	A309	20k dk sl grn *(lt bl)*	95	32
708	A309	30k brn vio *(red brn)*	95	70
709	A309	40k bl *(lt bl)*	1.65	70
710	A309	50k rose lake *(red brn)*	2.75	90
711	A309	80k gray ol *(lt bl)*	3.00	90
712	A315	1r dk bl *(lt bl)*	5.00	1.40
		Nos. 706-712 (7)	15.10	5.24

Issued as propaganda for "New Moscow." All designs are Moscow scenes. On 30k, denomination is at upper right.

1939, Mar.

713	A316	15k dark blue	55	30
a		Imperf.	20.00	

Statue on U.S.S.R. Pavilion — A317

U.S.S.R. Pavilion
A318

1939-40 Photo.

714	A317	30k ind & red	28	15
a		Imperf. ('40)	55	35
715	A318	50k bl & bis brn	32	24
a		Imperf. ('40)	60	45

Issued to commemorate Russia's participation in the New York World's Fair.

Paulina Osipenko
A318a

Marina Raskova
A318b

Design: 60k, Valentina Grizodubova.

1939, Mar.

718	A318a	15k green	1.25	60
719	A318b	30k brn vio	1.25	60
720	A318b	60k red	2.75	1.10

Issued to commemorate a non-stop record flight from Moscow to the Far East.

Exist imperf. Value, each $250.

Taras G. Shevchenko, Early Portrait
A319

Monument at Kharkov
A321

Design: 30k, Shevchenko portrait in later years.

1939, Mar. 9

721	A319	15k blk brn & blk	1.00	30
722	A319	30k dk red & blk	1.00	30
723	A321	60k grn & dk brn	2.75	1.25

Issued to commemorate the 125th anniversary of the birth of Taras G. Shevchenko (1814-1861), Ukrainian poet and painter.

Milkmaid with Prize Cow — A322

Tractor-plow at Work on Abundant Harvest
A323

Designs: 20k, Shepherd tending sheep. No. 727, Fair pavilion. No. 728, Fair emblem. 45k, Turkmen picking cotton. 50k, Drove of horses. 60k, Symbolizing agricultural wealth. 80k, Kolkhoz girl with sugar beets. 1r, Hunter with Polar foxes.

1939, Aug.

724	A322	10k rose pink	42	10
725	A323	15k red brn	42	10
726	A323	20k sl blk	42	10
727	A323	30k purple	42	10
728	A322	30k red org	42	15
729	A322	45k dk grn	55	35
730	A322	50k cop red	55	35
731	A322	60k brt pur	1.00	50
732	A322	80k dk vio	1.00	50
733	A322	1r dk bl	2.00	65
		Nos. 724-733 (10)	7.20	2.90

Issued to commemorate the Soviet Agricultural Fair.

Worker-Soldier-Aviator
A331 A332 A333

Arms of U.S.S.R.
A334 A335

1939-43 Unwmk. Typo. *Perf. 12*

734	A331	5k red	14	14
735	A332	15k dk grn	22	24
736	A333	30k dp bl	22	24
737	A334	60k fawn ('43)	60	24

Photo.

738	A335	60k rose car	48	35
		Nos. 734-738 (5)	1.66	1.21

No. 734 was re-issued in 1954-56 in slightly smaller format: 14x21½mm., instead of 14¾x22¼mm. Other values reissued in smaller format: 10k, 15k, 20k, 25k, 30k, 40k and 1r. (See notes following Nos. 622, 1260, 1347 and 1689.)

No. 416 Surcharged with New Value in Black

1939 Wmk. 170

743	A97	30k on 4k cl	6.00	5.00
a		Unwmk.	32.50	25.00

M.E. Saltykov (N. Shchedrin)
A336 A337

1939, Sept. Typo. Unwmk.

745	A336	15k claret	30	14
746	A337	30k dk grn	45	20
747	A336	45k ol gray	75	22
748	A337	60k dk bl	95	32

Issued to commemorate the 50th anniversary of the death of Mikhail E. Saltykov (1826-1889), writer and satirist who used pen name of N. Shchedrin.

Sanatorium of the State Bank — A338

Designs: 10k, 15k, Soviet Army sanatorium. 20k, Rest home, New Afyon. 30k, Clinical Institute. 50k, 80k, Sanatorium for workers in heavy industry. 60k, Rest home, Sukhumi.

1939, Nov. Photo. *Perf. 12*

749	A338	5k dl brn	35	18
750	A338	10k carmine	35	18
751	A338	15k yel grn	35	18
752	A338	20k dk sl grn	35	18
753	A338	30k bluish blk	35	18
754	A338	50k gray blk	75	28
755	A338	60k brn vio	90	40
756	A338	80k org red	1.10	55
		Nos. 749-756 (8)	4.50	2.13

Mikhail Lermontov in 1837 — A346

Portrait in 1838 — A347

Portrait in 1841 — A348

1939, Dec.

757	A346	15k ind & sep	80	22
758	A347	30k dk grn & dl blk	2.00	30
759	A348	45k brick red & ind	1.65	45

Issued to commemorate the 125th anniversary of the birth of Mikhail Y. Lermontov (1814-1841), poet and novelist.

Nikolai Chernyshevski
A349

Anton Chekhov
A350

1939, Dec. Photo.

760	A349	15k dk grn	35	22
761	A349	30k dl vio	35	45
762	A349	60k Prus grn	75	45

Issued to commemorate the 50th anniversary of the death of Nikolai Chernyshevski, scientist and critic.

1940, Feb. Unwmk. *Perf. 12*

Design: 20k, 30k, Portrait with hat.

763	A350	10k dk yel grn	25	22
764	A350	15k ultra	25	22
765	A350	20k violet	50	42
766	A350	30k cop brn	1.00	55

80th anniversary of birth of Anton Chekhov (1860-1904), playwright.

Welcome to Red Army by Western Ukraine and Western Byelorussia
A352

Designs: 30k, Villagers welcoming tank crew. 50k, 60k, Soldier giving newspapers to crowd. 1r, Crowd waving to tank column.

1940, Apr.

767	A352	10k dp rose	35	15
768	A352	30k myr grn	35	15
769	A352	50k gray blk	65	30
770	A352	60k indigo	65	30
771	A352	1r red	1.00	75
		Nos. 767-771 (5)	3.00	1.65

Issued to commemorate the liberation of the people of Western Ukraine and Western Byelorussia.

Ice-breaker "Josef Stalin," Captain Beloussov and Chief Ivan Papanin
A356

Vadygin and Papanin
A358

Map of the Drift of the Sedov and Crew Members — A359

Design: 30k, Icebreaker Georgi Sedov, Captain Vadygin and First Mate Trofimov.

1940, Apr.

772	A356	15k dl yel grn	1.40	55
773	A356	30k dl pur	2.75	55
774	A358	50k cop brn	2.25	55
775	A359	1r dk ultra	4.50	1.65

Heroism of the Sedov crew which drifted in the Polar Basin for 812 days.

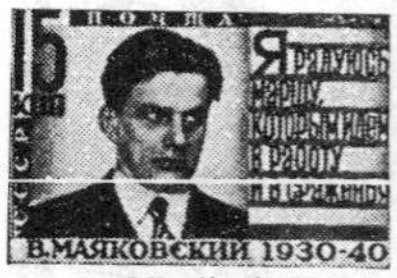

Vladimir V. Mayakovsky
A360 A361

1940, June

776	A360	15k dp red	24	14
777	A360	30k cop brn	42	22
778	A361	60k dk gray bl	50	32
779	A361	80k brt ultra	42	32

10th anniv. of the death of Mayakovsky, poet (1893-1930).

K.A. Timiryazev and Academy of Agricultural Sciences
A362

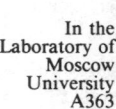

In the Laboratory of Moscow University
A363

Last Portrait
A364

Monument in Moscow — A365

1940, June

780	A362	10k indigo	30	18
781	A363	15k purple	30	25
782	A364	30k dk vio brn	30	25
783	A365	60k dk grn	1.25	50

Issued to commemorate the 20th anniversary of the death of K. A. Timiryasev, scientist and professor of agricultural and biological sciences.

Relay Race — A366

Sportswomen Marching
A367

Children's Sport Badge — A368

Skier — A369

Throwing the Grenade
A370

1940, July 21

784	A366	15k car rose	65	18
785	A367	30k sepia	1.40	18
786	A368	50k dk vio bl	1.50	45
787	A369	60k dk vio bl	2.00	45
788	A370	1r grysh grn	3.50	95
		Nos. 784-788 (5)	9.05	2.21

Issued to mark Russia's second All-Union Physical Culture Day.

Tchaikovsky Museum at Klin
A371

Tchaikovsky and Passage from his Fourth Symphony
A372

Tchaikovsky and Excerpt from Eugene Onegin — A373

1940, Aug. Unwmk. Typo. *Perf. 12*

789	A371	15k Prus grn	75	25
790	A372	20k brown	75	25
791	A372	30k dk bl	75	25
792	A371	50k rose lake	75	38
793	A373	60k red	90	60
		Nos. 789-793 (5)	3.90	1.73

Issued to commemorate the centenary of the birth of Peter Ilich Tchaikovsky (1840-1893), composer.

Volga Provinces Pavilion
A374

Northeast Provinces Pavilion — A376

Pavilions: 15k, Far East Provinces. No. 797, Central Regions. No. 798, Ukrainian. No. 799, Byelorussian. No. 800, Azerbaijan. No. 801, Georgian. No. 802, Armenian. No. 803, Uzbek. No. 804, Turkmen. No. 805, Tadzhik. No. 806, Kirghiz. No. 807, Kazakh. No. 808, Karelian Finnish. 50k, Main Building. 60k, Mechanizaton Pavilion and Stalin statue.

1940, Oct. Photo.

794	A374	10k multi	1.00	45
795	A374	15k multi	1.00	45
796	A376	30k grn, gray, buff & dk brn	1.00	60
797	A376	30k grn, gray bl, buff & red brn	1.00	60
798	A376	30k grn, dp bl, buff, red & blk brn	1.00	60
799	A376	30k grn, gray, buff & blk brn	1.00	60
800	A376	30k grn, gray, buff & blk brn	1.00	60
801	A374	30k grn, gray bl, buff & bis	1.00	60
802	A376	30k grn, gray bl, buff, dk brn & red	1.00	60
803	A376	30k grn, gray bl, buff, blk & red	1.00	60
804	A374	30k grn, pale, gray, buff & brn	1.00	60
805	A376	30k grn, gray, buff, org brn, brn & red	1.00	60
806	A376	30k grn, gray, buff, bis & dk brn	1.50	1.25
807	A376	30k grn, dp bl, buff, blk brn & red	1.50	1.25
808	A376	30k grn, dp bl, buff, brn, red & blk brn	1.50	1.25
809	A376	50k multi	2.00	1.25
810	A376	60k multi	2.25	1.25
		Nos. 794-810 (17)	20.75	13.15

Issued to commemorate the All-Union Agricultural Fair. Various vertical and horizontal se-tenant combinations of Nos. 796-808 are found because these stamps were printed together in one sheet.

Monument to Red Army Heroes
A391

Map of War Operations and M. V. Frunze
A393

Heroic Crossing of the Sivash
A394

Designs: 15k, Grenade thrower. 60k, Frunze's headquarters, Stroganovka. 1r, Victorious soldier.

1940 *Imperf.*

811	A391	10k dk grn	50	25
812	A391	15k org ver	50	25
813	A393	30k dl brn & car	50	25
814	A394	50k vio brn	50	32
815	A394	60k indigo	50	50
816	A391	1r gray blk	1.25	50
		Nos. 811-816 (6)	3.75	2.07

20th anniversary of battle of Perekop.

Nos. 811-816 were also issued perf. 12. Set price about 25% more.

Coal Miners
A397

Blast Furnace
A398

Bridge over Moscow-Volga Canal — A399

Three New Type Locomotives
A400

Workers on a Collective Farm — A401

Automobiles and Planes
A402

Oil Derricks — A403

1941, Jan. *Perf. 12*

817	A397	10k dp bl	25	16
818	A398	15k dk vio	25	16
819	A399	20k dp bl	25	16
820	A400	30k dk brn	32	20
821	A401	50k ol brn	32	40
822	A402	60k ol brn	52	52
823	A403	1r dk bl grn	1.00	80
		Nos. 817-823 (7)	2.91	2.40

Issued to publicize Soviet industries.

Troops on Skis — A404

Sailor — A405

Soldiers with Cannon
A406

Designs: 20k, Cavalry. 30k, 3r, Machine gunners. 45k, Army horsemen. 50k, Aviator. 1r, 3r, Marshal's Star.

1941-43

824	A404	5k dk vio	48	15
825	A405	10k dp bl	48	15
826	A406	15k brt yel grn	18	15
827	A404	20k vermilion	18	15
828	A404	30k dl brn	18	15
829	A406	45k gray grn	60	30
830	A404	50k dl bl	35	40
831	A404	1r dl bl grn	48	55
831A	A404	3r myr grn ('43)	1.90	1.10
		Nos. 824-831A (9)	4.83	3.10

Issued to commemorate the 23rd anniversary of the Army and Navy of the U.S.S.R.

Battle of Ismail
A412

Field Marshal Aleksandr Suvorov
A413

1941 Unwmk. *Perf. 12*

832	A412	10k dk grn	40	30
833	A412	15k car rose	55	45
834	A413	30k bl blk	80	65
835	A413	1r ol brn	1.65	90

Issued to commemorate the 150th anniversary of the capture of the Turkish fortress, Ismail.

Kirghiz Horse Breeder
A414

Kirghiz Miner — A415

1941, Mar.

836	A414	15k dl brn	90	45
837	A415	30k dl pur	1.25	60

Issued to commemorate the 15th anniversary of the Kirghizian Soviet Socialist Republic.

Prof. N. E. Zhukovski
A416

Zhukovski Lecturing
A418

Military Air Academy
A417

1941, Mar.

838	A416	15k dp bl	45	22
839	A417	30k car rose	45	35
840	A418	50k brn vio	75	42

20th anniv. of the death of Prof. Zhukovski, scientist (1847-1921).

Arms Type of 1938

Design: Arms of Karelian-Finnish Soviet Socialist Republic.

1941, Mar.

841	A252	30k rose	45	30
842	A252	45k dk bl grn	65	50

Issued to commemorate the first anniversary of the Karelian-Finnish Soviet Socialist Republic.

Spasski Tower, Kremlin
A420

Kremlin and Moscow River
A421

1941, May Typo. Unwmk.

843	A420	1r dl red	45	30
844	A421	2r brn org	1.10	60

"Suvorov's March through the Alps, 1799"
A422

Vasili Surikov, Self-portrait
A424

"Stepan Rasin on the Volga"
A423

1941, June Photo. *Perf. 12*

845	A422	20k black	90	38
846	A423	30k scarlet	1.50	65
847	A422	50k dk vio brn	3.00	1.10
848	A423	1r gray grn	4.00	1.25
849	A424	2r brown	7.50	1.50
		Nos. 845-849 (5)	16.90	4.88

Issued to commemorate the 25th anniversary of the death of Vasili Ivanovich Surikov (1848-1916), painter.

Mikhail Lermontov — A425

1941, July

850	A425	15k Prus grn	2.75	1.00
851	A425	30k dk vio	3.75	1.50

Issued to commemorate the centenary of the death of Mikhail Y. Lermontov, poet.

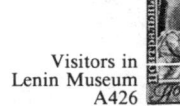

Visitors in Lenin Museum
A426

Lenin Museum
A427

1941-42

852	A426	15k rose red	1.10	70
853	A427	30k dk vio ('42)	4.25	1.40
854	A426	45k Prus grn	2.00	80
855	A427	1r org brn ('42)	5.50	1.40

Fifth anniversary of Lenin Museum.

Mother's Farewell to a Soldier Son ("Be a Hero!") — A428

1941, Aug.

856	A428	30k carmine	9.50	7.50

Alisher Navoi
A429

People's Militia
A430

1942, Jan.

857	A429	30k brown	1.75	1.50
858	A429	1r dk vio	2.75	2.50

Issued to commemorate the 500th anniversary of the birth of Alisher Navoi, Uzbekian poet.

1941, Dec. Typo.

859	A430	30k dull blue	18.00	17.00

Junior Lieutenant Talalikhin Ramming German Plane in Midair
A431

Captain Gastello and Burning Plane Diving into Enemy Gasoline Tanks — A432

Major General Dovator and Cossack Cavalry in Action
A433

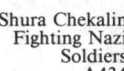

Shura Chekalin Fighting Nazi Soldiers
A434

Nazi Soldiers Leading Zoya Kosmodemjanskaja to her Death — A435

1942-44 Unwmk. Photo. *Perf. 12*

860	A431	20k bluish blk	65	20
860A	A431	30k Prus grn ('44)	65	20
861	A432	30k bluish blk	65	20
861A	A432	30k dp ultra ('44)	65	20
862	A433	30k black	65	20
863	A434	30k black	65	20
863A	A434	30k brt yel grn ('44)	65	20
864	A435	30k black	65	20
864A	A435	30k rose vio ('44)	65	20
865	A434	1r sl grn	3.00	1.75
866	A435	2r sl grn	4.50	2.50
		Nos. 860-866 (11)	13.35	6.05

Issued to honor Soviet heroes.

Anti-tank Artillery
A436

Signal Corps in Action
A437

Defense of Leningrad
A440

Guerrilla Fighters
A438

War Worker
A439

Red Army Scouts — A441

1942-43

867	A436	20k black	24	12
868	A437	30k sappire	40	12
869	A438	30k Prus grn ('43)	40	12
870	A439	30k dl red brn ('43)	40	12
871	A440	60k bl blk	1.00	40
872	A441	1r blk brn	1.75	60
		Nos. 867-872 (6)	4.19	1.48

Women Workers and Soldiers
A442

Flaming Tank A443

Women Preparing Food Shipments A444

Sewing Equipment for Red Army A445

Anti-Aircraft Battery in Action A446

1942-43 Typo. Unwmk.

873 A442	20k dk bl		40	12
874 A443	20k dl rose vio		40	12
875 A444	30k brn vio ('43)		40	12
876 A445	45k dl rose red		85	28
877 A446	45k dp dl bl ('43)		85	35
	Nos. 873-877 (5)		2.90	99

Manufacturing Explosives A447

Designs: 10k, Agriculture. 15k, Group of Fighters. 20k, Storming the Palace. 30k, Lenin and Stalin. 60k, Tanks. 1r, Lenin. 2r, Revolution scene.

Inscribed: "1917 XXV 1942".

1943, Jan. Photo. *Perf. 12*

878 A447	5k blk brn	15	12
879 A447	10k blk brn	15	12
880 A447	15k bl blk	15	12
881 A447	20k bl blk	24	12
882 A447	30k blk brn	24	12
883 A447	60k blk brn	35	20
884 A447	1r dl red brn	75	40
885 A447	2r black	1.75	70
	Nos. 878-885 (8)	3.78	1.90

25th anniversary of October Revolution.

Mount St. Elias, Alaska — A455

Bering Sea and Bering's Ship — A456

1943, Apr.

886 A455	30k chlky bl	40	15
887 A456	60k Prus grn	65	15
888 A455	1r yel grn	1.40	38
889 A456	2r bis brn	2.75	65

200th anniv. of the death of Vitus Bering, explorer (1681-1741).

Medical Corpsmen and Wounded Soldier — A457

Trench Mortar A458

Army Scouts — A459

Repulsing Enemy Tanks — A460

Snipers A461

1943

890 A457	30k myr grn	25	22
891 A458	30k brn bis	25	22
892 A459	30k myr grn	25	22
893 A460	60k myr grn	75	75
894 A461	60k chlky bl	75	75
	Nos. 890-894 (5)	2.25	2.16

Maxim Gorki (1868-1936), Writer — A462

1943, June

895 A462	30k green	35	14
896 A462	60k sl blk	45	22

Patriotic War Medal A463

Order of Field Marshal Suvorov A464

1943, July Engr.

897 A463	1r black	60	48
898 A464	10r dk ol grn	2.50	1.40

Sailors A465

Designs: 30k, Navy gunner and warship. 60k, Soldiers and tank.

1943, Oct. Photo.

899 A465	20k gldn brn	12	12
900 A465	30k dk myr grn	15	15
901 A465	60k brt yel grn	30	18
902 A465	3r chlky bl	85	40

Issued to commemorate the 25th anniversary of the Red Army and Navy.

Karl Marx A468

Vladimir V. Mayakovsky A469

1943, Sept.

903 A468	30k bl blk	30	12
904 A468	60k dk sl grn	40	15

Issued to commemorate the 125th anniversary of the birth of Karl Marx.

1943, Oct.

905 A469	30k red org	30	12
906 A469	60k dp bl	40	15

Issued to commemorate the 50th anniversary of the birth of V. V. Mayakovsky, poet.

Flags of U.S., Britain, and Russia — A470

1943, Nov.

907 A470	30k blk, dp red & dk bl	60	32
908 A470	3r sl bl, red & lt bl	2.50	85

The Tehran conference.

Ivan Turgenev (1818-83), Poet — A471

1943, Oct.

909 A471	30k myr grn	3.00	2.25
910 A471	60k dl pur	4.00	2.75

Map of Stalingrad A472

Harbor of Sevastopol and Statue of Lenin — A473

Leningrad A474

Odessa A475

1944, Mar. *Perf. 12*

911 A472	30k dl brn & car	25	14
912 A473	30k dk bl	25	14
913 A474	30k dk sl grn	25	14
914 A475	30k yel grn	25	14

Issued to honor the defenders of Stalingrad, Leningrad, Sevastopol and Odessa.

Souvenir sheet of four of No. 913 is listed as No. 959.

No. 911 measures 33x22mm. and also exists in smaller size: 32x21½mm.

Russian War Heroes — A476

1944, Apr.

915 A476	30k dp ultra	22	12

Sailor Loading Gun A477

Tanks A478

Soldier Bayoneting a Nazi A479

Infantryman A480

Soldier Throwing Hand Grenade — A481

1943-44 Photo.

916 A477	15k dp ultra	10	9
917 A478	20k red org ('44)	12	12
918 A479	30k dl brn & dk red ('44)	15	12
919 A480	1r brt yel grn	42	30
920 A481	2r Prus grn ('44)	65	60
	Nos. 916-920 (5)	1.44	1.23

Issued to commemorate the 25th anniversary of the Young Communist League (Komsomol).

Flags of U.S., Russia, Great Britain — A482

1944, May 30 Unwmk. *Perf. 12*

921 A482	60k blk, red & bl	60	30
922 A482	3r dk bl, red & lt bl	3.25	1.10

Issued to commemorate the Day of the Nations United Against Germany, June 14, 1944.

Patriotic War Order A483

Order of Prince Alexander Nevsky A484

Order of Field Marshal Suvorov A485

Order of Field Marshal Kutuzov A486

Paper with network as in parenthesis

1944 Typo. *Perf. 12, Imperf.*

923	A483	15k dl red *(rose)*	10	10
924	A484	20k bl *(lt bl)*	15	15
925	A485	30k grn *(grn)*	16	16
926	A486	60k dl red *(rose)*	35	35

Order of Patriotic War A487

Order of Prince, Alexander Nevski A488

Order of Field Marshal Kutuzov A489

Order of Field Marshal Suvorov A490

1944, June Unwmk. Engr. *Perf. 12*

927	A487	1r black	22	12
928	A488	3r bl blk	55	30
929	A489	5r dk ol grn	95	42
930	A490	10r dk red	1.65	50

Types of 1934, Inscribed 1924-1944 and

Lenin's Mausoleum — A491

Designs: 30k (No. 931), 3r, Lenin and Stalin. 50k, Lenin in middle age. 60k, Lenin, the orator.

1944, June Photo.

931	A190	30k org & car	12	8
932	A186	30k sl & blk	12	8
933	A187	45k sl & blk	18	8
934	A187	50k sl & blk	20	12
935	A187	60k sl & blk	22	12
936	A491	1r ind & brn blk	50	18
937	A190	3r bl blk & dl org	1.40	38
		Nos. 931-937 (7)	2.74	1.04

Issued to commemorate 20 years without Lenin.

Nikolai Rimski-Korsakov A492 A493

1944, June *Perf. 12, Imperf.*

938	A492	30k gray blk	15	10
939	A493	60k sl grn	25	10
940	A492	1r brt bl grn	32	15
941	A493	3r purple	52	20

Issued to commemorate the centenary of the birth of Nikolai Rimski-Korsakov (1844-1909), composer.

N.A. Schors A494

V. I. Chapayev A495

S. G. Lazho A496

Sergei A. Chaplygin A497

1944, Sept. *Perf. 12*

942	A494	30k gray blk	22	12
943	A495	30k dk sl grn	22	12
944	A496	30k brt yel grn	22	12

Issued to honor heroes of the 1918 civil war.
For 60k stamps of types A494 to A496, see Nos. 1209-1211. For 40k stamp of type A495, see No. 1403.

1944, Sept.

945	A497	30k gray	22	8
946	A497	1r lt brn	85	18

Issued to commemorate the 75th anniversary of the birth of Sergei A. Chaplygin, scientist and mathematician.

Khanpasha Nuradilov A498

A. Matrosov A499

F. Louzan A500

M. S. Polivanova and N. V. Kovshova A501

Pilot B. Safonov — A502

1944, July

947	A498	30k sl grn	15	15
948	A499	60k dl pur	30	24
949	A500	60k dl bl	30	24
950	A501	60k brt grn	30	24
951	A502	60k sl blk	45	24
		Nos. 947-951 (5)	1.50	1.11

Issued to honor Soviet war heroes.

Ilya E. Repin — A503

Ivan A. Krylov — A505

"Cossacks' Reply to Sultan Mohammed IV" — A504

1944, Nov. *Perf. 12 1/2, Imperf.*

952	A503	30k sl grn	24	15
953	A504	50k dk bl grn	35	15
954	A504	60k chlky bl	35	15
955	A503	1r dk org brn	50	18
956	A504	2r dk pur	1.00	24
		Nos. 952-956 (5)	2.44	87

Birth centenary of I. E. Repin (1844-1930), painter.

1944, Nov. *Perf. 12*

957	A505	30k yel brn	12	9
958	A505	1r dk vio bl	24	15

Issued to commemorate the centenary of the death of I. A. Krylov, fable writer.

Leningrad Type
Souvenir Sheet

1944, Dec. 6 *Imperf.*

959		Sheet of four	4.00	3.75
a.		A474 30k dk slate grn	40	40

Issued to commemorate the liberation of Leningrad, Jan. 27, 1944.

Partisan Medal A507

Order for Bravery A508

Order of Bogdan Chmielnicki A509

Order of Victory A510

Order of Ushakov A511

Order of Nakhimov A512

Paper with network as in parenthesis

Perf. 12 1/2, Imperf.

1945, Jan. Typo. Unwmk.

960	A507	15k blk *(grn)*	16	12
961	A508	30k dp bl *(lt bl)*	16	12
962	A509	45k dk bl	20	12
963	A510	60k dl rose *(pale rose)*	28	15
964	A511	1r dl bl *(grn)*	40	18
965	A512	1r yel grn *(bl)*	40	18
		Nos. 960-965 (6)	1.60	87

Aleksandr S. Griboedov A513

Red Army Soldier A514

1945, Jan. Photo. *Perf. 12 1/2*

966	A513	30k dk sl grn	28	18
967	A513	60k gray brn	55	28

Issued to commemorate the 150th anniversary of the birth of A. S. Griboedov (1795-1829), poet and statesman.

1945, Mar.

968	A514	60k gray blk & hn	38	55
969	A514	3r gray blk & hn	1.25	1.10

Souvenir Sheet

Imperf

970		Sheet of four	22.50	21.00
a.		A514 3r gray brn & hn	2.50	2.50

Second anniversary of victory at Stalingrad. No. 970 contains 4 stamps similar to No. 969.

Order for Bravery A516

Order of Bogdan Chmielnicki A517

The first value column gives the catalogue value of an unused stamp, the second that of a used stamp.

Order of Victory — A518

1945 **Engr.** ***Perf. 12***

971	A516	1r indigo	35	12
972	A517	2r black	75	20
973	A518	3r henna	1.25	32

See Nos. 1341-1342.

A519

A520

A521

A522

A523

Battle Scenes — A524

1945, Apr. **Photo.** ***Perf. 12½***

974	A519	20k sl grn, org red & blk	12	12
975	A520	30k bl blk & dl org	14	12
976	A521	30k bl blk	14	12
977	A522	60k org red	24	12
978	A523	1r sl grn & org red	38	32
979	A524	1r sl grn	38	32
		Nos. 974-979 (6)	1.40	1.12

Issued to commemorate the successes of the Red Army against Germany.

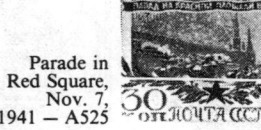

Parade in Red Square, Nov. 7, 1941 — A525

Designs: 60k, Soldiers and Moscow barricade, Dec. 1941. 1r, Air battle, 1941.

1945, June

980	A525	30k dk bl vio	12	8
981	A525	60k ol blk	22	12
982	A525	1r blk brn	70	20

Issued to commemorate the 3rd anniversary of the victory over the Germans before Moscow.

Elite Guard Badge and Cannons A528

Motherhood Medal A529

Motherhood Glory Order — A530

Mother-Heroine Order — A531

1945, Apr. **Typo.**

983	A528	60k red	40	12

1945 ***Perf. 12½, Imperf.***

Paper with network as in parenthesis

Size: 22x33¼mm.

984	A529	20k brn *(lt bl)*	12	12
985	A530	30k yel brn *(grn)*	22	15
986	A531	60k dl rose *(pale rose)*	40	15

Perf. 12½

Engr.

Size: 20x38mm.

986A	A529	1r blk brn *(grn)*	40	15
986B	A530	2r dp bl *(lt bl)*	89	32
986C	A531	3r brn red *(lt bl)*	1.00	60
		Nos. 984-986C (6)	3.03	1.49

Academy Building, Moscow A532

Academy at Leningrad and M. V. Lomonosov A533

1945, June **Photo.** ***Perf. 12½***

987	A532	30k bl vio	28	15
a.		Horiz. pair, imperf. between	3.25	
988	A533	2r grnsh blk	90	45

Issued to commemorate the 220th anniversary of the establishment of the Academy of Sciences.

Popov and his Invention A534

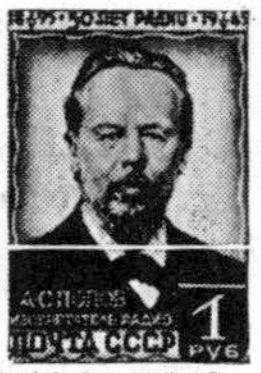
Aleksandr S. Popov A535

1945, July **Unwmk.**

989	A534	30k dp bl vio	42	16
990	A534	60k dk red	85	24
991	A535	1r yel brn	1.50	35

Issued to commemorate the 50th anniversary of the "invention of radio" by A. S. Popov.

No. 973 Overprinted in Blue

ПРАЗДНИК ПОБЕДЫ

9 мая 1945 года

1945, Aug. ***Perf. 12***

992	A518	3r henna	90	45

Issued to commemorate the Victory of the Allied Nations in Europe.

Iakovlev Fighter — A536

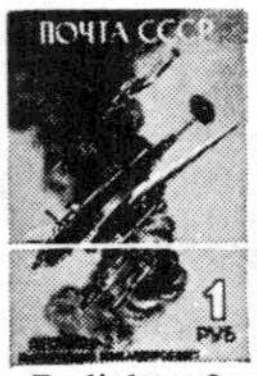
Petliakov-2 Dive Bombers A537

Iliushin-2 Bombers A538

Designs: Nos. 992A, 995, Iakovlev Fighter. Nos. 992B, 1000, Petliakov-2 dive bombers. Nos. 992C, 996, Ilyushin-2 bombers. Nos. 992D, 993, Petliakov-8 heavy bomber. Nos. 992E, 1001, Tupolev-2 bombers. Nos. 992F, 997, Ilyushin-4 bombers. Nos. 992G, 999, Polikarpov-2 biplane. Nos. 992H, 998, Lavochkin-7 fighters. Nos. 992I, 994, Iakovlev fighter in action.

1945-46 **Unwmk.** **Photo.** ***Perf. 12***

992A	A536	5k dk vio ('46)	22	10
992B	A537	10k hn brn ('46)	22	10
992C	A538	15k hn brn ('46)	30	10
992D	A536	15k Prus grn ('46)	30	10
992E	A538	20k gray brn ('46)	35	20
992F	A538	30k vio ('46)	35	20
992G	A538	30k brn ('46)	35	20
992H	A538	50k bl vio ('46)	70	45
992I	A536	60k dl bl vio ('46)	70	45
993	A536	1r gray blk	1.50	85
994	A536	1r hn brn	1.50	85
995	A536	1r brown	1.50	85
996	A538	1r dp brn	1.50	85
997	A538	1r int blk	1.50	85
998	A538	1r org ver	1.50	85
999	A538	1r brt grn	1.50	85
1000	A537	1r dp brn	1.50	85
1001	A538	1r vio bl	1.50	85
		Nos. 992A-1001 (18)	16.99	9.55

Issue dates: Nos. 992A-992I, Mar. 26. Nos. 993-1001, Aug. 19.

A545

A546

Lenin

Various Lenin Portraits Dated "1870-1945"

1945, Sept. ***Perf. 12½***

1002	A545	30k bluish blk	18	15
1003	A546	50k gray brn	22	15
1004	A546	60k org brn	28	18
1005	A546	1r grnsh blk	45	22
1006	A546	3r sepia	1.40	60
		Nos. 1002-1006 (5)	2.53	1.30

Issued to commemorate the 75th anniversary of the birth of Lenin.

Prince M. I. Kutuzov A550

Aleksandr Ivanovich Herzen A551

1945, Sept. 16

1007	A550	30k bl vio	30	15
1008	A550	60k brown	55	20

Issued to commemorate the bicentenary of the birth of Field Marshal Prince Mikhail Illarionovich Kutuzov (1745-1813).

1945, Oct. 26

1009	A551	30k dk brn	35	20
1010	A551	2r grnsh blk	1.10	40

Issued to commemorate the 75th anniversary of the death of A. I. Herzen, author and revolutionist.

Ilya Mechnikov A552

Friedrich Engels A553

1945, Nov. 27

1011	A552	30k brown	20	15
1012	A552	1r grnsh blk	40	25

Ilya I. Mechnikov, zoologist and bacteriologist (1845-1916).

1945, Nov. **Unwmk.** ***Perf. 12½***

1013	A553	30k dk brn	22	15
1014	A553	60k Prus grn	30	20

Issued to commemorate the 125th anniversary of the birth of Friedrich Engels, collaborator of Karl Marx.

Tank Leaving Assembly Line — A554

Designs: 30k, Harvesting wheat. 60k, Airplane designing. 1r, Moscow fireworks.

1945, Dec. 25 **Photo.**

1015	A554	20k ind & brn	20	15
1016	A554	30k blk & org brn	20	15
1017	A554	60k brn & grn	35	16
1018	A554	1r dk bl & org	65	24

Artillery Observer and Guns — A558

Heavy Field Pieces — A559

1945, Dec.

1019	A558	30k	brown	30	12
1020	A559	60k	sepia	65	30

Artillery Day, Nov. 19, 1945.

Catalogue values for unused stamps in this section, from this point to the end of the section, are for Never Hinged items.

Victory Medal — A560

Soldier with Victory Flag — A561

1946, Jan. 23

1021	A560	30k	dk vio	16	12
1022	A560	30k	brown	16	12
1023	A560	60k	grnsh blk	32	15
1024	A560	60k	henna	32	15
1025	A561	60k	blk & dl red	32	15
	Nos. 1021-1025 (5)			1.28	69

Arms of U.S.S.R. A562

Red Square A563

1946, Feb. 10

1026	A562	30k	henna	22	12
1027	A563	45k	henna	30	12
1028	A562	60k	grnsh blk	60	18

Issued to commemorate the elections to the Supreme Soviet of the U. S. S. R., February 10, 1946.

Artillery in Victory Parade — A564

Victory Parade — A565

1946, Feb. 23

1029	A564	60k	dk brn	30	20
1030	A564	2r	dl vio	65	25
1031	A565	3r	blk & red	90	40

Issued to publicize the Victory Parade held in Moscow, June 24, 1945.

Order of Lenin — A566

Order of Red Star — A567

Medal of Hammer and Sickle A568

Order of Token of Veneration A569

Gold Star Medal A570

Order of Red Banner A571

Order of the Red Workers' Banner — A572

Paper with network as in parenthesis

1946 Unwmk. Typo. *Perf. 12½x12*

1032	A566	60k	myr grn *(grn)*	35	30
1033	A567	60k	dk vio brn *(brn)*	35	30
1034	A568	60k	plum *(pink)*	35	30
1035	A569	60k	dp bl *(grn)*	35	30
1036	A570	60k	dk car *(sal)*	35	30
1037	A571	60k	red *(sal)*	35	30
1038	A572	60k	dk brn vio *(buff)*	35	30
	Nos. 1032-1038 (7)			2.45	2.10

See Nos. 1650-1654.

Medal for Workers' Achievement of Distinction A573

Medal for Workers' Gallantry A574

Marshal's Star A575

Medal for Defense of Soviet Trans-Arctic Regions A576

Medal for Meritorious Service in Battle A577

Medal for Defense of Caucasus A578

Medal for Defense of Moscow A579

Medal for Bravery A580

Paper with network as in parenthesis

1946

1039	A573	60k	choc *(sal)*	30	30
1040	A574	60k	brn *(sal)*	30	30
1041	A575	60k	bl *(pale bl)*	30	30
1042	A576	60k	dk grn *(grn)*	30	30
1043	A577	60k	dk bl *(grn)*	30	30
1044	A578	60k	dk yel grn *(grn)*	30	30
1045	A579	60k	car *(pink)*	30	30
1046	A580	60k	dk vio *(bl)*	30	30
	Nos. 1039-1046 (8)			2.40	2.40

A581

Maxim Gorki — A582

1946, June 18 **Photo.**

1047	A581	30k	brown	15	10
1048	A582	60k	dk grn	45	15

Issued to commemorate the 10th anniversary of the death of Maxim Gorki (Alexei M. Peshkov).

Mikhail Kalinin A583

Chebyshev A584

1946, June

1049	A583	20k	sepia	15	20

Death of Mikhail Ivanovich Kalinin (1875-1946).

1946, May 25

1050	A584	30k	brown	50	10
1051	A584	60k	gray brn	65	10

125th anniv. of the birth of Pafnuti Lvovich Chebyshev (1821-94), mathematician.

View of Sukhumi — A585

Sanatorium at Sochi — A587

Designs: 30k, Promenade at Gagri. 45k, New Afyon Sanatorium.

1946, June 18

1052	A585	15k	dk brn	25	12
1053	A585	30k	dk sl grn	30	12
1054	A587	30k	dk grn	30	12
1055	A585	45k	chnt brn	50	16

All-Union Parade of Physical Culturists — A589

1946, July 21

1056	A589	30k	dk grn	3.75	2.25

Tank Divisions in Red Square A590

1946, Sept. 8

1057	A590	30k	dk grn	60	32
1058	A590	60k	brown	95	48

Issued to honor Soviet tankmen.

Belfry of Ivan the Great, Kremlin A591

Bolshoi Theater, Moscow A592

Hotel Moscow A593

Red Square A597

Values quoted in this catalogue are for stamps graded at Fine-Very Fine and with no faults. An illustrated guide to grade is provided in introductory material, beginning on Page V.

Spasski Tower and Statues of Minin and Pozharski — A598

Designs: (Moscow scenes): 20k, Bolshoi Theater, Sverdlov Square. 45k, View of Kremlin. 50k, Lenin Museum.

1946, Sept. 5

1059	A591	5k brown	12	12
1060	A592	10k sepia	16	12
1061	A593	15k chestnut	16	12
1062	A593	20k lt brn	16	12
1063	A593	45k dk grn	28	15
1064	A593	50k brown	28	20
1065	A597	60k bl vio	40	20
1066	A598	1r chnt brn	55	20
		Nos. 1059-1066 (8)	2.11	1.23

Medal for Workers' Achievement of Distinction A599

Medal for Workers' Gallantry A600

Medal to the Partisan of the Patriotic War — A601

Medal for Defense of Soviet Trans-Arctic Regions — A602

Medal for Meritorious Service in Battle — A603

Medal for Defense of Caucasus — A604

Medal for Defense of Moscow — A605

Medal for Bravery — A606

1946, Sept. 5 **Engr.**

1067	A599	1r dk vio brn	45	18
1068	A600	1r dk car	45	18
1069	A601	1r carmine	45	18
1070	A602	1r bl blk	45	18
1071	A603	1r black	45	18
1072	A604	1r blk brn	45	18
1073	A605	1r ol blk	45	18
1074	A606	1r dp cl	45	18
		Nos. 1067-1074 (8)	3.60	1.44

See Nos. 1650-1654.

Give the Country Each Year: 127 Million Tons of Grain — A607

60 Million Tons of Oil — A608

60 Million Tons of Steel — A610

500 Million Tons of Coal — A609

50 Million Tons of Cast Iron — A611

Perf. 12½x12

1946, Oct. 6 **Photo.** **Unwmk.**

1075	A607	5k ol brn	7	9
1076	A608	10k dk sl grn	7	9
1077	A609	15k brown	12	12
1078	A610	20k dk bl vio	15	12
1079	A611	30k brown	32	16
		Nos. 1075-1079 (5)	73	58

Symbols of Transportation, Map and Stamps — A612

Early Soviet Stamp A613

Stamps of Soviet Russia — A614

1946, Nov. 6 ***Perf. 12½***

1080	A612	15k blk & dk red	65	35
a		Sheet of 4, imperf.	22.50	22.50
1081	A613	30k dk grn & brn	95	35
a		Sheet of 4, imperf.	32.50	32.50
1082	A614	60k dk grn & blk	1.40	45
a		Sheet of 4, imperf.	32.50	32.50

25th anniv. of the 1st Soviet postage stamp.

Lenin and Stalin — A615

1946 **Photo.** ***Perf. 12½, Imperf.***

1083	A615	30k dp brn org	1.25	1.25
a		Sheet of 4, imperf.	25.00	25.00
1084	A615	30k dk grn	1.25	1.25

29th anniversary of October Revolution.

Issue dates: Nos. 1083-1084 imperf., Nov. 6; perf., Dec. 18. No. 1083a, June, 1947.

Dnieprostroy Dam and Power Station — A616

1946, Dec. 23 ***Perf. 12½***

1085	A616	30k sepia	65	42
1086	A616	60k chlky bl	1.00	60

A. P. Karpinsky A617

Nikolai A. Nekrasov A618

1947, Jan. 17 **Unwmk.**

1087	A617	30k dk grn	65	30
1088	A617	50k sepia	1.00	45

Centenary of the birth of Aleksandr P. Karpinsky (1847-1936), geologist.

Canceled to Order

Canceled sets of new issues have long been sold by the government. Values in the second ("used") column are for these canceled-to-order stamps. Postally used copies are worth more.

1946, Dec. 4

1089	A618	30k sepia	35	12
1090	A618	60k brown	45	20

125th anniversary of birth of Nikolai A. Nekrasov (1821-1878), poet.

Lenin's Mausoleum A619

Lenin A620

1947, Jan. 21

1091	A619	30k sl bl	45	10
1092	A619	30k dk grn	45	10
1093	A620	50k dk brn	65	10

23rd anniversary of the death of Lenin.

See Nos. 1197-1199.

F. P. Litke and Sailing Vessel — A621

N. M. Przewalski, Mare and Foal — A622

1947, Jan. 27

1094	A621	20k bl vio	30	12
1095	A621	20k sepia	30	12
1096	A622	60k ol brn	65	25
1097	A622	60k sepia	65	25

Issued to commemorate the centenary of the Soviet Union Geographical Society.

Nikolai E. Zhukovski A623

1947, Jan. 17

1098	A623	30k sepia	42	10
1099	A623	60k bl vio	55	15

Birth centenary of N. E. Zhukovski (1847-1921), scientist.

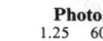

Stalin Prize Medal — A624

1946, Dec. 21 **Photo.**

1100	A624	30k blk brn	1.25	60

Russian Soldier A625

Military Instruction A626

Aviator, Sailor and Soldier A627

Perf. 12x12½, 12½x12, Imperf.

1947, Feb. 23 **Unwmk.**

1101	A625	20k sepia	25	20
1102	A626	30k sl bl	25	20
1103	A627	30k brown	25	20

29th anniversary of the Soviet Army.

Canceled-to-order stamps are often from remainders. Most collectors of canceled stamps prefer postally used specimens.

Arms of:

Russian Socialist Federated Soviet Republic A628

Armenian Socialist Soviet Republic A629

Azerbaijan S.S.R. A630

Byelorussian S.S.R. A631

Estonian S.S.R. — A632

Georgian S.S.R. — A633

Karelo Finnish S.S.R. A634

Kazakh S.S.R. A635

Kirghiz S.S.R. A636

Latvian S.S.R. A637

Lithuanian S.S.R. A638

Moldavian S.S.R. A639

Tadzhkistan S.S.R. A640

Turkmen S.S.R. A641

Ukrainian S.S.R. A642

Uzbek S.S.R. A643

Soviet Union — A644

1947 Unwmk. Photo. *Perf. 12½*

1104	A628	30k	hn brn	32	18
1105	A629	30k	chestnut	32	18
1106	A630	30k	ol brn	32	18
1107	A631	30k	ol grn	32	18
1108	A632	30k	vio blk	32	18
1109	A633	30k	dk vio brn	32	18
1110	A634	30k	dk vio	32	18
1111	A635	30k	dp org	32	18
1112	A636	30k	dk vio	32	18
1113	A637	30k	yel brn	32	18
1114	A638	30k	dk ol grn	32	18
1115	A639	30k	dk vio brn	32	18
1116	A640	30k	dk grn	32	18
1117	A641	30k	gray blk	32	18
1118	A642	30k	bl vio	35	18
1119	A643	30k	brown	28	18

Litho.

1120	A644	1r	dk brn, bl, gold & red	1.00	60
	Nos. 1104-1120 (17)			6.11	3.48

Aleksander S. Pushkin — A645

1947, Feb. Photo. *Perf. 12*

1121	A645	30k	sepia	55	18
1122	A645	50k	dk yel grn	75	20

Issued to commemorate the 110th anniversary of the death of Aleksander S. Pushkin (1799-1837), poet.

Classroom A646

Parade of Women — A647

1947, Mar. 11

1123	A646	15k	brt bl	75	45
1124	A647	30k	red	95	70

Issued to commemorate the International Day of Women, March 8, 1947.

Moscow Council Building A648

1947 *Perf. 12½*

1125	A648	30k	sep, gray bl & brick red	80	38

Issued to commemorate the 30th anniversary of the Moscow Soviet. Exists imperf. The imperf. exists also with gray blue omitted.

Both perf. and imperf. stamps exist in two sizes: 40x27mm. and 41x27mm.

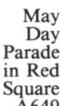

May Day Parade in Red Square A649

1947, June 10 *Perf. 12½*

1126	A649	30k	scarlet	35	30
1127	A649	1r	dk ol grn	90	45

Issued to publicize Labor Day, May 1, 1947.

Nos. 1062 and 1064 to 1066 Overprinted in Red: 800 лет Москвы 1147 – 1947 гг.

1947, Sept. *Perf. 12½x12*

1128	A593	20k	lt brn	35	12
1129	A593	50k	brown	50	18
1130	A597	60k	bl vio	75	20
1131	A598	1r	chnt brn	1.00	25

The overprint is arranged in four lines on No. 1131.

Crimes Bridge, Moscow — A650

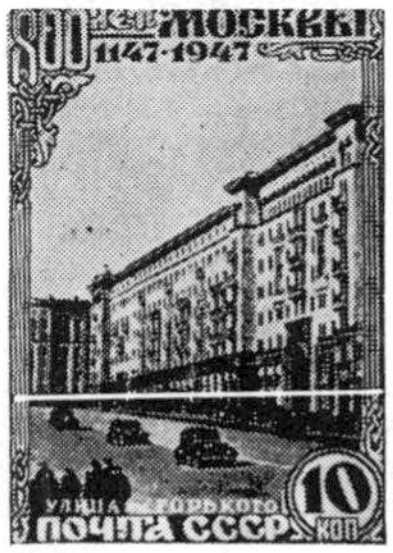
Gorki Street, Moscow A651

View of Kremlin, Moscow — A652

Designs: No. 1134, Central Telegraph Building. No. 1135, Kiev Railroad Station. No. 1136, Kazan Railroad Station. No. 1137, Kaluga St. No. 1138, Pushkin Square. 50k, View of Kremlin. No. 1141, Grand Kremlin Palace. No. 1142, "Old Moscow," by Vasnetsov. No. 1143, St. Basil Cathedral. 2r, View of Kremlin. 3r, View of Kremlin. 5r, Hotel Moscow and government building.

1947 Photo. *Perf. 12½*

Various Frames, Dated 1147-1947

1132	A650	5k	dk bl & dk brn	25	15
1133	A651	10k	red brn & brn blk	25	15
1134	A650	30k	brown	35	15
1135	A650	30k	dk Prus bl	35	15
1136	A650	30k	ultra	35	15
1137	A650	30k	dp yel grn	35	15
1138	A651	30k	yel grn	35	15
1139	A650	50k	dp yel grn	48	20
1140	A652	60k	red brn & brn blk	52	20
1141	A651	60k	gray bl	52	20
1142	A651	1r	dk vio	1.25	45

Typo.

Colors: Blue, Yellow and Red

1143	A651	1r	multi	1.25	45
1144	A651	2r	multi	2.25	90
1145	A650	3r	multi	4.00	90
a			Sheet of four, imperf.	24.00	20.00
1146	A650	5r	multi	6.75	1.75
	Nos. 1132-1146 (15)			19.27	6.10

Nos. 1128 to 1146 were issued to commemorate the 800th anniversary of the founding of Moscow.

Nos. 1143 to 1146 were printed in a single sheet containing a row of each denomination plus a row of labels.

No. 1145a is a souvenir sheet measuring 139½x172½mm., with national emblem and inscriptions in top and bottom margins.

Karamyshevsky Dam — A653

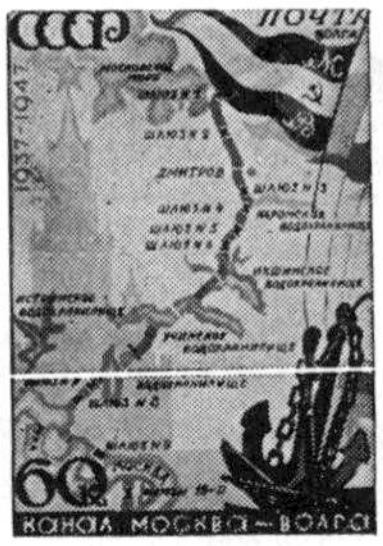
Map Showing Moscow-Volga Canal — A654

Designs: No. 1148, Direction towers, Yakromsky Lock. 45k, Yakromsky Pumping Station. 50k, Khimki Station. 1r, Lock No. 8.

1947, Sept. 7 Photo.

1147	A653	30k	sepia	52	15
1148	A653	30k	red brn	52	15
1149	A653	45k	hn brn	52	15
1150	A653	50k	brt ultra	52	15
1151	A654	60k	brt rose	52	15
1152	A653	1r	violet	75	28
	Nos. 1147-1152 (6)			3.35	1.03

Moscow-Volga Canal, 10th anniversary.

Elektrozavodskaya Station — A655

Mayakovsky Station A656

Planes and Flag A657

Designs (Moscow Subway scenes): No. 1154, Ismailovsky Station. No. 1155, Sokol Station. No. 1156, Stalinsky Station. No. 1158, Kiev Station.

1947, Sept.

1153	A655	30k	sepia	20	15
1154	A655	30k	bl blk	20	15
1155	A655	45k	yel brn	28	15
1156	A655	45k	dp vio	28	15
1157	A656	60k	hn brn	42	18
1158	A655	60k	dp yel grn	42	18
	Nos. 1153-1158 (6)			1.80	96

1947, Sept. 1

1159	A657	30k	dp vio	30	15
1160	A657	1r	brt ultra	70	18

Day of the Air Fleet. See Nos. 1246-1247.

Spasski Tower, Kremlin A658 — Agave Plant at Sukhumi A659

Gullripsh Sanatorium, Sukhumi A660

Perf. 12½

1947, Nov. Unwmk. Typo.

1161	A658	60k	dk red	1.75	42

See No. 1260.

1947, Nov. Photo.

Designs (Russian sanatoria): No. 1164, Peasants', Livadia. No. 1165, New Riviera. No. 1166, Abkhasia, New Afyon. No. 1167, Kemeri, near Riga. No. 1168, Kirov Memorial, Kislovodsk. No. 1169, Voroshilov Memorial, Sochi. No. 1170, Riza, Gagri. No. 1171, Zapadugol, Sochi.

1162	A659	30k	dk grn	25	9
1163	A660	30k	violet	25	9
1164	A660	30k	olive	25	9
1165	A660	30k	brown	25	9
1166	A660	30k	red brn	25	9
1167	A660	30k	blk vio	25	9
1168	A660	30k	brt ultra	25	9
1169	A660	30k	dk brn vio	25	9
1170	A659	30k	dk yel grn	25	9
1171	A660	30k	sepia	25	9
	Nos. 1162-1171 (10)			2.50	90

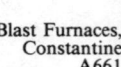

Blast Furnaces, Constantine A661

Maxim Gorki Theater, Stalingrad A666

Designs: 15k, No. 1174, Blast furnaces, Constantine. 20k, No. 1180, Kirov foundry, Makeevka. Nos. 1175, 1179, Agricultural machine plant, Rostov. Nos. 1176, 1181, Tractor plant, Kharkov. Nos. 1177, 1182, Tractor plant, Stalingrad.

1947, Nov. ***Perf. 12½, Imperf.***

1172	A661	15k	yel brn	15	15
1173	A661	20k	sepia	15	15
1174	A661	30k	vio brn	20	16
1175	A661	30k	dk grn	20	16
1176	A661	30k	brown	20	16
1177	A661	30k	blk brn	20	16
1178	A666	60k	vio brn	42	24
1179	A661	60k	yel brn	42	24
1180	A661	1r	org red	65	32
1181	A661	1r	red	65	32
1182	A661	1r	violet	65	32
	Nos. 1172-1182 (11)			3.89	2.38

Issued to commemorate the reconstruction of war-damaged cities and factories, and as Five-Year-Plan publicity.

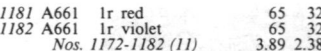

Revolutionists — A667

Designs: 30k, No. 1185, Revolutionists. 50k, 1r, Industry. No. 1186, 2r, Agriculture.

1947, Nov. ***Perf. 12½, Imperf.***
Frame in Dark Red

1183	A667	30k	grnsh blk	24	15
1184	A667	50k	bl blk	35	22
1185	A667	60k	brn blk	45	35
1186	A667	60k	brown	45	50
1187	A667	1r	black	75	60
1188	A667	2r	grnsh blk	1.50	85
	Nos. 1183-1188 (6)			3.74	2.67

30th anniversary of October Revolution.

Palace of the Arts (Winter Palace) A668 — Peter I Monument A669

Designs (Leningrad in 1947): 60k, Sts. Peter and Paul Fortress. 1r, Smolny Institute.

1948, Jan. 10 ***Perf. 12½***

1189	A668	30k	violet	55	18
1190	A669	50k	dk sl grn	90	24
1191	A668	60k	sepia	90	30
1192	A669	1r	dk brn vio	1.50	48

Issued to commemorate the 5th anniversary of the liberation of Leningrad from the German blockade.

Government Building, Kiev — A670

Designs: 50k, Dnieprostroy Dam. 60k, Wheat field and granary. 1r, Steel mill and coal mine.

1948, Jan. 25 ***Perf. 12½***

1193	A670	30k	indigo	32	18
1194	A670	50k	violet	42	22
1195	A670	60k	gldn brn	65	28
1196	A670	1r	sepia	1.00	45

Issued to commemorate the 30th anniversary of the Ukrainian Soviet Socialist Republic.

Lenin Types of 1947
Inscribed "1924-1948"

1948, Jan. 21 Unwmk.

1197	A619	30k	brn vio	35	24
1198	A619	60k	dk gray bl	75	30
1199	A620	60k	dp yel grn	75	30

24th anniversary of the death of Lenin.

Vasili I. Surikov A672 — Soviet Soldier and Artillery A675

Fliers and Planes — A676

1948, Feb. 15 Photo. ***Perf. 12***

1201	A672	30k	red brn	75	24
1202	A672	60k	dk grn	1.50	48

Issued to commemorate the centenary of the birth of Vasili Ivanovich Surikov, artist.

1948, Feb. 23

Designs: No. 1206, Soviet sailor. 60k, Military class.

1205	A675	30k	brown	52	25
1206	A675	30k	gray	52	24
1207	A676	30k	vio bl	52	24
1208	A676	60k	red brn	75	35

Hero Types of 1944

1948, Feb. 23

1209	A494	60k	dp grn	75	18
1210	A495	60k	yel brn	75	18
1211	A496	60k	vio bl	75	18

Nos. 1205 to 1211 were issued to commemorate the 30th anniversary of the Soviet army.

Karl Marx, Friedrich Engels and Communist Manifesto — A677

1948, Apr.

1212	A677	30k	black	22	12
1213	A677	50k	hn brn	35	18

Centenary of the Communist Manifesto.

Miner — A678 — Marine — A679

Aviator — A680 — Woman Farmer — A681

Arms of U.S.S.R. A682 — Scientist A683

Spasski Tower, Kremlin A684 — Soldier A685

1948 Photo.

1214	A678	5k	sepia	1.00	75
1215	A679	10k	violet	1.00	75
1216	A680	15k	brt bl	1.25	1.10
1217	A681	20k	brown	1.40	1.25
1218	A682	30k	hn brn	1.50	1.25
1219	A683	45k	brn vio	2.25	1.90
1220	A684	50k	brt bl	3.50	3.25
1221	A685	60k	brt grn	5.00	4.75
	Nos. 1214-1221 (8)			16.90	15.00

See Nos. 1306, 1343-1347, 1689.

May Day Parade in Red Square A686

1948, June 5 ***Perf. 12***

1222	A686	30k	dp car rose	32	14
1223	A686	60k	brt bl	60	20

Labor Day, May 1, 1948.

Vissarion G. Belinski (1811-48), Literary Critic — A687

1948, June 7 Unwmk. ***Perf. 12***

1224	A687	30k	brown	38	20
1225	A687	50k	dk grn	55	20
1226	A687	60k	purple	75	32

Aleksandr N. Ostrovski A690 A691

1948, June 10 Photo. ***Perf. 12***

1227	A690	30k	brt grn	70	15
1228	A691	60k	brown	90	22
1229	A691	1r	brn vio	1.40	35

Issued to commemorate the 125th anniversary of the birth of A. N. Ostrovski (1823-1886), playwright. Exist imperf. Value, set $100.

Ivan I. Shishkin — A692

"Field of Rye," by Shishkin
A693

Design: 60k, "Bears in a Forest," by Shishkin.

Photo. (30k, 1r), Typo. (50k, 60k)

1948, June 12

1230	A692	30k	dk grn & vio brn	90	55
1231	A693	50k	multi	1.10	55
1232	A693	60k	multi	1.75	70
1233	A692	1r	brn & bl blk	2.75	95

Issued to commemorate the 50th anniversary of the death of Ivan I. Shishkin (1832-1898), painter.

Industrial Expansion
A694

Public Gathering at Leningrad
A695

Photo., Frames Litho. in Carmine

1948, June 25

1234	A694	15k	red brn	24	18
1235	A695	30k	slate	35	25
1236	A694	60k	brn blk	60	38

Industrial five-year plan.

Planting Crops — A696

Designs: No. 1238, 1r, Gathering vegetables. 45k, No. 1241, Baling cotton. No. 1242, Harvesting grain.

1948, July 12 **Photo.**

1237	A696	30k	car rose	22	14
1238	A696	30k	bl grn	22	14
1239	A696	45k	red brn	40	20
1240	A696	50k	brn blk	50	20
1241	A696	60k	dk grn	50	20
1242	A696	60k	dk bl grn	50	20
1243	A696	1r	purple	85	32
			Nos. 1237-1243 (7)	3.19	1.40

Agricultural five-year plan.

Arms and Citizens of U.S.S.R.
A697

Soviet Miners
A698

Photo., Frames Litho. in Carmine

1948, July 25

1244	A697	30k	slate	90	48
1245	A697	60k	grnsh blk	1.10	65

Issued to commemorate the 25th anniversary of the Union of Soviet Socialist Republics.

Nos. 1159 and 1160 Overprinted in Red

ИЮЛЬ
1948
ГОДА

1948, Aug. 24 ***Perf. 12½***

1246	A657	30k	dp vio	1.75	90
1247	A657	1r	brt ultra	1.75	90

Air Fleet Day, 1948. On sale one day.

1948, Aug. **Photo.** ***Perf. 12½x12***

Designs: 60k, Scene in mine. 1r, Miner's badge.

1248	A698	30k	blue	20	15
1249	A698	60k	purple	40	20
1250	A698	1r	green	65	25

Miners' Day, August 29th.

A. A. Zhdanov
A699

Russian Sailor
A700

1948, Sept. 3

1251	A699	40k	slate	65	35

Issued in tribute to Andrei A. Zhdanov, statesman, 1896-1948.

1948, Sept. 12 ***Perf. 12***

1252	A700	30k	bl grn	30	18
1253	A700	60k	brt bl	60	28

Navy Day, Sept. 12.

Slalom
A701

Motorcyclist
A702

Designs: No. 1254, Foot race. 30k, Soccer game. 45k, Motorboat race. 50k, Diving.

1948, Sept. 15 ***Perf. 12½x12***

1253A	A701	15k	dk bl	85	24
1254	A702	15k	violet	85	24
1254A	A702	20k	dk sl bl	1.00	24
1255	A701	30k	brown	1.10	24
1256	A701	45k	sepia	1.25	24
1257	A702	50k	blue	2.00	32
			Nos. 1253A-1257 (6)	7.05	1.52

Tankmen Group — A703

Design: 1r, Tank parade.

1948, Sept. 25

1258	A703	30k	sepia	1.25	32
1259	A703	1r	rose	3.50	50

Day of the Tankmen, Sept. 25.

Spasski Tower Type of 1947

1948 **Litho.** ***Perf. 12x12½***

1260	A658	1r	brn red	1.10	30

No. 1260 was re-issued in 1954-56 in slightly smaller format: 14½x21½mm., instead of 14¾x22mm. and in a paler shade. See note after No. 738.

Train — A704

Designs: 60k, Auto and bus at intersection. 1r, Steamships at anchor.

1948, Sept. 30 **Photo.** ***Perf. 12½x12***

1261	A704	30k	brown	1.10	70
1262	A704	50k	dk grn	1.50	80
1263	A704	60k	blue	2.50	80
1264	A704	1r	bl vio	3.25	1.40

Transportation five-year plan.

Horses
A705

Design: 60k, Dairy farm.

1948, Sept. 30 ***Perf. 12***

1265	A705	30k	sl gray	1.10	50
1266	A705	60k	brt grn	2.00	75
1267	A705	1r	brown	2.75	1.00

Livestock five-year plan.

Pouring Molten Metal — A706

Designs: 60k, 1r, Iron pipe manufacture.

1948, Oct. 14 ***Perf. 12½***

1268	A706	30k	purple	85	50
1269	A706	50k	brown	1.00	65
1270	A706	60k	carmine	1.25	1.00
1271	A706	1r	dl bl	2.50	1.65

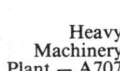

Heavy Machinery Plant — A707

Design: 60k, Pump station interior.

1948, Oct. 14

1272	A707	30k	purple	75	25
1273	A707	50k	sepia	1.40	65
1274	A707	60k	brown	2.00	75

Nos. 1268-1274 were issued to publicize the five-year plan for steel, iron and machinery industries.

Khachatur Abovian — A708

1948, Oct. 16 ***Perf. 12x12½***

1275	A708	40k	purple	1.50	70
1276	A708	50k	dp grn	1.75	70

Issued to commemorate the centenary of the death of Khachatur Abovian (1809-1848), Armenian writer and poet.

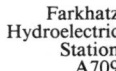

Farkhatz Hydroelectric Station
A709

Design: 60k, Zouiev Hydroelectric Station.

1948, Oct. 24 ***Perf. 12½***

1277	A709	30k	green	55	45
1278	A709	60k	red	1.25	75
1279	A709	1r	car rose	2.00	1.25

Electrification five-year plan.

Coal Mine — A710

Designs: No. 1282, 1r, Oil field and tank cars.

1948, Oct. 24

1280	A710	30k	sepia	95	35
1281	A710	60k	brown	1.10	50
1282	A710	60k	red brn	1.10	50
1283	A710	1r	bl grn	1.90	75

Five-year plan of coal mining and oil production.

Flying Model Planes — A712

Marching Pioneers
A713

Pioneers Saluting — A714

Designs: 60k, Pioneer bugler. 1r, Pioneers at campfire.

1948, Oct. 26 ***Perf. 12½***

1284	A712	30k	dk bl grn	1.75	1.25
1285	A713	45k	dk vio	2.00	1.65
1286	A714	45k	dp car	2.00	1.65
1287	A714	60k	dp ultra	2.75	2.25
1288	A713	1r	dp bl	6.50	4.00
			Nos. 1284-1288 (5)	15.00	10.80

Issued to honor the Young Pioneers, a Russian youth organization, and to publicize governmental supervision of children's summer vacations.

Marching Youths
A715

An enhanced introduction to the Scott Catalogue begins on Page V. A thorough understanding of the material presented there will greatly aid your use of the catalogue itself.

Farm Girl — A716

League Members and Flag — A717

Designs: 50k, Communist students. 1r, Flag and badges. 2r, Young worker.

1948, Oct. 29 ***Perf. 12½***
Inscribed: "1918 1948 XXX"

1289 A715	20k vio brn		55	48
1290 A716	25k rose red		85	60
1291 A717	40k brn & red		1.25	75
1292 A715	50k bl grn		2.00	95
1293 A717	1r multi		4.00	1.90
1294 A716	2r purple		8.00	4.00
	Nos. 1289-1294 (6)		16.65	8.68

Issued to commemorate the 30th anniversary of the Young Communist League (Komsomol).

Stage of Moscow Art Theater A719

K. S. Stanislavski V. I. Nemirovich Danchenko A720

1948, Nov. 1 ***Perf. 12½***

1295 A719	40k gray bl	1.25	65
1296 A720	1r vio brn	1.65	1.10

Issued to commemorate the 50th anniversary of the establishment of the Moscow Art Theater.

Flag and Moscow Buildings — A721

1948, Nov. 7 ***Perf. 12½***

1297 A721	40k red	1.50	90
1298 A721	1r green	2.25	1.40

31st anniversary of October Revolution.

House of Unions, Moscow A722

Player's Badge (Rook and Chessboard) A723

1948, Nov. 20 ***Perf. 12½***

1299 A722	30k grnsh bl	55	30
1300 A723	40k violet	1.25	38
1301 A722	50k org brn	1.65	45

16th Chess Championship.

Artillery Salute — A724

1948, Nov. 19 ***Perf. 12½***

1302 A724	30k blue	1.25	1.00
1303 A724	1r rose car	1.75	1.65

Artillery Day, Nov. 19, 1948.

V. P. Stasov A725

Stasov and Barracks of Paul's Regiment, Petrograd A726

1948, Nov. 27 **Unwmk.**

1304 A725	40k brown	85	50
1305 A726	1r sepia	1.65	75

Vasili Petrovich Stasov, architect (1769-1848).

Arms Type of 1948

1948 **Litho.** ***Perf. 12x12½***

1306 A682	40k brn red	3.50	20

Y. M. Sverdlov Monument A727

Design: 40k, Lenin Street, Sverdlovsk.

1948 **Photo.** ***Perf. 12½***

1307 A727	30k blue	15	9
1308 A727	40k purple	20	12
1309 A727	1r brt grn	50	15

Issued to commemorate the 225th anniversary of the city of Sverdlovsk (before 1924, Ekaterinburg). Exist imperf.

"Swallow's Nest," Crimea A729

Hot Spring, Piatigorsk A730

Shoreline, Sukhumi A731

Tree-lined Walk, Sochi A732

Formal Gardens, Sochi — A733

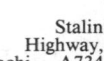

Stalin Highway, Sochi — A734

Colonnade, Kislovodsk A735

Seascape, Gagri — A736

1948, Dec. 30 ***Perf. 12½***

1310 A729	40k brown	52	15
1311 A730	40k brt red vio	52	15
1312 A731	40k dk grn	52	15
1313 A732	40k violet	52	15
1314 A733	40k dk pur	52	15
1315 A734	40k dk bl grn	52	15
1316 A735	40k brt bl	52	15
1317 A736	40k dk bl grn	52	15
	Nos. 1310-1317 (8)	4.16	1.20

Byelorussian S.S.R. Arms — A737

1949, Jan. 4

1318 A737	40k hn brn	1.00	48
1319 A737	1r bl grn	2.25	90

Issued to commemorate the 30th anniversary of the formation of the Ryelorussian Soviet Socialist Republic.

Mikhail V. Lomonosov A738

Lomonosov Museum, Leningrad A739

1949, Jan. 10

1320 A738	40k red brn	90	32
1321 A738	50k green	1.10	32
1322 A739	1r dp bl	2.25	75

Cape Dezhnev (East Cape) — A740

Design: 1r, Map and Dezhnev's ship.

1949, Jan. 30

1323 A740	40k ol grn	2.50	95
1324 A740	1r gray	4.25	1.90

Issued to commemorate the 300th anniversary of the discovery of the strait between Asia and America by S. I. Dezhnev.

Souvenir Sheet

A741

1949, Dec. ***Imperf.***

1325 A741	Sheet of four	72.50	100.00
a.	40k *Stalin's birthplace, Gorki*	12.00	18.00
b.	40k *Lenin & Stalin, Leningrad, 1917*	12.00	18.00
c.	40k *Lenin & Stalin, Gorki*	12.00	18.00
d.	40k *Marshal Stalin*	12.00	18.00

70th birthday of Joseph V. Stalin.

Lenin Mausoleum — A742

1949, Jan. 21 ***Perf. 12½***

1326 A742	40k ol grn & org brn	1.00	90
1327 A742	1r gray blk & org brn	2.00	1.40
a.	Sheet of four	87.50	87.50

25th anniversary of the death of Lenin. No. 1327a exists imperf. Value $475.

Admiral S. O. Makarov A743

Kirov Military Medical Academy A744

Professors Botkin, Pirogov and Sechenov A745

1949, Mar. 15

1328 A743	40k blue	1.25	90
1329 A743	1r red brn	1.75	1.40

Issued to commemorate the centenary of the birth of Admiral Stepan Osipovich Makarov, shipbuilder.

1949, Mar. 24

1330 A744	40k red brn	1.10	1.00
1331 A745	50k blue	1.50	1.50
1332 A744	1r bl grn	2.50	2.25

Issued to commemorate the 150th anniversary of the foundation of Kirov Military Medical Academy, Leningrad.

Soviet Soldier
A746

1949, Mar. 16 **Photo.**

1333	A746	40k rose red	4.00	4.00

31st anniversary of the Soviet army.

Textile Weaving A747 — Political Leadership A748

Designs: 25k, Preschool teaching. No. 1337, School teaching. No. 1338, Farm women. 1r, Women athletes.

1949, Mar. 8 ***Perf. 12½***
Inscribed: "8 МАРТА 1949г"

1334	A747	20k dk vio	15	12
1335	A747	25k blue	20	12
1336	A748	40k hn brn	32	12
1337	A747	50k sl gray	50	18
1338	A747	50k brown	50	18
1339	A747	1r green	1.10	30
1340	A748	2r cop red	1.75	95
		Nos. 1334-1340 (7)	4.52	1.97

International Women's Day, Mar. 8.

Medal Types of 1945

1948-49 **Engr.**

1341	A517	2r grn ('49)	1.75	85
1341A	A517	2r vio brn	6.75	9.00
1342	A518	3r brn car ('49)	2.25	85

Types of 1948

1949 **Litho.** ***Perf. 12x12½***

1343	A678	15k black	32	15
1344	A681	20k green	32	15
1345	A680	25k dk bl	50	15
1346	A683	30k brown	60	20
1347	A684	50k dp bl	1.50	55
		Nos. 1343-1347 (5)	3.24	1.20

The 20k, 25k and 30k were re-issued in 1954-56 in slightly smaller format. The 20k measures 14x21mm., instead of 15x22 mm.; 25k, 14½x21mm., instead of 14½x 21¾mm., and 30k, 14½x21mm., instead of 15x22mm.

The smaller-format 20k is olive green, the 25k, slate blue. The 15k was reissued in 1959 (?) in smaller format: 14x21mm., instead of 14½x22mm. See note after No. 738.

See No. 1709.

V. R. Williams
A749

1949, Apr. 18 **Photo.** ***Perf. 12½***

1348	A749	25k bl grn	65	65
1349	A749	50k brown	1.00	1.00

Issued to honor Vasili R. Williams (1863-1939), agricultural scientist.

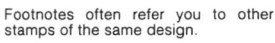

Footnotes often refer you to other stamps of the same design.

Russian Citizens and Flag
A750

A. S. Popov and Radio
A751

Popov Demonstrating Radio to Admiral Makarov
A752

1949, Apr. 30 ***Perf. 12½***

1350	A750	40k scarlet	1.00	65
1351	A750	1r bl grn	2.00	1.25

Labor Day, May 1, 1949.

1949, May **Unwmk.**

1352	A751	40k purple	1.25	48
1353	A752	50k brown	2.00	65
1354	A751	1r bl grn	4.00	1.25

Issued to commemorate the 54th anniversary of Popov's discovery of the principles of radio.

Soviet Publications
A753

Reading Pravda
A754

1949, May 4

1355	A753	40k crimson	1.00	95
1356	A754	1r dk vio	2.00	1.10

Issued to commemorate Soviet Press Day.

I. V. Michurin
A755

A. S. Pushkin, 1822
A756

Pushkin Reading Poem — A757

1949, July 28

1357	A755	40k bl gray	1.00	50
1358	A755	1r brt grn	2.25	1.10

Issued to honor Ivan Michurin (1855-1925), agricultural scientist.

1949, June **Unwmk.**

Designs: No. 1360, Pushkin portrait by Kiprensky, 1827. 1r, Pushkin Museum, Boldino.

1359	A756	25k ind & sep	50	22
1360	A756	40k org brn & sep	1.25	50
a		Souvenir sheet of 4	18.00	16.00
1361	A757	40k brn red & dk vio	1.25	65
1362	A757	1r choc & sl	2.75	1.25
1363	A757	2r brn & vio bl	4.50	2.00
		Nos. 1359-1363 (5)	10.25	4.62

Issued to commemorate the 150th anniversary of the birth of Aleksander S. Pushkin.

Horizontal rows of Nos. 1361 and 1363 contain alternate stamps and labels.

No. 1360a contains two each of Nos. 1359 and 1360, imperf., with marginal inscriptions and floral decorations in brown. Size: 110x142mm. Issued July 20.

River Tugboat
A758

Design: 1r, Freighter, motorship "Bolshaya Volga."

1949, July, 13

1364	A758	40k sl bl	2.00	1.10
1365	A758	1r red brn	3.00	1.65

Issued to commemorate the centenary of the establishment of the Sormovo Machine and Boat Works.

VCSPS No. 3, Kislovodsk
A759

State Sanatoria for Workers: No. 1367, Communications, Khosta. No. 1368, Sanatorium No. 3, Khosta. No. 1369, Electric power, Khosta. No. 1370, Sanatorium No. 1, Kislovodsk. No. 1371, State Theater, Sochi. No. 1372, Frunze Sanatorium, Sochi. No. 1373, Sanatorium at Machindzhaury. No. 1374, Clinical, Chaltubo. No. 1375, Sanatorium No. 41, Zheleznovodsk.

1949, Sept. 10 **Photo.** ***Perf. 12½***

1366	A759	40k violet	22	10
1367	A759	40k black	22	10
1368	A759	40k carmine	22	10
1369	A759	40k blue	22	10
1370	A759	40k vio brn	22	10
1371	A759	40k red org	22	10
1372	A759	40k dk brn	22	10
1373	A759	40k green	22	10
1374	A759	40k red brn	22	10
1375	A759	40k bl grn	22	10
		Nos. 1366-1375 (10)	2.20	1.00

Regatta
A760

Designs (Sports, "1949"): 25k, Kayak race. 30k, Swimming. 40k, Bicycling. No. 1380, Soccer. 50k, Mountain climbing. 1r, Parachuting. 2r, High jump.

1949, Aug. 7

1376	A760	20k brt bl	32	10
1377	A760	25k bl grn	40	10
1378	A760	30k violet	55	10
1379	A760	40k red brn	70	10
1380	A760	40k green	70	10
1381	A760	50k dk bl gray	75	10
1382	A760	1r car rose	1.25	50
1383	A760	2r gray blk	2.75	60
		Nos. 1376-1383 (8)	7.42	1.70

V. V. Dokuchayev and Fields — A761

1949, Aug. 8

1384	A761	40k brown	40	30
1385	A761	1r green	85	50

Issued to honor Vasili V. Dokuchayev (1846-1903), pioneer soil scientist.

Vasili Bazhenov and Lenin Library, Moscow
A762

1949, Aug. 14 **Photo.** ***Perf. 12½***

1386	A762	40k violet	70	28
1387	A762	1r red brn	1.25	40

Issued to commemorate the 150th anniversary of the death of Vasili Bazhenov, architect.

A. N. Radishchev
A763

Ivan P. Pavlov
A764

1949, Aug. 31

1388	A763	40k bl grn	70	52
1389	A763	1r gray	1.65	1.10

Issued to commemorate the 200th anniversary of the birth of Aleksandr N. Radishchev, writer.

1949, Sept. 30 **Unwmk.**

1390	A764	40k dp brn	50	16
1391	A764	1r gray blk	1.25	28

Issued to commemorate the centenary of the birth of Ivan P. Pavlov (1849-1936), Russian physiologist.

Globe Encircled by Letters
A765

1949, Oct. ***Perf. 12½***

1392	A765	40k org brn & ind	38	15
a		Imperf.	3.00	2.25
1393	A765	50k ind & gray vio	38	15
a		Imperf.	3.00	2.25

Issued to commemorate the 75th anniversary of the formation of the Universal Postal Union.

Cultivators
A766

Map of European Russia — A767

Designs: No. 1395, Peasants in grain field. 50k, Rural scene. 2r, Old man and children.

1949, Oct. 18 ***Perf. 12½***

1394	A766	25k green	40	38
1395	A766	40k violet	80	75
1396	A767	40k gray grn & blk	80	75
1397	A766	50k dp bl	1.10	95
1398	A766	1r gray blk	2.00	1.65
1399	A766	2r dk brn	4.50	4.00
		Nos. 1394-1399 (6)	9.60	8.48

Issued to encourage agricultural development.

Nos. 1394, 1398, 1399 measure 33x19mm. Nos. 1395, 1397 measure 33x22mm.

Maly (Little) Theater, Moscow
A768

M. N. Ermolova, I. S. Mochalov, A. N. Ostrovski, M. S. Shchepkin and P. M. Sadovsky
A769

1949, Oct. 27

1400	A768	40k green	70	18
1401	A768	50k red org	90	18
1402	A769	1r dp brn	1.65	35

Issued to commemorate the 125th anniversary of the Maly Theater (State Academic Little Theater).

Chapayev Type of 1944

1949, Oct. 22 **Photo.**

1403	A495	40k brn org	3.25	2.75

Portrait and outer frame same as type A495. Dates "1919 1949" are in upper corners. Other details differ.

Issued to commemorate the 30th anniversary of the death of V. I. Chapayev, a hero of the 1918 civil war.

Ivan S. Nikitin — A770

1949, Oct. 24 **Unwmk.**

1404	A770	40k brown	70	18
1405	A770	1r sl bl	95	30

125th anniv. of the birth of Ivan Savvich Nikitin, Russian poet (1824-1861).

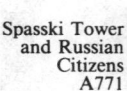

Spasski Tower and Russian Citizens
A771

1949, Oct. 29 ***Perf. 12½***

1406	A771	40k brn org	1.00	32
1407	A771	1r dp grn	1.75	52

October Revolution, 32nd anniversary.

Sheep, Cattle and Farm Woman — A772

1949, Nov. 2

1408	A772	40k chocolate	38	15
1409	A772	1r violet	75	28

Issued to encourage better cattle breeding in Russia.

Arms and Flag of U.S.S.R. — A773

1949, Nov. 30 **Engr.** ***Perf. 12***

1410	A773	40k carmine	3.75	3.75

Issued to commemorate Constitution Day.

Electric Trolley Car — A774

Ski Jump — A775

Designs: 40k, 1r, Diesel train. 50k, Steam train.

1949, Nov. 19 **Photo.** ***Perf. 12½***

1411	A774	25k red	65	10
1412	A774	40k violet	80	15
1413	A774	50k brown	1.25	15
1414	A774	1r Prus grn	2.75	32

1949, Nov. 12 **Unwmk.**

Designs: 40k, Girl on rings. 50k, Ice hockey. 1r, Weight lifter. 2r, Wolf hunt.

1415	A775	20k dk grn	60	12
1416	A775	40k org red	1.10	15
1417	A775	50k dp bl	1.75	15
1418	A775	1r red	2.25	25
1419	A775	2r violet	4.75	80
		Nos. 1415-1419 (5)	10.45	1.47

Textile Mills — A776

Designs: 25k, Irrigation system. 40k, 1r, Government buildings, Stalinabad. 50k, University of Medicine.

1949, Dec. 7 **Photo.** ***Perf. 12***

1420	A776	20k blue	30	12
1421	A776	25k green	35	12
1422	A776	40k red org	42	20
1423	A776	50k violet	60	24
1424	A776	1r gray blk	1.10	48
		Nos. 1420-1424 (5)	2.77	1.16

Tadzhik Republic, 20th anniv.

"Russia" versus "War" — A777

Byelorussians and Flag — A778

1949, Dec. 25

1425	A777	40k rose car	35	15
1426	A777	50k blue	42	22

Issued to portray Russia as the defender of world peace.

1949, Dec. 23 **Unwmk.**

Design: No. 1428, Ukrainians and flag.

Inscribed: "1939 1949"

1427	A778	40k org red	2.00	80
1428	A778	40k dp org	2.00	80

Issued to commemorate the 10th anniversary of the return of western territories to the Byelorussian and Ukrainian Republics.

Teachers College
A779

Designs: 25k, State Theater. No. 1431, Government House. No. 1432, Navol Street, Tashkent. 1r, Fergana Canal. 2r, Kuigonyarsk Dam.

1950, Jan. 3

1429	A779	20k blue	18	8
1430	A779	25k gray blk	18	8
1431	A779	40k red org	40	18
1432	A779	40k violet	40	18
1433	A779	1r green	95	30
1434	A779	2r brown	1.90	40
		Nos. 1429-1434 (6)	4.01	1.22

Uzbek Republic, 25th anniversary.

Lenin at Razliv — A780

Lenin's Office, Kremlin
A781

Design: 1r, Lenin Museum.

1950, Jan. Unwmk. Litho. ***Perf. 12***

1435	A780	40k dk grn & dk brn	30	9
1436	A781	50k dk brn, red brn & grn	52	20
1437	A781	1r dk brn, dk grn & cr	90	30

26th anniversary of the death of Lenin.

Textile Factory, Ashkhabad
A782

Designs: 40k, 1r, Power dam and Turkmenian arms. 50k, Rug making.

1950, Jan. 7 **Photo.**

1438	A782	25k gray blk	40	15
1439	A782	40k brown	60	20
1440	A782	50k green	80	30
1441	A782	1r purple	1.75	60

Turkmen Republic, 25th anniversary.

Motion Picture Projection
A783

1950, Feb.

1442	A783	25k brown	4.50	3.75

Issued to commemorate the 30th anniversary of the Soviet motion picture industry.

Voter
A784

Kremlin
A785

1950, Mar. 8

1443	A784	40k grn, *yel*	1.50	1.75
1444	A785	1r rose car	2.50	3.00

Issued to publicize the elections to the Supreme Soviet, March 12, 1950.

Pavlik Morozov Monument, Moscow
A786

Globes and Communication Symbols
A787

1950, Mar. 16 ***Perf. 12½***

1445	A786	40k blk brn & red	1.25	1.50
1446	A786	1r dk grn & red	2.75	2.25

Issued to mark the unveiling of a monument to Pavlik Morozov, Pioneer.

1950, Apr. 1

1447	A787	40k dp grn	1.75	1.75
1448	A787	50k dp bl	2.00	1.75

Issued to publicize the meeting of the Post, Telegraph, Telephone and Radio Trade Unions.

State Polytechnic Museum
A788

State Museum of Oriental Cultures
A789

State University Museum — A790

Pushkin Museum
A791

Museums: No. 1451, Tretiakov Gallery. No. 1452, Timiryazev Biologic Museum. No. 1453, Lenin Museum. No. 1454, Museum of the Revolution. No. 1456, State History Museum.

Inscribed: "MOCKBA 1949" in Top Frame

1950, Mar. 28 Litho. *Perf. 12½*
Multicolored Centers

1449	A788	40k dk bl	40	18
1450	A789	40k dk bl	40	18
1451	A789	40k green	40	18
1452	A789	40k dk brn	40	18
1453	A789	40k ol brn	40	18
1454	A789	40k claret	40	18
1455	A790	40k red	40	18
1456	A790	40k chocolate	40	18
1457	A791	40k brn vio	40	18
		Nos. 1449-1457 (9)	3.60	1.62

Russians of Three Races A792

A. S. Shcherbakov A793

Design: 1r, Four Russians and communist banner (horiz.).

1950, May 1 Photo. *Perf. 12½*

1458	A792	40k org red & gray	1.50	1.65
1459	A792	1r red & gray blk	3.00	3.25

Issued to publicize Labor Day, May 1, 1950.

1950, May Unwmk.

1460	A793	40k blk, *pale bl*	70	42
1461	A793	1r dk grn, *buff*	1.50	1.10

Shcherbakov, political leader (1901-1945).

Monument A794

Victory Medal A795

Wmk. 293- Hammer and Sickle, Multiple

Perf. 12x12½
1950 Photo. Wmk. 293

1462	A794	40k dk brn & red	2.50	2.25

Unwmk.

1463	A795	1r car rose	3.00	2.75

Issued to commemorate Russia's 5th International Victory Day, May 9, 1950.

A. V. Suvorov A796

Farmers Studying Agronomic Techniques A797

Designs: 50k, Suvorov crossing Alps, 32½x47mm. 60k, Badge, flag and marchers, 24x39½mm. 2r, Suvorov facing left, 19x33½ mm.

Various Designs and Sizes
Dated "1800 1950"

1950 *Perf. 12, 12½x12*

1464	A796	40k bl, *pink*	1.10	42
1465	A796	50k brn, *pink*	1.25	55
1466	A796	60k gray blk, *pale gray*	1.50	1.10
1467	A796	1r dk brn, *lem*	2.50	1.10
1468	A796	2r grnsh bl	4.50	3.00
		Nos. 1464-1468 (5)	10.85	6.17

Issued to commemorate the 150th anniversary of the death of Field Marshal Count Aleksandr V. Suvorov (1730-1800).

1950, June *Perf. 12½*

Designs: No. 1470, 1r, Sowing on collective farm.

1469	A797	40k dk grn, *pale grn*	85	60
1470	A797	40k gray blk, *buff*	85	60
1471	A797	1r bl, *lem*	2.25	1.50

George M. Dimitrov A798

Opera and Ballet Theater, Baku A799

1950, July 2

1472	A798	40k gray blk, *cit*	85	55
1473	A798	1r gray blk, *sal*	2.00	1.10

Issued to commemorate the first anniversary of the death of George M. Dimitrov (1882-1949), Bulgarian-born revolutionary leader and Comintern official.

1950, July Photo. *Perf. 12½*

Designs: 40k, Azerbaijan Academy of Science. 1r, Stalin Avenue, Baku.

1474	A799	25k dp grn, *cit*	25	16
1475	A799	40k brn, *pink*	60	28
1476	A799	1r gray blk, *buff*	1.75	1.10

Azerbaijan S.S.R., 30th anniversary.

Victory Theater A800

Lenin Street A801

Designs: 50k, Gorky Theater. 1r, Monument marking Stalingrad defense line.

1950, June

1477	A800	20k dk bl	48	32
1478	A801	40k green	90	65
1479	A801	50k red org	1.25	1.00
1480	A801	1r gray	2.75	2.00

Restoration of Stalingrad.

Moscow Subway Stations: "Park of Culture" A802

Designs: No. 1482, Kaluzskaya station. No. 1483, Taganskaya. No. 1484, Kurskaya. No. 1485, Paveletskaya. No. 1486, Park of Culture. No. 1487, Taganskaya.

1950, July 30
Size: 33½x23mm.

1481	A802	40k dp car	60	14
1482	A802	40k dk grn, *buff*	60	14
1483	A802	40k dp bl, *buff*	60	14
1484	A802	1r dk brn, *cit*	1.25	40
1485	A802	1r purple	1.25	40
1486	A802	1r dk grn, *cit*	1.25	40

Size: 33x18½mm.

1487	A802	1r blk, *pink*	1.10	28
		Nos. 1481-1487 (7)	6.65	1.90

Socialist Peoples and Flags A803

1950, Aug. 4 Unwmk. *Perf. 12½*

1488	A803	40k multi	45	14
1489	A803	50k multi	95	20
1490	A803	1r multi	1.10	30

Trade Union Building, Riga — A804

Opera and Ballet Theater, Riga -- A805

Designs: 40k, Latvian Cabinet building. 50k, Monument to Jan Rainis. 1r, Riga State Univ. 2r, Latvian Academy of Sciences.

1950 Photo. *Perf. 12½*

1491	A804	25k dk brn	40	20
1492	A804	40k scarlet	48	48
1493	A804	50k dk grn	1.10	48
1494	A805	60k dp bl	1.25	48
1495	A805	1r lilac	1.90	1.00
1496	A804	2r sepia	3.25	1.25
		Nos. 1491-1496 (6)	8.38	3.89

Issued to commemorate the 10th anniversary of the formation of the Latvian Soviet Socialist Republic.

Lithuanian Academy of Sciences A806

Marite Melnik A807

Design: 1r, Cabinet building.

1950

1497	A806	25k dp bl, *bluish*	45	32
1498	A807	40k brown	95	65
1499	A806	1r scarlet	1.90	1.65

Issued to commemorate the 10th anniversary of the formation of the Lithuanian Soviet Socialist Republic.

Stalingrad Square, Tallinn A808

Victor Kingisepp A809

Designs: 40k, Government building, Tallinn. 50k, Estonia Theater, Tallinn.

1950

1500	A808	25k dk grn	60	50
1501	A808	40k scarlet	70	65
1502	A808	50k bl, *yel*	1.10	1.00
1503	A809	1r brn, *bl*	2.00	2.00

Issued to commemorate the 10th anniversary of the formation of the Estonian Soviet Socialist Republic.

Citizens Signing Appeal for Peace A810

Children and Governess A811

Design: 50k, Peace Demonstration.

1950, Oct. 16 Photo.

1504	A810	40k red, *sal*	55	50
1505	A811	40k black	55	50
1506	A811	50k dk red	1.00	75
1507	A810	1r brn, *sal*	1.65	1.50

F. G. Bellingshausen, M. P. Lazarev and Globe — A812

Route of Antarctic Expedition — A813

1950, Oct. 25 Unwmk. *Perf. 12½*
Blue Paper

1508	A812	40k dk car	9.25	8.00
1509	A813	1r purple	18.00	8.00

Issued to commemorate the 130th anniversary of the Bellingshausen-Lazarev expedition to the Antarctic.

M. V. Frunze A814

M. I. Kalinin A815

1950, Oct. 31

1510	A814	40k bl, *buff*	1.90	1.50
1511	A814	1r brn, *bl*	3.50	3.50

Issued to commemorate the 25th anniversary of the death of M. V. Frunze, military strategist.

1950, Nov. 20 Engr.

1512	A815	40k dp grn	60	55
1513	A815	1r redsh brn	1.40	95
1514	A815	5r violet	3.25	1.90

Issued to commemorate the 75th anniversary of the birth of M. I. Kalinin, Soviet Russia's first president.

Gathering Grapes
A816

Armenian Government Building
A817

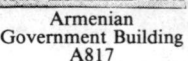

G. M. Sundukian
A818

1950, Nov. 29 **Photo.** ***Perf. 12½***

1515 A816 20k dp bl, *buff* 60 45
1516 A817 40k red org, *bl* 1.10 95
1517 A818 1r ol gray, *yel* 2.50 2.25

Issued to commemorate the 30th anniversary of the formation of the Armenian Republic. The 1 ruble also commemorates the birth of G. M. Sundukian, playwright.

Apartment Building, Koteljnicheskaya Quay — A819

Hotel, Kalanchevkaya Square — A820

Various Buildings

Inscribed: "Mockba, 1950"

1950, Dec. 2 **Unwmk.**

1518 A819 1r red brn, *buff* 18.00 21.00
1519 A819 1r gray blk 18.00 21.00
1520 A819 1r brn, *bl* 18.00 21.00
1521 A819 1r dk grn, *bl* 18.00 21.00
1522 A820 1r dp bl, *buff* 18.00 21.00
1523 A820 1r blk, *buff* 18.00 21.00
1524 A820 1r red org 18.00 21.00
1525 A819 1r dk grn, *yel* 18.00 21.00
Nos. 1518-1525 (8) 144.00 168.00

Skyscrapers planned for Moscow.

Spasski Tower, Kremlin — A821

1950, Dec. 4

1526 A821 1r dk grn, red brn & yel brn 5.50 4.00

October Revolution, 33rd anniversary.

Golden Autumn by Levitan
A822

I. I. Levitan
A823

1950, Dec. 6 **Litho.** ***Perf. 12½***

1527 A822 40k multi 2.75 55

Perf. 12

Photo.

1528 A823 50k red brn 3.75 55

I. I. Levitan, painter (1861-90).

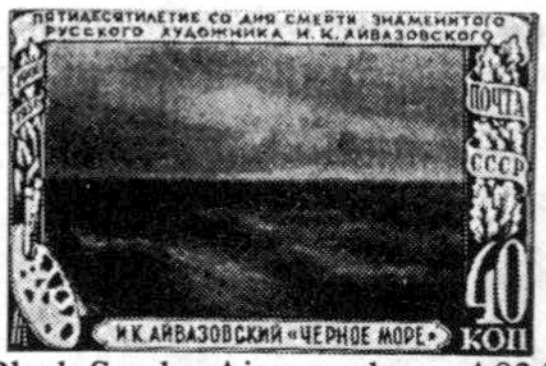

Black Sea by Aivazovsky — A824

I. K. Aivazovsky
A825

Design: 50k, "Ninth Surge."

1950, Dec. 6 **Litho.**

Multicolored Centers

1529 A824 40k chocolate 95 15
1530 A824 50k chocolate 95 30
1531 A825 1r indigo 1.25 70

50th anniversary of the death of Ivan K. Aivazovsky (1817-1900), painter.

Flags and Newspapers Iskra and Pravda
A826

Presidium of Supreme Soviet, Alma-Ata
A827

Design: 1r, Flag and profiles of Lenin and Stalin.

1950, Dec. 23 **Photo.**

1532 A826 40k gray blk & red 11.00 8.50
1533 A826 1r dk brn & red 14.00 11.00

50th anniversary of the first issue of the newspaper Iskra.

1950, Dec. 27

Design: 1r, Opera and Ballet Theater.

Inscribed: "ALMA-ATA" in Cyrillic

1534 A827 40k gray blk, *bl* 1.90 2.25
1535 A827 1r red brn, *yel* 2.50 2.75

Kazakh Republic, 30th anniversary. Cyrillic charcters for "ALMA-ATA" are above building in vignette on 40k, immediately below building on right on 1r.

Decembrists and Senatskaya Square, Leningrad — A828

1950, Dec. 30 **Unwmk.**

1536 A828 1r blk brn, *yel* 4.50 3.50

Issued to commemorate the 125th anniversary of the Decembrist revolution of 1825.

Lenin at Razliv
A829

Design: 1r, Lenin and young communists.

1951, Jan. 21 **Litho.** ***Perf. 12½***

Multicolored Centers

1537 A829 40k ol grn 75 24
1538 A829 1r indigo 1.25 52

27th anniversary of the death of Lenin.

Mountain Pasture
A830

Government Building, Frunze
A831

1951, Feb. 2 **Photo.** ***Perf. 12½***

1539 A830 25k dk brn, *bl* 1.50 80
1540 A831 40k dp grn, *bl* 1.75 1.10

Issued to commemorate the 25th anniversary of the formation of the Kirghiz Republic.

Government Building, Tirana — A832

1951, Jan. 6 **Unwmk.** ***Perf. 12***

1541 A832 40k grn, *bluish* 7.75 7.00

Issued to honor the Albanian People's Republic.

Bulgarians Greeting Russian Troops
A833

Lenin Square, Sofia — A834

Design: 60k, Monument to Soviet soldiers.

1951, Jan. 13

1542 A833 25k gray blk, *bluish* 80 52
1543 A834 40k org red, *sal* 1.50 1.00
1544 A834 60k blk brn, *sal* 2.25 1.40

Issued to honor the Bulgarian People's Republic.

Choibalsan State University — A835

State Theater, Ulan Bator
A836

Mongolian Republic Emblem and Flag — A837

1951, Mar. 12

1545 A835 25k pur, *sal* 55 45
1546 A836 40k dp org, *yel* 1.10 45
1547 A837 1r multi 2.75 1.50

Issued to honor the Mongolian People's Republic.

D. A. Furmanov (1891-1926) Writer
A838

Furmanov at Work
A839

1951, Mar. 17 ***Perf. 12½***

1548 A838 40k brown 1.00 65
1549 A839 1r gray blk, *buff* 1.40 1.00

Russian War Memorial, Berlin — A840

1951, Mar. 21 ***Perf. 12***

1550 A840 40k dk gray grn & dk red 2.25 1.25
1551 A840 1r brn blk & red 3.50 2.50

Stockholm Peace Conference.

Kirov Machine Works
A841

1951, May 19 **Photo.** ***Perf. 12½***

1552 A841 40k brn, *cr* 2.50 2.00

Issued to commemorate the 150th anniversary of the founding of the Kirov Machine Works.

Bolshoi Theater, Moscow — A842

Russian Composers A843

1951, May — **Unwmk.**

1553 A842 40k multi	3.50	42
1554 A843 1r multi	7.00	85

Issued to commemorate the 175th anniversary of the founding of the Bolshoi Theater, Moscow.

Liberty Bridge, Budapest A844

Monument to Liberators A845

Budapest Buildings: 40k, Parliament. 60k, National Museum.

1951, June 9 — ***Perf. 12***

1555 A844 25k emerald	45	15
1556 A844 40k brt bl	75	25
1557 A844 60k sepia	1.10	70
1558 A845 1r sep, *sal*	2.00	1.10

Issued to honor the Hungarian People's Republic.

Harvesting Wheat — A846

Designs: 40k, Apiary. 1r, Gathering citrus fruits. 2r, Cotton picking.

1951, June 25

1559 A846 25k dk grn	42	24
1560 A846 40k grn, *bluish*	55	24
1561 A846 1r brn, *yel*	1.40	65
1562 A846 2r dk grn, *sal*	3.00	1.00

Kalinin Museum, Moscow A847

Scott's editorial staff cannot undertake to identify, authenticate or appraise stamps and postal markings.

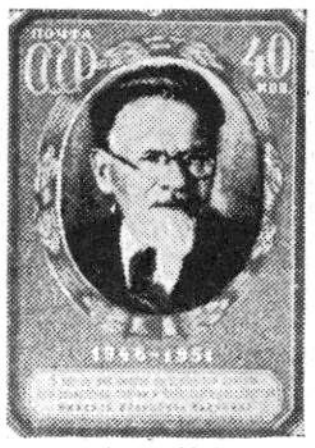
Mikhail I. Kalinin A848

F. E. Dzerzhinski A849

Design: 1r, Kalinin statue.

1951, Aug. 4 ***Perf. 12x12½, 12½x12***

1563 A847 20k org brn & blk	38	25
1564 A848 40k dp grn & choc	75	38
1565 A848 1r vio bl & gray	1.50	75

Issued to commemorate the 5th anniversary of the death of Mikhail I. Kalinin.

1951, Aug. 4 **Engr.** ***Perf. 12x12½***

Design: 1r, Profile of Dzerzhinski.

1566 A849 40k brn red	1.25	80
1567 A849 1r gray blk	1.90	1.25

Issued to commemorate the 25th anniversary of the death of F. E. Dzerzhinski.

Aleksandr M. Butlerov A850

A. A. Aliabiev A851

Portraits: No. 1569, A. Kovalevski, No. 1570 Sonya Kovalevskaya. No. 1571, P. K. Kozlov. No. 1572, S. P. Krasheninnikov. No. 1573, N. S. Kurnakov. No. 1574, P. N. Lebedev. No. 1575, N. I. Lobachevski. No. 1576, A. N. Lodygin. No. 1577, D. I. Mendeleev. No. 1578, N. N. Miklukho-Maklai. No. 1579, A. N. Svertzov. No. 1580, A. G. Stoletov. No. 1581, K. A. Timiryasev. No. 1582, K. E. Tsiolkovsky. No. 1583, P. N. Yablochkov.

1951, Aug. 15 **Photo.** ***Perf. 12½***

1568 A850 40k org red, *bluish*	1.00	25
1569 A850 40k dk bl, *sal*	65	15
1570 A850 40k pur, *sal*	65	15
1571 A850 40k org red	65	15
1572 A850 40k purple	65	15
1573 A850 40k brn, *sal*	65	15
1574 A850 40k blue	65	15
1575 A850 40k brown	65	15
1576 A850 40k green	65	15
1577 A850 40k dp bl	65	15
1578 A850 40k org red, *sal*	65	15
1579 A850 40k sep, *sal*	65	15
1580 A850 40k grn, *sal*	65	15
1581 A850 40k brn, *sal*	65	15
1582 A850 40k gray blk, *bl*	1.00	25
1583 A850 40k sepia	65	15
Nos. 1568-1583 (16)	11.10	2.60

Russian scientists.

1951, Aug. 28

Design: No. 1585, V. S. Kalinnikov.

1584 A851 40k brn, *sal*	3.00	2.00
1585 A851 40k gray, *sal*	3.00	2.00

Russian composers.

Opera and Ballet Theater, Tbilisi — A852

Gathering Citrus Fruit — A853

Designs: 40k, Principal street, Tbilisi. 1r, Picking tea.

1951 **Unwmk.** ***Perf. 12½***

1586 A852 20k dp grn, *yel*	45	32
1587 A853 25k pur, org & brn	60	32
1588 A853 40k dk brn, *bl*	1.25	65
1589 A853 1r red brn & dk grn	3.25	1.50

Georgian Republic, 30th anniversary.

Emblem of Aviation Society — A854

Planes and Emblem — A855

Designs: 60k, Flying model planes. 1r, Parachutists.

1951, Sept. 19 **Litho.** ***Perf. 12½***
Dated: "1951"

1590 A854 40k multi	55	20
1591 A854 60k emer, lt bl & brn	90	35
1592 A854 1r bl, sal & lil	1.40	55
1593 A855 2r multi	3.00	1.00

Issued to promote interest in aviation.

Victor M. Vasnetsov (1848-1926), Painter — A856

Three Heroes, by Vasnetsov — A857

1951, Oct. 15

1594 A856 40k dk bl, brn & buff	1.10	22
1595 A857 1r multi	1.75	95

Hydroelectric Station, Lenin and Stalin — A858

Design: 1r, Spasski Tower, Kremlin.

1951, Nov. 6 **Photo.** ***Perf. 12½***
Dated: "1917-1951"

1596 A858 40k bl vio & red	2.00	2.00
1597 A858 1r dk brn & red	3.25	3.25

34th anniversary of October Revolution.

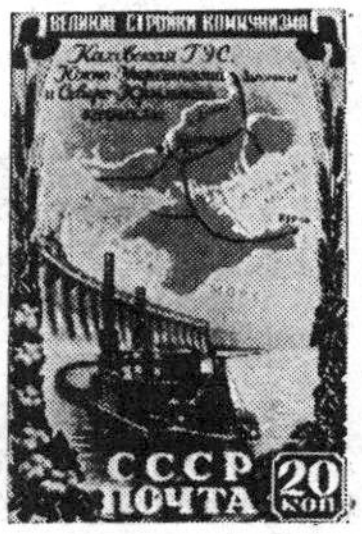
Map, Dredge and Khakhovsky Hydroelectric Station — A859

Map, Volga Dam and Tugboat A860

Designs (each showing map): 40k, Stalingrad Dam. 60k, Excavating Turkmenian canal. 1r, Kuibyshev dam.

1951, Nov. 28 ***Perf. 12½***

1598 A859 20k red brn, brn lil & car	1.40	1.25
1599 A860 30k brn, bl & dk bl	1.90	1.75
1600 A860 40k brn, aqua & red	2.75	2.75
1601 A860 60k dk bl, brn & red	3.50	3.25
1602 A860 1r multi	7.00	6.50
Nos. 1598-1602 (5)	16.55	15.50

Flag and Citizens Signing Peace Appeal A861

M. V. Ostrogradski A862

1951, Nov. 30 ***Perf. 12½***

1603 A861 40k gray & red	7.75	7.75

Third All-Union Peace Conference.

1951, Dec. 10 **Unwmk.**

1604 A862 40k blk brn, *pink*	4.50	3.75

Issued to commemorate the 150th anniversary of the birth of Mikhail V. Ostrogradski, mathematician.

Monument to Jan Zizka, Prague A863

Monument to Soviet Liberators A864

Designs: 25k, Monument to Soviet Soldiers, Ostrava. 40k, Julius Fucik. 60k, Smetana Museum, Prague.

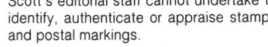

1951, Dec. 10 *Perf. 12½*

1605 A863 20k vio bl, *sal* 1.25 1.40
1606 A863 25k cop red, *yel* 1.50 1.75
1607 A863 40k red org, *sal* 1.90 2.00
1608 A863 60k brnsh gray, *buff* 2.50 3.00
1609 A864 1r brnsh gray, *buff* 5.50 6.00
Nos. 1605-1609 (5) 12.65 14.15

Soviet-Czechoslovakian friendship.

Volkhovski Hydroelectric Station and Lenin Statue — A865

1951, Dec. 19

1610 A865 40k dk bl, gray & yel 55 20
1611 A865 1r pur, gray & yel 1.25 55

Issued to commemorate the 25th anniversary of the opening of the Lenin Volkhovski hydroelectric station.

Lenin as a Schoolboy A866

Horizontal Designs: 60k, Lenin among children. 1r, Lenin and peasants.

1952, Jan. 24 **Photo.** *Perf. 12½*
Multicolored Centers

1612 A866 40k dk bl grn 1.10 25
1613 A866 60k vio bl 1.25 38
1614 A866 1r org brn 2.00 45

28th anniversary of the death of Lenin.

Petr P. Semenov A867

V. O. Kovalevski A868

1952, Feb. 1

1615 A867 1r sep, *bl* 3.00 2.50

Issued to commemorate the 125th anniversary of the birth of Petr Petrovich Semenov-Tianshanski (1827-1914), traveler and geographer who explored the Tian Shan mountains.

1952, Mar. 3 **Unwmk.**

1616 A868 40k sep, *yel* 3.25 2.75

Issued to honor V. O. Kovalevski (1843-1883), biologist and palaeontologist.

Skaters A869

Design: 60k, Skiers.

1952, Mar. 3

1617 A869 40k multi 1.00 22
1618 A869 60k multi 1.90 32

N. V. Gogol and Characters from "Taras Bulba" — A870

Designs: 60k, Gogol and V. G. Belinski. 1r, Gogol and Ukrainian peasants.

1952, Mar. 4
Dated: "1852-1952"

1619 A870 40k sep, *bl* 55 6
1620 A870 60k blk, dk brn & brn org 90 9
1621 A870 1r multi 1.10 24

Death centenary of N. V. Gogol, writer.

G. K. Ordzhonikidze A871

Workers and Soviet Flag A872

Workers' Rest Home A873

1952, Apr. 23 **Photo.** *Perf. 12½*

1622 A871 40k dp grn, *pink* 1.25 40
1623 A871 1r sep, *bl* 2.00 60

Issued to commemorate the 15th anniversary of the death of Grigori K. Ordzhonikidze, Georgian party worker.

1952, May 15 **Unwmk.**

Designs: No. 1626, Aged citizens. No. 1627, Schoolgirl.

1624 A872 40k red & blk, *cr* 3.50 3.25
1625 A873 40k red & dk grn, *pale gray* 3.50 3.25
1626 A873 40k red & brn, *pale gray* 3.50 3.25
1627 A872 40k red & blk, *pale gray* 3.50 3.25

15th anniversary of adoption of Stalin constitution.

A. S. Novikov-Priboy and Ship — A874

1952, June 5

1628 A874 40k blk, pale cit & bl grn 32 15

Issued to commemorate the 75th anniversary of the birth of A. S. Novikov-Priboy, writer.

Victor Hugo — A875

1952, June 5 **Unwmk.** *Perf. 12½*

1629 A875 40k brn org, gray & blk 40 15

150th anniversary of birth of Victor Hugo (1802-1855), French writer.

Salavat Julaev — A876

G. J. Sedov — A877

1952, June 28

1630 A876 40k rose red, *pink* 40 15

Issued to commemorate the 200th anniversary of the birth of Salavat Julaev, Bashkir hero who took part in the insurrection of 1773-1775.

1952, July 4

1631 A877 40k dk bl, dk brn & bl grn 4.00 2.50

Georgi Sedov, Arctic explorer (1877-1914).

Arms and Flag of Romania A878

University Square, Bucharest A879

Design: 60k, Monument to Soviet soldiers.

1952, July 26

1632 A878 40k multi 70 25
1633 A878 60k dk grn, *pink* 1.00 50
1634 A879 1r brt ultra 1.40 1.00

V. A. Zhukovski A880

N. P. Ogarev A881

Design: No. 1636, K.P. Bryullov.

1952, July 26 **Pale Blue Paper**

1635 A880 40k gray blk 65 28
1636 A880 40k brt bl grn 65 28

Zhukovski, poet, and Bryullov, painter (1799-1852).

1952, Aug. 29

1637 A881 40k dp grn 30 20

Issued to commemorate the 75th anniversary of the death of N. P. Ogarev, poet and revolutionary.

G. I. Uspenski A882

Admiral P. S. Nakhimov A883

1952, Sept. 4

1638 A882 40k ind & dk brn 30 15

Issued to commemorate the 50th anniversary of the death of Gleb Ivanovich Uspenski (1843-1902), writer.

1952, Sept. 9

1639 A883 40k multi 80 60

150th anniversary of birth of Adm. Paul S. Nakhimov (1802-1855).

University Building, Tartu — A884

1952, Oct. 2

1640 A884 40k blk brn, *sal* 1.65 60

Issued to commemorate the 150th anniversary of the enlargement of the University of Tartu, Estonia.

Kajum Nasyri A885

A. N. Radishchev A886

1952, Nov. 5

1641 A885 40k brn, *yel* 1.65 75

Issued to commemorate the 50th anniversary of the death of Kajum Nasyri (1825-1902), Tartar educator.

1952, Oct. 23

1642 A886 40k blk, brn & dk red 90 42

Issued to commemorate the 150th anniversary of the death of A. N. Radishchev, writer.

M.S. Joseph Stalin at Entrance to Volga-Don Canal — A887

Design: 1r, Lenin, Stalin and red banners.

1952, Nov. 6 *Perf. 12½*

1643 A887 40k multi 1.65 1.25
1644 A887 1r brn, red & yel 3.00 2.75

35th anniversary of October Revolution.

Pavel Fedotov
A888

V. D. Polenov
A889

"Moscow Courtyard" — A890

1953, Nov. 26

1645 A888 40k red brn & blk 38 20

Issued to commemorate the centenary of the death of Pavel Andreievitch Fedotov (1815-1852), artist.

1952, Dec. 6

1646 A889 40k red brn & buff 65 28
1647 A890 1r multi 1.65 50

Issued to commemorate the 25th anniversary of the death of V. D. Polenov, artist.

A. I. Odoyevski — A891

1952, Dec. 8

1648 A891 40k gray blk & red org 65 20

Odoyevski, poet (1802-39).

D. N. Mamin-Sibiryak — A892

1952, Dec. 15

1649 A892 40k dp grn, *cr* 65 20

Issued to commemorate the centenary of the birth of Dimitrii N. Mamin-Sibiryak (1852-1912), writer.

Composite Medal Types of 1946
Frames as A599-A606
Centers as Indicated

Medals: 1r, Token of Veneration. 2r, Red Star. 3r, Red Workers' Banner. 5r, Red Banner. 10r, Lenin.

1952-59 **Engr.** *Perf. 12½*

1650 A569 1r dk brn 3.75 2.75
1651 A567 2r red brn 45 18
1652 A572 3r dp bl vio 75 32
1653 A571 5r dk car ('53) 1.00 32
1654 A566 10r brt rose 1.90 65
a 10r dl red ('59) 2.50 2.00
Nos. 1650-1654 (5) 7.85 4.22

V. M. Bekhterev — A893

1952, Dec. 24 **Photo.**

1655 A893 40k vio bl, sl & blk 60 28

Issued to commemorate the 25th anniversary of the death of Vladimir M. Bekhterev (1857-1927), neuropathologist.

Byelorusskaya Station — A894

Designs (Moscow Subway stations): 40k, Botanical Garden Station. 40k, Novoslobodskaya Station. 40k, Komsomolskaya Station.

1952, Dec. 30
Multicolored Centers

1656 A894 40k dl vio 60 15
1657 A894 40k lt ultra 52 12
1658 A894 40k bl gray 52 12
1659 A894 40k dl grn 52 12

Nos. 1656-1659 were printed together in sheets of 20 (4x5), with each horizontal row consisting of one of each 40k.

USSR Emblem and Flags of 16 Union Republics A895

1952, Dec. 30

1660 A895 1r grn, dk red & brn 2.25 1.50

Issued to commemorate the 30th anniversary of the Union of Soviet Socialist Republics.

Lenin — A896

1953, Jan. 26
Multicolored Center

1661 A896 40k dk bl 3.50 2.75

Issued to commemorate 29 years without Lenin.

Foreign postal stationery (stamped envelopes, postal cards and air letter sheets) lies beyond the scope of this Catalogue, which is limited to adhesive postage stamps.

Stalin Peace Medal
A897

Valerian V. Kuibyshev
A898

1953, Apr. 30 *Perf. 12½*

1662 A897 40k red brn, bl & dl yel 8.00 8.00

1953, June 6

1663 A898 40k red brn & blk 75 55

Issued to commemorate the 65th anniversary of the birth of V. V. Kuibyshev (1888-1935), Bolshevik leader.

N. G. Chernyshevski
A899

1953, July 21

1664 A899 40k buff & dk brn 75 75

Issued to commemorate the 125th anniversary of the birth of Nikolai G. Chernyshevski (1828-1889), writer and radical leader; exiled to Siberia for 24 years.

V. V. Mayakovsky — A900

1953, July 19

1665 A900 40k ver & gray brn 75 35

Issued to commemorate the 60th anniversary of the birth of Vladimir V. Mayakovsky, poet.

Lock No. 9, Volga-Don Canal — A901

Designs: No. 1667, Lock 13. No. 1668, Lock 15. No. 1669, Volga River lighthouse. No. 1670, Tsymijanskaja Dam. No. 1671, M. S. "Joseph Stalin" in canal.

1953, Aug. 29 **Litho.**

1666 A901 40k multi 75 12
1667 A901 40k multi 75 12
1668 A901 405 multi 75 12
1669 A901 40k multi 75 12
1670 A901 40k multi 75 12
1671 A901 1r multi 1.75 40
Nos. 1666-1671 (6) 5.50 1.00

Issued to publicize the Volga-Don Canal.

V. G. Korolenko
A902

Leo N. Tolstoy
A903

1953, Aug. 29 **Photo.** *Perf. 12x12½*

1672 A902 40k brown 60 15

Issued to commemorate the centenary of the birth of V. G. Korolenko (1853-1921), writer.

1953, Sept. *Perf. 12*

1673 A903 1r dk brn 2.00 1.10

Issued to commemorate the 125th anniversary of the birth of Count Leo N. Tolstoy, writer.

Moscow University and Two Youths — A904

Nationalities of the Soviet Union — A905

Design: 1r, Komsomol badge and four orders.

1953, Oct. 29 *Perf. 12½x12*

1674 A904 40k multi 1.75 1.25
1675 A904 1r multi 3.75 1.75

Issued to commemorate the 35th anniversary of the Young Communist League (Komsomol).

1953, Nov. 6

Design: 60k, Lenin and Stalin at Smolny monastery.

1676 A905 40k multi 3.25 2.75
1677 A905 60k multi 6.50 5.50

36th anniversary of October Revolution.

No. 1676 measures 25½x38mm.; No. 1677, 25½x42mm.

Lenin and His Writings — A906

Design: 1r, Lenin facing left and pages of "What to Do."

1953

1678 A906 40k multi 3.00 3.00
1679 A906 1r dk brn, org brn & red 6.50 6.50

The 40k was issued on Nov. 12 to commemorate the 50th anniversary of the formation of the Communist Party. The 1r was issued Dec. 14 to commemorate the 50th anniversary of the 2nd congress of the Russian Socialist Party.

Lenin Statue — A907

Peter I Statue, Decembrists' Square — A908

Leningrad Views: Nos. 1681 & 1683, Admiralty building. Nos. 1685 & 1687, Smolny monastery.

1953, Nov. 23

1680 A907 40k brn blk, *yel* 1.50 1.25
1681 A907 40k vio brn, *yel* 1.50 1.25
1682 A907 40k dk brn, *pink* 1.50 1.25
1683 A907 40k brn blk, *cr* 1.50 1.25
1684 A908 1r dk brn, *bl* 3.50 3.25
1685 A908 1r dk grn, *pink* 3.50 3.25
1686 A908 1r vio, *yel* 3.50 3.25
1687 A908 1r blk brn, *bl* 3.50 3.25
Nos. 1680-1687 (8) 20.00 18.00

See Nos. 1944-1945, 1943a.

"Pioneers" and Model of Lomonosov Moscow University A909

A. S. Griboedov A910

1953, Dec. 22 Litho. *Perf. 12*

1688 A909 40k dk sl grn, dk brn & red 2.25 2.25

Arms Type of 1948

1954-57

1689 A682 40k scarlet 4.25 1.65
a 7 ribbon turns on wreath at left ('57) 1.00 25

No. 1689 was re-issued in 1954-56 typographed in slightly smaller format: 14½x21¾mm., instead of 14¾x21¾mm., and in a lighter shade. See note after No. 738.

No. 1689 has 8 ribbon turns on left side of wreath.

1954, Mar. 4 Photo.

1690 A910 40k dp cl, *cr* 52 20
1691 A910 1r blk, *grn* 1.00 32

Aleksandr S. Griboedov, writer (1795-1829).

Kremlin View A911

V. P. Chkalov A912

1954, Mar. 7 Litho. *Perf. 12½x12*

1692 A911 40k red & gray 1.10 1.10

1954 elections to the Supreme Soviet.

1954, Mar. 16 *Perf. 12*

1693 A912 1r gray, vio bl & dk brn 3.00 62

Issued to commemorate the 50th anniversary of the birth of Valeri P. Chkalov (1904-1938), airplane pilot.

Lenin — A913

Lenin at Smolny A914

Designs: No. 1696, Lenin's home (later museum), Ulyanovsk. No. 1697, Lenin addressing workers. No. 1698, Lenin among students, University of Kazan.

1954, Apr. 16 Photo.

1694 A913 40k multi 1.25 42

Size: 38x27½mm.

1695 A914 40k multi 1.25 42
1696 A914 40k multi 1.25 42

Size: 48x35mm.

1697 A914 40k multi 1.25 42
1698 A914 40k multi 1.25 42
Nos. 1694-1698 (5) 6.25 2.10

30th anniversary of the death of Lenin.
See No. 2060.

Joseph V. Stalin — A915

1954, Apr. 30 Unwmk. *Perf. 12*

1699 A915 40k dk brn 2.50 1.50

First anniversary of the death of Stalin.

Supreme Soviet Buildings in Kiev and Moscow A916

T. G. Shevchenko Statue, Kharkov — A917

Designs: No. 1701, University building, Kiev. No. 1702, Opera, Kiev. No. 1703, Ukranian Academy of Science. No. 1705, Bogdan Chmielnicki statue, Kiev. No. 1706 Flags of Soviet Russia and Ukraine. No. 1707, T. G. Shevchenko statue, Kanev. No. 1708, Chmielnicki proclaming reunion of Ukraine and Russia, 1654.

1954, May 10 Litho.

Size: 37½x26mm., 26x37½mm.

1700 A916 40k red brn, sal, cr & blk 65 10
1701 A916 40k ultra, vio bl & brn 65 10
1702 A916 40k red brn, buff, bl & brn 65 10
1703 A916 40k org brn, cr & grn 65 10
1704 A917 40k rose red, blk, yel & brn 75 10
1705 A917 60k multi 75 20
1706 A917 1r multi 1.90 32

Size: 42x28mm.

1707 A916 1r multi 1.25 32

Size: 45x29½mm.

1708 A916 1r multi, *pink* 1.90 32

300-ЛЕТИЕ

No. 1341 Overprinted in Carmine

ВОССОЕДИНЕНИЯ УКРАИНЫ С РОССИЕЙ

1709 A517 2r green 4.00 1.10
Nos. 1700-1709 (10) 13.15 2.76

Nos. 1700-1709 were issued to commemorate the 300th anniversary of the union between the Ukraine and Russia.

Sailboat Race A918

Basketball A919

Sports: No. 1711, Hurdle race. No. 1712, Swimmers. No. 1713, Cyclists. No. 1714, Track. No. 1715, Skier. No. 1716, Mountain climbing.

1954, May 29

Frames in Orange Brown

1710 A918 40k bl & blk 80 15
1711 A918 40k vio gray & blk 80 15
1712 A918 40k dk bl & blk 80 15
1713 A918 40k dk brn & buff 80 15
1714 A918 40k blk brn & buff 80 15
1715 A918 1r bl & blk 1.65 25
1716 A918 1r bl & blk 1.65 25
1717 A919 1r dk brn & brn 1.65 25
Nos. 1710-1717 (8) 8.95 1.50

See No. 2170.

Cattle A920

Designs: No. 1719, Potato planting and cultivation. No. 1720, Kolkhoz hydroelectric station.

1954, June 8

1718 A920 40k brn, cr, ind & bl gray 1.25 40
1719 A920 40k gray grn, buff & brn 1.25 40
1720 A920 40k blk, bl grn & vio bl 1.25 40

Anton P. Chekhov — A921

1954, July 15

1721 A921 40k grn & blk brn 42 20

Issued to commemorate the 50th anniversary of the death of Anton P. Chekhov, writer.

F. A. Bredichin, V. J. Struve, A. A. Belopolski and Observatory A922

1954, July 26

1722 A922 40k vio bl, blk & bl 4.75 1.25

Restoration of Pulkov Observatory.

Mikhail Glinka — A923

Pushkin and Zhukovsky Visiting Glinka A924

1954, July 26

1723 A923 40k dp cl, pink & blk brn 2.50 35
1724 A924 60k multi 3.00 60

Issued to commemorate the 150th anniversary of the birth of Mikhail I. Glinka, composer.

Nikolai A. Ostrovsky A925

Monument to Sunken Ships A926

Defenders of Sevastopol A927

1954, Sept. 29 Photo. *Perf. 12½x12*

1725 A925 40k brn, dk red & yel 65 20

Issued to commemorate the 50th anniversary of the birth of N. A. Ostrovsky (1904-1936), blind writer.

1954, Oct. 17 *Perf. 12½*

Design: 1r, Admiral P. S. Nakhimov.

1726	A926	40k bl grn, blk & ol brn	48	12
1727	A927	60k org brn, blk & brn	65	20
1728	A926	1r brn, blk & ol grn	1.25	35

Issued to commemorate the centenary of the defense of Sevastopol during the Crimean War.

Sculpture at Exhibition Entrance — A928

Agriculture Pavilion — A929

Designs: No. 1731, Cattle pavilion. No. 1732, Machinery pavilion. No. 1733, Main entrance. No. 1734, Main pavilion.

Perf. 12½, 12½x12, 12x12½

1954, Nov. 5 **Litho.**

Size: 26x37mm.

1729	A928	40k multi	30	12

Size: 40x29mm.

1730	A929	40k multi	30	12
1731	A929	40k multi	30	12
1732	A929	40k multi	30	12

Size: 40½x33mm.

1733	A929	1r multi	60	32

Size: 28½x40½mm.

1734	A928	1r multi	60	32
		Nos. 1729-1734 (6)	2.40	1.12

Issued to publicize the 1954 Agricultural Exhibition.

Marx, Engels, Lenin and Stalin — A930

1954, Nov. 6 **Photo.** *Perf. 12½x12*

1735	A930	1r dk brn, pale org & red	3.50	2.75

37th anniversary of October Revolution.

Kazan University Building A931

1954, Nov. 11 *Perf. 12x12½*

1736	A931	40k dp bl	50	25
1737	A931	60k claret	70	42

Issued to commemorate the 150th anniversary of the founding of Kazan University.

Salome Neris A932

1954, Nov. 17 *Perf. 12½x12*

1738	A932	40k red org & ol gray	50	10

Issued to commemorate the 50th anniversary of the birth of Salome Neris (1904-1945), Lithuanian poet.

Vegetables and Garden A933

Cultivating Flax — A934

Designs: No. 1741, Tractor plowing field. No. 1742, Loading ensilage.

1954, Dec. 12 **Litho.** *Perf. 12x12½*

1739	A933	40k multi	65	12
1740	A934	40k multi	65	12
1741	A933	40k multi	65	12
1742	A934	60k multi	95	24

Joseph Stalin — A935

Anton Rubinstein — A936

1954, Dec. 21 **Engr.** *Perf. 12½x12*

1743	A935	40k rose brn	60	48
1744	A935	1r dk bl	1.25	60

Issued to commemorate the 75th anniversary of the birth of Joseph V. Stalin.

1954, Dec. 30 **Photo.**

1745	A936	40k cl, gray & blk	1.65	35

Issued to commemorate the 125th anniversary of the birth of Anton G. Rubinstein, composer.

V. M. Garshin — A937

Lithographed and Photogravure

1955, Mar. 2 **Unwmk.** *Perf. 12*

1746	A937	40k buff, blk brn & grn	65	20

Issued to commemorate the centenary of the birth of Vsevolod M. Garshin (1855-1888), writer.

K. A. Savitsky and Painting A938

1955, Mar. 21 **Photo.**

1747	A938	40k multi	80	28
a.		Sheet of 4, black inscription	20.00	25.00
b.		Sheet of 4, red brn. inscription	20.00	25.00

Issued to commemorate the 50th anniversary of the death of K. A. Savitsky (1844-1905), painter.

Nos. 1747a and 1747b measure 152x108mm.

Globe and Clasped Hands — A939

1955, Apr. 9 **Litho.**

1748	A939	40k multi	30	10

Issued to publicize the International Conference of Public Service Unions, Vienna, April 1955.

Poets Pushkin and Mickiewicz A940

Brothers in Arms Monument, Warsaw — A941

Palace of Culture and Science, Warsaw A942

Copernicus, Painting by Jan Matejko (in Medallion) — A943

Unwmk.

1955, Apr. 22 **Photo.** *Perf. 12*

1749	A940	40k chlky bl, vio & blk	1.25	25
1750	A941	40k vio blk	1.25	25
1751	A942	1r brt red & gray blk	2.50	65
1752	A943	1r multi	2.50	65

Issued to commemorate the 10th anniversary of the Polish-USSR treaty of friendship.

Lenin at Shushinskoe — A944

Lenin at Secret Printing House A945

Friedrich von Schiller A946

Design: 1r, Lenin and Krupskaya with peasants at Gorki, 1921.

1955, Apr. 22

Frame and Inscription in Dark Red

1753	A944	60k multi	65	20
1754	A944	1r multi	90	22
1755	A945	1r multi	90	22

85th anniversary of the birth of Lenin.

1955, May 10

1756	A946	40k chocolate	35	12

Issued to commemorate the 150th anniversary of the death of Friedrich von Schiller, German poet.

A. G. Venezianov and "Spring on the Land" — A947

1955, June 21 **Photo.**

1757	A947	1r multi	1.75	60
a.		Souv. sheet of 4	12.50	12.50

Issued to commemorate the 175th anniversary of the birth of A. G. Venezianov, painter.

Anatoli K. Liadov A948

1955, July 5 **Litho.**

1758	A948	40k red brn, blk & lt brn	55	10

Issued to commemorate the centenary of the birth of Anatoli K. Liadov (1855-1914), composer.

Aleksandr Popov — A949

Lenin — A950

Storming the Winter Palace — A951

1955, Nov. 5
Portraits Multicolored
1759 A949 40k lt ultra 65 20
1760 A949 1r gray brn 1.25 35

Issued to commemorate the 60th anniversary of the construction of a coherer for detecting Hertzian electromagnetic waves by A. S. Popov, radio pioneer.

1955, Nov. 6

Design: 1r, Lenin addressing the people.

1761 A950 40k multi 75 30
1762 A951 40k multi 75 30
1763 A951 1r multi 1.90 65

38th anniversary of October Revolution.

Apartment Houses, Magnitogorsk — A952

1955, Nov. 29
1764 A952 40k multi 90 22

Issued to commemorate the 25th anniversary of the founding of the industrial center, Magnitogorsk.

Arctic Observation Post A953

Design: 1r, Scientist at observation post.

1955, Nov. 29 ***Perf. 12½x12***
1765 A953 40k multi 65 20
1766 A953 60k multi 1.10 30
1767 A953 1r multi 1.65 45
a Souv. sheet of 4 ('58) 17.50 25.00

Issued to publicize the Soviet scientific drifting stations at the North Pole.
In 1962, No. 1767a was overprinted in red "1962" on each stamp and, in the lower sheet margin, a three-line Russian inscription meaning "25 years from the beginning of the work of "NP-1" station."
Sheet value, $20 unused, $27.50 canceled.

Fedor Shubin — A954

1955, Dec. 22 ***Perf. 12***
1768 A954 40k grn & multi 30 10
1769 A954 1r brn & multi 60 20

Fedor Ivanovich Shubin, sculptor (1740-1805).

The lack of a value for a listed item does not necessarily indicate rarity.

Federal Socialist Republic Pavilion (R.S.F.S.R.) — A955

Designs: Pavilions.

1955 Litho. Unwmk.
Centers in Natural Colors; Frames in Blue Green and Olive
1770 A955 40k *shown* 25 10
a Sheet of four 10.00 9.50
1771 A955 40k *Tadzhik* 25 10
1772 A955 40k *Byelorussian* 25 10
a Sheet of four 10.00 9.50
1773 A955 40k *Azerbaijan* 25 10
1774 A955 40k *Georgian* 25 10
1775 A955 40k *Armenian* 25 10
1776 A955 40k *Turkmen* 25 10
1777 A955 40k *Uzbek* 25 10
1778 A955 40k *Ukrainian* 25 10
a Sheet of four 10.00 9.50
1779 A955 40k *Kazakh* 25 10
1780 A955 40k *Kirghiz* 25 10
1781 A955 40k *Karelo-Finnish* 25 10
1782 A955 40k *Moldavian* 25 10
1783 A955 40k *Estonian* 25 10
1784 A955 40k *Latvian* 25 10
1785 A955 40k *Lithuanian* 25 10
Nos. 1770-1785 (16) 4.00 1.60

All-Union Agricultural Fair.
Nos. 1773-1785 were printed in sheets containing various stamps, providing a variety of horizontal se-tenant pairs and strips.

Lomonosov Moscow State University A956

Design: 1r, New University buildings.

1955, June 9 ***Perf. 12***
1786 A956 40k multi 32 12
a Sheet of 4 ('56) 4.50 *11.50*
1787 A956 1r multi 65 25
a Sheet of 4 ('56) 9.00 *19.00*

Issued to commemorate the 200th anniversary of Lomonosov Moscow State University.

Vladimir Mayakovsky — A957

1955, May 31
1788 A957 40k multi 60 15

Issued to commemorate the 25th anniversary of the death of Vladimir V. Mayakovsky, poet.

Race Horse — A958

Trotter A959

1956, Jan. 9
1789 A958 40k dk brn 35 12
1790 A958 60k Prus grn & bl grn 60 18
1791 A959 1r dl pur & bl vio 1.10 30

Issued to commemorate the International Horse Races, Moscow, Aug. 14-Sept. 4, 1955.

Alexei N. Krylov — A960

Symbol of Spartacist Games, Stadium and Factories — A961

1956, Jan. 9
1792 A960 40k gray, brn & blk 38 12

Issued to commemorate the tenth anniversary of the death of Alexei N. Krylov (1863-1945), mathematician and naval architect.

1956, Jan. 18
1793 A961 1r red vio & lt grn 55 18

Issued to commemorate the fifth All-Union Spartacist Games of Soviet Trade Union sport clubs, Moscow, Aug. 12-18, 1955.

Atomic Power Station A962

Design: 60k, Atomic Reactor.

1956, Jan. 31
1794 A962 25k multi 30 10
1795 A962 60k multi 95 20
1796 A962 1r multi 1.65 30

Issued to commemorate the establishment of the first Atomic Power Station of the USSR Academy of Science. Inscribed in Russian: "Atomic Energy in the service of the people."

Statue of Lenin, Kremlin and Flags A963

Khachatur Abovian A964

1956, Feb.
1797 A963 40k multi 50 8
1798 A963 1r ol, buff & red org 70 18

Issued to commemorate the 20th Congress of the Communist Party of the Soviet Union.

1956, Feb. 25 Unwmk. ***Perf. 12***
1799 A964 40k blk brn, *bluish* 38 15

Issued to commemorate the 150th anniversary of the birth of Khachatur Abovian, Armenian writer.

Workers with Red Flag — A965

N. A. Kasatkin — A966

1956, Mar. 14
1800 A965 40k multi 38 15

Revolution of 1905, 50th anniversary.

1956, Apr. 30
1801 A966 40k car lake 30 15

Issued in honor of Nikolai A. Kasatkin (1859-1930), painter.

"On the Oka River" A967

1956, Apr. 30
Center Multicolored
1802 A967 40k bis & blk 95 15
1803 A967 1r ultra & blk 1.65 28

Issued in honor of A. E. Arkhipov, painter.

I. P. Kulibin — A968

V. G. Perov — A969

"Birdcatchers" — A970

1956, May 12
1804 A968 40k multi 38 15

Issued to commemorate the 220th anniversary of the birth of I. P. Kulibin, inventor.

1956, May 12

Painting: No. 1807, "Hunters at Rest."

Multicolored Centers
1805 A969 40k green 80 15
1806 A970 1r brown 1.90 30
1807 A970 1r org brn 1.90 30

Issued in honor of Vassili Grigorievitch Perov (1833-1882), painter.

Ural Pavilion A971

Pavilions: No. 1809, Tatar Republic. No. 1810, Volga District. No. 1811, Central Black Earth Area. No. 1812, Northeastern District. No. 1813, Northern Caucasus. No. 1814,

Bashkir Republic. No. 1815, Far East. No. 1816, Central Asia. No. 1817, Young Naturalists. No. 1818, Siberia. No. 1819, Leningrad and Northwestern District. No. 1820, Moscow, Tula, Kaluga, Ryazan and Bryansk Districts.

1956, Apr. 25

Multicolored Centers

1808 A971 1r yel grn & pale yel	60	12
1809 A971 1r bl grn & pale yel	60	12
1810 A971 1r dk bl grn & pale yel	60	12
1811 A971 1r dk bl grn & yel grn	60	12
1812 A971 1r dk bl grn & buff	60	12
1813 A971 1r ol gray & pale yel	60	12
1814 A971 1r ol & yel	60	12
1815 A971 1r ol grn & lem	60	12
1816 A971 1r ol brn & lem	60	12
1817 A971 1r ol brn & lem	60	12
1818 A971 1r brn & yel	60	12
1819 A971 1r redsh brn & yel	60	12
1820 A971 1r dk red brn & yel	60	12
Nos. 1808-1820 (13)	7.80	1.56

Issued to publicize the All-Union Agricultural Fair, Moscow.
Six of the Pavilion set were printed se-tenant in one sheet of 30 (6x5), the strip containing Nos. 1809, 1816, 1817, 1813, 1818 and 1810 in that order. Two others, Nos. 1819-1820, were printed as-tenant in one sheet of 35.

Lenin
A972

N. I. Lobachevski
A973

1956, May 25

1821 A972 40k lil & multi	1.40	40

86th anniversary of the birth of Lenin.

1956, June 4

1822 A973 40k blk brn	28	10

Issued to commemorate the centenary of the death of Nikolai Ivanovich Lobachevski (1793-1856), mathematician.

Nurse and Textile Factory A974

Design: 40k, First Aid instruction.

1956, June 4 **Unwmk.**

1823 A974 40k lt ol grn, grnsh bl & red	30	14
1824 A974 40k red brn, lt bl & red	30	14

Issued in honor of the Red Cross and Red Crescent. No. 1823 measures 37x25mm.; No. 1824, 40x28mm.

V. K. Arseniev
A975

I. M. Sechenov
A976

1956, June 15 **Litho.** ***Perf. 12***

1825 A975 40k vio, blk & rose	40	14

V. K. Arseniev (1872-1930), explorer and writer.

1956, June 15

1826 A976 40k multi	40	14

I. M. Sechenov (1829-1905), physiologist.

A. K. Savrasov — A977

1956, June 22

1827 A977 1r dl yel & brn	1.00	20

Issued in honor of A. K. Savrasov, painter.

I. V. Michurin A978

Design: 60k, I. V. Michurin with Pioneers.

1956, June 22

Center Multicolored

1828 A978 25k dk brn	60	9
1829 A978 60k grn & lt bl	90	12
1830 A978 1r lt bl	2.00	28

Issued to commemorate the centenary of the birth of I. V. Michurin, scientist.
Nos. 1828 and 1830 measure 32x25mm. No. 1829 measures 47x26mm.

Nadezhda K. Krupskaya A979

1956, June 28

1831 A979 40k brn, lt bl & pale brn	1.00	25

Issued to honor N. K. Krupskaya (1869-1939), teacher and wife of Lenin.
See Nos. 1862, 1886, 1983, 2028.

S. M. Kirov — A980

N. S. Leskov — A981

1956, June 28

1832 A980 40k red, buff & brn	32	10

Kirov, revolutionary (1886-1934).

1956, July 10

1833 A981 40k ol bis & brn	15	10
1834 A981 1r grn & dk brn	52	20

Issued to commemorate the 125th anniversary of the birth of Nikolai S. Leskov (1831-1895), novelist.

Aleksandr A. Blok — A982

1956, July 10

1835 A982 40k ol & brn, *cr*	25	10

Blok, poet (1880-1921).

Farm Machinery Factory A983

1956, July 23 ***Perf. 12½x12***

1836 A983 40k multi	22	10

Issued to commemorate the 25th anniversary of the Rostov Farm Machinery Works.

G. N. Fedotova A984

1956, July 23 **Unwmk.**

1837 A984 40k brn & rose vio	35	15

Issued to commemorate G. N. Fedotova (1846-1925), actress. See No. 2026.

P. M. Tretiakov and Art Gallery A985

"The Rooks Have Arrived" by A. K. Savrasov — A986

1956, July 31 ***Perf. 12***

1838 A985 40k multi	1.00	16
1839 A986 40k multi	1.00	16

Issued to commemorate the centenary of the Tretiakov Art Gallery. Moscow.

Relay Race — A987

For unused stamps, more recent issues are valued as never hinged, with the beginning point determined on a country-by-country basis. Notes to show the beginning points are prominently placed in the text.

Volleyball — A988

Designs: No. 1842, Rowing. No. 1843, Swimming. No. 1844, Medal with heads of man and woman. No. 1845, Tennis. No. 1846, Soccer. No. 1847, Fencing. No. 1848, Bicycle race. No. 1849, Stadium and flag. No. 1850, Diving. No. 1851, Boxing. No. 1852, Gymnast. 1r, Basketball.

1956, Aug. 5

1840 A987 10k car rose	14	5
1841 A988 25k dk org brn	24	5
1842 A988 25k brt grnsh bl	24	5
1843 A988 25k grn, bl & lt brn	24	5
1844 A988 40k org, pink, bis & yel	35	7
1845 A988 40k org brn	35	7
1846 A987 40k brt yel grn & dk brn	35	7
1847 A987 40k grn, brt grn & dk brn, *grnsh*	35	7
1848 A987 40k bl grn	35	7
1849 A988 40k brt yel grn & red	35	7
1850 A988 40k grnsh bl	35	7
1851 A988 60k violet	60	14
1852 A987 60k brt vio	60	14
1853 A987 1r red brn	1.00	28
Nos. 1840-1853 (14)	5.51	1.25

Issued to commemorate the All-Union Spartacist Games, Moscow, Aug. 5-16.

Parachute Landing A989

Building under Construction A990

1956, Aug. 5 ***Perf. 12x12½***

1854 A989 40k multi	40	14

Issued to commemorate the third World Parachute Championships, Moscow, July 1956.

1956 **Photo.** ***Perf. 12***

Designs: 60k, Building a factory. 1r, Building a dam.

1855 A990 40k dp org	15	7
1856 A990 60k brn car	28	9
1857 A990 1r int bl	42	12

Issued in honor of Builders' Day.

Ivan Franko A991

Makhmud Aivazov A992

1956, Aug. 27

1858 A991 40k dp cl	32	12
1859 A991 1r brt bl	65	18

Franko, writer (1856-1916).

1956, Aug. 27

Two types:
I. Three lines in panel with "148."

II. Two lines in panel with "148."

1860 A992 40k emer (II) 4.75 1.40
a Type I 20.00 17.50

Issued in honor of the 148th birthday of Russia's oldest man, an Azerbaijan collective farmer.

Robert Burns — A993

1956-57 **Photo.**

1861 A993 40k yel brn 1.50 1.25

Engr.

1861A A993 40k lt ultra & brn ('57) 1.50 85

Issued in honor of the 160th anniversary of the death of Robert Burns, Scottish poet. See No. 2174.

Portrait Type of 1956

Portrait: Lesya Ukrainka.

1956, Aug. 27 **Litho.**

1862 A979 40k ol, blk & brn 22 22

Issued in honor of Lesya Ukrainka (1871-1913), Ukrainian writer.

Statue of Nestor — A995

A. A. Ivanov — A996

1956, Sept. 22 ***Perf. 12x12½***

1863 A995 40k multi 42 12
1864 A995 1r multi 65 15

Issued to commemorate the 900th anniversary of the birth of Nestor, first Russian historian.

1956, Sept. 22 **Unwmk.**

1865 A996 40k gray & brn 32 15

Issued in honor of the 150th anniversary of the birth of Aleksandr Andreevich Ivanov (1806-1858), painter.

I. E. Repin and "Volga River Boatmen" — A997

"Cossacks Writing a Letter to the Turkish Sultan" — A998

1956, Aug. 21

Multicolored Centers

1866 A997 40k org brn & blk 2.50 50
1867 A998 1r chlky bl & blk 5.00 60

Issued to honor Ilya E. Repin (1844-1930), painter.

Chicken Farm A999

Designs: No. 1869, Harvest. 25k, Harvesting corn. No. 1871, Women in corn field. No. 1872, Farm buildings. No. 1873, Cattle. No. 1874, Farm workers, inscriptions and silos.

1956, Oct. 7

1868 A999 10k multi 12 10
1869 A999 10k multi 12 10
1870 A999 25k multi 24 15
1871 A999 40k multi 48 15
1872 A999 40k multi 48 15
1873 A999 40k multi 48 15
1874 A999 40k multi 48 15
Nos. 1868-1874 (7) 2.40 95

Nos. 1868, 1872 and 1873 measure 37x25½mm. Nos. 1869-1871 measure 37x27½mm. No. 1874 measures 37x21mm.

Benjamin Franklin — A1000

Portraits: No. 1876 Sesshu (Toyo Oda). No. 1877, Rembrandt. No. 1878, George Bernard Shaw. No. 1879, Mozart. No. 1880, Heinrich Heine. No. 1881, Fedor Dostoevski. No. 1882, Henrik Ibsen. No. 1883, Pierre Curie.

1956, Oct. 17 **Photo.**

Size: 25x37mm.

1875 A1000 40k cop brn 1.00 28
1876 A1000 40k brt org 80 14
1877 A1000 40k black 1.00 14
1878 A1000 40k black 80 14

Size: 21x32mm.

1879 A1000 40k grnsh bl 80 14
1880 A1000 40k violet 80 14
1881 A1000 40k green 80 14
1882 A1000 40k brown 80 14
1883 A1000 40k brt grn 1.00 28
Nos. 1875-1883 (9) 7.80 1.54

Issued in honor of great personalities of the world.

Antarctic Bases A1001

G. I. Kotovsky A1002

1956, Oct. 22 **Litho.** ***Perf. 12x12½***

1884 A1001 40k sl, grnsh bl & red 85 32

Issued to commemorate the Soviet Scientific Antarctic Expedition.

1956, Oct. 30

1885 A1002 40k magenta 50 15

Issued to commemorate the 75th anniversary of the birth of G. I. Kotovsky (1881-1925), military commander.

Portrait Type of 1956

Portrait: Julia A. Zemaite.

1956, Oct. 30 ***Perf. 12***

1886 A979 40k lt ol grn & brn 32 25

Julia A. Zemaite (1845-1921), Lithaunian novelist.

F. A. Bredichin A1004

1956, Oct. 30

1887 A1004 40k sep & ultra 2.50 65

Issued to commemorate the 125th anniversary of the birth of Fedor A. Bredichin (1831-1904), astronomer.

Aleksandr V. Suvorov — A1005

1956, Nov. 17 **Engr.**

1888 A1005 40k org & mar 20 10
1889 A1005 1r ol & dk red brn 40 15
1890 A1005 3r lt red brn & blk 1.10 65

Issued to commemorate the 225th anniversary of the birth of Field Marshal Count Aleksandr Suvorov (1730-1800).

Shatura Power Station A1006

1956 **Litho.** ***Perf. 12½x12***

1891 A1006 40k multi 25 10

Issued to commemorate the 30th anniversary of the Shatura power station.

Kryakutni's Balloon, 1731 A1007

1956, Nov. 17

1892 A1007 40k lt brn, sep & yel 28 10

Issued to commemorate the 225th anniversary of the first balloon ascension of the Russian inventor, Kryakutni.

Yuli M. Shokalski A1008

1956, Dec. 3 **Unwmk.** ***Perf. 12***

1893 A1008 40k ultra & brn 28 10

Issued to commemorate the centenary of the birth of Y. M. Shokalski (1856-1940), oceanographer and geodesist.

Vasnetsov and "Winter Scene" A1009

1956, Dec. 30

1894 A1009 40k multi 45 25

Issued to commemorate the centenary of the birth of Apollinari M. Vasnetsov (1856-1933), painter.

Indian Building and Books — A1010

Ivan Franko — A1011

1956, Dec. 26

1895 A1010 40k dp car 25 10

Issued to commemorate Kalidasa, 5th century Indian poet.

1956, Dec. 26 **Engr.**

1896 A1011 40k dk sl grn 25 10

Issued to commemorate Ivan Franko, Ukrainian writer. See Nos. 1858-1859.

Leo N. Tolstoy A1012

Portraits of Writers: No. 1898, Mikhail V. Lomonosov. No. 1899, Aleksander S. Pushkin. No. 1900, Maxim Gorki. No. 1901, Shota Rustaveli. No. 1902, Vissarion G. Belinski. No. 1903, Mikhail Y. Lermontov, poet, and Darjal Ravine in Caucasus.

1956-57 **Litho.** ***Perf. 12½x12***

Size: 37½x27½mm.

1897 A1012 40k brt grnsh bl & brn 25 10
1898 A1012 40k dk red, ol & brn ol 25 10

Size: 35½x25½mm.

1899 A1012 40k dk gray bl & brn 25 10
1900 A1012 40k blk & brn car 25 10
1901 A1012 40k ol, brn & ol gray 25 10
1902 A1012 40k bis, dl vio & brn ('57) 25 10
1903 A1012 40k ind & ol ('57) 25 10
Nos. 1897-1903 (7) 1.75 70

Issued in honor of famous Russian writers. See Nos. 1960-1962, 2031, 2112.

Fedor G. Volkov and Theater A1013

1956, Dec. 31 **Unwmk.**

1904 A1013 40k mag, gray & yel 25 10

Issued to commemorate the 200th anniversary of the founding of the St. Petersburg State Theater.

Vitus Bering and Map of Bering Strait A1016

1957, Feb. 6
1905 A1016 40k brn & bl 70 15

Issued to commemorate the 275th anniversary of the birth of Vitus Bering, Danish navigator and explorer.

Dmitri I. Mendeleev A1017

Mikhail I. Glinka A1018

1957, Feb. 6 ***Perf. 12x12½***
1906 A1017 40k gray & gray brn 60 50

Issued to commemorate the 50th anniversary of the death of D. I. Mendeleev (1834-1907), chemist.

1957, Feb. 23 ***Perf. 12***

Design: 1r, Scene from opera Ivan Susanin.

1907 A1018 40k dk red, buff & sep 40 12
1908 A1018 1r multi 65 20

Issued to commemorate the centenary of the death of Mikhail I. Glinka (1804-1857), composer.

Emblem A1019

Emblem A1020

1957, Feb. 23
1909 A1019 40k dk bl, red & ocher 25 10

All-Union festival of Soviet Youth, Moscow.

1957, Feb. 24 **Photo.**

Designs: 40k, Player. 60k, Goalkeeper.

1910 A1020 25k dp vio 38 10
1911 A1020 40k brt bl 38 12
1912 A1020 60k emerald 38 12

Issued to commemorate the 23rd Ice Hockey World Championship Games in Moscow.

Dove and Festival Emblem A1021

Assembly Line A1022

1957 **Litho.** ***Perf. 12***
1913 A1021 40k multi 25 12
1914 A1021 60k multi 35 15

6th World Youth Festival, Moscow. Exist imperf. Value, each $20.

1957, Mar. 15
1915 A1022 40k Prus grn & dp org 30 10

Moscow Machine Works centenary.

Black Grouse A1023

Axis Deer — A1024

Animals: 10k, Gray partridge. No. 1918, Polar bear. No. 1920, Bison. No. 1921, Mallard. No. 1922, European elk. No. 1923, Sable.

1957, Mar. 28
Center in Natural Colors

1916	A1024	10k	yel brn	35	12
1917	A1023	15k	brown	35	12
1918	A1023	15k	sl bl	38	12
1919	A1024	20k	red org	38	12
1920	A1023	30k	ultra	38	12
1921	A1023	30k	dk ol grn	38	12
1922	A1023	40k	dk ol grn	95	25
1923	A1024	40k	vio bl	95	25
			Nos. 1916-1923 (8)	4.12	1.22

See Nos. 2213-2219, 2429-2431.

Wooden Products, Hohloma A1025

National Handicrafts: No. 1925, Lace maker, Vologda. No. 1926, Bone carver, North Russia. No. 1927, Woodcarver, Moscow area. No. 1928, Rug weaver, Turkmenistan. No. 1929, Painting.

1957-58 **Unwmk.**

1924	A1025	40k	red org, yel & blk	48	12
1925	A1025	40k	brt car, yel & brn	48	12
1926	A1025	40k	ultra, buff & gray	48	12
1927	A1025	40k	brn, pale yel & hn brn	48	12
1928	A1025	40k	buff, brn, bl & org ('58)	60	25
1929	A1025	40k	multi ('58)	60	25
			Nos. 1924-1929 (6)	3.12	98

Aleksei N. Bach A1026

G. V. Plekhanov A1027

1957, Apr. 6 **Litho.** ***Perf. 12***
1930 A1026 40k ultra, brn & buff 32 10

Aleksei Nikolaievitch Bach, biochemist (1857-1946).

1957, Apr. 6 **Engr.**
1931 A1027 40k dl pur 28 10

Issued to commemorate the centenary of the birth of Georgi Valentinovich Plekhanov (1856-1918), political philosopher.

Leonhard Euler A1028

1957, Apr. 17 **Litho.**
1932 A1028 40k lil & gray 55 20

Issued to commemorate the 250th anniversary of the birth of Leonhard Euler (1707-1783), Swiss mathematician and physicist.

Lenin A1029

Youths of All Races Carrying Festival Banner A1030

Designs: No. 1934, Lenin talking to soldier and sailor. No. 1935, Lenin building barricades.

1957, Apr. 22
Multicolored Centers

1933 A1029 40k mag & bis 18 10
1934 A1029 40k mag & bis 18 10
1935 A1029 40k mag & bis 18 10

87th anniversary of the birth of Lenin.

1957, May 27 ***Perf. 12x12½***

Design: 20k, Sculptor with motherhood statue. 40k, Young couples dancing. 1r, Festival banner and fireworks over Moscow University.

1936	A1030	10k	emer, pur & yel	10	5
1937	A1030	20k	multi	15	7
1938	A1030	25k	emer, pur & yel	20	7
1939	A1030	40k	rose, bl grn & bis brn	30	7
1940	A1030	1r	multi	50	14
			Nos. 1936-1940 (5)	1.25	40

Issued to publicize the 6th World Youth Festival in Moscow. The 10k, 20k, and 1r exist imperf. Value each about $20.

Marine Museum Place and Neva A1031

Henry Fielding A1032

Designs: No. 1942, Lenin monument. No. 1943, Nevski Prospect and Admiralty.

1957, May 27 **Photo.** ***Perf. 12***
1941 A1031 40k bl grn 20 10
1942 A1031 40k redsh brn 20 10
1943 A1031 40k bluish vio 20 10
a Souvenir sheet of 3 6.00 4.00

250th anniversary of Leningrad.

No. 1943a contains three imperf. stamps similar to Nos. 1941, 1680 (in reddish brown) and 1943. This red-bordered sheet commemorates the 40th anniversary of the October Revolution, and shows a battleship in Leningrad Harbor. Size: 144x98mm. Issued Nov. 7, 1957. A similar sheet is listed as No. 2002a.

Type of 1953 Overprinted in Red **250 лет Ленинграда**

Designs: No. 1944, Peter I Statue, Decembrists' Square. No. 1945, Smolny Institute.

1957, May 27 ***Perf. 12½x12***
1944 A908 1r blk brn, *grnsh* 55 15
1945 A908 1r grn, *pink* 55 15

250th anniversary of Leningrad.
The overprint is in one line on No. 1945.

1957, June 20 **Litho.**
1946 A1032 40k multi 25 12

250th anniversary of the birth of Henry Fielding (1707-1754), English playwright and novelist.

William Harvey A1033

M. A. Balakirev A1034

1957, May 20 **Photo.**
1947 A1033 40k brown 15 12

Issued to commemorate the 300th anniversary of the death of the English physician William Harvey, discoverer of the blood circulation.

1957, May 20 **Engr.**
1948 A1034 40k bluish blk 25 12

Balakirev, composer (1836-1910).

A. I. Herzen and N. P. Ogarev A1035

1957, May 20 **Litho.**
1949 A1035 40k blk vio & dk ol gray 28 14

Centenary of newspaper Kolokol (Bell).

Kazakhstan Workers' Medal A1036

A. M. Liapunov A1037

1957, May 20
1950 A1036 40k lt bl, blk & yel 38 14

1957 **Photo.**

Portraits: No. 1952, V. Mickevicius Kapsukas, writer. No. 1953, G. Bashindchagian, Armenian painter. No. 1954, Yakub Kolas, Byelorussian poet. No. 1955, Carl von Linne, Swedish botanist.

Various Frames

1951	A1037	40k	dl red brn	1.00	65
1952	A1037	40k	sepia	1.00	65
1953	A1037	40k	sepia	1.00	65
1954	A1037	40k	gray	1.00	65
1955	A1037	40k	brn blk	1.00	65
	Nos. 1951-1955 (5)			5.00	3.25

See Nos. 2036-2038, 2059.

Bicyclist A1038

1957, June 20 **Litho.**

1956 A1038 40k cl & vio bl 20 12

10th Peace Bicycle Race.

Telescope — A1039

Designs: No. 1958, Comet and observatory. No. 1959, Rocket leaving earth.

1957, July 4

Size: 25½x37mm.

1957	A1039	40k	brn, ocher & bl	70	22
1958	A1039	40k	ind, lt bl & yel	70	22

Size: 14½x21mm.

1959 A1039 40k bl vio 70 22

Issued to publicize the International Geophysical Year, 1957-58. See Nos. 2089-2091.

Folksinger A1040

1957, May 20

1960 A1040 40k multi 20 12

Issued in honor of "The Song of Igor's Army," Russia's oldest literary work.

Taras G. Shevchenko A1041

Design: No. 1962, Nikolai G. Chernyshevski.

1957, July 20

1961	A1041	40k	grn & dk red brn	18	12
1962	A1041	40k	org brn & grn	18	12

Issued in honor of T. C. Shevchenko, Ukrainian poet. (No. 1961), and N. G. Chernyshevski, writer and politician (No. 1962).

Woman Gymnast — A1043

Designs: 25k, Wresting. No. 1965, Stadium. No. 1966, Youths of three races. 60k, Javelin thrower.

1957, July 15 **Litho.** ***Perf. 12***

1963	A1043	20k	bluish vio & org brn	12	7
1964	A1043	25k	brt grn & cl	12	7
1965	A1043	40k	Prus bl, ol & red	18	10
1966	A1043	40k	crim & vio	18	10
1967	A1043	60k	ultra & brn	25	12
	Nos. 1963-1967 (5)			85	46

Third International Youth Games, Moscow.

Javelin Thrower — A1044

Designs: No. 1969, Sprinter. 25k, Somersault. No. 1971, Boxers. No. 1972, Soccer players (horiz.). 60k, Weight lifter.

1957, July 20 **Unwmk.**

1968	A1044	20k	lt ultra & ol blk	12	7
1969	A1044	20k	brt grn, red vio & blk	12	7
1970	A1044	25k	org, ultra & blk	12	10
1971	A1044	40k	rose vio & blk	30	10
1972	A1044	40k	dp pink, bl, buff & blk	30	10
1973	A1044	60k	lt vio & brn	60	15
	Nos. 1968-1973 (6)			1.56	59

Issued to commemorate the success of Soviet athletes at the 16th Olympic Games, Melbourne.

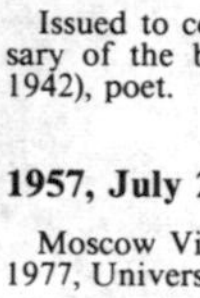

Yanka Kupala A1045

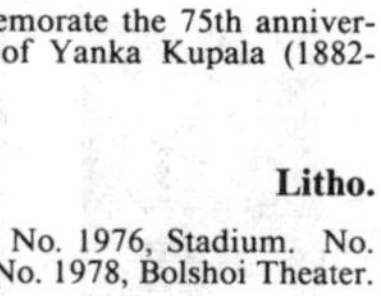

Kremlin A1046

1957, July 27 **Photo.**

1974 A1045 40k dk gray 60 60

Issued to commemorate the 75th anniversary of the birth of Yanka Kupala (1882-1942), poet.

1957, July 27 **Litho.**

Moscow Views: No. 1976, Stadium. No. 1977, University. No. 1978, Bolshoi Theater.

Center in Black

1975	A1046	40k	dl red brn	22	15
1976	A1046	40k	brn vio	22	15
1977	A1046	1r	red	52	20
1978	A1046	1r	brt vio bl	52	20

Sixth World Youth Festival, Moscow.

Lenin Library A1047

1957, July 27 **Photo.**

1979 A1047 40k brt grnsh bl 20 12

a. Souv. sheet of 2, light blue, imperf. 12.00 *15.00*

Intl. Phil. Exhib., Moscow, July 29-Aug. 11. No. 1979 exists imperf. Value $12.

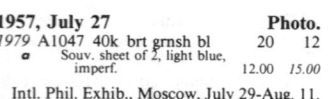

Pierre Jean de Beranger A1048

Globe, Dove and Olive Branch A1049

1957, Aug. 9

1980 A1048 40k brt bl grn 20 12

Death centenary of Pierre Jean de Beranger (1780-1857), French song writer.

1957, Aug. 8 **Litho.**

1981	A1049	40k	bl, grn & bis brn	42	30
1982	A1049	1r	vio, grn & brn	1.10	55

Publicity for world peace.

Portrait Type of 1956

1957, Aug. 9

Portrait: 40k, Clara Zetkin.

1983 A979 40k gray bl, brn & blk 40 20

Birth centenary of Clara Zetkin (1857-1933), German communist.

Krenholm Factory, Narva — A1050

1957, Sept. 8 **Photo.**

1984 A1050 40k blk brn 35 12

Issued to commemorate the centenary of Krenholm textile factory, Narva, Estonia.

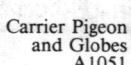

Carrier Pigeon and Globes A1051

1957, Sept. 26 **Unwmk.** ***Perf. 12***

1985	A1051	40k	blue	12	10
1986	A1051	60k	lilac	25	12

Issued to publicize International Letter Writing Week, Oct. 6-12.

Wyborshez Factory, Lenin Statue A1052

1957, Sept. 23 **Litho.**

1987 A1052 40k dk bl 25 10

Centenary of Krasny Wyborshez factory, Leningrad.

Vladimir V. Stasov — A1053

1957, Sept. 23 **Engr.**

1988	A1053	40k	brown	30	7
1989	A1053	1r	bluish blk	60	14

Issued to commemorate the 50th anniversary of the death of Vladimir Vasilievich Stasov (1824-1906), art and music critic.

Congress Emblem A1054

1957, Oct. 7 **Litho.** ***Perf. 12***

1990 A1054 40k gray bl & blk, *bluish* 25 10

Issued to publicize the fourth International Trade Union Congress, Leipzig, Oct. 4-15.

Konstantin E. Tsiolkovsky and Rockets A1055

1957, Oct. 7

1991 A1055 40k dk bl & pale brn 1.40 60

Centenary of the birth of Konstantin E. Tsiolkovsky (1857-1935), rocket and astronautics pioneer.

See No. 2021.

Sputnik 1 Circling Globe A1056

Turbine Wheel, Kuibyshev Hydroelectric Station A1057

1957 **Photo.**

1992	A1056	40k	ind, *bluish*	55	30
1993	A1056	40k	brt bl	55	30

Launching of first artificial earth satellite, Oct. 4. Issue dates: No. 1992, Nov. 5; No. 1993, Dec. 28.

1957, Nov. 20 **Litho.**

1994 A1057 40k red brn 18 10

All-Union Industrial Exhibition. See No. 2030.

Meteor A1058

Lenin A1059

1957, Nov. 20

1995 A1058 40k multi		40	12

Issued to commemorate the 10th anniversary of the falling of the Sihote Alinj meteor.

1957, Oct. 30 **Engr.**

Design: 60k, Lenin reading Pravda (horiz.).

1996 A1059 40k blue	30	7
1997 A1059 60k rose red	35	7

40th anniversary of October Revolution.

Students and Moscow University A1060

Worker and Railroad A1061

Designs: No. 1999, Red flag and Lenin. No. 2000, Lenin addressing workers and peasants. 60k, Harvester.

Perf. 12½x12, 12x12½, 12½

1957, Oct. 15 **Litho.**

1998 A1060 10k buff, sep & red	8	5
1999 A1060 40k buff, red, sep & yel	24	7
2000 A1060 40k red, blk & yel	24	7
2001 A1060 40k red, yel & grn	24	7
2002 A1060 60k red, ocher & vio brn	32	10
a Souvenir sheet of 3	5.50	3.50
Nos. 1998-2002 (5)	1.12	36

Issued to commemorate the 40th anniversary of the October Revolution. No. 2002a measures 144x98mm. and contains one each of Nos. 2000-2002 imperf. The sheet shows night view of Moscow and red ribbon. A similar sheet is listed as No. 1943a.

Nos. 1998-2002 exist imperf.

Federal Socialist Republic A1062

Uzbek Republic A1063

Designs (Republic): No. 2005, Tadzhik (Building and peasant girl). No. 2006, Byelorussia (Truck). No. 2007, Azerbaijan (Buildings). No. 2008, Georgia (Valley, palm and couple). No. 2009, Armenia, (Fruit, power line and mountains). No. 2010, Turkmen (couple and lambs). No. 2011, Ukraine (Farmers). No. 2012, Kazakh (Harvester and combine). No. 2013, Kirghiz, (Horseback rider and building). No. 2014, Moldavia (Automatic sorting machine). No. 2015, Estonia (Girl in national costume). No. 2016, Latvia (Couple, sea and field). No. 2017, Lithuania (Farm and farmer couple).

1957, Oct. 25

2003 A1062 40k multi	40	10
2004 A1063 40k multi	40	10
2005 A1062 40k multi	40	10
2006 A1062 40k multi	40	10
2007 A1062 40k multi	40	10
2008 A1062 40k multi	40	10
2009 A1062 40k multi	40	10
2010 A1062 40k multi	40	10
2011 A1063 40k multi	40	10
2012 A1062 40k multi	40	10
2013 A1062 40k multi	40	10
2014 A1062 40k multi	40	10
2015 A1063 40k multi	40	10
2016 A1062 40k multi	40	10
2017 A1062 40k multi	40	10
Nos. 2003-2017 (15)	6.00	1.50

40th anniversary of the October Revolution.

Artists and Academy of Art A1064

Red Army Monument, Berlin A1065

Monument: 1r, Worker and Peasant monument, Moscow.

1957, Dec. 16

2018 A1064 40k blk, *pale sal*	12	10
2019 A1065 60k black	15	10
2020 A1065 1r blk, *pink*	25	12

200th anniversary of the Academy of Arts, Leningrad. Artists on 40k are K. P. Bryulov, Ilya Repin and V. I. Surikov.

No. 1991 Overprinted in Black **4/X-57 г. Первый в мире искусств. спутник Земли**

1957, Nov. 28

2021 A1055 40k dk bl & pale brn	6.50	4.25

Launching of Sputnik 1.

Ukrainian Arms, Symbolic Figures A1066

1957, Dec. 24

2022 A1066 40k yel, red & bl	30	15

Issued to commemorate the 40th anniversary of the Ukrainian Soviet Republic.

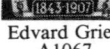

Edvard Grieg A1067

Giuseppe Garibaldi A1068

1957, Dec. 24 **Photo.**

2023 A1067 40k blk, *buff*	35	20

50th anniversary of the death of Edvard Grieg, Norwegian composer.

1957, Dec. 24 **Litho.**

2024 A1068 40k plum, lt grn & blk	35	15

150th anniversary of birth of Giuseppe Garibaldi, (1807-1882) Italian patriot.

V. L. Borovikovsky A1069

Kuibyshev Hydroelectric Station and Dam A1070

1957, Dec. 24 **Photo.**

2025 A1069 40k brown	35	15

Issued to commemorate the 200th anniversary of the birth of Vladimir Lukich Borovikovsky (1757-1825), painter.

Portrait Type of 1956

Portrait: 40k, Mariya Nikolayevna Ermolova (1853-1928), actress.

1957, Dec. 28 **Litho.**

2026 A984 40k red brn & brt vio	25	15

1957, Dec. 28

2027 A1070 40k dk bl, *buff*	35	15

Type of 1956

1958, Jan. 8

Portrait: 40k, Rosa Luxemburg (1870-1919), German socialist.

2028 A979 40k bl & brn	75	75

Chi Pai-shih A1070a

Flag and Symbols of Industry A1070b

1958, Jan. 8 **Photo.**

2029 A1070a 40k dp vio	35	15

Issued to honor Chi Pai-shih (1860-1957), Chinese painter.

1958, Jan. 8 **Litho.**

2030 A1070b 60k gray vio, red & blk	50	15

All-Union Industrial Exhibition. Exists imperf.

Aleksei N. Tolstoi A1071

1958, Jan. 28 **Photo.** ***Perf. 12***

2031 A1071 40k brn ol	30	15

Tolstoi, novelist and dramatist (1883-1945).

Symbolic Figure Greeting Sputnik 2 — A1072

1957-58 **Litho.**

Figure in Buff

2032 A1072 20k blk & rose	25	6
2033 A1072 40k blk & grn ('58)	35	12
2034 A1072 60k blk & lt brn ('58)	55	18
2035 A1072 1r blk & bl	70	24

Launching of Sputnik 2, Nov. 3, 1957.

Small Portrait Type of 1957

Portraits: No. 2036, Henry W. Longfellow, American poet. No. 2037, William Blake, English artist, poet, mystic. No. 2038, E. Sharents, Armenian poet.

1958, Mar. **Unwmk.** ***Perf. 12***

Various Frames

2036 A1037 40k gray blk	40	35
2037 A1037 40k gray blk	40	35
2038 A1037 40k sepia	40	35

Victory at Pskov A1073

Soldier and Civilian A1074

Designs: No. 2040, Airman, sailor and soldier. No. 2042, Sailor and soldier. 60k, Storming of Berlin Reichstag building.

1958, Feb. 21

2039 A1073 25k multi	7	5
2040 A1073 40k multi	12	7
2041 A1074 40k multi	12	7
2042 A1074 40k multi	12	7
2043 A1073 60k multi	22	10
Nos. 2039-2043 (5)	65	36

40th anniversary of Red Armed Forces.

Peter Ilich Tchaikovsky A1075

Swan Lake Ballet A1076

Design: 1r, Tchaikovsky, pianist and violinist.

1958, Mar. 18

2044 A1075 40k grn, bl, brn & red	24	10
2045 A1076 40k grn, ultra, red & yel	24	10
2046 A1075 1r lake & emer	65	25

Issued to honor Tchaikovsky and publicize the Tchaikovsky competitions for pianists and violinists. Exist imperf. Value, set $10.

Nos. 2044-2045 were printed in sheets of 30, including 15 stamps of each value and 5 se-tenant pairs.

V. F. Rudnev A1077

Maxim Gorki A1078

1958, Mar. 25 **Unwmk.**

2047 A1077 40k grn, blk & ocher	38	12

Issued in honor of V. F. Rudnev, naval commander.

1958, Apr. 3 **Litho.** ***Perf. 12***

2048 A1078 40k multi	18	12

Issued to commemorate the 90th anniversary of the birth of Maxim Gorki, writer.

Spasski Tower
A1079

Russian Pavilion, Brussels
A1080

1958, Apr. 9

2049 A1079 40k dp vio, *pnksh* 22 10
2050 A1079 60k rose red 32 15

Issued to publicize the 13th Congress of the Young Communist League (Komsomol).

1958, Apr.

2051 A1080 10k multi 12 5
2052 A1080 40k multi 30 10

Issued for the Universal and International Exhibition at Brussels. Exist imperf. Value $2.

Lenin
A1081

Jan A. Komensky (Comenius)
A1082

1958, Apr. 22 **Engr.**

2053 A1081 40k dk bl gray 30 7
2054 A1081 60k rose brn 40 10
2055 A1081 1r brown 70 14

88th anniversary of the birth of Lenin.

1958, May 5

Portrait: Nos. 2056-2058, Karl Marx.

2056 A1081 40k brown 15 7
2057 A1081 60k dk bl 30 10
2058 A1081 1r dk red 60 15

140th anniversary of the birth of Marx.

1958, Apr. 17 **Photo.**

2059 A1082 40k green 30 32

No. 1695 Overprinted in Blue **200 лет Академии художеств СССР. 1957**

1958, Apr. 22

2060 A914 40k multi 1.25 40

Issued to commemorate the 200th anniversary of the Academy of Arts, Moscow.

Lenin Order
A1083

Carlo Goldoni
A1084

1958, Apr. 30 **Litho.**

2061 A1083 40k brn, yel & red 28 10

1958, Apr. 28 **Photo.**

2062 A1084 40k bl & dk gray 28 10

Issued in honor of Carlo Goldoni, Italian dramatist.

Radio Tower, Ship and Planes
A1085

1958, May 7

2063 A1085 40k bl grn & red 1.00 25

Issued for Radio Day, May 7.

Globe and Dove
A1086

Ilya Chavchavadze
A1087

1958, May 6 **Litho.**

2064 A1086 40k bl & blk 16 10
2065 A1086 60k ultra & blk 25 10

Issued to publicize the 4th Congress of the International Democratic Women's Federation, June, 1958, at Vienna.

1958, May 12 **Photo.**

2066 A1087 40k blk & bl 25 10

Issued to commemorate the 50th anniversary of the death of Ilya Chavchavadze, Georgian writer.

Flags and Communication Symbols — A1088

1958-59 **Litho.**

2067 A1088 40k bl, red, yel & blk 2.50 85
a Red half of Czech flag at bottom 2.50 70

Issued to commemorate a communist ministers' meeting on social problems in Moscow, Dec. 1957.

On No. 2067, the Czech flag (center flag in vertical row of five) is incorrectly pictured with red stripe on top. This error is corrected on No. 2067a.

Bugler — A1089

Children of Three Races — A1090

Design: 25k, Boy with model plane.

1958, May 29 **Unwmk.** ***Perf. 12***

2068 A1089 10k ultra, red & red brn 10 5
2069 A1089 25k ultra, yel & red brn 12 10

Issued to honor the Pioneers.

1958, May 29

Design: No. 2071, Child and bomb.

2070 A1090 40k car, ultra & brn 15 10
2071 A1090 40k car & brn 15 10

Issued for the International Day for the Protection of Children.

Soccer Players and Globe
A1091

Nikolai A. Rimski-Korsakov
A1092

1958, June 5

2072 A1091 40k bl, red & buff 16 10
2073 A1091 60k bl, red & buff 35 12

Issued to commemorate the 6th World Soccer Championships, Stockholm, June 8-29. Exist imperf. Value $2.50.

1958, June 5 **Photo.**

2074 A1092 40k bl & brn 32 10

Issued to commemorate the 50th anniversary of the death of Nikolai Andreevich Rimski-Korsakov (1844-1908), composer.

Girl Gymnast — A1093

Design: No. 2076, Gymnast on rings and view.

1958, June 24 **Litho.**

2075 A1093 40k ultra, red & buff 30 10
2076 A1093 40k bl, red buff & grn 30 10

14th World Gymnastic Championships, Moscow, July 6-10.

Bomb, Globe, Atom, Sputniks, Ship
A1094

1958, July 1

2077 A1094 60k dk bl, blk & org 38 12

Issued to publicize a conference for peaceful uses of atomic energy, held at Stockholm.

Street Fighters — A1095

Congress Emblem — A1097

Moscow State University
A1096

1958, July 5

2078 A1095 40k red & vio blk 18 12

Issued to commemorate the 40th anniversary of the Communist Party in the Ukraine.

1958, July 8 ***Perf. 12***

2079 A1096 40k red & bl 22 10
2080 A1097 60k lt grn, bl & red 35 15
a Souv. sheet 4.50 5.50

Issued to commemorate the fifth Congress of the International Architects' Organization, Moscow.

No. 2080a contains one each of Nos. 2079-2080, imperf., with background design in yellow, brown, blue and red. Size 94½x144mm. Issued Sept. 8, 1958.

Young Couple
A1098

1958, June 25

2081 A1098 40k bl & ocher 15 8
2082 A1098 60k yel grn & ocher 28 10

Issued for the Day of Soviet Youth.

Sputnik 3 Leaving Earth
A1099

Sadriddin Aini
A1100

1958, June 16

2083 A1099 40k vio bl, grn & rose 60 20

Launching of Sputnik 3, May 15. Printed in sheets with alternating labels, giving details of launching.

1958, July 15

2084 A1100 40k rose, blk & buff 30 12

Issued to commemorate the 80th birthday of Sadriddin Aini, Tadzhik writer.

Emblem
A1101

1958, July 21 **Typo.** ***Perf. 12***

2085 A1101 40k lil & bl 25 12

Issued to publicize the first World Trade Union Conference of Working Youths, Prague, July 14-20.

Type of 1958-59 and

TU-104 and Globe
A1102

Design: 1r, Turbo-propeller liner AN-10.

1958, Aug. **Litho.**

2086 A1102 60k bl, red & bis 22 10
2087 A1123 1r yel, red & blk 38 14

Issued to honor Russian civil aviation. Exist imperf. Value, set $5.50. See Nos. 2147-2151.

L. A. Kulik — A1103

1958, Aug. 12
2088 A1103 40k sep, bl, yel & cl 60 15

Issued to commemorate the 50th anniversary of the falling of the Tungus meteor and the 75th anniversary of the birth of L. A. Kulik, meteorist.

IGY Type of 1957

1958, July 29

Designs: No. 2089, Aurora borealis and camera. No. 2090, Schooner "Zarja" exploring earth magnetism. No. 2091, Weather balloon and radar.

Size: 25½ x 37mm.

2089 A1039 40k bl & brt yel 38 10
2090 A1039 40k bl grn 38 10
2091 A1039 40k brt ultra 38 10

International Geophysical Year, 1957-58.

Crimea Observatory A1104

Moscow University A1105

Design: 1r, Telescope.

1958, Aug. **Photo.**
2092 A1104 40k brn & brt grnsh bl 35 12
2093 A1105 60k lt bl, vio & yel 50 15
2094 A1104 1r dp bl & org brn 60 18

Issued to publicize the 10th Congress of the International Astronomical Union, Moscow.

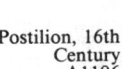

Postilion, 16th Century A1106

Designs: No. 2095, 15th century letter writer. No. 2097, A. L. Ordyn-Natshokin and sleigh mail coach, 17th century. No. 2098, Mail coach and post office, 18th century. No. 2099, Troika, 19th century. No. 2100, Lenin stamp, ship and Moscow University. No. 2101, Jet plane and postilion. No. 2102, Leningrad Communications Museum (vert.). No. 2103, V. N. Podbielski and letter carriers. No. 2104, Mail train. No. 2105, Loading mail on plane. No. 2106, Ship, plane, train and globe.

1958, Aug. Unwmk. Litho. ***Perf. 12***
2095 A1106 10k red, blk, yel & lil 8 5
2096 A1106 10k multi 8 5
2097 A1106 25k ultra & sl 18 5
2098 A1106 25k blk & ultra 18 5
2099 A1106 40k car lake & brn blk 22 7
2100 A1106 40k blk, mag & brn 22 7
2101 A1106 40k red, org & gray 22 7
2102 A1106 40k sal & brn 22 7
2103 A1106 60k grnsh bl & red lil 32 10
2104 A1106 60k grnsh bl & lil 32 10
2105 A1106 1r multi 48 15
2106 A1106 1r multi 48 15
Nos. 2095-2106 (12) 3.00 98

Centenary of Russian postage stamps.

Two imperf. souvenir sheets exist, measuring 155x106mm. One contains one each of Nos. 2095-2099, with background design in red, ultramarine, yellow and brown. The other contains one each of Nos. 2100, 2103-2106, with background design in blue, gray, ocher, pink and brown. Value for both, $10 unused, $6.50 canceled.

Nos. 2096, 2100-2101 exist imperf. Value each $2.50.

M. I. Chigorin A1107

Golden Gate, Vladimir A1108

1958, Aug. 30 **Photo.**
2107 A1107 40k blk & emer 30 12

Issued to commemorate the 50th anniversary of the death of M. I. Chigorin, chess player.

1958, Aug. 23 **Litho.**

Design: 60k, Gorki Street with trolley bus and truck.

2108 A1108 40k multi 12 6
2109 A1108 60k lt vio, yel & blk 25 10

Issued to commemorate the 850th anniversary of the city of Vladimir.

Nurse Bandaging Man's Leg — A1109

Design: No. 2111, Hospital and people of various races.

1958, Sept. 15
2110 A1109 40k multi 20 10
2111 A1109 40k ol, lem & red 20 10

Issued to honor 40 years of Red Cross-Red Crescent work.

Portrait Type of 1958

1958, Sept. 15

Portrait: M. E. Saltykov (Shchedrin).

2112 A1071 40k brn blk & mar 32 10

Issued to honor Mikhail E. Saltykov (Shchedrin), writer.

Rudagi A1110

V. V. Kapnist A1111

1958, Oct. 10 Litho. ***Perf. 12***
2113 A1110 40k multi 20 10

Issued to commemorate the 1100th anniversary of the birth of Rudagi, Persian poet.

1958, Sept. 30
2114 A1111 40k bl & gray 20 10

Issued to commemorate the 200th anniversary of the birth of V. V. Kapnist, poet and dramatist.

Book, Torch, Lyre, Flower A1112

1958, Oct. 4
2115 A1112 40k red org, ol & blk 20 10

Issued to commemorate the Conference of Asian and African Writers, Tashkent.

Chelyabinsk Tractor Factory A1113

Designs: No. 2117, Zaporozstal foundry. No. 2118, Ural machine building plant.

1958, Oct. 20 **Photo.**
2116 A1113 40k grn & yel 16 7
2117 A1113 40k brn red & yel 16 7
2118 A1113 40k blue 16 7

Issued to honor pioneers of Russian Industry.

Ancient Georgian on Horseback A1114

1958, Oct. 18 **Litho.**
2119 A1114 40k ocher, ultra & red 32 12

Issued to commemorate the 1500th anniversary of Tbilisi, capital of Georgia.

Red Square, Moscow — A1115

Cities: No. 2121, Lenin Square, Alma Ata. No. 2122, Lenin statue, Ashkhabad. No. 2123, Lenin statue, Tashkent. No. 2124, Lenin Square, Stalinabad. No. 2125, Rustaveli Ave., Tbilisi. No. 2126, View from Dvina River, Riga. No. 2127, University Square, Frunze. No. 2128, View, Yerevan. No. 2129, Communist Street, Baku. No. 2130, Lenin Prospect, Kishinev. No. 2131, Round Square, Minsk. No. 2132, Viru Gate, Tallinn. No. 2133, Main Street, Kiev. No. 2134, View, Vilnius.

1958 **Engr.**
2120 A1115 40k violet 16 10
2121 A1115 40k brt bl grn 16 10
2122 A1115 40k grnsh gray 16 10
2123 A1115 40k dk gray 16 10
2124 A1115 40k blue 16 10
2125 A1115 40k vio bl 16 10
2126 A1115 40k brn red 16 10
2127 A1115 40k dk bl gray 16 10
2128 A1115 40k brown 16 10
2129 A1115 40k purple 16 10
2130 A1115 40k olive 16 10
2131 A1115 40k gray brn 16 10
2132 A1115 40k emerald 16 10
2133 A1115 40k lil rose 16 10
2134 A1115 40k org ver 16 10
Nos. 2120-2134 (15) 2.40 1.50

Capitals of Soviet republics.
See No. 2836.

Young Civil War Soldier, 1919 — A1116

Designs: 20k, Industrial brigade. 25k, Youth in World War II. 40k, Girl farm worker. 60k, Youth building new towns. 1r, Students, fighters for culture.

1958, Oct. 25 **Litho.**
2135 A1116 10k multi 8 5
2136 A1116 20k multi 9 5
2137 A1116 25k multi 14 7
2138 A1116 40k multi 16 7
2139 A1116 60k multi 25 10
2140 A1116 1r multi 60 25
Nos. 2135-2140 (6) 1.32 59

Issued to commemorate the 40th anniversary of the Young Communist League (Komsomol).

Marx and Lenin A1117

Lenin, Intellectual, Peasant and Miner A1118

1958, Oct. 31
2141 A1117 40k multi 20 10
2142 A1118 1r multi 40 12

41st anniversary of Russian Revolution.

Torch, Wreath and Family A1119

Sergei Esenin A1120

1958, Nov. 5
2143 A1119 60k blk, beige & dl bl 30 10

Issued to commemorate the tenth anniversary of the Universal Declaration of Human Rights.

1958, Nov. 29
2144 A1120 40k multi 30 10

Sergei Esenin (1895-1925), poet.

G. K. Ordzhonikidze A1121

Kuan Han-ching A1122

1958, Dec. 12 ***Perf. 12***
2145 A1121 40k multi 22 10

G. K. Ordzhonikidze (1886-1937), Georgian party worker.

1958, Dec. 5
2146 A1122 40k dk bl & gray 22 10

Issued to commemorate the 700th anniversary of the theater of Kuan Han-ching, Chinese dramatist.

Airliner IL-14 and Globe — A1123

Designs: No. 2148, Jet liner TU-104. No. 2149, Turbo-propeller liner TU-114. 60k, Jet liner TU-110. 2r, Turbo-propeller liner IL-18.

1958-59

2147 A1123 20k ultra, blk & red 12 5
2148 A1123 40k bl grn, blk & red 20 7
2149 A1123 40k brt bl, blk & red 20 7
2150 A1123 60k rose car & blk 22 10
2151 A1123 2r plum, red & blk ('59) 55 20
Nos. 2147-2151 (5) 1.29 49

Issued to honor Russian civil aviation. Exist imperf.; value $8.50.

See Nos. 2086-2087.

Eleonora Duse A1124

John Milton A1125

1958, Dec. 26

2152 A1124 40k bl grn & gray 20 10

Issued to commemorate the centenary of the birth of Eleonora Duse, Italian actress.

1958, Dec. 17

2153 A1125 40k brown 20 10

350th birth anniversary of John Milton (1608-1674), English poet.

K. F. Rulye A1126

Fuzuli A1127

1958, Dec. 26

2154 A1126 40k ultra & blk 20 10

Issued to commemorate the centenary of the death of K. F. Rulye, educator.

1958, Dec. 23 **Photo.**

2155 A1127 40k grnsh bl & brn 20 10

Issued to commemorate the 400th anniversary of the death of Fuzuli (Mehmet Suleiman Oglou), Turkish poet.

Census Emblem and Family A1128

Lunik and Sputniks over Kremlin A1129

Design: No. 2157, Census emblem.

1958, Dec. **Litho.**

2156 A1128 40k multi 20 10
2157 A1128 40k yel, gray, bl & red 20 10

Issued to publicize the 1959 Russian census.

1959, Jan. **Unwmk.** ***Perf. 12***

Designs: 40k, Lenin and view of Kremlin. 60k, Workers and Lenin power plant on Volga.

2158 A1129 40k multi 28 15
2159 A1129 60k multi 42 18
2160 A1129 1r red, yel & vio bl 1.00 30

Issued to commemorate the 21st Congress of the Communist Party and to mark "the conquest of the cosmos by the Soviet people."

Lenin Statue, Minsk Buildings — A1130

Atomic Icebreaker "Lenin" A1131

1958, Dec. 20

2161 A1130 40k red, buff & brn 22 12

Issued to commemorate the 40th anniversary of the Byelorussian Republic.

1958, Dec. 31

Design: 60k, Diesel Locomotive "TE-3."

2162 A1131 40k multi 48 18
2163 A1131 60k multi 70 25

Shalom Aleichem A1132

Evangelista Torricelli A1133

1959, Feb. 10

2164 A1132 40k chocolate 22 15

Issued to commemorate the centenary of the birth of Shalom Aleichem, Yiddish writer.

1959, Feb.

Scientists: No. 2166, Charles Darwin, English biologist. No. 2167, N. F. Gamaleya, microbiologist.

Various Frames

2165 A1133 40k bl grn & blk 30 10
2166 A1133 40k chlky bl & brn 30 10
2167 A1133 40k dk red & blk 30 10

Issued to honor famous scientists.

Woman Skater A1134

Frederic Joliot-Curie A1135

1959, Feb. 5

2168 A1134 25k ultra, blk & ver 20 10
2169 A1134 40k ultra & blk 35 10

Women's International Ice Skating Championships, Sverdlovsk.

No. 1717 Overprinted in Orange Brown

Победа баскетбольной команды СССР. Чили 1959 г.

1959, Feb. 12

2170 A919 1r org brn, dk brn & brn 2.25 1.10

Issued to commemorate the "Victory of the U.S.S.R. Basketball Team - Chile 1959." However, the 3rd World Basketball Championship honors went to Bulgaria when the Soviet team was disqualified for refusing to play Nationalist China.

1959, Mar. 3 **Litho.** ***Perf. 12***

2171 A1135 40k turq bl & gray brn, *beige* 30 18

Frederic Joliot-Curie (1900-1958), French scientist.

Selma Lagerlöf A1136

Peter Zwirka A1137

1959, Feb. 26

2172 A1136 40k red brn & blk 25 10

Issued to commemorate the centenary of the birth of Selma Lagerlöf (1858-1940), Swedish writer.

1959, Mar. 3

2173 A1137 40k hn brn & blk, *yel* 25 10

Issued to commemorate the 50th anniversary of the birth of Peter Zwirka (1909-1947), Lithuanian writer.

No. 1861A Overprinted in Red: "1759 1959"

1959, Feb. 26 **Engr.**

2174 A993 40k lt ultra & brn 4.75 4.00

Issued to commemorate the 200th anniversary of the birth of Robert Burns, Scottish poet.

Type of 1958

Russian Writers: No. 2175, A. S. Griboedov. No. 2176, A. N. Ostrovski. No. 2177, Anton Chekhov. No. 2178, I. A. Krylov. No. 2178A, Nikolai V. Gogol, No. 2178B, S. T. Aksakov. No. 2178C, A. V. Koltzov. poet, and reaper.

1959 **Litho.**

2175 A1071 40k buff, cl, blk & vio 28 20
2176 A1071 40k vio & brn 28 20
2177 A1071 40k sl & hn brn 28 20
2178 A1071 40k ol bis & brn 28 20
2178A A1071 40k ol, gray & bis 28 20
2178B A1071 40k brn, vio & bis 28 20
2178C A1071 40k vio & blk 28 20
Nos. 2175-2178C (7) 1.96 1.40

No. 2178A commemorates the sesquicentennial of the birth of Nikolai V. Gogol, writer. No. 2178B commemorates the centenary of the death of S. T. Aksakov, writer.

A. S. Popov and Rescue from Ice Float — A1138

Design: 60k, Radio broadcasting "Peace" in five languages.

1959, Mar. 13

2179 A1138 40k brn, blk & dk bl 35 12
2180 A1138 60k multi 55 20

Issued to commemorate the centenary of the birth of A. S. Popov, pioneer in radio research.

M.S. Rossija at Odessa A1139

Ships: 10k, Steamer, Vladivostok-Petropavlovsk-Kamchatka line. 20k, M.S. Feliks Dzerzhinski, Odessa-Latakia line. No. 2184, Ship, Murmansk-Tyksi line. 60k, M.S. Mikhail Kalinin at Leningrad. 1r, M.S. Baltika, Leningrad-London line.

1959 **Litho.** **Unwmk.**

2181 A1139 10k multi 8 5
2182 A1139 20k red, lt grn & dk bl 16 8
2183 A1139 40k multi 20 8
2184 A1139 40k bl, buff & red 20 8
2185 A1139 60k bl grn, red & buff 32 8
2186 A1139 1r ultra, red & yel 48 12
Nos. 2181-2186 (6) 1.44 49

Issued to honor the Russian fleet.

Globe and Luna 1 — A1140

Design: No. 2188, Globe and route of Luna 1.

1959, Apr. 13

2187 A1140 40k red brn & rose 40 12
2188 A1140 40k ultra & bl 40 12

Luna 1, launched Jan. 2, 1959.

Saadi and "Gulistan" A1141

1959, Mar. 20 **Photo.**

2189 A1141 40k dk bl & blk 25 22

Issued to honor the Persian poet Saadi (Muslih-ud-Din) and to commemorate the 700th anniversary of his book, "Gulistan" (1258).

Suahan S. Orbeliani A1142

Drawing by Korin A1143

1959, Apr. 2

2190 A1142 40k dl rose & blk 20 18

Suahan S. Orbeliani (1658-1725), Georgian writer.

1959, Apr. 10 **Litho.**

2191 A1143 40k multi 18 18

Issued to honor Ogata Korin (1653?-1716), Japanese artist.

The Scott Catalogue value is a retail price, what you could expect to pay for the stamp in a grade of Fine-Very Fine. The value listed is a reference which reflects recent actual dealer selling price.

Lenin
A1144

Marcel
Cachin
A1146

1959, Apr. 17 **Engr.**

2192	A1144	40k sepia	18	18

89th anniversary of the birth of Lenin.

1959, Apr. 27 **Photo.**

2194	A1146	60k dk brn	18	18

Issued to commemorate Marcel Cachin (1869-1958), French Communist Party leader.

Joseph Haydn
A1147

Alexander
von
Humboldt
A1148

1959, May 8

2195	A1147	40k dk bl, gray & brn blk	18	10

Issued to commemorate the sesquicentennial of the death of Joseph Haydn, Austrian composer.

1959, May 6

2196	A1148	40k vio & brn	22	10

Issued to commemorate the centenary of the death of Alexander von Humboldt, German naturalist and geographer.

Three Races
Carrying Flag
of Peace
A1149

Mountain
Climber
A1150

1959, Apr. 30 **Litho.**

2199	A1149	40k multi	15	10

10th anniversary of World Peace Movement.

1959, May 15

Designs: No. 2201, Tourists reading map. No. 2202, Canoeing (horiz.). No. 2203, Skiers.

2200	A1150	40k multi	20	7
2201	A1150	40k multi	20	7
2202	A1150	40k multi	20	7
2203	A1150	40k multi	20	7

Issued to publicize sports and travel.

I. E. Repin
Statue,
Moscow
A1151

N. Y. Coliseum
and Spasski
Tower
A1152

Statues: No. 2205, Lenin, Ulyanovsk. 20k, V. V. Mayakovsky, Moscow. 25k, Alexander Pushkin, Leningrad. 60k, Maxim Gorki, Moscow. 1r, Tchaikovsky, Moscow.

1959 **Photo.** **Unwmk.**

2204	A1151	10k ocher & sep	8	6
2205	A1151	10k red & blk	8	6
2206	A1151	20k vio & sep	12	6
2207	A1151	25k grnsh bl & blk	12	6
2208	A1151	60k lt grn & sl	20	9
2209	A1151	1r lt ultra & gray	32	12
		Nos. 2204-2209 (6)	92	45

1959, June 25 **Litho.** ***Perf. 12***

2210	A1152	20k multi	22	8
2211	A1152	40k multi	30	12
a		Souvenir sheet	2.00	1.00

Issued to publicize the Soviet Exhibition of Science, Technology and Culture, New York, June 20-Aug. 10.

No. 2211a contains one imperf. copy of No. 2211. Size: 62x77mm. Issued July 20.

Animal Types of 1957

Animals: 20k, Hare. No. 2214, Siberian horse. No. 2215, Tiger. No. 2216, Red squirrel. No. 2217, Pine marten. No. 2218, Hazel hen. No. 2219, Mute swan.

1959-60 **Litho.** ***Perf. 12***

Center in Natural Colors

2213	A1023	20k vio bl ('60)	18	10
2214	A1023	25k bl blk	18	10
2215	A1023	25k brown	18	10
2216	A1023	40k dp grn	24	10
2217	A1023	40k dk grn	24	10
2218	A1024	60k dk grn	28	10
2219	A1023	1r brt bl	35	25
		Nos. 2213-2219 (7)	1.65	85

Louis Braille
A1153

Musa Djalil
A1154

1959, July 16

2220	A1153	60k bl grn, bis & brn	30	12

Issued to commemorate the 150th anniversary of the birth of Louis Braille, French educator of the blind.

1959, July 16 **Photo.**

2221	A1154	40k vio & blk	22	12

Issued to honor Musa Djalil, Tatar poet.

Sturgeon — A1155

Design: 60k, Chum salmon.

1959, July 16

2222	A1155	40k bl grn & blk	22	8
2223	A1155	60k vio bl & blk	30	12

See Nos. 2375-2377.

Gymnast
A1156

Athletes
Holding Trophy
A1157

Globe and
Hands
A1158

Designs: 25k, Runner. 60k, Water polo.

1959, Aug. 7

2224	A1156	15k lil rose & gray	10	5
2225	A1156	25k yel grn & red brn	12	7
2226	A1157	30k brt red & gray	12	7
2227	A1156	60k bl & org yel	20	14

2nd National Spartacist Games.

1959, Aug. 12 **Litho.**

2228	A1158	40k yel, bl & red	20	12

Issued to publicize the 2nd International Conference of Public Employees Unions.

Cathedral and
Modern Building
A1159

Schoolboys
in Workshop
A1160

1959, Aug. 21 **Unwmk.** ***Perf. 12***

2229	A1159	40k bl, ol, yel & red	20	12

Issued to commemorate the 1100th anniversary of the city of Novgorod.

1959, Aug. 27 **Photo.**

Design: 1r, Workers in night school.

2230	A1160	40k dk pur	16	8
2231	A1160	1r dk bl	52	10

Issued to stengthen the connection between school and life.

Glacier Survey
A1161

Rocket and
Observatory
A1162

Designs: 25k, Oceanographic ship "Vityaz" and map. 40k, Plane over Antarctica, camp and emperor penguin.

1959

2232	A1161	10k bl grn	8	5
2233	A1161	25k brt bl & red	16	7
2234	A1161	40k ultra & red	28	7
2235	A1162	1r ultra & buff	75	30

Issued to commemorate the International Geophysical Year. No. 2235 commemorates the first Russian rocket to reach the moon, Sept. 14, 1959.

Workers
and
Farmers
Holding
Atom
Symbol
A1163

1959, Sept. 23 **Litho.**

2236	A1163	40k red org & bis	25	10

All-Union Economic Exhibition, Moscow.

Russian and
Chinese
Students
A1164

Design: 40k, Russian miner and Chinese steel worker.

1959, Sept. 25 **Litho.** ***Perf. 12***

2237	A1164	20k multi	12	10
2238	A1164	40k multi	16	10

Issued to commemorate the 10th anniversary of the People's Republic of China.

Letter Carrier
A1165

Makhtumkuli
A1166

1959, Sept.

2239	A1165	40k dk car rose & blk	12	5
2240	A1165	60k bl & blk	30	10

Issued to publicize International Letter Writing Week, Oct. 4-10.

1959, Sept. 30 **Photo.**

2241	A1166	40k brown	25	10

Issued to commemorate the 225th anniversary of the birth of Makhtumkuli, Turkmen writer.

East German
Emblem and Workers
A1167

City Hall,
East Berlin
A1168

1959, Oct. 6 **Litho.**

2242	A1167	40k multi	22	5

Photo.

2243	A1168	60k dp cl & buff	35	10

Nos. 2242-43 issued to commemorate the 10th anniversary of the German Democratic Republic.

Steel Production — A1169

Designs (Industries): No. 2244, Chemicals. No. 2245, Spasski Tower, hammer and sickle. No. 2246, Home building. No. 2247, Meat production, woman with farm animals. No. 2248, Machinery. No. 2249, Grain production, woman tractor driver. No. 2250, Oil. No. 2251, Textiles. No. 2252, Steel. No. 2253, Coal. No. 2254, Iron. No. 2255, Electric power.

1959-60 **Litho.**

2244	A1169	10k	vio, grnsh bl & mar	8	5
2245	A1169	10k	org & dk car	8	5
2246	A1169	15k	brn, yel & red	12	6
2247	A1169	15k	brn, grn & mar	12	6
2248	A1169	20k	bl grn, yel & red	12	8
2249	A1169	20k	grn, yel & red	12	8
2250	A1169	30k	lil, sal & red	12	7
2251	A1169	30k	gldn brn, lil, red & grn ('60)	20	8
2252	A1169	40k	vio bl, yel & org	20	8
2253	A1169	40k	dk bl, pink & dp rose	20	8
2254	A1169	60k	org red, yel, bl & mar	28	9
2255	A1169	60k	ultra, buff & red	28	9
			Nos. 2244-2255 (12)	1.92	87

Seven-Year Production Plan.

Arms of Tadzhikistan A1170

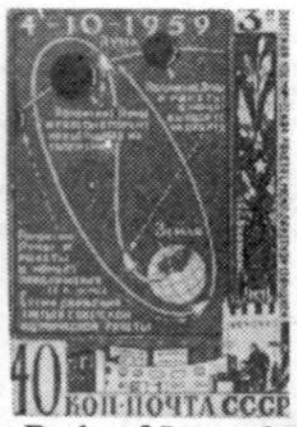
Path of Luna 3 and Electronics Laboratory A1171

1959, Oct. 13

2258	A1170	40k	red, emer, ocher & blk	16	7

Tadzhikistan statehood, 30th anniversary.

1959, Oct. 12

2259	A1171	40k	violet	48	22

Flight of Luna 3 around the moon, Oct. 4, 1959.

Red Square, Moscow A1172

1959, Oct. 26 **Engr.**

2260	A1172	40k	dk red	20	7

42nd anniversary of October Revolution.

U. S. Capitol, Globe and Kremlin A1173

1959, Oct. 27 **Photo.**

2261	A1173	60k	bl & yel	28	10

Issued to commemorate the visit of Premier Nikita Khrushchev to the United States, September, 1959.

Helicopter A1174

Designs: 25k, Diver. 40k, Motorcyclist. 60k, Parachutist.

1959, Oct. 28

2262	A1174	10k	vio bl & mar	8	6
2263	A1174	25k	bl & brn	12	6
2264	A1174	40k	red brn & ind	16	10
2265	A1174	60k	bl & ol bis	22	10

Issued to honor the voluntary aides of the army.

Moon, Earth and Path of Rocket A1175

Design: No. 2267, Kremlin and diagram showing rocket and positions of moon and earth.

1959, Nov. 1 **Litho.**

2266	A1175	40k	bl, dk bl, red & bis	28	12
2267	A1175	40k	gray, pink & red	28	12

Issued to commemorate the landing of the Soviet rocket on the moon, Sept. 14, 1959.

Sandor Petőfi A1176

Victory Statue and View of Budapest A1177

1959, Nov. 9 ***Perf. 12x12½, 12½x12***

2268	A1176	20k	gray & ol bis	12	8
2269	A1177	40k	multi	18	12

Soviet-Hungarian friendship. See No. 2308.

Manolis Glezos and Acropolis A1178

A. A. Voskresensky A1179

1959, Nov. 12 **Photo.** ***Perf. 12x12½***

2270	A1178	40k	ultra & brn	6.00	4.75

Issued to honor Manolis Glezos, Greek communist.

1959, Dec. 7 ***Perf. 12½x12***

2271	A1179	40k	ultra & brn	25	10

Issued to commemorate the 150th anniversary of the birth of A. A. Voskresensky, chemist.

Chusovaya River, Ural — A1180

Designs: No. 2273, Lake Ritza, Caucasus. No. 2274, Lena River, Siberia. No. 2275, Seashore, Far East. No. 2276, Lake Iskander, Central Asia. No. 2277, Lake Baikal, Siberia. No. 2278, Belukha Mountain, Altai range. No. 2279, Gursuf region, Crimea. No. 2280, Crimea.

1959, Dec. **Engr.** ***Perf. 12½***

2272	A1180	10k	purple	8	5
2273	A1180	10k	rose car	8	5
2274	A1180	25k	dk bl	12	7
2275	A1180	25k	olive	12	7
2276	A1180	25k	dk red	12	7
2277	A1180	40k	claret	20	7
2278	A1180	60k	Prus bl	24	15
2279	A1180	1r	ol grn	32	15
2280	A1180	1r	dp org	32	15
			Nos. 2272-2280 (9)	1.60	83

"Trumpeters of 1st Cavalry" by M. Grekov A1181

Farm Woman A1182

1959, Dec. 30 **Litho.** ***Perf. 12½x12***

2283	A1181	40k	multi	30	22

40th anniversary of the 1st Cavalry.

1958-60 **Engr.** ***Perf. 12½***

Designs: 25k, Architect. 60k, Steel worker.

2286	A1182	20k	sl grn ('59)	1.65	52
2287	A1182	25k	sep ('59)	1.65	85
2288	A1182	60k	carmine	15.00	4.25

Perf. 12x12½

Litho.

2290	A1182	20k	grn ('60)	15	10
2291	A1182	25k	sep ('60)	18	10
2292	A1182	60k	ver ('59)	45	15
2293	A1182	60k	bl ('60)	25	15
			Nos. 2286-2293 (7)	19.33	6.12

M. V. Frunze A1183

G. N. Gabrichevski A1184

1960, Jan. 25 **Photo.** ***Perf. 12½***

2295	A1183	40k	dk red brn	24	10

Issued to commemorate the 75th anniversary of the birth of Mikhail V. Frunze (1885-1925), revolutionary leader.

Perf. 12½x12

1960, Jan. 30 **Unwmk.**

2296	A1184	40k	brt vio & brn	24	10

Issued to commemorate the centenary of the birth of G. N. Gabrichevski, microbiologist.

Anton Chekhov and Moscow Home — A1185

Design: 40k, Chekhov in later years, and Yalta home.

1960, Jan. 20 **Litho.** ***Perf. 12x12½***

2297	A1185	20k	red, gray & vio bl	12	7
2298	A1185	40k	dk bl, buff & brn	20	7

Birth centenary of Anton P. Chekhov (1860-1904), playwright.

Vera Komissarzhevskaya A1186

Ice Hockey A1187

1960, Feb. 5 **Photo.** ***Perf. 12½x12***

2299	A1186	40k	chocolate	20	7

Issued to honor Vera Komissarzhevskaya (1864-1910), actress.

1960, Feb. 18 **Litho.** ***Perf. 11½***

Sports: 25k, Speed skating. 40k, Skier. 60k, Woman figure skater. 1r, Ski jumper.

2300	A1187	10k	ocher & vio bl	12	7
2301	A1187	25k	multi	16	7
2302	A1187	40k	org, rose lil & vio bl	24	10
2303	A1187	60k	vio, grn & buff	32	12
2304	A1187	1r	bl, grn & brn	48	20
			Nos. 2300-2304 (5)	1.32	56

Issued to commemorate the 8th Olympic Winter Games, Squaw Valley, Calif., Feb. 18-29.

Sword-into-Plowshare Statue, United Nations, N. Y. — A1188

1960 ***Perf. 12x12½***

2305	A1188	40k	grnsh bl, yel & brn,	32	10
a			Souvenir sheet	1.00	45

No. 2305a commemorated Premier Nikita Khrushchev's visit to the 15th General Assembly of the UN in NYC.

Women of Various Races — A1189

1960, Mar. 8

2306	A1189	40k	multi	20	10

Issued to commemorate 50 years of International Woman's Day, March 8.

Planes in Combat and Timur Frunze A1190

1960, Feb. 23 ***Perf. 12½x12***

2307	A1190	40k	multi	20	10

Issued to honor Lieutenant Timur Frunze, World War II hero.

No. 2269 Overprinted in Red

15 лет
освобождения
Венгрии

1960, Apr. 4
2308 A1177 40k vio, bl, yel & brn 1.40 1.00

15th anniversary of Hungary's liberation from the Nazis.

Lunik 3 Photographing Far Side of Moon — A1191

Design: 60k, Far side of the moon.

1960 Photo. *Perf. 12x12½*
2309 A1191 40k pale bl, dk bl & yel 45 15

Litho.
2310 A1191 60k lt bl, dk bl & cit 45 15

Issued to commemorate the photographing of the far side of the moon, Oct. 7, 1959.

Lenin as Child A1192

Various Lenin Portraits and: 20k, Lenin with children and Christmas tree. 30k, Flag, workers and ship. 40k, Kremlin, banners and marchers. 60k, Map of Russia, buildings and ship. 1r, Peace proclamation and globe.

1960, Apr. 10 Litho. *Perf. 12½x12*
2311 A1192 10k multi 7 5
2312 A1192 20k red, grn & blk 10 5
2313 A1192 30k multi 12 5
2314 A1192 40k multi 15 7
2315 A1192 60k multi 30 15
2316 A1192 1r red, vio bl & brn 45 15
Nos. 2311-2316 (6) 1.19 52

90th anniversary of the birth of Lenin.

Steelworker A1193

Government House, Baku A1194

1960, Apr. 30 Photo.
2317 A1193 40k brn & red 15 10

Issued to publicize the industrial overproduction by 50,000,000r during the first year of the 7-year plan.

1960, Apr. Litho. *Perf. 12x12½*
2318 A1194 40k bis & brn 28 22

Issued to commemorate the 40th anniversary of Azerbaijan. See No. 2898.

Brotherhood Monument, Prague — A1195

1960, Apr. 29 Photo. *Perf. 12½x12*

Design: 60k, Charles Bridge, Prague.

2319 A1195 40k brt bl & blk 15 7
2320 A1195 60k blk brn & yel 25 9

Issued to commemorate the 15th anniversary of the Czechoslovak Republic.

Radio Tower and Popov Central Museum of Communications, Leningrad — A1196

1960, May 6 Litho.
2321 A1196 40k bl, ocher & brn 18 9

Issued for Radio Day.

Gen. I. D. Tcherniakovski and Soldiers — A1197

1960, May 4
2322 A1197 1r multi 50 12

Issued to honor Gen. I. D. Tcherniakovski, World War II hero and his military school.

Robert Schumann A1198

Yakov M. Sverdlov A1199

1960, May 20 Photo. *Perf. 12x12½*
2323 A1198 40k ultra & blk 15 10

Issued to commemorate the 150th anniversary of the birth of Robert Schumann, German composer.

1960, May 24 *Perf. 12½x12*
2324 A1199 40k dk brn & org brn 15 10

Issued to commemorate the 75th anniversary of the birth of Y. M. Sverdlov (1885-1919), first President of the U.S.S.R.

Stamp of 1957 Under Magnifying Glass — A1200

1960, May 28 Litho. *Perf. 11½*
2325 A1200 60k grnsh bl, bl & bis brn 28 15

Issued for Stamp Day.

Karl Marx Avenue, Petrozavodsk, Karelian Autonomous Republic — A1201

Capitals, Soviet Autonomous Republics: No. 2327, Lenin street, Batum, Adzhar. No. 2328, Cultural Palace, Izhevsk, Udmurt. No. 2329, August street, Grozny, Chechen-Ingush. No. 2330, Soviet House, Cheboksary, Chuvash. No. 2331, Buinak Street, Makhachkala, Dagestan. No. 2332, Soviet street, Ioshkar Ola, Mari. No. 2333, Chkalov street, Dzaudzhikau, North Ossetia. No. 2334, October street, Yakutsk, Yakut. No. 2335, House of Ministers, Nukus, Kara-Kalpak.

1960 Engr. *Perf. 12½*
2326 A1201 40k Prus grn 25 12
2327 A1201 40k vio bl 25 12
2328 A1201 40k green 25 12
2329 A1201 40k maroon 25 12
2330 A1201 40k dl red 25 12
2331 A1201 40k carmine 25 12
2332 A1201 40k dk brn 25 12
2333 A1201 40k org brn 25 12
2334 A1201 40k dk bl 25 12
2335 A1201 40k brown 25 12
Nos. 2326-2335 (10) 2.50 1.20

See Nos. 2338-2344C.

No. 2326 Overprinted in Red

40 лет
КАССР
8.VI.1960

1960, June 4
2336 A1201 40k Prus grn 1.75 85

Issued to commemorate the 40th anniversary of the Karelian Autonomous Republic.

No. 2328 Overprinted in Red

40 лет Удмуртской АССР
4/XI 1960.

1960, Nov. 4
2337 A1201 40k green 1.75 85

Issued to commemorate the 40th anniversary of the Udmurt Autonomous Republic.

1961-62 *Perf. 12½, 12½x12*

Capitals, Soviet Autonomous Republics: No. 2338, Rustaveli Street, Sukhumi, Abkhazia. No. 2339, House of Soviets, Nalchik, Kabardino-Balkar. No. 2340, Lenin Street, Ulan-Ude, Buriat. No. 2341, Soviet Street, Syktyvkar, Komi. No. 2342, Lenin Street, Nakhichevan, Nakhichevan. No. 2343, Elista, Kalmyk. No. 2344, Ufa, Bashkir. No. 2344A, Lobachevsky Square, Kazan, Tartar. No. 2344B, Kizil, Tuvinia. No. 2344C, Saransk, Mordovia.

2338 A1201 4k org ver 20 10
2339 A1201 4k dk vio 20 10
2340 A1201 4k dk bl 20 10
2341 A1201 4k gray 20 10
2342 A1201 4k dk car rose 20 10
2343 A1201 4k ol grn 20 10
2344 A1201 4k dl pur 20 10
2344A A1201 4k grnsh blk ('62) 20 10
2344B A1201 4k cl ('62) 20 10
2344C A1201 4k dp grn ('62) 20 10
Nos. 2338-2344C (10) 2.00 1.00

Denominations of Nos. 2338-2344C are in the revalued currency.

Children's Friendship A1202

Drawings by Children: 20k, Collective farm (vert.). 25k, Winter joys. 40k, "In the Zoo."

Perf. 12x12½, 12½x12

1960, June 1 Litho.
2345 A1202 10k multi 7 7
2346 A1202 20k multi 10 7
2347 A1202 25k multi 12 7
2348 A1202 40k multi 15 10

Lomonosov University and Congress Emblem A1203

1960, June 17 Photo. *Perf. 12½x12*
2349 A1203 60k yel & dk brn 22 15

Issued to commemorate the first congress of the International Federation for Automation Control, Moscow.

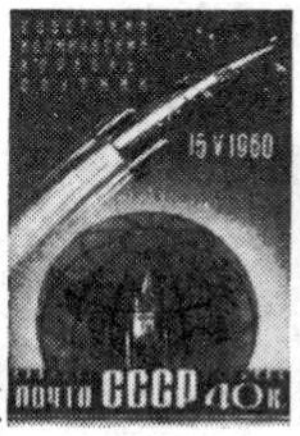

Sputnik 4 and Globe — A1204

1960, June 17 *Perf. 12x12½*
2350 A1204 40k vio bl & dp org 50 30

Launching on May 15, 1960, of Sputnik 4, which orbited the earth with a dummy cosmonaut.

Kosta Hetagurov A1205

1960, June 20 Litho. *Perf. 12½*
2351 A1205 40k gray bl & brn 20 15

Kosta Hetagurov (1859-1906), Ossetian poet.

Flag and Tallinn A1206

Designs: No. 2353, Flag and Riga. No. 2354, Flag and Vilnius.

Perf. 12x12½, 12½ (#1253)

1960 Photo.
2352 A1206 40k red & ultra 15 7

Typo.
2353 A1206 40k bl, gray & red 15 7

Litho.
2354 A1206 40k bl, red & grn 15 7

Issued to commemorate the 20th anniversary of the Soviet Republics of: No. 2352, Estonia. No. 2353, Latvia. No. 2354, Lithuania.

Cement Factory, Belgorod A1207

Design: 40k, Factory, Novy Krivoi.

1960, June 28 ***Perf. 12½x12***

2355	A1207	25k	ultra & blk	10	5
2356	A1207	40k	rose brn & blk	12	7

Issued to show "New buildings of the first year of the seven-year plan."

Automatic Production Line and Roller Bearing A1208

Design: No. 2358, Automatic production line and gear.

1960, June 13 ***Perf. 11½***

2357	A1208	40k	rose vio	12	7
2358	A1208	40k	Prus grn	12	7

Issued to publicize mechanization and automation of factories.

Running A1209

Sports: 10k, Wrestling. 15k, Basketball. 20k, Weight lifting. 25k, Boxing. No. 2364, Fencing. No. 2365, Diving. No. 2366, Women's gymnastics. 60k, Canoeing. 1r, Steeplechase.

1960, Aug. 1 **Litho.** ***Perf. 11½***

2359	A1209	5k	multi	7	7
2360	A1209	10k	brn, bl & yel	7	7
2361	A1209	15k	multi	10	7
2362	A1209	20k	blk, crim & sal	10	7
2363	A1209	25k	lake, sl & rose	12	7
2364	A1209	40k	vio bl, bl & bis	12	10
2365	A1209	40k	vio, gray & pink	12	10
2366	A1209	40k	multi	12	10
2367	A1209	60k	multi	25	12
2368	A1209	1r	brn, lil & pale grn	52	20
			Nos. 2359-2368 (10)	1.59	97

Issued to commemorate the 17th Olympic Games, Rome, Aug. 25-Sept. 11.

No. 2365 Overprinted in Red

Международная
ярмарка
в Риччоне

1960, Aug. 23

2369	A1209	40k	vio, gray & pink	2.00	2.00

12th San Marino-Riccione Stamp Fair.

Kishinev, Moldavian Republic A1210

1960, Aug. 2 ***Perf. 12x12½***

2370	A1210	40k	multi	20	10

20th anniversary of Moldavian Republic.

The Catalogue editors cannot undertake to appraise, identify or judge the genuineness or condition of stamps.

Tractor and Factory A1211

Book Museum, Hanoi A1212

Perf. 12x12½, 12½x12

1960, Aug. 25

2371	A1211	40k	grn, ocher & blk	12	7
2372	A1212	60k	bl, lil & brn	22	10

15th anniversary of North Viet Nam.

G. N. Minkh — A1213

1960, Aug. 25 **Photo.** ***Perf. 12½x12***

2373	A1213	60k	bis brn & dk brn	25	10

Issued to commemorate the 125th anniversary of the birth of Gregory N. Minkh, microbiologist.

"March," by I. I. Levitan A1214

1960, Aug. 29

2374	A1214	40k	ol bis & blk	32	10

Issued to commemorate the centenary of the birth of I. I. Levitan, painter.

Fish Type of 1959

Designs: 20k, Pikeperch. 25k, Fur seals. 40k, Ludogan whitefish.

1960, Sept. 3 ***Perf. 12½***

2375	A1155	20k	bl & blk	10	7
2376	A1155	25k	vio gray & red brn	12	7
2377	A1155	40k	rose lil & pur	15	10

Forest by I. I. Shishkin — A1215

1960, Aug. 29 **Engr.**

2378	A1215	1r	red brn	65	15

Issued to commemorate the 5th World Forestry Congress, Seattle, Wash., Aug. 29-Sept. 10.

Globe with USSR and Letter — A1216

1960, Sept. 10 **Litho.** ***Perf. 12x12½***

2379	A1216	40k	multi	10	7
2380	A1216	60k	multi	22	10

Issued for International Letter Writing Week, Oct. 3-9.

Farmer, Worker, Scientist A1217

1960, Oct. 4 **Typo.** ***Perf. 12½***

2381	A1217	40k	multi	15	7

Issued to commemorate the 40th anniversary of the Kazakh Soviet Socialist Republic.

Globes and Olive Branch — A1218

1960, Sept. 29 **Litho.** ***Perf. 12½x12***

2382	A1218	60k	pale vio, bl & gray	22	10

Issued to commemorate the 15th anniversary of the World Federation of Trade Unions.

Kremlin, Sputnik 5 and Dogs Belka and Strelka A1219

1960, Sept. 29 **Photo.**

2383	A1219	40k	brt pur & yel	42	10
2384	A1219	1r	bl & sal	70	22

Flight of Sputnik 5, Aug. 19-20, 1960.

Passenger Ship "Karl Marx" A1220

Ships: 40k, Turbo-electric ship "Lenin." 60k, Speedboat "Raketa" (Rocket).

1960, Oct. 24 **Litho.** ***Perf. 12x12½***

2385	A1220	25k	bl, blk, red & yel	12	7
2386	A1220	40k	bl, blk & red	20	10
2387	A1220	60k	bl, blk & rose	25	12

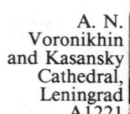

A. N. Voronikhin and Kasansky Cathedral, Leningrad A1221

1960, Oct. 24 **Photo.**

2388	A1221	40k	gray & brn blk	15	7

Issued to commemorate the 200th anniversary of the birth of A. N. Voronikhin, architect.

J. S. Gogebashvili A1222

1960, Oct. 29

2389	A1222	40k	dk gray & mag	20	7

Issued to commemorate the 120th anniversary of the birth of J. S. Gogebashvili, Georgian teacher and publicist.

Red Flag, Electric Power Station and Factory — A1223

1960, Oct. 29 **Litho.**

2390	A1223	40k	red, yel & brn	22	7

43rd anniversary of October Revolution.

Leo Tolstoy A1224

Designs: 40k, Tolstoy in Yasnaya Polyana. 60k, Portrait (vert.).

Perf. 12x12½, 12½x12

1960, Nov. 14

2391	A1224	20k	vio & brn	7	7
2392	A1224	40k	bl & lt brn	12	7
2393	A1224	60k	dp cl & sep	25	10

Issued to commemorate the 50th anniversary of the death of Count Leo Tolstoy, writer.

Yerevan, Armenian Republic A1225

1960, Nov. 14 ***Perf. 12x12½***

2394	A1225	40k	bl, red, buff & brn	15	7

Issued to commemorate the 40th anniversary of the Armenian Soviet Republic.

Friedrich Engels A1226

Badge of Youth Federation A1227

1960, Nov. 25 **Engr.** ***Perf. 12½***

2395	A1226	60k	slate	30	25

Issued to commemorate the 140th anniversary of the birth of Friedrich Engels.

1960, Nov. 2 **Litho.**

2396	A1227	60k	brt pink, blk & yel	30	12

Issued to commemorate the 15th anniversary of the International Youth Federation.

40-ton Truck MAL-530 A1228

Designs: 40k, "Volga" car. 60k, "Moskvitch 407" car. 1r, "Tourist LAS-697" Bus.

1960, Oct. 29 Photo. *Perf. 12x12½*
2397 A1228 25k ultra & gray 10 7
2398 A1228 40k ol bis & ultra 12 7
2399 A1228 60k Prus grn & dp car 20 10

Litho.
2400 A1228 1r multi 42 15

Automotive industry.

N. I. Pirogov
A1229

Friendship University and Students
A1230

1960, Dec. 13 Photo. *Perf. 12½x12*
2401 A1229 40k grn & brn blk 20 10

Issued to commemorate the 125th anniversary of the birth of N. I. Pirogov, surgeon.

1960, Nov. *Perf. 12x12½*
2402 A1230 40k brn car 20 10

Issued to publicize the completion of Friendship of Nations University in Moscow. See No. 2462.

Mark Twain
A1231

1960, Nov. 30 *Perf. 12½x12*
2403 A1231 40k dp org & brn 40 40

Issued to commemorate the 125th anniversary of the birth of Mark Twain.

Dove and Globe
A1232

Akaki Zeretely
A1233

1960, Oct. 29 Photo.
2404 A1232 60k mar & gray 25 15

Issued to commemorate the 15th anniversary of the International Democratic Women's Federation.

1960, Dec. 27
2405 A1233 40k vio & blk brn 25 15

Issued to commemorate the 120th anniversary of the birth of Akaki Zeretely, Georgian poet.

Frederic Chopin, after Delacroix
A1234

1960, Dec. 24 *Perf. 12x11½*
2406 A1234 40k bis & brn 25 12

Issued to commemorate the 150th anniversary of the birth of Frederic Chopin, Polish composer.

North Korean Flag and Flying Horse — A1235

Crocus — A1236

1960, Dec. 24 Litho. *Perf. 12½x12*
2407 A1235 40k multi 20 7

Issued to commemorate the 15th anniversary of "the liberation of the Korean people by the Soviet army."

1960 *Perf. 12x12½*

Asiatic Flowers: No. 2409, Tulip. No. 2410, Trollius. No. 2411, Tulip. No. 2412, Ginseng. No. 2413, Iris. No. 2414, Hypericum. 1r, Dog rose.

Flowers in Natural Colors
2408 A1236 20k grn & vio 10 5
2409 A1236 20k vio bl & blk 10 5
2410 A1236 25k gray 12 5
2411 A1236 40k ol bis & blk 15 7
2412 A1236 40k grn & blk, wmkd. 15 7
2413 A1236 60k yel, grn & red 20 10
2414 A1236 60k bluish grn & blk 20 10
2415 A1236 1r sl grn & blk 40 12
Nos. 2408-2415 (8) 1.42 61

The watermark on No. 2412 consists of vertical rows of chevrons.

Lithuanian Costumes
A1237

Regional Costumes: 60k, Uzbek.

Perf. 12½ (10k), 11½ (60k)
1960, Dec. 24 Typo. Unwmk.
2416 A1237 10k multi 10 7

Litho.
2417 A1237 60k multi 32 10

Currency Revalued

1961-62 Litho. *Perf. 11½*

Regional Costumes: No. 2418, Moldavia. No. 2419, Georgia. No. 2420, Ukrainia. No. 2421, White Russia. No. 2422, Kazakhstan. No. 2422A, Latvia. 4k, Koryak. 6k, Russia. 10k, Armenia. 12k, Estonia.

2418 A1237 2k buff, brn & ver 12 10
2419 A1237 2k red, brn, ocher & blk 12 10
2420 A1237 3k ultra, buff, red & brn 15 12
2421 A1237 3k red org, ocher & blk 15 12
2422 A1237 3k buff, brn, grn & red 15 12
2422A A1237 3k org red, gray ol & blk ('62) 15 12
2423 A1237 4k multi 32 12
2424 A1237 6k multi 42 20
2425 A1237 10k brn, ol bis & ver 65 25
2426 A1237 12k red, ultra & blk 85 32
Nos. 2418-2426 (10) 3.08 1.57

See Nos. 2723-2726.

Lenin and Map Showing Electrification — A1238

1961 *Perf. 12½x12*
2427 A1238 4k bl, buff & brn 12 12
2428 A1238 10k red org & bl blk 30 25

Issued to publicize the 40th anniversary (in 1960) of the State Electrification Plan.

Animal Types of 1957

1961, Jan. 7 *Perf. 12½*

Animals: 1k, Brown bear. 6k, Beaver. 10k, Roe deer.

Centers in Natural Colors.
2429 A1024 1k dk brn 10 10
2430 A1023 6k black 40 30
2431 A1023 10k black 50 42

Georgian Flag and Views
A1239

1961, Feb. 15 *Perf. 12½x12*
2432 A1239 4k multi 12 10

40th anniv. of Georgian SSR.

Nikolai D. Zelinski
A1240

N. A. Dobrolyubov
A1241

1961, Feb. 6 Photo. *Perf. 12x12½*
2433 A1240 4k rose vio 12 12

Issued to commemorate the centenary of the birth of N. D. Zelinski, chemist.

1961, Feb. 5 *Perf. 11½x12*
2434 A1241 4k brt bl & brn 12 12

Nikolai A. Dobrolyubov, journalist and critic (1836-1861).

Mechanization of Grain Harvest
A1242

"Labor" Holding Peace Flag
A1243

Designs: 3k, Cattle. 4k, Tractor in cornfield. 10k, Women picking apples.

1961 *Perf. 12x12½, 12x11½*
2435 A1242 3k bl & mag 10 7
2436 A1242 4k grn & dk gray 12 7
2437 A1242 6k vio bl & brn 20 7
2438 A1242 10k mar & ol grn 30 12

Agricultural development.

Perf. 12x12½; 12x11½ (Nos. 2439A, 2442 & 12k)
1961-65 Unwmk.

Designs: 2k, Harvester and silo. 3k, Space rockets. 4k, Arms and flag of U.S.S.R. 6k, Spasski tower. 10k, Workers' monument. 12k, Minin and Pozharsky Monument and Spasski tower. 16k, Plane over power station and dam.

Engr.
2439 A1243 1k ol bis 85 15

Litho.
2439A A1243 1k ol bis 32 10
2440 A1243 2k green 10 10
2441 A1243 3k dk vio 1.10 12

Engr.
2442 A1243 3k dk vio 2.00 85

Litho.
2443 A1243 4k red 35 12
2443A A1243 4k org brn ('65) 45 25
2444 A1243 6k vermilion 3.25 55
2445 A1243 6k dk car rose 90 10
2446 A1243 10k orange 1.65 12

Photo.
2447 A1243 12k brt mag 1.65 20

Litho.
2448 A1243 16k ultra 2.50 1.00
Nos. 2439-2448 (12) 15.12 3.66

V. P. Miroshnitchenko — A1244

1961, Feb. 23 Photo. *Perf. 12½x12*
2449 A1244 4k vio brn & sl 15 15

Issued to honor a soldier hero of World War II. See Nos. 2570-2571.

Taras G. Shevchenko and Birthplace
A1245

Shevchenko Statue, Kharkov
A1246

Andrei Rubljov
A1247

Design: 6k, Book, torch and Shevchenko with beard.

Perf. 12½, 11½x12
1961, Mar. Litho.; Photo. (4k)
2450 A1245 3k brn & vio 30 12
2451 A1246 4k red org & gray 60 20
2452 A1245 6k blk, grn & red brn 85 22

Issued to commemorate the centenary of the death of Taras G. Shevchenko, Ukrainian poet.

No. 2452 was printed with alternating green and black label, containing a quotation.

See No. 2852.

1961, Mar. 13 Litho. *Perf. 12½x12*
2453 A1247 4k ultra, bis & brn 12 7

Issued to commemorate the 600th anniversary of the birth of Andrei Rubljov, painter.

The indexes in each volume of the Scott Catalogue contain many listings which help to identify stamps.

N. V. Sklifosovsky A1248

Robert Koch A1249

1961, Mar. 26 Photo. *Perf. 11½x12*
2454 A1248 4k ultra & blk 15 10

Issued to commemorate the 125th anniversary of the birth of N. V. Sklifosovsky, surgeon.

1961, Mar. 26
2455 A1249 6k dk brn 15 10

Issued to commemorate the 50th anniversary of the death of Robert Koch, German microbiologist.

Globe and Sputnik 8 — A1250

Design: 10k, Space probe and its path to Venus.

1961, Apr. Litho. *Perf. 11½*
2456 A1250 6k dk & lt bl & org 40 20

Photo.
2457 A1250 10k vio bl & yel 55 30

Issued to commemorate the launching of the Venus space probe, Feb. 12, 1961.

Open Book and Globe A1251

1961, Apr. 7 Litho. *Perf. 12½x12*
2458 A1251 6k ultra & sep 30 10

Issued to commemorate the centenary of the children's magazine "Around the World."

Musician, Dancers and Singers A1252

1961, Apr. 7 Unwmk.
2459 A1252 4k yel, red & blk 12 12

Issued to commemorate the 50th anniversary of the Russian National Choir.

African Breaking Chains and Map A1253

Design: 6k, Globe, torch and black and white handshake.

1961, Apr. 15 *Perf. 12½*
2460 A1253 4k multi 10 7
2461 A1253 6k bl, pur & org 15 7

Issued for Africa Day and to commemorate the 3rd Conference of Independent African States, Cairo, March 25-31.

No. 2402 Surcharged in Red

4 коп. имени Патриса Лумумбы 1961 г.

1961, Apr. 15 Photo. *Perf. 12x12½*
2462 A1230 4k on 40k brn car 30 15

Issued to publicize the naming of Friendship University, Moscow, in memory of Patrice Lumumba, Premier of Congo.

Maj. Yuri A. Gagarin A1254

Designs: 6k, Kremlin, rockets and radar equipment. 10k, Rocket, Gagarin with helmet and Kremlin.

1961, Apr. *Perf. 11½(3k), 12½x12*
2463 A1254 3k Prus bl 15 10

Litho.
2464 A1254 6k bl, vio & red 25 15
2465 A1254 10k red, bl grn & brn 50 25

Issued to commemorate the first man in space, Yuri A. Gagarin, Apr. 12, 1961. No. 2464 printed with alternating light blue label with hammer and sickle emblem and quotation by Khrushchev in red.
Nos. 2463-2465 exist imperf. Value $1.75.

Lenin A1255

Rabindranath Tagore A1256

1961, Apr. 22 Litho. *Perf. 12x12½*
2466 A1255 4k dp car, sal & blk 12 10

91st anniversary of Lenin's birth.

1961, May 8 Engr. *Perf. 11½x12*
2467 A1256 6k bis, mar & blk 15 12

Issued to commemorate the birth centenary of Rabindranath Tagore, Indian poet.

The Hunchbacked Horse A1257

Fairy Tales: 1k, The Geese and the Swans. 3k, Fox, Hare and Cock. 6k, The Peasant and the Bear. 10k, Ruslan and Ludmilla.

1961 Litho. *Perf. 12½*
2468 A1257 1k multi 10 10
2469 A1257 3k multi 25 20
2470 A1257 4k multi 12 15
2471 A1257 6k multi 30 25
2472 A1257 10k multi 40 32
Nos. 2468-2472 (5) 1.17 1.02

"Man Conquering Space" — A1258

Design: 6k, Giuseppe Garibaldi.

1961, May 24 Photo.
2481 A1258 4k org brn 12 7
2482 A1258 6k lil & sal 25 12

International Labor Exposition, Turin.

Lenin A1259

Patrice Lumumba A1260

1961 Photo. *Perf. 12½x12*
Various Portraits of Lenin
Olive Bister Frame
2483 A1259 20k dk grn 65 65
2484 A1259 30k dk bl 1.50 1.50
2485 A1259 50k rose red 2.00 2.00

1961, May 29 Litho.
2486 A1260 2k yel & brn 7 7

Patrice Lumumba (1925-1961), premier of Congo.

Kindergarten — A1261

Designs: 3k, Young Pioneers in camp. 4k, Young Pioneers (vert.).

Perf. 12½x12, 12x12½
1961, May 31 Photo.
2487 A1261 2k org & ultra 7 7
2488 A1261 3k ol bis & pur 10 10
2489 A1261 4k red & gray 12 10

Issued for Children's Day, 1961.

Dog Zvezdochka and Sputnik 10 — A1263

Design: 4k, Dog Chernushka and Sputnik 9 (vert.).

1961, June 8 Litho. *Perf. 12½, 11½*
2491 A1263 2k vio, Prus bl & blk 12 10

Photo.
2492 A1263 4k Prus bl & brt grn 15 15

Sputniks 9 and 10.

A particular stamp may be scarce, but if few collectors want it, its market value may remain relatively low.

Vissarion G. Belinski A1265

Lt. Gen. D. M. Karbishev A1266

Engraved and Photogravure
1961, June 13 *Perf. 11½x12*
2493 A1265 4k car & blk 12 10

Issued to commemorate the 150th anniversary of the birth of Vissarion G. Belinski, author and critic.

1961, June 22 Litho. *Perf. 12½*
2494 A1266 4k blk, red & yel 12 10

Issued to honor Lt. Gen. D. M. Karbishev, who was tortured to death in the Nazi prison camp at Mauthausen, Austria.

Hydro-meteorological Map and Instruments — A1267

1961, June 21 *Perf. 12x12½*
2495 A1267 6k ultra & grn 15 10

Issued to commemorate the 40th anniversary of hydro-meteorological service in Russia.

Gliders — A1268

Designs: 6k, Motorboat race. 10k, Motorcycle race.

1961, July 5 Photo. *Perf. 12½*
2497 A1268 4k dk sl grn & crim 12 7

Litho.
2498 A1268 6k sl & ver 15 10
2499 A1268 10k sl & ver 30 12

USSR Technical Sports Spartakiad.

Javelin Thrower A1269

1961, Aug. 8 Photo. *Perf. 12½x12*
2500 A1269 6k dp car & pink 15 10

7th Trade Union Spartacist Games.

S. I. Vavilov A1270

Vazha Pshavela A1271

1961, July 25

2501	A1270	4k lt grn & sep	12	10

Issued to honor S. I. Vavilov, president of Academy of Science.

1961 Photo. *Perf. 11½x12*

2502	A1271	4k dk brn & cr	12	10

Issued to commemorate the centenary of the birth of Vazha Pshavela, Georgian poet.

Scientists at Control Panel for Rocket — A1272

Globe and Youth Activities A1273

Design: 2k, Men pushing tank into river.

1961 Unwmk. *Perf. 11½*

2503	A1273	2k org & sep	10	5
2504	A1272	4k lil & dk grn	20	7
2505	A1273	6k ultra & cit	25	10

International Youth Forum, Moscow.

Arms of Mongolian Republic and Sukhe Bator Statue A1274

1961, July 25 Litho. *Perf. 12½x12*

2506	A1274	4k multi	12	10

Issued to commemorate the 40th anniversary of the Mongol national revolution.

Knight Kalevipoeg A1275

Symbols of Biochemistry A1276

1961, July 31

2507	A1275	4k blk, bl & yel	12	10

Issued to commemorate the centenary of the first publication of "Kalevipoeg," Estonian national saga, recorded by R. K. Kreutzwald, Estonian writer.

1961, July 31

2508	A1276	6k multi	15	10

Issued to publicize the 5th International Biochemistry Congress, Moscow.

Major Titov and Vostok 2 — A1277

Design: 4k, Globe with orbit and cosmonaut.

1961, Aug. Photo. *Perf. 11½*

2509	A1277	4k vio bl & dp plum	20	10
2510	A1277	6k brn, grn & org	30	15

Issued to commemorate the first manned space flight around the world, Maj. Gherman S. Titov, Aug. 6-7, 1961. Nos. 2509-2510 exist imperf. Value, set $3.

A. D. Zacharov and Admiralty Building, Leningrad A1278

1961, Aug. 8 *Perf. 12x11½*

2511	A1278	4k bl, dk brn & buff	10	7

Issued to commemorate the 200th anniversary of the birth of A. D. Zacharov (1761-1811), architect.

Defense of Brest, 1941 A1279

Designs: No. 2512, Defense of Moscow. No. 2514, Defense of Odessa. No. 2514A, Defense of Sevastopol. No. 2514B, Defense of Leningrad. No. 2514C, Defense of Kiev. No. 2514D, Battle of the Volga (Stalingrad).

1961-63 Photo. *Perf. 12½x12*

2512	A1279	4k blk & red brn *(Moscow)*	30	12
		Litho.		
2513	A1279	4k multi *(Brest)*	30	12
2514	A1279	4k multi *(Odessa)*	30	12
2514A	A1279	4k multi *(Sevastopol; '62)*	30	12
2514B	A1279	4k brn, dl bl & bis *(Leningrad; '63)*	30	12
2514C	A1279	4k blk & multi *(Kiev; '63)*	30	12
2514D	A1279	4k dl org & multi *(Volga; '63)*	30	12
		Nos. 2512-2514D (7)	2.10	84

Issued to commemorate the "War of Liberation," 1941-1945. See Nos. 2757-2758.

Students' Union Emblem — A1280

1961, Aug. 8 Litho. *Perf. 12½*

2515	A1280	6k ultra & red	12	10

Issued to commemorate the 15th anniversary of the founding of the International Students' Union.

Soviet Stamps A1281

Stamps and Background Different on each Denomination

1961, Aug. *Perf. 12½x12*

2516	A1281	2k multi	12	12
2517	A1281	4k multi	20	20
2518	A1281	6k multi	25	25
2519	A1281	10k multi	40	32

40 years of Soviet postage stamps.

Nikolai A. Schors Statue, Kiev — A1282

Statue: 4k, Gregori I. Kotovski, Kishinev.

1961 Photo. *Perf. 11½x12*

2520	A1282	2k lt ultra & sep	10	7
2521	A1282	4k rose vio & sep	10	7

Letters and Means of Transportation — A1283

1961, Sept. 15 *Perf. 11½*

2522	A1283	4k dk car & blk	20	7

International Letter Writing Week.

Angara River Bridge, Irkutsk A1284

1961, Sept. 15 Litho. *Perf. 12½x12*

2523	A1284	4k ol bis, lil & blk	15	7

300th anniversary of Irkutsk.

Lenin, Marx, Engels and Marchers — A1285

Designs: 3k, Obelisk commemorating conquest of space and Moscow University. No. 2526, Harvester combine. No. 2527, Industrial control center. No. 2528, Worker pointing to globe.

1961 Litho.

2524	A1285	2k ver, yel & brn	7	7
2525	A1285	3k org & dp bl	20	15
2526	A1285	4k mar, bis & red brn	12	15
2527	A1285	4k car rose, brn, org & bl	12	15
2528	A1285	4k red & dk brn	12	15
		Nos. 2524-2528 (5)	63	67

Issued to commemorate the 22nd Congress of the Communist Party of the USSR, Oct. 17-31.

Soviet Soldier Monument, Berlin — A1286

1961, Sept. 28 Photo. *Perf. 12x12½*

2529	A1286	4k red & gray vio	10	7

Issued to commemorate the 10th anniversary of the International Federation of Resistance, FIR.

Workers Studying Mathematics — A1287

Designs: 2k, Communist labor team. 4k, Workers around piano.

1961, Sept. 28 Litho. *Perf. 12½x12*

2530	A1287	2k plum & red, *cr*	7	7
2531	A1287	3k brn & red, *yel*	10	7
2532	A1287	4k vio bl & red, *cr*	12	10

Issued to publicize the Communist labor teams in their efforts for labor, education and relaxation.

Rocket and Stars — A1288

Engraved on Aluminum Foil

1961, Oct. 17 *Perf. 12½*

2533	A1288	1r blk & red	4.00	4.00

Issued to commemorate Soviet scientific and technical achievements in exploring outer space.

Overprinted in Red XXII съезд КПСС

1961, Oct. 23

2534	A1288	1r blk & red	4.00	4.00

Issued to commemorate the 22nd Congress of the Communist Party of the USSR.

Amangaldi Imanov A1289

Franz Liszt A1290

1961, Oct. 25 Photo. *Perf. 11½x12*

2535	A1289	4k grn, buff & brn	12	7

Issued to honor Amangaldi Imanov (1873-1919), champion of Soviet power in Kazakhstan.

1961, Oct. 31 *Perf. 12x11½*
2536 A1290 4k mar, dk brn & ocher 12 7

Issued to commemorate the 150th anniversary of the birth of Franz Liszt, composer.

Flags and Slogans A1291

1961, Nov. 4 *Perf. 11½*
2537 A1291 4k red, yel & dk red 12 7

44th anniversary of October Revolution.

Hand Holding Hammer A1292

Congress Emblem A1293

Designs: Nos. 2538, 2542, Congress emblem. Nos. 2539, 2543, African breaking chains. No. 2541, Three hands holding globe.

1961, Nov. *Perf. 12, 12½, 11½*

2538	A1293	2k scar & bis	5	5
2539	A1293	2k dk pur & gray	5	5
2540	A1292	4k plum, org & bl	12	7
2541	A1292	4k blk, lt bl & pink	10	7
2542	A1293	6k grn, bis & red	22	7
2543	A1293	6k ind, dl yel & red	15	7
		Nos. 2538-2543 (6)	69	38

Issued to publicize the Fifth World Congress of Trade Unions, Moscow, Dec. 4-16.

Lomonosov Statue A1294

Hands Holding Hammer and Sickle A1295

Designs: 6k, Lomonosov at desk. 10k, Lomonosov, his birthplace and Leningrad Academy of Science (horiz.).

Perf. 11½x12, 12x11½
1961, Nov. 19 **Photo. & Engr.**

2544	A1294	4k Prus bl, yel grn & brn	10	7
2545	A1294	6k grn, yel & blk	15	10

Photo.

2546	A1294	10k mar, sl & brn	35	22

Issued to commemorate the 250th anniversary of the birth of M. V. Lomonosov, scientist and poet.

1961, Nov. 27 **Litho.** *Perf. 12x12½*
2547 A1295 4k red & yel 15 10

Issued to commemorate the 25th anniversary of the constitution of the USSR.

Romeo and Juliet Ballet — A1296

Linemen — A1297

Ballets: 2k, Red Flower. 3k, Paris Flame. 10k, Swan Lake.

1961-62 *Perf. 12x12½*

2548	A1296	2k brn, car & lt grn ('62)	10	7
2549	A1296	3k multi ('62)	12	7
2550	A1296	6k dk brn, bis & vio	20	7
2551	A1296	10k bl, pink & dk brn	32	10

Issued to honor the Russian Ballet.

1961 *Perf. 12½*

Designs: 4k, Welders. 6k, Surveyor.

2552	A1297	3k red, red brn & sl	7	5
2553	A1297	4k red, bl & brn	10	7
2554	A1297	6k red, gldn brn & sl	12	8

Issued to honor the self-sacrificing work of youth in the 7-year plan.

Andrejs Pumpurs A1298

1961, Dec. 20 *Perf. 12x11½*
2555 A1298 4k gray & cl 12 10

Issued to honor Andrejs Pumpurs (1841-1902), Latvian poet and satirist.

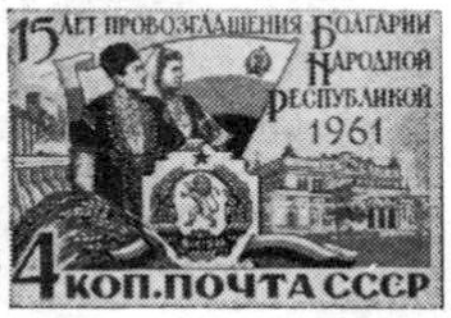

Bulgarian Couple, Flag, Emblem and Building A1299

1961, Dec. 28 *Perf. 12½x12*
2556 A1299 4k multi 12 10

Issued to commemorate the 15th anniversary of the proclamation of the Bulgarian People's Republic.

Fridtjof Nansen A1300

1961, Dec. 30 **Photo.** *Perf. 11½*
2557 A1300 6k dk bl & brn 60 52

Issued to commemorate the centenary of the birth of Fridtjof Nansen, Norwegian Polar explorer.

Mihael Ocipovich Dolivo-Dobrovolsky — A1301

1962, Jan. 25 *Perf. 12x11½*
2558 A1301 4k bis & dk bl 10 7

Issued to commemorate the centenary of the birth of Mihael Ocipovich Dolivo-Dobrovolsky, scientist and electrical engineer.

Woman and Various Activities A1302

1962, Jan. 26 *Perf. 11½*
2559 A1302 4k bis, blk & dp org 10 7

Issued to honor Russian Women.

Aleksander S. Pushkin — A1303

1962, Jan. 26 **Litho.** *Perf. 12½x12*
2560 A1303 4k buff, dk brn & ver 10 7

Issued to commemorate the 125th anniversary of the death of A. S. Pushkin, poet.

Dancers A1304

1962, Feb. 6 *Perf. 12x12½*
2561 A1304 4k bis & ver 10 7

Issued to commemorate the 25th anniversary of the State ensemble of folk dancers.

Speed Skating, Luzhniki Stadium A1305

Perf. 11½
1962, Feb. 17 **Unwmk.** **Photo.**
2562 A1305 4k org & ultra 32 10

Issued to publicize the International Winter Sports Championships, Moscow, 1962.

No. 2562 Overprinted: СОВЕТСКИЕ КОНЬКОБЕЖЦЫ— ЧЕМПИОНЫ МИРА

1962, Mar. 3
2563 A1305 4k org & ultra 60 32

Issued to commemorate the victories of I. Voronina and V. Kosichkin, world speed skating champions, 1962.

Ski Jump A1305a

Design: 10k, Woman long distance skier (vert.).

1962, May 31 *Perf. 11½*

2564	A1305a	2k ultra, brn & red	7	7
2565	A1305a	10k org, ultra & blk	25	10

Issued to commemorate the International Winter Sports Championships, Zakopane, 1962.

Hero Type of 1961

Designs: 4k, V. S. Shalandin. 6k, Magomet Gadgiev.

1962, Feb. 22 *Perf. 12½x12*

2570	A1244	4k dk bl & brn	1.00	65
2571	A1244	6k brn & sl grn	1.00	65

Soldier heroes of World War II.

Skier A1306

Designs: 6k, Ice hockey. 10k, Ice skating.

1962, Mar. 3 *Perf. 11½*

2572	A1306	4k pur & car	10	7
2573	A1306	6k Prus bl & plum	15	10
2574	A1306	10k bl, gray & red	32	12

First People's Winter Games, Sverdlovsk.

Aleksandr Ivanovich Herzen A1307

1962, Mar. 28 **Litho.** *Perf. 12x12½*
2575 A1307 4k ultra, blk & buff 20 10

Issued to commemorate the sesquicentennial of the birth of A. I. Herzen (1812-70), political writer.

Lenin A1308

Vostok 1 A1309

Design: 6k, Lenin (horiz.).

Perf. 12x12½, 12½x12
1962, Mar. 28

2576	A1308	4k brn, red & yel	10	8
2577	A1308	6k bl, org & brn	12	12

Issued to publicize the 14th congress of the Young Communist League (Komsomol).

1962, Apr. **Unwmk.** *Perf. 11x11½*
2578 A1309 10k multi 70 40

Issued to commemorate the first anniversary of Yuri A. Gagarin's flight into space.

No. 2578 was printed in sheets of 20 stamps alternating with 20 labels. Label shows globe with orbit, date and Gagarin's signature, and comes with blue or lilac background.

No. 2578 was also issued imperf. Value $2.50.

Bust of Tchaikovsky — A1310

Demand, as well as supply, determines a stamp's market value. One is as important as the other.

1962, Apr. 19 Photo. ***Perf. 11½x12***
2579 A1310 4k bl, blk & bis 10 7

Issued to commemorate the Second International Tchaikovsky Competition in Moscow.

Youths of 3 Races, Broken Chain, Globe A1311

1962, Apr. 19 ***Perf. 11½***
2580 A1311 6k blk, brn & yel 12 7

Issued for the International Day of Solidarity of Youth against Colonialism.

Ulyanov (Lenin) Family Portrait A1312

Lenin A1313

1962, Apr. 21 ***Perf. 12x11½***
2581 A1312 4k gray, red & dk brn 10 7

Typographed and Embossed

Perf. 12½

2582 A1313 10k dk red, gray & blk 25 10
a Souv. sheet of 2, perf. 12 ('64) 1.00 60

92nd anniversary of the birth of Lenin.
No. 2582a commemorated the 94th anniv. of the birth of Lenin. Issued Nov. 6, 1964.

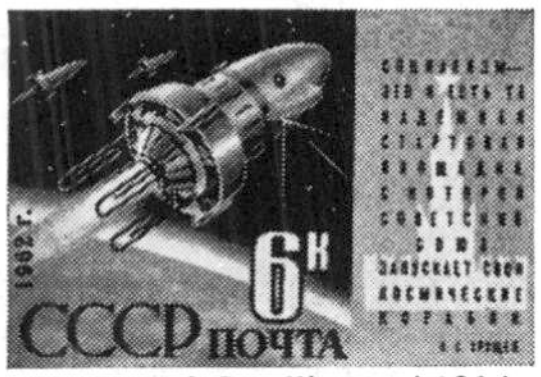

Kosmos 3 Satellite — A1314

1962, Apr. 26 Litho. ***Perf. 12½x12***
2586 A1314 6k blk, lt bl & vio 32 12

Issued to commemorate the launching of the Kosmos 3 earth satellite, Apr. 24.

Charles Dickens A1315

Karl Marx Monument, Moscow A1316

Portrait: No. 2589, Jean Jacques Rousseau.

1962, Apr. 29
2588 A1315 6k bl, brn & pur 15 10

Perf. 11½x12

Photo.

2589 A1315 6k gray, lil & brn 15 10

Issued to commemorate the 150th anniversary of the birth of Charles Dickens, English writer, and the 250th anniversary of the birth of Jean Jacques Rousseau, French writer.

1962, Apr. 29 ***Perf. 12x12½***
2590 A1316 4k dp ultra & gray 10 7

Issued to honor Karl Marx.

Pravda, Lenin, Revolutionists A1317

Lenin Reading Pravda A1318

Designs: No. 2592, Pravda, Lenin and rocket.

1962, May 4 **Litho.**
2591 A1317 4k blk, bis & red 10 7
2592 A1317 4k red, blk & ocher 12 7

Perf. 11½

Photo.

2593 A1318 4k ocher, dp cl & red 10 7

Issued to commemorate the 50th anniversary of Pravda, Russian newspaper founded by Lenin.

Malaria Eradication Emblem and Mosquito A1319

1962
2594 A1319 4k Prus bl, red & blk 10 7
2595 A1319 6k ol grn, red & blk 15 7

World Health Organization drive to eradicate malaria. Issue dates: 4k, May 6; 6k, June 23.
No. 2595 exists imperf. Value $1.25.

Pioneers Taking Oath before Lenin and Emblem A1320

Designs (Emblem and): 3k, Lenja Golikov and Valja Kotik. No. 2598, Pioneers building rocket model. No. 2599, Red Cross, Red Crescent and nurse giving health instruction. 6k, Pioneers of many races and globe.

1962, May 19 Litho. ***Perf. 12½x12***
2596 A1320 2k grn, red & brn 7 7
2597 A1320 3k multi 10 10
2598 A1320 4k multi 12 10
2599 A1320 4k multi 12 10
2600 A1320 6k multi 20 10
Nos. 2596-2600 (5) 61 47

Issued to commemorate the 40th anniversary of the All-Union Lenin Pioneers.

Mesrob A1321

Ivan A. Goncharov A1322

1962, May 27 Photo. ***Perf. 12½x12***
2601 A1321 4k yel & dk brn 10 10

Issued to commemorate the "1600th" anniversary of the birth of Bishop Mesrob (350?-439), credited as author of the Armenian and Georgian alphabets.

1962, June 18
2602 A1322 4k gray & brn 12 10

Issued to commemorate the 150th anniversary of the birth of Ivan Aleksandrovich Goncharov (1812-1891), novelist.

Volleyball A1323

Louis Pasteur A1324

Designs: 2k, Bicyclists (horiz.). 10k, Eight-man shell. 12k, Goalkeeper, soccer (horiz.). 16k, Steeplechase.

1962, June 27 ***Perf. 11½***
2603 A1323 2k lt brn, blk & ver 7 7
2604 A1323 4k brn org, blk & buff 10 7
2605 A1323 10k ultra, blk & yel 25 10
2606 A1323 12k lt bl, brn & yel 32 12
2607 A1323 16k lt grn, blk & red 40 15
Nos. 2603-2607 (5) 1.14 51

Issued to commemorate the International Summer Sports Championships, 1962.

1962, June 30 ***Perf. 12½x12***
2608 A1324 6k blk & brn org 15 7

Issued to commemorate the centenary of the invention of the sterilization process by Louis Pasteur, French chemist.

Library, 1862 A1325

Design: No. 2610, New Lenin Library.

1962, June 30 **Photo.**
2609 A1325 4k sl & blk 10 7
2610 A1325 4k sl & blk 10 7

Issued to commemorate the centenary of the Lenin Library, Moscow. Nos. 2609-2610 are printed se-tenant in the sheet.

Auction Building and Ermine — A1326

1962, June 30 **Litho.**
2611 A1326 6k multi 15 7

International Fur Auction, Leningrad.

Young Couple, Lenin, Kremlin A1327

Workers of Three Races and Dove A1328

1962, June 30 ***Perf. 12x12½***
2612 A1327 2k multi 7 5
2613 A1328 4k multi 10 5

Issued to publicize the program of the Communist Party of the Soviet Union for Peace and Friendship among all people.

Hands Breaking Bomb A1329

1962, July 7 ***Perf. 11½***
2614 A1329 6k bl, blk & ol 15 7

Issued to commemorate the World Congress for Peace and Disarmament, Moscow, July 9-14.

Yakub Kolas and Yanka Kupala A1330

1962, July 7 Photo. ***Perf. 12½x12***
2615 A1330 4k hn brn & buff 10 7

Issued to commemorate the 80th anniversary of the births of the Byelorussian poets. Yakub Kolas (1882-1956), and Yanka Kupala (1882-1942).

Alepker Sabir — A1331

Cancer Congress Emblem — A1332

1962, July 16 ***Perf. 11½***
2616 A1331 4k buff, dk brn & bl 10 7

Issued to commemorate the centenary of the birth of the Azerbaijan poet and satirist, Alepker Sabir (1862-1911).

1962, July 16 Litho. ***Perf. 12½***
2617 A1332 6k grnsh bl, blk & red 15 7

Issued to commemorate the Eighth Anti-Cancer Congress, Moscow, July 1962.

N. N. Zinin
A1333

1962, July 16 Photo. *Perf. 12x11½*
2618 A1333 4k vio & dk brn 10 7

Issued to commemorate the 150th anniversary of the birth of N. N. Zinin, chemist.

I. M. Kramskoy, Painter
A1334

I. D. Shadr, Sculptor
A1335

M. V. Nesterov, Painter
A1336

Perf. 11½x12, 12x12½
1962, July 28
2619 A1334 4k gray, mar & dk brn 10 7
2620 A1335 4k blk & red brn 10 7

Litho.
2621 A1336 4k multi 10 7

Vostok 2 Going into Space — A1337

Perf. 11½
1962, Aug. 7 Unwmk. Photo.
2622 A1337 10k blk, lil & bl 40 15
2623 A1337 10k blk, org & bl 40 15

Issued to commemorate the first anniversary of Gherman Titov's space flight. Issued imperf. on Aug. 6. Value, set $3.

Friendship House, Moscow — A1338

1962, Aug. 15 *Perf. 12x12½*
2624 A1338 6k ultra & gray 12 10

Kremlin and Atom Symbol — A1339

Design: 6k, Map of Russia, atom symbol and "Peace" in 10 languages.

1962, Aug. 15 Litho. *Perf. 12½x12*
2625 A1339 4k multi 10 7
2626 A1339 6k multi 15 10

Use of atomic energy for peace.

Andrian G. Nikolayev
A1340

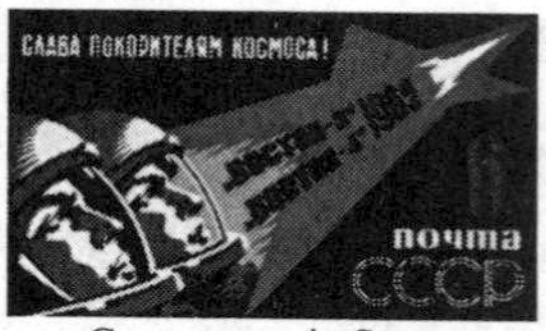

Cosmonauts in Space Helments — A1341

"To Space" Monument by G. Postnikov — A1342

Design: No. 2628, Pavel R. Popovich, with inscription at left and dated "12-15-VIII, 1962."

1962 Photo. *Perf. 11½*
2627 A1340 4k bl, brn & red 12 10
2628 A1340 4k bl, brn & red 12 10

Perf. 12½x12
Litho.
2629 A1341 6k dk bl, lt bl, org & yel 35 12

Perf. 11½
Photo.
2630 A1342 6k brt bl & multi 30 10
2631 A1342 10k vio & multi 35 12
Nos. 2627-2631 (5) 1.24 54

Souvenir Sheet

Design: 1r, Monument and portraits of Gagarin, Titov, Nikolayev and Popovich.

1962, Nov. 27 Litho. *Perf. 12½*
2631A A1342 1r brt bl, blk & sil 5.00 3.50

Nos. 2627-2631A honor the four Russian "conquerors of space," with Nos. 2627-2629 commemorating the first group space flight, by Vostoks 3 and 4, Aug. 11-15, 1962. Nos. 2627-2631A were also issued imperf.
Size of No. 2631A: 150x71mm.
See No. 2662.

Carp and Bream — A1343

Design: 6k, Freshwater salmon.

1962, Aug. 28 Photo. *Perf. 11½x12*
2632 A1343 4k bl & org 12 5
2633 A1343 6k bl & org 20 10

Fish preservation in USSR.

Feliks E. Dzerzhinski
A1344

1962, Sept. 6 Litho. *Perf. 12½x12*
2634 A1344 4k ol grn & dk bl 10 7

Issued to commemorate the 85th anniversary of the birth of Feliks E. Dzerzhinski (1877-1926), organizer of Soviet secret police.

O. Henry and New York Skyline
A1345

1962, Sept. 10 Photo. *Perf. 12x11½*
2635 A1345 6k yel, red brn & blk 15 10

Issued to commemorate the centenary of the birth of O. Henry (William Sidney Porter, 1862-1910), American writer.

Barclay de Tolly, Mikhail I. Kutuzov, Petr I. Bagration
A1346

Designs: 4k, Denis Davidov leading partisans. 6k, Battle of Borodino. 10k, Wasilisa Kozhina and partisans.

1962, Sept. 25 *Perf. 12½x12*
2636 A1346 3k org brn 10 7
2637 A1346 4k ultra 12 7
2638 A1346 6k bl gray 20 10
2639 A1346 10k violet 25 12

Issued to commemorate the 150th anniversary of the War of 1812 against the French.

Street in Vinnitsa
A1347

1962, Sept. 25 Photo.
2640 A1347 4k yel bis & blk 10 7

Issued to commemorate the 600th anniversary of the town of Vinnitsa, Ukraine.

"Mail and Transportation" — A1348

1962, Sept. 25 *Perf. 11½*
2641 A1348 4k bl grn, blk & lil 10 7

Issued for International Letter Writing Week, Oct. 7-13.

Cedar — A1349

Construction Worker — A1350

Plants: 4k, Canna. 6k, Arbutus. 10k, Chrysanthemum.

1962, Sept. 27 Engr. & Photo.
2642 A1349 3k ver, blk & grn 10 7
2643 A1349 4k multi 10 7
2644 A1349 6k multi 12 7
2645 A1349 10k multi 30 10

Issued to commemorate the 150th anniversary of the Nikitsky Botanical Gardens.

1962, Sept. 29 Litho. *Perf. 12x12½*

Designs: No. 2647, Hiker. No. 2648, Surgeon. No. 2649, Worker and lathe. No. 2650, Farmer's wife. No. 2651, Textile worker. No. 2652, Teacher.

2646 A1350 4k org, gray & vio bl 10 5
2647 A1350 4k yel, gray, grn & bl 10 5
2648 A1350 4k grn, gray & lil rose 10 5
2649 A1350 4k ver, gray & lil 10 5
2650 A1350 4k bl, gray & emer 10 5
2651 A1350 4k brt pink, gray & vio 10 5
2652 A1350 4k yel, gray, dp vio, red & brn 10 5
Nos. 2646-2652 (7) 70 35

Sputnik and Stars
A1351

1962, Oct. 4 *Perf. 12½x12*
2653 A1351 10k multi 40 12

5th anniversary, launching of Sputnik 1.

M. F. Ahundov — A1352

1962, Oct. 2 Photo.
2654 A1352 4k lt grn & dk brn 10 5

Issued to commemorate the 150th anniversary of the birth of M. F. Ahundov, Azerbaijan poet and philosopher.

Farm and Young Couple with Banner
A1353

Designs: No. 2656, Tractors, map and surveyor. No. 2657, Farmer, harvester and map.

1962, Oct. 18 Litho. *Perf. 12½x12*
2655 A1353 4k multi 25 22
2656 A1353 4k multi 25 22
2657 A1353 4k brn, yel & red 25 22

Issued to honor the pioneer developers of virgin soil.

N. N. Burdenko
A1354

V. P. Filatov
A1355

1962, Oct. 20 *Perf. 12½x12*
2658 A1354 4k red brn, lt brn & blk 10 7
2659 A1355 4k multi 10 7

Issued to honor N. N. Burdenko and V. P. Filatov, scientists and academicians.

Lenin Mausoleum, Red Square — A1356

1962, Oct. 26 **Litho.**

2660 A1356 4k multi 12 7

92nd anniversary of Lenin's birth.

Worker, Flag and Factories — A1357

1962, Oct. 29 ***Perf. 12x12½***

2661 A1357 4k multi 12 7

Issued to commemorate the 45th anniversary of the October Revolution.

No. 2631 Overprinted in Dark Violet

ЗЕМЛЯ—МАРС
1.XI.

1962, Nov. 3 **Photo.** ***Perf. 11½***

2662 A1342 10k vio & multi 1.10 85

Launching of a rocket to Mars.

Togolok Moldo A1358

Sajat Nova — A1359

1962, Nov. 17 ***Perf. 12x12½***

2663 A1358 4k brn red & blk 12 5
2664 A1359 4k ultra & blk 12 5

No. 2663 issued to commemorate the 20th anniversary of the death of Togolok Moldo (1860-1942), Kirghiz poet. No. 2664 commemorates the 250th anniversary of the birth of the Armenian poet, Sajat Nova (1712-1795).

Arms, Hammer & Sickle and Map of USSR A1360

1962, Nov. 17 ***Perf. 11½***

2665 A1360 4k red, org & dk red 10 5

Issued to commemorate the 40th anniversary of the founding of the U.S.S.R.

Space Rocket, Earth and Mars — A1361

1962, Nov. 17 ***Perf. 12½x12***
Size: 73x27mm.

2666 A1361 10k pur & org red 52 20

Issued to commemorate the launching of a space rocket to Mars, Nov. 1, 1962.

Electric Power Industry — A1362

Designs: No. 2668, Machines. No. 2669, Chemicals and oil. No. 2670, Factory construction. No. 2671, Transportation. No. 2672, Telecommunications and space. No. 2673, Metals. No. 2674, Grain farming. No. 2675, Dairy, poultry and meat.

Perf. 12½x12

1962, Nov.-Dec. **Litho.**

2667 A1362 4k ultra, red, blk & gray 10 5
2668 A1362 4k ultra, gray, yel & cl 10 5
2669 A1362 4k yel, pink, blk, gray & brn 10 5
2670 A1362 4k yel, bl, red brn & gray 10 5
2671 A1362 4k mar, yel, red & bl 10 5
2672 A1362 4k brt yel, bl & brn 10 5
2673 A1362 4k lil, org, yel & dk brn 10 5
2674 A1362 4k vio, bis, org red & dk brn 10 5
2675 A1362 4k emer, dk brn, brn & gray 10 5
Nos. 2667-2675 (9) 90 45

Issued to publicize "great decisions of the 22nd Communist Party Congress" and to show the Russian people at work.

Queen, Rook and Knight — A1363

Perf. 12½

1962, Nov. 24 **Unwmk.** **Photo.**

2676 A1363 4k org yel & blk 22 10

30th Russian Chess Championships.

Gen. Vasili Blucher A1364

1962, Nov. 27 ***Perf. 11½***

2677 A1364 4k multi 10 5

Issued to honor General Vasili Konstantinovich Blucher (1889-1938).

V. N. Podbelski A1365

1962, Nov. 27 ***Perf. 12½x12***

2678 A1365 4k red brn, gray & blk 10 5

Issued to commemorate the 75th anniversary of the birth of V. N. Podbelski (1887-1920), minister of posts.

A. Makharenko A1366

A. Gaidar A1367

1962, Nov. 30 ***Perf. 11½x12***

2679 A1366 4k multi 10 5
2680 A1367 4k multi 10 5

Issued to honor the writers A. S. Makharenko (1888-1939) and Arkadi Gaidar (1904-1941).

Dove and Globe — A1368

1962, Dec. 22 **Litho.** ***Perf. 12½x12***

2681 A1368 4k multi 15 10

Issued for New Year 1963 with alternating label inscribed "Happy New Year!" Issued imperf. on Dec. 20. Value 75 cents.

D. N. Prjanishnikov A1369

Rose-colored Starlings A1370

1962, Dec. 22 ***Perf. 12x12½***

2682 A1369 4k multi 10 7

Issued to honor D. N. Prjanishnikov, founder of Russian agricultural chemistry.

1962, Dec. 26 **Photo.** ***Perf. 11½***

Birds. 4k, Red-breasted geese. 6k, Snow geese. 10k, White storks. 16k, Greater flamingos.

2683 A1370 3k grn, blk & pink 7 5
2684 A1370 4k brn, blk & dp org 10 7
2685 A1370 6k gray, blk & red 12 7
2686 A1370 10k bl, blk & red 22 12
2687 A1370 16k lt bl, rose & blk 42 20
Nos. 2683-2687 (5) 93 51

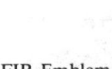

FIR Emblem A1371

1962, Dec. 26 ***Perf. 12x12½***

2688 A1371 4k vio & red 10 5
2689 A1371 6k grnsh bl & red 12 10

Issued to commemorate the 4th Congress of the International Federation of Resistance, FIR.

Map of Russia, Bank Book and Number of Savings Banks A1372

Design: 6k, as 4k, but with depositors.

1962, Dec. 30 **Litho.** ***Perf. 12½x12***

2690 A1372 4k multi 10 5
2691 A1372 6k multi 15 10

Issued to commemorate the 40th anniversary of Russian savings banks.

Rustavsky Fertilizer Plant — A1373

Hydroelectric Power Stations: No. 2693, Bratskaya. No. 2964, Volzhskaya.

1962, Dec. 30 **Photo.** ***Perf. 12½***

2692 A1373 4k ultra, lt bl & blk 10 5
2693 A1373 4k yel grn, bl grn & blk 10 5
2694 A1373 4k gray bl, brt bl & blk 10 5

Stanislavski A1374

A. S. Serafimovich A1375

Perf. 12½

1963, Jan. 15 **Unwmk.** **Engr.**

2695 A1374 4k sl grn 10 5

Issued to commemorate the centenary of the birth of Stanislavski, professional name of Konstantin Sergeevich Alekseev (1863-1938), actor, producer and founder of the Moscow Art Theater.

1963, Jan. 19 **Photo.** ***Perf. 11½***

2696 A1375 4k mag, dk brn & gray 10 5

Issued to commemorate the centenary of the birth of A. S. Serafimovich (1863-1949), writer.

Children in Nursery A1376

Designs: No. 2698, Kindergarten. No. 2699, Pioneers marching and camping. No. 2700, Young people studying and working.

1963, Jan. 31

2697 A1376 4k brn org, org red & blk 10 7
2698 A1376 4k bl, mag & org 10 7
2699 A1376 4k brt grn, red & brn 10 7
2700 A1376 4k multi 10 7

Wooden Dolls and Toys, Russia — A1377

National Handicrafts: 6k, Pottery, Ukraine. 10k, Bookbinding, Estonia. 12k, Metalware, Dagestan.

1963, Jan. 31 Litho. *Perf. 12x12½*
2701 A1377 4k multi 10 5
2702 A1377 6k multi 15 7
2703 A1377 10k multi 32 7
2704 A1377 12k ultra, org & blk 42 10

Gen. Mikhail N. Tukhachevski — A1378

Designs: No. 2706, U. M. Avetisian. No. 2707, A. M. Matrosov. No. 2708, J. V. Panfilov. No. 2709, Y. F. Fabriscius.

Perf. 12½x12
1963, Feb. Photo. Unwmk.
2705 A1378 4k bl grn & sl grn 10 7
2706 A1378 4k org brn & blk 10 7
2707 A1378 4k ultra & dk brn 10 7
2708 A1378 4k dp rose & blk 10 7
2709 A1378 4k rose lil & vio bl 10 7
Nos. 2705-2709 (5) 50 35

Issued to commemorate the 45th anniversary of the Soviet Army and to honor its heroes. No. 2705 commemorates the 70th anniversary of the birth of Gen. Mikhail Nikolaevich Tukhachevski (1893-1937).

M. A. Pavlov
A1379

E. O. Paton and Dnieper Bridge, Kiev
A1379a

Portraits: No. 2711, I. V. Kurchatov. No. 2712, V. I. Vernadski. No. 2713, Aleksei N. Krylov. No. 2714, V. A. Obrutchev, geologist.

1963 *Perf. 11½x12*
Size: 21x32mm.
2710 A1379 4k gray, buff & dk bl 10 5
2711 A1379 4k sl & brn 10 5
Perf. 12
2712 A1379 4k lil gray & lt brn 10 5
Perf. 11½
Size: 23x34½mm.
2713 A1379 4k dk bl, sep & red 10 5
2714 A1379 4k brn ol, gray & red 10 5
2715 A1379a 4k grnsh bl, blk & red 10 5
Nos. 2710-2715 (6) 60 30

Nos. 2710-2715 issued to honor members of the Russian Academy of Science. No. 2715 commemorates the 10th anniversary of the death of Eugene Oskarovich Paton (1870-1953), bridge building engineer.

Winter Sports
A1380

1963, Feb. 28 *Perf. 11½*
2716 A1380 4k brt bl, org & blk 15 10

Issued to commemorate the 5th Trade Union Spartacist Games. Printed in sheets of 50 (5x10) with every other row inverted.

No. 2573 Overprinted

Советские
хоккеисты-
чемпионы
мира
и Европы
Стокгольм
1963 г.

1963, Mar. 20
2717 A1306 6k Prus bl & plum 65 25

Issued to commemorate the victory of the Soviet ice hockey team in the World Championships, Stockholm. See No. 3612.

Victor Kingisepp
A1381

Rudolfs Blaumanis
A1382

1963, Mar. 24 *Perf. 12x12½*
2718 A1381 4k bl gray & choc 12 7

Issued to commemorate the 75th anniversary of the birth of Victor Kingisepp, communist party leader.

1963, Mar. 24 *Perf. 12½x12*
2719 A1382 4k ultra & dk red brn 12 7

Issued to commemorate the centenary of the birth of Rudolfs Blaumanis (1863-1908), Latvian writer.

Flower and Globe — A1383

Designs: 6k, Atom diagram and power line. 10k, Rocket in space.

1963, Mar. 26 *Perf. 11½*
2720 A1383 4k red, ultra & grn 10 7
2721 A1383 6k red, grn & lil 15 7
2722 A1383 10k red, vio & lt bl 20 10

Publicity for a "World without Arms and Wars."
The 10k exists imperf. Value $1.50.
See No. 2754.

Costume Type of 1960-62

Regional Costumes: 3k, Tadzhik. No. 2724, Kirghiz. No. 2725, Azerbaijan. No. 2726, Turkmen.

1963, Mar. 31 Litho. *Perf. 11½*
2723 A1237 3k blk, red, ocher & org 12 5
2724 A1237 4k brn, ver, ocher & ultra 15 5
2725 A1237 4k blk, ocher, red & grn 15 5
2726 A1237 4k red, lil, ocher & blk 15 5

Lenin
A1384

1963, Mar. 30 Engr. *Perf. 12*
2727 A1384 4k red & brn 12 5

93rd anniversary of the birth of Lenin.

Luna 4 Approaching Moon — A1385

1963, Apr. 2 Photo.
2728 A1385 6k blk, lt bl & red 25 15

Issued to commemorate Russia's rocket to the moon, Apr. 2, 1963. Exists imperforate. Value 85 cents.
See No. 3160.

Woman and Beach Scene
A1386

Designs: 4k, Young man's head and factory. 10k, Child's head and kindergarden.

1963, Apr. 7 Litho. *Perf. 12½x12*
2729 A1386 2k multi 7 5
2730 A1386 4k multi 10 5
2731 A1386 10k multi 22 10

15th anniversary of World Health Day.

Sputnik and Earth — A1387

Designs: No. 2733, Vostok 1, earth and moon. No. 2734, Rocket and Sun.

1963, Apr. 12
2732 A1387 10k blk, bl & lil rose 50 25
a "10k" bl 50 32
2733 A1387 10k lil rose, bl & blk 50 25
a "10k" lil rose 50 32
2734 A1387 10k blk, red & yel 50 25
a "10k" yel 50 32

Issued for Cosmonauts' Day. Nos. 2732-2734 and 2732a-2734a printed se-tenant. Alternate rows in sheets have colorless "10k."

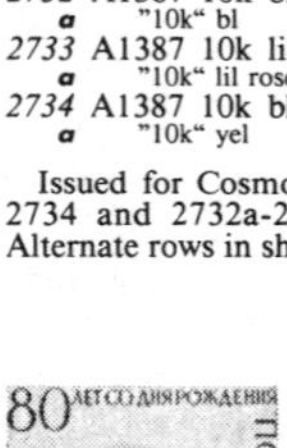

Demian Bednii
(1883-1945)
A1388

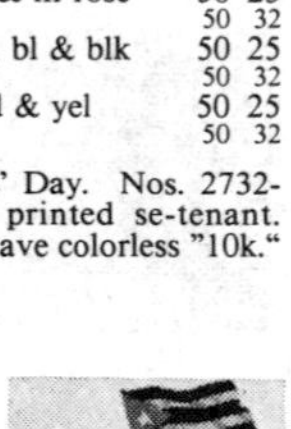

Soldiers on Horseback and Cuban Flag
A1389

1963, Apr. 13 Photo.
2735 A1388 4k brn & blk 10 5

Issued to commemorate the 80th anniversary of the birth of Demian Bednii, poet.

1963, Apr. 25 *Perf. 11½*

Designs: 6k, Cuban flag, hands with gun and book. 10k, Cuban and Russian flags and crane lifting tractor.

2736 A1389 4k blk, red & ultra 10 5
2737 A1389 6k blk, red & ultra 15 7
2738 A1389 10k red, ultra & blk 25 10

Soviet-Cuban friendship.

Karl Marx
A1390

Jaroslav Hasek
A1391

1963, May 9 *Perf. 12x12½*
2739 A1390 4k dk red brn & blk 10 5

145th anniversary of the birth of Marx.

1963, Apr. 29 *Perf. 11½x12*
2740 A1391 4k black 10 7

Issued to commemorate the 80th anniversary of the birth of Jaroslav Hasek (1883-1923), Czech writer.

Mascow P.O. for Foreign Mail
A1392

1963, May 9 *Perf. 11½*
2741 A1392 6k brt vio & red brn 15 7

Issued to commemorate the 5th Conference of Communications Ministers of Socialist countries, Budapest.

King and Pawn
A1393

Designs: 6k, Queen and bishop. 16k, Rook and knight.

1963, May 22 Photo.
2742 A1393 4k multi 10 5
2743 A1393 6k ultra, brt pink & grnsh bl 15 7
2744 A1393 16k brt plum, brt pink & blk 40 12

Issued to commemorate the 25th Championship Chess Match, Moscow. Imperforates exist, issued May 18. Value $2.

Richard Wagner
A1394

Boxers
A1395

Design: No. 2745A, Giuseppe Verdi.

1963 Unwmk. *Perf. 11½x12*
2745 A1394 4k blk & red 10 7
2745A A1394 4k red & vio brn 10 7

Issued to commemorate the 150th anniversaries of the births of Richard Wagner and Giuseppe Verdi, German and Italian composers.

1963, May 29 Litho. *Perf. 12½*

Design: 6k, Referee proclaiming victor.

2746 A1395 4k multi 10 5
2747 A1395 6k multi 15 10

Issued to commemorate the 15th European Boxing Championships, Moscow.

Valeri Bykovski — A1396

Valentina Tereshkova — A1397

Designs: No. 2749, Tereshkova. No. 2751, Bykovski. No. 2752, Symbolic man and woman fliers. No. 2753, Tereshkova (vert.).

Litho. (A1396); Photo. (A1397)
1963 ***Perf. 12½x12, 12x12½***

2748 A1396 4k multi 15 12
2749 A1396 4k multi 15 12
2750 A1397 6k grn & dk car rose 15 10
2751 A1397 6k pur & brn 12 10
2752 A1397 10k bl & red 32 15
2753 A1396 10k multi 60 20
Nos. 2748-2753 (6) 1.49 79

Issued to commemorate the space flights of Valeri Bykovski, June 14-19, and Valentina Tereshkova, first woman cosmonaut, June 16-19, 1963, in Vostoks 5 and 6.

Nos. 2748-2749 are printed se-tenant. Nos. 2750-2753 exist imperf. Value $3.

No. 2720 Overprinted in Red: Всемирный конгресс женщин.

1963, June 24 **Photo.** ***Perf. 11½***
2754 A1383 4k red, ultra & grn 25 10

Issued to publicize the International Women's Congress, Moscow, June 24-29.

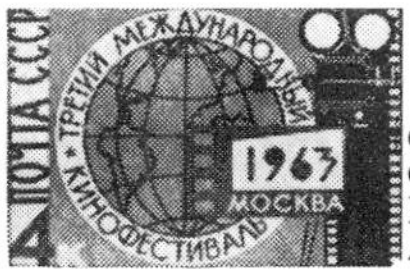

Globe, Camera and Film A1398

1963, July 7 **Photo.** ***Perf. 11½***
2755 A1398 4k gray & ultra 12 10

3rd International Film Festival, Moscow.

Vladimir V. Mayakovsky A1399

1963, July 19 **Engr.** ***Perf. 12½***
2756 A1399 4k red brn 15 10

Issued to commemorate the 70th anniversary of the birth of Vladimir V. Mayakovsky, poet.

The only foreign revenue stamps listed in this Catalogue are those authorized for prepayment of postage.

Tanks and Map A1400

Design: 6k, Soldier, tanks and flag.

1963, July **Litho.** ***Perf. 12½x12***
2757 A1400 4k sep & org 10 5
2758 A1400 6k org, sl grn & blk 15 10

Issued to commemorate the 20th anniversary of the Battle of Kursk in the "War of Liberation," 1941-1945.

Bicyclist — A1401

Sports: 4k, Long jump. 6k, Women divers (horiz.). 12k, Basketball. 16k, Soccer.

Perf. 12½x12, 12x12½
1963, July 27

2759 A1401 3k multi 7 7
2760 A1401 4k multi 12 7
2761 A1401 6k multi 20 10
2762 A1401 12k multi 32 10
2763 A1401 16k multi 40 12
a Souv. sheet of 4 2.00 50
Nos. 2759-2763 (5) 1.11 46

3rd Spartacist Games. Exist imperf. Value $2.50.

No. 2763a contains 4 imperf. stamps similar to the 3k, 4k, 12k and 16k, with colors changed. Bright green, orange and gray margin. Size: 155x104mm. Issued Dec. 22.

Ice Hockey — A1402

Lenin — A1403

1963, July 27 **Photo.**
2764 A1402 6k red & gray bl 15 7

Issued to commemorate the World Ice Hockey Championship, Stockholm.
See No. 3012.

1963, July 29
2765 A1403 4k red & blk 10 5

Issued to commemorate the 60th anniversary of the 2nd Congress of the Social Democratic Labor Party.

Freighter and Relief Shipment A1404

Design: 12k, Centenary emblem.

1963, Aug. 8 ***Perf. 12½***
2766 A1404 6k Prus grn & red 15 7
2767 A1404 12k dk bl & red 32 12

Centenary of International Red Cross.

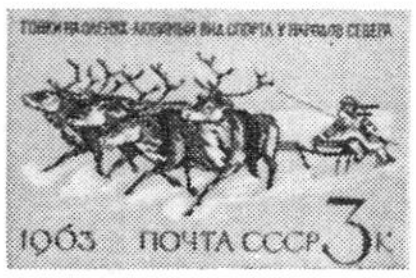

Lapp Reindeer Race A1405

Designs: 4k, Pamir polo (vert.). 6k, Burjat archery. 10k, Armenian wrestling (vert.).

1963, Aug. 8 ***Perf. 11½***
2768 A1405 3k lt vio bl, brn & red 7 5
2769 A1405 4k bis brn, red & blk 10 5
2770 A1405 6k yel, blk & red 15 10
2771 A1405 10k sep, blk & dk red 22 15

A. F. Mozhaisky (1825-1890), Pioneer Airplane Builder A1406

Designs: 10k, P. N. Nesterov (1887-1914), pioneer stunt flyer. 16k, N. E. Zhukovski (1847-1921), aerodynamics pioneer, and pressurized air tunnel.

1963, Aug. 18 **Engr. & Photo.**
2772 A1406 6k blk & brt bl 15 5
2773 A1406 10k blk & brt bl 22 10
2774 A1406 16k blk & brt bl 32 15

Issued to honor aviation pioneers.

Alexander S. Dargomyzhski and Scene from "Rusalka" — A1408

S. S. Gulak-Artemovsky and Scene from "Cossacks on the Danube" — A1409

Design: No. 2777, Georgi O. Eristavi and theater.

Perf. 11½x12, 12x12½
1963, Sept. 10 **Photo.**
2776 A1408 4k vio & blk 10 5
2777 A1408 4k gray vio & brn 10 5
2778 A1409 4k red & blk 10 5

Issued to commemorate the 150th anniversaries of the births of A. S. Dargomyzhski, Ukrainian composer; Georgi O. Eristavi, Georgian writer, and S. S. Gulak-Artemovsky, Ukrainian composer.

Map of Antarctica, Penguins, Research Ship and Southern Lights A1410

Designs: 4k, Map, southern lights and snocats (trucks). 6k, Globe, camp and various planes. 12k, Whaler and whales.

1963, Sept. 16 **Litho.** ***Perf. 12½x12***
2779 A1410 3k multi 7 5
2780 A1410 4k multi 10 7
2781 A1410 6k vio, bl & red 15 7
2782 A1410 12k multi 32 10

"The Antarctic - Continent of Peace."

Letters, Globe, Plane, Train and Ship A1411

1963, Sept. 20 **Photo.** ***Perf. 11½***
2783 A1411 4k vio, blk & org 10 5

International Letter Writing Week.

Denis Diderot A1412

Gleb Uspenski A1414

1963, Oct. 10 **Unwmk.** ***Perf. 11½***
2784 A1412 4k dk bl, brn & yel bis 10 7

Issued to commemorate the 250th anniversary of the birth of Denis Diderot (1713-84), French philosopher and encyclopedist.

1963, Oct. 10

Portraits: No. 2787, N. P. Ogarev. No. 2788, V. Brusov. No. 2789, F. Gladkov.

2786 A1414 4k buff, red brn & dk brn 12 5
2787 A1414 4k blk & pale grn 10 5
2788 A1414 4k car, brn & gray 10 5
2789 A1414 4k car, ol brn & gray 10 5

No. 2786 commemorates the 120th anniversary of the birth of Gleb Ivanovich Uspenski (1843-1902), historian and writer; No. 2787 the 150th anniversary of the birth of N. P. Ogarev, politician; No. 2788 the 90th anniversary of the birth of V. Brusov, poet, and No. 2789 the 80th anniversary of the birth of Fyodor Gladkov (1883-1958), writer.

"Peace" Worker, Student, Astronaut and Lenin — A1415

Kirghiz Academy and Spasski Tower — A1416

Designs: No. 2794, "Labor," automatic controls. No. 2795, "Liberty," painter, lecturer, newspaper man. No. 2796, "Equality," elections, regional costumes. No. 2797, "Brotherhood," Recognition of achievement. No. 2798, "Happiness," Family.

1963, Oct. 15 **Litho.** ***Perf. 12½x12***
2793 A1415 4k dk red, red & blk 10 5
2794 A1415 4k red, dk red & blk 10 5
2795 A1415 4k dk red, red & blk 10 5
2796 A1415 4k dk red, red & blk 10 5
2797 A1415 4k dk red, red & blk 10 5
2798 A1415 4k dk red, red & blk 10 5
a Strip of 6 85 60
Nos. 2793-2798 (6) 60 30

Issued to proclaim Peace, Labor, Liberty, Equality, Brotherhood and Happiness. Nos. 2793-2798 are printed se-tenant forming complete row in sheet.

1963, Oct. 22 ***Perf. 12x12½***
2799 A1416 4k red, yel & vio bl 10 5

Centenary of Russia's annexation of Kirghizia.

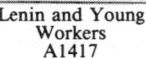

Lenin and Young Workers A1417

Olga Kobylyanskaya A1418

Design: No. 2801, Lenin and Palace of Congresses, the Kremlin.

1963, Oct. 24 Photo. *Perf. 11½*
2800 A1417 4k crime & blk 10 5
2801 A1417 4k car & blk 10 5

Issued to commemorate the 13th Congress of Soviet Trade Unions, held at Moscow.

1963, Oct. 24 *Perf. 11½x12*
2802 A1418 4k tan & dk car rose 10 5

Issued to commemorate the centenary of the birth of Olga Kobylyanskaya, Ukrainian novelist.

Ilya Mechnikov A1419

Cruiser Aurora and Rockets A1420

Designs: 6k, Louis Pasteur. 12k, Albert Calmette.

1963, Oct. 28 *Perf. 12*
2803 A1419 4k grn & bis 10 5
2804 A1419 6k pur & bis 15 10
2805 A1419 12k bl & bis 32 15

Issued to commemorate the 75th anniversary of the Pasteur Institute, Paris; the 12k commemorates the centenary of the birth of Albert Calmette (1863-1933), bacteriologist.

1963, Nov. 1
2806 A1420 4k mar, blk, gray & red org 15 10
2807 A1420 4k mar, blk, gray & brt rose red 15 10

Issued to publicize the development of the Armed Forces, and to commemorate the 46th anniversary of the October Revolution. The bright rose red ink of No. 2807 is fluorescent.

Mausoleum Gur Emi, Samarkand A1421

Designs (Architecture in Samarkand, Uzbekistan): No. 2809, Shahi-Zind Mosque. 6k, Registan Square.

1963, Nov. 14 Litho. *Perf. 12*
Size: 27½x27½mm.
2808 A1421 4k bl, yel & red brn 10 7
2809 A1421 4k bl, yel & red brn 10 7
Size: 55x27½mm.
2810 A1421 6k bl, yel & red brn 20 10

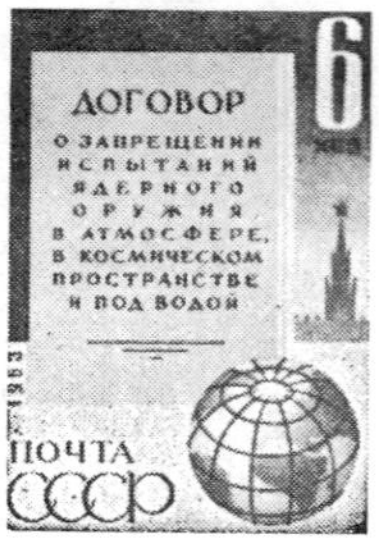

Proclamation, Spasski Tower and Globe — A1422

1963, Nov. 15 Photo. *Perf. 12x11½*
2811 A1422 6k pur & lt bl 20 10

Issued to commemorate the signing of the Nuclear Test Ban Treaty between the U.S.A. and the U.S.S.R.

Pushkin Monument, Kiev A1423

M. S. Shchepkin A1424

Portrait: No. 2814, V. L. Durov (1863-1934), circus clown.

1963 Engr. *Perf. 12x12½*
2812 A1423 4k dk brn 10 5
2813 A1424 4k brown 10 5
2814 A1424 4k brn blk 10 5

No. 2813 commemorates the 175th anniversary of the birth of M. S. Shchepkin, actor.

Yuri M. Steklov A1425

1963, Nov. 17 Photo. *Perf. 11½*
2815 A1425 4k blk & lil rose 10 5

Issued to commemorate the 90th anniversary of the birth of Yuri M. Steklov, first editor of Izvestia.

Vladimir G. Shuhov and Moscow Radio Tower — A1426

1963, Nov. 17 *Perf. 12½x12*
2816 A1426 4k grn & blk 10 5

Issued to commemorate the 110th anniversary of the birth of Vladimir G. Shuhov, scientist.

Russian and Czech Flags, Kremlin and Hradcany A1427

1963, Nov. 25 *Perf. 11½*
2817 A1427 6k red, ultra & brn 20 10

Issued to commemorate the 20th anniversary of the Russo-Czechoslovakian Treaty.

Fyodor A. Poletaev — A1428

1963, Nov. 25 Litho. *Perf. 12½x12*
2818 A1428 4k multi 12 5

Issued to honor F. A. Poletaev, Hero of the Soviet Union, National Hero of Italy, and holder of the Order of Garibaldi.

Julian Grimau and Worker Holding Flag — A1429

1963, Nov. 29 Photo. *Perf. 11½*
Flag and Name Panel Embossed
2819 A1429 6k vio blk, red & buff 15 10

Issued to honor the Spanish anti-fascist fighter Julian Grimau.

Rockets, Sky and Tree — A1430

"Happy New Year!" — A1431

1963, Dec. 12 Litho. *Perf. 12x12½*
2820 A1430 6k multi 15 10

Photogravure and Embossed
1963, Dec. 20 *Perf. 11½*
2821 A1431 4k grn, dk bl & red 10 5
2822 A1431 6k grn, dk bl & fluor. rose red 15 10

Nos. 2820-2822 issued for New Year 1964.

Mikas J. Petrauskas A1432

1963, Dec. 20 Photo. *Perf. 11½x12*
2823 A1432 4k brt grn & brn 10 5

Issued to commemorate the 90th anniversary of the birth of M. J. Petrauskas, Lithuanian composer.

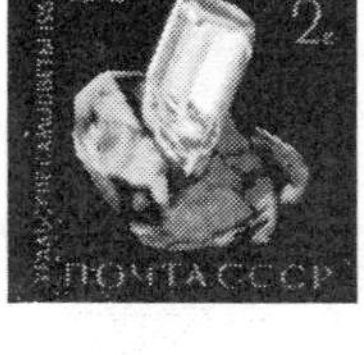

Topaz — A1433

Precious stones of the Urals: 4k, Jasper. 6k, Amethyst. 10k, Emerald. 12k, Rhodonite. 16k, Malachite.

1963, Dec. 26 Litho. *Perf. 12*
2824 A1433 2k brn, yel & bl 12 7
2825 A1433 4k multi 32 7
2826 A1433 6k red & pur 25 7
2827 A1433 10k multi 40 10
2828 A1433 12k multi 50 12
2829 A1433 16k multi 65 15
Nos. 2824-2829 (6) 2.24 58

Coat of Arms and Sputnik — A1434

Rockets: No. 2831, Luna I. No. 2832, Rocket around the moon. No. 2833, Vostok I, first man in space. No. 2834, Vostok III & IV. No. 2835, Vostok VI, first woman astronaut.

1963, Dec. 27 Litho. & Embossed
2830 A1434 10k red, gold & gray 32 16
2831 A1434 10k red, gold & gray 32 16
2832 A1434 10k red, gold & gray 32 16
2833 A1434 10k red, gold & gray 32 16
2834 A1434 10k red, gold & gray 32 16
2835 A1434 10k red, gold & gray 32 16
a Strip of 6 2.25 1.10
Nos. 2830-2835 (6) 1.92 96

Issued to publicize Russian achievements in space. Nos. 2830-2835 are printed se-tenant forming complete vertical row in sheet.

Dyushambe, Tadzhikistan — A1435

1963, Dec. 30 Engr.
2836 A1435 4k dl bl 10 5

No. 2836 was issued after Stalinabad was renamed Dyushambe. See No. 2943.

Flame, Broken Chain and Rainbow — A1436

1963, Dec. 30 Litho.
2837 A1436 6k multi 15 10

Issued to commemorate the 15th anniversary of the Universal Declaration of Human Rights.

F. A. Sergeev A1437

1963, Dec. 30 Photo. *Perf. 12x12½*
2838 A1437 4k gray & red 10 5

Issued to commemorate the 80th anniversary of the birth of the revolutionist Artjem (F. A. Sergeev).

Sun and Radar A1438

Designs: 6k, Sun and Earth (vert.). 10k, Earth and Sun.

1964, Jan. 1 Photo. *Perf. 11½*

2839	A1438	4k brt mag, org & blk	15	7
2840	A1438	6k org yel, red & bl	22	10
2841	A1438	10k bl, vio & org	25	15

International Quiet Sun Year, 1964-65.

Christian Donalitius A1439

1964, Jan. 1 Unwmk. *Perf. 12*

2842	A1439	4k grn & blk	12	7

Issued to commemorate the 250th anniversary of the birth of the Lithuanian poet Christian Donalitius (Donelaitis).

Women's Speed Skating A1440

Designs: 4k, Women's cross country skiing. 6k, 1964 Olympic emblem and torch. 10k, Biathlon. 12k, Figure skating pair.

1964, Feb. 4 *Perf. 11½, Imperf.*

2843	A1440	2k ultra, blk & lil rose	7	5
2844	A1440	4k lil rose, blk & ultra	10	7
2845	A1440	6k dk bl, red & blk	15	10
2846	A1440	10k grn, lil & blk	25	10
2847	A1440	12k lil, blk & grn	32	12
		Nos. 2843-2847 (5)	89	44

Issued to commemorate the 9th Winter Olympic Games, Innsbruck Jan. 29-Feb. 9, 1964. See Nos. 2865, 2867-2870.

Anna S. Golubkina A1441

1964, Feb. 4 Photo.

2848	A1441	4k gray, brn & buff	12	5

Issued to commemorate the centenary of the birth of Anna S. Golubkina (1864-1927), sculptor.

Ovpt. on No. 2450 in Red

150 років з дня народження. 1964 р.

Taras G. Shevchenko A1443

Designs: 4k, Shevchenko statue, Kiev. 10k, Shevchenko by Ilya Repin. (Portrait on 6k by I. Kremsko.)

1964 Litho. *Perf. 12*

2852	A1245	3k brn & vio	7	5
		Engr.		
2853	A1443	4k magenta	10	5
2854	A1443	4k dp grn	10	5
2855	A1443	6k red brn	15	7
2856	A1443	6k indigo	15	7
		Photo.		
2857	A1443	10k bis & brn	22	10
2858	A1443	10k buff & dl vio	22	10
		Nos. 2852-2858 (7)	1.01	49

150th anniv. of the birth of Taras G. Shevchenko, Ukrainian poet.

Issue dates: Nos. 2852, 2857-2858, Feb. 22. Others, Mar. 1.

K. S. Zaslonov A1444

Soviet Heroes: No. 2860, N. A. Vilkov. No. 2861, J. V. Smirnov. No. 2862, V. S. Khorujaia (heroine). No. 2862A, I. M. Sivko. No. 2862B, I. S. Polbin.

1964-65 Photo.

2859	A1444	4k hn brn & brn blk	10	7
2860	A1444	4k Prus bl & vio blk	10	7
2861	A1444	4k brn red & ind	10	7
2862	A1444	4k bluish gray & dk brn	10	7
2862A	A1444	4k lil & blk ('65)	10	7
2862B	A1444	4k bl & dk brn ('65)	10	7
		Nos. 2859-2862B (6)	60	42

Printer Inking Form, 16th Century A1445

Design: 6k, Statue of Ivan Fedorov, first Russian printer.

1964, Mar. 1 Litho. Unwmk.

2863	A1445	4k multi	10	7
2864	A1445	6k multi	12	7

Issued to commemorate the 400th anniversary of book printing in Russia.

Nos. 2843-2847 Overprinted and

Ice Hockey A1446

Olympic Gold Medal, "11 Gold, 8 Silver, 6 Bronze" A1447

1964, Mar. 9 Photo. *Perf. 11½*

2865	A1440	2k ultra, blk & lil rose	10	8
2866	A1446	3k blk, bl grn & red	12	8
2867	A1440	4k lil rose, blk & ultra	15	7
2868	A1440	6k dk bl, red & blk	25	8
2869	A1440	10k grn, lil & blk	30	8
2870	A1440	12k lil, blk & grn	35	15
		Perf. 12		
2871	A1447	16k org red & gldn brn	55	25
		Nos. 2865-2871 (7)	1.82	79

Issued to commemorate the Russian victories at the 9th Winter Olympic Games.

On Nos. 2865, 2867-2870 the black overprints commemorate victories in various events and are variously arranged in 3 to 6 lines, with "Innsbruck" in Russian added below "1964" on 2k, 4k, 10k and 12k.

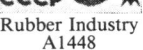

Rubber Industry A1448

Regular and Volunteer Militiamen A1449

Designs: No. 2873, Textile industry. No. 2874, Cotton, wheat, corn and helicopter spraying land.

1964 Litho. *Perf. 12x12½*

2872	A1448	4k org, lil, ultra & blk	10	5
2873	A1448	4k org, blk, grn & ultra	10	5
2874	A1448	4k dl yel, ol, red & bl	10	5

Issued to publicize the importance of the chemical industry for Russian economy.

Issue dates: No. 2872, Feb. 10. Nos. 2873-2874, Mar. 27.

1964, Mar. 27 Photo. *Perf. 12*

2875	A1449	4k red & dp ultra	12	5

Issued for the Day of the Militia.

Sailor and Odessa Lighthouse A1450

Liberation Monument, Minsk — A1451

Design: No. 2877, Lenin statue and Leningrad.

Perf. 12½x12

1964, Apr. 10-June 30 Litho.

2876	A1450	4k red, lt grn, ultra & blk	10	5
2877	A1450	4k red, yel, grn, brn & blk	10	5
2878	A1451	4k bl, gray, red & emer	10	5

Issued to commemorate the 20th anniversary of the liberation of Odessa (No. 2876), Leningrad (No. 2877) and Byelorussia (No. 2878).

First Soviet Sputniks A1452

F. A. Tsander A1453

Lenin A1454

Designs: 6k, Mars 1 spacecraft. No. 2886, Konstantin E. Tsiolkovsky. No. 2887, N. I. Kibaltchitch. No. 2888, Statue honoring 3 balloonists killed in 1934 accident. 12k, Gagarin and Kosmos 3.

Perf. 11½, Imperf.

1964, Apr. Photo.

2883	A1452	4k red org, blk & bl grn	12	7
2884	A1452	6k dk bl & org red	20	10
2885	A1453	10k grn, blk & fluor. pink	22	12
2886	A1453	10k dk bl grn, blk & fluor. pink	22	12
2887	A1453	10k lil, blk & lt grn	22	12
2888	A1453	10k bl & blk	22	12
2889	A1452	12k bl grn, org brn & blk	25	20
		Nos. 2883-2889 (7)	1.45	85

Issued to honor leaders in rocket theory and technique.

Engraved and Photogravure

1964-65 *Perf. 12x11½*

2890	A1454	4k blk, buff & lil rose	18	10
a		Re-engraved ('65)	48	12

94th anniversary of the birth of Lenin.

On No. 2890a, the portrait shading is much heavier. Lines on collar are straight and unbroken, rather than dotted. For 1964 Lenin's Birthday souvenir sheet, see No. 2582a.

William Shakespeare A1455

1964, Apr. 23 *Perf. 11½*

2891	A1455	10k gray & red brn	32	12

Issued to commemorate the 400th anniversary of the birth of William Shakespeare.

See Nos. 2985-2986.

"Irrigation" — A1456

1964, May 12 Litho. *Perf. 12x12½*

2892	A1456	4k multi	10	5

Y. B. Gamarnik A1457

Perf. 12½x11½

1964, May 12 Photo.

2893	A1457	4k bl & gray brn	10	5

Issued to commemorate the 70th anniversary of the birth of Y. B. Gamarnik, army commander.

D. I. Gulia — A1458

Portraits: No. 2895, Hamza Hakim-Zade Nijazi. No. 2896, Saken Seifullin. No. 2896A, M. M. Kotsyubinsky. No. 2896B, Stepanos Nazaryan. No. 2896C, Toktogil Satyiganov.

Engraved and Photogravure

1964 Unwmk. *Perf. 12x11½*

2894 A1458 4k grn, buff & blk 10 5
2895 A1458 4k red, buff & blk 10 5
2896 A1458 4k brn, ocher, buff & blk 10 5
2896A A1458 4k brn lake, blk & buff 10 5
2896B A1458 4k bl, pale bl, blk & buff 10 5
2896C A1458 4k red brn & blk 10 5
Nos. 2894-2896C (6) 60 30

No. 2894 commemorates the 90th anniversary of the birth of the Abkhazian poet Gulia; No. 2895 the 75th anniversary of the birth of the Uzbekian writer and composer Nijazi; No. 2896 the 70th anniversary of the birth of the Kazakian poet Seifullin; No. 2896A, birth centenary of Ukrainian writer M. M. Kotsyubinsky (1864-1913): No. 2896B, the 150th anniversary of the birth of Armenian writer Stefanos Nazaryan (1814-1879); No. 2896C, birth centenary of Kirghiz poet Toktogil Satylganov (1864-1933).

Arkadi Gaidar A1459

Design: No. 2897A, Nikolai Ostrovsky and battle scene (portrait at left).

1964 Photo. *Perf. 12*

2897 A1459 4k red org & gray 10 5

Engr.

2897A A1459 4k brn lake & blk 10 5

Issued to commemorate the 60th anniversaries of the birth of writers Arkadi Gaidar (1904-1941) and Nikolai A. Ostrovsky (1904-1936).

No. 2318 Surcharged:

150 лет вхождения
в состав России
1964

4
коп.

1964, May 27 Litho. *Perf. 12*

2898 A1194 4k on 40k bis & brn 45 10

Issued to commemorate the 150th anniversary of Azerbaijan's joining Russia.

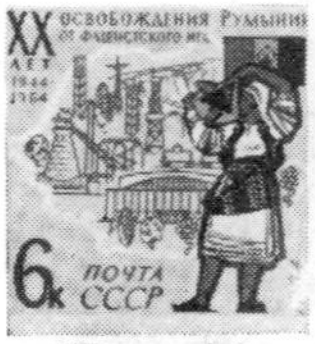

"Romania" A1460

Elephant A1461

Designs: No. 2900, "Poland," (map, Polish eagle, industrial and agricultural symbols). No. 2901, "Bulgaria" (flag, rose, industrial and agricultural symbols). No. 2902, Russian and Jugoslav soldiers and embattled Belgrade. No. 2903, "Czechoslovakia" (view of Prague, arms, Russian soldier and woman). No. 2903A, Map and flag of Hungary, Liberty statue. No. 2903B, Statue of Russian Soldier and Belvedere Palace, Vienna. No. 2904, Buildings under construction, Warsaw; Polish flag and medal.

1964-65 Litho. *Perf. 12*

2899 A1460 6k gray & multi 15 7
2900 A1460 6k ocher, red & brn 15 7
2901 A1460 6k tan, grn & red 15 7
2902 A1460 6k gray, blk, dl bl, ol & red 15 7
2903 A1460 6k ultra, blk & red ('65) 15 7
2903A A1460 6k brn, red & grn ('65) 15 7
2903B A1460 6k dp org, gray bl & blk ('65) 15 7
2904 A1460 6k bl, red, yel & bis ('65) 15 7
Nos. 2899-2904 (8) 1.20 56

Issued to commemorate the 20th anniversaries of liberation from German occupation of Romania, Poland, Bulgaria, Belgrade, Czechoslovakia, Hungary, Vienna and Warsaw.

Perf. 12x12½, 12½x12, Imperf.

1964 Photo.

Designs: 2k, Giant panda (horiz.). 4k, Polar bear. 6k, European elk. 10k, Pelican. 12k, Tiger. 16k, Lammergeier.

Size: 25x36mm., 36x25mm.

2905 A1461 1k red & blk 5 5
2906 A1461 2k tan & blk 7 5

Perf. 12

Size: 26x28mm.

2907 A1461 4k grnsh gray, blk & tan 10 6

Perf. 12x12½

Size: 25x36mm.

2908 A1461 6k ol, dk brn & tan 12 7

Perf. 12

Size: 26x28mm.

2909 A1461 10k ver, gray & blk 20 10

Perf. 12½x12, 12x12½

Size: 36x25mm., 25x36mm.

2910 A1461 12k brn, ocher & blk 35 12
2911 A1461 16k ultra, blk, bis & yel 32 15
Nos. 2905-2911 (7) 1.21 60

100th anniv. of the Moscow zoo.

Issue dates: Perf. set June 18. Imperf. set in May.

Leningrad Post Office A1462

1964, June 30 Litho. *Perf. 12*

2912 A1462 4k cit, blk & red 10 5

Issued to commemorate the 250th anniversary of Leningrad postal service.

Corn A1463

Maurice Thorez A1464

Designs: 3k, Wheat. 4k, Potatoes. 6k, Beans. 10k, Beets. 12k, Cotton. 16k, Flax.

1964 Photo. *Perf. 11½, Imperf.*

2913 A1463 2k ultra, yel & brn 5 5
2914 A1463 3k emer, yel & red brn 7 5
2915 A1463 4k brn, sl grn & lil 10 7
2916 A1463 6k ol bis, bis & grn 12 7
2917 A1463 10k dk car, grn, blk & tan 15 10
2918 A1463 12k lil, ap grn & blk 22 10
2919 A1463 16k lt bl, ol & red brn 32 12
Nos. 2913-2919 (7) 1.03 56

Issue dates: Perf. set July 10. Imperf. set June 25.

1964, July 31

2920 A1464 4k blk & red 25 10

Issued in memory of Maurice Thorez, chairman of the French Communist party.

Equestrian and Russian Olympic Emblem A1465

Designs: 4k, Weight lifter. 6k, High jump. 10k, Canoeing. 12k, Girl gymnast. 16k, Fencing.

1964, July *Perf. 11½, Imperf.*

2921 A1465 3k lt yel grn, red, brn & blk 7 5
2922 A1465 4k yel, blk & red 10 6
2923 A1465 6k lt bl, blk & red 12 7
2924 A1465 10k bl grn, red & blk 20 10
2925 A1465 12k gray, blk & red 22 12
2926 A1465 16k lt ultra, blk & red 32 15
Nos. 2921-2926 (6) 1.03 55

Issued for the 18th Olympic Games, Tokyo, Oct. 10-25, 1964.

Two 1r imperf. souvenir sheets exist, showing emblem, woman gymnast and stadium. Size: 91x71mm.

Value, red sheet, $4 unused, $1.75 canceled; green sheet, $165 unused, $225 canceled.

Three Races — A1466

Jawaharlal Nehru — A1467

1964, Aug. 8 Photo. *Perf. 12*

2929 A1466 6k org & blk 12 5

Issued to commemorate the International Congress of Anthropologists and Ethnographers, Moscow.

1964, Aug. 20 *Perf. 11½*

2930 A1467 4k brn & blk 12 5

Issued in memory of Prime Minister Jawaharlal Nehru of India (1889-1964).

Conquest of Space

A souvenir sheet, issued Aug. 20, 1964, celebrates the Conquest of Space. It carries six perforated, multicolored 10k stamps with different, interlocking designs picturing Soviet rockets and spacecraft. Size of sheet, 141x110mm. Value, $3 unused, $1.50 canceled. Sheet also exists on glossy paper. Value, $8.75 unused, $6 canceled.

Karl Marx and Friedrich Engels A1468

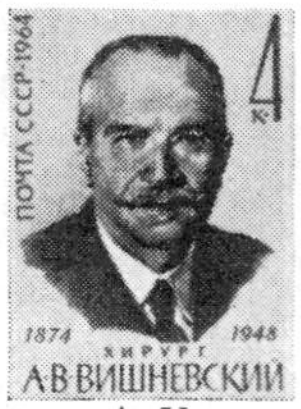

A. V. Vishnevsky A1469

Designs: No. 2932 Lenin and title page of "CPSS Program." No. 2933, Worker breaking chains around the globe. No. 2934, Title pages of "Communist Manifesto" in German and Russian. No. 2935, Globe and banner inscribed "Workers of the World Unite."

1964, Aug. 27 Photo. *Perf. 11½x12*

2931 A1468 4k red, dk red & brn 10 7
2932 A1468 4k red, brn & sl 10 7
2933 A1468 4k bl, fluor. brt rose & blk 10 7

Perf. 12½x12

Litho.

2934 A1468 4k ol blk, blk & red 10 7
2935 A1468 4k bl, red & ol bis 10 7
Nos. 2931-2935 (5) 50 35

Centenary of First Socialist International.

1964 Photo. *Perf. 11½*

Portraits: No. 2937, N. A. Semashko. No. 2938, D. Ivanovsky.

Size: 23½x35mm.

2936 A1469 4k gray & brn 10 5
2937 A1469 4k buff, sep & red 10 5

Litho.

Size: 22x32½mm.

2938 A1469 4k tan, gray & brn 10 5

Issued to commemorate the 90th anniversaries of the birth of A. V. Vishnevsky, surgeon, and N. A. Semashko, founder of the Russian Public Health Service; the centenary of the birth of D. Ivanovsky (1864-1920), physician.

Palmiro Togliatti — A1470

1964, Sept. 15 *Perf. 12½x12*

2939 A1470 4k blk & red 10 7

Issued to honor Palmiro Togliatti (1893-1964), General Secretary of the Italian Communist Party.

Letter, Aerogram and Globe A1471

1964, Sept. 20 Litho.

2940 A1471 4k tan, lil rose & ultra 10 7

Issued for International Letter Writing Week, Oct. 5-11.

Arms of German Democratic Republic, Factories, Ship and Train — A1472

1964, Oct. 7 *Perf. 12*

2942 A1472 6k blk yel, red & bis 12 7

Issued to commemorate the 15th anniversary of the German Democratic Republic.

No. 2836 Overprinted in Red

40 лет Советскому Таджикистану
1964 год

1964, Oct. 7 Engr.

2943 A1435 4k dl bl 30 32

40th anniversary of Tadzhik Republic.

Woman Holding Bowl of Grain and Fruit A1473

Uzbek Farm Couple and Arms A1474

Turkmen Woman Holding Arms A1475

1964, Oct. **Litho.**

2944 A1473 4k red, grn & brn 10 7
2945 A1474 4k red yel & cl 10 7
2946 A1475 4k red, blk & red brn 10 7

40th anniv. of the Moldavian, Uzbek and Turkmen Socialist Republics.
Issue dates: No. 2944, Oct. 7. Others, Oct. 26.

Soldier and Flags A1476

1964, Oct. 14

2947 A1476 4k red, bis, dk brn & bl 10 7

Issued to commemorate the 20th anniversary of the liberation of the Ukraine.

Mikhail Y. Lermontov A1477

Designs: 4k, Birthplace of Tarchany. 10k, Lermontov and Vissarion G. Belinski.

1964, Oct. 14 **Engr.; Litho. (10k)**

2948 A1477 4k vio blk 10 5
2949 A1477 6k black 12 7
2950 A1477 10k dk red brn & buff 25 7

Issued to commemorate the 150th anniversary of the birth of Mikhail Y. Lermontov (1814-41), poet.

Hammer and Sickle A1478

1964, Oct. 14 **Litho.**

2951 A1478 4k dk bl, red, ocher & yel 12 7

47th anniversary of October Revolution.

Col. Vladimir M. Komarov A1479

Komarov, Feoktistov and Yegorov — A1480

Designs: No. 2953, Boris B. Yegorov, M.D. No. 2954, Konstantin Feoktistov, scientist. 10k, Spacecraft Voskhod I and cosmonauts. 50k, Red flag with portraits of Komarov, Feoktistov and Yegorov, and trajectory around earth.

Perf. 11½ (A1479), 12½x12

1964 **Photo.**

2952 A1479 4k bl grn, blk & org 10 7
2953 A1479 4k bl grn, blk & org 10 7
2954 A1479 4k bl grn, blk & org 10 7

Size: 73x23mm.

2955 A1480 6k vio & dk brn 12 10
2956 A1480 10k dp ultra & pur 32 12

Miniature Sheet

Imperf

Litho.

Size: 90x45½mm.

2957 A1480 50k vio, red & gray 2.50 1.00
Nos. 2952-2957 (6) 3.24 1.43

Issued to commemorate the three-men space flight of Vladimir M. Komarov, Boris B. Yegorov and Konstantin Feoktistov, Oct. 12-13. Dates of issue: Nos. 2952-2954, Oct. 19; No. 2955, Oct. 17; No. 2956, Oct. 13; No. 2957, Nov. 20.

A. I. Yelizarova-Ulyanova A1482

Portrait: No. 2961, Nadezhda K. Krupskaya.

1964, Nov. 6 **Photo.** ***Perf. 11½***

2960 A1482 4k brn, org & ind 10 5
2961 A1482 4k ind, red & brn 10 5

Issued to commemorate the centenary of the birth of A. I. Yelizarova-Ulyanova, Lenin's sister and the 95th anniversary of the birth of Nadezhda Krupskaya, Lenin's wife.

Farm Woman, Sheep, Flag of Mongolia A1483

Mushrooms A1484

1964, Nov. 20 **Litho.** ***Perf. 12***

2962 A1483 6k multi 15 8

Issued to commemorate the 40th anniversary of the Mongolian People's Republic.

1964, Nov. 25 **Litho.** ***Perf. 12***

Designs: Various mushrooms.

2963 A1484 2k ol grn, red brn & yel 15 10
2964 A1484 4k grn & yel 15 10
2965 A1484 6k bluish grn, brn & yel 22 10
2966 A1484 10k grn, org red & brn 32 12
2967 A1484 12k ultra, yel & grn 55 15
Nos. 2963-2967 (5) 1.39 57

Nos. 2963-2967 exist varnished, printed in sheets of 25 with 10 labels in outside vertical rows. Issued Nov. 30. Value, set $1.65.

A. P. Dovzhenko A1485

Design: 6k, Scene from "Tchapaev" (man and boy with guns).

1964, Nov. 30 **Photo.** ***Perf. 12***

2968 A1485 4k gray & dp ultra 7 5
2968A A1485 6k pale ol & blk 10 7

Issued to commemorate the 70th anniversary of the birth of A. P. Dovzhenko (1894-1956), film producer, and the 30th anniversary of the production of the film "Tchapaev."

"Happy New Year" A1486

V. J. Struve A1487

Photogravure and Engraved

1964, Nov. 30 ***Perf. 11½***

2969 A1486 4k multi 12 7

Issued for New Year 1965. The bright rose ink is fluorescent.

1964-65 **Photo.** ***Perf. 12½x11½***

Portraits: No. 2971, N. P. Kravkov. No. 2971A, P. K. Sternberg. No. 2971B, Ch. Valikhanov. No. 2971C, V. A. Kistjakovski.

2970 A1487 4k sl bl & dk brn 20 7

Litho.

2971 A1487 4k brn, red & blk ('65) 10 7

Photo.

Perf. 11½

2971A A1487 4k dk bl & dk brn ('65) 10 7

Perf. 12

2971B A1487 4k rose vio & blk ('65) 10 7

Litho.

2971C A1487 4k brn vio, blk & cit ('65) 10 7
Nos. 2970-2971C (5) 60 35

Issued to commemorate the death centenary of astronomer V. J. Struve (1793-1864), founder of Pulkov Observatory; birth centenary of N. P. Kravkov (1865-1924), pharmacologist; birth centenary of P. K. Sternberg (1865-1920), astronomer; death centenary of Ch. Valikhanov (1835-1865), Kazakh scientist; birth centenary of V. A. Kistjakovski (1865-1952), chemist.

S. V. Ivanov and Skiers A1488

1964, Dec. 22 **Engr.** ***Perf. 12½***

2972 A1488 4k blk & brn 12 7

Issued to commemorate the centenary of the birth of the painter S. V. Ivanov (1864-1910).

Chemical Industry: Fertilizers and Pest Control — A1489

Design: 6k, Synthetics factory.

1964, Dec. 25 **Photo.** ***Perf. 12***

2973 A1489 4k ol & lil rose 12 5
2974 A1489 6k dp ultra & blk 14 10

Issued to publicize the importance of the chemical industry for national economy.

European Cranberries — A1490

Wild Berries: 3k, Huckleberries. 4k, Mountain ash. 10k, Blackberries. 16k, Cranberries.

1964, Dec. 25 ***Perf. 11½x12***

2975 A1490 1k pale grn & car 7 5
2976 A1490 3k gray, vio bl & grn 10 5
2977 A1490 4k gray, org red & brn 12 7
2978 A1490 10k lt grn, dk vio bl & cl 20 10
2979 A1490 16k gray, brt grn & car rose 25 12
Nos. 2975-2979 (5) 74 39

Academy of Science Library A1491

1964, Dec. 25 **Typo.** ***Perf. 12x12½***

2980 A1491 4k blk, pale grn & red 10 5

Issued to commemorate the 250th anniversary of the founding of the Academy of Science Library, Leningrad.

Congress Palace, Kremlin A1492

Khan Tengri A1493

1964, Dec. 25

2981 A1492 1r dk bl 1.75 70

1964, Dec. 29 **Photo.** ***Perf. 11½***

Mountains: 6k, Kazbek (horiz.). 12k, Twin peaks of Ushba.

2982 A1493 4k grnsh bl, vio bl & buff 8 7
2983 A1493 6k yel, dk brn & ol 15 7
2984 A1493 12k lt yel, grn & pur 30 10

Development of mountaineering in Russia.

Portrait Type of 1964

Design: 6k, Michelangelo. 12k, Galileo.

Engraved and Photogravure

1964, Dec. 30 ***Perf. 11½***

2985 A1455 6k sep, red brn & org 15 7
2986 A1455 12k dk brn & grn 30 10

Issued to commemorate the 400th anniversary of the death of Michelangelo Buonarotti, artist, and the 400th anniversary of the birth of Galileo Galilei, astronomer and physicist.

Helmet
A1494

Treasures from Kremlin Treasury: 6k, Saddle. 10k, Jeweled fur crown. 12k, Gold ladle. 16k, Bowl.

1964, Dec. 30 **Litho.**

2987 A1494	4k multi		7	5
2988 A1494	6k multi		10	7
2989 A1494	10k multi		15	10
2990 A1494	12k multi		22	10
2991 A1494	16k multi		25	12
	Nos. 2987-2991 (5)		79	44

Dante
A1495

Blood Donor
A1496

1965, Jan. 29 **Photo.** ***Perf. 11½***

2995 A1495	4k dk red brn & ol bis	10	5

Issued to commemorate the 700th anniversary of the birth of Dante Alighieri (1265-1321), Italian poet.

1965, Jan. 31 **Litho.** ***Perf. 12***

Design: No. 2997, Hand holding carnation, and donors' emblem.

2996 A1496	4k dk car, red, vio bl & bl	10	5
2997 A1496	4k brt grn, red & dk grn	10	5

Issued to honor the blood donors.

Bandy
A1497

Police Dog
A1498

Design: 6k, Figure skaters and Moscow Sports Palace.

1965, Feb. **Photo.** ***Perf. 11½x12***

2998 A1497	4k bl, red & yel	12	7
2999 A1497	6k grn, blk & red	15	7

The 4k was issued Feb. 21, to commemorate the victory of the Russian team in the World Bandy Championship, Moscow, Feb. 21-27; the 6k was issued, Feb. 12, to commemorate the European Figure Skating Championship. See No. 3017.

Perf. 12x11½, 11½x12 (Photo. stamps); 12x12½, 12½x12 (Litho.)
Photo., Litho. (1k, 10k, 12k, 16k)

1965, Feb. 26

Dogs: 1k, Russian hound. 2k, Irish setter. No. 3003, Pointer. No. 3004, Fox terrier. No. 3005, Sheepdog. No. 3006, Borzoi. 10k, Collie. 12k, Husky. 16k, Caucasian sheepdog. (1k, 2k, 4k, 12k and No. 3006 horizontal.)

3000 A1498	1k blk, yel & mar	6	5
3001 A1498	2k ultra, blk & red brn	7	5
3002 A1498	3k blk, ocher & org red	8	5
3003 A1498	4k org, yel grn & blk	12	6
3004 A1498	4k brn, blk & lt grn	12	6
3005 A1498	6k chlky bl, sep & red	15	7
3006 A1498	6k chlky bl, org brn & blk	15	7
3007 A1498	10k yel grn, ocher & red	22	10
3008 A1498	12k gray, blk & ocher	25	12
3009 A1498	16k multi	30	15
	Nos. 3000-3009 (10)	1.52	78

Richard
Sorge — A1499

1965, Mar. 6 **Photo.** ***Perf. 12x12½***

3010 A1499	4k hn brn & blk	10	5

Issued to commemorate the 70th anniversary of the birth of Richard Sorge (1895-1944), Russian spy and Hero of the Soviet Union.

Communications Symbols — A1500

1965, Mar. 6 ***Perf. 12½x12***

3011 A1500	6k grnsh bl, vio & brt pur	12	7

Centenary of the International Telecommunication Union.

No. 2764 Overprinted **ТАМПЕРЕ 1965 г.**

1965, Mar. 20 **Photo.** ***Perf. 12***

3012 A1402	6k red & gray bl	25	12

Issued to commemorate the Russian victory in the European and World Ice Hockey Championships.

Lt. Col. Alexei Leonov Taking Movies in Space — A1501

Design: 1r, Leonov walking in space and Voskhod 2.

1965, Mar. 23 **Photo.** ***Perf. 12***
Size: 73x23mm

3015 A1501	10k brt ultra, org & gray	25	12

First man walking in space, Lt. Col. Alexei Leonov, Mar. 17, 1965 ("18 March" on stamp).

Exists imperf. Value 50 cents.

Souvenir Sheet

1965, Apr. 12 **Litho.**

3016 A1501	1r multi	2.50	1.25

Issued to commemorate the space flight of Voskhod 2. No. 3016 contains one stamp (size: 81x27mm.), inscriptions and portraits of Lt. Col. Alexei Leonov and Col. Pavel Belyayev in margin. Size: 142x58mm.

No. 2999 Overprinted **Советские фигуристы— чемпионы мира в парном катании**

1965, Mar. 26 ***Perf. 11½x12***

3017 A1497	6k grn, blk & red	25	15

Issued to commemorate the Russian victory in the World Figure Skating Championships.

Flags of USSR and Poland — A1502

1965, Apr. 12 **Photo.** ***Perf. 12***

3018 A1502	6k bis & red	10	5

Issued to commemorate the 20th anniversary of the signing of the Polish-Soviet treaty of friendship, mutual assistance and postwar cooperation.

Tsiolkovsky Monument, Kaluga; Globe and Rockets
A1503

Rockets, Radio Telescope, TV Antenna
A1504

Designs: 12k, Space monument, Moscow. 16k, Cosmonauts' monument, Moscow. No. 3023, Globe with trajectories, satellite and astronauts.

1965, Apr. 12 ***Perf. 11½***

3019 A1503	4k pale grn, blk & brt rose	14	7
3020 A1503	12k vio, pur & brt rose	25	10
3021 A1503	16k multi	40	12

Lithographed on Aluminum Foil
Perf. 12½x12

3022 A1504	20k blk & red	1.50	40
3023 A1504	20k blk, bl & red	1.50	40
	Nos. 3019-3023 (5)	3.79	1.09

Nos. 3019-3023 issued to publicize National Cosmonauts' Day. On Nos. 3019-3021 the bright rose is fluorescent.

Lenin
A1505

1965, Apr. 16 **Engr.** ***Perf. 12***

3024 A1505	10k tan & ind	20	10

Issued to commemorate the 95th anniversary of the birth of Lenin.

Poppies
A1506

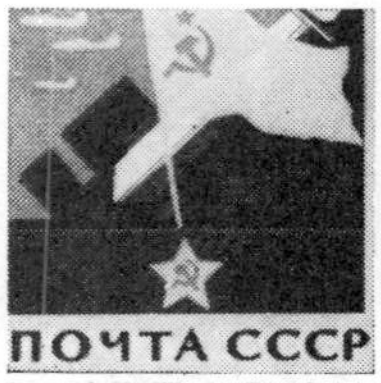

Russian Flag, Broken Swastikas, Fighting in Berlin
A1507

Flowers: 3k, Daisies. 4k, Peony. 6k, Carnation. 10k, Tulips.

1965, Apr. 23 **Photo.** ***Perf. 11***

3025 A1506	1k mar, red & grn	5	5
3026 A1506	3k dk brn, yel & grn	7	5
3027 A1506	4k blk, grn & lil	10	5
3028 A1506	6k dk sl grn, grn & red	14	7
3029 A1506	10k dk plum, yel & grn	20	10
	Nos. 3025-3029 (5)	56	32

1965 ***Perf. 11½***

Designs: 2k, "Fatherland Calling!" (woman with proclamation) by I. Toidze. 3k, "Attack on Moscow" by V. Bogatkin. No. 3033, "Rest after the Battle" by Y. Neprintsev. No. 3034, "Mother of Partisan" by S. Gerasimov. 6k, "Our Flag -Symbol of Victory" (soldiers with banner) by V. Ivanov. 10k, "Tribute to the Hero" (mourners at bier) by F. Bogorodsky. 12k, "Invincible Nation and Army" (worker and soldier holding shell) by V. Koretsky. 16k, "Victory celebration on Red Square" by K. Yuan. 20k, Soldier and symbols of war.

3030 A1507	1k red, blk & gold	5	5
3031 A1507	2k crim, blk & gold	5	5
3032 A1507	3k ultra & gold	7	5
3033 A1507	4k grn & gold	10	7
3034 A1507	4k vio & gold	10	7
3035 A1507	6k dp cl & gold	14	7
3036 A1507	10k plum & gold	20	10
3037 A1507	12k blk, red & gold	22	10
3038 A1507	16k lil rose & gold	25	10
3039 A1507	20k red, blk & gold	42	20
	Nos. 3030-3039 (10)	1.60	86

Issued to commemorate the 20th anniversary of the end of World War II. Issued Apr. 25-May 1.

Souvenir Sheet

From Popov's Radio to Space Telecommunications — A1508

1965, May 7 **Litho.** ***Perf. 11½***

3040 A1508	1r bl & multi	3.75	2.00

Issued to commemorate the 70th anniversary of Aleksandr S. Popov's radio pioneer work. No. 3040 contains 6 labels without denominations or country name. Size of sheet: 145x102mm.

Marx, Lenin and Crowd with Flags — A1509

1965, May 9 **Photo.** ***Perf. 12x12½***

3041 A1509	6k red & blk	14	7

Issued to commemorate the 6th conference of Postal Ministers of Communist Countries, Peking, June 21-July 15.

Bolshoi Theater, Moscow — A1510

1965, May 20 *Perf. 11x11½*

3042 A1510 6k grnsh bl, bis & blk 14 7

Issued for the International Theater Day.

Col. Pavel Belyayev A1511

Design: No. 3044, Lt. Col. Alexei Leonov.

1965, May 23 *Perf. 12x11½*

3043 A1511 6k mag & sil 14 7
3044 A1511 6k pur & sil 14 7

Issued to commemorate the space flight of Voskhod 2, March 18-19, 1965, and the first man walking in space, Lt. Col. Alexei Leonov.

Yakov M. Sverdlov A1512

Otto Grothewohl A1513

Portrait: No. 3046, Juldash Akhunbabaev.

Photogravure and Engraved

1965, May 30 *Perf. 11½x12*

3045 A1512 4k org brn & blk 10 5
3046 A1512 4k lt vio & blk 10 5

Issued to honor Yakov M. Sverdlov, 1885-1919, first president of U.S.S.R., and J. Akhunbabaev, 1885-1943, president of Uzbek Republic.

1965, June 12 **Photo.** *Perf. 12*

3051 A1513 4k blk & mag 10 5

Otto Grotewohl, prime minister of the German Democratic Republic (1894-1964).

Maurice Thorez A1514

Communication by Satellite A1515

1965, June 12

3052 A1514 6k brn & red 14 7

Issued to commemorate the 65th anniversary of the birth of Maurice Thorez, 1900-1964, chairman of the French Communist party.

1965, June 15 **Litho.**

Designs: No. 3054, Pouring ladle, steel mill and map of India. No. 3055, Stars, satellites and names of international organizations.

3053 A1515 3k ol, blk & gold 7 5
3054 A1515 6k emer, dk grn & gold 14 7
3055 A1515 6k vio bl, gold & blk 14 7

Issued to emphasize international cooperation through communication, economic cooperation and international organizations.

Symbols of Chemistry A1516

1965, June 15 **Photo.** *Perf. 11½*

3056 A1516 4k blk, brt rose & brt bl 14 7

Issued to publicize the 20th Congress of the International Union of Pure and Applied Chemistry (IUPAC), held at Moscow. The bright rose ink is fluorescent.

V. A. Serov A1517

Design: 6k, Full-length portrait of Feodor Chaliapin, the singer, by Serov.

1965, June 25 **Typo.** *Perf. 12½*

3057 A1517 4k red brn, buff & blk 10 7
3058 A1517 6k ol bis & blk 15 10

Issued to commemorate the centenary of the birth of V. A. Serov (1865-1911), historical painter.

Abay Kunanbaev, Kazakh Poet — A1518

Designs (writers and poets): No. 3060, Vsevolod Ivanov (1895-1963). No. 3060A, Eduard Vilde, Estonian writer. No. 3061, Mark Kropivnitsky, Ukrainian playwright. No. 3062, Manuk Apeghyan, Armenian writer and critic. No. 3063, Musa Djalil, Tartar poet. No. 3064, Hagop Hagopian, Armenian poet. No. 3064A, Djalil Mamedkulizade, Azerbaijan writer.

1965-66 **Photo.** *Perf. 12½x12*

3059 A1518 4k lt vio & blk 10 7
3060 A1518 4k rose lil & blk 10 7
3060A A1518 4k gray & blk 10 7
3061 A1518 4k blk & org brn 10 7

Perf. 12½

Typo.

3062 A1518 4k crim, bl grn & blk 10 7

Perf. 11½

Photogravure and Engraved

3063 A1518 4k blk & org brn ('66) 10 7
3064 A1518 4k grn & blk ('66) 10 7

Photo.

3064A A1518 4k Prus grn & blk ('66) 10 7
Nos. 3059-3064A (8) 80 56

Size: Nos. 3059-3062, 38x25mm. Nos. 3063-3064A, 35x23mm.

Jan Rainis A1518a

1965, Sept. 8 **Photo.** *Perf. 12½x12*

3064B A1518a 4k dl bl & blk 10 7

Issued to commemorate the birth centenary of Jan Rainis (1865-1929), Latvian playwright. "Rainis" was pseudonym of Jan Plieksans.

Film, Screen, Globe and Star A1519

1965, July 5 **Litho.** *Perf. 12*

3065 A1519 6k brt bl, gold & blk 14 7

Issued to commemorate the Fourth International Film Festival, Moscow: "For Humanism in Cinema Art, for Peace and Friendship among Nations."

Concert Bowl, Tallinn A1520

"Lithuania" A1521

"Latvia" A1522

1965, July *Perf. 12x11½, 11½x12*

3066 A1520 4k ultra, blk, red & ocher 10 5
3067 A1521 4k red & brn 10 5
3068 A1522 4k yel, red & bl 10 5

Nos. 3066-3068 commemorate the 25th anniversaries of Estonia, Lithuania and Latvia as Soviet Republics. Issue dates: No. 3066, July 7; No. 3067, July 14; No. 3068, July 16.

"Keep Peace" A1523

Protesting Women and Czarist Eagle A1524

1965, July 10 **Photo.** *Perf. 11x11½*

3069 A1523 6k yel, blk & bl 14 7

1965, July 20 **Litho.** *Perf. 11½*

Designs: No. 3071, Soldier attacking distributor of handbills. No. 3072, Fighters on barricades with red flag. No. 3073, Monument for sailors of Battleship "Potemkin," Odessa.

3070 A1524 4k blk, red & ol grn 10 5
3071 A1524 4k red, ol grn & blk 10 5
3072 A1524 4k red, blk & brn 10 5
3073 A1524 4k red & vio bl 10 5

60th anniversary of the 1905 revolution.

Gheorghe Gheorghiu-Dej A1525

1965, July 26 **Photo.** *Perf. 12*

3074 A1525 4k blk & red 10 5

Issued in memory of Gheorghe Gheorghiu-Dej (1901-1965), President of Romanian State Council (1961-1965).

Relay Race A1526

Sport: No. 3076, Bicycle race. No. 3077, Gymnast on vaulting horse.

1965, Aug. 5 **Litho.** *Perf. 12½x12*

3075 A1526 4k vio bl, bis brn & red brn 10 5
3076 A1526 4k buff, red brn, gray & mar 10 5
3077 A1526 4k bl, mar, buff & lt brn 10 5

8th Trade Union Spartacist Games.

Electric Power A1527

Designs: 2k, Metals in modern industry. 3k, Modern chemistry serving the people. 4k, Mechanization, automation and electronics. 6k, New materials for building industry. 10k, Mechanization and electrification of agriculture. 12k, Technological progress in transportation. 16k, Application of scientific discoveries to industry.

1965, Aug. 5 **Photo.** *Perf. 12x11½*

3078 A1527 1k ol, bl & blk 7 5
3079 A1527 2k org, blk & yel 7 5
3080 A1527 3k yel, vio & bis 7 5
3081 A1527 4k ultra, ind & red 10 7
3082 A1527 6k ultra & bis 14 7
3083 A1527 10k yel, org & red brn 20 10
3084 A1527 12k Prus bl & red 25 15
3085 A1527 16k rose lil, blk & vio bl 40 20
Nos. 3078-3085 (8) 1.30 74

Issued to publicize the creation of the material and technical basis of communism.

Values quoted in this catalogue are for stamps graded at Fine-Very Fine and with no faults. An illustrated guide to grade is provided in introductory material, beginning on Page V.

Gymnast A1528

Javelin and Running A1529

Design: 6k, Bicycling.

1965, Aug. 12 *Perf. 11½*

3086 A1528 4k multi & red 10 5
3087 A1528 6k grnsh bl, red & brn 14 7

9th Spartacist Games for school children.

1965, Aug. 27

Designs: 6k, High jump and shot put. 10k, Hammer throwing and hurdling.

3088 A1529 4k brn, lil & red 10 5
3089 A1529 6k brn, yel grn & red 14 7
3090 A1529 10k brn, chlky bl & red 22 10

Issued to commemorate the United States-Russian Track and Field Meet, Kiev.

Worker and Globe — A1530

Flag of North Viet Nam, Factory and Palm — A1531

Designs: No 3092, Heads of three races and torch. No. 3093, Woman with dove.

1965, Sept. 1

3091 A1530 6k dk pur & tan 14 7
3092 A1530 6k brt bl, brn & red org 14 7
3093 A1530 6k Prus grn & tan 14 7

Issued to commemorate the 20th anniversary of the International Federation of Trade Unions (No. 3091); the Federation of Democratic Youth (No. 3092); the Democratic Women's Federation (No. 3093).

1965, Sept. 1 **Litho.** *Perf. 12*

3094 A1531 6k red, yel, brn & gray 14 7

Issued to commemorate the 20th anniversary of the Republic of North Viet Nam.

Scene from Film "Potemkin" A1532

Film Scenes: 6k, "Young Guard." 12k, "Ballad of a Soldier."

1965, Sept. 29 **Litho.** *Perf. 12½x12*

3095 A1532 4k bl, blk & red 10 5
3096 A1532 6k multi 14 7
3097 A1532 12k multi 25 10

Post Rider, 16th Century — A1533

History of the Post: No. 3099, Mail coach, 17th-18th centuries. 2k, Train, 19th century. 4k, Mail truck, 1920. 6k, Train, ship and plane. 12k, New Moscow post office, helicopter, automatic sorting and cancelling machines. 16k, Lenin, airport and map of USSR.

1965 Photo. Unwmk. *Perf. 11½x12*

3098 A1533 1k org brn, dk gray & dk grn 5 5
3099 A1533 1k gray, ocher & dk brn 5 5
3100 A1533 2k dl lil, brt bl & brn 7 5
3101 A1533 4k bis, rose lake & blk 10 5
3102 A1533 6k pale brn, Prus grn & blk 14 7
3103 A1533 12k lt ultra, lt brn & blk 20 10
3104 A1533 16k gray, rose red & vio blk 25 14
Nos. 3098-3104 (7) 86 51

See No. 3175.

Atomic Icebreaker "Lenin" A1534

Designs: No. 3106, Icebreakers "Taimir" and "Vaigitch." 6k, Dickson Settlement. 10k, Sailing ships "Vostok" and "Mirni," Bellinghausen-Lazarew expedition, and icebergs. 16k, Vostok South Pole station.

1965, Oct. 23 **Litho.** *Perf. 12*

Size: 37x25mm.

3106 A1534 4k bl, blk & org 15 7
3107 A1534 4k bl, blk & org 15 7
3108 A1534 6k sep & dk vio 22 10

Size: 33x33mm.

3109 A1534 10k red, blk & buff 28 10

Size: 37x25mm.

3110 A1534 16k vio blk & red brn 40 15
Nos. 3106-3110 (5) 1.20 49

Issued to commemorate the scientific conquests of the Arctic and Antarctic. Nos. 3106-3107 printed se-tenant.

Souvenir Sheet

Basketball, Map of Europe and Flags A1535

1965, Oct. 29 **Litho.** *Imperf.*

3111 A1535 1r multi 3.75 90

Issued to commemorate the 14th European Basketball Championship, Moscow. Size: 65x89mm.

Timiryazev Agriculture Academy, Moscow — A1536

1965, Oct. 30 **Photo.** *Perf. 11*

3112 A1536 4k brt car, gray & vio bl 14 7

Issued to commemorate the centenary of the Agriculture Academy, Moscow.

Souvenir Sheet

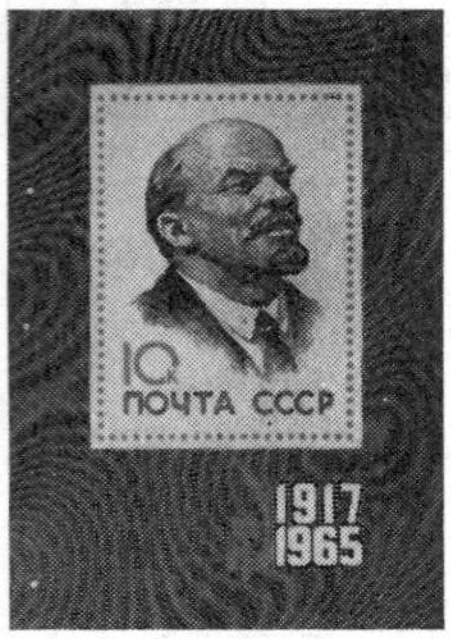

Lenin A1537

Lithographed and Engraved

1965, Oct. 30 *Imperf.*

3113 A1537 10k sil, blk & dp org 95 40

48th anniv. of the October Revolution.

Nicolas Poussin — A1538

1965, Nov. 16 **Photo.** *Perf. 11½*

3114 A1538 4k gray bl, dk bl & dk brn 14 7

Issued to commemorate the 300th anniversary of the death of Nicolas Poussin (1594-1665), French painter.

Kremlin A1539

1965, Nov. 16 *Perf. 12x11½*

3115 A1539 4k blk, ver & sil 14 7

Issued for New Year 1966.

Mikhail Ivanovich Kalinin A1540

1965, Nov. 19 *Perf. 12½*

3116 A1540 4k dp cl & red 14 7

Issued to commemorate the 90th anniversary of the birth of Mikhail I. Kalinin (1875-1946), president of U.S.S.R. (1923-1946).

Klyuchevskaya Sopka — A1541

Kamchatka Volcanoes: 12k, Karumski erupting (vert.). 16k, Koryakski snowcovered.

1965, Nov. 30 **Litho.** *Perf. 12*

3117 A1541 4k multi 14 7
3118 A1541 12k multi 25 10
3119 A1541 16k multi 40 14

October Subway Station, Moscow — A1542

Subway Stations: No. 3121, Lenin Avenue, Moscow. No. 3122, Moscow Gate, Leningrad. No. 3123, Bolshevik Factory, Kiev.

1965, Nov. 30 **Engr.**

3120 A1542 6k indigo 14 7
3121 A1542 6k brown 14 7
3122 A1542 6k gray brn 14 7
3123 A1542 6k sl grn 14 7

Buzzard — A1543

Birds: 2k, Kestrel. 3k, Tawny eagle. 4k, Red kite. 10k, Peregrine falcon. 12k, Golden eagle (horiz.). 14k, Lammergeier (horiz.). 16k, Gyrfalcon.

Perf. 11½x12

1965, Nov.-Dec. **Photo.**

3124 A1543 1k gray grn & blk 7 5
3125 A1543 2k pale brn & blk 10 5
3126 A1543 3k lt ol grn & blk 14 5
3127 A1543 4k lt gray brn & blk 16 7
3128 A1543 10k lt vio brn & blk 32 10
3129 A1543 12k bl & blk 40 14
3130 A1543 14k bluish gray & blk 45 16
3131 A1543 16k dl red brn & blk 50 22
Nos. 3124-3131 (8) 2.14 84

Red Star Medal, War Scene and View of Kiev A1544

Red Star Medal, War Scene and view of: No. 3133, Leningrad. No. 3134, Odessa. No. 3135, Moscow. No. 3136, Brest Litovsk. No. 3137, Volgograd (Stalingrad). No. 3138, Sevastopol.

1965, Dec. *Perf. 11½*

3132 A1544 10k red, gold & brn 20 7
3133 A1544 10k red, gold & dk bl 20 7
3134 A1544 10k red, gold & Prus bl 20 7
3135 A1544 10k red, gold & dk vio 20 7
3136 A1544 10k red, gold & dk brn 20 7
3137 A1544 10k red, gold & blk 20 7
3138 A1544 10k red, gold & gray 20 7
Nos. 3132-3138 (7) 1.40 49

Issued to honor the heroism of various cities during World War II. Nos. 3136-3138 issued Dec. 30, others, Dec. 20.

Map and Flag of Jugoslavia, and National Assembly Building — A1545

1965, Dec. 30 Litho. *Perf. 12*

3139 A1545 6k vio bl, red & bis 14 7

Issued to commemorate the 20th anniversary of the Republic of Jugoslavia.

Collective Farm Watchman by S.V. Gerasimov A1547

Painting: 16k, "Major's Courtship" by Pavel Andreievitch Fedotov (horiz.).

1965, Dec. 31 Engr.

3145 A1547 12k red & sep 25 14
3146 A1547 16k red & dk bl 30 16

No. 3145 commemorates the 80th anniversary of the birth of the painter S. V. Gerasimov; No. 3146 commemorates the 150th anniversary of the birth of the painter Pavel A. Fedotov (1815-52).

Microscope and Moscow University A1548

Congress Emblems: No. 3148, Turkeys, geese, chicken and globe. No. 3149, Crystals. No. 3150, Oceanographic instruments and ship No. 3151, Mathematical symbols.

1966 Photo. *Perf. 11½*

3147 A1548 6k dl bl, blk & red 14 7
3148 A1548 6k gray, pur & blk 14 7
3149 A1548 6k ol bis, blk & bl 14 7
3150 A1548 6k grnsh bl & blk 14 7
3151 A1548 6k dl yel, red brn & blk 14 7
Nos. 3147-3151 (5) 70 35

Issued to publicize international congresses to be held in Moscow: 9th Congress of Microbiology (No. 3147); 13th Congress on Poultry Raising (No. 3148); 7th Congress on Crystallography (No. 3149); 2nd International Congress of Oceanography (No. 3150); International Congress of Mathematicians (No. 3151).

See Nos. 3309-3310.

Mailman and Milkmaid, 19th Century Figurines — A1549

Design: 10k, Tea set.

1966, Jan. 28 Litho.

3152 A1549 6k multi 14 7
3153 A1549 10k gray, rose red & vio bl 22 10

Bicentenary of Dimitrov Porcelain Works.

Romain Rolland A1550

Portrait: No. 3155, Eugène Pottier.

1966 Photo. & Engr. *Perf. 11½*

3154 A1550 4k dk bl & brn org 10 10
3155 A1550 4k sl, red & dk red brn 10 5

Issued to commemorate the birth centenary of Romain Rolland (1866-1944), French writer (No. 3154); the 150th anniversary of the birth of Eugène Pottier (1816-1887), French poet and author of the "International" (No. 3155).

Horseback Rider, and Flags of Mongolia and Russia — A1551

1966, Jan. 31 Litho. *Perf. 12½x12*

3159 A1551 4k red, ultra & vio brn 10 5

Issued to commemorate the 20th anniversary of the signing of the Mongolian-Soviet treaty of friendship and mutual assistance.

No. 2728 Overprinted in Silver

„ЛУНА-9" —НА ЛУНЕ!
3.2. 1966

1966, Feb. 5 Photo. *Perf. 12*

3160 A1385 6k blk, lt bl & red 70 32

Issued to commemorate the first soft landing on the moon by Luna 9, Feb. 3, 1966.

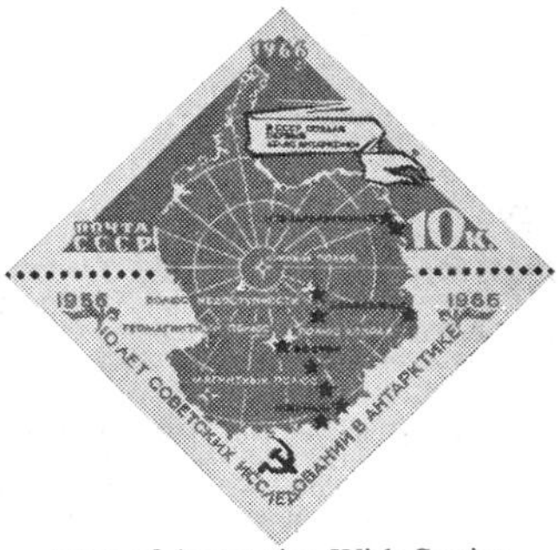

Map of Antarctica With Soviet Stations — A1552

Diesel Ship "Ob" and Emperor Penguins — A1553

Design: No. 3164, Snocat tractors and aurora australis.

1966, Feb. 14 Photo. *Perf. 11*

3162 A1552 10k sky bl, sil & dk car 30 10
3163 A1553 10k sil & dk car 30 10
3164 A1553 10k dk car, sil & sky bl 30 10

Issued to publicize ten years of Soviet explorations in Antarctica. Nos. 3162-3164 are printed in one sheet with Nos. 3163-3164 se-tenant at the base. No. 3162 has horizontal rows of perforation extending from either mid-side up to the map.

Lenin A1554

1966, Feb. 22 Photo. *Perf. 12x11½*

3165 A1554 10k grnsh blk & gold 22 10
3166 A1554 10k dk red & sil 22 10

96th anniversary of the birth of Lenin.

N.Y. Iljin, Guardsman A1555

Kremlin Congress Hall A1556

Portrait: No. 3168, Lt. Gen. G. P. Kravchenko. No. 3169, Pvt. Anatoli Uglovsky.

1966 *Perf. 11½x12*

3167 A1555 4k dp org & vio blk 10 5
3168 A1555 4k grnsh bl & dk pur 10 5
3169 A1555 4k grn & brn 10 5

Issued to honor Soviet heroes.

1966, Feb. 28 Typo. *Perf. 12*

3172 A1556 4k gold, red & lt ultra 10 5

23rd Communist Party Congress.

Hamlet and Queen from Film "Hamlet" A1557

Film Scene: 4k, Two soldiers from "The Quick and the Dead."

1966, Feb. 28 Litho.

3173 A1557 4k red, blk & ol 10 5
3174 A1557 10k ultra & blk 14 7

No. 3104 Overprinted

Учредительная конференция
Всесоюзного общества
филателистов. 1966

1966, Mar. 10 Photo. *Perf. 11½x12*

3175 A1533 16k gray, rose red & vio blk 85 52

Issued to commemorate the constituent assembly of the All-Union Society of Philatelists, 1966.

A little time given to the study of the arrangement of the Scott Catalogue can make it easier to use effectively.

Emblem and Skater — A1558

Designs: 6k, Emblem and ice hockey. 10k, Emblem and slalom skier.

1966, Mar. 11 *Perf. 11*

3176 A1558 4k ol, brt ultra & red 10 7
3177 A1558 6k bluish lil, red & dk brn 14 7
3178 A1558 10k lt bl, red & dk brn 20 10

Issued to commemorate the Second Winter Spartacist Games, Sverdlovsk. The label-like upper halves of Nos. 3176-3178 are separated from the lower halves by a row of perforation.

Electric Locomotive — A1559

Designs: 6k, Map of the Lenin Volga-Baltic Waterway, Admiralty, Leningrad, and Kremlin. 10k, Ship passing through lock in waterway (vert.). 12k, M.S. Aleksander Pushkin. 16k, Passenger liner and globe.

1966 Litho. *Perf. 12½x12, 12x12½*

3179 A1559 4k multi 10 7
3180 A1559 6k gray, ultra, red & blk 14 7
3181 A1559 10k Prus bl, gray brn & blk 32 10
3182 A1559 12k bl, ver & blk 30 14
3183 A1559 16k bl & multi 42 16
Nos. 3179-3183 (5) 1.28 54

Issued to publicize modern transportation. Dates of Issue: Nos. 3179-3181, Aug. 6; Nos. 3182-3183, Mar. 25.

Supreme Soviet Building, Frunze A1560

Sergei M. Kirov A1561

1966, Mar. 25 Photo. *Perf. 12*

3184 A1560 4k dp red 10 5

Issued to commemorate the 40th anniversary of the Kirghiz Republic.

1966 Engr. *Perf. 12*

Portraits: No. 3186, Grigori Ordzhonikidze. No. 3187, Ion Yakir.

3185 A1561 4k dk red brn 10 5
3186 A1561 4k sl grn 10 5
3187 A1561 4k dk gray vio 10 5

No. 3185 issued to commemorate the 80th anniversary of the birth of Sergei M. Kirov (1886-1934), revolutionist and Secretary of the Communist Party Central Committee; No. 3186, the 80th anniversary of the birth of Grigori Ordzhonikidze (1886-1937), a political leader of the Red Army and government official; No. 3187, the 70th anniversary of the

birth of Ion Yakir, military leader in October Revolution.
Issue dates: No. 3185, Mar. 27. No. 3186, June 22. No. 3187, July 30.

Souvenir Sheet

Lenin — A1563

Embossed and Typographed

1966, Mar. 29 ***Imperf.***

3188 A1563 50k red & sil 1.40 48

23rd Communist Party Congress.

Aleksandr E. Fersman (1883-1945), Mineralogist — A1564

Portraits: No. 3190, D. K. Zabolotny (1866-1929), microbiologist. No. 3191, M. A. Shatelen (1866-1957), physicist. No. 3191A, Otto Yulievich Schmidt (1891-1956), scientist and arctic explorer.

1966, Mar. 30 Litho. ***Perf. 12½x12***

3189 A1564 4k vio bl & multi 10 5
3190 A1564 4k red brn & multi 10 5
3191 A1564 4k lil & multi 10 5
3191A A1564 4k Prus bl & brn 10 5

Issued to honor Soviet scientists.

Luna 10 Automatic Moon Station — A1565

Overprinted in Red:

„Луна-10“—XXIII съезду КПСС

1966, Apr. 8 Typo. ***Imperf.***

3192 A1565 10k gold, blk, brt bl & brt rose 30 15

Issued to commemorate the launching of the first artificial moon satellite, Luna 10. The bright rose ink is fluorescent on Nos. 3192-3194.

Type A1565 Without Overprint

1966, Apr. 12 ***Perf. 12***

Design: 12k, Station on moon.

3193 A1565 10k multi 28 10
3194 A1565 12k multi 35 15

Day of Space Research, Apr. 12, 1966.

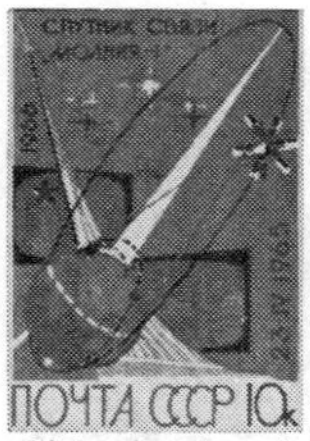

Lightning 1 and Television Screens A1566

Ernst Thälmann A1567

1966, Apr. 12 Litho. ***Perf. 12½***

3195 A1566 10k gold, blk, brt bl & red 25 15

Issued to commemorate the launching of the communications satellite "Lightning 1," Apr. 23, 1965.

1966-67 Engr. ***Perf. 12½x12***

Portraits: No. 3197, Wilhelm Pieck. No. 3198, Sun Yat-sen. No. 3199, Sen Katayama.

3196 A1567 6k rose cl 14 7
3197 A1567 6k bl vio 14 7
3198 A1567 6k redsh brn 14 7

Photo.

3199 A1567 6k gray grn ('67) 14 7

No. 3196 commemorates the 80th anniversary of the birth of Ernst Thälmann (1886-1944), German Communist leader; No. 3197, the 90th anniversary of the birth of Wilhelm Pieck (1876-1960), President of the German Democratic Republic; No. 3198, the centenary of the birth of Dr. Sun Yat-sen (1866-1925), leader of the Chinese revolution. No. 3199 honors Sen Katayama (1859-1933), who founded the Social Democratic Party in Japan in 1901.
Issue dates: No. 3196, Apr. 16, 1966. Nos. 3197-3198, June 22, 1966. No. 3199, Nov. 2, 1967.

Soldier, 1917, and Astronaut A1568

1966, Apr. 30 Litho. ***Perf. 11½***

3200 A1568 4k brt rose & blk 10 5

15th Congress of the Young Communist League (Komsomol).

Ice Hockey Player — A1569

1966, Apr. 30

3201 A1569 10k red, ultra, gold & blk 20 10

Issued to commemorate the Soviet victory in the World Ice Hockey Championships. For souvenir sheet see No. 3232.
See No. 3315.

Nicolai Kuznetsov — A1570

Portrait: No. 3203, Imant Sudmalis. No. 3204, Anya Morozova. No. 3205, Filipp Strelets. No. 3206, Tikhon Rumazhkov. (All designs include the Gold Star of Hero of the Soviet Union.)

1966, May 9 Photo. ***Perf. 12x12½***

3202 A1570 4k grn & blk 10 5
3203 A1570 4k ocher & blk 10 5
3204 A1570 4k bl & blk 10 5
3205 A1570 4k brt rose & blk 10 5
3206 A1570 4k vio & blk 10 5
Nos. 3202-3206 (5) 50 25

Issued to honor heroes of guerrilla warfare during World War II.

Peter I. Tchaikovsky A1571

Designs: 4k, Moscow State Conservatory and Tchaikovsky monument. 16k, Tchaikovsky House, Klin.

1966, May 26 Typo. ***Perf. 12½***

3207 A1571 4k red, yel & blk 7 5
3208 A1571 6k yel, red & blk 10 7
3209 A1571 16k red, bluish gray & blk 22 10

Issued to commemorate the Third International Tchaikovsky Contest, Moscow, May 30-June 29.

Runners — A1572

Designs: 6k, Weight lifters. 12k, Wrestlers.

1966, May 26 Photo. ***Perf. 11x11½***

3210 A1572 4k emer, ol & brn 10 5
3211 A1572 6k org, blk & lt brn 14 7
3212 A1572 12k grnsh bl, brn ol & blk 22 10

Issued to publicize: No. 3210, Znamensky Brothers International Track Competitions; No. 3211, International Weightlifting Competitions; No. 3212, International Wrestling Competitions for Ivan Poddubny Prize.

Jules Rimet World Soccer Cup, Ball and Laurel A1573

Chessboard, Gold Medal, Pawn and King — A1574

Designs: No. 3214, Soccer. 12k, Fencers. 16k, Fencer, mask, foil and laurel branch.

1966, May 31 Litho. ***Perf. 11½***

3213 A1573 4k rose red, gold & blk 10 8
3214 A1573 6k emer, tan, blk & red 14 7
3215 A1574 6k brn, gold, blk & white 14 8
3216 A1573 12k brt bl, ol & blk 32 10
3217 A1573 16k multi 35 16
Nos. 3213-3217 (5) 1.05 49

Nos. 3213-3214 commemorate the World Cup Soccer Championship, Wembley, England, July 11-30; No. 3215 the World Chess Title Match between Tigran Petrosian and Boris Spassky; Nos. 3216-3217 the World Fencing Championships. For souvenir sheet see No. 3232.

Sable and Lake Baikal, Map of Barguzin Game Reserve — A1575

Design: 6k, Map of Lake Baikal region and Game Reserve, brown bear on lake shore.

1966, June 25 Photo. ***Perf. 12***

3218 A1575 4k stl bl & blk 10 5
3219 A1575 6k rose lake & blk 14 7

Issued to commemorate the 50th anniversary of the Barguzin Game Reserve.

Pink Lotus — A1576

Designs: 6k, Palms and cypresses. 12k, Victoria cruziana.

1966, June 30 ***Perf. 11½***

3220 A1576 3k grn, pink & yel 10 7
3221 A1576 6k grnsh bl, ol brn & dk brn 16 7
3222 A1576 12k multi 32 10

Issued to commemorate the 125th anniversary of the Sukhum Botanical Garden.

Dogs Ugolek and Veterok after Space Flight A1577

Designs: No. 3224, Diagram of Solar System, globe and medal of Venus 3 flight. No. 3225, Luna 10, earth and moon.

1966, July 15 ***Perf. 12x11½***

3223 A1577 6k ocher, ind & org brn 16 7
3224 A1577 6k crim, blk & sil 16 7

Perf. 12x12½

3225 A1577 6k dk bl & bis brn 16 7

Russian achievements in space.

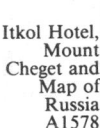

Itkol Hotel, Mount Cheget and Map of Russia A1578

Arch of General Headquarters, Winter Palace and Alexander Column — A1579

Resort Areas: 4k, Ship on Volga River and Zhigul Mountain. 10k, Castle, Kislovodsk. 12k, Ismail Samani Mausoleum, Bukhara, Uzbek. 16k, Hotel Caucasus, Sochi.

Perf. 12½x12, 12½ (6k)

1966 **Litho.**

3226	A1578	1k multi	5	5
3227	A1578	4k multi	7	5
3228	A1579	6k multi	10	7
3229	A1578	10k multi	16	7
3230	A1578	12k multi	25	10
3231	A1578	16k multi	35	14
		Nos. 3226-3231 (6)	98	48

Issue dates: 10k, Sept. 14. Others, July 20.

Souvenir Sheet

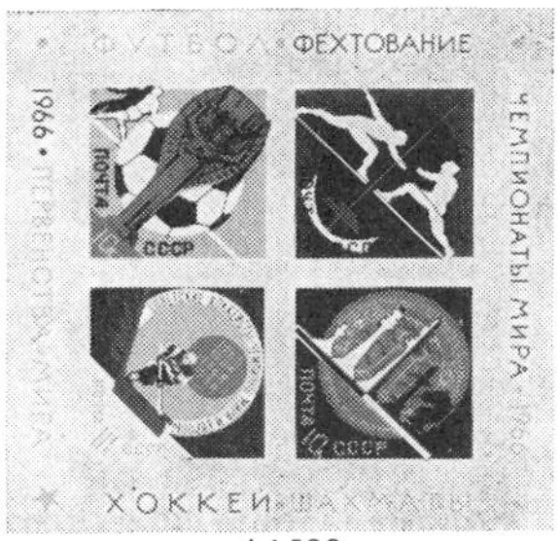

A1580

1966, July 26 **Litho.** ***Perf. 11½***

3232	A1580	Souv. sheet of 4	1.75	45
a		10k red, brnz & blk (fencers)	35	10
b		10k blk, sil & bl (chess)	35	10
c		10k bl, sil & blk (soccer cup)	35	10
d		10k red, blk, gold & bl (ice hockey)	35	10

World fencing, chess, soccer and ice hockey championships.

See Nos. 3201, 3213-3217.

Congress Emblem, Congress Palace and Kremlin Tower — A1581

1966, Aug. 6 **Photo.** ***Perf. 11½x12***

3233 A1581 4k brn & yel 10 5

Issued to commemorate the 7th Congress of Consumers' Cooperative Societies.

Dove, Crane, Russian and Japanese Flags A1582

1966, Aug. 9 ***Perf. 12½x11½***

3234 A1582 6k gray & red 14 7

Issued to publicize Soviet-Japanese friendship, and the second meeting of Russian and Japanese delegates at Khabarovsk.

"Knight Fighting with Tiger" by Rustaveli — A1583

Designs: 4k, Shota Rustaveli, bas-relief. 6k, "Avtandil at a Mountain Spring." 50k, Shota Rustaveli Monument and design of 3k stamp.

Perf. 11½x12½

1966, Aug. 31 **Engr.**

3235	A1583	3k *ol grn*	7	5
3236	A1583	4k brn, *yel*	7	5
3237	A1583	6k bluish blk, *lt ultra*	16	7

Souvenir Sheet

Imperf

Engraved and Photogravure

3238 A1583 50k sl grn & bis 1.90 90

Issued to commemorate the 800th anniversary of the birth of Shota Rustaveli, Georgian poet, author of "The Knight in the Tiger's Skin." No. 3238 contains one stamp (size: 32x49mm.); dark green margin with design of 6k stamp. Size: 97½x67mm.

Coat of Arms and Fireworks over Moscow A1584

Lithographed (Lacquered)

1966, Sept. 14 ***Perf. 11½***

3239 A1584 4k multi 10 5

49th anniversary of October Revolution.

Grayling A1585

Designs (Fish and part of design of 6k stamp): 4k, Sturgeon. 6k, Trawler, net and map of Lake Baikal (vert.). 10k, Two Baikal cisco. 12k, Two Baikal whitefish.

1966, Sept. 25 **Photo. & Engr.**

3240	A1585	2k multi	7	5
3241	A1585	4k multi	8	8
3242	A1585	6k multi	12	8
3243	A1585	10k multi	20	10
3244	A1585	12k gray, dk grn & red brn	22	14
		Nos. 3240-3244 (5)	69	45

Fish resources of Lake Baikal.

The first value column gives the catalogue value of an unused stamp, the second that of a used stamp.

Map of Russia and Symbols of Transportation and Communication — A1586

Designs (map of Russia and): No. 3246, Technological education. No. 3247, Agriculture and mining. No. 3248, Increased productivity through five-year plan. No. 3249, Technology and inventions.

1966, Sept. 29 **Photo.** ***Perf. 11½x12***

3245	A1586	4k ultra & sil	10	5
3246	A1586	4k car & sil	10	5
3247	A1586	4k red brn & sil	10	5
3248	A1586	4k red & sil	10	5
3249	A1586	4k dp grn & sil	10	5
		Nos. 3245-3249 (5)	50	25

Issued to publicize decisions of the 23rd Communist Party Congress.

Government House, Kishinev, and Moldavian Flag — A1587

1966, Oct. 8 **Litho.** ***Perf. 12½x12***

3250 A1587 4k multi 32 5

500th anniversary of Kishinev.

Symbolic Water Cycle A1588

1966, Oct. 12 ***Perf. 11½***

3251 A1588 6k multi 14 7

Hydrological Decade (UNESCO), 1965-1974.

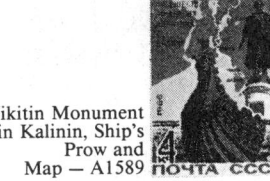

Nikitin Monument in Kalinin, Ship's Prow and Map — A1589

1966, Oct. 12 **Photo.**

3252 A1589 4k multi 10 5

Issued to commemorate the 500th anniversary of Afanasii Nikitin's trip to India.

Scene from Opera "Nargiz" by M. Magomayev A1590

Design: No. 3254, Scene from opera "Ker-ogli" by Y. Gadjubekov (knight on horseback and armed men).

1966, Oct. 12

3253	A1590	4k blk & ocher	14	7
3254	A1590	4k blk & bl grn	14	7

Issued to publicize Azerbaijan opera. Nos. 3253-3254 are printed se-tenant in checkerboard arrangement.

Fighters A1591

1966, Oct. 26

3255 A1591 6k red, blk & ol bis 14 7

30th anniversary of Spanish Civil War.

National Militia A1592

Protest Rally A1592a

1966, Oct. 26 **Litho.** ***Perf. 12x12½***

3256 A1592 4k red & dk brn 10 5

Issued to commemorate the 25th anniversary of the National Militia.

1966, Oct. 26 ***Perf. 12***

3256A A1592a 6k yel, blk & red 14 7

Issued to proclaim: "Hands off Viet Nam!"

Soft Landing on Moon, Luna 9 — A1593

Symbols of Agriculture and Chemistry — A1594

Designs: 1k, Congress Palace, Moscow, and map of Russia. 3k, Boy, girl and Lenin banner. 4k, Flag. 6k, Plane and Ostankino Television Tower. 10k, Soldier and Soviet star. 12k, Steel worker. 16k, "Peace," woman with dove. 20k, Demonstrators in Red Square, flags, carnation and globe. 50k, Newspaper, plane, train and Communications Ministry. 1r, Lenin and industrial symbols.

1966 **Litho.** ***Perf. 12***

Inscribed "1966"

3257	A1593	1k dk red brn	5	5
3258	A1593	2k violet	5	5
3259	A1593	3k red lil	5	5
3260	A1593	4k brt red	7	5
3261	A1593	6k ultra	10	5
3262	A1593	10k olive	16	6
3263	A1593	12k red brn	30	9
3264	A1593	16k vio bl	32	7

Perf. 11½

Photo.

3265	A1594	20k bis, red & dk bl	55	14
3266	A1594	30k dp grn & grn	70	20
3267	A1594	50k bl & vio bl	1.40	30
3268	A1594	1r blk & red	2.25	50
		Nos. 3257-3268 (12)	6.00	1.61

No. 3260 was issued on fluorescent paper in 1969.

See Nos. 3470-3481.

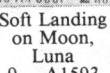

Ostankino Television Tower, Molniya 1 Satellite and Kremlin — A1595

1966, Nov. 19 Litho. *Perf. 12*

3273	A1595	4k multi	14	5

Issued for New Year, 1967, the 50th anniversary of the October Revolution.

Diagram of Luna 9 Flight — A1596

Arms of Russia and Pennant Sent to Moon — A1597

Design: No. 3276, Luna 9 and photograph of moonscape.

1966, Nov. 25 Typo. *Perf. 12*

3274	A1596	10k blk & sil	16	7
3275	A1597	10k red & sil	16	7
3276	A1596	10k blk & sil	16	7
a		Strip of 3	60	30

Issued to commemorate the soft landing on the moon by Luna 9, Jan. 31, 1966, and the television program of moon pictures on Feb. 2. Nos. 3274-3276 are printed se-tenant.

Battle of Moscow, 1941 — A1598

Details from "Defense of Moscow" Medal and Golden Star Medal A1599

Design: 10k, Sun rising over Kremlin. Ostankino Tower, chemical plant and rockets.

Perf. 12, 11½ (A1599)

1966, Dec. 1 Photo.

3277	A1598	4k red brn	10	8
3278	A1599	6k bis & brn	16	8
3279	A1598	10k dp bis & yel	25	10

25th anniversary of Battle of Moscow.

Cervantes and Don Quixote A1600

1966, Dec. 15 Photo. *Perf. 11½*

3280	A1600	6k gray & brn	16	10

Issued to commemorate the 350th anniversary of the death of Miguel Cervantes Saavedra (1547-1616), Spanish writer.

Bering's Ship and Map of Voyage to Commander Islands — A1601

Far Eastern Territories: 2k, Medny Island and map. 4k, Petropavlosk-Kamchatski Harbor. 6k, Geyser, Kamchatka (vert.). 10k, Avachinskaya Bay, Kamchatka. 12k, Fur seals, Bering Island. 16k, Guillemots in bird sanctuary, Kuril Islands.

1966, Dec. 25 Litho. *Perf. 12*

3281	A1601	1k bis & multi	5	5
3282	A1601	2k bis & multi	7	5
3283	A1601	4k dp bl & multi	10	5
3284	A1601	6k multi	14	7
3285	A1601	10k dp bl & multi	16	10
3286	A1601	12k ol & multi	25	10
3287	A1601	16k lt bl & multi	30	14
		Nos. 3281-3287 (7)	1.07	56

Communications Satellite, Molniya 1 — A1602

Design: No. 3289, Luna 11 moon probe, moon, earth and Soviet emblem.

1966, Dec. 29 Photo. *Perf. 12x11½*

3288	A1602	6k blk, vio bl & brt rose	20	7
3289	A1602	6k blk & brt rose	20	7

Issued to publicize space explorations. The bright rose is fluorescent.

Golden Stag, Scythia, 6th Century B.C. — A1603

Treasures from the Hermitage, Leningrad: 6k, Silver jug, Persia, 5th Century A.D. 10k, Statue of Voltaire by Jean Antoine Houdon. 12k, Malachite vase, Ural, 1840. 16k, "The Lute Player," by Michelangelo de Caravaggio. (6k, 10k, 12k are vertical).

1966, Dec. 29 Engr. *Perf. 12*

3290	A1603	4k yel & blk	10	5
3291	A1603	6k gray & blk	14	7
3292	A1603	10k dl vio & blk	20	10
3293	A1603	12k emer & blk	28	14
3294	A1603	16k ocher & blk	35	16
		Nos. 3290-3294 (5)	1.07	52

Sea Water Converter and Pavilion at EXPO '67 A1604

Designs (Pavilion and): 6k, Splitting atom (vert.). 10k, "Proton" space station. 30k, Russian pavilion.

1967, Jan. 25 Litho. *Perf. 12*

3295	A1604	4k multi	7	5
3296	A1604	6k multi	14	7
3297	A1604	10k multi	16	10

Souvenir Sheet

3298	A1604	30k multi	1.75	48

EXPO '67, Intl. Exhib., Montreal, Apr. 28-Oct. 27.

1st Lieut. B. I. Sizov A1605

Design: No. 3300, Sailor V. V. Khodyrev.

1967, Feb. 16 Photo. *Perf. 12x11½*

3299	A1605	4k dl yel & ocher	10	5
3300	A1605	4k gray & dk gray	10	5

Issued to honor heroes of World War II.

Woman's Head and Pavlov Shawl — A1606

1967, Feb. 16 *Perf. 11*

3301	A1606	4k vio, red & grn	10	7

International Woman's Day, Mar. 8.

Movie Camera and Film — A1607

1967, Feb. 16 Photo. *Perf. 11½*

3302	A1607	6k multi	14	7

Issued to publicize the 5th International Film Festival, Moscow, July 5-20.

Trawler Fish Factory and Fish — A1608

Designs: No. 3304, Refrigeration ship. No. 3305, Crab canning ship. No. 3306, Fishing trawler. No. 3307, Black Sea seiner.

1967, Feb. 28 Litho. *Perf. 12x11½*

Ships in Black and Red

3303	A1608	6k bl & gray	16	7
3304	A1608	6k bl & gray	16	7
3305	A1608	6k bl & gray	16	7
3306	A1608	6k bl & gray	16	7
3307	A1608	6k bl & gray	16	7
		Nos. 3303-3307 (5)	80	35

Issued to publicize the Russian fishing industry. Nos. 3303-3307 printed in vertical strips of five in sheets of 20 (4x5).

Newspaper Forming Hammer and Sickle, Red Flag — A1609

1967, Mar. 13 Litho. *Perf. 12x12½*

3308	A1609	4k cl brn, red, yel & brn	10	5

50th anniversary of newspaper Izvestia.

Congress Type of 1966

Congress Emblems and: No. 3309, Moscow State University, construction site and star. No. 3310, Pile driver, mining excavator, crossed hammers, globe and "V."

1967, Mar. 10 Photo. *Perf. 11½*

3309	A1548	6k ultra, brt bl & blk	14	7
3310	A1548	6k blk, org red & bl	14	7

Issued to publicize international congresses to be held in Moscow: 7th General Assembly Session of the International Standards Association (No. 3309); 5th International Mining Congress (No. 3310).

International Tourist Year Emblem and Travel Symbols — A1610

1967, Mar. 10 *Perf. 11*

3314	A1610	4k blk, sky bl & sil	10	5

International Tourist Year, 1967.

No. 3201 Overprinted: "BeHa-1967"

1967, Mar. 29 Litho. *Perf. 11½*

3315	A1569	10k multi	24	10

Issued to commemorate the victory of the Russian team in the Ice Hockey Championships, Vienna, March 18-29. Overprint reads: "Vienna-1967."

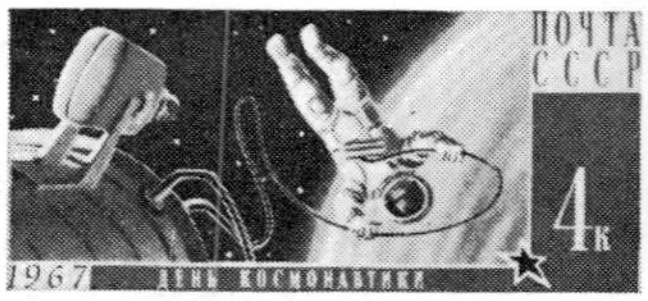

Space Walk — A1611

Designs: 10k, Rocket launching from satellite. 16k, Spaceship over moon, and earth.

1967, Mar. 30 Litho. *Perf. 12*

3316	A1611	4k bis & multi	10	7
3317	A1611	10k blk & multi	25	14
3318	A1611	16k lil & multi	40	20

National Cosmonauts' Day.

Lenin as Student, by V. Tsigal A1612

Sculptures of Lenin: 3k, Monument at Ulyanovsk by M. Manizer. 4k, Lenin in Razliv, by V. Pinchuk (horiz.). 6k, Head, by G. Neroda. 10k, Lenin as Leader, statue, by N. Andreyev.

1967 Photo. *Perf. 12x11½, 11½x12*

3319 A1612 2k ol grn, sep & buff 5 5
3320 A1612 3k mar & brn 7 5
3321 A1612 4k ol blk & gold 10 5
3322 A1612 6k dk bl, sil & blk 14 7
3323 A1612 10k sil, gray bl & blk 28 10
3323A A1612 10k gold, gray & blk 28 10
Nos. 3319-3323A (6) 92 42

97th anniversary of the birth of Lenin.
Issue dates: No. 3323A, Oct. 25. Others, Apr. 22.

Lt. M. S. Kharchenko and Battle Scenes A1613

Designs: No. 3325, Maj. Gen. S. V. Rudnev. No. 3326, M. Shmyrev.

1967, Apr. 24 *Perf. 12x11½*

3324 A1613 4k brt pur & ol bis 10 5
3325 A1613 4k ultra & ol bis 10 5
3326 A1613 4k org brn & ol bis 10 5

Issued to honor partisan heroes of World War II.

Marshal S. S. Biryuzov — A1614

1967, May 9 Photo. *Perf. 12*

3327 A1614 4k ocher & sl grn 10 5

Issued to honor Marshal S. S. Biryuzov, Hero of the Soviet Union.

Driver Crossing Lake Ladoga A1615

1967, May 9 *Perf. 11½*

3328 A1615 4k plum & bl gray 10 5

25th anniversary of siege of Leningrad.

Views of Old and New Minsk A1616

1967, May 9

3329 A1616 4k sl grn & blk 10 5

900th anniversary of Minsk.

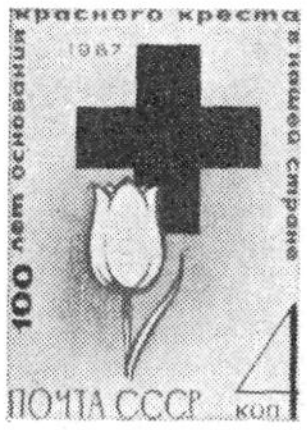

Red Cross and Tulip — A1617

1967, May 15 *Perf. 12*

3330 A1617 4k yel brn & red 10 5

Centenary of the Russian Red Cross.

Stamps of 1918 and 1967 A1618

1967 Photo. *Perf. 11½*

3331 A1618 20k bl & blk 50 22
a Souv. sheet of 2 1.50 70

Issued to publicize the All-Union Philatelic Exhibition "50 Years of the Great October," Moscow, Oct. 1-10. Printed se-tenant with light brown label showing exhibition emblem.

No. 3331a contains two black, imperf. stamps similar to No. 3331; red and gold margin with commemorative inscription. Size: 91x76mm.

Issue dates: 20k, May 25. Sheet, Oct. 1.

On Oct. 3 No. 3331 was re-issued with "Oct. 1-10" printed in blue on the label. Value 90 cents.

Komsomolsk-on-Amur and Map of Amur River — A1619

1967, June 12 *Perf. 12x12½*

3332 A1619 4k red & brn 14 5

Issued to commemorate the 35th anniversary of the Soviet youth town, Komsomolsk-on-Amur. Printed with red and brown label showing boy and girl of Young Communist League and tents.

Souvenir Sheet

Sputnik Orbiting Earth — A1620

1967, June 24 Litho. *Perf. 13x12*

3333 A1620 30k blk & multi 1.90 90

Issued to commemorate the 10th anniversary of the launching of Sputnik 1, the first artificial satellite, Oct. 4, 1957. No. 3333 contains one perforated stamp (size: 73x25mm).

Motorcyclist A1621

Photogravure and Engraved

1967, June 24 *Perf. 12x11½*

3334 A1621 10k multi 16 10

Issued to publicize the International Motor Rally, Moscow, July 19.

G. D. Gai — A1622

1967, June 30 Photo. *Perf. 12*

3335 A1622 4k red & blk 10 5

Issued in memory of G. D. Gai (1887-1937), Corps Commander of the First Cavalry, 1920.

Children's Games Emblem and Trophy A1623

1967, July 8 *Perf. 11½*

3336 A1623 4k sil, red & blk 10 5

Issued to commemorate the 10th National Athletic Games of School Children, Leningrad, July, 1967.

Games Emblem and Trophy A1624

Designs: No. 3338, Cup and dancer. No. 3339, Cup and bicyclists. No. 3340, Cup and diver.

1967, July 20

3337 A1624 4k sil, red & blk 10 5
3338 A1624 4k sil, red & blk 10 5
3339 A1624 4k sil, red & blk 10 5
3340 A1624 4k sil, red & blk 10 5

Issued to commemorate the 4th National Spartacist Games, celebrating the 50th anniversary of the USSR. Nos. 3337-3338 and Nos. 3339-3340 are printed se-tenant in 2 sheets of 50, in checkerboard arrangement.

V. G. Klochkov A1625

1967, July 20 *Perf. 12½x12*

3341 A1625 4k red & blk 10 5

Issued to honor V. G. Klochkov (1911-41), Hero of the Soviet Union. Printed with alternating red and black label showing citation.

Soviet Flag, Arms and Moscow Views A1626

Arms of U.S.S.R. and Laurel — A1627

Flag, Crest and Capital of Republic of: No. 3343, Armenia. No. 3344, Azerbaijan. No. 3345, Byelorussia. No. 3346, Estonia. No. 3347, Georgia. No. 3348, Kazakhstan. No. 3349, Kirghizia. No. 3350, Latvia. No. 3351, Lithuania. No. 3352, Moldavia. No. 3353, Tadzhikistan. No. 3354, Turkmenistan. No. 3355, Ukraine. No. 3356, Uzbekistan.

1967, Aug. 4 Litho. *Perf. 12½x12*

3342 A1626 4k multi 10 5
3343 A1626 4k multi 10 5
3344 A1626 4k multi 10 5
3345 A1626 4k multi 10 5
3346 A1626 4k multi 10 5
3347 A1626 4k multi 10 5
3348 A1626 4k multi 10 5
3349 A1626 4k multi 10 5
3350 A1626 4k multi 10 5
3351 A1626 4k multi 10 5
3352 A1626 4k multi 10 5
3353 A1626 4k multi 15 5
3354 A1626 4k multi 10 5
3355 A1626 4k multi 10 5
3356 A1626 4k multi 10 5
3357 A1627 4k red, gold & blk 10 5
Nos. 3342-3357 (16) 1.65 80

50th anniversary of October Revolution.

Communication Symbols — A1628

1967, Aug. 16 Photo. *Perf. 12*

3358 A1628 4k crim & sil 30 14

Development of communications in USSR.

Flying Crane, Dove and Anniversary Emblem A1629

1967, Aug. 20 *Perf. 12½x12*

3359 A1629 16k sil, red & blk 30 14

Issued to commemorate the 3rd Russo-Japanese Friendship Meeting, held at Khabarovsk. Emblem is for 50th anniversary of October Revolution.

Karl Marx and Title Page of "Das Kapital" — A1630

1967, Aug. 22 Engr. *Perf. 12½x12*

3360 A1630 4k sep & dk red 10 7

Issued to commemorate the centenary of the publication of "Das Kapital" by Karl Marx.

Russian Checkers Players A1631

Design: 6k, Woman gymnast.

Photogravure and Engraved

1967, Sept. 9 ***Perf. 12x11½***

3361	A1631	1k lt brn, dp brn & sl	7	5
3362	A1631	6k ol bis & mar	14	7

Issued to commemorate the World Championship of Russian Checkers (Shashki) at Moscow (1k), and the World Championship of Rhythmic Gymnastics (6k).

Javelin A1632

Sport: 3k, Running. 4k, Jumping.

1967, Sept. 9 **Engr.** ***Perf. 12x12½***

3363	A1632	2k brn red	7	5
3364	A1632	3k dp bl	7	5
3365	A1632	4k Prus bl	14	5

Issued to commemorate the Europa Cup Championships held at Kiev, Sept. 15-17.

Ice Skating and Olympic Emblem A1633

Designs: 3k, Ski jump. 4k, Emblem of Winter Olympics (vert.). 10k, Ice hockey. 12k, Long-distance skiing.

Photogravure and Engraved

1967, Sept. 20 ***Perf. 11½***

3366	A1633	2k gray, blk & bl	8	5
3367	A1633	3k bis, ocher, blk & grn	8	5
3368	A1633	4k gray, bl, red & blk	10	5
3369	A1633	10k bis, brn, bl & blk	25	7
3370	A1633	12k gray, blk, lil & grn	32	10
		Nos. 3366-3370 (5)	83	32

Issued to publicize the 10th Winter Olympic Games, Grenoble, France, Feb. 6-18, 1968.

Silver Fox A1634

Young Guards Memorial A1635

Fur-bearing Animals: 2k, Arctic blue fox (horiz.). 6k, Red fox (horiz.). 10k, Muskrat (horiz.). 12k, Ermine. 16k, Sable. 20k, Mink (horiz.).

1967, Sept. 20 **Photo.**

3371	A1634	2k brn, blk & gray bl	8	5
3372	A1634	4k tan, dk brn & gray bl	12	6
3373	A1634	6k gray grn, ocher & blk	16	8
3374	A1634	10k yel grn, dk brn & ocher	22	10
3375	A1634	12k lil, blk & bis	25	12
3376	A1634	16k org, brn & blk	30	14
3377	A1634	20k gray bl, blk & dk brn	40	20
		Nos. 3371-3377 (7)	1.53	75

International Fur Auctions in Leningrad.

1967, Sept. 23

3378	A1635	4k mag, org & blk	10	5

Issued to commemorate the 25th anniversary of the fight of the Young Guards at Krasnodon against the Germans.

Map of Cedar Valley Reservation and Snow Leopard — A1636

1967, Oct. 14 ***Perf. 12***

3379	A1636	10k ol bis & blk	20	10

Far Eastern Cedar Valley Reservation.

Planes and Emblem A1637

1967, Oct. 14 ***Perf. 11½***

3380	A1637	6k dp bl, red & gold	14	7

Issued to commemorate the 25th anniversary of the French Normandy-Neman aviators, who fought on the Russian Front.

Militiaman and Soviet Emblem A1638

1967, Oct. 14 ***Perf. 12½x12***

3381	A1638	4k ver & ultra	10	5

50th anniversary of the Soviet Militia.

Space Station Orbiting Moon — A1639

Science Fiction: 6k, Explorers on the moon (horiz.). 10k, Rocket flying to the stars. 12k, Landscape on Red Planet (horiz.). 16k, Satellites from outer space.

1967 **Litho.** ***Perf. 12x12½, 12½x12***

3382	A1639	4k multi	10	8
3383	A1639	6k multi	16	8
3384	A1639	10k multi	24	10
3385	A1639	12k multi	30	14
3386	A1639	16k multi	35	16
		Nos. 3382-3386 (5)	1.15	56

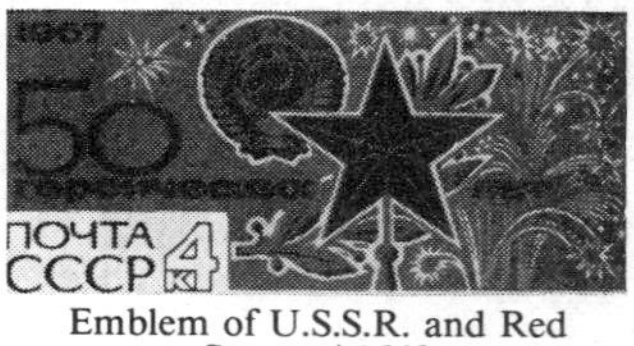

Emblem of U.S.S.R. and Red Star — A1640

Lenin Addressing 2nd Congress of Soviets, by V. A. Serov — A1641

Paintings: No. 3389, Lenin pointing to Map, by L. A. Schmatjko. No. 3390, The First Cavalry Army, by M. B. Grekov. No. 3391, Working Students on the March, by B. V. Yoganson. No. 3392, Russian Friendship for the World, by S. M. Karpov. No. 3393, Five-Year Plan Morning, by Y. D. Romas. No. 3394, Farmers' Holiday, by S. V. Gerasimov. No. 3395, Victory in the Great Patriotic War, by Y. K. Korolev. No. 3396, Builders of Communism, by L. M. Merpert and Y. N. Skripkov.

Lithographed and Embossed

1967, Oct. 25 ***Perf. 11½***

3387	A1640	4k gold, yel, red & dk brn	10	5
3388	A1641	4k gold & multi	10	5
3389	A1641	4k gold & multi	10	5
3390	A1641	4k gold & multi	10	5
3391	A1641	4k gold & multi	10	5
3392	A1641	4k gold & multi	10	5
3393	A1641	4k gold & multi	10	5
3394	A1641	4k gold & multi	10	5
3395	A1641	4k gold & multi	10	5
3396	A1641	4k gold & multi	10	5
a		Souv. sheet of 2	2.00	90
		Nos. 3387-3396 (10)	1.00	50

50th anniversary of October Revolution.

No. 3396a contains two 40k imperf. stamps similar to Nos. 3388 and 3396. Red margin contains Lenin portrait and first documents of the Soviet state. Size: 92x132mm. Issued Nov. 5.

Souvenir Sheet

Hammer, Sickle and Sputnik — A1642

1967, Nov. 5 **Engr.** ***Perf. 12½x12***

3397	A1642	1r lake	2.25	1.75

50th anniv. of the October Revolution. No. 3397 margin also contains "50" as a watermark.

Ostankino Television Tower — A1643

1967, Nov. 5 **Litho.** ***Perf. 11½***

3398	A1643	16k gray, org & blk	32	10

Jurmala Resort and Hepatica A1644

Health Resorts: 6k, Narva-Joesuu and Labrador tea. 10k, Druskininkai and cranberry blossoms. 12k, Zelenogradsk and Scotch heather (vert.). 16k, Svetlogorsk and club moss (vert.).

Perf. 12½x12, 12x12½

1967, Nov. 30 **Litho.**

Flowers in Natural Colors

3399	A1644	4k bl & blk	10	7
3400	A1644	6k ocher & blk	18	7
3401	A1644	10k grn & blk	20	10
3402	A1644	12k gray ol & blk	22	14
3403	A1644	16k brn & blk	32	14
		Nos. 3399-3403 (5)	1.02	52

Health resorts of Baltic region.

Emergency Commission Emblem — A1645

1967, Dec. 11 **Photo.** ***Perf. 11½***

3404	A1645	4k ultra & red	10	5

Issued to commemorate the 50th anniversary of the All-Russia Emergency Commission (later the State Security Commission).

Hotel Russia and Kremlin A1646

1967, Dec. 14

3405	A1646	4k sil, dk brn & brt pink	10	5

New Year 1968. The pink is fluorescent.

Soldiers, Sailors, Congress Building, Kharkov, and Monument to the Men of Arsenal — A1647

Designs: 6k, Hammer and sickle and scenes from industry and agriculture. 10k, Ukrainians offering bread and salt, monument of the Unknown Soldier, Kiev, and Lenin monument in Zaporozhye.

1967, Dec. 20 **Litho.** ***Perf. 12½***

3406	A1647	4k multi	10	5
3407	A1647	6k multi	14	5
3408	A1647	10k multi	16	7

Issued to commemorate the 50th anniversary of the Ukrainian Socialist Soviet Republic.

Three Kremlin Towers A1648

Kremlin: 6k, Cathedral of the Annunciation (horiz.). 10k, Konstantin and Elena, Nabatnaya and Spasski towers. 12k, Ivan the Great bell tower. 16k, Kutafya and Troitskaya towers.

Engraved and Photogravure
Perf. 12x11½, 11½x12

1967, Dec. 25

3409	A1648	4k dk brn & cl	10	5
3410	A1648	6k dk brn, yel & grn	12	5
3411	A1648	10k mar & sl	22	7
3412	A1648	12k sl grn, yel & vio	25	7
3413	A1648	16k brn, pink & red	30	10
		Nos. 3409-3413 (5)	99	34

Coat of Arms, Lenin's Tomb and Rockets A1649

Designs: No. 3415, Agricultural Progress: Wheat, reapers and silo. No. 3416, Industrial Progress: Computer tape, atom symbol, cogwheel and factories. No. 3417, Scientific Progress: Radar, microscope, university buildings. No. 3418, Communications progress: Ostankino TV tower, railroad bridge, steamer and Aeroflot emblem (vert.).

1967, Dec. 25 **Engr.** ***Perf. 12½***

3414	A1649	4k maroon	10	5
3415	A1649	4k green	10	5
3416	A1649	4k red brn	10	5
3417	A1649	4k vio bl	10	5
3418	A1649	4k dk bl	10	5
		Nos. 3414-3418 (5)	50	25

Issued to publicize the material and technical basis of Russian Communism.

Monument to the Unknown Soldier, Moscow — A1650

1967, Dec. 25

3419 A1650 4k carmine 10 5

Issued to commemorate the dedication of the Monument of the Unknown Soldier of World War II in the Kremlin Wall.

Seascape by Ivan Aivazovsky — A1651

Paintings: 3k, Interrogation of Communists by B. V. Yoganson. No. 3422, The Lacemaker, by V. A. Tropinin (vert.). No. 3423, Bread-makers, by T. M. Yablonskaya. No. 3424, Alexander Nevsky, by P. D. Korin (vert.). No. 3425, The Boyar Morozov Going into Exile by V. I. Surikov. No. 3426, The Swan Maiden, by M. A. Vrubel (vert.). No. 3427, The Arrest of a Propagandist by Ilya E. Repin. 16k, Moscow Suburb in February by G. G. Nissky.

Perf. 12½x12, 12x12½, 12, 11½

1967, Dec. 29 **Litho.**

Size: 47x33mm., 33x47mm.

3420	A1651	3k multi	8	5
3421	A1651	4k multi	8	5
3422	A1651	4k multi	8	5

Size: 60x35mm., 35x60mm.

3423	A1651	6k multi	10	8
3424	A1651	6k multi	10	8
3425	A1651	6k multi	10	8

Size: 47x33mm., 33x47mm.

3426	A1651	10k multi	22	12
3427	A1651	10k multi	22	12
3428	A1651	16k multi	28	18
		Nos. 3420-3428 (9)	1.26	81

Tretiakov Art Gallery, Moscow.

Globe, Wheel and Workers of the World — A1652

1968, Jan. 18 **Photo.** ***Perf. 12***

3429 A1652 6k ver & grn 14 7

14th Trade Union Congress.

Lt. S. Baikov and Velikaya River Bridge A1653

(War Memorial and): No. 3431. Lt. A. Pokalchuk. No. 3432, P. Gutchenko.

1968, Jan. 20 ***Perf. 12½x12***

3430	A1653	4k bl gray & blk	10	5
3431	A1653	4k rose & blk	10	5
3432	A1653	4k gray grn & blk	10	5

Issued to honor heroes of World War II.

Thoroughbred and Horse Race — A1654

Horses: 6k, Arab mare and dressage (vert.). 10k, Orlovski trotters. 12k, Altekin horse performing (vert.). 16k, Donskay race horse.

1968, Jan. 23 ***Perf. 11½***

3433	A1654	4k ultra, blk & red lil	10	5
3434	A1654	6k crim, blk & ultra	14	7
3435	A1654	10k grnsh bl, blk & org	22	10
3436	A1654	12k org brn, blk & ap grn	30	10
3437	A1654	16k ol grn, blk & red	40	14
		Nos. 3433-3437 (5)	1.16	46

Issued to publicize horse breeding.

Maria I. Ulyanova — A1655

1968, Jan. 30 ***Perf. 12x12½***

3438 A1655 4k ind & pale grn 10 5

Issued in memory of Maria I. Ulyanova (1878-1937), Lenin's sister.

Soviet Star and Flags of Army, Air Force and Navy — A1656

Lenin Addressing Troops in 1919 — A1657

Designs: No. 3441, Dneprostroi Dam and sculpture "On Guard." No. 3442, 1918 poster and marching volunteers. No. 3443, Red Army entering Vladivostok, 1922, and soldiers' monument in Primorie. No. 3444, Poster "Red Army as Liberator," Western Ukraine. No. 3445, Poster "Westward," defeat of German army. No. 3446, "Battle of Stalingrad" monument and German prisoners of war. No. 3447, Victory parade on Red Square, May 24, 1945, and Russian War Memorial, Berlin. Nos. 3448-3449, Modern weapons and Russian flag.

1968, Feb. 20 **Typo.** ***Perf. 12x12½***

3439 A1656 4k gold & multi 10 5

Photo.
Perf. 11½x12

3440	A1657	4k blk, red, pink & sil	10	5
3441	A1657	4k gold, blk & red	10	5

Litho.
Perf. 12½x12

3442	A1657	4k yel grn, blk, red & buff	10	5
3443	A1657	4k grn, dk brn, red & bis	10	5
3444	A1657	4k grn & multi	10	5
3445	A1657	4k yel grn & multi	10	5

Perf. 11½x12, 12x11½
Photo.

3446	A1657	4k blk, sil & red	10	5
3447	A1657	4k gold, blk, pink & red	10	5
3448	A1656	4k blk, red & sil	10	5
		Nos. 3439-3448 (10)	1.00	50

Souvenir Sheet

1968, Feb. 23 **Litho.** ***Imperf.***

3449 A1656 1r blk, sil & red 2.25 1.00

50th anniv. of the Armed Forces of the USSR. No. 3449 contains one stamp (size: 25x37½mm) with simulated perforations.

Maxim Gorki — A1658

1968, Feb. 29 **Photo.** ***Perf. 12***

3450 A1658 4k gray ol & dk brn 10 5

Birth centenary of Maxim Gorki (1868-1936), writer.

Fireman, Fire Truck and Boat — A1659

Link-up of Kosmos 186 and 188 Satellites — A1660

1968, Mar. 30 **Photo.** ***Perf. 12x12½***

3451 A1659 4k red & blk 10 5

50th anniversary of Soviet Fire Guards.

1968, Mar. 30 ***Perf. 11½***

3452 A1660 6k blk, dp lil rose & gold 16 5

First link-up in space of two satellites, Kosmos 186 and Kosmos 188, Oct. 30, 1967.

N. N. Popudrenko A1661

Design: No. 3453, P. P. Vershigora.

1968, Mar. 30 ***Perf. 12½x12***

3453	A1661	4k gray grn & blk	7	5
3454	A1661	4k lt pur & blk	7	5

Issued to honor partisan heroes of World War II.

Globe and Hand Shielding from War — A1662

1968, Apr. 11 ***Perf. 11½***

3455 A1662 6k sil, mar, ver & blk 16 5

Issued to publicize the emergency session of the World Federation of Trade Unions and to express solidarity with the people of Vietnam.

Space Walk — A1663

Designs: 6k, Docking operation of Kosmos 186 and Kosmos 188. 10k, Exploration of Venus.

1968, Apr. 12 **Litho.**

3456	A1663	4k multi	10	5
3457	A1663	6k multi	16	7
3458	A1663	10k multi	32	10

Issued to publicize National Astronauts' Day. Nos. 3456-3458 are printed in same sheet with alternating commemorative labels.

Lenin, 1919 — A1664

Lenin Portraits: No. 3460, Addressing crowd on Red Square, Nov. 7, 1918. No. 3461, Full-face portrait, taken in Petrograd, Jan. 1918.

Engraved and Photogravure

1968, Apr. 16 ***Perf. 12x11½***

3459	A1664	4k gold, brn & red	10	5
3460	A1664	4k gold, red & blk	10	5
3461	A1664	4k gold, brn, buff & red	10	5

98th anniversary of the birth of Lenin.

Alisher Navoi — A1665

1968, Apr. 29 Photo. *Perf. 12x12½*

3462	A1665	4k dp brn	10	5

Issued to commemorate the 525th anniversary of the birth of Alisher Navoi, Uzbek poet.

Karl Marx A1666

1968, May 5 Engr. *Perf. 11½x12*

3463	A1666	4k blk & red	10	5

Issued to commemorate the 150th anniversary of the birth of Karl Marx (1818-1883), political philosopher and writer.

Frontier Guard A1667

Jubilee Badge A1668

1968, May 22 Photo. *Perf. 11½*

3464	A1667	4k sl grn, ocher & red	10	5
3465	A1668	6k sl grn, blk & red brn	16	5

Issued to commemorate the 50th anniversary of the Russian Frontier Guards.

Crystal and Congress Emblem A1669

Congress Emblems and: No. 3467, Power lines and factories. No. 3468, Ground beetle. No. 3469, Roses and carbon rings.

1968, May 30

3466	A1669	6k bl, dk bl & grn	14	5
3467	A1669	6k org, gold & dk brn	14	5
3468	A1669	6k red brn, gold & blk	14	5
3469	A1669	6k lil rose, org & blk	14	5

International congresses to be held in Leningrad: 8th Congress for Mineral Research (No. 3466); 7th World Power Conference (No. 3467); 13th Entomological Congress (No. 3468); 4th Congress for the Study of Volatile Oils (No. 3469).

Types of 1966

Designs as Before

1968, June 20 Engr. *Perf. 12*

3470	A1593	1k dk red brn	7	5
3471	A1593	2k dp vio	7	5
3472	A1593	3k plum	10	5
3473	A1593	4k brt red	10	5
3474	A1593	6k blue	16	5
3475	A1593	10k olive	22	7
3476	A1593	12k red brn	30	7
3477	A1593	16k vio bl	35	10
		Perf. 12½		
3478	A1594	20k red	42	10
3479	A1594	30k brt grn	65	16
3480	A1594	50k vio bl	1.10	32
		Perf. 12x12½		
3481	A1594	1r gray, red brn & blk	2.25	50
		Nos. 3470-3481 (12)	5.79	1.57

Sadriddin Aini A1670

1968, June 30 Photo. *Perf. 12½x12*

3482	A1670	4k ol bis & mar	10	5

Issued to commemorate the 90th anniversary of the birth of Sadriddin Aini (1878-1954), Tadzhik poet.

Post Rider and C.C.E.P. Emblem A1671

Design: No. 3484, Modern means of communications (train, ship, planes and C.C.E.P. emblem).

1968, June 30

3483	A1671	6k gray & red brn	14	5
3484	A1671	6k org brn & bis	14	5

Issued to publicize the annual session of the Council of the Consultative Commission on Postal Investigation of the Universal Postal Union (C.C.E.P.), Moscow, Sept. 20-Oct. 5.

Bolshevik Uprising, Kiev — A1672

1968, July 5 *Perf. 11½*

3485	A1672	4k gold, red & plum	10	5

Issued to commemorate the 50th anniversary of the Ukrainian Communist Party.

Athletes A1673

1968, July 9

3486	A1673	4k yel, dp car & bis	10	5

Issued to publicize the First Youth Summer Sports Games celebrating the 50th anniversary of the Leninist Young Communists League.

Field Ball — A1674

Table Tennis A1675

Designs: 6k, 20th Baltic Regatta. 10k, Soccer player and cup. 12k, Scuba divers.

Perf. 12x12½, 12½x12

1968, July 18 Litho.

3487	A1674	2k red & multi	8	5
3488	A1675	4k pur & multi	8	5
3489	A1674	6k bl & multi	14	7
3490	A1674	10k multi	20	8
3491	A1675	12k grn & multi	28	10
		Nos. 3487-3491 (5)	78	35

Issued to publicize various European youth sports competitions.

Rhythmic Gymnast A1676

Olympic Sports: 6k, Weight lifting. 10k, Rowing. 12k, Women's hurdling. 16k, Fencing. 40k, Running.

1968, July 31 Photo. *Perf. 11½*

Gold Background

3492	A1676	4k bl & grn	12	5
3493	A1676	6k dp rose & pur	16	7
3494	A1676	10k yel grn & grn	25	7
3495	A1676	12k org & red brn	30	9
3496	A1676	16k ultra & pink	35	12
		Nos. 3492-3496 (5)	1.18	40

Souvenir Sheet

Perf. 12½x12

Lithographed and Photogravure

3497	A1676	40k gold, grn, org & gray	1.10	38

19th Olympic Games, Mexico City, Oct. 12-27.

Gediminas Tower, Vilnius — A1677

1968, Aug. 14 Photo. *Perf. 11½*

3498	A1677	4k mag, tan & red	10	5

Issued to commemorate the 50th anniversary of Soviet power in Lithuania.

Tbilisi State University A1678

1968, Aug. 14 *Perf. 12*

3499	A1678	4k sl grn & lt brn	10	5

50th anniversary of Tbilisi State University, Georgia.

Canceled-to-order stamps are often from remainders. Most collectors of canceled stamps prefer postally used specimens.

Laocoon — A1679

1968, Aug. 16 *Perf. 11½*

3500	A1679	6k sep, blk & mar	2.00	1.65

Issued to "promote solidarity with Greek democrats."

Red Army Man, Cavalry Charge and Order of the Red Banner of Battle — A1680

Designs: 3k, Young man and woman, Dneprostroi Dam and Order of the Red Banner of Labor. 4k, Soldier, storming of the Reichstag, Berlin, and Order of Lenin. 6k, "Restoration of National Economy" (workers), and Order of Lenin. 10k, Young man and woman cultivating virgin land and Order of Lenin. 50k, like 2k.

1968, Aug. 25 Litho. *Perf. 12½x12*

3501	A1680	2k gray, red & ocher	7	5
3502	A1680	3k multi	7	5
3503	A1680	4k org, ocher & rose car	10	5
3504	A1680	6k multi	14	5
3505	A1680	10k ol & multi	16	7
		Nos. 3501-3505 (5)	54	27

Souvenir Sheet

Imperf

3506	A1680	50k ultra, red & bis	1.10	50

50th anniv. of the Lenin Young Communist League, Komsomol.

Chemistry Institute and Dimeric Molecule A1681

1968, Sept. 3 Photo. *Perf. 11½*

3507	A1681	4k vio bl, dp lil rose & blk	14	7

50th anniversary of Kurnakov Institute for General and Inorganic Chemistry.

Letter, Compass Rose, Ship and Plane A1682

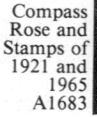

Compass Rose and Stamps of 1921 and 1965 A1683

1968, Sept. 16 Photo. *Perf. 11½*

3508	A1682	4k dk car rose, brn & brt red	10	5
3509	A1683	4k dk bl, blk & bis	10	5

No. 3508 issued for Letter Writing Week, Oct. 7-13, and No. 3509 for Stamp Day and the Day of the Collector.

The 26 Baku Commissars, Sculpture by Merkurov — A1684

1968, Sept. 20

3510	A1684	4k multi	14	5

Issued to commemorate the 50th anniversary of the shooting of the 26 Commissars, Baku, Sept. 20, 1918.

Toyvo Antikaynen — A1685

1968, Sept. 30 ***Perf. 12***

3511	A1685	6k gray & sep	14	7

Issued to commemorate the 70th anniversary of the birth of Toyvo Antikaynen (1898-1941), Finnish workers' organizer.

Russian Merchant Marine Emblem A1686

1968, Sept. 30 ***Perf. 12x11½***

3512	A1686	6k bl, red & ind	14	7

Issued to honor the Russian Merchant Marine.

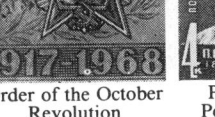

Order of the October Revolution A1687

Pavel P. Postyshev A1688

Typographed and Embossed

1968, Sept. 30 ***Perf. 12x12½***

3513	A1687	4k gold & multi	10	7

Issued to commemorate the 51st anniversary of the October Revolution. Printed with alternating label showing Supreme Soviet and Kremlin Senate Tower.

1968-70 **Engr.** ***Perf. 12½x12***

Designs: No. 3515, Stepan G. Shaumyan (1878-1918). No. 3516, Amkal Ikramov. (1898-1938). No. 3516A, N. G. Markin (1893-1918). No. 3516B, P. E. Dybenko (1889-1938). No. 3516C, S. V. Kosior (1889-1939). No. 3516D, Vasili Kikvidze (1895-1919).

Size: 21½x32½mm.

3514	A1688	4k bluish blk	14	5
3515	A1688	4k bluish blk	14	5
3516	A1688	4k gray blk	14	5
3516A	A1688	4k black	14	5
3516B	A1688	4k dk car ('69)	14	5
3516C	A1688	4k ind ('69)	14	5
3516D	A1688	4k dk brn ('70)	14	5
		Nos. 3514-3516D (7)	98	35

Issued to honor outstanding workers for the Communist Party and the Soviet State.

Issue dates: Nos. 3514-3516, Sept. 30, 1968. No. 3516A, Dec. 31, 1968. No. 3516D, Sept. 24, 1970. Others, May 15, 1969. See No. 3782.

American Bison and Zebra A1689

Designs: No. 3518, Purple gallinule and lotus. No. 3519, Great white egrets (vert.). No. 3520, Ostrich and golden pheasant (vert.). No. 3521, Eland and guanaco. No. 3522, European spoonbill and glossy ibis.

Perf. 12½x12, 12x12½

1968, Oct. 16 **Litho.**

3517	A1689	4k ocher, brn & blk	10	5
3518	A1689	4k ocher & multi	10	5
3519	A1689	6k ol & blk	14	8
3520	A1689	6k gray & multi	14	8
3521	A1689	10k dp grn & multi	22	8
3522	A1689	10k emer & multi	22	8
		Nos. 3517-3522 (6)	92	42

Issued to publicize the Askania Nova and Astrakhan state reservations.

Ivan S. Turgenev A1690

Warrior, 1880 B.C. and Mt. Ararat A1691

1968, Oct. 10 **Engr.** ***Perf. 12x12½***

3523	A1690	4k green	55	5

Issued to commemorate the 150th anniversary of the birth of Ivan S. Turgenev (1818-1883), writer.

Engraved and Photogravure

1968, Oct. 18 ***Perf. 11½***

Design: 12k, David Sasountsi monument, Yerevan, and Mt. Ararat.

3524	A1691	4k blk & dk bl, *gray*	7	5
3525	A1691	12k dk brn & choc, *bis*	20	10

2,750th anniversary of Yerevan, capital of Armenia.

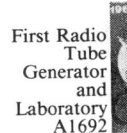

First Radio Tube Generator and Laboratory A1692

1968, Oct. 26 **Photo.** ***Perf. 11½***

3526	A1692	4k dk bl, dp bis & blk	10	5

50th anniversary of Russia's first radio laboratory at Gorki (Nizhni Novgorod).

Prospecting Geologist and Crystals A1693

Designs: 6k, Prospecting for metals: seismographic test apparatus with shock wave diagram, plane and truck. 10k, Oil derrick in the desert.

1968, Oct. 31 **Litho.** ***Perf. 11½***

3527	A1693	4k bl & multi	16	7
3528	A1693	6k multi	10	10
3529	A1693	10k multi	24	16

Issued for Geology Day. No. 3527 printed with alternating label with commemorative inscription, showing crystals, compass rose and geologist's hammer.

Borovoe, Kazakhstan — A1694

Landscapes: No. 3531, Djety-Oguz, Kirghizia (vert.). No. 3532, Issyk-kul Lake, Kirghizia. No. 3533, Borovoe, Kazakhstan (vert.).

Perf. 12½x12, 12x12½

1968, Nov. 20 **Typo.**

3530	A1694	4k dk red brn & multi	7	5
3531	A1694	4k gray & multi	7	5
3532	A1694	6k dk red brn & multi	14	5
3533	A1694	6k blk & multi	14	5

Issued to publicize recreational areas in the Kazakh and Kirghiz Republics.

Medals and Cup, Riccione, 1952, 1961 and 1965 — A1695

Designs: 4k, Medals, Eiffel Tower and Arc de Triomphe, Paris, 1964. 6k, Porcelain plaque, gold medal and Brandenburg Gate, Debria, Berlin, 1950, 1959. 12k, Medal and prize-winning stamp No. 2888, Buenos Aires. 16k, Cups and medals, Rome, 1952, 1954. 20k, Medals, awards and views, Vienna, 1961, 1965. 30k, Trophies, Prague, 1950, 1955, 1962.

1968, Nov. 27 **Photo.** ***Perf. 11½x12***

3534	A1695	4k dp cl, sil & blk	10	5
3535	A1695	6k dl bl, gold & blk	14	5
3536	A1695	10k lt ultra, gold & blk	20	7
3537	A1695	12k bl, sil & blk	24	7
3538	A1695	16k red, gold & blk	28	10
3539	A1695	20k brt bl, gold & blk	35	14
3540	A1695	30k org brn, gold & blk	52	20
		Nos. 3534-3540 (7)	1.83	68

This issue recalls awards to Russian post office at foreign stamp exhibitions.

Worker with Banner — A1696

V. K. Lebedinsky and Radio Tower — A1697

1968, Nov. 29 ***Perf. 12x12½***

3541	A1696	4k red & blk	10	7

Issued to commemorate the 50th anniversary of the Estonian Workers' Commune.

1968, Nov. 29 ***Perf. 11½x12***

3542	A1697	4k gray grn, blk & gray	10	7

Issued to commemorate the centenary of the birth of V. K. Lebedinsky (1868-1937), scientist.

Souvenir Sheet

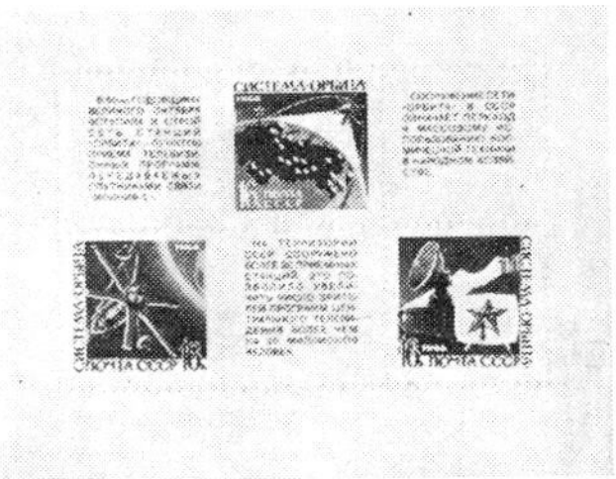

Communication via Satellite — A1698

1968, Nov. 29 **Litho.** ***Perf. 12***

3543	A1698	Souv. sheet of 3	1.50	50
a		16k *Molniya I*	35	14
b		16k *Map of Russia*	35	14
c		16k *Ground Station "Orbite"*	35	14

Issued to publicize television transmission throughout Russia with the aid of the earth satellite Molniya I.

Sprig, Spasski Tower, Lenin Univ. and Library A1699

1968, Dec. 1 ***Perf. 11½***

3544	A1699	4k ultra, sil, grn & red	7	7

Issued for New Year 1969.

Maj. Gen. Georgy Beregovoi — A1700

1968, Dec. 14 **Photo.** ***Perf. 11½***

3545	A1700	10k Prus bl, blk & red	16	7

Flight of Soyuz 3, Oct. 26-30.

Rail-laying and Casting Machines A1701

Design: 4k, Railroad map of the Soviet Union and Train.

1968, Dec. 14 ***Perf. 12½x12***

3546	A1701	4k rose mag & org	7	5
3547	A1701	10k brn & emer	16	7

Russian railroad transportation.

Newspaper Banner and Monument — A1702

1968, Dec. 23 ***Perf. 11½***

3548	A1702	4k tan, red & dk brn	7	7

Issued to commemorate the 50th anniversary of the communist party of Byelorussia.

The Reapers, by A. Venetzianov A1703

Knight at the Crossroads, by Viktor M. Vasnetsov — A1704

Paintings: 2k, The Last Day of Pompeii, by Karl P. Bryullov. 4k, Capture of a Town in Winter, by Vasili I. Surikov. 6k, On the Lake, by I.I. Levitan. 10k, Alarm, 1919 (family), by K. Petrov-Vodkin. 16k, Defense of Sevastopol, 1942, by A. Deineka. 20k, Sculptor with a Bust of Homer, by G. Korzhev. 30k, Celebration on Uristsky Square, 1920, by G. Koustodiev. 50k, Duel between Peresvet and Chelubey, by Mr. Avilov.

Perf. 12x12½, 12½

1968, Dec. 25 **Litho.**

3549 A1703 1k multi 7 5
3550 A1704 2k multi 10 5
3551 A1704 3k multi 12 5
3552 A1704 4k multi 14 5
3553 A1704 6k multi 20 6
3554 A1703 10k multi 30 7
3555 A1704 16k multi 35 12
3556 A1703 20k multi 38 8
3557 A1704 30k multi 52 22
3558 A1704 50k multi 95 35
Nos. 3549-3558 (10) 3.13 1.10

Russian State Museum, Leningrad.

House, Zaoneje, 1876 — A1705

Russian Architecture: 4k, Carved doors, Gorki Oblast, 1848. 6k, Castle, Kizhi, 1714. 10k, Fortress wall, Rostov-Yaroslav, 16th-17th centuries. 12k, Gate, Tsaritsino, 1785. 16k, Architect Rossi Street, Leningrad.

1968, Dec. 27 **Engr.** ***Perf. 12x12½***

3559 A1705 3k dp brn, *ocher* 10 5
3560 A1705 4k grn, *yel* 10 5
3561 A1705 6k vio, *gray vio* 14 7
3562 A1705 10k dl bl, *grnsh gray* 20 7
3563 A1705 12k car, *gray* 24 7
3564 A1705 16k blk, *yel* 30 10
Nos. 3559-3564 (6) 1.08 41

Banners of Young Communist League, October Revolution Medal — A1707

1968, Dec. 31 **Litho.** ***Perf. 12***

3566 A1707 12k red, yel & blk 20 7

Award of Order of October Revolution to the Young Communist League on its 50th anniversary.

Soldiers on Guard — A1708

1969, Jan. 1 ***Perf. 12x12½***

3567 A1708 4k org & cl 10 5

Issued to commemorate the 50th anniversary of the Latvian Soviet Republic.

Revolutionaries and Monument — A1709

Designs: 4k, Partisans and sword. 6k, Workers and Lenin Medals.

1969, Jan. **Photo.** ***Perf. 11½***

3568 A1709 2k ocher & rose cl 5 5
3569 A1709 4k ocher & red 7 5
3570 A1709 6k dk ol, mag & red 14 5

Issued to commemorate the 50th anniversary of the Byelorussian Soviet Republic.

Souvenir Sheet

Vladimir Shatalov, Boris Volynov, Alexei S. Elisseyev, Evgeny Khrunov — A1710

1969, Jan. 22 ***Imperf.***

3571 A1710 50k dp bis & dk brn 1.25 50

Issued to commemorate the first team flights of Soyuz 4 and 5, Jan. 16, 1969.

Leningrad University A1711

1969, Jan. 23 **Photo.** ***Perf. 12½x12***

3572 A1711 10k blk & mar 16 7

Issued to commemorate the 150th anniversary of the University of Leningrad.

Ivan A. Krylov A1712

Nikolai Filchenkov A1713

1969, Feb. 13 **Litho.** ***Perf. 12x12½***

3573 A1712 4k blk & multi 7 5

Issued to commemorate the bicentenary of the birth of Ivan A. Krylov (1769?-1844), fable writer.

1969 **Photo.**

Designs: No. 3575, Alexander Kosmodemiansky. No. 3575A, Otakar Yarosh, member of Czechoslovak Svoboda Battalion.

3574 A1713 4k dl rose & blk 7 5
3575 A1713 4k emer & dk brn 7 5
3575A A1713 4k bl & blk 7 5

Issued to honor heroes of World War II.
Issue dates: No. 3575A, May 9. Others, Feb. 23.

"Shoulder to the Wheel," Parliament, Budapest A1714

Design: "Shoulder to the Wheel" is a sculpture by Zigmond Kisfaludi-Strobl.

1969, Mar. 21 **Typo.** ***Perf. 11½***

3576 A1714 6k blk, ver & lt grn 10 5

Issued to commemorate the 50th anniversary of the Hungarian Soviet Republic.

Oil Refinery and Salavat Tualeyev Monument — A1715

1969, Mar. 22 **Litho.** ***Perf. 12***

3577 A1715 4k multi 14 7

50th anniv. of the Bashkir Autonomous Socialist Republic.

Sergei P. Korolev, Sputnik 1, Space Monument, Moscow — A1716

Vostok on Launching Pad — A1717

Designs: No. 3579, Zond 2 orbiting moon, and photograph of earth made by Zond 5. 80k, Spaceship Soyuz 3.

Perf. 12½x12, 12x12½

1969, Apr. 12 **Litho.**

3578 A1716 10k blk, vio & grn 16 7
3579 A1716 10k dk brn, yel & brn red 16 7
3580 A1717 10k multi 16 7

Souvenir Sheet

Perf. 12

3581 A1716 80k vio, grn & red 1.50 60

Issued for National Cosmonauts' Day.
No. 3581 contains one stamp (size: 37x24mm.); olive bister decorative margin with green inscription. Size: 90x67mm.

Lenin University, Kazan, and Kremlin A1718

Designs (Places Connected with Lenin): No. 3583, Lenin House, Kuibyshev. No. 3584, Lenin House, Pskov. No. 3585, Lenin House, Shushensko. No. 3586, Straw Hut, Razliv. No. 3587, Lenin Museum, Gorki. No. 3588, Smolny Institute, Leningrad. No. 3589, Lenin's room, Kremlin. No. 3590, Lenin Museum, Ulyanovsk. No. 3591, Lenin House, Ulyanovsk.

1969 **Photo.** ***Perf. 11½***

3582 A1718 4k pale rose & multi 7 5
3583 A1718 4k beige & multi 7 5
3584 A1718 4k bis brn & multi 7 5
3585 A1718 4k gray vio & multi 7 5
3586 A1718 4k vio & multi 7 5
3587 A1718 4k bl & multi 7 5
3588 A1718 4k brick red & multi 7 5
3589 A1718 4k rose red & multi 7 5
3590 A1718 4k lt red brn & multi 7 5
3591 A1718 4k dl grn & multi 7 5
Nos. 3582-3591 (10) 70 50

99th anniversary of the birth of Lenin.

Telephone, Transistor Radio and Trademark A1719

1969, Apr. 25 ***Perf. 12½x12***

3592 A1719 10k sep & dp org 14 7

50th anniversary of VEF Electrical Co.

ILO Emblem and Globe — A1720

1969, May 9 ***Perf. 11***

3593 A1720 6k car rose & gold 10 7

Issued to commemorate the 50th anniversary of the International Labor Organization.

Suleiman Stalsky A1721

1969, May 15 **Photo.** ***Perf. 12½x12***

3595 A1721 4k tan & ol grn 7 5

Birth centenary of Suleiman Stalsky (1869-1937), Dagestan poet.

Yasnaya Polyana Rose — A1722

Flowers: 4k, "Stroynaya" lily. 10k, Cattleya orchid. 12k, "Listopad" dahlia. 14k, "Ural Girl" gladioli.

1969, May 15 Litho. *Perf. 11½*

3596	A1722 2k gray & multi	7	5
3597	A1722 4k gold & multi	10	5
3598	A1722 10k gold & multi	16	7
3599	A1722 12k gold & multi	24	10
3600	A1722 14k gold & multi	24	10
	Nos. 3596-3600 (5)	81	37

Issued to publicize the work of the Botanical Gardens of the Academy of Sciences.

Ukrainian Academy of Sciences A1723

1969, May 22 Photo. *Perf. 12½x12*
3601 A1723 4k brn & yel 7 5

Issued to commemorate the 50th anniversary of the Ukrainian Academy of Sciences.

Film, Camera and Medal A1724

Ballet Dancers A1725

1969, June 3 Litho. *Perf. 12x12½*

3602	A1724 6k rose car, blk & gold	16	7
3603	A1725 6k dk brn & multi	16	7

No. 3602 commemorates the International Film Festival in Moscow, No. 3603 commemorates the 1st International Young Ballet Artists' Competitions.

Congress Emblem and Cell Division A1726

Estonian Singer and Festival Emblem A1727

1969, June 10 Photo. *Perf. 11½*
3605 A1726 6k dp cl, lt bl & yel 10 7

Issued to publicize the 3rd International Congress of Protozoologists, Leningrad.

1969, June 14 *Perf. 12x12½*
3606 A1727 4k ver & bis 7 7

Centenary of the Estonian Song Festival.

Mendeleev and Formula with Author's Corrections — A1728

Design: 30k, Dmitri Ivanovich Mendeleev (vert.).

Engraved and Lithographed

1969, June 20 *Perf. 12*
3607 A1728 6k brn & rose 16 10

Souvenir Sheet

3608 A1728 30k car rose 75 48

Issued to commemorate the centenary of the Periodic Law (classification of elements), formulated by Dimitri I. Mendeleev (1834-1907). No. 3608 contains one engraved stamp (size: 29x37mm.). Draft of Periodic Table from Mendeleev's workbook in gray on buff in margin. Size: 76½x102½mm.

Hand Holding Peace Banner and World Landmarks A1729

1969, June 20 Photo. *Perf. 11½*
3609 A1729 10k bl, dk brn & gold 16 7

20th anniversary of the Peace Movement.

Laser Beam Guiding Moon Rocket — A1730

1969, June 20
3610 A1730 4k sil, blk & red 10 7

Issued to commemorate the 50th anniversary of Soviet scientific inventions.

Ivan Kotlyarevski A1731

Typographed and Photogravure

1969, June 25 *Perf. 12½x12*
3611 A1731 4k blk, ol & lt brn 7 5

Issued to commemorate the 200th anniversary of the birth of Ivan Kotlyarevski (1769-1838), Ukrainian writer.

No. 2717 Overprinted in Vermilion Стокгольм. 1969

1969, June 25 Photo. *Perf. 11½*
3612 A1306 6k Prus bl & plum 90 55

Issued to commemorate the Russian victory in the Ice Hockey World Championships, Stockholm, 1969.

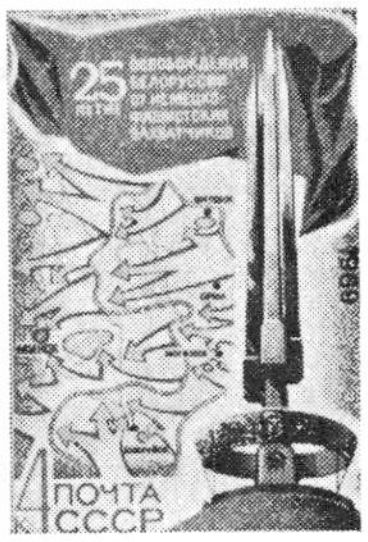

"Hill of Glory" Monument and Minsk Battle Map — A1732

1969, July 3 Litho. *Perf. 12x12½*
3613 A1732 4k red & ol 7 5

25th anniv. of the liberation of Byelorussia from the Germans.

Eagle, Flag and Map of Poland — A1733

Design: No. 3615, Hands holding torch, flags of Bulgaria and Russia, and Bulgarian coat of arms.

1969, July 10 Photo. *Perf. 12*
3614 A1733 6k red & bis 10 5

Litho.

3615 A1733 6k bis, red, grn & blk 10 5

No. 3614 issued to commemorate the 25th anniversary of the Polish Republic; 3615 commemorates the liberation of Bulgaria from the Germans.

Monument to 68 Heroes A1734

1969, July 15 Photo. *Perf. 12*
3616 A1734 4k red & mar 10 7

25th anniversary of the liberation of Nikolayev from the Germans.

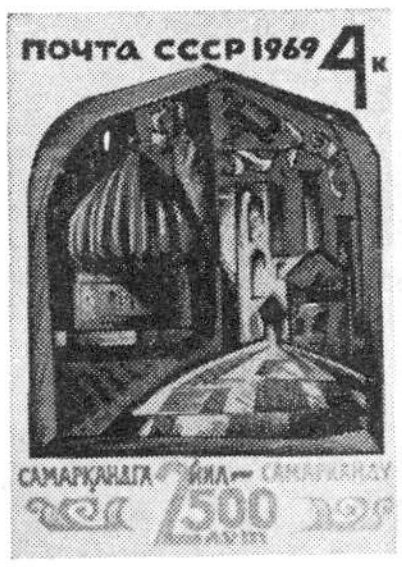

Old Samarkand A1735

Design: 6k, Intourist Hotel, Samarkand.

1969, July 15 Typo.

3617	A1735 4k multi	7	5
3618	A1735 6k multi	10	5

2500th anniversary of Samarkand.

Volleyball A1736

Munkascy and "Woman Churning Butter" A1737

Design: 6k, Kayak race.

Photogravure and Engraved

1969, July 20 *Perf. 11½*

3619	A1736 4k dp org & red brn	8	6
3620	A1736 6k multi	12	8

Issued to publicize the European Junior Volleyball Championships (4k) and the European Rowing Championships (6k).

1969, July 20 Photo.
3621 A1737 6k dk brn, blk & org 14 7

Issued to commemorate the 125th anniversary of the birth of Mihaly von Munkascy (1844-1900), Hungarian painter.

Miners' Monument — A1738

1969, July 30
3622 A1738 4k sil & mag 10 7

Issued to commemorate the centenary of the founding of the city of Donetsk, in the Donets coal basin.

Machine Gun Cart, by Mitrofan Grekov — A1739

1969, July 30 Engr. *Perf. 12½x12*
3623 A1739 4k red brn & brn red 10 7

Issued to commemorate the 50th anniversary of the First Mounted Army.

Barge Pullers Along the Volga, by Repin — A1740

An enhanced introduction to the Scott Catalogue begins on Page V. A thorough understanding of the material presented there will greatly aid your use of the catalogue itself.

Ilya E. Repin, Self-portrait
A1741

Repin Paintings: 6k, "Not Expected." 12k, Confession. 16k, Dnieper Cossacks.

Perf. 12½x12, 12x12½

1969, Aug. 5 **Litho.**

3624 A1740 4k multi		14	5
3625 A1740 6k multi		16	5
3626 A1741 10k bis, red brn & blk		20	7
3627 A1740 12k multi		28	7
3628 A1740 16k multi		35	10
	Nos. 3624-3628 (5)	1.13	34

Issued to commemorate the 125th anniversary of the birth of Ilya E. Repin (1844-1930), painter.

Runner
A1742

V. L. Komarov
A1743

Designs: 10k, Athlete on rings. 20k, Like 4k.

1969, Aug. 9 ***Perf. 12x12½***

3629 A1742 4k red, grn & blk	7	5
3630 A1742 10k grn, lt bl & blk	16	7

Souvenir Sheet

Imperf

3631 A1742 20k red, bis & blk	45	24

9th Trade Union Spartakiad, Moscow.

1969, Aug. 22 **Photo.** ***Perf. 12x11½***

3632 A1743 4k ol & brn	10	7

V. L. Komarov (1869-1945), botanist.

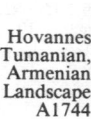

Hovannes Tumanian, Armenian Landscape
A1744

1969, Sept. 1 **Typo.** ***Perf. 12½x12***

3633 A1744 10k blk & pck bl	16	7

Birth centenary of Hovannes Tumanian (1869-1923), Armenian poet.

Turkmenian Wine Horn, 2nd Century
A1745

Mahatma Gandhi
A1746

Designs: 6k, Persian Simurg vessel (giant anthropomorphic bird), 13th century. 12k, Head of goddess Kannon, Korea, 8th century. 16k, Bodhisattva, Tibet, 7th century. 20k, Statue of Ebisu and fish (tai), Japan, 17th century.

1969, Sept. 3 **Litho.** ***Perf. 12x12½***

3634 A1745 4k bl & multi		12	5
3635 A1745 6k lil & multi		16	6
3636 A1745 12k red & multi		28	8
3637 A1745 16k bl vio & multi		30	10
3638 A1745 20k pale grn & multi		42	14
	Nos. 3634-3638 (5)	1.28	43

Issued to show treasures from the State Museum of Oriental Art.

1969, Sept. 10 **Engr.**

3639 A1746 6k dp brn	14	5

Issued to commemorate the centenary of the birth of Mohandas K. Gandhi (1869-1948), leader in India's fight for independence.

Black Stork Feeding Young
A1747

Designs: 6k, Doe and fawn (red deer). 10k, Fighting bison. 12k, Lynx and cubs. 16k, Wild pig and piglets.

1969, Sept. 10 **Photo.** ***Perf. 12***
Size: 75x23mm. (10k); 35x23mm. (others)

3640 A1747 4k blk, yel grn & red		7	6
3641 A1747 6k bl grn, dk brn & ocher		10	8
3642 A1747 10k dk brn, dl org & dp org		20	7
3643 A1747 12k dk & yel grn, brn & gray		20	8
3644 A1747 16k gray, yel grn & dk brn		24	10
	Nos. 3640-3644 (5)	81	39

Belovezhskaya Forest reservation.

Komitas
A1748

1969, Sept. 18 **Typo.** ***Perf. 12½x12***

3645 A1748 6k blk, gray & sal	10	7

Birth centenary of Komitas (S. N. Sogomonian (1869-1935)), Armenian composer.

Lisa Chaikina
A1749

A. Cheponis, J. Aleksonis and G. Borisa
A1750

Design: No. 3647, Major S. I. Gritsevets and fighter planes.

1969, Sept. 20 **Photo.** ***Perf. 12½x12***

3646 A1749 4k ol & brt grn	10	5
3647 A1749 4k gray & blk	10	5

Perf. 11½

3648 A1750 4k hn brn, brn & buff	10	7

Heroes of the Soviet Union.

Ivan P. Pavlov
A1751

East German Arms, TV Tower and Brandenburg Gate
A1752

1969, Sept. 26

3649 A1751 4k multi	7	7

Issued to commemorate the 120th anniversary of the birth of Ivan Petrovich Pavlov (1849-1936), physiologist.

1969, Oct. 7 **Litho.**

3650 A1752 6k red, blk & yel	10	7

Issued to commemorate the 20th anniversary of the German Democratic Republic.

Aleksei V. Koltsov — A1753

National Emblem — A1754

1969, Oct. 14 **Photo.** ***Perf. 12x12½***

3652 A1753 4k lt bl & brn	7	7

Issued to commemorate the 160th anniversary of the birth of Aleksei Vasilievich Koltsov (1809-1842), poet.

1969, Oct. 14 ***Perf. 12x11½***

3653 A1754 4k gold & red	7	7

Issued to commemorate the 25th anniversary of the liberation of the Ukraine from the Nazis.

Stars, Hammer and Sickle
A1755

1969, Oct. 21 **Typo.** ***Perf. 11½***

3654 A1755 4k vio bl, gold, yel & red	7	7

52nd anniversary of October Revolution.

Georgy Shonin and Valery Kubasov
A1756

Designs: No. 3656, Anatoly Filipchenko, Vladislav Volkov and Viktor Gorbatko. No. 3657, Vladimir Shatalov and Alexey Elisyev.

1969, Oct. 22 **Photo.** ***Perf. 12½x12***

3655 A1756 10k blk & gold	16	7
3656 A1756 10k blk & gold	16	7
3657 A1756 10k blk & gold	16	7

Issued to commemorate the group flight of the space ships Soyuz 6, Soyuz 7 and Soyuz 8, Oct. 11-13. Nos. 3655-3657 are printed se-tenant.

Lenin as a Youth
A1757

1969, Oct. 25 **Engr.** ***Perf. 11½***

3658 A1757 4k dk red, *pink*	7	7

Issued to publicize the First Russian Youth Philatelic Exhibition, Kiev, dedicated to Lenin's 100th birthday.

Emblem of Communications Unit of Army — A1758

1969, Oct. 30 **Photo.**

3659 A1758 4k dk red, red & bis	7	7

Issued to commemorate the 50th anniversary of the Communications Troops of Soviet Army.

Souvenir Sheet

Lenin and Quotation — A1759

Lithographed and Embossed

1969, Nov. 6 ***Imperf.***

3660 A1759 50k red, gold & pink	1.10	60

52nd anniv. of the October Revolution.

Cover of "Rules of the Kolkhoz" and Farm Woman's Monument — A1760

1969, Nov. 18 **Photo.** ***Perf. 12½x12***

3661 A1760 4k brn & gold	7	7

Issued to publicize the 3rd All Union Collective Farmers' Congress, Moscow, Nov.-Dec.

Vasilissa, the Beauty, by Ivan Y. Bilibin
A1761

Designs (Book Illustrations by Ivan Y. Bilibin): 10k, Marya Morevna. 16k, Finist, the Fine Fellow (horiz.). 20k, The Golden Cock. 50k, The Sultan and the Czar. The inscriptions on the 16k and 20k are transposed. 4k, 10k, 16k are fairy tales; 20k and 50k are tales by Pushkin.

1969, Nov. 20 Litho. *Perf. 12*

3662	A1761	4k gray & multi	10	6
3663	A1761	10k gray & multi	22	12
3664	A1761	16k gray & multi	30	16
3665	A1761	20k gray & multi	35	18
3666	A1761	50k gray & multi	90	30
		Nos. 3662-3666 (5)	1.87	82

Issued to honor the illustrator and artist Ivan Y. Bilibin.

Nos. 3662-3666 was printed se-tenant in strips of 5 with 16k turned sideway.

USSR Emblems Dropped on Venus, Radar Installation and Orbits A1762

Design: 6k, Interplanetary station, space capsule and orbits.

1969, Nov. 25 Photo. *Perf. 12x11½*

3667	A1762	4k bis, blk & red	7	5
3668	A1762	6k gray, lil rose & blk	10	5

Issued to commemorate the completion of the fights of the space stations Venera 5 and Venera 6.

Flags of Russia and Afghanistan A1763

Russian State Emblem and Star A1764

1969, Nov. 30 Photo. *Perf. 11½*

3669	A1763	6k red, blk & grn	10	5

Issued to commemorate the 50th anniversary of diplomatic relations between Russia and Afghanistan.

Coil Stamp

1969, Nov. 13 *Perf. 11x11½*

3670	A1764	4k red	14	10

MiG Jet and First MiG Fighter Plane — A1765

1969, Dec. 12 *Perf. 11½x12*

3671	A1765	6k red, blk & gray	14	7

Issued to honor Soviet aircraft builders.

Lenin and Flag — A1766

Typographed and Lithographed

1969, Dec. 25 *Perf. 11½*

3672	A1766	4k gold, bl, red & blk	7	7

Issued for "Happy New Year 1970, birth centenary of Lenin."

Antonov 2 — A1767

Aircraft: 3k, PO-2. 4k, ANT-9. 6k, TsAGI 1-EA. 10k, ANT-20 "Maxim Gorki." 12k, Tupolev-104. 16k, MiG-10 helicopter. 20k, Ilyushin-62. 50k, Tupolev-144.

Photogravure and Engraved

1969 *Perf. 11½x12*

3673	A1767	2k bis & multi	7	5
3674	A1767	3k multi	10	5
3675	A1767	4k multi	10	5
3676	A1767	6k multi	14	5
3677	A1767	10k lt vio & multi	20	7
3678	A1767	12k multi	24	10
3679	A1767	16k multi	30	10
3680	A1767	20k multi	35	14
		Nos. 3673-3680 (8)	1.50	61

Souvenir Sheet

Imperf

3681	A1767	50k bl & multi	1.50	70

Issued to publicize the history of national aeronautics and aviation. No. 3681 contains one stamp. In the margin is a quotation by N. E. Zhukovsky and the signs of the zodiac, partly overlapping the stamp. Size: 91x65mm.

Issue dates: Nos. 3679 and 3681, Dec. 31; others Dec. 25.

Photograph of Earth by Zond 7 — A1768

Designs: No. 3683a, same as 10k. No. 3683b, Photograph of moon.

1969, Dec. 26 Photo. *Perf. 12x11½*

3682	A1768	10k blk & multi	24	7

Souvenir Sheet

Imperf

Litho.

3683		Sheet of 2	2.00	1.65
a.	A1768	50k ind & multi	90	75
b.	A1768	50k dk brn & multi	90	75

Issued to publicize the space explorations of the automatic stations Zond 6, Nov. 10-17, 1968, and Zond 7, Aug. 8-14, 1969. No. 3683 contains 2 imperf. stamps (size: 27x40 mm.) with simulated perforations. Light blue margin showing trajectories around earth and moon and black commemorative inscription. Size: 116x79mm.

Model Aircraft — A1769

Technical Sports: 4k, Motorboats. 6k, Parachute jumping.

1969, Dec. 26 Engr. *Perf. 12½x12*

3684	A1769	3k brt mag	10	5
3685	A1769	4k dl bl grn	10	5
3686	A1769	6k red org	14	5

Romanian Arms and Soviet War Memorial, Bucharest A1770

1969, Dec. 31 Photo. *Perf. 11½*

3687	A1770	6k rose red & brn	14	5

Issued to commemorate the 25th anniversary of Romania's liberation from fascist rule.

Ostankino Television Tower, Moscow A1771

1969, Dec. 31 Typo. *Perf. 12*

3688	A1771	10k multi	16	7

Lenin, by N. Andreyev — A1772

Paintings: No. 3690, Lenin at Marxist Meeting, St. Petersburg, by A. Moravov. No. 3691, Lenin at Second Party Day, by Y. Vinogradov. No. 3692, First Day of Soviet Power, by F. Modorov. No. 3693, Conversation with Lenin, by A. Shirokov. No. 3694, Farmers' Delegation Meeting Lenin, by Modorov. No. 3695, With Lenin, by V. A. Serov. No. 3696, Lenin on May 1, 1920, by I. Brodsky. No. 3697, Builder of Communism, by a group of painters. No. 3698, Mastery of Space, by A. Deyneka.

1970, Jan. 1 Litho. *Perf. 12*

3689	A1772	4k multi	7	5
3690	A1772	4k multi	7	5
3691	A1772	4k multi	7	5
3692	A1772	4k multi	7	5
3693	A1772	4k multi	7	5
3694	A1772	4k multi	7	5
3695	A1772	4k multi	7	5
3696	A1772	4k multi	7	5
3697	A1772	4k multi	7	5
3698	A1772	4k multi	7	5
		Nos. 3689-3698 (10)	70	50

Centenary of birth of Lenin (1870-1924).

Map of Antarctic, "Mirny" and "Vostok" A1773

Design: 16k, Camp and map of the Antarctic with Soviet Antarctic bases.

1970, Jan. 27 Photo. *Perf. 11½*

3699	A1773	4k multi	7	5
3700	A1773	16k multi	28	7

Issued to commemorate the 150th anniversary of the Bellingshausen-Lazarev Antarctic expedition.

F. W. Sychkov and "Tobogganing" — A1774

1970, Jan. 27 *Perf. 12½x12*

3701	A1774	4k sep & vio bl	7	7

Birth centenary of F. W. Sychkov (1870-1958), painter.

Col. V. B. Borsoyev — A1775

Design: No. 3703, Sgt. V. Peshekhonov.

1970, Feb. 10 *Perf. 12x12½*

3702	A1775	4k brn ol & brn	7	5
3703	A1775	4k dk gray & plum	7	5

Issued to honor heroes of the Soviet Union.

Geographical Society Emblem and Globes A1776

Torch of Peace A1777

1970, Feb. 26 Photo. *Perf. 11½*

3704	A1776	6k bis, Prus bl & dk brn	10	7

Issued to commemorate the 125th anniversary of the Russian Geographical Society.

1970, Mar. 3 Litho. *Perf. 12*

3705	A1777	6k bl grn & tan	10	7

Issued to publicize International Women's Solidarity Day, March 8.

Symbols of Russian Arts and Crafts — A1778

Lenin — A1780

Footnotes often refer you to other stamps of the same design.

Lenin — A1779

Designs: 6k, Russian EXPO '70 pavilion. 10k, Boy holding model ship.

1970, Mar. 10 Photo. *Perf. 11½*

3706 A1778 4k dk bl grn, red & blk 7 5
3707 A1778 6k blk, sil & red 10 5
3708 A1778 10k vio bl, sil & red 16 7

Souvenir Sheet

Engr. & Litho.

Perf. 12x12½

3709 A1779 50k dk red 1.10 48

EXPO '70 International Exhibition, Osaka, Japan, Mar. 15-Apr. 13.

1970, Mar. 14 Photo. *Perf. 11½*

3710 A1780 4k red, blk & gold 7 7

Souvenir Sheet

Photogravure and Embossed

Imperf

3711 A1780 20k red, blk & gold 60 30

USSR Philatelic Exhibition dedicated to the centenary of the birth of Lenin.

Friendship Tree, Sochi A1781

1970, Mar. 18 Litho. *Perf. 11½*

3712 A1781 10k multi 20 7

Issued to publicize friendship among people. Printed with alternating yellow label with black inscription.

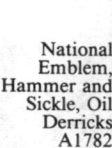

National Emblem, Hammer and Sickle, Oil Derricks A1782

1970, Mar. 18 Photo. *Perf. 11½*

3713 A1782 4k dk car rose & gold 7 5

Azerbaijan Republic, 50th anniversary.

Ice Hockey Players A1783

1970, Mar. 18

3714 A1783 6k bl & sl grn 14 7

Issued to commemorate the World Ice Hockey Championships in Sweden.

No. 3714 Overprinted in Upper Right Corner with Orange Cyrillic Inscription in 5 Vertical Lines

1970, Apr. 1 Photo. *Perf. 11½*

3715 A1783 6k bl & sl grn 14 7

Issued to honor Soviet hockey players as the tenfold world champions.

D. N. Medvedev A1784

Hungarian Arms, Budapest Landmarks A1786

Worker, Books, Globes and UNESCO Symbol A1785

Portrait: No. 3717, K. P. Orlovsky.

1970, Mar. 26 Engr. *Perf. 12x12½*

3716 A1784 4k chocolate 7 5
3717 A1784 4k dk redsh brn 7 5

Heroes of the Soviet Union.

1970, Mar. 26 Photo. *Perf. 12½x12*

3718 A1785 6k car lake & ocher 10 7

Issued to publicize the UNESCO-sponsored Lenin Symposium, Tampere, Finland, Apr. 6-10.

1970, Apr. 4 Typo. *Perf. 11½*

3719 A1786 6k multi 10 7

Issued to commemorate the 25th anniversary of the liberation of Hungary.
See No. 3738.

Cosmonauts' Emblem A1787

1970, Apr. 12 Litho. *Perf. 11½*

3720 A1787 6k buff & multi 10 7

Issued for Cosmonauts' Day.

Lenin, 1891 A1788

Order of Victory A1789

Designs: Various portraits of Lenin.

Lithographed and Typographed

1970, Apr. 15 *Perf. 12x12½*

3721 A1788 2k grn & gold 5 5
3722 A1788 2k ol gray & gold 5 5
3723 A1788 4k vio bl & gold 7 5
3724 A1788 4k lake & gold 7 5
3725 A1788 6k red brn & gold 12 5
3726 A1788 6k lake & gold 12 5
3727 A1788 10k dk brn & gold 16 7
3728 A1788 10k dk rose brn & gold 20 7
3729 A1788 12k blk, sil & gold 24 7

Photo.

3730 A1788 12k red & gold 24 7
Nos. 3721-3730 (10) 1.32 58

Souvenir Sheet

1970, Apr. 22 Litho. Typo.

3731 A1788 20k blk, sil & gold 50 28

Cent. of the birth of Lenin. Issued in sheets of 8 stamps surrounded by 16 labels showing Lenin-connected buildings, books, coats of arms and medals. No. 3731 contains one stamp in same design as No. 3729.

1970, May 8 Photo. *Perf. 11½*

Designs: 2k, Monument to the Unknown Soldier, Moscow. 3k, Victory Monument, Berlin-Treptow. 4k, Order of the Great Patriotic War. 10k, Gold Star of the Order of Hero of the Soviet Union and Medal of Socialist Labor. 30k, Like 1k.

3732 A1789 1k red lil, gold & gray 5 5
3733 A1789 2k dk brn, gold & red 5 5
3734 A1789 3k dk brn, gold & red 5 5
3735 A1789 4k dk brn, gold & red 7 5
3736 A1789 10k red lil, gold & red 16 7
Nos. 3732-3736 (5) 38 27

Souvenir Sheet

Imperf

3737 A1789 30k dk red, gold & gray 1.00 45

Issued to commemorate the 25th anniversary of victory in World War II. No. 3737 contains one stamp with simulated perforations. Gold and dark red margin with commemorative inscription and soldiers on parade. Size: 65x96mm.

Arms-Landmark Type of 1970

Design: Czechoslovakia arms and view of Prague.

1970, May 8 Typo. *Perf. 12½*

3738 A1786 6k dk brn & multi 10 7

Issued to commemorate the 25th anniversary of the liberation of Czechoslovakia from the Germans.

Young Fighters, and Youth Federation Emblem A1791

1970, May 20 Litho. *Perf. 12*

3739 A1791 6k bl & blk 10 7

Issued to commemorate the 25th anniversary of the World Federation of Democratic Youth.

Lenin A1792

1970, May 20 Photo. *Perf. 11½*

3740 A1792 6k red 10 7

Issued to commemorate the International Youth Meeting dedicated to the centenary of the birth of Lenin, United Nations, N.Y., June 1970.

Komsomol Emblem with Lenin A1793

1970, May 20 Litho. *Perf. 12*

3741 A1793 4k red, yel & pur 10 7

Issued to publicize the 16th Congress of the Young Communist League, May 26-30.

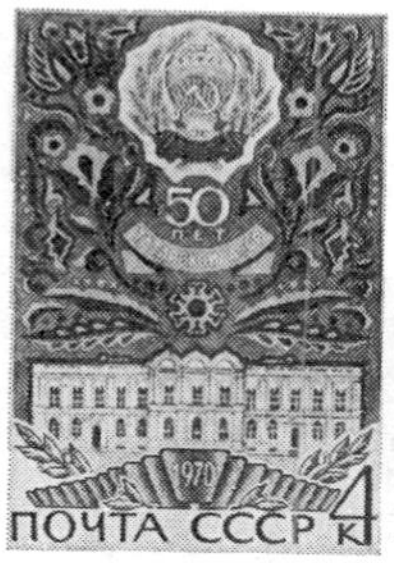

Hammer and Sickle Emblem and Building of Supreme Soviet in Kazan A1794

Designs (Hammer-Sickle Emblem and Supreme Soviet Building in): No. 3743, Petrozavodsk. No. 3744, Cheboksary. No. 3744A, Elista. No. 3744B, Izhevsk. No. 3744C, Yoshkar-Ola.

1970 Engr. *Perf. 12x12½*

3742 A1794 4k vio bl 7 5
3743 A1794 4k green 7 5
3744 A1794 4k dk car 7 5
3744A A1794 4k red 7 5
3744B A1794 4k dk grn 7 5
3744C A1794 4k dk car 7 5
Nos. 3742-3744C (6) 42 30

Issued to commemorate the 50th anniversaries of the Tatar (No. 3742), Karelian (No. 3743), Chuvash (No. 3744), Kalmyk (No. 3744A), Udmurt (No. 3744B) and Mari (No. 3744C) autonomous Soviet Socialist Republics.

Issue Dates: No. 3742, May 27; No. 3743, June 5; No. 3744, June 24; Nos. 3744A-3744B, Oct. 22; No. 3744C, Nov. 4.

See Nos. 3814-3823, 4286.

Soccer — A1795

Sword into Plowshare Statue, United Nations, N.Y. — A1796

Design: 10k, Woman athlete on balancing bar.

1970, May 31 Photo. *Perf. 11½*

3745 A1795 10k lt gray & brt rose 16 7
3746 A1795 16k dk grn & org brn 28 10

No. 3745 commemorates the 17th World Gymnastics Championships, Ljubljana, Oct. 22-27; No. 3746 the 9th World Soccer Championships for the Jules Rimet Cup, Mexico City, May 29-June 21.

1970, June 1 Litho. *Perf. 12x12½*

3747 A1796 12k gray & lake 20 7

25th anniversary of the United Nations.

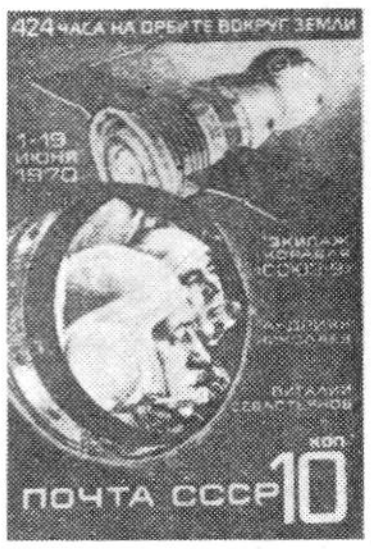

Soyuz 9, Andrian Nikolayev, Vitaly Sevastyanov
A1797

1970, June 7 Photo. *Perf. 12x11½*
3748 A1797 10k multi 20 7

Issued to commemorate the space flight of Soyuz 9, June 1-19, which lasted 424 hours.

Friedrich Engels
A1798

1970, June 16 Engr. *Perf. 12x12½*
3749 A1798 4k choc & ver 7 5

Issued to commemorate the sesquicentennial of the birth of Friedrich Engels (1820-1895), German socialist, collaborator with Karl Marx.

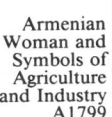

Armenian Woman and Symbols of Agriculture and Industry
A1799

Design: No. 3751, Kazakh woman and symbols of agriculture and industry.

1970, June 16 Photo. *Perf. 11½*
3750 A1799 4k red brn & sil 7 5
3751 A1799 4k brt rose lil & gold 7 5

Issued to commemorate the 50th anniversaries of the Armenian (No. 3750) and the Kazakh (No. 3751) Soviet Socialist Republics.

Missile Cruiser "Grozny" — A1800

Soviet Warships: 3k, Cruiser "Aurora." 10k, Cruiser "October Revolution." 12k, Missile cruiser "Varyag." 20k, Atomic submarine "Leninsky Komsomol."

1970, July 26 Photo. *Perf. 11½x12*
3752 A1800 3k lil, pink & blk 8 5
3753 A1800 4k yel & blk 12 6
3754 A1800 10k rose & blk 22 6
3755 A1800 12k buff & dk brn 22 8
3756 A1800 20k bl grn, dk brn & vio bl 30 12
Nos. 3752-3756 (5) 94 37

Issued for Navy Day.

Russian and Polish Workers and Flags
A1801

"History," Petroglyphs, Sputnik and Emblem
A1802

1970, July 26 *Perf. 12*
3757 A1801 6k red & sl 10 7

Issued to commemorate the 25th anniversary of the Treaty of Friendship, Collaboration and Mutual Assistance between Russia and Poland.

1970, Aug. 16 *Perf. 11½*
3758 A1802 4k red brn, buff & bl 7 5

Issued to publicize the 13th International Congress of Historical Sciences in Moscow.

Mandarin Ducks
A1803

Animals from the Sikhote-Alin Reserve: 6k, Pine marten. 10k, Asiatic black bear (vert.). 16k, Red deer. 20k, Ussurian tiger.

Perf. 12½x12, 12x12½
1970, Aug. 19 Litho.
3759 A1803 4k multi 10 6
3760 A1803 6k multi 14 6
3761 A1803 10k multi 16 8
3762 A1803 16k ultra & multi 24 12
3763 A1803 20k gray & multi 35 16
Nos. 3759-3763 (5) 99 48

Magnifying Glass over Stamp, and Covers — A1804

Pioneers' Badge — A1805

1970, Aug. 31 Photo. *Perf. 12x12½*
3764 A1804 4k red & sil 14 7

Issued to publicize the 2nd All-Union Philatelists' Congress in Moscow.

1970, Sept. 24 Photo. *Perf. 11½*

Designs: 2k, Lenin and Children, monument. 4k, Star and scenes from play "Zarnitsa."

3765 A1805 1k gray, red & gold 5 5
3766 A1805 2k brn red & sl grn 5 5
3767 A1805 4k lt ol, car & gold 10 5

Soviet general education.

Yerevan University
A1806

1970, Sept. 24 Photo. *Perf. 12½x12*
3768 A1806 4k ultra & sal pink 10 7

Issued to commemorate the 50th anniversary of Yerevan State University.

Library Bookplate, Vilnius University
A1807

Woman Holding Flowers
A1808

1970, Oct. Typo. *Perf. 12x12½*
3772 A1807 4k sil, gray & blk 7 7

Issued to commemorate the 400th anniversary of the Vilnius University Library.

1970, Oct. 30 Photo.
3773 A1808 6k bl & lt brn 10 7

Issued to commemorate the 25th anniversary of the International Democratic Federation of Women.

Farm Woman, Cattle Farm — A1809

Designs: No. 3775, Farmer and mechanical farm equipment. No. 3776, Farmer, fertilization equipment and plane.

1970, Oct. 30 *Perf. 11½x12*
3774 A1809 4k ol, yel & red 7 5
3775 A1809 4k ocher, yel & red 7 5
3776 A1809 4k lt vio, yel & red 7 5

Aims of the new agricultural 5-year plan.

Lenin — A1810

Lithographed and Embossed
1970, Nov. 3 *Perf. 12½x12*
3777 A1810 4k red & gold 7 7

Souvenir Sheet
3778 A1810 30k red & gold 1.00 28

53rd anniv. of the October Revolution.

No. 3389 Overprinted in Gold

50 лет
ленинскому плану
ГОЭЛРО • 1970

1970, Nov. 3 *Perf. 11½*
3779 A1641 4k gold & multi 10 7

Issued to commemorate the 50th anniversary of the GOELRO Plan for the electrification of Russia.

Spasski Tower and Fir Branch
A1811

A. A. Baykov
A1812

1970, Nov. 23 Litho. *Perf. 12x12½*
3780 A1811 6k multi 10 7

Issued for New Year, 1971.

1970, Nov. 25 Photo. *Perf. 12½x12*
3781 A1812 4k sep & gldn brn 10 7

Issued to commemorate the centenary of the birth of A. A. Baykov (1870-1946), metallurgist and academician.

Portrait Type of 1968

Portrait: No. 3782, A. D. Tsyurupa.

1970, Nov. 25 Photo. *Perf. 12x12½*
3782 A1688 4k brn & sal 10 7

Issued to commemorate the centenary of the birth of A. D. Tsyurupa (1870-1928), First Vice Chairman of the Soviet of People's Commissars.

Vasily Blazhenny Church, Red Square
A1813

Designs: 6k, Performance of Swan Lake. 10k, Two deer. 12k, Folk art. 14k, Sword into Plowshare statue, by E. Vouchetich, and museums. 16k, Automobiles and woman photographer.

Photogravure and Engraved
1970, Nov. 29 *Perf. 12x11½*
Frame in Brown Orange
3783 A1813 4k multi 7 5
3784 A1813 6k multi 10 5
3785 A1813 10k brn org & sl grn 16 7
3786 A1813 12k multi 20 7
3787 A1813 14k multi 24 10
3788 A1813 16k multi 30 10
Nos. 3783-3788 (6) 1.07 44

Tourist publicity.

Daisy
A1814

Flowers: 6k, Dahlia. 10k, Phlox. 12k, Aster. 16k, Clematis.

1970, Nov. 29 Litho. *Perf. 11½*

3789 A1814 4k grn & multi 7 6
3790 A1814 6k multi 10 8
3791 A1814 10k yel & multi 16 8
3792 A1814 12k multi 20 10
3793 A1814 16k multi 35 12
Nos. 3789-3793 (5) 88 44

U.N. Emblem, African Mother and Child, Broken Chain — A1815

1970, Dec. 10 Photo. *Perf. 12x12½*

3794 A1815 10k bl & dk brn 20 7

United Nations Declaration on Colonial Independence, 10th anniversary.

Ludwig van Beethoven A1816

1970, Dec. 16 Engr. *Perf. 12½x12*

3795 A1816 10k dp cl, *pink* 25 10

Bicentenary of the birth of Ludwig van Beethoven (1770-1827), composer.

Skating A1817

Luna 16 A1818

Design: 10k, Skiing.

1970, Dec. 18 Photo. *Perf. 11½*

3796 A1817 4k lt gray, ultra & dk red 10 5
3797 A1817 4k lt gray, brt grn & brn 20 7

Publicity for the 1971 Trade Union Winter Games.

1970, Dec. Photo. *Perf. 11½*

Designs: No. 3799, 3801b, Luna 16 leaving moon. No. 3800, 3801c, Capsule landing on earth. No. 3801a, like No. 3798.

3798 A1818 10k gray bl 16 7
3799 A1818 10k dk pur 16 7
3800 A1818 10k gray bl 16 7

Souvenir Sheet

3801 Sheet of 3 1.10 55
a. A1818 20k bl 28 12
b. A1818 20k dk pur 28 12
c. A1818 20k bl 28 12

Luna 16 unmanned, automatic moon mission, Sept. 12-24, 1970.

Nos. 3801a-3801c have attached labels (no perf. between vignette and label). Issue dates: No. 3801. Dec. 18; Nos. 3798-3800, Dec. 28.

For unused stamps, more recent issues are valued as never hinged, with the beginning point determined on a country-by-country basis. Notes to show the beginning points are prominently placed in the text.

The Conestabile Madonna, by Raphael A1819

Paintings: 4k, Apostles Peter and Paul, by El Greco. 10k, Perseus and Andromeda, by Rubens (horiz.). 12k, The Prodigal Son, by Rembrandt. 16k, Family Portrait, by van Dyck. 20k, The Actress Jeanne Samary, by Renoir. 30k, Woman with Fruit, by Gauguin. 50k, The Litte Madonna, by da Vinci. All paintings from the Hermitage in Leningrad, except 20k from Pushkin Museum, Moscow.

Perf. 12x12½, 12½x12

1970, Dec. 23 Litho.

3802 A1819 3k gray & multi 7 5
3803 A1819 4k gray & multi 10 7
3804 A1819 10k gray & multi 20 7
3805 A1819 12k gray & multi 20 10
3806 A1819 16k gray & multi 25 14
3807 A1819 20k gray & multi 35 14
3808 A1819 30k gray & multi 70 20
Nos. 3802-3808 (7) 1.87 77

Souvenir Sheet

Imperf

3809 A1819 50k gold & multi 1.00 55

Harry Pollyt and Shipyard A1820

1970, Dec. 31 Photo. *Perf. 12*

3810 A1820 10k mar & brn 20 7

80th anniversary of the birth of Harry Pollyt (1890-1960), British labor leader.

International Cooperative Alliance A1821

1970, Dec. 31 *Perf. 11½x12*

3811 A1821 12k yel grn & red 20 7

International Cooperative Alliance, 75th anniversary.

Lenin — A1822

1971, Jan. 1 *Perf. 12*

3812 A1822 4k red & gold 7 5

Year of the 24th Congress of the Communist Party of the Soviet Union.

Georgian Republic Flag — A1823

1971, Jan. 12 Litho. *Perf. 11½*

3813 A1823 4k ol bis & multi 7 5

Georgian Soviet Socialist Republic, 50th anniversary.

Republic Anniversaries Type of 1970

Designs (Hammer-Sickle Emblem and): No. 3814, Supreme Soviet Building, Makhachkala. No. 3815, Fruit, ship, mountain, conveyor. No. 3816, Grapes, refinery, ship. No. 3817, Supreme Soviet Building, Nalchik. No. 3818, Supreme Soviet Building, Syktyvkar, and lumber industry. No. 3819, Natural resources, dam, mining. No. 3820, Industrial installations and natural products. No. 3821, Ship, "industry." No. 3822, Grapes, pylons and mountains. No. 3823, Kazbek Mountain, industrial installations, produce.

1971-74 Engr. *Perf. 12x12½*

3814 A1794 4k dk bl grn 7 5
3815 A1794 4k rose red 7 5
3816 A1794 4k red 7 5
3817 A1794 4k blue 7 5
3818 A1794 4k green 7 5
3819 A1794 4k brt bl 7 5
3820 A1794 4k car rose 7 5
3821 A1794 4k brt ultra 7 5
3822 A1794 4k gldn brn 7 5

Litho.

3823 A1794 4k dk red 7 5
Nos. 3814-3823 (10) 70 50

Fiftieth anniversaries of Dagestan (No. 3814), Abkazian (No. 3815), Adzhar (No. 3816), Kabardino-Balkarian (No. 3817), Komi (No. 3818), Yakut (No. 3819), Checheno-Ingush (No. 3820), Buryat (No. 3821), Nakhichevan (No. 3822), and North Ossetian (No. 3823) autonomous Soviet Socialist Republics.

No. 3823 also commemorates the bicentenary of Ossetia's union with Russia.

Issue dates: No. 3814, Jan. 20. No. 3815, Mar. 3. No. 3816, June 16. Nos. 3817-3818, Aug. 17, 1971. No. 3819, Apr. 20. No. 3820, Nov. 22, 1972. No. 3821, May 24, 1973. No. 3822, Feb. 6, 1974. No. 3823, July 7, 1974.

Tower of Genoa, Cranes, Hammer and Sickle — A1824

Palace of Culture, Kiev — A1825

1971, Jan. 28 Typo. *Perf. 12*

3824 A1824 10k dk red, gray & yel 16 7

2500th anniversary of the founding of Feodosiya in the Crimea.

1971, Feb. 16 Photo. *Perf. 11½*

3825 A1825 4k red, bis & bl 7 7

24th Congress of the Ukrainian Communist Party.

N. Gubin, I. Chernykh, S. Kosinov A1826

1971, Feb. 16 *Perf. 12½x12*

3826 A1826 4k sl grn & vio brn 7 7

Heroes of the Soviet Union.

"Industry and Agriculture" A1827

Lesya Ukrayinka A1828

1971, Feb. 16 *Perf. 12x12½*

3827 A1827 6k ol bis & red 10 5

50th anniversary of the State Planning Organization.

1971, Feb. 25

3828 A1828 4k org red & bis 7 5

Birth centenary of Lesya Ukrayinka (1871-1913), Ukrainian poet.

"Summer" Dance — A1829

Dancers of Russian Folk Dance Ensemble: No. 3830, "On the Skating Rink." No. 3831, Ukrainian dance "Hopak." No. 3832, Adzharian dance. No. 3833, Gypsy dance.

1971, Feb. 25 Litho. *Perf. 12½x12*

3829 A1829 10k bis & multi 16 7
3830 A1829 10k ol & multi 16 7
3831 A1829 10k ol bis & multi 16 7
3832 A1829 10k gray & multi 16 7
3833 A1829 10k grnsh gray & multi 16 7
Nos. 3829-3833 (5) 80 35

Luna 17 on Moon A1830

Designs: No. 3835, Ground control. No. 3836, Separation of Lunokhod 1 and carrier. 16k, Lunokhod 1 in operation.

1971, Mar. 16 Photo. *Perf. 11½*

3834 A1830 10k dp vio & sep 16 7
3835 A1830 12k dk bl & sep 20 7
3836 A1830 12k dk bl & sep 20 10
3837 A1830 16k dp vio & sep 25 10
a Souvenir sheet of 4 1.00 45

Luna 17 unmanned, automated moon mission, Nov. 10-17, 1970. No. 3837a contains one each of Nos. 3834-3837.

Paris Commune A1831

Industry, Science, Culture A1832

1971, March 18 Litho. ***Perf. 12***
3838 A1831 6k red & blk 10 7

Centenary of the Paris Commune.

1971, Mar. 29 ***Perf. 11½***
3839 A1832 6k bis, brn & red 10 7

24th Communist Party Congress, March 30-Apr. 3.

Yuri Gagarin Medal A1833

1971, Mar. 30 Photo. ***Perf. 11½***
3840 A1833 10k brn & lem 20 7

Tenth anniversary of man's first flight into space.

Space Research A1834

1971, Mar. 30
3841 A1834 12k sl bl & vio brn 20 7

Cosmonauts' Day, Apr. 12.

E. Birznieks-Upitis A1835

Bee and Blossom A1836

1971, Apr. 1 ***Perf. 12x12½***
3842 A1835 4k red brn & gray 7 7

Centenary of the birth of E. Birznieks-Upitis (1871-1960), Latvian writer.

1971, Apr. 1 ***Perf. 11½***
3843 A1836 6k ol & multi 10 7

23rd International Bookeeping Congress, Moscow, Aug. 22-Sept. 2.

Souvenir Sheet

Cosmonauts and Spacecraft — A1837

Designs: 10k, Vostok. No. 3844b, Yuri Gagarin. No. 3844c, First man walking in space. 16k, First orbital station.

1971, Apr. 12 Litho. ***Perf. 12***
3844 A1837 Sheet of 4 1.25 50
a 10k vio brn 16 12
b 12k Prus grn 20 12
c 12k Prus grn 20 12
d 16k vio brn 24 12

Tenth anniversary of man's first flight into space. No 3844 has gray margin and commemorative inscription. Size of stamp: 26x19mm. Size of souvenir sheet: 91x76mm.

Lenin Memorial, Ulyanovsk — A1838

1971, Apr. 16 Photo. ***Perf. 12***
3845 A1838 4k cop red & ol bis 7 7

Lenin's birthday. Memorial was built for centenary celebration of his birth.

Lt. Col. Nikolai I. Vlasov — A1839

Khafiz Shirazi — A1840

1971, May 9 Photo. ***Perf. 12x12½***
3846 A1839 4k gray ol & brn 10 7

Hero of the Soviet Union.

1971, May 9 **Litho.**
3847 A1840 4k ol, brn & blk 10 7

650th anniversary of the birth of Khafiz Shirazi, Tadzhik-Persian poet.

GAZ-66 — A1841

Soviet Cars: 3k, BelAZ-540 truck. No. 3850, Moskvich-412. No. 3851, ZAZ-968. 10k, Volga.

1971, May 12 Photo. ***Perf. 11x11½***
3848 A1841 2k yel & multi 5 5
3849 A1841 3k lt bl & multi 7 5
3850 A1841 4k lt lil & multi 7 5
3851 A1841 4k lt gray & multi 7 5
3852 A1841 10k lt lil & multi 16 7
Nos. 3848-3852 (5) 42 27

A. A. Bogomolets A1842

Satellite A1843

1971, May 24 Photo. ***Perf. 12***
3853 A1842 4k org & blk 7 7

90th anniversary of the birth of A. A. Bogomolets, physician.

1971, June 9 ***Perf. 11½***
3854 A1843 6k bl & multi 10 7

15th General Assembly of the International Union of Geodesics and Geophysics.

Symbols of Science and History A1844

1971, June 9 ***Perf. 12***
3855 A1844 6k grn & gray 10 7

13th Congress of Science History.

Oil Derrick & Symbols A1845

1971, June 9 ***Perf. 11½***
3856 A1845 6k multi 14 7

8th World Oil Congress.

Sukhe Bator Monument — A1846

1971, June 16 Typo. ***Perf. 12***
3857 A1846 6k red, gold & blk 10 7

50th anniversary of Mongolian revolution.

Monument of Defenders of Liepaja A1847

1971, June 21 **Photo.**
3858 A1847 4k gray, blk & brn 7 7

30th anniversary of the defense of Liepaja (Libau) against invading Germans.

Map of Antarctica and Station A1848

Weather Map, Plane, Ship and Satellite A1849

Engraved and Photogravure

1971, June 21 ***Perf. 11½***
3859 A1848 6k blk, grn & ultra 14 7

Tenth anniversary of the Antarctic Treaty pledging peaceful uses of and scientific cooperation in Antarctica.

1971, June 21
3860 A1849 10k blk, red & ultra 20 7

50th anniversary of Soviet Hydrometeorological service.

FIR Emblem, "Homeland" by E. Vouchetich A1850

1971, June 21 Photo. ***Perf. 12x12½***
3861 A1850 6k dk red & sl 7 5

International Federation of Resistance Fighters (FIR), 20th anniversary.

Discus and Running A1851

Designs: 4k, Archery (women). 6k, Dressage. 10k, Basketball. 12k, Wrestling.

Lithographed and Engraved

1971, June 24 ***Perf. 11½***
3862 A1851 3k vio bl, *rose* 7 5
3863 A1851 4k sl grn, *pale pink* 10 5
3864 A1851 6k red brn, *ap grn* 14 5
3865 A1851 10k dk pur, *gray bl* 20 7
3866 A1851 12k red brn, *yel* 24 7
Nos. 3863-3866 (4) 68 24

5th Summer Spartakiad.

Benois Madonna, by da Vinci A1852

Paintings: 4k, Mary Magdalene, by Titian. 10k, The Washerwoman, by Jean Simeon Chardin (horiz.). 12k, Portrait of a Young Man, by Frans Hals. 14k, Tancred and Arminia, by Nicolas Poussin (horiz.). 16k, Girl with Fruit, by Murillo. 20k, Girl with Ball, by Picasso.

Perf. 12x12½, 12½x12

1971, July 7 **Litho.**
3867 A1852 2k bis & multi 7 5
3868 A1852 4k bis & multi 10 6
3869 A1852 10k bis & multi 20 8
3870 A1852 12k bis & multi 24 10
3871 A1852 14k bis & multi 28 12
3872 A1852 16k bis & multi 35 12
3873 A1852 20k bis & multi 42 18
Nos. 3867-3873 (7) 1.66 71

Foreign master works in Russian museums.

Kazakhstan Flag, Lenin Badge A1853

1971, July 7 Photo. ***Perf. 11½***
3874 A1853 4k bl, red & brn 7 7

50th anniversary of the Kazakh Communist Youth League.

Star Emblem and Letters A1854

1971, July 14
3875 A1854 4k ol, bl & blk 7 7

International Letter Writing Week.

Nikolai A. Nekrasov, by Ivan N. Kramskoi A1855

Portraits: No. 3877, Aleksandr Spendiarov, by M. S. Saryan. 10k, Fedor M. Dostoevski, by Vassili G. Perov.

1971, July 14 Litho. *Perf. 12x12½*
3876 A1855 4k cit & multi 7 5
3877 A1855 4k gray bl & multi 7 5
3878 A1855 10k multi 16 7

Sesquicentennial of the births of Nikolai Alekseevitch Nekrasov (1821-1877), poet, and of Fedor Mikhailovich Dostoevski (1821-1881), novelist; centenary of the birth of A. Spendiarov (1871-1928), Armenian composer (No. 3877).
See Nos. 4056-4057.

Z. Paliashvili and Score — A1856

1971, Aug. 3 Photo. *Perf. 12x12½*
3879 A1856 4k brown 7 5

Centenary of the birth of Zachary Paliashvili (1871-1933), Georgian composer.

Gorki Kremlin, Stag and Hydrofoil A1857

1971, Aug. 3 Litho. *Perf. 12*
3880 A1857 16k multi 28 16

750th anniversary of the founding of Gorki (formerly Nizhni Novgorod). See Nos. 3889, 3910-3914.

Federation Emblem and Students A1858

1971, Aug. 3 Photo. *Perf. 11½*
3881 A1858 6k ultra & multi 10 5

25th anniversary of the International Students Federation.

Common Dolphins A1859

Sea Mammals: 6k, Sea otter. 10k, Narwhals. 12k, Walrus. 14k, Ribbon seals.

Photogravure and Engraved

1971, Aug. 12 *Perf. 11½*
3882 A1859 4k sil & multi 10 5
3883 A1859 6k sil & multi 14 5
3884 A1859 10k sil & multi 20 7
3885 A1859 12k sil & multi 24 10
3886 A1859 14k sil & multi 28 10
Nos. 3882-3886 (5) 96 37

Miner's Star of Valor — A1860

1971, Aug. 17 Photo. *Perf. 11½*
3887 A1860 4k bis, blk & red 7 7

250th anniversary of the discovery of coal in the Donets Basin.

Ernest Rutherford and Diagram of Movement of Atomic Particles A1861

1971, Aug. 24 Photo. *Perf. 12*
3888 A1861 6k mag & dk ol 10 7

Centenary of the birth of Ernest Rutherford (1871-1937), British physicist.

Gorki and Gorki Statue — A1862

1971, Sept. 14 *Perf. 11½*
3889 A1862 4k stl bl & multi 7 7

750th anniversary of the founding of Gorki (Nizhni Novgorod).

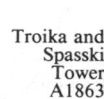

Troika and Spasski Tower A1863

1971, Sept. 14
3890 A1863 10k blk, red & gold 16 7

Issued for New Year 1972.

Automatic Production Center — A1864

Designs: No. 3892, Agricultural development. No. 3893, Family in shopping center. No. 3894, Hydro-generators, thermoelectric station. No. 3895, Marchers, flags, books inscribed Marx and Lenin.

1971, Sept. 29 Photo. *Perf. 12x11½*
3891 A1864 4k pur, red & blk 10 5
3892 A1864 4k ocher, red & brn 10 5
3893 A1864 4k yel, ol & red 10 5
3894 A1864 4k bis, red & brn 10 5
3895 A1864 4k ultra, red & sl 10 5
Nos. 3891-3895 (5) 50 25

Resolutions of 24th Soviet Union Communist Party Congress.

The Meeting, by Vladimir Y. Makovsky A1865

Ivan N. Kramskoi, Self-portrait A1866

Paintings: 4k, Woman Student, by Nikolai A. Yaroshenko. 6k, Woman Miner, by Nikolai A. Kasatkin. 10k, Harvest, by G. G. Myasoyedov (horiz.). 16k, Country Road, by A. K. Savrasov. 20k, Pine Forest, by I. I. Shishkin (horiz.).

Perf. 12x12½, 12½x12

1971, Oct. 14 Litho.

Frame in Light Gray

3896 A1865 2k multi 5 5
3897 A1865 4k multi 7 5
3898 A1865 6k multi 10 7
3899 A1865 10k multi 20 8
3900 A1865 16k multi 24 12
3901 A1865 20k multi 42 16
Nos. 3896-3901 (6) 1.08 53

Souvenir Sheet

Lithographed and Gold Embossed

3902 A1866 50k dk grn & multi 1.00 50

History of Russian painting. No. 3902 has marginal inscription commemorating the cent. of Russian Artists' Organization. Size: 93x67mm.

V. V. Vorovsky — A1867

1971, Oct. 14 Engr. *Perf. 12*
3903 A1867 4k red brn 7 7

Centenary of the birth of V. V. Vorovsky, Bolshevik party leader and diplomat.

Cosmonauts Dobrovolsky, Volkov and Patsayev — A1868

1971, Oct. 20 Photo. *Perf. 11½x12*
3904 A1868 4k blk, lil & org 7 7

In memory of cosmonauts Lt. Col. Georgi T. Dobrovolsky, Vladislav N. Volkov and Viktor I. Patsayev, who died during the Soyuz 11 space mission, June 6-30, 1971.

Order of October Revolution — A1869

1971, Oct. 20 Litho. *Perf. 12*
3905 A1869 4k red, yel & blk 7 7

54th anniversary of October Revolution.

E. Vakhtangov and "Princess Turandot" A1870

Dzhambul Dzhabayev A1871

Designs: No. 3907, Boris Shchukin and scene from "Man with Rifle (Lenin)" (horiz). No. 3908, Ruben Simonov and scene from "Cyrano de Bergerac" (horiz.).

Perf. 12x12½, 12½x12

1971, Oct. 26 Photo.
3906 A1870 10k mar & red brn 16 7
3907 A1891 10k brn & dl yel 16 7
3908 A1891 10k red brn & ocher 16 7

50th anniversary of Vakhtangov Theater, Moscow.

1971, Nov. 16 *Perf. 12x12½*
3909 A1871 4k org & brn 7 7

125th anniversary of the birth of Dzhambul Dzhabayev (1846-1945), Kazakh poet.

Gorki Kremlin Type, 1971

Designs: 3k, Pskov Kremlin and Velikaya River. 4k, Novgorod Kremlin and eternal flame memorial. 6k, Smolensk Fortress and liberation monument. 10k, Kolomna Kremlin and buses. 50k, Moscow Kremlin.

1971, Nov. 16 Litho. *Perf. 12*
3910 A1857 3k multi 7 5
3911 A1857 4k multi 7 5
3912 A1857 6k gray & multi 10 5
3913 A1857 10k ol & multi 16 7

Souvenir Sheet

Engraved and Lithographed

Perf. 11½
3914 A1857 50k yel & multi 1.00 50

Historic buildings. No. 3914 contains one stamp (21½x32mm).

William Foster, View of New York
A1872

1971 Litho. *Perf. 12*

3915	A1872 10k brown & blk ("-1961")		30	10
a	"-1964"		7.25	7.25

William Foster (1881-1961), chairman of Communist Party of U.S.A.

No. 3915a was issued Nov. 16 with incorrect death date (1964). No. 3915, with corrected date (1961), was issued Dec. 8.

Aleksandr Fadeyev and Cavalrymen — A1873

1971, Nov. 25 Photo. *Perf. 12½x12*

3916	A1873 4k sl & org	10	5

70th anniversary of the birth of Aleksandr Fadeyev (1901-1956), writer.

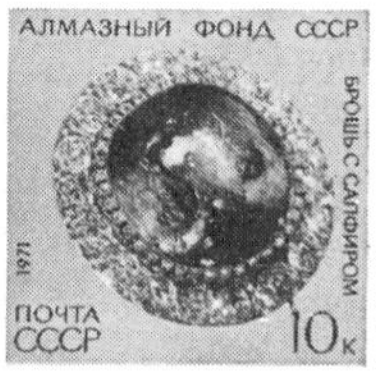

Amethyst and Diamond Brooch
A1874

Precious Jewels: No. 3918, Engraved Shakh diamond, India, 16th century. No. 3919, Diamond daffodils, 18th century. No. 3920, Amethyst and diamond pendant. No. 3921, Diamond rose made for centenary of Lenin's birth. 30k, Diamond and pearl pendant.

1971, Dec. 8 Litho. *Perf. 11½*

3917	A1874 10k brt bl & multi	16	7
3918	A1874 10k dk red & multi	16	7
3919	A1874 10k grnsh blk & multi	16	7
3920	A1874 20k grnsh blk & multi	32	16
3921	A1874 20k rose red & multi	32	16
3922	A1874 30k blk & multi	50	25
	Nos. 3917-3922 (6)	1.62	78

Souvenir Sheet

Workers with Banners, Congress Hall and Spasski Tower — A1875

1971, Dec. 15 Photo. *Perf. 11x11½*

3923	A1875 20k red, pale grn & brn	1.00	42

See note after No. 3895. No. 3923 contains one partially perforated stamp because the flag continues from the stamp into the margin. Pale green margin with brown inscription. Size: 90x65mm.

Vanda Orchid — A1876

Flowers: 2k, Anthurium. 4k, Flowering crab cactus. 12k, Amaryllis. 14k, Medinilla magnifica.

1971, Dec. 15 Litho. *Perf. 12x12½*

3924	A1876 1k ol & multi	5	5
3925	A1876 2k grn & multi	5	5
3926	A1876 4k bl & multi	7	7
3927	A1876 12k multi	24	10
3928	A1876 14k multi	28	14
	Nos. 3924-3928 (5)	69	41

Miniature Sheet

Perf. 12

3929	Sheet of 4	1.00	55
a	A1876 10k like 12k	22	10
b	A1876 10k like 1k	22	10
c	A1876 10k like 4k	22	10
d	A1876 10k like 14k	22	10

Nos. 3929a-3929d have white background, black frame line and inscription. Size of stamps 19x57mm. No. 3929 has pale violet margin with floral design. Size: 81x95mm.

Issue dates: Nos. 3924-3928, Dec. 15; No. 3929, Dec. 30.

Peter I Reviewing Fleet, 1723 — A1877

History of Russian Fleet: 4k, Oriol, first ship built in Eddinovo, 1668 (vert.). 10k, Battleship Poltava, 1712 (vert.). 12k, Armed ship Ingermanland, 1715 (vert.). 16k, Frigate Vladimir, 1848.

Engraved and Photogravure

Perf. 11½x12, 12x11½

1971, Dec. 15

3930	A1877 1k multi	5	5
3931	A1877 4k brn & multi	7	5
3932	A1877 10k multi	14	7
3933	A1877 12k multi	14	7
3934	A1877 16k lt grn & multi	24	10
	Nos. 3930-3934 (5)	64	34

Ice Hockey
A1878

1971, Dec. 15 Litho. *Perf. 12½*

3935	A1878 6k multi	16	7

25th anniversary of Soviet ice hockey.

Oil Rigs and Causeway in Caspian Sea — A1879

1971, Dec. 30 *Perf. 11½*

3936	A1879 4k dp bl, org & blk	10	7

Baku oil industry.

G. M. Krzhizhanovsky (1872-1959), Scientist and Co-worker with Lenin — A1880

1972, Jan. 5 Engr. *Perf. 12*

3937	A1880 4k yel brn	7	7

Alexander Scriabin
A1881

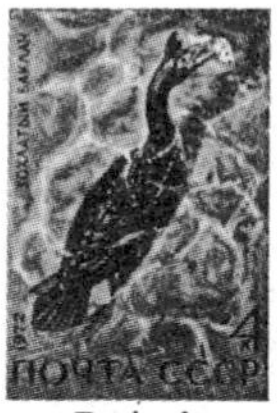

Bering's Cormorant
A1882

1972, Jan. 6 Photo. *Perf. 12x12½*

3938	A1881 4k ind & ol	7	7

Centenary of the birth of Alexander Scriabin (1872-1915), composer.

1972, Jan. 12 *Perf. 11½*

Birds: 6k, Ross' gull (horiz.). 10k, Barnacle geese. 12k, Spectacled eiders (horiz.). 16k, Mediterranean gull.

3939	A1882 4k dk grn, blk & yel	10	5
3940	A1882 6k ind, pink & blk	14	7
3941	A1882 10k grnsh bl, blk & brn	20	10
3942	A1882 12k multi	24	10
3943	A1882 16k ultra, gray & red	35	16
	Nos. 3939-3943 (5)	1.03	48

Waterfowl of Russia.

Speed Skating — A1883

Heart, Globe and Exercising Family — A1884

Designs (Olympic Rings and): 6k, Women's figure skating. 10k, Ice hockey. 12k, Ski jump. 16k, Long-distance skiing. 50k, Sapporo '72 emblem.

1972, Jan. 20 Litho. *Perf. 12x12½*

3944	A1883 4k bl grn, red & brn	7	5
3945	A1883 6k yel grn, bl & dp org	10	7
3946	A1883 10k vio, bl & dp org	20	7
3947	A1883 12k lt bl, bl & brick red	25	10
3948	A1883 16k gray, bl & brt rose	40	16
	Nos. 3944-3948 (5)	1.02	45

Souvenir Sheet

3949	A1883 50k multi	85	50

11th Winter Olympic Games, Sapporo, Japan, Feb. 3-13.

1972, Feb. 9 Photo.

3950	A1884 4k brt grn & rose red	7	7

Heart Week sponsored by the World Health Organization.

Leipzig Fair Emblem and Russian Pavilion
A1885

Hammer, Sickle and Cogwheel Emblem
A1886

1972, Feb. 22 *Perf. 11½*

3951	A1885 16k red & gold	25	10

50th anniversary of the participation of the USSR in the Leipzig Trade Fair.

1972, Feb. 29 *Perf. 12x12½*

3952	A1886 4k rose red & lt brn	7	5

15th USSR Trade Union Congress, Moscow, March 1972.

Aloe
A1887

Aleksandra Kollontai
A1888

Medicinal Plants: 2k, Horn poppy. 4k, Groundsel. 6k, Orthosiphon stamineus. 10k, Nightshade.

1972, Mar. 14 Litho. *Perf. 12x12½*

Flowers in Natural Colors

3953	A1887 1k ol bis	5	5
3954	A1887 2k sl grn	5	5
3955	A1887 4k brt pur	7	5
3956	A1887 6k vio bl	10	7
3957	A1887 10k dk brn	20	10
	Nos. 3953-3957 (5)	47	32

1972, Mar. 20 Engr. *Perf. 12½x12*

Portraits: No. 3959, Georgy Chicherin. No. 3960, Kamo (pseudonym of S.A. Ter-Petrosyan).

3958	A1888 4k red brn	7	5
3959	A1888 4k claret	7	5
3960	A1888 4k ol bis	7	5

Outstanding workers of the Communist Party of the Soviet Union and for the State.

Souvenir Sheet

No. 3949 Overprinted in Margin

СОВЕТСКИЕ СПОРТСМЕНЫ ЗАВОЕВАЛИ 8 ЗОЛОТЫХ МЕДАЛЕЙ, 5 СЕРЕБРЯНЫХ, 3 БРОНЗОВЫХ.

1972, Mar. 20 Litho. *Perf. 12x12½*

3961	A1883 50k multi	2.00	90

To commemorate the victories of Russian athletes in the 11th Winter Olympic Games. (8 gold, 5 silver and 3 bronze medals).

Foreign postal stationery (stamped envelopes, postal cards and air letter sheets) lies beyond the scope of this Catalogue, which is limited to adhesive postage stamps.

Orbital Station Salyut and Spaceship Soyuz Docking Above Earth — A1889

Designs: No. 3963, Mars 2 approaching Mars, and emblem dropped on Mars. 16k, Mars 3, which landed on Mars, Dec. 2, 1971.

1971, Apr. 5 Photo. *Perf. 11½x12*

3962 A1889 6k vio, bl & sil 10 5
3963 A1889 6k pur, ocher & sil 10 5
3964 A1889 16k pur, bl & sil 40 14

Cosmonauts' Day.

Shield and Products of Izhory Factory A1890

1972, Apr. 20 *Perf. 12½x12*

3965 A1890 4k pur & sil 10 7

250th anniversary of Izhory Factory, founded by Peter the Great.

Leonid Sobinov in "Eugene Onegin," by Tchaikovsky — A1891

1972, Apr. 20

3966 A1891 10k dp brn & buff 16 7

Centenary of the birth of Leonid Sobinov (1872-1934), opera singer.

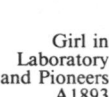

Book, Torch, Children and Globe A1892

1972, May 5 *Perf. 11½*

3967 A1892 6k brn, grnsh bl & buff 10 5

International Book Year 1972.

Girl in Laboratory and Pioneers A1893

Designs: 1k, Pavlik Morosov (Pioneer hero), Pioneers saluting and banner. 3k, Pioneers with wheelbarrow, Chukchi boy, and Chukotka Pioneer House. 4k, Pioneer Honor Guard and Parade. 30k, Pioneer Honor Guard (vert.).

1972, May 10

3968 A1893 1k red & multi 5 5
3969 A1893 2k multi 5 5
3970 A1893 3k multi 7 5
3971 A1893 4k gray & multi 10 5

Souvenir Sheet

Perf. 12x12½

3972 A1893 30k multi 1.00 40

50th anniversary of the Lenin Pioneer Organization of the USSR.

Pioneer Bugler A1894

1972, May 27 Photo. *Perf. 11½*

3973 A1894 4k red, ocher & plum 7 5

2nd Youth Philatelic Exhibition, Minsk, and 50th anniversary of Lenin Pioneer Organization.

M. S. Ordubady — A1895

1972, May 25 *Perf. 12x12½*

3974 A1895 4k org & rose brn 7 5

Centenary of the birth of M. S. Ordubady (1872-1950), Azerbaijan writer and social worker.

Globe A1896

1972, May 25 *Perf. 11½*

3975 A1896 6k multi 14 7

European Safety and Cooperation Conference, Brussels.

Cossack Leader, by Ivan Nikitin A1897

Paintings: 4k, Fedor G. Volkov (actor), by Anton Losenko. 6k, V. Majkov (poet), by Fedor Rokotov. 10k, Nikolai I. Novikov (writer), by Dimitri Levitsky. 12k, Gavriil R. Derzhavin (poet, civil servant), by Vladimir Borovikovsky. 16k, Peasants' Supper, by Mikhail Shibanov (horiz.). 20k, View of Moscow, by Fedor Alexeyev (horiz.).

Perf. 12x12½, 12½x12

1972, June 7 Litho.

3976 A1897 2k gray & multi 7 5
3977 A1897 4k gray & multi 10 5
3978 A1897 6k gray & multi 14 7
3979 A1897 10k gray & multi 20 7
3980 A1897 12k gray & multi 24 10
3981 A1897 16k gray & multi 35 16
3982 A1897 20k gray & multi 52 20
Nos. 3976-3982 (7) 1.62 70

History of Russian painting. See Nos. 4036-4042, 4074-4080, 4103-4109.

George Dimitrov A1898

Fencing, Olympic Rings A1899

1972, June 15 Photo. *Perf. 12½x12*

3983 A1898 6k brn & ol bis 10 7

90th anniversary of the birth of George Dimitrov (1882-1949), Bulgarian Communist Party leader and Premier.

1972, July 1 *Perf. 12x11½*

Designs (Olympic Rings and): 6k, Women's gymnastics. 10k, Canoeing. 14k, Boxing. 16k, Running. 50k, Weight lifting.

3984 A1899 4k brt mag & gold 7 5
3985 A1899 6k dp grn & gold 10 5
3986 A1899 10k brt bl & gold 20 7
3987 A1899 14k Prus bl & gold 25 10
3988 A1899 16k red & gold 35 14
Nos. 3984-3988 (5) 97 41

Souvenir Sheet

Perf. 11½

3989 A1899 50k gold & multi 1.25 55

20th Olympic Games, Munich, Aug. 26-Sept. 11. No. 3989 contains one stamp, size 25x35mm.

Congress Palace, Kiev — A1900

1972, July 1 Photo. & Engr.

3990 A1900 6k Prus bl & bis 10 7

9th World Gerontology Congress, Kiev, July 2-7.

Roald Amundsen, "Norway," Northern Lights A1901

1972, July 13 Photo. *Perf. 11½*

3991 A1901 6k vio bl & dp bis 10 7

Centenary of the birth of Roald Amundsen (1872-1928), Norwegian polar explorer.

17th Century House, Chernigov A1902

Designs: 4k, Market Square, Lvov (vert.). 10k, Kovnirov Building, Kiev. 16k, Fortress, Kamenets-Podolski (vert.).

Perf. 12x12½, 12½x12

1972, July 18 Litho.

3992 A1902 4k cit & multi 7 5
3993 A1902 6k gray & multi 10 5
3994 A1902 10k ocher & multi 16 7
3995 A1902 16k sal & multi 25 10

Historic and architectural treasures of the Ukraine.

Asoka Pillar, Indian Flag, Red Fort, New Delhi A1903

1972, July 27 Photo. *Perf. 11½*

3996 A1903 6k dk bl, emer & red 10 7

25th anniversary of India's independence.

Miners' Emblem A1904

1972, Aug. 10

3997 A1904 4k vio gray & red 10 7

25th Miners' Day.

Far East Fighters' Monument — A1905

Designs: 4k, Monument for Far East Civil War heroes, industrial view. 6k, Vladivostok rostral column, Pacific fleet ships.

1972, Aug. 10

3998 A1905 3k red org, car & blk 7 5
3999 A1905 4k yel, sep & blk 10 5
4000 A1905 6k pink, dk car & blk 14 7

50th anniversary of the liberation of the Far Eastern provinces.

Boy with Dog, by Murillo A1906

Perf. 12½x12, 12x12½

1972, Aug. 15 Litho.

4001 A1906 4k *Breakfast, Velazquez* (horiz.) 10 5
4002 A1906 6k *Milkmaid's Family, Louis Le Nain* (horiz.) 14 6
4003 A1906 10k *shown* 24 7
4004 A1906 16k *Sad Woman, Watteau* 35 12
4005 A1906 20k *Moroccan Saddling Steed, Delacroix* 52 18
Nos. 4001-4005 (5) 1.35 48

Souvenir Sheet

Perf. 12

4006 A1906 50k *Self-portrait, Van Dyck* 1.25 50

Paintings from the Hermitage, Leningrad.

Sputnik 1 — A1907

1972, Sept. 14 Litho. *Perf. 12x11½*

4007	A1907	6k	*shown*	14	5
4008	A1907	6k	*Launching of Vostok 2*	14	5
4009	A1907	6k	*Lenov floating in space*	14	5
4010	A1907	6k	*Lunokhod on moon*	14	5
4011	A1907	6k	*Venera 7 descending to Venus*	14	5
4012	A1907	6k	*Mars & descending to Mars*	14	5
			Nos. 4007-4012 (6)	84	30

15 years of space era. Sheets of 6.

Konstantin Mardzhanishvili A1908 К. МАРДЖАНИШВИЛИ კ. მარჯანიშვილი

1972, Sept. 20 Engr. *Perf. 12x12½*

4013 A1908 4k sl grn 10 7

Centenary of the birth of Konstantin Aleksandrovich Mardzhanishvili (1872-1933), theatrical producer.

Museum Emblem, Communications Symbols — A1909

1972, Sept. 20 Photo. *Perf. 11½*

4014 A1909 4k sl grn & multi 10 7

Centenary of the A. S. Popov Central Museum of Communications.

"Stamp" and Topical Collecting Symbols A1910

Engraved and Lithographed

1972, Oct. 4 *Perf. 12*

4015 A1910 4k yel, blk & red 10 7

Philatelic Exhibition in honor of 50th anniversary of the U.S.S.R.

Lenin A1911

1972, Oct. 12 Photo. *Perf. 11½*

4016 A1911 4k gold & red 10 7

55th anniversary of October Revolution.

Militia Badge — A1912

1972, Oct. 12

4017 A1912 4k gold, red & dk brn 10 5

55th anniversary of the Militia of the U.S.S.R.

Arms of U.S.S.R. A1913

1972, Oct. 28 *Perf. 12x11½*

4018	A1913	4k	*shown*	8	5
4019	A1913	4k	*Arms and industrial scene*	8	5
4020	A1913	4k	*Arms, Supreme Soviet, Kremlin*	8	5
4021	A1913	4k	*Lenin*	8	5
4022	A1913	4k	*Arms, worker, book (Constitution)*	8	5
			Nos. 4018-4022 (5)	40	25

Souvenir Sheet

Lithographed; Embossed

Perf. 12

4023 A1913 30k red & gold 70 40

50th anniversary of the Union of Soviet Socialist Republics. No. 4023 contains one horizontal stamp showing coat of arms and Spasski Tower. Multicolored margin with flags of the Republics. Size: 127x102mm.

Kremlin and Snowflake A1914

Savings Bank Book A1915

Engraved and Photogravure

1972, Nov. 15 *Perf. 11½*

4024 A1914 6k multi 14 5

New Year 1973.

1972, Nov. 15 Photo. *Perf. 12x12½*

4025 A1915 4k lil & sl 10 5

50th anniversary of savings banks in the USSR.

Soviet Olympic Emblem and Laurel A1916

Design: 30k, Soviet Olympic emblem and obverse of gold, silver and bronze medals.

1972, Nov. 15 *Perf. 11½*

4026 A1916 20k brn ol, red & gold 30 16
4027 A1916 30k dp car, gold & brn 42 24

Souvenir Sheet

No. 3989 Overprinted in Red

СЛАВА
СОВЕТСКИМ ОЛИМПИЙЦАМ,
ЗАВОЕВАВШИМ
50 ЗОЛОТЫХ, 27 СЕРЕБРЯНЫХ
И 22 БРОНЗОВЫЕ НАГРАДЫ!

4028 A1899 50k gold & multi 1.75 80

Soviet medalists at 20th Olympic Games.

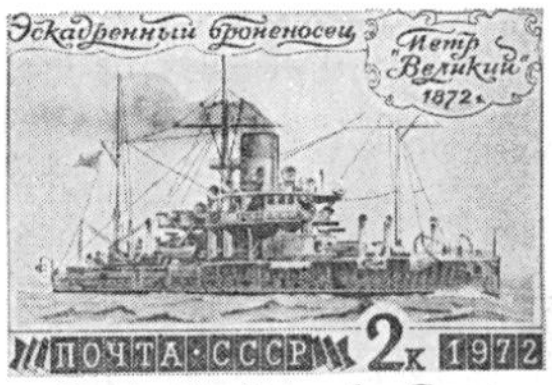
Battleship Peter the Great, 1872 — A1917

History of Russian Fleet: 3k, Cruiser Varyag, 1899. 4k, Battleship Potemkin, 1900. 6k, Cruiser Ochakov, 1902. 10k, Mine layer Amur, 1907.

Engraved and Photogravure

1972, Nov. 22 *Perf. 11½x12*

4029	A1917	2k	multi	7	5
4030	A1917	3k	multi	7	5
4031	A1917	4k	multi	10	7
4032	A1917	6k	multi	14	8
4033	A1917	10k	multi	25	10
			Nos. 4029-4033 (5)	63	35

Grigory S. Skovoroda A1918

Child Reading Traffic Rules A1919

1972, Dec. 7 Engr. *Perf. 12*

4034 A1918 4k dk vio bl 7 5

250th anniversary of the birth of Grigory S. Skovoroda (1722-1794), Ukrainian philosopher and humanist.

1972, Dec. 7 Photo. *Perf. 11½*

4035 A1919 4k Prus bl, blk & red 7 5

Traffic safety campaign.

Russian Painting Type of 1972

Paintings: 2k, Meeting of Village Party Members, by E. M. Cheptsov (horiz.). 4k, Pioneer Girl, by Nicolai A. Kasatkin. 6k, Woman Delegate, by G. G. Ryazhsky. 10k, Winter's End, by K. F. Yuon (horiz.). 16k, The Partisan A. G. Lunev, by N. I. Strunnikov. 20k, Igor E. Grabar, self-portrait. 50k, Blue Space (seascape with flying geese), by Arcadi A. Rylov (horiz.).

Perf. 12x12½, 12½x12

1972, Dec. 7 Litho.

4036	A1897	2k	ol & multi	7	5
4037	A1897	4k	ol & multi	7	6
4038	A1897	6k	ol & multi	10	7
4039	A1897	10k	ol & multi	20	10
4040	A1897	16k	ol & multi	35	14
4041	A1897	20k	ol & multi	52	16
			Nos. 4036-4041 (6)	1.31	58

Souvenir Sheet

Perf. 12

4042 A1897 50k multi 1.10 55

History of Russian painting. No.

Symbolic of Theory and Practice — A1920

Engraved and Photogravure

1972, Dec. 7 *Perf. 11½*

4043 A1920 4k sl grn, yel & red brn 7 5

Centenary of Polytechnic Museum, Moscow.

Venus 8 and Parachute A1921

Designs: No. 4045a, Venus 8. No. 4045b, Mars 3.

1972, Dec. 28 Photo. *Perf. 11½*

4044 A1921 6k dl cl, bl & blk 14 7

Souvenir Sheet

Imperf

4045	Sheet of 2	4.00	2.75
a	A1921 50k brn	1.25	75
b	A1921 50k brn	1.25	75

Soviet space research. No. 4045 contains 2 stamps with simulated perforations (size of stamps: 40x20mm.).

Globe, Torch and Palm — A1922

1973, Jan. 5 *Perf. 11x11½*

4046 A1922 10k tan, vio bl & red 24 10

15th anniversary of Afro-Asian Peoples' Solidarity Organization (AAPSO).

I. V. Babushkin A1923

"30," Map and Admiralty Tower, Leningrad A1924

1973, Jan. 10 Engr. *Perf. 12*

4047 A1923 4k grnsh blk 10 5

Centenary of the birth of I. V. Babushkin (1873-1906), revolutionary.

1973, Jan. 10 Photo. *Perf. 11½*

4048 A1924 4k pale brn, ocher & blk 10 5

30th anniversary of the breaking of the Nazi blockade of Leningrad.

TU-154 Turbojet Passenger Plane — A1925

1973, Jan. 10 Litho. *Perf. 12*
4049 A1925 6k multi 10 5

50th anniversary of Soviet Civil Aviation.

Gediminas Tower, Flag, Modern Vilnius A1926

1973, Jan. 10 Photo. *Perf. 11 1/2*
4050 A1926 10k gray, red & grn 20 7

650th anniversary of Vilnius.

Heroes' Memorial, Stalingrad — A1927

Designs (Details from Monument): 3k, Man with rifle and "Mother Russia" (vert.). 10k, Mourning mother and child. 12k, Arm with torch (vert.). No. 4055a, Red star, hammer and sickle emblem and statuary like 3k. No. 4055b, "Mother Russia" (vert.).

1973, Feb. 1 Litho. *Perf. 11 1/2*
4051 A1927 3k dp org & blk 5 5
4052 A1927 4k dp yel & blk 7 5
4053 A1927 10k ol & multi 14 7
4054 A1927 12k dp car & blk 16 7

Souvenir Sheet

Perf. 12x12 1/2, 12 1/2x12

4055 Sheet of 2 85 35
a A1927 20k multi 35 14
b A1927 20k multi 35 14

30th anniversary of the victory over the Germans at Stalingrad. No. 4055 contains 2 stamps (size: 40x18).

Large Portrait Type of 1971

Designs: 4k, Mikhail Prishvin. 10k, Fedor Chaliapin, by K. Korovin.

1973 Litho. *Perf. 11 1/2x12*
4056 A1855 4k pink & multi 7 5
4057 A1855 10k lt bl & multi 16 10

Birth centenaries of Mikhail Prishvin (1873-1954), author (4k) and Fedor Chaliapin (1873-1938), opera singer (10k). Issue dates: 4k, Feb. 1; 10k, Feb. 8.

"Mayakovsky Theater" A1928

"Mossovet Theater" A1929

1973, Feb. 1 Photo. *Perf. 11 1/2*
4058 A1928 10k red, gray & ind 16 7
4059 A1929 10k red, mag & gray 16 7

50th anniversary of the Mayakovsky and Mossovet Theaters in Moscow.

Copernicus and Solar System A1930

1973, Feb. 8 Engr. & Photo.
4060 A1930 10k ultra & sep 20 7

500th anniversary of the birth of Nicolaus Copernicus (1473-1543), Polish astronomer.

Ice Hockey A1931

Design: 50k, Two players (vert.).

1973, Mar. 14 Photo. *Perf. 11 1/2*
4061 A1931 10k gold, bl & sep 20 7

Souvenir Sheet

4062 A1931 50k bl grn, gold & sep 1.40 55

European and World Ice Hockey Championships, Moscow.

Athletes and Banners of Air, Land and Naval Forces A1932

Tank, Red Star and Map of Battle of Kursk A1933

1973, Mar. 14
4063 A1932 4k brt bl & multi 7 5

50th anniversary of the Sports Society of Soviet Army.

1973, Mar. 14
4064 A1933 4k gray, blk & red 7 5

30th anniversary of Soviet victory in the Battle of Kursk during World War II.

Nikolai E. Bauman (1873-1905), Bolshevist Revolutionary A1934

1973, Mar. 20 Engr. *Perf. 12 1/2x12*
4065 A1934 4k brown 7 5

Red Cross and Red Crescent — A1935

Designs: 6k, Theater curtain and mask. 16k, Youth Festival emblem and young people.

1973, Mar. 20 Photo. *Perf. 11*
4066 A1935 4k gray grn & red 7 5
4067 A1935 6k vio bl & red 10 7
4068 A1935 16k multi 25 10

50th anniversary of the Union of Red Cross and Red Crescent Societies of the USSR (4k); 15th Congress of the International Theater Institute (6k); 10th World Festival of Youth and Students, Berlin (16k).

Aleksandr N. Ostrovsky, by V. Perov A1936

1973, Apr. 5 Litho. *Perf. 12x12 1/2*
4069 A1936 4k tan & multi 7 5

Sesquicentennial of the birth of Aleksandr N. Ostrovsky (1823-1886), dramatist.

Earth Satellite "Interkosmos" A1937

Lunokhod 2 on Moon and Lenin Moon Plaque A1938

1973, Apr. 12 Photo. *Perf. 11 1/2*
4070 A1937 6k brn ol & dl cl 14 7
4071 A1938 6k vio bl & multi 14 7

Souvenir Sheets

Perf. 12x11 1/2

4072 Sheet of 3, pur & multi 1.50 65
a A1938 20k *Lenin plaque* 35 15
b A1938 20k *Lunokhod 2* 35 15
c A1938 20k *Telecommunications* 35 15
4073 Sheet of 3, sl grn & multi 1.50 65
a A1938 20k *Lenin plaque* 35 15
b A1938 20k *Lunokhod 2* 35 15
c A1938 20k *Telecommunications* 35 15

Cosmonauts' Day. No. 4070 commemorates cooperation in space research by European communist countries.
Souvenir sheets contain 3 horiz. stamps, size: 50x21mm.

Russian Painting Type of 1972

Paintings: 2k, Guitarist, V. A. Tropinin. 4k, Young Widow, by P. A. Fedotov. 6k, Self-portrait, by O. A. Kiprensky. 10k, Woman with Grapes ("An Afternoon in Italy") by K. P. Bryullov. 12k, Boy with Dog ("That was my Father's Dinner"), by A. Venetsianov. 20k, Soldiers ("Conquest of Siberia"), by V. I. Surikov (horiz.).

Perf. 12x12 1/2, 12 1/2x12

1973, Apr. 18 Litho.
4074 A1897 2k gray & multi 7 7
4075 A1897 4k gray & multi 10 7
4076 A1897 6k gray & multi 14 7
4077 A1897 10k gray & multi 20 14
4078 A1897 12k gray & multi 28 14
4079 A1897 16k gray & multi 35 16
4080 A1897 20k gray & multi 42 20
Nos. 4074-4080 (7) 1.56 85

Athlete, Ribbon of Lenin Order — A1939

1973, Apr. 18 Photo. *Perf. 11 1/2*
4081 A1939 4k bl, red & ocher 7 5

50th anniversary of Dynamo Sports Society.

No. 4062 with Blue Green Inscription and Ornaments Added in Margin
Souvenir Sheet

1973, Apr. 26 Photo. *Perf. 11 1/2*
4082 A1931 50k bl grn, gold & sep 85 55

Russian victory in European and World Ice Hockey Championships, Moscow. Size: 66 1/2x85mm.

"Mikhail Lermontov," Route Leningrad to New York A1940

1973, May 20 Photo. *Perf. 11 1/2*
4083 A1940 16k multi 35 14

Inauguration of transatlantic service Leningrad to New York.

Krenkel, Polar Stations and Ship Chelyuskin A1941

1973, May 20 Litho. & Engr.
4084 A1941 4k dl bl & ol 7 5

70th anniversary of birth of Ernest E. T. Krenkel (1903-1971), polar explorer.

Emblem and Sports — A1942

Singers — A1943

1973, May 20 Litho. *Perf. 12x12 1/2*
4085 A1942 4k multi 7 5

Sports Association for Labor and Defense.

1973, May 24
4086 A1943 10k multi 20 7

Centenary of Latvian Song Festival.

Throwing the Hammer — A1944

Designs: 3k, Athlete on rings. 4k, Woman diver. 16k, Fencing. 50k, Javelin.

1973, June 14 Litho. *Perf. 11 1/2*
4087 A1944 2k lem & multi 5 5
4088 A1944 3k bl & multi 7 5
4089 A1944 4k cit & multi 7 5
4090 A1944 16k lil & multi 35 10

Souvenir Sheet

4091 A1944 50k gold & multi 1.00 55

Universiad, Moscow, 1973.

Souvenir Sheet

Valentina Nikolayeva-Tereshkova — A1945

1973, June 14 Photo. *Perf. 12x11½*

4092 A1945 Sheet of 3 + label 2.50 65
- *a* 20k *as cosmonaut* 52 16
- *b* 20k *with Indian and African women* 52 16
- *c* 20k *with daughter* 52 16

10th anniversary of the flight of the first woman cosmonaut.

European Bison — A1946

1973, July 26 Photo. *Perf. 11x11½*

4093 A1946 1k *shown* 5 5
4094 A1946 3k *Ibex* 7 5
4095 A1946 4k *Caucasian snowcock* 10 7
4096 A1946 6k *Beaver* 18 7
4097 A1946 10k *Deer and fawns* 25 10
Nos. 4093-4097 (5) 65 34

Caucasus and Voronezh wildlife reserves.

Party Membership Card with Lenin Portrait — A1947

1973, July 26 Litho. *Perf. 11½*

4098 A1947 4k multi 10 7

70th anniversary of 2nd Congress of the Russian Social Democratic Workers' Party.

al-Biruni — A1948

1973, Aug. 9 Engr. *Perf. 12x12½*

4099 A1948 6k red brn 14 7

1000th anniversary of birth of abu-al-Rayhan al-Biruni (973-1048), Arabian (Persian) scholar and writer.

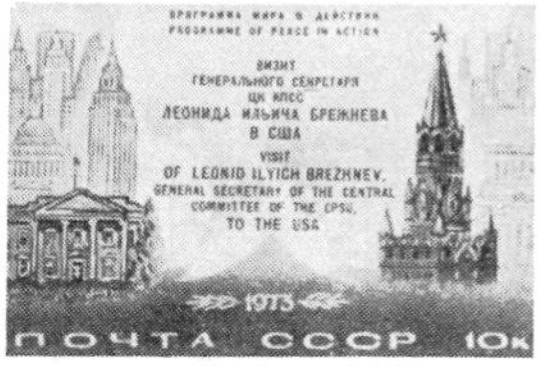

White House, Spasski Tower, Hemispheres — A1949

Designs: No. 4101, Eiffel Tower, Spasski Tower, globe. No. 4102, Schaumburg Palace, Bonn, Spasski Tower, globe. Stamps show representative buildings of Moscow, Washington, New York, Paris and Bonn.

1973, Aug. 10 Photo. *Perf. 11½x12*

4100 A1949 10k mag & multi 20 7
4101 A1949 10k brn & multi 20 7
4102 A1949 10k dp car & multi 20 7
- *a* Souvenir sheet of 3 1.00 50

Visit of General Secretary Leonid I. Brezhnev to Washington, Paris and Bonn. Nos. 4100-4102 each printed with se-tenant label with different statements by Brezhnev in Russian and English, French and German, respectively.

No. 4102a contains 4k stamps similar to Nos. 4100-4102 in changed colors, and 3 labels. Size: 133x138mm. Issued Nov. 26.

See Nos. 4161-4162.

Russian Painting Type of 1972

Paintings: 2k, S. T. Konenkov, sculptor, by P. D. Korin. 4k, Tractor Operators at Supper, by A. A. Plastov. 6k, Letter from the Front, by A. I. Laktionov. 10k, Mountains, by M. S. Saryan. 16k, Wedding on a Future Street, by Y. I. Pimenov. 20k, Ice Hockey, mosaic by A. A. Deineka. 50k, Lenin at 3rd Congress of Young Communist League, by B. V. Yoganson.

1973, Aug. 22 Litho. *Perf. 12x12½*
Frame in Light Gray

4103 A1897 2k multi 5 5
4104 A1897 4k multi 8 5
4105 A1897 6k multi 9 8
4106 A1897 10k multi 18 8
4107 A1897 16k multi 30 10
4108 A1897 20k multi 35 14
Nos. 4103-4108 (6) 1.05 50

Souvenir Sheet
Perf. 12

4109 A1897 50k multi 1.25 55

History of Russian Painting.

Museum, Tashkent A1950

Y. M. Steklov A1951

1973, Aug. 23 Photo. *Perf. 12x12½*

4110 A1950 4k multi 10 5

Lenin Central Museum, Tashkent branch.

1973, Aug. 27 Photo. *Perf. 11½x12*

4111 A1951 4k multi 10 5

Centenary of the birth of Y. M. Steklov (1873-1941), party worker, historian, writer.

Book, Pen and Torch — A1952

Echinopanax Elatum — A1953

1973, Aug. 31 *Perf. 11½*

4112 A1952 6k multi 10 5

Conference of Writers of Asia and Africa, Alma-Ata.

1973, Sept. 5 Litho. *Perf. 12x12½*

Medicinal Plants: 2k, Ginseng. 4k, Orchis maculatus. 10k, Arnica montana. 12k, Lily of the valley.

4113 A1953 1k yel & multi 5 5
4114 A1953 2k lt bl & multi 5 5
4115 A1953 4k gray & multi 7 5
4116 A1953 10k sep & multi 16 7
4117 A1953 12k grn & multi 24 7
Nos. 4113-4117 (5) 57 29

Imadeddin Nasimi — A1954

1973, Sept. 5 Engr.

4118 A1954 4k sepia 7 5

600th anniversary of the birth of Imadeddin Nasimi, Azerbaijani poet.

Cruiser Kirov — A1955

Soviet Warships: 4k, Battleship October Revolution. 6k, Submarine Krasnogvardeyets. 10k, Torpedo boat Soobrazitelny. 16k, Cruiser Red Caucasus.

Engraved and Photogravure
1973, Sept. 12 *Perf. 11½x12*

4119 A1955 3k vio & multi 7 5
4120 A1955 4k grn & multi 10 5
4121 A1955 6k multi 16 7
4122 A1955 10k bl grn & multi 25 10
4123 A1955 16k multi 40 16
Nos. 4119-4123 (5) 98 43

Globe and Red Flag Emblem — A1956

1973, Sept. 25 Photo. *Perf. 11½*

4124 A1956 6k gold, buff & red 14 7

15th anniversary of the international communist review "Problems of Peace and Socialism," published in Prague.

Emelyan I. Pugachev and Peasant Army — A1957

Engraved and Photogravure
1973, Sept. 25 *Perf. 11½x12*

4125 A1957 4k brn, bis & red 10 5

Bicentenary of peasant revolt of 1773-75 led by Emelyn Ivanovich Pugachev.

Crystal, Institute Emblem and Building A1958

1973, Oct. 5 *Perf. 11½*

4126 A1958 4k blk & multi 10 5

Bicentenary of the Leningrad Mining Institute.

Palm, Globe, Flower A1959

Elena Stasova A1960

1973, Oct. 5 Photo.

4127 A1959 6k red, gray & dk bl 14 7

World Congress of Peace-loving Forces, Moscow.

1973, Oct. 5 *Perf. 11½x12*

4128 A1960 4k dp cl 10 5

Centenary of the birth of Elena Dmitriyevna Stasova (1873-1966), communist party worker.

See Nos. 4228-4229.

Order of Friendship A1961

1973, Oct. 5 Litho. *Perf. 12*

4129 A1961 4k red & multi 10 5

56th anniversary of the October Revolution. Printed se-tenant with coupon showing Arms of USSR and proclamation establishing Order of Friendship of People, in 1972, on the 50th anniversary of the USSR.

Marshal Malinovsky A1962

Ural Man, Red Guard, Worker A1963

1973, Oct. 5 Engr.

4130 A1962 4k slate 10 5

75th anniversary of the birth of Marshal Rodion Y. Malinovsky (1898-1967).

See Nos. 4203-4205.

1973, Oct. 17 Photo. *Perf. 11½*

4131 A1963 4k red, gold & blk 10 5

250th anniversary of the city of Sverdlovsk.

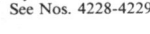

Dimitri Cantemir — A1964

1973, Oct. 17 Engr. *Perf. 12x12½*
4132 A1964 4k rose cl 10 5

300th anniversary of the birth of Dimitri Cantemir (1673-1723), Prince of Moldavia, writer.

Salvador Allende A1965

1973, Nov. 26 Photo. *Perf. 11½*
4133 A1965 6k rose brn & blk 14 7

Salvador Allende (1908-1973), President of Chile.

Spasski Tower, Kremlin A1966

Nariman Narimanov A1967

1973, Nov. 30 Litho. *Perf. 12x12½*
4134 A1966 6k brt bl & multi 14 7

New Year 1974.

1973, Nov. 30 Engr. *Perf. 12*
4135 A1967 4k sl grn 10 5

Nariman Narimanov (1870-1925), Chairman of Executive Committee of USSR.

Russo-Balt, 1909 — A1968

Designs: 3k, AMO-F15 truck, 1924. 4k, Spartak, NAMI-1 car, 1927. 12k, Ya-6 autobus, 1929. 16k, GAZ-A car, 1932.

1973, Nov. 30 Photo. *Perf. 12x11½*
4136 A1968 2k pur & multi 5 5
4137 A1968 3k ol & multi 7 5
4138 A1968 4k ocher & multi 10 7
4139 A1968 12k vio bl & multi 25 7
4140 A1968 16k red & multi 42 10
Nos. 4136-4140 (5) 89 34

Development of Russian automotive industry. See Nos. 4216-4220, 4325-4329, 4440-4444.

Still Life, by Frans Snyders — A1969

Paintings: 6k, Woman Trying on Earrings, by Rembrandt (vert.). 10k, Sick Woman and Physician, by Jan Steen (vert.). 12k, Still Life with Sculpture, by Jean-Baptiste Chardin. 14k, Lady in Garden, by Claude Monet. 16k, Young Love, by Jules Bastien-Lepage (vert.). 20k Girl with Fan, by Auguste Renoir (vert.). 50k, Flora, by Rembrandt (vert.).

Perf. 12x11½, 11½x12
1973, Dec. 12 Litho.
4141 A1969 4k bis & multi 10 8
4142 A1969 6k bis & multi 14 7
4143 A1969 10k bis & multi 24 7
4144 A1969 12k bis & multi 25 10
4145 A1969 14k bis & multi 30 14
4146 A1969 16k bis & multi 35 15
4147 A1969 20k bis & multi 45 16
Nos. 4141-4147 (7) 1.83 77

Souvenir Sheet
Perf. 12
4148 A1969 50k multi 1.25 55

Foreign paintings in Russian museums.

Pablo Picasso A1970

1973, Dec. 20 Photo. *Perf. 12x11½*
4149 A1970 6k gold, sl grn & red 14 7

Pablo Picasso (1881-1973), painter.

Organ Pipes and Dome, Riga — A1971

Designs: No. 4151, Small Trakai Castle, Lithuania. No. 4152, Great Sea Gate, Tallinn, Estonia. 10k, Town Hall and "Old Thomas" weather vane, Tallinn.

1973, Dec. 20 Engr. *Perf. 12x12½*
4150 A1971 4k blk, red & sl grn 7 5
4151 A1971 4k gray, red & buff 7 5
4152 A1971 4k blk, red & grn 7 5
4153 A1971 10k sep, grn, red & blk 24 7

Architecture of the Baltic area.

I. G. Petrovsky A1972

L. A. Artsimovich A1973

Portraits: No. 4154, I. G. Petrovsky (1901-1973), mathematician, rector of Moscow State University. No. 4155, L. A. Artsimovich (1909-1973), physician, academician. No. 4156, K. D. Ushinsky (1824-1874), teacher. No. 4157, M. D. Millionschikov (1913-1973), vice president of Academy of Sciences.

1973-74 Photo. *Perf. 11½*
4154 A1972 4k org & multi 7 5
4155 A1973 4k blk brn & ol 7 5

Engr.
Perf. 12½x12
4156 A1973 4k multi 7 5

Litho.
Perf. 12
4157 A1973 4k multi 7 5

Issue dates: No. 4154, Dec. 28, 1973. Others, Feb. 6, 1974.

Flags of India and USSR, Red Fort, Taj Mahal and Kremlin — A1974

Design: No. 4162, Flags of Cuba and USSR, José Martí Monument, Moncada Barracks and Kremlin.

1973-74 Litho. *Perf. 12*
4161 A1974 4k lt ultra & multi 7 5
4162 A1974 4k lt grn & multi ('74) 7 5

Visit of General Secretary Leonid I. Brezhnev to India and Cuba. Nos. 4161-4162 each printed with se-tenant label with different statements by Brezhnev in Russian and Hindi, and Russian and Spanish respectively.

Red Star, Soldier, Newspaper — A1975

1974, Jan. 1 Photo. *Perf. 11x11½*
4166 A1975 4k gold, red & blk 10 5

50th anniversary of the Red Star newspaper.

Victory Monument, Peter-Paul Fortress, Statue of Peter I — A1976

1974, Jan. 16 Litho. *Perf. 11½*
4167 A1976 4k multi 10 5

30th anniversary of the victory over the Germans near Leningrad.

Oil Workers, Refinery A1977

Comecon Building A1978

1974, Jan. 16 Photo. *Perf. 11½*
4168 A1977 4k dl bl, red & blk 10 5

10th anniversary of the Tyumen oilfields.

1974, Jan. 16 Photo. *Perf. 11½*
4169 A1978 16k red brn, ol & red 20 15

25th anniversary of the Council for Mutual Economic Assistance.

Skaters and Rink, Medeo A1979

1974, Jan. 28
4170 A1979 6k sl, brn red & bl 14 10

European Women's Skating Championships, Medeo, Alma-Ata.

Art Palace, Leningrad, Academy, Moscow A1980

Photogravure and Enbraved
1974, Jan. 30
4171 A1980 10k multi 20 15

25th anniversary of the Academy of Sciences of the USSR.

3rd Winter Spartiakad Emblem A1981

Young People and Emblem A1982

1974, Mar. 20 Photo. *Perf. 11½*
4172 A1981 10k gold & multi 20 15

Third Winter Spartiakad.

Photogravure and Engraved
1974, Mar. 20
4173 A1982 4k multi 10 5

Youth scientific-technical work.

Azerbaijan Theater — A1983

1974, Mar. 20 Photo. *Perf. 11½*
4174 A1983 6k org, red brn & brn 14 7

Centenary of Azerbaijan Theater.

Meteorological Satellite "Meteor" — A1984

Cosmonauts V. G. Lazarev and O. G. Makarov and Soyuz 12 — A1985

Design: No. 4177, Cosmonauts P. I. Klimuk and V. V. Lebedev, and Soyuz 13.

1974, Mar. 27 ***Perf. 11½***
4175 A1984 6k vio & multi 14 5

Perf. 12x11½
4176 A1985 10k grnsh bl & multi 20 7
4177 A1985 10k dl yel & multi 20 7

Cosmonauts' Day.

Odessa by Moonlight, by Aivazovski — A1986

Seascapes by Aivazovski: 4k, Battle of Chesma, 1848 (vert.). 6k, St. George's Monastery. 10k, Stormy Sea. 12k, Rainbow (shipwreck). 16k, Shipwreck. 50k, Portrait of Aivazovski, by Kramskoy (vert.).

Perf. 12x11½, 11½x12
1974, Mar. 30 **Litho.**
4178 A1986 2k gray & multi 5 5
4179 A1986 4k gray & multi 10 5
4180 A1986 6k gray & multi 16 8
4181 A1986 10k gray & multi 25 8
4182 A1986 12k gray & multi 30 12
4183 A1986 16k gray & multi 42 18
Nos. 4178-4183 (6) 1.28 56

Souvenir Sheet
4184 A1986 50k gray & multi 1.25 55

Ivan Konstantinovich Aivazovski (1817-1900), marine painter. Sheets of Nos. 4178-4183 each contain 2 labels with commemorative inscriptions.

Young Man and Woman, Banner A1987

1974, Mar. 30 **Litho.** ***Perf. 12½x12***
4185 A1987 4k red, yel & brn 7 5

17th Congress of the Young Communist League.

Lenin, by V. E. Tsigal A1988

1974, Mar. 30
4186 A1988 4k yel, red & brn 7 5

50th anniversary of naming the Komsomol (Young Communist League) after Lenin.

Souvenir Sheet

Lenin at the Telegraph, by Igor E. Grabar — A1989

1974, Apr. 16 **Litho.** ***Perf. 12***
4187 A1989 50k multi 1.10 55

104th anniv. of the birth of Lenin.

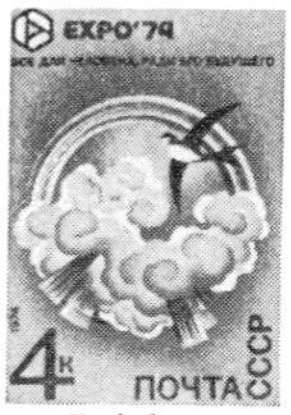

Rainbow, Swallow over Clouds A1990

Congress Emblem and Clover A1991

Designs (EXPO '74 Emblem and): 6k, Fish in water. 10k, Crystal. 16k, Rose. 20k, Fawn. 50k, Infant.

1974, Apr. 24 **Photo.** ***Perf. 11½***
4188 A1990 4k lil & multi 7 5
4189 A1990 6k multi 14 7
4190 A1990 10k multi 24 10
4191 A1990 16k bl & multi 35 14
4192 A1990 20k cit & multi 42 16
Nos. 4188-4192 (5) 1.22 52

Souvenir Sheet
Litho.
Perf. 12x12½
4193 A1990 50k bl & multi 1.10 55

EXPO '74 World's Fair, theme "Preserve the Environment," Spokane, Washington, May 4-Nov. 4.

1974, May 7 **Photo.** ***Perf. 11½***
4194 A1991 4k grn & multi 7 5

12th International Congress on Meadow Cultivation, Moscow, 1974.

"Cobblestones, Weapons of the Proletariat," by I. D. Shadra — A1992

1974, May 7
4195 A1992 4k gold, red & ol 7 5

50th anniversary of the Lenin Central Revolutionary Museum of the USSR.

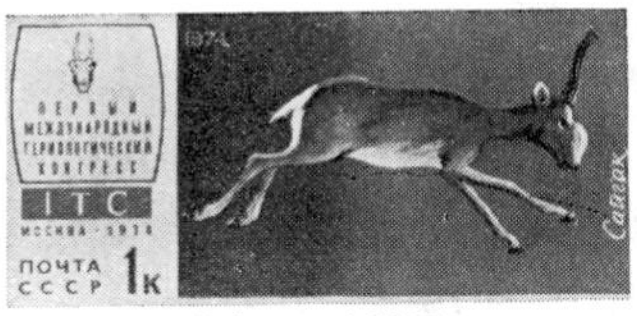

Saiga — A1993

Fauna of USSR: 3k, Koulan (wild ass). 4k, Desman. 6k, Sea lion. 10k, Greenland whale.

1974, May 22 **Litho.** ***Perf. 11½***
4196 A1993 1k ol & multi 5 5
4197 A1993 3k grn & multi 7 5
4198 A1993 4k multi 10 7
4199 A1993 6k multi 16 7
4200 A1993 10k multi 25 7
Nos. 4196-4200 (5) 63 31

Peter Ilich Tchaikovsky A1994

1974, May 22 **Photo.** ***Perf. 11½***
4201 A1994 6k multi 16 7

5th International Tchaikovsky Competition, Moscow.

Souvenir Sheet

Aleksander S. Pushkin, by O. A. Kiprensky — A1995

1974, June 4 **Litho.** ***Imperf.***
4202 A1995 50k multi 1.10 55

Aleksander S. Pushkin (1799-1837).

Marshal Type of 1973

1974 **Engr.** ***Perf. 12***
4203 A1962 4k ol grn 7 5
4204 A1962 4k indigo 7 5
4205 A1962 4k sl grn 7 5

Marshal F. I. Tolbukhin (1894-1949) (No. 4203). Admiral I. S. Isakov (1894-1967) (No. 4204); Marshal S. M. Budenny (1883-1973) (No. 4205).
Issue dates: No. 4203, June 5; No. 4204, July 18; No. 4205, Aug. 20.

Stanislavski and Nemirovich-Danchenko — A1996

1974, June 12 **Litho.** ***Perf. 12***
4211 A1996 10k yel, blk & dk red 24 7

75th anniversary of the Moscow Arts Theater.

Runner, Track, Open Book A1997

1974, June 12 **Photo.** ***Perf. 11½***
4212 A1997 4k multi 7 5

13th National School Spartakiad, Alma-Ata.

Railroad Car — A1998

1974, June 12
4213 A1998 4k multi 7 5

Centenary of the Egorov Railroad Car Factory.

Victory Monument, Minsk A1999

Liberation Monument, Poltava A2000

Design: No. 4215, Monument and Government House, Kiev.

1974, June 20
4214 A1999 4k vio, blk & yel 7 5
4215 A1999 4k bl, blk & yel 7 5

30th anniversary of liberation of Byelorussia (No. 4214), and of Ukraine (No. 4215).
Issue dates: No. 4214, June 20; No. 4215, July 18.

Automotive Type of 1973

Designs: 2k, GAZ AA truck, 1932. 3k, GAZ 03-30 bus, 1933. 4k, Zis 5 truck, 1933. 14k, Zis 8 bus, 1934. 16k, Zis 101 car, 1936.

1974, June 20 ***Perf. 12x11½***
4216 A1968 2k brn & multi 5 5
4217 A1968 3k multi 7 5
4218 A1968 4k org & multi 10 7
4219 A1968 14k multi 35 10
4220 A1968 16k multi 38 14
Nos. 4216-4220 (5) 95 41

Russian automotive industry.

1974, July 7 ***Perf. 11½***
4221 A2000 4k dl red & sep 10 5

800th anniversary of city of Poltava.

Nike Monument, Warsaw and Polish Flag A2001

1974, July 7 **Litho.** ***Perf. 12½x12***
4222 A2001 6k ol & red 14 7

Polish People's Republic, 30th anniversary.

Mine Layer — A2002

Soviet Warships: 4k, Landing craft. 6k, Anti-submarine destroyer and helicopter. 16k, Anti-submarine cruiser.

Engraved and Photogravure
1974, July 25 ***Perf. 11½x12***
4223 A2002 3k multi 9 5
4224 A2002 4k multi 10 7
4225 A2002 6k multi 18 7
4226 A2002 16k multi 35 14

The lack of a value for a listed item does not necessarily indicate rarity.

Pentathlon A2003

1974, Aug. 7 Photo. *Perf. 11½*
4227 A2003 16k gold, bl & brn 30 14

World Pentathlon Championships, Moscow.

Portrait Type of 1973

Portraits: No. 4228, Dimitri Ulyanov (1874-1943). Soviet official and Lenin's brother. No. 4229, V. Menzhinsky (1874-1934), Soviet official.

1974, Aug. 7 Engr. *Perf. 12½x12*
4228 A1960 4k sl grn 7 5

Litho.

Perf. 12x11½
4229 A1960 4k rose lake 7 5

Painting Type of 1974

Designs: 4k, Lilac, by W. Kontchalovski. 6k, "Towards the Wind" (sailboats), by E. Kalnins. 10k, "Spring" (girl and landscape), by O. Zardarjan. 16k, Northern Harbor, G. Nissky. 20k, Kirghiz Girl, by S. Tchnikov (vert.).

Perf. 12x11½, 11½x12
1974, Aug. 20 Litho.
4230 A1986 4k gray & multi 10 7
4231 A1986 6k gray & multi 14 7
4232 A1986 10k gray & multi 24 10
4233 A1986 16k gray & multi 38 10
4234 A1986 20k gray & multi 50 16
Nos. 4230-4234 (5) 1.36 50

Russian paintings. Printed in sheets of 18 stamps and 2 labels.

Page of First Russian Primer A2004

Monument, Russian and Romanian Flags A2005

1974, Aug. 20 Photo. *Perf. 11½*
4235 A2004 4k blk, red & gold 10 5

400th anniversary of the first printed Russian primer.

1974, Aug. 23
4236 A2005 6k dk bl, red & yel 14 7

Romania's liberation from Fascist rule, 30th anniversary.

Vitebsk A2006

1974, Sept. 4 Litho. *Perf. 12*
4237 A2006 4k dk car & ol 10 5

Millennium of city of Vitebsk.

Kirghiz Republic A2007

Designs: Flags, industrial and agricultural themes of various Republics. No. 4239, Moldavia. No. 4240, Turkmen. No. 4241, Uzbek. No. 4242, Tadzhik.

1974, Sept. 4 *Perf. 11½x11*
4238 A2007 4k vio bl & multi 10 5
4239 A2007 4k mar & multi 10 5
4240 A2007 4k yel & multi 10 5
4241 A2007 4k grn & multi 10 5
4242 A2007 4k lt bl & multi 10 5
Nos. 4238-4242 (5) 50 25

50th anniversary of the founding of the Kirghiz, Moldavian, Turkmenian, Uzbek and Tadzhik Soviet Socialist Republics.

Arms and Flag of Bulgaria — A2008

Photogravure and Engraved
1974, Sept. 4 *Perf. 11½*
4243 A2008 6k gold & multi 14 7

30th anniversary of the Bulgarian revolution.

Arms of DDR and Soviet War Memorial, Treptow A2009

1974, Sept. 4 Photo.
4244 A2009 6k multi 14 7

25th anniversary of the German Democratic Republic.

Souvenir Sheet

Russian Stamps and Exhibition Poster — A2010

1974, Sept. 4 Litho. *Perf. 12x12½*
4245 A2010 50k multi *3.00 2.00*

3rd Cong. of the Philatelic Soc. of the USSR.

Maly State Theater — A2011

1974, Oct. 3 Photo. *Perf. 11x11½*
4246 A2011 4k red, blk & gold 10 5

150th anniversary of the Lenin Academic Maly State Theater, Moscow.

"Guests from Overseas," by N. K. Roerich — A2012

1974, Oct. 3 Litho. *Perf. 12*
4247 A2012 6k multi 14 7

Birth centenary of Nicholas Konstantin Roerich (1874-1947), painter and sponsor of Roerich Pact and Banner of Peace.

UPU Monument, Bern, and Arms of USSR — A2013

Development of Postal Service — A2014

UPU Cent.: No. 4248, Ukrainian coat of arms, letters, UPU emblem and headquarters, Bern. No. 4249, Arms of Byelorussia, UPU emblem, letters, stagecoach and rocket.

Photogravure and Engraved
1974, Oct. 9 *Perf. 12x11½*
4248 A2013 10k red & multi 24 10
4249 A2013 10k red & multi 24 10
4250 A2013 10k red & multi 24 10

Souvenir Sheet

Typo.

Perf. 11½x12
4251 A2014 Sheet of 3 4.00 1.25
a 30k *Jet and UPU emblem* 1.00 35
b 30k *Mail coach and UPU emblem* 1.00 35
c 40k *UPU emblem* 1.00 35

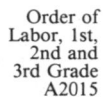

Order of Labor, 1st, 2nd and 3rd Grade A2015

KAMAZ Truck Leaving Kama Plant — A2016

Design: No. 4254, Nurek Hydroelectric Plant.

1974, Oct. 16 Litho. *Perf. 12½x12*
4252 A2015 4k multi 7 5
4253 A2016 4k multi 7 5
4254 A2016 4k multi 7 5

Space Stations Mars 4-7 over Mars — A2017

P. R. Popovitch, Y. P. Artyukhin and Soyuz 14 — A2018

Design: No. 4257, Cosmonauts G. V. Sarafanov and L. S. Demin, Soyuz 15, (horiz.).

Perf. 12x11½, 11½
1974, Oct. 28 Photo.
4255 A2017 6k multi 10 5
4256 A2018 10k multi 16 10
4257 A2018 10k multi 16 10

Russian explorations of Mars (6k); flight of Soyuz 14 (No. 4256) and of Soyuz 15, Aug. 26-28 (No. 4257).

Mongolian Flag and Arms A2019

1974, Nov. 14 Photo. *Perf. 11½*
4258 A2019 6k gold & multi 14 7

Mongolian People's Republic, 50th anniversary.

Guards' Ribbon, Estonian Government Building, Tower — A2020

1974, Nov. 14
4259 A2020 4k multi 10 5

Liberation of Estonia, 30th anniversary.

Tanker, Passenger and Cargo Ships A2021

1974, Nov. 14 Typo. *Perf. 12½x12*
4260 A2021 4k multi 10 5

USSR Merchant Marine, 50th anniversary.

Spasski Tower Clock A2022

1974, Nov. 14 Litho. *Perf. 12*
4261 A2022 4k multi 10 5

New Year 1975.

The Fishmonger, by Pieters
A2023

Paintings: 4k, The Marketplace, by Beukelaer, 1564 (horiz.). 10k, A Drink of Lemonade, by Gerard Terborch. 14k, Girl at Work, by Gabriel Metsu. 16k, Saying Grace, by Jean Chardin. 20k, The Spoiled Child, by Jean Greuze. 50k, Self-portrait, by Jacques Louis David.

Perf. 12x12½, 12½x12
1974 Nov. 20 Litho.

4262	A2023	4k	bis & multi	10	7
4263	A2023	6k	bis & multi	18	7
4264	A2023	10k	bis & multi	25	10
4265	A2023	14k	bis & multi	35	14
4266	A2023	16k	bis & multi	38	16
4267	A2023	20k	bis & multi	52	20
			Nos. 4262-4267 (6)	1.78	74

Souvenir Sheet
Perf. 12

4268 A2023 50k multi 1.10 50

Foreign paintings in Russian museums. Printed in sheets of 16 stamps and 4 labels.

Morning Glory
A2024

Ivan Nikitin
A2025

Designs: Flora of the USSR.

1974, Nov. 20 *Perf. 12x12½*

4269	A2024	1k	red brn & multi	5	5
4270	A2024	2k	grn & multi	6	5
4271	A2024	4k	multi	10	7
4272	A2024	10k	brn & multi	25	10
4273	A2024	12k	dk bl & multi	30	14
			Nos. 4269-4273 (5)	76	41

1974, Dec. 11 Photo. *Perf. 11½*
4274 A2025 4k gray grn, grn & blk 7 5

Sesquicentennial of the birth of Ivan S. Nikitin (1824-1861), poet.

Leningrad Mint — A2026

Photogravure and Engraved
1974, Dec. 11 *Perf. 11*
4275 A2026 6k sil & multi 14 7

250th anniversary of the Leningrad Mint.

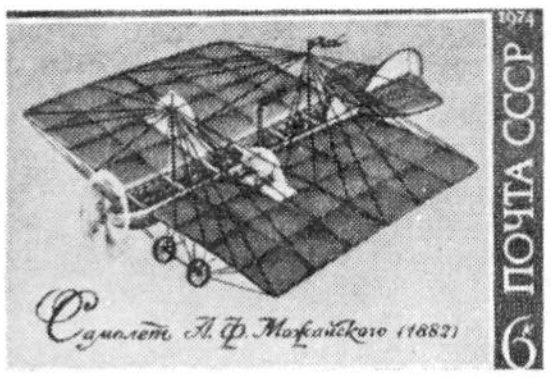
Mozhaisky Plane, 1882 — A2027

Early Russian Aircraft: No. 4277, Grizidubov-N biplane, 1910. No. 4278, Russia-A, 1910. No. 4279, Russian Vityaz (Sikorsky), 1913. No. 4280, Grigorovich flying boat, 1914.

1974, Dec. 25 Photo. *Perf. 11½x12*

4276	A2027	6k	ol & multi	16	7
4277	A2027	6k	ultra & multi	16	7
4278	A2027	6k	mag & multi	16	7
4279	A2027	6k	red & multi	16	7
4280	A2027	6k	brn & multi	16	7
			Nos. 4276-4280 (5)	80	35

Russian aircraft history, 1882-1914.

Souvenir Sheet

Sports and Sport Buildings, Moscow — A2028

1974, Dec. 25 *Perf. 11½*

4281	A2028		Sheet of 4	1.00	40
a		10k	*Woman gymnast*	20	7
b		10k	*Running*	20	7
c		10k	*Soccer*	20	7
d		10k	*Canoeing*	20	7

Moscow preparing for Summer Olympic Games, 1980.

Rotary Press, Masthead
A2029

1975, Jan. 20
4282 A2029 4k multi 7 5

50th anniv. of the newspaper Komsomolskaya Pravda.

Masthead and Pioneer Emblems
A2030

Spartakiad Emblem and Skiers
A2031

1975, Jan. 20
4283 A2030 4k red, blk & sil 7 5

50th anniversary of the newspaper Pioneers' Pravda.

1975, Jan. 20
4284 A2031 4k bl & multi 7 5

8th Winter Spartakiad of USSR Trade Unions.

Games' Emblem, Hockey Player and Skier
A2032

1975, Jan. 20
4285 A2032 16k multi 35 16

5th Winter Spartakiad of Friendly Armies, Feb. 23-Mar. 1.

Republic Anniversaries Type of 1970

Design (Hammer-Sickle Emblem and): No. 4286, Landscape and produce.

1975, Jan. 24 Engr. *Perf. 12x12½*
4286 A1794 4k green 7 5

50th anniversary of Karakalpak Autonomous Soviet Socialist Republic.

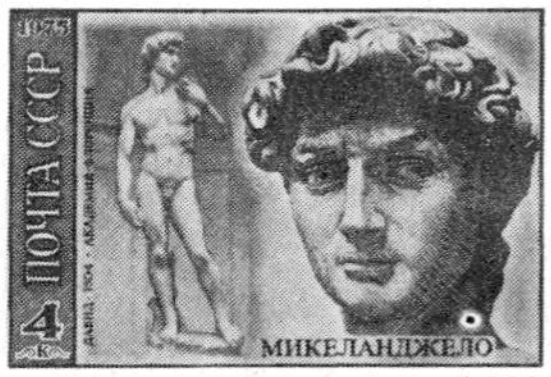
David, by Michelangelo — A2033

Michelangelo, Self-portrait
A2034

Designs (Works by Michelangelo): 6k, Squatting Boy. 10k, Rebellious Slave. 14k, The Creation of Adam. 20k, Staircase, Laurentian Library, Florence. 30k, The Last Judgment.

Lithographed and Engraved
1975, Feb. 27 *Perf. 12½x12*

4296	A2033	4k	sl grn & grn	10	7
4297	A2033	6k	red brn & bis	14	7
4298	A2033	10k	sl grn & grn	24	10
a			Miniature sheet of 6	1.25	50
4299	A2033	14k	red brn & bis	35	10
4300	A2033	20k	sl grn & grn	50	16
4301	A2033	30k	red brn & bis	70	24
a			Miniature sheet of 6	4.00	1.50
			Nos. 4296-4301 (6)	2.03	74

Souvenir Sheet
Perf. 12x11½

4302 A2034 50k gold & multi 1.25 50

500th birth anniversary of Michelangelo Buonarroti (1475-1564), Italian sculptor, painter and architect. Nos. 4296-4301 were issued only in miniature sheets of 6 with green and brown margins and inscriptions. No. 4298a contains 2 each of Nos. 4296-4298; No. 4301a contains 2 each of Nos. 4299-4301.

Mozhajski, Early Plane and Supersonic Jet TU-144 — A2035

1975, Feb. 27 Photo. *Perf. 12x11½*
4303 A2035 6k vio bl & ocher 14 7

A. F. Mozhajski (1825-1890), pioneer aircraft designer, birth sesquicentennial.

"Metric System"
A2036

1975, Mar. 14 *Perf. 11½*
4304 A2036 6k blk, vio bl & org 14 7

Centenary of International Meter Convention, Paris, 1875.

Spartakiad Emblem and Sports
A2037

1975, Mar. 14
4305 A2037 6k red, sil & blk 14 7

6th Summer Spartakiad.

Liberation Monument, Parliament, Arms — A2038

Charles Bridge Towers, Arms and Flags — A2039

1975, Mar. 14

4306	A2038	6k	gold & multi	14	7
4307	A2039	6k	gold & multi	14	7

30th anniversary of liberation from fascism, Hungary (No. 4306) and Czechoslovakia (No. 4307).

Flags of France and USSR
A2040

Yuri A. Gagarin, by L. Kerbel
A2041

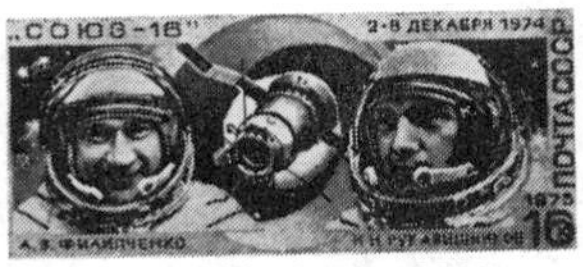
A. V. Filipchenko, N.N. Rukavishnikov, Russo-American Space Emblem, Soyuz 16 — A2042

1975, Mar. 25 Litho. *Perf. 12*
4308 A2040 6k lil & multi 14 7

50th anniversary of the establishment of diplomatic relations between France and USSR, first foreign recognition of Soviet State.

Perf. 11½x12, 12x11½
1975, Mar. 28 Photo.

Design: 10k, A. A. Gubarev, G. M. Grechko aboard Soyuz 17 and orbital station Salyut 4.

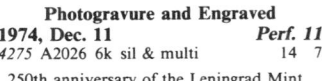

4309 A2041 6k bl, sil & red 10 5
4310 A2042 10k blk, bl & red 20 7
4311 A2042 16k multi 25 10

Cosmonauts' Day.

Warsaw Treaty Members' Flags — A2043

1975, Apr. 16 Litho. *Perf. 12*
4312 A2043 6k multi 14 7

20th anniversary of the signing of the Warsaw Treaty (Bulgaria, Czechoslovakia, German Democratic Rep., Hungary, Poland, Romania, USSR).

Lenin on Steps of Winter Palace, by V. G. Zyplakow A2044

1975, Apr. 22 *Perf. 12x12½*
4313 A2044 4k multi 10 5

105th anniversary of the birth of Lenin.

Communications Emblem and Exhibition Pavilion — A2045

1975, Apr. 22 *Perf. 11½*
4314 A2045 6k ultra, red & sil 14 7

International Communications Exhibition, Sokolniki Park, Moscow, May 1975.

Lenin and Red Flag A2046

War Memorial, Berlin-Treptow A2048

Order of Victory — A2047

1975, Apr. 22 Typo. *Perf. 12*
4315 A2046 4k *shown* 10 5
4316 A2046 4k *Eternal Flame and guard* 10 5
4317 A2046 4k *Woman munitions worker* 10 5
4318 A2046 4k *Partisans* 10 5
4319 A2046 4k *Soldier destroying swastika* 10 5
4320 A2046 4k *Soldier with gun and banner* 10 5
Nos. 4315-4320 (6) 60 30

Souvenir Sheet

Litho., Typo. & Photo.

Imperf

4321 A2047 50k multi 1.00 50

World War II victory, 30th anniversary.

1975, Apr. 25 Litho. *Perf. 12x12½*
4322 A2048 6k buff & multi 14 7

Souvenir Sheet

4323 A2048 50k dl bl & multi 1.00 50

Socfilex 75 Intl. Phil. Exhib. commemorating 30th anniv. of WW II victory, Moscow, May 8-18.

Soyuz-Apollo Docking Emblem and Painting by Cosmonaut A. A. Leonov — A2049

1975, May 8 Photo. *Perf. 12x11½*
4324 A2049 20k multi 50 25

Russo-American space cooperation.

Automobile Type of 1973

Designs: 2k, GAZ-M-I car, 1936. 3k, 5-ton truck, YAG-6, 1936. 4k, ZIZ-16, autobus, 1938. 12k, KIM-10 car, 1940. 16k, GAZ-67B jeep, 1943.

1975, May 23 Photo. *Perf. 12x11½*
4325 A1968 2k dp org & multi 5 5
4326 A1968 3k grn & multi 7 5
4327 A1968 4k dk grn & multi 10 7
4328 A1968 12k mar & multi 25 10
4329 A1968 16k ol & multi 38 10
Nos. 4325-4329 (5) 85 37

Canal, Emblem, Produce — A2050

1975, May 23 *Perf. 11½*
4330 A2050 6k multi 14 7

9th International Congress on Irrigation and Drainage, Moscow, and 25th anniversary of International Commission on Irrigation and Drainage.

Flags and Arms of Poland and USSR, Factories A2051

1975, May 23
4331 A2051 6k multi 14 7

Treaty of Friendship, Cooperation and Mutual Assistance between Poland and USSR, 30th anniversary.

Man in Space and Earth A2052

1975, May 23
4332 A2052 6k multi 14 7

First man walking in space, Lt. Col. Alexei Leonov, 10th anniversary.

Yakov M. Sverdlov — A2053

1975, June 4
4333 A2053 4k multi 10 5

Yakov M. Sverdlov (1885-1919), organizer and early member of Communist party, 90th anniversary of birth.

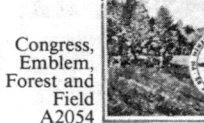

Congress, Emblem, Forest and Field A2054

1975, June 4
4334 A2054 6k multi 14 7

8th International Congress for Conservation of Plants, Moscow.

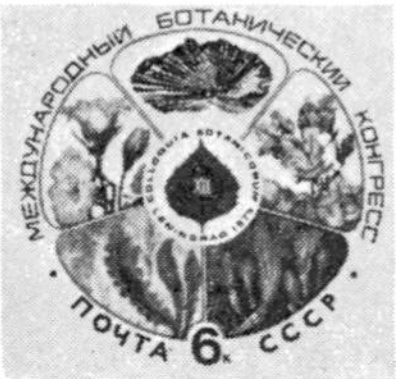

Symbolic Flower with Plants and Emblem A2055

1975, June 20 Litho. *Perf. 11½*
4335 A2055 6k multi 14 7

12th International Botanical Congress.

Souvenir Sheet

U.N. Emblem — A2056

1975, June 20 Photo. *Perf. 11½x12*
4336 A2056 50k gold & bl 1.00 50

30th anniversary of United Nations.

Globe and Film A2057

1975, June 20 Photo. *Perf. 11½*
4337 A2057 6k multi 14 7

9th International Film Festival, Moscow, 1975.

Russian and American Astronauts and Flags — A2058

Apollo and Soyuz After Link-up and Earth — A2059

Soyuz Launch — A2060

Designs: No. 4340, Spacecraft before link-up, earth and project emblem. 50k, Soviet Mission Control Center.

1975, July 15 Litho. *Perf. 11½*
4338 A2058 10k multi 20 10
4339 A2059 12k multi 35 14
4340 A2059 12k multi 35 14
4341 A2060 16k multi 40 20

Souvenir Sheet

Photo.

Perf. 12x11½

4342 A2058 50k multi 1.25 65

Apollo-Soyuz space test project (Russo-American space cooperation), launching, July 15; link-up July 17. Nos. 4339-4340 printed se-tenant vertically in sheets of 12 (3x4). See U.S. Nos. 1569-1570.

No. 4342 contains one stamp (50x21mm.); multicolored margin with Apollo-Soyuz project emblem. Portraits of participating U.S.S.R. and U.S. crews: Aleksei A. Leonov, Valery N. Kubasov, Thomas P. Stafford, Vance D. Brand and Donald K. Slayton.

Sturgeon, Caspian Sea, Oceanexpo 75 Emblem — A2061

Designs (Oceanexpo 75 Emblem and): 4k, Salt-water shell, Black Sea. 6k, Eel, Baltic Sea. 10k, Sea duck, Arctic Sea. 16k, Crab, Far Eastern waters. 20k, Chrisipther (fish), Pacific Ocean.

1975, July 22 Photo. *Perf. 11*
4343 A2061 3k multi 7 5
4344 A2061 4k multi 10 7
4345 A2061 6k grn & multi 16 7
4346 A2061 10k dk bl & multi 25 10

4347	A2061	16k pur & multi		40	14
4348	A2061	20k multi		50	20
		Nos. 4343-4348 (6)		1.48	63

Souvenir Sheet

Perf. 12x11½

4349		Sheet of 2, multi	1.50	65
a.	A2061 30k	*Dolphin rising*	60	20
b.	A2061 30k	*Dolphin diving*	60	20

Oceanexpo 75, 1st Intl. Oceanographic Exhib., Okinawa, July 20, 1975-Jan. 1976. No. 4349 contains 2 stamps. size: 55x25mm.

Parade, Red Square, 1941, by K. F. Yuon — A2062

Paintings: 2k, Morning of Industrial Moscow, by K. F. Yuon. 6k, Soldiers Inspecting Captured Artillery, by Y. Y. Lansere. 10k, Excavating Metro Tunnel, by Y. Y. Lansere. 16k, Pushkin and His Wife at Court Ball, by N. P. Ulyanov (vert.). 20k, De Lauriston at Kutuzov's Headquarters, by N. P. Ulyanov.

Perf. 12½x11½

1975, July 22 **Litho.**

4350	A2062	1k gray & multi	5	5
4351	A2062	2k gray & multi	5	5
4352	A2062	6k gray & multi	14	7
4353	A2062	10k gray & multi	24	10
4354	A2062	16k gray & multi	40	16
4355	A2062	20k gray & multi	50	20
		Nos. 4350-4355 (6)	1.38	63

Birth centenaries of Russian painters: Konstantin F. Yuon (1875-1958), Yevgeni Y. Lansere (1875-1946), Nikolai P. Ulyanov (1875-1949).

Finlandia Hall, Map of Europe, Laurel A2063

M. K. Chuyrlenis, Waves and Lighthouse A2064

1975, Aug. 18 **Photo.** ***Perf. 11½***

4356	A2063	6k brt bl, gold & blk	14	7

European Security and Cooperation Conference, Helsinki, July 30-Aug. 1. Printed se-tenant with label with quotation by Leonid I. Brezhnev, first secretary of Communist party.

1975, Aug. 20 **Photo. & Engr.**

4357	A2064	4k grn, ind & gold	10	5

M. K. Chuyrlenis, Lithuanian composer, birth centenary.

Avetik Isaakyan, by Martiros Sar'yan A2065

1975, Aug. 20 **Litho.** ***Perf. 12x12½***

4358	A2065	4k multi	10	5

Avetik Isaakyan (1875-1957), Armenian poet, birth centenary.

Jacques Duclos A2066

al-Farabi A2067

1975, Aug. 20 **Photo.** ***Perf. 11½x12***

4359	A2066	6k mar & sil	14	7

Jacques Duclos (1896-1975), French labor leader.

1975, Aug. 20 ***Perf. 11½***

4360	A2067	6k grnsh bl, brn & bis	14	7

Nasr al-Farabi (870 ?-950), Arab philosopher.

Male Ruffs A2068

1975, Aug. 25 **Litho.** ***Perf. 12½x12***

4361	A2068	1k *shown*	5	5
4362	A2068	4k *Altai roebuck*	10	7
4363	A2068	6k *Siberin marten*	14	7
4364	A2068	10k *Old squaw (duck)*	24	10
4365	A2068	16k *Badger*	38	14
		Nos. 4361-4365 (5)	91	43

Berezina River and Stolby wildlife reservations, 50th anniversary.

Flags of USSR, North Korea, Arms of N. K., Liberation Monument, Pyongyang A2069

Flags of USSR, North Viet Nam, Arms of N.V., Industrial Development A2070

1975, Aug. 28 ***Perf. 12***

4366	A2069	6k multi	14	7
4367	A2070	6k multi	14	7

Liberation of North Korea from Japanese occupation (No. 4366); and establishment of Democratic Republic of Viet Nam (No. 4367), 30th anniversaries.

P. Klimuk and V. Sevastyanov, Soyuz 18 and Salyut 4 Docking — A2071

1975, Sept. 12 **Photo.** ***Perf. 12x11½***

4368	A2071	10k ultra, blk & dp org	16	7

Docking of space ship Soyuz 18 and space station Salyut 4.

S. A. Esenin and Birches A2072

Photogravure and Engraved

1975, Sept. 12 ***Perf. 11½***

4369	A2072	6k brn & ocher	14	7

Sergei A. Esenin (1895-1925), poet, 50th death anniversary.

Standardization Symbols — A2073

1975, Sept. 12 **Photo.** ***Perf. 11½***

4370	A2073	4k red & multi	10	7

USSR Committee for Standardization of Communications Ministry, 50th anniversary.

Karakul Lamb A2074

1975, Sept. 22 **Photo.** ***Perf. 11½***

4371	A2074	6k blk, yel & grn	14	7

3rd International Symposium on astrakhan production, Samarkand, Sept. 22-27.

M. P. Konchalovsky A2075

Exhibition Emblem A2076

1975, Sept. 30 ***Perf. 11½x12***

4372	A2075	4k brn & red	10	7

Dr. M. P. Konchalovsky (1875-1942), physician, birth centenary.

1975, Sept. 30 ***Perf. 11½***

4373	A2076	4k dp bl & red	10	7

3rd All-Union Youth Philatelic Exhibition, Erevan.

IWY Emblem and Rose A2077

Jugoslavian Flag and Parliament A2078

1975, Sept. 30 **Litho.** ***Perf. 12x11½***

4374	A2077	6k multi	14	7

International Women's Year 1975.

1975, Sept. 30 **Photo.** ***Perf. 11½***

4375	A2078	6k gold, red & bl	14	7

30th anniversary of the proclamation of the Republic of Jugoslavia.

Illustration from 1938 Edition, by V. A. Favorsky A2079

Mikhail Ivanovich Kalinin A2080

1975, Oct. 20 **Typo.** ***Perf. 12***

4376	A2079	4k buff, red & blk	10	7

175th anniversary of the 1st edition of the old Russian saga "Slovo o polku Igoreve."

1975, Oct. 20 **Engr.** ***Perf. 12***

Portrait: No. 4378, Anatoli Vasilievich Lunacharski.

4377	A2080	4k sepia	10	5
4378	A2080	4k sepia	10	5

Birth Centenaries: M. I. Kalinin (1875-1946), chairman of Central Executive Committee and Presidium of Supreme Soviet; A. V. Lunacharski (1875-1933), writer, commissar for education.

Hand Holding Torch and Lenin Quotation — A2081

1975, Oct. 20 **Engr.**

4379	A2081	4k red & ol	10	5

70th anniversary of First Russian Revolution (1905).

Building Baikal-Amur Railroad A2082

Novolipetsk Metallurgical Plant A2083

Nevynomyssk Chemical Plant, Fertilizer Formula A2084

1975, Oct. 30 **Photo.** ***Perf. 11½***

4380	A2082	4k gold & multi	10	5
4381	A2083	4k red, gray & sl grn	10	5
4382	A2084	4k red, bl & sil	10	5

58th anniversary of October Revolution.

Bas-relief of Decembrists and "Decembrists at the Senate Square," by D. N. Kardovsky — A2085

1975, Nov. 12 Litho. & Engr.
4383 A2085 4k gray & multi 10 5

Sesquicentennial of Decembrist rising.

Star and "1976" — A2086

1975, Nov. 12 Litho. *Perf. 12x12½*
4384 A2086 4k grn & multi 10 5

New Year 1976.

Village Street, by F. A. Vasilev A2087

Paintings by Vasilev: 4k, Road in Birch Forest. 6k, After the Thunderstorm. 10k, Swamp (horiz.). 12k, In the Crimean Mountains. 16k, Meadow (horiz.). 50k, Self-portrait.

Perf. 12x12½, 12½x12
1975, Nov. 25

4385	A2087	2k gray & multi	8	5
4386	A2087	4k gray & multi	10	6
4387	A2087	6k gray & multi	16	7
4388	A2087	10k gray & multi	24	10
4389	A2087	12k gray & multi	30	12
4390	A2087	16k gray & multi	40	16
		Nos. 4385-4390 (6)	1.28	56

Souvenir Sheet
Perf. 12

4391 A2087 50k gray & multi 1.25 55

Fedor Aleksandrovich Vasilev (1850-1873), landscape painter, 125th birth anniversary. Nos. 4385-4390 printed in sheets of 7 stamps and one label with commemorative inscription. No. 4391 has black marginal inscription. Size: 63x93½mm.

Landing Capsule, Venus Surface, Lenin Banner A2088

1975, Dec. 8 Photo. *Perf. 11½*
4392 A2088 10k multi 24 7

Flights of Soviet interplanetary stations Venera 9 and Venera 10.

Gabriel Sundoukian A2089

1975, Dec. 8 Litho. *Perf. 12*
4393 A2089 4k multi 10 5

Gabriel Sundoukian (1825-1912), Armenian playright, birth sesquicentennial.

Polar Poppies, Taiga — A2090

Regional Flowers: 6k, Globeflowers, tundra. 10k, Buttercups, oak forest. 12k, Wood anemones, steppe. 16k, Eminium Lehmannii, desert.

Photogravure and Engraved
1975, Dec. 25 *Perf. 12x11½*

4394	A2090	4k blk & multi	10	7
4395	A2090	6k blk & multi	16	7
4396	A2090	10k blk & multi	24	10
4397	A2090	12k blk & multi	30	14
4398	A2090	16k blk & multi	40	16
		Nos. 4394-4398 (5)	1.20	54

A. L. Mints — A2091

1975, Dec. 31 Photo. *Perf. 11½x12*
4399 A2091 4k dp brn & gold 10 5

A. L. Mints (1895-1974), academician.

Demon, by A. Kochupalov A2092

Paintings: 6k, Vasilisa the Beautiful, by I. Vakurov. 10k, Snow Maiden, by T. Zubkova. 16k, Summer, by K. Kukulieva. 20k, The Fisherman and the Goldfish, by I. Vakurov (horiz.).

1975, Dec. 31 Litho. *Perf. 12*

4400	A2092	4k bis & multi	10	6
4401	A2092	6k bis & multi	16	7
4402	A2092	10k bis & multi	25	8
4403	A2092	16k bis & multi	38	12
4404	A2092	20k bis & multi	45	18
		Nos. 4400-4404 (5)	1.34	51

Palekh Art State Museum, Ivanov Region. Nos. 4400-4404 printed se-tenant in sheets of 20 (5x4).

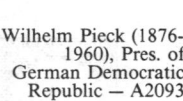

Wilhelm Pieck (1876-1960), Pres. of German Democratic Republic — A2093

1976, Jan. 3 Engr. *Perf. 12½x12*
4405 A2093 6k bluish blk 16 8

M. E. Saltykov-Shchedrin, by I.N. Kramskoi — A2094

1976, Jan. 14 Litho. *Perf. 12x12½*
4406 A2094 4k multi 10 7

Mikhail Evgrafovich Saltykov-Shchedrin (1826-1889), writer and revolutionist, birth sesquicentennial.

Congress Emblem A2095

Lenin Statue, Kiev A2096

1976, Feb. 2 Photo. *Perf. 11½*
4407 A2095 4k red, gold & mar 10 7

Souvenir Sheet
Perf. 11½x12

4408 A2095 50k red, gold & mar 1.25 55

25th Congress of the Communist Party of the Soviet Union.

1976, Feb. 2 *Perf. 11½*
4409 A2096 4k red, blk & bl 14 8

25th Congress of the Ukrainian Communist Party.

Ice Hockey, Games' Emblem A2097

Designs (Winter Olympic Games' Emblem and): 4k, Cross-country skiing. 6k, Figure skating, pairs. 10k, Speed skating. 20k, Luge. 50k, Winter Olympic Games' emblem (vert.).

1976, Feb. 4 Litho. *Perf. 12½x12*

4410	A2097	2k multi	8	5
4411	A2097	4k multi	10	7
4412	A2097	6k multi	16	7
4413	A2097	10k multi	24	10
4414	A2097	20k multi	50	20
		Nos. 4410-4414 (5)	1.08	49

Souvenir Sheet
Perf. 12x12½

4415 A2097 50k vio bl, org & red 1.10 55

12th Winter Olympic Games, Innsbruck, Austria, Feb. 4-15. No. 4415 contains one stamp; silver and violet blue margin showing designs of Nos. 4410-4414. Size: 90x80mm.

Souvenir Sheet
No. 4415 Overprinted in Red

1976, Mar. 24
4416 A2097 50k multi 2.00 1.00

Successful participation of Soviet athletes in 12th Winter Olympic Games. Translation of overprint: "Glory to Soviet Sport! The athletes of the USSR have won 13 gold, 6 silver and 8 bronze medals."

K.E. Voroshilov — A2098

1976, Feb. 4 Engr. *Perf. 12*
4417 A2098 4k sl grn 10 7

Kliment Efremovich Voroshilov (1881-1969), pres. of revolutionary military council, commander of Leningrad front, USSR pres. 1953-60. See Nos. 4487-4488.

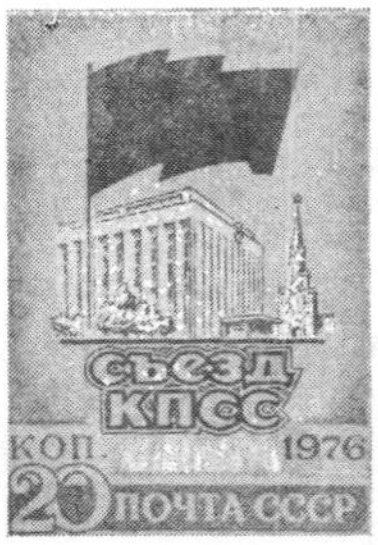

Flag over Kremlin Palace of Congresses, Troitskaya Tower A2099

Photogravure on Gold Foil
1976, Feb. 24 *Perf. 12x11½*
4418 A2099 20k gold, grn & red 1.40 70

25th Congress of the Communist Party of the Soviet Union (CPSU).

Lenin on Red Square, by P. Vasiliev — A2100

1976, Mar. 10 Litho. *Perf. 12½x12*
4419 A2100 4k yel & multi 14 8

106th anniversary of the birth of Lenin.

Atom Symbol and Dubna Institute — A2101

1976, Mar. 10 Photo. *Perf. 11½*
4420 A2101 6k vio bl, red & sil 16 8

Joint Institute of Nuclear Research, Dubna, 20th anniversary.

Bolshoi Theater — A2102

1976, Mar. 24 Litho. ***Perf. 11x11½***
4421 A2102 10k yel, bl & dk brn 16 8

Bicentenary of Bolshoi Theater.

Back from the Fair, by Konchalovsky — A2103

Paintings by P. P. Konchalovsky: 2k, The Green Glass. 6k, Peaches. 16k, Meat, Game and Vegetables. 20k, Self-portrait, 1943 (vert.).

1976, Apr. 6 ***Perf. 12½x12, 12x12½***
4422 A2103 1k yel & multi 5 5
4423 A2103 2k yel & multi 8 5
4424 A2103 6k yel & multi 16 7
4425 A2103 16k yel & multi 40 16
4426 A2103 20k yel & multi 50 20
Nos. 4422-4426 (5) 1.19 53

Birth centenary of P. P. Konchalovsky.

Vostok, Salyut-Soyuz Link-up — A2104

Yuri A. Gagarin A2105

Designs: 6k, Meteor and Molniya Satellites, Orbita Ground Communications Center. 10k, Cosmonauts on board Salyut space station and Mars planetary station. 12k, Interkosmos station and Apollo-Soyuz linking.

Lithographed and Engraved
1976, Apr. 12 ***Perf. 11½***
4427 A2104 4k multi 10 7
4428 A2104 6k multi 16 7
4429 A2104 10k multi 25 14
4430 A2104 12k multi 30 16

Souvenir Sheet

Engr. ***Perf. 12***
4431 A2105 50k black 3.50 1.00

1st manned flight in space, 15th anniv.

I. A. Dzhavakhishvili A2106

Samed Vurgun and Derrick A2107

1976, Apr. 20 Photo. ***Perf. 11½x12***
4432 A2106 4k multi 10 8

Dzhavakhishvili (1876-1940), scientist.

1976, Apr. 20 ***Perf. 11½***
4433 A2107 4k multi 10 8

Samed Vurgun (1906-1956), national poet of Azerbaijan, 70th birth anniversary.

USSR Flag, Worker and Farmer Monument A2108

1976, May 12 Litho. ***Perf. 11½x12***
4434 A2108 4k multi 10 8

1st All-Union Festival of Amateur Artists.

FIP Emblem — A2109

1976, May 12 Photo. ***Perf. 11½***
4435 A2109 6k ultra & car 12 8

International Federation of Philately, 50th anniversary.

Souvenir Sheet

V. A. Tropinin, Self-portrait — A2110

1976, May 12 Litho. ***Perf. 12***
4436 A2110 50k multi 1.00 65

Vasily Andreevich Tropinin (1776-1857), painter.

Emblem, Dnieper Bridge A2111

Dr. N. N. Burdenko A2112

1976, May 20 Photo. ***Perf. 11½***
4437 A2111 4k Prus bl, gold & blk 8 8

Bicentenary of Dnepropetrovsk.

1976, May 20 ***Perf. 11½x12***
4438 A2112 4k dp brn & red 8 8

N. N. Burdenko (1876-1946), neurosurgeon, birth centenary.

K. A. Trenev (1876-1945), Playwright — A2113

1976, May 20 ***Perf. 11½***
4439 A2113 4k blk & multi 8 8

Automobile Type of 1973

Designs: 2k, ZIS-110 passenger car. 3k, GAZ-51 Gorky truck. 4k, GAZ-M-20 Pobeda passenger car. 12k, ZIS-150 Moscow Motor Works truck. 16k, ZIS-154 Moscow Motor Works bus.

1976, June 15 Photo. ***Perf. 12x11½***
4440 A1968 2k grnsh bl & multi 6 5
4441 A1968 3k bis & multi 9 5
4442 A1968 4k dk bl & multi 8 6
4443 A1968 12k brn & multi 25 10
4444 A1968 16k dp car & multi 32 16
Nos. 4440-4444 (5) 80 42

Canoeing A2114

Designs (USSR National Olympic Committee Emblem and): 6k, Basketball (vert.). 10k, Greco-Roman wrestling. 14k, Women's discus (vert.). 16k, Target shooting. 50k, Olympic medal, obverse and reverse.

Perf. 12½x12, 12x12½
1976, June 23 Litho.
4445 A2114 4k red & multi 8 6
4446 A2114 6k red & multi 12 8
4447 A2114 10k red & multi 20 10
4448 A2114 14k red & multi 28 15
4449 A2114 16k red & multi 32 16
Nos. 4445-4449 (5) 1.00 55

Souvenir Sheet
4450 A2114 50k red & multi 1.00 65

21st Olympic Games, Montreal, Canada, July 17-Aug. 1.

Electric Trains, Overpass A2115

1976, June 23 Photo. ***Perf. 11½***
4451 A2115 4k multi 8 8

Electrification of USSR railroads, 50th anniversary.

L. Emilio Rekabarren A2116

1976, July 6
4452 A2116 6k gold, red & blk 12 8

Luis Emilio Rekabarren (1876-1924), founder of Chilean Communist Party, birth centenary.

L. M. Pavlichenko — A2117

1976, July 6
4453 A2117 4k dp brn, sil & yel 8 8

Ljudmilla Mikhajlovna Pavlichenko (1916-1974), WWII heroine, Komsomol, War Veterans and Women's Committee member.

New Partner, by P. A. Fedotov A2118

Paintings: 4k, The Fastidious Fiancée (horiz.). 6k, Aristocrat's Breakfast. 10k, Gamblers (horiz.). 16k, The Outing. 50k, Self-portrait.

Perf. 12x12½, 12½x12
1976, July 15 Litho.
4454 A2118 2k blk & multi 6 5
4455 A2118 4k blk & multi 8 8
4456 A2118 6k blk & multi 12 8
4457 A2118 10k blk & multi 20 10
4458 A2118 16k blk & multi 32 16
Nos. 4454-4458 (5) 78 47

Souvenir Sheet
Perf. 12
4459 A2118 50k multi 1.10 65

Pavel Andreevich Fedotov (1815-1852), painter. Nos. 4454-4458 each printed in sheets of 20 stamps and center label with black commemorative inscription.

S. S. Nametkin A2119

Squacco Heron A2120

1976, July 20 Photo. ***Perf. 11½x12***
4460 A2119 4k bl, blk & buff 8 8

Sergei Semenovich Nametkin (1876-1950), organic chemist, birth centenary.

1976, Aug. 18 Litho. ***Perf. 12x12½***

Waterfowl: 3k, Arctic loon. 4k, European coot. 6k, Atlantic puffin. 10k, Slender-billed gull.

4465	A2120	1k dk grn & multi	5	5
4466	A2120	3k ol grn & multi	9	5
4467	A2120	4k org & multi	8	6
4468	A2120	6k pur & multi	12	9
4469	A2120	10k brt bl & multi	20	10
		Nos. 4465-4469 (5)	54	35

Nature protection.

Peace Dove A2121

1976, Aug. 25 Photo. *Perf. 11½*

4470	A2121	4k sal, gold & bl	8	8

2nd Stockholm appeal and movement to stop arms race.

Resistance Movement Emblem A2122

1976, Aug. 25

4471	A2122	6k dk bl, blk & gold	12	9

International Resistance Movement Federation, 25th anniversary.

Souvenir Sheet

No. 4450 Overprinted in Gold in Margin Similar to No. 3961

1976, Aug. 25 Litho. *Perf. 12½x12*

4472	A2114	50k red & multi	1.10	65

Victories of Russian athletes in 21st Olympic Games (47 gold, 43 silver and 35 bronze medals).

Flags of India and USSR — A2123

UN, UNESCO Emblems, Open Book — A2124

1976, Sept. 8 *Perf. 12*

4473	A2123	4k multi	8	8

Friendship and cooperation between USSR and India.

1976, Sept. 8 Engr. *Perf. 12x12½*

4474	A2124	16k multi	32	16

UNESCO, 30th anniv.

B. V. Volynov, V. M. Zholobov, Star Circling Globe — A2125

1976, Sept. 8 Photo. *Perf. 12x11½*

4475	A2125	10k brn, bl & blk	28	16

Exploits of Soyuz 21 and Salyut space station.

"Industry" — A2126

1976, Sept. 17

4476	A2126	4k *shown*	8	8
4477	A2126	4k *Farm industry*	8	8
4478	A2126	4k *Science*	8	8
4479	A2126	4k *Transport & communications*	8	8
4480	A2126	4k *International cooperation*	8	8
		Nos. 4476-4480 (5)	40	40

25th Congress of the Communist Party of the Soviet Union.

Au (woman), by I. V. Markichev A2127

Paintings: 2k, Plower, by I. I. Golikov (horiz.). 12k, Firebird, by A. V. Kotuhin (horiz.). 14k, Festival, by A. I. Vatagin. 20k, Victory, by I. I. Vakurov.

Perf. 12½x12, 12x12½

1976, Sept. 22 Litho.

4481	A2127	2k blk & multi	6	5
4482	A2127	4k blk & multi	8	6
4483	A2127	12k blk & multi	25	14
4484	A2127	14k blk & multi	28	15
4485	A2127	20k blk & multi	42	20
		Nos. 4481-4485 (5)	1.09	60

Palekh Art State Museum, Ivanov Region.

Shostakovich, Score from 7th Symphony, Leningrad — A2128

1976, Sept. 25 Engr. *Perf. 12½x12*

4486	A2128	6k dk vio bl	12	8

Dimitri Dimitrievich Shostakovich (1906-1975), composer, 70th birth anniversary.

Voroshilov Type of 1976

Portraits: No. 4487, Georgi K. Zhukov. No. 4488, Konstantin K. Rokossovsky.

1976, Oct. 7 Engr. *Perf. 12*

4487	A2098	4k sl grn	8	6
4488	A2098	4k brown	8	6

Marshal Georgi Konstantinovich Zhukov (1896-1974), commander at Stalingrad and Leningrad and Deputy of Supreme Soviet; Marshal Konstantin K. Rokossovsky (1896-1968), commander at Stalingrad.

Interkosmos-14 A2129

Designs: 10k, India's satellite Arryabata. 12k, Soyuz-19 and Apollo before docking. 16k, French satellite Aureole and Northern Lights. 20k, Docking of Soyuz-Apollo, Interkosmos-14 and Aureole.

1976, Oct. 15 Photo. *Perf. 11½*

4489	A2129	6k blk & multi	10	7
4490	A2129	10k blk & multi	16	10
4491	A2129	12k blk & multi	20	10
4492	A2129	16k blk & multi	25	14
4493	A2129	20k blk & multi	32	16
		Nos. 4489-4493 (5)	1.03	57

Interkosmos Program for Scientific and Experimental Research.

Vladimir I. Dahl A2130

Photogravure and Engraved

1976, Oct. 15 *Perf. 11½*

4494	A2130	4k grn & dk grn	8	8

Vladimir I. Dahl (1801-1872), physician, writer, compiled Russian Dictionary.

Electric Power Industry A2131

Designs: No. 4496, Balashovo textile mill. No. 4497, Laying of drainage pipes and grain elevator.

1976, Oct. 20 Photo. *Perf. 11½*

4495	A2131	4k dk bl & multi	8	8
4496	A2131	4k rose brn & multi	8	8
4497	A2131	4k sl grn & multi	8	8

59th anniversary of the October Revolution.

Petrov Tumor Research Institute A2132

M. A. Novinski A2133

1976, Oct. 28

4498	A2132	4k vio bl & gold	8	6

Perf. 11½x12

4499	A2133	4k dk brn, buff & bl	8	6

Petrov Tumor Research Institute, 50th anniversary, and 135th birth anniversary of M. A. Novinski, cancer research pioneer.

Aviation Emblem, Gakkel VII — A2134

Designs (Russian Aviation Emblem and): 6k, Gakkel IX, 1912. 12k, I. Steglau No. 2, 1912. 14k, Dybovski's Dolphin, 1913. 16k, Iliya Muromets, 1914.

Lithographed and Engraved

1976, Nov. 4 *Perf. 12x12½*

4500	A2134	3k multi	8	5
4501	A2134	6k multi	12	8
4502	A2134	12k multi	25	14
4503	A2134	14k multi	28	15
4504	A2134	16k multi	32	16
		Nos. 4500-4504 (5)	1.05	58

Russian aircraft, 1911-1914. See Nos. C109-C120.

Saffron A2135

Flowers of the Caucasus: 2k, Pasqueflowers. 3k, Gentian. 4k, Columbine. 6k, Checkered lily.

1976, Nov. 17 *Perf. 12x11½*

4505	A2135	1k multi	5	5
4506	A2135	2k multi	6	5
4507	A2135	3k multi	7	5
4508	A2135	4k multi	8	6
4509	A2135	6k multi	12	7
		Nos. 4505-4509 (5)	38	28

Spasski Tower Clock, Greeting Card A2136

1976, Nov. 25 Litho. *Perf. 12½x12*

4510	A2136	4k multi	8	8

New Year 1977.

Parable of the Workers in the Vineyard, by Rembrandt — A2137

Rembrandt Paintings in Hermitage: 6k, birth anniversary. Nos. 4511 and 4515 14k, Holy Family (vert.). 20k, Rembrandt's brother Adrian, 1654 (vert.). 50k, Artaxerxes, Esther and Haman.

Perf. 12½x12, 12x12½

1976, Nov. 25 Photo.

4511	A2137	4k multi	8	6
4512	A2137	6k multi	12	7
4513	A2137	10k multi	20	10
4514	A2137	14k multi	28	14
4515	A2137	20k multi	40	20
		Nos. 4511-4515 (5)	1.08	57

Souvenir Sheet

4516	A2137	50k multi	3.25	1.00

Rembrandt van Rijn (1606-69). Nos. 4511 and 4515 printed in sheets of 7 stamps and decorative label.

Armed Forces Order — A2138

Worker and Farmer, by V. I. Muhina — A2139

Marx and Lenin, by Fridman and Belostotsky A2140

Council for Mutual Economic Aid Building A2141

Lenin, 1920 Photograph A2142

Globe and Sputnik Orbits A2143

Designs: 2k, Golden Star and Hammer and Sickle medals. 4k, Coat of arms and "CCCP." 6k, TU-154 plane, globe and airmail envelope. 10k, Order of Labor. 12k, Space exploration medal with Gagarin portrait. 16k, Lenin Prize medal.

1976		Engr.	Perf. 12	
4517	A2138	1k grnsh blk	5	5
4518	A2138	2k brt mag	6	5
4519	A2139	3k red	7	5
4520	A2138	4k brick red	8	5
4521	A2139	6k Prus bl	12	5
4522	A2138	10k ol grn	20	5
4523	A2139	12k vio bl	24	5
4524	A2139	16k dp grn	28	5
		Perf. 12½x12		
4525	A2140	20k brn red	35	6
4526	A2141	30k brick red	50	7
4527	A2142	50k brown	1.00	10
4528	A2143	1r dk bl	2.00	14
		Nos. 4517-4528 (12)	4.95	77

Issue dates: Nos. 4517-4524, Dec. 17. Nos. 4525-4528, Aug. 10.

See Nos. 4596-4607.

Luna 24 Emblem and Moon Landing A2144

1976, Dec. 17 Photo. *Perf. 11½*

4531 A2144 10k multi 20 10

Moon exploration of automatic station Luna 24.

Icebreaker "Pilot" — A2145

Icebreakers: 6k, Ermak (vert.). 10k, Fedor Litke. 16k, Vladimir Ilich (vert.). 20k, Krassin.

Perf. 12x11½, 11½x12

1976, Dec. 22		Litho. & Engr.		
4532	A2145	4k multi	8	6
4533	A2145	6k multi	12	7
4534	A2145	10k multi	20	10
4535	A2145	16k multi	32	16
4536	A2145	20k multi	40	20
		Nos. 4532-4536 (5)	1.12	59

See Nos. 4579-4585.

Soyuz 22 Emblem, Cosmonauts V. F. Bykofsky and V. V. Aksenov — A2146

1976, Dec. 28 Photo. *Perf. 12x11½*

4537 A2146 10k multi 20 10

Soyuz 22 space flight, Sept. 15-23.

Society Emblem — A2147

1977, Jan. 1 *Perf. 11½*

4538 A2147 4k multi 8 6

Red Banner Voluntary Society, supporting Red Army, Navy and Air Force, 50th anniversary.

S. P. Korolev, Vostok Rocket and Satellite A2148

1977, Jan. 12

4539 A2148 4k multi 8 6

Sergei Pavlovich Korolev (1907-1966), creator of first Soviet rocket space system.

Globe and Palm A2149

1977, Jan. 12

4540 A2149 4k multi 8 6

World Congress of Peace Loving Forces, Moscow, Jan. 1977.

Sedov and "St. Foka" A2150

1977, Jan. 25 Photo. *Perf. 11½*

4541 A2150 4k multi 8 6

G.Y. Sedov (1877-1914), polar explorer and hydrographer.

The Catalogue editors cannot undertake to appraise, identify or judge the genuineness or condition of stamps.

Worker and Farmer Monument and Izvestia Front Page — A2151

Ship Sailing Across the Oceans — A2152

1977, Jan. 25

4542 A2151 4k sil, blk & red 8 6

60th anniversary of newspaper Izvestia.

1977, Jan. 25

4543 A2152 6k dp bl & gold 12 7

24th International Navigation Congress, Leningrad.

Congress Hall and Troitskaya Tower, Kremlin A2153

Marshal Leonid A. Govorov (1897-1955) A2154

1977, Feb. 9 Photo. *Perf. 11½*

4544 A2153 4k red, gold & blk 8 8

16th Congress of USSR Trade Unions.

1977 Engr. *Perf. 12*

Portraits: No. 4546, Ivan S. Koniev. No. 4547, K. A. Merezhkov. No. 4548, W. D. Sokolovsky.

4545	A2154	4k brown	8	6
4546	A2154	4k sl grn	8	6
4547	A2154	4k brown	8	6
4548	A2154	4k black	8	6

Marshals of the Soviet Union.

Issue dates: No. 4545, Feb. 9. Nos. 4546-4548, June 7.

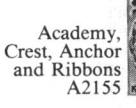

Academy, Crest, Anchor and Ribbons A2155

Photogravure and Engraved

1977, Feb. 9 *Perf. 11½*

4549 A2155 6k multi 12 8

A. A. Grechko Naval Academy, Leningrad, sesquicentennial.

Jeanne Labourbe A2156

Queen and Knights A2157

1977, Feb. 25 Photo. *Perf. 11½*

4550 A2156 4k multi 8 8

Jeanne Labourbe (1877-1919), leader of French communists in Moscow.

1977, Feb. 25

4551 A2157 6k multi 12 8

4th European Chess Championships.

Cosmonauts V. D. Zudov and V. I. Rozhdestvensky — A2158

1977, Feb. 25 *Perf. 12x11½*

4552 A2158 10k multi 14 10

Soyuz 23 space flight, Oct. 14-16, 1976.

A. S. Novikov-Priboy A2159

1977, Mar. 16 Photo. *Perf. 11½*

4553 A2159 4k multi 8 8

A. S. Novikov-Priboy (1877-1944), writer, birth centenary.

Welcome, by M. N. Soloninkin A2160

Paintings: 6k, Along the Street, by V. D. Antonov (horiz.). 10k, Northern Song, by J. V. Karapaev. 12k, Tale of Czar Saltan, by A. I. Kozlov. 14k, Summer Troika, by V. A. Nalimov (horiz.). 16k, Red Flower, by V. D. Lipitsky.

Perf. 12x12½, 12½x12

1977, Mar. 16		Litho.		
4554	A2160	4k blk & multi	2	5
4555	A2160	6k blk & multi	12	7
4556	A2160	10k blk & multi	20	10
4557	A2160	12k blk & multi	25	10
4558	A2160	14k blk & multi	28	14
4559	A2160	16k blk & multi	32	14
		Nos. 4554-4559 (6)	1.19	60

Folk tale paintings from Fedoskino artists' colony.

Lenin on Red Square, by K.V. Filatov — A2161

1977, Apr. 12 *Perf. 12½x11½*

4560	A2161	4k multi	8	8

107th anniversary of the birth of Lenin.

Electricity Congress Emblem A2162

1977, Apr. 12 Photo. *Perf. 11½*

4561	A2162	6k bl, red & gray	12	8

World Electricity Congress, Moscow 1977.

Yuri Gagarin, Sputnik, Soyuz and Salyut — A2163

1977, Apr. 12 *Perf. 12x11½*

4562	A2163	6k multi	12	8

Cosmonauts' Day.

N. I. Vavilov A2164

Feliks E. Dzerzhinski A2165

1977, Apr. 26 Photo. *Perf. 11½*

4563	A2164	4k multi	8	8

N. I. Vavilov (1887-1943), agricultural geneticist, 90th birth anniversary.

1977, May 12 Engr. *Perf. 12½x12*

4564	A2165	4k black	8	8

Feliks E. Dzerzhinski (1877-1926), organizer and head of secret police (OGPU).

Saxifraga Sibirica — A2166

Siberian Flowers: 3k, Dianthus repena. 4k, Novosieversia glactalis. 6k, Cerasticum maxinicem. 16k, Golden rhododendron.

1977, May 12 Litho. *Perf. 12x12½*

4565	A2166	2k multi	6	5
4566	A2166	3k multi	7	5
4567	A2166	4k multi	8	6
4568	A2166	6k multi	12	7
4569	A2166	16k multi	32	16
		Nos. 4565-4569 (5)	65	39

The Scott Catalogue value is a retail price, what you could expect to pay for the stamp in a grade of Fine-Very Fine. The value listed is a reference which reflects recent actual dealer selling price.

V. V. Gorbatko, Y. N. Glazkov, Soyuz 24 Rocket A2167

1977, May 16 Photo. *Perf. 12x11½*

4570	A2167	10k multi	20	10

Space explorations of cosmonauts on Salyut 5 orbital station, launched with Soyuz 24 rocket.

Film and Globe — A2168

1977, June 21 Photo. *Perf. 11½*

4571	A2168	6k multi	12	8

10th Intl. Film Festival, Moscow 1977.

Lion Hunt, by Rubens — A2169

Rubens Paintings, Hermitage, Leningrad: 4k, Lady in Waiting (vert.). 10k, Workers in Quarry. 12k, Alliance of Water and Earth (vert.). 20k, Landscape with Rainbow. 50k, Self-portrait.

Perf. 12x12½, 12½x12

1977, June 24 **Litho.**

4572	A2169	4k yel & multi	8	6
4573	A2169	6k yel & multi	12	7
4574	A2169	10k yel & multi	20	10
4575	A2169	12k yel & multi	25	12
4576	A2169	20k yel & multi	40	20
		Nos. 4572-4576 (5)	1.05	55

Souvenir Sheet

4577	A2169	50k yel & multi	1.00	65

Peter Paul Rubens (1577-1640), painter. Sheets of No. 4575 contain 2 labels with commemorative inscriptions and Atlas statue from Hermitage entrance.

Souvenir Sheet

Judith, by Giorgione A2170

1977, July 15 Litho. *Perf. 12x12½*

4578	A2170	50k multi	1.00	65

Il Giorgione (1478-1511), Venetian painter.

Icebreaker Type of 1976

Icebreakers: 4k, Aleksandr Sibiryakov. 6k, Georgi Sedov. 10k, Sadko. 12k, Dezhnev. 14k, Siberia. 16k, Lena. 20k, Amguyema.

Lithographed and Engraved

1977, July 27 *Perf. 12x11½*

4579	A2145	4k multi	8	6
4580	A2145	6k multi	12	7
4581	A2145	10k multi	20	10
4582	A2145	12k multi	25	12
4583	A2145	14k multi	28	14
4584	A2145	16k multi	32	16
4585	A2145	20k multi	40	20
		Nos. 4579-4585 (7)	1.65	85

Souvenir Sheet

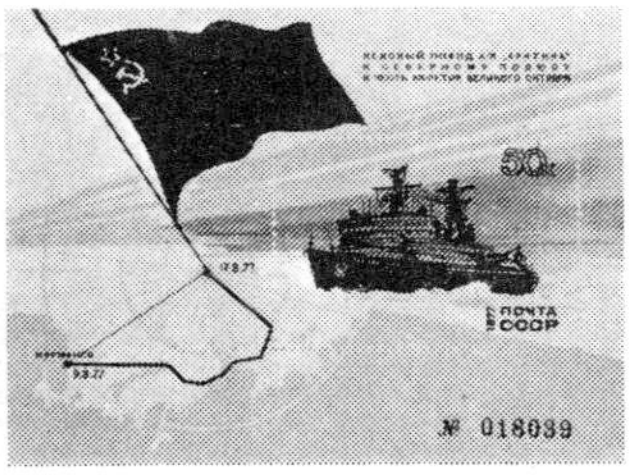

Icebreaker Arctica — A2171

Lithographed and Engraved

1977, Sept. 15 *Perf. 12½x12*

4586	A2171	50k multi	3.50	3.50

Arctica, first ship to travel from Murmansk to North Pole, Aug. 9-17.

View and Arms of Stavropol A2172

Stamps and Exhibition Emblem A2173

1977, Aug. 16 Photo. *Perf. 11½*

4587	A2172	6k multi	12	8

200th anniversary of Stavropol.

1977, Aug. 16

4588	A2173	4k multi	8	8

October Revolution Anniversary Philatelic Exhibition, Moscow.

Yuri A. Gagarin and Spacecraft — A2174

Designs: No. 4590, Alexei Leonov floating in space. No. 4591, Orbiting space station, cosmonauts at control panel. Nos. 4592-4594, Various spacecraft: No. 4592, International cooperation for space research; No. 4593, Interplanetary flights; No. 4594, Exploring earth's atmosphere. 50k, "XX," laurel, symbolic Sputnik with Red Star.

1977, Oct. 4 Photo. *Perf. 11½x12*

4589	A2174	10k sep & multi	16	10
4590	A2174	10k gray & multi	16	10
4591	A2174	10k gray grn & multi	16	10
4592	A2174	20k grn & multi	35	20
4593	A2174	20k vio bl & multi	35	20
4594	A2174	20k bis & multi	35	20
		Nos. 4589-4594 (6)	1.53	90

Souvenir Sheet

4595	A2174	50k cl & gold	*5.50*	*5.50*

20th anniv. of space research. No. 4595 contains one stamp, size 22x32mm.

Types of 1976

Designs: 15k, Communications emblem and globes; others as before.

1977-78 Litho. *Perf. 12*

4596	A2138	1k ol grn	5	5
4597	A2138	2k lil rose	6	5
4598	A2139	3k brick red	7	5
4599	A2138	4k vermilion	8	5
4600	A2139	6k Prus bl	12	5
4601	A2138	10k gray grn	20	5
4602	A2139	12k vio bl	25	5
4602A	A2139	15k bl ('78)	30	5
4603	A2139	16k sl grn	32	5
4604	A2140	20k brn red	40	6
4605	A2141	30k dl brick red	60	7
4606	A2142	50k brown	1.00	10
4607	A2143	1r dk bl	2.00	14
		Nos. 4596-4607 (13)	5.45	82

Nos. 4596-4602A, 4604-4607 were printed on dull and shiny paper.

Souvenir Sheet

Bas-relief, 12th Century, Cathedral of St. Dimitri, Vladimir — A2175

Designs: 6k, Necklace, Ryazan excavations, 12th century. 10k, Mask, Cathedral of the Nativity, Suzdal, 13th century. 12k, Archangel Michael, 15th century icon. 16k, Chalice by Ivan Fomin, 1449. 20k, St. Basil's Cathedral, Moscow, 16th century.

1977, Oct. 12 Litho. *Perf. 12*

4608		Sheet of 6	1.40	1.00
a	A2175	4k gold & blk	7	
b	A2175	6k gold & multi	8	
c	A2175	10k gold & multi	18	
d	A2175	12k gold & multi	25	
e	A2175	16k gold & multi	28	
f	A2175	20k gold & multi	35	

Masterpieces of old Russian culture.

Fir, Snowflake, Molniya Satellite — A2176

1977, Oct. 12 *Perf. 12x12½*

4609	A2176	4k multi	8	8

New Year 1978.

Cruiser Aurora and Torch A2177

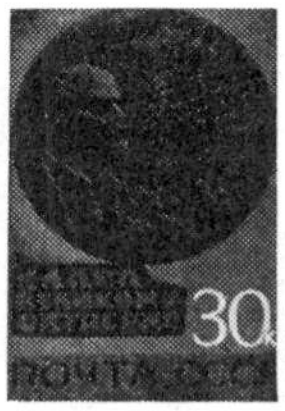

60th Anniversary of Revolution Medal — A2178

Designs: No. 4611, Lenin speaking at Finland Station (monument), 1917. No. 4612, 1917 Peace Decree, Brezhnev's book about Lenin. No. 4613, Kremlin tower with star and fireworks.

1977, Oct. 26 Photo. *Perf. 12x11½*

4610	A2177	4k gold, red & blk	8	6
4611	A2177	4k gold, red & blk	8	6
4612	A2177	4k gold, red & blk	8	6
4613	A2177	4k gold, red & blk	8	6

Souvenir Sheet

Perf. 11½

4614	A2178	30k gold, red & blk	1.00	60

60th anniversary of October Revolution.

Flag of USSR, Constitution (Book) with Coat of Arms — A2179

Designs: No. 4616, Red banner, people and cover of constitution. 50k, Constitution, Kremlin and olive branch.

1977, Oct. 31 Litho. *Perf. 12½x12*

4615	A2179	4k red, blk & yel	8	6
4616	A2179	4k red, blk & yel	8	6

Souvenir Sheet

Perf. 11½x12½

Lithographed and Embossed

4617	A2179	50k red, gold & yel	1.10	65

Adoption of new constitution. No. 4617 contains one stamp, size 70x50mm.

Souvenir Sheet

Leonid Brezhnev A2180

Lithographed and Embossed

1977, Nov. 2 *Perf. 11½x12*

4618	A2180	50k gold & multi	1.10	66

Adoption of new constitution, General Secretary Brezhnev, chairman of Constitution Commission.

Postal Official and Postal Code — A2181

Designs (Woman Postal Official and): No. 4620, Mail collection and Moskvich 430 car. No. 4621, Automatic letter sorting machine. No. 4622, Mail transport by truck, train, ship and planes. No. 4623, Mail delivery in city and country.

Lithographed and Engraved

1977, Nov. 16 *Perf. 12½x12*

4619	A2181	4k multi	8	6
4620	A2181	4k multi	8	6
4621	A2181	4k multi	8	6
4622	A2181	4k multi	8	6
4623	A2181	4k multi	8	6
		Nos. 4619-4623 (5)	40	30

Mail processing.

Capital, Asoka Pillar, Red Fort A2182

Proclamation Monument, Charkov A2183

1977, Dec. 14 Photo. *Perf. 11½*

4624	A2182	6k mar, gold & red	12	7

30th anniversary of India's independence.

1977, Dec. 14 Litho. *Perf. 12x12½*

4625	A2183	6k multi	12	7

60th anniversary of Soviet power in the Ukraine.

Lebetina Viper — A2184

Designs: 1k to 12k, Venomous snakes, useful for medicinal purposes. 16k, Polar bear and cub. 20k, Walrus and calf. 30k, Tiger and cub.

Photogravure and Engraved

1977, Dec. 16 *Perf. 11½x12*

4626	A2184	1k blk & multi	5	5
4627	A2184	4k blk & multi	8	6
4628	A2184	6k blk & multi	12	7
4629	A2184	10k blk & multi	20	10
4630	A2184	12k blk & multi	25	12
4631	A2184	16k blk & multi	32	16
4632	A2184	20k blk & multi	40	20
4633	A2184	30k blk & multi	60	30
		Nos. 4626-4633 (8)	2.02	1.06

Protected fauna.

Wheat, Combine, Silos — A2185

Congress Palace, Spasski Tower — A2186

1978, Jan. 27 Photo. *Perf. 11½*

4634	A2185	4k multi	8	6

Gigant collective grain farm, Rostov Region, 50th anniversary.

1978, Jan. 27 Litho. *Perf. 12x12½*

4635	A2186	4k multi	8	6

Young Communist League, Lenin's Komsomol, 60th anniversary and its 25th Congress.

Liberation Obelisk, Emblem, Dove — A2187

1978, Jan. 27 Photo. *Perf. 11½*

4636	A2187	6k multi	12	7

8th Congress of International Federation of Resistance Fighters, Minsk, Belorussia.

Soldiers Leaving for the Front — A2188

Designs: No. 4638, Defenders of Moscow Monument, Lenin banner. No. 4639, Soldier as defender of the people.

1978, Feb. 21 Litho. *Perf. 12½x12*

4637	A2188	4k red & multi	8	6
4638	A2188	4k red & multi	8	6
4639	A2188	4k red & multi	8	6

60th anniversary of USSR Military forces.

Morning, by Kustodiev — A2189

Kustodiev Paintings: 4k, Celebration in Village. 6k, Shrovetide (winter landscape). 12k, Merchant's Wife Drinking Tea. 20k, Bolshevik. 50k, Self-portrait (vert.).

1978, Mar. 3 *Perf. 11½*

Size: 70x33mm.

4640	A2189	4k lil & multi	8	6
4641	A2189	6k lil & multi	12	7

Size: 47x32mm.

Perf. 12½x12

4642	A2189	10k lil & multi	20	10
4643	A2189	12k lil & multi	25	12
4644	A2189	20k lil & multi	40	20
		Nos. 4640-4644 (5)	1.05	55

Souvenir Sheet

Perf. 11½x12½

4644A	A2189	50k lil & multi	1.00	65

Boris Mikhailovich Kustodiev (1878-1927), painter, birth centenary. Nos. 4640-4643 printed with se-tenant label showing museum where painting is kept. No. 4644A has label giving short biography; lilac margin with black inscription. Size: 92x71mm.

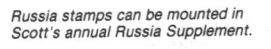

Russia stamps can be mounted in Scott's annual Russia Supplement.

Docking in Space, Intercosmos Emblem A2190

Designs: 6k, Rocket, Russian Cosmonaut Aleksei Gubarev and Czechoslovak Capt. Vladimir Remek on launching pad. 32k, Weather balloon, helicopter, Intercosmos emblem, Russian and Czechoslovakian flags.

1978, Mar. 10 Litho. *Perf. 12x12½*

4645	A2190	6k multi	12	7
4646	A2190	15k multi	30	14
4647	A2190	32k multi	65	32

Intercosmos, Soviet-Czechoslovak cooperative space program.

Festival Emblem — A2191

1978, Mar. 17 Litho. *Perf. 12x12½*

4648	A2191	4k bl & multi	8	6

11th Youth and Students' Congress, Havana.

Tulip, Bolshoi Theater A2192

Moscow Flowers: 2k, Rose "Moscow morning" and Lomonosov University. 4k, Dahlia "Red Star" and Spasski Tower. 10k, Gladiolus "Moscovite" and VDNH Building. 12k, Ilich anniversary iris and Lenin Central Museum.

1978, Mar. 17 *Perf. 12½x12*

4649	A2192	1k multi	5	5
4650	A2192	2k multi	6	5
4651	A2192	4k multi	8	6
4652	A2192	10k multi	20	10
4653	A2192	12k multi	25	12
		Nos. 4649-4653 (5)	64	38

IMCO Emblem and Waves — A2193

1978, Mar. 17 Litho. *Perf. 12x12½*

4654	A2193	6k multi	12	7

Intergovernmental Maritime Consultative Organization, 20th anniversary, and World Maritime Day.

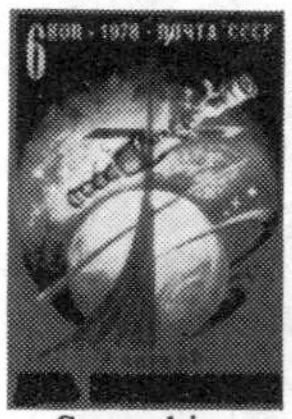

Spaceship, Orbits of Salyut 5, Soyuz 26 and 27
A2194

World Federation of Trade Unions Emblem
A2195

1978, Apr. 12 Photo. *Perf. 12*

4655	A2194	6k bl, dk bl & gold	12	7

Cosmonauts' Day, Apr. 12.

1978, Apr. 16 *Perf. 12*

4656	A2195	6k multi	12	7

9th World Trade Union Congress, Prague.

2-2-0 Locomotive, 1845, Petersburg and Moscow Stations — A2196

Locomotives: 1k, 1st Russian model by E. A. and M. W. Cherepanov (vert.). 2k, 1-3-0 freight, 1845. 16k, Aleksandrov 0-3-0, 1863. 20k, 2-2-0 passenger and Sergievsk Pustyn platform, 1863.

1978, Apr. 20 Litho. *Perf. 11½*

4657	A2196	1k org & multi	5	5
4658	A2196	2k ultra & multi	6	5
4659	A2196	3k yel & multi	9	5
4660	A2196	16k grn & multi	32	16
4661	A2196	20k rose & multi	40	20
		Nos. 4657-4661 (5)	92	51

Souvenir Sheet

Lenin, by V. A. Serov
A2197

1978, Apr. 22 *Perf. 12x12½*

4662	A2197	50k multi	1.00	65

108th anniversary of the birth of Lenin.

Soyuz and Salyut 6 Docking in Space — A2198

Y. V. Romanenko and G. M. Grechko — A2199

1978, June 15 *Perf. 12*

4663	A2198	15k multi	30	16
4664	A2199	15k multi	30	16

Photographic survey and telescopic observations of stars by crews of Soyuz 26, Soyuz 27 and Soyuz 28, Dec. 10, 1977-March 16, 1978. Nos. 4663-4664 printed se-tenant with label showing schematic pictures of various experiments.

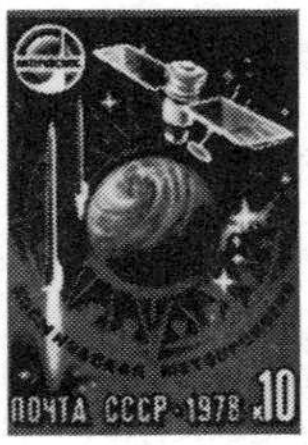

Space Meteorology, Rockets, Spaceship, Earth — A2200

Designs (Intercosmos Emblem and): No. 4666, Natural resources of earth and Soyuz. No. 4667, Space communications, "Orbita" Station and Molnyia satellite. No. 4668, Man, earth and Vostok. 50k, Study of magnetosphere, Prognoz over earth.

1978, June 23 *Perf. 12x12½*

4665	A2200	10k grn & multi	20	10
4666	A2200	10k bl & multi	20	10
4667	A2200	10k vio & multi	20	10
4668	A2200	10k rose lil & multi	20	10

Souvenir Sheet

Perf. 11½x12½

4669	A2200	50k multi	1.00	65

Space explorations of the Intercosmos program. No. 4669 contains one stamp size 36x51mm.

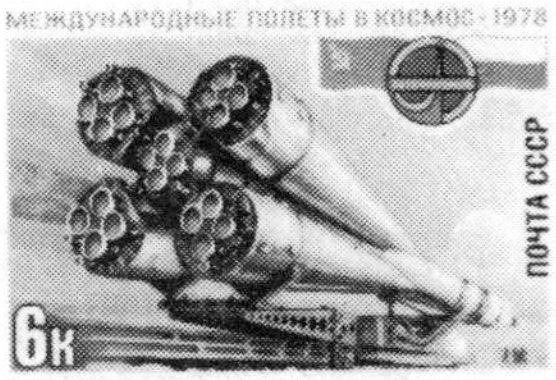

Soyuz Rocket on Carrier — A2201

Designs (Flags of USSR and Poland, Intercosmos Emblem): 15k, Crystal, spaceship (Sirena, experimental crystallogenesis in space). 32k, Research ship "Cosmonaut Vladimir Komarov", spaceship, world map and paths of Salyut 6, Soyuz 29-30.

1978, Litho. *Perf. 12½x12*

4670	A2201	6k multi	12	7
4671	A2201	15k multi	30	15
4672	A2201	32k multi	65	32

Intercosmos, Soviet-Polish cooperative space program. Issue dates: 6k, June 28. 15k, June 30. 32k, July 5.

Lenin, Awards Received by Komsomol
A2202

Kamaz Car, Train, Bridge, Hammer and Sickle
A2203

1978, July 5 *Perf. 12x12½*

4673	A2202	4k multi	8	6
4674	A2203	4k multi	8	6

Leninist Young Communist League (Komsomol), 60th anniversary (No. 4673); Komsomol's participation in 5-year plan (No. 4674).

M. V. Zaharov
A2204

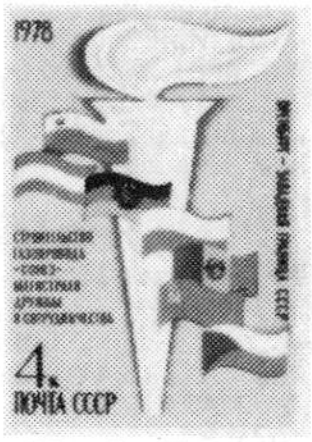

Torch, Flags of Participants
A2205

1978, July 5 Engr. *Perf. 12*

4675	A2204	4k sepia	8	6

M. V. Zaharov (1898-1972), Marshal of the Soviet Union.

1978, July 25 Litho. *Perf. 12x12½*

4676	A2205	4k multi	8	6

Construction of Soyuz gas-pipeline (Friendship Line), Orenburg. Flags of participating countries shown: Bulgaria, Hungary, German Democratic Republic, Poland, Romania, USSR, Czechoslovakia.

William Harvey
A2206

N. G. Chernyshevsky
A2207

1978, July 25 *Perf. 12*

4677	A2206	6k bl, blk & dp grn	12	7

Dr. William Harvey (1578-1657), discoverer of blood circulation, 400th birth anniversary.

1978, July 30 Engr. *Perf. 12x12½*

4678	A2207	4k brn, *yel*	8	6

Nikolai Gavilovich Chernyshevsky (1828-1889), revolutionary, birth sesquicentennial.

Whitewinged Petrel
A2208

Antarctic Fauna: 1k, Crested penguin (horiz.). 4k, Emperor penguin and chick. 6k, White-blooded pikes. 10k, Sea elephant (horiz.).

Perf. 12x11½, 11½x12

1978, July 30 Litho.

4679	A2208	1k multi	5	5
4680	A2208	3k multi	9	5
4681	A2208	4k multi	9	6
4682	A2208	6k multi	12	7
4683	A2208	10k multi	20	10
		Nos. 4679-4683 (5)	55	33

The Red Horse, by Petrov-Votkin — A2209

Paintings by Petrov-Votkin: 6k, Mother and Child, Petrograd, 1918. 10k, Death of the Commissar. 12k, Still-life with Fruit. 16k, Still-life with Teapot and Flowers. 50k, Self-portrait, 1918 (vert.).

1978, Aug. 16 Litho. *Perf. 12½x12*

4684	A2209	4k sil & multi	8	6
4685	A2209	6k sil & multi	12	7
4686	A2209	10k sil & multi	20	10
4687	A2209	12k sil & multi	25	12
4688	A2209	16k sil & multi	32	16
		Nos. 4684-4688 (5)	97	51

Souvenir Sheet

Perf. 11½x12

4689	A2209	50k sil & multi	1.00	65

Kozma Sergeevich Petrov-Votkin (1878-1939), painter. Nos. 4684-4688 have se-tenant silver and black labels with commemorative inscriptions. No. 4689 has label the size of stamp with inscription and silver margin.

Soyuz 31 in Shop, Intercosmos Emblem, USSR and DDR Flags
A2210

Designs (Intercosmos Emblem, Russian and German Democratic Republic Flags and): 15k, Pamir Mountains photographed from space; Salyut 6, Soyuz 29 and 31 complex and spectrum. 32k, Soyuz 31 docking, photographed from Salyut 6.

1978 Litho. *Perf. 12x12½*

4690	A2210	6k multi	12	7
4691	A2210	15k multi	30	14
4692	A2210	32k multi	65	35

Intercosmos, Soviet-East German cooperative space program.
Issue dates: 6k, Aug. 27. 15k, Aug. 31. 32k, Sept. 3.

PRAGA '78 Emblem, Plane, Radar, Spaceship
A2211

Photogravure and Engraved

1978, Aug. 29 *Perf. 11½*

4693	A2211	6k multi	12	7

PRAGA '78 International Philatelic Exhibition, Prague, Sept. 8-17.

Leo Tolstoi A2212

1978, Sept. 7 Engr. ***Perf. 12x12½***

4694	A2212	4k sl grn	8	6

Leo Tolstoi (1828-1910), novelist and philosopher.

Stag, Conference Emblem — A2213

1978 Photo. ***Perf. 11½***

4695	A2213	4k multi	8	6

14th General Assembly of the Society for Wildlife Preservation, Ashkhabad.

Bronze Figure, Erebuni, 8th Century A2214

Armenian Architecture: 6k, Etchmiadzin Cathedral, 4th century. 10k, Stone crosses, Dzaghkatzor, 13th century. 12k, Library, Erevan (horiz.). 16k, Lenin statue, Lenin Square, Erevan (horiz.).

1978 Litho. ***Perf. 12x12½, 12½x12***

4696	A2214	4k multi	8	6
4697	A2214	6k multi	12	7
4698	A2214	10k multi	20	10
4699	A2214	12k multi	25	12
4700	A2214	16k multi	32	16
	Nos. 4696-4700 (5)		97	51

Issue dates: 4k, 10k, 16k, Sept. 12; others, Oct. 14.

Memorial, Messina, Russian Warships A2215

1978, Sept. 12 Photo. ***Perf. 11½***

4701	A2215	6k multi	12	7

70th anniversary of aid given by Russian sailors during Messina earthquake.

Communications Emblem, Ostankino TV Tower — A2216

1978, Sept. 20 Photo. ***Perf. 11½***

4702	A2216	4k multi	8	6

Organization for Communication Cooperation of Socialist Countries, 20th anniv..

No. 4673 Overprinted

ФИЛВЫСТАВКА „60 лет ВЛКСМ"
МОСКВА. 1978

1978, Sept. 20 Litho. ***Perf. 12x12½***

4703	A2202	4k multi	8	6

Philatelic Exhibition for the Leninist Young Communist League.

Souvenir Sheet

Diana, by Paolo Veronese — A2217

1978, Sept. 28 Litho. ***Perf. 12x11½***

4704	A2217	50k multi	1.00	65

Veronese (1528-88), Italian painter.

Kremlin, Moscow A2218

S. G. Shauyan A2219

Souvenir Sheet

Lithographed and Embossed

1978, Oct. 7 ***Perf. 11½x12***

4705	A2218	30k gold & multi	1.00	65

Russian Constitution, 1st anniversary.

1978, Oct. 11 Engr. ***Perf. 12½x12***

4706	A2219	4k sl grn	8	6

Stepan Georgevich Shauyan (1878-1918), Communist Party functionary.

Ferry, Russian and Bulgarian Colors — A2220

Hammer and Sickle, Flags — A2221

1978, Oct. 14 Photo. ***Perf. 11½***

4707	A2220	6k multi	12	7

Opening of Ilychovsk-Varna Ferry.

1978, Oct. 26 Photo. ***Perf. 11½***

4708	A2221	4k gold & multi	8	6

61st anniversary of October Revolution.

Silver Gilt Cup, Novgorod, 12th Century — A2222

Old Russian Art: 10k, Pokrowna Nerli Church, 12th century (vert.). 12k, St. George Slaying the Dragon, icon, Novgorod, 15th century (vert.). 16k, The Czar, cannon, 1586.

Perf. 12½x12, 12x12½

1978, Nov. 28 Litho.

4709	A2222	6k multi	12	7
4710	A2222	10k multi	20	10
4711	A2222	12k multi	25	12
4712	A2222	16k multi	32	16

Oncology Institute, Emblem A2223

Savior Tower, Kremlin A2224

1978, Dec. 1 Photo. ***Perf. 11½***

4713	A2223	4k multi	8	6

75th anniv. of the P.A. Herzen Tumor Institute.

1978, Dec. 20 Litho. ***Perf. 12x12½***

4714	A2224	4k sil, bl & red	8	6

New Year 1979.

Nestor Pechersky, Chronicler, c. 885 — A2225

History of Postal Service: 6k, Birch bark letter and stylus. 10k, Messenger with trumpet and staff, from 14th century Psalm book. 12k, Winter traffic, from 16th century book by Sigizmund Gerberstein. 16k, Prikaz post office, from 17th century icon.

Lithographed and Engraved

1978, Dec. 20 ***Perf. 12½x12***

4715	A2225	4k multi	8	6
4716	A2225	6k multi	12	7
4717	A2225	10k multi	20	10
4718	A2225	12k multi	25	12
4719	A2225	16k multi	32	16
	Nos. 4715-4719 (5)		97	51

Kovalenok and Ivanchenkov, Salyut 6-Soyuz — A2226

1978, Dec. 20 Photo. ***Perf. 11½x12***

4720	A2226	10k multi	20	10

Cosmonauts V. V. Kovalenok and A. S. Ivanchenkov spent 140 days in space, June 15-Nov. 2, 1978.

Vasilii Pronchishchev — A2227

Icebreakers: 6k, Captain Belousov, 1954 (vert.). 10k, Moscow. 12k, Admiral Makarov, 1974. 16k, Lenin, 1959 (vert.). 20k, Nuclear-powered Arctica.

Perf. 11½x12, 12x11½

1978, Dec. 20 Photo. & Engr.

4721	A2227	4k multi	8	6
4722	A2227	6k multi	12	7
4723	A2227	10k multi	20	10
4724	A2227	12k multi	25	12
4725	A2227	16k multi	32	16
4726	A2227	20k multi	40	20
	Nos. 4721-4726 (6)		1.37	71

Souvenir Sheet

Mastheads and Globe with Russia — A2228

1978, Dec. 28 Litho. ***Perf. 12***

4727	A2228	30k multi	60	32

Distribution of periodicals through the Post and Telegraph Department, 60th anniversary.

Cuban Flags Forming Star — A2229

1979, Jan. 1 Photo. ***Perf. 11½***

4728	A2229	6k multi	12	7

Cuban Revolution, 20th anniversary.

Russian and Byelorussian Flags, Government Building, Minsk A2230

1979, Jan. 1
4729 A2230 4k multi 8 6

60th anniversaries of Byelorussian Soviet Socialist Republic and Byelorussian Community Party.

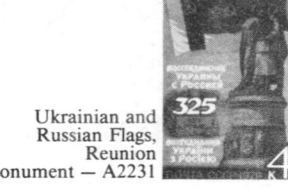

Ukrainian and Russian Flags, Reunion Monument — A2231

1979, Jan. 16
4730 A2231 4k multi 8 6

325th anniversary of reunion of Ukraine and Russia.

Old and New Vilnius University Buildings A2232

1979, Jan. 16 **Photo. & Engr.**
4731 A2232 4k blk & sal 8 6

400th anniversary of University of Vilnius.

Bulgaria No. 1 and Exhibition Hall A2233

1979, Jan. 25 **Litho.** ***Perf. 12½x12***
4732 A2233 15k multi 30 14

Filaserdica '79 Philatelic Exhibition, Sofia, commemorating centenary of Bulgarian postal service.

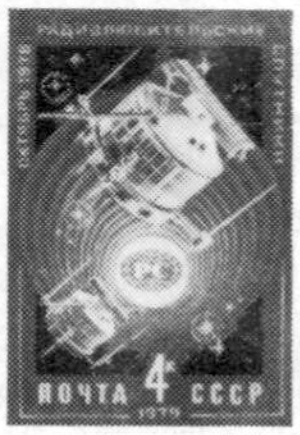
Sputniks, Soviet Radio Hams Emblem — A2234

1979, Feb. 23 **Photo.** ***Perf. 11½***
4733 A2234 4k multi 8 6

Sputnik satellites Radio 1 and Radio 2, launched, Oct. 1978.

1-3-0 Locomotive, 1878 — A2235

Locomotives: 3k, 1-4-0, 1912. 4k, 2-3-1, 1915. 6k, 1-3-1, 1925. 15k, 1-5-0, 1947.

1979, Feb. 23 **Litho.** ***Perf. 11½***

4734	A2235	2k multi	6	5
4735	A2235	3k multi	7	5
4736	A2235	4k multi	8	6
4737	A2235	6k multi	12	7
4738	A2235	15k multi	30	14
	Nos. 4734-4738 (5)		63	37

Souvenir Sheet

Medal for Land Development A2236

1979, Mar. 14 ***Perf. 11½x12½***
4739 A2236 50k multi 1.00 65

25th anniv. of drive to develop virgin lands.

Venera 11 and 12 over Venus — A2237

1979, Mar. 16 **Photo.** ***Perf. 11½***
4740 A2237 10k multi 20 10

Interplanetary flights of Venera 11 and Venera 12, December 1978.

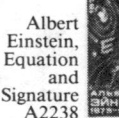

Albert Einstein, Equation and Signature A2238

1979, Mar. 16
4741 A2238 6k multi 12 7

Albert Einstein (1879-1955), theoretical physicist.

Congress Emblem A2239

1979, Mar. 16
4742 A2239 6k multi 12 7

21st World Veterinary Congress, Moscow.

"To Arms," by R. Berens A2240

1979, Mar. 21
4743 A2240 4k multi 8 6

60th anniversary of proclamation of Soviet Republic of Hungary.

Salyut 6, Soyuz, Research Ship, Letters — A2241

1979, Apr. 12 **Litho.** ***Perf. 11½x12***
4744 A2241 15k multi 30 14

Cosmonauts' Day.

Souvenir Sheet

Ice Hockey — A2242

1979, Apr. 14 **Photo.** ***Perf. 12x11½***
4745 A2242 50k multi 1.00 65

World and European Ice Hockey Championships, Moscow, Apr. 14-27.

Souvenir Sheet

Lenin A2243

1979, Apr. 18
4746 A2243 50k red, gold & brn 1.00 65

109th anniversary of the birth of Lenin.

Astronauts' Training Center A2244

Exhibition Emblem A2245

Design: 32k, Astronauts, landing capsule, radar, helicopter and emblem.

1979, Apr. 12 **Litho.** ***Perf. 11½***
4747 A2244 6k multi 12 7
4748 A2244 32k multi 65 32

Joint Soviet-Bulgarian space flight.

1979, Apr. 18 **Photo.** ***Perf. 11½***
4749 A2245 15k sil, red & vio bl 30 14

National USSR Exhibition in the United Kingdom. Se-tenant label with commemorative inscription.

Blast Furance, Pushkin Theater, "Tent" Sculpture — A2246

1979, May 24 **Photo.** ***Perf. 11½***
4750 A2246 4k multi 8 6

50th anniversary of Magnitogorsk City.

Souvenir Sheet

No. 4745 Overprinted in Margin in Red

СОВЕТСКИЕ ХОККЕИСТЫ—
ЧЕМПИОНЫ МИРА
И ЕВРОПЫ

1979, May 24 ***Perf. 12x11½***
4751 A2242 50k multi 1.25 65

Victory of Soviet team in World and European Ice Hockey Championships.

Infant, Flowers, IYC Emblem — A2247

1979, June **Litho.** ***Perf. 12x12½***
4752 A2247 4k multi 8 6

International Year of the Child.

Horn Player and Bears Playing Balalaika, Bogorodsk Wood Carvings — A2248

Folk Art: 3k, Decorated wooden bowls, Khokhloma. 4k, Tray decorated with flowers, Zhestovo. 6k, Carved bone boxes, Kholmogory. 15k, Lace, Vologda.

1979, June 14 **Litho.** ***Perf. 12½x12***

4753	A2248	2k multi	6	5
4754	A2248	3k multi	7	5
4755	A2248	4k multi	8	6
4756	A2248	6k multi	12	7
4757	A2248	15k multi	30	14
	Nos. 4753-4757 (5)		63	37

The indexes in each volume of the Scott Catalogue contain many listings which help to identify stamps.

V. A. Djanibekov, O. G. Makarov, Spacecraft
A2249

1979, June *Perf. 12x11½*

4758 A2249 4k multi		8	6

Flights of Soyuz 26-27 and work on board of orbital complex Salyut 26-27.

COMECON Building, Members' Flags
A2250

Scene from "Potemkin" and Festival Emblem
A2251

1979, June 26 *Perf. 12*

4759 A2250 16k multi	32	16

Council for Mutual Economic Aid of Socialist Countries, 30th anniversary.

Photogravure and Engraved

1979, July *Perf. 11½*

4760 A2251 15k multi	32	14

11th International Film Festival, Moscow, and 60th anniversary of Soviet film industry.

Lenin Square Station, Tashkent
A2252

1979, July Litho. *Perf. 12*

4761 A2252 4k multi	8	6

Tashkent subway.

Souvenir Sheets

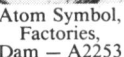

Atom Symbol, Factories, Dam — A2253

USSR Philatelic Society Emblem — A2254

1979, July 23 Photo. *Perf. 11½x12*

4762 A2253 30k multi	60	40

50th anniversary of 1st Five-Year Plan.

1979, July 25 Litho. *Perf. 12x12½*

4763 A2254 50k gray grn & red	1.00	65

4th Cong. of USSR Phil. Soc., Moscow.

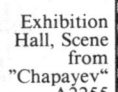

Exhibition Hall, Scene from "Chapayev"
A2255

1979, Aug. 8 Photo. *Perf. 11½*

4764 A2255 4k multi	8	8

60th anniversary of Soviet Film and Exhibition of History of Soviet Film.

Roses, by P. P. Konchalovsky, 1955 — A2256

Russian Flower Paintings: 1k, Flowers and Fruit, by I. F. Khrutsky, 1830. 2k, Phlox, by I. N. Kramskoi, 1884. 3k, Lilac, by K. A. Korovin, 1915. 15k, Bluebells, by S. V. Gerasimov, 1944. 2k, 3k, 15k, vert.

Perf. 12½x12, 12x12½

1979, Aug. 16 **Litho.**

4765 A2256 1k multi	5	5
4766 A2256 2k multi	6	5
4767 A2256 3k multi	9	6
4768 A2256 15k multi	30	20
4769 A2256 32k multi	65	45
Nos. 4765-4769 (5)	1.15	81

John McClean
A2257

Soviet Circus Emblem
A2258

1979, Aug. 29 Litho. *Perf. 11½*

4770 A2257 4k red & blk	8	8

John McClean (1879-1923), British Communist labor leader.

1979, Sept.

4771 A2258 4k multi	8	8

Soviet Circus, 60th anniversary.

Friendship — A2259

Children's Drawings: 3k, Children and Horses. 4k, Dances. 15k, The Excursion.

1979, Sept. 10 *Perf. 12½x12*

4772 A2259 2k multi	6	5
4773 A2259 3k multi	9	6
4774 A2259 4k multi	8	8
4775 A2259 15k multi	30	20

International Year of the Child.

Oriolus oriolus — A2260

Birds: 3k, Dendrocopus minor. 4k, Parus cristatus. 10k, Tyto alba. 15k, Caprimulgus europaeus.

1979, Sept. 18

4776 A2260 2k multi	6	5
4777 A2260 3k multi	9	6
4778 A2260 4k multi	8	8
4779 A2260 10k multi	20	14
4780 A2260 15k multi	30	20
Nos. 4776-4780 (5)	73	53

German Arms, Marx, Engels, Lenin, Berlin
A2261

1979, Oct. 7 Photo. *Perf. 11½*

4781 A2261 6k multi	12	8

German Democratic Republic, 30th anniversary.

Valery Ryumin, Vladimir Lyakhov, Salyut 6 — A2262

Design: No. 4783, Spacecraft.

1979, Oct. 10 *Perf. 12x11½*

4782 A2262 15k multi	30	20
4783 A2262 15k multi	30	20

175 days in space, Feb. 25-Aug. 19. Nos. 4782-4783 printed se-tenant in continuous design.

Star — A2264

Hammer and Sickle — A2265

1979, Oct. 18 *Perf. 11½*

4784 A2263 4k multi	8	8

USSR Armed Forces, 60th anniversary.

1979, Oct. 18

4785 A2264 4k multi	8	8

October Revolution, 62nd anniversary.

Katherina, by T. G. Shevchenko
A2266

Ukrainian Paintings: 3k, Working Girl, by K.K. Kostandi. 4k, Lenin's Return to Petrograd, by A.M. Lopuhov. 10k, Soldier's Return, by N.V. Kostesky 15k, Going to Work, by M.G. Belsky.

1979, Nov. 18 Litho. *Perf. 12x12½*

4786 A2266 2k multi	6	5
4787 A2266 3k multi	9	6
4788 A2266 4k multi	8	8
4789 A2266 10k multi	20	14
4790 A2266 15k multi	30	20
Nos. 4786-4790 (5)	73	53

Shabolovka Radio Tower, Moscow
A2267

Mischa Holding Stamp
A2268

1979, Nov. 28 Photo. *Perf. 12*

4791 A2267 32k multi	65	45

Radio Moscow, 50th anniversary.

1979, Nov. 28 *Perf. 12x12½*

4792 A2268 4k multi	8	8

New Year 1980.

Hand Holding Peace Message
A2269

Policeman, Patrol Car, Helicopter
A2270

Peace Program in Action: No. 4794, Hands holding cultural symbols. No. 4795, Hammer and sickle, flag.

1979, Dec. 5 Litho. *Perf. 12*

4793 A2269 4k multi	8	8
4794 A2269 4k multi	8	8
4795 A2269 4k multi	8	8

1979, Dec. 20 *Perf. 12x12½*

Traffic Safety: 4k, Car, girl and ball. 6k, Speeding cars.

4796 A2270 3k multi	9	6
4797 A2270 4k multi	8	8
4798 A2270 6k multi	12	8

Vulkanolog — A2271

Research Ships and Portraits: 2k, Professor Bogorov. 4k, Ernst Krenkel. 6k, Vladislav Volkov. 10k, Cosmonaut Yuri Gagarin. 15k, Academician E.B. Kurchatov.

Lithographed and Engraved

1979, Dec. 25 ***Perf. 12x11½***

4799	A2271	1k	multi	5	5
4800	A2271	2k	multi	6	5
4801	A2271	4k	multi	8	8
4802	A2271	6k	multi	12	8
4803	A2271	10k	multi	20	14
4804	A2271	15k	multi	30	20
	Nos. 4799-4804 (6)			81	60

See Nos. 4881-4886.

Souvenir Sheet

Explorers Raising Red Flag at North Pole — A2272

1979, Dec. 25 **Photo.** ***Perf. 11½x12***

4805 A2272 50k multi 1.00 65

Komsomolskaya Pravda North Pole expedition. Size: 66½x85mm.

Type of 1970

Design: 4k, Coat of arms, power line, factories.

1980, Jan. 10 **Litho.** ***Perf. 12x12½***

4806 A1794 4k carmine 8 8

Mordovian Autonomous Soviet Socialist Republic, 50th anniversary.

Freestyle Skating A2273

Perf. 12x12½, 12½x12

1980, Jan. 22

4807	A2273	4k	*Speed skating*	8	8
4808	A2273	6k	*shown*	12	8
4809	A2273	10k	*Ice hockey*	20	14
4810	A2273	15k	*Downhill skiing*	30	20
4811	A2273	20k	*Luge*, vert.	40	25
	Nos. 4807-4811 (5)			1.10	75

Souvenir Sheet

4812 A2273 50k *Cross-country skiing*, vert. 1.10 85

13th Winter Olympic Games, Lake Placid, N.Y., Feb. 12-24.

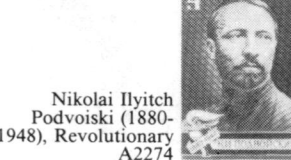

Nikolai Ilyitch Podvoiski (1880-1948), Revolutionary A2274

1980, Feb. 16 **Engr.** ***Perf. 12½x12***

4813 A2274 4k cl brn 8 8

Rainbow, by A.K. Savrasov — A2275

Paintings: No. 4815, Summer Harvest, by A.G. Venetsianov (vert.). No. 4816, Old Erevan, by M.S. Saryan.

1980, Mar. 4 **Litho.** ***Perf. 11½***

4814	A2275	6k	multi	12	8
4815	A2275	6k	multi	12	8
4816	A2275	6k	multi	12	8

Souvenir Sheet

Cosmonaut Alexei Leonov — A2276

1980, Mar. 18 **Litho.** ***Perf. 12½x12***

4817 A2276 50k multi 1.00 65

Man's first walk in space (Voskhod 2, Mar. 18-19, 1965), 15th anniversary.

Georg Ots, Estonian Artist A2277

Lenin Order, 50th Anniversary A2278

1980, Mar. 21 **Engr.**

4818 A2277 4k sl bl 8 8

1980, Apr. 6 **Photo.** ***Perf. 11½***

4819 A2278 4k multi 8 8

Souvenir Sheet

Cosmonauts, Salyut 6 and Soyuz — A2279

1980, Apr. 12 **Litho.** ***Perf. 12***

4820 A2279 50k multi 1.00 65

Intercosmos cooperative space program.

Flags and Arms of Azerbaijan, Government House A2280

"Mother Russia," Fireworks over Moscow A2282

Lenin, 110th Birth Anniversary — A2281

1980, Apr. 22 **Photo.**

4821 A2280 4k multi 8 8

Azerbaijan Soviet Socialist Republic, Communist Party of Azerbaijan. 60th anniv.

Souvenir Sheet

1980, Apr. 22 ***Perf. 12x11½***

4822 A2281 30k multi 65 50

1980, Apr. 25 **Litho.**

Designs: No. 4824, Soviet War Memorial, Berlin, raising of Red flag. No. 4825, Parade, Red Square, Moscow.

4823	A2282	4k	multi	8	8
4824	A2282	4k	multi	8	8
4825	A2282	4k	multi	8	8

35th anniv. of victory in World War II.

Workers' Monument A2283

"XXV" A2284

1980, May 12 **Litho.** ***Perf. 12***

4826 A2283 4k multi 8 8

Workers' Delegates in Ivanovo-Voznesensk, 75th anniversary.

1980, May 14 **Photo.** ***Perf. 11½***

4827 A2284 32k multi 65 45

Signing of Warsaw Pact (Bulgaria, Czechoslovakia, German Democratic Rep., Hungary, Poland, Romania, USSR), 25th anniversary.

YaK-24 Helicopter, 1953 — A2285

1980, May 15 **Litho.** ***Perf. 12½x12***

4828	A2285	1k	*shown*	5	5
4829	A2285	2k	*MI-8, 1962*	6	5
4830	A2285	3k	*KA-26, 1965*	7	6
4831	A2285	6k	*MI-6, 1957*	14	8
4832	A2285	15k	*MI-10*	30	20
4833	A2285	32k	*V-12*	65	45
	Nos. 4828-4833 (6)			1.27	89

David Anacht, Illuminated Manuscript A2286

Emblem, Training Lab A2287

1980, May 16 ***Perf. 12***

4834 A2286 4k multi 8 8

David Anacht, Armenian philosopher, 1500th birth anniversary.

1980, June 4

4835	A2287	6k	*shown*	14	8
4836	A2287	15k	*Cosmonauts meeting*	30	20
4837	A2287	32k	*Press conference*	65	45

Intercosmos cooperative space program (U.S.S.R.-Hungary).

Polar Fox A2288

1980, June 25 **Litho.** ***Perf. 12x12½***

4838	A2288	2k	*Dark silver fox*, vert.	6	5
4839	A2288	4k	*shown*	8	8
4840	A2288	6k	*Mink*	14	8
4841	A2288	10k	*Azerbaijan nutria*, vert.	20	14
4842	A2288	15k	*Black sable*	30	20
	Nos. 4838-4842 (5)			78	55

Factory, Buildings, Arms of Tatar A.S.S.R. A2289

1980, June 25 ***Perf. 12***

4843 A2289 4k multi 8 8

Tatar Autonomous Soviet Socialist Republic, 60th anniversary.

Bauman Technological College A2290

Ho Chi Minh A2291

1980, July 1 Photo. *Perf. 11½*

4844 A2290 4k multi 8 8

Bauman Technological College, Moscow, 150th anniversary.

1980, July 7

4845 A2291 6k multi 14 8

Red Flag, Lithuanian Arms, Flag, Red Guards Monument A2292

1980, July 12 Litho. *Perf. 12*

4846 A2292 4k multi 8 8

Lithuanian Soviet Socialist Republic, 40th anniversary.

Russian Flag and Arms, Latvian Flag, Monument, Buildings A2293

Design: No. 4848, Russian flag and arms, Estonian flag, monument, buildings.

1980, July 21 Litho. *Perf. 12*

4847 A2293 4k multi 8 8
4848 A2293 4k multi 8 8

Restoration of Soviet power.

Cosmonauts Boarding Soyuz A2294

1980, July 24 *Perf. 12x12½*

4849 A2294 6k *shown* 12 8
4850 A2294 15k *Working aboard spacecraft* 30 20
4851 A2294 32k *Return flight* 65 45

20th anniv. of Center for Cosmonaut Training.

Avicenna (980-1037), Philosopher and Physician — A2295

Photogravure and Engraved

1980, Aug. 16 *Perf. 11½*

4852 A2295 4k multi 8 8

Soviet Racing Car KHADI-7 — A2296

1980, Aug. 25 Litho. *Perf. 12*

4853 A2296 2k *shown* 6 5
4854 A2296 6k *KHADI-10* 12 6
4855 A2296 15k *KHADI-113* 30 20
4856 A2296 30k *KHADI-133* 60 40

Kazakhstan Republic, 60th Anniversary A2297

1980, Aug. 26

4857 A2297 4k multi 8 8

Ingres, Self-portrait, and Nymph A2298

1980, Aug. 29 *Perf. 12x12½*

4858 A2298 32k multi 65 45

Jean Auguste Dominique Ingres (1780-1867), French painter.

Morning on the Field of Kulikovo, by A. Bubnov — A2299

1980, Sept. 6 Litho. *Perf. 12*

4859 A2299 4k multi 8 8

Battle of Kulikovo, 600th anniversary.

Town Hall, Tartu — A2300

1980, Sept. 15 Photo. *Perf. 11½*

4860 A2300 4k multi 8 8

Tartu, 950th anniversary.

Y.V. Malyshev, V.V. Aksenov A2301

1980, Sept. 15 Litho. *Perf. 12x12½*

4861 A2301 10k multi 20 14

Soyuz T-2 space flight.

Flight Training, Yuri Gagarin — A2302

1980, Sept. 15 Photo. *Perf. 11½x12*

4862 A2302 6k *shown* 12 8
4863 A2302 15k *Space walk* 30 20
4864 A2302 32K *Endurance test* 65 40

Gagarin Cosmonaut Training Center, 20th anniversary.

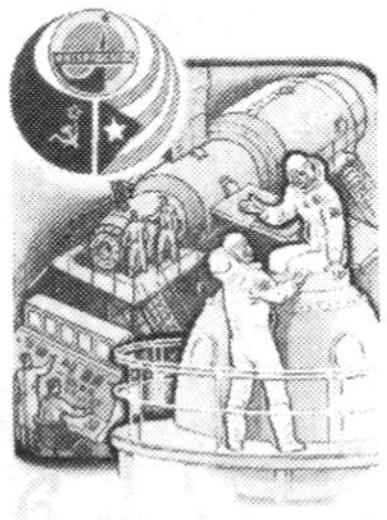

Cosmonauts Training A2303

Designs (Intercosmos Emblem, Flags of USSR and Cuba and): 15k, Inside weightless cabin. 32k, Landing.

1980, Sept. 15 Litho. *Perf. 12x12½*

4865 A2303 6k multi 12 6
4866 A2303 15k multi 30 20
4867 A2303 32k multi 65 40

Intercosmos cooperative space program (USSR-Cuba).

October Revolution, 63rd Anniversary A2304

1980, Sept. 20 Photo. *Perf. 11½*

4868 A2304 6k multi 12 8

David Gurumishvily (1705-1792), Poet — A2305

1980, Sept. 20

4869 A2305 6k multi 12 8

Family with Serfs, by N.V. Nevrev — A2305a

Design: No. 4869B. Countess Tarakanova, by K.D. Flavitsky (vert.)

1980, Sept. 25 Litho. *Perf. 11½*

4869A A2305a 6k multi 12 8
4869B A2305a 6k multi 12 8

N.V. Nevrev (1830-1904) and K.D. Flavitsky (1830-1866).

A.F. Joffe (1880-1960), Physicist — A2306

1980, Sept. 29

4870 A2306 4k multi 8 8

Siberian Pine A2307

1980, Sept. 29 Litho. *Perf. 12½x12*

4871 A2307 2k *shown* 6 5
4872 A2307 4k *Oak* 8 8
4873 A2307 6k *Lime tree*, vert. 12 8
4874 A2307 10k *Sea bucthorn* 20 14
4875 A2307 15k *European ash* 30 20
Nos. 4871-4875 (5) 76 55

A.M. Vasilevsky (1895-1977), Soviet Marshal — A2308

1980, Sept. 30 Engr. *Perf. 12*

4876 A2308 4k dk grn 8 8

Souvenir Sheet

Mischa Holding Olympic Torch — A2309

1980, Nov. 24 *Perf. 12x12½*

4877 A2309 1r multi 2.75 1.00

Completion of 22nd Summer Olympic Games, Moscow, July 19-Aug. 3.

A.V. Suvorov (1730-1800), General and Military Theorist A2310

1980, Nov. 24 Engr.

4878 A2310 4k slate 8 8

Armenian Soviet Socialist Republic and Armenian Communist Party, 60th Anniversary
A2311

1980, Nov. 24 Litho. *Perf. 12*
4879 A2311 4k multi 8 8

Aleksandr Blok (1880-1921), Poet — A2312

1980, Nov. 24
4880 A2312 4k multi 8 8

Research Ship Type of 1979

Lithographed and Engraved

1980, Nov. 24 *Perf. 12x11½*

4881	A2271	2k	Aju Dag, Fleet arms	6	5
4882	A2271	3k	Valerian Urywaev	7	6
4883	A2271	4k	Mikhail Somov	8	8
4884	A2271	6k	Sergei Korolev	12	8
4885	A2271	10k	Otto Schmidt	20	14
4886	A2271	15k	Ustislav Kelgysh	30	20
			Nos. 4881-4886 (6)	83	61

Russian Flag
A2313

Soviet Medical College, 50th Anniversary
A2314

1980, Dec. 1 Engr. *Perf. 12x12½*
4887 A2313 3k org red 7 6

1980, Dec. 1 Photo. *Perf. 11½*
4888 A2314 4k multi 8 8

New Year 1981
A2315

1980, Dec. 1 Litho. *Perf. 12*
4889 A2315 4k multi 8 8

Lenin, Electrical Plant
A2316

1980, Dec. 18
4890 A2316 4k multi 8 8

60th anniversary of GOELRO (Lenin's electro-economic plan).

Values quoted in this catalogue are for stamps graded at Fine-Very Fine and with no faults. An illustrated guide to grade is provided in introductory material, beginning on Page V.

A.N. Nesmeyanov (1899-1980), Chemist — A2317

1980, Dec. 19 *Perf. 12½x12*
4891 A2317 4k multi 8 8

Nagatinski Bridge, Moscow — A2318

Photogravure and Engraved

1980, Dec. 23 *Perf. 11½x12*

4892	A2318	4k	shown	8	8
4893	A2318	6k	Luzhniki Bridge	12	8
4894	A2318	15k	Kalininski Bridge	30	20

S.K. Timoshenko
A2319

Flags of India and U.S.S.R, Government House, New Delhi
A2320

1980, Dec. 25 Engr. *Perf. 12*
4895 A2319 4k rose lake 8 8

S.K. Timoshenko (1895-1970), Soviet marshal.

1980, Dec. 30 Litho. *Perf. 12x12½*
4896 A2320 4k multi 8 8

Visit of Pres. Brezhnev to India. Printed se-tenant with inscribed label.

Mirny Base — A2321

1981, Jan. 5 *Perf. 12*

4897	A2321	4k	shown	8	8
4898	A2321	6k	Earth station, rocket	12	8
4899	A2321	15k	Map, supply ship	30	20

Russian Antarctic research, 25th anniv.

Dagestan Soviet Socialist Republic, 60th Anniversary
A2322

1981, Jan. 20
4900 A2322 4k multi 8 8

Bandy World Championship, Cheborovsk — A2323

1981, Jan. 20
4901 A2323 6k multi 12 8

26th Congress of Ukrainian Communist Party.
A2324

1981, Jan. 23 Photo. *Perf. 11½*
4902 A2324 4k multi 8 8

Lenin, "XXVI"
A2325

Lenin and Congress Building — A2326

Banner and Kremlin — A2327

1981 Photo. *Perf. 11½*
4903 A2325 4k multi 8 8

Photogravure and Embossed

1982 *Perf. 11½x12*
4904 A2326 20k multi 1.25 65

Souvenir Sheet

Litho.

Perf. 12x12½
4905 A2327 50k multi 1.00 65

26th Communist Party Congress. Issue dates: 4k, 20k, Jan. 22; 50k, Feb. 16.

Mstislav V. Keldysh
A2328

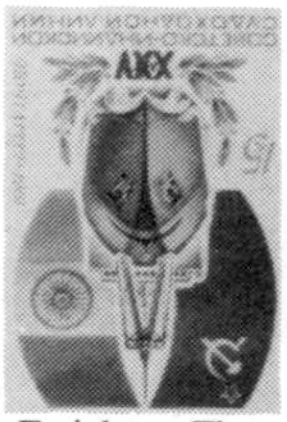

Freighter, Flags of USSR and India
A2329

Perf. 11½x12

1981, Feb. 10 Photo. Engr.
4906 A2328 4k multi 8 8

Mstislav Vsevolodovich Keldysh (1911-1978), mathematician.

1981, Feb. 10 Litho. *Perf. 12*
4907 A2329 15k multi 30 20

Russian-Indian Shipping Line, 25th anniv.

Baikal-Amur Railroad and Map — A2330

10th Five-Year Plan Projects (1976-1980): No. 4909, Gas plant, Urengoi. No. 4910, Enisei River power station. No. 4911, Atomic power plant. No. 4912, Paper mill. No. 4913, Coal mining, Ekibstyi.

1981, Feb. 18 *Perf. 12½x12*

4908	A2330	4k	multi	8	8
4909	A2330	4k	multi	8	8
4910	A2330	4k	multi	8	8
4911	A2330	4k	multi	8	8
4912	A2330	4k	multi	8	8
4913	A2330	4k	multi	8	8
			Nos. 4908-4913 (6)	48	48

Georgian Soviet Socialist Republic, 60th Anniv.
A2331

1981, Feb. 25 *Perf. 12*
4914 A2331 4k multi 8 8

Abkhazian Autonomous Soviet Socialist Republic, 60th Anniv. — A2332

1981, Mar. 4
4915 A2332 4k multi 8 8

Communications Institute
A2333

Satellite, Radio Operator
A2334

1981, Mar. 12 Photo. *Perf. 11½*
4916 A2333 4k multi 8 8

Moscow Electrotechnical Institute of Communications, 60th anniv.

1981, Mar. 12
4917 A2334 4k multi 8 8

30th All-Union Amateur Radio Designers Exhibition.

Cosmonauts L.I. Popov and V.V. Rumin A2335

1981, Mar. 20 Litho. *Perf. 12*
4918 A2335 15k shown 20 20
4919 A2335 15k Spacecraft complex 30 20

185-day flight of Cosmos 35-Salyut 6-Cosmos 37 complex, Apr. 9-Oct. 11, 1980. Nos. 4918-4919 se-tenant in continuous design and with label showing test and symbols.

Cosmonauts O. Makarov, L. Kizim and G. Strekalov — A2336

1981, Mar. 20 *Perf. 12½x12*
4920 A2336 10k multi 20 14

Soyuz T-3 flight, Nov. 27-Dec. 10, 1980.

Lift-Off, Baikonur Base — A2337

1981, Mar. 23
4921 A2337 6k shown 12 8
4922 A2337 15k Mongolians watching flight on TV 30 20
4923 A2337 32k Re-entry 65 42

Intercosmos cooperative space program (USSR-Mongolia).

Vitus Bering — A2338

Yuri Gagarin and Earth — A2339

Yuri Gagarin — A2340

1981, Mar. 25 Engr. *Perf. 12x12½*
4924 A2338 4k dk bl 8 8

Vitus Bering (1680-1741), Danish navigator, 300th birth anniv. (1980).

1981, Apr. 12 Photo. *Perf. 11½x12*
4925 A2339 6k shown 12 8
4926 A2339 15k S.P. Korolev (craft designer) 30 20
4927 A2339 32k Monument 65 42

Souvenir Sheet

4928 A2340 50k shown 1.75 90

Russian space flights, 20th anniversary. Nos. 4925-4927 each se-tenant with inscribed label.

Salyut Orbital Station, 10th Anniv. of Flight — A2341

1981, Apr. 19 Litho. *Perf. 12x12½*
4929 A2341 32k multi 65 42

Souvenir Sheet

111th Birth Anniv. of Lenin A2342

1981, Apr. 22 *Perf. 11½x12½*
4930 A2342 50k multi 1.00 50

Sergei Prokofiev (1891-1953), Composer A2343

New Hofburg Palace, Vienna A2344

1981, Apr. 23 Engr. *Perf. 12*
4931 A2343 4k dk pur 8 8

1981, May 5 Litho.
4932 A2344 15k multi 30 20

WIPA 1981 Philatelic Exhibition, Vienna, May 22-31.

Adzhar Autonomous Soviet Socialist Republic, 60th Anniv. A2345

1981, May 7
4933 A2345 4k multi 8 8

Centenary of Welding (Invented by N.N. Benardos) A2346

Lithographed and Engraved

1981, May 12 *Perf. 11½*
4934 A2346 6k multi 12 8

Intl. Architects Union, 14th Congress, Warsaw — A2347

1981, May 12 Photo.
4935 A2347 15k multi 30 20

Albanian Girl, by A.A. Ivanov A2348

Paintings: No. 4937, Horseman, by F.A. Roubeau. No. 4938, The Demon, by M.A. Wrubel (horiz.). No. 4939, Sunset over the Sea, by N.N. Ge (horiz.).

1981, May 15 Litho. *Perf. 12x12½*
4936 A2348 10k multi 20 14
4937 A2348 10k multi 20 14
4938 A2348 10k multi 20 14
4939 A2348 10k multi 20 14

Cosmonauts in Training A2349

1981, May 15
4940 A2349 6k shown 12 8
4941 A2349 15k In space 30 20
4942 A2349 32k Return 65 42

Intercosmos cooperative space program (USSR-Romania).

Dwarf Primrose A2350

Flowers of the Carpathian Mountains: 6k, Great carline thistle. 10k, Mountain parageum. 15k, Alpine bluebell. 32k, Rhododendron kotschyi.

1981, May 20 *Perf. 12*
4943 A2350 4k multi 8 8
4944 A2350 6k multi 12 8
4945 A2350 10k multi 20 14
4946 A2350 15k multi 30 20
4947 A2350 32k multi 65 42
Nos. 4943-4947 (5) 1.35 92

Luigi Longo, Italian Labor Leader, 1st Death Anniv. — A2351

1981, May 24 Photo. *Perf. 11½*
4948 A2351 6k multi 12 8

Nizami Gjanshevi (1141-1209), Azerbaijan Poet A2352

1981, May 25 Photo. & Engr.
4949 A2352 4k multi 8 8

Running A2353

Mongolian Revolution, 60th Anniv. A2354

1981, June 18 Litho. *Perf. 12*
4950 A2353 4k shown 8 8
4951 A2353 6k Soccer 12 8
4952 A2353 10k Discus throwing 20 14
4953 A2353 15k Boxing 30 20
4954 A2353 32k Diving 65 42
Nos. 4950-4954 (5) 1.35 92

1981, July 6
4955 A2354 6k multi 12 8

12th Intl. Film Festival, Moscow — A2355

1981, July 6 Photo. *Perf. 11½*
4956 A2355 15k multi 30 20

River Tour Boat Lenin A2356

1981, July 9 Litho. *Perf. 12½*
4957 A2356 4k shown 8 8
4958 A2356 6k Cosmonaut Gagarin 12 8
4959 A2356 15k Valerian Kuibyshev 30 20
4960 A2356 32k Freighter Baltijski 65 42

Icebreaker Maligin — A2357

Photogravure and Engraved

1981, July 9 *Perf. 11½x12*

4961	A2357	15k multi	30	20

26th Party Congress Resolutions (Intl. Cooperation) — A2358

1981, July 15 **Photo.** *Perf. 12x11½*

4962	A2358	4k shown	8	8
4963	A2358	4k Industry	8	8
4964	A2358	4k Energy	8	8
4965	A2358	4k Agriculture	8	8
4966	A2358	4k Communications	8	8
4967	A2358	4k Science	8	8
		Nos. 4962-4967 (6)	48	48

I.N. Ulyanov (Lenin's Father), 150th Anniv. of Birth — A2359

1981, July 25 **Engr.** *Perf. 11½*

4968	A2359	4k multi	8	8

Leningrad Theater, Sesquicentennial — A2360

1981, Aug. 12 **Photo.** *Perf. 11½*

4969	A2360	6k multi	12	8

A.M. Gerasimov, Artist, Birth Centenary A2361

1981, Aug. 12 **Litho.** *Perf. 12*

4970	A2361	4k multi	8	8

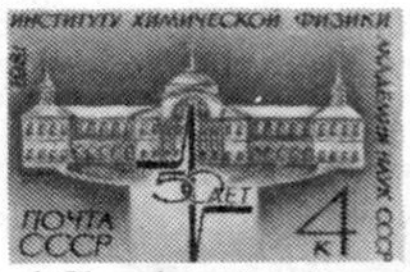

Physical Chemistry Institute, Moscow Academy of Science, 50th Anniv. A2362

1981, Aug. 12 **Photo.** *Perf. 11½*

4971	A2362	4k multi	8	8

Siberian Tit A2363

Designs: Song birds.

Perf. 12½x12, 12x12½

1981, Aug. 20 **Litho.**

4972	A2363	6k shown	12	8
4973	A2363	10k Tersiphone paradisi, vert.	20	14
4974	A2363	15k Emberiza jankovski	30	20
4975	A2363	20k Sutora webbiana, vert.	40	25
4976	A2363	32k Saxicola torquata, vert.	65	42
		Nos. 4972-4976 (5)	1.67	1.09

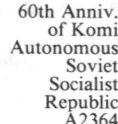

60th Anniv. of Komi Autonomous Soviet Socialist Republic A2364

1981, Aug. 22 *Perf. 12*

4977	A2364	4k multi	8	8

Svyaz-'81 Intl. Communications Exhibition — A2365

Photogravure and Engraved

1981, Aug. 22 *Perf. 11½*

4978	A2365	4k multi	8	8

60th Anniv. of Kabardino-Balkar Autonomous Soviet Socialist Republic — A2366

1981, Sept. 1 **Litho.** *Perf. 12*

4979	A2366	4k multi	8	8

War Veterans' Committee, 25th Anniv. — A2367

Schooner Kodor — A2368

1981, Sept. 1 **Photo.** *Perf. 11½*

4980	A2367	4k multi	8	8

Perf. 12½x12, 12x12½

1981, Sept. 18 **Litho.**

Designs: Training ships. 4k, 6k, 15k, 20k horiz.

4981	A2368	4k 4-masted bark Tovarich I	8	8
4982	A2368	6k Barkentine Vega I	12	8
4983	A2368	10k shown	20	14
4984	A2368	15k 3-masted bark Tovarich	30	20
4985	A2368	20k 4-masted bark Kruzenstern	40	25
4986	A2368	32k 4-masted bark Sedov	65	42
		Nos. 4981-4986 (6)	1.75	1.17

Kazakhstan's Union with Russia, 250th Anniv. A2369

Mikhail Alekseevich Lavrentiev (1900-1980), Mathematician A2370

1981, Oct. 10 *Perf. 12*

4987	A2369	4k multi	8	8

1981, Oct. 10 **Photo.** *Perf. 11½*

4988	A2370	4k multi	8	8

64th Anniv. of October Revolution — A2371

1981, Oct. 15 **Litho.**

4989	A2371	4k multi	8	8

Ekran Satellite TV Broadcasting System A2372

1981, Oct. 15 *Perf. 12*

4990	A2372	4k multi	8	8

A2373

A2374

1981, Oct. 15

4991	A2373	10k multi	20	14
4992	A2374	10k multi	20	14

Salyut 6-Soyuz flight of V.V. Kovalionok and V.P. Savinykh.

Souvenir Sheet

Birth Centenary of Pablo Picasso — A2375

1981, Oct. 25 *Perf. 12x12½*

4993	A2375	50k multi	1.65	85

Sergei Dmitrievich Merkurov (1881-1952), Artist — A2376

Photogravure and Engraved

1981, Nov. 5 *Perf. 11½*

4994	A2376	4k multi	8	8

Autumn, by Nino Pirosmanas, 1913 — A2377

Paintings: 6k, Guriyka, by M.G. Kokodze, 1921. 10k, Fellow Travelers, by U.M. Dzhaparidze, 1936 (horiz.). 15k, Shota Rustaveli, by S.S. Kobuladze, 1938. 32k, Collecting Tea, by V.D. Gudiashvili, 1964 (horiz.).

Perf. 12x12½, 12½x12

1981, Nov. 5 **Litho.**

4995	A2377	4k multi	8	8
4996	A2377	6k multi	12	8
4997	A2377	10k multi	20	14
4998	A2377	15k multi	30	20
4999	A2377	32k multi	65	42
		Nos. 4995-4999 (5)	1.35	92

New Year 1982 — A2378

1981, Dec. 2 **Litho.** *Perf. 12*

5000	A2378	4k multi	8	8

Public Transportation 19th-20th Cent. — A2379

Photogravure and Engraved

1981, Dec. 10 *Perf. 11½x12*

5001	A2379	4k Sled	8	8
5002	A2379	6k Horse-drawn trolley	12	8
5003	A2379	10k Coach	20	14
5004	A2379	15k Taxi, 1926	30	20

5005 A2379 20k Bus, 1926 40 25
5006 A2379 32k Trolley, 1912 65 42
Nos. 5001-5006 (6) 1.75 1.17

Souvenir Sheet

Kremlin and New Delhi Parliament — A2380

1981, Dec. 17 **Photo.**
5007 A2380 50k multi 1.00 50

1st direct telephone link with India. Labels show Brezhnev and Mrs. Gandhi talking on telephone.

60th Anniv. of Checheno-Ingush Autonomous Soviet Socialist Republic — A2381

60th Anniv. of Yakutsk Autonomous Soviet Socialist Republic — A2382

1982, Jan. 11 **Litho.** ***Perf. 12***
5008 A2381 4k multi 8 8
5009 A2382 4k multi 8 8

1500th Anniv. of Kiev — A2383

1982, Jan. 12 **Photo.** ***Perf. 11½x12***
5010 A2383 10k multi 20 14

S.P. Korolev (1907-1966), Rocket Designer A2384

Nazym Khikmet (1902-1963), Turkish Poet A2385

1982, Jan. 12 ***Perf. 11½***
5011 A2384 4k multi 8 8

1982, Jan. 20 **Litho.** ***Perf. 12***
5012 A2385 6k multi 12 8

10th World Trade Union Congress, Havana — A2386

1982, Feb. 1 **Photo.** ***Perf. 11½***
5013 A2386 15k multi 30 20

17th Soviet Trade Union Congress — A2387

1982, Feb. 10 **Litho.**
5014 A2387 4k multi 8 8

Edouard Manet (1832-1883) A2388

1982, Feb. 10 ***Perf. 12x12½***
5015 A2388 32k multi 65 42

Equestrian Sports A2389

1982, Feb. 16 **Photo.** ***Perf. 11½***
5016 A2389 4k Hurdles 8 8
5017 A2389 6k Riding 12 8
5018 A2389 15k Racing 30 20

2nd Death Anniv. of Marshal Tito of Jugoslavia A2390

1982, Feb. 25 **Litho.** ***Perf. 12***
5019 A2390 6k ol blk 12 8

350th Anniv. of State University of Tartu A2392

1982, Mar. 4 **Photo.** ***Perf. 11½***
5020 A2392 4k multi 8 8

9th Intl. Cardiologists Congress, Moscow — A2393

1982, Mar. 4
5021 A2393 15k multi 30 20

Souvenir Sheet

Biathlon, Speed Skating A2394

1982, Mar. 6 **Litho.** ***Perf. 12½x12***
5022 A2394 50k multi 1.00 65

5th Natl. Athletic Meet. Size: 96x67mm.

Blueberry Bush — A2395

Venera 13 and Venera 14 Flights — A2396

1982, Mar. 10 **Litho.** ***Perf. 12x12½***
5023 A2395 4k Blackberries 8 8
5024 A2395 6k shown 12 8
5025 A2395 10k Cranberries 20 14
5026 A2395 15k Cherries 30 20
5027 A2395 32k Strawberries 65 42
Nos. 5023-5027 (5) 1.35 92

1982, Mar. 10 **Photo.** ***Perf. 11½***
5028 A2396 10k multi 20 14

Marriage Ceremony, by W.W. Pukirev (1832-1890) A2397

Paintings: No. 5030, M.I. Lopuchino, by Vladimir Borowikowsky (1757-1825). No. 5031, E.W. Davidov, by O.A. Kiprensky (1782-1836). No.5032, Landscape.

1982, Mar. 18 ***Perf. 12***
5029 A2397 6k multi 12 8
5030 A2397 6k multi 12 8
5031 A2397 6k multi 12 8
5032 A2397 6k multi 12 8

The only foreign revenue stamps listed in this Catalogue are those authorized for prepayment of postage.

K.I. Tchukovsky (1882-1969), Writer — A2398

1982, Mar. 31 **Engr.**
5033 A2398 4k black 8 8

Cosmonauts' Day — A2399

1982, Apr. 12 **Photo.** ***Perf. 12x11½***
5034 A2399 6k multi 12 8

Souvenir Sheet

112th Birth Anniv. of Lenin — A2400

1982, Apr. 22 **Photo.** ***Perf. 11½x12***
5035 A2400 50k multi 1.00 65

V.P. Soloviev-Sedoi (1907-1979), Composer A2401

G. Dimitrov (1882-1949), 1st Bulgarian Prime Minister A2402

1982, Apr. 25 **Engr.** ***Perf. 12***
5036 A2401 4k brown 8 8

1982, Apr. 25
5037 A2402 6k green 12 8

Kremlin Tower, Moscow A2403

70th Anniv. of Pravda Newspaper A2404

1982 **Litho.** ***Perf. 12½x12***
5038 A2403 45k brown 95 60
a Engraved 95 60

Issue dates: No. 5038, Apr. 12. No. 5038a, Oct. 12.

1982, May 5 **Photo.** ***Perf. 12x11½***
5039 A2404 4k multi 8 8

U.N. Conference on Human Environment 10th Anniv. — A2405

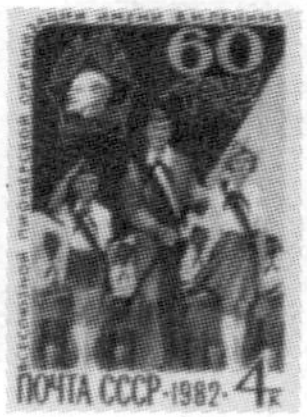

Pioneers' Org., 60th Anniv. — A2406

1982, May 10 *Perf. 11½*

5040 A2405 6k multi	12	8

1982, May 19

5041 A2406 4k multi	8	8

Communist Youth Org., 19th Congress A2407

ITU Delegates Conference, Nairobi A2408

1982, May 19

5042 A2407 4k multi	8	8

1982, May 19

5043 A2408 15k multi	30	20

TUL-80 Electric Locomotive — A2409

1982, May 20 *Perf. 12x11½*

5044 A2409 4k shown	8	8
5045 A2409 6k TEP-75 diesel	12	8
5046 A2409 10k TEP-7 diesel	20	14
5047 A2409 15k WL-82m electric	30	20
5048 A2409 32k EP-200 electric	65	42
Nos. 5044-5048 (5)	1.35	92

1982 World Cup — A2410

1982, June 4 *Perf. 11½x12*

5049 A2410 20k ol & pur	40	25

Grus Monacha — A2411

18th Ornithological Congress, Moscow: Rare birds.

1982, June 10 Litho. *Perf. 12x12½*

5050 A2411 2k shown	6	5
5051 A2411 4k Haliaeetus pelagicus	8	8
5052 A2411 6k Eurynorhynchus	12	8
5053 A2411 10k Eulabeia indica	20	14
5054 A2411 15k Chettusia gregaria	30	20
5055 A2411 32k Ciconia boyciana	65	42
Nos. 5050-5055 (6)	1.41	97

Komomolsk-on-Amur City, 50th Anniv. — A2412

Photogravure and Engraved

1982, June 10 *Perf. 11½*

5056 A2412 4k multi	8	8

Tatchanka, by M.B. Grekov (1882-1934) — A2413

1982, June 15 Litho. *Perf. 12½x12*

5057 A2413 6k multi	12	8

2nd UN Conference on Peaceful Uses of Outer Space, Vienna, Aug. 9-21 — A2414

1982, June 15 Photo. *Perf. 11½*

5058 A2414 15k multi	30	20

Intercosmos Cooperative Space Program (USSR-France) — A2415

1982 Litho. *Perf. 12½x12*

5059 A2415 6k Cosmonauts	12	8
5060 A2415 20k Rocket, globe	40	25
5061 A2415 45k Satellites	95	60

Souvenir Sheet

5062 A2415 50k Emblem, satellite	1.00	65

No. 5062 contains one stamp, size 41x29mm. Issue dates: 6k, 50k, June 24. 20k, 45k, July 2.

The Legend of the Goldfish, by P. Sosin, 1968 — A2416

Lacquerware Paintings, Ustera: 10k, Minin's Appeal to Count Posharski, by J. Phomitchev, 1953. 15k, Two Peasants, by A. Kotjagin, 1933. 20k, The Fisherman, by N. Klykov, 1933, 32k, The Arrest of the Propagandists, by N. Shishakov, 1968.

1982, July 6 Litho. *Perf. 12½x12*

5063 A2416 6k multi	12	8
5064 A2416 10k multi	20	14
5065 A2416 15k multi	30	20
5066 A2416 20k multi	40	25
5067 A2416 32k multi	65	42
Nos. 5063-5067 (5)	1.67	1.09

Telephone Centenary A2417

1982, July 13 *Perf. 12*

5068 A2417 4k Phone, 1882	8	8

P. Schilling's Electro-magnetic Telegraph Sesquicentennial — A2418

Photogravure and Engraved

1982, July 16 *Perf. 11½*

5069 A2418 6k Voltaic cells	12	8

Intervision Gymnastics Contest A2419

1982, Aug. 10 **Photo.**

5070 A2419 15k multi	30	20

Mastjahart Glider, 1923 — A2420

Gliders.

1982, Aug. 20 Litho. *Perf. 12½x12*

5071 A2420 4k shown	8	8
5072 A2420 6k Red Star, 1930	12	8
5073 A2420 10k ZAGI-1, 1934	20	14

Size: 60x28mm.

Perf. 11½x12

5074 A2420 20k Stakhanovets, 1939	40	14
5075 A2420 32k Troop carrier GR-29, 1941	65	42
Nos. 5071-5075 (5)	1.45	86

See Nos. 5118-5122.

Garibaldi (1807-1882) A2421

Intl. Atomic Energy Authority, 25th Anniv. A2422

1982, Aug. 25 Photo. *Perf. 11½*

5076 A2421 6k multi	12	8

1982, Aug. 30

5077 A2422 20k multi	40	25

Marshal B.M. Shaposhnikov (1882-1945) A2423

World Chess Championship A2424

1982, Sept. 10 Engr. *Perf. 12*

5078 A2423 4k red brn	8	8

1982, Sept. 10 Photo. *Perf. 11½*

5079 A2424 6k King	12	8
5080 A2424 6k Queen	12	8

See No. 5084.

African Natl. Congress 70th Anniv. A2425

S.P. Botkin (1832-1889), Physician A2426

1982, Sept. 10

5081 A2425 6k multi	12	8

1982, Sept. 17 Engr. *Perf. 12½x12*

5082 A2426 4k green	8	8

Souvenir Sheet

25th Anniv. of Sputnik — A2427

1982, Sept. 17 Litho. ***Perf. 12x12½***
5083 A2427 50k multi 1.75 75

No. 5079 Overprinted in Gold for Karpov's Victory

1982, Sept. 22 Photo. ***Perf. 11½***
5084 A2424 6k multi 12 8

World War II Warships — A2428

Photogravure and Engraved

1982, Sept. 22 ***Perf. 11½x12***
5085 A2428 4k Submarine S-56 8 8
5086 A2428 6k Minelayer Gremjashtsky 12 8
5087 A2428 15k Mine sweeper T-205 30 20
5088 A2428 20k Cruiser Red Crimea 40 25
5089 A2428 45k Sebastopol 95 60
Nos. 5085-5089 (5) 1.85 1.21

65th Anniv. of October Revolution A2429

1982, Oct. 12 Litho. ***Perf. 12***
5090 A2429 4k multi 8 8

House of the Soviets, Moscow — A2430

60th Anniv. of USSR: No. 5092, Dnieper Dam, Komosomol Monument, Statue of worker. No. 5093, Soviet War Memorial, resistance poster. No. 5094, Worker at podium, decree text. No. 5095, Workers' Monument, Moscow, Rocket, jet. No. 5096, Arms, Kremlin.

1982, Oct. 25 Photo. ***Perf. 11½x12***
5091 A2430 10k multi 20 14
5092 A2430 10k multi 20 14
5093 A2430 10k multi 20 14
5094 A2430 10k multi 20 14
5095 A2430 10k multi 20 14
5096 A2430 10k multi 20 14
Nos. 5091-5096 (6) 1.20 84

No. 5095 Overprinted in Red for All-Union Philatelic Exhibition, 1984.

1982, Nov. 10
5097 A2730 10k multi 20 14

An enhanced introduction to the Scott Catalogue begins on Page V. A thorough understanding of the material presented there will greatly aid your use of the catalogue itself.

Portrait of an Actor, by Domenico Fetti A2431

Paintings from the Hermitage: 10k, St. Sebastian, by Perugino. 20k, The Danae, by Titian (horiz.). 45k, Portrait of a Woman, by Correggio. No. 5102, Portrait of a Young Man, by Capriola. No. 5103, Portrait of a Young Woman, by Melzi.

1982, Nov. 25 Litho. ***Perf. 12x12½***
5098 A2431 4k multi 8 8
5099 A2431 10k multi 20 14
5100 A2431 20k multi 40 25
5101 A2431 45k multi 95 60
5102 A2431 50k multi 1.00 65
Nos. 5098-5102 (5) 2.63 1.72

Souvenir Sheet

5103 Sheet of 2 2.00 1.40
a A2431 50k multi 1.00 65

See Nos. 5129-5134, 5199-5204, 5233-5238, 5310-5315, 5335-5340.

New Year 1983 — A2432

60th Anniv. of USSR — A2433

1982, Dec. 1
5104 A2432 4k multi 8 8

Souvenir Sheet

1982, Dec. 3 ***Perf. 12½x12***
5105 A2433 50k multi 1.00 65

Souvenir Sheet

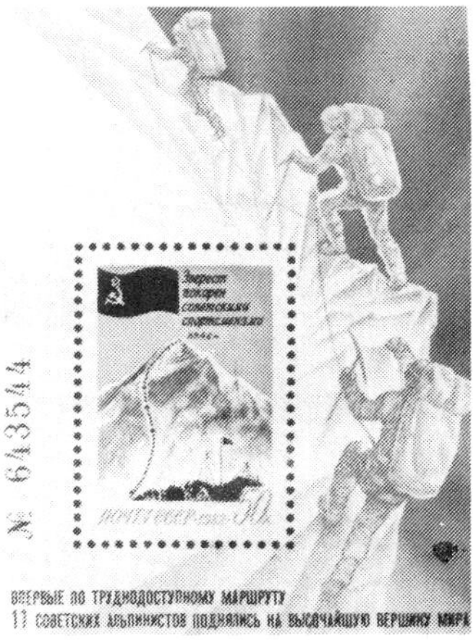

Mountain Climbers Reaching Mt. Everest — A2434

1982, Dec. 20 Photo. ***Perf. 11½x12***
5106 A2434 50k multi 2.00 90

Lighthouses A2435

Mail Transport A2436

1982, Dec. 29 Litho. ***Perf. 12***
5107 A2435 6k grn & multi 12 8
5108 A2435 6k lil & multi 12 8
5109 A2435 6k sal & multi 12 8
5110 A2435 6k lt gldn brn & multi 12 8
5111 A2435 6k lt brn & multi 12 8
Nos. 5107-5111 (5) 60 40

See Nos. 5179-5183, 5265-5269.

1982, Dec. 22 ***Perf. 12***
5112 A2436 5k grnsh bl 10 7

1983, May 20 Litho. ***Perf. 12***
5113 A2436 5k blue 10 7

Iskra Newspaper Masthead A2438

Fedor P. Tolstoi (1783-1873) Painter A2439

1983, Jan. 5 Litho. ***Perf. 12x12½***
5114 A2438 4k multi 8 8

80th anniv. of 2nd Social-Democratic Workers' Party.

1983, Jan. 5 Photo. ***Perf. 11½***
5115 A2439 4k multi 8 8

65th Anniv. of Armed Forces — A2440

60th Anniv. of Aeroflot Airlines — A2441

1983, Jan. 25 Litho. ***Perf. 12***
5116 A2440 4k multi 8 8

Souvenir Sheet

1983, Feb. 9 ***Perf. 12x12½***
5117 A2441 50k multi 1.00 90

Glider Type of 1982

1983, Feb. 10 ***Perf. 12½x12***
5118 A2420 2k A-9, 1948 6 5
5119 A2420 4k KAJ-12, 1957 8 8
5120 A2420 6k A-15, 1960 12 8
5121 A2420 20k SA-7, 1970 40 25
5122 A2420 45k LAJ-12, 1979 95 60
Nos. 5118-5122 (5) 1.61 1.06

Tashkent Bimillenium — A2442

1983, Feb. 17 ***Perf. 12½x12***
5123 A2442 4k View 8 8

B.N. Petrov (1913-1980), Scientist A2443

Holy Family, by Raphael A2444

1983, Feb. 17
5124 A2443 4k multi 8 8

1983, Feb. 17 ***Perf. 12x12½***
5125 A2444 50k multi 1.00 65

Soyuz T-7-Salyut 7-Soyuz T-5 Flight A2445

1983, Mar. 10 ***Perf. 12x12½***
5126 A2445 10k L. Popov, A. Serebrav, S. Savitskaya 20 14

Souvenir Sheet

World Communications Year — A2446

1983, Mar. 10 Photo. ***Perf. 11½***
5127 A2446 50k multi 90 65

A.W. Aleksandrov, Natl. Anthem Composer — A2447

1983, Mar. 22 Litho. ***Perf. 12***
5128 A2447 4k multi 8 8

Hermitage Type of 1982

Rembrandt Paintings, Hermitage, Leningrad: 10k, Portrait of a Learned Man. 20k, Old Warrior, 45k, Portrait of Mrs. B. Martens Doomer. No. 5133, Sacrifice of Abraham. No. 5134a, Portrait of an Old Man in a Red Garment.

1983, Mar. 25 ***Perf. 12x12½***

5129 A2431 4k multi 8 8
5130 A2431 10k multi 20 14
5131 A2431 20k multi 40 25
5132 A2431 45k multi 95 60
5133 A2431 50k multi 1.00 65
Nos. 5129-5133 (5) 2.63 1.72

Souvenir Sheet

Lithographed and Embossed

5134 Sheet of 2 + label *2.50* 1.40
a. A2431 50k multi 1.25 70

Souvenir Sheet

Cosmonauts' Day — A2449

1983, Apr. 12 **Litho.** ***Perf. 12½x12***

5135 A2449 50k Soyuz T *2.50* 1.00

Souvenir Sheet

113th Birth Anniv. of Lenin — A2450

Photogravure and Engraved

1983, Apr. 22 ***Perf. 11½x12***

5136 A2450 50k multi 1.00 65

A2451

Salyut 7-Soyuz 7 211-Day Flight — A2452

1983, Apr. 25 **Litho.** ***Perf. 12½x12***

5137 A2451 10k A. Berezovoy, V. Lebedev 20 14
5138 A2452 10k Spacecraft 20 14

Nos. 5137-5138 exist se-tenant with label.

Karl Marx (1818-1883) A2453

1983, May 5 ***Perf. 12x12½***

5139 A2453 4k multi 8 8

View of Rostov-on-Don — A2454

1983, May 5 **Photo.** ***Perf. 11½***

5140 A2454 4k multi 8 8

Buriat Autonomous Soviet Socialist Republic, 60th Anniv. A2455

1983, May 12 **Litho.** ***Perf. 12***

5141 A2455 4k multi 8 8

Kirov Opera and Ballet Theater, Leningrad, 200th Anniv. — A2456

Photogravure and Engraved

1983, May 12 ***Perf. 11½x12***

5142 A2456 4k multi 8 8

Emblem of Motorcycling, Auto Racing, Shooting, Motorboating, Parachuting Organization — A2457

1983, May 20 **Litho.** ***Perf. 11½***

5143 A2457 6k multi 12 8

A.I. Khachaturian (1903-1978), Composer — A2458

1983, May 25 **Engr.** ***Perf. 12½x12***

5144 A2458 4k vio brn 8 8

Chelyabinsk Tractor Plant, 50th Anniv. A2459

1983, June 1 **Photo.** ***Perf. 11½***

5145 A2459 4k multi 8 8

Simon Bolivar Bicentenary A2460

Photogravure and Engraved

1983, June 10 ***Perf. 12***

5146 A2460 6k brn & dk brn 12 8

City of Sevastopol, 200th Anniv. — A2461

1983, June 14 **Photo.** ***Perf. 11½x12***

5147 A2461 5k multi 10 7

Spring Flowers — A2462

1983, June 14 **Litho.** ***Perf. 12x12½***

5148 A2462 4k multi 8 8
5149 A2462 6k multi 12 8
5150 A2462 10k multi 20 14
5151 A2462 15k multi 30 20
5152 A2462 20k multi 40 25
Nos. 5148-5152 (5) 1.10 75

Valentina Tereshkova's Spaceflight, 20th Anniv. — A2463

1983, June 16 **Litho.** ***Perf. 12***

5153 A2463 10k multi 20 14

P.N. Pospelov (1898-1979), Academician A2464

10th European Congress of Rheumatologists A2465

Photogravure and Engraved

1983, June 20 ***Perf. 11½***

5154 A2464 4k multi 8 8

1983, June 21 **Photo.** ***Perf. 11½***

5155 A2565 4k multi 8 8

13th International Film Festival, Moscow — A2466

1983, July 7 **Litho.** ***Perf. 12***

5156 A2466 20k multi 40 25

Ships of the Soviet Fishing Fleet — A2467

Photogravure and Engraved

1983, July 20 ***Perf. 12x11½***

5157 A2467 4k Two trawlers 8 8
5158 A2467 6k Refrigerated trawler 12 8
5159 A2467 10k Large trawler 20 14
5160 A2467 15k Large refrigerated ship 30 20
5161 A2467 20k Base ship 40 25
Nos. 5157-5161 (5) 1.10 75

E.B. Vakhtangov (1883-1922), Actor and Producer — A2468

1983, July 20 **Photo.** ***Perf. 11½***

5162 A2468 5k multi 10 7

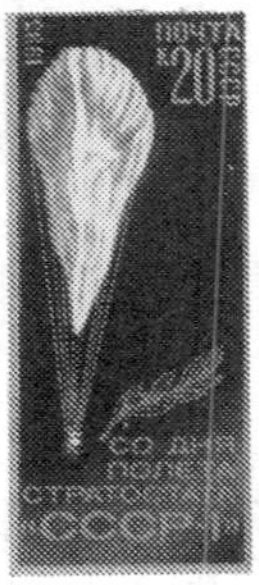

"USSR-1" Stratospheric Flight, 50th Anniv. — A2469

1983, July 25 **Photo.** ***Perf. 12***

5163 A2469 20k multi 40 25

Food Fish
A2470

Designs 4k, Oncorhynchus nerka. 6k, Perciformes. 15k, Anarhichas minor. 20k, Neogobius fluviatilis, 45k, Platichthys stellatus.

1983, Aug. 5 Litho. *Perf. 12½x12*

5164	A2470	4k multi		8	8
5165	A2470	6k multi		12	8
5166	A2470	15k multi		30	20
5167	A2470	20k multi		40	25
5168	A2470	45k multi		95	60
		Nos. 5164-5168 (5)		1.85	1.21

A2471

Moscow Skyline
A2472

1983, Aug. 18 Photo. *Perf. 11½*

5169 A2471 6k multi 12 8

Souvenir Sheet

5170 A2472 50k cob bl 1.00 65

SOZPHILEX '83 Philatelic Exhibition.

Miniature Sheet

First Russian Postage Stamp, 125th Anniv.
A2473

Photogravure and Engraved

1983, Aug. 25 *Perf. 11½x12*

5171 A2473 50k pale yel & blk 1.00 65

No. 5171 Ovptd. on Margin in Red for the 5th Philatelic Society Congress

Photogravure and Engraved

1984, Oct. 1 *Perf. 11½x12*

5171A A2473 50k pale yel & blk 1.00 65

Namibia Day
A2474

Palestinian Solidarity
A2475

1983, Aug. 26 Photo. *Perf. 11½*

5172 A2474 5k multi 10 7

1983, Aug. 29 Photo. *Perf. 11½*

5173 A2475 5k multi 10 7

1st European Championship of Radio-Telegraphy, Moscow — A2476

1983, Sept. 1 Photo. *Perf. 11½*

5174 A2476 6k multi 12 8

4th UNESCO Council on Communications Development — A2477

1983, Sept. 2 Photo. *Perf. 12x11½*

5175 A2477 10k multi 20 14

Muhammad Al-Khorezmi, Uzbek Mathematician, 1200th Birth Anniv. — A2478

Photogravure and Engraved

1983, Sept. 6 *Perf. 11½*

5176 A2478 4k multi 8 8

Marshal A.I. Egorov (1883-1939)
A2479

Union of Georgia and Russia, 200th Anniv.
A2480

1983, Sept. 8 Engr. *Perf. 12*

5177 A2479 4k brn vio 8 8

1983, Sept. 8 Photo. *Perf. 11½*

5178 A2480 6k multi 12 8

Lighthouse Type of 1982

Baltic Sea lighthouses.

1983, Sept. 19 Litho. *Perf. 12*

5179	A2435	1k Kipu		5	5
5180	A2435	5k Keri		10	7
5181	A2435	10k Stirsudden		20	14
5182	A2435	12k Tahkun		24	16
5183	A2435	20k Tallinn		40	25
		Nos. 5179-5183 (5)		99	67

Early Spring, by V.K. Bjalynitzky-Birulja, 1912 — A2481

Paintings by White Russians: 4k, Portrait of the Artist's Wife with Fruit and Flowers, by J.F. Krutzky, 1838. 15k, Young Partisan, by E.A. Zaitsev, 1943. 20k, Partisan Madonna, by M.A. Savitsky, 1967. 45k, Harvest, by V.K. Tsvirko, 1972. 15k, 20k vert.

Perf. 12½x12, 12x12½

1983, Sept. 28

5184	A2481	4k multi		8	8
5185	A2481	6k multi		12	8
5186	A2481	15k multi		30	20
5187	A2481	20k multi		40	25
5188	A2481	45k multi		95	60
		Nos. 5184-5188 (5)		1.85	1.21

Hammer and Sickle Steel Mill, Moscow, Centenary
A2482

1983, Oct. 1 Photo. *Perf. 11½*

5189 A2482 4k multi 8 8

Natl. Food Program
A2483

1983, Oct. 10

5190	A2483	5k Wheat production		10	7
5191	A2483	5k Cattle, dairy products		10	7
5192	A2483	5k Produce		10	7

October Revolution, 66th Anniv.
A2484

Ivan Fedorov
A2485

1983, Oct. 12 Litho. *Perf. 12*

5193 A2484 4k multi 8 8

1983, Oct. 12 Engr. *Perf. 12x12½*

5194 A2485 4k dk brn 8 8

Ivan Fedorov, first Russian printer (Book of the Apostles), 400th death anniv.

Urengoy-Uzgorod Transcontinental Gas Pipeline Completion — A2486

1983, Oct. 12 Photo. *Perf. 12x11½*

5195 A2486 5k multi 10 7

A.W. Sidorenko (1917-1982), Geologist
A2487

Campaign Against Nuclear Weapons
A2488

1983, Oct. 19 Litho. *Perf. 12*

5196 A2487 4k multi 8 8

1983, Oct. 19 Photo. *Perf. 11½*

5197 A2488 5k Demonstration 10 7

Machtumkuli, Turkmenistan Poet, 250th Birth Anniv. — A2489

1983, Oct. 27

5198 A2489 5k multi 10 7

Hermitage Painting Type of 1982

Paintings by Germans: 4k, Madonna and Child with Apple Tree, by Lucas Cranach the Elder. 10k, Self-portrait, by Anton R. Mengs. 20k, Self-portrait, by Jurgen Owen. 45k, Sailboat, by Caspar David Friedrich. No. 5203, Rape of the Sabines, by Johann Schoenfeld (horiz.). No. 5204, Portrait of a Young Man, by Hans Holbein.

Perf. 12x12½, 12½x12

1983, Nov. 10 Litho.

5199	A2431	4k multi		8	8
5200	A2431	10k multi		20	14
5201	A2431	20k multi		40	25
5202	A2431	45k multi		95	60
5203	A2431	50k multi		1.00	65
		Nos. 5199-5203 (5)		2.63	1.72

Souvenir Sheet

5204		Sheet of 2		2.00	1.40
a	A2431	50k multi		1.00	65

Physicians Against Nuclear War Movement
A2490

1983, Nov. 17 Photo. *Perf. 11½*

5205 A2490 5k Baby, dove, sun 10 7

Sukhe Bator (1893-1923), Mongolian People's Rep. Founder — A2491

1983, Nov. 17

5206 A2491 5k Portrait 10 7

New Year 1984
A2492

1983, Dec. 1
5207 A2492 5k Star, snowflakes 10 7

Newly Completed Buildings, Moscow — A2493

Perf. 12½x12, 12x12½

1983, Dec. 15 **Engr.**
5208 A2493 3k Children's Musical Theater 7 6
5209 A2493 4k Tourist Hotel, vert. 8 8
5210 A2493 6k Council of Ministers 12 8
5211 A2493 20k Ismaelovo Hotel 40 25
5212 A2493 45k Novosti Press Agency 95 60
Nos. 5208-5212 (5) 1.62 1.07

Souvenir Sheet

Environmental Protection Campaign A2494

1983, Dec. 20 **Photo.** ***Perf. 11½***
5213 A2494 50k multi 1.50 1.00

Moscow Local Broadcasting Network, 50th Anniv. — A2495

1984, Jan. 1
5214 A2495 4k multi 8 8

European Women's Skating Championships — A2496

1984, Jan. 1 ***Perf. 12x11½***
5215 A2496 5k multi 10 7

Cuban Revolution, 25th Anniv. A2497

1984, Jan. 1 ***Perf. 11½***
5216 A2497 5k Flag, "25" 10 7

World War II Tanks — A2498

1984, Jan. 25 **Litho.** ***Perf. 12½x12***
5217 A2498 10k KW 20 14
5218 A2498 10k IS-2 20 14
5219 A2498 10k T-34 20 14
5220 A2498 10k ISU-152 20 14
5221 A2498 10k SU-100 20 14
Nos. 5217-5221 (5) 1.00 70

1984 Winter Olympics — A2499

1984, Feb. 8 **Photo.** ***Perf. 11½x12***
5222 A2499 5k Biathlon 10 7
5223 A2499 10k Speed skating 20 14
5224 A2499 20k Hockey 40 25
5225 A2499 45k Figure skating 95 60

Moscow Zoo, 120th Anniv. — A2500

1984, Feb. 16 **Litho.** ***Perf. 12½x12***
5226 A2500 2k Mandrill 6 5
5227 A2500 3k Gazelle 7 6
5228 A2500 4k Snow leopard 8 8
5229 A2500 5k Crowned crane 10 7
5230 A2500 20k Macaw 40 25
Nos. 5226-5230 (5) 71 51

Yuri Gagarin (1934-68) — A2501

1984, Mar. 9 **Engr.** ***Perf. 12½x12***
5231 A2501 15k Portrait, Vostok 30 20

Souvenir Sheet

Mass Development of Virgin and Unused Land, 30th Anniv. — A2502

1984, Mar. 14 **Photo.** ***Perf. 11½x12***
5232 A2502 50k multi 1.00 75

Hermitage Painting Type of 1982

Paintings by English Artists: 4k, E.K. Vorontsova, by George Hayter. 10k, Portrait of Mrs. Greer, by George Romney. 20k, Approaching Storm, by George Morland (horiz.). 45k, Portrait of an Unknown Man, by Marcus Gheeraerts Jr. No. 5237, Cupid and Venus, by Joshua Reynolds. No. 5238, Portrait of a Lady in Blue, by Thomas Gainsborough.

Wmk. Cyrillic Letters in Shield (383)
Perf. 12x12½, 12½x12

1984, Mar. 20 **Litho.**
5233 A2431 4k multi 8 8
5234 A2431 10k multi 20 14
5235 A2431 20k multi 40 25
5236 A2431 45k multi 95 60
5237 A2431 50k multi 1.00 65
Nos. 5233-5237 (5) 2.63 1.72

Souvenir Sheet

5238 Sheet of 2 2.00 1.40
a A2431 50k multi 1.00 65

Nos. 5233-5237 each se-tenant with label showing text and embossed emblem.

S.V. Iljushin A2503

Andrei S. Bubnov A2504

Perf. 11½

1984, Mar. 23 **Photo.** **Unwmk.**
5239 A2503 5k Aircraft designer, (1894-1977) 10 7

1984, Apr. 3 ***Perf. 11½x12***
5240 A2504 5k Statesman, (1884-1940) 10 7

Intercosmos Cooperative Space Program (USSR-India) A2505

1984 ***Perf. 12x11½***
5241 A2505 5k Weather Station M-100 launch 10 7
5242 A2505 20k Geodesy (satellites, observatory) 40 25
5243 A2505 45k Rocket, satellites, dish antenna 95 60

Souvenir Sheet

5244 A2505 50k Flags, cosmonauts 1.00 65

No. 5244 contains one stamp, size 25x36mm. Issue dates: 50k, Apr. 5; others, Apr. 3.

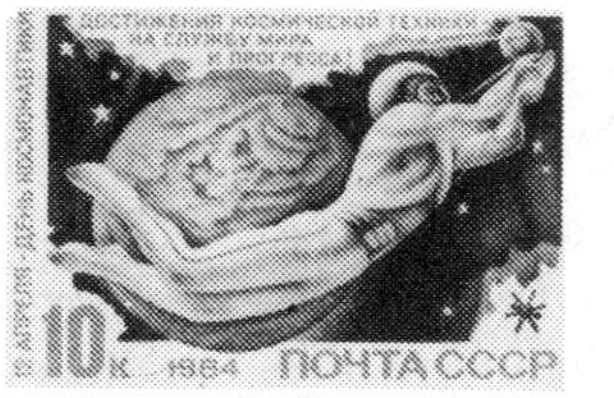

Cosmonauts' Day — A2506

1984, Apr. 12 ***Perf. 11½x12***
5245 A2506 10k Futuristic spaceman 20 14

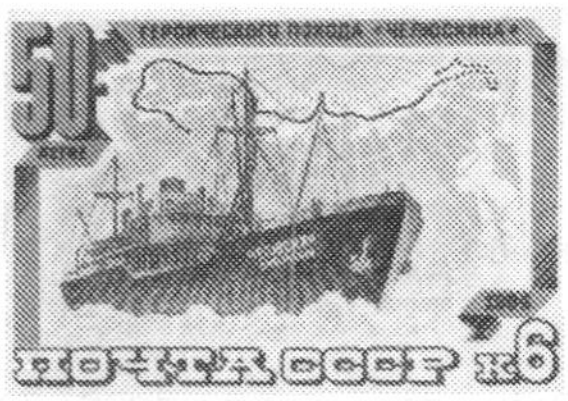

Tchelyuskin Arctic Expedition, 50th Anniv. — A2507

Photogravure and Engraved

1984, Apr. 13 ***Perf. 11½x12***
5246 A2507 6k Ship 12 8
5247 A2507 15k Shipwreck 30 20
5248 A2507 45k Rescue 95 60

Souvenir Sheet

Photo.

5249 A2507 50k Hero of Soviet Union medal 1.00 65

First HSU medal awarded to rescue crew. No. 5249 contains one stamp, size 27x39mm.

Souvenir Sheet

114th Birth Anniv. of Lenin A2508

Perf. 11½x12½

1984, Apr. 22 **Litho.**
5250 A2508 50k Portrait 1.00 65

Aquatic Plants — A2509

Soviet Peace Policy — A2510

1984, May 5 ***Perf. 12x12½, 12½x12***
5251 A2509 1k Lotus 5 5
5252 A2509 2k Euriola 6 5
5253 A2509 3k Water lilies, horiz. 7 6
5254 A2509 10k White nymphaea 20 14
5255 A2509 20k Marshflowers, horiz. 40 25
Nos. 5251-5255 (5) 78 55

1984, May 8 **Photo.** ***Perf. 11½***
5256 A2510 5k Marchers, banners (at left) 10 7
5257 A2510 5k Text 10 7
5258 A2510 5k Marchers, banners (at right) 10 7

Nos. 5256-5258 se-tenant.

The Scott Catalogue value is a retail price, what you could expect to pay for the stamp in a grade of Fine-Very Fine. The value listed is a reference which reflects recent actual dealer selling price.

50th Anniv. of E.O. Paton Institute of Electric Welding
A2511

25th Conference for Electric and Postal Communications Cooperation
A2512

1984, May 15 **Photo.** ***Perf. 11½***
5259 A2511 10k multi 20 14

1984, May 21
5260 A2512 10k multi 20 14

Maurice Bishop, Grenada Prime Minister (1944-1983)
A2513

60th Anniv. of V.I. Lenin Central Museum
A2514

1984, May 29
5261 A2513 5k vio brn 10 7

1984, May 31
5262 A2514 5k multi 10 7

City of Archangelsk, 400th Anniv. — A2515

1984, June 1 **Photo. & Engr.**
5263 A2515 5k multi 10 7

European Youth Soccer Championship
A2516

1984, June 1 **Photo.** ***Perf. 12x11½***
5264 A2516 15k multi 30 20

Lighthouse Type of 1982

Far Eastern seas lighthouses.

1984, June 14 **Litho.** ***Perf. 12***
5265 A2435 1k Petropavlovsk 5 5
5266 A2435 2k Tokarev 6 5
5267 A2435 4k Basargin 8 8
5268 A2435 5k Kronitsky 10 7
5269 A2435 10k Marekan 20 14
Nos. 5265-5269 (5) 49 39

Salyut 7-Soyuz T-9 150-Day Flight — A2517

1984, June 27 **Litho.** ***Perf. 12***
5270 A2517 15k multi 30 20

Morflot, Merchant and Transport Fleet, 60th Anniv.
A2518

Photogravure and Engraved
1984, July 1 ***Perf. 11½***
5271 A2518 10k multi 20 14

60th Anniv. of Awarding V.I. Lenin Name to Youth Communist League — A2519

1984, July 1 **Photo.** ***Perf. 11½x12***
5272 A2519 5k multi 10 7

Liberation of Byelorussia, 40th Anniv.
A2520

1984, July 3 **Photo.** ***Perf. 12x11½***
5273 A2520 5k multi 10 7

CMEA Conference, Moscow — A2521

1984, June 12 **Photo.** ***Perf. 11½***
5274 A2521 5k CMEA Building & Kremlin 10 7

27th Intl. Geological Congress, Moscow
A2522

People's Republic of Poland, 40th Anniv.
A2523

1984, July 20 **Photo.** ***Perf. 11½***
5275 A2522 5k Convention seal 10 7

1984, July 22 **Photo.** ***Perf. 11½***
5276 A2523 5k Arms, draped flag 10 7

B. V. Asafiev (1884-1949), Composer — A2524

1984, July 25 **Engr.** ***Perf. 12½x12***
5277 A2524 5k grnsh blk 10 7

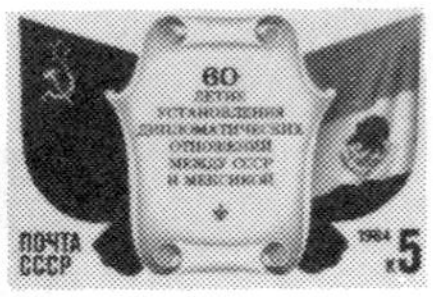

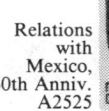

Relations with Mexico, 60th Anniv.
A2525

1984, Aug. 4 **Litho.** ***Perf. 12***
5278 A2525 5k Flags of U.S.S.R. and Mexico 10 7

Miniature Sheet

Russian Folk Tales
A2526

Designs: a. Three archers. b. Prince and frog. c. Old man and prince. d. Crowd and swans. e. Wolf and men. f. Bird and youth. g. Youth on white horse. h. Couple with Tsar. i. Village scene. j. Man on black horse. k. Old man. l. Young woman.

1984, Aug. 10 **Litho.** ***Perf. 12x12½***
5279 Sheet of 12 1.10 85
a.-l A2526 5k, any single 9 7

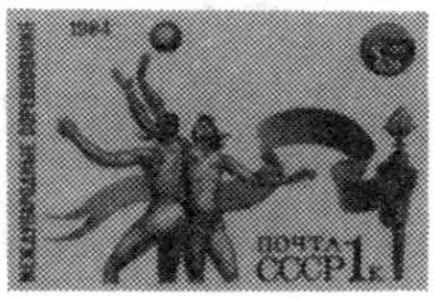

Friendship '84 Games
A2527

1984, Aug. 15 **Photo.** ***Perf. 11½***
5280 A2527 1k Basketball 5 5
5281 A2527 5k Gymnastics, vert. 10 7
5282 A2527 10k Weightlifting 20 14
5283 A2527 15k Wrestling 30 20
5284 A2527 20k High jump 40 25
Nos. 5280-5284 (5) 1.05 71

Liberation of Romania, 40th Anniv. — A2528

A2529

1984, Aug. 23 **Litho.** ***Perf. 12***
5285 A2528 5k Flag, monument 10 7

1984, Sept. 5 **Litho.** ***Perf. 12½x12***

Subjects: 35k, 3r, Environmental protection. 2r, Arctic development. 5r, World peace.

5286 A2529 35k Sable 55 40
5287 A2529 2r Ship, arctic map 3.00 2.00

Engr.

5288 A2529 3r Child and globe 4.50 3.00
5289 A2529 5r Palm frond and globe 7.50 5.00

World Chess Championships
A2530

Bulgarian Revolution 40th Anniv.
A2531

1984, Sept. 7 **Photo.** ***Perf. 11½***
5290 A2530 15k Motherland statue, Volgograd 28 16
5291 A2530 15k Spasski Tower, Moscow 28 16

1984, Sept. 9 **Photo.** ***Perf. 11½***
5292 A2531 5k Bulgarian arms 10 7

Ethiopian Revolution, 10th Anniv.
A2532

1984, Sept. 12 **Litho.** ***Perf. 12***
5293 A2532 5k Ethiopian flag, seal 10 7

Novokramatorsk Machinery Plant, 50th Anniv. — A2533

Photogravure and Engraved
1984, Sept. 20 ***Perf. 11½***
5294 A2533 5k Excavator 10 7

Nakhichevan ASSR, 60th Anniv.
A2534

1984, Sept. 20 **Litho.** ***Perf. 12***
5295 A2534 5k Arms 10 7

Television from Space, 25th Anniv.
A2535

1984, Oct. 4 **Photo.** ***Perf. 11½***
5296 A2535 5k Luna 3 10 7
5297 A2535 20k Venera 9 35 25
5298 A2535 45k Meteor satellite 85 52

Souvenir Sheet

Perf. 11½x12

5299	A2535	50k Camera, space walker, vert.		1.00	65

No. 5299 contains one stamp, size 26x37mm.

German Democratic Republic, 35th Anniv. A2536

1984, Oct. 7 Photo. *Perf. 11½*

5300	A2536	5k Flag, arms	10	7

Ukrainian Liberation, 40th Anniv. A2537

1984, Oct. 8 Photo. *Perf. 12x11½*

5301	A2537	5k Motherland statue, Kiev	10	7

Soviet Republics and Parties, 60th Anniv. A2538

Flags and Arms: No. 5302, Moldavian SSR. No. 5303, Kirgiz SSR. No. 5304, Tadzhik SSR. No. 5305, Uzbek SSR. No. 5306, Turkmen SSR.

1984 Litho. *Perf. 12*

5302	A2538	5k multi	10	7
5303	A2538	5k multi	10	7
5304	A2538	5k multi	10	7
5305	A2538	5k multi	10	7
5306	A2538	5k multi	10	7
		Nos. 5302-5306 (5)	50	35

Issue dates: No. 5302, Oct. 12; Nos. 5303-5304, Oct. 14, Nos. 5305-5306, Oct. 27.

October Revolution, 67th Anniv. A2539

M. Frunze Institute of Aviation and Cosmonautics A2540

1984, Oct. 23 Photo. *Perf. 11½*

5307	A2539	5k Kremlin, 1917 flag	10	7

1984, Nov. 6 Photo. *Perf. 11½*

5308	A2540	5k Aircraft, spacecraft	10	7

Baikal - Amur Railway Completion A2541

1984, Nov. 7 Photo. *Perf. 11½*

5309	A2541	5k Workers, map, engine	10	7

Hermitage Type of 1982

Paintings by French Artists: 4k, Girl in a Hat, by Jean Louis Voille. 10k, A Stolen Kiss, by Jean-Honore Fragonard. 20k, Woman Combing her Hair, by Edgar Degas. 45k, Pigmalion and Galatea, by Francois Boucher. 50k, Landscape with Polyphenus, by Nicholas Poussin.

Perf. 12x12½, 12½x12

1984, Nov. 20 Litho.

5310	A2431	4k multi	8	8
5311	A2431	10k multi, horiz.	18	14
5312	A2431	20k multi	35	25
5313	A2431	45k multi, horiz.	85	50
5314	A2431	50k multi, horiz.	90	60
		Nos. 5310-5314 (5)	2.36	1.57

Souvenir Sheet

5315		Sheet of 2	2.00	1.40
a	A2431	50k multi	1.00	60

No. 5315a depicts Child with a Whip, by Pierre-Auguste Renoir.

Mongolian Peoples' Republic, 60th Anniv. — A2542

1984, Nov. 26 Photo. *Perf. 11½*

5316	A2542	5k Mongolian flag, arms	10	7

New Year 1985 — A2543

1984, Dec. 4 Litho. *Perf. 11½*

5317	A2543	5k Kremlin, snowflakes	10	7

Souvenir Sheet

Environmental Protection — A2544

1984, Dec. 4 Litho. *Perf. 12½x12*

5318	A2544	50k Leaf, pollution sources	1.00	65

Russian Fire Vehicles — A2545

Photogravure and Engraved

1984, Dec. 12 *Perf. 12x11½*

5319	A2545	3k Crew wagon, 19th cent.	8	6
5320	A2545	5k Pumper, 19th cent.	10	7
5321	A2545	10k Ladder truck, 1904	18	14
5322	A2545	15k Pumper, 1904	28	18
5323	A2545	20k Ladder truck, 1913	35	25
		Nos. 5319-5323 (5)	99	70

See Nos. 5410-5414.

Intl. Venus-Halley's Comet Project — A2546

1984, Dec. 15 Photo. *Perf. 12x11½*

5324	A2546	15k Satellite, flight path	28	18

Indira Gandhi (1917-1984), Indian Prime Minister — A2547

1984, Dec. 28 Litho. *Perf. 12*

5325	A2547	5k Portrait	10	7

1905 Revolution A2548

1985, Jan. 22 Photo. *Perf. 11½*

5326	A2548	5k Flag, Moscow memorial	10	7

Patrice Lumumba Peoples' Friendship University 25th Anniv. — A2549

Mikhail Vasilievich Frunze (1885-1925), Party Leader — A2550

1985, Jan. 24

5327	A2549	5k multi	10	7

1985, Feb. 2

5328	A2550	5k bluish, blk & ocher	10	7

Karakalpak ASSR, 60th Anniv. A2551

1985, Feb. 16 *Perf. 12*

5329	A2551	5k Republic arms	10	7

10th Winter Spartakiad of Friendly Armies — A2552

1985, Feb. 23 *Perf. 11½*

5330	A2552	5k Hockey player, emblem	10	7

Kalevala, 150th Anniv. A2553

1985, Feb. 25 Litho. *Perf. 12*

5331	A2553	5k Rune singer, frontispiece	10	7

Finnish Kalevala, collection of Karelian epic poetry compiled by Elias Lonrot.

Yakov M. Sverdlov (1885-1919), Party Leader A2554

Pionerskaya Pravda, All-Union Children's Newspaper, 60th Anniv. A2555

1985, Mar. 3 Engr. *Perf. 12½x12*

5332	A2554	5k rose lake	10	7

1985, Mar. 6 Photo. *Perf. 11½*

5333	A2555	5k Pioneer badge, awards	10	7

Maria Alexandrovna Ulyanova (1835-1916), Lenin's Mother — A2556

1985, Mar. 6 Engr. *Perf. 12½x12*

5334	A2556	5k black	10	7

Hermitage Type of 1982

Paintings by Spanish artists: 4k, The Young Virgin Praying, vert., by Francisco de Zurbaran (1598-1664). 10k, Still-life, by Antonio Pereda (c. 1608-1678). 20k, The Immaculate Conception, vert., by Murillo (1617-1682). 45k, The Grinder, by Antonio Puga. No. 5339, Count Olivares, vert., by Diego Velazques (1599-1660). No. 5340, Portrait of the actress Antonia Zarate, vert., by Goya (1746-1828).

Perf. 12x12½, 12½x12

1985, Mar. 14 Litho. Wmk. 383

5335	A2431	4k multi	8	8
5336	A2431	10k multi	16	12
5337	A2431	20k multi	28	22
5338	A2431	45k multi	65	50
5339	A2431	50k multi	75	52
		Nos. 5335-5339 (5)	1.92	1.44

Souvenir Sheet

Lithographed and Embossed

5340		Sheet of 2 + label	1.90	1.40
a	A2431	50k multi	75	52

EXPO '85, Tsukuba, Japan A2557

Soviet exhibition, Expo '85 emblems and: 5k, Cosmonauts in space. 10k, Communications satellite. 20k, Alternative energy sources development. 45k, Future housing systems.

Perf. 12x11½

1985, Mar. 17 Photo. Unwmk.

5341 A2557 5k multi 10 7
5342 A2557 10k multi 16 12
5343 A2557 20k multi 28 22
5344 A2557 45k multi 65 50

Souvenir Sheet

5345 A2557 50k Soviet exhibition emblem, globe 75 52

Souvenir Sheet

Johann Sebastian Bach (1685-1750), Composer A2558

Photogravure and Engraved

1985, Mar. 21 *Perf. 12x11½*

5346 A2558 50k black 1.00 70

Hungary Liberated from German Occupation Forces, 40th Anniv. — A2559

1985, Apr. 4 Litho. *Perf. 12*

5347 A2559 5k Natl. crest, Budapest memorial 10 7

Society for Cultural Relations with Foreign Countries, 60th Anniv. — A2560

1985, Apr. 5 Photo. *Perf. 11½*

5348 A2560 15k Emblem 22 18

Victory over Fascism, 40th Anniv. A2561

Designs: No. 5349, Battle of Moscow, soldier, Kremlin, portrait of Lenin. No. 5350, Soldier, armed forces. No. 5351, Armaments production, worker. No. 5352, Partisan movement, cavalry. No. 5353, Berlin-Treptow war memorial, German Democratic Republic. No. 5354, Order of the Patriotic War, second class.

1985, Apr. 20 *Perf. 12x11½*

5349 A2561 5k multi 10 7
5350 A2561 5k multi 10 7
5351 A2561 5k multi 10 7
5352 A2561 5k multi 10 7
5353 A2561 5k multi 10 7
Nos. 5349-5353 (5) 50 35

Souvenir Sheet

Perf. 11½

5354 A2561 50k multi 75 52

No. 5354 contains one stamp, size: 28x40mm.

No. 5353 Ovptd. in Red for 40 Year Great Victory All-Union Philatelic Exhibition

1985, Apr. 29 Photo. *Perf. 12x11½*

5354A A2561 5k brn lake, gold & ver 10 7

Yuri Gagarin Center for Training Cosmonauts, 25th Anniv. — A2562

Cosmonauts day: Portrait, cosmonauts, Soyuz-T spaceship.

1985, Apr. 12 Photo. *Perf. 11½x12*

5355 A2562 15k multi 30 22

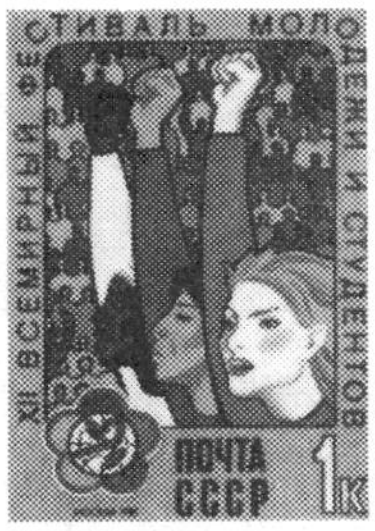

12th World Youth Festival, Moscow A2563

1985, Apr. 15 Litho. *Perf. 12x12½*

5356 A2563 1k Three youths 5 5
5357 A2563 3k African girl 8 8
5358 A2563 5k Girl, rainbow 10 8
5359 A2563 20k Asian youth, camera 40 30
5360 A2563 45k Emblem 90 65
Nos. 5356-5360 (5) 1.53 1.16

Souvenir Sheet

1985, July 4

5361 A2563 30k Emblem 60 45

115th Birth Anniv. of Lenin — A2564

Portrait and: No. 5362, Lenin Museum, Tampere, Finland. No. 5363, Memorial apartment, Paris, France.

1985, Apr. 22 Photo. *Perf. 11½x12*

5362 A2564 5k multi 10 7
5363 A2564 5k multi 10 7

Souvenir Sheet

Litho.

Perf. 12x12½

5364 A2564 30k Portrait 60 45

No. 5364 contains one stamp, size: 30x42mm.

Order of Victory — A2565

Photogravure and Engraved

1985, May 9 *Perf. 11½*

5365 A2565 20k sil, ryl bl, dk red & gold 40 30

Allied World War II victory over Germany and Japan, 40th anniv.

Liberation of Czechoslovakia from German Occupation Forces, 40th Anniv. — A2566

1985, May 9 Litho. *Perf. 12½x12*

5366 A2566 5k Arms 10 8

Warsaw Treaty Org., 30th Anniv. — A2567

1985, May 14 Photo. *Perf. 11½*

5367 A2567 5k Flags of member nations 10 8

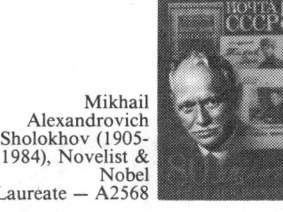

Mikhail Alexandrovich Sholokhov (1905-1984), Novelist & Nobel Laureate — A2568

Portraits and book covers: No. 5368, Tales from the Don, Quiet Flows the Don, A Human Tragedy. No. 5369, The Quiet Don, Virgin Lands Under the Plow, Thus They Have Fought for Their Homeland. No. 5370, Portrait.

1985, May 24 Litho. *Perf. 12½x12*

5368 A2568 5k reddish brn, cr & gold 10 8
5369 A2568 5k chnt, yel brn & gold 10 8

Photo.

Perf. 12x11½

Size: 37x52mm.

5370 A2568 5k brn, gold & blk 10 8

A little time given to the study of the arrangement of the Scott Catalogue can make it easier to use effectively.

INTERCOSMOS Project Halley-Venus — A2570

1985, June 11 Litho. *Perf. 12*

5372 A2570 15k Spacecraft, satellites, Venus 30 20

Artek Pioneer Camp, 60th Anniv. A2571

1985, June 14 Photo. *Perf. 11½*

5373 A2571 4k Camp, badges, Lenin Pioneers emblem 8 8

Mutiny on the Battleship Potemkin, 80th Anniv. — A2572

Photogravure and Engraved

1985, June 16 *Perf. 11½x12*

5374 A2572 5k dk red, gold & blk 10 7

Miniature Sheet

Soviet Railways Rolling Stock — A2573

Designs: a, Electric locomotive WL 80-R. b, Tanker car. c, Refrigerator car. d, Sleeper car. e, Tipper car. f, Box car. g, Shunting diesel locomotive. h, Mail car.

1985, June 15 Engr. *Perf. 12½x12*

5375 Sheet of 8 1.65 1.00
a.-h A2575 10k, Any single 20 12

Cosmonauts L. Kizim, V. Soloviov, O. Atkov and Salyut-7 Spacecraft — A2574

1985, June 25 Litho.

5376 A2574 15k multi 30 20

Soyuz T-10, Salyut-7 and Soyuz T-11 flights. Feb. 8-Oct. 2, 1984.

Beating Sword into Plowshares, Sculpture Donated to UN Hdqtrs. by USSR — A2575

Photogravure and Engraved

1985, June 26 *Perf. 11½*
5377 A2575 45k multi 90 60

UN 40th anniv.

Intl. Youth Year A2576

1985, June 26 Photo. *Perf. 12*
5378 A2576 10k multi 20 14

Medicinal Plants from Siberia — A2577

1985, July 10 Litho. *Perf. 12½x12*

5379	A2577	2k	O. dictiocarpum	6	5
5380	A2577	3k	Thermopsis lanceolata	7	6
5381	A2577	5k	Rosa acicularis lindi	10	7
5382	A2577	20k	Rhaponticum carthamoides	40	25
5383	A2577	45k	Bergenia crassifolia fritsch	90	60
			Nos. 5379-5383 (5)	1.53	1.03

Cosmonauts V. A. Dzhanibekov, S. E. Savistskaya, and I. P. Volk, Soyuz T-12 Mission, July 17-29, 1984 — A2578

1985, July 17
5384 A2578 10k multi 20 14

1st woman's free flight in space.

Caecilienhof Palace, Potsdam, Flags of UK, USSR, & USA A2579

Finlandia Hall, Helsinki A2580

1985, July 17
5385 A2579 15k multi 30 20

Potsdam Conference, 40th anniv.

1985, July 25 Photo. *Perf. 11½*
5386 A2580 20k multi 40 25

Helsinki Conference on European security and cooperation, 10th anniv.

The first value column gives the catalogue value of an unused stamp, the second that of a used stamp.

Flags of USSR, North Korea, Liberation Monument in Pyongyang A2581

1985, Aug. 1
5387 A2581 5k multi 10 7

Socialist Republic of North Korea, 40th anniv.

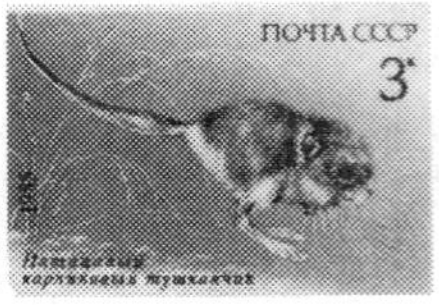

Endangered Wildlife A2582

Perf. 12x12½, 12½x12

1985, Aug. 15 **Litho.**

5388	A2582	2k	Sorex bucharensis, vert.	6	5
5389	A2582	3k	Cardiocranius paradoxus	7	6
5390	A2582	5k	Selevinia betpakdalensis, vert.	10	7

Size: 47x32mm.

5391	A2582	20k	Felis caracal	40	25
5392	A2582	45k	Gazella subgutturosa	90	60
			Nos. 5388-5392 (5)	1.53	1.03

Souvenir Sheet

5393 A2582 50k Panthera pardus 1.00 65

No. 5393 has multicolored margin continuing the design; black control number. Size: 90x66mm.

Youth World Soccer Cup Championships, Moscow — A2583

1985, Aug. 24 *Perf. 12*
5394 A2583 5k multi 10 7

Alexander G. Stakhanov, Coal Miner & Labor Leader A2584

1985, Aug. 30 Photo. *Perf. 11½*
5395 A2584 5k multi 10 7

Stakhanovite Movement for high labor productivity, 50th anniv.

Bryansk Victory Memorial, Buildings, Arms A2585

1985, Sept. 1
5396 A2585 5k multi 10 7

Millennium of Bryansk.

Socialist Republic of Vietnam, 40th Anniv. — A2586

1985, Sept. 2 Litho. *Perf. 12½x12*
5397 A2586 5k Arms 10 7

1985 World Chess Championship Match, A. Karpov Vs. G. Kasparov, Moscow — A2587

1985, Sept. 2 Photo. *Perf. 11½*
5398 A2587 10k multi 20 14

Lutsk City, Ukrainian S.S.R., 900th Anniv. — A2588

1985, Sept. 14
5399 A2588 5k Lutsk Castle 10 7

Open Book, the Weeping Jaroslavna and Prince Igor's Army — A2589

Photogravure and Engraved

1985, Sept. 14 *Perf. 11½x12*
5400 A2589 10k multi 20 14

The Song of Igor's Campaign, epic poem, 800th anniv.

Sergei Vasilievich Gerasimov (1885-1964), Painter A2590

1985, Sept. 26 *Perf. 12x11½*
5401 A2590 5k Portrait 10 7

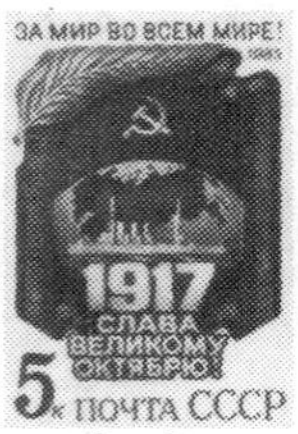

October Revolution, 68th Anniv. — A2591

UN 40th Anniv. — A2592

1985, Oct. 10 Photo. *Perf. 11½*
5402 A2591 5k multi 10 7

1985, Oct. 24
5403 A2592 15k multi 30 20

Krushjanis Baron (1835-1923), Latvian Folklorist — A2593

Lithographed and Engraved

1985, Oct. 31
5404 A2593 5k beige & blk 10 7

Lenin, Laborer Breaking Chains A2594

1985, Nov. 20 **Photo.**
5405 A2594 5k multi 10 7

Petersburg Union struggle for liberation of the working classes, founded by Lenin, 90th anniv.

Largest Soviet Telescope, 10th Anniv. — A2595

1985, Nov. 20 Engr. *Perf. 12½x12*
5406 A2595 10k dk bl 20 14

Soviet Observatory inauguration.

Angolan Independence, 10th Anniv. — A2596

Socialist Federal Republic of Jugoslavia, 40th Anniv. — A2597

1985, Nov. 25 **Photo.**
5407 A2596 5k multi 10 7

1985, Nov. 29 *Perf. 11½*
5408 A2597 5k multi 10 7

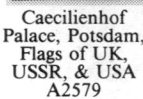

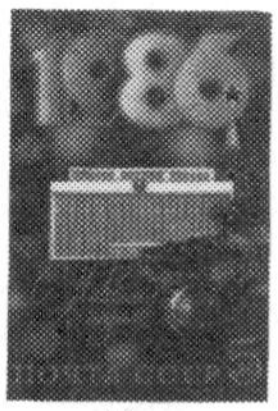

New Year — A2598

Samantha Smith — A2599

1985, Dec. 3 Litho. *Perf. 12*
5409 A2598 5k multi 10 7

Vehicle Type of 1984

1985, Dec. 18 Photo. *Perf. 12x11½*
5410 A2545 3k AMO-F15, 1926 7 5
5411 A2545 5k PMZ-1, 1933 10 7
5412 A2545 10k AC-40, 1977 20 14
5413 A2545 20k AL-30, 1970 40 25
5414 A2545 45k AA-60, 1978 90 60
Nos. 5410-5414 (5) 1.67 1.11

1985, Dec. 25 *Perf. 12*
5415 A2599 5k vio bl, choc & ver 10 7

American student invited to meet with Soviet leaders in 1984.

N.M. Emanuel (1915-1984), Chemist A2600

Family Leisure Activities A2601

1985, Dec. 30 Litho.
5416 A2600 5k multi 10 7

1985, Dec. 30
5417 A2601 5k Sightseeing 10 7
5418 A2601 5k Sports 10 7

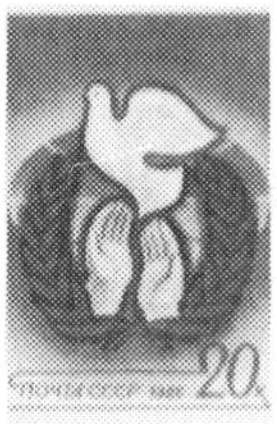

Intl. Peace Year — A2602

1986, Jan. 2 Photo. *Perf. 11½*
5419 A2602 20k brt bl, bluish grn & sil 40 25

Flags, Congress Palace, Carnation A2603

Lenin, Troitskaya Tower, Congress Palace A2604

Lenin — A2605

1986, Jan. 3
5420 A2603 5k multi 10 7

Photogravure and Engraved
Perf. 12x11½
5421 A2604 20k multi 40 25

Souvenir Sheet
Photo.
Perf. 11½
5422 A2605 50k multi 1.00 65

27th Communist Party Congress.

Modern Olympic Games, 90th Anniv. A2606

Flora of Russian Steppes A2607

1986, Jan. 10 *Perf. 11½x12*
5423 A2606 15k multi 30 20

Perf. 12½x12, 12x12½
1986, Jan. 15 Litho.
5424 A2607 4k multi 8 8
5425 A2607 5k multi, horiz. 10 7
5426 A2607 10k multi 20 14
5427 A2607 15k multi 30 20
5428 A2607 20k multi 40 25
Nos. 5424-5428 (5) 1.08 74

Vodovzvodnaya Tower, Grand Kremlin Palace — A2608

Voronezh City, 400th Anniv. — A2609

1986, Jan. 20 *Perf. 12½x12*
5429 A2608 50k grysh grn 1.00 65

1986, Feb. 20 *Perf. 11½*
5430 A2609 5k multi 10 7

Bela Kun (1886-1939), Hungarian Party Leader A2610

Karolis Pozhela (1896-1926), Lithuanian Party Founder A2611

1986, Feb. 20 Engr. *Perf. 12*
5431 A2610 10k bluish blk 20 14

1986, Feb. 28 *Perf. 12½x12*
5432 A2611 5k grysh blk 10 7

Intercosmos Project Halley, Final Stage — A2612

1986, Mar. 6 Litho. *Perf. 12*
5433 A2612 15k Vega probe, comet 30 20

Souvenir Sheet
Perf. 12½x12
5434 A2612 50k Vega I, comet 1.00 65

No. 5434 contains one stamp, size: 42x30mm.

Butterflies A2613

1986, Mar. 18 *Perf. 12x12½*
5435 A2613 4k Utetheisa pulchella 8 8
5436 A2613 5k Allancastria caucasica 10 8
5437 A2613 10k Zegris eupheme 20 14
5438 A2613 15k Catocala sponsa 30 20
5439 A2613 20k Satyrus bischoffi 40 25
Nos. 5435-5439 (5) 1.08 75

EXPO '86, Vancouver A2614

S.M. Kirov (1886-1934), Party Leader A2615

1986, Mar. 25 Photo. *Perf. 12x11½*
5440 A2614 20k Globe, space station 40 25

1986, Mar. 27 Engr. *Perf. 12½x12*
5441 A2615 5k black 10 7

Cosmonauts' Day — A2616

Designs: 5k, Konstantin E. Tsiolkovsky (1857-1935), aerodynamics innovator, and futuristic space station. 10k, Sergei P. Karolev (1906-1966), rocket scientist, and Vostok spaceship, vert. 15k, Yuri Gagarin, 1st cosmonaut, Sputnik I and Vega probe.

Perf. 12½x12, 12x12½
1986, Apr. 12 Litho.
5442 A2616 5k multi 10 7
5443 A2616 10k multi 20 14
5444 A2616 15k multi 30 20

No. 5444 printed se-tenant with label picturing Vostok and inscribed for the 25th anniv. of first space flight.

1986 World Ice Hockey Championships, Moscow — A2617

1986, Apr. 12 Photo. *Perf. 11½*
5445 A2617 15k multi 30 20

Ernst Thalmann (1886-1944), German Communist Leader — A2618

1986, Apr. 16 Engr. *Perf. 12½x12*
5446 A2618 10k dk red brn 20 14
5447 A2618 10k redsh brn 20 14

Lenin, 116th Birth Anniv. — A2619

Portraits and architecture: No. 5448, Socialist-Democratic People's House, Prague. No. 5449, Lenin Museum, Leipzig. No. 5450, Lenin Museum, Poronino, Poland.

1986, Apr. 22 Photo. *Perf. 11½x12*
5448 A2619 5k multi 10 7
5449 A2619 5k multi 10 7
5450 A2619 5k multi 10 7

Tambov City, 350th Anniv. A2620

1986, Apr. 27 *Perf. 11½*
5451 A2620 5k Buildings, city arms 10 7

Soviet Peace Fund, 25th Anniv.
A2621

1986, Apr. 27

5452	A2621	10k	lt chlky bl, gold & brt ultra	20	14

29th World Cycle Race, May 6-22
A2622

Toadstools
A2623

1986, May 6

5453	A2622	10k	multi	20	14

1986, May 15 **Litho.** ***Perf. 12***

5454	A2623	4k	Amanita phalloides	8	8
5455	A2623	5k	Amanita muscaria	10	8
5456	A2623	10k	Amanita pantherina	20	14
5457	A2623	15k	Tylopilus felleus	30	20
5458	A2623	20k	Hypholoma fasciculare	40	25
			Nos. 5454-5458 (5)	1.08	75

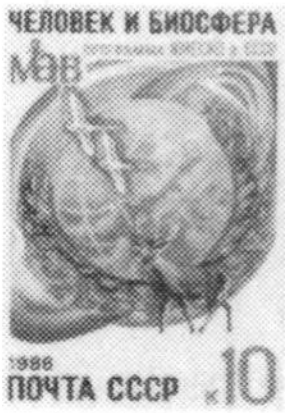

UNESCO Campaign, Man and Biosphere
A2624

9th Soviet Spartakiad
A2625

1986, May 19 **Photo.** ***Perf. 11½***

5459	A2624	10k	multi	20	14

1986, May 20

5460	A2625	10k	multi	20	14

City of Kuibyshev, 400th Anniv. — A2626

Design: Lenin's House, Eternal Glory and V. I. Chapaiev monuments, Gorky State Academic Drama Theater.

1986, May 24

5461	A2626	5k	multi	10	7

Canceled-to-order stamps are often from remainders. Most collectors of canceled stamps prefer postally used specimens.

"COMMUNICATION '86, Moscow" — A2627

1986, May 25

5462	A2627	5k	multi	10	7

1986 World Cup Soccer Championships, Mexico — A2628

Designs: 5k, 10k, Various soccer plays. 15k, World Cup on FIFA commemorative gold medal.

1986, May 31

5463	A2628	5k	multi	10	7
5464	A2628	10k	multi	20	14
5465	A2628	15k	multi	30	20

Paintings in the Tretyakov Gallery, Moscow — A2629

Designs: 4k, Lane in Albano, 1837, by M.I. Lebedev, vert. 5k, View of the Kremlin in Foul Weather, 1851, by A.K. Savrasov. 10k, Sunlit Pine Trees, 1896, by. I.I. Shishkin, vert. 15k, Return, 1896, by A.E. Arkhipov. 45k, Wedding Procession in Moscow, the 17th Century, 1901, by A.P. Ryabushkin.

Perf. 12x12½, 12½x12

1986, June 11 **Litho.**

5466	A2629	4k	multi	8	8
5467	A2629	5k	multi	10	8
5468	A2629	10k	multi	20	14

Size: 74x37mm

Perf. 11½

5469	A2629	15k	multi	30	20
5470	A2629	45k	multi	90	60
			Nos. 5466-5469 (4)	68	50

Irkutsk City, 300th Anniv. — A2630

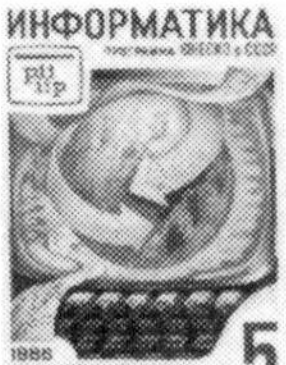

UNESCO Projects in Russia — A2632

Goodwill Games, Moscow, July 5-20
A2631

1986, June 28 **Photo.** ***Perf. 11½***

5471	A2630	5k	multi	10	7

1986, July 4 **Photo.** ***Perf. 11½***

5472	A2631	10k	Prus bl, gold & blk	20	14
5473	A2631	10k	brt bl, gold & blk	20	14

1986, July 15

Designs: 5k, Information sciences. 10k, Geological correlation. 15k, Inter-governmental oceanographic commission. 35k, Intl. hydrologic program.

5474	A2632	5k	multi	10	7
5475	A2632	10k	multi	20	14
5476	A2632	15k	multi	30	20
5477	A2632	35k	multi	65	45

Tyumen, 400th Anniv.
A2633

1986, July 27

5478	A2633	5k	multi	10	7

Olof Palme (1927-1986), Prime Minister of Sweden — A2634

1986, Aug. 1 **Photo.** ***Perf. 11½***

5479	A2634	10k	multi	20	14

10th World Women's Basketball Championships, Moscow, Aug. 15-17 — A2635

1986, Aug. 8

5480	A2613	15k	multi	30	20

Natl. Sports Committee Intl. Alpinist Camps — A2636

1986, Sept. 5 **Litho.** ***Perf. 12***

5481	A2636	4k	Mt. Lenin	8	8
5482	A2636	5k	Mt. E. Korzhenevskaya	10	8
5483	A2636	10k	Mt. Belukha	20	14
5484	A2636	15k	Mt. Communism	30	20
5485	A2636	30k	Mt. Elbrus	60	40
			Nos. 5481-5485 (5)	1.28	90

See Nos. 5532-5535.

Souvenir Sheet

Red Book, Rainbow, Earth
A2637

1986, Sept. 10 ***Perf. 11½***

5486	A2637	50k	multi	1.00	65

Nature preservation.

Chelyabinsk, 250th Anniv. — A2638

1986, Sept. 13 **Photo.**

5487	A2638	5k	multi	10	7

Mukran, DDR to Klaipeda, Lithuania, Train Ferry, Inauguration — A2639

1986, Sept. 23

5488	A2639	15k	multi	30	20

Siauliai, Lithuanian S.S.R., 750th Anniv. — A2640

1986, Sept. 26

5489	A2640	5k	multi	10	7

Trucks — A2641

1986, Oct. 15 ***Perf. 11½x12***

5490	A2641	4k	Ural-375D, 1964	8	8
5491	A2641	5k	GAZ-53A, 1965	10	8
5492	A2641	10k	KrAZ-256B, 1966	20	14
5493	A2641	15k	MAZ-515B, 1974	30	20
5494	A2641	20k	ZIL-133GY, 1979	40	25
			Nos. 5490-5494 (5)	1.08	75

October Revolution, 69th Anniv.
A2642

Mikhail Somov Trapped in the Antarctic
A2643

Design: Lenin Monument in October Square, Kremlin, Moscow.

1986, Oct. 1 Litho. *Perf. 12*
5495 A2642 5k multi 10 7

1986, Oct. 10 Photo. *Perf. 11½*
5496 A2643 5k Icebreaker, helicopters 10 7
5497 A2643 10k Mikhail Somov port side 20 14

Souvenir Sheet
Perf. 12½x11½
5498 A2643 50k Trapped in ice 1.00 65

Nos. 5496-5497 printed se-tenant in a continuous design picturing map of Russian Antarctic bases. No. 5498 contains one stamp, size: 51½x36½mm.

No. 4883 Ovptd. in Black for Rescue of the Mikhail Somov

15.III—26.VII.1985
Дрейф во льдах Антарктики

Lithographed & Engraved
1986, Oct. 10 *Perf. 12x11½*
5499 A2271 4k multi 15 8

Locomotives — A2644

1986, Oct. 15 Litho. *Perf. 12*
5500 A2644 4k EU 684-37, 1929 8 8
5501 A2644 5k FD 21-3000, 1941 10 8
5502 A2644 10k OV-5109, 1907 20 14
5503 A2644 20k C017-1613, 1944 40 25
5504 A2644 30k FDP 20-578, 1941 60 40
Nos. 5500-5504 (5) 1.38 95

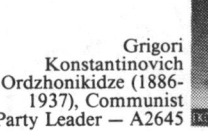

Grigori Konstantinovich Ordzhonikidze (1886-1937), Communist Party Leader — A2645

1986, Oct. 18 Engr. *Perf. 12½x12*
5505 A2645 5k dk bl grn 10 7

A.G. Novikov (1896-1984), Composer — A2646

1986, Oct. 30
5506 A2646 5k brn blk 10 7

UNESCO, 40th Anniv. A2647

Sun Yat-sen (1866-1925), Chinese Statesman A2648

1986, Nov. 4 Photo. *Perf. 11½*
5507 A2647 10k bl & sil 20 14

1986, Nov. 12
5508 A2648 5k lt grnsh gray & blk 10 7

Mikhail Vasilyevich Lomonosov, Scientist A2649

1986, Nov. 19 Engr. *Perf. 12x12½*
5509 A2649 5k dk vio brn 10 7

Aircraft by A.S. Yakovlev — A2650

1986, Nov. 25 Photo. *Perf. 11½x12*
5510 A2650 4k 1927 8 8
5511 A2650 5k 1935 10 8
5512 A2650 10k 1946 20 14
5513 A2650 20k 1972 40 25
5514 A2650 30k 1981 60 40
Nos. 5510-5514 (5) 1.38 95

New Year 1987 — A2651

27th Communist Party Congress, Feb. 25-Mar. 6 — A2652

1986, Dec. 4 Litho. *Perf. 11½*
5515 A2651 5k Kremlin towers 10 7

1986, Dec. 12 Photo. *Perf. 11½x12*

Red banner and: No. 5516, Computers. No. 5517, Engineer, computer, dish receivers. No. 5518, Aerial view of city. No. 5519, Council for Mutual Economic Assistance building, workers. No. 5520, Spasski Tower, Kremlin Palace.

5516 A2652 5k multi 10 7
5517 A2652 5k multi 10 7
5518 A2652 5k multi 10 7
5519 A2652 5k multi 10 7
5520 A2652 5k multi 10 7
Nos. 5516-5520 (5) 50 35

Alexander Yakovlevich Parkhomenko (1886-1921), Revolution Hero A2653

Samora Moises Machel (1933-1986) Pres. of Mozambique A2654

1986, Dec. 24 Engr. *Perf. 12½x12*
5521 A2653 5k black 10 7

1986, Dec. 25 Photo. *Perf. 11½*
5522 A2654 5k brn & buff 10 7

Miniature Sheet

Palace Museums in Leningrad — A2655

1986, Dec. 25 Engr. *Perf. 12*
5523 Sheet of 5 + label 2.00 1.25
a. A2655 5k State Museum, 1898 10 7
b. A2655 10k The Hermitage, 1764 20 14
c. A2655 15k Petrodvorets, 1728 30 20
d. A2655 20k Yekaterininsky, 1757 40 25
e. A2655 50k Pavlovsk, restored c. 1945 1.00 65

18th Soviet Trade Unions Congress, Feb. 24-28 — A2656

1987, Jan. 7 Photo. *Perf. 11½*
5524 A2656 5k multi 10 7

Butterflies A2657

1987, Jan. 15 Litho. *Perf. 12x12½*
5525 A2657 4k Atrophaneura alcinous 8 8
5526 A2657 5k Papilio machaon 10 8
5527 A2657 10k Papilio alexanor 20 14
5528 A2657 15k Papilio maackii 30 20
5529 A2657 30k Iphiclides podalirius 60 40
Nos. 5525-5529 (5) 1.28 90

Karlis Miyesniyek (1887-1977), Artist A2658

Stasis Shimkus (1887-1943), Composer A2659

1987, Jan. 31 *Perf. 12½x12*
5530 A2658 5k multi 10 7

1987, Feb. 4 *Perf. 12*
5531 A2659 5k buff & lake 10 7

Alpinist Camps Type of 1986

1987, Feb. 4
5532 A2636 4k Chimbulak Gorge 8 8
5533 A2636 10k Shavla Gorge 20 14
5534 A2636 20k Mts. Donguz-orun, Nakra-tau 40 25
5535 A2636 35k Mt. Kazbek 65 45

Vasily Ivanovich Chapayev (1887-1919), Revolution Hero — A2660

1987, Feb. 9 Engr.
5536 A2660 5k dk red brn 10 7

Heino Eller (1887-1970), Estonian Composer A2661

1987, Mar. 7 Litho. *Perf. 12*
5537 A2661 5k buff & brn 10 7

All-Union Leninist Young Communist League 20th Congress, Moscow A2662

Iosif Abgarovich Orbeli A2663

1987, Mar. 8 Photo. *Perf. 11½*
5538 A2662 5k multi 10 7

Souvenir Sheet
5539 A2662 50k "XX," and colored bands 1.00 65

No. 5539 contains one stamp, size: 26x37mm, perf. 11½x12).

Photogravure and Engraved
1987, Mar. 20 *Perf. 11½*
5540 A2663 5k buff & sep 10 7

Orbeli (1887-1961), first president of the Armenian Academy of Sciences.

World Wildlife Fund — A2664

Polar bears.

1987, Mar. 25 Photo. *Perf. 11½x12*

5541	A2664	5k	multi	10	7
5542	A2664	10k	multi	20	14
5543	A2664	20k	multi	40	25
5544	A2664	35k	multi	65	45

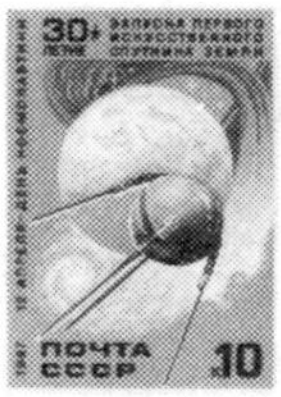

Cosmonauts' Day A2665

UN Emblem, ESCAP Headquarters, Bangkok A2666

1987, Apr. 12 *Perf. 11½*

5545	A2665	10k	Sputnik, 1957	20	14
5546	A2665	10k	Vostok 3 and 4, 1962	20	14
5547	A2665	10k	Mars 1, 1962	20	14

1987, Apr. 21

5548	A2666	10k	multi	20	14

UN Economic and Social Commission for Asia and the Pacific, 40th anniv.

Lenin, 117th Birth Anniv. — A2667

Paintings: No. 5549, Lenin's Birthday, by N.A. Sysoyev. No. 5550, Lenin with Delegates at the 3rd Congress of the Russian Young Communist League, by P.O. Belousov. No. 5551a, Lenin's Underground Activity (Lenin, lamp), by D.A. Nalbandyan. No. 5551b, Before the Assault (Lenin standing at table), by S.P. Viktorov. No. 5551c, We'll Show the Earth the New Way (Lenin, soldiers, flags), by A.G. Lysenko. No. 5551d, Lenin in Smolny, October 1917 (Lenin seated), by M.G. Sokolov. No. 5551e, Lenin, by N.A. Andreyev.

1987, Apr. 22 Litho. *Perf. 12½x12*

5549	A2667	5k	multi	10	7
5550	A2667	5k	multi	10	7

Souvenir Sheet

Perf. 12

5551	Sheet of 5	1.00	65
a.-e.	A2667 10k any single	20	12

No. 5551 contains 5 stamps (sizes: 40x28mm, Nos. 5551a-5551d; 40x56mm, No. 5551e). Size: 133x68mm.

European Gymnastics Championships, Moscow, May 18-26 — A2668

1987, May 5 Photo. *Perf. 11½*

5552	A2668	10k	multi	20	14

Bicycle Race A2669

Fauna A2670

1987, May 6

5553	A2669	10k	multi	20	14

40th Peace Bicycle Race, Poland-Czechoslovakia-German Democratic Republic, May.

Perf. 12½x12 (#5554), 12x12½

1987, May 15 Litho.

5554	A2670	5k	Menzbira marmot	10	7
5555	A2670	10k	Bald badger, horiz.	20	14

Size: 32x47mm.

5556	A2670	15k	Snow leopard	30	20

Passenger Ships — A2671

1987, May 20 Photo. *Perf. 12x11½*

5557	A2671	5k	Maxim Gorki	10	7
5558	A2671	10k	Alexander Pushkin	20	14
5559	A2671	30k	The Soviet Union	60	40

Paintings by Foreign Artists in the Hermitage Museum A2672

Designs: 4k, Portrait of a Woman, by Lucas Cranach Sr. (1472-1553). 5k, St. Sebastian, by Titian. 10k, Justice, by Durer. 30k, Adoration of the Magi, by Pieter Brueghel the Younger (c. 1564-1638). 50k, Ceres, by Rubens.

Perf. 12x12½, 12½x12

1987, June 5 Litho.

5560	A2762	4k	multi	8	8
5561	A2762	5k	multi	10	8
5562	A2762	10k	multi	20	14
5563	A2762	30k	multi	60	40
5564	A2762	50k	multi	1.00	65
			Nos. 5560-5564 (5)	1.98	1.35

Tolyatti City, 250th Anniv. — A2673

Design: Zhiguli car, Volga Motors factory, Lenin Hydroelectric plant.

1987, June 6 Photo. *Perf. 11½*

5565	A2673	5k	multi	10	7

Aleksander Pushkin (1799-1837), Poet — A2674

1987, June 6 Litho.

5566	A2674	5k	buff, yel brn & deep brn	10	7

No. 5566 printed se-tenant with label picturing manuscript, quote and Pushkin's signature.

Maj.-Gen. Sidor A. Kovpak (1887-1967), Vice-Chairman of the Ukranian SSR — A2675

Women's World Congress on Nuclear Disarmament, Moscow, June 23-27 — A2676

1987, June 7 Engr. *Perf. 12½x12*

5567	A2675	5k	blk	10	7

1987, June 23 Photo. *Perf. 11½*

5568	A2676	10k	multi	20	14

Tobolsk City, 400th Anniv. — A2677

Frelimo, 25th Anniv. — A2678

Design: Tobolsk kremlin, port, theater and Ermak Monument.

1987, June 25

5569	A2677	5k	multi	10	7

1987, June 25

5570	A2678	5k	Flag of Congo, man	10	7
5571	A2678	5k	Flags of Frelimo, USSR	10	7

Mozambique-USSR Peace Treaty, 10th anniv. Nos. 5570-5571 printed se-tenant in a continuous design.

Ferns — A2679

Kremlin and 2000 Year-old Coin of India — A2680

1987, July 2 Litho. *Perf. 12*

5572	A2679	4k	Scolopendrium vulgare	8	8
5573	A2679	5k	Ceterach officinarum	10	8
5574	A2679	10k	Salvinia natans, horiz.	20	14
5575	A2679	15k	Matteuccia struthiopteris	30	20
5576	A2679	50k	Adiantum pedatum	1.00	65
			Nos. 5572-5576 (5)	1.68	1.15

1987, July 3

5577	A2680	5k	shown	10	7
5578	A2680	5k	Red Fort, Delhi, Soviet hammer & sickle	10	7

Festivals 1987-88: India in the USSR (No. 5577) and the USSR in India (No. 5578). Nos. 5577-5578 printed se-tenant.

15th Intl. Film Festival, July 16-17, Moscow — A2681

1987, July 6 Photo. *Perf. 11½*

5579	2681	10k	multi	20	14

Joint Soviet-Syrian Space Flight A2682

Mir Space Station — A2683

Flags, Intercosmos emblem and: 5k, Cosmonaut training and launch. 10k, Mir space station, Syrian parliament and cosmonauts. 15k, Gagarin Memorial, satellite dishes and cosmonauts wearing space suits.

1987 Litho. *Perf. 12x12½*

5580	A2682	5k	multi	10	7
5581	A2682	10k	multi	20	14
5582	A2682	15k	multi	30	20

Souvenir Sheet

5583	A2683	50k	multi	1.00	65

Issue dates: 5k, July 22; 10k, July 24; 15k, 50k July 30.

Intl. Atomic Energy Agency, 30th Anniv. A2684

1987, July 29 Photo. *Perf. 11½*

5584	A2684	20k	multi	40	25

14th-16th Century Postrider — A2685

Designs: 5k, 17th cent. postman and 17th cent. kibitka (sled). 10k, 16th-17th cent. ship and 18th cent. packet. 30k, Railway station and 19th cent. mailcars. 35k, AMO-F-15 bus and car, 1905. 50k, Postal headquarters, Moscow, and modern postal delivery trucks.

Photo. & Engr.

1987, Aug. 25 ***Perf. 11½x12***

5585 A2685 4k buff & blk 8 8
5586 A2685 5k buff & blk 10 8
5587 A2685 10k buff & blk 20 14
5588 A2685 30k buff & blk 60 40
5589 A2685 35k buff & blk 65 45
Nos. 5585-5589 (5) 1.63 1.15

Souvenir Sheet

5590 A2685 50k pale yel, dull gray grn & blk 1.00 65

A2686

October Revolution, 70th Anniv. — A2687

Paintings by Russian artists: No. 5591, Long Live the Socialist Revolution! by V.V. Kuznetsov. No. 5592, V.I. Lenin Proclaims the Soviet Power (Lenin pointing), by V.A. Serov. No. 5593, V.I. Lenin (with pencil), by P.V. Vasiliev. No. 5594, On the Eve of the Storm (Lenin, Trotsky, Dzerzhinski), by V.V. Pimenov. No. 5585, Taking the Winter Palace by Storm, by V.A. Serov.

1987, Aug. 25 **Litho.** ***Perf. 12½x12***

5591 A2686 5k shown 10 7
5592 A2686 5k multi 10 7
5593 A2686 5k multi 10 7

Size: 70x33mm.

Perf. 11½

5594 A2686 5k multi 10 7
5595 A2686 5k multi 10 7
Nos. 5591-5595 (5) 50 35

Souvenir Sheet

Photo. & Engr.

Perf. 12x11½

5596 A2687 30k gold & blk 60 40

Souvenir Sheet

Battle of Borodino, 175th Anniv. — A2688

1987, Sept. 7 **Litho.** ***Perf. 12½x12***

5597 A2688 1r blk, yel brn & blue gray 2.00 1.25

Pavel Petrovich Postyshev (1887-1939), Party Leader — A2689

Moscow, 840th Anniv. — A2690

1987, Sept. 18 **Engr.**

5598 A2689 5k int blue 10 7

1987, Sept. 19 **Photo.** ***Perf. 11½***

Design: 5k, Monument to founder Yuri Dolgoruki, by sculptor S. Orlov, A. Antropov, N. Stamm and architect V. Andreyev, in Sovetskaya Square, and buildings in Moscow.

5599 A2690 5k dark red brn, cream & dark org 10 7

Scientists — A2691

Designs: No. 5600, Muhammed Taragai Ulugh Begh (1394-1449), Uzbek astronomer and mathematician. No. 5601, Sir Isaac Newton (1642-1727), English physicist and mathematician. No. 5602, Marie Curie (1867-1934), physicist, chemist, Nobel laureate.

1987, Oct. 3 **Photo. & Engr.**

5600 A2691 5k dark blue, org brn & blk 10 7
5601 A2691 5k dull grn, blk & dark ultra 10 7
5602 A2691 5k brn & deep blue 10 7

Nos. 5600-5602 each printed se-tenant with inscribed label.

Footnotes often refer you to other stamps of the same design.

Souvenir Sheet

COSPAS-SARSAT Intl. Satellite System for Tracking Disabled Planes and Ships — A2692

1987, Oct. 15 **Photo.**

5603 A2692 50k multi 1.00 65

No. 5603 has multicolored margin continuing the design and picturing American satellite in space, plane, ship, Earth and black control number. Size: 64x81mm.

No. 5595 Overprinted in Gold

Всесоюзная филателистическая выставка „70 лет Великого Октября"

1987, Oct. 17 **Litho.**

5604 A2686 5k multi 10 7

All-Union Philatelic Exhibition and the 70th Anniv. of the October Revolution.

My Quiet Homeland, by V.M. Sidorov — A2693

The Sun Above Red Square, by P.P. Ossovsky — A2694

Paintings by Soviet artists exhibited at the 7th Republican Art Exhibition, Moscow, 1985: 4k, There Will be Cities in the Taiga, by A.A. Yakovlev. 5k, Mother, by V.V. Shcherbakov. 30k, On Jakutian Soil, by A.N. Osipov. 35k, Ivan's Return, by V.I. Yerofeyev.

Perf. 12x12½, 12½x12

1987, Oct. 20

5605 A2693 4k multi, vert. 8 8
5606 A2693 5k multi, vert. 10 8
5607 A2693 10k shown 20 14
5608 A2693 30k multi 60 40
5609 A2693 35k multi 65 45
Nos. 5605-5609 (5) 1.63 1.15

Souvenir Sheet

Perf. 11½x12½

5610 A2694 50k multi 1.00 65

John Reed (1887-1920), American Journalist — A2695

1987, Oct. 22 ***Perf. 11½***

5611 A2695 10k buff & dark brn 20 14

Samuil Yakovlevich Marshak (1887-1964), Author — A2696

1987, Nov. 3 **Engr.** ***Perf. 12½x12***

5612 A2696 5k deep claret 10 7

Ilja Grigorjevich Chavchavadze (1837-1907), Georgian Author — A2697

1987, Nov. 8

5613 A2697 5k slate blue 10 7

Indira Gandhi (1917-1984) A2698

Vadim Nikolaevich Podbelsky (1887-1920), Revolution Leader A2699

1987, Nov. 19 **Photo.** ***Perf. 11½***

5614 A2698 5k blk & brn 10 7

1987, Nov. 25 ***Perf. 12½x12***

5615 A2699 5k blk 10 7

Nikolai Ivanovich Vavilov (1887-1943), Botantist A2700

Modern Science A2701

1987, Nov. 25

5616 A2700 5k dark blue gray 10 7

Photo. & Engr.

1987, Nov. 25 ***Perf. 11 ½***

Designs: 5k, TOKAMAK, a controlled thermonuclear reactor. 10k, Kola Project (Earth strata study). 20k, RATAN-600 radiotelescope.

5617	A2701	5k	grnsh gray & brn	10	7
5618	A2701	10k	dull grn, lt blue gray & dark blue	20	14
5619	A2701	20k	gray olive, blk & buff	40	25

US and Soviet Flags, Spasski Tower and US Capitol — A2702

1987, Dec. 17 **Photo.**

5620 A2702 10k multi 20 14

INF Treaty (eliminating intermediate-range nuclear missiles) signed by Gen.-Sec. Gorbachev and Pres. Reagan, Dec. 8.

New Year 1988 A2703

1987, Dec. 2 **Litho.** ***Perf. 12x12 ½***

5621 A2703 5k Kremlin 10 7

Marshal Ivan Khristoforovich Bagramyan (1897-1982) — A2704

1987, Dec. 2 **Engr.** ***Perf. 12 ½x12***

5622 A2704 5k blk 10 7

Miniature Sheet

18th-19th Cent. Naval Commanders and War Ships — A2705

Designs: 4k, Adm. Grigori Andreyevich Spiridov (1713-1790), Battle of Chesmen. 5k, Fedor Fedorovich Ushakov (1745-1817), Storming of Corfu. 10k, Adm. Dimitiri Nikolayevich Senyavin (1763-1831) and flagship at the Battle of Afon off Mt. Athos. 25k, Mikhail Petrovich Lazarev (1788-1851), Battle of Navarin. 30k, Adm. Pavel Stepanovich Nakhimov (1802-1855), Battle of Sinop.

1987, Dec. 22

5623		Sheet of 5 + label	1.50	1.00
a	A2705	4k dark blue & ind	8	8
b	A2705	5k mar & ind	10	8
c	A2705	10k mar & ind	20	14
d	A2705	25k dark blue & ind	50	32
e	A2705	30k dark blue & ind	60	40

No. 5623 contains corner label (LR) picturing ensign of period Russian Navy vessels and anchor.

Asia-Africa Peoples Solidarity Organization, 30th Anniv. — A2706

1987, Dec. 26 **Photo.** ***Perf. 11 ½***

5624 A2706 10k multi 20 14

First Soviet Postage Stamp, 70th Anniv. A2707

1988 Winter Olympics, Calgary A2708

1988, Jan. 4 **Photo.** ***Perf. 11 ½***

5625	A2707	10k	No. 149, No. 150 UR	20	14
5626	A2707	10k	No. 150, No. 149 UR	20	14

Nos. 5625-5626 are printed se-tenant. Lettering in brown on No. 5625, in blue on No. 5626.

1988, Jan. 4

5627	A2708	5k	Biathlon	10	7
5628	A2708	10k	Cross-country skiing	20	14
5629	A2708	15k	Slalom	30	20
5630	A2708	20k	Pairs figure skating	40	25
5631	A2708	30k	Ski jumping	60	40
			Nos. 5627-5631 (5)	1.60	1.06

Souvenir Sheet

5632 A2708 50k Ice hockey, horiz. 1.00 65

World Health Org., 40th Anniv. — A2709

1988, Jan. 7

5633 A2709 35k blue & gold 1.05 70

Lord Byron (1788-1824), English Poet — A2710

Photo. & Engr.

1988, Jan. 22 ***Perf. 12x11 ½***

5634 A2710 15k Prus blue, blk & grn blk 45 30

Cultural, Technical and Educational Agreement with the US, 30th Anniv. — A2711

G.I. Lomov-Oppokov (1888-1938), Party Leader — A2712

1988, Jan. 27 **Photo.** ***Perf. 11 ½***

5635 A2711 20k multi 60 40

1988, Feb. 5

5636 A2712 5k blk & tan 15 10

Animated Soviet Cartoons — A2713

1988, Feb. 18 **Litho.** ***Perf. 12 ½x12***

5637	A2713	1k	Little Humpback Horse, 1947	5	5
5638	A2713	3k	Winnie-the-Pooh, 1969	10	6
5639	A2713	4k	Gena, the Crocodile, 1969	12	8
5640	A2713	5k	Just you Wait! 1969	15	10
5641	A2713	10k	Hedgehog in the Mist, 1975	30	20
			Nos. 5637-5641 (5)	72	49

Souvenir Sheet

5642 A2713 30k Post, 1929 90 60

Mikhail Alexandrovich Bonch-Bruevich (1888-1940), Broadcast Engineer A2714

Intl. Red Cross and Red Crescent Organizations, 125th Annivs. A2715

1988, Feb. 21 **Photo.** ***Perf. 11 ½***

5643 A2714 10k buff & blk 30 20

1988, Feb. 25

5644 A2715 15k blk, brt blue & dark red 45 30

World Speed Skating Championships, Mar. 5-6, Alma-Ata — A2716

1988, Mar. 13 **Photo.** ***Perf. 11 ½***

5645 A2716 15k blk, vio & brt blue 45 30

No. 5645 printed se-tenant with label picturing Alma-Ata skating rink, Medeo.

Anton Semenovich Makarenko (1888-1939), Teacher, Youth Development Expert — A2717

1988, Mar. 13 **Litho.** ***Perf. 12 ½x12***

5646 A2717 10k dark olive grn 30 20

Franzisk Skorina (b. 1488), 1st Printer in Byelorussia A2718

1988, Mar. 17 **Engr.** ***Perf. 12x12 ½***

5647 A2718 5k gray blk 15 10

Labor Day A2719

Victor Eduardovich Kingisepp (1888-1922), Revolutionary A2720

1988, Mar. 22 **Photo.** ***Perf. 11 ½***

5648 A2719 5k multicolored 15 10

1988, Mar. 24 **Engr.** ***Perf. 12***

5649 A2720 5k dark grn 15 10

Organized Track and Field Events in Russia, Cent. A2721

1988, Mar. 24 **Photo.** ***Perf. 11 ½***

5650 A2721 15k multicolored 45 30

Marietta Sergeyevna Shaginyan (1888-1982), Author — A2722

1988, Apr. 2 **Litho.** ***Perf. 12 ½x12***

5651 A2722 10k brn 30 20

Soviet-Finnish Peace Treaty, 40th Anniv. — A2723

1988, Apr. 6 Photo. *Perf. 11½*
5652 A2723 15k multi 45 30

Cosmonaut's Day — A2724

Victory, 1948, Painted by P.A. Krivonogov — A2725

Design: MIR space station, Soyuz TM transport ship, automated cargo ship *Progress* and *Quant* module.

1988, Apr. 12 *Perf. 11½x12*
5653 A2724 15k multi 45 30

1988, Apr. 20 Litho. *Perf. 12x12½*
5654 A2725 5k multi 15 10

Victory Day (May 9).

Sochi City, 150th Anniv. A2726

1988, Apr. 20 Photo. *Perf. 11½*
5655 A2726 5k multi 15 10

Branches of the Lenin Museum — A2727

Portrait of Lenin and: No. 5656, Central museum, Moscow, opened May 15, 1926. No. 5657, Branch, Leningrad, opened in 1937. No. 5658, Branch, Kiev, opened in 1938. No. 5659, Branch, Krasnoyarsk, opened in 1987.

1988, Apr. 22 Litho. *Perf. 12*
5656 A2727 5k vio brn & gold 15 10
5657 A2727 5k brn vio, vio brn & gold 15 10
5658 A2727 5k deep brn olive & gold 15 10
5659 A2727 5k dark green & gold 15 10
a Block of 4, Nos. 5656-5659 60 40

Ivan Alexeyevich Akulov (1888-1939), Party Leader A2728

EXPO '88, Brisbane, Australia A2729

1988, Apr. 24 Photo. *Perf. 11½*
5660 A2728 5k blue blk 15 10

1988, Apr. 30
5661 A2729 20k multi 60 40

Karl Marx — A2730

1988, May 5 Engr. *Perf. 12*
5662 A2730 5k choc 15 10

Social and Economic Reforms — A2731

Designs: No. 5663, Cruiser *Aurora,* revolutionary soldiers, workers and slogans Speeding Up, Democratization, and Glasnost against Kremlin Palace. No. 5664, Worker, agriculture and industries.

1988, May 5 Photo. *Perf. 12x11½*
5663 A2731 5k multi 15 10
5664 A2731 5k multi 15 10

No. 5632 Ovptd. in Dark Red

Спортсмены СССР завоевали
11 золотых, 9 серебряных
и 9 бронзовых медалей!

1988, May 12 Photo. *Perf. 11½*
5665 A2708 50k multi 1.50 1.00

Victory of Soviet athletes at the 1988 Winter Olympics, Calgary. No. 5665 overprinted below stamp on souvenir sheet margin. Soviet sportsmen won 11 gold, 9 silver and 9 bronze medals.

Nikolai Mikhailovich Shvernik (1888-1970), Party Leader — A2732

1988, May 19 Engr. *Perf. 12*
5666 A2732 5k blk 15 10

Hunting Dogs — A2733

Designs: 5k, Russian borzoi, fox hunt. 10k, Kirghiz greyhound, falconry. 15k, Russian retrievers. 20k, Russian spaniel, duck hunt. 35k, East Siberian husky, bear hunt.

1988, May 20 Litho.
5667 A2733 5k multi 15 10
5668 A2733 10k multi 30 20
5669 A2733 15k multi 45 30
5670 A2733 20k multi 60 40
5671 A2733 35k multi 1.05 70
Nos. 5667-5671 (5) 2.55 1.70

Soviet-US Summit Conference, May 29-June 2, Moscow — A2734

1988, May 29 Photo. *Perf. 11½*
5672 A2734 5k multi 15 10

Valerian Vladimirovich Kuibyshev (1888-1935), Party Leader — A2735

Shipka '88, USSR-Bulgarian Joint Space Flight, June 7 — A2736

1988, June 6 Engr. *Perf. 12*
5673 A2735 5k brn blk 15 10

1988, June 7 Photo. *Perf. 11½*

Design: Flags, Mir space station and Soyuz TM spacecraft.

5674 A2736 15k multi 45 30

Soviet-Canada Transarctic Ski Expedition, May-Aug. A2737

For a World Without Nuclear Weapons A2738

Design: Natl. and Canadian flags, skis and globe.

1988, June 16
5675 A2737 35k multi 1.05 70

1988, June 16
5676 A2738 5k multi 15 10

A2739

A2740

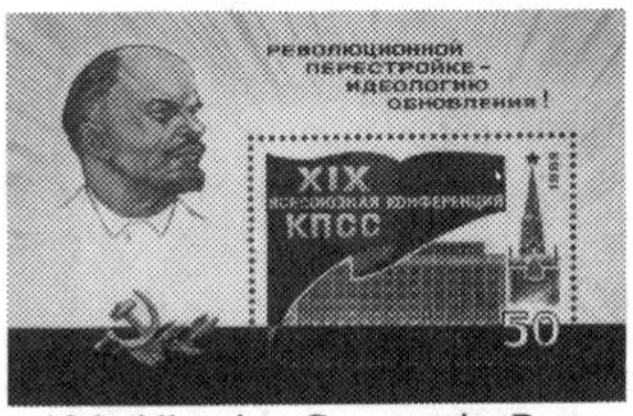

19th All-union Communist Party Conference, Moscow — A2741

1988, June 16 Litho. *Perf. 12*
5677 A2739 5k multi 15 10

Photo.
Perf. 11½
5678 A2740 5k multi 15 10

Souvenir Sheet
Perf. 11½x12
5679 A2741 50k multi 1.50 1.00

1988 Summer Olympics, Seoul A2742

1988, June 29 Litho. *Perf. 12*
5680 A2742 5k Hurdling 15 10
5681 A2742 10k Long jump 30 20
5682 A2742 15k Basketball 45 30
5683 A2742 20k Rhythmic gymnastics 60 40
5684 A2742 30k Swimming 90 60
Nos. 5680-5684 (5) 2.40 1.60

Souvenir Sheet
5685 A2742 50k Soccer 1.50 1.00

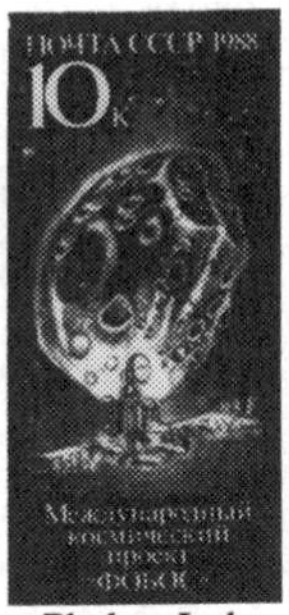

Phobos Intl. Space Project A2743

Flowers Populating Deciduous Forests A2744

1988, July 7 Photo. *Perf. 11½x12*
5686 A2743 10k Satellite, space probe 30 20

For the study of Phobos, a satellite of Mars.

1988, July 7 Litho. *Perf. 12*
5687 A2744 5k Campanula latifolia 15 10
5688 A2744 10k Orobus vernus, horiz. 30 20
5689 A2744 15k Pulmonaria obscura 45 30
5690 A2744 20k Lilium martagon 60 40
5691 A2744 35k Ficaria verna 1.05 70
Nos. 5687-5691 (5) 2.55 1.70

For unused stamps, more recent issues are valued as never hinged, with the beginning point determined on a country-by-country basis. Notes to show the beginning points are prominently placed in the text.

Leninist Young Communist League (Komsomol), 70th Anniv. A2745

Nelson Mandela (b. 1918), South African Anti-apartheid Leader A2746

1988, July 14 Photo. *Perf. 11½*
5692 A2745 5k multi 15 10

1988, July 18
5693 A2746 10k multi 30 20

Paintings in the Timiriazev Equestrian Museum of the Moscow Agricultural Academy — A2747

Paintings: 5k, *Light Gray Arabian Stallion,* by N.E. Sverchkov, 1860. 10k, *Konvoets, a Kabardian,* by M.A. Vrubel, 1882, vert. 15k, *Horsewoman Riding an Orlov-Rastopchinsky,* by N.E. Sverchkov. 20k, *Letuchya, a Gray Orlov Trotter,* by V.A. Serov, 1886, vert. 30k, *Sardar, an Akhaltekinsky Stallion,* by A.B. Villevalde, 1882.

1988, July 20 Litho. *Perf. 12½x12*
5694 A2747 5k multi 15 10
5695 A2747 10k multi 30 20
5696 A2747 15k multi 45 30
5697 A2747 20k multi 60 40
5698 A2747 30k multi 90 60
Nos. 5694-5698 (5) 2.40 1.60

No. 5692 Ovptd. for the All-Union Philatelic Exhibition, Moscow, Aug. 10-17

Филвыставка. Москва

1988, Aug. 10 Photo. *Perf. 11½*
5699 A2745 5k multi 15 10

Petr Lazarevich Voykov (1888-1927), Economic and Trade Union Plenipotentiary A2748

1988, Aug. 13 Engr. *Perf. 12½x12*
5700 A2748 5k blk 15 10

Intl. Letter-Writing Week — A2749

1988, Aug. 25 Photo. *Perf. 11½*
5701 A2749 5k blue grn & dark blue grn 15 10

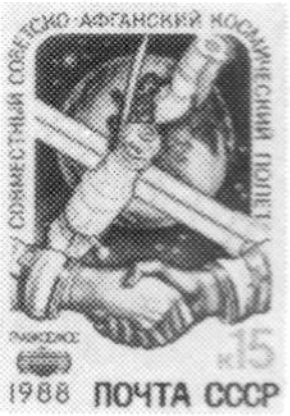

Soviet-Afghan Joint Space Flight — A2750

1988, Aug. 29
5702 A2750 15k Earth, Mir space station and Soyuz-TM 45 30

Problems of Peace and Socialism Magazine, 30th Anniv. A2751

Emmanuil Ionovich Kviring (1888-1937), Party Leader A2752

1988, Sept. 1 Photo. *Perf. 11½*
5703 A2751 10k multi 30 20

1988, Sept. 13 Engr. *Perf. 12*
5704 A2752 5k black 15 10

Folklore of the Soviet Republics — A2753

Designs: No. 5705, *Ilya Muromets,* Russian lore, vert. No. 5706, *Ballad of the Cossack Golota,* Ukrainian lore. No. 5707, *Musician-Magician,* a Byelorussian fairy tale, vert. No. 5708, *Koblandy-batyr,* a poem from Kazakh. No. 5709, *Alpamysh,* a fairy tale from Uzbek, vert.

Perf. 12x12½, 12½x12
1988, Sept. 22 Litho.
5705 A2753 10k multi 30 20
5706 A2753 10k multi 30 20
5707 A2753 10k multi 30 20
5708 A2753 10k multi 30 20
5709 A2753 10k multi 30 20
Nos. 5705-5709 (5) 1.50 1.00

Nos. 5705-5709 printed se-tenant with inscribed labels containing descriptive text.

Appeal of the Leader, 1947, by I.M. Toidze A2754

1988, Oct. 5 *Perf. 12x12½*
5710 A2754 5k multi 15 10

October Revolution, 71st anniv.

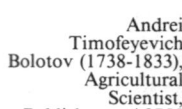

Andrei Timofeyevich Bolotov (1738-1833), Agricultural Scientist, Publisher — A2755

1988, Oct. 18 Engr. *Perf. 12*
5711 A2755 10k blk 30 20

Andrei Nikolayevich Tupolev (1888-1972), Aeronautical Engineer — A2756

1988, Oct. 18
5712 A2756 10k steel blue 30 20

North Pole Expedition (in 1987) A2757

Dmitry F. Ustinov (1908-1984), Minister of Defense A2758

Design: 20k, Map of expedition route, atomic icebreaker *Sibirj* and expedition members.

1988, Oct. 25 Litho.
5713 A2757 20k multi 60 40

1988, Oct. 30 Engr.
5714 A2758 5k brn blk 16 12

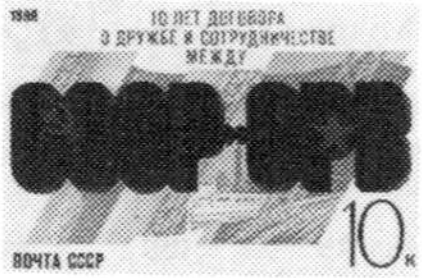

Soviet-Vietnamese Treaty, 10th Anniv. — A2759

1988, Nov. 3 Photo. *Perf. 11½*
5715 A2759 10k multi 30 20

State Broadcasting and Sound Recording Institute, 50th Anniv. A2760

1988, Nov. 3
5716 A2760 10k multi 30 20

U.N Declaration of Human Rights, 40th Anniv. A2761

1988, Nov. 21
5717 A2761 10k multi 30 20

New Year 1989 — A2762

Design: Preobrazhensky Regiment bodyguard riding to announce Peter the Great's decree to celebrate new year's eve as of January 1, 1700.

1988, Nov. 24 Litho. *Perf. 12x11½*
5718 A2762 5k multi 16 12

Soviet-French Joint Space Flight — A2763

1988, Nov. 26 Photo. *Perf. 11½*
5719 A2763 15k Space walkers 45 30

No. 4607 Overprinted in Red

★ КОСМИЧЕСКАЯ ПОЧТА

1988, Dec. 16 Litho. *Perf. 12½x12*
5720 A2143 1r dark blue 3.00 2.00

Space mail.

Martyn Ivanovich Latsis (1888-1938), Party Leader — A2764

1988, Dec. 16 Engr.
5721 A2764 5k slate grn 15 10

Souvenir Sheet

No. 5685 Ovptd. in Bright Blue

СПОРТСМЕНЫ СССР ЗАВОЕВАЛИ
55 ЗОЛОТЫХ, 31 СЕРЕБРЯНУЮ
И 46 БРОНЗОВЫХ МЕДАЛЕЙ
СЕУЛ • 1988

1988, Dec. 20 Litho. *Perf. 11½x12*
5722 A2741 50k multi 1.50 1.00

Victory of Soviet athletes at the 1988 Summer Olympics, Seoul. Overprint on margin of No. 5722 specifies that Soviet athletes won 55 gold, 31 silver and 46 bronze medals.

Post Rider A2765

Fountains of Petrodvorets A2766

Designs: 3k, Cruiser *Aurora.* 4k, Spasski Tower, Lenin Mausoleum. 5k, Natl. flag, crest. 10k, *The Worker and the Collective Farmer,* 1935, sculpture by V.I. Mukhina. 15k, Satellite dish. 20k, Lyre, art tools, quill pen, parchment (arts and literature). 25k, *Discobolus,* 5th cent. sculpture by Myron (c. 480-440 B.C.). 30k, Map of the Antarctic, penguins. 35k, *Mercury,* sculpture by Giambologna (1529-1608). 50k, White cranes (nature conservation). 1r, UPU emblem.

1988, Dec. 22 Engr. *Perf. 12x11 1/2*

5723	A2765	1k	dark brn	5	5
5724	A2765	3k	dark blue grn	9	6
5725	A2765	4k	indigo	12	8
5726	A2765	5k	red	15	10
5727	A2765	10k	claret	30	20
5728	A2765	15k	deep blue	45	30
5729	A2765	20k	olive gray	60	40
5730	A2765	25k	dark grn	75	50
5731	A2765	30k	dark blue	90	60
5732	A2765	35k	dark red brn	1.05	70
5733	A2765	50k	sapphire	1.50	1.00
5734	A2765	1r	blue gray	3.00	2.00
			Nos. 5723-5734 (12)	8.96	5.99

1988, Dec. 25 Engr. *Perf. 11 1/2x12*

Designs: 5k, Samson Fountain, 1723, and Great Cascade. 10k, Adam Fountain, 1722, and sculptures, 1718, by D. Bonazza. 15k, Golden Mountain Cascade, by N. Miketti (1721-1723) and M.G. Zemtsov. 30k, Roman Fountains, 1763. 50k, Oak Tree Fountain, 1735.

5735	A2766	5k	myrtle grn	15	10
5736	A2766	10k	myrtle grn	30	20
5737	A2766	15k	myrtle grn	45	30
5738	A2766	30k	myrtle grn	90	60
5739	A2766	50k	myrtle grn	1.50	1.00
a.			Pane of 5, Nos. 5735-5739	3.30	2.20
			Nos. 5735-5739 (5)	3.30	2.20

Nos. 5735-5739 se-tenant in panes of 5 with photogravure inscribed margin. Panes are printed bilaterally and separated in the center by perforations so that stamps in the 2nd pane are arranged in reverse order from the 1st pane.

19th Communist Party Congress — A2767

1988, Dec. 30 Photo. *Perf. 12x11 1/2*

5740	A2767	5k	multi & deep car (power)	15	10
5741	A2767	5k	multi & deep blue vio (industry)	15	10
5742	A2767	5k	multi & grn (land)	15	10

Souvenir Sheet

Inaugural Flight of the *Buran* Space Shuttle, Nov. 15 — A2768

1988, Dec. 30 *Perf. 11 1/2x12*

5743 A2768 50k multi 1.50 1.00

Luna 1, 30th Anniv. — A2769

1989, Jan. 2 Photo. *Perf. 11 1/2*

5744 A2769 15k multi 45 30

Jalmari Virtanen (1889-1939), Karelian Poet A2770

1989, Jan. 8

5745 A2770 5k olive brn 15 10

Council for Mutual Economic Assistance, 40th Anniv. A2771

1989, Jan. 8

5746 A2771 10k multi 30 20

Environmental Protection — A2772

1989, Jan. 18 Litho. *Perf. 12 1/2x12*

5747	A2772	5k	Forest	15	10
5748	A2772	10k	Arctic deer	30	20
5749	A2772	15k	Stop desert encroachment	45	30

Nos. 5747-5749 printed se-tenant with inscribed labels picturing maps.

Samovars — A2773

Samovars in the State Museum, Leningrad: 5k, Pear-shaped urn, late 18th cent. 10k, Barrel-shaped urn by Ivan Listisin, early 19th cent. 20k, "Kabachok" urn by the Sokolov Bros., Tula, c. 1830. 30k, Vase-shaped urn by the Nikolari Malikov Studio, Tula, c. 1840.

1989, Feb. 8 Photo. *Perf. 11 1/2*

5750	A2773	5k	multi	15	10
5751	A2773	10k	multi	30	20
5752	A2773	20k	multi	60	40
5753	A2773	30k	multi	90	60

Modest Petrovich Mussorgsky (1839-1881), Composer — A2774

1989, Feb. 15 Litho. *Perf. 12 1/2x12*

5754 A2774 10k dull vio & vio brn 30 20

P.E. Dybenko (1889-1938), Military Commander A2775

1989, Feb. 28 Engr. *Perf. 12*

5755 A2775 5k black 15 10

T.G. Shevchenko (1814-1861), Poet A2776

1989, Mar 6 Litho. *Perf. 11 1/2*

5756 A2776 5k pale grn, blk & brn 15 10

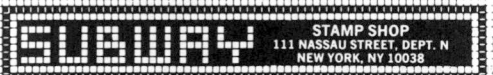

Cultivated Lilies — A2777

1989, Mar. 15 *Perf. 12 ½x12*

5757	A2777	5k	Lilium speciosum	15	10
5758	A2777	10k	African queen	30	20
5759	A2777	15k	Eclat du soir	45	30
5760	A2777	30k	White tiger	90	60

Souvenir Sheet

Labor Day, Cent. — A2778

1989, May 1 *Perf. 11 ½x12*

5761	A2778	30k	multi	90	60

SEMI-POSTAL STAMPS

Empire

Admiral Kornilov Monument, Sevastopol — SP1

Pozharski and Minin Monument, Moscow — SP2

Statue of Peter the Great, Leningrad — SP3

Alexander II Memorial and Kremlin, Moscow — SP4

Perf. 11 ½ to 13 ½ and Compound

1905 **Typo.** **Unwmk.**

B1	SP1	3k	red, brn & grn	2.75	2.25
a.			Perf. 13½x 11½	175.00	145.00
b.			Perf. 13½	27.00	27.50
c.			Perf. 11½x13½	200.00	165.00
B2	SP2	5k	lil, vio & straw	2.00	1.75
B3	SP3	7k	lt bl, dk bl & pink	2.75	2.25
a.			Perf. 13½	42.50	50.00
B4	SP4	10k	lt bl, dk bl & yel	4.00	3.25

These stamps were sold for 3 kopecks over face value. The surtax was donated to a fund for the orphans of soldiers killed in the Russo-Japanese war.

Ilya Murometz Legendary Russian Hero — SP5

Don Cossack Bidding Farewell to His Sweetheart — SP6

Symbolical of Charity — SP7

St. George Slaying the Dragon — SP8

1914 *Perf. 11 ½, 12 ½, 13 ½*

B5	SP5	1k	red brn & dk grn, *straw*	24	35
a.			Perf. 13½	30	45
B6	SP6	3k	mar & gray grn, *pink*	24	35
a.			Perf. 13½	27.50	32.50
B7	SP7	7k	dk brn & dk grn, *buff*	24	35
a.			Perf. 13½	24	45
B8	SP8	10k	dk bl & brn, *bl*	1.10	1.75
a.			Perf. 13½	5.80	7.25

1915 **White Paper**

B9	SP5	1k	org brn & gray	24	35
B10	SP6	3k	car & gray blk	30	45
B12	SP7	7k	dk brn & dk grn	4.25	
B13	SP8	10k	dk bl & brn	18	35

These stamps were sold for 1 kopeck over face value. The surtax was donated to charities connected with the war of 1914-17.

No. B12 not regularly issued.

Nos. B5-B13 exist imperf. Value each, $150 unused, $250 canceled.

Russian Soviet Federated Socialist Republic Volga Famine Relief Issue

Relief Work on Volga River — SP9

Administering Aid to Famine Victim — SP10

1921 **Litho.** *Imperf.*

B14	SP9	2250r	green	3.00	6.00
a.			Pelure paper	60.00	55.00
B15	SP9	2250r	dp red	2.50	4.25
a.			Pelure paper	7.50	12.50
B16	SP9	2250r	brown	2.50	10.00
B17	SP10	2250r	dk bl	6.00	12.50

Forged cancels and counterfeits of Nos. B14-B17 are plentiful.

Stamps of type A33 with this overprint were not charity stamps nor did they pay postage in any form.

They represent taxes paid on stamps exported from or imported into Russia. In 1925 the semi-postal stamps of 1914-15 were surcharged for the same purpose. Stamps of the regular issues 1918 and 1921 have also been surcharged with inscriptions and new values, to pay the importation and exportation taxes.

Nos. 149-150 Surcharged in Black, Red, Blue or Orange

Р. С. Ф. С. Р.
ГОЛОДАЮЩИМ
250 р.+250 р

1922, Feb. *Perf. 13 ½*

B18	A33		100r + 100r on 70k	60	1.00
a.			"100 p. + p. 100"	55.00	65.00
B19	A33		100r + 100r on 70k (R)	60	1.00
B20	A33		100r + 100r on 70k (Bl)	30	50
B21	A33		250r + 250r on 35k	30	50
B22	A33		250r + 250r on 35k (R)	60	1.00
B23	A33		250r + 250r on 35k (O)	1.10	2.00
			Nos. B18-B23 (6)	3.50	6.00

Issued to raise funds for Volga famine relief.

Nos. B18-B22 exist with surcharge inverted. Values $20 to $40.

Regular Issues of 1909-18 Overprinted

РСФСР
Филателия
—детям
19—8—22

1922, Aug. 19 *Perf. 14*

B24	A14	1k	orange	135.00	135.00
B25	A14	2k	green	10.50	*16.00*
B26	A14	3k	red	9.00	12.50
B27	A14	5k	claret	9.00	12.50
B28	A15	10k	dk bl	9.00	12.50

Imperf

B29	A14	1k	orange	135.00	150.00
			Nos. B24-B29 (6)	307.50	338.50

The overprint means "Philately for the Children". The stamps were sold at five million times their face values and 80% of the amount was devoted to child welfare. The stamps were sold only at Moscow and for one day.

Exist with overprint reading up. Counterfeits exist including those with overprint reading up. Reprints exist.

Worker and Peasant (Industry and Agriculture) — SP11

Allegory: Agriculture Will Help End Distress SP12

Star of Hope, Wheat and Worker-Peasant Handclasp — SP13

Sower — SP14

1922 **Litho.** *Imperf.*
Without Gum

B30	SP11	2t	(2000r) grn	7.25	20.00
B31	SP12	2t	(2000r) rose	12.00	32.50
B32	SP13	4t	(4000r) rose	12.00	32.50
B33	SP14	6t	(6000r) grn	12.00	32.50

Nos. B30-B33 exist with double impression. Value, each $100.

Counterfeits of Nos. B30-B33 exist.

Automobile SP15

Steamship SP16

Railroad Train SP17

Airplane SP18

1922 *Imperf.*

B34 SP15 lt vio 9 10
B35 SP16 violet 9 10
B36 SP17 gray bl 9 10
B37 SP18 bl gray 1.25 *3.00*

Inscribed "For the Hungry." Each stamp was sold for 200,000r postage and 50,000r charity.

Nos. 212, 183, 202 Surcharged in Bronze, Gold or Silver

1 мая 1923 г.
Филателия—
трудящимся.
2 р.+2 р.

1923 *Imperf.*

B38 A48 1r +1r on 10r 40.00 40.00
a. Invtd. surch. 250.00 250.00
B39 A48 1r +1r on 10r (G) 14.00 27.50
a. Invtd. surch. 250.00 250.00
B40 A43 2r +2r on 250r 16.00 32.50
a. Pelure paper 16.00 22.50
b. Invtd. surch. 200.00 200.00
c. Double surcharge

Wmk. Diamonds (171)

B41 A46 4r +4r on 5000r 14.00 22.50
a. Date spaced "1 923" 165.00 165.00
b. Invtd. surch. 265.00 265.00
B42 A46 4r +4r on 5000r (S) 225.00 225.00
a. Invtd. surch. 850.00 850.00
b. Date spaced "1 923" 850.00 850.00
c. As "b," invtd. surch. *3,200.*
Nos. B38-B42 (5) 309.00 347.50

The inscriptions mean "Philately's Contribution to Labor." The stamps were on sale only at Moscow and for one day. The surtax was for charitable purposes.
Counterfeits of No. B42 exist.

Leningrad Flood Issue

Nos. 181-182, 184-186 Surcharged

С. С. С. Р.
пострадавшему
от наводнения
Ленинграду.
7 К. + 20 К.

1924 Unwmk. *Imperf.*

B43 A40 3k + 10k on 100r 70 95
a. Pelure paper 3.00 4.00
b. Invtd. surcharge 85.00 85.00
B44 A40 7k + 20k on 200r 70 95
a. Invtd. surch. 105.00 105.00
B45 A40 14k + 30k on 300r 80 1.90
a. Pelure paper 215.00 215.00

Similar Surcharge in Red or Black

B46 A41 12k + 40k on 500r (R) 1.40 1.90
a. Double surch. *115.00 115.00*
b. Invtd. surch. 115.00 115.00
B47 A41 20k + 50k on 1000r 95 1.90
a. Thick paper 11.50 18.00
b. Pelure paper 20.00 25.00
c. Chalk surface paper 10.00 12.50
Nos. B43-B47 (5) 4.55 7.60

The surcharge on Nos. B43 to B45 reads: "S.S.S.R. For the sufferers by the inundation at Leningrad." That on Nos. B46 and B47 reads: "S.S.S.R. For the Leningrad Proletariat, 23, IX, 1924."
No. B46 is surcharged vertically, reading down, with the value as the top line.

Orphans SP19

Lenin as a Child SP20

1926 Typo. *Perf. 13½*

B48 SP19 10k brown 75 70
B49 SP20 20k dp bl 95 1.00

Wmk. Greek Border and Rosettes (170)

B50 SP19 10k brown 75 70
B51 SP20 20k dp bl 95 1.00

Two kopecks of the price of each of these stamps was donated to organizations for the care of indigent children.

Types of 1926 Issue

1927

B52 SP19 8k + 2k yel grn 40 35
B53 SP20 18k + 2k dp rose 95 1.00

The surtax was for child welfare.

Industrial Training SP21

Agricultural Training SP22

Perf. 10, 10½, 12½

1929-30 Photo. Unwmk.

B54 SP21 10k + 2k ol brn & org brn 1.90 1.90
a. Perf. 10½ 52.50 52.50
B55 SP21 10k + 2k ol grn ('30) 1.10 95
B56 SP22 20k + 2k blk brn & bl, perf. 10½ 1.65 1.65
a. Perf. 12½ 35.00 35.00
b. Perf. 10 10.00 10.00
B57 SP22 20k + 2k bl grn ('30) 1.65 1.65

Surtax was for child welfare.

Catalogue values for unused stamps in this section, from this point to the end of the section, are for Never Hinged items.

"Montreal Passing Torch to Moscow" SP23

Moscow '80 Olympic Games Emblem SP24

Designs: 16k+6k, like 10k+5k. 60k+30k, Aerial view of Kremlin and Moscow '80 emblem.

1976, Dec. 28 Litho. *Perf. 12x12½*

B58 SP23 4k + 2k multi 16 12
B59 SP24 10k + 5k multi 32 24
B60 SP24 16k + 6k multi 65 30

Souvenir Sheet

Photo.

Perf. 11½

B61 SP23 60k + 30k multi 2.00 1.65

22nd Olympic Games, Moscow, 1980.

Greco-Roman Wrestling — SP25

Moscow '80 Emblem and: 6k+3k, Free-style wrestling. 10k+5k, Judo. 16k+6k, Boxing. 20k+10k, Weight lifting.

1977, June 21 Litho. *Perf. 12½x12*

B62 SP25 4k + 2k multi 16 10
B63 SP25 6k + 3k multi 24 16
B64 SP25 10k + 5k multi 35 24
B65 SP25 16k + 6k multi 52 32
B66 SP25 20k + 10k multi 70 40
Nos. B62-B66 (5) 1.97 1.22

Perf. 12½x12, 12x12½

1977, Sept. 22

4k+2k, Bicyclist. 6k+3k, Woman archer (vert.). 10k+5k, Sharpshooting. 16k+6k, Equestrian. 20k+10k, Fencer. 50k+25k, Equestrian and fencer.

B67 SP25 4k + 2k multi 16 10
B68 SP25 6k + 3k multi 21 16
B69 SP25 10k + 5k multi 32 24
B70 SP25 16k + 6k multi 50 32
B71 SP25 20k + 10k multi 65 40
Nos. B67-B71 (5) 1.84 1.22

Souvenir Sheet

Perf. 12½x12

B72 SP25 50k + 25k multi 2.25 1.65

1978, Mar. 24 *Perf. 12½x12*

4k+2k, Swimmer at start. 6k+3k, Woman diver (vert.). 10k+5k, Water polo. 16k+ 6k, Canoeing. 20k+10k, Canadian single. 50k+25k, Start of double scull race.

B73 SP25 4k + 2k multi 14 7
B74 SP25 6k + 3k multi 20 10
B75 SP25 10k + 5k multi 30 16
B76 SP25 16k + 6k multi 45 24
B77 SP25 20k + 10k multi 60 35
Nos. B73-B77 (5) 1.69 92

Souvenir Sheet

B78 SP25 50k + 25k grn & blk 1.65 1.25

Star-class Yacht SP26

Women's Gymnastics SP27

Keel Yachts and Moscow '80 Emblem: 6k+3k, Soling class. 10k+5k, Centerboarder 470. 16k+6k, Finn class. 20k+ 10k, Flying Dutchman class. 50k+25k, Catamaran Tornado (horiz.).

1978, Oct. 26 Litho. *Perf. 12x12½*

B79 SP26 4k + 2k multi 14 7
B80 SP26 6k + 3k multi 20 10
B81 SP26 10k + 5k multi 30 16
B82 SP26 16k + 6k multi 45 24
B83 SP26 20k + 10k multi 60 32
Nos. B79-B83 (5) 1.69 89

Souvenir Sheet

Perf. 12½x12

B84 SP26 50k + 25k multi 1.75 1.25

1979, Mar. 21 Litho. *Perf. 12x12½*

6k+3k, Man on parallel bars. 10k+5k, Man on horizontal bar. 16k+6k, Woman on balance beam. 20k+10k, Woman on uneven bars. 50k+25k, Man on rings.

B85 SP27 4k + 2k multi 14 7
B86 SP27 6k + 3k multi 20 10
B87 SP27 10k + 5k multi 30 16
B88 SP27 16k + 6k multi 45 24
B89 SP27 20k + 10k multi 60 32
Nos. B85-B89 (5) 1.69 89

Souvenir Sheet

Perf. 12½x12

B90 SP25 50k + 25k multi 1.75 1.25

1979, June *Perf. 12½x12, 12x12½*

4k+2k, Soccer. 6k+3k, Basketball. 10k+5k, Women's volleyball. 16k+6k, Handball. 20k+10k, Field hockey.

B91 SP25 4k + 2k multi 12 7
B92 SP27 6k + 3k multi 18 10
B93 SP27 10k + 5k multi 30 16
B94 SP25 16k + 6k multi 45 24
B95 SP25 20k + 10k multi 60 32
Nos. B91-B95 (5) 1.65 89

22nd Olympic Games, Moscow, July 19-Aug. 3, 1980.

Running, Moscow '80 Emblem SP27a

1980 Litho. *Perf. 12½x12, 12x12½*

B96 SP27a 4k + 2k *shown* 12 7
B97 SP27a 4k + 2k *Pole vault* 12 7
B98 SP27a 6k + 3k *Discus* 18 10
B99 SP27a 6k + 3k *Hurdles* 18 10
B100 SP27a 10k + 5k *Javelin* 30 16
B101 SP27a 10k + 5k *Walking, vert.* 30 16
B102 SP27a 16k + 6k *Hammer throw* 45 24
B103 SP27a 16k + 6k *High jump* 45 24
B104 SP27a 20k + 10k *Shot put* 60 32
B105 SP27a 20k + 10k *Long jump* 60 32
Nos. B96-B105 (10) 3.30 1.78

Souvenir Sheet

B106 SP27a 50k + 25k *Relay race* 1.75 90

22nd Olympic Games, Moscow, July 19-Aug. 3. Issue dates: Nos. B96, B99, B101, B103, B105: Feb. 6; others, Mar. 12.

Moscow '80 Emblem, Relief from St. Dimitri's Cathedral, Arms of Vladimir — SP28

Moscow '80 Emblem and: No. B108, Bridge over Klyazma River and Vladimir Hotel. No. B109, Relief from Nativity Cathedral and coat of arms (falcon), Suzdal. No. B110, Tourist complex and Pozharski Monument, Suzdal. No. B111, Frunze Monument, Ivanovo, torch and spindle. No. B112, Museum of First Soviets, Fighters of the Revolution Monument, Ivanovo.

Photogravure and Engraved

1977, Dec. 30 *Perf. 11½x12*

B107 SP28 1r + 50k multi 2.00 90
B108 SP28 1r + 50k multi 2.00 90
B109 SP28 1r + 50k multi 2.00 90
B110 SP28 1r + 50k multi 2.00 90
B111 SP28 1r + 50k multi 2.00 90
B112 SP28 1r + 50k multi 2.00 90
Nos. B107-B112 (6) 12.00 5.40

"Tourism around the Golden Ring."

Fortifications and Arms of Zagorsk SP29

Moscow '80 Emblem, Coat of Arms and: No. B114, Gagarin Palace of Culture and new arms of Zagorsk. No. B115, Rostov Kremlin with St. John the Divine Church. No. B116, View of Rostov from Nero Lake. No. B117, Alexander Nevski and WWII soldiers' monuments, Pereyaslav. No. B118, Peter the Great monument, Pereyaslav. No. B119, Tower and wall of Monastery of the Transfiguration, Jaroslaw. No. B120, Dock and monument for Soviet heroes, Jaroslaw.

1978 *Perf. 12x11½*

B113	SP29	1r + 50k multi	1.90	80
B114	SP29	1r + 50k multi	1.90	80
B115	SP29	1r + 50k multi	1.90	80
B116	SP29	1r + 50k multi	1.90	80
B117	SP29	1r + 50k multi	1.90	80
B118	SP29	1r + 50k multi	1.90	80
B119	SP29	1r + 50k multi	1.90	80
B120	SP29	1r + 50k multi	1.90	80
		Nos. B113-B120 (8)	15.20	6.40

Issue dates: Nos. B113-B116, Oct. 16; Nos. B117-B120, Dec. 25.

1979 *Perf. 12x11½*

Moscow '80 Emblem and: No. B121, Narikaly Fortress, Tbilisi, 4th century. No. B122, Georgia Philharmonic Concert Hall, "Muse" sculpture, Tbilisi. No. B123, Chir-Dor Mosque, 17th century, Samarkand. No. B124, Peoples Friendship Museum, "Courage" monument, Tashkent. No. B125, Landscape, Erevan. B126, Armenian State Opera and Ballet Theater, Erevan.

B121	SP29	1r + 50k multi	2.50	1.25
B122	SP29	1r + 50k multi	2.50	1.25
B123	SP29	1r + 50k multi	2.50	1.25
B124	SP29	1r + 50k multi	2.50	1.25
B125	SP29	1r + 50k multi	2.50	1.25
B126	SP29	1r + 50k multi	2.50	1.25
		Nos. B121-B126 (6)	15.00	7.50

Issue dates: Nos. B121-B124, Sept. 5; Nos. B125-B126, Oct.

1980, Feb. 28 *Perf. 12x11½*

Moscow '80 Emblem, Coat of Arms and: No. B127, Kremlin. No. B128, Kalinin Prospect, Moscow.

B127	SP29	1r + 50k gold & multi	2.50	75
B128	SP29	1r + 50k gold & multi	2.50	75

1980 *Perf. 12x11½*

Moscow '80 Emblem and: No. B129, Admiralteistvo, St. Isaak Cathedral, Leningrad. No. B130, World War II Defense Monument, Leningrad. No. B131, Bogdan Khmelnitisky monument, St. Sophia's Monastery Kiev. No. B132, Metro Bridge, Dnieper River, Kiev. No. B133, Palace of Sports, obelisk, Minsk. No. B134, Republican House of Cinematography, Minsk. No. B135, Vyshgorodsky Castle, Town Hall, Tallinn. No. B136, Viru Hotel, Tallinn.

B129	SP29	1r + 50k multi	2.50	75
B130	SP29	1r + 50k multi	2.50	75
B131	SP29	1r + 50k multi	2.50	75
B132	SP29	1r + 50k multi	2.50	75
B133	SP29	1r + 50k multi	2.50	75
B134	SP29	1r + 50k multi	2.50	75
B135	SP29	1r + 50k multi	2.50	75
B136	SP29	1r + 50k multi	2.50	75
		Nos. B129-B136 (8)	20.00	6.00

Tourism. Issue dates: Nos. B129-B130, Mar. 25; Nos. B131-B136, Apr. 30.

Soviet Culture Fund — SP30

Art treasures: No. B137, *Z.E. Serebriakova,* 1910, by O.K. Lansere, vert. No. B138, *Boyar's Wife Examining an Embroidery Design,* 1905, by K.V. Lebedev. No. B139, *Talent,* 1910, by N.P. Bogdanov-Belsky, vert. No. B140, *Trinity,* 15th-16th cent., Novgorod School, vert.

Perf. 12x12½, 12½x12

1988, Aug. 22 **Litho.**

B137	SP30	10k +5k multi	45	22
B138	SP30	15k +7k multi	65	32
B139	SP30	30k +15k multi	1.35	68

Souvenir Sheet

B140	SP30	1r +50k multi	4.50	2.25

Zoo Relief Fund — SP31

1988, Oct. 20 **Litho.** ***Perf. 12***

B141	SP31	10k +5k Bear	45	22
B142	SP31	10k +5k Wolf	45	22
B143	SP31	20k +10k Fox	90	45
B144	SP31	20k +10k Boar	90	45
B145	SP31	20k +10k Lynx	90	45
a.		Block of 5+label, #B141-B145	3.75	1.80
		Nos. B141-B145 (5)	3.60	1.79

Se-tenant label pictures relief fund emblem. See Nos. B152-B156.

Lenin Children's Fund SP32

Children's drawings and fund emblem: No. B146, Skating Rink. No. B147, Rooster. No. B148, May (girl and flowers).

1988, Dec. 12 **Litho.** ***Perf. 12***

B146	SP32	5k +2k multi	22	11
B147	SP32	5k +2k multi	22	11
B148	SP32	5k +2k multi	22	11
a.		Block of 3+label, #B146-B148	68	35

Label pictures fund emblem and rainbow.

Armenian Earthquake Relief — SP33

Designs: No. B149, Tigranes I (c. 140-55 B.C.), king of Armenia, gold coin. No. B150, St. Ripsime Temple, c. 618. No. B151, *Virgin and Child,* fresco (detail) by Ovnat Ovnatanyan, 18th cent., Echmiadzin Cathedral.

1988, Dec. 27 ***Perf. 12½x12***

B149	SP33	20k +10k multi	90	45
B150	SP33	30k +15k multi	1.35	68
B151	SP33	50k +25k multi	2.25	1.15
a.		Block of 3+label, #B149-B151	4.50	2.25

Label pictures a Hachkar tombstone.

Zoo Relief Type of 1988

1989, Mar. 20 **Litho.** ***Perf. 12***

B152	SP34	10k +5k Marten	45	22
B153	SP34	10k +5k Squirrel	45	22
B154	SP34	20k +10k Hare	90	45
B155	SP34	20k +10k Hedgehog	90	45
B156	SP34	20k +10k Badger	90	45
a.		Block of 5+label, #B152-B156	3.60	1.80
		Nos. B152-B156 (5)	3.60	1.79

Label pictures relief fund emblem and text.

Foreign postal stationery (stamped envelopes, postal cards and air letter sheets) lies beyond the scope of this Catalogue, which is limited to adhesive postage stamps.

AIR POST STAMPS

AP1

Fokker F-111 — AP2

Plane Overprint in Red

1922 **Unwmk.** ***Imperf.***

C1	AP1	45r grn & blk	6.00	20.00

5th anniversary of October Revolution.

No. C1 was on sale only at the Moscow General Post Office. Counterfeits exist.

1923 **Photo.**

C2	AP2	1r red brn	2.75
C3	AP2	3r dp bl	3.25
C4	AP2	5r green	3.25
a.		Wide "5"	850.00
C5	AP2	10r carmine	2.25

Nos. C2 to C5 were not placed in use.

Nos. C2-C5 Surcharged **10 КОП. ЗОЛ.**

1924

C6	AP2	5k on 3r dp bl	1.25	1.25
C7	AP2	10k on 5r grn	1.25	1.25
a.		Wide "5"	425.00	425.00
b.		Invtd. surcharge	625.00	625.00
C8	AP2	15k on 1r red brn	1.25	1.25
a.		Inverted surch.	850.00	850.00
C9	AP2	20k on 10r car	1.25	1.25
a.		Invtd. surcharge	850.00	850.00

Airplane over Map of World AP3

1927, Sept. 1 **Litho.** ***Perf. 13x12***

C10	AP3	10k dk bl & yel brn	7.75	5.50
C11	AP3	15k dp red & ol grn	9.25	9.25

Commemorative of the first International Air Post Congress at The Hague, initiated by the U.S.S.R.

Graf Zeppelin and "Call to Complete 5-Year Plan in 4 Years" — AP4

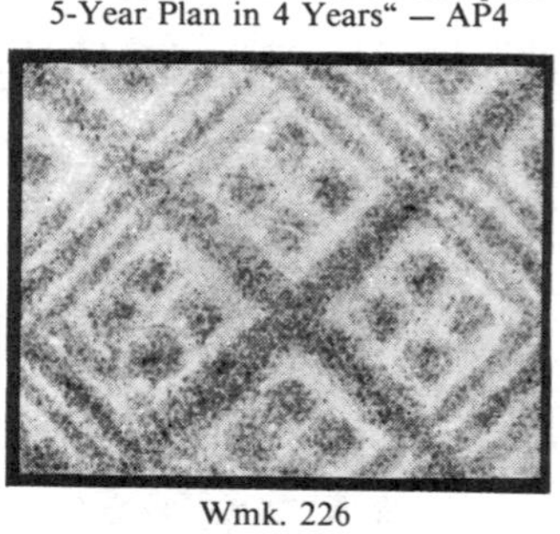

Wmk. 226

Wmk. Diamonds Enclosing Four Dots (226)

1930 **Photo.** ***Perf. 12½***

C12	AP4	40k dk bl & dl bl	20.00	16.00
a.		Perf. 10½	27.50	27.50
b.		Imperf.	*1,000.*	*1,000.*
C13	AP4	80k dk car & rose	22.50	20.00
a.		Perf. 10½	20.00	16.00
b.		Imperf.	*1,000.*	*1,000.*

Issued in connection with the flight of the Graf Zeppelin from Friedrichshafen to Moscow and return.

Symbolical of Airship Communication from the Tundra to the Steppes — AP5

Airship over Dneprostroi Dam — AP6

Airship over Lenin Mausoleum — AP7

Airship Exploring Arctic Regions — AP8

Constructing an Airship AP9

1931-32 **Wmk. 170** **Photo.** ***Imperf.***

C15	AP5	10k dk vio	7.00	7.75
		Litho.		
C16	AP6	15k gray bl	7.00	10.50
		Typo.		
C17	AP7	20k dk car	7.00	10.50
		Photo.		
C18	AP8	50k blk brn	7.00	10.50
C19	AP9	1r dk grn	7.00	10.50
		Nos. C15-C19 (5)	35.00	49.75

Perf. 10½, 12, 12½ and Compound

C20	AP5	10k dk vio	4.75	2.50
		Litho.		
C21	AP6	15k gray bl	9.00	3.75
		Typo.		
C22	AP7	20k dk car	6.50	2.00
a.		20k lt red	7.50	3.00
		Photo.		
C23	AP8	50k blk brn	4.75	2.00
a.		50k gray bl (error)	225.00	225.00
C24	AP9	1r dk grn	5.50	2.00

Perf. 12½

Unwmk.

Engr.

C25	AP6	15k gray blk ('32)	1.00	50
a.		Perf. 10½	600.00	110.00
b.		Perf. 14	57.50	37.50
c.		Imperf.	340.00	
		Nos. C20-C25 (6)	31.50	12.75

The 11½ perforation on Nos. C20-C25 is of private origin.

North Pole Issue

Graf Zeppelin and Icebreaker "Malygin" Transferring Mail — AP10

1931 Wmk. 170 *Imperf.*

C26	AP10	30k dk vio	10.00	7.25
C27	AP10	35k dk grn	10.00	7.25
C28	AP10	1r gray blk	10.00	7.25
C29	AP10	2r dp ultra	12.50	9.50

Perf. 12x12½

C30	AP10	30k dk vio	20.00	20.00
C31	AP10	35k dk grn	20.00	20.00
C32	AP10	1r gray blk	20.00	20.00
C33	AP10	2r dp ultra	20.00	20.00

Map of Polar Region, Airplane and Icebreaker "Sibiryakov" — AP11

1932 Wmk. 170 *Perf. 12, 10½*

C34	AP11	50k car rose	24.00	15.00
a.		Perf. 10½	775.00	775.00
b.		Perf. 10½x12		*1,200.*
C35	AP11	1r green	24.00	12.50
a.		Perf. 12	125.00	40.00

Issued to commemorate the second International Polar Year in connection with flight to Franz-Josef Land.

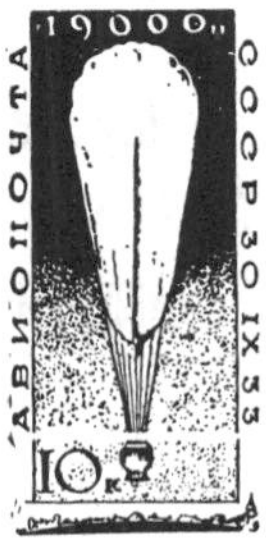

Stratostat "U.S.S.R." AP12

Furnaces of Kuznetsk AP13

1933 Photo. *Perf. 14.*

C37	AP12	5k ultra	52.50	10.50
a.		Vert. pair, imperf. btwn.		*625.00*
C38	AP12	10k carmine	52.50	10.50
a.		Horiz. pair, imperf. btwn.		*625.00*
C39	AP12	20k violet	30.00	10.50

Commemorating the ascent into the stratosphere by Soviet aeronauts on September 30th, 1933.

1933 Wmk. 170 *Perf. 14*

Designs: 10k, Oil wells. 20k, Collective farm. 50k, Map of Moscow-Volga Canal project. 80k, Arctic cargo ship.

C40	AP13	5k ultra	9.00	4.75
C41	AP13	10k green	9.00	4.75
C42	AP13	20k carmine	18.00	9.00
C43	AP13	50k dl bl	24.00	9.00
C44	AP13	80k purple	18.00	9.00
		Nos. C40-C44 (5)	78.00	36.50

Unwmk.

C45	AP13	5k ultra	12.00	3.50
C46	AP13	10k green	12.00	3.50
a.		Horizontal pair, imperf. between	375.00	150.00
C47	AP13	20k carmine	18.00	6.00
C48	AP13	50k dl bl	30.00	12.00
C49	AP13	80k purple	24.00	6.00
		Nos. C45-C49 (5)	96.00	31.00

Issued to commemorate the 10th anniversary of Soviet civil aviation and airmail service. Counterfeits exist.

I. D. Usyskin — AP18

Designs: 10k, A. B. Vasenko. 20k, P. F. Fedoseinko.

1934 Wmk. 170 *Perf. 11*

C50	AP18	5k vio brn	11.00	3.25
a.		Perf. 14	110.00	95.00
C51	AP18	10k brown	30.00	3.25
a.		Perf. 14	185.00	185.00
C52	AP18	20k ultra	30.00	3.25
a.		Perf. 14	225.00	225.00

Issued to honor victims of the stratosphere disaster. See Nos. C77-C79.

Airship "Pravda" — AP19

Airship Landing — AP20

Airship "Voroshilov" — AP21

Sideview of Airship — AP22

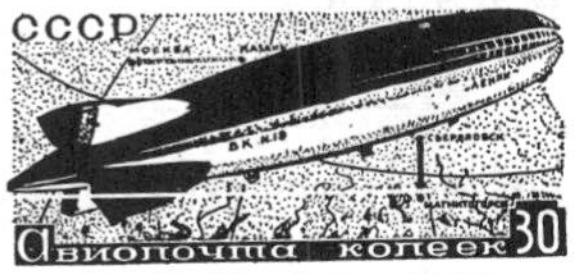

Airship "Lenin" — AP23

1934 *Perf. 14*

C53	AP19	5k red org	12.50	2.50
C54	AP20	10k claret	12.50	3.75
C55	AP21	15k brown	12.50	5.00
C56	AP22	20k black	27.50	7.75
C57	AP23	30k ultra	50.00	7.75
		Nos. C53-C57 (5)	115.00	26.75

Capt. V. Voronin and "Chelyuskin" — AP24

Prof. Otto Y. Schmidt AP25

A. V. Lapidevsky AP26

S. A. Levanevsky AP27

"Schmidt Camp" — AP28

Designs: 15k, M. G. Slepnev. 20k, I. V. Doronin. 25k, M. V. Vodopianov. 30k, V. S. Molokov. 40k, N. P. Kamanin.

1935 *Perf. 14*

C58	AP24	1k red org	5.00	3.25
C59	AP25	3k rose car	6.00	3.25
C60	AP26	5k emerald	5.00	3.25
C61	AP27	10k dk brn	6.00	3.25
C62	AP27	15k black	7.25	3.25
C63	AP27	20k dp claret	10.00	6.25
C64	AP27	25k indigo	25.00	12.50
C65	AP27	30k dl grn	35.00	15.00
C66	AP27	40k purple	25.00	9.25
C67	AP28	50k dk ultra	25.00	12.50
		Nos. C58-C67 (10)	149.25	71.75

Aerial rescue of ice-breaker Chelyuskin crew and scientific expedition.

No. C61 Surcharged in Red

Перелет Москва— Сан-Франциско через Сев. полюс 1935 1р.

1935, Aug.

C68	AP27	1r on 10k dk brn	150.00	225.00
a.		Invtd. surch.	*3,200.*	*3,200.*
b.		Small Cyrillic "f"	475.00	425.00

Issued in commemoration of the Moscow-San Francisco flight. Counterfeits exist.

Single-Engined Monoplane — AP34

Five-Engined Transport — AP35

Designs: 20k, Twin-engined cabin plane. 30k, Four-motored transport. 40k, Single-engined amphibian. 50k, Twin-motored transport. 80k, Eight-motored transport.

1937 Unwmk. *Perf. 12*

C69	AP34	10k yel brn & blk	1.25	85
a.		Imperf.		175.00
C70	AP34	20k gray grn & blk	1.25	85
C71	AP34	30k red brn & blk	1.50	85
C72	AP34	40k vio brn & blk	2.25	1.10
C73	AP34	50k dk vio & blk	3.75	1.75
C74	AP35	80k bl vio & brn	3.25	1.75
C75	AP35	1r blk, brn & buff	9.25	3.50
a.		Sheet of four, imperf.	42.50	85.00
		Nos. C69-C75 (7)	22.50	10.65

Jubilee Aviation Exhib., Moscow, Nov. 15-20.

Vertical pairs, imperf. between, exist for No. C71, value $100; No. C73, value $90.

Types of 1938 Regular Issue Overprinted in Various Colors

18 АВГУСТА ДЕНЬ АВИАЦИИ СССР

1939 Typo.

C76	A282	10k red (C)	1.65	50
C76A	A285	30k bl (R)	1.65	50
C76B	A286	40k dl grn (Br)	1.65	50
C76C	A287	50k dl vio (R)	2.50	65
C76D	A289	1r brn (Bl)	3.50	2.00
		Nos. C76-C76D (5)	10.95	4.15

Soviet Aviation Day, Aug. 18, 1939.

Types of 1934 with "30.1.1944" Added at Lower Left

Designs: No. C77, P. F. Fedoseinko. No. C78, I. D. Usyskin. No. C79, A. B. Vasenko.

1944 Photo. *Perf. 12.*

C77	AP18	1r dp bl	1.90	70
C78	AP18	1r sl grn	1.90	70
C79	AP18	1r brt yel grn	1.90	90

Issued to commemorate the 10th anniversary of the 1934 stratosphere disaster.

Nos. 860A and 861A Surcharged in Red

АВИАПОЧТА 1944 г. 1 РУБЛЬ

1944, May 25

C80	A431	1r on 30k Prus grn	50	14
C81	A432	1r on 30k dp ultra	50	14

Catalogue values for unused stamps in this section, from this point to the end of the section, are for Never Hinged items.

Planes and Soviet Air Force Flag — AP42

1948, Dec. 10 Litho. *Perf. 12½*

C82	AP42	1r dk bl	1.80	60

Air Force Day.

Plane over Zages, Caucasus AP43

Plane over Farm Scene AP44

Values quoted in this catalogue are for stamps graded at Fine-Very Fine and with no faults. An illustrated guide to grade is provided in introductory material, beginning on Page V.

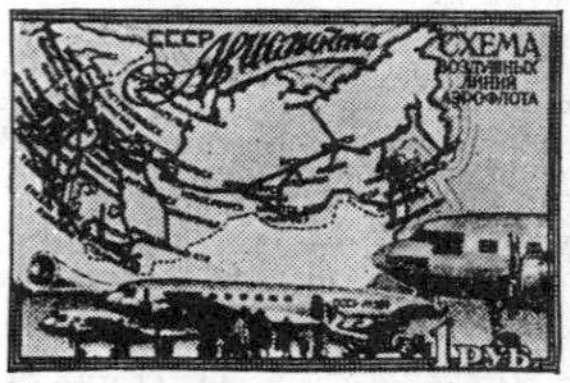

Map of Russian Air Routes and Transport Planes — AP45

Designs: No. C85, Sochi, Crimea. No. C86, Far East. No. C87, Leningrad. 2r, Moscow. 3r, Arctic.

Perf. 12x12½

1949, Nov. 9 Photo. Unwmk.

C83 AP43	50k red brn, *lem*	1.00	90
C84 AP44	60k sep, *pale buff*	2.00	1.75
C85 AP44	1r org brn, *yelsh*	2.00	1.75
C86 AP43	1r bl, *bluish*	2.00	1.75
C87 AP43	1r red brn, *pale fawn*	2.00	1.75
C88 AP45	1r blk, ultra & red, *gray*	4.25	3.00
C89 AP43	2r org brn, *bluish*	6.25	4.25
C90 AP43	3r dk grn, *bluish*	10.50	7.25
	Nos. C83-C90 (8)	30.00	22.40

Plane and Mountain Stream AP46

Globe and Plane AP47

Design: 1r, Plane over the Don.

1955 Litho. *Perf. 12½x12*

C91 AP46	1r multi	1.50	35
C92 AP46	2r blk & yel grn	2.25	55

1955, May 31 Photo.

C93 AP47	2r chocolate	1.75	55
C94 AP47	2r deep blue	1.75	55

Nos. C91 and C92 Overprinted in Red

„Сев. полюс"
— Москва
1955 г.

Perf. 12x12½

1955, Nov. 22 Litho. Unwmk.

C95 AP46	1r multi	2.50	2.25
C96 AP46	2r blk & yel grn	3.75	3.50

Issued for use at the scientific drifting stations North Pole-4 and North Pole-5. The inscription reads "North Pole-Moscow, 1955." Counterfeits exist.

Arctic Camp AP48

1956, June 8 *Perf. 12½x12*

C97 AP48	1r bl, grn, brn, yel & red	1.50	65

Issued to commemorate the opening of scientific drifting station North Pole-6.

The lack of a value for a listed item does not necessarily indicate rarity.

Helicopter over Kremlin AP49

Air Force Emblem and Arms of Normandy AP50

1960, Mar. 5 Photo. *Perf. 12*

C98 AP49	60k ultra	85	28

Surcharged with New Value, Bars and "1961"

1961, Dec. 20

C99 AP49	6k on 60k ultra	65	28

1962, Dec. 30 Unwmk. *Perf. 11½*

C100 AP50	6k bl grn, ocher & car	42	15

Issued to commemorate the 20th anniversary of the French Normandy-Neman Escadrille, which fought on the Russian front.

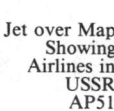

Jet over Map Showing Airlines in USSR AP51

Designs: 12k, Aeroflot emblem and globe. 16k, Jet over map showing Russian international airlines.

1963, Feb.

C101 AP51	10k red, blk & tan	45	14
C102 AP51	12k bl, red, tan & blk	60	16
C103 AP51	16k bl, blk & red	75	35

Issued to commemorate the 40th anniversary of Aeroflot, the civil air fleet.

Tupolev 134 at Sheremetyevo Airport, Moscow — AP52

Designs: 10k, An-24 (Antonov) and Vnukovo Airport, Moscow. 12k, Mi-10 (Mil helicopter) and Central Airport, Moscow. 16k, Be-10 (Beriev) and Chinki Riverport, Moscow. 20k, Antei airliner and Domodedovo Airport, Moscow.

1965, Dec. 31

C104 AP52	6k org, red & vio	24	9
C105 AP52	10k lt grn, org red & gray	38	9
C106 AP52	12k lil, dk sep & lt grn	38	12
C107 AP52	16k lil, lt brn, red & grn	60	15
C108 AP52	20k org red, pur & gray	75	18
	Nos. C104-C108 (5)	2.35	63

Issued to publicize civil aviation.

Aviation Type of 1976

Designs (Russian Aviation Emblem and): 4k, P-4 BIS biplane, 1917. 6k, AK-1 monoplane, 1924. 10k, R-3 (ANT-3) biplane, 1925. 12k, TB-1 (ANT-4) monoplane, 1925. 16k, R-5 biplane, 1929. 20k, Shcha-2 amphibian, 1930.

Lithographed and Engraved

1977, Aug. 16 *Perf. 12x11½*

C109 A2134	4k multi	12	10
C110 A2134	6k multi	15	10
C111 A2134	10k multi	20	12
C112 A2134	12k multi	24	15
C113 A2134	16k multi	35	20
C114 A2134	20k multi	45	25
	Nos. C109-C114 (6)	1.51	92

Russian Aviation 1917-1930.

1978, Aug. 10

Designs: 4k, PO-2 biplane, 1928. 6k, K-5 passenger plane, 1929. 10k, TB-3, cantilever monoplane, 1930. 12k, Stal-2, 1931. 16k, MBR-2 hydroplane, 1932. 20k, I-16 fighter plane, 1934.

C115 A2134	4k multi	12	6
C116 A2134	6k multi	15	9
C117 A2134	10k multi	22	9
C118 A2134	12k multi	25	12
C119 A2134	16k multi	35	15
C120 A2134	20k multi	42	18
	Nos. C115-C120 (6)	1.51	69

Russian aviation 1928-1934.

Jet and Compass Rose — AP53

1978, Aug. 4 Litho. *Perf. 12*

C121 AP53	32k dark blue	65	28

Aeroflot Plane AH-28 — AP54

Designs: Various Aeroflot planes.

Photogravure and Engraved

1979 *Perf. 11½x12*

C122 AP54	2k shown	7	6
C123 AP54	3k YAK-42	10	6
C124 AP54	10k T4-154	20	10
C125 AP54	15k IL76 transport	35	15
C126 AP54	32k IL86 jet liner	70	35
	Nos. C122-C126 (5)	1.42	72

AIR POST OFFICIAL STAMPS

Used on mail from Russian embassy in Berlin to Moscow. Surcharged on Consular Fee stamps. Currency: the German mark.

OA1

Surcharge in Carmine

1922, July Litho. *Perf. 13½*

Bicolored Burelage in Parenthesis

CO1 OA1	12m on 2.25r dp bl (grn & org)	67.50
CO2 OA1	24m on 3r dk grn (pink & grn)	67.50
CO3 OA1	120m on 2.25r dp bl (grn & org)	77.50
CO4 OA1	600m on 3r dk grn (pink & grn)	97.50
CO5 OA1	1200m on 10k brn (grn & org)	135.00
CO6 OA1	1200m on 50k grn (red & yel)	*3,200.*
CO7 OA1	1200m on 2.25r dp bl (grn & org)	375.00
CO8 OA1	1200m on 3r dk grn (pink & grn)	800.00

Three types of each denomination, distinguished by shape of "C" in surcharge and length of second line of surcharge. Used copies have pen or crayon cancel. Forgeries exist.

SPECIAL DELIVERY STAMPS

Motorcycle Courier — SD1

Express Truck — SD2

Design: 80k, Locomotive.

Perf. 12½x12, 12x12½

1932 Photo. Wmk. 170

E1 SD1	5k dull brown	7.50	7.25
E2 SD2	10k violet brown	9.75	7.25
E3 SD2	80k dull green	24.00	15.00

POSTAGE DUE STAMPS

Regular Issue of 1918 Surcharged in Red or Carmine

Доплата
3 коп.
золотом

1924-25 Unwmk. *Perf. 13½*

J1 A33	1k on 35k bl	10	*90*
J2 A33	3k on 35k bl	10	*90*
J3 A33	5k on 35k bl	10	*90*
a.	Imperf.	60.00	
J4 A33	8k on 35k bl ('25)	24	*90*
a.	Imperf.	40.00	
J5 A33	10k on 35k bl	15	*1.10*
a.	Pair, one without surcharge	25.00	
J6 A33	12k on 70k brn	12	*90*
J7 A33	14k on 35k bl ('25)	12	*90*
a.	Imperf.	65.00	
J8 A33	32k on 35k bl	12	*1.10*
J9 A33	40k on 35k bl	12	*1.10*
a.	Imperf.	60.00	
	Nos. J1-J9 (9)	1.17	*8.70*

Surcharge is found inverted on Nos. J1-J2, J4, J6-J9; value $25-$50. Double on Nos. J2, J4-J6; value, $40-$50.

Regular Issue of 1921 Surcharged in Violet

ДОПЛАТА
1 коп.

1924 *Imperf.*

J10 A40	1k on 100r org	3.50	*10.00*
a.	1k on 100r yel	4.00	*12.50*
b.	Pelure paper	4.00	*12.50*
c.	Invtd. surch.	67.50	

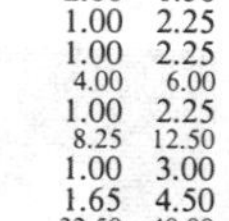

D1

Lithographed or Typographed

1925 *Perf. 12*

J11 D1	1k red	2.00	1.50
J12 D1	2k violet	1.00	2.25
J13 D1	3k lt bl	1.00	2.25
a.	Perf. 14½x14	4.00	6.00
J14 D1	7k orange	1.00	2.25
a.	Perf. 14½x14	8.25	12.50
J15 D1	8k green	1.00	3.00
J16 D1	10k dk bl	1.65	4.50
a.	Perf. 14½x14	32.50	40.00
J17 D1	14k brown	2.00	4.50
a.	Perf. 14½x14	2.25	3.50
	Nos. J11-J17 (7)	9.65	20.25

1925 Wmk. 170 Typo. *Perf. 12*

J18 D1	1k red	45	85
J19 D1	2k violet	45	85
J20 D1	3k lt bl	60	1.10
J21 D1	7k orange	60	1.10
J22 D1	8k green	60	1.10

J23	D1	10k dk bl	75	1.65
J24	D1	14k brown	1.10	2.25
		Nos. J18-J24 (7)	4.55	8.90

WENDEN (LIVONIA.)

A former district of Livonia, a province of the Russian Empire, which became part of Latvia, under the name of Vidzeme.

Used values for Nos. L2-L12 are for pen-canceled copies. Postmarked specimens sell for considerably more.

A1

1862 Unwmk. *Imperf.*

L1	A1	(2k) blue	3.50	
a.		Tete beche pair	17.50	

No. L1 was never put in use.

A2

A3

1863

L2	A2	(2k) rose & blk	150.00	150.00
a.		Background inverted	275.00	275.00
L3	A3	(4k) bl grn & blk	70.00	70.00
a.		(4k) yel grn & blk	150.00	150.00
b.		Half used as 2k on cover		1,800.
c.		Background inverted	150.00	150.00
d.		As "a," background inverted	210.00	210.00

The official imitations of Nos. L2 and L3 have a single instead of a double hyphen after "WENDEN".

Coat of Arms

A4 A5 A6

1863-71

L4	A4	(2k) rose & grn	27.50	14.00
a.		Yellowish paper		
b.		Grn frame around central oval	35.00	21.00
c.		Tete beche pair	1,800.	
L5	A5	(2k) rose & grn ('64)	70.00	52.50
L6	A6	(2k) rose & grn	21.00	21.00

Official imitations of Nos. L4b and L5 have a rose instead of a green line around the central oval. The first official imitation of No. L6 has the central oval 5½ instead of 6¼mm. wide; the second imitation is less clearly printed than the original and the top of the "f" of "Briefmarke" is too much hooked.

Coat of Arms

A7 A8

1872-75 *Perf. 12½*

L7	A7	(2k) red & grn	25.00	21.00
L8	A8	2k yel grn & red ('75)	7.00	7.00
a.		Numeral in upper right corner resembles an inverted "3"	27.50	27.50

Reprints of No. L8 have no horizontal lines in the background. Those of No. L8a have the impression blurred and only traces of the horizontal lines.

A9

Wenden Castle — A10

1878-80

L9	A9	2k grn & red	7.00	7.00
a.		Imperf.		
L10	A9	2k blk, grn & red ('80)	7.00	7.00
a.		Imperf. pair	27.50	

No. L9 has been reprinted in blue green and yellow green with perforation 11½ and in gray green with perforation 12½ or imperforate.

1884 *Perf. 11½*

L11	A9	2k blk, grn & red	2.00	2.00
a.		Grn arm omitted	21.00	
b.		Arm inverted	21.00	
c.		Arm double	27.50	
d.		Imperf. pair	21.00	

1901 Engr.

L12	A10	2k dk grn & brn	3.50	3.50
a.		Tete beche pair		
b.		Imperf. pair	20.00	

OCCUPATION STAMPS

Issued under Finnish Occupation

Finnish Stamps of 1917-18 Overprinted **Aunus**

1919 Unwmk. *Perf. 14*

N1	A19	5p green	12.50	12.50
N2	A19	10p rose	12.50	12.50
N3	A19	20p buff	12.50	12.50
N4	A19	40p red vio	12.50	12.50
N5	A19	50p org brn	100.00	100.00
N6	A19	1m dl rose & blk	105.00	105.00
N7	A19	5m vio & blk	325.00	325.00
N8	A19	10m brn & blk	575.00	575.00
		Nos. N1-N8 (8)	1,155.	1,155.

"Aunus" is the Finnish name for Olonets, a town of Russia.

Counterfeits exists of overprints on Nos. N1-N8.

Issued under German Occupation

Germany Nos. 506 to 523 Overprinted in Black **OSTLAND**

1941-43 Unwmk. Typo. *Perf. 14*

N9	A115	1pf gray blk	5	5
N10	A115	3pf lt brn	5	5
N11	A115	4pf slate	5	5
N12	A115	5pf dp yel grn	5	5
N13	A115	6pf purple	5	5
N14	A115	8pf red	5	5
N15	A115	10pf dk brn ('43)	14	1.00
N16	A115	12pf car ('43)	14	1.00
		Engr.		
N17	A115	10pf dk brn	20	25
N18	A115	12pf brt car	20	25
N19	A115	15pf brn lake	5	5
N20	A115	16pf pck grn	5	5
N21	A115	20pf blue	5	5
N22	A115	24pf org brn	5	5
N23	A115	25pf brt ultra	5	7
N24	A115	30pf ol grn	5	7
N25	A115	40pf brt red vio	5	7
N26	A115	50pf myr grn	5	7
N27	A115	60pf dk red brn	5	7
N28	A115	80pf indigo	7	10
		Nos. N9-N28 (20)	1.50	3.45

Issued for use in Estonia, Latvia and Lithuania.

Same Overprinted in Black **UKRAINE**

		Typo.		
N29	A115	1pf gray blk	5	5
N30	A115	3pf lt brn	5	5
N31	A115	4pf slate	5	5
N32	A115	5pf dp yel grn	5	5
N33	A115	6pf purple	5	5
N34	A115	8pf red	5	5
N35	A115	10pf dk brn ('43)	10	1.00
N36	A115	12pf car ('43)	10	1.00
		Engr.		
N37	A115	10pf dk brn	25	35
N38	A115	12pf brt car	25	35
N39	A115	15pf brn lake	5	5
N40	A115	16pf pck grn	5	5
N41	A115	20pf blue	5	5
N42	A115	24pf org brn	5	5
N43	A115	25pf brt ultra	5	7
N44	A115	30pf ol grn	5	7
N45	A115	40pf brt red vio	5	7
N46	A115	50pf myr grn	5	7
N47	A115	60pf dk red brn	5	7
N48	A115	80pf indigo	7	15
		Nos. N29-N48 (20)	1.52	3.70

ARMY OF THE NORTHWEST

(Gen. Nicolai N. Yudenich)

Russian Stamps of 1909-18 Overprinted in Black or Red **Сѣв.Зап. Армія**

On Stamps of 1909-12

Perf. 14 to 15 and Compound

1919, Aug. 1

1	A14	2k green	2.50	4.25
2	A14	5k claret	2.50	4.25
3	A15	10k dk bl (R)	2.75	5.00
4	A11	15k red brn & bl	2.75	5.00
5	A8	20k bl & car	5.00	7.50
6	A11	25k grn & gray vio	8.50	12.00
7	A8	50k brn vio & grn	5.00	6.25
		Perf. 13½		
8	A9	1r pale brn, dk brn & org	10.50	14.00
9	A13	10r scar, yel & gray	30.00	52.50
		On Stamps of 1917		
		Imperf		
10	A14	3k red	1.40	3.50
11	A12	3.50r mar & lt grn	17.50	27.50
12	A13	5r dk bl, grn & pale bl	14.00	25.00
13	A12	7r dk grn & pink	77.50	125.00
		No. 2 Surcharged		
		Perf. 14, 14½x15		
14	A14	10k on 5k cl	1.75	3.75
		Nos. 1-14 (14)	181.65	295.50

Nos. 1-14 exist with inverted overprint or surcharge. The 1, 3½, 5, 7 and 10 rubles with red overprint are trial printings (value $40 each). The 20k on 14k, perforated, and the 1, 2, 5, 15, 70k and 1r imperforate were overprinted but never placed in use. Value: $80, $30, $40, $40, $40, $40 and $60.

These stamps were in use from Aug. 1 to Oct. 15, 1919.

Counterfeits of Nos. 1-14 abound.

ARMY OF THE NORTH

A1 A2 A3

A4 A5

1919, Sept. Typo. *Imperf.*

1	A1	5k brn vio	15	70
2	A2	10k blue	15	70
3	A3	15k yellow	15	70
4	A4	20k rose	15	70
5	A5	50k green	15	70
		Nos. 1-5 (5)	75	3.50

The letters OKCA are the initials of Russian words meaning "Special Corps, Army of the North". The stamps were in use from about the end of September to the end of December, 1919.

(General Miller)

A set of seven stamps of this design was prepared in 1919, but not issued.

RUSSIAN OFFICES ABROAD

For various reasons the Russian Empire maintained Post Offices to handle its correspondence in several foreign countries. These were similar to the Post Offices in foreign countries maintained by other world powers.

OFFICES IN CHINA

100 Kopecks = 1 Ruble

100 Cents = 1 Dollar (1917)

Russian Stamps Overprinted in Blue or Red **КИТАЙ**

On Issues of 1889-92

Horizontally Laid Paper

1899-1904 Wmk. 168 *Perf. 14½x15*

1	A10	1k org (Bl)	50	65
2	A10	2k yel grn (R)	50	65
3	A10	3k car (Bl)	50	65
4	A10	5k red vio (Bl)	50	65
5	A10	7k dk bl (R)	1.25	2.00
6	A8	10k dk bl (R)	1.25	2.00
7	A8	50k vio & grn (Bl) ('04)	4.00	4.50
		Perf. 13½		
8	A9	1r lt brn, brn & org (Bl) ('04)	21.00	22.50
		Nos. 1-8 (8)	29.50	33.60

On Issues of 1902-05

Vertically Laid Paper

Perf. 14½ to 15 and Compound

1904-08

Overprinted in Black, Red or Blue

9	A8	4k rose red (Bl)	1.25	2.00
10	A10	7k dk bl (R)	8.00	11.50
11	A8	10k dk bl (R)	775.00	850.00
a.		Groundwork inverted	3,250.	
12	A11	14k bl & rose (R)	2.00	3.25
13	A11	15k brn vio & bl (Bl) ('08)	3.25	4.50
14	A8	20k bl & car (Bl)	1.00	2.00
15	A11	25k dl grn & lil (R) ('08)	5.00	6.50
16	A11	35k dk vio & grn (R)	2.00	3.25
17	A8	50k vio & grn (Bl)	42.50	55.00
18	A11	70k brn & org (Bl)	6.00	11.50
		Perf. 13½		
19	A9	1r lt brn, brn & org (Bl)	9.25	11.50
20	A12	3.50r blk & gray (R)	11.50	14.00
21	A13	5r dk bl, grn & pale bl (R) ('07)	6.50	8.00
22	A12	7r blk & yel (Bl)	11.50	13.00
23	A13	10r scar, yel & gray (Bl) ('07)	35.00	50.00
		Nos. 9-10,12-23 (14)	144.75	196.00

On Issues of 1909-12

Wove Paper

Lozenges of Varnish on Face

1910-16 Unwmk. *Perf. 14x14½*

24	A14	1k org yel (Bl)	25	32
25	A14	1k org yel (Bl Bk)	3.50	5.00
26	A14	2k grn (Bk)	25	32

27 A14 2k grn (Bl) 4.00 6.25
a. Double overprint (Bk and Bl)
28 A14 3k rose red (Bl) 25 32
29 A14 3k rose red (Bk) 7.25 10.00
30 A15 4k car (Bl) 25 32
31 A15 4k car (Bk) 5.00 7.25
32 A14 7k lt bl (Bk) 25 32
33 A15 10k bl (Bk) 25 32
34 A11 14k bl & rose (Bk) 55 65
35 A11 14k bl & rose (Bl) 3.25 4.50
36 A11 15k dl vio & bl (Bk) 32 65
37 A8 20k bl & car (Bk) 32 65
38 A11 25k grn & vio (Bl) 2.25 3.25
39 A11 25k grn & vio (Bk) 55 1.65
40 A11 35k vio & grn (Bk) 25 32
42 A8 50k vio & grn (Bl) 25 32
43 A8 50k brn vio & grn (Bk) 11.50 16.00
44 A11 70k lt brn & org (Bl) 25 32

Perf. 13½

45 A9 1r pale brn, brn & org (Bl) 1.00 1.10
47 A13 5r dk bl, grn & pale bl (R) 7.25 8.25
Nos. 24-47 (22) 48.99 68.08

Russian Stamps of 1902-12 Surcharged:

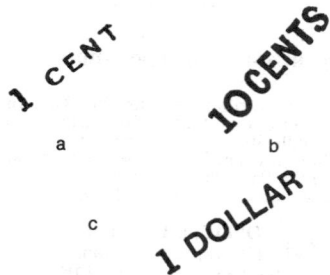

1 CENT

a

10CENTS

b

c

1 DOLLAR

On Stamps of 1909-12

1917 *Perf. 11½, 13½, 14, 14½x15*

50 A14(a) 1c on 1k dl org yel 50 4.00
51 A14(a) 2c on 2k dl grn 50 4.00
52 A14(a) 3c on 3k car 50 4.00
a. Invtd. surch. 65.00
b. Dbl. surch. 150.00
53 A15(a) 4c on 4k car 1.00 3.25
54 A14(a) 5c on 5k cl 1.00 11.50
55 A15(b) 10c on 10k dk bl 1.00 11.50
a. Invtd. surch. 85.00 85.00
b. Dbl. surch. 115.00
56 A11(b) 14c on 14k dk bl & car 1.00 8.50
a. Imperf. 6.00
b. Invtd. surch. 100.00
57 A11(a) 15c on 15k brn lil & dp bl 1.00 11.50
58 A8(b) 20c on 20k bl & car 1.00 11.50
59 A11(a) 25c on 25k grn & vio 1.00 11.50
60 A11(a) 35c on 35k brn vio & grn 1.25 11.50
a. Invtd. surch. 27.50
61 A8(a) 50c on 50k brn vio & grn 1.10 11.50
62 A11(a) 70c on 70k brn & red org 1.10 11.50
63 A9(c) $1 on 1r pale brn, brn & org 1.10 11.50
Nos. 50-63 (14) 13.05

On Stamps of 1902-05
Vertically Laid Paper
Perf. 11½, 13, 13½, 13½x11½
Wmk. Wavy Lines (168)

64 A12 $3.50 on 3.50r blk & gray 6.75 32.50
65 A13 $5 on 5r dk bl, grn & pale bl 6.75 32.50
66 A12 $7 on 7r blk & yel 6.75 32.50

On Stamps of 1915
Unwmk. ***Perf. 13½***
Wove Paper

68 A13 $5 on 5r ind, grn & lt bl 12.00 42.50
a. Invtd. surch. 125.00
70 A13 $10 on 10r car lake, yel & gray 12.50 100.00
Nos. 64-70 (5) 44.75

The surcharge on Nos. 64-70 is in larger type than on the $1.

Russian Stamps of 1909-18 Surcharged in Black or Red

2 Cent.

On Stamps of 1909-12

1920 ***Perf. 14, 14½x15***

72 A14 1c on 1k dl org yel 32.50 37.50
73 A14 2c on 2k dl grn (R) 16.00 15.00
74 A14 3c on 3k car 16.00 15.00
75 A15 4c on 4k car 16.00 15.00
a. Inverted surcharge 130.00
76 A14 5c on 5k cl 16.00 15.00
77 A15 10c on 10k dk bl (R) 95.00 57.50
78 A14 10c on 10k on 7k bl (R) 95.00 57.50

On Stamps of 1917-18
Imperf

79 A14 1c on 1k org 22.50 15.00
a. Inverted surcharge 45.00 75.00
80 A14 5c on 5k cl 30.00 30.00
a. Invtd. surch. 140.00
b. Double surcharge 200.00
c. Surcharged "Cent" only 95.00
Nos. 72-80 (9) 339.00

OFFICES IN THE TURKISH EMPIRE

Various powers maintained post offices in the Turkish Empire before World War I by authority of treaties which ended with the signing of the Treaty of Lausanne in 1923. The foreign post offices were closed Oct. 27, 1923.

100 Kopecks = 1 Ruble
40 Paras = 1 Piaster (1900)

Coat of Arms
A1

1863 Unwmk. Typo. *Imperf.*

1 A1 6k blue 330.00 1,000.
a. 6k lt bl, thin paper 350.00 1,350.
b. 6k dk bl, chlky paper 90.00

A2

A3

1865 **Litho.**

2 A2 (2k) brn & bl 700.00 625.00
3 A3 (20k) bl & red 900.00 850.00

Twenty-eight varieties of each.

A4

A5

A6

1866 **Horizontal Network**

4 A4 (2k) rose & pale bl 35.00 52.50
5 A5 (20k) dp bl & rose 55.00 62.50

1867 **Vertical Network**

6 A4 (2k) rose & pale bl 70.00 87.50
7 A4 (20k) dp bl & rose 100.00 150.00

The initials inscribed on Nos. 2 to 7 are those of the Russian Company of Navigation and Trade. Stamps of Russian Offices in the Turkish Empire overprinted with these initials were used in the Ukraine and are listed under that country.

The official imitations of Nos. 2 to 7 are on yellowish white paper. The colors are usually paler than those of the originals and there are minor differences in the designs.

Horizontally Laid Paper
Wmk. Wavy Lines (168)

1868 **Typo.** ***Perf. 11½***

8 A6 1k brown 35.00 19.00
9 A6 3k green 35.00 19.00
10 A6 5k blue 35.00 19.00
11 A6 10k car & grn 35.00 19.00

Colors of Nos. 8-11 dissolve in water.

1872-90 ***Perf. 14½x15***

12 A6 1k brown 6.25 3.00
a. Vertically laid 37.50 12.50
13 A6 3k green 20.00 2.00
a. Vertically laid 37.50 12.50
14 A6 5k blue 3.75 1.00
a. Vertically laid 37.50 12.50
15 A6 10k car & grn 11.00 3.75
a. Vertically laid 87.50 30.00
b. 10k pale red & grn ('90) 1.00 50

Nos. 12-15 exist imperf.

No. 15 Surcharged in Black or Blue:

8 7 7
a b c

1876

16 A6(a) 8k on 10k car & grn (Bk) 60.00 45.00
a. Vertically laid
b. Inverted surcharge 375.00
17 A6(a) 8k on 10k car & grn (Bl) 85.00 65.00
a. Vertically laid
b. Inverted surcharge

1879

18 A6(b) 7k on 10k car & grn (Bk) 85.00 72.50
a. Vertically laid
b. Inverted surcharge
19 A6(b) 7k on 10k car & grn (Bl) 100.00 85.00
a. Vertically laid
b. Inverted surcharge
19C A6(c) 7k on 10k car & grn (Bl) 700.00 550.00
19D A6(c) 7k on 10k car & grn (Bk) 550.00 500.00

Nos. 16-19D have been extensively counterfeited.

1879 ***Perf. 14½x15***

20 A6 1k blk & yel 3.00 1.50
a. Vertically laid 9.00 7.50
21 A6 2k blk & rose 4.50 4.25
a. Vertically laid 10.00 6.00
22 A6 7k car & gray 6.50 1.75
a. Vertically laid 27.50 12.50

1884

23 A6 1k orange 45 28
24 A6 2k green 70 40
25 A6 5k pale red vio 2.75 95
26 A6 7k blue 1.40 40

Nos. 23-26 imperforate are believed to be proofs.

No. 23 surcharged "40 PARAS" is bogus, though some copies were postally used.

A7

A8

A9

A10

A11

Surcharged in Blue, Black or Red

1900

Horizontally Laid Paper

27 A7 4pa on 1k org (Bl) 15 15
a. Invtd. surcharge 30.00 30.00
28 A7 4pa on 1k org (Bk) 15 15
a. Intd. surcharge 30.00 30.00
29 A7 10pa on 2k grn 22 22
a. Inverted surcharge
30 A8 1pi on 10k dk bl 50 60
a. Inverted surcharge

1903-05

Vertically Laid Paper

31 A7 10pa on 2k yel grn 30 45
a. Invtd. surcharge 70.00
32 A8 20pa on 4k rose red (Bl) 30 45
a. Invtd. surcharge 25.00
33 A8 1pi on 10k dk bl 30 45
a. Groundwork inverted 55.00 17.50
34 A8 2pi on 20k bl & car (Bk) 70 90
35 A8 5pi on 50k brn vio & grn 1.75 1.90
36 A9 7pi on 70k brn & org (Bl) 2.00 2.75

Perf. 13½

37 A10 10pi on 1r lt brn, brn & org (Bl) 3.25 4.25
38 A10 35pi on 3.50r blk & gray 9.75 12.00
39 A11 70pi on 7r blk & yel 11.20 14.00
Nos. 31-39 (9) 29.55 37.15

A12

A13

A14

Wove Paper
Lozenges of Varnish on Face

1909 **Unwmk.** ***Perf. 14½x15***

40 A12 5pa on 1k org 24 35
41 A12 10pa on 2k grn 30 52
a. Invtd. surcharge 7.25 8.50
42 A12 20pa on 4k car 60 90
43 A12 1pi on 10k bl 65 1.00
44 A12 5pi on 50k vio & grn 1.40 1.75
45 A12 7pi on 70k brn & org 2.00 2.75

Perf. 13½

46 A13 10pi on 1r brn & org 3.00 5.00
47 A14 35pi on 3.50r mar & lt grn 10.50 14.00
48 A14 70pi on 7r dk grn & pink 18.00 25.00
Nos. 40-48 (9) 36.69 51.27

50th anniv. of the establishing of the Russian Post Offices in the Levant.

Stamps of 1909 Overprinted with Names of Various Cities
Overprinted "Constantinople"
Black Overprint

1909-10 ***Perf. 14½x15***

61 A12 5pa on 1k org 12 28
a. "Consnantinople" 1.65
b. "Constantinopie" 1.65
62 A12 10pa on 2k grn 12 28
a. "Consnantinople" 1.25
b. "Constantinopie" 2.00
63 A12 20pa on 4k car 28 45
a. "Consnantinople" 2.00
b. "Constantinopie" 2.00
64 A12 1pi on 10k bl 30 52
a. "Consnantinople" 2.75
b. "Constantinopie" 2.75
65 A12 5pi on 50k vio & grn 60 90
a. "Consnantinople" 2.75
b. "Constantinopie" 2.75
66 A12 7pi on 70k brn & org 1.40 2.00
a. "Consnantinople" 5.00
b. "Constantinopie" 5.00

Perf. 13½

67 A13 10pi on 1r brn & org 5.50 8.75
a. "Constanttnople" 14.00
68 A14 35pi on 3.50r mar & lt grn 16.00 27.50
a. "Constautinople" 32.50
b. "Constantjnople" 32.50
69 A14 70pi on 7r dk grn & pink 30.00 42.50
a. "Constautinople" 60.00
b. "Constantjnople" 60.00

Blue Overprint

Perf. 14½x15

70 A12 5pa on 1k org 2.50 3.50
a. "Consnantinople" 8.00
Nos. 61-70 (10) 56.82 86.68

Overprinted "Jaffa"

Black Overprint

71 A12 5pa on 1k org 1.40 2.50
a. Invtd. overprint 11.50
72 A12 10pa on 2k grn 1.75 2.75
a. Invtd. overprint 11.50
73 A12 20pa on 4k car 2.00 3.50
a. Invtd. overprint 27.50
74 A12 1pi on 10k bl 2.50 3.50
a. Double overprint 32.50
75 A12 5pi on 50k vio & grn 6.00 7.00
76 A12 7pi on 70k brn & org 7.25 9.75

Perf. 13½

77 A13 10pi on 1r brn & org 24.00 37.50
78 A14 35pi on 3.50r mar & lt grn 60.00 87.50
79 A14 70pi on 7r dk grn & pink 80.00 125.00

Blue Overprint

Perf. 14½x15

80 A12 5pa on 1k org 4.00 6.25
Nos. 71-80 (10) 188.90 285.25

Overprinted "Ierusalem"

Black Overprint

81 A12 5pa on 1k org 1.25 1.75
a. Inverted overprint 13.00
b. "erusalem" 8.25
82 A12 10pa on 2k grn 1.75 2.50
a. Inverted overprint 13.00
b. "erusalem" 8.25
83 A12 20pa on 4k car 2.50 3.00
a. Inverted overprint 13.00
b. "erusalem" 8.25
84 A12 1pi on 10k bl 2.50 3.00
a. "erusalem" 11.50
85 A12 5pi on 50k vio & grn 4.25 6.00
a. "erusalem" 22.50
86 A12 7pi on 70k brn & org 9.00 10.50
a. "erusalem" 22.50

Perf. 13½

87 A13 10pi on 1r brn & org 32.50 42.50
88 A14 35pi on 3.50r mar & lt grn 75.00 90.00
89 A14 70pi on 7r dk grn & pink 90.00 125.00

Blue Overprint

Perf. 14½x15

90 A12 5pa on 1k org 4.50 6.50
Nos. 81-90 (10) 223.25 290.75

Overprinted "Kerassunde"

Black Overprint

91 A12 5pa on 1k org 28 42
a. Inverted overprint 8.75
92 A12 10pa on 2k grn 28 45
a. Inverted overprint 8.75
93 A12 20pa on 4k car 42 60
a. Inverted overprint 10.50
94 A12 1pi on 10k bl 52 70
95 A12 5pi on 50k vio & grn 1.00 1.25
96 A12 7pi on 70k brn & org 1.40 2.00

Perf. 13½

97 A13 10pi on 1r brn & org 5.50 7.75
98 A14 35pi on 3.50r mar & lt grn 17.50 21.00
99 A14 70pi on 7r dk grn & pink 25.00 30.00

Blue Overprint

Perf. 14½x15

100 A12 5pa on 1k org 3.75 5.50
Nos. 91-100 (10) 55.65 69.67

Overprinted "Mont Athos"

Black Overprint

101 A12 5pa on 1k org 30 60
a. "Mont Atho" 13.00
b. Inverted overprint 14.00
102 A12 10pa on 2k grn 30 60
a. "Mont Atho" 13.00
b. Inverted overprint 14.00
103 A12 20pa on 4k car 35 65
a. "Mont Atho" 13.00
b. Inverted overprint 15.00
104 A12 1pi on 10k bl 60 85
a. "Mont Atho" 20.00
b. Double ovpt. 22.50
c. Same as "a," double overprint 85.00
105 A12 5pi on 50k vio & grn 2.00 2.50
a. "Mont Atho" 27.50
106 A12 7pi on 70k brn & org 3.00 4.25
a. "Mont Atho" 40.00
b. Pair, one without "Mont Athos" 16.00

Perf. 13½

107 A13 10pi on 1r brn & org 10.00 12.50
108 A14 35pi on 3.50r mar & lt grn 22.50 27.50
109 A14 70pi on 7r dk grn & pink 40.00 55.00

Blue Overprint

Perf. 14½x15

110 A12 5pa on 1k org 3.50 6.25
a. "Mont Atho" 11.50
Nos. 101-110 (10) 82.55 110.70

Overprinted 

111 A12 5pa on 1k org 35 55
112 A12 10pa on 2k grn 35 55
113 A12 20pa on 4k car 45 90
114 A12 1pi on 10k bl 90 1.75
115 A12 5pi on 50k vio & grn 1.75 2.75
116 A12 7pi on 70k brn & org 3.00 5.00

Perf. 13½

117 A13 10pi on 1r brn & org 18.00 25.00
Nos. 111-117 (7) 24.80 36.50

The overprint is larger on No. 117.

Overprinted "Salonique"

Black Overprint

Perf. 14½x15

131 A12 5pa on 1k org 30 60
a. Inverted overprint 6.50
b. Pair, one without overprint
132 A12 10pa on 2k grn 45 90
a. Inverted overprint 10.00
133 A12 20pa on 4k car 60 90
a. Invtd. overprint 13.00
134 A12 1pi on 10k bl 60 90
135 A12 5pi on 50k vio & grn 1.25 1.75
136 A12 7pi on 70k brn & org 2.50 3.00

Perf. 13½

137 A13 10pi on 1r brn & org 12.00 15.00
138 A14 35pi on 3.50r mar & lt grn 27.50 32.50
139 A14 70pi on 7r dk grn & pink 40.00 50.00

Blue Overprint

Perf. 14½x15

140 A12 5pa on 1k org 6.00 7.25
Nos. 131-140 (10) 91.20 112.80

Overprinted "Smyrne"

Black Overprint

141 A12 5pa on 1k org 24 45
a. Double overprint
b. Invtd. overprint 5.00
c. "Smyrn" 3.50 4.00
142 A12 10pa on 2k grn 24 45
a. Inverted overprint 8.25
b. "Smyrn" 3.25 4.00
143 A12 20pa on 4k car 45 60
a. Invtd. overprint 10.00
b. "Smyrn" 3.25 4.00
144 A12 1pi on 10k bl 45 75
a. "Smyrn" 4.50 5.25
145 A12 5pi on 50k vio & grn 90 1.50
a. "Smyrn" 4.50 5.25
146 A12 7pi on 70k brn & org 1.75 3.00
a. "Smyrn" 6.50 6.50

Perf. 13½

147 A13 10pi on 1r brn & org 9.00 10.50
148 A14 35pi on 3.50r mar & lt grn 18.00 21.00
149 A14 70pi on 7r dk grn & pink 27.00 32.50

Blue Overprint

Perf. 14½x15

150 A12 5pa on 1k org 3.25 4.75
Nos. 141-150 (10) 61.28 75.50

Overprinted "Trebizonde"

Black Overprint

151 A12 5pa on 1k org 24 45
a. Invtd. ovpt. 4.50
152 A12 10pa on 2k grn 24 45
a. Invtd. ovpt. 6.50
b. Pair, one without "Trebizonde"
153 A12 20pa on 4k car 45 40
a. Invtd. ovpt. 10.00
154 A12 1pi on 10k bl 45 75
a. Pair, one without "Trebizonde" 27.50
155 A12 5pi on 50k vio & grn 1.00 1.50
156 A12 7pi on 70k brn & org 1.75 3.00

Perf. 13½

157 A13 10pi on 1r brn & org 9.00 10.50
158 A14 35pi on 3.50r mar & lt grn 18.00 21.00
159 A14 70pi on 7r dk grn & pink 27.50 32.50

Blue Overprint

Perf. 14½x15

160 A12 5pa on 1k org 3.25 4.75
Nos. 151-160 (10) 61.88 75.30

On Nos. 158 and 159 the overprint is spelled "Trebisonde".

Overprinted "Beyrouth"

Black Overprint

1910

161 A12 5pa on 1k org 22 45
162 A12 10pa on 2k grn 22 45
a. Invtd. ovpt. 20.00
163 A12 20pa on 4k car 40 60
164 A12 1pi on 10k bl 40 75
165 A12 5pi on 50k vio & grn 80 1.50
166 A12 7pi on 70k brn & org 1.65 3.00

Perf. 13½

167 A13 10pi on 1r brn & org 8.25 10.50
168 A14 35pi on 3.50r mar & lt grn 16.00 21.00
169 A14 70pi on 7r dk grn & pink 25.00 32.50
Nos. 161-169 (9) 52.94 70.75

Overprinted "Dardanelles"

Perf. 14½x15

171 A12 5pa on 1k org 22 45
172 A12 10pa on 2k grn 22 45
a. Pair, one without overprint
173 A12 20pa on 4k car 40 60
a. Invtd. ovpt. 10.00
174 A12 1pi on 10k bl 40 75
175 A12 5pi on 50k vio & grn 80 1.50
176 A12 7pi on 70k brn & org 1.65 3.00

Perf. 13½

177 A13 10pi on 1r brn & org 8.25 10.25
178 A14 35pi on 3.50r mar & lt grn 16.00 21.00
a. Center and overprint inverted
179 A14 70pi on 7r dk grn & pink 25.00 32.50
Nos. 171-179 (9) 52.94 70.50

Overprinted "Metelin"

Perf. 14½x15

181 A12 5pa on 1k org 28 60
a. Invtd. ovpt. 10.00
182 A12 10pa on 2k grn 28 60
a. Invtd. ovpt. 13.00
183 A12 20pa on 4k car 55 90
a. Invtd. ovpt. 13.00
184 A12 1pi on 10k bl 55 90
185 A12 5pi on 50k vio & grn 1.10 1.75
186 A12 7pi on 70k brn & org 2.25 3.50

Perf. 13½

187 A13 10pi on 1r brn & org 11.00 15.00
188 A14 35pi on 3.50r mar & lt grn 25.00 32.50
189 A14 70pi on 7r dk grn & pink 35.00 45.00
Nos. 181-189 (9) 76.01 100.75

Overprinted "Rizeh"

Perf. 14½x15

191 A12 5pa on 1k org 22 45
a. Invtd. ovpt. 6.50
192 A12 10pa on 2k grn 22 45
a. Invtd. ovpt. 10.00
193 A12 20pa on 4k car 40 60
a. Invtd. ovpt. 10.00
194 A12 1pi on 10k bl 40 60
195 A12 5pi on 50k vio & grn 80 1.50
196 A12 7pi on 70k brn & org 1.65 3.00

Perf. 13½

197 A13 10pi on 1r brn & org 8.25 10.50
198 A14 35pi on 3.50r mar & lt grn 16.00 21.00
199 A14 70pi on 7r dk grn & pink 25.00 32.50
Nos. 191-199 (9) 52.94 70.60

Nos. 61 to 199 were issued to commemorate the 50th anniversary of the establishing of Russian Post Offices in the Levant.

A15 A16 A17

Vertically Laid Paper

1910 **Wmk. 168** *Perf. 14½x15*

200 A15 20pa on 5k red vio (Bl) 38 50

Wove Paper

Vertical Lozenges of Varnish on Face

1910 **Unwmk.** *Perf. 14x14½*

201 A16 5pa on 1k org yel (Bl) 12 22
202 A16 10pa on 2k grn (R) 12 22
203 A17 20pa on 4k car rose (Bl) 12 22
204 A17 1pi on 10k bl (R) 12 22
205 A8 5pi on 50k vio & grn (Bl) 38 60
206 A9 7pi on 70k lt brn & org (Bl) 42 65

Perf. 13½

207 A10 10pi on 1r pale brn, brn & org (Bl) 50 75
Nos. 201-207 (7) 1.78 2.88

Russian Stamps of 1909-12 Surcharged in Black:

20 PARA
No. 208

1½PIASTRE
Nos. 209-212

1912 *Perf. 14x14½*

208 A14 20pa on 5k cl 12 20
209 A11 1½pi on 15k dl vio & bl 18 24
210 A8 2pi on 20k bl & car 18 30
211 A11 2½pi on 25k grn & vio 25 42
a. Double surch. 50.00 50.00
212 A11 3½pi on 35k vio & grn 38 55
Nos. 208-212 (5) 1.11 1.71

Russia Nos. 88-91, 93, 95-104 Surcharged:

PARA 5 PARA
c

10 PARA 10
d

1 1 PIASTRE
e

PIAS 1½ TRE
f

g

30 PIASTRES

1913 *Perf. 13½*

213 A16(c) 5pa on 1k 12 14
214 A17(d) 10pa on 2k 12 14
215 A18(c) 15pa on 3k 12 14
216 A19(c) 20pa on 4k 14 16
217 A21(e) 1pi on 10k 18 20
218 A23(f) 1½pi on 15k 40 52
219 A24(f) 2pi on 20k 40 52
220 A25(f) 2½pi on 25k 55 70
221 A26(f) 3½pi on 35k 1.10 1.40
222 A27(e) 5pi on 50k 1.40 1.75
223 A28(f) 7pi on 70k 5.50 7.00
224 A29(e) 10pi on 1r 5.50 7.00
225 A30(e) 20pi on 2r 1.10 1.40
226 A31(g) 30pi on 3r 1.65 2.00
227 A32(e) 50pi on 5r 47.50 62.50
Nos. 213-227 (15) 65.78 85.57

Romanov dynasty tercentenary.
Forgeries exist of overprint on No. 227.

Russia Nos. 75, 71, 72 Surcharged:

15 PARA
h

PIAS 50 TRES
i

Perf. 14x14½

Wove Paper

228 A14(h) 15pa on 3k 9 10

Perf. 13, 13½

230 A13(i) 50pi on 5r 4.50 10.00

Vertically Laid Paper

Wmk. Wavy Lines (168)

231 A13(i) 100pi on 10r 9.00 20.00
a. Double surcharge 24.00 40.00

No. 228 has lozenges of varnish on face but No. 230 has not.

Wrangel Issues

For the Posts of Gen. Peter Wrangel's army and civilian refugees from South Russia, interned in Turkey, Serbia, etc.

Russian Stamps of 1902-18 Surcharged in Blue, Red or Black

On Russia Nos. 69-70
Vertically Laid Paper

1921 Wmk. 168 *Perf. 13½*

232 A12 10,000r on 3.50r 8.25 8.25
233 A12 10,000r on 7r 6.50 6.50
234 A12 20,000r on 3.50r 13.00 13.00
235 A12 20,000r on 7r 6.50 6.50

On Russia Nos. 71-86, 87a, 117-118, 137-138
Wove Paper

Perf. 14x14½, 13½
Unwmk.

236 A14 1000r on 1k 20 20
237 A14 1000r on 2k (R) 20 20
237A A14 1000r on 2k (Bk) 2.75 2.75
238 A14 1000r on 3k 5 6
a. Inverted surcharge 65 64
239 A15 1000r on 4k 5 6
a. Inverted surcharge 65 65
240 A14 1000r on 5k 5 6
a. Inverted surcharge 65 65
241 A14 1000r on 7k 5 6
a. Inverted surcharge 65 65
242 A15 1000r on 10k 6 9
a. Inverted surcharge 65 65
243 A14 1000r on 10k on 7k 6 8
244 A14 5000r on 3k 5 7
245 A11 5000r on 14k 65 85
246 A11 5000r on 15k 5 5
a. "PYCCKIN" 1.25 1.25
247 A8 5000r on 20k 22 25
a. "PYCCKIN" 1.25 1.25
248 A11 5000r on 20k on 14k 22 25
249 A11 5000r on 25k 7 10
250 A11 5000r on 35k 6 8
a. Inverted surcharge 65 65
b. New value omitted
251 A8 5000r on 50k 6 8
a. Inverted surcharge
252 A11 5000r on 70k 6 6
a. Inverted surcharge 1.00 1.00
253 A9 10,000r on 1r (Bl) 7 10
254 A9 10,000r on 1r (Bk) 50 65
255 A12 10,000r on 3.50r 20 22
256 A13 10,000r on 5r 3.00 3.00
257 A13 10,000r on 10r 25 32
258 A9 20,000r on 1r 16 20
259 A12 20,000r on 3.50r 16 20
a. Inverted surcharge 3.25 3.25
b. New value omitted 27.50 27.50
260 A12 20,000r on 7r 6.00 6.00
261 A13 20,000r on 10r 20 25
Nos. 236-261 (27) 15.45 16.29

Very few of the Wrangel overprints were actually sold to the public, and many of the covers were made up later with the original cancels. Reprints abound.

On Russia No. 104

261A A32 20,000r on 5r

On Russia Nos. 119-123, 125-135

Imperf

262 A14 1000r on 1k 22 25
263 A14 1000r on 2k (R) 22 25
263A A14 1000r on 2k (Bk) 25 32
264 A14 1000r on 3k 22 25
265 A15 1000r on 4k 6.50 6.50
266 A14 1000r on 5k 25 30
267 A14 5000r on 3k 22 25
268 A11 5000r on 15k 25 30
268A A8 5000r on 20k 10.00
268B A11 5000r on 25k 10.00
269 A11 5000r on 35k 50 52
270 A8 5000r on 50k 50 52
271 A11 5000r on 70k 20 22
272 A9 10,000r on 1r (Bl) 5 7
a. Invtd. surcharge 1.00 65
273 A9 10,000r on 1r (Bk) 22 25
274 A12 10,000r on 3.50r 22 25
275 A13 10,000r on 5r 85 1.00
276 A12 10,000r on 7r 5.25 5.25
276A A13 10,000r on 10r *32.50*
277 A9 20,000r on 1r (Bl) 7 7
a. Invtd. surcharge 1.00 1.00
278 A9 20,000r on 1r (Bk) 22 25
279 A12 20,000r on 3.50r 85 1.00
280 A13 20,000r on 5r 16 20
281 A12 20,000r on 7r 4.00 4.00
281A A13 20,000r on 10r *32.50*
Nos. 262-268,269-276,277-281 (21) 21.22 22.02

A18

A19

On Postal Savings Stamps

Wmk. Diamonds (171)

Perf. 14½x15

282 A18 10,000r on 1k red, *buff* 16 20
283 A19 10,000r on 5k grn, *buff* 5 5
a. Inverted surcharge 2.75
284 A19 10,000r on 10k brn, *buff* 5 5
a. Inverted surcharge 2.75

On Stamps of Russian Offices in Turkey

On Issue of 1903-05

Vertically Laid Paper

Wmk. Wavy Lines (168)

284B A11 20,000r on 35pi on 3.50r blk & gray
284C A11 20,000r on 70pi on 7r blk & yel

On Issue of 1910

Vertically Laid Paper

284D A15 1000r on 20pa on 5k red vio 65 85

Wove Paper

Unwmk.

285 A16 1000r on 5pa on 1k org yel 20 22
286 A16 1000r on 10pa on 2k grn 20 22
287 A17 1000r on 20pa on 4k car rose 16 20
288 A17 1000r on 1pi on 10k bl 20 22
289 A8 5000r on 5pi on 50k vio & grn 22 25
290 A9 5000r on 7pi on 70k lt brn & org 22 25
291 A10 10,000r on 10pi on 1r pale brn, brn & org 85 1.00
a. Invtd. surcharge 2.75 2.75
b. Pair, one without surcharge 2.75 2.75
292 A10 20,000r on 10pi on 1r pale brn, brn & org 16 20
a. Invtd. surcharge 2.75 2.75
b. Pair, one without surcharge 2.75 2.75
Nos. 284D-292 (9) 2.86 3.41

On Issue of 1912

293 A14 1000r on 20pa on 5k cl 22 25
294 A11 5000r on 1½pi on 15k dl vio & bl 22 25
295 A8 5000r on 2pi on 20k bl & car 22 25
296 A11 5000r on 2½pi on 25k grn & vio 22 25
297 A11 5000r on 3½pi on 35k vio & grn 28 40
Nos. 293-297 (5) 1.16 1.40

On Issue of 1913

298 A14 1000r on 15pa on 3k car 22 25
299 A13 10,000r on 50pi on 5r dk bl, grn & pale bl 6.50 6.50
300 A13 10,000r on 100pi on 10r scar, yel & gray 8.00 8.00
301 A13 20,000r on 50pi on 5r dk bl, grn & pale bl 22 25
302 A13 20,000r on 100pi on 10r scar, yel & gray 8.00 8.00
Nos. 298-302 (5) 22.94 23.00

On Stamps of South Russia

Denikin Issue

Imperf.

303 A5 5000r on 5k org 5 6
a. Inverted surcharge
304 A5 5000r on 10k grn 5 6
305 A5 5000r on 15k red 5 6
306 A5 5000r on 35k lt bl 5 6
307 A5 5000r on 70k dk bl 5 6
307A A5 10,000r on 70k dk bl 5.25 5.25
308 A6 10,000r on 1r brn & red 16 20
309 A6 10,000r on 2r gray vio & yel 25 28
a. Inverted surcharge 1.25 1.25
310 A6 10,000r on 3r dl rose & grn 45 50
311 A6 10,000r on 5r sl & vio 50 55
312 A6 10,000r on 7r gray grn & rose 10.00 10.00
313 A6 10,000r on 10r red & gray 45 50
314 A6 20,000r on 1r brn & red 10 12
315 A6 20,000r on 2r gray vio & yel (Bl) 3.25 3.25
a. Inverted surcharge 5.00 5.00
315B A6 20,000r on 2r gray vio & yel (Bk) 20 22
316 A6 20,000r on 3r dl rose & grn (Bl) 5.25 5.25
316A A6 20,000r on 3r dl rose & grn (Bk) 2.75 2.75
317 A6 20,000r on 5r sl & vio 20 22
318 A6 20,000r on 7r gray grn & rose 6.50 6.50
319 A6 20,000r on 10r red & gray 20 22
Nos. 303-319 (20) 35.76 36.11

Trident Stamps of Ukraine Surcharged in Blue, Red, Black or Brown

1921 *Perf. 14, 14½x15*

320 A14 10,000r on 1k org 5 6
321 A14 10,000r on 2k grn 65 85
322 A14 10,000r on 3k red 5 5
a. Inverted surcharge 1.25 1.25
323 A15 10,000r on 4k car 5 5
324 A14 10,000r on 5k cl 20 22
325 A14 10,000r on 7k lt bl 5 6
a. Inverted surcharge 1.25 1.25
326 A15 10,000r on 10k dk bl 5 6
a. Inverted surcharge 1.25 1.25
327 A14 10,000r on 10k on 7k lt bl 7 8
a. Inverted surcharge 1.25 1.25
328 A8 20,000r on 20k bl & car (Br) 5 5
a. Inverted surcharge 1.25 1.25
329 A8 20,000r on 20k bl & car (Bk) 12 16
a. Inverted surcharge 1.25 1.25
330 A11 20,000r on 20k on 14k bl & rose 13 20
331 A11 20,000r on 35k red brn & grn 10.00 10.00
332 A8 20,000r on 50k brn vio & grn 5 5
a. Inverted surcharge 1.25 1.25
Nos. 320-332 (13) 11.52 11.89

Imperf

333 A14 10,000r on 1k org 5 8
a. Inverted surcharge 1.65
334 A14 10,000r on 2k grn 22 25
335 A14 10,000r on 3k red 7 8
336 A8 20,000r on 20k bl & car 12 16
337 A11 20,000r on 35k red brn & grn 2.75 2.75
338 A8 20,000r on 50k brn vio & grn 22 25
Nos. 333-338 (6) 3.43 3.57

There are several varieties of the trident surcharge on Nos. 320 to 338.

Same Surcharge on Russian Stamps

On Stamps of 1909-18

Perf. 14x14½

338A A14 10,000r on 1k dl org yel 25 25
339 A14 10,000r on 2k dl grn 25 25
340 A14 10,000r on 3k car 7 8
341 A15 10,000r on 4k car 7 8
342 A14 10,000r on 5k dk cl 8 10
343 A14 10,000r on 7k bl 10 12
344 A15 10,000r on 10k dk bl 25 30
344A A14 10,000r on 10k on 7k bl 50 55
344B A11 20,000r on 14k dk bl & car 2.75 2.75
345 A11 20,000r on 15k red brn & dp bl 10 12
346 A8 20,000r on 20k dl bl & dk car 8 10
347 A11 20,000r on 20k on 14k dk bl & car 50 55
348 A11 20,000r on 35k red brn & grn 20 22
349 A8 20,000r on 50k brn vio & grn 10 12
349A A11 20,000r on 70k brn & red org 25 32
Nos. 338A-349A (15) 5.55 5.91

On Stamps of 1917-18

Imperf.

350 A14 10,000r on 1k org 16 20
351 A14 10,000r on 2k gray grn 16 20
352 A14 10,000r on 3k red 16 20
353 A15 10,000r on 4k car 5.25 5.25
354 A14 10,000r on 5k cl 16 20
355 A11 20,000r on 15k red brn & dp bl 16 20
356 A8 20,000r on 50k brn vio & grn 50 55
357 A11 20,000r on 70k brn & org 25 32
Nos. 350-357 (8) 6.80 7.12

Same Surcharge on Stamps of Russian Offices in Turkey

On Stamps of 1909

Perf. 14½x15

358 A12 10,000r on 5pa on 1k org 1.65 1.65
359 A12 10,000r on 10pa on 2k grn 1.65 1.65
360 A12 10,000r on 20pa on 4k car 1.65 1.65
361 A12 10,000r on 1pi on 10k bl 1.65 1.65
362 A12 20,000r on 5pi on 50k vio & grn 1.65 1.65
363 A12 20,000r on 7pi on 70k brn & org 1.65 1.65
Nos. 358-363 (6) 9.90 9.90

On Stamps of 1910

364 A16 10,000r on 5pa on 1k yel org 32 32
365 A16 10,000r on 10pa on 2k grn 32 32
366 A17 10,000r on 20pa on 4k car rose 32 32
367 A17 10,000r on 1pi on 10k bl 32 32
368 A8 20,000r on 5pi on 50k vio & grn 32 32
369 A9 20,000r on 7pi on 70k lt brn & org 32 32
Nos. 364-369 (6) 1.92 1.92

On Stamps of 1912-13

370 A14 10,000r on 15pa on 3k car 20 20
371 A14 10,000r on 20pa on 5k cl 32 32
372 A11 20,000r on 1½pi on 15k dl vio & bl 32 32
373 A8 20,000r on 2pi on 20k bl & car 40
374 A11 20,000r on 2½pi on 25k grn & vio 40
375 A11 20,000r on 3½pi on 35k vio & grn 40

Same Surcharge on Stamp of South Russia, Crimea Issue

376 A8 20,000r on 5r on 20k bl & car 16.00
Nos. 370-376 (7) 18.04

RUSSIAN TURKESTAN

Russian stamps of 1917-18 surcharged as above are frauds.

RWANDA

(Rwandaise Republic)

LOCATION — Central Africa, adjoining the ex-Belgian Congo, Tanganyika, Uganda and Burundi.
GOVT. — Republic.
AREA — 10,169 sq. mi.
POP. — 5,650,000 (est. 1984).
CAPITAL — Kigali.

Rwanda was established as an independent republic on July 1, 1962. With Burundi, it had been a UN trusteeship territory administered by Belgium.

100 Centimes = 1 Franc

Catalogue values for all unused stamps in this country are for Never Hinged items.

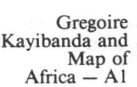

Gregoire Kayibanda and Map of Africa — A1

Design: 40c, 1.50fr, 6.50fr, 20fr, Rwanda map spotlighted, "R" omitted.

Perf. 11½

1962, July 1 Unwmk. Photo.

1	A1	10c brn & gray grn	5	5
2	A1	40c brn & rose lil	5	5
3	A1	1fr brn & bl	60	30
4	A1	1.50fr brn & lt brn	7	5
5	A1	3.50fr brn & dp org	10	5
6	A1	6.50fr brn & lt vio bl	18	7
7	A1	10fr brn & cit	20	8
8	A1	20fr brn & rose	42	16
		Nos. 1-8 (8)	1.67	81

Map of Africa and Symbolic Honeycomb A2

Ruanda-Urundi Nos. 151-152 Overprinted with Metallic Frame Obliterating Previous Inscription and Denomination. Black Commemorative Inscription and "REPUBLIQUE RWANDAISE." Surcharged with New Value.

1963, Jan. 28 Unwmk. *Perf. 11½*

9	A2	3.50fr sil, blk, ultra & red	10	10
10	A2	6.50fr brnz, blk, ultra & red	70	70
11	A2	10fr stl bl, blk, ultra & red	20	20
12	A2	20fr sil, blk, ultra & red	38	38

Rwanda's admission to UN, Sept. 18, 1962.

Stamps of Ruanda-Urundi, 1953, Overprinted

Littonia — A3

Designs as Before

1963, Mar. 21 Unwmk. *Perf. 11½*
Flowers in Natural Colors; Metallic and Black Overprint

13	A3	25c dk grn & dl org	5	5
14	A3	40c grn & sal	5	5
15	A3	60c bl grn & pink	5	5
16	A3	1.25fr dk grn & bl	70	70
17	A3	1.50fr vio & ap grn	55	55
18	A3	2fr on 1.50fr vio & ap grn	80	80
19	A3	4fr on 1.50fr vio & ap grn	80	80
20	A3	5fr dp plum & lt bl grn	80	80
21	A3	7fr dk grn & fawn	80	80
22	A3	10fr dp plum & pale ol	80	80
		Nos. 13-22 (10)	5.40	5.40

The overprint consists of silver panels with black lettering. The panels on No. 19 are bluish gray.

Imperforates exist of practically every issue, starting with Nos. 23-26, except Nos. 36, 55-69, 164-169.

Wheat Emblem, Bow, Arrow, Hoe and Billhook A4

1963, July 1 Photo. *Perf. 13½*

23	A4	2fr brn & grn	5	5
24	A4	4fr mag & ultra	10	5
25	A4	7fr red & gray	15	7
26	A4	10fr ol grn & yel	55	38

FAO "Freedom from Hunger" campaign.

The 20fr leopard and 50fr lion stamps of Ruanda-Urundi, Nos. 149-150, overprinted "Republique Rwandaise" at top and "Contre la Faim" at bottom, were intended to be issued Mar. 21, 1963, but were not placed in use.

Coffee A5

Designs: 10c, 40c, 4fr, Coffee. 20c, 1fr, 7fr, Bananas. 30c, 2fr, 10fr, Tea.

1963, July 1 *Perf. 11½*

27	A5	10c vio bl & brn	5	5
28	A5	20c sl & yel	5	5
29	A5	30c ver & grn	5	5
30	A5	40c dp grn & brn	5	5
31	A5	1fr mar & yel	5	5
32	A5	2fr dk bl & grn	55	42
33	A5	4fr red & brn	8	5
34	A5	7fr yel grn & yel	14	8
35	A5	10fr vio & grn	20	10
		Nos. 27-35 (9)	1.22	90

First anniversary of independence.

African Postal Union Issue
Common Design Type

1963, Sept. 8 Unwmk. *Perf. 12½*

36	CD114	14fr blk, ocher & red	55	50

Post Horn and Pigeon — A6

1963, Oct. 25 Photo. *Perf. 11½*

37	A6	50c ultra & rose	5	5
38	A6	1.50fr brn & bl	50	40
39	A6	3fr dp plum & gray	7	5
40	A6	20fr grn & yel	35	18

Rwanda's admission to the UPU, Apr. 6.

Scales, UN Emblem and Flame A7

1963, Dec. 10 Unwmk. *Perf. 11½*

41	A7	5fr crimson	14	7
42	A7	6fr brt pur	42	30
43	A7	10fr brt bl	22	14

15th anniversary of the Universal Declaration of Human Rights.

Children's Clinic — A8

Designs: 20c, 7fr, Laboratory examination (horiz.). 30c, 10fr, Physician examining infant. 40c, 20fr, Litter bearers (horiz.).

1963, Dec. Photo.

44	A8	10c yel org, red & brn blk	5	5
45	A8	20c grn, red & brn blk	5	5
46	A8	30c bl, red & brn blk	5	5
47	A8	40c red lil, red & brn	5	5
48	A8	2fr bl grn, red brn & blk	40	35
49	A8	7fr ultra, red & blk	12	9
50	A8	10fr red brn, red & brn blk	16	10
51	A8	20fr dp org, red & brn	32	12
		Nos. 44-51 (8)	1.20	86

Centenary of the International Red Cross.

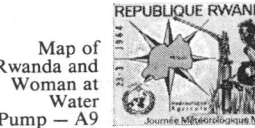

Map of Rwanda and Woman at Water Pump — A9

1964, May 4 Unwmk. *Perf. 11½*

52	A9	3fr lt grn, dk brn & ultra	5	50
53	A9	7fr pink, dk brn & ultra	20	12
54	A9	10fr yel, dk brn & ultra	28	20

Souvenir Sheet
Imperf

54A	A9	25fr lil, bl, brn & blk	1.75	1.75

UN 4th World Meteorological Day, Mar. 23.

Ruanda-Urundi Nos. 138-150, 153 Overprinted "REPUBLIQUE RWANDAISE", Some Surcharged, in Silver and Black

Buffaloes A10

Designs: 10c, 20c, 30c, Buffaloes. 40c, 2fr, Black-and-white colobus (monkey). 50c, 7.50fr, Impalas. 1fr, Mountain gorilla. 3fr, 4fr, 8fr, African elephants. 5fr, 10fr, Eland and zebras. 20fr, Leopard. 50fr, Lions. 40c, 1fr and 2fr are vertical.

1964, June 29 Photo. *Perf. 11½*
Size: 33x23mm, 23x33mm

55	A10	10c on 20c gray, ap grn & blk	5	5
56	A10	20c blk, gray & ap grn	5	5
57	A10	30c on 1.50fr blk, gray & org	5	5
58	A10	40c mag, blk & gray grn	5	5
59	A10	50c grn, org yel & brn	5	5
60	A10	1fr ultra, blk & brn	7	5
61	A10	2fr grnsh bl, ind & brn	7	5
62	A10	3fr brn, dp car & blk	8	5
63	A10	4fr on 3.50fr on 3fr brn, dp car & blk	16	5
64	A10	5fr brn, dl yel, grn & blk	15	5
65	A10	7.50fr on 6.50fr red, org yel & brn	30	8
66	A10	8fr bl, mag & blk	2.00	1.60
67	A10	10fr brn, dl yel, brt pink & blk	40	10

Size: 45x26½mm

68	A10	20fr hn brn, ocher & blk	65	35
69	A10	50fr dp bl & brn	1.10	80
		Nos. 55-69 (15)	5.23	3.43

Boy with Crutch and Gatagara Home — A11

Basketball — A12

Designs: 40c, 8fr, Girls with sewing machines (horiz.). 4fr, 10fr, Girl on crutches, map of Rwanda and Gatagara Home.

1964, Nov. 10 Photo. *Perf. 11½*

70	A11	10c lil blk brn	5	5
71	A11	40c bl & blk brn	5	5
72	A11	4fr org red & blk brn	8	6
73	A11	7.50fr yel grn & blk brn	15	12
74	A11	8fr bis & blk brn	75	50
75	A11	10fr mag & blk brn	22	14
		Nos. 70-75 (6)	1.30	92

Gatagara Home for handicapped children.

1964, Dec. 8 Litho. *Perf. 13½*

Sport: 10c, 4fr, Runner (horiz.). 30c, 20fr, High jump (horiz.). 40c, 50fr, Soccer.

Size: 26x38mm

76	A12	10c gray, sl & dk grn	5	5
77	A12	20c pink, sl & rose red	5	5
78	A12	30c lt grn, sl & grn	5	5
79	A12	40c buff, sl & brn	5	5
80	A12	4fr vio gray, sl & vio	5	5
81	A12	5fr pale grn, sl & yel grn	95	95
82	A12	20fr pale lil, sl & red lil	25	22
83	A12	50fr gray, sl & dk gray	60	50
a.		Souv. sheet of 4	2.50	2.50
		Nos. 76-83 (8)	2.05	1.92

18th Olympic Games, Tokyo, Oct. 10-25. No. 83a contains 4 stamps (10fr, soccer; 20fr, basketball; 30fr, high jump; 40fr, runner). Size of stamps: 28x38mm.

Quill, Books, Radical and Retort — A13

Medical School and Student with Microscope — A14

Designs: 30c, 10fr, Scales, hand, staff of Mercury and globe. 40c, 12fr, View of University.

1965, Feb. 22 Engr. *Perf. 11½*

84	A13	10c multi	5	5
85	A14	20c multi	5	5
86	A13	30c multi	5	5
87	A14	40c multi	5	5
88	A13	5fr multi	10	5
89	A14	7fr multi	14	9
90	A13	10fr multi	80	70
91	A14	12fr multi	22	14
		Nos. 84-91 (8)	1.46	1.18

National University of Rwanda at Butare.

Abraham Lincoln, Death Cent. — A15

1965, Apr. 15 Photo. *Perf. 13½*

92	A15	10c	emer & dk red	5	5
93	A15	20c	red brn & dk bl	5	5
94	A15	30c	brt vio & red	5	5
95	A15	40c	brt grnsh bl & red	5	5
96	A15	9fr	org brn & pur	12	10
97	A15	40fr	blk & brt grn	1.20	45
			Nos. 92-97 (6)	1.52	75

Souvenir Sheet

98	A15	50fr	red lil & red	1.40	1.40

Marabous A16

Zebras A17

Designs: 30c, Impalas. 40c, Crowned cranes, hippopotami and cattle egrets. 1fr, Cape buffalos. 3fr, Cape hunting dogs. 5fr, Yellow baboons. 10fr, Elephant and map of Rwanda with location of park. 40fr, Anhinga, great anad reed cormorants. 100fr, Lions.

1965, Apr. 28 Photo. *Perf. 11½*

Size: 32x23mm

99	A16	10c	multi	5	5
100	A17	20c	multi	5	5
101	A16	30c	multi	5	5
102	A17	40c	multi	5	5
103	A16	1fr	multi	5	5
104	A17	3fr	multi	7	5
105	A16	5fr	multi	2.50	90
106	A17	10fr	multi	16	7

Size: 45x26mm

107	A17	40fr	multi	65	25
108	A17	100fr	multi	1.60	20
			Nos. 99-108 (10)	5.23	1.72

Kagera National Park publicity.

Telstar and ITU Emblem A18

Design: 40c, 50fr, Syncom satellite. 60fr, old and new communications equipment.

1965 Unwmk. *Perf. 13½*

109	A18	10c	red brn, ultra & car	5	5
110	A18	40c	vio, emer & yel	5	5
111	A18	4.50fr	blk, car & dk bl	65	28
112	A18	50fr	dk brn, yel grn & brt grn	50	12

Souvenir Sheet

113	A18	60fr	blk brn, org brn & bl	1.25	1.25

ITU, centenary. Issue dates: No. 113, July 19. Others, May 17.

An enhanced introduction to the Scott Catalogue begins on Page V. A thorough understanding of the material presented there will greatly aid your use of the catalogue itself.

Papilio Bromius Chrapkowskii Suffert — A19

Cattle, ICY Emblem and Map of Africa — A20

Various butterflies and moths in natural colors.

1965-66 Photo. *Perf. 12½*

114	A19	10c	blk & yel	5	5
115	A19	15c	blk & dp org ('66)	5	5
116	A19	20c	blk & lil	5	5
117	A19	30c	blk & red lil	5	5
118	A19	35c	dk brn & dk bl ('66)	5	8
119	A19	40c	blk & Prus bl	5	5
120	A19	1.50fr	blk & grn ('66)	5	5
121	A19	3fr	dk brn & ol grn ('66)	1.40	55
122	A19	4fr	blk & red brn	80	40
123	A19	10fr	blk & pur ('66)	20	10
124	A19	50fr	blk & brn	60	22
125	A19	100fr	dk brn & bl ('66)	1.60	55
			Nos. 114-125 (12)	4.95	2.20

The 15c, 20c, 40c, 1.50fr, 10fr and 50fr are horizontal.

1965, Oct. 25 Unwmk. *Perf. 12*

ICY Emblem, Map of Africa and: 40c, Tree and lake. 4.50fr, Gazelle under tree. 45fr, Mount Ruwenzori.

126	A20	10c	ol bis & bl grn	5	5
127	A20	40c	lt ultra, red brn & grn	5	5
128	A20	4.50fr	brt grn, yel & brn	80	40
129	A20	45fr	rose cl	70	25

John F. Kennedy (1917-1963) — A21

1965, Nov. 22 Photo. *Perf. 11½*

130	A21	10c	brt grn & dk brn	5	5
131	A21	40c	brt pink & dk brn	5	5
132	A21	50c	dk bl & dk brn	5	5
133	A21	1fr	gray ol & dk brn	5	5
134	A21	8fr	vio & dk brn	90	65
135	A21	50fr	gray & dk brn	70	55
			Nos. 130-135 (6)	1.80	1.40

Souvenir Sheet

136			Sheet of two	4.50	4.50
a.	A21	40fr	org & dk brn	2.00	2.00
b.	A21	60fr	ultra & dk brn	2.00	2.00

Madonna — A22

1965, Dec. 20

137	A22	10c	gold & dk grn	5	5
138	A22	40c	gold & dk brn red	5	5
139	A22	50c	gold & dk bl	5	5
140	A22	4fr	gold & sl	50	45
141	A22	6fr	gold & vio	8	8
142	A22	30fr	gold & dk brn	42	40
			Nos. 137-142 (6)	1.15	1.08

Christmas.

Father Joseph Damien and Lepers — A23

Designs: 40c, 45fr, Dr. Albert Schweitzer and Hospital, Lambarene.

1966, Jan. 31 *Perf. 11½*

143	A23	10c	ultra & red brn	5	5
144	A23	40c	dk red & vio bl	7	5
145	A23	4.50fr	sl & brt grn	22	8
146	A23	45fr	brn & hn brn	1.50	80

Issued for World Leprosy Day.

Pope Paul VI, St. Peter's, UN Headquarters and Statue of Liberty — A24

Design: 40c, 50fr, Pope Paul VI, Papal arms and UN emblem.

1966, Feb. 28 Photo. *Perf. 12*

147	A24	10c	hn brn & sl	5	5
148	A24	40c	brt bl & sl	5	5
149	A24	4.50fr	lil & sl	1.10	1.10
150	A24	50fr	brt grn & sl	90	35

Visit of Pope Paul VI to the UN, New York City, Oct. 4, 1965.

Globe Thistle — A25

Flowers: 20c, Blood lily. 30c, Everlasting. 40c, Natal plum. 1fr, Tulip tree. 3fr, Rendle orchid. 5fr, Aloe. 10fr, Ammocharis tinneana. 40fr, Coral tree. 100fr, Caper. (20c, 40c, 1fr, 3fr, 5fr, 10fr are vertical).

1966, Mar. 14 *Perf. 11½*

Granite Paper

151	A25	10c	lt bl & multi	5	5
152	A25	20c	org & multi	5	5
153	A25	30c	car rose & multi	5	5
154	A25	40c	grn & multi	5	5
155	A25	1fr	multi	5	5
156	A25	3fr	ind & multi	5	5
157	A25	5fr	multi	2.00	1.25
158	A25	10fr	bl grn & multi	15	10
159	A25	40fr	brn & multi	50	25
160	A25	100fr	dk bl grn & multi	1.25	75
a.			Min. sheet	2.75	2.00
			Nos. 151-160 (10)	4.20	2.65

No. 160a contains one 100fr stamp in changed color, bright blue and multicolored.

Opening of WHO Headquarters, Geneva — A26

1966, May 1 Litho. *Perf. 12½x12*

161	A26	2fr	lt ol grn	5	5
162	A26	3fr	vermilion	16	16
163	A26	5fr	vio bl	8	8

Soccer — A27

Mother and Child, Planes Dropping Bombs — A28

Designs: 20c, 9fr, Basketball. 30c, 50fr, Volleyball.

1966, May 30 Photo. *Perf. 15x14*

164	A27	10c	dl grn, ultra & blk	5	5
165	A27	20c	crim, grn & blk	5	5
166	A27	30c	bl, brt rose lil & blk	5	5
167	A27	40c	yel bis, grn & blk	5	5
168	A27	9fr	gray, red lil & blk	16	14
169	A27	50fr	rose lil, Prus bl & blk	90	80
			Nos. 164-169 (6)	1.26	1.14

National Youth Sports Program.

1966, June 29 *Perf. 13½*

Design and Inscription Black and Red

170	A28	20c	rose lil	5	5
171	A28	30c	yel grn	5	5
172	A28	50c	lt ultra	5	5
173	A28	6fr	yellow	8	7
174	A28	15fr	bl grn	55	20
175	A28	18fr	lilac	50	35
			Nos. 170-175 (6)	1.28	77

Campaign against nuclear weapons.

Global Soccer Ball — A29

1966, July *Perf. 11½*

176	A29	20c	org & ind	5	5
177	A29	30c	lil & ind	5	5
178	A29	50c	brt grn & ind	5	5
179	A29	6fr	brt rose & ind	22	8
180	A29	12fr	lt vio brn & ind	65	25
181	A29	25fr	ultra & ind	80	50
			Nos. 176-181 (6)	1.82	98

World Soccer Cup Championship, Wembley, England, July 11-30.

Nyamilanga Falls — A30

Designs: 10c, Mikeno Volcano and crested shrike (horiz.). 4.50fr, Gahinga and Muhabura volcanoes and lobelias (horiz.). 55fr, Rusumu Falls.

1966, Oct. 24 Engr. *Perf. 14*

182	A30	10c	green	5	5
183	A30	40c	brn car	5	5
184	A30	4.50fr	vio bl	45	35
185	A30	55fr	red lil	50	35

UNESCO Emblem, African Artifacts and Musical Clef — A31

UNESCO Emblem and: 30c, 10fr, Hands holding primer showing giraffe and zebra. 50c, 15fr, Atom symbol and power drill. 1fr, 50fr, Submerged sphinexes and sailboat.

1966, Nov. 4 Photo. *Perf. 12*

186	A31	20c brt rose & dk bl	5	5
187	A31	30c grnsh bl & blk	5	5
188	A31	50c ocher & blk	5	5
189	A31	1fr vio & blk	5	5
190	A31	5fr yel grn & blk	7	7
191	A31	10fr brn & blk	16	16
192	A31	15fr red lil & dk bl	50	30
193	A31	50fr dl bl & blk	55	45
		Nos. 186-193 (8)	1.48	1.18

UNESCO, 20th anniversary.

Rock Python — A32

Snakes: 20c, 20fr, Jameson's mamba. 30c, 3fr, Rock python. 50c, Gabon viper. 1fr, Black-lipped spitting cobra. 5fr, African sand snake. 70fr, Egg-eating snake. (20c, 50c, 3fr and 20fr are horizontal.)

1967, Jan. 30 Photo. *Perf. 11½*

194	A32	20c red & blk	5	5
195	A32	30c bl, dk brn & yel	5	5
196	A32	50c yel grn & multi	5	5
197	A32	1fr lt lil, blk & bis	5	5
198	A32	3fr lt vio, dk brn & yel	10	7
199	A32	5fr yel & multi	16	10
200	A32	20fr pale pink & multi	80	60
201	A32	70fr pale vio, brn & blk	1.20	65
		Nos. 194-201 (8)	2.46	1.62

Ntaruka Hydroelectric Station and Tea Flowers — A33

Designs: 30c, 25fr, Transformer and chrysanthemums (pyrethrum). 50c, 50fr, Sluice and coffee.

1967, Mar. 6 Photo. *Perf. 13½*

202	A33	20c mar & dp bl	5	5
203	A33	30c blk & red brn	5	5
204	A33	50c brn & vio	5	5
205	A33	4fr dk grn & dp plum	5	5
206	A33	25fr vio & sl grn	30	30
207	A33	50fr dk bl & brn	90	90
		Nos. 202-207 (6)	1.40	1.40

Ntaruka Hydroelectric Station.

Souvenir Sheets

Cogwheels — A34

1967, Apr. 15 Engr. *Perf. 11½*

208	A34	100fr dk red brn	1.50	1.50
209	A34	100fr brt rose lil	1.50	1.50

7th "Europa" Phil. Exhib. and the Philatelic Salon of African States, Naples, Apr. 8-16.

Souvenir Sheet

African Dancers and EXPO '67 Emblem — A35

1967, Apr. 28 *Perf. 11½*

210	A35	180fr dk pur	2.25	2.25

EXPO '67, Intl. Exhib., Montreal, Apr. 28-Oct. 27.

A similar imperf. sheet has the stamp in violet brown.

St. Martin, by Van Dyck and Caritas Emblem A36

Paintings: 40c, 15fr, Rebecca at the Well, by Murillo (horiz.). 60c, 18fr, St. Christopher, by Dierick Bouts. 80c, 26fr, Job and his Friends, by Il Calabrese (Mattia Preti) (horiz.).

Perf. 13x11, 11x13

1967, May 8 Photo.

Black Inscription on Gold Panel

211	A36	20c dk pur	5	5
212	A36	40c bl grn	5	5
213	A36	60c rose car	5	5
214	A36	80c dp bl	5	5
215	A36	9fr redsh brn	50	28
216	A36	15fr org ver	18	10
217	A36	18fr dk ol grn	22	10
218	A36	26fr dk car rose	28	20
		Nos. 211-218 (8)	1.38	88

Issued to publicize the work of Caritas-Rwanda, Catholic welfare organization.

Round Table Emblem and Zebra — A37

Round Table Emblem and: 40c, Elephant. 60c, Cape buffalo. 80c, Antelope. 18fr, Wheat. 100fr, Palm tree.

1967, July 31 Photo. *Perf. 14*

219	A37	20c gold & multi	5	5
220	A37	40c gold & multi	5	5
221	A37	60c gold & multi	5	5
222	A37	80c gold & multi	5	5
223	A37	18fr gold & multi	28	16
224	A37	100fr gold & multi	1.60	65
		Nos. 219-224 (6)	2.08	1.01

Rwanda Table No. 9 of Kigali, a member of the Intl. Round Tables Assoc.

EXPO '67 Emblem, Africa Place and Dancers and Drummers — A38

EXPO '67 Emblem, Africa Place and: 30c, 3fr, Drum and vessels. 50c, 40fr, Two dancers. 1fr, 34fr, Spears, shields and bow.

1967, Aug. 10 Photo. *Perf. 12*

225	A38	20c brt bl & sep	5	5
226	A38	30c brt rose lil & sep	5	5
227	A38	50c org & sep	5	5
228	A38	1fr grn & sep	5	5
229	A38	3fr vio & sep	5	5
230	A38	15fr emer & sep	16	10
231	A38	34fr rose red & sep	50	35
232	A38	40fr grnsh bl & sep	65	38
		Nos. 225-232 (8)	1.56	1.08

Lions Emblem, Globe and Zebra — A39

1967, Oct. 16 Photo. *Perf. 13½*

233	A39	20c lil, bl & blk	5	5
234	A39	80c lt grn, bl & blk	5	5
235	A39	1fr rose car, bl & blk	5	5
236	A39	8fr bis, bl & blk	12	12
237	A39	10fr ultra, bl & blk	14	14
238	A39	50fr yel grn, bl & blk	90	65
		Nos. 233-238 (6)	1.31	1.06

50th anniversary of Lions International.

Woodland Kingfisher — A40

Birds: 20c, Red bishop (vert.). 60c, Red-billed quelea (vert.). 80c, Double-toothed barbet. 2fr, Pin-tailed whydah (vert.). 3fr, Solitary cuckoo. 18fr, Green wood hoopoe (vert.). 25fr, Blue-collared bee-eater. 80fr, Regal sunbird (vert.). 100fr, Red-shouldered widowbird.

1967, Dec. 18 *Perf. 11½*

239	A40	20c multi	5	5
240	A40	40c multi	5	5
241	A40	60c multi	5	5
242	A40	80c multi	5	5
243	A40	2fr multi	7	5
244	A40	3fr multi	8	5
245	A40	18fr multi	40	14
246	A40	25fr multi	45	16
247	A40	80fr multi	1.20	60
248	A40	100fr multi	1.75	70
		Nos. 239-248 (10)	4.15	1.90

Souvenir Sheet

Ski Jump, Speed Skating — A41

1968, Feb. 12 Photo. *Perf. 11½*

249		Souv. sheet of 2	1.25	1.25
a.	A41	50fr bl, blk & grn (skier)	50	50
b.	A41	50fr grn, blk & bl (skater)	50	50
c.		Souv. sheet of 2, #249a at right	1.25	1.25

10th Winter Olympic Games, Grenoble, France, Feb. 6-18.

Runner, Mexican Sculpture and Architecture — A42

Sport and Mexican Art: 40c, Hammer throw, pyramid and animal head. 60c, Hurdler and sculptures. 80c, Javelin and sculptures.

1968, May 27 Photo. *Perf. 11½*

250	A42	20c ultra & multi	5	5
251	A42	40c multi	5	5
252	A42	60c lil & multi	5	5
253	A42	80c org & multi	5	5

19th Olympic Games, Mexico City, Oct. 12-27.

Souvenir Sheet

19th Olympic Games, Mexico City — A43

Designs: 8fr, Soccer. 10fr, Mexican horseman and cactus. 12fr, Field hockey. 18fr, Cathedral, Mexico City. 20fr, Boxing. 30fr, Modern buildings, musical instruments and vase.

1967, May 27 Photo. *Perf. 11½*

Granite Paper

254	A43	Souv. sheet of 6	2.00	2.00
a.		8fr multi	14	14
b.		10fr multi	16	16
c.		12fr multi	20	20
d.		18fr multi	35	35

e.	20fr multi	40	40
f.	30fr multi	60	60

Three sets of circular gold "medal" overprints with black inscriptions were applied to the six stamps of No. 254 to honor 18 Olympic winners. Issued Dec. 12, 1968. Value $10.

Souvenir Sheet

Martin Luther King, Jr. — A44

1968, July 29 Engr. *Perf. 13½*

255 A44	100fr sepia	1.25	1.00

Rev. Dr. Martin Luther King, Jr. (1929-1968), American civil rights leader. See No. 406.

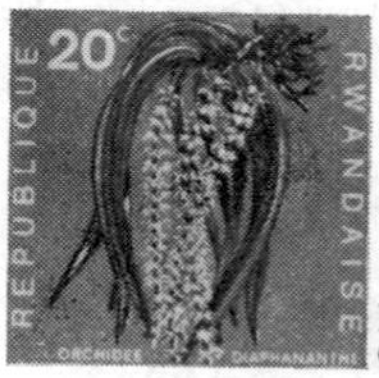

Diaphant Orchid — A45

Flowers: 40c, Pharaoh's scepter. 60c, Flower of traveler's-tree. 80c, Costus afer. 2fr, Banana tree flower. 3fr, Flower and fruit of papaw tree. 18fr, Clerodendron. 25fr, Sweet potato flowers. 80fr, Baobab tree flower. 100fr, Passion flower.

1968, Sept. 9 Litho. *Perf. 13*

256 A45	20c lil & multi	5	5
257 A45	40c multi	5	5
258 A45	60c bl grn & multi	5	5
259 A45	80c multi	5	5
260 A45	2fr brt yel & multi	5	5
261 A45	3fr multi	5	5
262 A45	18fr multi	25	14
263 A45	25fr gray & multi	35	16
264 A45	80fr multi	1.40	55
265 A45	100fr multi	1.60	70
	Nos. 256-265 (10)	3.90	1.85

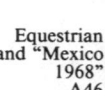

Equestrian and "Mexico 1968" A46

Designs: 40c, Wrestling and "Tokyo 1964." 60c, Fencing and "Rome 1960." 80c, High jump and "Berlin 1936." 38fr, Women's diving and "London 1908 and 1948." 60fr, Weight lifting and "Paris 1900 and 1924."

1968, Oct. 24 Litho. *Perf. 14x13*

266 A46	20c org & sep	5	5
267 A46	40c grnsh bl & sep	5	5
268 A46	60c car rose & sep	5	5
269 A46	80c ultra & sep	5	5
270 A46	38fr red & sep	55	25
271 A46	60fr emer & sep	1.00	50
	Nos. 266-271 (6)	1.75	95

19th Olympic Games, Mexico City, Oct. 12-27.

Tuareg, Algeria — A47

African National Costumes: 40c, Musicians, Upper Volta. 60c, Senegalese women. 70c, Girls of Rwanda going to market. 8fr, Young married couple from Morocco. 20fr, Nigerian officials in state dress. 40fr, Man and women from Zambia. 50fr, Man and woman from Kenya.

1968, Nov. 4 Litho. *Perf. 13*

272 A47	30c multi	5	5
273 A47	40c multi	5	5
274 A47	60c multi	5	5
275 A47	70c multi	5	5
276 A47	8fr multi	10	10
277 A47	20fr multi	30	16
278 A47	40fr multi	60	35
279 A47	50fr multi	70	50
	Nos. 272-279 (8)	1.90	1.31

Souvenir Sheet

Nativity, by Giorgione — A48

1968, Dec. 16 Engr. *Perf. 11½*

280 A48	100fr green	3.00	3.00

Christmas.

See Nos. 309, 389, 422, 494, 564, 611, 713, 787, 848, 894.

Singing Boy, by Frans Hals — A49

Paintings and Music: 20c, Angels' Concert, by van Eyck. 40c, Angels' Concert, by Matthias Grunewald. 60c, No. 283a, Singing Boy, by Frans Hals. 80c, Lute Player, by Gerard Terborch. 2fr, The Fifer, by Manet. 6fr, No. 286a, Young Girls at the Piano, by Renoir.

1969, Mar. 31 Photo. *Perf. 13*

281 A49	20c gold & multi	5	5
282 A49	40c gold & multi	5	5
283 A49	60c gold & multi	5	5
a.	Souv. sheet, 75fr	1.40	1.40
284 A49	80c gold & multi	5	5
285 A49	2fr gold & multi	7	5
286 A49	6fr gold & multi	14	10
a.	Souv. sheet, 75fr	1.40	1.40
	Nos. 281-286,C6-C7 (8)	3.11	2.33

Tuareg Men — A50

African Headdresses: 40c, Ovambo woman. South West Africa. 60c, Guinean man and Congolese woman. 80c, Dagger dancer, Guinean forest area. 8fr, Mohammedan Nigerians. 20fr, Luba dancer, Kabondo, Congo. 40fr, Senegalese and Gambian women. 80fr, Rwanda dancer.

1969, May 29 Litho. *Perf. 13*

287 A50	20c multi	5	5
288 A50	40c multi	5	5
289 A50	60c multi	5	5
290 A50	80c multi	5	5
291 A50	8fr multi	14	8
292 A50	20fr multi	30	16
293 A50	40fr multi	65	35
294 A50	80fr multi	1.40	60
	Nos. 287-294 (8)	2.69	1.39

See Nos. 398-405.

The Moneylender and his Wife, by Quentin Massys — A51

Design: 70fr, The Moneylender and his Wife, by Marinus van Reymerswaele.

1969, Sept. 10 Photo. *Perf. 13*

295 A51	30fr sil & multi	60	42
296 A51	70fr gold & multi	1.40	1.00

5th anniv. of the African Development Bank. Printed in sheets of 20 stamps and 20 labels with commemorative inscription.

Souvenir Sheet

First Man on the Moon — A52

1969, Oct. 9 Engr. *Perf. 11½*

297 A52	100fr bl gray	1.60	1.60

See note after Mali No. C80. See No. 407.

Camomile and Health Emblem — A53

Worker with Pickaxe and Flag — A54

Medicinal Plants and Health Emblem: 40c, Aloe. 60c, Cola. 80c, Coca. 3fr, Hagenia abissinica. 75fr, Cassia. 80fr, Cinchona. 100fr, Tephrosia.

1969, Nov. 24 Photo. *Perf. 13*

Flowers in Natural Colors

298 A53	20c gold, bl & blk	5	5
299 A53	40c gold, yel grn & blk	5	5
300 A53	60c gold, pink & blk	5	5
301 A53	80c gold, grn & blk	5	5
302 A53	3fr gold, org & blk	7	5
303 A53	75fr gold, yel & blk	1.40	55
304 A53	80fr gold, lil & blk	1.50	65
305 A53	100fr gold, dl yel & blk	1.75	80
	Nos. 298-305 (8)	4.92	2.25

1969, Nov. Photo. *Perf. 11½*

306 A54	6fr brt pink & multi	7	7
307 A54	18fr ultra & multi	38	20
308 A54	40fr brn & multi	70	42

10th anniversary of independence.

Souvenir Sheet

Christmas Type of 1968

Design: 100fr, "Holy Night" (detail), by Correggio.

1969, Dec. 15 Engr. *Perf. 11½*

309 A48	100fr ultra	1.75	1.75

The Cook, by Pierre Aertsen — A55

Paintings: 20c, Quarry Worker, by Oscar Bonnevalle (horiz.). 40c, The Plower, by Peter Brueghel (horiz.) 60c, Fisherman, by Constantin Meunier. 80c, Slipway, Ostende, by Jean van Noten (horiz.). 10fr, The Forge of Vulcan, by Velasquez (horiz.). 50fr, "Hiercheuse" (woman shoveling coal), by Meunier. 70fr, Miner, by Pierre Paulus.

1969, Dec. 22 Photo. *Perf. 13½*

310 A55	20c gold & multi	5	5
311 A55	40c gold & multi	5	5
312 A55	60c gold & multi	5	5
313 A55	80c gold & multi	5	5
314 A55	8fr gold & multi	20	8
315 A55	10fr gold & multi	22	10
316 A55	50fr gold & multi	1.00	55
317 A55	70fr gold & multi	1.40	70
	Nos. 310-317 (8)	3.02	1.63

ILO, 50th anniversary.

Napoleon Crossing St. Bernard, by Jacques L. David — A56

Paintings of Napoleon Bonaparte (1769-1821): 40c, Decorating Soldier before Tilsit, by Jean Baptiste Debret. 60c, Addressing Troops at Augsburg, by Claude Gautherot. 80c, First Consul, by Jean Auguste Ingres. 8fr, Battle of Marengo, by Jacques Auguste Pajou. 20fr, Napoleon Meeting Emperor Francis II, by Antoine Jean Gros. 40fr, Gen. Bonaparte at Arcole, by Gros. 80fr Coronation, by David.

1969, Dec. 29

318	A56	20c gold & multi	5	5
319	A56	40c gold & multi	5	5
320	A56	60c gold & multi	5	5
321	A56	80c gold & multi	5	5
322	A56	8fr gold & multi	18	8
323	A56	20fr gold & multi	38	20
324	A56	40fr gold & multi	70	42
325	A56	80fr gold & multi	1.50	80
		Nos. 318-325 (8)	2.96	1.70

Epsom Derby, by Gericault — A57

Paintings of Horses: 40c, Horses Emerging from the Sea, by Delacroix. 60c, Charles V at Muhlberg, by Titian (vert.). 80c, Amateur Jockeys, by Edgar Degas, 8fr, Horsemen at Rest, by Philips Wouwerman. 20fr, Imperial Guards Officer, by Gericault (vert.). 40fr, Friends of the Desert, by Oscar Bonnevalle. 80fr, Two Horses (detail from the Prodigal Son), by Rubens.

1970, Mar. 31 Photo. *Perf. 13½*

326	A57	20c gold & multi	5	5
327	A57	40c gold & multi	5	5
328	A57	60c gold & multi	5	5
329	A57	80c gold & multi	5	5
330	A57	8fr gold & multi	15	8
331	A57	20fr gold & multi	40	16
332	A57	40fr gold & multi	70	35
333	A57	80fr gold & multi	1.40	65
		Nos. 326-333 (8)	2.85	1.44

Souvenir Sheet

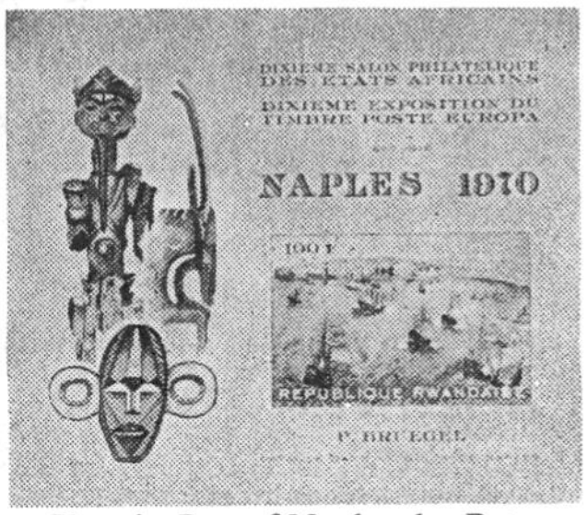

Fleet in Bay of Naples, by Peter Brueghel, the Elder — A58

1970, May 2 Engr. *Perf. 11½*

334 A58 100fr brt rose lil 2.00 2.00

10th Europa Phil. Exhib., Naples, Italy, May 2-10.

Copies of No. 334 were trimmed to 68x58mm and overprinted in silver or gold "NAPLES 1973" on the stamp, and "Salon Philatelique des Etats Africains / Exposition du Timbre-Poste Europa" in October, 1973.

Soccer and Mexican Decorations A59

Tharaka Meru Woman, East Africa A60

Designs: Various scenes from soccer game and pre-Columbian decorations.

1970, June 15 Photo. *Perf. 13*

335	A59	20c gold & multi	5	5
336	A59	30c gold & multi	5	5
337	A59	50c gold & multi	5	5
338	A59	1fr gold & multi	5	5
339	A59	6fr gold & multi	12	5
340	A59	18fr gold & multi	40	16
341	A59	30fr gold & multi	60	40
342	A59	90fr gold & multi	1.75	70
		Nos. 335-342 (8)	3.07	1.51

9th World Soccer Championships for the Jules Rimet Cup, Mexico City, May 30-June 21.

1970, June 1 Litho.

African National Costumes: 30c, Musician with wooden flute, Niger. 50c, Woman water carrier, Tunisia. 1fr, Ceremonial costumes, North Nigeria. 3fr, Strolling troubadour "Griot," Mali. 5fr, Quipongos women, Angola. 50fr, Man at prayer, Mauritania. 90fr, Sinehatiali dance costumes, Ivory Coast.

343	A60	20c multi	5	5
344	A60	30c multi	5	5
345	A60	50c multi	5	5
346	A60	1fr multi	5	5
347	A60	3fr multi	5	5
348	A60	5fr multi	8	8
349	A60	50fr multi	90	42
350	A60	90fr multi	1.60	70
		Nos. 343-350 (8)	2.83	1.45

Flower Arrangement, Peacock, EXPO '70 Emblem — A61

EXPO Emblem and: 30c, Torii and Camellias, by Yukihiko Yasuda. 50c, Kabuki character and Woman Playing Samisen, by Nampu Katayama. 1fr, Tower of the Sun, and Warrior Riding into Water. 3fr, Pavilion and Buddhist deity. 5fr, Pagoda and modern painting by Shuho Yamakawa. 20fr, Japanese inscription "Omatsuri" and Osaka Castle. 70fr, EXPO '70 emblem and Warrior on Horseback.

1970, Aug. 24 Photo. *Perf. 13*

351	A61	20c gold & multi	5	5
352	A61	30c gold & multi	5	5
353	A61	50c gold & multi	5	5
354	A61	1fr gold & multi	5	5
355	A61	3fr gold & multi	5	5
356	A61	5fr gold & multi	8	5
357	A61	20fr gold & multi	32	25
358	A61	70fr gold & multi	1.00	50
		Nos. 351-358 (8)	1.65	1.05

EXPO '70 International Exhibition, Osaka, Japan, Mar. 15-Sept. 13.

Young Mountain Gorillas — A62

Designs: Various Gorillas. 40c, 80c, 2fr, 100fr are vertical.

1970, Sept. 7

359	A62	20c ol & blk	5	5
360	A62	40c brt rose lil & blk	5	5
361	A62	60c bl, brn & blk	5	5
362	A62	80c org brn & blk	5	5
363	A62	1fr dp car & blk	5	5
364	A62	2fr blk & multi	5	5
365	A62	15fr sep & blk	30	16
366	A62	100fr brt bl & blk	1.90	1.10
		Nos. 359-366 (8)	2.50	1.56

Pierre J. Pelletier and Joseph B. Caventou A63

Designs: 20c, Cinchona flower and bark. 80c, Quinine powder and pharmacological vessels. 1fr, Anopheles mosquito. 3fr, Malaria patient and nurse. 25fr, "Malaria" (mosquito).

1970, Oct. 27 Photo. *Perf. 13*

367	A63	20c sil & multi	5	5
368	A63	80c sil & multi	5	5
369	A63	1fr sil & multi	5	5
370	A63	3fr sil & multi	7	5
371	A63	25fr sil & multi	50	25
372	A63	70fr sil & multi	1.40	60
		Nos. 367-372 (6)	2.12	1.05

150th anniv. of the discovery of quinine by Pierre Joseph Pelletier (1788-1842) and Joseph Bienaime Caventou (1795-1877), French pharmacologists.

Apollo Spaceship A64

Apollo Spaceship: 30c, Second stage separation. 50c, Spaceship over moon surface. 1fr, Landing module and astronauts on moon. 3fr, Take-off from moon. 5fr, Return to earth. 10fr, Final separation of nose cone. 80fr, Splashdown.

1970, Nov. 23 Photo. *Perf. 13*

373	A64	20c sil & multi	5	5
374	A64	30c sil & multi	5	5
375	A64	50c sil & multi	5	5
376	A64	1fr sil & multi	6	5
377	A64	3fr sil & multi	7	5
378	A64	5fr sil & multi	12	7
379	A64	10fr sil & multi	16	10
380	A64	80fr sil & multi	1.20	90
		Nos. 373-380 (8)	1.76	1.32

Conquest of space.

Franklin D. Roosevelt and Brassocattleya Olympia Alba — A65

Designs: Various portraits of Franklin D. Roosevelt and various orchids.

1970, Dec. 21 Photo. *Perf. 13*

381	A65	20c bl, blk & brn	5	5
382	A65	30c car rose, blk & brn	5	5
383	A65	50c dp org, blk & brn	5	5
384	A65	1fr grn, blk & brn	5	5
385	A65	2fr mar, blk & grn	5	5
386	A65	6fr lil & multi	8	5
387	A65	30fr bl, blk & sl grn	60	30
388	A65	60fr lil rose, blk & sl grn	1.25	50
		Nos. 381-388 (8)	2.18	1.10

Pres. Franklin D. Roosevelt, 25th death anniv.

Souvenir Sheet
Christmas Type of 1968

Design: 100fr, Adoration of the Shepherds, by Jose de Ribera (vert.).

1970, Dec. 24 Engr. *Perf. 11½*

389 A48 100fr Prus bl 2.00 2.00

Pope Paul VI — A66

Portraits of Popes: 20c, John XXIII, 1958-1963. 30c, Pius XII, 1939-1958. 40c, Pius XI, 1922-39. 1fr, Benedict XV, 1914-22. 18fr, St. Pius X, 1903-14. 20fr, Leo XIII, 1878-1903. 60fr, Pius IX, 1846-78.

1970, Dec. 31 Photo. *Perf. 13*

390	A66	10c gold & dk brn	5	5
391	A66	20c gold & dk grn	5	5
392	A66	30c gold & dp cl	5	5
393	A66	40c gold & ind	5	5
394	A66	1fr gold & dk pur	5	5
395	A66	18fr gold & pur	35	16
396	A66	20fr gold & org brn	42	25
397	A66	60fr gold & blk brn	1.10	60
		Nos. 390-397 (8)	2.12	1.26

Centenary of Vatican I, Ecumenical Council of the Roman Catholic Church, 1869-70.

Headdress Type of 1969

African Headdresses: 20c, Rendille woman. 30c, Young Toubou woman, Chad. 50c, Peul man, Niger. 1fr, Young Masai man, Kenya. 5fr, Young Peul girl, Niger. 18fr, Rwanda woman. 25fr, Man, Mauritania. 50fr, Rwanda women with pearl necklaces.

1971, Feb. 15 Litho. *Perf. 13*

398	A50	20c multi	5	5
399	A50	30c multi	5	5
400	A50	50c multi	5	5
401	A50	1fr multi	5	5
402	A50	5fr multi	7	5
403	A50	18fr multi	30	20
404	A50	25fr multi	45	25
405	A50	50fr multi	1.00	50
		Nos. 398-405 (8)	2.02	1.20

Souvenir Sheet
M. L. King Type of 1968

Design: 100fr, Charles de Gaulle (1890-1970), President of France.

1971, Mar. 15 Engr. *Perf. 13½*

406 A44 100fr ultra 1.75 1.25

Souvenir Sheet
Astronaut Type of 1969 Inscribed in Dark Violet with Emblem and: "APOLLO / 14 / SHEPARD / ROOSA / MITCHELL"

1971, Apr. 15 Engr. *Perf. 11½*

407 A52 100fr brn org 2.00 1.75

Apollo 14 U.S. moon landing, Jan. 31-Feb. 9. Size of No. 407: 94x109mm.

Beethoven, by Christian Horneman A67

Beethoven Portraits: 30c, Joseph Stieler. 50c, by Ferdinand Schimon. 3fr, by H. Best. 6fr, by W. Fassbender. 90fr, Beethoven's Funeral Procession, by Leopold Stöber.

1971, July 5 Photo. *Perf. 13*

408	A67	20c gold & multi	5	5
409	A67	30c gold & multi	5	5
410	A67	50c gold & multi	5	5
411	A67	3fr gold & multi	7	5
412	A67	6fr gold & multi	14	5
413	A67	90fr gold & multi	1.90	1.00
		Nos. 408-413 (6)	2.26	1.25

Ludwig van Beethoven (1770-1827), composer.

Equestrian — A68

Olympic Sports: 30c, Runner at start. 50c, Basketball. 1fr, High jump. 8fr, Boxing. 10fr, Pole vault. 20fr, Wrestling. 60fr, Gymnastics (rings).

1971, Oct. 25 Photo. *Perf. 13*

414	A68	20c gold & blk	5	5
415	A68	30c gold & dp rose lil	5	5
416	A68	50c gold & vio bl	5	5
417	A68	1fr gold & dp grn	5	5
418	A68	8fr gold & hn brn	16	9
419	A68	10fr gold & pur	22	12
420	A68	20fr gold & dp brn	40	22
421	A68	60fr gold & Prus bl	1.20	50
		Nos. 414-421 (8)	2.18	1.13

20th Summer Olympic Games, Munich, Aug. 26-Sept. 10, 1972.

Christmas Type of 1968
Souvenir Sheet

Design: 100fr, Nativity, by Anthony van Dyck (vert.).

1971, Dec. 20 Engr. *Perf. 11½*

422	A48	100fr indigo	1.65	1.65

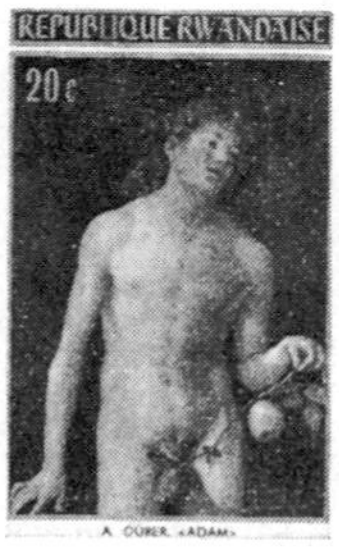

Adam by Dürer — A69

Paintings by Albrecht Dürer (1471-1528), German painter and engraver: 30c, Eve. 50c, Hieronymus Holzschuher, Portrait. 1fr, Lamentation of Christ. 3fr, Madonna with the Pear. 5fr, St. Eustace. 20fr, Sts. Paul and Mark. 70fr, Self-portrait, 1500.

1971, Dec. 31 Photo. *Perf. 13*

423	A69	20c gold & multi	5	5
424	A69	30c gold & multi	5	5
425	A69	50c gold & multi	5	5
426	A69	1fr gold & multi	5	5
427	A69	3fr gold & multi	7	5
428	A69	5fr gold & multi	10	6
429	A69	20fr gold & multi	42	22
430	A69	70fr gold & multi	1.40	90
		Nos. 423-430 (8)	2.19	1.43

A 600fr on gold foil honoring Apollo 15 was issued Jan. 15, 1972.

Guardsmen Exercising A70

National Guard Emblem and: 6fr, Loading supplies. 15fr, Helicopter ambulance. 25fr, Health Service for civilians. 50fr, Guardsman and map of Rwanda (vert.).

1972, Feb. 7 *Perf. 13½x14, 14x13½*

431	A70	4fr dp org & multi	7	5
432	A70	6fr yel & multi	8	7
433	A70	15fr lt bl & multi	22	15
434	A70	25fr red & multi	45	25
435	A70	50fr multi	90	60
		Nos. 431-435 (5)	1.72	1.12

"The National Guard serving the nation."

Ice Hockey, Sapporo Olympics Emblem A71

1972, Feb. 12 *Perf. 13x13½*

436	A71	20c shown	5	5
437	A71	30c Speed skating	5	5
438	A71	50c Ski jump	5	5
439	A71	1fr Men's figure skating	5	5
440	A71	6fr Cross-country skiing	8	7
441	A71	12fr Slalom	20	14
442	A71	20fr Bobsledding	38	22
443	A71	60fr Downhill skiing	1.10	70
		Nos. 436-443 (8)	1.96	1.33

11th Winter Olympic Games, Sapporo, Japan, Feb. 3-13.

Antelopes and Cercopithecus — A72

1972, Mar. 20 Photo. *Perf. 13*

444	A72	20c shown	5	5
445	A72	30c Buffaloes	5	5
446	A72	50c Zebras	5	5
447	A72	1fr Rhinoceroses	5	5
448	A72	2fr Wart hogs	5	5
449	A72	6fr Hippopotami	10	7
450	A72	18fr Hyenas	35	20
451	A72	32fr Guinea fowl	60	38
452	A72	60fr Antelopes	1.20	70
453	A72	80fr Lions	1.60	1.00
		Nos. 444-453 (10)	4.10	2.60

Akagera National Park.

Family Raising Flag of Rwanda — A73

1972, Apr. 4 *Perf. 13x12½*

454	A73	6fr dk red & multi	8	7
455	A73	18fr grn & multi	35	20
456	A73	60fr brn & multi	1.10	70

10th anniversary of the Referendum establishing Republic of Rwanda.

Common Waxbills and Hibiscus — A74

Birds: 30c, Collared sunbird. 50c, Variable sunbird. 1fr, Greater double-collared sunbird. 4fr, Ruwenzori puff-back flycatcher. 6fr, Red-billed fire finch. 10fr, Scarlet-chested sunbird. 18fr, Red-headed quelea. 60fr, Black-headed gonolek. 100fr, African golden oriole.

1972, May 17 Photo. *Perf. 13*

457	A74	20c dl grn & multi	5	5
458	A74	30c buff & multi	5	5
459	A74	50c yel & multi	5	5
460	A74	1fr lt bl & multi	5	5
461	A74	4fr dl rose & multi	7	5
462	A74	6fr lil rose & multi	8	7
463	A74	10fr pink & multi	16	10
464	A74	18fr gray & multi	35	20
465	A74	60fr multi	1.20	70
466	A74	100fr vio & multi	1.75	1.20
		Nos. 457-466 (10)	3.81	2.52

Belgica '72 Emblem, King Baudouin, Queen Fabiola, Pres. and Mrs. Kayibanda — A75

1972, June 24 Photo. *Perf. 13*

Size: 37x34mm

467	A75	18fr Rwanda landscape	38	20
468	A75	22fr Old houses, Bruges	45	22

Size: 50x34mm

469	A75	40fr shown	80	40

Belgica '72 Intl. Phil. Exhib., Brussels, June 24-July 9. Printed se-tenant in sheets of 15 (3x5).

Pres. Kayibanda Addressing Meeting — A76

Pres. Grégoire Kayibanda: 30c, promoting officers of National Guard. 50c, with wife and children. 6fr, casting vote. 10fr, with wife and dignitaries at Feast of Justice. 15fr, with Cabinet and members of Assembly. 18fr, taking oath of office. 50fr, Portrait (vert.).

1972, July 4

470	A76	20c gold & sl grn	5	5
471	A76	30c gold & dk pur	5	5
472	A76	50c gold & choc	5	5
473	A76	6fr gold & Prus bl	10	7
474	A76	10fr gold & dk pur	20	10
475	A76	15fr gold & dk bl	30	14
476	A76	18fr gold & brn	42	20
477	A76	50fr gold & Prus bl	1.00	60
		Nos. 470-477 (8)	2.17	1.26

10th anniversary of independence.

The indexes in each volume of the Scott Catalogue contain many listings which help to identify stamps.

Equestrian, Olympic Emblems A77

Olympic Emblems, Stadium, TV Tower and: 30c, Hockey. 50c, Soccer. 1fr, Broad jump. 6fr, Bicycling. 18fr, Yachting. 30fr, Hurdles. 44fr, Gymnastics, women's.

1972, Aug. 16 Photo. *Perf. 14*

478	A77	20c dk brn & gold	5	5
479	A77	30c vio bl & gold	5	5
480	A77	50c dk grn & gold	5	5
481	A77	1fr dp cl & gold	5	5
482	A77	6fr blk & gold	10	7
483	A77	18fr brn & gold	30	20
484	A77	30fr dk vio & gold	60	30
485	A77	44fr Prus bl & gold	80	40
		Nos. 478-485 (8)	2.00	1.17

20th Olympic Games, Munich, Aug. 26-Sept. 11.

Relay (Sport) and UN Emblem A78

1972, Oct. 23 Photo. *Perf. 13*

486	A78	20c shown	5	5
487	A78	30c Musicians	5	5
488	A78	50c Dancers	5	5
489	A78	1fr Operating room	5	5
490	A78	6fr Weaver & painter	10	7
491	A78	18fr Classroom	16	20
492	A78	24fr Laboratory	55	25
493	A78	50fr Hands of 4 races reaching for equality	1.00	60
		Nos. 486-493 (8)	2.01	1.32

Fight against racism.

Christmas Type of 1968
Souvenir Sheet

Design: 100fr, Adoration of the Shepherds, by Jacob Jordaens (vert.).

1972, Dec. 11 *Perf. 11½*

494	A48	100fr red brn	1.65	1.65

Phymateus Brunneri — A79

Designs: Various insects. 30c, 1fr, 6fr, 22fr, 100fr, vertical.

1973, Jan. 31 Photo. *Perf. 13*

495	A79	20c multi	5	5
496	A79	30c multi	5	5
497	A79	50c multi	5	5
498	A79	1fr multi	5	5
499	A79	2fr multi	5	5
500	A79	6fr multi	10	7
501	A79	18fr multi	35	20
502	A79	22fr multi	42	20
503	A79	70fr multi	1.40	80
504	A79	100fr multi	2.00	1.20
		Nos. 495-504 (10)	4.52	2.72

Souvenir Sheet
Perf. 14

505	A79	80fr like 20c	1.75	1.75

No. 505 contains one stamp 43½x33½mm.

Emile Zola, by Edouard Manet — A80

Paintings Connected with Reading, and Book Year Emblem: 30c, Rembrandt's Mother. 50c, St. Jerome Removing Thorn from Lion's Paw, by Colantonio. 1fr, Apostles Peter and Paul, by El Greco. 2fr, Virgin and Child with Book, by Roger van der Weyden. 6fr, St. Jerome in his Cell, by Antonella de Messina. 40fr, St. Barbara, by Master of Flemalle. No. 513, Don Quixote, by Otto Bonevalle. No. 514, Pres. Kayibanda reading book.

1973, Mar. 12 Photo. *Perf. 13*

506	A80	20c gold & multi	5	5
507	A80	30c gold & multi	5	5
508	A80	50c gold & multi	5	5
509	A80	1fr gold & multi	5	5
510	A80	2fr gold & multi	5	5
511	A80	6fr gold & multi	9	5
512	A80	40fr gold & multi	65	32
513	A80	100fr gold & multi	1.65	75
		Nos. 506-513 (8)	2.64	1.37

Souvenir Sheet

Perf. 14

514	A80	100fr gold, bl & ind	1.65	1.25

International Book Year.

Longombe — A81

Rubens and Isabella Brandt, by Rubens — A82

Designs: Musical instruments of Central and West Africa.

1973, Apr. 9 Photo. *Perf. 13½*

Gray and Multicolored

515	A81	20c shown	5	5
516	A81	30c Horn	5	5
517	A81	50c Xylophone	5	5
518	A81	1fr Harp	5	5
519	A81	4fr Alur horns	7	5
520	A81	6fr Drum, bells and horn	10	7
521	A81	18fr Large drums (Ngoma)	30	16
522	A81	90fr Toba	1.60	80
		Nos. 515-522 (8)	2.27	1.28

1973, May 11

Paintings from Old Pinakothek, Munich (IBRA Emblem and): 30c, Young Man, by Cranach. 50c, Woman Peeling Turnips, by Chardin. 1fr, The Abduction of Leucippa's Daughters, by Rubens. 2fr, Virgin and Child, by Filippo Lippi. 6fr, Boys Eating Fruit, by Murillo. 40fr, The Lovesick Woman, by Jan Steen. No. 530, Jesus Stripped of His Garments, by El Greco. No. 531, Oswalt Krehl, by Dürer.

523	A82	20c gold & multi	5	5
524	A82	30c gold & multi	5	5
525	A82	50c gold & multi	5	5
526	A82	1fr gold & multi	5	5
527	A82	2fr gold & multi	6	5
528	A82	6fr gold & multi	10	7
529	A82	40fr gold & multi	70	35
530	A82	100fr gold & multi	1.90	80
		Nos. 523-530 (8)	2.96	1.47

Souvenir Sheet

531	A82	100fr gold & multi	2.00	1.60

IBRA München 1973 Intl. Phil. Exhib., Munich, May 11-20. No. 531 contains one stamp 40x56mm.

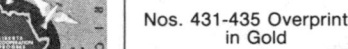

Map of Africa and Peace Doves A83

Design: 94fr, Map of Africa and hands.

1973, July 23 Photo. *Perf. 13½*

532	A83	6fr gold & multi	16	10
533	A83	94fr gold & multi	1.90	1.50

Org. for African Unity, 10th anniv.

Nos. 298-303 Overprinted in Blue, Black, Green or Brown: "SECHERESSE / SOLIDARITE AFRICAINE"

1973, Aug. 23 Photo. *Perf. 13*

534	A53	20c multi (Bl)	5	5
535	A53	40c multi (Bk)	5	5
536	A53	60c multi (Bl)	5	5
537	A53	80c multi (G)	5	5
538	A53	3fr multi (G)	5	5
539	A53	75fr multi (Br)	1.50	90
		Nos. 534-539,B1 (7)	4.25	3.40

African solidarity in drought emergency.

African Postal Union Issue

Common Design Type

1973, Sept. 12 Engr. *Perf. 13*

540	CD137	100fr dp brn, bl & brn	2.00	1.60

Six-lined Distichodus — A84

African Fish: 30c, Little triggerfish. 50c, Spotted upside-down catfish. 1fr, Nile mouthbreeder. 2fr, African lungfish. 6fr, Pareutropius mandevillei. 40fr, Congo characin. 100fr, Like 20c. 150fr, Julidochromis ornatus.

1973, Sept. 3 Photo. *Perf. 13*

541	A84	20c gold & multi	5	5
542	A84	30c gold & multi	5	5
543	A84	50c gold & multi	5	5
544	A84	1fr gold & multi	5	5
545	A84	2fr gold & multi	5	5
546	A84	6fr gold & multi	10	7
547	A84	40fr gold & multi	70	40
548	A84	150fr gold & multi	3.00	1.50
		Nos. 541-548 (8)	4.05	2.22

Souvenir Sheet

549	A84	100fr gold & multi	2.00	2.00

No. 549 contains one stamp 48x29mm.

Nos. 398-405 Overprinted in Black, Silver, Green or Blue

QUINZAINE AFRICAINE BRUXELLES 15/30 SEPT. 1973

1973, Sept. 15 Litho.

550	A50	20c multi (Bk)	5	5
551	A50	30c multi (S)	5	5
552	A50	50c multi (Bk)	5	5
553	A50	1fr multi (G)	5	5
554	A50	5fr multi (S)	12	5
555	A50	18fr multi (Bk)	35	20
556	A50	25fr multi (Bk)	50	25
557	A50	50fr multi (Bl)	1.20	55
		Nos. 550-557 (8)	2.37	1.25

Africa Weeks, Brussels, Sept. 15-30, 1973. On the 30c, 1fr and 25fr the text of the overprint is horizontal.

Nos. 431-435 Overprinted in Gold

Perf. 13½x14, 14x13½

1973, Oct. 31 Photo.

559	A70	4fr dp org & multi	10	7
560	A70	6fr yel & multi	15	10
561	A70	15fr lt bl & multi	42	27
562	A70	25fr red & multi	70	40
563	A70	50fr multi	1.50	80
		Nos. 559-563 (5)	2.87	1.64

25th anniv. of the Universal Declaration of Human Rights.

Christmas Type of 1968

Souvenir Sheet

Design: 100fr, Adoration of the Shepherds, by Guido Reni.

1973, Dec. 15 Engr. *Perf. 11½*

564	A48	100fr brt vio	1.50	1.50

Copernicus and Astrolabe A85

Pres. Juvénal Habyarimana A86

Designs: 30c, 18fr, 100fr, Portrait. 50c, 80fr, Copernicus and heliocentric system. 1fr, like 20c.

1973, Dec. 26 Photo. *Perf. 13*

565	A85	20c sil & multi	5	5
566	A85	30c sil & multi	5	5
567	A85	50c sil & multi	5	5
568	A85	1fr gold & multi	5	5
569	A85	18fr gold & multi	22	20
570	A85	80fr gold & multi	1.20	80
		Nos. 565-570 (6)	1.62	1.20

Souvenir Sheet

571	A85	100fr gold & multi	2.00	2.00

Nicolaus Copernicus (1473-1543), Polish astronomer.

1974, Apr. 8 Photo. *Perf. 11½*

Black Inscriptions

572	A86	1fr bis & sep	5	5
573	A86	2fr ultra & sep	5	5
574	A86	5fr rose red & sep	8	5
575	A86	6fr grnsh bl & sep	10	5
576	A86	26fr lil & sep	45	30
577	A86	60fr ol grn & sep	1.20	65
		Nos. 572-577 (6)	1.93	1.15

Souvenir Sheet

Christ Between the Thieves (Detail), by Rubens — A87

1974, Apr. 12 Engr. *Perf. 11½*

578	A87	100fr sepia	2.50	2.50

Easter.

Jugoslavia-Zaire Soccer Game — A88

Designs: Games' emblem and soccer games.

1974, July 6 Photo. *Perf. 13½*

579	A88	20c shown	5	5
580	A88	40c Netherlands-Sweden	5	5
581	A88	60c Germany (Fed.)-Australia	5	5
582	A88	80c Haiti-Argentina	5	5
583	A88	2fr Brazil-Scotland	5	5
584	A88	6fr Bulgaria-Uruguay	10	7
585	A88	40fr Italy-Poland	70	40
586	A88	50fr Chile-Germany (DDR)	1.00	65
		Nos. 579-586 (8)	2.05	1.37

World Cup Soccer Championship, Munich, June 13-July 7.

Marconi's Laboratory Yacht "Elletra" — A89

Designs: 30c, Marconi and steamer "Carlo Alberto." 50c, Marconi's wireless apparatus and telecommunications satellites. 4fr, Marconi and globes connected by communications waves. 35fr, Marconi's radio, and radar. 60fr, Marconi and transmitter at Poldhu, Cornwall. 50fr, like 20c.

1974, Aug. 19 Photo. *Perf. 13½*

587	A89	20c vio, blk & grn	5	5
588	A89	30c grn, blk & vio	5	5
589	A89	50c yel, blk & lil	5	5
590	A89	4fr sal, blk & bl	7	5
591	A89	35fr lil, blk & yel	60	40
592	A89	60fr bl, blk & brnz	1.20	70
		Nos. 587-592 (6)	2.02	1.30

Souvenir Sheet

593	A89	50fr gold, blk & lt bl	1.20	1.20

Guglielmo Marconi (1874-1937), Italian electrical engineer and inventor.

The Flute Player, by J. Leyster — A90

Messenger Monk — A91

Paintings: 20c, Diane de Poitiers, Fontainebleau School. 50c, Virgin and Child, by David. 1fr, Triumph of Venus, by Boucher. 10fr, Seated Harlequin, by Picasso. 18fr, Virgin and Child, 15th century. 20fr, Beheading of St. John, by Hans Fries. 50fr, Daughter of Andersdotter, by J. F. Höckert.

1974, Sept. 23 Photo. *Perf. 14x13*

594	A90	20c gold & multi	5	5
595	A90	30c gold & multi	5	5
596	A90	50c gold & multi	5	5
597	A90	1fr gold & multi	5	5
598	A90	10fr gold & multi	16	10
599	A90	18fr gold & multi	30	16

600 A90 20fr gold & multi 35 22
601 A90 50fr gold & multi 1.00 60
Nos. 594-601 (8) 2.01 1.28

INTERNABA 74 Intl. Phil. Exhib., Basel, June 7-10, and Stockholmia 74, Intl. Phil. Exhib., Stockholm, Sept. 21-29.

Six multicolored souvenir sheets exist containing two 15fr stamps each in various combinations of designs of Nos. 594-601. One souvenir sheet of four 25fr stamps exists with designs of Nos. 595, 597, 599 and 601.

1974, Oct. 9 ***Perf. 14***

UPU Emblem and Messengers: 30c, Inca. 50c, Morocco. 1fr, India. 18fr, Polynesia. 80fr, Rwanda.

602 A91 20c gold & multi 5 5
603 A91 30c gold & multi 5 5
604 A91 50c gold & multi 5 5
605 A91 1fr gold & multi 5 5
606 A91 18fr gold & multi 42 38
607 A91 80fr gold & multi 1.65 1.60
Nos. 602-607 (6) 2.27 2.18

Centenary of Universal Postal Union.

Nos. 306-308 Overprinted

15e ANNIVERSAIRE 1974

1974, Dec. 16 **Photo.** ***Perf. 11½***

608 A54 6fr brt pink & multi 3.50 3.50
609 A54 18fr ultra & multi 3.50 3.50
610 A54 40fr brn & multi 3.75 3.75

15th anniversary of independence.

Christmas Type of 1968
Souvenir Sheet

Design: 100fr, Adoration of the Kings, by Joos van Cleve.

1974, Dec. 23 **Engr.** ***Perf. 11½***

611 A48 100fr sl grn 3.50 3.50

Nos. 295-296 Overprinted: "1974 / 10e Anniversaire"

1974, Dec. 30 **Photo.** ***Perf. 13***

612 A51 30fr sil & multi 55 55
613 A51 70fr gold & multi 1.10 1.10

African Development Bank, 10th anniversary.

Uganda Kob — A92

Antelopes: 30c, Bongos (horiz.). 50c, Rwanda antelopes. 1fr, Young sitatungas (horiz.). 4fr, Greater kudus. 10fr, Impalas (horiz.). 34fr, Waterbuck. 40fr, Impalas. 60fr, Greater kudu. 100fr, Derby's elands (horiz.).

1975, Mar. 17 **Photo.** ***Perf. 13***

614 A92 20c multi 5 5
615 A92 30c multi 5 5
616 A92 50c multi 5 5
617 A92 1fr multi 5 5
618 A92 4fr multi 5 5
619 A92 10fr multi 12 8
620 A92 34fr multi 50 25
621 A92 100fr multi 1.65 75
Nos. 614-621 (8) 2.52 1.33

Miniature Sheets

622 A92 40fr multi 1.40 1.40
623 A92 60fr multi 1.40 1.40

Miniature Sheets

The Burial of Jesus, by Raphael — A93

1975, Apr. 1 **Photo.** ***Perf. 13x14***

624 A93 20fr shown 1.00 1.00
625 A93 30fr Pieta, by Cranach the Elder 1.20 1.20
626 A93 50fr by van der Weyden 1.20 1.20
627 A93 100fr by Bellini 1.20 1.20

Easter. Size of stamps: 40x52mm.

Souvenir Sheets

Prince Balthazar Charles, by Velazquez A94

Paintings: 30fr, Infanta Margaret of Austria, by Velazquez. 50fr, The Divine Shepherd, by Murillo. 100fr, Francisco Goya, by V. Lopez y Portana.

1975, Apr. 4 **Photo.** ***Perf. 13***

628 A94 20fr multi 1.00 1.00
629 A94 30fr multi 1.20 1.20
630 A94 50fr multi 1.20 1.20
631 A94 100fr multi 1.20 1.20

Espana 75 Intl. Phil. Exhib., Madrid, Apr. 4-13. Size of stamps: 38x48mm. See Nos. 642-643.

Pyrethrum (Insect Powder) — A95

1975, Apr. 14 ***Perf. 13***

632 A95 20c shown 5 5
633 A95 30c Tea 5 5
634 A95 50c Coffee (beans and pan) 5 5
635 A95 4fr Bananas 7 5
636 A95 10fr Corn 16 10
637 A95 12fr Sorghum 20 10
638 A95 26fr Rice 45 25
639 A95 47fr Coffee (workers and beans) 1.10 45
Nos. 632-639 (8) 2.13 1.10

Souvenir Sheets
Perf. 13½

640 A95 25fr like 50c 65 65
641 A95 75fr like 47fr 1.60 1.60

Year of Agriculture. Nos. 632-641 commemorate 10th anniversary of Office for Industrialized Cultivation.

Souvenir Sheets
Painting Type of 1975

Paintings: 75fr, Louis XIV, by Hyacinthe Rigaud. 125fr, Cavalry Officer, by Jean Gericault.

1975, June 6 **Photo.** ***Perf. 13***

642 A94 75fr multi 1.60 1.60
643 A94 125fr multi 3.00 3.00

ARPHILA 75, Intl. Philatelic Exhibition, Paris, June 6-16. Size of stamps: 38x48mm.

Nos. 390-397 Overprinted: "1975 / ANNEE / SAINTE"

1975, June 23 **Photo.** ***Perf. 13***

644 A66 10c gold & dk brn 5 5
645 A66 20c gold & dk grn 5 5
646 A66 30c gold & dp cl 5 5
647 A66 40c gold & ind 5 5
648 A66 1fr gold & dk pur 5 5
649 A66 18fr gold & pur 30 8
650 A66 20fr gold & org brn 40 20
651 A66 60fr gold & blk brn 1.50 80
Nos. 644-651 (8) 2.45 1.33

Holy Year 1975.

White Pelicans — A96

Designs: African birds.

1975, June 20

652 A96 20c shown 5 5
653 A96 30c Malachite kingfisher 5 5
654 A96 50c Goliath herons 5 5
655 A96 1fr Saddle-billed storks 5 5
656 A96 4fr African jacana 7 5
657 A96 10fr African anhingas 20 10
658 A96 34fr Sacred ibis 60 35
659 A96 80fr Hartlaub ducks 1.60 80
Nos. 652-659 (8) 2.67 1.50

Miniature Sheets

660 A96 40fr Flamingoes 1.20 1.20
661 A96 60fr Crowned cranes 1.60 1.60

Globe Representing Races and WPY Emblem — A97

The Bath, by Mary Cassatt and IWY Emblem — A98

Designs: 26fr, Population graph and emblem. 34fr, Globe with open door and emblem.

1975, Sept. 1 **Photo.** ***Perf. 13½x13***

662 A97 20fr dp bl & multi 38 20
663 A97 26fr dl red brn & multi 50 25
664 A97 34fr yel & multi 70 35

World Population Year.

1975, Sept. 15 ***Perf. 13***

IWY Emblem and: 30c, Mother and Infant Son, by Julius Gari Melchers. 50c, Woman with Milk Jug, by Jan Vermeer. 1fr, Water Carrier, by Goya. 8fr, Rwanda woman cotton picker. 12fr, Scientist with microscope. 18fr, Mother and child. 25fr, Empress Josephine, by Pierre-Paul Prud'hon. 40fr, Madame Vigee-Lebrun and Daughter, self-portrait. 60fr, Woman carrying child on back and water jug on head.

665 A98 20c gold & multi 5 5
666 A98 30c gold & multi 5 5
667 A98 50c gold & multi 5 5
668 A98 1fr gold & multi 5 5
669 A98 8fr gold & multi 14 8
670 A98 12fr gold & multi 20 12
671 A98 18fr gold & multi 30 18
672 A98 60fr gold & multi 1.20 60
Nos. 665-672 (8) 2.04 1.18

Souvenir Sheets
Perf. 13½

673 A98 25fr multi 1.60 1.60
674 A98 40fr multi 1.60 1.60

International Women's Year. Nos. 673-674 each contain one stamp 37x49mm.

Owl, Quill and Book — A99

Designs: 30c, Hygiene emblem. 1.50fr, Kneeling woman holding scales of Justice. 18fr, Chemist in laboratory. 26fr, Symbol of commerce and chart. 34fr, University Building.

1975, Sept. 29 ***Perf. 13***

675 A99 20c pur & multi 5 5
676 A99 30c ultra & multi 5 5
677 A99 1.50fr lil & multi 5 5
678 A99 18fr bl & multi 30 14
679 A99 26fr ol & multi 45 25
680 A99 34fr bl & multi 70 35
Nos. 675-680 (6) 1.60 89

National Univ. of Rwanda, 10th anniv.

Souvenir Sheets
Painting Type of 1975

Paintings by Jan Vermeer (1632-1675): 20fr, Man and Woman Drinking Wine. 30fr, Young Woman Reading Letter. 50fr, Painter in his Studio. 100fr, Young Woman Playing Virginal.

1975, Oct. 13 **Photo.** ***Perf. 13x14***

681 A93 20fr multi 40 40
682 A93 30fr multi 60 60
683 A93 50fr multi 1.00 1.00
684 A93 100fr multi 2.00 2.00

Size of stamps: 40x52mm.

Waterhole and Impatiens Stuhlmannii — A100

Designs: 30c, Antelopes, zebras, candelabra cactus. 50c, Brush fire, and tapinanthus prunifolius. 5fr, Bulera Lake and Egyptian white lotus. 8fr, Erosion prevention and protea madiensis. 10fr, Marsh and melanthera brownei. 26fr, Landscape, lobelias and senecons. 100fr, Sabyinyo Volcano and polystachya kermesina.

1975, Oct. 25 ***Perf. 13***

685 A100 20c blk & multi 5 5
686 A100 30c blk & multi 5 5
687 A100 50c blk & multi 5 5
688 A100 5fr blk & multi 8 5
689 A100 8fr blk & multi 14 8
690 A100 10fr blk & multi 16 10
691 A100 26fr blk & multi 50 25
692 A100 100fr blk & multi 1.90 1.00
Nos. 685-692 (8) 2.93 1.63

Nature protection.

Nos. 343-348 Overprinted

SECHERESSE
SOLIDARITE
1975

1975, Nov. 10 Litho. *Perf. 13*

693	A60	20c multi	5	5
694	A60	30c multi	5	5
695	A60	50c multi	5	5
696	A60	1fr multi	5	5
697	A60	3fr multi	7	5
698	A60	5fr multi	10	5
		Nos. 693-698,B2-B3 (8)	3.87	2.80

African solidarity in drought emergency.

Fork-lift Truck on Airfield A101

Designs: 30c, Coffee packing plant. 50c, Engineering plant. 10fr, Farmer with hoe (vert.). 35fr, Coffee pickers (vert.). 54fr, Mechanized harvester.

Wmk. JEZ Multiple (368)

1975, Dec. 1 Photo. *Perf. 14x13½*

699	A101	20c gold & multi	5	5
700	A101	30c gold & multi	5	5
701	A101	50c gold & multi	5	5
702	A101	10fr gold & multi	16	10
703	A101	35fr gold & multi	60	35
704	A101	54fr gold & multi	1.00	55
		Nos. 699-704 (6)	1.91	1.15

Basket Carrier and Themabelga Emblem — A102

Themabelga Emblem and: 30c, Warrior with shield and spear. 50c, Woman with beads. 1fr, Indian woman. 5fr, Male dancer with painted body. 7fr, Woman carrying child on back. 35fr, Male dancer with spear. 51fr, Female dancers.

1975, Dec. 8 Unwmk. *Perf. 13½*

705	A102	20c blk & multi	5	5
706	A102	30c blk & multi	5	5
707	A102	50c blk & multi	5	5
708	A102	1fr blk & multi	5	5
709	A102	5fr blk & multi	10	5
710	A102	7fr blk & multi	14	7
711	A102	35fr blk & multi	60	35
712	A102	51fr blk & multi	90	50
		Nos. 705-712 (8)	1.94	1.17

THEMABELGA Intl. Topical Philatelic Exhibition, Brussels, Dec. 13-21.

Christmas Type of 1968

Design: 100fr, Adoration of the Kings, by Peter Paul Rubens.

1975, Dec. 22 Engr. *Perf. 11½*

713	A48	100fr brt rose lil	2.25	2.25

Dr. Schweitzer, Keyboard, Score — A103

Albert Schweitzer and: 30c, 5fr, Lambarene Hospital. 50c, 10fr, Organ pipes from Strassbourg organ, and score. 1fr, 80fr, Dr. Schweitzer's house, Lambarene. 3fr, like 20c.

1976, Jan. 30 Photo. *Perf. 13½*

714	A103	20c mar & pur	5	5
715	A103	30c grn & pur	5	5
716	A103	50c brn org & pur	5	5
717	A103	1fr red lil & pur	5	5
718	A103	3fr vio bl & pur	7	5
719	A103	5fr brn & pur	10	5
720	A103	10fr bl & pur	20	10
721	A103	80fr ver & pur	1.40	80
		Nos. 714-721 (8)	1.97	1.20

World Leprosy Day.

Surrender at Yorktown A104

Paintings: 30c, Instruction at Valley Forge. 50c, Presentation of Captured Colors at Yorktown. 1fr, Washington at Fort Lee. 18fr, Washington Boarding British Warship. 26fr, Washington Studying Battle Plans at Night. 34fr, Washington Firing Cannon. 40fr, Washington Crossing the Delaware. 100fr, Sailing Ship "Bonhomme Richard" (vert.).

1976, Mar. 22 Photo. *Perf. 13x13½*

722	A104	20c gold & multi	5	5
723	A104	30c gold & multi	5	5
724	A104	50c gold & multi	5	5
725	A104	1fr gold & multi	5	5
726	A104	18fr gold & multi	35	16
727	A104	26fr gold & multi	42	22
728	A104	34fr gold & multi	60	35
729	A104	40fr gold & multi	65	40
		Nos. 722-729 (8)	2.22	1.33

Souvenir Sheet

Perf. 13½

730	A104	100fr gold & multi	2.00	2.00

American Bicentennial.

Sister Yohana, First Nun A105

Yachting A106

Designs: 30c, Abdon Sabakati, one of first converts. 50c, Father Alphonse Brard, first Superior of Save Mission. 4fr, Abbot Balthazar Gafuku, one of first priests. 10fr, Msgr. Bigirumwami, first bishop. 25fr, Save Church (horiz.). 60fr, Kabgayi Cathedral (horiz.).

Perf. 13x13½, 13½x13

1976, Apr. 26 Photo.

731	A105	20c multi	5	5
732	A105	30c multi	5	5
733	A105	50c multi	5	5
734	A105	4fr multi	12	7
735	A105	10fr multi	20	10
736	A105	25fr multi	45	25
737	A105	60fr multi	1.00	60
		Nos. 731-737 (7)	1.92	1.17

50th anniv. of the Roman Catholic Church of Rwanda.

1976, May 24 Photo. *Perf. 13x13½*

Montreal Games Emblem and: 30c, Steeplechase. 50c, Long jump. 1fr, Hockey. 10fr, Swimming. 18fr, Soccer. 29fr, Boxing. 51fr, Vaulting.

738	A106	20c gray & dk car	5	5
739	A106	30c gray & Prus bl	5	5
740	A106	50c gray & blk	5	5
741	A106	1fr gray & pur	5	5
742	A106	10fr gray & ultra	25	10
743	A106	18fr gray & dk brn	35	16
744	A106	29fr gray & blk	60	25
745	A106	51fr gray & sl grn	90	50
		Nos. 738-745 (8)	2.30	1.21

21st Olympic Games, Montreal, Canada, July 17-Aug. 1.

First Message, Manual Switchboard — A107

Designs: 30c, Telephone, 1876 and interested crowd. 50c, Telephone c. 1900, and woman making a call. 1fr, Business telephone exchange, c. 1905. 4fr, "Candlestick" phone, globe and A. G. Bell. 8fr, Dial phone and Rwandan man making call. 26fr, Telephone, 1976, satellite and radar. 60fr, Push-button telephone, Rwandan international switchboard operator.

1976, June 21 Photo. *Perf. 14*

746	A107	20c dl red & ind	5	5
747	A107	30c grnsh bl & ind	5	5
748	A107	50c brn & ind	5	5
749	A107	1fr org & ind	5	5
750	A107	4fr lil & ind	10	5
751	A107	8fr grn & ind	20	10
752	A107	26fr dl red & ind	50	25
753	A107	60fr vio & ind	1.10	60
		Nos. 746-753 (8)	2.10	1.20

Centenary of first telephone call by Alexander Graham Bell, Mar. 10, 1876.

Type of 1976 Overprinted in Silver with Bicentennial Emblem and "Independence Day"

Designs as before.

1976, July 4 *Perf. 13x13½*

754	A104	20c sil & multi	5	5
755	A104	30c sil & multi	5	5
756	A104	50c sil & multi	5	5
757	A104	1fr sil & multi	5	5
758	A104	18fr sil & multi	35	25
759	A104	26fr sil & multi	50	25
760	A104	34fr sil & multi	60	35
761	A104	40fr sil & multi	65	40
		Nos. 754-761 (8)	2.30	1.45

Independence Day.

Soccer, Montreal Olympic Emblem — A108

Montreal Olympic Games Emblem and: 30c, Shooting. 50c, Woman canoeing. 1fr, Gymnast. 10fr, Weight lifting. 12fr, Diving. 26fr, Equestrian. 50fr, Shot put.

1976, Aug. 1 Photo. *Perf. 13½x13*

762	A108	20c multi	5	5
763	A108	30c multi	5	5
764	A108	50c multi	5	5
765	A108	1fr multi	5	5
766	A108	10fr multi	16	10
767	A108	12fr multi	20	12
768	A108	26fr multi	42	25
769	A108	50fr multi	1.00	50
		Nos. 762-769 (8)	1.98	1.17

Souvenir Sheet

Designs: Various phases of hurdles race (horiz.).

770		Sheet of 4	3.00	3.00
a.	A108	20fr Start	35	35
b.	A108	30fr Sprint	55	55
c.	A108	40fr Hurdle	70	70
d.	A108	60fr Finish	1.00	1.00

21st Olympic Games, Montreal, Canada, July 17-Aug. 1.

Apollo and Soyuz Take-offs, Project Emblem A109

Designs: 30c, Soyuz in space. 50c, Apollo in space. 1fr, Apollo. 2fr, Spacecraft before docking. 12fr, Spacecraft after docking. 30fr, Astronauts visiting in docked spacecraft. 54fr, Apollo splashdown.

1976, Oct. 29 Photo. *Perf. 13½x14*

771	A109	20c multi	5	5
772	A109	30c multi	5	5
773	A109	50c multi	5	5
774	A109	1fr multi	5	5
775	A109	2fr multi	8	5
776	A109	12fr multi	25	12
777	A109	30fr multi	60	30
778	A109	54fr multi	90	55
		Nos. 771-778 (8)	2.03	1.22

Apollo Soyuz space test program (Russo-American cooperation), July 1975.

Eulophia Cucullata — A110

Orchids: 30c, Eulophia streptopetala. 50c, Disa Stairsii. 1fr, Aerangis kotschyana. 10fr, Eulophia abyssinica. 12fr, Bonatea steudneri. 26fr, Ansellia gigantea. 50fr, Eulophia angolensis.

1976, Nov. 22 Photo. *Perf. 14x13½*

779	A110	20c multi	5	5
780	A110	30c multi	5	5
781	A110	50c multi	5	5
782	A110	1fr multi	5	5
783	A110	10fr multi	16	10
784	A110	12fr multi	25	12
785	A110	26fr multi	50	25
786	A110	50fr multi	1.00	50
		Nos. 779-786 (8)	2.11	1.17

Souvenir Sheet
Christmas Type of 1968

Design: 100fr, Nativity, by Francois Boucher.

1976, Dec. 20 Engr. *Perf. 11½*

787	A48	100fr brt ultra	2.25	2.25

Nos. 714-721 Overprinted:
"JOURNEE / MONDIALE / 1977"

1977, Jan. 29 Photo. *Perf. 13½*

788	A103	20c mar & pur	5	5
789	A103	30c grn & pur	5	5
790	A103	50c brn org & pur	5	5
791	A103	1fr red lil & pur	5	5
792	A103	3fr vio bl & pur	8	5
793	A103	5fr brn & pur	16	7
794	A103	10fr bl & pur	25	10
795	A103	80fr ver & pur	1.40	80
		Nos. 788-795 (8)	2.09	1.22

World Leprosy Day.

Hands and Symbols of Learning — A111

Designs: 26fr, Hands and symbols of science. 64fr, Hands and symbols of industry.

1977, Feb. 7 Litho. *Perf. 12½*

796	A111	10fr multi	14	10
797	A111	26fr multi	35	25
798	A111	64fr multi	60	50

10th Summit Conference of the African and Malagasy Union, Kigali, 1976.

A particular stamp may be scarce, but if few collectors want it, its market value may remain relatively low.

Souvenir Sheets

Descent from the Cross, by Rubens A112

Easter: 25fr, Crucifixion, by Rubens.

1977, Apr. 27 Photo. *Perf. 13*

799	A112	25fr multi	60	60
800	A112	75fr multi	1.50	1.50

Size of stamp: 40x40mm.

Nos. 685-692 Overprinted

1977, May 2

801	A100	20c blk & multi	5	5
802	A100	30c blk & multi	5	5
803	A100	50c blk & multi	5	5
804	A100	5fr blk & multi	14	7
805	A100	8fr blk & multi	20	10
806	A100	10fr blk & multi	20	10
807	A100	26fr blk & multi	55	30
808	A100	100fr blk & multi	2.00	1.20
		Nos. 801-808 (8)	3.24	1.92

World Water Conference.

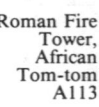

Roman Fire Tower, African Tom-tom A113

ITU Emblem and: 30c, Chappe's optical telegraph and postilion. 50c, Morse telegraph and code. 1fr, Tug Goliath laying cable in English Channel. 4fr, Telephone, radio, television. 18fr, Kingsport (US space exploration ship) and Marots communications satellite. 26fr, Satellite tracking station and O.T.S. satellite. 50fr, Mariner II, Venus probe.

1977, May 23 Litho. *Perf. 12½*

809	A113	20c multi	5	5
810	A113	30c multi	5	5
811	A113	50c multi	5	5
812	A113	1fr multi	5	5
813	A113	4fr multi	10	5
814	A113	18fr multi	38	18
815	A113	26fr multi	50	25
816	A113	50fr multi	1.00	50
		Nos. 809-816 (8)	2.18	1.18

World Telecommunications Day.

Souvenir Sheets

Amsterdam Harbor, by Willem van de Velde, the Younger A114

Design: 40fr, The Night Watch, by Rembrandt.

1977, May 26 Photo. *Perf. 13½*

817	A114	40fr multi	80	80
818	A114	60fr multi	1.20	1.20

AMPHILEX '277 Intl. Philatelic Exhibition, Amsterdam, May 27-June 5. Size of stamp: 38x49mm.

Road to Calvary, by Rubens — A115

Paintings by Peter Paul Rubens (1577-1640): 30c, Judgment of Paris (horiz.). 50c, Marie de Medicis. 1fr, Heads of Black Men (horiz.). 4fr, 26fr, Details from St. Ildefonso triptych. 8fr, Helene Fourment and her Children (horiz.). 60fr, Helene Fourment.

1977, June 13 *Perf. 14*

819	A115	20c gold & multi	5	5
820	A115	30c gold & multi	5	5
821	A115	50c gold & multi	5	5
822	A115	1fr gold & multi	5	5
823	A115	4fr gold & multi	10	5
824	A115	8fr gold & multi	20	10
825	A115	26fr gold & multi	50	25
826	A115	60fr gold & multi	1.20	60
		Nos. 819-826 (8)	2.20	1.20

Souvenir Sheet

Viking on Mars A116

1977, June 27 Photo. *Perf. 13*

827	A116	100fr multi	2.50	2.50

US Viking landing on Mars, first anniv.

Crested Eagle — A117

Birds of Prey: 30c, Snake eagle. 50c, Fish eagle. 1fr, Monk vulture. 3fr, Red-tailed buzzard. 5fr, Yellow-beaked kite. 20fr, Swallow-tailed kite. 100fr, Bateleur.

1977, Sept. 12 Litho. *Perf. 14*

828	A117	20c multi	5	5
829	A117	30c multi	5	5
830	A117	50c multi	5	5
831	A117	1fr multi	5	5
832	A117	3fr multi	7	5
833	A117	5fr multi	10	5
834	A117	20fr multi	42	22
835	A117	100fr multi	2.00	1.00
		Nos. 828-835 (8)	2.79	1.52

Nos. 771-778 Overprinted: "in memoriam / WERNHER VON BRAUN / 1912-1977"

1977, Sept. 19 Photo. *Perf. 13½x14*

836	A109	20c multi	5	5
837	A109	30c multi	5	5
838	A109	50c multi	5	5
839	A109	1fr multi	5	5
840	A109	2fr multi	7	5
841	A109	12fr multi	22	12
842	A109	30fr multi	60	30
843	A109	54fr multi	1.20	60
		Nos. 836-843 (8)	2.29	1.27

Wernher von Braun (1912-1977), space and rocket expert.

Souvenir Sheets
Nos. 628-631 Gold Embossed "ESPAMER '77" and ESPAMER Emblem

1977, Oct. 3 Photo. *Perf. 13*

844	A94	20fr multi	40	40
845	A94	30fr multi	60	60
846	A94	50fr multi	1.00	1.00
847	A94	100fr multi	2.00	2.00

ESPAMER '77, International Philatelic Exhibition, Barcelona, Oct. 7-13.

Souvenir Sheet
Christmas Type of 1968

Design: 100fr, Nativity, by Peter Paul Rubens.

1977, Dec. 12 Engr. *Perf. 13½*

848	A48	100fr vio bl	2.00	2.00

Marginal inscription typographed in red.

Boy Scout Playing Flute A118

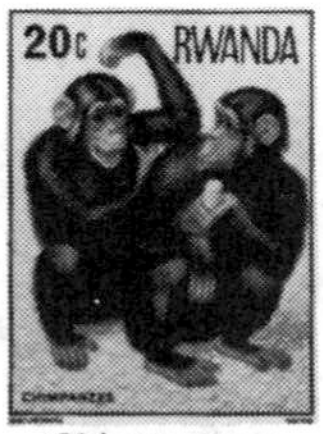

Chimpanzees A119

Designs: 30c, Campfire. 50c, Bridge building. 1fr, Scouts with unit flag. 10fr, Map reading. 18fr, Boating. 26fr, Cooking. 44fr, Lord Baden-Powell.

1978, Feb. 20 Litho. *Perf. 12½*

849	A118	20c yel grn & multi	5	5
850	A118	30c bl & multi	5	5
851	A118	50c lil & multi	5	5
852	A118	1fr bl & multi	5	5
853	A118	10fr pink & multi	20	12
854	A118	18fr lt grn & multi	38	18
855	A118	26fr org & multi	55	25
856	A118	44fr sal & multi	90	45
		Nos. 849-856 (8)	2.23	1.20

10th anniversary of Rwanda Boy Scouts.

1978, Mar. 20 Photo. *Perf. 13½x13*

Designs: 30c, Gorilla. 50c, Colobus monkey. 3fr, Galago. 10fr, Cercopithecus monkey (mone). 26fr, Potto. 60fr, Cercopithecus monkey (griuet). 150fr, Baboon.

857	A119	20c multi	5	5
858	A119	30c multi	5	5
859	A119	50c multi	5	5
860	A119	3fr multi	7	5
861	A119	10fr multi	20	12
862	A119	26fr multi	55	25
863	A119	60fr multi	1.20	55
864	A119	150fr multi	3.00	1.50
		Nos. 857-864 (8)	5.17	2.62

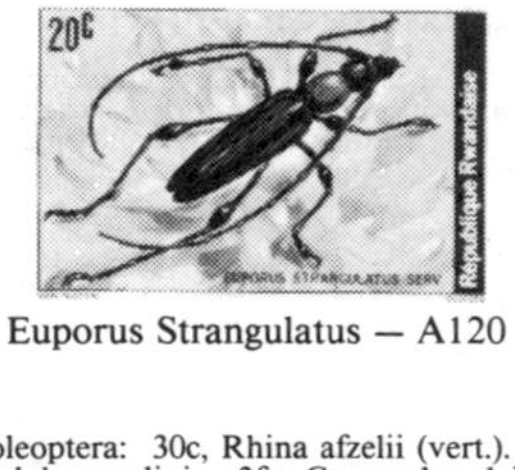

Euporus Strangulatus — A120

Coleoptera: 30c, Rhina afzelii (vert.). 50c, Pentalobus palini. 3fr, Corynodes dejeani (vert.). 10fr, Mecynorhina torquata. 15fr, Mecocerus rhombeus (vert.). 20fr, Macrotoma serripes. 25fr, Neptunides stanleyi (vert.). 26fr, Petrognatha gigas. 100fr, Eudicella gralli (vert.).

1978, May 22 Litho. *Perf. 14*

865	A120	20c multi	5	5
866	A120	30c multi	5	5
867	A120	50c multi	5	5
868	A120	3fr multi	7	5
869	A120	10fr multi	20	14
870	A120	15fr multi	30	20
871	A120	20fr multi	40	25
872	A120	25fr multi	50	28
873	A120	26fr multi	52	30
874	A120	100fr multi	2.00	1.40
		Nos. 865-874 (10)	4.14	2.77

Crossing "River of Poverty" A121

Emblem and: 10fr, 60fr, Men poling boat, facing right. 26fr, like 4fr.

1978, May 29 *Perf. 12½*

875	A121	4fr multi	8	5
876	A121	10fr multi	20	14
877	A121	26fr multi	52	30
878	A121	60fr multi	1.20	80

Natl. Revolutionary Development Movement (M.R.N.D.).

Soccer, Rimet Cup, Flags of Netherlands and Peru — A122

11th World cup, Argentina, June 1-25, (Various Soccer Scenes and Flags of): 30c, Sweden & Spain. 50c, Scotland & Iran. 2fr, Germany & Tunisia. 3fr, Italy & Hungary. 10fr, Brazil and Austria. 34fr, Poland & Mexico. 100fr, Argentina & France.

1978, June 19 *Perf. 13*

879	A122	20c multi	5	5
879A	A122	30c multi	5	5
879B	A122	50c multi	5	5
880	A122	2fr multi	5	5
881	A122	3fr multi	5	5
882	A122	10fr multi	15	10
883	A122	34fr multi	50	32
884	A122	100fr multi	1.50	1.00
		Nos. 879-884 (8)	2.40	1.67

Wright Brothers, Flyer I — A123

History of Aviation: 30c, Santos Dumont and Canard 14, 1906. 50c, Henry Farman and Voisin No. 1, 1908. 1fr, Jan Olieslaegers and Bleriot, 1910. 3fr, Marshal Balbo and Savoia S-17, 1919. 10fr, Charles Lindbergh and Spirit of St. Louis, 1927. 55fr, Hugo Junkers and Junkers JU52/3, 1932. 60fr, Igor Sikorsky and Sikorsky VS 300, 1939. 130fr, Concorde over New York.

1978, Oct. 30 Litho. *Perf. 13½x14*

885	A123	20c multi	5	5
886	A123	30c multi	5	5
887	A123	50c multi	5	5
888	A123	1fr multi	5	5
889	A123	3fr multi	7	5
890	A123	10fr multi	20	14
891	A123	55fr multi	1.10	70
892	A123	60fr multi	1.20	80
		Nos. 885-892 (8)	2.77	1.89

Souvenir Sheet

Perf. 13x13½

893	A123	130fr multi	2.25	2.25

No. 893 contains one stamp 47x35mm.

Souvenir Sheet
Christmas Type of 1968

Design: 200fr, Adoration of the Kings, by Albrecht Dürer (vert.).

1978, Dec. 11 Engr. *Perf. 11½*

894	A48	200fr brown	4.00	4.00

Nos. 532-533, Overprinted "1963 1978" in Black or Blue

1978, Dec. 18 Photo. *Perf. 13½*

895	A83	6fr multi (Bk)	16	7
896	A83	94fr multi (Bl)	1.90	1.25

Org. for African Unity, 15th anniv.

Goats A124

Designs: 20c, Ducks (vert.). 50c, Cock and chickens (vert.). 4fr, Rabbits. 5fr, Pigs (vert.). 15fr, Turkey. 50fr, Sheep and cattle (vert.). 75fr, Bull.

1978, Dec. 28 Litho. *Perf. 14*

897	A124	20c multi	5	5
898	A124	30c multi	5	5
899	A124	50c multi	5	5
900	A124	4fr multi	8	5
901	A124	5fr multi	10	7
902	A124	15fr multi	30	20
903	A124	50fr multi	1.00	65
904	A124	75fr multi	1.50	1.00
		Nos. 897-904 (8)	3.13	2.12

Husbandry Year.

Papilio Demodocus A125

Butterflies: 30c, Precis octavia. 50c, Charaxes smaragdalis. 4fr, Charaxes guderiana. 15fr, Colotis evippe. 30fr, Danaus limniace. 50fr, Byblia acheloia. 150fr, Utetheisa pulchella.

1979, Feb. 19 Photo. *Perf. 14½*

905	A125	20c multi	5	5
906	A125	30c multi	5	5
907	A125	50c multi	5	5
908	A125	4fr multi	8	5
909	A125	15fr multi	30	20
910	A125	30fr multi	60	40
911	A125	50fr multi	1.00	65
912	A125	150fr multi	3.00	2.00
		Nos. 905-912 (8)	5.13	3.45

Euphorbia Grantii, Weavers A126

Design: 60fr, Drummers and Intelsat IV-A.

1979, June 8 Photo. *Perf. 13*

913	A126	40fr multi	80	55
914	A126	60fr multi	1.20	80

Philexafrique II, Libreville, Gabon, June 8-17.

Entandrophragma Excelsum — A127

Trees and Shrubs: 20c, Polyscias fulva. 50c, Ilex mitis. 4fr, Kigelia Africana. 15fr, Ficus thonningi. 20fr, Acacia Senegal. 50fr, Symphonia globulifera. 110fr, Acacia sieberana. 20c, 50c, 15fr, 50fr, vertical.

1979, Aug. 27 *Perf. 14*

915	A127	20c multi	5	5
916	A127	30c multi	5	5
917	A127	50c multi	5	5
918	A127	4 fr multi	6	5
919	A127	15fr multi	22	15
920	A127	20fr multi	30	20
921	A127	50fr multi	75	50
922	A127	110fr multi	1.65	1.10
		Nos. 915-922 (8)	3.13	2.15

Black and White Boys, IYC Emblem A128

Designs: 26fr, 100fr, Children of various races, diff. (vert.).

Perf. 13½x13, 13x13½

1979, Nov. 19 Photo.

923	A128	Block of 8 multi	4.50	3.00
a.		26fr, any single	55	38
924	A128	42fr multi	80	55

Souvenir Sheet

925	A128	100fr multi	2.00	1.50

Intl. Year of the Child. No. 923 printed in sheets of 16 (4x4).

Basket Weaving A129

Perf. 12½x13, 13x12½

1979, Dec. 3 Litho.

926	A129	50c shown	5	5
927	A129	1.50fr Wood carving, vert.	5	5
928	A129	2fr Metal working	5	5
929	A129	10fr Jewelry, vert.	20	10
930	A129	20fr Straw plaiting	40	20
931	A129	26fr Wall painting, vert.	55	25
932	A129	40fr Pottery	80	40
933	A129	100fr Smelting, vert.	2.00	1.00
		Nos. 926-933 (8)	4.10	2.10

Souvenir Sheet

Children of Different Races, Christmas Tree — A130

1979, Dec. 24 Engr. *Perf. 12*

934	A130	200fr ultra & dp mag	4.25	2.00

Christmas; Intl. Year of the Child.

German East Africa No. N5, Hill A131

Sir Rowland Hill (1795-1879), originator of penny postage, and Stamps of Ruanda-Urundi or: 30c, German East Africa No. N23. 50c, German East Africa No. NB9. 3fr, No. 25. 10fr, No. 42. 26fr, No. 123. 100fr, No. B28.

1979, Dec. 31 Litho. *Perf. 14*

935	A131	20c multi	5	5
936	A131	30c multi	5	5
937	A131	50c multi	5	5
938	A131	3fr multi	7	5
939	A131	10fr multi	22	10
940	A131	26fr multi	65	25
941	A131	60fr multi	1.50	60
942	A131	100fr multi	2.50	1.00
		Nos. 935-942 (8)	5.09	2.15

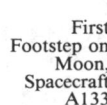

Sarothrura Pulchra A132

Birds of the Nyungwe Forest: 20c Ploceus alienus (vert.). 30c, Regal sunbird (vert.). 3fr, Tockus alboterminatus. 10fr, Pygmy owl (vert.). 26fr, Emerald cuckoo. 60fr, Finch (vert.). 100fr, Stepanoaetus coronatus (vert.).

Perf. 13½x13, 13x13½

1980, Jan. 7 Photo.

943	A132	20c multi	5	5
944	A132	30c multi	5	5
945	A132	50c multi	5	5
946	A132	3fr multi	7	5
947	A132	10fr multi	22	10
948	A132	26fr multi	65	25
949	A132	60fr multi	1.50	60
950	A132	100fr multi	2.50	1.00
		Nos. 943-950 (8)	5.09	2.15

First Footstep on Moon, Spacecraft A133

Spacecraft and Moon Exploration: 1.50fr, Descent onto lunar surface. 8fr, American flag. 30fr, Solar panels. 50fr, Gathering soil samples. 60fr, Adjusting sun screen. 200fr, Landing craft.

1980, Jan. 31 Photo. *Perf. 13x13½*

951	A133	50c multi	5	5
952	A133	1.50fr multi	5	5
953	A133	8fr multi	20	8
954	A133	30fr multi	70	30
955	A133	50fr multi	1.40	50
956	A133	60fr multi	1.50	60
		Nos. 951-956 (6)	3.90	1.58

Souvenir Sheet

957	A133	200fr multi	5.00	2.00

Apollo 11 moon landing, 10th anniv. (1979).

Globe, Butare and 1905 Chicago Club Emblems — A134

Rotary International, 75th Anniversary (Globe, Emblems of Butare or Kigali Clubs and): 30c, San Francisco, 1908. 50c, Chicago, 1910. 4fr, Buffalo, 1911. 15fr, London, 1911. 20fr, Glasgow, 1912. 50fr, Bristol, 1917. 60fr, Rotary International, 1980.

1980, Feb. 23 Litho. *Perf. 13*

958	A134	20c multi	5	5
959	A134	30c multi	5	5
960	A134	50c multi	5	5
961	A134	4fr multi	8	5
962	A134	15fr multi	30	15
963	A134	20fr multi	40	20
964	A134	50fr multi	1.00	50
965	A134	60fr multi	1.20	60
		Nos. 958-965 (8)	3.13	1.65

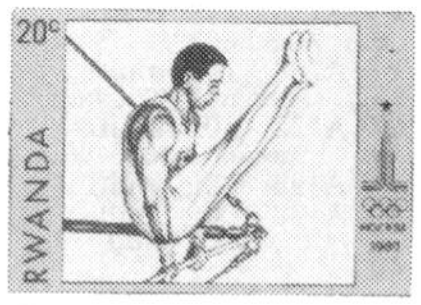

Gymnast, Moscow '80 Emblem A135

1980, Mar. 10 *Perf. 12½*

966	A135	20c shown	5	5
967	A135	30c Basketball	5	5
968	A135	50c Bicycling	5	5
969	A135	3fr Boxing	7	5
970	A135	20fr Archery	50	20
971	A135	26fr Weight lifting	65	25
972	A135	50fr Javelin	1.25	50
973	A135	100fr Fencing	2.50	1.00
		Nos. 966-973 (8)	5.12	2.15

22nd Summer Olympic Games, Moscow, July 19-Aug. 3.

Souvenir Sheet

Amalfi Coast, by Giacinto Gigante — A136

1980, Apr. 28 Photo. *Perf. 13½*

974	A136	200fr multi	5.00	2.00

20th Intl. Philatelic Exhibition, Europa '80, Naples, Apr. 26-May 4.

Geaster Mushroom A137

1980, July 21 Photo. *Perf. 13½*

975	A137	20c shown	5	5
976	A137	30c Lentinus atrobrunneus	5	5
977	A137	50c Gomphus stereoides	5	5
978	A137	4fr Cantharellus cibarius	10	5
979	A137	10fr Stilbothamnium dybowskii	22	10
980	A137	15fr Xeromphalina tenuipes	38	15
981	A137	70fr Podoscypha elegans	1.60	70
982	A137	100fr Mycena	2.25	1.00
		Nos. 975-982 (8)	4.70	2.15

Still Life, by Renoir — A138

Impressionist Painters: 30c, 26fr, At the Theater, by Toulouse-Lautrec (vert.). 50c, 10fr, Seaside Garden, by Monet. 4fr, Mother and Child, by Mary Cassatt (vert.). 5fr, Starry Night, by Van Gogh. 10fr, Dancers at their Toilet, by Degas (vert.). 50fr, The Card Players, by Cezanne. 70fr, Tahitian Women, by Gauguin (vert.). 75fr, like 20c. 100fr, In the Park, by Seurat.

1980, Aug. 4 Litho. *Perf. 14*

983	A138	20c multi	5	5
984	A138	30c multi	5	5
985	A138	50c multi	5	5
986	A138	4fr multi	10	5
a.		Sheet of 2 (4fr, 26fr)	70	70

987 A138 5fr multi 14 5
a. Sheet of 2 (5fr, 75fr) 2.00 2.00
988 A138 10fr multi 22 10
a. Sheet of 2 (10fr, 70fr) 2.00 2.00
989 A138 50fr multi 1.40 50
a. Sheet of 2 (50fr, 10fr) 1.50 1.50
990 A138 70fr multi 1.60 70
991 A138 100fr multi 2.25 1.00
Nos. 983-991 (9) 5.86 2.55

Souvenir Sheet

Virgin of the Harpies, by Andrea Del Sarto — A139

Photogravure and Engraved

1980, Dec. 22 ***Perf. 11½***
992 A139 200fr multi 4.00 2.00

Christmas.

Belgian War of Independence, Engraving — A140

Belgian Independence Sesquicentennial: Engravings of War of Independence.

1980, Dec. 29 **Litho.** ***Perf. 12½***
993 A140 20c pale grn & brn 5 5
994 A140 30c brn org & brn 5 5
995 A140 50c lt bl & brn 5 5
996 A140 9fr yel & brn 18 10
997 A140 10fr brt lil & brn 20 10
998 A140 20fr ap grn & brn 40 20
999 A140 70fr pink & brn 1.40 70
1000 A140 90fr lem & brn 1.75 90
Nos. 993-1000 (8) 4.08 2.15

Swamp Drainage A141

1980, Dec. 31 **Photo.** ***Perf. 13½***
1001 A141 20c shown 5 5
1002 A141 30c Fertilizer shed 5 5
1003 A141 1.50fr Rice fields 5 5
1004 A141 8fr Tree planting 16 8
1005 A141 10fr Terrace planting 20 10
1006 A141 40fr Farm buildings 80 40
1007 A141 90fr Bean cultivation 1.75 90
1008 A141 100fr Tea cultivation 2.00 1.00
Nos. 1001-1008 (8) 5.06 2.63

Soil Conservation Year.

Pavetta Rwandensis A142

1981, Apr. 6 **Photo.** ***Perf. 13x13½***
1009 A142 20c shown 5 5
1010 A142 30c Cyrtorchis praetermissa 5 5
1011 A142 50c Pavonia urens 5 5
1012 A142 4fr Cynorkis kassnerana 8 5
1013 A142 5fr Gardenia ternifolia 10 5
1014 A142 10fr Leptactina platyphylla 20 10
1015 A142 20fr Lobelia petiolata 40 20
1016 A142 40fr Tapinanthus brunneus 80 40
1017 A142 70fr Impatiens niamniamensis 1.40 70
1018 A142 150fr Dissotis rwandensis 3.00 1.50
Nos. 1009-1018 (10) 6.13 3.15

Girl Knitting — A143

SOS Children's Village: Various children.

1981, Apr. 27 ***Perf. 13***
1019 A143 20c multi 5 5
1020 A143 30c multi 5 5
1021 A143 50c multi 5 5
1022 A143 1fr multi 5 5
1023 A143 8fr multi 18 8
1024 A143 10fr multi 22 10
1025 A143 70fr multi 1.50 70
1026 A143 150fr multi 3.25 1.50
Nos. 1019-1026 (8) 5.35 2.58

Carolers, by Norman Rockwell A144

Designs: Saturday Evening Post covers by Norman Rockwell.

1981, May 11 **Litho.** ***Perf. 13½x14***
1027 A144 20c multi 5 5
1028 A144 30c multi 5 5
1029 A144 50c multi 5 5
1030 A144 1fr multi 5 5
1031 A144 8fr multi 16 8
1032 A144 20fr multi 40 20
1033 A144 50fr multi 1.00 50
1034 A144 70fr multi 1.40 70
Nos. 1027-1034 (8) 3.16 1.68

Cerval A145

Designs: Meat-eating animals.

1981, June 29 **Photo.** ***Perf. 13½x14***
1035 A145 20c shown 5 5
1036 A145 30c Jackals 5 5
1037 A145 2fr Genet 5 5
1038 A145 2.50fr Banded mongoose 5 5
1039 A145 10fr Zorille 20 10
1040 A145 15fr White-cheeked otter 30 15
1041 A145 70fr Golden wild cat 1.40 70
1042 A145 200fr Hunting dog, vert. 4.00 2.00
Nos. 1035-1042 (8) 6.10 3.15

Demand, as well as supply, determines a stamp's market value. One is as important as the other.

Drummer Sending Message — A146

1981, Sept. 1 **Litho.** ***Perf. 13***
1043 A146 20c shown 5 5
1044 A146 30c Map, communication waves 5 5
1045 A146 2fr Jet, radar screen 5 5
1046 A146 2.50fr Satellite, teletape 5 5
1047 A146 10fr Dish antenna 20 10
1048 A146 15fr Ship, navigation devices 30 15
1049 A146 70fr Helicopter 1.40 70
1050 A146 200fr Satellite with solar panels 4.00 2.00
Nos. 1043-1050 (8) 6.10 3.15

1500th Birth Anniv. of St. Benedict A147

Paintings and Frescoes of St. Benedict: 20c, Leaving his Parents, Mt. Oliveto Monastery, Maggiore. 30c, Oldest portrait, 10th cent., St. Chrisogone Church, Rome (vert.). 50c, Portrait, Virgin of the Misericord polyptich, Borgo San Sepolcro. 4fr, Giving the Rules of the order to his Monks, Mt. Oliveto Monastery. 5fr, Monks at their Meal, Mt. Oliveto Monastery. 20fr, Portrait, 13th cent., Lower Church of the Holy Spirit, Subiaco (vert.). 70fr, Our Lady in Glory with Sts. Gregory and Benedict, San Gimigniao (vert.). 100fr, Priest Carrying Easter Meal to St. Benedict, by Jan van Coninxloo, 16th cent.

Perf. 13½x13, 13x13½

1981, Nov. 30 **Photo.**
1051 A147 20c multi 5 5
1052 A147 30c multi 5 5
1053 A147 50c multi 5 5
1054 A147 4fr multi 8 5
1055 A147 5fr multi 10 5
1056 A147 20fr multi 40 20
1057 A147 70fr multi 1.40 65
1058 A147 100fr multi 2.00 2.00
Nos. 1051-1058 (8) 4.13 3.10

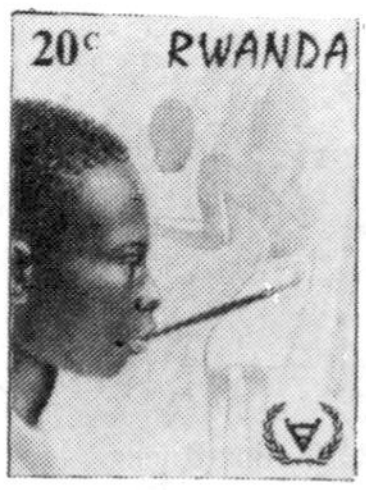

Intl. Year of the Disabled A148

1981, Dec. 7 **Litho.** ***Perf. 13***
1059 A148 20c Painting 5 5
1060 A148 30c Soccer 5 5
1061 A148 4.50fr Crocheting 10 5
1062 A148 5fr Painting vase 10 5
1063 A148 10fr Sawing 20 10
1064 A148 60fr Sign language 1.20 65
1065 A148 70fr Doing puzzle 1.40 80
1066 A148 100fr Juggling 2.00 1.10
Nos. 1059-1066 (8) 5.10 2.85

Souvenir Sheet

Christmas A149

Photo. & Engr.

1981, Dec. 21 ***Perf. 13½***
1067 A149 200fr Adoration of the Kings, by van der Goes 4.00 2.00

Natl. Rural Water Supply Year — A150

1981, Dec. 28 **Litho.** ***Perf. 12½***
1068 A150 20c Deer drinking 5 5
1069 A150 30c Women carrying water, vert. 5 5
1070 A150 50c Pipeline 5 5
1071 A150 10fr Filing pan, vert. 20 10
1072 A150 19fr Drinking 40 22
1073 A150 70fr Mother, child, vert. 1.40 65
1074 A150 100fr Lake pumping station, vert. 2.00 1.00
Nos. 1068-1074 (7) 4.15 2.12

World Food Day, Oct. 16, 1981 A151

1982, Jan. 25 **Litho.** ***Perf. 13***
1075 A151 20c Cattle 5 5
1076 A151 30c Bee 5 5
1077 A151 50c Fish 5 5
1078 A151 1fr Avocados 5 5
1079 A151 8fr Boy eating banana 16 10
1080 A151 20fr Sorghum 40 20
1081 A151 70fr Vegetables 1.40 65
1082 A151 100fr Balanced diet 2.00 1.00
Nos. 1075-1082 (8) 4.16 2.15

Hibiscus Berberidifolius — A152

1982, June 14 **Litho.** ***Perf. 13***
1083 A152 20c shown 5 5
1084 A152 30c Hypericum lanceolatum, vert. 5 5
1085 A152 50c Canarina eminii 5 5
1086 A152 4fr Polygala ruwenxoriensis 8 5
1087 A152 10fr Kniphofia grantii, vert. 20 10
1088 A152 35fr Euphorbia candelabrum, vert. 70 35
1089 A152 70fr Disa erubescens, vert. 1.40 65
1090 A152 80fr Gloriosa simplex 1.60 1.00
Nos. 1083-1090 (8) 4.13 2.30

20th Anniv. of Independence — A153

1982, June 28
1091 A153 10fr Flags 20 10
1092 A153 20fr Hands releasing doves 40 20
1093 A153 30fr Flag, handshake 60 30
1094 A153 50fr Govt. buildings 1.00 50

1982 World Cup — A154

Designs: Various soccer players.

1982, July 6 **Perf. 14x14½**

1095	A154	20c	multi	5	5
1096	A154	30c	multi	5	5
1097	A154	1.50fr	multi	5	5
1098	A154	8fr	multi	16	10
1099	A154	10fr	multi	20	10
1100	A154	20fr	multi	40	20
1101	A154	70fr	multi	1.40	65
1102	A154	90fr	multi	1.90	90
			Nos. 1095-1102 (8)	4.21	2.10

TB Bacillus Centenary — A155

1982, Nov. 22 **Litho.** **Perf. 14½**

1103	A155	10fr	Microscope, slide	20	10
1104	A155	20fr	Serum, slide	40	20
1105	A155	70fr	Lungs, slide	1.40	65
1106	A155	100fr	Koch	2.00	1.00

Souvenir Sheets

Madam Recamier, by David — A156

PHILEXFRANCE '82 Intl. Stamp Exhibition, Paris, June 11-21: No. 1108, St. Anne and Virgin and Child with Franciscan Monk, by H. van der Goes. No. 1109, Liberty Guiding the People, by Delacroix. No. 1110, Pygmalion, by P. Delvaux. Sizes: 130x90mm.

1982, Dec. 11 **Perf. 13½**

1107	A156	40fr	multi	80	42
1108	A156	40fr	multi	80	42
1109	A156	60fr	multi	1.20	55
1110	A156	60fr	multi	1.20	55

Souvenir Sheet

Rest During the Flight to Egypt, by Murillo A157

1982, Dec. 20 **Photo. & Engr.**

1111	A157	200fr	car rose	4.00	2.00

Christmas.

10th Anniv. of UN Conference on Human Environment — A158

1982, Dec. 27 **Litho.** **Perf. 14**

1112	A158	20c	Elephants	5	5
1113	A158	30c	Lion	5	5
1114	A158	50c	Flower	5	5
1115	A158	4fr	Bull	8	5
1116	A158	5fr	Deer	10	5
1117	A158	10fr	Flower, diff.	20	10
1118	A158	20fr	Zebras	40	20
1119	A158	40fr	Crowned cranes	80	40
1120	A158	50fr	Bird	1.00	50
1121	A158	70fr	Woman pouring coffee beans	1.40	65
			Nos. 1112-1121 (10)	4.13	2.10

Scouting Year A159

Perf. 13½x14½

1983, Jan. 17 **Photo.**

1122	A159	20c	Animal first aid	5	5
1123	A159	30c	Camp	5	5
1124	A159	1.50fr	Campfire	5	5
1125	A159	8fr	Scout giving sign	16	10
1126	A159	10fr	Knot	20	10
1127	A159	20fr	Camp, diff.	40	20
1128	A159	70fr	Chopping wood	1.40	65
1129	A159	90fr	Sign, map	1.75	90
			Nos. 1122-1129 (8)	4.06	2.10

Nectar-sucking Birds — A160

Perf. 14x14½, 14½x14

1983, Jan. 31 **Litho.**

1130	A160	20c	Angola nectar bird	5	5
1131	A160	30c	Royal nectar birds	5	5
1132	A160	50c	Johnston's nectar bird	5	5
1133	A160	4fr	Bronze nectar birds	8	5
1134	A160	5fr	Collared souimangas	10	5
1135	A160	10fr	Blue-headed nectar bird	30	10
1136	A160	20fr	Purple-bellied nectar bird	40	20
1137	A160	40fr	Copper nectar birds	80	40
1138	A160	50fr	Olive-bellied nectar birds	1.00	50
1139	A160	70fr	Red-breasted nectar bird	1.40	65
			Nos. 1130-1139 (10)	4.23	2.10

30c, 4fr, 10fr, 40fr, 70fr horiz. Inscribed 1982.

Soil Erosion Prevention A161

1983, Feb. 14 **Perf. 14½**

1140	A161	20c	Driving cattle	5	5
1141	A161	30c	Pineapple field	5	5
1142	A161	50c	Interrupted ditching	5	5
1143	A161	9fr	Hedges, ditches	18	10
1144	A161	10fr	Reafforestation	20	10
1145	A161	20fr	Anti-erosion barriers	40	20
1146	A161	30fr	Contour planting	60	30
1147	A161	50fr	Terracing	1.00	50
1148	A161	60fr	Protection of river banks	1.20	60
1149	A161	70fr	Fallow, planted strips	1.40	65
			Nos. 1140-1149 (10)	5.13	2.60

Cardinal Cardijn (1882-1967) A162

Gorilla A163

Young Catholic Workers Movement Activities. Inscribed 1982.

1983, Feb. 22 **Perf. 12½x13**

1150	A162	20c	Feeding ducks	5	5
1151	A162	30c	Harvesting tobacco	5	5
1152	A162	50c	Carrying melons	5	5
1153	A162	10fr	Teacher	20	10
1154	A162	19fr	Shoemakers	40	18
1155	A162	20fr	Growing millet	40	20
1156	A162	70fr	Embroidering	1.40	65
1157	A162	80fr	Cardinal Cardijn	1.60	80
			Nos. 1150-1157 (8)	4.15	2.08

1983, Mar. 14 **Perf. 14**

Various gorillas. Nos. 1158-1163 horiz.

1158	A163	20c	multi	5	5
1159	A163	30c	multi	5	5
1160	A163	9.50fr	multi	18	10
1161	A163	10fr	multi	20	14
1162	A163	20fr	multi	40	20
1163	A163	30fr	multi	60	30
1164	A163	60fr	multi	1.20	60
1165	A163	70fr	multi	1.40	65
			Nos. 1158-1165 (8)	4.08	2.09

Souvenir Sheet

The Granduca Madonna, by Raphael A164

Typo. & Engr.

1983, Dec. 19 **Perf. 11½**

1166	A164	200fr	multi	2.50	1.40

Christmas.

Local Trees — A165

1984, Jan. 15 **Litho.** **Perf. 13½x13**

1167	A165	20c	Hagenia abyssinica	5	5
1168	A165	30c	Dracaena steudneri	5	5
1169	A165	50c	Phoenix reclinata	5	5
1170	A165	10fr	Podocarpus milanjianus	14	7
1171	A165	19fr	Entada abyssinica	25	14
1172	A165	70fr	Parinari excelsa	90	45
1173	A165	100fr	Newtonia buchananii	1.40	65
1174	A165	200fr	Acacia gerrardi, vert.	2.50	1.40
			Nos. 1167-1174 (8)	5.34	2.86

World Communications Year — A166

1984, May 21 **Litho.** **Perf. 12½**

1175	A166	20c	Train	5	5
1176	A166	30c	Ship	5	5
1177	A166	4.50fr	Radio	7	5
1178	A166	10fr	Telephone	14	7
1179	A166	15fr	Mail	20	10
1180	A166	50fr	Jet	65	35
1181	A166	70fr	Satellite, TV screen	90	45
1182	A166	100fr	Satellite	1.40	65
			Nos. 1175-1182 (8)	3.46	1.77

1st Manned Flight Bicent. — A167

Historic flights: 20c, Le Martial, Sept. 19, 1783. 30c, La Montgolfiere, Nov. 21, 1783. 50c, Charles and Robert, Dec. 1, 1783, and Blanchard, Mar. 2, 1784. 9fr, Jean-Pierre Blanchard and wife in balloon. 10fr, Blanchard and Jeffries, 1785. 50fr, E. Demuyter, 1937. 80fr, Propane gas balloons. 200fr, Abruzzo, Anderson and Newman, 1978.

1984, June 4 **Litho.** **Perf. 13**

1183	A167	20c	multi	5	5
1184	A167	30c	multi	5	5
1185	A167	50c	multi	5	5
1186	A167	9fr	multi	12	7
1187	A167	10fr	multi	14	7
1188	A167	50fr	multi	65	35
1189	A167	80fr	multi	1.00	50
1190	A167	200fr	multi	2.50	1.40
			Nos. 1183-1190 (8)	4.56	2.54

1984 Summer Olympics — A168

1984, July 16 **Perf. 14**

1191	A168	20c	Equestrian	5	5
1192	A168	30c	Wind surfing	5	5
1193	A168	50c	Soccer	5	5
1194	A168	9fr	Swimming	12	7
1195	A168	10fr	Field hockey	14	7
1196	A168	40fr	Fencing	55	25
1197	A168	80fr	Running	1.10	55
1198	A168	200fr	Boxing	2.50	1.40
			Nos. 1191-1198 (8)	4.56	2.49

For unused stamps, more recent issues are valued as never hinged, with the beginning point determined on a country-by-country basis. Notes to show the beginning points are prominently placed in the text.

Zebras and Buffaloes A169

1984, Nov. 26 Litho. *Perf. 13*

1199	A169	20c	Zebra with colt	5	5
1200	A169	30c	Buffalo with calf, vert.	5	5
1201	A169	50c	Two zebras, vert.	5	5
1202	A169	9fr	Zebras fighting	12	7
1203	A169	10fr	Buffalo, vert.	14	7
1204	A169	80fr	Zebra herd	1.00	55
1205	A169	100fr	Zebra, vert.	1.25	60
1206	A169	200fr	Buffalo	2.50	1.25
			Nos. 1199-1206 (8)	5.16	2.69

Souvenir Sheet

Christmas 1984 A170

1984, Dec. 24 Typo. & Engr.

1207	A170	200fr	Virgin and Child, by Correggio	2.50	1.25

Gorilla Gorilla Beringei — A171

1985, Mar. 25 Litho. *Perf. 13*

1208	A171	10fr	Adults and young	14	7
1209	A171	15fr	Adults	20	10
1210	A171	25fr	Female holding young	35	16
1211	A171	30fr	Three adults	40	20

Souvenir Sheet

1212	A171	200fr	Baby climbing branch, vert.	2.50	1.40

No. 1212 contains one stamp 37x52mm, perf. 11½x12.

Self-Sufficiency in Food Production — A172

Designs: 20c, Raising chickens and turkeys. 30c, Pineapple harvest. 50c, Animal husbandry. 9fr, Grain products. 10fr, Education. 50fr, Sowing grain. 80fr, Food reserves. 100fr, Banana harvest.

1985, Mar. 30

1213	A172	20c	multi	5	5
1214	A172	30c	multi	5	5
1215	A172	50c	multi	5	5
1216	A172	9fr	multi	12	7
1217	A172	10fr	multi	14	7
1218	A172	50fr	multi	65	35
1219	A172	80fr	multi	1.00	50
1220	A172	100fr	multi	1.40	65
			Nos. 1213-1220 (8)	3.46	1.79

Natl. Redevelopment Movement, 10th Anniv. — A173

1985, July 5

1221	A173	10fr	multi	14	7
1222	A173	30fr	multi	40	20
1223	A173	70fr	multi	90	45

UN, 40th Anniv. A174

1985, July 25

1224	A174	50fr	multi	65	35
1225	A174	100fr	multi	1.40	65

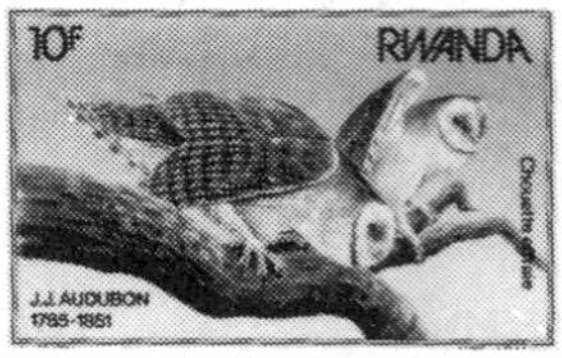

Audubon Birth Bicent. — A175

Illustrations of North American bird species by John J. Audubon.

1985, Sept. 18

1226	A175	10fr	Barn owl	14	7
1227	A175	20fr	White-faced owl	25	14
1228	A175	40fr	Red-breasted hummingbird	55	25
1229	A175	80fr	Warbler	1.00	50

Intl. Youth Year A176

1985, Oct. 14

1230	A176	7fr	Education and agriculture	10	5
1231	A176	9fr	Bicycling	12	7
1232	A176	44fr	Construction	55	28
1233	A176	80fr	Schoolroom	1.00	50

Nos. 1122-1129 Ovptd. in Green or Rose Violet with the Girl Scout Trefoil and "1910/1985"

1985, Nov. 25 *Perf. 13½x14½*

1234	A159	20c	multi	5	5
1235	A159	30c	multi (RV)	5	5
1236	A159	1.50fr	multi	5	5
1237	A159	8fr	multi (RV)	10	5
1238	A159	10fr	multi	14	7
1239	A159	20fr	multi	25	14
1240	A159	70fr	multi (RV)	90	45
1241	A159	90fr	multi	1.10	60
			Nos. 1234-1241 (8)	2.64	1.46

Natl. Girl Scout Movement, 75th anniv.

Souvenir Sheet

Adoration of the Magi, by Titian — A177

Photo. & Engr.

1985, Dec. 24 *Perf. 11½*

1242	A177	200fr	violet	2.50	1.40

Christmas.

Transportation and Communication — A178

1986, Jan. 27 Litho. *Perf. 13*

1243	A178	10fr	Articulated truck	14	7
1244	A178	30fr	Hand-canceling letters	40	20
1245	A178	40fr	Kigali Satellite Station	55	25

Size: 52x34mm

1246	A178	80fr	Kayibanda Airport, Kigali	1.00	50

Nos. 1141-1149 Surcharged or Ovptd. with Silver Bar and "ANNEE 1986 / INTENSIFICATION AGRICOLE"

1986, May 5 Litho. *Perf. 14½*

1247	A161	9fr	#1143	18	10
1248	A161	10fr	on 30c #1141	20	10
1249	A161	10fr	on 50c #1142	20	10
1250	A161	10fr	#1144	20	10
1251	A161	20fr	#1145	40	20
1252	A161	30fr	#1146	60	30
1253	A161	50fr	#1147	1.00	50
1254	A161	60fr	#1148	1.20	60
1255	A161	70fr	#1149	1.40	70
			Nos. 1247-1255 (9)	5.38	2.70

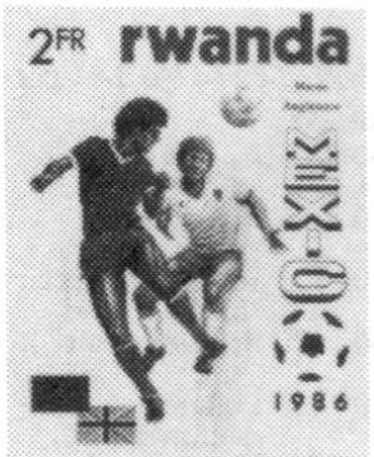

1986 World Cup Soccer Championships, Mexico — A179

Various soccer plays, natl. flags.

1986, June 16 *Perf. 13*

1256	A179	2fr	Morocco, England	5	5
1257	A179	4fr	Paraguay, Iraq	8	5
1258	A179	5fr	Brazil, Spain	10	5
1259	A179	10fr	Italy, Argentina	20	10
1260	A179	40fr	Mexico, Belgium	80	40
1261	A179	45fr	France, USSR	90	45
			Nos. 1256-1261 (6)	2.13	1.10

Akagera Natl. Park — A180

1986, Dec. 15 Litho. *Perf. 13*

1262	A180	4fr	Antelopes	8	5
1263	A180	7fr	Shoebills	14	8
1264	A180	9fr	Cape elands	18	10
1265	A180	10fr	Giraffe	20	10
1266	A180	80fr	Elephants	1.60	80
1267	A180	90fr	Crocodiles	1.80	90

Size: 48x34mm

1268	A180	100fr	Weaver birds	2.00	1.00
1269	A180	100fr	Pelican, zebras	2.00	1.00
			Nos. 1262-1269 (8)	8.00	4.03

Nos. 1268-1269 printed se-tenant in a continuous design with label picturing map on right.

Christmas, Intl. Peace Year — A181

1986, Dec. 24 Litho. *Perf. 13*

1270	A181	10fr	shown	20	10
1271	A181	15fr	Dove, Earth	30	15
1272	A181	30fr	like 10fr	60	30
1273	A181	70fr	like 15fr	1.40	70

UN Child Survival Campaign A182

1987, Feb. 13

1274	A182	4fr	Breast feeding	8	5
1275	A182	6fr	Rehydration therapy	12	6
1276	A182	10fr	Immunization	20	10
1277	A182	70fr	Growth monitoring	1.40	70

Year of Natl. Self-sufficiency in Food Production — A183

1987, June 15 Litho. *Perf. 13*

1278	A183	5fr	Farm	10	5
1279	A183	7fr	Storing produce	14	8
1280	A183	40fr	Boy carrying basket of fish, produce	80	40
1281	A183	60fr	Tropical fruit	1.20	60

Nos. 1279-1281 vert.

Natl. Independence, 25th Anniv. — A184

Designs: 10fr, Pres. Habyarimana, soldiers, farmers. 40fr, Pres. officiating government session. 70fr, Pres., Pope John Paul II. 100fr, Pres., vert..

1987, July 1

1283 A184 10fr multi 20 10
1284 A184 40fr multi 80 40
1285 A184 70fr multi 1.40 70
1286 A184 100fr multi 2.00 1.00

Fruit
A185

1987, Sept. 28

1287 A185 10fr Bananas, vert. 20 10
1288 A185 40fr Pineapples 80 40
1289 A185 80fr Papayas 1.60 80
1290 A185 90fr Avocados 1.80 90
1291 A185 100fr Strawberries, vert. 2.00 1.00
Nos. 1287-1291 (5) 6.40 3.20

Leopards — A186

1987, Nov. 18 **Litho.** ***Perf. 13***

1292 A186 50fr Female, cub 1.00 50
1293 A186 50fr Three cubs playing 1.00 50
1294 A186 50fr Adult attaching gazelle 1.00 50
1295 A186 50fr In tree 1.00 50
1296 A186 50fr Leaping from tree 1.00 50
a. Strip of 5, Nos. 1292-1296 5.00 2.50
Nos. 1291-1296 (6) 7.00 3.50

Intl. Year of the Volunteer — A187

1987, Dec. 12

1297 A187 5fr Constructing village water system 10 5
1298 A187 12fr Education, vert. 24 12
1299 A187 20fr Modern housing, vert. 40 20
1300 A187 60fr Animal husbandry, vert. 1.20 60

Souvenir Sheet

Virgin and Child, by Fra Angelico (c. 1387-1455) — A188

1987, Dec. 24 **Engr.** ***Perf. 11½***

1301 A188 200fr deep mag & dull blue 4.00 2.00

Christmas.

Maintenance of the Rural Economy Year — A189

1988, June 13 **Litho.** ***Perf. 13***

1302 A189 10fr Furniture store 26 14
1303 A189 40fr Dairy farm 1.05 52
1304 A189 60fr Produce market 1.60 80
1305 A189 80fr Fruit market 2.10 1.05

Primates, Nyungwe Forest — A190

1988 **Litho.** ***Perf. 13***

1306 A190 2fr Chimpanzee 5 5
1307 A190 3fr Black and white colobus 8 5
1308 A190 10fr Pygmy galago 25 12
1309 A190 90fr Cercopithecidae ascagne 2.35 1.20

1988 Summer Olympics, Seoul A191

1988

1310 A191 5fr Boxing 14 8
1311 A191 7fr Relay 18 10
1312 A191 8fr Table tennis 22 12
1313 A191 10fr Women's running 28 14
1314 A191 90fr Hurdles 2.35 1.20
Nos. 1310-1314 (5) 3.17 1.64

Organization of African Unity, 25th Anniv. — A192

1988, Nov. 30 **Litho.** ***Perf. 13***

1315 A192 5fr shown 14 8
1316 A192 7fr Handskake, map 18 10
1317 A192 8fr "OAU" in brick, map 20 10
1318 A192 90fr Slogan 2.35 1.20

Souvenir Sheet

Detail of The Virgin and the Soup, by Paolo Veronese — A193

1988, Dec. 23 **Typo.** ***Perf. 13½***

1319 A193 200fr lt vio, grnsh bl & lake 5.25 5.25

Christmas.

Intl. Red Cross and Red Crescent Organizations, 125th Annivs. — A194

1988, Dec. 30 **Litho.** ***Perf. 13***

1320 A194 10fr Refugees 25 12
1321 A194 30fr First aid 78 40
1322 A194 40fr Elderly 1.05 52
1323 A194 100fr Travelling doctor 2.60 1.30

Nos. 1322-1323 vert.

Medicinal Plants — A195

1989, Feb. 15 **Litho.** ***Perf. 13***

1324 A195 5fr Plectranthus barbatus 14 7
1325 A195 10fr Tetradenia riparia 28 14
1326 A195 20fr Hygrophila auriculata 55 28
1327 A195 40fr Datura stramonium 1.10 55
1328 A195 50fr Pavetta ternifolia 1.40 70
Nos. 1324-1328 (5) 3.47 1.74

SEMI-POSTAL STAMPS

No. 305 Surcharged in Black and Overprinted in Brown: "SECHERESSE/SOLIDARITE AFRICAINE"

1973, Aug. 23 **Photo.** ***Perf. 13***

B1 A53 100fr + 50fr multi 2.50 2.25

African solidarity in drought emergency.

Nos. 349-350 Surcharged and Overprinted Like Nos. 693-698

1975, Nov. 10 **Litho.** ***Perf. 13***

B2 A60 50fr + 25fr multi 1.50 1.00
B3 A60 90fr + 25fr multi 2.00 1.50

African solidarity in drought emergency.

AIR POST STAMPS

African Postal Union Issue, 1967
Common Design Type

1967, Sept. 18 **Engr.** ***Perf. 13***

C1 CD124 6fr brn, rose cl & gray 12 8
C2 CD124 18fr brt lil, ol brn & plum 40 30
C3 CD124 30fr grn, dp bl & red 65 55

PHILEXAFRIQUE Issue

Alexandre Lenoir, by Jacques L. David
AP1

1968, Dec. 30 **Photo.** ***Perf. 12½***

C4 AP1 100fr emer & multi 1.90 80

Issued to publicize PHILEXAFRIQUE, Philatelic exhibition in Abidjan, Feb. 14-23, 1969. Printed with alternating emerald label.

2nd PHILEXAFRIQUE Issue

Ruanda-Urundi No. 123, Cowherd and Lake Victoria — AP2

1969, Feb. 14 **Litho.** ***Perf. 14***

C5 AP2 50fr multi 90 80

Issued to commemorate the opening of PHILEXAFRIQUE, Abidjan, Feb. 14.

Painting Type of Regular Issue

Paintings and Music: 50fr, The Music Lesson, by Fragonard. 100fr, Angels' Concert, by Memling (horiz.).

1969, Mar. 31 **Photo.** ***Perf. 13***

C6 A49 50fr gold & multi 80 38
C7 A49 100fr gold & multi 1.90 1.60

African Postal Union Issue, 1971
Common Design Type

Design: 100fr, Woman and child of Rwanda and UAMPT Building, Brazzaville, Congo.

1971, Nov. 13 ***Perf. 13x13½***

C8 CD135 100fr bl & multi 1.75 1.75

No. C8 Overprinted in Red

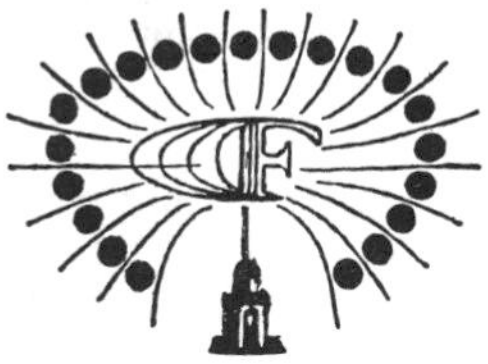

a

LIÈGE
ACCUEILLE
LES PAYS
DE LANGUE
FRANCAISE
1973
b

1973, Sept. 17 Photo. *Perf. 13x13½*

C9	CD135(a) 100fr multi	2.00	2.00
C10	CD135(b) 100fr multi	2.00	2.00

3rd Conference of French-speaking countries, Liege, Sept. 15-Oct. 14. Overprints alternate checkerwise in same sheet.

Sassenage Castle, Grenoble — AP3

1977, June 20 Litho. *Perf. 12½*

C11	AP3 50fr multi	1.00	80

10th anniversary of International French Language Council.

Philexafrique II-Essen Issue
Common Design Types

Designs: No. C12, Okapi and Rwanda No. 239. No. C13, Woodpecker and Oldenburg No. 4.

1978, Nov. 1 Litho. *Perf. 12½*

C12	CD138 30fr multi	60	50
C13	CD139 30fr multi	60	50

Nos. C12-C13 printed se-tenant.

RYUKYU ISLANDS

LOCATION — Chain of 63 islands between Japan and Formosa, separating the East China Sea from the Pacific Ocean.
GOVT. — Semi-autonomous under United States administration.
AREA — 848 sq. mi.
POP. — 945,465 (1970).
CAPITAL — Naha, Okinawa.

The Ryukyus were part of Japan until American forces occupied them in 1945. The islands reverted to Japan May 15, 1972.

Before the general issue of 1948, a number of provisional stamps were used. These included a mimeographed-handstamped adhesive for Kume Island, and various current stamps of Japan handstamped with the personal chops of the postmasters of Okinawa, Amami, Miyako and Yaeyama. Although authorized by American authorities, these provisionals were local in nature, so are omitted in the listings that follow. They are listed in Scott's United States Specialized Catalogue.

100 Sen = 1 Yen
100 Cents = 1 Dollar (1958)

Catalogue values for all unused stamps in this country are for Never Hinged items.

Cycad — A1

Lily — A2

Sailing Ship
A3

Farmer
A4

Wmk. 257

1948-49 Wmk. 257 Typo. *Perf. 13*
Second Printing

1	A1	5s magenta	1.25	1.25
2	A2	10s yel grn	3.25	2.75
3	A1	20s yel grn	2.25	2.00
4	A3	30s vermilion	1.25	1.25
5	A2	40s magenta	1.25	1.25
6	A3	50s ultra	2.75	2.75
7	A4	1y ultra	3.00	3.00
		Nos. 1-7 (7)	15.00	14.25

First Printing

1a	A1	5s magenta	2.25	4.00
2a	A2	10s yel grn	1.40	2.50
3a	A1	20s yel grn	1.40	2.50
4a	A3	30s vermilion	2.25	3.50
5a	A2	40s magenta	45.00	45.00
6a	A3	50s ultra	2.25	4.00
7a	A4	1y ultra	250.00	225.00
		Nos. 1a-7a (7)	304.55	286.50

First printing: thick yellow gum, dull colors, rough perforations, grayish paper. Second printing (1949): white gum, sharp colors, cleancut perforations, white paper.

Roof
Tiles — A5

Ryukyu
University — A6

Designs: 1y, Ryukyu girl. 2y, Shuri Castle. 3y, Guardian dragon. 4y, Two women. 5y, Sea shells.

1950 Unwmk. Photo. *Perf. 13x13½*

8	A5	50s dk car rose	20	20
9	A5	1y dp bl	2.25	2.00
10	A5	2y rose vio	8.25	5.00
11	A5	3y car rose	16.00	5.00
12	A5	4y grnsh gray	10.00	4.25
13	A5	5y bl grn	4.50	3.75
		Nos. 8-13 (6)	41.20	20.20

A 1958 printing of No. 8 is on whiter paper with colorless gum and has an 8-character imprint in the sheet margin. The original 1950 printing is on toned paper with yellowish gum and has a 5-character imprint.

1951, Feb. 12 *Perf. 13½x13*

14	A6	3y red brn	37.50	12.00

Opening of Ryukyu University, Feb. 12.

Pine Tree — A7

1951, Feb. 19 *Perf. 13*

15	A7	3y dk grn	32.50	10.00

Reforestation Week, Feb. 18-24.

Nos. 8 and 10
Surcharged in Black

Three types of 10y surcharge:
I - Narrow-spaced rules, "10" normal spacing.
II - Wide-spaced rules, "10" normal spacing.
III - Rules and "10" both wide-spaced.

1952 *Perf. 13x13½*

16	A5	10y on 50s dk car rose (II)	8.00	8.00
a.		Type I	24.00	24.00
b.		Type III	30.00	30.00
17	A5	100y on 2y rose vio	1,750.	1,250.

There are two types of surcharge on No. 17.

Dove, Bean
Sprout and
Map — A8

Madanbashi
Bridge — A9

1952, Apr. 1 *Perf. 13½x13*

18	A8	3y dp plum	57.50	18.00

Establishment of the Government of the Ryukyu Islands (GRI), Apr. 1, 1952.

1952-53

Designs: 2y, Main Hall, Shuri Castle. 3y, Shurei Gate. 6y, Stone Gate, Sogenji temple, Naha. 10y, Benzaiten-do temple. 30y, Sonohan Utaki (altar) at Shuri Castle. 50y, Tamaudum (royal mausoleum), Shuri. 100y, Stone Bridge, Hosho Pond.

19	A9	1y red	20	20
20	A9	2y green	28	28
21	A9	3y aqua	35	35
22	A9	6y blue	1.40	2.10
23	A9	10y crim rose	2.25	35
24	A9	30y ol grn	7.75	5.00
a.		30y light olive grn ('58)	27.50	
25	A9	50y rose vio	6.75	4.00
26	A9	100y claret	8.50	2.50
		Nos. 19-26 (8)	27.48	14.78

Issue dates: 1y, 2y and 3y, Nov. 20, 1952. Others, Jan. 20, 1953.

Reception at
Shuri
Castle — A10

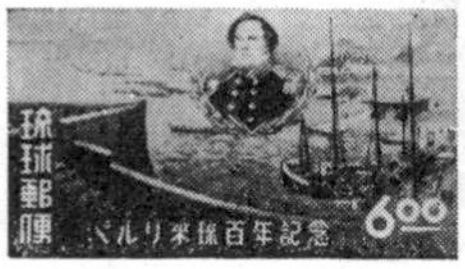

Perry and
American
Fleet
A11

Perf. 13½x13, 13x13½
1953, May 26

27	A10	3y dp mag	7.50	4.25
28	A11	6y dl bl	70	70

Centenary of the arrival of Commodore Matthew Calbraith Perry at Naha, Okinawa.

Chofu Ota and
Pencil-shaped
Matrix — A12

Shigo Toma
and
Pen — A13

1953, Oct. 1 *Perf. 13½x13*

29	A12	4y yel brn	6.75	2.50

3rd Newspaper Week.

1954, Oct. 1

30	A13	4y blue	7.25	3.50

4th Newspaper Week.

Ryukyu
Pottery
A14

Noguni Shrine
and Sweet
Potato Plant
A15

Designs: 15y, Lacquerware. 20y, Textile design.

1954-55 Photo. *Perf. 13*

31	A14	4y brown	65	32
32	A14	15y ver ('55)	2.25	1.65
33	A14	20y yel org ('55)	1.65	1.40

1955, Nov. 26

34	A15	4y blue	8.00	4.00

350th anniv. of the introduction of the sweet potato to the Ryukyu Islands.

Stylized Trees
A16

Willow
Dance
A17

1956, Feb. 18 Unwmk.

35	A16	4y bluish grn	8.00	4.00

Arbor Week, Feb. 18-24.

1956, May 1 *Perf. 13*

Design: 8y, Straw hat dance. 14y, Dancer in warrior costume with fan.

36	A17	5y rose lil	70	40
37	A17	8y vio bl	1.75	1.40
38	A17	14y redsh brn	2.00	1.75

Telephone — A18

1956, June 8

39	A18	4y vio bl	11.50	5.75

Establishment of dial telephone system.

Garland of Pine, Bamboo and Plum — A19

Map of Okinawa and Pencil Rocket — A20

1956, Dec. 1 *Perf. 13½x13*

40	A19	2y multi	1.65	80

New Year, 1957.

1957, Oct. 1 Photo. *Perf. 13½x13*

41	A20	4y dp vio bl	50	50

7th annual Newspaper Week, Oct. 1-7.

Phoenix — A21

1957, Dec. 1 Unwmk. *Perf. 13*

42	A21	2y multi	25	25

New Year, 1958.

Ryukyu Stamps — A22

1958, July 1 *Perf. 13½*

43	A22	4y multi	80	60

10th anniversary of first Ryukyu stamps.

Yen Symbol and Dollar Sign — A23

1958, Sept. 16 Typo. *Perf. 11*
Without Gum

44	A23	½c orange	42	42
a.		Imperf., pair	*950.00*	
b.		Horiz. pair, imperf. btwn.	*80.00*	
c.		Vert. pair, imperf. btwn.	*100.00*	
45	A23	1c yel grn	85	55
a.		Horiz. pair, imperf. btwn.	*120.00*	
b.		Vert. pair, imperf. btwn.	*90.00*	
46	A23	2c dk bl	1.10	1.00
a.		Horiz. pair, imperf. btwn.	*150.00*	
b.		Vert. pair, imperf. btwn.	*1,200.*	
47	A23	3c dp car	85	55
a.		Horiz. pair, imperf. btwn.	*120.00*	
b.		Vert. pair, imperf. btwn.	*90.00*	
48	A23	4c brt grn	95	85
a.		Horiz. pair, imperf. btwn.	*500.00*	
b.		Vert. pair, imperf. btwn.	*150.00*	
49	A23	5c orange	1.90	1.90
a.		Horiz. pair, imperf. btwn.	*125.00*	
b.		Vert. pair, imperf. btwn.	*750.00*	
50	A23	10c aqua	2.75	2.75
a.		Horiz. pair, imperf. btwn.	*200.00*	
b.		Vert. pair, imperf. btwn.	*150.00*	
51	A23	25c brt vio bl	3.75	3.75
a.		Gummed paper ('61)	6.00	
b.		Horiz. pair, imperf. btwn.	*1,400.*	
c.		Vert. pair, imperf. btwn.	*1,000.*	
52	A23	50c gray	9.00	6.00
a.		Gummed paper ('61)	8.25	
b.		Horiz. pair, imperf. btwn.	*1,200.*	
53	A23	$1 rose lil	7.50	2.25
a.		Horiz. pair, imperf. btwn.	*350.00*	
b.		Vert. pair, imperf. btwn.	*1,200.*	
		Nos. 44-53 (10)	29.07	20.02

Printed locally. Perforation, paper and shade varieties exist.

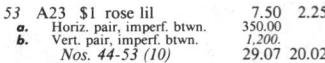

Gate of Courtesy — A24

1958, Oct. 15 Photo. *Perf. 13½*

54	A24	3c multi	1.25	1.00

Restoration of Shureimon, Gate of Courtesy, on road leading to Shuri City.

Lion Dance A25

Trees and Mountains A26

1958, Dec. 10 Unwmk. *Perf. 13½*

55	A25	1½c multi	20	20

New Year, 1959.

1959, Apr. 30 Litho. *Perf. 13½x13*

56	A26	3c bl, yel grn, grn & red	60	55
a.		Red omitted		

"Make the Ryukyus Green" movement.

Yonaguni Moth A27

1959, July 23 Photo. *Perf. 13*

57	A27	3c multi	95	60

Meeting of the Japanese Biological Education Society in Okinawa.

Hibiscus A28

Toy (Yakaji) A29

Designs: 3c, Fish (Moorish idol). 8c, Sea shell (Phalium bandatum). 13c, Butterfly (Kallima Inachus Eucerca), denomination at left, butterfly going up. 17c, Jellyfish (Dactylometra pacifera Goette).

Inscribed 琉球郵便

1959, Aug. 10 *Perf. 13x13½*

58	A28	½c multi	20	20
59	A28	3c multi	75	38
60	A28	8c lt ultra, blk & ocher	6.00	5.25
61	A28	13c lt bl, gray & org	2.10	1.75
62	A28	17c vio bl, red & yel	14.00	7.50
		Nos. 58-62 (5)	23.05	15.08

Four-character inscription measures 10x2mm on ½c; 12x3mm on 3c, 8c; 8½x2mm on 13c, 17c. See Nos. 76-80.

1959, Dec. 1 **Litho.**

63	A29	1½c gold & multi	55	28

New Year, 1960.

University Badge A30

1960, May 22 Photo. *Perf. 13*

64	A30	3c multi	95	48

Opening of Ryukyu University, 10th anniv.

Dancer — A31

Designs: Various Ryukyu Dances.

1960, Nov. 1 Photo. *Perf. 13*
Dark Gray Background

65	A31	1c yel, red & vio	1.00	65
66	A31	2½c crim, bl & yel	2.00	65
67	A31	5c dk bl, yel & red	65	75
68	A31	10c dk bl, yel & car	65	65

See Nos. 81-87, 220.

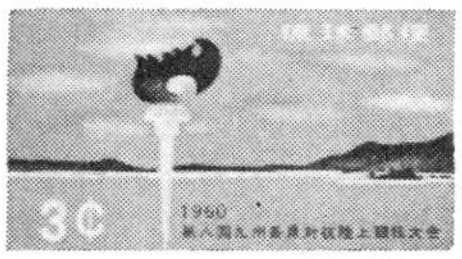

Torch and Nago Bay A32

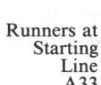

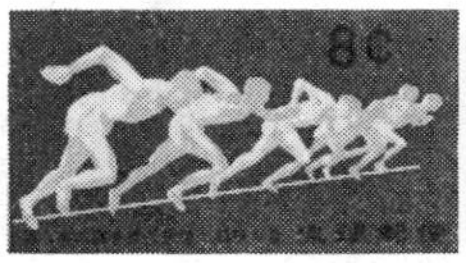

Runners at Starting Line A33

1960, Nov. 8

72	A32	3c lt bl, grn & red	5.25	2.25
73	A33	8c org & sl grn	75	75

8th Kyushu Inter-Prefectural Athletic Meet, Nago, Northern Okinawa, Nov. 6-7.

Little Egret and Rising Sun A34

1960, Dec. 1 Unwmk. *Perf. 13*

74	A34	3c redsh brn	5.00	2.50

National census.

Okinawa Bull Fight — A35

1960, Dec. 10 *Perf. 13½*

75	A35	1½c bis, dk bl & red brn	1.75	65

New Year, 1961.

Type of 1959 With Japanese Inscription Redrawn:

琉球郵便

1960-61 Photo. *Perf. 13x13½*

76	A28	½c multi ('61)	28	22
77	A28	3c multi ('61)	75	22
78	A28	8c lt ultra, blk & ocher	75	38
79	A28	13c bl, brn & red	95	65
80	A28	17c vio bl, red & yel	6.00	3.50
		Nos. 76-80 (5)	8.73	4.97

Size of Japanese inscription on Nos. 78-80 is 10½x11½mm. On No. 79 the denomination is at right, butterfly going down.

Dancer Type of 1960 with "RYUKYUS" Added

1961-64 *Perf. 13*

81	A31	1c multi	12	9
82	A31	2½c multi ('62)	18	9
83	A31	5c multi ('62)	22	18
84	A31	10c multi ('62)	40	30
84A	A31	20c multi ('64)	1.00	75
85	A31	25c multi ('62)	75	75
86	A31	50c multi	2.00	60
87	A31	$1 multi	2.75	12
		Nos. 81-87 (8)	7.42	2.88

Pine Tree — A36

1961, May 1 Photo. *Perf. 13*

88	A36	3c yel grn & red	1.50	1.25

"Make the Ryukyus Green" movement.

Naha, Steamer and Sailboat A37

1961, May 20

89	A37 3c aqua	2.10 1.10

40th anniversary of Naha.

White Silver Temple A38

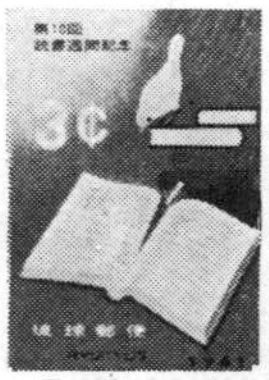

Books and Bird A39

1961, Oct. 1 Typo. *Perf. 11*

90	A38 3c red brn	1.25 1.10
a.	Horiz. pair, imperf. between	*450.00*
b.	Vert. pair, imperf. between	*550.00*

Merger of townships Takamine, Kanegushiku and Miwa with Itoman.

1961, Nov. 12 Litho. *Perf. 13*

91	A39 3c multi	1.10 80

Issued for Book Week.

Rising Sun and Eagles — A40

Symbolic Steps, Trees and Government Building — A41

1961, Dec. 10 Photo. *Perf. 13½*

92	A40 1½c gold, ver & blk	2.00 1.75

New Year, 1962.

1962, Apr. 1 Unwmk. *Perf. 13½*

Design: 3c, Government Building.

93	A41 1½c multi	42 45
94	A41 3c brt grn, red & gray	70 55

10th anniv. of the Government of the Ryukyu Islands (GRI).

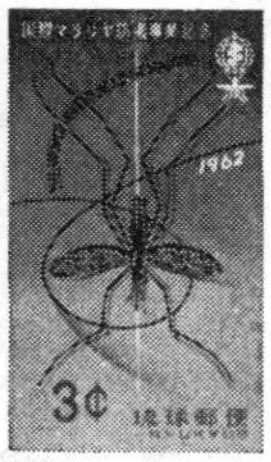

Anopheles Hyrcanus Sinensis — A42

Design: 8c, Malaria eradication emblem and Shurei gate.

1962, Apr. 7 *Perf. 13½x13*

95	A42 3c multi	45 48
96	A42 8c multi	90 60

WHO drive to eradicate malaria.

Dolls and Toys A43

Linden or Sea Hibiscus A44

1962, May 5 Litho. *Perf. 13½*

97	A43 3c red, blk, bl & buff	1.10 65

Issued for Children's Day.

1962, June 1 Photo.

Flowers: 3c, Indian coral tree. 8c, Iju (Schima liukiuensis Nakai). 13c, Touch-me-not (garden balsam). 17c, Shell flower (Alpinia speciosa).

98	A44 ½c multi	8 8
99	A44 3c multi	30 12
100	A44 8c multi	35 35
101	A44 13c multi	55 48
102	A44 17c multi	75 75
	Nos. 98-102 (5)	2.03 1.78

See Nos. 107 and 114 for 1½c and 15c flower stamps.

Earthenware A45

1962, July 5 *Perf. 13½x13*

103	A45 3c multi	3.75 3.00

Issued for Philatelic Week.

Japanese Fencing (Kendo) A46

1962, July 25 *Perf. 13*

104	A46 3c multi	4.00 3.00

All-Japan Kendo Meeting, Okinawa, July 25.

Rabbit Playing near Water, Bingata Cloth Design — A47

Young Man and Woman, Stone Relief — A48

1962, Dec. 10 *Perf. 13x13½*

105	A47 1½c gold & multi	1.25 1.00

New Year, 1963.

1963, Jan. 15 Photo. *Perf. 13½*

106	A48 3c gold, blk & bl	80 65

Issued for Adult Day.

Gooseneck Cactus A49

Trees and Wooded Hills A50

1963, Apr. 5 *Perf. 13x13½*

107	A49 1½c dk bl, grn, yel & pink	10 10

1963, Mar. 25 *Perf. 13½x13*

108	A50 3c ultra, grn & red brn	80 80

"Make the Ryukyus Green" movement.

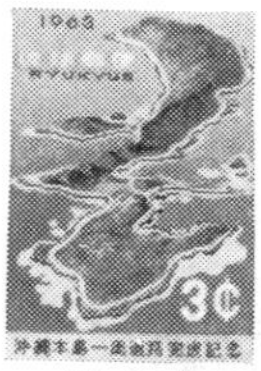

Map of Okinawa A51

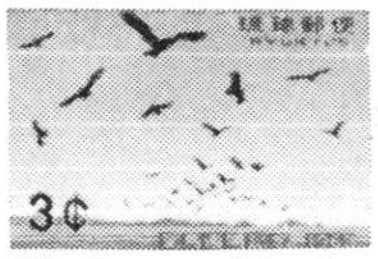

Hawks over Islands A52

1963, Apr. 30 Unwmk. *Perf. 13½*

109	A51 3c multi	1.00 1.00

Opening of the Round Road on Okinawa.

1963, May 10 Photo.

110	A52 3c multi	95 95

Issued for Bird Day, May 10.

Shioya Bridge — A53

1963, June 5

111	A53 3c multi	95 95

Opening of Shioya Bridge over Shioya Bay.

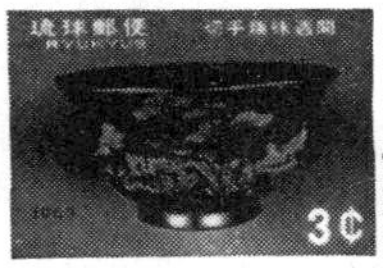

Tsuikin-wan Lacquerware Bowl — A54

1963, July 1 Unwmk. *Perf. 13½*

112	A54 3c multi	2.75 2.25

Issued for Philatelic Week.

Map of Far East and JCI Emblem A55

1963, Sept. 16 Photo. *Perf. 13½*

113	A55 3c multi	70 48

Meeting of the Intl. Junior Chamber of Commerce (JCI), Naha, Okinawa, Sept. 16-19.

Mamaomoto A56

Site of Nakagusuku Castle A57

1963, Oct. 15 *Perf. 13x13½*

114	A56 15c multi	80 40

1963, Nov. 1 *Perf. 13½x13*

115	A57 3c multi	70 42

Protection of national cultural treasures.

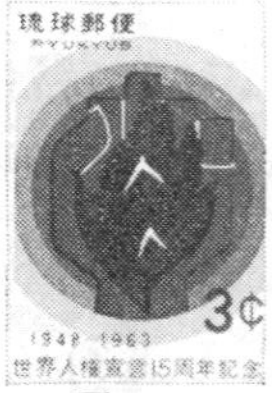

Flame A58

Dragon (Bingata Pattern) A59

1963, Dec. 10 *Perf. 13½*

116	A58 3c red, dk bl & yel	70 42

15th anniversary of the Universal Declaration of Human Rights.

1963, Dec. 10 Photo.

117	A59 1½c multi	40 25

New Year, 1964.

Carnation A60

Pineapples and Sugar Cane A61

1964, May 10 *Perf. 13½*

118	A60 3c bl, yel, blk & car	40 35

Issued for Mother's Day.

1964, June 1

119	A61 3c multi	40 35

Agricultural census.

Minsah Obi (Sash Woven of Kapok) — A62

1964, July 1 Unwmk. *Perf. 13½*

120 A62 3c dp bl, rose pink & ocher	55 42
a. 3c dp bl, dp car & ocher	70 60

Issued for Philatelic Week.

Girl Scout and Emblem A63

1964, Aug. 31 Photo.

121 A63 3c multi	40 30

10th anniversary of Ryukyuan Girl Scouts.

Shuri Relay Station — A64

Parabolic Antenna and Map — A65

1964, Sept. 1 Unwmk. *Perf. 13½*
Black Overprint

122 A64 3c dp grn	65 65
a. Figure "1" inverted	22.50 22.50
123 A65 8c ultra	1.25 1.25

Opening of the Ryukyu Islands-Japan microwave system carrying telephone and telegraph messages between the Ryukyus and Japan. Nos. 122-123 not issued without overprint.

Gate of Courtesy, Olympic Torch and Emblem — A66

1964, Sept. 7 Photo. *Perf. 13½x13*

124 A66 3c ultra, yel & red	20 15

Relaying of the Olympic torch on Okinawa en route to Tokyo.

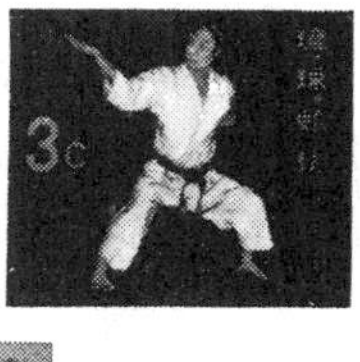

"Naihanchi," Karate Stance — A67

"Makiwara," Strengthening Hands and Feet — A68

"Kumite," Simulated Combat — A69

1964-65 Photo. *Perf. 13½*

125 A67 3c dl cl, yel & blk	48 30
126 A68 3c yel & multi ('65)	38 30
127 A69 3c gray, red & blk ('65)	38 30

Karate, Ryukyuan self-defense sport.

Miyara Dunchi A70

Snake and Iris (Bingata) A71

1964, Nov. 1 *Perf. 13½*

128 A70 3c multi	22 18

Protection of national cultural treasures. Miyara Dunchi was built as a residence by Miyara-pechin Toen in 1819.

1964, Dec. 10 Photo.

129 A71 1½c multi	25 20

New Year, 1965.

Boy Scouts — A72

1965, Feb. 6 *Perf. 13½*

130 A72 3c lt bl & multi	42 28

10th anniversary of Ryukyuan Boy Scouts.

Main Stadium, Onoyama A73

1965, July 1 *Perf. 13x13½*

131 A73 3c multi	20 18

Inauguration of the main stadium of the Onoyama athletic facilities.

Samisen of King Shoko — A74

1965, July 1 Photo. *Perf. 13½*

132 A74 3c buff & multi	42 30

Issued for Philatelic Week.

Kin Power Plant — A75

ICY Emblem, Ryukyu Map — A76

1965, July 1

133 A75 3c grn & multi	20 18

Completion of Kin power plant.

1965, Aug. 24 Photo. *Perf. 13½*

134 A76 3c multi	18 14

UN, 20th anniv.; Intl. Cooperation Year, 1964-65.

Naha City Hall — A77

1965, Sept. 18 Unwmk. *Perf. 13½*

135 A77 3c bl & multi	18 14

Completion of Naha City Hall.

Chinese Box Turtle A78

Horse (Bingata) A79

Turtles: No. 137, Hawksbill turtle (denomination at top, country name at bottom). No. 138, Asian terrapin (denomination and country name on top).

1965-66 Photo. *Perf. 13½*

136 A78 3c gldn brn & multi	30 30
137 A78 3c blk, yel & brn ('66)	30 30
138 A78 3c gray & multi ('66)	30 30

Issue dates: No. 136, Oct. 20, 1965. No. 137, Jan. 20, 1966. No. 138, Apr. 20, 1966.

1965, Dec. 10 Photo. *Perf. 13½*

139 A79 1½c multi	12 10
a. Gold omitted	*1,200. 1,200.*

New Year, 1966.

Nature Conservation Issue

Noguchi's Okinawa Woodpecker A80

Sika Deer A81

Design: No. 142, Dugong.

1966 Photo. *Perf. 13½*

140 A80 3c bl grn & multi	20 20
141 A81 3c bl, red, blk, brn & grn	24 24
142 A81 3c bl, yel grn, blk & red	24 24

Issue dates: No. 140, Feb. 15. No. 141, Mar. 15. No. 142, Apr. 20.

Ryukyu Bungalow Swallow — A82

1966, May 10 Photo. *Perf. 13½*

143 A82 3c sky bl, blk & brn	14 14

4th Bird Week, May 10-16.

Lilies and Ruins A83

1966, June 23 *Perf. 13x13½*

144 A83 3c multi	14 14

Memorial Day, commemorating the end of the Battle of Okinawa, June 23, 1945.

University of the Ryukyus A84

1966, July 1

145 A84 3c multi	14 14

Transfer of the University of the Ryukyus from United States' authority to the Ryukyu Government.

Lacquerware, 18th Century A85

Tile-Roofed House and UNESCO Emblem A86

1966, Aug. 1 *Perf. 13½*

146 A85 3c gray & multi	14 14

Issued for Philatelic Week.

1966, Sept. 20 Photo. *Perf. 13½*

147 A86 3c multi	14 14

UNESCO, 20th anniv.

Government Museum and Dragon Statue — A87

1966, Oct. 6

148 A87 3c multi	14 14

Completion of the GRI (Government of the Ryukyu Islands) Museum, Shuri.

Tomb of Nakasone-Tuimya Genga, Ruler of Miyako — A88

1966, Nov. 1 Photo. *Perf. 13½*

149 A88 3c multi	14 14

Protection of national cultural treasures.

Ram in Iris Wreath (Bingata) A89

Clown Fish A90

1966, Dec. 10 Photo. *Perf. 13½*

150 A89 1½c dk bl & multi	14 14

New Year, 1967.

1966-67

Fish: No. 152, Young boxfish (white numeral at lower left). No. 153, Forceps fish (pale buff numeral at lower right). No. 154, Spotted triggerfish (orange numeral). No. 155, Saddleback butterflyfish (carmine numeral, lower left).

151 A90 3c org red & multi	18	14
152 A90 3c org yel & multi ('67)	18	14
153 A90 3c multi ('67)	25	22
154 A90 3c multi ('67)	25	22
155 A90 3c multi ('67)	28	22
Nos. 151-155 (5)	1.14	94

Issue dates: No. 151, Dec. 20, 1966. No. 152, Jan. 10, 1967. No. 153, Apr. 10, 1967. No. 154, May 25, 1967. No. 155, June 10, 1967.

Tsuboya Urn — A91

Episcopal Miter — A92

1967, Apr. 20

156 A91 3c yel & multi	20	16

Issued for Philatelic Week.

1967-68 Photo. *Perf. 13½*

Seashells: No. 158, Venus comb murex. No. 159, Chiragra spider. No. 160, Green turban. No. 161, Euprotomus bulla.

157 A92 3c lt grn & multi	18	14
158 A92 3c grnsh bl & multi	18	14
159 A92 3c emer & multi ('68)	22	18
160 A92 3c lt bl & multi ('68)	22	18
161 A92 3c brt bl multi ('68)	40	28
Nos. 157-161 (5)	1.20	92

Issue dates: 1967, No. 157, July 20; No. 158, Aug. 30. 1968, No. 159, Jan. 18; No. 160, Feb. 20; No. 161, June 5.

Red-tiled Roofs and ITY Emblem — A93

1967, Sept. 11 Photo. *Perf. 13½*

162 A93 3c multi	18	18

International Tourist Year.

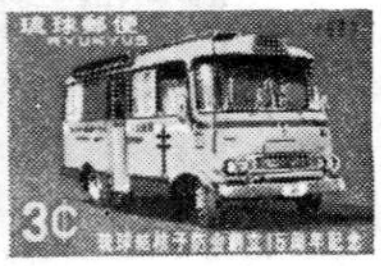
Mobile TB Clinic — A94

1967, Oct. 13 Photo. *Perf. 13½*

163 A94 3c lil & multi	18	18

Anti-Tuberculosis Society, 15th anniv.

Hojo Bridge, Enkaku Temple, 1498 — A95

1967, Nov. 1

164 A95 3c bl grn & multi	18	18

Protection of national cultural treasures.

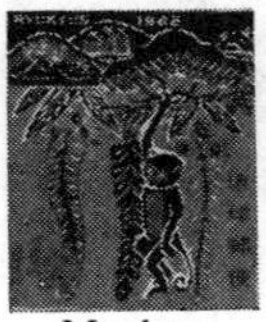
Monkey (Bingata) A96

TV Tower and Map A97

1967, Dec. 11 Photo. *Perf. 13½*

165 A96 1½c sil & multi	18	18

New Year 1968.

1967, Dec. 22

166 A97 3c multi	18	18

Opening of Miyako and Yaeyama television stations.

Dr. Kijin Nakachi and Helper — A98

Pill Box (Inro) — A99

1968, Mar. 15 Photo. *Perf. 13½*

167 A98 3c multi	18	18

120th anniv. of the first vaccination in the Ryukyu Islands, performed by Dr. Kijin Nakachi.

1968, Apr. 18

168 A99 3c gray & multi	45	42

Philatelic Week.

Young Man, Library, Book and Map of Ryukyu Islands A100

1968, May 13

169 A100 3c multi	25	22

10th International Library Week.

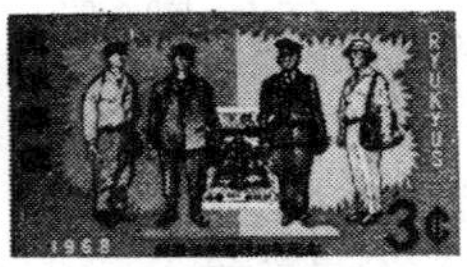
Mailmen's Uniforms and Stamp of 1948 — A101

1968, July 1 Photo. *Perf. 13x13½*

170 A101 3c multi	25	22

1st Ryukyuan postage stamps, 20th anniv.

Main Gate, Enkaku Temple A102

Photo. & Engr.

1968, July 15 *Perf. 13½*

171 A102 3c multi	25	22

Restoration of the main gate of the Enkaku Temple, built 1492-1495, and destroyed during WWII.

Old Man's Dance — A103

1968, Sept. 15 Photo. *Perf. 13½*

172 A103 3c gold & multi	25	22

Issued for Old People's Day.

Mictyris Longicarpus A104

Crabs: No. 174, Uca dubia stimpson. No. 175, Baptozius vinosus. No. 176, Cardisoma carnifex. No. 177, Ocypode ceratophthalma pallas.

1968-69 Photo. *Perf. 13½*

173 A104 3c bl, ocher & blk	30	25
174 A104 3c lt bl grn & multi ('69)	35	25
175 A104 3c lt grn & multi ('69)	35	25
176 A104 3c lt ultra & multi ('69)	45	30
177 A104 3c lt ultra & multi ('69)	45	30
Nos. 173-177 (5)	1.90	1.35

Issue dates: No. 173, Oct. 10, 1968. No. 174, Feb. 5, 1969. No. 175, Mar. 5, 1969. No. 176, May 15, 1969; No. 177, June 2, 1969.

Saraswati Pavilion A105

1968, Nov. 1 Photo. *Perf. 13½*

178 A105 3c multi	24	18

Restoration of the Saraswati Pavilion (in front of Enkaku Temple), destroyed during WWII.

Tennis Player A106

Cock and Iris (Bingata) A107

1968, Nov. 3 Photo. *Perf. 13½*

179 A106 3c grn & multi	40	30

35th All-Japan East-West Men's Soft-ball Tennis Tournament, Naha City, Nov. 23-24.

1968, Dec. 10

180 A107 1½c org & multi	14	14

New Year, 1969.

The only foreign revenue stamps listed in this Catalogue are those authorized for prepayment of postage.

Boxer — A108

Ink Slab Screen — A109

1969, Jan. 3

181 A108 3c gray & multi	25	22

20th All-Japan Amateur Boxing Championships, University of the Ryukyus, Jan. 3-5.

1969, Apr. 17 Photo. *Perf. 13½*

182 A109 3c sal, ind & red	25	18

Philatelic Week.

Box Antennas and Map of Radio Link A110

Gate of Courtesy and Emblems A111

1969, July 1 Photo. *Perf. 13½*

183 A110 3c multi	14	12

Opening of the UHF (radio) circuit system between Okinawa and the outlying Miyako-Yaeyama Islands.

1969, Aug. 1 Photo. *Perf. 13½*

184 A111 3c Prus bl, gold & ver	14	12

22nd All-Japan Formative Education Study Conference, Naha, Aug. 1-3.

Folklore Issue

Tug of War Festival A112

Hari Boat Race A113

Izaiho Ceremony, Kudaka Island A114

Mortardrum Dance — A115

Sea God Dance A116

1969-70 Photo. *Perf. 13*

185 A112 3c multi	28	22
186 A113 3c multi	35	22
187 A114 3c multi	35	22

188 A115 3c multi ('70) 50 35
189 A116 3c multi ('70) 50 35
Nos. 185-189 (5) 1.98 1.36

Issue dates: No. 185, Aug. 1; No. 186, Sept. 5; No. 187, Oct. 3; No. 188, Jan. 20, 1970; No. 189, Feb. 27, 1970.

No. 99 Surcharged 改訂½¢

1969, Oct. 15 Photo. *Perf. 13½*
190 A44 ½c on 3c multi 12 12

Nakamura-ke Farm House, Built 1713-51
A117

1969, Nov. 1 Photo. *Perf. 13½*
191 A117 3c multi 14 10

Protection of national cultural treasures.

Statue of Kyuzo Toyama, Maps of Hawaiian and Ryukyu Islands
A118

1969, Dec. 5 Photo. *Perf. 13½*
192 A118 3c lt ultra & multi 22 20
a. Without overprint *2,500.*
b. Wide-spaced bars *725.00*

Ryukyu-Hawaii emigration led by Kyuzo Toyama, 70th anniversary.
The overprint -"1969" at lower left and bars across "1970" at upper right- was applied before No. 192 was issued.

Dog and Flowers (Bingata)
A119

Sake Flask Made from Coconut
A120

1969, Dec. 10
193 A119 1½c pink & multi 12 12

New Year, 1970.

1970, Apr. 15 Photo. *Perf. 13½*
194 A120 3c multi 22 20

Philatelic Week.

Classic Opera Issue

"The Bell" (Shushin Kaneiri)
A121

Child and Kidnapper (Chu-nusudu)
A122

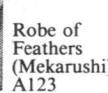

Robe of Feathers (Mekarushi)
A123

Vengeance of Two Young Sons (Nidotichiuchi)
A124

The Virgin and the Dragon (Kokonomaki)
A125

1970 Photo. *Perf. 13½*
195 A121 3c dl bl & multi 40 38
196 A122 3c lt bl & multi 40 38
197 A123 3c bluish grn & multi 40 38
198 A124 3c dl bl grn & multi 40 38
199 A125 3c multi 40 38
Nos. 195-199 (5) 2.00 1.90
195a-199a, 5 sheets of 4 16.00 17.00

Underwater Observatory and Tropical Fish — A126

1970, May 22
200 A126 3c bl grn & multi 28 25

Completion of the underwater observatory at Busena-Misaki, Nago.

Noboru Jahana (1865-1908), Politician
A127

Map of Okinawa and People
A128

Portraits: No. 202, Saion Gushichan Bunjaku (1682-1761), statesman. No. 203, Choho Giwan (1823-1876), regent and poet.

1970-71 Engr. *Perf. 13½*
201 A127 3c rose cl 48 30
202 A127 3c dl bl grn 75 55
203 A127 3c blk ('71) 48 30

Issue dates: No. 201, Sept. 25, 1970. No. 202, Dec. 22, 1970. No. 203, Jan. 22, 1971.

1970, Oct. 1 Photo.
204 A128 3c red & multi 18 15

Oct. 1, 1970 census.

Great Cycad of Une — A129

1970, Nov. 2 Photo. *Perf. 13½*
205 A129 3c gold & multi 22 20

Protection of national treasures.

Japanese Flag, Diet and Map of Ryukyus
A130

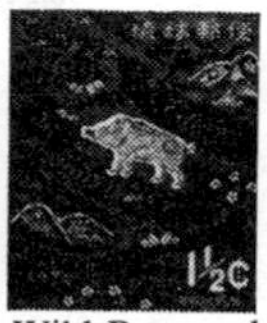
Wild Boar and Cherry Blossoms (Bingata)
A131

1970, Nov. 15 Photo. *Perf. 13½*
206 A130 3c ultra & multi 70 50

Citizens' participation in national administration according to Japanese law of Apr. 24, 1970.

1970, Dec. 10
207 A131 1½c multi 14 14

New Year, 1971.

Low Hand Loom (Jibata)
A132

Farmer Wearing Palm Bark Raincoat and Kuba Leaf Hat — A133

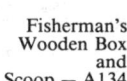

Fisherman's Wooden Box and Scoop — A134

Designs: No. 209, Woman running a filature (reel). No. 211, Woman hulling rice with cylindrical "Shiri-ushi."

1971 Photo. *Perf. 13½*
208 A132 3c lt bl & multi 28 22
209 A132 3c pale grn & multi 28 22
210 A133 3c lt bl & multi 35 24
211 A132 3c yel & multi 40 30
212 A134 3c gray & multi 35 24
Nos. 208-212 (5) 1.66 1.22

Issue dates: No. 208, Feb. 16; No. 209, Mar. 16; No. 210, Apr. 13; No. 211, May 20; No. 212, June 15.

Water Carrier (Taku) — A135

1971, Apr. 15 Photo. *Perf. 13½*
213 A135 3c bl grn & multi 35 25

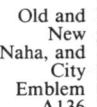

Philatelic Week.

Old and New Naha, and City Emblem
A136

1971, May 20 *Perf. 13*
214 A136 3c ultra & multi 22 20

50th anniversary of Naha as a municipality.

Caesalpinia Pulcherrima — A137

Design: 2c, Madder (Sandanka).

1971 Photo. *Perf. 13*
215 A137 2c gray & multi 12 8
216 A137 3c gray & multi 16 12

Issue dates: 2c, Sept. 30; 3c, May 10.

Government Park Series

View from Mabuni Hill — A138

Mt. Arashi from Haneji Sea — A139

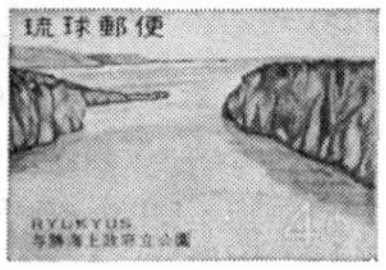
Yabuchi Island from Yakena Port — A140

1971-72
217 A138 3c grn & multi 20 15
218 A139 3c bl & multi 20 15
219 A140 4c multi ('72) 25 15

Issue dates: No. 217, July 30; No. 218, Aug. 30, 1971; No. 219, Jan. 20, 1972.

Dancer
A141

Deva King, Torinji Temple
A142

1971, Nov. 1 Photo. *Perf. 13*
220 A141 4c Prus bl & multi 14 12

1971, Dec. 1
221 A142 4c dp bl & multi 18 18

Protection of national cultural treasures.

Rat and Chrysanthemums
A143

Student Nurse
A144

1971, Dec. 10
222 A143 2c brn org & multi 14 14

New Year 1972.

1971, Dec. 24
223 A144 4c lil & multi 20 15

Nurses' training, 25th anniversary.

Birds on Seashore A145

Sun over Islands A147

Coral Reef — A146

1972 Photo. *Perf. 13*

224	A145	5c brt bl & multi	35	24
225	A146	5c gray & multi	35	24
226	A147	5c ocher & multi	35	24

Issue dates: No. 224, Apr. 14; No. 225, Mar. 30; No. 226, Mar. 21.

Dove, US and Japanese Flags — A148

1972, Apr. 17 Photo. *Perf. 13*

227	A148	5c brt bl & multi	55	38

Ratification of the Reversion Agreement with US under which the Ryukyu Islands were returned to Japan.

Antique Sake Pot (Yushibin) — A149

1972, Apr. 20

228	A149	5c ultra & multi	40	25

Philatelic Week.

Ryukyu stamps were replaced by those of Japan after May 15, 1972.

AIR POST STAMPS

Dove and Map of Ryukyus — AP1

1950 Unwmk. Photo. *Perf. 13x13½*

C1	AP1	8y brt blue	62.50	50.00
C2	AP1	12y green	22.50	20.00
C3	AP1	16y rose car	18.00	15.00

Heavenly Maiden AP2

1951-54

C4	AP2	13y blue	1.50	1.40
C5	AP2	18y green	2.10	2.10
C6	AP2	30y cerise	3.25	1.10
C7	AP2	40y red vio ('54)	5.25	5.00
C8	AP2	50y yel org ('54)	6.50	5.75
		Nos. C4-C8 (5)	18.60	15.35

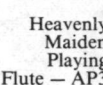

Heavenly Maiden Playing Flute — AP3

1957, Aug. 1 Engr. *Perf. 13½*

C9	AP3	15y blue grn	3.75	2.00
C10	AP3	20y rose car	6.00	3.50
C11	AP3	35y yel grn	11.00	5.50
C12	AP3	45y reddish brn	12.00	8.00
C13	AP3	60y gray	16.00	9.50
		Nos. C9-C13 (5)	48.75	28.50

Same Surcharged in Brown Red or Light Ultramarine

改訂 9¢

1959, Dec. 20

C14	AP3	9c on 15y bl grn (BrR)	2.00	1.40
a.		Inverted surcharge	750.00	
C15	AP3	14c on 20y rose car (LU)	2.50	2.10
C16	AP3	19c on 35y yel grn (BrR)	4.50	3.50
C17	AP3	27c on 45y redsh brn (LU)	8.50	5.00
C18	AP3	35c on 60y gray (BrR)	10.00	6.50
		Nos. C14-C18 (5)	27.50	18.50

改訂

Nos. 31-33, 36 and 38 Surcharged in Black, Brown, Red, Blue or Green

9¢

1960, Aug. 3 Photo. *Perf. 13*

C19	A14	9c on 4y brn	2.25	1.40
a.		Inverted surcharge	*12,000.*	*15,000.*
C20	A17	14c on 5y rose lil (Br)	2.25	1.40
C21	A14	19c on 15y ver (R)	1.75	1.00
C22	A17	27c on 14y redsh brn (Bl)	5.00	2.75
C23	A14	35c on 20y yel org (G)	4.50	3.75
		Nos. C19-C23 (5)	15.75	10.30

Wind God — AP4

Designs: 9c, Heavenly Maiden (as on AP2). 14c, Heavenly Maiden (as on AP3). 27c, Wind God at right. 35c, Heavenly Maiden over treetops.

1961, Sept. 21 Photo. *Perf. 13½*

C24	AP4	9c multi	28	12
C25	AP4	14c multi	45	45
C26	AP4	19c multi	48	45
C27	AP4	27c multi	1.90	30
C28	AP4	35c multi	1.25	60
		Nos. C24-C28 (5)	4.36	1.92

Jet over Gate of Courtesy — AP5

Jet Plane — AP6

1963, Aug. 28 *Perf. 13x13½*

C29	AP5	5½c multi	14	14
C30	AP6	7c multi	18	20

SPECIAL DELIVERY STAMP

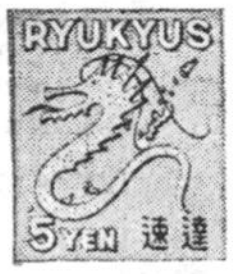

Dragon and Map of Ryukyus — SD1

1950 Unwmk. Photo. *Perf. 13x13½*

E1	SD1	5y brt bl	16.00	22.50

SAAR

LOCATION — On the Franco-German border southeast of Luxembourg.
GOVT. — A German state.
POP. — 1,400,000 (1959).
AREA — 991 sq. mi.
CAPITAL — Saarbrücken.

A former German territory, the Saar was administered by the League of Nations 1920-35. After a January 12, 1935, plebiscite, it returned to Germany, and the use of German stamps was resumed. After World War II, France occupied the Saar and later established a protectorate. The provisional semi-independent State of Saar was established Jan. 1, 1951. France returned the Saar to the German Federal Republic Jan. 1, 1957.

Saar stamps were discontinued in 1959 and replaced by stamps of the German Federal Republic.

100 Pfennig = 1 Mark
100 Centimes = 1 Franc (1921)

German Stamps of 1906-19 Overprinted **Sarre**

Perf. 14, 14½

1920, Jan. 30 Wmk. 125

1	A22	2pf gray	55	*1.25*
a.		Inverted overprint	75.00	*125.00*
b.		Double overprint	725.00	*1,200.*
2	A22	2½pf gray	90	*1.75*
a.		Inverted ovpt.	110.00	*180.00*
3	A16	3pf brown	40	*85*
a.		Inverted ovpt.	100.00	*160.00*
4	A16	5pf green	12	*18*
a.		Inverted ovpt.	200.00	*325.00*
b.		Double overprint	240.00	*400.00*
5	A22	7½pf orange	22	*35*
a.		Invtd. overprint	150.00	*240.00*
6	A16	10pf carmine	12	*18*
a.		Inverted overprint	150.00	*240.00*
b.		Double overprint	240.00	*400.00*
7	A22	15pf dk vio	9	12
a.		Double overprint	225.00	*360.00*
8	A16	20pf bl vio	12	*18*
a.		Double overprint	180.00	*300.00*
9	A16	25pf org & blk, *yel*	5.50	6.00
a.		Inverted overprint	275.00	*475.00*
10	A16	30pf org & blk, *buff*	10.00	15.00
11	A22	35pf red brn	12	15
a.		Invtd. overprint	135.00	*225.00*
12	A16	40pf lake & blk	20	22
a.		Invtd. overprint	130.00	*200.00*
13	A16	50pf pur & blk, *buff*	15	22
a.		Inverted ovpt.	150.00	*240.00*
14	A16	60pf red vio	22	25
15	A16	75pf grn & blk	20	22
a.		Inverted overprint	72.50	*125.00*
16	A16	80pf lake & blk, *rose*	150.00	110.00

Three types of overprint exist on Nos. 1-5, 12, 13; two types on Nos. 6-11, 14-16.

Saar stamps can be mounted in Scott's Germany Part II Album.

Overprinted **Sarre**

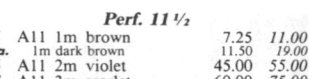

17	A17	1m car rose	12.00	*15.00*
a.		Inverted ovpt.	325.00	*525.00*
b.		Double overprint	450.00	*725.00*
		Nos. 1-17 (17)	180.91	151.92

The 3m type A19 exists with this overprint but was not issued.

Overprint forgeries exist.

Bavarian Stamps of 1914-16 Overprinted **Sarre**

Perf. 14x14½

1920, Mar. 1 Wmk. 95

19	A10	2pf gray	*1,000.*	*4,000.*
20	A10	3pf brown	100.00	*525.00*
21	A10	5pf yel grn	32	*70*
a.		Double ovpt.	400.00	*900.00*
22	A10	7½pf green	25.00	*150.00*
23	A10	10pf car rose	32	*75*
a.		Double ovpt.	150.00	*265.00*
24	A10	15pf vermilion	6.00	*18.00*
a.		Double ovpt.	175.00	*315.00*
25	A10	15pf carmine	32	*75*
26	A10	20pf blue	32	*75*
a.		Double ovpt.	150.00	*265.00*
27	A10	25pf gray	3.75	*7.00*
28	A10	30pf orange	3.25	*5.00*
30	A10	40pf ol grn	4.50	*7.00*
31	A10	50pf red brn	45	*75*
a.		Double ovpt.	100.00	*150.00*
32	A10	60pf dk grn	1.25	*3.00*

Overprinted **Sarre**

Perf. 11½

35	A11	1m brown	7.25	*11.00*
a.		1m dark brown	11.50	*19.00*
36	A11	2m violet	45.00	*55.00*
37	A11	3m scarlet	60.00	*75.00*

Overprinted **SARRE**

38	A12	5m dp bl	500.00	*900.00*
39	A12	10m yel grn	90.00	*135.00*
a.		Double ovpt.	*9,000.*	*15,000.*

Nos. 19, 20 and 22 were not officially issued, but were available for postage. Examples are known legitimately used on cover. The 20m type A12 was also overprinted in small quantity.

Overprint forgeries exist.

German Stamps of 1906-20 Overprinted **SAARGEBIET**

Perf. 14, 14½

1920, Mar. 26 Wmk. 125

41	A16	5pf green	14	*20*
a.		Inverted ovpt.	12.50	*125.00*
42	A16	5pf red brn	28	25
43	A16	10pf carmine	14	*20*
a.		Inverted ovpt.	13.00	
44	A16	10pf orange	20	15
a.		Inverted ovpt.	8.50	
45	A22	15pf dk vio	14	*20*
a.		Inverted ovpt.	13.00	*175.00*
46	A16	20pf bl vio	14	*20*
a.		Inverted ovpt.	12.50	
47	A16	20pf green	30	25
a.		Double ovpt.		
48	A16	30pf org & blk, *buff*	18	20
a.		Double ovpt.	55.00	
b.		Inverted ovpt.		
49	A16	30pf dl bl	40	38
50	A16	40pf lake & blk	18	20
a.		Inverted ovpt.		

51 A16 40pf car rose 60 38
52 A16 50pf pur & blk, *buff* 20 20
a. Double ovpt. 55.00
b. Inverted ovpt.
53 A16 60pf red vio 32 22
a. Inverted ovpt. 35.00 *150.00*
54 A16 75pf grn & blk 32 22
a. Dbl. overprint 90.00
b. Inverted ovpt. 90.00
55 A17 1.25m green 90 65
a. Inverted ovpt. 70.00
56 A17 1.50m yel brn 90 65
a. Inverted ovpt. 60.00
57 A21 2.50m lil rose 2.75 *5.50*
58 A16 4m blk & rose 5.00 *8.00*
a. Double ovpt. 20.00
Nos. 41-58 (18) 13.09 *18.05*

On No. 57 the overprint is placed vertically at each side of the stamp.

Counterfeit overprints exist.

Germany No. 90 Surcharged in Black

20
SAARGEBIET

1921, Feb.

65 A16 20pf on 75pf grn & blk 30 75
a. Inverted surcharge 16.00 *25.00*
b. Double surcharge 42.50 *70.00*

Mark 5 Mark

Germany No. 120 Surcharged

66 A22 5m on 15pf vio brn 3.25 *8.75*
67 A22 10m on 15pf vio brn 4.00 *10.00*

Forgeries exist of Nos. 66-67.

Old Mill near Mettlach — A3

Miner at Work — A4

Entrance to Reden Mine — A5

Saar River Traffic — A6

Saar River near Mettlach — A7

Slag Pile at Völklingen — A8

Signal Bridge, Saarbrücken A9

Church at Mettlach A10

"Old Bridge," Saarbrücken A11

Cable Railway at Ferne A12

Colliery Shafthead — A13

Saarbrücken City Hall — A14

Pottery at Mettlach — A15

St. Ludwig's Cathedral — A16

Presidential Residence, Saarbrücken A17

Burbach Steelworks, Dillingen A18

1921 Unwmk. Typo. *Perf. 12½*

68 A3 5pf ol grn & vio 16 12
a. Tete beche pair 3.50 *8.75*
c. Center inverted 50.00
69 A4 10pf org & ultra 16 12
70 A5 20pf grn & sl 22 15
a. Tete beche pair 5.50 *15.00*
c. Perf. 10½ 11.50 *55.00*
d. As "c," tete beche pair 60.00 *190.00*
71 A6 25pf brn & dk bl 25 18
a. Tete beche pair 6.50 *17.50*
72 A7 30pf gray grn & brn 22 20
a. Tete beche pair 5.50 *15.00*
c. 30pf ol grn & blk 1.40 *7.75*
d. As "c", tete beche pair 10.50 *27.50*
e. As "c," imperf., pair 175.00 *350.00*
73 A8 40pf vermilion 22 20
a. Tete beche pair 13.00 *37.50*
74 A9 50pf gray & blk 35 *85*
75 A10 60pf red & dk brn 85 *85*
76 A11 80pf dp bl 32 38
a. Tete beche pair 18.00 *50.00*
77 A12 1m lt red & blk 32 35
a. 1m grn & blk *675.00*
78 A13 1.25m lt brn & dk grn 48 *55*
79 A14 2m red & blk 1.50 *1.65*
80 A15 3m brn & dk ol 1.90 *3.50*
a. Center inverted 85.00
81 A16 5m yel & vio 4.00 *7.50*
82 A17 10m grn & red brn 6.25 *9.50*
83 A18 25m ultra, red & blk 16.00 *27.50*
Nos. 68-83 (16) 33.20 *53.60*

Values for tete beche are for vertical pair. Horizontal pairs sell for about twice as much.

The ultramarine ink on No. 69 appears to be brown where it overlays the orange.

Exist imperf. but were not regularly issued.

Nos. 70-83 Surcharged in Red, Blue or Black

5 cent. (a) 1 Fr. (b)

5 FRANKEN (c)

1921, May 1

85 A5(a) 3c on 20pf (R) 18 12
a. Tete beche pair 3.50 *10.00*
d. Perf. 10½ 3.25 *15.00*
e. As "d," tete beche pair 15.00 *37.50*
86 A6(a) 5c on 25pf (R) 15 *32*
a. Tete beche pair 60.00 *190.00*
87 A7(a) 10c on 30pf (Bl) 20 20
a. Tete beche pair 3.50 *10.00*
b. Invtd. surch. 80.00 *225.00*
88 A8(a) 15c on 40pf (Bk) 30 20
a. Tete beche pr. 55.00 *190.00*
b. Inverted surcharge 80.00 *225.00*
89 A9(a) 20c on 50pf (R) 18 10
90 A10(a) 25c on 60pf (Bl) 24 14
91 A11(a) 30c on 80pf (Bk) 90 28
a. Tete beche pair 9.00 *25.00*
c. Inverted surcharge 80.00 *225.00*
d. Dbl. surch. 80.00 *225.00*
92 A12(a) 40c on 1m (Bl) 1.40 28
a. Inverted surcharge 80.00 *225.00*
93 A13(a) 50c on 1.25m (Bk) 2.00 48
b. Perf. 10½ 45.00 *75.00*
94 A14(a) 75c on 2m (Bl) 2.00 65
95 A15(b) 1fr on 3m (Bl) 2.00 1.00
96 A16(b) 2fr on 5m (Bl) 7.25 3.00
97 A17(b) 3fr on 10m (Bk) 7.50 *9.50*
b. Dbl. surch. 165.00 *375.00*
98 A18(c) 5fr on 25m (Bl) 12.00 *16.00*
Nos. 85-98 (14) 36.30 *32.27*

In these surcharges the period is occasionally missing and there are various wrong font and defective letters.

Values for tete beche are for vertical pairs. Horizontal pairs sell for about twice as much.

Nos. 85-89, 91, 93, 97-98 exist imperf. but were not regularly issued.

Cable Railway, Ferne — A19

Miner at Work — A20

"Old Bridge," Saarbrücken A21

Saarbrücken City Hall — A22

Slag Pile at Völklingen A23

Pottery at Mettlach — A24

Saar River Traffic — A25

St. Ludwig's Cathedral — A26

Colliery Shafthead — A27

Mettlach Church — A28

Burbach Steelworks, Dillingen A29

Perf. 12½x13½, 13½x12½

1922-23 Typo.

99 A19 3c ol grn & straw 24 20
100 A20 5c org & blk 24 8
101 A21 10c bl grn 24 8
102 A19 15c dp brn 40 8
103 A19 15c org ('23) 3.00 22
104 A22 20c dk bl & lem 2.25 8
105 A22 20c brt bl & straw ('23) 3.00 22
106 A22 25c red & yel 2.75 1.00
107 A22 25c mag & straw ('23) 2.25 15
108 A23 30c car & yel 40 30
109 A24 40c brn & yel 65 6
110 A25 50c dk bl & straw 65 6
111 A24 75c dp grn & straw 7.00 *10.00*
112 A24 75c blk & straw ('23) 19.00 1.25
113 A26 1fr brn red 1.65 22
114 A27 2fr dp vio 2.75 1.10
115 A28 3fr org & dk grn 2.25 1.25
116 A29 5fr brn & red brn 14.00 *24.00*
Nos. 99-116 (18) 62.72 *40.35*

Nos. 99 to 116 exist imperforate but were not regularly issued in that condition.

Madonna of Blieskastel — A30

1925, Apr. 9 Photo. *Perf. 13½x12½*

Size: 23x27mm

118 A30 45c lake brn 1.90 1.40

Size: 31½x36mm

Perf. 12

119 A30 10fr blk brn 7.25 *24.00*

Nos. 118-119 exist imperf. but were not regularly issued.

Market Fountain, St. Johann A31

View of Saar Valley A32

Colliery Shafthead A35

Burbach Steelworks A36

Designs: 15c, 75c, View of Saar Valley. 20c, 40c, 90c, Scene from Saarlouis fortifications. 25c, 50c, Tholey Abbey.

1927-32 *Perf. 13½*

120	A31	10c	dp brn	45	6
121	A32	15c	ol blk	30	*38*
122	A32	20c	brn org	28	6
123	A32	25c	bluish sl	35	18
124	A31	30c	ol grn	45	12
125	A32	40c	ol brn	35	6
126	A32	50c	magenta	45	6
127	A35	60c	red org ('30)	85	10
128	A32	75c	brn vio	35	9
129	A35	80c	red org	1.90	*3.75*
130	A32	90c	dp red ('32)	4.75	*10.00*
131	A35	1fr	violet	1.50	18
132	A36	1.50fr	sapphire	2.25	18
133	A36	2fr	brn red	2.25	18
134	A36	3fr	dk ol grn	5.50	38
135	A36	5fr	dp brn	7.25	2.75
			Nos. 120-135 (16)	29.23	*18.53*

60 cent.

Nos. 126 and 129 Surcharged

1930-34

136	A32	40c on 50c	mag ('34)	75	65
137	A35	60c on 80c	red org	75	*1.10*

Plebiscite Issue

Stamps of 1925-32 Overprinted in Various Colors

VOLKSABSTIMMUNG
1935

Perf. 13½, 13½x13, 13x13½

1934, Nov. 1

139	A31	10c	brn (Br)	40	32
140	A32	15c	blk grn (G)	40	32
141	A32	20c	brn org (O)	32	20
142	A32	25c	bluish sl (Bl)	55	*70*
143	A31	30c	ol grn (G)	30	30
144	A32	40c	ol brn (Br)	32	35
145	A32	50c	mag (R)	70	70
146	A35	60c	red org (O)	32	28
147	A32	75c	brn vio (V)	70	*75*
148	A32	90c	dp red (R)	70	*75*
149	A35	1fr	vio (V)	85	*75*
150	A36	1.50fr	saph (Bl)	1.25	*1.65*
151	A36	2fr	brn red (R)	1.75	*2.00*
152	A36	3fr	dk ol grn (G)	3.00	*4.00*
153	A36	5fr	dp brn (Br)	14.00	*15.00*

Size: 31½x36mm

Perf. 12

154	A30	10fr	blk brn (Br)	18.00	*27.50*
			Nos. 139-154 (16)	43.56	*55.57*

French Administration

Miner — A37

Steel Workers — A38

Harvesting Sugar Beets — A39

Mettlach Abbey — A40

Marshal Ney — A41

Saar River near Mettlach A42

1947 Unwmk. Photo. *Perf. 14*

155	A37	2pf	gray	5	*12*
156	A37	3pf	orange	6	*30*
157	A37	6pf	dk Prus grn	5	*15*
158	A37	8pf	scarlet	5	*15*
159	A37	10pf	rose vio	5	*15*
160	A38	15pf	brown	6	*30*
161	A38	16pf	ultra	5	*15*
162	A38	20pf	brn rose	5	*15*
163	A38	24pf	dp brn org	5	*15*
164	A39	25pf	cerise	30	*10.00*
165	A39	30pf	lt ol grn	10	*30*
166	A39	40pf	org brn	10	*30*
167	A39	50pf	bl vio	30	*10.00*
168	A40	60pf	violet	30	*10.00*
169	A40	80pf	dp org	5	*22*
170	A41	84pf	brown	5	*22*
171	A42	1m	gray grn	6	*30*
			Nos. 155-171 (17)	1.73	

Nos. 155-162, 164-171 exist imperf.

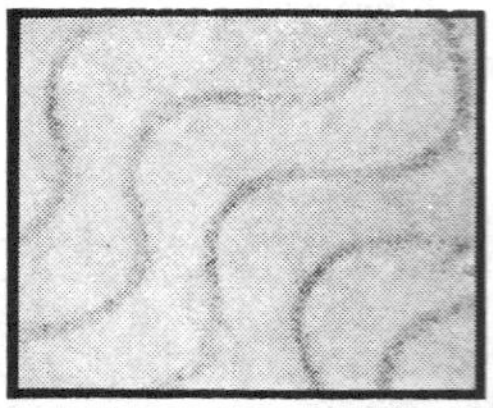
Wmk. 285- Marbleized Pattern

Types of 1947

1947 **Wmk. 285**

172	A37	12pf	ol grn	5	*15*
173	A39	45pf	crimson	20	*7.50*
174	A40	75pf	brt bl	6	*20*

Nos. 172-174 exist imperf.

Types of 1947 Surcharged with New Value, Bars and Ornament in Black or Red

1947, Nov. 27 **Unwmk.**

Printing II

175	A37	10c on 2pf gray	6	*25*
176	A37	60c on 3pf org	6	*25*
177	A37	1fr on 10pf rose vio	6	*25*
178	A37	2fr on 12pf ol grn	5	*75*
179	A38	3fr on 15pf brn	5	*25*
180	A38	4fr on 16pf ultra	10	*2.00*
181	A38	5fr on 20pf brn rose	8	*50*
182	A38	6fr on 24pf dp brn org	8	*25*
183	A39	9fr on 30pf lt ol grn	22	*3.00*
184	A39	10fr on 50pf bl vio (R)	28	*5.00*
185	A40	14fr on 60pf vio	35	*2.50*
186	A41	20fr on 84pf brn	25	*3.75*
187	A42	50fr on 1m gray grn	95	*6.25*
		Nos. 175-187 (13)	2.59	

Printing I

175a	A37	10c on 2pf gray	75.00	*200.00*
176a	A37	60c on 3pf org	60.00	*525.00*
177a	A37	1fr on 10pf rose vio	5.00	*8.75*
178a	A37	2fr on 12pf ol grn, wmk. 285	25	*50*
179a	A38	3fr on 15pf brn	400.00	*1,200.*
180a	A38	4fr on 16pf ultra	9.00	*65.00*
181a	A38	5fr on 20pf brn rose	35.00	*2,000.*
182a	A38	6fr on 24pf dp brn org	25	*1.00*
183a	A39	9fr on 30pf lt ol grn	37.50	*475.00*
184a	A39	10fr on 50pf bl vio (R)	380.00	*4,000.*
185a	A40	14fr on 60pf vio	90.00	*575.00*
186a	A41	20fr on 84pf brn	2.00	*3.75*
187a	A42	50fr on 1m gray grn	35.00	*275.00*
		Nos. 175a-187a (13)	1,129.	

Printing I was surcharged on Nos. 155-171. The crossbar of the A's in SAAR is high on the 10c, 60c, 1fr, 2fr, 9fr and 10fr; numeral "1" has no base serif on the 3fr and 4fr; wide space between vignette and SAAR panel; 1m inscribed "1M."

Printing II was surcharged on a special printing of the basic stamps, with details of design that differ on each denomination. The "A" crossbar is low on 10c, 60c, 1fr, 2fr, 9fr, 10fr; numeral "1" has base serif on 3fr and 4fr; narrow space between vignette and SAAR panel; 1m inscribed "1SM."

Inverted surcharges exist on Nos. 175-187 and 175a-187a.

French Protectorate

Clasped Hands A43

Colliery Shafthead A44

Designs: 2fr, 3fr, Worker. 4fr, 5fr, Girl gathering wheat. 6fr, 9fr, Miner. 14fr, Smelting. 20fr, Reconstruction. 50fr, Mettlach Abbey portal.

Perf. 14x13, 13

1948, Apr. 1 Engr. Unwmk.

188	A43	10c	hn brn	22	*85*
189	A43	60c	dk Prus grn	22	*85*
190	A43	1fr	brn blk	10	9
191	A43	2fr	rose car	12	6
192	A43	3fr	blk brn	14	6
193	A43	4fr	red	14	6
194	A43	5fr	red vio	14	8
195	A43	6fr	hn brn	20	8
196	A43	9fr	dk Prus grn	1.65	12
197	A44	10fr	dk bl	90	18
198	A44	14fr	dk vio brn	1.25	45
199	A44	20fr	hn brn	2.25	45
200	A44	50fr	bl blk	5.00	1.40
			Nos. 188-200 (13)	12.33	4.73

Map of the Saar A45

Caduceus, Microscope, Bunsen Burner and Book A46

1948, Dec. 15 Photo. *Perf. 13½x13*

201	A45	10fr	dk red	85	*1.10*
202	A45	25fr	dp bl	1.25	*2.50*

Issued to commemorate the first anniversary of the establishment of the French Protectorate.

1949, Apr. 2 *Perf. 13x13½*

203	A46	15fr	carmine	1.75	18

Issued to honor Saar University.

Ludwig van Beethoven A47

Laborer Using Spade A51

Saarbrücken A52

Designs: 10c, Building trades. 1fr, 3fr, Gears, factories. 5fr, Dumping mine waste. 6fr, 15fr, Coal mine interior. 8fr, Communications symbols. 10fr, Emblem of printing. 12fr, 18fr, Pottery. 25fr, Blast furnace worker. 45fr, Rock formation "Great Boot." 60fr, Reden Colliery, Landsweiler. 100fr, View of Weibelskirchen.

1949-51 Unwmk. *Perf. 13x13½*

204	A47	10c	vio brn	12	*85*
205	A47	60c	gray ('51)	12	*85*
206	A47	1fr	car lake	60	10
207	A47	3fr	brn ('51)	2.75	22
208	A47	5fr	dp vio ('50)	80	10
209	A47	6fr	Prus grn ('51)	4.25	20
210	A47	8fr	ol grn ('51)	28	20
211	A47	10fr	org ('50)	1.50	10
212	A47	12fr	dk grn	5.25	10
213	A47	15fr	red ('50)	2.75	10
214	A47	18fr	brn car ('51)	1.00	*2.50*

Perf. 13½

215	A51	20fr	gray ('50)	65	14
216	A51	25fr	vio bl	6.50	14
217	A52	30fr	red brn ('51)	5.50	30
218	A52	45fr	rose lake ('51)	1.90	32
219	A51	60fr	dp grn ('51)	1.90	75
220	A51	100fr	brown	2.75	1.00
			Nos. 204-220 (17)	38.62	*7.97*

Peter Wust — A54

St. Peter — A55

1950, Apr. 3

221	A54	15fr	car rose	1.75	*3.25*

10th anniversary of death of Peter Wust (1884-1940), Catholic philosopher.

1950, June 29 Engr. *Perf. 13*

222	A55	12fr	dp grn	1.75	*4.00*
223	A55	15fr	red brn	2.00	*4.00*
224	A55	25fr	blue	3.75	*7.50*

Holy Year, 1950.

Street in Ottweiler A56

Symbols of the Council of Europe A57

1950, July 10 Photo. *Perf. 13x13½*

225	A56	10fr	org brn	1.50	*4.00*

Issued to commemorate the 400th anniversary of the founding of Ottweiler.

1950, Aug. 8 *Perf. 13½*

226	A57	25fr	dp bl	18.00	4.25

Issued to commemorate the Saar's admission to the Council of Europe. See No. C12.

Post Rider and Guard — A62

1951, Apr. 29 Engr. *Perf. 13*

227	A62	15fr	dk vio brn	3.00	*6.00*

Issued to publicize Stamp Day, 1951.

A little time given to the study of the arrangement of the Scott Catalogue can make it easier to use effectively.

"Agriculture and Industry" and Fair Emblem
A63

Tower of Mittelbexbach and Flowers
A67

1951, May 12 Photo. *Perf. 13x13½*

228 A63 15fr dk gray grn	85	*3.00*

Issued to publicize the 1951 fair at Saarbrücken.

1951, June 9 Engr. *Perf. 13*

229 A67 15fr dk grn	85	60

Issued to publicize the Exhibition of Gardens and Flowers, Bexbach, 1951.

Refugees
A68

Globe & Stylized Fair Building
A69

1952, May 2 Unwmk. *Perf. 13*

230 A68 15fr brt red	1.00	60

Issued to honor the Red Cross.

1952, Apr. 26

231 A69 15fr red brn	1.00	60

Issued to publicize the 1952 fair at Saarbrücken.

Mine Shafts
A70

Ludwig's Gymnasium
A71

General Post Office
A72

Reconstruction of St. Ludwig's Cathedral
A73

"SM" Monogram
A74

Designs: 3fr, 18fr, Bridge building. 6fr, Transporter bridge, Mettlach. 30fr, Saar University Library.

1952-55 Engr.

232	A70	1fr dk bl grn ('53)	8	6
233	A71	2fr pur ('53)	8	6
234	A72	3fr dk car rose ('53)	8	6
235	A72	5fr dk grn (no inscription)	1.90	10
236	A72	5fr dk grn ("Hauptpostamt Saarbrücken") ('54)	8	6
237	A72	6fr vio brn ('53)	14	6
238	A71	10fr brn ol ('53)	20	6
239	A72	12fr grn ('53)	20	6
240	A70	15fr blk brn (no inscription)	2.75	10
241	A70	15fr blk brn ("Industrie-Landschaft") ('53)	1.25	10
242	A70	15fr dp car ('55)	8	6
243	A72	18fr dk rose brn ('55)	90	*1.90*
244	A72	30fr ultra ('53)	28	*40*
245	A73	500fr brn car ('53)	4.75	*19.00*
		Nos. 232-245 (14)	12.77	*22.08*

1953, Mar. 23

246 A74 15fr dk ultra	1.00	75

1953 fair at Saarbrücken.

Bavarian and Prussian Postilions
A75

1953, May 3

247 A75 15fr deep blue	1.75	*3.50*

Stamp Day.

Fountain and Fair Buildings — A76

1954, Apr. 10

248 A76 15fr dp grn	85	50

1954 International Fair at Saarbrücken.

Post Coach and Post Bus of 1920 — A77

1954, May 9 Engr.

249 A77 15fr red	1.65	*4.50*

Stamp Day, May 9, 1954.

Madonna and Child, Holbein
A78

Designs: 10fr, Sistine Madonna, Raphael. 15fr, Madonna and Child with pear, Durer.

1954, Aug. 14

250 A78 5fr dp car	32	*1.25*
251 A78 10fr dk grn	45	*1.65*
252 A78 15fr dp vio bl	70	*2.25*

Issued to commemorate the centenary of the promulgation of the Dogma of the Immaculate Conception.

Cyclist and Flag — A79

Symbols of Industry and Rotary Emblem — A80

1955, Feb. 28 Photo. *Perf. 13x13½*

253 A79 15fr multi	15	*32*

Issued to publicize the world championship cross country bicycle race.

1955, Feb. 28

254 A80 15fr org brn	15	*32*

Rotary International, 50th anniversary.

Flags of Participating Nations — A81

1955, Apr. 18 Photo. *Perf. 13x13½*

255 A81 15fr multi	15	*32*

1955 International Fair at Saarbrücken.

Postman at Illingen
A82

Unwmk.

1955, May 8 Engr. *Perf. 13*

256 A82 15fr deep claret	30	*1.10*

Issued to publicize Stamp Day, 1955.

Nos. 242-244 Overprinted "VOLKSBEFRAGUNG 1955"

1955, Oct. 22

257 A70 15fr dp car	6	*20*
258 A72 18fr dk rose brn	8	*22*
259 A72 30fr ultra	8	*42*

Plebiscite, Oct. 23, 1955.

Symbols of Industry and the Fair
A83

Radio Tower, Saarbrücken
A84

1956, Apr. 14 Photo. *Perf. 11½*

260 A83 15fr dk brn red & yel grn	12	*25*

Issued to publicize the International Fair at Saarbrücken, April 14-29, 1956.

1956, May 6

Granite Paper

261 A84 15fr grn & grnsh bl	12	*25*

Stamp Day.

German Administration

Arms of Saar — A85

Pres. Theodor Heuss — A86

Perf. 13x13½

1957, Jan. 1 Litho. Wmk. 304

262 A85 15fr brick red & bl	8	*20*

Return of the Saar to Germany.

1957 Typo. *Perf. 14*

Size: 18x22mm

263	A86	1(fr) brt grn	5	6
264	A86	2(fr) brt vio	5	6
265	A86	3(fr) bis brn	5	6
266	A86	4(fr) red vio	10	*38*
267	A86	5(fr) lt ol grn	5	6
268	A86	6(fr) vermilion	8	*30*
269	A86	10(fr) gray	5	*18*
270	A86	12(fr) dp org	6	6
271	A86	15(fr) lt bl grn	10	6
272	A86	18(fr) car rose	28	*75*
273	A86	25(fr) brt lil	15	*30*

Engr.

274	A86	30(fr) pale pur	15	*38*
275	A86	45(fr) gray ol	48	*1.25*
276	A86	50(fr) vio brn	48	*55*
277	A86	60(fr) dl rose	65	*1.40*
278	A86	70(fr) red org	1.25	*2.25*
279	A86	80(fr) ol grn	48	*1.40*
280	A86	90(fr) dk gray	1.10	*2.25*

Size: 24x29mm

281	A86	100(fr) dk car	90	*3.75*
282	A86	200(fr) violet	2.75	*10.50*
		Nos. 263-282 (20)	9.26	*26.00*

See Nos. 289-308.

Steel Industry — A87

Merzig Arms and St. Peter's Church — A88

Perf. 13x13½

1957, Apr. 20 Litho. Wmk. 304

284 A87 15fr gray & mag 8 *20*

The 1957 Fair at Saarbrücken.

1957, May 25 ***Perf. 14***

285 A88 15fr blue 8 *20*

Centenary of the town of Merzig.

Europa Issue, 1957

"United Europe" — A89

Lithographed; Tree Embossed

Perf. 14x13½

1957, Sept. 16 Unwmk.

286	A89	20fr org & yel	15	*55*
287	A89	35fr vio & pink	25	*65*

Issued to publicize a united Europe for peace and prosperity.

Carrier Pigeons — A90

Wmk. 304

1957, Oct. 5 Litho. ***Perf. 14***

288 A90 15fr dp car & blk 8 12

Issued for International Letter Writing Week, Oct. 6-12.

Redrawn Type of 1957; "F" added after denomination

1957 Wmk. 304 Litho. ***Perf. 14***

Size: 18x22mm

289	A86	1fr gray grn	5	10
290	A86	3fr blue	5	10
291	A86	5fr olive	5	10
292	A86	6fr lt brn	6	*30*
293	A86	10fr violet	6	*18*
294	A86	12fr brn org	6	*18*
295	A86	15fr dl grn	18	18
296	A86	18fr gray	75	*2.25*
297	A86	20fr lt ol grn	42	*1.25*
298	A86	25fr org brn	28	*30*
299	A86	30fr rose lil	35	30
300	A86	35fr brown	85	*1.25*
301	A86	45fr lt bl grn	60	*1.75*
302	A86	50fr dk red brn	35	*85*
303	A86	70fr brt grn	1.65	*2.25*
304	A86	80fr chlky bl	1.10	*2.25*
305	A86	90fr rose car	1.90	*3.75*

Engr.

Size: 24x29mm

306	A86	100fr orange	1.65	*3.25*
307	A86	200fr brt grn	3.25	*10.00*
308	A86	300fr blue	3.75	*12.50*
		Nos. 289-308 (20)	17.41	*43.09*

"Max and Moritz" — A91

Design: 15fr, Wilhelm Busch.

Perf. 13½x13

1958, Jan. 9 Litho. Wmk. 304

309	A91	12fr lt ol grn & blk	6	*12*
310	A91	15fr red & blk	12	*22*

Issued to commemorate the 50th anniversary of the death of Wilhelm Busch, humorist.

"Prevent Forest Fires" — A92

1958, Mar. 5 ***Perf. 14***

311 A92 15fr brt red & blk 8 *20*

Issued to aid in the prevention of forest fires.

Rudolf Diesel A93

1958, Mar. 18 Engr.

312 A93 12fr dk bl grn 8 *20*

Issued to commemorate the centenary of the birth of Rudolf Diesel, inventor.

Fair Emblem and City Hall, Saarbrücken A94

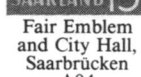

View of Homburg A95

1958, Apr. 10 Litho. ***Perf. 14***

313 A94 15fr dl rose 8 *20*

1958 Fair at Saarbrücken.

1958, June 14 Engr. Wmk. 304

314 A95 15fr gray grn 8 *20*

400th anniversary of Homburg.

Turner Emblem A96

Herman Schulze-Delitzsch A97

1958, July 21 Litho. ***Perf. 13½x14***

315 A96 12fr gray, blk & dl grn 8 *20*

Issued to commemorate 150 years of German Turners and on the occasion of the 1958 Turner Festival.

1958, Aug. 29 Engr. Wmk. 304

316 A97 12fr yel grn 8 *20*

150th anniv. of the birth of Schultze-Delitzsch, founder of German trade organizations.

Europa Issue, 1958

Common Design Type

1958, Sept. 13 Litho.

Size: 24½x30mm

317	CD1	12fr yel grn & bl	25	*50*
318	CD1	30fr lt bl & red	32	*65*

Issued to show the European Postal Union at the service of European integration.

Jakob Fugger — A98

Old and New City Hall and Burbach Mill — A99

Perf. 13x13½

1959, Mar. 6 Wmk. 304

319 A98 15fr dk red & blk 8 *20*

500th anniv. of the birth of Jakob Fugger the Rich, businessman and banker.

1959, Apr. 1 Engr. ***Perf. 14x13½***

320 A99 15fr lt bl 8 *20*

Greater Saarbrucken, 50th anniversary.

Hands Holding Merchandise A100

Alexander von Humboldt A101

1959, Apr. 1 Litho.

321 A100 15fr dp rose 10 *20*

Issued to publicize the 1959 Fair at Saarbrucken.

1959, May 6 Engr. ***Perf. 13½x14***

322 A101 15fr blue 10 *20*

Cent. of the death of Alexander von Humboldt, naturalist and geographer.

SEMI-POSTAL STAMPS

Red Cross Dog Leading Blind Man — SP1

Nurse and Invalid — SP2

Children Getting Drink at Spring — SP3

Maternity Nurse with Child — SP4

Perf. 13½

1926, Oct. 25 Photo. Unwmk.

B1	SP1	20c + 20c dk ol grn	4.75	*11.00*
B2	SP2	40c + 40c dk brn	5.00	*12.00*
B3	SP3	50c + 50c red org	5.00	*11.00*
B4	SP4	1.50fr + 1.50fr brt bl	10.00	*27.50*

Nos. B1-B4 Overprinted **1927-28**

1927, Oct. 1

B5	SP1	20c + 20c dk ol grn	10.00	*9.50*
B6	SP2	40c + 40c dk brn	8.50	*14.00*
B7	SP3	50c + 50c red org	8.00	*8.50*
B8	SP4	1.50fr + 1.50fr brt bl	12.00	*27.50*

"The Blind Beggar" by Dyckmans — SP5

"Almsgiving" by Schiestl — SP6

"Charity" by Raphael — SP7

1928, Dec. 23 Photo.

B9	SP5	40c (+40c) blk brn	7.75	*15.00*
B10	SP5	50c (+50c) brn rose	7.75	*15.00*
B11	SP5	1fr (+1fr) dl vio	7.75	*15.00*
B12	SP6	1.50fr (+1.50fr) cob bl	7.75	*15.00*
B13	SP6	2fr (+2fr) red brn	9.50	*17.50*
B14	SP6	3fr (+3fr) dk ol grn	9.50	*17.50*
B15	SP7	10fr (+10fr) dk brn	325.00	*4,000.*
		Nos. B9-B15 (7)	375.00	

"Orphaned" by Kaulbach — SP8

"St. Ottilia" by Feuerstein — SP9

"Madonna" by Ferruzzio — SP10

1929, Dec. 22

B16	SP8	40c (+15c) ol grn	1.75	*3.00*
B17	SP8	50c (+20c) cop red	3.50	*4.75*
B18	SP8	1fr (+50c) vio brn	3.50	*6.25*
B19	SP9	1.50fr (+75c) Prus bl	3.50	*6.25*
B20	SP9	2fr (+1fr) brn car	3.50	*6.25*
B21	SP9	3fr (+2fr) sl grn	6.00	*13.00*
B22	SP10	10fr (+8fr) blk brn	40.00	*75.00*
		Nos. B16-B22 (7)	61.75	

"The Safety-Man" SP11

"The Good Samaritan" SP12

"In the Window" — SP13

1931, Jan. 20

B23	SP11	40c (+15c) org brn	7.25	*15.00*
B24	SP11	60c (+20c) org red	7.25	*15.00*
B25	SP12	1fr (+50c) rose car	7.25	*24.00*
B26	SP11	1.50fr (+75c) sl bl	10.00	*24.00*
B27	SP12	2fr (+1fr) brn	10.00	*24.00*
B28	SP12	3fr (+2fr) ol grn	14.00	*24.00*
B29	SP13	10fr (+10fr) org brn	65.00	*150.00*
		Nos. B23-B29 (7)	120.75	

St. Martin of Tours — SP14

"Charity" — SP15

"The Widow's Mite" — SP16

1931, Dec. 23

B30	SP14	40c (+15c) blk brn	10.50	*17.50*
B31	SP14	60c (+20c) org red	10.50	*17.50*
B32	SP14	1fr (+50c) vio brn	12.50	*30.00*
B33	SP15	1.50fr (+75c) dp bl	15.00	*30.00*
B34	SP15	2fr (+1fr) rose car	16.00	*30.00*
B35	SP15	3fr (+2fr) ol grn	22.50	*65.00*
B36	SP16	5fr (+5fr) org brn	67.50	*175.00*
		Nos. B30-B36 (7)	154.50	

Ruins at Kirkel SP17

Illingen Castle, Kerpen SP23

Designs: 60c, Church at Blie. 1fr, Castle Ottweiler. 1.50fr, Church of St. Michael, Saarbrucken. 2fr, Statue of St. Wendel. 3fr, Church of St. John, Saarbrucken.

1932, Dec. 20

B37	SP17	40c (+15c) blk brn	7.75	*12.50*
B38	SP17	60c (+20c) brn org	7.75	*12.50*
B39	SP17	1fr (+50c) dp vio	11.50	*22.50*
B40	SP17	1.50fr (+75c) dp bl	18.00	*27.50*
B41	SP17	2fr (+1fr) car rose	18.00	*27.50*
B42	SP17	3fr (+2fr) ol grn	42.50	*92.50*
B43	SP23	5fr (+5fr) red brn	75.00	*175.00*
		Nos. B37-B43 (7)	180.50	

Scene of Neunkirchen Disaster SP24

1933, June 1

B44	SP24	60c (+ 60c) org red	12.50	15.00
B45	SP24	3fr (+ 3fr) ol grn	30.00	*40.00*
B46	SP24	5fr (+ 5fr) org brn	32.50	*60.00*

The surtax was for the aid of victims of the explosion at Neunkirchen, Feb. 10.

"Love" SP25

"Anxiety" SP26

"Peace" SP27

"Solace" SP28

"Welfare" SP29

"Truth" SP30

Figure on Tomb of Duchess Elizabeth of Lorraine — SP31

1934, Mar. 15 **Photo.**

B47	SP25	40c (+15c) blk brn	5.00	*8.00*
B48	SP26	60c (+20c) red org	5.00	*8.00*
B49	SP27	1fr (+50c) dl vio	6.75	*10.00*
B50	SP28	1.50fr (+75c) bl	12.50	*19.00*
B51	SP29	2fr (+1fr) car rose	11.50	*17.50*
B52	SP30	3fr (+2fr) ol grn	12.50	*19.00*
B53	SP31	5fr (+5fr) red brn	27.50	*42.50*
		Nos. B47-B53 (7)	80.75	

Nos. B47-B53 Overprinted like Nos. 139-154 in Various Colors Reading up

1934, Dec. 1 ***Perf. 13x13½***

B54	SP25	40c (+15c) blk brn (Br)	3.75	*9.00*
B55	SP26	60c (+20c) red org (R)	3.75	*9.00*
B56	SP27	1fr (+50c) dl vio (V)	7.25	*16.00*
B57	SP28	1.50fr (+75c) bl (Bl)	7.25	*16.00*
B58	SP29	2fr (+1fr) car rose (R)	9.25	*22.50*
B59	SP30	3fr (+2fr) ol grn (G)	8.50	*20.00*
B60	SP31	5fr (+5fr) red brn (Br)	14.00	*27.50*
		Nos. B54-B60 (7)	53.75	

French Protectorate

Various Flood Scenes
SP32 SP33

Perf. 13½x13, 13x13½

1948, Oct. 12 **Photo.**

Inscribed "Hochwasser-Hilfe 1947-48"

B61	SP32	5fr + 5fr dl grn	1.65	*16.00*
B62	SP33	6fr + 4fr dk vio	1.65	*16.00*
B63	SP32	12fr + 8fr red	2.00	*22.50*
B64	SP33	18fr + 12fr bl	3.00	*27.50*
a.		Souv. sheet of 4, #B61-B64, imperf.	265.00	*2,000.*
		Nos. B61-B64,CB1 (5)	23.30	

The surtax was for flood relief.

Hikers and Ludweiler Hostel SP34

Designs: No. B66, Hikers approaching Weisskirchen Hostel.

1949, Jan. 11 ***Perf. 13½x13***

B65	SP34	8fr + 5fr dk brn	1.25	*3.50*
B66	SP34	10fr + 7fr dk grn	1.25	*2.75*

The surtax aided youth hostels.

Mare and Foal — SP35

Design: No. B68, Jumpers.

1949, Sept. 25 ***Perf. 13½***

B67	SP35	15fr + 5fr brn red	5.75	*20.00*
B68	SP35	25fr + 15fr bl	7.25	*21.00*

Day of the Horse, Sept. 25, 1949.

Detail from "Moses Striking the Rock" — SP36

Designs: No. B70, "Christ at the Pool of Bethesda." No. B71, "The Sick Child." No. B72, "St. Thomas of Villeneuve." No. B73, Madonna of Blieskastel.

1949, Dec. 20 **Engr.** ***Perf. 13***

B69	SP36	8fr + 2fr ind	3.50	*24.00*
B70	SP36	12fr + 3fr dk grn	4.25	*26.00*
B71	SP36	15fr + 5fr brn lake	6.00	*42.50*
B72	SP36	25fr + 10fr dp ultra	9.00	*67.50*
B73	SP36	50fr + 20fr choc	16.00	*95.00*
		Nos. B69-B73 (5)	38.75	

The first value column gives the catalogue value of an unused stamp, the second that of a used stamp.

Adolph Kolping SP37

Relief for the Hungry SP38

1950, Apr. 3 **Photo.** ***Perf. 13x13½***

B74	SP37	15fr + 5fr car rose	13.00	*50.00*

Engraved and Typographed

1950, Apr. 28 ***Perf. 13***

B75	SP38	25fr + 10fr dk brn car & red	13.00	*37.50*

Stagecoach — SP39

1950, Apr. 22 **Engr.**

B76	SP39	15fr + 15fr brn red & dk brn	25.00	*85.00*

Issued to commemorate "Stamp Day," April 27, 1950. Sold at the exhibition and to advance subscribers.

Lutwinus Seeking Admission to Abbey SP40

Designs: 12fr+3fr, Lutwinus Building Mettlach Abbey. 15fr+5fr, Lutwinus as Abbot. 25fr+10fr, Bishop Lutwinus at Rheims. 50fr+20fr, Aid to the poor and sick.

1950, Nov. 10 **Unwmk.** ***Perf. 13***

B77	SP40	8fr + 2fr dk brn	3.25	*14.00*
B78	SP40	12fr + 3fr dk grn	3.25	*14.00*
B79	SP40	15fr + 5fr red brn	4.00	*20.00*
B80	SP40	25fr + 10fr bl	6.00	*32.50*
B81	SP40	50fr + 20fr brn car	8.25	*50.00*
		Nos. B77-B81 (5)	24.75	

The surtax was for public assistance.

Mother and Child — SP41

John Calvin and Martin Luther — SP42

1951, Apr. 28

B82	SP41	25fr + 10fr dk grn & car	12.00	*35.00*

The surtax was for the Red Cross.

1951, Apr. 28

B83	SP42	15fr + 5fr blk brn	90	*3.50*

Issued to commemorate the 375th anniversary of the Reformation in Saar.

"Mother" SP43

Runner with Torch SP44

Paintings: 15fr+5fr, "Before the Theater." 18fr+7fr, "Sisters of Charity." 30fr+10fr, "The Good Samaritan." 50fr+ 20fr, "St. Martin and Beggar."

1951, Nov. 3

B84 SP43	12fr + 3fr dk grn	2.75	*9.00*
B85 SP43	15fr + 5fr pur	2.75	*9.00*
B86 SP43	18fr + 7fr dk red	3.25	*11.50*
B87 SP43	30fr + 10fr dp bl	5.25	*18.00*
B88 SP43	50fr + 20fr blk brn	12.50	*37.50*
	Nos. B84-B88 (5)	26.50	

1952, Mar. 29 Unwmk. *Perf. 13*

Design: 30fr+5fr, Hand with olive branch, and globe.

Inscribed: "Olympische Spiele 1952"

B89 SP44	15fr + 5fr dp grn	1.40	*5.50*
B90 SP44	30fr + 5fr dp bl	1.65	*7.75*

XV Olympic Games, Helsinki, 1952.

Postrider Delivering Mail — SP45

1952, Mar. 30

B91 SP45	30fr + 10fr dk bl	4.75	*12.50*

Stamp Day, Mar. 29, 1952.

Count Stroganoff as a Boy SP46

Henri Dunant SP47

Portraits: 18fr+7fr, The Holy Shepherd by Murillo. 30fr+10fr, Portrait of a Boy by Georg Melchior Kraus.

1952, Nov. 3

B92 SP46	15fr + 5fr dk brn	1.90	*6.75*
B93 SP46	18fr + 7fr brn lake	2.50	*9.25*
B94 SP46	30fr + 10fr dp bl	2.75	*10.50*

The surtax was for child welfare.

1953, May 3 Cross in Red

B95 SP47	15fr + 5fr blk brn	1.00	*4.00*

Clarice Strozzi by Titian — SP48

Children of Rubens SP49

Portrait: 30fr+10fr, Rubens' son.

1953, Nov. 16

B96 SP48	15fr + 5fr pur	90	*3.00*
B97 SP49	18fr + 7fr dp cl	90	*3.50*
B98 SP48	30fr + 10fr dp ol grn	1.75	*5.50*

The surtax was for child welfare.

St. Benedict Blessing St. Maurus SP50

Child and Cross SP51

1953, Dec. 18 Litho.

B99 SP50	30fr + 10fr blk	1.00	*4.50*

The surtax was for the abbey at Tholey.

1954, May 10 Engr.

B100 SP51	15fr + 5fr choc	1.25	*3.75*

The surtax was for the Red Cross.

Street Urchin with Melon, Murillo — SP52

Nurse Holding Baby — SP53

Paintings: 10fr+5fr, Maria de Medici, Bronzino. 15fr+7fr, Baron Emil von Maucler, Dietrich.

1954, Nov. 15

B101 SP52	5fr + 3fr red	18	*50*
B102 SP52	10fr + 5fr dk grn	22	*60*
B103 SP52	15fr + 7fr pur	28	*75*

The surtax was for child welfare.

Perf. 13x13½

1955, May 5 Photo. Unwmk.

B104 SP53	15fr + 5fr blk & red	15	*45*

The surtax was for the Red Cross.

Dürer's Mother, Age 63 — SP54

Etchings by Dürer: 10fr+5fr, Praying hands. 15fr+7fr, Old man of Antwerp.

1955, Dec. 10 Engr. *Perf. 13*

B105 SP54	5fr + 3fr dk grn	20	*45*
B106 SP54	10fr + 5fr ol grn	40	*90*
B107 SP54	15fr + 7fr ol bis	50	*1.10*

The surtax was for public assistance.

First Aid Station, Saarbrücken, 1870 — SP55

1956, May 7

B108 SP55	15fr + 5fr dk brn	12	*30*

The surtax was for the Red Cross.

"Victor of Benevent" SP56

Winterberg Monument SP57

1956, July 25 Unwmk. *Perf. 13*

B109 SP56	12fr + 3fr dk yel grn & bl grn	12	*28*
B110 SP56	15fr + 5fr brn vio & brn	12	*28*

Issued to publicize the forthcoming 16th Olympic Games at Melbourne, Nov. 22-Dec. 8, 1956.

1956, Oct. 29

B111 SP57	5fr + 2fr grn	6	*15*
B112 SP57	12fr + 3fr red lil	8	*28*
B113 SP57	15fr + 5fr brn	8	*28*

The surtax was for the rebuilding of monuments.

"La Belle Ferronnière" by da Vinci — SP58

Designs: 10fr + 5fr, "Saskia" by Rembrandt. 15fr+7fr, "Family van Berchem," by Frans Floris. (Detail: Woman playing Spinet.)

1956, Dec. 10

B114 SP58	5fr + 3fr dp bl	8	*12*
B115 SP58	10fr + 5fr dp cl	12	*24*
B116 SP58	15fr + 7fr dk grn	14	*40*

The surtax was for charitable works.

German Administration

Miner with Drill — SP59

"The Fox who Stole the Goose" — SP60

Designs: 6fr+4fr, Miner. 15fr+7fr, Miner and conveyor. 30fr+10fr, Miner and coal elevator.

Wmk. 304

1957, Oct. 1 Litho. *Perf. 14*

B117 SP59	6fr + 4fr bis brn & blk	8	*14*
B118 SP59	12fr + 6fr blk & yel grn	8	*16*
B119 SP59	15fr + 7fr blk & red	12	*38*
B120 SP59	30fr + 10fr blk & bl	18	*45*

The surtax was for independent welfare organizations.

1958, Apr. 1 Wmk. 304 *Perf. 14*

Design: 15fr+7fr, "A Hunter from the Palatinate."

B121 SP60	12fr + 6fr brn red, grn & blk	8	*18*
B122 SP60	15fr + 7fr grn, red, blk & gray	8	*24*

The surtax was to finance young peoples' study trip to Berlin.

Friedrich Wilhelm Raiffeisen SP61

Dairy Maid SP62

Designs: 15fr+7fr, Girl picking grapes. 30fr+10fr, Farmer with pitchfork.

1958, Oct. 1 Wmk. 304 *Perf. 14*

B123 SP61	6fr + 4fr gldn brn & dk brn	8	12
B124 SP62	12fr + 6fr grn, red & yel	8	14
B125 SP62	15fr + 7fr red, yel & bl	18	*30*
B126 SP62	30fr + 10fr bl & ocher	22	*40*

The surtax was for independent welfare organizations.

AIR POST STAMPS

Airplane over Saarbrücken AP1

Perf. 13½

1928, Sept. 19 Unwmk. Photo.

C1 AP1	50c brn red	2.25	1.40
C2 AP1	1fr dk vio	3.00	1.90

Saarbrücken Airport and Church of St. Arnual AP2

1932, April 30

C3 AP2	60c org red	4.00	2.50
C4 AP2	5fr dk brn	35.00	*60.00*

Nos. C1-C4 Overprinted like Nos. 139-154 in Various Colors

1934, Nov. 1 *Perf. 13½, 13½x13*

C5 AP1	50c brn red (R)	4.00	*4.75*
C6 AP2	60c org red (O)	2.75	*2.25*
C7 AP1	1fr dk vio (V)	6.00	*6.50*
C8 AP2	5fr dk brn (Br)	8.50	*8.75*

French Protectorate

Shadow of Plane over Saar River AP3

Unwmk.

1948, Apr. 1 Engr. *Perf. 13*

C9 AP3	25fr red	2.00	1.90
C10 AP3	50fr dk Prus grn	1.25	95
C11 AP3	200fr rose car	12.00	*16.00*

Symbols of the Council of Europe
AP4

1950, Aug. 8 Photo. *Perf. 13½*

C12 AP4 200fr red brn 85.00 *130.00*

Issued to commemorate the Saar's admission to the Council of Europe.

AIR POST SEMI-POSTAL STAMPS

French Protectorate

Flood Scene
SPAP1

Perf. 13½x13

1948, Oct. 12 Photo. Unwmk.

CB1 SPAP1 25fr + 25fr sep 15.00 *80.00*
a. Souv. sheet of 1 250.00 *1,500.*

The surtax was for flood relief.

OFFICIAL STAMPS

Regular Issue of 1922-1923 Overprinted Diagonally in Red or Blue

DIENSTMARKE

Perf. 12½x13½, 13½x12½

1922-23 Unwmk.

O1 A19 3c ol grn & straw (R) 52 *19.00*
O2 A20 5c org & blk (R) 25 18
O3 A21 10c bl grn (R) 25 12
O4 A19 15c dp brn (Bl) 25 14
O5 A19 15c org (Bl) ('23) 1.65 22
O6 A22 20c dk bl & lem (R) 25 14
O7 A22 20c brt bl & straw (R) ('23) 1.65 22
O8 A22 25c red & yel (Bl) 2.50 60
O9 A22 25c mag & straw (Bl) ('23) 1.65 22
O10 A23 30c car & yel (Bl) 25 12
O11 A24 40c brn & yel (Bl) 42 14
O12 A25 50c dk bl & straw (R) 42 14
O13 A24 75c dp grn & straw (R) 10.50 11.00
O14 A24 75c blk & straw (R) ('23) 3.00 1.00
O15 A26 1fr brn red (Bl) 4.50 1.25
Nos. O1-O15 (15) 28.06 *34.49*

Inverted overprints exist on 10c, 20c, 30c, 50c and 1fr. Double overprints exist on Nos. O4, O6 and 1fr.

Regular Issue of 1927-30 Overprinted in Various Colors

DIENSTMARKE

1927-34 *Perf. 13½*

O16 A31 10c dp brn (Bl) ('34) 1.00 1.10
O17 A32 15c ol blk (Bl) ('34) 1.50 *4.25*
O18 A32 20c brn org (Bk) ('31) 1.00 80
O19 A32 25c bluish sl (Bl) 1.50 *2.75*
O20 A31 30c ol grn (C) 85 14
O21 A32 40c ol brn (C) 85 14
O22 A32 50c mag (Bl) 85 14
O23 A35 60c red org (Bk) ('30) 60 18
O24 A32 75c brn vio (C) 70 32
O25 A35 1fr vio (RO) 1.50 14
O26 A36 2fr brn red (Bl) 1.50 22
Nos. O16-O26 (11) 11.85 *10.18*

The overprint listed is at a 23 to 25-degree angle. Also at 32-degree angle on Nos. O20-O22, O24-O26.

The overprint on Nos. O16 and O20 is known only inverted. Nos. O21-O26 exist with double overprint.

French Protectorate

Arms — O1

1949, Oct. 1 Engr. *Perf. 14x13*

O27 O1 10c dp car 20 *9.75*
O28 O1 30c bl blk 14 *9.75*
O29 O1 1fr Prus grn 14 15
O30 O1 2fr org red 85 55
O31 O1 5fr blue 25 22
O32 O1 10fr black 40 50
O33 O1 12fr red vio 3.25 *3.75*
O34 O1 15fr indigo 40 20
O35 O1 20fr green 90 55
O36 O1 30fr vio rose 1.10 *2.00*
O37 O1 50fr purple 1.10 *1.90*
O38 O1 100fr red brn 40.00 *100.00*
Nos. O27-O38 (12) 48.73

STE.-MARIE DE MADAGASCAR

LOCATION — An island off the east coast of Madagascar.
GOVT. — French Possession.
AREA — 64 sq. mi.
POP. — 8,000 (approx.).

In 1896 Ste.-Marie de Madagascar was attached to the colony of Madagascar for administrative purposes.

100 Centimes = 1 Franc

Navigation and Commerce — A1

1894 Unwmk. Typo. *Perf. 14x11½*

Name of Colony in Blue or Carmine

1 A1 1c blk, *lil bl* 55 55
2 A1 2c brn, *buff* 60 60
3 A1 4c claret, *lav* 2.40 2.00
4 A1 5c grn, *grnsh* 5.50 4.00
5 A1 10c blk, *lavender* 5.50 4.25
6 A1 15c blue 11.00 11.00
7 A1 20c red, *grn* 10.00 7.00
8 A1 25c blk, *rose* 8.00 6.00
9 A1 30c brn, *bis* 5.50 4.50
10 A1 40c red, *straw* 5.75 4.50
11 A1 50c car, *rose* 22.50 18.00
12 A1 75c vio, *org* 40.00 20.00
13 A1 1fr brnz grn, *straw* 20.00 14.00
Nos. 1-13 (13) 137.30 96.40

These stamps were replaced by those of Madagascar.

ST. PIERRE & MIQUELON

LOCATION — Two small groups of islands off the southern coast of Newfoundland.
GOVT. — Former French overseas territory.
AREA — 93 sq. mi.
POP. — 5,450 (est. 1974).
CAPITAL — St. Pierre.

The territory of St. Pierre and Miquelon became a Department of France in July 1976.

100 Centimes = 1 Franc

Catalogue values for unused stamps in this country are for Never Hinged items, beginning with Scott 300 in the regular postage section, Scott B13 in the semi-postal section, Scott C1 in the airpost section, and Scott J68 in the postage due section.

Stamps of French Colonies Handstamp Surcharged in Black

05
SPM

1885 Unwmk. *Imperf.*

1 A8 05c on 40c ver, *straw* 45.00 22.50
2 A8 10c on 40c ver, *straw* 11.00 9.00
a "M" inverted 110.00 75.00
3 A8 15c on 40c ver, *straw* 11.00 9.00

Nos. 2 and 3 exist with "SPM" 17mm wide instead of 15½mm.

Nos. 1-3 exist with surcharge inverted and with it doubled.

Handstamp Surcharged in Black

05 SPM — b
25 S P M — c
25 S P M — d

1885

4 A8 (b) 05c on 35c blk, *yel* 55.00 40.00
5 A8 (b) 05c on 75c car, *rose* 150.00 90.00
6 A8 (b) 05c on 1fr brnz grn, *straw* 12.00 11.00
7 A8 (c) 25c on 1fr brnz grn, *straw* *5,750.* *1,600.*
8 A8 (d) 25c on 1fr brnz grn, *straw* *2,100.* *1,100.*

Nos. 7 and 8 exist with surcharge inverted, and with it vertical. No. 7 exists with "S P M" above "25" (the handstamping was done in two steps).

1885 *Perf. 14x13½*

9 A9 (c) 5c on 2c brn, *buff* *4,250.* *1,750.*
10 A9 (d) 5c on 4c cl, *lav* 225.00 150.00
11 A9 (b) 05c on 20c red, *grn* 12.00 11.00

No. 9 surcharge is always inverted. No. 10 exists with surcharge inverted.

P D
5
A15

1886 Typo. *Imperf.*

12 A15 5c black 650.00
13 A15 10c black 800.00
14 A15 15c black 500.00

"P D" are the initials for "Payéa destination." Excellent forgeries of Nos. 12 to 14 exist.

Stamps of French Colonies Surcharged in Black

15 c. SPM — e
15 c. SPM — f

1891 *Perf. 14x13½*

15 A9 (e) 15c on 30c brn, *bis* 17.50 15.00
a Inverted surcharge 120.00 90.00
16 A9 (e) 15c on 35c blk, *org* 325.00 225.00
a Inverted surcharge 350.00 325.00
17 A9 (f) 15c on 35c blk, *org* 800.00 500.00
a Inverted surcharge 1,400. 800.00
18 A9 (e) 15c on 40c red, *straw* 40.00 32.50
a Inverted surcharge 100.00 90.00

Nos. 7, 8, 10, 16 and 17 have been reprinted. Originals are surcharged in dull black, the reprints in deep or glossy black.

Stamps of French Colonies Overprinted in Black or Red

ST-PIERRE M-ON

1891

19 A9 1c blk, *lil bl* 4.50 4.00
a Inverted overprint 12.50 12.50
20 A9 1c blk, *lil bl* (R) 4.25 4.25
a Inverted overprint 9.00 9.00
21 A9 2c brn, *buff* 4.50 4.00
a Inverted overprint 12.50 12.50
22 A9 2c brn, *buff* (R) 10.00 10.00
a Inverted overprint 27.50 27.50
23 A9 4c cl, *lav* 4.50 4.00
a Inverted overprint 14.00 14.00
24 A9 4c cl, *lav* (R) 8.00 8.00
a Inverted overprint 22.50 22.50
25 A9 5c grn, *grnsh* 4.50 4.00
a Double surcharge 40.00
26 A9 10c blk, *lav* 14.00 11.00
a Inverted overprint 32.50 32.50
27 A9 10c blk, *lav* (R) 7.00 7.00
a Inverted overprint 22.50 22.50
28 A9 15c blk, *blue* 9.00 6.25
29 A9 20c red, *grn* 27.50 25.00
30 A9 25c blk, *rose* 11.00 9.00
31 A9 30c brn, *bis* 45.00 37.50
32 A9 35c vio, *org* 225.00 165.00
33 A9 40c red, *straw* 35.00 25.00
a Double surcharge 82.50
34 A9 75c car, *rose* 45.00 40.00
a Inverted overprint 100.00 100.00
35 A9 1fr brnz grn, *straw* 27.50 25.00
a Inverted overprint 82.50 82.50

Numerous varieties of mislettering occur in the preceding overprint: "S," "ST," "P," "M," "ON," or "-" missing; "-" instead of "ON"; "=" instead of "-" These varieties command values double or triple those of normal stamps.

Surcharged in Black

1 ST-PIERRE M-ON cent.

1891-92

36 A9 1c on 5c grn, *grnsh* 4.25 4.00
37 A9 1c on 10c blk, *lav* 5.25 4.25
38 A9 1c on 25c blk, *rose* ('92) 4.00 3.25
39 A9 2c on 10c blk, *lav* 4.00 3.25
a Double surcharge 42.50
40 A9 2c on 15c bl 3.00 3.00
41 A9 2c on 25c blk, *rose* ('92) 3.00 3.00
42 A9 4c on 20c red, *grn* 3.00 3.00
43 A9 4c on 25c blk, *rose* ('92) 3.00 3.00

44	A9	4c on 30c brn, *bis*	9.00	8.00
45	A9	4c on 40c red, *straw*	12.00	7.00

See note after No. 35.

Surcharged

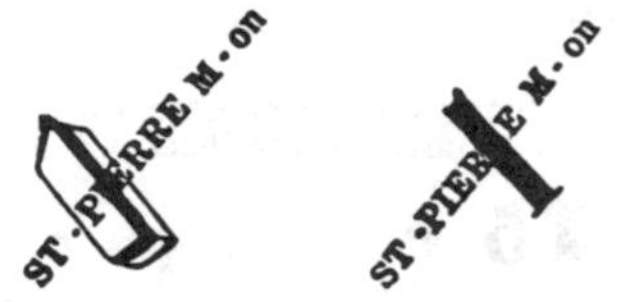

j k

1892

46	A9 (j)	1c on 5c grn, *grnsh*	5.00	4.25
47	A9 (j)	2c on 5c grn, *grnsh*	5.00	4.25
48	A9 (j)	4c on 5c grn, *grnsh*	5.00	4.25
49	A9 (k)	1c on 25c blk, *rose*	2.50	2.50
50	A9 (k)	2c on 25c blk, *rose*	2.50	2.50
51	A9 (k)	4c on 25c blk, *rose*	2.50	2.50

See note after No. 35.

Postage Due Stamps of French Colonies Overprinted in Red

1892 ***Imperf.***

52	D1	10c black	15.00	15.00
53	D1	20c black	9.00	9.00
54	D1	30c black	10.00	10.00
55	D1	40c black	10.00	10.00
56	D1	60c black	45.00	45.00

Black Overprint

57	D1	1fr brown	65.00	65.00
58	D1	2fr brown	120.00	120.00
59	D1	5fr brown	225.00	225.00

See note after No. 35.

Navigation and Commerce — A16

1892-1908 Typo. *Perf. 14x13½*

60	A16	1c blk, *lil bl*	40	40
61	A16	2c brn, *buff*	40	40
62	A16	4c cl, *lav*	80	70
63	A16	5c grn, *grnsh*	1.00	1.00
64	A16	5c yel grn ('08)	1.65	1.40
65	A16	10c blk, *lav*	2.50	2.25
66	A16	10c red ('00)	2.25	80
67	A16	15c bl, quadrille paper	3.25	1.40
68	A16	15c gray, *lt gray* ('00)	42.50	25.00
69	A16	20c red, *grn*	11.00	8.25
70	A16	25c blk, *rose*	4.00	1.20
71	A16	25c blue ('00)	7.00	5.00
72	A16	30c brn, *bis*	4.00	2.00
73	A16	35c blk, *yel* ('06)	3.75	3.00
74	A16	40c red, *straw*	3.50	2.00
75	A16	50c car, *rose*	21.00	16.00
76	A16	50c brn, *az* ('00)	16.00	14.00
77	A16	75c vio, *org*	14.00	11.00
78	A16	1fr brnz grn, *straw*	11.00	6.00
		Nos. 60-78 (19)	150.00	101.80

Fisherman A17

Fulmar Petrel — A18

Fishing Schooner A19

1909-30

79	A17	1c org red & ol	5	5
80	A17	2c ol & dp bl	5	5
81	A17	4c vio & ol	5	5
82	A17	5c bl grn & ol grn	20	10
83	A17	5c bl & blk ('22)	5	5
84	A17	10c car rose & red	20	20
85	A17	10c bl grn & ol grn ('22)	10	10
86	A17	10c bis & mag ('25)	20	20
86A	A17	15c dl vio & rose ('17)	20	10
87	A17	20c bis brn & vio brn	45	45
88	A18	25c dp bl & bl	80	60
89	A18	25c ol brn & bl grn ('22)	22	22
90	A18	30c org & vio brn	45	45
91	A18	30c rose & dl red ('22)	12	12
92	A18	30c red brn & bl ('25)	5	5
93	A18	30c gray grn & bl grn ('26)	28	28
94	A18	35c ol grn & vio brn	20	20
95	A18	40c vio brn & ol grn	1.25	80
96	A18	45c vio & ol grn	28	28
97	A18	50c ol & ol grn	55	55
98	A18	50c bl & pale bl ('22)	45	45
99	A18	50c yel brn & mag ('25)	25	25
100	A18	60c dk bl & ver ('25)	28	28
101	A18	65c vio & org brn ('28)	50	50
102	A18	75c brn & ol	55	55
103	A18	90c brn red & org red ('30)	10.00	10.00
104	A19	1fr ol grn & dp bl	1.40	1.20
105	A19	1.10fr bl grn & org red ('28)	1.50	1.50
106	A19	1.50fr bl & dp bl ('30)	4.00	4.00
107	A19	2fr vio & brn	1.40	1.25
108	A19	3fr red vio ('30)	4.00	4.00
109	A19	5fr vio brn & ol grn	4.50	3.00
		Nos. 79-109 (32)	34.58	31.88

Stamps of 1892-1906 Surcharged in Carmine or Black

05 **10**

1912

110	A16	5c on 2c brn, *buff*	80	80
111	A16	5c on 4c cl, *lav* (C)	15	15
112	A16	5c on 15c bl (C)	15	15
113	A16	5c on 20c red, *grn*	15	15
114	A16	5c on 25c blk, *rose* (C)	15	15
115	A16	5c on 30c brn, *bis* (C)	25	25
116	A16	5c on 35c blk, *yel* (C)	40	40
117	A16	10c on 40c red, *straw*	15	15
118	A16	10c on 50c car, *rose*	28	28
119	A16	10c on 75c dp vio, *org*	65	65
120	A16	10c on 1fr brnz grn, *straw*	80	80
		Nos. 110-120 (11)	3.93	3.93

Two spacings between the surcharged numerals are found on Nos. 110 to 120.

Stamps and Types of 1909-17 Surcharged with New Value and Bars in Black, Blue (Bl) or Red

1924-27

121	A17	25c on 15c dl vio & rose ('25)	20	20
a		Double surcharge	70.00	
b		Triple surcharge	70.00	
122	A19	25c on 2fr vio & lt brn (Bl)	20	20
123	A19	25c on 5fr brn & ol grn (Bl)	20	20
a		Triple surcharge	65.00	
124	A18	65c on 45c vio & ol grn ('25)	45	45
125	A18	85c on 75c brn & ol ('25)	45	45
126	A18	90c on 75c brn red & dp org ('27)	80	80
127	A19	1.25fr on 1fr dk bl & ultra (R) ('26)	70	70
128	A19	1.50fr on 1fr ultra & dk bl ('27)	1.40	1.40
129	A19	3fr on 5fr ol brn & red vio ('27)	80	80
130	A19	10fr on 5fr ver & ol grn ('27)	6.50	6.50
131	A19	20fr on 5fr vio & ver ('27)	9.00	9.00
		Nos. 121-131 (11)	20.70	20.70

Colonial Exposition Issue

Common Design Types

1931 Engr. *Perf. 12½*

Name of Country in Black

132	CD70	40c dp grn	90	90
133	CD71	50c violet	90	90
134	CD72	90c red org	90	90
135	CD73	1.50fr dull blue	90	90

Map and Fishermen — A20

Lighthouse and Fish — A21

Fishing Steamer and Sea Gulls — A22

Perf. 13½x14, 14x13½

1932-33 Typo.

136	A20	1c red brn & ultra	5	5
137	A21	2c blk & dk grn	5	5
138	A22	4c mag & ol brn	10	10
139	A22	5c vio & dk brn	10	10
140	A21	10c red brn & blk	12	12
141	A21	15c dk bl & vio	40	40
142	A20	20c blk & red org	40	40
143	A20	25c lt vio & lt grn	40	40
144	A22	30c ol grn & bl grn	40	40
145	A22	40c dp bl & dk brn	55	55
146	A21	45c ver & dp grn	55	55
147	A21	50c dk brn & dk grn	55	55
148	A22	65c ol brn & org	65	65
149	A20	75c grn & red org	65	65
150	A20	90c dl red & red	70	70
151	A22	1fr org brn & org red	55	55
152	A20	1.25fr dp bl & lake ('33)	70	70
153	A20	1.50fr dp bl & bl	70	70
154	A22	1.75fr blk & dk brn ('33)	90	90
155	A22	2fr bl blk & Prus bl	3.75	3.75
156	A21	3fr dp grn & dk brn	4.50	4.50
157	A21	5fr brn red & dk brn	9.00	9.00
158	A22	10fr dk grn & vio	27.50	27.50
159	A20	20fr ver & dp grn	27.50	27.50
		Nos. 136-159 (24)	80.77	80.77

Cartier Issue

Stamps of 1932-33 Overprinted in Black, Red or Blue

JACQUES CARTIER

JACQUES CARTIER

1534 - 1934 1534-1934

p q

1934

160	A21(p)	50c dk brn & dk grn (Bk)	80	80
161	A20(q)	75c grn & red org (Bk)	1.20	1.20
162	A20(p)	1.50fr dp bl & bl (Bk)	1.20	1.20
163	A22(p)	1.75fr blk & dk brn (R)	1.50	1.50
164	A21(p)	5fr brn red & dk brn (Bl)	12.00	12.00
		Nos. 160-164 (5)	16.70	16.70

400th anniv. of the landing of Jacques Cartier.

Paris International Exposition Issue

Common Design Types

1937 *Perf. 13*

165	CD74	20c dp vio	65	65
166	CD75	30c dk grn	65	65
167	CD76	40c car rose	65	65
168	CD77	50c dk brn & bl	65	65
169	CD78	90c red	65	65
170	CD79	1.50fr ultra	65	65
		Nos. 165-170 (6)	3.90	3.90

Colonial Arts Exhibition Issue

Souvenir Sheet

Common Design Type

1937 *Imperf.*

171	CD78	3fr dk ultra	2.25	2.25

Dog Team A23

Port St. Pierre A24

Tortue Lighthouse A25

Soldiers' Bay at Langlade A26

1938-40 Photo. *Perf. 13½x13*

172	A23	2c dk bl grn	5	5
173	A23	3c brn vio	5	5
174	A23	4c dk red vio	5	5
175	A23	5c car lake	5	5
176	A23	10c bis brn	5	5
177	A23	15c red vio	5	5
178	A23	20c bl vio	10	10
179	A23	25c Prus bl	80	80
180	A24	30c dk red vio	10	10
181	A24	35c dp grn	20	20
182	A24	40c slate bl ('40)	5	5
183	A24	45c dp grn ('40)	20	20
a		Value omitted	35.00	
184	A24	50c car rose	5	5
185	A24	55c Prus bl	1.00	1.00
186	A24	60c vio ('39)	20	20
187	A24	65c brown	1.65	1.65
188	A24	70c org yel ('39)	20	20
189	A25	80c violet	35	35
190	A25	90c ultra ('39)	20	20
191	A25	1fr brt pink	4.00	4.00
192	A25	1fr pale ol grn ('40)	20	20
193	A25	1.25fr brt rose ('39)	60	60
194	A25	1.40fr dk brn ('40)	15	15
195	A25	1.50fr bl grn	20	20
196	A25	1.60fr rose vio ('40)	25	25
197	A25	1.75fr dp bl	55	55
198	A26	2fr rose vio	12	12
199	A26	2.25fr brt bl ('39)	28	28
200	A26	2.50fr org yel ('40)	45	45
201	A26	3fr gray brn	15	15
202	A26	5fr hn brn	40	40
203	A26	10fr dk bl, *bluish*	55	55
204	A26	20fr sl grn	65	65
		Nos. 172-204 (33)	13.95	13.95

New York World's Fair Issue

Common Design Type

1939 Engr. *Perf. 12½x12*

205	CD82	1.25fr car lake	40	40
206	CD82	2.25fr ultra	40	40

Lighthouse on Cliff A27

1941 Engr. *Perf. 12½x12*

206A	A27	1fr dl lil	25	
206B	A27	2.50fr blue	25	

Nos. 206A-206B were issued by the Vichy government and were not placed on sale in the colony.

Stamps of types A23 and A26 without "RF" monogram were issued in 1941-1944 by the Vichy government, but were not sold in the colony.

> Free French Administration
> The circumstances surrounding the overprinting and distribution of these stamps were most unusual. Practically all of the stamps issued in small quantities, with the exception of Nos. 260 to 299, were obtained by speculators within a few days after issue. At a later date, the remainders were taken over by the Free French Agency in Ottawa, Canada, by whom they were sold at a premium for the benefit of the Syndicat des Oeuvres Sociales.
> Excellent counterfeits of these surcharges and overprints are known.

Nos. 86 and 92 Overprinted in Black

FRANCE LIBRE
a
F. N. F. L.

1942 Unwmk. *Perf. 14x13½*

206C	A17	10c bis & mag	600.00	600.00
206D	A18	30c red brn & bl	600.00	600.00

The letters "F. N. F. L." are the initials of "Forces Navales Francaises Libres" or "Free French Naval Forces."

Same Overprint in Black on Stamps of 1932-33

207	A21	2c blk & Prus bl	125.00	125.00
208	A22	4c mag & ol brn	22.50	22.50
208A	A22	5c vio & dk brn	450.00	450.00
209	A22	40c dp bl & dk brn	7.00	7.00
a		Inverted overprint	300.00	
210	A21	45c ver & dp grn	90.00	90.00
211	A21	50c dk brn & dp grn	3.50	3.50
212	A22	65c ol brn & org	16.00	16.00
213	A22	1fr org brn & org red	165.00	165.00
214	A22	1.75fr blk & dk brn	3.50	3.50
215	A22	2fr bl blk & Prus bl	3.50	3.50
216	A22	5fr brn red & dk brn	150.00	150.00

Stamps of 1932-33 Overprinted in Black

FRANCE
LIBRE
F N F L

Perf. 13½x14

216A	A20	20c blk & red org	175.00	175.00
217	A20	75c grn & red org	9.00	9.00
218	A20	1.25fr dp bl & lake	9.00	9.00
218A	A20	1.50fr dp bl & bl	225.00	225.00

Same Surcharged with New Value and Bars

219	A20	10fr on 1.25fr dp bl & lake	18.00	18.00
220	A20	20fr on 75c grn & red org	25.00	25.00

> Canceled-to-order stamps are often from remainders. Most collectors of canceled stamps prefer postally used specimens.

No. 154 Surcharged in Red

5 fr
FRANCE LIBRE
F. N. F. L.

Perf. 14x13½

221	A22	5fr on 1.75fr blk & dk brn	5.00	5.00

Stamps of 1938-40 Overprinted type "a" in Black

Perf. 13½x13

222	A23	2c dk bl grn	275.00	275.00
223	A23	3c brn vio	70.00	70.00
224	A23	4c dk red vio	57.50	57.50
225	A23	5c car lake	450.00	450.00
226	A23	10c bis brn	4.50	4.50
227	A23	15c red vio	1,050.	1,050.
228	A23	20c bl vio	95.00	95.00
229	A23	25c Prus bl	4.50	4.50
230	A24	35c dp grn	450.00	450.00
a		Double overprint	1,000.	
231	A24	40c slate bl	4.50	4.50
232	A24	45c dp grn	4.50	4.50
233	A24	55c Prus bl	6,000.	6,000.
234	A24	60c violet	350.00	350.00
235	A24	65c brown	8.50	8.50
236	A24	70c org yel	17.50	17.50
237	A25	80c violet	265.00	265.00
238	A25	90c ultra	6.75	6.75
a		Inverted overprint	300.00	300.00
239	A25	1fr pale ol grn	5.00	5.00
240	A25	1.25fr brt rose	5.00	5.00
241	A25	1.40fr dk brn	5.00	5.00
a		Inverted overprint	300.00	300.00
242	A25	1.50fr bl grn	475.00	475.00
243	A25	1.60fr rose vio	4.50	4.50
244	A26	2fr rose vio	30.00	30.00
245	A26	2.25fr brt bl	4.50	4.50
246	A26	2.50fr org yel	5.00	5.00
247	A26	3fr gray brn	7,000.	7,000.
248	A26	5fr henna brn	1,500.	1,500.
248A	A26	20fr slate grn	600.00	600.00

Stamps of 1938-39 Surcharged in Black

FRANCE LIBRE
F. N. F. L.
20 c

249	A23	20c on 10c bis brn	3.50	3.50
250	A23	30c on 10c bis brn	3.50	3.50
251	A25	60c on 90c ultra	4.25	4.25
252	A25	1.50fr on 90c ultra	7.00	7.00
253	A23	2.50fr on 10c bis brn	7.00	7.00
254	A23	10fr on 10c bis brn	30.00	30.00
255	A25	20fr on 90c ultra	32.50	32.50

New York World's Fair Issue Overprinted type "a" in Black

Perf. 12½x12

256	CD82	1.25fr car lake	4.75	4.75
257	CD82	2.25fr ultra	4.75	4.75
a		Inverted overprint	350.00	

Same, Surcharged

2 fr 50
FRANCE LIBRE
F. N. F. L.

258	CD82	2.50fr on 1.25fr car lake	6.25	6.25
259	CD82	3fr on 2.25fr ultra	6.25	6.25

Stamps of 1938-40 Overprinted in Carmine

Noël 1941
FRANCE LIBRE
F. N. F. L.

1941 *Perf. 13½x13*

260	A23	10c bis brn	17.50	17.50
261	A23	20c bl vio	17.50	17.50
262	A23	25c Prus bl	17.50	17.50
263	A24	40c slate bl	17.50	17.50
264	A24	45c dp grn	17.50	17.50
265	A24	65c brown	17.50	17.50
266	A24	70c org yel	17.50	17.50
267	A25	80c violet	17.50	17.50
268	A25	90c ultra	17.50	17.50
269	A25	1fr pale ol grn	17.50	17.50
270	A25	1.25fr brt rose	17.50	17.50
271	A25	1.40fr dk brn	17.50	17.50
272	A25	1.60fr rose vio	20.00	20.00
273	A25	1.75fr brt bl	20.00	20.00
274	A26	2fr rose vio	20.00	20.00
275	A26	2.25fr brt bl	20.00	20.00
276	A26	2.50fr org yel	20.00	20.00
277	A26	3fr gray brn	20.00	20.00

Same Surcharged in Carmine with New Values

278	A23	10fr on 10c bis brn	35.00	35.00
279	A25	20fr on 90c ultra	35.00	35.00
		Nos. 260-279 (20)	400.00	400.00

Stamps of 1938-40 Overprinted in Black

280	A23	10c bis brn	22.50	22.50
281	A23	20c bl vio	22.50	22.50
282	A23	25c Prus bl	22.50	22.50
283	A24	40c sl bl	22.50	22.50
284	A24	45c dp grn	22.50	22.50
285	A24	65c brn	22.50	22.50
286	A24	70c org yel	22.50	22.50
287	A25	80c violet	22.50	22.50
288	A25	90c ultra	22.50	22.50
289	A25	1fr pale ol grn	22.50	22.50
290	A25	1.25fr brt rose	22.50	22.50
291	A25	1.40fr dk brn	22.50	22.50
292	A25	1.60fr rose vio	22.50	22.50
293	A25	1.75fr brt bl	400.00	400.00
294	A26	2fr rose vio	22.50	22.50
295	A26	2.25fr brt bl	22.50	22.50
296	A26	2.50fr org yel	22.50	22.50
297	A26	3fr gray brn	22.50	22.50

Same Surcharged in Black with New Values

298	A23	10fr on 10c bis brn	65.00	65.00
299	A25	20fr on 90c ultra	65.00	65.00
		Nos. 280-299 (20)	912.50	912.50

Christmas Day plebiscite ordered by Vice Admiral Emile Henri Muselier, commander of the Free French naval forces (Nos. 260-299).

> **Catalogue values for unused stamps in this section, from this point to the end of the section, are for Never Hinged items.**

St. Malo Fishing Schooner A28

1942 Photo. *Perf. 14x14½*

300	A28	5c dk bl	5	5
301	A28	10c dl pink	5	5
302	A28	25c brt grn	5	5
303	A28	30c slate blk	5	5
304	A28	40c brt grnsh bl	5	5
305	A28	60c brn red	5	5
306	A28	1fr dk vio	20	20
307	A28	1.50fr brt red	40	40
308	A28	2fr brown	20	20
309	A28	2.50fr brt ultra	40	40
310	A28	4fr dk org	20	20
311	A28	5fr dp plum	20	20
312	A28	10fr lt ultra	45	45
313	A28	20fr dk grn	65	65
		Nos. 300-313 (14)	3.00	3.00

Stamps of 1942 Surcharged in Carmine or Black

50c

1945

314	A28	50c on 5c dk bl (C)	5	5
315	A28	70c on 5c dk bl (C)	5	5
316	A28	80c on 5c dk bl (C)	15	15
317	A28	1.20fr on 5c dk bl (C)	10	10
318	A28	2.40fr on 25c brt grn	10	10
319	A28	3fr on 25c brt grn	15	15
320	A28	4.50fr on 25c brt grn	35	15
321	A28	15fr on 2.50fr brt ultra (C)	60	60
		Nos. 314-321 (8)	1.55	1.35

Eboue Issue

Common Design Type

1945 Engr. *Perf. 13*

322	CD91	2fr black	28	28
323	CD91	25fr Prus grn	45	45

Nos. 322 and 323 exist imperforate.

Soldiers' Bay — A29

Fishing Industry Symbols A30

Fishermen A31

Weighing the Catch A32

Fishing Boat and Dinghy A33

Storm-swept Coast — A34

1947 Engr. *Perf. 12½*

324	A29	10c chocolate	5	5
325	A29	30c violet	5	5
326	A29	40c rose lil	5	5
327	A29	50c intense bl	5	5
328	A30	60c carmine	15	15
329	A30	80c brt ultra	15	15
330	A30	1fr dk grn	15	15
331	A31	1.20fr blue grn	22	22
332	A31	1.50fr black	22	22
333	A31	2fr red brn	22	22
334	A32	3fr rose vio	70	70
335	A32	3.60fr dp brn org	45	45
336	A32	4fr sepia	45	45
337	A33	5fr orange	40	40
338	A33	6fr blue	55	55
339	A33	10fr Prus grn	70	70
340	A34	15fr dk sl grn	90	90
341	A34	20fr vermilion	80	80
342	A34	25fr dk blue	90	90
		Nos. 324-342 (19)	7.16	7.16

> Imperforates
> Most stamps of St. Pierre and Miquelon from 1947 onward exist imperforate in issued and trial colors, and also in small presentation sheets in issued colors.

Silver Fox — A35

1952 Unwmk. *Perf. 13*

343	A35	8fr dk brn	80	65
344	A35	17fr blue	1.00	80

Military Medal Issue
Common Design Type

1952 **Engr. & Typo.**
345 CD101 8fr multi 2.25 2.25

Fish Freezing Plant — A36

1955-56 **Engr.**
346 A36 30c ultra & dk bl ('56) 12 12
347 A36 50c gray, blk & sep ('56) 12 12
348 A36 3fr pur ('56) 22 22
349 A36 40fr Prus bl 1.20 1.20

FIDES Issue

Fish Freezer "Le Galantry" A37

1956 **Unwmk.** ***Perf. 13x12½***
350 A37 15fr blk brn & chnt 80 60

See note in Common Design section after CD103.

Codfish A38

Design: 4fr, 10fr, Lighthouse and fishing fleet.

1957 ***Perf. 13***
351 A38 40c dk brn & grnsh bl 10 10
352 A38 1fr brn & grn 12 12
353 A38 2fr ind & dl bl 20 15
354 A38 4fr mar, car & pur 25 20
355 A38 10fr grnsh bl, dk bl & brn 55 40
Nos. 351-355 (5) 1.22 97

Human Rights Issue
Common Design Type

1958 **Engr.** ***Perf. 13***
356 CD105 20fr red brn & dk bl 90 70

Flower Issue
Common Design Type

Design: Spruce.

1959 **Photo.** ***Perf. 12½x12***
357 CD104 5fr red, yel grn & vio 65 45

Ice Hockey A39

Mink — A40

1959 **Engr.** ***Perf. 13***
358 A39 20fr multi 65 50
359 A40 25fr ind, yel grn & brn 1.10 70

Cypripedium Acaule — A41

Eider Ducks — A42

Flower: 50fr, Calopogon pulchellus.

1962, Apr. 24 **Unwmk.** ***Perf. 13***
360 A41 25fr grn, org & car rose 65 50
361 A41 50fr grn & car lake 1.25 90

See No. C24.

1963, Mar. 4 ***Perf. 13***

Birds: 1fr, Rock ptarmigan. 2fr, Ringed plovers. 6fr, Blue-winged teal.

362 A42 50c blk, ultra & ocher 15 12
363 A42 1fr red brn, ultra & rose 22 15
364 A42 2fr blk, dk bl & bis 40 25
365 A42 6fr multi 90 60

Albert Calmette A43

1963, Aug. 5 **Engr.**
366 A43 30fr dk brn & dk bl 1.20 90

Birth cent. of Albert Calmette, bacteriologist.

Red Cross Centenary Issue
Common Design Type

1963, Sept. 2 **Unwmk.** ***Perf. 13***
367 CD113 25fr ultra, gray & car 90 65

Human Rights Issue
Common Design Type

1963, Dec. 10 **Unwmk.** ***Perf. 13***
368 CD117 20fr org, bl & dk brn 90 65

Philatec Issue
Common Design Type

1964, Apr. 4 **Engr.**
369 CD118 60fr choc, grn & dk bl 2.25 2.25

Rabbits A44

Designs: 4fr, Fox. 5fr, Roe deer. 34fr, Charolais bull.

1964, Sept. 28 ***Perf. 13***
370 A44 3fr grn, dk brn & red brn 25 20
371 A44 4fr dk bl, dk brn & grn 25 20
372 A44 5fr dk brn, dk bl & red brn 60 40
373 A44 34fr grn, bl & red brn 1.50 1.20

Airport and Map of St. Pierre and Miquelon A45

Designs: 40fr, Television tube and tower, and map. 48fr, Map of new harbor of St. Pierre.

1967 **Engr.** ***Perf. 13***
374 A45 30fr ind, bl & dk red 80 55
375 A45 40fr sl grn, ol & dk red 1.00 60
376 A45 48fr dk red, brn & sl bl 1.20 80

Issue dates: 30fr, Oct. 23; 40fr, Nov. 20; 48fr, Sept. 25.

WHO Anniversary Issue
Common Design Type

1968, May 4 **Engr.** ***Perf. 13***
377 CD126 10fr multi 1.00 55

René de Chateaubriand and Map of Islands — A46

Designs: 4fr, J. D. Cassini and map. 15fr, Prince de Joinville, Francois F. d'Orleans (1818-1900), ships and map. 25fr, Admiral Gauchet, World War I warship and map.

1968, May 20 **Photo.** ***Perf. 12½x13***
378 A46 4fr multi 70 55
379 A46 6fr multi 1.00 60
380 A46 15fr multi 1.40 80
381 A46 25fr multi 1.60 1.20

Human Rights Year Issue
Common Design Type

1968, Aug. 10 **Engr.** ***Perf. 13***
382 CD127 20fr bl, ver & org yel 60 45

Belle Riviere, Langlade A47

Design: 15fr, Debon Brook, Langlade.

1969, Apr. 30 **Engr.** ***Perf. 13***
Size: 36x22mm
383 A47 5fr bl, sl grn & brn 50 30
384 A47 15fr brn, bl & dl grn 65 45

See Nos. C41-C42.

Treasury A48

Designs: 25fr, Scientific and Technical Institute of Maritime Fishing. 30fr, Monument to seamen lost at sea. 60fr, St. Christopher College.

1969, May 30 **Engr.** ***Perf. 13***
385 A48 10fr brt bl, cl & blk 40 22
386 A48 25fr dk bl, brt bl & brn red 70 45
387 A48 30fr bl, grn & gray 1.20 60
388 A48 60fr brt bl, brn red & blk 1.60 1.00

Ringed Seals — A49

Designs: 3fr, Sperm whales. 4fr, Pilot whales. 6fr, Common dolphins.

1969, Oct. 6 **Engr.** ***Perf. 13***
389 A49 1fr lil, vio brn & red brn 60 40
390 A49 3fr bl grn, ind & red 60 40
391 A49 4fr ol, gray grn & mar 70 55
392 A49 6fr brt grn, pur & red 1.00 60

L'Estoile and Granville, France A50

Designs: 40fr, "La Jolie" and St. Jean de Luz, France, 1750. 48fr, "Le Juste" and La Rochelle, France, 1860.

1969, Oct. 13 **Engr.** ***Perf. 13***
393 A50 34fr grn, mar & sl grn 1.20 80
394 A50 40fr brn red, lem & sl grn 1.50 1.20
395 A50 48fr multi 2.25 1.60

Historic ships connecting St. Pierre and Miquelon with France.

ILO Issue
Common Design Type

1969, Nov. 24
396 CD131 20fr org, gray & ocher 70 55

UPU Headquarters Issue
Common Design Type

1970, May 20 **Engr.** ***Perf. 13***
397 CD133 25fr dk car, brt bl & brn 65 55
398 CD133 34fr mar, brn & gray 1.10 70

Rowers and Globe — A51

1970, Oct. 13 **Photo.** ***Perf. 12½x12***
399 A51 20fr lt grnsh bl & brn 60 45

World Rowing Championships, St. Catherine.

Blackberries A52

Fruit: 4fr, Strawberries. 5fr, Raspberries. 6fr, Blueberries.

1970, Oct. 20 **Engr.** ***Perf. 13***
400 A52 3fr brn org & multi 30 16
401 A52 4fr red & multi 40 22
402 A52 5fr pur & multi 45 30
403 A52 6fr brt pink & multi 55 40

Ewe and Lamb — A53

Designs: 30fr, Animal quarantine station. 34fr, Charolais bull. 48fr, Refrigeration ship and slaughterhouse.

1970 **Engr.** ***Perf. 13***
404 A53 15fr plum, grn & ol 80 45
405 A53 30fr sl, bis brn & ap grn 90 45
406 A53 34fr red lil, org brn & emer 1.60 1.20
407 A53 48fr multi 1.20 80

Issue dates: 48fr, Nov. 10; others, Dec. 8.

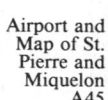

Footnotes often refer you to other stamps of the same design.

Saint François d'Assise 1900 — A54

Ships: 35fr, Sainte Jehanne, 1920. 40fr, L'Aventure, 1950. 80fr, Commandant Bourdais, 1970.

1971, Aug. 25

408	A54	30fr Prus bl & hn brn	80	60
409	A54	35fr Prus bl, lt grn & ol brn	1.20	70
410	A54	40fr sl grn, bl & dk brn	1.50	1.00
411	A54	80fr dp grn, bl & blk	1.60	1.40

Deep-sea fishing fleet.

"Aconit" and Map of Islands — A55

Ships: 25fr, Alysse. 50fr, Mimosa.

1971, Sept. 27 Engr. *Perf. 13*

412	A55	22fr bl, blk & brt grn	1.50	80
413	A55	25fr bl & multi	2.00	1.40
414	A55	50fr vio bl, blk & Prus bl	3.00	1.60

Rallying of the Free French forces, 30th anniv.

Ship's Bell — A56

Design: 45fr, Old chart and sextants (horiz.).

1971, Oct. 25 Photo. *Perf. 12½x13*

415	A56	20fr gray & multi	65	55
416	A56	45fr red brn & multi	1.00	70

St. Pierre Museum.

De Gaulle Issue

Common Design Type

Designs: 35fr, Gen. de Gaulle, 1940. Pres. de Gaulle, 1970.

1971, Nov. 9 Engr. *Perf. 13*

417	CD134	35fr ver & blk	1.60	1.50
418	CD134	45fr ver & blk	2.50	2.00

Haddock A57

Fish: 3fr, Hippoglossoides platessoides. 5fr, Sebastes mentella. 10fr, Codfish.

1972, Mar. 7

419	A57	2fr vio bl, ind & pink	35	20
420	A57	3fr grn & gray ol	38	25
421	A57	5fr Prus bl & brick red	42	30
422	A57	10fr grn & sl grn	65	42

Oldsquaws — A58

Birds: 10c, 70c, Puffins. 20c, 90c, Snow owl. 40c, Like 6c. Identification of birds on oldsquaw and puffin stamps transposed.

1973, Jan. 1 Engr. *Perf. 13*

423	A58	6c Prus bl, pur & brn	12	12
424	A58	10c Prus bl, blk & org	20	20
425	A58	20c ultra, bis & dk vio	20	20
426	A58	40c pur, sl grn & brn	50	32
427	A58	70c brt grn, blk & org	65	55
428	A58	90c Prus bl, bis & pur	1.50	90
		Nos. 423-428 (6)	3.17	2.29

Indoor Swimming Pool — A59

Design: 1fr, Cultural Center of St. Pierre.

1973, Sept. 25 Engr. *Perf. 13*

429	A59	60c brn, brt bl & dk car	45	35
430	A59	1fr bl grn, ocher & choc	65	60

Opening of Cultural Center of St. Pierre.

Map of Islands, Weather Balloon and Ship, WMO Emblem A60

1974, Mar. 23 Engr. *Perf. 13*

431	A60	1.60fr multi	1.50	1.20

World Meteorological Day.

Gannet Holding Letter — A61

1974, Oct. 9 Engr. *Perf. 13*

432	A61	70c bl & multi	55	42
433	A61	90c red & multi	65	50

Centenary of Universal Postal Union.

Clasped Hands over Red Cross — A62

Hands Putting Money into Fish-shaped Bank — A63

1974, Oct. 15 Photo. *Perf. 12½x13*

434	A62	1.50fr multi	1.00	70

Honoring blood donors.

1974, Nov. 15 Engr. *Perf. 13*

435	A63	50c ocher & vio bl	45	35

St. Pierre Savings Bank centenary.

Church of St. Pierre and Seagulls A64

Designs: 10c, Church of Miquelon and fish. 20c, Church of Our Lady of the Sailors, and fishermen.

1974, Dec. 9 Engr. *Perf. 13*

436	A64	6c multi	16	16
437	A64	10c multi	16	16
438	A64	20c multi	35	35

Danaus Plexippus A65

Design: 1fr, Vanessa atalanta (vert.).

1975, July 17 Litho. *Perf. 12½*

439	A65	1fr bl & multi	80	60
440	A65	1.20fr grn & multi	1.00	70

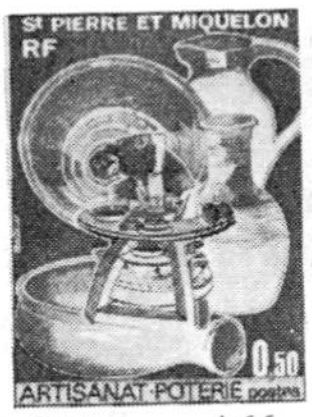

Pottery — A66

Mother and Child, Wood Carving — A67

1975, Oct. 20 Engr. *Perf. 13*

441	A66	50c ol, brn & choc	60	45
442	A67	60c bl & dl yel	60	45

Local handicrafts.

Pointe Plate Lighthouse and Murres A68

Designs: 10c, Galantry lighthouse and Atlantic puffins. 20c, Cap Blanc lighthouse, whale and squid.

1975, Oct. 21

443	A68	6c vio bl, blk & lt grn	12	12
444	A68	10c lil rose, blk & dk ol	16	16
445	A68	20c bl, ind & brn	28	28

Pompidou Type of Wallis and Futuna Islands

1976, Feb. 17 Engr. *Perf. 13*

446	A11	1.10fr brn & sl	80	60

Georges Pompidou (1911-1974), President of France.

The Scott Catalogue value is a retail price, what you could expect to pay for the stamp in a grade of Fine-Very Fine. The value listed is a reference which reflects recent actual dealer selling price.

Washington and Lafayette, American Flag — A69

1976, July 12 Photo. *Perf. 13*

447	A69	1fr multi	80	60

American Bicentennial.

Woman Swimmer and Maple Leaf — A70

Design: 70c, Basketball and maple leaf (vert.).

1976, Aug. 10 Engr. *Perf. 13*

448	A70	70c multi	60	40
449	A70	2.50fr multi	1.60	1.20

21st Olympic Games, Montreal, Canada, July 17-Aug. 1.

Vigie Dam — A71

1976, Sept. 7 Engr. *Perf. 13*

450	A71	2.20fr multi	2.00	1.25

Croix de Lorraine — A72

Design: 1.40fr, Goelette.

1976, Oct. 5 Photo. *Perf. 13*

451	A72	1.20fr multi	1.00	70
452	A72	1.40fr multi	1.25	1.00

Fishing vessels.

France Nos. 1783-1784, 1786-1789, 1794, 1882, 1799, 1885, 1802, 1889, 1803-1804 and 1891 Ovptd. "SAINT PIERRE / ET / MIQUELON"

1986, Feb. 4 Engr. *Perf. 13*

453	A915	5c dk grn	5	5
454	A915	10c dl red	5	5
455	A915	20c brt grn	6	6
456	A915	30c orange	8	8
457	A915	40c brown	12	12
458	A915	50c lilac	14	14
459	A915	1fr ol grn	28	28
460	A915	1.80fr emerald	50	50
461	A915	2fr brt yel grn	55	55
462	A915	2.20fr red	60	60
463	A915	3fr choc brn	85	85
464	A915	3.20fr sapphire	90	90
465	A915	4fr brt car	1.10	1.10
466	A915	5fr gray bl	1.40	1.40
467	A915	10fr purple	2.75	2.75
		Nos. 453-467 (15)	9.43	9.43

Discovery of St. Pierre & Miquelon by Jacques Cartier, 450th Anniv. — A73

1986, June 11 Engr. *Perf. 13*
476 A73 2.20fr sep, sage grn & redsh brn 60 60

Statue of Liberty, Cent. — A74

1986, July 4
477 A74 2.50fr Statue, St. Pierre Harbor 70 70

Fishery Resources A75

Holy Family, Stained Glass by J. Balmet A76

1986, Oct. 22 Engr. *Perf. 13*
478 A75 1fr brt red 32 32
479 A75 1.40fr violet 45 45

See Nos. 487-488.

1986, Dec. 10 Litho. *Perf. 13*
480 A76 2.20fr multi 68 68

Christmas.

Hygrophorus Pratensis — A77

1987, Feb. 14 Engr. *Perf. 12½*
481 A77 2.50fr dk brn & yel brn 75 75

See Nos. 492, 503.

Dr. François Dunan (1884-1961), Clinic A78

1987, May 5 Engr. *Perf. 13*
482 A78 2.20fr brt bl, blk & dk red brn 75 75

Transat Yacht Race, Lorient to St. Pierre to Lorient A79

1987, May 18
483 A79 5fr dp ultra, dk rose brn & brt bl 1.75 1.75

Visit of Pres. Mitterand A80

1987, May 29 Litho. *Perf. 12½x13*
484 A80 2.20fr dl ultra, gld & scar 75 75

Marine Slip, Cent. — A81

1987, June 20 Litho. *Perf. 13*
485 A81 2.50fr pale sal & dark red brn 80 80

Stern Trawler La Normande — A82

1987, Oct. 14 Photo.
486 A82 3fr multi 1.05 1.05

See No. 499.

Fishery Resources Type of 1986

1986, Oct. 19 Engr.
487 A75 1.10fr brt org 38 38
488 A75 1.50fr brt ultra 52 52

St. Christopher and the Christ Child, Stained Glass Window,and Scout Emblem — A83

1987, Dec. 9 Litho. *Perf. 13*
489 A83 2.20fr multi 80 80

Christmas, Scout movement in St. Pierre & Miquelon, 50th anniv.

The Great Barachoise Nature Reserve — A84

1987, Dec. 16 Engr. *Perf. 13x12½*
490 A84 3fr Horses, waterfowl 1.15 1.15
491 A84 3fr Waterfowl, seals 1.15 1.15

Nos. 491-492 printed se-tenant with center label in a continuous design.

Mushroom Type of 1987

Litho. & Engr.

1988, Jan. 29 *Perf. 12½*
492 A77 2.50fr Russula paludosa britz 90 90

1988 Winter Olympics, Calgary A86

1988, Mar. 5 Engr. *Perf. 13*
493 A86 5fr brt ultra & dark red 1.80 1.80

Louis Thomas (1887-1976), Photographer A87

1988, May 4 Engr. *Perf. 13*
494 A87 2.20fr blk, dk ol bis & Prus bl 78 78

France No. 2105 Overprinted "ST-PIERRE ET MIQUELON"

1988, July 25 Engr. *Perf. 13*
495 A1107 2.20fr ver, blk & violet blue 78 78

Fishery Resources Type of 1986

1988, Aug. 7
496 A75 1.30fr dark red 42 42
497 A75 1.60fr emer green 52 52

Seizure of Schooner Nellie J. Banks, 50th Anniv. A88

1988, Aug. 7
498 A88 2.50fr brn, vio blue & brt blue 82 82

The Nellie J. Banks was seized by Canada for carrying prohibited alcohol in 1938.

Trawler Type of 1987

1988, Sept. 28 Litho. *Perf. 13*
499 A82 3fr Le Marmouset 95 95

Conservation Type of 1987

Designs: 2.20fr, Ross Cove. 13.70fr, Cape Perce.

1988, Nov. 2 Engr. *Perf. 13x12½*
500 A84 2.20fr brt blue, brn & dark blue 75 75
501 A84 13.70fr brt blue, brn & dark blue 4.60 4.60

Nos. 500-501 printed se-tenant with center label picturing whale jumping out of water near The Cliffs.

Christmas — A89

1988, Dec. 17 Litho. *Perf. 13*
502 A89 2.20fr multi 70 70

Mushroom Type of 1987

1989, Jan. 30 Litho. & Engr. *Perf.*
503 A77 2.50fr Tricholoma virgatum 80 80

Judo Competitions in St. Pierre & Miquelon, 25th Anniv. — A90

1989, Mar. 4 Engr. *Perf. 13*
504 A90 5fr brn org, blk & yel grn 1.65 1.65

French Revolution Bicent.; 40th Anniv. of the UN Declaration of Human Rights (in 1988) — A91

1989 Engr. *Perf. 12½x13*
505 A91 2.20fr Liberty 72 72
506 A91 2.20fr Equality 72 72
507 A91 2.20fr Fraternity 72 72

Issue dates: No. 505, Mar. 28; No. 506, May 9; No. 507, June 19.

SEMI-POSTAL STAMPS

Regular Issue of 1909-17 Surcharged in Red **+ 5c**

1915-17 Unwmk. *Perf. 14x13½*
B1 A17 10c + 5c car rose & red 35 35
B2 A17 15c + 5c dl vio & rose ('17) 45 45

Curie Issue

Common Design Type

1938 Engr. *Perf. 13*
B3 CD80 1.75fr + 50c brt ultra 5.25 5.25

French Revolution Issue
Common Design Type

1939 **Photo.**
Name and Value Typo. in Black

B4	CD83	45c + 25c grn	3.00	3.00
B5	CD83	70c + 30c brn	3.00	3.00
B6	CD83	90c + 35c red org	3.00	3.00
B7	CD83	1.25fr + 1fr rose pink	3.00	3.00
B8	CD83	2.25fr + 2fr bl	3.00	3.00
		Nos. B4-B8 (5)	15.00	15.00

Common Design Type and

Sailor of Landing Force — SP1

Dispatch Boat "Ville d'Ys" — SP2

1941 **Photo.** ***Perf. 13½***

B8A	SP1	1fr + 1fr red	60
B8B	CD86	1.50fr + 3fr mar	60
B8C	SP2	2.50fr + 1fr bl	60

Nos. B8A-B8C were issued by the Vichy government, and were not placed on sale in the colony.

Nos. 206A-206B were surcharged "OEUVRES COLONIALES" and surtax (including change of denomination of the 2.50fr to 50c). These were issued in 1944 by the Vichy government and not placed on sale in the colony.

Regular Stamps of 1942 With Additional Surcharge in Carmine

+ 50c

ŒUVRES SOCIALES

1942 **Unwmk.** ***Perf. 13½x13***

B9	A25	1fr + 50c pale ol grn	15.00	15.00
B10	A26	2.50fr + 1fr org yel	15.00	15.00

Catalogue values for unused stamps in this section, from this point to the end of the section, are for Never Hinged items.

Red Cross Issue
Common Design Type

1944 ***Perf. 14½x14***

B13	CD90	5fr + 20fr dp ultra	40	40

Surtax for the French Red Cross and national relief.

Tropical Medicine Issue
Common Design Type

1950 **Engr.** ***Perf. 13***

B14	CD100	10fr + 2fr red brn & red	2.00	2.00

The surtax was for charitable work.

AIR POST STAMPS

Catalogue values for unused stamps in this section, from this point to the end of the section, are for Never Hinged items.

Common Design Type
Perf. 14½x14

1942, Aug. 17 **Photo.** **Unwmk.**

C1	CD87	1fr dk org		10	10
C2	CD87	1.50fr brt red		12	12
C3	CD87	5fr brn red		16	16
C4	CD87	10fr black		25	25
C5	CD87	25fr ultra		30	30
C6	CD87	50fr dk grn		45	45
C7	CD87	100fr plum		70	70
		Nos. C1-C7 (7)		2.08	2.08

Victory Issue
Common Design Type

1946, May 8 **Engr.** ***Perf. 12½***

C8	CD92	8fr dp cl	42	42

Chad to Rhine Issue
Common Design Types

1946, June 6

C9	CD93	5fr brn red	50	50
C10	CD94	10fr lil rose	50	50
C11	CD95	15fr gray blk	65	65
C12	CD96	20fr violet	65	65
C13	CD97	25fr chocolate	1.00	1.00
C14	CD98	50fr grnsh blk	1.00	1.00
		Nos. C9-C14 (6)	4.30	4.30

Plane, Sailing Vessel and Coast — AP2

AP3

AP4

1947, Oct. 6

C15	AP2	50fr yel grn & rose	2.00	1.50
C16	AP3	100fr dk bl grn	3.00	2.25
C17	AP4	200fr bluish blk & brt rose	6.00	3.25

UPU Issue
Common Design Type

1949, July 4 **Engr.** ***Perf. 13***

C18	CD99	25fr multi	3.75	3.75

Liberation Issue
Common Design Type

1954, June 6

C19	CD102	15fr sep & red	2.00	2.00

10th anniversary of the liberation of France.

Plane over St. Pierre Harbor — AP6

1956, Oct. 22

C20	AP6	500fr ultra & ind	22.50	12.50

Dog and Village — AP7

Design: 100fr, Caravelle over archipelago.

1957, Nov. 4 **Unwmk.** ***Perf. 13***

C21	AP7	50fr gray, brn blk & bl	14.00	9.00
C22	AP7	100fr blk & gray	6.00	4.50

Anchors and Torches — AP8

1959, Sept. 14 **Engr.** ***Perf. 13***

C23	AP8	200fr dk pur, grn & cl	4.50	3.00

Approval of the constitution and the vote which confirmed the attachment of the islands to France.

Pitcher Plant — AP9

1962, Apr. 24 **Unwmk.** ***Perf. 13***

C24	AP9	100fr grn, org & car	3.25	1.50

Gulf of St. Lawrence and Submarine "Surcouf" — AP10

Perf. 13½x12½
1962, July 24 **Photo.**

C25	AP10	500fr dk red & bl	70.00	60.00

20th anniv. of St. Pierre & Miquelon's joining the Free French.

Telstar Issue
Common Design Type

1962, Nov. 22 **Engr.** ***Perf. 13***

C26	CD111	50fr Prus grn & bis	3.00	2.25

Arrival of Governor Dangeac, 1763 — AP11

1963, Aug. 5 **Unwmk.** ***Perf. 13***

C27	AP11	200fr dk bl, sl grn & brn	5.25	3.50

Bicentenary of the arrival of the first French governor.

Jet Plane and Map of Maritime Provinces and New England — AP12

1964, Sept. 28 **Engr.** ***Perf. 13***

C28	AP12	100fr choc & Prus bl	4.25	3.00

Inauguration of direct airmail service between St. Pierre and New York City.

ITU Issue
Common Design Type

1965, May 17

C29	CD120	40fr org brn, dk bl & lil rose	5.00	3.50

French Satellite A-1 Issue
Common Design Type

Designs: 25fr, Diamant rocket and launching installations. 30fr, A-1 satellite.

1966, Jan. 24 **Engr.** ***Perf. 13***

C30	CD121	25fr dk brn, dk bl & rose cl	2.75	2.00
C31	CD121	30fr dk bl, rose cl & dk brn	2.75	2.00
a.		Strip of 2 + label	6.00	4.50

No. C31a contains one each of Nos. C30-C31 and dark brown label with commemorative inscription. Each sheet contains 16 triptychs (2x8).

French Satellite D-1 Issue
Common Design Type

1966, May 23 **Engr.** ***Perf. 13***

C32	CD122	48fr brt grn, ultra & rose cl	3.25	2.25

Arrival of Settlers — AP13

1966, June 22 **Photo.** ***Perf. 13***

C33	AP13	100fr multi	3.00	2.25

150th anniv. of the return of the islands of St. Pierre and Miquelon to France.

Front Page of Official Journal and Printing Presses — AP14

1966, Oct. 20 **Engr.** ***Perf. 13***

C34	AP14	60fr dk bl, lake & dk pur	2.00	1.25

Centenary of the Government Printers and the Official Journal.

Map of Islands, Old and New Fishing Vessels — AP15

Design: 100fr, Cruiser Colbert, maps of Brest, St. Pierre and Miquelon.

1967, July 20 Engr. *Perf. 13*

C35	AP15	25fr dk bl, gray & crim	11.00 7.00
C36	AP15	100fr multi	20.00 15.00

Visit of President Charles de Gaulle.

Speed Skater and Olympic Emblem — AP16

Design: 60fr, Ice hockey goalkeeper and Olympic emblem.

1968, Apr. 22 Photo. *Perf. 13*

C37	AP16	50fr ultra & multi	1.60 1.20
C38	AP16	60fr grn & multi	2.25 1.50

10th Winter Olympic Games, Grenoble, France, Feb. 6-18.

War Memorial, St. Pierre — AP17

1968, Nov. 11 Photo. *Perf. 12½*

C39	AP17	500fr multi	12.50 10.00

Wrld War I armistice, 50th anniv.

Concorde Issue

Common Design Type

1969, Apr. 17 Engr. *Perf. 13*

C40	CD129	34fr dk brn & ol	7.00 5.00

Scenic Type of Regular Issue, 1969.

Designs: 50fr, Grazing horses, Miquelon. 100fr, Gathering driftwood on Mirande Beach, Miquelon.

1969, Apr. 30 Engr. *Perf. 13*

Size: 47½x27mm

C41	A47	50fr ultra, brn & ol	3.00 2.00
C42	A47	100fr dk brn, bl & sl	5.50 4.50

L'Esperance Leaving Saint-Malo, 1600 — AP18

1969, June 16 Engr. *Perf. 13*

C43	AP18	200fr blk, grn & dk red	6.00 3.00

Pierre Loti and Sailboats — AP19

1969, June 23

C44	AP19	300fr lem, choc & Prus bl	9.00 6.00

Loti (1850-1923), French novelist and naval officer.

EXPO Emblem and "Mountains" by Yokoyama Taikan — AP20

Design: 34fr, Geisha, rocket and EXPO emblem (vert.).

1970, Sept. 8 Engr. *Perf. 13*

C45	AP20	34fr dp cl, ol & ind	1.50 1.00
C46	AP20	85fr org, ind & car	3.00 2.00

EXPO '70 Intl. Exposition, Osaka, Japan, Mar. 15-Sept. 13.

Etienne François Duke of Choiseul and his Ships — AP21

Designs: 50fr, Jacques Cartier, ship and landing party. 60fr, Sebastien Le Gonrad de Sourdeval, ships and map of islands.

1970, Nov. 25

Portrait in Lake

C47	AP21	25fr lil & Prus bl	1.20 60
C48	AP21	50fr sl grn & red lil	2.25 1.50
C49	AP21	60fr red lil & sl grn	3.00 1.50

De Gaulle, Cross of Lorraine, Sailor, Soldier, Coast Guard — AP22

1972, June 18 Engr. *Perf. 13*

C50	AP22	100fr lil, brn & grn	4.50 3.00

Charles de Gaulle (1890-1970), French pres.

Louis Joseph de Montcalm — AP23

Designs: 2fr, Louis de Buade Frontenac (vert.). 4fr, Robert de La Salle.

1973, Jan. 1

C51	AP23	1.60fr Prus bl, blk & pur	1.20 60
C52	AP23	2fr vio, sl grn & dp mag	1.50 80
C53	AP23	4fr sl grn, brn ol & rose cl	3.50 1.60

Scott's editorial staff cannot undertake to identify, authenticate or appraise stamps and postal markings.

Transall C 160 over St. Pierre — AP24

1973, Oct. 16 Engr. *Perf. 13*

C54	AP24	10fr multi	12.50 7.00

Arms and Map of Islands, Fish and Bird — AP25

1974, Nov. 5 Photo. *Perf. 13*

C55	AP25	2fr gold & multi	1.60 1.00

Copernicus, Kepler, Newton and Einstein — AP26

1974, Nov. 26 Engr.

C56	AP26	4fr multi	3.50 2.00

Nicolaus Copernicus (1473-1543), Polish astronomer.

Type of 1909, Cod and ARPHILA Emblem AP27

1975, Aug. 5 Engr. *Perf. 13*

C57	AP27	4fr ultra, red & ind	4.00 2.50

ARPHILA 75, International Philatelic Exhibition, Paris, June 6-16.

Judo, Maple Leaf, Olympic Rings AP28

1975, Nov. 18 Engr. *Perf. 13*

C58	AP28	1.90fr red, bl & vio	1.60 1.20

Pre-Olympic Year.

Concorde — AP29

1976, Jan. 21 Engr. *Perf. 13*

C59	AP29	10fr red, blk & sl	9.00 6.00

1st commercial flight of supersonic jet Concorde from Paris to Rio, Jan. 21.

A. G. Bell, Telephone and Satellite AP30

1976, June 22 Litho. *Perf. 12½*

C60	AP30	5fr vio bl, org & red	4.00 2.75

Centenary of first telephone call by Alexander Graham Bell, Mar. 10, 1876.

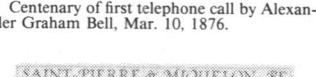

Aircraft — AP31

1987, June 30 Engr. *Perf. 13*

C61	AP31	5fr Hawker-Siddeley H. S. 748, 1987	1.75 1.75
C62	AP31	10fr Latecoere 522, 1939	3.35 3.35

Hindenburg — AP32

Designs: 10fr, Douglas DC3, 1948-1988.

1988, June 22 Engr. *Perf. 13*

C63	AP32	5fr brt blue, blk & rose vio	1.65 1.65
C64	AP32	10fr brt blue, blk & rose vio	3.35 3.35

AIR POST SEMI-POSTAL STAMPS

V4

Stamps of the design shown above and stamp of Cameroun type V10 inscribed "St. Pierre-et-Miquelon" were issued in 1942 by the Vichy Government, but were not placed on sale in the Colony.

POSTAGE DUE STAMPS

Postage Due Stamps of French Colonies Overprinted in Red

ST.-PIERRE M.-on

1892 Unwmk. *Imperf.*

J1 D1 5c black 25.00 25.00
J2 D1 10c black 6.25 6.25
J3 D1 15c black 6.25 6.25
J4 D1 20c black 6.25 6.25
J5 D1 30c black 6.25 6.25
J6 D1 40c black 6.25 6.25
J7 D1 60c black 27.50 27.50

Black Overprint

J8 D1 1fr brown 55.00 55.00
J9 D1 2fr brown 55.00 55.00

These stamps exist with and without hyphen.

See note after No. 59.

Postage Due Stamps of France, 1893-1924, Overprinted

SAINT-PIERRE
-ET-
MIQUELON

1925-27 *Perf. 14x13½*

J10 D2 5c blue 20 20
J11 D2 10c dk brn 20 20
J12 D2 20c ol grn 28 28
J13 D2 25c rose 28 28
J14 D2 30c red 40 40
J15 D2 45c bl grn 40 40
J16 D2 50c brn vio 80 80
J17 D2 1fr red brn, *straw* 1.00 1.00
J18 D2 3fr mag ('27) 3.50 3.50

Surcharged

SAINT-PIERRE
-ET-MIQUELON
2
francs
à percevoir

J19 D2 60c on 50c buff 80 80
J20 D2 2fr on 1fr red 1.25 1.25
Nos. J10-J20 (11) 9.11 9.11

Newfoundland Dog — D3

1932 Typo.

J21 D3 5c dk bl & blk 60 60
J22 D3 10c grn & blk 60 60
J23 D3 20c red & blk 80 80
J24 D3 25c red vio & blk 80 80
J25 D3 30c org & blk 1.50 1.50
J26 D3 45c lt bl & blk 1.50 1.50
J27 D3 50c bl grn & blk 3.00 3.00
J28 D3 60c brt rose & blk 4.00 4.00
J29 D3 1fr yel brn & blk 9.00 9.00
J30 D3 2fr dp vio & blk 15.00 15.00
J31 D3 3fr dk brn & blk 15.00 15.00
Nos. J21-J31 (11) 51.80 51.80

Codfish — D4

1938 Photo. *Perf. 13*

J32 D4 5c gray blk 5 5
J33 D4 10c dk red vio 5 5
J34 D4 15c slate grn 5 5
J35 D4 20c deep bl 5 5
J36 D4 30c rose car 9 9
J37 D4 50c dk bl grn 9 9
J38 D4 60c dk blue 20 20
J39 D4 1fr henna brn 25 25
J40 D4 2fr gray brn 1.10 1.10
J41 D4 3fr dl vio 1.50 1.50
Nos. J32-J41 (10) 3.43 3.43

Type of Postage Due Stamps of 1932 Overprinted in Black

FRANCE LIBRE
F. N. F. L.

1942 Unwmk. *Perf. 14x13½*

J42 D3 25c red vio & blk 100.00 100.00
J43 D3 30c org & blk 100.00 100.00
J44 D3 50c bl grn & blk 400.00 400.00
J45 D3 2fr dp vio & bl blk 15.00 15.00

Same Surcharged in Black

3 fr
FRANCE LIBRE
F. N. F. L.

J46 D3 3fr on 2fr dp vio & blk 9.00 9.00
a. "F.N.F.L." omitted 4.00 4.00
Nos. J42-J46 (5) 624.00 624.00

Postage Due Stamps of 1938 Overprinted in Black

NOËL 1941
F N F L

1942 *Perf. 13*

J48 D4 5c gray blk 10.00 10.00
J49 D4 10c dk red vio 10.00 10.00
J50 D4 15c slate grn 10.00 10.00
J51 D4 20c deep bl 10.00 10.00
J52 D4 30c rose car 10.00 10.00
J53 D4 50c dk bl grn 17.50 17.50
J54 D4 60c dk blue 45.00 45.00
J55 D4 1fr henna brn 55.00 55.00
J56 D4 2fr gray brn 55.00 55.00
J57 D4 3fr dl vio 62.50 62.50
Nos. J48-J57 (10) 285.00 285.00

Christmas Day plebiscite ordered by Vice Admiral Emile Henri Muselier, commander of the Free French naval forces.

Postage Due Stamps of 1938 Overprinted in Black

FRANCE
LIBRE
F N F L

1942

J58 D4 5c gray blk 15.00 15.00
J59 D4 10c dk red vio 2.00 2.00
J60 D4 15c sl grn 2.00 2.00
J61 D4 20c dp bl 2.00 2.00
J62 D4 30c rose car 2.00 2.00
J63 D4 50c dk bl grn 2.00 2.00
J64 D4 60c dk bl 2.00 2.00
J65 D4 1fr hn brn 6.00 6.00
J66 D4 2fr gray brn 6.00 6.00
J67 D4 3fr dl vio 225.00 225.00
Nos. J58-J67 (10) 264.00 264.00

Catalogue values for unused stamps in this section, from this point to the end of the section, are for Never Hinged items.

Arms and Fishing Schooner — D5

1947 Engr. *Perf. 13*

J68 D5 10c dp org 5 5
J69 D5 30c dp ultra 5 5
J70 D5 50c dk bl grn 10 10
J71 D5 1fr dp car 15 15
J72 D5 2fr dk grn 15 15
J73 D5 3fr violet 35 35
J74 D5 4fr chocolate 40 40
J75 D5 5fr yel grn 40 40
J76 D5 10fr blk brn 45 45
J77 D5 20fr org red 55 55
Nos. J68-J77 (10) 2.65 2.65

Newfoundland Dog — D6

1973, Jan. 1 Engr. *Perf. 13*

J78 D6 2c brn & blk 10 10
J79 D6 10c pur & blk 15 15
J80 D6 20c grnsh bl & blk 35 35
J81 D6 30c dk car & blk 80 80
J82 D6 1fr bl & blk 2.00 2.00
Nos. J78-J82 (5) 3.40 3.40

France Nos. J106-J115 Overprinted "ST - PIERRE ET MIQUELON" Reading Up in Red

1986, Sept. 15 Engr. *Perf. 13*

J83 D8 10c multi 5 5
J84 D8 20c multi 6 6
J85 D8 30c multi 10 10
J86 D8 40c multi 12 12
J87 D8 50c multi 15 15
J88 D8 1fr multi 30 30
J89 D8 2fr multi 60 60
J90 D8 3fr multi 90 90
J91 D8 4fr multi 1.20 1.20
J92 D8 5fr multi 1.50 1.50
Nos. J83-J92 (10) 4.98 4.98

PARCEL POST STAMPS

No. 65 Overprinted

COLIS
POSTAUX

1901 Unwmk. *Perf. 14x13½*

Q1 A16 10c blk, *lav* 40.00 40.00
a. Inverted overprint

No. 66 Overprinted

Colis Postaux

Q2 A16 10c red 7.00 7.00

Nos. 84 and 87 Overprinted

Colis Postaux

1917-25

Q3 A17 10c car rose & red 80 80
a. Double overprint 22.50
Q4 A17 20c bis brn & vio brn ('25) 65 65
a. Double overprint 40.00 40.00

No. Q4 with Additional Overprint in Black

FRANCE LIBRE
F. N. F. L.

1942

Q5 A17 20c bis brn & vio brn 250.00 250.00

ST. THOMAS AND PRINCE ISLANDS

Democratic Republic of Sao Tome and Principe

LOCATION — Two islands in the Gulf of Guinea, 125 miles off the west coast of Africa.
GOVT. — Republic.
AREA — 372 sq. mi.
POP. — 102,000 (est. 1984).
CAPITAL — Sao Tome.

This colony of Portugal became a province, later an overseas territory, and achieved independence on July 12, 1975.

1000 Reis = 1 Milreis
100 Centavos = 1 Escudo (1913)
100 Cents = 1 Dobra (1978)

Catalogue values for unused stamps in this country are for Never Hinged items, beginning with Scott 353 in the regular postage section, Scott J52 in the postage due section, and Scott RA4 in the postal tax section.

Portuguese Crown — A1

King Luiz — A2

FIVE, TWENTY-FIVE, FIFTY REIS:
Type I - "5" is upright.
Type II - "5" is slanting.

TEN REIS:
Type I - "1" has short serif at top.
Type II - "1" has long serif at top.

FORTY REIS:
Type I - "4" is broad.
Type II - "4" is narrow.

Perf. 12½, 13½

1869-75 Unwmk. **Typo.**

1 A1 5r blk, I 2.00 1.65
a. Type II 2.00 1.65
2 A1 10r yel, I 14.00 8.50
a. Type II 14.00 8.50
3 A1 20r bister 3.25 2.50
4 A1 25r rose, I 1.25 1.10
a. 25r red 3.00 1.10
5 A1 40r bl ('75) I 4.75 3.50
a. Type II 4.75 3.50
6 A1 50r gray grn, II 8.00 7.75
a. Type I 15.00 14.00
7 A1 100r gray lil 6.00 5.00
8 A1 200r red org ('75) 7.75 6.25
9 A1 300r choc ('75) 7.75 6.25

1881-85

10 A1 10r gray grn, I 8.00 6.00
a. Type II 8.00 6.00
b. Perf. 13½ 9.00 6.00
11 A1 20r car rose ('85) 3.50 3.00
12 A1 25r vio ('85) II 2.25 1.75
13 A1 40r yel buff, II 5.00 4.00
a. Perf. 13½ 6.00 4.50
14 A1 50r dk bl, I 2.50 2.25
a. Type II 2.50 2.25

Nos. 1 to 14 inclusive have been reprinted on stout white paper, ungummed, with rough perforation 13½, also on ordinary paper with shiny white gum and clean-cut perforation 13½ with large holes. Value of lowest-cost reprint, $1.

Typo., Head Embossed

1887 *Perf. 12½, 13½*

15 A2 5r black 3.00 2.50
16 A2 10r green 4.25 2.50
17 A2 20r brt rose 4.25 3.00
a. Perf. 12½ 55.00 55.00
18 A2 25r violet 4.25 1.65
19 A2 40r brown 4.25 2.25
20 A2 50r blue 4.25 1.90
21 A2 100r yel brn 4.25 2.00
22 A2 200r gray lil 15.00 10.50
23 A2 300r orange 15.00 10.50

Nos. 15, 16, 19, 21, 22, and 23 have been reprinted in paler colors than the originals, with white gum and cleancut perforation 13½. Value $1.50 each.

Nos. 16-17, 19 Surcharged:

5 — 5 réis (a)
5 cinco réis (b)
R.$50 (c)

1889-91 **Without Gum**

24 A2(a) 5r on 10r grn 30.00 20.00
25 A2(b) 5r on 20r rose 25.00 20.00
26 A2(c) 50r on 40r brn ('91) 100.00 70.00

Varieties of Nos. 24-26, including inverted and double surcharges, "5" inverted, "Cinoc" and "Cinco," were deliberately made and unofficially issued.

King Carlos
A6 A7

1895 **Typo.** ***Perf. 11½, 12½***

27 A6 5r yellow 60 45
28 A6 10r red lil 95 75
29 A6 15r red brn 1.40 1.10
30 A6 20r lavender 1.50 1.10
31 A6 25r green 1.50 50
32 A6 50r light bl 1.65 50
a. Perf. 13½ 2.00 1.25
33 A6 75r rose 3.75 3.25
34 A6 80r yel grn 7.25 6.25
35 A6 100r brn, *yel* 3.50 3.00
36 A6 150r car, *rose* 6.00 5.00
37 A6 200r dk bl, *bl* 7.75 6.00
38 A6 300r dk bl, *sal* 8.50 7.75

1898-1903 ***Perf. 11½***
Name and Value in Black except 500r

39 A7 2½r gray 25 25
40 A7 5r orange 25 20
41 A7 10r lt grn 25 20
42 A7 15r brown 2.00 1.75
43 A7 15r gray grn ('03) 1.10 1.10
44 A7 20r gray vio 90 50
45 A7 25r sea green 50 25
46 A7 25r car ('03) 1.10 30
47 A7 50r blue 65 30
48 A7 50r brn ('03) 4.50 4.50
49 A7 65r dull bl ('03) 10.00 8.00
50 A7 75r rose 10.00 6.50
51 A7 75r red lil ('03) 1.75 1.40
52 A7 80r brt vio 5.00 5.00
53 A7 100r dk blue, *bl* 2.50 2.00
54 A7 115r org brn, *pink* ('03) 7.00 6.00
55 A7 130r brn, *straw* ('03) 7.00 6.00
56 A7 150r brn, *buff* 2.75 2.25
57 A7 200r red lil, *pnksh* 4.00 2.00
58 A7 300r dk bl, *rose* 5.50 5.00
59 A7 400r dl bl, *straw* ('03) 10.00 7.50
60 A7 500r blk & red, *bl* ('01) 6.00 5.00
61 A7 700r vio, *yelsh* ('01) 16.00 12.00
Nos. 39-61 (23) 99.00 78.00

Stamps of 1869-95 Surcharged in Red or Black

65
RÉIS

1902

On Stamp of 1887

62 A2 130r on 5r blk (R) 6.00 5.00
a. Perf. 13½ 27.50 27.50

On Stamps of 1869

63 A1 115r on 50r grn 10.00 7.50
64 A1 400r on 10r yel 37.50 25.00
a. Double surcharge

On Stamps of 1887

65 A2 65r on 20r rose 6.25 4.00
a. Perf. 13½ 6.75 5.50
66 A2 65r on 25r vio 4.50 4.00
a. Inverted surcharge
67 A2 65r on 100r yel brn 4.50 4.00
68 A2 115r on 10r bl grn 4.50 4.00
69 A2 115r on 300r org 4.50 4.00
70 A2 130r on 200r gray lil 6.00 4.25
71 A2 400r on 40r brn 8.00 6.00
72 A2 400r on 50r bl 14.00 12.00
a. Perf. 13½ 100.00 80.00

On Stamps of 1895

73 A6 65r on 5r yel 4.00 3.00
74 A6 65r on 10r red vio 4.00 3.00
75 A6 65r on 15r choc 4.00 3.00
76 A6 65r on 20r lav 4.00 3.00
77 A6 115r on 25r grn 4.00 3.00
78 A6 115r on 150r car, *rose* 4.00 3.00
79 A6 115r on 200r bl, *bl* 4.00 3.00
80 A6 130r on 75r rose 4.00 3.00
81 A6 130r on 100r brn, *yel* 4.00 3.50
a. Double surcharge
82 A6 130r on 300r bl, *sal* 4.00 3.00
83 A6 400r on 50r lt bl 1.10 95
a. Perf. 13½ 1.50 1.25
84 A6 400r on 80r yel grn 2.00 1.50

On Newspaper Stamp No. P12

85 N3 400r on 2½r brn 1.10 95
a. Double surcharge
Nos. 62-85 (24) 149.95 113.65

Reprints of Nos. 63, 64, 67, 71, and 72 have shiny white gum and clean-cut perf. 13½. Value $1 each.

Stamps of 1898 Overprinted PROVISORIO

1902

86 A7 15r brown 2.00 1.25
87 A7 25r sea grn 2.00 1.25
88 A7 50r blue 2.25 1.25
89 A7 75r rose 5.00 3.50

No. 49 Surcharged in Black

50
RÉIS

1905

90 A7 50r on 65r dl bl 3.25 2.75

Stamps of 1898-1903 Overprinted in Carmine or Green

REPUBLICA

1911

91 A7 2½r gray 25 20
a. Inverted overprint 4.50 3.00
92 A7 5r orange 25 20
93 A7 10r lt grn 25 20
a. Inverted overprint 4.00 3.50
94 A7 15r gray grn 25 20
95 A7 20r gray vio 25 20
96 A7 25r car (G) 60 20
97 A7 50r brown 25 20
a. Inverted overprint 4.50 4.50
98 A7 75r red lil 25 20
99 A7 100r dk bl, *bl* 60 50
a. Inverted overprint 4.25 3.25
100 A7 115r org brn, *pink* 1.10 95
101 A7 130r brn, *straw* 1.10 95
102 A7 200r red lil, *pnksh* 6.00 3.75
103 A7 400r dl bl, *straw* 1.40 1.00
104 A7 500r blk & red, *bl* 1.40 1.00
105 A7 700r vio, *yelsh* 1.40 1.00
Nos. 91-105 (15) 15.35 10.75

King Manuel II — A8

Overprinted in Carmine or Green

1912 ***Perf. 11½, 12***

106 A8 2½r violet 15 15
a. Double overprint 5.00 5.00
b. Double overprint, one inverted
107 A8 5r black 15 15
108 A8 10r gray grn 15 15
a. Double overprint 5.00 5.00
109 A8 20r car (G) 1.00 75
110 A8 25r vio brn 60 45
111 A8 50r dk bl 60 55
112 A8 75r bis brn 90 55
113 A8 100r brn, *lt grn* 1.10 50
114 A8 200r dk grn, *sal* 2.00 1.40
115 A8 300r blk, *azure* 2.00 1.75
Nos. 106-115 (10) 8.65 6.40

Stamps of 1898-1905 Overprinted in Black

REPUBLICA

1913

On Stamps of 1898-1903

116 A7 2½r gray 1.00 1.00
a. Inverted overprint 5.00 5.00
b. Double overprint 4.00 4.00
117 A7 5r orange 1.25 1.00
118 A7 15r gray grn 22.50 17.50
a. Inverted overprint
119 A7 20r gray vio 1.25 1.00
a. Inverted overprint
120 A7 25r carmine 5.00 4.00
a. Inverted overprint
b. Double overprint
121 A7 75r red lil 5.00 5.00
122 A7 100r bl, *bluish* 8.50 6.50
123 A7 115r org brn, *pink* 30.00 27.50
a. Double overprint 50.00 40.00
124 A7 130r brn, *straw* 11.00 10.00
125 A7 200r red lil, *pnksh* 12.00 11.00
126 A7 400r dl bl, *straw* 11.00 10.00
127 A7 500r blk & red, *gray* 27.50 25.00
128 A7 700r vio, *yelsh* 45.00 35.00

On Provisional Issue of 1902

129 A1 115r on 50r grn 72.50 65.00
a. Inverted overprint
129B A1 400r on 10r yel 155.00 140.00
130 A2 115r on 10r bl grn 2.75 2.50
a. Inverted overprint
131 A2 400r on 50r bl 50.00 40.00
132 A6 115r on 25r grn 2.00 1.75
a. Inverted overprint
133 A6 115r on 150r car, *rose* 35.00 30.00
a. Inverted overprint
134 A6 115r on 200r bl, *bl* 2.50 2.00
135 A6 130r on 75r rose 2.25 2.00
a. Inverted overprint
136 A6 400r on 50r lt bl 3.25 3.25
a. Perf. 13½ 5.00 5.00
137 A6 400r on 80r yel grn 4.00 3.75

Same Overprint on Nos. 86, 88 and 90

138 A7 15r brown 2.00 1.75
139 A7 50r blue 2.25 2.00
140 A7 50r on 65r dl bl 12.00 10.00

No. 123-125, 130-131 and 137 were issued without gum.

Stamps of 1898-1905 Overprinted in Black

REPUBLICA

On Stamps of 1898-1903

141 A7 2½r gray 60 50
a. Inverted overprint 4.50
b. Double overprint 4.50 4.50
c. Double overprint inverted
142 A7 5r orange 25.00 20.00
143 A7 15r gray grn 1.75 1.50
a. Inverted overprint
144 A7 20r gray vio 70.00 45.00
a. Inverted overprint
145 A7 25r carmine 30.00 20.00
a. Inverted overprint
146 A7 75r red lil 2.00 1.50
a. Inverted overprint
147 A7 100r bl, *bl* 2.25 1.75
148 A7 115r org brn, *pink* 8.00 7.00
a. Inverted overprint
149 A7 130r brn, *straw* 8.00 7.00
a. Inverted overprint
150 A7 200r red lil, *pnksh* 2.50 1.75
a. Inverted overprint
151 A7 400r dl bl, *straw* 10.00 8.00
152 A7 500r blk & red, *gray* 9.00 8.00
153 A7 700r vio, *yelsh* 9.00 8.00

On Provisional Issue of 1902

154 A1 115r on 50r grn 100.00 80.00
155 A2 115r on 10r bl grn 2.50 2.25
156 A2 115r on 300r org 100.00 90.00
157 A2 130r on 5r blk 100.00 90.00
158 A2 400r on 50r bl 75.00 60.00
159 A6 115r on 25r grn 2.00 1.50
160 A6 115r on 150r car, *rose* 2.50 2.25
a. "REPUBLICA" inverted
161 A6 115r on 200r bl, *bl* 2.50 2.25
162 A6 130r on 75r rose 2.25 2.00
a. Inverted surcharge
163 A6 130r on 100r brn, *yel* 200.00 175.00
164 A6 400r on 50r lt bl 2.50 2.25
a. Perf. 13½ 20.00 7.50
165 A6 400r on 80r yel grn 2.50 2.25
166 N3 400r on 2½r brn 2.00 1.75

Same Overprint on Nos. 86, 88 and 90

167 A7 15r brown 1.50 1.25
a. Inverted overprint
168 A7 50r blue 1.50 1.25
a. Inverted overprint
169 A7 50r on 65r dl bl 2.25 1.50

Most of Nos. 141-169 were issued without gum.

Foreign postal stationery (stamped envelopes, postal cards and air letter sheets) lies beyond the scope of this Catalogue, which is limited to adhesive postage stamps.

Vasco da Gama Issue of Various Portuguese Colonies Surcharged as

REPUBLICA
S.TOMÉ E PRINCIPE
¼ C.

On Stamps of Macao

170 CD20 ¼c on ½a bl grn 2.00 2.00
171 CD21 ½c on 1a red 2.00 2.00
172 CD22 1c on 2a red vio 2.00 2.00
173 CD23 2½c on 4a yel grn 2.00 2.00
174 CD24 5c on 8a dk bl 2.00 2.00
175 CD25 7½c on 12a vio brn 2.75 2.75
176 CD26 10c on 16a bis brn 2.00 2.00
177 CD27 15c on 24a bis 2.00 2.00
Nos. 170-177 (8) 16.75 16.75

On Stamps of Portuguese Africa

178 CD20 ¼c on 2½r bl grn 1.40 1.40
179 CD21 ½c on 5r red 1.40 1.40
180 CD22 1c on 10r red vio 1.40 1.40
181 CD23 2½c on 25r yel grn 1.40 1.40
182 CD24 5c on 50r dk bl 1.40 1.40
183 CD25 7½c on 75r vio brn 1.75 1.75
184 CD26 10c on 100r bis brn 1.40 1.40
185 CD27 15c on 150r bis 1.40 1.40
Nos. 178-185 (8) 11.55 11.55

On Stamps of Timor

186 CD20 ¼c on ½a bl grn 1.75 1.50
187 CD21 ½c on 1a red 1.75 1.50
188 CD22 1c on 2a red vio 1.75 1.50
a. Double surcharge
189 CD23 2½c on 4a yel grn 1.75 1.50
190 CD24 5c on 8a dk bl 1.75 2.00
191 CD25 7½c on 12a vio brn 2.25 2.00
192 CD26 10c on 16a bis brn 1.75 1.50
193 CD27 15c on 24a bis 1.75 1.50
Nos. 186-193 (8) 14.50 13.00

Ceres — A9

A10

1914-26 **Typo.** ***Perf. 12x11½, 15x14***
Name and Value in Black

194 A9 ¼c ol brn 15 15
195 A9 ½c black 15 15
196 A9 1c bl grn 50 50
197 A9 1c yel grn ('22) 15 15
198 A9 1½c lil brn 15 15
199 A9 2c carmine 15 15
200 A9 2c gray ('26) 20 20
201 A9 2½c lt vio 15 15
202 A9 3c org ('22) 20 20
203 A9 4c rose ('22) 20 20
204 A9 4½c gray ('22) 20 20
205 A9 5c deep bl 45 35
206 A9 5c brt bl ('22) 20 20
207 A9 6c lilac ('22) 20 20
208 A9 7c ultra ('22) 20 20
209 A9 7½c yel brn 20 20
210 A9 8c slate 20 20
211 A9 10c org brn 25 25
212 A9 12c bl grn ('22) 50 45
213 A9 15c plum 1.65 1.25
214 A9 15c brn rose ('22) 25 25
215 A9 20c yel grn 1.75 1.10
216 A9 24c ultra ('26) 3.50 3.00
217 A9 25c choc ('26) 3.50 3.00
218 A9 30c brn, *grn* 1.75 1.50
219 A9 30c gray grn ('22) 50 40
220 A9 40c brn, *pink* 2.00 1.75
221 A9 40c turq bl ('22) 55 50
222 A9 50c org, *sal* 4.50 3.50
223 A9 50c lt vio ('26) 75 60
224 A9 60c dk bl ('22) 1.25 90
225 A9 60c rose ('26) 2.00 2.00
226 A9 80c brt rose ('22) 1.65 50
227 A9 1e grn, *bl* 4.00 3.50
228 A9 1e pale rose ('22) 2.25 1.40
229 A9 1e bl ('26) 1.50 1.25
230 A9 2e dk vio ('22) 2.75 1.65
231 A9 5e buff ('26) 20.00 10.00
232 A9 10e pink ('26) 30.00 17.50
233 A9 20e pale turq ('26) 55.00 45.00
Nos. 194-233 (40) 145.50 104.80

Perforation and paper variations command a premium for some of Nos. 194-233.

Preceding Issues Overprinted in Carmine

REPUBLICA

1915

On Provisional Issue of 1902

234 A2 115r on 10r grn 2.25 2.00
235 A2 115r on 300r org 2.25 1.75
236 A2 130r on 5r blk 4.00 3.00
237 A2 130r on 200r gray lil 1.50 1.25
238 A6 115r on 25r grn 60 45
239 A6 115r on 150r car, *rose* 60 45
240 A6 115r on 200r bl, *bl* 60 45
241 A6 130r on 75r rose 60 45
242 A6 130r on 100r brn, *yel* 1.40 1.40
243 A6 130r on 300r bl, *sal* 1.10 90

Same Overprint on Nos. 88 and 90

244 A7 50r blue 90 60
245 A7 50r on 65r dl bl 90 60
Nos. 234-245 (12) 16.70 13.30

1919

246 A10 2½c on 15r brn 60 55

No. 91 Surcharged in Black ½ C.

247 A7 ½c on 2½r gray 3.00 2.50
248 A7 1c on 2½r gray 2.25 2.00
249 A7 2½c on 2½r gray 1.10 65

No. 194 Surcharged in Blue ½

250 A9 ½c on ¼c ol brn 2.00 1.50
251 A9 2c on ¼c ol brn 2.25 1.50
252 A9 2½c on ¼c ol brn 6.00 5.00

No. 201 Surcharged in Black $04 Centavos

253 A9 4c on 2½c lt vio 90 75
Nos. 246-253 (8) 18.10 14.45

Nos. 246-253 were issued without gum.

Stamps of 1898-1905 Overprinted in Green or Red REPUBLICA

1920

On Stamps of 1898-1903

255 A7 75r red lil (G) 55 50
256 A7 100r bl, *bl* (R) 60 55
257 A7 115r org brn, *pink* (G) 1.65 1.25
258 A7 130r brn, *straw* (G) 25.00 20.00
259 A7 200r red lil, *pnksh* (G) 1.65 1.00
260 A7 500r blk, & red, *gray* (G) 1.10 1.00
261 A7 700r vio, *yelsh* (G) 1.65 1.00

On Stamps of 1902

262 A6 115r on 25r grn (R) 90 60
263 A6 115r on 200r bl, *bl* (R) 1.10 1.00
264 A6 130r on 75r rose (G) 1.65 1.00

On Nos. 88-89

265 A7 50r bl (R) 1.25 1.10
266 A7 75r rose (G) 7.50 7.00

On No. 90

267 A7 50r on 65r dl bl (R) 8.00 6.00
Nos. 255-267 (13) 52.60 42.00

Provisional Issue of 1915 Surcharged in Blue or Red DEZ CENTAVOS

1923 **Without Gum**

268 A6 10c on 115r on 25r grn (Bl) 50 40
269 A6 10c on 115r on 150r car, *rose* (Bl) 50 40
270 A6 10c on 115r on 200r bl, *bl* (R) 50 40
271 A6 10c on 130r on 75r rose (Bl) 50 40
272 A6 10c on 130r on 100r brn, *yel* (Bl) 50 40
273 A6 10c on 130r on 300r bl, *sal* (R) 50 40
Nos. 268-273 (6) 3.00 2.40

Nos. 268-273 are usually stained and discolored.

Nos. 84-85 Surcharged República 40 C.

1925

274 A6 40c on 400r on 80r yel grn 90 45
275 N3 40c on 400r on 2½r brn 90 45

Nos. 228 and 230 Surcharged 70 C.

1931

281 A9 70c on 1e pale rose 2.00 1.25
282 A9 1.40e on 2e dk vio 2.75 2.50

Ceres — A11

1934 **Typo.** **Wmk. 232** ***Perf. 12x11½***

283 A11 1c bister 20 20
284 A11 5c ol brn 20 20
285 A11 10c violet 20 20
286 A11 15c black 25 20
287 A11 20c gray 25 20
288 A11 30c dk grn 35 30
289 A11 40c red org 35 30
290 A11 45c brt bl 40 30
291 A11 50c brown 40 30
292 A11 60c ol grn 40 30
293 A11 70c brn org 40 30
294 A11 80c emerald 40 30
295 A11 85c dp rose 2.00 1.50
296 A11 1e maroon 75 60
297 A11 1.40e dk bl 2.25 1.25
298 A11 2e dk vio 2.50 1.50
299 A11 5e ap grn 7.50 4.25
300 A11 10e ol bis 17.50 8.00
301 A11 20e orange 60.00 25.00
Nos. 283-301 (19) 96.30 45.20

Common Design Types
Inscribed "S. Tome"

1938 **Unwmk.** ***Perf. 13½x13***

Name and Value in Black

302 CD34 1c gray grn 15 15
303 CD34 5c org brn 20 20
304 CD34 10c dk car 30 30
305 CD34 15c dk vio brn 30 30
306 CD34 20c slate 30 30
307 CD35 30c rose vio 30 30
308 CD35 35c brt grn 55 45
309 CD35 40c brown 55 45
310 CD35 50c brt red vio 55 45
311 CD36 60c gray blk 55 45
312 CD36 70c brn vio 55 45
313 CD36 80c orange 55 45
314 CD36 1e red 1.50 80
315 CD37 1.75e blue 1.75 1.00
316 CD37 2e brn car 11.00 6.50
317 CD37 5e ol grn 11.00 6.50
318 CD38 10e bl vio 14.00 6.50
319 CD38 20e red brn 22.50 8.00
Nos. 302-319 (18) 66.60 33.55

Marble Column and Portuguese Arms with Cross — A12

1938 ***Perf. 12½***

320 A12 80c bl grn 1.40 1.10
321 A12 1.75e dp bl 6.50 3.25
322 A12 20e brown 25.00 12.00

Visit of the President of Portugal in 1938.

Common Design Types
Inscribed "S. Tomé e Principe"

1939 ***Perf. 13½x13***

Name and Value in Black

323 CD34 1c gray grn 18 14
324 CD34 5c org brn 18 14
325 CD34 10c dk car 18 14
326 CD34 15c dk vio brn 18 14
327 CD34 20c slate 18 14
328 CD35 30c rose vio 22 14
329 CD35 35c brt grn 22 14
330 CD35 40c brown 22 14
331 CD35 50c brt red vio 22 18
332 CD36 60c gray blk 22 18
333 CD36 70c brn vio 32 28
334 CD36 80c orange 32 28
335 CD36 1e red 70 40
336 CD37 1.75e blue 95 50
337 CD37 2e brn car 1.90 1.40
338 CD37 5e ol grn 3.75 2.75
339 CD38 10e bl vio 8.50 3.50
340 CD38 20e red brn 11.00 5.75
Nos. 323-340 (18) 29.44 16.34

Cola Nuts A13

UPU Symbols A14

Designs: 10c, Breadfruit. 30c, Annona. 50c, Cacao pods. 1e, Coffee. 1.75e, Dendem. 2e, Avocado. 5e, Pineapple. 10e, Mango. 20e, Coconuts.

1948 **Litho.** ***Perf. 14½***

341 A13 5c blk & yel 30 30
342 A13 10c blk & buff 40 30
343 A13 30c ind & gray 1.50 1.25
344 A13 50c brn & yel 1.50 1.25
345 A13 1e red & rose 3.00 1.50
346 A13 1.75e bl & gray 4.00 3.00
347 A13 2e blk & grn 3.00 1.50
348 A13 5e brn & lil rose 7.00 4.00
349 A13 10e blk & pink 10.00 7.50
350 A13 20e blk & gray 35.00 15.00
a. Sheet of ten, #341-350 80.00 80.00
Nos. 341-350 (10) 65.70 35.60

No. 350a sold for 42.50 escudos.

Lady of Fatima Issue

Common Design Type

1948, Dec. **Unwmk.**

351 CD40 50c purple 5.25 4.50

Catalogue values for unused stamps in this section, from this point to the end of the section, are for Never Hinged items.

1949 **Unwmk.** ***Perf. 14***

352 A14 3.50e blk & gray 7.50 5.00

UPU, 75th anniv.

Holy Year Issue

Common Design Types

1950 ***Perf. 13x13½***

353 CD41 2.50e blue 2.75 1.50
354 CD42 4e orange 4.50 3.50

Holy Year Extension Issue

Common Design Type

1951 ***Perf. 14***

355 CD43 4e ind & bl gray 2.75 2.00

Medical Congress Issue

Common Design Type

Design: Clinic.

1952 ***Perf. 13½***

356 CD44 10c choc & bl 30 30

Joao de Santarem A15

Jeronymos Convent A16

Portraits: 30c, Pero Escobar. 50c, Fernao de Po 1e, Alvaro Esteves. 2e, Lopo Goncalves. 3.50e, Martim Fernandes.

1952 **Unwmk.** **Litho.** ***Perf. 14***

Centers Multicolored

357 A15 10c cr & choc 10 6
358 A15 30c pale grn & dk grn 10 6
359 A15 50c gray & dk gray 10 6
360 A15 1e gray bl & dk bl 60 8
361 A15 2e lil gray & vio brn 45 15
362 A15 3.50e buff & choc 60 25
Nos. 357-362 (6) 1.95 66

1953 ***Perf. 13x13½***

363 A16 10c dk brn & gray 15 12
364 A16 50c brn org & org 50 40
365 A16 3e bl blk & gray blk 2.00 80

Exhib. of Sacred Missionary Art, Lisbon, 1951.

Stamp Centenary Issue

Stamp of Portugal and Arms of Colonies — A17

1953 **Photo.** ***Perf. 13***

Stamp and Arms Multicolored

366 A17 50c buff & org brn 75 60

Centenary of Portugal's first postage stamps.

Presidential Visit Issue

Map and Plane — A18

1954 **Typo. & Litho.** ***Perf. 13½***

367 A18 15c blk, bl, red & grn 20 15
368 A18 5e brn, grn & red 1.10 80

Visit of Pres. Francisco H. C. Lopes.

Sao Paulo Issue

Common Design Type

1954 **Litho.**

369 CD46 2.50e bl, gray bl & blk 55 35

Fair Emblem, Globe and Arms — A19

1958 **Unwmk.** ***Perf. 12x11½***

370 A19 2.50e multi 60 50

World's Fair at Brussels.

Tropical Medicine Congress Issue

Common Design Type

Design: Cassia occidentalis.

1958 ***Perf. 13½***

371 CD47 5e pale grn, brn, yel, grn & red 2.00 1.75

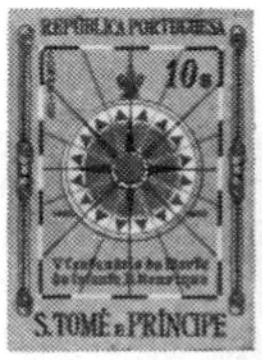

Compass Rose — A20

Going to Church — A21

1960 Litho. *Perf. 13½*
372 A20 10e gray & multi 1.00 40

500th death anniv. of Prince Henry the Navigator.

1960 *Perf. 14½*
373 A21 1.50e multi 40 30

10th anniv. of the Commission for Technical Co-operation in Africa South of the Sahara (C.C.T.A.).

Sports Issue
Common Design Type

Sports: 50c, Angling. 1e, Gymnast on rings. 1.50e, Handball. 2e, Sailing. 2.50e, Sprinting. 20e, Skin diving.

1962, Jan. 18 Litho. *Perf. 13½*
Multicolored Design

374 CD48 50c gray grn 5 5
a. "$50 CORREIOS" omitted
375 CD48 1e lt lil 60 22
376 CD48 1.50e salmon 60 22
377 CD48 2e blue 75 35
378 CD48 2.50e gray grn 95 50
379 CD48 20e dk bl 2.25 1.65
Nos. 374-379 (6) 5.20 2.99

On No. 374a, the blue impression, including imprint, is missing.

Anti-Malaria Issue
Common Design Type

Design: Anopheles gambiae.

1962 Unwmk. *Perf. 13½*
380 CD49 2.50e multi 1.15 80

Airline Anniversary Issue
Common Design Type

1963 Unwmk. *Perf. 14½*
381 CD50 1.50e pale bl & multi 60 50

National Overseas Bank Issue
Common Design Type

Design: 2.50e, Francisco de Oliveira Chamico.

1964, May 16 *Perf. 13½*
382 CD51 2.50e multi 70 50

ITU Issue
Common Design Type

1965, May 17 Litho. *Perf. 14½*
383 CD52 2.50e tan & multi 1.50 1.00

Infantry Officer, 1788 — A22

Designs: 35c, Sergeant with lance, 1788. 40c, Corporal with pike, 1788. 1e, Private with musket, 1788. 2.50e, Artillery officer, 1806. 5e, Private, 1811. 7.50e, Private, 1833. 10e, Lancer officer, 1834.

1965, Aug. 24 Litho. *Perf. 13½*
384 A22 20c multi 16 12
385 A22 35c multi 16 12
386 A22 40c multi 22 16
387 A22 1e multi 1.10 50
388 A22 2.50e multi 1.10 50
389 A22 5e multi 1.65 1.25
390 A22 7.50e multi 2.00 1.90
391 A22 10e multi 2.50 2.00
Nos. 384-391 (8) 8.89 6.55

National Revolution Issue
Common Design Type

Design: 4e, Arts and Crafts School and Anti-Tuberculosis Dispensary.

1966, May 28 Litho. *Perf. 11½*
392 CD53 4e multi 75 50

Navy Club Issue
Common Design Type

Designs: 1.50e, Capt. Campos Rodrigues and ironclad corvette Vasco da Gama. 2.50e, Dr. Aires Kopke, microscope and tsetse fly.

1967, Jan. 31 Litho. *Perf. 13*
393 CD54 1.50e multi 90 50
394 CD54 2.50e multi 1.40 75

Valinhos Shrine, Children and Apparition A23

Cabral Medal, from St. Jerome's Convent A24

1967, May 13 Litho. *Perf. 12½x13*
395 A23 2.50e multi 30 25

50th anniv. of the apparition of the Virgin Mary to 3 shepherd children, Lucia dos Santos, Francisco and Jacinta Marto, at Fatima.

1968, Apr. 22 Litho. *Perf. 14*
396 A24 1.50e bl & multi 45 30

500th birth anniv. of Pedro Alvares Cabral, navigator who took possession of Brazil for Portugal.

Admiral Coutinho Issue
Common Design Type

Design: 2e, Adm. Coutinho, Cago Coutinho Island and monument (vert.).

1969, Feb. 17 Litho. *Perf. 14*
397 CD55 2e multi 50 35

Vasco da Gama's Fleet — A25

Manuel Portal of Guarda Episcopal See — A26

1969, Aug. 29 Litho. *Perf. 14*
398 A25 2.50e multi 75 50

Vasco da Gama (1469-1524), navigator.

Administration Reform Issue
Common Design Type

1969, Sept. 25 Litho. *Perf. 14*
399 CD56 2.50e multi 50 35

1969, Dec. 1 Litho. *Perf. 14*
400 A26 4e multi 50 35

500th birth anniv. of King Manuel I.

The lack of a value for a listed item does not necessarily indicate rarity.

Pero Escobar, Joao de Santarem and Map of Islands — A27

Pres. Américo Rodrigues Thomaz — A28

1970, Jan. 25 Litho. *Perf. 14*
401 A27 2.50e lt bl & multi 35 30

500th anniv. of the discovery of St. Thomas and Prince Islands.

1970 Litho. *Perf. 12½*
402 A28 2.50e multi 35 30

Visit of Pres. Américo Rodrigues Thomaz of Portugal.

Marshal Carmona Issue
Common Design Type

Design: 5e, Antonio Oscar Carmona in dress uniform.

1970, Nov. 15 Litho. *Perf. 14*
403 CD57 5e multi 75 55

Coffee Plant and Stamps — A29

Designs: 1.50e, Postal Administration Building and stamp No. 1 (horiz.). 2.50e, Cathedral of St. Thomas and stamp No. 2.

1970, Dec. *Perf. 13½*
404 A29 1e multi 25 10
405 A29 1.50e multi 35 15
406 A29 2.50e multi 60 20

Centenary of St. Thomas and Prince Islands postage stamps.

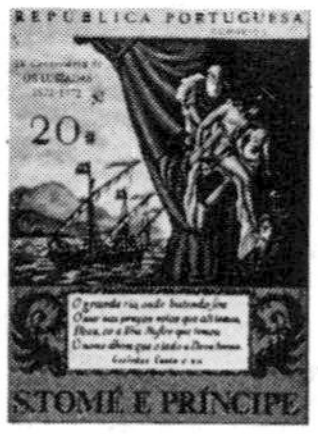

Descent from the Cross — A30

1972, May 25 Litho. *Perf. 13*
407 A30 20e lil & multi 2.25 1.25

4th centenary of publication of The Lusiads by Luiz Camoens.

Olympic Games Issue
Common Design Type

Design: 1.50e, Track and javelin, Olympic emblem.

1972, June 20 *Perf. 14x13½*
408 CD59 1.50e multi 35 25

Lisbon-Rio de Janeiro Flight Issue
Common Design Type

Design: 2.50e, "Lusitania" flying over warship at St. Peter Rocks.

1972, Sept. 20 Litho. *Perf. 13½*
409 CD60 2.50e multi 35 25

WMO Centenary Issue
Common Design Type

1973, Dec. 15 Litho. *Perf. 13*
410 CD61 5e dl grn & multi 60 50

Republic

Flags of Portugal and St. Thomas & Prince A31

1975, July 12 Litho. *Perf. 13½*
411 A31 3e gray & multi 40 40
412 A31 10e yel & multi 1.00 30
413 A31 20e lt bl & multi 2.00 50
414 A31 50e sal & multi 3.50 2.25

Argel Agreement, granting independence, Argel, Sept. 26, 1974.

Man and Woman with St. Thomas & Prince Flag — A32

1975, Dec. 21
415 A32 1.50e pink & multi 15 10
416 A32 4e multi 40 20
417 A32 7.50e org & multi 75 40
418 A32 20e bl & multi 1.75 1.00
419 A32 50e ocher & multi 4.00 2.00
Nos. 415-419 (5) 7.05 3.70

Proclamation of Independence, Dec. 7, 1975.

Chart and Hand — A33

1975, Dec. 21 Litho. *Perf. 13½*
420 A33 1e ocher & multi 15 10
421 A33 1.50e multi 20 12
422 A33 2.50e org & multi 30 15

National Reconstruction Fund.

****

Stamps of 1952-1973 Overprinted **Rep. Democr.**

12–7–75

1977 Litho. *Perf. 13½, 14, 13*
423 A15 10c multi (#357)
424 A22 20c multi (#384)
425 A15 30c multi (#358)
426 A22 35c multi (#385)
427 A22 40c multi (#386)
428 A15 50c multi (#359)
429 A15 1e multi (#360)
430 CD56 2.50e multi (#399)
431 A27 2.50e multi (#401)
432 A15 3.50e multi (#362)
433 A26 4e multi (#400)
434 CD61 5e multi (#410)
435 A22 7.50e multi (#390)
436 A20 10e multi (#372)
Nos. 423-436 (14) 10.00

The 10c, 30c, 50c, 1e, 3.50e, 10e issued with glassine interleaving stuck to back.

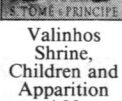

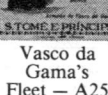

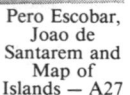

Pres. Manuel Pinto da Costa and Flag — A34

Designs: 3.50e, 4.50e, Portuguese Governor handing over power. 12.50e, like 2e.

1977, Jan. *Perf. 13½*

437	A34	2e yel & multi		20	10
438	A34	3.50e bl & multi		25	12
439	A34	4.50e red & multi		35	15
440	A34	12.50e multi		90	35

1st anniversary of independence.

Pairs of Nos. 358-359, 357, 362, 384-386 Overprinted Alternately in Black

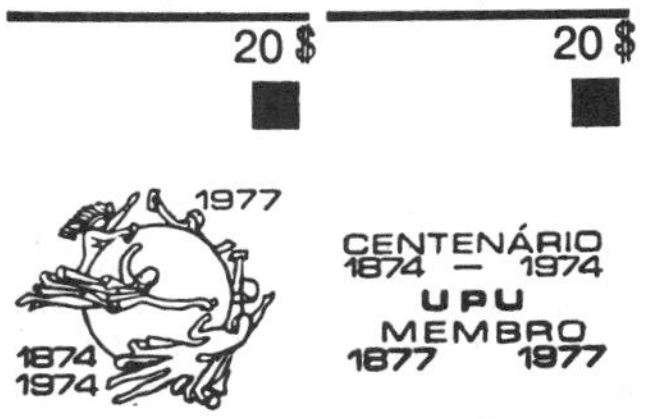

a b

1977, Oct. 19 **Litho.** *Perf. 14, 13½*

442	A15(a)	3e on 30c multi	
443	A15(b)	3e on 30c multi	
444	A15(a)	5e on 50c multi	
445	A15(b)	5e on 50c multi	
446	A15(a)	10e on 10c multi	
447	A15(b)	10e on 10c multi	
448	A15(a)	15e on 3.50e multi	
449	A15(b)	15e on 3.50e multi	
450	A22(a)	20e on 20c multi	
451	A22(b)	20e on 20c multi	
452	A22(a)	35e on 35c multi	
453	A22(b)	35e on 35c multi	
454	A22(a)	40e on 40c multi	
455	A22(b)	40e on 40c multi	

Centenary of membership in UPU. Overprints "a" and "b" alternate in sheets. Nos. 442-449 issued with glassine interleaving stuck to back.

These overprints exist in red on Nos. 444-445, 450-455 and on 1e on 10c, 3.50e and 30e on 30c.

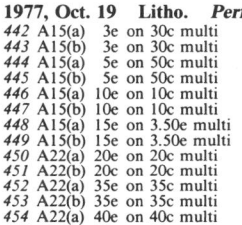

Mao Tse-tung (1893-1976), Chairman, People's Republic of China — A36

1977, Dec. **Litho.** *Perf. 13½x14*

461	A36	50d multi	4.00
a.		Souvenir sheet	4.50

Lenin — A37

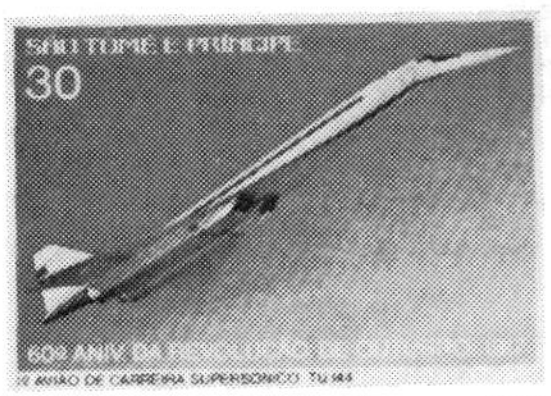

Russian Supersonic Plane — A38

Designs: 40d, Rowing crew. 50d, Cosmonaut Yuri A. Gagarin.

1977, Dec. *Perf. 13½x14, 14x13½*

462	A37	15d multi	75
463	A38	30d multi	1.50
464	A38	40d multi	2.00
465	A37	50d red & blk	2.50

60th anniv. of Russian October Revolution.

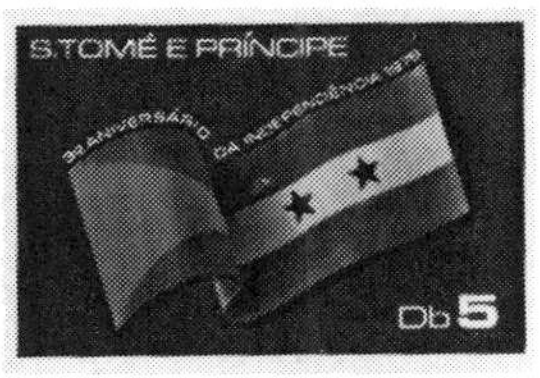

Flag of St. Thomas and Prince Islands — A39

Designs: Nos. 479, 479a, Map of Islands (vert.). No. 480, Coat of arms (vert.).

Perf. 14x13½, 13½x14

1978, July 12

478	A39	5d multi	40
479	A39	5d multi	40
a.		Souvenir sheet, 50d	4.25
480	A39	5d multi	40

Third anniversary of independence. Nos. 478-480 printed se-tenant in sheets of 9. No. 479a contains one imperf. stamp.

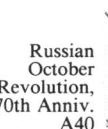

Russian October Revolution, 70th Anniv. A40

1988 **Litho.** *Perf. 12*

481	A40	25d Lenin addressing revolutionaries	1.20

AIR POST STAMPS

Common Design Type
Inscribed "S. Tome"

1938 *Perf. 13½x13*

Name and Value in Black

C1	CD39	10c scarlet	40.00	30.00
C2	CD39	20c purple	20.00	15.00
C3	CD39	50c orange	1.50	1.25
C4	CD39	1e ultra	2.50	2.00
C5	CD39	2e lil brn	3.75	3.00
C6	CD39	3e dk grn	5.75	4.00
C7	CD39	5e red brn	7.50	6.50
C8	CD39	9e rose car	8.50	6.50
C9	CD39	10e magenta	8.50	6.50
		Nos. C1-C9 (9)	98.00	74.75

Common Design Type
Inscribed "S. Tomé e Principe"

1939 **Engr.** **Unwmk.**

Name and Value Typo. in Black

C10	CD39	10c scarlet	25	25
C11	CD39	20c purple	25	25
C12	CD39	50c orange	25	25
C13	CD39	1e dp ultra	25	25
C14	CD39	2e lil brn	1.40	1.10
C15	CD39	3e dk grn	1.65	1.25
C16	CD39	5e red brn	2.75	1.75
C17	CD39	9e rose car	4.75	2.50
C18	CD39	10e magenta	4.75	2.50
		Nos. C10-C18 (9)	16.30	10.10

No. C16 exists with overprint "Exposicao International de Nova York, 1939-1940" and Trylon and Perisphere.

POSTAGE DUE STAMPS

"S. Thomé" — D1

1904 **Unwmk.** **Typo.** *Perf. 12*

J1	D1	5r yel grn	55	55
J2	D1	10r slate	65	65
J3	D1	20r yel brn	65	65
J4	D1	30r orange	65	65
J5	D1	50r gray brn	1.40	1.40
J6	D1	60r red brn	1.75	1.65
J7	D1	100r red lil	2.75	1.75
J8	D1	130r dl bl	4.00	3.25
J9	D1	200r carmine	4.00	3.50
J10	D1	500r gray vio	6.50	5.00
		Nos. J1-J10 (10)	22.90	19.05

Overprinted in Carmine or Green

REPUBLICA

1911

J11	D1	5r yel grn	25	25
J12	D1	10r slate	25	25
J13	D1	20r yel brn	25	25
J14	D1	30r orange	25	25
J15	D1	50r gray brn	25	25
J16	D1	60r red brn	60	60
J17	D1	100r red lil	70	70
J18	D1	130r dl bl	70	70
J19	D1	200r car (G)	70	70
J20	D1	500r gray vio	1.10	1.10
		Nos. J11-J20 (10)	5.05	5.05

Nos. J1-J10 Overprinted in Black

REPUBLICA

1913 **Without Gum**

J21	D1	5r yel grn	2.50	2.50
J22	D1	10r slate	3.50	3.00
J23	D1	20r yel brn	2.50	2.50
J24	D1	30r orange	2.50	2.50
J25	D1	50r gray brn	2.50	2.50
J26	D1	60r red brn	3.00	3.00
J27	D1	100r red lil	5.00	4.00
J28	D1	130r dl bl	17.50	17.50
a.		Inverted overprint	30.00	30.00
J29	D1	200r carmine	25.00	20.00
J30	D1	500r gray vio	27.50	25.00
		Nos. J21-J30 (10)	91.50	82.50

Nos. J1-J10 Overprinted in Black

REPUBLICA

1913 **Without Gum**

J31	D1	5r yel grn	1.75	1.75
a.		Inverted overprint		
J32	D1	10r slate	1.75	1.75
J33	D1	20r yel brn	1.75	1.75
J34	D1	30r orange	1.75	1.75
a.		Inverted overprint		
J35	D1	50r gray brn	1.75	1.75
J36	D1	60r red brn	2.75	2.25
J37	D1	100r red lil	2.75	2.25
J38	D1	130r dl bl	2.75	2.25
J39	D1	200r carmine	4.50	3.50
J40	D1	500r gray vio	13.00	13.00
		Nos. J31-J40 (10)	34.50	32.00

No. J5 Overprinted "Republica" in Italic Capitals like Regular Issue in Green

1920 **Without Gum**

J41	D1	50r gray brn	40.00	30.00

"S. Tomé" — D2

1921 **Typo.** *Perf. 11½*

J42	D2	½c yel grn	20	15
J43	D2	1c slate	20	15
J44	D2	2c org brn	20	15
J45	D2	3c orange	20	15
J46	D2	5c gray brn	20	15
J47	D2	6c lt brn	20	15
J48	D2	10c red vio	20	15
J49	D2	13c dl bl	25	20
J50	D2	20c carmine	25	20
J51	D2	50c gray	35	40
		Nos. J42-J51 (10)	2.25	1.85

In each sheet one stamp is inscribed "S. Thome" instead of "S. Tomé." Value, set of 10, $60.

Catalogue values for unused stamps in this section, from this point to the end of the section, are for Never Hinged items.

Common Design Type

Photo. & Typo.

1952 **Unwmk.** *Perf. 14*

Numeral in Red, Frame Multicolored

J52	CD45	10c chocolate	10	10
J53	CD45	30c red brn	10	10
J54	CD45	50c dk bl	10	10
J55	CD45	1e dk bl	25	25
J56	CD45	2e ol grn	60	60
J57	CD45	5e blk brn	1.25	1.25
		Nos. J52-J57 (6)	2.40	2.40

NEWSPAPER STAMPS

N1

N2

Perf. 11½, 12½ and 13½

1892 **Without Gum** **Unwmk.**

Black Surcharge

P1	N1	2½r on 10r grn	60.00	50.00
P2	N1	2½r on 20r rose	75.00	50.00
P3	N2	2½r on 10r grn	75.00	50.00
P4	N2	2½r on 20r rose	75.00	50.00

Green Surcharge

P5	N1	2½r on 5r blk	60.00	35.00
P6	N1	2½r on 20r rose	75.00	50.00
P8	N2	2½r on 5r blk	100.00	50.00
P9	N2	2½r on 10r grn	75.00	50.00
P10	N2	2½r on 20r rose	85.00	65.00

Both surcharges exist on No. 18 in green.

N3

PROVISORIO

d

1893 **Typo.** *Perf. 11½, 13½*

P12	N3	2½r brown	45	40

No. P12 Overprinted Type "d" in Blue

1899

Without Gum

P13 N3 2½r brown 25.00 16.00

POSTAL TAX STAMPS

Pombal Issue
Common Design Types

1925 Unwmk. *Perf. 12½*

RA1 CD28 15c org & blk 45 45
RA2 CD29 15c org & blk 45 45
RA3 CD30 15c org & blk 45 45

Certain revenue stamps (5e, 6e, 7e, 8e and other denominations) were surcharged in 1946 "Assistencia", 2 bars and new values (1e or 1.50e) and used as postal tax stamps.

Catalogue values for unused stamps in this section, from this point to the end of the section, are for Never Hinged items.

PT1

1948-58 Typo. *Perf. 12x11½*

Denomination in Black

RA4 PT1 50c yel grn 3.00 75
RA5 PT1 1e car rose 3.50 1.00
RA6 PT1 1e emer ('58) 1.50 50
RA7 PT1 1.50e bis brn 2.00 1.25

Denominations of 2e and up were used only for revenue purposes. No. RA6 lacks "Colonia de" below coat of arms.

Type of 1958 Surcharged

um escudo

Um escudo

1$00 1$00

m n

1964-65 Typo. *Perf. 12x11½*

RA8 PT1(m) 1e on 5e org yel 12.00 12.00
RA9 PT1(n) 1e on 5e org yel ('65) 4.50 4.50

The basic 5e orange yellow does not carry the words "Colonia de."

No. RA6 Surcharged: "Um escudo"

1965

RA10 PT1 1e emerald 2.00 2.00

1$00

Type of 1948 Surcharged

UM ESCUDO

1965 Typo. *Perf. 12x11½*

RA11 PT1 1e emerald 40 40

POSTAL TAX DUE STAMPS

Pombal Issue
Common Design Types

1925 Unwmk. *Perf. 12½*

RAJ1 CD31 30c org & blk 75 75
RAJ2 CD32 30c org & blk 75 75
RAJ3 CD33 30c org & blk 75 75

SALVADOR, EL

LOCATION — On the Pacific coast of Central America, between Guatemala, Honduras and the Gulf of Fonseca.
GOVT. — Republic.
AREA — 8,236 sq. mi.
POP. — 5,300,000 (est. 1984).
CAPITAL — San Salvador.

8 Reales = 100 Centavos = 1 Peso
100 Centavos = 1 Colón

Catalogue values for unused stamps in this country are for Never Hinged items, beginning with Scott 589 in the regular postage section, Scott C85 in the airpost section, and Scott O362 in the official section.

Volcano San Miguel — A1

1867 Unwmk. Engr. *Perf. 12*

1 A1 ½r blue 65 75
2 A1 1r red 65 65
3 A1 2r green 1.50 2.00
4 A1 4r bister 3.50 3.00

Nos. 1 to 4 when overprinted "Contra Sello" and shield with 14 stars, are telegraph stamps.

Nos. 1-4 Handstamped

1874

5 A1 ½r blue 5.00 3.50
6 A1 1r red 5.00 3.50
7 A1 2r green 5.00 3.50
8 A1 4r bister 18.75 17.50

Nos. 1-4 Handstamped

9 A1 ½r blue 2.50 2.00
10 A1 1r red 2.50 2.00
11 A1 2r green 2.50 2.00
12 A1 4r bister 7.50 6.25

The overprints on Nos. 5-12 exist double. Counterfeits are plentiful.

Coat of Arms
A2 A3

A4

A5

A6

1879 Litho. *Perf. 12½.*

13 A2 1c green 1.25 90
a Inverted "V" for second "A" in "SALVADOR" 2.50 2.00
b Inverted "V" for "A" in "REPUBLICA" 2.00 2.00
c Inverted "V" for "A" in "UNIVERSAL" 2.00 2.00
14 A3 2c rose 2.00 1.50
a Inverted scroll in upper left corner 6.00 5.00
15 A4 5c blue 3.50 1.25
a 5c ultra 6.00 4.00
16 A5 10c black 7.00 3.50
17 A6 20c violet 17.50 10.00
Nos. 13-17 (5) 31.25 17.15

There are fifteen varieties of the 1c and 2c, twenty-five of the 5c and five each of the 10 and 20c.

In 1881 the 1c, 2c and 5c were redrawn, the 1c in fifteen varieties and the 2c and 5c in five varieties each.

These stamps, when overprinted "Contra sello" and arms, are telegraph stamps.

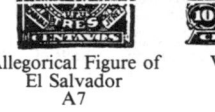

Allegorical Figure of El Salvador
A7

Volcano
A8

1887 Engr. *Perf. 12.*

18 A7 3c brown 38 18
a Imperf., pair 2.50 2.50
19 A8 10c orange 2.50 90

El Salvador — A9

1888 *Rouletted.*

20 A9 5c dp bl 30 25

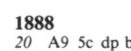

A10

A11

1889 *Perf. 12*

21 A10 1c green 12
22 A10 2c scarlet 12
23 A11 1c green 30 25
24 A11 2c scarlet 30

Nos. 21, 22 and 24 were never placed in use.

A12

Type I, thick numerals, heavy serifs.
Type II, thin numerals, straight serifs.

25 A12 1c on 3c brn, type II 65 40
a Double surcharge 1.50
b Triple surcharge 3.50
c Type I 65

The 1c on 2c scarlet is bogus.

Handstamped **1889.**

1889

Violet Handstamp.

25D A2 1c green 12.50 12.50
25E A6 20c violet 30.00 30.00
26 A11 1c green 1.00 90
26C A12 1c on 3c brn 20.00 20.00
27 A7 3c brown 1.00 90
28 A8 10c orange 5.00 4.00

Black Handstamp.

28A A2 1c green 15.00 14.00
28B A3 2c rose 17.50 17.50
28C A6 20c violet 30.00 30.00
29 A11 1c green 90 75
30 A7 3c brown 1.00 90
31 A12 1c on 3c brn 17.50 17.50
32 A8 10c orange 4.50 3.50

Rouletted.

Black Handstamp.

35 A9 5c dp bl 90 75

Violet Handstamp.

36 A9 5c dp bl 90 75

The 1889 handstamps as usual, are found double, inverted, etc. Counterfeits are plentiful.

A13

A14

1890 Engr. *Perf. 12*

38 A13 1c green 12 12
39 A13 2c bis brn 12 12
40 A13 3c yellow 12 12
41 A13 5c blue 12 12
42 A13 10c violet 12 12
43 A13 20c orange 12 20
44 A13 25c red 12 *30*
45 A13 50c claret 12 *65*
46 A13 1p carmine 12 *1.50*
Nos. 38-46 (9) 1.08 *3.25*

The issues of 1890 to 1898 inclusive were printed by the Hamilton Bank Note Co., New York, to the order of N. F. Seebeck, who held a contract for stamps with the government of El Salvador. This contract gave the right to make reprints of the stamps and such were subsequently made in some instances, as will be found noted in italic type.

Used values of 1890-1898 issues are for stamps with genuine cancellations applied while the stamps were valid. Various counterfeit cancellations exist.

1891

47 A14 1c vermilion 12 12
48 A14 2c yel grn 12 12
49 A14 3c violet 12 12
50 A14 5c car lake 12 12
51 A14 10c blue 12 12
52 A14 11c violet 12 12
53 A14 20c green 12 *32*
54 A14 25c yel brn 12 *38*
55 A14 50c dk bl 12 *90*
56 A14 1p dk brn 12 *1.50*
Nos. 47-56 (10) 1.20 *3.82*

Nos. 47 and 56 have been reprinted in thick toned paper with dark gum.

A15

Nos. 48, 49 Surcharged in Black or Violet:

UN CENTAVO b

5 CENTAVOS c

1891

57	A15 1c on 2c yel grn		2.00	1.75
a	Inverted surch.		3.00	
58	A14 (b) 1c on 2c yel grn		1.50	1.40
59	A14 (c) 5c on 3c vio		3.50	3.00

Landing of Columbus — A18

1892 **Engr.**

60	A18	1c bl grn	12	12
61	A18	2c org brn	12	12
62	A18	3c ultra	12	12
63	A18	5c gray	12	12
64	A18	10c vermilion	12	12
65	A18	11c brown	12	38
66	A18	20c orange	12	38
67	A18	25c maroon	12	45
68	A18	50c yellow	12	90
69	A18	1p car lake	12	1.25
		Nos. 60-69 (10)	1.20	3.96

Issued to commemorate the 400th anniversary of the discovery of America by Columbus.

A19

A20

Surcharged in Black, Red or Yellow.

1892

70	A19 1c on 5c gray (Bk) (down)	75	65
a	Surcharge reading up	1.25	1.10
72	A19 1c on 5c gray (R) (up)	75	65
a	Surcharge reading down		
73	A20 1c on 20c org (Bk)	90	75
a	Inverted surcharge	2.50	2.50
b	"V" of "CENTAVO" inverted	2.50	2.50

Similar Surcharge in Yellow or Blue, "centavo" in lower case letters.

74	A20 1c on 25c mar (Y)	1.50	1.00
a	Inverted surcharge	2.50	2.50
75	A20 1c on 25c mar (Bl)	200.00	200.00
a	Double surcharge (Bl + Bk)	225.00	225.00

Counterfeits exist of Nos. 75 and 75a.

Gen. Carlos Ezeta — A21

1893 **Engr.**

76	A21	1c blue	12	12
77	A21	2c brn red	12	12
78	A21	3c purple	12	12
79	A21	5c dp brn	12	12
80	A21	10c org brn	12	12
81	A21	11c vermilion	12	22
82	A21	20c green	12	28
83	A21	25c dk ol gray	12	38
84	A21	50c red org	12	50
85	A21	1p black	12	75
		Nos. 76-85 (10)	1.20	2.73

Founding City of Isabela — A22

Columbus Statue, Genoa — A23

Departure from Palos — A24

1893

86	A22	2p green	75
87	A23	5p violet	75
88	A24	10p orange	75

Nos. 86 to 88 commemorated the discoveries by Columbus. No. 86 is known on cover, but experts are not positive that Nos. 87 and 88 were postally used.

No. 77 Surcharged "UN CENTAVO"

1893

89	A21 1c on 2c brn red	50	42
a	"CENTNVO"	3.00	3.00

Liberty A26

Columbus before Council of Salamanca A27

Columbus Protecting Indian Hostages A28

Columbus Received by Ferdinand and Isabella — A29

1894, Jan.

91	A26	1c brown	12	12
92	A26	2c blue	12	12
93	A26	3c maroon	12	12
94	A26	5c org brn	12	12
95	A26	10c violet	12	12
96	A26	11c vermilion	12	25
97	A26	20c dk bl	12	32
98	A26	25c orange	12	38
99	A26	50c black	12	65
100	A26	1p sl bl	12	90
101	A27	2p dp bl	75	
102	A28	5p car lake	75	
103	A29	10p dp brn	75	
		Nos. 91-103 (13)	3.45	

Nos. 101 to 103 commemorated the discoveries by Columbus. Experts are not positive that these were postally used.

Liberty A30

Coat of Arms A31

1894, Dec.

104	A30 1c on 11c ver	1.00	65
a	"Ccntavo"	2.00	2.00
b	Double surcharge		

Arms Overprint in Second Color. Various Frames

1895, Jan. 1

105	A31	1c ol & grn	12	12
106	A31	2c dk grn & bl	12	12
a		2c dk grn & grn	75	60
107	A31	3c brn & brn	12	12
108	A31	5c bl & brn	12	12
109	A31	10c org & brn	12	18
110	A31	12c mag & brn	12	30
111	A31	15c ver & ver	12	35
112	A31	20c yel & brn	12	42
a		Inverted overprint	1.50	
113	A31	24c vio & brn	10	45
114	A31	30c dp bl & bl	12	50
115	A31	50c car & brn	12	65
116	A31	1p blk & brn	12	90
		Nos. 105-116 (12)	1.42	4.23

As printed, Nos. 105-116 portrayed Pres. Antonio Ezeta, brother of Gen. Carlos Ezeta. Before issuance, Ezeta's overthrow caused the government to obliterate his features with the national arms overprint. The stamps exist without overprint. Value 15c each.

Reprints of 2c are in dark yellow green on thick paper. Value 15 cents.

Coat of Arms — A32

1895 **Engr.** ***Perf. 12***

117	A32	1c olive	42	50
118	A32	2c dk bl grn	15	12
119	A32	3c brown	15	12
120	A32	5c blue	15	12
121	A32	10c orange	65	30
122	A32	12c claret	65	30
123	A32	15c vermilion	12	30
124	A32	20c dp grn	18	50
125	A32	24c violet	18	50
126	A32	30c dp bl	12	45
127	A32	50c car lake	1.00	1.25
128	A32	1p gray blk	1.25	1.75
		Nos. 117-128 (12)	5.02	6.21

The reprints are on thicker paper than the originals, and many of the shades differ. Value 15c each.

Nos. 122, 124-126 Surcharged in Black or Red:

UN centavo

1895

129	A32 1c on 12c cl (Bk)	1.00	90
130	A32 1c on 24c vio	1.00	90
131	A32 1c on 30c dp bl	1.00	90
132	A32 2c on 20c dp grn	1.00	90
133	A32 3c on 30c dp bl	1.25	1.10
a	Double surcharge	4.50	
	Nos. 129-133 (5)	5.25	4.70

"Peace" — A45

1896, Jan. 1 **Engr.** **Unwmk.**

134	A45	1c blue	12	12
135	A45	2c dk brn	12	12
136	A45	3c bl grn	12	15
137	A45	5c brn ol	12	15
138	A45	10c yellow	12	20
139	A45	12c dk bl	75	90
140	A45	15c bl vio	10	20
141	A45	20c magenta	65	50
142	A45	24c vermilion	12	25
143	A45	30c orange	12	42
144	A45	50c blk brn	12	50
145	A45	1p rose lake	12	90
		Nos. 134-145 (12)	2.58	4.41

The frames of Nos. 134 to 145 differ slightly on each denomination.

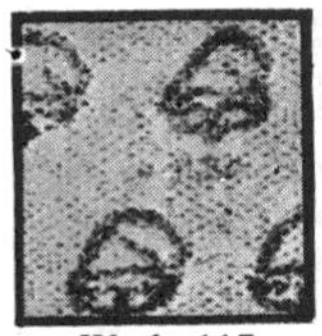

Wmk. 117

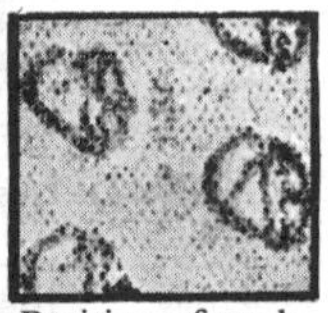

Position of wmk. on reprints

Wmk. Liberty Cap. (117)

145B	A45	2c dk brn	12	12

The 1c, 2c, 12c, 20c, 30c, 50c and 1p on unwatermarked paper and the 2c on watermarked have been reprinted. The paper is thicker than that of the originals and the shades are different. The watermark is always upright on original stamps of Salvador, sideways on the reprints. Value 15c each.

Coat of Arms A46

"White House" A47

Locomotive A48

Mt. San Miguel A49

Ocean Steamship A50 A51

Post Office A52

Lake Ilopango A53

Atehausillas Waterfall A54

Coat of Arms A55

Coat of Arms A56

Columbus A57

1896

146 A46 1c emerald 12 12
147 A47 2c lake 12 12
148 A48 3c yel brn 12 12
149 A49 5c dp bl 12 12
150 A50 10c brown 12 12
151 A51 12c slate 12 *15*
152 A52 15c bl grn 12 *25*
153 A53 20c car rose 12 *30*
154 A54 24c violet *10* *38*
155 A55 30c dp grn 12 38
156 A56 50c orange 12 *38*
157 A57 100c dk bl 12 *90*
Nos. 146-157 (12) 1.42 *3.34*

Unwmk.

157B A46 1c emerald 12 12
157C A47 2c lake 12 12
157D A48 3c yel brn 12 12
157E A49 5c dp bl 12 12
157F A50 10c brown 18 18
157G A51 12c slate 12 *18*
157I A52 15c bl grn 22 *25*
157J A53 20c car rose 12 *38*
157K A54 24c violet 50 *90*
157M A55 30c dp grn 12 *65*
157N A56 50c orange 12 *65*
157O A57 100c dk bl 12 *1.10*

The 15c, 30c, 50c and 100c have been reprinted on watermarked and the 1c, 2c, 3c, 5c, 12c, 20c, 24c and 100c on unwatermarked paper. The papers of the reprints are thicker than those of the originals and the shades are different. Value 10c each.

A58

Black Surcharge on Nos. 154, 157K

1896 **Wmk. 117**

158 A58 15c on 24c vio 3.00 3.00
a. Double surcharge
b. Inverted surch. 6.25

Unwmk.

158D A58 15c on 24c vio 3.00 3.00

Types of 1896.

1897 **Engr.** **Wmk. 117**

159 A46 1c scarlet 12 12
160 A47 2c yel grn 12 12
161 A48 3c bis brn 12 12
162 A49 5c orange 12 12
163 A50 10c bl grn 12 12
164 A51 12c blue 42 30
165 A52 15c black 2.50 2.00
166 A53 20c slate 12 12
167 A54 24c yellow 12 25
168 A55 30c rose 12 20
169 A56 50c violet 18 50
170 A57 100c brn lake 2.50 2.00
Nos. 159-170 (12) 6.56 5.97

Unwmk.

170A A46 1c scarlet 12 12
170B A47 2c yel grn 12 12
170C A48 3c bis brn 12 12
170D A49 5c orange 12 12
170E A50 10c bl grn 75 50
170F A51 12c blue 75 75
170G A52 15c black 2.00 2.00
170H A53 20c slate 12 *25*
170I A54 24c yellow 12 *50*
170J A55 30c rose 1.90 1.25
170K A56 50c violet 90 90
170L A57 100c brn lake 6.25 6.25
Nos. 170A-170L (12) 13.27 12.88

The 1c, 2c, 3c, 5c, 12c, 15c, 50c and 100c have been reprinted on watermarked and the entire issue on unwatermarked paper. The papers of the reprints are thicker than those of the originals. Value 10c each.

Surcharged in Red or Black **TRECE centavos**

1897 **Wmk. 117**

171 A54 13c on 24c yel (R) 2.50 2.25
172 A55 13c on 30c rose (Bk) 2.50 2.25
173 A56 13c on 50c vio (Bk) 2.50 2.25
174 A57 13c on 100c brn lake (Bk) 2.50 2.25

Unwmk.

174A A54 13c on 24c yel (R) 2.50 2.25
174B A55 13c on 30c rose (Bk) 2.50 2.25
174C A56 13c on 50c vio (Bk) 2.50 2.25

Coat of Arms of "Republic of Central America" — A59

ONE CENTAVO.

Originals: The mountains are outlined in red and blue. The sea is represented by short red and dark blue lines on a light blue background.

Reprints: The mountains are outlined in red only. The sea is printed in green and dark blue, much blurred.

FIVE CENTAVOS.

Originals: The sea is represented by horizontal and diagonal lines of dark blue on a light blue background.

Reprints: The sea is printed in green and dark blue, much blurred. The inscription in gold is in thicker letters.

1897 **Litho.**

175 A59 1c bl, gold, rose & grn 50 *1.00*
176 A59 5c rose, gold, bl & grn 50 *1.50*

Issued to commemorate the forming of the "Republic of Central America".

Stamps of type A59 formerly listed as "Type II" are now known to be reprints.

Allegory of Central American Union — A60

1898 **Engr.** **Wmk. 117**

177 A60 1c org ver 12 12
178 A60 2c rose 12 12
179 A60 3c pale yel grn 12 12
180 A60 5c bl grn 10 10
181 A60 10c gray bl 12 12
182 A60 12c violet 15 20
183 A60 13c brn lake 12 12
184 A60 20c dp bl 12 *18*
185 A60 24c dp ultra 12 *22*
186 A60 26c bis brn 12 *30*
187 A60 50c orange 12 *65*
188 A60 1p yellow 12 *75*
Nos. 177-188 (12) 1.45 *3.00*

The entire set has been reprinted on unwatermarked paper and all but the 12c and 20c on watermarked paper. The shades of the reprints are not the same as those of the originals, and the paper is thicker. Value 10c each.

No. 180 Overprinted Vertically, up or down in Black, Violet, Red, Magenta and Yellow **Transito Territorial**

1899

189 A60 5c bl grn (Bk) 7.50 6.25
a. Italic 3rd "r" in "Territorial" 12.50 12.50
b. Dbl. ovpt. (Bk + Y) 37.50 37.50
190 A60 5c bl grn (V) *82.50* *82.50*
191 A60 5c bl grn (R) *70.00* *70.00*
191A A60 5c bl grn (M) *70.00* *70.00*
191B A60 5c bl grn (Y) *75.00* *75.00*

Counterfeits exist.

Nos. 177-184 Overprinted in Black 

1899

192 A60 1c org ver 75 38
193 A60 2c rose 1.00 75
194 A60 3c pale yel grn 1.00 38
195 A60 5c bl grn 1.10 38
196 A60 10c gray bl 1.50 1.00
197 A60 12c violet 2.50 2.00
198 A60 13c brn lake 2.50 2.00
198A A60 20c dp bl 100.00 82.50
Nos. 192-198A (8) 110.35 89.39

Counterfeits exist of the "wheel" overprint used in 1899-1900.

Ceres ("Estado") — A61

Inscribed: "Estado de El Salvador".

1899 **Unwmk.** **Litho.** ***Perf. 12.***

199 A61 1c brown 10
200 A61 2c gray grn 10
201 A61 3c blue 10
202 A61 5c brn org 10
203 A61 10c chocolate 10
204 A61 12c dk grn 10
205 A61 13c dp rose 10
206 A61 24c lt bl 10
207 A61 26c car rose 10
208 A61 50c org red 10
209 A61 100c violet 10
Nos. 199-209 (11) 1.10

Nos. 208-209 were probably not placed in use.

Same, Overprinted 

Red Overprint.

210 A61 1c brown 37.50 32.50

Blue Overprint.

211 A61 1c brown 38 15
212 A61 5c brn org 38 20
212A A61 10c chocolate 5.00 3.50

Black Overprint.

213 A61 1c brown 38 15
214 A61 2c gray grn 50 12
215 A61 3c blue 50 18
216 A61 5c brn org 25 12
217 A61 10c chocolate 38 15
218 A61 12c dk grn 1.00 50
219 A61 13c dp rose 75 65
220 A61 24c lt bl 10.00 8.75
221 A61 26c car rose 2.50 2.00
222 A61 50c org red 2.50 2.00
223 A61 100c violet 2.50 2.00
Nos. 213-223 (11) 21.26 16.62

No. 177 Handstamped **1900**

1900 **Wmk. 117**

224 A60 1c org ver 1.00 75

No. 177 Overprinted **1900**

225 A60 1c org ver 12.50 11.50

Stamps of 1898 Surcharged in Black **1900 1 centavo**

1900

226 A60 1c on 10c gray bl 3.50 3.00
a. Inverted surcharge 5.00 4.50
227 A60 1c on 13c brn lake *275.00*
228 A60 2c on 12c vio 14.00 10.00
a. "eentavo"
b. Inverted surcharge
c. "centavos" 25.00
d. Same as "c", double surcharge
e. Vertical surcharge
229 A60 2c on 13c brn lake 1.50 1.40
a. "eentavo" 2.50 2.00
b. Inverted surcharge 3.50 3.00
c. "1900" omitted
230 A60 2c on 20c dp bl 1.50 1.50
a. Inverted surcharge 2.50 2.50
230B A60 2c on 26c bis brn *175.00* *175.00*
231 A60 3c on 12c vio *37.50* *37.50*
a. "eentavo"
b. Inverted surcharge *35.00* *35.00*
c. Double surcharge
232 A60 3c on 50c org 12.50 12.50
a. Inverted surcharge 12.50 12.50
233 A60 5c on 12c vio
234 A60 5c on 24c ultra 11.25 11.25
a. "eentavo"
b. "centavos" 11.25
235 A60 5c on 26c bis brn *37.50* *37.50*
a. Inverted surcharge *35.00* *35.00*
236 A60 5c on 1p yel 15.00 15.00
a. Inverted surcharge 15.00 15.00

With Additional Overprint in Black 

237 A60 2c on 12c vio 1.75 1.75
a. Inverted surcharge 1.75 1.75
b. "eentavo" 6.00
c. "centavos" 75.00
d. "1900" omitted
237H A60 2c on 13c brn lake
238 A60 3c on 12c vio 42.50 42.50
a. "eentavo" 35.00 35.00
239 A60 5c on 26c bis brn 67.50 67.50
a. Inverted surcharge

Vertical Surcharge.

"Centavos" in the Plural.

240 A60 2c on 12c vio 95.00 95.00
b. Without wheel
240A A60 5c on 24c dp ultra 95.00 95.00

With Additional Overprint in Black 

241 A60 5c on 12c vio 17.50 17.50
a. Surcharge reading downward

Counterfeits exist of the surcharges on Nos. 226-241 and the "wheel" overprint on Nos. 237-239, 241.

Same Surcharge on Stamps of 1898 Without Wheel.

1900 **Unwmk.**

242 A61 1c on 13c dp rose 30 30
a. Inverted surcharge 55 55
b. "eentavo" 55 55
c. "ecntavo" 90 55
d. "1 centavo 1" 3.00 2.00
e. Double surcharge
243 A61 2c on 12c dk grn 1.25 1.25
a. Inverted surcharge 1.75 1.75
b. "eentavo"
244 A61 2c on 13c dp rose 65 50
a. "eentavo" 75 75
b. "ecntavo" 90 90
c. Inverted surcharge
245 A61 3c on 12c dk grn 65 50
a. Inverted surcharge 1.50 1.10
b. "eentavo" 3.00 3.00
c. Double surcharge 1.50

With Additional Overprint in Black 

246 A61 1c on 2c gray grn 18 12
a. "eentavo" 65 65
b. Inverted surcharge 3.00 3.00
247 A61 1c on 13c dp rose 75 65
a. "eentavo" 3.00
b. "1 centavo 1"
248 A61 2c on 12c dk grn 1.00 75
a. "eentavo" 3.00
b. Inverted surcharge 90 90
c. Double surcharge 1.50
249 A61 2c on 13c dp rose 42.50
a. "eentavo"
b. Double surcharge 75.00 75.00
250 A61 3c on 12c dk grn 1.00 65
a. Inverted surcharge 1.10 90
b. "eentavo" 1.90 1.75
c. Date double 3.00
251 A61 5c on 24c lt bl 1.90 90
a. "eentavo" 3.00 3.00
252 A61 5c on 26c car rose 75 65
a. Inverted surcharge 3.00 1.75
b. "eentavo" 1.25 1.10
252D A61 5c on 1c on 26c car rose
Nos. 246-248,250-252 (6) 5.58 3.72

Counterfeits exist of the surcharges on Nos. 242-252D and the "wheel" overprint on Nos. 246-252D.

Ceres ("Republica") — A63

There are two varieties of the 1c, type A63, one with the word "centavo" in the middle of the label, the other with "centavo" nearer the left end than the right.

The stamps of type A63 are found in a great variety of shades. Stamps of type A63 without handstamp were not regularly issued.

Handstamped in Violet or Black

Inscribed: "Republica de El Salvador"

1900

253	A63	1c bl grn	12	12
a		1c yel grn	12	12
254	A63	2c rose	18	12
255	A63	3c gray blk	12	12
256	A63	5c pale bl	38	25
a		5c dp bl	38	25
257	A63	10c dp bl	42	30
258	A63	12c yel grn	42	30
259	A63	13c yel brn	38	30
260	A63	24c gray	3.00	2.50
261	A63	26c yel brn	1.25	1.10
262	A63	50c rose red	1.25	1.10
		Nos. 253-262 (10)	7.52	6.21

Handstamped in Violet or Black

263	A63	1c lt grn	1.10	75
264	A63	2c pale rose	1.10	38
265	A63	3c gray blk	1.10	38
266	A63	5c sl bl	1.10	25
267	A63	10c dp bl	50.00	42.50
268	A63	13c yel brn	12.50	8.75
269	A63	50c dl rose	1.25	1.10
		Nos. 263-269 (7)	68.15	54.11

Handstamped on 1898 Stamps.

Wmk. Liberty Cap. (117)

269A	A60	2c rose	30.00	30.00
269B	A60	10c gray bl	30.00	30.00

The overprints on Nos. 253 to 269B are handstamped and, as usual with that style of overprint, are to be found double, inverted, omitted, etc.

Stamps of Type A63 Overprinted in Black

1900 **Unwmk.**

270	A63	1c lt grn	12	12
271	A63	2c rose	12	12
272	A63	3c gray blk	12	12
273	A63	5c pale bl	12	12
a		5c dk bl	12	12
274	A63	10c dp bl	25	15
a		10c pale bl	20	15
275	A63	12c lt grn	25	20
276	A63	13c yel brn	12	12
277	A63	24c gray	30	25
278	A63	26c yel brn	38	30
		Nos. 270-278 (9)	1.78	1.50

This overprint is known double, inverted, etc.

Nos. 271-273 Surcharged in Black

1902

280	A63	1c on 2c rose	2.00	1.50
281	A63	1c on 3c black	1.50	1.00
282	A63	1c on 5c blue	1.00	75

Morazán Monument — A64

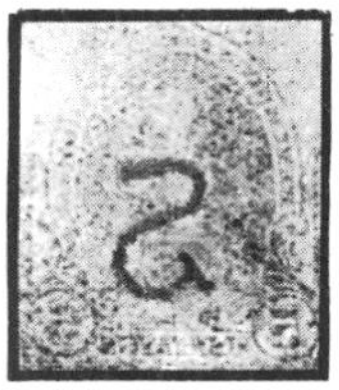

Wmk. 173- S

Perf. 14, 14½

1903 **Engr.** **Wmk. 173**

283	A64	1c green	25	15
284	A64	2c carmine	25	15
285	A64	3c orange	75	50
286	A64	5c dk bl	25	15
287	A64	10c dl vio	25	15
288	A64	12c slate	30	15
289	A64	13c red brn	30	18
290	A64	24c scarlet	1.75	90
291	A64	26c yel brn	1.75	75
292	A64	50c bister	1.00	50
293	A64	100c grnsh bl	3.75	1.50
		Nos. 283-293 (11)	10.60	5.08

Stamps of 1900 with Shield in Black Overprinted:

1905 (5¾x13½mm.) a

1905 (5x14¾mm.) b

1905 (4½x16mm.) c

1905 (4½x13½mm.) d

(5x14½mm.) — e 1905

1905-06 **Unwmk.** ***Perf. 12***

Blue Overprint.

293A	A63 (a)	2c rose		
294	A63 (a)	3c gray blk	3.00	2.00
a		Without shield		
295	A63 (a)	5c blue	3.50	2.00

Purple Overprint.

296	A63 (b)	3c gray blk (Shield in purple)	3.50	3.00
296A	A63 (b)	5c bl (Shield in purple)	2.50	2.00
297	A63 (b)	3c gray blk	4.50	3.50
298	A63 (b)	5c blue	3.00	2.00

Black Overprint.

298A	A63 (b)	5c blue		

Blue Overprint.

299	A63 (c)	1c green	3.50	2.00
299B	A63 (c)	2c rose	30	25
c		"1905" vert.	65	
300	A63 (c)	5c blue	90	38
301	A63 (c)	10c dp bl	50	38

Black Overprint.

302	A63 (c)	2c rose	2.00	75
303	A63 (c)	5c blue	10.00	8.00
304	A63 (c)	10c dp bl	3.00	2.50

Blue Overprint.

305	A63 (d)	1c green	4.00	2.50
306	A63 (d)	2c rose (ovpt. vert.)	2.00	1.00
a		Ovpt. horiz.		
306B	A63 (d)	3c gray blk	3.75	1.25
307	A63 (d)	5c blue	1.75	65

Blue Overprint.

311	A63 (e)	2c rose	1.75	1.25
a		Without shield	3.00	2.25

Black Overprint.

311B	A63 (e)	5c blue	20.00	19.00

These overprints are found double, inverted, omitted, etc. Counterfeits exist.

Regular Issue of 1903 Surcharged with New Values:

UN CENTAVO f

5 CENTAVOS g

1 1

1CENTAVO1 h

1905-06 **Wmk. 173** ***Perf. 14, 14½***

Black Surcharge.

312	A64 (f)	1c on 2c car	30	25
a		Double surcharge	3.00	

Red Surcharge.

312B	A64 (g)	5c on 12c sl	65	50
c		Double surcharge		
d		Blk. surcharge	3.50	3.50
e		As "d", double surcharge		

Blue Handstamped Surcharge.

313	A64 (h)	1c on 2c car	18	15
314	A64 (h)	1c on 10c vio	18	15
315	A64 (h)	1c on 12c sl ('06)	65	50
316	A64 (h)	1c on 13c red brn	3.00	2.50

No. 271 with Handstamped Surcharge in Blue.

Unwmk.

317	A63 (h)	1c on 2c rose	42.50	37.50

The "h" is handstamped in strips of four stamps each differing from the others in the size of the upper figures of value and in the letters of the word "CENTAVO", particularly in the size of the "N" and the "O" of that word. The surcharge is known inverted, double, etc.

Regular Issue of 1903 with Handstamped Surcharge:

5 5 i

5 5 5 5 j

5 5 5 5 k

Wmk. 173

Red Handstamped Surcharge.

318	A64 (i)	5c on 12c sl	1.50	90
319	A64 (j)	5c on 12c sl	1.50	1.10
a		Blue surcharge		

Blue Handstamped Surcharge.

320	A64 (k)	5c on 12c sl	2.00	1.75

One or more of the numerals in the handstamped surcharges on Nos. 318, 319 and 320 are frequently omitted, inverted, etc.

Surcharged:

6 6 6CENTAVOS6 l

1 1 ● ● m

Blue Handstamped Surcharge.

321	A64 (l)	6c on 12c slate	38	30
322	A64 (l)	6c on 13c red brn	65	42

Red Handstamped Surcharge.

323	A64 (l)	6c on 12c slate	14.00	11.25

Type "l" is handstamped in strips of four varieties, differing in the size of the numerals and letters. The surcharge is known double and inverted.

Black Surcharge.

324	A64 (m)	1c on 13c red brn	1.00	1.00
a		Double surcharge	3.00	3.00
b		Right "1" & dot omitted		
c		Both numerals omitted		
325	A64 (m)	3c on 13c red brn	38	38

Stamps of 1900, with Shield in Black, Overprinted — n 01905

1905 **Unwmk.** ***Perf. 12.***

Blue Overprint.

326	A63 (n)	1c green	3.00	2.50
a		Invtd. ovpt.		
327	A63 (n)	2c rose	2.50	2.50
a		Vertical overprint	4.50	4.00
327B	A63 (n)	3c black	22.50	20.00
327C	A63 (n)	5c blue	10.00	7.50
328	A63 (n)	10c dp bl	4.50	3.50

Black Overprint.

328A	A63 (n)	10c dp bl	4.50	3.00

Counterfeits of Nos. 326-335 abound.

Stamps of 1900, with Shield in Black Surcharged or Overprinted:

1906

● ● 2 2 o

1906 p 1906 q

1906

Blue and Black Surcharge.

329	A63 (o)	2c on 26c brn org	30	25
a		"2" & dot double	5.50	5.50
330	A63 (o)	3c on 26c brn org	3.00	2.50
a		"3" & dot double		

Black Surcharge or Overprint.

331	A63 (o)	3c on 26c brn org	2.00	1.75
a		Disks and numerals omitted		
b		"3" and disks double		
c		"1906" omitted		
333	A63 (p)	10c dp bl	1.25	1.00
334	A63 (q)	10c dp bl	90	75
334A	A63 (q)	26c brn org	17.50	15.00
b		"1906" in blue		

No. 257 Overprinted in Black.

335	A63 (q)	10c dp bl (Shield in violet)	14.00	12.50
a		Overprint type "p"		

There are numerous varieties of these surcharges and overprints.

Pres. Pedro José Escalón — A65

1906 **Engr.** ***Perf. 11½***

Glazed Paper.

336	A65	1c grn & blk	10	10
a		Thin paper	75	15
337	A65	2c red & blk	10	10
338	A65	3c yel & blk	10	10
339	A65	5c ultra & blk	10	10
a		5c dk bl & blk	10	10
340	A65	6c car & blk	10	10
341	A65	10c vio & blk	10	10
342	A65	12c vio & blk	10	10
343	A65	13c dk brn & blk	10	10
345	A65	24c car & blk	25	25
346	A65	26c choc & blk	25	25
347	A65	50c yel & blk	25	38
348	A65	100c bl & blk	75	75
		Nos. 336-348 (12)	2.30	2.43

All values of this set are known imperforate but are not believed to have been issued in this condition.

The entire set has been reprinted. The shades of the reprints differ from those of the originals, the paper is thinner, the gum whiter and the perforation 12. Value 10c each.

Nos. 336-338 Overprinted in Black

1907

349	A65	1c grn & blk	18	15
a		Shield in red	2.50	
350	A65	2c red & blk	18	15
a		Shield in red	2.50	
351	A65	3c yel & blk	18	15

Reprints of Nos. 349 to 351 have the same characteristics as the reprints of the preceding issue. Value 5c each.

Stamps of 1906 Surcharged with Shield and **1**

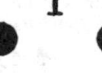

352	A65	1c on 5c ultra & blk	8	8
a		1c on 5c dk bl & blk	10	8
b		Inverted surcharge		
c		Double surcharge		
352D	A65	1c on 6c rose & blk	15	12
e		Double surcharge	1.00	1.00
353	A65	2c on 6c rose & blk	1.50	65
354	A65	10c on 6c rose & blk	38	25

The above surcharges are frequently found with the shield double, inverted, or otherwise misplaced.

National Palace — A66

Overprinted with Shield in Black.

1907 Engr. Unwmk.

Paper with or without colored dots.

355	A66	1c grn & blk	10	6
356	A66	2c red & blk	10	8
357	A66	3c yel & blk	10	8
358	A66	5c bl & blk	10	6
a		5c ultra & blk	10	6
359	A66	6c ver & blk	10	8
a		Shield in red	2.50	
360	A66	10c vio & blk	10	8
361	A66	12c vio & blk	10	8
362	A66	13c sep & blk	10	6
363	A66	24c rose & blk	10	8
364	A66	26c yel brn & blk	25	12
365	A66	50c org & blk	38	20
a		50c yel & blk	2.50	
366	A66	100c turq bl & blk	75	38
		Nos. 355-366 (12)	2.28	1.36

Most values exist without shield, also with shield inverted, double, and otherwise misprinted. Many of these were never sold to the public.

See Nos. 369-373, 397-401.

No. 356 With Additional Surcharge in Black **UN CENTAVO**

1908

367	A66	1c on 2c red & blk	25	20
a		Double surcharge	1.00	1.00
b		Inverted surcharge	50	50
c		Double surcharge, one inverted	50	50
d		Red surcharge		

Same Surcharged in Black or Red **UN CENTAVO**

368	A66	1c on 2c red & blk	19.00	17.50
368A	A66	1c on 2c red & blk (R)	27.50	25.00

Counterfeits exist of the surcharges on Nos. 368-368A.

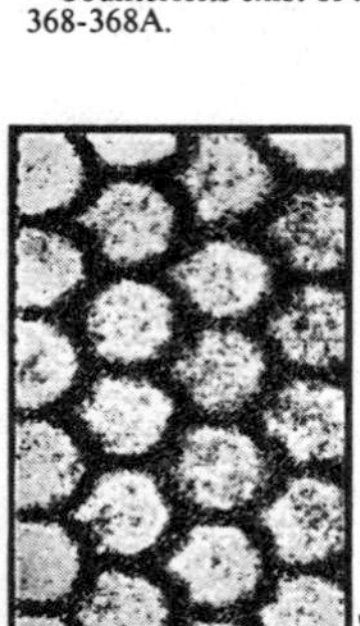
Wmk. 172-Honeycomb

Type of 1907

1909 Engr. Wmk. 172

369	A66	1c grn & blk	10	10
370	A66	2c rose & blk	10	10
371	A66	3c yel & blk	15	10
372	A66	5c bl & blk	15	10
373	A66	10c vio & blk	18	15
		Nos. 369-373 (5)	68	55

The note after No. 366 will apply here also.

Nos. 355, 369 Overprinted in Red **1821 15 septiembre 1909**

1909, Sept. Unwmk.

374	A66	1c grn & blk	1.50	1.10
a		Inverted overprint		

Wmk. 172

375	A66	1c grn & blk	1.25	1.10
a		Inverted overprint		

88th anniv. of El Salvador's independence.

Nos. 362, 364 Surcharged **2 CENTAVOS 1909**

1909 Unwmk.

376	A66	2c on 13c sep & blk	1.00	90
a		Inverted surcharge		
377	A66	3c on 26c yel brn & blk	1.25	1.00
a		Inverted surcharge		

Pres. Fernando Figueroa — A67

1910 Engr. Wmk. 172

378	A67	1c sep & blk	10	8
379	A67	2c dk grn & blk	10	9
380	A67	3c org & blk	10	9
381	A67	4c car & blk	10	9
a		4c scar & blk	15	15
382	A67	5c pur & blk	10	9
383	A67	6c scar & blk	10	9
384	A67	10c pur & blk	15	12
385	A67	12c dp bl & blk	15	12
386	A67	17c ol grn & blk	15	12
387	A67	19c brn red & blk	15	12
388	A67	29c choc & blk	15	12
389	A67	50c yel & blk	10	9
390	A67	100c turq bl & blk	15	12
		Nos. 378-390 (13)	1.60	1.34

José Matias Delgado A68

Manuel José Arce A69

Centenary Monument — A70

1911 Unwmk.

Paper with colored dots.

391	A68	5c dp bl & brn	10	10
392	A69	6c org & brn	10	10
393	A70	12c vio & brn	10	10

Wmk. 172

394	A68	5c dp bl & brn	8	8
395	A69	6c org & brn	8	8
396	A70	12c vio & brn	8	8
		Nos. 391-396 (6)	54	54

Centenary of the insurrection of 1811.

Palace Type of 1907 without Shield.

1911

Paper without colored dots.

397	A66	1c scarlet	5	5
398	A66	2c chocolate	25	25
a		Paper with brown dots		
399	A66	13c dp grn	10	10
400	A66	24c yellow	15	15
401	A66	50c dk brn	15	15
		Nos. 397-401 (5)	70	70

José Matias Delgado A71

Manuel José Arce A72

Francisco Morazán A73

Rafael Campo A74

Trinidad Cabanas A75

Monument of Gerardo Barrios A76

Centenary Monument A77

National Palace A78

Rosales Hospital — A79

Coat of Arms — A80

1912 Unwmk. Perf. 12

402	A71	1c dp bl & blk	12	8
403	A72	2c bis brn & blk	15	10
404	A73	5c scar & blk	15	10
405	A74	6c dk grn & blk	12	10
406	A75	12c ol grn & blk	65	18
407	A76	17c vio & sl	38	15
408	A77	19c scar & sl	75	20
409	A78	29c org & sl	90	20
410	A79	50c bl & sl	1.10	38
411	A80	1col blk & sl	1.75	75
		Nos. 402-411 (10)	6.07	2.24

Juan Manuel Rodriguez A81

Pres. Manuel E. Araujo A82

1914 Perf. 11½

412	A81	10c org & brn	1.75	75
413	A82	25c pur & brn	1.75	75

Type of 1907 without Shield Overprinted in Black. **1915**

1915

Paper overlaid with colored dots.

414	A66	1c gray grn	10	8
415	A66	2c red	10	8
416	A66	5c ultra	10	6
417	A66	6c pale bl	10	6
418	A66	10c yellow	42	30
419	A66	12c brown	30	15
420	A66	50c violet	15	12
421	A66	100c blk brn	90	90
		Nos. 414-421 (8)	2.17	1.75

Varieties such as center omitted, center double, center inverted, imperforate exist with or without date, date inverted, date double, etc., but are believed to be entirely unofficial.

Preceding the stamps with the "1915" overprint a quantity of stamps of this type was overprinted with the letter "S". Evidence is lacking that they were ever placed in use. The issue was demonetized in 1916.

National Theater — A83

Various Frames.

1916 Engr. Perf. 12

431	A83	1c dp grn	8	5
432	A83	2c vermilion	10	8
433	A83	5c dp bl	12	8
434	A83	6c gray vio	18	9
435	A83	10c blk brn	18	9
436	A83	12c violet	1.75	50
437	A83	17c orange	25	10
438	A83	25c dk brn	50	20
439	A83	29c black	3.75	75
440	A83	50c slate	1.25	65
		Nos. 431-440 (10)	8.16	2.59

Watermarked letters which occasionally appear are from the papermaker's name.

Nos. O324-O325 with "OFICIAL" Barred out in Black.

1917

441	O3	2c red	30	20
a		Double bar		
442	O3	5c ultra	38	25
a		Double bar		

Regular Issue of 1915 Overprinted "OFICIAL" and Re-overprinted In Red **CORRIENTE**

443	A66	6c pale bl	50	38
a		Double bar		
444	A66	12c brown	65	50
a		Double bar		
b		"CORRIENTE" inverted		

Same Overprint in Red On Nos. O323-O327

445	O3	1c gray grn	1.25	1.00
a		"CORRIENTE" inverted		
b		Double bar		
c		"CORRIENTE" omitted		
446	O3	2c red	1.25	1.00
a		Double bar		
447	O3	5c ultra	7.50	5.00
a		Double bar, both in black		
448	O3	10c yellow	75	50
a		Double bar		
b		"OFICIAL" and bar omitted		
449	O3	50c violet	50	38
a		Double bar		
		Nos. 443-449 (7)	12.40	8.76

Nos. O334-O335 Overprinted or Surcharged in Red:

1 Corriente — a

1 1 CORRIENTE Un Centavo — b

450	A83 (a)	5c dp bl	1.25	1.00
a		"CORRIENTE" double		
451	A83 (b)	1c on 6c gray vio	65	50
a		"CORRIERTE"		
b		"CORRIENRE"		
c		"CORRIENTE" double		

A84

1918

Black Surcharge.

452 A84 1c on 6c gray vio 1.25 1.00
a Double surcharge
b Inverted surcharge

No. 434 Surcharged in Black

1
1 Centavo *1*

1918

453 A83 1c on 6c gray vio 1.00 75
a "Centado" 1.50 1.50
b Double surcharge 1.75 1.75
c Inverted surcharge

No. 434 Surcharged in Black or Red

1 CENTAVO 1

454 A83 1c on 6c gray vio 3.00 2.50
a Double surcharge
b Inverted surcharge 3.50 3.50
455 A83 1c on 6c gray vio (R) 3.00 2.50
a Double surcharge
b Inverted surcharge 3.50 3.50

Counterfeits exist of Nos. 454-455.

Pres. Carlos Meléndez — A85

1919 **Engr.**

456 A85 1col dk bl & blk 50 45

No. 437 Surcharged in Black

1
1 Centavo 1

1919

457 A83 1c on 17c org 15 8
a Inverted surcharge 50 50
b Double surcharge 50 50

A86

A87

A88

A89

Black or Blue Surcharge.

1920-21

458 A86 1c on 12c vio 12 10
a Double surcharge 1.00 1.00
459 A87 2c on 10c dk brn 18 10
460 A88 5c on 50c sl ('21) 30 12
461 A89 6c on 25c dk brn (Bl) ('21) 30 20

Same Surcharge in Black on No. O337

462 A86 1c on 12c vio 65 65
a Double surcharge

No. 460 surcharged in yellow and 461 surcharged in red are essays.

No. 462 is due to some sheets of Official Stamps being mixed with the ordinary 12c stamps at the time of surcharging. The error stamps were sold to the public and used for ordinary postage.

A90

Surcharged in Red:

15 15 15 15
I II III IV

463 A90 15c on 29c blk (III) ('21) 1.00 38
a Double surcharge 2.00
b Type I 1.50 1.00
c Type II 1.00 75
d Type IV 2.50

A91

A92

Surcharged in Blue or Black.

464 A91 26c on 29c blk (Bl) 75 38
a Double surcharge
466 A92 35c on 50c sl (Bk) 65 42

One stamp in each row of ten of No. 464 has the "t" of "cts" inverted and one stamp in each row of No. 466 has the letters "c" in "cinco" larger than the normal.

No. 464 surcharged in green or yellow and the 35c on 29c black are essays.

No. 456 Surcharged in Red

60
CENTAVOS

467 A85 60c on 1col dk bl & blk 30 25

Setting includes three types of numerals and "CENTAVOS" measuring from 16mm. to 20mm. wide.

A93

1921

468 A93 1c on 1c ol grn 5 5
a Double surcharge 75
469 A93 1c on 5c yel 5 5
a Inverted surcharge
b Double surcharge
470 A93 1c on 10c bl 10 8
a Double surcharge 50
471 A93 1c on 25c grn 5 5
a Double surcharge
472 A93 1c on 50c ol 12 12
a Double surcharge
473 A93 1c on 1p gray blk 18 18
a Double surcharge
Nos. 468-473 (6) 55 53

The frame of No. 473 differs slightly from the illustration.

Setting includes many wrong font letters and numerals.

Francisco Menendez
A94

Manuel José Arce
A95

Confederation Coin — A96

Delgado Addressing Crowd
A97

Coat of Arms of Confederation
A98

Francisco Morazán
A99

Independence Monument
A100

Columbus — A101

1921 **Engr.** ***Perf. 12***

474 A94	1c	green	18	5
475 A95	2c	black	20	5
476 A96	5c	orange	65	12
477 A97	6c	car rose	38	8
478 A98	10c	dp bl	38	8
479 A99	25c	ol grn	1.65	12
480 A100	60c	violet	4.00	38
481 A101	1col	blk brn	7.50	50
	Nos. 474-481 (8)		14.94	1.38

Nos. 474-477 Overprinted in Red, Black or Blue

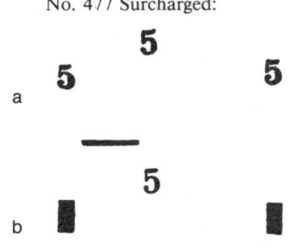

CENTENARIO CENTENARIO
a b

1921

481A A94 (a) 1c grn (R) 3.00 2.50
481B A95 (a) 2c blk (R) 3.00 2.50
481C A96 (b) 5c org (Bk) 3.00 2.50
481D A97 (b) 6c car rose (Bl) 3.00 2.50

Centenary of independence.

No. 477 Surcharged:

a 5 5 5
b 5

1923

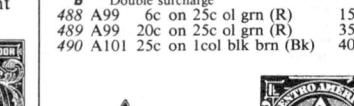

482 A97 (a) 5c on 6c 25 15
483 A97 (b) 5c on 6c 20 15
484 A97 (b) 20c on 6c 25 25

Nos. 482-484 exist with double surcharge.

No. 475 Surcharged in Red

10

1923

485 A95 10c on 2c blk 38 15

José Simeón Cañas y Villacorta — A102

1923 **Engr.** ***Perf. 11½***

486 A102 5c blue 38 25

Centenary of abolition of slavery.

Nos. 479, 481 Surcharged in Red or Black

6 6
Seis centavos

1924 ***Perf. 12***

487 A99 1c on 25c ol grn (R) 12 10
a Numeral at right invtd.
b Double surcharge
488 A99 6c on 25c ol grn (R) 15 12
489 A99 20c on 25c ol grn (R) 35 25
490 A101 25c on 1col blk brn (Bk) 40 38

A103

A104

1924

491 A103 1c on 5c org (Bk) 25 20
492 A104 6c on 10c dp bl (R) 25 20

Nos. 491-492 exist with double surcharge.

A stamp similar to No. 492 but with surcharge "6 centavos 6" is an essay.

No. 476 Surcharged

2
Dos centavos

493 A96 2c on 5c org 25 25
a Top ornament omitted 1.50 1.50

A105

1924

Red Surcharge.

494 A105 5c on 60c vio 4.50 3.00
a "1781" for "1874" 10.00 8.75
b "1934" for "1924" 10.00 8.75

Universal Postal Union, 50th anniversary.

This stamp with black surcharge is an essay. Copies have been passed through the post.

The Catalogue editors cannot undertake to appraise, identify or judge the genuineness or condition of stamps.

Daniel Hernandez Monument A106

National Gymnasium A107

Atlacatl A108

Conspiracy of 1811 A109

Bridge over Lempa River A110

Map of Central America A111

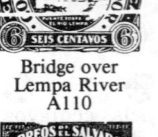

Balsam Tree — A112

Tulla Serra — A114

Columbus at La Rabida — A115

Coat of Arms — A116

Photogravure; Engraved (35c, 1col)

1924-25 *Perf. 12½; 14 (35c, 1col)*

495	A106	1c red vio	8	5
496	A107	2c dk red	20	8
497	A108	3c chocolate	15	8
498	A109	5c on blk	15	8
499	A110	6c grnsh bl	20	6
500	A111	10c orange	50	15
a		"ATLANT CO"	5.00	4.50
501	A112	20c dp grn	75	25
502	A114	35c scar & grn	1.75	38
503	A115	50c org brn	1.50	30
504	A116	1col grn & vio ('25)	2.25	30
		Nos. 495-504 (10)	7.53	1.73

A117

Red Surcharge

1925, Aug. *Perf. 12*

506	A117	2c on 60c vio	1.25	1.10

Issued to commemorate the 400th anniversary of the city of San Salvador.

The variety with dates in black is an essay.

View of San Salvador — A118

1925 **Photo.** *Perf. 12½*

507	A118	1c blue	65	65
508	A118	2c dp grn	65	65
509	A118	3c Mahogany red	65	65

No. 506 and Nos. 507 to 509 were issued to commemorate the fourth centenary of the founding of the City of San Salvador.

A119

A120

Black Surcharge

1928, July 17

510	A119	3c on 10c org	65	50
a		"ATLANT CO"	12.50	12.50

Industrial Exhibition, Santa Ana, July 1928.

Red Surcharge.

1928

511	A120	1c on 5c ol blk	25	20
a		Bar instead of top left "1"	38	25

Pres. Pío Romero Bosque, Salvador, and Pres. Lazaro Chacon, Guatemala A121

1929 **Litho.** *Perf. 11½.*

Portraits in Dark Brown

512	A121	1c dl vio	25	20
a		Center inverted	12.50	12.50
513	A121	3c bis brn	25	20
a		Center inverted	37.50	37.50
514	A121	5c gray grn	25	20
515	A121	10c orange	25	20

Issued to celebrate the opening of the international railroad connecting El Salvador and Guatemala.

Nos. 512-515 exist imperforate. No. 512 in the colors of No. 515.

Tomb of Menendez A122

1930, Dec. 3

516	A122	1c violet	2.50	2.25
517	A122	3c brown	2.50	2.25
518	A122	5c dk grn	2.50	2.25
519	A122	10c yel brn	2.50	2.25

Issued to commemorate the centenary of the birth of General Francisco Menendez.

Stamps of 1924-25 Issue Overprinted **1932**

1932 *Perf. 12½, 14*

520	A106	1c dp vio	10	6
521	A107	2c dk red	15	10
522	A108	3c chocolate	20	8
523	A109	5c ol blk	20	6
524	A110	6c dp bl	25	6
525	A111	10c orange	65	15
a		"ATLANT CO"	7.50	6.25
526	A112	20c dp grn	1.10	32
527	A114	35c scar & grn	1.50	50
528	A115	50c org brn	2.25	75
529	A116	1col grn & vio	4.00	1.50
		Nos. 520-529 (10)	10.40	3.58

Values are for the overprint measuring 7½x3mm. It is found in two other sizes: 7½x3¼mm. and 8x3mm.

Types of 1924-25.
Surcharged with New Values in Red or Black.

1934 *Perf. 12½*

530	A109	2(c) on 5c grnsh blk (R)	10	8
a		Double surcharge		
531	A111	3(c) on 10c org	12	8
a		"ATLANT CO"	4.00	4.00

Stamps of 1924-25 Surcharged with New Values in Black.

Perf. 12½, 14½

532	A115	2(c) on 50c org brn	20	12
a		Double surcharge	3.00	
533	A116	8(c) on 1col grn & vio	10	10
534	A114	15(c) on 35c scar & grn	20	18
		Nos. 530-534 (5)	72	56

Police Barracks — A123

Wmk. 240-REPUBLICA DE EL SALVADOR in Sheet

Two types of the 2c.

Type I. The clouds have heavy lines of shading.

Type II. The lines of shading have been removed from the clouds.

Wmk. 240

1934-35 **Litho.** *Perf. 12½*

535	A123	2c gray brn, type I	12	8
a		2c brn (type II)	12	8
536	A123	5c car, type II	12	8
537	A123	8c lt ultra, type II	12	8
		Nos. 535-537,C33-C35 (6)	2.33	1.34

Discus Thrower A124

1935, Mar. 16 **Engr.** **Unwmk.**

538	A124	5c carmine	2.50	1.50
539	A124	8c blue	2.75	1.75
540	A124	10c org yel	3.50	2.00
541	A124	15c bister	4.00	2.75
542	A124	37c green	5.00	4.00
		Nos. 538-542 (5)	17.75	12.00

Issued to commemorate the 3rd Central American Games. See Nos. C36-C40.

Same Overprinted **HABILITADO** in Black

1935, June 27

543	A124	5c carmine	3.50	2.50
544	A124	8c blue	5.00	2.50
545	A124	10c org yel	5.00	3.00
546	A124	15c bister	5.00	3.00
547	A124	37c green	8.00	5.00
		Nos. 543-547 (5)	26.50	16.00

See Nos. C41-C45.

Values quoted in this catalogue are for stamps graded at Fine-Very Fine and with no faults. An illustrated guide to grade is provided in introductory material, beginning on Page V.

Flag of El Salvador A125

Tree of San Vicente A126

1935, Oct. 26 **Litho.** **Wmk. 240**

548	A125	1c gray bl	8	5
549	A125	2c blk brn	8	5
550	A125	3c plum	10	8
551	A125	5c rose car	18	8
552	A125	8c ultra	20	10
553	A125	15c fawn	25	12
		Nos. 548-553,C46 (7)	1.27	63

1935, Dec. 26

Numerals in Black, Tree in Yellow Green

554	A126	2c blk brn	20	18
555	A126	3c dk bl grn	25	20
556	A126	5c rose red	35	25
557	A126	8c dk bl	35	30
558	A126	15c brown	45	38
		Nos. 554-558 (5)	1.60	1.31

Tercentenary of San Vicente. See Nos. C47-C51.

Volcano of Izalco — A127

Wharf at Cutuco — A128

Doroteo Vasconcelos A129

Parade Ground A130

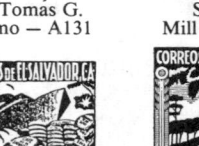

Dr. Tomás G. Palomo — A131

Sugar Mill — A132

Coffee at Pier A133

Gathering Balsam A134

Pres. Manuel E. Araujo — A135

1935, Dec. **Engr.** **Unwmk.**

559	A127	1c dp vio	10	5
560	A128	2c chestnut	10	5
561	A129	3c green	10	5
562	A130	5c carmine	30	6
563	A131	8c dl bl	12	5
564	A132	10c orange	18	8
565	A133	15c dk ol bis	30	15

566 A134 50c indigo 1.50 75
567 A135 1col black 3.75 2.25
Nos. 559-567 (9) 6.45 3.49

Paper has faint imprint "El Salvador" on face.

Stamps of 1935 Surcharged with New Value in Black.

1938 ***Perf. 12½***
568 A130 1c on 5c car 10 8
569 A132 3c on 10c org 10 8
570 A133 8c on 15c dk ol bis 12 10

No. 486 Surcharged with New Value in Red.

1938 ***Perf. 11½***
571 A102 3c on 5c bl 18 18

Issued to commemorate the centenary of the death of Jose Simeon Canas, liberator of slaves in Latin America.

Map of Flags of US and El Salvador — A136

Engraved and Lithographed

1938, Apr. 21 ***Perf. 12***
572 A136 8c multi 38 30

150th anniv. of US Constitution. See No. C61.

No. 560 Surcharged with New Value in Black.

1938 ***Perf. 12½.***
573 A128 1c on 2c chnt 8 8

Indian Sugar Mill — A137

Designs; 2c, Indian women washing. 3c, Indian girl at spring. 5c, Indian plowing. 8c, Izote flower. 10c, Champion cow. 20c, Extracting balsam. 50c, Maquilishuat in bloom. 1col, Post Office, San Salvador.

1938-39 **Engr.** ***Perf. 12***
574 A137 1c dk vio 12 5
575 A137 2c dk grn 12 5
576 A137 3c dk brn 18 5
577 A137 5c scarlet 18 5
578 A137 8c dk bl 1.00 15
579 A137 10c yel org ('39) 1.75 15
580 A137 20c bis brn ('39) 1.50 20
581 A137 50c dl blk ('39) 2.00 45
582 A137 1col blk ('39) 1.75 75
Nos. 574-582 (9) 8.60 1.90

25 Sept.
1839 1939

Nos. 566-567, 504 Surcharged in Red

BATALLA
SAN PEDRO PERULAPAN
₵ 0.50

1939, Sept. 25 ***Perf. 12½, 14***
583 A134 8c on 50c ind 25 15
584 A135 10c on 1col blk 38 15
585 A116 50c on 1col grn & vio 2.50 2.00

Issued to commemorate the 100th anniversary of the battle of San Pedro Perulapan.

Sir Rowland Hill — A146

1940, Mar. 1 ***Perf. 12½***
586 A146 8c dk bl, lt bl & blk 2.50 50

Issued to commemorate the centenary of the postage stamp. See Nos. C69-C70.

Statue of Christ and San Salvador Cathedral A147

A148

Wmk. 269- REPUBLICA DE EL SALVADOR

Wmk. 269

1942, Nov. 23 **Engr.** ***Perf. 14***
587 A147 8c deep blue 50 20

Souvenir Sheet

Imperf

Without Gum

Lilac Tinted Paper

588 A148 Sheet of four 11.25 11.25
a 8c dp bl 2.50 2.50
b 30c red org 2.50 2.50

Nos. 587-588 were issued to commemorate the first Eucharistic Congress of Salvador. See No. C85.

No. 588 contains two No. 587 and two No. C85, imperf.

Catalogue values for unused stamps in this section, from this point to the end of the section, are for Never Hinged items.

Cuscatlan Bridge, Pan-American Highway — A149

Arms Overprint at Right in Carmine.

Perf. 12½

1944, Nov. 24 **Unwmk.** **Engr.**
589 A149 8c dk bl & blk 12 10

See No. C92.

Gen. Juan José Canas — A150

1945, June 9
590 A150 8c blue 10 5

No. 575 Surcharged in Black

1 1
a *b*

1944-46
591 A137(a) 1(c) on 2c dk grn 10 6
592 A137(b) 1(c) on 2c dk grn ('46) 10 6

Lake of Ilopango A151

Ceiba Tree A152

Water Carriers — A153

1946-47 **Litho.** **Wmk. 240**
593 A151 1c bl ('47) 8 5
594 A152 2c lt bl grn ('47) 18 8
595 A153 5c carmine 10 5

Isidro Menéndez — A154

Designs: 2c, Cristano Salazar. 3c, Juan Bertis.5c, Francisco Duenas, 8c, Ramon Belloso. 10c, Jose Presentacion Trigueros. 20c, Salvador Rodriguez Gonzalez. 50c, Francisco Castaneda. 1col, David Castro.

1947 **Unwmk.** **Engr.** ***Perf. 12***
596 A154 1c car rose 5 5
597 A154 2c dp org 5 5
598 A154 3c violet 6 5
599 A154 5c sl gray 6 5
600 A154 8c dp bl 8 5
601 A154 10c bis brn 12 8
602 A154 20c green 20 9
603 A154 50c black 50 20
604 A154 1col scarlet 1.10 25
Nos. 596-604 (9) 2.22 87

Manuel José Arce — A163

1948, Feb. 25 ***Perf. 12½***
605 A163 8c deep blue 20 10

See Nos. C108-C110.

President Roosevelt Presenting Awards for Distinguished Service — A164

President Franklin D. Roosevelt A165

A166

Designs: 8c, Pres. and Mrs. Roosevelt. 15c, Mackenzie King, Roosevelt and Winston Churchill. 20c, Roosevelt and Cordell Hull. 50c, Funeral of Pres. Roosevelt.

1948, Apr. 12

Various Frames; Center in Black

606 A164 5c dk bl 8 5
607 A164 8c green 10 8
608 A164 12c violet 15 10
609 A164 15c vermilion 18 10
610 A164 20c car lake 20 20
611 A164 50c gray 55 45
Nos. 606-611 (6) 1.26 98

Souvenir Sheet

Perf. 13½

1948, Apr. 1
612 A166 1col ol grn & brn 1.40 1.40

3rd anniv. of the death of F. D. Roosevelt. See Nos. C111-C117.

Torch and Winged Letter — A167

Perf. 12½

1949, Oct. 9 **Unwmk.** **Engr.**
613 A167 8c blue 32 15

75th anniv. of the UPU. See Nos. C122-C124.

Workman and Soldier Holding Torch — A168

Wreath and Open Book — A169

1949, Dec. 15 Litho. *Perf. 10½*

614	A168	8c blue	22	8

Issued to commemorate the 1st anniversary of the Revolution of Dec. 14, 1948. See Nos. C125-C129.

Perf. 11½

1952, Feb. 14 Photo. Unwmk.

Wreath in Dark Green

615	A169	1c yel grn	5	5
616	A169	2c magenta	5	5
617	A169	5c brn red	5	5
618	A169	10c yellow	8	6
619	A169	20c gray grn	15	10
620	A169	1col dp car	75	50
		Nos. 615-620 (6)	1.13	81

Constitution of 1950. See Nos. C134-C141.

Nos. 598, 600 and 603 Surcharged with New Values in Various Colors.

1952-53 *Perf. 12½.*

621	A154	2c on 3c vio (C)	8	5
622	A154	2c on 8c dp bl (C)	10	5
623	A154	3c on 8c dp bl (G)	10	5
624	A154	5c on 8c dp bl (O)	10	8
625	A154	7c on 8c dp bl (Bk)	10	8
626	A154	10c on 50c blk (O) ('53)	15	10
		Nos. 621-626 (6)	63	41

Nos. C106 and C107 Surcharged and "AEREO" Obliterated in Various Colors.

1952-53 Wmk. 240

627	AP31	2c on 12c choc (Bl)	10	5
628	AP32	2c on 14c dk bl (R) ('53)	10	5
629	AP31	5c on 12c choc (Bl)	10	8
630	AP32	10c on 14c dk bl (C)	10	10

José Marti — A170

Perf. 10½

1953, Feb. 27 Litho. Unwmk.

631	A170	1c rose red	8	5
632	A170	2c bl grn	10	5
633	A170	10c dk vio	12	8
		Nos. 631-633,C142-C144 (6)	1.04	76

Issued to commemorate the centenary of the birth of José Marti, Cuban patriot.

No. 598 Overprinted in Carmine "IV Congreso Médico Social Panamericano 15 / 19 Abril, 1953"

1953, June 19 *Perf. 12½*

634	A154	3c violet	15	8

Issued to commemorate the 4th Pan-American Congress of Social Medicine, San Salvador, April 16-19, 1953. See No. C146.

Signing of Act of Independence A171

Capt. Gen. Gerardo Barrios A172

1953, Sept. 15 Litho. *Perf. 11½*

635	A171	1c rose pink	5	5
636	A171	2c dp bl grn	5	5
637	A171	3c purple	5	5
638	A171	5c dp bl	6	6
639	A171	7c lt brn	8	8
640	A171	10c ocher	15	9
641	A171	20c dp org	20	15
642	A171	50c green	45	20
643	A171	1col gray	90	75
		Nos. 635-643,C147-C150 (13)	2.76	2.10

Issued to commemorate the 132nd anniversary of the Act of Independence, Sept. 15, 1821.

1953, Dec. 1 *Perf. 11½*

Portrait: 3c, 7c, 10c, 22c, Francisco Morazan, (facing left).

Black Overprint ("C de C").

644	A172	1c green	5	5
645	A172	2c blue	5	5
646	A172	3c green	5	5
647	A172	5c carmine	8	5
648	A172	7c blue	10	6
649	A172	10c carmine	12	8
650	A172	20c violet	15	12
651	A172	22c violet	20	15
		Nos. 644-651 (8)	80	61

The overprint "C de C" is a control indicating "Tribunal of Accounts". A double entry of this overprint occurs twice in each sheet of each denomination.

Coastal Bridge — A173

Motherland and Liberty A174

Census Allegory A175

Balboa Park A176

Designs: Nos. 653 and 664, Fishing boats. Nos. 654 and 655, National Palace. Nos. 658 and 662, Gen. Arce. Nos. 659 and 665, Izalco Volcano. Nos. 660 and 661, Guayabo dam. No. 666, Lake Ilopango. Nos. 667 and 672, ODECA officials and flag. No. 668, Motherland and Liberty. No. 669, Housing development. Nos. 670 and 673, Coast guard boat. No. 671, Modern highway.

Perf. 11½

1954, June 1 Unwmk. Photo.

652	A173	1c car rose & brn	6	5
653	A173	1c ol & bl gray	6	5
654	A173	1c pur & pale lil	6	5
655	A173	2c yel grn & lt gray	10	6
656	A174	2c car lake	10	6
657	A175	2c org red	10	6
658	A175	3c maroon	10	6
659	A173	3c bl grn & bl	12	6
660	A174	3c dk gray & vio	10	6
661	A174	5c red vio & vio	10	6
662	A175	5c emerald	10	6
663	A176	7c mag & buff	12	8
664	A173	7c bl grn & gray bl	12	8
665	A173	7c org brn & org	12	8
666	A173	10c car lake	12	8
667	A174	10c red, dk brn & bl	12	8
668	A174	10c dk bl grn	12	8
669	A174	20c org & cr	25	12
670	A173	22c gray vio	25	25
671	A176	50c dk gray & brn	50	28
672	A174	1col brn org, dk brn & bl	90	50
673	A173	1col brt bl	90	50
		Nos. 652-673 (22)	4.52	2.76

Capt. Gen. Gerardo Barrios — A177

Coffee Picker — A178

Wmk. 269

1955, Dec. 20 Engr. *Perf. 12½*

674	A177	1c red	8	8
675	A177	2c yel grn	10	8
676	A177	3c vio bl	12	8
677	A177	20c violet	15	12
		Nos. 674-677,C166-C167 (6)	75	61

Perf. 13½

1956, June 20 Litho. Unwmk.

678	A178	3c bis brn	8	5
679	A178	5c red org	9	5
680	A178	10c dk bl	12	9
681	A178	2col dk red	1.25	1.00
		Nos. 678-681,C168-C172 (9)	4.77	3.57

Centenary of Santa Ana Department.

Map of Chalatenango — A179

1956, Sept. 14

682	A179	2c blue	8	5
683	A179	7c rose red	20	18
684	A179	50c yel brn	35	30
		Nos. 682-684,C173-C178 (9)	2.25	1.87

Centenary of Chalatenango Department (in 1955).

Coat of Arms of Nueva San Salvador — A180

Wmk. 269

1957, Jan. 3 Engr. *Perf. 12½*

685	A180	1c rose red	5	5
686	A180	2c green	5	5
687	A180	3c violet	5	5
688	A180	7c red org	25	25
689	A180	10c ultra	8	6
690	A180	50c pale brn	30	30
691	A180	1col dl red	65	65
		Nos. 685-691,C179-C183 (12)	4.08	3.10

Issued to commemorate the centenary of the founding of the city of Nueva San Salvador (Santa Tecla).

Nos. 664-665, 683 and 688 Surcharged with New Value in Black.

1957 Unwmk. Photo. *Perf. 11½*

692	A173	6c on 7c bl grn & gray bl	22	16
693	A173	6c on 7c org brn & org	22	16

1957 Litho. *Perf. 13½*

694	A179	6c on 7c rose red	15	10

Wmk. 269

1957-58 Engr. *Perf. 12½*

695	A180	5c on 7c red org ('58)	20	14
696	A180	6c on 7c red org	25	16
		Nos. 692-696 (5)	1.04	72

El Salvador Intercontinental Hotel — A181

Perf. 11½

1958, June 28 Unwmk. Photo.

Granite Paper.

Vignette in Green, Dark Blue & Red

697	A181	3c brown	7	7
698	A181	6c crim rose	7	7
699	A181	10c brt bl	10	7
700	A181	15c brt grn	16	10
701	A181	20c lilac	25	16
702	A181	30c brt yel grn	35	22
		Nos. 697-702 (6)	1.00	69

Presidents Eisenhower and Lemus and Flags A182

1959, Dec. 14

Design in Ultramarine, Dark Brown, Light Brown and Red

Granite Paper

703	A182	3c pink	14	7
704	A182	6c green	14	7
705	A182	10c crimson	20	7
		Nos. 703-705,C184-C186 (6)	1.03	60

Issued to commemorate the visit of Pres. Jose M. Lemus of El Salvador to the United States, Mar. 9-21.

No. 686 Overprinted: "5 Enero 1960 XX Aniversario Fundacion Sociedad Filatelica de El Salvador"

1960 Wmk. 269 Engr. *Perf. 12½*

706	A180	2c green	10	8

Issued to commemorate the 20th anniversary of the Philatelic Association of El Salvador.

Apartment Houses A183

1960 Unwmk. Photo. *Perf. 11½*

Multicolored Centers; Granite Paper.

707	A183	10c scarlet	8	7
708	A183	15c brt pur	12	8
709	A183	25c brt yel grn	20	14
710	A183	30c Prus bl	22	16
711	A183	40c olive	35	25
712	A183	80c dk bl	65	45
		Nos. 707-712 (6)	1.62	1.15

Issued to publicize the erection of multi-family housing projects in 1958.

No. 686 Surcharged with New Value.

1960 Wmk. 269 Engr. *Perf. 12½*

713	A180	1c on 2c grn	10	8

Poinsettia — A184

Perf. 11½

1960, Dec. Unwmk. Photo.

Granite Paper

Design in Slate Green, Red and Yellow

714 A184 3c yellow 10 8
715 A184 6c salmon 15 8
716 A184 10c grnsh bl 20 10
717 A184 15c pale vio bl 25 14
Nos. 714-717,C188-C191 (8) 1.82 1.17

Miniature Sheet

718 A184 40c silver 50 50

Nos. 718 and C192 exist with overprints for: (1.) First Central American Philatelic Congress, July, 1961. (2.) Death of General Barrios, 96th anniversary. (3.) Centenary of city of Ahuachapan. (4.) Football (soccer) games. (5.) 4th Latin American Congress of Pathological Anatomy and 10th Central American Medical Congress, December, 1963. (6.) Second anniversary of the Alliance for Progress.

Fathers Nicolas, Vicente and Manuel Aguilar
A185

Parish Church, San Salvador, 1808
A186

Designs: 5c, 6c, Manuel José Arce, José Matias Delgado and Juan Manuel Rodriguez. 10c, 20c, Pedro Pablo Castillo, Domingo Antonio de Lara and Santiago José Celis. 50c, 80c, Monument to the Fathers, Plaza Libertad.

Perf. 11½

1961, Nov. 5 Unwmk. Photo.

719 A185 1c gray & dk brn 7 7
720 A185 2c rose & dk brn 7 7
721 A185 5c pale brn & dk ol grn 14 5
722 A185 6c brt pink & dk brn 14 8
723 A185 10c bl & dk brn 14 7
724 A185 20c vio & dk brn 22 10
725 A186 30c brt bl & vio 35 16
726 A186 40c brn org & sep 50 20
727 A186 50c bl grn & sep 65 40
728 A186 80c gray & ultra 1.00 60
Nos. 719-728 (10) 3.28 1.80

Issued to commemorate the sesquicentennial of the first cry for Independence in Central America.

No. 651 Overprinted: "III Exposición Industrial Centroamericana Diciembre de 1962"

1962, Dec. 21 Litho. *Perf. 11½*

729 A172 22c violet 20 15

Issued to publicize the 3rd Central American Industrial Exposition. See Nos. C193-C195.

Nos. 708, 726-728 and 673 Surcharged.

1962-63 Photo.

730 A183 6c on 15c brt pur & multi ('63) 22 8
731 A186 6c on 40c brn org & sep ('63) 22 8
732 A186 6c on 50c bl grn & sep ('63) 22 8
733 A183 10c on 15c brt pur & multi 22 8
734 A186 10c on 50c dl grn & sep ('63) 22 8
735 A186 10c on 80c gray & ultra ('63) 22 8
736 A173 10c on 1col brt bl ('63) 22 8
Nos. 730-736 (7) 1.54 56

Surcharge includes bars on Nos. 731-734, 736; dot on Nos. 730, 735.

No. 726 Overprinted in Arc: "CAMPAÑA MUNDIAL CONTRA EL HAMBRE"

1963, Mar. 21

737 A186 40c brn org & sep 60 40

FAO "Freedom from Hunger" campaign.

Coyote
A187

Christ on Globe
A188

Designs: 2c, Spider monkey (vert.). 3c, Raccoon. 5c, King vulture (vert.). 6c, Brown coati. 10c, Kinkajou.

1963 Photo. *Perf. 11½*

738 A187 1c lil, blk, ocher & brn 5 5
739 A187 2c lt grn & blk 5 5
740 A187 3c fawn, dk brn & buff 5 5
741 A187 5c gray grn, ind, red & buff 8 5
742 A187 6c rose lil, blk, brn & buff 8 5
743 A187 10c lt bl, brn & buff 8 5
Nos. 738-743 (6) 39 30

See Nos. C200-C207.

1964-65 *Perf. 12x11½*

744 A188 6c bl & brn 6 5
745 A188 10c bl & bis 8 5

Miniature Sheets

Imperf

746 A188 60c bl & brt pur 45 42
a Marginal ovpt. (La Union) 90 90
b Marginal ovpt. (Usulutan) 90 90
c Marginal ovpt. (La Libertad) 90 90

2nd Natl. Eucharistic Cong., San Salvador, Apr. 16-19. See Nos. C208-C210.

Nos. 746a, 746b and 746c commemorate the centenaries of the Departments of La Union, Usulutan and La Libertad.

Issue dates: Nos. 744-746, Apr. 16, 1964. Nos. 746a-746b, June 22, 1965, No. 746c, Jan. 28, 1965.

Pres. John F. Kennedy
A189

Perf. 11½x12

1964, Nov. 22 Unwmk.

747 A189 6c buff & blk 8 5
748 A189 10c tan & blk 12 5
749 A189 50c pink & blk 38 22
Nos. 747-749,C211-C213 (6) 1.18 76

Miniature Sheet

Imperf

750 A189 70c dp grn & blk 50 50

President John F. Kennedy (1917-1963).

Water Lily — A190

Flowers: 5c, Maquilishuat. 6c, Cinco negritos. 30c, Hortensia. 50c, Maguey. 60c, Geranium.

1965, Jan. 6 Photo. *Perf. 12x11½*

751 A190 3c dl grn, brn yel & org 5 5
752 A190 5c ol gray & car rose 5 5
753 A190 6c multi 5 5
754 A190 30c ol bis, vio & grn 15 10
755 A190 50c dk bl, yel grn & brn 45 18
756 A190 60c multi 50 20
Nos. 751-756 (6) 1.25 63

See Nos. C215-C220.

ICY Emblem
A191

1965, Apr. 27 Photo. *Perf. 11½x12*

Design in Brown and Gold

757 A191 5c dp yel 5 5
758 A191 6c dp rose 5 5
759 A191 10c gray 8 5
Nos. 757-759,C221-C223 (6) 66 53

International Cooperation Year.

No. 728 Overprinted in Red: "1er. Centenario Muerte / Cap. Gral. Gerardo Barrios / 1865 1965 / 29 de Agosto"

1965 Unwmk. *Perf. 11½*

760 A186 80c gray & ultra 50 30

Issued to commemorate the centenary of the death of Capt. Gen. Gerardo Barrios.

Francisco Antonio Gavidia
A192

Fair Emblem
A193

Perf. 11½x12

1965, Sept. 24 Photo. Unwmk.

Portrait in Natural Colors

761 A192 2c blk & rose vio 10 8
762 A192 3c blk & org 12 8
763 A192 6c blk & lt ultra 12 8
Nos. 761-763,C224-C226 (6) 1.56 94

Issued to honor Francisco Antonio Gavidia, philosopher.

No. 759 Overprinted in Carmine: "1865 / 12 de Octubre / 1965 / Dr. Manuel Enrique Araujo"

1965, Oct. 12

764 A191 10c brn, gray & gold 8 5

Issued to commemorate the centenary of the birth of Manuel Enrique Araujo, president of Salvador, 1911-1913. See No. C227.

1965, Nov. 5 Photo. *Perf. 12x11½*

765 A193 6c yel & multi 6 5
766 A193 10c multi 9 5
767 A193 20c pink & multi 15 10
Nos. 765-767,C228-C230 (6) 3.42 2.95

Issued to publicize the International Fair of El Salvador, Nov. 5-Dec. 4, 1965.

WHO Headquarters, Geneva — A194

1966, May 20 Photo. Unwmk.

768 A194 15c beige & multi 12 8

Issued to commemorate the inauguration of World Health Organization Headquarters, Geneva. See No. C231.

No. 728 Overprinted in Red: "Mes de Conmemoracion / Civica de la Independencia / Centroamericana / 19 Sept. / 1821 1966"

1966, Sept. 19 Photo. *Perf. 11½*

769 A186 80c gray & ultra 40 35

Issued to publicize the month of civic commemoration of Central American independence.

UNESCO Emblem
A195

1966, Nov. 4 Unwmk. *Perf. 12*

770 A195 20c gray, blk & vio bl 12 9
771 A195 1col emer, blk & vio bl 65 40

20th anniv. of UNESCO. See Nos. C233-C234.

Map of Central America, Flags and Cogwheels
A196

1966, Nov. 27 Litho. *Perf. 12*

772 A196 6c multi 6 5
773 A196 10c multi 8 6
Nos. 772-773,C235-C237 (5) 79 54

Issued to commemorate the 2nd International Fair of El Salvador, Nov. 5-27.

José Simeon Cañas Pleading for Indian Slaves — A197

1967, Feb. 18 Litho. *Perf. 11½*

774 A197 6c yel & multi 8 5
775 A197 10c lil rose & multi 9 5

Issued to commemorate the bicentenary of the birth of Father Jose Simeon Canas y Villacorta, D.D. (1767-1838), emancipator of the Central American slaves.
See Nos. C239-C240.

No. 726 Overprinted in Red: "XV Convencion de Clubes / de Leones, Region de / El Salvador-11 y 12 / de Marzo de 1967"

1967 Photo.

776 A186 40c brn org & sep 35 15

Issued to publicize the 15th Convention of Lions Clubs of El Salvador, March 11-12.

Volcano San Miguel
A198

1967, Apr. 14 Photo. *Perf. 13*

777 A198 70c lt rose lil & brn 75 45

Centenary of stamps of El Salvador. See No. C241.

No. 768 Overprinted in Red: "VIII CONGRESO / CENTROAMERICANO DE / FARMACIA Y BIOQUIMICA / 5 di 11 Noviembre de 1967"

1967, Oct. 26 Photo. *Perf. 12x11½*
778 A194 15c multi 12 8

Issued to publicize the 8th Central American Congress for Pharmacy and Biochemistry. See No. C242.

No. 751 Overprinted in Red: "I Juegos / Centroamericanos y del / Caribe de Basquetbol / 25 Nov. al 3 Dic. 1967"

1967, Nov. 15
779 A190 3c dl grn, brn, yel & org 6 5

Issued to publicize the First Central American and Caribbean Basketball Games, Nov. 25-Dec. 3. See No. C243.

No. 757 Overprinted in Carmine: "1968 / AÑO INTERNACIONAL DE / LOS DERECHOS HUMANOS"

1968, Jan. 2 Photo. *Perf. 11½x12*
780 A191 5c dp yel, brn & gold 6 5

Issued for International Human Rights Year 1968. See No. C244.

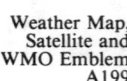

Weather Map, Satellite and WMO Emblem A199

1968, Mar. 25 Photo. *Perf. 11½x12*
781 A199 1c multi 8 5
782 A199 30c multi 22 12

World Meteorological Day, Mar. 25.

No. 768 Overprinted in Red: "1968 / XX ANIVERSARIO DE LA / ORGANIZACION MUNDIAL / DE LA SALUD"

1968, Apr. 7 *Perf. 12x11½*
783 A194 15c multi 15 8

20th anniv. of WHO. See No. C245.

No. 765 Overprinted in Red: "1968 / Año / del Sistema / del Crédito / Rural"

1968, May 6 Photo. *Perf. 12x11½*
784 A193 6c yel & multi 8 5

Rural credit system. See No. C246.

Alberto Masferrer — A200

Scouts Helping to Build — A201

1968, June 22 Litho. *Perf. 12x11½*
785 A200 2c multi 5 5
786 A200 6c multi 8 5
787 A200 25c vio & multi 25 10
Nos. 785-787,C247-C248 (5) 56 31

Issued to commemorate the centenary of the birth of Alberto Masferrer, philosopher and scholar.

1968, July 26 Litho. *Perf. 12*
788 A201 25c multi 18 12

Issued to publicize the 7th Inter-American Boy Scout Conference, July-Aug., 1968. See No. C249.

Map of Central America, Flags and Presidents of U.S., Costa Rica, Salvador, Guatemala, Honduras and Nicaragua — A202

1968, Dec. 5 Litho. *Perf. 14½*
789 A202 10c tan & multi 8 5
790 A202 15c multi 12 6

Issued to commemorate the meeting of Pres. Lyndon B. Johnson with the presidents of the Central American republics (J. J. Trejos, Costa Rica; Fidel Sanchez Hernandez, Salvador; J. C. Mendez Montenegro, Guatemala; Osvaldo Lopez Arellano, Honduras; Anastasio Somoza Debayle, Nicaragua), San Salvador, July 5-8, 1968. See Nos. C250-C251.

Heliconius Charithonius — A203

Various Butterflies.

1969 Litho. *Perf. 12*
791 A203 5c bluish lil, blk & yel 5 5
792 A203 10c beige & multi 8 5
793 A203 30c lt grn & multi 18 10
794 A203 50c tan & multi 30 18
Nos. 791-794,C252-C255 (8) 8.48 4.99

Red Cross Activities A204

1969 Litho. *Perf. 12*
795 A204 10c lt bl & multi 5 5
796 A204 20c pink & multi 10 6
797 A204 40c lil & multi 20 12
Nos. 795-797,C256-C258 (6) 3.68 2.08

Issued to commemorate the 50th anniversary of the League of Red Cross Societies.

No. 749 Overprinted in Green: "Alunizaje / Apolo-11 / 21 Julio / 1969"

1969, Sept. Photo. *Perf. 11½x12*
798 A189 50c pink & blk 30 20

Issued to commemorate man's first landing on the moon, July 20, 1969. See note after U.S. No. C76.

The same overprint in red brown and pictures of the landing module and the astronauts on the moon were applied to the margin of No. 750.

See No. C259.

Social Security Hospital A205

1969, Oct. 24 Litho. *Perf. 11½*
799 A205 6c multi 5 5
800 A205 10c multi 6 5
801 A205 30c multi 20 10
Nos. 799-801,C260-C262 (6) 5.46 2.90

ILO Emblem — A206

1969 Litho. *Perf. 13*
802 A206 10c yel & multi 8 5

50th anniv. of the ILO. See No. C263.

Chorros Spa A207

Views: 40c, Jaltepeque Bay. 80c, Fountains, Amapulapa Spa.

1969, Dec. 19 Photo. *Perf. 12x11½*
803 A207 10c blk & multi 6 6
804 A207 40c blk & multi 25 18
805 A207 80c blk & multi 50 35
Nos. 803-805,C264-C266 (6) 1.51 95

Tourism.

Euchroma Gigantea — A208

Insects: 25c, Grasshopper. 30c, Digger wasp.

1970, Feb. 24 Litho. *Perf. 11½x11*
806 A208 5c lt bl & multi 5 5
807 A208 25c dl yel & multi 15 6
808 A208 30c dl rose & multi 20 12
Nos. 806-808,C267-C269 (6) 6.05 3.33

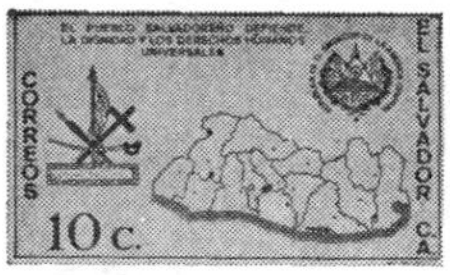

Map and Arms of Salvador, National Unity Emblem A209

1970, Apr. 14 Litho. *Perf. 14*
809 A209 10c yel & multi 8 5
810 A209 40c pink & multi 35 10

Issued to publicize Salvador's support of universal human rights. See Nos. C270-C271.

Soldiers with Flag — A210

Design: 30c, Anti-aircraft gun.

1970, May 7 *Perf. 12*
811 A210 10c grn & multi 8 5
812 A210 30c lem & multi 22 10
Nos. 811-812,C272-C274 (5) 1.02 48

Issued for Army Day, May 7.

The indexes in each volume of the Scott Catalogue contain many listings which help to identify stamps.

National Lottery Headquarters A211

1970, July 15 Litho. *Perf. 12*
813 A211 20c lt vio & multi 12 5

National Lottery centenary. See No. C291.

U.N. and Education Year Emblems A212

1970, Sept. 11 Litho. *Perf. 12*
814 A212 50c multi 30 12
815 A212 1col multi 65 30

Issued for International Education Year. See Nos. C292-293.

Map of Salvador, Globe and Cogwheels A213

1970, Oct. 28 Litho. *Perf. 12*
816 A213 5c pink & multi 5 5
817 A213 10c buff & multi 9 5

4th International Fair, San Salvador. See Nos. C294-C295.

Beethoven — A214

1971, Feb. 22 Litho. *Perf. 13½*
818 A214 50c ol, brn & yel 38 20

Second International Music Festival. See No. C296.

No. 787 Overprinted: "Año / del Centenario de la / Biblioteca Nacional / 1970"

1970, Nov. 25 *Perf. 12x11½*
819 A200 25c vio & multi 15 12

Cent. of the National Library. See No. C297.

Maria Elena Sol A215

Pietà, by Michelangelo A216

1971, Apr. 1 Litho. *Perf. 14*

820 A215 10c lt grn & multi 8 5
821 A215 30c multi 20 10

Maria Elena Sol, Miss World Tourism, 1970-71. See Nos. C298-C299.

1971, May 10

822 A216 10c sal & vio brn 6 5

Mother's Day, 1971. See No. C300.

No. 810 Overprinted in Red

1867
CIV Aniversario*
Fundación de la
Policía Nacional
6-Julio
1971

1971, July 6 Litho. *Perf. 14*

823 A209 40c pink & multi 35 18

104th anniversary of National Police. See No. C301.

Tiger Sharks — A217

Design: 40c, Swordfish.

1971, July 28

824 A217 10c multi 6 5
825 A217 40c grn & multi 20 12

See Nos. C302-C303.

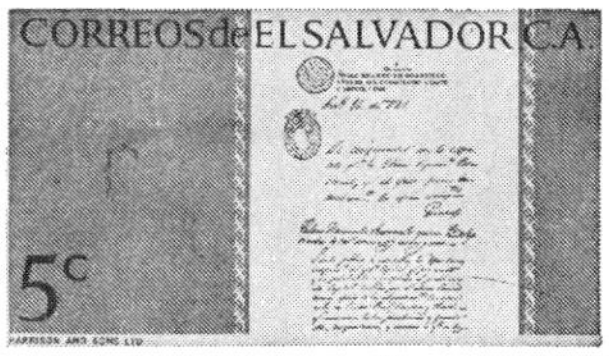

Declaration of Independence — A218

Designs: Various sections of Declaration of Independence of Central America.

1971 *Perf. 13½x13*

826 A218 5c yel grn & blk 5 5
827 A218 10c brt rose & blk 6 5
828 A218 15c dp org & blk 9 5
829 A218 20c dp red lil & blk 12 6
Nos. 826-829,C304-C307 (8) 1.70 89

Sesquicentennial of independence of Central America.

Izalco Church A219

Design: 30c, Sonsonate Church.

1971, Aug. 21 Litho. *Perf. 13x13½*

830 A219 20c blk & multi 20 8
831 A219 30c pur & multi 30 10

See Nos. C308-C309.

No. 821 Overprinted in Carmine: "1972 Año de Turismo / de las Américas"

1972, Nov. 15 Litho. *Perf. 14*

832 A215 30c multi 20 8

Tourist Year of the Americas, 1972.

No. 818 Overprinted in Red

III Festival
Internacional de
Música 9-25-
Febrero - 1973.

1973, Feb. 5 Litho. *Perf. 13½*

833 A214 50c ol, brn & yel 25 12

3rd International Music Festival, Feb. 9-25. See No. C313.

Lions International Emblem — A220

1973, Feb. 20 Litho. *Perf. 13*

834 A220 10c pink & multi 5 5
835 A220 25c lt bl & multi 10 6

31st Lions International District "D" Convention, San Salvador, May 1972. See Nos. C314-C315.

No. 812 Overprinted: "1923 1973 / 50 AÑOS FUNDACION / FUERZA AEREA"

1973, Mar. 20 Litho. *Perf. 12*

836 A210 30c lem & multi 18 8

50th anniversary of Salvadorian Air Force.

Hurdling A221

Designs (Olympic Emblem and): 10c, High jump. 25c, Running. 60c, Pole vault.

1973, May 21 Litho. *Perf. 13*

837 A221 5c lil & multi 5 5
838 A221 10c dl org & multi 5 5
839 A221 25c bl & multi 10 6
840 A221 60c ultra & multi 28 15
Nos. 837-840,C316-C319 (8) 3.20 1.51

20th Olympic Games, Munich, Aug. 26-Sept. 11, 1972.

No. 777 Surcharged:

10
CTS.

1973, Dec. Photo. *Perf. 13*

841 A198 10c on 70c multi 5 5

See No. C320.

Nos. 774, C240 Surcharged with New Value and Overprinted "1823-1973 / 150 Aniversario Liberación / Esclavos en Centroamérica"

1973-74 Litho. *Perf. 11½*

841A A197 5c on 6c multi ('74) 5 5
842 A197 10c on 45c multi 5 5

Sesquicentennial of the liberation of the slaves in Central America. On No. 841A two bars cover old denomination. On No. 842 "Aereo" is obliterated with a bar and old denomination with two bars.

Nos. 747 and 786 Surcharged:

5
CTS.

1974 Photo. *Perf. 11½x12*

843 A189 5c on 6c buff & blk 8 5

Litho. *Perf. 12x11½*

843A A200 5c on 6c multi 8 5

No. 843A has one obliterating rectangle and sans-serif "5".

Issue dates: No. 843, Apr. 22. No. 843A, June 21.

Rehabilitation Institute Emblem A222

1974, Apr. 30 Litho. *Perf. 13*

844 A222 10c multi 5 5

10th anniversary of the Salvador Rehabilitation Institute. See No. C324.

INTERPOL Headquarters, Saint-Cloud, France — A223

1974, Sept. 2 Litho. *Perf. 12½*

845 A223 10c multi 5 5

50th anniv. of Intl. Criminal Police Organization (INTERPOL). See No. C341.

UN and FAO Emblems A224

1974, Sept. 2 Litho. *Perf. 12½*

846 A224 10c bl, dk bl & gold 5 5

World Food Program, 10th anniversary. See No. C342.

25c Silver Coin, 1914 A225

Coins: 15c, 50c silver, 1953. 25c, 25c silver, 1943. 30c, 1c copper, 1892.

1974, Nov. 19 Litho. *Perf. 12½x13*

848 A225 10c multi 5 5
849 A225 15c multi 6 5
850 A225 25c multi 10 8
851 A225 30c multi 12 9
Nos. 848-851,C343-C346 (8) 1.01 78

No. 763 Surcharged

XII Serie
Ajedrez de
Centro America
y del Caribe
Oct. 1974
5
cts.

1974, Oct. 14 Photo. *Perf. 11½x12*

852 A192 5c on 6c multi 6 5

12th Central American and Caribbean Chess Tournament, Oct. 1974.

No. 762 and 771 Surcharged

₵ 0.10

1974-75 *Perf. 11½x12, 12*

853 A192 10c on 3c multi 6 5
853A A195 25c on 1col multi ('75) 10 5

Bar and surcharge on one line on No. 853A.

Issue dates: No. 853, Dec. 19, 1974. No. 853A, Jan. 13, 1975.

UPU Emblem A226

1975, Jan. 22 Litho. *Perf. 13*

854 A226 10c bl & multi 5 5
855 A226 60c bl & multi 24 18

Cent. of UPU. See Nos. C356-C357.

Acajutla Harbor A227

1975, Feb. 17

856 A227 10c bl & multi 5 5

See No. C358.

No. 799 Surcharged

₵ 0.05

1975 Litho. *Perf. 11½*

857 A205 5c on 6c multi 6 5

Central Post Office, San Jose — A228

1975, Apr. 25 Litho. *Perf. 13*

858 A228 10c bl & multi 5 5

See No. C359.

A particular stamp may be scarce, but if few collectors want it, its market value may remain relatively low.

Map of Americas and El Salvador, Trophy
A229

1975, June 25 Litho. *Perf. 12½*

859 A229 10c red org & multi	8	5
860 A229 40c yel & multi	25	18

El Salvador, site of 1975 Miss Universe Contest. See Nos. C360-C361.

Claudia Lars, Poet, and IWY Emblem — A230

1975, Sept. 4 Litho. *Perf. 12½*

861 A230 10c yel & bl blk	5	5

International Women's Year 1975. See Nos. C362-C363.

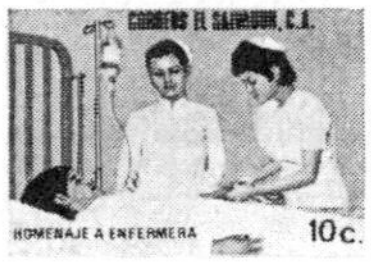

Nurses Attending Patient — A231

1975, Oct. 24 Litho. *Perf. 12½*

862 A231 10c lt grn & multi	8	5

Nurses' Day. See No. C364.

Congress Emblem — A232

1975, Nov. 19 Litho. *Perf. 12½*

863 A232 10c yel & multi	5	5

15th Conference of Inter-American Federation of Securities Enterprises, San Saalvador, Nov. 16-20. See No. C365.

No. 768 Overprinted in Red: "XVI / CONGRESO MEDICO / CENTROAMERICANO / SAN SALVADOR, / EL SALVADOR, / DIC. 10-13, 1975"

1975, Nov. 26 Photo. *Perf. 12x11½*

864 A194 15c beige & multi	12	8

16th Central American Medical Congress, San Salvador, Dec. 10-13.

Flags of Participants, Arms of Salvador — A233

1975, Nov. 28 Litho. *Perf. 12½*

865 A233 15c blk & multi	6	5
866 A233 50c brn & multi	20	15

8th Ibero-Latin-American Dermatological Congress, San Salvador, Nov. 28-Dec. 3. See Nos. C366-C367.

Jesus and Caritas Emblem — A234

1975, Dec. 18 Litho. *Perf. 13½*

867 A234 10c dl red & mar	5	5

7th Latin American Charity Congress, San Salvador, Nov. 1971. See No. C368.

No. 862 Overprinted: "III CONGRESO / ENFERMERIA / CENCAMEX 76"

1976, May 10 Litho. *Perf. 12½*

868 A231 10c lt grn & multi	6	5

CENCAMEX 76, 3rd Nurses' Congress.

Map of El Salvador
A235

1976, May 18

869 A235 10c vio bl & multi	5	5

10th Congress of Revenue Collectors (Centro Interamericano de Administradores Tributarios, CIAT), San Salvador, May 16-22. See No. C382.

Flags of Salvador and U.S., Torch, Map of Americas
A236

The Spirit of '76, by Archibald M. Willard — A237

1976, June 30 Litho. *Perf. 12½*

870 A236 10c yel & multi	5	5
871 A237 40c multi	16	12

American Bicentennial. See Nos. C383-C384.

American Crocodile — A238

Reptiles: 20c, Green iguana. 30c, Iguana.

1976, Sept. 23 Litho. *Perf. 12½*

872 A238 10c multi	5	5
873 A238 20c multi	8	6
874 A238 30c multi	12	9
Nos. 872-874,C385-C387 (6)	65	51

Post-classical Vase, San Salvador
A239

Pre-Columbian Art: 15c, Brazier with classical head, Tazumal. 40c, Vase with classical head, Tazumal.

1976, Oct. 11 Litho. *Perf. 12½*

875 A239 10c multi	5	5
876 A239 15c multi	6	5
877 A239 40c multi	16	12
Nos. 875-877,C388-C390 (6)	81	65

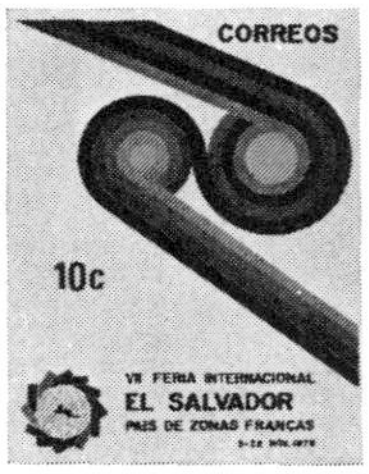

Fair Emblem
A240

1976, Oct. 25 Litho. *Perf. 12½*

878 A240 10c multi	5	5
879 A240 30c gray & multi	12	9

7th International Fair, Nov. 5-22. See Nos. C391-C392.

Child under Christmas Tree — A241

1976, Dec. 16 Litho. *Perf. 11*

880 A241 10c yel & multi	5	5
881 A241 15c buff & multi	6	5
882 A241 30c vio & multi	12	9
883 A241 40c pink & multi	16	12
Nos. 880-883,C393-C396 (8)	1.23	94

Christmas 1976.

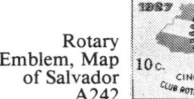

Rotary Emblem, Map of Salvador
A242

1977, June 20 Litho. *Perf. 11*

884 A242 10c multi	8	5
885 A242 15c multi	10	8

San Salvador Rotary Club, 50th anniversary. See Nos. C397-C398.

Cerron Grande Hydroelectric Station — A243

Designs: No. 887, 15c, Central sugar refinery, Jiboa. 30c, Radar station, Izalco (vert.).

1977, June 29 *Perf. 12½*

886 A243 10c multi	5	5
887 A243 10c multi	5	5
888 A243 15c multi	6	5
889 A243 30c multi	12	9
Nos. 886-889,C399-C401 (7)	88	69

Industrial development. Nos. 886-889 have colorless overprint in multiple rows: GOBIERNO DEL SALVADOR.

Nos. 785 and 774 Surcharged with New Value and Bar

1977, June 30 *Perf. 12x11½, 11½*

890 A200 15c on 2c multi	6	5
891 A197 25c on 6c multi	10	8

Microphone, ASDER Emblem — A244

1977, Sept. 14 Litho. *Perf. 14*

892 A244 10c multi	8	5
893 A244 15c multi	10	8

Broadcasting in El Salvador, 50th anniversary (Asociacion Salvadoreno de Empresa Radio). See Nos. C406-C407.

Wooden Drum
A245

Design: 10c, Flute and recorder.

1978, Aug. 29 Litho. *Perf. 12½*

894 A245 5c multi	5	5
895 A245 10c multi	5	5
Nos. 894-895,C433-C435 (5)	72	57

"Man and Engineering"
A246

1978, Sept. 12 Litho. *Perf. 13½*

896 A246 10c multi	5	5

4th National Engineers' Congress, San Salvador, Sept. 18-23. See No. C436.

Izalco Station
A247

1978, Sept. 14 *Perf. 12½*

897 A247 10c multi	5	5

Inauguration of Izalco satellite earth station, Sept. 15, 1978. See No. C437.

Fair Emblem A248

1978, Oct. 30 Litho. *Perf. 12½*

898 A248 10c multi 5 5
899 A248 20c multi 8 6

8th International Fair, Nov. 3-20. See Nos. C440-C441.

Henri Dunant, Red Cross Emblem A249

1978, Oct. 30 *Perf. 11*

900 A249 10c multi 5 55

Henri Dunant (1828-1910), founder of the Red Cross. See No. C442.

World Map and Cotton Boll A250

1978, Nov. 22 *Perf. 12½*

901 A250 15c multi 6 5

International Cotton Consulting Committee, 37th Meeting, San Salvador, Nov. 27-Dec. 2. See No. C443.

Nativity, Stained-glass Window A251

1978, Dec. 5 Litho. *Perf. 12½*

902 A251 10c multi 5 5
903 A251 15c multi 6 5

Christmas 1978. See Nos. C444-C445.

Athenaeum Coat of Arms — A252

1978, Dec. 20 Litho. *Perf. 14*

904 A252 5c multi 5 5

Millennium of Castilian language. See No. C446.

Postal Service and UPU Emblems A253

1979, Apr. 2 Litho. *Perf. 14*

905 A253 10c multi 5 5

Centenary of Salvador's membership in Universal Postal Union. See No. C447.

"75," Health Organization and WHO Emblems — A254

1979, Apr. 7 *Perf. 14x14½*

906 A254 10c multi 5 5

Pan-American Health Organization, 75th anniversary. See No. C448.

Flame and Pillars — A255

1979, May 25 Litho. *Perf. 12½*

907 A255 10c multi 5 5
908 A255 15c multi 6 5

Social Security 5-year plan, 1978-1982. See Nos. C449-C450.

Pope John Paul II, Map of Americas A256

1979, July 12 Litho. *Perf. 14½x14*

909 A256 10c multi 5 5
910 A256 20c multi 8 6

See Nos. C454-C455.

Mastodon A257

1979, Sept. 7 Litho. *Perf. 14*

911 A257 10c *shown* 5 5
912 A257 20c *Saber-toothed tiger* 8 6
913 A257 30c *Toxodon* 12 9
Nos. 911-913,C458-C460 (6) 1.21 93

Salvador Flag, JoséAberiz and Proclamation — A258

1979, Sept. 14 *Perf. 14½x14*

914 A258 10c multi 5 5

National anthem centenary. See No. C461.

Cogwheel around Map of Americas — A259

1979, Oct. 19 Litho. *Perf. 14½x14*

915 A259 10c multi 5 5

8th COPIMERA Congress (Mechanical, Electrical and Allied Trade Engineers), San Salvador, Oct. 22-27. See No. C462.

Children of Various Races, IYC Emblem A260

Children and Nurses, IYC Emblem A261

Perf. 14x14½, 14½x14

1979, Oct. 29

916 A260 10c multi 5 5
917 A261 15c multi 6 5

International Year of the Child.

Map of Central and South America, Congress Emblem — A262

1979, Nov. 1 Litho. *Perf. 14½x14*

918 A262 10c multi 5 5

5th Latin American Clinical Biochemistry Congress, San Salvador, Nov. 5-10. See No. C465.

Coffee Bushes in Bloom, Coffee Association Emblem A263

Salvador Coffee Association, 50th Anniversary: 30c, Planting coffee bushes (vert.). 40c, Coffee berries.

Perf. 14x14½, 14½x14

1979, Dec. 18

919 A263 10c multi 5 5
920 A263 30c multi 12 9
921 A263 40c multi 16 12
Nos. 919-921,C466-C468 (6) 1.23 93

Children, Dove and Star — A264

1979, Dec. 18 *Perf. 14½x14*

922 A264 10c multi 5 5

Christmas 1979.

Hoof and Mouth Disease Prevention A265

1980, June 3 Litho. *Perf. 14½x14*

923 A265 10c multi 5 5

See No. C469.

Anadara Grandis A266

1980, Aug. 12 *Perf. 14x14½*

924 A266 10c *shown* 5 5
925 A266 30c *Ostrea iridescens* 12 9
926 A266 40c *Turitello leucostoma* 16 12
Nos. 924-926,C470-C473 (7) 1.19 91

Quetzal (Pharomachrus mocino) — A267

1980, Sept. 10 Litho. *Perf. 14x14½*

927 A267 10c shown 5 5
928 A267 20c Penelopina nigra 8 6
Nos. 927-928,C474-C476 (5) 73 56

Local Snakes A268

1980, Nov. 12 Litho. *Perf. 14x14½*

929 A268 10c Tree snake 5 5
930 A268 20c Water snake 8 6

See Nos. C477-C478.

Corporation of Auditors, 50th Anniv. — A269

1980, Nov. 26 Litho. *Perf. 14*
931 A269 15c multi 6 5
932 A269 20c multi 8 6

See Nos. C479-C480.

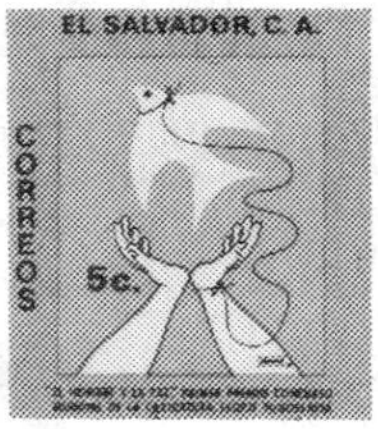

Christmas 1980 — A270

1980, Dec. 5 Litho. *Perf. 14*
933 A270 5c multi 5 5
934 A270 10c multi 5 5

See Nos. C481-C482.

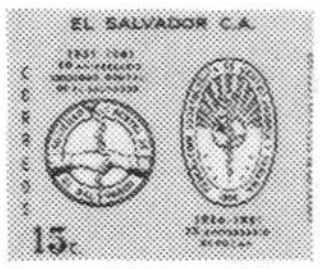

Dental Association Emblems — A271

1981, June 18 Litho. *Perf. 14*
935 A271 15c lt yel grn & blk 6 5

Dental Society of Salvador, 50th anniv.; Odontological Federation of Central America and Panama, 25th anniv. See No. C494.

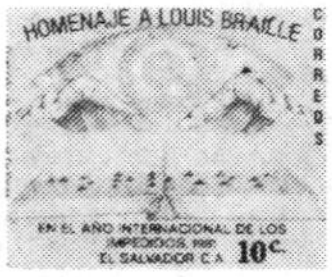

Hands Reading Braille Book — A272

1981, Aug. 14 Litho. *Perf. 14x14½*
936 A272 10c multi 5 5
Nos. 936,C495-C498 (5) 1.05 80

Intl. Year of the Disabled.

Roberto Quinonez Natl. Agriculture College, 25th Anniv. — A273

1981, Aug. 28 Litho. *Perf. 14x14½*
937 A273 10c multi 5 5

See No. C499.

World Food Day — A274

1981, Sept. 16 Litho. *Perf. 14x14½*
938 A274 10c multi 5 5

See No. C500.

1981 World Cup Preliminaries — A275

1981, Nov. 27 Litho. *Perf. 14x14½*
939 A275 10c shown 5 5
940 A275 40c Cup soccer ball, flags 16 12

See Nos. C505-C506.

Salvador Lyceum (High School), 100th Anniv. — A276

1981, Dec. 17 Litho. *Perf. 14*
941 A276 10c multi 5 5

Pre-Columbian Stone Sculptures A277

1982, Jan. 22 Litho. *Perf. 14*
942 A277 10c Axe with bird's head 5 5
943 A277 20c Sun disc 8 6
944 A277 40c Stele Carving with effigy 16 12
Nos. 942-944,C508-C510 (6) 83 64

Scouting Year — A278

1982, Mar. 17 Litho. *Perf. 14½x14*
945 A278 25c Baden-Powell 10 8
946 A278 30c Girl Scout helping woman 12 9

See Nos. C511-C512.

Armed Forces A279

1982, May 7 Litho. *Perf. 14x13½*
947 A279 10c multi 5 5

See No. C514.

1982 World Cup A280

1982, July 14 *Perf. 14x14½*
948 A280 10c Team, emblem 5 5

See Nos. C518-C520.

10th International Fair — A281

1982, Oct. 14 Litho. *Perf. 14*
949 A281 10c multi 5 5

See No. C524.

Christmas 1982 — A282

1982, Dec. 14 Litho. *Perf. 14*
950 A282 5c multi 5 5

See No. C528.

Dancers, Pre-Colombian Ceramic Design — A283

1983, Feb. 18 Litho. *Perf. 14*
951 A283 10c shown 5 5
952 A283 20c Sower 8 6
953 A283 25c Flying Man 10 8
954 A283 60c Hunters 25 20
955 A283 60c Hunters, diff. 25 20
956 A283 1col Procession 40 30
957 A283 1col Procession, diff. 40 30
Nos. 951-957 (7) 1.53 1.19

Nos. 953-957 airmail. Stamps of same denomination se-tenant.

Visit of Pope John Paul II — A284

1983, Mar. 4 Litho. *Perf. 14*
958 A284 25c shown 10 8
959 A284 60c Monument to the Divine Savior, Pope 25 20

Salvadoran Air Force, 50th Anniv. A285

1983, Mar. 24 Litho. *Perf. 14*
960 A285 10c Ricardo Aberle 5 5
961 A285 10c Air Force Emblem 5 5
962 A285 10c Enrico Massi 5 5
a Strip of 3 (#960-962) 15 15
963 A285 10c Juan Ramon Munes 5 5
964 A285 10c American Air Force Cooperation Emblem 5 5
965 A285 10c Belisario Salazar 5 5
a Strip of 3 (#963-965) 15 15

Arranged se-tenant horizontally with two Nos. 960 or 963 at left and two Nos. 962 or 965 at right.

Local Butterflies A286

1983, May 31 Litho. *Perf. 14*
966 Pair 10 10
a A286 5c Papilio torquatus 5 5
b A286 5c Metamorpha steneles 5 5
967 Pair 10 10
a A286 10c Papilio torquatus, diff. 5 5
b A286 10c Anaea marthesia 5 5
968 Pair 12 10
a A286 15c Prepona brooksiana 6 5
b A286 15c Caligo atreus 6 5
969 Pair 20 16
a A286 25c Morpho peleides 10 8
b A286 25c Dismorphia praxinoe 10 8
970 Pair 40 30
a A286 50c Morpho polyphemus 20 15
b A286 50c Metamorphia epaphus 20 15
Nos. 966-970 (5) 92 76

Simon Bolivar, 200th Birth Anniv. — A287

1983, June 23 Litho. *Perf. 14*
971 A287 75c multi 30 22

Salvador Medical College, 40th Anniv. — A288

1983, July 21 Litho. *Perf. 14*
972 A288 10c Dr. Jose Mendoza, college emblem 5 5

Centenary of David J. Guzman National Museum — A289

Perf. 13½x14, 14x13½
1983, Oct. 30 Litho.
973 A289 10c multi 5 5
974 A289 50c multi, horiz. 20 15

50c airmail.

World Communications Year — A290

Designs: 10c, Gen. Juan Jose Canas, Francisco Duenas (organizers of First natl. telegraph service), Morse key, 1870. 25c, Mailman delivering letters (vert.). 50c, Post Office sorting center, San Salvador. 25c, 50c airmail.

Perf. 14x13½, 13½x14

1983, Nov. 23 **Litho.**

975	A290	10c multi	5	5
976	A290	25c multi	10	8
977	A290	50c multi	20	15

Christmas 1983 — A291

Perf. 13½x14, 14x13½

1983, Nov. 30

978	A291	10c Dove over globe	5	5
979	A291	25c Creche figures, horiz.	10	8

25c airmail.

Environmental Protection A292

1983, Dec. 13

980	A292	10c Vehicle exhaust	5	5
981	A292	15c Fig tree	6	5
982	A292	25c Rodent	10	8

15c, 25c airmail.

Philatelists' Day — A293

1984, Jan. 5 ***Perf. 14x13½***

983	A293	10c No. 1	5	5

Corn — A294

1984, Feb. 21 **Litho.** ***Perf. 14½x14***

984	A294	10c shown	5	5
985	A294	15c Cotton	6	5
986	A294	25c Coffee beans	10	8
987	A294	50c Sugar cane	20	15
988	A294	75c Beans	30	22
989	A294	1col Agave	40	30
990	A294	5col Balsam	2.00	1.50
		Nos. 984-990 (7)	3.11	2.35

See Nos. 1047-1051.

Caluco Church, Sonsonate A295

1984, Mar. 30 ***Perf. 14x13½***

991	A295	5c shown	5	5
992	A295	10c Salcoatitan, Sonsonate	5	5
993	A295	15c Huizucar, La Libertad	6	5
994	A295	25c Santo Domingo, Sonsonate	10	8
995	A295	50c Pilar, Sonsonate	20	15
996	A295	75c Nahuizalco, Sonsonate	30	22
		Nos. 991-996 (6)	76	60

Nos. 993-996 airmail.

Central Reserve Bank of Slavador, 50th Anniv. A296

1984, July 17 **Litho.** ***Perf. 14x14½***

997	A296	10c First reserve note	5	5
998	A296	25c Bank, 1959	10	8

25c airmail.

1984 Summer Olympics A297

Perf. 14x13½, 13½x14

1984, July 20

999	A297	10c Boxing	5	5
1000	A297	25c Running, vert.	10	8
1001	A297	40c Bicycling	16	12
1002	A297	50c Swimming	20	15
1003	A297	75c Judo, vert.	30	22
1004	A297	1col Pierre de Coubertin	40	30
		Nos. 999-1004 (6)	1.21	92

Nos. 1000-1004 airmail.

Govt. Printing Office Building Opening A298

1984, July 27 ***Perf. 14x13½***

1005	A298	10c multi	5	5

5th of November Hydroelectric Plant A299

Designs: 55c, Cerron Grande Plant. 70c, Ahuachapan Geothermal Plant. 90c, Mural. 2col, 15th of September Plant. 7c, 90c, 2 col airmail.

1984, Sept. 13 **Litho.** ***Perf. 14x14½***

1006	A299	20c multi	8	6
1007	A299	55c multi	22	18
1008	A299	70c multi	28	22
1009	A299	90c multi	36	28
1010	A299	2col multi	80	60
		Nos. 1006-1010 (5)	1.74	1.34

Boys Playing Marbles — A300

1984, Oct. 16 ***Perf. 14½x14***

1011	A300	55c shown	22	18
1012	A300	70c Spinning top	28	22
1013	A300	90c Flying kite	36	28
1014	A300	2col Top, diff.	80	60

11th International Fair — A301

1984, Oct. 31 **Litho.** ***Perf. 14x14½***

1015	A301	25c shown	10	8
1016	A301	70c Fairgrounds	28	22

70c airmail.

Los Chorros Tourist Center A302

1984, Nov. 23 **Litho.** ***Perf. 14x14½***

1017	A302	15c shown	6	5
1018	A302	25c Plaza las Americas	10	8
1019	A302	70c El Salvador International Airport	28	22
1020	A302	90c El Tunco Beach	36	28
1021	A302	2col Sihuatehuacan Tourist Center	80	60
		Nos. 1017-1021 (5)	1.60	1.23

The Paper of Papers, 1979, by Roberto A. Galicia (b. 1945) A302a

Paintings by natl. artists: 20c, The White Nun, 1939, by Salvador Salazar Arrue (b. 1899), vert. 70c, Supreme Elegy to Masferrer, 1968, by Antonio G. Ponce (b. 1938), vert. 90c, Transmutation, 1979, by Armando Solis (b. 1940). 2 col, Figures at Theater, 1959, by Carlos Canas (b. 1924), vert.

1984, Dec. 10 **Litho.** ***Perf. 14***

1021A	A302a	20c multi	8	6
1021B	A302a	55c multi	22	16
1021C	A302a	70c multi	28	22
1021D	A302a	90c multi	35	26
1021E	A302a	2col multi	75	60
		Nos. 1021A-1021E (5)	1.68	1.30

Nos. 1021B-1021E are airmail. 70c and 2col issued with overprinted silver bar and corrected inscription in black; copies exist without overprint.

Christmas 1984 — A303

1984, Dec. 19 **Litho.**

1022	A303	25c Glass ornament	10	8
1023	A303	70c Ornaments, dove	28	22

No. 1023 airmail.

Birds — A304

1984, Dec. 21 **Litho.** ***Perf. 14½x14***

1024	A304	15c Lepidocolaptes affinis	6	5
1025	A304	25c Spodiornis rusticus barriliensis	10	8
1026	A304	55c Claravis mondetoura	22	18
1027	A304	70c Hylomanes momotula	28	22
1028	A304	90c Xenotriccus calizonus	36	28
1029	A304	1col Cardellina rubrifrons	45	35
		Nos. 1024-1029 (6)	1.47	1.16

Nos. 1026-1029 airmail.

Salvador Bank Centenary A305

1985, Feb. 6 **Litho.** ***Perf. 14***

1030	A305	25c Stock certificate	10	8

Mortgage Bank, 50th Anniv. — A306

1985, Feb. 20 **Litho.** ***Perf. 14***

1031	A306	25c Mortgage	10	8

Intl. Youth Year A307

1985, Feb. 28 **Litho.** ***Perf. 14***

1032	A307	25c IYY emblem	10	8
1033	A307	55c Woodcrafting	22	18
1034	A307	70c Professions symbolized	28	22
1035	A307	1.50col Youths marching	60	45

Nos. 1033-1035 airmail.

Archaeology
A308

1985, Mar. 6 Litho. *Perf. 14½x14*

1036 A308 15c Pre-classical figure 6 5
1037 A308 20c Engraved vase 8 6
1038 A308 25c Post-classical ceramic 10 8
1039 A308 55c Post-classical figure 22 18
1040 A308 70c Late post-classical deity 28 22
1041 A308 1col Late post-classical figure 40 30
Nos. 1036-1041 (6) 1.14 89

Souvenir Sheet

Rouletted 13½

1042 A308 2col Tazumal ruins, horiz. 80 60

Nos. 1039-1041 airmail. No. 1042 has enlargement of stamp design in margin.

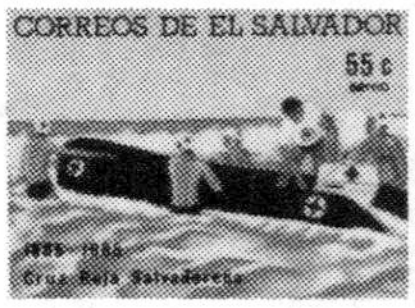

Natl. Red Cross, Cent.
A309

1985, Mar. 13 Litho. *Perf. 14*

1043 A309 25c Anniv. emblem vert. 9 7
1044 A309 55c Sea rescue 20 15
1045 A309 70c Blood donation service 25 20
1046 A309 90c First aid, ambulance, vert. 35 26

Nos. 1044-1046 are airmail.

Agriculture Type of 1984

1985 *Perf. 14½x14*

1047 A294 55c Cotton 20 15
1048 A294 70c Corn 25 20
1049 A294 90c Sugar cane 35 26
1050 A294 2col Beans 75 60
1051 A294 10col Agave 4.00 3.00
Nos. 1047-1051 (5) 5.55 4.21

Issue dates: 55c, 70c, 90c, Apr. 4. 2col, 10col, Sept. 4.

Child Survival
A310

Children's drawings.

1985, May 3 Litho. *Perf. 14x14½*

1052 A310 25c Hand, houses 9 7
1053 A310 55c House, children 20 15
1054 A310 70c Boy, girl holding hands 25 20
1055 A310 90c Oral vaccination 35 28

Nos. 1053-1055 are airmail.

Salvador Army
A311

1985, May 17 *Perf. 14*

1056 A311 25c Map 9 7
1057 A311 70c Recruit, natl. flag 25 20

No. 1057 is airmail.

Inauguration of Pres. Duarte, 1st Anniv. — A312

1985, June 28 *Perf. 14½x14*

1058 A312 25c Flag, laurel, book 9 7
1059 A312 70c Article I, Constitution 25 20

Inter-American Development Bank, 25th Anniv. — A313

Bank emblem and: 25c, Central Hydroelectric Dam, power station. 70c, Map of Salvador. 1col, Natl. arms.

1985, July 5 *Perf. 14x13½*

1060 A313 25c multi 9 7
1061 A313 70c multi 25 20
1062 A313 1col multi 38 30

Nos. 1061-1062 are airmail.

Fish
A314

1985, Sept. 30 *Perf. 14x14½*

1064 A314 25c Cichlasoma trimaculatum 9 7
1065 A314 55c Rhamdia guatemalenis 20 15
1066 A314 70c Poecilia sphenops 25 20
1067 A314 90c Cichlasoma nigrofasciatum 35 28
1068 A314 1col Astyanax fasciatus 38 30
1069 A314 1.50col Dormitator latifrons 60 42
Nos. 1064-1069 (6) 1.87 1.42

Nos. 1065-1069 are airmail.

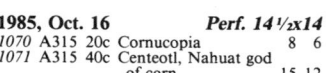

UNFAO, 40th Anniv. — A315

1985, Oct. 16 *Perf. 14½x14*

1070 A315 20c Cornucopia 8 6
1071 A315 40c Centeotl, Nahuat god of corn 15 12

Dragonflies
A316

1985, Dec. 9 *Perf. 14x14½*

1072 A316 25c Cordulegaster godmani mc-lachlan 9 7
1073 A316 55c Libellula herculea karsch 20 15
1074 A316 70c Cora marina selys 25 20
1075 A316 90c Aeshna cornigera braver 35 28
1076 A316 1col Mecistogaster ornata rambur 38 30
1077 A316 1.50col Hetaerina smaragdalis de marmels 60 42
Nos. 1072-1077 (6) 1.87 1.42

Nos. 1073-1077 are airmail.

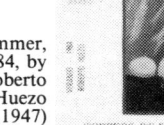

Summer, 1984, by Roberto Huezo (b.1947)
A317

Paintings by natl. artists: 25c, Profiles, 1978, by Rosa Mena Valenzuela (b. 1924), vert. 70c, The Deliverance, 1984, by Fernando Llort (b. 1949). 90c, Making Tamale, 1975, by Pedro A. Garcia (b. 1930). 1col, Warm Presence, 1984, by Miguel A. Orellana (b. 1929), vert. Nos. 1079-1082 are airmail.

1985, Dec. 18 *Perf. 14*

1078 A317 25c multi 9 7
1079 A317 55c multi 20 15
1080 A317 70c multi 25 20
1081 A317 90c multi 35 26
1082 A317 1col multi 38 30
Nos. 1078-1082 (5) 1.27 98

San Vincente de Austria y Lorenzana City, 350th Anniv.
A318

1985, Dec. 20

1083 A318 15c Tower, vert. 6 5
1084 A318 20c Cathedral 8 6

Intl. Peace Year 1986 — A319

1986, Feb. 21 Litho. *Perf. 14*

1085 A319 15c multi 12 8
1086 A319 70c multi 50 38

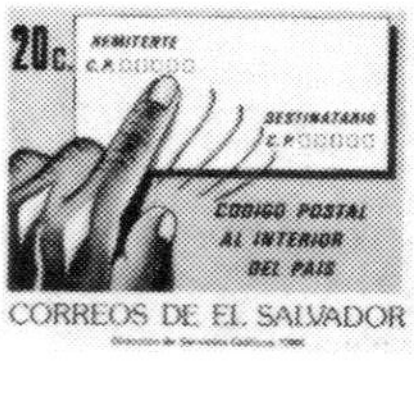

Postal Code Inauguration
A320

1986, Mar. 14 Litho. *Perf. 14x14½*

1087 A320 20c Domestic mail 16 12
1088 A320 25c Intl. mail 18 14

Radio El Salvador, 60th Anniv.
A321

1986, Mar. 21

1089 A321 25c Microphone 18 14
1090 A321 70c Map 50 38

No. 1090 is airmail.

Mammals
A322

1986, May 30 Litho. *Perf. 14x14½*

1091 A322 15c Tigrillo 12 10
1092 A322 20c Oso hormiguero 16 12
1093 A322 1col Armadillo 80 60
1094 A322 2col Tunco de monte 1.60 1.20

Nos. 1093-1094 are airmail.

1986 World Cup Soccer Championships, Mexico — A323

Designs: 70c, Flags, mascot. 1col, Players, Soccer Cup, vert. 2col, Natl. flag, player dribbling, vert. 5col, Goal, emblem.

1986, June 6 *Perf. 14x14½, 14½x14*

1095 A323 70c multi 55 42
1096 A323 1col multi 80 60
1097 A323 2col multi 1.60 1.20
1098 A323 5col multi 4.00 3.00

Teachers
A324

1986, June 30 Litho. *Perf. 14½x14*

1099 A324 20c Dario Gonzalez 10 8
1100 A324 20c Valero Lecha 10 8
1101 A324 40c Marcelino G. Flamenco 20 15
1102 A324 40c Camilo Campos 20 15
1103 A324 70c Saul Flores 32 24
1104 A324 70c Jorge Larde 32 24
1105 A324 1col Francisco Moran 48 35
1106 A324 1col Mercedes M. De Luarca 48 35
Nos. 1099-1106 (8) 2.20 1.64

Stamps of the same denomination printed se-tenant. Nos. 1103-1106 are airmail.

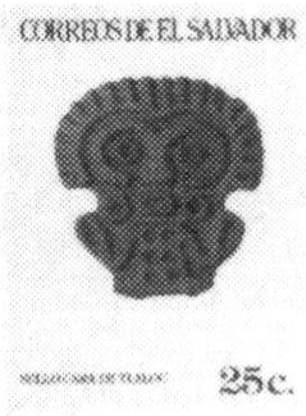

Pre-Hispanic Ceramic Seal, Cara Sucia, Ahuachapan, Tlaloc Culture (300 B.C.-A.D. 1200) — A325

1986, July 23 Litho. *Perf. 13½*

1107 A325	25c	org & brn	12	10
1108 A325	55c	grn, org & brn	25	18
1109 A325	70c	pale gray, org & brn	32	24
1110 A325	90c	pale yel, org & brn	45	32
1111 A325	1col	pale grn, org & brn	48	35
1112 A325	1.50col	pale pink, org & brn	70	52
		Nos. 1107-1112 (6)	2.32	1.71

Nos. 1108-1112 are airmail.

World Food Day A326

1986, Oct. 30 Litho. *Perf. 14x14½*

1113 A326	20c	multi	16	12

Flowers A327

1986, Sept. 30 *Perf. 14*

1114 A327	20c	Spathiphyllum phryniifolium, vert.	10	8
1115 A327	25c	Asclepias curassavica	12	10
1116 A327	70c	Tagetes tenuifolia	32	24
1117 A327	1col	Ipomoea tiliacea, vert.	48	35

Nos. 1116-1117 are airmail.

Christmas A328

Perf. 14x14½, 14½x14

1986, Dec. 10 Litho.

1118 A328	25c	Candles, vert.	12	10
1119 A328	70c	Doves	32	24

No. 1119 is airmail.

Crafts A329

1986, Dec. 18

1120 A329	25c	Basket-making	12	10
1121 A329	55c	Ceramicware	25	18
1122 A329	70c	Guitars, vert.	32	24
1123 A329	1col	Baskets, diff.	48	35

Christmas A330

Paintings: 25c, Church, by Mario Araujo Rajo, vert. 70c, Landscape, by Francisco Reyes.

1986, Dec. 22

1124 A330	25c	multi	12	10
1125 A330	70c	multi	32	24

No. 1125 is airmail.

Publicity of Philately A331

1987, Mar. 10 Litho. *Perf. 14½x14*

1126 A331	25c	multi	12	10

Intl. Aid Following Earthquake, Oct. 10, 1986 — A332

1987, Mar. 25

1127 A332	15c	multi	8	6
1128 A332	70c	multi	32	24
1129 A332	1.50col	multi	70	52
1130 A332	5col	multi	2.40	1.80

See Nos. 1186-1189.

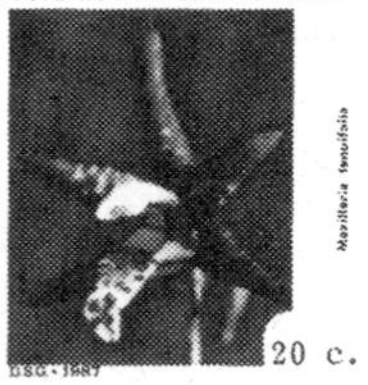

Orchids A333

1987, June 8 Litho. *Perf. 14½x14*

1131 A333	20c	Maxillaria tenuifolia	10	8
1132 A333	20c	Ponthieva maculata	10	8
1133 A333	25c	Meiracyllium trinasutum	12	10
1134 A333	25c	Encyclia vagans	12	10
1135 A333	70c	Encyclia cochleata	32	24
1136 A333	70c	Maxillaria atrata	32	24
1137 A333	1.50col	Sobrialia xantholeuca	70	52
1138 A333	1.50col	Encyclia microcharis	70	52
		Nos. 1131-1138 (8)	2.48	1.88

Nos. 1133-1138 horiz. Stamps of the same denomination printed se-tenant. Nos. 1135-1138 are airmail.

Teachers A334

Designs: No. 1139, C. de Jesus Alas, music. No. 1140, Luis Edmundo Vasquez, medicine. No. 1141, David Rosales, law. No. 1142, Guillermo Trigueros, medicine. No. 1143, Manuel Farfan Castro, history. No. 1144, Iri Sol, voice. No. 1145, Carlos Arturo Imendia, primary education. No. 1146, Benjamin Orozco, chemistry.

1987, June 30 Litho. *Perf. 14½x14*

1139 A334	15c	greenish blue & blk	8	6
1140 A334	15c	greenish blue & blk	8	6
1141 A334	20c	beige & blk	10	8
1142 A334	20c	beige & blk	10	8
1143 A334	70c	yel org & blk	32	24
1144 A334	70c	yel org & blk	32	24
1145 A334	1.50col	lt blue grn & blk	70	52
1146 A334	1.50col	lt blue grn & blk	70	52
		Nos. 1139-1146 (8)	2.40	1.80

Stamps of the same denomination printed se-tenant. Nos. 1143-1146 are airmail.

10th Pan American Games, Indianapolis A335

Perf. 14½x14, 14x14½

1987, July 31

1147 A335	20c	Emblem, vert.	10	8
1148 A335	20c	Table tennis, vert.	10	8
1149 A335	25c	Wrestling	12	10
1150 A335	25c	Fencing	12	10
1151 A335	70c	Softball	32	24
1152 A335	70c	Equestrian	32	24
1153 A335	5col	Weight lifting, vert.	2.35	1.75
1154 A335	5col	Hurdling, vert.	2.35	1.75
		Nos. 1147-1154 (8)	5.78	4.34

Stamps of the same denomination are printed se-tenant. Nos. 1151-1154 are airmail.

Prior Nicolas Aguilar (1742-1818) A336

Famous men: 20c, Domingo Antonio de Lara (1783-1814), aviation pioneer. 70c, Juan Manuel Rodrigues (1771-1837), president who abolished slavery. 1.50col, Pedro Pablo Castillo (1780-1814), patriot.

1987, Sept. 11 Litho. *Perf. 14½x14*

1155 A336	15c	multi	8	6
1156 A336	20c	multi	10	8
1157 A336	70c	multi	32	24
1158 A336	1.50col	multi	70	52

Nos. 1157-1158 are airmail.

World Food Day A337

1987, Oct. 16 *Perf. 14x14½*

1159 A337	50c	multi	24	18

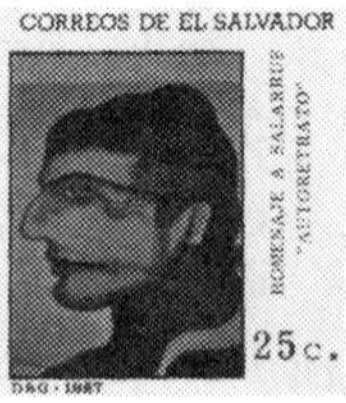

Paintings by Salarrue A338

Perf. 14½x14, 14x14½

1987, Nov. 30

1160 A338	25c	Self-portrait	12	10
1161 A338	70c	Lake	32	24

No. 1161 is airmail.

Christmas 1987 — A339

Designs: 25c, Virgin of Perpetual Sorrow, stained-glass window. 70c, The Three Magi, figurines.

1987, Nov. 18 *Perf. 14x14½*

1162 A339	25c	multi	12	10
1163 A339	70c	multi	32	24

No. 1163 is airmail.

Pre-Columbian Musical Instruments — A340

Designs: 20c, Pottery drum worn around neck. No. 1165, Frieze picturing pre-Columbian musicians, from a Salua culture ceramic vase, c. 700-800 A.D. (left side), vert. No. 1166, Frieze (right side), vert. 1.50col, Conch shell trumpet.

Perf. 14x14½, 14½x14

1987, Dec. 14 Litho.

1164 A340	20c	multi	10	8
1165 A340	70c	multi	32	24
1166 A340	70c	multi	32	24
1167 A340	1.50col	multi	70	52

Nos. 1165-1167 are airmail. Nos. 1165-1166 are printed se-tenant in a continuous design.

Promotion of Philately — A341

1988, Jan. 20 Litho. *Perf. 14*

1168 A341	25c	multi	12	10

An enhanced introduction to the Scott Catalogue begins on Page V. A thorough understanding of the material presented there will greatly aid your use of the catalogue itself.

Young Entrepreneurs of El Salvador — A342

1988 *Perf. 14x14½*
1169 A342 25c multi 12 10

St. John Bosco (1815-88) A343

1988, Mar. 15 Litho. *Perf. 14x14½*
1170 A343 20c multi 10 8

Environmental Protection — A344

1988, June 3 Litho. *Perf. 14x14½*
1171 A344 20c Forests 10 8
1172 A344 70c Forests and rivers 35 28

No. 1172 is airmail.

1988-1992 Summer Olympics, Seoul and Barcelona A345

1988, Aug. 31 Litho. *Perf. 13½*
1173 A345 1col High jump
1174 A345 1col Javelin
1175 A345 1col Shooting
1176 A345 1col Wrestling
1177 A345 1col Basketball
a. Strip of 5, Nos. 1173-1177
b. Min. sheets of 5+5 labels

Souvenir Sheets

1178 A345 2col Torch

Printed in sheets of 10 containing 2 each Nos. 1173-1177.

No. 1177b exists in 2 forms: 1st contains labels picturing 1988 Summer Games emblem or character trademark; 2nd contains labels picturing the 1992 Summer Games emblem or character trademark.

No. 1178 exists in 2 forms: 1st contains 1988 Games emblem; 2nd contains 1992 Games emblem.

World Food Day — A346

1988, Oct. 11 Litho. *Perf. 14x14½*
1179 A346 20c multi 10 8

13th Intl. Fair, Nov. 23-Dec. 11 — A347

1988, Oct. 25 *Perf. 14½x14*
1180 A347 70c multi 35 28

Child Protection A348

1988, Nov. 10
1181 A348 15c Flying kite 8 6
1182 A348 20c Child hugging adult's leg 10 8

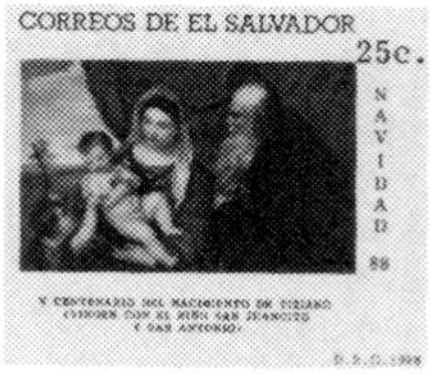

Christmas A349

Paintings by Titian: 25c, *Virgin and Child with the Young St. John and St. Anthony.* 70c, *Virgin and Child in Glory with St. Francis and St. Alvise,* vert.

Perf. 14x14½, 14½x14

1988, Nov. 15
1183 A349 25c multi 12 9
1184 A349 70c multi 35 28

70c is airmail.

Return to Moral Values — A350

1988, Nov. 22 *Perf. 14½x14*
1185 A350 25c multi 12 9

Art Type of 1987

Paintings by Salvadoran artists: 40c, *Esperanza de los Soles,* by Victor Rodriguez Preza. 1col, *Shepherd's Song,* by Luis Angel Salinas, horiz. 2col, *Children,* by Julio Hernandez Aleman, horiz. 5col, *El Nino de Las Alcancias,* by Camilo Minero. Nos. 1187-1189 are airmail.

Perf. 14½x14, 14x14½

1988, Nov. 30
1186 A338 40c multi 20 15
1187 A338 1col multi 50 38
1188 A338 2col multi 1.00 75
1189 A338 5col multi 2.50 1.90

A351

Discovery of America, 500th Anniv. (in 1992) — A352

Ruins and artifacts: a. El Tazumul. b. Multicolored footed bowl. c. San Andres. d. Two-color censer. e. Sihuatan. f. Carved head of the God of Lluvia. g. Cara Sucia. h. Man-shaped vase. i. San Lorenzo. j. Multicolored pear-shaped vase. 2col, Christopher Columbus.

1988, Dec. 21 *Perf. 14x14½*
1190 Sheet of 10 5.00 3.80
a.-j. A351 1col any single 50 38

Souvenir Sheet

Roulette 13½

1191 A352 2col ver 1.00 75

U.N. Declaration of Human Rights, 40th Anniv. A353

1988, Dec. 9 *Perf. 14½x14, 14x14½*
1192 A353 25c Family, map, emblem, vert. 12 9
1193 A353 70c shown 35 28

70c is airmail.

World Wildlife Fund — A354

Felines: No. 1194a, *Felis wiedii* laying on tree branch. No. 1194b, *Felis wiedii* sitting on branch. No. 1194c, *Felis pardalis* laying in brush. No. 1194d, *Felis pardalis* standing on tree branch.

1988 *Perf. 14½x14*
1194 Strip of 4 82 60
a.-b. A354 25c any single 12 9
c.-d. A354 55c any single 28 21

World Meteorological Organization, 40th Anniv. — A355

1989, Feb. 3 Litho. *Perf. 14½x14*
1195 A355 15c shown 8 6
1196 A355 20c Wind gauge 10 8

Meteorology in El Salvador, cent.

AIR POST STAMPS

Regular Issue of 1924-25 Overprinted in Black or Red

Servicio Aéreo

First Printing.
15c on 10c: "15 QUINCE 15" measures 22½ mm.
20c: Shows on the back of the stamp an albino impression of the 50c surcharge.
25c on 35c: Original value canceled by a long and short bar.
40c on 50c: Only one printing.
50c on 1col: Surcharge in dull orange red.

Perf. 12½, 14

1929, Dec. 28 **Unwmk.**
C1 A112 20c dp grn (Bk) 3.25 2.50
a Red overprint 350.00 350.00

Counterfeits exist of No. C1a.

With Additional Surcharge of New Values and Bars in Black or Red.

C3 A111 15c on 10c org 50 50
a "ALTANT CO" 17.50 17.50
C4 A114 25c on 35c scar & grn 1.25 1.25
a Bars inverted 7.50 7.50
C5 A115 40c on 50c org brn 50 35
C6 A116 50c on 1col grn & vio (R) 8.00 5.50

Second Printing.
15c on 10d: "15 QUINCE 15" measures 20½ mm.
20c: Has not the albino impression on the back of the stamp.
25c on 35c: Original value cancelled by two bars of equal length.
50c on 1col: Surcharge in carmine rose.

1930, Jan. 10
C7 A112 20c dp grn 45 45
C8 A111 15c on 10c org 45 45
a "ATLANT CO" 17.50
b Double surcharge 10.00
c As "a" double surcharge 75.00
d Pair, one without surch. 175.00
C9 A114 25c on 35c scar & grn 38 38
C10 A116 50c on 1col grn & vio (C) 90 90
a Without bars over "UN COLON" 2.50
b As "a" and without block over "1" 2.50

Numerous wrong font and defective letters exist in both printings of the surcharges.
No. C10 with black surcharge is bogus.

Mail Plane over San Salvador AP1

1930, Sept. 15 Engr. *Perf. 12½*
C11 AP1 15c dp red 12 8
C12 AP1 20c emerald 18 8
C13 AP1 25c brn vio 18 8
C14 AP1 40c ultra 32 6

Simón Bolivar — AP2

1930, Dec. 17 Litho. *Perf. 11½*
C15 AP2 15c dp red 4.50 3.50
a "15" double 82.50
C16 AP2 20c emerald 4.50 3.50
C17 AP2 25c brn vio 4.50 3.50
a Vert. pair, imperf. between 110.00
b Imperf., pair
C18 AP2 40c dp ultra 4.50 3.50

Centenary of death of Simón Bolivar. Counterfeits of Nos. C15-C18 exist.

No. 504 Overprinted in Red 

1931, June 29 Engr. *Perf. 14*

C19 A116 1col grn & vio 2.50 2.00

Tower of La Merced Church — AP3

1931, Nov. 5 Litho. *Perf. 11½*

C20 AP3 15c dk red 3.00 2.50
a Imperf., pair 50.00
C21 AP3 20c bl grn 3.00 2.50
C22 AP3 25c dl vio 3.00 2.50
a Vert. pair, imperf. btwn. 110.00
C23 AP3 40c ultra 3.00 2.50
a Imperf., pair 60.00

120th anniv. of the 1st movement toward the political independence of El Salvador. In the tower of La Merced Church (AP3) hangs the bell which José Matias Delgado-called the Father of his Country-rang to initiate the movement for liberty.

José Matias Delgado AP4

Airplane and Caravels of Columbus AP5

1932, Nov. 12 Wmk. 271 *Perf. 12½*

C24 AP4 15c dl red & vio 90 90
C25 AP4 20c bl grn & bl 1.25 1.25
C26 AP4 25c dl vio & brn 1.25 1.25
C27 AP4 40c ultra & grn 1.50 1.50

Issued in commemoration of the first centenary of the death of Father José Matias Delgado, who is known as the Father of El Salvadoran Political Emancipation.

Nos. C24 to C27 show cheek without shading in the 72nd stamp of each sheet.

1933, Oct. 12 Wmk. 240 *Perf. 13*

C28 AP5 15c red org 90 90
C29 AP5 20c bl grn 1.75 1.75
C30 AP5 25c lilac 1.75 1.75
C31 AP5 40c ultra 1.75 1.75
C32 AP5 1col black 1.75 1.75
Nos. C28-C32 (5) 7.90 7.90

Commemorative of the 441st anniversary of the sailing of Chistopher Columbus from Palos, Spain, for the New World.

Police Barracks — AP6

1934, Dec. 16 *Perf. 12½*

C33 AP6 25c lilac 30 15
C34 AP6 30c brown 42 30
a Imperf. (pair) 42.50
C35 AP6 1col black 1.25 65

Runner AP7

1935, Mar. 16 Engr. Unwmk.

C36 AP7 15c carmine 3.50 3.50
C37 AP7 25c violet 3.50 3.50
C38 AP7 30c brown 3.00 2.50
C39 AP7 55c blue 14.00 12.50
C40 AP7 1col black 11.00 10.00
Nos. C36-C40 (5) 35.00 32.00

Issued in commemoration of the Third Central American Games.

Same Overprinted in Black HABILITADO

1935, June 27

C41 AP7 15c carmine 3.50 1.50
C42 AP7 25c violet 3.50 1.50
C43 AP7 30c brown 3.50 1.50
C44 AP7 55c blue 22.50 19.00
C45 AP7 1col black 7.50 1.00
Nos. C41-C45 (5) 40.50 24.50

Flag of El Salvador AP8

Tree of San Vicente AP9

1935, Oct. 26 Litho. Wmk. 240

C46 AP8 30c blk brn 38 15

1935, Dec. 26 *Perf. 12½*

Numerals in Black, Tree in Yellow Green.

C47 AP9 10c yellow 85 70
C48 AP9 15c brown 85 70
C49 AP9 20c dk bl grn 85 70
C50 AP9 25c dk pur 85 70
C51 AP9 30c blk brn 85 70
Nos. C47-C51 (5) 4.25 3.50

Tercentenary of San Vicente.

No. 565 Overprinted in Red AEREO

1937 Engr. Unwmk.

C52 A133 15c dk ol bis 20 15
a Double ovpt. 25.00

No. C44 Surcharged in Red 30

C53 AP7 30c on 55c bl 1.75 75

Panchimalco Church AP10

1937, Dec. 3 Engr. *Perf. 12*

C54 AP10 15c org yel 15 12
C55 AP10 20c green 15 10
C56 AP10 25c violet 15 10
C57 AP10 30c brown 15 5
C58 AP10 40c blue 25 20
C59 AP10 1col black 65 25
C60 AP10 5col rose car 2.50 2.00
Nos. C54-C60 (7) 4.00 2.82

U.S. Constitution Type of Regular Issue

1938, Apr. 22 Engr. & Litho.

C61 A136 30c multi 60 50

José Simeón Cañas Villacorta — AP12

1938, Aug. 18 Engr.

C62 AP12 15c orange 90 90
C63 AP12 20c brt grn 1.10 90
C64 AP12 30c redsh brn 1.10 65
C65 AP12 1col black 3.75 3.00

Issued to commemorate the centenary of the death of José Simeón Cañas y Villacorta (1767-1838), liberator of slaves in Central America.

Golden Gate Bridge, San Francisco Bay AP13

1939, Apr. 14 *Perf. 12½*

C66 AP13 15c dl yel & blk 20 10
C67 AP13 30c dk brn & blk 25 10
C68 AP13 40c dk bl & blk 38 20

Golden Gate International Exposition, San Francisco.

Sir Rowland Hill — AP14

1940, Mar. 1 Engr.

C69 AP14 30c dk brn, buff & blk 4.00 1.50
C70 AP14 80c org red & blk 10.00 7.50

Centenary of the postage stamp. Covers postmarked Feb. 29 were predated. Actual first day was Mar. 1.

Map of the Americas, Figure of Peace, Plane — AP15

1940, May 22 *Perf. 12*

C71 AP15 30c brn & bl 25 20
C72 AP15 80c dk rose & blk 50 42

Pan American Union, 50th anniversary.

Demand, as well as supply, determines a stamp's market value. One is as important as the other.

Coffee Tree in Bloom — AP16

Coffee Tree with Ripe Berries — AP17

1940, Nov. 27

C73 AP16 15c yel org 75 18
C74 AP16 20c dp grn 90 10
C75 AP16 25c dk vio 1.25 38
C76 AP17 30c cop brn 1.50 18
C77 AP17 1col black 5.00 45
Nos. C73-C77 (5) 9.40 1.29

Juan Lindo, Gen. Francisco Mallespin and New National University of El Salvador — AP18

Designs (portraits changed): 40c, 80c, Narciso Monterey and Antonio José Cañas. 60c, 1col, Isidro Menéndez and Chrisanto Salazar.

1941, Feb. 16 *Perf. 12½*

C78 AP18 20c dk grn & rose lake 75 65
C79 AP18 40c ind & brn org 75 65
C80 AP18 60c dl pur & brn 75 65
C81 AP18 80c hn brn & dk bl grn 2.00 1.75
C82 AP18 1col blk & org 2.00 1.75
C83 AP18 2col yel org & rose vio 2.00 1.75
a Min. sheet of 6, #C78-C83, perf. 11½ 11.50 11.50
Nos. C78-C83 (6) 8.25 7.20

Centenary of University of El Salvador.

Stamps from No. C83a, perf. 11½, sell for about the same values as the perf. 12½stamps.

Catalogue values for unused stamps in this section, from this point to the end of the section, are for Never Hinged items.

Map of El Salvador AP20

Wmk. 269

1942, Nov. 25 Engr. *Perf. 14*

C85 AP20 30c red org 38 30
a Horiz. pair, imperf. between 100.00

First Eucharistic Congress of El Salvador. See No. 588.

Nos. C66 to C68 Surcharged with New Values in Dark Carmine 15

1943 Unwmk. *Perf. 12½.*

C86 AP13 15c on 15c dl yel & blk 20 18
C87 AP13 20c on 30c dk brn & blk 30 20
C88 AP13 25c on 40c dk bl & blk 50 30

Nos. C66 to C68 Surcharged with New Values in Dark Carmine 15

1944

C89	AP13	15c on 15c dl yel & blk	25	22
C90	AP13	20c on 30c dk brn & blk	40	25
C91	AP13	25c on 40c dk bl & blk	50	30

Bridge Type of Regular Issue Arms Overprint at Right in Blue Violet.

1944, Nov. 24 **Engr.**

C92	A149	30c crim rose & blk	25	12

No. C92 exists without overprint, but was not issued in that form.

Presidential Palace AP22

National Theater AP23

National Palace AP24

1944, Dec. 22 ***Perf. 12½***

C93	AP22	15c red vio	10	8
C94	AP23	20c dk bl grn	12	8
C95	AP24	25c dl vio	15	8

No. 582 Overprinted in Red **Aéreo**

1945, Aug. 23 ***Perf. 12***

C96	A137	1col black	45	22

Juan Ramon Uriarte — AP25

Wmk. 240

1946, Jan. 1 **Typo.** ***Perf. 12½***

C97	AP25	12c dk bl	12	8
C98	AP25	14c dp org	12	5

Mayan Pyramid, St. Andres Plantation AP26

Municipal Children's Garden, San Salvador AP27

Civil Aeronautics School, Ilopango Airport AP28

1946, May 1 **Unwmk.**

C99	AP26	30c rose car	12	8
C100	AP27	40c dp ultra	12	8
C101	AP28	1col black	65	30

Alberto Masferrer — AP29

1946, July 19 **Litho.** **Wmk. 240**

C102	AP29	12c carmine	15	10
C103	AP29	14c dl grn	15	8
a		Imperf., pair	12.50	

Souvenir Sheets

AP30

Designs: 40c, Charles I of Spain. 60c, Juan Manuel Rodriguez. 1col, Arms of San Salvador. 2col, Flag of El Salvador.

Perf. 12, Imperf.

1946, Nov. 8 **Engr.** **Unwmk.**

C104	AP30	Sheet of four	1.75	1.75
a		40c brn	32	32
b		60c car	32	32
c		1col grn	32	32
d		2col ultra	32	32

4th cent. of San Salvador's city charter. The imperf. sheets are without gum.

Felipe Soto AP31

Alfredo Espino AP32

Wmk. 240

1947, Sept. 11 **Litho.** ***Perf. 12½***

C106	AP31	12c chocolate	15	10
C107	AP32	14c dk bl	12	8

Arce Type of Regular Issue

1948, Feb. 26 **Engr.** **Unwmk.**

C108	A163	12c green	12	10
C109	A163	14c rose car	18	10
C110	A163	1col violet	1.65	1.40

Cent. of the death of Manuel José Arce (1783-1847). "Father of Independence" and 1st pres. of the Federation of Central America.

Roosevelt Types of Regular Issue

Designs: 12c, Pres. Franklin D. Roosevelt. 14c, Pres. Roosevelt presenting awards for distinguished service. 20c, Roosevelt and Cordell Hull. 25c, Pres. and Mrs. Roosevelt. 1col, Mackenzie King, Roosevelt and Winston Churchill. 2col, Funeral of Pres. Roosevelt. 4col, Pres. and Mrs. Roosevelt.

1948, Apr. 12 **Engr.** ***Perf. 12½***

Various Frames; Center in Black.

C111	A165	12c green	25	20
C112	A164	14c olive	25	20
C113	A164	20c chocolate	25	25
C114	A164	25c carmine	25	25
C115	A164	1col vio brn	1.00	75
C116	A164	2col bl vio	1.75	1.25
		Nos. C111-C116 (6)	3.75	2.90

Souvenir Sheet.

Perf. 13½.

C117	A166	4col gray & brn	3.00	3.00

Nos. 599, 601 and 604 Overprinted in Carmine or Black **Aéreo**

1948, Sept. 7 ***Perf. 12½***

C118	A154	5c sl gray	8	5
C119	A154	10c bis brn	10	6
C120	A154	1col scar (Bk)	90	50

No. C99 Surcharged in Black

1949, July 23

C121	AP26	10(c) on 30c rose car	12	5

UPU Type of Regular Issue

1949, Oct. 9 **Engr.** ***Perf. 12½***

C122	A167	5c brown	10	8
C123	A167	10c black	15	5
C124	A167	1col purple	5.00	5.00

Flag and Arms of El Salvador — AP38

1949, Dec. 15 ***Perf. 10½***

Flag and Arms in Blue, Yellow and Green.

C125	AP38	5c ocher	10	5
C126	AP38	10c dk grn	15	5
a		Yellow omitted	20.00	
C127	AP38	15c violet	20	5
C128	AP38	1col rose	45	40
C129	AP38	5col red vio	3.75	3.75
		Nos. C125-C129 (5)	4.65	4.30

Issued to commemorate the 1st anniversary of the Revolution of Dec. 14, 1948.

Isabella I of Spain — AP39

Flag, Torch and Scroll — AP40

1951, Apr. 28 **Litho.** **Unwmk.**

Background in Ultramarine, Red and Yellow.

C130	AP39	10c green	25	8
C131	AP39	20c purple	25	15
a		Horiz. pair, imperf. between	25.00	
C132	AP39	40c rose car	25	15
C133	AP39	1col blk brn	90	50

Issued to commemorate the 500th anniversary of the birth of Queen Isabella I of Spain. Nos. C130-C133 exist imperforate.

1952, Feb. 14 **Photo.** ***Perf. 11½***

Flag in Blue.

C134	AP40	10c brt bl	8	5
C135	AP40	15c chocolate	12	8
C136	AP40	20c dp bl	12	6
C137	AP40	25c gray	12	8
C138	AP40	40c purple	25	20
C139	AP40	1col red org	50	38
C140	AP40	2col org brn	1.75	1.50
C141	AP40	5col vio bl	1.75	90
		Nos. C134-C141 (8)	4.69	3.25

Constitution of 1950.

Marti Type of Regular Issue Inscribed "Aereo"

1953, Feb. 27 **Litho.** ***Perf. 10½***

C142	A170	10c dk pur	12	10
C143	A170	20c dl brn	12	10
C144	A170	1col dl org	50	38

Issued to commemorate the centenary of the birth of José Marti, Cuban patriot.

No. C95 Surcharged "C 0.20" and Obliterations in Red.

1953, Mar. 20 ***Perf. 12½***

C145	AP24	20c on 25c dl vio	20	15

No. C95 Overprinted in Carmine **"IV Congreso Medico Social Panamericano 16/19 Abril, 1953"**

1953, June 19

C146	AP24	25c dl vio	30	18

See note after No. 634.

Bell Tower, La Merced Church — AP42

1953, Sept. 15 ***Perf. 11½***

C147	AP42	5c rose pink	6	6
C148	AP42	10c dp bl grn	6	6
C149	AP42	20c blue	15	12
C150	AP42	1col purple	50	38

Issued to commemorate the 132nd anniversary of the Act of Independence, September 15, 1821.

Fishing Boats — AP43

Gen. Manuel José Arce — AP44

Balboa Park — AP45

ODECA Officials and Flag AP46

Designs: No. C152, Census allegory. No. C155, National Palace. No. C157, Coast guard boat. No. C158, Lake Ilopango. No. C159, Coastal bridge. No. C160, Guayabo dam. No. C161, Housing development. No. C162, Modern highway. No. C163, and C165, Motherland and Liberty. No. C164, Izalco volcano.

Perf. 11½

1954, June 1 **Unwmk.** **Photo.**

C151	AP43	5c org brn & cr	15	5
C152	AP44	5c brt car	15	5
C153	AP44	10c gray bl	18	5
C154	AP45	10c pur & lt brn	18	5
C155	AP43	10c ol & bl gray	18	5
C156	AP46	10c bl grn, dk grn & bl	18	5
C157	AP43	10c rose car	22	6
C158	AP43	15c dk gray	28	10
C159	AP43	20c pur & gray	32	12
C160	AP46	25c bl grn & bl	32	14
C161	AP46	30c mag & sal	35	14
C162	AP45	40c brt org & brn	50	25
C163	AP46	80c red brn	1.00	90
C164	AP43	1col mag & sal	1.25	90
C165	AP46	2col orange	2.25	90
		Nos. C151-C165 (15)	7.51	3.81

Barrios Type of Regular Issue, 1955

Wmk. 269

1955, Dec. 20 **Engr.** ***Perf. 12½***

C166	A177	20c brown	12	10
C167	A177	30c dp red lil	18	15

Santa Ana Type of Regular Issue, 1956.

Perf. 13½

1956, June 20 **Unwmk.** **Litho.**

C168	A178	5c org brn	5	5
C169	A178	10c green	5	5
C170	A178	40c red lil	18	15
C171	A178	80c emerald	45	38
C172	A178	5col gray bl	2.50	1.75
		Nos. C168-C172 (5)	3.23	2.38

Chalatenango Type of Regular Issue, 1956.

1956, Sept. 14

C173	A179	10c brt rose	8	6
C174	A179	15c orange	12	8
C175	A179	20c lt ol grn	12	9
C176	A179	25c dl pur	25	18

C177 A179 50c org brn 40 28
C178 A179 1col brt vio bl 65 65
Nos. C173-C178 (6) 1.62 1.34

Nueva San Salvador Type of Regular Issue, 1957

Wmk. 269

1957, Jan. 3 Engr. *Perf. 12½*

C179 A180 10c pink 10 6
C180 A180 20c dl red 15 6
C181 A180 50c pale org red 25 22
C182 A180 1col lt grn 65 45
C183 A180 2col org red 1.50 90
Nos. C179-C183 (5) 2.65 1.69

Lemus' Visit Type of Regular Issue, 1959.

Perf. 11½

1959, Dec. 14 Unwmk. Photo.

Granite Paper

Design in Ultramarine, Dark Brown Light Brown and Red.

C184 A182 15c red 15 9
C185 A182 20c green 18 12
C186 A182 30c carmine 22 18

No. C169 Overprinted in Red: "ANO MUNDIAL DE LOS REFUGIADOS 1959-1960."

1960, Apr. 7 Litho. *Perf. 13½*

C187 A178 10c green 18 15

Issued to publicize World Refugee Year, July 1, 1959-June 30, 1960.

Type of Regular Issue, 1960 Poinsettia

Perf. 11½

1960, Dec. 17 Unwmk. Photo.

Granite Paper

Design in Slate Green, Red and Yellow

C188 A184 20c rose lil 20 12
C189 A184 30c gray 25 20
C190 A184 40c lt gray 25 20
C191 A184 50c sal pink 42 25

Miniature Sheet

Imperf

C192 A184 60c gold 50 25

No. C192 contains one stamp and is inscribed: "REPUBLICA DE EL SALVADOR, C.A." Size: 99x74mm.

See note after No. 718.

Nos. 672, 691 and C183 Overprinted: "III Exposición Industrial Centroamericana Diciembre de 1962" with "AEREO" Added on Nos. 672, 691.

1962, Dec. 21 *Perf. 11½, 12½*

C193 A174 1col brn org, dk brn & bl 75 75
C194 A180 1col dl red 38 32
C195 A180 2col org red 75 65

Issued to publicize the 3rd Central American Industrial Exposition.

Nos. C189, C194, C182 and C195 Surcharged

1963

C196 A184 10c on 30c multi 12 8
C197 A180 10c on 1col dl red 12 9
C198 A180 10c on 1col lt grn 85 9
C199 A180 10c on 2col org red 85 8

Surcharges include: "X" on No. C196; two dots and bar at bottom on No. C197. Heavy bar at bottom on No. C198. On No. C199, the four-line "Exposition" overprint is lower than on No. C195.

Turquoise-browed Motmot — AP49

Birds: 5c, King vulture (vert., like No. 741). 6c, Yellow-headed parrot (vert.). 10c, Spotted-breasted oriole. 30c, Greattailed grackle. 40c, Great curassow (vert.). 50c, Magpie-jay. 80c, Golden-fronted woodpecker (vert.).

1963 Unwmk. Photo. *Perf. 11½*

Birds in Natural Colors

C200 AP49 5c gray grn & blk 5 5
C201 AP49 6c tan & bl 6 6
C202 AP49 10c lt bl & blk 9 6
C203 AP49 20c gray & brn 18 9
C204 AP49 30c ol bis & blk 25 15
C205 AP49 40c pale & dk vio 38 20
C206 AP49 50c lt grn & blk 42 25
C207 AP49 80c vio bl & blk 75 40
Nos. C200-C207 (8) 2.18 1.26

Type of Regular Issue, 1964 (Eucharistic Congress)

1964-65 *Perf. 12x11½*

C208 A188 10c sl grn & bl 8 5
C209 A188 25c red & bl 15 12

Miniature Sheets

Imperf

C210 A188 80c bl & grn 50 50
a Marginal ovpt. (La Union) 65 65
b Marginal ovpt. (Usulutan) 65 65
c Marginal ovpt. (La Libertad) 65 65

See note after No. 746.

Issue dates: Nos. C208-C210, Apr. 16, 1964. Nos. C210a-C210b, June 22, 1965, 210c, Jan. 28, 1965.

Kennedy Type of Regular Issue

1964, Nov. 22 *Perf. 11½x12*

C211 A189 15c gray & blk 12 10
C212 A189 20c sage grn & blk 18 12
C213 A189 40c yel & blk 30 22

Miniature Sheet

Imperf

C214 A189 80c grnsh bl & blk 75 75

Flower Type of Regular Issue

Flowers: 10c, Rose. 15c, Platanillo. 25c, San Jose. 40c, Hibiscus. 45c, Veranera. 70c, Fire flower.

1965, Jan. 6 Photo. *Perf. 12x11½*

C215 A190 10c lt grn, ol & dp car 8 5
C216 A190 15c multi 10 8
C217 A190 25c bl, yel & grn 15 12
C218 A190 40c gray, car rose & grn 20 18
C219 A190 45c sl, lil & grn 30 20
C220 A190 70c multi 42 32
Nos. C215-C220 (6) 1.25 95

ICY Type of Regular Issue

Perf. 11½x12

1965, Apr. 27 Photo. Unwmk.

Design in Brown and Gold

C221 A191 15c lt bl 8 6
C222 A191 30c dl lil 15 10
C223 A191 50c ocher 25 22

Gavidia Type of Regular Issue

1965, Sept. 24 Photo. Unwmk.

Portraits in Natural Colors

C224 A192 10c blk & grn 12 8
C225 A192 20c blk & bis 20 12
C226 A192 1col blk & rose 90 50

No. C223 Overprinted in Green: "1865 / 12 de Octubre / 1965 / Dr. Manuel Enrique Araujo"

1965, Oct. 12 *Perf. 11½x12*

C227 A191 50c brn, ocher & gold 32 22

See note after No. 764.

Fair Type of Regular Issue, 1965

1965, Nov. 5 *Perf. 12x11½*

C228 A193 20c bl & multi 12 8
C229 A193 80c multi 50 42
C230 A193 5col multi 2.50 2.25

WHO Type of Regular Issue

1966, May 20 Photo. Unwmk.

C231 A194 50c multi 32 22

No. C209 Overprinted in Dark Green: "1816 1966 / 150 anos / Nacimiento / San Juan Bosco"

1966, Sept. 3 Photo. *Perf. 12x11½*

C232 A188 25c red & bl 25 18

150th anniv. of the birth of St. John Bosco (1815-88), Italian priest, founder of the Salesian Fathers and Daughters of Mary.

UNESCO Type of Regular Issue

1966, Nov. 4 Photo. *Perf. 12*

C233 A195 30c tan, blk & vio bl 25 12
C234 A195 2col emer, blk & vio bl 1.25 85

Fair Type of Regular Issue, 1966

1966, Nov. 27 Litho. *Perf. 12*

C235 A196 15c multi 12 8
C236 A196 20c multi 15 10
C237 A196 60c multi 38 25

No. C209 Overprinted: "IX-Congreso / Interamericano / de Educacion / Catolica / 4 Enero 1967"

1967, Jan. 4 Photo. *Perf. 12x11½*

C238 A188 25c red & bl 25 15

Issued to publicize the 9th Inter-American Congress for Catholic Education.

Cañas Type of Regular Issue

1967, Feb. 18 Litho. *Perf. 11½*

C239 A197 5c multi 8 5
C240 A197 45c lt bl & multi 42 25

Volcano Type of Regular Issue

1967, Apr. 14 Photo. *Perf. 13*

C241 A198 50c ol gray & brn 38 22

No. C231 Overprinted in Red: "VIII CONGRESO / CENTROAMERICANO DE / FARMACIA & B10QUIMICA / 5 di 11 Noviembre de 1967"

1967, Oct. 26 Photo. *Perf. 12x11½*

C242 A194 50c multi 32 22

Issued to publicize the 8th Central American Congress for Pharmacy and Biochemistry.

No. C217 Overprinted in Red: "I Juegos / Centroamericanos y del / Caribe de Basquetbol / 25 Nov. al 3 Dic. 1967"

1967, Nov. 15

C243 A190 25c bl, yel & grn 18 12

First Central American and Caribbean Basketball Games, Nov. 25-Dec. 3.

No. C222 Overprinted in Carmine: "1968 / AÑO INTERNACIONAL DE / LOS DERECHOS HUMANOS"

1968, Jan. 2 Photo. *Perf. 11½x12*

C244 A191 30c dl lil, brn & gold 30 18

International Human Rights Year 1968.

No. C231 Overprinted in Red: "1968 / XX ANIVERSARIO DE LA / ORGANIZACION MUNDIAL / DE LA SALUD"

1968, Apr. 7 *Perf. 12x11½*

C245 A194 50c multi 38 20

20th anniv. of WHO.

No. C229 Overprinted in Red: "1968 / Año / del Sistema / del Credito / Rural"

1968, May 6 Photo. *Perf. 12x11½*

C246 A193 80c multi 50 30

Rural credit system.

Masferrer Type of Regular Issue

1968, June 22 Litho. *Perf. 12x11½*

C247 A200 5c brn & multi 8 5
C248 A200 15c grn & multi 10 6

Scouts Hiking AP50

1968, July 26 Litho. *Perf. 12*

C249 AP50 10c multi 8 5

Issued to publicize the 7th Inter-American Boy Scout Conference, July-Aug., 1968.

Presidents' Meeting Type of Regular Issue

1968, Dec. 5 Litho. *Perf. 14½*

C250 A202 20c sal & multi 10 6
C251 A202 1col lt bl & multi 55 38

Butterfly Type of Regular Issue

Designs: Various butterflies.

1969 Litho. *Perf. 12*

C252 A203 20c multi 12 6
C253 A203 1col multi 50 35
C254 A203 2col multi 1.25 70
C255 A203 10col gray & multi 6.00 3.50

Red Cross, Crescent and Lion and Sun Emblems AP51

1969 Litho. *Perf. 11*

C256 AP51 30c yel & multi 18 10
C257 AP51 1col multi 65 35
C258 AP51 4col multi 2.50 1.40

Issued to commemorate the 50th anniversary of the League of Red Cross Societies.

No. C213 Overprinted in Green: "Alunizaje / Apolo-11 / 21 Julio / 1969"

1969, Sept. Photo. *Perf. 11½x12*

C259 A189 40c yel & blk 22 15

Issued to commemorate man's first landing on the moon, July 20, 1969. See note after U.S. No. C76.

The same overprint in red brown and pictures of the landing module and the astronauts on the moon were applied to the margin of No. C214.

Hospital Type of Regular Issue

Design: Benjamin Bloom Children's Hospital.

1969, Oct. 24 Litho. *Perf. 11½*

C260 A205 1col multi 65 35
C261 A205 2col multi 1.25 70
C262 A205 5col multi 3.25 1.65

ILO Type of Regular Issue

1969 Litho. *Perf. 13*

C263 A206 50c lt bl & multi 30 18

Tourist Type of Regular Issue

Views: 20c, Devil's Gate. 35c, Ichanmichen Spa. 60c, Aerial view of Acajutla Harbor.

1969, Dec. 19 Photo. *Perf. 12x11½*

C264 A207 20c blk & multi 12 6
C265 A207 35c blk & multi 20 10
C266 A207 60c blk & multi 38 20

Insect Type of Regular Issue, 1970

Insects: 2col, Bee. 3col, Elaterida. 4col, Praying mantis.

1970, Feb. 24 Litho. *Perf. 11½x11*

C267 A208 2col multi 1.25 70
C268 A208 3col multi 1.90 1.00
C269 A208 4col org & multi 2.50 1.40

Human Rights Type of Regular Issue

Design: 20c, 80c, Map and arms of Salvador and National Unity emblem similar to A209, but vertical.

1970, Apr. 14 Litho. *Perf. 14*

C270 A209 20c bl & multi 12 6
C271 A209 80c bl & multi 60 28

Army Type of Regular Issue

Designs: 20c, Fighter plane. 40c, Gun and crew. 50c, Patrol boat.

1970, May 7 *Perf. 12*

C272 A210 20c gray & multi 12 6
C273 A210 40c grn & multi 28 12
C274 A210 50c bl & multi 32 15

Brazilian Team, Jules Rimet Cup — AP52

Designs: Soccer teams and Jules Rimet Cup.

1970, May 25 Litho. *Perf. 12*
C275 AP52 1col *Belgium* 75 65
C276 AP52 1col *Brazil* 75 65
C277 AP52 1col *Bulgaria* 75 65
C278 AP52 1col *Czechoslovakia* 75 65
C279 AP52 1col *Germany (Fed. Rep.)* 75 65
C280 AP52 1col *Britain* 75 65
C281 AP52 1col *Israel* 75 65
C282 AP52 1col *Italy* 75 65
C283 AP52 1col *Mexico* 75 65
C284 AP52 1col *Morocco* 75 65
C285 AP52 1col *Peru* 75 65
C286 AP52 1col *Romania* 75 65
C287 AP52 1col *Russia* 75 65
C288 AP52 1col *Salvador* 75 65
C289 AP52 1col *Sweden* 75 65
C290 AP52 1col *Uruguay* 75 65
Nos. C275-C290 (16) 12.00 10.40

Issued to publicize the 9th World Soccer Championships for the Jules Rimet Cup, Mexico City, May 30-June 21, 1970.

Lottery Type of Regular Issue

1970, July 15 Litho. *Perf. 12*
C291 A211 80c multi 50 25

Education Year Type of Regular Issue

1970, Sept. 11 Litho. *Perf. 12*
C292 A212 20c pink & multi 12 6
C293 A212 2col buff & multi 1.25 65

Fair Type of Regular Issue

1970, Oct. 28 Litho. *Perf. 12*
C294 A213 20c multi 18 6
C295 A213 30c yel & multi 25 9

Music Type of Regular Issue

Design: 40c, Johann Sebastian Bach, harp, horn and music.

1971, Feb. 22 Litho. *Perf. 13½*
C296 A214 40c gray & multi 38 18

No. C247 Overprinted: "Año / del Centenario de la / Biblioteca Nacional / 1970"

1970, Nov. 25 *Perf. 12x11½*
C297 A200 5c brn & multi 5 5

Miss Tourism Type of Regular Issue

1971, Apr. 1 Litho. *Perf. 14*
C298 A215 20c lil & multi 12 8
C299 A215 60c gray & multi 45 18

Pietà Type of Regular Issue

1971, May 10
C300 A216 40c lt yel grn & vio brn 32 15

No. C270 Overprinted in Red Like No. 823

1971, July 6 Litho. *Perf. 14*
C301 A209 20c bl & multi 18 8

Fish Type of Regular Issue

Designs: 30c, Smalltooth sawfish. 1col, Atlantic sailfish.

1971, July 28
C302 A217 30c lil & multi 18 9
C303 A217 1col multi 65 30

Independence Type of Regular Issue

Designs: Various sections of Declaration of Independence of Central America.

1971 Litho. *Perf. 13½x13*
C304 A218 30c bl & blk 20 10
C305 A218 40c brn & blk 30 15
C306 A218 50c yel & blk 38 18
C307 A218 60c gray & blk 50 25
a Souvenir sheet of 8 1.75 1.65

No. C307a contains 8 stamps with simulated perforations similar to Nos. 826-829, C304-C307.

Church Type of Regular Issue

Designs: 15c, Metapan Church. 70c, Panchimalco Church.

1971, Aug. 21 Litho. *Perf. 13x13½*
C308 A219 15c ol & multi 12 5
C309 A219 70c multi 55 22

No. C274 Overprinted in Red

1951-12 Octubre-1971
XX Aniversario
MARINA NACIONAL

1971, Oct. 12 Litho. *Perf. 12*
C310 A210 50c bl & multi 38 15

National Navy, 20th anniversary.

No. C229 Overprinted: "V Feria / Internacional / 3-20 Noviembre / de 1972"

1972, Nov. 3 Photo. *Perf. 12x11½*
C311 A193 80c multi 90 30

5th Intl. Fair, El Salvador, Nov. 3-20.

No. C223 Overprinted in Red

1972 - XXX Aniversario
Creacion Instituto
Interamericano de
Ciencias Agricolas

1972, Nov. 30 Photo. *Perf. 11½x12*
C312 A191 50c ocher, brn & gold 42 20

30th anniversary of the Inter-American institute for Agricultural Sciences.

No. C296 Overprinted

III Festival
Internacional de
Música 9-25-
Febrero - 1973.

1973, Feb. 5 Litho. *Perf. 13½*
C313 A214 40c gray & multi 30 15

3rd International Music Festival, Feb. 9-29.

Lions Type of Regular Issue

Designs: 20c, 40c, Map of El Salvador and Lions International Emblem.

1973, Feb. 20 Litho. *Perf. 13*
C314 A220 20c gray & multi 15 6
C315 A220 40c multi 30 12

Olympic Type of Regular Issue

Designs: 20c, Javelin, women's. 80c, Discus, women's. 1col, Hammer throw. 2col, Shot put.

1973, May 21 Litho. *Perf. 13*
C316 A221 20c lt grn & multi 12 6
C317 A221 80c sal & multi 55 24
C318 A221 1col ultra & multi 65 30
C319 A221 2col multi 1.40 60

No. C241 Surcharged Like No. 841

1973, Dec. Photo. *Perf. 13*
C320 A198 25c on 50c multi 10 8

Souvenir Sheet
No. C307a Overprinted: "Centenario / Cuidad / Santiago de Maria / 1874 1974"

1974, Mar. 7 Litho. *Imperf.*
C321 A218 Sheet of 8 1.00

Centenary of the City Santiago de Maria. The overprint is so arranged that each line appears on a different pair of stamps. Size of sheet: 172x190mm.

No. C231 Surcharged in Red

25 cts.

1974, Apr. 22 Photo. *Perf. 12x11½*
C322 A194 25c on 50c multi 12 8

No. C229 Surcharged

10
CTS.

1974, Apr. 24
C323 A193 10c on 80c multi 8 5

Rehabilitation Type of 1974

1974, Apr. 30 Litho. *Perf. 13*
C324 A222 25c multi 10 8

Nos. C275-C290 Overprinted

ALEMANIA 1974

1974, June 4 Litho. *Perf. 12*
C325 AP52 1col *Belgium* 65 40
C326 AP52 1col *Brazil* 65 40
C327 AP52 1col *Bulgaria* 65 40
C328 AP52 1col *Czechoslovakia* 65 40
C329 AP52 1col *Germany* 65 40
C330 AP52 1col *Britain* 65 40
C331 AP52 1col *Israel* 65 40
C332 AP52 1col *Italy* 65 40
C333 AP52 1col *Mexico* 65 40
C334 AP52 1col *Morocco* 65 40
C335 AP52 1col *Peru* 65 40
C336 AP52 1col *Romania* 65 40
C337 AP52 1col *Russia* 65 40
C338 AP52 1col *Salvador* 65 40
C339 AP52 1col *Sweden* 65 40
C340 AP52 1col *Uruguay* 65 40
Nos. C325-C340 (16) 10.40 6.40

World Cup Soccer Championship, Munich, June 13-July 7.

INTERPOL Type of 1974

1974, Sept. 2 Litho. *Perf. 12½*
C341 A223 25c multi 10 8

FAO Type of 1974

1974, Sept. 2 Litho. *Perf. 12½*
C342 A224 25c bl, dk bl & gold 10 8

Coin Type of 1974

1974, Nov. 19 Litho. *Perf. 12½x13*

Coins: 20c, 1p sliver, 1892. 40c, 20c, silver, 1828. 50c, 20p gold, 1892. 60c, 20col gold, 1925.

C343 A225 20c multi 8 6
C344 A225 40c multi 16 12
C345 A225 50c multi 20 15
C346 A225 60c multi 24 18

Souvenir Sheet
No. C307a Overprinted: "X ASAMBLEA GENERAL DE LA CONFERENCIA / INTERAMERICANA DE SEGURIDAD SOCIAL Y XX / REUNION DEL COMITE PERMANENTE INTERAMERICANO / DE SEGURIDAD SOCIAL, 24 -- 30 NOVIEMBRE 1974"

1974, Nov. 18 Litho. *Imperf.*
C347 A218 Sheet of 8 1.75

Social Security Conference, El Salvador, Nov. 24-30. The overprint is so arranged that each line appears on a different pair of stamps. Size: 172x190mm.

Issues of 1965-69 Surcharged

₡0.10 a
₡0.10 b
₡0.25 c
₡0.25 d

1974-75
C348 A190(a) 10c on 45c #C219 8 5
C349 A190(a) 10c on 70c #C220 8 5
C350 A198(b) 10c on 50c #C241 5 5
C351 AP51(d) 25c on 1col #C257 15 10
C352 A195(c) 25c on 2col #C234 ('75) 32 18
C353 A203(d) 25c on 2col #C254 ('75) 15 10
C354 AP51(d) 25c on 4col #C258 15 10
C355 A205(d) 25c on 5col #C262 15 10
Nos. C348-C355 (8) 1.13 73

No. C353 has new value at left and 6 vertical bars. No. C355 has 7 vertical bars.

UPU Type of 1975

1975, Jan. 22 Litho. *Perf. 13*
C356 A226 25c bl & multi 10 8
C357 A226 30c bl & multi 12 9

Acajutla Harbor Type of 1975

1975, Feb. 17
C358 A227 15c bl & multi 6 5

Post Office Type of 1975

1975, Apr. 25 Litho. *Perf. 13*
C359 A228 25c bl & multi 10 8

Miss Universe Type of 1975

1975, June 25 *Perf. 12½*
C360 A229 25c multi 18 10
C361 A229 60c lil & multi 38 25

Women's Year Type and

IWY Emblem — AP53

1975, Sept. 4 Litho. *Perf. 12½*
C362 A230 15c bl & bl blk 6 5
C363 AP53 25c yel grn & blk 10 8

International Women's Year 1975.

Nurse Type of 1975

1975, Oct. 24 Litho. *Perf. 12½*
C364 A231 25c lt bl & multi 18 10

Printers' Congress Type of 1975

1975, Nov. 19 Litho. *Perf. 12½*
C365 A232 30c grn & multi 12 9

Dermatologists' Congress Type, 1975

1975, Nov. 28
C366 A233 20c bl & multi 8 6
C367 A233 30c red & multi 12 9

Caritas Type of 1975

1975, Dec. 18 Litho. *Perf. 13½*
C368 A234 20c bl & vio bl 8 6

UNICEF Emblem — AP54

1975, Dec. 18
C369 AP54 15c lt grn & sil 8 5
C370 AP54 20c dl rose & sil 10 8

UNICEF, 25th anniv. (in 1971).

Nos. C267-C269 Surcharged

25c.

1976, Jan. 14 *Perf. 11½x11*
C371 A208 25c on 2col multi 12 8
C372 A208 25c on 3col multi 12 8
C373 A208 25c on 4col multi 12 8

Caularthron Bilamellatum AP55

Designs: Orchids.

1976, Feb. 19 Litho. *Perf. 12½*
C374 AP55 25c *shown* 15 8
C375 AP55 25c *Oncidium oliganthum* 15 8

C376 AP55 25c *Epidendrum radicans* 15 8
C377 AP55 25c *Epidendrum vitellinum* 15 8
C378 AP55 25c *Cyrtopodium punctatum* 15 8
C379 AP55 25c *Pleurothallis schiedei* 15 8
C380 AP55 25c *Lycaste cruenta* 15 8
C381 AP55 25c *Spiranthes speciosa* 15 8
Nos. C374-C381 (8) 1.20 64

CIAT Type of 1976

1976, May 18 Litho. *Perf. 12½*
C382 A235 50c org & multi 20 15

Bicentennial Types of 1976

1976, June 30 Litho. *Perf. 12½*
C383 A236 25c multi 10 8
C384 A237 5col multi 2.00 1.50

Reptile Type of 1976

Reptiles: 15c, Green fence lizard. 25c, Basilisk. 60c, Star lizard.

1976, Sept. 23 Litho. *Perf. 12½*
C385 A238 15c multi 6 5
C386 A238 25c multi 10 8
C387 A238 60c multi 24 18

Archaeology Type of 1976

Pre-Columbian Art: 25c, Brazier with pre-classical head, El Trapiche. 50c, Kettle with pre-classical head, Atiquizaya. 70c, Classical whistling vase, Tazumal.

1976, Oct. 11 Litho. *Perf. 12½*
C388 A239 25c multi 10 7
C389 A239 50c multi 20 14
C390 A239 70c multi 24 22

Fair Type of 1976

1976, Oct. 25 Litho. *Perf. 12½*
C391 A240 25c multi 10 8
C392 A240 70c yel & multi 28 22

Christmas Type of 1976

1976, Dec. 16 Litho. *Perf. 11*
C393 A241 25c bl & multi 10 8
C394 A241 50c multi 20 15
C395 A241 60c multi 24 18
C396 A241 75c red & multi 30 22

Rotary Type of 1977

1977, June 20 Litho. *Perf. 11*
C397 A242 25c multi 18 10
C398 A242 1col multi 65 38

Industrial Type of 1977

Designs: 25c, Radar station, Izalco (vert.). 50c, Central sugar refinery, Jiboa. 75c, Cerron Grande hydroelectric station.

1977, June 29 *Perf. 12½*
C399 A243 25c multi 10 8
C400 A243 50c multi 20 15
C401 A243 75c multi 30 22

Nos. C399-C401 have colorless overprint in multiple rows: GOBIERNO DEL SALVADOR.

Nos. C271 and C239 Surcharged with New Value and Bar

1977 *Perf. 14, 11½*
C402 A209 25c on 80c multi 22 12
C403 A197 30c on 5c multi 15 10
C404 A197 40c on 5c multi 18 12
C405 A197 50c on 5c multi 20 15

Broadcasting Type of 1977

1977, Sept. 14 Litho. *Perf. 14*
C406 A244 20c multi 15 8
C407 A244 25c multi 20 10

Symbolic Chessboard and Emblem — AP56

1977, Oct. 20 Litho. *Perf. 11*
C408 AP56 25c multi 10 8
C409 AP56 50c multi 20 16

El Salvador's victory in International Chess Olympiad, Tripoli, Libya, Oct. 24-Nov. 15, 1976.

Soccer — AP57

Boxing AP58

1977, Nov. 16 Litho. *Perf. 16*
C410 AP57 10c *shown* 5 5
C411 AP57 10c *Basketball* 5 5
C412 AP57 15c *Javelin* 6 5
C413 AP57 15c *Weight lifting* 6 5
C414 AP57 20c *Volleyball* 8 6
C415 AP58 20c *shown* 8 6
C416 AP57 25c *Baseball* 10 8
C417 AP58 25c *Softball* 10 8
C418 AP58 30c *Swimming* 12 9
C419 AP58 30c *Fencing* 12 9
C420 AP58 40c *Bicycling* 16 12
C421 AP58 50c *Rifle shooting* 20 15
C422 AP58 50c *Women's tennis* 20 15
C423 AP57 60c *Judo* 24 18
C424 AP58 75c *Wrestling* 30 22
C425 AP58 1col *Equestrian hurdles* 40 30
C426 AP58 1col *Woman gymnast* 40 30
C427 AP58 2col *Table tennis* 80 60
Nos. C410-C427 (18) 3.52 2.68

Imperf.
Size: 100x119mm
C428 AP57 5col *Games' poster* 2.00

2nd Central American Olympic Games, San Salvador, Nov. 25-Dec. 4.

No. C390 Overprinted in Red: "CENTENARIO / CIUDAD DE / CHALCHUAPA / 1878-1978"

1978, Feb. 13 Litho. *Perf. 12½*
C429 A239 70c multi 24 22

Centenary of Chalchuapa.

Map of South America, Argentina '78 Emblem AP59

1978, Aug. 15 Litho. *Perf. 11*
C430 AP59 25c multi 10 8
C431 AP59 60c multi 24 18
C432 AP59 5col multi 2.00 1.50

11th World Cup Soccer Championship, Argentina, June 1-25.

Musical Instrument Type of 1978

Designs: 25c, Drum (vert.). 50c, Hollow rattles. 80c, Xylophone.

1978, Aug. 29 *Perf. 12½*
C433 A245 25c multi 10 8
C434 A245 50c multi 20 15
C435 A245 80c multi 32 24

Engineering Type of 1978

1978, Sept. 12 Litho. *Perf. 13½*
C436 A246 25c multi 10 8

Izalco Station Type of 1978

1978, Sept. 14 *Perf. 12½*
C437 A247 75c multi 30 22

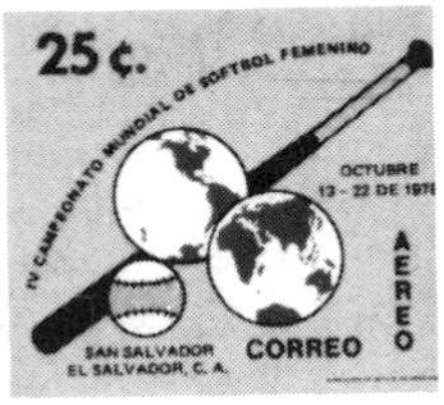

Softball, Bat and Globes AP60

1978, Oct. 17 Litho. *Perf. 12½*
C438 AP60 25c pink & multi 10 8
C439 AP60 1col yel & multi 40 30

4th World Softball Championship for Women, San Salvador, Oct. 13-22.

Fair Type, 1978

1978, Oct. 30 Litho. *Perf. 12½*
C440 A248 15c multi 6 5
C441 A248 25c multi 10 8

Red Cross Type, 1978

1978, Oct. 30 Litho. *Perf. 11*
C442 A249 25c multi 10 8

Cotton Conference Type, 1978

1978, Nov. 22 *Perf. 12½*
C443 A250 40c multi 16 12

Christmas Type, 1978

1978, Dec. 5 Litho. *Perf. 12½*
C444 A251 25c multi 10 8
C445 A251 1col multi 40 30

Athenaeum Type 1978

1978, Dec. 20 Litho. *Perf. 14*
C446 A252 25c multi 10 8

UPU Type of 1979

1979, Apr. 2 Litho. *Perf. 14*
C447 A253 75c multi 30 22

Health Organization Type of 1979

1979, Apr. 7 *Perf. 14x14½*
C448 A254 25c multi 10 8

Social Security Type of 1979

1979, May 25 Litho. *Perf. 12½*
C449 A255 25c multi 10 8
C450 A255 1col multi 40 30

Games Emblem AP61

1979, July 12 Litho. *Perf. 14½x14*
C451 AP61 25c multi 10 8
C452 AP61 40c multi 16 12
C453 AP61 70c multi 28 20

8th Pan American Games, Puerto Rico, July 1-15.

Pope John Paul II Type of 1979

Design: 60c, 5col, Pope John Paul II and pyramid (horiz.).

1979, July 12
C454 A256 60c multi 24 18
C455 A256 5col multi 2.00 1.50

"25," Family and Map of Salvador — AP62

1979, May 14 Litho. *Perf. 14x14½*
C456 AP62 25c blk & bl 10 8
C457 AP62 60c blk & lil rose 24 18

Social Security, 25th anniversary.

Pre-Historic Animal Type, 1979

1979, Sept. 7 Litho. *Perf. 14*
C458 A257 15c *Mammoth* 6 5
C459 A257 25c *Giant anteater (vert.)* 10 8
C460 A257 2 col *Hyenas* 80 60

National Anthem Type, 1979

1979, Sept. 14 *Perf. 14½x14*
C461 A258 40c *Jose Aberiz, score* 16 12

COPIMERA Type, 1979

1979, Oct. 19 Litho. *Perf. 14½x14*
C462 A259 50c multi 20 15

Circle Dance, IYC Emblem AP63

Children's Village and IYC Emblems AP64

Perf. 14½x14, 14x14½
1979, Oct. 29
C463 AP63 25c multi 10 8
C464 AP64 30c vio & blk 12 9

International Year of the Child.

Biochemistry Type of 1979

1979, Nov. 1 Litho. *Perf. 14½x14*
C465 A262 25c multi 10 8

Coffee Type of 1979

50c, Picking coffee. 75, Drying coffee beans. 1col, Coffee export.

Perf. 14x14½, 14½x14
1979, Dec. 18
C466 A263 50c multi 20 15
C467 A263 75c multi 30 22
C468 A263 1 col multi 40 30

Hoof and Mouth Disease Type of 1980

1980, June 3 Litho. *Perf. 14½x14*
C469 A265 60c multi 24 18

Shell Type of 1980

1980, Aug. 12 *Perf. 14x14½*
C470 A266 15c *Hexaplex regius* 6 5
C471 A266 25c *Polinices helicoides* 10 8
C472 A266 75c *Jenneria pustulata* 30 22
C473 A266 1 col *Pitar lupanaria* 40 30

Birds Type

1980, Sept. 10 Litho. *Perf. 14x14½*
C474 A267 25c Aulacorhynchus prasinus 10 8
C475 A267 50c Strix varia fulvescens 20 15
C476 A267 75c Myadestes unicolor 30 22

Snake Type of 1980

1980, Nov. 12 Litho. *Perf. 14x14½*
C477 A268 25c Rattlesnake 10 8
C478 A268 50c Coral snake 20 15

Auditors Type

1980, Nov. 26 Litho. *Perf. 14*
C479 A269 50c multi 20 15
C480 A269 75c multi 30 22

Christmas Type

1980, Dec. 5 Litho. *Perf. 14*
C481 A270 25c multi 10 8
C482 A270 60c multi 24 18

Intl. Women's Decade, 1976-85 — AP65

1981, Jan. 30 *Perf. 14½x14*
C483 AP65 25c org & blk 10 8
C484 AP65 1 col ol grn & blk 40 30

Protected Animals AP66

1981, Mar. 20 Litho. *Perf. 14x14½*
C485 AP66 25c Ateles geoffroyi 10 8
C486 AP66 40c Lepisosteus tropicus 16 12
C487 AP66 50c Iguana iguana 20 15
C488 AP66 60c Eretmochelys imbricata 24 18
C489 AP66 75c Spizaetus ornatus 30 22
Nos. C485-C489 (5) 1.00 75

Heinrich von Stephan, 150th Birth Anniv. — AP67

1981, May 18 Litho. *Perf. 14½x14*
C490 AP67 15c multi 6 5
C491 AP67 2 col multi 80 60

Nos. C435, C453 Surcharged
Perf. 12½, 14½x14
1981, May 18 **Litho.**
C492 AP59 50c on 80c, #C435 20 15
C493 AP61 1 col on 70c, #C453 40 30

Dental Associations Type
1981, June 18 Litho. *Perf. 14*
C494 A271 5 col bl & blk 2.00 1.50

IYD Type of 1981
1981, Aug. 14 Litho. *Perf. 14x14½*
C495 A272 25c like #936 10 8
C496 A272 50c Emblem 20 15
C497 A272 75c like #936 30 22
C498 A272 1 col like # C496 40 30

Quinonez Type
1981, Aug. 28 Litho. *Perf. 14x14½*
C499 A273 50c multi 20 15

World Food Day Type
1981, Sept. 16 Litho. *Perf. 14x14½*
C500 A274 25c multi 10 8

Land Registry Office, 100th Anniv. — AP68

1981, Oct. 30 Litho. *Perf. 14x14½*
C501 AP68 1 col multi 40 30

TACA Airlines, 50th Anniv. AP69

1981, Nov. 10 Litho. *Perf. 14*
C502 AP69 15c multi 6 5
C503 AP69 25c multi 10 8
C504 AP69 75c multi 30 22

World Cup Preliminaries Type
1981, Nov. 27 Litho. *Perf. 14x14½*
C505 A275 25c Like No. 939 10 8
C506 A275 75c Like No. 940 30 22

Lyceum Type
1981, Dec. 17 Litho. *Perf. 14*
C507 A276 25c multi 10 8

Sculptures Type
1982, Jan. 22 Litho. *Perf. 14*
C508 A277 25c Palm leaf with effigy 10 8
C509 A277 30c Jaguar mask 12 9
C510 A277 80c Mayan flint carving 32 24

Scouting Year Type of 1982
1982, Mar. 17 Litho. *Perf. 14½x14*
C511 A278 25c Baden-Powell 10 8
C512 A278 50c Girl Scout, emblem 20 15

TB Bacillus Centenary — AP70

1982, Mar. 24 *Perf. 14*
C513 AP70 50c multi 20 15

Armed Forces Type of 1982
1982, May 7 Litho. *Perf. 14x13½*
C514 A279 25c multi 10 8

Symbolic Design — AP71

1982, May 14 *Perf. 14*
C515 AP71 75c multi 30 22

25th anniv. of Latin-American Tourist Org. Confederation (COTAL).

14th World Telecommunications Day — AP72

1982, May 17 *Perf. 14x14½*
C516 AP72 15c multi 6 5
C517 AP72 2col multi 80 65

World Cup Type of 1982
1982, July 14
C518 A280 25c Team, emblem 10 8
C519 A280 60c Map, cup 25 18

Size: 67x47mm
Perf. 11½
1982, July 1
C520 A280 2col Team, emblem, diff. 80 65

1982 World Cup — AP73

Flags or Arms of Participating Countries; C521a, C522a, Italy. C521b, C522c, Germany. C521c, C522e, Argentina. C521d, C522m, England. C521e, C522o, Spain. C521f, C522q, Brazil. C521g, C522b, Poland. C521h, C522d, Algeria. C521i, C522f, Belgium. C521j, C522n, France. C521k, C522p, Honduras. C521l, C522r, Russia. C521m, C522g, Peru. C521n, C522i, Chile. C521o, C522k, Hungary. C521p, C522s, Czechoslovakia. C521q, C522u, Jugoslavia. C521r, C522w, Scotland. C521s, C522h, Cameroun. C521t, C522j, Austria. C521u, C522l, Salvador. C521v, C522t, Kuwait. C521w, C522v, Ireland. C521x, C522x, New Zealand.

1982, Aug. 26
C521 Sheet of 24 1.50
a.-x AP73 15c Flags 6 5
C522 Sheet of 24 2.50
a.-x AP73 25c Arms 10 8

Salvador Team, Cup, Flags — AP74

1982, Aug. 26 Litho. *Perf. 11½*
C523 AP74 5col multi 2.00 1.50

International Fair Type
1982, Oct. 14 Litho. *Perf. 14*
C524 A281 15c multi 6 5

World Food Day — AP75

1982, Oct. 21 Litho. *Perf. 14*
C525 AP75 25c multi 10 8

St. Francis of Assisi, 800th Birth Anniv. AP76

Natl. Labor Campaign AP77

1982, Nov. 10 Litho. *Perf. 14*
C526 AP76 1col multi 40 30

1982, Nov. 30 Litho. *Perf. 14x14½*
C527 AP77 50c multi 20 15

Christmas Type
1982, Dec. 14 Litho. *Perf. 14*
C528 A282 25c multi, horiz. 10 8

Salvadoran Paintings AP78

Designs: No. C529, The Pottery of Paleca, by Miguel Ortiz Villacorta. No. C530, The Rural School, by Luis Caceres Madrid. No. C531, To the Wash, by Julia Diaz. No. C532, "La Pancha" by Jose Mejia Vides. No. C533, Boats Near The Beach, by Raul Elas Reyes. No. C534, The Muleteers, by Canjura.

Perf. 14x13½, 13½x14
1983, Oct. 18 **Litho.**
C529 AP78 25c multi 10 8
C530 AP78 25c multi 10 8
C531 AP78 75c multi, vert. 30 22
C532 AP78 75c multi, vert. 30 22
C533 AP78 1col multi, vert. 40 30
C534 AP78 1col multi, vert. 40 30
Nos. C529-C534 (6) 1.60 1.20

Stamps of the same denomination are se-tenant.

Fishing Industry — AP79

1983, Dec. 20 Litho. *Perf. 14½x14*
C535 AP79 25c Fisherman 10 8
C536 AP79 75c Feeding fish 30 22

No. 999 Surcharged

¢1.00
aereo

1985, Apr. 10 Litho. *Perf. 14*
C536A A297 1col on 10c multi 40 30

Natl. Constitution, Cent. — AP80

1986, Aug. 29 Litho. *Perf. 14*
C537 AP80 1col multi 48 35

Hugo Lindo (1917-1985), Writer — AP81

1986, Nov. 10 Litho. *Perf. 14½x14*
C538 AP81 1col multi 48 35

Central American Economic Integration Bank, 25th Anniv. AP82

1986, Nov. 20
C539 AP82 1.50col multi 70 52

12th Intl. Fair, Feb. 14-Mar. 1
AP83

1987, Jan. 20 Litho. *Perf. 14½x14*

C540	AP83	70c multi	32	24

Intl. Year of Shelter for the Homeless
AP84

Perf. 14x14½, 14½x14

1987, July 15 Litho.

C541	AP84	70c shown	32	24
C542	AP84	1col Emblem, vert.	45	35

Miniature Sheet

Discovery of America, 500th Anniv. (in 1992)
AP85

15th cent. map of the Americas (details) and: a. Ferdinand. b. Isabella. c. Caribbean. d. Ships, coat of arms. e. Base of flagstaff. f. Ships, g. Pre-Columbian statue. h. Compass. i. Anniv. emblem. j. Columbus rose.

1987, Dec. 21 Litho. *Perf. 14*

C543		Sheet of 10	4.50	3.50
a.-j.	AP85	1col any single	45	35

No. 1075 Surcharged

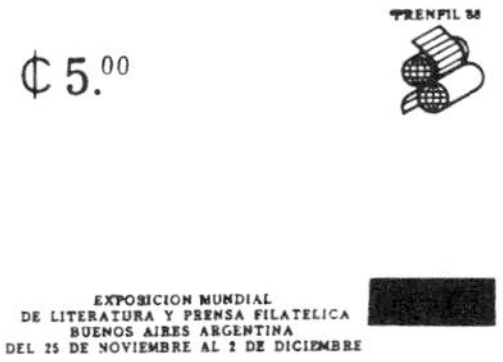

1988, Oct. 28 Litho. *Perf. 14x14½*

C544	A316	5col on 90c multi	2.35	1.75

PRENFIL '88, Nov. 25-Dec. 2, Buenos Aire.

Organization of American States 18th General Assembly, Nov. 14-19
AP86

1988, Nov. 19

C545	AP86	70c multi	38	28

REGISTRATION STAMPS

Gen. Rafael Antonio Gutierrez — R1

Wmk. Liberty Cap. (117)

1897 Engr. *Perf. 12*

F1	R1	10c dk bl	*125.00*	
F2	R1	10c brn lake	15	

Unwmk.

F3	R1	10c dk bl	20	
F4	R1	10c brn lake	15	

Nos. F1 and F3 were probably not placed in use without the overprint "FRANQUEO OFICIAL" (Nos. O127-O128).

The reprints are on thick unwatermarked paper. Value 8c each.

ACKNOWLEDGMENT OF RECEIPT STAMPS

AR1

Wmk. Liberty Cap. (117)

1897 Engr. *Perf. 12*

H1	AR1	5c dk grn	8	

Unwmk.

H2	AR1	5c dk grn	10	

No. H2 has been reprinted on thick paper. Value 8c.

POSTAGE DUE STAMPS

D1

1895 Unwmk. Engr. *Perf. 12*

J1	D1	1c ol grn	10	10
J2	D1	2c ol grn	10	10
J3	D1	3c ol grn	10	10
J4	D1	5c ol grn	10	10
J5	D1	10c ol grn	10	10
J6	D1	15c ol grn	10	12
J7	D1	25c ol grn	10	18
J8	D1	50c ol grn	15	25
		Nos. J1-J8 (8)	85	1.05

1896 Wmk. d. Liberty Cap. (117)

J9	D1	1c red	10	10
J10	D1	2c red	10	10
J11	D1	3c red	10	12
J12	D1	5c red	12	12
J13	D1	10c red	12	12
J14	D1	15c red	15	15
J15	D1	25c red	10	15
J16	D1	50c red	18	18
		Nos. J9-J16 (8)	97	1.04

Unwmk.

J17	D1	1c red	10	10
J18	D1	2c red	10	10
J19	D1	3c red	10	10
J20	D1	5c red	10	10
J21	D1	10c red	10	10
J22	D1	15c red	10	15
J23	D1	25c red	10	15
J24	D1	50c red	10	18
		Nos. J17-J24 (8)	80	98

Nos. J17 to J24 exist imperforate.

1897

J25	D1	1c dp bl	10	10
J26	D1	2c dp bl	10	10
J27	D1	3c dp bl	10	10
J28	D1	5c dp bl	10	10
J29	D1	10c dp bl	10	12
J30	D1	15c dp bl	10	12
J31	D1	25c dp bl	10	15
J32	D1	50c dp bl	10	20
		Nos. J25-J32 (8)	80	99

1898

J33	D1	1c violet	10	
J34	D1	2c violet	10	
J35	D1	3c violet	10	
J36	D1	5c violet	10	
J37	D1	10c violet	18	
J38	D1	15c violet	10	
J39	D1	25c violet	10	
J40	D1	50c violet	20	
		Nos. J33-J40 (8)	98	

Reprints of Nos. J1 to J40 are on thick paper, often in the wrong shades and usually with the impression somewhat blurred. They exist on both watermarked and unwatermarked paper. Value 5c each.

Wmk. Liberty Cap Sideways. (117)

1899

J41	D1	1c orange	10	
J42	D1	2c orange	10	
J43	D1	3c orange	10	
J44	D1	5c orange	10	
J45	D1	10c orange	10	
J46	D1	15c orange	10	
J47	D1	25c orange	10	
J48	D1	50c orange	10	
		Nos. J41-J48 (8)	80	

Unwmk.

Thick Porous Paper.

J49	D1	1c orange	10	
J50	D1	2c orange	10	
J51	D1	3c orange	10	
J52	D1	5c orange	10	
J53	D1	10c orange	10	
J54	D1	15c orange	10	
J55	D1	25c orange	10	
J56	D1	50c orange	10	
		Nos. J49-J56 (8)	80	

Nos. J41-J56 were probably not put in use without the wheel overprint.

Nos. J49-J56 Overprinted in Black

1900

J57	D1	1c orange	38	
J58	D1	2c orange	38	
J59	D1	3c orange	38	
J60	D1	5c orange	50	
J61	D1	10c orange	75	
J62	D1	15c orange	75	
J63	D1	25c orange	90	
J64	D1	50c orange	1.10	
		Nos. J57-J64 (8)	5.14	

See note after No. 198A.

Morazán Monument — D2

Wmk. S. (173)

1903 Engr. *Perf. 14, 14½.*

J65	D2	1c yel grn	1.25	75
J66	D2	2c carmine	2.00	1.25
J67	D2	3c orange	2.00	1.25
J68	D2	5c dk bl	2.00	1.25
J69	D2	10c dl vio	2.00	1.25
J70	D2	25c bl grn	2.00	1.25
		Nos. J65-J70 (6)	11.25	7.00

Nos. 355, 356, 358 and 360 Overprinted

DEFICIENCIA
DE FRANQUEO

1908 Unwmk. *Perf. 11½.*

J71	A66	1c grn & blk	38	30
J72	A66	2c red & blk	30	25
J73	A66	5c bl & blk	75	50
J74	A66	10c vio & blk	1.10	1.00

Same Overprint on No. O275

J75	O3	3c yel & blk	75	65
		Nos. J71-J75 (5)	3.28	2.70

Nos. 355-358, 360 Overprinted

Deficiencia de
franqueo

J76	A66	1c grn & blk	25	25
J77	A66	2c red & blk	30	30
J78	A66	3c yel & blk	35	35
J79	A66	5c bl & blk	50	50
J80	A66	10c vio & blk	1.00	1.00
		Nos. J76-J80 (5)	2.40	2.40

It is now believed that stamps of type A66, on paper with Honeycomb watermark, do not exist with genuine overprints of the types used for Nos. J71 to J80.

Pres. Fernando Figueroa — D3

Wmk. Honeycomb. (172)

1910 Engr.

J81	D3	1c sep & blk	9	9
J82	D3	2c dk grn & blk	9	9
J83	D3	3c org & blk	9	9
J84	D3	4c scar & blk	9	9
J85	D3	5c pur & blk	9	9
J86	D3	12c dp bl & blk	9	9
J87	D3	24c brn red & blk	9	9
		Nos. J81-J87 (7)	63	63

OFFICIAL STAMPS

Regular Issues Overprinted

FRANQUEO
OFICIAL

1896 Unwmk. *Perf. 12*

O1	A45	1c blue	10	
O2	A45	2c dk brn	10	
a.		Double overprint		
O3	A45	3c bl grn	30	
O4	A45	5c brn ol	10	
O5	A45	10c yellow	10	
O6	A45	12c dk bl	10	
O7	A45	15c bl vio	10	
O8	A45	20c magenta	30	
O9	A45	24c vermilion	10	
O10	A45	30c orange	30	
O11	A45	50c blk brn	18	
O12	A45	1p rose lake	10	
		Nos. O1-O12 (12)	1.88	

The 1c has been reprinted on thick unwatermarked paper. Value 10c.

Wmk. Liberty Cap. (117)

O13	A46	1c emerald	10	
O14	A47	2c lake	10	
O15	A48	3c yel brn	10	
a.		Inverted overprint	65	
O16	A49	5c dp bl	12	
O17	A50	10c brown	10	
a.		Inverted overprint	1.25	
O18	A51	12c slate	15	
O19	A52	15c bl grn	15	
O20	A53	20c car rose	15	
a.		Inverted overprint		
O21	A54	24c violet	15	
O22	A55	30c dp grn	10	
O23	A56	50c orange	15	
O24	A57	100c dk bl	20	
		Nos. O13-O24 (12)	1.57	

Unwmk.

O25	A46	1c emerald	10	
a.		Double overprint		
O26	A47	2c lake	10	
O27	A48	3c yel brn	10	
O28	A49	5c dp bl	85	
O29	A50	10c brown	12	
a.		Inverted overprint		
O30	A51	12c slate	15	
O31	A52	15c bl grn	22	
O32	A53	20c car rose	15	
a.		Inverted overprint		
O33	A54	24c violet	42	
O34	A55	30c dp grn	12	

O35	A56	50c orange	85	
O36	A57	100c dk bl	1.10	
		Nos. O25-O36 (12)	4.28	

The 3, 5, 10, 12, 15, 20, 24, 30 and 100c have been reprinted on thick unwatermarked paper and the 15c, 50c and 100c on thick watermarked paper. Value 10c each.

Nos. 134-145 Handstamped in Black or Violet

1896

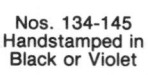

O37	A45	1c blue	7.50	
O38	A45	2c dk brn	7.50	
O39	A45	3c bl grn	7.50	
O40	A45	5c brn ol	7.50	
O41	A45	10c yellow	8.75	
O42	A45	12c dk bl	11.50	
O43	A45	15c bl vio	11.50	
O44	A45	20c magenta	11.50	
O45	A45	24c vermilion	11.50	
O46	A45	30c orange	11.50	
O47	A45	50c blk brn	15.00	
O48	A45	1p rose lake	15.00	
		Nos. O37-O48 (12)	126.25	

Reprints of the 1c and 2c on thick paper exist with this handstamp. Value 10c each.

Forged overprints exist of Nos. O37-O78, O103-O126 and of the higher valued stamps of O141-O214.

Same Overprint Handstamped on Nos. 146-157F, 157I-157O, 158D in Black or Violet

1896 **Wmk. 117**

O49	A46	1c emerald	6.25	
O50	A47	2c lake	6.25	
O51	A48	3c yel brn	6.25	
O52	A49	5c dp bl	6.25	
O53	A50	10c brown	6.25	
O54	A51	12c slate	10.00	
O55	A52	15c bl grn	11.50	
O56	A53	20c car rose	11.50	
O57	A54	24c violet	11.50	
O58	A55	30c dp grn	11.50	
O59	A56	50c orange	11.50	
O60	A57	100c dk bl	11.50	
		Nos. O49-O60 (12)	110.25	

Unwmk.

O61	A46	1c emerald	6.25	
O62	A47	2c lake	6.25	
O63	A48	3c yel brn	6.25	
O64	A49	5c dp bl	6.25	
O65	A50	10c brown	8.75	
O66	A52	15c bl grn	11.50	
O67	A58	15c on 24c vio	11.50	
O68	A53	20c car rose	11.50	
O69	A54	24c violet	11.50	
O70	A55	30c dp grn	11.50	
O71	A56	50c orange	12.50	
O72	A57	100c dk bl	12.50	
		Nos. O61-O72 (12)	116.25	

Nos. 175-176 Overprinted in Black

1897

O73	A59	1c bl, gold, rose & grn	20	
O74	A59	5c rose, gold, bl & grn	20	

These stamps were probably not officially issued.

Nos. 175-176 Handstamped in Black or Violet

1900

O75	A59	1c bl, gold, rose & grn	17.50	
O76	A59	5c rose, gold, bl & grn	17.50	

Nos. 159-170L Overprinted in Black

1897 **Wmk. 117**

O79	A46	1c scarlet	10	
O80	A47	2c yel grn	1.25	
O81	A48	3c bis brn	38	
O82	A49	5c orange	10	10
O83	A50	10c bl grn	12	
O84	A51	12c blue	18	
O85	A52	15c black	18	50
O86	A53	20c slate	12	
O87	A54	24c yellow	18	
a.		Inverted overprint		
O88	A55	30c rose	38	
O89	A56	50c violet	1.25	1.00
O90	A57	100c brn lake	1.75	
		Nos. O79-O90 (12)	5.99	

Unwmk.

O91	A46	1c scarlet	5	
O92	A47	2c yel grn	30	
O93	A48	3c bis brn	12	
O94	A49	5c orange	12	18
O95	A50	10c bl grn	65	
O96	A51	12c blue	65	
O97	A52	15c black	75	
O98	A53	20c slate	12	38
O99	A54	24c yellow	12	38
O100	A55	30c rose	12	38
O101	A56	50c violet	65	
O102	A57	100c brn lake	38	1.00
		Nos. O91-O102 (12)	4.03	

All values have been reprinted on thick paper without watermark and the 1c, 12c, 15c and 100c on thick paper with watermark. Value 10c each.

Nos. 159-170L Handstamped in Violet or Black

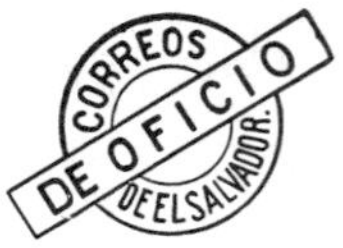

1897 **Wmk. 117**

O103	A46	1c scarlet	7.50	
O104	A47	2c yel grn	7.50	
O105	A48	3c bis brn	7.50	
O106	A49	5c orange	7.50	
O107	A50	10c bl grn	8.75	
O108	A51	12c blue		
O109	A52	15c black		
O110	A53	20c slate	15.00	
O111	A54	24c yellow	17.50	
O112	A55	30c rose		
O113	A56	50c violet		
O114	A57	100c brn lake		

Unwmk.

O115	A46	1c scarlet	7.50	
O116	A47	2c yel grn	7.50	
O117	A48	3c bis brn	7.50	
O118	A49	5c orange	7.50	
O119	A50	10c bl grn	7.50	
O120	A51	12c blue		
O121	A52	15c black		
O122	A53	20c slate		
O123	A54	24c yellow		
O124	A55	30c rose	15.00	
O125	A56	50c violet		
O126	A57	100c brn lake	17.50	

Reprints of the 1 and 15c on thick watermarked paper and the 12, 30, 50 and 100c on thick unwatermarked paper are known with this overprint. Value 10c each.

Registration Stamps Overprinted in Red

Wmk. Liberty Cap. (117)

O127	R1	10c dk bl	10	

Unwmk.

O128	R1	10c dk bl	15	

The reprints are on thick paper. Value 10c.
Originals of the 10c brown lake Registration Stamp and the 5c Acknowledgment of Receipt stamp are believed not to have been issued with the "FRANQUEO OFICIAL" overprint. They are believed to exist only as reprints.

Nos. 177-188 Overprinted

1898 **Wmk. 117**

O129	A60	1c org ver	10	
O130	A60	2c rose	10	
O131	A60	3c pale yel grn	1.40	
O132	A60	5c bl grn	10	
O133	A60	10c gray bl	10	
O134	A60	12c violet	1.40	
O135	A60	13c brn lake	10	
O136	A60	20c dp bl	10	
O137	A60	24c ultra	10	
O138	A60	26c bis brn	10	
O139	A60	50c orange	10	
O140	A60	1p yellow	10	
		Nos. O129-O140 (12)	3.80	

Reprints of the above set are on thick paper with and without watermark. Value 10c each.

No. 177 Handstamped in Violet

O141	A60	1c org ver	30.00	

Same, with Additional Overprint in Black

O142	A60	1c org ver		

Counterfeits exist of the "wheel" overprint.

Nos. 204-205, 207 and 209 Overprinted

1899 **Unwmk.**

O143	A61	12c dk grn		
O144	A61	13c dp rose		
O145	A61	26c car rose		
O146	A61	100c violet		

Nos. 204-205 Overprinted and Punched with 12 small holes

O147	A61	12c dk grn		
O148	A61	13c dp rose		

Official stamps punched with twelve small holes were issued and used for ordinary postage.

Nos. 199-209 Overprinted

1899

Blue Overprint.

O149	A61	1c brown	10	
O150	A61	2c gray grn	10	
O151	A61	3c blue	10	
O152	A61	5c brn org	10	
O153	A61	10c chocolate	10	
O154	A61	13c dp rose	10	
O155	A61	26c car rose	10	
O156	A61	50c org red	10	
O157	A61	100c violet	10	

Black Overprint.

O158	A61	3c blue	10	
O159	A61	12c dk grn	10	
O160	A61	24c lt bl	10	
		Nos. O149-O160 (12)	1.20	

Nos. O149 to O160 were probably not placed in use.

With Additional Overprint in Black

O161	A61	1c brown	30	25
O162	A61	2c gray grn	45	38
O163	A61	3c blue	30	25
O164	A61	5c brn org	30	25
O165	A61	10c chocolate	38	30
O166	A61	12c dk grn		
O167	A61	13c dp rose	75	65
O168	A61	24c lt bl	12.50	11.50
O169	A61	26c car rose	38	30
O170	A61	50c org red	75	65
O171	A61	100c violet	75	65
		Nos. O161-O165,O167-O171 (10)	16.86	15.18

Regular Issue of 1899 Overprinted and Punched with 12 Small Holes

Blue Overprint.

O172	A61	1c brown	62	15
O173	A61	2c gray grn	75	15
O174	A61	3c blue	1.00	90
O175	A61	5c brn org	1.25	45
O176	A61	10c chocolate	1.75	1.25
O177	A61	13c dp rose	1.75	65
O177A	A61	24c lt bl		
O178	A61	26c car rose	20.00	8.75

Black Overprint.

O179	A61	12c dk grn	1.25	90
		Nos. O172-O177,O178-O179 (8)	28.37	13.20

It is stated that Nos. O172-O214 inclusive were issued for ordinary postage and not for use as official stamps.

With Additional Overprint in Black

O180	A61	1c brown	1.00	90
O180A	A61	2c gray grn		
O181	A61	3c blue		
O182	A61	5c brn org	90	
O182A	A61	10c chocolate		
O182B	A61	12c dk grn		
O183	A61	13c dp rose	3.00	1.25
O184	A61	26c car rose		

Overprinted in Black

O185	A61	100c violet		

Postage Due Stamps Nos. J49 to J56 Overprinted in Black

1900

O186	D1	1c orange	15.00	
O187	D1	2c orange	15.00	
O188	D1	3c orange	15.00	
O189	D1	5c orange	15.00	
O190	D1	10c orange	15.00	
O191	D1	15c orange	32.50	
O192	D1	25c orange	32.50	
O193	D1	50c orange	32.50	
		Nos. O186-O193 (8)	172.50	

With Additional Overprint in Black

O194	D1	1c orange		
O195	D1	2c orange		7.50
O196	D1	3c orange		
O197	D1	5c orange		
O198	D1	15c orange	7.50	
O199	D1	25c orange	8.75	
O200	D1	50c orange	82.50	

Overprinted in Black and Punched with 12 Small Holes

O201	D1	1c orange	15.00	
O202	D1	2c orange	15.00	
O203	D1	3c orange	15.00	
O204	D1	5c orange	15.00	

With Additional Overprint in Black

O205	D1	1c orange	5.50	4.00
O206	D1	2c orange		4.00
O207	D1	3c orange		4.00
O208	D1	5c orange	5.50	3.50

Overprinted like Nos. O186-O193 in Violet and with "Wheel" in Black.

O209 D1 2c orange 12.50
 a. Inverted overprint
O210 D1 3c orange
O211 D1 10c orange 3.00

With Additional Handstamp in Violet

O212 D1 1c orange 7.50 5.00
O213 D1 2c orange 7.50 5.50
O214 D1 3c orange 7.50 5.50

See note after No. O48.

Type of Regular Issue of 1900 Overprinted in Black

FRANQUEO OFICIAL

O223 A63 1c lt grn 25 25
 a. Inverted overprint
O224 A63 2c rose 30 25
 a. Inverted overprint 1.75
O225 A63 3c gray blk 20 20
 a. Overprint vertical
O226 A63 5c blue 20 20
O227 A63 10c blue 50 50
 a. Inverted overprint
O228 A63 12c yel grn 50 50
O229 A63 13c yel brn 50 50
O230 A63 24c gray blk 38 50
O231 A63 26c yel brn 17.50 15.00
 a. Inverted overprint
O232 A63 50c dl rose 50 50
 a. Inverted overprint
 Nos. O223-O231 (9) 20.33 17.90

With Additional Overprint in Violet

O233 A63 1c lt grn 3.50 3.00
O234 A63 2c rose
 a. "FRANQUEO OFICIAL" inverted
O235 A63 26c yel brn 38 38
O236 A63 50c dl rose 50 42

Overprinted in Black

FRANQUEO OFICIAL

O237 A63 1c lt grn 3.50 3.50
O238 A63 3c gray blk
O239 A63 5c blue
O240 A63 10c blue
O241 A63 12c yel grn

Violet Overprint.

O242 A63 50c dl rose 10.00

The shield overprinted on No. O242 is of the type on No. O212.

O1

1903 Wmk. S. (173) *Perf. 14, 14½*

O243 O1 1c yel grn 25 18
O244 O1 2c carmine 25 12
O245 O1 3c orange 75 60
O246 O1 5c dk bl 25 12
O247 O1 10c dl vio 38 25
O248 O1 13c red brn 38 25
O249 O1 15c yel brn 2.50 1.25
O250 O1 24c scarlet 25 25
O251 O1 50c bister 38 18
O252 O1 100c grnsh bl 38 60
 Nos. O243-O252 (10) 5.77 3.80

No. 285 Handstamped in Black

CORREOS DE OFICIO DE EL SALVADOR

1904

O253 A64 3c orange 35.00

Nos. O246-O248 Surcharged in Black

2 2

1905

O254 O1 2c on 5c dk bl 2.50 2.00
O255 O1 3c on 5c dk bl
 a. Double surcharge
O256 O1 3c on 10c dl vio 5.50 4.50
O257 O1 3c on 13c red brn 65 50

A 2c surcharge of this type exists on No. O247.

No. O225 Overprinted in Blue

1905 a   1905 b

1905 Unwmk.

O258 A63(a) 3c gray blk 1.50 1.25
O259 A63(b) 3c gray blk 1.25 1.00

Nos. O224-O225 Overprinted in Blue

1906 c   1906 d

1906

O260 A63(c) 2c rose 11.25 10.00
O261 A63(c) 3c gray blk 90 75
 a. Overprint "1906" in blk
O262 A63(d) 3c gray blk 1.00 90

Escalón — O2

National Palace — O3

1906 Engr. *Perf. 11½*

O263 O2 1c grn & blk 10 7
O264 O2 2c car & blk 10 7
O265 O2 3c yel & blk 10 6
O266 O2 5c bl & blk 10 32
O267 O2 10c vio & blk 10 7
O268 O2 13c dk brn & blk 10 8
O269 O2 15c red org & blk 15 8
O270 O2 24c car & blk 18 16
O271 O2 50c org & blk 18 65
O272 O2 100c dk bl & blk 20 2.00
 Nos. O263-O272 (10) 1.31 3.56

The centers of these stamps are also found in blue black.

Nos. O263 to O272 have been reprinted. The shades differ, the paper is thinner, the gum whiter and the perforation 12. Value 5c each.

1908

O273 O3 1c grn & blk 8 8
O274 O3 2c red & blk 8 8
O275 O3 3c yel & blk 8 8
O276 O3 5c bl & blk 8 8
O277 O3 10c vio & blk 8 8
O278 O3 13c vio & blk 10 10
O279 O3 15c pale brn & blk 10 10
O280 O3 24c rose & blk 10 10
O281 O3 50c yel & blk 10 10
O282 O3 100c turq bl & blk 20 10
 Nos. O273-O282 (10) 1.00 90

Same Overprinted in Black

O283 O3 1c grn & blk 65
O284 O3 2c red & blk 75
O285 O3 3c yel & blk 75
O286 O3 5c bl & blk 1.00
O287 O3 10c vio & blk 1.00
O288 O3 13c vio & blk 1.10
O289 O3 15c pale brn & blk 1.25
O290 O3 24c rose & blk 1.40
O291 O3 50c yel & blk 1.50
O292 O3 100c turq & blk 1.75
 Nos. O283-O292 (10) 11.15

Pres. Figueroa — O4

1910 Engr. Wmk. 172

O293 O4 2c dk grn & blk 9 9
O294 O4 3c org & blk 9 9
O295 O4 4c scar & blk 9 9
 a. 4c car & blk
O296 O4 5c pur & blk 9 9
O297 O4 6c scar & blk 9 9
O298 O4 10c pur & blk 9 9
O299 O4 12c dp bl & blk 9 9
O300 O4 17c ol grn & blk 9 9
O301 O4 19c brn red & blk 9 9
O302 O4 29c choc & blk 9 9
O303 O4 50c yel & blk 9 9
O304 O4 100c turq & blk 9 9
 Nos. O293-O304 (12) 1.08 1.08

Regular Issue, Type A63, Overprinted or Surcharged:

OFICIAL a

OFICIAL 3 b

OFICIAL UN COLON c

1911 Unwmk.

O305 A63(a) 1c lt grn 8 8
O306 A63(b) 3c on 13c yel brn 8 8
O307 A63(b) 5c on 10c dp bl 8 8
O308 A63(a) 10c dp bl 8 8
O309 A63(a) 12c lt grn 8 8
O310 A63(a) 13c yel brn 8 8
O311 A63(b) 50c on 10c dp bl 8 8
O312 A63(c) 1col on 13c yel brn 12 12
 Nos. O305-O312 (8) 68 68

O5

O6

1914 Typo. *Perf. 12*

Background in Green, Shield and "Provisional" in Black.

O313 O5 2c yel brn 8 8
O314 O5 3c yellow 8 8
O315 O5 5c dk bl 8 8
O316 O5 10c red 8 8
O317 O5 12c green 8 8
O318 O5 17c violet 8 8
O319 O5 50c brown 8 8
O320 O5 100c dl rose 8 8
 Nos. O313-O320 (8) 64 64

Stamps of this issue are known imperforate or with parts of the design omitted or misplaced. These varieties were not regularly issued.

1914 Typo.

O321 O6 2c bl grn 8 8
O322 O6 3c orange 8 8

Type of Official Stamps of 1908 Overprinted

1915 OFICIAL

1915

O323 O3 1c gray grn 20 15
 a. "1915" double
 b. "OFICIAL" inverted
O324 O3 2c red 20 15
O325 O3 5c ultra 20 15
O326 O3 10c yellow 20 18
 a. Date omitted
O327 O3 50c violet 45 38
O328 O3 100c blk brn 90 90
 Nos. O323-O328 (6) 2.15 1.91

Same Overprint on Nos. 414, 417, 429.

O329 A66 1c gray grn 1.25 1.25
O330 A66 6c pale bl 38 30
 a. 6c ultra
O331 A66 12c brown 45 45

Nos. O323-O327, O329-O331 exist imperforate.

Nos. O329-O331 exist with "OFICIAL" inverted and double. See note after No. 421.

Nos. 431-440 Overprinted in Blue or Red

OFICIAL

1916

O332 A83 1c dp grn 8 6
O333 A83 2c vermilion 25 15
O334 A83 5c dp bl (R) 18 15
O335 A83 6c gray vio (R) 8 6
O336 A83 10c blk brn 8 6
O337 A83 12c violet 30 25
O338 A83 17c orange 8 6
O339 A83 25c dk brn 8 6
O340 A83 29c blk (R) 8 6
O341 A83 50c sl (R) 8 97
 Nos. O332-O341 (10) 1.29 97

Nos. 474-481 Overprinted

OFICIAL a   OFICIAL b

1921

O342 A94(a) 1c green 10 8
O343 A95(a) 2c black 10 8
 a. Invtd. ovpt.
O344 A96 (b) 5c orange 15 12
O345 A97(a) 6c car rose 12 8
O346 A98(a) 10c dp bl 20 15
O347 A99(a) 25c ol grn 50 25
O348 A100(a) 60c violet 62 38
O349 A101(a) 1col blk brn 65 45
 Nos. O342-O349 (8) 2.44 1.59

Nos. 498 and 500 Overprinted in Black or Red

OFICIAL

1925

O350 A109 5c ol blk 25 10
O351 A111 10c org (R) 50 12
 a. "ATLANT CO" 7.50 6.25

Inverted overprints exist.

Regular Issue of 1924-25 Overprinted in Black or Red

OFICIAL

1927

O352 A106 1c red vio 12 8
O353 A107 2c dk red 25 8
O354 A109 5c ol blk (R) 25 9
O355 A110 6c dp bl (R) 2.50 2.00
O356 A111 10c orange 25 12
 a. "ATLANT CO" 12.50 11.50
O357 A116 1col grn & vio (R) 1.25 75
 Nos. O352-O357 (6) 4.62 3.12

Inverted overprints exist on 1c, 2c, 5c and 10c.

Regular Issue of 1924-25 Overprinted in Black **OFICIAL**

1932			*Perf. 12½.*	
O358	A106	1c dp vio	12	6
O359	A107	2c dk red	25	6
O360	A109	5c ol blk	12	5
O361	A111	10c orange	50	12
a.		"ATLANT CO"	14.00	12.50

Catalogue values for unused stamps in this section, from this point to the end of the section, are for Never Hinged items.

Regular Issue of 1947 Overprinted in Black or Red **OFICIAL**

1948	Unwmk.	Engr.	*Perf. 12*	
O362	A154	1c car rose	32.50	19.00
O363	A154	2c dp org	32.50	19.00
O364	A154	5c sl gray (R)	32.50	19.00
O365	A154	10c bis brn (R)	32.50	19.00
O366	A154	20c grn (R)	32.50	19.00
O367	A154	50c blk (R)	32.50	19.00
		Nos. O362-O367 (6)	195.00	114.00

No. 602 Surcharged in Carmine and Black

1 CTS

X X

OFICIAL

1964(?)

O368 A154 1c on 20c grn

The X's are black, the rest carmine.

PARCEL POST STAMPS

Mercury
PP1

1895	Unwmk.	Engr.	*Perf. 12*
Q1	PP1	5c brn org	18
Q2	PP1	10c dk bl	18
Q3	PP1	15c red	18
Q4	PP1	20c orange	18
Q5	PP1	50c bl grn	18
		Nos. Q1-Q5 (5)	90

POSTAL TAX STAMPS

Nos. 503, 501 Surcharged **EDIFICIOS POSTALES 1**

1931	Unwmk.		*Perf. 12½*	
RA1	A115	1c on 50c org brn	12	10
a.		Double surcharge	1.50	1.50
RA2	A112	2c on 20c dp grn	12	10

Nos. 501, 503 Surcharged **EDIFICIOS POSTALES ₡ 0.01**

RA3	A112	1c on 20c dp grn	12	10
RA4	A115	2c on 50c org brn	12	10
a.		Without period in "0.02"	75	

The use of these stamps was obligatory, in addition to the regular postage, on letters and other postal matter. The money obtained from their sale was to be used to erect a new post office in San Salvador.

Samoa German Dominion Stamps can be mounted in Scott's Germany Part II Album.

SAMOA

LOCATION — An archipelago in the South Pacific Ocean, east of Fiji.
GOVT. — Former monarchy and (partially) former German possession.
AREA — 1,130 sq. mi.
POP. — 39,000 (est. 1910).
CAPITAL — Apia.

In 1861-99, Samoa was an independent kingdom under the influence of the United States, to which the harbor of Pago Pago had been ceded, and that of Great Britain and Germany. In 1898 a disturbance arose, resulting in the withdrawal of Great Britain, and the partitioning of the islands between Germany and the United States. Early in World War I the islands under German domination were occupied by New Zealand troops and in 1920 the League of Nations declared them a mandate to New Zealand. See Vol. I for British issues.

12 Pence = 1 Shilling
20 Shillings = 1 Pound
100 Pfennig = 1 Mark (1900)

Issues of the Kingdom

A1

Type I - Line above "X" is usually unbroken. Dots over "SAMOA" are uniform and evenly spaced. Upper right serif of "M" is horizontal.

Type II - Line above "X" is usually broken. Small dot near upper right serif of "M".

Type III - Line above "X" roughly retouched. Upper right serif of "M" bends down.

Type IV - Speck of color on curved line below center of "M".

Perf. 12, 12½

1877-82		Litho.	Unwmk.	
1	A1	1p bl (III) ('79)	30.00	35.00
a.		1p ultra (III) ('79)	32.50	45.00
b.		1p ultra (II) ('78)	115.00	110.00
c.		1p ultra (I) ('77)	315.00	135.00
2	A1	2p lil rose (IV) ('82)	30.00	
3	A1	3p ver (III) ('79)	32.50	35.00
a.		3p brt scar (III) ('79)	32.50	35.00
b.		3p scarlet (II)	340.00	110.00
c.		3p dp scarlet (I) ('77)	145.00	110.00
4	A1	6p vio (III) ('79)	32.50	35.00
a.		6p violet (II) ('78)	225.00	125.00
b.		6p violet (I) ('77)	315.00	135.00
5	A1	9p yel brn (IV) ('80)	55.00	135.00
a.		9p orange brn (IV) ('80)	55.00	135.00
6	A1	1sh org yel (II) ('78)	100.00	100.00
a.		1sh dull yel (I) ('77)	50.00	55.00
7	A1	2sh dp brn (III) ('79)	125.00	135.00
a.		2sh red brown (II) ('78)	315.00	275.00
b.		2sh brown (II) ('78)	315.00	275.00
8	A1	5sh yel grn (III) ('79)	625.00	750.00
a.		5sh deep grn (III) ('79)	625.00	750.00
b.		5sh gray grn (II) ('78)	1,000.	1,350.

The 1p often has a period after "PENNY." The 2p was never placed in use.

Imperforates of this issue are proofs.

Sheets of the first issue were not perforated around the outer sides. All values except the 2p were printed in sheets of 10 (2x5). The 1p, 3p and 6p type I and the 1p type III were also printed in sheets of 20 (4x5), and six stamps on each of these sheets were perforated all around. The 2p was printed in sheets of 21 (3x7) and five stamps in the second row were perforated all around. These are the only varieties of the original stamps which have not one or two imperforate edges.

Reprints are of type IV and nearly always perforated on all sides. They have a spot of color at the edge of the panel below the "M". This spot is not on any originals except the 2p, which may be distinguished by its color, and the 9p which may be distinguished by having a rough blind perf. 12.

Palms — A2

King Malietoa Laupepa — A3

Wmk. 62 - NZ and Star Wide Apart

1895-99	Typo.	Wmk. 62	*Perf. 11*	
9	A2	½p brn vio ('95)	90	1.75
10	A2	½p grn ('99)	65	80
11	A2	1p grn ('95)	1.40	1.75
12	A2	1p red brn ('99)	60	75
13	A2	2p brt yel ('95)	1.40	1.40
14	A3	2½p rose ('92)	1.10	1.10
15	A3	2½p blk, perf. 10x11 ('96)	1.50	1.50
a.		Perf. 11 ('95)	135.00	110.00
16	A2	4p bl ('95)	1.40	1.75
17	A2	6p mar ('95)	1.50	4.50
18	A2	1sh rose ('95)	2.00	6.75
19	A2	2sh6p red vio ('95)	6.75	13.00
c.		Vert. pair, imperf. between	600.00	
		Nos. 9-19 (11)	19.20	35.05

1886-92			*Perf. 12½*	
9a	A2	½p brn vio	15.00	25.00
11a	A2	1p green	9.00	18.00
13a	A2	2p orange	9.00	18.00
14a	A3	2½p rose ('92)	1.50	3.25
16a	A2	4p blue	8.00	8.00
17a	A2	6p maroon		900.00
18a	A2	1sh rose	32.50	12.50
c.		Diag. half used as 6p on cover		375.00
19a	A2	2sh6p purple	50.00	35.00
		Nos. 9a-16a,18a-19a (7)	125.00	119.75

1887-92			*Perf. 12x11½*	
9b	A2	½p brn vio	30	30
11b	A2	1p green	7.25	1.75
13b	A2	2p brn org	9.00	2.75
14b	A3	2½p rose ('92)	275.00	4.50
16b	A2	4p blue	135.00	5.50
17b	A2	6p maroon	18.00	9.00
18b	A2	1sh rose	13.00	4.50
19b	A2	2sh6p red vio	14.00	2.25
		Nos. 9b-19b (8)	471.55	30.55

Three forms of watermark 62 are found on stamps of type A2: 1. Wide "N Z" and wide star, 6mm apart (used 1886-87). 2. Wide "N Z" and narrow star, 4mm apart (1890). 3. Narrow "NZ" and narrow star, 7mm apart (1890-1900). The 2½p has only the last form.

No. 14a Handstamp Surcharged in Black or Red

FIVE PENCE
a

FIVE PENCE
b

5d
c

1893			*Perf. 12x11½*	
20	A2(a)	5p on 4p bl (bar 16mm)	60.00	60.00
21	A2(b)	5p on 4p bl	80.00	90.00
22	A2(c)	5p on 4p bl (R)	18.00	18.00

As the surcharges on Nos. 20-21 were handstamped in two steps and on No. 22 in three steps, various varieties exist.

Flag Design — A7

1894-95	Typo.		*Perf. 11½x12*	
23	A7	5p vermilion	9.00	4.50
a.		Perf. 11 ('95)	1.40	6.25

Types of 1887-1895 Surcharged in Blue, Black, Red or Green:

Surcharged 1½d.
d

R 3d.
e

1895			*Perf. 11*	
24	A2(d)	1½p on 2p org (Bl)	1.40	1.40
a.		1½p on 2p brn org, perf. 12x11½ (Bl)	2.75	2.75
b.		1½p on 2p yel, "2" ends with vertical stroke	1.40	1.40
25	A2(e)	3p on 2p org (Bk)	2.75	3.00
a.		3p on 2p brn org, perf. 12x11½ (Bk)	4.00	4.00
b.		3p on 2p yel, perf. 11 (Bk)	52.50	52.50
c.		Vert. pair, imperf. btwn.	450.00	

1898-1900			*Perf. 11*	
26	A2(d)	2½p on 1sh rose (Bk)	1.50	1.50
a.		Double surcharge	450.00	
27	A2(d)	2½p on 2sh6p vio (Bk)	5.75	9.00
28	A2(d)	2½p on 1p bl grn (R)	65	1.40
a.		Inverted surcharge		450.00
29	A2(d)	2½p on 1sh rose (R)	10.00	10.00
30	A2(e)	3p on 2p org (G)	1.00	

No. 30 was a re-issue, available for postage.

Stamps of 1886-99 Overprinted in Red or Blue **PROVISIONAL GOVT.**

1899				
31	A2	½p grn (R)	30	35
32	A2	1p red brn (Bl)	30	35
33	A2	2p org (R)	55	70
a.		2p yellow	70	80
34	A2	4p bl (R)	55	70
35	A7	5p scar (Bl)	65	65
36	A2	6p mar (Bl)	85	1.10
37	A2	1sh rose (Bl)	2.00	2.25
38	A2	2sh6p vio (R)	3.50	4.00
		Nos. 31-38 (8)	8.70	10.10

In 1900 the Samoan islands were partitioned between the United States and Germany. The part which became American has since used US stamps.

Issued under German Dominion

A10

A11

Stamps of Germany Overprinted in Black

1900	Unwmk.		*Perf. 13½x14½*	
51	A10	3pf dk brn	9.25	8.50
52	A10	5pf green	13.00	10.50
53	A11	10pf carmine	9.25	*10.50*
54	A11	20pf ultra	18.00	*18.00*
55	A11	25pf orange	45.00	*47.50*
56	A11	50pf red brn	45.00	*40.00*
		Nos. 51-56 (6)	139.50	*135.00*

Kaiser's Yacht "Hohenzollern"
A12 A13

1900 Typo. *Perf. 14*

57	A12 3pf brown	1.00	65
58	A12 5pf green	1.25	65
59	A12 10pf carmine	1.25	65
60	A12 20pf ultra	80	*1.25*
61	A12 25pf org & blk, *yel*	1.40	*10.00*
62	A12 30pf org & blk, *sal*	1.25	*10.00*
63	A12 40pf lake & blk	1.25	*10.00*
64	A12 50pf pur & blk, *sal*	1.50	*10.00*
65	A12 80pf lake & blk, *rose*	3.25	*22.50*

Perf. 14½x14

Engr.

66	A13 1m carmine	3.50	*45.00*
67	A13 2m blue	4.75	*70.00*
68	A13 3m blk vio	7.25	*100.00*
69	A13 5m sl & car	150.00	*415.00*
	Nos. 57-69 (13)	178.45	

Wmk. Lozenges (125)

1915 Typo. *Perf. 14*

70	A12 3pf brown	1.25
71	A12 5pf green	1.75
72	A12 10pf carmine	1.75

Perf. 14½x14

Engr.

73	A13 5m sl & car	22.50

Nos. 70-73 were never put in use.

Stamps issued under British dominion and those of Western Samoa are listed in Volume I.

SAN MARINO

LOCATION — Eastern Italy, about 20 miles inland from the Adriatic Sea.
GOVT. — Republic.
AREA — 24.1 sq. mi.
POP. — 21,622 (1981).
CAPITAL — San Marino.

100 Centesimi = 1 Lira

Catalogue values for unused stamps in this country are for Never Hinged items, beginning with Scott 446 in the regular postage section, Scott B39 in the semi-postal section, Scott C11 in the airpost section, Scott E26 in the special delivery section, and Scott Q40 inthe parcel post section.

Values of San Marino Nos. 1-28, 72 are for specimens in fine condition with original gum. Very fine to superb stamps sell at higher prices. Copies without gum or with perforations cutting into the design sell at lower prices, depending on the condition of the individual specimen.

Coat of Arms
A1 A2

Wmk. 140 - Crown

1877-99 Typo. Wmk. 140 *Perf. 14*

1	A1 2c green	3.50	1.00
2	A1 2c blue ('94)	3.00	1.75
3	A1 2c claret ('95)	2.50	1.75
4	A2 5c org ('90)	27.50	3.75
5	A2 5c ol grn ('92)	1.75	85
6	A2 5c grn ('99)	1.50	65
7	A2 10c ultra	27.50	3.75
a	10c blue ('90)	110.00	16.00
8	A2 10c dk grn ('92)	1.90	1.00
9	A2 10c claret ('99)	1.50	90
10	A2 15c claret ('94)	45.00	11.00
11	A2 20c vermilion	4.50	1.50
12	A2 20c lilac ('95)	1.90	1.50
13	A2 25c maroon ('90)	27.50	5.00
14	A2 25c blue ('99)	1.65	1.10
15	A2 30c brown	165.00	16.00
16	A2 30c org yel ('92)	2.50	1.75
17	A2 40c violet	165.00	16.00
18	A2 40c dk brn ('92)	1.75	1.75
19	A2 45c gray grn ('92)	1.90	1.75
20	A2 65c red brn ('92)	2.25	1.75
21	A2 1 l car & yel ('92)	900.00	225.00
22	A2 1 l lt blue ('95)	800.00	200.00
23	A2 2 l brn & yel ('94)	24.00	20.00
24	A2 5 l vio & grn ('94)	55.00	55.00

See Nos. 911-915.

Nos. 7a, 15, 11 Surcharged in Black — Cmi. 5

1892

25	A2 5c on 10c blue	21.00	5.00
a	Inverted surcharge	21.00	5.00
b	5c on 10c ultramarine	*6,750.*	*1,250.*
c	As "b," inverted surch.	*6,750.*	*1,250.*
26	A2 5c on 30c brown	175.00	22.50
a	Inverted surcharge	175.00	22.50
b	Double surch., one inverted	175.00	50.00
c	Dbl. invtd. surcharge	175.00	35.00
27	A2 10c on 20c ver	13.00	1.00
a	Inverted surcharge	16.00	1.90
b	Double surch., one inverted	15.00	7.00
c	Double surcharge	15.00	7.00

Ten to twelve varieties of each surcharge.

No. 11 Surcharged 10 10

28	A2 10c on 20c ver	75.00	1.75

Government Palace and Portraits of Regents, Tonnini and Marcucci
A6 A7

Portraits of Regents and View of Interior of Palace — A8

Wmk. 174 - Coat of Arms

Wmk. 174

1894, Sept. 30 Litho. *Perf. 15½*

29	A6 25c bl & dk brn	1.50	38
30	A7 50c dl red & dk brn	4.50	1.00
31	A8 1 l grn & dk brn	4.50	1.00

Opening of the new Government Palace and the installation of the new Regents.

Statue of Liberty — A9

Wmk. 140

1899-1922 Typo. *Perf. 14*

32	A9 2c brown	55	45
33	A9 2c claret ('22)	8	8
34	A9 5c brn org	1.00	90
35	A9 5c ol grn ('22)	8	8
36	A9 10c brn org ('22)	8	8
37	A9 20c dp brn ('22)	14	14
38	A9 25c ultra ('22)	18	18
39	A9 45c red brn ('22)	45	45
	Nos. 32-39 (8)	2.56	2.36

Numeral of Value — A10

Mt. Titano — A11

1903-25 *Perf. 14, 14½x14*

40	A10 2c violet	4.50	60
41	A10 2c org brn ('21)	6	6
42	A11 5c blue grn	1.50	30
43	A11 5c ol grn ('21)	8	8
44	A11 5c red brn ('25)	6	10
45	A11 10c claret	1.50	30
46	A11 10c brn org ('21)	8	8
47	A11 10c ol grn ('25)	6	10
48	A11 15c bl grn ('22)	10	10
49	A11 15c brn vio ('25)	10	10
50	A11 20c brn org	25.00	7.25
51	A11 20c brown ('21)	10	10
52	A11 20c bl grn ('25)	10	10
53	A11 25c blue	5.50	1.25
54	A11 25c gray ('21)	14	14
55	A11 25c violet ('25)	10	10
56	A11 30c brn red	2.25	2.50
57	A11 30c claret ('21)	16	16
58	A11 30c orange ('25)	3.75	45
59	A11 40c org red	3.50	3.00
60	A11 40c dp rose ('21)	18	18
61	A11 40c brown ('25)	16	16
62	A11 45c yellow	3.50	3.00
63	A11 50c brn vio ('23)	28	28
64	A11 50c gray blk ('25)	16	16
65	A11 60c brn red ('25)	18	18
66	A11 65c chocolate	3.50	3.00
67	A11 80c blue ('21)	32	32
68	A11 90c brown ('23)	32	32
69	A11 1 l ol grn	7.75	4.00
70	A11 1 l ultra ('21)	32	32
71	A11 1 l lt bl ('25)	22	22
72	A11 2 l violet	300.00	90.00
73	A11 2 l orange ('21)	7.00	7.25
74	A11 2 l lt grn ('25)	1.00	1.00
75	A11 5 l slate	50.00	40.00
76	A11 5 l ultra ('25)	5.00	5.00
	Nos. 40-76 (37)	428.53	172.26

No. 50 Surcharged — 1905 15

1905, Sept. 1

77	A11 15c on 20c brn org	2.75	1.50
a	Large "5" in "1905"	13.00	7.75

Coat of Arms
A12 A13

Two types:
I - Width 18½mm.
II - Width 19mm.

1907-10 Unwmk. Engr. *Perf. 12*

78	A12 1c brn, II ('10)	75	55
a	Type I	1.50	75
79	A13 15c gray, I	6.00	1.10
a	Type II ('10)	65.00	5.00

No. 79a Surcharged in Brown — Cent. 20 1918

1918, Mar. 15

80	A13 20c on 15c gray	1.25	1.25

St. Marinus — A14

Perf. 14½x14, 14x14½

1923, Aug. 11 Typo. Wmk. 140

81	A14 30c dk brn	20	28

San Marino Intl. Exhib. of 1923. Proceeds from the sale of this stamp went to a mutual aid society.

Italian Flag and Views of Arbe and Mt. Titano A15

1923, Aug. 6

82	A15 50c olive grn	20	28

Presentation to San Marino of the Italian flag which had flown over the island of Arbe, the birthplace of the founder of San Marino. Inscribed on back: "V. Moraldi dis. Blasi inc. Petiti impr.-Roma".

Mt. Titano and Sword — A16

1923, Sept. 29 *Perf. 14x14½*

83	A16 1 l dk brn	3.00	3.00

In honor of the San Marino Volunteers who were killed or wounded in WWI.

Giuseppe Garibaldi
A17

Allegory-San Marino Sheltering Garibaldi
A18

1924, Sept. 25 *Perf. 14*

84	A17 30c dark vio	32	32
85	A17 50c olive brn	32	32
86	A17 60c dull red	90	90
87	A18 1 l deep blue	1.50	1.50
88	A18 2 l gray grn	1.75	1.75
	Nos. 84-88 (5)	4.79	4.79

75th anniv. of Garibaldi's taking refuge in San Marino.

Semi-Postal Stamps of 1918 Surcharged with New Values and Bars

Cmi 30

1924, Oct. 9

89	SP1	30c on 45c yel brn & blk	20	20

Surcharged

LIRE UNA

90	SP2	60c on 1 l bl grn & blk	1.90	1.90
91	SP2	1 l on 2 l vio & blk	4.50	4.50
92	SP2	2 l on 3 l red brn & blk	4.00	4.00

Nos. 67 and 68 Surcharged in Black or Red

Lire 1,20

1926, July 1

93	A11	75c on 80c bl	30	30
94	A11	1.20 l on 90c brn	30	30
95	A11	1.25 l on 90c brn (R)	1.00	1.00
96	A11	2.50 l on 80c bl (R)	1.40	1.40

Antonio Onofri — A19

A20

Unwmk.

1926, July 29 Engr. *Perf. 11*

97	A19	10c dk bl & blk	8	8
98	A19	20c ol grn & blk	45	40
99	A19	45c dk vio & blk	22	22
100	A19	65c grn & blk	22	22
101	A19	1 l org & blk	1.40	1.40
102	A19	2 l red vio & blk	1.40	1.40
		Nos. 97-102 (6)	3.77	3.72

Perf. 14½x14

1926, Nov. 25 Wmk. 140

103	A20	1.85 l on 60c vio	30	30

Nos. 101 and 102 Surcharged

1,25

1927, Mar. 10 Unwmk. *Perf. 11*

104	A19	1.25 l on 1 l org & blk	95	95
105	A19	2.50 l on 2 l red vio & blk	2.75	2.75
106	A19	5 l on 2 l red vio & blk	15.00	15.00

Type of Special Delivery Stamp of 1923 Surcharged

L. 1,75

1927, Sept. 15 Wmk. 140 *Perf. 14*

107	A11	1.75 l on 50c on 25c vio	45	45

The 50c on 25c violet was not issued without 1.75-lire surcharge.

War Memorial A21

Unwmk.

1927, Sept. 28 Engr. *Perf. 12*

108	A21	50c brn vio	60	60
109	A21	1.25 l blue	1.10	1.10
110	A21	10 l gray	8.25	8.25

Erection of a cenotaph in memory of the San Marino volunteers in WWI.

Capuchin Church and Convent A22

Design: 2.50 l, 5 l, Death of St. Francis.

1928, Jan. 2

111	A22	50c red	6.00	1.25
112	A22	1.25 l dp bl	1.00	1.00
113	A22	2.50 l dk brn	1.00	1.00
114	A22	5 l dl vio	8.25	8.25

7th centenary of the death of St. Francis of Assisi.

The Rocca (State Prison) — A24

Government Palace — A25

Statue of Liberty — A26

Wmk. 217 - Three Plumes

1929-35 Wmk. 217

115	A24	5c vio brn & ultra	6	7
116	A24	10c bl gray & red vio	30	8
117	A24	15c dp org & emer	6	7
118	A24	20c dk bl & org red	6	8
119	A24	25c grn & gray blk	6	7
120	A24	30c gray brn & red	6	7
121	A24	50c red vio & ol gray	6	8
122	A24	75c dp red & gray blk	6	7
123	A25	1 l dk brn & emer	6	7
124	A25	1.25 l dk bl & blk	6	7
125	A25	1.75 l grn & org	15	15
126	A25	2 l bl gray & red	8	8
127	A25	2.50 l car rose & ultra	8	8
128	A25	3 l dp org & bl	8	8
129	A25	3.70 l ol blk & red brn ('35)	18	18
130	A26	5 l dk vio & dk grn	20	20
131	A26	10 l bis brn & dk bl	95	95
132	A26	15 l grn & red vio	7.25	7.25
133	A26	20 l dk bl & red	125.00	125.00
		Nos. 115-133 (19)	134.81	134.70

General Post Office — A27

San Marino-Rimini Electric Railway — A28

1932, Feb. 4

134	A27	20c blue grn	1.75	85
135	A27	50c dark red	2.75	1.75
136	A27	1.25 l dark bl	85.00	45.00
137	A27	1.75 l dark brn	27.50	24.00
138	A27	2.75 l dark vio	9.00	9.00
		Nos. 134-138 (5)	126.00	80.60

Opening of new General Post Office.

1932, June 11

139	A28	20c deep grn	55	55
140	A28	50c dark red	80	80
141	A28	1.25 l dark bl	1.40	1.40
142	A28	5 l deep brn	16.00	16.00

Opening of the new electric railway between San Marino and Rimini.

Giuseppe Garibaldi A29

Garibaldi's Arrival at San Marino — A30

1932, July 30

143	A29	10c vio brn	60	60
144	A29	20c violet	28	28
145	A29	25c green	52	52
146	A29	50c yel brn	1.25	1.25
147	A30	75c dk red	1.25	1.25
148	A30	1.25 l dark blue	1.90	1.90
149	A30	2.75 l brn org	9.00	9.00
150	A30	5 l olive grn	110.00	110.00
		Nos. 143-150 (8)	124.80	124.80

Garibaldi (1807-1882), Italian patriot.

Nos. 138 and 137 Surcharged

50 CENT

28 MAGGIO 1933

CONVEGNO FILATELICO

1933, May 27

151	A27	25c on 2.75 l dk vio	45	45
152	A27	50c on 1.75 l dk brn	1.75	1.75
153	A27	75c on 2.75 l dk vio	7.00	7.00
154	A27	1.25 l on 1.75 l dk brn	125.00	125.00

Convention of philatelists, San Marino, May 28.

Nos. 134-137 Surcharged in Black

0,50

12-27 APRILE 1934

MOSTRA FILATELICA

1934, Apr. 12

155	A27	25c on 1.25 l dk bl	45	45
156	A27	50c on 1.75 l dk brn	65	65
157	A27	75c on 50c dk red	1.90	1.90
158	A27	1.25 l on 20c bl grn	12.50	12.50

San Marino's participation (with a philatelic pavilion) in the 15th annual Trade Fair at Milan, Apr. 12-27.

Nos. 136 and 138 Surcharged Wheel and New Value

1934, Apr. 12

159	A27	3.70 l on 1.25 l dk bl	37.50	37.50
160	A27	3.70 l on 2.75 l dk vio	37.50	37.50

Ascent to Mt. Titano A31

Unwmk.

1935, Feb. 7 Engr. *Perf. 14*

161	A31	5c choc & blk	7	7
162	A31	10c dk vio & blk	7	7
163	A31	20c org & blk	7	7
164	A31	25c green & blk	7	7
165	A31	50c ol bis & blk	20	20
166	A31	75c brn red & blk	1.25	1.25
167	A31	1.25 l blue & blk	2.50	2.50
		Nos. 161-167 (7)	4.23	4.23

12th anniv. of the founding of the Fascist Movement.

Melchiorre Delfico — A32

Statue of Delfico — A33

1935, Apr. 15 Wmk. 217 *Perf. 12*

Center in Black

169	A32	5c brn lake	7	7
170	A32	7½c lt brn	7	7
171	A32	10c dk bl grn	7	7
172	A32	15c rose car	3.75	80
173	A32	20c orange	7	7
174	A32	25c green	10	7
175	A33	30c dl vio	10	10
176	A33	50c ol grn	60	52
177	A33	75c red	3.25	3.25
178	A33	1.25 l dark bl	75	75
179	A33	1.50 l dk brn	9.00	9.00
180	A33	1.75 l brn org	14.00	14.00
		Nos. 169-180 (12)	31.83	28.77

Melchiorre Delfico (1744-1835), historian.

Nos. 99-100 Surcharged in Black

80

1936, Apr. 14 Unwmk. *Perf. 11*

181	A19	80c on 45c dk vio & blk	1.10	1.10
182	A19	80c on 65c grn & blk	1.10	1.10

Nos. 112-113 Surcharged in Black

L. 2,05

1936, Aug. 23 *Perf. 12*

183	A22	2.05 l on 1.25 l dp bl	3.00	3.00
184	A22	2.75 l on 2.50 l dk brn	12.50	12.50

The only foreign revenue stamps listed in this Catalogue are those authorized for prepayment of postage.

Souvenir Sheet

Design from Base of Roman Column — A34

1937, Aug. 23 Engr. Wmk. 217

185 A34 5 l steel bl	7.00	7.00

Unveiling of the Roman Column at San Marino. The date "1636 d. F. R." means the 1,636th year since the founding of the republic.
No. 185 was privately surcharged "+ 10 L 1941."

Souvenir Sheets

Abraham Lincoln — A35

1938, Apr. 7 Wmk. 217 *Perf. 13*

186 A35 3 l dark blue	75	75
187 A35 5 l rose red	8.75	8.75

Dedication of a Lincoln bust, Sept. 3, 1937.

No. 49 and Type of 1925 Surcharged with New Value in Black

1941 Wmk. 140 *Perf. 14*

188 A11 10c on 15c brn vio	12	12
189 A11 10c on 30c brn org	55	40

Flags of Italy and San Marino — A36

Harbor of Arbe — A37

1942 Photo.

190 A36 10c yel brn & brn org	6	8
191 A36 15c brn & red brn	6	8
192 A36 20c gray grn & gray blk	6	8
193 A36 25c grn & bl	6	8
194 A36 50c brn red & brn	6	8
195 A36 75c red & gray blk	6	8
196 A37 1.25 l bl & gray bl	15	15
197 A37 1.75 l brn & grnsh blk	22	22
198 A37 2.75 l bis brn & gray bl	38	38
199 A37 5 l grn & brn	2.25	2.25
Nos. 190-199 (10)	3.36	3.48

Return of the Italian flag to Arbe.

No. 190 Surcharged in Black

1942, July 30

200 A36 30c on 10c yel brn & brn org	28	28

Rimini-San Marino Stamp Day, Aug. 3.

No. 192 Surcharged with New Value and Bars in Black

1942, Sept. 14

201 A36 30c on 20c gray grn & gray blk	20	20

No. 177 Surcharged with New Value in Black

1942, Sept. 28 Wmk. 217 *Perf. 12*

202 A33 20 l on 75c red & blk	6.75	6.75

Printing Press and Newspaper A38

Newspapers — A39

Wmk. 140

1943, Apr. 12 Photo. *Perf. 14*

203 A38 10c deep grn	6	8
204 A38 15c bister	6	8
205 A38 20c dk org brn	6	8
206 A38 30c dk rose vio	6	8
207 A38 50c blue blk	6	8
208 A38 75c red org	6	8
209 A39 1.25 l blue	6	8
210 A39 1.75 l deep vio	12	12
211 A39 5 l slate	18	18
212 A39 10 l dark brn	1.75	1.75
Nos. 203-212 (10)	2.47	2.61

Nos. 206 and 207 Overprinted in Red

1943, July 1

213 A38 30c dk rose vio	10	10
214 A38 50c bl blk	10	10

Rimini-San Marino Stamp Day, July 5.

A40

A41

Overprinted in Black: "28 LVGLIO 1943 1642 F. R."

1943, Aug. 27

215 A40 5c brown	6	8
216 A40 10c org red	6	8
217 A40 20c ultra	6	8
218 A40 25c dp grn	6	8
219 A40 30c brn car	6	8
220 A40 50c dp vio	6	8
221 A40 75c car rose	6	8
222 A41 1.25 l sapphire	6	8
223 A41 1.75 l red org	15	15
224 A41 2.75 l dk red brn	18	18
225 A41 5 l green	45	45
226 A41 10 l violet	75	75
227 A41 20 l slate bl	1.90	1.90
Nos. 215-227 (13)	3.91	4.07

This series was prepared to commemorate the 20th anniversary of fascism, but as Mussolini was overthrown July 25, 1943, it was converted by overprinting to commemorate the downfall of fascism.
Overprint on Nos. 222-227 adds "d." before "F.R."
Nos. 215-227 exist without overprint (not regularly issued). Value of set $45.
See Nos. C26-C33.

A42

A43

Overprinted "Governo Provvisorio" in Black

1943, Aug. 27

228 A42 5c brown	6	8
229 A42 10c org red	6	8
230 A42 20c ultra	6	8
231 A42 25c dp grn	6	8
232 A42 30c brn car	6	8
233 A42 50c dp vio	6	8
234 A42 75c car rose	6	8
235 A43 1.25 l sapphire	6	8
236 A43 1.75 l red org	30	30
237 A43 5 l green	55	55
238 A43 20 l slate bl	1.90	1.90
Nos. 228-238 (11)	3.23	3.39

See Nos. C34-C39.

Souvenir Sheets

A44

Perf. 14, Imperf.

1945, Mar. 15 Photo. Unwmk.

239 A44 Sheet of three	25.00	25.00
a 10 l dull blue	5.50	5.50
b 15 l dull green	5.50	5.50
c 25 l dull red brown	5.50	5.50

Sheets contain a papermaker's watermark, "Hammermill Bond, Made in U.S.A."
Nos. 239, 241 and C40 were issued to commemorate the 50th anniv. of the reconstruction of the Government Palace.

Government Palace — A45

1945, Mar. 15 Wmk. 140 *Perf. 14*

241 A45 25 l brn vio	3.00	3.00

Coats of Arms

Faetano A46

Montegiardino A47

San Marino A48

Fiorentino A49

Borgomaggiore A50

Serravalle A51

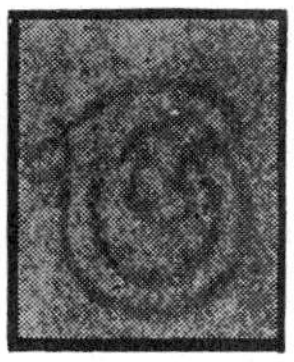

Wmk. 277 - Winged Wheel

1945-46 Wmk. 277

242 A46 10c dark bl	8	8
243 A47 20c vermilion	8	8
244 A48 40c dp org	8	8
245 A47 60c slate blk	8	8
246 A49 80c dk grn	8	8
247 A46 1 l dk car rose	8	8
248 A46 1.20 l dp vio	8	8
249 A49 2 l chestnut	9	8
250 A49 3 l dp bl ('46)	8	8
250A A49 4 l red org ('46)	9	15
251 A48 5 l dk brn	8	8
251A A46 15 l dp bl ('46)	65	1.10

Lithographed and Engraved

252 A50 10 l brt red & brn	1.50	1.10
253 A51 20 l brt red & ultra	2.75	1.65
254 A51 20 l org brn & ultra ('46)	2.75	1.65
a Vert. pair, imperf. between	175.00	
255 A47 25 l hn brn & ultra ('46)	2.75	1.90

Size: 22x27mm

256 A48 50 l ol brn & ultra ('46)	3.00	5.75
Nos. 242-256 (17)	14.30	14.10

Nos. 252-256 are in sheets of 10 (2x5). Values: Nos. 252, 254-255, $60 each. No. 253, $90, No. 256, $200.

"Dawn of New Hope" — A52

Engr. & Litho.

1946 Unwmk. *Perf. 14*

257 A52 100 l dl yel & brn vio	3.25	3.25
i Vertical pair, imperf. betwn.	175.00	

UN Relief and Rehabilitation Administration. Sheets of 10 with blue coat of arms in top margin.

Franklin D. Roosevelt and Flags of San Marino and U.S. — A52a

Designs: 1 l, 50 l, Quotation on Liberty, from Franklin D. Roosevelt. 2 l, 100 l, Roosevelt portrait (vert.). 5 l, 15 l, Roosevelt and flags (as shown).

Wmk. 277

1947, May 3		**Photo.**	***Perf. 14***	
257A	A52a	1 l bis & brn	6	6
257B	A52a	2 l bl & sep	6	6
257C	A52a	5 l vio & multi	6	6
257D	A52a	15 l grn & multi	9	6
257E	A52a	50 l ver & brn	45	45
257F	A52a	100 l vio & sep	65	65
		Nos. 257A-257F (6)	1.37	1.34

Franklin D. Roosevelt (1882-1945), 32nd president of the US. See Nos. C51A-C51H.

Nos. 257A-257C Surcharged with New Value

1947, June 16				
257G	A52a	3 l on 1 l bis & brn	25	25
257H	A52a	4 l on 2 l bl & sep	25	25
257I	A52a	6 l on 5 l vio & multi	25	25
		Nos. 257G-257I,C51I-C51K (6)	1.50	1.50

No. 250A Surcharged with New Value in Black

1947, June 16		**Wmk. 277**		
258	A49	6(l) on 4 l red org	12	10

No. 250A Surcharged in Black

21

259	A49	21 l on 4 l red org	50	60

"St. Marinus Raising the Republic" by Girolamo Batoni — A53

Wmk. 217

1947, July 18		**Engr.**	***Perf. 12***	
260	A53	1 l brt grn & vio	6	10
261	A53	2 l pur & ol	6	10
262	A53	4 l vio brn & dk bl grn	6	10
263	A53	10 l org & bl blk	6	10
264	A53	25 l car & pur	40	55
265	A53	50 l dk bl grn & brn	9.00	8.25
		Nos. 260-265,C52-C53 (8)	12.64	12.20

United States 1847 Stamp A54

United States Stamps of 1847 and 1869 — A55

A56

Wmk. 277

1947, Dec. 24		**Photo.**	***Perf. 14***	
266	A54	2 l red vio & dk brn	6	8
267	A55	3 l sl gray, dp ultra & car	6	8
268	A54	6 l dp bl & dk gray grn	6	8
269	A56	15 l vio, dp ultra & car	18	22
270	A55	35 l dk brn, dp ultra & car	60	60
271	A56	50 l sl grn, dp ultra & car	85	90
		Nos. 266-271,C55 (7)	5.81	5.96

1st United States postage stamps, cent.

Laborer and San Marino Flag — A57

1948, June 3				
272	A57	5 l brown	10	12
273	A57	8 l green	12	18
274	A57	30 l crimson	18	24
275	A57	50 l red brn & rose lil	1.25	1.25
		Engr.		
276	A57	100 l dk bl & dp vio	17.00	17.00
		Nos. 272-276 (5)	18.65	18.79

See Nos. 373-374.

No. 172 Surcharged with New Value and Ornaments in Black

1948		**Wmk. 217**	***Perf. 12***	
277	A32	100 l on 15c rose car & blk	21.00	21.00

Government Palace — A58

Mt. Titano, Distant View — A59

Various Views of San Marino.

1949-50		**Wmk. 277 Photo.**	***Perf. 14***	
278	A58	1 l blk & bl	6	6
279	A58	2 l vio & car	6	6
280	A58	3 l vio & ultra	6	6
281	A58	4 l blk & vio	6	6
282	A58	5 l vio & brn	6	6
283	A58	6 l dp bl & sep	10	18
284	A59	8 l blk brn & yel brn	14	24
285	A59	10 l brn blk & bl	14	15
286	A58	12 l brt rose & vio	35	52
287	A58	15 l vio & brt rose	52	75
288	A58	20 l dp bl & brn ('50)	3.25	1.00
289	A58	35 l grn & vio	1.90	1.90
290	A58	50 l brt rose & yel brn	75	1.00
291	A58	55 l dp bl & dl grn ('50)	10.50	11.00
		Perf. 14x13½		
		Engr.		
292	A59	100 l blk brn & dk grn	42.50	22.50
293	A59	200 l dp bl & brn	47.50	32.50
		Nos. 278-293 (16)	107.95	72.04

Nos. 260 and 261 Overprinted in Black

Giornata Filatelica
San Marino-Riccione
28-6-1949

1949, June 28		**Wmk. 217**		
294	A53	1 l brt grn & vio	10	9
295	A53	2 l pur & ol	10	9

San Marino-Riccione Stamp Day, June 28.

Francesco Nullo — A60

Designs: 1 l, 20 l, Francesco Nullo. 2 l, 5 l, Anita Garibaldi. 3 l, 50 l, Giuseppe Garibaldi. 4 l, 15 l, Ugo Bassi.

Wmk. 277

1949, July 31		**Photo.**	***Perf. 14***	
		Size: 22x28mm		
296	A60	1 l blk & car lake	8	8
297	A60	2 l red brn & bl	8	8
298	A60	3 l car lake & dk grn	8	8
299	A60	4 l vio & dk brn	8	8
		Size: 26½x36½mm		
300	A60	5 l pur & dk brn	8	14
301	A60	15 l car lake & gray bl	60	60
302	A60	20 l vio & car lake	1.00	1.00
303	A60	50 l red brn & vio	10.50	10.50
		Nos. 296-303 (8)	12.50	12.56

Centenary of Garibaldi's escape to San Marino.
See Nos. C57-C61, 404-410.

Stagecoach on Road from San Marino A61

1949, Dec. 29			**Engr.**	
304	A61	100 l bl & gray vio	5.00	5.00
		Sheet of 6	100.00	100.00

UPU, 75th anniversary.

A62

A63a

A63

Perf. 13½x14, 14x13½

1951, Mar. 15		**Engr.**	**Wmk. 277**	
		Sky and Cross in Carmine		
305	A62	25 l dk brn & red vio	2.50	2.50
306	A63	75 l org brn & dk brn	3.00	3.00
307	A63a	100 l dk brn & gray blk	4.50	4.50

Issued to honor the San Marino Red Cross.

Christopher Columbus — A64

Designs: 2 l, 25 l, Columbus on his ship. 3 l, 10 l, 20 l, Landing of Columbus. 4 l, 15 l, 80 l, Pioneers trading with Indians. 5 l, 200 l, Columbus and map of Americas.

1952, Jan. 28		**Photo.**	***Perf. 14***	
308	A64	1 l brn org & dk grn	8	8
309	A64	2 l dk brn & vio	8	8
310	A64	3 l vio & dk brn	8	8
311	A64	4 l bl & org brn	8	8
312	A64	5 l grn & dk bl grn	8	8
313	A64	10 l dk brn & blk	12	20
314	A64	15 l car & blk	18	18
		Engr.		
315	A64	20 l dp bl & dk bl grn	30	35
316	A64	25 l vio brn & blk brn	1.25	1.00
317	A64	60 l choc & vio bl	3.00	3.00
318	A64	80 l gray & blk	6.00	6.00
319	A64	200 l Prus grn & dp ultra	14.00	14.00
		Nos. 308-319,C80 (13)	37.75	37.63

Issued to honor Christopher Columbus.

Type of 1952 in New Colors Overprinted in Black or Red

FIERA DI TRIESTE
1952

1952, June 29			**Photo.**	
320	A64	1 l vio & dk brn	8	8
321	A64	2 l car & blk	8	8
322	A64	3 l grn & dk bl grn (R)	8	8
323	A64	4 l dk brn & blk	8	8
324	A64	5 l pur & vio	10	20
325	A64	10 l bl & org brn (R)	1.00	1.00
326	A64	15 l org brn & bl	2.75	2.75
		Nos. 320-326,C81 (8)	14.67	14.77

4th Intl. Sample Fair of Trieste.

Discobolus — A65

Tennis A66

Model Airplane — A67

Designs: 3 l, Runner. 4 l, Cyclist. 5 l, Soccer. 25 l, Shooting. 100 l, Roller skating.

1953, Apr. 20		**Wmk. 277**	***Perf. 14***	
327	A65	1 l dk brn & blk	8	8
328	A66	2 l blk & brn	8	8
329	A65	3 l blk & grnsh bl	8	8
330	A66	4 l blk & brt bl	8	8
331	A66	5 l dk brn & sl grn	8	12
332	A67	10 l dp bl & crim	15	28
333	A67	25 l blk & dk brn	1.10	1.10
334	A66	100 l dk brn & sl	2.75	2.75
		Nos. 327-334,C90 (9)	39.40	39.57

See No. 438.

Type of 1953 in New Colors Overprinted in Black

GIORNATA FILATELICA
S. MARINO • RICCIONE
24 AGOSTO 1953

1953, Aug. 24				
335	A66	100 l grn & dk bl grn	10.50	10.50

San Marino-Riccione Stamp Day, Aug. 24.

Narcissus A68

Flowers: 2 l, Tulips. 3 l, Oleanders. 4 l, Cornflowers. 5 l, Carnations. 10 l, Irises. 25 l, Cyclamen. 80 l, Geraniums. 100 l, Roses.

1953, Dec. 28			**Photo.**	
336	A68	1 l multi	8	8
337	A68	2 l multi	8	8
338	A68	3 l multi	8	8
339	A68	4 l multi	8	8
340	A68	5 l multi	8	8
341	A68	10 l multi	12	24
342	A68	25 l multi	1.65	1.65

343	A68	80 l multi	8.00	8.00
344	A68	100 l multi	10.00	10.00
		Nos. 336-344 (9)	20.17	20.29

Walking Racer — A69

Fencing A70

Sports: 3 l, Boxing. 4 l, 200 l, 250 l, Gymnastics. 5 l, Motorcycling. 8 l, Javelin-throwing. 12 l, Automobiling. 25 l, Wrestling. 80 l, Walking racer.

1954-55 Photo. Wmk. 277

345	A69	1 l vio & cer	8	8
346	A70	2 l dk grn & vio	8	8
347	A70	3 l brn & brn org	8	8
348	A69	4 l dk bl & brt bl	8	8
349	A70	5 l dk grn & dk brn	8	8
350	A70	8 l lil rose & pur	10	20
351	A70	12 l blk & crim	10	20
352	A69	25 l bl & dk bl grn	18	20
353	A69	80 l dk bl & bl grn	35	35
354	A69	200 l vio & brn	2.00	2.00

Perf. 12½x13

Engr.

355	A69	250 l multi ('55)	25.00	25.00
		Sheet of 4 (#355)	180.00	180.00
		Nos. 345-355 (11)	28.13	28.35

Liberty Statue and Government Palace — A71

1954, Dec. 16 ***Perf. 13x13½***

356	A71	20 l choc & bl	20	22
357	A71	60 l car & dk grn	75	75

See No. C92.

Sailboat — A72

Wmk. 303 - Multiple Stars

1955, Aug. 27 Wmk. 303 ***Perf. 14***

358	A72	100 l gray blk & bl	2.50	2.50

7th San Marino-Riccione Stamp Fair. See No. 385.

Murata Nuova Bridge — A73

View of La Rocca — A74

Design: 15 l, Government Palace.

1955, Nov. 15 ***Perf. 14***

Size: 22x27½mm; 27½x22mm

359	A73	5 l blue & brn	8	8
360	A74	10 l org & bl grn	8	8
361	A74	15 l Prus grn & car	8	8
362	A73	25 l dk brn & vio	9	9
363	A74	35 l vio & red car	14	14
		Nos. 359-363 (5)	47	47

See Nos. 386-388, 636-638.

Ice Skater — A75

Skier — A76

Designs: 3 l, 50 l, Tobogganing. 4 l, Skier going downhill. 5 l, 100 l, Ice Hockey player. 10 l, Girl ice skater.

1955, Dec. 15 Wmk. 303 ***Perf. 14***

364	A75	1 l brn & yel	8	8
365	A76	2 l brt bl & red	8	8
366	A76	3 l blk brn & lt brn	8	8
367	A75	4 l brn & grn	8	8
368	A76	5 l ultra & sal pink	8	8
369	A75	10 l ultra & pink	12	12
370	A76	25 l gray blk & red	60	60
371	A76	50 l brn & ind	1.40	1.40
372	A76	100 l blk & Prus grn	3.25	3.25
		Nos. 364-372,C95 (10)	14.77	14.77

7th Winter Olympic Games at Cortina d'Ampezzo, Jan. 26-Feb. 5, 1956.

Type of 1948 Inscribed: "50th Anniversario Arengo 25 Marzo 1906"

1956, Mar. 24 Wmk. 303 ***Perf. 14***

373	A57	50 l sapphire	5.00	5.00

50th anniv. of the meeting of the heads of families (Arengo), the beginning of the democratic era in San Marino.

Type of 1948 inscribed: "Assistenza Invernale"

1956, Mar. 24 Photo.

374	A57	50 l dk grn	5.00	5.00

Issued to publicize the Winterhelp charity.

Pointer and Arms A77

Dogs: 2 l, Russian greyhound. 3 l, Sheep dog. 4 l, English greyhound. 5 l, Boxer. 10 l, Great Dane. 25 l, Irish setter. 60 l, German shepherd. 80 l, Scotch collie. 100 l, Hunting hound.

1956, June 8 Wmk. 303 ***Perf. 14***

375	A77	1 l ultra & brn	8	8
376	A77	2 l car lake & bl gray	8	8
377	A77	3 l ultra & brn	8	8
378	A77	4 l grnsh bl & gray vio	8	8
379	A77	5 l car lake & dk brn	8	8
380	A77	10 l ultra & brn	10	10
381	A77	25 l dk bl & multi	18	18
382	A77	60 l car lake & multi	1.40	1.40
383	A77	80 l dk bl & multi	1.75	1.75
384	A77	100 l car lake & multi	2.75	2.75
		Nos. 375-384 (10)	6.58	6.58

Sailboat Type of 1955

1956 Wmk. 303 ***Perf. 14***

385	A72	100 l brn & bl grn	1.75	1.75

8th San Marino-Riccione Stamp Fair.

Types of 1955 with added inscription: "Congresso Internaz. Periti Filatelici San Marino-Salsomaggiore 6-8 Ottobre 1956."

Designs: 20 l, La Rocca. 80 l, Murata Nuova Bridge. 100 l, Government palace.

1956, Oct. 6 ***Perf. 14***

Size: 26x36mm; 36x26mm

386	A74	20 l bl & brn	38	28
387	A73	80 l vio & red car	1.50	1.40
388	A74	100 l org & bl grn	1.65	1.65

Intl. Philatelic Congress, San Marino, Oct. 6-8.

Street and Borgo Maggiore Church — A78

Hospital Street — A79

Views: 3 l, Gate tower. 20 l, Covered Market of Borgo Maggiore. 125 l, View from South Bastion.

1957, May 9 Photo. Wmk. 303

389	A78	2 l dk grn & rose red	8	8
390	A78	3 l bl & brn	8	8
391	A78	20 l dk bl grn	18	15
392	A79	60 l brn & bl vio	75	65

Engr.

393	A78	125 l dk bl & blk	32	28
		Nos. 389-393 (5)	1.41	1.24

See Nos. 473-476, 633-635.

Daisies and View of San Marino — A80

Flowers: 2 l, Primrose. 3 l, Lily. 4 l Orchid. 5 l, Lily of the Valley. 10 l, Poppy. 25 l, Pansy. 60 l, Gladiolus. 80 l, Wild Rose. 100 l, Anemone.

Wmk. 303

1957, Aug. 31 Photo. ***Perf. 14***

Flowers in Natural Colors

394	A80	1 l dk vio bl	8	8
395	A80	2 l dk vio bl	8	8
396	A80	3 l dk vio bl	8	8
397	A80	4 l dk vio bl	8	8
398	A80	5 l dk vio bl	8	8
399	A80	10 l bl, buff & lil	8	8
400	A80	25 l bl, yel & lil	8	10
401	A80	60 l bl, yel & dl red brn	28	24
402	A80	80 l bl & dl red brn	40	35
403	A80	100 l bl, yel & dl red brn	90	90
		Nos. 394-403 (10)	2.14	2.07

Type of 1949 Inscribed: "Commemorazione 150 Nascita G. Garibaldi."

Portraits: 2 l, 50 l, Anita Garibaldi. 3 l, 25 l, Francesco Nullo. 5 l, 100 l, Giuseppe Garibaldi. 15 l, Ugo Bassi.

1957, Dec. 12 Wmk. 303 ***Perf. 14***

Size: 22x28mm

404	A60	2 l vio & dl bl	6	6
405	A60	3 l lake & dk grn	6	6
406	A60	5 l brn & ol gray	6	6

Size: 26½x37mm

407	A60	15 l bl & vio	10	15
408	A60	25 l grn & dk gray	24	30
409	A60	50 l vio & brn	1.65	1.50
410	A60	100 l brn & vio	1.65	1.50
		Nos. 404-410 (7)	3.82	3.63

Nos. 409-410 are printed se-tenant. Birth of Giuseppe Garibaldi, 150th anniv.

Panoramic View A81

1958, Feb. 27 Engr. ***Perf. 14***

411	A81	500 l grn & blk	35.00	35.00
		Sheet of 6	275.00	250.00

Fair Emblem and San Marino Peaks — A82

1958, Apr. 12 Photo. ***Perf. 14***

412	A82	40 l yel grn & brn	22	15
413	A82	60 l brt bl & mar	30	28

World's Fair, Brussels, Apr. 17-Oct. 19.

Madonna and Fair Entrance A83

Design: 60 l, View of Fair Grounds.

1958, Apr. 12

414	A83	15 l yel, grn & bl	20	14
415	A83	60 l grn & rose red	70	60

San Marino's 10th participation in the Milan Fair. See No. C97.

Wheat — A84

Designs: 2 l, 125 l, Corn. 3 l, 80 l, Grapes. 4 l, 25 l, Peaches. 5 l, 40 l, Plums.

1958, Aug. 30 Wmk. 303 ***Perf. 14***

416	A84	1 l dk bl & yel org	6	6
417	A84	2 l dk grn & red org	6	6
418	A84	3 l bl & ocher	6	6
419	A84	4 l grn & rose car	6	6
420	A84	5 l bl, yel & grn	8	8
421	A84	15 l ultra & brn org	9	9
422	A84	25 l multi	9	9
423	A84	40 l multi	32	22
424	A84	80 l multi	65	45
425	A84	125 l bl, grn & org ver	2.75	1.75
		Nos. 416-425 (10)	4.22	2.92

Bay and Stamp of Naples A85

1958, Oct. 8 **Photo.**

426	A85	25 l lil & red brn	32	30

Centenary of the stamps of Naples. See No. C100.

Pierre de Coubertin — A86

Portraits: 3 l, Count Alberto Bonacossa. 5 l, Avery Brundage. 30 l, Gen. Carlo Montu. 60 l, J. Sigfrid Edstrom. 80 l, Henri de Baillet Latour.

1959, May 19 **Wmk. 303** ***Perf. 14***

427	A86	2 l brn org & blk	5	6
428	A86	3 l lil & gray brn	5	6
429	A86	5 l bl & dk grn	5	6
430	A86	30 l vio & blk	8	8
431	A86	60 l dk grn & gray brn	22	18
432	A86	80 l car rose & dp grn	22	18
		Nos. 427-432,C106 (7)	1.67	1.47

Leaders of the Olympic movement; 1960 Olympic Games, Rome.

Lincoln and his Praise of San Marino, May 7, 1861 — A87

Lincoln Portraits and: 10 l, Map of San Marino. 15 l, Government palace. 70 l, San Marino peaks (vert.).

1959, July 1 ***Perf. 14***

433	A87	5 l brn & blk	8	8
434	A87	10 l bl grn & ultra	8	8
435	A87	15 l gray & grn	12	12

Perf. 13x13½

Engr.

436	A87	70 l violet	95	75

Birth sesquicentennial of Abraham Lincoln. See No. C108.

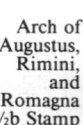

Arch of Augustus, Rimini, and Romagna ½b Stamp A88

1959, Aug. 29 **Photo.** ***Perf. 14***

437	A88	30 l blk & brn	22	16

Issued to commemorate the centenary of the first stamps of Romagna. See No. C109.

Type of 1953 Inscribed: "Universiade Torino"

1959, Aug. 29 **Wmk. 303** ***Perf. 14***

438	A65	30 l red org	60	40

Turin University Sports Meet, Aug. 27-Sept. 6.

Messina Cathedral Portal and Stamp of Sicily 1859 — A89

Stamp of Sicily and: 2 l, Greek temple, Selinus. 3 l, Erice Church. 4 l, Temple of Concordia, Agrigento. 5 l, Ruins of Castor and Pollux Temple, Agrigento. 25 l, San Giovanni degli Eremiti Church. 60 l, Greek theater, Taormina (horiz.).

1959, Oct. 16

439	A89	1 l ocher & dk brn	5	6
440	A89	2 l ol & dk red	5	6
441	A89	3 l bl & slate	5	6
442	A89	4 l red & brn	5	6
443	A89	5 l dl bl & rose lil	5	6
444	A89	25 l multi	22	18
445	A89	60 l multi	25	22
		Nos. 439-445,C110 (8)	1.97	1.45

Centenary of stamps of Sicily.

Catalogue values for unused stamps in this section, from this point to the end of the section, are for Never Hinged items.

Golden Oriole A90

Nightingale A91

Shot Put A92

Birds: 3 l, Woodcock. 4 l, Hoopoe. 5 l, Red-legged partridge. 10 l, Goldfinch. 25 l, European Kingfisher. 60 l, Ringnecked pheasant. 80 l, Green woodpecker. 110 l, Red-breasted flycatcher.

1960, Jan. 28 **Photo.** ***Perf. 14***

Centers in Natural Colors

446	A90	1 l blue	8	8
447	A91	2 l grn & red	8	8
448	A90	3 l grn & red	8	8
449	A91	4 l dk grn & red	8	8
450	A90	5 l dk grn	8	8
451	A91	10 l bl & red	8	8
452	A91	25 l grnsh bl	24	18
453	A90	60 l bl & red	1.25	90
454	A91	80 l Prus bl & red	2.00	1.75
455	A91	110 l bl & red	2.50	2.00
		Nos. 446-455 (10)	6.47	5.31

1960, May 23 **Wmk. 303** ***Perf. 14***

Sports: 2 l, Gymnastics. 3 l, Walking. 4 l, Boxing. 5 l, Fencing (horiz.). 10 l, Bicycling. 15 l, Hockey (horiz.). 25 l, Rowing (horiz.). 60 l, Soccer. 110 l, Equestrian (horiz.).

456	A92	1 l car rose & vio	6	6
457	A92	2 l gray & org	6	6
458	A92	3 l brn ol & pur	6	6
459	A92	4 l rose red & brn	6	6
460	A92	5 l brn & bl	6	6
461	A92	10 l red brn & bl	6	6
462	A92	15 l emer & lil	6	6
463	A92	25 l bl grn & org	9	9
464	A92	60 l dp grn & org	10	10
465	A92	110 l emer, red & blk	14	14
		Set of 3 souvenir sheets	7.00	7.00
		Nos. 456-465,C111-C114 (14)	2.11	1.89

Issued to commemorate the 17th Olympic Games, Rome, Aug. 25-Sept. 11.

Souvenir sheets are: (1.) Sheet of 4, one each of 1 l, 2 l, 3 l and 60 l, all printed in deep green and brown. (2.) Sheet of 4, one each of 4 l and 10 l plus a 20 l and 40 l in designs of Nos. C111-C112 but without "Posta Aerea" inscribed-all 4 printed in rose red and brown. (3.) Sheet of 6, one each of 5 l, 15 l, 25 l and 110 l plus an 80 l and 125 l in designs of Nos. C113-C114 but without "Posta Aerea"-all 6 printed in emerald and brown.

San Marino stamps can be mounted in Scott's annual San Marino Supplement.

Mt. Titano — A93

Founder Melvin Jones and Lions Headquarters — A94

Designs (Lions Emblem and): 60 l, Government Palace and statue of Liberty. 115 l, Clarence L. Sturm, president. 150 l, Finis E. Davis, vice president.

1960, July 1 **Photo.** **Wmk. 303**

466	A93	30 l red brn & dk bl	14	14
467	A94	45 l bl vio & bis brn	50	50
468	A93	60 l dl rose & bl	14	14
469	A94	115 l grn & blk	50	50
470	A94	150 l brn & dk bl	3.50	2.75
		Nos. 466-470,C115 (6)	9.78	8.03

Lions Intl.; founding of the Lions Club of San Marino.

Beach of Riccione and San Marino Peaks A95

1960, Aug. 27 ***Perf. 14***

471	A95	30 l multi	45	32

12th San Marino-Riccione Stamp Day, Aug. 27. See No. C116.

Boy with Basket of Fruit, by Caravaggio — A96

1960, Dec. 29 **Wmk. 303** ***Perf. 14***

472	A96	200 l multi	5.75	4.75

350th anniversary of the death of Michelangelo da Caravaggio (Merisi), painter.

Types of 1957

Views: 1 l, Hospital street. 4 l, Government building. 80 l, Gate tower. 115 l, Covered market of Borgo Maggiore.

1961, Feb. 16 ***Perf. 14***

473	A79	1 l dk bl grn	5	5
474	A78	4 l dk bl & blk	8	8
475	A78	30 l brt vio & brn	70	28
476	A78	115 l brn & bl	42	35

Hunting Roebuck A97

Hunting Scenes (16th-18th century): 2 l, Falconer (vert.). 3 l, Wild boar hunt. 4 l, Duck shooting with crossbow. 5 l, Stag hunt. 10 l, Mounted falconer (vert.). 30 l, Hunter with horn and dogs. 60 l, Hunter with rifle and dog (vert.). 70 l, Hunter and beater. 115 l, Duck hunt.

Wmk. 303

1961, May 4 **Photo.** ***Perf. 14***

477	A97	1 l lil rose & vio bl	8	8
478	A97	2 l gray, dk red & blk	8	8
479	A97	3 l red org, brn & blk	8	8
480	A97	4 l lt bl, red & blk	8	8
481	A97	5 l yel grn & brn	8	8
482	A97	10 l org, blk, brn & vio	9	9
483	A97	30 l yel, bl & dk grn	10	10
484	A97	60 l ocher, brn, blk & red	18	18
485	A97	70 l grn, blk & car	28	28
486	A97	115 l brt pink, blk & dk bl	50	50
		Nos. 477-486 (10)	1.55	1.55

Mt. Titano and Cancelled Stamp of Sardinia, 1862 — A98

Photogravure and Embossed

1961, Sept. 5 **Wmk. 303** ***Perf. 13***

487	A98	30 l multi	60	60
488	A98	70 l multi	1.25	1.25
489	A98	200 l multi	65	65

Centenary of Independence Phil. Exhib., Turin, 1961.

Europa Issue, 1961

View of San Marino A99

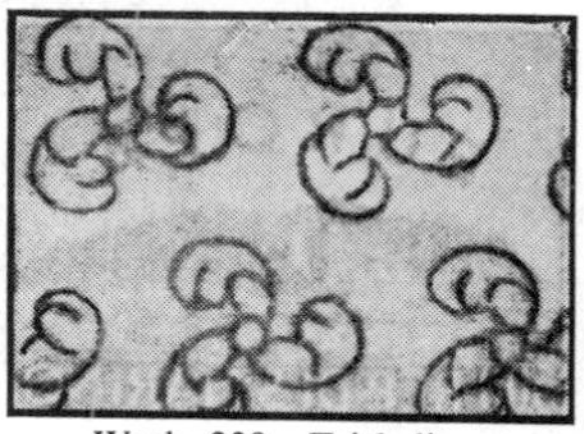

Wmk. 339 - Triskelion

Wmk. 339

1961, Oct. 20 **Photo.** ***Perf. 13***

490	A99	500 l brn & bl grn	9.75	9.75
		Sheet of 6	55.00	55.00

King Enzo's Palace and Neptune Fountain, Bologna — A100

Views of Bologna: 70 l, Loggia dei Mercanti. 100 l, Two Towers.

1961, Nov. 25 **Wmk. 339** ***Perf. 14***

491	A100	30 l grnsh bl & blk	8	8
492	A100	70 l dk ol grn & blk	14	14
493	A100	100 l red brn & blk	18	18

Bophilex, philatelic exhibition, Bologna.

Duryea, 1892 A101

Automobiles (pre-1910): 2 l, Panhard-Levassor. 3 l, Peugeot. 4 l, Daimler. 5 l, Fiat (vert.). 10 l, Decauville. 15 l, Wolseley. 20 l, Benz. 25 l, Napier. 30 l, White (vert.). 50 l, Oldsmobile. 70 l, Renault (vert.). 100 l, Isotta Fraschini. 115 l, Bianchi. 150 l, Alfa.

1962, Jan. 23 Wmk. 303 *Perf. 14*

494	A101	1 l red brn & bl	7	7
495	A101	2 l ultra & org brn	7	7
496	A101	3 l blk, brn & org	7	7
497	A101	4 l gray & dk red	7	7
498	A101	5 l vio & org	7	7
499	A101	10 l blk & org	7	7
500	A101	15 l blk & ver	7	7
501	A101	20 l blk & ultra	12	12
502	A101	25 l gray & org	12	12
503	A101	30 l blk & ocher	12	12
504	A101	50 l blk & brt pink	18	18
505	A101	70 l blk, gray & grn	18	18
506	A101	100 l blk, yel & car	18	18
507	A101	115 l blk, org & bl grn	18	18
508	A101	150 l multi	45	45
		Nos. 494-508 (15)	2.02	2.02

Wright Plane, 1904 A102

Historic Planes (1907-1910): 2 l, Ernest Archdeacon. 3 l, Albert and Emile Bonnet-Labranche. 4 l, Glenn Curtiss. 5 l, Farman. 10 l, Louis Blériot. 30 l, Hubert Latham. 60 l, Alberto Santos Dumont. 70 l, Alliott Verdon Roe. 115 l, Faccioli.

Wmk. 339

1962, Apr. 4 Photo. *Perf. 14*

509	A102	1 l blk & dl yel	7	7
510	A102	2 l red brn & grn	7	7
511	A102	3 l red brn & gray grn	7	7
512	A102	4 l brn & blk	7	7
513	A102	5 l mag & bl	7	7
514	A102	10 l ocher & bl grn	7	7
515	A102	30 l ocher & ultra	10	10
516	A102	60 l blk & ocher	22	22
517	A102	70 l dp org & blk	30	30
518	A102	115 l blk, grn & ocher	75	75
		Nos. 509-518 (10)	1.79	1.79

Mountaineer Descending A103

Designs: 2 l, View of Sassolungo. 3 l, Mt. Titano. 4 l, Three Peaks of Javaredo. 5 l, Matterhorn. 15 l, Skier on downhill run. 30 l, Climbing an overhang. 40 l, Cutting steps in ice. 85 l, Giant's Tooth. 115 l, Mt. Titano.

1962, June 14 Wmk. 339 *Perf. 14*

519	A103	1 l bis brn & blk	5	5
520	A103	2 l Prus grn & blk	5	5
521	A103	3 l lil & blk	5	5
522	A103	4 l brt bl & blk	5	5
523	A103	5 l dp org & blk	5	5
524	A103	15 l org yel & blk	10	10
525	A103	30 l car & blk	10	10
526	A103	40 l grnsh bl & blk	10	10
527	A103	85 l lt grn & blk	18	18
528	A103	115 l vio bl & blk	25	25
		Nos. 519-528 (10)	98	98

Hunter with Dog A104

Modern Hunting Scenes: 2 l, Hound master on horseback (vert.). 3 l, Duck hunt. 4 l, Stag hunt. 5 l, Partridge hunt. 15 l, Lapwing (hunt). 50 l, Wild duck hunt. 70 l, Duck hunt from boat. 100 l, Boar hunt. 150 l, Pheasant hunt (vert.).

1962, Aug. 25 Photo. *Perf. 14*

529	A104	1 l brn & yel grn	6	6
530	A104	2 l dk bl & org	6	6
531	A104	3 l blk & Prus bl	6	6
532	A104	4 l blk & brn	6	6
533	A104	5 l brn & yel grn	6	6
534	A104	15 l blk & org brn	8	8
535	A104	50 l brn, dp grn & blk	12	12
536	A104	70 l grn, sal pink & blk	15	15
537	A104	100 l blk, brick red & sep	18	18
538	A104	150 l grn lil & blk	22	22
		Nos. 529-538 (10)	1.05	1.05

Europa Issue, 1962

Mt. Titano and "Europa" A105

1962, Oct. 25 Wmk. 339

539	A105	200 l gray & car	2.25	2.25
		Sheet of 6	15.00	15.00

Egyptian Cargo Ship A106

Ancient Ships: 2 l, Greece, 2nd Cent. B.C. 3 l, Roman galley. 4 l, Vikings, 10th Cent. 5 l, "Santa Maria," 1492. 10 l, Cypriote galleon (vert.). 30 l, Galley, 1600. 60 l, "Sovereign of the Seas," 1637 (vert.). 70 l, Danish ship, 1750 (vert.). 115 l, Frigate, 1850.

1963, Jan. 10

540	A106	1 l bl & org yel	7	7
541	A106	2 l mag, tan & brn	7	7
542	A106	3 l brn & lil rose	7	7
543	A106	4 l vio brn & gray	7	7
544	A106	5 l brn & yel	7	7
545	A106	10 l brn & brt yel grn	10	10
546	A106	30 l blk, bl & sep	60	45
547	A106	60 l lt vio bl & yel grn	45	45
548	A106	70 l blk, gray & dl red	45	45
549	A106	115 l blk, brn & gray bl	1.25	1.40
		Nos. 540-549 (10)	3.20	3.20

Lady with Veil, by Raphael — A107

Jousting with "Saracen," Arezzo — A108

Paintings by Raphael: 70 l, Self-portrait. 100 l, St. Barbara from Sistine Madonna. 200 l, Portrait of a Young Woman (Maddalena Strozzi).

Wmk. 339

1963, Mar. 28 Photo. *Perf. 14*

Size: 26½x37mm

550	A107	30 l multi	40	40
551	A107	70 l multi	15	15
552	A107	100 l multi	25	25

Size: 26½x44mm

553	A107	200 l multi	48	48

1963, June 22 Wmk. 339 *Perf. 14*

Medieval "Knightly Games": 2 l, French knights (horiz.). 3l, Crossbow contest. 4 l, English knight receiving lance (horiz.). 5 l, Tournament, Florence. 10 l, Jousting with "Quintana," Ascoli Piceno. 30 l, "Quintana," Foligno (horiz.). 60 l, Race through Siena. 70 l, Tournament, Malpaga (horiz.). 115 l, Knights challenging.

554	A108	1 l lilac rose	8	8
555	A108	2 l slate	8	8
556	A108	3 l black	8	8
557	A108	4 l violet	8	8
558	A108	5 l rose vio	8	8
559	A108	10 l dull grn	8	8
560	A108	30 l red brown	8	8
561	A108	60 l Prussian grn	10	8
562	A108	70 l brown	10	10
563	A108	115 l black	10	10
		Nos. 554-563 (10)	86	84

Butterfly — A109

St. Marinus Statue, Government Palace — A110

Designs: Various Butterflies (70 l, 115 l, horiz.).

Wmk. 339

1963, Aug. 31 Photo. *Perf. 14*

564	A109	25 l multi	8	8
565	A109	30 l multi	8	8
566	A109	60 l multi	9	9
567	A109	70 l multi	10	10
568	A109	115 l multi	16	16
		Nos. 564-568 (5)	51	51

1963, Aug. 31

569	A110	100 l shown	25	25
570	A110	100 l Modern fountain	25	25

San Marino-Riccione Stamp Fair.

Europa Issue, 1963

Flag and "E" — A111

1963, Sept. 21 Wmk. 339 *Perf. 14*

571	A111	200 l bl & brn org	40	40

Women's Hurdles A112

Sports: 2 l, Pole vaulting (vert.). 3 l, Women's relay race. 4 l, Men's high jump. 5 l, Soccer. 10 l, Women's high jump. 30 l, Women's discus throw (vert.). 60 l, Women's javelin throw. 70 l, Water polo. 115 l, Hammer throw.

1963, Sept. 21

572	A112	1 l org & red brn	5	5
573	A112	2 l lt grn & dk brn	5	5
574	A112	3 l bl & dk brn	5	5
575	A112	4 l dp bl & dk brn	5	5
576	A112	5 l red & dk brn	5	5
577	A112	10 l lil rose & cl	5	5
578	A112	30 l gray & red brn	5	5
579	A112	60 l brt yel & dk brn	6	6
580	A112	70 l brt bl & dk brn	6	6
581	A112	115 l grn & dk brn	8	8
		Nos. 572-581 (10)	55	55

Publicity for 1964 Olympic Games.

Modern Pentathlon A113

Designs: 1 l, Runner (vert.). 2 l, Woman gymnast (vert.). 3 l, Basketball (vert.). 5 l, Dual rowing. 15 l, Broad jumper. 30 l, Swimmer in racing dive. 70 l, Woman sprinter. 120 l, Bicycle racers (vert.). 150 l, Fencers (vert.).

Inscribed "Tokio, 1964"

1964, June 25 Wmk. 339 *Perf. 14*

582	A113	1 l brn & yel grn	9	9
583	A113	2 l blk & red brn	9	9
584	A113	3 l blk & brn	9	9
585	A113	4 l blk & org red	9	9
586	A113	5 l blk & brt bl	9	9
587	A113	15 l dk brn & org	9	9
588	A113	30 l dk vio & bl	10	10
589	A113	70 l red brn & grn	12	12
590	A113	120 l brn & brt bl	12	12
591	A113	150 l blk & crim	14	14
		Nos. 582-591 (10)	1.02	1.02

18th Olympic Games, Tokyo, Oct. 10-25.

Same Inscribed "Verso Tokio"

1964, June 25 Photo.

592	A113	30 l ind & lil	14	14
593	A113	70 l brn & Prus grn	20	20

"Verso Tokyo" Stamp Exhibition at Rimini, Italy, June 25-July 6.

Murray-Blenkinsop Locomotive, 1812 — A114

History of Locomotive: 2 l, Puffing Billy, 1813. 3 l, Locomotion I, 1825. 4 l, Rocket, 1829. 5 l, Lion, 1838. 15 l, Bayard, 1839. 20 l, Crampton, 1849. 50 l, Little England, 1851. 90 l, Spitfire, c. 1860. 110 l, Rogers, c. 1865.

1964, Aug. 29 Wmk. 339 *Perf. 14*

594	A114	1 l blk & buff	7	7
595	A114	2 l blk & grn	7	7
596	A114	3 l blk & rose lil	7	7
597	A114	4 l blk & yel	7	7
598	A114	5 l blk & salmon	7	7
599	A114	15 l blk & yel grn	7	7
600	A114	20 l blk & dp pink	7	7
601	A114	50 l blk & pale bl	14	14
602	A114	90 l blk & yel org	42	42
603	A114	110 l blk & brt bl	70	70
		Nos. 594-603 (10)	1.75	1.75

Baseball Players A115

Design: 70 l, Pitcher.

1964, Aug. 29 Photo.

604	A115	30 l blk, dp grn & gray	18	18
605	A115	70 l blk & dp carmine	20	20

8th European Baseball Championship, Milan.

Europa Issue, 1964

"E" and Globe A116

1964, Oct. 15 Wmk. 339 *Perf. 14*

606	A116	200 l dk bl & red	55	55

President John F. Kennedy (1917-1963) A117

Design: 130 l, John F. Kennedy and American flag (vert.).

1964, Nov. 22 Photo. *Perf. 14*

607 A117 70 l multi 15 15
608 A117 130 l multi 22 22

Start of Bicycle Race from Government Palace A118

Rooks on Chessboard A120

Brontosaurus — A119

Designs: 70 l, Cyclists (going right) and view of San Marino. 200 l, Cyclists (going left) and view of San Marino.

1965, May 15 Photo. Wmk. 339

609 A118 30 l sepia 8 8
610 A118 70 l dp claret 10 10
611 A118 200 l rose red 22 22

48th Bicycle Tour of Italy.

1965, June 30 Wmk. 339 *Perf. 14*

Dinosaurs: 2 l, Brachiosaurus (vert.). 3 l, Pteranodon. 4 l, Elasmosaurus. 5 l, Tyrannosaurus. 10 l, Stegosaurus. 75 l, Thaumatosaurus victor. 100 l, Iguanodon. 200 l, Triceratops.

612 A119 1 l dk brn & emer 8 8
613 A119 2 l blk & sl bl 8 8
614 A119 3 l sl grn, ol grn & yel 8 8
615 A119 4 l brn & sl bl 8 8
616 A119 5 l claret & grn 8 8
617 A119 10 l claret & grn 10 10
618 A119 75 l dk bl & bl grn 35 35
619 A119 100 l grn & claret 35 35
620 A119 200 l brn & grn 50 50
Nos. 612-620 (9) 1.70 1.70

Europa Issue, 1965

1965, Aug. 28 Photo. *Perf. 14*

621 A120 200 l brn & multi 28 28

Dante by Gustave Dore A121

Doré's Illustrations for Divina Commedia: 90 l, Charon ferrying boat across Acheron. 130 l, Eagle carrying Dante from Purgatory to Paradise. 140 l, Dante with Beatrice examined by Sts. Peter, James and John on faith.

Perf. 14x14½

1965, Nov. 20 Engr. Wmk. 339

Center in Brown Black

622 A121 40 l indigo 12 12
623 A121 90 l car rose 12 12
624 A121 130 l red brn 12 12
625 A121 140 l ultra 18 18

Dante Alighieri (1265-1321), poet.

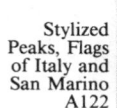

Stylized Peaks, Flags of Italy and San Marino A122

1965, Nov. 25 Photo. *Perf. 14*

626 A122 115 l grn, red, ocher & bl 18 18

Visit of Giuseppe Saragat, president of Italy.

Trotter A123

Horses: 20 l, Cross Country (vert.). 40 l, Hurdling. 70 l, Gallop. 90 l, Steeplechase. 170 l, Polo (vert.).

Perf. 14x13, 13x14

1966, Feb. 28 Photo. Wmk. 339

627 A123 10 l multi 8 8
628 A123 20 l multi 8 8
629 A123 40 l multi 8 8
630 A123 70 l multi 10 10
631 A123 90 l multi 12 12
632 A123 170 l multi 18 18
Nos. 627-632 (6) 64 64

Scenic Types of 1955-57

Designs: 5 l, Hospital Street. 10 l, Gate tower. 15 l, View from South Bastion. 40l, Murata Nuova Bridge. 90 l, View of La Rocca. 140 l, Government Palace.

1966, Mar. 29 Wmk. 339 *Perf. 14*

633 A79 5 l blue & brn 6 6
634 A78 10 l dk sl grn & bl grn 6 6
635 A78 15 l dk brn & vio 6 6
636 A73 40 l dk pur & brick red 8 8
637 A74 90 l blk & dl bl 12 12
638 A74 140 l vio & org 15 15
Nos. 633-638 (6) 53 53

"Bella" by Titian A124

Titian Paintings: 90 l, 100 l, Details from "The Education of Love." 170 l, Detail from "Sacred and Profane Love."

1966, June 16 Wmk. 339 *Perf. 14*

639 A124 40 l multi 8 8
640 A124 90 l multi 12 12
641 A124 100 l multi 12 12
642 A124 170 l multi 22 22

Stone Bass A125

Fish: 2 l, Cuckoo wrasse. 3 l, Dolphin. 4 l, John Dory. 5 l, Octopus (vert.). 10 l, Orange scorpionfish. 40 l, Electric ray (vert.). 90 l, Jellyfish (vert.). 115 l, Sea Horse (vert.). 130 l, Dentex.

Perf. 14x13½, 13½x14

1966, Aug. 27 Photo. Wmk. 339

643 A125 1 l multi 8 8
644 A125 2 l multi 8 8
645 A125 3 l multi 8 8
646 A125 4 l multi 8 8
647 A125 5 l multi 8 8
648 A125 10 l multi 8 8
649 A125 40 l multi 8 8
650 A125 90 l multi 8 8
651 A125 115 l multi 9 9
652 A125 130 l multi 12 12
Nos. 643-652 (10) 85 85

Europa Issue, 1966

Our Lady of Europe A126

1966, Sept. 24 Wmk. 339 *Perf. 14*

653 A126 200 l multi 25 25

Peony and Mt. Titano — A127

Flowers and Various Views of Mt. Titano: 10 l, Bell flowers. 15 l, Pyrenean poppy. 20 l, Purple nettle. 40 l, Day lily. 140 l, Gentian. 170 l, Thistle.

Wmk. 339

1967, Jan. 12 Photo. *Perf. 14*

654 A127 5 l multi 8 8
655 A127 10 l multi 8 8
656 A127 15 l multi 8 8
657 A127 20 l multi 8 8
658 A127 40 l multi 8 8
659 A127 140 l multi 15 15
660 A127 170 l multi 15 15
Nos. 654-660 (7) 70 70

St. Marinus — A128

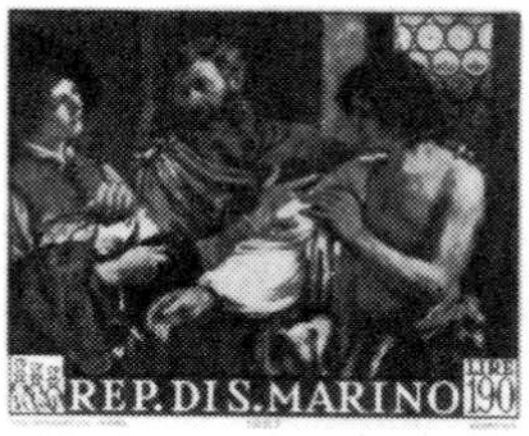

The Return of the Prodigal Son — A129

Design: 170 l, St. Francis. The paintings are by Giovanni Francesco Barbieri (1591-1666).

Wmk. 339

1967, March 16 Photo. *Perf. 14*

661 A128 40 l multi 8 8
662 A128 170 l multi 18 18
663 A129 190 l multi 20 20
Strip of 3, #661-663 48 48

Nos. 661-663 printed as triptychs. Each sheet contains 10 triptychs (2x5).

Map Showing Members of CEPT — A130

Amanita Caesarea — A131

Europa Issue, 1967

1967, May 5 Wmk. 339 *Perf. 14*

664 A130 200 l sl grn & brn org 25 20

1967, June 15 Photo. *Perf. 14*

Various Mushrooms.

665 A131 5 l multi 8 8
666 A131 15 l multi 8 8
667 A131 20 l multi 8 8
668 A131 40 l multi 8 8
669 A131 50 l multi 8 8
670 A131 170 l multi 15 15
Nos. 665-670 (6) 55 55

Amiens Cathedral A132

Designs: 40 l, Siena Cathedral. 80 l, Toledo Cathedral. 90 l, Salisbury Cathedral. 170 l, Cologne Cathedral.

Wmk. 339

1967, Sept. 21 Engr. *Perf. 14*

671 A132 20 l dk vio, *bister* 8 8
672 A132 40 l slate grn, *bis* 8 8
673 A132 80 l slate bl, *bis* 12 12
674 A132 90 l sepia, *bis* 12 12
675 A132 170 l deep plum, *bis* 16 16
Nos. 671-675 (5) 56 56

Crucifix of Santa Croce, by Cimabue A133

1967, Dec. 5 Wmk. 339 *Perf. 15*

676 A133 300 l brn & vio bl 40 40

The Crucifix of Santa Croce, by Giovanni Cimabue (1240-1302), was severely damaged in the Florentine flood of Nov. 1966.

Coat of Arms — A134

Coats of Arms: 3 l, Penna Rossa. 5 l, Fiorentino. 10 l, Montecerreto. 25 l, Serravalle. 35 l, Montegiardino. 50 l, Faetano. 90 l, Borgo Maggiore. 180 l, Montelupo. 500 l, State arms of San Marino.

Perf. 13x13½

1968, Mar. 14 Litho. Wmk. 339

677	A134	2 l multi	6	6
678	A134	3 l multi	6	6
679	A134	5 l multi	6	6
680	A134	10 l multi	6	6
681	A134	25 l multi	6	6
682	A134	35 l multi	8	8
683	A134	50 l multi	9	9
684	A134	90 l multi	9	9
685	A134	180 l multi	14	14
686	A134	500 l multi	48	48
		Nos. 677-686 (10)	1.18	1.18

Europa Issue, 1968

Common Design Type

1968, Apr. 29 Engr. *Perf. 14x13½*

Size: 37x27½mm

687	CD11	250 l cl brn	38	38

"Battle of San Romano" (Detail), by Paolo Uccello — A135

Designs: Details from "The Battle of San Romano," by Paolo Uccello (1397-1475). 90 l is vertical.

Photogravure and Engraved

1968, June 14 Wmk. 339 *Perf. 14*

688	A135	50 l pale pink & blk	6	6
689	A135	90 l pale lil & blk	10	10
690	A135	130 l pale lil & blk	14	14
691	A135	230 l pale pink & blk	30	30

The Mystic Nativity, by Botticelli, Detail A136

Wmk. 339

1968, Dec. 5 Engr. *Perf. 14*

692	A136	50 l dark blue	9	9
693	A136	90 l dp claret	12	12
694	A136	180 l sepia	25	25

Christmas.

"Peace" by Lorenzetti A137

Designs: 80 l, "Justice." 90 l, "Moderation." 180 l, View of Siena, 14th century (horiz.). All designs are from the "Good Government" frescoes by Ambrogio Lorenzetti in the Town Hall of Siena.

Wmk. 339

1969, Feb. 13 Engr. *Perf. 14*

695	A137	50 l dark blue	7	7
696	A137	80 l brown	10	10
697	A137	90 l dk bl vio	10	10
698	A137	180 l magenta	22	22

Young Soldier, by Bramante — A138

Designs: 90 l, Old Soldier, by Bramante. Designs are from murals in the Pinakotheke of Brear, Milan.

1969, Apr. 28 Photo. *Perf. 14*

699	A138	50 l multi	10	10
700	A138	90 l multi	12	12

Bramante (1444-1514), Italian architect and painter.

Europa Issue, 1969

Common Design Type

1969, Apr. 28 Engr. *Perf. 14x13*

Size: 37x27mm

701	CD12	50 l dl green	14	14
702	CD12	180 l rose claret	18	18

Charabanc A139

Coaches, 19th Century: 10 l, Barouche. 25 l, Private drag. 40 l, Hansom cab. 50 l, Curricle. 90 l, Wagonette. 180 l, Spider phaeton.

Perf. 14½x14

1969, June 25 Photo. Unwmk.

703	A139	5 l blk, ocher & dk bl	6	6
704	A139	10 l blk, grn & pur	6	6
705	A139	25 l dk grn, pink & brn	6	6
706	A139	40 l ind, lil & lt brn	10	10
707	A139	50 l blk, dl yel & dk bl	10	10
708	A139	90 l blk, yel grn & brn	10	10
709	A139	180 l multi	12	12
		Nos. 703-709 (7)	60	60

Pier at Rimini A140

Paintings by R. Viola: 20 l, Mt. Titano. 200 l, Pier at Riccione (horiz.).

1969, Sept. 17 Unwmk. *Perf. 14*

710	A140	20 l multi	8	8
711	A140	180 l multi	20	20
712	A140	200 l multi	24	24

"Faith" by Raphael — A141

Designs: 180 l, "Hope" by Raphael. 200 l, "Charity" by Raphael.

Perf. 13½x14

1969, Dec. 10 Engr. Wmk. 339

713	A141	20 l dl pur & sal	8	8
714	A141	180 l dl pur & lt grn	20	20
715	A141	200 l dp pur & bis	24	24

Aries A142

Signs of the Zodiac: 2 l, Taurus. 3 l, Gemini. 4 l, Cancer. 5 l, Leo. 10 l, Virgo. 15 l, Libra. 20 l, Scopio. 70 l, Sagittarius. 90 l, Capricorn. 100 l, Aquarius. 180 l, Pisces.

Perf. 14x13½

1970, Feb. 18 Photo. Unwmk.

716	A142	1 l blk & yel	8	8
717	A142	2 l blk & pink	8	8
718	A142	3 l blk & lil	8	8
719	A142	4 l blk & dp yel grn	8	8
720	A142	5 l blk & blue	8	8
721	A142	10 l blk & sale	8	8
722	A142	15 l blk & dl yel	8	8
723	A142	20 l blk & ocher	8	8
724	A142	70 l blk & bister	8	8
725	A142	90 l blk & brt pink	9	9
726	A142	100 l blk & rose	9	9
727	A142	180 l blk & gray bl	24	24
		Nos. 716-727 (12)	1.14	1.14

Fleet in Bay of Naples, by Peter Brueghel, the Elder — A143

Unwmk.

1970, Apr. 30 Photo. *Perf. 14*

728	A143	230 l multi	40	40

10th Europa Phil. Exhib., Naples, May 2-10.

Europa Issue, 1970

Common Design Type

1970, Apr. 30 *Perf. 14x13½*

Size: 36x27mm

729	CD13	90 l brt yel grn & red	14	14
730	CD13	180 l ocher & red	20	20

For unused stamps, more recent issues are valued as never hinged, with the beginning point determined on a country-by-country basis. Notes to show the beginning points are prominently placed in the text.

St. Francis' Gate and Rotary Emblem — A144

Woman with Mandolin, by Tiepolo — A145

Design: 220 l, Rocca (State Prison) and Rotary emblem.

1970, June 25 Photo. *Perf. 13½x14*

731	A144	180 l multi	25	25
732	A144	220 l multi	30	30

65th anniv. of Rotary Intl.; 10th anniv. of the San Marino Rotary Club.

1970, Sept. 10 Unwmk. *Perf. 14*

Paintings by Tiepolo: 180 l, Woman with Parrot. 220 l, Rinaldo and Armida Surprised (horiz.).

Size: 26½x37½mm

733	A145	50 l multi	15	15
734	A145	180 l multi	22	22

Size: 56x37½mm

735	A145	220 l multi	30	30
		Strip of 3, #733-735	70	70

Giambattista Tiepolo (1696-1770), Venetian painter. Nos. 733-735 printed as triptychs. Each sheet contains 10 triptychs (2x5).

Black Pete — A146

Walt Disney and Jungle Book Scene A147

Disney Characters: 2 l, Gyro Gearloose. 3 l, Pluto. 4 l, Minnie Mouse. 5 l, Donald Duck. 10 l, Goofy. 15 l, Scrooge McDuck. 50 l, Huey, Louey and Dewey. 90 l, Mickey Mouse.

Perf. 13x14, 14x13

1970, Dec. 22 Photo.

736	A146	1 l multi	6	6
737	A146	2 l multi	6	6
738	A146	3 l multi	6	6
739	A146	4 l multi	6	6
740	A146	5 l multi	6	6
741	A146	10 l multi	6	6
742	A146	15 l multi	6	6
743	A146	50 l multi	20	20
744	A146	90 l multi	38	38
745	A147	220 l multi	4.50	4.50
		Nos. 736-745 (10)	5.50	5.50

Honoring Walt Disney (1901-1966), cartoonist and film maker.

Customhouse Dock, by Canaletto — A148

Paintings by Canaletto: 180 l, Grand Canal between Balbi Palace and Rialto Bridge. 200 l, St. Mark's and Doges' Palace.

1971, Mar. 23 Unwmk. *Perf. 14*

746	A148	20 l multi	6	6
747	A148	180 l multi	30	30
748	A148	200 l multi	32	32

Save Venice campaign.

Europa Issue, 1971

Common Design Type

1971, May 29 *Perf. 13½x14*

Size: 27½x23mm

749	CD14	50 l org & blue	15	15
750	CD14	90 l blue & org	18	18

Congress Emblem and Hall, San Marino Flag — A149

Design: 90 l, Detail from Government Palace door, Congress and San Marino emblems (vert.).

1971, May 29 Photo. *Perf. 12*

751	A149	20 l vio & multi	8	8
752	A149	90 l ol & multi	12	12
753	A149	180 l multi	22	22

Italian Philatelic Press Union Congress, San Marino, May 29-30.

Duck-shaped Jug with Flying Lasa — A150

Etruscan Art, 6th-3rd Centuries B.C.: 80 l, Head of Mercury (vert.). 90 l, Sarcophagus of a married couple (vert.). 180 l, Chimera.

Photo. & Engr.

1971, Sept. 16 *Perf. 14*

754	A150	50 l blk & org	12	12
755	A150	80 l blk & lt grn	12	12
756	A150	90 l blk & lt bl	12	12
757	A150	180 l blk & org	22	22

Tiger Lily A151

Venus, by Botticelli A152

Flowers: 2 l, Phlox. 3 l, Carnations. 4 l, Globe flowers. 5 l, Thistles. 10 l, Peonies. 15 l, Hellebore. 50 l, Anemones. 90 l, Gaillardia. 220 l, Asters.

1971, Dec. 2 Photo. *Perf. 11½*

758	A151	1 l brt yel & multi	5	5
759	A151	2 l lt bl & multi	5	5
760	A151	3 l yel & multi	5	5
761	A151	4 l multi	5	5
762	A151	5 l multi	5	5
763	A151	10 l gray & multi	5	5
764	A151	15 l pink & multi	5	5
765	A151	50 l pale bl & multi	8	8
766	A151	90 l tan & multi	8	8
767	A151	220 l multi	20	20
		Nos. 758-767 (10)	71	71

1972, Feb. 23 *Perf. 14, 13x14 (180 l)*

Details from La Primavera, by Sandro Botticelli: 180 l, Three Graces. 220 l, Spring.

Sizes: 50 l, 220 l, 21x37mm; 180 l, 27x37mm

768	A152	50 l gold & multi	12	12
769	A152	180 l gold & multi	18	18
770	A152	220 l gold & multi	25	25

Europa Issue 1972

Common Design Type

1972, Apr. 27 *Perf. 11½*

Granite Paper

Size: 22½x33mm

771	CD15	50 l org & multi	15	15
772	CD15	90 l lt bl & multi	15	15

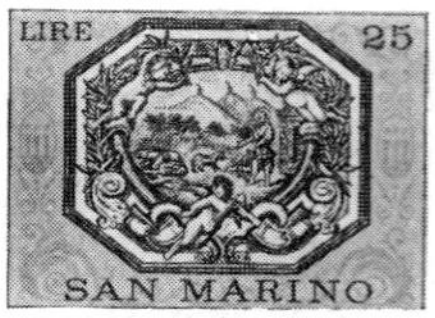

St. Marinus Taming Bear A153

Designs: 55 l, Donna Felicissima asking St. Marinus for mercy for her sons. 100 l, St. Marinus turning archers to stone. 130 l, Felicissima giving mountains to St. Marinus to establish Republic.

Photo. & Engr.

1972, Apr. 27 *Perf. 14*

773	A153	25 l dl yel & blk	8	8
774	A153	55 l sal pink & blk	8	8
775	A153	100 l dl bl & blk	10	10
776	A153	130 l citron & blk	12	12

Allegories of San Marino after 16th century paintings.

Italian House Sparrow — A154

1972, June 30 Photo. *Perf. 11½*

Granite Paper

777	A154	1 l shown	5	5
778	A154	2 l Firecrest	5	5
779	A154	3 l Blue tit	5	5
780	A154	4 l Ortolan bunting	5	5
781	A154	5 l White-spotted bluethroat	5	5
782	A154	10 l Bullfinch	5	5
783	A154	25 l Linnet	5	5
784	A154	50 l Black-eared wheater	12	12
785	A154	90 l Sardinian warbler	12	12
786	A154	220 l Greenfinch	24	24
		Nos. 777-786 (10)	83	83

Young Man, Heart, Emblem — A155

Italian Philatelic Federation Emblem — A156

Design: 90 l, Heart disease victim (horiz.).

Perf. 13½x14, 14x13½

1972, Aug. 26

787	A155	50 l lt bl & multi	12	12
788	A155	90 l ocher & multi	16	16

World Heart Month.

1972, Aug. 26 *Perf. 13½x14*

789	A156	25 l gold & ultra	15	15

Honoring veterans of Philately.

5c Coin, 1864 A157

Coins: 10 l, 10c coin, 1935. 15 l, 1 lira, 1906. 20 l, 5 lire, 1898. 25 l, 5 lire, 1937. 50 l, 10 lire, 1932. 55 l, 20 lire, 1938. 220 l, 20 lire, 1925.

1972, Dec. 15 Litho. *Perf. 12½x13*

790	A157	5 l gray, blk & brn	5	5
791	A157	10 l org, blk & sil	5	5
792	A157	15 l brt rose, blk & sil	8	8
793	A157	20 l lil, blk & sil	8	8
794	A157	25 l vio, blk & sil	8	8
795	A157	50 l brt bl, blk & sil	8	8
796	A157	55 l ocher, blk & sil	10	10
797	A157	220 l emer, blk & gold	22	22
		Nos. 790-797 (8)	74	74

New York, 1673 A158

Design: 300 l, View of New York from East River, 1973.

1973, Mar. 9 Photo. *Perf. 11½*

Granite Paper

798	A158	200 l bis, ocher & ol grn	32	32
799	A158	300 l bl, lil & blk	40	40
		Pair, #798-799	80	80

New York, 300th anniv. Nos. 798-799 printed se-tenant checkerwise in sheets of 50.

Rotary Press, San Marino Towers — A159

Gymnasts and Olympic Rings — A160

1973, May 10 Photo. *Perf. 13x14*

800	A159	50 l multi	15	15

Tourist Press Congress, San Marino.

1973, May 10 Unwmk.

801	A160	100 l grn & multi	18	18

5th Youth Games.

Europa Issue 1973

Common Design Type

1973, May 10 *Perf. 11½*

Size: 32½x23mm

802	CD16	20 l sal & multi	28	28
803	CD16	180 l lt bl & multi	1.40	1.40

Grapes — A161

1973, July 11 Photo. *Perf. 11½*

804	A161	1 l shown	5	5
805	A161	2 l Tangerines	5	5
806	A161	3 l Apples	5	5
807	A161	4 l Plums	5	5
808	A161	5 l Strawberries	5	5
809	A161	10 l Pears	6	6
810	A161	25 l Cherries	8	8
811	A161	50 l Pomegranate	10	10
812	A161	90 l Apricots	10	10
813	A161	220 l Peaches	14	14
		Nos. 804-813 (10)	73	73

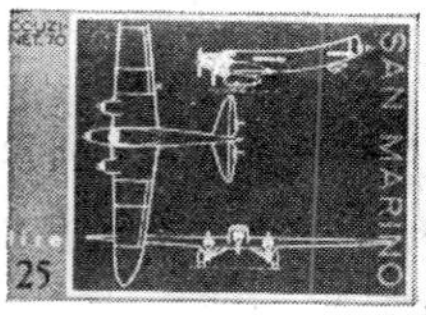

Arc-en-Ciel, France A162

Famous Aircraft: 55 l, Macchi Castoldi, Italy. 60 l, Antonov, USSR. 90 l, Spirit of St. Louis, USA. 220 l, Handley Page, Great Britain.

1973, Aug. 31 Photo. *Perf. 14x13½*

814	A162	25 l ocher, vio bl & gold	8	8
815	A162	55 l gray, vio bl & gold	8	8
816	A162	60 l rose, vio bl & gold	8	8
817	A162	90 l lem, vio bl & gold	10	10
818	A162	220 l org, vio bl & gold	22	22
		Nos. 814-818 (5)	56	56

Crossbowman, Serravalle Castle — A163

Designs: 10 l, Crossbowman, Pennarossa Castle. 15 l, Drummer, Montegiardino Castle. 20 l, Trumpeter, Fiorentino Castle. 30 l, Crossbowman, Borga Maggiore Castle. 50 l, Trumpeter, Guaita Castle. 80 l, Crossbowman, Faetano Castle. 200 l, Crossbowman, Montelupo Castle.

1973, Nov. 7 Photo. *Perf. 13½*

819	A163	5 l blk & multi	5	5
820	A163	10 l blk & multi	6	6
821	A163	15 l blk & multi	6	6
822	A163	20 l blk & multi	8	8
823	A163	30 l blk & multi	8	8
824	A163	40 l blk & multi	8	8
825	A163	50 l blk & multi	14	14
826	A163	80 l blk & multi	14	14
827	A163	200 l blk & multi	20	20
		Nos. 819-827 (9)	89	89

San Marino victories in the Crossbow Tournament, Massa Marittima, July 15, 1973.

Attendants, by Gentile Fabriano — A164

1973, Dec. 19 Photo. *Perf. 11½*

Christmas: Details from Adoration of the Kings, by Gentile Fabriano (1370-1427).

828	A164	5 l shown	8	8
829	A164	30 l King	8	8
830	A164	115 l King	14	14
831	A164	250 l Horses	22	22

Shield, 16th Century — A165

16th Century Armor: 5 l, Round shield. 10 l, German full armor. 15 l, Helmet with intricate etching. 20 l, Horse's head armor "Massimiliano." 30 l, Decorated helmet with Sphinx statuette on top. 50 l, Pommeled sword and gauntlets. 80 l, Sparrow-beaked helmet. 250 l, Sforza round shield.

Engr. & Litho.

1974, Mar. 12 ***Perf. 13***

832	A165	5 l blk, lt grn & buff	5	5
833	A165	10 l blk, buff & bl	6	6
834	A165	15 l blk, bl & ultra	6	6
835	A165	20 l blk, tan & ultra	8	8
836	A165	30 l blk & lt bl	8	8
837	A165	50 l blk, rose & ultra	12	12
838	A165	80 l blk, gray & grn	12	12
839	A165	250 l blk & yel	22	22
		Nos. 832-839 (8)	79	79

Europa Issue 1974

Head of Woman, by Emilio Greco — A166

Design: 200 l, Nude, by Emilio Greco (head shown on 100 l).

Engr. & Litho.

1974, May 9 ***Perf. 13x14***

840	A166	100 l buff & blk	16	16
841	A166	200 l pale grn & blk	32	32

Yachts at Riccione and San Marino Peaks A167

1974, July 18 **Photo.** ***Perf. 11½***

Granite Paper

842	A167	50 l ultra & multi	18	18

26th San Marino-Riccione Stamp Day.

Arms of San Sepolcro — A168

Designs: Coats of arms of participating cities.

1974, July 18 ***Perf. 12***

843	A168	15 l shown	90	90
844	A168	20 l Massa Marittima	90	90
845	A168	50 l San Marino	90	90
846	A168	115 l Gubbio	90	90
847	A168	300 l Lucca	90	90
		Strip of 5, #843-847	4.75	4.75
		Nos. 843-847 (5)	4.50	4.50

9th Crossbow Tournament, San Marino. Nos. 843-847 printed se-tenant in sheets of 25 (5x5).

UPU Emblem — A169

1974, Oct. 9 **Photo.** ***Perf. 11½***

Granite Paper

848	A169	50 l multi	10	10
849	A169	90 l grn & multi	12	12

Centenary of Universal Postal Union.

Mt. Titano and Hymn by Tommaseo A170

Niccolo Tommaseo A171

1974, Dec. 12 **Photo.** ***Perf. 13½x14***

850	A170	50 l lt grn, blk & red	6	6
851	A171	150 l yel, grn & blk	18	18

Tommaseo (1802-1874), Italian writer.

Virgin and Child, 14th Century Wood Panel — A172

1974, Dec. 12 ***Perf. 11½***

852	A172	250 l gold & multi	28	28

Christmas.

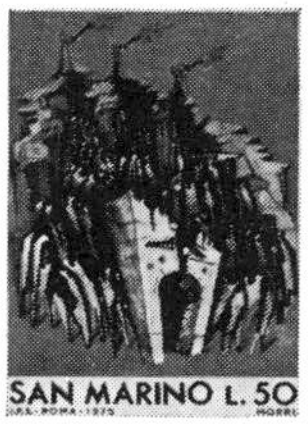

"Refuge in San Marino" — A173

1975, Feb. 20 **Photo.** ***Perf. 13½x14***

853	A173	50 l multi	15	15

Flight of 100,000 refugees from Romagna to San Marino, 30th anniversary.

Musicians, from Leopard Tomb, Tarquinia — A174

Etruscan Art: 30 l, Chariot race, from Tomb on the Hill, Chiusi. 180 l, Achilles and Troilus, from Bulls' Tomb, Tarquinia. 220 l, Dancers, from Triclinium Tomb, Tarquinia.

Litho. & Engr.

1975, Feb. 20 ***Perf. 14***

854	A174	20 l multi	7	7
855	A174	30 l multi	8	8
856	A174	180 l multi	15	15
857	A174	220 l multi	25	25

Europa Issue 1975

St. Marinus, by Guercino (Francesco Barbieri)
A175 A176

1975, May 14 **Photo.** ***Perf. 11½***

Granite Paper

858	A175	100 l multi	14	14
859	A176	200 l multi	25	25

The Lamentation, by Giotto — A177

Frescoes by Giotto (details): 40 l, Mary and Jesus (Flight into Egypt). 50 l, Heads of four angels (Flight into Egypt). 100 l, Mary Magdalene (Noli Me Tangere) (horiz.). 500 l, Angel and the elect (Last Judgment) (horiz.).

1975, July 10 **Photo.** ***Perf. 11½***

Granite Paper

860	A177	10 l gold & multi	5	5
861	A177	40 l gold & multi	9	9
862	A177	50 l gold & multi	9	9
863	A177	100 l gold & multi	14	14
864	A177	500 l gold & multi	42	42
		Nos. 860-864 (5)	79	79

Holy Year.

Tokyo, 1835, Woodcut by Hiroshige — A178

Design: 300 l, Tokyo, Business District, 1975.

1975, Sept. 5 **Photo.** ***Perf. 11½***

Granite Paper

865	A178	200 l multi	24	24
866	A178	300 l multi	35	35

Nos. 865-866 printed se-tenant checkerwise in sheets of 50.

Aphrodite A179

1975, Sept. 19 **Photo.** ***Perf. 11½***

867	A179	50 l vio, blk & gray	20	20

Europa '75 Philatelic Exhibition, Naples.

Multiple Crosses A180

1975, Sept. 19

868	A180	100 l blk, dp org & vio	18	18

EUROCOPHAR Intl. Pharmaceutical Cong.

Angel — A181

Doni Madonna — A182

Design: 100 l, Head of Virgin, from Doni Madonna by Michelangelo.

1975, Dec. 3 **Photo.** ***Perf. 11½***

Granite Paper

869	A181	50 l multi	15	12
870	A181	100 l multi	15	15
871	A182	250 l multi	60	60
		Strip of 3	80	80

Christmas. Nos. 869-871 printed se-tenant in sheets of 30 (6x5).

Woman on Balcony, by Gentilini — A183

Two Women, by Gentilini A184

Design: 230 l, Woman (same as right head on 150 l) and IWY emblem, by Franco Gentilini.

1975, Dec. 3

Granite Paper

872	A183	70 l bl & multi	8	8
873	A184	150 l multi	15	15
874	A183	230 l multi	25	25

International Women's Year.

Modesty, by Emilio Greco — A185

Capitol, Washington, D.C. — A186

"Civic Virtues": 20 l, Temperance. 50 l, Fortitude. 100 l, Altruism. 150 l, Hope. 220 l, Prudence. 250 l, Justice. 300 l, Faith. 500 l, Honesty. 1000 l, Industry. Designs show drawings of women's heads by Emilio Greco.

1976, Mar. 4 Photo. *Perf. 11½*
Granite Paper

875	A185	10 l	buff & blk	5	5
876	A185	20 l	pink & blk	5	5
877	A185	50 l	grnsh & blk	8	8
878	A185	100 l	salmon & blk	12	12
879	A185	150 l	lilac & blk	16	16
880	A185	220 l	gray & blk	25	25
881	A185	250 l	yel & multi	35	35
882	A185	300 l	gray & blk	38	38
883	A185	500 l	yel & blk	60	60
884	A185	1000 l	gray & blk	1.25	1.25
			Nos. 875-884 (10)	3.29	3.29

See Nos. 900-905, 931-933.

1976, May 29 Photo. *Perf. 11½*

Arms of San Marino and: 150 l, Statue of Liberty. 180 l, Independence Hall, Philadelphia.

885	A186	70 l	multi	12	12
886	A186	150 l	multi	16	16
887	A186	180 l	multi	22	22

American Bicentennial.

Montreal Olympic Games Emblem A187

1976, May 29

888	A187	150 l	crim & blk	20	20

21st Olympic Games, Montreal, Canada, July 17-Aug. 1.

Europa Issue 1976

Decorated Plate — A188

Design: 180 l, Seal of San Marino.

1976, July 8 Photo. *Perf. 11½*
Granite Paper

889	A188	150 l	multi	22	22
890	A188	180 l	bl, sil & blk	22	22

"Unity" — A189

"Peaks of San Marino" — A190

1976, July 8 *Perf. 13½x14*

891	A189	150 l	vio blk, yel & red	22	22

United Mutual Aid Society, centenary.

1976, Oct. 14 Photo. *Perf. 13x14*

892	A190	150 l	blk & multi	22	22

ITALIA 76 Intl. Phil. Exhib., Milan, Oct. 14-24.

A little time given to the study of the arrangement of the Scott Catalogue can make it easier to use effectively.

Children and UNESCO Emblem A191

1976, Oct. 14 *Perf. 11½*
Granite Paper

893	A191	181 l	multi	22	22
894	A191	220 l	multi	25	25

UNESCO, 30th anniv.

Annunciation (detail), by Titian — A192

Design: 300 l, Virgin and Child, by Titian.

Litho. & Engr.
1976, Dec. 15 *Perf. 13x14*

895	A192	150 l	multi	15	15
896	A192	300 l	multi	42	42

Christmas. Nos. 895-896 printed se-tenant.

Exhibition Emblem A193

1977, Jan. 28 Photo. *Perf. 11½*
Granite Paper

897	A193	80 l	multi	9	9
898	A193	170 l	multi	15	15
899	A193	200 l	multi	24	24

San Marino 77 Phil. Exhib. See No. C133.

Civic Virtues Type of 1976

Designs: 70 l, Fortitude. 90 l, Prudence. 120 l, Altruism. 160 l, Temperance. 170 l, Hope. 320 l, Faith.

1977, Apr. 14 Photo. *Perf. 11½*
Granite Paper

900	A185	70 l	pink & blk	7	7
901	A185	90 l	buff & blk	10	10
902	A185	120 l	lt bl & blk	12	12
903	A185	160 l	lt grn & blk	22	22
904	A185	170 l	cream & blk	22	22
905	A185	320 l	lil & blk	40	40
			Nos. 900-905 (6)	1.13	1.13

Europa Issue 1977

San Marino, after Ghirlandaio A194

Design: 200 l, San Marino, detail from painting by Guercino.

1977, Apr. 14
Granite Paper

906	A194	170 l	multi	22	22
907	A194	200 l	multi	25	25

Vertical Flying Machine, by da Vinci — A195

Litho. & Engr.
1977, June 6 *Perf. 13x14*

908	A195	120 l	multi	18	18

Centenary of Enrico Forlanini's experiments with vertical flight.

University Square, Bucharest, 1877 — A196

Design: 400 l, National Theater and Intercontinental Hotel, 1977.

1977, June 6 Photo. *Perf. 11½*
Granite Paper

909	A196	200 l	bis & multi	28	28
910	A196	400 l	lt bl & multi	40	40

Centenary of Romanian independence. Nos. 909-910 printed checkerwise in sheets of 50.

Type A2 of 1877 — A197

1977, June 15 Engr. *Perf. 15x14½*

911	A197	40 l	slate grn	6	6
912	A197	70 l	deep blue	10	10
913	A197	170 l	red	32	32
914	A197	500 l	brown	55	55
915	A197	1000 l	purple	1.10	1.10
			Nos. 911-915 (5)	2.13	2.13

Centenary of San Marino stamps.

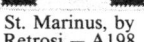

St. Marinus, by Retrosi — A198

Medicinal Plants — A199

Souvenir Sheet
1977, Aug. 28 Photo. *Perf. 11½*
Granite Paper

916	A198		Sheet of 5	8.50	8.50
a.		1000 l	single stamp	1.65	1.65

Centenary of San Marino stamps; San Marino '77 Phil. Exhib., Aug. 28-Sept. 4.

1977, Oct. 19 Photo. *Perf. 11½*

917	A199	170 l	multi	22	22

Congress of Italian Pharmacists' Union. Design shows high mallow, tilia, camomile, borage, centaury and juniper.

Woman Attacked by Octopus, Emblem A200

1977, Oct. 19

918	A200	200 l	multi	25	25

World Rheumatism Year.

Virgin Mary — A201

San Francisco Gate — A202

Christmas: 230 l, Palm, olive and star. 300 l, Angel.

1977, Dec. 5 Photo. *Perf. 11½*

919	A201	170 l	sil, gray & blk	20	20
920	A201	230 l	sil, gray & blk	25	25
921	A201	300 l	sil, gray & blk	30	30

Nos. 919-921 printed se-tenant.

Europa Issue 1978

Design: 200 l, Ripa Gate.

1978, May 30 Photo. *Perf. 11½*

922	A202	170 l	lt bl & dk bl	20	20
923	A202	200 l	buff & brn	28	28

Baseball Player and Diamond A203

Feather, WHO Emblem A204

1978, May 30

924	A203	90 l	multi	12	12
925	A203	120 l	multi	18	18

World Baseball Championships.

1978, May 30

926	A204	320 l	multi	38	38

Fight against hypertension.

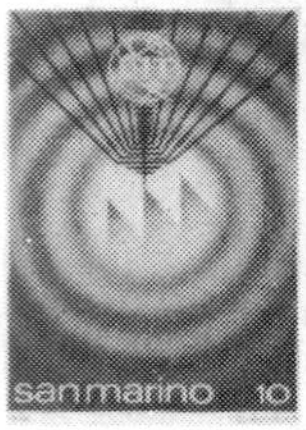

ITU Emblem, Waves Coming from 3 Peaks — A205

1978, July 26 Photo. *Perf. 11½*

927	A205	10 l	car & yel	5	5
928	A205	200 l	vio bl & lt bl	30	30

Membership in ITU.

Seagull and Falcon, 3 Peaks A206

1978, July 26

929 A206 120 l multi 14 14
930 A206 170 l multi 22 22

30th San Marino-Riccione Stamp Day.

Civic Virtues Type of 1976

Drawings by Emilio Greco: 5 l, Wisdom. 35 l, Love. 2000 l, Faithfulness.

1978, Sept. 28 Photo. *Perf. 11½*
Granite Paper

931 A185 5 l lt vio & blk 5 5
932 A185 35 l gray & blk 10 10
933 A185 2000 l yel & blk 2.25 2.25

Holly Leaves A207

Christmas: 120 l, Stars. 170 l, Snowflakes.

1978, Dec. 6 Photo. *Perf. 14x13½*

941 A207 10 l multi 5 5
942 A207 120 l multi 12 12
943 A207 170 l multi 24 24

Globe and Woman Holding Torch — A208

1978, Dec. 6 *Perf. 11½x12*

944 A208 200 l multi 22 22

Universal Declaration of Human Rights, 30th anniversary.

Europa Issue 1979

First San Marino Autobus, 1915 A209

Design: 220 l, Mail coach, 1895.

1979, Mar. 29 Photo. *Perf. 11½x12*

945 A209 170 l multi 24 24
946 A209 220 l multi 30 30

Albert Einstein (1879-1955), Theoretical Physicist A210

1979, Mar. 29 *Perf. 11½*

947 A210 120 l gray, lt & dk brn 30 30

San Marino Crossbow Federation Emblem A211

Maigret A212

1979, July 12 Litho. *Perf. 14x13*

948 A211 120 l multi 20 20

14th Crossbow Tournament.

Litho. & Engr.
1979, July 12 *Perf. 13x14*

Fictional Detectives: 80 l, Perry Mason. 150 l, Nero Wolfe. 170 l, Ellery Queen. 220 l, Sherlock Holmes.

949 A212 10 l multi 5 5
950 A212 80 l multi 15 15
951 A212 150 l multi 20 20
952 A212 170 l multi 20 20
953 A212 220 l multi 32 32
Nos. 949-953 (5) 92 92

Girl Holding Bird — A213

IYC Emblem, Paintings by Marina Busignani: 120 l, 170 l, 220 l, Children and birds (diff.). 350 l, Mother nursing child.

1979, Sept. 6 Litho. *Perf. 11½*

954 A213 20 l multi 6 6
955 A213 120 l multi 10 10
956 A213 170 l multi 20 20
957 A213 220 l multi 24 24
958 A213 350 l multi 35 35
Nos. 954-958 (5) 95 95

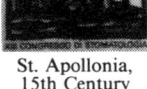

St. Apollonia, 15th Century Woodcut — A214

Chestnut Tree, Deer — A216

Waterskier A215

1979, Sept. 6 Photo.

959 A214 170 l multi 20 20

13th Biennial Intl. Congress of Stomatology.

1979, Sept. 6

960 A215 150 l multi 20 20

European Waterskiing Championship.

1979, Oct. 25 Photo. *Perf. 11½*

Protected Trees and Animals or Birds: 10 l, Cedar of Lebanon, falcon. 35 l, Dogwood, racoon. 50 l, Banyan, tiger. 70 l, Umbrella pine, hoopoe. 90 l, Siberian spruce, marten. 100 l, Eucalyptus, koala bear. 120 l, Date palm, camel. 150 l, Sugar maple, beaver. 170 l, Adansonia, elephant.

961 A216 5 l multi 5 5
962 A216 10 l multi 5 5
963 A216 35 l multi 6 6
964 A216 50 l multi 7 7
965 A216 70 l multi 8 8
966 A216 90 l multi 10 10
967 A216 100 l multi 10 10
968 A216 120 l multi 15 15
969 A216 150 l multi 18 18
970 A216 170 l multi 22 22
Nos. 961-970 (10) 1.06 1.06

Holy Family, by Antonio Alberto de Ferrara, 15th Century Fresco — A217

Christmas (de Ferrara Fresco): 80 l, St. Joseph. 170 l, Infant Jesus. 220 l, One of the Three Kings.

1979, Dec. 6 Photo. *Perf. 12*

971 A217 80 l multi 10 10
972 A217 170 l multi 24 24
973 A217 220 l multi 28 28
974 A217 320 l multi 32 32

Disturbing Muses, by Giorgio de Chirico — A218

Chirico Paintings:

1979, Dec.

975 A218 40 l shown 9 9
976 A218 150 l Ancient horses 18 18
977 A218 170 l Self-portrait 22 22

Giorgio de Chirico, Italian surrealist painter.

St. Benedict, 15th Century Fresco — A219

Fight Against Cigarette Smoking — A220

1980, Mar. 27 Photo. *Perf. 12x11½*
Granite Paper

978 A219 170 l multi 22 22

St. Benedict of Nursia, 1500th birth anniversary.

1980, Mar. 27

Designs: Sketches of smokers and cigarettes by Giuliana Consilivio.

979 A220 120 l multi 12 12
980 A220 220 l multi 40 40
981 A220 520 l multi 65 65

Naples, 17th Century Engraving A221

1980, Mar. 27 *Perf. 14x13½*

982 A221 170 l multi 25 25

20th Intl. Phil. Exhib., Europa '80, Naples, Apr. 26-May 4.

View of London, 1850 — A222

1980, May 8 *Perf. 11½x12*

983 A222 200 l shown 24 24
984 A222 400 l London, 1980 55 55

London 1980 Intl. Stamp Exhib., May 6-14. Nos. 983-984 printed se-tenant checkerwise in sheets of 50.

Europa Issue 1980

Giovanbattista Belluzzi (1506-1554), Military Architect A223

Designs: 220 l, Antonio Orafo (1460-1552), goldsmith and jeweler.

1980, May 8 *Perf. 11½*

985 A223 170 l multi 20 20
986 A223 220 l multi 28 28

Bicycling — A224

1980, July 7 Photo. *Perf. 11½*
Granite Paper

987 A224 70 l shown 10 10
988 A224 90 l Basketball 10 10
989 A224 170 l Running 28 28
990 A224 350 l Gymnast 42 42
991 A224 450 l High jump 55 55
Nos. 987-991 (5) 1.45 1.45

22nd Summer Olympic Games, Moscow, July 19-Aug. 3.

Ancient Fortifications A225

Weight Lifting A226

Photogravure and Engraved

1980, Sept. 18 ***Perf. 13½x14***

992	A225	220 l multi	32	32

World Tourism Conf., Manila, Sept. 27.

1980, Sept. 18 **Photo.** ***Perf. 14x13½***

993	A226	170 l multi	22	22

European Junior Weight Lifting Championship, Sept.

Robert Stolz, "Philatelic Waltz" Score A227

Photo. & Engr.

1980, Sept. 18 ***Perf. 14***

994	A227	120 l lt bl & blk	22	22

Robert Stolz (1880-1975) composer.

Madonna of the Harpies, by Andrea Del Sarto — A228

Annunciation by Del Sarto (Details): 250 l, Virgin Mary. 500 l Angel.

1980, Dec. 11 ***Perf. 13½***

995	A228	180 l multi	25	25
996	A228	250 l multi	38	38
997	A228	500 l multi	75	75

Christmas; 450th death anniv. of Del Sarto.

St. Joseph's Eve Bonfire A229

Intl. Year of the Disabled A230

Europa Issue 1981

1981, Mar. 24 **Photo.** ***Perf. 12***

Granite Paper

998	A229	200 l shown	24	24
999	A229	300 l San Marino Day fireworks	40	40

1981, May 15 **Photo.** ***Perf. 11½***

Granite Paper

1000	A230	300 l multi	38	38

St. Charles' Square, Vienna, by Jakob Alt, 1817 — A231

1981, May 15

Granite Paper

1001	A231	200 l shown	28	28
1002	A231	300 l Vienna, 1981	38	38

WIPA '81 Intl. Phil. Exhib., Vienna, May 22-31. Nos. 1001-1002 se-tenant.

Woman Playing Flute — A232

Grand Prix Motorcycle Race — A233

Designs: Drawings based on Roman sculptures.

1981, July 10 **Photo.** ***Perf. 11½***

Granite Paper

1003	A232	300 l shown	48	48
1004	A232	550 l Soldier	80	80
1005	A232	1500 l Shepherd	1.40	1.40
a		Souvenir sheet of 3, #1003-1005	4.00	4.00

Virgil's birth bimillennium. Nos. 1003-1005 in continuous design.

1981, July 10 **Litho.** ***Perf. 14x15***

1006	A233	200 l multi	22	22

Natl. Urban Development Plan (Housing) — A234

1981, Sept. 22 **Photo.**

Granite Paper

1007	A234	20 l shown	5	5
1008	A234	80 l Parks	10	10
1009	A234	400 l Energy plants	45	45

European Junior Judo Championship, Oct. 30-Nov. 1 — A235

1981, Sept. 22 **Photo.** ***Perf. 11½***

Granite Paper

1010	A235	300 l multi	42	42

World Food Day — A236

1981, Oct. 23

Granite Paper

1011	A236	300 l multi	42	42

Child Holding a Dove, by Pablo Picasso (1881-1973) A237

Designs: 200 l, Homage to Picasso, by Renato Guttuso.

1981, Oct. 23

Granite Paper

1012	A237	150 l multi	20	20
1013	A237	200 l multi	28	24

One of the Three Kings with Goblet, by Garafalo — A238

Christmas; 500th Birth Anniv. of Benvenuto Tisi da Garafalo (Adoration of the Kings and St. Bartholomew): 300 l, King with a Jar. 600 l, Virgin and Child.

Photo. & Engr.

1981, Dec. 15 ***Perf. 13½***

1014	A238	200 l multi	24	24
1015	A238	300 l multi	35	35
1016	A238	600 l multi	75	75

Postal Cover Centenary A239

1982, Feb. 19 **Photo.** ***Perf. 12***

1017	A239	200 l multi	22	22

Savings Bank Centenary A240

1982, Feb. 19

1018	A240	300 l multi	38	38

Europa 1982 — A241

Designs: 300 l, Convocation of the Assembly of Heads of Families, 1906. 450 l, Napoleons's Treaty of Friendship offer, 1797.

1982, Apr. 21 **Photo.** ***Perf. 11½***

Granite Paper

1019	A241	300 l multi	40	40
1020	A241	450 l multi	60	60

Archimedes A242

800th Birth Anniv. of St. Francis of Assisi A243

1982, Apr. 21 **Photo.** ***Perf. 14x13½***

1021	A242	20 l shown	5	5
1022	A242	30 l Copernicus	5	5
1023	A242	40 l Newton	8	8
1024	A242	50 l Lavoisier	8	8
1025	A242	60 l Marie Curie	10	10
1026	A242	100 l Robert Koch	10	10
		Litho. & Engr.		
1027	A242	200 l Thomas Edison	16	16
1028	A242	300 l Guglielmo Marconi	38	38
1029	A242	450 l Hippocrates	75	75
		Engr.		
1030	A242	5000 l Galileo	6.00	6.00
		Nos. 1021-1030 (10)	7.75	7.75

See Nos. 1041-1046.

1982, June 10 **Photo.**

1031	A243	200 l multi	25	25

Notre Dame, 1806 — A244

1982, June 10

1032	A244	300 l shown	35	35
1033	A244	450 l 1982	55	55

PHILEXFRANCE '82 Stamp Exhibition, Paris, June 11-21. Nos. 1032-1033 se-tenant.

Visit of Pope John Paul II A245

Natl. Flags of ASCAT Members A246

1982, Aug. 29 Litho. *Perf. 13½x14*
1034 A245 900 l multi 1.00 1.00

1982, Sept. 1 Photo. *Perf. 11½*
Granite Paper
1035 A246 300 l multi 40 40

Inaugural Meeting of ASCAT (Assoc. of Editors of Philatelic Catalogues), 1977.

15th Amnesty Intl. Congress, Rimini, Italy, Sept. 9-15 — A247

Christmas — A248

1982, Sept. 1 Unwmk.
1036 A247 700 l blk & red 80 80

Photo. & Engr.
1982, Dec. 15 *Perf. 13½*

Paintings by Gregorio Sciltian (b. 1900).

1037 A248 200 l Angel 24 24
1038 A248 300 l Virgin and Child 35 35
1039 A248 450 l Angel, diff. 52 52

Secondary School Centenary — A249

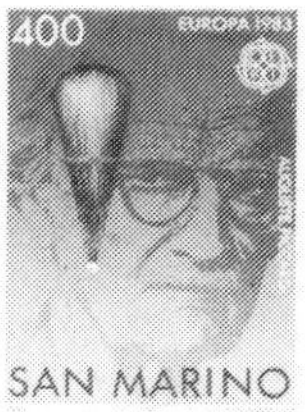

Auguste Piccard — A251

3rd Formula One Grand Prix A250

1983, Feb. 24 Photo. *Perf. 13½x14*
1040 A249 300 l Begni Building 35 35

Scientist Type of 1982

1983, Apr. 21 *Perf. 14x13½*
1041 A242 150 l Alexander Fleming 15 15
1042 A242 250 l Alessandro Volta 35 35
1043 A242 350 l Evangelista Torricelli 52 52
1044 A242 400 l Carolus Linnaeus 55 55
1045 A242 1000 l Pythagoras 1.00 1.00
1046 A242 1400 l Leonardo da Vinci 1.50 1.50
Nos. 1041-1046 (6) 4.07 4.07

1983, Apr. 20 Photo. *Perf. 14x13½*
1047 A250 50 l multi 10 10
1048 A250 350 l multi 40 40

Europa Issue 1983
1983, Apr. 20 *Perf. 12x11½*
Granite Paper
1049 A251 400 l Aerostat 75 75
1050 A251 500 l Bathyscaph 95 95

Piccard (1884-1962), Swiss scientist.

World Communications Year — A252

1983, Apr. 28 Engr. *Perf. 14x13*
1051 A252 400 l Ham radio operator 50 50
1052 A252 500 l Mailman 60 60

Manned Flight Bicentenary A253

Lithographed and Engraved
1983, May 22 *Perf. 13½x14*
1053 A253 500 l Montgolfiere, 1783 60 60

Botafogo Bay and Monte Corcovado, Rio de Janeiro — A254

1983, July 29 Photo. *Perf. 11½x12*
Granite Paper
1054 A254 400 l 1845 50 50
1055 A254 1400 l 1983 1.65 1.65

Se-tenant. BRASILIANA '83 Intl. Stamp Show, Rio de Janeiro, July 29-Aug. 7.

20th Anniv. of World Food Program A255

1983, Sept. 29 Photo. *Perf. 14x13½*
1056 A255 500 l multi 60 60

Christmas A256

Flag-wavers Group, 2nd Anniv. A257

Paintings, Raphael (1483-1520): 300 l, Our Lady of the Grand Duke. 400 l, Our Lady of the Goldfinch. 500 l, Our Lady of the Chair.

Photo. & Engr.
1983, Dec. 1 *Perf. 13½*
1057 A256 300 l multi 38 38
1058 A256 400 l multi 45 45
1059 A256 500 l multi 55 55

Olympic Type of 1959

IOC Presidents: 300 l, Demetrius Vikelas, 1894-96. 400 l, Lord Killanin. 550 l, Antonio Samaranch, 1984.

1984, Feb. 8 Photo. *Perf. 14x13½*
1060 A86 300 l multi 35 35
1061 A86 400 l multi 48 48
1062 A86 550 l multi 65 65

Litho. & Engr.
1984, Apr. 27 *Perf. 13x14*
1063 A257 300 l Flag 35 35
1064 A257 400 l Flags 48 48

Europa (1959-1984) A258

1984, Apr. 27 Photo. *Perf. 11½*
Granite Paper
1065 A258 400 l multi 65 65
1066 A258 550 l multi 80 80

Motorcross Grand Prix, Baldasserona A259

1984, June 14 Photo. *Perf. 13½x14*
1067 A259 450 l multi 55 55

Souvenir Sheet

1984 Summer Olympics A260

1984, June 14 Litho. *Perf. 13x14*
1068 Sheet of 2 2.00 2.00
a A260 550 l Man 70 70
b A260 1000 l Woman 1.25 1.25

Ausipex '84 — A261

Views of Melbourne. Se-tenant.

1984, Sept. 21 Photo. *Perf. 11½*
Granite Paper
1069 A261 1500 l 1839 2.00 2.00
1070 A261 2000 l 1984 2.75 2.75

Visit of Italian Pres. Pertini A262

1984, Oct. 20 Photo. *Perf. 14x13½*
1071 A262 1950 l multi 2.75 2.75

School and Philately A263

Christmas A264

Sketches by Jacovitti.

1984, Oct. 30 *Perf. 13½x14*
1072 A263 50 l Universe 7 7
1073 A263 100 l Evolution 12 12
1074 A263 150 l Environment 24 24
1075 A263 200 l Mankind 25 25
1076 A263 450 l Science 60 60
1077 A263 550 l Philosophy 70 70
Nos. 1072-1077 (6) 1.98 1.98

1984, Dec. 5 Litho. *Perf. 13½x14*

Details of Madonna of San Girolamo by Correggio, 1527.

1078 A264 400 l multi 55 55
1079 A264 450 l multi 60 60
1080 A264 550 l multi 80 80

Composers and Music — A265

Olympiad of the Small States, May 23-26 — A266

Europa Issue 1985

Designs: 450 l, Johann Sebastian Bach (1685-1750), Toccata and Fugue. 600 l, Vincenzo Bellini (1801-1835), Norma.

1985, Mar. 18 Photo. *Perf. 12*
1081 A265 450 l ocher & gray blk 80 80
1082 A265 600 l yel grn & gray blk 1.00 1.00

1985, May 16 Litho. *Perf. 13½x14*

Sportphilex '85: Natl. Olympic Committee and Sportphilex '85 emblems, flags of Andorra, Cyprus, Iceland, Liechtenstein, Luxembourg, Malta, Monaco, San Marino.

1083 A266 50 l Diving 5 5
1084 A266 350 l Running 45 45
1085 A266 400 l Rifle shooting 52 52
1086 A266 450 l Cycling 60 60
1087 A266 600 l Handball 80 80
Nos. 1083-1087 (5) 2.42 2.42

Emigration A267

Intl. Youth Year A268

1985, May 16
1088 A267 600 l Birds migrating 80 80

1985, June 24 Photo. *Perf. 12*
Granite Paper
1089 A268 400 l Boy, dove 55 55
1090 A268 600 l Girl, dove, horse 85 85

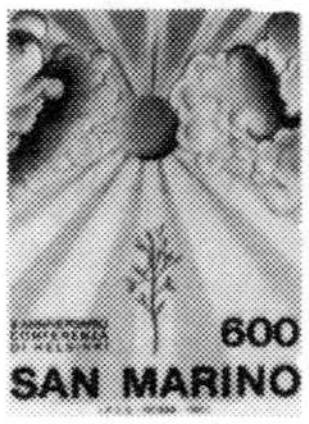

Helsinki Conference, 10th Anniv. — A269

City Hall, by Renzo Bonelli, Camera Lens. — A270

1985, June 24 *Perf. 13 ½x14*

1091 A269 600 l Sapling, sunburst, clouds 80 80

1985, June 24 *Perf. 13 ½x14 ½*

1092 A270 450 l multi 60 60

Intl. Fed. of Photographic Art, 18th Congress.

World Angling Championships, Arno River, Florence, Sept. 14-15 — A271

1985, Sept. 11 Photo. *Perf. 14 ½x15*

1093 A271 600 l Hooked fish 80 80

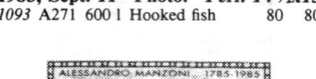

Alessandro Manzoni (1785-1873), Novelist & Poet — A272

19th century engravings from Manzoni's I Promessi Sposi (1825-27): 400 l, Don Abbondio encounters Don Rodrigo's henchmen. 450 l, The attempt to force the curate to perform a dubious marriage ceremony. 600 l, The Plague at Milan.

1985, Sept. 11 Engr. *Perf. 14x13 ½*

1094 A272 400 l multi 55 55
1095 A272 450 l multi 60 60
1096 A272 600 l multi 85 85

Intl. Feline Fed. Congress A273

Mosaic detail: Cat, Natl. Museum, Naples.

1985, Oct. 25 Photo. *Perf. 12*
Granite Paper

1097 A273 600 l multi 70 70

ITALIA '85 — A274

Views of the Colosseum, Rome. Se-tenant.

1985, Oct. 25 *Perf. 11 ½x12*
Granite Paper

1098 A274 1000 l multi 1.25 1.25
1099 A274 1500 l multi 1.90 1.90

Christmas A275

Photo. & Engr.

1985, Dec. 3 *Perf. 14*

1100 A275 400 l Angel 48 48
1101 A275 450 l Mother and Child 55 55
1102 A275 600 l Angel, diff. 70 70

Se-tenant.

Hospital, Cailungo A276

1986, Mar. 6 Photo. *Perf. 12x11 ½*

1103 A276 450 l multi 60 60
1104 A276 650 l multi 85 85

Natl. social security org., ISS, 30th anniv., and World Health Day.

Halley's Comet — A277

Designs: 550 l, Giotto space probe. 1000 l, Adoration of the Magi, by Giotto (1276-1337).

1986, Mar. 6 *Perf. 11 ½x12*

1105 A277 550 l multi 75 75
1106 A277 1000 l multi 1.35 1.35

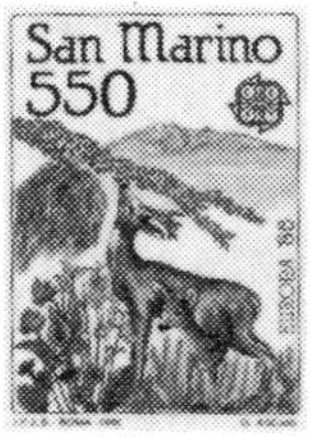

Deer A278

3rd Veterans World Table Tennis Championships A279

Europa Issue 1986

1986, May 22 Photo. *Perf. 13 ½x14*

1107 A278 550 l shown 75 75
1108 A278 650 l Falcon 90 90

1986, May 22 **Engr.**

1109 A279 450 l dp mag, dk chlky bl & ultra 62 62

AMERIPEX '86, Chicago, May 22-June 1 — A280

Views of Old Water Tower, Chicago: 2000 l, Lithograph, 1870, by Charles Shober. 3000 l, Photograph, 1986. Printed se-tenant.

Perf. 11 ½x12

1986, May 22 Photo. Unwmk.

1110 A280 2000 l multi 2.75 2.75
1111 A280 3000 l multi 4.25 4.25

Intl. Peace Year — A281

1986, July 10 Photo. *Perf. 11 ½x12*

1112 A281 550 l multi 75 75

Souvenir Sheet

Terra Cotta Statuary, Tomb of Emperor Qin Shi Huang Di (259-210 B.C.) — A282

Litho. & Engr.

1986, July 10 *Perf. 13 ½*

1113 Sheet of 3 4.50 4.50
a. A282 550 l Bearded man 75 75
b. A282 650 l Horse, horiz. 88 88
c. A282 2000 l Bearded man, diff. 2.75 2.75

Normalization of diplomatic relations with the People's Republic of China, 15th anniv.

UNICEF, 40th Anniv. A283

European Boccie Championships A284

1986, Sept 16 Photo. *Perf. 12*

1114 A283 650 l multi 95 95

1986, Sept. 16 *Perf. 14x15*

1115 A284 550 l multi 80 80

The first value column gives the catalogue value of an unused stamp, the second that of a used stamp.

Choral Society, 25th Anniv. — A285

Christmas — A286

Painting (detail): Apollo Dancing with the Muses, by Giulio Romano (1492-1546).

1986, Sept. 16

1116 A285 450 l multi 65 65

Photo. & Engr.

1986, Nov. 26 *Perf. 14*

Design: Oil on wood triptych, 15th cent., by Hans Memling (1435-1494), Kunsthistorisches Museum, Vienna.

1117 A286 450 l St. John the Baptist 68 68
1118 A286 550 l Virgin and Child 82 82
1119 A286 650 l St. John the Evangelist 98 98

Printed se-tenant.

Europa Issue 1987

Our Lady of Consolation Church, Borgomaggiore A287

Church designed by Giovanni Michelucci, architect: 600 l, Architect's sketch of interior. 700 l, Actual interior.

1987, Mar. 12 Photo. *Perf. 12*

1120 A287 600 l multi 95 95
1121 A287 700 l multi 1.10 1.10

Motoring Events A288

Designs: 500 l, 80th anniv., Peking-Paris Race. 600 l, 15th San Marino Rally. 700 l, Mille Miglia Race, 60th anniv.

1987, Mar. 12 *Perf. 11 ½*

1122 A288 500 l multi 80 80
1123 A288 600 l multi 95 95
1124 A288 700 l multi 1.10 1.10

Sculptures, Open-air Museum A289

Seventh Natl. Art Biennale A290

Perf. 14 ½x13 ½

1987, June 13 **Photo.**

1125 A289 50 l Reffi Busignani 8 8
1126 A289 100 l Bini 16 16

1127 A289 200 l Guguianu 32 32
1128 A289 300 l Berti 48 48
1129 A289 400 l Crocetti 62 62
1130 A289 500 l Berti, diff. 78 78
1131 A289 600 l Messina 90 90
1132 A289 1000 l Minguzzi 1.50 1.50
1133 A289 2200 l Greco 3.50 3.50
1134 A289 10000 l Sassu 15.50 15.50
Nos. 1125-1134 (10) 23.84 23.84

1987, June 13 ***Perf. 11½***
Granite Paper

Abstract works: 500 l, Dal Diario del Brasile-foresta Vergine, by Emilio Vedova. 600 l, Invenzione Cromatica con Brio, by Corrado Cagli.

1135 A290 500 l multi 78 78
1136 A290 600 l multi 90 90

Air Club of San Marino Ultra-lightweight Aircraft — A291

1987, June 13
Granite Paper

1137 A291 600 l multi 90 90

Mahatma Gandhi A292

1987, Aug. 2 **Photo.** ***Perf. 14x13½***

1138 A292 500 l Gandhi Square, bust 78 78

OLYMPHILEX '87, Rome — A293

1987, Aug. 29 ***Perf. 12***
Granite Paper

1139 A293 600 l Olympic emblem, athlete 90 90

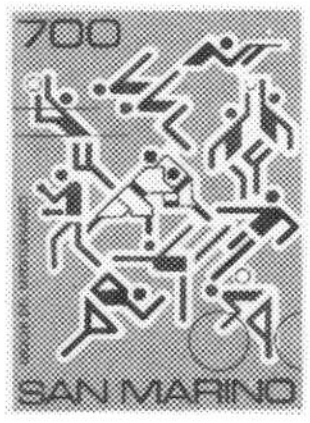

First Representation of San Marino at the Mediterranean Games, Syria, Sept. 11-15 — A294

1987, Aug. 29 **Granite Paper**

1140 A294 700 l ultra, blk & red 1.05 1.05

HAFNIA '87 — A295

Views of Copenhagen (1836-1986), as seen from the Round Tower. Se-tenant.

1987, Oct. 16 **Photo.** ***Perf. 11½x12***
Granite Paper

1141 A295 1200 l multi 1.85 1.85
1142 A295 2200 l multi, diff. 3.35 3.35

Christmas A296

High Speed Train A297

Details from Triptych of Cortona and The Annunciation, by Fra Angelico (c. 1400-1455), Diocesan Museum of Cortona: No. 1143, Angel. No. 1144, Madonna and child. No. 1145, Saint. Printed se-tenant.

Photo. & Engr.
1987, Nov. 12 ***Perf. 13½***

1143 A296 600 l multi 98 98
1144 A296 600 l multi 98 98
1145 A296 600 l multi 98 98

Europa Issue 1988
1988, Mar. 17 **Photo.** ***Perf. 12***
Granite Paper

1146 A297 600 l shown 98 98
1147 A297 700 l Fiber optics 1.15 1.15

Promote Stamp Collecting A298

Stamps, cancellations, covers: 50 l, Nos. 81, B25 and 859. 150 l, No. C11. 300 l, Nos. 349 and 1006. 350 l, Nos. 944 and 1031. 1000 l, Nos. 303, 1081 and 308.

1988, Mar. 17 ***Perf. 11½***
Granite Paper

1148 A298 50 l multi 8 8
1149 A298 150 l multi 24 24
1150 A298 300 l multi 50 50
1151 A298 350 l multi 58 58
1152 A298 1000 l multi 1.60 1.60
Nos. 1148-1152 (5) 3.00 3.00

Bologna University, 900th Anniv. — A299

Historic sites and distinguished professors: 550 l, Carlo Malagola. 650 l, Pietro Ellero. 1300 l, Giosue Carducci (1835-1907), professor of literary history, 1861-1904, and Nobel Prize winner for literature, 1906. 1700 l, Giovanni Pascoli (1855-1912), lyric poet, Pascoli's successor as professor at Bologna.

1988, May 7 **Photo.** ***Perf. 13½x14***

1153 A299 550 l multi 92 92
1154 A299 650 l multi 1.10 1.10
1155 A299 1300 l multi 2.15 2.15
1156 A299 1700 l multi 2.80 2.80

Posters from Fellini Films — A300

Designs: 300 l, La Strada. 900 l, La Dolce Vita. 1200 l, Amarcord.

1988, July 8 **Photo.** ***Perf. 13½x14***

1157 A300 300 l multi 45 45
1158 A300 900 l multi 1.35 1.35
1159 A300 1200 l multi 1.80 1.80

Federico Fellini, Italian film director and winner of the 1988 San Marino Prize.

Mt. Titano and Sand Dunes of the Adriatic Coast A301

1988, July 8 ***Perf. 14x13½***

1160 A301 750 l multi 1.10 1.10

40th Stamp Fair, Riccione.

Souvenir Sheet

1988 Summer Olympics, Seoul — A302

1988, Sept. 19 **Photo.** ***Perf. 13½x14***

1161 A302 Sheet of 3 4.00 4.00
a. 650 l Running 95 95
b. 750 l Hurdles 1.10 1.10
c. 1300 l Gymnastics 1.90 1.90

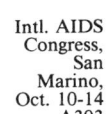

Intl. AIDS Congress, San Marino, Oct. 10-14 A303

1988, Sept. 19 ***Perf. 14x13½***

1162 A303 250 l shown 38 38
1163 A303 350 l "AIDS" 52 52
1164 A303 650 l Virus, knot 95 95
1165 A303 1000 l Newspaper 1.50 1.50

Kurhaus Scheveningen, The Hague — A304

1988, Oct. 18 **Photo.** ***Perf. 11½x12***
Granite Paper

1166 A304 1600 l Lithograph, c. 1885 2.35 2.35
1167 A304 3000 l 1988 4.40 4.40

FILACEPT '88, Holland. Printed se-tenant.

Christmas A305

Paintings by Melozzo da Forli (1438-1494): No. 1168, Angel with Violin, Vatican Art Gallery. No. 1169, Angel of the Annunciation, Uffizi Gallery, Florence. No. 1170, Angel with Mandolin, Vatican Art Gallery.

1988, Dec. 9 **Photo.** ***Perf. 13½***
Size of No. 1169: 21x40mm

1168 A305 650 l multi 1.05 1.05
1169 A305 650 l multi 1.05 1.05
1170 A305 650 l multi 1.05 1.05

Europa Issue 1989
Souvenir Sheet

Children's Games — A306

1989, Mar. 31 **Photo.** ***Perf. 13½x14***

1171 A306 Sheet of 2 2.05 2.05
a. 650 l Sledding 95 95
b. 750 l Hopscotch 1.10 1.10

Nature Conservation — A307

Illustrations by contest-winning youth: 200 l, Federica Sparagna. 500 l, Giovanni Monteduro. 650 l, Rosa Mannarino.

1989, Mar. 31 ***Perf. 14x13½***

1172 A307 200 l multi 30 30
1173 A307 500 l multi 75 75
1174 A307 650 l multi 95 95

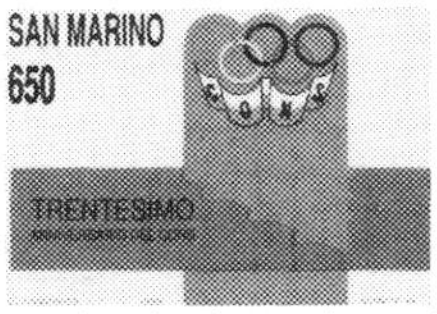

Sporting Anniversaries and Events — A308

1989, May 13 **Photo.** ***Perf. 12***
Granite Paper

1175 A308 650 l Olympics 98 98
1176 A308 750 l Soccer 1.15 1.15
1177 A308 850 l Tennis 1.25 1.25
1178 A308 1300 l Car racing 1.95 1.95

Natl. Olympic Committee, 30th anniv. (650 l); admission of San Marino Soccer Federation to the UEFA and FIFA (750 l); San

Marino '89, the tennis grand prix (850 l); Grand Prix of San Marino, Imola (1300 l).

Stamp Collecting Type of 1988

Covers and canceled stamps (postal history): 100 l, No. 916a with Iserravalle cancel, Sept. 1, 1977. 200 l, No. 1151 with Montegiardino cancel, May 3, 1986. 400 l, Italy No. 47 canceled on San Marino parcel card #422, 1895. 500 l, Type SP3 essay proposed by Martin Riester di Parigi, March 1865. 1000 l, Stampless cover, 1862.

1989, May 13 *Perf. 12*

Granite Paper

1179	A298	100 l multi	15	15
1180	A298	200 l multi	30	30
1181	A298	400 l multi	60	60
1182	A298	500 l multi	75	75
1183	A298	1000 l multi	1.50	1.50
		Nos. 1179-1183 (5)	3.30	3.30

SEMI-POSTAL STAMPS

Regular Issue of 1903 Surcharged:

1917 1917

Pro combattenti Pro combattenti

=25 Cent. 50

a b

1917, Dec. 15 **Wmk. 140** *Perf. 14*

B1	A10(a)	25c on 2c vio	80	80
B2	A11(b)	50c on 2 l vio	11.50	11.50

Statue of Liberty — SP1

View of San Marino SP2

1918, June 1 **Typo.**

B3	SP1	2c dl vio & blk	10	10
B4	SP1	5c bl grn & blk	10	10
B5	SP1	10c lake & blk	10	10
B6	SP1	20c brn org & blk	10	10
B7	SP1	25c ultra & blk	22	22
B8	SP1	45c yel brn & blk	22	22
B9	SP2	1 l bl grn & blk	5.00	5.00
B10	SP2	2 l vio & blk	3.75	3.75
B11	SP2	3 l claret & blk	3.75	3.75
		Nos. B3-B11 (9)	13.34	13.34

These stamps were sold at an advance of 5c each over face value, the receipts from that source being devoted to the support of a hospital for Italian soldiers.

Nos. B6-B8 Overprinted

3
Novembre
1918

1918, Dec. 12

B12	SP1	20c brn org & blk	60	60
B13	SP1	25c ultra & blk	60	60
B14	SP1	45c yel brn & blk	60	60

Overprinted **3 Novembre 1918**

B15	SP2	1 l bl grn & blk	60	60
B16	SP2	2 l vio & blk	3.75	3.75
B17	SP2	3 l claret & blk	3.75	3.75
		Nos. B12-B17 (6)	9.90	9.90

Celebration of Italian Victory over Austria.
Inverted overprints were privately produced.

Coat of Arms SP3

Liberty SP4

1923, Sept. 20 **Engr.**

B18	SP3	5c + 5c ol grn	12	12
B19	SP3	10c + 5c orange	12	12
B20	SP3	15c + 5c dk grn	12	12
B21	SP3	25c + 5c brn lake	40	40
B22	SP3	40c + 5c vio brn	70	70
B23	SP3	50c + 5c gray	50	25
B24	SP4	1 l + 5c blk & bl	1.25	1.25
		Nos. B18-B24 (7)	3.21	2.96

St. Marinus SP5

Wmk. 140

1944, Apr. 25 **Photo.** *Perf. 14*

B25	SP5	20 l + 10 l gldn brn	90	50
		Sheet of 8	27.50	27.50

The surtax was used for workers' houses. See No. CB1.

No. 256 Surcharged in Red "L. 10"

1946, Aug. 24 **Unwmk.**

B26	A48	50 l + 10 l ol brn & ultra	5.00	5.00
		Sheet of 10	*575.00*	*575.00*

Third Philatelic Day, Rimini. The surtax was for the exhibition.

Air Post Types of 1946 Surcharged "CONVEGNO FILATELICO / 30 NOVEMBRE 1946 / + LIRE 25" (or "LIRE 50") in Red or Violet

1946, Nov. 30 **Wmk. 277**

B26A	AP7	3 l + 25 l dk brn (R)	25	18
B26B	AP8	5 l + 25 l red org (V)	25	18
B26C	AP6	10 l + 50 l ultra (R)	2.75	2.50

Inscription "Posta Aerea" does not appear on these stamps.

No. 260 Surcharged in Black "+ 1"

1947, Nov. 13 **Wmk. 217** *Perf. 12*

B27	A53	1 l + 1 l brt grn & vio	6	8
B28	A53	1 l + 2 l brt grn & vio	6	8
B29	A53	1 l + 3 l brt grn & vio	6	8
B30	A53	1 l + 4 l brt grn & vio	6	8
B31	A53	1 l + 5 l brt grn & vio	6	8

Surcharged on No. 261

B32	A53	2 l + 1 l pur & ol	6	8
B33	A53	2 l + 2 l pur & ol	6	8
B34	A53	2 l + 3 l pur & ol	6	8
B35	A53	2 l + 4 l pur & ol	6	8
B36	A53	2 l + 5 l pur & ol	6	8

Surcharged on No. 262

B37	A53	4 l + 1 l vio brn & dk bl grn	3.00	3.25
B38	A53	4 l + 2 l vio brn & dk bl grn	3.00	3.25
		Nos. B27-B38 (12)	6.60	7.30

Surcharges on Nos. B27-B38 are arranged consecutively, changing from ascending to descending order of denomination on alternate rows in the sheet.

Catalogue values for unused stamps in this section, from this point to the end of the section, are for Never Hinged items.

Refugee Boy — SP6

1982, Dec. 15 **Photo.** *Perf. 11½*

B39	SP6	300 l + 100 l multi	48	48

Surcharge was for refugee support.

AIR POST STAMPS

View of San Marino AP1

Wmk. 217

1931, June 11 **Engr.** *Perf. 12*

C1	AP1	50c bl grn	45	45
C2	AP1	80c red	65	65
C3	AP1	1 l bis brn	65	65
C4	AP1	2 l brt vio	90	90
C5	AP1	2.60 l Prus bl	7.00	7.00
C6	AP1	3 l dk gray	7.00	7.00
C7	AP1	5 l ol grn	1.75	1.75
C8	AP1	7.70 l dk brn	2.25	2.25
C9	AP1	9 l dp org	2.75	2.75
C10	AP1	10 l dk bl	135.00	135.00
		Nos. C1-C10 (10)	158.40	158.40

Nos. C1 to C10 exist imperforate.

Catalogue values for unused stamps in this section, from this point to the end of the section, are for Never Hinged items.

Graf Zeppelin Issue

Stamps of Type AP1 Surcharged in Blue or Black

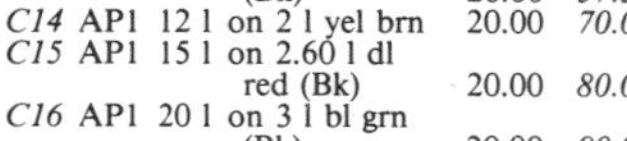

ZEPPELIN
1933

L. 3.

1933, Apr. 28

C11	AP1	3 l on 50c org	52	*45.00*
C12	AP1	5 l on 80c ol grn	20.00	*45.00*
C13	AP1	10 l on 1 l dk bl (Bk)	20.00	*57.50*
C14	AP1	12 l on 2 l yel brn	20.00	*70.00*
C15	AP1	15 l on 2.60 l dl red (Bk)	20.00	*80.00*
C16	AP1	20 l on 3 l bl grn (Bk)	20.00	*90.00*
		Nos. C11-C16 (6)	100.52	*387.50*

Nos. C11 to C16 exist imperforate.

Nos. C1 and C2 Surcharged

C. 75

1936, Apr. 14

C17	AP1	75c on 50c bl grn	2.75	2.75
C18	AP1	75c on 80c red	7.75	7.75

Nos. C5 and C6 Surcharged with New Value and Bars

1941, Jan. 12

C19	AP1	10 l on 2.60 l Prus blue	85.00	85.00
C20	AP1	10 l on 3 l dk gray	21.00	21.00

View of Arbe — AP2

Wmk. 140

1942, Mar. 16 **Photo.** *Perf. 14*

C21	AP2	25c brn & gray blk	12	12
C22	AP2	50c grn & brn	15	15
C23	AP2	75c gray bl & red brn	16	16
C24	AP2	1 l ocher & brn	28	28
C25	AP2	5 l bis brn & bl	3.50	3.50
		Nos. C21-C25 (5)	4.21	4.21

Return of the Italian flag to Arbe.

San Marino Map, Fasces and Wing AP3 AP4

Overprinted "28 LVGLIO 1943 1642 d. F. R." in Black

1943, Aug. 27

C26	AP3	25c yel org	8	9
C27	AP3	50c car rose	8	9
C28	AP3	75c dark brn	8	9
C29	AP3	1 l dk rose vio	8	9
C30	AP3	2 l sapphire	8	92
C31	AP3	5 l org red	28	28
C32	AP3	10 l deep grn	75	75
C33	AP3	20 l black	2.25	2.75
		Nos. C26-C33 (8)	3.68	5.06

See footnote after No. 227. Nos. C26-C33 exist without overprint (not regularly issued). Value $2,250.

Overprinted "GOVERNO PROVVISORIO"

1943, Aug. 27

C34	AP4	25c yel org	8	8
C35	AP4	50c car rose	8	8
C36	AP4	75c dark brn	8	8
C37	AP4	1 l dk rose vio	8	8
C38	AP4	5 l org red	38	38
C39	AP4	20 l black	1.90	1.90
		Nos. C34-C39 (6)	2.60	2.60

Government Palace AP5

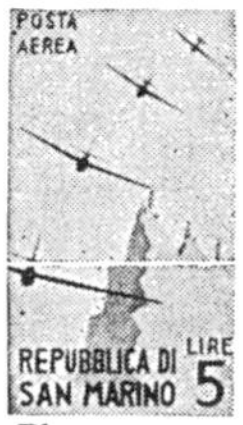
Planes over Mt. Titano AP8

Gulls and San Marino Skyline AP6

Plane and View of San Marino AP7

Plane over Globe AP9

1945, Mar. 15 **Photo.**
C40 AP5 25 l bis brn 2.50 2.50

See note after No. 239.

Photo., Engr. (20 l, 50 l)
1946-47 **Unwmk.** ***Perf. 14***

C41	AP6	25c bl blk	8	8
C42	AP7	75c red org	8	8
C43	AP6	1 l brown	8	8
C44	AP7	2 l dl grn	8	8
C45	AP7	3 l violet	8	8
C46	AP8	5 l vio bl	8	10
C47	AP6	10 l crimson	10	16
C48	AP8	20 l brn lake	1.40	1.75
C49	AP8	35 l org red	3.25	3.00
C50	AP8	50 l dk yel grn	3.25	3.00
C51	AP9	100 l sepia ('47)	1.10	1.10
		Nos. C41-C51 (11)	9.58	9.51

Some values exist imperforate.
Issue dates: 35 l, Nov. 3, 1946; 100 l, Mar. 27, 1947; others, Aug. 8, 1946.

Roosevelt Type of Regular Issue, 1947

F. D. Roosevelt and: 1 l, 31 l, 50 l, Eagle. 2 l, 20 l, 100 l, San Marino arms. 5 l, 200 l, Flags of San Marino and US (vert.).

Wmk. 277
1947, May 3 **Photo.** ***Perf. 14***

C51A	A52a	1 l dp ultra & sep	8	8
C51B	A52a	2 l org red & sep	8	8
C51C	A52a	5 l multi	8	8
C51D	A52a	20 l choc & sep	9	14
C51E	A52a	31 l org & sep	25	28
C51F	A52a	50 l dk car & sep	32	40
C51G	A52a	100 l bl & sep	55	85
C51H	A52a	200 l multi	8.50	6.50
		Nos. C51A-C51H (8)	9.95	8.41

Nos. C51A-C51E, C51H exist imperf. Value, set $105.

Nos. C51A-C51C Surcharged

1947, June 16

C51I	A52a	3 l on 1 l dp ultra & sep	25	25
C51J	A52a	4 l on 2 l org red & sep	25	25
C51K	A52a	6 l on 5 l multi	25	25

St. Marinus Type of Regular Issue, 1947

Wmk. 217
1947, July 18 **Engr.** ***Perf. 12***
Center in Bright Blue

C52	A53	25 l deep org	1.00	1.00
C53	A53	50 l red brn	2.00	2.00

No. C51 Overprinted in Red

Giornata Filatelica
Rimini - San Marino
18 Luglio 1947

1947, July 18 **Unwmk.** ***Perf. 14***

C54	AP9	100 l sepia	70	70
a.		Double overprint	22.50	
b.		Inverted overprint	65.00	

Rimini Phil. Exhib., July 18-20.

US No. 1 and Mt. Titano AP11

Wmk. 277
1947, Dec. 24 **Engr.** ***Perf. 14***

C55	AP11	100 l dk pur & dk brn	4.00	4.00
a.		Imperf.	47.50	
		Sheet of 10	*1,250.*	

1st US postage stamps, cent.

No. 264 Surcharged "POSTA AEREA" and New Value in Black

1948, Oct. 9 **Wmk. 217** ***Perf. 12***
C56 A53 200 l on 25 l car & pur 10.00 10.00

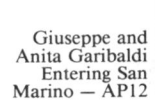

Giuseppe and Anita Garibaldi Entering San Marino — AP12

Wmk. 277
1949, June 28 **Photo.** ***Perf. 14***
Size: 27½x22mm

C57	AP12	2 l brn red & ultra	8	10
C58	AP12	3 l dk grn & sep	8	10
C59	AP12	5 l dk bl grn & ultra	10	20

Size: 37x22mm

C60	AP12	25 l dk grn & vio	1.00	1.00
C61	AP12	65 l grnsh blk & gray blk	5.00	5.00
		Nos. C57-C61 (5)	6.26	6.40

Garibaldi's escape to San Marino, cent.

Stagecoach on Road from San Marino AP13

1950, Feb. 9 **Engr.** ***Perf. 14***

C62	AP13	200 l deep bl	1.40	1.40
a.		Perf. 13½x14 ('51)	2.75	2.75
		As "a," sheet of 6	22.50	22.50
b.		Imperf ('51)	11.50	11.50
		As "b," sheet of 6	90.00	90.00

UPU, 75th anniv. No. C62 was issued in sheets of 25; Nos. C62a and C62b in sheets of 6. See No. C75.

AP14

AP15

AP16

Various Views of San Marino.

1950, Apr. 12 **Photo.** ***Perf. 14***
Size: 27½x21½mm, 21½x27½mm

C63	AP14	2 l vio & dp grn	5	5
C64	AP14	3 l bl & brn	5	5
C65	AP15	5 l brn blk & rose red	5	5
C66	AP14	10 l grnsh blk & bl	18	24
C67	AP14	15 l grnsh blk & vio	20	30

Size: 36x26½mm, 26½x36mm

C68	AP15	55 l dp bl & dp grn	7.75	6.50
C69	AP14	100 l car & gray	2.00	2.00
C70	AP15	250 l vio & brn	7.75	6.50

Engr.

C71	AP16	500 l bl, dk grn & vio brn	50.00	50.00
		Nos. C63-C71 (9)	68.03	65.69

See No. C78.

Types of 1950 Overprinted in Black, Blue or Brown

XXVIII FIERA
INTERNAZIO-
NALE DI
MILANO
APRILE
1950

1950, Apr. 12 **Photo.**
New Colors; Sizes as Before

C72	AP15	5 l dp bl & dp grn	8	10
C73	AP14	15 l car & gray (Bl)	60	55
C74	AP15	55 l vio & brn (Br)	2.50	2.50

The overprint is arranged differently on each denomination.
San Marino's participation in the 28th Intl. Fair of Milan, Apr., 1950.

Stagecoach Type of 1950

1951, Jan. 31 **Engr.** ***Perf. 13½x14***

C75	AP13	300 l cl, brn & dk brn	10.00	10.00
a.		Imperf.	350.00	
		Sheet of 6	100.00	100.00

No. C71 Surcharged in Black "Giornata Filatelica San Marino-Riccione 20-8-1951," New Value and Bars

1951, Aug. 20 ***Perf. 14***
C76 AP16 300 l on 500 l bl, dk grn & vio brn 20.00 20.00

Flag and Plane AP17

Perf. 13½x14
1951, Nov. 22 **Engr.** **Wmk. 277**

C77	AP17	1000 l blk brn, bl & vio brn	200.00	200.00
		Sheet of 6	*5,250.*	*4,250.*

Type of 1950

1951, Apr. 28 **Photo.** ***Perf. 14***
Size: 36x26½mm

C78	AP16	500 l dk grn & brn	60.00	60.00
		Sheet of 6	1,000.	1,000.

Canceled-to-order stamps are often from remainders. Most collectors of canceled stamps prefer postally used specimens.

No. C70 Surcharged in Black

Pro-alluvionati
italiani
1951
100

1951, Dec. 6
C79 AP15 100 l on 250 l vio & brn 3.75 3.75

Issued to raise funds for flood victims in northern Italy.

Columbus, Globe, Statue of Liberty and Buildings AP18

1952, Jan. 28 **Engr.**
C80 AP18 200 l dk bl & blk 12.50 12.50

Issued to honor Christopher Columbus.

Type of 1952 Overprinted in Red

FIERA DI TRIESTE
1952

1952, June 29
C81 AP18 200 l blk brn & choc 10.50 10.50

4th Intl. Sample Fair of Trieste.

Cyclamen — AP19

Flowers and Seacoast — AP20

Designs: 2 l, As Nos. C85 to C87 with flowers omitted. 3 l, Rose.

1952, Aug. 25 **Photo.** ***Perf. 10x14***

C82	AP19	1 l pur & lil rose	8	8
C83	AP19	2 l bl & bl grn	8	8
C84	AP19	3 l dk brn & red	8	8

Perf. 14

C85	AP20	5 l rose lil & brn	8	8
C86	AP20	25 l vio & bl grn	20	30

Perf. 13
Engr.

C87	AP20	200 l multi	21.00	21.00
		Sheet of 6 (C87)	325.00	325.00
		Nos. C82-C87 (6)	21.52	21.62

Riccione Phil. Exhib., Aug. 25, 1952.

Plane Making Photographic Survey — AP21

Design: 75 l, Aerial survey, seen through window.

1952, Nov. 17 Photo. *Perf. 14*
C88 AP21 25 l ol grn 90 90
C89 AP21 75 l red brn & pur 3.50 3.50

Aerial photographic survey of San Marino, 1952.

Skier AP22

1953, Apr. 20 Engr.
C90 AP22 200 l bl grn & dk grn 35.00 35.00
Sheet of 6 600.00 600.00

Plane and Arms of San Marino AP23

1954, April 5
C91 AP23 1000 l dk bl & brn 55.00 55.00
Sheet of 6 575.00 575.00

Type of Regular Issue, 1954

1954, Dec. 16 Photo. *Perf. 13*
C92 A71 120 l dp bl & red brn 1.10 1.10

Hurdler AP25

Design: 120 l, Relay.

1955, June 26 Wmk. 303 *Perf. 14*
C93 AP25 80 l shown 85 65
C94 AP25 120 l Relay 85 90

San Marino's first Intl. Exhib. of Olympic Stamps, June.

Ski Jumper AP26

1955, Dec. 15
C95 AP26 200 l blk & red org 9.00 9.00

7th Winter Olympic Games at Cortina d'Ampezzo, Jan. 26-Feb. 5, 1956.

No. 372 Overprinted in Upper Right Corner with Plane and "Posta Aerea"

1956, Dec. 10
C96 A76 100 l blk & Prus grn 1.25 1.25

Helicopter, Plane and Modernistic Building — AP27

Wmk. 303

1958, April 12 Photo. *Perf. 14*
C97 AP27 125 l lt bl & brn 2.00 2.00

10th participation in Milan Fair.

View of San Marino AP28

Design: 300 l, Road from Mt. Titano.

Wmk. 303

1958, June 23 Engr. *Perf. 13*
C98 AP28 200 l brn & dk bl 2.00 2.00
C99 AP28 300 l mag & vio 2.00 2.00
a. Strip, Nos. C98, C99 + label 4.50 4.50

Printed in sheets containing 20 each of Nos. C98 and C99 flanking a center label with San Marino coat of arms. Nos. C98 and C99 also come se-tenant in sheet.

Naples Stamps Type of Regular Issue, 1958

Design: Bay of Naples and 50g stamp of Naples.

1958, Oct. 8 Photo. *Perf. 14*
C100 A85 125 l brn & red brn 1.65 1.65

Sea Gull AP29

Birds: 10 l, Falcon. 15 l, Mallard. 120 l, Stock dove. 250 l, Barn swallow.

1959, Feb. 12 *Perf. 14*
C101 AP29 5 l grn & gray 8 8
C102 AP29 10 l bl & org brn 8 8
C103 AP29 15 l red & multi 8 9
C104 AP29 120 l rose red, yel & gray blk 45 35
C105 AP29 250 l dp grn, yel & blk 1.25 1.10
Nos. C101-C105 (5) 1.94 1.70

Pierre de Coubertin AP30

Wmk. 303

1959, May 19 Engr. *Perf. 13*
C106 AP30 120 l sepia 1.00 85

Pierre de Coubertin; 1960 Olympic Games in Rome.

Alitalia Viscount Over San Marino AP31

1959, June 3 Photo. *Perf. 14*
C107 AP31 120 l brt vio 1.75 1.10

First flight San Marino-Rimini-London.

Lincoln Type of Regular Issue, 1959

Design: Abraham Lincoln and San Marino peaks.

1959, July 1 Engr. *Perf. 14x13*
C108 A87 200 l dk bl 3.50 2.50

Romagna Stamps Type of Regular Issue, 1959

Design: Bologna view; 3b, Romagna stamp.

Wmk. 303

1959, Aug. 29 Photo. *Perf. 14*
C109 A88 120 l blk & bl grn 2.25 1.65

Sicily Stamps Type of Regular Issue, 1959

Design: Fishing boats, Monte Pellegrino and 50g stamp of Sicily (horiz.).

1959, Oct. 16
C110 A89 200 l multi 1.25 75

Olympic Games Type of Regular Issue, 1960

Sports: 20 l, Basketball. 40 l, Sprint race. 80 l, Swimming (horiz.). 125 l, Target shooting (horiz.).

1960, May 23 Wmk. 303 *Perf. 14*
C111 A92 20 l lilac 18 18
C112 A92 40 l bis brn & dk red 28 28
C113 A92 80 l ultra & buff 40 38
C114 A92 125 l ver & dk brn 50 30

Souvenir sheets are valued and described below No. 465.

Lions Intl. Type of Regular Issue, 1960

Design: 200 l, Globe and Lions emblem.

1960, July 1 Photo.
C115 A94 200 l ol grn, brn & ultra 5.00 4.00

12th Stamp Fair Type of Regular Issue, 1960

1960, Aug. 27 Wmk. 303 *Perf. 14*
C116 A95 125 l multi 1.40 1.25

Helicopter and Mt. Titano AP32

1961, July 6 Engr. *Perf. 14*
C117 AP32 1000 l rose car 35.50 27.50
Sheet of 6 210.00 150.00

Tupolev TU-104A AP33

Planes: 10 l, Boeing 707 (vert.). 15 l, Douglas DC-8. 25 l, Boeing 707. 50 l, Vickers Viscount 837. 75 l, Caravelle (vert.). 120 l, Vickers VC10. 200 l, D. H. Comet 4C. 300 l, Boeing 727. 500 l, Rolls Royce Dart turboprop. 1000 l, Boeing 707.

1963-65 Wmk. 339 Photo. *Perf. 14*
C118 AP33 5 l bl & vio brn 8 8
C119 AP33 10 l org & dk bl 8 8
C120 AP33 15 l vio & red 8 8
C121 AP33 25 l vio & car 10 10
C122 AP33 50 l grnsh bl & red 10 10
C123 AP33 75 l emer & dp org 10 10
C124 AP33 120 l vio bl & red 28 28
C125 AP33 200 l brt yel & blk 22 22
C126 AP33 300 l org & blk 25 25

Perf. 13
C127 AP33 500 l multi ('65) 3.75 3.75
Sheet of 4 14.00 14.00
C128 AP33 1000 l lil rose, ultra & yel ('64) 2.50 2.50
Sheet of 4 21.00 21.00
Nos. C118-C128 (11) 7.54 7.54

Dates of issue: Nos. C118-C126, Dec. 5, 1963. No. C127, Mar. 4, 1965. No. C128, Mar. 12, 1964.

Mt. Titano and Flight Symbolized AP34

1972, Oct. 25 Unwmk. *Perf. 11½*
Granite Paper
C129 AP34 1000 l multi 1.00 90

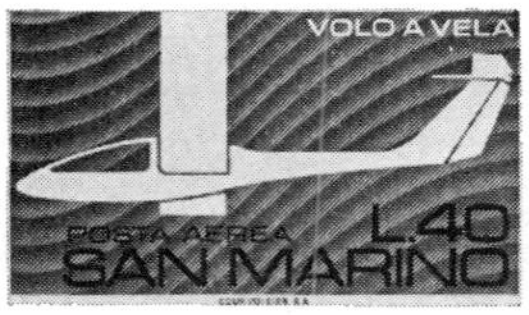

Glider AP35

Designs: Each stamp shows a different type of air current in background.

1974, Oct. 9 Photo. *Perf. 11½*
Granite Paper
C130 AP35 40 l multi 8 8
C131 AP35 120 l multi 14 14
C132 AP35 500 l multi 50 50

50th anniversary of gliding in Italy.

San Marino 77 Type of 1977

1977, Jan. 28 Photo. *Perf. 11½*
C133 A193 200 l multi 22 22

Wright Brothers' Flyer A — AP36

1978, Sept. 28 Photo. *Perf. 11½*
C134 AP36 10 l multi 5 5
C135 AP36 50 l multi 8 8
C136 AP36 200 l multi 22 22

75th anniversary of first powered flight.

AIR POST SEMI-POSTAL STAMP

View of San Marino APSP1

Wmk. 140

1944, Apr. 25 Photo. *Perf. 14*
CB1 APSP1 20 l + 10 l ol grn 90 90
Sheet of 8 22.50 22.50

The surtax was used for workers' houses.

SPECIAL DELIVERY STAMPS

SD1

Unwmk.

1907, Apr. 25 Engr. *Perf. 12*
E1 SD1 25c carmine 5.25 2.50

Type of Regular Issue of 1903 Overprinted ESPRESSO

Perf. 14½x14
1923, May 30 Wmk. 140
E2 A11 60c violet 30 30

Type of 1907 Issue Surcharged

Cent. 60

1923, July 26 *Perf. 14*
E3 SD1 60c on 25c car 30 30
a. Vert. pair, imperf. between 20.00

No. E2 Surcharged Lire 1,25

1926, Nov. 25 *Perf. 14½x14*
E4 A11 1.25 l on 60c vio 45 45

No. E3 Surcharged

L 1,25

1927, Sept. 15
E5 SD1 1.25 l on 60c on 25c brn car 35 35
a. Inverted surcharge 8.50
b. Vert. pair, imperf. between 42.50
c. Double surcharge 65.00

Statue of Liberty and View of San Marino — SD2

Wmk. 217
1929, Aug. 29 Engr. *Perf. 12*
E6 SD2 1.25 l green 16 16

Overprinted in Red UNION POSTALE UNIVERSELLE

E7 SD2 2.50 l deep blue 55 55

Arms of San Marino SD3

Wmk. 140
1943, Sept. Photo. *Perf. 14*
E8 SD3 1.25 l green 10 10
E9 SD3 2.50 l reddish org 12 12

View of San Marino SD4

Pegasus SD5

1945-46 Photo. Wmk. 140
E12 SD4 2.50 l deep grn 10 10
E13 SD4 5 l deep org 12 12
Unwmk.
E14 SD4 5 l car rose 70 50
Wmk. 277
E15 SD4 10 l saph ('46) 1.75 1.25
Engr.
Unwmk.
E16 SD5 30 l dp ultra ('46) 4.00 4.00
Nos. E12-E16 (5) 6.67 5.97

See Nos. E22-E23.

Nos. E14 and E15 Surcharged in Black

L. 15

1947 Unwmk. *Perf. 14*
E17 SD4 15 l on 5 l car rose 25 20
Wmk. 277
E18 SD4 15 l on 10 l saph 25 20

No. E16 Surcharged with New Value and Bars in Carmine

1947-48 Unwmk.
E19 SD5 35 l on 30 l dp ultra ('48) 16.00 16.00
E20 SD5 60 l on 30 l dp ultra 2.75 2.75
E21 SD5 80 l on 30 l dp ultra ('48) 7.50 9.00

Types of 1945-46

1950, Dec. 11 Photo. Wmk. 277
E22 SD4 60 l rose brn 3.50 3.50
E23 SD5 80 l deep blue 3.50 3.50

Nos. E22-E23 Surcharged with New Value and Three Bars

1957, Dec. 12 *Perf. 14*
E24 SD4 75 l on 60 l rose brn 1.50 1.50
E25 SD5 100 l on 80 l dp bl 1.50 1.50

Catalogue values for unused stamps in this section, from this point to the end of the section, are for Never Hinged items.

Crossbow SD6

Design: No. E27, "Espresso" at left; crossbow casts two shadows.

1965, Aug. 28 Photo. Wmk. 339
E26 SD6 120 l on 75 l blk, gray & yel 15 15
E27 SD6 135 l on 100 l blk & org 18 18

Without Surcharge

Design: 80 l, 100 l, "Espresso" at left; crossbow casts two shadows.

1966, Mar. 29
E28 SD6 75 l blk, gray & yel 10 10
E29 SD6 80 l blk & lil 15 15
E30 SD6 100 l blk & org 18 18

SEMI-POSTAL SPECIAL DELIVERY STAMP

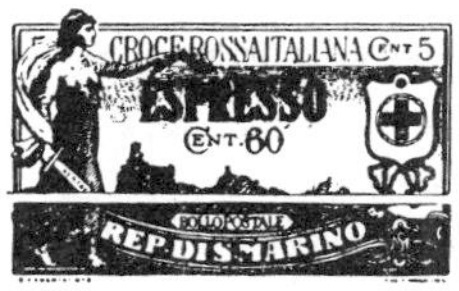

SPSD1

Wmk. 140
1923, Sept. 20 Engr. *Perf. 14*
EB1 SPSD1 60c + 5c brn red 75 75

POSTAGE DUE STAMPS

D1

D2

D3

D4

D5

Wmk. 140
1897-1920 Typo. *Perf. 14*
J1 D1 5c bl grn & dk brn 8 8
J2 D2 10c bl grn & dk brn 9 9
a. Numerals inverted 12.00 12.00
J3 D2 30c bl grn & dk brn 14 14
J4 D2 50c bl grn & dk brn 45 45
a. Numerals inverted 12.00 12.00
J5 D2 60c bl grn & dk brn 1.40 1.75
J6 D3 1 l cl & dk brn 90 90
J7 D4 3 l cl & brn ('20) 2.75 3.25
J8 D4 5 l cl & dk brn 12.50 11.00
J9 D5 10 l cl & dk brn 4.50 5.50
Nos. J1-J9 (9) 22.81 23.16

1924
J10 D1 5c rose & brn 6 8
J11 D2 10c rose & brn 6 8
J12 D2 30c rose & brn 9 9
J13 D2 50c rose & brn 9 9
J14 D2 60c rose & brn 1.10 1.10
J15 D3 1 l grn & brn 1.40 1.40
J16 D4 3 l grn & brn 5.50 5.50
J17 D4 5 l grn & brn 6.50 5.50
J18 D5 10 l grn & brn 55.00 55.00
Nos. J10-J18 (9) 69.80 68.84

1925-39 *Perf. 14*
J19 D1 5c bl & brn 5 5
a. Numerals inverted 14.00 14.00
J20 D2 10c bl & brn 5 5
a. Numerals inverted 14.00 14.00
J21 D2 15c bl & brn ('39) 6 6
J22 D2 20c bl & brn ('39) 6 6
J23 D2 25c bl & brn ('39) 14 14
J24 D2 30c bl & brn 6 6
J25 D2 40c bl & brn ('39) 90 90
J26 D2 50c bl & brn 10 10
a. Numerals inverted 14.00 14.00
J27 D2 60c bl & brn 45 45
J28 D3 1 l buff & brn 1.10 45
J29 D4 2 l buff & brn ('39) 45 65
J30 D4 3 l buff & brn 15.00 11.50
J31 D4 5 l buff & brn 4.50 2.25
J32 D5 10 l buff & brn 7.50 3.50
J33 D4 15 l buff & brn ('28) 45 45
J34 D4 25 l buff & brn ('28) 12.00 9.00
J35 D4 30 l buff & brn ('28) 2.25 4.00
J36 D4 50 l buff & brn ('28) 3.50 4.50
Nos. J19-J36 (18) 48.62 38.17

Postage Due Stamps of 1925 Surcharged in Black and Silver C. 15

1931, May 18
J37 D1 15c on 5c bl & brn 9 9
J38 D2 15c on 10c bl & brn 9 9
J39 D2 15c on 30c bl & brn 9 9
J40 D1 20c on 5c bl & brn 8 8
J41 D2 20c on 10c bl & brn 8 8
J42 D2 20c on 30c bl & brn 8 8
J43 D1 25c on 5c bl & brn 40 22
J44 D2 25c on 10c bl & brn 40 22
J45 D2 25c on 30c bl & brn 4.50 2.75
J46 D1 40c on 5c bl & brn 28 14
J47 D2 40c on 10c bl & brn 32 14
J48 D2 40c on 30c bl & brn 32 14
J49 D1 2 l on 5c bl & brn 11.50 11.50
J50 D2 2 l on 10c bl & brn 25.00 16.00
J51 D2 2 l on 30c bl & brn 21.00 13.00
Nos. J37-J51 (15) 64.23 44.62

Postage Due Stamps of 1925-39 Surcharged in Black Lire 1

Perf. 14, 14½x14
1936-40 Wmk. 140
J52 D1 10c on 5c bl & brn ('38) 45 45
J53 D2 25c on 30c bl & brn ('38) 3.50 3.50
J54 D1 50c on 5c bl & brn ('37) 3.50 3.25
J55 D2 1 l on 30c bl & brn 11.00 2.75
J56 D2 1 l on 40c bl & brn ('40) 3.50 2.50
J57 D4 1 l on 3 l buff & brn ('37) 9.00 90
J58 D4 1 l on 25 l buff & brn ('39) 22.50 5.50
J59 D4 2 l on 15 l buff & brn ('38) 11.00 6.50
J60 D4 3 l on 20c bl & brn ('40) 12.00 11.00
Nos. J52-J60 (9) 76.45 36.35

D6

Coat of Arms — D7

1939 Typo. *Perf. 14*
J61 D6 5c blue & brown 6 6

Nos. J61 and J36 Surcharged with New Values and Bars

1940-43
J62 D6 10c on 5c bl & brn 38 38
J63 D6 50c on 5c bl & brn 1.50 75
J64 D4 25 l on 50 l buff & brn ('43) 1.75 1.75

Unwmk.
1945, June 7 Photo. *Perf. 14*
J65 D7 5c dk grn 5 5
J66 D7 10c org brn 5 5
J67 D7 15c rose red 6 5
J68 D7 20c dp ultra 6 5
J69 D7 25c dk pur 6 5
J70 D7 30c rose lake 6 5
J71 D7 40c bister 6 5
J72 D7 50c slate blk 6 5
J73 D7 60c chestnut 6 5
J74 D7 1 l dp org 6 5
J75 D7 2 l carmine 8 8
J76 D7 5 l dl vio 8 10
J77 D7 10 l dk blue 15 22
J78 D7 20 l dk grn 4.25 3.75
J79 D7 25 l red org 4.25 3.75
J80 D7 50 l dk brn 4.25 3.75
Nos. J65-J80 (16) 13.64 12.15

PARCEL POST STAMPS

These stamps were used by affixing them to the way bill so that one half remained on it following the parcel, the other half staying on the receipt given the sender. Most used halves are right halves. Complete stamps were and are obtainable canceled, probably to order. Both unused and used values are for complete stamps.

PP1

Engraved, Typographed
1928, Nov. 22 Unwmk. *Perf. 12*
Pairs are imperforate between
Q1 PP1 5c blk brn & bl 15 15
a. Imperf. 12.00
Q2 PP1 10c dk bl & bl 15 15
Q3 PP1 20c gray blk & bl 15 15
a. Imperf. 12.00
Q4 PP1 25c car & bl 15 15
Q5 PP1 30c ultra & bl 15 15
Q6 PP1 50c org & bl 15 15
Q7 PP1 60c rose & bl 15 15
Q8 PP1 1 l vio & brn 15 15
a. Imperf. 12.00
Q9 PP1 2 l grn & brn 22 22
Q10 PP1 3 l bis & brn 30 30
Q11 PP1 4 l gray & brn 38 38
Q12 PP1 10 l rose lil & brn 75 75

Q13	PP1	12 l red brn & brn	3.00	3.00
Q14	PP1	15 l ol grn & brn	6.00	6.00
a.		Imperf.	12.00	
Q15	PP1	20 l brn vio & brn	6.50	6.50
		Nos. Q1-Q15 (15)	18.35	18.35

Halves Used

Q1-8	5
Q9-Q10	10
Q11	15
Q12	35
Q13	65
Q14	2.75
Q15	3.00

1945-46 Wmk. 140 *Perf. 14*

Pairs are perforated between

Q16	PP1	5c rose vio & red org	5	5
Q17	PP1	10c red org & blk	5	5
Q18	PP1	20c dk red & grn	5	5
Q19	PP1	25c yel & blk	5	5
Q20	PP1	30c red vio & org red	5	5
Q21	PP1	50c dl pur & blk	5	5
Q22	PP1	60c rose lake & blk	5	5
Q23	PP1	1 l brn & dp bl	5	5
Q24	PP1	2 l dk brn & dk bl	5	5
Q25	PP1	3 l ol brn & brn	5	5
Q26	PP1	4 l bl grn & brn	5	5
Q27	PP1	10 l blk & brt pur	10	10
Q28	PP1	12 l myr grn & dl bl	1.65	1.10
Q29	PP1	15 l grn & pur	1.50	95
Q30	PP1	20 l rose lil & brn	1.10	75
Q31	PP1	25 l dp car & ultra ('46)	21.00	20.00
Q32	PP1	50 l yel & dp org ('46)	24.00	24.00
		Nos. Q16-Q32 (17)	49.90	47.45

Halves Used

Q16-Q27	5
Q28	8
Q29	10
Q30	15
Q31	25
Q32	50

Nos. Q32 and Q31 Surcharged with New Value and Wavy Lines in Black

1948-50

Q33	PP1	100 l on 50 l yel & dp org	30.00	32.50
		Half, used		1.00
Q34	PP1	200 l on 25 l dp car & ultra ('50)	60.00	65.00
		Half, used		1.00

1953, Mar. 5 Wmk. 277 *Perf. 13½*

Pairs Perforated Between

Q35	PP1	10 l dk grn & rose lil	14.00	5.00
		Half, used		1.00
Q36	PP1	300 l pur & lake	95.00	95.00
		Half, used		1.00

1956 Wmk. 303 *Perf. 13½*

Q37	PP1	10 l gray & brt pur	35	30
		Half, used		5
Q38	PP1	50 l yel & dp org	1.10	1.00
		Half, used		10

No. Q38 Surcharged with New Value and Wavy Lines In Black

Q39	PP1	100 l on 50 l yel & dp org	1.25	1.10
		Half, used		25

Catalogue values for unused stamps in this section, from this point to the end of the section, are for Never Hinged items.

1960-61

Q40	PP1	300 l vio & brn	37.50	30.00
		Half, used		50
Q41	PP1	500 l dk brn & car ('61)	3.25	3.00
		Half, used		5

1965-72 Wmk. 339 *Perf. 13½*

Pairs Perforated Between

Q42	PP1	10 l gray & brt pur	8	8
Q43	PP1	50 l yel & red org	8	8
Q44	PP1	100 l on 50 l yel & red org	1.50	1.50
Q45	PP1	300 l vio & brn	50	50
Q46	PP1	500 l brn & red ('72)	9.25	9.25
Q47	PP1	1000 l bl grn & lt red brn ('67)	1.00	1.00
		Nos. Q42-Q47 (6)	12.41	12.41

Halves Used

Q42-Q43	5
Q44-Q45	10
Q46	20
Q47	45

SASENO

LOCATION — An island in the Adriatic Sea, lying at the entrance of Valona Bay, Albania.
GOVT. — Former Italian possession.
AREA — 2 sq. mi.

Italy occupied this Albanian islet in 1914, and returned it to Albania in 1947.

100 Centesimi = 1 Lira

Italian Stamps of 1901-22 Overprinted SASENO

1923 Wmk. Crown (140) *Perf. 14*

1	A48	10c claret	2.50	*8.25*
2	A48	15c slate	2.50	*8.25*
3	A50	20c brn org	2.50	*8.25*
4	A49	25c blue	2.50	*8.25*
5	A49	30c yel brn	2.50	*8.25*
6	A49	50c violet	2.50	*8.25*
7	A49	60c carmine	2.50	*8.25*
8	A46	1 l brn & grn	2.50	*8.25*
a.		Double ovpt.	70.00	
		Nos. 1-8 (8)	20.00	

Nos. 1 to 8 were superseded by postage stamps of Italy.

SAUDI ARABIA

LOCATION — Southwestern Asia, on the Arabian Peninsula between the Red Sea and the Persian Gulf.
GOVT. — Kingdom
AREA — 927,000 sq. mi.
POP. — 8,400,000 (est. 1984)
CAPITAL — Riyadh

In 1916 the Grand Sherif of Mecca declared the Sanjak of Hejaz independent of Turkish rule. In 1925, Ibn Saud, then Sultan of the Nejd, captured the Hejaz after a prolonged siege of Jedda, the last Hejaz stronghold.

The resulting Kingdom of the Hejaz and Nejd was renamed Saudi Arabia in 1932.

40 Paras = 1 Piaster = 1 Guerche (Garch, Grouche or Qirsh)
11 Guerche = 1 Riyal (1928)
110 Guerche = 1 Sovereign (1931)
440 Guerche = 1 Sovereign (1952)
20 Piasters (Guerche) = 1 Riyal (1960)
100 Halalas = 1 Riyal (1976)

Catalogue values for unused stamps in this country are for Never Hinged items, beginning with Scott 178 in the regular postage section, Scott C1 in the airpost section, Scott J28 in the postage due section, Scott O7 in official section, and Scott RA6 in the postal tax section.

HEJAZ

Sherifate of Mecca

Adapted from Carved Door Panels of Mosque El Salih Talay, Cairo — A1

Taken from Page of Koran in Mosque of El Sultan Barquq, Cairo — A2

Taken from Details of an Ancient Prayer Niche in the Mosque of El Amri at Qus in Upper Egypt — A3

1916 Unwmk. Typo. *Perf. 10, 12*

L1	A1	¼pi green	45.00	35.00
L2	A2	½pi red	40.00	32.50
a.		Perf. 10	120.00	100.00
L3	A3	1pi blue	12.00	12.00
a.		Perf. 12	150.00	150.00
b.		Perf. 10x12		850.00

Exist imperf.

Central Design Adapted from a Koran Design for a Tomb. Background is from Stone Carving on Entrance Arch to the Ministry of Wakfs — A4

1916-17 *Roulette 20*

L4	A4	⅛pi org ('17)	3.00	1.50
L5	A1	¼pi green	3.00	1.50
L6	A2	½pi red	3.00	1.50
L7	A3	1pi blue	3.00	1.50

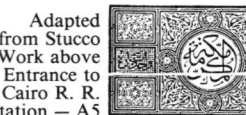

Adapted from Stucco Work above Entrance to Cairo R. R. Station — A5

Adapted from First Page of the Koran of Sultan Farag — A6

1917 *Serrate Roulette 13*

L8	A5	1pa lil brn	3.00	1.50
L9	A4	⅛pi orange	3.00	1.50
L10	A1	¼pi green	3.00	1.50
L11	A2	½pi red	3.00	1.50
L12	A3	1pi blue	3.00	1.50
L13	A6	2pi magenta	20.00	10.00
		Nos. L8-L13 (6)	35.00	17.50

Designs A1-A6 are inscribed "Hejaz Postage."

Kingdom of the Hejaz

Stamps of 1917-18 Overprinted in Black, Red or Brown:

1921, Dec. 21 *Serrate Roulette 13*

L14	A5	1pa lil brn	30.00	15.00
L15	A4	⅛pi orange	30.00	17.50
a.		Inverted overprint	100.00	
b.		Double overprint	200.00	
c.		Roulette 20	600.00	
d.		As "c", invtd. overprint		*1,500.*
L16	A1	¼pi green	12.00	6.00
a.		Invtd. overprint	100.00	
b.		Double overprint	200.00	
c.		Roulette 20	600.00	
L17	A2	½pi red	15.00	7.50
a.		Inverted overprint	150.00	85.00
b.		Roulette 20	600.00	
L18	A3	1pi bl (R)	12.00	7.00
a.		Brown ovpt.	25.00	20.00
b.		Black ovpt.	35.00	30.00
c.		As "b", invtd. ovpt.	400.00	
d.		Roulette 20	700.00	
L19	A6	2pi magenta	17.50	10.00
		Nos. L14-L19 (6)	116.50	63.00

Nos. L15-L17, L18b and L19 exist with date (1340) omitted at one or both sides.

With Additional Surcharge:

a b

L22	A5(a)	½pi on 1pa lil brn	275.00	140.00
L23	A5(b)	1pi on 1pa lil brn	275.00	140.00

Stamps of 1917-18 Overprinted in Black

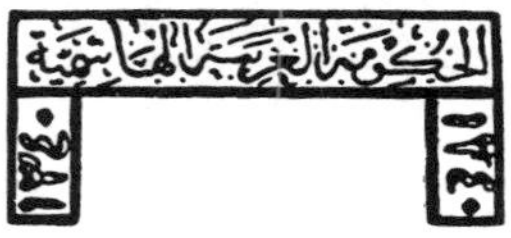

1922, Jan. 7

L24	A5	1pa lil brn	3.25	3.00
a.		Inverted ovpt.	150.00	
b.		Double overprint	100.00	
c.		Double overprint, one inverted	200.00	
L25	A4	⅛pi orange	10.00	7.00
a.		Inverted ovpt.	100.00	
b.		Double overprint, one inverted	200.00	
L26	A1	¼pi green	3.25	3.00
a.		Inverted ovpt.	100.00	
b.		Double overprint, one inverted	200.00	
L27	A2	½pi red	2.50	2.00
a.		Inverted ovpt.	100.00	
b.		Double overprint, one inverted	200.00	
L28	A3	1pi blue	2.50	50
a.		Double overprint	90.00	
b.		Inverted ovpt.	200.00	
L29	A6	2pi magenta	6.50	5.00
a.		Double overprint	150.00	

With Additional Surcharge of New Value

L30	A5(a)	½pi on 1pa lil brn	22.50	15.00
L31	A5(b)	1pi on 1pa lil brn	2.50	1.00
a.		Inverted surch.	100.00	
b.		Double surch.	90.00	
c.		Double surcharge, one inverted		
		Nos. L24-L31 (8)	53.00	36.50

The 1921 and 1922 overprints read: "The Government of Hashemite Arabia, 1340."

The overprint on Nos. L24-L31 in red is bogus.

Arms of Sherif of Mecca — A7

1922 Typo. *Perf. 11½*

L32	A7	⅛pi red brn	2.00	50
L34	A7	½pi red	2.00	50
L35	A7	1pi dk bl	2.00	50
L36	A7	1½pi violet	2.00	50
L37	A7	2pi orange	2.00	50
L38	A7	3pi ol brn	2.00	50
L39	A7	5pi ol grn	2.00	60
		Nos. L32-L39 (7)	14.00	3.60

Numerous shades exist. Exist imperf.

Stamps of 1922 Surcharged with New Values in Arabic:

c d

1923

L40	A7(c)	¼pi on ½pi org brn	25.00	5.00
a.		Double surcharge		
b.		Double inverted surcharge		
c.		Double surcharge, one inverted		
d.		Invtd. surch.	175.00	
L41	A7(d)	10pi on 5pi ol grn	30.00	10.00
a.		Double surcharge, one inverted		
b.		Inverted surch.		

Caliphate Issue

Stamps of 1922 Overprinted in Gold

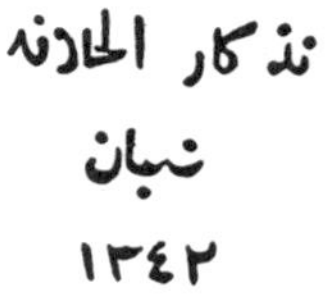

1924

L42	A7	1/8pi org brn	3.50	1.75
L43	A7	1/2pi red	3.50	1.75
L44	A7	1pi dk bl	3.50	1.75
L45	A7	1 1/2pi violet	3.50	1.75
L46	A7	2pi orange	3.50	1.75
L47	A7	3pi ol brn	4.00	2.00
L48	A7	5pi ol grn	4.00	1.75
		Nos. L42-L48 (7)	25.50	12.50

The overprint reads "In commemoration of the Caliphate, Shaaban, 1342." The issue commemorates the assumption of the Caliphate by King Hussein in March, 1924.

The overprint was typographed in black and dusted with "gold" powder while wet. It exists inverted on the 1pi, 2pi and 5pi. The several settings differ in spacing and alignment. Forgeries exist.

This overprint is also known on Nos. LJ11-LJ13.

Type of 1922 and

Arms of Sherif of Mecca — A8

1924 *Perf. 11 1/2*

L48A	A7	1/4pi yel grn	5.00	90
b.		Tete beche pair	15.00	
L49	A7	3pi brn red	10.00	4.00
a.		3pi dl red	5.00	2.00
L50	A8	10pi vio & dk brn	5.00	4.00
a.		Center inverted	30.00	15.00
b.		Center omitted	27.50	
c.		10pi pur & sep	4.50	4.00

Nos. L48A, L50, L50a exist imperf.

See Jordan for various overprints on 1922-25 issues of Hejaz.

Jedda Issues

Stamps of 1916-17 Overprinted

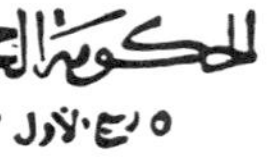

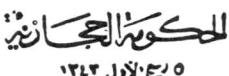

The control overprints on Nos. L51-L185 read: "Hukumat al Hageziet, 5 Rabi al'awwal 1343" (The Hejaz Government, October 4, 1924). This is the date of the accession of King Ali.

Counterfeits exist of all Jedda overprints.

Red Overprint

1925, Jan. *Roulette 20*

L51	A4	1/8pi orange	15.00	8.00
a.		Inverted overprint	100.00	
b.		Overprinted on face and back	200.00	
L52	A1	1/4pi green	15.00	8.00
a.		Inverted overprint	40.00	
b.		Double overprint	50.00	
c.		Double overprint, one invtd.	150.00	
L53	A2	1/2pi red	60.00	37.50
a.		Inverted overprint	100.00	
L54	A3	1pi blue	35.00	17.50
a.		Inverted overprint	75.00	
b.		Double overprint, one inverted	120.00	

Serrate Roulette 13

L55	A5	1pa lil brn	12.00	6.00
a.		Inverted overprint	50.00	
b.		Double overprint	50.00	
c.		Overprinted on face and back	100.00	
L56	A4	1/8pi orange	30.00	15.00
a.		Inverted overprint	60.00	
L57	A1	1/4pi green	18.00	10.00
a.		Pair, one without overprint	500.00	
b.		Inverted overprint	45.00	
c.		Double overprint, one inverted	300.00	
L58	A2	1/2pi red	25.00	10.00
a.		Inverted overprint	40.00	
L59	A3	1pi blue	27.50	15.00
a.		Inverted overprint	65.00	
L60	A6	2pi magenta	35.00	17.50
a.		Inverted overprint	50.00	

Gold Overprint

Roulette 20

L61	A1	1/4pi green	*2,500.*	*2,500.*

Serrate Roulette 13

L62	A1	1/4pi green	20.00	12.50
a.		Inverted overprint	75.00	

The overprint on No. L61 was typographed in red or blue (No. L62 only in red) and dusted with "gold" powder while wet.

Blue Overprint

Roulette 20

L63	A1	1/4pi green	25.00	12.50
a.		Inverted overprint	60.00	
b.		Overprinted on face and back	90.00	
L64	A2	1/2pi red, invtd. ovpt.	90.00	75.00
a.		Upright overprint	150.00	

Serrate Roulette 13

L65	A1	1/4pi green	18.00	18.00
a.		Inverted overprint	50.00	
b.		Vertical overprint	800.00	
L66	A2	1/2pi red	30.00	10.50
a.		Inverted overprint	75.00	
L66B	A6	2pi mag, invtd. ovpt.	*1,500.*	

Blue overprint on No. L55 is bogus.

Same Overprint in Blue on Provisional Stamps of 1922 Overprinted on No. L17

L67	A2	1/2pi red	*3,000.*	

Overprinted on Nos. L24-L29

L68	A5	1pa lil brn	60.00	27.50
L69	A4	1/8pi orange	*3,000.*	750.00
a.		Inverted overprint		
L70	A1	1/4pi green	60.00	30.00
a.		Inverted overprint	750.00	
L71	A2	1/2pi red	60.00	30.00
a.		Inverted overprint	1,000.	
L72	A3	1pi blue	80.00	32.50
L73	A6	2pi magenta	80.00	45.00
a.		Inverted overprint	650.00	

Same Overprint on Nos. L30 and L31

L74	A5(a)	1/2pi on 1pa lil brn	100.00	60.00
L75	A5(b)	1pi on 1pa lil brn	85.00	60.00
a.		Inverted overprint	600.00	

Same Overprint in Blue Vertically, Reading Up or Down, on Stamps of 1922-24

Perf. 11 1/2

L76	A7	1/2pi red	*850.00*	*850.00*
L76A	A8	10pi vio & dk brn	*1,500.*	*1,500.*

Nos. L5, L10 Overprinted in Blue or Red

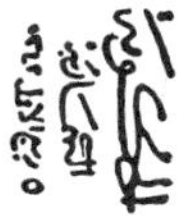

Roulette 20

L77	A1	1/4pi grn (Bl)	*200.00*	*200.00*
L78	A1	1/4pi grn (R)	*125.00*	*125.00*

Serrate Roulette 13

L79	A1	1/4pi grn (Bl)	75.00	75.00
L80	A1	1/4pi grn (R)	50.00	50.00

Nos. L77-L80 exist with overprint reading up or down. It reads up in illustration.

Nos. L10, L32-L39 Overprinted

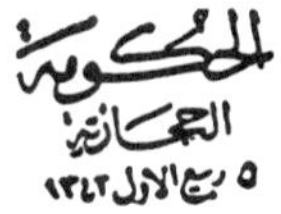

Serrate Roulette 13

Red Overprint (vertical)

L81	A1	1/4pi green	*800.00*	

Overprint on No. L81 also exists horizontal and inverted.

Perf. 11 1/2

Blue Overprint

L82	A7	1/8pi red brn	4.50	3.00
a.		Inverted overprint	50.00	
L83	A7	1/2pi red	8.00	8.00
a.		Double overprint	50.00	
b.		Inverted overprint	50.00	10.00
c.		Double overprint, one inverted	25.00	
d.		Vertical overprint		
L84	A7	1pi dk bl		
a.		Inverted overprint		
L85	A7	1 1/2pi violet	12.00	10.00
a.		Inverted overprint	50.00	15.00
L86	A7	2pi orange	12.00	8.00
a.		Double overprint, one inverted	25.00	
b.		Inverted overprint	50.00	
c.		Double overprint	50.00	
L87	A7	3pi ol brn	10.00	7.00
a.		Inverted overprint	50.00	
b.		Double overprint, one inverted	35.00	
c.		Vertical overprint	175.00	
d.		Dbl. ovpt., both invtd.	35.00	
L88	A7	3pi dl red	12.00	8.00
a.		Inverted overprint	50.00	
b.		Double overprint, one inverted	35.00	
L89	A7	5pi ol grn	12.00	8.00
a.		Inverted overprint	50.00	

Black Overprint

L90	A7	1/8pi red brn		
a.		Inverted overprint		
L91	A7	1/2pi red	5.00	4.00
a.		Inverted overprint	50.00	
L92	A7	1pi dk bl		
a.		Inverted overprint		
L93	A7	1 1/2pi violet	14.00	14.00
a.		Inverted overprint	75.00	
L94	A7	2pi orange	4.50	3.50
a.		Inverted overprint	50.00	
L95	A7	3pi ol brn	6.00	5.00
a.		Inverted overprint	50.00	15.00
L96	A7	3pi dl red	6.00	5.00
a.		Inverted overprint	50.00	
L97	A7	5pi ol grn	7.50	6.00
a.		Inverted overprint	50.00	

Red Overprint

L98	A7	1/8pi red brn, invtd.		
L99	A7	1/4pi yel grn	17.50	12.50
a.		Tete beche pair	30.00	
b.		Inverted overprint	50.00	
L100	A7	1/2pi red		
a.		Inverted overprint		
L101	A7	1pi dk bl	9.00	8.00
a.		Inverted overprint	50.00	
b.		Double overprint, one invtd.	35.00	
L102	A7	1 1/2pi violet	3.50	3.00
a.		Inverted overprint	50.00	
L103	A7	2pi orange	13.00	9.00
a.		Inverted overprint	50.00	
b.		Vertical overprint	175.00	
L104	A7	3pi ol brn	13.00	9.00
a.		Inverted overprint	50.00	
L105	A7	3pi dl red, invtd.		
L106	A7	5pi ol grn	8.00	6.00
a.		Inverted overprint	50.00	
b.		Vertical overprint		
L107	A8	10pi vio & dk brn	17.50	15.00
a.		Inverted overprint	50.00	
b.		Center inverted	30.00	
c.		As "b," invtd. ovpt.	*125.00*	

Double overprint is also found on Nos. L87-L88, L94-L95, L100, L103-L105.

Gold Overprint

L108	A7	1/2pi red brn	20.00	20.00
a.		Inverted overprint	30.00	
L109	A7	1/2pi red	20.00	20.00
L110	A7	1pi dk bl	20.00	20.00
L111	A7	1 1/2pi violet	85.00	85.00
L112	A7	2pi orange	70.00	70.00
L113	A7	3pi ol brn	25.00	25.00
L114	A7	3pi dl red	75.00	75.00
L115	A7	5pi ol grn	65.00	65.00

Same Overprint on Nos. L42-L48

Blue Overprint

L116	A7	1/8pi red brn	8.00	8.00
a.		Double ovpt., one inverted	50.00	
b.		Inverted overprint	25.00	
L117	A7	1/2pi red	15.00	15.00
a.		Inverted overprint	25.00	
L118	A7	1pi dk bl	10.00	10.00
L119	A7	1 1/2pi violet	12.00	12.00
L120	A7	2pi orange	50.00	50.00
a.		Inverted overprint	82.50	
L121	A7	3pi ol brn	20.00	20.00
a.		Inverted overprint	35.00	
L122	A7	5pi ol grn	8.00	8.00
a.		Inverted overprint	40.00	

Black Overprint

L123	A7	1/8pi red brn	8.00	8.00
a.		Inverted overprint	75.00	
L124	A7	1/2pi red		
a.		Inverted overprint		
L125	A7	1 1/2pi violet	100.00	100.00
a.		Inverted overprint	200.00	
L127	A7	3pi ol brn	65.00	65.00
a.		Inverted overprint	100.00	

L128	A7	5pi ol grn	10.00	10.00
a.		Inverted overprint	50.00	

Red Overprint

L129	A7	1pi dk bl	20.00	20.00
L130	A7	1½pi violet	75.00	75.00
L131	A7	2pi orange	20.00	20.00

Experts question the authenticity of the ½pi red and 3pi brown with red overprint.

Stamps of 1922-24 Surcharged

a 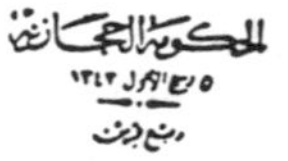

and Handstamped

b 

1925 Litho. *Perf. 11½*

L135	A7	¼pi on ⅛pi red brn	32.50	32.50
b.		1 pi on ¼ pi on ⅛ pi red brn		
L136	A7	¼pi on ½pi red	20.00	20.00
a.		¼pi on 1pi on ½pi, surch invtd.	20.00	
c.		1pi on ¼pi on ½pi	60.00	60.00
L138	A7	1pi on 1pi on 2pi org	20.00	20.00
a.		¼pi on ¼pi on 2pi org		
b.		10pi on 1pi on 2pi org	100.00	
c.		¼pi on 1pi on 2pi org	50.00	
d.		1pi on ¼pi on 2pi org	*100.00*	
L139	A7	1pi on 1pi on 3pi ol brn	14.00	14.00
L140	A7	1pi on 1pi on 3pi dl red	22.50	22.50
b.		¼ pi on 1 pi on 3 pi dl red		
L141	A7	10pi on 10pi on 5pi ol grn	11.00	11.00
b.		1pi on 10 pi on 5 pi		
		Nos. L135-L141 (6)	120.00	120.00

The printed surcharge (a) reads "The Hejaz Government. October 4, 1924." with new denomination in third line. This surcharge alone was used for the first issue (Nos. L135a-L141a). The new denomination was so small and indistinct that its equivalent in larger characters was soon added by handstamp (b) at bottom of each stamp for the second issue (Nos. L135-L141).

The handstamped surcharge (b) is found double, inverted, etc. It is also known in dark violet.

Without Handstamp "b"

L135a	A7	¼pi on ⅛pi red brn	25.00
L136b	A7	¼pi on ½pi red	25.00
L138e	A7	1pi on 2pi org	25.00
L139a	A7	1pi on 3pi ol brn	25.00
L140a	A7	1pi on 3pi dl red	25.00
L141a	A7	10pi on 5pi ol grn	25.00
		Nos. L135a-L141a (6)	150.00

Stamps of 1922-24 Surcharged

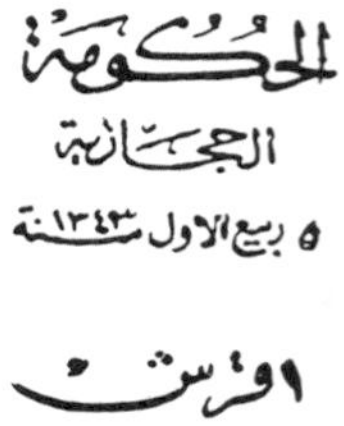

Black Surcharge

L142	A7	⅛pi on ½pi red	6.00	6.00
a.		Inverted surcharge	25.00	
L143	A7	¼pi on ½pi red	6.00	6.00
a.		Inverted surcharge	25.00	
L144	A7	1pi on ½pi red	6.00	6.00
a.		Inverted surcharge	15.00	
L145	A7	1pi on 1½pi vio	6.00	6.00
a.		Inverted surcharge	15.00	
L146	A7	1pi on 2pi org	6.00	6.00
a.		"10pi"	75.00	
b.		Inverted surcharge	25.00	
L147	A7	1pi on 3pi ol brn	6.00	6.00
a.		"10pi"	75.00	
b.		Inverted surcharge	35.00	
L148	A7	10pi on 5pi ol grn	15.00	12.50
a.		Inverted surcharge	25.00	

Blue Surcharge

L149	A7	⅛pi on ½pi red	12.00	12.00
a.		Inverted surcharge	25.00	
L150	A7	¼pi on ½pi red	12.00	12.00
a.		Inverted surcharge	25.00	
L151	A7	1pi on ½pi red	12.00	12.00
a.		Inverted surcharge	25.00	
b.		Double surcharge		
L152	A7	1pi on 1½pi vio	12.00	12.00
a.		Inverted surcharge	25.00	
L153	A7	1pi on 2pi org	12.00	12.00
a.		"10pi"	30.00	
b.		Inverted surcharge	25.00	
L154	A7	1pi on 3pi ol brn	25.00	20.00
a.		"10pi"	60.00	
b.		Inverted surcharge	40.00	
L155	A7	10pi on 5pi ol grn	35.00	15.00
a.		Inverted surcharge	60.00	

Red Surcharge

L156	A7	1pi on 1½pi vio	25.00	25.00
a.		Inverted surcharge	50.00	
L157	A7	1pi on 2pi org	25.00	25.00
a.		"10pi"	60.00	
b.		Inverted surcharge	50.00	
L158	A7	1pi on 3pi ol brn	25.00	25.00
a.		"10pi"	50.00	
b.		Inverted surcharge	40.00	
L159	A7	10pi on 5pi ol grn	25.00	25.00
a.		Inverted surcharge	75.00	

The "10pi" surcharge is found inverted on Nos. L146a, L147a, L153a, L154a, L157a and L158a.

King Ali Issue

A9

A10

A11

A12

1925, May-June *Perf. 11½*

Black Overprint

L160	A9	⅛pi chocolate	1.00	60
L161	A9	¼pi ultra	1.00	60
L162	A9	½pi car rose	1.00	60
L163	A10	1pi yel grn	1.25	75
L164	A10	1½pi orange	1.25	75
L165	A10	2pi blue	1.50	90
L166	A11	3pi dk grn	1.50	1.00
L167	A11	5pi org brn	1.50	1.00
L168	A12	10pi red & grn	3.00	2.00
a.		Center inverted	35.00	

Red Overprint

L169	A9	⅛pi chocolate	1.00	60
L170	A9	¼pi ultra	60	60
L171	A10	1pi yel grn	75	75
L172	A10	1½pi orange	75	75
L173	A10	2pi dp bl	90	90
L174	A11	3pi dk grn	1.00	1.00
a.		Horiz. pair, imperf. vert.		
L175	A11	5pi org brn	1.00	1.00
L176	A12	10pi red & grn	2.00	2.00

Blue Overprint

L177	A9	⅛pi chocolate	1.00	1.00
L179	A9	½pi car rose	1.00	1.00
L180	A10	1pi yel grn	1.00	1.00
L181	A10	1½pi orange	1.00	1.00
L182	A11	3pi dk grn	1.00	1.00
L183	A11	5pi org brn	3.00	2.00
L184	A12	10pi red & grn	4.00	3.00
L185	A12	10pi red & org	275.00	*125.00*

Without Overprint

L186	A12	10pi red & grn	2.00	2.00
a.		Double impression of center	*100.00*	

The overprint in the tablets on Nos. L160-L185 reads: "5 Rabi al'awwal, 1343" (Oct. 5, 1924), the date of the accession of King Ali.

The tablet overprints vary slightly in size. Each is found reading upward or downward and at either side of the stamp. These control overprints were first applied in Jedda by the government press. They were later made from new plates by the stamp printer in Cairo. In the Jedda overprint, the bar over the "0" figure extends to the left. The lines of the Cairo overprinting are generally heavier and the bar is at center right. Imperforates exist.

Nos. L160-L168 are known with the overprints spaced as on type D3 and aligned horizontally.

Copies of these stamps (perforated or imperforate) without the overprint, except No. L186 were not regularly issued and not available for postage.

No. L185 without overprint is a proof. Two sheets were overprinted by error and were put on sale with the ordinary stamps.

The ¼ pi with blue overprint is bogus.

NEJD

Handstamped in Blue, Red, Black or Violet

The overprint reads: "1343. Barid al Sultanat at Nejdia" (1925. Post of the Sultanate of Nejd).

The overprints on this and succeeding issues are handstamped and, as usual, are found double, inverted, etc. These variations are scarce.

1925, Mar.-Apr. Unwmk. *Perf. 12*

On Stamp of Turkey, 1915, With Crescent and Star in Red

1	A22	5pa ocher (Bl)	30.00	30.00
2	A22	5pa ocher (R)	22.50	22.50
3	A22	5pa ocher (Bk)	25.00	25.00
4	A22	5pa ocher (V)	20.00	20.00

On Stamp of Turkey, 1913

5	A28	10pa grn (Bl)	18.00	18.00
6	A28	10pa grn (R)	14.00	14.00

On Stamps of Hejaz, 1922-24

Perf. 11½

7	A7	⅛pi red brn (R)	25.00	25.00
8	A7	⅛pi red brn (Bk)	35.00	35.00
9	A7	⅛pi red brn (V)	25.00	25.00
10	A7	⅛pi car (R)	30.00	30.00
11	A7	⅛pi car (Bk)	35.00	35.00
12	A7	⅛pi car (V)	*20.00*	*20.00*
13	A7	½pi red (Bl)	15.00	15.00
14	A7	½pi red (V)	12.50	12.50
15	A7	1½pi vio (R)	17.50	17.50
16	A7	2pi yel buff (R)	60.00	60.00
a.		2pi org (R)	40.00	
17	A7	2pi yel buff (V)	60.00	60.00
a.		2pi org (V)	35.00	35.00
18	A7	3pi brn red (Bl)	30.00	30.00
19	A7	3pi brn red (R)	22.50	22.50
20	A7	3pi brn red (V)	25.00	25.00

Many Hejaz stamps of the 1922 type were especially printed for this and following issues. The re-impressions are usually more clearly printed, in lighter shades than the 1922 stamps, and some are in new colors.

Counterfeits exist.

Arabic Inscriptions
R1 R2

On Hejaz Bill Stamp

22	R1	1pi vio (R)	12.50	12.50

On Hejaz Notarial Stamps

23	R2	1pi vio (R)	15.00	15.00
24	R2	2pi bl (R)	25.00	25.00
25	R2	2pi bl (V)	20.00	20.00

Locomotive — R3

On Hejaz Railway Tax Stamps

26	R3	1pi bl (R)	22.50	10.00
27	R3	2pi ocher (R)	25.00	15.00
28	R3	2pi ocher (V)	20.00	15.00
29	R3	3pi lil (R)	22.50	22.50
		Nos. 1-20,22-29 (28)	704.50	677.00

There are two types of basic stamps.

Pilgrimage Issue.

Various Stamps Handstamp Surcharged in Blue and Red in Types "a" and "b" and with Tablets with New Values

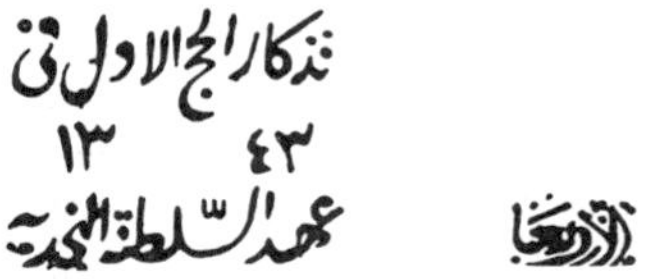

a b

Surcharge "a" reads: "Tezkar al Hajj al Awwal Fi 'ahd al Sultanat al Nejdia, 1343". (Commemorating the first pilgrimage under the Nejdi Sultanate, 1925).

Surcharge "b" reads: "Al Arba" (Wednesday.)

1925, July 1 *Perf. 12*

On Stamps of Turkey, 1913

30	A28	1pi on 10pa grn (Bl & R)	60.00	60.00
31	A30	5pi on 1pi bl (Bl & R)	60.00	60.00

On Stamps of Hejaz, 1917-18

Serrate Roulette 13

32	A5	2pi on 1pa lil brn (R & Bl)	85.00	75.00
33	A4	4pi on ⅛pi org (R & Bl)	350.00	350.00

On Hejaz Railway Tax Stamp

Perf. 11½

34	R3	3pi lil (Bl & R)	45.00	40.00
		Nos. 30-34 (5)	600.00	585.00

Handstamped in Blue, Red, Black or Violet

This overprint has practically the same meaning as that described over No. 1. The Mohammedan year (1343) is omitted.

1925, July-Aug. *Perf. 12*

On Stamp of Turkey, 1915, with Crescent and Star in Red

35	A22	5pa ocher (Bl)	25.00	25.00

On Stamps of Turkey, 1913

36	A28	10pa grn (Bl)	15.00	15.00
a.		Black ovpt.	80.00	

On Stamps of Hejaz, 1922 (Nos. L28-L29)

Serrate Roulette 13

37	A3	1pi bl (R)	60.00	*75.00*
38	A6	2pi mag (Bl)	60.00	*75.00*

On Stamps of Hejaz, 1922-24

Perf. 11½

38A	A7	⅛pi red brn (Bk)	*2,250.*	
38B	A7	⅛pi red brn (Bl)	*3,000.*	
39	A7	½pi red (Bl)	10.00	10.00
a.		Imperf., pair	18.00	18.00
39B	A7	½pi red (Bk)	50.00	50.00
c.		Imperf., pair	17.50	17.50
40	A7	1pi gray vio (R)	30.00	30.00
a.		1pi blk vio (R)	*45.00*	
b.		Imperf., pair	50.00	
41	A7	1½pi dk red (Bk)	30.00	30.00
a.		1½pi brick red (Bk)	50.00	
42	A7	2pi yel buff (Bl)	35.00	35.00
a.		2pi org (Bl)	60.00	60.00
43	A7	2pi dp vio (Bl)	30.00	30.00
a.		Imperf., pair		
44	A7	3pi brn red (Bl)	22.50	22.50
a.		Imperf., pair		
45	A7	5pi scar (Bl)	27.50	27.50
a.		Imperf., pair		
		Nos. 35-38,39-45 (12)	395.00	*425.00*

With Additional Surcharge of New Value Typo. in Black:

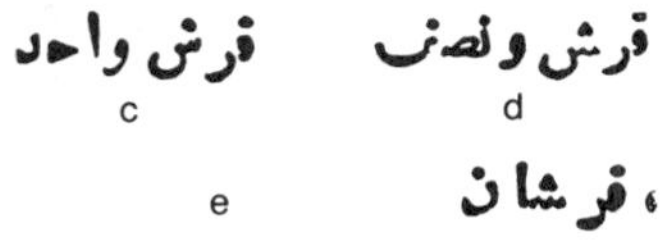

c d e

Color in parenthesis is that of overprint on basic stamp.

46	A7(c)	1pi on ½pi red (Bl)	10.00	2.00
a.		Imperf. pair	17.00	
b.		Ovpt. & surch. invtd.		
47	A7(d)	1½pi on ½pi red (Bl)	15.00	8.00
a.		Imperf., pair	30.00	
b.		Black ovpt.	14.00	
48	A7(e)	2pi on 3pi brn red (Bl)	15.00	15.00

Several variations in type settings of "c," "d" and "e" exist, including inverted letters and values.

On Hejaz Notarial Stamp

49	R2	2pi bl (Bk)	16.00	16.00

On Hejaz Railway Tax Stamps

50	R3	1pi bl (R)	25.00	25.00
51	R3	1pi bl (Bk)	30.00	30.00
52	R3	2pi ocher (Bl)	27.50	27.50
53	R3	3pi lil (Bl)	22.50	22.50
54	R3	5pi grn (Bl)	15.00	15.00

Hejaz Railway Tax Stamp Handstamped in Black

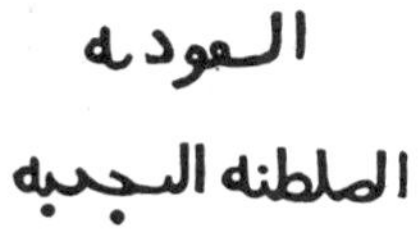

This overprint reads: "Al Saudia. - Al Sultanat al Nejdia." (The Saudi Sultanate of Nejd.)

1925-26

55	R3	1pi blue	100.00	75.00

On Nos. L34, L36-L37, L41

55A	A7	½ pi red	*375.00*	
56	A7	1½pi violet	*375.00*	
a.		Violet overprint	*375.00*	
57	A7	2pi orange	*375.00*	
57A	A7	10pi on 5pi ol grn	*375.00*	

On Nos. L95 and L97

Color in parentheses is that of rectangular overprint on basic stamp

58	A7	3pi ol brn (Bk)	*375.00*	
58A	A7	5pi ol grn (Bk)	*375.00*	

On Nos. L162-L163, L173

Perf. 11½

58B	A9	½pi car rose (Bk)	*375.00*	
58C	A10	1pi yel grn (Bk)	*210.00*	
58D	A10	2pi bl (R)	*375.00*	

Nos. 55-58D were provisionally issued at Medina after its capitulation.

Specialists question the status of unused examples of Nos. 55A-58D.

This overprint exists on Nos. L160-L161, L164-L172, L174-L175, L180-L183. These 17 are known as bogus items, but may exist genuine.

No. L161 (¼pi) is known with a similar but larger overprint.

Lithographed overprints are forgeries.

The illustrated overprint is not genuine.

Medina Issue

Hejaz Railway Tax Stamps Handstamped

and Handstamp Surcharged in Various Colors

The large overprint reads: "The Nejdi Posts - 1344 - Commemorating Medina, the Illustrious". The tablet shows the new value.

1925

59	R3	1pi on 10pi vio (Bk & V)	50.00	60.00
60	R3	2pi on 50pi lt bl (R & Bl)	50.00	60.00
61	R3	3pi on 100pi red brn (Bl & Bk)	50.00	60.00
62	R3	4pi on 500pi dl red (Bl & Bk)	50.00	60.00
63	R3	5pi on 1000pi dp red (Bl & Bk)	50.00	60.00
		Nos. 59-63 (5)	250.00	300.00

Jedda Issue

Hejaz Railway Tax Stamps Handstamped and Tablet with New Value in Various Colors

This handstamp reads: "Commemorating Jedda - 1344 - The Nejdi Posts".

1925

64	R3	1pi on 10pi vio (Bk & Bl)	50.00	60.00
65	R3	2pi on 50pi lt bl (R & Bk)	50.00	60.00
66	R3	3pi on 100pi red brn (R & Bl)	50.00	60.00
67	R3	4pi on 500pi dl red (Bk & Bl)	50.00	60.00
68	R3	5pi on 1000pi dp red (Bk & Bl)	50.00	60.00
		Nos. 64-68 (5)	250.00	300.00

Nos. 59-63 and 64-68 were prepared in anticipation of the surrender of Medina and Jedda.

Kingdom of Hejaz-Nejd

Arabic Inscriptions and Value — A1

A2

Inscriptions in upper tablets: "Barid al Hejaz wa Nejd" (Posts of the Hejaz and Nejd)

1926, Feb. Typo. Unwmk. *Perf. 11*

69	A1	¼pi violet	9.25	9.25
70	A1	½pi gray	9.25	9.25
71	A1	1pi dp bl	12.50	11.00
72	A2	2pi bl grn	10.00	9.00
73	A2	3pi carmine	12.50	10.00
74	A2	5pi maroon	6.25	6.25
		Nos. 69-74 (6)	59.75	54.75

Nos. 69-71, 74 exist imperf. Value, each $25.

1926, Mar. *Perf. 11*

75	A1	¼pi orange	6.25	3.50
76	A1	½pi bl grn	2.50	1.50
77	A1	1pi carmine	1.90	1.25
78	A2	2pi violet	2.50	1.50
79	A2	3pi dk bl	2.50	1.50
80	A2	5pi lt brn	6.25	3.50
a.		5pi ol brn		
		Nos. 75-80 (6)	21.90	12.75

Nos. 75-80 also exist with perf. 14, 14x11, 11x14 and imperf. All of these sell for 10 times the values quoted.

Counterfeits of types A1 and A2 are perf. 11½. They exist with and without overprints.

Types A1 and A2 in colors other than listed are proofs.

Footnotes often refer you to other stamps of the same design.

Pan-Islamic Congress Issue

Stamps of 1926 Handstamped

1926 *Perf. 11*

92	A1	¼pi orange	3.25	3.00
93	A1	½pi bl grn	3.25	3.00
94	A1	1pi carmine	3.25	3.00
95	A2	2pi violet	3.25	3.00
96	A2	3pi dk bl	3.25	3.00
97	A2	5pi lt brn	3.25	3.00
		Nos. 92-97 (6)	19.50	18.00

The overprint reads: "al Mootamar al Islami 20 Zilkada, Sanat 1344". (The Islamic Congress, June 1, 1926.)

See counterfeit note after No. 80.

Tughra of King Abdul Aziz — A3

1926-27 Typo. *Perf. 11½*

98	A3	⅛pi ocher	3.50	50
99	A3	¼pi gray grn	4.00	1.25
100	A3	½pi dl red	4.00	1.25
101	A3	1pi dp vio	4.00	1.25
102	A3	1½pi gray bl	12.00	2.00
103	A3	3pi ol grn	10.00	4.00
104	A3	5pi brn org	20.00	5.00
105	A3	10pi dk brn	60.00	6.00
		Nos. 98-105 (8)	117.50	21.25

Inscription at top reads: "Al Hukumat al Arabia" (The Arabian Government). Inscription below tughra reads: "Barid al Hejaz wa Nejd" (Post of the Hejaz and Nejd).

Stamps of 1926-27 Handstamped in Black or Red

1927

107	A3	⅛pi ocher	10.00	5.00
108	A3	¼pi gray grn	10.00	5.00
109	A3	½pi dl red	10.00	5.00
110	A3	1pi dp vio	10.00	5.00
111	A3	1½pi gray bl (R)	10.00	5.00
112	A3	3pi ol grn	10.00	5.00
113	A3	5pi brn org	10.00	5.00
114	A3	10pi dk brn	10.00	5.00
		Nos. 107-114 (8)	80.00	40.00

The overprint reads: "In commemoration of the Kingdom of Nejd and Dependencies, 25th Rajab 1345".

Turkey No. 258 Surcharged in Violet

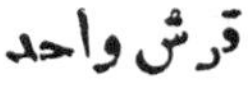

1927 (?) *Perf. 12*

115	A28	1g on 10pa grn		

Similar surcharges of 6g and 20g were made in red, but were not known to have been issued.

A4

A5

1929-30 Typo. *Perf. 11½*

117	A4	1¾g gray bl	20.00	2.50
119	A4	20g violet	25.00	4.50
120	A4	30g green	40.00	12.50

1930 *Perf. 11, 11½*

125	A5	½g rose	10.00	3.00
126	A5	1½g violet	10.00	2.00
127	A5	1¾g ultra	10.00	2.50
128	A5	3½g emerald	10.00	4.00
129	A5	5g blk brn	15.00	6.00
		Nos. 125-129 (5)	55.00	17.50

Issued in commemoration of the anniversary of King Ibn Saud's accession to the throne of the Hejaz, January 8, 1926.

A6

A7

1931-32 *Perf. 11½*

130	A6	⅛g ocher ('32)	12.00	2.50
131	A6	¼g bl grn	12.00	2.00
133	A6	1¾g ultra	18.00	2.50

1932 *Perf. 11, 11½*

135	A7	¼g bl grn	6.00	2.00
136	A7	½g scarlet	14.00	3.00
137	A7	2¼g ultra	35.00	5.00

Kingdom of Saudi Arabia

A8

1934, Jan. *Perf. 11½, Imperf.*

138	A8	¼g yel grn	9.00	8.00
139	A8	½g red	9.00	8.00
140	A8	1½g lt bl	18.00	15.00
141	A8	3g bl grn	18.00	15.00
142	A8	3½g ultra	35.00	6.00
143	A8	5g yellow	45.00	30.00
144	A8	10g red org	90.00	
145	A8	20g brt vio	110.00	
146	A8	¼s claret	225.00	
147	A8	30g dl vio	135.00	
148	A8	½s chocolate	500.00	
149	A8	1s vio brn	1,000.	
		Nos. 138-149 (12)	2,194.	

Proclamation of Emir Saud as Heir Apparent of Arabia. Perf. and imperf. stamps were issued in equal quantities.

Tughra of King Abdul Aziz — A9

1934-57 *Perf. 11, 11½*

159	A9	⅛g yellow	3.50	40
160	A9	¼g yel grn	3.50	40
161	A9	½g rose red ('43)	2.75	10
a.		½g dk car	13.00	1.50
162	A9	⅞g lt bl ('56)	4.50	50
163	A9	1g bl grn	3.50	40
164	A9	2g ol grn ('57)	7.25	2.00
a.		2g ol bis ('57)	27.50	8.00
165	A9	2⅞g vio ('57)	4.50	50
166	A9	3g ultra ('38)	4.50	20
a.		3g lt bl	22.50	2.00
167	A9	3½g lt ultra	18.00	2.00
168	A9	5g orange	4.50	50
169	A9	10g violet	13.00	1.50
170	A9	20g pur brn	18.00	1.00
a.		20g pur blk	22.50	2.50
171	A9	100g red vio ('42)	72.50	4.50
172	A9	200g vio brn ('42)	90.00	6.00
		Nos. 159-172 (14)	250.00	20.00

The ½g has two types differing in position of the tughra.

No. 162 measures 31x22mm. No. 164 30½x21½mm. No. 165, 30½x22mm. No. 166 30x21mm. No. 171, 31x22mm. No. 172, 30½x21½mm. Rest of set, 29x20½mm. Grayish paper was used in 1946-49 printings.

Yanbu Harbor near Radwa — A10

1945 **Typo.** *Perf. 11½*

173	A10	½g brt car	6.50	25
174	A10	3g lt ultra	8.25	1.00
175	A10	5g purple	25.00	1.25
176	A10	10g dk brn vio	55.00	3.00

Meeting of King Abdul Aziz and King Farouk of Egypt at Jebal Radwa, Saudi Arabia, Jan. 24, 1945.

Map of Saudi Arabia Type I (Flag inscriptions intact) — A11

Type II (Flag inscriptions scratched out)

1946 **Unwmk.** *Perf. 11½*

177	A11	½g mag (II)	15.00	1.00
a.		Type I	60.00	1.00
b.		Type I, perf. 11	50.00	10.00
c.		Type II, perf. 11	50.00	

Return of King Ibn Saud from Egypt.

Catalogue values for unused stamps in this section, from this point to the end of the section, are for Never Hinged items.

Arms of Saudi Arabia and Afghanistan A12

1950, Mar. *Perf. 11*

178	A12	½g carmine	7.50	1.00
179	A12	3g vio bl	12.50	1.00

Visit of Zahir Shah of Afghanistan, March 1950. On 3g in each sheet inscribed POSTFS, value $50.

Old City Walls, Riyadh A13

1950

Center in Red Brown

180	A13	½g magenta	3.50	10
181	A13	1g lt bl	6.75	10
182	A13	3g violet	10.00	50
183	A13	5g vermilion	22.50	1.00
184	A13	10g green	40.00	2.50
a.		Singular "guerche" in Arabic	250.00	40.00
		Nos. 180-184 (5)	82.75	4.20

Issued to commemorate the 50th lunar anniversary of King Ibn Saud's capture of Riyadh, Jan. 16, 1902.

No. 184a: On the 3g, 5g and 10g the currency is expressed in the plural in both French (grouche) and Arabic. One stamp in each sheet of 20 (4x5), position 11, of the 10g shows the Arabic characters in the singular form of "guerche," as on the ½g and 1g.

Arms of Saudi Arabia and Jordan — A14

1951, Nov. *Perf. 11*

185	A14	½g carmine	6.00	1.00
a.		"BOYAUME"	200.00	
186	A14	3g vio bl	18.00	1.50
a.		"BOYAUME"	200.00	

Visit of King Tallal of Jordan, Nov. 1951.

Bedouins and Train — A15

1952, June **Engr.** *Perf. 12*

187	A15	½q redsh brn	5.00	75
188	A15	1q dp grn	5.00	75
189	A15	3q violet	10.00	50
190	A15	10q rose pink	20.00	3.50
191	A15	20q blue	40.00	7.50
		Nos. 187-191 (5)	80.00	13.00

Issued to commemorate the inaugural trip over the Saudi Government Railroad between Riyadh and Dammam.

Saudi Arabia Arms and Lebanon Emblem — A16

1953, Feb. **Typo.** *Perf. 11*

192	A16	½g carmine	6.00	1.00
193	A16	3g vio bl	12.00	1.50

Issued to commemorate the visit of President Camille Chamoun of Lebanon.

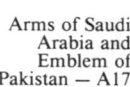

Arms of Saudi Arabia and Emblem of Pakistan — A17

1953, Mar.

194	A17	½g dk car	8.00	1.00
195	A17	3g vio bl	17.00	1.50

Visit of Gov.-Gen. Ghulam Mohammed of Pakistan.

Arms of Saudi Arabia and Jordan — A18

1953, July **Unwmk.**

196	A18	½g carmine	5.00	1.00
a.		"GOERCHE"	125.00	
197	A18	3g vio bl	15.00	1.50

Visit of King Hussein of Jordan, July, 1953.

Globe — A18a

1955, July **Litho.**

198	A18a	½g emerald	3.00	50
199	A18a	3g violet	8.00	1.00
200	A18a	4g orange	12.00	2.50

Issued to commemorate the founding of the Arab Postal Union, July 1, 1954.

Ministry of Communications Building, Riyadh — A19

1960, Apr. 12 **Photo.** *Perf. 13*

201	A19	2p brt bl	70	15
202	A19	5p dp cl	1.40	20
203	A19	10p dk grn	3.50	50

Arab Postal Union Conference, at Riyadh, Apr. 11. Imperfs. exist.

Arab League Center, Cairo A20

1960, Mar. 22 *Perf. 13x13½*

204	A20	2p dl grn & blk	1.75	20

Issued to commemorate the opening of the Arab League Center and the Arab Postal Museum in Cairo. Exists imperf.

Radio Tower and Waves A21

1960, June 4

205	A21	2p red & blk	1.65	25
206	A21	5p brn blk & mar	2.50	30
207	A21	10p bluish blk & ultra	4.00	70

Issued to commemorate the first international radio station in Saudi Arabia.

Map of Palestine, Refugee Camp and WRY Emblem — A22

1960, Oct. 30 **Litho.** *Perf. 13*

208	A22	2p dk bl	40	8
209	A22	8p lilac	40	12
210	A22	10p green	1.25	20

World Refugee Year, July 1, 1959-June 30, 1960. Imperfs. exist.

Wadi Hanifa Dam, near Riyadh — A23

Gas-Oil Separating Plant, Buqqa — A24

Type I (Saud Cartouche) (Illustrated over No. 286)

1960-62 **Unwmk.** **Photo.** *Perf. 14*

Size: 27½x22mm.

211	A23	½p bis brn & org	1.10	10
212	A23	1p ol bis & pur	1.10	10
213	A23	2p bl & sep	1.10	8
214	A23	3p sep & bl	1.10	6
215	A23	4p sep & ocher	1.10	8
216	A23	5p blk & dk vio	1.10	10
217	A23	6p brn blk & car rose ('62)	1.10	20
a.		6p blk & car rose	1.25	35
218	A23	7p red & gray ol	1.10	15
219	A23	8p dk bl & brn blk	1.10	30
220	A23	9p org brn & scar	1.10	30
c.		9p yel brn & metallic red	1.25	50
221	A23	10p emer grn & mar ('62)	1.25	35
a.		10p bl grn & mar	1.65	75
222	A23	20p brn & grn	3.25	35
223	A23	50p blk & brn	16.00	1.00
224	A23	75p brn & gray	52.50	2.25
225	A23	100p dk bl & grn bl	42.50	2.50
226	A23	200p lil & grn	67.50	6.50
		Nos. 211-226 (16)	194.00	14.42

1960-61

227 A24 ½p mar & org 1.10 10
228 A24 1p bl & red org 1.10 10
229 A24 2p ver & bl 1.10 10
230 A24 3p lil & brt grn 1.10 10
231 A24 4p yel grn & lil 1.10 8
232 A24 5p dk gray & brn red 1.10 10
233 A24 6p brn org & dk vio 1.10 10
234 A24 7p vio & dl grn 1.10 12
235 A24 8p bl grn & gray 1.10 20
236 A24 9p ultra & sep 3.25 20
237 A24 10p dk bl & rose 1.75 35
238 A24 20p org brn & blk 6.50 50
239 A24 50p red & brn grn 18.00 1.50
240 A24 75p red & blk brn 27.50 3.00
241 A24 100p dk bl & red brn 42.50 2.75
242 A24 200p dk gray & ol grn 72.50 6.50
Nos. 227-242 (16) 181.90 15.80

Nos. 211-212, 214-221, 227-230, 233-242 exist imperf; probably not regularly issued.
See Nos. 258-273, 286-341, 393-450, 461-483.

Dammam Port — A25

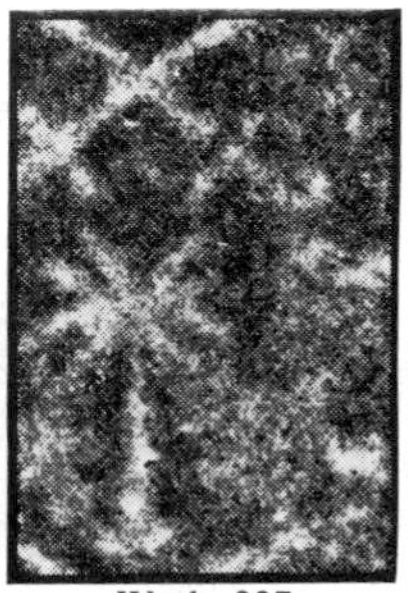

Wmk. 337

Wmk. Crossed Swords and Palm Tree (337)

1961, Aug. 16 Litho. *Perf. 13*

243 A25 3p lilac 1.65 20
244 A25 6p lt bl 2.50 30
245 A25 8p dk grn 4.00 40

Expansion of the port of Dammam. Imperf min. sheets of 4 exist. Set value, $300.

Globe, Radio and Telegraph — A26

Perf. 13x13½

1961, Aug. 7 Photo. Unwmk.

246 A26 3p dl pur 1.40 15
247 A26 6p gray blk 2.25 30
248 A26 8p brown 3.50 50

Arab Union of Telecommunications. Imperfs. exist.

Arab League Building, Cairo A27

Malaria Eradication Emblem A28

1962, Apr. 22 Wmk. 337 *Perf. 13*

249 A27 3p olive grn 1.00 20
250 A27 6p car rose 2.00 30
251 A27 8p slate bl 3.00 40

Arab League Week, Mar. 22-28.

Imperforate or missing-color varieties of Nos. 249-285 and 344-353 were not regularly issued, except No. 255a.

1962, May 7 Litho. Wmk. 337

252 A28 3p red org & bl 1.00 15
253 A28 6p emer & Prus bl 1.50 25
254 A28 8p blk & lil rose 2.25 40
a. Souv. sheet of 3, #252-254, imperf. 17.50 17.50

WHO drive to eradicate malaria.

Nos. 252-254 are known unofficially overprinted with new dates only or with "AIR MAIL" and two plane silhouettes.

A 4p exists as an essay.

Koran A29

1963, Mar. 12 Wmk. 337 *Perf. 11*

255 A29 2½p lil rose & pink 1.00 15
a. Pink background omitted *150.00*
256 A29 7½p bl & pale grn 2.00 35
257 A29 9½p grn & gray 3.00 40

First anniversary of the Islamic Institute, Medina. A 3p exists as an essay.

Dam Type of 1960 Redrawn
Type I (Saud Cartouche)

Perf. 13½x13

1963-65 Wmk. 337 Litho.

Size: 28½x23mm.

258 A23 ½p bis brn & org 9.25 75

Nos. 258, 264-265 are widely spaced in the sheet, producing large margins.

Perf. 14

Photo.

Size: 27½x22mm.

259 A23 ½p bis brn & org ('65) 15.00 1.50
260 A23 3p sep & bl 6.00 60
261 A23 4p sep & ocher ('64) 8.00 80
262 A23 5p blk & dk vio 8.00 80
263 A23 20p dk car & grn 15.00 1.50
Nos. 258-263 (6) 61.25 5.95

A 1p was prepared but not issued. It is known only imperf.

Gas-Oil Plant Type of 1960 Redrawn
Type I (Saud Cartouche)

Perf. 13½x13

1963-65 Wmk. 337 Litho.

Size: 28½x23mm.

264 A24 ½p mar & org 7.00 1.00
265 A24 1p bl & red org ('64) 3.25 30

Photo.

Perf. 14

Size: 27½x22mm.

266 A24 ½p mar & org ('64) 5.25 50
267 A24 1p bl & red org 4.25 30
268 A24 3p lil & brt grn 10.50 1.00
269 A24 4p yel grn & lil 6.25 50
270 A24 5p dk gray & brn red 6.25 50
271 A24 6p brn org & dk vio ('65) 8.50 70
272 A24 8p dl grn & blk 15.00 1.25
273 A24 9p bl & sep 15.00 1.50
Nos. 264-273 (10) 81.25 7.55

The 3p, 4p and 6p exist imperf.

Hands Holding Wheat Emblem A30

1963, Mar. 21 Litho. *Perf. 11*

274 A30 2½p lil rose & rose 1.00 10
275 A30 7½p brt lil & pink 1.00 30
276 A30 9p red brn & lt bl 2.00 35

FAO "Freedom from Hunger" campaign. The 3p imperf. in this design is an essay.

Jet over Dhahran Airport — A31

Flame — A32

1963, July 27 Litho. *Perf. 13*

277 A31 1p bl gray & ocher 1.00 10
278 A31 3½p ultra & emer 2.00 20
279 A31 6p emer & rose 3.50 25
a. "Thahran" for "Dharan" in Arabic 7.50
280 A31 7½p lil rose & lt bl 3.50 30
281 A31 9½p ver & dl vio 5.00 40
Nos. 277-281 (5) 15.00 1.25

Opening of the US-financed terminal of the Dhahran Airport and inauguration of international jet service

On No. 279a the misspelling consists of an omitted dot over character near top left in one horiz. row of five.

1964, Apr. Wmk. 337 *Perf. 13x13½*

282 A32 3p lil, pink & Prus bl 3.00 15
283 A32 6p yel grn, lt bl & Prus bl 4.00 25
284 A32 9p brn, buff & Prus bl 8.00 40

Issued to commemorate the 15th anniversary of the signing of the Universal Declaration of Human Rights.

King Faisal and Arms of Saudi Arabia A33

1964, Nov. Litho. *Perf. 13*

285 A33 4p dk bl & emer 3.00 15

Issued to commemorate the installation of Prince Faisal ibn Abdul Aziz as King, Nov. 2, 1964.

King Saud's Cartouche Type I

King Faisal's Cartouche Type II

Redrawn Dam Type of 1960
Type I (Saud Cartouche)

1965-70 Litho. Unwmk. *Perf. 14*

Size: 27x22mm

286 A23 1p ol bis & pur 20.00 1.00
287 A23 2p dk bl & sep ('66) 4.00 25
288 A23 3p sep & bl 4.00 30
289 A23 4p sep & ocher ('66) 7.00 20
290 A23 5p blk & dk vio 5.00 20
291 A23 6p blk & car rose ('68) 8.75 60
292 A23 7p brn & gray ('68) 12.00 30
293 A23 8p dk bl & gray ('68) *65.00* 5.00
294 A23 9p org brn & scar ('68) *60.00* 4.00
295 A23 10p bl grn & mar ('66) *50.00* 3.00
296 A23 11p red & yel grn ('66) 5.25 30
297 A23 12p org & dk bl ('66) 4.75 30
298 A23 13p dk ol & rose ('66) 4.75 40
299 A23 14p org brn & yel grn ('66) 4.75 40
300 A23 15p sep & gray grn ('66) 4.75 40
301 A23 16p dk red & dl vio ('66) 5.50 45
302 A23 17p rose lil & dk bl ('66) 5.50 45
303 A23 18p grn & brt bl ('66) 5.50 45
304 A23 19p blk & bis ('66) 7.25 50
305 A23 20p brn & grn ('66) 10.00 50
306 A23 23p mar & lil 7.25 50
307 A23 24p ver & bl 7.25 60
308 A23 26p ol & yel 8.75 75
309 A23 27p ultra & red brn 8.75 75
310 A23 31p gray & dl bl 8.75 80
311 A23 33p ol grn & lil 8.75 80
312 A23 100p dk bl & grnsh bl ('70) *325.00* *50.00*
313 A23 200p dl lil & grn ('70) *325.00* *50.00*
Nos. 286-313 (28) *993.25* *123.20*

A 50p exists but was never placed in use.

Redrawn Gas-Oil Plant Type of 1960
Type I (Saud Cartouche)

1964-70 Litho. Unwmk.

Size: 27x22mm

314 A24 1p bl & red org ('66) 6.50 20
315 A24 2p ver & bl ('66) 8.75 20
316 A24 3p lil & brt grn 6.00 10
317 A24 4p yel grn & lil ('65) 7.25 20
318 A24 5p dl gray vio & dk red brn ('66) 26.00 2.00
319 A24 6p brn org & dk vio ('68) 55.00 5.00
320 A24 7p vio & dl grn ('68) 30.00 2.00
321 A24 8p bl grn & gray ('65) 6.75 30
322 A24 9p ultra & sep ('65) 14.00 80
323 A24 10p dk bl & rose *325.00* 35.00
324 A24 11p ol & org ('66) 4.50 30
325 A24 12p bis & grn ('66) 5.50 30
326 A24 13p rose red & dk bl ('66) 5.50 40
327 A24 14p vio & lt brn ('66) 6.00 40
328 A24 15p rose red & sep ('67) 6.00 50
329 A24 16p grn & rose red ('66) 6.75 50
330 A24 17p car rose & red brn ('66) 12.50 1.50
331 A24 18p gray & ultra ('66) 7.00 60
332 A24 19p brn & yel ('66) 7.00 60
333 A24 20p dl org & dk gray ('66) 25.00 2.00
334 A24 23p org & car ('65) 7.00 70
335 A24 24p emer & org yel ('65) 7.75 80
336 A24 26p lil & red brn ('65) 10.00 80
337 A24 27p ver & dk gray ('65) 10.00 80
338 A24 31p dl grn & car ('65) 21.00 1.50
339 A24 33p red brn & gray ('65) 19.00 1.50
340 A24 50p red brn & dl grn ('69) *250.00* *50.00*
341 A24 200p dk gray & ol gray ('70) *250.00* *50.00*
Nos. 314-341 (28) *1,145.* *159.00*

A 100p exists but was never placed in use.

Holy Ka'aba, Mecca — A34

1965, Apr. 17 Wmk. 337 *Perf. 13*

344 A34 4p sal & blk 3.00 20
345 A34 6p brt pink & blk 4.75 25
346 A34 10p yel grn & blk 6.75 40

Issued to commemorate the Mecca Conference of the Moslem World League.

Arms of Saudi Arabia and Tunisia A35

1965, Apr. Litho.

347	A35	4p car rose & sil	2.50	20
348	A35	8p red lil & sil	3.25	35
349	A35	10p ultra & sil	4.75	40

Issued to commemorate the visit of Pres. Habib Bourguiba of Tunisia, Feb. 22-26.

Highway, Hejaz Mountains — A36

1965, June 2 Wmk. 337 *Perf. 13*

350	A36	2p red & blk	1.65	30
351	A36	4p bl & blk	2.75	40
352	A36	6p lil & blk	3.75	50
353	A36	8p brt grn & blk	5.50	60

Opening of highway from Mecca to Tayif.

ICY Emblem A37

1965, Nov. 13 Unwmk. *Perf. 13*

354	A37	1p yel & dk brn	1.40	5
355	A37	2p org & ol grn	1.40	10
356	A37	3p lt bl & gray	1.40	10
357	A37	4p yel grn & dk sl grn	1.40	20
358	A37	10p org & mag	3.75	50
		Nos. 354-358 (5)	9.35	95

International Cooperation Year, 1965.

ITU Emblem, Old and New Communication Equipment — A38

1965, Dec. 22 Litho. *Perf. 13*

359	A38	3p bl & blk	1.75	10
360	A38	4p lil & dk grn	1.75	10
361	A38	8p emer & dk brn	1.75	35
362	A38	10p dl org & dk grn	1.75	40

Issued to commemorate the centenary of the International Telecommunication Union.

Library Aflame and Lamp A39

1966, Jan. Litho. *Perf. 12x12½*

363	A39	1p orange	1.40	15
364	A39	2p dk red	1.40	15
365	A39	3p red vio	2.00	15
366	A39	4p violet	2.75	20
367	A39	5p lil rose	4.75	35
368	A39	6p vermilion	8.00	50
		Nos. 363-368 (6)	20.30	1.50

Issued to commemorate the burning of the Library of Algiers, June 2, 1962. Nos. 363-368 were withdrawn from sale Jan. 26, 1966, due to incorrect Arabic inscriptions. Later some values were inadvertently again placed in use.

Scott's editorial staff cannot undertake to identify, authenticate or appraise stamps and postal markings.

Arab Postal Union Emblem — A40

Dagger in Map of Palestine — A41

1966, Mar. 15 Litho. *Perf. 14*

369	A40	3p dl pur & ol	1.10	15
370	A40	4p dp bl & ol	1.10	15
371	A40	6p mar & ol	4.25	25
372	A40	7p dp grn & ol	4.25	35

Issued to commemorate the 10th anniversary (in 1964) of the Arab Postal Union. Printed in sheets of two panes, so horizontal gutter pairs exist.

1966, Mar. 19 Litho. *Perf. 13*

373	A41	2p yel grn & blk	1.25	15
374	A41	4p lt brn & blk	2.50	15
375	A41	6p dl bl & blk	3.75	25
376	A41	8p ocher & blk	5.00	35

Deir Yassin massacre, Apr. 9, 1948.

Emblems of World Boy Scout Conference and Saudi Arabian Scout Association A42

1966, Mar. 23 Unwmk.

377	A42	4p yel, blk, grn & gray	5.75	50
378	A42	8p yel, blk, org & lt bl	5.75	50
379	A42	10p yel, blk, sal & bl	11.00	75

Arab League Rover Moot (Boy Scout Jamboree).

WHO Headquarters, Geneva, and Flag — A43

1966, May Litho. *Perf. 13*

380	A43	4p aqua & multi	1.25	15
381	A43	6p yel brn & multi	2.50	25
382	A43	10p pink & multi	5.00	40

Opening of the WHO Headquarters, Geneva.

UNESCO Emblem — A44

1966, Sept. Unwmk. *Perf. 12*

383	A44	1p ap grn & multi	1.40	5
384	A44	2p dl org & multi	1.40	10
385	A44	3p lil rose & multi	1.90	10
386	A44	4p pale grn & multi	1.90	15
387	A44	10p gray & multi	2.75	40
		Nos. 383-387 (5)	9.35	80

20th anniv. of UNESCO.

Radio Tower, Telephone and Map of Arab Countries — A45

1966, Nov. 7 Litho. *Perf. 12½*
Design in Black, Carmine & Yellow

388	A45	1p vio bl	1.50	10
389	A45	2p bluish lil	1.50	15
390	A45	4p rose lil	3.00	15
391	A45	6p lt ol grn	3.00	30
392	A45	7p gray grn	4.00	40
		Nos. 388-392 (5)	13.00	1.10

Issued to publicize the 8th Congress of the Arab Telecommunications Union, Riyadh.

Redrawn Dam Type of 1960
Type II (Faisal Cartouche) (Illustrated over No. 286)

1966-76 Litho. Unwmk. *Perf. 14*
Size: 27x22mm

393	A23	1p ol bis & pur	*165.00*	*52.50*
394	A23	2p dk bl & sep ('67)	19.00	1.65
395	A23	3p blk & dk bl ('68)	11.50	90
396	A23	4p sep & ocher ('68)	17.50	45
397	A23	5p blk & dk vio ('69)	37.50	8.25
398	A23	6p blk & car rose ('68)	37.50	7.50
399	A23	7p sep & gray ('68)	19.00	2.00
400	A23	8p dk bl & gray ('69)	13.00	50
401	A23	9p org brn & scar ('70)	8.00	90
402	A23	10p bl grn & mar ('67)	17.50	1.50
403	A23	11p red & yel grn ('73)	13.00	1.50
404	A23	12p org & dk bl ('72)	9.50	1.50
405	A23	13p blk & rose ('75)	25.00	1.50
406	A23	14p org brn & yel grn ('75)	20.00	1.50
407	A23	15p sep & gray grn ('72)	20.00	2.00
408	A23	16p dk red & dl vio ('72)	30.00	3.50
409	A23	17p rose lil & dk bl ('74)	35.00	2.00
410	A23	18p grn & brt bl ('76)	32.50	2.75
411	A23	19p blk & bis ('75)	6.00	90
412	A23	20p brn & grn ('68)	65.00	*50.00*
413	A23	23p mar & lil ('70)	325.00	*35.00*
414	A23	24p ver & bl ('75)	60.00	6.00
415	A23	26p ol & yel ('75)	7.75	80
416	A23	27p ultra & red brn ('75)	7.75	80
417	A23	33p ol grn & lil ('75)	50.00	2.50
419	A23	50p blk & brn ('74)	200.00	*40.00*
420	A23	100p dk bl & grnsh bl ('74)	325.00	*50.00*
421	A23	200p dl lil & grn ('74)	325.00	*80.00*
		Nos. 393-421 (28)	*1,902.*	*358.40*

A 31p has been reported.

Redrawn Gas-Oil Plant Type of 1960
Type II (Faisal Cartouche)

1966-78 Unwmk.
Size: 27x22mm.

422	A24	1p bl & red org	75.00	*3.00*
423	A24	2p ver & dl bl	8.75	30
424	A24	3p lil & brt grn	11.50	60
425	A24	4p grn & dl lil	7.75	30
426	A24	5p dl gray vio & dk red brn ('68)	30.00	2.00
427	A24	6p brn org & dl pur ('68)	26.00	4.00
428	A24	7p vio & dl grn ('68)	26.00	2.00
429	A24	8p bl grn & grnsh gray ('68)	6.75	30
430	A24	9p ultra & sep ('68)	4.00	30
431	A24	10p dk bl & rose	6.75	60
432	A24	11p ol & org ('70)	80.00	8.00
433	A24	12p bis & grn ('75)	4.25	80
434	A24	13p rose red & dk bl ('73)	40.00	30
435	A24	14p vio & lt brn ('70)	35.00	2.50
436	A24	15p car & sep ('68)	10.50	70
437	A24	16p grn & rose red ('68)	15.00	80
438	A24	17p car rose & red brn ('75)	8.00	60
439	A24	18p gray & ultra ('73)	15.00	1.65
440	A24	19p brn & yel ('74)	18.00	1.65
441	A24	20p brn org & gray ('67)	13.00	1.65
442	A24	23p org & car	24.00	2.00
443	A24	24p emer & org yel ('73)	9.00	80
444	A24	26p lil & red brn ('78)	*200.00*	
445	A24	27p ver & dk gray ('75)	40.00	4.00
446	A24	31p grn & rose car ('75)	12.00	80
447	A24	33p brn & gray ('75)	18.00	1.25
448	A24	50p red brn & dl grn ('74)	375.00	*72.50*
449	A24	100p dk bl & red brn ('69)	325.00	*45.00*
450	A24	200p dk gray & ol gray ('70)	400.00	*62.50*
		Nos. 422-450 (29)	1,844.	

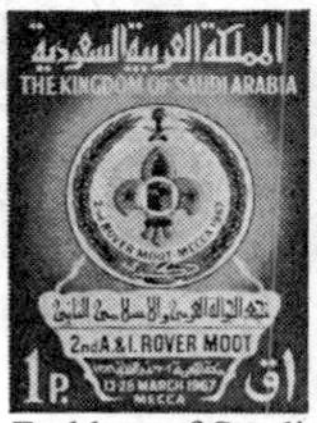

Emblem of Saudi Arabian Scout Association A46

Meteorological Instruments and WMO Emblem A47

1967, Mar. 28 Litho. *Perf. 13½*
Emblem in Green, Red, Yellow & Black

451	A46	1p dk bl & blk	2.50	15
452	A46	2p bl grn & blk	2.50	15
453	A46	3p lt bl & blk	3.50	15
454	A46	4p rose brn & blk	4.75	15
455	A46	10p brn & blk	10.50	50
		Nos. 451-455 (5)	23.75	1.10

2nd Arabic League Rover Moot, Mecca, March 13-28.

1967, July Unwmk. *Perf. 13*

456	A47	1p brt mag	1.00	5
457	A47	2p violet	2.00	10
458	A47	3p olive	2.00	10
459	A47	4p bl grn	6.00	10
460	A47	10p blue	8.50	35
		Nos. 456-460 (5)	19.50	70

Issued for World Meteorological Day.

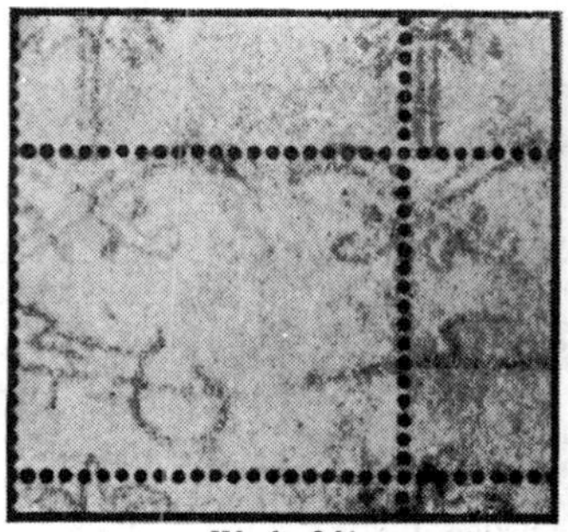

Wmk. 361

Redrawn Dam Type of 1960
Type II (Faisal Cartouche)

Wmk. Crossed Swords, Palm Tree and Arabic Inscription (361)

1968-76 Litho. *Perf. 14*

461 A23 1p ol bis & pur ('71) *800.00 300.00*
462 A23 2p dk bl & sep 24.00 *2.00*
463 A23 3p blk & dk bl ('69) 22.50 *1.00*
464 A23 4p sep & ocher ('73) 200.00 *32.50*
465 A23 5p blk & dk vio ('71) 27.50 *2.00*
466 A23 6p blk & car rose ('72) 26.00 *1.50*
467 A23 7p sep & gray ('72) 40.00 *3.00*
468 A23 8p dk bl & gray ('70) 20.00 1.00
469 A23 9p org brn & ver ('76) 62.50 *7.00*
470 A23 10p bl grn & mar 45.00 *4.00*
471 A23 11p red & yel grn ('72) 60.00 *6.00*
472 A23 12p org & sl bl ('72) 40.00 *5.00*
473 A23 13p blk & rose ('74) 62.50 *7.50*

Redrawn Gas-Oil Plant Type of 1960
Type II (Faisal Cartouche)

1968-76 *Perf. 14*

474 A24 1p bl & red org 10.50 1.00
475 A24 2p ver & dl bl 6.25 50
476 A24 4p grn & dl lil 80.00 *8.00*
477 A24 5p dk brn & red brn ('73) 22.50 1.50
478 A24 6p brn org & dk vio ('73) 27.50 2.00
479 A24 9p dk bl & sep ('76) 45.00 4.00
480 A24 10p dk bl & rose 9.50 70
481 A24 11p ol & org ('72) 32.50 2.00
482 A24 12p bis & grn ('72) 35.00 3.00
483 A24 23p org & car ('74) 65.00 3.00
Nos. 474-483 (10) 333.75 *25.70*

Map Showing Dammam to Jedda Road, and Dates — A48

Wmk. 361

1968, Aug. Litho. *Perf. 14*

484 A48 1p yel & multi 1.50 5
485 A48 2p org & multi 1.50 10
486 A48 3p multi 3.00 10
487 A48 4p multi 3.00 10
488 A48 10p multi 9.00 40
Nos. 484-488 (5) 18.00 75

Issued to commemorate the completion of the trans-Saudi Arabia highway in 1967.

Prophet's Mosque, Medina A49

New Arcade, Mecca Mosque A50

Perf. 13½x14

1968-76 Litho. Wmk. 361

489 A49 1p org & grn, wmk. 337 ('70) 3.00 30
490 A49 2p red brn & grn ('72) 4.75 40
a. Wmk. 337 ('71) 7.00 30
b. As "a," redrawn *200.00*
491 A49 3p vio & grn ('72) 4.25 40
a. Wmk. 337 ('70) 3.00 30
492 A49 4p ocher & grn 4.75 40
a. Wmk. 337 ('71) 6.00 50
b. As "a," redrawn
493 A49 5p dp lil rose & grn, wmk. 337 ('71) 10.00 1.00
494 A49 6p blk & grn ('73) 12.00 1.00
a. 6p gray & grn ('76) 20.00 1.00
495 A49 10p brn & grn 15.00 1.00
a. Redrawn
496 A49 20p dk brn & grn ('70) 20.00 2.00
a. Redrawn
497 A49 50p sep & grn ('75) 25.00 6.50
498 A49 100p dk bl & grn ('75) 20.00 5.00
499 A49 200p red & grn ('75) 25.00 7.00
Nos. 489-499 (11) 143.75 25.00

1968-69

500 A50 3p dp org & gray ('69) 425.00 50.00
501 A50 4p grn & gray 5.75 50
502 A50 10p mag & gray 9.25 1.00

Expansion of Prophet's Mosque A51

Madayin Saleh A52

1968-76

503 A51 1p org & grn ('72) 5.00 25
a. Wmk. 337 5.50 40
504 A51 2p brn & grn ('72) 8.00 25
a. Wmk. 337 ('70) 7.50 35
b. As "a," redrawn 40.00
505 A51 3p blk & grn ('69) 7.00 40
a. Wmk. 337 ('71) 8.00 80
b. 3p gray & grn ('76) 20.00 2.00
c. As No. 505, redrawn
d. As "a," redrawn
506 A51 4p org & grn ('70) 7.00 50
a. Wmk. 337 ('72) 5.00 50
b. As "a," redrawn 10.00
507 A51 5p red & grn ('74) 7.50 75
a. Wmk. 337 ('70) 5.00 50
508 A51 6p Prus bl & grn ('72) 10.00 1.00
a. Wmk. 337 ('72) 7.00 60
509 A51 8p rose red & grn ('76) 25.00 2.00
510 A51 10p brn red & grn ('70) 9.25 60
a. Wmk. 337 ('70) 12.00 70
b. 10p org & grn ('76) 20.00 1.00
c. As "a," redrawn
511 A51 20p vio & grn ('74) 20.00 2.50
a. Wmk. 337 ('72) 9.25 80
Nos. 503-511 (9) 98.75 8.25

1968-75

512 A52 2p ultra & bis brn ('70) 22.50 4.00
513 A52 4p dk & lt brn 5.50 80
514 A52 7p org & lt brn ('75) 55.00 *10.00*
515 A52 10p sl grn & lt brn 14.00 2.00
516 A52 20p lil rose & brn ('71) 14.00 1.50

Arabian Stallion — A53

Camels and Oil Derrick — A54

517 A53 4p mag & org brn 5.50 80
518 A53 10p blk & org brn 15.00 3.00
519 A53 14p bl & ocher ('71) 30.00 6.00
520 A53 20p ol grn & ocher ('71) 12.50 2.00

1969-71

521 A54 4p dk pur & redsh brn ('71) 20.00 4.00
522 A54 10p ultra & hn brn 15.00 3.00

Holy Ka'aba, Mecca — A55

Numeral & "Postage" on Gray Background, 8p on White

1969-75

523 A55 4p dp grn & blk ('70) 10.00 80
a. Value corner white ('74) 20.00 2.00
b. As "a," redrawn ('75)
524 A55 6p dp lil rose & blk ('71) 6.00 40
a. Value corner white ('74) 30.00 3.00
525 A55 8p red & blk ('75) 35.00 3.00
526 A55 10p org & blk ('69) 20.00 1.50
a. Value corner white ('74) 20.00 2.00
b. As "a," redrawn ('75)

On the original stamps the knob-shaped Arabic letter, located under the two square dots in the middle of the top panel, has a small central dot. The dot often is missing.

On the redrawn stamps the dot has been enlarged into a conspicuous irregular oval. The 3p also has a period added after the value and the 4p has the "4" under the "T" instead of the "S." There are other small differences.

Rover Moot Badge — A56

Perf. 13½x14

1969, Feb. 19 Litho. Wmk. 337

607 A56 1p org & multi 2.00 10
608 A56 4p dl pur & multi 6.00 20
609 A56 10p org brn & multi 16.00 60

3rd Arab League Rover Moot, Mecca, Feb. 19-Mar. 3.

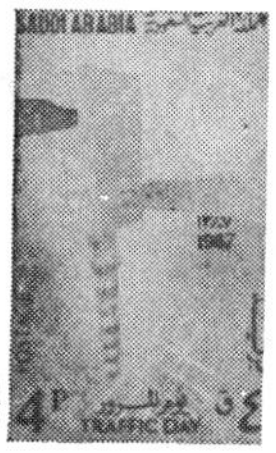

Traffic Light and Intersection — A57

1969, Feb. Wmk. 361 *Perf. 13½*

610 A57 3p dl bl, red & brt bl grn 2.00 15
a. 3p dl bl, red & gray grn 8.00
611 A57 4p org brn, red & gray grn 2.00 15
612 A57 10p dl pur, red & gray grn 4.00 50

Issued for Traffic Day.

WHO Emblem — A58

1969 Wmk. 337 *Perf. 14*

613 A58 4p lt bl, vio bl & yel 7.50 15

20th anniv. (in 1968) of WHO.

Foreign postal stationery (stamped envelopes, postal cards and air letter sheets) lies beyond the scope of this Catalogue, which is limited to adhesive postage stamps.

Islamic Conference Emblem A59

1970, Mar. 23 Litho. Wmk. 361

614 A59 4p bl & blk 2.75 15
615 A59 10p yel bis & blk 4.25 45

Islamic Conference of Foreign Ministers, Jedda, March 1970.

Open Book and Satellite Earth Receiving Station — A60

Perf. 14x13½

1970, Aug. 1 Litho. Wmk. 337

616 A60 4p vio bl & multi 5.25 15
617 A60 10p grn & multi 10.50 50

World Telecommunications Day.

Steel Rolling Mill, Jedda A61

1970, Oct. 26 Wmk. 337 *Perf. 13½*

618 A61 3p yel org & multi 2.25 10
619 A61 4p vio & multi 3.50 15
620 A61 10p brt grn & multi 6.00 50

Inauguration of 1rst steel mill in Saudi Arabia.

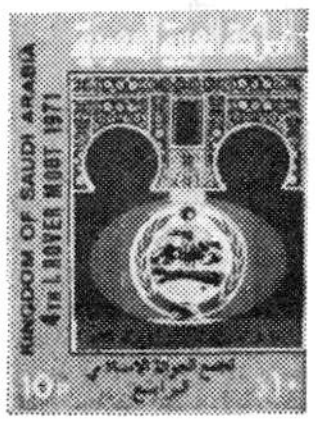

Rover Moot Emblem — A62

1971, Feb. Litho. *Perf. 14*

621 A62 10p brt bl & multi 5.75 75

4th Arab League Rover Moot, 1971.

Telecommunications Symbol — A63

1971, May 17 Wmk. 337 *Perf. 14*

622 A63 4p bl & blk 1.75 15
623 A63 10p lil & blk 3.50 40

World Telecommunications Day.

University Minaret
A64

Arab League Emblem
A65

Wmk. 337; Wmk. 361 (4p)

1971, Aug. **Litho.** ***Perf. 14***

624 A64	3p brt grn & blk	1.40	10
625 A64	4p brn & blk	2.75	15
626 A64	10p bl & blk	5.50	50

King Abdul Aziz National University.

1971, Nov. **Wmk. 337** ***Perf. 13½***

627 A65 10p multi		4.50	40

Arab League Week.

Education Year Emblem
A66

OPEC Emblem
A67

1971, Nov. **Litho.**

628 A66 4p ap grn & brn red		4.25	15

International Education Year 1970.

1971, Dec. ***Perf. 14***

629 A67 4p lt bl		9.00	15

10th anniversary of OPEC (Organization of Petroleum Exporting Countries).

Globe
A68

1972, Aug. **Wmk. 361** ***Perf. 14***

630 A68 4p multi		5.75	12

4th World Telecommunications Day.

Telephone — A69

1972, Oct. **Wmk. 337, 361 (5p)**

631 A69	1p red, blk & grn	2.25	5
632 A69	4p dk grn, blk & grn	2.25	15
633 A69	5p lil, blk & grn	4.50	20
634 A69	10p tan, blk & grn	9.00	50

Inauguration of automatic telephone system (1969).

Writing Hand — A70

1972, Sept. 8 **Litho.** **Wmk. 361**

635 A70 10p multi		5.50	35

World Literacy Day, Sept. 8.

Holy Ka'aba and Grand Mosque, Mecca
A71

Designs (Rover Moot Emblem and): 4p, Prophet's Mosque, Medina. 10p, Plains of Arafat.

1973

636 A71	4p lt bl & multi	3.25	20
637 A71	6p lil & multi	6.50	30
638 A71	10p sal & multi	10.00	60

5th Arab League Rover Moot.

Globe and Map of Palestine
A71a

1973 **Litho.** **Wmk. 361** ***Perf. 14***

639 A71a	4p blk, yel & red	2.25	15
640 A71a	10p bl, yel & red	4.50	40

Palestine Week.

Leaf and Emblem — A72

1973

641 A72 4p yel & multi		5.00	25

International Hydrological Decade 1965-74.

Arab Postal Union Emblem — A73

1973, Dec. **Litho.** ***Perf. 14***

642 A73	4p sep & multi	5.25	25
643 A73	10p pur & multi	10.50	50

25th anniversary (in 1971) of the Conference of Sofar, Lebanon, establishing the Arab Postal Union.

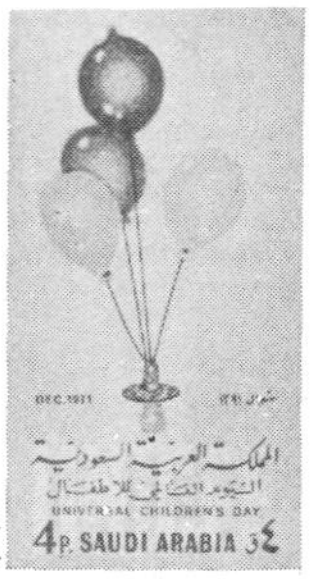

Balloons and Pacifier — A74

1973, Dec.

644 A74 4p lt bl & multi		5.75	15

Universal Children's Day (stamp dated 1971).

Arab Postal and UPU Emblems
A75

1974, July 7 **Wmk. 361** ***Perf. 14***

645 A75	3p yel & multi	*30.00*	2.50
646 A75	4p rose & multi	*40.00*	5.00
647 A75	10p lt grn & multi	*50.00*	7.50

Centenary of the Universal Postal Union.

Handshake and UNESCO Emblem — A76

1974, May 21 ***Perf. 13½***

648 A76	4p org & multi	3.00	25
649 A76	10p grn & multi	12.50	75

International Book Year, 1972.

Desalination Plant — A77

1974, Sept. 3 **Wmk. 361** ***Perf. 14***

650 A77	4p dp org & bl	2.25	15
651 A77	6p emer & vio	4.75	25
652 A77	10p rose red & blk	7.25	50

Opening (in 1971) of sea water desalination plant, Jedda.

INTERPOL Emblem — A78

1974, Nov. 1

653 A78	4p ocher & ultra	5.25	20
654 A78	10p emer & ultra	10.50	50

50th anniversary (in 1973) of International Criminal Police Organization.

APU Emblem, Tower and Letter — A79

1974, Oct. 26 **Litho.** **Wmk. 361**

655 A79 4p multi		6.75	15

Arab Consultative Council for Postal Studies, 3rd session.

UPU Headquarters, Bern — A80

1974, Nov. 15 ***Perf. 13½***

656 A80	3p org & multi	2.75	25
657 A80	4p lil & multi	5.75	50
658 A80	10p bl & multi	8.25	1.25

Opening of new Universal Postal Union Headquarters, Bern, May 1970.

Tank, Planes, Rockets and Flame
A81

1974, Dec. 15 ***Perf. 14***

659 A81	3p sl & multi	2.00	15
660 A81	4p brn & multi	4.00	25
661 A81	10p lil & multi	12.00	75

King Faisal Military Cantonment, 1971.

Red Crescent Flower — A82

1974, Dec. 17 ***Perf. 14x14½***

662 A82	4p gray & multi	2.00	25
663 A82	6p lt grn & multi	5.00	50
664 A82	10p lt bl & multi	10.00	1.00

Saudi Arabian Red Crescent Society, 10th anniversary (in 1973).

Saudi Arabian Scout Emblem and Minarets
A83

1974, Dec. 23 Wmk. 361 *Perf. 14*

665 A83 4p brn & multi 4.25 20
666 A83 6p bl blk & multi 8.50 30
667 A83 10p pur & multi 12.50 60

6th Arab League Rover Moot, Mecca.

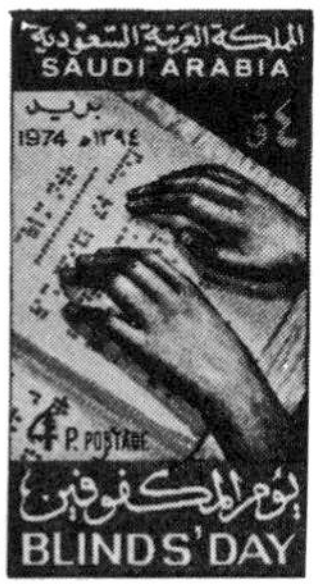

Reading Braille — A84

1975, Mar. 31 *Perf. 14x13½*

668 A84 4p multi 2.50 25
669 A84 10p multi 6.00 50

Day of the Blind.

Anemometer and Weather Balloon with UN Emblem — A85

Perf. 13½x14

1975, May 8 Litho. Wmk. 361

670 A85 4p multi 5.25 25

Centenary (in 1973) of International Meteorological Cooperation.

King Faisal — A86

Conference Emblem — A87

1975, July 6 Unwmk. *Perf. 14*

671 A86 4p grn & rose brn 3.00 25
672 A86 16p vio & grn 4.00 75
673 A86 23p dk grn & vio 8.00 1.25

Miniature Sheet

Imperf

674 A86 40p Prus bl & ocher *600.00*

King Faisal ibn Abdul-Aziz Al Saud (1906-1975). Size of No. 674: 71x80mm.

1975, July 11 *Perf. 14*

675 A87 10p rose brn & blk 3.75 50

6th Islamic Conference of Foreign Ministers, Jedda, July 12.

Wheat and Sun — A88

1975, Sept. 17 Litho. Wmk. 361

676 A88 4p lil & multi 2.25 20
677 A88 10p bl & multi 6.75 40

Charity Society, 20th anniversary.

Holy Ka'aba, Globe, Clasped Hands — A89

1975, Sept. 17 *Perf. 14*

678 A89 4p ol bis & multi *5.00* 15
679 A89 10p org & multi *10.00* 35

Conference of Moslem Organizations, Mecca, Apr. 6-10, 1974.

Saudia Tri-Star and DC-3 — A90

1975, Sept. Litho. Unwmk.

680 A90 4p buff & multi *6.25* 25
681 A90 10p lt bl & multi *12.00* 50

Saudia, Saudi Arabian Airline, 30th anniversary.

Conference Centers in Mecca and Riyadh A91

1975, Sept. *Perf. 14*

682 A91 10p multi *7.00* 50

Friday Mosque, Medina, and Juwatha Mosque, al-Hasa — A92

1975, Oct. 26 Litho. Unwmk.

683 A92 4p grn & multi *5.75* 25
684 A92 10p ver & multi *7.75* 50

Ancient Islamic holy places.

FAO Emblem — A93

1975, Oct. 26

685 A93 4p gray & multi 3.00 20
686 A93 10p buff & multi 8.50 50

World Food Program, 10th anniversary (in 1973). Stamps are dated 1973.

Conference Emblem — A94

1976, Mar. 20 Unwmk. *Perf. 14*

687 A94 4p multi 14.00 25

Islamic Solidarity Conference of Science and Technology.

Saudi Arabia Map, Transmission Tower, TV Screen — A95

1976, May 26 Litho. *Perf. 14*

688 A95 4p multi 14.00 25

Saudi Arabian television, 10th anniversary.

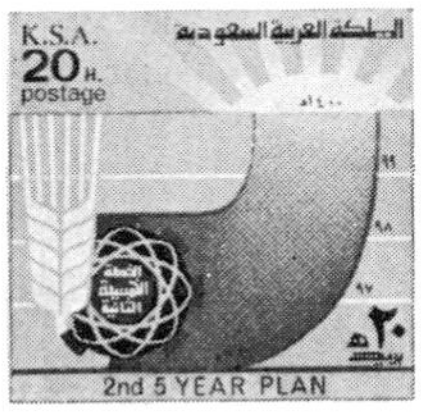

Grain, Atom Symbol, Graph A96

1976, June 28 Litho. *Perf. 14*

689 A96 20h yel & multi 4.00 25
690 A96 50h yel & multi 7.00 50

Second Five-year Plan.

Holy Ka'aba A97

Two types:
I. "White" minarets. Gray vignette.
II. Black minarets and vignette. Design redrawn, strengthened, darkened, clarified.

1976-79 Litho. Wmk. 361 *Perf. 14*

Type II

691 A97 5h lil & blk ('78) 12 5
692 A97 10h lt vio & blk ('78) 20 10
693 A97 15h sal & blk ('78) 28 10
a. Type I 3.50 20
694 A97 20h lt bl & blk, I ('77) 4.50 20
a. Type II 3.50 20
695 A97 25h yel & blk ('78) 90 10
696 A97 30h gray grn & blk ('78) 1.25 15
697 A97 35h bis & blk ('78) 70 15
698 A97 40h lt grn & blk ('78) 2.75 20
a. Type I ('77) 5.50 30
b. Imperf. pair, II *125.00*
699 A97 45h dl rose & blk ('78) 80 15
700 A97 50h pink & blk ('78) 90 15
703 A97 65h gray bl & blk ('79) 1.10 15
710 A97 1r lt yel grn & blk ('78) 1.75 20
711 A97 2r grn & blk ('79) 6.25 35
Nos. 691-711 (13) 21.50 2.05

Imperfs of Nos. 691-711 other than No. 698b were not regularly issued.

See Nos. 872-882, 961-968

Quba Mosque, Medina, built 622 — A98

1976-77

719 A98 20h org & blk 2.25 10
720 A98 50h emer & lil ('77) 4.25 20

Reissued in 1978 in different shades

Globe, Telephones 1876 and 1976 A100

1976, July 17 Unwmk. *Perf. 13½*

721 A100 50h multi *4.75* 30

Centenary of first telephone call by Alexander Graham Bell, Mar. 10, 1876.

Arab Leaders A101

1976, Oct. 30 Litho. *Perf. 14*

722 A101 20h ultra & emer *3.75* 25

Arab Summit Conference, Riyadh, October. Leaders pictured: Pres. Elias Sarkis, Lebanon; Pres. Anwar Sadat, Egypt; Pres. Hafez al Assad, Syria; King Khalid, Saudi Arabia; Amir Sabah, Kuwait; Yasir Arafat, Palestine Liberation Organization chairman.

WHO Emblem and Eye A102

1976, Nov. 28 Litho. *Perf. 14*

723 A102 20h multi *9.50* 15

World Health Day; Prevention of Blindness.

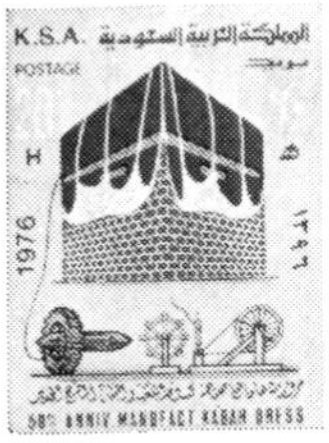

Holy Ka'aba — A103

1976, Nov. 28 Unwmk.

724 A103 20h multi *4.50* 20

50th anniversary of installation of new covering of Holy Ka'aba, Mecca.

Conference Emblem A104

Unwmk.

1977, Feb. 18 Litho. *Perf. 14*

725	A104	20h multi	*5.50*	15

Islamic Jurisprudence Conference, Riyadh, Oct. 24-Nov. 2, 1976.

Sharia College Emblem — A105

1977, Feb. 25 *Perf. 14*

726	A105	4p multi	*4.00*	15

25th anniversary (in 1974) of the founding of Sharia (Islamic Law) College, Mecca.

King Khalid ibn Abdul-Aziz A106

1977

727	A106	20h dk brn & brt grn	2.00	15
a.		Incorrect date	22.50	
728	A106	80h bl blk & brt grn	4.00	50
a.		Incorrect date	22.50	

2nd anniversary of installation of King Khalid ibn Abdul-Aziz. Nos. 727a-728a (illustrated), issued Mar. 3, have incorrect Arabic date in bottom panel, last characters of 2nd and 3rd rows identical "ir." Stamps withdrawn after a few days and replaced Aug. 14 with corrected date, last characters in 3rd row changed to "ro."

Diesel Train and Map of Route A107

1977, May 23 Litho. *Perf. 14*

729	A107	20h multi	*13.00*	15

Dammam-Riyadh railroad, 25th anniversary.

Values quoted in this catalogue are for stamps graded at Fine-Very Fine and with no faults. An illustrated guide to grade is provided in introductory material, beginning on Page V.

Arabic Ornament and Names — A108

Designs (Names from Left to Right): UL, Malik Ben Anas (715-795). UR, Mohammad Ben Idris Al-Shafi'i (767-820). LL, Abu Hanifa an-Nu'man (699-767). LR, Ahmed Ben Hanbal (780-855).

1977, Aug. 15 Litho. *Perf. 14*

730	A108	Block of 4, multi	*21.00*	2.25
a.		20h, single stamp	*3.00*	25

Famous Imams (7th-9th centuries), founders of traditional schools of Islamic jurisprudence. Sheets of 60.

Al Khafji Oil Rig — A109

1976-80 Wmk. 361

731	A109	5h vio bl & org	7	5
732	A109	10h yel grn & org	10	5
733	A109	15h brn & org	14	5
734	A109	20h grn & org	20	10
735	A109	25h dk pur & org	25	10
736	A109	30h bl & org	28	10
737	A109	35h sep & org	35	15
a.		Imperf, pair	*160.00*	
738	A109	40h mag & org	35	15
a.		40h dl pur & org	*200.00*	
739	A109	45h vio & org	45	20
740	A109	50h rose & org	52	20
a.		50h dl org & org (error)	*57.50*	*7.50*
741	A109	55h grnsh bl & org	19.00	4.00
743	A109	65h sep & org	1.00	35
750	A109	1r gray & org	1.25	60
751	A109	2r dk vio & org ('80)	2.50	1.00
		Nos. 731-751 (14)	26.46	7.10

All values exist with extra dot in Arabic "Al Khafji." The 20, 25, 50, 65h and 1r were retouched to remove the dot.

Color of flame varies from light orange to vermilion. See Nos. 885-892.

Mohenjo-Daro Ruins — A110

1977, Oct. 23 Litho. Unwmk.

761	A110	50h multi	4.25	30

UNESCO campaign to save Mohenjo-Daro excavations in Pakistan.

Idrisi's World Map, 1154 — A111

1977, Nov. 1 Litho. *Perf. 14*

762	A111	20h multi	1.50	15
763	A111	50h multi	3.00	35

First International Symposium on Studies in the History of Arabia at the University of Riyadh, Apr. 23-26, 1977.

King Faisal Specialist Hospital, Riyadh — A112

1977, Nov. 13 Litho. Unwmk.

764	A112	20h multi	2.25	20
765	A112	50h multi	3.50	35

Conference Emblem — A113

1977 Litho. *Perf. 14*

766	A113	20h vio bl & yel	3.25	15

1st World Conf. on Moslem Education.

APU Emblem, Members' Flags A114

1977

767	A114	20h multi	1.25	15
768	A114	80h multi	2.75	50

25th anniversary of Arab Postal Union.

Taif-Abha-Gizan Highway — A115

1978, Oct. 15 Litho. *Perf. 14*

769	A115	20h multi	1.65	10
770	A115	80h multi	3.25	40

Inauguration of Taif-Abha-Gizan highway.

Pilgrims, Mt. Arafat and Holy Ka'aba — A116

Unwmk.

1978, Nov. 6 Litho. *Perf. 14*

771	A116	20h multi	1.25	10
772	A116	80h multi	2.50	40

Pilgrimage to Mecca.

Gulf Postal Organization Emblem — A117

1979, Feb. 6 Litho. *Perf. 14*

773	A117	20h multi	1.10	10
774	A117	50h multi	2.25	25

First Conference of Gulf Postal Organization, Baghdad.

Saudi Arabia No. 129, King Abdul Aziz ibn Saud A118

Unwmk.

1979, June 4 Litho. *Perf. 14*

775	A118	20h multi	1.25	10
776	A118	50h multi	2.50	25
777	A118	115h multi	4.25	58

Souvenir Sheet

Imperf

778	A118	100h multi	*60.00*	

First commemorative stamp, 50th anniversary. No. 778 contains one stamp with simulated perforations; marginal inscription and portrait of King. Size: 101x76mm.

Crown Prince Fahd A119

1979, June 25 *Perf. 14*

779	A119	20h multi	1.50	10
780	A119	50h multi	3.00	25

Crown Prince Fahd ibn Abdul Aziz.

Dome of the Rock, Jerusalem A120

1979, July 2 Wmk. 361

781	A120	20h multi (shades)	1.00	25

See No. 866.

Gold Door, Holy Ka'aba — A121

1979, Oct. 13 **Litho.** ***Perf. 14***
782 A121 20h multi 95 10
783 A121 80h multi 2.25 40

Installation of new gold doors.

Pilgrims at Holy Ka'aba, Mecca Mosque — A122

1979, Oct. 27
784 A122 20h multi 85 10
785 A122 50h multi 1.90 25

Pilgrimage to Mecca.

Birds in Trees, IYC Emblem — A123

IYC Emblem and: 50h, Child's drawing.

1980, Feb. 17 **Litho.** ***Perf. 14***
786 A123 20h multi *11.00* 10
787 A123 50h multi *18.00* 25

International Year of the Child (1979).

King Abdul Aziz ibn Saud on Horseback, Saudi Flag A124

1980, Apr. 5 **Litho.** ***Perf. 14***
788 A124 20h multi 1.50 10
789 A124 80h multi 3.50 40

Saudi Arabian Army, 80th anniv. (1979).

Arab League, 35th Anniversary A125

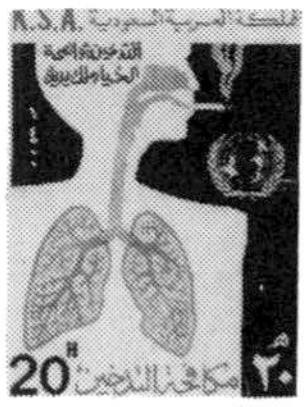

Smoke Entering Lungs, WHO Emblem A127

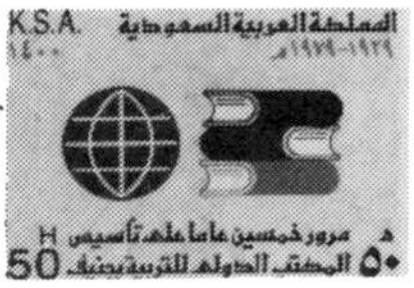

International Bureau of Education, 50th Anniversary A126

1980, Apr. 27 **Litho.** ***Perf. 14***
790 A125 20h multi 90 10

1980, May 4
791 A126 50h multi *1.65* 25

1980, May 20
792 A127 20h *shown* 60 10
793 A127 50h *Cigarette,* horiz. 1.40 25

Anti-smoking campaign.

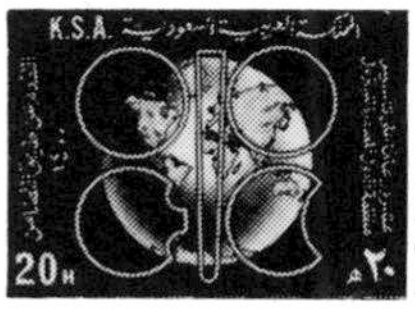

20th Anniversary of OPEC A128

Design: 50h, Workers holding OPEC emblem (Organization of Petroleum Exporting Countries).

1980, Sept. 1 **Litho.** ***Perf. 14***
794 A128 20h multi 1.00 10
795 A128 50h multi, vert. 2.00 25

Pilgrims Arriving at Jedda Airport A129

1980, Oct. 18
796 A129 20h multi 90 10
797 A129 50h multi 1.75 25

Pilgrimage to Mecca.

Conference Emblem A130

Holy Ka'aba, Mecca Mosque — A131

1981, Jan. 25 **Litho.** ***Perf. 14***
798 A130 20h shown 75 10
799 A131 20h shown 75 10
800 A131 20h Prophet's Mosque, Medina 75 10
801 A131 20h Dome of the Rock, Jerusalem 75 10

Third Islamic Summit Conference, Mecca.

Hegira, 1500th Anniv. A132

1981, Jan. 26
802 A132 20h multi 50 10
803 A132 50h multi 1.00 25
804 A132 80h multi 2.00 40

Souvenir Sheet

805 A132 300h multi

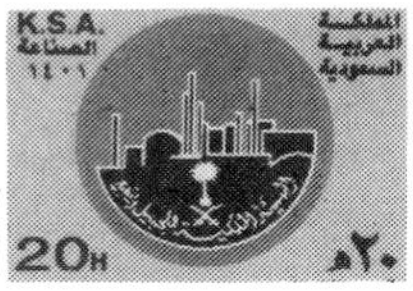

Industry Week A133

1981, Feb. 21
806 A133 20h multi 60 10
807 A133 80h multi 1.90 40

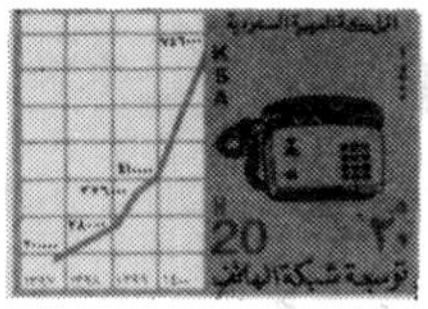

Line Graph and Telephone A134

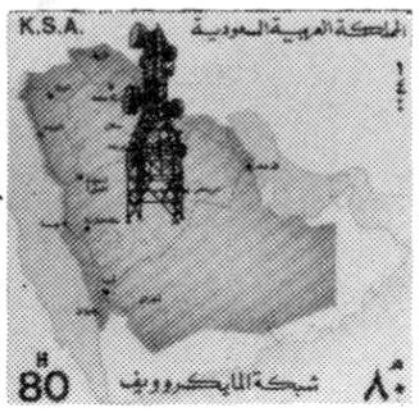

Map of Saudi Arabia, Microwave Tower A135

1981, Feb. 28
808 A134 20h shown 15 10
809 A135 80h shown 1.25 40
810 A134 115h Earth satellite station 1.40 55

Souvenir Sheets

811 A134 100h like #808
812 A135 100h like #809
813 A134 100h like #810

Ministry of Posts and Telecommunications achievements.

Arab City Day — A135a

1981, Apr. 2 **Litho.** ***Perf. 14***
814 A135a 20h multi 25 10
815 A135a 65h multi 80 32
816 A135a 80h multi 1.00 40
817 A135a 115d multi 1.40 60

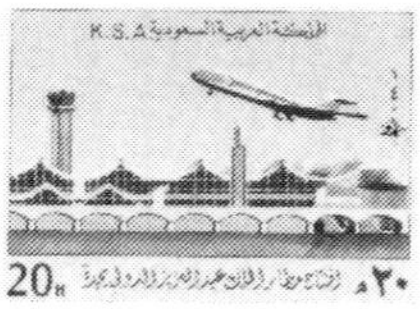

Jedda Airport Opening A136

1981, Apr. 12
818 A136 20h shown 60 10
819 A136 80h Plane over airport, diff. 2.25 40

1982 World Cup Soccer Preliminary Games — A137

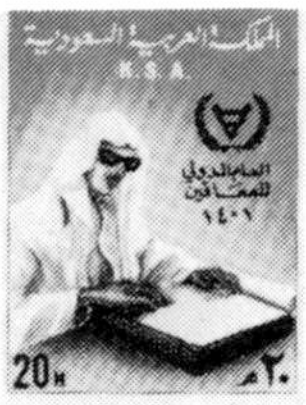

Intl. Year of the Disabled — A138

1981, July 26 **Litho.** ***Perf. 14***
820 A137 20h multi *1.90* 10
821 A137 80h multi *3.50* 40

1981, Aug. 5
822 A138 20h Reading braille *2.25* 10
823 A138 50h Man weaving rug *3.50* 25

3rd Five-year Plan (1981-1985) A139

1981, Sept. 5
824 A139 20h multi 90 10

King Abdul Aziz, Map of Saudi Arabia A140

1981, Sept. 23 **Litho.** ***Perf. 14***
825 A140 5h multi 6 5
826 A140 10h multi 12 5
827 A140 15h multi 18 8
828 A140 20h multi 25 10
829 A140 50h multi 65 25
830 A140 65h multi 85 32
831 A140 80h multi 2.25 40
832 A140 115h multi 2.75 58
Nos. 825-832 (8) 7.11 1.83

Souvenir Sheet

Imperf

833 A140 10r multi *80.00*

50th anniv. of kingdom. No. 833 shows king, map, document. Size: 100x75mm.

Pilgrimage to Mecca A141

1981, Oct. 7
834 A141 20h multi *2.00* 10
835 A141 65h multi *4.00* 32

World Food Day — A142

1981, Oct. 16
836 A142 20h multi 90 10

2nd Session of the Gulf Cooperative Council Summit Conference, Riyadh, Nov. 10 — A143

1981, Nov. 10 **Litho.** ***Perf. 14***
837 A143 20h multi 50 10
838 A143 80h multi 1.50 40

King Saud University, 25th Anniv. A144

1982, Mar. 10 Litho. *Perf. 14*

839 A144 20h multi 50 10
840 A144 50h multi 1.00 25

New Regional Postal Centers A145

1982, July 14 Litho. *Perf. 14*

841 A145 20h Riyadh P.O. 22 10
842 A145 65h Jedda 75 32
843 A145 80h Dammam 95 40
844 A145 115h Automated sorting 1.25 58

Four 300h souvenir sheets exist in same designs as Nos. 841-844 respectively.

Riyadh Television Center — A146

1982, Sept. 4

845 A146 20h multi 1.00 10

25th Anniv. of King's Soccer Cup — A147

1982, Sept. 8

846 A147 20h multi 95 10
847 A147 65h multi 1.90 32

30th Anniv. of Arab Postal Union A148

1982, Sept. 8

848 A148 20h Emblem 48 10
849 A148 65h Map, vert. 1.25 32

Pilgrimage to Mecca A149

1982, Sept. 26

850 A149 20h multi 60 10
851 A149 50h multi 1.25 25

The lack of a value for a listed item does not necessarily indicate rarity.

World Standards Day A150

1982, Oct. 14

852 A150 20h multi 90 10

World Food Day — A151

1982, Oct. 16

853 A151 20h multi 90 10

Coronation of King Fahd, June 14, 1982 A152

Installation of Crown Prince Abdullah, June 14, 1982 — A153

1983, Feb. 12 Litho. *Perf. 14*

854 A152 20h multi 22 10
855 A153 20h multi 22 10
856 A152 50h multi 50 25
857 A153 50h multi 50 25
858 A152 65h multi 70 32
859 A153 65h multi 70 32
860 A152 80h multi 90 40
861 A153 80h multi 90 40
862 A152 115h multi 1.25 60
863 A153 115h multi 1.25 60
Nos. 854-863 (10) 7.14 3.34

Two one-stamp souvenir sheets contain Nos. 862-863, perf. 12½.

6th Anniv. of United Arab Shipping Co. — A154

Various freighters.

1983, Aug. 9 Litho. *Perf. 14*

864 A154 20h multi 12 6
865 A154 65h multi 40 20

Dome of the Rock, Jerusalem A155

Perf. 13½x12

1983, Sept. Litho. Wmk. 361

866 A155 20h multi 12 6

See No. 781.

Pilgrimage to Mecca A156

1983, Sept. 16 Litho. *Perf. 14*

867 A156 20h brt bl & multi 12 6
868 A156 65h dk blk & multi 40 20

World Communications Year — A157

1983, Oct. 8 Litho. *Perf. 14*

869 A157 20h Post and UPU emblems 12 6
870 A157 80h Telephone and ITU emblems 48 24

Holy Ka'ba Type of 1976
Type II

Perf. 14x13½

1982-86 Litho. Wmk. 361

Size: 26x21mm

872 A97 10h lt vio & blk ('83) 10 5
a. Perf. 12, unwmkd. ('87) 10 5
873 A97 15h sal & blk, perf. 12 ('85) 8 5
874 A97 20h lt bl & blk 20 5
a. Perf. 12 ('84) 20 5
b. Perf. 12, unwmkd. 12 6
880 A97 50h pink & blk ('83) 50 10
a. Perf. 13½ 50 10
b. Perf. 12 ('86) 30 15
881 A97 65h gray bl & blk 65 15
a. Perf. 13½ 65 15
b. Perf. 12 ('84) 65 15
882 A97 1r lt yel grn & blk 1.00 20
a. Perf. 13½ 1.00 20
b. Perf. 12 ('83) 1.00 20
Nos. 872-882 (6) 2.53 60

Counterfeits of the 1r are perf. 11.

Al Khafji Oil Rig Type of 1976

Perf. 14x13½

1982-84 Litho. Wmk. 361

Size: 26x21mm

885 A109 5h vio bl & org 5 5
a. Perf. 13½ 5 5
886 A109 10h yel grn & org 6 5
a. Perf. 13½ 6 5
b. Perf. 12 ('83) 6 5
887 A109 15h bis brn & org 10 5
a. Perf. 13½ 10 5
b. Perf. 12 ('83) 10 5
888 A109 20h grn & org 12 6
a. Perf. 13½ 12 6
b. Perf. 12 ('83) 12 6
889 A109 25h dk pur & org, perf. 12 ('83) 15 8
890 A109 50h rose & org 30 15
a. Perf. 13½ 30 15
b. Perf. 12 ('83) 30 15
891 A109 65h sep & org, perf. 13½ ('84) 40 20
a. Perf. 14x13½ 3.00 1.50
b. Perf. 12 ('83) 40 20
892 A109 1r gray & org 60 30
a. Perf. 13½ 60 30
b. Perf. 12 ('83) 60 30
Nos. 885-892 (8) 1.78 94

Opening of King Khalid International Airport — A158

1983, Nov. 16 Litho. *Perf. 13½x14*

893 A158 20h shown 12 6
894 A158 65h bl & multi 40 20

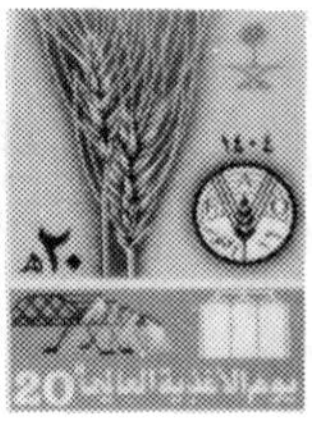

World Food Day — A159

1983, Nov. 29 Litho. *Perf. 14*

895 A159 20h Wheat, Irrigation, Silos 12 6

Aqsa Mosque, Jerusalem A160

1983, Dec. 13 Litho. *Perf. 14*

896 A160 20h multi 12 6

Old and Modern Riyadh — A161

Shobra Palace, Taif — A162

Old and New Jedda (Waterfront) — A163

1984-89 Litho. Wmk. 361 *Perf. 12*

900 A161 20h lil rose & multi 12 6
901 A162 20h Prus grn & multi 12 6
907 A161 50h blk & multi 30 15
908 A162 50h brn & multi ('87) 75 38

Unwmk.

909 A163 50h multi ('89) 1.00 50
910 A162 150h grn & multi ('87) 1.65 82
911 A161 150h pink & multi ('88) 1.65 82

Dates of issue: No. 900, June 27. No. 901, Oct. 13. 50h, Aug. 29 No. 908, Mar. 10. No. 909, Jan. 31. No. 910, Sept. 3. No. 911, May 4.

Estate Development Fund, 10th Anniv. — A165

1984, July 28 **Litho.** ***Perf. 12***
912 A165 20h multi 35 6

Opening of Solar Village, near Al-Eyenah A166

1984, Aug. 14 **Litho.** ***Perf. 12***
913 A166 20h multi 15 6
914 A166 80h Stylized sun, solar panels 60 24

Imperf

Size: 81x81mm

915 A166 100h like 20h 60 30
916 A166 100h like 80h 60 30

Pilgrimage to Mecca — A167

Perf. 14, 12 (65h)

1984, Sept. 4 **Litho.**
917 A167 20h brn & multi 25 6
918 A167 65h ol gray & multi 80 20

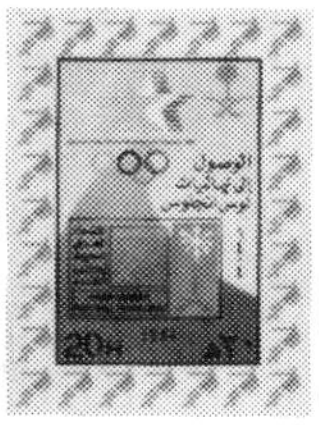

Participation of Saudi Arabian Soccer Team in 1984 Olympics — A168

1984, Sept. 25 **Litho.** ***Perf. 12***
919 A168 20h bl & multi 25 6
920 A168 115h grn & multi 1.00 35

"Games" and "Olympiad" are misspelled on both stamps.

World Food Day — A169

1984, Oct. 16 **Litho.** ***Perf. 12***
921 A169 20h multi 35 6

Beginning with Nos. 922-923 some issues are printed in sheets that have labels inscribed in Arabic. Generally there are from 2 to 6 labels per sheet. Stamps with label attached command a premium.

90th Anniv. International Olympic Committee — A170

1984, Dec. 23 **Litho.** ***Perf. 12***
922 A170 20h multi 12 6
923 A170 50h multi 60 15

Launch of ARABSAT — A171

1985, Feb. 9 **Litho.** ***Perf. 12***
924 A171 20h ARABSAT, view of Earth 90 6

7th Holy Koran Competition — A172

1985, Feb. 10 **Litho.** ***Perf. 12***
925 A172 20h multi 25 6
926 A172 65h multi 75 20

4th Five-Year Development Plan, 1985-1990 — A173

Portrait of King Fahd, industry emblems and: 20h, Dhahran Harbor, Jubail. 50h, Television tower, earth receiver, microwave tower. 65h, Agriculture. 80h, Harbor, Yanbu.

1985, Mar. 23 **Litho.** ***Perf. 13x12***
927 A173 20h multi 48 6
928 A173 50h multi 1.25 15
929 A173 65h multi 1.40 20
930 A173 80h multi 1.90 22
a. Block of 4, Nos. 927-930 5.00 75

Intl. Youth Year — A174

1985, May 4 ***Perf. 12***
931 A174 20h multi 18 6
932 A174 80h multi 70 22

Self-sufficiency in Wheat Production A175

1985, May 4
933 A175 20h multi 48 6

East-West Pipeline — A176

1985, June 9
934 A176 20h Tanker loading berth, Yanbu 25 6
935 A176 65h Pipeline, map 75 20

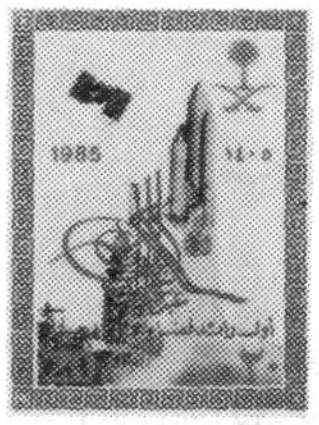

Shuttle Launch — A177

Shuttle, Missions Emblem — A178

1985, July 7
936 A177 20h multi 25 6
937 A178 115h multi 1.25 32

Prince Sultan Ibn Salman Al-Saud, 1st Arab-Moslem astronaut, on Discovery 51-G.

UN, 40th Anniv. A179

1985, July 15
938 A179 20h multi 48 6

Highway, Map, Holy Ka'aba in Mecca to Prophet's Mosque in Medina — A180

1985, July 22
939 A180 20h multi 25 6
940 A180 65h multi 75 20

Mecca-Medina Highway opening, Oct. 11, 1984.

Post Code Inauguration — A181

1985, July 24
941 A181 20h Covers 25 6

1984 Asian Soccer Cup Victory A182

1985, July 30
942 A182 20h multi 18 6
943 A182 65h multi 48 20
944 A182 115h multi 1.00 32

Pilgrimage to Mecca — A183

1985, Aug. 25 **Litho.** ***Perf. 12***
945 A183 10h multi 6 5
946 A183 15h multi 20 5
947 A183 20h multi 25 6
948 A183 65h multi 75 20

1st Gulf Olympics Day, Riyadh, May 2 — A184

1985, Sept. 8
949 A184 20h multi 25 6
950 A184 115h multi 1.25 32

World Food Day A185

1985, Oct. 16
951 A185 20h multi 20 6
952 A185 65h multi 65 20

King Abdul Aziz, Masmak Fort and Horsemen — A186

1985, Dec. 1
953 A186 15h multi 10 5
954 A186 20h multi 12 6
955 A186 65h multi 38 20
956 A186 80h multi 45 22

Intl. Conference on the History of King Abdul Aziz Al-Sa'ud, Riyadh. An imperf. souvenir sheet showing smaller versions of Nos. 953-956 and the conference emblem exists. Sold for 10r.

King Fahd Koran Publishing Center, Medina — A187

1985, Dec. 18
957 A187 20h multi 15 6
958 A187 65h multi 52 20

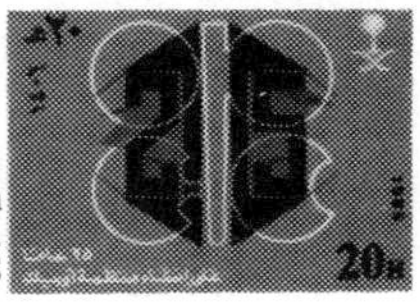
OPEC, 25th Anniv. A188

1985, Dec. 24
959 A188 20h multi 15 6
960 A188 65h multi 52 20

Holy Ka'aba Type of 1976
Type II
Booklet Stamps

1986, Feb. 17 Litho. *Perf. 12*
Size: 29x19mm.
961 A97 10h lt vio & blk 6 5
a. Bklt. pane of 4 *10.00* 12
965 A97 20h bluish grn & blk 12 6
968 A97 50h pink & blk 28 14
a. Bklt. pane of 4, #961, 2 #965, #968 *15.00* 24

Intl. Peace Year — A189

1986, Jan. 8 Litho. *Perf. 12*
971 A189 20h multi 12 6

Riyadh Municipality, 50th Anniv. — A190

1986, Mar. 24 *Perf. 14, 12 (65h)*
972 A190 20h multi 12 6
a. Perf. 12 12 6
973 A190 65h multi 38 20

UN Child Survival Campaign A191

1986, Apr. 21 *Perf. 12*
974 A191 20h multi 12 6
975 A191 50h multi 28 14

General Establishment for Electric Power, 10th Anniv. — A192

1986, Apr. 26
976 A192 20h multi 12 6
977 A192 65h multi 38 20

Continental Maritime Cable Inauguration — A193

1986, June 1 Litho. *Perf. 12*
978 A193 20h multi 12 6
979 A193 50h multi 28 14

Natl. Guard Housing Project, Riyadh, Inauguration A194

1986, July 19
980 A194 20h multi 12 6
981 A194 65h multi 38 20

Islamic Arch, Holy Ka'aba — A195

1986, Aug. 5 Litho. *Perf. 12*
984 A195 30h blk & bluish grn 18 8
985 A195 40h blk & lil rose 22 10

Pilgrimage to Mecca — A196

Designs of: a, A116. b, A129. c, A156. d, A149. e, A141. f, A122. g, A183. h, A167.

1986, Aug. 13 Litho. *Perf. 12*
1002 Block of 8 *12.00 12.00*
a.-h. A196 20h, any single

Discovery of Oil, 50th Anniv. — A197

World Food Day — A198

1986, Sept. 16
1003 A197 20h Well, refinery 12 6
1004 A197 65h Well, map 38 18

1986, Oct. 18
1005 A198 20h shown 12 6
1006 A198 115h Stylized plant 65 32

Massacre of Palestinian Refugees, Sept. 17, 1982 — A199

1986, Nov. 1 Litho. *Perf. 12*
1007 A199 80h multi 65 32
1008 A199 115h multi 95 48

Saudi Universities

Imam Mohammed ibn Saud — A200

Umm al-Qura — A201

King Abdul Aziz — A202

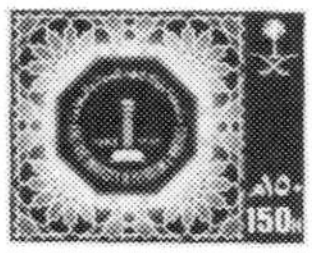
King Fahd Petroleum and Minerals — A203

King Faisal — A204

King Saud — A205

Medina Islamic — A206

1986-89

1009	A200	15h	sage grn & blk	12	6
1010	A200	20h	ultra & blk	16	8
1011	A200	65h	brt bl & blk	52	25
1012	A200	100h	rose & blk	80	40
1013	A200	150h	rose claret & blk ('89)	1.40	70
1014	A201	50h	ultra & blk	55	28
1015	A201	65h	brt blue & blk ('89)	75	25
1017	A201	100h	dull rose & blk	1.10	55
1018	A201	150h	rose claret & blk	1.65	82
1022	A202	100h	dull rose & blk	1.10	55
1025	A203	50h	ultra & blk ('89)	45	22
1027	A203	150h	rose claret & blk ('89)	1.40	70
1029	A204	50h	ultra & blk ('89)	45	22
1033	A205	50h	ultra & blk ('89)	45	22
1037	A206	150h	rose claret & blk ('89)	1.40	22
			Nos. 1009-1037 (15)	12.30	5.52

Issue dates: Nos. 1009-1012, Nov. 26. No. 1017, Mar. 29. No. 1022, July 22. Nos. 1014, 1018, Aug. 8. Nos. 1013, 1027, 1037, Jan. 31. Nos. 1025, 1029, 1033, Feb. 25.

Saudi-Bahrain Highway Inauguration — A207

1986, Nov. 26 *Perf. 14*
1039 Strip of 2 32 16
a.-b. A207 20h, any single 16 8

Printed se-tenant in a continuous design.

1st Modern Olympic Games, Athens, 90th Anniv. A208

1986, Dec. 27
1040 A208 20h multi 16 8
1041 A208 100h multi 80 40

General Petroleum and Minerals Organization (Petromin), 25th Anniv. A209

Unwmk.
1987, Feb. 23 Litho. *Perf. 12*
1042 A209 50h multi 55 28
1043 A209 100h multi 1.10 55

Restoration and Expansion of Quba Mosque, Medina — A210

Design: View of mosque and model of expanded mosque.

1987, Mar. 21
1044 A210 50h multi 55 28
1045 A210 75h multi 82 40

Vocational Training A211

Designs: No. 1046a, Welding. No. 1046b, Drill press operation. No. 1046c, Lathe operation. No. 1046d, Electrician.

Unwmk.
1987, Apr. 8 Litho. *Perf. 12*
1046 Block of 4 5.60 2.80
a.-d. A211 50h any single 1.40 70

Cairo Exhibition — A212

Design: Desert fortifications in silhouette, Riyadh television tower, King Khalid Intl. Airport hangars and pyramid of Giza.

Unwmk.
1987, June 17 Litho. *Perf. 12*
1047 A212 50h multi 58 30
1048 A212 75h multi 88 45

A213

Inauguration of King Fahd Telecommunications Center, Jedda — A214

1987, July 21

1049 A213 50h multi	58	30
1050 A214 75h multi	88	45

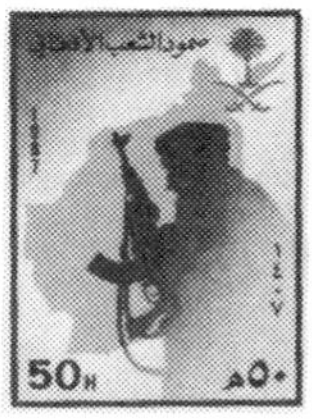
Afghan Resistance Movement — A215

1987, July 25

1051 A215 50h multi	55	28
1052 A215 100h multi	1.10	55

Pilgrimage to Mecca — A216

Design: View of Ihram and Meqat Wadi Muhrim Mosque from Wadi Muhrim Meqat.

1987, Aug. 3

1053 A216 50h multi	58	30
1054 A216 75h multi	88	45
1055 A216 100h multi	1.15	58

Home for Disabled Children, 1st Anniv. — A217

1987, Oct. 3

1056 A217 50h multi	52	25
1057 A217 75h multi	78	40

World Post Day — A218

1987, Oct. 10

1058 A218 50h multi	55	28
1059 A218 150h multi	1.60	80

World Food Day A219

1987, Oct. 17

1060 A219 50h multi	52	25
1061 A219 75h multi	78	40

Social Welfare Society, 25th Anniv. — A220

Dome of the Rock — A221

1987, Oct. 26

1062 A220 50h multi	60	30
1063 A220 100h multi	1.20	60

1987, Dec. 5

1064 A221 75h multi	85	42
1065 A221 150h multi	1.70	85

Restoration and Expansion of the Prophet's Mosque, Medina — A222

1987, Dec. 15 ***Perf. 14***

1066 A222 50h multi	52	25
1067 A222 75h multi	78	40
1068 A222 150h multi	1.55	78

An imperf. 300h souvenir sheet exists.

Battle of Hattin, 800th Anniv. A223

Design: Warriors in silhouette and Dome of the Rock.

1987, Dec. 21 ***Perf. 12***

1069 A223 75h multi	82	40
1070 A223 150h multi	1.65	82

Saladin's conquest of Jerusalem.

8th Session of the Supreme Council of the Gulf Cooperation Council — A224

1987, Dec. 26

1071 A224 50h multi	60	30
1072 A224 75h multi	88	45

3rd Regional Highways Conference of the Middle East — A225

1988, Feb. 13 **Litho.** ***Perf. 12***

1073 A225 50h multi	1.00	50
1074 A225 75h multi	1.50	75

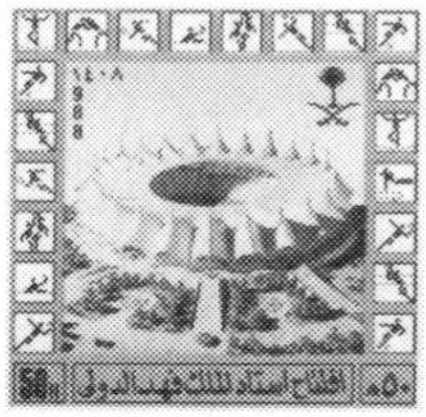
A226

Inauguration of King Fahd Intl. Stadium — A227

1988, Mar. 2

1075 A226 50h multi	62	30
1076 A227 150h multi	1.85	95

Blood Donation — A228

1988, Apr. 12 **Litho.** ***Perf. 12***

1077 A228 50h multi	62	30
1078 A228 75h multi	92	45

WHO, 40th Anniv. — A229

1988, Apr. 17

1079 A229 50h multi	62	30
1080 A229 75h multi	92	45

King Fahd, Custodian of the Holy Mosques — A230

Design: King Fahd and mosques at Medina and Mecca.

1988, Apr. 23 Litho. *Perf. 12*

1081	A230	50h multi	50	25
1082	A230	75h multi	75	38
1083	A230	150h multi	1.50	75

A 75h souvenir sheet exists containing an enlarged version of No. 1082. Sold for 3r.

Environmental Protection — A231

1988, June 5

1084	A231	50h multi	52	25
1085	A231	75h multi	78	40

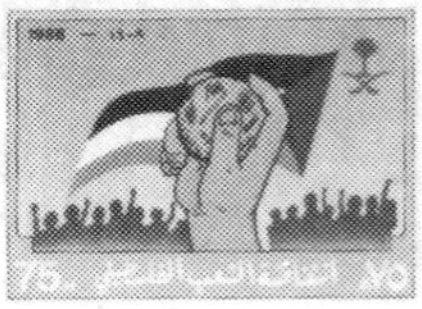

Palestinian Uprising, Gaza and the West Bank A232

1988, July 10

1086	A232	75h multi	75	38
1087	A232	150h multi	1.50	75

Pilgrimage to Mecca — A233

1988, July 23 Litho. *Perf. 12*

1088	A233	50h multi	62	30
1089	A233	75h multi	92	45

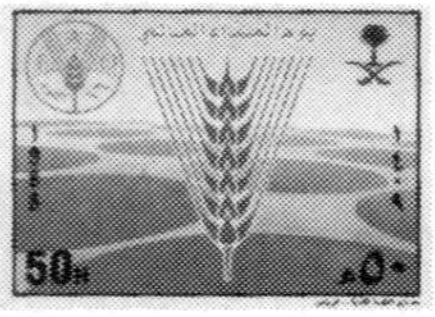

World Food Day A234

1988, Oct. 16 Litho. *Perf. 12*

1090	A234	50h multi	52	25
1091	A234	75h multi	78	40

Qiblatain Mosque Expansion — A235

1988, Nov. 9

1092	A235	50h multi	52	25
1093	A235	75h multi	80	40

AIR POST STAMPS

Catalogue values for unused stamps in this section, from this point to the end of the section, are for Never Hinged items.

Airspeed Ambassador Airliner — AP1

1949-58 Unwmk. Typo. *Perf. 11*

C1	AP1	1g bl grn	2.00	10
C2	AP1	3g ultra	2.50	10
a.		3g bl ('58)	10.00	1.00
C3	AP1	4g orange	2.50	10
C4	AP1	10g purple	6.75	15
C5	AP1	20g chocolate	12.50	50
a.		20g brn vio ('58?)	6.00	20
C6	AP1	100g vio rose	60.00	7.00
		Nos. C1-C6 (6)	86.25	7.95

Imperfs. exist.

The 1st printings are on greyish paper and sell for more.

Saudi Airlines Convair 440 — AP2

Type I (Saud Cartouche)
(Illustrated over No. 286)

1960-61 Photo. *Perf. 14*

C7	AP2	1p dl pur & grn	60	5
C8	AP2	2p grn & dl pur	60	5
C9	AP2	3p brn red & bl	60	5
C10	AP2	4p bl & dl pur	60	10
C11	AP2	5p grn & rose red	60	10
C12	AP2	6p ocher & sl	1.00	20
C13	AP2	8p rose & gray ol	1.25	20
C14	AP2	9p pur & red brn	1.75	20
C15	AP2	10p blk & dl red brn	5.00	45
C16	AP2	15p bl & bis brn	5.00	20
C17	AP2	20p bis brn & emer	5.00	40
C18	AP2	30p sep & Prus grn	12.50	1.00
C19	AP2	50p grn & ind	25.00	75
C20	AP2	100p gray & dk brn	50.00	2.00
C21	AP2	200p dk vio & blk	75.00	3.00
		Nos. C7-C21 (15)	184.50	8.75

The 5p, 9p, 10p, 15p and 20p exist imperf; probably not regularly issued.

1963-64 Photo. Wmk. 337
Size: 27½x22mm.

C24	AP2	1p lil & grn	2.00	10
C25	AP2	2p grn & dl pur	8.00	20
C26	AP2	4p bl & dl pur	3.00	15
C27	AP2	6p ocher & sl	8.00	80
C28	AP2	8p rose & gray ol	15.00	1.50
C29	AP2	9p pur & red brn ('64)	10.00	1.00
		Nos. C24-C29 (6)	46.00	3.75

Redrawn

Perf. 13½x13
1964 Wmk. 337 Litho.
Size: 28½x23mm.

C30	AP2	3p brn red & dl bl	4.50	50
C31	AP2	10p blk & dk red brn	7.00	80
C32	AP2	20p bis brn & emer	15.00	1.75

Nos. C30-C32 are widely spaced in the sheet, producing large margins.

Saudi Airline Boeing 720-B Jet — AP3

Type I (Saud Cartouche)
(Illustrated over No. 286)

1965-70 Unwmk. Litho. *Perf. 14*

C33	AP3	1p lil & grn ('66)	*70.00*	3.00
C34	AP3	2p grn & dl pur ('70)	*800.00*	*100.00*
C35	AP3	3p rose lil & dl bl ('66)	8.00	10
C36	AP3	4p bl & dl pur	6.00	10
C37	AP3	5p ol & rose red ('69)	*800.00*	*2,500.*
C38	AP3	6p ocher & sl ('70)	*95.00*	*2.00*
C39	AP3	7p rose & ol gray ('66)	7.00	40
C40	AP3	8p rose & gray ol ('70)	*90.00*	*2.00*
C41	AP3	9p pur & red brn	7.50	30
C42	AP3	10p blk & dk red brn ('66)	*100.00*	*6.00*
C43	AP3	11p grn & bis ('69)	*90.00*	*20.00*
C44	AP3	12p org & gray ('66)	7.00	30
C45	AP3	13p dk grn & yel grn ('66)	7.00	30
C46	AP3	14p dk bl & org ('66)	7.00	40
C47	AP3	15p bl & bis brn ('70)	*82.50*	*6.00*
C48	AP3	16p blk & ultra ('66)	10.00	50
C49	AP3	17p bis & sep ('66)	7.50	40
C50	AP3	18p dk bl & yel grn ('66)	7.50	40
C51	AP3	19p car & dp org ('66)	8.75	50
C52	AP3	20p bis brn & emer ('70)	*150.00*	*7.00*
C53	AP3	23p ol & bis	*165.00*	*12.00*
C54	AP3	24p dk bl & sep	7.50	50
C55	AP3	26p ver & bl grn	7.50	50
C56	AP3	27p ol brn & ap grn	7.75	50
C57	AP3	31p car rose & rose red	8.00	60
C58	AP3	33p red & dl pur	13.00	60

The 50p, 100p and 200p exist but were not placed in use.

Type II (Faisal Cartouche)

1966-78 Unwmk. Litho. *Perf. 14*

C59	AP3	1p dl pur & grn	*21.00*	*1.00*
C60	AP3	2p grn & dl pur	*22.50*	*1.50*
C61	AP3	3p brn red & dl bl	*18.50*	50
C62	AP3	4p bl & dl pur ('68)	10.00	25
C63	AP3	5p ol & rose red	*800.00*	*350.00*
C64	AP3	6p ocher & sl ('71)	140.00	*10.00*
C65	AP3	7p rose & ol gray ('69)	62.50	*7.00*
C66	AP3	8p rose & gray ol ('70)	100.00	*12.50*
C67	AP3	9p pur & red brn ('70)	6.75	60
C68	AP3	10p blk & dl red brn	18.00	1.00
C69	AP3	11p grn & bis	10.00	50
C70	AP3	12p org & gray ('75)	*62.50*	*4.00*
C71	AP3	13p dk grn & yel grn ('71)	16.00	1.00
C72	AP3	14p dk bl & org ('75)	18.00	1.65
C73	AP3	15p bl & bis brn ('75)	12.00	80
C74	AP3	16p blk & ultra ('71)	*15.00*	3.00
C75	AP3	17p bis & sep ('75)	*15.00*	1.50
C76	AP3	18p dk bl & yel grn ('76)	*15.00*	2.50
C77	AP3	19p car & org ('75)	*15.00*	1.00
C78	AP3	20p brn & brt grn ('70)	*200.00*	*14.00*
C79	AP3	23p ol & bis	17.00	3.00
C80	AP3	24p dk bl & blk ('75)	*30.00*	3.00
C83	AP3	31p car rose & rose red ('78)	*750.00*	
C84	AP3	33p red & dl pur ('68)	12.00	50
C85	AP3	50p emer & ind ('74)	*650.00*	*200.00*
C86	AP3	100p gray & dk brn ('78)	*850.00*	*300.00*
C87	AP3	200p dk vio & blk ('74)	*1,000.*	*200.00*

The existence of 26p and 27p denominations has been reported.

1968-71 Wmk. 361 Litho. *Perf. 14*

C88	AP3	1p lil & grn	8.25	20
C89	AP3	2p grn & lil	8.25	20
C90	AP3	3p rose lil & dl bl ('69)	37.50	*2.00*
C91	AP3	4p bl & dl pur ('70)	13.00	1.25
C92	AP3	7p rose & gray ('71)	13.00	1.65
C93	AP3	8p red & gray ol ('71)	*42.50*	*6.50*
C94	AP3	9p pur & red brn ('71)	*57.50*	*8.00*
C95	AP3	10p blk & dl red brn ('69)	*40.00*	4.00

Falcon — AP4

Perf. 13½x14
1968-71 Litho. Wmk. 361

C96	AP4	1p grn & red brn	4.75	15
C97	AP4	4p dk red & red brn	*25.00*	*12.00*
C98	AP4	10p bl & red brn	14.00	3.00
C99	AP4	20p grn & red brn ('71)	37.50	6.00

Nine other denominations were printed but are not known to have been issued.

POSTAGE DUE STAMPS

HEJAZ

From Old Door at El Ashraf Barsbai in Shari el Ashrafiya, Cairo — D1

Serrate Roulette 13
1917, June 27 Typo. Unwmk.

LJ1	D1	20pa red	3.00	2.25
LJ2	D1	1pi blue	3.00	2.25
LJ3	D1	2pi magenta	3.00	2.25

a

b

Nos. LJ1-LJ3 Overprinted Type "a" in Black or Red

1921, Dec.

LJ4	D1	20pa red	20.00	3.00
a.		Double overprint, one at left	150.00	
b.		Ovpt. at left	27.50	22.50
LJ5	D1	1pi bl (R)	6.00	4.00
LJ6	D1	1pi bl, ovpt. at left	30.00	20.00
a.		Ovpt. at right	30.00	35.00
LJ7	D1	2pi magenta	11.00	8.00
a.		Double overprint, one at left	70.00	
b.		Ovpt. at left	30.00	

Nos. LJ1-LJ3 Overprinted Type "b" in Black

1922, Jan.

LJ8	D1	20pa red	25.00	30.00
a.		Ovpt. at left	40.00	
LJ9	D1	1pi blue	3.50	3.50
a.		Ovpt. at left	50.00	
LJ10	D1	2pi magenta	3.50	3.50
a.		Ovpt. at left	35.00	

Regular issue of 1922 Overprinted

Black Overprint

1923 *Perf. 11½*

LJ11	A7	½pi red	4.00	1.50
LJ12	A7	1pi dk bl	6.00	1.50
LJ13	A7	2pi orange	4.00	2.00

1924

Blue Overprint

LJ14	A7	½pi red	17.50	3.00
LJ15	A7	1pi dk bl	40.00	3.00
LJ16	A7	2pi orange	30.00	5.00

This overprint reads "Mustahaq" (Due).

Jedda Issues

Nos. LJ1-LJ3 Overprinted in Red or Blue (Overprint reads up in illustration)

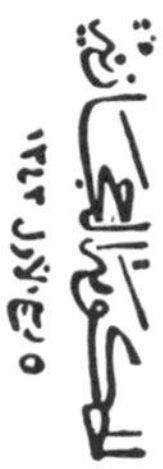

1925, Jan. *Serrate Roulette 13*

LJ17 D1 20pa red (R) 400.00 200.00
a. Ovpt. reading down 600.00 300.00
LJ18 D1 20pa red, ovpt. reading down (Bl) 500.00
LJ19 D1 1pi bl (R) 20.00 20.00
a. Ovpt. reading down 20.00 20.00
LJ20 D1 1pi bl (Bl) 27.50 15.00
a. Ovpt. reading down 75.00 90.00
LJ21 D1 2pi mag (Bl) 16.00 16.00
a. Ovpt. reading down 60.00 50.00

Nos. LJ1-LJ3 Overprinted in Blue or Red

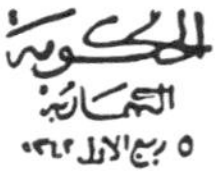

1925

LJ22 D1 20pa red (Bl) 350.00 300.00
a. Inverted overprint 350.00 250.00
LJ24 D1 1pi bl (R) 25.00 30.00
a. Inverted overprint 20.00 30.00
LJ25 D1 2pi mag (Bl) 20.00 20.00
a. Inverted overprint 30.00 50.00
b. Double overprint 400.00

No. LJ2 with this overprint in blue is bogus.

Regular Issues of 1922-24 Overprinted

a

and Handstamped

b

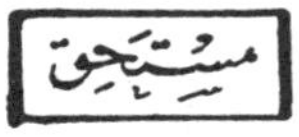

1925 *Perf. 11½*

LJ26 A7 ⅛pi red brn 20.00 5.00
LJ27 A7 ½pi red 27.50 7.50
LJ28 A7 1pi dk bl 20.00 6.00
LJ29 A7 1½pi violet 20.00 6.00
LJ30 A7 2pi orange 22.50 12.00
LJ31 A7 3pi ol brn 22.50 10.00
LJ32 A7 3pi dl red 50.00 15.00
LJ33 A7 5pi ol grn 22.50 8.00
LJ34 A7 10pi vio & dk brn 30.00 9.00
Nos. LJ26-LJ34 (9) 235.00 78.50

The printed overprint *(a)*, consisting of the three top lines of Arabic, was used alone for the first issue (Nos. LJ26a-LJ34a). The "postage due" box was so small and indistinct that its equivalent in larger characters was added by boxed handstamp *(b)* at bottom of each stamp for the second issue (Nos. LJ26-LJ34).

The handstamped overprint *(b)* is found double, inverted, etc.

Counterfeits exist of both overprint and handstamp.

Without Boxed Handstamp "b"

LJ26a A7 ⅛pi red brn 40.00
LJ27a A7 ½pi red 40.00
LJ28a A7 1pi dk bl 40.00
LJ29a A7 1½pi violet 40.00
LJ30a A7 2pi orange 40.00
LJ31a A7 3pi ol brn 40.00
LJ32a A7 3pi dl red 40.00
LJ33a A7 5pi ol grn 50.00
LJ34a A7 10pi vio & dk brn 50.00
Nos. LJ26a-LJ34a (9) 380.00

Regular Issue of 1922 Overprinted

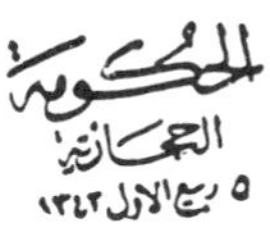

and Handstamped

LJ35 A7 ½pi red 150.00 75.00
LJ36 A7 1½pi violet 150.00 75.00
a. Ovpt. in red, boxed handstamp vio 1,500.
LJ37 A7 2pi orange 200.00 100.00
LJ38 A7 3pi ol brn 150.00 75.00
LJ39 A7 5pi ol grn 150.00 75.00
Nos. LJ35-LJ39 (5) 800.00 400.00

Counterfeits exist of Nos. LJ4-LJ39.

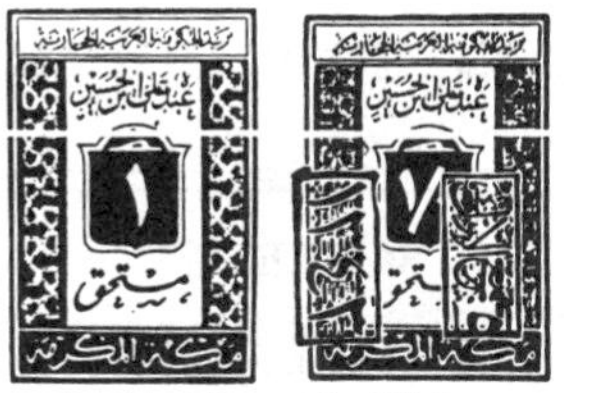

Arabic Numeral of Value
D2 D3

1925, May-June *Perf. 11½*

LJ40 D2 ½pi lt bl 3.00
LJ41 D2 1pi orange 3.00
LJ42 D2 2pi lt brn 3.00
LJ43 D2 3pi pink 3.00

Nos. LJ40-LJ43 exist imperforate. Impressions in colors other than issued are trial color proofs.

Black Overprint

1925

LJ44 D3 ½pi lt bl 3.00
LJ45 D3 1pi orange 3.00
LJ46 D3 2pi lt brn 3.00
LJ47 D3 3pi pink 4.00

Nos. LJ44-LJ47 exist imperforate.

Red Overprint

LJ48 D3 ½pi lt bl 4.00
LJ49 D3 1pi orange 4.00
LJ50 D3 2pi lt brn 4.00
LJ51 D3 3pi pink 4.00

Blue Overprint

LJ52 D3 ½pi lt bl 4.00
LJ53 D3 1pi orange 4.00
LJ54 D3 2pi lt brn 4.00
LJ55 D3 3pi pink 4.00
Nos. LJ40-LJ55 (16) 57.00

Nos. LJ44-LJ55 exist with either Jedda or Cairo overprints and the tablets normally read upward. Values are for Cairo overprints; Jedda overprints, especially the red and blue, sell for more.

Nejd

Handstamped in Blue, Red or Black

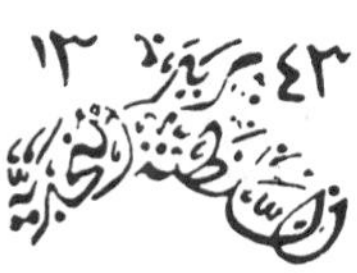

On Hejaz Postage Due Stamps
Typographed or Handstamped in Black

Perf. 11½

1925, April-June **Unwmk.**

J1 A7 ½pi red (Bl) 15.00 15.00
J2 A7 1pi lt bl (R) 15.00 15.00
a. 1pi dk bl (R) 25.00 25.00
J3 A7 2pi yel buff (Bl) 17.50 17.50
a. 2pi org (Bl) 25.00 25.00

Same, with Postage Due Overprint in Blue

J4 A7 ½pi red (Bl) *27.50*
J5 A7 1pi dk bl (R) *375.00*
J6 A7 2pi org (Bl) *110.00*

On Hejaz Stamps of 1922-24

Handstamped in Blue

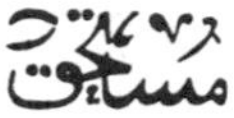

J7 A7 ½pi red (Bl & Bl) 10.00 10.00
J8 A7 3pi brn red (Bl & Bl) 10.00 10.00

Handstamped in Blue, Black or Violet

On Hejaz No. LJ9
Serrate Roulette 13½

J9 D1 1pi bl (V) 40.00 30.00

Same Overprint on Hejaz Stamps of 1924 with additional Handstamp in Black, Blue or Red

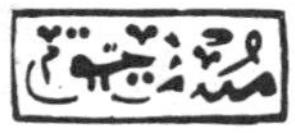

Perf. 11½

J10 A7 3pi brn red (Bl & Bk) 12.00 12.00
J11 A7 3pi brn red (Bk & Bl) 12.00 12.00

Same Handstamps on Hejaz Railway Tax Stamps

J12 R3 1pi bl (Bk & R) 10.00 10.00
J13 R3 2pi ocher (Bl & Bk) 10.00 10.00
J14 R3 5pi grn (Bk & R) 15.00 15.00
J15 R3 5pi grn (V & BK) 15.00 10.00

The second handstamp, which is struck on the lower part of the Postage Due Stamps, is the word Mustahaq (Due) in various forms.

No. J13 exists with second handstamp in blue.

Hejaz-Nejd

D1

1926 **Typo.** *Perf. 11*

J16 D1 ½pi carmine 1.65 75
J17 D1 2pi orange 1.65 75
J18 D1 6pi lt brn 1.65 75

Nos. J16-J18 exist with perf. 14, 14x11 and 11x14, and imperf. These sell for six times the values quoted.

Nos. J16-J18 in colors other than listed (both perf. and imperf.) are proofs.

Counterfeit note after No. 80 also applies to Nos. J16-J21.

Pan-Islamic Congress Issue
Postage Due Stamps of 1926 Handstamped like Regular Issue

J19 D1 ½pi carmine 3.25 3.25
J20 D1 2pi orange 3.25 3.25
J21 D1 6pi lt brn 3.25 3.25

D2

1927 *Perf. 11½*

J22 D2 1pi slate 12.50 50
a. Inscription reads "2 piastres" in upper right circle 110.00 110.00
J23 D2 2pi dk vio 3.75 50

There are two types of No. J22.

Saudi Arabia

Saudi Arabia No. 161 Handstamped in Black

1935

J24 A9 ½g dk car 150.00

Two types of overprint.

D3 D4

1937-39 **Unwmk.**

J25 D3 ½g org brn ('39) 10.50 1.50
J26 D3 1g lt bl 10.50 1.50
J27 D3 2g rose vio ('39) 16.00 3.00

Catalogue values for unused stamps in this section, from this point to the end of the section, are for Never Hinged items.

1961 **Litho.** *Perf. 13x13½*

J28 D4 1p purple 6.50 1.00
J29 D4 2p green 11.00 1.00
J30 D4 4p rose red 13.00 2.00

The use of Postage Due stamps ceased in 1963.

OFFICIAL STAMPS

Official stamps were normally used only on external correspondence.

O1 O2

1939 **Unwmk.** **Typo.** *Perf. 11, 11½*

O1 O1 3g dp ultra 4.00 1.50
O2 O1 5g red vio 5.00 2.00
O3 O1 20g brown 10.00 4.00
O4 O1 50g bl grn 20.00 8.00
O5 O1 100g ol grn 80.00 35.00
O6 O1 200g purple 60.00 25.00
Nos. O1-O6 (6) 179.00 75.50

Catalogue values for unused stamps in this section, from this point to the end of the section, are for Never Hinged items.

1961 **Litho.** *Perf. 13x13½*
Size: 18x22-22½mm.

O7 O2 1p black 1.25 20
O8 O2 2p dk grn 1.90 30
O9 O2 3p bister 2.50 40
O10 O2 4p dk bl 3.00 50
O11 O2 5p rose red 3.75 60
O12 O2 10p maroon 6.25 2.00
O13 O2 20p vio bl 11.00 3.50

O14	O2	50p dl brn	30.00	10.00
O15	O2	100p dl grn	55.00	18.00
		Nos. O7-O15 (9)	114.65	35.50

Nos. O11-O15 exist imperf.

1964-65 Wmk. 337 *Perf. 13½x13*
Size: 21x26mm.

O16	O2	1p black	1.00	40
O17	O2	2p grn ('65)	2.00	80
O18	O2	3p bister	7.00	2.75
O19	O2	4p dk bl	5.00	2.00
O20	O2	5p rose red	6.00	1.25
		Nos. O16-O20 (5)	21.00	7.20

1965-70 Wmk. 337 Typo. *Perf. 11*

O21	O2	1p dk brn	4.00	1.50
O22	O2	2p green	4.00	1.50
O23	O2	3p bister	4.00	1.50
O24	O2	4p dk bl	4.00	1.50
O25	O2	5p dp org	7.50	2.00
O26	O2	6p red lil	7.50	2.00
O27	O2	7p emerald	7.50	2.00
O28	O2	8p car rose	7.50	2.00
O29	O2	9p red	30.00	
O30	O2	10p red brn	30.00	2.00
O31	O2	11p pale grn	*60.00*	
O32	O2	12p violet	*250.00*	
O33	O2	13p blue	10.00	3.00
O34	O2	14p purple	10.00	3.00
O35	O2	15p orange	*100.00*	1.00
O36	O2	16p black	*100.00*	
a.		"19" instead of "16"	*500.00*	
O37	O2	17p gray grn	*100.00*	
O38	O2	18p yellow	*100.00*	
O39	O2	19p dp red lil	*100.00*	
O39A	O2	20p lt bl grn		
O40	O2	23p ultra	*250.00*	
O41	O2	24p yel grn	*100.00*	
O42	O2	26p bister	*100.00*	
O43	O2	27p pale lil	*100.00*	
O44	O2	31p pale sal	*150.00*	
O45	O2	33p yel grn	*100.00*	
O46	O2	50p ol bis	*400.00*	
O47	O2	100p ol gray ('70)	*900.00*	
		Nos. O21-O39,O40-O47 (27)	*3,036.*	

Nos. O21-O30 and O33-O34 were released to the philatelic trade in 1964. Nos. O21-O47 were printed from new plates; lines of the design are heavier. The numerals have been enlarged and the P's are smaller. Head of "P" 2mm. wide on 1964-65 issue, 1 mm. wide on 1965-70 issue.

O3

Wmk. 361, 337 (7p, 8p, 9p, 11p)
1970-72 Litho. *Perf. 13½x14*

O48	O3	1p red brn	3.00	1.00
O49	O3	2p dp grn	3.00	1.00
O50	O3	3p rose red	4.00	1.50
O51	O3	4p brt bl	5.00	2.00
O52	O3	5p brick red	5.00	2.00
O53	O3	6p orange	5.00	2.00
a.		Wmk. 337	*200.00*	*50.00*
O54	O3	7p dp sal	*90.00*	
O55	O3	8p violet		
O56	O3	9p dk bl grn		
O57	O3	10p blue	7.00	3.00
O58	O3	11p ol grn		
O58A	O3	12p blk brn		
O59	O3	20p gray vio	15.00	5.00
a.		Wmk. 337	*200.00*	*100.00*
O59B	O3	23p ocher ('72)	*425.00*	
O60	O3	31p dp plum	*50.00*	*20.00*
O61	O3	50p lt brn		
O62	O3	100p green		

Use of official stamps ceased in 1974.

NEWSPAPER STAMPS

Nos. 8, 9 and 14 with Additional Overprint in Black

1925 Unwmk. *Perf. 11½*

P1	A7	⅛pi red brn (Bk)	*2,000.*	*2,000.*
P2	A7	⅛pi red brn (V)	*1,500.*	*1,000.*
P3	A7	½pi red (V)	*3,000.*	*2,000.*

Overprint reads: "Matbu'a" (Newspaper), but these stamps were normally used for regular postage. Counterfeits exist.

POSTAL TAX STAMPS

PT1

1934, June Unwmk. *Perf. 11½*

RA1	PT1	⅛g scarlet	*150.00*	5.00

No. RA1 collected a "war tax" to aid wounded of the 1934 Saudi-Yemen war.

General Hospital, Mecca PT2

1936, Oct.
Size: 37x20mm

RA2	PT2	⅛g scarlet	*500.00*	10.00

Nos. RA2-RA8 raised funds for public health purposes.

Type of 1936, Redrawn

1937-42
Size: 30½x18mm

RA3	PT2	⅛g scarlet	45.00	1.00
a.		⅛g rose ('39)	*100.00*	2.00
b.		⅛g rose car, perf. 11 ('42)	*150.00*	*7.50*

General Hospital, Mecca — PT3

1943 Typo. *Perf. 11½, 11*
Grayish Paper

RA4	PT3	⅛g car rose	*25.00*	10
a.		⅛g scar	*40.00*	15

Type of 1943, Redrawn

1948-53 Litho. *Perf. 10*

RA5	PT3	⅛g rose brn ('53)	*15.00*	20
a.		⅛g car, perf. 10 ('53)		
b.		⅛g rose, perf. 10 ('53)		
c.		As RA5, perf. 11x10	30.00	20

Catalogue values for unused stamps in this section, from this point to the end of the section, are for Never Hinged items.

1950 *Rouletted*

RA6	PT3	⅛g red brown	6.00	10
a.		⅛g rose	8.00	20
b.		⅛g carmine	10.00	25

All lines in lithographed design considerably finer; some shading in center eliminated.

Type of 1943

1955-56 Photo. *Perf. 11*

RA7	PT3	⅛g rose car	4.00	10
RA8	PT3	¼g car rose ('56)	3.00	10

Nos. RA4-RA8 exist imperf., part perf. and in various shades.

The tax on postal matter was discontinued in May, 1964.

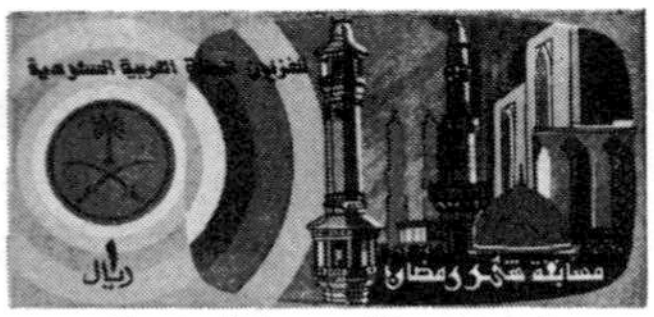
Coat of Arms, Waves and View — PT4

Wmk. 361
1974, Oct. Litho. *Perf. 14*

RA9	PT4	1r bl & multi	*70.00*	

Obligatory on all mailed entries in a government television contest during month of Ramadan in 1974 and 1975. The tax aided a benevolent society.

SCHLESWIG

LOCATION — In the northern part of the former Schleswig-Holstein Province, in northern Germany.

Schleswig was divided into North and South Schleswig after the Versailles Treaty, and plebiscites were held in 1920. North Schleswig (Zone 1) voted to join Denmark, South Schleswig to stay German.

100 Pfennig = 1 Mark
100 Ore = 1 Krone

Schleswig stamps can be mounted in Scott's Germany Part II Album.

Plebiscite Issue

Arms A11

View of Schleswig A12

Wmk. 114 - Multiple Crosses

Perf. 14x15
1920, Jan. 25 Typo. Wmk. 114

1	A11	2½pf gray	8	8
2	A11	5pf green	8	8
3	A11	7½pf yel brn	12	10
4	A11	10pf dp rose	15	12
5	A11	15pf red vio	8	8
6	A11	20pf dp bl	18	14
7	A11	25pf orange	30	24
8	A11	35pf brown	40	35
9	A11	40pf violet	24	20
10	A11	75pf grnsh bl	40	35
11	A12	1m dk brn	40	35
12	A12	2m dp bl	55	52
13	A12	5m green	85	70
14	A12	10m red	1.50	1.25
		Nos. 1-14 (14)	5.33	4.56

The colored portions of type A11 are white, and the white portions are colored, on Nos. 7-10.

Types of 1920 Overprinted in Blue **1. ZONE**

1920, May 20

15	A11	1o dk gray	8	*65*
16	A11	5o green	8	*32*
17	A11	7o yel brn	8	*50*
18	A11	10o rose red	10	*65*
19	A11	15o lil rose	10	*65*
20	A11	20o dk bl	8	*85*
21	A11	25o orange	20	*3.00*
22	A11	35o brown	85	*6.50*
23	A11	40o violet	30	*2.25*
24	A11	75o grnsh bl	40	*4.00*
25	A12	1k dk brn	55	*4.00*
26	A12	2k dp bl	4.00	*22.50*
27	A12	5k green	2.75	*22.50*
28	A12	10k red	6.00	*45.00*
		Nos. 15-28 (14)	15.57	

OFFICIAL STAMPS

Nos. 1-14 Overprinted **C·I·S**

1920 Wmk. 114 *Perf. 14x15*

O1	A11	2½pf gray	52.50	75.00
O2	A11	5pf green	52.50	80.00
O3	A11	7½pf yel brn	52.50	75.00
O4	A11	10pf dp rose	50.00	80.00
O5	A11	15pf red vio	32.50	42.50
O6	A11	20pf dp bl	47.50	52.50
O7	A11	25pf orange	105.00	115.00
a.		Inverted overprint	*1,250.*	
O8	A11	35pf brown	105.00	125.00
O9	A11	40pf violet	82.50	75.00
O10	A11	75pf grnsh bl	90.00	180.00
O11	A12	1m dk brn	90.00	180.00
O12	A12	2m dp bl	145.00	190.00
O13	A12	5m green	215.00	315.00
O14	A12	10m red	380.00	425.00
		Nos. O1-O14 (14)	1,500.	2,010.

The letters "C.I.S." are the initials of "Commission Interalliée Slesvig," under whose auspices the plebiscites took place.

Counterfeit overprints exist.

SENEGAL

LOCATION — West coast of Africa, bordering on the Atlantic Ocean.
GOVT. — Republic
AREA — 76,000 sq. mi.
POP. — 6,300,000 (est. 1984)
CAPITAL — Dakar

The former French colony of Senegal became part of French West Africa in 1943. The Republic of Senegal was established November 25, 1958. From April 4, 1959, to June 20, 1960, the Republic of Senegal and the Sudanese Republic together formed the Mali Federation. After its breakup, Senegal resumed issuing its own stamps in 1960.

100 Centimes = 1 Franc

Catalogue values for unused stamps in this country are for Never Hinged items, beginning with Scott 195 in the regular postage section, Scott B16 in the in the semi-postal section, Scott C26 in the airpost section, Scott CB2 in the airpost semi-postal section, Scott J32 in the postage due section, and Scott O1 in the official section.

French Colonies Nos. 48, 49, 51, 52, 55, type A9, Surcharged:

5 5 5 5 5
a b c d e

1887 Unwmk. *Perf. 14x13½*
Black Surcharge

1	(a)	5c on 20c red, *grn*	90.00	90.00
a		Double surcharge		
2	(b)	5c on 20c red, *grn*	140.00	140.00
3	(c)	5c on 20c red, *grn*	600.00	600.00
4	(d)	5c on 20c red, *grn*	125.00	120.00
5	(e)	5c on 20c red, *grn*	225.00	225.00
6	(a)	5c on 30c brn, *bis*	175.00	175.00
7	(b)	5c on 30c brn, *bis*	700.00	700.00
8	(d)	5c on 30c brn, *bis*	200.00	200.00

10 10 10 10
f g h i

10 10 10 10
j k l m

9	(f)	10c on 4c cl, *lav*	65.00	65.00
10	(g)	10c on 4c cl, *lav*	90.00	90.00
11	(h)	10c on 4c cl, *lav*	35.00	35.00

12	(i)	10c on 4c cl, *lav*	250.00	250.00
a		"1" without top stroke		
13	(f)	10c on 20c red, *grn*	400.00	400.00
14	(g)	10c on 20c red, *grn*	400.00	400.00
15	(h)	10c on 20c red, *grn*	350.00	350.00
16	(i)	10c on 20c red, *grn*	*2,250.*	*2,250.*
17	(j)	10c on 20c red, *grn*	400.00	400.00
18	(k)	10c on 20c red, *grn*	400.00	400.00
19	(l)	10c on 20c red, *grn*	400.00	400.00
20	(m)	10c on 20c red, *grn*	400.00	400.00

15 15 15 15 15
n o p q r

15 15 15 15
s t u v

15
w

21	(n)	15c on 20c red, *grn*	50.00	50.00
22	(o)	15c on 20c red, *grn*	40.00	40.00
23	(p)	15c on 20c red, *grn*	35.00	35.00
24	(q)	15c on 20c red, *grn*	62.50	62.50
25	(r)	15c on 20c red, *grn*	40.00	40.00
26	(s)	15c on 20c red, *grn*	40.00	40.00
27	(t)	15c on 20c red, *grn*	120.00	120.00
28	(u)	15c on 20c red, *grn*	32.50	32.50
29	(v)	15c on 20c red, *grn*	45.00	45.00
30	(w)	15c on 20c red, *grn*	200.00	200.00

Counterfeits exist of Nos. 1-34.

Surcharged:

x y

1892

Black Surcharge

31	A9	75c on 15c bl	225.00	90.00
32	A9	1fr on 5c grn, *grnsh*	225.00	120.00

"SENEGAL" in Red

33	A9	75c on 15c bl	*6,500.*	*2,750.*
34	A9	1fr on 5c grn, *grnsh*	*3,250.*	*700.00*

Navigation and Commerce — A24

1892-1900 **Typo.**

Name of Colony in Blue or Carmine

35	A24	1c blk, *lil bl*	25	25
36	A24	2c brn, *buff*	70	65
37	A24	4c cl, *lav*	60	50
38	A24	5c grn, *grnsh*	60	50
39	A24	5c yel grn ('00)	50	35
40	A24	10c blk, *lav*	2.75	2.50
41	A24	10c red ('00)	1.40	35
42	A24	15c bl, quadrille paper	2.75	60
43	A24	15c gray ('00)	1.20	80
44	A24	20c red, *grn*	4.00	2.50
45	A24	25c blk, *rose*	6.00	2.50
46	A24	25c bl ('00)	15.00	12.00
47	A24	30c brn, *bis*	6.00	2.50
48	A24	40c red, *straw*	9.00	8.00
49	A24	50c car, *rose*	15.00	11.00
50	A24	50c brn, *az* ('00)	18.00	16.00
51	A24	75c vio, *org*	7.00	6.25
52	A24	1fr brnz grn, *straw*	7.00	6.25
		Nos. 35-52 (18)	97.75	73.50

Stamps of 1892 Surcharged:

5 10

1903

53	A24	5c on 40c red, *straw*	5.00	5.00
54	A24	10c on 50c car, *rose*	7.00	7.00
55	A24	10c on 75c vio, *org*	7.00	7.00
56	A24	10c on 1fr brnz grn, *straw*	32.50	30.00

General Louis Faidherbe A25

Oil Palms — A26

Dr. Noel Eugene Ballay A27

1906 **Typo.**

"SÉNÉGAL" in Red or Blue

57	A25	1c slate	25	25
a		"SENEGAL" omitted	40.00	40.00
58	A25	2c choc (R)	35	35
58A	A25	2c choc (Bl)	65	65
59	A25	4c choc, *gray bl*	50	50
60	A25	5c green	60	25
61	A25	10c car (Bl)	3.00	25
a		"SENEGAL" omitted	150.00	150.00
62	A25	15c violet	2.50	1.60
63	A26	20c blk, *az*	3.00	1.60
64	A26	25c bl, *pnksh*	70	60
65	A26	30c choc, *pnksh*	2.50	2.00
66	A26	35c blk, *yellow*	9.00	90
67	A26	40c car, *az* (Bl)	3.75	3.00
67A	A26	45c choc, *grnsh*	8.00	6.00
68	A26	50c dp vio	3.25	3.00
69	A26	75c bl, *org*	2.50	1.60
70	A27	1fr blk, *az*	11.00	8.00
71	A27	2fr bl, *pink*	15.00	12.50
72	A27	5fr car, *straw* (Bl)	30.00	25.00
		Nos. 57-72 (18)	96.55	68.05

Stamps of 1892-1900 Surcharged in Carmine or Black

05 10

1912

73	A24	5c on 15c gray (C)	35	35
74	A24	5c on 20c red, *grn*	55	55
75	A24	5c on 30c brn, *bis* (C)	55	55
76	A24	10c on 40c red, *straw*	55	55
77	A24	10c on 50c car, *rose*	1.50	1.50
78	A24	10c on 75c vio, *org*	3.00	3.00
		Nos. 73-78 (6)	6.50	6.50

Two spacings between the surcharged numerals found on Nos. 73 to 78.

Senegalese Preparing Food — A28

1914-33 **Typo.**

79	A28	1c ol brn & vio	5	5
80	A28	2c blk & bl	5	5
81	A28	4c gray & brn	5	5
82	A28	5c yel grn & bl grn	10	10
83	A28	5c blk & rose ('22)	5	5
84	A28	10c org red & rose	10	10
85	A28	10c yel grn & bl grn ('22)	12	12
86	A28	10c red brn & bl ('25)	5	5
87	A28	15c red org & brn vio ('17)	5	5
88	A28	20c choc & blk	5	5
89	A28	20c grn & bl grn ('26)	5	5
90	A28	20c db & lt bl ('27)	12	12
91	A28	25c ultra & bl	10	10
92	A28	25c red & blk ('22)	5	5
93	A28	30c blk & rose	10	5
94	A28	30c red org & rose ('22)	12	12
95	A28	30c gray & bl ('26)	15	15
96	A28	30c dl grn & dp grn ('28)	20	12
97	A28	35c org & vio	5	5
98	A28	40c vio & grn	35	10
99	A28	45c bl & ol brn	55	55
100	A28	45c rose & bl ('22)	15	15
101	A28	45c rose & ver ('25)	15	15
102	A28	45c ol brn & org ('28)	1.20	42
103	A28	50c vio brn & bl	35	12
104	A28	50c ultra & bl ('22)	70	65
105	A28	50c red org & grn ('26)	15	12
106	A28	60c vio, *pnksh* ('26)	15	15
107	A28	65c rose red & dp grn ('28)	50	50
108	A28	75c gray & rose	40	28
109	A28	75c dk bl & lt bl ('25)	25	15
110	A28	75c rose & gray bl ('26)	60	20
111	A28	90c brn red & rose ('30)	2.00	1.90
112	A28	1fr vio & blk	45	20
113	A28	1fr bl ('26)	25	15
114	A28	1fr blk & gray bl ('26)	50	15
115	A28	1.10fr bl grn & blk ('28)	1.20	1.20
116	A28	1.25fr dp grn & dp org ('33)	35	32
117	A28	1.50fr dk bl & bl ('30)	80	80
118	A28	1.75fr dk brn & Prus bl ('33)	3.00	35
119	A28	2fr car & bl	80	55
120	A28	2fr lt bl & brn ('22)	90	20
121	A28	3fr red vio ('30)	1.90	75
122	A28	5fr grn & vio	1.90	40
		Nos. 79-122 (44)	21.16	11.99

Nos. 79, 82, 84 and 97 are on both ordinary and chalky paper.

Stamps and Type of 1914 Surcharged:

60 60

1922-25

123	A28	60c on 75c vio, *pnksh*	35	35
124	A28	65c on 15c red org & dl vio ('25)	55	55
125	A28	85c on 15c red org & dl vio ('25)	55	55
126	A28	85c on 75c gray & rose ('25)	60	60

No. 87 Surcharged in Various Colors

0,01 0,01

1922

127	A28	1c on 15c (Bk)	15	15
128	A28	2c on 15c (Bl)	15	15
129	A28	4c on 15c (G)	15	15
130	A28	5c on 15c (R)	15	15
		Nos. 123-130 (8)	2.65	2.65

Stamps and Type of 1914 Surcharged with New Value and Bars in Black or Red

1924-27

131	A28	25c on 5fr grn & vio	20	20
132	A28	90c on 75c brn red & cer ('27)	40	35
a		Double surcharge	40.00	40.00
133	A28	1.25fr on 1fr bl & lt bl (R) ('26)	20	20
134	A28	1.50fr on 1fr dk bl & ultra ('27)	30	25
135	A28	3fr on 5fr mag & ol brn ('27)	70	35
136	A28	10fr on 5fr dk bl & red org ('27)	2.50	80
137	A28	20fr on 5fr vio & ol bis ('27)	3.50	2.25
		Nos. 131-137 (7)	7.80	4.40

Colonial Exposition Issue

Common Design Types

Name of Country Typographed in Black

1931 **Engr.** ***Perf. 12½***

138	CD70	40c dp grn	1.20	1.20
139	CD71	50c violet	1.20	1.20
140	CD72	90c red org	1.20	1.20
a		"SENEGAL" double	50.00	
141	CD73	1.50fr dl bl	1.20	1.20

Faidherbe Bridge, St. Louis A29

Diourbel Mosque A30

1935-40 ***Perf. 12½x12***

142	A29	1c vio bl	5	5
143	A29	2c brown	5	5
144	A29	3c vio ('40)	5	5
145	A29	4c gray bl	5	5
146	A29	5c org red	5	5
147	A29	10c violet	5	5
148	A29	15c black	5	5
149	A29	20c dk car	5	5
150	A29	25c blk brn	5	5
151	A29	30c green	5	5
152	A29	40c rose lake	8	8
153	A29	45c dk bl grn	8	8
154	A30	50c red org	5	5
155	A30	60c vio ('40)	12	12
156	A30	65c dk vio	12	12
157	A30	70c red brn ('40)	20	20
158	A30	75c brown	25	25
159	A30	90c rose car	80	65
160	A30	1fr violet	3.25	80
161	A30	1.25fr redsh brn	40	25
162	A30	1.25fr rose car ('39)	35	35
163	A30	1.40fr dk bl grn ('40)	20	20
164	A30	1.50fr dk blue	12	12
165	A30	1.60fr pck bl ('40)	25	25
166	A30	1.75fr dk bl grn	12	12
167	A30	2fr blue	12	12
168	A30	3fr green	12	12
169	A30	5fr blk brn	30	20
170	A30	10fr rose lake	40	30
171	A30	20fr grnsh sl	40	30
		Nos. 142-171 (30)	8.23	5.18

Nos. 143, 148 and 156 surcharged with new values are listed under French West Africa.

Paris International Exposition Issue

Common Design Types

1937 ***Perf. 13***

172	CD74	20c dp vio	35	35
173	CD75	30c dk grn	35	35
174	CD76	40c car rose	35	35
175	CD77	50c dk brn	42	42
176	CD78	90c red	42	42
177	CD79	1.50fr ultra	65	65
		Nos. 172-177 (6)	2.54	2.54

Common Design Types pictured in section at front of book

Colonial Arts Exhibition Issue

Souvenir Sheet

Common Design Type

1937 **Unwmk.** ***Imperf.***

178	CD76	3fr rose vio	1.90	1.90

Senegalese Woman — A31

1938-40 ***Perf. 12x12½, 12½x12***

179	A31	35c green	25	16
180	A31	55c chocolate	25	20
181	A31	80c violet	40	16
182	A31	90c lt rose vio ('39)	14	14
183	A31	1fr car lake	80	42
184	A31	1fr cop brn ('40)	12	12
185	A31	1.75fr ultra	25	16
186	A31	2.25fr ultra ('39)	25	25
187	A31	2.50fr blk ('40)	38	38
		Nos. 179-187 (9)	2.84	1.99

Caillié Issue
Common Design Type

1939 **Engr.** ***Perf. 12½x12***
188 CD81 90c org brn & org 28 28
189 CD81 2fr brt vio 42 42
190 CD81 2.25fr ultra & dk bl 42 42

For No. 188 surcharged 20fr and 50fr, see French West Africa.

New York World's Fair Issue
Common Design Type

1939 ***Perf. 12½x12***
191 CD82 1.25fr car lake 30 30
192 CD82 2.25fr ultra 30 30

Diourbel Mosque and Marshal Pétain A32

1941 **Engr.**
193 A32 1fr green 22
194 A32 2.50fr blue 22

Nos. 193-194 were issued by the Vichy government, but it is doubtful whether they were placed on sale in Senegal.
Stamps of types A29, A30 and A31, without "RF", were issued in 1943 by the Vichy Government, but were not placed on sale in the colony.

Catalogue values for unused stamps in this section, from this point to the end of the section, are for Never Hinged items.

Republic

Roan Antelope — A33

Animals: 10fr, Savannah buffalo (horiz.). 15fr, Wart hog. 20fr, Giant eland. 25fr, Bushbuck (horiz.). 85fr, Defassa waterbuck.

1960 **Unwmk.** **Engr.** ***Perf. 13***
195 A33 5fr brn, grn & cl 10 5
196 A33 10fr grn & brn 16 8
197 A33 15fr blk, cl & org brn 20 10
198 A33 20fr brn, grn, ocher & sal 25 10
199 A33 25fr brn, lt grn & org 35 16
200 A33 85fr brn, grn, ol & bis 1.10 50
Nos. 195-200 (6) 2.16 99

Imperforates
Most Senegal stamps from 1960 onward exist imperforate in issued and trial colors, and also in small presentation sheets in issued colors.

Allegory of Independent State — A34

1961, Apr. 4
201 A34 25fr bl, choc & grn 22 14

Independence Day, Apr. 4.

Wrestling A35

Designs: 1fr, Pirogues racing. 2fr, Horse race. 30fr, Male tribal dance. 45fr, Lion game.

1961, Sept. 30 ***Perf. 13***
202 A35 50c ol, bl & choc 5 5
203 A35 1fr grn, bl & mar 5 5
204 A35 2fr ultra, bis & sep 5 5
205 A35 30fr car & cl 30 18
206 A35 45fr ind & brn org 40 25
Nos. 202-206 (5) 85 58

UN Headquarters, New York and Flag — A36

1962, Jan. 6 **Engr.** ***Perf. 13***
207 A36 10fr grn, ocher & car 14 10
208 A36 30fr car, ocher & grn 30 20
209 A36 85fr grn, ocher & car 70 42

1st anniv. of Senegal's admission to the United Nations, Sept. 28, 1960.

Map of Africa, ITU Emblem and Man with Telephone A37

1962, Jan. 22 **Photo.** ***Perf. 12½x12***
210 A37 25fr blk, grn, red & ocher 25 20

Meeting of the Commission for the Africa Plan of the ITU, Dakar.

African and Malgache Union Issue
Common Design Type

1962, Sept. 8 **Unwmk.**
211 CD110 30fr grn, bluish grn, red & gold 40 35

Boxing — A38

Charaxes Varanes — A40

UPU Monument, Bern — A39

Designs: 15fr, Diving (horiz.). 20fr, High jump (horiz.). 25fr, Soccer. 30fr, Basketball. 85fr, Running.

1963, Apr. 11 **Engr.** ***Perf. 13***
Athletes in Dark Brown
212 A38 10fr ver & emer 14 8
213 A38 15fr dk bl & bis 16 10
214 A38 20fr ver & dk bl 22 14
215 A38 25fr grn & dk bl 25 16
216 A38 30fr ver & grn 35 20
217 A38 85fr vio bl 90 60
Nos. 212-217 (6) 2.02 1.28

Friendship Games, Dakar, Apr. 11-21.

1963, June 14 **Unwmk.** ***Perf. 13***
218 A39 10fr grn & ver 16 14
219 A39 15fr dk bl & red brn 20 16
220 A39 30fr red brn & dk bl 35 22

2nd anniv. of Senegal's admission to the UPU.

1963, July 20 **Photo.** ***Perf. 12½x13***
Butterflies in Natural Colors

Butterflies: 45fr, Papilio nireus. 50fr, Colotis danae. 85fr, Epiphora bauhiniae. 100fr, Junonia hierta. 500fr, Danaus chrysippus.

221 A40 30fr bl gray & blk 40 16
222 A40 45fr org & blk 55 22
223 A40 50fr brt yel & blk 65 30
224 A40 85fr red & blk 1.00 55
225 A40 100fr bl & blk 1.10 65
226 A40 500fr emer & blk 4.25 2.25
Nos. 221-226 (6) 7.95 4.13

Prof. Gaston Berger (1896-1960), Philosopher, and Owl — A41

1963, Nov. 13 ***Perf. 12½x12***
227 A41 25fr multi 22 14

Scales, Globe, Flag and UNESCO Emblem A42

1963, Dec. 10
228 A42 60fr multi 55 30

15th anniv. of the Universal Declaration of Human Rights.

Flag, Mother and Child — A43

1963, Dec. 21 ***Perf. 12x12½***
229 A43 25fr multi 30 22

Issued for the Senegalese Red Cross.

Dredging of Titanium-bearing Sand — A44

Designs: 10fr, Titanium extraction works. 15fr, Cement works at Rufisque. 20fr, Phosphate quarry at Pallo. 25fr, Extraction of phosphate ore at Taiba. 85fr, Mineral dock, Dakar.

1964, July 4 **Engr.** ***Perf. 13***
230 A44 5fr grnsh bl, car & dk brn 7 5
231 A44 10fr ocher, grn & ind 10 5
232 A44 15fr dk bl, brt grn & dk brn 14 7
233 A44 20fr ultra, ol & pur 16 10
234 A44 25fr dk bl, yel & blk 25 5
235 A44 85fr bl, red & brn 80 42
Nos. 230-235 (6) 1.52 74

Cooperation Issue
Common Design Type

1964, Nov. 7 **Engr.** ***Perf. 13***
236 CD119 100fr dk grn, dk brn & car 90 60

St. Theresa's Church, Dakar A45

Designs: 10fr, Mosque, Touba. 15fr, Mosque, Dakar (vert.).

1964, Nov. 28 **Unwmk.** ***Perf. 13***
237 A45 5fr bl, grn & red brn 8 7
238 A45 10fr dk bl, ocher & blk 12 8
239 A45 15fr brn, bl & sl grn 16 12

Leprosy Examination — A46

Leprosarium, Peycouk Village — A47

1965, Jan. 30 **Engr.** ***Perf. 13***
240 A46 20fr brn red, grn & blk 22 20
241 A47 65fr org, dk bl & grn 65 40

Issued to publicize the fight against leprosy.

Upper Casamance Region A48

Views: 30fr, Sangalkam. 45fr, Forest along Senegal River.

1965, Feb. 27 **Unwmk.** ***Perf. 13***
Size: 36x22mm
242 A48 25fr red brn, sl bl & grn 22 14
243 A48 30fr ind & lt brn 25 14
244 A48 45fr yel grn, red brn & dk brn 40 22

Abdoulaye Seck A49

Berthon-Ader Telephone A51

General Post Office, Dakar A50

1965, Apr. 24 **Unwmk.** ***Perf. 13***
245 A49 10fr dk brn & blk 10 7
246 A50 15fr brn & dk sl grn 16 9

1965, May 17 **Engr.**

Designs: 60fr, Cable laying ship "Alsace." 85fr, Picard's cable relay for submarine telegraph.

247 A51 50fr bl grn & org brn 50 30
248 A51 60fr mag & dk bl 60 38
249 A51 85fr ver, bl & red brn 90 50

ITU, centenary.

Plowing with Ox Team A52

Designs: 60fr, Harvesting millet (vert.). 85fr, Men working in rice field.

1965, July 3 **Unwmk.** ***Perf. 13***

250 A52 25fr dk ol grn, brn & pur 25 16
251 A52 60fr ind, sl grn & dk brn 55 22
252 A52 85fr dp car, sl grn & brt grn 80 38

Gorée Sailboat A53 — Cashew A54

Designs: 20fr, Large Seumbediou canoe. 30fr, Fadiouth one-man canoe. 45fr, One-man canoe on Senegal River.

1965, Aug. 7 **Photo.** ***Perf. 12½x13***

253 A53 10fr multi 10 7
254 A53 20fr multi 16 10
255 A53 30fr multi 30 16
256 A53 45fr multi 42 25

1965 **Photo.** ***Perf. 12½***

257 A54 10fr shown 14 7
258 A54 15fr Papaya 16 10
259 A54 20fr Mango 20 12
260 A54 30fr Peanuts 30 8

Dates of issue: Nov. 6, 10fr, 15fr, 20fr. Dec. 18, 30fr.

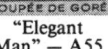

"Elegant Man" — A55 — Drummer and Map of Africa — A56

Dolls of Gorée: 2fr, "Elegant Woman." 3fr, Woman peddling fruit. 4fr, Woman pounding grain.

1966, Jan. 22 **Engr.** ***Perf. 13***

261 A55 1fr brn, rose car & ultra 5 5
262 A55 2fr brn, bl & org 5 5
263 A55 3fr brn, red & bl 5 5
264 A55 4fr brn, lil & emer 8 8

1966

Designs: 15fr, Sculpture; mother and child. No. 267, Music; stringed instrument. 75fr, Dance; carved antelope headpiece (Bambara). 90fr, Ideogram.

265 A56 15fr dk red brn, bl & ocher 14 14
266 A56 30fr brn, red & grn 30 18
267 A56 30fr dk red brn, bl & yel 30 18
268 A56 75fr dk red brn, bl & blk 70 42
269 A56 90fr dk red brn, org & sl grn 90 55
a Souv. sheet of 4, #265, 267-269 2.50 2.50
Nos. 265-269 (5) 2.34 1.47

Intl. Negro Arts Festival, Dakar, Apr. 1-24.

Dates of issue: No. 266, Feb. 5. Others, Apr. 2. See No. 364.

Tuna A57

Fish: 30fr, Merou. 50fr, Girella. 100fr, Parrot fish.

1966, Feb. 26 **Photo.** ***Perf. 12½x13***

270 A57 20fr pale grn & multi 22 14
271 A57 30fr bl & multi 35 16
272 A57 50fr pink & multi 55 30
273 A57 100fr buff & multi 1.10 50

Arms of Senegal — A58 — Mexican Poppy — A59

1966, July 2 **Litho.** ***Perf. 13x12½***

274 A58 30fr multi 25 8

1966, Nov. 19 **Photo.** ***Perf. 11½***

Flowers: 55fr, Mimosa. 60fr, Haemanthus. 90fr, Baobab.

Flowers in Natural Colors

275 A59 45fr dp brn & brt grn 42 18
276 A59 55fr yel grn & brt pur 50 20
277 A59 60fr grnsh bl 60 22
278 A59 90fr dp bl & lt ultra 80 38

Harbor, Gorée Island A60

Designs: 25fr, S.S. France in roadstead, Dakar and seagulls. 30fr, Hotel and tourist village, N'Gor. 50fr, Hotel and bay, N'Gor.

1966, Dec. 25 **Engr.** ***Perf. 13***

279 A60 20fr mar & vio bl 20 14
280 A60 25fr red, grn & blk 22 14
281 A60 30fr dk red & dp bl 25 16
282 A60 50fr brn, sl grn & emer 45 20

Laying Urban Water Pipes — A61

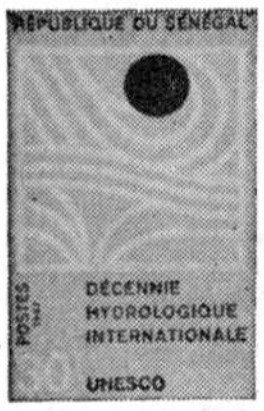

Symbolic Water Cycle — A62

Designs: 20fr, Cattle at water trough. 50fr, Village well.

1967, Mar. 25 **Engr.** ***Perf. 13***

283 A61 10fr org brn, grn & dk bl 14 10
284 A61 20fr grn, brt bl & org brn 25 20

Typo.

Perf. 13x14

285 A62 30fr sky bl, blk & org 35 10

Engr.

Perf. 13

286 A62 50fr brn red, brt bl & bis 55 20

Intl. Hydrological Decade (UNESCO), 1965-74.

Lions Emblem A63

1967, May 27 **Photo.** ***Perf. 12½x13***

287 A63 30fr lt ultra & multi 30 16

50th anniversary of Lions International.

Blaise Diagne A64

1967, June 10 **Engr.** ***Perf. 13***

288 A64 30fr ocher, sl grn & dk red brn 30 20

Blaise Diagne (1872-1934), member of French Chamber of Deputies and Colonial Minister.

City Hall and Arms, Dakar A65

1967, June 10

289 A65 90fr bl, dk grn & blk 80 38

Eagle and Antelope Carvings — A66

Design: 150fr, Flags, maple leaf and EXPO '67 emblem.

1967, Sept. 2 **Photo.** ***Perf. 13x12½***

290 A66 90fr red & blk 60 30
291 A66 150fr red & multi 1.00 50

EXPO '67 Intl. Exhib., Montreal, Apr. 28-Oct. 27.

International Tourist Year Emblem — A67

Tourist Photographing Hippopotamus and Siminti Hotel — A68

1967, Oct. 7 **Typo.** ***Perf. 14x13***

292 A67 50fr blk & bl 55 38

Perf. 13

Engr.

293 A68 100fr blk, sl grn & ocher 1.10 50

International Tourist Year.

Monetary Union Issue

Common Design Type

1967, Nov. 4 **Engr.** ***Perf. 13***

294 CD125 30fr multi 25 10

5th anniv. of the West African Monetary Union.

Lyre-shaped Megalith, Kaffrine A69

Design: 70fr, Ancient covered bowl, Bandiala.

1967, Dec. 2 **Engr.** ***Perf. 13***

295 A69 30fr grn, grnsh bl & red brn 25 10
296 A69 70fr red brn, ocher & brt bl 60 25

Nurse Feeding Child — A70 — Human Rights Flame — A71

1967, Dec. 23

297 A70 50fr bl grn, red & red brn 45 22

Issued for the Senegalese Red Cross.

1968, Jan. 20 **Photo.** ***Perf. 13x12½***

298 A71 30fr brt grn & gold 30 14

International Human Rights Year.

Parliament, Dakar A72

1968, Apr. 16 **Photo.** ***Perf. 12½x13***

299 A72 30fr car rose 25 14

Inter-Parliamentary Union Meeting, Dakar.

Pied Kingfisher A73 — Goose Barnacles A74

Designs: 10fr, Green lobster. 15fr, African jacana. 20fr, Sea cicada. 35fr, Shrimp. African anhinga.

1968-69 **Photo.** ***Perf. 11½***

Dated "1968" or (70fr) "1969"

Granite Paper

300 A73 5fr brn & multi 7 5
301 A74 10fr red & multi 10 7
302 A73 15fr yel & multi 16 9
303 A74 20fr ultra & multi 20 10
304 A74 35fr car rose & ol grn 30 20

305 A73 70fr Prus bl & multi ('69) 65 35
306 A74 100fr yel grn & multi 90 50
Nos. 300-306 (7) 2.38 1.36

Dates of issue: 5fr, July 13, 1968; 15fr, Dec. 21, 1968; 70fr, Apr. 26, 1969, others May 18, 1968. See Nos. C53-C57.

Steer and Hypodermic Syringe A75

1968, Aug. 17 Engr. *Perf. 13*
307 A75 30fr dk grn, dp bl & brn red 22 16

Campaign against cattle plague.

Boy and WHO Emblem A76

Bambara Antelope Symbol A77

1968, Nov. 16 Engr. *Perf. 13*
308 A76 30fr blk, grn & car 25 14
309 A76 45fr red brn, grn & blk 40 20

WHO, 20th anniversary.

1969, Jan. 13 Engr. *Perf. 13*

Design: 30fr, School of Medicine and Pharmacology, Dakar (horiz.).

310 A77 30fr emer, brt bl & ind 25 16
311 A77 50fr red, gray ol & bl grn 40 20

6th Medical Meeting, Dakar, Jan. 13-18.

Panet, Camels and Mogador-St. Louis Route — A78

1969, Feb. 15 Engr. *Perf. 13*
312 A78 75fr ultra, Prus bl & brn 60 25

Leopold Panet (1819-1859), first explorer of the Mauritanian Sahara.

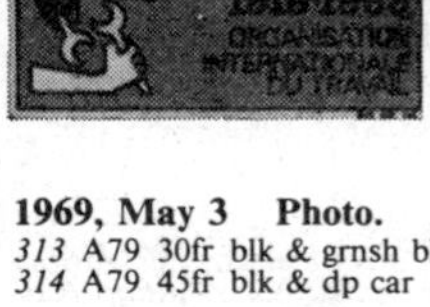
ILO Emblem A79

1969, May 3 Photo. *Perf. 12½x13*
313 A79 30fr blk & grnsh bl 22 10
314 A79 45fr blk & dp car 40 18

ILO, 50th anniversary.

The Catalogue editors cannot undertake to appraise, identify or judge the genuineness or condition of stamps.

Arms of Casamance A80

Mahatma Gandhi A81

Design: 20fr, Arms of Gorée Island.

1969, July 26 Litho. *Perf. 13½*
315 A80 15fr rose & multi 10 5
316 A80 20fr bl & multi 14 7

Development Bank Issue
Common Design Type

1969, Sept. 10 Engr. *Perf. 13*
317 CD130 30fr gray, grn & ocher 25 16
318 CD130 45fr brn, grn & ocher 40 20

1969, Oct. 2 Engr. *Perf. 13*
319 A81 50fr multi 42 20
a Min. sheet of 4 1.90 1.90

Mohandas K. Gandhi (1869-1948), leader in India's fight for independence.

Rotary Emblem and Symbolic Ship — A82

1969, Nov. 29 Photo. *Perf. 12½x13*
320 A82 30fr ultra, yel & blk 35 20

Dakar Rotary Club, 30th anniversary.

ASECNA Issue
Common Design Type

1969, Dec. 12 Engr. *Perf. 13*
321 CD132 100fr dk gray 65 35

Tourist Issue

Niokolo-Koba Campsite — A83

Designs: 20fr, Cape Skiring, Casamance. 35fr, Elephants at Niokolo-Koba National Park. 45fr, Millet granaries, pigs and boats, Fadiouth Island.

1969, Dec. 27
322 A83 20fr bl, red brn & ol 16 10
323 A83 30fr bl, red brn & ocher 25 10
324 A83 35fr grnsh bl, blk & ocher 30 16
325 A83 45fr vio bl & hn brn 35 16

Bottle-nosed Dolphins A84

Lenin (1870-1924) A85

1970, Feb. 21 Photo. *Perf. 12x12½*
326 A84 50fr dl bl, blk & red 40 20

1970, Apr. 22 Photo. *Perf. 11½*
327 A85 30fr brn, buff & ver 22 16
a A85 50fr souvenir sheet 40 40

No. 327a contains one stamp 32x48mm, perf. 12x11½.

UPU Headquarters Issue
Common Design Type

1970, May 20 Engr. *Perf. 13*
328 CD133 30fr dk red, ind & dp cl 22 14
329 CD133 45fr dl brn, dk car & bl grn 40 18

Textile Plant, Thies — A86

Design: 45fr, Fertilizer plant, Dakar.

1970, Nov. 21 Engr. *Perf. 13*
330 A86 30fr grn, brt bl & brn red 25 14
331 A86 45fr brn red & brt bl 40 18

Industrialization of Senegal.

Boy Scouts — A87

Three Heads and Sun — A88

Design: 100fr, Lord Baden-Powell, map of Africa with Dakar, and fleur-de-lis.

1970, Dec. 11 Photo. *Perf. 11½*
332 A87 30fr multi 22 14
333 A87 100fr multi 80 38

1st African Boy Scout Conf., Dakar, Dec. 11-14.

1970, Dec. 19 Engr. *Perf. 13*

Design: 40fr, African man and woman, globe with map of Africa.

334 A88 25fr ultra, org & vio brn 25 14
335 A88 40fr brn ol, dk brn & org 45 20

International Education Year.

Senegal Arms A89

Refugees and UN Emblem A90

1970-76 Photo. *Perf. 12*
336 A89 30fr yel grn & multi 20 10
336A A89 35fr brt pink & multi ('71) 22 10
b Bklt. pane of 10 ('72) 2.50
336C A89 50fr bl & multi ('75) 25 10
336D A89 65fr lil rose & multi ('76) 35 10

The booklet pane has a control number in the margin.
See No. 654.

1971, Jan. 16 *Perf. 12½x12*
337 A90 40fr ver, blk, yel & grn 35 16

High Commissioner for Refugees, 20th anniversary. See No. C94.

Mare "Mbayang" A91

Horses: 25fr, Mare Madjiguene. 100fr, Stallion Pass. 125fr, Stallion Pepe.

1971 Photo. *Perf. 11½*
338 A91 25fr multi 20 7
339 A91 40fr multi 35 16
340 A91 100fr multi 70 40
341 A91 125fr multi 90 40

Improvements in horse breeding.

UN Emblem, Black and White Children A92

Globe and Telephone A94

UN Emblem, Four Races A93

Perf. 13x12½, 12½x11
1971, Mar. 21 Litho.
342 A92 30fr multi 22 10
343 A93 50fr multi 40 20

Intl. Year against Racial Discrimination.

1971, May 17 Engr. *Perf. 13*

Design: 40fr, Radar, satellite, orbits.

344 A94 30fr pur, grn & brn 22 14
345 A94 40fr Prus bl, dk brn & red brn 30 14

3rd World Telecommunications Day.

Drummer (Hayashida) — A95

Jamboree Emblem and: 50fr, Dwarf Japanese quince and grape hyacinth. 65fr, Judo. 75fr, Mt. Fuji.

1971, Aug. 7 Photo. *Perf. 13½*
346 A95 35fr lt ultra & multi 25 14
347 A95 50fr yel & multi 40 20
348 A95 65fr dp org & multi 50 22
349 A95 75fr grn & multi 60 35

13th Boy Scout World Jamboree, Asagiri Plain, Japan, Aug. 2-10.

Map of West Africa with Senegal, UNICEF Emblem A97

Design: 100fr, Nurse, children and UNICEF emblem.

1971, Oct. 30 *Perf. 12½*

352 A97 35fr dl bl, org & blk 25 14
353 A97 100fr multi 80 38

UNICEF, 25th anniv.

Basketball and Games' Emblem — A98

Designs: 40fr, Basketball and emblem. 75fr, Games' emblem.

1971, Dec. 24 Photo. *Perf. 13½x13*

354 A98 35fr lt vio & multi 30 16
355 A98 40fr emer & multi 35 18
356 A98 75fr ocher & multi 65 38

6th African Basketball Championships, Dakar, Dec. 25, 1971-Jan. 2, 1972.

"The Exile of Albouri" — A99

Design: 40fr, "The Merchant of Venice."

1972, Mar. 25 *Perf. 13x12½*

357 A99 35fr dk red & multi 30 16
358 A99 40fr dk red & multi 38 20

Intl. Theater Day. See No. C112.

WHO Emblem and Heart A100

Design: 40fr, Physician with patient, WHO emblem and electrocardiogram.

1972, Apr. 7 Engr. *Perf. 13*

359 A100 35fr brt bl & red brn 25 14
360 A100 40fr sl grn & brn 30 16

"Your heart is your health," World Health Month.

Containment of the Desert, Environment Emblem — A101

1972, June 3 Photo. *Perf. 13x12½*

361 A101 35fr multi 30 16

UN Conference on Human Environment, Stockholm, June 5-16. See No. C113.

Tartarin Shooting the Lion — A102

Design: 100fr, Alphonse Daudet.

1972, June 24 Engr. *Perf. 13*

362 A102 40fr brt grn, rose car & brn 35 14
363 A102 100fr Prus bl, bl & brn 80 35

Alphonse Daudet (1840-1897), French novelist, and centenary of the publication of his "Tartarin de Tarascon."

Souvenir Sheet

Stringed Instrument — A103

1972, July 1 Engr. *Perf. 11½*

364 A103 150fr rose red 1.25 1.00

Belgica 72, Intl. Phil. Exhib., Brussels, June 24-July 9. No. 364 contains one stamp in design similar to No. 267.

Wrestling, Olympic Rings — A104

1972, July 22 Photo. *Perf. 14x13½*

365 A104 15fr shown 14 8
366 A104 20fr 100-meter dash 16 10
367 A104 100fr Basketball 65 35
368 A104 125fr Judo 80 40

Souvenir Sheet

Perf. 13½x14½

369 A104 240fr Torchbearer and Munich 1.90 1.60

20th Olympic Games, Munich, Aug. 26-Sept. 11.

Book Year Emblem, Children Reading A105

Senegalese Fashion A106

1972, Sept. 16 Photo. *Perf. 13*

370 A105 50fr gray & multi 38 16

International Book Year.

1972-76 **Engr.**

371 A106 25fr black 16 5
a Booklet pane of 5 1.60
b Booklet pane of 10 3.50
372 A106 40fr brt ultra 25 5
a Booklet pane of 5 2.50
b Booklet pane of 10 5.50
372C A106 60fr brt grn ('76) 35 5
372D A106 75fr lil rose 50 20

See Nos. 563-568.

Aleksander Pushkin A107

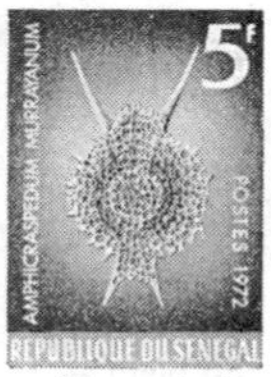

Amphicrasphedum Murrayanum A108

1972, Oct. 28 Photo. *Perf. 11½*

373 A107 100fr sal & pur 80 40

Aleksander Pushkin (1799-1837), Russian writer.

West African Monetary Union Issue

Common Design Type

Design: 40fr, African couple, city, village and commemorative coin.

1972, Nov. 2 Engr. *Perf. 13*

374 CD136 40fr ol brn, bl & gray 30 16

1972-73 Photo. *Perf. 11½*

Marine Life: 10fr, Pterocanium tricolpum. 15fr, Ceratospyris polygona. 20fr, Cortiniscus typicus. 30fr, Theopera cortina.

375 A108 5fr multi 5 5
376 A108 10fr multi 8 5
377 A108 15fr multi 14 5
378 A108 20fr multi ('73) 14 7
379 A108 30fr multi ('73) 16 7
Nos. 375-379,C115-C118 (9) 2.67 1.34

Issue dates: Nos. 375-377, Nov. 25, 1972. Nos. 378-379, July 28, 1973.

No. 288 Surcharged in Vermilion

1872-1972
100F
=

1972, Dec. 9 Engr. *Perf. 13*

380 A64 100fr on 30fr multi 60 30

Blaise Diagne (1872-1934).

Melchior — A109

Black and White Men Carrying Emblem — A110

1972, Dec. 23 Photo. *Perf. 13x13½*

381 A109 10fr shown 8 5
382 A109 15fr Caspar 10 5
383 A109 40fr Balthasar 22 12
384 A109 60fr Joseph 30 20
385 A109 100fr Virgin and Child 50 32
Nos. 381-385 (5) 1.20 74

Christmas. Nos. 381-385 printed se-tenant with continuous design, showing traditional Gorée dolls.

Europafrica Issue

1973, Jan. 20 Engr. *Perf. 13*

386 A110 65fr blk & grn 42 22

Radar Station, Gandoul A111

1973, May 17 Engr. *Perf. 13*

387 A111 40fr multi 25 16

Phases of Solar Eclipse A112

Designs: 65fr, Moon between earth and sun casting shadow on earth. 150fr, Diagram of areas of partial and total eclipse, satellite in space.

1973, June 30 Photo. *Perf. 13x14*

388 A112 35fr dk bl & multi 22 14
389 A112 65fr dk bl & multi 38 25
390 A112 150fr dk bl & multi 90 60

Total solar eclipse over Africa, June 30.

Men Holding Torch over Africa — A113

1973, July 7 *Perf. 12½x13*

391 A113 75fr multi 42 30

Org. for African Unity, 10th anniv.

No. 338 Surcharged with New Value, 2 Bars, and Overprinted in Ultramarine: "SECHERESSE / SOLIDARITE AFRICAINE"

1973, July 21 Photo. *Perf. 11½*

392 A91 100fr on 25fr multi 60 40

African solidarity in drought emergency.

African Postal Union Issue

Common Design Type

1973, Sept. 12 Engr. *Perf. 13*

393 CD137 100fr dk grn, vio & dk red 60 30

Child, Map of Senegal, WMO Emblem A114

1973, Sept. 22

394 A114 50fr multi 30 10

Intl. meteorological cooperation, cent.

INTERPOL Headquarters, Paris — A115

1973, Oct. 6 Engr. *Perf. 13*

395 A115 75fr ultra, bis & sl grn 42 25

50th anniv. of Intl. Criminal Police Org.

Souvenir Sheet

John F. Kennedy (1917-1963) A116

1973, Nov. 22 Engr. *Perf. 13*
396 A116 150fr ultra 1.00 1.00

Amilcar Cabral — A117

Victorious Athletes and Flag — A118

1973, Dec. 15 Photo. *Perf. 12½x13*
397 A117 75fr multi 42 35

Cabral (1924-1973), leader of anti-Portuguese guerrilla movement in Portuguese Guinea.

1974, Apr. 6 Photo. *Perf. 12½x13*

Design: 40fr, Folk theater.

398 A118 35fr multi 22 14
399 A118 40fr multi 30 20

National Youth Week.

Soccer Cup, Jugoslavia-Brazil Game, Our Lady's Church, Munich — A119

Soccer Cup and Games: 40fr, Australia-Germany (Fed. Rep.) and Belltower, Hamburg. 65fr, Netherlands-Uruguay and Tower, Hanover. 70fr, Zaire-Italy and Church, Stuttgart.

1974, June 29 Photo. *Perf. 13x14*
400 A119 25fr car & multi 16 8
401 A119 40fr car & multi 25 16
402 A119 65fr car & multi 40 16
403 A119 70fr car & multi 42 18

World Cup Soccer Championship, Munich, June 13-July 7.

UPU Emblem, Envelopes and Means of Transportation — A120

1974, Oct. 9 Engr. *Perf. 13*
404 A120 100fr multi 60 40

Centenary of Universal Postal Union.

Fair Emblem — A121

1974, Nov. 28 Engr. *Perf. 12½x13*
405 A121 100fr bl, org & dk brn 55 35

Dakar International Fair.

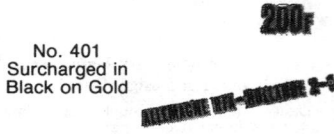

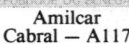

No. 401 Surcharged in Black on Gold

1975, Feb. 1 Photo. *Perf. 13x14*
406 A119 200fr on 40fr multi 1.10 65

World Cup Soccer Championships, 1974, victory of German Federal Republic.

Pres. Senghor and King Baudouin A122

1975, Feb. 28 Photo. *Perf. 13x13½*
407 A122 65fr lil & dk bl 35 20
408 A122 100fr org & grn 55 35

Visit of King Baudouin of Belgium.

ILO Emblem A123

1975, Apr. 30 Photo. *Perf. 13½x13*
409 A123 125fr multi 65 38

International Labor Festival.

Globe, Stamp, Letters, España 75 Emblem — A124

1975, June 6 Engr. *Perf. 13*
410 A124 55fr ind, grn & red 30 20

Espana 75 Intl. Phil. Exhib., Madrid, Apr. 4-13.

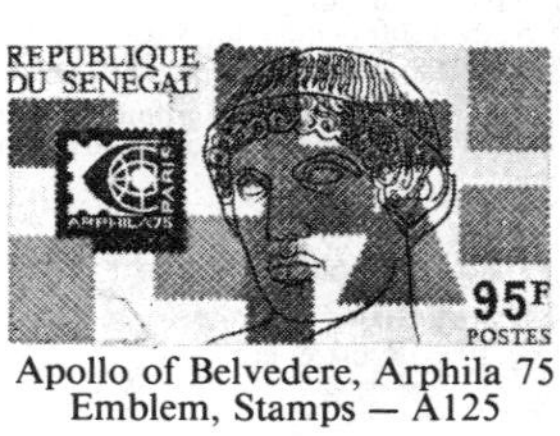

Apollo of Belvedere, Arphila 75 Emblem, Stamps — A125

1975, June 6
411 A125 95fr dk brn, brn & bis 50 35

Arphila 75 International Philatelic Exhibition, Paris, June 6-16.

Professional Instruction — A126

1975, June 28 Engr. *Perf. 13*
412 A126 85fr multi 45 25

Dr. Albert Schweitzer (1875-1965), Medical Missionary, Lambarene Hospital — A127

1975, July 5
413 A127 85fr grn & vio brn 45 25

Senegalese Soldier, Batallion Flag, Map of Sinai — A128

1975, July 10 Litho. *Perf. 12½*
414 A128 100fr multi 55 25

Senegalese Battalion of the United Nations' Sinai Service, 1973-1974.

Women and Child — A129

Design: 55fr, Women pounding grain, IWY emblem (vert.).

1975, Oct. 18 Photo. *Perf. 13½*
415 A129 55fr sil & multi 30 15
416 A129 75fr sil & multi 40 20

International Women's Year.

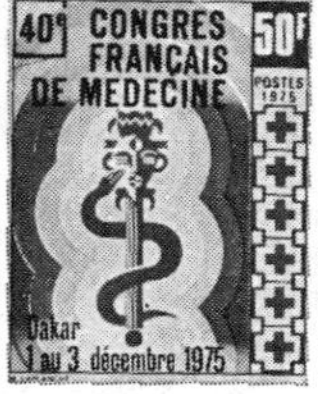

Staff of Aesculapius and African Mask — A130

1975, Dec. 1 Photo. *Perf. 12½x13*
417 A130 50fr multi 25 10

40th French Medical Cong., Dakar, Dec. 1-3.

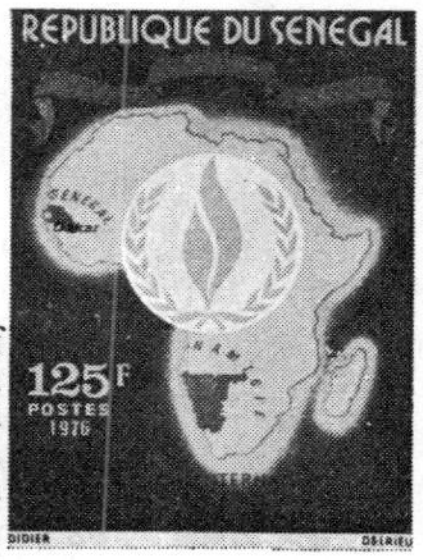

Map of Africa with Senegal and Namibia, UN Emblem A131

1976, Jan. 5 Photo. *Perf. 13*
418 A131 125fr vio bl & multi 65 35

International Human Rights and Namibia Conference, Dakar, Jan. 5-8.

Sailfish Fishing A132

Design: 200fr, Racing yachts and Oceanexpo 75 emblem.

1976, Jan. 28 Photo. *Perf. 13½x13*
419 A132 140fr multi 70 38
420 A132 200fr multi 1.10 55

Oceanexpo 75, 1st Intl. Oceanographic Exhib., Okinawa, July 20, 1975-Jan. 1976.

Servals — A133

Designs: 3fr, Black-tailed godwits. 4fr, River hogs. 5fr, African fish eagles. No. 425, Okapis. No. 426, Sitatungas.

1976, Feb. 26 Photo. *Perf. 13*
421 A133 2fr gold & multi 5 5
422 A133 3fr gold & multi 5 5
423 A133 4fr gold & multi 5 5
424 A133 5fr gold & multi 5 5
425 A133 250fr gold & multi 1.40 65
426 A133 250fr gold & multi 1.40 65
Strip of 2 + label 3.00
Nos. 421-426 (6) 3.00 1.50

Basse Casamance National Park. Nos. 425-426 printed se-tenant and with label showing map with location of park.
See Nos. 473-478.

A. G. Bell, Telephone, ITU Emblem — A134

1976, Mar. 31 Litho. *Perf. 12½x13*
427 A134 175fr multi 90 42

Centenary of first telephone call by Alexander Graham Bell, Mar. 10, 1876.

The indexes in each volume of the Scott Catalogue contain many listings which help to identify stamps.

Map of African French-speaking Countries — A135

1976, Apr. 12 Litho. *Perf. 13½*

428 A135 60fr yel grn & multi 35 20

Scientific and Cultural Meeting of the African Dental Association, Dakar, Apr. 12-17.

Family and Graph A136

1976, Apr. 26

429 A136 65fr multi 35 20

1st population census in Senegal, Apr. 1976.

Thomas Jefferson and 13-star Flag — A137

1976, June 19 Engr. *Perf. 13*

430 A137 50fr bl, red & blk 25 14

American Bicentennial.

Planting Seedlings — A138

1976, Aug. 21 Litho. *Perf. 12*

431 A138 60fr yel & multi 35 16

Reclamation of Sahel region.

Campfire A139

Jamboree Emblem, Map of Africa — A140

1976, Aug. 30 Litho. *Perf. 12½*

432 A139 80fr multi 42 35
433 A140 100fr multi 55 40

1st All Africa Scout Jamboree, Sherehills, Jos, Nigeria, Apr. 2-8, 1977.

Mechanized Tomato Harvest A141

1976, Oct. 23 Photo. *Perf. 13*

434 A141 180fr multi 1.00 42

Map of Dakar and Goree A142

Designs: 60fr, Star over Africa. 70fr, Students in laboratory and library. 200fr, Handshake over world map, Pres. Senghor.

1976, Oct. 9 Litho. *Perf. 13½x14*

435 A142 40fr multi 14 12
436 A142 60fr multi 20 16
437 A142 70fr multi 20 20
438 A142 200fr multi 58 55

70th birthday of Pres. Leopold Sedar Senghor.

Scroll with Map of Africa, Senegalese People — A143

1977, Jan. 8 *Perf. 12½*

439 A143 60fr multi 35 16

Day of the Black People.

Joe Frazier and Muhammad Ali — A144

Design: 60fr, Ali and Frazier in ring (vert.).

1977, Jan. 7 Photo. *Perf. 13x13½*

440 A144 60fr bl & blk 65 16
441 A144 150fr emer & blk 1.20 40

World boxing champion Muhammad Ali.

Dancer and Musician A145

Festival Emblem and: 75fr, Wood carving and masks. 100fr, Dancers and ancestor statuette.

1977, Feb. 10 Litho. *Perf. 12½*

442 A145 50fr yel & multi 25 14
443 A145 75fr grn & multi 40 20
444 A145 100fr rose & multi 55 25

2nd World Black and African Festival, Lagos, Nigeria, Jan. 15-Feb. 12.

Cogwheels and Symbols of Industry — A146

1977, Mar. 28 Engr. *Perf. 13*

445 A146 70fr yel grn & ocher 38 18

Dakar Industrial Zone, 1st anniversary.

Burning Match and Burnt Trees — A147

Design: 60fr, Burnt trees and house, firetruck (horiz.).

1977, Apr. 30 Litho. *Perf. 12½*

446 A147 40fr grn & multi 20 10
447 A147 60fr sl & multi 35 16

Prevention of forest fires.

Drummer, Telephone, Agriculture and Industry — A148

Electronic Tree and ITU Emblem — A149

1977, May 17 Litho. *Perf. 13*

448 A148 80fr multi 35 22
449 A149 100fr multi 40 25

World Telecommunications Day.

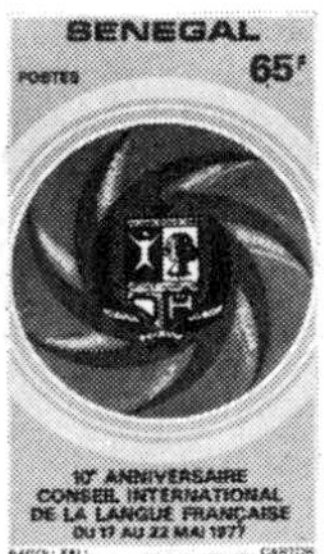

Symbol of Language Studies — A150

Sassenage Castle, Grenoble — A151

Perf. 12x12½, 12½

1977, May 21 Litho.

450 A150 65fr multi 22 18
451 A151 250fr multi 1.00 65

10th anniv. of Intl. French Language Council.

Woman in Boat, Wooden Shoe A152

Design: 125fr, Senegalese woman, symbolic tulip and stamp (vert.).

1977, June 4 *Perf. 13½x14, 14x13½*

452 A152 50fr bl grn & multi 25 14
453 A152 125fr ocher & multi 65 35

Amphilex '77 International Philatelic Exhibition, Amsterdam, May 26-June 5.

Adult Reading Class A153

Design: 65fr, Man learning to read.

1977, Sept. 10 Litho. *Perf. 12½*

454 A153 60fr multi 35 16
455 A153 65fr multi 38 16

National Literacy Week, Sept. 8-14.

Mercury, by Rubens — A154

Paintings: 25fr, Daniel in the Lions' Den, by Peter Paul Rubens (1577-1640). 40fr, The Empress, by Titian (1477-1576). 60fr, Flora, by Titian. 65fr, Jo, the Beautiful Irish Woman, by Gustave Courbet (1819-1877). 100fr, The Painter's Studio, by Courbet.

1977, Nov. Photo. *Perf. 13x13½*

456 A154 20fr multi 10 5
457 A154 25fr multi 14 7
458 A154 40fr multi 20 10
459 A154 60fr multi 30 16
460 A154 65fr multi 35 18
461 A154 100fr multi 55 25
Nos. 456-461 (6) 1.64 81

An enhanced introduction to the Scott Catalogue begins on Page V. A thorough understanding of the material presented there will greatly aid your use of the catalogue itself.

Adoration by People of Various Races — A155

Designs: 25fr, Decorated arch and procession. 40fr, Christmas tree, mother and child. 100fr, Adoration of the Kings (horiz.).

1977, Dec. 22 Litho. *Perf. 12½*

462 A155 20fr multi 10 5
463 A155 25fr multi 14 7
464 A155 40fr multi 20 10
465 A155 100fr multi 55 25

Christmas.

Regatta at Soumbedioun A156

Designs: 10fr, Senegalese wrestlers. 65fr, Regatta at Soumbedioun (horiz.). 100fr, Dancers (horiz.).

1978, Jan. 7 Litho. *Perf. 12½*

466 A156 10fr multi 7 5
467 A156 30fr multi 16 8
468 A156 65fr multi 35 18
469 A156 100fr multi 55 25

Tourist publicity.

Acropolis, Athens, and African Buildings A157

1978, Jan. 30

470 A157 75fr multi 40 20

UNESCO campaign to save world's cultural heritage.

Solar-powered Pump, Field and Sheep — A158

Design: 95fr, Pylon bringing electricity to villages and factories.

1978, Feb. 25

471 A158 50fr multi 25 14
472 A158 95fr multi 50 25

Energy in Senegal.

Park Type of 1976

Designs: 5fr, Caspian terns in flight, royal terns on ground. 10fr, Pink-backed pelicans. 15fr, Wart hog and gray heron. 20fr, Greater flamingoes, nests, eggs and young. No. 477, Gray heron and royal terns. No. 478, Abyssinian ground hornbill and wart hog.

1978, Apr. 22 Photo. *Perf. 13*

473 A133 5fr gold & multi 5 5
474 A133 10fr gold & multi 7 5
475 A133 15fr gold & multi 10 5
476 A133 20fr gold & multi 14 5
477 A133 150fr gold & multi 1.00 65
478 A133 150fr gold & multi 1.00 65
Strip of 2 + label 2.00
Nos. 473-478 (6) 2.36 1.50

Salum Delta National Park. Nos. 477-478 printed se-tenant and with label showing map with location of park.

Dome of the Rock, Jerusalem — A159

1978, May 15 Litho. *Perf. 12½*

479 A159 60fr multi 40 15

Palestinian fighters and their families.

Vaccination, Dr. Jenner, WHO Emblem — A160

1978, June 3

480 A160 60fr multi 40 15

Eradication of smallpox.

Soccer, Flags: Argentina, Hungary, France, Italy — A161

Mahatma Gandhi — A162

Soccer, Cup, Argentina '78 Emblem and Flags of: 40fr, No. 486a, Poland, German Democratic Rep., Tunisia, Mexico. 65fr, 125fr, Austria, Spain, Sweden, Brazil. 75fr, No. 484, Netherlands, Iran, Peru, Scotland. 150fr, like 25fr.

1978, June 24 Photo. *Perf. 13*

481 A161 25fr multi 12 5
482 A161 40fr multi 20 8
483 A161 65fr multi 32 14
484 A161 100fr multi 50 22

Souvenir Sheets

485 Sheet of 2 1.10
a A161 75fr multi 38
b A161 125fr multi 65
486 Sheet of 2 1.40
a A161 100fr multi 50
b A161 150fr multi 75

11th World Cup Soccer Championship, Argentina, June 1-25.

1978, June 27 *Perf. 12*

Design: 150fr, No. 489a, Martin Luther King. No. 489b, like 125fr.

487 A162 125fr multi 80 35
488 A162 150fr multi 1.00 40

Souvenir Sheet

489 Sheet of 2 3.00
a A162 200fr multi 1.40
b A162 200fr multi 1.40

Mahatma Gandhi and Martin Luther King, advocates of non-violence.

Homes and Industry — A163

1978, Aug. 5 Litho. *Perf. 12½*

490 A163 110fr multi 70 30

3rd Intl. Fair, Dakar, Nov. 28-Dec. 10.

Wright Brothers and Flyer — A164

Designs: 150fr, like 75fr. 100fr, 250fr, Yuri Gagarin and spacecraft. 200fr, 300fr, US astronauts Frank Borman, William Anders, James Lovell Jr. and spacecraft.

1978, Sept. 25 Litho. *Perf. 13½x14*

491 A164 75fr multi 50 20
492 A164 100fr multi 65 28
493 A164 200fr multi 1.40 55

Souvenir Sheet

494 Sheet of 3, multi 4.00
a A164 150fr multi 60
b A164 250fr multi 1.40
c A164 300fr multi 2.00

75th anniv. of 1st powered flight; 10th anniv. of the death of Yuri Gagarin, first man in space; 10th anniv. of Apollo 8 flight around moon.

Henri Dunant (1828-1910), Founder of Red Cross, and Patients — A165

Design: 20fr, Henri Dunant, First Aid station, Red Cross flag.

1978, Oct. 28 Photo. *Perf. 11½*

495 A165 5fr brt bl & red 5 5
496 A165 20fr multi 14 5

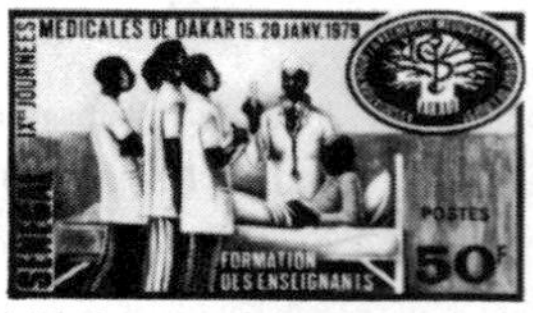

Bedside Lecture and Emblem — A166

Design: 100fr, Pollution, fish and mercury bottles.

1979, Jan. 15 Litho. *Perf. 13½x13*

497 A166 50fr multi 35 14
498 A166 100fr multi 65 25

9th Medical Days, Dakar, Jan. 15-20.

Map of Senegal with Shortwave Stations A167

Designs: 60fr, Children on vacation, ambulance, soccer player. 65fr, Rural mobile post office.

1978, Dec. 27 Litho. *Perf. 13½x13*

499 A167 50fr multi 35 14
500 A167 60fr multi 40 16
501 A167 65fr multi 42 18

Achievements of postal service.

Farmer A168

Design: 150fr, Factories, communication, transportation, fish, physician and worker.

1979, Feb. 17 Litho. *Perf. 12½*

502 A168 30fr multi 20 8
503 A168 150fr multi 1.00 40

Pride in workmanship.

Children's Village and Children — A169

Design: 60fr, Different view of village.

1979, Mar. 30 *Perf. 12x12½*

504 A169 40fr multi 25 10
505 A169 60fr multi 40 16

Children's SOS villages.

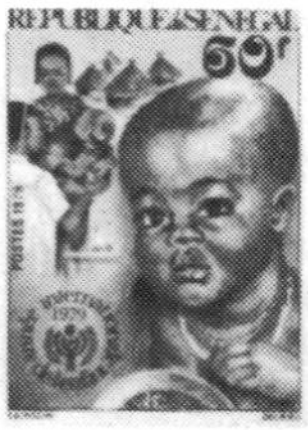

Infant, Physician Vaccinating Child, IYC Emblem — A170

Design: 65fr, Boys with book and globe, IYC emblem.

1979, Apr. 24 Litho. *Perf. 13½x13*

506 A170 60fr multi 40 16
507 A170 65fr multi 42 18

International Year of the Child.

Drum, Carrier Pigeon, Satellite A171

Design: 60fr, Baobab tree and flower, Independence monument with lion (vert.).

1979, June 8 *Perf. 12½x13*

Size: 36x48mm

508 A171 60fr multi 40 16

Perf. 12½

Size: 36x36mm

509 A171 150fr multi 1.00 40

Philexafrique II, Libreville, Gabon, June 8-17. Nos. 508, 509 each printed with labels showing UAPT '79 emblem.

People Walking through Open Book A172

1979, Sept. 15 Photo. *Perf. 11½x12*

510 A172 250fr multi 1.90 65

Intl. Bureau of Education, Geneva, 50th anniv.

Sir Rowland Hill (1795-1879), Originator of Penny Postage, Type AP3 with Exhibition Cancel — A173

1979, Oct. 9 *Perf. 11½*

511 A173 500fr multi 3.50 1.40

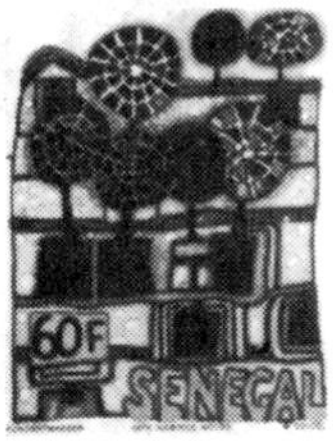

Black Trees, by Hundertwasser A174

Litho. & Engr.

1979, Dec. 10 *Perf. 13½x14*

512 A174 60fr shown 40 16
a Souvenir sheet of 4 1.90 80
513 A174 100fr Head of a man 65 25
a Souvenir sheet of 4 3.00 1.20
514 A174 200fr Rainbow windows 1.40 55
a Souvenir sheet of 4 5.75 2.25

Paintings by Friedensreich Hundertwasser, pseudonym of Friedrich Stowasser (b. 1928).

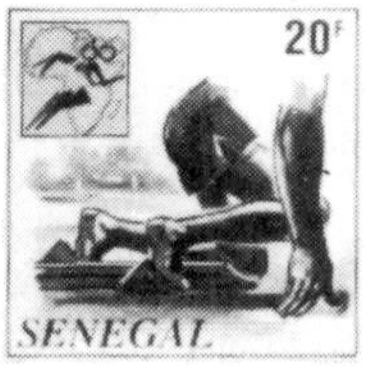

Running, Championship Emblem A175

1980, Jan. 14 Litho. *Perf. 13*

515 A175 20fr shown 14 5
516 A175 25fr Javelin 16 7
517 A175 50fr Relay race 35 14
518 A175 100fr Discus 80 25

1st African Athletic Championships.

Musicians A176

1980, Mar. 22 Photo. *Perf. 14*

519 A176 50fr shown 35 14
520 A176 100fr Dancers, festival building 65 25
521 A176 200fr Drummer, dancers 1.40 55

Mudra Afrique Arts Festival.

Lions Emblem, Map of Dakar Harbor A177

1980, May 17 Litho. *Perf. 13*

522 A177 100fr multi 80 25

22nd Congress, Lions Intl. District 403, Dakar.

Chimpanzees — A178

1980, June 2 Photo. *Perf. 13½*

523 A178 40fr shown 25 10
524 A178 60fr Elephants 40 16
525 A178 65fr Derby's elands 42 18
526 A178 100fr Hyenas 65 25
527 Pair 2.50 1.10
a A178 200fr Herd 1.25 55
b A178 200fr Guest house 1.25 55
Nos. 523-527 (5) 4.22 1.79

Souvenir Sheet

528 Sheet of 4 4.00 1.40
a A178 125fr like #523 1.00 35
b A178 125fr like #524 1.00 35
c A178 125fr like #525 1.00 35
d A178 125fr like #526 1.00 35

Niokolo Koba National Park. No. 527 printed in continuous design with label showing location of park.

Tree Planting Year — A179

1980, June 27 Litho. *Perf. 13*

529 A179 60fr multi 40 16
530 A179 65fr multi 42 18

Rural Women Workers A180

Designs: Rural women workers. 50fr, 200fr, horiz.

1980, July 19

531 A180 50fr multi 35 14
532 A180 100fr multi 65 25
533 A180 200fr multi 1.40 55

Wrestling, Moscow '80 Emblem — A181

1980, Aug. 21 *Perf. 14½*

534 A181 60fr shown 40 16
535 A181 65fr Running 42 18
536 A181 70fr Sports, map showing Moscow 45 20
537 A181 100fr Judo 80 25
538 A181 200fr Basketball 1.60 55
Nos. 534-538 (5) 3.67 1.34

Souvenir Sheet

539 Sheet of 2 1.50
a A181 75fr like #534 50 22
b A181 125fr like #535 80 35
540 Sheet of 2 1.50
a A181 75fr like #527 50 22
b A181 125fr like #538 80 35

22nd Summer Olympic Games, Moscow, July 19-Aug. 3.

Caspian Tern and Sea Gulls, Kalissaye Bird Sanctuary A182

National Park Wildlife: 70fr, Laughing gulls and Hansel's tern, Barbarie Spit. 85fr, Turtle and crab, Madeleine Islands. 150fr, Cormorant, Madeleine Islands.

1981, Jan. 31 Litho. *Perf. 14½x14*

541 A182 50fr multi 50 14
542 A182 70fr multi 65 20
543 A182 85fr multi 75 22
544 A182 150fr multi 1.20 40

Souvenir Sheet

545 Sheet of 4 4.00 1.40
a A182 125fr like #541 1.00 35
b A182 125fr like #542 1.00 35
c A182 125fr like #543 1.00 35
d A182 125fr like #544 1.00 35

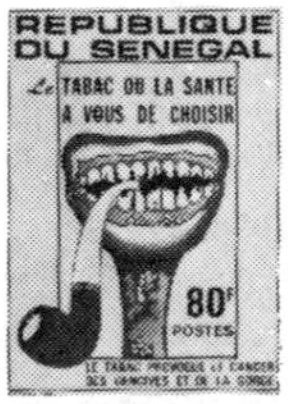

Anti-Tobacco Campaign — A183

1981, June 20 Litho. *Perf. 13*

546 A183 75fr Healthy people 50 20
547 A183 80fr shown 55 22

4th Intl. Dakar Fair, Nov. 25-Dec. 7 — A184

1981, Sept. 19 Litho. *Perf. 12½*

548 A184 80fr multi 55 22

Natl. Hero Lat Dior A185

1982, Jan. 11 Photo. *Perf. 14*

549 A185 80fr Portrait, vert. 55 22
550 A185 500fr Battle 3.50 1.40

Local Flora — A186

1982, Feb. 1 *Perf. 11½*

551 A186 50fr Nymphaea lotus 35 14
552 A186 75fr Strophanthus sarmentosus 50 20
553 A186 200fr Crinum moorei 1.40 55
554 A186 225fr Cochlospermum tinctorium 1.50 60

Inscribed 1981.

Euryphrene Senegalensis — A187

1982, Feb. 27 Litho. *Perf. 14*

555 A187 45fr shown 30 10
556 A187 55fr Hypolimnas salmacis 38 15
557 A187 75fr Cymothoe caenis 50 20
558 A187 80fr Precis cebrene 55 22

Souvenir Sheet

Perf. 14½

559 Sheet of 4 6.00 2.00
a A187 100fr like 45fr 65 25
b A187 150fr like 55fr 1.00 40
c A187 200fr like 75fr 1.40 55
d A187 250fr like 80fr 1.60 65

Destructive Insects — A188 Banner and Stamp — A189

Various insects. 80fr, 100fr horiz.

1982, Apr. 7 Litho. *Perf. 14*

560 A188 75fr multi 50 20
561 A188 80fr multi 55 22
562 A188 100fr multi 65 25

Fashion Type of 1972

1982-84 Engr. *Perf. 13*

563 A106 5fr Prus bl 5 5
564 A106 10fr dl red 7 5
565 A106 15fr orange 10 5
566 A106 20fr dk pur 14 5
567 A106 30fr hn brn 20 10
568 A106 90fr brt car ('84) 25 10
Nos. 563-568 (6) 81 40

Issue dates: 5-30fr, Apr. 30. 90fr, Dec.

1982, Dec. 30 Photo. *Perf. 13*

575 A189 100fr shown 50 25
576 A189 500fr Stamp, arrows 3.00 1.40

PHILEXFRANCE Intl. Stamp Exhibition, Paris, June 11-21.

Senegambia Confederation, Feb. 1 — A190

1982, Nov. 15 Litho. *Perf. 12½*

577	A190	225fr	Map, flags	1.00	65
578	A190	350fr	Arms	1.60	1.00

Local Birds — A191

1982 World Cup — A192

1982, Dec. 1 Photo. *Perf. 11½*

Granite Paper

579	A191	45fr	Godwit	30	12
580	A191	75fr	Jabiru	50	20
581	A191	80fr	Francolin	55	22
582	A191	500fr	Eagle	3.50	1.40

1982, Dec. 11 Litho. *Perf. 12½x13*

583	A192	30fr	Player	20	8
584	A192	50fr	Player, diff.	35	14
585	A192	75fr	Ball	50	20
586	A192	80fr	Cup	55	22

Souvenir Sheets

Perf. 12½

587	A192	75fr	like 30fr	50	25
588	A192	100fr	like 50fr	65	35
589	A192	150fr	like 75fr	1.00	50
590	A192	200fr	like 80fr	1.40	65

Dakar '82 Stamp Exhibition — A193

Designs: 60fr, Exhibition poster, viewers, horiz. 70fr, Simulated butterfly stamps. 90fr, Simulated stamps under magnifying glass. 95fr, Coat of Arms over Exhibition Building.

1983, Aug. 6 Litho. *Perf. 12½*

591	A193	60fr	multi	20	10
592	A193	70fr	multi	22	12
593	A193	90fr	multi	30	15
594	A193	95fr	multi	32	16

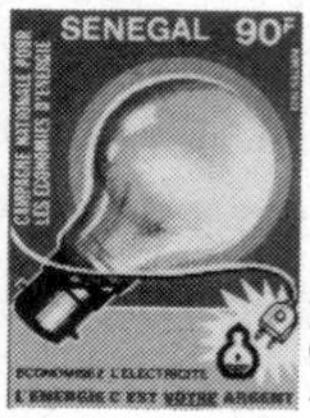

Energy Conservation A194

1983, Oct. 25 Litho. *Perf. 12½x13*

595	A194	90fr	Electricity	30	15
596	A194	95fr	Gasoline	32	16
597	A194	260fr	Coal, wood	90	42

Namibia Day — A195

1983, Nov. 14 Litho. *Perf. 13½x13*

598	A195	90fr	Torch	30	15
599	A195	95fr	Chain, fist	32	16
600	A195	260fr	Woman bearing torch	90	42

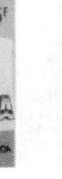

West African Monetary Union, 20th Anniv. — A196

Dakar Alizes Rotary Club, First Anniv. — A197

Designs: 60fr, Mask emblem, Ziguinchor Agency building, Dakar (horiz.). 65fr, Monetary Union headquarters, emblem.

Perf. 13½x13, 13x13½

1983, Nov. 28

601	A196	60fr	multi	20	10
602	A196	65fr	multi	20	12

1983, Dec. 5 *Perf. 13x13½*

603	A197	70fr	grn & multi	22	12
604	A197	500fr	bl & multi	1.60	80

Customs Cooperation Council, 30th Anniv. — A198

Fconomic Comm. for Africa, 25th Anniv. — A199

1983, Dec. 23 *Perf. 12½x13*

605	A198	90fr	multi	30	15
606	A198	300fr	multi	1.00	50

1984, Jan. 10 *Perf. 12½*

607	A199	90fr	multi	30	15
608	A199	95fr	multi	32	16

SOS Children's Village A200

Perf. 13½x13, 13x13½

1984, Mar. 29

609	A200	90fr	Village	30	15
610	A200	95fr	Mother & child, vert.	32	16
611	A200	115fr	Brothers & sisters	40	20
612	A200	260fr	House, vert.	90	42

Scouting Year A201

1984, May 28 Litho. *Perf. 13*

613	A201	60fr	Sign	20	10
614	A201	70fr	Emblem	22	12
615	A201	90fr	Scouts	30	15
616	A201	95fr	Baden-Powell	32	16

1984 Olympic Games — A202

1984, July 28 Litho. *Perf. 13*

617	A202	90fr	Javelin	30	15
618	A202	95fr	Hurdles	35	16
619	A202	165fr	Soccer	55	30

Souvenir Sheet

Perf. 13x12½

620			Sheet of 3	1.90	1.00
a	A202	125fr	like 90fr	40	20
b	A202	175fr	like 95fr	60	30
c	A202	250fr	like 165fr	80	45

World Food Day A203

Perf. 13x12½, 12½x13

1984, Dec. 16 Litho.

621	A203	65fr	Food production	18	10
622	A203	70fr	Cooking, vert.	18	10
623	A203	225fr	Dining	60	30

No. 612 Overprinted "AIDE AU SAHEL 84"

1984, Dec. *Perf. 13x13½*

624	A200	260fr	multi	70	35

Drought relief.

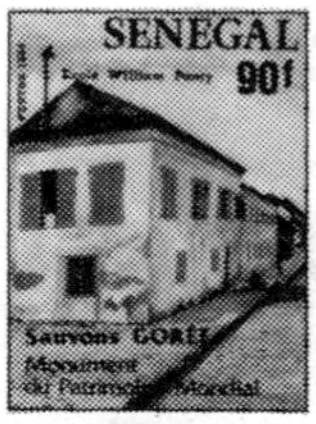

UNESCO World Heritage Campaign A204

Water Emergency Plan A205

1984, Dec. 6 Litho. *Perf. 13½*

625	A204	90fr	William Ponty School	25	14
626	A204	95fr	Island map, horiz.	25	14
627	A204	250fr	History Museum	65	35
628	A204	500fr	Slave Prison, horiz.	1.40	65

Souvenir Sheet

Perf. 13x12½, 12½x13

629			Sheet of 4	3.50	1.90
a	A204	125fr	like No. 625	30	16
b	A204	150fr	like No. 626	40	20
c	A204	325fr	like No. 627	90	40
d	A204	675fr	like No. 628	1.90	90

Restoration of historic sites, Goree Island.

Perf. 13x12½, 12½x13

1985, Mar. 28

630	A205	40fr	Well and pump	10	5
631	A205	50fr	Spigot and crops	14	7
632	A205	90fr	Water tanks, livestock	25	14
633	A205	250fr	Women at well	65	35

Nos. 631-633 horiz.

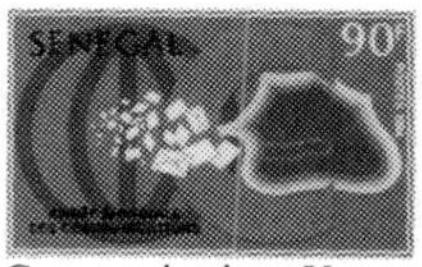

World Communications Year — A206

Designs: 95fr, Maps of Africa and Senegal, transmission tower. 350fr Globe, pigeon with letter.

1985, Apr. 13 Litho. *Perf. 13*

634	A206	90fr	multi	25	14
635	A206	95fr	multi	25	14
636	A206	350fr	multi	90	45

Traditional Musical Instruments A207

Designs: 50fr, Gourd fiddle and bamboo flute. 85fr, Drums and stringed instrument. 125fr, Musician playing balaphone, drums. 250fr, Rabab, shawm and single-string fiddles.

1985, May 4 *Perf. 12½x13, 13x12½*

637	A207	50fr	multi	14	7
638	A207	85fr	multi	22	12
639	A207	125fr	multi	35	16
640	A207	250fr	multi	65	35

Nos. 638-640 vert.

PHILEXAFRICA '85, Lome, Togo, Nov. 16-24 — A208

1985, Oct. 21 *Perf. 13*

641	A208	100fr	Political and civic education	35	16
642	A208	125fr	Vocational training	42	20
643	A208	150fr	Culture, space exploration	55	25
644	A208	175fr	Self-sufficiency in food production	60	30

Intl. Youth Year A209

1985, Nov. 30 *Perf. 14*

645	A209	40fr	Vocational training	14	7
646	A209	50fr	Communications	16	8
647	A209	90fr	World peace	30	15
648	A209	125fr	Cultural exchange	42	20

Senegal Arms Type of 1970

1985, Dec. Litho. *Perf. 13*

Background Color

654	A89	95fr	brt org	35	16

Fishing at Kayar A210

1986, Jan. 28 Litho. *Perf. 14*

659	A210	40fr	Hauling boat	20	10
660	A210	50fr	Women on beach	25	12
661	A210	100fr	Fisherman, catch	52	25

662 A210 125fr Women buying fish 68 35
663 A210 150fr Unloading fish 80 40
Nos. 659-663 (5) 2.45 1.22

Nos. 661-662 vert.

Folk Costumes — A211

1985, Dec. 28 Litho. *Perf. 13½*

664 A211 40fr multi 15 8
665 A211 95fr multi, vert., diff. 35 16
666 A211 100fr multi, vert., diff. 38 18
667 A211 150fr multi, vert., diff. 55 28

Coiffures A212

1986 Africa Soccer Cup, Cairo A213

1986, Mar. 3 *Perf. 13*

668 A212 90fr Perruque, Ceeli 50 25
669 A212 125fr Ndungu, Kearly, Rasta 68 35
670 A212 250fr Jamono Kura, Kooraa 1.35 68
671 A212 300fr Mbaram, Jeere 1.65 82

1986, Mar. 7 *Perf. 13½*

672 A213 115fr Soccer ball, flags 62 32
673 A213 125fr Athlete, map 68 35
674 A213 135fr Pyramid, heraldic lion 75 38
675 A213 165fr Flag, lions, map 90 45

No. 638 Surcharged with Lions Intl. Emblem, Two Bars, and "Ve CONVENTION / MULTI-DISTRICT / 403 / 8-10 / MAI / 1986" in Dark Ultramarine

1986, May 8 Litho. *Perf. 13x12½*

676 A207 165fr on 85fr multi 1.00 50

World Wildlife Fund — A214

Ndama gazelles.

1986, June 30 *Perf. 13*

677 A214 15fr multi 8 5
678 A214 45fr multi 25 12
679 A214 85fr multi 48 24
680 A214 125fr multi 70 35

UN Child Survival Campaign — A215

1986, Sept. 5 Litho. *Perf. 14*

681 A215 50fr Immunization 32 16
682 A215 85fr Nutrition 50 25

1986 World Cup Soccer Championships, Mexico — A216

Various plays, world cup and artifacts: 125fr, Ceremonial vase. 135fr, Mayan mask, Palenque. 165fr, Gold breastplate. 340fr, Porcelain mask, Teofihuacan, 7th cent. B.C.

1986, Nov. 17 *Perf. 12½x12*

683 A216 125fr multi 80 40
684 A216 135fr multi 85 42
685 A216 165fr multi 1.10 55
686 A216 340fr multi 2.25 1.10

Nos. 683-686 Overprinted "ARGENTINE 3 / R.F.A. 2" in Scarlet

1986, Nov. 17

687 A216 125fr multi 80 40
688 A216 135fr multi 85 42
689 A216 165fr multi 1.10 55
690 A216 340fr multi 2.25 1.10

Guembeul Nature Reserve A217

1986, Dec. 4 Litho. *Perf. 13½*

691 A217 50fr Ostriches 28 14
692 A217 65fr Kob antelopes 38 20
693 A217 85fr Giraffes 48 24
694 A217 100fr Ostrich, buffalo, kob, giraffe 55 28
695 A217 150fr Buffaloes 85 42
Nos. 691-695 (5) 2.54 1.28

Christmas A218

1986, Dec. 22 Litho. *Perf. 14*

696 A218 70fr Puppet, vert. 40 20
697 A218 85fr Folk musicians 48 24
698 A218 150fr Outdoor celebration, vert. 82 40
699 A218 250fr Boy praying, creche 1.40 70

Inscribed 1985.

Statue of Liberty, Cent. — A219

1986, Dec. 30 Litho. *Perf. 12½*

700 A219 225fr multi 1.30 65

Marine Life A220

1987, Jan. 2 *Perf. 14*

701 A220 50fr Jellyfish, coral 28 14
702 A220 85fr Sea urchin, starfish 48 24
703 A220 100fr Spiny lobster 55 28
704 A220 150fr Dolphin 85 42
705 A220 200fr Octopus 1.15 58
Nos. 701-705 (5) 3.31 1.66

Senegal Stamp Cent. — A221

1987, Apr. 8 *Perf. 13*

706 A221 100fr Intl. express mail 55 28
707 A221 130fr No. 37 75 38
708 A221 140fr similar to No. 201 80 40
709 A221 145fr No. 151, similar to No. 154 82 40
710 A221 320fr No. 27 1.80 90
Nos. 706-710 (5) 4.72 2.36

Designs of Nos. 37, 151 and 27 same as originally released but perfs simulated.

Paris-Dakar Rally — A222

1987, Jan. 22 *Perf. 14*

711 A222 115fr Motorcycle, truck, vert. 65 32
712 A222 125fr Official, race 72 35
713 A222 135fr Sabine, truck 78 40
714 A222 340fr Eiffel Tower, Dakar huts, vert. 1.95 95

Homage to Thierry Sabine. Inscribed 1986.

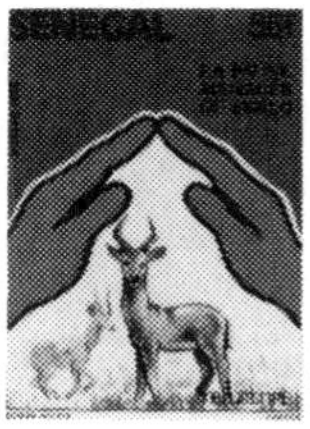

Ferlo Nature Reserve — A223

1987, Feb. 5 *Perf. 13½*

715 A223 55fr Antelope 30 15
716 A223 70fr Ostrich 40 20
717 A223 85fr Warthog 48 24
718 A223 90fr Elephant 52 25

Inscribed 1986.

Agena-Gemini 8 Link-up in Outer Space, 20th Anniv. — A224

1987, Feb. 27 Litho. *Perf. 13*

719 A224 320fr multi 1.75 90

Souvenir Sheet

Perf. 12½

720 A224 500fr multi 2.75 1.40

Nos. 719-720 inscribed 1986 and have erroneous "10e Anniversaire" inscription.

Solidarity Against South African Apartheid — A225

1987, July 31 Litho. *Perf. 13*

721 A225 130fr shown 85 42
722 A225 140fr Mandela, hand, broken chain, vert. 92 45
723 A225 145fr Mandela, dove, death 95 48

Inscribed 1986.

Intelsat, 20th Anniv. A226

1987, Aug. 31 *Perf. 14*

724 A226 50fr Emblem 32 16
725 A226 125fr Satellite 85 42
726 A226 150fr Emblem, globe 1.00 50
727 A226 200fr Earth, satellite in space 1.35 68

Inscribed 1985. Nos. 726-727 vert.

West African Union, 10th Anniv. — A227

Dakar Rotary Club, 45th Anniv. — A228

1987, Sept. 7

728 A227 40fr shown 30 15
729 A227 125fr Emblem, handshake 90 45

Inscribed 1985.

1987, Sept. 29 *Perf. 13*

730 A228 500fr multi 3.60 1.80

Inscribed 1985.

United Nations, 40th Anniv. — A229

1987, Oct. 8 *Perf. 14*

731 A229 85fr Emblem, New York office 62 30
732 A229 95fr Emblem 70 35
733 A229 150fr Hands, emblem 1.10 55

Inscribed 1985.

Cathedral of African Memory, 50th Anniv. A230

Designs: 130fr, Statue of saint, Fr. Daniel Brottier, vert.

Perf. 12½x13, 13x12½

1987, Oct. 16

734 A230 130fr multi 95 48
735 A230 140fr multi 1.00 50

Inscribed 1986.

Lat Dior, King of Cayor (d. 1887) A231

1987, Oct. 27 Litho. *Perf. 14*

736 A231 130fr Battle of Dekhele 95 48
737 A231 260fr Lat Dior 1.90 95

World Food Day — A232

1987, Oct. 30 Litho. *Perf. 12½*

738 A232 130fr Earth storing grain, vert. 90 45
739 A232 140fr shown 98 48
740 A232 145fr Emblem, vert. 1.00 50

Inscribed 1986.

SENEGAL A233

Fauna, Casamance Reefs Natl. Park — A234

1987, Nov. 9 *Perf. 13*

741 A233 115fr Felis servaline 82 40
742 A233 135fr Galagoides demi-dovii 95 48
743 A233 150fr Potamochoerus porcus 1.10 55
744 A233 250fr Panthera pardus 1.80 90
745 A234 300fr Aigrette 2.15 1.10
746 A234 300fr Guepier 2.15 1.10
Nos. 741-746 (6) 8.97 4.53

Inscribed 1986. Nos. 745-746 printed se-tenant in continuous design with corner label picturing map of Senegal with park highlighted.

A particular stamp may be scarce, but if few collectors want it, its market value may remain relatively low.

Traditional Wrestling A235

Birds in Djoudj Natl. Park A236

Various moves.

1987, Nov. 30 Litho. *Perf. 14*

747 A235 115fr multi, horiz. 82 40
748 A235 125fr multi, diff., horiz. 90 45
749 A235 135fr multi, diff. 95 48
750 A235 165fr multi, diff. 1.20 60

1987, Dec. 4

751 A236 115fr Stork 82 40
752 A236 125fr Pink flamingos, horiz. 90 45
753 A236 135fr White pelicans, horiz. 95 48
754 A236 300fr Pelicans in water 2.15 1.10
755 A236 350fr like 125fr, horiz. 2.50 1.25
756 A236 350fr like 135fr, horiz. 2.50 1.25
Nos. 751-756 (6) 9.82 4.93

Nos. 755-756 printed se-tenant with center label picturing map of Senegal with park highlighted.

Christmas A237

Designs: 145fr, Youth dreaming of presents. 150fr, Madonna and child. 180fr, Holy Family, congregation praying. 200fr, Holy Family, candle and Christmas tree.

1987, Dec. 24 *Perf. 12½x13*

757 A237 145fr multi 1.05 52
758 A237 150fr multi 1.10 55
759 A237 180fr multi 1.30 65
760 A237 200fr multi 1.45 72

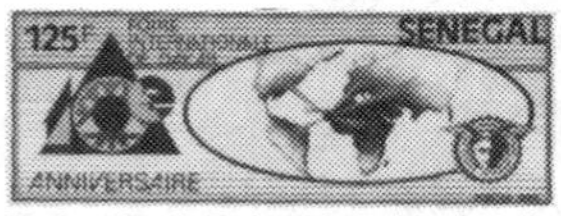

Dakar Intl. Fair, 10th Anniv. (in 1985) — A238

1988, Feb. 27 Litho. *Perf. 13*

761 A238 125fr multi 90 45

Inscribed 1985.

Fish A239

1988, Feb. 29 Litho. *Perf. 13*

762 A239 5fr Amelurus nebulosus 5 5
763 A239 100fr Heniochus acuminatus 72 35
764 A239 145fr Anthias anthias 1.05 52
765 A239 180fr Cyprinus carpio 1.30 65

World Meteorology Day — A240

1988, Mar. 15 *Perf. 13½*

766 A240 145fr multi 1.05 52

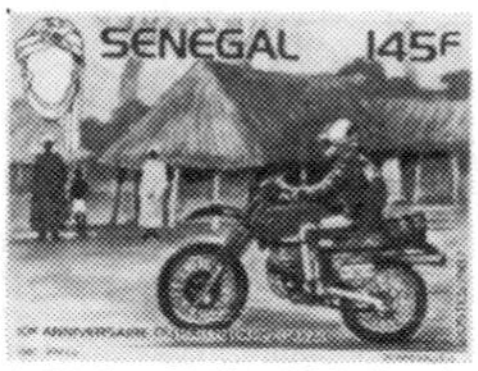

Paris-Dakar Rally, 10th Anniv. (in 1987) — A241

Various motorcycle and automobile entries in desert settings.

1988

767 A241 145fr Motorcycle 1.05 52
768 A241 180fr Race car 1.30 65
769 A241 200fr Race car, truck 1.45 72
770 A241 410fr Thierry Sabine 2.90 1.45

Inscribed 1987.

Mollusks A242

1988, Apr. 20 *Perf. 12½*

771 A242 10fr Squid 8 5
772 A242 20fr Donax trunculus 15 8
773 A242 145fr Achatina fulica, vert. 1.05 52
774 A242 165fr Helix nemoralis 1.20 60

1988 African Soccer Cup Championships, Rabat — A243

1988, May 10 Litho. *Perf. 13*

775 A243 80fr Cameroun (winner) 55 28
776 A243 100fr Kick, CAF emblem 70 35
777 A243 145fr Map, players, final score 1.00 50
778 A243 180fr Trophy 1.25 62

Nos. 776-778 vert.

US Peace Corps in Senegal, 25th Anniv. — A244

1988, May 11 Litho. *Perf. 13*

779 A244 190fr multi 1.25 62

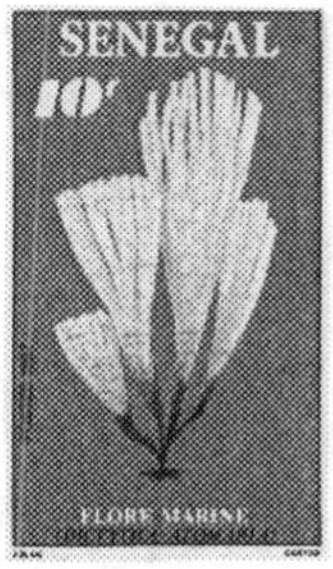

Marine Flora — A245

1988, June 13 Litho. *Perf. 12½*

780 A245 10fr Dictyota atomaria 6 5
781 A245 65fr Agarum gmelini 45 22
782 A245 145fr Saccorrhiza bulbosa 95 48
783 A245 180fr Rhodymenia palmetta 1.20 60

Inscribed 1987.

No. 710 Overprinted

RICCIONE 88 27-29-08-89

1988, Aug. 27 Litho. *Perf. 13*

784 A221 320fr multi 2.20 1.10

Stamp Fair, Riccione, Aug. 27-29, 1988. Stamp incorrectly overprinted "89," instead of "88."

ENDA — A246

1988 Litho. *Perf. 13*

785 A246 125fr Thierno Saidou Nourou Tall Center 80 40

1988 Summer Olympics, Seoul — A247

1988, Sept. 17 Litho. *Perf. 13*

786 A247 5fr shown 5 5
787 A247 75fr Running, swimming, soccer 50 25
788 A247 300fr Character trademark, torch 2.00 1.00
789 A247 410fr Emblems, running 2.75 1.40

Industries
A248

Indigenous
Flowers
A250

Postcards, c. 1900 — A249

1988, Nov. 7 Litho. *Perf. 13*

790 A248 5fr Phosphate, Thies 5 5
791 A248 20fr I.C.S. 14 6
792 A248 145fr Seib Mill, Diourbel 92 45
793 A248 410fr Mbao refinery 2.60 1.30

1988, Nov. 26

Designs: 20fr, Boys, Government Palace. 145fr, Wrestlers, St. Louis Great Mosque. 180fr, Dakar Depot, young woman in folk costume. 200fr, Governor's Residence, housewife using mortar and pestle.

794 A249 20fr red brn & blk 14 6
795 A249 145fr red brn & blk 92 45
796 A249 180fr red brn & blk 1.15 58
797 A249 200fr red brn & blk 1.30 65

1988, Dec. 4 *Perf. 13x12½*

798 A250 20fr Packia biglobosa 14 6
799 A250 60fr Eurphorbia pulcherrima 38 20
800 A250 65fr Cyrtosperma senegalense 42 20
801 A250 410fr Bombax costatum 2.60 1.30

11th Paris-
Dakar Rally
A251

1989, Jan. 13 Litho. *Perf. 13½*

802 A251 10fr Mask, vehicle, Eiffel Tower 7 5
803 A251 145fr Helmet, desert scene 95 48
804 A251 180fr Turban, rallyist in desert 1.20 60
805 A251 220fr Thierry Sabine 1.45 72

Tourism
A252

1989, Feb. 15 *Perf. 13*

806 A252 10fr Teranga 7 5
807 A252 80fr Campement 52 25
808 A252 100fr Saly 65 32
809 A252 350fr Dior 2.25 1.15

Inscribed 1988.

Tourism — A253

1989, Mar. 11

810 A253 130fr Natl. tourism emblem, vert. 85 42
811 A253 140fr Visiting rural community 92 45
812 A253 145fr Sport fishing 95 48
813 A253 180fr Water skiing, polo 1.20 60

Inscribed 1987.

SEMI-POSTAL STAMPS

No. 84 Surcharged in Red **+ 5c**

1915 Unwmk. *Perf. 14x13½*

B1 A28 10c + 5c org red & rose 35 35

No. B1 is on both ordinary and chalky paper.

Same Surcharge on No. 87

1918

B2 A28 15c + 5c red org & brn vio 38 38

Curie Issue
Common Design Type

1938 Engr. *Perf. 13*

B3 CD80 1.75fr + 50c brt ultra 4.00 4.00

French Revolution Issue
Common Design Type

Photo., Name & Value Typo. in Black

1939

B4 CD83 45(c) + 25(c) grn 3.00 3.00
B5 CD83 70(c) + 30(c) brn 3.00 3.00
B6 CD83 90(c) + 35(c) red org 3.00 3.00
B7 CD83 1.25fr + 1fr rose pink 3.00 3.00
B8 CD83 2.25fr + 2fr bl 3.00 3.00
Nos. B4-B8 (5) 15.00 15.00

Stamps of 1935-38 Surcharged in Red or Black **SECOURS + 1 fr. NATIONAL**

1941 *Perf. 12x12½, 12*

B9 A30 50c + 1fr red org (Bk) 40
B10 A31 80c + 2fr vio (R) 1.60
B11 A30 1.50fr + 2fr dk bl (Bk) 2.25
B12 A30 2fr + 3fr bl (Bk) 2.25

Common Design Type and

Bambara
Sharpshooter
SP1

Colonial
Soldier
SP2

1941 Photo. *Perf. 13½*

B13 SP1 1fr + 1fr red 50
B14 CD86 1.50fr + 3fr mar 50
B15 SP2 2.50fr + 1fr bl 50

The surtax was for the defense of the colonies.

Nos. B13-B15 were issued by the Vichy government, but it is doubtful whether they were placed in use in Senegal.

Stamps of type A32 surcharged "OEUVRES COLONIALES" and new values were issued in 1944 by the Vichy Government, but were not placed on sale in the colony.

Catalogue values for unused stamps in this section, from this point to the end of the section, are for Never Hinged items.

Republic
Anti-Malaria Issue
Common Design Type
Perf. 12½x12

1962, Apr. 7 Engr. Unwmk.

B16 CD108 25fr + 5fr brt grn 40 40

Freedom from Hunger Issue
Common Design Type

1963, Mar. 21 *Perf. 13*

B17 CD112 25fr + 5fr dp vio, grn & brn 35 35

AIR POST STAMPS

Landscape
AP1

Caravan
AP2

Perf. 12½x12, 12x12½

1935 Engr. Unwmk.

C1 AP1 25c dk brn 12 12
C2 AP1 50c red org 35 25
C3 AP1 1fr rose lil 12 12
C4 AP1 1.25fr yel grn 12 12
C5 AP1 2fr blue 12 12
C6 AP1 3fr ol grn 12 12
C7 AP2 3.50fr violet 12 12
C8 AP2 4.75fr orange 35 28
C9 AP2 6.50fr dk bl 55 45
C10 AP2 8fr black 80 60
C11 AP2 15fr rose lake 55 42
Nos. C1-C11 (11) 3.32 2.72

No. C8 surcharged "ENTR' AIDE FRANCAIS + 95f 25" in green, red violet or blue, was never issued in this colony.

Common Design Type

1940 Engr. *Perf. 12½x12*

C12 CD85 1.90fr ultra 20 20
C13 CD85 2.90fr dk red 20 20
C14 CD85 4.50fr dk gray grn 28 28
C15 CD85 4.90fr yel bis 35 35
C16 CD85 6.90fr dp org 35 35
Nos. C12-C16 (5) 1.38 1.38

Common Design Types

1942

C17 CD88 50c car & bl 5
C18 CD88 1fr brn & blk 20
C19 CD88 2fr dk grn & red brn 20
C20 CD88 3fr dk bl & scar 40
C21 CD88 5fr vio & brn red 22

Frame Engr., Center Typo.

C22 CD89 10fr ultra, ind & hn 22
C23 CD89 20fr rose car, mag & choc 25
C24 CD89 50fr yel grn, dl grn & yel 55 70

Engr. & Photo.
Size: 47x26mm

C25 CD88 100fr dk red & bl 1.00 1.00
Nos. C17-C25 (9) 3.09

There is doubt whether Nos. C17 to C23 were officially placed in use.

Catalogue values for unused stamps in this section, from this point to the end of the section, are for Never Hinged items.

Republic

Abyssinian Roller — AP3

Designs: 50fr, Carmine bee-eater (vert.). 200fr, Violet touraco (vert.). 250fr, Red bishop (vert.). 500fr, Fish eagle (vert.).

Perf. 12½x13, 13x12½

1960-63 Photo. Unwmk.

Birds in Natural Colors

C26 AP3 50fr blk & gray bl ('61) 65 20
C27 AP3 100fr blk, yel & lil 1.40 45
C28 AP3 200fr blk, grn & bl ('61) 2.50 1.50
C29 AP3 250fr blk & pale grn ('63) 3.50 1.90
C30 AP3 500fr blk & bl 5.50 2.50
Nos. C26-C30 (5) 13.55 6.55

Air Afrique Issue
Common Design Type

1962, Feb. 17 Engr. *Perf. 13*

C31 CD107 25fr vio brn, sl grn & ocher 30 16

African Postal Union Issue
Common Design Type

1963, Sept. 8 Photo. *Perf. 12½*

C32 CD114 85fr choc, ocher & red 65 42

Air Afrique Issue, 1963
Common Design Type

1963, Nov. 19 Unwmk. *Perf. 13x12*

C33 CD115 50fr multi 70 50

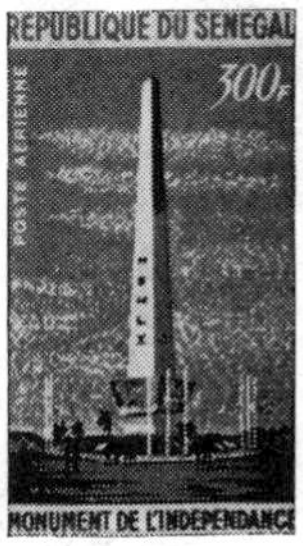

Independence
Monument — AP4

1964, Apr. 4 Photo. *Perf. 12x13*

C34 AP4 300fr ultra, tan, ocher & grn 2.00 1.00

Symbolic European and African
Cities — AP5

1964, Apr. 18 Engr. *Perf. 13*

C35 AP5 150fr grn, brn red & blk 1.60 1.00

Congress of the Intl. Federation of Twin Cities, Dakar.

Europafrica Issue, 1964

Peanuts, Globe, Factory, Figures of "Africa," and "Europe" — AP6

1964, July 20 Photo. *Perf. 13x12*
C36 AP6 50fr multi 65 50

See note after Madagascar No. 357.

Basketball — AP7

Launching of Syncom 2 — AP8

Design: 100fr, Pole vault.

1964, Aug. 22 Engr. *Perf. 13*
C37 AP7 85fr org brn & bl 65 42
C38 AP7 100fr dk grn, red brn & dk brn 90 50

18th Olympic Games, Tokyo, Oct. 10-25.

1964, Oct. 24 Unwmk. *Perf. 13*
C39 AP8 150fr grn, red brn & ultra 1.10 55

Communication through space.

Pres. John F. Kennedy (1917-1963) AP9

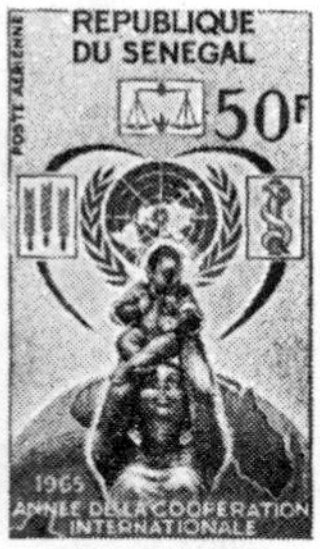

Mother and Child, Globe and Emblems AP10

1964, Dec. 5 Photo. *Perf. 13*
C40 AP9 100fr brt yel, dk grn & brn red 90 75
a. Souv. sheet of 4 4.00 4.00

Scenic Type of Regular Issue, 1965

View: 100fr, Shore of Gambia River in Eastern Senegal.

1965, Feb. 27 Engr. *Perf. 13*
Size: 48x27mm
C41 A48 100fr brn blk, grn & bis 1.00 42

1965, Sept. 25 Unwmk. *Perf. 13*
C42 AP10 50fr choc, brt bl & grn 45 25

International Cooperation Year.

Demand, as well as supply, determines a stamp's market value. One is as important as the other.

A-1 Satellite and Earth — AP11

Designs: No. C44, Diamant rocket. 90fr, Scout rocket and FR-1 satellite.

1966, Feb. 19 Engr. *Perf. 13*
C43 AP11 50fr yel brn, dk grn & blk 38 20
C44 AP11 50fr Prus bl, lt red brn & car rose 38 20
C45 AP11 90fr dk red brn, dk gray & Prus bl 80 42

French achievements in space.

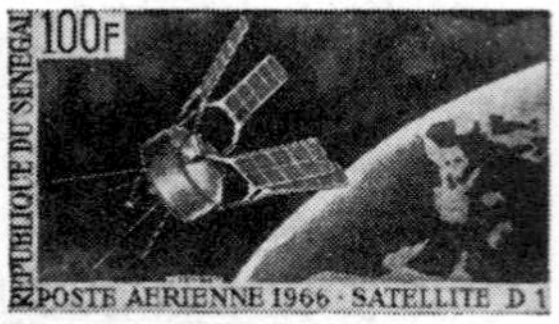

D-1 Satellite over Globe — AP12

1966, June 11 Engr. *Perf. 13*
C46 AP12 100fr dk car, sl & vio 1.00 55

Launching of the D-1 satellite at Hammaguir, Algeria, Feb. 17, 1966.

Air Afrique Issue, 1966
Common Design Type

1966, Aug. 31 Photo. *Perf. 13*
C47 CD123 30fr red brn, blk & lem 30 14

Mermoz Plane "Arc-en-Ciel" — AP13

Jean Mermoz — AP14

Designs: 35fr, Latecoère 300 "Croix du Sud." 100fr, Map showing last flight from Dakar to Brazil.

1966, Dec. 7 Engr. *Perf. 13*
C48 AP13 20fr bl, rose lil & ind 22 16
C49 AP13 35fr sl, brn & grn 38 20
C50 AP13 100fr grn, lt grn & mar 1.00 42
C51 AP14 150fr blk, ultra & mar 1.50 70

Jean Mermoz (1901-36), French aviator, on the 30th anniv. of his last flight.

Dakar-Yoff Airport — AP15

1967, Apr. 22 Engr. *Perf. 13*
C52 AP15 200fr red brn, ind & brt bl 1.10 38

Knob-billed Goose — AP16

Flowers and Birds: 100fr, Mimosa. 150fr, Flowering cactus. 250fr, Village weaver. 500fr, Bateleur.

1967-69 Photo. *Perf. 11½*
Granite Paper
Dated "1967"
C53 AP16 100fr gray, yel & grn 1.10 45
C54 AP16 150fr multi 1.60 65

Dated "1969"
C55 AP16 250fr gray & multi 2.00 1.00

Dated "1968"
C56 AP16 300fr brt bl & multi 3.00 1.25
C57 AP16 500fr org & multi 4.25 1.90
Nos. C53-C57 (5) 11.95 5.25

Issue dates: 100fr, 150fr, June 24, 1967; 500fr, July 13, 1968; 300fr, Dec. 21, 1968; 250fr, Apr. 26, 1969.

The Girls from Avignon, by Picasso AP17

1967, July 22 *Perf. 12x13*
C59 AP17 100fr multi 1.20 80

African Postal Union Issue, 1967
Common Design Type

1967, Sept. 9 Engr. *Perf. 13*
C60 CD124 100fr brt grn, vio & car lake 90 45

Konrad Adenauer AP18

Weather Balloon, Vegetation and WMO Emblem AP19

1968, Feb. 17 Photo. *Perf. 12½*
C61 AP18 100fr dk red, ol & blk 1.10 55
a. Souv. sheet of 4 4.50 4.50

Konrad Adenauer (1876-1967), chancellor of West Germany (1949-63).

1968, Mar. 23 Engr. *Perf. 13*
C62 AP19 50fr blk, ultra & bl grn 45 22

8th World Meteorological Day, Mar. 23.

19th Olympic Games, Mexico City, Oct. 12-27 — AP20

1968, Oct. 12 Engr. *Perf. 13*
C63 AP20 20fr Hurdling 20 8
C64 AP20 30fr Javelin 22 16
C65 AP20 50fr Wrestling 42 18
C66 AP20 75fr Basketball 60 22

PHILEXAFRIQUE Issue

Young Woman Reading Letter, by Jean Raoux AP21

1968, Oct. 26 Photo. *Perf. 12½*
C67 AP21 100fr buff & multi 1.10 1.00

PHILEXAFRIQUE, Phil. Exhib. in Abidjan, Feb. 14-23, 1969. Printed with alternating buff label.

2nd PHILEXAFRIQUE Issue
Common Design Type

Design: 50fr, Senegal No. 160 and Boulevard, Dakar.

1969, Feb. 14 Engr. *Perf. 13*
C68 CD128 50fr grn, gray & pur 60 50

Tourist Emblem with Map of Africa and Dove — AP22

1969 Photo. *Perf. 13*
C69 AP22 100fr red, lt grn & lt bl 70 35

Year of African Tourism, 1969.

Pres. Lamine Gueye (1891-1968) AP23

Design: 45fr, Pres. Gueye wearing fez.

1969, June 10 Photo. *Perf. 12½*
C70 AP23 30fr brn, org & blk 22 14
C71 AP23 45fr brn, lt grnsh bl & blk 35 16
a. Min. sheet of 4, 2 each #C70-C71 1.25 1.25

"Transmission of Thought" Tapestry by Ousmane Faye — AP24

Fari, Tapestry by Allaye N'Diaye — AP25

1969, Oct. 25 Photo. *Perf. 12½*

C72 AP24 25fr multi 22 14

Perf. 12x12½

C73 AP25 50fr multi 45 22

Europafrica Issue

Baila Bridge — AP26

1969, Nov. 15 Photo. *Perf. 13x12*

C74 AP26 100fr multi 70 38

Emile Lécrivain, Plane and Toulouse-Dakar Route — AP27

1970, Jan. 31 Engr. *Perf. 13*

C75 AP27 50fr grn, sl & rose brn 40 22

50th anniv. of the disappearance of the aviator Emile Lécrivain (1897-1929).

René Maran, Martinique AP28

Portraits: 45fr, Marcus Garvey, Jamaica. 50fr, Dr. Price Mars, Haiti.

1970, Mar. 21 Photo. *Perf. 12½*

C76 AP28 30fr red brn, lt grn & blk 22 10

C77 AP28 45fr bl, pink & blk 38 16

C78 AP28 50fr grn, buff & blk 40 16

Issued to honor prominent Negro leaders.

"One People, One Purpose, One Faith" AP29

1970, Apr. 3 Photo. *Perf. 11½*

C79 AP29 500fr gold & multi 4.00 1.90

a. Souvenir sheet 4.50 4.50

10th anniv. of independence. No. C79 sold for 600fr.

Bay of Naples and Dakar Post Office — AP30

1970, May 2 Photo. *Perf. 13x12½*

C80 AP30 100fr multi 80 55

10th Europa Phil. Exhib., Naples, May 2-10.

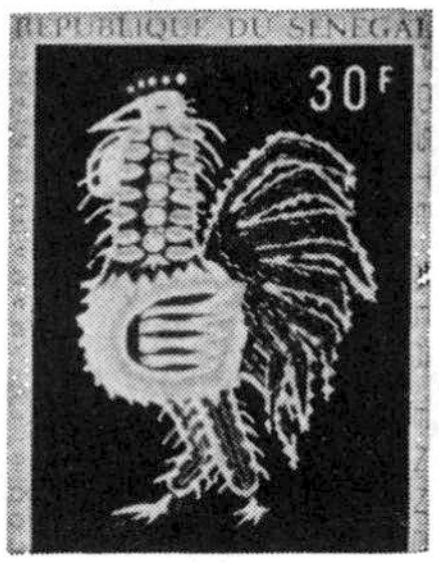

Blue Cock, by Mamadou Niang AP31

Tapestries: 45fr, Fairy. 75fr, "Lunaris," by Jean Lurçat.

1970, June 20 Photo. *Perf. 12½x12*

C81 AP31 30fr blk & multi 20 12

C82 AP31 45fr dk red brn & multi 35 15

C83 AP31 75fr yel & multi 50 30

Head of the Courtesan Nagakawa, by Chobunsai Yeishi, and Mt. Fuji, by Hokusai — AP32

EXPO Emblem and: 25fr, Woman Playing Guitar, by Hokusai, and Sun Tower (vert.). 150fr, "One of the Present-day Beauties of Nanboku" by Katsukawa Shuncho (vert.).

1970, July 18 Engr. *Perf. 13*

C84 AP32 25fr red & grn 20 14

C85 AP32 75fr yel grn, dk bl & red brn 55 22

C86 AP32 150fr bl, red brn & ocher 1.10 55

EXPO '70 Intl. Exhib., Osaka, Japan, Mar. 15-Sept. 13.

Tuna, Processing Plant and Ship — AP33

Urban Development in Dakar — AP34

1970, Aug. 22 Engr. *Perf. 13*

C87 AP33 30fr dl red, blk & brt bl 22 14

C88 AP34 100fr choc & grn 70 40

Progress in industrialization and urbanization in Dakar.

Beethoven; Napoleon and Allegory of Eroica Symphony AP35

Design: 100fr, Beethoven holding quill.

1970, Sept. 26 Engr. *Perf. 13*

C89 AP35 50fr ol, brn & ocher 42 22

C90 AP35 100fr Prus grn & dp cl 80 50

Ludwig van Beethoven (1770-1827), composer.

Globe, Scales and Women of Four Races — AP36

1970, Oct. 24 Engr. *Perf. 13*

C91 AP36 100fr grn, ocher & red 90 55

25th anniversary of United Nations.

De Gaulle, Map of Africa, Symbols — AP37

Phillis Wheatley, American Poet — AP39

"A Roof for Every Refugee" — AP38

Design: 100fr, Charles de Gaulle and map of Senegal.

1970, Dec. 31 Photo. *Perf. 12½*

C92 AP37 50fr multi 45 35

C93 AP37 100fr bl & multi 1.00 65

Honoring Pres. Charles de Gaulle as liberator of the colonies.

1971, Jan. 16

C94 AP38 100fr multi 80 42

High Commissioner for Refugees, 20th anniv.

1971, Apr. 10 Photo. *Perf. 12½*

Prominent Blacks: 40fr, James E. K. Aggrey, Methodist missionary, Ghana. 60fr, Alain Le Roy Locke, American educator. 100fr, Booker T. Washington, American educator.

C95 AP39 25fr multi 16 10

C96 AP39 40fr blk, bl & bis 30 16

C97 AP39 60fr blk, bl & emer 45 18

C98 AP39 100fr blk, bl & red 70 38

Napoleon as First Consul, by Ingres AP40

Designs: 25fr, Napoleon in 1809, by Robert Lefevre. 35fr, Napoleon on his death bed, by Georges Rouget. 50fr, Awakening into Immortality, sculpture by Francois Rude.

1971, June 19 Photo. *Perf. 13*

C99 AP40 15fr gold & multi 25 20

C100 AP40 25fr gold & multi 40 25

C101 AP40 35fr gold & multi 45 35

C102 AP40 50fr gold & multi 65 60

Napoleon Bonaparte (1769-1821).

Gamal Abdel Nasser AP41

Alfred Nobel AP41a

1971, July 17 *Perf. 12½*

C103 AP41 50fr multi 40 20

Nasser (1918-1970), President of Egypt.

1971, Sept. 25 Photo. *Perf. 13½x13*

C103A AP41a 100fr multi 80 45

Alfred Nobel (1833-1896), inventor of dynamite who established the Nobel Prizes.

Iranian Flag and Senegal Coat of Arms — AP42

1971, Oct. 15 ***Perf. 13x12½***
C104 AP42 200fr multi 1.50 65

2500th anniversary of the founding of the Persian empire by Cyrus the Great.

African Postal Union Issue, 1971
Common Design Type

Design: 100fr, Arms of Senegal and UAMPT Building, Brazzaville, Congo.

1971, Nov. 13 ***Perf. 13x13½***
C105 CD135 100fr bl & multi 70 30

Louis Armstrong (1900-1971), American Jazz Musician AP43

1971, Nov. 27 **Photo.** ***Perf. 12½***
C106 AP43 150fr gold & dk brn 1.20 80

Sapporo Olympic Emblem and Speed Skating — AP44

Sapporo '72 Emblem and: 10fr, Bobsledding. 125fr, Skiing.

1972, Jan. 22 ***Perf. 13***
C107 AP44 5fr multi 5 5
C108 AP44 10fr multi 8 5
C109 AP44 125fr multi 90 40

11th Winter Olympic Games, Sapporo, Japan, Feb. 3-13.

Fonteghetto della Farina, by Canaletto — AP45

Design: 100fr, San Giorgio Maggiore, by Giovanni Antonio Guardi (vert.).

1972, Feb. 26
C110 AP45 50fr gold & multi 40 20
C111 AP45 100fr gold & multi 80 40

UNESCO campaign to save Venice.

Theater Type of Regular Issue

Design: 150fr, Daniel Sorano as Shylock (vert.).

1972, Mar. 25 **Photo.** ***Perf. 12½x13***
C112 A99 150fr multi 1.40 70

Environment Type of Regular Issue

Design: 100fr, Protection of the ocean (oil slick).

1972, June 3 **Photo.** ***Perf. 13x12½***
C113 A101 100fr multi 80 45

Emperor Haile Selassie, Ethiopian and Senegalese Flags — AP46

1972, July 23 **Photo.** ***Perf. 13½x13***
C114 AP46 100fr gold & multi 80 40

80th birthday of Emperor Haile Selassie of Ethiopia.

Swordfish — AP47

Designs: 65fr, Killer whale. 75fr, Rhincodon. 125fr, Common rorqual (whale).

1972-73 **Photo.** ***Perf. 11½***
C115 AP47 50fr multi 35 10
C116 AP47 65fr multi ('73) 40 18
C117 AP47 75fr multi ('73) 45 22
C118 AP47 125fr multi 90 55

Issue dates: Nos. C115, C118, Nov. 25, 1972. Nos. C116-C117, July 28, 1973.

Palace of the Republic — AP48

1973, Apr. 3 **Photo.** ***Perf. 13***
C119 AP48 100fr multi 60 35

Hotel Teranga, Dakar — AP49

1973, May 26 **Photo.** ***Perf. 13***
C120 AP49 100fr multi 60 35

Emblem of African Lions Club — AP50

1973, June 2
C121 AP50 150fr multi 1.00 65

15th Congress of Lions Intl., District 403, Dakar, June 1-2.

"Couple with Mimosa," by Marc Chagall AP51

1973, Aug. 11 **Photo.** ***Perf. 13***
C122 AP51 200fr multi 1.60 90

Map of Italy with Riccione AP52

Human Rights Flame and People AP54

Raoul Follereau and World Map — AP53

1973, Aug. 25 **Engr.**
C123 AP52 100fr dk grn, red & pur 60 38

Intl. Phil. Exhib., Riccione 1973.

1973, Dec. 22 **Engr.** ***Perf. 13***

Design: 100fr, Dr. Armauer G. Hansen and leprosy bacilli.

C124 AP53 40fr sl grn, pur & red brn 25 14
C125 AP53 100fr sl grn, mag & plum 65 40

Centenary of the discovery of the Hansen bacillus, the cause of leprosy.

1973, Dec. 15 **Photo.** ***Perf. 13½***

Design: 65fr, Human Rights flame and drummer.

C126 AP54 35fr grn & multi 20 14
C127 AP54 65fr org & multi 25 22

25th anniv. of the Universal Declaration of Human Rights.

Men of Four Races, Arms of Dakar, Congress Emblem — AP55

Design: 50fr, Key joining twin cities and emblem (vert.).

1973, Dec. 26 **Photo.**
C128 AP55 50fr org & multi 35 20
C129 AP55 125fr red & multi 80 45

8th Congress of the World Federation of Twin Cities, Dakar, Dec. 26-29.

Finfoots — AP56

1974, Feb. 9 **Photo.** ***Perf. 13***
C130 AP56 1fr shown 5 5
C131 AP56 2fr Spoonbills 5 5
C132 AP56 3fr Crested cranes 5 5
C133 AP56 4fr Egrets 5 5
C134 AP56 250fr Flamingos 1.40 90
C135 AP56 250fr Flamingos 1.40 90
Strip of 2 + label 3.00
Nos. C130-C135 (6) 3.00 2.00

Djoudj Park bird sanctuary. Nos. C134-C135 printed se-tenant with label showing map of Senegal. Denomination in gold on No. C134, in black on No. C135.

Tiger Attacking Wild Horse, by Delacroix — AP57

Design: 200fr, Tiger Hunt, by Eugène Delacroix (1798-1863).

1974, Mar. 23 **Photo.** ***Perf. 13***
C136 AP57 150fr gold & multi 90 60
C137 AP57 200fr gold & multi 1.20 65

A Dakar Fair set of 2 was issued in 1974.

Soyuz and Apollo, Space Docking Emblem — AP58

1975, May 23 **Engr.** ***Perf. 13***
C138 AP58 125fr multi 50 35

Russo-American space cooperation.

Senegal Type D6, Tuscany Type A1, Map of Italy AP59

1975, Aug. 23 **Engr.** ***Perf. 13***
C139 AP59 125fr org, vio & dk red 65 35

Intl. Phil. Exhib., Riccione 1975.

No. C138 Overprinted: "JONCTION / 17 Juil. 1975"

1975, Oct. 21 Engr. *Perf. 13*

C140	AP58 125fr multi	50	35

Apollo-Soyuz link-up in space, July 17, 1975.

Boston Massacre — AP60

Design: 500fr, Lafayette, Washington, Rochambeau and Battle of Yorktown.

1975, Dec. 20 Engr. *Perf. 13*

C141	AP60 250fr ultra, red & brn	1.40	65
C142	AP60 500fr bl & ver	2.50	1.40

American Bicentennial.

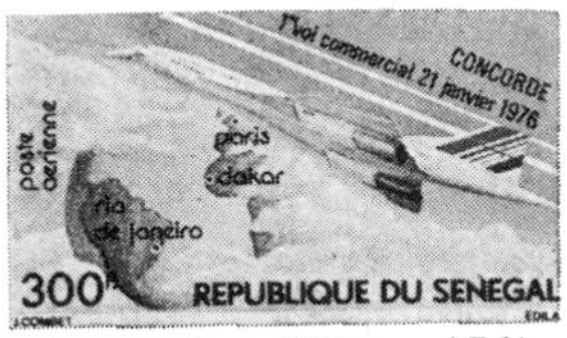

Concorde and Map — AP61

1976, Jan. 21 Litho. *Perf. 13*

C143	AP61 300fr multi	1.60	80

First commercial flight of supersonic jet Concorde, Paris to Rio de Janeiro, Jan. 21.

Spaceship and Control Room — AP62

1977, June 25 Litho. *Perf. 12½*

C144	AP62 300fr multi	1.60	80

Viking space mission to Mars.

No. C143 Overprinted in Red: "22.11.77 / PARIS NEW-YORK"

1977, Nov. 22 *Perf. 13*

C145	AP61 300fr multi	1.60	80

Concorde, first commercial flight, Paris to New York.

Philexafrique II-Essen Issue

Common Design Types

Designs: No. C146, Lion and Senegal No. C28. No. C147, Capercaillie and Schleswig-Holstein No. 1.

1978, Nov. 1 Litho. *Perf. 12½*

C146	CD138 100fr multi	65	28
C147	CD139 100fr multi	65	28

Nos. C146-C147 printed se-tenant.

J. Dabry, L. Gimie, and J. Mermoz, Airplane, Map of Route (St. Louis-Natal) — AP63

1980, Dec. Photo. *Perf. 13*

C148	AP63 300fr multi	2.25	80

1st airmail crossing of South Atlantic, 50th anniversary.

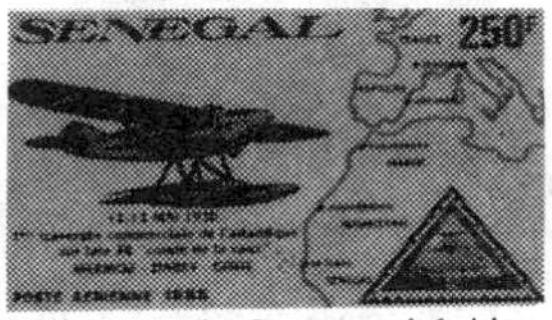

1st Transatlantic Commercial Airmail Flight, 55th Anniv. — AP64

1985, May 12 Litho. *Perf. 13*

C149	AP64 250fr multi	65	35

AIR POST SEMI-POSTAL STAMPS

French Revolution Issue

Common Design Type

1939 Unwmk. Photo. *Perf. 13*

Name and Value Typo. in Orange

CB1	CD83 4.75 + 4fr brn blk	4.25	4.25

Surtax used for the defense of the colonies.

Stamps of types of Dahomey V1, V2, V3, and V4 inscribed "Senegal" were issued in 1942 by the Vichy Government, but were not placed on sale in the colony.

Catalogue values for unused stamps in this section, from this point to the end of the section, are for Never Hinged items.

Republic

Nile Gods Uniting Upper and Lower Egypt (Abu Simbel) — SPAP1

1964, Mar. 7 Engr. *Perf. 13*

CB2	SPAP1 25fr + 5fr Prus bl, red brn & sl grn	80	60

UNESCO campaign to save historic monuments in Nubia.

POSTAGE DUE STAMPS

Postage Due Stamps of French Colonies Surcharged **10**

1903 Unwmk. *Imperf.*

J1	D1 10c on 50c lil	40.00	40.00
J2	D1 10c on 60c brn, *buff*	40.00	40.00
J3	D1 10c on 1fr rose, *buff*	190.00	190.00

D2

D3

1906 Typo. *Perf. 14x13½*

J4	D2 5c grn, *grnsh*	2.00	2.00
J5	D2 10c red brn	2.50	2.50
J6	D2 15c dk bl	2.75	2.75
J7	D2 20c blk, *yellow*	3.25	3.25
J8	D2 30c red, *straw*	3.50	3.25
J9	D2 50c violet	3.50	3.25
J10	D2 60c blk, *buff*	4.50	4.50
J11	D2 1fr blk, *pinkish*	8.00	7.50
	Nos. J4-J11 (8)	30.00	29.00

1914

J12	D3 5c green	12	12
J13	D3 10c rose	20	20
J14	D3 15c gray	20	20
J15	D3 20c brown	30	20
J16	D3 30c blue	50	42
J17	D3 50c black	60	55
J18	D3 60c orange	80	65
J19	D3 1fr violet	80	65
	Nos. J12-J19 (8)	3.52	2.99

Type of 1914 Issue Surcharged **2F.**

1927

J20	D3 2fr on 1fr lil rose	2.25	1.90
J21	D3 3fr on 1fr org brn	2.25	1.90

D4

1935 Engr. *Perf. 12½x12*

J22	D4 5c yel grn	5	5
J23	D4 10c red org	5	5
J24	D4 15c violet	5	5
J25	D4 20c ol grn	5	5
J26	D4 30c redsh brn	9	9
J27	D4 50c rose lil	30	30
J28	D4 60c orange	50	50
J29	D4 1fr black	35	35
J30	D4 2fr dk bl	35	35
J31	D4 3fr dk car	42	42
	Nos. J22-J31 (10)	2.21	2.21

Catalogue values for unused stamps in this section, from this point to the end of the section, are for Never Hinged items.

Republic

D5

Lion — D6

1961, Feb. 20 Typo. *Perf. 14x13½*

J32	D5 1fr org & red	5	5
J33	D5 2fr ultra & red	10	10
J34	D5 5fr brn & red	12	12
J35	D5 20fr grn & red	50	50
J36	D5 25fr red lil & red	55	55
	Nos. J32-J36 (5)	1.32	1.32

1966-83 Typo. *Perf. 14x13*

Lion in Gold

J37	D6 1fr red & blk	5	5
J38	D6 2fr yel brn & blk	5	5
J39	D6 5fr red lil & blk	9	9
J40	D6 10fr brt bl & blk	20	20
J41	D6 20fr emer & blk	32	32
J42	D6 30fr gray & blk	55	55
J43	D6 60fr bl & blk ('83)	28	28
J44	D6 90fr rose & blk ('83)	42	42
	Nos. J37-J44 (8)	1.96	1.96

Issue dates: 1fr-30fr, Dec. 1, 1966. Others, Oct. 1983.

OFFICIAL STAMPS

Catalogue values for unused stamps in this section, from this point to the end of the section, are for Never Hinged items.

Arms O1

Baobab Tree O2

Perf. 14x13½

1961, Sept. 18 Typo. Unwmk.

Denominations in Black

O1	O1 1fr sep & bl	5	5
O2	O1 2fr dk bl & org	10	9
O3	O1 5fr mar & grn	10	10
O4	O1 10fr ver & bl	12	12
O5	O1 25fr vio bl & ver	35	12
O6	O1 50fr ver & gray	65	35
O7	O1 85fr lil & org	1.20	62
O8	O1 100fr ver & yel grn	1.60	90
	Nos. O1-O8 (8)	4.17	2.35

1966-77 Typo. *Perf. 14x13*

O9	O2 1fr yel & blk	5	5
O10	O2 5fr org & blk	10	5
O11	O2 10fr red & blk	10	10
O12	O2 20fr dp red lil & blk	15	10
O13	O2 25fr dp lil & blk ('75)	12	5
O14	O2 30fr bl & blk	28	12
O15	O2 35fr bl & blk ('73)	40	12
O16	O2 40fr grnsh bl & blk ('75)	25	5
O17	O2 55fr emer & blk	65	45
O18	O2 60fr emer & blk ('77)	32	5
O19	O2 90fr dk bl grn & blk	1.00	22
O20	O2 100fr brn & blk	1.20	22
	Nos. O9-O20 (12)	4.62	1.58

No. O17 Surcharged with New Value and Two Bars

1969

O21	O2 60fr on 55fr emer & blk	1.00	15

Type of 1966

1983, Oct. Typo. *Perf. 14x13*

O22	O2 90fr dk grn & blk ('83)	42	5

SENEGAMBIA & NIGER

A French Administrative unit for the Senegal and Niger possessions in Africa during the period when the French possessions in Africa were being definitely divided into colonies and protectorates. The name was dropped in 1904 when this territory was consolidated with part of French Sudan, under the name Upper Senegal and Niger.

100 Centimes = 1 Franc

Navigation and Commerce — A1

1903 Unwmk. Typo. *Perf. 14x13½*

Name of Colony in Blue or Carmine

1	A1 1c black, *lil bl*	85	85
2	A1 2c brown, *buff*	1.00	1.00
3	A1 4c cl, *lav*	1.90	1.90
4	A1 5c yel grn	2.50	2.50
5	A1 10c red	2.50	2.50
6	A1 15c gray	5.00	5.00
7	A1 20c red, *green*	5.00	5.00
8	A1 25c blue	7.00	7.00
9	A1 30c brn, *bister*	7.00	7.00
10	A1 40c red, *straw*	10.00	10.00
11	A1 50c brn, *azure*	20.00	20.00
12	A1 75c dp vio, *org*	22.50	22.50
13	A1 1fr brnz grn, *straw*	30.00	30.00
	Nos. 1-13 (13)	115.25	115.25

SERBIA

LOCATION — In southeastern Europe, bounded by Romania and Bulgaria on the east, the former Austro-Hungarian Empire on the north, Greece on the south, and Albania and Montenegro on the west.

GOVT. — A former Kingdom.

AREA — 18,650 sq. mi.
POP. — 2,911,701 (1910).
CAPITAL — Belgrade.

Following World War I, Serbia united with Montenegro, Bosnia and Herzegovina, Croatia, Dalmatia and Slovenia to form the kingdom (later republic) of Jugoslavia.

100 Paras = 1 Dinar

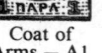

Coat of Arms — A1

Prince Michael (Obrenovich III) — A2

1866 Unwmk. Typo. *Imperf.*
Paper colored Through

1 A1 1p dk grn, *dk vio rose* 45.00

Surface Colored Paper, Thin or Thick

2 A1 1p dk grn, *lil rose* 50.00
- *a.* 1p olive green, *rose* 50.00
- *b.* 1p yel grn, *pale rose* (thick paper) 300.00

3 A1 2p red brn, *lil* 60.00
- *a.* 2p red brn, *lil gray* (thick paper) 250.00
- *b.* 2p dl grn, *lil gray* (thick paper) 800.00

Vienna Printing
Perf. 12

4 A2 10p orange 750.00 500.00
5 A2 20p rose 425.00 17.50
6 A2 40p blue 475.00 125.00
- *a.* Half used as 20p on cover

Belgrade Printing
Perf. 9½

7 A2 1p green 15.00
8 A2 2p bis brn 22.75
9 A2 20p rose 15.00 11.50
- *a.* Pair, imperf. between

10 A2 40p ultra 150.00 150.00
- *a.* Half used as 20p on cover

Pelure Paper

11 A2 10p orange 65.00 70.00
12 A2 20p rose 60.00 8.75
- *a.* Pair, imperf. between

13 A2 40p ultra 35.00 20.00
- *a.* Pair, imperf. between
- *b.* Half used as 20p on cover

Nos. 1-3, 7-8, 14-16, 25-26 were used only as newspaper tax stamps.

1868-69 Ordinary Paper *Imperf.*

14 A2 1p green 35.00
- *a.* 1p olive grn ('69) *2,000.*

15 A2 2p brown 50.00
- *a.* 2p bister brn ('69) 150.00

Counterfeits of type A2 are common.

Prince Milan (Obrenovich IV)
A3 A4

1869-78 *Perf. 9½, 12 and Compound*

16 A3 1p yellow 2.25 *95.00*
17 A3 10p red brn 7.50 3.75
- *a.* 10p yellow brown *350.00* 35.00

18 A3 10p org ('78) 1.25 3.25
19 A3 15p orange 85.00 15.00
20 A3 20p gray bl 1.50 2.50
- *a.* 20p ultramarine 3.25 2.00
- *b.* Half used as 10p on cover

21 A3 25p rose 1.50 5.75
22 A3 35p lt grn 2.75 3.50
23 A3 40p violet 1.40 2.75
- *a.* Half used as 20p on cover

24 A3 50p bl grn 3.25 3.50
Nos. 16-24 (9) 106.40 *135.00*

The first setting, which included all values except No. 18, had the stamps 2-2½mm apart. A new setting, introduced in 1878, had the stamps 3-4mm apart, providing wider margins. Only Nos. 17, 18, 20 and 21 exist in this new setting, which differs also in shades from the earlier setting. The narrow-spaced Nos. 17, 20 and 21 are rarer, especially unused, as are the early shades of Nos. 23 and 24. All values except Nos. 19 and 24 are known in various partly perforated varieties.
Counterfeits exist.

1872-79 *Imperf.*

25 A3 1p yellow 3.50 7.75
- *a.* Tête bêche pair

26 A4 2p blk, thin paper ('79) 35 35
- *a.* Thick paper ('73) 1.50 *4.00*

Used value of No. 26 is for canceled-to-order.

King Milan I — A5

King Alexander (Obrenovich V) — A6

1880 *Perf. 13x13½*

27 A5 5p green 40 15
- *a.* 5p olive green 475.00 1.50

28 A5 10p rose 60 15
29 A5 20p orange 42 20
- *a.* 20p yellow 2.75 1.10

30 A5 25p ultra 60 25
- *a.* 25p blue 1.75 70

31 A5 50p brown 42 *1.65*
- *a.* 50p brown violet 60.00 2.50

32 A5 1d violet 5.25 5.25
Nos. 27-32 (6) 7.69 *7.65*

1890

33 A6 5p green 15 10
34 A6 10p rose red 35 10
35 A6 15p red vio 35 10
36 A6 20p orange 28 10
37 A6 25p blue 42 15
38 A6 50p brown 1.75 1.40
39 A6 1d dl lil 9.00 7.75
Nos. 33-39 (7) 12.30 9.70

King Alexander — A7

1894-96 *Perf. 13x13½*
Granite Paper

40 A7 5p green 3.75 12
- *a.* Perf. 11½ 3.50 38

41 A7 10p car rose 3.50 12
- *b.* Perf. 11½ 37.50 75

42 A7 15p violet 4.50 12
43 A7 20p orange 52.50 30
- *a.* Half used as 10p on cover *375.00*

44 A7 25p blue 10.50 22
45 A7 50p brown 11.00 45
46 A7 1d dk grn 1.50 2.50
47 A7 1d red brn, *bl* ('96) 11.00 3.75
Nos. 40-47 (8) 98.25 7.58

1898-1900 *Perf. 13x13½, 11½*
Ordinary Paper

48 A7 1p dl red 15 25
49 A7 5p green 1.00 20
50 A7 10p rose 42.50 20
51 A7 15p violet 7.00 20
52 A7 20p orange 6.25 25
53 A7 25p dp bl 7.00 28
54 A7 50p brown 12.50 3.00
Nos. 48-54 (7) 76.40 4.38

Nos. 49-54 exist imperf. Nos. 49-51, 53 and 56-57 exist with perf. 13x13½x 11½x13½.

Type of 1900 Stamp Surcharged **10 ПАРА**

1900

56 A7 10p on 20p rose 1.25 15

Same, Surcharged **10 ПАРА**

1901

57 A7 10p on 20p rose 1.75 10
58 A7 15p on 1d red brn, *bl* 3.75 1.00
- *a.* Inverted surcharge *100.00 110.00*

King Alexander (Obrenovich V)
A8 A9

1901-03 Typo. *Perf. 11½*

59 A8 5p green 10 8
60 A8 10p rose 10 8
61 A8 15p red vio 10 8
62 A8 20p orange 10 8
63 A8 25p ultra 10 8
64 A8 50p bister 12 12
65 A9 1d brown 55 60
66 A9 3d brt rose 6.75 5.75
67 A9 5d dp vio 5.25 5.75
Nos. 59-67 (9) 13.17 12.62

Counterfeits of Nos. 66-67 exist. Nos. 59-67 imperf. value of set of pairs, $100.

Arms of Serbia on Head of King Alexander — A10

Two Types of the Overprint

Type I - Overprint 12mm wide. Bottom of mantle defined by a single line. Wide crown above shield.

Type II - Overprint 10mm wide. Double line at bottom of mantle. Smaller crown above shield.

Arms Overprinted in Blue, Black, Red and Red Brown

1903-04 Type I *Perf. 13½*

68 A10 1p red lil & blk (Bl) 35 38
- *a.* Inverted overprint 6.75

69 A10 5p yel grn & blk (Bl) 20 6
70 A10 10p car & blk (Bk) 12 6
- *a.* Double overprint 8.25

71 A10 15p ol gray & blk (Bk) 12 6
- *a.* Double overprint 8.25

72 A10 20p org & blk (Bk) 20 12
73 A10 25p bl & blk (Bk) 20 12
- *a.* Double overprint 9.25

74 A10 50p gray & blk (R) 1.25 65

There were two printings of the type I overprint on Nos. 68-74, one typographed and one lithographed.

Type II

75 A10 1d bl grn & blk (Bk) 5.00 1.50

Nos. 68-75 with overprint omitted, value, set $75.

Perf. 11½.
Type I

75A A10 5p yel grn & blk (Bl) 15 25
75B A10 50p gray & blk (R) 40 1.00
75C A10 1d bl grn & blk (Bk) 75 1.75

Type II

76 A10 3d vio & blk (R Br) 85 85
- *a.* Perf. 13½ *95.00 95.00*

77 A10 5d lt brn & blk (Bl) 85 85

Type I With Additional Surcharge **1 ПАРА 1**

78 A10 1p on 5d lt brn & blk (R) 75 2.75
- *a.* Perf. 13½ *265.00 265.00*

Nos. 68-78 (14) 11.19 10.40

Karageorge and Peter I — A11

Insurgents, 1804 — A12

1904 Typo.

79 A11 5p yel grn 7 7
80 A11 10p rose red 7 7
81 A11 15p red vio 7 7
82 A11 25p blue 7 7
83 A11 50p gray brn 22 22
84 A12 1d bister 90 1.10
85 A12 3d bl grn 90 1.25
86 A12 5d violet 1.50 1.65
Nos. 79-86 (8) 3.80 4.50

Centenary of the Karageorgevich dynasty and the coronation of King Peter. Counterfeits of Nos. 79-86 exist.

King Peter I Karageorgevich
A13 A14

Perf. 11½, 12x11½
1905 Wove Paper

87 A13 1p gray & blk 12 7
88 A13 5p yel grn & blk 24 7
89 A13 10p red & blk 85 7
90 A13 15p red lil & blk 1.00 7
91 A13 20p yel & blk 1.65 10
92 A13 25p ultra & blk 2.50 10
93 A13 30p sl grn & blk 1.65 10
94 A13 50p dk brn & blk 2.50 20
95 A13 1d bis & blk 32 25
96 A13 3d bl grn & blk 32 50
97 A13 5d vio & blk 1.25 85
Nos. 87-97 (11) 12.40 2.38

Counterfeits of Nos. 87-97 abound.
The stamps of this issue may be found on both thick and thin paper.

1908 Laid Paper

98 A13 1p gray & blk 28 10
99 A13 5p yel grn & blk 2.25 10
100 A13 10p red & blk 6.75 10
101 A13 15p red lil & blk 6.75 20
102 A13 20p yel & blk 7.25 20
103 A13 25p ultra & blk 6.75 20
104 A13 30p gray grn & blk 10.00 20
105 A13 50p dk brn & blk 13.00 60
Nos. 98-105 (8) 53.03 1.70

Nos. 90, 98-100, 102-104 are known imperforate but are not believed to have been issued in this condition.
Values of Nos. 98-105 are for horizontally laid paper. Four values also exist on vertically laid paper (1p, 5p, 10p, 30p).

1911-14
Thick Wove Paper

108 A14 1p sl grn 5 5
109 A14 2p dk vio 5 5
110 A14 5p green 7 5
111 A14 5p pale yel grn ('14) 5 5
112 A14 10p carmine 7 5
113 A14 10p red ('14) 5 5
114 A14 15p red vio 14 7
115 A14 15p sl blk ('14) 10 7
- *a.* 15p red (error)

116 A14 20p yellow 20 7
117 A14 20p brn ('14) 35 20
118 A14 25p dp blue 30 5
119 A14 25p indigo ('14) 5 5
120 A14 30p bl grn 14 5
121 A14 30p ol grn ('14) 5 5
122 A14 50p dk brn 16 5
123 A14 50p brn red ('14) 7 5
124 A14 1d orange 14.00 *25.00*
125 A14 1d slate ('14) 2.00 *2.75*
126 A14 3d lake 27.50 *77.50*
127 A14 3d ol yel ('14) 77.50 *475.00*
128 A14 5d violet 27.50 *42.50*
129 A14 5d dk vio ('14) 2.00 *14.00*
Nos. 108-129 (22) 152.40

Counterfeits exist.

Serbia Austrian Occupation stamps can be mounted in Scott's Austria Album.

King Peter and Military Staff — A15

1915 — *Perf. 11½*

132	A15	5p	yel grn	10	1.00
133	A15	10p	scarlet	10	1.00
134	A15	15p	slate	1.50	
135	A15	20p	brown	45	
136	A15	25p	blue	3.25	
137	A15	30p	ol grn	2.00	
138	A15	50p	org brn	16.00	
			Nos. 132-138 (7)	23.40	

Nos. 134-138 were prepared but not issued for postal use. Instead they were permitted to be used as wartime emergency currency. Some are known imperf. The 15p also exists in blue; value $250.

POSTES SERBES

Stamps of France, 1900-1907, with this handstamped control were issued in 1916-1918 by the Serbian Postal Bureau, in the Island of Corfu, during a temporary shortage of Serbian stamps. On the 1c to 35c, the handstamp covers 2 or 3 stamps. It was applied after the stamps were on the cover, and frequently no further cancellation was used.

King Peter and Prince Alexander — A16

1918-20 — **Typo.** — *Perf. 11, 11½*

155	A16	1p	black	7	7
156	A16	2p	ol brn	7	7
157	A16	5p	apple grn	7	7
158	A16	10p	red	7	7
159	A16	15p	blk brn	7	7
160	A16	20p	red brn	8	7
161	A16	20p	vio ('20)	3.00	1.50
162	A16	25p	deep bl	8	7
163	A16	30p	olive grn	8	7
164	A16	50p	violet	8	7
165	A16	1d	vio brn	22	7
166	A16	3d	slate grn	70	60
167	A16	5d	red brn	1.10	65
			Nos. 155-167 (13)	5.69	3.45

Nos. 157-160, 164 exist imperf. Value each $6.

1920 — **Pelure Paper** — *Perf. 11½*

169	A16	1p	black	10	15
170	A16	2p	olive brn	10	15

POSTAGE DUE STAMPS

Coat of Arms
D1 D2

1895 — **Unwmk.** — **Typo.** — *Perf. 13x13½*

Granite Paper

J1	D1	5p	red lilac	1.40	60
J2	D1	10p	blue	1.40	42
J3	D1	20p	orange brn	42.50	2.75
J4	D1	30p	green	20	35
J5	D1	50p	rose	28	42
a.			Cliche of 5p in plate of 50p	75.00	95.00

No. J1 exists imperf. Value $35.

1898-1904

Ordinary Paper

J6	D1	5p	mag ('04)	70	70
J7	D1	20p	brown	3.00	70
a.			Tete beche pair	115.00	115.00
J8		20p	dp brn ('04)	3.00	70

1906 — **Granite Paper** — *Perf. 11½*

J9	D1	5p	magenta	5.25	1.00

1909

Laid Paper

J10	D1	5p	magenta	65	65
J11	D1	10p	pale bl	2.25	1.65
J12	D1	20p	pale brn	40	40

1914

White Wove Paper

J13	D1	5p	rose	25	32
J14	D1	10p	dp bl	1.50	2.25

1918-20 — *Perf. 11*

J15	D2	5p	red	40	85
J16	D2	5p	red brn ('20)	40	85
J17	D2	10p	yel grn	40	85
J18	D2	20p	ol brn	40	85
J19	D2	30p	sl grn	40	85
J20	D2	50p	chocolate	80	1.25
			Nos. J15-J20 (6)	2.80	5.50

NEWSPAPER STAMPS

N1

Overprinted with Crown-topped Shield in Black

1911 — **Unwmk.** — **Typo.** — *Perf. 11½*

P1	N1	1p	gray	45	45
P2	N1	5p	green	45	45
P3	N1	10p	orange	45	45
a.			Cliche of 1p in plate of 10p	200.00	
P4	N1	15p	violet	45	45
P5	N1	20p	yellow	45	45
a.			Cliche of 50p in plate of 20p	75.00	125.00
P6	N1	25p	blue	45	45
P7	N1	30p	slate	5.25	5.25
P8	N1	50p	brown	4.50	4.50
P9	N1	1d	bister	4.50	4.50
P10	N1	3d	rose red	4.50	4.50
P11	N1	5d	gray vio	4.50	4.50
			Nos. P1-P11 (11)	25.95	25.95

ISSUED UNDER AUSTRIAN OCCUPATION

100 Heller = 1 Krone

Stamps of Bosnia, 1912-14, Overprinted

SERBIEN

1916 — **Unwmk.** — *Perf. 12½*

1N1	A23	1h	olive grn	1.50	2.00
1N2	A23	2h	brt blue	1.50	2.00
1N3	A23	3h	claret	1.50	2.00
1N4	A23	5h	green	35	55
1N5	A23	6h	dk gray	70	1.10
1N6	A23	10h	rose car	35	65
1N7	A23	12h	dp ol grn	70	1.10
1N8	A23	20h	org brn	42	70
1N9	A23	25h	ultra	42	70
1N10	A23	30h	org red	42	70
1N11	A24	35h	myrtle grn	42	70
1N12	A24	40h	dk vio	42	70
1N13	A24	45h	olive brn	42	70
1N14	A24	50h	slate bl	42	70
1N15	A24	60h	brn vio	42	70
1N16	A24	72h	dk bl	42	70
1N17	A25	1k	brn vio, *straw*	65	90
1N18	A25	2k	dk gray, *bl*	65	90
1N19	A26	3k	car, *grn*	65	90
1N20	A26	5k	dk vio, *gray*	65	90
1N21	A25	10k	dk ultra, *gray*	9.25	14.00
			Nos. 1N1-1N21 (21)	22.23	33.30

Stamps of Bosnia, 1912-14, Overprinted "SERBIEN" Horizontally at Bottom

1916

1N22	A23	1h	olive grn	4.50	5.25
1N23	A23	2h	brt blue	4.50	5.25
1N24	A23	3h	claret	4.50	5.25
1N25	A23	5h	green	45	45
1N26	A23	6h	dk gray	4.50	5.25
1N27	A23	10h	rose car	45	45
1N28	A23	12h	dp ol grn	4.50	5.25
1N29	A23	20h	org brn	4.50	5.25
1N30	A23	25h	ultra	4.50	5.25
1N31	A23	30h	org red	4.50	5.25
1N32	A24	35h	myrtle grn	4.50	5.25
1N33	A24	40h	dk vio	4.50	5.25
1N34	A24	45h	olive brn	4.50	5.25
1N35	A24	50h	slate bl	4.50	5.25
1N36	A24	60h	brn vio	4.50	5.25
1N37	A24	72h	dk blue	4.50	5.25
1N38	A25	1k	brn vio, *straw*	11.00	13.00
1N39	A25	2k	dk gray, *bl*	11.00	13.00
1N40	A26	3k	car, *grn*	11.00	13.00
1N41	A26	5k	dk vio, *gray*	19.00	21.00
1N42	A25	10k	dk ultra, *gray*	27.50	30.00
			Nos. 1N22-1N42 (21)	143.40	164.40

Nos. 1N22 to 1N42 were prepared in 1914, at the time of the first Austrian occupation of Serbia. They were not issued at that time because of the retreat. The stamps were put on sale in 1916, at the same time as Nos. 1N1 to 1N21.

ISSUED UNDER GERMAN OCCUPATION

In occupied Serbia, authority was ostensibly in the hands of a government created by the former Jugoslav General, Milan Nedich, supported by the Chetniks, a nationalist organization which turned fascist. Actually the German military ran the country.

Types of Jugoslavia, 1939-40, Overprinted in Black

SERBIEN

1941 — **Unwmk.** — **Typo.** — *Perf. 12½*

Paper with colored network

2N1	A16	25p	blk *(lt grn)*	10	1.25
2N2	A16	50p	org *(pink)*	10	25
2N3	A16	1d	yel grn *(lt grn)*	10	25
2N4	A16	1.50d	red *(pink)*	10	25
2N5	A16	2d	dp mag *(pink)*	10	25
2N6	A16	3d	dl red brn *(pink)*	90	5.00
2N7	A16	4d	ultra *(lt grn)*	15	75
2N8	A16	5d	dk bl *(lt grn)*	50	2.00
2N9	A16	5.50d	dk vio brn *(pink)*	50	2.00
2N10	A16	6d	sl bl *(pink)*	50	2.00
2N11	A16	8d	sep *(lt grn)*	70	3.00
2N12	A16	12d	brt vio *(lt grn)*	70	3.00
2N13	A16	16d	dl vio *(pink)*	1.10	10.00
2N14	A16	20d	bl *(lt grn)*	1.10	12.50
2N15	A16	30d	brt pink *(lt grn)*	5.75	75.00
			Nos. 2N1-2N15 (15)	12.40	

Double overprints exist on 50p, 1d, 5d, 5.50d and 12d. Value, each $125 to $250.

Stamps of Jugoslavia, 1939-40, Overprinted in Black

SERBIEN

Paper with colored network

2N16	A16	25p	blk *(lt grn)*	10	3.75
2N17	A16	50p	org *(pink)*	10	75
2N18	A16	1d	yel grn *(lt grn)*	12	50
2N19	A16	1.50d	red *(pink)*	12	75
2N20	A16	2d	dp mag *(pink)*	12	50
2N21	A16	3d	dl red brn *(pink)*	30	3.00
2N22	A16	4d	ultra *(lt grn)*	20	50
2N23	A16	5d	dk bl *(lt grn)*	20	1.25
2N24	A16	5.50d	dk vio brn *(pink)*	40	3.00
2N25	A16	6d	sl bl *(pink)*	40	3.00
2N26	A16	8d	sep *(lt grn)*	60	3.75
2N27	A16	12d	brt vio *(lt grn)*	1.00	3.75
2N28	A16	16d	dl vio *(pink)*	1.00	12.50
2N29	A16	20d	bl *(lt grn)*	1.00	20.00
2N30	A16	30d	brt pink *(lt grn)*	5.25	65.00
			Nos. 2N16-2N30 (15)	10.91	

Lazaritza Monastery — OS1

Ruins of Manassia Monastery OS4

Designs: 1d, Kalenica Monastery. 1.50d, Ravanica Monastery. 3d, Ljubostinja Monastery. 4d, Sopocane Monastery. 7d, Tsitsa Monastery. 12d, Goriak Monastery. 16d, Studenica Monastery.

1942-43 — **Typo.** — *Perf. 11½*

2N31	OS1	50p	brt vio	8	15
2N32	OS1	1d	red	8	10
2N33	OS1	1.50d	red brn	65	2.00
2N34	OS1	1.50d	grn ('43)	8	20
2N35	OS4	2d	dl rose vio	6	15
2N36	OS4	3d	brt bl	65	2.00
2N37	OS4	3d	rose pink ('43)	6	12
2N38	OS4	4d	ultra	8	18
2N39	OS4	7d	dk sl grn	8	18
2N40	OS1	12d	lake	15	1.25
2N41	OS1	16d	grnsh blk	85	1.50
			Nos. 2N31-2N41 (11)	2.82	

Post Rider — OS10 — Post Wagon — OS11

Designs: 9d, Mail train. 30d, Mail truck. 50d, Mail plane.

1943, Oct. 15 — **Photo.** — *Perf. 12½*

2N42	OS10	3d	cop red & gray lil	28	1.00
2N43	OS11	8d	vio rose & gray	28	1.00
2N44	OS10	9d	dk bl grn & sep	28	1.00
2N45	OS10	30d	chnt & sl grn	28	1.00
2N46	OS10	50d	dp bl & red brn	28	1.00
			Nos. 2N42-2N46 (5)	1.40	

Centenary of postal service in Serbia. Printed in sheets of 24 containing 4 of each stamp and 4 labels.

OCCUPATION SEMI-POSTAL STAMPS

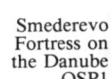

Smederevo Fortress on the Danube OSP1

Refugees OSP2

Perf. 11½x12½

1941, Sept. 22 Typo. Unwmk.

2NB1	OSP1	50p + 1d dk brn	20	*65*
2NB2	OSP2	1d + 2d dk gray grn	20	*85*
2NB3	OSP2	1.50d + 3d dp cl	42	*1.50*
a.		Perf. 12½	3.75	*6.25*
2NB4	OSP1	2d + 4d dk bl	60	*2.00*

Souvenir Sheets

Perf. 11½x12½

2NB5		Sheet of two	22.50	*100.00*
a.	OSP2	1d + 49d rose lake	6.75	*17.50*
b.	OSP1	2d + 48d gray	6.75	*17.50*

Imperf

2NB6		Sheet of two	22.50	*100.00*
a.	OSP2	1d + 49d gray	6.75	*17.50*
b.	OSP1	2d + 48d rose lake	6.75	*17.50*

The surtax aided the victims of an explosion at Smederevo and was used for the reconstruction of the town.

Christ and Virgin Mary — OSP4

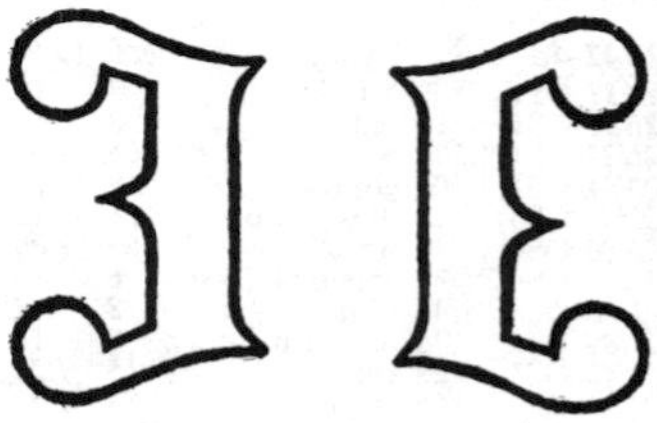
a b

1941, Dec. 5 Photo. *Perf. 11½*

With Rose Burelage

2NB7	OSP4	50p + 1.50d brn red	22	*3.75*
a.		With symbol (a) outlined in cerise	6.75	*37.50*
b.		With symbol (b) outlined in cerise	6.75	*37.50*
c.		Without burelage	1.25	*12.00*
2NB8	OSP4	1d + 3d sl grn	22	*3.75*
a.		With symbol (a) outlined in cerise	6.75	*37.50*
b.		With symbol (b) outlined in cerise	6.75	*37.50*
c.		Without burelage	1.25	*12.50*
2NB9	OSP4	2d + 6d dp red	22	*3.75*
a.		With symbol (a) outlined in cerise	6.75	*37.50*
b.		With symbol (b) outlined in cerise	6.75	*37.50*
c.		Without burelage	1.25	*12.50*
2NB10	OSP4	4d + 12d dp bl	22	*3.75*
a.		With symbol (a) outlined in cerise	6.75	*37.50*
b.		With symbol (b) outlined in cerise	6.75	*37.50*
c.		Without burelage	1.25	*12.50*

These stamps were printed in sheets of 50, divided into two panes of 25. In these panes, Nos. 8, 12, 13, 14 and 18, forming a cross, are without burelage. Nos. 7 and 17 are of type "a". Nos. 9, and 19 are of type "b". Sixteen of the 25 units have the over-all burelage.

The surtax aided prisoners of war.

1942, Mar. 26

Thicker Paper, Without Burelage

2NB11	OSP4	50p + 1.50d brn	60	*2.75*
2NB12	OSP4	1d + 3d bl grn	60	*2.75*
2NB13	OSP4	2d + 6d mag	60	*2.75*
2NB14	OSP4	4d + 12d ultra	60	*3.00*

OSP5

OSP6

OSP7

OSP8

Designs: Anti-Masonic symbolisms.

1942, Jan. 1

2NB15	OSP5	50p + 50p yel brn	14	*65*
2NB16	OSP6	1d + 1d dk grn	14	*65*
2NB17	OSP7	2d + 2d rose car	24	*1.25*
2NB18	OSP8	4d + 4d ind	24	*1.25*

Anti-Masonic Exposition of Oct. 22, 1941. The surtax was used for anti-Masonic propaganda.

Mother and Children — OSP9

1942

2NB19	OSP9	2d + 6d brt pur	90	*2.50*
2NB20	OSP9	4d + 8d dp bl	90	*2.50*
2NB21	OSP9	7d + 13d dk bl grn	90	*2.50*
2NB22	OSP9	20d + 40d dp rose lake	90	*2.50*

Nos. 2NB19-2NB22 were issued in sheets of 16 consisting of a block of four of each denomination. The surtax aided war orphans.

Broken Sword — OSP10

Wounded Flag-bearer OSP11

Designs: 1.50d+48.50d, Broken sword. 3d+5d, 2d+48d, Wounded soldier. 3d+47d, Wounded flag-bearer. 4d+10d, 4d+46d, Tending casualty.

1943

2NB23	OSP10	1.50d + 1.50d dk brn	42	*1.25*
2NB24	OSP11	2d + 3d dk bl grn	42	*1.25*
2NB25	OSP11	3d + 5d dp rose vio	60	*2.00*
2NB26	OSP10	4d + 10d dp bl	1.00	*3.00*

Souvenir Sheets

Thick Paper

2NB27		Sheet of two	25.00	*550.00*
a.	OSP10	1.50d + 48.50d dk brn	10.00	*225.00*
b.	OSP10	4d + 46d dp bl	10.00	*225.00*
2NB28		Sheet of two	25.00	*550.00*
a.	OSP11	2d + 48d dk bl grn	10.00	*225.00*
b.	OSP11	3d + 47d dp rose vio	10.00	*225.00*

The sheets measure 150x110mm. The surtax aided war victims.

Stamps of 1942-43 Surcharged in Black

За пострадале
од англо-америчког
терор. бомбардовања
Ниша — 20-X-1943
+ 9

1943, Dec. 11

Pale Green Burelage

2NB29	OS1	50p + 2d brt vio	8	*2.50*
2NB30	OS1	1d + 3d red	8	*2.50*
2NB31	OS1	1.50d + 4d dp grn	8	*2.50*
2NB32	OS4	2d + 5d dl rose vio	10	*2.50*
2NB33	OS4	3d + 7d rose pink	10	*2.50*
2NB34	OS4	4d + 9d ultra	10	*2.50*
2NB35	OS4	7d + 15d dk sl grn	32	*2.50*
2NB36	OS1	12d + 25d lake	32	*12.50*
2NB37	OS1	16d + 33d grnsh blk	55	*12.50*
		Nos. 2NB29-2NB37 (9)	1.73	

The surtax aided victims of the bombing of Nisch.

OCCUPATION AIR POST STAMPS

Types of Jugoslavia, 1937-40, Overprinted in Carmine or Maroon

a SERBIEN

b SERBIEN

1941 Unwmk. *Perf. 12½*

Paper with colored network

2NC1	AP6(a)	50p brn (C)	2.50	*25.00*
2NC2	AP7(a)	1d yel grn (C)	2.50	*25.00*
2NC3	AP8(a)	2d bl gray (C)	2.50	*25.00*
2NC4	AP9(b)	2.50d rose red (M)	2.50	*25.00*
2NC5	AP6(a)	5d brn vio (C)	2.50	*25.00*
2NC6	AP7(a)	10d brn lake (M)	2.50	*25.00*
2NC7	AP8(a)	20d dk grn (C)	2.50	*25.00*
2NC8	AP9(b)	30d ultra (C)	2.50	*25.00*
2NC9	AP10(a)	40d Prus grn & pale grn (C)	5.50	*125.00*
2NC10	AP11(b)	50d sl bl & gray bl (C)	7.00	*190.00*
		Nos. 2NC1-2NC10 (10)	32.50	

Nos. 2NC1-2NC2 exist without network.

Same Surcharged in Maroon or Carmine with New Values and Bars

Without colored network

2NC11	AP7	1d on 10d brn lake (M)	2.00	*15.00*
2NC12	AP8	3d on 20d dk grn (C)	2.00	*15.00*
2NC13	AP9	6d on 30d ultra (C)	2.00	*15.00*
2NC14	AP10	8d on 40d Prus grn & pale grn (C)	2.25	*30.00*
2NC15	AP11	12d on 50d sl bl & gray bl (C)	4.50	*75.00*
		Nos. 2NC11-2NC15 (5)	12.75	

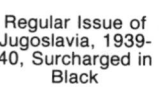

Regular Issue of Jugoslavia, 1939-40, Surcharged in Black

14 СРБИЈА

1942

Green Network

2NC16	A16	2d on 2d dp mag	12	*1.25*
2NC17	A16	4d on 4d ultra	12	*1.25*
2NC18	A16	10d on 12d brt vio	12	*2.00*
2NC19	A16	14d on 20d blue	12	*2.00*
2NC20	A16	20d on 30d brt pink	30	*10.00*
		Nos. 2NC16-2NC20 (5)	78	

OCCUPATION POSTAGE DUE STAMPS

OD1

OD2

1941 Unwmk. Typo. *Perf. 12½*

2NJ1	OD1	50p violet	60	*3.75*
2NJ2	OD1	1d lake	60	*3.75*
2NJ3	OD1	2d dk bl	60	*3.75*
2NJ4	OD1	3d red	85	*5.00*
2NJ5	OD2	4d lt bl	1.10	*12.50*
2NJ6	OD2	5d orange	1.10	*12.50*
2NJ7	OD2	10d violet	2.50	*25.00*
2NJ8	OD2	20d green	7.25	*75.00*
		Nos. 2NJ1-2NJ8 (8)	14.60	

OD3

OD4

1942 *Perf. 12½*

2NJ9	OD3	1d mar & grn	9	*1.25*
2NJ10	OD3	2d dk bl & red	9	*1.25*
2NJ11	OD3	3d ver & bl	16	*2.50*
2NJ12	OD4	4d bl & red	16	*2.50*
2NJ13	OD4	5d org & bl	18	*3.00*
2NJ14	OD4	10d vio & red	20	*7.50*
2NJ15	OD4	20d grn & red	90	*22.50*
		Nos. 2NJ9-2NJ15 (7)	1.78	

OD5

2NJ16	OD5	50p black	10	*1.25*
2NJ17	OD5	3d violet	10	*1.25*
2NJ18	OD5	4d blue	10	*1.25*
2NJ19	OD5	5d dk sl grn	10	*1.25*
2NJ20	OD5	6d orange	18	*3.75*
2NJ21	OD5	10d red	32	*6.25*
2NJ22	OD5	20d ultra	90	*15.00*
		Nos. 2NJ16-2NJ22 (7)	1.80	

OCCUPATION OFFICIAL STAMP

OOS1

1943 Unwmk. Typo. *Perf. 12½*
2NO1 OOS1 3d red lil 55 *1.25*

SHANGHAI

LOCATION — A city on the Whangpoo River, Kiangsu Province, China.
POP. — 3,489,998.

A British settlement was founded there in 1843 and by agreement with China settlements were established by France and the United States. Special areas were set aside for the foreign settlements and a postal system independent of China was organized which was continued until 1898.

16 Cash = 1 Candareen
100 Candareens = 1 Tael
100 Cents = 1 Dollar (1890)

Values for Nos. 1-71 are for fine stamps without gum. Stamps of higher grade are worth more.

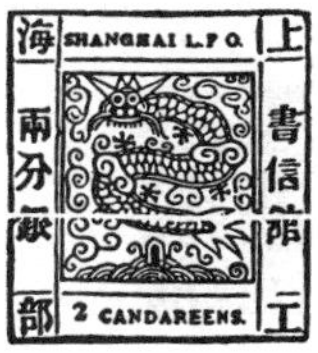
Dragon — A1

1865-66 Unwmk. Typo. *Imperf.*

Antique Numerals
Roman "I" in "I6"
"Candareens" in the Plural
Wove Paper

1 A1 2ca black 140.00
a. Pelure paper 125.00
2 A1 4ca yellow 90.00
a. Pelure paper 65.00
b. Double impression
3 A1 8ca green 150.00
a. 8ca yellow green 150.00
4 A1 16ca scarlet 200.00
a. 16ca vermilion 200.00
b. Pelure paper 200.00

Antique Numerals
"Candareens" in the Plural
Pelure Paper

5 A1 2ca black 115.00
a. Wove paper 75.00
6 A1 4ca yellow 115.00
7 A1 8ca deep green 115.00

Antique Numerals
"Candareen" in the Singular
Laid Paper

8 A1 1ca blue 125.00
a. 1ca dark blue 140.00
9 A1 2ca black 1,500.
10 A1 4ca yellow 350.00

Wove Paper

11 A1 1ca blue 250.00
12 A1 2ca black 130.00
13 A1 4ca yellow 140.00
14 A1 8ca olive green 140.00
15 A1 16ca vermilion 140.00
a. "1" of "16" omitted

Only one copy of No. 15a is known.

Antique Numerals
Roman "I"
"Candareens" in the Plural Except on 1ca
Wove Paper

16 A1 1ca blue 250.00
17 A1 12ca fawn 165.00
18 A1 12ca chocolate 165.00

Antique Numerals
"Candareens" in the Plural Except on 1ca
Wove Paper

19 A1 1ca indigo 125.00
a. Pelure paper 110.00
20 A1 3ca orange brn 140.00
a. Pelure paper 140.00
21 A1 6ca red brown 70.00
22 A1 6ca fawn 350.00
23 A1 6ca vermilion 100.00
24 A1 12ca orange brn 75.00
25 A1 16ca vermilion 75.00
a. "1" of "16" omitted 225.00

Antique Numerals
Roman "I"
"Candareens" in the Plural Except on 1ca
Laid Paper

26 A1 1ca blue *11,000.*
27 A1 2ca black 1,100.
28 A1 3ca red brown *7,000.*

Modern Numerals
"Candareen" in the Singular

29 A1 1ca dark blue 70.00
a. 1ca slate blue 70.00
30 A1 3ca red brown 70.00

"Candareens" in the Plural Except the 1c

31 A1 2ca black 40.00
32 A1 3ca red brown 65.00

Coarse Porous Wove Paper

33a A1 1ca blue 50.00
34a A1 2ca black 55.00
b. grayish paper 55.00
35a A1 3ca red brown 55.00
36a A1 4ca yellow 55.00
37a A1 6ca olive green 55.00
38a A1 8ca emerald 55.00
39a A1 12ca org vermilion 55.00
40a A1 16ca red 65.00
41a A1 16ca red brown 75.00

Nos. 1, 2, 11 and 32 exist on thicker paper, usually toned. Most authorities consider these four stamps and Nos. 33a-41a to be official reprints made to present sample sets to other post offices. The tone in this paper is an acquired characteristic, due to various causes. Many shades and minor varieties exist of Nos. 1-41a.

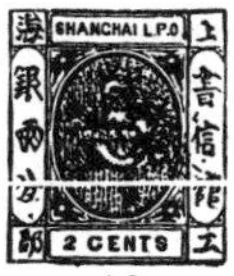
A2

A3

A4

A5

1866 Litho. *Perf. 12*
42 A2 2c rose 8.00 6.00
43 A3 4c lilac 17.50 14.00
44 A4 8c gray blue 17.50 14.00
45 A5 16c green 40.00 27.50

Nos. 42-45 imperforate are proofs.

A6

A7

A8

A9

1866 *Perf. 15*
46 A6 1ca brown 4.00 3.00
a. "CANDS" 32.50 30.00
47 A7 3ca orange 15.00 14.00
48 A8 6ca slate 16.00 12.00
49 A9 12ca olive gray 40.00 27.50

1872
50 A2 2c rose 60.00 32.50

Handstamp Surcharged in Blue, Red or Black

a

1873 *Perf. 12*
51 A2 1ca on 2c rose 15.00 11.00
52 A3 1ca on 4c lil 12.50 7.00
53 A3 1ca on 4c lil (R) *1,150.* *1,150.*
54 A3 1ca on 4c lil (Bk) 11.00 10.00
55 A4 1ca on 8c gray bl 15.00 12.50
56 A4 1ca on 8c gray bl (R) *2,500.* *2,500.*
57 A5 1ca on 16c grn *800.00* *800.00*
58 A5 1ca on 16c grn (R) *2,750.* *2,750.*

Perf. 15
59 A2 1ca on 2c rose 12.00 10.00

1875 *Perf. 12*
60 A2 3ca on 2c rose 40.00 35.00
61 A5 3ca on 16c grn *800.00* *750.00*

Perf. 15
62 A7 1ca on 3ca org *2,500.* *2,500.*
63 A8 1ca on 6ca sl 125.00 100.00
64 A8 1ca on 6ca sl (R) *1,500.* *1,500.*
65 A9 1ca on 12ca ol gray 150.00 135.00
66 A9 1ca on 12ca ol gray (R) *1,750.* *1,250.*
67 A2 3ca on 2c rose 125.00 100.00
68 A9 3ca on 12ca ol gray *1,500.* *1,000.*

Counterfeits exist of Nos. 51-68.

Types of 1866

1875 *Perf. 15*
69 A6 1ca yel, *yel* 18.00 20.00
70 A7 3ca rose, *rose* 18.00 20.00

Perf. 11½
71 A6 1ca yel, *yel* 150.00 140.00

1876 *Perf. 15*
72 A6 1ca yellow 4.50 4.50
73 A7 3ca rose 25.00 22.50
74 A8 6ca green 55.00 40.00
75 A9 9ca blue 65.00 50.00
76 A9 12ca lt brn 90.00 70.00

1877 Engr. *Perf. 12½*
77 A6 1ca rose 700.00 450.00

Stamps of 1875-76 Surcharged type "a" in Blue or Red

1877 Litho. *Perf. 15*
78 A7 1ca on 3ca rose, *rose* 165.00 140.00
79 A7 1ca on 3ca rose 27.50 20.00
80 A8 1ca on 6ca grn 27.50 22.50
81 A9 1ca on 9ca bl 125.00 125.00
82 A9 1ca on 12ca lt brn 600.00 600.00
83 A9 1ca on 12ca lt brn (R) *2,250.* *2,000.*

Counterfeits exist of Nos. 78-83.

A11

A12

A13

A14

1877 *Perf. 15*
84 A11 20 cash violet 4.50 3.00
a. 20 cash blue violet 4.50 3.00
85 A12 40 cash rose 6.00 4.50
86 A13 60 cash green 8.00 6.50
87 A14 80 cash blue 14.00 10.00
88 A14 100 cash brown 14.00 10.00

Handstamp Surcharged in Blue

b

1879 *Perf. 15*
89 A12 20 cash on 40c rose 14.00 11.00
90 A14 60 cash on 80c bl 17.50 17.50
91 A14 60 cash on 100c brn 17.50 17.50

Types of 1877

1880 *Perf. 11½*
92 A11 20 cash violet 4.50 4.00
93 A12 40 cash rose 2.25 2.00
94 A13 60 cash green 2.25 2.00
95 A14 80 cash blue 6.00 5.25
96 A14 100 cash brown 7.00 6.25

Perf. 15x11½
97 A11 20 cash lilac 18.00 16.00

Surcharged type "b" in Blue

1884 *Perf. 11½*
98 A12 20 cash on 40c rose 5.00 5.00
99 A14 60 cash on 80c bl 9.00 9.00
100 A14 60 cash on 100c brn 10.00 10.00

Types of 1877

1884
101 A11 20 cash green 3.00 3.00

1885 *Perf. 15*
102 A11 20 cash green 2.25 2.00
103 A12 40 cash brown 3.00 3.00
104 A13 60 cash violet 5.50 4.75
a. 60 cash red violet 9.00 8.25
105 A14 80 cash buff 5.00 4.25
106 A14 100 cash yellow 5.00 5.00

Perf. 11½x15
107 A11 20 cash green 2.25 2.00
108 A13 60 cash red vio 5.00 5.00

Surcharged type "b" in Blue

1886 *Perf. 15*
109 A14 40 cash on 80c buff 3.00 3.00
110 A14 60 cash on 100c yel 4.00 4.00

Types of 1877

1888 *Perf. 15*
111 A11 20 cash gray 3.00 3.00
112 A12 40 cash black 3.00 3.00
113 A13 60 cash rose 3.50 3.50
a. Third character at left lacks dot at top 5.75 4.75
114 A14 80 cash green 4.00 4.00
115 A14 100 cash lt blue 5.25 4.50

Handstamp Surcharged in Blue or Red Type "b" or:

c

d

1888 *Perf. 15*
116 A14(b) 40 cash on 100c yel 3.00 5.00
117 A14(b) 40 cash on 100c yel (R) 4.00 4.00
118 A12(c) 20 cash on 40c brn 7.00 7.00
119 A14(c) 20 cash on 80c buff 2.00 2.00
120 A12(d) 20 cash on 40c brn 7.00 7.00

Inverted surcharges exist on Nos. 116-120; double on Nos. 116, 119, 120; omitted surcharges paired with normal stamp on Nos. 116, 119.

Handstamp Surcharged in Black and Red or Red

e

1889 Unwmk.
121 A14(e) 100 cash on 20c on 100c yel 20.00 17.50
a. Without the surcharge "100 cash" 125.00
b. Blue & red surcharge

122 A14(c) 20 cash on 80c grn (R) 4.00 5.00
123 A14(c) 20 cash on 100c bl (R) 4.00 5.00

Counterfeits exist of Nos. 116-123.

Shield with Dragon Supporters — A20

Wmk. 175 - Kung Pu (Municipal Council)

1889 Wmk. 175 *Perf. 15*

124 A11 20 cash gray 1.25 1.25
125 A12 40 cash black 2.25 1.90
126 A13 60 cash rose 2.75 2.50
a. Third character at left lacks dot at top 5.50 4.75

Perf. 12

127 A14 80 cash grn 2.50 2.25
128 A14 100 cash dk bl 6.50 5.75

Nos. 124-126 are sometimes found without watermark. This is caused by the sheet being misplaced in the printing press, so that the stamps are printed on the unwatermarked margin of the sheet.

1890 Unwmk. Litho. *Perf. 15*

129 A20 2c brown 1.00 1.00
130 A20 5c rose 3.50 3.50
131 A20 15c blue 3.50 3.50

Nos. 129-131 imperforate are proofs.

Wmk. 175

132 A20 10c black 4.00 3.25
133 A20 15c blue 7.00 5.50
134 A20 20c violet 3.00 2.50

1891 *Perf. 12*

135 A20 2c brown 1.25 1.25
136 A20 5c rose 2.25 2.25

1892

137 A20 2c green 1.00 1.00
138 A20 5c red 1.25 1.25
139 A20 10c orange 3.00 3.00
140 A20 15c violet 4.00 3.00
141 A20 20c brown 4.00 3.00

No. 130 Handstamp Surcharged in Blue

2 Cts.
f
時先式

1892 Unwmk. *Perf. 15*

142 A20 2c on 5c rose 14.00 11.00

Counterfeits exist of Nos. 142-152.

Stamps of 1892 Handstamp Surcharged in Blue:

銀分半 HALF CENT. g
銀分壹 ONE CENT. h

1893 Wmk. 175 *Perf. 12*

143 A20 ½c on 15c violet 4.00 4.00
144 A20 1c on 20c brown 4.00 4.00
a. ½c on 20c brown (error) 3,000.

Surcharged in Blue or Red on Halves of Stamps:

½Ct. i ½Ct. j ½Ct. k 1Ct. m

145 A20(i) ½c on half of 5c rose 4.00 2.00
146 A20(j) ½c on half of 5c rose 4.00 3.00
147 A20(k) ½c on half of 5c rose 40.00
148 A20(i) ½c on half of 5c red 4.00 2.00
149 A20(j) ½c on half of 5c red 4.00 3.00
150 A20(k) ½c on half of 5c red 40.00
151 A20(m) 1c on half of 2c brn 1.50 1.25
c. Dbl. surch., one in green 250.00
d. Dbl. surch., one in black 250.00
152 A20(m) 1c on half of 2c grn (R) 9.00 7.00

The ½c surcharge setting of 20 (2x10) covers a vertical strip of 10 unsevered stamps, with horizontal gutter midway. This setting has 11 of type "i," 8 of type "j" and 1 of type "k." Nos. 145-152 are perforated vertically down the middle.

Inverted surcharges exist on Nos. 145-151. Double surcharges, one inverted, are also found in this issue.

Handstamped provisionals somewhat similar to Nos. 145-152 were issued in Foochow by the Shanghai Agency.

Coat of Arms — A24

Mercury — A26

1893 Litho. *Perf. 13½x14*
Frame Inscriptions in Black

153 A24 ½c org, typo. 25 25
a. ½c orange, litho. 4.00 4.00
154 A24 1c brn, typo. 25 25
a. 1c brown, litho. 4.00 4.00
155 A24 2c vermilion 50 50
a. Imperf.
156 A24 5c blue 25 25
a. Black inscriptions inverted 600.00
157 A24 10c grn, typo. & litho. 35 35
a. 10c green, litho. 2.00 2.00
158 A24 15c yellow 40 40
159 A24 20c lil, typo. & litho. 50 50
a. 20c lilac, litho. 2.00 2.00
Nos. 153-159 (7) 2.50 2.50

On Nos. 157 and 159, frame inscriptions are lithographed, rest of design typographed.

Stamps of 1893 Overprinted in Black

1843 Jubilee 1893

1893, Dec. 14

160 A24 ½c org & blk 45 45
161 A24 1c brn & blk 55 55
a. Double overprint 9.00
162 A24 2c ver & blk 65 65
a. Inverted overprint 35.00
163 A24 5c bl & blk 2.25 2.25
a. Inverted overprint
164 A24 10c grn & blk 3.25 2.75
165 A24 15c yel & blk 3.25 2.75
166 A24 20c lil & blk 5.50 4.50
Nos. 160-166 (7) 15.90 13.90

50th anniv. of the first foreign settlement in Shanghai.

1893, Nov. 11 Litho. *Perf. 13½*

167 A26 2c ver & black 50 50

Nos. 158 and 159 Handstamp Surcharged in Black

FOUR CENTS.
分四

1896 *Perf. 13½x14*

168 A24 4c on 15c yel & blk 5.00 5.00
169 A24 6c on 20c lil & blk 5.00 5.00

Surcharge occurs inverted or double on Nos. 168-169.

Arms Type of 1893

1896

170 A24 2c scarlet & blk 25 40
a. Black inscriptions inverted 60.00
171 A24 4c org & blk, *yel* 32 50
172 A24 6c car & blk, *rose* 65 1.00

POSTAGE DUE STAMPS

Postage Stamps of 1890-92 Handstamped in Black, Red or Blue

Postage Due.

1892 Unwmk. *Perf. 15*

J1 A20 2c brown (Bk) 100.00 75.00
J2 A20 5c rose (Bk) 2.25 2.25
J3 A20 15c blue (Bk) 17.50 17.50

Wmk. 175

J4 A20 10c black (R) 6.00 6.00
J5 A20 15c blue (Bk) 6.00 5.00
J6 A20 20c violet (Bk) 2.25 2.50

1892-93 *Perf. 12*

J7 A20 2c brown (Bk) 50 50
J8 A20 2c brown (Bl) 50 50
J9 A20 5c rose (Bl) 1.50 2.00
J10 A20 10c orange (Bk) 50.00 40.00
J11 A20 10c orange (Bl) 2.00 1.50
J12 A20 15c violet (R) 5.00 5.00
J13 A20 20c brown (R) 5.00 5.00

D2

Perf. 14x13½, 13½ (½c)

1893 Litho.

J14 D2 ½c orange & blk 30 25
J15 D2 1c brown & blk 30 25
J16 D2 2c ver & black 30 25
J17 D2 5c blue & blk 30 30
J18 D2 10c green & blk 50 40
J19 D2 15c yellow & blk 50 40
J20 D2 20c violet & blk 50 40
Nos. J14-J20 (7) 2.70 2.25

Stamps of Shanghai were discontinued in 1898.

SIBERIA

LOCATION — A vast territory of Russia lying between the Ural Mountains and the Pacific Ocean.

The anti-Bolshevist provisional government set up at Omsk by Adm. Aleksandr V. Kolchak issued Nos. 1-10 in 1919. The monarchist, anti-Soviet government in Priamur province issued Nos. 51-118 in 1921-22.

(Stamps of the Czechoslovak Legion are listed under Czechoslovakia.)

100 Kopecks = 1 Ruble

Russian Stamps of 1909-18 Surcharged

35 a
1 рубль b

On Stamps of 1909-12

1919 Unwmk. *Perf. 14x14½*
Wove Paper
Lozenges of Varnish on Face

1 A14(a) 35k on 2k dl grn 45 1.10
a. Inverted surcharge 32.50
2 A14(a) 50k on 3k car 45 1.25
a. Inverted surcharge 32.50
3 A14(a) 70k on 1k dl org yel 90 3.00
a. Inverted surcharge 32.50
4 A15(b) 1r on 4k car 90 1.75
a. Dbl. surch., one inverted 52.50
b. Inverted surcharge 52.50
5 A14(b) 3r on 7k bl 1.50 3.50
a. Double surcharge 25.00
b. Inverted surcharge 20.00
6 A11(b) 5r on 14k dk bl & car 2.50 5.50
a. Double surcharge 25.00
b. Inverted surcharge 22.50

On Stamps of 1917

Imperf.

7 A14(a) 35k on 2k gray grn 90 1.75
8 A14(a) 50k on 3k red 90 1.75
a. Inverted surcharge 100.00
9 A14(a) 70k on 1k org 75 1.40
a. Inverted surcharge 25.00
10 A15(b) 1r on 4k car 4.50 7.75
Nos. 1-10 (10) 13.75 28.75

Nos. 1-10, were first issued in Omsk during the regime of Admiral Kolchak. Later they were used along the line of the Trans-Siberian railway to Vladivostok.

Some experts question the postal use of most off-cover canceled copies of Nos. 1-10.

25 P 1-

Similar surcharges, handstamped as above are bogus.

Priamur Government Issues
Nikolaevsk Issue

A5

A6

A7

Russian Stamps Handstamp Surcharged or Overprinted On Stamps of 1909-17

1921 Unwmk. *Perf. 14x14½, 13½*

51 A5 10k on 4k carmine
52 A5 10k on 10k dark blue
53 A6 15k on 14k dk blue & car
54 A6 15k on 15k red brn & dp bl
55 A6 15k on 35k red brn & grn
56 A6 15k on 50k brn vio & grn
57 A6 15k on 70k brn & red org
58 A6 15k on 1r brn & orange
59 A5 on 20k dl bl & dk car
60 A5 on 20k on 14k dk bl & car (No. 118)
a. 15k on 20k on 14k dk bl & car (error)
61 A7 20k on 3½r mar & lt grn
62 A7 20k on 5r ind, grn & lt bl
63 A7 20k on 7r dk grn & pink

Nos. 59-60 are overprinted with initials but original denominations remain.

A 10k on 5k claret (Russia No. 77) and a 15k on 20k blue & carmine (Russia No. 82a) were not officially issued. Some authorities consider them bogus.

Any postmark except the Vladivostok arrival cancel is bogus.

Reprints exist.

On Semi-Postal Stamp of 1914

64 SP6 20k on 3k mar & gray grn, *pink*

On Stamps of 1917

Imperf.

65 A5 10k on 1k orange
66 A5 10k on 2k gray green
67 A5 10k on 3k red

68 A5 10k on 5k claret
69 A6 15k on 1r pale brn, brn & red org
70 A7 20k on 1r pale brn, brn & red org
71 A7 20k on 3½r mar & lt grn
72 A7 20k on 7r dk grn & pink

The letters of the overprint are the initials of the Russian words for "Nikolaevsk on Amur Priamur Provisional Government".

As the surcharges on Nos. 51-72 are handstamped, a number exist inverted or double.

A 20k blue & carmine (Russia No. 126) with Priamur overprint and a 15k on 20k (Russia No. 126) were not officially issued. Some authorities consider them bogus.

Priamur Commemorative Issue

Stamps of Far Eastern Republic Overprinted

1922

78	A2	2k gray grn	32.50	32.50
a.		Inverted overprint	125.00	
79	A2a	4k rose	32.50	32.50
a.		Inverted overprint	*115.00*	
80	A2	5k claret	32.50	32.50
81	A2a	10k blue	32.50	32.50

Anniv. of the overthrow of the Bolshevik power in the Priamur district.

The letters of the overprint are the initials of "Vremeno Priamurski Pravitel'stvo" i. e. Provisional Priamur Government, 26th May.

Priamur Issue

Russian Stamps of 1909-21 Overprinted in Dark Blue or Vermilion

Приамур.
Земскій
Край

On Stamps of 1909-18

1922 ***Perf. 14x14½***

85	A14	1k dl org yel	32.50	40.00
86	A14	2k dull green	60.00	65.00
87	A14	3k carmine	15.00	20.00
88	A15	4k carmine	9.00	12.00
89	A14	5k dk claret	20.00	22.50
90	A14	7k blue (V)	20.00	22.50
91	A15	10k dark bl (V)	25.00	32.50
92	A11	14k dk bl & car	40.00	50.00
93	A11	15k red brn & dp bl	9.00	12.00
94	A8	20k dl bl & dk car	9.00	12.00
95	A11	20k on 14k dk bl & car	52.50	65.00
96	A11	25k dl grn & dk vio (V)	18.00	25.00
97	A11	35k red brn & grn	5.00	8.25
a.		Inverted overprint	60.00	
98	A8	50k brn vio & grn	6.50	9.00
99	A11	70k brn & red org	15.00	20.00

On Stamps of 1917

Imperf.

100	A14	1k orange	3.25	5.00
a.		Inverted overprint	65.00	85.00
101	A14	2k gray green	7.75	9.00
102	A14	3k red	8.25	12.00
103	A15	4k carmine	50.00	65.00
104	A14	5k claret	12.00	15.00
105	A11	15k red brn & dp bl	65.00	100.00
106	A8	20k blue & car	32.50	40.00
107	A9	1r pale brn, brn & red org	9.00	15.00

On Stamps of Siberia, 1919

Perf. 14½x15

108	A14	35k on 2k grn	32.50	40.00

Imperf

109	A14	70k on 1k org	45.00	60.00

On Stamps of Far Eastern Republic, 1921

110	A2	2k gray green	4.75	5.50
111	A2a	4k rose	4.75	5.50
112	A2	5k claret	4.75	5.50
a.		Inverted overprint	100.00	
113	A2a	10k bl (R)	3.00	3.50

Same, Surcharged with New Values

114	A2	1k on 2k gray grn	3.00	3.50
115	A2a	3k on 4k rose	3.00	3.50

The overprint is in a rectangular frame on stamps of 1k to 10k and 1r; on the other values the frame is omitted. It is larger on the 1 ruble than on the smaller stamps.

The overprint reads "Priamurski Zemski Krai", Priamur Rural Province.

Far Eastern Republic Nos. 30-32 Overprinted in Blue

ПЗК.

Perf. 14½x15

116	A14	35k on 2k green	5.00	6.50

Imperf

117	A14	35k on 2k grn	60.00	85.00
118	A14	70k on 1k org	8.25	11.50

Counterfeits of Nos. 51-118 abound.

SOMALIA

(Somali Democratic Republic) (Italian Somaliland) (Benadir)

LOCATION — Eastern Africa, bordering on the Indian Ocean and the Gulf of Aden.
GOVT. — Republic
AREA — 246,201 sq. mi.
POP. — 3,862,000 (est. 1982)
CAPITAL — Mogadiscio

The former Italian colony which included the territory west of the Juba River became known as Oltre Giuba (Trans-Juba), was absorbed into Italian East Africa in 1936. It was under British military administration from 1941-49. Italian trusteeship took effect in 1950, with a U.N. Advisory Council helping the administrator. On July 1, 1960, the former Italian colony merged with Somaliland Protectorate (British) to form the independent Republic of Somalia.

4 Besas = 1 Anna
16 Annas = 1 Rupee
100 Besas = 1 Rupee (1922)
100 Centesimi = 1 Lira (1905, 1925)
100 Centesimi = 1 Somalo (1950)
100 Centesimi = 1 Somali Shilling (1961)

Catalogue values for unused stamps in this country are for Never Hinged items, beginning with Scott 170 in the regular postage section, Scott B52 in the semi-postal section, Scott C17 in the airpost section, Scott CB11 in the airpost semi-postal section, Scott CE1 in the airpost special delivery section, Scott E8 in the special delivery section, Scott J55 in the postage due section, and Scott Q56 in the parcel post section.

Italian Somaliland

Elephant — A1

Lion — A2

Wmk. 140 - Crown

Wmk. 140

1903, Oct. **Typo.** ***Perf. 14***

1	A1	1b brown	20.00	3.00
2	A1	2b blue green	1.25	1.00
3	A2	1a claret	1.25	1.75
4	A2	2a org brown	2.50	7.25
5	A2	2½a blue	1.25	2.50
6	A2	5a orange	2.50	8.50
7	A2	10a lilac	2.50	8.50
		Nos. 1-7 (7)	31.25	*32.50*

Surcharged Centesimi 15

1905, Dec. 29

8	A2	15c on 5a orange	*1,100.*	175.00
9	A2	40c on 10a lilac	175.00	65.00

Surcharged C. 2

1906-07

10	A1	2c on 1b brown	2.00	*7.25*
11	A1	5c on 2b blue grn	2.00	*5.00*

Surcharged C. ~~~ 10

12	A2	10c on 1a claret	2.00	*3.50*
13	A2	15c on 2a brn org ('06)	2.00	*4.00*
14	A2	25c on 2½a blue	3.50	*4.00*
15	A2	50c on 5a yellow	5.50	*8.50*

Surcharged 1 LIRA 1

16	A2	1 l on 10a lilac	5.50	*12.00*
		Nos. 10-16 (7)	22.50	*44.25*

Nos. 15 and 16 with bars over former Surcharge and C. 5

1916, May

18	A2	5c on 50c on 5a yel	6.50	8.50
19	A2	20c on 1 l on 10a dl lil	3.00	6.00

No. 4 Surcharged C. ~~~ 20

20	A2	20c on 2a org brn	5.00	1.50

Stamps of 1906-07 Surcharged:

3 3 (a) 6 BESA 6 (b)

1922, Feb. 1

22	A1(a)	3b on 5c on 2b bl grn	3.50	*8.50*
23	A2(b)	6c on 10c on 1a cl	3.50	*7.25*
24	A2(b)	9b on 15c on 2a brn org	3.50	*6.00*
25	A2(b)	15b on 25c on 2½a bl	4.00	*7.25*
26	A2(b)	30b on 50c on 5a yel	5.50	*12.50*
27	A2(b)	60b on 1 l on 10a lil	7.25	*20.00*
		Nos. 22-27 (6)	27.25	*61.50*

Victory Issue

Italy Nos. 136-139 Surcharged SOMALIA ITALIANA BESA 3

1922, Apr.

28	A64	3b on 5c ol grn	35	*2.00*
29	A64	6b on 10c red	35	*2.00*
30	A64	9b on 15c sl grn	60	*3.00*
31	A64	15b on 25c ultra	60	*3.00*

Stamps of 1906-07 Surcharged with Bars and

2 2 (c) 5 BESA 5 (d)

1923, July 1

40	A1	1b brown	2.00	*7.25*
41	A1(c)	2b on 2c on 1b brn	2.00	*7.25*
42	A1(c)	3b on 2c on 1b brn	2.00	*7.25*
43	A2(d)	5b on 50c on 5a yel	2.00	*6.00*
44	A1(c)	6b on 5c on 2b bl grn	3.00	3.50
45	A2(d)	18b on 10c on 1a rose red	3.00	3.50
46	A2(d)	20b on 15c on 2a brn org	3.50	5.00
47	A2(d)	25b on 15c on 2a brn org	3.50	5.00
48	A2(d)	30b on 25c on 2½a bl	4.50	6.75
49	A2(d)	60b on 1 l on 10a lil	5.50	*14.00*
50	A2(d)	1r on 1 l on 10a lil	6.75	*20.00*
		Nos. 40-50 (11)	37.75	*85.50*

No. 40 is No. 10 with bars over the 1907 surcharge.

Propagation of the Faith Issue

Italy Nos. 143-146 Surcharged

SOMALIA ITALIANA
besa 6

1923, Oct. 24 **Wmk. 140**

51	A68	6b on 20c ol grn & brn org	1.10	*5.50*
52	A68	13b on 30c cl & brn org	1.10	*5.50*
53	A68	20b on 50c vio & brn org	85	*4.50*
54	A68	30b on 1 l bl & brn org	85	*4.50*

Fascisti Issue

Italy Nos. 159-164 Surcharged in Red or Black

SOMALIA ITALIANA
BESA 30

1923, Oct. 29 **Unwmk.** ***Perf. 14***

55	A69	3b on 10c dk grn (R)	1.25	*5.00*
56	A69	13b on 30c dk vio (R)	1.25	*5.00*
57	A69	20b on 50c brn car	1.25	*5.00*

Wmk. 140

58	A70	30b on 1 l bl	1.25	*5.00*
59	A70	1r on 2 l brn	1.25	*5.00*
60	A71	3r on 5 l blk & bl (R)	2.00	*10.00*
		Nos. 55-60 (6)	8.25	*35.00*

Manzoni Issue

Italy Nos. 165-170 Surcharged in Red

SOMALIA ITALIANA
besa 9

1924, Apr. 1

61	A72	6b on 10c brn red & blk	50	*5.00*
62	A72	9b on 15c bl grn & blk	50	*5.00*
63	A72	13b on 30c blk & sl	50	*5.00*
64	A72	20b on 50c org brn & blk	50	*5.00*

Surcharged

SOMALIA ITALIANA rupie 3

65	A72	30b on 1 l bl & blk	8.00	*55.50*
66	A72	3r on 5 l vio & blk	175.00	*1,000.*
		Nos. 61-66 (6)	185.00	*1,075.*

Victor Emmanuel Issue

Italy Nos. 175-177 Overprinted SOMALIA ITALIANA

1925-26 **Unwmk.** ***Perf. 13½***

67	A78	60c brn car	20	*2.00*
a.		Perf. 11	8.50	*35.00*
68	A78	1 l dk bl, perf. 11	32	*2.00*
a.		Perf. 13½	1.75	*14.00*
69	A78	1.25 l dk bl ('26)	30	*6.00*
a.		Perf. 11	85.00	*200.00*

Stamps of 1907-16 with Bars over Original Values

1926, Mar. 1 Wmk. 140 *Perf. 14*

70	A1	2c on 1b brn	6.00	*17.00*
71	A1	5c on 2b bl grn	5.50	*12.50*
72	A2	10c on 1a rose red	2.50	2.75
73	A2	15c on 2a org brn	2.50	3.50
74	A2	20c on 2a org brn	3.00	4.00
75	A2	25c on 2½a bl	3.00	*5.00*
76	A2	50c on 5a yel	3.50	*10.00*
77	A2	1 l on 10a dl lil	4.00	*12.50*
		Nos. 70-77 (8)	30.00	*67.25*

Saint Francis of Assisi Issue

Italy Nos. 178-180 Overprinted — SOMALIA ITALIANA

1926, Apr. 12 *Perf. 14*

78	A79	20c gray grn	60	*3.00*
79	A80	40c dk vio	60	*3.00*
80	A81	60c red brn	60	*3.00*

Italy Nos. 182 and Type of 1926 Overprinted in Red — **Somalia**

Unwmk. *Perf. 11*

81	A82	1.25 l dk bl	60	*3.00*

Perf. 14

82	A83	5 l + 2.50 l ol grn	1.50	*5.50*
		Nos. 78-82 (5)	3.90	*17.50*

Italian Stamps of 1901-26 Overprinted — SOMALIA ITALIANA

1926-30 Wmk. 140

83	A43	2c org brn	85	1.50
84	A48	5c green	1.00	1.50
85	A48	10c claret	35	30
86	A49	20c vio brn	50	42
87	A46	25c grn & pale grn	30	24
88	A49	30c gray ('30)	2.00	4.00
89	A49	60c brn org	50	70
90	A46	75c dk red & rose	16.00	3.50
91	A46	1 l brn & grn	60	35
92	A46	1.25 l bl & ultra	1.25	85
93	A46	2 l dk grn & org	2.00	1.50
94	A46	2.50 l dk grn & org	2.50	2.00
95	A46	5 l bl & rose	10.50	7.25
96	A51	10 l gray grn & red	10.50	8.50
		Nos. 83-96 (14)	48.85	32.61

Volta Issue

Type of Italy, 1927, Overprinted — **Somalia Italiana**

1927, Oct. 10

97	A84	20c purple	2.00	*7.25*
98	A84	50c dp org	2.50	*5.00*
a.		Double overprint	12.50	
99	A84	1.25 l brt bl	3.00	*7.25*

Italian Stamps of 1927-28 Overprinted in Black or Red — SOMALIA ITALIANA

1928-30

100	A86	7½c lt brn (Bk)	3.50	*12.50*
a.		Double overprint	85.00	
101	A85	50c brn & sl (R)	2.50	*3.50*
102	A86	50c brt vio (Bk) ('30)	6.00	*12.50*

Perf. 11

Unwmk.

103	A85	1.75 l dp brn	6.00	6.00

Monte Cassino Issue

Types of Monte Cassino Issue of Italy Overprinted in Red or Blue — SOMALIA ITALIANA

1929, Oct. 14 Wmk. 140 *Perf. 14*

104	A96	20c dk grn (R)	1.10	*5.00*
105	A96	25c red org (Bl)	1.10	*5.00*
106	A98	50c + 10c crim (Bl)	1.10	*7.25*
107	A98	75c + 15c ol brn (R)	1.10	*7.25*
108	A96	1.25 l + 25c dk vio (R)	2.00	*7.25*
109	A98	5 l + 1 l saph (R)	2.00	*7.25*

Overprinted in Red — **Somalia Italiana**

Unwmk.

110	A100	10 l + 2 l gray brn	2.00	*10.00*
		Nos. 104-110 (7)	10.40	*49.00*

Royal Wedding Issue

Type of Italian Royal Wedding Stamps of 1930 Overprinted — SOMALIA ITALIANA

1930, Mar. 17 Wmk. 140

111	A101	20c yel grn	50	*2.00*
112	A101	50c + 10c dp org	35	*2.50*
113	A101	1.25 l + 25c rose red	35	*3.00*

Ferrucci Issue

Types of Italian Stamps of 1930 Overprinted in Red or Blue — SOMALIA ITALIANA

1930, July 26

114	A102	20c vio (R)	35	*1.50*
115	A103	25c dk grn (R)	35	*1.50*
116	A103	50c blk (R)	35	*1.50*
117	A103	1.25 l dp bl (R)	35	*1.50*
118	A104	5 l + 2 l dp car (bl)	1.50	*3.00*
		Nos. 114-118 (5)	2.90	*9.00*

Virgil Issue

Types of Italian Stamps of 1930 Overprinted in Red or Blue — S O M A L I A

1930, Dec. 4 Photo. Wmk. 140

119	A106	15c vio bl	24	*1.50*
120	A106	20c org brn	24	*1.50*
121	A106	25c dk grn	24	*1.25*
122	A106	30c lt brn	24	*1.50*
123	A106	50c dl vio	24	*1.25*
124	A106	75c rose red	24	*1.50*
125	A106	1.25 l gray bl	24	*1.50*

Engr.

Unwmk.

126	A106	5 l + 1.50 l dk vio	1.25	*6.00*
127	A106	10 l + 2.50 l ol brn	1.25	*6.00*
		Nos. 119-127 (9)	4.18	

Saint Anthony of Padua Issue

Types of Italian Stamps of 1931 Overprinted in Blue or Red

S O M A L I A

1931, May 7 Photo. Wmk. 140

129	A116	20c brn (Bl)	50	*2.00*
130	A116	25c grn (R)	50	*2.00*
131	A118	30c gray brn (Bl)	50	*2.00*
132	A118	50c dl vio (Bl)	50	*1.50*
133	A120	1.25 l sl bl (R)	50	*2.00*

Overprinted in Red or Black — **Somalia**

Engr. Unwmk.

134	A121	75c black (R)	50	*2.00*
135	A122	5 l + 2.50 l dk brn (Bk)	1.50	*7.25*
		Nos. 129-135 (7)	4.50	

Italy Nos. 218, 221 Overprinted in Red — SOMALIA ITALIANA

1931 Wmk. 140

136	A94	25c dk grn (R)	1.65	2.50
137	A95	50c purple (R)	2.75	1.00

Lighthouse at Cape Guardafui — A3

Tower at Mnara Ciromo — A4

The only foreign revenue stamps listed in this Catalogue are those authorized for prepayment of postage.

Governor's Palace at Mogadishu — A5

Termite Nest — A6

Ostrich A7

Hippopotamus A8

Greater Kudu — A9

Lion — A10

1932 Wmk. 140 Photo. *Perf. 12*

138	A3	5c dp brn	1.25	60
139	A3	7½c violet	1.50	*3.50*
140	A3	10c gray blk	2.00	30
141	A3	15c ol grn	70	30
142	A4	20c carmine	18.00	20
143	A4	25c dp grn	70	14
144	A4	30c dk brn	2.50	30
145	A5	35c dk bl	2.00	1.65
146	A5	50c violet	27.50	8
147	A5	75c carmine	85	42
148	A6	1.25 l dk bl	85	35
149	A6	1.75 l red org	1.25	35
150	A6	2 l carmine	70	42
151	A7	2.55 l indigo	7.25	*14.00*
152	A7	5 l carmine	3.00	1.10
153	A8	10 l violet	7.25	5.00
154	A9	20 l dk grn	17.00	17.00
155	A10	25 l dark blue	25.00	25.00
		Nos. 138-155 (18)	119.30	*70.71*

1934-37 *Perf. 14*

138a	A3	5c dp brn	14	14
139a	A3	7½c violet	14	*1.00*
140a	A3	10c gray blk	14	14
141a	A3	15c ol grn	14	24
142a	A4	20c carmine	14	5
143a	A4	25c dp grn	14	5
144a	A4	30c dk brn	24	24
145a	A5	35c dk bl	50	1.25
146a	A5	50c violet	2.50	5
147a	A5	75c carmine	85	20
148a	A6	1.25 l dk bl	6.00	30
149a	A6	1.75 l red org	20.00	24
150a	A6	2 l carmine	7.25	30
151a	A7	2.55 l indigo	100.00	85.00
152a	A7	5 l carmine	1.50	85
153a	A8	10 l violet	35.00	12.50
154a	A9	20 l dk grn	*4,000.*	*275.00*
155a	A10	25 l dk bl	100.00	100.00
		Nos. 138a-153a,155a (17)	274.68	202.55

Eleven denominations in the foregoing series exist perf. 12x14 or 14x12.

Types of 1932 Issue Overprinted in Black or Red — ONORANZE AL DUCA DEGLI ABRUZZI

1934, May *Perf. 14*

156	A3	10c brn (Bk)	1.25	*4.50*
157	A4	25c green	1.25	*4.50*
158	A5	50c dl vio (Bk)	1.25	*4.50*
159	A6	1.25 l blue	1.25	*4.50*
160	A7	5 l brn blk	2.00	*5.00*
161	A8	10 l car rose (Bk)	2.00	*5.00*
162	A9	20 l dl bl	2.00	*5.00*
163	A10	25 l dk grn	2.00	*5.00*
		Nos. 156-163 (8)	13.00	*38.00*

Duke of the Abruzzi (Luigi Amadeo, 1873-1933).

Mother and Child A11

1934, Oct.

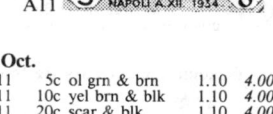

164	A11	5c ol grn & brn	1.10	*4.00*
165	A11	10c yel brn & blk	1.10	*4.00*
166	A11	20c scar & blk	1.10	*4.00*
167	A11	50c dk vio & brn	1.10	*4.00*
168	A11	60c org brn & blk	1.10	*4.00*
169	A11	1.25 l dk bl & grn	1.10	*4.00*
		Nos. 164-169 (6)	6.60	*24.00*

Second Colonial Arts Exhibition, Naples.

Catalogue values for unused stamps in this section, from this point to the end of the section, are for Never Hinged items.

Somalia

Tower at Mnara Ciromo — A12

Governor's Palace, Mogadishu — A13

Design: 5c, 20c, 60c, Ostrich.

Wmk. 277

1950, Mar. 24 Photo. *Perf. 14*

170	A12	1c gray blk	8	8
171	A12	5c car rose	8	5
172	A13	6c violet	8	8
173	A12	8c Prus grn	8	8
174	A13	10c dk grn	8	5
175	A12	20c bl grn	8	6
176	A12	35c red	20	20
177	A13	55c brt blue	25	14
178	A12	60c purple	32	14
179	A12	65c brown	42	14
180	A13	1s dp org	65	12
		Nos. 170-180,E8-E9 (13)	3.97	2.99

Council in Session A14

1951, Oct. 4

181	A14	20c dk grn & brn	1.65	24
182	A14	55c brn & vio	3.25	3.00

Meeting of First Territorial Council. See Nos. C27A-C27B.

Somali Tiger, Palm Tree and Minaret — A16

Mother and Child — A17

1952, Sept. 14 Wmk. 277 *Perf. 14*

185	A16	25c red & dk brn	1.25	1.75
186	A16	55c bl & dk brn	1.25	1.75

1st Somali Fair, Mogadishu, Sept. 14-28. See No. C28.

1953, May 27
Center in Dark Brown

187 A17 5c rose vio 7 10
188 A17 25c rose 10 14
189 A17 50c blue 50 70

Anti-tuberculosis campaign. See No. C29.

Laborer at Fair Entrance A18

1953, Sept. 28 Unwmk. *Perf. 11½*

190 A18 25c dk grn & gray 15 24
191 A18 60c bl & gray 32 50

2nd Somali Fair, Mogadishu, Sept. 28-Oct. 12. See Nos. C30-C31.

Map and Stamps of 1903 A19

Perf. 13x13½
1953, Dec. 16 Engr. Wmk. 277
"Stamps" in Brown and Rose Carmine

192 A19 25c dp mag 15 24
193 A19 35c dk grn 15 24
194 A19 60c orange 15 24
Nos. 192-194,C32-C33 (5) 1.09 1.72

50th anniv. of the 1st Somali postage stamps.

Somalia Brushwood A20

Perf. 12½x13½
1954, June 1 Photo. Unwmk.

195 A20 25c dp bl & dk gray 20 30
196 A20 60c org brn & brn 20 32

Convention of Nov. 11, 1953, with the Sovereign Military Order of Malta, providing for the care of lepers. See Nos. C37-C38.

Somali Flag A21

Adenium Somalense A22

Perf. 13½x13
1954, Oct. 12 Litho. Wmk. 277

197 A21 25c blk, grn, bl, red & yel 20 30

Adoption of a Somali flag. See No. C39.

1955, Feb. Photo. *Perf. 13*

Flowers: 5c, Haemanthus multiflorus martyn. 10c, Grinum scabrum. 25c, Poinciana elata. 60c, Calatropis procera. 1s, Pancratium. 1.20s, Sesamothamnus bussernus.

198 A22 1c bl, dp rose & dk ol brn 8 12
199 A22 5c bl, rose lil & grn 8 12
200 A22 10c lil & grn 20 12
201 A22 25c vio brn, yel & grn 32 18
202 A22 60c blk, car & grn 8 18
203 A22 1s red brn & grn 12 22
204 A22 1.20s dk brn, yel & grn 12 22
Nos. 198-204 (7) 1.00 1.16

See Nos. 216-220, E10-E11.

Weaver at Loom A23

Design: 30c, Cattle fording stream.

Perf. 13½x14
1955, Sept. 24 Wmk. 303

205 A23 25c dk brown 20 30
206 A23 30c dk green 20 30

3rd Somali Fair, Mogadishu, Sept. 1955. See Nos. C46-C47.

Casting Ballots — A24

Arms of Somalia — A25

1956, Apr. 30 *Perf. 14*

207 A24 5c brn & gray grn 8 12
208 A24 10c brn & ol bis 8 12
209 A24 25c brn & brn red 8 12
Nos. 207-209,C48-C49 (5) 48 71

Opening of the territory's first democratically elected Legislative Assembly.

1957, May 6 Wmk. 303 *Perf. 13½*
Coat of Arms in Dull Yellow, Blue and Black

210 A25 5c lt red brn 8 8
211 A25 25c carmine 12 18
212 A25 60c bluish vio 12 18
Nos. 210-212,C50-C51 (5) 59 88

Issued in honor of the new coat of arms.

Dam at Falcheiro A26

Designs: 10c, Juba River Bridge. 25c, Silos at Margherita.

1957, Sept. 28 Photo. *Perf. 14*

213 A26 5c brn & pur 8 8
214 A26 10c bis & bl grn 8 10
215 A26 25c car & bl 10 14
Nos. 213-215,C52-C53 (5) 62 88

Fourth Somali Fair and Film Festival.

Flower Type of 1955

Flowers: 1c, Adenium Somalense. 10c, Grinum scabrum. 15c, Adansonia digitata. 25c, Poinciana elata. 50c, Gloriosa virescens.

1956-59 Wmk. 303 Photo. *Perf. 13*

216 A22 1c bl, dp rose & dk ol brn 8 8
217 A22 10c lil, grn & yel ('59) 10 14
218 A22 15c red, grn & yel ('58) 12 20
219 A22 25c dl lil, grn & yel ('59) 10 14
220 A22 50c bl, grn, red & yel ('58) 20 30
Nos. 216-220 (5) 60 86

Runner — A27

Soccer Player A28

Designs: 5c, Discus thrower. 6c, Motorcyclist. 8c, Fencer. 10c, Archer. 25c, Boxers.

1958, Apr. 28 Wmk. 303 *Perf. 14*

221 A27 2c violet 6 8
222 A28 4c green 6 8
223 A27 5c vermilion 6 8
224 A28 6c gray 6 8
225 A27 8c vio bl 6 8
226 A28 10c orange 6 8
227 A28 25c dk grn 10 10
Nos. 221-227,C54-C56 (10) 80 1.08

Book and Assembly Palace — A29

White Stork — A30

1959, June 19

228 A29 5c grn & ultra 10 14
229 A29 25c ocher & ultra 10 14

Opening of Somalia's Constituent Assembly. See Nos. C59-C60 and souvenir sheet No. C60a.

1959, Sept. 4 Photo. *Perf. 14*

Birds: 10c, Saddle-billed stork. 15c, Sacred ibis. 25c, Pink-backed pelican.

230 A30 5c yel, blk & red 7 10
231 A30 10c brn, red & yel 7 10
232 A30 15c org & blk 7 10
233 A30 25c dk car, blk & org 7 10
Nos. 230-233,C61-C62 (6) 66 98

Incense Bush — A31

Arms of University Institute — A32

Design: 60c, Girl burning incense.

1959, Sept. 28 Wmk. 303

234 A31 20c org & blk 10 14
235 A31 60c blk, org & dk red 14 22

5th Somali Fair, Mogadishu. See Nos. C63-C64.

1960, Jan. 14 Photo. *Perf. 14*

Designs: 50c, Map of Africa and arms (horiz.). 80c, Arms of University Institute.

236 A32 5c brn & sal 8 8
237 A32 50c lt vio bl, brn & blk 10 14
238 A32 80c brt red & blk 24 24
Nos. 236-238,C65-C66 (5) 1.01 1.05

Opening of the University Institute of Somalia.

Globe and Uprooted Oak Emblem A33

Palm — A34

Design: 60c, Like 10c but with inscription and emblem rearranged.

1960, Apr. 7 *Perf. 14*

239 A33 10c yel brn, grn & blk 8 8
240 A33 60c dp bis & blk 8 10
241 A34 80c pink, grn & blk 8 10

World Refugee Year. July 1, 1959-June 30, 1960. See No. C67.

Republic

No. 217 Overprinted **Somaliland Independence 26 June 1960**

Wmk. 303
1960, June 26 Photo. *Perf. 13*

242 A22 10c lil, grn & yel 6.00 6.50

Independence of British Somaliland, which became part of the Republic of Somalia. See Nos. C68-C69

Gazelle and Map of Africa — A36

Design: 25c, New York skyline, UN Building and UN flag.

1960, July 1 *Perf. 14*

243 A36 5c lil & brn 12 8
244 A36 25c blue 15 12

Somalia independence. See Nos. C70-C71.

Boy Drawing Giraffe A37

Designs: 15c, Zebra. 25c, Black rhinoceros.

1960, Nov. 24

245 A37 10c bl grn, blk & brn 8 5
246 A37 15c dp car, blk & yel grn 8 6
247 A37 25c multi 8 8

See No. C72.

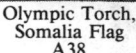

Olympic Torch, Somalia Flag
A38

Girl Harvesting Papaya
A39

Designs: 10c, Runners, flag and Olympic rings.

1960 Wmk. 303 *Perf. 14*

248	A38	5c grn & bl	8	5
249	A38	10c yel & bl	8	6

17th Olympic Games, Rome, Aug. 25-Sept. 11. See Nos. C73-C74.

1961, July 5 Photo.

Girl harvesting: 10c, Durrah (sorghum). 20c, Cotton. 25c, Sesame. 40c, Sugar cane. 50c, Bananas. 75c, Peanuts (horiz.). 80c, Grapefruit (horiz.).

250	A39	5c multi	6	5
251	A39	10c multi	6	5
252	A39	20c multi	8	6
253	A39	25c multi	8	8
254	A39	40c multi	8	8
255	A39	50c multi	15	8
256	A39	75c multi	20	8
257	A39	80c multi	32	8
		Nos. 250-257 (8)	1.03	56

Shield, Bow and Quiver
A40

Pomacanthus Semicirculatus
A41

Design: 45c, Pottery and incense jug.

1961, Sept. 28

258	A40	25c blk, car & ocher	8	8
259	A40	45c blk, bl grn & ocher	12	8

6th Somali Fair, Mogadishu. See Nos. C82-C83.

1962, Apr. 26 Photo.

Fish: 15c, Girl embroidering fish on cloth. 40c, Novaculichthys taeniourus.

260	A41	15c brn, blk & pink	8	8
261	A41	25c org, blk & ultra	12	8
262	A41	40c grn, blk & rose	28	15

See No. C84.

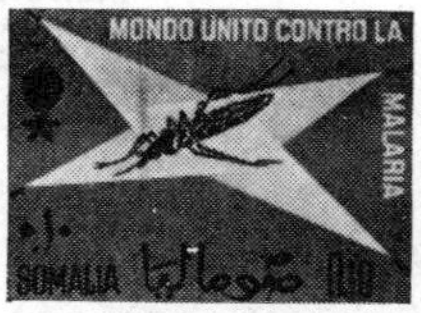

Mosquito Trapped by Sprays
A42

Design: 25c, Man with spray gun and malaria eradication emblem (vert.).

1962, Oct. 25 Wmk. 303 *Perf. 14*

263	A42	10c org red & grn	8	8
264	A42	25c rose lil, brn & blk	12	8

WHO drive to eradicate malaria. See Nos. C85-C86.

Police Auxiliary Woman
A43

Designs: 10c, Army auxiliary woman. 25c, Radio police car. 75c, First aid army auxiliary (vert.).

1963, May 15 Wmk. 303 *Perf. 14*

265	A43	5c multi	5	5
266	A43	10c blk & org	8	8
267	A43	25c multi	12	8
268	A43	75c multi	24	12
		Nos. 265-268,C87-C88 (6)	1.41	65

Women's auxiliary forces.

Carved Fork and Spoon and Wheat Emblem
A44

1963, June 25 Photo.

269	A44	75c grn & red brn	20	12

FAO "Freedom from Hunger" campaign. See No. C89.

Pres. Aden Abdulla Osman — A45

1963, Sept. 15 Wmk. 303 *Perf. 14*

270	A45	25c bl, dk brn, org & lt bl	20	12

3rd anniv. of independence. See Nos. C90-C91.

Dunes Theater
A46

Design: 55c, African Merchants' and Artisans' Exhibit.

1963, Sept. 28 Photo.

271	A46	25c bl grn	12	8
272	A46	55c car rose	15	12

7th Somali Fair, Mogadishu. See No. C92.

Somali Credit Bank Building
A47

1964, May 16 Wmk. 303 *Perf. 14*

273	A47	60c ind, red lil & yel	28	12

10th anniv. of the Somali Credit Bank. See Nos. C93-C94.

Running — A48

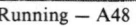

ITU Emblem and Map of Africa — A50

DC-3 — A49

Design: 25c, High jump.

1964, Oct. 10 Wmk. 303 *Perf. 14*

274	A48	10c org brn & bl	8	8
275	A48	25c org brn & bl	12	8

18th Olympic Games, Tokyo, Oct. 10-25. See Nos. C95-C96.

1964, Nov. 8 Photo. *Perf. 14*

Design: 20c, Passengers leaving DC-3.

276	A49	5c dk bl & lil rose	8	5
277	A49	20c bl & org	32	8

Establishment of Somali Air Lines. See Nos. C97-C98.

1965, May 17 Wmk. 303 *Perf. 14*

278	A50	25c dp bl & dp org	20	6

ITU, centenary. See Nos. C99-C100.

Tanning Industry
A51

Designs: 25c, Meat industry; cannery and cattle. 35c, Fishing industry; cannery and fishing boats.

1965, Sept. 28 Photo. *Perf. 14*

279	A51	10c sep & buff	8	5
280	A51	25c sep & pink	8	8
281	A51	35c sep & lt bl	12	8
		Nos. 279-281,C101-C102 (5)	1.43	60

8th Somali Fair, Mogadishu.

Hottentot Fig and Gazelle
A52

Designs: 60c, African tulip and giraffes. 1sh, Ninfea and flamingos. 1.30sh, Pervincia and ostriches. 1.80sh, Bignonia and zebras.

1965, Nov. 1 Wmk. 303 *Perf. 14*

Flowers in Natural Colors

282	A52	20c blk & brt bl	8	5
283	A52	60c blk & dk gray	12	8
284	A52	1sh blk, sl grn & ol grn	24	12
285	A52	1.30sh blk & dp grn	50	15
286	A52	1.80sh blk & brt bl	70	24
		Nos. 282-286 (5)	1.64	64

Narina's Trogon
A53

Birds: 35c, Bateleur eagle (vert.). 50c, Vulture. 1.30sh, European roller. 2sh, Vulturine guinea fowl (vert.).

1966, June 1 Photo. Wmk. 303

287	A53	25c multi	8	6
288	A53	35c brt bl & multi	8	8
289	A53	50c multi	12	8
290	A53	1.30sh multi	32	20
291	A53	2sh multi	50	24
		Nos. 287-291 (5)	1.10	66

Globe and UN Emblem — A54

UN emblem and: 1sh, Map of Africa. 1.50sh, Map of Somalia.

1966, Oct. 24 Litho. *Perf. 13x12½*

292	A54	35c bl, pur & brt bl	8	8
293	A54	1sh brn, yel & brick red	15	15
294	A54	1.50sh grn, blk, bl & yel	28	28

21st anniversary of United Nations.

Woman Sitting on Crocodile
A55

Paintings: 1sh, Woman and warrior. 1.50sh, Boy leading camel. 2sh, Women pounding grain.

Wmk. 303

1966, Dec. 1 Photo. *Perf. 14*

295	A55	25c multi	8	6
296	A55	1sh multi	12	12
297	A55	1.50sh multi	20	15
298	A55	2sh multi	24	20

Somali art, exhibited in the Garesa Museum, Mogadishu.

UNESCO Emblem
A56

1966, Dec. 20 Wmk. 303 *Perf. 14*

299	A56	35c blk, dk red & gray	8	8
300	A56	1sh blk, emer & yel	12	12
301	A56	1.80sh blk, ultra & red	28	24

UNESCO, 20th anniv.

Haggard's Oribi
A57

Dancers
A58

Gazelles: 60c, Long-snouted dik-dik. 1sh, Gerenuk. 1.80s, Soemmering's gazelle.

1967, Feb. 20 Photo. *Perf. 14*

302	A57	35c	blk, ultra & bis	8	8
303	A57	60c	blk, org & brn	8	8
304	A57	1sh	blk, red & brn	12	12
305	A57	1.80sh	blk, yel grn & brn	28	24

Unwmk.

1967, July 15 Litho. *Perf. 13*

Designs: Various Folk Dances.

306	A58	25c	multi	8	8
307	A58	50c	multi	8	8
308	A58	1.30sh	multi	20	20
309	A58	2sh	multi	24	24

Boy Scout Giving Scout Sign — A59

Designs: 50c, Boy Scouts with flags. 1sh, Boy Scout cooking and tent. 1.80sh, Jamboree emblem.

1967, Aug. 15

310	A59	35c	multi	8	8
311	A59	50c	multi	8	8
312	A59	1sh	multi	24	12
313	A59	1.80sh	multi	52	32

12th Boy Scout World Jamboree, Farragut State Park, Idaho, Aug. 1-9.

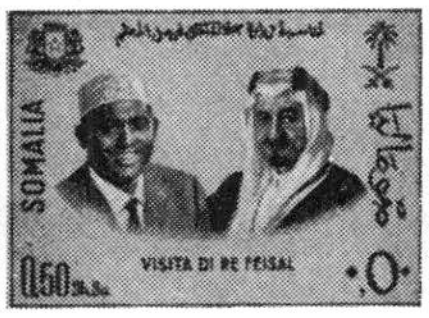

Pres. Abdirascid Ali Scermarche and King Faisal A60

Designs: 1sh, Clasped hands, flags of Somalia and Saudi Arabia.

Wmk. 303

1967, Sept. 21 Photo. *Perf. 14*

314	A60	50c	blk & lt bl	8	8
315	A60	1sh	multi	15	12

Visit of King Faisal of Saudi Arabia. See No. C103.

Gaterin Gaterinus A61

Tropical Fish: 50c, Chaetodon semilarvatus. 1sh, Priacanthus hamrur. 1.80sh, Epinephelus summana.

1967, Nov. 15 Litho. *Perf. 14*

316	A61	35c	dk bl, yel & blk	8	8
317	A61	50c	brt bl, ocher & blk	8	8
318	A61	1sh	emer, org, brn & blk	24	15
319	A61	1.80sh	pur, yel & blk	50	42

Physician Treating Infant — A62

Waterbuck — A64

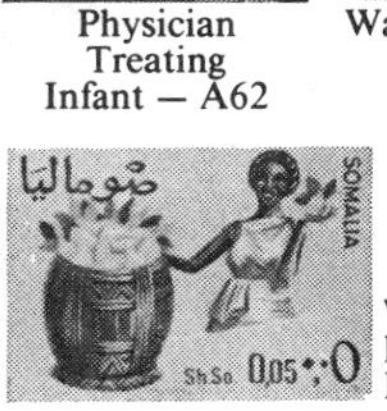

Woman and Basket with Lemons — A63

Designs: 1sh, Physician examining boy, and nurse. 1.80sh, Physician and nurse treating patient.

Wmk. 303

1968, Mar. 20 Photo. *Perf. 14*

320	A62	35c	blk, scar, bl & brn	8	8
321	A62	1sh	blk, grn & brn	12	12
322	A62	1.80sh	blk, org & brn	32	24

WHO, 20th anniversary.

1968 Litho. *Perf. 11½*

Designs: 10c, Oranges. 25c, Coconuts. 35c, Papayas. 40c, Limes. 50c, Grapefruit. 1sh, Bananas. 1.30sh, Cotton bolls. 1.80sh, Speke's gazelle. 2sh, Lesser kudu. 5sh, Hunter's hartebeest. 10sh, Clark's gazelle (dibatag).

323	A63	5c	lt bl & multi	5	5
324	A63	10c	yel & multi	5	5
325	A63	25c	lt lil & multi	8	5
326	A63	35c	sal & multi	8	6
327	A63	40c	buff & multi	8	8
328	A63	50c	multi	8	8
329	A63	1sh	lt bl & multi	15	15
330	A63	1.30sh	gray & multi	24	24
331	A64	1.50sh	lt bl & multi	20	15
332	A64	1.80sh	multi	28	24
333	A64	2sh	pink & multi	32	24
334	A64	5sh	multi	1.00	80
335	A64	10sh	multi	2.75	1.25
			Nos. 323-335 (13)	5.36	3.44

Issue dates: Nos. 323-330, Apr. 25; Nos. 331-335, May 10.

Javelin A65

Woman Grinding Grain, Statuette A66

Sports: 50c, Running. 80c, High jump. 1.50sh, Basketball.

Wmk. 303

1968, Oct. 12 Photo. *Perf. 14*

336	A65	35c	blk, yel & brn	8	8
337	A65	50c	blk, rose red & brn	8	8
338	A65	80c	blk, brt rose lil & brn	12	8
339	A65	1.50sh	blk, brt grn & brn	24	15
a.			Souv. sheet of 4, #336-339	70	60

19th Olympic Games, Mexico City, Oct. 12-27. No. 339a sold for 3.65sh.

Perf. 11½x12

1968, Dec. 1 Litho. Unwmk.

Statuettes: 35c, Woman potter. 2.80sh, Woman mat maker.

340	A66	25c	rose lil, blk & brn	8	5
341	A66	35c	brick red, blk & brn	8	8
342	A66	2.80sh	grn, blk & brn	52	35

Cornflower and Rhinoceros A67

Flowers: 80c, Sunflower and elephant. 1sh, Oleander and antelopes. 1.80sh, Chrysanthemums and storks.

Perf. 13x12½

1969, Mar. 25 Litho. Unwmk.

343	A67	40c	red & multi	8	8
344	A67	80c	vio & multi	12	8
345	A67	1sh	bl & multi	15	12
346	A67	1.80sh	yel & multi	28	24

ILO Emblem and Blacksmiths A68

Designs: 1sh, Oxdrawn plow. 1.80sh, Drawing water from well.

Wmk. 303

1969, May 10 Photo. *Perf. 14*

347	A68	25c	dk red, dp bis & blk	8	5
348	A68	1sh	car rose, brn & blk	15	12
349	A68	1.80sh	multi	28	24

ILO, 50th anniversary.

Mahatma Gandhi — A69

Designs: 1.50sh, Gandhi, globe and hands releasing dove (horiz.). 1.80sh, Gandhi seated.

Unwmk.

1969, Oct. 2 Photo. *Perf. 13*

Size: 25x35½mm

350	A69	35c	brn vio	8	8

Perf. 14½x14

Size: 37½x20mm

351	A69	1.50sh	bis brn	20	20

Perf. 13

Size: 25x35½mm

352	A69	1.80sh	ol gray	24	24

Mohandas K. Gandhi (1869-1948), leader in India's fight for independence.

A Space Exploration (US) set of 7, plus souvenir sheet, was issued Feb. 14, 1970.

Nivprale Vevanes A70

Butterflies: 50c, Leschenault. 1.50sh, Papilio (ornytoptera) aeacus. 2sh, Urania riphaeus.

Perf. 12½x13

1970, Mar. 25 Litho. Unwmk.

353	A70	25c	multi	8	8
354	A70	50c	multi	8	8
355	A70	1.50sh	org & multi	20	20
356	A70	2sh	yel & multi	28	28

Somali Democratic Republic

Lenin Addressing Crowd — A71

Designs: 25c, Lenin walking with children. 1.80sh, Lenin in his study (horiz.).

Perf. 12x12½, 12½x12

1970, Apr. 22 Litho. Unwmk.

357	A71	25c	multi	8	5
358	A71	1sh	multi	20	14
359	A71	1.80sh	multi	22	18

Lenin (1870-1924), Russian communist leader.

Bird Feeding Young A72

Designs: 35c, Monument and Battle of Dagahtur. 1sh, Arms of Somalia and UN emblem (vert.). 2.80sh, Boy milking camel, and star (vert.).

Perf. 14x13½, 13½x14

1970, July 28 Photo. Wmk. 303

360	A72	25c	bl & multi	8	8
361	A72	35c	sl & multi	8	8
362	A72	1sh	vio & multi	20	20
363	A72	2.80sh	bl & multi	65	50

10th anniversary of independence.

"Agriculture" — A73

Designs: 40c, Soldier and flag. 1sh, Hand on open book. 1.80sh, Grain, scales of justice and dove.

Perf. 14x13½

1970, Oct. 21 Photo. Wmk. 303

364	A73	35c	grn & multi	8	8
365	A73	40c	ultra & blk	8	8
366	A73	1sh	red brn & blk	20	12
367	A73	1.80sh	multi	42	22

First anniversary of Oct. 21st Revolution.

Snake Strangling Black Man, Map of South Africa A74

Design: 1.80sh, Concentration camp and symbols of justice holding scales.

Perf. 14x13½

1971, June 20 Photo. Wmk. 303

368	A74	1.30sh	multi	30	20
369	A74	1.80sh	gray, red & blk	45	32

Against racial discrimination in South Africa.

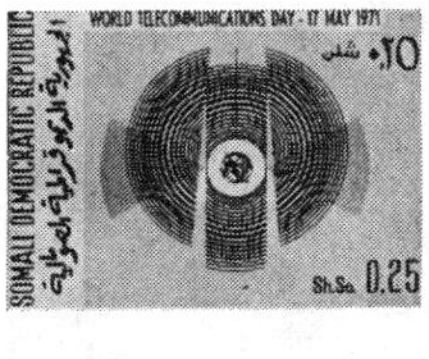

Waves A75

Design: 2.80sh, Waves and globe.

1971, June 30

370	A75	25c	blk & bl	8	6
371	A75	2.80sh	blk, grn & bl	60	42

3rd World Telecommunications Day, May 17.

Map of Africa and Telecommunications System — A76

Design: 1.50sh, Map of Africa and telecommunications system (different design).

1971, July 25

372	A76	1sh blk, lt bl & grn	20 14
373	A76	1.50sh blk & yel	32 25

Pan-African Telecommunications system.

White Rhinoceros A77

Wild Animals: 1sh, Cheetahs. 1.30sh, Zebras. 1.80sh, Lion attacking camel.

1971, Aug. 25

374	A77	35c ocher & multi	12 8
375	A77	1sh vio & multi	22 14
376	A77	1.30sh vio & multi	42 18
377	A77	1.80sh multi	52 25

Headquarters, Mogadishu, Flag, Map of Africa — A78

Design: 1.30sh, Desert Fort.

1971, Oct. 18

378	A78	1.30sh blk & red org	22 22
379	A78	1.50sh blk, bl & yel	30 25

East and Central African Summit Conference.

Revolution Monument A79

Designs: 1sh, Field workers. 1.35sh, Building workers.

1971, Oct. 21

380	A79	10c blk & bl	5 5
381	A79	1sh blk, yel brn & grn	18 18
382	A79	1.35sh blk, dp brn & yel	35 20

2nd anniversary of 1969 revolution.

Vaccination of Cow — A80

Design: 1.80sh, Veterinarian vaccinating cow.

Perf. 14x13½

1971, Nov. 28 Photo. Wmk. 303

383	A80	40c blk, red & bl	40 8
384	A80	1.80sh lt grn & multi	45 35

Rinderpest campaign.

Postal Union Emblem, Dove and Letter A81

1972, Jan. 25 Unwmk.

385	A81	1.50sh multi	52 45

10th anniv. of APU. See No. C108.

Children and UNICEF Emblem A82

Design: 50c, Mother and child (vert.).

1972, Mar. 30 *Perf. 13x14, 13x13*

386	A82	50c blk, bis brn & dk brn	12 12
387	A82	2.80sh lt bl & multi	70 52

UNICEF, 25th anniv. (in 1971).

Camel A83

Designs: 10c, Cattle and cargo ship. 20c, Bull. 40c, Sheep. 1.70sh, Goat.

1972, Apr. 10 *Perf. 14x13*

388	A83	5c grn & multi	6 5
389	A83	10c multi	8 6
390	A83	20c multi	8 8
391	A83	40c org red & blk	14 8
392	A83	1.70sh dl grn & blk	85 45
		Nos. 388-392 (5)	1.21 72

Hands Holding Infant A84

Designs: 1sh, Youth Corps emblem, marchers with flags. 1.50sh, Woman, man, tent and tractor.

1972, Oct. 21 Photo. *Perf. 14x13½*

393	A84	70c yel & multi	18 12
394	A84	1sh red & multi	22 18
395	A84	1.50sh lt bl & multi	35 30

3rd anniversary of October 21 Revolution.

Folk Dance A85

Folk Dances: 40c, Man and woman (vert.). 1sh, Group dance (vert.). 2sh, Two men and a woman.

1973 Photo. *Perf. 14x13½, 13½x14*

396	A85	5c dl bl & multi	5 5
397	A85	40c brn & multi	8 8
398	A85	1sh yel & multi	22 15
399	A85	2sh brick red & multi	45 30

Hand Writing Somali Script A86

Designs: 40c, Flame and "FAR SOMALI" inscription (vert.). 1sh, Woman and sunburst with Somali script.

Perf. 13½x14, 14x13½

1973, Oct. 21 Photo.

400	A86	40c red & multi	8 8
401	A86	1sh bl & multi	20 14
402	A86	2sh yel & multi	45 30

Publicity for use of Somali script.

Map of Africa and Emblem — A87

Map of Africa with Target on Somalia — A88

1974, June 12 *Perf. 13½x14*

403	A87	40c multi	12 6
404	A88	2sh multi	52 30

OAU Meeting, Mogadishu.

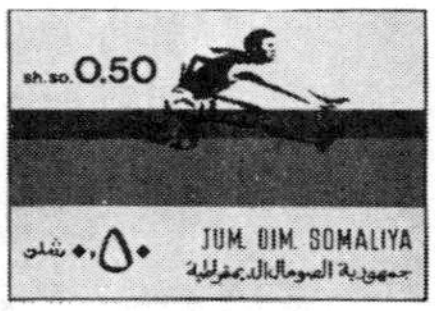

Hurdler A89

Designs: 1sh, Runners. 1.40sh, Netball (vert.).

1974, Aug. 1 *Perf. 14x13, 13x14*

405	A89	50c blk & org	12 8
406	A89	1sh blk & grn	22 18
407	A89	1.40sh blk & ol	35 22

Victory Pioneers — A90

Pioneers Helping Woman — A91

1974, Aug. 25 Photo. *Perf. 13x14*

408	A90	40c multi	8 8
409	A91	2sh multi	40 30

Victory Pioneers, founded Aug. 24, 1972, to defend Socialist Revolution.

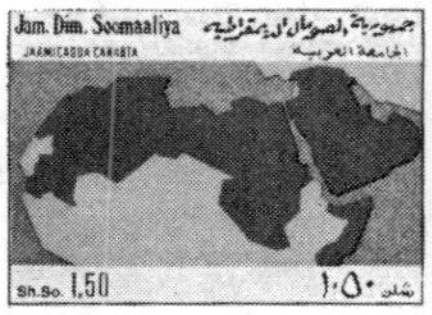

Map of Arab Countries A92

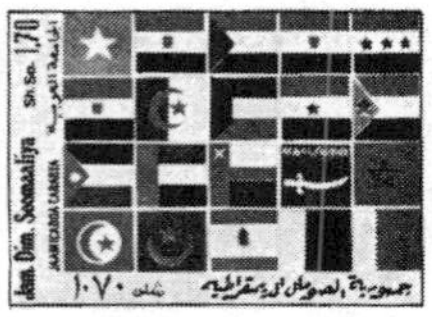
Flags of Arab Countries A93

1974, Sept. 1 *Perf. 14x13*

410	A92	1.50sh multi	35 20
411	A93	1.70sh multi	42 22

Somalia's admission to the Arab League, Feb. 14, 1974.

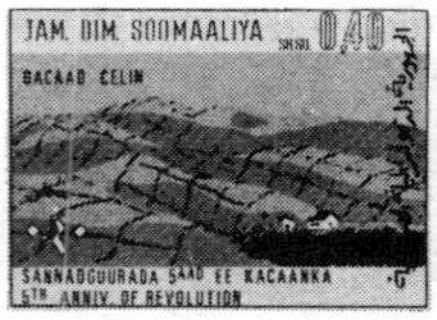

Tank Tracks in Desert A94

Somalis Reading Books — A95

Perf. 14x13½, 13½x14

1974, Oct. 21 Litho.

412	A94	40c multi	12 8
413	A95	2sh multi	52 30

5th anniversary of the Oct. 21st Revolution.

Carrier Pigeons A96

Design: 3sh, Postrider.

1975, Feb. 15 Litho. *Perf. 14x13½*

414	A96	50c bl & multi	22 12
415	A96	3sh multi	1.25 45

UPU centenary (in 1974).

Africa A97

Design: 1.50sh, Carrier pigeons.

1975, Apr. 10

416	A97	1sh multi	30 14
417	A97	1.50sh multi	50 22

African Postal Union.

Somali Warrior — A98

Designs: Traditional costumes of Somali men (1sh, 10sh) and women (40c, 50c, 5sh).

1975, Oct. 27 Photo. *Perf. 13½*

418	A98	10c yel & multi	5	5
419	A98	40c lt bl & multi	8	6
420	A98	50c multi	12	8
421	A98	1sh grn & multi	22	12
422	A98	5sh cl & multi	1.25	65
423	A98	10sh rose & multi	2.50	1.75
		Nos. 418-423 (6)	4.22	2.71

Monument — A99

IWY Emblem A100

1975, Dec. 10 Litho. *Perf. 13½x14*

424	A99	50c blk & red org	12	8
425	A100	2.30sh blk, pink & mag	50	40

International Women's Year.

Abdulla Hassan Monument A101

Abdulla Hassan with Warriors — A102

Designs: 1.50sh, Abdulla Hassan speaking to his men. 2.30sh, Attacking horsemen (horiz.).

Perf. 14x13½, 13½x14

1976, Nov. 30 Photo.

426	A101	50c multi	10	8
427	A102	60c multi	12	8
428	A102	1.50sh multi	30	22
429	A102	2.30sh multi	50	35

Sayid Mohammed Abdulla Hassan (1864-1920), poet and military leader.

Cypraea Gracilis A103

Sea Shells: 75c, Charonia bardayi. 1sh, Chlamys townsendi. 2sh, Cymatium ranzanii. 2.75sh, Conus argillaceus. 2.90sh, Strombus oldi.

1976, Dec. 15 Photo. *Perf. 14x13½*

430	A103	50c bl & multi	12	8
431	A103	75c bl & multi	14	10
432	A103	1sh bl & multi	22	14
433	A103	2sh bl & multi	45	32
434	A103	2.75sh bl & multi	65	45
435	A103	2.90sh bl & multi	75	45
a.		Souvenir sheet of 6, #430-435	3.25	3.25
		Nos. 430-435 (6)	2.33	1.54

No. 435a sold for 11sh.

Benin Head and Hunters — A104

Benin Head and: 75c, Handicrafts. 2sh, Dancers. 2.90sh, Musicians.

1977, Aug. 30 Photo. *Perf. 14x13½*

436	A104	50c multi	12	8
437	A104	75c multi	14	10
438	A104	2sh multi	45	32
439	A104	2.90sh multi	60	42

2nd World Black and African Festival, FESTAC '77, Lagos, Nigeria, Jan. 15-Feb. 12.

Arms of Somalia A105

Designs: 75c, Somali flags (vert.). 1.50sh, Pres. Mohammed Siad Barre and globe. 2sh, Arms over rising sun and flags (vert.).

Perf. 13½x14, 14x13½

1977, Sept. 30 Photo.

440	A105	75c multi	18	12
441	A105	1sh multi	20	14
442	A105	1.50sh multi	25	20
443	A105	2sh multi	45	35

Somali Socialist Revolutionary Party, established July 1, 1976.

Licaon Pictus A106

Protected Animals: 75c, Bush baby. 1sh, Somali ass. 1.50sh, Aardwolf. 2sh, Greater kudu. 3sh, Giraffe.

1977, Nov. 25 Photo. *Perf. 14x13½*

444	A106	50c multi	12	8
445	A106	75c multi	14	12
446	A106	1sh multi	22	18
447	A106	1.50sh multi	35	25
448	A106	2sh multi	50	35
449	A106	3sh multi	70	60
a.		Souvenir sheet of 6, #444-449	2.50	2.50
		Nos. 444-449 (6)	2.03	1.58

Leonardo da Vinci's Flying Machine A107

ICAO Emblem and: 1.50sh, Montgolfier's balloon. 2sh, Wright brothers' plane. 2.90sh, Somali Airlines' turbojet.

1977, Dec. 23 Photo. *Perf. 14x13½*

450	A107	1sh multi	22	18
451	A107	1.50sh multi	35	22
452	A107	2sh multi	45	40
453	A107	2.90sh multi	70	45
a.		Souvenir sheet of 4, #450-453	2.25	2.25

ICAO, 30th anniv. No. 453a sold for 10sh.

Dome of the Rock — A108

Lithographed and Engraved

1978, Apr. 30 *Perf. 13x14*

454	A108	75c multi	18	12
455	A108	2sh multi	45	35

Palestinian fighters and their families.

Stadium and Soccer Player — A109

Designs: 4.90sh, Stadium and goalkeeper. 5.50sh, Stadium and player.

1978, Aug. 5 Litho. *Perf. 14x13½*

456	A109	1.50sh multi	35	22
457	A109	4.90sh multi	1.10	90
458	A109	5.50sh multi	1.25	1.10
a.		Souvenir sheet of 3, #456-458	3.75	3.75

11th World Cup Soccer Championship, Argentina, June 1-25. No. 458a sold for 14sh.

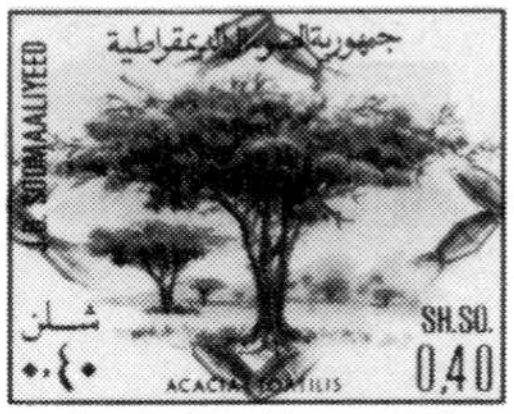

Acacia Tortilis — A110

Trees: 50c, Ficus sycomorus (vert.). 75c, Terminalia catapa (vert.). 2.90sh, Baobab.

1978, Sept. 5 Photo. *Perf. 14*

459	A110	40c multi	12	8
460	A110	50c multi	14	12
461	A110	75c multi	20	14
462	A110	2.90sh multi	45	35

Forest conservation.

Hibiscus — A111

Flowers of Somalia: 1sh, Cassia baccarinii. 1.50sh, Kigelia somalensis. 2.30sh, Dichrostachys glomerata.

1978, Dec. 15 Photo. *Perf. 13½x14*

463	A111	50c multi	12	8
464	A111	1sh multi	22	18
465	A111	1.50sh multi	30	25
466	A111	2.30sh multi	52	35
a.		Souvenir sheet of 4, #463-466, perf. 14	2.00	2.00

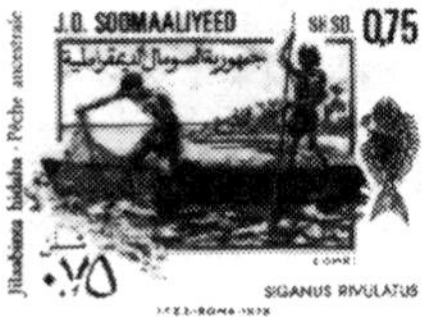

Huri and Siganus Rivulatus A112

Fishery Development: 80c, Sail huri, gaterin gaterinus. 2.30sh, Fishing boats, hypacanthus amia. 2.50sh, Motorized fishing boat, mackerel.

1979, Sept. 1 Photo. *Perf. 14x13½*

467	A112	75c multi	12	12
468	A112	80c multi	14	14
469	A112	2.30sh multi	42	42
470	A112	2.50sh multi	45	45

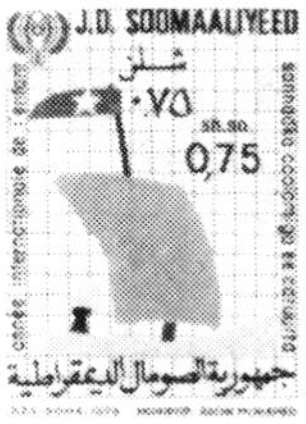

Sailing, IYC Emblem — A113

IYC Emblem, Children's Drawings: 50c, Schoolboy. 1.50sh, Houses. 3sh, Bird and flower.

1979, Sept. 10 Photo. *Perf. 13½x14*

471	A113	50c multi	8	8
472	A113	75c multi	14	14
473	A113	1.50sh multi	25	25
474	A113	3sh multi	52	52
a.		Souvenir sheet of 4, #471-474	1.75	1.75

International Year of the Child.

University Students, Outdoor Classrooms — A114

Flower and: 50c, Housing construction. 75c, Children's recreation. 1sh, Doctor examining child, woman and man carrying grain and fish. 2.40sh, Woman and children carrying produce over bridge. 3sh, Dish antenna.

1979, Nov. 30 Litho. *Perf. 14x13½*

475	A114	20c multi	6	5
476	A114	50c multi	12	8
477	A114	75c multi	14	8
478	A114	1sh multi	18	12
479	A114	2.40sh multi	45	25
480	A114	3sh multi	52	32
		Nos. 475-480 (6)	1.47	90

Oct. 21 revolution, 10th anniversary.

Barbopsis Devecchii A115

Freshwater Fish: 90c, Phreatichthys andruzzii. 1sh, Uegitglanis zammaranoi. 2.50sh, Pardi's catfish.

1979, Dec. 12

481	A115	50c multi	18	8
482	A115	90c multi	22	12
483	A115	1sh multi	25	12
484	A115	2.50sh multi	65	32
a.		Souvenir sheet of 4, #481-484	2.00	2.00

No. 484a sold for 10sh.

Taleh Fortress, Congress Emblem — A116

1980, June 1 Photo. *Perf. 14x13½*

485 A116 2.25sh multi 48 35
486 A116 3.50sh multi 75 55

1st International Congress of Somalian Studies, Mogadishu, July 6-13.

View of Marka — A117

1980, July 1 Litho. *Perf. 14*

487 A117 75c shown 15 12
488 A117 1sh Gandershe 20 14
489 A117 2.30sh Afgooye 50 35
490 A117 3.50sh Muqdisho 75 55

Nos. 487-490 each se-tenant with label showing regional map. See Nos. 502-505, 527-530.

Batis Perkeo — A118

1980, July 30 Photo. *Perf. 13½x14*

491 A118 1sh shown 22 14
492 A118 2.25sh Rynchostruthus socotranus louisae 22 35
493 A118 5sh Laniarius ruficeps 1.25 80
a. Souvenir sheet of 3, #491-493 1.75 1.25

World Food Day — A119

Perf. 13½x14, 14x13½

1981, Oct. 16 Litho.

494 A119 75c Globe, grain 15 12
495 A119 3.25sh Emblem, horiz. 65 52
496 A119 5.50sh like No. 494 1.25 90

13th World Telecommunications Day — A120

1981, Oct. 10 *Perf. 13½x14*

497 A120 1sh Shepherdess, sheep, dish antenna 24 14
498 A120 3sh Emblems 85 50
499 A120 4.60sh like No. 498 85 52

Hegira, 1500th Anniv. — A121

1982 World Cup — A122

1981, Oct. Photo. *Perf. 13½x14*

500 A121 1.50sh multi 30 20
501 A121 3.80sh multi 85 65

View Type of 1980

1982, May 31 Litho. *Perf. 13½x14*

502 A117 2.25sh Balcad 48 35
503 A117 4sh Jowhar 90 65
504 A117 5.50sh Golaleey 1.25 90
505 A117 8.30sh Muqdisho 1.75 1.25

Nos. 502-505 each se-tenant with label showing regional map.

1982, June 13

Designs: Various soccer players.

506 A122 1sh multi 25 15
507 A122 1.50sh multi 42 22
508 A122 3.25sh multi 90 52
a. Souvenir sheet of 3, #506-508 1.65 1.00

ITU Plenipotentiaries Conference, Nairobi, Sept. — A123

1982, Oct. 15 Photo. *Perf. 14x13½*

509 A123 75c grn & multi 15 12
510 A123 3.25sh org & multi 65 52
511 A123 5.50sh bl & multi 1.10 90

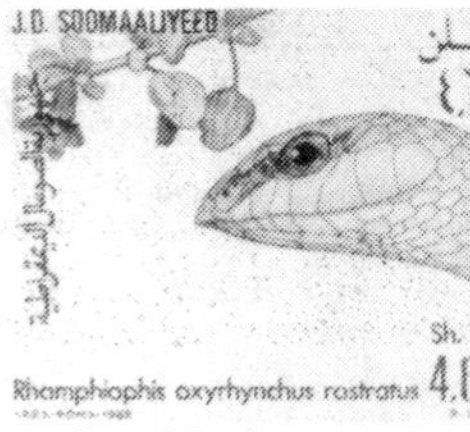

Local Snakes — A124

Designs: 2.80sh, Bitis arietans. 3.20sh, Psammophis punctulatus. 4.60sh, Rhamphiophis oxyrhynchus. 8.60sh, Sphalerosophis josephscorteccii.

1982, Dec. 20 Photo. *Perf. 14*

512 A124 2.80sh multi 60 42
513 A124 3.20sh multi 65 50
514 A124 4.60sh multi 1.00 65

Souvenir Sheet

515 A124 8.60sh multi 3.00 2.25

Somali Woman — A125

1982, Dec. 30 *Perf. 14x13½*

516 A125 1sh yel & multi 15 12
517 A125 5.20sh lil & multi 90 85
518 A125 5.80sh org & multi 1.00 90
519 A125 6.40sh bl & multi 1.10 1.00
520 A125 9.40sh lt brn & multi 1.65 1.50
521 A125 25sh grn & multi 4.25 4.00
Nos. 516-521 (6) 9.05 8.37

World Communications Year — A126

1983, July 20 *Perf. 13½x14*

522 A126 5.20sh multi 85 65
523 A126 6.40sh multi 90 85

2nd Intl. Congress of Somali Studies, Hamburg — A127

Various views of Hamburg.

1983, Aug. 1 *Perf. 14*

524 A127 5.20sh multi 85 65
525 A127 6.40sh multi 1.00 85

Military Uniforms — A128

Designs: a. Air Force. b. Women's Auxiliary Corps. c. Border Police. d. People's Militia. e. Army Infantry. f. Custodial Corps. g. Police. h. Navy.

1983, Oct. 21 Litho. *Perf. 13½x14*

526 Strip of 8, multi 2.00
a.-h. A128 3.20sh, any single 25 20

View Type of 1980

1983

527 A117 2.80sh Barawe 25 15
528 A117 3.20sh Bur Hakaba 30 20
529 A117 5.50sh Baydhabo 50 32
530 A117 8.60sh Dooy Nuunaay 85 50

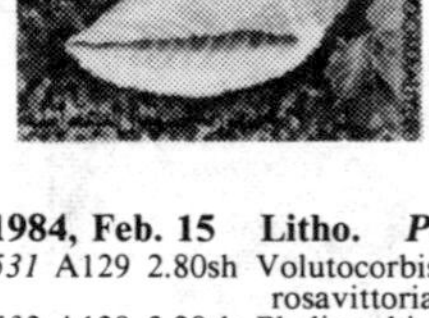

Sea Shells A129

1984, Feb. 15 Litho. *Perf. 14x13½*

531 A129 2.80sh Volutocorbis rosavittoriae 22 15
532 A129 3.20sh Phalium bituberculosum 25 20
533 A129 5.50sh Conus milneedwarsi 42 32

Souvenir Sheet

Perf. 14

534 A129 15sh Cypraea broderipi 1.25 90

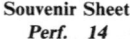

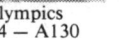

Olympics 1984 — A130

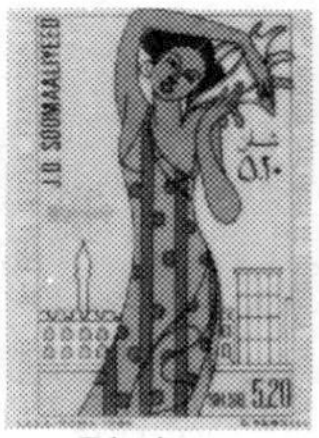

Riccione Fair — A131

1984, Sept. Litho. *Perf. 13½x14*

535 A130 1.50sh Runners 12 9
536 A130 3sh Discus 24 15
537 A130 8sh Pole vaulting 65 45
a. Souvenir sheet of 3, #535-537 1.25 90

No. 537a sold for 15sh.

1984, Sept. Litho. *Perf. 13½x14*

538 A131 5.20sh multi 42 30
539 A131 6.40sh multi 52 40

Animals A132

1984, Sept. Litho. *Perf. 14x13½*

540 A132 1sh Hystrix cristata 9 7
541 A132 1.50sh Ichneumia albicauda 12 9
542 A132 2sh Mungos mungo 15 12
543 A132 4sh Mellivora capensis 35 22
a. Souvenir sheet of 4, #540-543 90 60

No. 543a sold for 10sh.

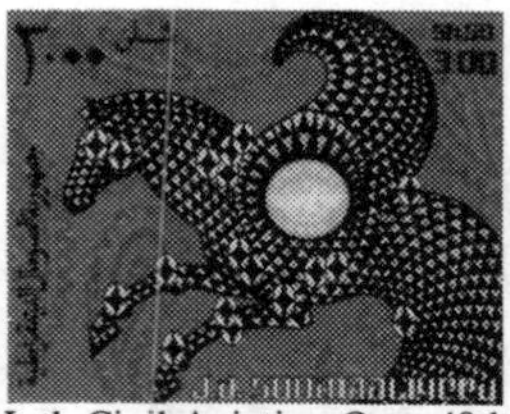

Intl. Civil Aviation Org., 40th Anniv. — A133

1984, Nov. 20 Litho. *Perf. 14*

544 A133 3sh multi 10 8
545 A133 6.40sh multi 22 15

Souvenir Sheet

546 Sheet of 2 35 35
e. A133 3sh like No. 544 12 12
f. A133 6.40sh like No. 545 24 24

No. 546 contains 2 stamps 49½x46mm. Sold for 10sh.

Dove — A134

Constellations from the Book of Fixed Stars, by Abd al-Rahman al-Sufi.

1985, Aug. 10 Litho. *Perf. 13½x14*

547 A134 4.30sh shown 45 30
548 A134 11sh Bull 1.10 75
549 A134 12.50sh Rams 1.25 90
550 A134 13.80sh Archer 1.50 1.00

Architecture — A135

1985, Sept. Litho. Perf. 13½x14

551	A135 2sh Ras Kiambone		20	14
552	A135 6.60sh Hannassa		60	42
553	A135 10sh Mnarani		1.50	1.10
554	A135 18.60sh Ras Kiambone, diff.		2.75	1.75

Nos. 551-554 each printed se-tenant with decorative label. See Nos. 572-575.

Lady Somalia Seated in Posthorn A136

1985, Oct. Perf. 14x14½

555	A136 2sh multi	20	14
556	A136 20sh multi	2.00	1.50
a.	Souvenir sheet of 2, #555-556, perf. 13½	3.25	3.25

ITALIA '85, Rome. No. 556a sold for 30sh.

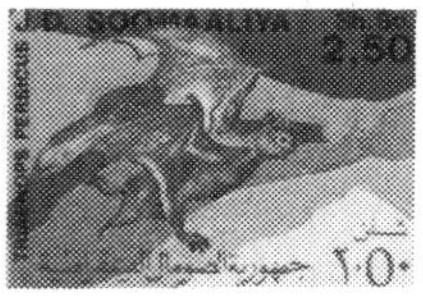
Bats — A137

1985, Dec. 25 Litho. Perf. 14x13½

557	A137 2.50sh Triaenops persicus	9	7
558	A137 4.50sh Cardioderma cor	15	12
559	A137 16sh Tadarida condylura	55	40
560	A137 18sh Coleura afra	65	45

Souvenir Sheet

561	Sheet of 4	1.75	1.75
a.	A137 2.50sh like #552	12	12
b.	A137 4.50sh like #553	20	20
c.	A137 16sh like #554	70	70
d.	A137 18sh like #555	80	80

Nos. 561a-561d printed in continuous design. No. 561 sold for 50sh.

Economic Trade Agreement with Kenya — A138

Design: Presidents Arap Moi and Barre, satellite communications.

1986, Feb. 15 Perf. 14

562	A138 9sh multi	32	22
563	A138 14.50sh multi	52	35

EUROFLORA Flower Exhibition, Genoa — A139

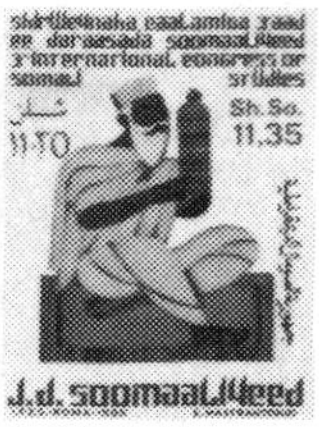

3rd Intl. Congress on Somali Studies — A140

1986, Apr. 25 Perf. 13½x14

564	A139 10sh Flower arrangement	35	24
565	A139 15sh Arrangement, diff.	52	38
a.	Souv. sheet of 2, #564-565	1.25	1.25

No. 565a sold for 30sh.

1986, May 26

566	A140 11.35sh multi	40	30
567	A140 20sh multi	70	50

1986 World Cup Soccer Championships, Mexico — A141

Various soccer plays.

1986, June Perf. 14x13½

568	A141 3.60sh multi	12	9
569	A141 4.80sh multi	18	12
570	A141 6.80sh multi	24	18
571	A141 22.60sh multi	85	55
a.	Souv. sheet of 4, #568-571	1.75	1.75

No. 571a sold for 50sh.

Architecture Type of 1985

1986 Litho. Perf. 13½x14

572	A135 10sh Bulaxaar	35	30
573	A135 15sh Saylac	52	40
574	A135 20sh Saylac, diff.	70	55
575	A135 31sh Jasiiradaha Jawaay	1.10	85

Nos. 572-575 each printed se-tenant with decorative label.

Red Crescent - Red Cross Rehabilitation Center, Mogadishu — A143

1987, May 8 Litho. Perf. 13½x13

576	A143 56sh multi	2.00	1.65

Souvenir Sheet

577	A143 56sh multi, diff.	2.25	2.25

See Norway No. 908. No. 577 sold for 60sh.

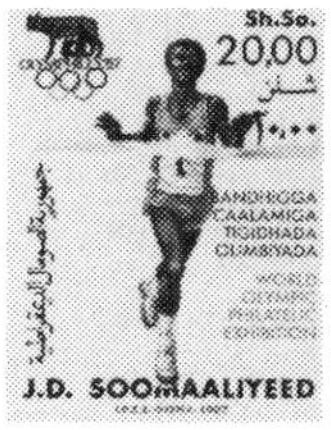

OLYMPHILEX '87, Rome — A144

1987, Sept. 27 Litho. Perf. 13½x14

578	A144 20sh Running	90	70
579	A144 48sh Javelin	2.00	1.65
a.	Souv. sheet of 2, #578-579	3.50	3.50

No. 579a sold for 75sh.

Intl. Year of Shelter for the Homeless A145

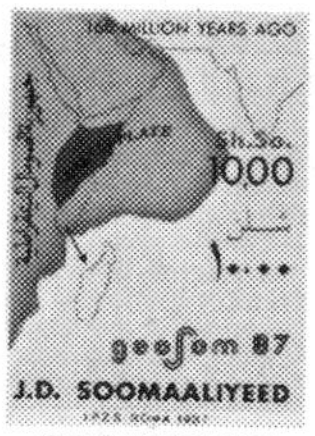

GEOSOM '87 A146

1987, Oct. 5 Photo. Perf. 13½x14½

580	A145 53sh multi	1.40	1.10
581	A145 72sh multi	1.90	1.40

1987, Nov. 24 Litho. Perf. 13½x14

Maps: 10sh, 160 millions years ago. 20sh, 60 millions years ago. 40sh, 15 millions years ago. 50sh, Today.

582	A146 10sh multi	25	20
583	A146 20sh multi, diff.	52	40
584	A146 40sh multi, diff.	1.00	75
585	A146 50sh multi, diff.	1.25	1.00

Symposium on the Geology of Somalia, Mogadishu, Nov. 24-Dec. 1.

SEMI-POSTAL STAMPS

Italy Nos. B1-B4 Overprinted **SOMALIA**

1916 Wmk. 140 Perf. 14

B1	SP1 10c + 5c rose	1.65	*3.00*
B2	SP2 15c + 5c slate	4.50	*8.50*
B3	SP2 20c + 5c orange	1.65	*4.00*
B4	SP2 20c on 15c + 5c sl	4.50	*8.50*

Holy Year Issue

Italy Nos. B20-B25 Surcharged in Black or Red

= SOMALIA ITALIANA =
Besa 13

Besa 6
= =

1925, June 1 Perf. 12

B5	SP4 6b + 3b on 20c + 10c dk grn & brn	65	*3.00*
B6	SP4 13b + 6b on 30c + 15c dk brn & brn	65	*3.00*
B7	SP4 15b + 8b on 50c + 25c vio & brn	65	*3.00*
B8	SP4 18b + 9b on 60c + 30c dp rose & brn	65	*3.00*
B9	SP8 30b + 15b on 1 l +50c (R)	65	*3.00*
B10	SP8 1r + 50b on 5 l +2.50 l (R)	65	*3.00*
	Nos. B5-B10 (6)	3.90	

Colonial Institute Issue

"Peace" Substituting Spade for Sword — SP10

1926, June 1 Typo. Perf. 14

B11	SP10 5c + 5c brown	15	*1.65*
B12	SP10 10c + 5c ol grn	15	*1.65*
B13	SP10 20c + 5c blue grn	15	*1.65*
B14	SP10 40c + 5c brn red	15	*1.65*
B15	SP10 60c + 5c orange	15	*1.65*
B16	SP10 1 l + 5c blue	15	*1.65*
	Nos. B11-B16 (6)	90	

The surtax of 5c on each stamp was for the Italian Colonial Institute.

Types of Italian Semi-Postal Stamps of 1926 Overprinted **SOMALIA ITALIANA**

1927, Apr. 21 Unwmk. Perf. 11½

B17	SP10 40c + 20c dk brn & blk	65	*3.50*
B18	SP10 60c + 30c brn red & ol brn	65	*3.50*
B19	SP10 1.25 l + 60c dp bl & blk	65	*3.50*
B20	SP10 5 l + 2.50 l dk grn & blk	1.00	*4.50*

The surtax was for the charitable work of the Voluntary Militia for Italian National Defense.

Allegory of Fascism and Victory — SP11

1928, Oct. 15 Wmk. 140 Perf. 14

B21	SP11 20c + 5c bl grn	50	*2.50*
B22	SP11 30c + 5c red	50	*2.50*
B23	SP11 50c + 10c purple	50	*2.50*
B24	SP11 1.25 l + 20c dk bl	50	*2.50*

46th anniv. of the Societa Africana d'Italia. The surtax aided that society.

Types of Italian Semi-Postal Stamps of 1928 Overprinted **SOMALIA ITALIANA**

1929, Mar. 4 Unwmk. Perf. 11

B25	SP10 30c + 10c red & blk	85	*3.50*
B26	SP10 50c + 20c vio & blk	85	*3.50*
B27	SP10 1.25 l + 50c brn & bl	1.00	*5.00*
B28	SP10 5 l + 2 l ol grn & blk	1.00	*5.00*

The surtax was for the charitable work of the Voluntary Militia for Italian National Defense.

Types of Italian Semi-Postal Stamps of 1926 Overprinted in Black or Red **SOMALIA ITALIANA**

1930, Oct. 20 Perf. 14

B29	SP10 30c + 10c dk grn & bl grn (Bk)	2.50	*10.00*
B30	SP10 50c + 10c dk grn & vio (R)	2.50	*10.00*
B31	SP10 1.25 l + 30c ol brn & red brn (R)	2.50	*10.00*
B32	SP10 5 l + 1.50 l ind & grn (R)	8.00	*32.50*

The surtax was for the charitable work of the Voluntary Militia for Italian National Defense.

Irrigation Canal SP14

1930, Nov. 27 Photo. Wmk. 140

B33	SP14 50c + 20c ol brn	70	*4.00*
B34	SP14 1.25 l + 20c dp bl	70	*4.00*
B35	SP14 1.75 l + 20c green	70	*4.00*

B36	SP14	2.55 l + 50c pur	1.10	*4.00*
B37	SP14	5 l + 1 l dp car	1.10	*4.00*
		Nos. B33-B37 (5)	4.30	

25th anniv. of the Italian Colonial Agricultural Institute. The surtax was for the aid of that institution.

SP15

King Victor Emmanuel III — SP16

1935, Jan. 1

B38	SP15	5c + 5c blk brn	60	*2.50*
B39	SP15	7½c + 7½c vio	60	*2.50*
B40	SP15	15c + 10c ol blk	60	*2.50*
B41	SP15	20c + 10c rose red	60	*2.50*
B42	SP15	25c + 10c dp grn	60	*2.50*
B43	SP15	30c + 10c brn	60	*2.50*
B44	SP15	20c + 10c pur	60	*2.50*
B45	SP15	75c + 15c rose car	60	*2.50*
B46	SP15	1.25 l + 15c dp bl	60	*2.50*
B47	SP15	1.75 l + 25c red org	60	*2.50*
B48	SP15	2.75 l + 25c gray	6.00	*25.00*
B49	SP15	5 l + 1 l dp cl	6.00	*25.00*
B50	SP15	10 l + 1.80 l red brn	6.00	*25.00*
B51	SP16	25 l + 2.75 l brn & red	40.00	*70.00*
		Nos. B38-B51 (14)	64.00	

Visit of King Victor Emmanuel III.

Catalogue values for unused stamps in this section, from this point to the end of the section, are for Never Hinged items.

Somalia

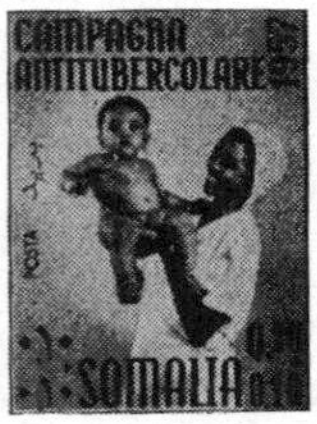

Nurse Holding Infant — SP17

1957, Nov. 30 Wmk. 303 *Perf. 14*

B52	SP17	10c + 10c red & brn	12	20
B53	SP17	25c + 10c grn & brn	12	20

The surtax was for the fight against tuberculosis. See Nos. CB11-CB12.

Republic

Refugees SP18

1964, Dec. 12 Photo. *Perf. 14*

B54	SP18	25c + 10c vio bl & red	24	8

The surtax was to help refugees. See Nos. CB13-CB14.

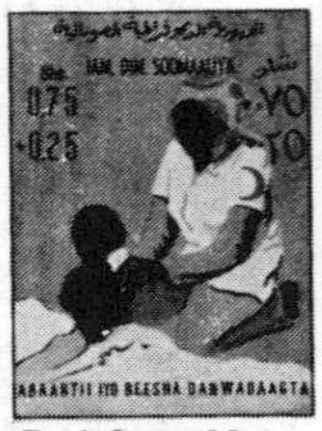

Red Cross Nurse Feeding Child SP19

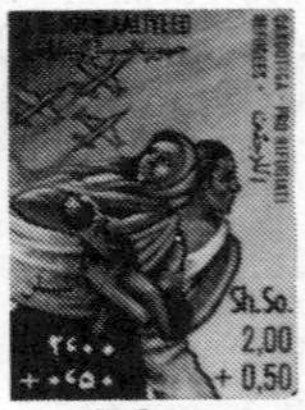

Refugees SP20

Designs: 80c+20c, Nomad in parched land (horiz.). 2.40sh+10c, Family with fish and produce. 2.90sh+10c, Physician and Aid Society emblem (horiz.).

1976, Dec. 10 *Perf. 13x14, 14x13*

B55	SP19	75c + 25c multi	25	25
B56	SP19	80c + 20c multi	25	25
B57	SP19	2.40sh + 10c multi	52	52
B58	SP19	2.90sh + 10c multi	70	70

Famine relief.

1981, Dec. 15 Photo. *Perf. 13½x14*

B59	SP20	2sh + 50c multi	52	40
B60	SP20	6.80sh + 50c multi	1.50	60
a.		Souvenir sheet of 2, #B59-B60	3.00	1.65

TB Bacillus Centenary — SP31

1982, Dec. 30 Photo. *Perf. 14*

B61	SP31	4.60sh + 60c multi	1.25	85
B62	SP31	5.80sh + 60c multi	1.25	1.00

AIR POST STAMPS

View of Coast — AP1

Cheetahs AP2

Wmk. 140

1934, Oct. Photo. *Perf. 14*

C1	AP1	25c sl bl & red org	1.10	*4.00*
C2	AP1	50c dk grn & blk	1.10	*4.00*
C3	AP1	75c brn & red org	1.10	*4.00*
a.		Imperf.		
C4	AP2	80c org brn & blk	1.10	*4.00*
C5	AP2	1 l scar & blk	1.10	*4.00*
C6	AP2	2 l dk bl & brn	1.10	*4.00*
		Nos. C1-C6 (6)	6.60	

2nd Colonial Arts Exhibition, Naples.

Banana Tree and Airplane AP3

Designs: 25c, 1.50 l, Banana tree andplane. 50c, 2 l, Plane over cotton field. 60c, 5 l, Plane over orchard. 75c, 10 l, Plane over field workers. 1 l, 3 l, Small girl watching plane.

1936 Photo.

C7	AP3	25c sl grn	70	*1.65*
C8	AP3	50c brown	24	20
C9	AP3	60c red org	1.00	*3.50*
C10	AP3	75c org brn	60	70
C11	AP3	1 l deep bl	8	5
C12	AP3	1.50 l purple	60	30
C13	AP3	2 l slate bl	1.25	70
C14	AP3	3 l cop red	4.00	1.65
C15	AP3	5 l yel grn	4.00	2.00
C16	AP3	10 l dp rose red	4.00	*6.75*
		Nos. C7-C16 (10)	16.47	*17.50*

Catalogue values for unused stamps in this section, from this point to the end of the section, are for Never Hinged items.

Somalia

AP8

1950-51 Wmk. 277

C17	AP8	30c yel brn	10	*30*
C18	AP8	45c dk car	10	*30*
C19	AP8	65c dk bl vio	10	*30*
C20	AP8	70c dull blue	10	*30*
C21	AP8	90c olive brn	10	*30*
C22	AP8	1s lil rose	18	30
C23	AP8	1.35s violet	25	*70*
C24	AP8	1.50s bl grn	35	*60*
C25	AP8	3s blue	2.50	2.50
C26	AP8	5s chocolate	3.00	3.00
C27	AP8	10s red org ('51)	3.25	2.50
		Nos. C17-C27 (11)	10.03	

Scene in Mogadishu AP8a

1951, Oct. 4

C27A	AP8a	1s vio & Prus bl	85	1.00
C27B	AP8a	1.50s ol grn & chnt brn	1.65	3.00

First Territorial Council meeting.

Plane, Palm Tree and Minaret AP9

Mother and Child AP10

1952, Sept. 14

C28	AP9	1.20s ol bis & dp bl	1.00	2.00

1st Somali Fair, Mogadishu, Sept. 14-28.

1953, May 27

C29	AP10	1.20s dk grn & dk brn	60	85

Somali anti-tuberculosis campaign.

Fair Entrance AP11

1953, Sept. 28 Unwmk. *Perf. 11½*

C30	AP11	1.20s brn car & pink	32	50
C31	AP11	1.50s yel brn & buff	32	50

2nd Somali Fair, Mogadishu, Sept. 28-Oct. 12, 1953.

Plane over Map and Stamps of 1903 AP12

Perf. 13x13½

1953, Dec. 16 Engr. Wmk. 277

Early Stamps in Brown and Rose Carmine

C32	AP12	60c org brn	32	50
C33	AP12	1s grnsh blk	32	50

50th anniv. of the first Somali postage stamps.

"UPU" among Constellations — AP13

Perf. 11½

1953, Dec. 16 Photo. Unwmk.

C34	AP13	1.20s red & cr	24	35
C35	AP13	1.50s brn & cr	32	50
C36	AP13	2s grn & lt bl	32	50

UPU, 75th anniv. (in 1949).

Alexander Island Juba River — AP14

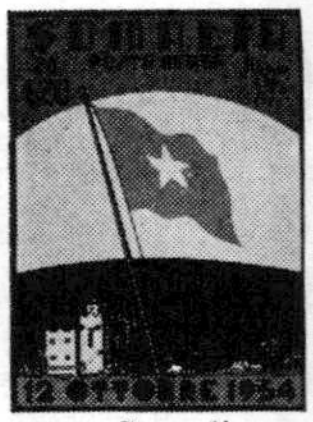

Somali Flag — AP15

1954, June 1 *Perf. 13½x12½*

C37	AP14	1.20s dk grn & brn	35	50
C38	AP14	2s dk car & pur	42	60

See note after No. 196.

Perf. 13½x13

1954, Oct. 12 Litho. Wmk. 277

C39	AP15	1.20s multi	20	30

Adoption of Somali flag.

Haggard's Oribi — AP16

Designs: 45c, Phillip's dik-dik. 50c, Speke's gazelle. 75c, Gerenuk. 1.20s, Soemmering's gazelle. 1.50s, Waterbuck.

Wmk. 277

1955, Apr. 12 Photo. *Perf. 13½*

Antelopes in Natural Colors

Size: 22x33mm

C40	AP16	35c gray grn & blk	15	20
C41	AP16	45c lil & blk	42	35
C42	AP16	50c rose lil & blk	15	20
C43	AP16	75c red	24	24
C44	AP16	1.20s dk gray grn	24	24
C45	AP16	1.50s bright bl	42	50
	Nos. C40-C45 (6)		1.62	1.73

See Nos. C57-C58.

Caravan at Water Hole AP17

Design: 1.20s, Village well.

Perf. 13½x14

1955, Sept. 24 Wmk. 303

C46	AP17	45c brn & org	20	30
C47	AP17	1.20s saph & pink	25	40

3rd Somali Fair, Mogadishu, Sept. 1955.

Ballot Type of Regular Issue

1956, Apr. 30 Photo. *Perf. 14*

C48	A24	60c brn & ultra	12	15
C49	A24	1.20s brn & org	12	20

Opening of the territory's first democratically elected Legislative Assembly.

Arms Type of Regular Issue

1957, May 6 Wmk. 303 *Perf. 13½*

Coat of Arms in Dull Yellow, Blue and Black

C50	A25	45c blue	12	20
C51	A25	1.20s bluish grn	15	24

Issued in honor of the new coat of arms.

Type of Regular Issue, 1957 and

Oil Well — AP18

Design: 60c, Irrigation canal construction.

1957, Sept. 28 *Perf. 14*

C52	A26	60c bl & brn	18	28
C53	AP18	1.20s blk & ver	18	28

Fourth Somali Fair and Film Festival.

Sport Type of Regular Issue

Designs: 60c, Runner. 1.20s, Bicyclist. 1.50s, Basketball player.

1958, Apr. 28 Wmk. 303 *Perf. 14*

C54	A27	60c brown	10	14
C55	A27	1.20s blue	12	18
C56	A27	1.50s rose car	12	18

Animal Type of 1955

Designs: 3s, Lesser kudu. 5s, Hunter's hartebeest.

1958-59 Photo.

Size: 20½x36½mm

C57	AP16	3s ocher & sep	60	85
C58	AP16	5s gray, blk & yel ('59)	60	85

See No. CE1.

Police Bugler AP19

1959, June 19 Photo.

C59	AP19	1.20s ocher & ultra	20	30
C60	AP19	1.50s ol grn & ultra	20	30
a.		Souvenir sheet of 4	2.00	2.00

Opening of the Constituent Assembly of Somalia.

No. C60a contains one each of Nos. 228-229 and C59-C60.

Marabou AP20

Design: 2s, Great egret.

1959, Sept. 4 Wmk. 303

C61	AP20	1.20s vio, blk & red	18	28
C62	AP20	2s bl, gray & red	20	30

Incense Shipment, 15th Century B.C. AP21

Design: 2s, Incense burner and view of Mogadishu harbor.

1959, Sept. 28 *Perf. 14*

C63	AP21	1.20s red & blk	20	30
C64	AP21	2s bl, blk & org	30	45

5th Somali Fair, Mogadishu.

University Institute and Arms AP22

Design: 1.20s, Front view of Institute.

1960, Jan. 14

C65	AP22	45c grn, blk & org brn	24	24
C66	AP22	1.20s bl, ultra & blk	35	35

Opening of the University Institute of Somalia.

Stork and Uprooted Oak Emblem — AP23

1960, Apr. 7 Wmk. 303 *Perf. 14*

C67	AP23	1.50s lt grn, bl & red	24	24

World Refugee Year, July 1, 1959-June 30, 1960.

Republic

Nos. C42 and C44 Overprinted Like No. 242

Wmk. 277

1960, June 26 Photo. *Perf. 13½*

Antelopes in Natural Colors

C68	AP16	50c rose lil & blk	6.00	5.75
C69	AP16	1.20s dk gray grn	10.50	5.75

See note after No. 242.

Parliament and Italian Flag AP25

Design: 1.80s, Somali flag and assembly building.

1960, July 1 Wmk. 303 *Perf. 14*

C70	AP25	1s org red, grn & red	28	15
C71	AP25	1.80s red org, ultra & blk	60	32

Somalia's independence.

Animal Type of Regular Issue

Design: 3s, Leopard.

1960, Nov. 24

C72	A37	3s multi	60	50

Olympic Games Type of Regular Issue

Designs: 45c, Runner, flag and Olympic rings. 1.80s, Long distance runner, flag & Olympic rings.

1960, Nov. 24

C73	A38	45c lil & bl	15	15
C74	A38	1.80s org ver & bl	30	30

17th Olympic Games, Rome, Aug. 25-Sept. 11.

Amauris Fenestrata and Jet Plane AP26

Various Butterflies.

1961, Sept. 9

C75	AP26	60c bl, brn & yel	12	12
C76	AP26	90c yel, blk & grn	15	12
C77	AP26	1s multi	1.65	12
C78	AP26	1.80s org, blk & red	40	24
C79	AP26	3s multi	52	40
C80	AP26	5s ver, blk & brt bl	1.25	70
C81	AP26	10s multi	2.50	1.25
	Nos. C75-C81 (7)		6.59	2.95

Wooden Headrest, Comb and Cap AP27

Design: 1.80sh, Camel, metal sculpture.

1961, Sept. 28 Wmk. 303 *Perf. 14*

C82	AP27	1sh blk, ultra & ocher	24	15
C83	AP27	1.80sh blk, yel & brn	40	28

6th Somali Fair, Mogadishu.

Fish Type of Regular Issue

Fish: 2.70sh, Lutianus sebae.

1962, Apr. 26

C84	A41	2.70sh ultra, brn & rose brn	90	60

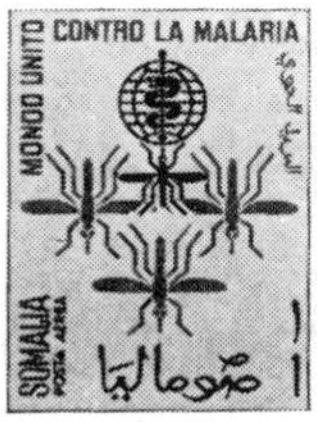

Mosquitoes and Malaria Eradication Emblem — AP28

Police Auxiliary Women — AP29

Wmk. 303

1962, Oct. 25 Photo. *Perf. 14*

C85	AP28	1sh bis brn & blk	28	15
C86	AP28	1.80sh lt grn & blk	60	28

WHO drive to eradicate malaria.

1963, May 15 Wmk. 303 *Perf. 14*

Design: 1.80sh, Army auxiliary women with flag.

C87	AP29	1sh dk bl, yel & org	32	12
C88	AP29	1.80sh multi	60	20

Women's auxiliary forces.

Freedom from Hunger Type of Regular Issue

Design: 1sh, Sower and wheat.

1963, June 25

C89	A44	1sh dk brn, yel & bl	42	20

President Osman Type of Regular Issue, 1963

1963, Sept. 15 Wmk. 303 *Perf. 14*

C90	A45	1sh multi	55	20
C91	A45	1.80sh multi	52	28

Somali Fair Type of Regular Issue, 1963

Design: 1.80sh, Government Pavilion.

1963, Sept. 28 Photo.

C92	A46	1.80sh blue	85	40

Map of Somalia, Animals and Globe AP30

Design: 1.80sh, Somali Credit Bank emblem.

1964, May 16 Wmk. 303 *Perf. 14*

C93	AP30	1sh multi	32	15
C94	AP30	1.80sh blk, bl & yel	70	32

10th anniversary of Somali Credit Bank.

Olympic Type of Regular Issue, 1964

Designs: 90c, Diving. 1.80sh, Soccer.

1964, Oct. 10 Photo.

C95	A48	90c org brn & bl	35	20
C96	A48	1.80sh org brn & bl	52	32

Elephants and DC-3 AP31

Design: 1.80sh, Plane over Mogadishu.

1964, Nov. 8 Photo. *Perf. 14*

C97	AP31	1sh brn & grn	60	24
C98	AP31	1.80sh blk & bl	1.25	40

Establishment of Somali Air Lines.

ITU Type of Regular Issue

1965, May 17 Wmk. 303 *Perf. 14*
C99 A50 1sh dp grn & blk 40 12
C100 A50 1.80sh rose lil & brn 80 40

Somali Fair Type of Regular Issue, 1965

Designs: 1.50sh, Sugar industry; harvesting sugar cane and refinery. 2sh, Dairy industry; bottling plant and milk cow.

1965, Sept. 28 Photo. *Perf. 14*
C101 A51 1.50sh sep & pale bl 40 15
C102 A51 2sh sep & rose 75 24

Faisal Type of Regular Issue

Design: 1.80sh, Ka'aba, Mecca, Pres. Abdirascid Ali Scermarche and King Faisal.

1967, Sept. 21 Wmk. 303 *Perf. 14*
C103 A60 1.80sh blk, dp rose & org 28 20

Egret — AP32

Birds: 1sh, Southern carmine bee-eater. 1.30sh, Bruce's green pigeon. 1.80sh, Broad-tailed paradise whydah.

Perf. 11½
1968, Nov. 1 Unwmk. Litho.
C104 AP32 35c bl & multi 8 8
C105 AP32 1sh grn & multi 20 12
C106 AP32 1.30sh vio bl & multi 24 20
C107 AP32 1.80sh yel & multi 28 24

Somali Democratic Republic

Postal Union Type of Regular Issue

Design: 1.30sh, Postal Union emblem and letter.

Perf. 14x13½
1972, Jan. 25 Photo. Unwmk.
C108 A81 1.30sh multi 42 35

AIR POST SEMI-POSTAL STAMPS

King Victor Emmanuel III
SPAP1

Wmk. 140
1934, Nov. 5 Photo. *Perf. 14*
CB1 SPAP1 25c + 10c gray grn 1.25 *5.00*
CB2 SPAP1 50c + 10c brn 1.25 *5.00*
CB3 SPAP1 75c + 15c rose red 1.25 *5.00*
CB4 SPAP1 80c + 15c blk brn 1.25 *5.00*
CB5 SPAP1 1 l + 20c red brn 1.25 *5.00*
CB6 SPAP1 2 l + 20c brt bl 1.25 *5.00*
CB7 SPAP1 3 l + 25c pur 10.50 *40.00*
CB8 SPAP1 5 l + 25c org 10.50 *40.00*
CB9 SPAP1 10 l + 30c rose vio 10.50 *40.00*
CB10 SPAP1 25 l + 2 l dp grn 10.50 *40.00*
Nos. CB1-CB10 (10) 49.50 *190.00*

65th birthday of King Victor Emmanuel III; non-stop flight from Rome to Mogadishu.

Catalogue values for unused stamps in this section, from this point to the end of the section, are for Never Hinged items.

Somalia

Type of Semi-Postal Stamps, 1957

1957, Nov. 30 Wmk. 303 *Perf. 14*
CB11 SP17 55c + 20c dk bl & brn 15 24
CB12 SP17 1.20s + 20c vio & brn 22 32

The surtax was for the fight against tuberculosis.

Type of Semi-Postal Issue, 1964

Designs: 75c+20c, Destroyed Somali village. 1.80sh+50c, Soldier aiding children, and map of Somalia (vert.).

1964, Dec. 12 Photo. *Perf. 14*
CB13 SP18 75c + 20c blk, org red & brn 40 15
CB14 SP18 1.80sh + 50c blk, ol bis & sl 90 32

AIR POST SPECIAL DELIVERY STAMP

Catalogue values for the stamp in this section is for a Never Hinged item.

Antelopes
APSD1

Wmk. 303
1958, Oct. 4 Photo. *Perf. 14*
CE1 APSD1 1.70s org ver & blk 60 85

AIR POST OFFICIAL STAMP

No. C1 Overprinted

11 NOV. 1934-XIII
SERVIZIO AEREO
SPECIALE

Wmk. 140
1934, Nov. 11 Photo. *Perf. 14*
CO1 AP1 25c sl bl & red org *700.00 1,050.*

Forgeries of this overprint exist.

AIR POST SEMI-POSTAL OFFICIAL STAMP

Type of Air Post Semi-Postal Stamps, 1934 Overprinted Crown and "SERVIZIO DI STATO" in Black

1934, Nov. 5 Wmk. 140 *Perf. 14*
CBO1 SPAP1 25 l + 2 l cop red 1,050. *2,250.*

SPECIAL DELIVERY STAMPS

Italy No. E3 Surcharged

BESA 30 Somalia Italiana

1923, July 16 Wmk. 140 *Perf. 14*
E1 SD1 30b on 60c dl red 7.25 *10.00*

Italy, Type of 1908 Special Delivery Stamp Surcharged

60 BESA 60 SOMALIA ITALIANA

E2 SD2 60b on 1.20 l bl & red 10.00 *12.50*

"Italia"
SD3

1924, June Engr. Unwmk.
E3 SD3 30b dk red & brn 3.00 4.00
E4 SD3 60b dk bl & red 4.00 5.00

Nos. E3-E4 Surcharged in Black or Red with Bars and

CENT 70

1926, Oct.
E5 SD3 70c on 30b dk red & brn (Bk) 3.00 4.00
E6 SD3 2.50 l on 60b dk bl & red (R) 4.00 5.00
a. Imperf., pair 150.00

Same Surcharge on No. E3

1927 *Perf. 11*
E7 SD3 1.25 l on 30b dk red & brn 3.00 4.00
a. Perf. 14 100.00 175.00
b. Imperf., pair 150.00

Catalogue values for unused stamps in this section, from this point to the end of the section, are for Never Hinged items.

Somalia

Bananas, Grant's Gazelles
SD4

Wmk. 277
1950, Apr. 24 Photo. *Perf. 14*
E8 SD4 40c blue green 65 60
E9 SD4 80c violet 1.00 1.25

Gardenias
SD5

Design: 1s, Eryrhina melanocantha.

1955, Feb. *Perf. 13*
E10 SD5 50c lilac & green 20 30
E11 SD5 1s bl, rose brn & grn 42 60

AUTHORIZED DELIVERY STAMP

Italy No. EY2 Overprinted in Black — SOMALIA ITALIANA

1941 Wmk. 140 *Perf. 14*
EY1 AD2 10c dark brown 12

No. EY1 was prepared but not issued.

POSTAGE DUE STAMPS

Postage Due Stamps of Italy Overprinted — Somalia Italiana Meridionale

1906-08 Wmk. 140 *Perf. 14*
J1 D3 5c buff & mag 2.00 *10.00*
J2 D3 10c buff & mag 13.00 14.00
J3 D3 20c org & mag 8.50 *14.00*
J4 D3 30c buff & mag 6.00 *14.00*
J5 D3 40c buff & mag 8.50 *14.00*
J6 D3 50c buff & mag 8.50 *14.00*
J7 D3 60c buff & mag ('08) 10.50 *17.00*
J8 D3 1 l bl & mag 165.00 60.00
J9 D3 2 l bl & mag 150.00 65.00
J10 D3 5 l bl & mag 150.00 65.00
J11 D3 10 l bl & mag 35.00 *85.00*
Nos. J1-J11 (11) 557.00 *372.00*

Postage Due Stamps of Italy Overprinted at Top of Stamps — Somalia Italiana

1909-19
J12 D3 5c buff & mag 1.50 *3.00*
J13 D3 10c buff & mag 1.50 *3.00*
J14 D3 20c buff & mag 2.50 *6.00*
J15 D3 30c buff & mag 5.00 *8.50*
J16 D3 40c buff & mag 5.00 *8.50*
J17 D3 50c buff & mag 5.00 *8.50*
J18 D3 60c buff & mag ('19) 5.00 *8.50*
J19 D3 1 l bl & mag 12.50 10.00
J20 D3 2 l bl & mag 20.00 *32.50*
J21 D3 5 l bl & mag 25.00 *45.00*
J22 D3 10 l bl & mag 3.50 *14.00*
Nos. J12-J22 (11) 86.50 *147.50*

Same with Overprint at Bottom of Stamps

1920
J12a D3 5c buff & mag 25.00 21.00
J13a D3 10c buff & mag 25.00 21.00
J14a D3 20c buff & mag 27.50 21.00
J15a D3 30c buff & mag 20.00 21.00
J16a D3 40c buff & mag 20.00 21.00
J17a D3 50c buff & mag 20.00 21.00
J18a D3 60c buff & mag 25.00 21.00
J19a D3 1 l bl & mag 27.50 21.00
J20a D3 2 l bl & mag 27.50 21.00
J21a D3 5 l bl & mag 32.50 21.00
Nos. J12a-J21a (10) 250.00 210.00

D4

D5

1923, July 1
J23 D4 1b buff & blk 50 *1.25*
J24 D4 2b buff & blk 50 *1.25*
a. Invtd. numeral and ovpt. 62.50
J25 D4 3b buff & blk 50 *1.25*
J26 D4 5b buff & blk 60 *1.25*
J27 D4 10b buff & blk 60 *1.25*
J28 D4 20b buff & blk 60 *1.25*
J29 D4 40b buff & blk 60 *1.25*
J30 D4 1r bl & blk 1.25 *2.00*
Nos. J23-J30 (8) 5.15 *10.75*

Type of Postage Due Stamps of Italy Overprinted — Somalia Italiana

1926, Mar. 1
J31 D3 5c buff & blk 5.00 3.00
J32 D3 10c buff & blk 4.00 3.00
a. Numerals and ovpt. invtd. 14.00
J33 D3 20c buff & blk 4.00 3.00
a. Numerals and ovpt. invtd. 110.00
J34 D3 30c buff & blk 4.00 3.00
a. Numerals and ovpt. invtd. 14.00
J35 D3 40c buff & blk 4.00 3.00
a. Numerals and ovpt. invtd. 14.00
J36 D3 50c buff & blk 7.25 3.00
a. Numerals and ovpt. invtd. 14.00
J37 D3 60c buff & blk 7.25 3.00
a. Numerals and ovpt. invtd. 14.00
J38 D3 1 l blue & blk 10.00 4.00
J39 D3 2 l blue & blk 13.00 4.00
J40 D3 5 l blue & blk 13.00 4.00
J41 D3 10 l blue & blk 13.00 4.00
Nos. J31-J41 (11) 84.50 37.00

Postage Due Stamps of Italy, 1934, Overprinted in Black — SOMALIA ITALIANA

1934, May 12

J42	D6	5c brown	60	*1.50*
J43	D6	10c blue	60	*1.50*
J44	D6	20c rose red	1.65	2.00
J45	D6	25c green	1.65	2.00
J46	D6	30c red org	3.00	*4.00*
J47	D6	40c blk brn	3.00	*5.00*
J48	D6	50c violet	3.50	1.50
J49	D6	60c black	6.00	*10.00*
J50	D7	1 l red org	8.50	3.50
J51	D7	2 l green	12.50	*14.00*
J52	D7	5 l violet	14.00	*25.00*
J53	D7	10 l blue	14.00	*27.50*
J54	D7	20 l carmine	15.00	*30.00*
		Nos. J42-J54 (13)	84.00	*127.50*

Catalogue values for unused stamps in this section, from this point to the end of the section, are for Never Hinged items.

Somalia

1950 Wmk. 277 Photo. *Perf. 14*

J55	D5	1c dk gray vio	15	24
J56	D5	2c deep blue	15	24
J57	D5	5c blue green	15	24
J58	D5	10c rose lilac	15	24
J59	D5	40c violet	65	1.00
J60	D5	1s dark brown	1.10	1.65
		Nos. J55-J60 (6)	2.35	3.61

PARCEL POST STAMPS

These stamps were used by affixing them to the way bill so that one half remained on it following the parcel, the other half staying on the receipt given the sender. Most used halves are right halves. Complete stamps were and are obtainable canceled, probably to order. Both unused and used values are for complete stamps.

Parcel Post Stamps of Italy, 1914-17, Overprinted SOMALIA ITALIANA

1917-19 Wmk. 140 *Perf. 13½*

Q1	PP2	5c brown	1.00	2.50
a.		Double overprint	70.00	
Q2	PP2	10c blue	1.00	2.50
Q3	PP2	20c black ('19)	27.50	40.00
Q4	PP2	25c red	2.50	6.00
a.		Double overprint	150.00	
Q5	PP2	50c orange	18.00	20.00
Q6	PP2	1 l lilac	10.00	*14.00*
Q7	PP2	2 l green	10.50	*15.00*
Q8	PP2	3 l bister	13.00	*20.00*
Q9	PP2	4 l slate	14.00	*25.00*
		Nos. Q1-Q9 (9)	97.50	*145.00*

Halves Used

Q1, Q4	10
Q2	7
Q3, Q5	2.75
Q6-Q7	32
Q8	52
Q9	1.25

Nos. Q5-Q9 were overprinted in 1922 with a slightly different type in which the final "A" of SOMALIA is directly over the final "A" of ITALIANA. They were not regularly issued. Value for set, $400.

Parcel Post Stamps of Italy, 1914-17, Overprinted SOMALIA

1923

Q10	PP2	25c red	14.00	*25.00*
Q11	PP2	50c orange	12.50	*25.00*
Q12	PP2	1 l violet	13.00	*25.00*
Q13	PP2	2 l green	13.00	*25.00*
Q14	PP2	3 l bister	15.00	25.00
Q15	PP2	4 l slate	20.00	25.00
		Nos. Q10-Q15 (6)	87.50	*150.00*

Halves Used

Q10	1.10
Q11, Q12	32
Q13	40
Q14	85
Q15	1.65

Parcel Post Stamps of Italy, 1914-17, Surcharged

BESA SOMALIA ITALIANA   SOMALIA ITALIANA BESA 5

1923

Q16	PP2	3b on 5c brn	2.00	2.50
Q17	PP2	5b on 5c brn	2.00	2.50
Q18	PP2	10b on 10c bl	2.50	3.25
Q19	PP2	25b on 25c red	3.00	4.00
Q20	PP2	50b on 50c org	6.00	7.25
Q21	PP2	1r on 1 l lil	7.25	10.00
Q22	PP2	2r on 2 l grn	10.00	14.00
Q23	PP2	3r on 3 l bis	10.50	20.00
Q24	PP2	4r on 4 l sl	12.50	25.00
		Nos. Q16-Q24 (9)	55.75	88.50

Halves Used

Q16-Q17	12
Q18-Q19	20
Q20-Q21	32
Q22	60
Q23	1.10
Q24	1.65

No. Q16 has the numeral "3" at the left also.

Parcel Post Stamps of Italy, 1914-22 Overprinted SOMALIA ITALIANA

1926-31

Red Overprint

Q25	PP2	5c brown	6.00	*10.00*
Q26	PP2	10c blue	6.00	*10.00*
Q27	PP2	20c black	10.50	*14.00*
Q28	PP2	25c red	10.50	*14.00*
Q29	PP2	50c orange	10.50	*14.00*
Q30	PP2	1 l violet	10.50	*14.00*
Q31	PP2	2 l green	15.00	14.00
Q32	PP2	3 l yellow	5.00	*10.00*
Q33	PP2	4 l slate	5.00	*10.00*
Q34	PP2	10 l vio brn ('30)	6.00	*14.00*
Q35	PP2	12 l red brn ('31)	6.00	*14.00*
Q36	PP2	15 l olive ('31)	6.00	*14.00*
Q37	PP2	20 l dl vio ('31)	6.00	*14.00*
		Nos. Q25-Q37 (13)	103.00	*166.00*

Halves Used

Q25-Q26	32
Q27-Q28, Q33	70
Q29, Q34	90
Q30-Q31	52
Q32	40
Q35-Q36	1.10
Q37	1.25

Nos. Q25-Q31 come with two types of overprint: I - The first "I" and last "A" of ITALIANA extend slightly at both sides of SOMALIA. II - Only the "I" extends. These seven stamps with type I overprint were not regularly issued, and Nos. Q27-Q31 (type I) sell for less than with type II overprint.

Black Overprint

Q38	PP2	10 l vio brn	13.00	7.25
Q39	PP2	12 l red brn	8.50	7.25
Q40	PP2	15 l olive	8.50	7.25
Q41	PP2	20 l dull vio	8.50	7.25

Halves Used

Q38	45
Q39-Q41	30

Same Overprint on Parcel Post Stamps of Italy, 1927-38

Black Overprint

1928-39

Q42	PP3	25c red ('31)	17.50	*25.00*
Q43	PP3	30c ultra	24	1.50
Q43A	PP3	50c orange	*7,500.*	*3,000.*
Q44	PP3	60c red	24	1.50
Q45	PP3	1 l lilac ('31)	8.50	*17.50*
Q46	PP3	2 l green ('31)	8.50	*17.50*
Q47	PP3	3 l bister	30	2.50
Q48	PP3	4 l gray blk	35	3.00
Q49	PP3	10 l rose lil ('34)	100.00	*150.00*
Q50	PP3	20 l lil brn ('34)	100.00	*150.00*
		Nos. Q42-Q43,Q44-Q50 (9)	235.63	*368.50*

Halves Used

Q42, Q50	1.00
Q43, Q44	20
Q43A	40.00
Q45-Q48	32
Q49	2.00

The 25c, 1 l and 2 l come with both types of overprint (see note below No. Q37). Both types were regularly issued. Values are for type I on 25c, type II on 1 l and 2 l.

Red Overprint

Q51	PP3	5c brn ('39)	7.25	
Q52	PP3	3 l bister ('30)	5.00	*14.00*
		Half stamp		32
Q53	PP3	4 l gray blk ('30)	5.00	*14.00*
		Half stamp		32

Same Overprint in Black on Italy Nos. Q24-Q25

1940 *Perf. 13*

Q54	PP3	5c brown	70	2.50
		Half stamp		7
Q55	PP3	10c deep blue	1.00	3.00
		Half stamp		10

Catalogue values for unused stamps in this section, from this point to the end of the section, are for Never Hinged items.

Somalia

PP1

1950 Wmk. 277 Photo. *Perf. 14*

Q56	PP1	1c cerise	20	*50*
Q57	PP1	3c dk gray vio	20	*50*
Q58	PP1	5c rose lil	20	*50*
Q59	PP1	10c red org	20	*50*
Q60	PP1	20c dark brn	20	*50*
Q61	PP1	50c blue grn	30	*70*
Q62	PP1	1s violet	1.25	*3.00*
Q63	PP1	2s brown	1.65	*4.00*
Q64	PP1	3s blue	1.75	*4.50*
		Nos. Q56-Q64 (9)	5.95	*14.70*

Halves Used

Q56-Q58	5
Q59-Q60	8
Q61	10
Q62	12
Q63	30
Q64	50

SOMALI COAST

(Djibouti)

LOCATION — In eastern Africa, bordering on the Gulf of Aden.
GOVT. — French Overseas Territory.
AREA — 8,500 sq. mi.
POP. — 86,000 (est. 1963).
CAPITAL — Djibouti (Jibuti).

The port of Obock, which issued postage stamps in 1892-1894, was included in the territory and began to use stamps of Somali Coast in 1902. See Obock in Vol. III.

On Mar. 19, 1967, the territory changed its name to the French Territory of the Afars and Issas. The Republic of Djibouti was proclaimed June 27, 1977.

100 Centimes = 1 Franc

Catalogue values for unused stamps in this country are for Never Hinged items, beginning with Scott 224 in the regular postage section, Scott B13 in the semi-postal section, Scott C1 in the airpost section, Scott CB1 in the airpost semi-postal section, and Scott J39 in the postage due section.

Navigation and Commerce
A1 A2

A3

For unused stamps, more recent issues are valued as never hinged, with the beginning point determined on a country-by-country basis. Notes to show the beginning points are prominently placed in the text.

Camel and Rider A4

Obock Nos. 32-33, 35, 45 with Overprint or Surcharge Handstamped in Black, Blue or Red

1894 Unwmk. *Perf. 14x13½*

1	A1	5c grn & red, *grnsh* (with bar)	65.00	60.00
a.		Without bar	700.00	400.00
2	A2	25c on 2c brn & bl, *buff* (Bl & Bk)	200.00	100.00
a.		"25" omitted	600.00	450.00
b.		"DJIBOUTI" omitted	600.00	450.00
c.		"DJIBOUTI" inverted	625.00	600.00
3	A3	50c on 1c blk & red, *bl* (R & Bl)	225.00	160.00
a.		"5" instead of "50"	700.00	525.00
b.		"0" instead of "50"	700.00	525.00
c.		"DJIBOUTI" omitted	700.00	525.00

Imperf

4	A4	1fr on 5fr car	400.00	300.00
5	A4	5fr carmine	900.00	800.00

The overprint on No. 1 includes a bar to obliterate "OBOCK."

"DJIBOUTI" is in blue on No. 2, in red on No. 3.

Counterfeits exist of Nos. 4-5.

View of Djibouti, Somali Warriors — A5

French Gunboat A7

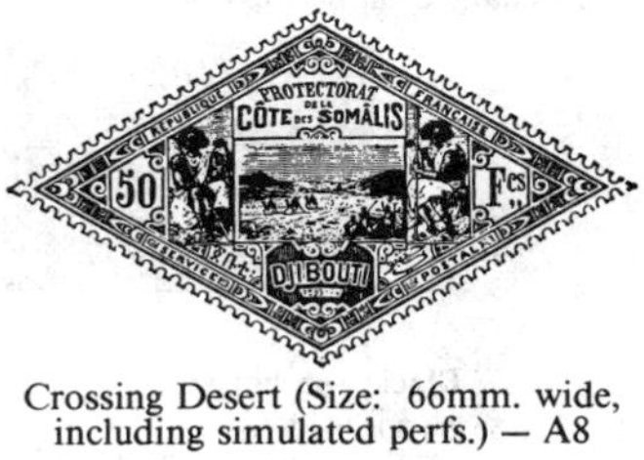

Crossing Desert (Size: 66mm. wide, including simulated perfs.) — A8

Designs: 15c, 25c, 30c, 40c, 50c, 75c, Different views of Djibouti. 1fr, 2fr, Djibouti quay.

Imperf. (Simulated Perforations in Frame Color)

1894-1902 Typo.

Quadrille Lines Printed on Paper

6	A5	1c blk & cl	1.50	1.50
7	A5	2c cl & blk	1.50	1.50
8	A5	4c vio brn & bl	5.00	3.75
9	A5	5c bl grn & red	5.00	3.75
10	A5	5c grn & yel grn ('02)	4.50	4.50
11	A5	10c brn & grn	7.00	3.75
a.		Half used as 5c on cover		65.00
12	A5	15c vio & grn	7.00	3.75
13	A5	25c rose & bl	11.00	6.00
14	A5	30c gray brn & rose	9.00	6.00
a.		Half used as 15c on cover		250.00
15	A5	40c org & bl ('00)	35.00	25.00
16	A5	50c bl & rose	11.00	9.00
a.		Half used as 25c on cover		800.00
17	A5	75c vio & org	20.00	17.50
18	A5	1fr ol grn & blk	12.00	9.00
19	A5	2fr gray brn & rose	50.00	40.00
20	A7	5fr rose & bl	100.00	60.00

21 A8 25fr rose & bl 500.00 500.00
22 A8 50fr bl & rose 750.00 750.00

High values are found with the overprint "S" (Specimen) erased and, usually, a cancellation added.

A9

1899

Black Surcharge

23 A9 40c on 4c brn & bl *2,250.* 10.00
a. Double surcharge *4,000.* 700.00

Surcharged **0.05**

1902 **Blue Surcharge**

24 A5 0.05c on 75c vio & org 25.00 16.00
a. Inverted surcharge 375.00 325.00
25 A5 0.10c on 1fr ol grn & blk 35.00 27.50
a. Inverted surcharge 300.00 225.00
26 A5 0.40c on 2fr gray brn & rose 225.00 150.00

Black Surcharge

27 A7 0.75c on 5fr rose & bl 300.00 250.00
a. Inverted surcharge 1,750. 1,500.

Obock No. 57 Surcharged in Blue

27B A7 0.05c on 75c gray lil & org 1,000. 700.00

A10

Nos. 15-16 Surcharged in Black

28 A10 5c on 40c org & bl 2.50 2.00
a. Double surcharge 55.00 55.00
29 A10 10c on 50c bl & rose 11.00 11.00
a. Inverted surch. 300.00 300.00

Surcharged on Stamps of Obock

Group of Warriors A11

Black Surcharge

30 A11 5c on 30c bis & yel grn 5.00 3.75
a. Inverted surcharge 140.00 110.00
b. Double surcharge 120.00 110.00

A12

Red Surcharge

31 A12 10c on 25c blk & bl 5.50 4.50
a. Inverted surcharge 150.00 140.00
b. Double surcharge 150.00 125.00
c. Triple surcharge 900.00 900.00

A little time given to the study of the arrangement of the Scott Catalogue can make it easier to use effectively.

A13

Black Surcharge

32 A13 10c on 10fr org & red vio 14.00 12.00
a. Double surcharge 140.00 120.00
b. Triple surcharge, one inverted 500.00 500.00

A14

Black Surcharge

33 A14 10c on 2fr dl vio & org 25.00 20.00
a. "DJIBOUTI" inverted 160.00 140.00
b. Large "0" in "10" 65.00 60.00
c. Double surcharge 250.00 225.00

Same Surcharge on Obock No. 53 in Red

33D A7 10c on 25c blk & bl *25,000.* *14,500.*

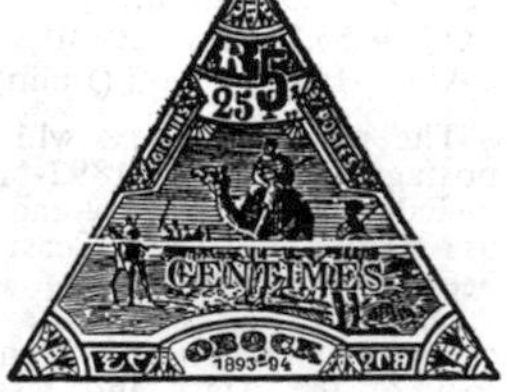

A14a

Black Surcharge on Obock Nos. 63-64

33E A14a 5c on 25fr brn & bl 27.50 22.50
33F A14a 10c on 50fr red vio & grn 32.50 25.00
g. "01" instead of "10" 125.00 110.00
h. "CENTIMES" inverted 1,750. 1,750.
i. Double surcharge 1,600. 1,600.

Tadjoura Mosque A15

Somalis on Camel A16

Warriors — A17

1902 **Engr.** ***Perf. 11½***

34 A15 1c brn vio & org 40 35
35 A15 2c yel brn & yel grn 40 35
36 A15 4c bl & carmine 1.10 65
37 A15 5c bl grn & yel grn 80 55
38 A15 10c car & red org 3.00 1.60
39 A15 15c brn org & bl 2.75 1.60
40 A16 20c vio & green 4.00 3.50
41 A16 25c blue 7.00 6.00
a. 25c indigo & bl ('03) 10.00 8.00
42 A16 30c red & blk 2.50 1.90
43 A16 40c org & blue 6.00 4.00
44 A16 50c grn & red org 20.00 19.00
45 A16 75c org & vio 2.00 1.60
46 A17 1fr red org & vio 7.00 6.00
47 A17 2fr yel grn & car 15.00 12.00
a. Without names of designer and engraver at bottom 82.50 82.50
48 A17 5fr org & blue 10.00 6.25
Nos. 34-48 (15) 81.95 65.35

1903

49 A15 1c brn vio & blk 40 40
50 A15 2c yel brn & blk 55 55
51 A15 4c lake & blk 65 55
a. 4c red & black 70 60
52 A15 5c bl grn & blk 1.40 1.10
53 A15 10c car & blk 3.50 1.25
54 A15 15c org brn & blk 7.00 4.00
55 A16 20c dl vio & blk 9.00 8.00
56 A16 25c ultra & blk 4.00 3.50
58 A16 40c org & blk 4.00 3.50
59 A16 50c grn & blk 7.00 6.00
60 A16 75c buff & blk 5.00 4.25
a. 75c brn org & blk 40.00 35.00
61 A17 1fr org & blk 7.00 6.00
62 A17 2fr yel grn & blk 3.50 3.00
a. Without names of designer and engraver at bottom 25.00 25.00
63 A17 5fr red org & blk 7.00 6.00
a. 5fr ocher & blk 7.25 7.25
Nos. 49-63 (14) 60.00 48.10

Imperforates, transposed colors and inverted centers exist in the 1902 and 1903 issues. Most of these were issued from Paris and some are said to have been fraudulently printed.

Tadjoura Mosque A18

Somalis on Camel — A19

Warriors — A20

1909 **Typo.** ***Perf. 14x13½***

64 A18 1c maroon & brn 35 30
65 A18 2c vio & ol gray 35 30
66 A18 4c ol gray & bl 45 40
67 A18 5c grn & gray grn 55 30
68 A18 10c car & ver 1.40 55
69 A18 20c blk & red brn 2.75 2.50
70 A19 25c bl & pale bl 1.90 1.50
71 A19 30c brn & scar 2.50 2.00
72 A19 35c vio & grn 2.75 2.25
73 A19 40c rose & vio 3.50 2.00
74 A19 45c brn & bl grn 3.50 2.50
75 A19 50c mar & brn 3.50 3.00
76 A19 75c scar & grn 6.25 5.00
77 A20 1fr vio & brn 9.00 8.25
78 A20 2fr brn & rose 15.00 14.00
79 A20 5fr vio brn & bl grn 25.00 20.00
Nos. 64-79 (16) 78.75 64.85

Drummer A21

Somali Girl A22

Djibouti-Addis Ababa Railroad Bridge — A23

1915-33 ***Perf. 13½x14***

Chalky Paper

80 A21 1c brt vio & red brn 5 5
81 A21 2c ocher & ind 5 5
82 A21 4c dk brn & red 9 9
83 A21 5c yel grn & grn 28 25
84 A21 5c org & dl red ('22) 28 28
85 A22 10c car & dk red 35 32
86 A22 10c ap grn & grn ('22) 40 40
87 A22 10c ver & grn ('25) 10 10
88 A22 15c brn vio & car 22 22
89 A22 20c org & blk brn 15 15
90 A22 20c dp grn & bl grn ('25) 10 10
91 A22 20c dk grn & red ('27) 20 15
92 A22 25c ultra & dl bl 25 22
93 A22 25c blk & bl grn ('22) 40 40
94 A22 30c blk & bl grn 55 45
95 A22 30c rose & red brn ('22) 40 40
96 A22 30c vio & ol grn ('25) 15 15
97 A22 30c grn & dl grn ('27) 15 15
98 A22 35c lt grn & dl rose 28 25
99 A22 40c bl & brn vio 28 25
100 A22 45c red brn & dk bl 40 32
101 A22 50c car rose & blk 4.00 2.50
102 A22 50c ultra & ind ('24) 55 55
103 A22 50c dk brn & red vio ('25) 15 9
104 A22 60c ol grn & red vio ('25) 15 15
105 A22 65c car rose & ol grn ('25) 20 15
106 A22 75c dl vio & choc 40 28
107 A22 75c ind & ultra ('25) 15 15
108 A22 75c brt vio & ol brn ('27) 70 45
109 A22 85c vio brn & bl grn ('25) 60 38
110 A22 90c brn red & brt red ('30) 3.25 2.25
111 A23 1fr bis brn & red 80 38
112 A23 1.10fr lt brn & ultra ('28) 2.00 2.00
113 A23 1.25fr dk bl & blk brn ('33) 3.75 3.25
114 A23 1.50fr lt bl & dk bl ('30) 60 45
115 A23 1.75fr gray grn & lt red ('33) 2.50 2.00
116 A23 2fr bl vio & blk 1.25 80
117 A23 3fr red vio ('30) 4.00 2.50
118 A23 5fr rose red & blk 2.50 1.10
Nos. 80-118 (39) 32.68 24.18

No. 99 is on ordinary paper.

Stamps of 1915 Surcharged in Green or Blue **1922 0f50**

1922

119 A21 10c on 5c yel grn & grn (G) 28 28
a. Double surcharge 40.00 40.00
120 A22 50c on 25c ultra & bl (Bl) 28 28

Type of 1915 Surcharged in Various Colors **0,01**

1922

121 A22 0,01c on 15c vio & rose (Bk) 15 15
122 A22 0,02c on 15c vio & rose (Bl) 15 15
123 A22 0,04c on 15c vio & rose (G) 15 15
124 A22 0,05c on 15c vio & rose (R) 15 15

Stamps and Type of 1915 Surcharged **60**

1923-27

125 A22 60c on 75c ol grn & vio 12 12
126 A22 65c on 15c brn vio & car ('25) 40 40
127 A22 85c on 40c bl & brn vio ('25) 50 50
128 A22 90c on 75c brn red & red ('27) 2.25 2.25

Stamps and Type of 1915-17 Surcharged with New Value and Bars in Black or Red

1924-27

129	A23	25c	on 5fr rose red & blk	40	40
130	A23	1.25fr	on 1fr dk bl & ultra (R) ('26)	40	40
131	A23	1.50fr	on 1fr lt bl & dk bl ('27)	55	55
132	A23	3fr	on 5fr ver & red vio ('27)	1.50	1.50
133	A23	10fr	on 5fr brn red & ol brn ('27)	4.00	4.00
134	A23	20fr	on 5fr gray grn & lil rose ('27)	6.25	6.25
			Nos. 129-134 (6)	13.10	13.10

Colonial Exposition Issue
Common Design Types
Engr., Name of Country Typo. in Black

1931 *Perf. 12½*

135	CD70	40c	dp grn	2.25	2.25
136	CD71	50c	violet	2.25	2.25
137	CD72	90c	red org	2.25	2.25
138	CD73	1.50fr	dull blue	2.25	2.25

Paris International Exposition Issue
Common Design Types

1937 **Engr.** *Perf. 13*

139	CD74	20c	dp vio	55	55
140	CD75	30c	dk grn	60	60
141	CD76	40c	car rose	55	55
142	CD77	50c	dk brn & bl	60	60
143	CD78	90c	red	90	90
144	CD79	1.50fr	ultra	90	90
			Nos. 139-144 (6)	4.10	4.10

Colonial Arts Exhibition Issue
Souvenir Sheet
Common Design Type

1937 *Imperf.*

145	CD75	3fr	dl vio	2.25	2.25

Mosque of Djibouti
A24

Somali Warriors
A25

Governor Léonce Lagarde — A26

View of Djibouti — A27

1938-40 *Perf. 12x12½, 12½*

146	A24	2c	dl red vio	5	5
147	A24	3c	slate grn	5	5
148	A24	4c	dl red brn	5	5
149	A24	5c	carmine	5	5
150	A24	10c	bl gray	5	5
151	A24	15c	slate blk	9	9
152	A24	20c	dk org	9	9
153	A25	25c	dk brn	20	15
154	A25	30c	dk blue	15	15
155	A25	35c	ol grn	35	28
156	A24	40c	org brn ('40)	5	5
157	A24	45c	dl grn ('40)	9	9
158	A25	50c	red	15	15
159	A25	55c	dl red vio	40	35
160	A25	60c	blk ('40)	35	35
161	A25	65c	org brn	28	28
162	A25	70c	lt vio ('40)	55	55
163	A26	80c	gray blk	65	55
164	A25	90c	rose vio ('39)	65	65
165	A26	1fr	carmine	80	55
166	A26	1fr	blk ('40)	22	22
167	A26	1.25fr	mag ('39)	40	40
168	A26	1.40fr	pck bl ('40)	40	40
169	A26	1.50fr	dl grn	42	35
170	A26	1.60fr	brn car ('40)	40	40
171	A26	1.75fr	ultra	42	35
172	A26	2fr	dk org	42	35
173	A26	2.25fr	ultra ('39)	60	60
174	A26	2.50fr	org brn ('40)	80	80
175	A26	3fr	dl vio	42	35
176	A27	5fr	brn & pale cl	80	65
177	A27	10fr	ind & pale bl	80	65
178	A27	20fr	car lake & gray	1.10	1.10
			Nos. 146-178 (33)	12.30	11.20

New York World's Fair Issue
Common Design Type

1939 **Engr.** *Perf. 12½x12*

179	CD82	1.25fr	car lake	60	60
180	CD82	2.25fr	ultra	60	60

Mosque of Djibouti and Marshal Petain — A28

1941 **Engr.** *Perf. 12x12½*

181	A28	1fr	yel brn	30
182	A28	2.50fr	blue	30

Nos. 181-182 were issued by the Vichy government, but it is doubtful whether they were placed in use in Somali Coast.

Stamps of types A24, A25 and A26, without "RF", were issued in 1944 by the Vichy Government, but were not placed on sale in the colony.

Stamps of 1915-33 Overprinted in Black or Red

a FRANCE LIBRE

Perf. 13½x14, 14x13½

1943 **Unwmk.**

183	A21	1c	brt vio & red brn	40	40
184	A21	2c	ocher & ind	55	55
185	A21	4c	dk brn & red	11.00	11.00
186	A21	5c	org & dl red	55	55
187	A22	15c	brn vio & car	2.50	2.50
188	A22	20c	dk grn & red	55	55
189	A22	30c	grn & dl grn	55	55
190	A22	50c	dk brn & red vio	50	50
191	A22	65c	car rose & ol grn	65	65
192	A23	1.50fr	lt bl & dk bl (R)	65	65
193	A23	1.75fr	gray grn & lt red	3.00	3.00
			Nos. 183-193 (11)	20.90	20.90

Stamps of 1938-40 Overprinted in Black or Red

France Libre
b

FRANCE LIBRE
c

France Libre
d

FRANCE LIBRE
e

1943 *Perf. 12x12½, 12½*

194	A24(b)	2c	dl red vio	80	80
195	A24(b)	3c	sl grn (R)	80	80
196	A24(b)	4c	dl red brn	80	80
197	A24(b)	5c	carmine	80	80
198	A24(b)	10c	bl gray (R)	40	40
199	A24(b)	15c	sl blk (R)	80	80
200	A24(b)	20c	dk org	80	80
201	A25(c)	25c	dk brn (R)	1.00	1.00
202	A25(c)	30c	dk bl (R)	35	35
203	A25(c)	35c	ol (R)	1.00	1.00
204	A24(b)	40c	brn org	35	35
205	A24(b)	45c	dl grn	80	80
206	A25(b)	55c	dl red vio (R)	80	80
207	A25(c)	60c	blk (R)	40	40
208	A25(b)	70c	lt vio (R)	35	35
a.			Inverted overprint	90.00	90.00
209	A26(d)	80c	gray blk (R)	42	42
210	A25(c)	90c	rose vio (R)	35	35
211	A26(d)	1.25fr	magenta	42	42
212	A26(d)	1.40fr	pck bl (R)	35	35
213	A26(d)	1.50fr	dl grn	42	42
214	A26(d)	1.60fr	brn car	45	45
215	A26(d)	1.75fr	ultra (R)	3.75	3.75
216	A26(d)	2fr	dk org	35	35
217	A26(d)	2.25fr	ultra (R)	55	55
218	A26(d)	2.50fr	chestnut	55	55
219	A26(d)	3fr	dl vio (R)	80	80
220	A27(e)	5fr	brn & pale cl	3.50	3.50
221	A27(e)	10fr	ind & pale bl	70.00	70.00
222	A27(e)	20fr	car lake & gray	2.25	2.25

The space between surcharge on Nos. 206 and 208 measures 10½mm

FRANCE LIBRE

No. 161 Surcharged in Black

50c.

=

223	A25	50c	on 65c org brn	35	35
			Nos. 194-223 (30)	94.76	94.76

Catalogue values for unused stamps in this section, from this point to the end of the section, are for Never Hinged items.

Locomotive and Palms — A29

1943 **Unwmk.** **Photo.** *Perf. 14½x14*

224	A29	5c	ryl bl	5	5
225	A29	10c	pink	5	5
226	A29	25c	emerald	15	15
227	A29	30c	gray blk	10	10
228	A29	40c	violet	10	10
229	A29	80c	red brn	15	15
230	A29	1fr	aqua	20	20
231	A29	1.50fr	scarlet	15	15
232	A29	2fr	brown	22	22
233	A29	2.50fr	ultra	28	28
234	A29	4fr	brt org	35	35
235	A29	5fr	dp rose lil	35	35
236	A29	10fr	lt ultra	55	55
237	A29	20fr	green	60	60
			Nos. 224-237 (14)	3.30	3.30

Eboue Issue
Common Design Type

1945 **Engr.** *Perf. 13*

238	CD91	2fr	black	28	28
239	CD91	25fr	Prus grn	65	65

Nos. 238 and 239 exist imperforate.

Nos. 224, 226 and 233 Surcharged with New Values and Bars in Carmine or Black

1945 *Perf. 14½x14*

240	A29	50c	on 5c ryl bl (C)	28	28
241	A29	60c	on 5c ryl bl (C)	12	12
242	A29	70c	on 5c ryl bl (C)	12	12
a.			Inverted surcharge	65.00	
243	A29	1.20fr	on 5c ryl bl (C)	35	35
244	A29	2.40fr	on 25c emer	40	40
a.			Inverted surcharge	60.00	
245	A29	3fr	on 25c emer	28	28
246	A29	4.50fr	on 25c emer	40	40
a.			Inverted surcharge	60.00	
247	A29	15fr	on 2.50fr ultra (C)	60	60
			Nos. 240-247 (8)	2.55	2.55

Danakil Tent — A30

Khor-Angar Outpost
A31

Obock-Tadjouran Road — A32

Somali Woman
A33

Somali Village
A34

Djibouti Mosque
A35

1947 **Unwmk.** **Photo.** *Perf. 13*

248	A30	10c	vio bl & org	5	5
249	A30	30c	ol brn & org	5	5
250	A30	40c	dp plum & org	5	5
251	A31	50c	bl grn & org	5	5
252	A31	60c	choc & dp yel	10	12
253	A31	80c	vio bl & org	12	12
254	A32	1fr	bl & choc	12	12
255	A32	1.20fr	bl grn & ol grn	42	42
256	A32	1.50fr	org & vio bl	15	15
257	A33	2fr	red lil & bl gray	35	28
258	A33	3fr	dp bl & brn org	45	40
259	A33	3.60fr	car rose & cop red	80	70
260	A33	4fr	choc & bl gray	70	50
261	A34	5fr	org & choc	40	28
262	A34	6fr	gray bl & int bl	55	35
263	A34	10fr	gray bl & red lil	55	38
264	A35	15fr	choc, gray bl & pink	70	45
265	A35	20fr	dk bl, gray bl & org	80	55
266	A35	25fr	vio brn, lil rose & gray bl	1.40	1.35
			Nos. 248-266 (19)	7.81	6.37

Military Medal Issue
Common Design Type

1952 **Engraved and Typographed**

267	CD101	15fr	blk, grn, yel & dk pur	2.00	2.00

Imperforates
Most stamps of Somali Coast from 1956 onward exist imperforate in issued and trial colors, and also in small presentation sheets in issued colors.

FIDES Issue
Common Design Type and

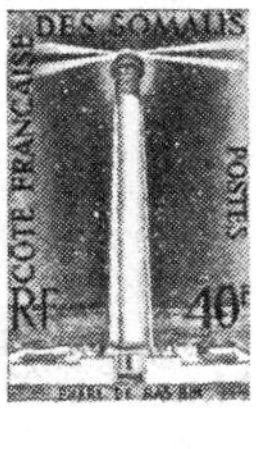

Lighthouse, Ras-Bir — A36

Design: 15fr, Loading ship and map, Djibouti.

1956 Unwmk. Engr. *Perf. 13*
268 CD103 15fr purple 70 38
269 A36 40fr dp ultra & gray 1.50 1.00

Flower Issue
Common Design Type

Design: 10fr, Haemanthus (horiz.).

1958 Photo. *Perf. 12½x12*
270 CD104 10fr grn, red & yel 1.40 65

Wart Hog — A37

Designs: 40c, Cheetah. 50c, Gerenuk (vert.).

1958 Engr. *Perf. 13*
271 A37 30c red brn & sep 15 8
272 A37 40c brn & ol 15 12
273 A37 50c brn, grn & gray 25 20

See No. C21.

Human Rights Issue
Common Design Type

1958 Unwmk.
274 CD105 20fr brt pur & dk bl 1.00 1.00

Universal Declaration of Human Rights, 10th anniv.

Parrotfish A38

Designs: Various Tropical Fish.

1959 Engr. *Perf. 13*
275 A38 1fr brt bl, brn & red org 16 16
276 A38 2fr blk, lt bl, yel & grn 18 16
277 A38 3fr vio & blk brn 18 16
278 A38 4fr brt grnsh bl, org & lt brn 40 30
279 A38 5fr brt grnsh bl & blk 42 28
280 A38 20fr brt bl, dl red brn & rose 90 70
281 A38 25fr red, grn & ultra 1.50 1.00
282 A38 60fr bl & dk grn 3.50 1.60
Nos. 275-282 (8) 7.24 4.36

No. 276 is vertical.

Flamingo — A39

Birds: 15fr, Bee-eater (horiz.). 30fr, Sacred ibis (horiz.). 75fr, Pink-backed pelican.

1960 Unwmk. *Perf. 13*
283 A39 10fr bluish grn, bis & cl 35 25
284 A39 15fr rose lil, grn & yel 50 30
285 A39 30fr bl, blk, org & brn 1.25 90
286 A39 75fr grn, sl grn & yel 3.00 1.75

Dragon Tree — A40

Klipspringer A41

Meleagrina Margaritifera A42

Designs: 4fr, Cony. 6fr, Large flatfish. 25fr, Fennecs. 40fr, Griffon vulture.

1962, Mar. 24 Engr. *Perf. 13*
287 A40 2fr grn, yel, org & brn 50 25
288 A40 4fr ocher & choc 50 25
289 A40 6fr brn, mar, grn & yel 85 50
290 A40 25fr red brn, ocher & grn 1.25 1.00
291 A40 40fr dk bl, brn & gray 2.00 1.50
292 A41 50fr bis, bl & lil 3.00 2.00
Nos. 287-292 (6) 8.10 5.50

1962, Nov. 24 Photo.

Sea Shells: 10fr, Tridacna squamosa (horiz.). 25fr, Strombus tricornis (horiz.). 30fr, Trochus dentatus.

Shells in Natural Colors
293 A42 8fr red & blk 40 30
294 A42 10fr car rose & blk 40 30
295 A42 25fr dp bl & brn 1.40 65
296 A42 30fr rose lil & brn 1.10 60

See Nos. C28-C29.

Red Cross Centenary Issue
Common Design Type

1963, Sept. 2 Engr. *Perf. 13*
297 CD113 50fr org brn, gray & car 2.50 2.50

Astraea Coral — A43

Design: 6fr, Organ-pipe coral.

1963, Nov. 30 Photo. *Perf. 13x13½*
298 A43 5fr multi 40 35
299 A43 6fr multi 40 35

See Nos. C26-C27, C30.

Human Rights Issue
Common Design Type

1963, Dec. 20 Engr. *Perf. 13*
300 CD117 70fr dk brn & ultra 3.50 3.50

Philatec Issue
Common Design Type

1964, Apr. 7 Unwmk. *Perf. 13*
301 CD118 80fr dp lil rose, grn & brn 3.50 3.50

Houri (Somali Sailboats) A44

Design: 25fr, Sambouk (Somali sailboats).

1964, June 9 Engr.
302 A44 15fr multi 50 42
303 A44 25fr multi 90 70

View of Dadwayya and Map of Somali Coast A45

Design: 20fr, View of Tadjourah and map of Somali Coast.

1965, Oct. 20 Engr. *Perf. 13*
304 A45 6fr ultra, sl grn & red brn 40 30
305 A45 20fr ultra, org brn & brt grn 40 35

Senna — A46

Designs: 8fr, Poinciana. 25fr, Aloe.

1966 Engr. *Perf. 13*
306 A46 5fr red brn, sl grn & org 40 30
307 A46 8fr brn, dk grn & org 40 30
308 A46 25fr sl grn, ver & ind 60 50

See No. C41.

Desert Monitor A47

1967, May 8 Engr. *Perf. 13*
309 A47 20fr red brn, ocher & sep 1.00 70

Stamps of Somali Coast were replaced in 1967 by those of the French Territory of the Afars and Issas.

SEMI-POSTAL STAMPS

Somali Girl — SP1

Perf. 13½x14
1915 Unwmk. Chalky Paper
B1 SP1 10c + 5c car & dk red 3.00 3.00

Curie Issue
Common Design Type

1938 Engr. *Perf. 13*
B2 CD80 1.75fr + 50c brt ultra 3.00 3.00

French Revolution Issue
Common Design Type

Photo., Name and Value Typo. in Black

1939
B3 CD83 45(c) + 25(c) grn 3.00 3.00
B4 CD83 70(c) + 30(c) brn 3.00 3.00
B5 CD83 90(c) + 35(c) red org 3.00 3.00
B6 CD83 1.25fr + 1fr rose pink 3.25 3.25
B7 CD83 2.25fr + 2fr bl 3.75 3.75
Nos. B3-B7 (5) 16.00 16.00

Common Design Type and

Somali Guard — SP2

Local Police — SP3

1941 Photo. *Perf. 13½*
B8 SP2 1fr + 1fr red 62
B9 CD86 1.50fr + 3fr maroon 62
B10 SP3 2.50fr + 1fr blue 62

Nos. B8-B10 were issued by the Vichy government, but were not placed in use in the colony.

Nos. 181-182 surcharged "OEUVRES COLONIALES" and surtax were issued in 1944 by the Vichy Government, but were not placed on sale in the colony.

Catalogue values for unused stamps in this section, from this point to the end of the section, are for Never Hinged items.

Red Cross Issue
Common Design Type
Inscribed "Djibouti"

1944 *Perf. 14½x14*
B13 CD90 5fr + 20fr emer 80 80

The surtax was for the French Red Cross and national relief.

Tropical Medicine Issue
Common Design Type

1950 Engr. *Perf. 13*
B14 CD100 10fr + 2fr red brn & red 2.00 2.00

The surtax was for charitable work.

Anti-Malaria Issue
Common Design Type

1962, Apr. 7 Unwmk. *Perf. 13*
B15 CD108 25fr + 5fr aqua 3.25 3.25

Infant, Sun, Chest and Skulls SP4

1965, Dec. 10 Engr. *Perf. 13*
B16 SP4 25fr + 5fr ocher, sl & brt grn 1.20 1.20

Campaign against tuberculosis.

AIR POST STAMPS

Catalogue values for unused stamps in this section, from this point to the end of the section, are for Never Hinged items.

The first value column gives the catalogue value of an unused stamp, the second that of a used stamp.

V1

Stamps of the design shown above were issued in 1943 by the Vichy Government, but were not placed on sale in the colony.

Common Design Type
Inscribed "Djibouti"

1944	**Unwmk.**	**Photo.**	***Perf. 14½x14***		
C1	CD87	1fr dk org		35	35
C2	CD87	1.50fr brt red		35	35
C3	CD87	5fr brn red		50	50
C4	CD87	10fr black		55	55
C5	CD87	25fr ultra		90	90
C6	CD87	50fr dk grn		80	80
C7	CD87	100fr plum		1.40	1.40
		Nos. C1-C7 (7)		4.85	4.85

Victory Issue
Common Design Type

1946	**Engr.**	***Perf. 12½***		
C8	CD92	8fr deep blue	50	50

Chad to Rhine Issue
Common Design Types

1946				
C9	CD93	5fr gray blk	45	45
C10	CD94	10fr dp org	40	40
C11	CD95	15fr vio brn	40	40
C12	CD96	20fr brt vio	40	40
C13	CD97	25fr bl grn	70	70
C14	CD98	50fr lt ultra	1.00	1.00
		Nos. C9-C14 (6)	3.35	3.35

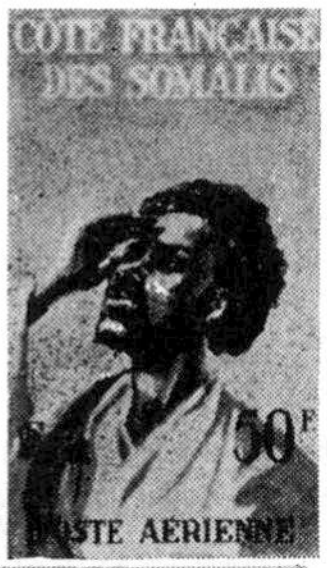

Somali Gazing Skyward — AP1

Frontier Post, Loyada — AP2

Governor's Mansion, Djibouti — AP3

Perf. 12½x13, 13x12½

1947	**Photo.**	**Unwmk.**		
C15	AP1	50fr gray bl & choc	1.75	75
C16	AP2	100fr ol grn, org yel & gray bl	2.00	1.00
C17	AP3	200fr gray bl, org yel & ol grn	3.25	1.75

UPU Issue
Common Design Type

1949	**Engr.**	***Perf. 13***		
C18	CD99	30fr bl, dp bl, brn red & grn	2.75	2.75

Liberation Issue
Common Design Type

1954, June 6				
C19	CD102	15fr ind & pur	2.50	2.50

Somali Woman and Map of Djibouti — AP4

1956, Feb. 20		**Unwmk.**		
C20	AP4	500fr dk vio & rose vio	25.00	15.00

Mountain Reedbucks — AP5

1958, July 7	**Engr.**	***Perf. 13***		
C21	AP5	100fr ultra, lt grn & dk red brn	1.60	1.25

Albert Bernard, Flag and Troops — AP6

1960, Jan. 18				
C22	AP6	55fr ultra, sep & car	80	55

25th death anniv. of Administrator Albert Bernard at Moraito.

Great Bustard — AP7

1960, Oct. 24	**Unwmk.**	***Perf. 13***		
C23	AP7	200fr brn, org & sl	4.25	2.50

Salt Dealers' Caravan at Assal Lake — AP8

1962, Jan. 6	**Engr.**	***Perf. 13***		
C24	AP8	500fr dk bl, red brn, pink & blk	5.00	3.00

Obock — AP9

1962, Mar. 11	**Unwmk.**	***Perf. 13***		
C25	AP9	100fr bl & org brn	1.50	1.00

Centenary of the founding of Obock.

Rostellaria Magna — AP10

Designs: 40fr, Millepore coral. 55fr, Brain coral. 100fr, Lambis bryonia (seashell). 200fr, Branch coral.

1962-63	**Photo.**	***Perf. 13½x12½***		
C26	AP10	40fr multi ('63)	65	40
C27	AP10	55fr multi ('63)	1.20	60
C28	AP10	60fr multi	1.20	60
C29	AP10	100fr multi	1.50	1.00
C30	AP10	200fr multi ('63)	2.50	1.50
		Nos. C26-C30 (5)	7.05	4.10

Telstar Issue
Common Design Type

1963, Feb. 9	**Engr.**	***Perf. 13***		
C31	CD111	20fr dp cl & dk grn	40	40

Zaroug (Somali Sailboats) — AP11

Designs: 50fr, Sambouk (boat) building. 300fr, Zeima sailboat.

1964-65	**Engr.**	***Perf. 13***		
C32	AP11	50fr bl, ocher & choc	1.10	65
C33	AP11	85fr dk Prus grn, dk brn & mag	1.40	1.10
C34	AP11	300fr ultra, lt brn & bl grn ('65)	4.50	2.50

Discus Thrower — AP12

1964, Oct. 10		**Engr.**		
C35	AP12	90fr rose lil, red brn & blk	3.50	2.75

18th Olympic Games, Tokyo, Oct. 10-25.

ITU Issue
Common Design Type

C36	CD120	95fr lil rose, brt bl & lt brn	5.00	3.50

Camels in Ghoubet Kharab and Map of Somali Coast — AP13

Design: 45fr, Abbé Lake.

1965	**Engr.**	***Perf. 13***		
C37	AP13	45fr Prus bl, bl & red brn	90	45
C38	AP13	65fr bl, choc & yel	1.00	70

Issue dates: 45fr, Oct. 20; 65fr, July 16.

French Satellite A-1 Issue
Common Design Type

Designs: 25fr, Diamant rocket and launching installations. 30fr, A-1 satellite.

1966, Jan. 28	**Engr.**	***Perf. 13***		
C39	CD121	25fr redsh brn, ol brn & dl red	90	90
C40	CD121	30fr ol brn, dl red & redsh brn	90	90
a.		Strip of 2 + label	1.90	1.90

No. C40a contains one each of Nos. C39-C40 and reddish brown label with commemorative inscription. Each sheet contains 16 triptychs (2x8).

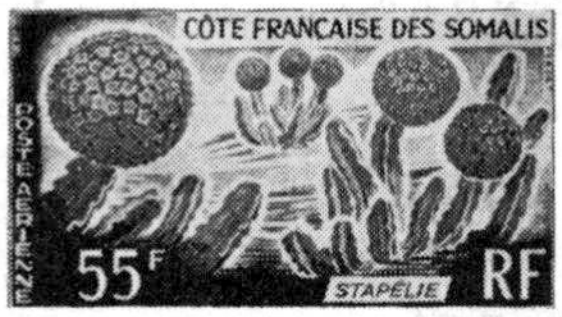

Stapelia — AP14

1966	**Engr.**	***Perf. 13***		
C41	AP14	55fr sl grn, dl mag & emer	1.20	70

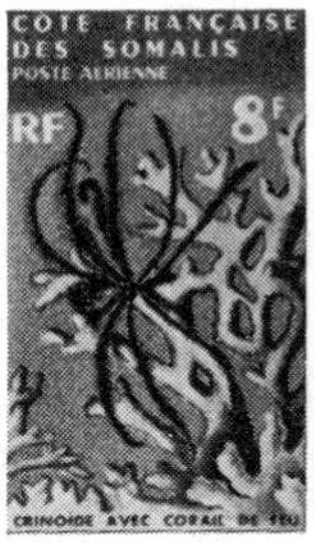

Feather Starfish and Coral — AP15

Fish: 25fr, Regal angelfish. 40fr, Pomocanthops filamentosus. 50fr, Amphiprion ephippium. 70fr, Squirrelfish. 80fr, Surgeonfish. 100fr, Pterois lunulatus.

1966	**Photo.**	***Perf. 13***		
C42	AP15	8fr multi	40	40
C43	AP15	25fr multi	80	80
C44	AP15	40fr multi	1.20	1.20
C45	AP15	50fr multi	1.90	1.90
C46	AP15	70fr multi	2.25	2.25
C47	AP15	80fr multi	2.50	2.50
C48	AP15	100fr multi	3.00	3.00
		Nos. C42-C48 (7)	12.05	12.05

French Satellite D-1 Issue
Common Design Type

1966, June 10	**Engr.**	***Perf. 13***		
C49	CD122	48fr dk brn, brt bl & grn	1.20	80

AIR POST SEMI-POSTAL STAMPS

Catalogue values for unused stamps in this section, from this point to the end of the section, are for Never Hinged items.

V2

Stamps of the design shown above and stamp of Cameroun type V10 inscribed "Cote Frcs. des Somalis" were issued in 1942 by the Vichy Government, but were not placed on sale in the colony.

Pharaoh Sacrificing before Horus and Hathor — SPAP1

Unwmk.

1964, Aug. 28 Engr. *Perf. 13*

CB1 SPAP1 25fr + 5fr Prus grn, dk red & brn 3.25 3.25

UNESCO world campaign to save historic monuments in Nubia.

POSTAGE DUE STAMPS

D1

D2

Perf. 14x13½

1915 Unwmk. Typo.

Chalky Paper

J1 D1 5c dp ultra 12 12
J2 D1 10c brn red 20 20
J3 D1 15c black 20 20
J4 D1 20c purple 38 38
J5 D1 30c orange 50 50
J6 D1 50c maroon 1.10 1.10
J7 D1 60c green 1.90 1.90
J8 D1 1fr dk bl 2.50 2.50
Nos. J1-J8 (8) 6.90 6.90

Type of 1915 Issue Surcharged **2F.**

1927

J9 D1 2fr on 1fr lt red 2.50 2.50
J10 D1 3fr on 1fr lil rose 2.50 2.50

Type of 1915

1938 Engr. *Perf. 12½x13*

J11 D1 5c lt ultra 5 5
J12 D1 10c dk car 5 5
J13 D1 15c brn blk 5 5
J14 D1 20c violet 10 10
J15 D1 30c org yel 35 35
J16 D1 50c brown 25 25
J17 D1 60c emerald 50 50
J18 D1 1fr indigo 1.10 1.10
J19 D1 2fr red 28 28
J20 D1 3fr dk brn 50 50
Nos. J11-J20 (10) 3.23 3.23

Nos. J11 to J20 are inscribed "Inst de Grav" below design.

Postage Due Stamps of 1915 Overprinted in Red or Black **FRANCE** **LIBRE**

1943 Unwmk. *Perf. 14x13½*

J21 D1 5c ultra (R) 30 30
J22 D1 10c brn red 30 30
J23 D1 15c blk (R) 30 30
J24 D1 20c purple 30 30
J25 D1 30c orange 30 30
J26 D1 50c maroon 30 30
J27 D1 60c green 30 30
J28 D1 1fr dk bl (R) 1.75 1.75
Nos. J21-J28 (8) 3.85 3.85

Postage Due Stamps of 1938 Overprinted in Red or Black **France** **Libre**

1943 *Perf. 12½x13*

J29 D1 5c lt ultra (R) 25 25
J30 D1 10c dk car 25 25
J31 D1 15c brn blk (R) 25 25
J32 D1 20c violet 25 25
J33 D1 30c org yel 35 35
J34 D1 50c brown 35 35
J35 D1 60c emerald 35 35
J36 D1 1fr ind (R) 35 35
J37 D1 2fr red 2.00 2.00
J38 D1 3fr dk brn (R) 2.50 2.50
Nos. J29-J38 (10) 6.90 6.90

In 1944 the Vichy Government issued five stamps of type D1, but without "RF," which were not placed on sale in the colony. The stamps were engraved, with the value numerals typographed, some in different color inks. Denominations: 30c, 50c, 60c, 2fr, 3fr.

Catalogue values for unused stamps in this section, from this point to the end of the section, are for Never Hinged items.

1947 Photo. *Perf. 13½x13*

J39 D2 10c purple 5 5
J40 D2 30c brown 5 5
J41 D2 50c green 5 5
J42 D2 1fr dp org 10 10
J43 D2 2fr lil rose 15 15
J44 D2 3fr dk org brn 15 15
J45 D2 4fr blue 25 25
J46 D2 5fr org red 25 25
J47 D2 10fr ol grn 30 30
J48 D2 20fr bl vio 50 50
Nos. J39-J48 (10) 1.85 1.85

SOUTH KASAI

This part of a Congo province declared itself an autonomous state and in 1961 issued several series of stamps, some of which were overprints on Congo (ex-Belgian) stamps. Established nations did not recognize South Kasai as an independent state.

SOUTH MOLUCCAS

(Republik Maluku Selatan)

On the basis of information received from the Republic of Indonesia, it appears that stamps of the so-called republic of South Moluccas were privately issued and had no postal use. Accordingly, they are not recognized as postage stamps.

SOUTH RUSSIA

LOCATION — An area in southern Russia bordering on the Caspian and Black Seas.

A provisional government set up and maintained by General Denikin in opposition to the Bolshevik forces in Russia following the downfall of the Empire. The stamps were used in the field postal service established for carrying on communication between the various armies united in the revolt. These armies included the Don Cossacks, the Kuban Cossacks, and also the neighboring southern Russian people in favor of the counter-revolution against the Bolsheviks.

100 Kopecks = 1 Ruble

Values for used stamps are for canceled to order copies. Postally used specimens sell for considerably more.

DON GOVERNMENT.

(Novocherkassk)
Rostov Issue

Russian Stamps of 1909-17 Surcharged **25**

1918 Unwmk. *Perf. 14x14½*

1 A14 25k on 1k dl org yel 1.25 1.45
a. Inverted surcharge 20.00 40.00
2 A14 25k on 2k dl grn 45 60
a. Inverted surcharge 16.00 35.00
3 A14 25k on 3k car 45 75
a. Double surcharge 30.00 55.00
4 A15 25k on 4k car 1.75 2.50
a. Inverted surcharge 16.00 35.00
5 A14 50k on 7k bl 3.00 4.25

Imperf

6 A14 25k on 1k org 45 60
a. Inverted surcharge 16.00 40.00
7 A14 25k on 2k gray grn 4.75 6.50
8 A14 25k on 3k red 1.40 1.90
Nos. 1-8 (8) 13.50 18.55

Counterfeits exist of Nos. 1-8.

Ermak, Cossack Leader — A1

Inscription on Back

1919 *Perf. 11½*

10 A1 20k green 30.00 85.00

This stamp was available for both postage and currency.

Novocherkassk Issue

25 1P. 1P.

Russian stamps with these surcharges are bogus.

Kuban Government
Ekaterinodar Issues

Russian Stamps of 1909-17 Surcharged:

—25 —70к. —1 р.
d e f

1 р. —3— рубля 10 рублей
g h i

1918-20 Unwmk. *Perf. 14x14½*

20 A14(d) 25k on 1k dl org yel 50 65
a. Inverted surcharge 20.00 27.50
b. Dbl. surch., one inverted 16.00 27.50
21 A14(d) 50k on 2k dl grn 4.50 6.00
a. Inverted surcharge 16.00 27.50
b. Double surcharge 10.50 13.00
c. Double surcharge inverted 10.50 13.00
22 A14(e) 70k on 5k dk cl 65 85
23 A14(f) 1r on 3k car 1.50 2.00
a. Inverted surcharge 11.50 16.00
b. Double surcharge 5.25 10.00
c. Pair, one without surcharge 5.25 10.00
24 A14(g) 1r on 3k car 65 1.00
a. Inverted surcharge 8.00 13.00
b. Double surcharge 8.00 13.00
c. Pair, one without surcharge 11.50 13.00
25 A15(h) 3r on 4k rose 10.00 11.50
b. Inverted surcharge 27.50 50.00
c. Double surcharge 30.00 52.50
d. Double surcharge inverted 30.00 52.50
26 A15(i) 10r on 4k rose 3.25 4.00
a. 10r on 4k car 8.00 13.00
b. Inverted surcharge 32.50 50.00
27 A11(i) 10r on 15k red brn & dp bl 1.10 1.00
a. Surcharged on face and back 13.00 13.00
b. Dbl. surch., one inverted 30.00 60.00
28 A14(i) 25r on 3k car 2.25 1.65
a. Inverted surcharge 4.50 10.00
29 A14(i) 25r on 7k bl 22.50 27.50
a. Inverted surcharge 40.00 52.50
30 A11(i) 25r on 14k bl & car 45.00 65.00
a. Inverted surcharge 52.50 70.00
31 A11(i) 25r on 25k dl grn & dk vio 30.00 42.50
a. Inverted surcharge 52.50 70.00

Imperf

35 A14(d) 25d on 1k org 1.10 2.00
36 A14(d) 50k on 2k gray grn 24 32
a. Inverted surcharge 20.00 22.50
b. Double surcharge 20.00 22.50
c. Pair, one without surcharge 20.00 27.50
37 A14(e) 70k on 5k cl 2.25 3.25
38 A14(f) 1r on 3k red 1.50 2.00
a. Inverted surcharge 13.00 16.00
b. Double surcharge 7.25 11.50
c. Pair, one without surcharge 4.00 8.00
39 A14(g) 1r on 3k red 40 65
a. Double surcharge 7.25 16.00
b. Pair, one without surch. 7.25 16.00
c. As "a," inverted 21.00 40.00
40 A11(i) 10r on 15k red brn & dp bl 2.25 3.25
41 A14(i) 25r on 3k red 5.25 3.25
a. Inverted surcharge 42.50

South Russia stamps can be mounted in Scott's Soviet Republics Part I Album.

Russian Stamps of 1909-17 Surcharged **70 коп.**

1919 *Perf. 14, 14½x15*

45 A14 70k on 1k dl org yel 1.00 1.00

Imperf.

46 A14 70k on 1k org 1.00 1.00
a. Inverted surcharge 10.50 14.00
b. Dbl. surch., one inverted 14.00 20.00

The 1k postal savings stamp with this surcharge inverted is a proof.

Counterfeits exist of Nos. 20-46.

Postal Savings Stamps Surcharged for Postal Use

A2

Wmk. 171 - Diamonds

1919 Wmk. 171 *Perf. 14½x15*

47 A2 10r on 1k red, *buff* 14.00 21.00
a. Inverted surcharge 70.00
48 A2 10r on 5k grn, *buff* 32.50 40.00
a. Double surcharge 110.00
49 A2 10r on 10k brn, *buff* 80.00 100.00

Counterfeits exist of Nos. 47-49.

Crimea

Russian Stamp of 1917 Surcharged **35 коп.**

1919 Unwmk. *Imperf.*

51 A14 35k on 1k org 32 1.00
a. Comma, instead of period in surcharge 85

A3

Paper with Buff Network
Inscription on Back

1919 *Imperf.*

52 A3 50k brown 32.50 65.00

Available for both postage and currency.

Russian Stamps of 1909-17 Surcharged **5 ПЯТЬ рублей.**

1920 *Perf. 14x14½*

53 A14 5r on 5k dk cl 1.50 2.75
a. Inverted surcharge 35.00
b. Double surcharge 42.50
54 A8 5r on 20k dl bl & dk car 1.50 2.75
a. Inverted surcharge 14.00
b. Double surcharge 35.00
c. "5" omitted 14.00

Imperf

55	A14 5r on 5k cl	1.50	2.75
a.	Double surcharge	14.00	

Same Surcharge on Stamp of Denikin Issue.

57	A5 5r on 35k lt bl	9.25	13.00
a.	Double surcharge	65.00	

A4

1920 ***Perf. 14x14½***

58	A4 100r on 1k dl org yel	3.25	
a.	"10" in place of "100"	50.00	
b.	Inverted surcharge	22.50	
c.	Double surcharge	50.00	

Imperf

59	A4 100r on 1k org	2.75	

Nos. 53-57 were issued at Sevastopol during the occupation by General Wrangel's army. Nos. 58-59 were prepared but not used.

Denikin Issue

A5

St. George — A6

1919 **Unwmk.** ***Imperf.***

61	A5 5k orange	12	24
62	A5 10k green	12	24
63	A5 15k red	18	35
64	A5 35k light bl	12	24
65	A5 70k dk blue	12	35
a.	Tete beche pair	65.00	
66	A6 1r brn & red	35	50
67	A6 2r gray vio & yel	35	75
68	A6 3r dl rose & grn	35	75
a.	Perf. 11½	1.25	1.25
69	A6 5r slate & vio	75	1.10
a.	Perf. 11½	1.75	1.75
70	A6 7r gray grn & rose	1.10	2.75
71	A6 10r red & gray	75	2.00
a.	Perf. 11½	1.40	1.65
	Nos. 61-71 (11)	4.31	9.27

Nos. 61-71 were issued at Ekaterinodar and used in all parts of South Russia that were occupied by the People's Volunteer Army under Gen. Anton Ivanovich Denikin. The inscription on the stamps reads "United Russia."

Stamps of type A6 with rosettes instead of numerals in the small circles at the sides are private and fraudulent. So are perforated copies of Nos. 61-67 and 70.

SPAIN

LOCATION — Southwestern Europe, Iberian Peninsula.
GOVT. — Monarchy
AREA — 194,884 sq. mi.
POP. — 38,219,534 (est. 1983)
CAPITAL — Madrid

Spain was a monarchy until about 1931, when a republic was established. After the Civil War (1936-39), the Spanish State of Gen. Francisco Franco was recognized. The monarchy was restored in 1975.

32 Maravedis = 8 Cuartos = 1 Real
1000 Milesimas = 100 Centimos = 1 Escudo (1866) 100 Milesimas = 1 Real 4 Reales = 1 Peseta 100 Centimos = 1 Peseta (1872)

Catalogue values for unused stamps in this country are for Never Hinged items, beginning with Scott 909 in the regular postage section, Scott B139 in the semi-postal section, Scott C159 in the airpost section, and Scott E21 in the special delivery section.

Values of early Spanish stamps vary according to condition. Quotations for Nos. 1-73 are for fine copies. Very fine to superb specimens sell at much higher prices, and inferior or poor copies sell at reduced prices, depending on the condition of the individual specimen.

Stamps punched with a small round hole have done telegraph service. In this condition they sell for 5 cents to $1 apiece.

Stamps of 1854 to 1882 cancelled with three parallel horizontal bars are remainders. Most of these are valued through No. 101.

Kingdom

Queen Isabella II
A1 A2

6 CUARTOS.
Type I. "T" and "O" of CUARTOS separated.
Type II. "T" and "O" joined.

Unwmk.

1850, Jan. 1 **Litho.** ***Imperf.***

1	A1 6c blk, thin paper (II)	165.00	7.50
a	Thick paper (II)	200.00	10.50
b	6c blk, thick paper (I)	190.00	9.50
c	Thin paper (I)	205.00	13.00
2	A2 12c lilac	2,000.	135.00
a	Thin paper	*2,750.*	150.00
3	A2 5r red	1,500.	125.00
4	A2 6r blue	2,750.	275.00
5	A2 10r green	3,600.	1,500.

Stamps of types A2, A3, A4, A6, A7a and A8 are inscribed "FRANCO" on the cuarto values and "CERTIFICADO," "CERTIFO" or "CERT DO" on the reales values.

A3

A4

1851, Jan. 1 **Typo.**

Thin Paper

6	A3 6c black	125.00	1.25
a	Thick paper	225.00	6.00
7	A3 12c lilac	2,750.	100.00
8	A3 2r red	*12,500.*	*5,500.*
9	A3 5r rose	2,000.	70.00
a	5r red brn (error)	*15,000.*	*7,000.*
10	A3 6r blue	3,000.	300.00
a	Cliche of 2r in plate of 6r		*110,000.*
11	A3 10r green	2,000.	165.00

1852, Jan. 1

Thick Paper

12	A4 6c rose	135.00	1.00
a	Thin paper	150.00	1.50
13	A4 12c lilac	1,350.	70.00
a	12c gray lil	1,750.	90.00
14	A4 2r pale red	*11,000.*	*3,500.*
15	A4 5r green	1,350.	70.00
16	A4 6r grnsh bl	*2,500.*	275.00
a	6r bl	*3,250.*	360.00

Arms of Madrid
A5

Isabella II
A6

1853, Jan. 1

Thin Paper

17	A5 1c bronze	1,750.	225.00
18	A5 3c bronze	*11,000.*	*4,500.*
19	A6 6c car rose	180.00	70
a	Thick paper	275.00	5.50
b	bluish thick paper	400.00	6.75
20	A6 12c red vio	1,350.	60.00
21	A6 2r vermilion	*9,000.*	*2,250.*
22	A6 5r lt grn	1,350.	70.00
23	A6 6r dp bl	2,000.	240.00

Nos. 17-18 were issued for use on Madrid city mail only. *They were reprinted on this white paper in duller colors.*

Coat of Arms of Spain
A7 A7a A8

1854

Thin White Paper.

24	A7 2c green	1,500.	200.00
25	A7a 4c carmine	165.00	1.00
a	Thick paper	190.00	3.25
	Bar cancellation		3.75
26	A8 6c carmine	150.00	75
a	Thick paper	400.00	10.00
	Bar cancellation		1.40
27	A7a 1r indigo	2,000.	150.00
	Bar cancellation		7.00
28	A8 2r scarlet	1,000.	55.00
a	2r ver	1,250.	70.00
	Bar cancellation		3.50
29	A8 5r green	1,000.	70.00
	Bar cancellation		6.00
30	A8 6r blue	1,750.	135.00
	Bar cancellation		10.00

See boxed note on bar cancellation below country heading.

Thick Bluish Paper.

31	A7 2c green	*12,500.*	*1,000.*
32	A7a 4c carmine	190.00	3.25
33	A7a 1r pale bl	*25,000.*	*7,000.*
	Bar cancellation		110.00
34	A8 2r dl red	*4,500.*	415.00

The 2c on paper watermarked loops is a proof.

Isabella II — A9

Wmk. 104

Wmk. 105

1855, Apr. 1 **Wmk. Loops. (104)**

Blue Paper.

36	A9 2c green	*2,250.*	55.00
a	2c yel grn	*2,750.*	100.00
	Bar cancellation		4.00
37	A9 4c brn red	125.00	35
a	4c car	135.00	40
b	4c lake	135.00	95
	Bar cancellation		80
38	A9 1r grn bl	500.00	8.00
a	1r bl	900.00	10.00
b	Cliché of 2r in plate of 1r	*15,000.*	*2,750.*
	Bar cancellation		2.25
39	A9 2r brn vio	325.00	7.00
a	2r red vio	450.00	7.75
	Bar cancellation		2.25

Wmk. Crossed Lines. (105)

1856, Jan. 1

Rough Yellowish Paper.

40	A9 2c green	*2,500.*	100.00
	Bar cancellation		6.75
41	A9 4c rose	5.50	1.00
	Bar cancellation		70
42	A9 1r grnsh bl	*2,500.*	90.00
a	1r dl bl	*3,250.*	90.00
	Bar cancellation		4.00
43	A9 2r brn vio	225.00	11.50
a	2r redsh vio	275.00	25.00
	Bar cancellation		3.25

1856, Apr. 11 **Unwmk.**

White Smooth Paper.

44	A9 2c bl rn	200.00	16.00
a	2c yel grn	250.00	25.00
	Bar cancellation		3.25
45	A9 4c rose	1.90	28
a	4c car	30.00	14.00
46	A9 1r blue	11.00	6.00
a	1r grnsh bl	16.00	10.50
	Bar cancellation		1.65
47	A9 2r brn lil	32.50	9.75
a	2r dl lil	45.00	12.00
	Bar cancellation		2.25

Three types of No. 45.

1859

48	A9 12c orange	100.00	
	Bar cancellation		15.00

No. 48 was never put in use.

A10

A11

1860-61

Tinted Paper.

49 A10 2c grn, *grn* 150.00 9.00
Bar cancellation 1.10
50 A10 4c org, *grn* 22.50 60
51 A10 12c car, *buff* 150.00 6.00
Bar cancellation 2.25
52 A10 19c brn, *buff* ('61) 2,000. 800.00
53 A10 1r bl, *grn* 100.00 5.00
Bar cancellation 1.90
54 A10 2r lil, *lil* 135.00 5.00
Bar cancellation 1.90

1862, July 16

55 A11 2c dp bl, *yel* 19.00 5.50
56 A11 4c dk brn, *redsh buff* 1.00 28
a 4c brn, *white* 12.50 3.25
57 A11 12c bl, *pnksh* 25.00 4.50
Bar cancellation 1.75
58 A11 19c car, *lil* 85.00 85.00
a 19c car, *white* 150.00 110.00
59 A11 1r brn, *yel* 25.00 10.00
Bar cancellation 1.90
60 A11 2r grn, *pnksh* 16.00 6.00
Bar cancellation 1.65

A12

A13

1864, Jan. 1

61 A12 2c dk bl, *lil* 19.00 9.50
62 A12 4c rose, *redsh buff* 95 28
a 4c car, *redsh buff* 10.00
63 A12 12c grn, *pnksh* 25.00 8.25
64 A12 19c vio, *pnksh* 95.00 95.00
65 A12 1r brn, *grn* 80.00 35.00
Bar cancellation 2.75
66 A12 2r dp bl, *pnksh* 22.50 6.00
Bar cancellation 2.25

1865, Jan. 1 ***Imperf.***

67 A13 2c rose 105.00 115.00
68 A13 4c blue *2,500.*
69 A13 12c bl & rose 160.00 11.00
a Frame invtd. *10,000.* 900.00
Bar cancellation 2.75
70 A13 19c brn & rose 1,250. 325.00
Bar cancellation 40.00
71 A13 1r yel grn 175.00 27.50
Bar cancellation 5.50
72 A13 2r red lil 200.00 16.00
Bar cancellation 4.00
73 A13 2r rose 275.00 25.00
a 2r sal 245.00 30.00
Bar cancellation 6.75

No. 68 may not have been regularly issued.

1865, Jan. 1 ***Perf. 14***

74 A13 2c rose red 400.00 47.50
Bar cancellation 6.00
75 A13 4c blue 24.00 60
76 A13 12c bl & rose 275.00 24.00
Bar cancellation 4.50
a Frame invtd. *15,000.* *2,250.*
As "a," bar cancel 425.00
77 A13 19c brn & rose *3,000.* *2,000.*
78 A13 1r yel grn 1,250. 200.00
Bar cancellation 12.00
79 A13 2r violet 900.00 125.00
Bar cancellation 9.00
80 A13 2r rose 1,000. 150.00
a 2r sal 1,000. 150.00
b 2r dl org 1,000. 150.00
Bar cancellation 15.00

A14

A14a

1866, Jan. 1

81 A14 2c rose 135.00 10.50
Bar cancellation 2.50
82 A14 4c blue 20.00 45
83 A14 12c orange 125.00 7.25
a 12c org yel 165.00 12.00
84 A14 19c brown 350.00 140.00
Bar cancellation 21.00

1866

85 A14 10c green 150.00 11.00
Bar cancellation 1.40
86 A14 20c lilac 105.00 10.00
Bar cancellation 1.40
87 A14a 20c dl lil 425.00 27.50
Bar cancellation 1.65

A15

A15a

A15b

A15c

1867-68

88 A15 2c yel brn 195.00 18.00
89 A15a 4c blue 13.00 45
90 A15b 12c org yel 115.00 3.25
a 12c dk org 150.00 6.00
b 12c red org ('68) 550.00 42.50
91 A15c 19c rose 1,000. 200.00
Bar cancellation 21.00

A15d

A15e

92 A15d 10c bl grn 135.00 12.00
Bar cancellation 1.25
93 A15e 20c lilac 60.00 4.75
Bar cancellation 1.25

A16

A17

A18

A19

94 A16 5m green 24.00 7.25
Bar cancellation 1.25
95 A17 10m brown 24.00 6.00
a Tete beche pair *15,000.* *5,000.*
96 A18 25m bl & rose 135.00 11.00
a Frame inverted *12,500.*
Bar cancellation 3.00
97 A18 50m bis brn 12.00 30

1868-69

98 A18 25m blue 150.00 7.50
Bar cancellation 1.75
99 A19 50m violet 12.00 30
100 A15b 100m brown 235.00 35.00
Bar cancellation 1.25
101 A15c 200m green 90.00 4.00
Bar cancellation 90
102 A15c 19c brown 1,600. 275.00

Provisional Government.

Excellent counterfeits exist of the provisional and provincial overprints.

Regular Issues Handstamped in Black — HABILITADO POR LA NACION.

1868-69

116 A15d 10c green 24.00 13.00
117 A15e 20c lilac 18.00 6.00
118 A16 5m green 12.00 4.50
119 A17 10m brown 10.50 4.50
120 A18 25m bl & rose 30.00 12.00
121 A18 25m blue 24.00 7.50
122 A18 50m bis brn 6.00 3.50
123 A19 50m violet 6.00 3.00
124 A15b 100m brown 75.00 24.00
125 A15c 200m green 24.00 7.50
126 A15b 12c orange 27.50 6.00
127 A15c 19c rose 240.00 90.00
128 A15c 19c brown 450.00 125.00

Nos. 116-128 exist with handstamp in blue, a few in red. These sell for more.

For Andalusian Provinces.

Regular Issues Handstamped Vertically in Blue — HABILITADO POR LA NACION.

114a A15 2c brown 60.00 24.00
115a A15a 4c blue 22.50 10.00
116a A15d 10c green 30.00 12.00
117a A15e 20c lilac 21.00 10.00
118a A16 5m green 15.00 6.50
119a A17 10m brown 10.50 4.50
120a A18 25m bl & rose 35.00 12.00
b Frame inverted
121a A18 25m blue 27.50 10.00
122a A18 50m bis brn 7.50 4.50
123a A19 50m violet 7.50 3.00
124a A15b 100m brown 75.00 27.50
125a A15c 200m green 25.00 10.00
126a A15b 12c orange 30.00 7.50
127a A15c 19c rose 275.00 135.00
128a A15c 19c brown 550.00 175.00

For Valladolid Province.

Regular Issues Handstamped in Black — HABILITADO POR LA NACION.

(Two types of overprint)

116c A15d 10c green 32.50 15.00
117c A15e 20c lilac 24.00 10.50
120c A18 25m bl & rose 45.00 12.00
121c A18 25m blue 35.00 12.00
122c A18 50m bis brn 12.00 7.50
123c A19 50m violet 12.00 6.00
124c A15b 100m brown 90.00 30.00
125c A15c 200m green 30.00 12.00
126c A15b 12c orange 32.50 10.50
127c A15c 19c rose *300.00* *150.00*
128c A15c 19c brown *850.00* *210.00*

For Asturias Province.

Regular Issues Handstamped in Black — *Habilitado por la Junta Revolucionaria*

117d A15e 20c lilac 150.00 105.00
122d A18 50m bis brn 165.00 105.00

For Teruel Province.

Regular Issues Handstamped in Black — HPN

117e A15e 20c lilac 60.00 45.00
120e A18 25m bl & rose 75.00 45.00
122e A18 50m bis brn 55.00 27.50
123e A19 50m violet 55.00 27.50
124e A15b 100m brown 125.00 60.00
125e A15c 200m green 90.00 35.00
126e A15b 12c orange 75.00 45.00

For Salamanca Province.

Regular Issues Handstamped in Blue — HABILITADO POR LA NACION

117f A15e 20c lilac 60.00 45.00
119f A17 10m brown 55.00 35.00
122f A18 50m bis brn 60.00 35.00

Duke de la Torre Regency.

"España" — A20

1870, Jan. 1 **Typo.**

159 A20 1m brn lil, *buff* 5.50 4.25
a 1m brn lil, *buff* 6.00 4.75
b 1m brn lil, *pnksh buff* 6.00 4.75
161 A20 2m blk, *pinkish* 6.00 4.75
a 2m blk, *buff* 6.50 5.50
163 A20 4m bis brn 10.50 9.00
164 A20 10m rose 12.00 4.50
a 10m car 15.00 5.00
165 A20 25m gray lil 30.00 6.00
a 25m lil 30.00 6.00
b 25m anil vio 45.00 7.50
166 A20 50m ultra 7.50 30
a 50m dl bl 90.00 4.50
167 A20 100m red brn 18.00 4.50
a 100m cl 21.00 6.50
b 100m org brn 21.00 6.50
168 A20 200m pale brn 18.00 4.50
169 A20 400m green 180.00 12.00
170 A20 1e60m dl lil 1,000. 300.00
171 A20 2e blue 900.00 175.00
172 A20 12c red brn 135.00 6.00
173 A20 19c yel grn 175.00 125.00

Kingdom.

A21

A22

King Amadeo
A23 A24

1872, Oct. 1 ***Imperf.***

174 A21 ¼c ultra 2.00 2.00
a Complete 1c (block four ¼c) 35.00 40.00

See No. 221A.

1872-73 ***Perf. 14***

176 A22 2c gray lil 15.00 6.00
a 2c vio 21.00 10.00
b Imperf. 50.00
177 A22 5c green 75.00 30.00
a Imperf., pair 225.00
178 A23 5c rose ('73) 15.00 3.50
179 A23 6c blue 75.00 12.00
180 A23 10c brn lil 165.00 60.00
181 A23 10c ultra ('73) 4.50 45
182 A23 12c gray lil 10.00 90
183 A23 20c gray vio ('73) 75.00 24.00
184 A23 25c brown 25.00 6.00
185 A23 40c pale red brn 40.00 6.00
186 A23 50c dp grn 60.00 6.00
187 A24 1p lilac 60.00 18.00
188 A24 4p red brn 300.00 200.00
189 A24 10p dp grn 1,250. 1,000.

First Republic.

Mural Crown
A25

"España"
A26

1873, July 1 ***Imperf.***

190 A25 ¼c green 90 60
a Complete 1c (block four ¼c) 24.00 12.00

1873, July 1 ***Perf. 14***

191 A26 2c orange 9.00 4.50
192 A26 5c claret 21.00 4.50
193 A26 10c green 6.00 30
a Tete beche pair *24,000.*
194 A26 20c black 45.00 15.00
195 A26 25c dp brn 21.00 5.50
196 A26 40c brn vio 22.50 5.50
197 A26 50c ultra 10.00 5.50
198 A26 1p gray lil 30.00 12.00
199 A26 4p red brn 240.00 210.00
200 A26 10p vio brn 1,250. 1,100.

"Justice"
A27

Coat of Arms
A28

1874, July 1

201 A27 2c yellow 15.00 5.50
202 A27 5c violet 21.00 5.50
a 5c red vio 21.00 7.50
203 A27 10c ultra 7.50 30
a Imperf., pair 24.00
204 A27 20c dk grn 90.00 21.00
205 A27 25c red brn 21.00 5.50
a 25c lil (error) 300.00 325.00
b Imperf., pair 80.00
206 A27 40c violet 210.00 5.50
a 40c brn (error) 150.00
b Imperf., pair 275.00
207 A27 50c yellow 60.00 4.75
a Imperf., pair 150.00
208 A27 1p yel grn 45.00 12.00
a 1p emer 55.00 20.00
b Imperf., pair 175.00
209 A27 4p rose 350.00 200.00
a 4p car 450.00 250.00
210 A27 10p black 1,900. 1,100.

1874, Oct. 1

211 A28 10c red brn 12.00 60
a 10c brn 12.00 60
b Imperf., pair 175.00

Kingdom

King Alfonso XII — A29

1875, Aug. 1

Blue Framed Numbers on Back, 1 to 100 on Each Sheet.

212 A29 2c org brn 12.00 4.50
a 2c choc brn 15.00 8.50
b Imperf., pair 90.00 90.00
213 A29 5c lilac 35.00 7.50
a Imperf., pair 125.00 125.00
214 A29 10c blue 3.00 30
a Imperf., pair 30.00 30.00
215 A29 20c brn org 150.00 45.00
216 A29 25c rose 30.00 3.50
217 A29 40c dp brn 60.00 18.00
a Imperf., pair 240.00 240.00
218 A29 50c gray lil 90.00 15.00
219 A29 1p black 105.00 30.00
220 A29 4p dk grn 175.00 150.00
221 A29 10p ultra 1,000. 900.00

1876, June 1 ***Imperf.***

221A A21 ¼c green 22 8
b Complete 1c (block four ¼c) 1.00 30
c Block of four with two ¼c sideways 110.00 110.00
d Tete beche (block 4 with both upper ¼c invtd.) 110.00 110.00
e Tete beche (block 4 with upper left ¼c invtd.) 1,000. 350.00

King Alfonso XII
A30 A31

Wmk. 178- Castle

ONE PESETA:
Type I. Thin figures of value and "PESETA" in thick letters.
Type II. Thick figures of value and "PESETA" in thin letters.

Wmk. 178

1876, June 1 Engr. ***Perf. 14***

222 A30 5c yel brn 6.00 1.50
a Imperf. 10.00
223 A30 10c blue 3.00 30
a Imperf. 4.50
224 A30 20c dk grn 8.50 6.00
225 A30 25c brown 6.00 2.00
a Imperf. 10.00
226 A30 40c blk brn 40.00 21.00
227 A30 50c green 10.00 3.25
a Imperf. 12.00
228 A30 1p dp bl, I 12.00 6.00
a 1p ultra, II 16.00 6.50
b Imperf. 18.00
229 A30 4p brn vio 30.00 21.00
a Imperf. 60.00
230 A30 10p vermilion 75.00 75.00
a Imperf. 150.00

Two plates each were used for the 5c, 10c, 25c, 50c, 1p and 10p. The 1p plates are most easily distinguished.

Unwmk.

1878, July 1 Typo. ***Perf. 14***

232 A31 2c lilac 15.00 4.50
a Imperf. 40.00
233 A31 5c orange 24.00 4.50
234 A31 10c brown 6.00 30
235 A31 20c black 105.00 45.00
a Imperf. 160.00
236 A31 25c ol bis 15.00 1.75
237 A31 40c red brn 90.00 60.00
238 A31 50c bl grn 45.00 6.00
239 A31 1p gray 40.00 12.00
240 A31 4p violet 105.00 60.00
241 A31 10p blue 180.00 180.00
a Imperf. 250.00

A32 A33

1879, May 1

242 A32 2c black 6.00 45
243 A32 5c gray grn 7.50 45
244 A32 10c rose 6.50 30
245 A32 20c red brn 70.00 7.50
246 A32 25c bluish gray 7.50 30
247 A32 40c brown 15.00 2.50
248 A32 50c dl buff 60.00 2.50
a 50c vel 85.00 5.00
249 A32 1p brt rose 60.00 1.25
250 A32 4p lil gray 275.00 15.00
251 A32 10p ol bis 1,250. 135.00

1882, Jan. 1

252 A33 15c salmon 5.50 30
a 15c org 15.00 60
253 A33 30c red lil 135.00 2.00
254 A33 75c gray lil 135.00 2.00
a Imperf. 210.00

King Alfonso XIII
A34 A35

1889-99

255 A34 2c bl grn 2.50 30
256 A34 2c blk ('99) 13.00 2.00
257 A34 5c blue 4.50 12
258 A34 5c bl grn ('99) 42.50 60
259 A34 10c red brn 6.50 12
260 A34 10c red ('99) 85.00 1.75
261 A34 15c vio brn 1.75 12
262 A34 20c yel grn 16.00 1.75
263 A34 25c blue 5.75 12
264 A34 30c ol gray 22.50 1.25
265 A34 40c brown 22.50 90
266 A34 50c rose 22.50 60
267 A34 75c orange 65.00 1.40
268 A34 1p dk vio 18.00 30
269 A34 4p car rose 325.00 13.00
270 A34 10p org red 550.00 32.50

The 15c yellow, type A34 is an official stamp listed as No. O9.
Nos. 256-261, 263-264, 266-268 exist imperf.

Control Number on Back

1900-05 Engr. Unwmk.

272 A35 2c bis brn 1.90 8
a Imperf. 11.00
273 A35 5c dk grn 4.00 8
a Imperf. 14.00
274 A35 10c rose red 5.50 8
a Imperf. 16.00
275 A35 15c bl blk 11.00 8
a Imperf. 37.50
276 A35 15c dl lil ('02) 5.50 8
a Imperf. 14.00
277 A35 15c pur ('05) 4.00 8
a Imperf. 11.00
278 A35 20c grnsh blk 19.00 60
a Imperf. 40.00
279 A35 25c blue 3.25 8
a Imperf. 11.00
b 25c grn (error) 3,200.
280 A35 30c bl grn 17.50 22
a 30c dp grn 20.00 22
b Imperf. 32.50
281 A35 40c ol bis 67.50 2.00
a Imperf. 135.00
282 A35 40c rose ('05) 135.00 80
a Imperf. 250.00
283 A35 50c sl bl 22.50 22
a Imperf. 55.00
b 50c bl grn (error) 1,250. 1,000.
284 A35 1p lake 22.50 22
a Imperf. 35.00
285 A35 4p dk vio 135.00 8.25
a Imperf. 225.00
286 A35 10p brn org 135.00 32.50
a Imperf. 200.00
Nos. 272-286 (15) 589.15 45.37

Don Quixote Starts Forth A36

Designs: 10c, Don Quixote attacks windmill. 15c, Meets country girls. 25c, Sancho Panza tossed in blanket. 30c, Don Quixote knighted. 40c, Tilting at sheep. 50c, On Wooden horse. 1p, Adventure with lions. 4p, In bullock cart, 10p, The Enchanted Lady.

Control Number on Back

1905, May 1 Typo.

287 A36 5c dk grn 1.10 90
a Imperf. 24.00
288 A36 10c org red 1.65 90
289 A36 15c violet 1.65 90
a Imperf. 24.00
290 A36 25c dk bl 4.25 1.25
291 A36 30c dk bl grn 21.00 4.50
292 A36 40c brt rose 42.50 12.00
293 A36 50c slate 8.50 2.50
294 A36 1p rose red 125.00 32.50
295 A36 4p dk vio 45.00 35.00
296 A36 10p brn org 85.00 70.00
Nos. 287-296 (10) 335.65 160.45

300th anniversary of the publication of Cervantes' "Don Quixote".
Counterfeits exist of Nos. 287-296.

Six stamps picturing King Alfonso XIII and Queen Victoria Eugenia were issued Oct. 1, 1907, at the Madrid Industrial Exhibition. They were not valid for postage.

Alfonso XIII — A46 A47

Blue Control Number on Back

Perf. 13x12½, 13, 13½x13, 14.

1909-22 Engr.

297 A46 2c dk brn 60 5
a No control number 60 30
298 A46 5c green 1.25 5
299 A46 10c carmine 1.25 5
300 A46 15c violet 6.00 5
301 A46 20c ol grn 30.00 30
302 A46 25c dp bl 3.00 5
303 A46 30c bl grn 6.00 10
304 A46 40c rose 9.00 30
305 A46 50c sl bl 7.50 30
a 50c bl ('22) 9.00 30
306 A46 1p lake 21.00 12
307 A46 4p dp vio 60.00 4.50
309 A46 10p orange 65.00 10.50
Nos. 297-309 (12) 210.60 16.37

Nos. 297-309 exist imperforate.
The 5c exists in carmine (value $300); the 15c in blue (value $525); the 4p in lake (value $1,250). The 4p lake is known only with perfin "B.H.A." (Banco Hispano-Americano).

Control Number on Back in Red or Orange.

1917

310 A46 15c yel ocher 3.00 24
a Control number in bl 10.50 85

Control Number on Back in Blue.

1918

313 A46 40c lt red 90.00 4.50

1920 Typo. ***Imperf.***

314 A47 1c bl grn 30 12

Perf. 13x12½, 14.

Litho.

315 A46 2c bister 3.50 12
316 A46 20c violet 35.00 6

Nos. 314-315 have no control number on back.

1921 Engr.

317 A46 20c violet 24.00 10

Madrid Post Office — A48

1920, Oct. 1 Typo. ***Perf. 13½***

Center and Portrait in Black.

318 A48 1c bl grn 25 24
319 A48 2c ol bis 25 24

Control Number on Back

320 A48 5c green 55 60
321 A48 10c red 55 48
322 A48 15c yellow 85 75
323 A48 20c violet 1.10 60
324 A48 25c gray bl 1.10 1.25
325 A48 30c dk grn 3.50 2.50
326 A48 40c rose 15.00 3.50
327 A48 50c brt bl 18.00 10.50
328 A48 1p brn red 21.00 9.00
329 A48 4p brn vio 52.50 37.50
330 A48 10p orange 115.00 75.00
Nos. 318-330 (13) 229.65 142.16

Universal Postal Union Congress, Madrid, Oct. 10-Nov. 30.
Nos. 318-330 exist imperforate. Values: 3 times those of perforated stamps.

King Alfonso XIII
A49 A49a

FIFTEEN CENTIMOS.
Die I. Narrow "5".
Die II. Wide "5".

TWENTY FIVE CENTIMOS.
Die I. "25" is 2¾mm. high. Vertical stroke of "5" is 1 mm long.
Die II. "25" is 3 mm. high. Vertical stroke of "5" is 1½ mm. long.

Perf. 11 to 14, Compound

1922-26 Engr. Unwmk.

331 A49 2c ol grn 24 5
a 2c dp org (error) 75.00 90.00

Control Number on Back

332 A49 5c red vio 2.50 5
333 A49 5c claret 1.25 5
334 A49 10c carmine 1.25 90
335 A49 10c yel grn 1.65 5
a 10c bl grn ('23) 1.90 12
336 A49 15c sl bl (I) 4.00 5
a 15c blk grn (II) 16.00 1.65
337 A49 20c violet 2.50 6
338 A49 25c car (I) 2.50 5
a 25c rose red (II) 3.25 9
b 25c lil rose (error) 60.00 75.00
339 A49 30c blk brn ('26) 6.50 18
340 A49 40c dp bl 2.75 6
341 A49 50c orange 11.00 8
a 50c org red 20.00 1.50
342 A49a 1p bl blk 13.00 8
343 A49a 4p lake 45.00 3.00
344 A49a 10p brown 21.00 6.50
Nos. 331-344 (14) 115.14 11.16

Nos. 331, 334, 336-344 exist imperf.
The 5c exists in vermilion (value $120); the 25c in dark blue (value $180). The 50c exists in red brown, the 4p in brown and 10p in lake; value, each $125. These five were not regularly issued.

"Santa Maria" and View of Seville — A50

Herald of Barcelona
A51

Exposition Buildings
A52

King Alfonso XIII and View of Barcelona
A53

1929, Feb. 15 *Perf. 11*

345	A50	1c	grnsh bl	20	30
346	A51	2c	pale yel grn	20	30
347	A52	5c	rose lake	42	60

Control Number on Back

348	A53	10c	green	60	60
349	A50	15c	Prus bl	42	30
350	A51	20c	purple	60	60
351	A50	25c	brt rose	60	60
352	A52	30c	blk brn	3.00	2.50
353	A53	40c	dk bl	4.00	2.50
354	A51	50c	dp org	2.00	1.75
355	A52	1p	bl blk	6.00	4.50
356	A53	4p	dp rose	16.00	12.00
357	A53	10p	brown	35.00	27.50
	Nos. 345-357,E2 (14)			78.04	62.30

Perf. 14

345a	A50	1c	grnsh bl	60	60
348a	A53	10c	green	21.00	21.00
350a	A51	20c	purple	21.00	21.00
351a	A50	25c	brt rose	21.00	21.00
352a	A52	30c	blk brn	21.00	21.00
353a	A53	40c	dk bl	42.50	42.50
354a	A51	50c	dp org	21.00	21.00
355a	A52	1p	bl blk	21.00	21.00
356a	A53	4p	dp rose	21.00	21.00
357a	A53	10p	brown	75.00	75.00
	Nos. 345a-357a,E2a (11)			285.10	285.10

Seville and Barcelona Exhibitions.

Nos. 345-357 exist imperf. Values about 6 times those of perf. stamps. See note after No. 432.

Nos. 314, 331, 333, 335-344 Overprinted in Red or Blue

Sociedad
de las Naciones
LV reunión
del Consejo
Madrid.

1929, June 10 *Imperf.*

358	A47	1c	bl grn	55	60

Perf. 13½x12½

359	A49	2c	ol grn	55	60
360	A49	5c	cl (Bl)	55	60
361	A49	10c	yel grn	55	60
362	A49	15c	sl bl	55	60
363	A49	20c	violet	55	60
364	A49	25c	car (Bl)	35	30
365	A49	30c	blk brn	1.75	1.50
366	A49	40c	dp bl	1.75	1.50
367	A49	50c	org (Bl)	1.75	1.50
368	A49a	1p	bl blk	5.50	6.00
369	A49a	4p	lake (Bl)	7.25	7.25
370	A49a	10p	brn (Bl)	24.00	30.00
	Nos. 358-370,E4 (14)			54.65	60.65

55th assembly of League of Nations at Madrid June 10-16. The stamps were available for postal use only on those days.

Exposition Building — A54

1930 **Litho.** *Perf. 11.*

371	A54	5c	dk bl & sal	4.25	3.50
372	A54	5c	dk vio & bl	4.25	3.50

Barcelona Philatelic Congress and Exhibition. "C. F. y E. F." are the initials of "Congreso Filatelico y Exposicion Filatelica." For each admission ticket, costing 2.75 pesetas, the holder was allowed to buy one of each of these stamps.

Locomotives
A55 A56

1930, May 10 *Perf. 14*

373	A55	1c	lt bl	22	50
374	A55	2c	ap grn	22	50

Control Number on Back

375	A55	5c	lake	22	50
376	A55	10c	yel grn	22	50
377	A55	15c	bluish gray	22	50
378	A55	20c	purple	22	50
379	A55	25c	brt rose	12	24
380	A55	30c	ol gray	85	65
381	A55	40c	dk bl	70	65
382	A55	50c	dk org	1.75	2.25
383	A56	1p	dk gray	2.00	2.75
384	A56	4p	dp rose	22.50	25.00
385	A56	10p	bis brn	140.00	140.00
	Nos. 373-385,C12-C17,E6 (20)			236.49	244.04

11th International Railway Congress, Madrid, 1930.

These stamps were on sale May 10-21, 1930, exclusively at the Palace of the Senate in Madrid and at the Barcelona and Seville expositions.

Francisco de Goya at 80 ("1746 1828") ("1828 1928")
A57 A59

"La Maja Desnuda" — A58

1930, June 15 **Litho.** *Perf. 12½*
Inscribed "Correos Espana"

386	A57	1c	yellow	10	8
387	A57	2c	bis brn	10	8
388	A57	5c	lil rose	10	8
389	A57	10c	green	12	20

Engr.

390	A57	15c	lt bl	10	10
391	A57	20c	brn vio	10	10
392	A57	25c	red	22	20
393	A57	30c	brown	3.50	4.00
394	A57	40c	dk bl	3.50	4.00
395	A57	50c	vermilion	3.50	4.00
396	A57	1p	black	4.50	5.00
397	A58	1p	dk vio	65	1.00
398	A58	4p	sl gray	45	65
399	A58	10p	red brn	8.50	10.00

Inscribed "1828 Goya 1928"

Litho.

400	A59	2c	ol grn	10	8
401	A59	5c	gray vio	10	8

Engr.

402	A59	25c	rose car	22	20
	Nos. 386-402,C18-C30,CE1,E7 (32)			37.51	42.78

To commemorate the death of Francisco de Goya y Lucientes, painter and engraver.

Nos. 386-399 were issued in connection with the Spanish-American Exposition at Seville.

Nos. 386-402 exist imperf. Values about 6 times those of perf. stamps.

See note after No. 432.

King Alfonso XIII — A61

Two types of the 40c:

Type I

Type II

1930 *Perf. 11½, 12x11½*

406	A61	2c	red brn	9	5

Control Number on Back

407	A61	5c	blk brn	42	5
408	A61	10c	green	2.00	5
409	A61	15c	sl grn	6.50	5
410	A61	20c	dk vio	2.75	45
411	A61	25c	carmine	42	5
412	A61	30c	brn lake	7.50	90
413	A61	40c	dk bl (I)	11.50	60
a.	Type II			15.00	60
414	A61	50c	orange	11.50	1.10
	Nos. 406-414 (9)			42.68	3.30

Nos. 406-414 exist imperf. Value for set, $325.

Bow of "Santa Maria" — A63

Stern of "Santa Maria" — A64

"Santa Maria," "Nina," "Pinta" — A65

Columbus Leaving Palos — A66

Columbus Arriving in America — A67

1930, Sept. 29 **Litho.** *Perf. 12½*

418	A63	1c	ol gray	8	9
419	A64	2c	ol grn	8	9
420	A63	2c	ol grn	8	9
421	A64	5c	red brn	8	9
422	A63	5c	red brn	8	9
423	A64	10c	bl grn	45	50
424	A63	15c	ultra	45	65
425	A64	20c	violet	65	65

Engr.

426	A65	25c	dk red	65	75
427	A66	30c	bis brn, bl & blk brn	2.75	3.00
428	A65	40c	ultra	2.25	2.50
429	A66	50c	dk vio, bl & vio brn	2.75	3.00
430	A65	1p	black	2.75	3.00
431	A67	4p	blk & dk bl	3.00	3.50
432	A67	10p	red brn & dk brn	13.00	15.00
	Nos. 418-432,E8 (16)			29.85	33.75

Christopher Columbus tribute.

Nos. 418 to 432 were privately produced. Their promoters presented a certain quantity of these labels to the Spanish Postal Authorities, who placed them on sale and allowed them to be used for three days, retaining the money obtained from the sale.

This note will also apply to Nos. 345-357, 386-402, 433-448, 557-571, B1-B105, C18-C57, C73-C87, CB1-CB5, CE1, E2, E7-E9, E15 and EB1.

Many so-called "errors" of color and perforation are known.

Nos. 418-432 exist imperf. Values about 5 times those of perf. stamps.

Arms of Spain, Bolivia, Paraguay
A68

Pavilion and Map of Central America — A69

Exhibition Pavilion of Ecuador — A70

Colombia Pavilion — A71

Dominican Republic Pavilion
A72

Uruguay Pavilion
A73

Argentina Pavilion
A74

Chile Pavilion A75

Brazil Pavilion A76

Mexico Pavilion A77

Cuba Pavilion A78

Peru Pavilion A79

U.S. Pavilion A80

Exhibition Pavilion of Portugal — A81

King Alfonso XIII and Queen Victoria — A82

Unwmk.

1930, Oct. 10 Photo. *Perf. 14*

433	A68	1c	bl grn	12	25
434	A69	2c	bis brn	12	25
435	A70	5c	ol brn	12	25
436	A71	10c	dk grn	25	25
437	A72	15c	indigo	25	25
438	A73	20c	violet	25	25
439	A74	25c	car rose	25	25
440	A75	25c	car rose	25	25
441	A76	30c	rose lil	75	1.40
442	A77	40c	sl bl	42	75
443	A78	40c	sl bl	42	75
444	A79	50c	brn org	75	1.40
445	A80	1p	ultra	1.40	1.75
446	A81	4p	brn vio	6.00	7.50
447	A82	10p	brown	75	1.40

Engr. *Perf. 11, 14.*

448	A82	10p	org brn	18.00	15.00
	Nos. 433-448,E9 (17)			30.35	32.20

Spanish-American Union Exhibition, Seville. See Nos. C50-C57.

The note after No. 432 will also apply to Nos. 433 to 448. All values exist imperforate.

Reprints of Nos. 433-448 have blurred colors, yellowish paper and an inferior, almost invisible gum. They sell for 5c to 10c each.

Revolutionary Issues. Madrid Issue.

Regular Issues of 1920-30 Overprinted in Black, Green or Red

REPUBLICA

On No. 314

1931 *Imperf.*

449	A47	1c	bl grn	8	8

On Nos. 406-411

Perf. 11½.

450	A61	2c	red brn (G)	18	22
451	A61	5c	blk brn (R)	18	22
452	A61	10c	green	35	42
453	A61	15c	sl grn (R)	90	1.10
454	A61	20c	dk vio (R)	90	1.10
455	A61	25c	car (G)	1.10	1.25
	Nos. 449-455 (7)			3.69	4.39

First Barcelona Issue.

Regular Issues of 1920-30 Overprinted in Black or Red

REPUBLICA

On No. 314

1931 *Imperf.*

457	A47	1c	bl grn	10	10

On Nos. 406-414

Perf. 11½.

458	A61	2c	red brn	10	10
459	A61	5c	blk brn	10	10
460	A61	10c	green	32	40
461	A61	15c	sl grn (R)	35	45
462	A61	20c	dk vio (R)	35	45
463	A61	25c	carmine	35	45
464	A61	30c	brn lake	2.50	3.00
465	A61	40c	dk bl (R)	85	1.10
466	A61	50c	orange	85	1.10

On Stamp of 1922-26.

467	A49a	1p	bl blk (R)	4.75	6.00
	Nos. 457-467 (11)			10.62	13.25

Nos. 457 to 467 are known both with and without accent over "U".

Second Barcelona Issue.

Regular Issues of 1920-30 Overprinted in Black or Red

REPUBLICA

On No. 314

Imperf.

468	A47	1c	bl grn	10	10

On Nos. 406-414

Perf. 11½

469	A61	2c	red brn	10	10
470	A61	5c	blk brn (R)	18	22
471	A61	10c	green	18	22
472	A61	15c	sl grn (R)	90	1.10
473	A61	20c	dk vio (R)	25	32
474	A61	25c	carmine	25	32
475	A61	30c	brn lake	4.00	5.00
476	A61	40c	dk bl (R)	90	1.10
477	A61	50c	orange	3.00	4.00
	Nos. 468-477 (10)			9.86	12.48

General Issue of the Republic

Nos. 406-414, 342 Overprinted in Blue or Red

República Española.

1931, May 27

478	A61	2c	red brn	16	5
479	A61	5c	blk brn (R)	25	5
480	A61	10c	grn (R)	25	5
481	A61	15c	sl grn (R)	2.25	24
482	A61	20c	dk vio (R)	1.25	60
483	A61	25c	carmine	16	8
484	A61	30c	brn lake	3.50	60
485	A61	40c	dk bl (R)	3.50	30
486	A61	50c	orange	5.75	30
487	A49a	1p	bl blk (R)	32.50	60
	Nos. 478-487 (10)			49.57	2.87

The setting contained 18 repetitions of "Republica Espanola" for each vertical row of 10 stamps. According to its sheet position, a stamp received different parts of the overprinted words.

Overprint position varieties include: reading down on 25c, 30c, 40c and 50c; double on 1p; double, both reading down, on 25c, 40c and 50c.

Fountain of Lions, The Alhambra, Granada A84

Interior of Mosque, Cordoba — A85

Alcántara Bridge and Alcazar, Toledo A86

Francisco García y Santos A87

Puerta del Sol, Madrid, on April 14, 1931 as Republic Was Proclaimed A88

Perf. 12½

1931, Oct. 10 Unwmk. Engr.

491	A84	5c	vio brn	18	30
492	A85	10c	bl grn	28	30
493	A86	15c	dk vio	28	30
494	A85	25c	dp red	35	30
495	A87	30c	ol grn	35	30
496	A84	40c	indigo	65	60
497	A85	50c	org red	65	60
498	A86	1p	black	1.10	1.25
499	A88	4p	red vio	4.25	5.50
500	A88	10p	red brn	15.00	13.00
	Nos. 491-500 (10)			23.09	22.45

Third Pan-American Postal Union Congress, Madrid. See Nos. C62-C67, C01-C06.

Nos. 491-500 exist imperforate. Values about 5 times those of perforated stamps.

Symbolical of Montserrat Cut With a Saw — A89

Abbott Oliva and Monastery Workman — A90

Canceled-to-order stamps are often from remainders. Most collectors of canceled stamps prefer postally used specimens.

"Black Virgin"
A91 A92

Montserrat Monastery — A93

1931, Dec. 9 *Perf. 11, 14*

501	A89	1c	myr grn	1.65	1.50
a	Perf. 14			16.00	21.00
502	A89	2c	red brn	1.00	90
a	Perf. 14			12.50	15.00

Control Number on Back

503	A89	5c	blk brn	1.25	1.25
a	Perf. 14			12.50	15.00
504	A89	10c	yel grn	1.25	1.25
a	Perf. 14			12.50	15.00
505	A90	15c	myr grn	1.50	1.50
a	Perf. 14			16.00	21.00
506	A91	20c	dk vio	2.50	2.00
a	Perf. 11			105.00	125.00
507	A92	25c	lake	3.75	3.00
a	Perf. 14			5.00	6.00
508	A91	30c	dp red	30.00	30.00
a	Perf. 14			40.00	55.00
509	A93	40c	dl bl	21.00	15.00
a	Perf. 11			150.00	150.00
510	A90	50c	dk org	40.00	35.00
a	Perf. 14			55.00	65.00
511	A92	1p	gray blk	40.00	35.00
a	Perf. 11			80.00	90.00
512	A93	4p	lil rose	300.00	275.00
a	Perf. 14			550.00	900.00
513	A92	10p	dp brn	240.00	225.00
a	Perf. 14			550.00	900.00
	Nos. 501-513,E13 (14)			699.90	647.40

Commemorative of the building of the old Monastery at Montserrat, started in 1031, and of the image of the Black Virgin (said to have been carved by St. Luke) which was crowned by Pope Leo XIII in 1881.

Nos. 501-513 exist imperforate. Values about 3 times those of perforated stamps.

See Nos. C68-C72.

Francisco Pi y Margall A95

Joaquin Costa A96

Nicolas Salmeron A97

Pablo Iglesias A99

Emilio Castelar — A100

1931-32 *Perf. 11½.*

Control Number on Back

516	A95	5c	brnsh blk	1.90	30
517	A96	10c	yel grn	4.50	30
518	A97	15c	sl grn	3.25	6
520	A99	25c	lake	15.50	60
b	Imperf.			45.00	
521	A99	30c	car rose	4.75	6
c	Imperf.			45.00	

522	A100	40c dk bl	27.50	2.75
523	A97	50c orange	35.00	4.50
		Nos. 516-523 (7)	92.40	8.57

See Nos. 532, 538, 550, 579, 579a.

Without Control Number

516a	A95	5c brnsh blk ('32)	3.50	8
b		Imperf.	7.25	
517a	A96	10c yel grn ('32)	3.25	8
b		Imperf.	9.50	
518a	A97	15c sl grn ('32)	55	6
b		Imperf.	5.75	
520a	A99	25c lake	25.00	6
c		Imperf.	6.00	
521a	A99	30c car rose	1.65	9
b		Imperf.	5.75	
522a	A100	40c dk bl ('32)	9	8
b		Imperf.	10.50	
523a	A97	50c org ('32)	25.00	45
b		Imperf.	70.00	
		Nos. 516a-523a (7)	59.04	90

Blasco Ibanez A103

Manuel Ruiz-Zorrilla A104

Without Control Number

1931-34 *Perf. 11 1/2*

526	A103	2c red brn ('32)	9	5
a		Imperf.	9.50	
528	A103	5c choc ('34)	8	8
a		Imperf.	2.50	
532	A95	20c dk vio	28	8
a		Imperf.	5.75	
534	A104	25c lake ('34)	45	5
a		Imperf.	2.00	
538	A100	60c ap grn ('32)	9	8
a		Imperf.	5.75	
		Nos. 526-538 (5)	99	34

Cliff Houses, Cuenca A105

Alcazar of Segovia A106

Gate of the Sun at Toledo — A107

1932-38 *Perf. 10*

539	A105	1p gray blk ('38)	10	6
a		Imperf.	1.75	2.50
b		Perf. 11 1/2	16	9
540	A106	4p mag ('38)	32	25
a		Imperf.	4.50	6.00
b		Perf. 11 1/2	65	60
541	A107	10p dp brn ('38)	50	55
a		Perf. 11 1/2	1.50	1.75
b		Imperf.	2.75	5.50

Numeral A108

Santiago Ramon y Cajal A109

1933 Unwmk. Typo. *Imperf.*

542	A108	1c bl grn	8	8

Perf. 11 1/2

543	A108	2c buff	24	8
a		Perf. 13 1/2x13	45	9

See Nos. 592-597.

1934 Engr. *Perf. 11 1/2x11*

545	A109	30c blk brn	7.50	1.00
a		Perf. 14	18.00	27.50
b		Imperf.	35.00	

Type of 1931 and

Mariana Pineda A110

Concepcion Arenal A111

Gumersindo de Azcarate A112

Gaspar Melchor de Jovellanos A113

1935

546	A110	10c green	8	6
a		Imperf.	2.75	
547	A111	15c green	20	10
a		Imperf.	2.75	
548	A112	30c car rose	6.50	15
a		Imperf.	21.00	
549	A113	30c rose red	8	8
a		Imperf.	3.00	
550	A97	50c dk bl	75	30
a		Imperf.	22.50	
		Nos. 546-550 (5)	7.61	69

Shades exist.

Lope's Bookplate A116

Lope de Vega A117

Alcantara and Alcazar, Toledo A118

Perf. 11 1/2x11, 11x11 1/2

1935, Oct. 12

552	A116	15c myr grn	4.75	30
a		Imperf.	125.00	
553	A117	30c rose red	1.75	30
a		Imperf.	6.50	
b		Perf. 14	9.00	10.00
554	A117	50c dk bl	9.50	1.75
a		Imperf.	35.00	
b		Perf. 14	20.00	27.50
555	A118	1p bl blk	16.00	1.25
a		Imperf.	27.50	
b		Perf. 14	22.50	30.00

Issued in commemoration of the 300th anniversary of the death of Lope Felix de Vega Carpio (1562-1635), Spanish dramatist and poet.

Map of Amazon by Bartolomeo Oliva, 16th Century — A119

1935, Oct. 12 *Perf. 11 1/2*

556	A119	30c rose red	1.75	60
a		Perf. 14	15.00	15.00
b		Imperf.	24.00	

Issued in commemoration of the proposed Iglesias Amazon Expedition.

Miguel Moya — A120

Torcuato Luca de Tena — A121

Jose Francos Rodriguez A122

Alejandro Lerroux A123

Nazareth School and Rotary Press — A124

1936, Feb. 14 Photo. *Perf. 12 1/2*

Size: 22x26mm.

557	A120	1c crimson	8	8
558	A121	2c org brn	8	8
559	A122	5c blk brn	8	8
560	A123	10c emerald	8	8

Size: 24x28 1/2mm.

561	A120	15c bl grn	8	8
562	A121	20c violet	8	8
563	A122	25c red vio	8	8
564	A123	30c crimson	8	8

Size: 25 1/2x30 1/2mm.

565	A120	40c orange	42	32
566	A121	50c ultra	20	8
567	A122	60c ol grn	42	32
568	A123	1p gray blk	60	32
569	A124	2p lt bl	5.25	2.25
570	A124	4p lil rose	6.25	4.00
571	A124	10p red brn	10.00	6.50
		Nos. 557-571,E15 (16)	24.08	14.75

Madrid Press Association, 40th anniversary.
Nos. 557-571 exist imperf. Values about 7 times those of perf. stamps.
See note after No. 432. See Nos. C73-C87.

Arms of Madrid — A125

1936, Apr. 2 Engr. *Imperf.*

572	A125	10c brn blk	27.50	27.50
573	A125	15c dk grn	27.50	27.50

Issued in commemoration of the first National Philatelic Exhibition which opened in Madrid, April 2nd, 1936.

"Republica Espanola" A126

Gregorio Fernandez A127

1936 Litho. *Perf. 11 1/2, 13 1/2x13*

574	A126	2c org brn	8	5

1936, Mar. 10 Engr. *Perf. 11 1/2*

576	A127	30c carmine	1.00	65
a		Perf. 14	10.00	10.00
b		Imperf.	14.00	

Issued to commemorate the tercentenary of the death of Gregorio Fernandez, sculptor.

Type of 1931 and

Pablo Iglesias
A128 A129

Velazquez A130

Fermin Salvoechea A131

1936-38 *Perf. 11, 11 1/2, 11 1/2x11*

577	A128	30c rose red	9	7
578	A129	30c car rose	1.00	30
579	A100	40c car rose ('37)	1.00	30
580	A129	45c car ('37)	15	6
581	A130	50c dk bl	9	6
582	A131	60c ind ('37)	65	60
583	A131	60c dp org ('38)	4.25	3.50
		Nos. 577-583 (7)	7.23	4.89

Perf. 14

577a	A128	30c rose red	6.00
578a	A129	30c car rose	6.50
579a	A100	40c car rose	6.00
580a	A129	45c carmine	4.75
582a	A131	60c indigo	5.75
583a	A131	60c dp org	10.50
		Nos. 577a-583a (6)	39.50

Nos. 577-583 exist imperf. Value, set $70.

Statue of Liberty, Spanish and U.S. Flags A132

1938, June 1 Photo. *Perf. 11 1/2*

585	A132	1p multi	9.00	9.00
a		Imperf., pair	57.50	57.50
b		Imperf. vert., pair	67.50	67.50
c		Souv. sheet of 1	18.00	20.00
d		As "c," imperf.	200.00	200.00

150th anniv. of the Constitution of the US.
Nos. 585c, 585d have control numbers on front. Size: 102x104mm.

No. 289 Surcharged in Black

14 ABRIL 1938
VII Aniversario
de la República
45 cts.

1938 *Perf. 14*

586	A36	45c on 15c vio	8.00	8.00

7th anniversary of the Republic.

No. 289 Surcharged in Black:

a

Fiesta del Trabajo
1 MAYO
b **1938**
1 Peseta

1938, May 1

587	A36	45c on 15c vio	2.50	3.00
588	A36	1p on 15c vio	3.50	4.50

Issued to commemorate Labor Day.

No. 507 Surcharged in Black

2'50 PTAS.

1938, Nov. 10 *Perf. 11 ½*

589	A92	2.50p on 25c lake	12	14
b		Perf. 14	1.90	3.50

Types of 1933-36 Surcharged in Blue or Red

45 céntimos.

1938 *Perf. 10, 11, 13 ½x13, 13x14.*

590	A108	45c on 1c grn (R)	30	18
b		Imperf.	4.50	4.50
590A	A108	45c on 2c buff (Bl)	24.00	16.00
591	A126	45c on 2c org brn (Bl)	10	5

Numeral Type of 1933

1938-39 **Litho.** *Perf. 11 ½, 13*

White or Gray Paper.

592	A108	5c gray brn	10	6
593	A108	10c yel grn	10	6
594	A108	15c sl grn	10	6
595	A108	20c vio, gray paper	10	6
596	A108	25c red vio	10	6
597	A108	30c scarlet	10	6
		Nos. 592-597 (6)	60	36

"Republic" — A133

1938 *Perf. 11 ½*

598	A133	40c rose red	10	5
599	A133	45c car rose	10	5
a		Printed on both sides	10.00	10.00
600	A133	50c ultra	10	5
601	A133	60c dp ultra	40	60

Nos. 598-601 exist imperf. Value for set $16.50.

Machine Gunners A134

Infantry — A135

Perf. 11 ½x11, 11x11 ½, Imperf.

1938, Sept. 1 **Photo.**

602	A134	25c dk grn	5.00	8.25
603	A135	45c red brn	5.00	8.25

Issued in commemoration of the 43rd Division of the Republican Army. Sold only at the Philatelic Agency and for foreign exchange.

Blast Furnace A136

Steel Mill and Sculpture, "Defenders of Numantia" A137

1938, Aug. 9 *Perf. 16*

604	A136	45c black	15	15
605	A137	1.25p dk bl	15	15

Issued in honor of the workers of Sagunto.

"Correo Submarino"

A set of six stamps and souvenir sheet inscribed "Correo Submarino" was issued Aug. 11, 1938. It was sold at double face value and only at the Philatelic Agency. The stamps and sheet were used on 300 agency-prepared covers carried on a single submarine voyage from Barcelona to Mahon, Minorca. Value for set of six, perf. $475, imperf. $525; souvenir sheet, $400.

Riflemen A138

Machine Gunners A139

Bomb Throwing — A140

1938, Nov. 25 **Engr.** *Perf. 10*

606	A138	5c sepia	1.90	2.75
607	A138	10c dp vio	1.90	2.75
608	A138	25c bl grn	1.90	2.75
609	A139	45c rose red	1.50	2.25
610	A139	60c dk bl	3.25	3.50
611	A139	1.20p black	75.00	75.00
612	A140	2p orange	24.00	25.00
613	A140	5p dk brn	125.00	105.00
614	A140	10p dk bl grn	27.50	24.00
		Nos. 606-614 (9)	261.95	243.00

Issued in honor of the Militia. Sold only at the Philatelic Agency and for foreign exchange. Exist imperf.

Spanish State

Arms of Spain — A141

1936 **Litho.** *Imperf.*

Thin Transparent Paper.

615	A141	30c blue	180.00
616	A141	30c pale grn	180.00

Perf. 11.

Thick Wove Paper.

617	A141	30c dk bl	450.00	75.00

Issued in Granada during siege. After the city was liberated, these stamps were used throughout the province of Granada.

A143

Cathedral of Burgos A145

University of Salamanca A146

Cathedral del Pilar, Zaragoza A147

"La Giralda," Seville A148

Xavier Castle, Navarre — A149

Court of Lions, Alhambra at Granada — A150

Mosque, Córdoba — A151

Alcántara Bridge and Alcázar, Toledo — A152

Soldier Carrying Flag — A153

Troops Landing at Algeciras — A154

Two types of 30c:

Type I: Imprint 12 mm. long; "3" does not touch frame.

Type II: Imprint 8 mm. long; "3" touches frame.

1936 **Unwmk.** **Litho.** *Imperf.*

623	A143	1c green	3.25	3.00

Perf. 11 ½.

624	A143	2c org brn	60	45
625	A145	5c gray brn	65	60
626	A146	10cgreen	50	30
627	A147	15cdl grn	50	30
628	A148	25crose lake	85	30
629	A149	30ccar (I)	85	45
a		Type II	1.10	60
630	A150	50cdp bl	10.00	7.50
631	A151	60cyel grn	1.00	60
632	A152	1p black	4.00	2.50
633	A153	4p rose vio, red & yel	35.00	21.00
634	A154	10plt brn	42.50	18.00
		Nos. 623-634 (12)	99.70	55.00

Nos. 624-634 exist imperf. Value, set $375.

Nos. 625-631, 633-634 were privately overprinted "VIA AEREA" and plane, supposedly for use in Ifni.

Nos. 542-543 Surcharged "Habilitado 0'05 ptas." in Two Lines

1936 *Imperf., Perf. 11 ½*

634A	A108	5c on 1c bl grn	2.75	2.75
634B	A108	5c on 2c buff	2.75	2.75
634C	A108	10c on 1c bl grn	2.75	2.75
634D	A108	15c on 2c buff	2.75	2.75

Issued in the Balearic Islands to meet a shortage of these values. Nos. 634A and 634C are imperf., Nos. 634B and 634D are perf. 11 ½.

St. James of Compostela — A155

St. James Cathedral A156

Pórtico de la Gloria A157

Two types of 30c:

I. No dots in "1937".

II. Dot before and after "1937".

1937 *Perf. 11 ½, 11x11 ½*

635	A155	15c vio brn	1.25	1.10
636	A156	30c rose red (I)	4.00	50
a		Type II	12.00	12.50
637	A157	1p bl & org	12.50	3.00
a		Center invtd.	475.00	225.00

Holy Year of Compostela. Nos. 635-637 exist imperf. Value for set $140.

"Estado Espanol" A159 A160

"El Cid" — A161

Isabella I — A162

Two types of 5c, 30c and 10p:
5 Centimos: Type I Imprint 9½ mm. long. Type II Imprint 14 mm. long.
30 Centimos: Type I Imprint, "Hija De B. Fournier Burgos". Type II Imprint, "Fournier Burgos".
10 Pesetas: Type I "10" 2½ mm. high. Type II "10" 3 mm. high.

With Imprint

1936-40 ***Imperf.***

638	A159	1c green	7	5

Perf. 11.

639	A159	1c green	7	7
640	A160	2c brown	7	5

Perf. 11, 11½, 11½x11, 11½x10½.

641	A161	5c brn (I)	45	10
642	A161	5c brn (II)	8	5
643	A161	10c green	12	5

Perf. 11, 11x11½.

644	A162	15c gray blk	14	5
645	A162	20c dk vio	30	8
646	A162	25c brn lake	15	5
647	A162	30c rose (I)	40	5
648	A162	30c rose (II)	12.50	1.25
649	A162	40c orange	1.00	8
650	A162	50c dk bl	1.00	8
651	A162	60c yellow	25	8
652	A162	1p blue	10.50	32
653	A162	4p magenta	15.00	3.00
654	A161	10p dk bl (I) ('37)	50.00	30.00
655	A161	10p dp bl (II) ('40)	25.00	10.00
		Nos. 638-655 (18)	117.10	45.41

No. 639 is said to have been privately perforated. See Nos. 662-667.

Ferdinand the Catholic A163

Emblem of the Falange A164

1938 ***Perf. 10½, 11½x11***

Imprint: "Lit Fournier Vitoria".

656	A163	15c dp grn	2.00	7
657	A163	30c dp red	4.00	7

Imprint: "Fournier Vitoria"

Perf. 10

658	A163	15c dp grn	1.25	6
659	A163	20c purple	8.25	1.10
660	A163	25c brn car	65	6
661	A163	30c dp red	4.00	6
		Nos. 656-661 (6)	20.15	1.42

Nos. 656-661 exist imperf.; value for set, $60. Part-perf. varieties exist.

Without Imprint

1938-48 ***Perf. 11, 13½***

Two types of the 15 Centimos.
Type I. Medieval style numerals with diagonal line through "5".
Type II. Modern numerals. Narrower "5" without diagonal line.

662	A159	1c grn, imperf.	8	8
663	A160	2c brn (18½x22mm;'40)	8	8
a		2c bis brn (17½x21mm;'48)	8	8
664	A161	5c gray brn ('39)	20	8
665	A161	10c dk car	30	8
a		10c rose	70	10
666	A161	15c dk grn (I)	1.00	8
666A	A161	15c dk grn (II)	1.00	8
667	A162	70c dk bl ('39)	60	12
		Nos. 662-667 (7)	3.26	60

1938, July 17 ***Perf. 10***

668	A164	15c bl grn & lt grn	3.75	4.00
669	A164	25c rose red & rose	3.75	4.00
670	A164	30c bl & lt bl	1.75	2.00
671	A164	1p brn & yel	60.00	50.00

Second anniversary of the Civil War.

Isabella I — A165

Gen. Francisco Franco — A166

1938-39 **Litho.** ***Perf. 10***

672	A165	20c brt vio ('39)	42	10
673	A165	25c brn car	5.50	52
674	A165	30c rose red	28	15
675	A165	40c dl vio	28	6
676	A165	50c ind ('39)	22.50	2.00
677	A165	1p dp bl	7.75	70
		Nos. 672-677 (6)	36.73	3.53

Imprint: "Sanchez Toda"

1939-40 ***Perf. 10.***

678	A166	20c brt vio	20	8
679	A166	25c rose lake	20	8
680	A166	30c rose car	15	8
681	A166	40c sl grn	15	8
682	A166	45c ver ('40)	1.10	1.50
683	A166	50c indigo	15	8
684	A166	60c orange	1.65	2.00
685	A166	70c blue	20	8
686	A166	1p black	6.50	8
687	A166	2p dk brn	10.00	1.00
688	A166	4p dk vio	50.00	10.00
689	A166	10p lt brn	22.50	22.50
		Nos. 678-689 (12)	92.80	37.56

Nos. 686 to 689 have value and "Pta." on one line while Nos. 702 to 705 have value and "Pta." on two lines.

Without Imprint.

Perf. 9½x10½, 12½x13

1939-51 **Litho.** **Unwmk.**

690	A166	5c dl brn vio ('40)	50	12
691	A166	10c brn org	1.65	60
692	A166	15c lt grn	50	15
693	A166	20c brt vio	50	8
694	A166	25c dp cl	50	8
695	A166	30c blue	50	8
696	A166	35c aqua ('51)	40	5
697	A166	40c Prus grn ('40)	65	8
a		40c grnsh blk	50	5
698	A166	45c ultra ('41)	50	9
699	A166	50c ind ('40)	32	8
a		Perf. 11½ ('47)	6.00	3.00
700	A166	60c dl org ('40)	42	20
701	A166	70c bl ('40)	50	8
702	A166	1p gray blk ('40)	4.00	8
703	A166	2p dl brn ('40)	6.00	20
704	A166	4p dl rose ('40)	15.00	20
705	A166	10p lt brn ('40)	115.00	2.50
		Nos. 690-705 (16)	146.94	4.67

The 40c exists in three types, with variations in the value tablet: I. "CTS" does not touch bottom line. II. Light background in tablet. "CTS" touches bottom line. III. As type I, but with well defined lines of white and color around rectangle.

The 60c exists in two types: I. Top and left side of value tablet touch rest of design. II. Tablet separated from rest of design by white lines.

Five values exist with perf. 10: 5c, 10c, 45c, 4p and 10p.

The imperforate 10c dull claret, type A166, without imprint, is a postal tax stamp, RA14.

1944 **Redrawn**

706	A166	1p gray	40.00	60

"PTS" instead of "PTA" as No. 702.
Nos. 690-706 exist imperforate.

The value reads "PTAS" instead of "PTS".

1944 **Unwmk.** ***Perf. 9½x10½, 13***

709	A166	10p brown	12.00	30

General Franco A167

St. John of the Cross A168

1942-48 **Engr.** ***Perf. 12½x13***

712	A167	40c chestnut	32	12
713	A167	75c dk bl, perf. 9½x10½ ('46)	2.00	30
714	A167	90c dk grn ('48)	20	8
a		Perf. 9½x10½ ('47)	85	12
715	A167	1.35p pur ('48)	20	8
a		Perf. 9½x10½ ('46)	65	30

1942 **Litho.** ***Perf. 9½x10½***

721	A168	20c violet	42	12
722	A168	40c salmon	1.25	60
723	A168	75c ultra	1.25	1.25

400th birth anniversary of St. John of the Cross (1542-1591).
Nos. 721 to 723 exist imperforate.

Holy Year Issues.

Statue in St. James Cathedral A169

St. James of Compostela A170

Incense Burner — A171

Perf. 9½x10½

1943, Oct. **Litho.** **Unwmk.**

724	A169	20c dp bl	18	12
725	A170	40c dk red brn	45	20
726	A171	75c dp bl	1.90	1.50

Carvings in St. James Cathedral
A172 A174

St. James — A173

St. James' Casket — A175

East Portal of Cathedral A176

St. James Cathedral A177

1943-44 ***Perf. 9½x10½, 10½x9½***

727	A172	20c rose red ('44)	18	12
728	A173	40c dl grn	40	20
729	A174	75c dk bl ('44)	2.50	1.90

1944

730	A175	20c red vio	18	12
731	A176	40c dl brn	50	20
732	A177	75c brt bl	22.50	21.00

Millenium of Castile Issues.

Arms of Soria A178

Arms of Castile A179

Arms of Avila A180

Fortress A181

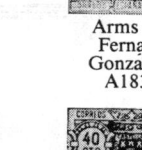

Arms of Segovia A182

Arms of Fernan Gonzalez A183

Arms of Avila A184

Arms of Burgos A185

Arms of Santander — A186

Perf. 9½x10½

1944 **Unwmk.** **Litho.**

733	A178	20c violet	18	15
734	A179	40c dl brn	2.50	45
735	A180	75c blue	2.50	2.50

1944

736	A181	20c rose vio	18	15
737	A182	40c dl brn	2.50	28
738	A183	75c dl bl	2.25	2.50

1944

739	A184	20c red vio	18	15
740	A185	40c dl brn	1.90	28
741	A186	75c blue	3.00	3.00
		Nos. 733-741 (9)	15.19	9.46

Francisco de Quevedo — A187

1945, Sept. 8 **Engr.** ***Perf. 10***

742	A187	40c dk brn	65	52

Issued to commemorate the 300th anniversary of the death of Francisco Gomez de Quevedo y Villegas (1580-1645), writer.

Type of Semi-Postal Stamp, 1940, Without Imprint at Lower Left and Right.

1946, Jan. 1 **Litho.** ***Perf. 11***

743	SP20	50c (40c + 10c) sl grn & rose vio	1.50	20

No. 743 was used as an ordinary postage stamp of 50c denomination.

Elio Antonio de Nebrija A188

University of Salamanca and Signature of Francisco de Vitoria A189

1946, Oct. 12 Engr. *Perf. 9½x10*

744	A188	50c dp plum	30	30
745	A189	75c dp bl	40	45

Issued in connection with Stamp Day and the Day of the Race, Oct. 12, 1946. See No. C121.

Francisco de Goya — A190

Benito Jeronimo Feijoo y Montenegro — A191

1946, Oct 26

746	A190	25c dp plum	7	7
747	A190	50c green	7	7
748	A190	75c dk bl	35	35

Issued to commemorate the bicentenary of the birth of Francisco de Goya.

1947, June 1 Unwmk.

749	A191	50c dp grn	40	30

Don Quixote Reading A192

"Don Quixote" by Zuloaga A193

1947, Oct. 9 Engr. *Perf. 9½x10½*

750	A192	50c sepia	24	18
751	A193	75c dk bl	48	38

Issued to commemorate Stamp Day and the 400th anniversary of the birth of Miguel de Cervantes Saavedra. See No. C122.

General Franco
A194 A195

1948 Litho. *Perf. 12½x13*

752	A194	15c green	12	10
753	A195	50c rose vio	1.00	10

See Nos. 760-768, 780, 801-803.

Hernando Cortez A196

Mateo Aleman A197

Perf. 12½x13, 9½x10½(70c)

1948, June 15 Engr.

754	A196	35c black	24	15
755	A197	70c dk vio brn	1.75	1.75
a		Perf. 12½x13	22.50	27.50

Ferdinand III (The Saint) A198

Grandson of Adm. Ramon de Bonifaz A199

1948, Sept. 20 Litho. *Perf. 12½x13*

756	A198	25c rose vio	20	10
757	A199	30c scarlet	16	10

Issued to commemorate the 700th anniversary of the Spanish navy and of the capture of Seville by Ferdinand the Saint.

Jose de Salamanca y Mayol A200

Train Crossing Pancorbo Viaduct A201

Perf. 12½x13, 13x12½.

1948, Oct. 9 Unwmk.

758	A200	50c brown	42	10
759	A201	5p dp grn	1.25	15

Issued to commemorate the centenary of Spanish railroads. See No. C125.

Franco Types of 1948.

1948-49 Litho. *Perf. 12½x13*

760	A194	5c brown	6	6
761	A195	25c vermilion	6	6
762	A195	35c bl grn	6	6
763	A195	40c red brn	40	6
764	A195	45c car rose ('49)	28	8
765	A194	50c bister	18	9
766	A195	70c pur ('49)	1.25	22
767	A195	75c dk vio bl	1.25	22
768	A195	1p rose pink	3.25	6
		Nos. 760-768 (9)	6.79	91

No. 761 exists imperforate.

Symbols of U.P.U. A202

1949, Oct. 9

769	A202	50c red brn	40	15
770	A202	75c vio bl	40	40

75th anniv. of the UPU. See No. C126.

St. John of God — A203

Pedro Calderon de la Barca — A204

1950, Mar. 8 Engr. Unwmk.

771	A203	1p dk vio	9.25	2.75

Issued to commemorate the 400th anniversary of the death of St. John of God, humanitarian.

1950-53 Photo. *Perf. 12½*

Designs: 10c Lope de Vega. 15c, Tirso de Molina. 20c, Juan Ruiz de Alarcon, dramatist. 50c, St. Antonio Maria Claret y Clara.

772	A204	5c brn ('51)	10	8
773	A204	10c dp rose brn ('51)	10	8
773A	A204	15c dk sl grn ('53)	20	8
774	A204	20c violet	22	8

Engr. *Perf. 12½x13.*

775	A204	50c dk bl ('51)	3.50	1.50
		Nos. 772-775 (5)	4.12	1.82

Stamp of 1850 — A205

Queen Isabella I — A206

1950, Oct. 12 Engr. *Imperf.*

776	A205	50c purple	6.00	6.00
777	A205	75c ultra	6.00	6.00
778	A205	10p dk sl grn	80.00	90.00
779	A205	15p red	80.00	90.00
		Nos. 776-779,C127-C130 (8)	268.50	298.50

Centenary of Spain's stamps.

Franco Type of 1948.

1950 Litho. *Perf. 12½x13*

780	A195	45c red	75	15

1951, Apr. 22 Photo. *Perf. 12½*

781	A206	50c brown	35	32
782	A206	75c blue	60	32
783	A206	90c rose brn	35	25
784	A206	1.50p orange	7.25	5.00
785	A206	2.80p ol grn	13.00	13.00
		Nos. 781-785 (5)	21.55	18.89

Issued to commemorate the 500th anniversary of the birth of Queen Isabella I. See Nos. C132-C136.

Ferdinand, the Catholic A210

Maria Michaela Dermaisieres A211

1952, May 10 Photo. *Perf. 13*

787	A210	50c green	45	35
788	A210	75c indigo	2.50	1.25
789	A210	90c rose brn	28	35
790	A210	1.50p orange	5.50	4.75
791	A210	2.80p brown	9.50	10.50
		Nos. 787-791 (5)	18.23	17.20

Issued to commemorate the 500th anniversary of the birth of Ferdinand the Catholic of Spain. See Nos. C139-C143.

1952, May 26 *Perf. 12½x13*

792	A211	90c claret	20	15

Issued to publicize the 35th International Eucharistic Congress, Barcelona, 1952. See No. C137.

Dr. Santiago Ramon y Cajal — A212

Portrait: 4.50p, Dr. Jaime Ferran y Clua.

1952, July 8 Photo.

793	A212	2p brt bl	14.00	32
794	A212	4.50p red brn	50	52

Issued to commemorate the centenary of the births of Dr. Santiago Ramon y Cajal and Dr. Jaime Ferran y Clua.

University Seal — A213

Luis de Leon — A214

Cathedral of Salamanca A215

Perf. 12½x13, 13x12½

1953, Oct. 12

795	A213	50c dp mag	35	22
796	A214	90c dk ol gray	1.65	1.65
797	A215	2p brown	11.50	2.50

Issued in connection with Stamp Day, Oct. 12, 1953, to commemorate the 700th anniversary of the founding of the University of Salamanca.

The Magdalene — A216

1954, Jan. 10 *Perf. 12½x13*

798	A216	1.25p dp mag	12	12

Issued to commemorate the 300th anniversary of the death of Jose de Ribera, painter.

St. James of Compostela A217

St. James Cathedral A218

1954, Mar. 1

799	A217	50c dk brn	15	15
800	A218	3p blue	26.00	1.75

Holy Year of Compostela, 1954.

Franco Types of 1948

1954 Litho. *Perf. 12½*

801	A194	5c ol gray	12	5
802	A195	30c dp grn	12	12
803	A194	80c dl car rose	2.00	15

Virgin by Alonso Cano A219

Marcelino Menendez y Pelayo A220

Virgins: 15c, Begoña. 25c, Of the Abandoned. 30c, Black. 50c, Of the Pillar. 60c,

Covadonga. 80c, Kings'. 1p, Almudena. 2p, Africa. 3p, Guadalupe.

1954, July 18 Photo. *Perf. 12½x13*

804	A219	10c dk car rose	8	7
805	A219	15c ol grn	8	7
806	A219	25c purple	16	7
807	A219	30c brown	18	7
808	A219	50c brn ol	60	7
809	A219	60c gray	18	7
810	A219	80c grnsh gray	2.72	7
811	A219	1p lil gray	2.75	7
812	A219	2p red brn	85	7
813	A219	3p brt bl	75	75
		Nos. 804-813 (10)	8.35	1.38

Issued to publicize the Marian Year.

1954, Oct. 12

814	A220	80c dk gray grn	5.00	30

Issued to publicize Stamp Day, October 12, 1954.

Gen. Franco — A221

Imprint: "F.N.M.T."

1954-56 *Perf. 12½x13*

815	A221	10c dk car lake	7	5
816	A221	15c bister	7	5
817	A221	20c dk ol grn ('55)	7	5
818	A221	25c bl vio	7	5
819	A221	30c brown	7	5
820	A221	40c rose vio ('55)	7	5
821	A221	50c dk brn ol	7	5
822	A221	60c dk vio brn	8	5
823	A221	70c dk grn	12	5
824	A221	80c dk bl grn	8	5
825	A221	1p dp org	8	5
826	A221	1.40p lil rose ('56)	14	12
827	A221	1.50p lt bl grn ('56)	8	5
828	A221	1.80p emer ('56)	14	12
829	A221	2p red	17.50	80
830	A221	2p red lil ('56)	8	5
831	A221	3p Prus bl	12	5
832	A221	5p dk red brn	22	5
833	A221	6p dk gray ('55)	22	12
834	A221	8p brt vio ('56)	12	10
835	A221	10p yel grn ('55)	35	10
		Nos. 815-835 (21)	19.82	2.11

Coils: The 1.50p, No. 830, the 3p and the 6p were issued in coils in brighter tones (the 3p in 1974, others in 1973). Every fifth stamp has a black control number on the back.
See Nos. 937-938, 1852-1855.

St. Ignatius of Loyola — A222

St. Ignatius and Loyola Palace A223

Perf. 13x12½, 12½x13
1955, Oct. 12 Photo. Unwmk.

836	A222	25c dl pur	15	12
837	A223	60c bister	65	45
838	A222	80c Prus grn	2.75	25

Issued to mark the fourth centenary of the death of St. Ignatius of Loyola, founder of the Jesuit Order and to publicize the Day of the Stamp, 1955.

Footnotes often refer you to other stamps of the same design.

Symbols of Telegraph and Radio Communication A224

St. Vincent Ferrer A225

1955, Dec. 8 *Perf. 13x12½*

839	A224	15c dk ol bis	40	15
840	A224	80c Prus grn	6.50	25
841	A224	3p brt bl	12.50	1.25

Spanish telegraph system centenary.

1955, Dec. 20 *Perf. 13*

842	A225	15c ol bis	40	25

Canonization of St. Vincent Ferrer, fifth centenary.

"Holy Family" by El Greco A226

Marching Soldiers and Dove A227

1955, Dec. 24 *Perf. 13x12½*

843	A226	80c dk grn	3.00	50

1956, July 17 Unwmk.

844	A227	15c ol bis & brn	10	6
845	A227	50c lt ol grn & ol	60	28
846	A227	80c mag & grnsh blk	5.00	22
847	A227	3p ultra & dp bl	5.00	1.40

20th anniversary of Civil War.

Ciudad de Toledo A228

1956, Aug. 3 *Perf. 12½x13*

848	A228	3p blue	4.00	1.50

Issued to publicize the voyage of the S. S. Ciudad de Toledo to Central and South America carrying the First Floating (Industrial) Exposition.

Black Virgin of Montserrat A229

Archangel Gabriel by Fra Angelico A230

Design: 60c, Monastery of Montserrat, mountains and crucifix.

1956, Sept. 11 *Perf. 13x12½*

849	A229	15c bister	7	7
850	A229	60c vio blk	15	20
851	A229	80c bl grn	35	42

Issued to commemorate the 75th anniversary of the coronation of the Black Virgin of Montserrat.

1956, Oct. 12 Engr.

852	A230	80c dl grn	90	45

Stamp Day, Oct. 12.

Statistical Chart A231

1956, Nov. 3 *Perf. 12½x13*

853	A231	15c dk ol bis	32	28
854	A231	80c green	3.25	55
855	A231	1p red org	3.25	55

Centenary of Spanish Statistics.

Hermitage and Monument A232

1956, Dec. 4

856	A232	80c dl bl grn	3.00	25

Issued to commemorate the 20th anniversary of the nomination of Gen. Franco as chief of state and commander in chief of the army.

Hungarian Children A233

St. Marguerite Alacoque's Vision of Jesus A234

1956, Dec. 17 *Perf. 13x12½*

857	A233	10c brn lake	6	6
858	A233	15c dk bis	14	6
859	A233	50c ol gray	30	12
860	A233	80c dk bl grn	2.00	10
861	A233	1p red org	2.25	10
862	A233	3p brt bl	6.00	1.50
		Nos. 857-862 (6)	10.75	1.94

Issued in sympathy to the children of Hungary.

1957, Oct. 12 Photo. Unwmk.

863	A234	15c dk ol bis	7	10
864	A234	60c vio blk	25	15
865	A234	80c dk bl grn	28	15

Issued to commemorate the centenary of the feast of the Sacred Heart of Jesus and for Stamp Day 1957.

Gonzalo de Cordoba — A235

1958, Feb. 28 Engr. *Perf. 13x12½*

866	A235	1.80p yel grn	22	10

Issued in honor of El Gran Capitan, 15th century military leader.

"The Parasol," by Goya — A236

"Wife of the Bookseller of Carretas Street" — A237

Goya Paintings: 50c, Duke of Fernan-Nunez. 60c, The Crockery Seller. 70c, Isabel Cobos de Porcel. 80c, Goya by Vicente Lopez. 1p, "El Pelele" (Carnival Doll). 1.80p, Goya's grandson Marianito. 2p, The Vintage. 3p, The Drinker.

1958, Mar. 24 Photo. *Perf. 13*
Gold Frame.

867	A236	15c bister	8	6
868	A237	40c plum	8	6
869	A237	50c ol gray	8	6
870	A237	60c vio gray	8	6
871	A237	70c dp yel grn	8	8
872	A237	80c dk sl grn	8	8
873	A237	1p org red	12	8
874	A237	1.80p brt grn	12	8
875	A237	2p red lil	25	28
876	A236	3p brt bl	40	50
		Nos. 867-876 (10)	1.37	1.34

Issued to honor Francisco Jose de Goya and for the "Day of the Stamp," March 24.
See Nos. 1111-1114.

Exhibition Emblem and Globe — A238

1958, June 7 *Perf. 13x12½*

877	A238	80c car, dk brn & gray	18	15
a.		Souvenir sheet, imperf.	22.50	22.50
878	A238	3p car, vio blk & bl	85	75
a.		Souvenir sheet, imperf.	22.50	22.50

No. 877a sold for 2p, No. 878a sold for 5p.
Issued for the Universal and International Exposition at Brussels.

Charles V A239

Various Portraits of Charles V: 50c, 1.80p, with helmet. 70c, 2p, facing left. 80c, 3p, with beret.

1958, July 30 Photo. *Perf. 13*

879	A239	15c buff & brn	8	6
880	A239	50c lt grn & ol brn	8	6
881	A239	70c gray, grn & blk	18	15
882	A239	80c pale brn & Prus grn	16	6
883	A239	1p bis & brick red	18	6
884	A239	1.80p pale grn & brt grn	16	12

885 A239 2p gray & lil 40 48
886 A239 3p pale brn & brt bl 1.10 1.00
Nos. 879-886 (8) 2.34 1.99

Issued to commemorate the 400th anniversary of the death of Charles V (Carlos I of Spain.)

Escorial and Streamlined Train — A240

Designs: 60c, 2p, Railroad bridge at Despenaperros (vert.). 80c, 3p, Train and Castle de La Mota.

1958, Sept. 29 *Perf. 12½x13*
887 A240 15c dk ol bis 7 7
888 A240 60c dk pur 7 7
889 A240 80c dk bl grn 12 7
890 A240 1p red org 35 7
891 A240 2p red lil 35 7
892 A240 3p blue 1.65 65
Nos. 887-892 (6) 2.61 1.00

International Railroad Congress, Madrid, Sept. 28-Oct. 7.

Velazquez Self-portrait A240a

Velazquez Paintings: 15c, The Drinkers (horiz.). 40c, The Spinners. 50c, Surrender of Breda. 60c, The Little Princesses. 70c, Prince Balthazar. 1p, The Coronation of Our Lady. 1.80p, Aesop. 2p, Vulcan's Forge. 3p, Menippus.

1959, Mar. 24 **Photo.** *Perf. 13*
Gold Frame
893 A240a 15c dk brn 7 7
894 A240a 40c rose vio 7 7
895 A240a 50c olive 7 7
896 A240a 60c blk brn 7 7
897 A240a 70c dp yel grn 7 7
898 A240a 80c dk sl grn 10 7
899 A240a 1p org red 12 7
900 A240a 1.80p emerald 7 7
901 A240a 2p red lil 14 15
902 A240a 3p brt bl 32 42
Nos. 893-902 (10) 1.10 1.13

Issued to honor Diego de Silva Velazquez (1599-1660) and for Stamp Day, Mar. 24.

Civil War Memorial — A241

1959, Apr 1. **Litho.** **Unwmk.**
903 A241 80c yel grn & dk sl grn 12 8

Issued to commemorate the inauguration of the war memorial at the monastery of the Holy Cross in the Valley of the Fallen.

Louis XIV and Philip II — A242

1959, Oct. 24 **Photo.** *Perf. 13x12½*
904 A242 1p gold & rose brn 12 8

Issued to commemorate the 300th anniversary of the signing of the Treaty of the Pyrenees. Design shows the French-Spanish meeting at Isle des Faisans in 1659, as pictured in the Lebrun Tapestry, Versailles.

Monastery of Guadalupe A243

Designs: 80c, Monastery, different view. 1p, Portals.

1959, Nov. 16 **Engr.** *Perf. 12½x13*
905 A243 15c lt red brn 8 10
906 A243 80c slate 15 10
907 A243 1p rose red 15 10

Issued to commemorate the 50th anniversary of the entrance of the Franciscan Brothers into Guadalupe monastery.

Holy Family, by Goya — A244

1959, Dec. 10 **Photo.** *Perf. 13x12½*
908 A244 1p org brn 18 8

Catalogue values for unused stamps in this section, from this point to the end of the section, are for Never Hinged items.

Lidian Bull A245

Bullfighter, 19th Century — A246

Designs: 20c, Rounding up bulls. 25c, Running with the bulls, Pamplona. 30c, Bull entering arena. 50c, Bullfighting with cape. 70c, Bullfighting with banderillas. 80c, 1p, 1.40p, 1.50p, Fighting with muleta, various poses. 1.80p, Mounted bullfighter placing banderillas.

Perf. 12½x13, 13x12½
1960, Feb. 29 **Engr.** **Unwmk.**
909 A245 15c sep & bis 12 10
910 A245 20c vio & bl vio 12 10
911 A246 25c gray 12 10
912 A246 30c sep & bis 12 10
913 A246 50c dl vio & sep 18 10
914 A246 70c sep & sl grn 18 10
915 A246 80c bl grn & grn 12 10
916 A246 1p red & brn 30 10
917 A246 1.40p brn & lake 12 10
918 A246 1.50p grnsh bl & grn 12 10
919 A245 1.80p grn & dk grn 12 10
920 A246 5p brn & brn car 65 45
Nos. 909-920,C159-C162 (16) 3.46 2.20

Murillo Self-portrait A246a

Christ of Lepanto A247

Murillo Paintings: 25c, The Good Shepherd. 40c, Rebecca and Eliezer. 50c, Virgin of the Rosary. 70c, Immacualte Conception. 80c, Children with Shell. 1.50p, Holy Family with Bird (horiz.). 2.50p, Children Playing Dice. 3p, Children Eating. 5p, Children counting Money.

1960, Mar. 24 **Photo.** *Perf. 13*
Gold Frame
921 A246a 25c dl vio 12 10
922 A246a 40c plum 12 10
923 A246a 50c ol gray 15 10
924 A246a 70c dp yel grn 15 10
925 A246a 80c dp grn 15 10
926 A246a 1p vio brn 15 10
927 A246a 1.50p bl grn 15 10
928 A246a 2.50p rose car 22 10
929 A246a 3p brt bl 1.50 80
930 A246a 5p dp red brn 65 20
Nos. 921-930 (10) 3.36 1.80

Issued to honor Bartolome Esteban Murillo (1617-1682) and for Stamp Day, Mar. 24.

1960, Mar. 27 *Perf. 13x12½*

Designs: 80c, 2.50p, 10p, Holy Family Church, Barcelona.

931 A247 70c brn car & grn 2.50 2.00
932 A247 80c blk & ol grn 2.50 2.00
933 A247 1p cl & brt red 2.50 2.00
934 A247 2.50p brt vio & gray vio 2.50 2.00
935 A247 5p sep & bis 2.50 2.00
936 A247 10p sep & bis 2.50 2.00
Nos. 931-936,C163-C166 (10) 37.00 28.00

Issued to commemorate the First International Congress of Philately, Barcelona, March 26-Apr. 5. Nos. 931-936 could be bought at the exhibition upon presentation of 5p entrance ticket.

Franco Type of 1954-56.
Imprint: "F.N.M.T.-B"
1960, Mar. 31 **Photo.** *Perf. 13*
937 A221 1p dp org 2.50 1.00
938 A221 5p dk red brn 2.50 1.00

Printed and issued at the International Congress of Philately in Barcelona.

St. Juan de Ribera — A248

St. Vincent de Paul — A249

1960, Aug. 16 **Photo.** *Perf. 13*
939 A248 1p org red 40 14
940 A248 2.50p lil rose 10 12

Canonization of St. Juan de Ribera.

Europa Issue, 1960
Common Design Type
1960, Sept. 19 *Perf. 12½x13*
Size: 38½x21½mm.
941 CD3 1p sl grn & ol bis 1.50 20
942 CD3 5p choc & sal 1.50 60

1960, Sept. 27 **Unwmk.** *Perf. 13*
943 A249 25c violet 12 10
944 A249 1p org red 38 10

Issued to commemorate the 3rd centenary of the death of St. Vincent de Paul.

Pedro Menendez de Aviles A250

Runner A251

Portraits: 70c, 2.50p, Hernando de Soto. 80c, 3p, Juan Ponce de Leon. 1p, 5p, Alvar Nunez Cabeza de Vaca.

1960, Oct. 12 *Perf. 13x12½*
945 A250 25c vio bl, *bl* 12 7
946 A250 70c sl grn, *pink* 12 7
947 A250 80c dk grn, *pale brn* 12 7
948 A250 1p org brn, *yel* 16 7
949 A250 2p dk car rose, *pink* 30 7
950 A250 2.50p lil rose, *buff* 60 7
951 A250 3p dk bl, *grnsh* 2.75 50
952 A250 5p dk brn, *cit* 2.25 85
Nos. 945-952 (8) 6.42 1.77

Issued to commemorate the fourth centenary of Florida's discovery and colonization.

Perf. 13x12½, 12½x13
1960, Oct. 31 **Photo.**

Sports: 40c, 2p, Bicycling (horiz.). 70c, 2.50p, Soccer (horiz.). 80c, 3p, Athlete with rings. 1p, 5p, Hockey on roller skates (horiz.).

953 A251 25c dk vio, brn & blk 9 7
954 A251 40c pur, org & blk 9 7
955 A251 70c brt grn & red 30 8
956 A251 80c dp grn, car & blk 22 7
957 A251 1p red org, brt grn & blk 55 7
958 A251 1.50p Prus grn, brn & blk 38 7
959 A251 2p red lil, emer & blk 1.10 7
960 A251 2.50p lil rose & grn 38 7
961 A251 3p ultra, red & blk 75 15
962 A251 5p red brn, bl & blk 75 35
Nos. 953-962,C167-C170 (14) 7.41 2.33

Isaac Albeniz — A252

1960, Nov. 7 *Perf. 13*
963 A252 25c dk gray 9 7
964 A252 1p org red 40 10

Issued to commemorate the centenary of the birth of Isaac Albeniz, composer.

Courtyard of Samos Monastery A253

Designs: 1p, Fountain (vert.). 5p, Facade (vert.).

Perf. 12½x13, 13x12½
1960, Nov. 21 **Engr.**
965 A253 80c bl grn & Prus grn 12 6
966 A253 1p org brn & car rose 1.65 10
967 A253 5p sep & ocher 1.65 45

Issued in honor of the reconstructed Benedictine monastery at Samos, Lugo.

Adoration, by Velazquez — A254

1960, Dec. 1 Photo. *Perf. 13x12½*

968	A254	1p org red	50	10

Flight into Egypt by Francisco Bayeu A255

1961, Jan. 23 *Perf. 12½x13*

969	A255	1p cop red	38	10
970	A255	5p dl red brn	80	15

World Refugee Year.

Leandro F. de Moratin, by Goya — A256

St. Peter by El Greco — A257

1961, Feb. 13 *Perf. 13*

971	A256	1p hn brn	28	8
972	A256	1.50p dk bl grn	12	10

Issued to commemorate the 200th anniversary of the birth of Leandro Fernandez de Moratin (1760-1828), poet and dramatist.

1961, Mar. 24 *Perf. 13*

El Greco Paintings: 40c, Virgin Mary. 70c, Head of Christ. 80c, Knight with Hand on Chest. 1p, Self-portrait. 1.50p, Baptism of Christ. 2.50p, Holy Trinity. 3p, Burial of Count Orgaz. 5p, Christ Stripped of His Garments. 10p, St. Mauritius and the Theban Legion.

Gold Frame

973	A257	25c vio blk	20	15
974	A257	40c lilac	20	10
975	A257	70c green	25	20
976	A257	80c Prus grn	25	10
977	A257	1p chocolate	2.00	10
978	A257	1.50p grnsh bl	25	10
979	A257	2.50p dk car rose	38	10
980	A257	3p brt bl	1.00	45
981	A257	5p blk brn	3.00	1.40
982	A257	10p purple	50	28
		Nos. 973-982 (10)	8.03	2.98

Issued in honor of El Greco and for Stamp Day, March 24.

Diego Velazquez A258

Canceled Stamp A259

Velazquez Paintings: 1p, Duke de Olivares. 2.50p, Infanta Margarita. 10p, Detail from The Spinners (horiz.).

Unwmk.

1961, Apr. 17 Engr. *Perf. 13*

983	A258	80c dk bl & sl grn	85	35
a		Souvenir sheet	11.00	5.50
984	A258	1p brn red & choc	2.50	35
a		Souvenir sheet	11.00	5.50
985	A258	2.50p vio bl & bl	60	42
a		Souvenir sheet	11.00	5.50
986	A258	10p grn & yel grn	2.75	1.10
a		Souvenir sheet	11.00	5.50

Issued to commemorate the 300th anniversary (in 1960) of the death of Velazquez, painter.

Each souvenir sheet contains one imperf. stamp with marginal inscriptions and red control numbers. Size: 73x86mm. The colors of the stamps have been changed: 80c, red brown & slate; 1p, blue & violet; 2.50p, green & blue; 10p, slate blue & greenish blue. The sheets were sold at a premium.

1961, May 6 Photo. *Perf. 13x12½*

987	A259	25c gray & red	16	10
988	A259	1p org & blk	1.40	10
989	A259	10p ol grn & brn	1.40	65

Issued for International Stamp Day.

Juan Vazquez de Mella — A260

Flag, Angel and Peace Doves — A261

1961, June 8 Unwmk. *Perf. 13*

990	A260	1p hn brn	75	8
991	A260	2.30p red lil	15	15

Issued to commemorate the centenary of the birth of Juan Vazquez de Mella y Fanjul, politician and writer.

1961, July 10

Designs: 80c, Ships and Strait of Gibraltar. 1p, Alcazar and horseman. 1.50p, Ruins and triumphal arch. 2p, Horseman over Ebro. 2.30p, Victory parade. 2.50p, Ship building. 3p, Steel industry. 5p, Map of Spanish irrigation dams and statue (horiz.). 6p, Dama de Elche statue and power station. 8p, Mining development. 10p, General Franco.

992	A261	70c multi	8	6
993	A261	80c multi	8	6
994	A261	1p multi	20	6
995	A261	1.50p gold, pink & brn	12	6
996	A261	2p gold, gray & bl	12	6
997	A261	2.30p multi	16	9
998	A261	2.50p multi	16	6
999	A261	3p gold, red & dk gray	40	24
1000	A261	5p bl grn, ol gray & pink	2.50	1.10
1001	A261	6p multi	1.25	75
1002	A261	8p gold, ol & sep	80	55
1003	A261	10p gold, gray & grn	80	55
		Nos. 992-1003 (12)	6.67	3.64

25th anniversary of national uprising.

Christ, San Clemente, Tahull A262

Luis de Argote y Gongora A263

Designs: 25c, Bas-relief, Compostela Cathedral. 1p, Cloister of Silos. 2p, Virgin of Irache.

1961, July 24 Unwmk. *Perf. 13*

Gold Frame

1004	A262	25c bl vio	38	10
1005	A262	1p org brn	55	10
1006	A262	2p dp plum	75	10
1007	A262	3p grnsh bl, sal & blk	95	40

Issued to publicize the Seventh Exposition of the Council of Europe dedicated to Romanesque art, Barcelona-Santiago de Compostela, July 10-Oct. 10, 1961.

1961, Aug. 10 Photo. *Perf. 13*

1008	A263	25c vio blk	12	10
1009	A263	1p hn brn	50	12

Issued to commemorate the 400th anniversary of the birth of Luis de Argote y Gongora, poet.

Europa Issue, 1961

Common Design Type

1961, Sept. 18 *Perf. 12½x13*

Size: 37½x21½mm.

1010	CD4	1p brt ver	12	7
1011	CD4	5p brown	52	30

Cathedral at Burgos A264

Sebastian de Belalcazar A265

1961, Oct. 1 *Perf. 13*

1012	A264	1p gold & ol grn	18	8

Issued to commemorate the 25th anniversary of the nomination of Gen. Francisco Franco as Head of State.

Builders of the New World

1961, Oct. 12 Photo. *Perf. 13x12½*

Portraits: 70c, 2.50p, Blas de Lezo. 80c, 3p, Rodrigo de Bastidas. 1p, 5p, Nuflo de Chaves.

1013	A265	25c ind, *grn*	16	10
1014	A265	70c grn, *cr*	16	10
1015	A265	80c sl grn, *pnksh*	16	10
1016	A265	1p dk bl, *sal*	60	15
1017	A265	2p dk car, *bluish*	4.25	15
1018	A265	2.50p lil, *pale lil*	85	38
1019	A265	3p bl, *grysh*	2.00	60
1020	A265	5p brn, *yel*	2.25	75
		Nos. 1013-1020 (8)	10.43	2.33

Issued to honor the discoverers and conquerors of Colombia and Bolivia.

See Nos. 1131-1138, 1187-1194, 1271-1278, 1316-1323, 1377-1384, 1489-1496, 1548, 1550, 1587-1588, 1632-1633.

Patio of the Kings, Escorial — A266

Views of Escorial: 80c, Patio. 1p, Garden of the Monks and Escorial (horiz.). 2.50p, Staircase. 5p, General view of Escorial (horiz.). 6p, Main altar.

Perf. 13x12½, 12½x13

1961, Oct. 31 Engr. Unwmk.

1021	A266	70c bl grn & ol grn	16	10
1022	A266	80c Prus grn & ind	16	10
1023	A266	1p ocher & dk red	60	10
1024	A266	2.50p cl & dl vio	60	15
1025	A266	5p bis & dk brn	1.90	75
1026	A266	6p sl bl & dl pur	2.50	1.65
		Nos. 1021-1026 (6)	5.92	2.85

Alfonso XII Monument, Retiro Park — A267

Church of St. Mary, Naranco — A268

Designs: 1p, King Philip II. 2p, Town hall (horiz.). 2.50p, Cibeles fountain (horiz.). 3p, Alcala gate (horiz.). 5p, Cervantes memorial, Plaza de Espagna.

Photogravure (25c, 2p, 5p) Engraved (1p, 2.50p, 3p)

1961, Nov. 13 Unwmk. *Perf. 13*

1027	A267	25c gray & dl pur	16	10
1028	A267	1p bis brn & gray	42	10
1029	A267	2p cl & gray	42	10
1030	A267	2.50p blk & lil	35	10
1031	A267	3p sl & ind	85	42
1032	A267	5p Prus grn & beige	1.65	75
		Nos. 1027-1032 (6)	3.85	1.57

Issued to commemorate the 400th anniversary of Madrid as capital of Spain.

1961, Nov. 27

Designs: 1p, King Fruela I, founder of Oviedo. 2p, Cross of the Angels. 2.50p, King Alfonso II. 3p, King Alfonso III. 5p, Apostles from Oviedo Cathedral (sculpture).

1033	A268	25c pur & gray grn	18	10
1034	A268	1p bis brn & brn	45	10
1035	A268	2p dk brn & pale pur	90	10
1036	A268	2.50p cl & ind	45	10
1037	A268	3p sl & ind	90	65
1038	A268	5p ol & ol grn	1.65	75
		Nos. 1033-1038 (6)	4.53	1.80

Issued to commemorate the 1200th anniversary of the founding of Oviedo, capital of Asturia.

Nativity Sculptured by JoseGines A269

"La Cierva" Autogiro A270

1961, Dec. 1 Photo. *Perf. 13x12½*

1039	A269	1p dl pur	38	10

1961, Dec. 11 Unwmk. *Perf. 13*

Designs: 2p, Hydroplane "Plus Ultra." (horiz.). 3p, "Jesus del Gran Poder," plane of Madrid-Manila flight (horiz.). 5p, Bustard hunt by plane. 10p, Madonna of Loretto, patron saint of Spanish airmen.

1040	A270	1p ind & bl	16	6
1041	A270	2p grn, dl pur & blk	16	12
1042	A270	3p blk & ol grn	1.90	35
1043	A270	5p dl pur, gray bl & blk	3.75	90
1044	A270	10p blk, lt bl & ol gray	2.00	60
		Nos. 1040-1044 (5)	7.97	2.03

50th anniversary of Spanish aviation.

Provincial Arms Issue

Alava — A271

Arms of Spain — A271a

1962 Photo. *Perf. 13*

1045	A271	5p	Alava	20	15
1046	A271	5p	Albacete	20	15
1047	A271	5p	Alicante	35	40
1048	A271	5p	Almeria	35	40
1049	A271	5p	Avila	35	40
1050	A271	5p	Badajoz	20	15
1051	A271	5p	Baleares	30	15
1052	A271	5p	Barcelona	20	15
1053	A271	5p	Burgos	1.00	40
1054	A271	5p	Caceres	55	25
1055	A271	5p	Cadiz	70	35
1056	A271	5p	(Castellon de la Plana	5.50	1.50
			Nos. 1045-1056 (12)	9.90	4.45

1963

1057	A271	5p	Ciudad Real	70	35
1058	A271	5p	Cordoba	5.25	1.25
1059	A271	5p	Coruna	90	35
1060	A271	5p	Cuenca	90	35
1061	A271	5p	Fernando Po	1.25	75
1062	A271	5p	Gerona	16	15
1063	A271	5p	Gran Canaria	16	15
1064	A271	5p	Granada	35	25
1065	A271	5p	Guadalajara	90	35
1066	A271	5p	Guipuzcoa	25	15
1067	A271	5p	Huelva	16	15
1068	A271	5p	Huesca	16	15
			Nos. 1057-1068 (12)	11.14	4.40

1964

1069	A271	5p	Ifni	15	15
1070	A271	5p	Jaen	15	15
1071	A271	5p	Leon	15	15
1072	A271	5p	Lerida	15	15
1073	A271	5p	Logrono	15	15
1074	A271	5p	Lugo	15	15
1075	A271	5p	Madrid	15	15
1076	A271	5p	Malaga	15	15
1077	A271	5p	Murcia	15	15
1078	A271	5p	Navarra	20	15
1079	A271	5p	Orense	20	15
1080	A271	5p	Oviedo	20	15
			Nos. 1069-1080 (12)	1.95	1.80

1965

1081	A271	5p	Palencia	20	15
1082	A271	5p	Pontevedra	20	15
1083	A271	5p	Rio Muni	20	15
1084	A271	5p	Sahara	20	15
1085	A271	5p	Salamanca	20	15
1086	A271	5p	Santander	20	15
1087	A271	5p	Segovia	20	15
1088	A271	5p	Seville	20	15
1089	A271	5p	Soria	14	15
1090	A271	5p	Tarragona	20	15
1091	A271	5p	Tenerife	15	15
1092	A271	5p	Teruel	14	15
			Nos. 1081-1092 (12)	2.23	1.80

1966

1093	A271	5p	Toledo	14	12
1094	A271	5p	Valencia	14	12
1094A	A271	5p	Valladolid	12	12
1094B	A271	5p	Vizcaya	14	12
1094C	A271	5p	Zamora	12	12
1094D	A271	5p	Zaragoza	12	12
1094E	A271	5p	Ceuta	12	12
1094F	A271	5p	Melilla	12	12
1094G	A271a	10p	black	25	15
			Nos. 1093-1094G (9)	1.27	1.11
			Nos. 1045-1094G (57)	26.49	13.56

Zurbaran Self-portrait A272

Zurbaran Paintings: 25c, Martyr (horiz.). 40c, Burial of St. Catherine. 70c, St. Casilda. 80c, Jesus crowning St. Joseph. 1.50p, St. Jerome. 2.50p, Virgin of Grace. 3p, The Apotheosis of St. Thomas Aquinas. 5p, The Virgin as a child. 10p, The Immaculate Virgin.

Unwmk.

1962, Mar. 24 Photo. *Perf. 13*

Gold Frame

1095	A272	25c	ol gray	25	7
1096	A272	40c	purple	25	7
1097	A272	70c	green	40	8
1098	A272	80c	Prus grn	25	7
1099	A272	1p	chocolate	6.00	7
1100	A272	1.50p	brt bl grn	65	7
1101	A272	2.50p	dk car rose	65	7
1102	A272	3p	brt bl	75	30
1103	A272	5p	dp brn	2.00	60
1104	A272	10p	ol grn	2.00	60
			Nos. 1095-1104 (10)	13.20	2.00

Issued to honor Francisco de Zurbaran (1598-1664) and for Stamp Day, March 24.

San Jose Convent, Avila — A272a

St. Theresa (by Velazquez?) A273

Mercury A274

Design: 1p, St. Theresa by Bernini.

1962, Apr. 10 *Perf. 13*

1105	A272a	25c	bluish blk	8	8
1106	A272a	1p	brown	16	12

Perf. 13x12½

1107	A273	3p	brt bl	1.65	28

Issued to commemorate the 4th centenary of St. Theresa's reform of the Carmelite order.

1962, May 7

1108	A274	25c	vio, rose & mag	8	8
1109	A274	1p	brn, org & lt brn	30	8
1110	A274	10p	dp grn, ol grn & brt grn	2.75	80

International Stamp Day, May 7.

Painting Type of 1958

Rubens Paintings: 25c, Ferdinand of Austria. 1p, Self-portrait. 3p, Philip II.10p, Duke of Lerma on horseback.

1962, May 28 *Perf. 13*

Gold Frame

Size: 25x30mm.

1111	A237	25c	vio blk	42	16
1112	A237	1p	chocolate	3.75	12
1113	A237	3p	blue	3.50	1.10

Perf. 13x12½

Size: 26x38mm.

1114	A237	10p	sl grn	2.50	1.50

St. Benedict A275

El Cid, Statue by Cristobal A276

Berruguete Sculptures: 80c, Apostle. 1p, St. Peter. 2p, St. Christopher carrying Christ Child. 3p, Ecce Homo (Christ). 10p, St. Sebastian.

1962, July 9 *Perf. 13x12½*

1115	A275	25c	lt bl & plum	16	8
1116	A275	80c	sal & ol gray	40	8
1117	A275	1p	gray & red	60	8
1118	A275	2p	gray & mag	4.75	8
1119	A275	3p	brn pink & dk bl	1.75	1.25
1120	A275	10p	rose & brn	1.75	70
			Nos. 1115-1120 (6)	9.41	2.27

Issued to commemorate the 400th anniversary of the death of Alonso Berruguete (1486-1561), architect, sculptor and painter.

Perf. 13x12½, 12½x13

1962, July 30 Engr.

Designs: 2p, Equestrian statue by Anna Huntington. 3p, El Cid's treasure chest (horiz.). 10p, Oath-taking ceremony at Santa Gadea (horiz.).

1121	A276	1p	lt grn & gray	24	7
1122	A276	2p	brn & choc	1.50	7
1123	A276	3p	bl & sl grn	4.75	1.10
1124	A276	10p	lt grn & sl grn	3.00	60

Issued to commemorate El Cid Campeador (Rodrigo Diaz de Vivar, 1040-99), Spain's national hero.

Europa Issue, 1962

Bee and Honeycomb — A277

1962, Sept. 13 Photo. *Perf. 12½x13*

1125	A277	1p	dp rose	35	7
1126	A277	5p	dl grn	1.40	30

Discus Thrower A278

UPAE Emblem A279

Sports: 80c, Runner. 1p, Hurdler. 3p, Sprinter at start.

1962, Oct. 7 *Perf. 13x12½*

1127	A278	25c	pale pink & vio blk	10	8
1128	A278	80c	pale yel & dk grn	30	8
1129	A278	1p	pale rose & brn	20	8
1130	A278	3p	pale bl & dk bl	40	20

Issued to commemorate the Second Spanish-American Games, Madrid, Oct. 7-12.

Builders of the New World

Portrait Type of 1961

Portraits: 25c, 2p, Alonso de Mendoza. 70c, 2.50p, Jimenez de Quesada. 80c, 3p, Juan de Garay. 1p, 5p, Pedro de la Gasca.

1962, Oct. 12 Unwmk.

1131	A265	25c	rose lil, *gray*	20	10
1132	A265	70c	grn, *pale pink*	1.50	15
1133	A265	80c	dk grn, *pale yel*	1.00	15
1134	A265	1p	red brn, *gray*	2.00	15
1135	A265	2p	car, *lt bl*	4.50	15
1136	A265	2.50p	dk vio, *pnksh*	1.00	25
1137	A265	3p	dp bl, *pale pink*	10.00	1.40
1138	A265	5p	brn, *pale yel*	5.00	1.65
			Nos. 1131-1138 (8)	25.20	4.00

1962, Oct. 20 Engr. *Perf. 13*

1139	A279	1p	sep & grn	20	10

Issued to commemorate the 50th anniversary of the founding of the Postal Union of the Americas and Spain, UPAE.

The Annunciation, by Murillo — A280

Holy Family by Pedro de Mena — A281

Mysteries of the Rosary: 70c, The Visitation, Correa. 80c, Nativity, Murillo. 1p, The Presentation, Pedro de Campana. 1.50p, The Finding in the Temple, (unknown painter). 2p, The Agony in the Garden, Gianquinto. 2.50p, The Scourging at the Pillar, Alonso Cano. 3p, The Crowning with Thorns, Tiepolo. 5p, Carrying of the Cross, El Greco. 8p, The Crucifixion, Murillo. 10p, The Resurrection, Murillo.

1962, Oct. 26

1140	A280	25c	lil & brn	12	8
1141	A280	70c	grn & dk bl grn	12	8
1142	A280	80c	ol & dk bl grn	12	8
1143	A280	1p	grn & gray	4.00	65
1144	A280	1.50p	grn & dk bl	12	8
1145	A280	2p	brn & vio	1.10	52
1146	A280	2.50p	dk brn & rose cl	35	15
1147	A280	3p	lil & gray	35	15
1148	A280	5p	brn & dk car	55	35
1149	A280	8p	vio brn & blk	55	25
1150	A280	10p	grn & yel grn	90	25
			Nos. 1140-1150,C171-C174 (15)	10.80	3.65

1962, Dec. 6 Photo. *Perf. 13x12½*

1151	A281	1p	ol gray	58	15

Malaria Eradication Emblem A282

1962, Dec. 21 *Perf. 12½x13*

1152	A282	1p	blk, yel grn & yel	32	10

Issued for the World Health Organization drive to eradicate malaria.

Pope John XXIII and St. Peter's, Rome A283

1962, Dec. 29 Engr.

1153	A283	1p	dp plum & blk	42	20

Issued to commemorate Vatican II, the 21st Ecumenical Council of the Roman Catholic Church. See also No. 1199.

St. Paul, by El Greco A284

Courtyard, Poblet Monastery A285

1963, Jan. 25 *Perf. 13*

1154	A284	1p	brn, blk & ol	60	15

Issued to commemorate the 1,900th anniversary of St. Paul's visit to Spain.

Perf. 12½x13, 13x12½

1963, Feb. 25 **Unwmk.**

Designs: 1p, Royal sepulcher. 3p, View of monastery (horiz.). 5p, Gothic arch.

1155	A285	25c choc & sl grn	12	8
1156	A285	1p org ver & rose car	50	10
1157	A285	3p vio bl & dk bl	1.50	12
1158	A285	5p brn & ocher	3.00	90

Issued in honor of the Cistercian monastery of Santa Maria de Poblet.

José de Ribera, Self-portrait A285a

Coach A286

Ribera Paintings: 25c, Archimedes. 40c, Jacob's Flock. 70c, Triumph of Bacchus. 80c, St. Christopher. 1.50p, St. Andrew. 2.50p, St. John the Baptist. 3p, St. Onofre. 5p, St. Peter. 10p, The Immaculate Virgin.

Unwmk.

1963, Mar. 24 **Photo.** ***Perf. 13***

Gold Frame

1159	A285a	25c	violet	18	7
1160	A285a	40c	red lil	20	7
1161	A285a	70c	green	50	7
1162	A285a	80c	dk grn	50	7
1163	A285a	1p	brown	50	7
1164	A285a	1.50p	bl grn	50	7
1165	A285a	2.50p	car rose	1.50	12
1166	A285a	3p	dk bl	1.65	30
1167	A285a	5p	olive	5.50	1.25
1168	A285a	10p	dl red brn	2.00	90
	Nos. 1159-1168 (10)			13.03	2.99

Issued to honor José de Ribera (1588-1652) and for Stamp Day, Mar. 24.

1963, May 3 ***Perf. 13x12½***

1169 A286 1p multi 20 10

Issued to commemorate the centenary of the first International Postal Conference, Paris, 1863.

Globe A287

1963, May 8 ***Perf. 12½x13***

1170	A287	25c multi	14	6
1171	A287	1p multi	20	6
1172	A287	10p multi	1.40	40

Issued for International Stamp Day, 1963.

"Give us this Day our Daily Bread..." A288

1963, June 1 **Unwmk.**

1173 A288 1p multi 12 10

FAO "Freedom from Hunger" campaign.

The Scott Catalogue value is a retail price, what you could expect to pay for the stamp in a grade of Fine-Very Fine. The value listed is a reference which reflects recent actual dealer selling price.

"Pillars of Hercules" and Globes — A289

Seal of Council of San Sebastian — A290

Designs: 80c, Fleet of Columbus. 1p, Columbus and compass rose.

1963, June 4 ***Perf. 13***

1174	A289	25c multi	10	10
1175	A289	80c brn, lt grn & gold	15	10
1176	A289	1p sl grn, sep & gold	25	10

Issued to publicize the Congress of Institutions of Spanish Culture, June 5-15.

1963, June 27 **Photo.**

Designs: 80c, Burning of city, 1813. 1p, View, 1836.

1177	A290	25c vio, grn & blk	10	10
1178	A290	80c dk brn, gray & red	15	10
1179	A290	1p dk grn, grn & ol	30	10

150th anniversary of the rebuilding of San Sebastian.

Europa Issue, 1963

Our Lady of Europe — A291

1963, Sept. 16 **Engr.** ***Perf. 13x12½***

1180	A291	1p bis brn & choc	20	10
1181	A291	5p bluish grn & blk	90	45

Arms of Order of Mercy — A292

King James I — A293

Designs: 1p, Our Lady of Mercy. 1.50p, St. Pedro Nolasco. 3p, St. Raimundo de Penafort.

1963, Sept. 24 **Photo.** ***Perf. 13***

1182 A292 25c blk, car rose & gold 10 10

Engr.

1183	A293	80c sep & grn	15	10
1184	A293	1p gray vio & brn vio	15	10
1185	A293	1.50p dl bl & blk	15	10
1186	A293	3p gray & blk	25	20
	Nos. 1182-1186 (5)		80	60

Issued to commemorate the 75th anniversary of the coronation of Our Lady of Mercy.

Builders of the New World

Portrait Type of 1961.

Portraits: 25c, 2p, Father Junipero Serra. 70c, 2.50p, Vasco Nuñez de Balboa. 80c, 3p, Jose de Galvez. 1p, 5p, Diego Garcia de Paredes.

1963, Oct. 12 ***Perf. 13x12½***

1187	A265	25c vio bl, *bl*	20	10
1188	A265	70c grn, *pale rose*	20	10
1189	A265	80c dk grn, *yel*	60	10
1190	A265	1p dk bl, *pale rose*	75	10
1191	A265	2p mag, *lt bl*	2.25	10
1192	A265	2.50p vio blk, *dl rose*	1.50	10
1193	A265	3p brt bl, *pink*	3.00	50
1194	A265	5p brn, *yel*	4.00	1.90
	Nos. 1187-1194 (8)		12.50	3.00

The Good Samaritan — A294

1963, Oct. 28 **Unwmk.**

1195 A294 1p gold, pur & brt car 18 10

Centenary of International Red Cross.

Holy Family by Alonso Berruguete (1486-1561) A295

Father Raymond Lully A296

1963, Dec. 2 **Photo.** ***Perf. 13x12½***

1196 A295 1p dk grn 18 10

Christmas 1963. See No. 1279.

1963, Dec. 5 **Engr.**

Portrait: 1.50p, Cardinal Luis Antonio de Belluga (1662-1743).

1197	A296	1p dk vio & blk	28	5
1198	A296	1.50p sep & dl vio	18	5

See Nos. C175-C176.

Papal Type of 1962

Design: 1p, Pope Paul VI and St. Peter's, Rome.

1963, Dec. 30 ***Perf. 12½x13***

1199 A283 1p dk grn & blk 18 10

Issued to commemorate the second session of Vatican II, the 21st Ecumenical Council of the Roman Catholic Church.

Tourist Issue, 1964

Alcazar, Segovia — A297

Dragon Caves, Majorca — A298

Designs: 40c, Potes, Santander. 50c, Leon Cathedral. No. 1202, Crypt of San Isidro at Leon. No. 1203, Costa Brava. 80c, Christ of the Lanterns, Cordova. No. 1206, Court of Lions, Alhambra, Granada. No. 1208, Interior of La Mezquita, Cordova. 1.50p, View of Gerona.

1964 **Engr.** ***Perf. 13***

1200	A297	40c sep & bl	8	8
1201	A298	50c gray & sep	8	8
1202	A297	70c ind & dk bl grn	16	8
1203	A298	70c vio & brn	8	8
1204	A298	80c dp ultra & blk	16	8
1205	A297	1p vio bl & pur	16	8
1206	A297	1p rose red & dl pur	20	8
1207	A298	1p dk grn & blk	8	8
1208	A298	1p brn vio & rose	8	8
1209	A297	1.50p gray grn, brn & blk	16	8
	Nos. 1200-1209 (10)		1.24	80

See Nos. 1280-1289.

Santa Maria de Huerta Monastery A299

Joaquin Sorolla, Self-portrait A300

Designs: 1p, Great Hall. 5p, View of monastery with apse (horiz.).

Perf. 13x12½, 12½x13

1964, Feb. 24

1212	A299	1p gray grn & grn	12	10
1213	A299	2p grnsh bl & sep	28	10
1214	A299	5p dk bl	2.00	45

8th century of Santa Maria Monastery, Huerta.

1964, Mar. 24 **Photo.** ***Perf. 13***

Sorolla Paintings: 25c, The Jug (woman and child). 40c, Oxen and Driver (horiz.). 70c, Man and Woman from La Mancha. 80c, Fisher Woman of Valencia. 1p, Self-portrait. 1.50p, Round up (horiz.). 2.50p, Fishermen (horiz.). 3p, Children at the Beach (horiz.). 5p, Unloading the Boat. 10p, Man and Woman on Horseback, Valencia.

Gold Frame

1215	A300	25c	violet	10	10
1216	A300	40c	purple	10	10
1217	A300	70c	dp yel grn	10	10
1218	A300	80c	bluish grn	10	10
1219	A300	1p	brown	10	10
1220	A300	1.50p	Prus bl	15	10
1221	A300	2.50p	dk car rose	20	10
1222	A300	3p	vio bl	65	25
1223	A300	5p	chocolate	1.25	75
1224	A300	10p	dp grn	75	25
	Nos. 1215-1224 (10)			3.50	1.95

Issued to honor Joaquin Sorolla y Bastida (1863-1923) and for Stamp Day, March 24.

"Peace" — A301

"Sport" — A302

Designs: 40c, Radio and television. 50c, New apartments. 70c, Agriculture. 80c, Reforestation. 1p, Economic development. 1.50p, Modern architecture. 2p, Transportation. 2.50p, Hydroelectric development. 3p, Electrification. 5p, Scientific achievements. 6p, Buildings, tourism. 10p, Generalissimo Franco.

1964, Apr. 1

1225	A301	25c blk, emer & gold	8	8
1226	A302	30c blk, bl & sal pink	8	8
1227	A301	40c gold & blk	8	8
1228	A302	50c multi	8	8
1229	A301	70c multi	8	8
1230	A301	80c multi	8	8
1231	A302	1p multi	24	8
1232	A302	1.50p multi	16	8
1233	A301	2p multi	16	8
1234	A302	2.50p multi	16	8
1235	A301	3p gold, blk & red	1.00	65
1236	A302	5p gold, grn & red	30	24
1237	A301	6p multi	65	48
1238	A302	10p multi	65	48
	Nos. 1225-1238 (14)		3.80	2.65

Issued to commemorate 25 years of peace.

Bullfight and Unisphere A303

Stamp of 1850 and Modern Stamps A304

Designs: 1p, Spanish pavilion (horiz.). 2.50p, La Mota castle, Medina de Campo. 5p, Spanish dancer. 50p, Jai alai.

Perf. 12½x13, 13x12½

1964, Apr. 23 **Engr.**

1239 A303 1p bl grn & yel grn 30 7
1240 A303 1.50p car & brn 12 7
1241 A303 2.50p dk bl & sl grn 20 7
1242 A303 5p car & dk car rose 40 30
1243 A303 50p vio bl & dk bl 1.40 40
Nos. 1239-1243 (5) 2.42 91

New York World's Fair, 1964-65.

1964, May 6 ***Perf. 13x12½***

1244 A304 25c dk car rose & dl pur 12 10
1245 A304 1p yel grn & dk bl 28 10
1246 A304 10p org & rose red 85 35

Issued for International Stamp Day, 1964.

Virgin of Hope — A305

Santa Maria — A306

1964, May 31 **Photo.** ***Perf. 13x12½***

1247 A305 1p dk grn 18 10

Issued to commemorate the canonical coronation of the Virgin of Hope (La Macarena) in St. Gil's Church, Seville, May 31.

1964, July 16 ***Perf. 13***

Designs (ships): 15c, 13th cent. ship of King Alfonso X, from medieval manuscript (vert.). 25c, Carrack, from 15th cent. engraving (vert.). 50c, Galley. 70c, Galleon. 80c, Xebec. 1p, Warship, Santisima Trinidad (vert.). 1.50p, 18th cent. corvette, Atrevida (vert.). 2p, Steamer, Isabel II. 2.50p, Frigate, Numancia, Spain's 1st armored ship. 3p, Destroyer. 5p, Submarine of Isaac Peral. 6p, Cruiser, Baleares. 10p, Training ship, Juan Sebastian Elcano.

1248 A306 15c dp rose & vio blk 12 10
1249 A306 25c org yel & gray grn 12 10
1250 A306 40c ultra & dk bl 12 10
1251 A306 50c sl grn & dk bl 12 10
1252 A306 70c vio & dk bl 12 10
1253 A306 80c dl bl grn & ultra 12 10
1254 A306 1p org & vio brn 12 10
1255 A306 1.50p car & sep 12 10
1256 A306 2p blk & sl grn 1.10 10
1257 A306 2.50p rose car & dl vio 25 10
1258 A306 3p sep & ind 25 10
1259 A306 5p dk bl, lt grn & vio 1.25 45
1260 A306 6p lt grn & vio 60 40
1261 A306 10p org yel & rose red 50 20
Nos. 1248-1261 (14) 4.91 2.15

Issued to honor the Spanish Navy.

Europa Issue, 1964
Common Design Type

1964, Sept. 14 **Photo.** ***Perf. 12½x13***
Size: 21½x39mm.

1262 CD7 1p bis, red & grn 40 10
1263 CD7 5p brt bl, mag & grn 1.65 45

Madonna of Alcazar — A307

Shot Put — A308

1964, Oct. 9 **Photo.** ***Perf. 13***

1264 A307 25c bis & brn 10 5
1265 A307 1p gray & ind 15 5

700th anniversary of the reconquest of Jerez de la Frontera.

1964, Oct. 10

Sport: 80c, Broad jump. 1p, Slalom. 3p, Judo. 5p, Discus.

Gold Olympic Rings

1266 A308 25c org red & blk 10 10
1267 A308 80c emer & blk 10 10
1268 A308 1p brt bl & ind 10 10
1269 A308 3p bis & ind 18 15
1270 A308 5p lil & ind 22 18
Nos. 1266-1270 (5) 70 63

1964 Olympic Games.

Builders of the New World
Portrait Type of 1961

Portraits: 25c, 2p, Diego de Almagro. 70c, 2.50p, Francisco de Toledo. 80c, 3p, Archbishop Toribio de Mogrovejo. 1p, 5p, Francisco Pizarro.

1964, Oct. 12 ***Perf. 13x12½***

1271 A265 25c pale grn & vio 12 10
1272 A265 70c pink & ol gray 12 10
1273 A265 80c buff & Prus grn 50 10
1274 A265 1p buff & gray vio 50 10
1275 A265 2p pale bl & ol gray 50 10
1276 A265 2.50p pale grn & cl 38 25
1277 A265 3p gray & dk bl 3.25 70
1278 A265 5p yel & brn 2.00 90
Nos. 1271-1278 (8) 7.37 2.35

Christmas Type of 1963

Design: Nativity by Francisco de Zurbaran (1598-1664).

1964, Dec. 4 **Photo.**

1279 A295 1p ol blk 20 10

Tourist Issue, 1965
Types of 1964

Designs: 25c, Columbus monument, Barcelona. 30s, Facade of Santa Maria, Burgos. 50c, Santa Maria la Blanca (medieval synagogue), Toledo. 70c, Bridge, Zamora. 80c, La Giralda (tower) and Cathedral of Seville. 1p, Boat and nets in Cudillero harbor. No. 1286, Cathedral of Burgos, interior. No. 1287, View of Mogrovejo, Santander. 3p, Bridge, Cambados, Pontevedra. 6p, Silk merchants' hall (Lonja), Valencia, interior.

1965 **Engr.** ***Perf. 13***

1280 A298 25c dk bl & blk 15 5
1281 A298 30c dl grn & sep 18 5
1282 A298 50c cl & rose car 12 5
1283 A297 70c vio bl & ind 15 5
1284 A298 80c rose cl & dk pur 12 5
1285 A298 1p dp cl, car & blk 15 5
1286 A298 2.50p brn vio & bis 15 5
1287 A297 2.50p dl bl & gray 12 5
1288 A298 3p rose car & dk brn 18 5
1289 A298 6p sl & blk 22 8
Nos. 1280-1289 (10) 1.54 53

Foreign postal stationery (stamped envelopes, postal cards and air letter sheets) lies beyond the scope of this Catalogue, which is limited to adhesive postage stamps.

Alfonso X, the Wise (1232-84) A309

Julio Romero de Torres, Self-portrait A310

Portraits: 25c, Juan Donoso-Cortes (1809-53). 2.50p, Gaspar M. Jovellanos (1744-1810). 5p, St. Dominic de Guzman (1170-1221).

1965, Feb. 25 **Engr.** ***Perf. 13x12½***

1292 A309 25c sl bl & blk 10 8
1293 A309 70c bl & ind 16 10
1294 A309 2.50p sl grn & sep 24 8
1295 A309 5p dl grn & sl grn 40 18

1965, Mar. 24 **Photo.** ***Perf. 13***

De Torres Paintings: 25c, Girl with Jar. 40c, "The Song" (girl with guitar). 70c, Madonna of the Lanterns. 80c, Girl with guitar. 1.50p, "The Poem of Cordova" (pensive woman). 2.50p, Martha and Mary. 3p, "The Poem of Cordova" (two women holding statue of angel). 5p, Girl with the Charcoal. 10p, Back of woman's head.

Gold Frame

1296 A310 25c dl pur 12 10
1297 A310 40c purple 12 10
1298 A310 70c ol grn 12 10
1299 A310 80c sl grn 12 10
1300 A310 1p dk red brn 15 10
1301 A310 1.50p bl grn 15 10
1302 A310 2.50p lil rose 20 10
1303 A310 3p dk bl 25 10
1304 A310 5p brown 38 15
1305 A310 10p sl grn 60 20
Nos. 1296-1305 (10) 2.21 1.15

Issued to honor Julio Romero de Torres (1880-1930) and for Stamp Day, March 24.

Bull and Symbolic Stamps — A311

1965, May 6 ***Perf. 13x12½***

1306 A311 25c multi 12 10
1307 A311 1p org & multi 18 10
1308 A311 10p multi 75 25

Issued for International Stamp Day, 1965.

ITU Emblem, Old and New Communication Equipment — A312

1965, May 17 ***Perf. 12½x13***

1309 A312 1p sal, blk & red 12 10

Issued to commemorate the centenary of the International Telecommunication Union.

Pilgrim — A313

Explorer, Royal Flag of Spain and Ships — A314

Design: 2p, Pilgrim (profile).

1965, July 25 **Photo.** ***Perf. 13***

1310 A313 1p multi 10 6
1311 A313 2p multi 10 6

Issued to commemorate the Holy Year of St. James of Compostela, patron saint of Spain.

1965, Aug. 28 ***Perf. 13x12½***

1312 A314 3p red, blk & yel 15 10

400th anniv. of the settlement of Florida, and the 1st permanent European settlement in the continental US, St. Augustine, Fla. See US No. 1271.

St. Benedict A315

Sports Palace, Madrid A316

Europa Issue, 1965

1965, Sept. 27 **Engr.** ***Perf. 13x12½***

1313 A315 1p yel grn & sl grn 20 12
1314 A315 5p lil & vio 70 18

1965, Oct. 9 **Photo.** ***Perf. 13***

1315 A316 1p gray, gold & dk brn 12 8

Issued to commemorate the meeting of the International Olympic Committee in Madrid.

Builders of the New World
Portrait Type of 1961

Portraits: 25c, 2p, Don Fadrique de Toledo. 70c, 2.50p, Father José de Anchieta. 80c, 3p, Francisco de Orellana. 1p, 5p, St. Luis Beltran.

1965, Oct. 12 **Photo.** ***Perf. 13x12½***

1316 A265 25c pale grn & dp pur 12 8
1317 A265 70c pink & brn 12 8
1318 A265 80c cr & Prus grn 12 8
1319 A265 1p buff & dk vio 12 8
1320 A265 2p lt bl & dk ol grn 12 8
1321 A265 2.50p lt bl & pur 12 8
1322 A265 3p gray & dk bl 90 25
1323 A265 5p yel & brn 1.10 30
Nos. 1316-1323 (8) 2.72 1.03

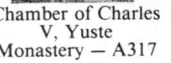

Chamber of Charles V, Yuste Monastery — A317

Stamp of 1865 (No. 78) — A318

Yuste Monastery: 1p, Courtyard (horiz.). 5p, View of monastery (horiz.).

Perf. 12½x13, 13x12½

1965, Nov. 15 **Engr.**

1324	A317	1p	bl gray & blk	10	10
1325	A317	2p	red brn & brn blk	25	10
1326	A317	5p	grysh bl & grn	40	20

Monastery of Yuste, Estremadura.

1965, Nov. 22 ***Perf. 13x12½***

Designs: 1p, Stamp of 1865 (No. 77). 5p, Stamp of 1865 (No. 80).

1327	A318	80c	blk & yel grn	10	5
1328	A318	1p	plum, brn & rose	10	7
1329	A318	5p	sep & org brn	10	10

Issued to commemorate the centenary of the first Spanish perforated postage stamps.

Nativity A319

1965, Dec. 1 **Photo.** ***Perf. 12½x13***

1330	A319	1p	brt grn	12	10

Virgin of Peace, Antipolo A320

Globe and Four Beasts of Apocalypse A321

Design: 3p, Father Andres de Urdaneta.

1965, Dec. 3 ***Perf. 13x12½***

1331	A320	1p	pale sal & ol brn	7	7
1332	A320	3p	gray & dp bl	18	10

400th anniv. of the Christianization of the Philippines.

1965, Dec. 29 **Photo.** ***Perf. 13x12½***

1333	A321	1p	grnsh bl, yel & brn	18	10

Issued to commemorate Vatican II, the 21st Ecumenical Council of the Roman Catholic Church, Oct. 11, 1962-Dec. 8, 1965.

Adm. Alvaro de Bazan (1526-88) — A322

Exhibition Emblem; Type Block "P" — A323

Portrait: 2p, Daza de Valdes, scientist (17th century).

1966, Feb. 26 **Engr.** ***Perf. 13x12½***

1334	A322	25c	dl bl & gray	16	5
1335	A322	2p	mag & vio	25	8

See Nos. C177-C178.

1966, Mar. 4 **Photo.** ***Perf. 13***

1336	A323	1p	red, grn & vio bl	12	10

Issued to publicize the Graphic Arts and Advertising Packaging Exhibition "Graphispack," Barcelona, March 4-13.

José Maria Sert, Self-portrait A324

Santa Maria Church, Guernica A325

Sert Paintings: 25c, The Magic Ball. 40c, Evocation of Toledo (horiz.). 70c, Christ on the Cross. 80c, Parachutists. 1.50p, "Audacity." 2.50p, "Justice." 3p, Jacob Wrestling with the Angel. 5p, "The Five Continents." 10p, Sts. Peter and Paul.

1966, Mar. 24

Gold Frame

1337	A324	25c	dk pur	10	6
1338	A324	40c	dp mag	10	6
1339	A324	70c	green	10	5
1340	A324	80c	dk ol grn	10	5
1341	A324	1p	cl brn	10	5
1342	A324	1.50p	dl bl	10	5
1343	A324	2.50p	dk red	10	6
1344	A324	3p	dp bl	10	10
1345	A324	5p	sepia	10	10
1346	A324	10p	black	15	15
		Nos. 1337-1346 (10)		1.05	73

Issued to honor José Maria Sert (1876-1945) and for Stamp Day, March 24.

1966, Apr. 28 **Photo.** ***Perf. 13***

Designs: 1p, Arms of Guernica and Luno. 3p, Tree of Guernica.

1347	A325	80c	bl, sep & grn	8	6
1348	A325	1p	yel grn & multi	8	8
1349	A325	3p	bl, grn & vio brn	8	8

Issued to commemorate the 6th centenary of the founding of Guernica and Luno.

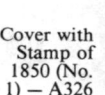

Cover with Stamp of 1850 (No. 1) — A326

Designs (covers): 1p, 5r (No. 3). 10p, 10r (No. 5).

1966, May 6 ***Perf. 12½x13***

1350	A326	25c	rose vio, blk & red	6	5
1351	A326	1p	red brn, org & blk	6	5
1352	A326	10p	ol grn, grn & org	25	10

Issued for International Stamp Day, 1966.

Tourist Issue, 1966

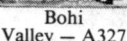

Bohi Valley — A327

Torla, Huesca — A328

Designs: 40c, Portal of Sigena Monastery, Huesca. 50c, Santo Domingo Church, Soria. 80c, Torre del Oro, Seville. 1p, Palm and view, Pico de Teyde, Santa Cruz de Tenerife. 1.50p, Monastery of Guadalupe, Caceres. 2p, Alcala de Henares University. 3p, Seo Cathedral, Lerida. 10p, Courtyard of St. Gregorio, Valladolid.

1966 **Engr.** ***Perf. 13***

1353	A327	10c	gray grn & bl grn	6	5
1354	A328	15c	gray grn & brn	6	5
1355	A327	40c	bis brn & brn	6	5
1356	A327	50c	car rose & dp cl	6	5
1357	A327	80c	lil & rose vio	6	5
1358	A327	1p	vio bl & bl grn	6	5
1359	A328	1.50p	dk bl & blk	6	5
1360	A328	2p	sl bl & sep	6	5
1361	A328	3p	ultra & blk	15	6
1362	A327	10p	brt bl & grnsh bl	15	5
		Nos. 1353-1362 (10)		78	51

Tree and Globe A329

1966, June 6 **Photo.** ***Perf. 12½x13***

1363	A329	1p	brn & dk grn	15	10

Issued to commemorate the 6th International Forestry Congress, Madrid, June 6-18.

Navy Emblem — A330

1966, July 1 **Photo.** ***Perf. 13***

1364	A330	1p	gray & dk bl	15	10

Naval Week, Barcelona, July 1-8.

Guadamur Castle — A331

Castles: 25c, Alcazar, Segovia. 40c, La Mota. 50c, Olite. 70c, Monteagudo. 80c, Butron (vert.). 1p, Manzanares. 3p, Almansa (vert.).

1966, Aug. 13 **Engr.** ***Perf. 13***

1365	A331	10c	grysh bl & sep	6	5
1366	A331	25c	vio & pur	6	5
1367	A331	40c	grnsh bl & bl grn	6	5
1368	A331	50c	grnsh bl & ultra	6	5
1369	A331	70c	vio bl & ind	6	5
1370	A331	80c	vio & sl grn	6	5
1371	A331	1p	ol bis & gray	8	5
1372	A331	3p	rose & red lil	8	5
		Nos. 1365-1372 (8)		52	40

Don Quixote, Dulcinea and Aldonza Lorenzo — A332

1966, Sept. 5 **Photo.** ***Perf. 13***

1373	A332	1.50p	sal, lt grn & blk	12	10

4th World Congress of Psychiatry, Madrid.

Europa Issue, 1966

The Rape of Europa A333

1966, Sept. 28 **Photo.** ***Perf. 12½x13***

1374	A333	1p	multi	12	10
1375	A333	5p	multi	30	20

Don Quixote and Sancho Panza on Clavileno A334

Title Page of "Dotrina Christiana" A335

1966, Oct. 9 ***Perf. 13x12½***

1376	A334	1.50p	sl bl, red brn & dk brn	15	10

Issued to commemorate the 17th Congress of the International Astronautical Federation.

Builders of the New World

Types of 1961 and A335

Designs: 30c, Antonio de Mendoza. 1p, José A. Manso de Velasco. 1.20p, Coins of Lima, 1699. 1.50p, Manuel de Castro y Padilla. 3p, Portal of Oruro Convent, Bolivia. 3.50p, Manuel de Amat. 6p, Inca courier, El Chasqui.

1966, Oct. 12

1377	A265	30c	pale pink & brn	8	6
1378	A335	50c	pale bis & brn	8	6
1379	A265	1p	gray & vio	10	6
1380	A335	1.20p	gray & sl	10	6
1381	A265	1.50p	pale grn & dp grn	10	6
1382	A335	3p	pale gray & dp bl	10	6
1383	A265	3.50p	pale lil & pur	12	10
1384	A265	6p	buff & sep	12	6
		Nos. 1377-1384 (8)		80	52

Ramon del Valle Inclan — A336

Portraits: 3p, Carlos Arniches. 6p, Jacinto Benavente y Martinez.

1966, Nov. 7 **Photo.** ***Perf. 13***

1385	A336	1.50p	blk & grn	10	10
1386	A336	3p	blk & gray vio	10	8
1387	A336	6p	blk & sl	10	10

Issued to honor Spanish writers.

Carthusian Monastery, Jerez — A337

St. Mary Carthusian Monastery: 1p, Portal (vert.). 5p, Entrance gate.

Perf. 13x12½, 12½x13

1966, Nov. 24 **Engr.**

1388	A337	1p	grnsh bl & sl bl	8	7
1389	A337	2p	grn & yel grn	12	10
1390	A337	5p	lil & cl	20	12

Nativity, Sculpture by Pedro Duque Cornejo A338

1966, Dec. 5 **Photo.** ***Perf. 12½x13***

1391	A338	1.50p	multi	12	10

Regional Costumes Issue

Woman from Alava — A339

1967 Photo. *Perf. 13*

1392	A339	6p	*shown*	10	10
1393	A339	6p	*Albacete*	10	10
1394	A339	6p	*Alicante*	10	10
1395	A339	6p	*Almeria*	12	10
1396	A339	6p	*Avila*	10	10
1397	A339	6p	*Badajoz*	10	10
1398	A339	6p	*Baleares*	10	10
1399	A339	6p	*Barcelona*	10	10
1400	A339	6p	*Burgos*	10	10
1401	A339	6p	*Caceres*	12	10
1402	A339	6p	*Cadiz*	10	10
1403	A339	6p	*Castellon de la Plana*	10	10
			Nos. 1392-1403 (12)	1.24	1.20

1968

1404	A339	6p	*Ciudad Real*	10	10
1405	A339	6p	*Cordoba*	12	10
1406	A339	6p	*Coruna*	12	10
1407	A339	6p	*Cuenca*	12	10
1408	A339	6p	*Fernando Po*	12	10
1409	A339	6p	*Gerona*	10	10
1410	A339	6p	*Gran Canaria, Las Palmas*	12	10
1411	A339	6p	*Granada*	12	10
1412	A339	6p	*Guadalajara*	12	10
1413	A339	6p	*Guipuzcoa*	12	10
1414	A339	6p	*Huelva*	12	10
1415	A339	6p	*Huesca*	12	10
			Nos. 1404-1415 (12)	1.40	1.20

1969

1416	A339	6p	*Ifni*	12	10
1417	A339	6p	*Jaen*	12	10
1418	A339	6p	*Leon*	12	10
1419	A339	6p	*Lerida*	12	10
1420	A339	6p	*Logrono*	12	10
1421	A339	6p	*Lugo*	12	10
1422	A339	6p	*Madrid*	12	10
1423	A339	6p	*Malaga*	12	10
1424	A339	6p	*Murcia*	12	10
1425	A339	6p	*Navarra*	12	10
1426	A339	6p	*Orense*	12	10
1427	A339	6p	*Oviedo*	12	10
			Nos. 1416-1427 (12)	1.44	1.20

1970

1428	A339	6p	*Palencia*	12	10
1429	A339	6p	*Pontevedra*	12	10
1430	A339	6p	*Sahara*	12	10
1431	A339	6p	*Salamanca*	12	10
1432	A339	6p	*Santa Cruz de Tenerife*	12	10
1433	A339	6p	*Santander*	12	10
1434	A339	6p	*Segovia*	12	10
1435	A339	6p	*Seville*	12	15
1436	A339	6p	*Soria*	12	10
1437	A339	6p	*Tarragona*	14	10
1438	A339	6p	*Teruel*	14	10
1439	A339	6p	*Toledo*	14	10
			Nos. 1428-1439 (12)	1.50	1.25

1971

1440	A339	6p	*Valencia*	20	12
1441	A339	8p	*Valladolid*	25	12
1442	A339	8p	*Vizcaya*	25	12
1443	A339	8p	*Zamora*	25	12
1444	A339	8p	*Zaragoza*	25	12
			Nos. 1440-1444 (5)	1.20	60
			Nos. 1392-1444 (53)	6.78	5.45

Archers A340

Ornament A341

Designs: 50c, Boar hunt. 1.20p, Bison. 1.50p, Hands. 2p, Warrior. 2.50p, Deer. 3.50p, Archers. 4p, Hunters and gazelle. 6p, Hunters and deer herd.

1967, Mar. 27 Photo. *Perf. 13*
Gold Frame

1449	A340	40c	ocher & car rose	8	5
1450	A340	50c	gray & dk red	8	5
1451	A341	1p	ocher & org ver	10	5
1452	A340	1.20p	gray & rose brn	10	5
1453	A340	1.50p	gray & red	10	5
1454	A341	2p	lt brn & dk car rose	10	5
1455	A341	2.50p	sky bl & rose brn	10	5
1456	A340	3.50p	yel & blk	10	8
1457	A341	4p	cit & red	10	10
1458	A341	6p	ol & red	12	10
			Nos. 1449-1458 (10)	98	63

Issued for Stamp Day, 1967. The designs are from paleolithic and mesolithic wall paintings found in Spanish caves.

Palma Cathedral and Conference Emblem — A342

1967, Mar. 28

1459	A342	1.50p	brt bl grn	15	10

Issued to publicize the Congress of the Interparliamentary Union, Palma de Mallorca.

W. K. Röntgen, X-ray Tube and Atom — A343

1967, Apr. 3 Photo. *Perf. 13*

1460	A343	1.50p	green	15	10

Issued to publicize the 7th Congress of Latin Radiologists and the 1st Congress of European Radiologists, Barcelona, Apr. 2-8.

Averroes (1120-1198), Physician and Philosopher — A344

Portraits: 3.50p, Josede Acosta (1539-1600), Jesuit, historian, poet. 4p, Moses ben Maimonides (1135-1204), Jewish philosopher and physician. 25p, Andres Laguna, 16th century physician.

1967, Apr. 6 Engr. *Perf. 13x12½*

1461	A344	1.20p	lil & dl vio	10	5
1462	A344	3.50p	mag & dl pur	12	7
1463	A344	4p	brn & sep	12	8
1464	A344	25p	dl bl & blk	32	10

Europa Issue, 1967
Common Design Type

1967, May 2 Photo. *Perf. 13*
Size: 25x31mm.

1465	CD10	1.50p	sl grn, red brn & dl red	12	12
1466	CD10	6p	vio, brt bl & brn	35	20

Exhibition Building and Fountain, Valencia — A345

1967, May 3

1467	A345	1.50p	gray grn	12	10

Issued to commemorate the 50th anniversary of the International Fair at Valencia.

Numeral Postmark No. 3 of 1850 — A346

Guardian Angel Over Indigent Sleeper — A347

Designs: 1.50p, No. 2, 12c stamp of 1850 with crowned M postmark of Madrid. 6p, No. 4, 6r stamp of 1850 with 1r postmark.

1967, May 6

1468	A346	40c	brn org, dl bl & blk	7	5
1469	A346	1.50p	brn, grn & blk	7	5
1470	A346	6p	bl, red & blk	10	10

International Stamp Day, 1967. See Nos. 1527-1528.

1967, May 16 *Perf. 13*

1471	A347	1.50p	bl, blk, brn & red	12	10

Issued for National Caritas Day to honor Caritas, Catholic welfare organization.

Tourist Issue, 1967

Betanzos Church, Coruna — A348

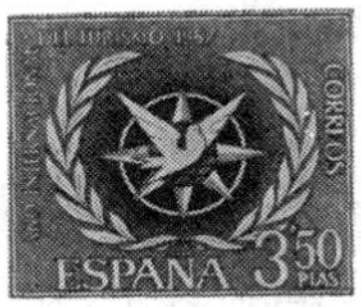

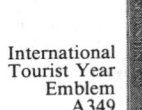

International Tourist Year Emblem A349

Designs: 1p, Tower of St. Miguel Church, Palencia. 1.50p, Human pyramid (Castellers). 2.50p, Columbus monument, Huelva. 5p, The Enchanted City, Cuenca. 6p, Church of Our Lady, Sanlucar, Cadiz.

1967, July 26 Engr. *Perf. 13*

1472	A348	10c	ultra & blk	8	6
1473	A348	1p	dl bl & blk	8	6
1474	A348	1.50p	lt brn & blk	8	6
1475	A348	2.50p	grnsh bl & dk bl	8	6
1476	A349	3.50p	dl pur & dk bl	8	6
1477	A348	5p	yel grn & dk grn	12	6
1478	A348	6p	red lil & dl lil	12	6
			Nos. 1472-1478 (7)	64	42

Balsareny Castle — A350

Castles: 1p, Jarandilla. 1.50p, Almodovar. 2p, Ponferrada (vert.). 2.50p, Peniscola. 5p, Coca. 6p, Loarre. 10p, Belmonte.

1967, Aug. 11 Engr.

1479	A350	50c	gray & lt brn	8	8
1480	A350	1p	bl gray & dl pur	8	8
1481	A350	1.50p	bl gray & sage grn	8	8
1482	A350	2p	brick red & bis brn	8	8
1483	A350	2.50p	grnsh bl & sep	8	8
1484	A350	5p	rose vio & vio bl	12	8
1485	A350	6p	bis brn & gray brn	12	10
1486	A350	10p	aqua & sl	16	10
			Nos. 1479-1486 (8)	80	68

Globe, Snowflake and Thermometer A351

Galleon, Map of Americas, Spain and Philippines A352

1967, Aug. 30 Photo.

1487	A351	1.50p	brt bl	12	10

Issued to publicize the 12th International Refrigeration Congress, Madrid, Sept. 4-8.

1967, Oct. 10 Photo. *Perf. 13*

1488	A352	1.50p	red lil	12	10

Issued to commemorate the 4th Congress of Spanish, Portuguese, American and Philippine Municipalities, Barcelona, Oct. 6-12.

Builders of the New World

Type of 1961 and

Nootka Settlement A353

Designs: 40c, Francisco de la Bodega. 50c, Old map of Nootka coast (vert.). 1p, Francisco Antonio Mourelle. 1.50p, Esteban Jose Martinez. 3p, Old maps of coast of Northern California. 3.50p, Cayetano Valdes. 6p, Ships, San Elias, Alaska.

1967, Oct. 12

1489	A265	40c	pink & grnsh gray	8	5
1490	A353	50c	dk brn	8	5
1491	A265	1p	pale bl & red lil	8	5
1492	A353	1.20p	dk ol grn	8	5
1493	A265	1.50p	pale pink & bl grn	8	5
1494	A353	3p	buff & vio blk	8	8
1495	A265	3.50p	pale pink & bl	10	10
1496	A353	6p	red brn, *bluish*	15	8
			Nos. 1489-1496 (8)	73	51

Issued to honor the explorers of the Northwest coast of North America.

Roman Statue and Gate A354

José Bethencourt A355

Designs: 3.50p, Ancient plower with ox team (horiz.). 6p, Roman coins of Caceres.

1967, Oct. 31 Photo. *Perf. 13*

1497	A354	1.50p	multi	8	8
1498	A354	3.50p	multi	12	10
1499	A354	6p	multi	18	15

Issued to commemorate the 2000th anniversary of the founding of Caceres by the Romans.

1967, Nov. 15

Portraits: 1.50p, Enrique Granados (composer). 3.50p, Ruben Dario (poet). 6p, St. Ildefonso.

1500 A355 1.20p gray & red brn 8 6
1501 A355 1.50p blk & grn 8 6
1502 A355 3.50p brn & pur 8 6
1503 A355 6p blk & sl 8 8

Issued to honor famous Spanish men.

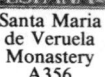

Santa Maria de Veruela Monastery A356

St. José Receiving Last Unction, by Goya A357

Designs: 3.50p, Aerial view of monastery (horiz.). 6p, Inside view (horiz.).

1967, Nov. 24 Engr. *Perf. 13*
1504 A356 1.50p ultra & ind 8 8
1505 A356 3.50p grn & blk 12 10
1506 A356 6p rose vio & bis brn 22 15

1967, Nov. 27 Photo.
1507 A357 1.50p multi 12 10

Issued to commemorate the 200th anniversary of the canonization of St. José de Calasanz (1556-1648), founder of the first Christian Schools in Rome.

Nativity, by Francisco Salzillo — A358

1967, Dec. 5
1508 A358 1.50p multi 12 10

Christmas, 1967.

Slalom A359

Designs: 3.50p, Bobsled (vert.). 6p, Ice hockey.

1968, Feb. 6 Photo. *Perf. 13*
1509 A359 1.50p multi 10 10
1510 A359 3.50p multi 12 10
1511 A359 6p multi 16 10

Issued to commemorate the 10th Winter Olympic Games, Grenoble, France, Feb. 6-18.

Mariano Fortuny, Self-portrait A360

Fortuny Paintings: 40c, The Vicariate (horiz.). 50c, "Fantasy" (pianist). 1p, "Idyll" (piper and sheep). 1.20p, The Print Collector (horiz.). 2p, Old Man in the Sun. 2.50p, Calabrian Man. 3.50p, Lady with Fan. 4p, Battle of Tetuan, 1860. 6p, Queen Christina in Carriage (horiz.).

1968, Mar. 25 Photo. *Perf. 13*
Gold Frame
1512 A360 40c dp red lil 6 6
1513 A360 50c dk bl grn 6 6
1514 A360 1p brown 8 5
1515 A360 1.20p dp vio 8 6
1516 A360 1.50p dp grn 8 5
1517 A360 2p org brn 8 5
1518 A360 2.50p car rose 8 6
1519 A360 3.50p dk red brn 16 8
1520 A360 4p dk ol 8 6
1521 A360 6p brt bl 8 8
Nos. 1512-1521 (10) 84 61

Issued to honor Mariano Fortuny y Carbo (1838-74), and for Stamp Day.

Beatriz Galindo A361

Famous Women: 1.50p, Agustina de Aragon. 3.50p, Maria Pacheco. 6p, Rosalia de Castro.

1968, Apr. 8 Engr. *Perf. 12½x13*
1522 A361 1.20p yel brn & blk brn 10 9
1523 A361 1.50p bl grn & dk bl 10 8
1524 A361 3.50p lt vio & dk vio 12 10
1525 A361 6p gray bl & blk 18 10

Europa Issue, 1968
Common Design Type

1968, Apr. 29 Photo. *Perf. 13*
Size: 38x22mm.
1526 CD11 3.50p brt bl, gold & brn 22 15

Spain No. 1 with Galicia Puebla Postmark — A362

Map of Leon and Seal — A363

Design: 3.50p, Spain No. 4 with Serena postmark.

1968, May 6 Photo. *Perf. 13*
1527 A362 1.50p blk, bl & ocher 10 10
1528 A362 3.50p bl, dk grn & blk 10 10

Issued for Stamp Day, 1968. See Nos. 1568-1569, 1608, 1677, 1754.

Perf. 13x12½, 12½x13
1968, June 15 Photo.
Size: 25x38½mm.

Designs: 1.50p, Roman legionary. 3.50p, Emperor Galba coin (horiz.).

1529 A363 1p lil, red brn & yel 8 8

Size: 25x47½mm.
1530 A363 1.50p brn, dk brn & buff 8 8

Size: 37½x26mm.
1531 A363 3.50p ocher & sl grn 22 10

Issued to commemorate the 1900th anniversary of the founding of Leon by the Roman Legion VII Gemina.

Human Rights Emblem A364

Benavente Palace, Baeza A365

1968, June 25 Photo. *Perf. 13x12½*
1532 A364 3.50p bl, red & grn 15 10

International Human Rights Year, 1968.

Tourist Issue, 1968

Designs: 1.20p, View of Salamanca with Tormes River Bridge (horiz.). 1.50p, Statuary group from St. Vincent's Church, Avila (The Adoration of the Magi). 2p, Tomb of Martin Vazquez de Arce, Cathedral of Sigüenza (horiz.). 3.50p, Portal of St. Mary's Church, Sangüesa, Navarre.

1968, July 15 Engr. *Perf. 13*
1533 A365 50c dp rose & brn 8 6
1534 A365 1.20p emer & sl grn 8 6
1535 A365 1.50p dp grn & ind 8 6
1536 A365 2p lil rose & blk 16 6
1537 A365 3.50p brt lil & rose lil 12 6
Nos. 1533-1537 (5) 52 30

Escalona Castle, Toledo — A366

Castles: 1.20p, Fuensaldaña, Valladolid. 1.50p, Peñafiel, Valladolid. 2.50p, Villasobroso, Pontevedra. 6p, Frias, Burgos (vert.).

1968, July 29 Engr. *Perf. 13*
1538 A366 40c dk bl & sep 8 8
1539 A366 1.20p vio brn & vio blk 8 8
1540 A366 1.50p ol & blk 8 6
1541 A366 2.50p ol grn & blk 12 5
1542 A366 6p vio bl & bl grn 25 8
Nos. 1538-1542 (5) 61 35

Rifle Shooting A367

Designs: 1.50p, Horse jumping. 3.50p, Bicycling. 6p, Sailing (vert.).

Perf. 12½x13, 13x12½
1968, Sept. 24 Photo.
1543 A367 1p multi 7 6
1544 A367 1.50p multi 8 8
1545 A367 3.50p multi 15 10
1546 A367 6p multi 10 10

Issued to publicize the 19th Olympic Games, Mexico City, Oct. 12-27.

Builders of the New World
Type of 1961 and

Map of Capuchin Missions along Orinoco River, 1732 — A368

Designs: 1p, Diego de Losada. 1.50p, de Henares. 6p, Map of Caracas, drawn by Diego de Henares, 1578 (horiz.).

1968, Oct. 12 Photo. *Perf. 13*
1547 A368 40c grnsh bl, *bluish* 7 6
1548 A265 1p red lil, *gray* 7 6
1549 A368 1.50p sl, *pale rose* 10 7
1550 A265 3.50p dk bl, *pnksh* 20 14
1551 A368 6p dk ol bis 28 16
Nos. 1547-1551 (5) 72 49

Issued to commemorate the Christianization of Venezuela and the founding of Caracas.

St. Maria del Parral Monastery, Segovia — A369

Designs: 3.50p, Monastery, inside view. 6p, Madonna and Child, statue from main altar.

1968, Nov. 25 Engr. *Perf. 13*
1552 A369 1.50p gray bl & rose vio 18 6
1553 A369 3.50p brn & red brn 25 18
1554 A369 6p rose cl & brn 25 12

Nativity, by Federico Fiori da Urbino A370

Alonso Cano by Velázquez A371

1968, Dec. 2 Photo. *Perf. 13x12½*
1555 A370 1.50p gold & multi 10 10

Christmas, 1968.

1969, Mar. 24 Photo. *Perf. 13*

Cano Paintings: 40c, St. Agnes. 50c, St. John. 1p, Jesus and Angel. 2p, Holy Family. 2.50p, Circumcision of Jesus. 3p, Jesus and the Samaritan Woman. 3.50p, Madonna and Child. 4p, Sts. John Capistrano and Bernardino (horiz.). 6p, Vision of St. John the Baptist.

Gold Frame
1556 A371 40c dp plum 10 10
1557 A371 50c green 10 10
1558 A371 1p sepia 10 10
1559 A371 1.50p sl grn 10 10
1560 A371 2p red brn 10 10
1561 A371 2.50p dp red lil 10 10
1562 A371 3p ultra 10 10
1563 A371 3.50p dk rose brn 10 10
1564 A371 4p dl lil 10 10
1565 A371 6p sl bl 12 12
Nos. 1556-1565 (10) 1.02 1.02

Issued to honor Alonso Cano (1601-1667), and for Stamp Day.

DNA (Genetic Code) Molecule and Chart A372

1969, Apr. 7 Photo. *Perf. 13*
1566 A372 1.50p gray & multi 12 10

Issued to publicize the 6th European Congress of Biochemistry, Madrid, Apr. 7-11.

Europa Issue, 1969
Common Design Type

1969, Apr. 28
Size: 38x22mm.
1567 CD12 3.50p multi 22 15

Stamp Day Type of 1968

Design: 1.50p, Spain No. 6 with crowned M postmark. 3.50p, Spain No. 11 with Corvera postmark.

1969, May 6 Photo. *Perf. 13*
1568 A362 1.50p blk, red & grn 10 10
1569 A362 3.50p grn, bl & red 12 10

Issued for Stamp Day, 1969.

Spectrum A373

1969, May 26

1570	A373	1.50p	blk & multi	12	10

Issued to publicize the 15th International Spectroscopy Colloquium, Madrid, May 26-30.

World Map, Red Crescent, Cross, Lion and Sun Emblems A374

1969, May 30

1571	A374	1.50p	multi	12	10

Issued to commemorate the 50th anniversary of the League of Red Cross Societies.

Last Supper, Finial from Lugo Cathedral — A375

1969, June 4

1572	A375	1.50p	grn, brn & blk	12	10

Issued to commemorate the 300th anniversary of the dedication of Galicia Province to the reign of Jesus.

Turegano Castle, Segovia — A376

Father Junipero Serra — A377

Castles: 1.50p, Villalonso, Zamora. 2.50p, Velez Blanco, Almeria. 3.50p, Castilnovo, Segovia. 6p, Torrelobaton, Valladolid.

1969, June 24 Engr. *Perf. 13*

1573	A376	1p	dl grn & sl	10	10
1574	A376	1.50p	bluish lil & dk bl	22	15
1575	A376	2.50p	bl vio & bluish lil	10	10
1576	A376	3.50p	red brn & ol grn	25	15
1577	A376	6p	gray grn & dl brn	16	12
			Nos. 1573-1577 (5)	83	62

1969, July 16 Photo. *Perf. 13*

1578	A377	1.50p	multi	12	10

Bicentenary of San Diego, Calif.

Rock of Gibraltar A378

Dama de Elche A379

Design: 2p, View of Gibraltar across the Bay of Algeciras.

1969, July 18

1579	A378	1.50p	bl grn	16	10
1580	A378	2p	brt rose lil	12	10

Tourist Issue, 1969

Designs: 1.50p, Alcañiz Castle, Teruel (horiz.). 3p, Murcia Cathedral. 6p, St. Maria de la Redonda, Logrono.

1969, July 23 Engr. *Perf. 13*

1581	A379	1.50p	dl grn & blk	18	10
1582	A379	3p	yel grn & bl grn	15	10
1583	A379	3.50p	gray bl & dk bl	18	10
1584	A379	6p	yel grn & vio blk	28	10

Builders of the New World
Type of 1961 and

Santo Domingo Church, Santiago, Chile — A380

Designs: 1.50p, Casa de Moneda de Chile (horiz.). 2p, Ambrosio O'Higgins. 3.50p, Pedro de Valdivia. 6p, First large bridge over Mapocho River (horiz.).

1969, Oct. 12 Photo. *Perf. 13*

1585	A380	40c	lt bl & dk red brn	12	10
1586	A380	1.50p	pale rose & dk vio	12	10
1587	A265	2p	pale pink & ol	25	10
1588	A265	3.50p	pale yel & dk Prus grn	30	18
1589	A380	6p	pale yel & blk brn	35	15
			Nos. 1585-1589 (5)	1.14	63

Exploration and development of Chile. See Nos. 1630-1631, 1634.

Adoration of the Magi, by Juan Bautista Mayno — A381

Christmas: 2p, Nativity, bas-relief from altar of Cathedral of Gerona.

1969, Nov. 3

1590	A381	1.50p	multi	10	8
1991	A381	2p	multi	12	10

Tomb of Alfonso VIII and Wife, Las Huelgas Monastery, Burgos A382

Designs: 1.50p, Las Huelgas Monastery. 6p, Inside view (vert.).

1969, Nov. 22 Engr.

1592	A382	1.50p	lt bl grn & ind	25	10
1593	A382	3.50p	ultra & vio bl	25	16
1594	A382	6p	ol & yel grn	38	16

See Nos. 1639-1641.

St. Juan de Avila, by El Greco — A383

St. Stephen, by Luis de Morales — A384

Design: 50p, Bishop Rodrigo Ximenez de Rada, Juan de Borgona mural.

1970, Feb. 25 Engr. *Perf. 13*

1595	A383	25p	pale pur & ind	3.50	15
1596	A383	50p	brn org & brn	2.75	40

1970, Mar. 24 Photo. *Perf. 13*

Morales Paintings: 1p, Annunciation. 1.50p, Madonna and Child with St. John. 2p, Madonna and Child. 3p, Presentation at the Temple. 3.50p, St. Jerome. 4p, St. John de Ribera. 5p, Ecce Homo. 6p, Pieta. 10p, St. Francis of Assisi.

1597	A384	50c	gold & multi	12	8
1598	A384	1p	gold & multi	12	8
1599	A384	1.50p	gold & multi	30	8
1600	A384	2p	gold & multi	30	8
1601	A384	3p	gold & multi	12	8
1602	A384	3.50p	gold & multi	12	10
1603	A384	4p	gold & multi	16	10
1604	A384	5p	gold & multi	12	10
1605	A384	6p	gold & multi	12	10
1606	A384	10p	gold & multi	25	20
			Nos. 1597-1606 (10)	1.73	1.00

Issued to honor Luis de Morales, "El Divino" (1509-1586), and for Stamp Day.

Europa Issue, 1970
Common Design Type

1970, May 4 Photo. *Perf. 13x12½*
Size: 37½x22mm.

1607	CD13	3.50p	brt bl & gold	25	12

Stamp Day Type of 1968

Design: 2p, Spain No. 51 with "Ferro Carril de Langreo" postmark.

1970, May 4 *Perf. 13x12½*

1608	A362	2p	dl red, grn & blk	15	10

Issued for Stamp Day, 1969.

Barcelona Fair Building A385

1970, May 27 *Perf. 13*

1609	A385	15p	multi	40	15

Barcelona Trade Fair, 50th anniversary.

Miguel Primo de Rivera — A386

1970, June 6 Photo. *Perf. 13*

1610	A386	2p	buff, brn & ol grn	20	10

Issued to commemorate the centenary of the birth of Gen. Miguel Primo de Rivera (1870-1930), Spanish dictator, 1923-1930.

Valencia de Don Juan Castle — A387

Castles: 1.20p, Monterrey. 3.50p, Mombeltran. 6p, Sadaba. 10p, Bellver.

1970, June 24 Engr.

1611	A387	1p	blk & dl bl	55	12
1612	A387	1.20p	lt grnsh bl & vio	15	8
1613	A387	3.50p	pale grn & brn	22	9
1614	A387	6p	sep & dl pur	38	15
1615	A387	10p	fawn & sep	1.25	22
			Nos. 1611-1615 (5)	2.55	66

Tourist Issue, 1970

Alcazaba Castle, Almeria — A388

Designs: 1p, Malaga Cathedral. 1.50p, St. Mary of the Assumption, Lequeitio (vert.). 2p, Cloister of St. Francis of Orense. 3.50p, Market (Lonja), Zaragoza (vert.). 5p, The Gate of Vitoria (vert.).

1970, July 23 Engr. *Perf. 13*

1616	A388	50c	bluish gray & dl pur	10	8
1617	A388	1p	red brn & ocher	20	8
1618	A388	1.50p	bluish gray & sl grn	20	8
1619	A388	2p	sl & dk bl	60	8
1620	A388	3.50p	pur & vio bl	30	15
1621	A388	5p	gray grn & red brn	1.25	20
			Nos. 1616-1621 (6)	2.65	67

Tailor, from Book Published in Madrid, 1589 A389

1970, Aug. 18 Photo. *Perf. 13*

1622	A389	2p	mag, brn & dl vio	15	10

Issued to publicize the 14th International Tailoring Congress, Madrid.

Diver and Map of Europe A390

1970, Aug. 25

1623	A390	2p	grn & brt bl	15	10

Issued to publicize the 12th European Championships in Swimming, Diving and Water Polo, Barcelona.

Concha Espina — A391

Portraits: 1p, Guillen de Castro. 1.50p, Juan Ramon Jimenez. 2p, Gustavo Adolfo Becquer. 2.50p, Miguel de Unamuno. 3.50p, Jose M. Gabriel y Galan.

1970, Sept. 21 Photo. *Perf. 13x12½*

1624	A391	50c	brn, vio bl & pale rose	8	8
1625	A391	1p	sl grn, dp rose lil & gray	10	8

1626	A391	1.50p	dk bl, brt grn & gray	10	8
1627	A391	2p	grn, dk ol & buff	30	8
1628	A391	2.50p	pur, rose lake & buff	12	8
1629	A391	3.50p	brn, dk red & gray	20	15
			Nos. 1624-1629 (6)	90	55

Issued to honor Spanish writers.

Builders of the New World

Portrait Type of 1961 and Building Type of 1969.

Designs: 40c, Ecala House, Queretaro, Mexico. 1.50p, Mexico Cathedral (horiz.). 2p, Vasco de Quiroga. 3.50p, Brother Juan de Zumarraga. 6p, Cathedral Towers, Morelia, Mexico.

1970, Oct. 12 Photo. *Perf. 13*

1630	A380	40c	lt bl & ol gray	10	8
1631	A380	1.50p	lt bl & brn	20	8
1632	A265	2p	buff & dk vio	52	8
1633	A265	3.50p	pale grn & dk grn	20	15
1634	A380	6p	pale pink & Prus bl	40	15
			Nos. 1630-1634 (5)	1.42	54

Exploration and development of Mexico.

Map of Western Mediterranean — A392

1970, Oct. 20 Photo. *Perf. 13*

1635	A392	2p	multi	15	10

Issued to commemorate the centenary of the Geographical and Statistical Institute.

Adoration of the Shepherds, by El Greco — A393

Christmas: 2p, Adoration of the Shepherds, by Murillo.

1970, Oct. 30

1636	A393	1.50p	multi	10	8
1637	A393	2p	multi	10	8

U.N. Emblem and Headquarters — A394

1970, Nov. 3

1638	A394	8p	multi	25	10

25th anniversary of the United Nations.

Monastery Type of 1969

Ripoll Monastery: 2p, Portal. 3.50p, View of monastery. 5p, Inside court.

1970, Nov. 12 Engr.

1639	A382	2p	vio & pur	95	12
1640	A382	3.50p	org & mar	38	12
1641	A382	5p	Prus grn & yel grn	1.50	15

Map with Main European Pilgrimage Routes — A395

Cathedral of St. David, Wales A396

Designs: No. 1643, Map of main pilgrimage routes. No. 1644, St. Bridget statue, Vadstena, Sweden. No. 1645, Santiago Cathedral. No. 1646, Tower of St. Jacques, Paris. No. 1647, Pilgrim before entering Santiago de Compostela. No. 1648, St. James statue, Pistoia, Italy. No. 1649, Lugo Cathedral. 2.50p, Villafranca del Bierzo church. No. 1652, Astorga Cathedral. 3.50p, San Marcos de Leon. No. 1654, Charlemagne, bas-relief, Aachen Cathedral, Germany. No. 1655, San Tirso de Sahagun. 5p, San Martin de Fromista. 6p, Bas-relief, King's Hospital, Burgos. 7p, Portal of Santo Domingo de la Calzada. 7.50p, Cloister, Najera. 8p, Puente de la Reina (Christ on the Cross and portal). 9p, Santa Maria de Eunate. 10p, Cross of Roncesvalles.

1971 Engr. *Perf. 13*

1642	A395	50c	grnsh bl & sep	15	8
1643	A396	50c	bl & dl vio	12	10
1644	A335	1p	brn & sl grn	20	8
1645	A395	1p	grn & sl grn	15	8
1646	A395	1.50p	dl grn & dp plum	38	8
1647	A396	1.50p	vio bl & lil	20	8
1648	A395	2p	dk pur & blk	30	15
1649	A395	2p	sl grn & dk bl	1.25	8
1650	A396	2.50p	vio brn & dl vio	25	15
1651	A396	3p	ultra & dk bl	38	15
1652	A395	3p	dl red & rose lil	65	8
1653	A396	3.50p	dp org & gray grn	38	20
1654	A396	4p	ol grn	65	20
1655	A395	4p	grnsh bl & brn	38	15
1656	A396	5p	lt grn & blk	1.00	15
1657	A395	6p	lt ultra	38	10
1658	A395	7p	lil & dl vio	35	30
1659	A396	7.50p	car lake & dl vio	35	30
1660	A395	8p	grn & vio blk	35	20
1661	A396	9p	grn & vio	35	25
1662	A395	10p	grn & brn	50	20
			Nos. 1642-1662 (21)	8.72	3.16

Holy Year of Compostela, 1971.

Ignacio Zuloaga, Self-portrait A397

Amadeo Vives, Composer A398

Zuloaga Paintings: 50c, "My Uncle Daniel." 1p, View of Segovia (horiz.). 1.50p, Countess of Alba. 3p, Juan Belmonte. 4p, Countess of Noailles. 5p, Pablo Uranga. 8p, Cobblers' Houses at Lerma (horiz.).

1971, Mar. 24 Photo. *Perf. 13*

1663	A397	50c	gold & multi	10	8
1664	A397	1p	gold & multi	10	8
1665	A397	1.50p	gold & multi	10	8
1666	A397	2p	gold & multi	22	10
1667	A397	3p	gold & multi	22	10
1668	A397	4p	gold & multi	10	10
1669	A397	5p	gold & multi	22	15
1670	A397	8p	gold & multi	42	25
			Nos. 1663-1670 (8)	1.48	94

Ignacio Zuloaga (1870-1945). Stamp Day.

1971, Apr. 20

Portraits: 2p, St. Teresa of Avila. 8p, Benito Perez Galdos, writer. 15p, Ramon Menendez Pidal, writer.

1671	A398	1p	multi	28	8
1672	A398	2p	multi	28	8
1673	A398	8p	multi	35	18
1674	A398	15p	multi	45	18

Europa Issue, 1971

Common Design Type

1971, Apr. 29 Photo. *Perf. 13*

Size: 37x26mm.

1675	CD14	2p	lt bl, brn & vio bl	1.10	12
1676	CD14	8p	lt grn, dk brn & dk grn	60	25

Stamp Day Type of 1968

Design: 2p, Spain No. 1 with blue "A" cancellation.

1971, May 6

1677	A362	2p	blk, bl & ol	18	10

Stamp Day, 1971.

Gymnast — A399

Design: 2p, Gymnast on bar.

1971, May 14

1678	A399	1p	ocher & multi	20	12
1679	A399	2p	lt bl & multi	20	8

9th European Gymnastic Championships for Men, Madrid, May 14-15.

Great Bustard A400

Designs: 2p, Pardine lynx. 3p, Brown bear. 5p, Red-legged partridge (vert.). 8p. Spanish ibex (vert.).

1971, May 24

1680	A400	1p	multi	20	10
1681	A400	2p	multi	28	10
1682	A400	3p	multi	35	10
1683	A400	5p	multi	70	25
1684	A400	8p	multi	90	35
			Nos. 1680-1684 (5)	2.43	90

Legionnaires — A401

Designs: 2p, Legionnaires on dress parade. 5p, Memorial service. 8p, Desert fighter and tank column.

1971, June 21 Photo. *Perf. 13*

1685	A401	1p	multi	22	10
1686	A401	2p	multi	45	10
1687	A401	5p	multi	45	10
1688	A401	8p	multi	45	32

50th anniversary of the Legion, a voluntary military organization.

UNICEF Emblem, Children of Various Races — A402

1971, Sept. 10

1689	A402	8p	multi	20	15

25th anniv. of UNICEF.

Don Juan of Austria, Fleet Commander A403

Hockey Players, Hockey League and Games Emblems A404

Designs: 5p, Battle of Lepanto (horiz.). 8p, Holy League banner in Cathedral.

1971, Oct. 7 Engr. *Perf. 13*

1690	A403	2p	sep & sl grn	95	12
1691	A403	5p	chocolate	1.10	12
1692	A403	8p	rose car & vio bl	1.10	35

400th anniversary of the Battle of Lepanto against the Turks.

1971, Oct. 15 Photo.

1693	A404	5p	multi	1.10	20

First World Hockey Cup, Barcelona, Oct. 15-24.

De Havilland DH-9 over Seville A405

Design: 15p, Boeing 747 over Plaza de la Cibeles, Madrid.

1971, Oct. 25

1694	A405	2p	multi	52	12
1695	A405	15p	multi	60	22

50th anniversary of Spanish air mail service.

Nativity, Avia Altarpiece A406

Emilia Pardo Bazan A407

Design: 8p, Nativity, Sagas altarpiece.

1971, Nov. 4 ***Perf. 12½x13***
1696 A406 2p multi 15 8
1697 A406 8p multi 30 15

Christmas 1971.

1972, Jan. 27 Engr. ***Perf. 13***

Portraits: 25p, José de Espronceda. 50p, King Fernan Gonzalez.

1698 A407 15p brn & sl grn 40 15
1699 A407 25p lt grn & sl grn 40 15
1700 A407 50p cl & dp brn 70 35

Honoring Emilia Pardo Bazan (1852-1921), novelist (15p); José de Espronceda (1808-1842), poet (25p); Fernan Gonzalez (910-970), first King of Castile (50p).

Figure Skating — A408

Don Quixote Title Page, 1605 — A409

Design: 2p, Ski jump and Sapporo Olympic emblem (horiz.).

1972, Feb. 10 **Photo.**
1701 A408 2p gray & multi 38 8
1702 A408 15p bl & multi 55 22

11th Winter Olympic Games, Sapporo, Japan, Feb. 3-13.

1972, Feb. 24 Engr. ***Perf. 13x12½***
1703 A409 2p brn & cl 15 8

International Book Year 1972.

José Gutierrez Solana with Wife and Child — A410

Gutierrez Solana Paintings: 1p, Clowns (horiz.). 3p, Balladier. 4p, Fisherman. 5p, Mask makers. 7p, The book collector. 10p, Merchant marine captain. 15p, Afterdinner speaker (horiz.).

1972, Mar. 24 Photo. ***Perf. 13***
1704 A410 1p gold & multi 38 20
1705 A410 2p gold & multi 38 8
1706 A410 3p gold & multi 38 10
1707 A410 4p gold & multi 38 12
1708 A410 5p gold & multi 1.25 15
1709 A410 7p gold & multi 75 15
1710 A410 10p gold & multi 75 25
1711 A410 15p gold & multi 55 20
Nos. 1704-1711 (8) 4.82 1.25

José Gutierrez Solana (1886-1945). Stamp Day 1972.

Fir — A411

1972, Apr. 21
1712 A411 1p *shown* 50 10
1713 A411 2p *Strawberry tree* 50 12
1714 A411 3p *Cluster pine* 50 12
1715 A411 5p *Evergreen oak* 50 18
1716 A411 8p *Juniper* 50 22
Nos. 1712-1716 (5) 2.50 74

Europeans Interlocking A412

Pre-stamp Cordoba Postmark (1824-42) A413

Europa, 1972
Common Design Type and Type A412

1972, May 2
1717 A412 2p dl grn & ocher 3.25 15

Size: 25x38mm.
1718 CD15 8p multi 1.40 30

1972, May 6 ***Perf. 12½x13***
1719 A413 2p dl yel, blk & car 15 8

Stamp Day 1972.

Santa Catalina Castle, Jaen — A414

Castles: 1p, Sajazarra, Rioja (vert.). 3p, Biar, Alicante. 5p, San Servando, Toledo. 10p, Pedraza, Segovia.

1972, June 22 Engr. ***Perf. 13***
1720 A414 1p dl bl grn & brn 65 20
1721 A414 2p gray ol & grn 1.10 15
1722 A414 3p rose car & red brn 1.10 15
1723 A414 5p vio bl & dl grn 1.10 25
1724 A414 10p sl & lil 3.50 25
Nos. 1720-1724 (5) 7.45 1.00

Weight Lifting, Olympic Emblems — A415

1972, Aug. 26 Photo. ***Perf. 13***
1725 A415 1p *Olympic emblems, fencing,* horiz. 18 10
1726 A415 2p *shown* 38 10
1727 A415 5p *Sculling* 28 20
1728 A415 8p *Pole vaulting* 28 25

20th Olympic Games, Munich, Aug. 26-Sept. 11.

Egyptian Mongoose A416

1972, Sept. 14
1729 A416 1p *Aquatic mole,* vert. 20 15
1730 A416 2p *Chamois* 50 15
1731 A416 3p *Wolf* 70 15
1732 A416 5p *shown* 70 20
1733 A416 7p *Spotted genet* 70 20
Nos. 1729-1733 (5) 2.80 85

Brigadier M.A. de Ustariz — A417

San Juan, 1870 A418

1972, Oct. 12 Photo. ***Perf. 13***
1734 A417 1p *shown* 35 10
1735 A418 2p *shown* 45 10
1736 A418 5p *San Juan, 1625* 45 15
1737 A418 8p *Map of Plaza and Bay, 1792* 45 40

450th anniversary of San Juan.

St. Tomas Monastery, Avila — A419

Designs: 8p, Inside view. 15p, Cloister (horiz.).

1972, Oct. 26 **Engr.**
1738 A419 2p Prus bl & gray grn 1.25 12
1739 A419 8p gray & cl 1.25 25
1740 A419 15p vio & red lil 1.10 25

Teatro del Liceo, Barcelona A420

1972, Nov. 7 ***Perf. 12½x13***
1741 A420 8p ultra & sep 55 20

125th anniversary of the Gran Teatro del Liceo in Barcelona.

Annunciation — A421

Design: 8p, Angel and shepherds. Designs are from Romanesque murals in the Collegiate Basilica of San Isidro, Leon.

1972, Nov. 14 Photo. ***Perf. 13***
1742 A421 2p gold & multi 25 8
1743 A421 8p gold & multi 15 8

Christmas 1972.

Juan de Herrera and Escorial A422

Designs: 10p, Juan de Villanueva and Prado. 15p, Ventura Rodriguez and Apollo Fountain.

1973, Jan. 29 Engr. ***Perf. 12½x13***
1744 A422 8p sep & sl grn 85 15
1745 A422 10p blk brn & bluish blk 1.65 25
1746 A422 15p brt grn & ind 85 10

Great Spanish architects.

Myrica Faya — A423

Europa, Roman Mosaic — A424

Designs: Flora of Canary Islands.

1973, Mar. 21 Photo. ***Perf. 13***
1747 A423 1p *Apollonias canariensis,* horiz. 30 10
1748 A423 2p *shown* 75 10
1749 A423 4p *Palms* 30 10
1750 A423 5p *Holly* 75 10
1751 A423 15p *Dracaena draco* 80 22
Nos. 1747-1751 (5) 2.90 62

Europa Issue
Common Design Type and A424

1973, Apr. 30 Photo. ***Perf. 13***
1752 A424 2p multi 1.25 20

Size: 37x26mm.
1753 CD16 8p lt bl, blk & red 1.00 25

Stamp Day Type of 1968

Design: 2p, Spain No. 23 with red Madrid, 1853, cancellation.

1973, May 5
1754 A362 2p blk, bl & red 18 8

Stamp Day 1973.

Iznajar Dam on Genil River — A425

1973, June 9 Photo. ***Perf. 12½x13***
1755 A425 8p multi 22 12

11th Congress of the International Commission on High Dams, Madrid, June 11-15.

Oñate University, Guipuzcoa A426

Designs: 2p, Plaza del Campo and fountain, Lugo. 3p, Plaza de Llerena and fountain, Badajoz (vert.). 5p, House of Columbus, Las Palmas. 8p, Windmills, La Mancha.

1973, June 11 Engr. ***Perf. 13***
1756 A426 1p gray & sep 38 10
1757 A426 2p brt grn & sl grn 70 10
1758 A426 3p dk brn & org brn 70 10
1759 A426 5p dk gray & vio blk 1.65 15
1760 A426 8p dk gray & car 95 35
Nos. 1756-1760 (5) 4.38 80

The lack of a value for a listed item does not necessarily indicate rarity.

Azure-winged Magpie — A427

Knight, Holy Fraternity of Castile, 1488 — A428

Birds: 1p, Black-bellied sand grouse (horiz.). 2p, Black stork (horiz.). 7p, Imperial eagle (horiz.). 15p, Red-crested pochard.

1973, July 3 Photo. *Perf. 13*

1761	A427	1p multi	32	10
1762	A427	2p multi	60	10
1763	A427	5p multi	85	10
1764	A427	7p multi	1.10	10
1765	A427	15p multi	75	35
		Nos. 1761-1765 (5)	3.62	75

1973, July 17

Uniforms: 2p, Knight, Castile, 1493 (horiz.). 3p, Harquebusier, 1534. 7p, Mounted rifleman, 1560. 8p, Infantry sergeants, 1567.

1766	A428	1p multi	40	12
1767	A428	2p multi	80	10
1768	A428	3p multi	1.00	12
1769	A428	7p multi	60	10
1770	A428	8p multi	80	25
		Nos. 1766-1770 (5)	3.60	69

See Nos. 1794-1798, 1824-1828, 1869-1873, 1902-1906, 1989-1993, 2020-2024, 2051-2055, 2078-2082.

Fish in Net — A429

1973, Sept. 12 Photo. *Perf. 13*

1771	A429	2p multi	20	10

6th International Fishing Exhibition, Vigo, Sept. 12-19.

Conference Hall A430

1973, Sept. 14

1772	A430	8p multi	22	10

Plenipotentiary Conference of the International Telecommunications Union, Torremolinos, Sept. 1973.

Vicente López, Self-portrait A431

Paintings by Vicente López: 1p, King Ferdinand VII. 3p, Senora de Carvallo. 4p, Marshal Castelldosrrius. 5p, Queen Isabella II. 7p, Francisco Goya. 10p, Maria Amalia de Sajonia. 15p, The organist Felix López.

1973, Sept. 29 Photo. *Perf. 13*

1773	A431	1p gold & multi	20	8
1774	A431	2p gold & multi	30	8
1775	A431	3p gold & multi	30	8
1776	A431	4p gold & multi	20	10
1777	A431	5p gold & multi	20	10
1778	A431	7p gold & multi	20	10
1779	A431	10p gold & multi	30	12
1780	A431	15p gold & multi	40	20
		Nos. 1773-1780 (8)	2.10	86

Vicente Lopez y Portana (1772-1850), painter. Stamp Day 1973.

Leon Cathedral, Nicaragua A432

Designs: 2p, Subtiava Church. 5p, Portal of Governor's House (vert.). 8p, Rio San Juan Castle.

1973, Oct. 12

1781	A432	1p multi	22	8
1782	A432	2p multi	35	10
1783	A432	5p multi	45	10
1784	A432	8p multi	45	10

Hispanic-American buildings in Nicaragua.

Pope Gregory XI and Pedro Fernandez Pecha — A433

1973, Oct. 26

1785	A433	2p multi	18	8

600th anniversary of the founding of the Order of the Hermites of St. Jerome by Pedro Fernandez Pecha.

St. Domingo de Silos Monastery A434

Nativity, Column Capital, Silos Church A435

Designs: 8p, Cloister walk (horiz.). 15p, Three saints, sculpture.

Perf. 13x12½, 12½x13

1973, Oct. 26 Engr.

1786	A434	2p brn & rose mag	48	8
1787	A434	8p dk bl & pur	38	15
1788	A434	15p Prus grn & ind	55	15

St. Domingo de Silos Monastery, Burgos.

1973, Nov. 6 Photo. *Perf. 13*

Design: 8p, Adoration of the Kings, Butrera Church (horiz.).

1789	A435	2p multi	20	8
1790	A435	8p multi	20	15

Christmas 1973.

Map of Spain and Americas with Dates of First Printings A436

Designs: 7p, Teacher and Pupils, woodcut from "Libros de los Suenos," Valencia, 1474 (vert.). 15p, Title page from "Los Sinodales," Segovia, 1472.

1973, Dec. 11 Engr. *Perf. 13*

1791	A436	1p ind & sl grn	52	8
1792	A436	7p vio bl & pur	30	12
1793	A436	15p pur & blk	60	25

500 years of Spanish printing.

Uniform Type of 1973

Uniforms: 1p, Harquebusier on horseback, 1603. 2p, Harquebusiers, 1632. 3p, Cuirassier, 1635. 5p, Mounted drummer of the Dragoons, 1677. 9p, Two Musketeers, 1694.

1974, Jan. 5 Photo. *Perf. 13*

1794	A428	1p multi	42	10
1795	A428	2p multi	85	10
1796	A428	3p multi	1.00	10
1797	A428	5p multi	1.50	20
1798	A428	9p multi	1.25	25
		Nos. 1794-1798 (5)	5.02	75

Nautical Chart of Western Europe and North Africa — A437

1974, Jan. 26

1799	A437	2p multi	15	8

50th anniversary of the Superior Geographical Council of Spain. The chart is from a 14th century Catalan atlas.

M. Biada and Steam Engine A438

1974, Apr. 2 Photo. *Perf. 13*

1800	A438	2p multi	18	8

125th anniversary of Barcelona-Mataro Railroad.

Young Collector, Album, Magnifier A439

Exhibition Emblem — A440

Design: 8p, Emblem, globe and arrows.

1974, Apr. 4 *Perf. 13*

1801	A439	2p lil rose & multi	25	12

Perf. 12½

1802	A440	5p buff, blk & dl bl	50	12
1803	A440	8p dl grn & multi	40	18

Espana 75, International Philatelic Exhibition, Madrid, Apr. 4-13, 1975.

Woman with Offering — A441

Europa: 8p, Woman from Baza, painted sculpture.

1974, Apr. 29 Photo. *Perf. 13*

1804	A441	2p multi	1.40	12
1805	A441	8p multi	50	35

No. 28 and 1854 "Sevilla" Cancel A442

1974, May 6

1806	A442	2p blk, bl & red	15	8

World Stamp Day.

Father Jaime Balmes A443

Designs: 10p, Father Pedro Poveda. 15p, Jorge Juan y Santacilla.

1974, May 28 Engr. *Perf. 13*

1807	A443	8p bl gray & sep	28	20
1808	A443	10p red brn & dk brn	80	15
1809	A443	15p brn & sl	38	15

Famous Spaniards: Jaime Balmes (1810-1848), mathematician; death centenary of Pedro Poveda, pedagogue; Don Jorge Juan (1712-1773), explorer and writer.

Templeto, by Bramante, Rome — A444

1974, June 4 Photo.

1810	A444	5p multi	40	12

Centenary of the Spanish Academy of Fine Arts, Rome.

Aqueduct, Segovia A445

Designs: 2p, Tajo Bridge, Alcantara. 3p, Marcus Valerius Martial lecturing. 4p, Triumphal Arch, Tarragona (vert.). 5p, Theater, Merida. 7p, Bishop Ossius of Cordoba preaching. 8p, Tribunal Arch, Talavera Forum (vert.). 9p, Emperor Trajan (vert.).

1974, June 25 Engr.

1811	A445	1p brn & blk	12	10
1812	A445	2p gray grn & sep	50	10
1813	A445	3p lt & dk brn	12	10
1814	A445	4p grn & ind	12	10
1815	A445	5p gray bl & choc	22	10
1816	A445	7p gray grn & lil	22	10

1817	A445	8p dk brn & grn	22	20
1818	A445	9p brt red lil & cl	22	20
		Nos. 1811-1818 (8)	1.74	1.00

Roman architecture and history in Spain.

Greek Tortoise A446

Reptiles: 2p, Common chameleon. 5p, Wall gecko. 7p, Emerald lizard. 15p, Blunt-nosed viper.

1974, July 3 **Photo.**

1819	A446	1p multi	32	10
1820	A446	2p multi	42	10
1821	A446	5p multi	55	25
1822	A446	7p multi	42	22
1823	A446	15p multi	42	20
		Nos. 1819-1823 (5)	2.13	87

Uniform Type of 1973

Uniforms: 1p, Hussar and horse, 1705. 2p, Artillery officers, 1710. 3p, Piper and drummer, Granada Regiment, 1734. 7p, Mounted standard-bearer, Numancia Dragoons, 1737. 8p, Standard-bearer and soldier, Zamora Regiment, 1739.

1974, July 17

1824	A428	1p multi	20	10
1825	A428	2p multi	60	10
1826	A428	3p multi	70	12
1827	A428	7p multi	60	18
1828	A428	8p multi	80	22
		Nos. 1824-1828 (5)	2.90	72

Life Saving A447

1974, Sept. 5 **Photo.** ***Perf. 13***

1829	A447	2p multi	22	8

18th World Life Saving Championships, Barcelona, Sept. 1974.

Eduardo Rosales, by Federico Madrazo — A448

Eduardo Rosales Paintings: 1p, Tobias and the Angel. 3p, The Last Will of Isabella the Catholic (horiz.). 4p, Nena (little girl). 5p, Presentation of John of Austria to Charles I (horiz.). 7p, The First Step (horiz.). 10p, St. John the Evangelist. 15p, St. Matthew.

1974, Sept. 29 **Photo.** ***Perf. 13***

1830	A448	1p gold & multi	15	10
1831	A448	2p gold & multi	15	10
1832	A448	3p gold & multi	15	10
1833	A448	4p gold & multi	20	10
1834	A448	5p gold & multi	25	10
1835	A448	7p gold & multi	25	10
1836	A448	10p gold & multi	45	15
1837	A448	15p gold & multi	45	25
		Nos. 1830-1837 (8)	2.05	1.00

Eduardo Rosales (1836-1873). Stamp Day 1974.

Values quoted in this catalogue are for stamps graded at Fine-Very Fine and with no faults. An illustrated guide to grade is provided in introductory material, beginning on Page V.

"International Mail" — A449 UPU Monument, Bern — A450

1974, Oct. 9

1838	A449	2p dk bl & multi	28	12
1839	A450	8p red & multi	22	20

Centenary of Universal Postal Union.

Sobremonte House, Cordoba, Argentina — A451

Ruins of San Ignacio de Mini, 18th Century — A452 The Gaucho Martin Fierro — A453

Design: 2p, Municipal Council Building, Buenos Aires, 1829.

1974, Oct. 12

1840	A451	1p multi	20	8
1841	A451	2p multi	40	8
1842	A452	5p multi	40	8
1843	A453	10p multi	40	18

Cultural ties with Latin America.

Nativity, Valdavia Church A454

Adoration of the Kings, Valcobero Church — A455

1974 **Photo.** ***Perf. 13***

1844	A454	2p multi	10	8
1845	A455	3p lt bl & multi	20	8
1846	A455	8p ol & multi	20	10

Christmas 1974.
Issue dates: 2p, 8p, Nov. 4; 3p, Dec. 2.

Teucriun Lanigerum — A456

Flowers: 2p, Hypericum ericoides. 4p, Thymus longiflorus. 5p, Anthyllis onobrychioides. 8p, Helianthemun paniculatum.

1974, Nov. 8

1847	A456	1p multi	25	8
1848	A456	2p multi	38	8
1849	A456	4p multi	25	8
1850	A456	5p multi	38	8
1851	A456	8p multi	50	12
		Nos. 1847-1851 (5)	1.76	44

Franco Type of 1954-56
Imprint: "F.N.M.T."

1974-1975 **Photo.** ***Perf. 12½x13***

1852	A221	4p rose car ('75)	12	5
1853	A221	7p brt ultra	18	5
1854	A221	12p bl grn	22	5
1855	A221	20p rose car	55	12

Leyre Monastery A457

Designs: 8p, Column and bas-relief (vert.). 15p, Crypt.

1974, Dec. 10 **Engr.** ***Perf. 12½x13***

1862	A457	2p slate	55	8
1863	A457	8p carmine	32	15
1864	A457	15p grnsh blk	55	12

Leyre Monastery, Navarre.

Spain Nos. 1 and 1802 — A458

Mail Coach, 1850 A459

Designs: 8p, Mail ship of Indian Service. 10p, Chapel of St. Mark.

Perf. 12½x13, 13x12½

1975, Jan. 2 **Engr.**

1865	A458	2p sl bl	35	15
1866	A459	3p ol & brn	90	25
1867	A459	8p lil & sl bl	90	28
1868	A458	10p brn & sl grn	90	35

125th anniversary of Spanish postage stamps.

Uniform Type of 1973

Uniforms: 1p, Sergeant and grenadier, Toledo Regiment, 1750. 2p, Royal Artillery, 1762. 3p, Queen's Regiment, 1763. 5p, Fusiliers, Vitoria Regiment, 1766. 10p, Dragoon, Sagunto Regiment, 1775.

1975, Jan. 7 **Photo.** ***Perf. 13***

1869	A428	1p multi	75	10
1870	A428	2p multi	75	10
1871	A428	3p multi	2.25	15
1872	A428	5p multi	1.00	15
1873	A428	10p multi	2.25	18
		Nos. 1869-1873 (5)	7.00	68

Antonio Gaudi A460

Designs: 10p, Antonio Palacios and Casa Guell, Barcelona. 15p, Secundino Zuazo.

1975, Feb. 25 **Engr.** ***Perf. 13***

1874	A460	8p grn & blk	30	18
1875	A460	10p car & dp cl	60	12
1876	A460	15p brn & blk	40	12

Contemporary Spanish architects.

Souvenir Sheets

Spanish Goldsmiths' Works — A461

Designs: 2p, Agate box, 9th century. 3p, Votive crown of Recesvinto. 8p, Cover of Evangelistary, Roncesvalles Collegiate Church, 12th century. 10p, Chalice of Infanta Donna Urraca, 11th century. 12p, Processional monstrance, St. Domingo de Silos, 16th century. 15p, Sword of Boabdil, 15th century. 25p, Sword and head of Charles V (Carlos I of Spain). 50p, Earring and bracelet from Aliseda, 6th-4th centuries B.C. 3p, 10p, 12p, 25p vertical (No. 1878).

1975, Apr. 4 **Engr.** ***Perf. 13***

1877	A461	Sheet of 4	14.00	14.00
a		2p gray & Prus bl	1.50	1.50
b		8p brn & Prus bl	2.50	2.50
c		15p gray & dk car	2.50	2.50
d		50p dk car & gray	7.00	7.00
1878	A461	Sheet of 4	14.00	14.00
a		3p sl grn & gray	1.50	1.50
b		10p sep & sl	2.50	2.50
c		12p gray & bluish blk	2.50	2.50
d		25p sep & bluish blk	4.75	4.75

Espana 75 Intl. Phil. Exhib., Madrid, Apr. 4-13.

Pomegranates A462 Woman Gathering Honey, Arana Cave A463

1975, Apr. 21 **Photo.**

1879	A462	1p *Almonds, nuts and blossoms* (horiz.)	20	8
1880	A462	2p *shown*	40	8
1881	A462	3p *Oranges*	40	8
1882	A462	4p *Chestnuts*	32	8
1883	A462	5p *Apples*	32	8
		Nos. 1879-1883 (5)	1.64	40

Europa Issue 1975

Design: 12p, Horse (horiz.), wall painting from Tito Bustillo Cave.

1975, Apr. 28 **Photo.** ***Perf. 13***

1884	A463	3p brn & multi	1.00	15
1885	A463	12p brn & multi	75	20

Pre-stamp León Cancellation A464

1975, May 6 *Perf. 12½x13*
1886 A464 3p multi 12 8

World Stamp Day.

World Tourism Organization Emblem — A465

1975, May 12 **Photo.** *Perf. 13*
1887 A465 3p dk bl 15 8

First General Assembly of the World Tourism Organization, Madrid, May 1975.

Fair Emblem, Agricultural Symbols — A466

1975, May 14
1888 A466 3p multi 15 8

25th Agricultural Fair.

Equality Between Men and Women A467

1975, June 3
1889 A467 3p multi 15 8

International Women's Year.

Virgin of Cabeza Sanctuary A468

1975, June 18 **Photo.** *Perf. 13*
1890 A468 3p multi 15 8

Virgin of Cabeza Sanctuary, site of siege during Civil War, 1937.

Tourist Issue, 1975

Cervantes' Prison Cell, Argamasilla de Alba — A469

Designs: 2p, Bridge of St. Martin, Toledo. 3p, Church of St. Peter, Tarrasa. 4p, Arch, Alhambra, Granada (vert.). 5p, Street, Mijas, Malaga (vert.). 7p, Church of St. Mary, Tarrasa (vert.).

1975, June 25 **Engr.** *Perf. 13*
1891 A469 1p pur & blk 10 8
1892 A469 2p red brn & brn 15 8
1893 A469 3p sl & sep 15 8
1894 A469 4p org & cl 15 8
1895 A469 5p sl grn & ind 20 12
1896 A469 7p vio bl & ind 75 12
Nos. 1891-1896 (6) 1.50 56

Salamander — A470

Designs: 2p, Newt. 3p, Tree toad. 6p, Midwife toad. 7p, Leaf frog.

1975, July 9 **Photo.** *Perf. 13*
1897 A470 1p ol & multi 25 8
1898 A470 2p lt bl & multi 38 8
1899 A470 3p gray & multi 38 8
1900 A470 6p vio bl & multi 25 15
1901 A470 7p bl grn & multi 25 15
Nos. 1897-1901 (5) 1.51 54

Uniform Type of 1973

Uniforms: 1p, Cavalry officer, 1788. 2p, Fusilier, Asturias Regiment, 1789. 3p, Infantry Colonel, 1802. 4p, Artillery standard-bearer, 1803. 7p, Sapper, 1809.

1975, July 17
1902 A428 1p multi 22 8
1903 A428 2p multi 60 8
1904 A428 3p multi 22 8
1905 A428 4p multi 22 12
1906 A428 7p multi 60 12
Nos. 1902-1906 (5) 1.86 48

Infant and Children Playing A471

1975, Sept. 9 **Photo.** *Perf. 13*
1907 A471 3p multi 12 8

"Defend Life."

Scroll and Emblem A472

1975, Sept. 25
1908 A472 3p multi 15 8

13th International Congress of Latin Notaries, Barcelona, Sept. 26-Oct. 4.

Blessing of the Birds A473

Designs (Scenes from Apocalypse): 2p, Angel at River of Life. 3p, Angel Guarding Gate of Paradise. 4p, Fox carrying cock. 6p, Daniel with wild bulls. 7p, The Last Judgment. 10p, Four horsemen of the Apocalypse. 12p, Bird holding snake. 2p, 3p, 7p, 10p, 12p are vertical.

1975, Sept. 29
1909 A473 1p gold & multi 12 8
1910 A473 2p gold & multi 20 8
1911 A473 3p gold & multi 20 8
1912 A473 4p gold & multi 12 8
1913 A473 6p gold & multi 12 8
1914 A473 7p gold & multi 24 12
1915 A473 10p gold & multi 28 12
1916 A473 12p gold & multi 32 18
Nos. 1909-1916 (8) 1.60 82

Millenium Gerona Cathedral.

Symbols of Industry A474

1975, Oct. 7 **Engr.** *Perf. 13*
1917 A474 3p vio & lil 12 8

Spanish industrialization.

Pioneers' Covered Wagon A475

Designs: 1p, El Cabildo, meeting house of 1st Uruguayan Government. 3p, Fort St. Theresa over River Plate. 8p, Montevideo Cathedral (vert.).

1975, Oct. 12 **Photo.**
1918 A475 1p multi 12 8
1919 A475 2p multi 22 8
1920 A475 3p multi 22 8
1921 A475 8p multi 18 8

Cultural ties with Latin America; sesquicentennial of Uruguay's independence.

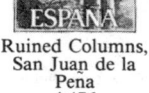

Ruined Columns, San Juan de la Pena A476

Madonna, Mosaic, Navarra Cathedral A477

Designs: 3p, Monastery (horiz.). 8p, Cloister (horiz.).

Perf. 13x12½, 12½x13

1975, Oct. 28 **Engr.**
1922 A476 3p sl grn & brn 30 8
1923 A476 8p vio & brt lil 25 8
1924 A476 10p dp mag & car 42 18

San Juan de la Pena Monastery.

1975, Nov. 4 **Photo.** *Perf. 13*

Design: 12p, Flight into Egypt, carved capital, Navarra Cathedral (horiz.).

1925 A477 3p multi 20 8
1926 A477 12p multi 20 12

Christmas 1975.

King Juan Carlos I — A478

Queen Sofia and King — A479

Designs: No. 1928, Queen Sofia. 12p, like No. 1929.

1975, Dec. 29 **Photo.** *Perf. 13x12½*
1927 A478 3p multi 12 6
1928 A478 3p multi 12 6

Perf. 12½

1929 A479 3p multi 12 6
1930 A479 12p multi 25 8

King Juan Carlos I, accession to the throne.

Pilgrim Virgin, Pontevedra A480

Mountains and Center Emblem A481

1976, Jan. 2 **Engr.** *Perf. 13*
1931 A480 3p rose & brn 18 10

Holy Year of St. James of Compostela, patron saint of Spain.

1976, Feb. 10 **Photo.**
1932 A481 6p multi 20 10

Catalunya Excursion Center, centenary.

Cosme Damian Churruca — A482

Navigators: 12p, Luis de Requesens. 50p, Juan Sebastian Elcano (horiz.).

1976, Mar. 1 **Engr.** *Perf. 13*
1933 A482 7p vio brn & grnsh blk 1.65 12
1934 A482 12p lt bl & vio 32 12
1935 A482 50p dp brn & gray ol 70 18

A. G. Bell, Radar and Telephone A483

1976, Mar. 10 **Photo.**
1936 A483 3p multi 20 10

Centenary of first telephone call by Alexander Graham Bell, March 10, 1876.

"Watch at Street Crossings" A484

Designs: 3p, "Don't pass when in doubt" (vert.). 5p, "Wear seat belts."

1976, Apr. 6 **Photo.** *Perf. 13*
1937 A484 1p org & multi 18 5
1938 A484 3p gray & multi 55 6
1939 A484 5p lil & multi 38 12

Road safety.

St. George, Alcoy Cathedral A485

1976, Apr. 23

1940	A485	3p multi	20	8

7th centenary of the apparition of St. George in Alcoy.

Europa Issue 1976

Talavera Pottery A486

Design: 12p, Lace making.

1976, May 3 Photo. *Perf. 13*

1941	A486	3p multi	1.25	10
1942	A486	12p multi	1.75	20

17th Conference of European Postal and Telecommunications Administrations.

6r Stamp of 1851 with Coruna Cancel — A487

1976, May 6

1943	A487	3p bl, org & blk	20	8

World Stamp Day.

Coin of Caesar Augustus A488

Designs: 7p, Map of Roman camp on banks of Ebro, and coin. 25p, Orpheus, mosaic from Roman era (vert.).

1976, May 26 Engr. *Perf. 13*

1944	A488	3p dk brn & mar	3.00	12
1945	A488	7p dk brn & bl	1.65	12
1946	A488	25p brn & blk	1.25	18

2000th anniversary of the founding of Saragossa.

Spanish-made Rifle, 1757 — A489

Designs (Bicentennial Emblem and): 3p, Bernardo de Galvez, Spanish governor. 5p, Dollar bank note, Richmond, 1861. 12p, Spanish capture of Pensacola from English.

1976, May 29

1947	A489	1p dk brn & vio bl	24	8
1948	A489	3p sl grn & dk brn	1.10	12
1949	A489	5p dk brn & sl grn	50	12
1950	A489	12p sl grn & dk brn	85	18

American Bicentennial.

Old Customs House, Cadiz A490

Customs Houses: 3p, Madrid. 7p, Barcelona.

1976, June 9

1951	A490	1p blk & mar	24	8
1952	A490	3p sep & grn	85	12
1953	A490	7p red brn & vio brn	1.25	12

Postal Savings Box with Symbols A491

Railroad Post Office A492

Rural Mailman in Winter A493

Design: 10p, Automatic letter sorting machine.

1976, June 16 Photo.

1954	A491	1p multi	18	8
1955	A492	3p multi	55	8
1956	A493	6p multi	28	12
1957	A493	10p multi	48	12

Postal service.

King and Queen, Map of Americas A494

1976, June 25

1958	A494	12p multi	35	15

Visit of King Juan Carlos I and Queen Sofia to the Americas, June 1976.

San Marcos, Leon A495

Greco-Roman Wrestling A496

Tourist Issue, 1976

Designs (Famous Hotels): 2p, Las Canadas, Tenerife. 3p, Portal of R. R. Catolicos, Santiago (vert.). 4p, Cruz de Tejeda, Las Palmas. 7p, Gredos, Avila. 12p, La Arruzafa, Cordoba.

1976, June 30 Engr. *Perf. 13*

1959	A495	1p sl & sep	15	8
1960	A495	2p grn & ind	52	8
1961	A495	3p brn & red brn	35	8
1962	A495	4p sep & sl	35	8
1963	A495	7p sl & sep	70	8
1964	A495	12p rose brn & pur	1.25	12
		Nos. 1959-1964 (6)	3.32	52

1976, July 9 Photo.

Designs (Montreal Olympic Emblem and): 1p, Men's rowing (horiz.). 2p, Boxing (horiz.). 12p, Basketball.

1965	A496	1p multi	18	8
1966	A496	2p lil & multi	38	8
1967	A496	3p multi	28	8
1968	A496	12p multi	28	18

21st Olympic Games, Montreal, Canada, July 17-Aug. 1.

King Juan Carlos I — A497

1976-77 Photo. *Perf. 13*

1969	A497	10c org ('77)	5	5
1970	A497	25c ap grn ('77)	5	5
1971	A497	30c dp bl ('77)	5	5
1972	A497	50c pur ('77)	5	5
1973	A497	1p emer ('77)	5	5
1974	A497	1.50p scarlet	5	5
1975	A497	2p dp bl	5	5
1976	A497	3p dp grn	5	5
1977	A497	4p bl grn ('77)	6	5
1978	A497	5p dp car rose	8	5
1979	A497	6p brt grn ('77)	12	5
1980	A497	7p olive	12	5
1982	A497	8p brt bl ('77)	18	5
1983	A497	10p lil rose ('77)	20	5
1984	A497	12p gldn brn	20	5
1985	A497	15p vio bl ('77)	28	5
1986	A497	20p brt red lil ('77)	35	5
		Nos. 1969-1986 (17)	1.99	85

See Nos. 2185-2194

Uniform Type of 1973

Uniforms: 1p, Trumpeter, Alcantara Regiment, 1815. 2p, Sapper, 1821. 3p, Engineer in dress uniform, 1825. 7p, Artillery infantry, 1828. 25p, Infantry riflemen, 1830.

1976, July 17

1989	A428	1p multi	18	8
1990	A428	2p multi	95	8
1991	A428	3p multi	28	8
1992	A428	7p multi	28	12
1993	A428	25p multi	38	25
		Nos. 1989-1993 (5)	2.07	61

Blood Donors A498

Mosaic, Batitales A499

1976, Sept. 7 Engr. *Perf. 13*

1994	A498	3p car & blk	18	8

Give blood, save a life!

1976, Sept. 22

Designs: 3p, Lugo city wall. 7p, Obverse and reverse of Roman 1st Legion coin.

1995	A499	1p blk & pur	12	8
1996	A499	3p blk & dp brn	30	12
1997	A499	7p grn & mag	55	12

2000th anniversary of Lugo City.

Parliament, Madrid — A500

1976, Sept. 23

1998	A500	12p grn & sep	20	8

63rd Conference of Inter-parliamentary Union, Madrid.

Still Life, by L. E. Menendez A501

St. Christopher Carrying Christ Child A502

Luis Eugenio Menendez Paintings: 2p, Peaches and jar. 3p, Pears, melon and barrel. 4p, Brace of pigeons and basket. 6p, Sea bream and oranges (horiz.). 7p, Water melon and bread (horiz.). 10p, Figs, bread and jug (horiz.). 12p, Various fruits (horiz.).

1976, Sept. 29 Photo. *Perf. 13*

1999	A501	1p gold & multi	12	5
2000	A501	2p gold & multi	12	5
2001	A501	3p gold & multi	12	5
2002	A501	4p gold & multi	12	5
2003	A501	6p gold & multi	15	8
2004	A501	7p gold & multi	15	8
2005	A501	10p gold & multi	28	10
2006	A501	12p gold & multi	28	10
		Nos. 1999-2006 (8)	1.34	56

Luis Eugenio Menendez (1716-1780). Stamp Day 1976.

1976, Oct. 8

Design: 3p, Nativity (horiz.). Both designs after painted wood carvings.

2007	A502	3p multi	1.00	8
2008	A502	12p multi	1.50	8

Christmas 1976.

Nicoya Church, Costa Rica A503

Juan Vazquez de Coronado A504

Designs: 3p, Orosi Mission, Costa Rica (horiz.). 12p, Tomas de Acosta.

1976, Oct. 12

2009	A503	1p multi	9	8
2010	A504	2p multi	15	8
2011	A503	3p multi	20	8
2012	A504	12p multi	32	10

Spain's link with Costa Rica.

Map of South and Central America, Santa Maria, King and Queen A505

1976, Oct. 12

2013	A505	12p multi	30	15

Visit of King Juan Carlos I and Queen Sofia to Latin America.

St. Peter of Alcantara Monastery A506

Tomb of Peter of Alcantara A507

St. Peter of Alcantara A508

1976, Oct. 29 **Engr.** ***Perf. 13***

2014	A506	3p dp brn & sep	28	12
2015	A507	7p dk pur & blk	28	18
2016	A508	20p brn & dk brn	50	22

St. Peter of Alcantara (1499-1562), Franciscan reformer.

Hand Releasing Doves A509

1976, Nov. 23 **Litho.** ***Perf. 13***

2017	A509	3p multi	12	8

11th Philatelic Exhibition of the National Association of the Handicapped.

Casals and Cello A510

Design: 5p, Manuel de Falla and Fire Dance from El Amor Brujo.

1976, Dec. 29 **Engr.** ***Perf. 13***

2018	A510	3p blk & vio bl	15	8
2019	A510	5p sl grn & car	15	12

Birth centenaries of Pablo Casals (1876-1973), cellist and composer, and of Manuel de Falla (1876-1946), composer.

Uniform Type of 1973

Uniforms: 1p, Outrider, Calatrava Lancers, 1844. 2p, Sapper, 1850. 3p, Corporal, Light Infantry, 1861. 4p, Drum Major, 1861. 20p, Artillery Captain, Mounted, 1862.

1977, Jan. 5 **Photo.** ***Perf. 13***

2020	A428	1p multi	15	5
2021	A428	2p multi	30	5
2022	A428	3p multi	15	5
2023	A428	4p multi	22	12
2024	A428	20p multi	30	12
		Nos. 2020-2024 (5)	1.12	39

King James I A511

1977, Feb. 10 **Engr.** ***Perf. 13***

2025	A511	4p pur & ocher	12	7

James I, El Conquistador (1208-1276), King of Aragon, 700th death anniversary.

Jacinto Verdaguer — A512

Portraits: 7p, Miguel Servet. 12p, Pablo Sarasate. 50p, Francisco Tarrega.

1977, Feb. 22

2026	A512	5p pur & dk red	25	6
2027	A512	7p ol & sl grn	22	8
2028	A512	12p dk bl & bl grn	25	8
2029	A512	50p lt grn & brn	75	25

Honoring Jacinto Verdaguer (1845-1902), Catalan poet; Miguel Servet (1511-1553), physician and theologian; Pablo Sarasate (1844-1908), violinist and composer; Francisco Tarrega (1854-1909), creator of modern Spanish guitar music.

Marquis de Penaflorida A513

1977, Feb. 24 **Engr.** ***Perf. 13***

2030	A513	4p dl grn & brn	12	6

Bicentenary of the Economic Society of the Friends of the Land (agricultural improvements).

Trout A514

Fish: 1p, Salmon (vert.). 3p, Eel. 4p, Carp. 6p, Barbel.

1977, Mar. 8 **Photo.**

2031	A514	1p multi	12	5
2032	A514	2p multi	12	5
2033	A514	3p multi	16	5
2034	A514	4p multi	12	10
2035	A514	6p multi	22	10
		Nos. 2031-2035 (5)	74	35

Slalom A515

1977, Mar. 24 **Engr.** ***Perf. 13***

2036	A515	5p multi	12	6

World Ski Championships, Granada, Sierra Nevada, Mar. 24-27.

La Cuadra, 1900 A516

Spanish Pioneer Automobiles: 4p, Hispano Suiza, 1916. 5p, Elizalde, 1915. 7p, Abadal, 1914.

1977, Apr. 23 **Photo.** ***Perf. 13***

2037	A516	2p multi	8	5
2038	A516	4p multi	10	5
2039	A516	5p multi	14	12
2040	A516	7p multi	16	12

Europa Issue 1977

Ordesa National Park A517

Design: 3p, Tree in Doñana National Park.

1977, May 2 **Litho.**

2041	A517	3p multi	22	5
2042	A517	12p multi	25	12

Plaza Mayor, Spanish Stamps, Tongs A518 A518

1977, May 7 **Engr.** ***Perf. 13***

2043	A518	3p multi	12	5

50th anniversary of Philatelic Market on Plaza Mayor, Madrid.

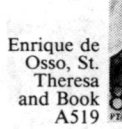

Enrique de Osso, St. Theresa and Book A519

1977, June 7 **Photo.** ***Perf. 13***

2044	A519	8p multi	18	10

Centenary of the founding by Enrique de Osso of the Society of St. Theresa of Jesus.

Tourist Issue 1977

Toledo Gate, Ciudad Real — A520

Designs: 2p, Roman aqueduct, Almunecar. 3p, Cathedral, Jaen (vert.). 4p, Ronda Gorge, Malaga (vert.). 7p, Ampudia Castle, Palencia. 12p, Bisagra Gate, Toledo.

1977, June 24 **Engr.** ***Perf. 13***

2045	A520	1p org & brn	8	5
2046	A520	2p sep & sl	8	5
2047	A520	3p vio & pur	8	5
2048	A520	4p brt & dk grn	8	5
2049	A520	7p brn & blk	15	8
2050	A520	12p vio & org brn	15	12
		Nos. 2045-2050 (6)	62	40

Uniform Type of 1973

Uniforms: 1p, Military Administration official, 1875. 2p, Cavalry lancers, 1883. 3p, General Staff Commander, 1884. 7p, Trumpeter, Divisional Artillery, 1887. 25p, Medical Corps official, 1895.

1977, July 16 **Photo.**

2051	A428	1p multi	9	5
2052	A428	2p multi	18	5
2053	A428	3p multi	18	5
2054	A428	7p multi	18	8
2055	A428	25p multi	22	15
		Nos. 2051-2055 (5)	85	38

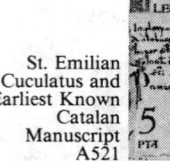

St. Emilian Cuculatus and Earliest Known Catalan Manuscript A521

1977, Sept. 9 **Engr.** ***Perf. 13***

2056	A521	5p vio, grn & brn	12	5

Millennium of Catalan language.

The Boy Florez, by Madrazo — A522

Federico Madrazo Portraits: 2p, Duke of San Miguel. 3p, Senora Coronado. 4p, Campoamor. 6p, Marquesa de Montelo. 7p, Rivadeneyra. 10p, Countess de Vilches. 15p, Senora Gomez de Avellaneda.

1977, Sept. 29 **Photo.** ***Perf. 13***

2057	A522	1p gold & multi	10	8
2058	A522	2p gold & multi	10	8
2059	A522	3p gold & multi	10	8
2060	A522	4p gold & multi	10	8
2061	A522	6p gold & multi	10	8
2062	A522	7p gold & multi	10	8
2063	A522	10p gold & multi	16	10
2064	A522	15p gold & multi	16	14
		Nos. 2057-2064 (8)	92	72

Federico Madrazo (1815-1894).

Sailing Ship and Mail Routes, 18th Century — A523

1977, Oct. 7 **Engr.**

2065	A523	15p blk, brn & grn	50	35

ESPAMER '77 Philatelic Exhibition, Barcelona, Oct. 7-13, and for the Bicentenary for regular mail routes to the Indies (Central and South America). No. 2065 issued in sheets of 8 stamps and 8 labels showing exhibition emblem.

Church of St. Francis, Guatemala City A524

Designs (Guatemala City): 3p, Modern buildings. 7p, Government Palace. 12p, Columbus Square and monument.

1977, Oct. 12 **Photo.** ***Perf. 13***

2066	A524	1p multi	7	5
2067	A524	3p multi	7	5
2068	A524	7p multi	12	8
2069	A524	12p multi	15	10

Spain's link with Guatemala.

San Pedro Monastery, Cardena A525

Designs: 7p, Cloister. 20p, Tomb of El Cid and Dona Gimena.

1977, Oct. 28 **Engr.**

2070	A525	3p vio bl & sl	10	5
2071	A525	7p brn & mar	10	8
2072	A525	20p grn & sl	30	18

San Pedro Monastery, Cardena, Bugos.

Adoration of the Kings A526

Design: 12p, Flight into Egypt (vert.). Designs from Romanesque paintings in Jaca Cathedral Museum.

1977, Nov. 3 **Photo.**

2073	A526	5p multi	10	5
2074	A526	12p multi	18	8

Christmas 1977.

Old and New Iberia Planes A527

1977, Nov. 3

2075	A527	12p multi	20	10

IBERIA, Spanish Airlines, 50th anniversary.

Felipe de Borbon, Prince of Asturias — A528

Judo, Games Emblem — A529

1977, Dec. 22 **Photo.** ***Perf. 13***

2076	A528	5p multi	12	6

Felipe de Borbon, Spanish crown prince.

1977, Dec. 29

2077	A529	3p multi	12	5

10th World Judo Championships, Taiwan.

Uniform Type of 1973

Uniforms: 1p, Flag bearer, 1908. 2p, Lieutenant Colonel, Hussar, 1909. 3p, Mounted artillery lieutenant, 1912. 5p, Engineers' captain, 1921. 12p, Captain General, 1925.

1978, Jan. 5

2078	A428	1p multi	8	5
2079	A428	2p multi	8	5
2080	A428	3p multi	12	6
2081	A428	5p multi	16	8
2082	A428	12p multi	16	10
		Nos. 2078-2082 (5)	60	34

Hilarión Eslava and Score A530

Designs: 8p, José Clara and sculpture. 25p, Pio Baroja and farm. 50p, Antonio Machado Ruiz and castle.

1978, Feb. 20 **Engr.** ***Perf. 13***

2083	A530	5p blk & dk pur	12	5
2084	A530	8p bl grn & blk	16	6
2085	A530	25p yel grn & blk	35	15
2086	A530	50p dk pur & dk brn	55	25

Miguel Hilarión Eslava (1807-1878), composer; José Clara, sculptor; Pio Baroja (1872-1956), author and physician; Antonio Machado Ruiz (1875-1939), poet and playwright.

Burial of Christ, by de Juni — A531

Detail from Burial of Christ — A532

Designs: No. 2089, Juan de Juni. No. 2090, Rape of Sabine Women, by Rubens. No. 2091, Rape (detail) and Rubens portrait. No. 2092, Rubens signature and palette. No. 2093, Judgment of Paris, by Titian. No. 2094, Judgment and Titian portrait. No. 2095, Initial "TF" and palette.

1978, Mar. 28 **Engr.** ***Perf. 12½x13***

2087	A532	3p multi	10	5
2088	A531	3p multi	10	5
2089	A532	3p multi	10	5
2090	A532	5p multi	10	6
2091	A531	5p multi	10	6
2092	A532	5p multi	10	6
2093	A532	8p multi	12	6
2094	A531	8p multi	12	6
2095	A532	8p multi	12	6
		Nos. 2087-2095 (9)	96	51

Juan de Juni (1507-77), sculptor, (3p); Peter Paul Rubens (1577-1640), painter, (5p); Titian (1477-1576), painter, (8p). Stamps of same denomination printed se-tenant.

Edelweiss in Pyrenees — A533

Designs: 5p, Fish and duck, wetlands. 7p, Forest, and forest destroyed by fire. 12p, Waves, oil rig, tanker and city. 20p, Sea gulls and seals (vert.).

1978, Apr. 4 **Photo.** ***Perf. 13***

2096	A533	3p multi	10	5
2097	A533	5p multi	10	6
2098	A533	7p multi	12	8
2099	A533	12p multi	18	8
2100	A533	20p multi	28	12
		Nos. 2096-2100 (5)	78	39

Protection of the environment.

Europa Issue 1978

Palace of Charles V, Granada A534

Design: 12p, The Lonja, Seville.

1978, May 2 **Engr.** ***Perf. 13***

2101	A534	5p dl grn & sl grn	12	5
2102	A534	12p dl grn & car rose	20	12

"España" — A535

1978, May 5 **Photo.** ***Perf. 12½***

2103	A535	12p multi	18	8

Spain's admission to the Council of Europe.

Symbols and Emblems of Postal Service A536

1978, June 27 **Engr.** ***Perf. 13***

2104	A536	5p sl grn	12	5

Stamp Day.

Map of Las Palmas, 16th Century A537

Designs: 5p, Hermitage of Columbus Church (vert.). 12p, View of Las Palmas, 16th century.

1978, June 23 **Photo.**

2105	A537	3p multi	7	5
2106	A537	5p multi	10	5
2107	A537	12p multi	15	8

500th anniversary of the founding of Las Palmas.

Pablo Picasso, Self-portrait A538

Picasso Paintings: 3p, Señora Canals. 8p, Jaime Sabartes. 10p, End of the Act (actress). 12p, Science and Charity (woman patient, doctor, nurse and child; horiz.). 15p, "Las Mennas" (blue period; horiz.). 20p, The Sparrows. 25p, The Painter and his Model (horiz.).

1978, Sept. 29 **Photo.** ***Perf. 13***

2108	A538	3p gold & multi	10	6
2109	A538	5p gold & multi	10	6
2110	A538	8p gold & multi	10	8
2111	A538	10p gold & multi	15	8
2112	A538	12p gold & multi	20	8
2113	A538	15p gold & multi	25	8
2114	A538	20p gold & multi	25	12
2115	A538	25p gold & multi	35	15
		Nos. 2108-2115 (8)	1.50	71

Pablo Picasso (1881-1973). Stamp Day 1978.

José de San Martin A539

Design: 12p, Simon Bolivar.

1978, Oct. 12 **Engr.** ***Perf. 13***

2116	A539	7p sep & car	10	6
2117	A539	12p vio & car	18	10

José de San Martin (1778-1850) and Simon Bolivar (1783-1830), South American liberators.

Flight into Egypt, Capital from St. Mary de Nieva A540

Design: 12p, Annunciation, capital from St. Mary de Nieva.

1978, Nov. 3 **Photo.** ***Perf. 13***

2118	A540	5p multi	10	6
2119	A540	12p multi	18	10

Christmas 1978.

Mexican Calendar Stone A541

Designs (King Juan Carlos I, Queen Sofia and): No. 2121, Machu Picchu. No. 2122, Calchaqui jars from Tucuman and Angalgala.

1978

2120	A541	5p multi	10	6
2121	A541	5p multi	10	6
2122	A541	5p multi	10	6

Royal visits to Mexico, Peru and Argentina.
Issue dates: No. 2120 (Mexico), Nov. 17; No. 2121 (Peru), Nov. 22; No. 2122 (Argentina), Nov. 26.

King Philip V — A542

Rulers of Spain: No. 2124, Louis I. 8p, Ferdinand VI. 10p, Carlos III. 12p, Carlos IV. 15p, Ferdinand VII. 20p, Isabella II. 25p, Alfonso XII. 50p, Alfonso XIII. 100p, Juan Carlos I.

1978, Nov. 22 **Engr.** ***Perf. 13***

2123	A542	5p dk bl & rose red	8	6
2124	A542	5p ol & dl grn	8	6
2125	A542	8p vio bl & red brn	12	8
2126	A542	10p bl grn & blk	16	8

2127	A542	12p brn & mar	20	8
2128	A542	15p blk & ind	20	10
2129	A542	20p ol & ind	30	10
2130	A542	25p ultra & vio brn	30	14
2131	A542	50p ver & brn	60	20
2132	A542	100p ultra & vio blk	1.25	55
		Nos. 2123-2132 (10)	3.29	1.45

Spanish Flag, Preamble to Constitution, Parliament — A543

1978, Dec. Photo. *Perf. 13*

2133	A543	5p multi	12	6

Proclamation of New Constitution.

Illuminated Pages from Bible and Codex — A544

1978, Dec. 27

2134	A544	5p multi	12	6

Millennium of the consecration of the Basilica of Santa Maria de Ripoll.

Car and Drop of Oil — A545

Designs: 8p, Insulated house and thermometer. 10p, Hand pulling plug.

1979, Jan. 24 Photo. *Perf. 13*

2135	A545	5p multi	8	6
2136	A545	8p multi	12	6
2137	A545	10p multi	12	6

Energy conservation.

De La Salle, Students A546

1979, Feb. 14 Photo. *Perf. 13*

2138	A546	5p multi	12	6

Institute of Christian Brothers, founded by Jean-Baptiste de la Salle, centenary.

Jorge Manrique — A547

Portraits: 8p, Fernan Caballero (pen name of Cecilia Böhl de Faber). 10p, Francisco Villaespesa. 20p, Gregorio Maranon.

1979, Feb. 28 Engr.

2139	A547	5p grn & brn	10	6
2140	A547	8p dk red & bl	10	6
2141	A547	10p brn & pur	16	8
2142	A547	20p grn & ol	24	12

Jorge Manrique, poet, 500th death anniversary; Fernan Caballero, Francisco Villaespesa, and Gregorio Maranon, writers, birth centenaries.

Running and Jumping A548

Sport for All: 8p, Children kicking ball and skipping rope, jogging and bicycling. 10p, Family jogging, and dog.

1979, Mar. 14 Photo. *Perf. 13*

2143	A548	5p multi	6	6
2144	A548	8p multi	12	6
2145	A548	10p multi	14	6

Children in Library A549

1979, Apr. 27 Photo. *Perf. 13*

2146	A549	5p multi	12	6

International Year of the Child.

Manuel Ysasi (1810-1855) Postal Reformer — A550

Europa: 5p, Mounted messenger and postilion, 1761 engraving (vert.).

1979, Apr. 30 Engr.

2147	A550	5p brn & sep	12	6
2148	A550	12p red brn & sl grn	20	8

Radar and Satellite A551

Design: 5p, Symbolic people and cables (vert.).

1979, May 17 Photo. *Perf. 13*

2149	A551	5p multi	8	6
2150	A551	8p multi	14	6

World Telecommunications Day, May 17.

Bulgaria No. 1, Sofia Opera House, Housing Development — A552

1979, May 18

2151	A552	12p multi	20	10

Philaserdica '79, International Philatelic Exhibition, Sofia, Bulgaria, May 18-27.

Tank, Jet and Destroyer A553

1979, May 25

2152	A553	5p multi	12	6

Armed Forces Day.

Messenger Handing Letter to King — A554

1979, June 15 Litho. & Engr.

2153	A554	5p multi	12	6

Stamp Day 1979.

Daroca Gate, Zaragoza — A555

Architecture: 8p, Gerona Cathedral. 10p, Interior, Carthusian Monastery Church, Granada. 20p, Portal, Palace of the Marques de Dos Aguas, Valencia.

1979, June 27 Engr.

2154	A555	5p vio bl & lil brn	12	6
2155	A555	8p dk bl & sep	12	8
2156	A555	10p blk & grn	12	8
2157	A555	20p brn & sep	28	12

Turkey Sponge A556

Fauna: 7p, Crayfish. 8p, Scorpion. 20p, Starfish. 25p, Sea anemone.

1979, July 11 Photo. *Perf. 13*

2158	A556	5p multi	14	6
2159	A556	7p multi	14	6
2160	A556	8p multi	14	6
2161	A556	20p multi	20	12
2162	A556	25p multi	20	12
		Nos. 2158-2162 (5)	82	42

Gen. Antonio Gutierrez and Battle A557

1979, Aug. Engr.

2163	A557	5p multi	12	6

Naval defense of Tenerife, 18th century.

Immaculate Conception, by Juanes — A558

Juan de Juanes Paintings: 10p, Holy Family. 15p, Ecce Homo. 20p, St. Stephen in the Synagogue. 25p, The Last Supper (horiz.). 50p, Adoration of the Mystic Lamb (horiz.).

1979, Sept. 28 Photo. *Perf. 13x13½*

2164	A558	8p multi	12	8
2165	A558	10p multi	12	10
2166	A558	15p multi	25	12
2167	A558	20p multi	38	12
2168	A558	25p multi	38	12
2169	A558	50p multi	75	22
		Nos. 2164-2169 (6)	2.00	76

Zaragoza Cathedral, Mother and Child Statue — A559

1979, Oct. 3 Photo. *Perf. 13x13½*

2170	A559	5p multi	12	6

8th Mariology and 15th International Marianist Congresses, Zaragoza, Oct. 3-12.

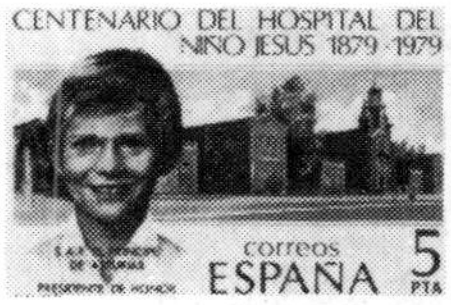

Felipe de Borbon, Hospital A560

1979, Oct. *Perf. 13½x13*

2171	A560	5p multi	12	6

Hospital of the Child Jesus, centenary.

St. Bartholomew College, Bogota — A561

Design: 12p, University of St. Mark, Lima, coat of arms.

1979, Oct. 12 Engr. *Perf. 13*

2172	A561	7p multi	12	6
2173	A561	12p multi	20	12

Hispanidad 79.

Clasped Hands, Badge, Governor's Palace — A562

Design: No. 2175, Statute book (vert.).

Lithographed and Engraved

1979, Oct. 27 *Perf. 13*

2174	A562	8p multi	10	6
2175	A562	8p multi	10	6

Catalonian and Basque autonomy statute.

Type A54, Barcelona Coat of Arms A563

Photogravure and Engraved

1979, Nov. 6 *Perf. 13½x13*

2176	A563	5p multi	12	6

Barcelona Philatelic Congress and Exhibition, 50th anniversary.

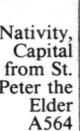

Nativity, Capital from St. Peter the Elder A564

Christmas 1979: 19p, Flilght into Egypt, column from St. Peter the Elder, Huesca.

1979, Nov. 14 **Photo.**

2177	A564	8p multi	12	6
2178	A564	19p multi	24	12

Carlos I, Coat of Arms A565

Kings of the House of Austria (Hapsburg Dynasty): 20p, Philip II. 25p, Philip III. 50c, Philip IV. 100p, Carlos II.

1979, Nov. 22 **Engr.** *Perf. 13*

2179	A565	15p sl grn & dk bl	20	8
2180	A565	20p dk bl & mag	28	8
2181	A565	25p vio & yel bis	52	12
2182	A565	50p brn & sl grn	55	18
2183	A565	100p mag & brn	1.25	45
		Nos. 2179-2183 (5)	2.80	91

2nd International Olive Oil Year — A566

1979, Dec. 4 **Photo.** *Perf. 13½x13*

2184	A566	8p multi	15	6

King Juan Carlos I Type of 1976

1980-84 **Photo.** *Perf. 13*

2185	A497	13p dk red brn ('81)	30	5
2186	A497	14p red org ('82)	25	5
2187	A497	16p sepia	30	5
2188	A497	17p bluish gray ('84)	30	8
2189	A497	19p orange	50	8
2190	A497	30p dk grn ('81)	55	5
2191	A497	50p org ver ('81)	75	8
2192	A497	60p bl ('81)	1.00	8
2193	A497	75p brt yel grn ('81)	1.00	8
2194	A497	85p gray ('81)	1.50	8
		Nos. 2185-2194 (10)	6.45	68

Train and People A567

Public Transportation: 4p, Bus. 5p, Subway.

1980, Feb. 20 **Engr.** *Perf. 13½*

2200	A567	3p car rose & brn	8	5
2201	A567	4p dk bl & brn	10	5
2202	A567	5p sl & brn	12	6

Steel Export A568

1980, Mar. 15 **Photo.** *Perf. 13½x13*

2203	A568	5p *shown*	8	6
2204	A568	8p *Ships*	12	6
2205	A568	13p *Shoes*	20	8
2206	A568	19p *Machinery*	20	8
2207	A568	25p *Technology*	30	22
		Nos. 2203-2207 (5)	90	50

Europa Issue 1980

Federico Garcia Lorca (1899-1936) — A569

Design: 19p, José Ortega y Gasset (1883-1955), philosopher and statesman.

1980, Apr. 28 **Engr.** *Perf. 13½*

2208	A569	8p vio & ol grn	15	6
2209	A569	19p brn & dk grn	25	12

Armed Forces Day A570

1980, May 24 **Photo.** *Perf. 13½x13*

2210	A570	8p multi	20	6

Soccer Players A571

1980, May 23

2211	A571	8p *shown*	16	8
2212	A571	19p *Soccer ball, flags*	24	12

World Soccer Cup 1982.

Bourbon Arms, Ministry of Finance A572

1980, June 9 **Engr.** *Perf. 13½*

2213	A572	8p dk brn	20	6

Public Finances in Bourbon Spain Exhibition.

Helen Keller, Sign Language A573

1980, June 27

2214	A573	19p dk yel grn & rose lake	28	12

Helen Keller (1880-1968), deaf mute writer and lecturer.

Mounted Postman, 12th Century Panel, Barcelona — A574

Lithographed and Engraved

1980, June 28 *Perf. 13x12½*

2215	A574	8p multi	20	6

Stamp Day.

King Alfonso and Count of Maceda at 1930 National Exhibition A575

1980, July 1 **Photo.** *Perf. 13½*

2216	A575	8p multi	20	6

1st National Stamp Exhibition, Barcelona, 50th anniversary.

Altar of the Virgin, La Palma Cathedral — A576

1980, July 12 **Engr.** *Perf. 13*

2217	A576	8p blk & brn	20	6

Appearance of the Virgin of the Snow at La Palma, 300th anniversary.

Perez de Ayala — A577

1980, Aug. 9 **Engr.** *Perf. 13*

2218	A577	100p sl & sep	1.40	25

Ramon Perez de Ayala (1881-1962), novelist and diplomat.

Souvenir Sheet

La Atlantida Ruins, Mexican Bonampak Musicians — A578

Designs: b, Sun Gate, Tiahuanaco; Roman arch, Medinaceli. c, Alonso de Ercilla, Garcilaso de la Vega; title pages from La Arauca and Commentario Reales. d, Virgin of Quito, Virgin of Seafarers.

1980, Oct. 3 **Engr.** *Perf. 13*

2219		Sheet of 4	3.00	3.00
a	A578	25p multi	38	38
b	A578	25p multi	38	38
c	A578	50p multi	55	55
d	A578	100p multi	1.25	1.25

ESPAMER '80 Stamp Exhibition, Madrid, Oct. 3-12. No. 2219 has 2 labels showing exhibition emblem.

400th Anniversary of Buenos Aires — A579

1980, Oct. 24

2220	A579	19p multi	30	12

Miniature Sheet

The Creation, Tapestry, Gerona Cathedral — A580

1980, Nov. **Litho.** *Perf. 13½x13*

2221	A580	Sheet of 6	3.00	2.75
a		25p multi	30	20
b		25p multi	30	20
c		25p multi	30	20
d		50p multi	48	28
e		50p multi	48	28
f		50p multi	48	28

Conference Building, Flags of Participants A581

Holy Family Church of Santa Maria, Cuina A582

1980, Nov. 11 **Photo.** *Perf. 13½*

2222	A581	22p multi	32	12

1980, Nov. 12

Christmas 1980, 22p, Adoration of the Kings, portal, Church of Santa Maria, Cuina (horiz.).

2223	A582	10p multi	14	5
2224	A582	22p multi	25	10

Pedro Vives and His Airplane A583

Designs: Aviation pioneers.

1980, Dec. 10
2225 A583 5p *shown* 10 6
2226 A583 10p *Benito Loygorri* 15 6
2227 A583 15p *Alfonso De Orleans* 25 10
2228 A583 22p *Alfredo Kindelan* 38 12

Winter University Games A584

1981, Mar. 4 ***Perf. 13½x13***
2229 A584 30p multi 50 12

Picasso's Birth Centenary Emblem, by Joan Miro — A585

1981, Mar. 27 ***Perf. 13***
2230 A585 100p multi 1.75 30

Pablo Picasso (1881-1973).

Galician Autonomy — A586

Perf. 13
1981, Mar. 27 **Photo.** **Engr.**
2231 A586 12p multi 25 8

Homage to the Press A587

1981, Aug. 8 **Photo.** ***Perf. 13½x13***
2232 A587 12p multi 30 8

International Year of the Disabled — A588

1981, Apr. 29 **Litho.**
2233 A588 30p multi 50 12

Soccer Players A589

1981, May 2 **Photo.**
2234 A589 12p Soccer players, diff., vert. 25 8
2235 A589 30p shown 50 12

1982 World Cup Soccer.

Europa Issue 1981

La Jota Folkdance A590

1981, May 4 **Engr.**
2236 A590 12p shown 20 6
2237 A590 30p Virgin of Rocio procession 42 12

Armed Forces Day — A591

Gabriel Miro (1879-1930), Writer — A592

1981, May 29 **Photo.** ***Perf. 13x13½***
2238 A591 12p multi 18 8

1981, June 17 **Engr.**

Famous Men: 12p, Francisco de Quevedo (1580-1645), writer. 30p, St. Benedict (480-543), patron saint of Europe.

2239 A592 6p pur & dk grn 18 5
2240 A592 12p brn & pur 12 5
2241 A592 30p dk grn & brn 35 12

Mail Messenger, 14th Cent., Woodcut — A593

Photogravure and Engraved
1981, June 19 ***Perf. 12½x13***
2242 A593 12p multi 18 8

Stamp Day

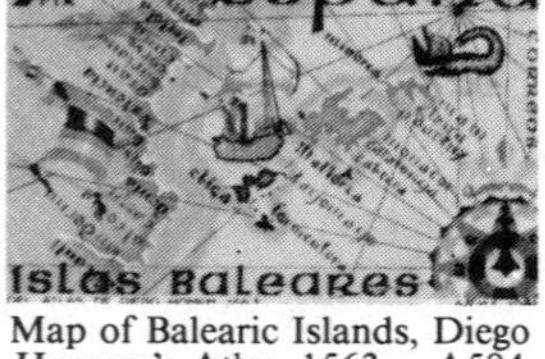

Map of Balearic Islands, Diego Homem's Atlas, 1563 — A594

1981, July 8 **Photo.** ***Perf. 13x12½***
2243 A594 7p shown 15 6
2244 A594 12p Canary Islds., Prunes map, 1563 25 6

Kings Alfonso XII and Juan Carlos, Advocates Arms A595

1981, July 27 **Engr.** ***Perf. 13½x13***
2245 A595 50p multi 65 12

Chamber of Advocates of State (Public Prosecutor) centenary.

King Sancius VI of Navarre with City Charter, 12th Cent. Miniature A596

1981, Aug. 5 **Photo.** ***Perf. 12½x13***
2246 A596 12p multi 18 8

Vitoria, 800th anniv.

Exports A597

1981, Sept. 30 **Photo.** ***Perf. 13½x13***
2247 A597 6p Fruit 12 5
2248 A597 12p Wine 15 8
2249 A597 30p Vehicles 38 12

Congress Palace, Buenos Aires A598

1981, Oct. 12 **Engr.** ***Perf. 13½x13***
2250 A598 12p dk bl & car rose 20 8

ESPAMER '81 Intl. Stamp Exhibition, Buenos Aires, Nov. 13-22.

World Food Day A599

1981, Oct. 16
2251 A599 30p multi 50 12

Souvenir Sheet

Guernica, by Pablo Picasso (1881-1973) — A600

1981, Oct. 25 **Photo.**
2252 A600 200p multi 3.00 3.00

Adoration of the Kings, Cervera de Pisuerga, Palencia — A601

1981, Nov. 18 **Litho.** ***Perf. 13***
2253 A601 12p shown 25 8
2254 A601 30p Nativity, Paredes de Nava 50 12

Christmas 1981.

King Juan Carlos I — A602

1981, Oct. 21 **Engr.** ***Perf. 13x12½***
2268 A602 100p brown 1.50 15
2269 A602 200p dk grn 3.50 25
2270 A602 500p dk bl 8.50 90

Postal Museum, Madrid — A603

1981, Nov. 30 **Engr.** ***Perf. 13***
2273 A603 7p Telegraph operator 18 5
2274 A603 12p Coach 25 5

Souvenir Sheet

2275 Sheet of 4 2.50 2.50
c. A603 50p Emblem 75 48
d. A603 100p Cap, posthorn, pouch 1.50 80

No. 2275 contains Nos. 2273, 2274, 2275a, 2275b.

Royal Mint Building, Seville A604

1981, Dec. 4 **Engr.** ***Perf. 13***
2276 A604 12p blk & brn 25 8

Spanish Administration of the Bourbons in the Indies.

Iparraguirre (1820-1881) A605

Designs: 30p, Juan Ramon Jimenez (1881-1958), writer. 50p, Pedro Calderon (1600-1681), playwright.

1981-82

2277 A605 12p blk & dk bl 25 8
2278 A605 30p dk bl & dk grn 60 8
2279 A605 50p blk & vio 1.00 12

Issue dates: 12p, Dec. 16. 30p, 50p, Mar. 10, 1982.

Espana '82 World Cup Soccer — A606

Andres Bello (1782-1865), Writer — A607

1982, Feb. 24 **Photo.**

2280 A606 14p Poster by Joan Miro 25 8
2281 A606 33p Cup, emblem 60 12

1982, Mar. 10 **Engr.**

2282 A607 30p grn & dk grn 60 8

Holy Year of Compostelo — A608

1982, Mar. 31 **Photo.** ***Perf. 13***

2283 A608 14p St. John of Compostelo 20 8

A609

Manuel Fernandez Caballero (1835-1906) and Scene from his Gigantes and Cabezudos — A610

Designs: Operetta composers and scenes from their works. Stamps of same denomination se-tenant.

Lithographed and Engraved

1982, Apr. 28 ***Perf. 13***

2284 A609 3p shown 8 5
2285 A610 3p shown 8 5
2286 A609 6p Amadeo Vives Roig (1871-1932) 12 6
2287 A610 6p Dona Francisquita 12 6
2288 A609 8p Tomas Breton Hernandez (1850-1923) 18 6
2289 A610 8p Verbena of Paloma 18 6
Nos. 2284-2289 (6) 76 34

Europa 1982 — A611

1982, May 3 **Engr.** ***Perf. 12½***

2290 A611 14p Unification, 1512 25 8
2291 A611 33p Discovery of New World, 1492 60 8

Armed Forces Day — A612

1982, May 28 **Photo.** ***Perf. 13***

2292 A612 14p multi 25 8

1982 World Cup A613

Designs: Soccer players.

1982, June 13 ***Perf. 13***

2293 A613 14p multi 30 8
2294 A613 33p multi 60 12

Souvenir Sheets

2295 Sheets of 4, #2293-2294, 9p, 100p 3.00 3.00
a. A613 9p Captains' handshake 20 12
b. A613 100p Player holding cup 2.00 1.75

No. 2295 has two types of multicolored margin, each showing seven arms of the 14 host cities. Size: 164x106mm.

One sheet has 3 blue coats of arms, the other has 2.

Stamp Day — A614

Perf. 12½

1982, July 16 **Litho.** **Engr.**

2296 A614 14p Map, postal code 30 8

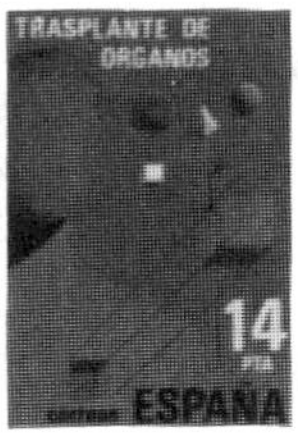

Organ Transplants A615

1982, July 28 **Photo.** ***Perf. 13***

2297 A615 14p Symbolic organs 30 8

Storks and Express Train — A616

Locomotive, 1850 — A617

Perf. 12½, 13 (A617)

1982, Sept. 27 **Photo.**

2298 A616 9p shown 15 8
2299 A617 14p shown 25 8
2300 A617 33p Santa Fe locomotive 60 12

23rd Intl. Railways Congress, Malaga.

ESPAMER '82 Intl. Stamp Exhibition, San Juan, Oct. 12-17 — A618

1982, Oct. 12 **Engr.** ***Perf. 13½x13***

2301 A618 33p dk bl & pur 60 12

St. Teresa of Avila (1515-1582) — A619

1982, Oct. 15

2302 A619 33p Statue by Gregorio Hernandez 60 12

Visit of Pope John Paul II, Oct. 31-Nov. 9 — A620

1982, Oct. 31 **Engr.** ***Perf. 12½***

2303 A620 14p multi 30 8

Water Wheel, Alcantarilla A621

Landscapes and Monuments. 6p horiz.

1982, Nov. 5 ***Perf. 13x12½, 12½x13***

2304 A621 4p shown 10 6
2305 A621 6p Bank of Spain, 19th cent. 12 6
2306 A621 9p Crucifixion 20 8
2307 A621 14p St. Martin's Tower, Teruel 30 8
2308 A621 33p St. Andrew's Gate, Zamora 55 12
Nos. 2304-2308 (5) 1.27 40

Christmas 1982 A622

1982, Nov. 17 **Photo.** ***Perf. 13½***

2309 A622 14p Nativity, wood carving, by Gil de Siloe 25 5
2310 A622 33p Flight into Egypt 55 8

Pablo Gargallo, Sculptor, Birth Centenary A623

Salesian Fathers in Spain, Centenary A624

1982, Dec. 9 **Engr.** ***Perf. 13***

2311 A623 14p bl & dk grn 30 8

1982, Dec. 16 **Photo.** ***Perf. 12½x13***

2312 A624 14p multi 30 8

Arms of King Juan Carlos I A625

1983, Feb. 9 **Photo.** ***Perf. 12½***

2313 A625 14p multi 30 5

Andalusia Autonomy Statute A626

1983 **Litho.** **Engr.** ***Perf. 13½***

2314 A626 14p shown 25 8
2315 A626 14p Cantabria 25 8

Issue dates: No. 2314, Feb. 28; No. 2315, Mar. 15.

State Security Forces A627

1983, Mar. 23 **Photo.**
2316 A627 9p Natl. Police Force 18 8
2317 A627 14p Civil Guard 25 12
2318 A627 33p Superior Police Corps 55 12

Operetta Type of 1982

Designs: 4p, Francisco Alonso Lopez (1887-1948), La Parranda. 6p, Jacinto Guerrero y Torres (1895-1951), La Rosa del Azafran. 9p, Jesus de Guridi Bidaola (1886-1961), El Caserio.

Lithographed and Engraved
1983, Apr. 22 ***Perf. 13***
2319 A610 4p multi 8 5
2320 A609 4p multi 8 5
2321 A609 6p multi 10 5
2322 A610 6p multi 10 5
2323 A609 9p multi 18 12
2324 A610 9p multi 18 12
Nos. 2319-2324 (6) 72 44

Europa 1983 — A628

Designs: 16p, Scene from Don Quixote, by Miguel Cervantes. 38p, L. Torres Quevedo's Niagara Spanish aerocar.

1983, May 5 **Engr.** ***Perf. 13x12½***
Granite Paper
2325 A628 16p dk grn & brn red 30 6
2326 A628 38p brown 75 18

Francisco Salzillo Alvarez (1707-83), Painter — A629

World Communications Year — A630

Designs: 38p, Antonio Soler Ramos (1729-1783), composer. 50p, Joaquin Turina Perez (1882-1949), composer. 100p, St. Isidro Labrador (1082-1170), patron saint of Madrid.

1983, May 14 ***Perf. 13***
2327 A629 16p pur & dk grn 30 6
2328 A629 38p bl & brn 75 12
2329 A629 50p bl grn & dk brn 1.00 22
2330 A629 100p red brn & pur 1.75 30

1983, May 17 **Photo.** ***Perf. 13***
2331 A630 38p multi 65 18

Rioja Autonomous Region — A631

Lithographed and Engraved
1983, May 25 ***Perf. 13***
2332 A631 16p multi 30 12

Spain stamps can be mounted in Scott's annual Spain and Spanish Andorra Supplement.

Armed Forces Day — A632

1983, May 26 **Photo.**
2333 A632 16p multi 30 12

Intl. Canine Exhibition, Madrid, June 1984 A633

Lithographed and Engraved
1983, June 8 ***Perf. 13½***
2334 A633 10p Pointer 25 5
2335 A633 16p Mastiff 38 12
2336 A633 26p Iberian hound 50 18
2337 A633 38p Navarro pointer 75 30

Discovery of Tungsten Bicentenary A634

Scouting Year A635

400th Anniv. of University of Zaragoza A636

1983, June 22 **Photo.** ***Perf. 13***
2338 A634 16p Elhuyar brothers 30 12
2339 A635 38p multi 65 30
2340 A636 50p multi 85 45

Murcia Autonomous Region — A637

Photogravure and Engraved
1983, July 8 ***Perf. 13½***
2341 A637 16p Arms 35 12

Asturias Autonomous Region — A638

Lithographed and Engraved
1983, Sept. 8 ***Perf. 13***
2342 A638 14p Victory Cross, Covadonga Basilica 35 12

Intl. Institute of Statistics, 44th Congress, Madrid, Sept. 12-22 A639

1983, Sept. 12 **Photo.** ***Perf. 13***
2343 A639 38p Institute building 85 18

Stamp Day — A640

Lithographed and Engraved
1983, Oct. 8 ***Perf. 13x12½***
2344 A640 16p Roman mail cart 75 50

No. 2344 se-tenant with label publicizing ESPAÑA '84 Philatelic Exhibition, April 27-May 6, 1984.

Valencia Automony Statute, 1st Anniv. A641

Lithographed and Engraved
1983, Oct. 10 ***Perf. 13***
2345 A641 16p multi 38 10

View of Sevilla, 16th cent. — A642

1983, Oct. 12 **Engr.** ***Perf. 12½x13***
2346 A642 38p multi 70 18

Spanish-American trade in 17th century.

Stained-glass Windows A643

Designs: 10p King, Leon Cathedral. 16p, Epiphany, Gerona Cathedral. 38p, Apostle Santiago, Royal Hospital Chapel, Santiago.

Lithographed and Engraved
1983, Oct. 28 ***Perf. 12½x13***
2347 A643 10p multi 18 12
2348 A643 16p multi 28 12
2349 A643 38p multi 65 18

Church at Llivia, Gerona — A644

Designs: 6p, Temple, Santa Maria del Mar, Barcelona. 16p, Cathedral, Ceuta. 38p, Gate of the Santiago Bridge, Melila. 50p, Charity Hospital, Seville.

1983, Nov. 9 **Engr.** ***Perf. 13x12½***
2350 A644 3p dk bl gray & grn 10 5
2351 A644 6p dk bl gray 10 5
2352 A644 16p red brn & dl vio 28 6
2353 A644 38p bis brn & rose car 65 12
2354 A644 50p brn & org red 85 22
Nos. 2350-2354 (5) 1.98 50

Christmas 1983 — A645

Indalecio Prieto (1883-1962), Patriot — A646

1983, Nov. 23 **Photo.** ***Perf. 13x13½***
2355 A645 16p The Nativity, Tortosa 28 6
2356 A645 38p The Adoration, Vich 65 12

1983, Dec. 14 **Engr.** ***Perf. 13***
2357 A646 16p red brn & blk 38 6

Industrial Accident Prevention A647

1984, Jan. 25 **Photo.** ***Perf. 13½***
2358 A647 7p Construction worker 12 5
2359 A647 10p Fire 18 5
2360 A647 16p Electrical plug, pliers 28 12

Extremadura Statute of Autonomy, First Anniv. — A648

Lithographed and Engraved
1984, Feb. 25 ***Perf. 13***
2361 A648 16p multi 28 6

1500th Anniv. of City of Burgos A649

1984, Mar. 1 **Engr.**
2362 A649 16p multi 28 6

Carnivals A650

1984 Photo. *Perf. 13½x13*

2363 A650 16p Santa Cruz de Tenerife 28 6
2364 A650 16p Valencia Fallas 28 6

Issue dates: No. 2363, Mar. 5; No. 2364, Mar. 16.

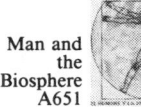

Man and the Biosphere A651

1984, Apr. 11

2365 A651 38p da Vinci's Study of Man 70 12

Aragon Statute of Autonomy, 2nd Anniv. — A652

Lithographed and Engraved

1984, Apr. 23 *Perf. 13x13½*

2366 A652 16p Map 28 6

Juan Carlos — A653 Congress Emblem — A654

Souvenir Sheet

Espana '84 (Spanish Royal Family): b. Sofia of Greece. c. Cristina de Borbon. d. Prince of Asturias Felipe de Borbon. e. Elene de Borbon.

1984, Apr. 27 *Perf. 12½x13*

2367 Sheet of 5 5.00 5.00
a.-e. A653 38p, any single 85 85

1984, May 3 Engr. *Perf. 13x13½*

2368 A654 38p pur & red 70 12

World Philatelic Federation, 53rd Congress, Madrid, May 7-9.

Europa (1959-84) A655

1984, May 5

2369 A655 16p orange 28 6
2370 A655 38p dk bl 65 22

Armed Forces Day A656

Design: 17p, Monument to Hunters Regiment of Caceres, by Mariano Benlliure.

1984, May 19 Photo. *Perf. 13½x13*

2371 A656 17p multi 30 6

Canary Islds. Statute of Autonomy A657 Castilla-La Mancha Statute of Autonomy A658

Lithographed and Engraved

1984, May 29 *Perf. 13*

2372 A657 16p Arms, map 28 6

1984, May 31 *Perf. 13*

2373 A658 17p Arms 30 6

King Alfonso X (1252-84) A659

Design: 38p, Ignacio Barroquer (1884-1965), ophthalmologist

1984, June 20 Engr. *Perf. 13*

2374 A659 16p multi 28 6
2375 A659 38p multi 65 12

Balearic Islds. Statute of Autonomy — A660

1984, June 29 Litho. & Engr.

2376 A660 17p multi 30 6

Feast of San Fermin of Pamplona A661

1984, July 5 Photo.

2377 A661 17p Bullfighters 30 6

Operetta Type of 1982

Designs: No. 2378, El Nino Judio. No. 2379, Pablo Luna (1880-1942). No. 2380, La Revoltosa. No. 2381, Ruperto Chapi (1851-1909). No. 2382, La Reina Mora. No. 2383, Jose Serrano (1873-1941).

Lithographed and Engraved

1984, July 20 *Perf. 13*

2378 A610 6p multi 10 5
2379 A609 6p multi 10 5
2380 A610 7p multi 12 5
2381 A609 7p multi 12 5
2382 A610 10p multi 18 5
2383 A609 10p multi 18 5
Nos. 2378-2383 (6) 80 30

1984 Summer Olympics A662

Greek or Roman sculptures.

1984, July 27 Photo.

2384 A662 1p Chariot race 5 5
2385 A662 2p Diving, vert. 5 5
2386 A662 5p Wrestling 10 5
2387 A662 8p Discus, vert. 15 5

Navarra Statute of Automony A663

Lithographed and Engraved

1984, Aug. 16 *Perf. 13*

2388 A663 17p multi 30 6

Intl. Bicycling Championship, Barcelona, Aug. 27-Sept. 2 — A664

1984, Aug. 27 Photo.

2389 A664 17p multi 30 6

Castilla and Leon Statute of Autonomy A665

1984, Sept. 5 Litho. & Engr.

2390 A665 17p multi 30 6

Jerez Vintage Feast — A666

1984, Sept. 20 Photo. *Perf. 13*

2391 A666 17p Women picking grapes 30 6

Journey to the Holy Land by Sister Egeria, 1600th Anniv. — A667

1984, Sept. 26

2392 A667 40p Map, Sister Egeria 70 12

Stamp Day — A668

1984, Oct. 5 Litho. & Engr.

2393 A668 17p Arab postrider 30 6

Father Junipero Serra (1713-84), Mission Founder in California A669

1984, Oct. 12 Engr. *Perf. 13*

2394 A669 40p Map, Serra, mission 70 8

Christmas 1984 A670

1984, Nov. 21 Photo.

2395 A670 17p Nativity 30 6
2396 A670 40p Adoration of the Kings, vert. 70 8

Madrid Autonomy Statue A671

1984, Nov. 28 Litho. & Engr.

2397 A671 17p Arms, buildings 30 6

Andean Pact, 15th Anniv. A672

Condor, Flags of Bolivia, Colombia, Ecuador, Peru and Venezuela.

1985, Jan. 16 Photo. *Perf. 13*

2398 A672 17p multi 20 5

An enhanced introduction to the Scott Catalogue begins on Page V. A thorough understanding of the material presented there will greatly aid your use of the catalogue itself.

The Virgin of Louvain, by Jan Gossaert (c. 1478-1536) A673

Santa Cruz College, Valladolid University, 500th Anniv. A674

1985, Jan. 21 *Perf. 13½*
2399 A673 40p multi 48 12

EUROPALLA '85. See Belgium No. 1185.

1985, Feb. 20 **Litho. & Engr.**
2400 A674 17p Main gateway 20 5

OLYMPHILEX '85, Lausanne, Switz. — A675

1985, Mar. 18 **Photo.**
2401 A675 40p multi 48 12

ESPAMER '85, Cuba — A676

1985, Mar. 20 **Engr.**
2402 A676 40p Cathedral, Havana 48 12

Fairs A677

Perf. 13½, 13½x14 (#2405)

1985 **Photo.**
2403 A677 17p Seville 22 6
2404 A677 17p Alcoy 22 6
2405 A677 17p Arriondas-Ribadesella 22 6
2406 A677 18p Toledo, vert. 24 6

Issue dates: No. 2403, Apr. 16. No. 2404, Apr. 22. No. 2405, Aug. 2. No. 2406, June 6.

Intl. Youth Year — A678

1985, Apr. 17 **Engr.** *Perf. 13½*
2407 A678 17p blk, hn brn & dk grn 22 6

Europa '85 A680

Designs: 18p, Antonio de Cabezon (1510-1566), organist and composer, court Musician to Felipe II. 45p, Natl. Youth Orchestra.

1985, May 3 **Engr.**
2408 A680 18p dk bl, dk red & blk, *buff* 22 6
2409 A680 45p ol grn, dk red & blk, *buff* 55 14

Armed Forces Day A681

1985, May 24 **Photo.**
2410 A681 18p multi 22 6

Natl. Flag Bicent. — A682

Designs: No. 2411, Arms of King Carlos III, text of 1785 Decree, sailing ship Santisima Trinidad. No. 2412, Natl. arms, Article No. 4 from 1978 Constitution, lion ornament from Chamber of Deputies Building.

Lithographed and Engraved

1985, May 28 *Perf. 13x13½*
2411 A682 18p multi 22 6
2412 A682 18p multi 22 6

Nos. 2411-2412 printed se-tenant.

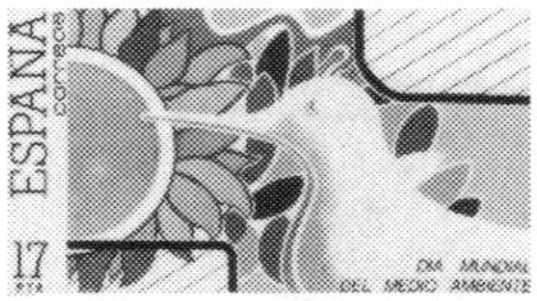

Intl. Environment Day — A683

1985, June 5 **Photo.**
2413 A683 17p multi 20 5

Juan Carlos I — A684

1985-87		Photo.	*Perf. 14*	
2416	A684	1p brt bl	5	5
2417	A684	2p dk grn ('86)	5	5
2418	A684	3p chnt brn ('86)	5	5
2419	A684	4p ol grn ('86)	6	5
2421	A684	5p brt rose lil	6	5
2421A	A684	6p brn blk ('87)	10	5
2422	A684	7p brt vio	8	5
2423	A684	7p ap grn	8	5
2424	A684	8p gray blk	10	5
2425	A684	10p lake ('86)	14	5
2427	A684	12p red	15	5
2432	A684	17p yel bis	22	6
2433	A684	18p brt grnsh bl	24	6
2434	A684	19p vio brn ('86)	30	8
a		Bklt. pane of 6	1.80	
2435	A684	20p brt pink ('87)	32	8
2435A	A684	30p ultra ('87)	48	12
2436	A684	45p brt grn	58	14
		Nos. 2416-2436 (17)	3.06	1.09

Issue dates: 1p, 5p, 8p, 12p, 18p, 45p, June 12. Nos. 2422, 2423, 17p, July 16. 2p, 3p, 4p, 10p, Apr. 3. 19p, Sept. 27. 6p, 20p, 30p, Jan. 26.

Astrophysical Observatory Opening, La Palma, Canary Islands — A685

1985, June 25 **Photo.** *Perf. 14*
2441 A685 45p multi 58 14

European Music Year — A686

Designs: 12p, Ataulfo Argenta, conductor. 17p, Tomas Luis de Victoria, composer. 45p, Fernando Sor, composer.

1985, June 26 **Litho. Engr.** *Perf. 13*
2442 A686 12p multi 15 5
2443 A686 17p multi 22 6
2444 A686 45p multi 58 14

Bernal Diaz del Castillo (1492-1585), Historian — A687

Famous men: 12p, Esteban Terradas (1883-1950), mathematician. 17p, Vicente Aleixandre (1898-1984), 1977 Nobel laureate in literature. 45p, Leon Felipe Camino (1884-1968), poet.

1985, July 24 **Engr.** *Perf. 13½*
2445 A687 7p dk red, blk & dk grn, *buff* 10 5
2446 A687 12p brt ver, dk bl & blk, *buff* 15 5
2447 A687 17p blk, dk grn & dk red, *buff* 22 6
2448 A687 45p bis, blk & dk grn, *buff* 58 14

Monastic Mail Delivery, 1122 — A688

Lithographed and Engraved

1985, Sept. 27 *Perf. 13*
2449 A688 17p multi 22 6

Stamp Day 1985.

12th Rhythmic Gymnastics World Championships, Valladolid — A689

1985, Oct. 9 **Photo.** *Perf. 13x13½*
2450 A689 17p Ribbon exercise 22 6
2451 A689 45p Hoop exercise 58 14

Souvenir Sheet

Prado Museum, La Alcachofa Fountain — A690

Lithographed and Engraved

1985, Oct. 18 *Perf. 13*
2452 A690 17p multi 22 6

EXFILNA '85, Madrid, Oct. 18-27.

Virgin and Child, Seville Cathedral A691

Stained glass windows: 12p, Monk, by Peter Boniface, Toledo Cathedral. 17p, King Henry II of Castile, Alcazar of Segovia.

1985, Oct. 24 *Perf. 12½x13*
2453 A691 7p multi 10 5
2454 A691 12p multi 16 5
2455 A691 17p multi 24 6

Christmas 1985 A692

14th-15th century paintings in the Episcopal Museum, Vich: 17p, Nativity, Guimera Altarpiece retable, 14th cent., by Ramon de Mur. 45p, Epiphany, from an embroidered frontal, 15th cent.

1985, Nov. 27 **Photo.** *Perf. 13½*
2456 A692 17p multi 24 6
2457 A692 45p multi 60 15

Birds — A693

1985, Dec. 4 **Litho. & Engr.**

2458	A693	6p	Sylvia cantillans	8	5
2459	A693	7p	Monticola saxatilis	10	5
2460	A693	12p	Sturnus unicolor	16	5
2461	A693	17p	Panurus biarmicus	24	6

Wildlife conservation.

Count of Penaflorida (1729-1785) — A694

1985, Dec. 11 **Engr.** ***Perf. 13½***

2462	A694	17p	dk bl	24	6

Francisco Javier de Munibe e Idiaguez, founded Natl. Economic Society of Friends in 1765.

Government Palace, Madrid, and Accession Agreement Text — A695

Designs: 17p, Map and flags of EEC countries. 30p, Hall of Columns, Royal Palace. 45p, Member flags.

1986, Jan 7. **Litho.** ***Perf. 13½x13***

2463	A695	7p	multi	10	5
2464	A695	17p	multi	25	6
2465	A695	30p	multi	42	10
2466	A695	45p	multi	62	16
a			Bklt. pane of 4, Nos. 2463-2466	1.40	

Admission of Spain and Portugal to European Economic Community. See Portugal Nos. 1661-1662.

Tourism — A696

Historic sites: 12p, Inner courtyard, La Lupiana Monastery, Guadalajara. 35p, Balcony of Europe, Nerja.

1986, Jan. 20 **Engr.** ***Perf. 13x12½***

2467	A696	12p	dk rose, brn & gray brn	18	5
2468	A696	35p	brt bl & sep	48	12

2nd World Conference on Merino Sheep A697

1986, Jan. 27 **Photo.** ***Perf. 13½***

2469	A697	45p	multi	65	16

Masquerade, 19th Cent., by F. Hohenleiter — A698

1986, Feb. 5

2470	A698	17p	multi	24	6

Cadiz Carnival.

Intl. Peace Year — A699

Lithographed and Engraved

1986, Feb. 12 ***Perf. 13x13½***

2471	A699	45p	multi	65	16

Festival of Religious Music, Cuenca A700

1986, Mar. 26 **Photo.** ***Perf. 13½***

2472	A700	17p	multi	25	6

Chamber of Commerce, Cent. A701

Painting detail: Swearing in of the Regent, Queen Maria Christina, Before the Spanish Parliament, 1886, by Francisco Jover and Joaquin Sorolla y Bastida, Senate Palace, Madrid.

1986, Apr. 9 **Engr.** ***Perf. 13½***

2473	A701	17p	sage grn & grnsh blk	25	6

Emigration of Spaniards — A702

1986, Apr. 22 **Photo.**

2474	A702	45p	multi	65	16

Europa 1986 — A703

Lithographed and Engraved

1986, May 5 ***Perf. 13x13½***

2475	A703	17p	Youth feeding birds	25	6
2476	A703	45p	Girl watering tree	65	16

Our Lady of the Dew Festival, Almonte A704

1986, May 14 **Photo.** ***Perf. 13½x13***

2477	A704	17p	multi	25	6

Army Day A705

Design: Captains-General Building, Canary Islands.

1986, May 16 **Engr.** ***Perf. 13½***

2478	A705	17p	pale yel brn, sep & red	25	6

Rodrigo City Cathedral A706

1986, June 16 ***Perf. 12½x13½***

2479	A706	12p	shown	18	5
2480	A706	35p	Calella Lighthouse	50	12

10th World Basketball Championships, July 5-20 — A707

1986, July 4 **Photo.** ***Perf. 12½***

2481	A707	45p	multi	65	16

Famous Men — A708

Mystery of the Virgin's Death Festival Elche — A709

Designs: 7p, Francisco Loscos Bernal (1823-1886), botanist. 11p, Salvador Espriu (1913-1985), author. 17p, Jose Martinez Ruiz (Azorin, 1873-1967), artist. 45p, Jose Vitoriano Gonzalez (Juan Gris, 1887-1927), painter.

1986, July 16 **Engr.** ***Perf. 13***

2482	A708	7p	ol grn & bl	10	5
2483	A708	11p	brt rose & blk	18	5
2484	A708	17p	dk brn vio & blk	25	6
2485	A708	45p	org, red vio & blk	68	18

1986, Aug. 11 **Photo.** ***Perf. 13x13½***

2486	A709	17p	Angels carrying soul	25	6

5th World Swimming, Water Polo, Diving and Synchronized Swimming Championships — A710

1986, Aug. 13 **Engr.** ***Perf. 13½***

2487	A710	45p	multi	68	18

10th World Pelota Championships — A711

1986, Sept. 12

2488	A711	17p	multi	25	6

Stamp Day — A712

Design: Messenger, The Husband's Return, Song 63, TI1 Codex, 1979 edition, Spanish Royal Academy.

1986, Sept. 27 **Litho.** ***Perf. 13x12½***

2489	A712	17p	multi	28	8

Souvenir Sheet

EXFILNA '86, Cordova, Oct. 9-18 — A713

1986, Oct. 7 **Litho. & Engr.**

2490	A713	17p	Man, Cordova "Mosque"	28	28

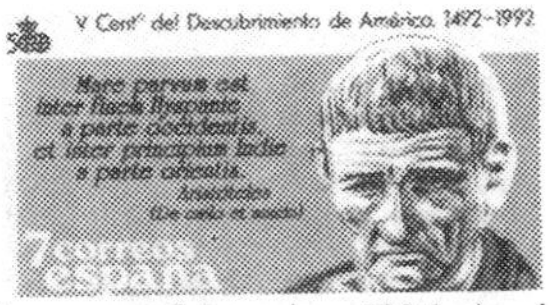

Discovery of America, 500th Anniv. (in 1992) — A714

Men and text: 7p, Aristotle, text from De Cielo et Mundo. 12p, Seneca, text from Medea. 17p, San Isidoro, text from Etimologias. 30p, Pedro de Ailly, text from Imago Mundi. 35p, Mayan, prophesy from Libros de Chilam Balam. 45p, European, prophesy from Libros de Chilam Balam.

Lithographed and Engraved

1986, Oct. 15 ***Perf. 13x13½***

2491	A714	7p	multi	12	5
2492	A714	12p	multi	20	5
2493	A714	17p	multi	28	8
2494	A714	30p	multi	48	12
2495	A714	35p	multi	55	14
2496	A714	45p	multi	70	18
a			Bklt. pane of 6, #2491-2496	2.35	
			Nos. 2491-2496 (6)	2.33	62

The Catalogue editors cannot undertake to appraise, identify or judge the genuineness or condition of stamps.

Caspar de Portola y Rovira (1717-1786), Pioneer of California — A715

1986, Nov. 6 *Perf. 13½*
2497 A715 22p multi 32 8

Christmas A716

Wood carving details: 19p, The Holy Family, by Diego de Siloe (c. 1495-1563), Natl. Sculpture Museum, Valladolid, vert. 48p, Nativity, Toledo Cathedral altarpiece, by Felipe de Borgona (c. 1475-1543).

1986, Nov. 19 Photo. *Perf. 13½*
2498 A716 19p multi 30 8
2499 A716 48p multi 75 18

Spanish-Islamic Cultural Heritage — A717

Famous men: 7p, Abd Al Rahman II (792-852), 4th independent emir of Cordoba. 12p, Ibn Hazm (994-1064), scholar. 17p, Al-Zarqali (1061-1100), astronomer. 45p, Alfonso VII, scholar, Toledo School of Translators.

1986, Dec. 3 **Engr.**
2500 A717 7p org red & dk red brn 12 5
2501 A717 12p brn blk & red org 20 5
2502 A717 17p blk & dk bl 28 8
2503 A717 45p grn & blk 70 18

Alfonso R. Castelao (1886-1950), Artist, Writer — A718

Lithographed and Engraved
1986, Dec. 11 *Perf. 13x13½*
2504 A718 32p El Buen Cura, 1917 50 12

Globe, Chateau de la Muette A719

Lithographed and Engraved
1987, Jan. 14 *Perf. 14*
2505 A719 48p multi 75 18

Organization for Economic Cooperation and Development, OECD, 25th anniv.

EXPO '92, Seville A720

1987, Jan. 21 **Photo.**
2506 A720 19p Geometric shapes 30 8
2507 A720 48p Earth, Moon's surface 75 18

See Nos. 2540-2541, 2550-2551.

Portrait of Vitoria, by Vera Fajardo A721

1987, Feb. 11 **Engr.**
2508 A721 48p dk rose brn 75 18

Francisco de Vitoria (c. 1486-1546), theologian, teacher and a founder of intl. law.

Marine Corps, 450th Anniv. A722

Design: 18th Cent. 74-gun man-of-war, period standard bearer, corps insignia.

1987, Feb. 25
2509 A722 19p multi 30 8

Deusto University, Cent. — A723

1987, Feb. 26 Engr. *Perf. 14x13½*
2510 A723 19p blk, hn brn & dk grn 30 8

UN Child Survival Campaign A724

1987, Mar. 4 *Perf. 13½x14*
2511 A724 19p red brn & blk 30 8

Constitution of Cadiz, 175th Anniv. — A725

Nos. 2512a-2512c in a continuous design: The Promulgation of 1812, by Salvador Viniegra. No. 2512d, Anniv. emblem.

1987, Mar. 18 Litho. *Perf. 13½*
2512 Strip of 4 1.60 40
a.-d A725 25p, any single 40 10

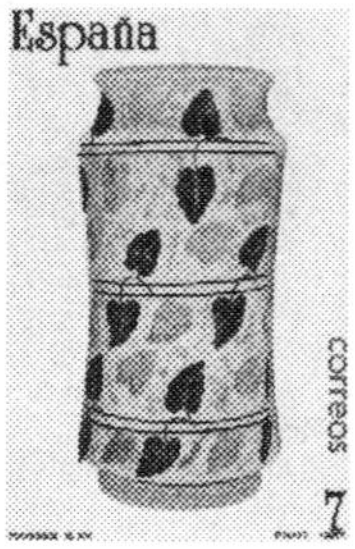

Ceramicware A726

Designs: 7p, Pharmaceutical jar, 15th cent., Manises of Valencia. 14p, Abstract figurine, 20th cent., Sargadelos of Galicia. 19p, Neo-classical lidded urn, 18th cent., Buen Retiro of Madrid. 32p, Water jar, 20th cent., Salvatierra of Extremadura. 40p, Pitcher, 18th cent., Talavera of Toledo. 48p, Pitcher, 18th-19th cent., Granada of Andalucia.

Lithographed and Engraved
1987, Mar. 20 *Perf. 12½x13*
2513 Block of 6 + 3 labels 2.60 68
a A726 7p multi 12 5
b A726 14p multi 22 5
c A726 19p multi 30 8
d A726 32p multi 52 14
e A726 40p multi 65 16
f A726 48p multi 78 20

See No. 2552.

Passion Week in Zamora and Seville A727

Paintings: 19p, The Amanecer Procession, by Gallego Marquina, vert. 48p, Jesus Carrying the Cross, by Martinez Montanes, and the Gate of Forgiveness, Seville Cathedral.

1987, Apr. 13 Photo. *Perf. 14x13½*
2514 A727 19p multi 32 8
2515 A727 48p multi 80 20

Tourism A728

Designs: 14p, Rock of Ifach, Calpe. 19p, Nave of Santa Marina d'Ozo Church, Pontevedra, before restoration. 40p, Sonanes Palace, Villacarriedo. 48p, Monastery of St. Joan de les Abadesses, Gerona, vert.

1987 Engr. *Perf. 12½x13*
2515A A728 14p dp bl & sage grn 24 6
2516 A728 19p dp grn & grnh blk 32 8
2516A A728 40p dp clar 68 18
2517 A728 48p black 80 20

Issue dates: 19p, 48p, Apr. 21. 14p, 40p, June 10.

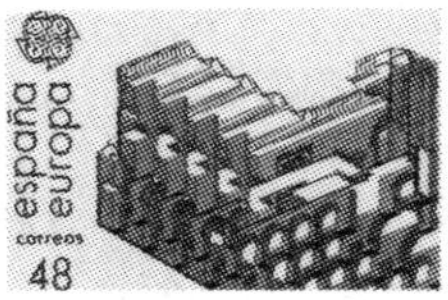

Europa 1987 A729

Modern architecture: 19p, Bilbao Bank, Madrid, designed by Saenz de Oiza, vert. 48p, Natl. Museum of Roman Art, Merida, designed by Rafael Moneo.

Lithographed and Engraved
1987, May 4 *Perf. 14x13½*
2518 A729 19p multi 32 8
2519 A729 48p multi 80 20

Horse Fair, Jerez de La Frontera A730

1987, May 6 Photo. *Perf. 13½x14*
2520 A730 19p multi 32 8

Ramon Carande (1887-1986), Historian — A731

1987, May 29 **Engr.**
2521 A731 40p blk & dk vio brn 68 18

Postal Code Inauguration — A732

1987, June 1 Litho. *Perf. 14*
2522 A732 19p multi 32 8

Eibar Weaponry School, 75th Anniv. A733

1987, July 2 Litho. *Perf. 14*
2523 A733 20p multi 32 8

1992 Summer Olympics, Barcelona A734

1987, July 15 **Photo.**
2524 A734 32p Casa de Battlo masonry 52 12
2525 A734 65p Athletes 1.05 28

25th Folk Festival of the Pyrenees, Jaca — A735

1987, July 22
2526 A735 50p multi 80 20

Monturiol and Submarine Designs A736

1987, Sept. 9 Engr. *Perf. 13½x14*
2527 A736 20p black brown 35 8

Narcis Monturiol (d. 1887), inventor of the submarine Ictineos.

Stamp Day — A737

Illuminated codex from *Constitutiones Jacobi II Regis Majoricum,* 14th cent., King Albert I Royal Library, Brussels.

Litho & Engr.

1987, Sept. 16 *Perf. 13*
2528 A737 20p multi 35 8

Postal service of Mallorca under James II.

ESPAMER '87 — A738

Designs: 8p, Handstamped letter that traveled from La Coruna to Havana, Cuba, 18th cent. 12p, La Coruna Harbor, 19th cent., engraving. 20p, Illustration of Havana harbor from *Viaje Alrededor da La Isla de Cuba,* by Francisco Mialche, 18th cent. 50p, West Indies packets.

1987, Oct. 2 Litho. & Engr. *Perf. 13*

2529	Sheet of 4	3.25	3.25
a	A738 8p blk, brt blue & red	28	28
b	A738 12p brt blue, red & blk	42	42
c	A738 20p blk, brt blue & red	75	75
d	A738 50p blk, brt blue & red	1.80	1.80

No. 2529 printed se-tenant (rouletted between) with ESPAMER entrance ticket. Sold for 180p. Size: 150x83mm (including ticket).

Souvenir Sheet

EXFILNA '87, Gerona, Oct. 24-Nov. 1 — A739

Design: Greek statue, Emporion, Olympic torch-bearer.

1987, Oct. 24 Photo. *Perf. 13x12½*
2530 A739 20p multi 35 35

No. 2530 has multicolored margin continuing the design, picturing exhibition emblem, architecture, coastline, and containing control number. Size: 121x80mm.

Discovery of America, 500th Anniv. (in 1992) — A740

Ships and: 14p, Amerigo Vespucci (1454-1512), Italian navigator. 20p, Ferdinand and Isabella. 32p, Friar Juan Perez, Queen's confessor. 40p, Juan de la Cosa (c. 1460-1510), master of the Santa Maria, cartographer who made first map of the New World. 50p, Christopher Columbus. 65p, Vicente Yanez Pinzon (c. 1460-1523) and Martin Alonso Pinzon (c. 1441-1493), brothers, navigators and ship owners, accompanied Columbus on voyage.

Litho. & Engr.

1987, Oct. 30 *Perf. 13*

2531	A740 14p multi	25	6
2532	A740 20p multi	35	8
2533	A740 32p multi	58	15
2534	A740 40p multi	72	18
2535	A740 50p multi	90	22
2536	A740 65p multi	1.20	30
a	Bklt. pane of 6, Nos. 2531-2536	4.00	
	Nos. 2531-2536 (6)	4.00	99

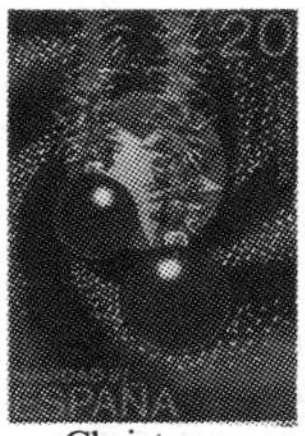

Christmas A741

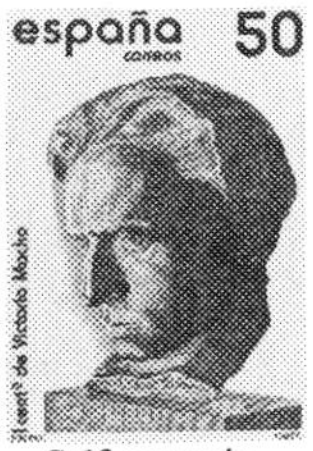

Self-portrait, Sculpture by Victorio Macho (1887-1966) A742

1987, Nov. 17 Photo. *Perf. 14x13½*
2537 A741 20p Ornaments 38 10
2538 A741 50p Zambomba, tambourine 92 24

1987, Dec. 23 Engr.
2539 A742 50p brn blk 92 24

EXPO '92 Type of 1987

1987, Dec. 29 Photo. *Perf. 13½x14*
2540 A720 20p like No. 2506 38 10
2541 A720 50p like No. 2507 92 24

HRH Sofia and Juan Carlos, 50th Birth Anniv. — A743

1987, Jan. 5 *Perf. 13x13½*
2542 A743 20p Sofia 38 10
2543 A743 20p Juan Carlos 38 10

Nos. 2542-2543 printed se-tenant with inscribed center.

Clara Campoamor (b. 1888), Suffragette — A744

1988, Feb. 12 Photo. *Perf. 14*
2544 A744 20p multi 38 10

1988 Winter Olympics, Calgary — A745

Passion Week in Valladolid and Malaga — A746

1988, Feb. 15 *Perf. 14*
2545 A745 45p Speed skater 85 22

Designs: 20p, Valladolid Cathedral and 17th cent. statue of Christ at the column by Gregorio Fernandez. 50p, Christ carrying the cross along Malaga procession route.

1988, Mar. 30 Photo. *Perf. 14*
2546 A746 20p multi 38 10
2547 A746 50p multi 92 24

Tourism A747

1988, Apr. 7
2548 A747 18p Paella pan, ingredients 35 8
2549 A747 45p Covadonga Natl. Park 85 22

EXPO '92 Type of 1987

Era of Discoveries: 8p, Road to globe, rays of light, vert. 45p, Compass rose, globe.

1988, Apr. 12
2550 A720 8p multi 15 5
2551 A720 45p multi 85 22

Art Type of 1987

Glassware: a. Chalice, Valencia, 18th cent. b. Cadalso de los Vidrios, Madrid, 18th cent. c. Candy dish, La Granja de San Ildefonso, 18th cent. d. Castril double-handled jar, Andalucia, 18th cent. e. Jug, Catalina, 17th cent. f. Bottle, Baleares, 20th cent.

Litho. & Engr.

1988, Apr. 13 *Perf. 12½x13*
2552 Block of 6+6 labels 2.30 60
a.-f A726 20p any single 38 10

Stamp Day 1988 — A748

Francis de Tassis, postmaster by royal appointment (1505) in charge of establishing communications between Spain, France, Germany, Rome, Naples.

1988, Apr. 29 Engr. *Perf. 12½x13*
2553 A748 20p dark vio & dark brn 38 10

General Workers' Union (UGT), Cent. A749

Emblem and Pablo Iglesias, union pioneer.

1988, May 1 Photo. *Perf. 14*
2554 A749 20p multi 38 10

Europa 1988 — A750

Transport and communication: 20p, Locomotive made in Spain and operated in Cuba, 1837. 50p, Spanish telegraph in the Philippines linking Plaza de Manila and Bagumbayan Camp, 1818.

1988, May 5 Engr. *Perf. 13*
2555 A750 20p blk & dark red 38 10
2556 A750 50p blk & dark grn 95 24

Jean Monnet (1888-1979), Economist — A751

1988, May 9 *Perf. 14x13½*
2557 A751 45p blue blk 85 22

Universal Exposition, Barcelona, Cent. A752

1988, May 31 Photo. *Perf. 13½x14*
2558 A752 50p multi 88 22

Intl. Music and Dance Festival, Granada — A753

1988, June 1 *Perf. 14x13½*
2559 A753 50p multi 88 22

World Expo '88, Brisbane, Australia A754

1988, June 14 *Perf. 13½x14*
2560 A754 50p Bull 88 22

For unused stamps, more recent issues are valued as never hinged, with the beginning point determined on a country-by-country basis. Notes to show the beginning points are prominently placed in the text.

Coronation of the Virgin of Hope — A755

1988, June 18 *Perf. 14x13½*

2561 A755 20p multi 35 8

Holy Week in Malaga.

Souvenir Sheet

EXFILNA '88, June 25-July 3, Madrid — A756

1988, June 25 *Perf. 13x12½*

2562 A756 20p Ciudadela Fortress floor plan 35 35

Tourism A757

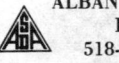

1988, July 11 Engr. *Perf. 13½x14*

2563 A757 18p Cantabrian Coast storehouse 32 8

2564 A757 45p Dulzaina (wind instrument) 78 20

28th World Roller Hockey Championships, La Coruna — A758

1988, Sept. 7 Photo. *Perf. 13½x14*

2565 A758 20p multi 35 8

1st World Cong. of Spanish Regional Shelters — A759

1988 Summer Olympics, Seoul — A760

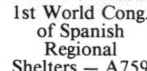

1988, Sept. 9 *Perf. 14*

2566 A759 20p multi 35 8

1988, Sept. 10 **Litho.**

2567 A760 50p Yachting 85 22

Catalonia Millennium — A761

1988, Sept. 21 Photo. *Perf. 12½*

2568 A761 20p multi 35 8

1st Call to Session of the Cortes de Leon, 800th Anniv. — A762

Design: Illumination and seal of Alfonso IX, King of Leon.

1988, Sept. 26 Photo. *Perf. 12½x13*

2569 A762 20p multi 35 8

Federation of Spanish Philatelic Societies, 25th Anniv. A763

1988, Sept. 27 *Perf. 14x13½*

2570 A763 20p multi 35 8

1992 Summer Olympics, Barcelona — A764

1988, Oct. 3 Photo. *Perf. 14*

2571 A764 8p multi 14 5

See Nos. B139-B141.

Reconquest of Valencia by King James I, 750th Anniv. — A765

Design: Castle in Valencia and royal seal of James I, 13th cent.

1988, Oct. 7 *Perf. 14x13½*

2572 A765 20p multi 35 8

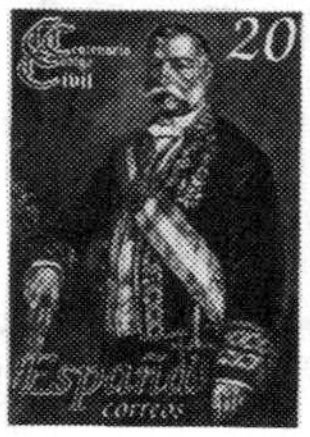

Civil Law, Cent. — A766

1988, Oct. 10 *Perf. 13x13½*

2573 A766 20p multi 35 8

Discovery of America (in 1992), 500th Anniv. — A767

Conquerors, exporers and symbols: No. 2574, Hernando Cortez, conqueror of Mexico, and serpent Quetzalcoatl. No. 2575, Vasco Nunez de Balboa, discoverer of the Pacific Ocean, and sun setting over sea. No. 2576, Francisco Pizarro, conqueror of Peru, and llama. No. 2577, Portuguese navigator Ferdinand Magellan, Juan de Elcano (c. 1476-1526) and globe symbolizing circumnavigation of the world. No. 2578, Alvar Nunez Cabeza de Vaca (c. 1490-1560), explorer, and sunrise. No. 2579, Andres de Urdaneta (1498-1568), and symbol of the west-to-east route between the Philippines and America that he discovered.

1988, Oct. 13 Engr. *Perf. 13x13½*

2574 A767 10p brick red, mar & ultra 18 5

2575 A767 10p brick red, mar & ultra 18 5

2576 A767 20p brick red, mar & ultra 35 8

2577 A767 20p brick red, mar & ultra 35 8

2578 A767 50p brick red, mar & ultra 88 22

2579 A767 50p brick red, mar & ultra 88 22

a. Bklt. pane of 6, Nos. 2574-2579 3.00

Nos. 2574-2579 (6) 2.82 70

Henry III of Castile, 1st Prince of Asturias — A768

1988, Oct. 26 Photo. *Perf. 13*

2580 A768 20p multi 35 8

1st Bestowal of the title Prince of Asturias, 600th anniv., guaranteeing that the throne would continue to be inherited according to primogeniture.

Christmas — A769

1988, Nov. 24 Photo. *Perf. 14*

2581 A769 20p Snowflakes 38 10

2582 A769 50p Shepherd, vert. 92 22

Sites and Cities Appearing on the UNESCO World Patrimony List — A770

1988, Dec. 1 Engr. *Perf. 12½x13*

2583 A770 18p Mosque de Cordoba, vert. 35 8

2584 A770 20p Burgos Cathedral, vert. 38 10

2585 A770 45p El Escorial Monastery 82 20

2586 A770 50p The Alhambra, Granada 92 22

Natl. Constitution, 10th Anniv. — A771

1988, Dec. 7 Photo. *Perf. 14*

2587 A771 20p multi 38 10

Souvenir Sheet

Charles III (1759-1788) and the Enlightenment — A772

1988, Dec. 14 Engr. *Perf. 13x12½*
2588 A772 45p blk & dk grn 80 80

Natl. Organization for the Blind, 50th Anniv. — A773

1988, Dec. 27 Photo. *Perf. 14*
2589 A773 20p multi 38 10

Fr. Luis de Granada (1504-1588) A774

1988, Dec. 31
2590 A774 20p multi 38 10

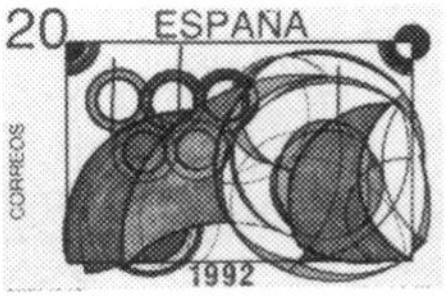

1992 Summer Olympics, Barcelona A775

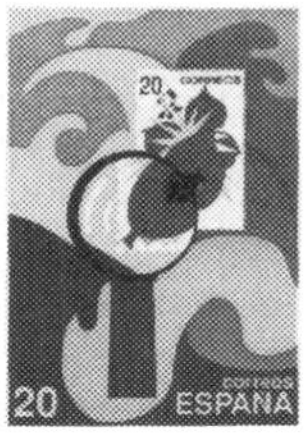

Stamp Collecting A776

1989, Jan. 3
2591 A775 20p multi 38 10
2592 A776 20p multi 38 10

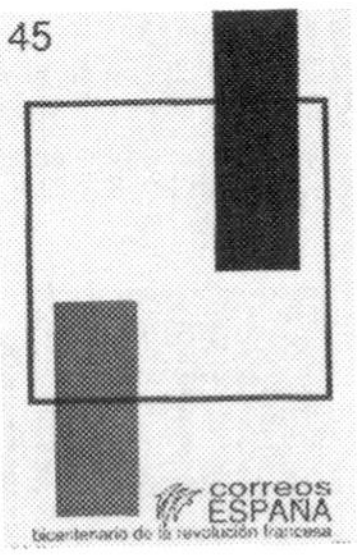

French Revolution, Bicent. A777

1989, Jan. 24 Photo. *Perf. 13*
2593 A777 45p multi 78 20

Maria de Maeztu (b. 1882), Educator A778

1989, Feb. 7 Photo. *Perf. 14x13½*
2594 A778 20p multi 35 8

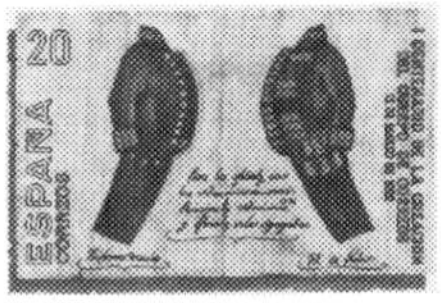

Postal Service, Cent. A779

Litho. & Engr.
1989, Mar. 11 *Perf. 13½x14*
2595 A779 20p Uniform, 1889 35 8

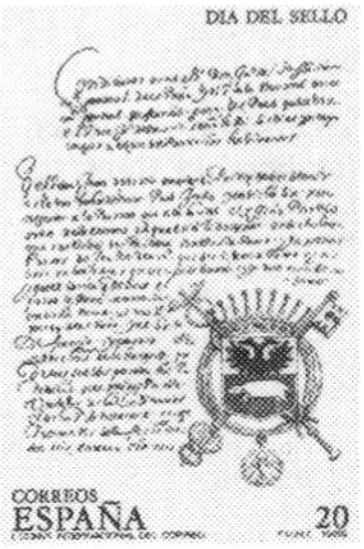

Stamp Day — A780

Design: Intl. postal treaty negotiated with France and Italy by Franz von Taxis, 1601.

1989, Apr. 4 Engr. *Perf. 13*
2596 A780 20p black 35 8

Casa del Cordon, Burgos — A781

1989, Apr. 22 *Perf. 14x13½*
2597 A781 20pblack 35 8

Europa 1989 — A782

Children's toys.

1989, May 5 Photo. *Perf. 13x13½*
2598 A782 40p shown 70 15
2599 A782 50p Top 88 18

Spain's Presidency of the European Economic Community — A783

1989, May 9 *Perf. 13½x14*
2600 A783 45p multi 80 16

SEMI-POSTAL STAMPS

Red Cross Issue

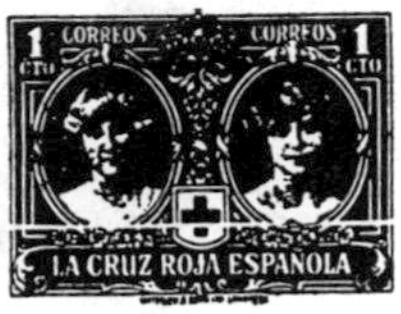

Princesses Maria Cristina and Beatrice SP1

Queen as a Nurse — SP2

Queen Victoria Eugenia — SP3

Prince of Asturias — SP4

King Alfonso XIII — SP5

Perf. 12½
1926, Sept. 15 Unwmk. Engr.
B1 SP1 1c black 1.40 1.00
B2 SP2 2c ultra 1.40 1.00
B3 SP3 5c vio brn 3.00 1.90
B4 SP4 10c green 2.50 1.90
B5 SP1 15c indigo 1.00 75
B6 SP4 20c dl vio 1.00 1.00
a. 20c vio brn (error) 190.00
B7 SP5 25c rose red 30 48
B8 SP1 30c bl grn 20.00 20.00
B9 SP3 40c dk bl 13.00 9.50
B10 SP2 50c red org 11.00 8.50
B11 SP4 1p slate 75 1.25
B12 SP3 4p magenta 30 48
B13 SP5 10p brown 48 75
Nos. B1-B13,EB1 (14) 62.13 54.51

The 20c was printed in violet brown for use in three colonies (Cape Juby, Spanish Guinea and Spanish Sahara). No. B6a, the missing overprint error, is listed here because it is not known to which colony it belongs.

Airplane and Map of Madrid-Manila Flight — SP6

1926, Sept. 15
B14 SP6 15c dp ultra & org 20 30
B15 SP6 20c car & yel grn 20 30
B16 SP6 30c dk brn & ultra 20 30
B17 SP6 40c dk grn & brn org 20 30
B18 SP6 4p mag & yel 47.50 45.00
Nos. B14-B18 (5) 48.30 46.20

Madrid to Manila flight of Captains Eduardo G. Gallarza and Joaquim Loriga y Taboada.

Nos. B1-B18, CB1-CB5 and EB1 were used for regular postage on Sept. 15, 16, 17, 1926. Subsequently the unsold stamps were given to the Spanish Red Cross Society, by which they were sold uncanceled but they then had no franking power.

Coronation Silver Jubilee Issue.

Red Cross Stamps of 1926 Overprinted "ALFONSO XIII", Dates and Ornaments in Various Colors

1927, May 27
B19 SP1 1c blk (R) 2.75 3.50
B20 SP2 2c ultra (Bl) 4.00 6.00
B21 SP3 5c vio brn (R) 1.10 1.50
a. Double overprint 32.50
B22 SP4 10c grn (Bl) 24.00 30.00
B23 SP1 15c ind (R) 85 1.25
B24 SP4 20c dl vio (Bl) 1.65 2.00
B25 SP5 25c rose red (Bl) 28 60
B26 SP1 30c bl grn (Bl) 55 90
B27 SP3 40c dk bl (R) 55 90
B28 SP2 50c red org (Bl) 55 90
B29 SP4 1p sl (R) 85 1.50
B30 SP3 4p mag (Bl) 4.75 6.00
B31 SP5 10p brn (G) 16.00 24.00
Nos. B19-B31 (13) 57.88 79.05

Same with Additional Surcharges of New Values.

B32 SP2 3c on 2c (G) 7.25 7.50
B33 SP2 4c on 2c (Bk) 7.25 7.50
B34 SP5 10c on 25c (Bk) 35 30
B35 SP5 25c on 25c (Bl) 35 45
B36 SP2 55c on 2c (R) 75 90
B37 SP4 55c on 10c (Bk) 35.00 30.00
B38 SP4 55c on 20c (Bk) 35.00 30.00
B39 SP1 75c on 15c (R) 55 60
B40 SP1 75c on 30c (R) 105.00 105.00
B41 SP3 80c on 5c (R) 32.50 30.00
B42 SP3 2p on 40c (R) 75 90
B43 SP4 2p on 1p (R) 75 90
B44 SP2 5p on 50c (G) 1.50 1.75
B45 SP3 5p on 4p (Bk) 1.75 2.50
B46 SP5 10p on 10p (G) 14.00 15.00
Nos. B32-B46 (15) 242.75 233.30

Nos. B14-B18 Overprinted

17 MAYO 17
1902 1927
ALFONSO XIII.

B47 SP6 15c (Br) 18 32
a. Double overprint 22.50
B48 SP6 20c (Bl) 18 32
a. Brown overprint (error) 52.50
b. Inverted overprint 22.50
B50 SP6 30c (R) 18 32
a. Blue overprint (error) 52.50
b. Dbl. ovpt. 22.50
B52 SP6 40c (Br) 18 32
a. Invtd. ovpt. 22.50
b. Dbl. ovpt. (Bl + Br) 82.50
B53 SP6 4p (Bl) 45.00 40.00
a. Inverted overprint 150.00

Semi-Postal Special Delivery Stamp of 1926 Overprinted "ALFONSO XIII", Dates and Ornaments in Violet.

B54 SPSD1 20c red vio & vio brn 3.00 4.00
Nos. B47-B54 (6) 48.72 45.28

Nos. CB1-CB5 Overprinted in Various Colors

17-V-1902 17-V-1927
A A
XIII XIII

B55 SPAP1 5c (R) 1.10 1.10
a. Inverted overprint 22.50
B56 SPAP1 10c (R) 1.10 1.25
a. Inverted overprint 22.50
B57 SPAP1 25c (Bl) 15 28
B58 SPAP1 50c (Bl) 15 28
a. Double overprint, one inverted 65.00
B59 SPAP1 1p (R) 1.10 1.25
a. Inverted overprint 85.00

Same with Additional Surcharges of New Values.

B60 SPAP1 75c on 5c (R) 3.00 2.75
a. Inverted surcharge 22.50
B61 SPAP1 75c on 10c (R) 11.00 10.00
a. Inverted surcharge 22.50
B62 SPAP1 75c on 25c (Bl) 20.00 20.00
a. Double surcharge 30.00
B63 SPAP1 75c on 50c (Bl) 10.00 10.00
Nos. B55-B63 (9) 47.60 46.91

Nos. B54 to B63 inclusive were available for ordinary postage.

Stamps of Spanish Offices in Morocco and Spanish Colonies, 1926 (Spain Types SP3, SP5) Surcharged in Various Colors with New Values and

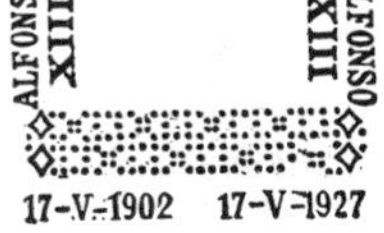

On Spanish Morocco

B64 SP3 55c on 4p bis (Bl) 4.75 6.00

B65 SP5 80c on 10p vio (Br) 4.75 6.00

On Spanish Tangier

B66 SP5 1p on 10p vio (Br) 15.00 24.00
B67 SP3 4p bis (G) 7.50 9.00

On Cape Juby

B68 SP3 5p on 4p bis (R) 11.50 15.00
B69 SP5 10p on 10p vio (R) 7.50 9.00

On Spanish Guinea

B70 SP5 1p on 10p vio (Bl) 4.75 6.00
B71 SP3 2p on 4p bis (G) 4.75 6.00

On Spanish Sahara

B72 SP5 80c on 10p vio (R) 6.50 9.00
B73 SP3 2p on 4p bis (R) 4.75 6.00
Nos. B64-B73 (10) 71.75 96.00

Nos. B64 to B73 inclusive were available for postage in Spain only.

Nos. B19 to B73 were issued to commemorate the 25th year of the reign of King Alfonso XIII.

Catacombs Restoration Issues.

Pope Pius XI and King Alfonso XIII SP7

1928, Dec. 23 Engr. *Perf. 12½*

Santiago Issue.

B74 SP7 2c vio & blk 28 30
B75 SP7 2c lake & blk 35 60
B76 SP7 3c bl blk & vio 28 30
B77 SP7 3c dl bl & vio 35 60
B78 SP7 5c ol grn & vio 75 90
B79 SP7 10c yel grn & blk 1.10 1.25
B80 SP7 15c bl grn & vio 3.25 3.50
B81 SP7 25c dp rose & vio 3.25 3.50
B82 SP7 40c ultra & blk 18 30
B83 SP7 55c ol brn & vio 18 30
B84 SP7 80c red & blk 18 30
B85 SP7 1p gray blk & vio 18 30
B86 SP7 2p red brn & blk 3.50 4.50
B87 SP7 3p pale rose & vio 3.50 4.50
B88 SP7 4p vio brn & blk 3.50 4.50
B89 SP7 5p grnsh blk & vio 3.50 4.50

Toledo Issue

B90 SP7 2c bl blk & car 28 30
B91 SP7 2c ultra & car 35 60
B92 SP7 3c bis brn & ultra 28 30
B93 SP7 3c ol grn & ultra 35 55
B94 SP7 5c red vio & car 75 90
B95 SP7 10c yel grn & ultra 1.10 1.25
B96 SP7 15c sl bl & car 3.25 3.50
B97 SP7 25c red brn & ultra 3.25 3.50
B98 SP7 40c ultra & car 18 30
B99 SP7 55c dk brn & ultra 18 30
B100 SP7 80c blk & car 18 30
B101 SP7 1p yel & car 18 30
B102 SP7 2p dk gray & ultra 3.50 4.50
B103 SP7 3p vio & car 3.50 4.50
B104 SP7 4p vio brn & car 3.50 4.50
B105 SP7 5p bis & ultra 3.50 4.50
Nos. B74-B105 (32) 48.66 60.25

Nos. B74 to B105 inclusive replaced the stamps of the regular issue from Dec. 23, 1928 to Jan. 6, 1929 inclusive. The proceeds from their sale were given to a fund to restore the catacombs of Saint Damasus and Saint Praetextatus at Rome.

Issues of the Republic

SP13

1938, Apr. 15 *Perf. 11½*

B106 SP13 45c + 2p bl & grnsh bl 45 60
a. Imperf., pair 9.00 9.00
b. Souv. sheet of 1 15.00 18.00
c. Souv. sheet of 1, imperf. 150.00 180.00

The surtax was used to benefit the defenders of Madrid.

See No. CB6.

Nurse and Orderly Carrying Wounded Soldier — SP14

1938, June 1 Engr. *Perf. 10*

B107 SP14 45c + 5p cop red 45 60
a. Imperf., pair 30.00

See No. CB7.

No. B106 Overprinted in Black

SEGUNDO ANIVERSARIO DE LA
7 NOV. 1938
HEROICA DEFENSA DE MADRID

1938, Nov. 7 *Perf. 11½*

B108 SP13 45c + 2p bl & grnsh bl 2.50 4.00

Defense of Madrid, 2nd anniversary.

A similar but larger overprint was applied to cover blocks of four. Value $17.50.

Spanish State

Souvenir Sheets

Alcazar, Toledo — SP15

Design: No. B108C, A patio of Alcazar after Civil War fighting.

1937 Unwmk. Photo. *Perf. 11½*

Control Numbers on Back

B108A SP15 2p org brn 14.00 15.00
b. Imperf. 200.00 200.00
B108C SP15 2p dk grn 14.00 15.00
d. Imperf. 200.00 200.00

Nos. B108A-B108C sold for 4p each.

SP16

Designs: 20c, Covadongas Cathedral. 30c, Palma Cathedral, Majorca. 50c, Alcazar of Segovia. 1p, Leon Cathedral.

1938 Unwmk. Engr. *Perf. 12½*

Control Numbers on Back

B108E SP16 Sheet of four 32.50 32.50
f. 20c dl vio 4.50 5.00
g. 30c rose red 4.50 5.00
h. 50c brt bl 4.50 5.00
i. 1p grnsh gray 4.50 5.00
j. Imperf. sheet 65.00 65.00

Each sheet sold for 4p.

The indexes in each volume of the Scott Catalogue contain many listings which help to identify stamps.

SP17

Designs, alternating in sheet: Flag bearer. Battleship "Admiral Cervera." Soldiers in trenches. Moorish guard.

1938, July 1 Unwmk. *Perf. 13*

Control Numbers on Back

B108K SP17 Sheet of 20 16.00 22.50
l. Imperf. sheet 120.00 130.00

Sheet measures 175x132mm. Consists of five vertical rows of four 2c violet, 3c deep blue, 5c olive gray, 10c deep green and 30c red orange, with each denomination appearing in two different designs. Marginal inscription: "Homenaje al Ejercito y a la Marina" (Honoring the Army and Navy). Sold for 4p, or double face value.

Souvenir Sheets

Don Juan of Austria — SP18

Battle of Lepanto SP19

Perf. 12½

1938, Dec. 15 Unwmk. Engr.

Control Numbers on Back

B108M SP18 30c dk car 7.50 9.00
B108N SP19 50c bl blk 7.50 9.00

Imperf

B108O SP18 30c blk vio 200.00 250.00
B108P SP19 50c dk sl grn 200.00 250.00

Issued to commemorate the victory over the Turks in the Battle of Lepanto, 1571.

Nos. B108M-B108P contain one stamp. The dates "1571-1938" appear in the lower sheet margin. Size: 89x74mm. Sold for 10p a pair.

LOCAL CHARITY STAMPS.

Hundreds of different charity stamps were issued by local organizations and cities during the Civil War, 1936-39. Some had limited franking value, but most were simply charity labels. They are of three kinds: 1. Local semipostals. 2. Obligatory surtax stamps. 3. Propaganda or charity labels.

Ruins of Belchite SP20

Miracle of Calanda — SP21

Designs: 10c+5c, 70c+20c, Ruins of Belchite. 15c+10c, 80c+20c, The Rosary. 20c+10c, 1.50p+50c, El Pilar Cathedral. 25c+10c, 1p+30c, Mother Raffols praying. 40c+10c, 2.50p+50c, The Little Chamber. 45c+15c, 1.40p+40c, Oath of the Besieged. 10p+4p, The Apparition.

Perf. 10½, 11½x10½, 11½.

1940, Jan. 29 Litho. Unwmk.

B109 SP20 10c + 5c dp bl & vio brn 9 9
B110 SP20 15c + 10c rose vio & dk grn 15 15
B111 SP20 20c + 10c vio & dp bl 15 15
B112 SP20 25c + 10c dp rose & vio brn 15 15
B113 SP20 40c + 10c sl grn & rose vio 9 9
B114 SP20 45c + 15c vio & dp rose 28 25
B115 SP20 70c + 20c multi 28 25
B116 SP20 80c + 20c dp rose & vio 28 25
B117 SP20 1p + 30c dk sl grn & pur 28 25
B118 SP20 1.40p + 40c pur & gray blk 16.00 16.00
B119 SP20 1.50p + 50c lt bl & brn vio 55 85
B120 SP20 2.50p + 50c choc & bl 55 85
B121 SP21 4p + 1p rose lil & sl grn 9.00 9.50
a. 4p + 1p vio & sl grn 25.00 37.50
B122 SP21 10p + 4p ultra & chnt 75.00 100.00
a. 10p + 4p ultra & brn vio 25.00 37.50
Nos. B109-B122,EB2 (15) 103.20 129.15

19th centenary of the Virgin of the Pillar.

The surtax was used to help restore the Cathedral at Zaragoza, damaged during the Civil War.

Nos. B109-B122 exist imperf. Value, 1½ times that of perf. set.

See No. 743, CB8-CB17.

General Franco — SP23

Knight and Lorraine Cross — SP24

1940, Dec. 23 Unwmk. *Perf. 10*

B123 SP23 20c + 5c dk grn & red 30 45
B124 SP23 40c + 10c dk bl & red 55 30

The surtax was for the tuberculosis fund. See also Nos. RA15, RAC1.

Stamps of 10c denomination, types SP23 to SP28, are postal tax issues.

1941, Dec. 23

B125 SP24 20c + 5c bl vio & red 35 30
B126 SP24 40c + 10c sl grn & red 35 30

The surtax was used to fight tuberculosis. See Nos. RA16, RAC2.

Cross of Lorraine
SP25 SP26

1942, Dec. 23 Litho.

B127 SP25 20c + 5c pale brn & rose red 90 1.25
B128 SP25 40c + 10c lt bluish grn & rose red 85 32

The surtax was used to fight tuberculosis. See Nos. RA17, RAC3.

1943, Dec. 23 Photo. *Perf. 11½*

B129 SP26	20c + 5c dl sl grn & dl red	3.25	1.25
B130 SP26	40c + 10c brt bl & dl red	2.00	1.00

The surtax was used to fight tuberculosis. See Nos. RA18, RAC4.

Dragon Slaying SP27

St. George Slaying the Dragon SP28

Perf. 9½x10

1944, Dec. 23 Litho. Unwmk.

B131 SP27	20c + 5c sl grn & red	30	20
B132 SP27	40c + 10c dl vio & red	65	15
B133 SP27	80c + 10c ultra & rose	6.50	7.25

The surtax was used to fight tuberculosis. See Nos. RA19, RAC5.

1945, Dec. 23

Lorraine Cross in Red

B134 SP28	20c + 5c dl gray grn	18	14
B135 SP28	40c + 10c vio	35	22
B136 SP28	80c + 10c ultra	7.25	7.50

The surtax was used to fight tuberculosis. See Nos. RA20, RAC6.

Nos. 753 and 768 Surcharged in Blue

VISITA DEL CAUDILLO A CANARIAS OCTUBRE 1950 SOBRETASA: DIEZ CTS

1950, Oct. 23

B137 A195	50c + 10c rose vio	25.00	35.00
a.	"Caudillo" 14¼mm wide	80.00	80.00
B138 A195	1p + 10c rose pink	20.00	35.00
a.	"Caudillo" 14¼mm wide	60.00	60.00

Visit of General Franco to Canary Islands. First printing was issued in Canary Islands. Second printing was issued in Madrid Feb. 22, 1951. See No. CB18.

Catalogue values for unused stamps in this section, from this point to the end of the section, are for Never Hinged items.

Barcelona '92 Olympics Type of 1988

1988, Oct. 3 Photo. *Perf. 14*

B139 A764	20p +5p Track and field	45	22
B140 A764	45p +5p Badminton	88	45
B141 A764	50p +5p Basketball	95	48

EXPO '92, Seville — SP29

Globes and sites of previous exhibitions: No. B142, Crystal Palace, London, 1851. No. B143, Eiffel Tower, Paris, 1889. No. B144, "The Atom," Brussels, 1958. No. B145, Monument, Osaka, 1970.

1989, Feb. 9 Photo. *Perf. 14x13½*

B142 SP29	8p +5p multi	24	12
B143 SP29	8p +5p multi	24	12
B144 SP29	20p +5p multi	45	22
B145 SP29	20p +5p multi	45	22

1992 Summer Olympics, Barcelona — SP30

1989, Mar. 7 Photo. *Perf. 14*

B146 SP30	8p +5p Handball	24	12
B147 SP30	18p +5p Boxing	42	20
B148 SP30	20p +5p Cycling	45	22
B149 SP30	45p +5p Equestrian	90	45

AIR POST STAMPS

Regular Issue of 1909-10 Overprinted in Red or Black **CORREO AEREO**

Perf. 13x12½, 14

1920, Apr. 4 Unwmk.

C1 A46	5c grn (R)	55	65
a.	Imperf. (pair)	70.00	70.00
b.	Double overprint	25.00	25.00
c.	Inverted ovpt.	52.50	65.00
d.	Double overprint, one inverted	18.00	21.00
e.	Triple overprint	18.00	21.00
C2 A46	10c car (Bk)	90	65
a.	Imperf. (pair)	70.00	70.00
b.	Double overprint	21.00	25.00
d.	Double overprint, one inverted	18.00	21.00
C3 A46	25c dp bl (R)	1.50	90
a.	Invtd. ovpt.	65.00	85.00
b.	Double overprint	25.00	25.00
C4 A46	50c sl bl (R)	5.00	3.50
a.	Imperf. (pair)	70.00	90.00
C5 A46	1p lake (Bk)	17.50	11.00
a.	Imperf. (pair)	225.00	225.00
	Nos. C1-C5 (5)	25.45	16.70

The overprint and its varieties have been counterfeited.

A 30c green was authorized, but not issued. Value $1,100.

"Spirit of St. Louis" over Coast of Europe — AP1

Plane and Congress Seal — AP2

Seville-Barcelona Exposition Issue

Control Numbers on Back

1929, Feb. 15 Engr. *Perf. 11*

C6 AP1	5c brown	3.50	4.00
C7 AP1	10c rose	3.50	4.50
C8 AP1	25c dk bl	4.00	5.00
C9 AP1	50c purple	5.25	6.50
C10 AP1	1p green	25.00	22.50
C11 AP1	4p black	28.00	16.00
	Nos. C6-C11 (6)	69.25	58.50

Nos. C6 to C11 exist imperforate. Values about four times those of perforated stamps.

The so-called errors of color of Nos. C10, C18-C21, C23-C24, C28-C31, C37, C40, C42, C44, C46, C48, C50, C52, C55, C62-C67 are believed to have been irregularly produced.

Railway Congress Issue.

Control Numbers on Back.

1930, May 10 Litho. *Perf. 14*

C12 AP2	5c bis brn	3.00	3.75
a.	Imperf., pair	85.00	
C13 AP2	10c rose	3.00	3.75
C14 AP2	25c dk bl	3.00	3.75
C15 AP2	50c purple	6.75	6.75
a.	Vert.pair, imperf. between	210.00	
C16 AP2	1p yel grn	12.50	12.50
C17 AP2	4p black	15.00	15.00
	Nos. C12-C17 (6)	43.25	45.50

The note after No. 385 will apply here also. Dangerous counterfeits exist.

Goya Issue

Fantasy of Flight AP3

1930, June 15 Engr. *Perf. 12½*

C18 AP3	5c brn red & yel	10	14
C19 AP3	15c blk & red org	10	14
C20 AP3	25c brn car & dp red	12	14

Asmodeus and Cleofas — AP4

C21 AP4	5c ol grn & grnsh bl	6	8
C22 AP4	10c sl grn & yel grn	10	14
C23 AP4	20c ultra & rose red	12	14
C24 AP4	40c vio bl & lt bl	35	40

Fantasy of Flight AP5

C25 AP5	30c brn & vio	35	40
C26 AP5	50c ver & grn	35	40
C27 AP5	4p brn car & blk	1.50	1.65

Fantasy of Flight — AP6

C28 AP6	1p vio brn & vio	35	40
C29 AP6	4p bl blk & sl grn	1.50	1.65
C30 AP6	10p blk brn & bis brn	6.25	6.75
	Nos. C18-C30,CE1 (14)	11.45	12.63

Nos. C18-C30 exist imperf. Value for set, $250.

Christopher Columbus Issue.

La Rábida Monastery — AP7

Martín Alonso Pinzón — AP8

Vicente Yanez Pinzón — AP9

Columbus in His Cabin — AP10

1930, Sept. 29 Litho.

C31 AP7	5c lt red brn	20	15
C32 AP7	5c ol bis	20	15
C33 AP7	10c bl grn	20	15
C34 AP7	15c dk vio	20	15
C35 AP7	20c ultra	20	15
	Engr.		
C36 AP8	25c car rose	20	15
C37 AP9	30c dp red brn	1.25	1.65
C38 AP8	40c indigo	1.25	1.65
C39 AP9	50c orange	1.25	1.65
C40 AP8	1p dl vio	1.25	1.65
C41 AP10	4p ol grn	1.25	1.65
C42 AP10	10p lt brn	6.00	8.25
	Nos. C31-C42 (12)	13.45	17.40

Nos. C31-C42 exist imperf. Value for set, $210.

Spanish-American Issue.

AP11

Columbus — AP12

Columbus and Pinzon Brothers AP13

1930, Sept. 29 Litho.

C43 AP11	5c lt red	20	18
C44 AP11	10c dl grn	20	18
	Engr.		
C45 AP12	25c scarlet	20	18
C46 AP12	50c sl gray	1.40	1.50
C47 AP12	1p fawn	1.65	1.50
C48 AP13	4p sl bl	1.65	1.50
C49 AP13	10p brn vio	7.25	6.00
	Nos. C43-C49 (7)	12.55	11.04

Nos. C43-C49 exist imperf. Value for set, $225.

Spanish-American Exhibition Issue.

Santos-Dumont and First Flight of His Airplane — AP14

Teodoro Fels and His Airplane AP15

Dagoberto Godoy and Pass over Andes AP16

Sacadura Cabral and Gago Coutinho and Their Airplane AP17

Sidar of Mexico and Map of South America — AP18

Ignacio Jiménez and Francisco Iglesias — AP19

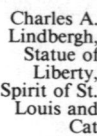

Charles A. Lindbergh, Statue of Liberty, Spirit of St. Louis and Cat AP20

Santa Maria, Plane and Torre del Oro, Seville AP21

1930, Oct. 10 Photo. *Perf. 14*

C50	AP14	5c gray blk	30	30
C51	AP15	10c dk ol grn	30	30
C52	AP16	25c ultra	30	30
C53	AP17	50c bl gray	60	60
C54	AP18	50c black	60	60
C55	AP19	1p car lake	1.25	90
a.		1p brn vio	30.00	30.00
C56	AP20	1p dp grn	1.25	90
C57	AP21	4p sl bl	3.25	3.25
		Nos. C50-C57 (8)	7.85	7.15

Exist imperf. Value, set $100.

Note after No. 432 also applies to Nos. C31-C57.

Reprints of Nos. C50-C57 have blurred impressions, yellowish paper. Value, one-tenth of originals.

Nos. C1-C4 Overprinted in Red or Black

REPUBLICA

1931 *Perf. 13x12½*

C58	A46	5c grn (R)	6.00	7.50
C59	A46	10c car (Bk)	6.00	7.50
C60	A46	25c dp bl (R)	7.50	9.00
C61	A46	50c sl bl (R)	16.00	21.00

Counterfeits of overprint exist.

Plane and Royal Palace, Madrid AP22

Madrid Post Office and Cibeles Fountain AP23

Plane over Calle de Alcala, Madrid AP24

1931, Oct. 10 Engr. *Perf. 12*

C62	AP22	5c brn vio	20	30
C63	AP22	10c dp grn	20	30
C64	AP22	25c dl red	20	30
C65	AP23	50c dp bl	30	40
C66	AP23	1p dp vio	40	40
C67	AP24	4p black	4.00	5.50
		Nos. C62-C67 (6)	5.30	7.20

Issued to commemorate the 3rd Pan-American Postal Union Congress, Madrid.

Exist imperf. Value, set $60.

Montserrat Issue.

Plane over Montserrat Pass — AP25

1931, Dec. 9 *Perf. 11½*

Control Number on Back

C68	AP25	5c blk brn	1.10	1.00
a.		Perf. 14	6.50	13.00
C69	AP25	10c yel grn	2.00	2.00
a.		Perf. 14	27.50	32.50
C70	AP25	25c dp rose	6.25	8.25
a.		Perf. 14	40.00	60.00
C71	AP25	50c orange	21.00	22.50
a.		Perf. 14	40.00	60.00
C72	AP25	1p gray blk	14.00	16.00
f.		Perf. 14	40.00	60.00
		Nos. C68-C72 (5)	44.35	49.75

Issued to commemorate the 900th anniversary of Montserrat Monastery.

Nos. C68-C72 exist imperf. Values about 7 times those quoted for perf. 11½stamps.

Autogiro over Seville — AP26

1935-39 *Perf. 11½*

C72A	AP26	2p gray bl	16.00	3.00
g.		Imperf., pair	165.00	

Re-engraved

C72B	AP26	2p dk bl ('38)	20	20
c.		Imperf., pair	18.00	
d.		Perf. 10 ('39)	1.00	1.00
e.		Perf. 14	6.50	6.50

The sky has heavy horizontal lines of shading. Entire design is more heavily shaded than No. C72A.

Eagle and Newspapers — AP27

Press Building, Madrid — AP28

Don Quixote and Sancho Panza Flying on the Wooden Horse — AP29

Design: 15c, 30c, 50c, 1p, Autogiro over House of Nazareth.

1936, Mar. 11 Photo. *Perf. 12½*

C73	AP27	1c rose car	7	7
C74	AP28	2c dk brn	7	7
C75	AP27	5c blk brn	7	7
C76	AP28	10c dk yel grn	7	7
C77	AP28	15c Prus bl	12	7
C78	AP27	20c violet	12	7
C79	AP28	25c magenta	12	7
C80	AP28	30c red org	7	7
C81	AP27	40c orange	35	12
C82	AP28	50c lt bl	18	12
C83	AP28	60c ol grn	52	32
C84	AP28	1p brnsh blk	52	50
C85	AP29	2p brt ultra	2.75	2.25
C86	AP29	4p lil rose	3.00	2.75
C87	AP29	10p vio brn	7.25	6.50
		Nos. C73-C87 (15)	15.28	13.12

Madrid Press Association, 40th anniv.

Exist imperf. Value, set $525.

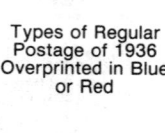

See note after No. 432.

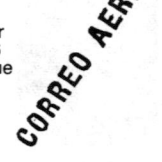

Types of Regular Postage of 1936 Overprinted in Blue or Red

CORREO AEREO

1936 *Imperf.*

C88	A125	10c dk red (Bl)	85.00	85.00
C89	A125	15c dk bl (R)	85.00	85.00

Issued in commemoration of the first National Philatelic Exhibition which opened in Madrid, April 2nd, 1936.

No. 577 Overprinted in Black

VUELO :-:-:
:-: MANILA
MADRID :-:
1936
ARNAIZ -:-:
:-:-: CALVO

1936, Aug. 1 *Perf. 11½*

C90	A128	30c rose red	3.50	1.00
a.		Perf. 14	42.50	42.50
b.		Imperf., pair	110.00	

Issued in commemoration of the flight of aviators Antonio Arnaiz and Juan Calvo from Manila to Spain.

No. 288 Surcharged in Black

CORREO AÉREO
14 Abril 1938
VII Aniversario
de la República
2'50 pts.

1938, Apr. 13 *Perf. 14*

C91	A36	2.50p on 10c org red	75.00	85.00

7th anniversary of the Republic.

No. 507 Surcharged in Various Colors

CORREO AEREO 50 CTS. CORREO AEREO

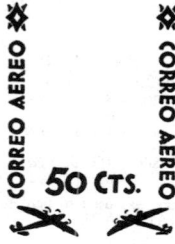

1938, Aug. *Perf. 11½*

C92	A92	50c on 25c (Bk)	18.00	16.00
C93	A92	1p on 25c (G)	1.10	1.25
C94	A92	1.25p on 25c (R)	1.10	1.25
C95	A92	1.50p on 25c (Bl)	1.10	1.25
C96	A92	2p on 25c (Bk & R)	18.00	16.00
		Nos. C92-C96 (5)	39.30	35.75

No. 585 Surcharged

AEREO + 5 Pts.

1938, June 1 *Perf. 11*

C97	A132	5p on 1p multi	100.00	100.00
a.		Imperf., pair	400.00	475.00
b.		Inverted surcharge	165.00	200.00
c.		Souv. sheet	500.00	500.00
d.		Souvenir sheet, imperf.	3,000.	3,500.
e.		Dbl. surch.	275.00	300.00

Type of 1938-39 Overprinted in Red or Carmine

Correo Aereo

1938, May *Perf. 10, 10½*

C98	A163	50c ind (R)	65	40
C99	A163	1p dk bl (C)	2.00	40

Exist imperf. Value, each $80.

Exist without overprint. Value, each $100.

Juan de la Cierva and his Autogiro over Madrid AP30

1939, Jan. Unwmk. Litho. *Perf. 11*

C100	AP30	20c red org	35	20
C101	AP30	25c dk car	24	10
C102	AP30	35c brt vio	35	20
C103	AP30	50c dk brn	35	14
C105	AP30	1p blue	35	14
C107	AP30	2p green	1.65	90
C108	AP30	4p dl bl	2.75	1.65
		Nos. C100-C108 (7)	6.04	3.33

Exist imperf. Value, set $600.

1941-47 *Perf. 10.*

C109	AP30	20c dk red org	15	8
C110	AP30	25c redsh brn	15	7
C111	AP30	35c lil rose	1.10	42
C112	AP30	50c brown	24	5
C113	AP30	1p chlky bl	90	5
C114	AP30	2p lt gray grn	1.10	12
C115	AP30	4p gray bl	2.25	30
C116	AP30	10p brt pur ('47)	2.00	60
		Nos. C109-C116 (8)	7.89	1.69

Issued in honor of Juan de la Cierva (1895-1936), inventor of the autogiro.

Exist imperf. Value, set $75.

The overprint "EXPOSICION NACIONAL DE FILATELIA 1948 SAN SEBASTIAN" multiple, in parallel horizontal lines, on Nos. C109 to C113 and other airmail stamps, was privately applied.

Correo Aéreo   Correo Aéreo

Nos. 625-634, 660, 676 and 677 with either of these overprints have not been established as issues of the Spanish government.

Mariano Pardo de Figueroa (Dr. Thebussem) AP31

1944, Oct. 12 Engr. *Perf. 10*
C117 AP31 5p brt ultra 12.00 11.00

Issued to commemorate "Stamp Day" and "Day of the Race," October 12, 1944. Valid for franking air mail correspondence one day only.

Mail Coach, Plane and Count of St. Louis AP32

1945, Oct. 12 Unwmk.
C118 AP32 10p yel grn 12.00 11.00

Issued to commemorate "Stamp Day" and "Day of the Race," October 12, 1945, and to honor Luis Jose Sartorius, Count of St. Louis, who issued the decree for Spain's first postage stamps. No. C118 was valid for franking air mail correspondence one day only.

Maj. Joaquin Garcia Morato AP33

1945, Nov. 27
C119 AP33 10p dp cl 12.00 4.75

Capt. Carlos Haya Gonzalez AP34

Bartolomé de las Casas AP35

1945, Dec. 14
C120 AP34 4p red 6.75 4.00

1946, Oct. 12 *Perf. 11½x11*
C121 AP35 5.50p green 1.75 2.25

Stamp Day and Day of the Race. Exists imperf. Value $15.

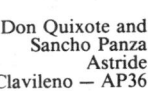

Don Quixote and Sancho Panza Astride Clavileno — AP36

1947, Oct. 9 *Perf. 10*
C122 AP36 5.50p purple 3.25 3.00

Issued to commemorate Stamp Day and the 400th anniversary of the birth of Miguel de Cervantes Saavedra.

Manuel de Falla AP37

Ignacio Zuloaga AP38

1947, Dec. 1 *Perf. 9½x10½*
Control Number on Back
C123 AP37 25p dk vio & brn 24.00 15.00
C124 AP38 50p dk car 95.00 24.00

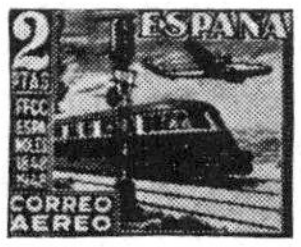
Train and Plane — AP39

1948, Oct. 9 Litho. *Perf. 13x12½*
C125 AP39 2p scarlet 1.75 1.25

Issued to commemorate the centenary of Spanish railroads and Stamp Day.

UPU Type of Regular Issue with Pedestal and Propeller Added

1949, Oct. 9 *Perf. 12½x13*
C126 A202 4p dk ol grn 30 40

Stamp Day and the 75th anniv. of the UPU.

Stamp of 1850 — AP40

Map of Western Hemisphere — AP41

1950, Oct. 12 Engr. *Imperf.*
C127 AP40 1p rose brn 3.25 3.25
C128 AP40 2.50p brn org 3.25 3.25
C129 AP40 20p dk bl 45.00 50.00
C130 AP40 25p green 45.00 50.00

Centenary of Spanish postage stamps.

1951, Apr. 16 Photo. *Perf. 12½*
C131 AP41 1p blue 3.50 1.50

Issued to commemorate the 6th Congress of the Postal Union of the Americas and Spain.

Isabella I AP42

1951, Oct. 12 Engr. *Perf. 13*
C132 AP42 60c dk gray grn 5.00 40
C133 AP42 90c orange 50 55
C134 AP42 1.30p plum 4.00 4.00
C135 AP42 1.90p sepia 3.75 4.00
C136 AP42 2.30p dk bl 2.25 2.75
Nos. C132-C136 (5) 15.50 11.70

Issued to publicize Stamp Day, Oct. 12, 1951, and to commemorate the 500th anniversary of the birth of Queen Isabella I.

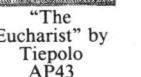

"The Eucharist" by Tiepolo AP43

St. Francis Xavier AP44

1952, May 26 Photo. *Perf. 12½x13*
C137 AP43 1p gray grn 3.50 60

Issued to publicize the 35th International Eucharistic Congress, Barcelona, 1952.

1952, July 3 Engr.
C138 AP44 2p dp bl 24.00 14.00

Issued to commemorate the 400th anniversary of the death of St. Francis Xavier.

Ferdinand the Catholic and Columbus Presenting Natives AP45

1952, Oct. 12
C139 AP45 60c dl grn 18 18
C140 AP45 90c orange 18 18
C141 AP45 1.30p plum 35 30
C142 AP45 1.90p sepia 1.50 2.00
C143 AP45 2.30p dp bl 7.50 9.50
Nos. C139-C143 (5) 9.71 12.16

Issued to commemorate the 500th anniversary of the birth of Ferdinand the Catholic and to publicize Stamp Day.

Joaquin Sorolla Bastida AP46

Miguel Lopez de Legazpi AP47

1953, Oct. 9 *Perf. 13x12½*
C144 AP46 50p dk vio 200.00 20.00

Issued to honor Joaquin Sorolla y Bastida (1863-1923), impressionist painter.

1953, Nov. 5
C145 AP47 25p gray blk 90.00 20.00

Issued to commemorate the Spanish-Philippine Postal Convention of 1951.

Leonardo Torres Quevedo — AP48

Perf. 13x12½.
1955, Sept. 6 Engr. Unwmk.
C146 AP48 50p bluish gray & blk 6.00 90

Issued in honor of Leonardo Torres Quevedo (1852-1939), mathematician and inventor.

Plane and Caravel AP49

1955-56 Photo. *Perf. 12½x13*
C147 AP49 20c gray grn ('56) 8 8
C148 AP49 25c gray vio 8 8
C149 AP49 50c ol gray ('56) 8 8
C150 AP49 1p red org 8 8
C151 AP49 1.10p emer ('56) 12 8
C152 AP49 1.40p rose car 15 8
C153 AP49 3p brt bl ('56) 12 8
C154 AP49 4.80p yellow 16 12
C155 AP49 5p redsh brn 1.25 12
C156 AP49 7p lil ('56) 35 14
C157 AP49 10p lt ol grn ('56) 40 22
Nos. C147-C157 (11) 2.87 1.16

Mariano Fortuny — AP50

1956, Jan. 10 Engr. *Perf. 13x12½*
C158 AP50 25p grnsh blk 16.00 80

Issued in honor of Mariano Fortuny y Carbo (1838-1874), painter.

Catalogue values for unused stamps in this section, from this point to the end of the section, are for Never Hinged items.

Bullfight Type of Regular Issue

Designs: 25c, Small town arena. 50c, Fighting with cape. 1p, Dedication of the bull. 5p, Bull ring.

Perf. 13x12½, 12½x13
1960, Feb. 29 Engr. Unwmk.
C159 A246 25c brn car & dl lil 12 10
C160 A245 50c blue 12 10
C161 A246 1p red & dl red 30 10
C162 A245 5p red lil & vio 65 35

Jai Alai AP51

1960, Mar. 27 Photo. *Perf. 12½x13*
C163 AP51 1p brt red & dk brn 5.50 4.00
C164 AP51 5p dl brn & mag 5.50 4.00
C165 AP51 6p vio blk & mag 5.50 4.00
C166 AP51 10p grn, mag & dk brn 5.50 4.00

Issued to commemorate the first International Congress of Philately, Barcelona. March 26-Apr. 5. Nos. C163-C166 could be bought at the exhibition upon presentation of 5p entrance ticket.

Sport Type of Regular Issue, 1960

Sports: 1.25p, 6p, Steeplechase (horiz.). 1.50p, 10p, Basque ball game.

Perf. 12½x13, 13x12½
1960, Oct. 31 Unwmk.
C167 A251 1.25p choc & car 30 8
C168 A251 1.50p pur, brn & blk 30 8
C169 A251 6p vio blk & car 95 55
C170 A251 10p ol grn, red & blk 1.25 55

Rosary Type of Regular Issue, 1962

Mysteries of the Rosary: 25c, The Ascension, Bayeu. 1p, The Descent of the Holy Ghost, El Greco. 5p, The Assumption, Mateo Cerezo. 10p, The Coronation of the Virgin Mary, El Greco.

1962, Oct. 26 Engr. *Perf. 13*

C171	A280	25c vio & dl gray vio	22	8
C172	A280	1p ol & brn	35	16
C173	A280	5p brn & rose cl	55	25
C174	A280	10p bluish grn & yel grn	1.40	52

Recaredo I, Visigothic King, 586-601 — AP52

Portrait: 50p, Francisco Cardinal Jimenez de Cisneros (1436-1517).

1963, Dec. 5 Engr. *Perf. 13x12½*

C175	AP52	25p dl pur	1.50	28
C176	AP52	50p grn & blk	2.00	65

1966, Feb. 26

Portraits: 25p, Seneca (4 B.C.-65 A.D.). 50p, Pope St. Damasus I (304?-384).

C177	AP52	25p yel grn & dk grn	1.65	18
C178	AP52	50p sky bl & gray bl	2.50	50

Plaza de Espana, Seville AP53

1981, Nov. 26 Engr. *Perf. 13*

C179	AP53	13p shown	25	6
C180	AP53	20p Rande River Bridge, Pontevedra	45	6

St. Thomas, by El Greco — AP54

1982, July 7 Photo. *Perf. 13*

C181	AP54	13p Sts. Andrew and Francis	25	5
C182	AP54	20p shown	35	12

Bowling AP55

1983, Apr. 13 Photo. *Perf. 13*

C183	AP55	13p Bicycling, vert.	25	6
C184	AP55	20p shown	50	12

AIR POST SEMI-POSTAL STAMPS

Red Cross Issue.

Ramon Franco's Plane Plus Ultra SPAP1

Perf. 12½, 13

1926, Sept. 15 Engr. Unwmk.

CB1	SPAP1	5c blk & vio	1.00	90
CB2	SPAP1	10c ultra & blk	1.00	90
CB3	SPAP1	25c car & blk	15	22
CB4	SPAP1	50c red org & blk	15	22
CB5	SPAP1	1p blk & grn	1.50	1.40
		Nos. CB1-CB5 (5)	3.80	3.64

No. B106 Surcharged in Black AEREO ◆ 5 Pts.

1938, Apr. 15 *Perf. 11½*

CB6	SP13	45c + 2p + 5p	100.00	100.00
a.		Imperf., pair	600.00	600.00
b.		Souvenir sheet of 1	*3,750.*	*4,250.*
c.		Souvenir sheet, imperf.	*3,250.*	*4,000.*
d.		Souv. sheet, surch. invtd.	*3,250.*	*4,000.*

The surtax was used to benefit the defenders of Madrid.

No. B107 Surcharged +3Pts Aereo

1938, June 1 *Perf. 10*

CB7	SP14	45c + 5p + 3p	6.00	6.00

Monument SPAP2

Caravel Santa Maria SPAP3

Dome Fresco by Goya, Cathedral of Zaragoza SPAP6

Designs: SPAP4, The Ascension. SPAP5, The Coronation, SPAP7, Bombardment of Cathedral of Zaragoza.

Perf. 10½, 11½x10½, 11½.

1940, Jan. 29 Litho. Unwmk.

Bicolored

CB8	SPAP2	25c + 5c	18	18
CB9	SPAP3	50c + 5c	18	18
CB10	SPAP4	65c + 15c	18	18
CB11	SPAP2	70c + 15c	18	18
CB12	SPAP4	90c + 20c	18	18
CB13	SPAP5	1.20p + 30c	18	18
CB14	SPAP3	1.40p + 40c	35	30
CB15	SPAP5	2p + 50c	35	30
CB16	SPAP6	4p + 1p sl grn & rose lil	6.50	8.25
a.		4p + 1p sl grn & vio	32.50	45.00
CB17	SPAP7	10p + 4 chnt & ultra	110.00	130.00
a.		10p + 4p red vio & ultra	32.50	45.00
		Nos. CB8-CB17 (10)	118.28	139.93

Issued in commemoration of the 19th centenary of the Pillar Virgin. The surtax was used to help restore the Cathedral at Zaragoza, damaged during the Civil War.

Exist imperf. Value, set $575.

A particular stamp may be scarce, but if few collectors want it, its market value may remain relatively low.

No. C123 Surcharged in Black

Correspondencia por avión
VISITA DEL CAUDILLO A CANARIAS
OCTUBRE 1950
Sobretasa:
DIEZ CTS

1950-51 *Perf. 9½x10½*

Control Number on Back

CB18	AP37	25p + 10c	250.00	150.00
a.		Without control number	*1,800.*	250.00

Issued to commemorate the visit of General Franco to the Canary Islands, October, 1950.

No. CB18a is from the first printing of the surcharge issued Oct. 23, 1950. The control number was printed on the gum, and regummed copies of No. CB18 are frequently offered as No. CB18a.

No. CB18 was issued Feb. 22, 1951.

AIR POST SPECIAL DELIVERY STAMP

Goya Commemorative Issue.

Type of Air Post Stamp of 1930 Overprinted URGENTE

1930 Unwmk. *Perf. 12½*

CE1	AP4	20c bl blk & lt brn (Bk)	20	20
a.		Blue overprint	9.00	10.00
b.		Ovpt. omitted	14.00	15.00

See note after No. 432.

AIR POST OFFICIAL STAMPS

Pan-American Postal Union Congress Issue

Types of Air Post Stamps of 1931 Overprinted in Red or Blue

OFICIAL

1931 Unwmk. *Perf. 12*

CO1	AP22	5c red brn (R)	8	7
CO2	AP22	10c bl grn (Bl)	8	7
CO3	AP22	25c rose (Bl)	8	7
CO4	AP23	50c lt bl (R)	8	7
a.		50c dp bl (R)	24.00	22.50
CO5	AP23	1p vio (R)	8	7
CO6	AP24	4p gray blk (R)	2.75	3.00
		Nos. CO1-CO6 (6)	*3.15*	3.35

SPECIAL DELIVERY STAMPS

Pegasus and Coat of Arms SD1

1905-25 Unwmk. Typo. *Perf. 14*

Control Number on Back

E1	SD1	20c dp red	24.00	30
a.		20c rose red, litho. ('25)	26.50	30
b.		Imperf., pair	125.00	
c.		As "a", imperf., pair	100.00	

Gazelle SD2

Pegasus SD3

1929 Engr. *Perf. 11*

Control Number on Back

E2	SD2	20c dull red	9.00	8.25
a.		Perf. 14	20.00	20.00

Seville and Barcelona Exhibitions. See note after No. 432.

1929-32 *Perf. 13½x12½, 11½*

Control Number on Back

E3	SD3	20c red	9.00	60
a.		Imperf., pair	60.00	
b.		Without control number, perf. 11½ ('32)	48.00	90
c.		As "b", imperf., pair	*500.00*	

No. E3 Overprinted like Nos. 358-370

E4	SD3	20c red (Bl)	9.00	9.00

League of Nations 55th assembly.

No. E3 Overprinted in Blue URGENCIA

1930 *Perf. 13½x12½, 11½*

E5	SD3	20c red	9.00	60

Railway Congress Issue.

Electric Locomotive — SD4

1930, May 10 Litho. *Perf. 14*

Control Number on Back

E6	SD4	20c brn org	24.00	24.00

The note after No. 385 will apply here also.

Goya Issue.

Type of Regular Issue of 1930 Overprinted URGENTE

1930 *Perf. 12½*

E7	A57	20c lil rose	20	30

Christopher Columbus Issue.

Type of Regular Issue of 1930 Overprinted URGENTE

1930 Sept. 29

E8	A64	20c brn vio	75	75

Spanish-American Exhibition Issue.

View of Seville Exhibition — SD5

1930, Oct. 10 Photo. *Perf. 14*

E9	SD5	20c orange	25	25

The note after No. 432 will apply to Nos. E8 and E9, also to No. E15.

Madrid Issue.

No. E5 Overprinted in Green REPUBLICA

1931 *Perf. 11½.*

E10	SD3	20c red	2.00	2.50

Barcelona Issue.

No. E3 Overprinted REPUBLICA

E11	SD3	20c red	2.75	3.00

No. E11 also exists with accent over "U".

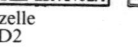

No. E3 Overprinted in Blue — República Española.

E12	SD3 20c red	6.00	90

Montserrat Issue.

Pegasus — SD6

1931 Engr. *Perf. 11*
Control Number on Back

E13	SD6 20c vermilion	16.00	21.00
a.	Perf. 14	40.00	45.00

SD7

1934 *Perf. 10*

E14	SD7 20c vermilion	20	8
a.	Imperf., pair	4.25	

Newsboy SD8

Pegasus SD9

1936 Photo. *Perf. 12½*

E15	SD8 20c rose car	30	32

Issued in commemoration of the 40th anniversary of the Madrid Press Association.
See note after No. 432.

Spanish State

1937-38 Unwmk. Litho. *Perf. 11.*
With imprint "Hija. deB Fournier-Burgos".

E16	SD9 20c vio brn	5.00	2.25
a.	Imperf., pair	50.00	

Without Imprint.

E17	SD9 20c dk vio brn ('38)	1.00	22
a.	Imperf., pair	32.50	

No. 645 Overprinted in Black — CORRESPONDENCIA URGENTE

1937

E18	A162 20c dk vio	7.25	7.25

Pegasus SD10

1939-42 *Perf. 10½*
Imprint: "SANCHEZ TODA"

E19	SD10 25c carmine	3.25	65
a.	Imperf., pair	30.00	

Without Imprint.
Perf. 10

E20	SD10 25c car ('42)	20	12
a.	Imperf., pair	5.75	

Catalogue values for unused stamps in this section, from this point to the end of the section, are for Never Hinged items.

"Flight" SD11

Centaur — SD12

Perf. 12½x13, 13x12½
1956, Feb. 12 Photo. Unwmk.

E21	SD11 2p scarlet	15	8
E22	SD12 4p blk & mag	20	12

1965-66

E23	SD11 3p dp car	25	12
E24	SD11 5p dp org ('66)	12	10
E25	SD12 6.50p dk vio & rose brn ('66)	20	10
	Nos. E21-E25 (5)	*92*	*52*

Chariot SD13

Mail Circling Globe — SD14

1971, June 1 Photo. *Perf. 13*

E26	SD13 10p red & yel grn	20	10
E27	SD14 15p red, bl & blk	30	12

SEMI-POSTAL SPECIAL DELIVERY STAMPS

Red Cross Issue.

Royal Family Group SPSD1

1926 Unwmk. Engr. *Perf. 12½, 13.*

EB1	SPSD1 20c red vio & vio brn	6.00	6.00

See notes after Nos. 432 and B18.

Motorcyclist and Zaragoza Cathedral SPSD2

1940 Litho. *Perf. 11½.*

EB2	SPSD2 25c + 5c rose red & buff	35	32

Issued in commemoration of the 19th centenary of the Pillar Virgin. The surtax was used to help restore the Cathedral at Zaragoza, damaged during the Civil War.

DELIVERY TAX STAMPS

D1

1931 Unwmk. Litho. *Perf. 11½*

ER1	D1 5c black	5.00	20

No. ER1 Overprinted in Red — REPUBLICA

1931

ER2	D1 5c black	1.10	1.25

No. ER2 also exists with accent over "U".

No. ER1 Overprinted in Red — REPUBLICA

ER3	D1 5c black	2.75	2.75

These stamps were originally issued for Postage Due purpose but were later used as regular postage stamps.

WAR TAX STAMPS

These stamps did not pay postage but represented a fiscal tax on mail matter in addition to the postal fees. Their use was obligatory.

Coat of Arms
WT1 WT2

Unwmk.
1874, Jan. 1 Typo. *Perf. 14*

MR1	WT1 5c black	5.50	52
a.	Imperf. pair	12.00	
MR2	WT1 10c pale bl	7.50	1.75
a.	Imperf., pair	52.50	

1875, Jan. 1

MR3	WT2 5c green	3.75	55
a.	Imperf., pair	25.00	
MR4	WT2 10c lilac	8.25	1.65
a.	Imperf., pair	50.00	

King Alfonso XII
WT3 WT4

1876, June 1

MR5	WT3 5c pale grn	1.40	45
MR6	WT3 10c blue	1.40	45
a.	Cliche of 5c in plate of 10c	11.00	9.75
MR7	WT3 25c black	16.00	5.50
MR8	WT3 1p lilac	180.00	32.50
MR9	WT3 5p rose	225.00	100.00

Nos. MR5-MR9 exist imperforate.

1877, Sept. 1

MR10	WT4 15c claret	6.75	40
a.	Imperf., pair	67.50	
MR11	WT4 50c yellow	225.00	30.00

WT5

WT6

1879

MR12	WT5 5c blue	27.50	
MR13	WT5 10c rose	16.00	
MR14	WT5 15c violet	9.75	
MR15	WT5 25c brown	16.00	
MR16	WT5 50c ol grn	11.00	
MR17	WT5 1p bister	16.00	
MR18	WT5 5p gray	65.50	

Nos. MR12-MR18 were never placed in use.

Inscribed "1897 A 1898"

1897 *Perf. 14*

MR19	WT6 5c green	2.75	80
MR20	WT6 10c green	2.75	80
MR21	WT6 15c green	325.00	100.00
MR22	WT6 20c green	6.75	2.50

Nos. MR19-MR22 exist imperf. Value for set $600.

Inscribed "1898-99"

1898

MR23	WT6 5c black	1.10	55
MR24	WT6 10c black	1.40	55
MR25	WT6 15c black	32.50	8.25
MR26	WT6 20c black	2.75	1.40

Nos. MR23-MR26 exist imperf. Value about $150 a pair.

King Alfonso XIII — WT7

1898

MR27	WT7 5c black	5.50	30
a.	Imperf., pair	55.00	

OFFICIAL STAMPS

Coat of Arms
O1 O2

Unwmk.
1854, July 1 Typo. *Imperf.*

O1	O1 ½o blk, *yellow*	1.50	60
O2	O1 1o blk, *rose*	2.50	90
a.	1o blk, *bl*	24.00	
O3	O1 4o blk, *green*	6.00	1.50
O4	O1 1 l blk, *blue*	40.00	30.00

1855-63

O5	O2 ½o blk, *yellow*	1.25	60
a.	½o blk, *straw* ('63)	1.50	75
O6	O2 1o blk, *rose*	1.25	60
a.	1o blk, *sal rose*	3.00	1.75
O7	O2 4o blk, *green*	3.00	1.25
a.	4o blk, *yel grn*	3.50	1.50
O8	O2 1 l blk, *gray bl*	10.50	6.00

The "value indication" on Nos. O1-O8 actually is the weight of the mail in onzas (ounces, "o") and libras (pounds, "l") for which they were valid.

Type of Regular Issue of 1889.

1895 ***Perf. 14***

O9 A34 15c yellow	6.00	75
a. Imperf., pair	6.00	

Coat of Arms — O5

1896-98

O10 O5 rose	4.50	75
a. Imperf., pair	50.00	
O11 O5 dk bl ('98)	13.00	3.50

Cervantes Issue

Chamber of Deputies O6

Statue of Cervantes O7

Cervantes O9

National Library O8

1916, Apr. 22 **Engr.** ***Perf. 12***

For the Senate.

O12 O6 grn & blk	90	75
O13 O7 brn & blk	90	75
O14 O8 car & blk	90	75
O15 O9 brn & blk	90	75

For the Chamber of Deputies.

O16 O6 vio & blk	90	75
O17 O7 car & blk	90	75
O18 O8 grn & blk	90	75
O19 O9 vio & blk	90	75
Nos. O12-O19 (8)	7.20	6.00

Nos. O12-O19 exist imperf. Value $300 for set of pairs.

Nos. O12-O19 exist with centers inverted. Value for set, $100.

Pan-American Postal Union Congress Issue

Types of Regular Issue of 1931 Overprinted in Red or Blue **Oficial.**

1931 ***Perf. 12½***

O20 A84 5c dk brn (R)	10	12
O21 A85 10c brt grn (Bl)	10	12
O22 A86 15c dl vio (R)	10	12
O23 A85 25c dp rose (Bl)	10	12
O24 A87 30c ol grn (Bl)	10	12
O25 A84 40c ultra (R)	22	25
O26 A85 50c dp org (Bl)	22	25
O27 A86 1p bl blk (R)	22	25
O28 A88 4p mag (Bl)	3.75	3.75
O29 A88 10p lt brn (R)	10.00	10.00
Nos. O20-O29 (10)	14.91	15.10

Nos. O22-O29 exist imperf. Values about 5 times those quoted.

Demand, as well as supply, determines a stamp's market value. One is as important as the other.

POSTAL TAX STAMPS

PT5

PT6

Perf. 10½x11½

1937, Dec. 23 **Litho.**

RA11 PT5 10c blk, pale bl & red	3.50	2.00
a. Imperf. pair	60.00	

The tax was for the tuberculosis fund.

1938, Dec. 23 ***Perf. 11½***

RA12 PT6 10c multi	3.00	1.50
a. Imperf. pair	40.00	

The tax was for the tuberculosis fund.

"Spain" Holding Wreath of Peace over Marching Soldiers PT7

1939, July 18 ***Perf. 11***

RA13 PT7 10c blue	25	20
a. Imperf. pair	72.50	

Type of Regular Issue, 1939. Without Imprint.

Unwmk.

1939, Dec. 23 **Litho.** ***Imperf.***

RA14 A166 10c dl cl	25	20

Tuberculosis Fund Issues.

Types of Corresponding Semi-Postal Stamps.

1940, Dec. 23 ***Perf. 10***

RA15 SP23 10c vio & red	20	20

1941, Dec. 23

RA16 SP24 10c blk & red	20	18

1942, Dec. 23

RA17 SP25 10c dl sal & rose red	30	18

1943, Dec. 23 **Photo.** ***Perf. 11***

RA18 SP26 10c pur & dl red	55	50

Perf. 9½x10

1944, Dec. 23 **Litho.** **Unwmk.**

RA19 SP27 10c sal & rose	30	15

1945, Dec. 23

RA20 SP28 10c sal & car	30	15

Mother and Child — PT8

1946, Dec. 22 **Litho.** ***Perf. 9½x10½***

RA21 PT8 5c vio & red	20	15
RA22 PT8 10c grn & red	20	15

See No. RAC7.

Lorraine Cross PT9

Tuberculosis Sanatorium PT10

Perf. 9½x10½

1947, Dec. 22 **Unwmk.**

RA23 PT9 5c dk brn & red	15	12
RA24 PT10 10c vio bl & red	18	12

See No. RAC8.

Aesculapius PT11

"El Cid" PT11a

Photogravure; Cross Engraved

1948, Dec. 22 **Unwmk.** ***Perf. 12½***

RA25 PT11 5c brn & car	18	12
RA26 PT11 10c dp grn & car	18	12

The tax on Nos. RA15-RA26 was used to fight tuberculosis. See Nos. RAB1, RAC9.

1949, Feb. 1 **Litho.** ***Perf. 10½x9½***

RA27 PT11a 5c violet	32	12

The tax aided displaced children. Valid for ordinary postage after Dec. 24, 1949.

Tuberculosis Fund Issues

Galleon and Lorraine Cross — PT12

Pine Branch and Candle — PT13

Photogravure; Cross Engraved

1949, Dec. 22 ***Perf. 12½***

RA28 PT12 5c vio & red	8	8
RA29 PT12 10c yel grn & red	10	10

See Nos. RAB2, RAC10.

1950, Dec. 22

Cross in Carmine.

RA30 PT13 5c rose vio	12	8
RA31 PT13 10c dp grn	12	8

See Nos. RAB3, RAC11.

Children at Seashore PT14

Nurse and Baby PT15

1951, Oct. 1

Cross in Carmine.

RA32 PT14 5c rose brn	18	10
RA33 PT14 10c dl grn	50	18

See No. RAC12.

1953, Oct. 1

Cross in Carmine.

RA34 PT15 5c car lake	60	12
RA35 PT15 10c gray bl	85	18

See No. RAC13.

The tax on RA28-RA35 was used to fight tuberculosis.

POSTAL TAX SEMI-POSTAL STAMPS

Types of Corresponding Postal Tax Stamps.

Photogravure; Cross Engraved

1948 **Unwmk.** ***Perf. 12½***

RAB1 PT11 50c + 10c red brn & car	1.25	1.50

1949

RAB2 PT12 50c + 10c dk ol bis & red	1.00	50

1950

RAB3 PT13 50c + 10c brn & car	3.75	2.00

The surtax on Nos. RAB1-RAB3 was used to fight tuberculosis. Combines domestic letter rate and tax obligatory from December 22 until January 3.

POSTAL TAX AIR POST STAMPS

Tuberculosis Fund Issues.

General Franco — PTAP1

Knight and Lorraine Cross — PTAP2

Unwmk.

1940, Dec. 23 **Litho.** ***Perf. 10***

RAC1 PTAP1 10c brt pink & red	40	30

1941, Dec. 23

RAC2 PTAP2 10c bl & red	40	30

Lorraine Cross and Doves PTAP3

1942, Dec. 23

RAC3 PTAP3 10c dl sal & rose	1.00	60

Cross of Lorraine PTAP4

Tuberculosis Sanatorium PTAP5

1943, Dec. 23 **Photo.** ***Perf. 11***

RAC4 PTAP4 10c vio & dl red	1.00	1.25

1944, Dec. 23 **Litho.** ***Perf. 10x9½***

RAC5 PTAP5 25c sal & rose	5.00	5.00

Lorraine Cross and Eagle — PTAP6

1945, Dec. 23 ***Perf. 10***

RAC6 PTAP6 25c red & car	1.65	1.50

Eagle — PTAP7

1946, Dec. 22
RAC7 PTAP7 25c red & car 40 25

Tuberculosis Sanatorium PTAP8

Plane over Sanatorium PTAP9

1947, Dec. 22 ***Perf. 11½***
RAC8 PTAP8 25c red vio 25 20

Photogravure; Cross Engraved
1948, Dec. 22 ***Perf. 12½***
RAC9 PTAP9 25c ultra & car 25 30

Bell and Lorraine Cross PTAP10

Dove and Flowers PTAP11

1949, Dec. 22
RAC10 PTAP10 25c mar & red 22 30

1950, Dec. 22
RAC11 PTAP11 25c dk bl & car 1.00 50

Mother and Child PTAP12

Tobias and Archangel PTAP13

1951, Oct. 1
RAC12 PTAP12 25c brn & car 1.00 20

1953, Oct. 1
RAC13 PTAP13 25c brn & car 4.00 3.00

FRANCHISE STAMPS

F1

F2

1869 Unwmk. Litho. *Imperf.*
S1 F1 blue 42.50 32.50
a. Tete beche pair 90.00 90.00

The franchise of No. S1 was granted to Diego Castell to use in distributing his publications on Spanish postal history.

1881
S2 F2 blk, *buff* 30.00 12.00

The franchise of No. S2 was granted to Antonio Fernandez Duro for his book, "Resena historico-descriptiva de los sellos correos de Espana."

Reprints of No. S2 have been made on carmine, blue, gray, fawn and yellow paper.

CARLIST STAMPS

From the beginning of the Civil War (April 21, 1872) until separate stamps were issued on July 1, 1873, stamps of France were used on all mail from the provinces under Carlist rule.

King Carlos VII — A1

Tilde on N — A1a

Unwmk.
1873, July 1 Litho. *Imperf.*
X1 A1 1r blue 425.00 425.00
X2 A1a 1r blue 225.00 225.00

These stamps were reprinted three times in 1881 and once in 1887. The originals have 23 white lines and dots in the lower right spandrel. They are thin and of even width and spacing. The first reprint has 17 to 20 lines in the spandrel, most of them thick and of irregular width and length. The second and third reprints have 21 very thin lines, the second from the bottom being almost invisible. In the fourth reprint the lower right spandrel is an almost solid spot of color.

Originals of type A1 have the curved line above "ESPANA" broken at the left of the "E." All reprints of this type have the curved line continuous.

The reprints exist in various shades of blue, rose, red, violet and black.

King Carlos VII
A2 A3

A4

A5

1874
X3 A2 1r violet 150.00 165.00
X4 A3 16m rose 4.25 *60.00*
X5 A4 ½r rose 47.50 47.50

Nos. X3 and X6-X7 were for use in the Basque Provinces and Navarra; No. X4 in Catalonia, and No. X5 in Valencia.

Two types of No. X5, alternating in each sheet.

No. X4 with favor cancellation (lozenge of dots) sells for same price as unused.

1875
White Paper
X6 A5 50c green 4.75 *45.00*
a. 50c bl grn 21.00 *82.50*
b. bluish paper 35.00
X7 A5 1r brown 4.75 *45.00*
a. bluish paper 35.00

Fake cancellations exist on Nos. X1-X7.

REVOLUTIONARY OVERPRINTS

Issued by the Nationalist (Revolutionary) Forces

Many districts or cities made use of the stamps of the Republic overprinted in various forms. Most such overprinting was authorized by military or postal officials but some were without official sanction. These overprints were applied in patriotic celebration and partly as a protection from the use of unoverprinted stamps seized or stolen by soldiers.

BURGOS ISSUE AIR POST STAMPS

RAP1

Revenue Stamps Overprinted in Red, Blue or Black.

1936, Dec. 1 Unwmk. *Perf. 11½*
Control Number on Face of Stamp.
7LC1 RAP1 25c gray grn & blk (R) 16.00 16.00
a. Blue ovpt. 22.50 22.50
7LC2 RAP1 1.50p bl & blk (R) 3.25 3.25
7LC3 RAP1 3p rose & blk (Bl) 3.25 3.25

RAP2

RAP4

Perf. 13½.
Blue Control Number on Back.
7LC4 RAP2 15c grn (R) 2.25 2.25
7LC5 RAP2 25c bl (R) 20.00 20.00

Perf. 11½.
Without Control Number.
Overprint in Black
7LC6 RAP4 1.50p dk bl 4.00 4.00
7LC7 RAP4 3p carmine 4.00 4.00

RAP5

RAP6

Overprint in Black
Perf. 13½, 11½.
7LC8 RAP5 1.20p green 16.00 16.00

Perf. 14
Control Number on Back
7LC9 RAP6 1.20p green 16.00 16.00
7LC10 RAP6 2.40p green 16.00 16.00

No. 7LC9 is inscribed "CLASE 8a".

RAP7

1937 Unwmk. *Perf. 11½*
Control Number on Back.
7LC11 RAP7 25c ultra (R) 180.00 180.00

Stamps of Spain, 1931-36, Overprinted in Red

¡VIVA ESPAÑA!
Correo
Aéreo

Perf. 11, 11½, 11x11½
1937, Apr. 1 Unwmk.
Overprint 15mm high
7LC12 A100 40c blue 65 65
7LC13 A97 50c dk bl 65 65
7LC14 AP26 2p gray bl 16.00 16.00

1937, May 1
Overprint 13mm high
7LC15 A100 40c dk bl 65 65
7LC16 A97 50c dk bl 1.00 1.00
7LC17 A130 50c dk bl 1.00 1.00
7LC18 A100 60c ap grn 1.25 1.25
7LC19 AP26 2p gray bl 20.00 20.00

Spain No. 576 Overprinted in Black or Blue

¡VIVA ESPAÑA!
CORREO
AÉREO

1937, May *Perf. 11½x11*
7LC20 A127 30c car (Bk) 1.25 1.25
7LC21 A127 30c car (Bl) 65 65

Spain No. 578 Overprinted in Black or Blue

¡VIVA ESPAÑA!
CORREO
AÉREO

Perf. 11x11½
7LC22 A129 30c car rose (Bk) 1.25 1.25
7LC23 A129 30c car rose (Bl) 65 65

BURGOS ISSUE SPECIAL DELIVERY STAMPS

Pair of Spain No. 546 Overprinted in Black

Correspondencia
URGENTE

1936 Unwmk. *Perf. 11½x11*
7LE3 A110 20c (10c+10c) emer 3.00 3.00
a. Overprint invtd. 10.00

Type of Regular Stamp of 1931 Overprinted in Red

CORRESPONDENCIA
URGENTE

7LE4 A95 20c dk vio 7.25 7.25

Type of Delivery Tax Stamp of 1931 Overprinted in Red on four 5c stamps

HABILITA
DO PARA
LA CO-
RRESPON-
DENCIA
URGENTE

Perf. 11½.

7LE5 D1 20c black 7.25 7.25

Same Overprinted in Red on four 5c stamps

Habilitado
para la co-
rrespond
urgente

7LE6 D1 20c black 14.00 14.00

SD1

1936 Unwmk. ***Perf. 11½.***

7LE7 SD1 20c grn & blk 5.00 5.00
7LE8 SD1 20c grn & red 5.00 5.00

Nos. 7LE7-7LE8 exist with control number on back. Value $37.50 each.

CADIZ ISSUE SEMI-POSTAL STAMPS

Stamps of Spain, 1931-36, Surcharged in Black or Red

1936 Unwmk. ***Imperf.***

8LB1 A108 1c + 5c bl grn 14 14

Perf. 11½x11, 11½

8LB2 A108 2c + 5c org brn 14 14
8LB3 A103 5c + 5c choc (R) 32 32
8LB4 A110 10c + 5c grn 32 32
8LB5 A111 15c + 5c Prus grn (R) 2.00 2.00
8LB6 A95 20c + 5c dk vio (R) 2.00 3.50
8LB7 A104 25c + 5c lake 2.00 2.00
8LB8 A113 30c + 5c rose red 50 50
8LB9 A100 40c + 5c dk bl (R) 2.25 2.25
8LB10 A97 50c + 5c dk bl (R) 5.00 5.00
Nos. 8LB1-8LB10 (10) 14.67 16.17

CANARY ISLANDS AIR POST STAMPS

Issued for Use via the Lufthansa Service.

Stamps of Spain, 1932-34, Surcharged in Blue

VIVA ESPAÑA
18 JULIO 1936
HABILITADO
AVIÓN
Pts. 0'50

1936, Oct. 27 Unwmk. ***Imperf.***

9LC1 A108 50c on 1c bl grn 13.00 6.50

Perf. 11½x11

9LC2 A108 80c on 2c buff 6.50 2.75
9LC3 A103 1.25p on 5c choc 18.00 11.50

The date July 18, 1936, in the overprints of Nos. 9LC1-9LC22 marks the beginning of the Franco regime.

Spain Nos. 542, 543, 528 and 641 Surcharged in Black, Red or Green

VIVA ESPAÑA
18 JULIO 1936
HABILITADO
AVIÓN
CANARIAS
50 Cts.

1936-37 ***Imperf.***

9LC4 A108 50c on 1c ol grn 2.75 2.00
9LC5 A108 50c on 1c bl grn (R) ('37) 3.25 2.00

Perf. 11, 11½x11

9LC6 A108 80c on 2c buff 1.10 1.00
9LC7 A108 80c on 2c buff (G) ('37) 2.75 1.25
9LC8 A103 1.25 Pts on 5c choc (R) 3.25 2.75
9LC9 A103 Pts 1.25 on 5c choc (R) ('37) 8.25 4.50
9LC10 A161 1.25p on 5c brn (G) ('37) 2.75 1.25
Nos. 9LC4-9LC10 (7) 24.10 14.75

Spain Nos. 542, 543 and 641 Surcharged in Blue

CANARIAS
A
FRANCO
18 JULIO 1936
AVION
50 Cts.

1937, Mar. 31 ***Imperf.***

9LC11 A108 50c on 1c bl grn 2.75 1.65

Perf. 11

9LC12 A108 80c on 2c buff 2.00 1.25
9LC13 A161 1.25p on 5c brn 2.25 1.25

Stamps of Spain, 1931-1936, Surcharged in Blue or Red

VÍVA ESPAÑA
18 JULIO 1936
AVIÓN
CANARIAS
+ 80

1937

9LC14 A104 25c + 50c lake 22.50 11.50
9LC15 A162 30c + 80c rose 6.50 5.25
9LC16 A162 30c + 1.25p rose 10.00 6.50
9LC17 A97 50c + 1.25p dp bl (R) 16.00 11.50
9LC18 A100 60c + 80c ap grn 10.00 7.25
9LC19 A105 1p + 1.25p bl blk (R) 27.50 14.00
Nos. 9LC14-9LC19 (6) 92.50 56.00

The surcharge represents the airmail rate and the basic stamp the postage rate.

Spain Nos. 542, 624 and 641 Surcharged in Black

ARRIBA ESPAÑA
18 JULIO 1936
CANARIAS
AVION
50 Cts.

1937, May 25 Unwmk. ***Imperf.***

9LC20 A108 50c on 1c bl grn 3.25 1.50

Perf. 11½, 11½x11

9LC21 A143 80c on 2c org brn 2.25 1.10
9LC22 A161 1.25p on 5c gray brn 2.25 1.10

Stamps of Spain, 1933-36, Surcharged in Black

CANARIAS
CORREO AÉREO
50 Cts.

1937, July ***Perf. 13½x13, 11, 11½***

9LC23 A143 50c on 2c org brn 65 42
9LC24 A126 80c on 2c org brn 200.00 110.00
9LC25 A161 80c on 5c gray brn 1.10 65
9LC26 A108 1.25p on 1c bl grn 1.50 65
9LC27 A161 2.50p on 10c grn 6.50 4.00

Spain Nos. 647, 650 and 652 Surcharged in Black or Red

CANARIAS
CORREO AÉREO
+80

Perf. 11.

9LC28 A162 30c + 80c rose 65 42
9LC29 A162 50c + 1.25p dk bl (R) 4.00 2.00
9LC30 A162 1p + 1.25p bl (R) 8.25 4.00

See note after No. 9LC19.

Wmk. 116

AP1

Wmk. Crosses and Circles. (116)

1937, July 16 ***Perf. 14x13½***

Surcharge in Various Colors.

9LC31 AP1 50c on 5c ultra (Br) 2.25 2.75
9LC32 AP1 80c on 5c ultra (G) 1.25 1.65
9LC33 AP1 1.25p on 5c ultra (V) 1.65 2.00

Spain Nos. 641, 643 and 640 Surcharged in Green or Orange

50 Cts.
CORREO AEREO
CANARIAS

1937, Oct. 29 Unwmk. ***Perf. 11***

9LC34 A161 50c on 5c (G) 8.50 3.25
9LC35 A161 80c on 10c (O) 2.75 1.65
9LC36 A160 1.25p on 2c (G) 10.00 5.00

Spain Nos. 638, 640 and 643 Surcharged in Red, Blue or Violet

CANARIAS
50 Cts.
Correo Aéreo

1937, Dec. 23 ***Imperf.***

9LC37 A159 50c on 1c (R) 6.50 3.25

Perf. 11, 11x11½

9LC38 A160 80c on 2c (Bl) 2.00 1.65
9LC39 A161 1.25p on 10c (V) 6.50 3.25

Spain Nos. 647, 650 to 652 Surcharged in Black, Green or Brown

CANARIAS
Correo Aereo
+30 C

1937, Dec. 29

9LC40 A162 30c + 30c rose 1.25 1.25
9LC41 A162 50c + 2.50p dk bl (G) 21.00 14.00
9LC42 A162 60c + 2.30p yel (G) 21.00 14.00
9LC43 A162 1p + 5p bl (Br) 21.00 14.00

See note after No. 9LC19.

Stamps of Spain, 1936, Surcharged in Black, Green, Blue or Red

CANARIAS
Via Aérea
50 C

1938, Feb. 2 ***Perf. 11, 11½, 11x11½***

9LC44 A160 50c on 2c brn 2.00 1.00
9LC45 A161 80c on 5c brn (G) 2.00 1.00
9LC46 A162 80c on 30c rose (Bl) 1.65 85
9LC47 A161 1.25p on 10c grn (Bl) 2.00 1.00
9LC48 A162 1.25p on 50c dk bl (R) 2.25 1.00
Nos. 9LC44-9LC48 (5) 9.90 4.85

Spain Nos. 645, 646 and 649 Surcharged in Brown, Green or Violet

Vía Aerea
CANARIAS
2'50 Pts.

1938, Feb. 14

9LC51 A162 2.50p on 20c (Br) 30.00 20.00
9LC52 A162 5p on 25c (G) 30.00 20.00
9LC53 A162 10p on 40c (V) 30.00 20.00

MALAGA ISSUE

Stamps of 1920-36 Overprinted in Black or Red

¡Arriba España!
Málaga
Liberada
8-2-1937

1937 Unwmk. ***Imperf.***

10L1 A47 1c bl grn (Bk) 10 10
10L2 A108 1c bl grn (Bk) 10 10
10L3 A108 1c lt grn (R) 10 10

Perf. 13½, 13½x13, 11, 11½x11.

10L4 A108 2c org brn (Bk) 5.00 5.00
10L5 A126 2c org brn (Bk) 10 10
10L6 A103 5c choc (R) 10 10
10L7 A96 10c yel grn (Bk) 10.00 10.00
10L8 A110 10c emer (Bk) 10 10
10L9 A111 15c Prus grn (R) 32 32
10L10 A97 15c bl grn (R) 32 32
10L11 A95 20c dk vio (R) 20 20
10L12 A99 25c lake (Bk) 1.00 1.00
10L13 A104 25c lake (Bk) 20 20
10L14 A113 30c car (Bk) 10 10
10L15 A129 30c car rose (Bk) 85 85
10L16 A100 40c bl (R) 10 10
10L17 A97 50c dk bl (R) 1.00 1.00
10L18 A100 60c ap grn (Bk) 65 65
10L19 A105 1p blk (R) 1.00 1.00
Nos. 10L1-10L19 (19) 21.34 21.34

Stamps of 1932-35 Overprinted in Red or Black in panes of 25, reading down. "8.2.37" and "!Arriba Espana!" form the lower half of all overprints. The upper half varies.

First and second rows "MALAGA AGRADECIDA A TRANQUILLO-BIANCHI".

Third row "MALAGA A SU SALVADOR QUEIPO DE LLANO".

Fourth and fifth rows "MALAGA A SU CAUDILLO FRANCO".

1937 ***Perf. 11½.***

10L20 A111 15c Prus grn (R) 1.00 1.00
10L21 A113 30c rose red (Bk) 1.00 1.00
10L22 A97 50c dk bl (R) 1.75 1.75
10L23 A100 60c ap grn (Bk) 1.75 1.75

SPECIAL DELIVERY STAMP

Same Overprint on Type of Special Delivery Stamp of 1934.

1936 ***Perf. 10.***

10LE1 SD7 20c rose red (Bk) 40 40

ORENSE ISSUE

Stamps of 1931-36 Overprinted in Red, Blue or Black

¡VIVA ESPAÑA!

1936 ***Imperf.***

11L1	A108	1c bl grn (Bl)	40	40
		Perf. 11½, 13½x13.		
11L2	A108	2c org brn (Bk)	2.50	2.50
11L3	A126	2c org brn (Bk)	40	40
11L4	A103	5c brn (R)	85	85
11L5	A110	10c lt grn (Bl)	1.65	1.65
11L6	A111	15c Prus grn (R)	1.65	1.65
11L7	A95	20c vio (Bl)	1.65	1.65
11L8	A104	25c lake (Bk)	2.50	2.50
11L9	A113	30c rose red (Bl)	1.90	1.90
11L10	A100	40c bl (R)	2.75	2.75
a.		Imperf., pair	8.00	8.00
11L11	A97	50c dk bl (R)	4.50	4.50
11L12	A100	60c ap grn (R)	3.75	3.75
a.		Imperf., pair	6.75	6.50
		Nos. 11L1-11L12 (12)	24.50	24.50

SEMI-POSTAL STAMPS

Stamps of Spain, 1931-36, Surcharged in Blue on front and on back of stamp

¡VIVA ESPAÑA! + 5 cts.

1936-37 **Unwmk.** ***Imperf.***

11LB1	A47	1c + 5c bl grn	65	65
11LB2	A108	1c + 5c grn	32	32
		Perf. 13½x13, 11½, 11½x11		
11LB3	A108	2c + 5c org brn	40	40
11LB4	A126	2c + 5c red brn	40	40
11LB5	A103	5c + 5c choc	60	60
11LB6	A110	10c + 5c emer	60	60
11LB7	A111	15c + 5c Prus grn	85	85
11LB8	A95	20c + 5c vio	60	60
11LB9	A104	25c + 5c lake	85	85
11LB10	A113	30c + 5c rose red	2.00	2.00
11LB11	A117	30c + 5c rose red	30.00	30.00
		Nos. 11LB1-11LB11 (11)	37.27	37.27

SPECIAL DELIVERY STAMPS

Type of Special Delivery Stamp of 1934 Overprinted "!VIVA ESPANA!" in Blue or Black

1936 ***Perf. 10***

11LE1	SD7	20c rose red (Bl)	1.75	1.75
11LE2	SD7	20c rose red (Bk)	3.75	3.75

Same with Surcharge "+ 5 cts."

11LE3	SD7	20c + 5c rose red	90	90

Same Surcharge, Overprint Repeated at Right.

11LE4	SD7	20c + 5c rose red	1.00	1.00

SAN SEBASTIAN ISSUE

For Use in Province of Guipuzcoa

Stamps of 1931-36 Overprinted in Red or Blue

¡¡ARRIBA ESPAÑA!! 1936

1937 **Unwmk.** ***Imperf.***

12L1	A108	1c bl grn (R)	42	42
		Perf. 11, 13½.		
12L2	A108	2c buff (Bl)	65	65
12L3	A126	2c org brn (Bl)	65	65
12L4	A95	5c choc (R)	4.00	4.00
12L5	A103	5c choc (R)	65	65
12L6	A110	10c emer (R)	1.00	1.00
12L7	A111	15c Prus grn (R)	1.10	1.10
12L8	A95	20c dk vio (R)	1.50	1.50
12L9	A104	25c car lake (Bl)	1.50	1.50
12L10	A113	30c rose red (Bl)	1.00	1.00
12L11	A100	40c bl (R)	3.00	3.00
12L12	A97	50c dk bl (R)	3.00	3.00
		Nos. 12L1-12L12 (12)	18.47	18.47

SANTA CRUZ DE TENERIFE ISSUE

Stamps of Spain, 1931-36 Overprinted in Black or Red

Viva España 18 Julio 1936

1936 **Unwmk.** ***Imperf.***

13L1	A108	1c bl grn (R)	70	70
13L2	A108	1c bl grn (Bk)	2.00	2.00
		Perf. 11, 13½.		
13L3	A108	2c buff (Bk)	5.00	5.00
13L4	A126	2c org brn (Bk)	70	70
13L5	A103	5c choc (R)	2.75	2.75
13L6	A110	10c grn (R)	2.50	2.50
13L7	A104	25c lake (Bk)	5.00	5.00
13L8	A100	40c dk bl (R)	2.00	2.00
13L9	A107	10p dp brn (Bk)	200.00	200.00
		Nos. 13L1-13L9 (9)	220.65	220.65

SEVILLE ISSUE

Stamps of Spain, 1931-36, Overprinted in Black or Red

Sevilla "VIVA ESPAÑA" Julio-1936

1936 ***Imperf.***

14L1	A108	1c bl grn (Bk)	20	20
		Perf. 13½x13, 11, 11½x11		
14L2	A126	2c org brn (Bk)	20	20
14L3	A103	5c choc (R)	32	32
14L4	A110	10c emer (Bk)	42	42
14L5	A111	15c Prus grn (R)	85	85
14L6	A95	20c vio (R)	85	85
14L7	A104	25c lake (Bk)	85	85
14L8	A113	30c car (Bk)	85	85
14L9	A128	30c rose red (Bk)	6.75	6.75
14L10	A100	40c bl (R)	4.50	4.50
14L11	A97	50c dk bl (R)	4.50	4.50
14L12	A100	60c ap grn (Bk)	5.50	5.50
		Nos. 14L1-14L12 (12)	25.79	25.79

Stamps of Spain, 1931-36, Handstamped in Black

SEVILLA "VIVA ESPAÑA" JULIO-1936

Imperf.

14L13	A108	1c bl grn	20	20
		Perf. 13½x13, 11, 11x11½, 11½x11		
14L14	A126	2c org brn	32	32
14L15	A103	5c chocolate	32	32
14L16	A110	10c emerald	32	32
14L17	A111	15c Prus grn	42	42
14L18	A95	20c violet	32	32
14L19	A104	25c lake	32	32
14L20	A113	30c carmine	32	32
14L21	A128	30c rose red	2.00	2.00
14L22	A100	40c blue	70	70
14L23	A97	50c dk bl	2.00	2.00
14L24	A100	60c ap grn	70	70
14L25	A105	1p black	2.00	2.00
14L26	AP26	2p gray bl	11.00	11.00
14L27	A106	4p magenta	4.00	4.00
14L28	A107	10p dp brn	8.25	8.25
		Nos. 14L13-14L28,14LE1 (17)	33.59	33.59

The date "Julio-1936" in the overprints of Nos. 14L1-14L28 and 14LE1 marks the beginning of the Franco regime.

SPECIAL DELIVERY STAMP

Same Overprint on Type of Special Delivery Stamp of 1934.

1936 ***Perf. 10.***

14LE1	SD7	20c rose red	1.40	1.40

SPANISH GUINEA

LOCATION — In western Africa, bordering on the Gulf of Guinea.
GOVT. — Spanish Colony
AREA — 10,852 sq. mi.
POP. — 212,000 (est. 1957)
CAPITAL — Santa Isabel

Spanish Guinea Nos. 1-84 were issued for and used only in the continental area later called Rio Muni. From 1909 to 1960, Spanish Guinea also included Fernando Po, Elobey, Annobon and Corisco.

Fernando Po and Rio Muni united in 1968 to become the Republic of Equatorial Guinea.

100 Centimos = 1 Peseta

Catalogue values for unused stamps in this country are for Never Hinged items, beginning with Scott 319 in the regular postage section, Scott B13 in the semi-postal section, and Scott C13 in the airpost section.

King Alfonso XIII
A1 A2

1902 **Unwmk.** **Typo.** ***Perf. 14***

Blue Control Numbers on Back

1	A1	5c dark green	5.00	1.00
2	A1	10c indigo	5.00	1.00
3	A1	25c claret	35.00	8.25
4	A1	50c deep brown	35.00	6.50
5	A1	75c violet	35.00	6.50
6	A1	1p carmine rose	60.00	6.50
7	A1	2p olive green	65.00	11.50
8	A1	5p dull red	100.00	35.00
		Nos. 1-8 (8)	340.00	76.25

Revenue Stamps Surcharged

HABILITADO PARA CORREOS 10 cen de peseta

1903 ***Imperf.***

Blue or Black Control Numbers on Back

8A	10c on 25c blk (R)	415.00	175.00
8B	10c on 50c org (Bl)	110.00	32.50
8D	10c on 1p 25c car (Bk)	500.00	300.00
8F	10c on 2p cl (Bk)	900.00	450.00
g.	Blue surcharge	1,250.	65.00
8H	10c on 2p 50c red brn (Bl)	1,250.	550.00
8J	10c on 5p ol blk (R)	1,250.	375.00

Nos. 8A-8J are surcharged on stamps inscribed "Posesiones Espanolas de Africa Occidental" and "1903," with arms at left.

This surcharge was also applied to revenue stamps of 10, 15, 25, 50, 75 and 100 pesetas. See Nos. 98-101C.

1903 **Typo.** ***Perf. 14***

Blue Control Numbers on Back

9	A2	¼c black	65	15
10	A2	½c blue green	65	15
11	A2	1c claret	65	12
12	A2	2c dark olive	65	12
13	A2	3c dark brown	65	12
14	A2	4c vermilion	65	12
15	A2	5c black brown	65	12
16	A2	10c red brown	1.00	15
17	A2	15c dark blue	3.50	1.00
18	A2	25c orange buff	3.50	1.50
19	A2	50c carmine lake	6.25	2.25
20	A2	75c violet	9.25	2.25
21	A2	1p blue green	11.50	3.50
22	A2	2p dark green	11.50	3.50
23	A2	3p scarlet	30.00	4.00
24	A2	4p dull blue	40.00	7.50
25	A2	5p dark violet	65.00	11.50
26	A2	10p carmine rose	115.00	14.00
		Nos. 9-26 (18)	301.05	52.05

1905

Same, Dated "1905"

Blue Control Numbers on Back

27	A2	1c black	12	10
28	A2	2c blue grn	12	10
29	A2	3c claret	12	10
30	A2	4c bronze grn	12	10
31	A2	5c dark brn	12	10
32	A2	10c red	65	50
33	A2	15c blk brn	2.25	1.50
34	A2	25c chocolate	2.25	1.50
35	A2	50c dark blue	4.75	3.25
36	A2	75c org buff	5.25	3.25
37	A2	1p car rose	5.25	3.25
38	A2	2p violet	11.50	5.00
39	A2	3p blue grn	27.50	10.00
40	A2	4p dark grn	27.50	12.50
40A	A2	5p vermilion	47.50	12.50
41	A2	10p dull blue	72.50	40.00
		Nos. 27-41 (16)	207.50	93.75

Stamps of Elobey, 1905, Overprinted in Violet or Blue

1906

42	A1	1c rose	3.25	1.50
43	A1	2c deep vio	3.25	1.50
44	A1	3c black	3.25	1.50
45	A1	4c org red	3.25	1.50
46	A1	5c deep grn	3.25	1.50
47	A1	10c blue grn	7.25	4.00
48	A1	15c violet	13.00	6.50
49	A1	25c rose lake	13.00	6.50
50	A1	50c org buff	18.00	8.50
51	A1	75c dark blue	22.50	10.50
52	A1	1p red brn	42.50	18.00
53	A1	2p blk brn	62.50	13.00
54	A1	3p vermilion	90.00	30.00
55	A1	4p dark brn	325.00	105.00
56	A1	5p bronze grn	325.00	105.00
57	A1	10p claret	*2,000.*	*750.00*
		Nos. 42-54 (13)	285.00	104.50

King Alfonso XIII
A3 A4

1907 **Typo.**

Blue Control Numbers on Back

58	A3	1c dark grn	40	10
59	A3	2c dull blue	40	10
60	A3	3c violet	40	10
61	A3	4c yel grn	40	10
62	A3	5c car lake	40	10
63	A3	10c orange	2.00	42
64	A3	15c brown	1.10	25
65	A3	25c dark blue	1.10	25
66	A3	50c blk brn	1.10	25
67	A3	75c blue grn	1.10	30
68	A3	1p red	2.50	50
69	A3	2p dark brn	4.00	1.65
70	A3	3p olive gray	4.00	1.65
71	A3	4p maroon	5.00	1.65
72	A3	5p green	5.75	2.75
73	A3	10p red vio	8.25	3.00
		Nos. 58-73 (16)	37.90	13.17

Issue of 1907 Surcharged in Black or Red

HABILITADO PARA 05CTMS

1908-09

74	A3	05c on 1c dk grn (R)	1.75	1.25
75	A3	05c on 2c blue (R)	1.75	1.25
76	A3	05c on 3c violet	1.75	1.25
77	A3	05c on 4c yel grn	1.75	1.25
78	A3	05c on 10c orange	2.25	1.25
a.		Red surcharge	6.00	2.75
84	A3	15c on 10c orange	10.00	5.75
		Nos. 74-84 (6)	19.25	12.00

Many stamps of this issue are found with the surcharge inverted, sideways, double and in both black and red. Other stamps of the 1907 issue are known with this surcharge but are not believed to have been put in use. Value, each $15.

1909 **Typo.** ***Perf. 14½***

Blue Control Numbers on Back

85	A4	1c org brn	12	6
86	A4	2c rose	12	6
87	A4	5c dark grn	75	12
88	A4	10c vermilion	25	8
89	A4	15c dark brn	25	8
90	A4	20c violet	40	18
91	A4	25c dull blue	45	18
92	A4	30c chocolate	48	15
93	A4	40c lake	30	12
94	A4	50c dark vio	30	12
95	A4	1p blue grn	7.75	2.75
96	A4	4p orange	1.90	1.50
97	A4	10p red	1.90	1.50
		Nos. 85-97 (13)	14.97	6.90

Revenue Stamps Surcharged like Nos. 8A-8J in Black

1909 ***Imperf.***

With or Without Control Numbers on Back

98	10c on 50c bl grn	72.50	50.00
a.	Red or violet surcharge	90.00	65.00
99	10c on 1p 25c violet	90.00	60.00
100	10c on 2p dk brn	550.00	350.00
100A	10c on 5p dk vio	550.00	350.00
101	10c on 25p red brn	*1,000.*	*675.00*
101A	10c on 50p brn lil	*2,500.*	*1,800.*
101B	10c on 75p carmine	*2,500.*	*1,800.*
101C	10c on 100p orange	*2,500.*	*1,800.*

Nos. 98-101C are surcharged on undated stamps, arms centered. Stamps inscribed: "Territorios Espanoles del Africa Occidental." Basic revenue stamps similar to Rio de Oro type A3.

Stamps of 1909 Overprinted with Handstamp in Black, Blue, Green or Red

1911

102	A4	1c org brn (Bl)	20	12
103	A4	2c rose (G)	20	12
104	A4	5c dk grn (R)	65	12
105	A4	10c vermilion	52	20
106	A4	15c dk brn (R)	65	32
107	A4	20c violet	1.00	45
108	A4	25c dull bl (R)	1.10	85
109	A4	30c choc (Bl)	1.50	1.00
110	A4	40c lake (Bl)	1.65	1.10
111	A4	50c dark vio	2.25	2.00
112	A4	1p bl grn (R)	22.50	5.00
113	A4	4p org (R)	10.50	4.50
114	A4	10p red (G)	14.00	7.25
		Nos. 102-114 (13)	56.72	23.03

The date "1911" is missing from the overprint on the first stamp in each row, or ten times in each sheet of 100 stamps. This variety occurs on all stamps of the series.

King Alfonso XIII
A5 A6

1912 **Typo.** ***Perf. 13½***

Blue Control Numbers on Back

115	A5	1c black	12	8
116	A5	2c dark brn	12	8
117	A5	5c deep grn	12	8
118	A5	10c red	18	8
119	A5	15c claret	22	8
120	A5	20c red	35	10
121	A5	25c dull blue	22	8
122	A5	30c lake	2.00	85
123	A5	40c car rose	95	50
124	A5	50c brn org	80	20
125	A5	1p dark vio	1.25	52
126	A5	4p lilac	1.90	1.10
127	A5	10p blue grn	6.50	3.25
		Nos. 115-127 (13)	14.73	7.00

1914 ***Perf. 13***

Blue Control Numbers on Back

128	A6	1c dull vio	12	10
129	A6	2c car rose	12	12
130	A6	5c deep grn	12	10
131	A6	10c vermilion	15	12
132	A6	15c dark vio	15	12
133	A6	20c dark brn	50	20
134	A6	25c dark blue	22	16
135	A6	30c brn org	85	24
136	A6	40c blue grn	85	24
137	A6	50c dp claret	30	16
138	A6	1p vermilion	85	75
139	A6	4p maroon	3.50	1.75
140	A6	10p olive blk	4.00	2.75
		Nos. 128-140 (13)	11.73	6.81

Stamps with these or similar overprints are unauthorized and fraudulent.

Stamps of 1912 Overprinted 1917

1917 ***Perf. 13½***

141	A5	1c black	42.50	10.50
142	A5	2c dark brn	42.50	10.50
143	A5	5c deep grn	38	15
144	A5	10c red	38	15
145	A5	15c claret	38	15
146	A5	20c red	38	12
147	A5	25c dull blue	15	12
148	A5	30c lake	38	15
149	A5	40c car rose	52	24
150	A5	50c brn org	30	15
151	A5	1p dark vio	52	24
152	A5	4p lilac	4.50	2.00
153	A5	10p blue grn	6.00	2.00
		Nos. 141-153 (13)	98.89	26.47

Nos. 143-153 exist with overprint double, inverted, in dark blue, reading "9117" and in pairs one without overprint.

Stamps of 1917 Surcharged

HTADO

15 Cents.

1918

154	A5	5c on 40c car rose	20.00	6.50
155	A5	10c on 4p lilac	21.00	6.50
156	A5	15c on 20c red	40.00	11.50
157	A5	25c on 10p bl grn	40.00	11.50
a.		"52" for "25"	265.00	225.00

The varieties "Gents" and "Censt" occur on Nos. 154-157. Values 50 percent more.

King Alfonso XIII
A7 A8

1919 **Typo.** ***Perf. 13***

Blue Control Numbers on Back

158	A7	1c lilac	65	15
159	A7	2c rose	65	15
160	A7	5c vermilion	65	15
161	A7	10c violet	1.00	15
162	A7	15c brown	1.00	20
163	A7	20c blue	1.00	32
164	A7	25c green	1.00	32
a.		25c blue (error)	50.00	
165	A7	30c orange	1.00	32
166	A7	40c orange	2.75	32
167	A7	50c red	2.75	32
168	A7	1p light green	2.75	65
169	A7	4p claret	6.00	2.75
170	A7	10p brown	10.50	4.00
		Nos. 158-170 (13)	31.70	9.80

1920

Blue Control Numbers on Back

171	A8	1c brown	12	8
172	A8	2c dull rose	12	8
173	A8	5c gray green	15	12
174	A8	10c dull rose	15	8
175	A8	15c orange	15	12
176	A8	20c yellow	15	12
177	A8	25c dull blue	40	12
178	A8	30c greenish bl	21.00	6.25
179	A8	40c light brn	32	12
180	A8	50c lilac	1.00	12
181	A8	1p light red	1.00	12
182	A8	4p bright rose	3.25	1.65
183	A8	10p gray lilac	4.50	3.00
		Nos. 171-183 (13)	32.31	11.98

A9

Nipa House — A10

1922

Blue Control Numbers on Back

184	A9	1c dark brn	32	6
185	A9	2c claret	32	6
186	A9	5c blue grn	32	6
187	A9	10c pale red	2.00	30
188	A9	15c orange	32	6
189	A9	20c lilac	1.25	28
190	A9	25c dark blue	2.25	30
191	A9	30c violet	2.00	35
192	A9	40c turq bl	1.10	18
193	A9	50c deep rose	1.10	18
194	A9	1p myrtle grn	1.10	20
195	A9	4p red brown	4.50	2.75
196	A9	10p yellow	12.00	4.75
		Nos. 184-196 (13)	28.58	9.53

1924

Blue Control Numbers on Back

197	A10	5c choc & bl	20	15
198	A10	10c gray grn & bl	20	15
199	A10	15c rose & blk	24	25
200	A10	20c vio & blk	20	15
201	A10	25c org red & blk	40	35
202	A10	30c org & blk	40	25
203	A10	40c dl bl & blk	40	25
204	A10	50c cl & blk	40	25
205	A10	60c red brn & blk	40	25
206	A10	1p dk vio & blk	1.25	25
a.		Center inverted	225.00	100.00
207	A10	4p brt bl & blk	4.00	2.00
208	A10	10p bl grn & blk	7.25	4.75
		Nos. 197-208 (12)	15.34	9.05

Seville-Barcelona Exhibition Issue

Seville-Barcelona Issue of Spain, 1929, Overprinted in Red or Blue

GUINEA

1929 ***Perf. 11***

209	A52	5c rose lake	6	6
210	A53	10c green (R)	6	6
211	A50	15c Prus bl (R)	6	6
212	A51	20c purple (R)	6	6
213	A50	25c brt rose	6	6
214	A52	30c black brn	6	6
215	A53	40c dk bl (R)	12	12
216	A51	50c dp orange	9	9
217	A52	1p bl blk (R)	1.00	85
218	A53	4p deep rose	2.50	1.75
219	A53	10p brown	3.50	2.75
		Nos. 209-219 (11)	7.57	5.92

Porter A11

Drummers A12

King Alfonso XIII and Queen Victoria — A13

1931 **Engr.** ***Perf. 14***

220	A11	1c blue grn	7	6
221	A11	2c red brn	7	6

Blue Control Numbers on Back

222	A11	5c brn blk	10	6
223	A11	10c light grn	10	6
224	A11	15c dark grn	16	7
225	A11	20c deep vio	16	7
226	A12	25c carmine	16	7
227	A12	30c lake	20	7
228	A12	40c dark blue	52	35
229	A12	50c red org	1.25	40
230	A13	80c blue vio	2.00	1.10
231	A13	1p black	3.50	2.75
232	A13	4p vio rose	25.00	10.50
233	A13	5p dark brn	10.50	8.00
		Nos. 220-233 (14)	43.79	23.62

Exist imperf. Value for set, $300.

Stamps of 1931 Overprinted

REPUBLICA

ESPAÑOLA

1931

234	A11	1c blue grn	12	7
235	A11	2c red brn	12	7
236	A11	5c brn blk	15	7
237	A11	10c light grn	15	7
238	A11	15c dark grn	15	7
239	A11	20c deep vio	15	7
240	A12	25c carmine	15	7
241	A12	30c lake	38	16
242	A12	40c dark blue	1.10	35
243	A12	50c red org	6.75	3.75
244	A13	80c blue vio	2.25	1.00
245	A13	1p black	7.50	2.25
246	A13	4p vio rose	13.00	6.75
247	A13	5p dark brn	13.00	6.75
		Nos. 234-247 (14)	44.97	21.50

Stamps of 1931 Overprinted in Red or Blue

República
Española

1933

248	A11	1c bl grn (R)	10	7
249	A11	2c red brn (Bl)	10	7
250	A11	5c brn blk (R)	14	7
251	A11	10c lt grn (Bl)	14	7
252	A11	15c dk grn (R)	14	7
253	A11	20c dp vio (R)	35	7
254	A12	25c carmine (Bl)	28	16
255	A12	30c lake (Bl)	28	16
256	A12	40c dk blue (R)	2.00	50
257	A12	50c red org (Bl)	7.00	2.50
258	A13	80c bl vio (R)	3.75	2.25
259	A13	1p black (R)	8.00	2.25
260	A13	4p vio rose (Bl)	27.50	7.75
261	A13	5p dk brn (Bl)	27.50	10.50
		Nos. 248-261 (14)	77.28	26.49

Types of 1931
Without Control Number

1934-35 **Engr.** ***Perf. 10***

262	A11	1c blue grn ('35)	6.00	14
263	A11	2c red brn ('35)	6.00	14
264	A11	5c blk brn	1.00	7
265	A11	10c light grn	1.00	7
266	A11	15c dark grn	2.00	7
267	A12	30c rose red	2.50	7
268	A12	50c indigo ('35)	6.00	52
		Nos. 262-268 (7)	24.50	1.08

Types of 1931

1941 **Litho.** ***Unwmk.***

269	A11	5c olive gray	1.25	12
270	A11	20c violet	1.25	12
271	A12	40c gray green	55	12

Stamps of 1931-33 Surcharged in Black

HABILITADO

30 Cts.
a

1
peseta.
b

1936-37 ***Perf. 10, 14***

272	A12	30c on 40c dk bl (#228)	2.50	1.50
273	A12	30c on 40c dk bl (#242)	10.00	2.25
274	A12	30c on 40c dk bl (#256)	37.50	10.50

The surcharge on Nos. 272-274 exists in two types, differing in the "3" which is scarcer in italic.

No. 268 Surcharged Type "b" in Red

275	A12	1p on 50c indigo	14.00
276	A12	4p on 50c indigo	52.50
277	A12	5p on 50c indigo	27.50

Stamps of Spain, 1936, Overprinted in Black or Carmine

Territorios
Españoles del
Golfo de Guinea

1938 ***Perf. 11***

278	A161	10c gray green	1.25	32
279	A162	15c gray blk (C)	1.25	32
280	A162	20c dark vio	2.75	90
281	A162	25c brown lake	2.75	90

Stamps of 1931-33, Surcharged in Black — **Habilitado 40 cts.**

1939

282 A13 40c on 80c bl vio (#244) 8.00 4.00
283 A13 40c on 80c bl vio (#258) 8.00 2.50

A14

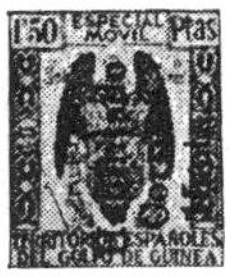
A15

Revenue Stamps Surcharged in Black

1940-41 ***Perf. 11½***

284 A14 5c on 35c pale grn 5.25 1.75
285 A14 25c on 60c org brn 5.25 2.00
286 A14 50c on 75c blk brn 7.25 2.25

Red Surcharge

287 A15 10c on 75c blk brn 7.25 2.25
288 A15 15c on 1.50p lt vio 5.25 2.00
289 A15 25c on 60c org brn 9.00 3.00

A16

A17

Black or Carmine Surcharge

Perf. 11

290 A16 1p on 17p deep red 40.00 12.00
291 A17 1p on 40p yel grn (C) 10.00 3.25

A18

A19

Black Surcharge

Perf. 11, 13x12½

292 A18 5c carmine 5.00 1.25
293 A19 1p yellow 80.00 30.00

A20

General Francisco Franco — A21

Black Surcharge

294 A20 1p on 15c gray grn 10.50 3.50

1940 ***Perf. 11½, 13½***

295 A21 5c olive brown 2.00 32
296 A21 40c blue 3.00 32
297 A21 50c green 3.50 32
a. 50c greenish gray 13.00 5.75

Nos. 295-297 exist imperf. Values twice those quoted.

No. 270 Surcharged in Black — **Habilitado 3 Pesetas**

1942

298 A11 3p on 20c vio 8.25 1.10

Spain, Nos. 702 and 704 Overprinted in Carmine or Black — Golfo de Guinea.

1942 ***Perf. 9½x10½***

299 A166 1p gray blk (C) 35 15
300 A166 4p dl rose (Bk) 4.00 55

The overprint on No. 299 exists in two types: Spacing between lines of 2mm, and spacing of 3mm. The 3mm spacing sells for about twice as much.

Spain, No. 703 Overprinted in Carmine — Territorios españoles del Golfo de Guinea.

1943

301 A166 2p dull brown 85 15

Nos. 299 and 301 Surcharged in Green — Habilitado para quince cts.

1949 **Unwmk.** ***Perf. 9½x10½***

302 A166 5c (cinco) on 1p gray blk 15 7
303 A166 15c on 2p dl brn 15 7

The two types of No. 299, described in footnote, also exist on No. 302.

Men Poling Canoe A22

1949, Oct. 9 **Litho.** ***Perf. 12½x13***

304 A22 4p dk vio 1.25 70

UPU, 75th anniversary.

San Carlos Bay — A23

Designs: Various Views

1949-50 ***Perf. 12½x13***

305	A23	2c	brown	15	6
306	A23	5c	rose vio	15	6
307	A23	10c	Prussian bl	15	6
308	A23	15c	dp ol gray	20	6
309	A23	25c	red brown	20	6
309A	A23	30c	brt yel ('50)	15	6
310	A23	40c	olive gray	15	6
311	A23	45c	rose lake	15	6
312	A23	50c	brn orange	15	6
312A	A23	75c	ultra ('50)	15	6
313	A23	90c	dl bl grn	20	6
314	A23	1p	gray	1.25	18
315	A23	1.35p	violet	5.25	90
316	A23	2p	sepia	12.50	1.25
317	A23	5p	lilac rose	18.00	3.25
318	A23	10p	light brn	50.00	15.00
			Nos. 305-318 (16)	88.80	21.24

Catalogue values for unused stamps in this section, from this point to the end of the section, are for Never Hinged items.

Surveyor A24

1951, Dec. 5

319 A24 50c orange 40 5
320 A24 5p indigo 8.00 1.75

Intl. Conference of West Africans, 1951.

Drummer A25

1952, Mar. 10

321 A25 5c red brown 6 5
322 A25 50c olive gray 6 6
323 A25 5p violet 2.50 6

Musician A26

Design: 60c, Musician facing right.

1953, July 1 **Photo.**

324 A26 15c sepia 6 6
325 A26 60c brown 10 6

See Nos. B25-B26.

Woman and Dove A27

Drummer A28

1953, Sept. 5 ***Perf. 13x12½***

326 A27 5c orange 6 5
327 A27 10c brt lilac rose 6 5
328 A27 60c brown 15 5
329 A28 1p dull purple 1.00 6
330 A28 1.90p greenish blk 2.75 40
Nos. 326-330 (5) 4.02 61

Tragocephala Nobilis — A29

Butterfly: 60c, Papilio antimachus.

1953, Nov. 23

331 A29 15c dark green 32 20
332 A29 60c brown 32 20

Colonial Stamp Day. See Nos. B27-B28.

Hunter A30

Design: 60c, Hunter and elephant.

1954, June 10 ***Perf. 12½x13***

333 A30 15c dark gray green 6 6
334 A30 60c dark brown 28 12

See Nos. B29-B30.

The only foreign revenue stamps listed in this Catalogue are those authorized for prepayment of postage.

Swimming Turtle A31

Design: 60c, Shark.

1954, Nov. 23

335 A31 15c gray green 6 6
336 A31 60c orange brown 28 12

Colonial Stamp Day. See Nos. B31-B32.

Manuel Iradier y Bulfy A32

1955, Jan. 18

337 A32 60c orange brown 15 8
338 A32 1p dark violet 3.50 32

Birth cent. (in 1954) of Manuel Iradier y Bulfy.

Priest Saying Mass — A33

1955, June 1 **Photo.** ***Perf. 13x12½***

339 A33 50c olive gray 20 6

Centenary of the establishment of an Apostolic Prefecture at Fernando Po. See Nos. B33-B34.

Palace of Pardo A34

1955, July 18 ***Perf. 12½x13***

340 A34 5c ol brn 5 5
341 A34 15c brn lake 5 5
342 A34 80c Prus grn 15 5

Treaty of Pardo, 1778.

Red-eared Guenons A35

Orchid A36

1955, Nov. 23 ***Perf. 13x12½***

343 A35 70c gray grn & bl 24 20

Colonial Stamp Day. See Nos. B35-B36.

1956, June 1 **Unwmk.**

Flower: 50c, Strophantus Kombe.

344 A36 20c bluish green 16 8
345 A36 50c brown 16 8

See Nos. 360-361, B37-B38, B53-B54.

Arms of Santa Isabel — A37

African Gray Parrot — A38

1956, Nov. 23 *Perf. 13x12½*

346 A37 70c lt ol grn	8	5

Colonial Stamp Day. See Nos. B39-B40.

1957, June 1 **Photo.**

347 A38 70c ol grn	20	8

See Nos. B41-B42.

Elephants A39

Design: 70c, Elephant (vertical).

Perf. 12½x13, 13x12½

1957, Nov. 23

348 A39 20c blue green	8	8
349 A39 70c emerald	16	10

Colonial Stamp Day. See Nos. B43-B44.

Boxing A40

Basketball A41

Preaching Missionary A42

Various Sports: 15c, 2.30p, Jumping. 80c, 3p, Runner at finish line.

1958, Apr. 10 **Photo.** **Unwmk.**

350 A40 5c violet brn	5	5
351 A41 10c orange brn	5	5
352 A40 15c brown	5	5
353 A41 80c green	6	5
354 A40 1p orange red	6	5
355 A41 2p rose lilac	28	5
356 A40 2.30p dl violet	50	6
357 A41 3p brt blue	50	6
Nos. 350-357 (8)	1.55	42

1958, June 1 *Perf. 13x12½*

Design: 70c, Crucifix and missal.

358 A42 20c blue green	5	5
359 A42 70c green	15	5

75th anniversary of Catholic missions in Spanish Guinea. See Nos. B48-B49.

Type of 1956 Inscribed: "Pro-Infancia 1959"

Plants: 20c, Castor bean. 70c, Digitalis.

1959, June 1 *Perf. 13x12½*

360 A36 20c blue green	6	6
361 A36 70c green	10	8

Issued to promote child welfare. See Nos. B53-B54.

Stamps of Spanish Guinea were succeeded by those of Fernando Po and Rio Muni in 1960.

SEMI-POSTAL STAMPS

Red Cross Issue

Types of Semi-Postal Stamps of Spain, 1926, Overprinted in Black or Blue

GUINEA ESPAÑOLA

1926 **Unwmk.** *Perf. 12½, 13*

B1 SP3 5c black brn	1.90	1.50
B2 SP4 10c dark grn	1.90	1.50
B3 SP1 15c dark vio (Bl)	65	55
B4 SP4 20c vio brown	65	55
B5 SP5 25c dp carmine	65	55
B6 SP1 30c olive grn	65	55
B7 SP3 40c ultra	15	10
B8 SP2 50c red brown	15	10
B9 SP5 60c myrtle grn	15	10
B10 SP4 1p vermilion	15	10
B11 SP3 4p bister	55	42
B12 SP5 10p lt violet	1.00	90
Nos. B1-B12 (12)	8.55	6.92

Catalogue values for unused stamps in this section, from this point to the end of the section, are for Never Hinged items.

Allegory SP1

Leopard SP2

1950, Dec. 1 **Photo.** *Perf. 13x12½*

B13 SP1 50c + 10c ultra	40	25
B14 SP1 1p + 25c dk grn	12.50	5.75
B15 SP1 6.50p + 1.65p dp org	3.00	2.50

The surtax was to help the native population.

1951, Nov. 23

B16 SP2 5c + 5c brown	6	6
B17 SP2 10c + 5c red orange	6	6
B18 SP2 60c + 15c olive brn	40	25

Colonial Stamp Day, Nov. 23.

Love Lily — SP3

Brown-cheeked Hornbill — SP4

1952, June 1

B19 SP3 5c + 5c brown	6	6
B20 SP3 50c + 10c gray	6	6
B21 SP3 2p + 30c blue	1.50	1.10

The surtax was to help the native population.

1952, Nov. 23 *Perf. 12½*

B22 SP4 5c + 5c brown	7	6
B23 SP4 10c + 5c brown car	20	12
B24 SP4 60c + 15c dk brown	45	30

Colonial Stamp Day, Nov. 23.

Music Type of Regular Issue

Designs: 5c+5c, Musician facing left. 10c+5c, Musician facing right.

1953, July 1 *Perf. 12½x13*

B25 A26 5c + 5c lt rose brn	6	6
B26 A26 10c + 5c red violet	6	6

The surtax was to help the native population.

Insect Type of Regular Issue

Designs: 5c+5c, Beetle. 10c+5c, Butterfly.

1953, Nov. 23 *Perf. 13x12½*

B27 A29 5c + 5c dark blue	6	6
B28 A29 10c + 5c brt red vio	6	6

Hunter Type of Regular Issue

Designs: 5c+5c, Hunter with bow and arrow. 10c+5c, Hunter and elephant.

1954, June 10 *Perf. 12½x13*

B29 A30 5c + 5c rose brown	6	6
B30 A30 10c + 5c violet	6	6

The surtax was to help the native population.

Type of Regular Issue

Designs: 5c+5c, Turtle. 10c+5c, Shark.

1954, Nov. 23

B31 A31 5c + 5c org ver	6	6
B32 A31 10c + 5c mag	6	6

Type of Regular Issue and

Baptism — SP5

Design: 10c+5c, Priest.

Perf. 13x12½

1955, June 1 **Photo.** **Unwmk.**

B33 A33 10c + 5c red vio	6	6
B34 SP5 25c + 10c vio	6	6

Centenary of the establishment of an Apostolic Prefecture at Fernando Po.

Type of Regular Issue and

Red-eared Guenons SP6

Design: 5c+5c, Talapoin monkeys (vert.).

Perf. 13x12½, 12½x13

1955, Nov. 23

B35 A35 5c + 5c redsh brn & rose car	20	15
B36 SP6 15c + 5c rose car & blk brn	20	15

Colonial Stamp Day.

Flower Type of Regular Issue

Design: 15c+5c, Strophantus Kombe.

1956, June 1 *Perf. 13x12½*

B37 A36 5c + 5c greenish gray	6	6
B38 A36 15c + 5c bister	6	6

The tax was for native welfare work.

Type of Regular Issue and

Drummers and Arms of Bata — SP7

Design: 5c+5c, Arms of Santa Isabel.

Perf. 13x12½, 12½x13

1956, Nov. 23

B39 A37 5c + 5c red brown	10	6
B40 SP7 15c + 5c blue vio	10	6

Colonial Stamp Day.

Type of Regular Issue and

African Gray Parrot SP8

Design: 5c+5c, African gray parrot (vert.).

Perf. 13x12½, 12½x13

1957, June 1 **Photo.** **Unwmk.**

B41 A38 5c + 5c brn car	6	6
B42 SP8 15c + 5c bister	6	6

The surtax was for child welfare.

Type of Regular Issue, 1957

Designs: 10c+5c, Elephants (horizontal). 15c+5c, Elephant (vertical).

Perf. 12½x13, 13x12½

1957, Nov. 23

B43 A39 10c + 5c lil rose	6	6
B44 A39 15c + 5c bister	6	6

Pigeons and Arms of Valencia and Santa Isabel SP9

1958, Mar. 6 *Perf. 12½x13*

B45 SP9 10c + 5c org brn	6	6
B46 SP9 15c + 10c bister	6	6
B47 SP9 50c + 10c ol gray	15	10

The surtax was to aid the victims of the Valencia flood, Oct., 1957.

Type of Regular Issue, 1958

Designs: 10c+5c, Preaching missionary. 15c+5c, Crucifix and missal.

1958, June 1 **Photo.** *Perf. 13x12½*

B48 A42 10c + 5c red brown	5	5
B49 A42 15c + 5c dp bister	5	5

The surtax was to help the native population.

Butterflies SP10

Early Bicycle SP11

1958, Nov. 23 **Unwmk.**

Various Butterflies

B50 SP10 10c + 5c brown red	5	5
B51 SP10 25c + 10c brt pur	6	6
B52 SP10 50c + 10c gray olive	15	6

Stamp Day.

Type of Regular Issue 1956 Inscribed: "Pro-Infancia 1959"

Plants: 10c+5c, Digitalis. 15c+5c, Castor bean.

1959, June 1 **Photo.** *Perf. 13x12½*

B53 A36 10c + 5c rose brn	5	5
B54 A36 15c + 5c bister	5	5

The surtax was for child welfare.

1959, Nov. 23

Designs: 20c+5c, Bicycle race. 50c+20c, Bicyclist winning race.

B55	SP11 10c + 5c lt rose brn	5	5
B56	SP11 20c + 5c turq blue	5	5
B57	SP11 50c + 20c olive gray	15	6

Stamp Day.

AIR POST STAMPS

AP1

Revenue Stamp Surcharged "Habilitado para / Correo Aereo / Intercolonial / Una Peseta"

Type I - "Correo Aereo," 20½mm.
Type II - "Correo Aereo," 22 mm.

1941 **Unwmk.** ***Perf. 11***

C1	AP1 1p on 17p dp red, I	30.00	6.50
a.	Type II	40.00	9.25

Spain No. C113 Overprinted in Red — **Golfo de Guinea.**

1942, June 23

C2	AP30 1p chalky blue	1.50	25

No. 300 Overprinted in Green — Correo Aéreo / Viaje Ministerial / 10-19 Enero 1948

1948, Jan. 15 ***Perf. 10½x9½***

C3	A166 4p dull rose	7.25	2.00

The overprint exists in two types: I - The numeral 1's are lower case L's. II - The numeral 1's are actual ones.

Count of Argelejo and Frigate Catalina at Fernando Po, 1778
AP2

1949, Nov. 23 Photo. ***Perf. 12½x13***

C4	AP2 5p dk sl grn	1.50	75

Stamp Day, Nov. 23, 1949.

Manuel Iradier and Native Products — AP3

Woman Holding Dove — AP5

Benito Rapids AP4

1950, Nov. 23 **Unwmk.** ***Perf. 12½***

C5	AP3 5p dk brn	2.50	75

Stamp Day, Nov. 23, 1950.

1951, Mar. 1 Litho. ***Perf. 12½x13***
Various Views

C6	AP4	25c ocher		6	5
C7	AP4	50c lilac rose		6	5
C8	AP4	1p green		6	5
C9	AP4	2p brt blue		22	6
C10	AP4	3.25p rose lilac		70	12
C11	AP4	5p gray brown		3.25	1.65
C12	AP4	10p rose red		20.00	4.50
		Nos. C6-C12 (7)		24.35	6.48

Catalogue values for unused stamps in this section, from this point to the end of the section, are for Never Hinged items.

1951, Apr. 22 **Engr.** ***Perf. 10***

C13	AP5 5p dark blue	17.50	2.50

500th birth anniv. of Queen Isabella I.

Ferdinand the Catholic AP6

Soccer Players AP7

1952, July 18 Photo. ***Perf. 13x12½***

C14	AP6 5p red brn	25.00	6.00

500th birth anniv. of Ferdinand the Catholic of Spain.

1955-56 **Unwmk.**

C15	AP7	25c bl vio ('56)	6	6
C16	AP7	50c olive ('56)	6	6
C17	AP7	1.50p brown ('56)	85	6
C18	AP7	4p rose car ('56)	2.75	35
C19	AP7	10p yel grn	1.50	35
		Nos. C15-C19 (5)	5.22	88

Planes and Arm Holding Spear — AP8

1957, Sept. 19 ***Perf. 13x12½***

C20	AP8 25p bis & sep	6.75	75

30th anniv. of the Atlantida Squadron flight to Spanish Guinea.

SPECIAL DELIVERY STAMP

View of Fernando Po — SD1

Perf. 12½x13
1951, Mar. 1 **Litho.** **Unwmk.**

E1	SD1 25c rose car	30	20

SPANISH MOROCCO

LOCATION — Northwest coast of Africa
GOVT. — Former Spanish Protectorate
AREA — 17,398 sq. mi. (approx.)
POP. — 1,010,117 (1950)
CAPITAL — Tetuán

Spanish Morocco was a Spanish Protectorate until 1956 when it, along with the French and Tangier zones of Morocco, became the independent country, Morocco.

100 Centimos = 1 Peseta

Catalogue values for unused stamps in this country are for Never Hinged items, beginning with Scott 280 in the regular postage section, Scott B27 in the semi-postal section, Scott C24 in the airpost section, and Scott E11 in special delivery section.

Spanish Offices in Morocco

Spain No. 221A Overprinted in Carmine — CORREO ESPAÑOL MARRUECOS

1903-09 **Unwmk.** ***Imperf.***

1	A21 ¼c blue green	30	10

Stamps of Spain Overprinted in Carmine or Blue

a — CORREO ESPAÑOL MARRUECOS

On Stamps of 1900
Perf. 14

2	A35	2c bis brn	60	40
3	A35	5c green	75	20
4	A35	10c rose red (Bl)	85	10
5	A35	15c brt vio	1.10	22
6	A35	20c grnsh blk	3.50	90
7	A35	25c blue	42	22
8	A35	30c bl grn	1.75	90
9	A35	40c rose (Bl)	4.25	1.00
10	A35	50c slate grn	2.50	1.00
11	A35	1p lake (Bl)	3.50	2.00
12	A35	4p dull vio	12.00	3.50
13	A35	10p brn org (Bl)	12.00	6.50
		Nos. 1-13 (13)	43.52	17.04

Many varieties of overprint exist. Nos. 7-13 exist imperf.

On Stamps of 1909-10
1909-10 ***Perf. 13x12½, 14***

14	A46	2c dark brn	28	6
15	A46	5c green	1.10	6
16	A46	10c car (Bl)	1.40	6
17	A46	15c violet	3.25	12
18	A46	20c olive grn	6.50	22
19	A46	25c deep bl	67.50	
20	A46	30c blue grn	2.50	12
21	A46	40c rose (Bl)	2.50	12
22	A46	50c slate bl	4.50	1.75
23	A46	1p lake (Bl)	9.00	3.75
24	A46	4p deep vio	67.50	
25	A46	10p org (Bl)	67.50	
		Nos. 14-18,20-23 (9)	31.03	6.26

The stamps overprinted "Correo Espanol Marruecos" were used in all Morocco until the year 1914. After the issue of special stamps for the Protectorate the "Correo Espanol" stamps were continued in use solely in the city of Tangier.

Many varieties of overprint exist.

Nos. 19, 24 and 25 were not regularly issued.

Spanish Morocco

Spain No. 221A Overprinted in Carmine — MARRUECOS

1914 ***Imperf.***

26	A21 ¼c green	6	6

Stamps of Spain 1909-10 Overprinted in Carmine or Blue — MARRUECOS

Perf. 13x12½, 14

27	A46	2c dk brn (C)	6	6
28	A46	5c green (C)	15	12
29	A46	10c carmine (Bl)	15	12
30	A46	15c violet (C)	60	45
31	A46	20c ol grn (C)	90	65
32	A46	25c dp bl (C)	90	45
33	A46	30c bl grn (C)	2.00	90
34	A46	40c rose (Bl)	4.50	1.40
35	A46	50c slate bl (C)	2.50	90
36	A46	1p lake (Bl)	2.50	1.40
37	A46	4p dp vio (C)	11.50	7.75
38	A46	10p org (Bl)	13.00	9.00
		Nos. 26-38,E1 (14)	40.82	24.26

Many varieties of overprint exist, including inverted.

Nos. 27-38 exist imperf. Value for set, $475

Stamps of Spain 1876 and 1909-10 Overprinted in Red or Blue — PROTECTORADO ESPAÑOL EN MARRUECOS

1915 ***Imperf.***

39	A21 ¼c bl grn (R)	18	8

Perf. 13x12½, 14

40	A46	2c dk brn (R)	10	6
41	A46	5c green (R)	20	8
42	A46	10c carmine (Bl)	20	5
43	A46	15c violet (R)	24	10
44	A46	20c ol grn (R)	60	15
45	A46	25c deep bl (R)	60	15
46	A46	30c bl grn (R)	75	22
47	A46	40c rose (Bl)	1.10	22
48	A46	50c slate bl (R)	1.90	15
49	A46	1p lake (Bl)	1.90	22
50	A46	4p dp vio (R)	11.00	8.75
51	A46	10p org (Bl)	17.50	10.50
		Nos. 39-51,E2 (14)	37.77	21.48

One stamp in the setting on Nos. 39-51 has the first "R" of "PROTECTORADO" inverted. Many other varieties of overprint exist, including double and inverted.

Nos. 40-51 exist imperf. Value, set $700.

Stamps of Spain 1877 and 1909-10 Overprinted in Red or Blue

b — ZONA DE PROTECTORADO ESPAÑOL EN MARRUECOS

1916-18 ***Imperf.***

52	A21 ¼c bl grn (R)	60	10

Perf. 13x12½, 14

53	A46	2c dk brn (R)	60	10
54	A46	5c green (R)	2.25	10
55	A46	10c carmine (Bl)	3.00	15
56	A46	15c violet (R)	125.00	
57	A46	20c ol grn (R)	125.00	
58	A46	25c dp bl (R)	6.50	65
59	A46	30c bl grn (R)	12.00	5.25
60	A46	40c rose (Bl)	14.00	32
61	A46	50c sl bl (R)	6.00	12
62	A46	1p lake (Bl)	14.00	65
63	A46	4p dp vio (R)	25.00	10.00
64	A46	10p org (Bl)	52.50	27.50
		Nos. 52-55,58-64 (11)	136.45	44.94

Nos. 56-57 were not regularly issued.

Varieties of overprint, including double and inverted, exist for several denominations.

The 5c exists in olive brown. Value $475.

Same Overprint on Spain No. 310

1920

65	A46 15c ocher (Bl)	3.50	10

Exists imperf.; also with overprint inverted.

Stamps of 1915 Perforated through the middle and each half Surcharged "10 centimos" in Red

1920

66	A46 10c on half of 20c ol grn	3.50	2.00
67	A46 15c on half of 30c bl grn	8.00	6.00

No. E2 Divided and Surcharged in Black

68	SD1	10c on half of 20c red	10.00	8.00
a.		"10/cts." surch. added	50.00	18.00

Values of Nos. 66-68 are for pairs, both halves of the stamp. Varieties were probably made deliberately.

"Justice" — A1

Revenue Stamps Perforated through the Middle and each half Surcharged with New Value in Red or Green

1920 *Perf. 11½*

69	A1	5c on 5p lt bl (R)	8.00	2.25
70	A1	5c on 10p grn (R)	25	15
71	A1	10c on 25p dk grn (R)	25	15
a.		Inverted surcharge	10.00	9.00
72	A1	10c on 50p ind (R)	50	40
73	A1	15c on 100p red (G)	50	40
74	A1	15c on 500p cl (G)	11.00	6.75
		Nos. 69-74 (6)	20.50	10.10

Values of Nos. 69-74 are for pairs, both halves of the stamp.

Stamps of Spain 1917-20 Overprinted Type "a" in Blue or Red

1921-24 *Perf. 13*

75	A46	15c ocher (Bl)	1.10	10
76	A46	20c violet (R)	1.75	10

Stamps of Spain 1920-21 Overprinted Type "b" in Red

Imperf

77	A47	1c blue grn	90	10

Engr.

Perf. 13

78	A46	20c violet	6.00	10

Stamps of Spain, 1922 Overprinted Type "a" in Red or Blue

1923-28 *Perf. 13½ x 12½*

79	A49	2c ol grn (R)	2.00	10
80	A49	5c red vio (Bl)	2.00	10
81	A49	10c yel grn (R)	2.25	10
82	A49	20c violet (R)	3.50	60

Same Overprinted Type "b"

1923-25

83	A49	2c ol grn (R)	35	6
84	A49	5c red vio (Bl)	35	5
85	A49	10c yel grn (R)	1.40	5
86	A49	15c blue (R)	1.40	6
87	A49	20c violet (R)	2.75	5
88	A49	25c car (Bl)	4.75	45
89	A49	40c dp blue (R)	6.00	1.40
90	A49	50c org (Bl)	14.00	1.65
91	A49a	1p bl blk (R)	19.00	1.40
		Nos. 83-91 (9)	50.00	5.17

Spain No. 314 Overprinted Type "a" in Red

1927 *Imperf.*

92	A47	1c blue grn	14	6

Mosque of Alcazarquivir A2

Moorish Gateway at Larache A3

Well at Alhucemas A4

View of Xauen — A5

View of Tetuan — A6

1928-32 **Engr.** *Perf. 14, 14½*

93	A2	1c red ("Cs")	8	8
94	A2	1c car rose ("Ct") ('32)	20	12
95	A2	2c dk vio	8	8
96	A2	5c dp blue	8	8
97	A2	10c dk grn	8	8
98	A2	15c org brn	24	8
99	A3	20c olive grn	24	8
100	A3	25c cop red	24	8
102	A3	30c blk brn	85	8
103	A3	40c dull bl	1.10	8
104	A3	50c brn vio	2.00	6
105	A4	1p yel grn	3.25	15
106	A5	2.50p red vio	10.50	2.25
107	A6	4p ultra	7.25	1.65
		Nos. 93-107,E4 (15)	28.19	6.05

Seville-Barcelona Issue of Spain, 1929, Overprinted in Red or Blue

PROTECTORADO
MARRUECOS

1929 *Perf. 11, 14*

108	A50	1c greenish bl	7	7
109	A51	2c pale yel grn	7	7
110	A52	5c rose lake (Bl)	7	7
111	A53	10c green	7	7
112	A50	15c Prussian bl	7	7
113	A51	20c purple	7	7
114	A50	25c brt rose (Bl)	7	7
115	A52	30c blk brn (bl)	22	20
116	A53	40c dark blue	22	20
117	A51	50c dp org (Bl)	22	20
118	A52	1p blue blk	1.65	1.25
119	A53	4p dp rose (Bl)	4.00	3.25
120	A53	10p brn (Bl)	6.50	4.50
		Nos. 108-120 (13)	13.30	10.09

Stamps of Spain, 1922-31, Overprinted Type "a" in Black, Blue or Red

1929-34 *Perf. 11½, 13x12½*

121	A49	5c claret (Bk)	1.75	6
122	A61	10c green (R)	1.90	15
123	A61	15c sl grn (R)	57.50	48
124	A61	20c vio (R)	2.00	20
125	A61	30c brn lake (Bl)	2.25	45
126	A61	40c dk bl (R)	8.50	1.50
127	A49	50c org (Bl)	13.00	1.25
128	A49a	10p brn (Bl)	2.00	2.00
		Nos. 121-128 (8)	88.90	6.09

Stamps of Spain, 1922-26, overprinted diagonally as above, and with no control number, or with "A000,000" on back, were not issued but were presented to the delegates at the 1929 UPU Congress in London.

Stamps of Spain 1931-32, Overprinted in Black **MARRUECOS**

1933-34 *Imperf.*

130	A108	1c bl grn	14	7

Perf. 11½

131	A108	2c buff	14	7
132	A95	5c brnsh blk	14	7
133	A96	10c yel grn	14	7
134	A97	15c sl grn	14	7
135	A95	20c dk vio	14	7
136	A104	25c lake	14	7
137	A99	30c car rose	27.50	1.90
138	A100	40c dk blue	30	7
139	A97	50c orange	70	7
140	A100	60c apple grn	70	7
141	A105	1p blue blk	70	7
142	A106	4p magenta	1.90	1.10
143	A107	10p deep brn	2.50	1.90
		Nos. 130-143,E7 (15)	36.38	5.87

Street Scene in Tangier A7

View of Xauen A8

Gate in Town Wall, Arzila — A9

Street Scene in Tangier A10

Mosque of Alcazarquivir A11

Caliph and His Guard A12

View of Tangier A13

Green Control Numbers Printed on Gum

1933-35 **Photo.** *Perf. 14, 13½*

144	A7	1c brt rose	7	6
145	A8	2c grn ('35)	7	6
146	A9	5c mag ('35)	10	6
147	A10	10c dark green	15	6
148	A11	15c yel ('35)	85	7
149	A7	20c slate grn	32	6
150	A12	25c crim ('35)	8.50	15
151	A10	30c red brown	2.50	5
152	A13	40c deep blue	5.25	10
153	A13	50c red org	14.00	1.75
154	A8	1p sl blk ('35)	6.00	10
155	A9	2.50p brn ('35)	10.00	1.75
156	A11	4p yel grn ('35)	10.00	1.75
157	A12	5p black ('35)	13.00	1.75
		Nos. 144-157,E5 (15)	71.66	7.87

Mosque A14

Landscape A15

Green Control Numbers Printed on Gum

1935

158	A14	25c violet	44	6
159	A15	30c crimson	5.50	6
160	A14	40c orange	3.25	12
161	A15	50c bright bl	3.25	12
162	A14	60c dk bl grn	3.25	12
163	A15	2p brn lake	15.00	2.25
		Nos. 158-163 (6)	30.69	2.73

See No. 174.

Regular Issue and Special Delivery Stamp of 1928, Surcharged in Blue, Green or Red with New Values and Ornaments

1936

164	A6	1c on 4p ultra (Bl)	15	7
165	A5	2c on 2.50p red vio (G)	15	7
166	A3	5c on 25c cop red (R)	10	7
167	A4	10c on 1p yel grn (G)	4.00	2.25
168	SD2	15c on 20c blk (Bl)	3.25	1.10
		Nos. 164-168 (5)	7.65	3.56

Caliph and Viziers A16

View of Bokoia A17

View of Alcazarquivir A18

Sidi Saida Mosque A19

Caliph and Procession A20

Without Control Numbers

1937 **Photo.** *Perf. 13½*

169	A16	1c green	7	6
170	A17	2c red vio	7	6
171	A18	5c orange	12	6
172	A16	15c violet	12	6
173	A19	30c red	32	7
174	A14	1p ultra	2.75	12
175	A20	10p brown	27.50	8.50
		Nos. 169-175 (7)	30.95	8.93

See Nos. 192-193, souvenir sheets.

Harkeno Rifleman A21

Troops Marching A22

Designs: 2c, Legionnaires. 5c, Cavalryman leading his mount. 10c, Moroccan phalanx. 15c, Legion flag-bearer. 20c, Colonial soldier. 25c, Ifni sharpshooters. 30c, Mounted trumpeters. 40c, Cape Juby Dromedary Corps. 50c, Regular infantry. 60c, Caliphate guards. 1p, Orderly on guard. 2p, Sentry. 2.50p, Regular cavalry. 4p, Orderly.

1937 *Perf. 13½*

176	A21	1c dull blue	6	6
177	A21	2c org brn	6	6
178	A21	5c cerise	6	6
179	A21	10c emerald	6	6
180	A21	15c brt blue	6	6
181	A21	20c red brn	6	6
182	A21	25c magenta	6	6
183	A21	30c red org	6	6
184	A21	40c orange	10	10
185	A21	50c ultra	10	10
186	A21	60c yel grn	10	10
187	A21	1p blue vio	10	10
188	A21	2p Prus blue	3.75	3.00
189	A21	2.50p gray blk	3.75	3.00

190	A21	4p	dark brn	3.75	3.00
191	A21	10p	black	3.75	3.00
	Nos. 176-191,E6 (17)			15.98	12.98

First Year of Spanish Civil War.

Souvenir Sheets

1937 ***Perf. 13½***

192	Sheet of 4, #169-171, 174	10.00	6.25
193	Sheet of 4, #170-173	10.00	6.25

1st year of the Spanish Civil War.

Nos. 192-193 were privately overprinted "TANGER" in black on each stamp in the sheet for "use" in the International City of Tangier, and "GUINEA" for "use" in Spanish Guinea.

Spanish Quarter — A25

Designs: 10c, Moroccan quarter. 15c, Street scene, Larache. 20c, Tetuan.

1939 Unwmk. Photo. *Perf. 13½*

194	A25	5c	orange	15	6
195	A25	10c	brt blue grn	15	6
196	A25	15c	golden brn	35	6
197	A25	20c	brt ultra	35	6

Postman A26

Mail Box A27

Landscape A28

Street Scene, Alcazarquivir A29

View of Xauen A30

Sentry Guarding Palace at Sat A31

The Chieftain A32

Market Place, Larache A33

Tetuan A34

Ancient Gateway at Xauen A35

Scene in Alcazarquivir A36

Post Office A37

Spanish War Veterans A38

Victory Flag Bearers A39

Cavalry A40

Day of Court A41

1940 Unwmk. Photo. *Perf. 11½x11*

198	A26	1c	dark brn	7	6
199	A27	2c	olive grn	7	6
200	A28	5c	dk blue	12	5
201	A29	10c	dk red lil	12	5
202	A30	15c	dk green	12	5
203	A31	20c	purple	12	5
204	A32	25c	blk brn	12	5
205	A33	30c	brt grn	12	5
206	A34	40c	slate grn	1.10	5
207	A35	45c	org ver	45	8
208	A36	50c	brn org	45	6
209	A37	70c	sapphire	45	6
210	A38	1p	ind & brn	1.25	8
211	A39	2.50p	choc & dk grn	6.50	1.75
212	A40	5p	dk cer & sep	1.25	15
213	A41	10p	dk ol grn & brn org	12.00	3.00
	Nos. 198-213,E8 (17)			24.56	5.80

"ZONA" printed in black on back.

Stamps of 1937 Overprinted in Various Colors

17-VII-940
4º ANIVERSARIO

1940 Unwmk. *Perf. 13½*

214	A21	1c	dl bl (Bk)	45	45
215	A21	2c	org brn (Bk)	45	45
216	A21	5c	cerise (Bk)	45	45
217	A21	10c	emerald (Bk)	45	45
218	A21	15c	brt bl (Bk)	45	45
219	A21	20c	red brn (Bk)	45	45
220	A21	25c	magenta (Bk)	45	45
221	A21	30c	red org (V)	45	45
222	A21	40c	orange (V)	75	75
223	A21	50c	ultra (Bk)	75	75
224	A21	60c	yel grn (Bk)	75	75
225	A21	1p	bl vio (V)	75	75
226	A21	2p	Prus bl (Bl)	21.00	21.00
227	A21	2.50p	gray blk (V)	21.00	21.00
228	A21	4p	dk brn (Bl)	21.00	21.00
229	A22	10p	black (R)	21.00	21.00
	Nos. 214-229,E10 (17)			97.10	97.10

4th anniversary of Spanish Civil War.

Larache A42

Alcazarquivir A43

Market Place, Larache — A44

Tangier
A45 A46

1941 Unwmk. Photo. *Perf. 10½*

230	A42	5c	dk brn & brn	7	7
231	A43	10c	dp rose & ver	12	6
232	A44	15c	sl grn & yel grn	12	5
233	A45	20c	vio bl & dp bl	30	6
234	A46	40c	dp plum & cl	85	6
	Nos. 230-234 (5)			1.46	30

1943 ***Perf. 12x12½***

234A	A43	5c	dark blue	7	5
235	A44	40c	dl vio brn	13.00	12

Plowing A47

Harvesting A48

Returning from Work — A49

Transporting Wheat — A50

Vegetable Garden A51

Picking Oranges A52

Goat Herd — A53

1944 Unwmk. Photo. *Perf. 12½*

236	A47	1c	choc & lt bl	9	6
237	A48	2c	sl grn & lt grn	9	6
238	A49	5c	choc & grnsh blk	9	6
239	A50	10c	brt ultra & red org	9	6
240	A51	15c	sl grn & lt grn	9	6
241	A52	20c	dp cl & blk	9	6
242	A53	25c	lt bl & choc	12	6
243	A47	30c	yel grn & brt ultra	12	6
244	A48	40c	choc & red vio	9	6
245	A49	50c	brt ultra & red brn	25	6
246	A50	75c	yel grn & brt ultra	30	6
247	A51	1p	brt ultra & choc	30	5
248	A52	2.50p	blk & brt ultra	2.50	1.25
249	A53	10p	sal & gray blk	5.50	2.50
	Nos. 236-249 (14)			9.72	4.46

Potters A54

Dyers A55

Blacksmiths A56

Cobblers A57

Weavers A58

Metal Workers A59

1946 Unwmk. Litho. *Perf. 10½x10*

250	A54	1c	pur & brn	6	5
251	A55	2c	dk Prus grn & vio blk	6	5
252	A54	10c	dp org & vio bl	6	5
253	A55	15c	dk bl & bl grn	6	5
254	A54	25c	yel grn & ultra	6	5
255	A56	40c	dk bl & brn, perf. 12½	6	5
256	A55	45c	blk & rose	40	6
257	A57	1p	dk Prus grn & dp bl	50	6
258	A58	2.50p	dp org & gray	1.50	50
259	A59	10p	dk bl & gray	2.50	1.25
	Nos. 250-259 (10)			5.26	2.17

Control letter "Z" in circle in black on back.

A60

Sanitorium — A61

1946, Sept. 1 *Perf. 11½x10½, 10½*

260	A60	10c crim & bl grn	7	6
261	A61	25c crim & brn	7	6
		Nos. 260-261,B14-B16 (5)	1.05	54

Issued to aid anti-tuberculosis work.

A62

A63

1947 *Perf. 10*

262	A62	10c car & blue	7	7
263	A63	25c red & choc	7	7
		Nos. 262-263,B17-B19 (5)	98	81

Issued to aid anti-tuberculosis work.

Commerce by Railroad A64

Commerce by Truck — A65

Urban Market A66

Country Market A67

Caravan A68

Maritime Commerce A69

1948 **Litho.** *Perf. 10, 10x10½*

264	A64	2c pur & brn	6	6
265	A65	5c dp cl & vio	6	6
266	A66	15c brt ultra & bl grn	6	6
267	A67	25c blk & Prus grn	6	6
268	A65	35c brt ultra & gray blk	6	6
269	A68	50c red & vio	6	6
270	A66	70c dk gray grn & ultra	6	6
271	A67	90c cer & dk gray grn	15	6
272	A68	1p brt ultra & vio	55	6
273	A64	2.50p vio brn & sl grn	1.40	40
274	A69	10p blk & dp ultra	2.50	1.10
		Nos. 264-274 (11)	5.02	2.04

Emblem of Tuberculosis Association
A70 A71

Design: 25c, Plane over sanatorium.

1948, Oct. 1 *Perf. 10*

275	A70	10c car & green	6	6
276	A70	25c car & grnsh gray	1.25	60
		Nos. 275-276,B20-B23 (6)	19.86	7.36

1949

Designs: 10c, Road of Health. 25c, Minaret and Palm.

Black Control Number on Back

277	A71	5c car & green	6	6
278	A71	10c car & dk vio	6	6
279	A71	25c car & black	55	24
		Nos. 277-279,B25-B26 (5)	2.02	68

Catalogue values for unused stamps in this section, from this point to the end of the section, are for Never Hinged items.

Mail Transport, 1890 — A72

Herald — A73

Designs: 5c, 50c, 90c, Mail transport, 1890. 10c, 45c, 1p, Mail transport, 1906. 15c, 1.50p, Mail transport, 1913. 35c, 75c, 5p, Mail transport, 1914. 10p, Mail transport, 1918.

1950 **Litho.** *Perf. 10½*

280	A72	5c choc & vio bl	6	6
281	A72	10c deep bl & sep	6	6
282	A72	15c grnsh blk & emer	6	6
283	A72	35c pur & gray blk	9	8
284	A72	45c dp car & rose lil	12	12
285	A72	50c emer & dk brn	6	6
286	A72	75c dk vio bl & bl	9	8
287	A72	90c grnsh blk & rose car	6	5
288	A72	1p blk brn & gray	6	6
289	A72	1.50p car & blue	30	9
290	A72	5p blk & vio brn	60	12
291	A72	10p pur & blue	12.00	9.00
		Nos. 280-291,E11 (13)	25.56	18.84

UPU, 75th anniv. (in 1949).
Nos. 280-291 exist imperf. Value $350.

1950 **Unwmk.** *Perf. 10*

Designs: 10c, Old fort. 25c, Sanatorium.

Frame and Device in Carmine
Black Control Number on Back

292	A73	5c gray blk	6	5
293	A73	10c blue grn	6	6
294	A73	25c vio blue	60	30
		Nos. 292-294,B27-B28 (5)	1.54	77

Issued to aid anti-tuberculosis work.

Boar Hunt — A74

Designs: 10c and 1p, Hunters and hounds. 50c, Boar hunt. 5p, Fishermen. 10p, Moorish fishing boat.

1950, Dec. 30 *Perf. 10½x10*
Black Control Number on Back

295	A74	5c dk brn & rose vio	6	5
296	A74	10c car & gray	6	5
297	A74	50c grn & sepia	6	5
298	A74	1p bl vio & cl	35	5
299	A74	5p dp cl & bl vio	60	8
300	A74	10p grnsh blk & dp cl	1.75	30
		Nos. 295-300 (6)	2.88	58

Emblem — A75

Designs: 10c, Patients expressing gratitude. 25c, Plane in the Clouds.

Dated "1951"

1951 **Litho.** *Perf. 12*
Frame and Device in Carmine
Black Control Number on Back

301	A75	5c green	8	6
302	A75	10c blue vio	8	6
303	A75	25c gray blk	55	30
		Nos. 301-303,B29-B32 (7)	7.78	4.50

Issued to aid anti-tuberculosis work.

Armed Attack — A76

Designs: 10c, Horses on parade. 15c, Holiday procession. 20c, Road to market. 25c, "Brother-hoods." 35c, "Offering." 45c, Soldiers. 50c, On the rooftop. 75c, Teahouse. 90c, Wedding. 1p, Pilgrimage. 5p, Storyteller. 10p, Market corner.

1952 *Perf. 11*
Black Control Number on Back

304	A76	5c dk bl & brn	6	6
305	A76	10c dk brn & lil rose	6	6
306	A76	15c black & emer	6	6
307	A76	20c ol grn & red vio	6	6
308	A76	25c red & lt bl	6	6
309	A76	35c ol & org	6	6
310	A76	45c red & rose red	6	6
311	A76	50c rose car & gray grn	6	6
312	A76	75c pur & ultra	6	6
313	A76	90c dk bl & rose vio	6	6
314	A76	1p dk bl & red brn	6	6
315	A76	5p red & bl	1.40	25
316	A76	10p dk grn & gray blk	2.00	40
		Nos. 304-316,E12 (14)	4.14	1.39

Worship — A77

Designs: 10c, Distributing alms. 25c, Prickly pear.

1952, Oct. 1 **Dated "1952"**
Black Control Number on Back

317	A77	5c car & dk ol grn	6	6
318	A77	10c car & dk brn	6	6
319	A77	25c car & deep bl	32	20
		Nos. 317-319,B33-B37 (8)	6.10	3.37

Semi-Postal Types of 1948-49 Dated "1953"

Designs: 10c, As No. B26. 25c, As No. B23.

1953 **Litho.** *Perf. 10*
Black Control Number on Back

320	SP7	5c car & bl grn	6	6
321	SP9	10c car & pur	6	6
322	SP7	25c car & grn	48	32
		Nos. 320-322,B38-B42 (8)	7.75	4.91

Issued to aid anti-tuberculosis work.

A78

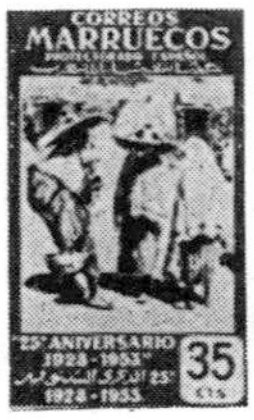
Mountain Women — A79

1953, Nov. 15
Black Control Number on Back

323	A78	5c red	15	6
324	A78	10c gray grn	15	6

1953, Dec. 15 **Photo.**

Designs: 50c and 2.50p, Water carrier. 90c and 2p, Mountaineers and donkey. 1p and 4.50p, Moorish women and child. 10p, Mounted dignitary.

Black Control Number on Back

334	A79	35c grn & rose vio	6	6
335	A79	50c red & green	6	6
336	A79	90c dk bl & org	6	6
337	A79	1p dk brn & grn	6	6
338	A79	1.25p dk grn & car rose	9	6
339	A79	2p dk rose vio & bl	18	18
340	A79	2.50p blk & org	42	20
341	A79	4.50p brt car rose & dk grn	1.75	30
342	A79	10p grn & blk	2.25	55
		Nos. 334-342,E13 (10)	5.08	1.68

25th anniv. of Spanish Morocco's first definitive postage stamps.

Zauia — A80

Queen's Gate — A81

Designs: 10c, "The Family." 25c, Plane and Spanish coast.

1954, Nov. 1 **Dated "1954"**
Black Control Number on Back

343	A80	5c car & bl grn	6	6
344	A80	10c car & dk brn	6	6
345	A80	25c car & blue	14	14
		Nos. 343-345,B43-B45 (6)	5.07	3.92

1955 **Litho.** *Perf. 11*

Gates: 25c and 1p, Saida. 80c, Queen's. 15p, Ceuta.

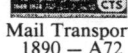

Black Control Number on Back
Frames in Black

346 A81	15c green	6	6
347 A81	25c vio brown	6	6
348 A81	80c blue	6	6
349 A81	1p car rose	15	6
350 A81	15p Prussian grn	2.50	65
	Nos. 346-350,E14 (6)	3.03	1.04

Honor Guard — A82

Designs: 25c, 80c, 3p, Caliph Moulay Hassan ben el-Medi. 30c, 1p, 5p, Caliph and procession. 15p, Coat of arms.

Perf. 13x12½
1955, Nov. 8 Photo. Unwmk.

351 A82	15c ol brn & ol	6	6
352 A82	25c lil & dp rose	6	6
353 A82	30c brn blk & Prus grn	6	6
354 A82	70c Prus grn & yel grn	6	6
355 A82	80c ol & ol brn	6	6
356 A82	1p dk bl & redsh brn	12	6
357 A82	1.80p blk & bl vio	18	6
358 A82	3p blue & gray	18	6
359 A82	5p dk grn & brn	1.25	45
	Engr.		
360 A82	15p red brn & yel grn	2.75	1.65
	Nos. 351-360 (10)	4.78	2.58

30th anniv. of accession to throne by Caliph Moulay Hassan ben el-Medi ben Ismail.

Succeeding issues, released under the Kingdom, are listed under Morocco.

SEMI-POSTAL STAMPS.

Types of Semi-Postal Stamps of Spain, 1926, Overprinted in Black or Blue

ZONA PROTECTORADO ESPAÑOL

1926 Unwmk. *Perf. 12½, 13*

B1 SP1	1c orange	1.90	1.65
B2 SP2	2c rose	2.75	1.90
B3 SP3	5c black brn	1.25	75
B4 SP4	10c dark grn	1.25	75
B5 SP1	15c dk vio (Bl)	30	30
B6 SP4	20c vio brn	30	30
B7 SP5	25c deep car	30	30
B8 SP1	30c olive grn	30	30
B9 SP3	40c ultra	9	9
B10 SP2	50c red brn	9	9
B11 SP4	1p vermilion	9	9
B12 SP3	4p bister	30	30
B13 SP5	10p light vio	75	60
	Nos. B1-B13,EB1 (14)	10.32	8.02

Tuberculosis Fund Issues

SP1

SP2

SP3

Perf. 10½, 11½x10½
1946, Sept. 1 Litho. Unwmk.

B14 SP1	25c + 5c crim & rose vio	7	6
B15 SP2	50c + 10c crim & blue	24	12
B16 SP3	90c + 10c crim & gray brn	60	24

Medical Center
SP4

Nurse and Children
SP5

"Protection"
SP6

Herald
SP7

1947 *Perf. 10*

B17 SP4	25c + 5c red & vio	7	7
B18 SP5	50c + 10c red & bl	22	15
B19 SP6	90c + 10c red & sep	55	45

1948, Oct. 1

Designs: No. B21, Protection. No. B22, Sun bath. No. B23, Plane over Ben Karrich.

B20 SP7	50c + 10c car & dk vio	15	10
B21 SP7	90c + 10c car & dk gray	90	35
B22 SP7	2.50p + 50c car & brn	7.00	2.50
B23 SP7	5p + 1p car & vio bl	10.50	3.75

Moulay Hassan ben el-Medi ben Ismail — SP8

Flag — SP9

1949, May 15

B24 SP8	50c + 10c lil rose	22	18

Wedding of the Caliph at Tetuan, June 5.

Tuberculosis Fund Issues
1949

Design: No. B26, Fight with dragon.

Black Control Numbers on Back

B25 SP9	50c + 10 car & brown	35	8
B26 SP9	90c + 10 car & grnsh gray	1.00	24

Catalogue values for unused stamps in this section, from this point to the end of the section, are for Never Hinged items.

A little time given to the study of the arrangement of the Scott Catalogue can make it easier to use effectively.

Crowd at Fountain of Life
SP10

Warrior
SP11

Design: 90c+10c, Mohammedan hermit's tomb.

1950, Oct. 1 Litho. *Perf. 10*
Black Control Numbers on Back
Frame and Cross in Carmine

B27 SP10	50 + 10c dk brown	22	6
B28 SP10	90 + 10c dk green	60	30

Dated "1951"
1951 Unwmk. *Perf. 12*

Designs: 90c+10c, Fort. 1p+5p, Port of Salvation. 1.10p+25c, Road to market.

Black Control Numbers on Back

B29 SP11	50c + 10c car & brn	8	6
B30 SP11	90c + 10c car & bl	24	12
B31 SP11	1p + 5p car & gray	4.25	2.50
B32 SP11	1.10p + 25p car & gray	2.50	1.40

Pilgrimage
SP12

Armed Horseman in Action
SP13

Designs: 60c+25c, Palmettos. 90c+10c, Fort. 1.10p+25c, Agave. 5p+2p, Warrior.

1952 Dated "1952" *Perf. 11.*
Black Control Numbers on Back

B33 SP12	50 + 10c car & gray	6	6
B34 SP12	60 + 25c car & dk grn	55	32
B35 SP12	90 + 10c car & vio brn	55	32
B36 SP12	1.10p + 25p car & pur	1.25	70
B37 SP12	5p + 2p car & gray	3.25	1.65
	Nos. B33-B37 (5)	5.66	3.05

1953 Dated "1953" *Perf. 10*

Designs: 60c+25c, As No. 276. 1.10p+25c, Plane and clouds.

Black Control Numbers on Back

B38 SP13	50c + 10c car & vio	8	8
B39 A70	60c + 25c car & brn	1.10	65
B40 SP11	90c + 10c car & blk	32	24
B41 SP13	1.10p + 25c car & vio brn	1.65	1.00
B42 A73	5p + 2p car & bl	4.00	2.50
	Nos. B38-B42 (5)	7.15	4.47

Stork — SP14

Designs: 50c+10c, Father & Child. 5p+2p, Tomb.

Dated "1954"
1954 Photo.
Black Control Numbers on Back

B43 SP14	5c + 5c car & rose vio	6	6
B44 SP14	50c + 10c car & gray grn	50	35
B45 SP14	5p + 2p car & gray	4.25	3.25

AIR POST STAMPS.

Mosque de Baja and Plane — AP1

View of Tetuan and Plane — AP2

Designs: 10c, Stork of Alcazar. 25c, Shore scene and plane. 40c, Desert tribesmen watching plane. 75c, View of shoreline at Larache. 1p, Arab mailman and plane above. 1.50p, Arab farmers and stork. 2p, Plane at twilight. 3p, Shadow of plane over city.

1938 Unwmk. Photo. *Perf. 13½*

C1 AP1	5c red brn	7	6
C2 AP1	10c emerald	10	7
C3 AP1	25c crimson	7	5
C4 AP1	40c dull blue	1.50	45
C5 AP2	50c cerise	7	5
C6 AP2	75c ultra	7	5
C7 AP1	1p dk brn	10	5
C8 AP1	1.50p purple	50	30
C9 AP1	2p brn lake	32	6
C10 AP1	3p gray blk	1.25	22
	Nos. C1-C10 (10)	4.05	1.36

Nos. C1-C10 exist imperf. Value of set, $275.

Landscape, Ketama
AP3

Mosque, Tangier
AP4

Velez
AP5

Sanjurjo
AP6

Strait of Gibraltar
AP7 AP8

1942 *Perf. 12½*

C11 AP3	5c deep blue	6	6
C12 AP4	10c org brn	6	6
C13 AP5	15c grnsh blk	6	6
C14 AP6	90c dark rose	6	6
C15 AP7	5p black	1.00	70
	Nos. C11-C15 (5)	1.24	94

Nos. C11-C15 exist imperf. Value of set, $90.

1949 Litho. *Perf. 10*

Designs: 5c, 1.75p, Strait of Gibraltar. 10c, 20c, 3p, Market day. 30c, 4p, Kebira Fortress. 6.50p, Airmail arrival. 8p, Horseman.

C16	AP8	5c vio brn & brt grn	6	6
C17	AP8	10c blk & rose lil	6	6
C18	AP8	30c dk vio bl & grnsh gray	6	6
C19	AP8	1.75p car & bl vio	10	6
C20	AP8	3p dk bl & gray	15	6
C21	AP8	4p grnsh blk & car rose	30	18
C22	AP8	6.50p brt grn & brn	1.00	22
C23	AP8	8p rose lil & bl vio	1.75	38
		Nos. C16-C23 (8)	3.48	1.08

Nos. C16-C23 exist imperf. Value of set, $150.

Catalogue values for unused stamps in this section, from this point to the end of the section, are for Never Hinged items.

Road to Tetuan AP9

Designs: 4p, Arrival of mail from Spain. 8p, Greeting plane. 16p, Shadow of plane.

1952 *Perf. 11*
Black Frames and Inscriptions
Black Control Numbers on Back

C24	AP9	2p brt bl	10	6
C25	AP9	4p scarlet	25	7
C26	AP9	8p dk ol grn	40	22
C27	AP9	16p vio brn	2.00	85

Part of the proceeds was used toward the establishment of a postal museum at Tetuan.

Plane over Boat — AP10

Designs: 60c, Mosques, Sidi Saidi. 1.10p, Plowing. 4.50p, Fortress, Xauen.

1953 *Perf. 10*

C28	AP10	35c dp bl & car rose	12	6
C29	AP10	60c dk car & sl grn	12	6
C30	AP10	1.10p dp bl & blk	22	10
C31	AP10	4.50p dk car & dk brn	85	30

Nos. C28-C31 exist imperf. Value of set, $75.

No. C6 Surcharged with New Value in Black

50 Type I   50 Type II

1953 *Perf. 13½*

C32	AP2	50c on 75c ultra (I)	45	15
a.		50c on 75c ultra (II)	45	15
b.		Vert. gutter pair, types (I) and (II)	2.50	

Sheets of 2 panes, 25 stamps each, with gutter between. Upper pane surcharged type I, lower type II.

The Scott Catalogue value is a retail price, what you could expect to pay for the stamp in a grade of Fine-Very Fine. The value listed is a reference which reflects recent actual dealer selling price.

AIR POST SEMI-POSTAL STAMPS

No. 150 Surcharged in Black

18-7-36

= 0'25 + 2'00 =

1936 Unwmk. *Perf. 14*

CB1	A12	25c + 2p on 25c crim	9.00	4.00
a.		Bars at right omitted	30.00	30.00
b.		Blue surcharge	21.00	10.50

25c was for postage, 2p for air post.

Nos. C1 to C10 surcharged "Lucha Antituberculosa," a Lorraine cross and surtax are stated to be bogus.

Crowd at Palace — SPAP1

1949, May 15 Unwmk. *Perf. 10*

CB2 SPAP1 1p + 10c gray blk 65 30

Wedding of the Caliph at Tetuan, June 5.

SPECIAL DELIVERY STAMPS.

Special Delivery Stamp of Spain Overprinted in Blue

MARRUECOS

1914 Unwmk. *Perf. 14*

E1 SD1 20c red 2.00 1.00

Special Delivery Stamp of Spain Overprinted in Blue

PROTECTORADO ESPAÑOL EN MARRUECOS

1915

E2 SD1 20c red 1.50 75

Special Delivery Stamp of Spain Overprinted in Blue

ZONA DE PROTECTORADO ESPAÑOL EN MARRUECOS

1923

E3 SD1 20c red 6.00 2.75

Mounted Courier SD2

1928 Engr. *Perf. 14, 14½*

E4 SD2 20c black 2.00 1.10

Moorish Postman SD3

Mounted Courier SD4

1935 Photo. *Perf. 14*
Green Control Number on Back

E5 SD3 20c vermilion 85 10

See No. E9.

1937 *Perf. 13½*

E6 SD4 20c brt car 10 10

1st Year of the Spanish Civil War.

Spain No. E14 Overprinted in Black

MARRUECOS

1938 *Perf. 10*

E7 SD7 20c vermilion 1.10 20

Arab Postman SD5

Airmail 1935 SD6

1940 Photo. *Perf. 11½x11*

E8 SD5 25c scarlet 25 15

"ZONA" printed on back in black.

Type of 1935

1940 Litho. *Perf. 10*

E9 SD3 20c blk brn 1.25

No. E9 was prepared but not issued.

No. E6 Surcharged with New Value, Bars and

17-VII-940 4° ANIVERSARIO

1940 *Perf. 13½*

E10 SD4 25c on 20c brt car 6.50 6.50

4th anniversary of Spanish Civil War.

Catalogue values for unused stamps in this section, from this point to the end of the section, are for Never Hinged items.

1950 Unwmk. Litho. *Perf. 10½*

E11 SD6 25c car & gray 12.00 9.00

UPU, 75th anniv. (in 1949).

Moorish Postrider SD7

1952 *Perf. 11*
Black Control Number on Back

E12 SD7 25c car & rose car 8 8

Rider with Special Delivery Mail SD8

Gate of Tangier SD9

1953 Photo. *Perf. 10*
Black Control Number on Back

E13 SD8 25c dk bl & car rose 15 15

25th anniv. of Spanish Morocco's first definitive postage stamps.

1955 Litho. *Perf. 11*
Black Control Number on Back

E14 SD9 2p vio & blk 20 15

SEMI-POSTAL SPECIAL DELIVERY STAMP.

Type of Semi-Postal Special Delivery Stamp of Spain, 1926, Overprinted

ZONA PROTECTORADO ESPAÑOL

1926 Unwmk. *Perf. 12½, 13*

EB1 SPSD1 20c ultra & blk 65 60

POSTAL TAX STAMPS.

General Francisco Franco PT1   PT3

Soldiers PT2

1937-39 Unwmk. Photo. *Perf. 12½*

RA1	PT1	10c sepia	32	7
a.		Sheet of 4, imperf.	1.75	1.25
RA2	PT1	10c cop brn ('38)	32	7
a.		Sheet of 4, imperf.	1.75	1.25
RA3	PT1	10c bl ('39)	32	7
a.		Sheet of 4, imperf.	1.75	1.25

The tax was used for the disabled soldiers in North Africa.

1941 Litho. *Perf. 13½*

RA4	PT2	10c brt grn	1.50	15
RA5	PT2	10c rose pink	1.50	15
RA6	PT2	10c henna brn	1.50	15
RA7	PT2	10c ultra	1.50	15

The tax was used for the disabled soldiers in North Africa.

1943 Photo. *Perf. 10*

RA8	PT3	10c chalky bl	2.50	10
RA9	PT3	10c slate bl	2.50	10
RA10	PT3	10c dl gray brn	2.50	10
RA11	PT3	10c blue vio	2.50	12

1944 *Perf. 12*

RA12	PT3	10c dp mag & brn	2.50	12
RA13	PT3	10c dp org & dk grn	2.50	12

1946 **Litho.**

RA14	PT3	10c ultra & brown	2.50	12
RA15	PT3	10c gray blk & rose lil	2.50	12

TANGIER

For the International City of Tangier
Seville-Barcelona Issue of Spain, 1929, Overprinted in Blue or Red

TANGER

1929 ***Perf. 11***

L1	A52	5c rose lake	8	6
L2	A53	10c green (R)	8	6
L3	A50	15c Prus bl (R)	8	6
L4	A51	20c purple (R)	8	6
L5	A50	25c brt rose	8	6
L6	A52	30c blk brn	8	6
L7	A53	40c dk blue (R)	20	18
L8	A51	50c deep org	20	18
L9	A52	1p bl blk (R)	1.65	1.25
L10	A53	4p deep rose	3.75	3.25
L11	A53	10p brown	5.75	4.25
		Nos. L1-L11 (11)	12.03	9.47

Overprints of 1937-39
The following overprints on stamps of Spain exist in black or in red:
"TANGER" vertically on Nos. 517-518, 522-523, 528, 532, 534, 539-543, 549.
"Correo Espanol Tanger" horizontally or vertically in three lines on Nos. 540, 592-597 (gray paper), 598-601.
"Tanger" horizontally on Nos. 539-541, 592-601.
"Correo Tanger" horizontally in two lines on five consular stamps.

Woman — A1

Palm Tree — A2

Man — A3

Old Map of Tangier — A4

Tangier Street A5

Moroccan Women A6

Head of Moor — A7

Perf. 9½x10½, 12½x13 (1c, 2c, 10c, 20c)
Engr., Photo. (1c, 2c)

1948-51 **Unwmk.**

L12	A1	1c bl grn ('51)	6	6
L13	A1	2c red org ('51)	6	6
L14	A2	5c vio brn ('49)	6	5
L15	A3	10c deep bl ('51)	6	6
L16	A3	20c gray ('51)	6	6
L17	A2	25c grn ('51)	6	6
L18	A4	30c dk sl grn	24	5
L19	A5	45c car rose	24	5
L20	A6	50c dp claret	24	5
L21	A7	75c dp blue	48	5
L22	A7	90c green	35	6
L23	A4	1.35p org ver	1.50	18
L24	A6	2p purple	2.75	18
L25	A5	10p dk grnsh bl ('49)	3.25	35
		Nos. L12-L25,LE1 (15)	10.01	1.52

Nos. L18-L25, LE1 exist imperf. Value, set $250.

TANGIER SEMI-POSTAL STAMPS.

Types of Semi-Postal Stamps of Spain, 1926, Overprinted

CORREO ESPAÑOL
TANGER

1926 ***Perf. 12½, 13***

LB1	SP1	1c orange	1.50	1.40
LB2	SP2	2c rose	1.50	1.40
LB3	SP3	5c blk brn	75	65
LB4	SP4	10c dk grn	75	65
LB5	SP1	15c dk vio	35	35
LB6	SP4	20c vio brn	35	35
LB7	SP5	25c dp car	35	35
LB8	SP1	30c ol grn	35	35
LB9	SP3	40c ultra	12	12
LB10	SP2	50c red brn	12	12
LB11	SP4	1p vermilion	18	18
LB12	SP3	4p bister	18	18
LB13	SP5	10p lt vio	75	65
		Nos. LB1-LB13,LEB1 (14)	8.00	7.40

TANGIER AIR POST STAMPS.

Overprints of 1939
The following overprints on stamps of Spain exist in black or in red:
"Correo Aereo Tanger" in two lines on Nos. 539-541, 596 (gray paper), 600, C72B.
"Via Aerea Tanger" in three lines on Nos. 539-540, 592-597 (gray paper), 599, 601, E14.
"Correo Aereo Tanger" in three lines on four consular stamps.
"Correo Espanol Tanger" in three lines on No. C72B.
"Tanger" on No. C72B.

Plane over Shore — AP1

Twin-Engine Plane — AP2

Passenger Plane in Flight — AP3

Perf. 11x11½, 11½
1949-50 **Engr.** **Unwmk.**

LC1	AP1	20c vio brown ('50)	24	6
LC2	AP2	25c bright red	24	6
LC3	AP3	35c dull green	24	6
LC4	AP1	1p violet ('50)	75	5
LC5	AP2	2p deep blue	1.40	22
LC6	AP3	10p brown violet	2.50	75
		Nos. LC1-LC6 (6)	5.37	1.20

Nos. LC1, LC4-LC6 exist imperf. Value $50 each.

TANGIER SPECIAL DELIVERY STAMP.

Arab Postrider — SD1

1949 **Unwmk.** **Engr.** ***Perf. 13***

LE1	SD1	25c red	60	20

TANGIER SEMI-POSTAL SPECIAL DELIVERY STAMP

Type of Semi-Postal Special Delivery Stamp of Spain, 1926, Overprinted

CORREO ESPAÑOL
TANGER

1926 **Unwmk.** ***Perf. 12½, 13***

LEB1	SPSD1	20c ultra & blk	75	65

TETUAN

Stamps of Spanish Offices in Morocco, 1903-09, Handstamped in Black, Blue or Violet

TETUAN

1908 **Unwmk.** ***Imperf.***

1	A21	¼c bl grn	8.25	5.25
		Perf. 14		
2	A35	2c bis brn	90.00	50.00
3	A35	5c green	65.00	22.50
4	A35	10c rose red	85.00	22.50
5	A35	20c grnsh blk	200.00	90.00
6	A35	25c blue	75.00	27.50
		Nos. 1-6 (6)	523.25	217.75

Same Handstamp On Stamps of Spain, 1877 and 1900-05, in Black, Blue or Violet

1908 ***Imperf.***

7	A21	¼c dp grn	6.00	2.75
		Perf. 14		
8	A35	2c bis brn	22.50	8.00
9	A35	5c dk grn	27.50	13.00
10	A35	10c rose red	27.50	13.00
11	A35	15c purple	35.00	18.00
12	A35	20c grnsh blk	115.00	90.00
13	A35	25c blue	42.00	22.50
14	A35	30c bl grn	125.00	52.50
15	A35	40c ol bis	125.00	90.00
		Nos. 7-15 (9)	525.50	309.75

Counterfeits of this overprint are plentiful.

SPANISH SAHARA

(Spanish Western Sahara)

LOCATION — Northwest Africa, bordering on the Atlantic
GOVT. — Former Spanish possession.
AREA — 102,703 sq. mi.
POP. — 76,425 (1970)
CAPITAL — Aaiún.

Spanish Sahara is a subdivision of Spanish West Africa. It includes the colony of Rio de Oro and the territory of Saguiet el Hamra. Spanish Sahara was formerly known as Spanish Western Sahara, which superseded the older title of Rio de Oro.

In 1976, Spanish Sahara was divided between Morocco and Mauritania.

100 Centimos = 1 Peseta

Catalogue values for unused stamps in this country are for Never Hinged items, beginning with Scott 105 in the regular postage section, Scott B58 in the semi-postal section, Scott C17 in the airpost section, and Scott E3 in the special delivery section.

Tuareg and Camel — A1

1924 **Unwmk.** **Typo.** ***Perf. 13***
Control Number on Back

1	A1	5c blue grn	1.25	30
2	A1	10c gray grn	1.25	30
3	A1	15c turq bl	1.25	30
4	A1	20c dark vio	1.25	38
5	A1	25c red	1.25	38
6	A1	30c red brn	1.25	38
7	A1	40c dark bl	1.25	38
8	A1	50c orange	1.25	38
9	A1	60c violet	1.25	38
10	A1	1p rose	5.75	1.65
11	A1	4p chocolate	27.50	9.00
12	A1	10p claret	57.50	24.00
		Nos. 1-12 (12)	102.00	37.83

Nos. 1-12 were for use in La Aguera and Rio de Oro.
A set of 10, similar to Nos. 3-12, exists with perf. 10 and no control number except on 50c.

Seville-Barcelona Issue of Spain, 1929 Overprinted in Blue or Red

SAHARA

1929 ***Perf. 11***

13	A52	5c rose lake	7	7
14	A53	10c green (R)	7	7
15	A50	15c Prus bl (R)	7	7
16	A51	20c purple (R)	7	7
17	A50	25c brt rose	7	7
18	A52	30c blk brn	7	7
19	A53	40c dk blue (R)	16	14
20	A51	50c dp org	16	14
21	A52	1p bl blk (R)	90	55
22	A53	4p dp rose	5.50	4.25
23	A53	10p brown	11.00	7.50
		Nos. 13-23 (11)	18.14	13.00

Stamps of 1924 Overprinted in Red or Blue

República
Española

1931 ***Perf. 13***

24	A1	5c bl grn (R)	32	20
25	A1	10c gray grn (R)	32	20
26	A1	15c turq bl (R)	32	20
27	A1	20c dk vio (R)	32	20
28	A1	25c red	40	20
29	A1	30c red brn	40	20
30	A1	40c dk bl (R)	1.65	32
31	A1	50c orange	1.65	65
32	A1	60c violet	1.65	65
33	A1	1p rose	1.65	65
34	A1	4p chocolate	18.00	6.00
35	A1	10p claret	32.50	10.00
		Nos. 24-35 (12)	59.18	19.47

The stamps of the 1931 issue exist with the overprint reading upward, downward or horizontally.

Stamps of Spain, 1936-40, Overprinted in Carmine or Blue

SAHARA
ESPAÑOL

1941-46 **Unwmk.** ***Imperf.***

36	A159	1c green	1.10	1.00
		Perf. 10 to 11		
37	A160	2c org brn (Bl)	1.10	1.00
38	A161	5c gray brn	35	35
39	A161	10c dk car (Bl)	1.10	1.00

40	A161	15c dk grn		35	35
41	A166	20c brt vio		35	35
42	A166	25c dp claret		70	52
43	A166	30c lt blue		70	75
44	A166	40c Prus grn		35	35
45	A166	50c indigo		3.50	75
46	A166	70c blue		2.50	1.25
47	A166	1p gray blk		11.00	1.75
48	A166	2p dl brn		60.00	37.50
49	A166	4p dl rose (Bl)		130.00	70.00
50	A166	10p lt brn		350.00	130.00
		Nos. 36-50 (15)		563.10	246.92

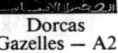

Dorcas Gazelles — A2

Caravan — A3

Camel Troops — A4

1943 Unwmk. *Perf. 12½*

51	A2	1c brn & lil rose	6	6
52	A3	2c yel brn & sl bl	6	6
53	A4	5c mag & vio	6	6
54	A2	15c sl grn & grn	7	7
55	A3	20c vio & red brn	7	7
56	A2	40c rose vio & vio	10	10
57	A3	45c brn vio & red	15	15
58	A4	75c indigo & bl	15	15
59	A2	1p red & brn	65	65
60	A3	3p bl vio & sl grn	1.25	1.25
61	A4	10p blk brn & blk	16.00	14.00
		Nos. 51-61,E1 (12)	19.27	17.27

Nos. 51-61, E1 exist imperf. Value for set, $100.

Gen. Franco and Desert Scene — A5

1951 Photo. *Perf. 12½x13*

62	A5	50c deep org	10	6
63	A5	1p chocolate	35	28
64	A5	5p blue grn	30.00	12.50

Visit of Gen. Francisco Franco, 1950.

Allegorical Figure and Globe A6

Woman Musician A7

1953, Mar. 2 *Perf. 13x12½*

65	A6	5c red org	6	6
66	A6	35c dk sl grn	6	6
67	A6	60c brown	25	10

75th anniv. of the founding of the Royal Geographical Society.

1953, June 1

Design: 60c, Man musician.

68	A7	15c ol gray	6	6
69	A7	60c brown	20	6

See Nos. B25-B26.

Orange Scorpionfish — A8

Fish: 60c, Banded sargo.

1953, Nov. 23 *Perf. 12½x13*

70	A8	15c dk ol grn	15	10
71	A8	60c orange	25	10

Colonial Stamp Day. See Nos. B27-B28.

Hurdlers A9

Runner — A10

1954, June 1 *Perf. 12½x13, 13x12½*

72	A9	15c gray grn	15	6
73	A10	60c brown	15	6

See Nos. B29-B30.

Atlantic Flyingfish A11

Fish: 60c, Gilthead.

1954, Nov. 23 *Perf. 12½x13*

74	A11	15c dk ol grn	10	6
75	A11	60c red brown	25	8

Colonial Stamp Day. See Nos. B31-B32.

Emilio Bonelli A12

1955, June 1 Photo. Unwmk.

76	A12	50c ol gray	15	6

Birth cent. of Emilio Bonelli, explorer. See Nos. B33-B34.

Scimitar-horned Oryx — A13

1955, Nov. 23

77	A13	70c green	25	6

Colonial Stamp Day. See Nos. B35-B36.

Antirrhinum Romosissimum — A14

Design: 50c, Sesiviun portulacastrum.

1956, June 1 *Perf. 13x12½*

78	A14	20c bluish grn	10	6
79	A14	50c brown	15	6

See Nos. B37-B38.

Arms of Aaiun and Camel Rider A15

1956, Nov. 23 *Perf. 12½x13*

80	A15	70c ol grn & sep	15	6

Colonial Stamp Day. See Nos. B39-B40.

Dromedaries A16

Golden Eagle A17

Designs: 15c, 80c, Ostrich. 50c, 1.80p, Mountain gazelle.

1957, Apr. 10 *Perf. 13x12½*

81	A16	5c purple	6	5
82	A16	15c bister	6	5
83	A16	50c dk olive	6	5
84	A16	70c yel green	95	12
85	A16	80c blue green	95	12
86	A16	1.80p lilac rose	95	22
		Nos. 81-86 (6)	3.03	61

1957, June 1 Photo. Unwmk.

87	A17	70c dark grn	25	10

See Nos. B41-B42.

Striped Hyena — A18

Design: 70c, Striped Hyena (horiz.).

Perf. 13x12½, 12½x13

1957, Nov. 23

88	A18	20c slate grn	6	5
89	A18	70c yellowish grn	20	8

Stamp Day. See Nos. B43-B44.

Don Quixote and the Lion A19

Cervantes A20

Gray Heron A21

1958, June 1 *Perf. 12½x13, 13x12½*

90	A19	20c bis brn & grn	6	5
91	A20	70c dk grn & yel grn	15	6

See Nos. B48-B49.

Cervantes Type of 1958

Designs: 20c, Actor as "Peribanez," by Lope de Vega. 70c, Lope de Vega.

1959, June Photo. *Perf. 13x12½*

92	A20	20c lt grn & brn	10	6
93	A20	70c yel grn & sl grn	10	6

Issued to promote child welfare. See Nos. B53-B54.

1959, Oct. 15 *Perf. 13x12½*

Birds: 50c, 1.50p, 5p, Sparrowhawk. 75c, 2p, 10p, Sea gull. 1p, 3p, As 25c.

94	A21	25c dl vio	8	5
95	A21	50c dk olive	8	5
96	A21	75c dk brown	8	5
97	A21	1p red org	8	5
98	A21	1.50p brt grn	8	5
99	A21	2p brt red lil	75	5
100	A21	3p blue	75	6
101	A21	5p red brn	1.40	15
102	A21	10p olive grn	6.50	3.00
		Nos. 94-102 (9)	9.80	3.51

Scene from "The Pilferer Don Pablos" by Quevedo — A22

Francisco Gomez de Quevedo A23

1960, June *Perf. 13x12½, 12½x13*

103	A22	35c slate grn	12	5
104	A23	80c Prussian grn	12	5

Francisco Gomez de Quevedo, writer. See Nos. B58-B59.

Catalogue values for unused stamps in this section, from this point to the end of the section, are for Never Hinged items.

Houbara Bustard A24

Map of Spanish Sahara A25

Gen. Franco and Camel Rider A26

Design: 50c, 1p, 2p, 5p, Doves.

1961, Apr. 18 Photo. *Perf. 13x12½*

105	A24	25c	blue vio	6	5
106	A24	50c	olive gray	6	5
107	A24	75c	brn vio	6	5
108	A24	1p	org ver	6	5
109	A24	1.50p	blue grn	6	6
110	A24	2p	magenta	90	6
111	A24	3p	dark blue	1.00	6
112	A24	5p	red brn	1.25	35
113	A24	10p	olive	3.00	1.10
			Nos. 105-113 (9)	6.45	1.83

1961, Oct. 1 *Perf. 13x12½, 12½x13*

Design: 70c, Chapel of Aaiun.

114	A25	25c	gray vio	10	5
115	A26	50c	ol brn	10	5
116	A25	70c	brt grn	10	5
117	A26	1p	red org	15	5

25th anniv. of the nomination of Gen. Francisco Franco as Chief of State.

Neurada Procumbres A27

Clock Fish A28

Designs: 50c, 1.50p, 10p, Anabasis articulata, flower. 70c, 2p, Euphorbia resinifera, cactus.

1962, Feb. 26 *Perf. 13x12½*

118	A27	25c	blk vio	5	5
119	A27	50c	dark brn	5	5
120	A27	70c	brt green	5	5
121	A27	1p	org ver	6	6
122	A27	1.50p	blue grn	32	5
123	A27	2p	red lilac	1.10	6
124	A27	3p	slate	1.75	28
125	A27	10p	olive	4.00	95
			Nos. 118-125 (8)	7.38	1.55

Perf. 13x12½, 12½x13

1962, July 10 Photo.

Design: 50c, Avia fish (horiz.).

126	A28	25c	vio black	5	5
127	A28	50c	dk green	6	5
128	A28	1p	org brown	20	6

Goats A29

Design: 35c, Sheep.

1962, Nov. 23 *Perf. 12½x13*

129	A29	15c	yel green	5	5
130	A29	35c	magenta	5	5
131	A29	1p	org brown	20	5

Issued for Stamp Day.

Seville Cathedral Tower — A30

1963, Jan. 29 *Perf. 13x12½*

132	A30	50c	olive	10	5
133	A30	1p	brown org	15	5

Issued to help Seville flood victims.

Camel Riders — A31

Hands Releasing Dove and Arms — A32

Design: 50c, Tuareg and camel.

1963, June 1 Unwmk.

134	A31	25c	deep vio	10	7
135	A31	50c	gray	10	7
136	A31	1p	orange red	15	7

Issued for child welfare.

1963, July 12

137	A32	50c	Prussian grn	10	5
138	A32	1p	orange brn	10	5

Issued for Barcelona flood relief.

John Dory A33

Fish: 50c, Plain bonito (vert.).

Perf. 12½x13, 13x12½

1964, Mar. 6 Photo.

139	A33	25c	purple	5	5
140	A33	50c	ol grn	5	5
141	A33	1p	brn red	15	5

Issued for Stamp Day 1963.

Moth and Flowers A34

Design: 50c, Two moths (vert.).

Perf. 12½x13, 13x12½

1964, June 1 Unwmk.

142	A34	25c	dull vio	10	5
143	A34	50c	brn blk	10	5
144	A34	1p	org red	15	5

Issued for child welfare.

Camel Rider and Microphone A35

Squirrel A36

Designs: 50c, 1.50p, 3p, Boy with flute and camels. 70c, 2p, 10p, Woman with drum.

1964, Sept. Photo. *Perf. 13x12½*

145	A35	25c	dull pur	5	5
146	A35	50c	olive	5	5
147	A35	70c	green	5	5
148	A35	1p	dl red brn	6	6
149	A35	1.50p	brt grn	7	6
150	A35	2p	Prus grn	15	10
151	A35	3p	dark blue	28	14
152	A35	10p	car lake	1.75	90
			Nos. 145-152 (8)	2.46	1.41

1964, Nov. 23 Unwmk.

Design: 1p, Squirrel's head (horiz.).

153	A36	50c	ol gray	10	5
154	A36	1p	brn car	10	5
155	A36	1.50p	green	15	6

Issued for Stamp Day.

Tuareg Girl — A37

Wellhead and Camel Rider — A38

Design: 1p, Physician examining patient (horiz.).

Perf. 13x12½, 12½x13

1965, Feb. 22 Photo.

156	A37	50c	blk brn	10	5
157	A38	1p	dk red	10	5
158	A38	1.50p	dp bl	15	6

25 years of peace.

Anthia Sexmaculata — A39

Design: 1p, 3p, Blepharopsis mendica, vert.

Perf. 12½x13, 13x12½

1965, June 1 Photo. Unwmk.

159	A39	50c	slate blue	5	5
160	A39	1p	blue grn	5	5
161	A39	1.50p	brown	6	6
162	A39	3p	dark blue	1.25	70

Issued for child welfare.

Basketball A40

Arms and Camels A41

1965, Nov. 23 *Perf. 13x12½*

163	A40	50c	rose claret	10	5
164	A41	1p	deep magenta	10	5
165	A40	1.50p	slate blue	15	6

Issued for Stamp Day.

Ship "Rio de Oro" A42

Design: 1.50p, S.S. Fuerte Ventura.

1966, June 1 Photo. *Perf. 12½x13*

166	A42	50c	olive	10	5
167	A42	1p	dk red brn	10	6
168	A42	1.50p	blue grn	15	6

Issued for child welfare.

Ocean Sunfish — A43

A44

Designs: 10c, 1.50p, Bigeye tuna (horiz.).

1966, Nov. 23 Photo. *Perf. 13*

169	A43	10c	bl gray & cit	5	5
170	A43	40c	slate & pink	5	5
171	A43	1.50p	brn & olive	6	6
172	A43	4p	rose vio & gray	25	15

Issued for Stamp Day.

1967, June 1 Photo. *Perf. 13*

Designs: 40c, 4p, Flower and leaves.

173	A44	10c	blk, ocher & gray grn	5	5
174	A44	40c	emer & lilac	5	5
175	A44	1.50p	dk grn & yel grn	6	6
176	A44	4p	brt bl & org	25	15

Issued for child welfare.

Aaiun Harbor A45

Design: 4p, Villa Cisneros Harbor.

1967, Sept. 28 Photo. *Perf. 12½x13*

177	A45	1.50p	brt bl & red brn	6	6
178	A45	4p	brt bl & bis brn	20	10

Modernization of harbor installations.

Ruddy Sheldrake — A46

Designs: 1.50p, Flamingo (vert.). 3.50p, Rufous bush robin.

1967, Nov. 23 Photo. *Perf. 13*

179	A46	1p	bis brn & grn	6	6
180	A46	1.50p	brt rose & gray	6	6
181	A46	3.50p	brn red & sep	30	20

Issued for Stamp Day.

Scorpio A47

Mailman A48

Zodiac Issue

Signs of the Zodiac: 1.50p, Aries. 2.50p, Virgo.

1968, Apr. 25 Photo. *Perf. 13*

182	A47	1p brt mag, *lt yel*	6	6
183	A47	1.50p brn, *pink*	6	6
184	A47	2.50p dk vio, *yel*	30	20

Issued for child welfare.

1968, Nov. Photo. *Perf. 13x12½*

Designs: 1p, Post horn, pigeon, letter and Spain No. 1. 1.50p, Letter, canceller and various stamps of Spain and Ifni.

185	A48	1p dp lil rose & dk bl	6	6
186	A48	1.50p green & sl grn	6	6
187	A48	2.50p dp org & dk bl	25	15

Issued for Stamp Day.

Dorcas Gazelle — A49

Designs: 1.50p, Doe and fawn. 2.50p, Gazelle and camel. 6p, Leaping gazelle.

1969, June 1 Photo. *Perf. 13*

188	A49	1p gldn brn & blk	5	5
189	A49	1.50p gldn brn & blk	6	6
190	A49	2.50p gldn brn & blk	15	6
191	A49	6p gldn brn & blk	40	30

Child welfare. See Nos. 196-199, 209-212.

Woman Playing Drum — A50

Designs: 1.50p, Man with flute. 2p, Drum and camel rider (horiz.). 25p, Flute (horiz.).

1969, Nov. 23 Photo. *Perf. 13*

192	A50	50c brn red & lt ol	5	5
193	A50	1.50p dk bl grn & grnsh gray	6	6
194	A50	2p ind & bis brn	6	6
195	A50	25p brn & lt bl grn	1.40	45

Issued for Stamp Day.

Animal Type of 1969

Fennec: 50c, Sitting. 2p, Running. 2.50p, Head. 6p, Vixen and pups.

1970, June 1 Photo. *Perf. 13*

196	A49	50c dp bis & blk	5	5
197	A49	2p org brn & blk	8	6
198	A49	2.50p dp bis & blk	20	6
199	A49	6p dp bis & blk	32	15

Issued for child welfare.

Grammodes Boisdeffrei — A51

Designs: 1p, like 50c. 2p, 5p, Danaus chrysippus. 8p, Celerio euphorbiae.

1970, Nov. 23 Photo. *Perf. 12½*

200	A51	50c red & multi	5	5
201	A51	1p car & multi	6	6
202	A51	2p grn & multi	6	6
203	A51	5p Prus bl & multi	30	10
204	A51	8p dk bl & multi	45	20
		Nos. 200-204 (5)	92	47

Issued for Stamp Day. See Nos. 233-234.

Gazelle, Arms of Aaiun A52

Smara Mosque A53

Designs: 2p, Inn (horiz.). 5p, Assembly building, Aaiun (horiz.).

Perf. 12½x13, 13x12½

1971, June 1 Photo.

205	A52	1p multi	6	5
206	A53	2p gray grn & ol	6	6
207	A53	5p lt bl & lt red brn	12	6
208	A53	25p lt bl & grnsh gray	85	18

Issued for child welfare.

Animal Type of 1969

Birds: 1.50p, 2p, Trumpeter bullfinch. 5p, Cream-colored courser. 10p, Lanner (falcon).

1971, Nov. 23 Photo. *Perf. 12½*

209	A49	1.50p blk & multi	6	6
210	A49	2p bl & multi	6	6
211	A49	5p grn & multi	15	7
212	A49	24p blk & multi	85	20

Stamp Day.

Saharan Woman — A55

Tuareg Woman — A56

Designs: 1.50p, 2p, Saharan man. 5p, as 1p. 8p, 10p, Man's head. 12p, Woman. 15p, Soldier. 24p, Dancer.

1972, Feb. 18 Photo. *Perf. 13*

213	A55	1p bl, pink & brn	5	5
214	A55	1.50p brn, lil & blk	6	6
215	A55	2p grn, buff & sep	6	6
216	A55	5p grn, pur & vio brn	10	8
217	A55	8p blk, lt grn & vio	22	10
218	A55	10p blk, gray & Prus bl	35	10
219	A55	12p multi	42	20
220	A55	15p multi	52	24
221	A55	24p multi	1.10	40
		Nos. 213-221 (9)	2.88	1.29

1972, June 1 Photo. *Perf. 13*

Design: 12p, Tuareg man.

222	A56	8p multi	32	8
223	A56	12p multi	48	20

Child welfare.

The first value column gives the catalogue value of an unused stamp, the second that of a used stamp.

Mother and Child — A57

1972, Nov. 23 Photo. *Perf. 13*

224	A57	4p shown	24	6
225	A57	15p Saharan man	55	24

Stamp Day. See No. 229.

Dunes A58

Design: 7p, Old Market and Gate, Aaiun.

1973, June 1 Photo. *Perf. 13*

226	A58	2p multi	6	6
227	A58	7p multi	30	15

Child welfare.

Type of 1972 and

View of Villa Cisneros A59

1973, Nov. 23 Photo. *Perf. 13*

228	A59	2p shown	6	6
229	A57	7p Tuareg man	30	15

Stamp Day.

UPU Monument, Bern — A60

Gate, Smara Mosque — A61

1974, May Photo. *Perf. 13*

230	A60	15p multi	65	20

Centenary of the Universal Postal Union.

1974, May

Design: 2p, Court and Minaret, Villa Cisneros Mosque.

231	A61	1p multi	10	5
232	A61	2p multi	10	5

Child welfare.

Animal Type of 1970

1974, Nov. Photo. *Perf. 13*

233	A51	2p Desert eagle owl	10	5
234	A51	5p Lappet-faced vulture	20	15

Stamp Day.

Espana 75 Emblem, Spain No. 1084 — A63

Old Man — A65

Children A64

1975, Apr. 4 Photo. *Perf. 13*

235	A63	8p olive, blk & bl	25	10

Espana 75 Intl. Phil. Exhib., Madrid, Apr. 4-13.

1975 Photo. *Perf. 13*

236	A64	1.50p shown	10	5
237	A64	3p Children's village	10	6

Child welfare.

1975, Nov. 7 Photo. *Perf. 13*

238	A65	3p blk, lt grn & mar	20	6

SEMI-POSTAL STAMPS

Red Cross Issue

Types of Semi-Postal Stamps of Spain, 1926, Overprinted

SAHARA ESPAÑOL

1926 Unwmk. *Perf. 12½, 13*

B1	SP3	5c black brn	2.00	1.65
B2	SP4	10c dark grn	2.00	1.65
B3	SP1	15c dark vio	90	70
B4	SP4	20c vio brn	90	70
B5	SP5	25c deep car	90	70
B6	SP1	30c olive grn	90	70
B7	SP3	40c ultra	8	7
B8	SP2	50c red brn	8	7
B9	SP5	60c myrtle grn	8	7
B10	SP4	1p vermilion	8	7
B11	SP3	4p bister	65	60
B12	SP5	10p light vio	1.65	1.10
		Nos. B1-B12 (12)	10.22	8.08

Shepherd and Lamb — SP1

Dromedary and Calf — SP2

1950, Oct. 20 Photo. *Perf. 13x12½*

B13	SP1	50c + 10c brown	20	15
B14	SP1	1p + 25c rose brn	9.25	4.75
B15	SP1	6.50p + 1.65p dk gray grn	4.50	1.65

The surtax was for child welfare.

1951, Nov. 23

B16	SP2	5c + 5c brown	6	6
B17	SP2	10c + 5 red org	6	6
B18	SP2	60c + 15c olive brn	24	9

Colonial Stamp Day, Nov. 23.

Child and Protector
SP3

Ostrich
SP4

1952, June 1

B19 SP3 5c + 5c brn 9 6
B20 SP3 50c + 10c gray 9 12
B21 SP3 2p + 30c bl 1.50 75

The surtax was for child welfare.

1952, Nov. 23 ***Perf. 12½***

B22 SP4 5c + 5c brn 10 10
B23 SP4 10c + 5c brn car 10 10
B24 SP4 60c + 15c dk grn 30 15

Colonial Stamp Day, Nov. 23.

Musician Type of Regular Issue

Designs: 5c+5c, Woman musician. 10c+5c, Man musician.

1953, June 1 ***Perf. 13x12½***

B25 A7 5c + 5c lawn 6 6
B26 A7 10c + 5c dp red vio 6 6

The surtax was for child welfare.

Fish Type of Regular Issue

Fish: 5c+5c, Orange scorpionfish. 10c+5c, Banded sargo.

1953, Nov. 23 ***Perf. 12½x13***

B27 A8 5c + 5c violet 10 10
B28 A8 10c + 5c green 10 10

Athlete Types of Regular Issue

1954, June 1 ***Perf. 12½x13, 13x12½***

B29 A9 5c + 5c brn org 10 6
B30 A10 10c + 5c purple 10 6

The surtax was to help the native population.

Fish Type of Regular Issue

Designs: 5c+5c, Atlantic flyingfish. 10c+5c, Gilthead.

1954, Nov. 23 ***Perf. 12½x13***

B31 A11 5c + 5c vermilion 6 6
B32 A11 10c + 5c plum 6 6

Type of Regular Issue and

Emilio Bonelli
SP5

Design: 10c+5c, Bonelli's head at right.

1955, June 1 **Photo.** **Unwmk.**

B33 A12 10c + 5c red vio 6 6
B34 SP5 25c + 10c violet 6 6

Birth cent. of Emilio Bonelli, explorer. The surtax was for child welfare.

Antelope Type of Regular Issue

Design: 15c+5c, Head of scimitar-horned oryx.

1955, Nov. 23 ***Perf. 12½x13***

B35 A13 5c + 5c org brn 6 6
B36 A13 15c + 5c ol bis 6 6

Flower Type of Regular Issue

Design: 15c+5c, Sesivium portulacastrum.

1956, June 1 ***Perf. 13x12½***

B37 A14 5c + 5c grnsh gray 10 6
B38 A14 15c + 5c bis 10 6

The tax was for the children.

Aaiun Type of Regular Issue and

Arms of Villa Cisneros and Man — SP6

Design: 5c+5c, Arms of Aaiun and camel rider.

Perf. 12½x13, 13x12½

1956, Nov. 23 **Unwmk.**

B39 A15 5c + 5c pur & blk 10 6
B40 SP6 15c + 5c bis & grn 10 6

Stamp Day.

Eagle Type of Regular Issue

Design: 15c+5c, Lesser spotted eagle in flight.

1957, June 1 ***Perf. 13x12½***

B41 A17 5c + 5c red brown 6 6
B42 A17 15c + 5c golden brn 6 6

The surtax was for child welfare.

Hyena Type of Regular Issue

Designs: 10c+5c, Striped Hyena (vert.). 15c+5c, Striped Hyena (horiz.).

Perf. 13x12½, 12½x13

1957, Nov. 23

B43 A18 10c + 5c red vio 6 6
B44 A18 15c + 5c bister 6 6

Stork and Arms of Valencia and Aaiun
SP7

1958, Mar. 6 **Photo.** ***Perf. 12½x13***

B45 SP7 10c + 5c org brn 6 6
B46 SP7 15c + 10c bister 6 6
B47 SP7 50c + 10c brn ol 15 6

The surtax was to aid the victims of the Valencia flood, Oct., 1957.

Cervantes Type of Regular Issue

Designs: 10c+5c, Cervantes. 15c+5c, Don Quixote and Sancho Panza.

1958, June 1 ***Perf. 13x12½***

B48 A20 10c + 5c hn brn & chnt brn 5 5
B49 A20 15c + 5c dp org & sl grn 5 5

The surtax was for child welfare.

Hoopoe Lark
SP8

Mailman
SP9

Designs: 25c+10c, Hoopoe larks (horiz.). 50c+10c, Bird.

Perf. 13x12½, 12½x13

1958, Nov. 23 **Photo.** **Unwmk.**

B50 SP8 10c + 5c brn red 10 6
B51 SP8 25c + 10c brt pur 10 6
B52 SP8 50c + 10c olive 15 6

Cervantes Type of Regular Issue, 1958

Designs: 10c+5c, Lope de Vega. 15c+5c, Actress from "Star of Seville," by Lope de Vega.

1959, June ***Perf. 13x12½***

B53 A20 10c + 5c org brn & ol gray 10 5
B54 A20 15c + 5c dp ocher & choc 10 5

The surtax was for child welfare.

1959, Nov. 23 **Photo.**

Designs: 20c+5c, Mailman. 50c+20c, Mailman on camel.

B55 SP9 10c + 5c rose & brn 7 7
B56 SP9 20c + 5c lt grn & brn 7 7
B57 SP9 50c + 20c ol gray & sl 14 6

Stamp Day.

Catalogue values for unused stamps in this section, from this point to the end of the section, are for Never Hinged items.

Quevedo Type of Regular Issue

1960, June 1 ***Perf. 12½x13, 13x12½***

Designs: 10c+5c, Francisco Gomez de Quevedo. 15c+5c, Winged wheel and hourglass, symbolic of "Hora de Todas."

B58 A23 10c + 5c maroon 12 5
B59 A22 15c + 5c bis brn 12 5

The surtax was for child welfare.

Leopard
SP10

Alonso Fernandez de Lugo
SP11

Designs: 20c+5c, Desert fox. 30c+10c, Eagle and leopard. 50c+20c, Sand fox.

1960, Nov. 23 **Photo.** ***Perf. 13x12½***

B60 SP10 10c + 5c rose lilac 5 5
B61 SP10 20c + 5c dk slate grn 5 5
B62 SP10 30c + 10c chocolate 6 5
B63 SP10 50c + 20c ol gray 20 5

Issued for Stamp Day, 1960.

Animal Type of 1961 inscribed: "Pro-Infancia 1961"

Designs: Various Mountain Gazelles.

1961, June 21 **Unwmk.**

B64 SP10 10c + 5c rose brn 5 5
B65 SP10 25c + 10c gray vio 5 5
B66 SP10 80c + 20c dk grn 15 5

The surtax was for child welfare.

1961, Nov. 23 ***Perf. 13x12½***

Design: 25c+10c, 1p+10c, Diego de Herrera.

B67 SP11 10c + 5c org red 10 6
B68 SP11 25c + 10c dk pur 10 6
B69 SP11 30c + 10c dk red brn 10 6
B70 SP11 1p + 10c red org 15 6

Stamp Day, 1961.

AIR POST STAMPS

In 1942, seven air post stamps of Spain, Nos. C100 to C108, were overprinted "SAHARA ESPANOL", but satisfactory information regarding their status is not available.

Ostriches
AP1

Desert Scene
AP2

1943 **Unwmk.** **Litho.** ***Perf. 12½***

C8 AP1 5c cer & vio brn 7 7
C9 AP2 25c yel grn & ol grn 7 7
C10 AP1 50c ind & turq grn 10 10
C11 AP2 1p pur & grnsh bl 10 10
C12 AP1 1.40p gray grn & bl 10 10
C13 AP2 2p mag & org brn 85 85
C14 AP1 5p brn & pur 1.10 1.00
C15 AP2 6p brt bl & gray grn 18.00 14.00
Nos. C8-C15 (8) 20.39 16.29

Nos. C8-C15 exist imperf. Value of set $125.

Diego Garcia de Herrera
AP3

1950, Nov. 23 **Photo.**

C16 AP3 5p rose vio 3.00 80

Stamp Day.

Catalogue values for unused stamps in this section, from this point to the end of the section, are for Never Hinged items.

Woman Holding Dove — AP4

1951, Apr. 22 **Engr.** ***Perf. 10***

C17 AP4 5p dp grn 17.50 5.00

500th birth anniv. of Queen Isabella I.

Helmet and Trappings
AP5

Plane and Camel Rider
AP6

1952, July 18 **Photo.** ***Perf. 13x12½***

C18 AP5 5p brown 24.00 4.00

500th birth anniv. of Ferdinand the Catholic, of Spain.

1961, May 16 **Unwmk.**

C19 AP6 25p gray brn 2.75 85

SPECIAL DELIVERY STAMPS

Type A4 Inscribed "URGENTE"

1943 **Unwmk.** ***Perf. 12½***

E1	A4 25c dk grn & car	65	65

Catalogue values for unused stamps in this section, from this point to the end of the section, are for Never Hinged items.

Messenger on Motorcycle — SD1

Unwmk.

1971, Sept. 6 **Photo.** ***Perf. 13***

E2	SD1 10p brt rose & ol	40	22

SPANISH WEST AFRICA

LOCATION — Northwest Africa bordering on the Atlantic Ocean.
GOVT. — Spanish administration.
AREA — 117,000 sq. mi.
POP. — 95,000 (1950).
CAPITAL — Sidi Ifni.

Spanish West Africa was the major political division of Spanish areas in northwest Africa. It included Spanish Sahara (Rio de Oro and Saguiet el Hamra) Ifni and, for administrative purposes, Southern Morocco. Separate stamp issues have been used for Rio de Oro, Ifni and La Aguera.

Catalogue values for all unused stamps in this country are for Never Hinged items.

Native — A1

Perf. 13x12½

1949, Oct. **Litho.** **Unwmk.**

1	A1 4p dk gray grn	1.90	90

UPU, 75th anniversary.

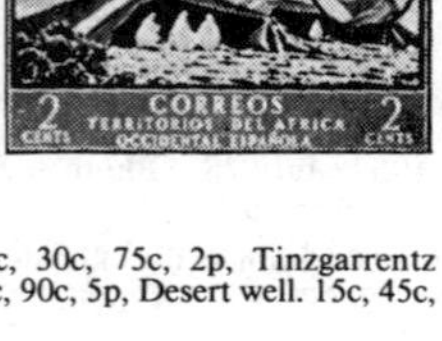

Nomad Camp — A2

Designs: 5c, 30c, 75c, 2p, Tinzgarrentz Oasis. 10c, 40c, 90c, 5p, Desert well. 15c, 45c, 1p, Caravan.

1950, June 5 ***Perf. 12½x13***

2	A2	2c brown	5	5
3	A2	5c rose violet	5	5
4	A2	10c Prussian bl	5	5
5	A2	15c dp ol gray	12	7
6	A2	25c red brown	12	6
7	A2	30c brt yellow	7	6
8	A2	40c olive gray	7	6
9	A2	45c rose lake	7	6
10	A2	50c brn orange	7	6
11	A2	75c ultra	12	10
12	A2	90c dl bl grn	6	6
13	A2	1p gray	6	6
14	A2	1.35p violet	60	32
15	A2	2p sepia	1.10	65
16	A2	5p lilac rose	9.25	2.00
17	A2	10p light brn	18.00	12.50
		Nos. 2-17 (16)	29.86	16.21

AIR POST STAMPS

Isabella the Catholic, Queen of Castile — AP1

Perf. 13x12½

1949, Nov. 23 **Photo.** **Unwmk.**

C1	AP1 5p yel brn	1.50	80

Stamp Day, Nov. 23, 1949.

Desert Camp AP2

Designs: Various Desert Scenes.

1951, Mar. 1 **Litho.** ***Perf. 12½x13***

C2	AP2	25c ocher	15	6
C3	AP2	50c lil rose	10	6
C4	AP2	1p green	20	6
C5	AP2	2p brt bl	52	6
C6	AP2	3.25p rose lil	1.10	40
C7	AP2	5p gray brn	8.25	50
C8	AP2	10p rose red	20.00	11.50
		Nos. C2-C8 (7)	30.32	12.64

SPECIAL DELIVERY STAMP

Tilimenzo Pass and Franco SD1

Perf. 12½x13

1951, Mar. 1 **Litho.** **Unwmk.**

E1	SD1 25c rose car	32	20

SURINAM

(Dutch Guiana)

LOCATION — On the northeast coast of South America, bordering on the Atlantic Ocean.
GOVT. — Republic
AREA — 70,087 sq. mi.
POP. — 370,000 (est. 1984)
CAPITAL — Paramaribo

The Dutch colony of Surinam became an integral part of the Kingdom of the Netherlands under the Constitution of 1954. It became an independent state November 25, 1975.

100 Cents = 1 Gulden

Catalogue values for unused stamps in this country are for Never Hinged items, beginning with Scott 168 in the regular postage section, Scott B34 in the semi-postal section, Scott C23 in the airpost section, Scott CB1 in the airpost semi-postal section, and Scott J33 in the postage due section.

Canceled-to-order stamps are often from remainders. Most collectors of canceled stamps prefer postally used specimens.

King William III — A1

Numeral of Value — A2

Perf. 11½, 11½x12, 12½x12, 13½, 14

1873-88 **Typo.** **Unwmk.**

1	A1	1c lil gray ('85)	1.25	1.25
2	A1	2c yel ('85)	50	50
3	A1	2½c rose	50	32
b		Perf. 14, small holes	8.25	10.00
4	A1	3c green	8.50	6.50
b		Perf. 14, small holes	10.00	14.00
5	A1	5c dl vio	10.50	3.50
b		Perf. 14, small holes	11.50	11.50
6	A1	10c bister	2.00	1.65
b		Perf. 14, small holes	12.00	16.00
7	A1	12½c sl bl ('85)	8.50	3.25
8	A1	15c gray ('88)	10.50	3.50
9	A1	20c grn ('88)	20.00	16.00
10	A1	25c grnsh bl	47.50	4.50
11	A1	25c ultra	170.00	11.50
b		Perf. 14, small holes	170.00	40.00
12	A1	30c red brn ('88)	20.00	18.00
13	A1	40c dk brn ('88)	17.50	16.00
14	A1	50c brn org	20.00	11.50
b		Perf. 14, small holes	32.50	30.00
15	A1	1g red brn & gray ('88)	32.50	27.50
16	A1	2.50g grn & org ('79)	52.50	47.50

The paper of Nos. 3-6, 11 and 14 sometimes has an accidental bluish tinge of varying strength. During its manufacture a chemical whitener (bluing agent) was added in varying quantities. No particular printing was made on bluish paper.

Nos. 1-16 were issued without gum.

For surcharges, see Nos. 23, 31-35, 39-42.

1890 ***Perf. 11½x11, 12½***

17	A2	1c gray	50	52
18	A2	2c yel brn	1.10	1.00
19	A2	2½c carmine	1.50	85
20	A2	3c green	3.50	2.75
21	A2	5c ultra	18.00	1.25

For surcharges, see Nos. 63-64.

A3

1892 ***Perf. 10½***

22	A3 2½c blk & org	85	50
a	First and fifth vertical words have fancy "F"	22.50	14.00
b	Imperf.	1.10	
c	Same as "a" imperf.	22.50	

No. 22 was issued without gum.

No. 14 Surcharged in Black

2½
CENT.

1892, Aug. 1 ***Perf. 14***

23	A1 2½c on 50c brn org	200.00	8.25
a	Perf. 12½x12	225.00	8.25
b	Perf. 11½x12	325.00	11.50
c	Double surcharge	275.00	250.00

Nos. 23-23c were issued without gum.

Queen Wilhelmina — A5

1892-93 **Typo.** ***Perf. 12½***

25	A5	10c bister	27.50	1.65
26	A5	12½c rose lilac	32.50	3.25
27	A5	15c gray	1.25	70
28	A5	20c green	1.75	1.10
29	A5	25c blue	7.25	3.00
30	A5	30c red brn	2.00	1.25

Nos. 25-30 were issued without gum.

For surcharges, see Nos. 65-66.

Nos. 7-12 Surcharged

10
CENT

1898 ***Perf. 11½x12, 12½x12, 13½***

31	A1 10c on 12½c sl bl	20.00	2.25
32	A1 10c on 15c gray	50.00	42.50
33	A1 10c on 20c green	2.50	2.25
34	A1 10c on 25c grnsh bl	5.75	3.50
34A	A1 10c on 25c ultra	425.00	400.00
b	Perf. 11½x12	500.00	450.00
35	A1 10c on 30c red brn	2.25	2.25
a	Double surcharge	225.00	

Nos. 31-35 were issued without gum.

Dangerous counterfeits exist.

Netherlands Nos. 80, 83-84 Surcharged

50 Ct 2.50 2.50

SURINAME SURINAME
c d

1900 ***Perf. 11½x11, 12½***

36	A11(c) 50c on 50c brnz grn & red brn	18.00	5.75
37	A12(d) 1g on 1g dk grn	14.00	10.00
38	A12(d) 2.50g on 2½g brn lil	11.50	8.25

Nos. 36-38 were issued without gum. For surcharge, see No. 67.

Nos. 13-16 Surcharged

25 cent

Perf. 11½, 11½x12, 12½x12, 14

1900

39	A1 25c on 40c dk brn	1.75	2.50
40	A1 25c on 50c brn org	1.10	1.10
a	Perf. 14, small holes	115.00	115.00
b	Perf. 11½x12	2.75	3.25
41	A1 50c on 1g red brn & gray	18.00	18.00
42	A1 50c on 2.50g grn & org	115.00	125.00

Nos. 39-42 were issued without gum.

Counterfeits of No. 42 exist.

A9

Queen Wilhelmina
A10 A11

1902-08 Typo. *Perf. 11, 12½*

44	A9	½c violet	55	50
45	A9	1c olive grn	90	70
46	A9	2c yel brn	6.50	2.25
47	A9	2½c blue grn	2.00	20
48	A9	3c orange	3.00	2.25
49	A9	5c red	4.00	20
50	A9	7½c gray ('08)	10.50	5.75
51	A10	10c slate	7.25	70
52	A10	12½c deep blue	1.00	12
53	A10	15c dp brown	18.00	6.50
54	A10	20c olive grn	18.00	3.75
55	A10	22½c brn & ol grn	13.00	8.25
56	A10	25c violet	14.00	1.00
57	A10	30c org brn	27.50	10.50
58	A10	50c lake brn	18.00	5.00
59	A11	1g violet	35.00	8.75
60	A11	2½g slate bl	32.50	32.50
		Nos. 44-60 (17)	211.70	88.92

Nos. 44-50, and possibly 59-60, were issued without gum.

A12

1909 *Serrate Roulette 13½*

61	A12	5c red	8.25	7.25
a.		Tete beche pair	115.00	100.00

Perf. 11½x10½

62	A12	5c red	10.00	8.50
a.		Tete beche pair	85.00	70.00

Nos. 61-62 were issued without gum.

Nos. 17-18, 29-30, 38 Surcharged in Red

1/
/2
cent
f

15 cent.
g

h

30 cent

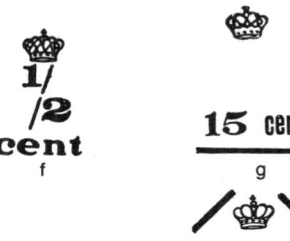

1911 *Perf. 12½ and 11½x11*

63	A2(f)	½c on 1c gray	65	65
64	A2(f)	½c on 2c yel brn	5.75	6.50
65	A5(g)	15c on 25c bl	52.50	50.00
66	A5(g)	20c on 30c red brn	5.75	6.00
67	A12(h)	30c on 2.50g on 2½g brn lil	90.00	90.00
		Nos. 63-67 (5)	154.65	153.15

Nos. 63-67 were issued without gum.

A13

1912, July Typeset *Perf. 11½*

70	A13	½c lilac	55	55
a.		Horiz. pair, imperf. btwn.	150.00	
71	A13	2½c dk grn	65	55
72	A13	5c pale red	6.25	5.50
a.		Vert. pair, imperf. btwn.	200.00	
73	A13	12½c dp bl	8.50	8.25

Nos. 70-73 were issued without gum.

Numeral of Value — A14

Queen Wilhelmina
A15 A16

Perf. 11x11½, 11½, 12½

1913-31 Typo.

74	A14	½c violet	20	24
75	A14	1c olive grn	20	12
76	A14	1½c blue ('21)	20	12
77	A14	2c yel brn	85	1.00
78	A14	2½c green	40	10
79	A14	3c yellow	50	40
80	A14	3c green ('26)	2.00	2.00
81	A14	4c chlky bl ('26)	6.50	3.50
82	A14	5c rose	90	10
83	A14	5c green ('22)	90	70
84	A14	5c lilac ('26)	90	12
85	A14	6c bis ('26)	2.00	2.00
86	A14	6c red org ('31)	1.65	20
87	A14	7½c drab	65	15
88	A14	7½c org ('27)	90	30
89	A14	7½c yel ('31)	2.25	7.25
90	A14	10c vio ('22)	2.75	2.75
91	A14	10c rose ('26)	2.50	30
92	A15	10c car rose	1.10	50
93	A15	12½c blue	1.25	40
94	A15	12½c red ('22)	1.25	1.65
95	A15	15c olive grn	40	40
96	A15	15c lt bl ('26)	5.00	3.75
97	A15	20c green	2.75	2.75
98	A15	20c bl ('22)	2.00	1.25
99	A15	20c ol grn ('26)	2.25	1.75
100	A15	22½c orange	1.65	2.00
101	A15	25c red vio	2.75	30
102	A15	30c slate	3.75	90
103	A15	32½c vio & org ('22)	12.00	14.00
104	A15	35c sl & red ('26)	3.75	3.50

Perf. 11, 11½, 11½x11, 12½

Engr.

105	A16	50c green	2.50	40
a.		Perf. 12½ ('32)	10.50	1.00
106	A16	1g brown	3.25	30
a.		Perf. 12½ ('32)	11.50	40
107	A16	1½g dp vio ('26)	27.50	27.50
108	A16	2½g carmine	20.00	20.00
a.		Perf. 11½x11	27.50	27.50
		Nos. 74-108 (35)	119.40	102.70

All stamps issued in 1913 were without gum.

For surcharges, see Nos. 116-120, 139.

Queen Wilhelmina — A17

1923 *Perf. 11, 11x11½, 11½*

109	A17	5c green	50	55
110	A17	10c car rose	70	1.25
111	A17	20c indigo	1.65	2.25
112	A17	50c brown org	10.50	16.00
113	A17	1g brown vio	16.00	11.50
114	A17	2½g gray blk	50.00	*175.00*
115	A17	5g brown	65.00	*200.00*
		Nos. 109-115 (7)	144.35	*406.55*

25th anniv. of the assumption of the government of the Netherlands by Queen Wilhelmina, at age 18.

Values for Nos. 114-115 used are for copies clearly dated before July 15, 1924.

Nos. 83, 93-94, 98 Surcharged in Black or Red:

3
j

10 CENT
k

15
CENT
m

1925

116	A14	3c on 5c green	70	85
117	A15	10c on 12½c red	1.50	1.50
118	A15	15c on 12½c bl (R)	1.10	1.10
119	A15	15c on 20c blue	1.10	1.10

No. 100 Surcharged in Blue

12½ Ct.

1926

120	A15	12½c on 22½c org	20.00	21.00

Postage Due Stamps Nos. J14 and J29 Surcharged in Blue or Black:

Frankeerzegel
12½ Cent
SURINAME
o

Frankeerzegel
12½
CENT
SURINAME
p

121	D2(o)	12½c on 40c lil & blk (Bl)	1.65	1.65
122	D2(p)	12½c on 40c lil (Bk)	21.00	21.00

Queen Wilhelmina — A21

1927-30 Engr. *Perf. 11½*

123	A21	10c carmine	65	30
124	A21	12½c red org	1.25	1.50
125	A21	15c dark blue	1.65	50
126	A21	20c indigo	1.65	40
127	A21	21c dk brn ('30)	13.00	13.00
128	A21	22½c brown ('28)	7.25	8.25
129	A21	25c dk vio	2.25	55
130	A21	30c dk green	2.25	90
131	A21	35c blk brn	2.50	2.50
		Nos. 123-131 (9)	32.45	27.90

Types of Netherlands Marine Insurance Stamps Inscribed "SURINAME" and Surcharged

FRANKEER
= ZEGEL =
10
CENT

1927, Oct. 26

132	MI1	3c on 15c dk grn	12	18
133	MI1	10c on 60c car rose	15	20
134	MI1	12½c on 75c gray brn	20	12
135	MI2	15c on 1.50 dk bl	1.75	1.75
136	MI2	25c on 2.25g org brn	4.00	4.00
137	MI3	30c on 4½g blk	9.25	7.25
138	MI3	50c on 7½g red	4.00	4.00
		Nos. 132-138 (7)	19.47	17.50

Nos. 135-137 have "FRANKEERZEGEL" in small capitals in one line. Nos. 135 and 136 have a heavy bar across the top of the stamp.

No. 88 Surcharged

6

1930, Mar. 1 *Perf. 12½*

139	A14	6c on 7½c org	1.50	85

Prince William I (Portrait by Van Key) — A22

1933, Apr. 19 Photo.

141	A22	6c dp org	5.00	1.25

400th birth anniv. of Prince William I, Count of Nassau and Prince of Orange, frequently referred to as William the Silent.

Van Walbeeck's Ship
A23

Queen Wilhelmina
A24

1936-42 Litho. *Perf. 13½x12½*

142	A23	½c yel brn	15	20
143	A23	1c lt yel grn	25	10
144	A23	1½c brt bl	40	32
145	A23	2c blk brn	50	20
146	A23	2½c green	10	12
a.		Perf. 13 ('41)	12.00	4.50
147	A23	3c dk ultra	42	32
148	A23	4c orange	50	55
149	A23	5c gray	50	15
150	A23	6c red	2.00	1.50
151	A23	7½c red vio	10	10
a.		7½c plum, perf. 13 ('41)	4.00	40

Engr.

Perf. 14, 12½

Size: 20x30mm

152	A24	10c vermilion	65	8
a.		Perf. 12½ ('39)	42.50	8.25
153	A24	12½c dull grn	2.75	1.00
154	A24	15c dark blue	1.00	50
155	A24	20c yel org	1.65	50
156	A24	21c dk gray	2.50	2.50
a.		Perf. 12½ ('39)	2.50	2.50
157	A24	25c brn lake	1.75	85
158	A24	30c brn vio	2.75	70
159	A24	35c olive brn	3.25	3.00

Perf. 12½x14

Size: 22x33mm

160	A24	50c dl yel grn	3.25	1.50
161	A24	1g dull blue	5.75	1.75
162	A24	1.50g blk brn	16.00	13.00
163	A24	2.50g rose lake	10.00	6.50
		Nos. 142-163 (22)	56.22	35.44

For surcharges, see Nos. 181-183, B37-B40.

Queen Wilhelmina — A25

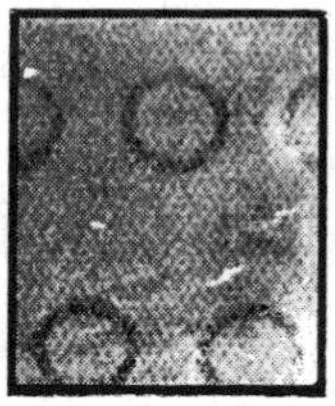

Wmk. 202 - Circles

Perf. 12½x12

1938, Aug. 30 Photo. Wmk. 202

164	A25	2c dull pur	50	40
165	A25	7½c red org	1.00	90
166	A25	15c royal bl	3.00	2.25

Reign of Queen Wilhelmina, 40th anniv.

Catalogue values for unused stamps in this section, from this point to the end of the section, are for Never Hinged items.

Van Walbeeck's Ship A26

Queen Wilhelmina A27

1941 Unwmk. Litho. *Perf. 12*

168	A26	1c lt yel grn	55	15
169	A26	2c blk brn	1.25	1.25

Type A26 is similar to type A23 except for the white side frame lines which extend to the base.

For surcharges, see No. 180.

1941-46 Photo. *Perf. 13½x12½*

Size: 18x22½mm

174	A27	12½c royal bl ('46)	24	15

Perf. 12½

175	A27	15c ultra	16.00	5.75

Royal Family — A28

1943, Nov. 2 Engr. *Perf. 13½x13*

176	A28	2½c dp org	24	32
177	A28	7½c red	24	15
178	A28	15c black	1.75	1.50
179	A28	40c dp bl	2.25	1.75

Issued in honor of Princess Margriet Francisca of the Netherlands.

Nos. 151, 152 and 168 Surcharged with New Values and Bars in Black

1945 Unwmk. *Perf. 13, 13½, 12*

180	A26	½c on 1c lt yel grn	8	15
181	A23	2½c on 7½c red vio	1.65	1.75
182	A24	5c on 10c ver	55	40
183	A24	7½c on 10c ver	65	40
a.		Double surcharge	150.00	165.00

Bauxite Mine, Moengo A29

Queen Wilhelmina A30 A31

Designs: 1½c, Bush Negroes on Cottica River near Moengo. 2c, Waterfall in interior. 2½c, Road scene, Coronie District. 3c, Surinam River near Berg en Dahl Plantation. 4c, Government Square, Paramaribo. 5c, Mining gold. 6c, Street in Paramaribo. 7½c, Sugar cane train.

1945 Engr. *Perf. 12*

184	A29	1c rose car	24	24
185	A29	1½c rose lake	90	90
186	A29	2c violet	40	32
187	A29	2½c olive brn	40	32
188	A29	3c dull grn	90	50
189	A29	4c brown	90	50
190	A29	5c blue	90	24
191	A29	6c olive	1.65	1.10
192	A29	7½c deep org	55	24
193	A30	10c blue	1.00	10
194	A30	15c brown	1.10	20
195	A30	20c dull grn	2.00	14
196	A30	22½c gray	2.25	65
197	A30	25c carmine	6.50	3.00
198	A30	30c olive grn	5.25	40
199	A30	35c brt bl grn	12.00	6.00
200	A30	40c rose lake	5.25	22
201	A30	50c red org	5.25	20
202	A30	60c violet	5.25	55
203	A31	1g red brn	4.50	24
204	A31	1.50g lilac	4.75	55
205	A31	2.50g olive brn	10.00	65
206	A31	5g rose car	22.50	8.50
207	A31	10g red org	35.00	13.00
		Nos. 184-207 (24)	129.44	38.76

For surcharges, see Nos. 240, CB2-CB3. For types surcharged, see Nos. B41-B46.

Nos. 151 and 152 Surcharged with New Value and Bar in Blue or Black

1947 *Perf. 13½x12½, 14*

209	A23	1½(c) on 7½c red vio (Bl)	8	*15*
a.		Double surcharge	125.00	
210	A24	2½c on 10c ver (Bk)	85	24

Numeral A32

Queen Wilhelmina A33

Perf. 12½x13½

1948 Unwmk. Photo.

211	A32	1c dk red	8	8
212	A32	1½c plum	12	12
213	A32	2c purple	20	8
214	A32	2½c ol grn	1.10	12
215	A32	3c dk grn	12	10
216	A32	4c red brn	15	12

Perf. 13½x12½

217	A33	5c dp blue	32	12
218	A33	6c dk olive	85	55
219	A33	7½c scarlet	32	15
220	A33	10c blue	50	8
221	A33	12½c dark bl	90	85
222	A33	15c henna brn	1.25	28
223	A33	17½c dk vio brn	1.50	1.10
224	A33	20c dk bl grn	1.10	12
225	A33	22½c slate bl	1.10	55
226	A33	25c crimson	1.10	22
227	A33	27½c car lake	1.10	15
228	A33	30c ol green	1.50	14
229	A33	37½c olive brn	2.25	1.50
230	A33	40c lil rose	1.65	22
231	A33	50c red org	1.65	22
232	A33	60c purple	1.75	32
233	A33	70c black	2.00	42
		Nos. 211-233 (23)	22.61	7.61

See Nos. 241-242.

Queen Wilhelmina — A34

1948 Engr. *Perf. 12½x13½*

234	A34	7½c vermilion	65	55
235	A34	12½c dp bl	65	55

Reign of Queen Wilhelmina, 50th anniv.

Queen Juliana — A35

1948 Wmk. 202 Photo. *Perf. 14x13*

236	A35	7½c dp org	2.50	2.50
237	A35	12½c ultra	2.50	2.50

Investiture of Queen Juliana, Sept. 6, 1948. For surcharges, see Nos. B53-B54.

Post Horns Entwined — A36

1949 Unwmk. *Perf. 11½x12½*

238	A36	7½c brn red	4.75	2.25
239	A36	27½c dull blue	4.00	1.65

UPU, 75th anniversary.

No. 192 Surcharged with New Value, Square and Bar in Black

1950 *Perf. 12*

240	A29	1c on 7½c dp org	55	55

Numeral Type of 1948

1951 *Perf. 12½x13½*

241	A32	5c dp bl	1.10	8
242	A32	7½c dp org	2.50	1.00

Queen Juliana A37 A38

1951 *Perf. 13½x12½*

243	A37	10c blue	32	8
244	A37	15c henna brn	85	20
245	A37	20c dk bl grn	2.00	10
246	A37	25c crimson	1.25	32
247	A37	27½c car lake	1.25	12
248	A37	30c olive grn	1.25	30
249	A37	35c ol brown	1.50	1.25
250	A37	40c lil rose	1.65	32
251	A37	50c red org	2.00	32

Engr.

252	A38	1g red brn	21.00	25
		Nos. 243-252 (10)	33.07	3.26

For surcharge, see No. 271.

Shooting Fish A39

Plowing with Water Buffalo A40

Designs: 2½c, Fisherman. 5c, Bauxite mining. 6c, Log raft. 10c, Woman picking fruit. 12½c, Armored catfish. 15c, Macaw. 17½c, Armadillo. 20c, Poling canoe. 25c, Common iguana.

1953-55 Photo. *Perf. 14x13, 13x14*

253	A39	2c ol grn ('53)	8	8
254	A40	2½c blue green	22	15
255	A40	5c gray	24	10
256	A40	6c bright bl	1.25	1.00
257	A40	7½c pur ('53)	12	8
258	A40	10c brt red ('53)	15	8
259	A40	12½c dk gray bl	1.50	1.10
260	A40	15c crimson	50	20
261	A40	17½c red brn	2.25	1.65
262	A40	20c Prus brn ('53)	40	8
263	A40	25c olive grn	2.00	65
a.		Miniature sheet of 4, #259-261, 263 ('55)	30.00	25.00
		Nos. 253-263 (11)	8.71	5.17

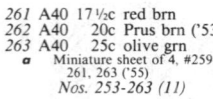

Queen Juliana — A41

1954, Dec. 15 *Perf. 13½*

264	A41	7½c dk red brn	65	60

Charter of the Kingdom, adopted Dec. 15, 1954.

Harvesting Bananas — A46

Globe and Mercury's Rod — A47

Designs: 7½c, Pounding rice. 10c, Preparing cassava. 15c, Fishing.

1955, May *Perf. 14x13*

265	A46	2c dark grn	1.25	1.00
266	A46	7½c dull yel	2.25	1.65
267	A46	10c org brn	2.25	1.65
268	A46	15c ultra	2.25	1.65

4th anniv. of the establishment of the Caribbean Tourist Assoc.

1955, Sept. 19 Unwmk. *Perf. 13x12*

269	A47	5c brt ultra	32	25

Paramaribo Trade Fair, Oct. 1955.

Flags and Map of Caribbean — A48

1956, Dec. 6 Litho. *Perf. 12½x14*

270	A48	10c lt bl & red	24	24

10th anniv. of Caribbean Commission.

No. 247 Surcharged **8 C**

1958 Photo. *Perf. 13½x12½*

271	A37	8c on 27½c car lake	10	10

Queen Juliana A49

Symbolic Flowers A50

1959 Unwmk. Litho. *Perf. 12½x12*

272 A49	1g magenta		1.25	8
273 A49	1.50g olive bis		2.00	40
274 A49	2.50g dk carmine		2.75	24
275 A49	5g dull blue		5.75	24

1959 *Perf. 12½x13*

276 A50	20c multi	2.25	1.25

5th anniv. of the constitution. Flowers in design symbolize Netherlands, Surinam and Netherlands Antilles.

Charles Lindbergh's Plane — A51

Designs: 10c, De Snip plane. 15c, Cessna 170B. 20c, Super Constellation. 40c, Boeing 707 Jet.

1960, Mar. 12 Litho. *Perf. 12½*

277 A51	8c chalky bl	1.00	1.00
278 A51	10c brt grn	1.50	1.50
279 A51	15c rose red	1.50	1.50
280 A51	20c pale vio	1.75	1.75
281 A51	40c light brn	2.50	2.50
	Nos. 277-281 (5)	8.25	8.25

Inauguration of Zanderij Airport, Mar. 12. Nos. 277-281 show 25 years of Surinam's civil aviation.

Flag of Surinam and Map — A52

Arms of Surinam — A53

1960, July 1 *Perf. 12½x13*

282 A52	10c multi	50	50
283 A53	15c multi	50	50

Day of Freedom, July 1.

Bananas — A54

Finance Building — A55

Designs: 2c, Citrus fruit. 3c, Cacao. 4c, Sugar cane. 5c, Coffee. 6c, Coconuts. 8c, Rice.

1961, Mar. 1 Litho. *Perf. 13½*

284 A54	1c sl, yel & blk	8	8
285 A54	2c bis, grn & blk	8	8
286 A54	3c dl red brn, blk & ocher	8	8
287 A54	4c lt ultra, blk & lem	8	8
288 A54	5c brn, blk & crim	8	8
289 A54	6c yel, grn, blk & bis	8	8
290 A54	8c ultra, blk & yel	8	8
	Nos. 284-290 (7)	56	56

1961 Unwmk. *Perf. 13½*

Buildings: 15c, Court of Justice. 20c, Concordia Lodge (Masons). 25c, Neve Shalom Synagogue, Paramaribo (horiz.). 30c, Old Dutch lock in New Amsterdam. 35c, Government office (horiz.). 40c, Governor's palace (horiz.). 50c, Legislative Council (horiz.). 60c, Old Dutch Reformed Church (horiz.). 70c, Zeelandia Fortress (horiz.).

291 A55	10c multi	8	8
292 A55	15c multi	15	8
293 A55	20c multi	24	14
294 A55	25c multi	50	28
295 A55	30c multi	1.25	1.10
296 A55	35c multi	1.25	1.25
297 A55	40c multi	65	50
298 A55	50c multi	65	24
299 A55	60c multi	70	70
300 A55	70c multi	90	90
	Nos. 291-300 (10)	6.37	5.27

Dag Hammarskjold (1905-1961) — A56

1962, Jan. 2 Litho. *Perf. 12, 12½*

301 A56	10c brt bl & blk	12	12
302 A56	20c lil & blk	20	20

Dag Hammarskjold, Secretary General of the United Nations, 1953-61. Printed in sheets of 12 (3x4).

Sheets exist either with or without extension of perforations through the margins.

Queen Juliana and Prince Bernhard A56a

1962, Jan. 31 Photo. *Perf. 14x13*

303 A56a	20c ol grn	24	24

Silver wedding anniversary of Queen Juliana and Prince Bernhard.

Malaria Eradication Emblem — A57

Perf. 13x14

1962, Apr. 7 Unwmk. Litho.

304 A57	8c brt red	12	12
305 A57	10c blue	20	20

WHO drive to eradicate malaria.

Stoelmans Guesthouse — A58

Design: 15c, Torarica Hotel.

1962, July 10 *Perf. 13½*

306 A58	10c multi	32	32
307 A58	15c multi	32	32

Opening of the Torarica Hotel in Paramaribo and Stoelmans Guesthouse on Stoelman Island.

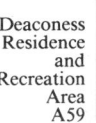

Deaconess Residence and Recreation Area A59

Design: 20c, Deaconess Hospital.

1962, Nov. 30

308 A59	10c multi	32	32
309 A59	20c multi	32	32

Hands Holding Wheat Emblem A60

Design: 20c, Farmer harvesting and wheat emblem (vert.).

Perf. 13½x13, 13x13½

1963, Mar. 21 Photo.

310 A60	10c dp car	12	12
311 A60	20c dk bl	12	12

FAO "Freedom from Hunger" campaign.

Broken Chain — A61

1963, July 1 Litho. *Perf. 13½x13*

312 A61	10c red & blk	12	12
313 A61	20c grn & blk	12	12

Centenary of emancipation of the slaves.

Prince William of Orange Landing at Scheveningen A61a

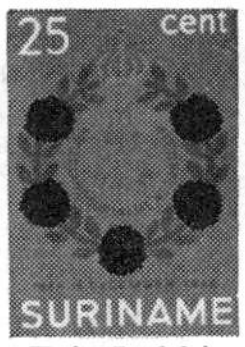

Faja Lobbi Wreath A62

1963, Nov. 21 Photo. *Perf. 13x14*

Size: 26x26mm

314 A61a	10c dl bl, blk & brn	8	8

Founding of the Kingdom of the Netherlands, 150th anniv.

1964, Dec. 15 Litho. *Perf. 12½x13*

315 A62	25c multi	20	20

Charter of the Kingdom of the Netherlands, 10th anniv.

Abraham Lincoln (1809-1865) — A63

1965, Apr. 14 Litho. *Perf. 12½x13*

316 A63	25c ol bis & brn	10	10

ICY Emblem A64

1965, May 26 *Perf. 13x12½*

317 A64	10c org & bl	5	5
318 A64	15c red & vio bl	8	8

International Cooperation Year.

Bauxite Mine, Moengo A65

Red-breasted Blackbird A66

Designs: 15c, Alum Pottery Works, Paranam. 20c, Hydroelectric plant, Afobaka. 25c, Aluminum smeltery, Paranam.

1965, Oct. 9 Photo. Unwmk.

319 A65	10c ocher	5	5
320 A65	15c dk grn	8	8
321 A65	20c dk bl	8	8
322 A65	25c carmine	8	8

Opening of the Brokopondo Power Station.

1966, Feb. 16 Litho. *Perf. 13x14*

Birds: 2c, Great kiskadee. 3c, Silver-beaked tanager. 4c, Ruddy ground dove. 5c, Blue-gray tanager. 6c, Glittering-throated emerald (hummingbird). 8c, Turquoise tanager. 10c, Pale-breasted robin.

323 A66	1c brt grn, blk & red	8	8
324 A66	2c lt ultra, yel & brn	8	8
325 A66	3c multi	8	8
326 A66	4c lt ol grn, red brn & blk	8	8
327 A66	5c org, ultra & blk	8	8
328 A66	6c multi	8	8
329 A66	8c gray, vio bl & blk	8	8
330 A66	10c multi	8	8
	Nos. 323-330 (8)	64	64

Central Hospital A67

Design: 15c, Hospital, side view.

1966, Mar. 9 Litho. *Perf. 13x12½*

331 A67	10c multi	8	8
332 A67	15c multi	8	8

Opening of Central Hospital, Paramaribo.

Father Petrus Donders — A68

Designs: 10c, Church and parsonage, Batavia. 15c, Msgr. Joannes B. Swinkels. 25c, Cathedral, Paramaribo.

1966, Mar. 26 Photo. *Perf. 12½x13*

333 A68	4c org brn & blk	5	5
334 A68	10c rose brn & blk	8	8
335 A68	15c yel brn & blk	8	8
336 A68	25c lt vio & blk	8	8

Centenary of the Redemptorist Mission in Surinam (Congregation of the Most Holy Redeemer).

100-Year-Old Tree — A69

1966, May 9 Litho. *Perf. 13x12½*

337 A69	25c grn, dp org & blk	10	10
338 A69	30c red org, grn & blk	10	10

Centenary of the Surinam Parliament.

Television Transmitter, Eye and Globe — A70

1966, Oct. 20 Litho. ***Perf. 12½x13***

339 A70 25c dk bl & ver 10 10
340 A70 30c brn & ver 10 10

Inauguration of television service.

Bauxite Industry, 1916 — A71

Design: 25c, Bauxite industry, 1966.

1966, Dec. 19 Litho. ***Perf. 13x12½***

341 A71 20c yel, org & blk 10 10
342 A71 25c org, bl & blk 10 10

50th anniversary of bauxite industry.

Central Bank, Paramaribo A72

Design: 25c, Central Bank, different view.

1967, Apr. 1 Litho. ***Perf. 13x12½***

343 A72 10c dp yel & blk 10 10
344 A72 25c lil & blk 10 10

Central Bank of Surinam, 10th anniv.

Amelia Earhart, Lockheed Electra and Paramaribo A73

1967, June 3 Photo. ***Perf. 13x12½***

345 A73 20c yel & dk car 10 10
346 A73 25c yel & grn 10 10

30th anniv. of Amelia Earhart's visit to Surinam, June 3-4, 1937.

Siva Nataraja, God of Dance, and Ballerina's Foot — A74

Design: 25c, Drummer's mask "Bashi Lele," and scroll of violin.

1967, June 21 ***Perf. 12½x13***

347 A74 10c yel grn & bl 10 10
348 A74 25c yel grn & brn 10 10

20th anniv. of the Surinam Cultural Center Foundation.

Surinam stamps can be mounted in Scott's annual Netherlands Supplement.

New Amsterdam, 1660 (New York City) — A75

Designs after 17th Century Engravings: 10c, Fort Zeelandia, Paramaribo, 1670. 25c, Breda Castle, Netherlands, 1667.

1967, July 31 Litho. ***Perf. 13½x13***

349 A75 10c yel, blk & bl 15 15
350 A75 20c red brn, yel & blk 15 15
351 A75 25c bl grn, yel & blk 15 15

300th anniv. of the Treaty of Breda between Britain, France and the Netherlands.

WHO Emblem A76

1968, Apr. 7 Litho. ***Perf. 13x12½***

352 A76 10c mag & dk bl 8 8
353 A76 25c bl & dk pur 15 15

WHO, 20th anniversary.

Chandelier and Christian Symbols A77

Design: 15c, like 10c, reversed. Brass chandelier from the Reformed Church, Paramaribo.

1968, May 29 Litho. ***Perf. 13x12½***

354 A77 10c dk bl 8 8
355 A77 25c dp yel grn 15 15

300th anniv. of the Reformed Church of Paramaribo.

Missionary Store, 1768 — A78

Designs: 25c, Main Church and store, Paramaribo, 1868. 30c, C. Kersten & Co., 1968.

1968, June 29 Litho. ***Perf. 13x12½***

356 A78 10c yel & blk 8 8
357 A78 25c lt grnsh bl & blk 15 15
358 A78 30c lil rose & blk 15 15

200th anniv. of C. Kersten & Co., which is partially owned by the Evangelical Brotherhood Missionary Society.

Joden Savanne Synagogue A79

Mahatma Gandhi A81

Spectacled Caiman A80

Designs: 20c, Map of Joden Savanne and Surinam River. 30c, Gravestone, 1733. The Hebrew inscriptions are quotations from the Bible: 20c, Joshua 24:2; 25c, Isaiah 56:7; 30c, Genesis 31:52.

1968, Aug. 28 ***Perf. 12½x13***

359 A79 20c multi 32 32
360 A79 25c multi 32 32
361 A79 30c multi 32 32

Founding of the first synagogue in the Western Hemisphere in 1685 in Joden Savanne, Surinam.

Perf. 13x12½, 12½x13

1969, Aug. 20 Litho.

Designs: 20c, Squirrel monkey (vert.). 25c, Armadillo.

362 A80 10c grn & multi 32 32
363 A80 20c bl gray & multi 32 32
364 A80 25c vio & multi 32 32

1969, Oct. 2 Litho. ***Perf. 12½x13***

365 A81 25c red & blk 24 24

Mohandas K. Gandhi (1869-1948), leader in India's fight for independence.

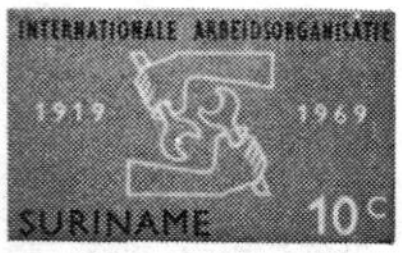

ILO Emblem A82

1969, Oct. 29 Litho. ***Perf. 13x12½***

366 A82 10c brt bl grn & blk 15 15
367 A82 25c red & blk 24 24

ILO, 50th anniversary.

Queen Juliana and Rising Sun — A82a

1969, Dec. 15 Photo. ***Perf. 14x12½***

368 A82a 25c bl & multi 24 24

15th anniv. of the Charter of the Kingdom of the Netherlands. Phosphorescent paper.

"1950-1970" A83

1970, Apr. 3 Photo. ***Perf. 13x12½***

369 A83 10c brn, grn & org 8 8
370 A83 25c emer, dk bl & org 15 15

20th anniv. of secondary education in Surinam.

Inauguration of UPU Headquarters, Bern — A84

Design: 25c, UPU Headquarters, sideview and UPU emblem.

1970, May 20 Litho. ***Perf. 13x12½***

371 A84 10c sky bl & dk pur 12 12
372 A84 25c red & blk 20 20

"UNO" A85

Plane over Paramaribo A86

1970, June 26 Litho. ***Perf. 12x13***

373 A85 10c ocher & yel 12 12
374 A85 25c dp bl & ultra 20 20

25th anniversary of the United Nations.

1970, July 15

Designs: 20c, Plane over map of Totness, 25c, Plane over Nieuw-Nickerie.

375 A86 10c bl, vio bl & gray 24 24
376 A86 20c yel, red & gray 24 24
377 A86 25c pink, dk red & gray 24 24

40th anniv. of domestic airmail service.

Plan of Soccer Field and Ball — A87

Morse Key — A89

Cocoi Heron — A88

Designs: Plan of soccer field with ball in different positions.

1970, Oct. 1 Litho. ***Perf. 12x13***

378 A87 4c yel, red brn & blk 8 8
379 A87 10c pale lem, red brn & blk 15 15
380 A87 15c lt yel grn, red brn & blk 15 15
381 A87 25c lt grn, red brn & blk 24 24

50th anniv. of the Soccer Assoc. of Surinam.

1971, Feb. 14 Litho. ***Perf. 13x12½***

Birds in Flight: 20c, Flamingo. 25c, Scarlet macaw.

382 A88 15c gray & multi 32 32
383 A88 20c ultra & multi 32 32
384 A88 25c pale grn & multi 32 32

25th anniversary of regular air service between the Netherlands, Surinam and Netherlands Antilles.

1971, May 17 Litho. ***Perf. 12½x13***

Designs: 20c, Telephone. 25c, Lunar landing module, telescope.

385 A89 15c lt grn & multi 35 35
386 A89 20c bl & multi 42 42
387 A89 25c lil & multi 50 50

3rd World Telecommunications Day.

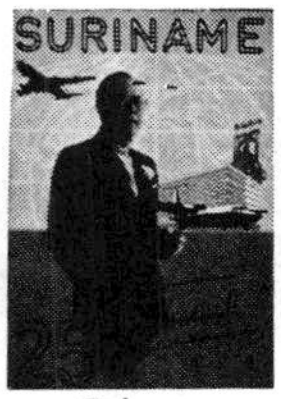

Prince Bernhard, Fokker F27, Boeing 747B — A89a

Map of Surinam, Population Chart — A90

1971, June 29 Photo. *Perf. 13x14*

388 A89a 25c multi 24 24

60th birthday of Prince Bernhard.

1971, July 31 Litho. *Perf. 12½x13*

Design: 30c, Map of Surinam and individual registration population.

389 A90 15c gray bl, blk & ver 15 15
390 A90 30c ver, gray bl & blk 24 24

50th anniv. of the first census; introduction of civil registration in Surinam.

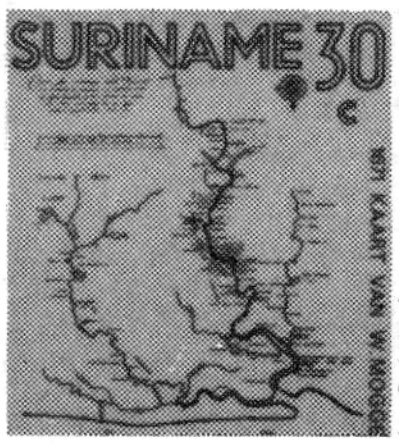

William Mogge's Map of Surinam A91

1971, Oct. 27 *Perf. 11½x11*

391 A91 30c dl yel & dk brn 40 40

300th anniv. of the first map of Surinam.

Map of Albina — A92

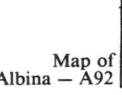

August Kappler A93

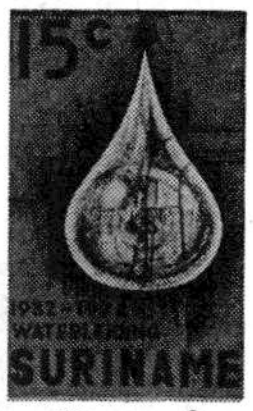

Drop of Water A94

Design: 20c, View of Albina from Maroni River.

Perf. 13x12½, 12½x13

1971, Dec. 13

392 A92 15c saph & blk 32 32
393 A92 20c brt grn & blk 32 32
394 A93 25c yel & blk 32 32

125th anniv. of the founding of Albina by August Kappler (1815-1887).

1972, Feb. 2 *Perf. 12½x13*

Design: 30c, Faucet and water tower.

395 A94 15c vio & blk 24 24
396 A94 30c bl & blk 32 32

Surinam water works, 40th anniversary.

Air Mail Envelope A95

1972, Aug. 2 Litho. *Perf. 13x12½*

397 A95 15c red & bl 15 15
398 A95 30c bl & red 24 24

50th anniversary of the arrival of the first airmail in Surinam, carried by Capt. Dutertre from French Guiana.

Giant Tree — A96

Designs: 20c, Wood transport by air lift. 30c, Hands tending seedling.

1972, Dec. 20 Photo. *Perf. 12½x13*

399 A96 15c yel & dk brn 15 15
400 A96 20c bl & dp brn 15 15
401 A96 30c brt grn & dp brn 32 32

Surinam Forestry Commission, 25th anniv.

Hindu Woman in Rice Field — A97

Designs: 25c, J. F. A. Cateau van Rosevelt with map of Surinam and ship "Lalla Rookh." 30c, Symbolic bird, flower, sun, flag and factories.

1973, May 23 Litho. *Perf. 13x13½*

402 A97 15c pur & yel 24 24
403 A97 25c mar & gray 24 20
404 A97 30c yel & lt bl 32 32

1st immigrants from India, cent.

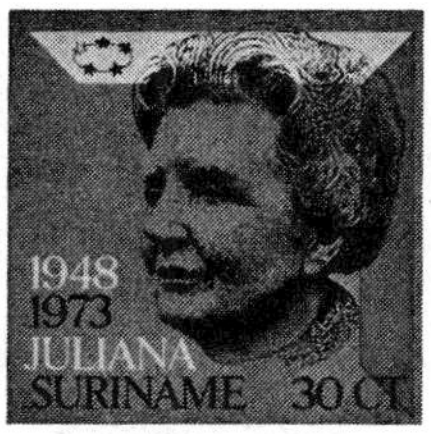

Queen Juliana, Surinam and House of Orange Colors A97a

Engr. & Litho.

1973, Sept. 4 *Perf. 12½*

405 A97a 30c sil, blk & org 50 50

25th anniversary of reign of Queen Juliana.

INTERPOL Emblem A98

Mailman A99

Design: 30c, INTERPOL emblem, Surinam visa handstamp.

1973, Nov. 7 Litho. *Perf. 14x14½*

406 A98 15c vio bl & multi 15 15
407 A98 30c lt bl, lil & blk 24 24

50th anniv. of Intl. Criminal Police Org.

1973, Dec. 12 Litho. *Perf. 12½*

Designs: 15c, Pigeons carrying Letters. 30c, Map of Surinam, plane, ship, train and truck.

408 A99 15c lt yel grn & bl 15 15
409 A99 25c sal, blk & bl 24 24
410 A99 30c ver & multi 40 40

Centenary of stamps of Surinam.

Patient and Blood Transfusion A100

Design: 30c, Cross section of tissue and oscilloscope.

1974, June 1 Litho. *Perf. 14½x14*

411 A100 15c red brn & multi 15 15
412 A100 30c lem & multi 24 24

75th anniversary of the Medical College.

Crop Dusting A101

1974, July 17 Litho. *Perf. 13½*

413 A101 15c shown 15 15
414 A101 30c Fertilizer plant 24 24

Foundation for Development of Mechanical Agriculture in Surinam, 25th anniv.

Old Title Page — A102

1974, Aug. 12 *Perf. 14x14½*

415 A102 15c multi 15 15
416 A102 30c multi 24 24

Bicentenary of the "Weekly Wednesday Surinam Newspaper." First editor was Beeldsnijder Matroos.

Paramaribo Main Post Office A103

Design: 30c, Post Office, different view.

1974, Sept. 11 Litho. *Perf. 14½x14*

417 A103 15c brn & blk 15 15
418 A103 30c bl & blk 24 24

Centenary of Universal Postal Union.

Gold Panner A104

Design: 30c, Modern excavator.

1975, Feb. 5 Litho. *Perf. 13x12½*

419 A104 15c brn & ol bis 15 15
420 A104 30c ver & mar 24 24

Centenary of prospecting policy granting concessions for winning of raw materials.

Symbolic Design A105

1975, June 25 Litho. *Perf. 13x12½*

421 A105 15c grn & multi 32 32
422 A105 25c bl & multi 32 32
423 A105 30c red & multi 32 32

Cent. of Intl. Meter Convention, Paris, 1875.

Hands Holding Saw — A106

Designs: 50c, Book with notes and letter "a". 75c, Hands holding ball.

1975, Nov. 25 Litho. *Perf. 13x14*

424 A106 25c yel, red & brn 22 22
425 A106 50c yel, red & pur 42 42
426 A106 75c dk bl, org & emer 65 65

Independence. Sheets of 10 (5x2) with ornamental margins.

Oncidium Lanceanum A107

Central Bank, Paramaribo A109

Orchids: 2c, Epidendrum stenopetalum. 3c, Brassia lanceana. 4c, Epidendrum ibaguense. 5c, Epidendrum fragrans.

1975-76 Litho. *Perf. 14½x13½*

427 A107 1c multi 5 5
428 A107 2c multi 5 5
429 A107 3c multi 5 5
430 A107 4c multi 5 5
431 A107 5c multi 8 5

Perf. 13½x13

436 A109 1g rose lil & blk 90 25
437 A109 1½g brn, dp org & blk 1.25 25
438 A109 2½g red brn, org red & blk 2.75 32
439 A109 5g grn, yel grn & blk 5.00 52
440 A109 10g dk vio bl & blk 10.00 1.10
Nos. 427-431,436-440 (10) 20.18 2.69

Issue dates: Nos. 436-439, Nov. 25, 1975. Nos. 427-431, Feb. 18, 1976. No. 440, May 6, 1976.

For surcharges, see Nos. 772-774, 810.

Flag of Surinam — A110

1976, Mar. 3 *Perf. 14x13*

Design: 35c, Coat of Arms.

445	A110	25c emer & multi	22	22
446	A110	35c red org & multi	32	32

Sheets of 12 (6x2) with ornamental margins.

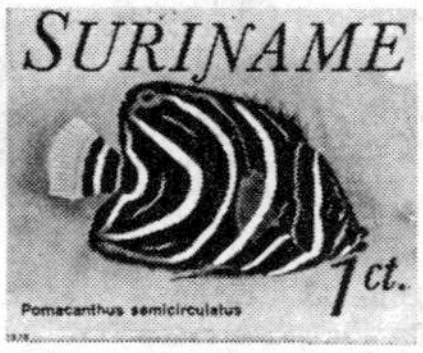

Pomacanthus Semicirculatus — A111

Fish: 2c, Adioryx diadema. 3c, Pogonoculius zebra. 4c, Balistes vetula. 5c, Myripristis jacobus.

1976, June 2 Litho. *Perf. 12½x13*

447	A111	1c multi	5	5
448	A111	2c multi	5	5
449	A111	3c multi	5	5
450	A111	4c multi	5	5
451	A111	5c multi	8	8
		Nos. 447-451,C55-C57 (8)	1.95	1.95

See Nos. 471-475, 504-508, C72-C74, C85-C87.

19th Century Switchboard and Telephone — A112

Design: 35c, Satellite, globe and 1976 telephone.

1976, Aug. 5 Litho. *Perf. 13x13½*

452	A112	20c yel & multi	70	20
453	A112	35c ultra & multi	40	40

Centenary of first telephone call by Alexander Graham Bell, Mar. 10, 1876.

The Story of Anansi Tori, by A. Baag — A113

Designs: 30c, "Surinam Now" (young people), by R. Chang. 35c, Lamentation, by Nola Hatterman (vert.). 50c, Chess Players, by Q. Jan Telting.

Perf. 13x13½, 13½x13

1976, Sept. 29 **Photo.**

454	A113	20c multi	22	22
455	A113	30c multi	32	32
456	A113	35c multi	40	40
457	A113	50c multi	55	55

Paintings by Surinam artists.

Franklin's Divided Snake Poster, 1754 — A114

1976, Nov. 10 Litho. *Perf. 13x13½*

458	A114	20c green & blk	20	20
459	A114	60c orange & blk	65	65

American Bicentennial.

Ionopsis Utricularioides A115

Surinam Costume A116

Orchids: 30c, Rodriguezia secunda. 35c, Oncidium pusillum. 55c, Sobralia sessilis. 60c, Octomeria surinamensis.

1977, Jan. 19 Litho. *Perf. 14½x13*

460	A115	20c ver & multi	22	22
461	A115	30c ultra & multi	32	32
462	A115	35c mag & multi	40	40
463	A115	55c yel & multi	60	60
464	A115	60c grn & multi	65	65
		Nos. 460-464 (5)	2.19	2.19

1977, Mar. 2 Photo. *Perf. 14x13½*

Designs: Various Surinamese women's costumes.

465	A116	10c brt bl & multi	15	10
466	A116	15c grn & multi	15	15
467	A116	35c vio & multi	35	35
468	A116	60c org & multi	65	65
469	A116	75c ultra & multi	80	80
470	A116	1g yel & multi	1.10	1.10
		Nos. 465-470 (6)	3.20	3.15

Fish Type of 1976

1977, June 8 Litho. *Perf. 12½x13*

Tropical Fish: 1c, Liopropoma carmabi. 2c, Holacanthus ciliaris. 3c, Opistognathus aurifrons. 4c, Anisotremus virginicus. 5c, Gramma loreto.

471	A111	1c multi	5	5
472	A111	2c multi	5	5
473	A111	3c multi	5	5
474	A111	4c multi	6	6
475	A111	5c multi	8	8
		Nos. 471-475,C72-C74 (8)	3.09	3.09

Edison's Phonograph, 1877 — A117

Design: 60c, Modern turntable.

1977, Aug. 24 Litho. *Perf. 13½x14*

476	A117	20c multi	20	20
477	A117	60c multi	65	65

Invention of the phonograph, cent.

Packet Curacao, 1827 — A118

Designs: 15c, Hellevoetsluis Harbor and postmark, 1827. 30c, Sea chart and technical details of packet Curacao. 35c, Logbook and compass rose. 60c, Map of Paramaribo harbor and 1852 postmark. 95c, Modern liner Stuyvesant.

1977, Sept. 28 Litho. *Perf. 14x13½*

478	A118	5c grnsh bl & dk bl	8	8
479	A118	15c org & mar	15	15
480	A118	30c lt brn & blk	32	32
481	A118	35c ol & blk	40	40
482	A118	60c lil & blk	65	65
483	A118	95c yel grn & dk grn	1.10	1.10
		Nos. 478-483 (6)	2.70	2.70

Regular steamer connection between the Netherlands and Surinam, 150th anniversary.

Passiflora Quadrangularis A119

Javanese Costume A120

Flowers: 30c, Centropogon surinamensis. 55c, Gloxinia perennis. 60c, Hydrocleis nymphoides. 75c, Clusia grandiflora.

1978, Feb. 8 Litho. *Perf. 13x14*

484	A119	20c multi	20	20
485	A119	30c multi	30	30
486	A119	55c multi	55	55
487	A119	60c multi	60	60
488	A119	75c multi	75	75
		Nos. 484-488 (5)	2.40	2.40

1978, Mar. 1 Photo. *Perf. 14x13*

People of Surinam, Costumes: 20c, Forest black. 35c, Chinese. 60c, Creole. 75c, Aborigine Indian. 1g, Hindustani.

489	A120	10c multi	10	10
490	A120	20c multi	20	20
491	A120	35c multi	32	32
492	A120	60c multi	60	60
493	A120	75c multi	75	75
494	A120	1g multi	1.10	1.10
		Nos. 489-494 (6)	3.07	3.07

Air Post Stamps of 1972 Surcharged

1978 Litho. *Perf. 13x13½*

495	AP6	1c on 25c #C44	5	5
496	AP6	4c on 15c #C42	6	6
497	AP6	4c on 30c #C45	6	6
498	AP6	5c on 40c #C47	8	8
499	AP6	10c on 75c #C54	10	10
		Nos. 495-499 (5)	35	35

"Luchtpost" obliterated with 2 bars.

Old Municipal Church A121

Johannes King — A122

Designs: 55c, New Municipal Church. 60c, Johannes Raillard.

1978, May 31 Litho. *Perf. 14x13*

500	A121	10c bl, blk & gray	10	10
501	A122	20c gray & blk	24	24
502	A121	55c rose lil & blk	55	55
503	A122	60c org & blk	65	65

Evangelical Brothers Community Church, Paramaribo, bicentenary.

Tropical Fish Type of 1976

Tropical Fish: 1c, Nannacara Anomala. 2c, Leporinus fasciatus. 3c, Pristella riddlei. 4c, Nannostomus beckfordi. 5c, Rivulus agilae.

1978, June 21 *Perf. 12½x13*

504	A111	1c multi	5	5
505	A111	2c multi	5	5
506	A111	3c multi	5	5
507	A111	4c multi	5	5
508	A111	5c multi	6	5
		Nos. 504-508,C85-C87 (8)	3.26	3.25

Souvenir Sheet

Commewijne River Development A124

Designs: 60c, Map of Surinam and dam. 95c, Planes and world map.

1978, Oct. 18 Litho. *Perf. 13½x14*

509		Sheet of 3	1.65	1.65
a	A124	20c multi	15	15
b	A124	60c multi	50	50
c	A124	95c multi	75	75

Development.

Coconuts — A125

1978-85 Photo. *Perf. 13x12½*

510	A125	5c shown	6	6
a		Bklt. pane of 12 (4 #510, 3 #511, 5 #515) ('80)	1.75	
511	A125	10c Oranges	8	8
512	A125	15c Papayas	12	12
a		Bklt. pane of 11 + label (5 #512, 6 #514) ('79)	1.75	
513	A125	20c Bananas	15	15
514	A125	25c Soursop	20	20
514A	A125	30c Cocoa beans ('85)	20	20
b		Bklt. pane of 7 + label (6 #514A, 1 #513) ('85)	1.25	1.25
515	A125	35c Watermelon	28	28
		Nos. 510-515 (7)	1.09	1.09

Wright Brothers' Flyer 1 — A126

Designs: 20c, Daedalus and Icarus (vert.). 95c, DC 8. 125c, Concorde.

Perf. 13x14, 14x13

1978, Dec. 13 **Litho.**

516	A126	20c multi	15	15
517	A126	60c multi	50	50
518	A126	95c multi	75	75
519	A126	125c multi	1.00	1.00

75th anniversary of 1st powered flight.

Rodriguezia Candida A127

Javanese Dancer A128

Flowers: 20c, Stanhopea grandiflora. 35c, Scuticaria steelei. 60c, Bollea violacea.

1979, Feb. 7 Photo. *Perf. 12½x14*

520	A127	10c multi	8	8
521	A127	20c multi	15	15
522	A127	35c multi	28	28
523	A127	60c multi	50	50

1979, Feb. 28

Dancing Costumes: 10c, Forest Negro. 15c, Chinese. 20c, Creole. 25c, Aborigine Indian. 35c, Hindustani.

524	A128	5c multi	6	6
525	A128	10c multi	8	8
526	A128	15c multi	15	15
527	A128	20c multi	14	14
528	A128	25c multi	20	20
529	A128	35c multi	28	28
		Nos. 524-529 (6)	91	91

Equetus Pulchellus A129

Tropical Fish: 2c, Apogon binotatus. 3c, Anisotremus virginicus. 5c, Bodianus rufus. 35c, Microspathodon chrysurus.

1979, May 30 Photo. *Perf. 14x13*

530 A129 1c multi 5 5
531 A129 2c multi 5 5
532 A129 3c multi 5 5
533 A129 5c multi 6 6
534 A129 35c multi 28 28
Nos. 530-534,C89-C91 (8) 2.67 2.67

See Nos. 557-561, C92-C94.

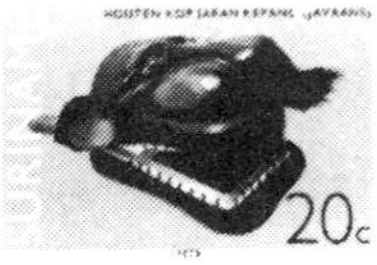

Javanese Wooden Head — A130

Folkart: 35c, Head ornament, Indian. 60c, Horse's head, Javanese.

1979, Aug. 29 Litho. *Perf. 14x13*

535 A130 20c multi 15 15
536 A130 35c multi 28 28
537 A130 60c multi 50 50

Sir Rowland Hill A131

Javanese Girl's Costume A133

SOS Emblem, House A132

1979, Oct. 3 Litho. *Perf. 13x14*

538 A131 1g yel & olive 80 80

Sir Rowland Hill (1795-1879), originator of penny postage.

1979, Oct. 3 *Perf. 14x13*

Design: 60c, SOS emblem and buildings.

539 A132 20c multi 15 15
540 A132 60c multi 50 50

Intl. Year of the Child; SOS Children's Villages, 30th anniv.

1980, Feb. 6 Photo. *Perf. 13x14*

541 A133 10c shown 8 8
542 A133 15c Forest Black boy 12 12
543 A133 25c Chinese girl 20 20
544 A133 60c Creole girl 50 50
545 A133 90c Indian girl 70 70
546 A133 1g Hindustani boy 80 80
Nos. 541-546 (6) 2.40 2.40

Rotary Intl., 75th Anniversary A134

Design: 20c, Handshake, Rotary emblem (vert.).

Perf. 13x14, 14x13

1980, Feb. 23 Litho.

547 A134 20c ultra & yel 15 15
548 A134 60c ultra & yel 50 50

Rowland Hill — A135

Weight Lifting — A136

1980, May 6 Litho. *Perf. 13x14*

549 A135 50c Mailcoach 40 40
550 A135 1g shown 80 80
a Souvenir sheet 80 80
551 A135 2g People mailing letters 1.65 1.65

London 1980 Intl. Stamp Exhibition, May 6-14. No. 550a contains No. 550 in changed colors. Blue and black margin shows designs of Nos. 549, 551, London 1980 emblem. (No. 550 in lilac rose and multicolored; stamps of No. 550a in light green and multicolored).

1980, June 17

552 A136 20c shown 15 15
553 A136 30c Diving 24 24
554 A136 50c Gymnast 40 40
555 A136 75c Basketball 60 60
556 A136 150c Running 1.25 1.25
a Souvenir sheet of 3, #554-556 2.25 2.25
Nos. 552-556 (5) 2.64 2.64

22nd Summer Olympic Games, Moscow, July 19-Aug. 3.

Fish Type of 1979

Tropical Fish: 10c, Osteoglossum bicirrhosum. 15c, Colossoma species. 25c, Hemigrammus pulcher. 30c, Petitella georgiae. 45c, Copeina guttata.

1980, Sept. 10 Photo. *Perf. 14x13*

557 A129 10c multi 8 8
558 A129 15c multi 12 12
559 A129 25c multi 20 20
560 A129 30c multi 24 24
561 A129 45c multi 35 35
Nos. 557-561,C92-C94 (8) 2.74 2.74

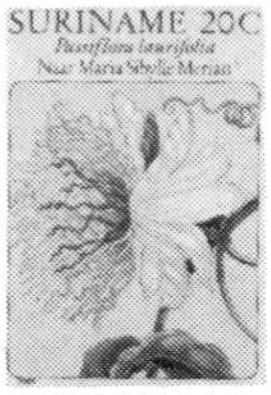

Open Hands (Reflection) A137

Passiflora Laurifolia A138

Souvenir Sheet

1980, Nov. 19 Litho. *Perf. 13x14*

562 Sheet of 3 2.75 2.75
a A137 50c shown 40 40
b A137 1g Shaking hands (cooperation) 70 70
c A137 2g Victory sign 1.65 1.65

5th anniv. of independence.

1981, Jan. 14 Litho. *Perf. 13x14*

Designs: Flower paintings by Maria Sibylle Merian (1647-1717).

563 A138 20c shown 15 15
564 A138 30c Aphelandra pectinata 24 24
565 A138 60c Caesalpinia pulcherrima 50 50
566 A138 75c Hibiscus mutabilis 60 60
567 A138 1.25g Hippeastrum puniceum 1.10 1.10
Nos. 563-567 (5) 2.59 2.59

Renovation of the Economic Order — A139

1981, Feb. 25 *Perf. 14x13*

568 A139 30c shown 24 24
569 A139 60c Educational Order 50 50
570 A139 75c Social Order 60 60
571 A139 1g Political Order 80 80
a Souvenir sheet of 2, #569, 571

Government renovation.

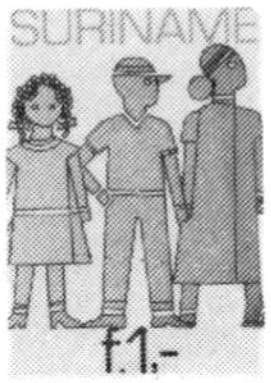

Youths — A140

1981, Apr. 29 Litho. *Perf. 13½*

572 Sheet of 2 2.00 2.00
a A140 1g shown 80 80
b A140 1.50g Youths, diff. 80 80

Youth and its future. Entire sheet in continuous design; multicolored margin also shows map of Surinam. Size: 117x70mm.

Souvenir Sheet

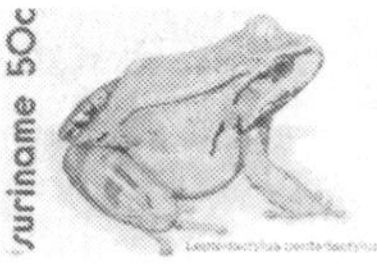

No. 424, Exhibition Hall — A141

1981, May 22 Litho. *Perf. 13½x14*

573 Sheet of 3 2.75 2.75
a A141 50c shown 40 40
b A141 1g Penny Black 80 80
c A141 2g Austria #5 1.65 1.65

WIPA '81 Intl. Philatelic Exhibition, Vienna, May 22-31.

Leptodactylus Pentadactylus A142

1981, June 24 Photo. *Perf. 14x13*

574 A142 40c Phyllomedusa hypochondrialis 32 32
575 A142 50c shown 40 40
576 A142 60c Hyla boans 50 50
Nos. 574-576,C95-C97 (6) 3.62 3.62

Child Wearing Earphones A143

1981, Sept. 16 Litho. *Perf. 14x13*

580 A143 50c shown 40 40
581 A143 100c Child reading Braille 80 80
582 A143 150c Woman in wheelchair 1.25 1.25

Intl. Year of the Disabled.

Planter's House on Parakreek River — A144

Designs: Illustrations from Voyage to Surinam, by P.I. Benoit.

1981, Oct. 21 Photo. *Perf. 14x13*

583 A144 20c shown 15 15
584 A144 30c Sarameca St., Paramaribo 22 22
585 A144 75c Negro Hamlet, Paramaribo 60 60
586 A144 1g Fish Market, Paramaribo 80 80
a Miniature sheet of 1 85 85
587 A144 1.25g Blaauwe Berg Cascade 1.00 1.00
Nos. 583-587 (5) 2.77 2.77

Research and Peaceful Uses of Space A145

1982, Jan. 13 Litho.

588 A145 35c Satellites 25 25
589 A145 65c Columbia space shuttle 50 50
590 A145 1g Apollo-Soyuz 80 80

Caretta Caretta A146

1982, Feb. 17 Photo. *Perf. 14x13*

591 A146 5c shown 6 6
592 A146 10c Chelonia mydas 8 8
593 A146 20c Dermochelys coriacea 15 15
594 A146 25c Eretmochelys imbricata 20 20
595 A146 35c Lepidochelys olivacea 25 25
Nos. 591-595,C98-C100 (8) 2.84 2.84

25th Anniv. of Lions Intl. in Surinam A147

1982, May 7 Litho.

596 A147 35c multi 25 25
597 A147 70c multi 52 52

Beatification of Father Petrus Donders, May 23 — A148

1982, May 18 Litho. *Perf. 13x14*

598 A148 35c Helping the sick 25 25
599 A148 65c Birthplace, map 50 50
a Souvenir sheet 50 50

PHILEXFRANCE '82 Stamp Exhibition, Paris, June 11-21 — A149

1982, June 9 Litho. *Perf. 13x14*

600 A149 50c Stamp designing 40 40
601 A149 100c Printing 85 85
602 A149 150c Collecting 1.25 1.25
a Souvenir sheet of 3, #600-602 2.50 2.50

Nos. 600-602 in continuous design.

TB Bacillus Centenary
A150

1982, Sept. 15 Litho. *Perf. 14x13*

603 A150 35c Text 25 25
604 A150 65c Microscope 50 50
605 A150 150c Bacillus 1.25 1.25

Marienburg Sugar Co. Centenary
A151

1982, Oct. 20

606 A151 35c Mill 25 25
607 A151 65c Gathering cane 50 50
608 A151 100c Rail transport 80 80
609 A151 150c Gears 1.25 1.25

EBG Missionaries, 250th Anniv. in Caribbean
A152

Inga Edulis
A153

Designs: 35c, Municipal Church, horiz. 65c, St. Thomas Monastery, horiz. 150c, Johan Leonhardt Dober (1706-1766).

Perf. 14x13, 13x14

1982, Dec. 13 Litho.

610 A152 35c multi 25 25
611 A152 65c multi 50 50
612 A152 150c multi 1.25 1.25

1983, Jan. 12

Flower Paintings by Maria Sibylle Merian (1647-1717). Nos. 613-618 horiz.

613 A153 1c Erythrina fusca 5 5
614 A153 2c Ipomoea acuminata 5 5
615 A153 3c Heliconia psittacorum 5 5
616 A153 5c Ipomoea 6 6
617 A153 10c Herba non denominata 8 8
618 A153 15c Anacardium occidentale 12 12
619 A153 20c shown 15 15
620 A153 25c Abelmoschus moschatus 20 20
621 A153 30c Argemone mexicana 24 24
622 A153 35c Costus arabicus 28 28
623 A153 45c Muellera frutescens 35 35
624 A153 65c Punica granatum 52 52
Nos. 613-624 (12) 2.15 2.15

Scouting Year — A154

500th Birth Anniv. of Raphael — A155

1983, Feb. 22 Litho. *Perf. 13x14*

625 A154 40c Anniv. emblem 32 32
626 A154 65c Baden-Powell 50 50
627 A154 70c Tent, campfire 52 52
628 A154 80c Ax in log 65 65

1983, Apr. 13 Photo.

Crayon sketches.

629 A155 5c multi 6 6
630 A155 10c multi 8 8
631 A155 40c multi 32 32
632 A155 65c multi 50 50
633 A155 70c multi 52 52
634 A155 80c multi 65 65
Nos. 629-634 (6) 2.13 2.13

1982 Coins and Banknotes
A156

1983, June 1 Litho. *Perf. 14x13*

635 A156 5c 1-cent coin 6 6
636 A156 10c 5-cent coin 8 8
637 A156 40c 10-cent coin 32 32
638 A156 65c 25-cent coin 50 50
639 A156 70c 1g note 55 55
640 A156 80c 2.50g note 65 65
Nos. 635-640 (6) 2.16 2.16

For surcharge, see No. 751. For overprints see Nos. J59-J60.

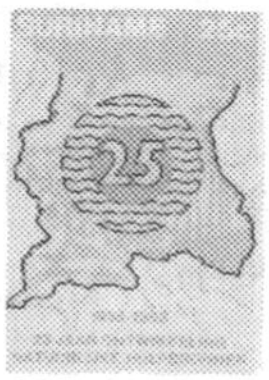

25th Anniv. of Dept. of Construction
A157

Manned Ballooning, 200th Anniv.
A159

Local Butterflies
A158

1983, June 15 Litho. *Perf. 13x14*

641 A157 25c Map 20 20
642 A157 50c Map, bulldozers 40 40

Perf. 13x14, 14x13

1983, Sept. 14 Litho.

Drawings by Maria Sibylle Merian (1647-1717). Nos. 643-648 vert.

643 A158 1c Papile anchisiades esper 5 5
644 A158 2c Urania leilus 5 5
645 A158 3c Morpho deidamia 5 5
646 A158 5c Thysania aguippina 6 6
647 A158 10c Morpho sp. 8 8
648 A158 15c Metamorpha dido 12 12
649 A158 20c Morpho menelaus 15 15
650 A158 25c Manduca rustica 20 20
651 A158 30c Rothschildia sp. 24 24
652 A158 35c Catopsilia ebule 30 30
653 A158 45c Pailio androgeos 40 40
654 A148 65c Eumorpha vitis 60 60
Nos. 643-654 (12) 2.30 2.30

1983, Oct. 19 Litho. *Perf. 13x14*

Designs: 5c, 1783, sheep, cock and duck. 10c, first manned flight, d'Arlandes and Pilatre de Rozier. 40c, first hydrogen balloon, Jacques Charles. 65c, 1870, Paris flight, minister Gambetta. 70c, Double Eagle II, transatlantic flight. 80c, Intl. Balloon Festival, Albuquerque.

655 A159 5c multi 6 6
656 A159 10c multi 8 8
657 A159 40c multi 32 32
658 A159 65c multi 50 50
659 A159 70c multi 55 55
660 A159 80c multi 65 65
Nos. 655-660 (6) 2.16 2.16

Martin Luther, 500th Birth Anniv. — A160

1983, Dec. 7 Litho.

661 A160 25c Portrait 20 20
662 A160 50c Engraving 40 40

Local Flowers — A161

Local Seashells — A162

1984, Jan. 11 Litho.

663 A161 5c Catasetum discolor 6 6
664 A161 10c Menadenium labiosum 8 8
665 A161 40c Comparettia falcata 32 32
666 A161 50c Rodriquezia decora 50 50
667 A161 70c Oncidium papilio 55 55
668 A161 75c Epidendrum porpax 60 60
Nos. 663-668 (6) 2.11 2.11

1984, Feb. 22 Litho.

669 A162 40c Arca zebra 32 32
670 A162 65c Trachycardium egmontianum 55 55
671 A162 70c Tellina radiata 55 55
672 A162 80c Vermicularia knorrii 65 65

Intl. Civil Aviation Org., 40th Anniv.
A163

1984, May 16 Litho. *Perf. 14x13*

673 A163 35c Sea plane 28 25
674 A163 65c Surinam Airways jet 55 55

1984 Summer Olympics — A164

Greek Art and Artifacts: Ancient Games.

1984, June 13 *Perf. 13x14*

675 A164 2c Running 5 5
676 A164 3c Javelin, discus, long jump 5 5
677 A164 5c Massage 6 6
678 A164 10c Ointment massage 8 8
679 A164 15c Wrestling 12 12
680 A164 20c Boxing 15 15
681 A164 30c Horse racing 24 24
682 A164 35c Chariot racing 28 28
683 A164 45c Temple of Olympia 35 35
684 A164 50c Crypt entrance 42 42
685 A164 65c Olympia Stadium 55 55
686 A164 75c Zeus (bust) 60 60
a Miniature sheet of 3 (#675, 682, 686) 1.00 1.00
Nos. 675-686 (12) 2.95 2.95

Intl. Council of Military Sports Basketball Championship
A165

1984, Sept. 18 Litho. *Perf. 13x14*

687 A165 50c Ball, net 42 42
688 A165 90c Ball in net 70 70

World Chess Championship, Moscow
A166

1984, Oct. 10 Litho. *Perf. 14x13*

689 A166 10c Red Square 8 8
690 A166 15c Knight, king, pawn 12 12
691 A166 30c Kasparov 24 24
692 A166 50c Board 42 42
693 A166 75c Karpov 65 65
a Souvenir sheet of 3 (30c, 50c, 75c) 1.25 1.25
694 A166 90c Game 70 70
Nos. 689-694 (6) 2.21 2.21

For surcharges, see Nos. 742, 796.

World Food Day, Oct. 16 — A167

1984, Oct. 10

695 A167 50c Children receiving milk 42 42
696 A167 90c Food 70 70

Cacti
A168

Independence, 5th Anniv.
A169

1985, Jan. 9 Litho. *Perf. 13x14*

697 A168 5c Leaf 6 6
698 A168 10c Melon 8 8
699 A168 30c Pillar 22 22
700 A168 50c Fig 35 35
701 A168 75c Nightqueen 55 55
702 A168 90c Segment 65 65
Nos. 697-702 (6) 1.91 1.91

1985, Feb. 22 Litho. *Perf. 12½x14*

Designs, 5c, Star, red stripe from national flag. 30c, Unified labor. 50c, Perpetual flowering plant. 75c, Growth of agriculture. 90c, Peace dove and plant.

703 A169 5c multi 5 5
704 A169 30c multi 20 20
705 A169 50c multi 32 32
a Miniature sheet of 3 (2 #703, 1 #705) 42
706 A169 75c multi 50 50
707 A169 90c multi 60 60
Nos. 703-707 (5) 1.67 1.67

Values quoted in this catalogue are for stamps graded at Fine-Very Fine and with no faults. An illustrated guide to grade is provided in introductory material, beginning on Page V.

Chamber of Commerce and Industry, 75th Anniv. — A170

UN Emblem, Natl. Coat of Arms — A171

1985, Apr. 17 Litho. *Perf. 14x12½*
708 A170 50c Chamber emblem 32 32
709 A170 90c Chamber, factories 60 60

1985, Apr. 29 Litho. *Perf. 13x14*
710 A171 50c multi 32 32
711 A171 90c multi 60 60

UN, 40th anniv.

Trains — A172

1985, June 5 Litho. *Perf. 13½*
712 A172 5c No. 192 5 5
713 A172 5c Monaco, No. J50 5 5
714 A172 10c Locomotive "Dam" 8 8
715 A172 10c Diesel locomotive 8 8
716 A172 20c Steam locomotive "No. 3737" 12 12
717 A172 20c Netherlands locomotive "IC III" 12 12
718 A172 30c Stephenson's locomotive "Rocket" 20 20
719 A172 30c French Railways high-speed TGV 20 20
720 A172 50c Stephenson's locomotive "Adler" 32 32
721 A172 50c French Railways commuter train 32 32
722 A172 75c Locomotive "General" 50 50
723 A172 75c Japanese bullet train "Shinkansen" 50 50
Nos. 712-723 (12) 2.54 2.54

Stamps of the same denomination se-tenant. For surcharges, see Nos. 749-750, 808-809.

Birds — A173

1985-86 Litho. *Perf. 14x13*
729 A173 1g American purple fowl 65 65
a Miniature sheet of 1 65 65
730 A173 1.50g Tiger bird 1.00 1.00
732 A173 2.50g Red ibis 1.65 1.65
734 A173 5g Guyana red cockerel ('86) 3.25 3.25
735 A173 10g Harpy eagle ('86) 7.50 7.50
Nos. 729-735 (5) 14.05 14.05

Issue dates: Nos. 729, 729a, 1.50g, 2.50g, Aug. 21. 5g, Jan. 2, 1986. 10g, Oct. 1, 1986.
For overprint, see No. J63.

Mailboxes A174

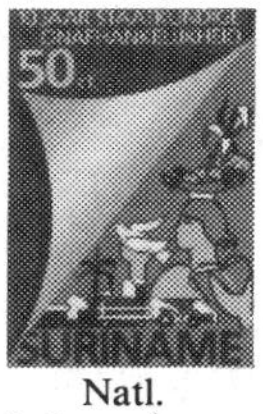
Natl. Independence, 10th Anniv. A175

1985, Oct. 2 Litho. *Perf. 13x14*
736 A174 15c Germany, 1900 10 10
737 A174 30c France, 1900 20 20
738 A174 50c England, 1932 32 32
739 A174 90c Netherlands, 1850 60 60

1985, Nov. 22
740 A175 50c Agriculture 32 32
741 A175 90c Industry 60 60
a Miniature sheet of 2, #740-741 95 95

No. 691 Ovptd. in Red

КАСПАРОВ
Wereldkampioen
9 nov. 1985

1985, Nov. 22 Litho. *Perf. 14x13*
742 A166 30c multi 22 22

World Wildlife Fund — A177

Orchids.

1986, Feb. 19 Litho. *Perf. 14x13*
743 A177 5c Epidendrum ciliare 5 5
744 A177 15c Cycnoches chlorochilon 10 10
745 A177 30c Epidendrum anceps 20 20
746 A177 50c Epidendrum vespa 32 32

Halley's Comet — A178

Designs: 50c, The Bayeux Tapestry, c. 1092, France. 110c, Halley's Comet.

1986, Mar. 5 Litho. *Perf. 14x12½*
747 A178 50c multi 32 32
748 A178 110c multi 70 70

Nos. 720-721 Surcharged in Red

1986, May 28 Litho. *Perf. 13½*
749 A172 15c on 50c #720 12 12
750 A172 15c on 50c #721 12 12

No. 639 Surcharged

30c

150 jaar FINANCIËNGEBOUW

1986, June 25 Litho. *Perf. 14x13*
751 A156 30c on 70c multi 22 22

Finance Building, Paramaribo, 150th anniv.

Surinam Shipping Co., 50th Anniv. A179

1986, Sept. 1 Litho. *Perf. 14x13*
752 A179 50c Emblem 38 38
753 A179 110c Freighter Saramacca 85 85

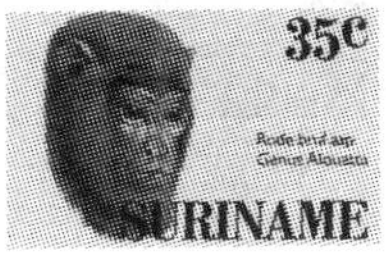
Monkeys A180

1987, Jan. 7 Litho.
755 A180 35c Alouatta 25 25
756 A180 60c Aotus 42 42
757 A180 110c Saimiri 85 85
758 A180 120c Cacajao 90 90

Esperanto, Cent. A181

1987, Feb. 4 Litho.
759 A181 60c shown 42 42
760 A181 110 World map, doves 85 85
761 A181 120c L.L. Zamenhof 90 90

10th Pan-American Games, Indianapolis, July 23 — A182

Forestry Commission, 40th Anniv. — A183

1987, June 3 Litho. *Perf. 13x14*
763 A182 90c Soccer 65 65
764 A182 110c Swimming 85 85
765 A182 150c Basketball 1.10 1.10

1987, July 21 Litho. *Perf. 13x14*
766 A183 90c Emblem 65 65
767 A183 120c Logging 90 1.10
768 A183 150c Parrot in virgin forest 1.10 1.10

Intl. Year of Shelter for the Homeless A184

1987, Sept. 2 Litho. *Perf. 14x13*
769 A184 90c Distressed boy, encampment 65 65
770 A184 120c Man, ghetto 90 90

Founders Catherine and William Booth A185

1987, Sept. 2 *Perf. 14x13*
771 A185 150c multi 1.10 1.10

Salvation Army in the Caribbean, cent.

Nos. 436-438 Surcharged

35 ct

1987, Mar. Litho. *Perf. 13½x13*
772 A109 35c on 1g rose lil & blk 25 25
773 A109 50c on 1.50g brn, dp org & blk 38 38
774 A109 60c on 2.50g red brn, org red & blk 45 45

Fruits — A186

Perf. 12½x13½
1987, Oct. 14 Litho.
775 A186 10c Bananas 8 8
776 A186 15c Cacao 12 12
777 A186 20c Pineapple 15 15
778 A186 25c Papaya 20 20
779 A186 35c Oranges 28 28
Nos. 775-779 (5) 83 83

Aircraft and Aircraft on Stamps — A187

1987, Oct. 14 Litho. *Perf. 13½*
784 A187 25c Degen, 1808 20 20
785 A187 25c Ultra Light 20 20
786 A187 35c J.C.H. Ellehammer, 1906 28 28
787 A187 35c Concorde jet 28 28
788 A187 60c Fokker F7, 1924 48 48
789 A187 60c Fokker F28 jet 48 48
790 A187 90c Spin Fokker, 1910 70 70
791 A187 90c DC-10 70 70
792 A187 110c Orion, 1932 90 90
793 A187 110c Boeing 747 90 90
794 A187 120c No. 346 95 95
795 A187 120c No. 518 95 95
Nos. 784-795 (12) 7.02 7.02

Stamps of the same denominaion printed se-tenant.

Souvenir Sheet

No. 693a Overprinted "3e match sevilla 1987" on Stamps in 3 or 4 Lines and with Bar and "sevilla 1987" in Sheet Margin

1987, Nov. 2 Litho. *Perf. 14x13*
796 Sheet of 3
a. A166 30c Kasparov
b. A166 50c Board
c. A166 75c Karpov

Alligators and Crocodiles A188

1988, Jan. 20 Litho. *Perf. 14x13*
797 A188 50c Gavialis gangeticus 40 40
798 A188 60c Crocodylus niloticus 48 48
799 A188 90c Melanosuchus niger 70 70
800 A188 110c Mississippi alligator 90 90

Traditional Wedding Costumes — A189

1988, Feb. 24 Litho. *Perf. 13x14*
801 A189 35c Javanese 28 28
802 A189 60c Bushman 48 48
803 A189 80c Chinese 65 65
804 A189 110c Creole 90 90
805 A189 120c Indian 95 95
806 A189 130c Hindustan 1.10 1.10
Nos. 801-806 (6) 4.36 4.36

Nos. 722-723 and 440 Surcharged in Black or Silver

60 c
a

125 c
b

Perf. 13½x13, 13½
1988, Mar. 23 Litho.
808 A172(a) 60c on 75c No. 722
809 A172(a) 60c on 75c No. 723

810 A109(b) 125c on 10g No. 440 (S)

Nos. 808-809 printed se-tenant.

1988 Summer Olympics, Seoul — A190

Abolition of Slavery, 125th Anniv. — A191

1988, May 4 Litho. *Perf. 13x14*

812	A190	90c	Relay	65	65
813	A190	110c	Soccer	85	85
814	A190	120c	Pole vault	90	90
a.			Souv. sheet of 3, #812-814	2.50	2.50
815	A190	250c	Women's tennis	1.90	1.90

1988, June 29 Litho.

816	A191	50c	Abaisa Monument	58	58
817	A191	110c	Kwakoe Monument	1.25	1.25
818	A191	120c	Home of Anton de Kom	1.35	1.35

See Netherlands Antilles Nos. 597-598.

Intl. Fund for Agricultural Development (IFAD), 10th Anniv. A192

1988, Sept. 21 *Perf. 14x13*

819	A192	105c	Crop harvest	1.20	1.20
820	A192	110c	Net fishing	1.25	1.25
821	A192	125c	Agricultural research	1.40	1.40

FILACEPT '88, The Netherlands, Oct. 18-23 — A193

1988, Oct. 18 Litho. *Perf. 13*

822	A193	120c	Egypt No. 49	1.15	1.15
823	A193	150c	Netherlands No. 334	1.40	1.40
824	A193	250c	Surinam No. 238	2.35	2.35

Souvenir Sheet

Same Types, Colors Changed (120c, 150c)

825	Sheet of 3	5.00	5.00
a.	A193 120c Egypt Type A23 (4m grn)	1.15	1.15
b.	A193 150c Netherlands Type A81 (10c red brn)	1.40	1.40
c.	A193 250c Surinam No. 239	2.35	2.35

Stylized Butterfly Stroke A194

1988, Nov. 1 Litho. *Perf. 14x13*

826 A194 110c multi 1.25 1.25

Anthony Nesty, swimmer and 1st Olympic gold medalist from Surinam.

Otters — A195

1989, Jan. 18 Litho. *Perf. 14x13*

827	A195	10c	Otter	11	11
828	A195	20c	Two on land	22	22
829	A195	25c	Two crossing log	28	28
830	A195	30c	Fishing	35	35
			Nos. 827-830,C107 (5)	3.01	3.01

SEMI-POSTAL STAMPS

Green Cross

SP1 SP2 SP3

1927 Unwmk. Photo. *Perf. 12½*

B1	SP1	2c (+ 2c)	bl blk & grn	90	90
B2	SP2	5c (+ 3c)	vio & grn	90	90
B3	SP3	10c (+ 3c)	ver & grn	1.50	1.50

Surtax was given to the Green Cross Society, an organization similar to the Red Cross Society in other countries.

Nurse and Patient SP4

Good Samaritan SP5

1928, Dec. 1 *Perf. 11½*

B4	SP4	1½c (+ 1½c)	ultra	4.00	4.00
B5	SP4	2c (+ 2c)	bl grn	4.00	4.00
B6	SP4	5c (+ 3c)	vio	4.00	4.00
B7	SP4	7½c (+ 2½c)	ver	4.00	4.00

The surtax on these stamps was for a fund to combat indigenous diseases.

1929, Dec. 1 *Perf. 12½*

B8	SP5	1½c (+ 1½c)	grn	5.50	5.50
B9	SP5	2c (+ 2c)	scar	5.50	5.50
B10	SP5	5c (+ 3c)	ultra	5.50	5.50
B11	SP5	6c (+ 4c)	blk	5.50	5.50

The surtax on these stamps was for the benefit of the Green Cross Society.

Surinam Mother and Child — SP6

1931, Dec. 14

B12	SP6	1½c (+ 1½c)	blk	4.00	4.00
B13	SP6	2c (+ 2c)	car rose	4.00	4.00
B14	SP6	5c (+ 3c)	ultra	4.00	4.00
B15	SP6	6c (+ 4c)	dp grn	4.00	4.00

The surtax was for Child Welfare Societies.

Footnotes often refer you to other stamps of the same design.

Designs Symbolical of the Creed of the Moravians

SP7 SP8

1935, Aug. 1 *Perf. 12½x13½*

B16	SP7	1c (+ ½c)	dk brn	2.00	1.65
B17	SP7	2c (+ 1c)	dp ultra	2.25	1.65
B18	SP8	3c (+ 1½c)	grn	2.75	2.75
B19	SP8	4c (+ 2c)	red org	2.75	2.75
B20	SP8	5c (+ 2½c)	blk brn	2.75	3.00
B21	SP7	10c (+ 5c)	car	2.75	3.00
			Nos. B16-B21 (6)	15.25	14.80

200th anniv. of the founding of the Moravian Mission in Surinam.

Surinam Child — SP9

1936, Dec. 14 *Perf. 12½*

B22	SP9	2c (+ 1c)	dk grn	2.75	2.75
B23	SP9	3c (+ 1½c)	dk bl	2.75	2.75
B24	SP9	5c (+ 2½c)	brn blk	3.25	3.25
B25	SP9	10c (+ 5c)	lake	3.25	3.25

"Emancipation" SP10

Surinam Girl SP11

1938, June 1 Litho. *Perf. 12½x12*

B26 SP10 2½c (+ 2c) dk bl grn 1.75 1.50

Photo.

B27	SP11	3c (+ 2c)	vio blk	1.75	1.50
B28	SP11	5c (+ 3c)	dk brn	1.75	1.75
B29	SP11	7½c (+ 5c)	ind	1.75	1.75

75th anniv. of the abolition of slavery in Surinam.

Creole Woman SP12

Javanese Woman SP13

Hindustani Woman SP14

American Indian Woman SP15

1940 Engr. *Perf. 12½x14*

B30	SP12	2½c (+ 2c)	dk grn	2.25	1.75
B31	SP13	3c (+ 2c)	red org	2.25	1.75
B32	SP14	5c (+ 3c)	dp bl	2.25	1.75
B33	SP15	7½c (+ 5c)	hn brn	2.25	1.75

Catalogue values for unused stamps in this section, from this point to the end of the section, are for Never Hinged items.

Netherlands Coat of Arms and Inscription, "Netherlands Shall Rise Again" — SP16

1941, Aug. 30 Typo. *Perf. 12½*

B34	SP16	7½c + 7½c dp org, ultra & blk	2.25	2.25
B35	SP16	15c + 15c scar, ultra & blk	2.75	2.75
B36	SP16	1g + 1g gray & ultra	18.00	14.00

The surtax was used to buy bombers for Dutch pilots in the Royal Air Force of Great Britain.

Stamps of 1936-41 Surcharged in Red:

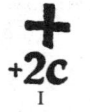

+2c I

+2c II

+5c III +5c IV +5c V

1942, Jan. 2

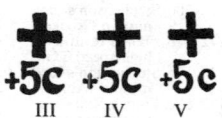

B37	A23	2c + 2c blk brn, I	1.65	1.65
a		Type II	1.65	1.65
B38	A26	2c + 2c blk brn, I	42.50	35.00
a		Type II	42.50	35.00
B39	A23	2½c + 2c green, I	1.65	1.65
a		Type II	1.65	1.65
B40	A23	7½c + 5c red vio, III	1.65	1.65
a		Type IV	6.50	6.50
b		Type V	16.00	16.00

The surtax was for the Red Cross.

In type III, the "c" may be "large," as illustrated, or "small," as in type II. Value is the same.

The distinctive feature of type IV is the pointed ending of the lower part of the "5."

Types of Regular Issue of 1945 Surcharged in Black

5 CENT VOOR HET NATIONAAL STEUNFONDS

Unwmk.

1945, July 23 Engr. *Perf. 12*

B41	A29	7½c + 5c	dp org	2.75	1.65
B42	A30	15c + 10c	brn	2.00	1.65
B43	A30	20c + 15c	dl grn	2.00	1.65
B44	A30	22½c + 20c	gray	2.00	1.65
B45	A30	40c + 35c	rose lake	2.00	1.65
B46	A30	60c + 50c	vio	2.00	1.65
			Nos. B41-B46 (6)	12.75	9.90

Surtax for the National Welfare Fund.

Star SP17

Marie Curie SP18

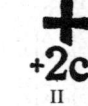

Perf. 13½x12½

1947, Dec. 16 **Photo.**

B47	SP17	7½c + 12½c red org	2.00	2.00
B48	SP17	12½c + 37½c bl	2.00	2.00

The surtax was used to combat leprosy. See Nos. CB4-CB5.

1950, May 15 *Perf. 14x13*

Designs: 7½c+22½c, 27½c+12½c, William Roentgen.

B49	SP18	7½c + 7½c lil	10.00	6.50
B50	SP18	7½c + 22½c dl bl grn	10.00	6.50
B51	SP18	27½c + 12½c dp gray bl	10.00	6.50
B52	SP18	27½c + 97½c red brn	10.00	6.50

The surtax was used to combat cancer.

12½c + 7½c

Nos. 236-237 Surcharged in Black or Red

STORMRAMP NEDERLAND 1953

Perf. 14x13

1953, Feb. 18 **Wmk. 202**

B53	A35	12½c + 7½c on 7½c dl org	2.50	2.25
B54	A35	20c + 10c on 12½c ultra (R)	2.50	2.25

The surtax was for flood relief in the Netherlands.

Stadium, Paramaribo — SP19

Perf. 13½

1953, Aug. 29 **Unwmk.** **Photo.**

B55	SP19	10c + 5c claret	8.25	6.00
B56	SP19	15c + 7½c brn	8.25	6.00
B57	SP19	30c + 15c dk grn	8.25	6.00

Issued to publicize Sport Week, 1953.

Surinam Children — SP20

Doves — SP21

1954, Nov. 1 *Perf. 13x14*

B58	SP20	7½c + 3c sep	5.75	4.50
B59	SP20	10c + 5c bl grn	5.75	4.50
B60	SP20	15c + 7½c red brn	5.75	4.50
B61	SP20	30c + 15c bl	5.75	4.50

The surtax was for the youth center of the Moravian Church.

1955, May 5 *Perf. 14x13*

B62	SP21	7½c + 3½c brt red	2.50	2.50
B63	SP21	15c + 8c ultra	2.50	2.50

The Netherlands' liberation, 10th anniv.

Queen Juliana and Prince Bernhard SP22

1955, Oct. 27 **Unwmk.**

B64	SP22	7½c + 2½c dk ol	50	50

Royal visit to Surinam, 1955.

Theater, 1837 — SP23

Designs: 10c+5c, Theater and car, circa 1920. 15c+7½c, Theater and car, circa 1958. 20c+10c, Theater interior.

1958, Feb. 15 **Litho.** *Perf. 13x12½*

B65	SP23	7½c + 3c lt bl & blk	40	40
B66	SP23	10c + 5c rose lil & blk	40	40
B67	SP23	15c + 7½c lt grn & blk	40	40
B68	SP23	20c + 10c org & blk	40	40

120th anniv. of the "Thalia" theatrical society.

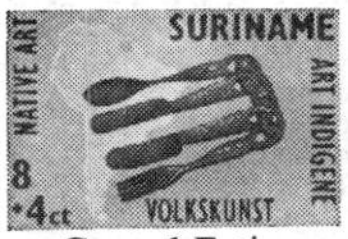

Carved Eating Utensils and Map of South America — SP24

Uprooted Oak Emblem of WRY — SP25

Native Art (Map of So. America and): 10c+5c, Feather headgear. 15c+7c, Clay pottery. 20c+10c, Carved wooden stool.

1960, Jan. 15

B69	SP24	8c + 4c multi	85	85
B70	SP24	10c + 5c sal, red & bl	85	85
B71	SP24	15c + 7c red org, grn & sep	85	85
B72	SP24	20c + 10c lt bl, ultra & bis	85	85

1960, Apr. 7 *Perf. 12½x13½*

B73	SP25	8c + 4c choc & grn	15	15
B74	SP25	10c + 5c vio bl & ol grn	15	15

World Refugee Year, July 1, 1959-June 30, 1960. The surtax was for aid to refugees.

Putting the Shot — SP26

Sports: 10c+5c, Basketball. 15c+7c, Runner. 20c+10c, Swimmer. 40c+20c, Soccer.

1960, Aug. 10 **Photo.** *Perf. 14x13*

B75	SP26	8c + 4c gray, brn & blk	55	55
B76	SP26	10c + 5c red org & blk	55	55
B77	SP26	15c + 7c vio, bis & blk	85	85
B78	SP26	20c + 10c bl, bis & blk	85	85
B79	SP26	40c + 20c emer, brn & blk	85	85
		Nos. B75-B79 (5)	3.65	3.65

17th Olympic Games, Rome, Aug. 25-Sept. 11.

Girl Scout Signaling SP27

Designs: 10c+3c, Scout Saluting (vert.). 15c+4c, Brownies around toadstool. 20c+5c, Scouts around campfire (vert.). 25c+6c, Scouts cooking outdoors.

Perf. 14x13, 13x14

1961, Aug. 19 **Litho.**

Multicolored Designs

B80	SP27	8c + 2c bl	32	32
B81	SP27	10c + 3c lil	32	32
B82	SP27	15c + 4c yel	32	32
B83	SP27	20c + 5c brn red	40	40
B84	SP27	25c + 6c aqua	40	40
		Nos. B80-B84 (5)	1.76	1.76

Caribbean Girl Scout Jamborette.

Hibiscus SP28

Flowers: 10c+5c, Caesalpinia pulcherrima. 15c+6c, Heliconia psittacorum. 20c+10c, Lochnera rosea. 25c+12c, Ixora macrothyrsa.

1962, Mar. 7 **Photo.** *Perf. 14x13½*

Cross in Red

B85	SP28	8c + 4c dk ol & scar	25	25
B86	SP28	10c + 5c dk bl & org	25	25
B87	SP28	15c + 6c multi	25	25
B88	SP28	20c + 10c multi	25	25
B89	SP28	25c + 12c dk bl grn, red & yel	25	25
		Nos. B85-B89 (5)	1.25	1.25

The surtax was for the Red Cross.

Hands Protecting Duck — SP29

American Indian Girl — SP30

Designs: 8c+2c, Dog. 10c+3c, Donkey. 15c+4c, Horse.

1962, Dec. 15 **Litho.** *Perf. 13x14*

B90	SP29	2c + 1c chlky bl & red	8	8
B91	SP29	8c + 2c blk & red	15	15
B92	SP29	10c + 3c dl grn & blk	15	15
B93	SP29	15c + 4c red & blk	24	24

The surtax was for the Organization for Animal Protection.

1963, Oct. 30 **Photo.** **Unwmk.**

Girls: 10c+4c, Negro. 15c+10c, East Indian. 20c+10c, Indonesian. 40c+20c, Caucasian.

B94	SP30	8c + 3c Prus grn	8	8
B95	SP30	10c + 4c red brn	8	8
a		Minature sheet of 4	1.10	1.10
B96	SP30	15c + 10c dp bl	24	24
B97	SP30	20c + 10c brn red	24	24
B98	SP30	40c + 20c red vio	32	32
		Nos. B94-B98 (5)	96	96

The surtax was for Child Welfare. No. B95a contains two each of Nos. B94-B95.

X-15 — SP31

Designs: 8c+4c, Flag of the Aeronautical and Astronautical Foundation. 10c+5c, 20c+10c, Agena B Ranger rocket.

1964, Apr. 14 *Perf. 13x12½*

B99	SP31	3c + 2c blk & rose lake	15	15
B100	SP31	8c + 4c blk, ultra & lt ultra	15	15
B101	SP31	10c + 5c blk & grn	15	15
B102	SP31	15c + 7c blk & yel brn	15	15
B103	SP31	20c + 10c blk & vio	15	15
		Nos. B99-B103 (5)	75	75

Surtax for the Aeronautical and Astronautical Foundation of Surinam.

Stylized Campfire amid Trees — SP32

Girls Skipping Rope — SP33

1964, July 29 *Perf. 13x14*

B104	SP32	3c + 1c brn ol, yel bis & lem	8	8
B105	SP32	8c + 4c bluish blk, vio bl & yel bis	8	8
B106	SP32	10c + 5c dk red, red & yel bis	15	15
B107	SP32	20c + 10c grnsh blk, ol grn & yel bis	15	15

Jamborette at Paramaribo, Aug. 20-30, marking the 40th anniv. of the Surinam Boy Scout Association.

1964, Nov. 30 **Photo.** *Perf. 14x13*

Designs: 10c+4c, Children on swings. 15c+9c, Girl on scooter. 20c+10c, Boy rolling hoop.

B108	SP33	8c + 3c dk bl	8	8
B109	SP33	10c + 4c red	8	8
a		Minature sheet of 4	42	42
B110	SP33	15c + 9c ol grn	8	8
B111	SP33	20c + 10c mag	15	15

Issued for Child Welfare. No. B109a contains 2 each of Nos. B108-B109.

Mother and Child — SP34

Designs: 4c+2c, Pregnant woman. 15c+7c, Child. 25c+12c, Old man.

1965, Feb. 27 **Photo.** *Perf. 13x14*

B112	SP34	4c + 2c grn	8	8
B113	SP34	10c + 5c brn & grn	12	12
B114	SP34	15c + 7c Prus bl & grn	15	15
B115	SP34	25c + 12c brt pur & grn	20	20

50th anniv. of the Green Cross Assoc. which promotes public health services.

Girl with Leopard and Spider SP35

Designs: 10c+5c, Boy with monkey and spider. 15c+7c, Girl with tortoise and spider. 25c+10c, Boy with rabbit and spider.

Perf. 13x12½

1965, Nov. 26 **Litho.** **Unwmk.**

B116	SP35	4c + 4c lt grn & blk	8	8
B117	SP35	10c + 5c ocher & blk	8	8
B118	SP35	15c + 7c dp org & blk	8	8
a		Minature sheet of 4	42	42
B119	SP35	25c + 10c lt ultra & blk	8	8

Issued for Child Welfare. No. B118a contains 2 each of Nos. B116 and B118.

"Help them to a safe haven" SP35a

1966, Jan. 31 Photo. *Perf. 14x13*

B120	SP35a 10c + 5c blk & grn	10	10
B121	SP35a 25c + 10c blk & rose brn	10	10
a	Min. sheet of 3	42	42

The surtax was for the Intergovernmental Committee for European Migration (ICEM). The message on the stamps was given and signed by Queen Juliana. No. B121a contains two Nos. B120 and one No. B121.

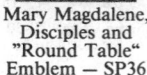

Mary Magdalene, Disciples and "Round Table" Emblem — SP36

"New Year's Eve" Boys with Bamboo Gun — SP37

Mary Magdalene (John 20:18), and Service Club Emblems: 15c+8c, Toastmasters International. 20c+10c, Junior Chamber, Surinam. 25c+12c, Rotary International. 30c+15c, Lions International.

1966, Apr. 13 Photo. *Perf. 12½x13*

B122	SP36 10c + 5c dp crim, blk & gold	15	15
B123	SP36 15c + 8c dp vio, blk & bl	15	15
B124	SP36 20c + 10c yel org, blk & ultra	15	15
B125	SP36 25c + 12c grn, blk & gold	15	15
B126	SP36 30c + 15c ultra, blk & gold	15	15
	Nos. B122-B126 (5)	75	75

Easter.

1966, Nov. 25 Litho. *Perf. 12½x13*

Designs: 15c+8c, "The End of Lent," boys pouring paint over each other. 20c+10c, "Liberation Day," parading children. 25c+12c, "Queen's Birthday," children on hobbyhorses. 30c+15c, "Christmas," Children decorating room with star.

B127	SP37 10c + 5c multi	8	8
B128	SP37 15c + 8c multi	15	15
B129	SP37 20c + 10c multi	8	8
a	Minature sheet of 3	32	32
B130	SP37 25c + 12c multi	15	15
B131	SP37 30c + 15c multi	15	15
	Nos. B127-B131 (5)	61	61

Child welfare. No. B129a contains two No. B127 and one No. B129.

Good Samaritan Giving His Coat SP38

Children Stilt-walking SP39

The Good Samaritan: 15c+8c, Dressing the wounds. 20c+10c, Feeding the poor man. 25c+12c, Poor man riding Samaritan's horse. 30c+15c, Samaritan taking poor man to the inn.

1967, Mar. 22

B132	SP38 10c + 5c yel & blk	8	8
B133	SP38 15c + 8c lt bl & blk	15	15
B134	SP38 20c + 10c buff & blk	15	15
B135	SP38 25c + 12c pale rose & blk	15	15
B136	SP38 30c + 15c grn & blk	15	15
	Nos. B132-B136 (5)	68	68

Easter.

1967, Nov. 27 Litho. *Perf. 12½x13*

Children's Games: 15c+8c, Boys playing with marbles. 20c+10c, Girl playing dibs (five stones). 25c+12c, Boy making kite. 30c+15c, Girls play-cooking.

B137	SP39 10c + 5c multi	7	7
B138	SP39 15c + 8c multi	15	15
B139	SP39 20c + 10c multi	15	15
a	Minature sheet of 3	42	42
B140	SP39 25c + 12c multi	15	15
B141	SP39 30c + 15c multi	15	15
	Nos. B137-B141 (5)	67	67

Child welfare. No. B139a contains two No. B137 and one No. B139.

Cross, Ash Wednesday SP40

Hopscotch SP41

Easter Symbols: 15c+8c, Palms, Palm Sunday. 20c+10c, Bread and Wine, Maundy Thursday. 25c+12c, Cross, Good Friday. 30c+15c, Chrismon, Easter Sunday.

1968, Apr. 10 Litho. *Perf. 12½x13*

B142	SP40 10c + 5c lil & gray	8	8
B143	SP40 15c + 8c brick red & grn	15	15
B144	SP40 20c + 10c yel & dk grn	15	15
B145	SP40 25c + 12c gray & blk	15	15
B146	SP40 30c + 15c brt yel & brn	15	15
	Nos. B142-B146 (5)	68	68

1968, Nov. 22 Photo. *Perf. 12½x13*

Designs: 15c+8c, Balancing pyramid. 20c+10c, Handball. 25c+12c, Handicraft. 30c+15c, Tug-of-war.

B147	SP41 10c + 5c fawn & blk	8	8
B148	SP41 15c + 8c lt ultra & blk	15	15
B149	SP41 20c + 10c pink & blk	15	15
a	Min. sheet of 3	50	50
B150	SP41 25c + 12c yel grn & blk	24	24
B151	SP41 30c + 15c bluish lil & blk	32	32
	Nos. B147-B151 (5)	94	94

Child welfare. No. B149a contains two No. B147 and one No. B149.

Globe with Map of South America SP42

Pillow Fight SP43

Easter Issue

1969, Apr. 2 Litho. *Perf. 12½x13*

B152	SP42 10c + 5c bl & lt bl	25	25
B153	SP42 15c + 8c sl grn & yel	25	25
B154	SP42 20c + 10c sl grn & gray grn	25	25
B155	SP42 25c + 12c brn & bis	25	25
B156	SP42 30c + 15c vio & gray	25	25
	Nos. B152-B156 (5)	1.25	1.25

1969, Nov. 21 Litho. *Perf. 12½x13*

Designs: 15c+8c, Eating contest. 20c+10c, Pole climbing. 25c+12c, Sack race. 30c+15c, Obstacle race.

B157	SP43 10c + 5c lt ultra & mag	8	8
B158	SP43 15c + 8c yel & brn	24	24
B159	SP43 20c + 10c gray & dp bl	15	15
a	Min. sheet of 3	70	70
B160	SP43 25c + 12c pink & brt bl	24	24
B161	SP43 30c + 15c emer & brn	24	24
	Nos. B157-B161 (5)	95	95

Child welfare. No. B159a contains two No. B157 and one No. B159.

Flower SP44

Ludwig van Beethoven, 1786 SP45

Designs: 15c+8c, Butterfly. 20c+10c, Flying bird. 25c+12c, Sun. 30c+15c, Star.

1970, Mar. 25 Litho. *Perf. 12½x13*

B162	SP44 10c + 5c multi	52	52
B163	SP44 15c + 8c multi	52	52
B164	SP44 20c + 10c multi	52	52
B165	SP44 25c + 12c multi	52	52
B166	SP44 30c + 15c multi	52	52
	Nos. B162-B166 (5)	2.60	2.60

Easter.

1970, Nov. 25 Litho. *Perf. 12½x13*

Various Portraits of Beethoven: 15c+8c, In 1804. 20c+10c, In 1812. 25c+12c, In 1814. 30c+15c, In 1827 (death mask).

Portrait and Inscription in Gray and Ocher

B167	SP45 10c + 5c grn	52	52
B168	SP45 15c + 8c scar	52	52
B169	SP45 20c + 10c bl	52	52
a	Minature sheet of 3	1.65	1.65
B170	SP45 25c + 12c red org	52	52
B171	SP45 30c + 15c pur	52	52
	Nos. B167-B171 (5)	2.60	2.60

Ludwig van Beethoven (1770-1827), composer. The surtax was for child welfare. No. B169a contains 2 No. B167 and one No. B169.

Donkey and Palm — SP46

Leapfrog, by Peter Brueghel — SP47

Easter: 15c+8c, Cock. 20c+10c, Lamb of God. 25c+12c, Cross and Crown of Thorns. 30c+15c, Sun.

1971, Apr. 7 Litho. *Perf. 12½x13*

B172	SP46 10c + 5c multi	52	52
B173	SP46 15c + 8c bl & multi	52	52
B174	SP46 20c + 10c multi	52	52
B175	SP46 25c + 12c multi	52	52
B176	SP46 30c + 15c multi	52	52
	Nos. B172-B176 (5)	2.60	2.60

1971, Nov. 24 Photo. *Perf. 13½x14*

Children's Games, by Peter Brueghel: 15c+8c, Girl strewing flowers. 20c+10c, Spinning the hoop. 25c+12c, Ball players. 30c+15c, Stilt walker.

B177	SP47 10c + 5c multi	55	55
B178	SP47 15c + 8c multi	55	55
B179	SP47 20c + 10c multi	55	55
a	Minature sheet of 3	1.75	1.75
B180	SP47 25c + 12c multi	55	55
B181	SP47 30c + 15c multi	55	55
	Nos. B177-B181 (5)	2.75	2.75

Child welfare. No. B179a contains 2 No. B177 and one No. B179.

Easter Candle SP48

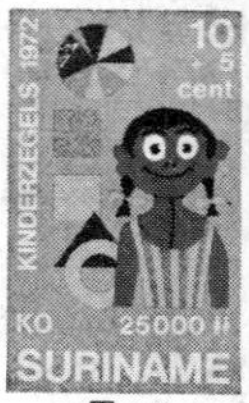

Toys SP49

Easter: 15c+8c, Christ teaching Apostles, and crosses. 20c+10c, Cup and folded hands. 25c+12c, Fish in net. 30c+15c, Judas' bag of silver.

1972, Mar. 29 Litho. *Perf. 12x13*

B182	SP48 10c + 5c multi	40	40
B183	SP48 15c + 8c multi	40	40
B184	SP48 20c + 10c multi	40	40
B185	SP48 25c + 12c multi	40	40
B186	SP48 30c + 15c multi	40	40
	Nos. B182-B186 (5)	2.00	2.00

1972, Nov. 29 Litho. *Perf. 12½x13*

Designs: 15c+8c, Abacus and clock. 20c+10c, Pythagorean theorem. 25c+12c, Model of molecule. 30c+15c, Monkey wrench and drill. Each design represents a different stage of education.

B187	SP49 10c + 5c multi	45	45
B188	SP49 15c + 8c multi	45	45
B189	SP49 20c + 10c multi	45	45
a	Minature sheet of 3	1.40	1.40
B190	SP49 25c + 12c multi	45	45
B191	SP49 30c + 15c multi	45	45
	Nos. B187-B191 (5)	2.25	2.25

Child welfare. No. B189a contains 2 No. B187 and one No. B189.

Jesus Calming the Waves — SP50

Easter: 15c+8c, The washing of the feet. 20c+10c, Jesus carrying Cross. 25c+12c, Cross and "ELI, ELI, LAMA SABACHTHANI?" 30c+15c, on the road to Emmaus.

1973, Apr. 4 Litho. *Perf. 12½x13*

B192	SP50 10c + 5c multi	35	35
B193	SP50 15c + 8c multi	35	35
B194	SP50 20c + 10c multi	35	35
B195	SP50 25c + 12c multi	35	35
B196	SP50 30c + 15c multi	35	35
	Nos. B192-B196 (5)	1.75	1.75

Red Cross and Florence Nightingale SP51

1973, Oct. 3 Litho. *Perf. 15x14*

B197	SP51 30c + 10c multi	65	65

30th anniversary of Surinam Red Cross.

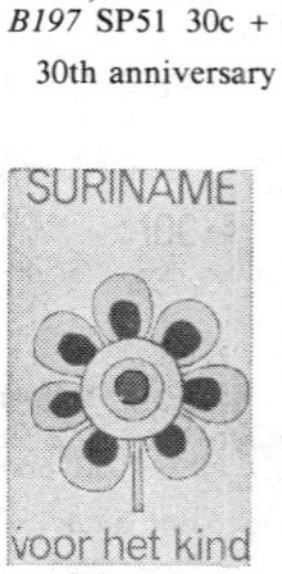

Flower SP52

Bitterwood SP53

1973, Nov. 28 Litho. *Perf. 14x14½*

B198 SP52 10c + 5c shown	24	24
B199 SP52 15c + 8c Tree	40	40
B200 SP52 20c + 10c Dog	32	32
a Minature sheet of 3	1.00	1.00
B201 SP52 25c + 12c House	50	50
B202 SP52 30c + 15c Girl	50	50
Nos. B198-B202 (5)	1.96	1.96

Child welfare. No. B200a contains two No. B198 and one No. B200.

1974, Apr. 3 Litho. *Perf. 14x14½*

Tropical Flowers: 15c+8c, Passion flower. 20c+10c, Wild angelica. 25c+12c, Candlestick senna. 30c+15c, Blood flower.

B203 SP53 10c + 5c multi	40	40
B204 SP53 15c + 8c multi	40	40
B205 SP53 20c + 10c multi	40	40
B206 SP53 25c + 12c multi	40	40
B207 SP53 30c + 15c multi	40	40
Nos. B203-B207 (5)	2.00	2.00

Easter charities.

Boy Scout, Tent and Trees — SP54

Designs: 15c+8c, 5th Caribbean Jamboree emblem. 20c+10c, Scouts and emblem.

1974, Aug. 21 Litho. *Perf. 14x14½*

B208 SP54 10c + 5c multi	32	32
B209 SP54 10c + 8c multi	32	32
B210 SP54 20c + 10c multi	32	32

50th anniversary of Surinam Boy Scouts.

Fruit — SP55

Designs: 15c+8c, Children, birds and nest (security). 20c+10c, Flower, mother and child (protection). 25c+12c, Child and corn (good food). 30c+15c, Dancing children (child care).

1974, Nov. 27 Litho. *Perf. 14½x14*

B211 SP55 10c + 5c multi	24	24
B212 SP55 15c + 8c multi	32	32
B213 SP55 20c + 10c multi	32	32
a Miniature sheet of 3	90	90
B214 SP55 25c + 12c multi	50	50
B215 SP55 30c + 15c multi	55	55
Nos. B211-B215 (5)	1.93	1.93

Child welfare. No. B213a contains two No. B211 and one No. B213.

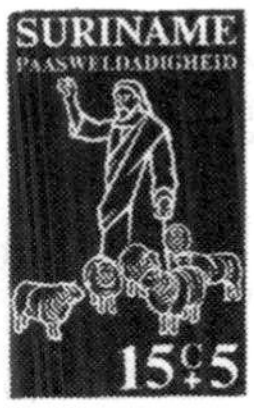

The Good Shepherd SP56

Woman and IWY Emblem SP57

Designs: 20c+10c, Peter's denial. 30c+15c, The Women at the Tomb. 35c+20c, Jesus showing His wounds to Thomas.

1975, Mar. 26 Litho. *Perf. 12½x13*

B216 SP56 15c + 5c yel grn & grn	50	50
B217 SP56 20c + 10c org & dk bl	65	65
B218 SP56 30c + 15c yel & red	65	65
B219 SP56 35c + 20c bl & pur	65	65

Easter charities.

1975, May 14 Photo. *Perf. 12½x13*

B220 SP57 15c + 5c multi	65	55
B221 SP57 30c + 15c multi	65	55

International Women's Year.

Carib Indian Water Jug — SP58

Feeding the Hungry — SP59

Designs: 20c+10c, 35c+20c, Indian arrow head (diff.). 30c+15c, Wayana board with animal figures.

1975, Nov. 12 Litho. *Perf. 12½x13*

B222 SP58 15c + 5c multi	15	15
B223 SP58 20c + 10c multi	50	50
a Miniature sheet of 3	1.50	1.50
B224 SP58 30c + 15c multi	85	70
B225 SP58 35c + 20c multi	85	85

Child welfare. No. B223a contains 2 No. B222 and one No. B223.

1976, Apr. 14 Photo. *Perf. 14x13*

Paintings: 25c+15c, Visiting the Sick. 30c+15c, Clothing the Naked. 35c+15c, Burying the Dead. 50c+25c, Giving Water to the Thirsty. Designs after panels in Alkmaar Church, 1504.

B226 SP59 20c + 10c multi	25	25
B227 SP59 25c + 15c multi	32	32
B228 SP59 30c + 15c multi	40	40
a Souvenir sheet of 3	1.00	1.00
B229 SP59 35c + 15c multi	42	42
B230 SP59 50c + 25c multi	65	65
Nos. B226-B230 (5)	2.04	2.04

Easter. No. B228a contains 2 No. B226 and one No. B228.

Pekingese and Boy's Head — SP60

Child's Head and: 25c+10c, German shepherd. 30c+15c, Dachshund. 35c+15c, Retriever. 50c+25c, Terrier.

1976 Litho. *Perf. 13½*

B231 SP60 20c + 10c multi	25	25
B232 SP60 25c + 10c multi	35	35
B233 SP60 30c + 15c multi	40	40
a Miniature sheet of 3	1.00	1.00
B234 SP60 35c + 15c multi	42	42
B235 SP60 50c + 25c multi	65	65
Nos. B231-B235 (5)	2.07	2.07

Surtax was for child welfare. No. B233a contains 2 No. B231 and one No. B233.

St. Veronica's Veil — SP61

Descent from the Cross — SP62

Easter: Religious scenes, side panels, front and back, from triptych by Jan Mostaert (1473-1555).

1977, Apr. 6 Litho. *Perf. 13½x14*

B236 SP61 20c + 10c multi	25	25
B237 SP61 25c + 15c multi	35	35
B238 SP61 30c + 15c multi	40	40
B239 SP62 35c + 15c multi	42	42
B240 SP61 50c + 25c multi	65	65
Nos. B236-B240 (5)	2.07	2.07

Dog and Girl's Head — SP63

Crosses, Luke 23:43 — SP64

Child's Head and: 25c+15c, Monkey. 30c+15c, Rabbit. 35c+15c, Cat. 50c+25c, Parrot.

1977, Nov. 23 Litho. *Perf. 13x14*

B241 SP63 20c + 10c multi	25	25
B242 SP63 25c + 15c multi	35	35
B243 SP63 30c + 15c multi	40	40
a Miniature sheet of 3	1.00	1.00
B244 SP63 35c + 15c multi	42	42
B245 SP63 50c + 25c multi	65	65
Nos. B241-B245 (5)	2.07	2.07

Surtax was for child welfare. No. B243a contains 2 No. B241 and one No. B243.

1978, Mar. 22 Litho. *Perf. 12½x14*

Easter: 25c+15c, Serpent and Cross, John 3:14. 30c+15c, Lamb and blood, Exodus 12:13. 35c+15c, Passover plate, chalice and bread. 60c+30c, Cross and solar eclipse.

B246 SP64 20c + 10c multi	32	32
B247 SP64 25c + 15c multi	42	42
B248 SP64 30c + 15c multi	50	50
B249 SP64 35c + 15c multi	52	52
B250 SP64 60c + 30c multi	1.00	1.00
Nos. B246-B250 (5)	2.76	2.76

Child's Head and White Cat SP65

Church, Cross and Chalice SP66

Designs: Child's head and cats in various positions.

1978, Nov. 22 Litho. *Perf. 14x13*

B251 SP65 20c + 10c multi	22	22
B252 SP65 25c + 15c multi	32	32
B253 SP65 30c + 15c multi	35	35
a Miniature sheet of 3	90	90
B254 SP65 35c + 15c multi	40	40
B255 SP65 60c + 30c multi	70	70
Nos. B251-B255 (5)	1.99	1.99

Surtax was for child welfare. No. B253a contains 2 No. B251 and one No. B253.

1979, Apr. 11 Litho. *Perf. 13x14*

Easter: Cross, chalice and various churches.

B256 SP66 20c + 10c multi	22	22
B257 SP66 30c + 15c multi	35	35
B258 SP66 35c + 15c multi	40	40
B259 SP66 40c + 20c multi	45	45
B260 SP66 60c + 30c multi	70	70
Nos. B256-B260 (5)	2.12	2.12

Boy, Bird, Red Cross, Blood Transfusion Bottle — SP67

1979, Nov. 21 Litho. *Perf. 13x14*

B261 SP67 20c + 10c multi	22	22
B262 SP67 30c + 15c multi	35	35
B263 SP67 35c + 15c multi	40	40
a Miniature sheet of 3	1.00	1.00
B264 SP67 40c + 20c multi	45	45
B265 SP67 60c + 30c multi	70	70
Nos. B261-B265 (5)	2.12	2.12

Surtax was for child welfare. No. B263a contains 2 No. B261 and one No. B263.

Cross SP68

Anansi SP69

Easter: Various symbols.

1980, Mar. 26 Litho. *Perf. 13x14*

B266 SP68 20c + 10c multi	22	22
B267 SP68 30c + 15c multi	35	35
B268 SP68 40c + 20c multi	45	45
B269 SP68 50c + 25c multi	60	60
B270 SP68 60c + 30c multi	70	70
Nos. B266-B270 (5)	2.32	2.32

1980, Nov. 5 Litho. *Perf. 13x14*

Designs: Characters from Anansi and His Creditors.

B271 SP69 20c + 10c shown	22	22
B272 SP69 25c + 15c Ba Tigri	28	28
B273 SP69 30c + 15c Kakafowroe	35	35
B274 SP69 35c + 15c Ontiman	40	40
B275 SP69 60c + 30c Mat Kalaka	70	70
a Miniature sheet of 3	1.25	1.25
Nos. B271-B275 (5)	1.95	1.95

Surtax was for child welfare. No. B275a contains 2 No. B271 and No. B275.

Woman Reading SP70

1980, Dec. 10 *Perf. 14x13*

B276 SP70 25c + 10c shown	28	28
B277 SP70 50c + 15c Gardening	50	50
B278 SP70 75c + 20c With grandchildren	75	75

Surtax was for the elderly.

Crucifixion — SP71

Easter: Scenes from the Passion of Christ.

1981, Apr. 8 Litho. *Perf. 13x14*

B279 SP71 20c + 10c multi	22	22
B280 SP71 30c + 15c multi	35	35
B281 SP71 50c + 25c multi	60	60
B282 SP71 60c + 30c multi	65	65
B283 SP71 75c + 35c multi	75	75
Nos. B279-B283 (5)	2.57	2.57

Surtax was for the elderly.

Indian Girl — SP72

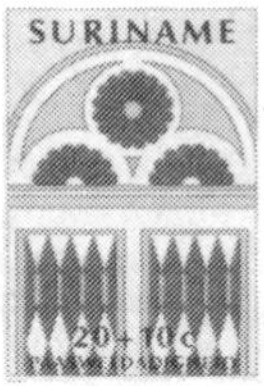

Easter — SP73

1981, Nov. 26 **Litho.**

B284	SP72	20c + 10c shown	22	22
B285	SP72	30c + 15c Black	35	35
B286	SP72	50c + 25c Hindustani	60	60
B287	SP72	60c + 30c Javanese	65	65
B288	SP72	75c + 35c Chinese	75	75
a		Souvenir sheet of 3	1.50	1.50
		Nos. B284-B288 (5)	2.57	2.57

Surtax was for child welfare. No. B288a contains 2 No. B285, No. B288.

1982, Apr. 7 **Litho.** ***Perf. 13x14***

Designs: Stained-glass windows, Sts. Peter and Paul Church, Paramaribo.

B289	SP73	20c + 10c multi	22	22
B290	SP73	35c + 15c multi	40	40
B291	SP73	50c + 25c multi	60	60
B292	SP73	65c + 30c multi	70	70
B293	SP73	75c + 35c multi	80	80
		Nos. B289-B293 (5)	2.72	2.72

Man Pushing Wheelbarrow SP74

Easter SP75

Children's Drawings of City Cleaning Activities.

1982, Nov. 17 **Litho.**

B294	SP74	20c + 10c multi	22	22
B295	SP74	35c + 15c multi	40	40
B296	SP74	50c + 25c multi	60	60
B297	SP74	65c + 30c multi	70	70
B298	SP74	75c + 35c multi	80	80
a		Souvenir sheet of 3	1.65	1.65
		Nos. B294-B298 (5)	2.72	2.72

Surtax was for child welfare. No. B298a contains 2 No. B295, No. B298.

1983, Mar. 23 **Litho.** ***Perf. 13x14***

Mosaic Symbols.

B299	SP75	10c + 5c Dove	12	12
B300	SP75	15c + 5c Bread	14	14
B301	SP75	25c + 10c Fish	25	25
B302	SP75	50c + 25c Eye	60	60
B303	SP75	65c + 30c Wine cup	70	70
		Nos. B299-B303 (5)	1.81	1.81

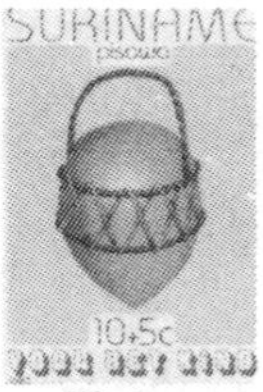

Pitcher SP76

Easter SP77

1983, Nov. 16 **Litho.** ***Perf. 13x14***

B304	SP76	10c + 5c shown	12	12
B305	SP76	15c + 5c Headdress	14	14
B306	SP76	25c + 10c Medicine rattle	25	25
B307	SP76	50c + 25c Sieve	60	60
B308	SP76	65c + 30c Basket	70	70
a		Miniature sheet of 3 (# B305, B306, B308)	1.10	1.10
		Nos. B304-B308 (5)	1.81	1.81

1984, Apr. 4 **Litho.** ***Perf. 13x14***

B309	SP77	10c + 5c Cross, rose	12	12
B310	SP77	15c + 15c Cemetery	14	14
B311	SP77	25c + 10c Candles	25	25
B312	SP77	50c + 25c Cross, crown of thorns	60	60
B313	SP77	65c + 30c Candle	70	70
		Nos. B309-B313 (5)	1.81	1.81

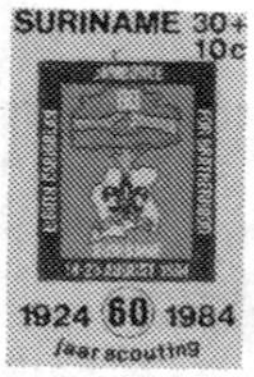

Boy Scouts in Surinam, 60th Anniv. — SP78

Designs: 30c+10c, 8th Caribbean Jamboree emblem. 35c+10c, Salute. 50c+10c, Gardening. 90c+10c, Campfire in map of Surinam. Surtax was for Boy Scouts.

1984, Aug. 15 **Litho.** ***Perf. 13x14***

B314	SP78	30c + 10c multi	30	30
B315	SP78	35c + 10c multi	35	35
B316	SP78	50c + 10c multi	45	45
B317	SP78	90c + 10c multi	75	75

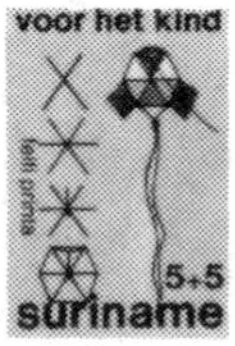

Children's Games — SP79

Easter — SP80

1984, Nov. 14 **Litho.** ***Perf. 13x14***

B318	SP79	5c + 5c Kites	8	8
B319	SP79	10c + 5c Kites, diff.	12	12
B320	SP79	30c + 10c Pingi-pingi-kasi	30	30
B321	SP79	50c + 25c Cricket	60	60
a		Souvenir sheet of 3 (#B319-B321)	1.10	1.10
B322	SP79	90c + 30c Peroen, peroen	90	90
		Nos. B318-B322 (5)	2.00	2.00

Surtax was for child welfare.

1985, Mar. 27 **Litho.** ***Perf. 12½x14***

B323	SP80	5c + 5c multi	7	7
B324	SP80	10c + 5c multi	10	10
B325	SP80	30c + 15c multi	30	30
B326	SP80	50c + 25c multi	50	50
B327	SP80	90c + 30c multi	80	80
		Nos. B323-B327 (5)	1.77	1.77

Surtax for child welfare.

Map, Emblem SP81

Literacy SP82

1985, Oct. 22 **Litho.** ***Perf. 13x14***

B328	SP81	30c + 10c shown	25	25
B329	SP81	50c + 10c Crucifix, missionaries	40	40
B330	SP81	90c + 20c Scroll	70	70

Evangelical Brotherhood Mission in Surinam, 250th anniv. Surtax for mission medical and social work.

1985, Nov. 6

B331	SP82	5c + 5c Boy reading	7	7
B332	SP82	10c + 5c Learning alphabet	10	10
B333	SP82	30c + 10c Writing	25	25
B334	SP82	50c + 25c Girl reading	50	50
a		Miniature sheet of 3, #B332-B334	90	90
B335	SP82	90c + 30c Studying	80	80
		Nos. B331-B335 (5)	1.72	1.72

Surtax for child welfare.

Easter — SP83

Sts. Peter and Paul Cathedral, Cent. — SP84

1986, Mar. 19 **Litho.**

B336	SP83	5c + 5c multi	7	7
B337	SP83	10c + 5c multi	10	10
B338	SP83	30c + 15c multi	30	30
B339	SP83	50c + 25c multi	50	50
B340	SP83	90c + 30c multi	75	75
		Nos. B336-B340 (5)	1.72	1.72

1986, May 28 **Litho.**

B341	SP84	30c + 10c Exterior	30	30
B342	SP84	50c + 10c Saints, bas-relief	42	42
B343	SP84	110c + 30c Baptismal font	1.10	1.10

Ancient Order of Foresters Court Charity, Cent. — SP85

1986, July 29 **Litho.** ***Perf. 14x13***

B344	SP85	50c + 20c Foresters emblem	52	52
B345	SP85	110c + 30c Court building	1.10	1.10

Youth Activities SP86

1986, Nov. 5 **Litho.** ***Perf. 14x13***

B346	SP86	5c + 5c Hopscotch	8	8
B347	SP86	10c + 5c Ballet	12	12
B348	SP86	30c + 10c Mobile library	30	30
B349	SP86	50c + 25c Crafts	55	55
a		Miniature sheet of 3, #B347-B349	1.00	1.00
B350	SP86	110c + 30c Education	1.10	1.10
		Nos. B346-B350 (5)	2.15	2.15

Surtax for Children's Charities.

Easter SP87

Natl. Girl Guides Movement, 40th Anniv. SP88

Stations of the cross.

1987, Apr. 9 **Litho.** ***Perf. 13x14***

B351	SP87	5c + 5c Crucifixion	8	8
B352	SP87	10c + 5c Christ on cross	12	12
B353	SP87	35c + 15c Descent from cross	38	38
B354	SP87	60c + 30c Funeral procession	65	65
B355	SP87	110c + 50c Entombment	1.10	1.10
		Nos. B351-B355 (5)	2.33	2.33

Surtax for annual Easter Charity programs.

1987, May 7 **Litho.**

Designs: 15c+10c, Mushroom, Brownie's emblem. 60c+10c, Clover, Guides' emblem. 110c+10c, Campfire, Rangers' emblem. 120c+10c, Ivy, Captain's emblem.

B356	SP88	15c + 10c multi	20	20
B357	SP88	60c + 10c multi	52	52
B358	SP88	110c + 10c multi	90	90
B359	SP88	120c + 10c multi	95	95

Surtax for the Surinam Girl Guides.

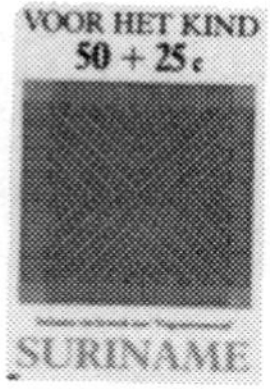

Caribbean Manari — SP89

Easter — SP90

1987, Nov. 4 **Litho.** ***Perf. 13x14***

B360	SP89	50c + 25c Herring bone	60	60
B361	SP89	60c + 30c Tortoise-back	70	70
B362	SP89	110c + 50c Whirlpool (squares)	1.25	1.25
a		Miniature sheet of 2, #B360, B362	2.50	2.50

Surtax to benefit child welfare organizations.

1988, Mar. 23 ***Perf. 13x13½***

B363	SP90	50c + 25c multi	52	52
B364	SP90	60c + 30c multi	65	65
B365	SP90	110c + 50c multi	1.25	1.25

Surtax for annual Easter Charity programs.

Intl. Red Cross and Red Crescent Organizations, 125th Annivs. — SP91

1988, Oct. 26 **Litho.** ***Perf. 13x14***

B366	SP91	60c + 30c shown	1.00	1.00
B367	SP91	120c + 60c Anniv. and blood donation emblems	2.00	2.00

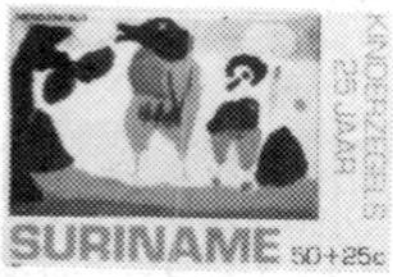

Children's Drawings SP92

1988, Dec. 5 **Litho.** ***Perf. 14x13***

B368	SP92	50c + 25c Man and animal	85	85
B369	SP92	60c + 30c Children and nature	1.00	1.00
B370	SP92	110c + 50c Stop drugs	1.80	1.80
a.		Souv. sheet of 3, Nos. B368-B370	3.75	3.75

Surtax to benefit children's charities.

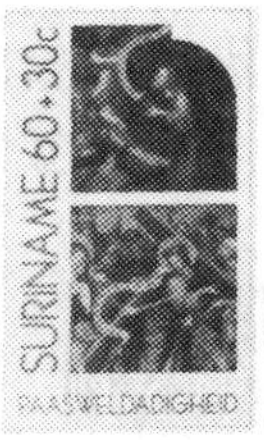

Easter 1989 — SP93

Details from Hungarian altarpieces: 60c+30c, Scenes of the Passion, by M.S., 1506. 105c+50c, Crucifixion, by Tamas of Koszvar, 1427. 110c+55c, Miracles, by Tamas of Koszvar, 1427.

1989, Mar. 21 Litho. *Perf.*
Size: (No. B372)

B371 SP93 60c + 30c multi 1.00 1.00
B372 SP93 105c + 50c multi 1.75 1.75
B373 SP93 110c + 55c multi 1.85 1.85

Surtax for annual East Charity programs.

AIR POST STAMPS

Allegory of Flight — AP1

1930 Unwmk. Engr. *Perf. 12½*

C1 AP1 10c dl red 3.00 40
C2 AP1 15c ultra 3.00 55
C3 AP1 20c dl grn 8 15
C4 AP1 40c orange 15 28
C5 AP1 60c brn vio 40 32
C6 AP1 1g gray blk 1.10 1.25
C7 AP1 1½g dp brn 1.25 1.50
Nos. C1-C7 (7) 8.98 4.45

Nos. C1-C7 Overprinted in Black or Red

Vlucht
Do. X
1931

1931

C8 AP1 10c red (Bk) 15.00 10.50
a. Double overprint 300.00
C9 AP1 15c ultra (Bk) 15.00 10.50
C10 AP1 20c dl grn (R) 15.00 10.50
C11 AP1 40c org (Bk) 22.50 15.00
a. Double overprint 300.00
C12 AP1 60c brn vio (R) 45.00 40.00
C13 AP1 1g gray blk (R) 55.00 45.00
C14 AP1 1½g dp brn (Bk) 55.00 47.50
Nos. C8-C14 (7) 222.50 179.00

The variety with period omitted after "Do" occurs twice on each sheet.

Type of 1930
Thick Paper

1941 Litho. *Perf. 13*

C15 AP1 20c lt grn 1.75 70
C16 AP1 40c lt org 8.50 4.00
C17 AP1 2½g yellow 10.50 8.50
C18 AP1 5g bl grn 225.00 225.00
C19 AP1 10g lt bis 25.00 35.00
Nos. C15-C19 (5) 270.75 273.20

The lines of shading on Nos. C15 and C16 are not as heavy as on Nos. C3 and C4. For surcharges, see Nos. C24-C25.

Type of 1930

1941 Redrawn *Perf. 12*

C20 AP1 10c lt red 1.50 24
C21 AP1 60c dl brn vio 1.00 32
C22 AP1 1g black 20.00 15.00

Redrawn stamps have three horizontal lines through post horn and many minor variations. For surcharges, see Nos. C23, CB1.

Catalogue values for unused stamps in this section, from this point to the end of the section, are for Never Hinged items.

Nos. C17, C19 and C21 Surcharged with New Values and Bars in Carmine

1945 *Perf. 13, 12*

C23 AP1 22½c on 60c dl brn vio 32 50
a. Inverted surcharge 215.00 215.00
C24 AP1 1g on 2½g yel 8.50 10.50
C25 AP1 5g on 10g lt bis 14.00 16.00

Women of Netherlands and Surinam AP2

Globe and Winged Post Horn AP3

Perf. 12x12½

1949, May 10 Photo. Unwmk.

C26 AP2 27½c hn brn 5.00 2.50

Valid only on first flight of Paramaribo-Amsterdam service.

1954, Sept. 25 *Perf. 13½x12½*

C27 AP3 15c dp ultra & ultra 1.10 1.00

Establishment of airmail service in Surinam, 25th anniv.

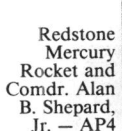

Redstone Mercury Rocket and Comdr. Alan B. Shepard, Jr. — AP4

Design: 15c, Cosmonaut Gagarin in capsule and globe.

1961, July 3 Litho. *Perf. 12*

C28 AP4 15c multi 85 85
C29 AP4 20c multi 85 85

"Man in Space," Major Yuri A. Gagarin, USSR, and Comdr. Alan B. Shepard, Jr., USA.

Printed in sheets of 12 (4x3) with ornamental borders and inscriptions.

Water Tower — AP5

Eucyane Bicolor — AP6

Designs: 15c, 65c, Brewery. 20c, Boat on lake. 25c, 75c, Wood industry. 30c, Bauxite mine. 35c, 50c, Poelepantje bridge. 40c, Ship in harbor. 45c, Wharf.

1965, July 31 Photo. *Perf. 14x13½*
Size: 25x18mm

C30 AP5 10c olive grn 8 6
C31 AP5 15c ocher 8 6
C32 AP5 20c slate grn 8 6
C33 AP5 25c vio blue 15 6
C34 AP5 30c bl green 15 15
C35 AP5 35c red org 24 15
C36 AP5 40c orange 24 15
C37 AP5 45c dk car 24 24
C38 AP5 50c vermilion 24 24
C39 AP5 55c emerald 24 24
C40 AP5 65c bister 32 32
C41 AP5 75c blue 32 32
Nos. C30-C41 (12) 2.38 2.05

See Nos. C75-C84.

1972, July 26 Litho. *Perf. 13x13½*

C42 AP6 15c shown 12 12
C43 AP6 20c Helicopis cupido 15 12
C44 AP6 25c Papilio thoas thoas 18 12
C45 AP6 30c Urania leilus 20 8
C46 AP6 35c Stalachtis calliope 20 28
C47 AP6 40c Stalachtis phlegia 24 20
C48 AP6 45c Victorina steneles 28 8
C49 AP6 50c Papilio neophilus 35 8
C50 AP6 55c Anartia amathea 40 42
C51 AP6 60c Adelpha cytherea 45 65
C52 AP6 65c Heliconius doris metharmina 42 42
C53 AP6 70c Nessaea obrinus 52 52
C54 AP6 75c Ageronia feronia 50 40
Nos. C42-C54 (13) 4.01 3.49

Surinam butterflies. Valid for regular postage also. For surcharges, see Nos. 495-499.

Fish Type of 1976

Fish: 35c, Chaetodon unimaculatus. 60c, Centropyge loriculus. 95c, Caetodon collare.

1976, June 2 Litho. *Perf. 12½x13*

C55 A111 35c multi 30 30
C56 A111 60c multi 52 52
C57 A111 95c multi 85 85

Black-headed Sugarbird AP7

Birds of Surinam: 20c, Leistes militaris. 30c, Paradise tangara. 40c, Whippoorwill. 45c, Hemitraupis flavicollis. 50c, White-tailed gold-throated hummingbird. 55c, Saberwing. 60c, Blackcap parrot (vert.). 65c, Toucan (vert.). 70c, Manakin (vert.). 75c, Collared parrot (vert.). 80c, Cayenne cotinga (vert.). 85c, Trogon (vert.). 95c, Black-striped tropical tree owl (vert.).

1977 Litho. *Perf. 14x12½, 12½x14*

C58 AP7 20c multi 20 20
C59 AP7 25c multi 25 25
C60 AP7 30c multi 28 28
a. Miniature sheet of 4 1.25 1.25
C61 AP7 40c multi 42 42
C62 AP7 45c multi 45 45
C63 AP7 50c multi 52 52
C64 AP7 55c multi 60 60
C65 AP7 60c multi 65 65
C66 AP7 65c multi 70 70
C67 AP7 70c multi 75 75
C68 AP7 75c multi 85 85
C69 AP7 80c multi 85 85
C70 AP7 85c multi 90 90
C71 AP7 95c multi 1.10 1.10
Nos. C58-C71 (14) 8.52 8.52

No. C60a contains 2 each of Nos. C59-C60, perf. 13½. Size: 108x75mm.

A souvenir sheet of 4 with same stamps and perf. as No. C60a has marginal inscription "Amphilex 77" with magnifier over No. 424. Sold only canceled in folder at philatelic exhibition in Amsterdam May 26-June 5, 1977.

See Nos. C88, C101. For surcharges, see Nos. C102-C105. For overprints, see Nos. J58, J62.

Fish Type of 1976

Tropical Fish: 60c, Chaetodon striatus. 90c, Bodianus pulchellus. 120c, Centropyge argi.

1977, June 8 Litho. *Perf. 12½x13*

C72 A111 60c multi 60 60
C73 A111 90c multi 95 95
C74 A111 120c multi 1.25 1.25

Type of 1965 Redrawn

Designs: 5c, Brewery. 10c, Water tower. 20c, Boat on lake. 25c, Wood industry. 30c, Bauxite mine. 35c, Poelepantje bridge. 40c, Ship in harbor. 60c, Wharf.

1977-78 Photo. *Perf. 12½x13½*
Size: 22x18mm

C75 AP5 5c ocher ('78) 8 5
a. Bklt. pane of 7 + label (4 #C75, 3 #C84) 2.00
C76 AP5 10c ol grn 10 8
a. Bklt. pane of 5 + label (1 #C76, 4 #C80) 1.50
C77 AP5 20c sl grn 20 10
a. Bklt. pane of 6 (2 #C77, 2 #C78, 2 #C79) 1.50
b. Bklt. pane of 8 (6 #C77, 2 #C81) ('78) 2.00
C78 AP5 25c vio bl 22 12
C79 AP5 30c bl grn 35 12
C80 AP5 35c red org 32 15
C81 AP5 40c org ('78) 42 20
C84 AP5 60c dk car ('78) 65 3.25

Nos. C75-C84 issued in booklets only. Nos. C75a and C77b have inscribed selvage the size of 4 stamps; Nos. C76a and C77a the size of 6 stamps.

Fish Type of 1976

Tropical Fish: 60c, Astyanax species. 90c, Corydoras wotroi. 120c, Gasteropelecus sternicla.

1978, June 21 Litho. *Perf. 12½x13*

C85 A111 60c multi 65 65
C86 A111 90c multi 1.10 1.10
C87 A111 120c multi 1.25 1.25

Bird Type of 1977

Design: 5g, Crested curassow (vert.).

1979, Jan. 10 Engr. *Perf. 13x13½*

C88 AP7 5g violet 4.00 4.00

Fish Type of 1979

Tropical Fish: 60c, Cantherinus macrocerus. 90c, Holocenthrus rufus. 120c, Holacanthus tricolor.

1979, May 30 Photo. *Perf. 14x13*

C89 A129 60c multi 48 48
C90 A129 90c multi 70 70
C91 A129 120c multi 1.00 1.00

Fish Type of 1979

Tropical Fish: 60c, Symphysodon discus. 75c, Aeqidens curviceps. 90c, Catoprion mento.

1980, Sept. 10 Photo. *Perf. 14x13*

C92 A129 60c multi 45 45
C93 A129 75c multi 60 60
C94 A129 90c multi 70 70

Frog Type of 1981

1981, June 24 *Perf. 13x14*

C95 A142 75c Phyllomedusa burmeisteri, vert. 60 60
C96 A142 1g Dendrobates tinctorius, vert. 80 80
C97 A142 1.25g Bufo guttatus, vert. 1.00 1.00

Turtle T pe of 1982

1982, Feb. 17 Photo. *Perf. 14x13*

C98 A146 65c Platemys platycephala 50 50
C99 A146 75c Phrynops gibba 60 60
C100 A146 125c Rhinoclemys punctularia 1.00 1.00

Bird Type of 1977

1985, Jan. 9 Litho. *Perf. 13x14*

C101 AP7 90c Venezuelan Amazon, vert. 65 65

For overprint, see No. J61.

No. C60 Surcharged

1986, Oct. 1 Litho. *Perf. 14x13*

C102 AP7 15c on 30c multi 12 12

Nos. C70-C71 and C67 Surcharged

10 ct

1987, Mar. Litho. *Perf. 12½x14*

C103 AP7 10c on 85c No. C70 8 8
C104 AP7 10c on 95c No. C71 8 8
C105 AP7 25c on 70c No. C67 20 20

Otter Type of 1989

1989, Jan. 18 Litho. *Perf. 13x14*

C107 A195 185c Otters, vert. 2.05 2.05

AIR POST SEMI-POSTAL STAMPS

Catalogue values for unused stamps in this section, from this point to the end of the section, are for Never Hinged items.

No. C20 Surcharged in Red like No. B40

1942, Jan. 2 Unwmk. *Perf. 12*

CB1 AP1 10c + 5c lt red, III 4.00 4.00
a. Type IV 6.50 6.50
b. Type V 18.00 21.00

The surtax was for the Red Cross.

See note on types III and IV below No. B40.

Nos. 193 and 194 Surcharged in Carmine

1946

CB2	A30 10c + 40c blue	1.00	1.00
CB3	A30 15c + 60c brown	1.00	1.00

The surtax was used for the prevention of tuberculosis.

Star — SPAP1

1947 Photo. *Perf. 13½x12½*

CB4	SPAP1 22½c + 27½c gray	2.25	2.00
CB5	SPAP1 27½c + 47½c grn	2.25	2.00

The surtax was used to combat leprosy.

POSTAGE DUE STAMPS

D1

D2

Type I - 34 loops. "T" of "BETALEN" over center of loop; top branch of "E" of "TE" shorter than lower branch.

Type II - 33 loops. "T" of "BETALEN" over space between two loops.

Type III - 32 loops. "T" of "BETALEN" slightly to the left of center of loop; top branch of first "E" of "BETALEN" shorter than lower branch.

Type IV - 37 loops and letters of "PORT" larger than in the other three types.

Value in Black

1886 Typo. Unwmk. *Perf. 12½x12*

J1	D1 2½c lilac (III)	1.65	1.65
a.	2½c lilac (I)	3.00	3.00
b.	2½c lilac (II)	2.50	2.50
J2	D1 5c lilac (III)	4.50	4.50
a.	5c lilac (I)	5.50	5.50
b.	5c lilac (II)	4.75	4.75
J3	D1 10c lilac (III)	70.00	45.00
a.	10c lilac (I)	85.00	55.00
b.	10c lilac (II)	1,250.	1,250.
c.	10c lilac (IV)	350.00	200.00
J4	D1 20c lilac (III)	4.50	4.50
a.	20c lilac (I)	11.50	11.50
b.	20c lilac (II)	4.75	4.75
J5	D1 25c lilac (III)	6.50	6.50
a.	25c lilac (I)	8.50	8.50
b.	25c lilac (II)	275.00	275.00
c.	25c lilac (IV)	105.00	105.00
J6	D1 30c lilac (III)	1.10	1.10
a.	30c lilac (I)	11.50	11.50
b.	30c lilac (II)	55.00	55.00
J7	D1 40c lilac (III)	3.00	3.00
a.	40c lilac (I)	6.50	6.50
b.	40c lilac (II)	265.00	265.00
c.	40c lilac (IV)	105.00	105.00
J8	D1 50c lilac (III)	1.50	1.50
a.	50c lilac (I)	2.00	2.00
b.	50c lilac (II)	2.50	2.50

Nos. J1-J16 were issued without gum. For surcharges, see Nos. J15-J16.

1892-96 *Perf. 12½*

Value in Black

J9	D2 2½c lilac (III)	20	20
a.	2½c lilac (I)	20	20
b.	2½c lilac (II)	40	45
J10	D2 5c lilac (III)	65	50
a.	5c lilac (I)	1.00	1.00
b.	5c lilac (II)	1.50	1.50
J11	D2 10c lilac (III)	12.00	11.50
a.	10c lilac (I)	11.50	10.00
b.	10c lilac (II)	22.50	22.50
J12	D2 20c lilac (III)	1.25	1.10
a.	20c lilac (I)	2.50	2.50
b.	20c lilac (II)	65.00	65.00
J13	D2 25c lilac (III)	5.00	5.00
a.	25c lilac (I)	6.50	6.50
b.	25c lilac (II)	70.00	75.00
J14	D2 40c lilac (I)	1.65	2.25

For surcharges, see Nos. 121-122.

Stamps of 1886 Surcharged in Red

1911

J15	D1 10c on 30c lil (III)	62.50	62.50
a.	10c on 30c lilac (I)	150.00	175.00
b.	10c on 30c lilac (II)	*1,800.*	*1,800.*
J16	D1 10c on 50c lil (III)	85.00	85.00
a.	10c on 50c lilac (I)	90.00	90.00
b.	10c on 50c lilac (II)	90.00	90.00

D3

D4

Type I

Value in Color of Stamp

1912-31 *Perf. 12½, 13½x12½*

J17	D2 ½c lilac ('30)	8	8
J18	D2 1c lilac ('31)	8	12
J19	D2 2c lilac ('31)	14	14
J20	D2 2½c lilac	8	8
J21	D2 5c lilac	8	8
J22	D2 10c lilac	12	10
J23	D2 12c lilac ('31)	12	14
J24	D2 12½c lilac ('22)	12	8
J25	D2 15c lilac ('26)	20	20
J26	D2 20c lilac	40	20
J27	D2 25c lilac	15	8
J28	D2 30c lilac ('26)	15	30
J29	D2 40c lilac	8.25	8.25
J30	D2 50c lilac ('26)	65	55
J31	D2 75c lilac ('26)	70	70
J32	D3 1g lilac ('26)	90	70
	Nos. J17-J32 (16)	12.22	11.80

Catalogue values for unused stamps in this section, from this point to the end of the section, are for Never Hinged items.

1945 Litho. *Perf. 12*

J33	D4 1c lt brn vio	15	15
J34	D4 5c lt brn vio	2.75	1.00
J35	D4 25c lt brn vio	6.25	15

D5

D6

Perf. 13½x12½

1950 Unwmk. Photo.

J36	D5 1c purple	1.25	1.10
J37	D5 2c purple	2.00	1.00
J38	D5 2½c purple	1.75	1.10
J39	D5 5c purple	2.25	24
J40	D5 10c purple	1.25	24
J41	D5 15c purple	3.25	1.50
J42	D5 20c purple	1.10	2.00
J43	D5 25c purple	6.50	15
J44	D5 50c purple	11.50	85
J45	D5 75c purple	27.50	21.00
J46	D5 1g purple	10.00	4.00
	Nos. J36-J46 (11)	68.35	33.18

1956

J47	D6 1c purple	8	8
J48	D6 2c purple	32	15
J49	D6 2½c purple	32	15
J50	D6 5c purple	32	15
J51	D6 10c purple	32	15
J52	D6 15c purple	50	30
J53	D6 20c purple	50	35
J54	D6 25c purple	55	15
J55	D6 50c purple	1.50	20
J56	D6 75c purple	2.00	65
J57	D6 1g purple	2.75	50
	Nos. J47-J57 (11)	9.16	2.83

Stamps of 1977-1985 Overprinted "TE BETALEN"

Perf. 13x14, 14x13

1987, July Litho.

J58	AP7 65c No. C66	48	48
J59	A156 65c No. 638	48	48
J60	A156 80c No. 640	60	60
J61	AP7 90c No. C101	65	65
J62	AP7 95c No. C71	70	70
J63	A173 1g No. 729	75	75
	Nos. J58-J63 (6)	3.66	3.66

SWEDEN

LOCATION — Northern Europe, occupying the eastern half of the Scandinavian Peninsula.
GOVT. — Republic
AREA — 173,341 sq. mi.
POP. — 8,330,577 (est. 1983)
CAPITAL — Stockholm

48 skilling banco = 1 rixdaler banco (until 1858)

100 öre = 1 rixdaler (1858 to 1874)
100 öre = 1 krona (since 1874)

Catalogue values for unused stamps in this country are for Never Hinged items, beginning with Scott 358 in the regular postage section, and Scott B37 in the semi-postal section.

Coat of Arms
A1 A2

1855 Unwmk. Typo. *Perf. 14*

1	A1 3s bl grn	*4,500.*	*2,500.*
a.	3s org (error)		
2	A1 4s lt bl	900.00	67.50
a.	4s gray bl	*6,000.*	*200.00*
3	A1 6s gray	*6,000.*	725.00
a.	6s gray brn	*7,250.*	800.00
b.	Imperf.		*8,000.*
4	A1 8s orange	3,000.	475.00
a.	8s yel org	3,800.	525.00
b.	8s em yel	4,000.	875.00
c.	Imperf.		
5	A1 24s dl red	*4,750.*	*2,000.*

Nos. 1-5 were reprinted two or three times perf. 14, once perf. 13. Value of the lowest cost perf. 14 reprints, $400 each. Perf. 13, $350 each.

The reprints were made after Nos. 1-5 were withdrawn, but before being demonitized. Used copies are known.

1858-61 *Perf. 14*

6	A2 5o green	125.00	16.00
a.	5o dp grn	275.00	110.00
7	A2 9o violet	300.00	175.00
a.	9o lil	325.00	200.00
8	A2 12o blue	125.00	2.75
9	A2 12o ultra ('61)	225.00	9.00
10	A2 24o orange	210.00	20.00
a.	24o yel	300.00	32.50
11	A2 30o brown	195.00	22.50
a.	30o red brn	195.00	25.00
12	A2 50o rose	250.00	62.50
a.	50o car	315.00	65.00

Nos. 6 and 8 exist with double impressions. No. 8 is known printed on both sides. No. 11 exists imperf.

Nos. 6-8, 10-12 were reprinted in 1885, perf. 13. Value $120 each. Also reprinted in 1963, perf. 13½, with lines in stamp color crossing denominations, and affixed to book page. Value $17.50 each.

Lion and Arms
A3 A4

1862-69

13	A3 3o bis brn	55.00	16.00
a.	Printed on both sides		*2,000.*
14	A4 17o red vio ('66)	300.00	140.00
15	A4 17o gray ('69)	350.00	500.00
16	A4 20o ver ('66)	125.00	15.00

Nos. 13, 15-16 were reprinted in 1885, perf. 13. Value $120 each.

Numeral of Value — A5

Coat of Arms — A6

1872-77 *Perf. 14.*

17	A5 3o bis brn	32.50	5.25
18	A5 4o gray ('76)	180.00	80.00
19	A5 5o bl grn	165.00	3.00
a.	5o emer	165.00	12.00
20	A5 6o violet	165.00	13.00
a.	6o dk vio	165.00	13.00
21	A5 6o gray ('74)	500.00	32.50
22	A5 12o blue	80.00	90
23	A5 20o vermilion	325.00	4.50
a.	20o dl org yel ('75)	1,750.	16.00
b.	Dbl. impression, dl yel & ver ('76)	2,500.	17.50
24	A5 24o orange	325.00	17.50
a.	24o yel	325.00	20.00
25	A5 30o pale brn	250.00	5.50
a.	30o blk brn	250.00	6.00
26	A5 50o rose	265.00	22.50
a.	50o car	265.00	22.50
27	A6 1rd bis & bl	525.00	45.00
a.	1rd bis & ultra	325.00	45.00

1877-79 *Perf. 13*

28	A5 3o yel brn	40.00	2.50
a.	Imperf., pair	675.00	
29	A5 4o gray ('79)	90.00	2.25
a.	Imperf., pair	675.00	
30	A5 5o dk grn	75.00	75
a.	Imperf., pair	675.00	
31	A5 6o lilac	100.00	3.75
a.	6o red lil	100.00	5.50
b.	Imperf., pair	675.00	
32	A5 12o blue	17.50	48
a.	Imperf., pair	675.00	
33	A5 20o vermilion	125.00	1.10
a.	"TRETIO" instead of "TJUGO" ('79)	6,750.	6,000.
b.	Imperf., pair	675.00	
34	A5 24o org ('78)	45.00	10.00
a.	24o yel	45.00	10.00
b.	Imperf., pair	675.00	
35	A5 30o pale brn	150.00	1.45
a.	30o blk brn	150.00	1.10
b.	Imperf., pair	675.00	
36	A5 50o car ('78)	150.00	4.50
a.	Imperf., pair	675.00	
37	A6 1rd bis & bl	1,000.	350.00
38	A6 1k bis & bl ('78)	275.00	9.00
a.	Imperf., pair ('78)	675.00	

See Nos. 40-44, 46-49.

No. 37 has been reprinted in yellow brown and dark blue; perforated 13. Value, $225.

King Oscar II — A7

Coat of Arms — A8

1885 Typo.

39	A7 10o dl rose	130.00	50
a.	Imperf., pair		*1,750.*

Numeral Type with Post Horn on Back

1886-91

40	A5 2o org ('91)	3.25	3.75
a.	Period before "FRIMARKE"	5.00	5.50
b.	Imperf., pair	525.00	
41	A5 3o yel brn ('87)	9.00	9.75
42	A5 4o gray	26.00	60
43	A5 5o green	42.50	45
44	A5 6o red lil ('88)	24.00	18.00
a.	6o vio	27.50	18.00
45	A7 10o pink	52.50	12
a.	10o rose	52.50	12
b.	Imperf.		2,250.
46	A5 20o vermilion	75.00	45
47	A5 30o pale brn	115.00	85
48	A5 50o rose	100.00	3.25
49	A6 1k bis & dk bl	65.00	1.90
a.	Imperf., pair	525.00	

Nos. 32, 34 with Blue Surcharge

1889, Oct. 1

50	A8 10o on 12o bl	3.00	3.00
51	A8 10o on 24o org	18.00	*25.00*

A9

A10

King Oscar II — A11

Wmk. 180- Crown

Wmk. 180

1891-1904 Typo. *Perf. 13*

52	A9	1o brn & ultra ('92)	1.50	25
a.		Imperf., pair ('92)	75.00	
53	A9	2o bl & yel org	6.00	15
a.		Imperf., pair	*210.00*	
54	A9	3o brn & org ('92)	1.00	75
a.		Imperf., pair	*225.00*	
55	A9	4o car & ultra ('92)	10.00	6
a.		Imperf., pair ('92)	200.00	

Engr.

56	A10	5o yel grn	3.50	5
a.		5o bl grn	7.50	6
b.		Imperf. 5o yel grn, pair	70.00	
c.		Imperf. 5o bl grn, pair	175.00	
d.		5o brn (error)	*6,250.*	
e.		Booklet pane of 6	45.00	
57	A10	8o red vio ('03)	5.25	60
a.		Imperf., pair	265.00	
58	A10	10o carmine	6.00	5
b.		Imperf., pair	35.00	
c.		Booklet pane of 6	52.50	
59	A10	15o red brn ('96)	24.00	15
a.		Imperf., pair	265.00	
60	A10	20o blue	25.00	6
a.		Imperf., pair	100.00	
61	A10	25o red org ('96)	30.00	22
a.		Imperf., pair	315.00	
62	A10	30o brown	42.50	18
a.		Imperf., pair	315.00	
63	A10	50o slate	67.50	35
a.		Imperf., pair	315.00	
64	A10	50o ol gray ('04)	60.00	28
a.		Imperf., pair	250.00	
65	A11	1k car & sl ('00)	100.00	1.25
a.		Imperf., pair	350.00	
		Nos. 52-65 (14)	382.25	4.40

See Nos. 75-76.

Stockholm Post Office — A12

1903, Oct. 26

66	A12	5k blue	275.00	20.00
a.		Imperf., pair	1,750.	

Opening of the new General Post Office at Stockholm.

Arms A13

Gustaf V A14

Perf. 13, 13x13½.

1910-14 Typo. Wmk. 180

67	A13	1o blk ('11)	90	1.00
68	A13	2o org ('10)	3.25	1.75
69	A13	4o vio ('10)	5.00	85

Engr.

70	A14	5o grn ('11)	11.00	*21.00*
71	A14	10o car ('10)	17.50	35
72	A14	1k *yel* ('11)	90.00	30
73	A14	5k cl, *yel* ('14)	2.75	1.75
		Nos. 67-73 (7)	130.40	*27.00*

See Nos. 95-98. See Nos. Q1-Q2 for No. 73 surcharged "Kr 1.98" or "Kr 2.12."

1911 Unwmk.

75	A10	20o blue	15.00	6.75
76	A10	25o red org	18.00	2.50

1910-19

77	A14	5o grn ('11)	2.75	5
a.		Bklt. pane of 10	200.00	
b.		Bklt. pane of 4	105.00	
78	A14	7o gray grn ('18)	25	12
a.		Bklt. pane of 10	8.00	
79	A14	8o mag ('12)	25	24
80	A14	10o car ('10)	3.75	5
a.		Bklt. pane of 10	200.00	
b.		Bklt. pane of 4	105.00	
81	A14	12o rose lake ('18)	25	10
a.		Bklt. pane of 10	8.00	
82	A14	15o red brn ('11)	7.75	5
a.		Bklt. pane of 10	300.00	
83	A14	20o dp bl ('11)	11.50	5
a.		Bklt. pane of 10	315.00	
84	A14	25o org red ('11)	45	8
85	A14	27o pale bl ('18)	70	70
86	A14	30o cl brn ('11)	22.50	5
87	A14	35o dk vio ('11)	27.50	14
88	A14	40o ol grn ('17)	42.50	7
89	A14	50o gray ('12)	45.00	7
90	A14	55o pale bl ('18)	1,500.	3,150.
91	A14	65o pale ol grn ('18)	1.10	1.75
92	A14	80o blk ('18)	1,500.	3,150.
93	A14	90o gray grn ('18)	1.40	42
94	A14	1k *yel* ('19)	90.00	28
		Nos. 77-89,91,93-94 (16)	257.65	4.22

Excellent forgeries of Nos. 90 and 92 exist.

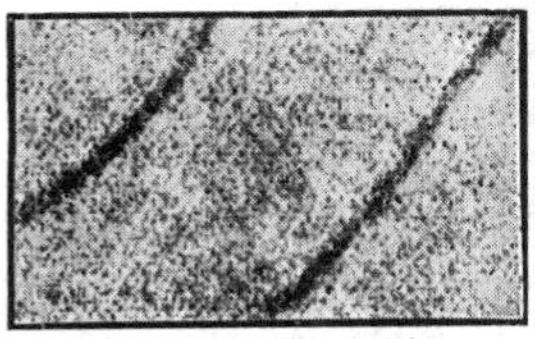

Wmk. 181- Wavy Lines

1911-19 Typo. Wmk. 181 *Perf. 13*

95	A13	1o black	15	15
96	A13	2o orange	15	15
97	A13	3o pale brn ('19)	15	15
98	A13	4o pale vio	15	15

Stamps of these and many later issues are frequently found with watermark showing parts of the words "Kungl Postverket" in double-lined capitals. This watermark is normally located in the margins of the sheets of unwatermarked paper or paper watermarked wavy lines or crown.

Remainders of Nos. 95-98 received various private overprints, mostly as publicity for stamp exhibitions. They were not postally valid.

Stamps of 1910-18 Surcharged:

7 a **7** **12** b **12**

1918 Unwmk.

99	A14(a)	7o on 10o car	38	22
100	A14(b)	12o on 25o red org	2.75	30
a.		Inverted surcharge	150.00	250.00
101	A14(a)	12o on 65o pale ol grn	2.00	70
102	A14(a)	27o on 55o pale bl	95	1.10
103	A14(a)	27o on 65o pale ol grn	2.00	2.25
104	A14(a)	27o on 80o blk	80	1.10
		Nos. 99-104 (6)	8.88	5.67

Arms A15

Heraldic Lion Supporting Arms of Sweden A16

Two types each of 5o green, 5o copper red and 10o violet, type A16.

Perf. 10 Vertically.

1920-25 Engr. Unwmk.

115	A15	3o cop red	25	20
116	A16	5o green	3.50	6
117	A16	5o cop red ('21)	5.75	8
118	A16	10o grn ('21)	16.00	8
a.		Tete beche pair	*1,000.*	*1,250.*
119	A16	10o vio ('25)	3.50	6
120	A16	25o org ('21)	17.50	25
121	A16	30o brown	50	20

Wmk. Wavy Lines. (181)

122	A16	5o green	1.40	15
123	A16	5o cop red ('22)	7.50	42
124	A16	10o grn ('22)	2.00	30
125	A16	30o brown	4.25	2.25
		Nos. 115-125 (11)	62.15	4.05

Coil Stamps

Unless part of a booklet pane any stamp perforated only horizontally or vertically is a coil stamp.

1920-26 Unwmk. *Perf. 10*

126	A16	5o green	4.00	42
a.		Booklet pane of 10	50.00	
127	A16	10o grn ('21)	9.50	2.00
a.		Booklet pane of 10	105.00	
128	A16	10o vio ('25)	5.00	28
a.		Booklet pane of 10	55.00	
129	A16	30o brown	27.50	3.00

Wmk. Wavy Lines. (181)

130	A16	5o green	9.50	9.75
131	A16	10o grn ('21)	21.00	25.00
a.		Bklt. pane of 10	300.00	

Perf. 13 Vertically

Unwmk.

132	A16	5o grn ('25)	4.00	70
133	A16	5o cop red ('21)	200.00	90.00
134	A16	10o vio ('26)	12.00	15.00

Wmk. Wavy Lines. (181)

135	A16	5o grn ('25)	1.75	1.00
136	A16	5o cop red ('22)	1.75	1.50
137	A16	10o grn ('24)	6.00	8.50
138	A16	10o vio ('25)	4.00	6.00
		Nos. 126-138 (13)	306.00	163.15

The paper used for the earlier printings of types A16, A17, A18, A18a and A20 is usually tinted by the color of the stamp. Printings of 1934 and later are on white paper in slightly different shades.

King Gustaf V — A17

1920-21 Unwmk. *Perf. 10 Vertically*

139	A17	10o rose	17.50	20
140	A17	15o claret	30	18
141	A17	20o blue	25.00	20

Perf. 10

142	A17	10o rose	10.50	3.00
143	A17	20o bl ('21)	21.00	3.50
a.		Booklet pane of 10	300.00	
		Nos. 139-143 (5)	74.30	7.08

Wmk. Wavy Lines. (181)

144	A17	20o blue	*2,000.*	

Crown and Post Horn A18 A18a

See note after No. 138 regarding paper. There are 2 types of the 35, 40, 45 and 60o.

1920-34 Unwmk. *Perf. 10 Vert.*

145	A18	35o yel ('22)	25.00	32
146	A18	40o ol grn	25.00	40
147	A18	45o brn ('22)	1.10	40
148	A18	60o claret	17.50	12
149	A18	70o red brn ('22)	80	90
150	A18	80o dp grn	70	20
151	A18	85o myr grn ('29)	2.75	32
152	A18	90o lt bl ('25)	37.50	12
153	A18a	1kr dp org ('21)	6.00	12
154	A18	110o ultra	70	12
155	A18	115o red brn ('29)	7.00	25
156	A18	120o gray blk ('25)	47.50	35
157	A18	120o lil rose ('33)	6.00	52
158	A18	140o gray blk	95	20
159	A18	145o brt grn ('30)	5.75	52

Wmk. Wavy Lines. (181)

160	A18	35o yel ('23)	35.00	1.75
161	A18	60o red vio	47.50	45.00
162	A18	80o bl grn	4.00	1.45
163	A18	110o ultra	2.75	1.50
		Nos. 145-163 (19)	273.50	54.56

Gustavus Adolphus
A19

King Gustaf V
A20

Perf. 10 Vertically.

1920, July 28 **Unwmk.**

164	A19	20o dp bl	3.00	40

Wmk. Wavy Lines. (181)

165	A19	20o blue	70.00	10.00

Unwmk. ***Perf. 10***

166	A19	20o blue	6.00	1.50
a.		Bklt. pane of 10	75.00	

Tercentenary of Swedish post which first ran between Stockholm and Hamburg.

1921-36 **Unwmk.** ***Perf. 10 Vert.***

See note after No. 138 regarding paper.
There are two types each of the 15o rose and 40o olive green.

167	A20	15o vio ('22)	13.00	8
168	A20	15o rose ('25)	6.50	6
169	A20	15o brn ('36)	4.75	6
170	A20	20o violet	28	6
171	A20	20o rose ('22)	15.00	28
172	A20	20o org ('25)	28	35
174	A20	25o rose red ('22)	45	70
175	A20	25o dk bl ('25)	15.00	8
176	A20	25o dk ultra ('34)	15.00	20
177	A20	25o yel org ('36)	25.00	10
178	A20	30o bl ('23)	15.00	20
179	A20	30o brn ('25)	25.00	10
180	A20	30o lt ultra ('36)	5.50	20
181	A20	35o red vio ('30)	10.50	14
182	A20	40o blue	40	55
183	A20	40o ol grn ('29)	25.00	60
184	A20	45o brn ('29)	3.50	28
185	A20	50o gray	1.75	14
186	A20	85o myr grn ('25)	9.00	1.25
187	A20	115o brn red ('25)	10.00	1.25
188	A20	145o ap grn ('25)	6.25	1.25
		Nos. 167-188 (21)	207.16	7.93

Wmk. Wavy Lines. (181)

189	A20	15o vio ('22)	1,500.	400.00
189A	A20	20o violet		1,150.

1922-36 **Unwmk.** ***Perf. 10***

190	A20	15o violet	18.00	25
a.		Booklet pane of 10	300.00	
191	A20	15o rose red ('25)	20.00	12
a.		Booklet pane of 10	315.00	
192	A20	15o brn ('36)	4.50	12
a.		Booklet pane of 10	72.50	
193	A20	20o vio ('22)	45	50
a.		Booklet pane of 10	7.25	

Gustavus Vasa — A21

1921, June ***Perf. 10 Vertically.***

194	A21	20o violet	8.25	10.50
195	A21	110o ultra	50.00	3.00
196	A21	140o gray blk	27.50	2.75

400th anniversary of Gustavus Vasa's war of independence from the Danes.

Universal Postal Union Congress

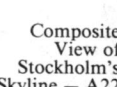

Composite View of Stockholm's Skyline — A22

King Gustaf V — A23

1924, July 4 **Unwmk.** ***Perf. 10***

197	A22	5o red brn	2.00	1.75
198	A22	10o green	2.00	1.75
199	A22	15o dk vio	2.00	1.75
200	A22	20o rose red	11.00	9.50
201	A22	25o dp org	17.50	12.00
202	A22	30o dp bl	15.00	13.00
a.		30o grnsh bl	75.00	55.00
203	A22	35o black	21.00	19.00
204	A22	40o ol grn	22.50	22.50
205	A22	45o dp brn	22.50	19.00
206	A22	50o gray	25.00	22.50
207	A22	60o vio brn	50.00	42.50
208	A22	80o myr grn	40.00	27.50
209	A23	1k green	90.00	70.00
210	A23	2k rose red	160.00	175.00
211	A23	5k dp bl	350.00	375.00

Wmk. Wavy Lines. (181)

212	A22	10o green	15.00	17.50
		Nos. 197-212 (16)	845.50	830.25

Universal Postal Union Issue.

Postrider Watching Airplane
A24

Carrier Pigeon and Globe — A25

1924, Aug. 16 **Engr.** **Unwmk.**

213	A24	5o red brn	2.75	2.50
214	A24	10o green	3.50	2.50
215	A24	15o dk vio	3.00	2.25
216	A24	20o rose red	16.00	16.00
217	A24	25o dp org	20.00	12.50
218	A24	30o dp bl	20.00	13.00
a.		30o grnsh bl	90.00	35.00
219	A24	35o black	21.00	21.00
220	A24	40o ol grn	25.00	21.00
221	A24	45o dp brn	35.00	22.50
222	A24	50o gray	37.50	30.00
223	A24	60o vio brn	50.00	37.50
224	A24	80o myr grn	47.50	26.00
225	A25	1k green	85.00	72.50
226	A25	2k rose red	150.00	72.50
227	A25	5k dp bl	350.00	175.00

Wmk. Wavy Lines. (181)

228	A24	10o green	20.00	18.00
		Nos. 213-228 (16)	886.25	544.75

Royal Palace at Stockholm — A26

Death of Gustavus Adolphus — A27

1931, Nov. 26 **Unwmk.** ***Perf. 10***

229	A26	5k dk grn	92.50	5.25
a.		Bklt. pane of 10	1,750.	

1932, Nov. 1

230	A27	10o dk vio	2.00	1.75
a.		Booklet pane of 10	27.50	
231	A27	15o dk red	3.00	1.00
a.		Bklt. pane of 10	52.50	

Perf. 10 Vertically

232	A27	10o dk vio	2.00	18
233	A27	15o dk red	2.00	18
234	A27	25o dk bl	5.75	60
235	A27	90o dk grn	18.00	1.65
		Nos. 230-235 (6)	32.75	5.36

300th anniv. of the death of King Gustavus Adolphus II who was killed on the battlefield of Lützen, Nov. 6, 1632.

Catching Sunlight in Bowl — A28

1933, Dec. 6 ***Perf. 10.***

236	A28	5o green	2.75	60
a.		Booklet pane of 10	37.50	

There are two types of No. 236.

Perf. 10 Vertically.

237	A28	5o green	2.75	12

Perf. 13 Vertically.

238	A28	5o green	3.50	3.00

50th anniv. of the Swedish Postal Savings Bank.

The Old Law Courts — A29

Stock Exchange — A30

Parish Church (Storkyrkan)
A31

House of The Nobility
A32

House of Parliament — A33

The "Four Estates" and Arms of Engelbrekt — A34

1935, Jan. 10 ***Perf. 10***

239	A29	5o green	2.50	50
a.		Bklt. pane of 10	45.00	
240	A30	10o dl vio	2.50	2.25
a.		Booklet pane of 10	45.00	
241	A31	15o carmine	3.50	1.10
a.		Booklet pane of 10	67.50	

Perf. 10 Vertically

242	A29	5o green	1.25	10
243	A30	10o dl vio	4.75	10
244	A31	15o carmine	1.90	10
245	A32	25o ultra	9.00	50
246	A33	35o dp cl	14.00	1.40
247	A34	60o dp cl	18.00	1.40
		Nos. 239-247 (9)	57.40	7.45

500th anniv. of the Swedish Parliament.

Chancellor Axel Oxenstierna
A35

Post Runner
A36

Mounted Courier — A37

Old Sailing Packet — A38

Mail Paddle Steamship
A39

Mail Coach
A40

1855 Stamp Model — A41

Mail Train — A42

Postmaster General A. W. Roos — A43

Mail Truck and Trailer — A44

Modern Swedish Liner A45

Junkers Plane with Pontoons A46

1936, Feb. 20 Engr. *Perf. 10.*

248	A35	5o green	1.90	35
a.		Bklt. pane of 18	95.00	
249	A36	10o dk vio	2.00	1.40
a.		Bklt. pane of 18	110.00	
250	A37	15o dk car	3.50	35
a.		Bklt. pane of 18	205.00	

Perf. 10 Vertically.

251	A35	5o green	1.90	18
252	A36	10o dk vio	1.90	18
253	A37	15o dk car	1.90	18
254	A38	20o lt bl	9.00	2.25
255	A39	25o lt ultra	6.00	35
256	A40	30o yel brn	22.50	1.65
257	A41	35o plum	6.50	1.10
258	A42	40o ol grn	6.00	1.40
259	A43	45o myr grn	9.25	1.65
260	A44	50o gray	24.00	1.65
261	A45	60o maroon	30.00	48
262	A46	1k dp bl	9.25	4.00
		Nos. 248-262 (15)	135.60	17.17

300th anniv. of the Swedish Postal Service.
See Nos. 946-950, B55-B56.

Airplane over Bromma Airport A47

Emanuel Swedenborg A48

1936, May 23 *Perf. 10 Vert.*

263	A47	50o ultra	6.00	6.25

Opening of Bromma Airport near Stockholm.

Swedish Booklets

Before 1940, booklets were hand-made and usually held two panes of 10 stamps (2x5). About every third booklet contained one row of stamps with straight edges at right or left side. Se-tenant pairs may be obtained with one stamp perforated on 4 sides and one perforated on 3 sides.

Starting in 1940, booklet stamps have one or more straight edges.

1938, Jan. 29 *Perf. 12½.*

264	A48	10o violet	90	12
a.		Perf. on 3 sides	12.00	2.00
b.		Bklt. pane of 10	20.00	

Perf. 12½ Vertically.

266	A48	10o violet	90	8
267	A48	100o green	6.00	75

250th anniv. of the birth of Emanuel Swedenborg, scientist, philosopher and religious writer.

Johann Printz and Indian Chief A49

"Kalmar Nyckel" Sailing from Gothenburg A50

Symbolizing the Settlement of New Sweden — A51

Holy Trinity Church, Wilmington, Del. — A52

Queen Christina — A53

1938, Apr. 8 *Perf. 12½ Vert.*

268	A49	5o green	60	8
269	A50	15o brown	60	6
270	A51	20o red	3.00	40
271	A52	30o ultra	6.50	60
272	A53	60o brn lake	9.75	14

Perf. 12½.

273	A49	5o green	95	48
a.		Perf. on 3 sides	11.00	3.50
b.		Bklt. pane of 18	57.50	
274	A50	15o brown	1.65	40
a.		Perf. on 3 sides	16.00	3.25
b.		Bklt. pane of 18	80.00	
		Nos. 268-274 (7)	23.05	2.16

Tercentenary of the Swedish settlement at Wilmington, Del. See No. B54.

King Gustaf V — A54

1938, June 16 *Perf. 12½ Vert.*

275	A54	5o green	60	8
276	A54	15(o) brown	60	6
277	A54	30(o) ultra	16.00	55

Perf. 12½.

278	A54	5o green	95	25
a.		Perf. on 3 sides	20.00	2.50
b.		Bklt. pane of 10	22.50	
279	A54	15(o) brown	1.25	18
a.		Perf. on 3 sides	27.50	80
b.		Bklt. pane of 10	27.50	
		Nos. 275-279 (5)	19.40	1.12

80th birthday of King Gustaf V.

King Gustaf V A55

Three Crowns A56

1939 *Perf. 12½ Vertically*

280	A55	10o violet	1.00	8
281	A55	20o carmine	1.75	25
282	A56	60o lake	3.25	6
283	A56	85o dk grn	1.00	15
284	A56	90o pck bl	2.25	6
285	A56	1k orange	75	5
286	A56	1.15k hn brn	90	6
287	A56	1.20k brt rose vio	3.25	10
288	A56	1.45k lt yel grn	4.25	40

Perf. 12½.

289	A55	10o violet	2.00	1.75
a.		Perf. on 3 sides	40.00	40.00
b.		Bklt. pane of 10, perf. on 4 sides	21.00	
		Nos. 280-289 (10)	20.40	2.96

See Nos. 394-398, 416-417, 425-426, 431, 439-441, 473, 588-591, 656-664.

Per Henrik Ling — A57

1939, Feb. 25 *Perf. 12½ Vert.*

290	A57	5o green	15	5
291	A57	25(o) brown	1.00	20

Perf. 12½.

292	A57	5o green	85	32
a.		Perf. on 3 sides	16.00	2.00
b.		Bklt. pane of 10	13.00	

Issued in commemoration of the centenary of the death of P. H. Ling, father of Swedish gymnastics.

J. J. Berzelius A58

Carl von Linne A59

Perf. 12½ Vertically.

1939, June 2 Engr.

293	A58	10o violet	1.75	8
294	A59	15o fawn	42	8
295	A58	30o ultra	12.50	25
296	A59	50o gray	11.00	50

Perf. 12½.

297	A58	10o violet	1.75	38
a.		Perf. on 3 sides	85.00	22.50
b.		Booklet pane of 10	30.00	
298	A59	15o fawn	2.75	15
a.		Perf. on 3 sides	16.00	15
b.		Booklet pane of 10	52.50	
c.		As "a," bklt. pane of 20	550.00	
		Nos. 293-298 (6)	30.17	1.44

200th anniv. of the founding of the Royal Academy of Science at Stockholm.

King Gustaf V — A60

Type A55 Re-engraved

1939-46 *Perf. 12½*

299	A60	5o dp grn ('46)	25	5
a.		Booklet pane of 20, perf. on 4 sides	250.00	
b.		Perf. on 3 sides ('41)	35	5
c.		As "b," bklt. pane of 20	11.00	
300	A60	10(o) vio ('46)	25	5
a.		Booklet pane of 10, perf. on 4 sides	32.50	
b.		Booklet pane of 20, perf. on 4 sides	250.00	
c.		Perf. on 3 sides	1.00	15
i.		As "c," bklt. pane of 20	55.00	
300D	A60	15(o) chnt ('46)	25	12
e.		Booklet pane of 20, perf. on 4 sides	60.00	
f.		Perf. on 3 sides ('45)	50	35
j.		As "f," bklt. pane of 20	8.00	
300G	A60	20(o) red ('42)	35	5
h.		Booklet pane of 20	8.00	

No. 300 differs slightly from the original due to deeper engraving. No. 300G was issued only in booklets; all copies have one straight edge.

1940-42 *Perf. 12½ Vertically*

301	A60	5o dp grn ('41)	18	5
302	A60	10(o) violet	18	5
302A	A60	15(o) chnt ('42)	22	5
303	A60	20(o) red	18	5
304	A60	25(o) orange	1.10	5
305	A60	30(o) ultra	52	5
306	A60	35(o) red vio ('41)	95	8
307	A60	40(o) ol grn	95	5
308	A60	45(o) dk brn	95	8
309	A60	50(o) gray blk ('41)	3.50	10
		Nos. 301-309 (10)	8.73	61

Numerals measure 4½mm high. Less shading around head gives a lighter effect. Horizontal lines only as background for "SVERIGE."

See Nos. 391-393, 399.

Karl Mikael Bellman A61

Tobias Sergel A62

1940, Feb. 4 Engr. ***Perf. 12½ Vert.***

310 A61 5o green 12 8
311 A61 35(o) rose red 75 18

Perf. 12½.

312 A61 5o green 1.00 28
a. Perf. on 3 sides 9.00 50
b. Booklet pane of 10 21.00
c. As "a," bklt. pane of 20 475.00

Bellman (1740-95), lyric poet.

1940, Sept. 5 ***Perf. 12½ on 3 Sides.***

313 A62 15o lt brn 5.00 25
a. Bklt. pane of 20 300.00

Perf. 12½ Vertically.

314 A62 15o lt brn 2.00 6
315 A62 50o gray blk 18.00 50

Bicentenary of birth of Johan Tobias von Sergel (1740-1814), sculptor.

Reformers Presenting Bible to Gustavus Vasa A63

View of Skansen A64

1941, May 11 ***Perf. 12½ on 3 Sides***

316 A63 15o brown 1.90 30
a. Bklt. pane of 18 100.00

Perf. 12½ Vertically.

317 A63 15o brown 25 8
318 A63 90o ultra 16.00 48

400th anniv. of the 1st authorized version of the Bible in Swedish.

1941, June 18 ***Perf. 12½ on 3 Sides***

319 A64 10o violet 2.00 40
a. Bklt. pane of 20 70.00

Perf. 12½ Vertically

320 A64 10o violet 1.25 10
321 A64 60o red lil 11.50 30

50th anniv. of Skansen, an open air extension of the Nordic Museum.

Royal Palace at Stockholm A65

Artur Hazelius A66

1941 ***Perf. 12½ on 3 Sides***

322 A65 5k blue 2.00 30
a. Perf. on 4 sides 30.00 1.00
b. Bklt. pane 20, perf. 3 sides 50.00
c. Bklt. pane 10, perf. 4 sides 575.00

For coil stamp see No. 537.

1941, Aug. 30 ***Perf. 12½ on 3 Sides.***

323 A66 5o lt grn 2.50 35
a. Bklt. pane of 20 100.00

Perf. 12½ Vertically.

324 A66 5o lt grn 18 6
325 A66 1k lt org 11.00 1.90

Issued to honor Artur Hazelius, founder of Skansen, Nordic museum.

St. Bridget of Sweden — A67

Perf. 12½ on 3 Sides.

1941, Oct. 7 **Engr.**

326 A67 15o dp brn 1.65 28
a. Bklt. pane of 18 47.50

Perf. 12½ Horiz.

327 A67 15o dp brn 35 8
328 A67 1.20k red vio 32.50 8.25

King Gustavus III A68

K. G. Tessin, Architect A69

1942, June 29 ***Perf. 12½ on 3 Sides***

329 A68 20o red 1.25 28
a. Bklt. pane of 20 42.50

Perf. 12½ Vertically

330 A68 20o red 60 6
331 A69 40o ol grn 24.00 80

Issued to commemorate the sesquicentennial of the Swedish National Museum, Stockholm.

Torsten Rudenschold and Nils Mansson — A70

1942, July 1 ***Perf. 12½ Horiz.***

332 A70 10o magenta 45 25
a. Booklet pane of 10 4.50

Perf. 12½ Vertically

333 A70 10o magenta 40 25
334 A70 90o lt bl 4.00 4.00

Issued to commemorate the 100th anniversary of the Swedish Public School System.

Carl Wilhelm Scheele — A71

King Gustaf V — A72

1942, Dec. 9 ***Perf. 12½ on 3 Sides***

335 A71 5o green 1.40 50
a. Bklt. pane of 20 45.00

Perf. 12½ Vertically.

336 A71 5o green 15 8
337 A71 60o dp mag 10.00 25

200th anniv. of the birth of Carl Wilhelm Scheele, chemist.

Perf. 12½ Horizontally.

1943, June 16

338 A72 20o red 60 18
339 A72 30o ultra 1.40 1.65
340 A72 60o brt red vio 2.25 2.50

Perf. 12½ on 3 Sides.

341 A72 20o red 6.50 42
a. Bklt. pane of 20 275.00

85th birthday of King Gustaf V, June 16.

Rifle Federation Emblem A73

Oscar Montelius A74

1943, July 22 ***Perf. 12½ Vert.***

342 A73 10o rose vio 18 6
343 A73 90o dp ultra 6.00 30

Perf. 12½ on 3 Sides.

344 A73 10o rose vio 42 42
a. Booklet pane of 20 10.00

Issued to commemorate the 50th anniversary of the Swedish Voluntary Rifle Associations.

1943, Sept. 9 Engr. ***Perf. 12½ Vert.***

345 A74 5o green 12 8
346 A74 1.20k brt red vio 10.00 1.65

Perf. 12½ on 3 Sides

347 A74 5o green 55 28
a. Booklet pane of 20 14.00

Birth centenary of Oscar Montelius (1843-1921), archaeologist.

Johan Mansson's Chart of Baltic, 1644 — A75

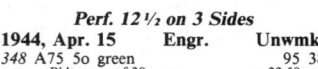

Perf. 12½ on 3 Sides

1944, Apr. 15 Engr. Unwmk.

348 A75 5o green 95 38
a. Bklt. pane of 20 22.50

Perf. 12½ Vertically.

349 A75 5o green 12 6
350 A75 60o lake 6.50 25

Issued to commemorate the tercentenary of the first Swedish Marine Chart.

"The Lion of Smaland" A76

Clas Fleming A77

"Kung Karl" — A78

"Gustaf V" — A80

Stern of "Amphion," Flagship of Gustavus III — A79

1944, Oct. 13 ***Perf. 12½ Vert.***

351 A76 10o purple 30 18
352 A77 20o red 45 8
353 A78 30o blue 60 40
354 A79 40o ol grn 75 55
355 A80 90o gray blk 9.75 1.00

Perf. 12½ on 3 Sides.

356 A76 10o purple 75 55
a. Booklet pane of 20 19.00
357 A77 20o red 2.50 25
a. Booklet pane of 20 90.00
Nos. 351-357 (7) 15.10 3.01

Issued to honor the Swedish Fleet and mark the tercentenary of the Swedish naval victory at Femern, 1644.

See Nos. B53, B57-B58.

Catalogue values for unused stamps in this section, from this point to the end of the section, are for Never Hinged items.

Red Cross — A81

Torch and Quill Pen — A82

1945, Feb. 27 ***Perf. 12½ Vert.***

358 A81 20o red 1.10 8

Perf. 12½ on 3 Sides

359 A81 20o red 3.50 50
a. Bklt. pane of 20 92.50

Issued to commemorate the 80th anniversary of the Swedish Red Cross Society.

1945, May 29 ***Perf. 12½ Vert.***

360 A82 5o green 25 8
361 A82 60o car rose 9.75 28

Perf. 12½ on 3 Sides

362 A82 5o green 50 35
a. Booklet pane of 20 10.00

Tercentenary of Swedish press.

Viktor Rydberg A83

Oak Tree A84

1945, Sept. 21 ***Perf. 12½ Vert.***

363 A83 20o red 45 5
364 A83 90o blue 12.00 35

Perf. 12½ on 3 Sides.

365 A83 20o red 2.00 25
a. Bklt. pane of 20 57.50

Viktor Rydberg (1828-95), author.

1945, Oct. 27 ***Perf. 12½ Vert.***

366 A84 10o violet 32 25
367 A84 40o olive 1.65 95

Perf. 12½ on 3 Sides.

368 A84 10o violet 65 50
a. Booklet pane of 20 14.00

Issued to commemorate the 125th anniversary of the Savings Bank movement.

Angel and Lund Cathedral — A85

View of Lund Cathedral — A86

Perf. 12½ Vertically.

1946, May 28 Unwmk.

369 A85 15o org brn 1.00 24
370 A86 20o red 32 5
371 A85 90o ultra 11.00 60

Perf. 12½ on 3 Sides.

372 A85 15o org brn 1.10 75
a. Bklt. pane of 20 27.50
373 A86 20o red 2.25 18
a. Bklt. pane of 20 57.50
Nos. 369-373 (5) 15.67 1.82

Lund Cathedral, 800th anniversary.

Mare and Colt — A87

Esaias Tegner — A88

1946, June 8 *Perf. 12½ Vert.*
374 A87 5o green 18 8
375 A87 60o car rose 7.00 40

Perf. 12½ on 3 Sides
376 A87 5o green 38 45
a. Booklet pane of 20 8.00

Issued to commemorate the centenary of Swedish agricultural shows.

Perf. 12½ Vertically
1946, Nov. 2 **Engr.** **Unwmk.**
377 A88 10o dp vio 18 10
378 A88 40o dk ol grn 2.00 38

Perf. 12½ on 3 Sides.
379 A88 10o dp vio 38 32
a. Booklet pane of 20 7.75

Death centenary of Esaias Tegner (1782-1846), poet.

Alfred Nobel A89

Erik Gustaf Geijer A90

1946, Dec. 10 *Perf. 12½ Vert.*
380 A89 20o red 70 8
381 A89 30o ultra 2.50 55

Perf. 12½ on 3 Sides.
382 A89 20o red 2.25 18
a. Booklet pane of 20 52.50

Issued to commemorate the 50th anniversary of the death of Alfred Nobel, inventor and philanthropist.

1947, Apr. 23 *Perf. 12½ Vert.*
383 A90 5o dk yel grn 15 8
384 A90 90o ultra 5.50 15

Perf. 12½ on 3 Sides.
385 A90 5o dk yel grn 35 20
a. Booklet pane of 20 7.50

Issued to commemorate the centenary of the death of Erik Gustaf Geijer, historian, philosopher and poet.

King Gustaf V — A91

1947, Dec. 8 **Engr.** *Perf. 12½ Horiz.*
386 A91 10o dp vio 14 14
387 A91 20o red 20 18
388 A91 60o red vio 1.50 1.25

Perf. 12½ on 3 Sides
389 A91 10o dp vio 15 18
a. Booklet pane of 20 3.00
390 A91 20o red 42 28
a. Booklet pane of 20 8.50
Nos. 386-390 (5) 2.41 2.03

40th anniv. of the reign of King Gustaf V.

King and 3-Crown Types of 1939

1948 Unwmk. *Perf. 12½ Vertically.*
391 A60 5o orange 25 5
392 A60 10o green 30 5
393 A60 25o violet 1.00 10
394 A56 55o org brn 4.50 15
395 A56 80o ol grn 1.50 8
396 A56 1.10k violet 11.00 5
397 A56 1.40k dk bl grn 1.50 8
398 A56 1.75k brt grnsh bl 35.00 6.50

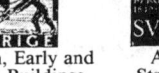

Perf. 12½ on 3 Sides.
399 A60 10o green 25 12
a. Booklet pane of 20 7.00
Nos. 391-399 (9) 55.30 7.18

Plowman, Early and Modern Buildings A92

August Strindberg A93

1948, Apr. 26 *Perf. 12½ Vert.*
400 A92 15o org brn 28 12
401 A92 30o ultra 1.00 32
402 A92 1k orange 2.75 55

Perf. 12½ on 3 Sides
403 A92 15o org brn 55 30
a. Booklet pane of 20 11.00

Issued to commemorate the centenary of the Swedish pioneers' settlement in the United States.

1949, Jan. 22 *Perf. 12½ Vert.*
404 A93 20o red 45 8
405 A93 30o blue 1.00 45
406 A93 80o ol grn 2.75 35

Perf. 12½ on 3 Sides.
407 A93 20o red 1.00 18
a. Booklet pane of 20 20.00

Birth centenary of August Strindberg (1849-1912), author and playwright.

Girl and Boy Gymnasts — A94

Perf. 12½ Horiz.
1949, July 27 **Engr.**
408 A94 5o ultra 20 16
409 A94 15o brown 24 16

Perf. 12½ on 3 Sides.
410 A94 15o brown 55 55
a. Bklt. pane of 20 10.50

Issued to publicize the second Lingiad or World Gymnastics Festival, Stockholm, July-August 1949.

A95

Symbols of UPU — A96

1949, Oct. 9 *Perf. 12½ Vert.*
411 A95 10o green 20 12
412 A95 20o red 25 10

Perf. 12½ Horizontally.
413 A96 30o lt bl 60 32

Perf. 12½ on 3 sides.
414 A95 10o green 25 15
a. Booklet pane of 20 4.00
415 A95 20o red 30 12
a. Booklet pane of 20 4.75
Nos. 411-415 (5) 1.60 81

75th anniv. of the formation of the UPU.

Three-Crown Type of 1939.

Perf. 12½ Vertically.
1949, Nov. 11 **Unwmk.**
416 A56 65o lt yel grn 1.25 12
417 A56 70o pck bl 7.25 95

Gustaf VI Adolf (Letters in color) A97

Christopher Polhem A98

1951, June 6 *Perf. 12½ Vert.*
Without Imprint
418 A97 10o dl grn 24 5
419 A97 15o chnt brn 35 10
420 A97 20o car rose 35 15
421 A97 25o gray 80 5
422 A97 30o ultra 48 15

Perf. 12½ on 3 sides.
423 A97 10o dl grn 24 15
a. Booklet pane of 20 6.00
424 A97 25o gray 48 15
a. Booklet pane of 20 11.00
Nos. 418-424 (7) 2.94 80

See Nos. 435-438, 442-443, 456-461, 502, 505-509, 515-517.

Three-Crown Type of 1939.

1951, June 1 *Perf. 12½ Vert.*
425 A56 85o org brn 9.00 1.25
426 A56 1.70k red 1.65 6

1951, Aug. 30 *Perf. 12½ Vert.*
427 A98 25o gray 70 15
428 A98 45o brown 55 55

Perf. 12½ on 3 sides.
429 A98 25o gray 50 50
a. Booklet pane of 20 11.00

Issued to commemorate the 200th anniversary of the death of Christopher Polhem, engineer and technician.

Numeral (Lettering in color) A99

Olaus Petri Preaching A100

Type A99 and 3-Crown Type of 1939

1951, Nov. **Engr.** *Perf. 12½ Vert.*
430 A99 5o rose car 24 6
431 A56 1.50k red vio 2.25 1.10

For other stamps similar to type A99, see type A115a, Nos. 503-504, 513-514, 570, 580, 666-667.

1952, Apr. 19 *Perf. 12½ Horiz.*
432 A100 25o gray blk 30 9
433 A100 1.40k brown 4.00 60

Perf. 12½ on 3 sides.
434 A100 25o gray blk 2.00 1.50
a. Booklet pane of 20 52.50

400th anniversary of death of Olaus Petri (1493-1552), Lutheran clergyman, historian and Bible translator.

King and 3-Crown Types of 1951 and 1939.

1952 *Perf. 12½ Vertically.*
Without Imprint
435 A97 20o gray 35 5
436 A97 25o car rose 2.50 5
437 A97 30o dk brn 45 20
438 A97 40o blue 90 14
439 A56 50o gray 10.00 12
440 A56 75o org brn 5.50 45
441 A56 2k red vio 1.40 5

Perf. 12½ on 3 sides
442 A97 20o gray 70 22
a. Booklet pane of 20 14.00
443 A97 25o car rose 90 14
a. Bklt pane of 20 18.00
Nos. 435-443 (9) 22.70 1.42

Ski Jump A101

Ice Hockey A102

Designs: 40o, Woman throwing slingball. 1.40kr, Wrestlers.

Perf. 12½ Vert. (V), Horiz. (H)
1953, May 27
444 A101 10o grn (V) 55 22
445 A102 15o brn (H) 90 40
446 A102 40o dp bl (H) 1.40 95
447 A101 1.40k red vio (V) 4.00 80

Perf. 12½ on 3 sides.
448 A101 10o green 1.10 70
a. Booklet pane of 20 22.50
Nos. 444-448 (5) 7.95 3.07

50th anniv. of Swedish Athletic Association.

Old Stockholm A103

Original and Present Seals of Stockholm A104

1953, June 17 *Perf. 12½ Vert.*
449 A103 25o blue 30 5
450 A104 1.70k red 4.25 45

Perf. 12½ on 3 sides.
451 A103 25o blue 85 22
a. Booklet pane of 20 22.50

Issued to commemorate the 700th anniversary of the founding of Stockholm.

"Telephone" — A105

Designs: 40o, "Radio." 60o, "Telegraph."

1953, Nov. 22 *Perf. 12½ Horiz.*
452 A105 25o dp ultra 30 5
453 A105 40o ol grn 1.25 85
454 A105 60o dp car 1.75 1.25

Perf. 12½ on 3 sides.
455 A105 25o dp ultra 80 18
a. Booklet pane of 20 18.00

Issued to commemorate the centenary of the foundation of the Swedish Telegraph Service.

King Type of 1951.

1954 *Perf. 12½ Vertically*
Without Imprint
456 A97 10o dk brn 12 5
457 A97 25o ultra 25 5
458 A97 30o red 25.00 15
459 A97 40o ol grn 85 15

Perf. 12½ on 3 sides
460 A97 10o dk brn 22 15
a. Bklt. pane of 10 9.00
b. Bklt. pane of 20 7.00
461 A97 25o ultra 22 5
a. Bklt. pane of 4 14.00
b. Bklt. pane of 8 125.00
c. Bklt. pane of 20 12.00
Nos. 456-461 (6) 26.66 60

The booklet pane of 4 contains two copies of No. 461 which are perforated on two adjoining sides.

Skier
A106

Anna Maria Lenngren
A107

Design: 1k, Girl skier.

1954, Feb. 13 *Perf. 12½ Vert.*
462 A106 20o gray 60 24
463 A106 1k blue 13.00 90

Perf. 12½ on 3 sides.
464 A106 20o gray 2.00 1.25
a. Bklt. pane of 20 45.00

Issued to publicize the World Ski Championship Matches, 1954.

1954, June 18 *Perf. 12½ Horiz.*
465 A107 20o gray 35 15
466 A107 65o dk brn 9.00 1.65

Perf. 12½ on 3 sides
467 A107 20o gray 2.00 1.00
a. Bklt. pane of 20 45.00

Issued to commemorate the 200th anniversary of the birth of Anna Maria Lenngren, author.

Rock Carvings
A108

Coat of Arms
A109

1954, Nov. 8 *Perf. 12½ Vert.*
468 A108 50o gray 40 5
469 A108 60o dp car 40 5
470 A108 65o dk ol grn 2.00 20
471 A108 75o dk brn 3.25 20
472 A108 90o dk bl 1.00 8
Nos. 468-472 (5) 7.05 58

See Nos. 510-512, 655.

Three-Crown Type of 1939
1954, Dec. 10 *Perf. 12½ Vert.*
473 A56 2.10k dp ultra 12.00 12

1955, May 16 *Perf. 12½ Vert.*
474 A109 25o blue 15 5
475 A109 40o green 1.65 25

Perf. 12½ on 3 sides
476 A109 25o blue 15 10
a. Bklt. pane of 4 9.00
b. Bklt. pane of 20 5.00

Issued to commemorate the centenary of Sweden's first postage stamps.
The booklet pane of 4 contains two copies of No. 476 which are perforated on two adjoining sides.

Crown and Flag — A110

Perf. 12½
1955, June 6 **Unwmk.** **Litho.**
477 A110 10o grn, bl & yel 20 12
478 A110 15o lake, bl & yel 24 15

National Flag Day.

Foreign postal stationery (stamped envelopes, postal cards and air letter sheets) lies beyond the scope of this Catalogue, which is limited to adhesive postage stamps.

A111

Wmk. 307

Wmk. Crown and 1955 (307)
1955, July 1 **Typo.** *Perf. 13*
479 A111 3o yel grn 3.50 4.00
480 A111 4o blue 3.50 4.00
481 A111 6o gray 3.50 4.00
482 A111 8o org yel 3.50 4.00
483 A111 24o salmon 3.50 4.00
Nos. 479-483 (5) 17.50 20.00

Cent. of the 1st Swedish postage stamps. Nos. 479-483 were printed in sheets of nine. They were sold in complete sets at the Stockholmia Philatelic Exhibition, July 1-10, 1955. A set cost 45 ore (face value) plus 2k (entrance fee). Value for set of 5 sheets, $150 unused, $200 canceled.

Per Atterbom
A112

Greek Horseman
A113

Perf. 12½ Horizontally.
1955, July 21 **Engr.** **Unwmk.**
484 A112 20o dk bl 32 20
485 A112 1.40k sepia 4.50 55

Perf. 12½ on 3 sides.
486 A112 20o dk bl 1.65 1.00
a. Booklet pane of 20 37.50

Cent. of the death of Per Daniel Amadeus Atterbom, poet.

1956, Apr. 16 *Perf. 12½ Vert.*
487 A113 20o carmine 20 10
488 A113 25o ultra 20 10
489 A113 40o gray grn 1.75 1.00

Perf. 12½ on 3 sides.
490 A113 20o carmine 42 30
a. Booklet pane of 20 8.75
491 A113 25o ultra 42 18
a. Booklet pane of 20 8.75
Nos. 487-491 (5) 2.99 1.68

Issued to publicize the Olympic Equestrian Competitions, Stockholm, June 10-17, 1956.

Northern Countries Issue.

Whooper Swans — A113a

Perf. 12½ Vertically
1956, Oct. 30 **Engr.** **Unwmk.**
492 A113a 25o rose red 60 9
493 A113a 40o ultra 2.25 48

See footnote after Norway No. 354.

Railroad Builders — A114

Ship in Distress and Lifeboat — A115

Designs: 25o, First Swedish locomotive and passenger car. 40o, Express train crossing Arsta bridge.

1956, Dec. 1 *Perf. 12½ Vert.*
494 A114 10o ol grn 48 15
495 A114 25o ultra 32 10
496 A114 40o orange 2.25 2.00

Perf. 12½ on 3 sides.
497 A114 10o ol grn 48 35
a. Booklet pane of 20 10.00
498 A114 25o ultra 60 45
a. Booklet pane of 20 15.00
Nos. 494-498 (5) 4.13 3.05

Centenary of Swedish railroads.

Perf. 12½ Vertically
1957, June 1 **Engr.** **Unwmk.**
499 A115 30o blue 6.25 10
500 A115 1.40k dp rose 8.00 75

Perf. 12½ on 3 sides
501 A115 30o blue 2.00 75
a. Bklt. pane of 20 50.00

Issued to commemorate the 50th anniversary of the Swedish Life Saving Society.

King Type of 1951.
1957, June 1 *Perf. 12½ Vert.*
Without Imprint
502 A97 25o dk brn 1.65 1.65

Re-engraved Types of 1951 and 1954 with Imprint, and

Numeral (Letters in white) — A115a

1957-64 *Perf. 12½ Vertically*
503 A115a 5o red ('61) 10 5
a. 5o dk red 15 15
504 A115a 10o bl ('61) 15 5
a. 10o dk bl 30 15
505 A97 15o dk red 32 5
506 A97 20o gray 32 5
507 A97 25o brown 1.10 5
508 A97 30o blue 60 5
509 A97 40o ol grn 1.40 12
510 A108 55o vermilion 1.50 18
511 A108 70o orange 1.10 12
512 A108 80o yel grn 1.10 6

Perf. 12½ on 3 sides
513 A115a 5o red ('61) 10 5
a. Bklt. pane of 20 ('64) 2.00
b. 5o dk red 1.25 20
c. Bklt. pane of 10 (5 No. 513b + 5 No. 515) 9.50
514 A115a 10o bl ('61) 15 6
a. 10o dk bl 12.00 2.00
b. Bklt. pane of 4 (1 No. 514a + 3 No. 517) 30.00
515 A97 15o dk red 65 12
a. Bklt. pane of 20 14.00
516 A97 20o gray 1.10 32
a. Bklt. pane of 20 30.00
517 A97 30o blue 1.40 5
a. Bklt. pane of 20 35.00
Nos. 503-517 (15) 11.09 1.38

In the redrawn Numeral type A99, "Sverige, ore" and the "g" tail flourishes are white instead of in color.
Booklet pane including No. 513 is listed as No. 581b.
The booklet pane of 4, No. 514b, contains two copies of No. 517 which are imperf. on two adjoining sides. No. 514a was issued only in booklet pane No. 514b.
See Nos. 570, 580, 580a, 581b, 584b, 586b-586c, 668a, 669b-669c.

Helicopter Mail Service — A116

Modern and 17th Century Vessels — A117

Perf. 12½ Vertically
1958, Feb. 10 **Engr.** **Unwmk.**
518 A116 30o blue 20 8
519 A116 1.40k brown 7.25 50

Perf. 12½ on 3 sides
520 A116 30o blue 1.10 30
a. Booklet pane of 20 22.50

Issued to commemorate the 10th anniversary of helicopter mail service to the Stockholm archipelago, Feb. 10.

1958, Feb. 10 *Perf. 12½ Vert.*
521 A117 15o dk red 35 20
522 A117 40o gray ol 6.00 2.50

Perf. 12½ on 3 sides
523 A117 15o dk red 60 52
a. Booklet pane of 20 12.00

Issued to commemorate three centuries of transatlantic mail service.

Soccer Player — A118

1958, May 8 *Perf. 12½ Vert.*
524 A118 15o vermilion 30 15
525 A118 20o yel grn 35 15
526 A118 1.20k dk bl 1.50 70

Perf. 12½ on 3 sides.
527 A118 15o vermilion 50 32
a. Bklt. pane of 20 10.00
528 A118 20o yel grn 50 35
a. Bklt. pane of 20 10.00
Nos. 524-528 (5) 3.15 1.67

Issued to publicize the 6th World Soccer Championships, Stockholm, June 8-29.

Bessemer Converter
A119

Selma Lagerlof
A120

Perf. 12½ Horizontally
1958, June 18 **Engr.** **Unwmk.**
529 A119 30o gray bl 30 8
530 A119 1.70k dl red brn 4.00 55

Perf. 12½ on 3 sides
531 A119 30o gray bl 90 38
a. Bklt. pane of 20 20.00

Issued to commemorate the centenary of the first successful Bessemer blow in Sweden, July 18, 1858.

1958, Nov. 20 *Perf. 12½ Horiz.*
532 A120 20o dk red 20 14
533 A120 30o blue 20 12
534 A120 80o gray ol 1.00 75

Perf. 12½ on 3 Sides
535 A120 20o dk red 60 40
a. Bklt. pane of 20 13.00
536 A120 30o blue 60 40
a. Bklt. pane of 20 13.00
Nos. 532-536 (5) 2.60 1.81

Issued to commemorate the centenary of the birth of Selma Lagerlof, writer.

Palace Type of 1941
1958, Sept. 17 *Perf. 12½ Vert.*
537 A65 5k blue 3.00 18

Electric Power Line — A121

Hydroelectric Plant and Dam — A122

Perf. 12½ Horiz. (H), Vert. (V)
1959, Jan. 20 **Unwmk.**
538 A121 30o ultra (H) 50 8
539 A122 90o car rose (V) 4.00 1.65

Perf. 12½ on 3 sides
540 A121 30o ultra 70 32
a. Bklt. pane of 20 16.00

50th anniv. of the establishment of the State Power Board.

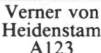

Verner von Heidenstam A123

Forest A124

Perf. 12½ Horizontally

1959, July 6 Engr. Unwmk.

541 A123 15o rose car 1.00 10
542 A123 1k slate 6.50 55

Perf. 12½ on 3 Sides

543 A123 15o rose car 90 45
a. Bklt. pane of 20 18.00

Issued to commemorate the centenary of the birth of Verner von Heidenstam, poet.

1959, Sept. 4 ***Perf. 12½ Horiz.***

Design: 1.40k, Felling tree.

544 A124 30o green 1.50 8
545 A124 1.40k brn red 5.00 45

Perf. 12½ on 3 sides.

546 A124 30o green 1.10 65
a. Booklet pane of 20 25.00

Centenary of administration of crown lands and forests.

Svante Arrhenius A125

Anders Zorn A126

Perf. 12½ Horizontally

1959, Dec. 10 Engr. Unwmk.

547 A125 15o dl red brn 35 10
548 A125 1.70k dk bl 4.50 30

Perf. 12½ on 3 sides

549 A125 15o dl red brn 60 30
a. Bklt. pane of 20 12.00

Birth centenary of Svante Arrhenius (1859-1927), chemist and physicist.

1960, Feb. 18 ***Perf. 12½ Horiz.***

550 A126 30o gray 28 12
551 A126 80o sepia 3.50 90

Perf. 12½ on 3 sides

552 A126 30o gray 1.65 30
a. Booklet pane of 20 35.00

Birth centenary of Anders Zorn (1860-1920), painter and sculptor.

Uprooted Oak Emblem — A127

People of Various Races, WRY Emblem — A128

Perf. 12½ Vert. (V), Horiz. (H)

1960, Apr. 7 Engr. Unwmk.

553 A127 20o red brn (V) 12 10
554 A128 40o pur (H) 45 42

Perf. 12½ on 3 sides

555 A127 20o red brn 45 38
a. Booklet pane of 20 10.00

Issued to publicize World Refugee Year, July 1, 1959-June 30, 1960.

Target Shooting A129

Gustaf Froding A130

Design: 90o, Parade of riflemen.

1960, June 30 ***Perf. 12½ Vert.***

556 A129 15o rose car 28 14
557 A129 90o grnsh bl 3.00 1.25

Perf. 12½ on 3 sides

558 A129 15o rose car 48 38
a. Booklet pane of 20 10.00

Issued to commemorate the centenary of the founding of the Voluntary Shooting Organization.

1960, Aug. 22 ***Perf. 12½ Horiz.***

559 A130 30o red brn 28 10
560 A130 1.40k sl grn 3.75 25

Perf. 12½ on 3 sides

561 A130 30o red brn 55 18
a. Booklet pane of 20 12.00

Birth centenary of Gustaf Froding (1860-1911), poet.

Europa Issue, 1960

Common Design Type

1960, Sept. 19 ***Perf. 12½ Vert.***

Size: 27x21mm.

562 CD3 40o blue 20 16
563 CD3 1k red 48 40

Hjalmar Branting — A131

Perf. 12½ Horiz.

1960, Nov. 23 Engr.

564 A131 15o rose car 16 10
565 A131 1.70k sl bl 5.00 35

Perf. 12½ on 3 sides

566 A131 15o rose car 35 20
a. Booklet pane of 20 7.25

Issued to commemorate the centenary of the birth of Hjalmar Branting (1860-1925), Labor Party leader and Prime Minister.

SAS Issue

DC-8 Airliner — A131a

Perf. 12½ Vertically

1961, Feb. 24 Unwmk.

567 A131a 40o blue 28 15

Perf. 12½ on 3 sides

568 A131a 40o blue 1.10 65
a. Booklet pane of 10 11.50

Issued to commemorate the 10th anniversary of the Scandinavian Airlines System, SAS.

Numeral Type of 1957, Three-Crown Type of 1939 and

Gustaf VI Adolf (Letters, numerals in white) A132

Rune Stone, Oland, 11th Century A133

1961-1965 ***Perf. 12½ Vert.***

570 A115a 15o grn ('62) 28 8
571 A132 15o red 32 8
572 A132 20o gray 32 5
573 A132 25o brown 32 5
574 A132 30o ultra 4.50 8
575 A132 30o lil ('62) 55 5
576 A132 35o lilac 55 5
577 A132 35o ultra ('62) 1.10 8
578 A132 40o emerald 1.00 5
579 A132 50o gray grn ('62) 1.40 8

Perf. 12½ on 3 sides

580 A115a 15o grn ('65) 28 15
a. Bklt. pane of 6 (2 each #514, 580, 583) 2.25
581 A132 15o red 22 15
a. Bklt. pane of 20 5.00
b. Bklt. pane of 10 (5 each #513, 581) 2.50
582 A132 20o gray 90 75
a. Bklt. pane of 20 17.50
583 A132 25o brn ('62) 32 20
a. Bklt. pane of 20 15.00
b. Bklt. pane of 4 2.25
584 A132 30o ultra 65 20
a. Bklt. pane of 20 15.00
b. Bklt. pane of 4 (1 No. 514 + 3 No. 584) 4.00
585 A132 30o lil ('64) 65 30
a. Bklt. pane of 20 14.00
586 A132 35o ultra ('62) 55 5
a. Bklt. pane of 20 16.00
b. Bklt. pane of 5 (3 No. 514 + 2 No. 586 + blank label) 5.00
c. Bklt. pane of 5 (3 No. 514 + 2 No. 586 + inscribed label) 3.50

Perf. 12½ Vertically

588 A56 1.05k Prus grn ('62) 3.50 50
589 A56 1.50k brn ('62) 2.50 50
590 A56 2.15k dk sl grn ('62) 14.00 60
591 A56 2.50k emerald 1.90 10

Perf. 12½ on 3 sides

592 A133 10k dl red brn 16.00 1.00
a. Bklt. pane of 10 ('68) 190.00
b. Bklt. pane of 20 475.00
Nos. 570-592 (22) 51.81 5.15

Booklet panes of 4, 5 or 6 (Nos. 580a, 583b, 584b, 586b, 586c) contain two stamps which are imperf. on two adjoining sides.

Combination panes (Nos. 580a, 581b, 584b, 586b, 586c) come in different arrangements of the denominations.

The label of No. 586c is inscribed "ett brev / betyder / sa / mycket" ("a letter means so much"). The label inscription "nord 63 / 5-13 oktober / GÖTEBORG" was privately applied to No. 586b by the Gothenburg Philatelic Society to raise funds for Nord 63 Philatelic Exhibition in Gothenburg. The pane was sold for the equivalent of $1 U.S., 5 times face value.

See Nos. 648-654A, 666a, 668-672F.

K.-G. Pilo, Self-portrait A134

Jonas Alstromer A135

1961, Apr. 17 ***Perf. 12½ Horiz.***

594 A134 30o brown 25 10
595 A134 1.40k Prus bl 5.00 70

Perf. 12½ on 3 sides

596 A134 30o brown 1.25 30
a. Bkt. pane of 20 30.00

250th anniversary of birth of Karl-Gustaf Pilo (1711-1793), painter. Self-portrait from "The Coronation of Gustavus III."

1961, June 2 ***Perf. 12½ Vert.***

597 A135 15o dl cl 18 15
598 A135 90o grnsh bl 1.50 1.10

Perf. 12½ on 3 sides

599 A135 15o dl cl 35 35
a. Bklt. pane of 20 7.25

Issued to commemorate the 200th anniversary of the birth of Jonas Alstromer, pioneer of agriculture and industry.

17th Century Printer and Student in Library — A136

Roentgen, Prudhomme, von Behring, van't Hoff — A137

Perf. 12½ Vert.

1961, Sept. 22 Engr.

600 A136 20o dk red 20 12
601 A136 1k blue 14.00 75

Perf. 12½ on 3 sides

602 A136 20o dk red 35 28
a. Bklt. pane of 20 7.25

Issued to commemorate the 300th anniversary of the regulation requiring copies of all Swedish printed works to be deposited in the Royal Library.

1961, Dec. 9 ***Perf. 12½ Vertically***

603 A137 20o vermilion 18 12
604 A137 40o blue 18 12
605 A137 50o green 28 12

Perf. 12½ on 3 sides

606 A137 20o vermilion 35 24
a. Bklt. pane of 20 7.00

Issued to commemorate the winners of the 1901 Nobel Prize; Wilhelm K. Roentgen, Rene Sully Prudhomme, Emil von Behring, Jacob van't Hoff.

Footsteps and Postmen's Badges — A138

1962, Jan. 29 Engr. ***Perf. 12½ Vert.***

607 A138 30o lilac 32 10
608 A138 1.70k rose red 4.75 25

Perf. 12½ on 3 sides

609 A138 30o lilac 55 35
a. Bklt. pane of 20 11.00

Issued to commemorate the centenary of local mail delivery service in Sweden.

Voting Tool (Budkavle), Codex of Law and Gavel — A139

1962, Mar. 21 ***Perf. 12½ Horiz.***

610 A139 30o dk bl 32 8
611 A139 2k red 4.75 25

Perf. 12½ on 3 sides

612 A139 30o dk bl 55 35
a. Bklt. pane of 20 11.00

Issued to commemorate the centenary of the municipal reform laws.

An enhanced introduction to the Scott Catalogue begins on Page V. A thorough understanding of the material presented there will greatly aid your use of the catalogue itself.

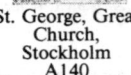

St. George, Great Church, Stockholm
A140

Skokloster Castle
A141

Perf. 12½ Horiz. (H), Vert. (V)

1962, Sept. 24

613	A140 20o rose lake (H)		28	12
614	A141 50o dk sl grn (V)		45	18

Perf. 12½ on 3 sides

615 A140 20o rose lake	28	18
a. Booklet pane of 20	6.00	
616 A141 50o dk sl grn	1.00	65
a. Booklet pane of 10	10.00	

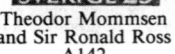

Theodor Mommsen and Sir Ronald Ross
A142

Ice Hockey
A143

Design: 50o, Hermann Emil Fischer, Pieter Zeeman and Hendrik Antoon Lorentz.

1962, Dec. 10 ***Perf. 12½ Vert.***

617 A142 25o dk red	38	22
618 A142 50o blue	38	20

Perf. 12½ on 3 sides

619 A142 25o dk red	75	60
a. Booklet pane of 20	15.00	

Winners of the 1902 Nobel Prize. See Nos. 689-692, 710, 712, 769-772, 805, 807.

1963, Feb. 15 ***Perf. 12½ Horiz.***

620 A143 25o green	20	12
621 A143 1.70k vio bl	3.50	48

Perf. 12½ on 3 sides

622 A143 25o green	40	40
a. Bklt. pane of 20	8.00	

1963 Ice Hockey World Championships.

Wheat Emblem and Stylized Hands — A144

Engineering and Industry Symbols — A145

1963, Mar. 21 ***Perf. 12½ Vertically***

623 A144 35o lil rose	20	7
624 A144 50o violet	32	24

Perf. 12½ on 3 sides

625 A144 35o lil rose	32	24
a. Bklt. pane of 20	6.50	

FAO "Freedom from Hunger" campaign.

1963, May 27 ***Perf. 12½ Vertically***

626 A145 50o gray	40	24
627 A145 1.05k orange	3.50	2.00

Perf. 12½ on 3 sides

628 A145 50o gray	2.75	2.25
a. Bklt. pane of 10	27.50	

The lack of a value for a listed item does not necessarily indicate rarity.

Gregoire François Du Reitz
A146

Hammarby, Home of Carl von Linne (Linnaeus)
A147

Perf. 12½ Vertically

1963, Sept. 16 **Engr.** **Unwmk.**

629 A146 25o brown	38	30
630 A146 30o dk bl	22	9
631 A146 2k dk red	4.75	48

Perf. 12½ on 3 sides

632 A146 25o brown	95	70
a. Booklet pane of 20	20.00	
633 A146 35o dk bl	45	20
a. Bklt. pane of 20	10.00	
Nos. 629-633 (5)	6.75	1.77

Issued to commemorate the 300th anniversary of the Swedish Board of Health. Dr. Du Rietz (1607-1682) was first president of the "Collegium Medicorum," forerunner of the Board of Health.

1963, Oct. 25 ***Perf. 12½ Vert.***

634 A147 20o org red	18	15
635 A147 50o yel grn	30	15

Perf. 12½ on 3 sides

636 A147 20o org red	30	35
a. Bklt. pane of 20	6.00	

Svante Arrhenius, Niels Finsen, Bjornstjerne Bjornson
A148

"The Assumption of Elijah"
A149

Design: 50o, Antoine Henri Becquerel, Pierre and Marie Curie.

Perf. 12½ Vertically

1963, Dec. 10 **Engr.** **Unwmk.**

637 A148 25o gray ol	50	42
638 A148 50o chocolate	50	24

Perf. 12½ on 3 sides

639 A148 25o gray ol	75	90
a. Bklt. pane of 20	15.00	

Winners of the 1903 Nobel Prize. See Nos. 711, 713, 804, 806.

1964, Feb. 3 ***Perf. 12½ Horiz.***

640 A149 35o lt ultra	80	10
641 A149 1.05k dl red	7.25	2.50

Perf. 12½ on 3 sides

642 A149 35o lt ultra	48	35
a. Bklt. pane of 20	10.00	

Issued to commemorate the centenary of the birth of the poet Erik Axel Karlfeldt (1864-1931).

Seal of Archbishop Stephen — A150

1964, June 12 ***Perf. 12½ Horiz.***

643 A150 40o sl grn	20	15
644 A150 60o org brn	32	24

Perf. 12½ Vertically

645 A150 40o sl grn	20	15
a. Bklt. pane of 10	2.00	
646 A150 60o org brn	32	24
a. Bklt. pane of 10	3.25	

Issued to commemorate the 800th anniversary of the Archbishopric of Uppsala. Nos. 645-646 are from the booklet panes.

Types of Regular Issues, 1939-61, and

Post Horns
A151

Ship Grave, Skane (Bronze Age)
A152

1964-71 **Engr.** ***Perf. 12½ Vert.***

647	A151	20o sl bl & org yel ('65)	16	5
648	A132	35o gray	70	22
649	A132	40o ultra	90	8
650	A132	45o orange	90	8
651	A132	45o vio bl ('67)	90	8
652	A132	50o grn ('68)	60	5
652A	A132	55o dk red ('69)	60	5
653	A132	60o rose car	1.25	75
653A	A132	65o dl grn ('71)	1.40	8
654	A132	70o lil rose ('67)	70	22
654A	A132	85o dp cl ('71)	1.40	35
655	A108	95o violet	8.75	4.50
656	A56	1.20k lt bl	11.00	2.50
657	A56	1.80k dk bl ('67)	4.00	52
658	A56	1.85k bl ('67)	12.00	1.10
659	A56	2k dp car ('69)	80	8
660	A56	2.30k choc ('65)	32.50	25
661	A56	2.55k red	10.00	2.50
662	A56	2.80k red ('67)	6.25	18
663	A56	2.85k org ('65)	8.00	5.25
664	A56	3k brt ultra	2.75	12
665	A152	3.50k grnsh gray ('66)	2.00	18

Perf. 12½ on 3 Sides

666	A115a	10o brown	24	22
a.		Bklt. pane of 6 (2 each #666, 667, 583)	3.00	
667	A115a	15o brown	52	48
668	A132	30o rose red, perf. on 2 adjoining sides ('66)	1.25	95
a.		Bklt. pane of 6 (2 each #513, 580, 668)	3.00	
b.		Perf. on 3 sides	2.00	1.50
c.		Bklt. pane of 10 (2 each #513-514, 580, 668b-669)	7.00	
669	A132	40o ultra	48	8
a.		Bklt. pane of 20	15.00	
b.		Bklt. pane of 4 (2 each #514, 669)	2.75	
670	A132	45o org ('67)	48	15
a.		Bklt. pane of 20	12.00	
671	A132	45o vio bl ('67)	60	8
a.		Bklt. pane of 20	14.00	
672	A132	50o grn ('69)	65	52
a.		Bklt. pane of 10	7.25	
672B	A132	55o dk red ('69)	65	8
c.		Bklt. pane of 10	7.25	
672D	A132	65o dl grn ('71)	1.00	52
e.		Bklt. pane of 10	11.00	
672F	A132	85o dp cl ('71)	1.25	95
g.		Bklt. pane of 10	14.00	
		Nos. 647-672F (32)	114.68	23.22

Some combination booklet panes of 4, 6 or 10 contain two stamps which are imperf. on two adjoining sides. Combination panes come in different arrangements of the denominations.

Fluorescent Paper
Starting in 1967, fluorescent paper was used in printing both definitive and commemorative issues. Its use was gradually eliminated starting in 1976. Numerous definitives and a few commemoratives were printed on both ordinary and fluorescent paper.

Echegaray, Mistral and Strutt
A153

Visby Town Wall
A154

Designs: 30o, José Echegaray y Eizaguirre, Frédéric Mistral and John William Strutt, Lord Rayleigh. 40o, Sir William Ramsey and Ivan Petrovich Pavlov.

Perf. 12½ Vertically

1964, Dec. 10 **Engr.**

673 A153 30o blue	50	35
674 A153 40o red	55	8

Perf. 12½ on 3 Sides

675 A153 30o blue	70	50
a. Bklt. pane of 20	14.00	
676 A153 40o red	80	14
a. Bklt. pane of 20	18.00	

Winners of the 1904 Nobel Prize.

1965, Apr. 5 ***Perf. 12½ Horiz.***

677 A154 30o dk car rose	18	8
678 A154 2k brt ultra	4.00	20

Perf. 12½ on 3 Sides

679 A154 30o dk car rose	38	30
a. Bklt. pane of 20	7.75	

Antenna
A155

Prince Eugen
A156

1965, May 17 ***Perf. 12½ Horiz.***

680 A155 60o lilac	38	28
681 A155 1.40k bluish blk	3.75	1.00

Perf. 12½ on 3 Sides

682 A155 60o lilac	80	90
a. Bklt. pane of 10	8.00	

Issued to commemorate the centenary of the International Telecommunication Union.

1965, July 5 ***Perf. 12½ Horiz.***

683 A156 40o black	22	6
684 A156 1k brown	2.50	30

Perf. 12½ on 3 Sides

685 A156 40o black	38	12
a. Bklt. pane of 20	7.75	

Issued to commemorate the centenary of the birth of Prince Eugen (1865-1947), painter and patron of the arts.

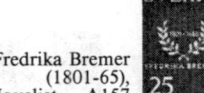

Fredrika Bremer (1801-65), Novelist — A157

Perf. 12½ Vertically

1965, Oct. 25 **Engr.**

686 A157 25o violet	16	6
687 A157 3k gray grn	8.50	35

Perf. 12½ on 3 Sides

688 A157 25o violet	25	18
a. Bklt. pane of 20	5.00	

Nobel Prize Winners Type of 1962.

Designs: 30o, Philipp von Lenard and Adolf von Baeyer. 40o, Robert Koch and Henryk Sienkiewicz.

Perf. 12½ Vertically

1965, Dec. 10 **Unwmk.**

689 A142 30o ultra	50	15
690 A142 40o dk red	40	6

Perf. 12½ on 3 Sides

691 A142 30o ultra 70 35
a. Booklet pane of 20 14.00
692 A142 40o dk red 75 12
a. Booklet pane of 20 15.00

Winners of the 1905 Nobel Prize.

Nathan Soderblom A158

Speed Skater A159

1966, Jan. 15 ***Perf. 12½ Horiz.***

693 A158 60o brown 40 20
694 A158 80o green 1.00 12

Perf. 12½ on 3 Sides

695 A158 60o brown 60 50
a. Bklt. pane of 10 6.00

Issued to commemorate the centenary of the birth of Nathan Soderblom (1866-1931), Protestant theologian, who worked for the union of Christian churches and received 1930 Nobel Peace Prize.

Perf. 12½ on 3 Sides

1966, Feb. 18 **Engr.**

696 A159 5o rose red 10 12
697 A159 25o sl grn 15 18
698 A159 40o dk bl 60 50
a. Bklt. pane of 10 (4 #696, 4 #697, 2 #698) 2.25

World Speed Skating Championships for Men, Gothenburg, Feb. 18-20, and 75th anniversary of World Skating Championships.

National Museum, Staircase, 1866 — A160

Baron Louis Gerhard De Geer — A161

1966, Mar. 26 ***Perf. 12½ Vert.***

699 A160 30o violet 15 15
a. Bklt. pane of 10 1.50
700 A160 2.30k ol grn 1.00 1.00
a. Bklt. pane of 10 10.00

Issued to commemorate the centenary of the National Gallery, Blasieholmen, Stockholm. The design is from an 1866 woodcut showing the inauguration of the Museum.

Perf. 12½ Vertically

1966, May 12 **Engr.**

701 A161 40o dk bl 48 6
702 A161 3k brn car 6.50 55

Perf. 12½ on 3 Sides

703 A161 40o dk bl 48 30
a. Bklt. pane of 20 10.00

Issued to commemorate the centenary of the reform of the Representative Assembly under the leadership of Minister of Justice (1858-1870) Baron Louis Gerhard De Geer (1818-1896).

Stage, Drottningholm Court Theater A162

Carl J. L. Almqvist and Wild Rose A163

Perf. 12½ on 3 Sides

1966, June 15 **Engr.**

Salmon Paper

704 A162 5o vermilion 10 10
705 A162 25o ol bis 12 12
706 A162 40o dk pur 65 65
a. Bklt. pane of 10 (4 #704, 4 #705, 2 #706) 2.50

Issued to commemorate the 200th anniversary of the Drottningholm Court Theater.

Perf. 12½ Horizontally

1966, Sept. 26 **Engr.**

707 A163 25o magenta 30 8
708 A163 1k green 3.50 20

Perf. 12½ on 3 Sides

709 A163 25o magenta 35 20
a. Bklt. pane of 20 7.00

Issued to commemorate the centenary of the death of Carl Jonas Love Almqvist (1793-1866), writer and poet.

Nobel Prize Winner Types of 1962-63

Designs: 30o, Joseph John Thomson and Giosue Carducci. 40o, Henri Moissan, Camillo Golgi and Santiago Ramon y Cajal.

Perf. 12½ Vertically

1966, Dec. 10 **Engr.**

710 A142 30o rose lake 60 20
711 A148 40o dk grn 40 6

Perf. 12½ on 3 Sides

712 A142 30o rose lake 60 35
a. Bklt. pane of 20 12.00
713 A148 40o dk grn 60 35
a. Bklt. pane of 20 12.00

Winners of the 1906 Nobel Prize.

Field Ball Player — A164

Perf. 12½ Horizontally

1967, Jan. 12

714 A164 45o dk vio bl 20 16
715 A164 2.70k dp rose lil 3.50 1.25

Perf. 12½ on 3 Sides

716 A164 45o dk vio bl 32 12
a. Bklt. pane of 20 6.50

Issued to publicize the World Field Ball Championships, Jan. 12-21.

EFTA Emblem — A165

1967, Feb. 15 ***Perf. 12½ Horiz.***

717 A165 70o orange 60 35

Perf. 12½ on 3 Sides

718 A165 70o orange 1.50 1.40
a. Bklt. pane of 10 16.00

European Free Trade Association. Tariffs were abolished Dec. 31, 1966, among EFTA members: Austria, Denmark, Finland, Great Britain, Norway, Portugal, Sweden, Switzerland.

"The Fjeld," by Sixten Lundbohm A166

Lion Fortress, Gothenburg A167

Uppsala Cathedral A168

Gripsholm Castle A169

1967 **Engr.** ***Perf. 12½ Vert.***

719 A166 35o dl bl & blk brn 20 7

Perf. 12½ Horiz.

720 A167 3.70k violet 3.00 10
721 A168 4.50k dl red 2.75 10

Perf. 12½ Vert.

722 A169 7k vio bl & rose red 5.50 30

Perf. 12½ on 3 Sides

723 A166 35o dl bl & blk brn 25 8
a. Bklt. pane of 10 2.50
Nos. 719-723 (5) 11.70 65

Issue Dates: Nos. 719, 721, 723, Mar. 15; No. 720, Feb. 15; No. 722, Apr. 11.

Table Tennis — A170

1967, Apr. 11 ***Perf. 12½ Horiz.***

724 A170 35o brt mag 20 14
725 A170 90o grnsh bl 1.00 42

Perf. 12½ on 3 Sides

726 A170 35o brt mag 35 24
a. Bklt. pane of 20 7.00

Issued to publicize the World Table Tennis Championships, Stockholm.

Man with Axe and Fettered Beast — A171

Double Mortise Corner — A172

Designs: 15o, Man fighting two bears. 30o, Warrior disguised as wolf pursuing enemy. 35o, Two warriors with swords and lances. The designs are taken from 6th century bronze plates (1¾in. x 2½in.) used to decorate helmets; now in Swedish Museum of National Antiquities.

Perf. 12½ on 3 Sides

1967, May 17 **Engr.**

727 A171 10o dk brn & dp bl 7 6
728 A171 15o dp bl & dk brn 20 9
729 A171 30o brt pink & dk brn 22 12
730 A171 35o dk brn & brt pink 22 12
a. Bklt. pane of 10 (4 #727, 2 each #728-730) 1.75

Lithographed and Photogravure

1967, June 16 ***Perf. 12½***

731 A172 10o ol & multi 20 12
732 A172 35o dk bl multi 25 12
a. Bklt. pane of 10 (6 #731, 4 #732) 2.60

Issued to honor generations of Finnish settlers in Sweden.

Right-hand Driving as Seen Through Windshield — A173

1967, Sept. 2 **Engr.** ***Perf. 12½ Vert.***

733 A173 35o dp bl, ocher & blk 15 25
734 A173 45o yel grn, ocher & blk 15 15

Perf. 12½ Horiz.

735 A173 35o dp bl, ocher & blk 24 25
a. Bklt. pane of 10 2.50
736 A173 45o yel grn, ocher & blk 24 15
a. Bklt. pane of 10 2.50

Issued to publicize the introduction of right-hand driving in Sweden, Sept. 3, 1967.

Postrider A174

Griffin A174a

Rocky Isles in Bloom, by Harald Lindberg A175

Dalsland Canal A176

Gothenburg Harbor — A176a

Nils Holgersson Riding Wild Goose — A176b

Elk — A177

Mail Coach, by Eigil Schwab A177a

SVERIGE 140

Illustration from Lapponia, by Johannes Schefferus A177b

Blood-money Coins and Old Map of Sweden A177c

Great Seal, 1439 (St. Erik with Banner and Shield) A177d

Designs: 10o, Merchant vessel in Oresund, 1661. 15o, The Prodigal Son, 13th cent., Rada Church. 20o, St. Stephen as a boy tending horses, medallion from Dädesio Church. No. 742, Lion, from Grodinge tapestry, 15th cent. 45o, Log roller. 60o, Horse-drawn timber sled. 75o, Windmills, Öland Island. 80o, Steamer Storskar and Royal Palace, Stockholm. 95o, Roe deer. 1k, Dancing cranes. 2.55k, Seal of Magnus Ladulas, 1285 (King Magnus Birgersson on throne with lily scepter and orb). 3k, Seal of Duke Erik Magnusson, 1306 (Duke on horseback with standard of Folkunga dynasty). 6k, Gustavus Vasa's silver daler.

1967-72 ***Perf. 12½ Horiz. or Vert.***

737 A174 5o red & blk 10 8
738 A174 10o bl & blk 10 5
739 A177d 15o sl grn, *grnsh* ('71) 18 8
740 A174 20o sep, *buff* ('70) 18 8
741 A174a 25o bis & blk ('71) 22 8
742 A174a 25o blk & bis ('71) 22 8
743 A175 30o ultra & ver 18 8
744 A176 40o blk, dk grn & ultra ('68) 18 6
745 A177 45o bl & brn blk ('70) 22 8
746 A176a 55o bl & vio, perf. 12½ vert. ('71) 35 15
747 A176 60o blk brn ('71) 28 8
747A A176b 65o brt bl ('71) 32 8
748 A177 75o sl grn ('71) 45 8
749 A176 80o bl & blk ('71) 35 8
750 A177 90o sep & bl gray 40 12
750A A175 95o sep ('72) 45 12
751 A177 1k sl grn ('68) 45 8
751A A177a 1.20k multi ('71) 55 15
751B A177b 1.40k lt bl & red ('72) 65 18
752 A177d 2.55k brt bl ('70) 1.75 55
753 A177d 3k dk gray bl ('70) 1.10 15
754 A177c 4k blk ('71) 1.75 15
755 A177d 5k Prus grn ('70) 2.25 15
755A A177c 6k ind ('72) 2.25 15

Nos. 741-742 printed se-tenant.

Perf. 12½ on 3 Sides

756 A174 5o red & blk 6 6
a. Bklt. pane of 20 1.20
757 A174 10o bl & blk ('69) 7 6
a. Bklt. pane of 20 1.40
758 A175 30o ultra & ver 22 12
a. Bklt. pane of 10 3.00
759 A176 40o blk, dk grn & ultra ('68) 35 25
a. Bklt. pane of 10 3.50
760 A176 45o bl & brn blk ('70) 35 15
a. Bklt. pane of 10 3.50
761 A176a 55o bl & vio, perf. 12½horiz. ('71) 35 15
a. Bklt. pane of 10 3.50
762 A176b 65o brt bl ('71) 35 15
a. Bklt. pane of 10 3.50
763 A177 75o sl grn ('72) 1.40 8
a. Bklt. pane of 10 14.00
764 A177 90o sep & bl gray 1.40 75
a. Bklt. pane of 10 14.00
Nos. 737-764 (33) 19.48 4.71

King Gustaf VI Adolf — A178

Perf. 12½ Horiz.

1967, Nov. 11 **Engr.**

765 A178 45o lt ultra 22 8
766 A178 70o green 30 12

Perf. 12½ on 3 Sides

767 A178 45o lt ultra 25 18
a. Bklt. pane of 20 5.00
768 A178 70o green 65 55
a. Bklt. pane of 10 6.50

85th birthday of King Gustaf VI Adolf.

Nobel Prize Winners Type of 1962

Designs: 35o, Eduard Buchner (Chemistry) & Albert A. Michelson (Physics). 45o, Charles L. A. Laveran (Medicine) & Rudyard Kipling (Literature).

1967, Dec. 9 ***Perf. 12½ Vert.***

769 A142 35o vermilion 65 40
770 A142 45o dk bl 35 10

Perf. 12½ on 3 Sides

771 A142 35o vermilion 65 60
a. Bklt. pane of 10 6.50
772 A142 45o dk bl 60 40
a. Bklt. pane of 10 6.00

Winners of the 1907 Nobel Prize.

Franz Berwald, Violin and His Music — A179

National Bank Seal — A180

1968, Apr. 3 ***Perf. 12½ Horiz.***

773 A179 35o blk & red 28 30
774 A179 2k blk, vio bl & org yel 3.50 80

Perf. 12½ on 3 Sides

775 A179 35o blk & red 48 40
a. Bklt. pane of 10 5.00

Issued to commemorate the centenary of the death of Franz Berwald (1796-1868), composer. Design includes opening bar of overture to his opera, "The Queen of Golconda."

Perf. 12½ Vertically

1968, May 15 **Engr.**

776 A180 45o dl bl 25 6
777 A180 70o blk, *pink* 40 12

Perf. 12½ on 3 Sides

778 A180 45o dl bl 50 30
a. Bklt. pane of 10 5.00
779 A180 70o blk, *pink* 80 50
a. Bklt. pane of 10 8.00

Issued to commemorate the 300th anniversary of the National Bank of Sweden. Nos. 777 and 779 are on non-fluorescent paper.

Seal of Lund University A181

Butterfly Orchid A182

1968, June 4 ***Perf. 12½ on 3 sides***

780 A181 10o dp bl 12 15
781 A181 35o red 50 40
a. Bklt. pane of 10 (6 #780, 4 #781) 3.00

300th anniversary of University of Lund.

1968, June 4

Nordic Wild Flowers: No. 783, Wood anemone. No. 784, Dog rose. No. 785, Prune Cherry. No. 786, Lily of the valley.

782 A182 45o sl grn 70 40
783 A182 45o gray grn 70 40
784 A182 45o sl grn & rose car 70 40
785 A182 45o gray grn 70 40
786 A182 45o sl grn 70 40
a. Bklt. pane of 10 (2 each Nos. 782-786) 9.00
Nos. 782-786 (5) 3.50 2.00

World Council of Churches' Emblem A183

Electron Orbits A184

1968, July 4 ***Perf. 12½ Horiz.***

787 A183 70o plum 35 30
788 A183 90o Prus grn 1.00 18

Perf. 12½ on 3 Sides

789 A183 70o plum 60 50
a. Bklt. pane of 10 6.00

Issued to commemorate the 4th General Assembly of the World Council of Churches, Uppsala, July 4-19.

Perf. 12½ Horizontally

1968, Aug. 9 **Engr.**

790 A184 45o rose car 32 10
791 A184 2k dk bl 3.00 25

Perf. 12½ on 3 Sides

792 A184 45o rose car 45 50
a. Bklt. pane of 10 4.50

Issued to commemorate the centenary of the establishment of the first three People's Colleges.

"Orienteer" Finding Way through Forest A185

"Fingerkrok" by Axel Petersson A186

Perf. 12½ Horizontally

1968, Sept. 5 **Engr.**

793 A185 40o vio & red brn 32 18
794 A185 2.80k grn & vio 4.50 2.50

Perf. 12½ on 3 Sides

795 A185 40o vio & red brn 65 42
a. Bklt. pane of 10 6.50

Issued to publicize the World Championships in Orienteering, Linkoping, Sept. 28-29.

Perf. 12½ on 3 Sides

1968, Oct. 28 **Engr.**

796 A186 5o green 12 12
797 A186 25o sepia 1.10 1.10
798 A186 45o blk brn & red brn 24 25
a. Bklt. pane of 8 (3 #796, 2 #797, 3 #798) 3.50

Issued to commemorate the centenary of the birth of Axel Petersson, called "Doderhultarn" (1868-1925), sculptor.

Black-backed Gull — A187

Designs: No. 799, Varying hare. No. 801, Red fox. No. 802, Hooded crows harassing golden eagle. No. 803, Weasel.

Perf. 12½ on 3 Sides

1968, Nov. 9 **Engr.**

799 A187 30o blue 60 60
800 A187 30o black 60 60
801 A187 30o dk brn 60 60
802 A187 30o black 60 60
803 A187 30o blue 60 60
a. Bklt. pane of 10 (2 each #799-803) 7.00
Nos. 799-803 (5) 3.00 3.00

See Nos. 873-877.

Nobel Prize Winners Types of 1962 and 1963

Designs: 35o, Elie Metchnikoff, Paul Ehrlich and Ernest Rutherford. 45o, Gabriel Lippmann and Rudolf Eucken.

1968, Dec. 10 ***Perf. 12½ Vertically***

804 A148 35o maroon 45 25
805 A142 45o dk grn 35 12

Perf. 12½ on 3 Sides

806 A148 35o maroon 75 45
a. Bklt. pane of 10 7.50
807 A142 45o dk grn 55 25
a. Bklt. pane of 10 5.50

Nordic Cooperation Issue

Five Ancient Ships — A187a

1969, Feb. 28 **Engr.** ***Perf. 12½ Vert.***

808 A187a 45o dk gray 48 20
809 A187a 70o blue 60 50

Perf. 12½ on 3 Sides

810 A187a 45o dk gray 1.25 1.00
a. Bklt. pane of 10 12.50

See footnote after Norway No. 524.

Worker, by Albin Amelin — A188

Perf. 12½ Horiz.

1969, Mar. 31 **Engr.**

811 A188 55o dk car rose 25 12
812 A188 70o dk bl 75 40

Perf. 12½ on 3 Sides

813 A188 55o dk car rose 45 15
a. Bklt. pane of 10 4.50

50th anniv. of the ILO.

Europa Issue, 1969

Common Design Type

1969, Apr. 28 **Photo.** ***Perf. 14 Vert.***

Size: 27x22mm.

814 CD12 70o org & multi 60 40
815 CD12 1k vio bl & multi 60 16

Perf. 14 on 3 Sides

816 CD12 70o org & multi 2.00 1.65
a. Bklt. pane of 10 20.00

Not fluorescent.

Albert Engstrom with Owl, Self-portrait A189

Perf. 12½ Vert.

1969, May 12 **Engr.**

817 A189 35o blk brn 30 25
818 A189 55o bl gray 30 12

Perf. 12½ on 3 Sides

819 A189 35o blk brn 42 30
a. Bklt. pane of 10 4.25
820 A189 55o bl gray 35 20
a. Bklt. pane of 10 3.50

Issued to commemorate the centenary of the birth of Albert Engstrom (1869-1940), cartoonist.

Souvenir Sheet

Paintings by Ivan Agueli — A190

1969, June 6 **Litho.** ***Perf. 13½***

821 A190 Sheet of 6, multi 2.25 *3.25*
a. 45o *Landscape* 35 *42*
b. 45o *Still life* 35 *42*
c. 45o *Near East town* 35 *42*
d. 55o *Young woman* 35 *42*
e. 55o *Sunny landscape* 35 *42*
f. 55o *Street at night* 35 *42*

Ivan Agueli (1869-1917), painter. Size: a-c: 35x28mm. d-e, 28x44mm. f, 48x44mm. Not fluorescent.

Tjorn Bridges — A191

Designs: 15o, 30o, Various bridges.

Perf. 12½ on 3 Sides

1969, Sept. 3 **Engr.**

Size: 20x19mm.

Bluish Paper

822 A191 15o dp bl 3.00 50
823 A191 30o dk grn & blk 3.00 50

Size: 41x19mm.

824 A191 55o blk & dp bl 3.50 60
a. Bklt. pane of 6 (2 each #822-824) 22.50

Issued to publicize the Tjorn highway bridges connecting the Islands of Orust and Tjorn in the Gothenburg Archipelago with the mainland.

Man's Head, Woodcarving A192

Warship Wasa, 1628 A193

Designs: No. 826, Crowned lion. No. 827, Great Swedish coat of arms. No. 828, Lion, front view. No. 829, Man's head (different from No. 825).

1969, Sept. 3 ***Perf. 12½ on 3 Sides***

825 A192 55o dk red 50 12
826 A192 55o brown 50 12
827 A192 55o dk bl 50 25
828 A192 55o brown 50 12
829 A192 55o dk red 50 12
830 A192 55o dk bl 50 25
a. Bklt. pane of 10 (#827, #830, 2 each #825-826, 828-829) 5.00
Nos. 825-830 (6) 3.00 98

Issued to publicize the salvaging of the warship Wasa, sunk on her maiden voyage, Aug. 10, 1628, and salvaged in 1961.

Hjalmar Soderberg A194

Bo Bergman A195

Perf. 12½ Horiz.

1969, Oct. 13 **Engr.**

831 A194 45o brn, *buff* 24 12

Perf. 12½ Vert.

832 A195 55o grn, *grnsh* 24 12

Perf. 12½ on 3 Sides

833 A194 45o brn, *buff* 48 35
a. Bklt. pane of 10 5.00
834 A195 55o grn, *grnsh* 48 35
a. Bklt. pane of 10 5.00

Nos. 831 and 833 commemorate the centenary of the birth of Hjalmar Soderberg (1869-1941), writer; Nos. 832 and 834 of Bo Bergman (1869-1967), poet.

Lever Light, Lightship, Landsort and Svenska Lighthouses — A196

Perf. 12½ Vert.

1969, Nov. 17 **Photo.**

835 A196 30o gray, blk & pink 24 20
836 A196 55o lt bl, blk & brn 24 15

Issued to commemorate the 300th anniversary of Swedish lighthouses.

Pelle's New Suit — A197

The Adventures of Nils — A198

Swedish Fairy Tales: No. 839, Pippi Longstocking (little girl, horse and monkey). No. 840, Vill-Vallareman (boy blowing horn). No. 841, Kattresan (child riding on back of cat).

Perf. 12½ on 3 Sides

1969, Nov. 17 **Engr.**

837 A197 35o org, red & dk brn 2.00 1.25
838 A198 35o dk brn 2.00 1.25
839 A197 35o org, red & dk brn 2.00 1.25
840 A198 35o dk brn 2.00 1.25
841 A197 35o org, red & dk brn 2.00 1.25
a. Bklt. pane of 10 (2 each #837-841) 22.50
Nos. 837-841 (5) 10.00 6.25

Issued for use in Christmas cards.

Dr. Emil T. Kocher and Wilhelm Ostwald — A199

Designs: 55o, Selma Lagerlof and open book. 70o, Guglielmo Marconi and Carl Ferdinand Braun.

1969, Dec. 10 ***Perf. 12½ Vert.***

842 A199 45o dl grn 75 30
843 A199 55o blk, *pale sal* 60 12
844 A199 70o black 70 50

Perf. 12½ on 3 Sides

845 A199 45o dl grn 70 50
a. Bklt. pane of 10 7.00
846 A199 50o blk, *pale sal* 60 35
a. Bklt. pane of 10 6.00
Nos. 842-846 (5) 3.35 1.77

Winners of the 1909 Nobel Prize.

Weather Vane, Soderala Church A200

Door with Iron Fittings, Bjorksta Church, Vastmanland A201

Swedish Art Forgings: 10o, like 5o, facing right. 30o, Memorial cross, Ekshärad churchyard, Varmland.

Perf. 12½ on 3 sides

1970, Feb. 9 **Engr.**

847 A200 5o sl grn & brn 55 15
848 A200 10o sl grn & brn 55 15
849 A200 30o blk & sl grn 55 15

Perf. 12½ Vert.

850 A201 55o brn & sl grn 55 15
a. Bklt. pane of 8 (2 each #847-850) 5.00

Ljusman River Rapids A202

Perf. 12½ Vert.

1970, May 11 **Engr.**

851 A202 55o blk & multi 55 8
852 A202 70o blk & multi 1.00 55

Issued to publicize the European Nature Conservation Year, 1970.

Skiing — A203

"Around the Arctic Circle": No. 853, View of Kiruna. No. 855, Boat on mountain lake in Stora Sjofellet National Park. No. 856, Reindeer herd and herdsman. No. 857, Rocket probe under northern lights.

Perf. 12½ Horiz.

1970, June 5 **Engr.**

853 A203 45o sepia 55 50
854 A203 45o vio bl 55 50
855 A203 45o dl grn 55 50
856 A203 45o sepia 55 50
857 A203 45o vio bl 55 50
a. Bklt. pane of 10 (2 each #853-857) 5.50
Nos. 853-857 (5) 2.75 2.50

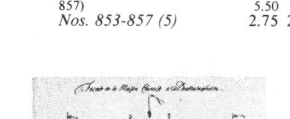

China Palace, Drottningholm Park, 1769 — A204

Perf. 12½ Vert.

1970, Aug. 28 **Photo.**

858 A204 2k yel, grn & pink 2.00 15

Glimmingehus, Skane Province, 15th Century — A205

Perf. 12½ Horiz.

1970, Aug. 28 **Engr.**

859 A205 55o gray grn 30 8

Perf. 12½ on 3 Sides

860 A205 55o gray grn 45 25
a. Booklet pane of 10 4.50

Timber Industry — A206

Shipping Industry — A207

Miner — A208

Designs: No. 863, Heavy industry (propeller). No. 864, Hydroelectric power (dam and diesel). No. 865, Mining (freight train and mine). No. 866, Technical research.

Perf. 12½ on 3 sides

1970, Sept. 28 **Engr.**

861 A206 70o ind & lt brn 5.00 3.00
862 A207 70o ind, lt brn & dp plum 5.00 3.00
863 A206 70o ind & dp plum 5.00 3.00
864 A206 70o ind & dp plum 5.00 3.00
865 A207 70o ind & dp plum 5.00 3.00
866 A206 70o dp plum & lt brn 5.00 3.00
a. Bklt. pane of 6 (#861-866) 30.00
867 A208 1k blk, *buff* 42 12
a. Booklet pane of 10 4.25

Perf. 12½ Vertically

868 A208 1k blk, *buff* 65 10
Nos. 861-868 (8) 31.07 18.22

Issued to publicize Swedish trade and industry.

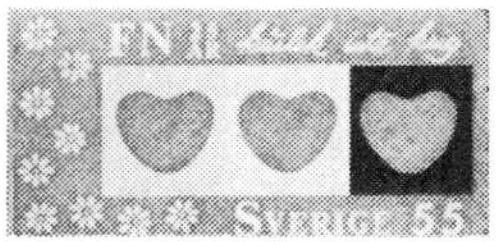

"Love, Not War" A209

Design: 70o, Four-leaf clovers symbolizing efforts for equality and brotherhood.

Engraved and Lithographed

1970, Oct. 24 ***Perf. 12½ Horiz.***

869 A209 55o rose red, yel & blk 38 10
a. Booklet pane of 4 1.65
870 A209 70o emer, yel & blk 52 30
a. Booklet pane of 4 2.25

Perf. 12½ Vert.

871 A209 55o rose red, yel & blk 25 8
872 A209 70o emer, yel & blk 52 25

25th anniversary of the United Nations.

Bird Type of 1968

Birds: No. 873, Blackbird. No. 874, Great titmouse. No. 875, Bullfinch. No. 876, Greenfinch. No. 877, Blue titmouse.

Perf. 12½ on 3 Sides

1970, Nov. 20 **Photo.**

873 A187 30o bl grn & multi 1.00 60
874 A187 30o bis & multi 1.00 60
875 A187 30o bl & multi 1.00 60
876 A187 30o pink & multi 1.00 60
877 A187 30o org yel & multi 1.00 60
a. Bklt. pane of 10 (2 each #873-877) 12.00
Nos. 873-877 (5) 5.00 3.00

Paul Johann Ludwig Heyse A210

Kerstin Hesselgren A211

Designs: 55o, Otto Wallach and Johannes Diderik van der Waals. 70o, Albrecht Kossel.

Perf. 12½ Horiz.

1970, Dec. 10 **Engr.**

878 A210 45o violet 90 45
879 A210 55o sl bl 70 12
880 A210 70o gray 1.25 65

Perf. 12½ on 3 Sides

881 A210 45o violet 1.00 60
a. Booklet pane of 10 10.00
882 A210 55o sl bl 1.25 35
a. Booklet pane of 10 12.50
Nos. 878-882 (5) 5.10 2.17

Winners of the 1910 Nobel Prize.

Perf. 12½ Horiz.

1971, Feb. 19 **Engr.**

883 A211 45o dp cl, *gray* 32 20
884 A211 1k dp brn, *buff* 75 12

Perf. 12½ on 3 Sides

885 A211 45o dp cl, *gray* 50 50
a. Booklet pane of 10 5.00

50th anniversary of woman suffrage; Kerstin Hesselgren, was first woman member of Swedish Upper House.

Terns in Flight — A212

Abstract Music, by Ingvar Lidholm — A213

1971, Mar. 26 *Perf. 13½ Vert.*

886 A212 40o dk red 42 18
887 A212 55o vio bl 95 12

Perf. 12½ on 3 Sides

888 A212 55o vio bl 1.10 18
a. Booklet pane of 10 11.00

Joint northern campaign for the benefit of refugees.

Perf. 12½ Horiz.

1971, Aug. 27 **Engr.**

889 A213 55o dp lil 35 12
890 A213 85o green 55 25

Perf. 12½ on 3 Sides

891 A213 55o dp lil 35 20
a. Booklet pane of 10 3.50

The Three Kings, Grotlingbo Church — A214

Flight into Egypt, Stanga Church A215

Designs: 10o, Adam and Eve, Gammelgarn Church. 55o, Saint on horseback and Samson with the lion, Hogrân Church.

Perf. 12½ on 3 Sides

1971, Sept. 28 **Engr.**

892 A214 50o vio & brn 60 20
893 A214 10o vio & sl grn 60 20

Perf. 12½ Horiz.

894 A215 55o sl grn & brn 80 20
895 A215 65o brn & vio blk 35 12
a. Bklt. pane of 5 (#892-894, 2 #895) 3.00

Art of medieval stonemasons in Gotland.

Toddler and Automobile Wheel — A216

1971, Oct. 20 *Perf. 12½ Vert.*

896 A216 35o blk & red 24 15
897 A216 65o dp bl & multi 35 8

Perf. 12½ on 3 Sides

898 A216 65o dp bl & multi 90 25
a. Booklet pane of 10 9.00

Publicity for road safety.

King Gustavus Vasa's Sword, c. 1500 — A217

Swedish Crown Regalia: No. 900, Scepter. No. 901, Crown. No. 902, Orb (Scepter, crown and orb were made in 1561 for Erix XIV). No. 903, Karl IX's anointing horn, 1606.

Perf. 12½ on 3 Sides

1971, Oct. 20 **Engr.**

899 A217 65o lt bl & multi 60 45
900 A217 65o lt ol grn & multi 60 45
901 A217 65o dk bl & multi 60 45
902 A217 65o lt ol grn & multi 60 45
903 A217 65o lt bl & multi 60 45
a. Bklt. pane of 10 (2 each #899-903) 6.00
Nos. 899-903 (5) 3.00 2.25

Christmas Elf and Goat Bringing Gifts — A218

Christmas Customs (Old Prints): No. 905, Christmas market. No. 906, Dancing children and father playing fiddle. No. 907, Ice-skating on frozen waterways in Stockholm. No. 908, Sleigh ride to church.

1971, Nov. 10

904 A218 35o dp car 1.65 90
905 A218 35o vio bl 1.65 90
906 A218 35o vio brn 1.65 90
907 A218 35o vio bl 1.65 90
908 A218 35o sl grn 1.65 90
a. Bklt. pane of 10 (2 each #904-908) 17.00
Nos. 904-908 (5) 8.25 4.50

Maurice Maeterlinck — A219

Designs: 65o, Wilhelm Wien and Allvar Gullstrand. 85o, Marie Sklodovska Curie.

1971, Dec. 10 *Perf. 12½ Horiz.*

909 A219 55o orange 55 25
910 A219 65o green 55 12
911 A219 85o dk car 1.00 65

Perf. 12½ on 3 Sides

912 A219 55o orange 70 90
a. Booklet pane of 10 7.00
913 A219 65o green 70 25
a. Booklet pane of 10 7.00
Nos. 909-913 (5) 3.50 2.17

Winners of the 1911 Nobel Prize.

Figure Skating — A220

Women Athletes: No. 915, Tennis. No. 916, Gymnastics. No. 917, Diving. No. 918, Fencing.

1972, Feb. 23 *Perf. 12½ on 3 Sides*

914 A220 55o indigo 75 60
915 A220 55o lilac 75 60
916 A220 55o dp grn 75 60
917 A220 55o vio bl 75 60
918 A220 55o dp lil 75 60
a. Bklt. pane of 10 (2 each #914-918) 7.50
Nos. 914-918 (5) 3.75 3.00

Lars Johan Hierta, by Christian Eriksson A221

Frans Michael Franzen, by Soderberg and Hultstrom A222

Hugo Alfven, by Carl Milles A223

Georg Stiernhielm, by David K. Ehrenstrahl A224

Photo., Perf 12½ Horiz. (35, 85o); Engr., Perf. 12½ Vert. (50, 65o)

1972 Feb. 23

919 A221 35o multi 25 20
920 A222 50o violet 30 8
921 A223 65o bluish blk 45 8
922 A224 85o multi 40 20

Hierta (1801-72), journalist (35o). Franzen (1772-1847), poet (50o). Alfven (1872-1960), composer (65o). Stiernhielm (1598-1672), poet, writer, scientist (85o).

Glass Blower A225

Swedish Glassmaking: No. 923, Lifting molten glass. No. 925, Decorating vase. No. 926, Annealing vase. No. 927, Polishing jug.

Perf. 12½ Horiz.

1972, Mar. 22 **Engr.**

923 A225 65o black 1.30 60
924 A225 65o vio bl 1.30 60
925 A225 65o carmine 1.30 60
926 A225 65o black 1.30 60
927 A225 65o vio bl 1.30 60
a. Bklt. pane of 10 (2 each #923-927) 13.00
Nos. 923-927 (5) 6.50 3.00

Horses and Ruin of Borgholm Castle A226

Designs: No. 929, Oland Island Bridge. No. 930, Kalmar Castle. No. 931, Salmon fishing. No. 932, Schooner Falken, Karlskrona.

1972, May 8 *Perf. 12½ Horiz.*

928 A226 55o chocolate 50 45
929 A226 55o dk vio bl 50 45
930 A226 55o chocolate 50 45
931 A226 55o bl grn 50 45
932 A226 55o dk vio bl 50 45
a. Bklt. pane of 10 (2 each #928-932) 5.00
Nos. 928-932 (5) 2.50 2.25

Tourist attractions in Southeast Sweden.

"Only one Earth" Environment Emblem — A227

"Spring," Bror Hjorth — A228

1972, June 5 **Engr.** *Perf. 12½ Vert.*

933 A227 65o bl & car 35 12

Perf. 12½ Horiz.

934 A227 65o bl & car 35 12
a. Booklet pane of 10 3.50

Perf. 12½ Vert.

935 A228 85o brn & multi 75 60
a. Booklet pane of 4 3.00

U.N. Conference on Human Environment, Stockholm, June 5-16.

Junkers JU52 — A229

Historic Planes: 5o, Junkers F13. 25o, Friedrichshafen FF49. 75o, Douglas DC-3.

1972, Sept. 8 *Perf. 12½ on 3 Sides*

Size: 20x19mm.

936 A229 5o lilac 18 8

Size: 44x19mm.

937 A229 15o blue 35 12
938 A229 25o blue 35 15
939 A229 75o gray grn 65 15
a. Bklt. pane of 6 (#937-938, 2 #936, 2 #939) 2.50

Lady with Veil, by Alexander Roslin — A230

Amphion Figurehead, by Per Ljung — A231

Stockholm from the South, by Johan Fredrik Martin — A232

Designs: No. 941, (Queen) Sofia Magdalena, by Carl Gustaf Pilo. No. 943, Quadriga, by Johan Tobias von Sergel. No. 945, Anchor Forge, by Pehr Hillestrom.

Perf. 12½ on 2 Sides, or on 3 Sides (#942-943)

1972, Oct. 7 **Engr.**

940 A230 75o dk brn, blk & dk car 50 30
941 A230 75o dk brn, blk & dk car 50 30
942 A231 75o dk car 50 30
943 A231 75o dk car 50 30

944	A232	75o dk brn	50	30
945	A232	75o prnsh blk	50	30
a.		Bklt. pane of 6 (#940-945)	3.00	
		Nos. 940-945 (6)	3.00	1.80

18th century Swedish art.

Types of 1936
Imprint: "1972"

1972, Oct. 7 ***Perf. 12½ on 3 Sides***

946	A36	10o dk car	40	40
947	A37	15o yel grn	40	40
948	A42	40o dp bl	40	40
949	A44	50o dp cl	40	40
950	A45	60o dp bl	40	40
a.		Bklt. pane of 10 (2 each #946-950)	4.00	
		Nos. 946-950 (5)	2.00	2.00

Centenary of the birth of Olle Hjortzberg (1872-1959), stamp designer. Value of booklet was 5k of which 1.50k was for "Stockholmia 74," International Philatelic Exhibition, Sept. 21-29, 1973.

Santa Claus — A233

St. Lucia Singers A234

Design: No. 952, Candles.

Perf. 14 on 3 Sides

1972, Nov. 6 **Photo.**

951	A233	45o red & multi	35	20
952	A233	45o vio bl & multi	35	28
a.		Bklt. pane of 10 (5 each #951-952)	3.50	

Perf. 12½ Vert.

953	A234	75o gray & multi	55	10

Christmas 1972 (children's drawings).

Horse A235

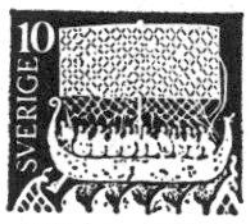

Viking Ship A236

Willows, by Peter A. Persson A237

Trosa, by Reinhold Ljunggren A238

Spring Birches, by Oskar Bergman A239

King Gustaf VI Adolf — A240

Perf. 12½ Horiz. or Vert.

1972-73 **Engr.**

954	A235	5o mar ('73)	10	8
955	A236	10o dk bl ('73)	10	8
956	A237	40o sep ('73)	20	8
957	A238	50o blk & brn ('73)	40	8
958	A239	55o yel grn ('73)	40	10
959	A240	75o indigo	50	8
960	A240	1k dp car	75	8

1973 ***Perf. 12½ on 3 Sides***

961	A235	5o maroon	6	6
a.		Booklet pane of 20	1.20	
962	A236	10o dk bl	6	6
a.		Booklet pane of 20	1.20	
963	A240	75o indigo	50	8
a.		Booklet pane of 10	5.00	
		Nos. 954-963 (10)	3.07	78

King Gustaf VI Adolf A245

Chinese Objects A246

Designs: No. 983, King opening Parliament. No. 984, Etruscan vase and dish. No. 985, King with flowers.

1972, Nov. 11 ***Perf. 12½ Vert.***

981	A245	75o vio bl	3.25	5.00
982	A246	75o sl grn	3.25	5.00
983	A245	75o maroon	3.25	5.00
984	A246	75o vio bl	3.25	5.00
985	A245	75o sl grn	3.25	5.00
a.		Bklt. pane of 5 (#981-985)	17.00	
		Nos. 981-985 (5)	16.25	25.00

90th birthday of King Gustaf VI Adolf. Booklet sold for 4.75k of which 1k was for the King Gustaf VI Adolf Foundation for Swedish Cultural Activities.

Paul Sabatier and Victor Grignard A247

Dr. Alexis Carrel A248

Designs: 75o, Nils Gustaf Dalen. 1k, Gerhart Hauptmann.

1972, Dec. 8 **Engr.** ***Perf. 12½ Vert.***

986	A247	60o ol bis	65	30

Perf. 12½ Horiz.

987	A248	65o dk bl	80	30
988	A248	75o violet	1.10	8
989	A248	1k redsh brn	1.40	15

Winners of the 1912 Nobel Prize.

Mail Coach, 1923 — A249

Design: 70o, Postal autobus, 1972.

Perf. 12½ on 3 Sides

1973, Jan. 18 **Engr.**

990	A249	60o blk, *yel*	30	18
a.		Booklet pane of 10	3.00	

Perf. 12½ Vert.

991	A249	70o bl, org & grn	38	10

Tintomara, by Lars Johan Werle — A250

Orpheus and Eurydice, by Christoph W. Gluck — A251

1973, Jan. 18 ***Perf. 12½ Horiz.***

992	A250	75o green	32	8

Booklet Stamp

993	A251	1k red lil	50	20
a.		Booklet pane of 5	2.50	

Bicentenary of the Royal Theater in Stockholm. The 75o shows a stage setting by Bo-Ruben Hedwall for Tintomara, a new opera, performed for the bicentenary celebration. The 1k shows painting by Pehr Hillestrom of Orpheus and Eurydice, which was first opera performed in Royal Theater.

Vaasa Ski Race, Dalecarlia A252

Designs: No. 995, "Going to Church in Mora" (church boats), by Anders Zorn. No. 996, Church stables, Rättvig. No. 997, Falun copper mine. No. 998, Midsummer Dance, by Bengt Nordenberg.

1973, Mar. 2 ***Perf. 12½ Horiz.***

994	A252	65o sl grn	40	30
995	A252	65o sl grn	40	30
996	A252	65o black	40	30
997	A252	65o sl grn	40	30
998	A252	65o claret	40	30
a.		Bklt. pane of 10 (2 each #994-998)	4.00	
		Nos. 994-998 (5)	2.00	1.50

Tourist attractions in Dalecarlia.

Worker, Confederation Emblem A253

Observer Reading Temperature A254

1973, Apr. 26 ***Perf. 12½ Vert.***

999	A253	75o dk car	45	8
1000	A253	1.40k sl bl	80	12

75th anniversary of the Swedish Confederation of Trade Unions (LO).

Perf. 12½ Vert.

1973, May 24 **Engr.**

Design: No. 1002, Clouds, photographed by US weather satellite.

1001	A254	65o sl grn	1.65	25
1002	A254	65o blk & ultra	1.65	25

Centenary of the Swedish Weather Organization and of International Meteorological Cooperation. Nos. 1001-1002 printed se-tenant.

Nordic Cooperation Issue 1973

Nordic House, Reykjavik A254a

1973, June 26 ***Perf. 12½ Vert.***

1003	A254a	75o multi	70	12
1004	A254a	1k multi	1.10	20

A century of postal cooperation among Denmark, Finland, Iceland, Norway and Sweden and in connection with the Nordic Postal Conference, Reykjavik, Iceland.

Carl Peter Thunberg (1743-1828) — A255

Designs: No. 1006, Anders Sparrman (1748-1820) and Polynesian double canoe. No. 1007, Nils Adolf Erik Nordenskjold (1832-1901) and ship in pack ice. No. 1008, Salomon August Andrée (1854-1897) and balloon on snow field. No. 1009, Sven Hedin (1865-1952) and camel riders.

Perf. 12½ Horiz.

1973, Sept. 22 **Engr.**

1005	A255	1k sl grn, bl & brn	1.25	1.25
1006	A255	1k bl, sl grn & brn	1.25	1.25
1007	A255	1k bl, sl grn & brn	1.25	1.25
1008	A255	1k blk & multi	1.25	1.25
1009	A255	1k blk & multi	1.25	1.25
a.		Bklt. pane of 5 (#1005-1009)	6.25	
		Nos. 1005-1009 (5)	6.25	6.25

Swedish explorers.

Plower with Ox Team A256

Designs: No. 1011, Woman working flax brake. No. 1012, Farm couple planting potatoes. No. 1013, Women baking bread. No. 1014, Man with horse-drawn sower.

Perf. 12½ Horiz.

1973, Oct. 24 **Engr.**

1010	A256	75o grnsh blk	3.25	25
1011	A256	75o red brn	3.25	25
1012	A256	75o grnsh blk	3.25	25
1013	A256	75o plum	3.25	25
1014	A256	75o red brn	3.25	25
a.		Bklt. pane of 10 (2 each #1010-1014)	32.50	
		Nos. 1010-1014 (5)	16.25	1.25

Centenary of Nordic Museum, Stockholm.

Gray Seal A257

King Gustaf VI Adolf A258

Protected Animals: 20o, Peregrine falcon. 25o, Lynx. 55o, Otter. 65o, Wolf. 75o, White-tailed sea eagle.

1973, Oct. 24 ***Perf. 12½ on 3 Sides***

1015	A257	10o sl grn	8	6
1016	A257	20o violet	8	6
1017	A257	25o Prus grn	9	6
1018	A257	55o Prus grn	20	14
1019	A257	65o violet	24	20
1020	A257	75o sl grn	30	20
a.		Bklt. pane of 12 (2 each #1015-1020)	1.65	
		Nos. 1015-1020 (6)	99	72

1973, Oct. 24 ***Perf. 12½ Vert.***

1021	A258	75o dk vio bl	32	10
1022	A258	1k purple	50	15

King Gustaf VI Adolf (1882-1973).

The Three Kings A259

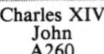

Charles XIV John A260

The Goosegirl, by Josephson A261

Designs: No. 1024, Merry country dance. No. 1026, Basket with stylized Dalecarlian gourd plant.

Perf. 14 Horiz.

1973, Nov. 12 **Photo.**

1023	A259	45o multi	60	15
1024	A259	45o multi	60	15
a.		Bklt. pane of 10 (5 each #1023-1024)	6.00	

Coil Stamps

1025	A260	75o multi	2.50	10
1026	A260	75o multi	2.50	10

Christmas 1973. Designs are from Swedish peasant paintings. Nos. 1025-1026 printed se-tenant.

Perf. 12½ Horiz.

1973, Nov. 12 **Engr.**

1027	A261	10k multi	3.75	35

Ernst Josephson (1851-1906), painter.

Alfred Werner and Heike Kamerlingh-Onnes A262

Charles Robert Richet A263

Design: 1.40k, Rabindranath Tagore.

1973, Dec. 10 **Engr.** ***Perf. 12½ Vert.***

1028	A262	75o dk vio	45	8

Perf. 12½ Horiz.

1029	A263	1k dk brn	75	15
1030	A263	1.40k green	1.00	15

Winners of 1913 Nobel Prize.

Ski Jump A264

Skiing: No. 1032, Cross-country race. No. 1033, Relay race. No. 1034, Slalom. No. 1035, Women's cross-country race.

Perf. 12½ Horiz.

1974, Jan. 23 **Engr.**

1031	A264	65o sl grn	60	70
1032	A264	65o vio bl	60	70
1033	A264	65o sl grn	60	70
1034	A264	65o dk car	60	70
1035	A264	65o vio bl	60	70
a.		Bklt. pane of 10 (2 each #1031-1035)	6.00	
		Nos. 1031-1035 (5)	3.00	3.50

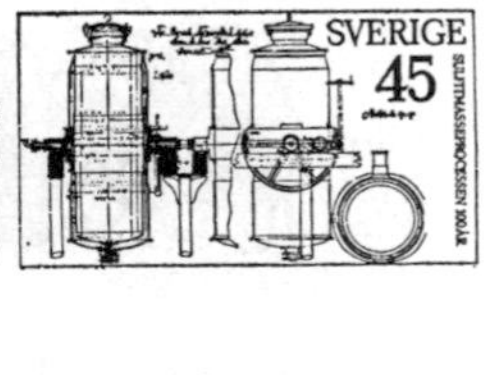

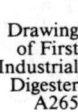

Drawing of First Industrial Digester A265

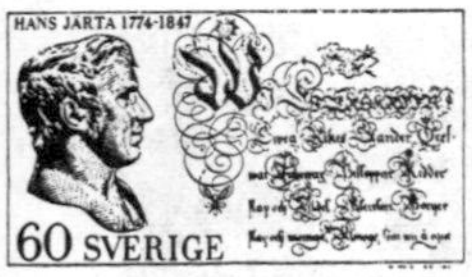

Hans Järta and Quotation from 1809 A266

Samuel Owen and 19th Century Factory A267

1974, Mar. 5 **Engr.** ***Perf. 12½ Vert.***

1036	A265	45o sepia	30	12
1037	A266	60o green	30	20
1038	A267	75o dl red	38	10

Issued to commemorate: Centenary of sulphite pulp process (45o); Bicentenary of the birth of Hans Järta (1774-1847), statesman responsible for the Instrument of Government Act of 1809 (60o); bicentenary of the birth of Samuel Owen (1774-1854), English-born industrialist who introduced new production methods (75o).

Stora Sjofallet (Great Falls) — A268

Street in Ystad — A269

1974, Apr. 2 ***Perf. 12½ Horiz.***

1039	A268	35o bl grn & blk	25	12

Perf. 12½ on 3 Sides

1040	A269	75o dl cl	40	8
a.		Booklet pane of 10	4.50	

UPU Type of 1924 A270

1974 **Engr.** ***Perf. 12½ on 3 Sides***

1041	A270	20o green	20	25
1042	A270	25o ultra	20	25
1043	A270	30o dk brn	20	25
1044	A270	35o dk red	20	25
a.		Bklt. pane of 8 (2 each #1041-1044)	1.75	

Miniature Sheets

Perf. 12½

1045	Sheet of 4	1.90	1.90
a.	A270 20o ocher, single stamp	45	45
1046	Sheet of 4	1.90	1.90
a.	A270 25o dk vio, single stamp	45	45
1047	Sheet of 4	1.90	1.90
a.	A270 30o dk red, single stamp	45	45
1048	Sheet of 4	1.90	1.90
a.	A270 35o yel grn, single stamp	45	45

Stockholmia 74 philatelic exhibition, Stockholm, Sept. 21-29. Booklet sold for 3k with surtax going toward financing the exhibition.

Nos. 1045-1048 sold during exhibition in folder with 5k entrance ticket.

Issue dates: Nos. 1041-1044, Apr. 2. Nos. 1045-1048, Sept. 21.

Europa Issue 1974

"Man in Storm," by Bror Marklund — A271

Design: 1k, Sculpture by Picasso, Lake Vanern, Kristinehamm.

Perf. 12½ Horiz.

1974, Apr. 29 **Engr.**

1049	A271	75o vio brn	95	10
1050	A271	1k sl grn	1.00	10

King Karl XVI Gustaf — A272

1974-78 **Engr.** ***Perf. 12½ Vert.***

1068	A272	75o sl grn	60	5
1069	A272	90o brt bl ('75)	75	6
1070	A272	1k maroon	38	6
1071	A272	1.10k rose red ('75)	40	6
1072	A272	1.30k grn ('76)	48	6
1073	A272	1.40k vio bl ('77)	60	18
1074	A272	1.50k red lil ('80)	45	6
1075	A272	1.70k org ('78)	65	18
1076	A272	2k dk brn ('80)	75	18

Perf. 12½ on 3 Sides

1077	A272	75o sl grn	60	5
a.		Booklet pane of 10	6.00	
1078	A272	90o brt bl ('75)	60	8
a.		Booklet pane of 10	6.00	
1079	A272	1k mar ('76)	38	5
a.		Booklet pane of 10	4.00	
1080	A272	1.10k rose red ('77)	40	6
a.		Booklet pane of 10	4.00	
1081	A272	1.30k grn ('78)	48	12
a.		Booklet pane of 10	5.00	
1082	A272	1.50k red lil ('80)	45	6
a.		Booklet pane of 10	4.50	
		Nos. 1068-1082 (15)	7.97	1.31

Central Post Office, Stockholm A273 A274

Mailman, Northernmost Rural Delivery Route — A275

Perf. 12½ on 3 Sides

1974, June 7 **Engr.**

1084	A273	75o vio brn	1.50	18
1085	A274	75o vio brn	1.50	18
a.		Bklt. pane of 10 (5 each #1084-1085)	15.00	

Perf. 12½ Vert.

1086	A275	1k sl grn	75	15

Centenary of Universal Postal Union.

Regatta A276

Scenes from Sweden's West Coast: No. 1088, Vinga Lighthouse. No. 1089, Varberg Fortress. No. 1090, Seine fishing. No. 1091, Fishing village Mollosund.

1974, June 7 ***Perf. 12½ Horiz.***

1087	A276	65o crimson	38	35
1088	A276	65o blue	38	35
1089	A276	65o dk ol grn	38	35
1090	A276	65o sl grn	38	35
1091	A276	65o brown	38	35
a.		Bklt. pane of 10 (2 each #1087-1091)	4.00	
		Nos. 1087-1091 (5)	1.90	1.75

Mr. Simmons, by Axel Fridell A277

Thread and Spool A278

Perf. 12½ on 3 Sides

1974, Aug. 28 **Engr.**

1092	A277	45o black	30	20
a.		Booklet pane of 10	3.00	

Perf. 12½ Horiz.

1093	A277	1.40k dp cl	60	12

Swedish Publicists' Club, centenary.

1974, Aug. 28 ***Perf. 12½ Horiz.***

Design: No. 1094, Sewing machines (abstract).

1094	A278	85o dp vio	38	30
1095	A278	85o blk & org	38	30

Swedish textile and clothing industries. Nos. 1094-1095 printed se-tenant.

Tugs in Stockholm Harbor — A279

Designs: No. 1097, Skane Train Ferry, Trelleborg-Sassnitz. No. 1098, Ice breakers Tor and Atle. No. 1099, Liner "Snow Storm." No. 1100, Tanker.

Perf. 12½ Horiz.

1974, Nov. 16 **Engr.**

1096	A279	1k dk bl	1.00	60
1097	A279	1k dk bl	1.00	60
1098	A279	1k dk bl	1.00	60
1099	A279	1k dk bl	1.00	60
1100	A279	1k dk bl	1.00	60
a.		Bkt. pane of 5 (#1096-1100)	5.00	
		Nos. 1096-1100 (5)	5.00	3.00

Swedish shipping industry.

Miniature Sheet

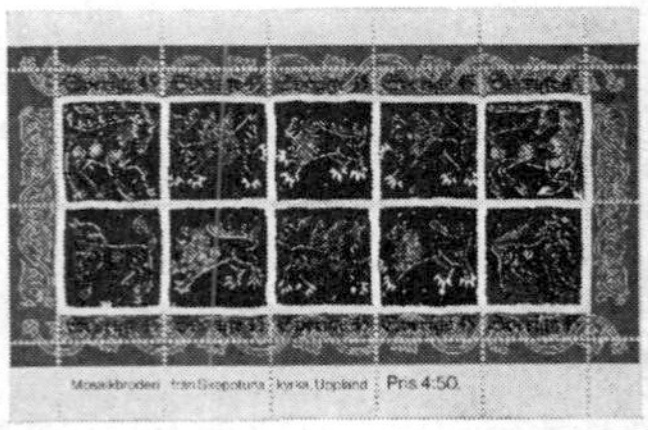

Quilt from Skepptuna Church — A280

Deer, Quilt from Hog Church — A281

Designs are from woolen quilts, 15th-16th centuries. Motifs shown on No. 1101 are stylized deer, griffins, lions, unicorn and horses.

1974, Nov. 16 **Photo.** ***Perf. 14***

1101	A280	Sheet of 10	11.00	12.50
a.-j.		45o, single stamp	1.10	1.10

Perf. 13 Horiz.

1102	A281	75o bl blk, red & yel	35	10

Max von Laue — A282

Designs: 70o, Theodore William Richards. 1k, Robert Barany.

1974, Dec. 10 Engr. *Perf. 12½ Vert.*
1103 A282 65o rose red 60 25
1104 A282 70o slate 60 25
1105 A282 1k indigo 60 12

Winners of 1914 Nobel Prize.

Sven Jerring's Children's Program — A283

Televising Parliamentary Debate — A284

1974, Dec. 10 *Perf. 12½ Vert.*
1106 A283 75o dk bl & brn 1.50 18
1107 A284 75o brn & dk bl 1.50 18

Swedish Broadcasting Corporation, 50th anniversary. Nos. 1106-1107 printed se-tenant.

Account Holder's Envelope A285

Photogravure and Engraved
1975, Jan. 21 *Perf. 14 Vert.*
1108 A285 1.40k ocher & blk 60 12

Swedish Postal Giro Office, 50th anniv.

Male and Female Architects, New Parliament A286

Jenny Lind (1820-87), by J. O. Sodermark A287

Perf. 12½ Vert.
1975, Mar. 25 Engr.
1109 A286 75o sl grn 28 8

Perf. 12½ Horiz.
1110 A287 1k claret 55 12

Perf. 12½ on 3 Sides
1111 A286 75o sl grn 30 18
a. Booklet pane of 10 3.00

International Women's Year 1975.

Horseman, Helmet Decoration A288

"Gold Men" A289

Designs: 15o, Scabbard and hilt. 20o, Shield buckle. 55o, Iron helmet.

1975, Mar. 25 *Perf. 12½ Vert.*
1112 A288 10o dl red 5 5
1113 A288 15o sl grn 8 5
1114 A288 20o violet 10 6
1115 A288 55o vio brn 27 12
a. Bklt. pane of 8 (2 each #1112-1115) 1.00

Perf. 12½ Horiz.
1116 A289 25o dp yel 18 8

Treasures from tombs of the Vendel period (550-800A.D.), and "gold men" (25o) from Eketorp II excavations (400-700A.D.).

Europa Issue 1975

New Year's Eve at Skansen, by Eric Hallstrom — A290

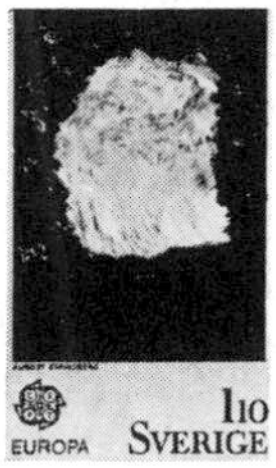

Inferno, by August Strindberg — A291

Perf. 12½ Vert.
1975, Apr. 28 Photo.
1117 A290 90o multi 48 20

Perf. 12½ Horiz.
1118 A291 1.10k multi 65 25

Capercaillie A292

Rok Stone, 9th Century A293

Perf. 12½ Vert.
1975, May 20 Engr.
1119 A292 170o indigo 70 12

Perf. 12½ Horiz.
1120 A293 2k dp cl 70 12

Metric Tape Measure — A294

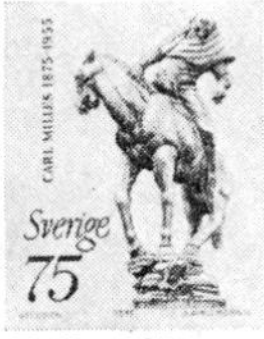

Folke Filbyter Statue, by Milles — A296

Hernqvist by Per Krafft the Younger — A295

1975, May 20 *Perf. 12½ Vert.*
1121 A294 55o dp bl 30 20
1122 A295 70o yel brn & dk brn 30 12

Perf. 12½ Horiz.
1123 A296 75o violet 30 18

Cent. of Intl. Meter Convention, Paris, 1875; bicent. of Swedish veterinary medicine, founded by Peter Hernqvist (1726-1808); Carl Milles (1875-1955), sculptor.

Officers' Mess, Rommehed, 1798 — A297

Designs: No. 1125, Falun Mine pithead gear, 1852. No. 1126, Gunpowder Tower, Visby. No. 1127, Foundry and furnace, Engelsberg, 18th century. No. 1128, Skelleftea Church Village, 17th century.

1975, June 13 *Perf. 12½ Horiz.*
1124 A297 75o vio bl 30 25
1125 A297 75o dk car 30 25
1126 A297 75o black 30 25
1127 A297 75o dk car 30 25
1128 A297 75o black 30 25
a. Bklt. pane of 10 (2 each #1124-1128) 3.00
Nos. 1124-1128 (5) 1.50 1.25

European Architectural Heritage Year 1975.

Rescue at Sea: Helicopter over Ice-covered Tanker — A298

Designs: No. 1130, Hospital Service: patient arriving by ambulance. No. 1131, Police: Officer talking to boy on bridge. No. 1132, Customs narcotics service: trained dogs checking cargo. No. 1133, Fire fighters: firemen fighting fire.

1975, Aug. 27 *Perf. 12½ Horiz.*
1129 A298 90o green 45 25
1130 A298 90o dk bl 45 25
1131 A298 90o dk car rose 45 25
1132 A298 90o dk bl 45 25
1133 A298 90o dk car rose 45 25
a. Bklt. pane of 10 (2 each #1129-1133) 4.50
Nos. 1129-1133 (5) 2.25 1.25

Public service organizations watching, guarding, helping.

"Fryckstad" A299

"Gotland" A300

Design: 90o, "Prins August."

1975, Aug. 27 *Perf. 12½ on 3 Sides*
Size: 20x19mm
1134 A299 5o green 16 10
1135 A300 5o dk bl 16 10

Size: 45x19mm
1136 A299 90o sl grn 80 15
a. Bklt. pane of 6 (2 each #1134-1136) 2.50

Scouts Around Campfire — A301

Scouts in Canoes — A302

1975, Oct. 11 Photo. *Perf. 14 Vert.*
1137 A301 90o multi 1.10 20
1138 A302 90o multi 1.10 20

Nordjamb 75, 14th World Boy Scout Jamboree, Lillehammer, Norway, July 29-Aug. 7. Nos. 1137-1138 printed setenant.

Hedgehog — A303

Old Man Playing Key Fiddle — A304

Romeo and Juliet Ballet — A305

1975, Oct. 11 Engr. *Perf. 12½ Vert.*
1139 A303 55o black 30 12
1140 A304 75o dk red 32 12

Perf. 12½ Horiz.
1141 A305 7k bl grn 2.00 20

Perf. 12½ on 3 Sides
1142 A303 55o black 35 20
a. Booklet pane of 10 3.50

Virgin Mary, 12th Cent. Statue A306

Chariot of the Sun, from 12th Cent. Altar A307

Mourning Mary, c. 1280 — A308

Jesse at Foot of Genealogical Tree, c. 1510 — A309

Design: No. 1145, Nativity, from 12th century gilt-copper altar. No. 1148, like No. 1147.

Perf. 14 Horiz.
1975, Nov. 11 Photo.
1143 A306 55o multi 30 12

Perf. 12½ on 3 Sides
1144 A307 55o gold & multi 45 20
1145 A307 55o gold & multi 45 20
a. Bklt. pane of 10 (5 each #1144-1145) 4.50

Perf. 12½ Horiz.
Engr.
1146 A308 90o brown 50 12

Perf. 12½ on 3 Sides
1147 A309 90o red 1.25 20
1148 A309 90o blue 1.25 20
a. Bklt. pane of 10 (5 each #1147-1148) 12.50

Christmas 1975.

No. 1145a was issued with top row of 5 either No. 1144 or No. 1145.

William H. and William L. Bragg — A310

Designs: 90o, Richard Willstätter. 1.10k, Romain Rolland.

1975, Dec. 10 Engr. *Perf. 12½ Vert.*

1149 A310 75o claret 30 18
1150 A310 90o vio bl 45 12
1151 A310 1.10k sl grn 52 20

Winners of 1915 Nobel Prize.

Cave of the Winds, by Eric Grate — A311

1976, Jan. 27 *Perf. 12½ Vert.*

1152 A311 1.90k sl grn 65 15

The sculpture by Eric Grate (b. 1896) stands in front of the Town Hall of Vasteras.

Razor-billed Auks and Black Guillemot A312

Bobbin Lace Maker from Vadstena A313

Perf. 12½ Vert.

1976, Mar. 10 Engr.

1153 A312 85o dk bl 42 12

Perf. 12½ Horiz.

1154 A313 1k cl brn 40 10

Perf. 12½ on 3 Sides

1155 A312 85o dk bl 40 20
a. Booklet pane of 10 4.00
1156 A313 1k cl brn 40 12
a. Booklet pane of 10 4.00

Old and New Telephones, Relays — A314

1976, Mar. 10 *Perf. 12½ Vert.*

1157 A314 1.30k brt vio 48 25
1158 A314 3.40k red 1.25 50

Centenary of first telephone call by Alexander Graham Bell, March 10, 1876.

Europa Issue 1976

Lapp Elk Horn Spoon — A315

Tile Stove — A316

Perf. 14½ Horiz.

1976, May 3 Photo.

1159 A315 1k multi 60 15
1160 A316 1.30k multi 60 30

Wheat and Cornflower Seeds — A317

Viable and Nonviable Seedlings — A318

1976, May 3 Engr. *Perf. 12½ Vert.*

1161 A317 65o brown 38 20
1162 A318 65o choc & grn 38 20

Swedish seed testing centenary. Nos. 1161-1162 printed se-tenant.

King Karl XVI Gustaf and Silvia Sommerlath A319

Perf. 12½ Vert.

1976, June 19 Engr.

1163 A319 1k rose car 38 12
1164 A319 1.30k sl grn 52 20

Perf. 12½ on 3 Sides

1165 A319 1k rose car 38 12
a. Booklet pane of 10 4.00

Wedding of King Karl XVI Gustaf and Silvia Sommerlath.

View from Ringkallen, by Helmer Osslund — A320

Views in Angermanland Province: No. 1167, Tugboat pulling timber. No. 1168, Hay-drying racks. No. 1169, Granvagsnipan slope, Angerman River. No. 1170, Seine fishing.

1976, June 19 *Perf. 12½ Horiz.*

1166 A320 85o sl grn 32 30
1167 A320 85o vio bl 32 30
1168 A320 85o dp brn 32 30
1169 A320 85o vio bl 32 30
1170 A320 85o brn red 32 30
a. Bklt. pane of 10 (2 each #1166-1170) 3.25
Nos. 1166-1170 (5) 1.60 1.50

Roman Cross and Ship's Wheel — A321

1976, June 19 *Perf. 12½ Horiz.*

1171 A321 85o brt bl & bl 40 20

Swedish Seamen's Church, centenary.

Torgny Segerstedt and 1917 Page of Gothenburg Journal — A322

1976, June 19 *Perf. 12½ Vert.*

1172 A322 1.90k brn & blk 85 20

Torgny Segerstedt (1876-1945), editor in chief of the Gothenburg Journal of Commerce and Shipping, birth centenary.

Coiled Snake, Bronze Buckle — A323

Pilgrim's Badge, Adoration of the Magi — A324

Drinking Horn, 14th Century A325

Chimney Sweep A326

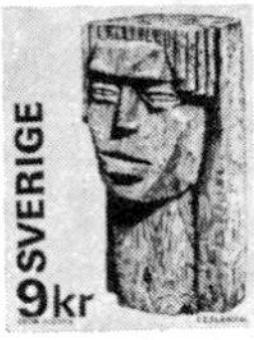

Girl's Head, by Bror Hjorth, 1922 — A327

Perf. 12½ Horiz., Vert. (30o)

1976, Sept. 8 Engr.

1173 A323 15o bister 12 8
1174 A324 20o green 12 8
1175 A325 30o dk rose brn 12 6
1176 A326 90o indigo 35 10
1177 A327 9k yel grn & sl grn 2.75 25
Nos. 1173-1177 (5) 3.46 57

John Ericsson, Ship Propeller and "Monitor" — A328

Designs: No. 1179, Helge Palmcrantz (1842-1880) and reaper. No. 1180, Lars Magnus Ericsson (1846-1926) and switchboard. No. 1181, Sven Wingquist (1876-1953) and ball bearing. No. 1182, Gustaf de Laval (1845-1913) and milk separator.

1976, Oct. 9 Engr. *Perf. 12½ Horiz.*

1178 A328 1.30k multi 1.10 80
1179 A328 1.30k multi 1.10 80
1180 A328 1.30k multi 1.10 80
1181 A328 1.30k multi 1.10 80
1182 A328 1.30k multi 1.10 80
a. Bklt. pane of 5 (#1178-1182) 5.50
Nos. 1178-1182 (5) 5.50 4.00

Swedish inventors and their technological inventions.

Hands and Cogwheels A329

Verner von Heidenstam, Lake Vattern A330

1976, Oct. 9 *Perf. 12½ Vert.*

1183 A329 85o org & dk vio 42 18
1184 A329 1k yel grn & brn 42 12

Industrial safety.

Perf. 12½ Vert.

1976, Nov. 17 Engr.

1185 A330 1k yel grn 60 20
1186 A330 1.30k blue 75 25

Verner von Heidenstam (1859-1940), Swedish poet, 1916 Nobel Prize winner.

Archangel Michael A331

Virgin Mary Visiting St. Elizabeth A332

Designs: No. 1189, like No. 1187. No. 1190, St. Nicholas saving 3 children. No. 1191, like No. 1188. No. 1192, Illuminated page, prayer to Virgin Mary. 65o stamps are from Flemish prayer book, c. 1500. 1k stamps are from Austrian prayer book, late 15th century.

Perf. 12½ Horiz.

1976, Nov. 17 Photo.

1187 A331 65o bl & multi 25 12
1188 A332 1k gold & multi 40 12

Perf. 12½ on 3 Sides

1189 A331 65o bl & multi 25 20
1190 A331 65o bl & multi 25 20
a. Bklt. pane of 10 (5 each #1189-1190) 2.50

Perf. 12½ Vert.

1191 A332 1k gold & multi 40 12
1192 A332 1k gold & multi 40 12
a. Bklt. pane of 10 (5 each #1191-1192) 4.00

Christmas 1976.

Five Water Lilies — A333

Tailor — A334

Photogravure and Engraved

1977, Feb. 2 *Perf. 12½ Horiz.*

1193 A333 1k brt grn & multi 52 12
1194 A333 1.30k ultra & multi 42 50

Nordic countries cooperation for protection of the environment and 25th Session of Nordic Council, Helsinki, Feb. 19.

1977, Feb. 24 *Perf. 12½ Vert.*

1195 A334 2.10k red brn 85 12

Longdistance Skating — A335

Designs: No. 1197, Swimming. No. 1198, Bicycling. No. 1199, Jogging. No. 1200, Badminton.

Perf. 12½ Horiz.

1977, Mar. 24 Engr.

1196 A335 95o blue 40 30
1197 A335 95o sl grn 40 30
1198 A335 95o red 40 30
1199 A335 95o sl grn 40 30

1200 A335 95o blue 40 30
a. Bklt. pane of 10 (2 each #1196-1200) 4.00
Nos. 1196-1200 (5) 2.00 1.50

Physical fitness.

Politeness, by "OA," 1905 — A336

1977, Mar. 24 ***Perf. 12½ on 3 Sides***
1201 A336 75o black 35 20
a. Booklet pane of 10 3.50

Perf. 12½ Horiz.
1202 A336 3.80k red 1.50 45

Oskar Andersson (1877-1906), cartoonist.

Calle Schewen — A337

Designs: No. 1204, Seagull. No. 1205, Dancers and accordionist. No. 1206, Fishermen in boat. No. 1207, Tree on shore at sunset. Designs are illustrations for poem The Calle Schewen Waltz, by Evert Taube, and include bars of music of this song.

Perf. 12½ Horiz.
1977, May 2 **Engr.**
1203 A337 95o sl grn 40 25
1204 A337 95o vio bl 40 25
1205 A337 95o grn & blk 40 25
1206 A337 95o dk bl 40 25
1207 A337 95o red 40 25
a. Bklt. pane of 10 (2 each #1203-1207) 4.00
Nos. 1203-1207 (5) 2.00 1.25

Tourist publicity for Roslagen (archipelago) and to honor Evert Taube (1890-1976), poet.

Gustavianum, Uppsala University A338

1977, May 2 **Photo.** ***Perf. 12½ Vert.***
1208 A338 1.10k multi 50 12

Perf. 12½ on 3 Sides
1209 A338 1.10k multi 50 12
a. Booklet pane of 10 5.00

Uppsala University, 500th anniversary.

Europa Issue 1977

Forest in Snow A339

Rapadalen Valley — A340

1977, May 2 ***Perf. 12½ Vert.***
1210 A339 1.10k multi 55 12
1211 A340 1.40k multi 80 40

Owl A341

Cast-iron Stove Decoration A342

Gotland Ponies — A343

1977, Sept. 8 **Engr.** ***Perf. 12½ Vert.***
1212 A341 45o dk sl grn 30 25

Perf. 12½ Horiz.
1213 A342 70o dk vio bl 30 25

Booklet Stamp
1214 A343 1.40k brown 45 30
a. Bklt. pane of 5 2.25

Blackberry — A344

Designs: Wild berries.

Perf. 14 on 3 Sides
1977, Sept. 8 **Photo.**
1215 A344 75o *shown* 35 25
1216 A344 75o *Cranberry* 35 25
1217 A344 75o *Raspberry* 35 25
1218 A344 75o *Whortleberry* 35 25
1219 A344 75o *Alpine strawberry* 35 25
a. Bklt. pane of 10 (2 each #1215-1219) 3.50
Nos. 1215-1219 (5) 1.75 1.25

Horse-drawn Trolley — A345

Designs: Public transportation.

1977, Oct. 8 **Engr.** ***Perf. 12½ Horiz.***
1220 A345 1.10k *shown* 45 30
1221 A345 1.10k *Electric trolley* 45 30
1222 A345 1.10k *Ferry* 45 30
1223 A345 1.10k *Tandem bus* 45 30
1224 A345 1.10k *Subway* 45 30
a. Bklt. pane of 5 (#1220-1224) 2.25
Nos. 1220-1224 (5) 2.25 1.50

Putting up Sheaf for the Birds — A346

Preparing Dried Soaked Fish — A347

Traditional Christmas Preparations: No. 1227, Children baking ginger snaps. No. 1228, Bringing in Yule tree. No. 1229, Making straw goat. No. 1230, Candle dipping.

Perf. 12½ horiz.
1977, Nov. 17 **Engr.**
1225 A346 75o violet 30 15
1226 A347 1.10k yel grn 45 15

Perf. 12½ on 3 Sides
1227 A346 75o ocher 30 25
1228 A346 75o sl grn 30 25
a. Booklet pane of 10 (5 each #1227-1228) 3.00
1229 A347 1.10k dk red 40 12
1230 A347 1.10k dk bl 40 12
a. Booklet pane of 10 (5 each #1229-1230) 4.00
Nos. 1225-1230 (6) 2.15 1.04

Christmas 1977.

Henrik Pontoppidan, Karl Adolph Gjellerup — A348

Design: 1.40k, Charles Glover Barkla.

1977, Nov. 17 ***Perf. 12½ Vert.***
1231 A348 1.10k red brn 50 70
1232 A348 1.40k yel grn 70 45

1917 Nobel Prize winners: Henrik Pontoppidan (1857-1943) and Karl Adolph Gjellerup (1857-1919), Danish writers; Charles Glover Barkla (1877-1944), English X-ray pioneer.

Space Without Affiliation, by Arne Jones — A349

Brown Bear — A350

1978, Jan. 25 ***Perf. 12½ Horiz.***
1233 A349 2.50k vio bl 90 10

1978, Apr. 11 ***Perf. 12½ Horiz.***
1234 A350 1.15k dk brn 50 12

Europa Issue 1978

Örebro Castle — A351

Arch and Stairs — A352

1978, Apr. 11 ***Perf. 12½ Vert.***
1235 A351 1.30k sl grn 65 12

Perf. 12½ Horiz.
1236 A352 1.70k dl red 80 45

Pentecostal Preacher and Congregation A353

Free Churches: No. 1238, Swedish Missionary Society. No. 1239, Evangelical National Missionary Society. No. 1240, Baptist Society. No. 1241, Salvation Army.

1978, Apr. 11 ***Perf. 12½ on 3 sides***
1237 A353 90o purple 40 40
1238 A353 90o slate 40 40
1239 A353 90o violet 40 40
1240 A353 90o slate 40 40
1241 A353 90o purple 40 40
a. Booklet pane of 10 (2 each #1237-1241) 4.00
Nos. 1237-1241 (5) 2.00 2.00

Independent Christian Associations.

Brosarp Hills — A354

Grindstone Production A355

Red Limestone Cliff A356

Designs: No. 1243, Avocets. No. 1245, Linnaea borealis (Linné's favorite flower.) No. 1247, Linne with Lapp drum, wearing Lapp clothes and Dutch doctor's hat.

Perf. 12½ Horiz.
1978, May 23 **Engr.**
1242 A354 1.30k gray grn 55 30
1243 A354 1.30k vio bl 55 30

Perf. 12½ on 3 Sides
1244 A355 1.30k vio brn 55 30
1245 A355 1.30k brn red 55 30
1246 A356 1.30k vio bl 55 30
1247 A356 1.30k vio brn 55 30
a. Bklt. pane of 6 (#1242-1247) 3.30
Nos. 1242-1247 (6) 3.30 1.80

Travels of Carl von Linné (1707-1778), botanist.

Cranes, Lake Hornborgasjon — A357

Designs: No. 1248, Gliding School, Alleberg. No. 1250, Skara Church, Lacko Island. No. 1251, Ancient rock tomb, Luttra. No. 1252, Cloth merchants, sculpture by Nils Sjogren.

1978, May 23 ***Perf. 12½ Horiz.***
1248 A357 1.15k dl grn 42 30
1249 A357 1.15k maroon 42 30
1250 A357 1.15k vio bl 42 30
1251 A357 1.15k dk gray grn 42 30
1252 A357 1.15k brn & gray grn 42 30
a. Booklet pane of 10 (2 each #1284-1252) 4.25
Nos. 1248-1252 (5) 2.10 1.50

Tourist publicity for Vastergotland.

Laurel and Scroll — A358

1978, May 23 ***Perf. 12½ Vert.***
1253 A358 2.50k gray & sl grn 1.10 25

Stockholm University, centenary.

The Catalogue editors cannot undertake to appraise, identify or judge the genuineness or condition of stamps.

Homecoming, by Carl Kylberg — A359

Nude, by Karl Isakson
A360

Self-portrait, by Ivar Arosenius
A361

1978, Sept. 5 Engr. *Perf. 12½ Vert.*
1254 A359 90o multi 48 18

Perf. 12½ Horiz.
1255 A360 1.15k multi 48 18
1256 A361 4.50k multi 1.90 40

Swedish painters: Carl Kylberg (1878-1952); Karl Isakson (1878-1922); Ivar Arosenius (1878-1909).

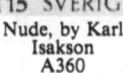

North Arrow (Compass Rose), Map, 1769 — A362

1978, Sept. 5 *Perf. 12½ Horiz.*
1257 A362 10k lilac 2.75 20

Coronation Coach, 1699 — A363

1978, Oct. 7 Engr. *Perf. 12½ Horiz.*
1258 A363 1.70k dk red, *yel* 75 60
a. Booklet pane of 5 3.75

Orange Russula — A364

Designs: Edible mushrooms.

1978, Oct. 7 *Perf. 12½ on 3 Sides*
1259 A364 1.15k *shown* 45 40
1260 A364 1.15k *Common puff ball* 45 40
1261 A364 1.15k *Parasol mushroom* 45 40
1262 A364 1.15k *Chanterelle* 45 40
1263 A364 1.15k *Boletus edulis* 45 40
1264 A364 1.15k *Ramaria botrytis* 45 40
a. Booklet pane of 6 (#1259-1264) 2.75
Nos. 1259-1264 (6) 2.70 2.40

The indexes in each volume of the Scott Catalogue contain many listings which help to identify stamps.

Toy Ferris Wheel — A365

Rider Drawing Water Cart — A366

Toys: No. 1266, Teddy bear. No. 1267, Dalecarlian wooden horse. No. 1268, Doll. No. 1270, Spinning tops.

Perf. 12½ Horiz.
1978, Nov. 14 Engr.
1265 A365 90o dk red & grn 35 12
1266 A365 1.30k brt ultra 42 12

Perf. 12½ on 3 Sides
Photo.
1267 A365 90o multi 35 18
1268 A365 90o multi 35 18
a. Booklet pane of 10 (5 each #1267-1268) 3.50
1269 A366 1.30k multi 42 12
1270 A366 1.30k multi 42 12
a. Booklet pane of 10 (5 each 1269-1270) 4.25
Nos. 1265-1270 (6) 2.31 84

Christmas 1978.

Fritz Haber — A367

Design: 1.70k, Max Planck.

Perf. 12½ Vert.
1978, Nov. 14 Engr.
1271 A367 1.30k dk brn 60 20
1272 A367 1.70k dk vio bl 80 45

1918 Nobel Prize winners: Fritz Haber (1868-1934), German chemist; Max Planck (1858-1947), German physicist.

Bandy — A368

1979, Jan. 25 Engr. *Perf. 12½ Vert.*
1273 A368 1.05k vio bl 45 12
1274 A368 2.50k orange 85 12

Child Wearing Gas Mask in Heavy Traffic — A369

1979, Mar. 13 *Perf. 12½ Vert.*
1275 A369 1.70k dk bl 75 60

International Year of the Child.

Drill-weave Tapestry, c. 1855-1860
A370

Carrier Pigeon, Hand with Quill
A371

1979, Mar. 13 *Perf. 12½ Horiz.*
1276 A370 4k gray & red 1.10 12

Perf. 14x14½ on 3 Sides
1979, Apr. 2 Photo.
1277 A371 (1k) ultra & yel 60 10
a. Booklet pane of 20 12.00

Every Swedish household received during April, 1979, 2 coupons for the purchase of 2 discount booklets. The stamps were for use on post cards and letters within Sweden. Price of booklet 20k.

Europa Issue 1979

Mail Service by Boat, Grisslehamn to Echero
A372

Design: 1.70k, Hand on telegraph.

1979, May 7 Engr. *Perf. 12½ Vert.*
1278 A372 1.30k sl grn & blk 65 12
1279 A372 1.70k ocher & blk 80 50

Woodcutter, Winter — A373

Designs: No. 1281, Sowing, spring. No. 1282, Grazing cattle, summer. No. 1283, Harvester, summer. No. 1284, Plowing, autumn.

1979, May 7 *Perf. 12½ Horiz.*
1280 A373 1.30k multi 48 12
1281 A373 1.30k sl grn & dk brn 48 12
1282 A373 1.30k dk brn & sl grn 48 12
1283 A373 1.30k sl grn & ocher 48 12
1284 A373 1.30k multi 48 12
a. Booklet pane of 10 (2 each #1280-1284) 5.00
Nos. 1280-1284 (5) 2.40 60

Tourist Steamer Juno — A374

Roller Bridge, Hajstorp — A375

Sailing Ship — A376

Gota Canal: No. 1286, Borenshult Lock. No. 1288, Hand-drawn gate. No. 1290, Rowboat in Forsvik lock.

1979, May 7 *Perf. 12½ Horiz.*
1285 A374 1.15k vio bl 50 40
1286 A374 1.15k sl grn 50 40

Perf. 12½ on 3 Sides
1287 A375 1.15k dl pur 50 40
1288 A375 1.15k carmine 50 40

Perf. 12½ on 2 Sides
1289 A376 1.15k vio bl 50 40
1290 A376 1.15k sl grn 50 40
a. Booklet pane of 6 (#1285-1290) 3.00
Nos. 1285-1290 (6) 3.00 2.40

Strikers and Sawmill
A377

Temperance Movement Banner — A378

Jons Jacob Berzelius — A379

Johan Olof Wallin — A380

1979, Sept. 6 Engr. *Perf. 12½ Vert.*
1291 A377 90o car & dp brn 38 15

Perf. 12½ Horiz.
Litho.
1292 A378 1.30k multi 50 20

Engr.
1293 A379 1.70k brn & grn 70 50
1294 A380 4.50k sl bl 1.90 50

Centenaries of Sundsvall strike and Swedish Temperance Movement; birth bicentennials of Jons Jacob Berzelius (1779-1848), physician and chemist; Johan Olof Wallin (1779-1839), Archbishop and poet.

Dragonfly
A381

Green Spotted Toad
A383

Pike
A382

1979, Sept. 6 *Perf. 12½ Horiz.*
1295 A381 60o violet 55 18

Perf. 12½ Vert.
1296 A382 65o gray 55 20
1297 A383 80o ol grn 55 24

Potpourri Pot — A384

Portrait, by Johan Henrik Scheffel — A385

Designs: 1.30k, Silver coffeepot. 1.70k, Bust of Carl Johan Cronstedt.

Souvenir Sheet

Engraved and Photogravure

1979, Oct. 6 *Perf. 12x12½*

1298 Sheet of 4 2.75 3.00
a. A384 90o multi 65 70
b. A385 1.15k multi 65 70
c. A384 1.30k multi 65 70
d. A385 1.70k multi 65 70

Swedish Rococo. No. 1298 has marginal inscription. Sold for 6k; surcharge was for philately. Size: 144x63mm.

Herrings, Age Determination — A386

Sea Research: No. 1300, Acoustic survey of sea bottom. No. 1301, Water bloom of algae in Baltic Sea. No. 1302, Computer map of herring distribution in South Baltic Sea. No. 1303, Research ship Argos.

1979, Oct. 6 Engr. *Perf. 12½ Horiz.*

1299 A386 1.70k multi 65 50
1300 A386 1.70k sepia 65 50
1301 A386 1.70k multi 65 50
1302 A386 1.70k sepia 65 50
1303 A386 1.70k multi 65 50
a. Booklet pane of 5 (#1299-1303) 3.25
Nos. 1299-1303 (5) 3.25 2.50

Brooch from Jamtland A387

Ljusdal Costume A388

Christmas 1979 (Costumes and Jewelry from): No. 1305, Pendant, Smaland. No. 1307, Osteraker. No. 1308, Goinge. No. 1309, Mora.

Perf. 12½ Horiz.

1979, Nov. 15 **Engr.**

1304 A387 90o dk Prus bl 30 8
1305 A387 1.30k dl red 45 12

Perf. 12½ on 3 Sides

Photo.

Size: 22x27mm

1306 A388 90o multi 30 18
1307 A388 90o multi 30 18
a. Booklet pane of 10 (5 each #1306-1307) 3.00

Perf. 12½ Vert.

Size: 26x44mm

1308 A388 1.30k multi 45 12
1309 A388 1.30k multi 45 12
a. Booklet pane of 10 (5 each #1308-1309) 4.50
Nos. 1304-1309 (6) 2.25 80

Nobel Prize Winner Type of 1978

1919 Nobel Prize Winners: 1.30k, Jules Bordet (1870-1961), Belgian bacteriologist. 1.70k, Johannes Stark (1874-1957), German physicist. 2.50k, Carl Spitteler (1845-1924), Swiss poet.

Perf. 12½ Vert.

1979, Nov. 15 **Engr.**

1310 A367 1.30k lilac 55 12
1311 A367 1.70k ultra 70 45
1312 A367 2.50k ol grn 1.10 20

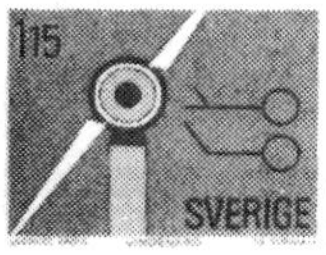

Wind Power — A389

Renewable Energy Sources: No. 1314, Biodegradable material. No. 1315, Solar energy. No. 1316, Geothermal energy. No. 1317, Hydro power.

1980, Jan. 29 *Perf. 12½ on 3 sides*

1313 A389 1.15k dk bl 45 40
1314 A389 1.15k dk grn & bis 45 40
1315 A389 1.15k yel org 45 40
1316 A389 1.15k dk grn 45 40
1317 A389 1.15k dk bl & dk grn 45 40
a. Bklt. pane of 10 (2 each #1313-1317) 4.50
Nos. 1313-1317 (5) 2.25 2.00

Crown Princess Victoria and King Karl XVI Gustaf — A390

1980, Feb. 26 *Perf. 12½ on 3 sides*

1318 A390 1.30k brt bl 65 12
a. Bklt. pane of 10 6.50

Perf. 12½ Vert.

1319 A390 1.30k brt bl 65 12
1320 A390 1.70k car rose 85 40

Child Holding Adult's Hand — A391

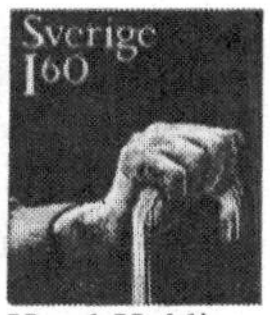

Hand Holding Cane — A392

1980, Apr. 22 *Perf. 12½ Horiz.*

1321 A391 1.40k red brn 55 12
1322 A392 1.60k sl grn 55 20

Parents' insurance system; care for the elderly.

Squirrel — A393

Perf. 15 on 3 Sides

1980, May 12 **Photo.**

1323 A393 (1k) ultra & yel 50 8
a. Bklt. pane of 20 10.00

See note after No. 1277.

Europa Issue 1980

Elise Ottesen-Jensen (1886-1973), Journalist A394

Design: 1.70k, Joe Hill (1879-1915), member of American Workers' Movement and poet.

1980, June 4 Engr. *Perf. 12½ Vert.*

1324 A394 1.30k green 65 12
1325 A394 1.70k red 85 60

Banga Farm, Alfta, Halsingland Province — A395

Tourism (Halsingland Province): No. 1327, Iron Works, Iggesund. No. 1328, Blaxas Ridge, Forsa. No. 1329, Tybling farm, Tyby. No. 1330, Sunds Canal, Hudiksvall.

1980, June 4 *Perf. 12½ Horiz.*

1326 A395 1.15k red 40 30
1327 A395 1.15k dk bl 40 30
1328 A395 1.15k dk grn 40 30
1329 A395 1.15k chocolate 40 30
1330 A395 1.15k dk bl 40 30
a. Bklt. pane of 10 (2 each #1326-1330) 4.00
Nos. 1326-1330 (5) 2.00 1.50

Booklet Panes

Panes consisting of blocks, strips or pairs removed from large sheets of regular issue and fastened or enclosed within a cover or folder, often by stapling or sewing in the sheet margin, are no longer being listed. Such panes contain no straight edges and can easily be made privately.

Chair, Scania, 1831 — A396

Cradle, North Bothnia, 19th Century — A397

Perf. 12½ Horiz.

1980, Sept. 9 **Engr.**

1331 A396 1.50k grnsh bl 65 14

Perf. 12½ Vert.

1332 A397 2k dk red brn 85 30

Norden 80.

Scene from "Diagonal Symphony," 1924 — A398

1980, Sept. 9 *Perf. 12½ Horiz.*

1333 A398 3k dk bl 1.10 12

Viking Eggeling (1880-1925), artist and film maker.

Souvenir Sheet

Gustaf Erikson's Carriage — A399

Vabis, 1909 A400

Swedish Automobile History: 1.30k, Thulin, 1923. 1.40k, Scania, 1903. 1.50k, Tidaholm, 1917. 1.70k, Volvo, 1927.

Photogravure and Engraved

1980, Oct. 11 *Perf. 12½*

1334 Sheet of 6 3.25 3.25
a. A399 90o lt bl & dk brn 45 50
b. A400 1.15k cr & dk brn 45 50
c. A399 1.30k lt bl & dk brn 45 50
d. A399 1.40k lt bl & dk brn 45 50
e. A400 1.50k cr & dk brn 45 50
f. A399 1.70k lt bl & dk brn 45 50

No. 1334 sold for 9k.

Bamse the Bear — A401

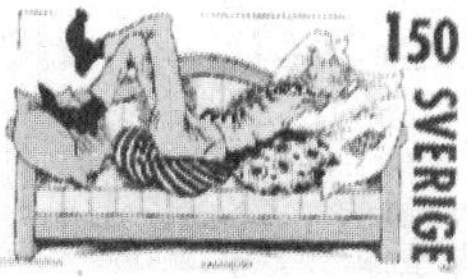

Farmer Kronblom — A402

Christmas 1980 (Comic Strip Characters): No. 1336, Mandel Karlsson (vert.). No. 1337, Adamson (vert.).

1980, Oct. 11 Engr. *Perf. 12½ Vert.*

1335 A401 1.15k multi 45 10

Perf. 12½ on 3 sides

Photo.

1336 A401 1.15k multi 45 10
a. Bklt. pane of 10 4.50

Perf. 12½ Horiz.

Engr.

1337 A401 1.50k black 65 12

Photo.

1338 A402 1.50k multi 65 12
a. Bklt. pane of 10 6.50

Angel Blowing Horn A403

Necken, by Ernst Josephson A404

Perf. on 3 Sides

1980, Nov. 18 **Engr.**

1339 A403 1.25k multi 60 20
a. Bklt. pane of 12 7.20

Christmas 1980.

1980, Nov. 18 *Perf. 12½ Horiz.*

1340 A404 8k multi 2.25 25

Nobel Prize Winner Type of 1978

1920 Nobel Prize Winners: No. 1341, Knut Hamsun (1859-1953), Norwegian writer. No. 1342, August Krogh (1874-1949), Danish Physiologist. No. 1343, Charles-Edouard Guillaume (1861-1938), French chemist. No. 1344, Walther Nernst (1864-1941), German physicist.

1980, Nov. 18 *Perf. 13 on 3 Sides*

1341 A367 1.40k dk bl gray 52 20
1342 A367 1.40k red 52 20
a. Bklt. pane of 10 (5 each #1341-1342) 5.25
1343 A367 2k green 60 35
1344 A367 2k brown 60 35
a. Bklt. pane of 10 (5 each #1343-1344) 6.00

Ernst Wigforss (1881-1977), Politician & Writer A405

Freya (Fertility Goddess) A406

1981, Jan. 29 Engr. *Perf. 12½ Vert.*

1345 A405 5k rose car 1.90 30

1981, Jan. 29 ***Perf. 12½ on 3 Sides***

Norse Mythological Characters: 10o, Thor (thunder god). 15o, Heimdall (rainbow god). 50o, Frey (god of peace, fertility, weather). 1k, Odin.

1346	A406	10o bl blk	5	5
1347	A406	15o dk car	6	5
1348	A406	50o dk car	20	8
1349	A406	75o dp grn	30	12
1350	A406	1k bl blk	40	18
a.		Bklt. pane of 10 (2 each #1346-1350)	2.00	
		Nos. 1346-1350 (5)	1.01	48

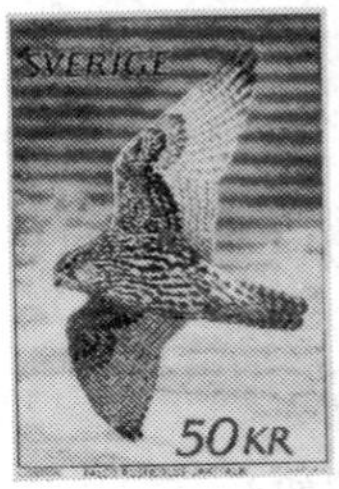

Gyrfalcon A407

1981, Feb. 26 **Engr.** ***Perf. 12½ Vert.***

1351	A407	50k multi	15.00	4.00
a.		Bklt. pane of 4	60.00	

Troll Chasing Boy — A408

Intl. Year of the Disabled — A409

Europa: 2k, Lady of the Woods.

1981, Apr. 28 **Engr.**

1352	A408	1.50k dk bl & red	60	14
1353	A408	2k dk grn & red	80	25

1981, Apr. 28

1354	A409	1.50k dk grn	55	12
1355	A409	3.50k purple	1.25	25

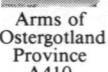

Arms of Ostergotland Province A410

Sail Boat, Bohuslan A411

Perf. 14½ on 3 Sides

1981, May 18 **Photo.**

1356	A410	1.40k shown	60	12
1357	A410	1.40k Jamtland	60	12
1358	A410	1.40k Dalarna	60	12
1359	A410	1.40k Bohuslan	60	12
a.		Bklt pane of 20 (5 each #1356-1359)	12.00	

See note after No. 1277. See Nos. 1403-1406, 1456-1459, 1492-1495, 1534-1537, 1592-1595.

Perf. 12½ on 3 Sides

1981, May 26 **Engr.**

1360	A411	1.65k shown	65	25
1361	A411	1.65k Blekinge	65	25
1362	A411	1.65k Norrbotten	65	25
1363	A411	1.65k Halsingland	65	25
1364	A411	1.65k Gotland	65	25
1365	A411	1.65k Skane	65	25
a.		Bklt. pane of 6 (#1360-1365)	4.00	
		Nos. 1360-1365 (6)	3.90	1.50

King Karl XVI Gustaf A412

Queen Silvia A413

1981-1984 ***Perf. 12½ Vert.***

1366	A412	1.65k dk grn	45	15
1367	A413	1.75k dk bl	90	25
1368	A412	1.80k dk bl	60	15
1369	A412	1.90k red ('84)	60	15
1370	A412	2.40k vio brn	75	25
1371	A413	2.40k grnsh blk ('84)	75	30
1372	A412	2.70k brt lil	75	30
1373	A413	3.20k red	90	30
		Nos. 1366-1373 (8)	5.70	1.85

Day and Night A414

Scene from Par Lagerkvist's Autobiography Guest of Reality A415

Perf. 12½ on 3 Sides

1981, Sept. 9 **Engr.**

1376	A414	1.65k purple	55	15
a.		Bklt. pane of 10	5.50	

1981, Sept. 9

1377	A415	1.50k dk grn	42	12

Conductor Sixten Ehrling and Opera Singer Birgit Nilsson — A416

Bjorn Borg, Tennis Player A417

Baker's Sign A418

Designs: No. 1378, Electric locomotive. No. 1379, Trucks. No. 1381, Oil rig. No. 1383, Ingemar Stenmark, skier.

1981, Sept. 9

1378	A416	2.40k rose car	85	60
1379	A416	2.40k red	85	60
1380	A416	2.40k rose lil	85	60
1381	A416	2.40k dp vio	85	60
1382	A417	2.40k dk bl	85	60
1383	A417	2.40k dk bl	85	60
a.		Bklt. pane of 6 (4 #1378-1381, #1382-1383)	5.25	
		Nos. 1378-1383 (6)	5.10	3.60

1981, Sept. 9 ***Perf. 12½ Vert.***

1384	A418	2.30k shown	75	15
1385	A418	2.30k Pewter shop sign	75	15

Nos. 1384-1385 se-tenant.

Ingrid Bergman and Gosta Ekman in Intermezzo A419

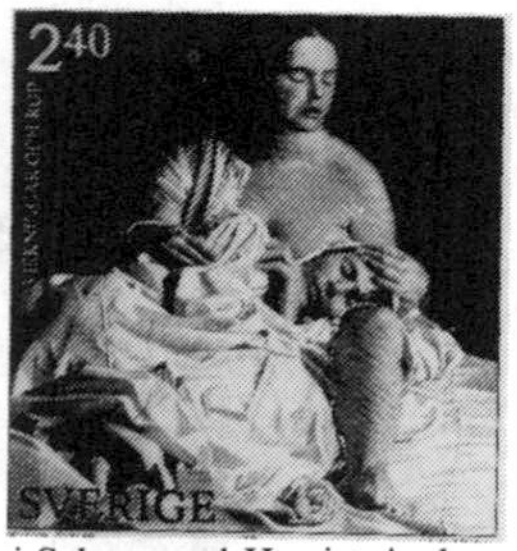

Kari Sylwan and Harriet Andersson in Cries and Whispers — A420

Swedish Films: a, Olof Ahs in The Coachman. c, Greta Garbo in The Gosta Berling Saga, d, Stig Jarrel and Alf Kjellin in Persecution.

Photogravure and Engraved

1981, Oct. 10 ***Perf. 13½***

1386		Sheet of 5	3.50	3.25
a.	A419	1.50k multi	70	55
b.	A419	1.50k multi	70	55
c.	A419	1.65k multi	70	55
d.	A419	1.65k multi	70	55
e.	A420	2.40k multi	70	55

No. 1386 sold for 10k.

Nobel Prize Winner Type of 1978

1921 Winners: 1.35k, Albert Einstein (1879-1955), German physicist 1.65k, Anatole France (1844-1924), French writer. Frederick Soddy (1877-1956), British chemist.

Perf. 12½ Vert.

1981, Nov. 24 **Engr.**

1387	A367	1.35k red	55	30
1388	A367	1.65k green	55	15
1389	A367	2.70k blue	85	45

Christmas 1981 — A421

Designs: Wooden birds.

1981, Nov. 24 ***Perf. 12½ on 3 Sides***

1390	A421	1.40k red	48	25
1391	A421	1.40k green	48	25
a.		Bklt pane of 10 (5 each #1390-1391)	5.00	

Knight on Horseback, by John Bauer A422

John Bauer (1882-1918), Fairytale Illustrator: No. 1393, "What a Miserable Little Paleface, said the Troll Mother." No. 1394, Marsh Princess. No. 1395, Now the Dusk of the Night is already Upon Us.

Perf. 12x12½ on 3 sides

1982, Feb. 16 **Engr.**

1392	A422	1.65k multi	55	40
1393	A422	1.65k multi	55	40
1394	A422	1.65k multi	55	40
1395	A422	1.65k multi	55	40
a.		Bklt. pane of 4 (#1392-1395)	2.25	

Impossible Figures — A423

Designs: Geometric figures.

1982, Feb. 16 ***Perf. 12½ Horiz.***

1396	A423	25o vio brn	16	10
1397	A423	50o brn ol	16	10
1398	A423	75o dk bl	25	10

Newspaper Distributor, by Svenolov Ehren A424

Graziella, by Carl Larsson A425

1982, Feb. 16

1399	A424	1.35k dp vio	50	18
1400	A425	5k vio brn	1.50	15

Europa Issue 1982

Land Reform, 19th Cent. A426

Anders Celsius (1701-1744), Inventor of Temperature Scale — A427

1982, Apr. 26 **Engr.** ***Perf. 12½ Vert.***

1401	A426	1.65k dk ol grn	90	15

Perf. 12½ on 3 Sides

1402	A427	2.40k dk grn	1.25	75
a.		Bklt. pane of 6	7.50	

Provincial Arms Type of 1981

Perf. 14 on 3 Sides

1982, Apr. 26 **Photo.**

1403	A410	1.40k Dalsland	55	8
1404	A410	1.40k Halsingland	55	8
1405	A410	1.40k Vastmandland	55	8
1406	A410	1.40k Oland	55	8
a.		Bklt. pane of 20 (5 each #1403-1406)	11.00	

See note after No. 1277.

Elin Wagner (1882-1949), Writer — A428

Perf. 12½ Horiz.

1982, June 3 **Engr.**

1407	A428	1.35k Sketch by Siri Derkert	50	30

Burgher House — A429

Embroidered Lace Ribbon, 19th Cent. — A430

1982, June 3 ***Perf. 12½ Vert.***

1408	A429	1.65k brown	55	12

Perf. 12½ Horiz.

1409	A430	2.70k bister	90	40

Cent. of Museum of Cultural History, Lund.

1982 Intl. Buoyage System A431

Designs: Various buoy signals.

1982, June 3 ***Perf. 13 Horiz.***
1410 A431 1.65k shown 60 20
1411 A431 1.65k Ferry 60 20
1412 A431 1.65k Six sailboats 60 20
1413 A431 1.65k One-globed buoy 60 20
1414 A431 1.65k Two-globed buoy 60 20
a. Bklt. pane of 10 (2 each #1410-1414) 6.00
Nos. 1410-1414 (5) 3.00 1.00

Vietnamese Workers in Sweden — A432

Living Together: Swedish emigration and immigration.

1982, Aug. 26 **Engr.** ***Perf. 13 Horiz.***
1415 A432 1.65k Leaving Sweden, 1880 60 20
1416 A432 1.65k shown 60 20
1417 A432 1.65k Local voting right 60 20
1418 A432 1.65k Girls 60 20
a. Bklt. pane of 8 (2 each #1415-1418) 4.80

Early Purple Orchid — A433

Photogravure and Engraved

1982, Oct. 9 ***Perf. 12x13***
1419 Sheet of 4 4.50 4.00
a. A433 1.65k shown 1.10 1.00
b. A433 1.65k Lady's-slipper 1.10 1.00
c. A433 2.40k Marsh helleborine 1.10 1.00
d. A433 2.70k Elder-flowered orchid 1.10 1.00

Wild orchids. Sold for 10k for benefit of stamp collecting.

Christmas 1982 — A434

Stained-glass Windows, Church at Lye, Gotland, 14th cent.

Perf. 13 on 3 Sides

1982, Nov. 24 **Photo.**
1420 A434 1.40k Angel 60 45
1421 A434 1.40k Child in the Temple 60 45
1422 A434 1.40k Adoration of the Kings 60 45
1423 A434 1.40k Tidings to the Shepherds 60 45
1424 A434 1.40k Birth of Christ 60 45
a. Bklt. pane of 10 (2 each #1420-1424) 6.00
Nos. 1420-1424 (5) 3.00 2.25

Signature, Atomic Model — A435

Nobel Prizewinners in Physics (Quantum Mechanics): Various atomic models.

1982, Nov. 24 **Engr.** ***Perf. 13 Horiz.***
1425 A435 2.40k Niels Bohr, Denmark, 1922 1.00 50
1426 A435 2.40k Erwin Schrodinger, Austria, 1933 1.00 50
1427 A435 2.40k Louis de Broglie, France, 1929 1.00 50
1428 A435 2.40k Paul Dirac, England, 1933 1.00 50
1429 A435 2.40k Werner Heisenberg, Germany, 1932 1.00 50
a. Bklt. pane of 5 (#1425-1429) 5.00
Nos. 1425-1429 (5) 5.00 2.50

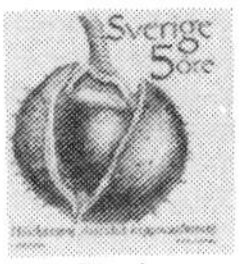

Fruit A436

Crown and Posthorn A436a

King Karl XVI Gustaf A436b

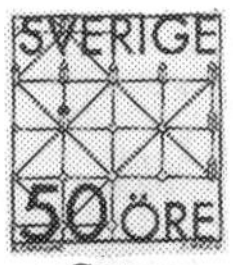

Games A436c

Games A436d

1983-85 **Engr.** ***Perf. 12½ Vert.***
1430 A436 5o Horse chestnut 5 5
1431 A436 10o Norway maple 5 5
1432 A436 15o Dogrose 8 5
1433 A436 20o Sloe 10 6
1434 A436c 50o Fox and cheese 18 5
1435 A436c 60o Dominoes 20 5
1436 A436c 70o Ludo 24 5
1437 A436c 80o Chinese checkers 28 5
1438 A436c 90o Backgammon 30 5
1439 A436a 1.60k dp bl ('85) 45 8
1440 A436b 2k bis ('85) 60 10
1441 A436a 2.50k bis ('85) 75 12
1442 A436b 2.70k dl red brn ('85) 80 12
1443 A436d 3k Chess 90 15
1444 A436b 3.20k brt bl ('85) 1.00 15
1445 A436a 4k dp car ('85) 1.25 20
Nos. 1430-1445 (16) 7.23 1.38

Issue dates: Nos. 1430-1433, Feb. 10, 1983. Nos. 1434-1438, 1443, Oct. 12, 1985. Nos. 1439-1442, 1444-1445, Jan. 24, 1985.

See Nos. 1573-1580.

Peace Movement Centenary A437

1983, Feb. 10
1446 A437 1.35k blue 50 25

Nils Ferlin (1898-1961), Poet — A438

1983, Feb. 10
1447 A438 6k dk grn 1.65 35

500th Anniv. of Printing in Sweden — A439

1983, Feb. 10 ***Perf. 13 Horiz.***
1448 A439 1.65k Lead type 60 20
1449 A439 1.65k Dialogus Creaturarum, 1483 60 20
1450 A439 1.65k Carolus XII Bible, 1793 60 20
1451 A439 1.65k ABC Books, 1760s 60 20
1452 A439 1.65k Laser photo composition 60 20
a. Bklt. pane of 10 (2 each #1448-1452) 6.00
Nos. 1448-1452 (5) 3.00 1.00

Sweden-US Relations Bicentenary — A440

1983, Mar. 24
1453 A440 2.70k Benjamin Franklin, Swedish Arms 1.10 40
a. Bklt. pane of 5 5.50

See U.S. No. 2036.

Nordic Cooperation Issue — A441

Perf. 12½ Horiz.

1983, Mar. 24 **Engr.**

Size: 21x27mm.

1454 A441 1.65k Bicycling 60 15

Perf. 13 Vert.

1455 A441 2.40k Sailing 90 50

Provincial Arms Type of 1981

1983, Apr. 25 **Photo.** ***Perf. 14½x14***
1456 A410 1.60k Gotland 60 8
1457 A410 1.60k Gastrikland 60 8
1458 A410 1.60k Medelpad 60 8
1459 A410 1.60k Vastergotland 60 8
a. Bklt. pane of 20 (5 each #1456-1459) 12.00

See note after No. 1277.

Europa 1983 — A442

Perf. 12½ Horiz.

1983, Apr. 25 **Engr.**
1460 A442 1.65k Swedish Ballet Co. 90 15
1461 A442 2.70k Sliding-jaw spanner 1.25 50

STOCKHOLMIA Intl. Stamp Exhibition, Aug. 28-Sept. 7, 1986 — A443

Designs: 1k, 3k, 10-ore King Oscar II definitive essays, 1884. 2k, No. 39. 4k, No. 58.

1983, May 25 ***Perf. 12½***
1462 A443 1k blue 35 30
1463 A443 2k red 70 50
1464 A443 3k blue 1.10 95
1465 A443 4k green 1.50 1.25
a. Bklt. pane of 4 (#1462-1465) 3.75

Red Cross A444

Greater Karlso A445

Perf. 12½ Horiz.

1983, Aug. 24 **Engr.**
1466 A444 1.50k red 55 15
1467 A445 1.60k dk bl 55 15

Planorbis Snail A446

Arctic Fox A447

Perf. 12½ on 3 Sides, Horiz.

1983, Aug. 24
1468 A446 1.80k green 60 15
a. Bklt. pane of 10 6.00
1469 A447 2.10k grnsh blk 65 15

Hjalmar Bergman (1883-1931), Writer — A448

1983, Aug. 24 ***Perf. 13 Horiz.***
1470 A448 1.80k Portrait 70 12
1471 A448 1.80k Jac the Clown illustration by Nisse Skoog 70 12

Se-tenant.

View of Helgeandsholmen, Stockholm, by Franz Hogenberg, 1580 — A449

1983, Aug. 24 *Perf. 12½ Vert.*
1472 A449 2.70k dl pur & dk bl 95 35

Wilhelm Stenhammar Composer and Pianist — A450

Hins-Anders, Violinist — A451

Photogravure and Engraved

1983, Oct. 1 *Perf. 13½*
1473 Sheet of 5 4.50 3.25
a. A450 1.80k shown 75 55
b. A450 1.80k Aniara (opera) 75 55
c. A450 1.80k Lars Gullin jazz saxophonist 75 55
d. A450 1.80k ABBA pop music group 75 55
e. A451 2.70k shown 1.25 90

Sold for 11.50k.

Christmas 1983 — A452

Postcard designs: No. 1474, Christmas Gnomes around the tree. No. 1475, on straw goats. No. 1476, Folk children, Christmas porridge and gingerbread. No. 1477, shown.

Perf. 12½ on 3 sides

1983, Nov. 22 **Photo.**
1474 A452 1.60k multi 55 18
1475 A452 1.60k multi 55 18
1476 A452 1.60k multi 55 18
1477 A452 1.60k multi 55 18
a. Bklt. pane of 12 (3 each #1474-1477) 7.25

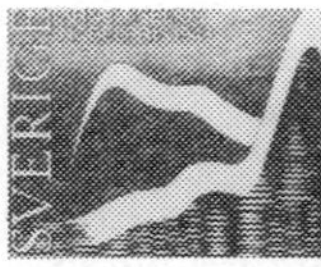

Chemistry, Nobel Prize Winners — A453

Designs: No. 1478, Arne Tiselius (1902-1971), Electrophoresis Studies. No. 1479, George De Hevsy (1885-1966), Radioactive isotope tracers. No. 1480 Svante Arrenius (1859-1927), Theory of Electrolytic Dissociation. No. 1481, Theodor Svedberg (1884-1971), Colloid Studies. No. 1482, Hans Von Euler-Chelpin (1873-1964). Enzyme and Vitamin Structures.

Photogravure and Engraved

1983, Nov. 22 *Perf. 12½ horiz.*
1478 A453 2.70k slate 1.10 45
1479 A453 2.70k dp bl vio 1.10 45
1480 A453 2.70k grnsh blk 1.10 45
1481 A453 2.70k bl blk 1.10 45
1482 A453 2.70k red lil 1.10 45
a. Bklt. pane of 5 (#1478-1482) 5.50 2.00
Nos. 1478-1482 (5) 5.50 2.25

Postal Savings Centenary — A454

Design: 100o, Three crowns.

1984, Feb. 9 Engr. *Perf. 12½ Vert.*
1483 A454 100o orange 35 15
1484 A454 1.60k purple 55 15
1485 A454 1.80k pink 65 15

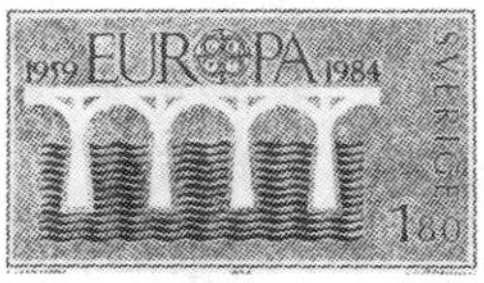

Europa 1984 A455

Design: Symbolic bridge of communications exchange.

1984, Feb. 9 *Perf. 12½ horiz.*
1486 A455 1.80k red 85 15
a. Bklt. pane of 10 8.50

Perf. 13 Vert.
1487 A455 2.70k dp ultra 1.10 45

Lemmings A456

Angelica A457

1984, Mar. 27 *Perf. 12½ on 3 Sides*
1488 A456 1.90k shown 65 12
1489 A456 1.90k Musk ox 65 12
a. Bklt. pane of 10 (5 each #1488-1489) 6.50

Perf. 12½ Horiz.
1490 A457 2k shown 70 12
1491 A457 2.25k Alpine birch 80 18

Provincial Arms Type of 1981

1984, Apr. 24 Photo. *Perf. 14½x14*
1492 A410 1.60k Skane 55 8
1493 A410 1.60k Blekinge 55 8
1494 A410 1.60k Sodermanland 55 8
1495 A410 1.60k Vasterbotten 55 8
a. Bklt. pane of 20 (5 each #1492-1495) 11.00

See note after No. 1277.

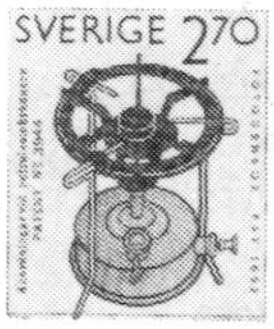

Swedish Patent System Centenary — A458

Designs: No. 1496, Paraffin stove, F.W. Lindquist, 1892. No. 1497, Industrial robot ASEA-IRB 6. No. 1498, Fan suction vacuum cleaner, Axel Wennergren, 1912. No. 1499, Inboard-outboard motor, AQ-200, No. 1500, SLIC integrated electronic circuit. No. 1501, Tetrahedron container, 1948, 1951.

Perf. 12½ on 3 Sides

1984, June 6 **Engr.**
1496 A458 2.70k red 1.00 50
1497 A458 2.70k sepia 1.00 50
1498 A458 2.70k green 1.00 50
1499 A458 2.70k green 1.00 50
1500 A458 2.70k sepia 1.00 50
1501 A458 2.70k blue 1.00 50
a. Bklt. pane of 6 (#1496-1501) 6.00
Nos. 1496-1501 (6) 6.00 3.00

Famous Letters — A459

Stockholmia '86: 1k, Erik XIV's marriage proposal to Queen Elizabeth I, 1561. 2k, Erik Dahlbergh to Sten Bielke, 1684. 3k, Feather letter, 1834. 4k, August Strindberg to Harriet Bosse, 1905.

Lithographed and Engraved

1984, June 6 *Perf. 12½*
1502 A459 1k multi 40 40
1503 A459 2k multi 80 80
1504 A459 3k multi 1.25 1.25
1505 A459 4k multi 1.65 1.65
a. Bklt. pane of 4 (#1502-1505) 4.25 4.25

Fredrika Bremer Assn. (Women's Rights) Centenary A460

Perf. 12½ Vert.

1984, Aug. 28 **Engr.**
1506 A460 1.50k pink 60 15
1507 A460 6.50k red 2.25 60

Medieval Towns A461

Engravings by E. Dahlbergh or M. Karl.

1984, Aug. 28 *Perf. 12½x13*
1508 A461 1.90k Jonkoping 60 25
1509 A461 1.90k Karlstad 60 25
1510 A461 1.90k Gavle 60 25
1511 A461 1.90k Sigtuna 60 25
1512 A461 1.90k Norrkoping 60 25
1513 A461 1.90k Vadstena 60 25
a. Bklt. pane of 6 (#1508-1513) 3.75
Nos. 1508-1513 (6) 3.60 1.50

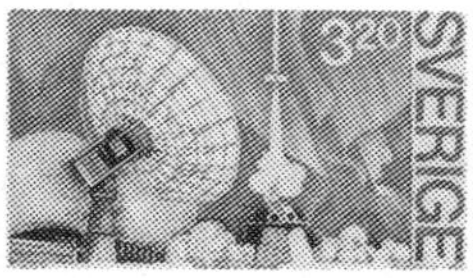

Viking Satellite, 1985 A462

1984, Oct. 13 *Perf. 12½ Vert.*
1514 A462 1.90k Satellite 60 12
1515 A462 3.20k Receiving station 1.00 40

Souvenir Sheet

Thulin D Two-Seater, 1915 — A463

For unused stamps, more recent issues are valued as never hinged, with the beginning point determined on a country-by-country basis. Notes to show the beginning points are prominently placed in the text.

Carl Nyberg's Flugan, 1900 — A464

Swedish Aviation History: b. SAAB-90 Scandia, 1946. c. Carl Gustaf Cederstrom (1867-1918, "The Flying Baron"), Bleriot, 1910. d. Tomten, 1927. Sold for 12k.

1984, Oct. 13 *Perf. 12½*
1516 Sheet of 5 4.50 4.00
a.-d. A463 1.90k, any single 85 75
e. A464 2.70k, multi 1.10 1.00

Christmas 1984 — A465

Birds.

Lithographed and Engraved

1984, Nov. 29 *Perf. 12½ on 3 Sides*
1517 A465 1.60k Coccothraustes coccothraustes 55 25
1518 A465 1.60k Bombycilla garrulus 55 25
1519 A465 1.60k Dendrocopos major 55 25
1520 A465 1.60k Sitta europaea 55 25
a. Bklt. pane of 12 (3 each #1517-1520) 6.75

Inner Ear A466

Nobel Prize Winners in Physiology or Medicine: No. 1521, Georg von Bekesy, 1961, hearing. No. 1522, John Eccles, Alan Hodgkin & Andrew Huxley, 1963, Nerve cell activation. No. 1523, Julius Axelrod, Bernard Katz & Ulf von Euler, 1970, nerve cell storage and release. No. 1524, Roger Sperry, Hubel, Wiesel, 1981, brain functions. No. 1525, David Hubel, Torsten Wiesel, 1981, Visual information processing.

Perf. 12½ Horiz.

1984, Nov. 29 **Engr.**
1521 A466 2.70k shown 1.00 40
1522 A466 2.70k Nerve, arrows 1.00 40
1523 A466 2.70k Nerve (front, side) 1.00 40
1524 A466 2.70k Brain halves 1.00 40
1525 A466 2.70k Eye 1.00 40
a. Bklt. pane of 5 (#1521-1525) 5.00
Nos. 1521-1525 (5) 5.00 2.00

World Wildlife Fund — A467

Perf. 13 on 3 Sides

1985, Mar. 14 **Engr.**
1526 A467 2k Muscardinus avellanarius 60 8
1527 A467 2k Salvelinus salvelinus 60 8
a. Bklt. pane of 10 (5 each #1526-1527) 6.00

Perf. 12½ Vert.

1528 A467 2.20k Nigritella nigra 60 20
1529 A467 3.50k Nymphaea alba 1.10 20

World Table Tennis Championships A468

1985, Mar. 14 ***Perf. 12½ Vert.***

1530 A468 2.70k Jan-Ove Waldner, Sweden 1.00 25
1531 A468 3.20k Cai Zhenhua, China 1.25 25

Clavichord — A469

Key Harp — A470

1985, Apr. 24 ***Perf. 13 Vert.***

1532 A469 2k bluish blk, *buff* 70 8

Perf. 13 on 3 Sides

1533 A470 2.70k dl red brn, *buff* 95 30
a. Bklt. pane of 6 6.00

Europa 1985.

Provincial Arms Type of 1981

Perf. 14½x14 on 3 Sides

1985, Apr. 24 **Photo.**

1534 A410 1.80k Narke 60 8
1535 A410 1.80k Angermanland 60 8
1536 A410 1.80k Varmland 60 8
1537 A410 1.80k Smaland 60 8
a. Bklt. pane of 20 (5 each #1534-1537) 12.00

See note after No. 1277.

St. Cnut's Land Grant to Lund Cathedral, 900th Anniv. A471

Seal of St. Cnut and: No. 1538, Lund Cathedral. No. 1539, City of Helsingdorg.

Perf. 12½ on 3 Sides

1985, May 21 **Engr.**

1538 A471 2k bluish blk & blk 70 8
1539 A471 2k blk & dk red 70 8
a. Bklt. pane of 10 (5 each, #1538-1539) 7.00

See Denmark Nos. 777-778.

Stockholmia '86 — A472

Paintings of old Stockholm: No. 1540, A View of Slussen, by Sigrid Hjerten (1919). No. 1541, Skeppsholmen, Winter, by Gosta Adrian-Nilsson (1919). No. 1542, A Summer's Night by the Riddarholmen, by Hilding Linnquist (1945). No. 1543, Klara Church Tower, by Otte Skold (1927).

Lithographed and Engraved

1985, May 21 ***Perf. 12½***

1540 A472 2k multi 70 45
1541 A472 2k multi 70 45
1542 A472 3k multi 1.25 85
1543 A472 4k multi 1.65 1.00
a. Bklt. pane of 4 (Nos. 1540-1543) 4.50

Swedish Touring Club Cent. — A473

Designs: No. 1544, Af Chapman Hostel, Stockholm. No. 1545, Touring Club Syl Station (c. 1920).

Perf. 12½ Vert.

1985, May 21 **Engr.**

1544 A473 2k blk & dp bl 65 12

Size: 62x27mm

1545 A473 2k dp bl & blk 65 12

Se-tenant.

Trade Signs — A474

Perf. 12½ on 3 Sides

1985, Aug. 28 **Engr.**

1546 A474 10o Music Shop, Slottsgatan 5 5
1547 A474 20o Furrier, Stockholm 6 5
1548 A474 20o Coppersmith, Landskrona 6 5
1549 A474 50o Haberdasher, Stockholm 18 15
1550 A474 2k Shoemaker, Norrkoping 70 15
a. Bklt. pane of 6 (#1546-1549, 2 #1550) 1.75
Nos. 1546-1550 (5) 1.05 45

The Dying Spartan Hero, Otryades, 1779, by Johan Tobias Sergel A475

Baron Carl Frederik Adelcrantz, Academy Pres., 1754, by Alexander Roslin (1718-1793) — A476

1985, Aug. 28 ***Perf. 12½ Vert.***

1551 A475 2k sl bl 70 15

Perf. 12½ Horiz.

1552 A476 7k dk red brn 2.50 35

Royal Academy of Fine Arts, 250th anniv.

Intl. Youth Year — A477

Children's drawings: 2k, Participation, by Marina Karlsson. 2.70k, Development, by Madeleine Andersson. 3.20k, Peace, by Charlotta Ankar.

Lithographed and Engraved

1985, Oct. 12 ***Perf. 12½x13***

1553 Sheet of 3 3.00 3.25
a. A477 2k multi 90 1.00
b. A477 2.70k multi 90 1.00
c. A477 3.20k multi 90 1.00

Sold for 10k.

Prime Minister Per Albin Hansson (1885-1946) — A478

Birger Sjoberg (1885-1929), Journalist, Novelist, Poet — A479

1985, Oct. 12 **Engr.** ***Perf. 12½ Vert.***

1556 A478 1.60k blk & red 55 15

Perf. 12½ Horiz.

1557 A479 4k dk bl grn 1.25 1.25

Christmas 1985 — A480

15th cent. religious paintings by Albertus Pictor.

Perf. 13x12½ on 3 Sides

1985, Nov. 21 **Engr.**

1558 A480 1.80k Annunciation 65 30
1559 A480 1.80k Birth of Christ 65 30
1560 A480 1.80k Adoration of the Magi 65 30
1561 A480 1.80k Mary as the Apocalyptic Virgin 65 30
a. Bklt. pane of 12 (3 each, Nos. 1558-1561) 8.00

Nobel Laureates in Literature A481

Authors: No. 1562, William Faulkner (1897-1962), 1949, Southern United States. No. 1563, Halldor Kiljan Laxness (b.1902), 1955, Iceland. No. 1564, Miguel Angel Asturias (1899-1974), 1967, Guatemala. No. 1565, Yasunari Kawabata (1899-1972), 1968, Japan. No. 1566, Patrick White (b. 1912), 1973, Australia.

Lithographed and Engraved

1985, Nov. 21 ***Perf. 13 Horiz.***

1562 A481 2.70k myr grn 95 30
1563 A481 2.70k dp brn, chlky bl & myr grn 95 30
1564 A481 2.70k myr grn & tan 95 30
1565 A481 2.70k chlky bl & myr grn 95 30
1566 A481 2.70k chlky bl & ocher 95 30
a. Blkt. pane of 5, Nos. 1562-1566 4.75
Nos. 1562-1566 (5) 4.75 1.50

Types of 1983-85 and

Queen Sylvia — A482

1986-89 **Engr.** ***Perf. 12½ Vert.***

1567 A436a 1.70k dk vio 52 10
1568 A436a 1.80k brt vio ('87) 48 10
1569 A436b 2.10k dk bl 55 10
1570 A436b 2.20k int blue ('88) 65 12
1571 A436b 2.30k dk ol grn ('89) 78 12
1572 A436a 2.80k emerald 75 15
1573 A436b 2.90k dk grn 80 15
1574 A436b 3.10k dk brn ('87) 90 18
1575 A436a 3.20k yel brn ('87) 90 18
1576 A436b 3.30k dk rose brn ('89) 1.10 18
1577 A482 3.40k dk red 90 18
1578 A482 3.60k grn ('87) 1.00 20
1579 A482 3.90k vio bl ('89) 1.65 35
1580 A436a 6k bl grn ('87) 2.00 35
Nos. 1567-1580 (14) 12.98 2.46

Issue dates: 2.10, 2.90, 3.40k, Jan. 23. 1.70, 2.80k, Feb. 20. 1.80, 3.10, 3.20, 3.60, 6k, Jan. 27. 2.20k, Jan. 29. 2.30, 3.30, 3.90k, Apr. 20.

Waterbirds — A484

Perf. 13 on 2 or 3 Sides

1986, Jan. 23 **Engr.**

1582 A484 2.10k Eider 70 15
1583 A484 2.10k Smaspov 70 15
a. Bklt. pane of 10 (5 each, #1582-1583) 7.00
1584 A484 2.30k Storiom 75 30

STOCKHOLMIA '86 — A485

Lithographed and Engraved

1986, Jan. 23 ***Perf. 13***

1585 A485 2k No. 33a, cancel 70 70
1586 A485 2k Stamp engraver 70 70
1587 A485 3k Nos. 268, 271, US No. 836 1.10 1.10
1588 A485 4k Boy soaking stamps 1.40 1.40
a. Bklt. pane of 4, #1585-1588 4.00

See U.S. Nos. 2198-2201a.

Swedish PO, 350th Anniv. — A486

Sundial — A487

Lithographed and Engraved

1986, Feb. 20 ***Perf. 13x12½***

1589 A486 2.10k org yel & dk bl 70 15
a. Bklt pane of 8 5.75

1986, Feb. 20 **Engr.** ***Perf. 13 Horiz.***

Design: No. 1591, Motto of the Swedish Academy.

1590 A487 1.70k dk bl & lake, *gray* 55 15
1591 A487 1.70k grn & dk red, *gray* 55 15

Royal Swedish Academy of Letters, History and Antiquities, and Swedish Academy, bicents. Nos. 1590-1591 se-tenant.

Provincial Arms Type of 1981

Perf. 15x14½ on 3 Sides

1986, Apr. 23 **Photo.**

1592 A410 1.90k Harjedalen 60 15
1593 A410 1.90k Uppland 60 15
1594 A410 1.90k Halland 60 15

1595 A410 1.90k Lappland 60 15
a. Bklt. pane of 20 (5 each #1592-1595) 12.00

See note after No. 1277.

King Carl XVI Gustaf A488

Royal Cipher A489

40th birthday: No. 1598, King presenting No. bel Prize for literature to Czeslaw Milosz, 1980. No. 1600, Royal family at Soldien palace

Lithographed and Engraved

1986, Apr. 23 *Perf. 12 on 3 Sides*

1596 A488 2.10k grnsh blk & pale grn 70 18
1597 A489 2.10k dk bl, pink & gold 70 18
1598 A488 2.10k dk bl & pale bl 70 18
1599 A489 2.10k dk bl, pale grn & gold 70 18
1600 A488 2.10k blk & pale pink 70 18
a. Bklt. pane (2 each #1596-1600) 7.00

Olof Palme (1927-1986), Prime Minister — A490

Perf. 13 on 3 Sides

1986, Apr. 11 **Engr.**

1601 A490 2.10k dk lil rose 85 40
1602 A490 2.90k grnsh blk 1.10 60
a. Bklt. pane of 10, 5 each #1601-1602 10.00

Nordic Cooperation Issue — A491

Europa 1986 — A492

Sister towns.

1986, May 27 Engr. *Perf. 13 Vert.*

1603 A491 2.10k Uppsala 70 15
1604 A491 2.90k Eskilstuna 1.00 40

1986, May 27 *Perf. 13 Horiz.*

1605 A492 2.10k Automotive pollutants 70 15

Perf. 13 on 3 Sides.

1606 A492 2.90k Industrial pollutants 1.00 40
a. Bklt. pane of 6 6.00

STOCKHOLMIA '86 — A493

Designs: No. 1607, Mail handling terminal, Tomteboda, 1986. No. 1608, Railroad mail car, 19th cent. No. 1609, Post Office, 18th cent. No. 1610, Postman, 17th cent.

Lithographed and Engraved

1986, Aug. 29 *Perf. 13*

1607 A493 2.10k multi 6.25 5.00
1608 A493 2.10k multi 6.25 5.00
1609 A493 2.90k multi 6.25 5.00
1610 A493 2.90k multi 6.25 5.00
a. Bklt. pane of 4, #1607-1610 25.00

Bklt. sold for 40k, including 30k ticket to STOCKHOLMIA '86.

Souvenir Sheet

World Class Athletes in Track and Field — A494

Designs: a, Ann-Louise Skoglund, 400-meter hurdle, 1982. b, Dag Wennlund, 1986, and Eric Lemming, c. 1900, javelin. c, Standing high jumper and Patrik Sjoberg, high jump, 1985. d, Anders Garderud, 300-meter steeplechase record-holder.

1986, Oct. 18 Engr. *Perf. 12 1/2*

1611 Sheet of 4 3.75 3.75
a.-d. A494 2.10k, any single 85 85

No. 1611 sold for 11k to benefit philatelic organizations.

Intl. Peace Year — A495

Amnesty Intl., 25th Anniv. — A496

1986, Oct. 18 *Perf. 13 Vert.*

1612 A495 3.40k bluish blk & emer grn 1.10 40
1613 A496 3.40k dk red & bluish blk 1.10 40
a. Pair, #1612-1613 2.50 2.25

Christmas — A497

Winter village scenes.

Lithographed and Engraved

Perf. 13x12 1/2 on 3 Sides

1986, Nov. 25

1614 A497 1.90k Postal van 65 38
1615 A497 1.90k Postman on motorcycle 65 38
1616 A497 1.90k Children, sled 65 38
1617 A497 1.90k Child mailing letter 65 38
a. Block of 4, #1614-1617 2.75 1.60
b. Bklt. pane of 12, 3 #1617a 8.50

Nos. 1614-1617 printed se-tenant in a continuous design.

Demand, as well as supply, determines a stamp's market value. One is as important as the other.

Nobel Peace Prize Laureates — A498

Designs: No. 1618, Bertha von Suttner, 1905. No. 1619, Carl von Ossietzky, 1935. No. 1620, Albert Luthuli, 1960, No. 1621, Martin Luther King, Jr., 1964. No. 1622, Mother Teresa, 1979.

1986, Nov. 25 Engr. *Perf. 13 Horiz.*

1618 A498 2.90k brt bl, blk & hn brn 1.00 50
1619 A498 2.90k blk & hn brn 1.00 50
1620 A498 2.90k brt bl, blk & brn blk 1.00 50
1621 A498 2.90k brn blk & hn brn 1.00 50
1622 A498 2.90k blk, brt bl & hn brn 1.00 50
a. Bklt pane of 5 #1618-1622 5.00

Fauna and Flora — A499

Perf. 13 on 3 Sides

1987, Mar. 10 **Engr.**

1623 A499 2.10k Parnassius mnemosyne 70 35
1624 A499 2.10k Gentianella campestris 70 35
a. Booklet pane of 5 each #1623-1624 7.00

Perf. 13 Horiz.

1625 A499 2.50k Osmoderma eremita 85 32
1626 A499 4.20k Arnica montana 1.40 70

Swedish Aviation Industry A500

1987, Mar. 10 *Perf. 13 Vert.*

1627 A500 25k Saab SF340 6.75 3.50

Europa 1987 — A501

Designs: Nos. 1628-1629, City Library, Asplund. No. 1630, Lewerentz Marcus Church.

1987, May 14 Engr. *Perf. 13 Vert.*

1628 A501 2.10k int blk & grn 68 35

Perf. 13 on 3 Sides

1629 A501 3.10k emer grn & red brn 1.00 50
1630 A501 3.10k emer grn & sep 1.00 50
a. Bklt. pane of 6 (3 #1629, 3 #1630) 6.00

Illustrations from Children's Novels by Astrid Lindgren (b. 1907) — A502

Perf. 13x12 1/2 on 3 Sides

1987, May 14 **Litho. & Engr.**

1631 A502 1.90k Karlsson Pa Taket 60 30
1632 A502 1.90k Barnen and Bullerbyn 60 30
1633 A502 1.90k Madicken 60 30
1634 A502 1.90k Mio, Min Mio 60 30
1635 A502 1.90k Nils Karlsson-Pyssling 60 30
1636 A502 1.90k Emil and Lonneberga 60 30
1637 A502 1.90k Ronja Rovardotter 60 30
1638 A502 1.90k Pippi Longstocking 60 30
1639 A502 1.90k Broderna Lejonhjarta 60 30
1640 A502 1.90k Lotta Pa Brakmakargatan 60 30
a. Bklt. pane of 20, 2 each #1631-1640 12.00
Nos. 1631-1640 (10) 6.00 3.00

Medieval Towns — A503

Designs: No. 1641, Hans Brask, Bishop of Linkoping, 16th cent. No. 1642, Nykopingshus Castle.

Perf. 12 1/2 Vert.

1987, May 14 **Engr.**

1641 A503 2.10k blk, dk vio & yel bis 68 35
1642 A503 2.10k dk vio, blk & yel bis 68 35

Nos. 1641-1642 printed se-tenant.

Swedes in the Service of Mankind A504

Designs: No. 1643, Raoul Wallenberg, Swedish diplomat in Budapest during World War II. No. 1644, Dag Hammarskjold (1905-1961), UN secretary-general. No. 1645, Folke Bernadotte af Wisborg (1895-1948), organizer of the Red Cross operation that saved thousands from Nazi death camps.

Perf. 12 1/2 Horiz.

1987, Aug. 10 **Engr.**

1643 A504 3.10k 1.00 50
1644 A504 3.10k 1.00 50
1645 A504 3.10k 1.00 50
a. Bklt. pane of 6 (2 each #1643-1645) 6.00

Gripsholm Castle, 450th Anniv. — A505

Paintings from the Royal Castle Collection, Gripsholm: No. 1646, King Gustav I Vasa (d. 1560), artist unknown. No. 1647, Blue Tiger, 1673, favorite horse of King Charles XI, by D.K. Ehrenstrahl. No. 1648, Hedvig Charlotta Nordenflycht (1718-1763), poet, by Kopia J.H. Scheffel. No. 1649, Gripsholm Castle Outer Courtyard, 17th Cent., 19th cent. lithograph by C.J. Billmark.

1987, Aug. 10 *Perf. 13 Vert.*

1646 A505 2.10k multi 68 35
1647 A505 2.10k multi 68 35
1648 A505 2.10k multi 68 35
1649 A505 2.10k multi 68 35
a. Bklt. pane of 8 (2 strips of #1646-1649 with gutter btwn.) 5.50

Botanical Gardens
A506

Designs: No. 1650, Victoria cruziana (water lily), Victoria House, Bergian Garden, c. 1790, Stockholm University. No. 1651, Layout of baroque palace garden, by Carl Harleman (1700-1753), Uppsala University. No. 1652, White anemones, rock garden, Gothenberg Botanical Gardens, 1923. No. 1653, Tulip tree blossoms, Academy Garden, c. 1860, Lund University.

1987, Oct. 10 Engr. *Perf. 13 Vert.*

1650 A506 2.10k multi 68 35
1651 A506 2.10k multi 68 35
1652 A506 2.10k multi 68 35
1653 A506 2.10k multi 68 35
a. Bklt. pane of 8 (2 each #1650-1653 with gutter between) 5.50

The Circus in Sweden, Bicent.
A507

Litho. & Engr.

1987, Oct. 10 *Perf. 13*

1654 A507 2.10k Juggler, clown 85 42
1655 A507 2.10k High wire 85 42
1656 A507 2.10k Equestrian 85 42
a. Bklt. pane of 3 (#1654-1656) 2.55

Stamp Day. Sold for 8k.

Christmas
A508

Customs: No. 1657, Putting porridge in the stable for the gray Christmas elf. No. 1658, Watering horses at a north-running stream on Boxing Day. No. 1659, Sled-race home from church on Christmas Day. No. 1660, Hanging out sheaves of wheat to foretell a good harvest.

Perf. 13 on 3 Sides

1987, Nov. 25 Litho.

1657 A508 2k multi 65 38
1658 A508 2k multi 65 38
1659 A508 2k multi 65 38
1660 A508 2k multi 65 38
a. Bklt. pane of 12 (3 each Nos. 1657-1660) 7.80

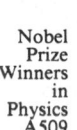

Nobel Prize Winners in Physics
A509

Space and diagram or formula: No. 1661, Antony Hewish, Great Britain, 1974. No. 1662, Subrahmanyan Chandrasekhar, US, 1983. No. 1663, William Fowler, US, 1983. No. 1664, Arno Penzias and Robert Wilson, US, 1978. No. 1665, Martin Ryle, Great Britain, 1974.

1987, Nov. 25 Engr. *Perf. 13*

1661 A509 2.90k dark blue 95 48
1662 A509 2.90k blk 95 48
1663 A509 2.90k dark blue 95 48
1664 A509 2.90k dark blue 95 48
1665 A509 2.90k blk 95 48
a. Bklt. pane of 5, Nos. 1661-1665 4.75

Inland Boats
A510

1988, Jan. 29 Engr. *Perf. 13*

1666 A510 3.10k Skiff, Lake Hjalmaren 90 45
1667 A510 3.10k Village boat, Lake Vattern 90 45
1668 A510 3.10k Rowboat, Byske 90 45
1669 A510 3.10k Flat-bottomed rowboat, Asnen 90 45
1670 A510 3.10k Ice boat, Lake Vanern 90 45
1671 A510 3.10k Church boat, Lake Locknesjon 90 45
a. Bklt. pane of 6, Nos. 1666-1671 5.50

A511

A512

Settling of New Sweden, 350th Anniv. — A513

Designs: No. 1672, 17th Cent. European settlers negotiating with American Indians, map of New Sweden, the Swedish ships *Kalmar Nyckel* and *Fogel Grip,* based on an 18th cent. illustration from a Swedish book about the American Colonies. No. 1673, Bishop Hill and painter Olof Krans. No. 1674, Carl Sandburg (1878-1967), author, and Jenny Lind (1820-1867), opera singer known as the "Swedish Nightingale." No. 1675, Charles Lindbergh (1902-1974), and *The Spirit of St. Louis.* No. 1676, American astronaut with Swedish Hasselblad camera on the Moon. No. 1677, The New York Rangers playing ice hockey with Swedish national team.

Perf. 13x12½ on 2 or 3 Sides

Litho. & Engr. (#1674-1675)

1988, Mar. 29

1672 A511 3.60k multi 1.20 60
1673 A511 3.60k multi 1.20 60
1674 A512 3.60k brn 1.20 60
1675 A512 3.60k dk bl & brn 1.20 60
1676 A513 3.60k dk bl & yel 1.20 60
1677 A513 3.60k dk red, dk bl & blk 1.20 60
a. Bklt. pane of 6, Nos. 1672-1677 7.20
Nos. 1672-1677 (6) 7.20 7.20

See US No. C117 and Finland No. 768.

Species Inhabiting Coastal Waters — A514

Perf. 13 on 3 Sides

1988, Mar. 29 Engr.

1678 A514 2.20k Haliaetus albicilla 72 35
1679 A514 2.20k Halichoerus grypus 72 35
a. Bklt. pane of 10, 5 each Nos. 1678-1679 7.20

Perf. 13 Horiz.

1680 A514 4.40k Anguilla anguilla 1.45 72

Midsummer Celebration
A515

Skara Township Millennium
A516

Perf. on 3 Sides

1988, May 17 Litho. & Engr.

1681 A515 2k Wildflowers in meadow 70 35
1682 A515 2k Rowing 70 35
1683 A515 2k Children making wreaths 70 35
1684 A515 2k Raising maypole 70 35
1685 A515 2k Fiddlers 70 35
1686 A515 2k Ferry 70 35
1687 A515 2k Dancing 70 35
1688 A515 2k Accordion player 70 35
1689 A515 2k Maypole, residence 70 35
1690 A515 2k Bouquet of flowers 70 35
a. Bklt. pane of 20, 2 each Nos. 1681-1690 14.00

1988, May 17 *Perf. 13 Horiz.*

Design: Detail from Creation, a Skara Cathedral stained-glass window by Bo Beskow, 20th cent.

1691 A516 2.20k multi 78 40

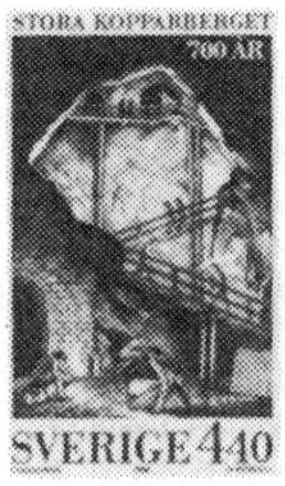

Stora Mining Co., 700th Anniv. — A517

Royal Dramatic Theater, Stockholm, Founded by King Gustav III in 1788 — A518

1988, May 17 Engr.

1692 A517 4.40k Mine, 18th cent. 1.60 80

1988, May 17

Design: Scene from *The Queen's Diamond Ornament,* about the murder of King Gustav III at the Royal Opera in 1792.

1693 A518 8k grn, red & blk 2.80 1.40

Self-portrait, 1923, by Nils Dardel (1888-1943) — A519

Paintings: No. 1695, *Old Age Home in Autumn,* c. 1930, by Vera Nilsson (1888-1979). No. 1696, *Self-portrait,* 1912, by Isaac Grunewald (1899-1979). No. 1697, *Visit of an Eccentric Lady,* 1921, by Dardel. No. 1698, *Soap Bubbles,* 1927, by Nilsson. No. 1699, *The Fair,* 1915, by Grunewald.

Perf. on 3 Sides

1988, Aug. 25 Litho. & Engr.

Size: 33x35mm (Nos. 1695, 1698)

1694 A519 2.20k shown 72 35
1695 A519 2.20k multi 72 35
1696 A519 2.20k multi 72 35
1697 A519 2.20k multi 72 35
1698 A519 2.20k multi 72 35
1699 A519 2.20k multi 72 35
a. Bklt. pane of 6, #1694-1699 4.50

Europa
A520

Transport and communication.

1988, Aug. 25 Engr. *Perf. 13 Vert.*

1700 A520 2.20k like No. 1701 72 35

Perf. 13 on 3 Sides

1701 A520 3.10k X2 high-speed train 1.00 50
1702 A520 3.10k Steam locomotive, 1887 1.00 50
a. Bklt. pane of 6, 3 each #1701-1702 6.00

Common Swift — A521

1988, Aug. 25 *Perf. 12½ Vert.*

1703 A521 20k brt vio & dk vio 6.50 3.25

Dan Andersson (1888-1920), Poet, and Manuscript
A522

Forest and Pond, Finnmarken — A523

1988, Oct. 8 Engr. *Perf. 13 Vert.*

1704 A522 2.20k vio, dk bl & dk bl grn 70 35
1705 A523 2.20k vio, dk bl & dk bl grn 70 35

Printed se-tenant.

Soccer — A524

Match scenes: No. 1706, Dribble (Torbjorn Nilsson representing local club matches). No. 1707, Heading the ball (Ralf Edstrom of the national league). No. 1708, Kick (Pia Sundhage, women's soccer).

1988, Oct. 8 Litho. & Engr. *Perf. 13*

1706	A524	2.20k multi	1.20	60
1707	A524	2.20k multi	1.20	60
1708	A524	2.20k multi	1.20	60
a.		Bklt. pane of 3, #1706-1708	3.60	

No. 1708a sold for 8.50k; surtax benefited stamp collecting.

Nobel Laureates in Chemistry A525

Designs: No. 1709, Willard F. Libby, US, 1960, carbon-14 method of dating artifacts. No. 1710, Karl Ziegler, West Germany, and Guilio Natta, Italy, 1963, catalysts. No. 1711, Aaron Klug, South Africa, 1982, electron microscopy. No. 1712, Ilya Prigogine, Belgium, 1977, proof that molecular order can occur spontaneously out of chaos.

Perf. 12½ Vert.

1988, Nov. 29 Litho. & Engr.

1709	A525	3.10k multi	1.05	52
1710	A525	3.10k multi	1.05	52
1711	A525	3.10k multi	1.05	52
1712	A525	3.10k multi	1.05	52
a.		Bklt. pane of 8 (2 each #1709-1712)	8.50	

Christmas — A526

Story of Christ's birth according to Luke (2:7-20): No. 1713, Angels appear to inform shepherds of Christ's birth. No. 1714, Star of Bethlehem, angel, horse. No. 1715, Birds singing. No. 1716, Magi offering gifts. No. 1717, Holy family. No. 1718, Shepherds with palm offering.

Perf. 12½x13 on 3 Sides

1988, Nov. 29

1713	A526	2k multi	65	32
1714	A526	2k multi	65	32
1715	A526	2k multi	65	32
1716	A526	2k multi	65	32
1717	A526	2k multi	65	32
1718	A526	2k multi	65	32
a.		Bklt. pane of 12 (2 each Nos. 1713-1718)	7.80	

Nos. 1713 and 1716, 1714 and 1717, 1715 and 1718 printed se-tenant in continuous designs.

Lighthouses A527

Designs: 1.90k, Twin masonry lighthouses, 1832, and concrete lighthouse, 1946, Nidingen, Kattegat Is. 2.70k, Soderarm, Uppland, 1839. 3.80k, Sydostbrotten, Gulf of Bothnia, 1963. 3.90k, Sandhammaren, Skane, c. 1860.

1989, Jan. 31 Engr. *Perf. 13 Vert.*

1719	A527	1.90k multi	65	32
1720	A527	2.70k multi	90	45
1721	A527	3.80k multi	1.25	62
1722	A527	3.90k multi	1.30	65

Endangered Species — A528

1989, Jan. 31 *Perf. 13 on 3 Sides*

1723	A528	2.30k *Gulo gulo*	75	38
1724	A528	2.30k *Strix uralensis*	75	38
a.		Bklt. pane of 10, 5 each Nos. 1723-1724	7.50	

Perf. 13 Horiz.

1725	A528	2.40k *Dendrocopos minor*	80	40
1726	A528	2.60k *Calidris alpina schinzii*	88	45
1727	A528	3.30k *Hyla arborea*	1.10	55
1728	A528	4.60k *Ficedula parva*	1.55	78
		Nos. 1723-1728 (6)	5.83	2.94

Opening of The Globe Arena, Stockholm — A529

Perf. 13 Horiz.

1989, Apr. 14 Litho. & Engr.

1729	A529	2.30k Exterior	75	38
1730	A529	2.30k Ice hockey	75	38
1731	A529	2.30k Gymnastics	75	38
1732	A529	2.30k Concert	75	38
a.		Bklt. pane of 4, #1729-1732	3.00	

Nordic Cooperation Issue — A530

Folk costumes.

Perf. 13 Horiz.

1989, Apr. 20 Litho. & Engr.

1733	A530	2.30k Woman's wool waist	75	38
1734	A530	3.30k Belt pouch	1.10	55

Natl. Labor Movement, Cent. — A531

Europa 1989 — A532

1989, May 17 Engr. *Perf. 13 Horiz.*

1735	A531	2.30k dk red & blk	75	38

1989, May 17 *Perf. 13 Vert.*

Children's games: 2.30k, No. 1738, Sailing toy boats. No. 1737, Kick-sledding.

1736	A532	2.30k car lake	75	38

Perf. 13

1737	A532	3.30k lilac	1.10	55
1738	A532	3.30k greenish bl	1.10	55
a.		Bklt. pane of 6, (3 each #1737-1738)	6.60	

Summer — A533

Perf. 13 on 3 Sides

1989, May 17 Litho.

1739	A533	2.10k Sailing	68	35
1740	A533	2.10k Beach ball	68	35
1741	A533	2.10k Cycling	68	35
1742	A533	2.10k Canoeing	68	35
1743	A533	2.10k Angling	68	35
1744	A533	2.10k Camping	68	35
1745	A533	2.10k Croquet	68	35
1746	A533	2.10k Badminton	68	35
1747	A533	2.10k Gardening	68	35
1748	A533	2.10k Sand sculpture	68	35
a.		Bklt. pane of 20 (2 each Nos. 1739-1748)	13.60	
		Nos. 1739-1748 (10)	6.80	3.50

SEMI-POSTAL STAMPS

Type of 1872-91 Issues Surcharged in Dark Blue

Wmk. Wavy Lines. (181)

1916, Dec. 21 *Perf. 13x13½.*

B1	A5	5o + 5o on 2o org	4.50	5.50
B2	A5	5o + 5o on 3o yel brn	4.50	5.50
B3	A5	5o + 5o on 4o gray	4.50	5.50
B4	A5	5o + 5o on 5o grn	4.50	5.50
B5	A5	5o + 5o on 6o lil	4.50	5.50
B6	A5	10o + 10o on 12o pale bl	4.50	5.50
B7	A5	10o + 10o on 20o red org	4.50	5.50
B8	A5	10o + 10o on 24o yel	4.50	5.50
B9	A5	10o + 10o on 30o brn	4.50	5.50
B10	A5	10o + 10o on 50o rose red	4.50	5.50
		Nos. B1-B10 (10)	45.00	55.00

The surtax on Nos. B1-B31 was for the militia. See note after No. B21.

No. 66 Surcharged in Dark Blue

1916, Dec. 21 Wmk. 180 *Perf. 13*

B11	A12	10o + 4.90k on 5k dl bl	140.00	250.00

Postage Due Stamps of 1877 Surcharged in Dark Blue

1916, Dec. 21 Unwmk. *Perf. 13*

B12	D1	5o + 5o on 1o blk	5.50	5.00
B13	D1	5o + 5o on 3o rose	2.25	3.25
B14	D1	5o + 5o on 5o brn	2.25	3.25
B15	D1	5o + 10o on 6o yel	3.00	4.75
B16	D1	5o + 15o on 12o pale red	22.50	15.00
B17	D1	10o + 20o on 20o pale bl	9.00	12.00
B18	D1	10o + 40o on 24o lil	40.00	62.50
B19	D1	10o + 20o on 30o grn	3.00	4.75
B20	D1	10o + 40o on 50o yel brn	20.00	27.50

B21 D1 10o + 90o on 1kr bl & yel brn	105.00	*250.00*
Nos. B12-B21 (10)	212.50	*388.00*

The surtax on Nos. B12-B21 is indicated not in figures, but in words at bottom of surcharge: Fem, 5; Tio, 10; Femton, 15; Tjugo, 20; Fyrtio, 40; Nittio, 90.

Nos. B1-B10 Surcharged

1918, Dec. 18 — **Wmk. 181**

B22 A5 7o + 3o on #B1	6.50	6.50
B23 A5 7o + 3o on #B2	1.90	1.40
B24 A5 7o + 3o on #B3	1.90	1.40
B25 A5 7o + 3o on #B4	1.90	1.40
B26 A5 7o + 3o on #B5	1.90	1.40
B27 A5 12o + 8o on #B6	1.90	1.40
B28 A5 12o + 8o on #B7	1.90	1.40
B29 A5 12o + 8o on #B8	1.90	1.40
B30 A5 12o + 8o on #B9	1.90	1.40
B31 A5 12o + 8o on #B10	1.90	1.40
Nos. B22-B31 (10)	23.60	19.10

The 12o+8o surcharge exists on Nos. B1-B5 and the 7o+3o surcharge exists on Nos. B6-B10. Value, each $65.

Nos. B24, B26, B28 and B30 exist with surcharge inverted. Value unused, each $125.

King Gustaf V
SP1 SP2

Unwmk.

1928, June 16 — **Engr.** — ***Perf. 10***

B32 SP1 5o (+ 5o) yel grn	3.00	4.50
a. Booklet pane of 8	115.00	
B33 SP1 10o (+ 5o) dk vio	3.00	4.50
a. Booklet pane of 8	115.00	
B34 SP1 15o (+ 5o) car	3.00	4.50
a. Booklet pane of 8	115.00	
B35 SP1 20o (+ 5o) org	4.75	2.00
B36 SP1 25o (+ 5o) dk bl	4.75	2.00
Nos. B32-B36 (5)	18.50	17.50

70th birthday of King Gustaf V. The surtax was used for anti-cancer work.

Catalogue values for unused stamps in this section, from this point to the end of the section, are for Never Hinged items.

1948, June 16 — ***Perf. 12½ Vertically***

B37 SP2 10o + 10o grn	55	60
B38 SP2 20o + 10o red	80	75
B39 SP2 30o + 10o ultra	55	60

Perf. 12½ on 3 Sides.

B40 SP2 10o + 10o grn	65	50
a. Bklt. pane of 20	13.00	
B41 SP2 20o + 10o red	80	55
a. Booklet pane of 20	16.00	
Nos. B37-B41 (5)	3.35	3.00

90th anniv. of the birth of King Gustaf V. The surtax provided aid for Swedish youth.

King Gustaf VI Adolf
SP3

Henri Dunant
SP4

1952, Nov. 11 — ***Perf. 12½ Horiz.***

B42 SP3 10o + 10o grn	25	25
B43 SP3 25o + 10o car rose	32	32
B44 SP3 40o + 10o ultra	45	45

Perf. 12½ on 3 Sides

B45 SP3 10o + 10o grn	25	32
a. Booklet pane of 20	5.00	
B46 SP3 25o + 10o car rose	32	32
a. Booklet pane of 20	6.50	
Nos. B42-B46 (5)	1.59	1.66

70th birthday of King Gustaf VI Adolf. The surtax was used to promote Swedish culture.

1959, May 8 — ***Perf. 12½ Horizontally***

B47 SP4 30o + 10o red	80	90

Perf. 12½ on 3 Sides

B48 SP4 30o + 10o red	1.00	1.10
a. Bklt. pane of 20	20.00	

Issued to commemorate the centenary of the Red Cross idea. The surtax went to the Swedish Red Cross.

King Gustav VI Adolf — SP5

Perf. 12½ Vertically

1962, Nov. 10 — **Engr.** — **Unwmk.**

Size: 58x24mm

B49 SP5 20o + 10o brn	15	22
B50 SP5 35o + 10o bl	15	22

Perf. 12½ Horizontally

B51 SP5 20o + 10o brn	28	38
a. Bklt. pane of 10	2.75	
B52 SP5 35o + 10o bl	28	38
a. Bklt. pane of 10	2.75	

Issued to commemorate the 80th birthday of King Gustav VI Adolf. The surtax went to the King Gustav VI Adolf 80th anniversary Foundation for Swedish Cultural Activities.

Ship Types of Regular Issues, 1936-44
Imprint: "1966"

Designs (Ships): 10o, "The Lion of Smaland." 15o, "Kalmar Nyckel." 20o, Old Sailing Packet. 25o, Mail Paddle Steamship. 30o, "Kung Karl." 40o, Stern of "Amphion."

1966, Nov. 15 — ***Perf. 12½ on 3 Sides***

B53 A76 10o vermilion	30	30
B54 A50 15o vermilion	30	30
B55 A38 20o sl grn	30	30
B56 A39 25o ultra	20	14
B57 A78 30o vermilion	30	30
B58 A79 40o vermilion	30	30
a. Bklt. pane of 10 (#B53-B54, B57-B58, 2 #B55, 4 #B56)	2.75	
Nos. B53-B58 (6)	1.70	1.64

The booklet sold for 3.50k and the surtax of 1.15k went to the National Cancer Fund.

AIR POST STAMPS

Official Stamps Surcharged in Dark Blue

1920, Sept. 17 — **Wmk. 181** — ***Perf. 13***

C1 O3 10o on 3o brn	3.50	5.50
a. Inverted surcharge	115.00	200.00
C2 O3 20o on 2o org	7.25	8.50
a. Inverted surcharge	115.00	200.00
C3 O3 50o on 4o vio	27.50	27.50
a. Inverted surcharge	115.00	200.00

Wmk. Crown (180)

C4 O3 20o on 2o org	1,350.	1,400.
C5 O3 50o on 4o vio	125.00	125.00

Airplane over Stockholm — AP2

Flying Swans — AP3

Perf. 10 Vertically.

1930, May 9 — **Engr.** — **Unwmk.**

C6 AP2 10o dp bl	30	65
C7 AP2 50o dk vio	70	1.00

1942-53 — ***Perf. 12½ on 3 Sides***

C8 AP3 20k brt ultra ('53)	5.00	65
a. Bklt. pane of 20 ('53)	600.00	
b. Bklt. pane of 10 ('68)	50.00	
c. Perf. on 4 sides	65.00	7.50
d. As "c", bklt. pane of 10	1,200.	

Issue dates: No. C8c, May 4, 1942. No. C8, July 7.

POSTAGE DUE STAMPS

D1

1874 — **Unwmk.** — **Typo.** — ***Perf. 14***

J1 D1 1o black	18.00	15.00
J2 D1 3o rose	18.00	15.00
J3 D1 5o brown	18.00	15.00
J4 D1 6o yellow	40.00	37.50
J5 D1 12o pale red	4.50	4.00
J6 D1 20o blue	27.50	18.00
J7 D1 24o violet	175.00	110.00
J8 D1 24o gray	21.00	17.00
J9 D1 30o dk grn	22.50	21.00
J10 D1 50o brown	40.00	22.50
J11 D1 1k bl & bis	75.00	35.00

1877-86 — ***Perf. 13***

J12 D1 1o blk ('80)	2.00	2.50
J13 D1 3o rose	3.50	3.50
J14 D1 5o brown	3.50	3.50
J15 D1 6o yellow	3.50	3.50
a. Printed on both sides	600.00	
J16 D1 12o pale red ('82)	6.25	6.50
J17 D1 20o pale bl ('78)	3.75	2.50
J18 D1 24o red lil ('86)	9.00	9.00
a. 24o violet ('84)	9.00	9.00
J19 D1 24o gray lil ('82)	60.00	52.50
J20 D1 30o yel grn	3.25	2.75
J21 D1 50o yel brn	5.75	3.75
J22 D1 1k bl & bis	25.00	15.00

Nos. J12-J17, J19-J22 exist imperf. Value, pairs, each $300.

STAMPS FOR CITY POSTAGE

S1

Perf. 14x13½

1856-62 — **Typo.** — **Unwmk.**

LX1 S1 (1sk or 3o) blk	425.00	250.00
LX2 S1 (3o) bis brn ('62)	225.00	200.00

From 1856 to 1858 No. LX1 was sold at 1sk, from 1858 to 1862 at 3o.

No. LX1 was reprinted three times with perf. 14, once with perf. 13. No. LX2 was reprinted once with each perforation. Value of lowest-cost Perf. 14 reprints, $200 each. Perf. 13, $160 each.

OFFICIAL STAMPS

O1

O3

1874-77 Unwmk. Typo. *Perf. 14*

O1	O1	3o bister	35.00	11.50
a.		Imperf., pair	175.00	
O2	O1	4o gray ('77)	115.00	17.50
a.		Imperf., pair	215.00	
O3	O1	5o yel grn	115.00	17.50
a.		Imperf., pair	225.00	
O4	O1	6o lilac	175.00	20.00
a.		Imperf., pair	200.00	
O5	O1	6o gray	275.00	65.00
O6	O1	12o blue	65.00	1.75
a.		Imperf., pair	350.00	
O7	O1	20o pale red	375.00	32.50
a.		Imperf., pair	1,000.	
O8	O1	24o yellow	375.00	14.00
a.		24o org	375.00	14.00
b.		Imperf., pair	1,000.	
O9	O1	30o pale brn	200.00	17.50
a.		Imperf., pair	200.00	
O10	O1	50o rose	300.00	60.00
a.		Imperf., pair	800.00	
O11	O1	1k bl & bis	900.00	30.00
a.		Imperf., pair	1,500.	

1881-93 *Perf. 13*

O12	O1	2o org ('91)	1.25	1.25
a.		Imperf., pair	180.00	
O13	O1	3o bis brn	1.25	2.00
O14	O1	4o gray blk ('93)	2.00	30
a.		4o gray ('82)	5.00	60
O15	O1	5o grn ('84)	2.00	20
O16	O1	6o red lil ('82)	20.00	17.50
a.		6o lil ('81)	20.00	17.50
O17	O1	10o car ('85)	2.50	12
a.		Imperf., pair	180.00	
b.		10o rose	17.50	85
c.		Imperf., pair (rose)	180.00	
O18	O1	12o blue	25.00	8.00
O19	O1	20o ver ('82)	70.00	1.50
O20	O1	20o dk bl ('91)	2.50	25
a.		Imperf., pair	32.50	
O21	O1	24o yellow	32.50	9.00
a.		24o orange	32.50	9.00
O22	O1	30o brown	14.00	40
O23	O1	50o pale rose	100.00	12.00
O24	O1	50o pale gray ('93)	12.00	1.50
a.		Imperf., pair	180.00	
O25	O1	1k dk bl & yel brn	12.00	1.50

Surcharged in Dark Blue

1889

O26	O1	10o on 12o blue	10.50	14.00
a.		Inverted surcharge	275.00	475.00
b.		Perf. 14	*2,750.*	*1,500.*
O27	O1	10o on 24o yel	13.00	13.00
a.		Inverted surcharge	*900.00*	*1,000.*
b.		Perf. 14	*1,500.*	*1,400.*

1910-12 Wmk. 180 Typo.

O28	O3	1o black	20	22
O29	O3	2o orange	1.45	2.25
O30	O3	4o pale vio	2.50	3.25
O31	O3	5o green	65	80
O32	O3	8o claret	65	80
O33	O3	10o red	13.00	65
O34	O3	15o red brn	85	80
O35	O3	20o dp bl	7.25	80
O36	O3	25o red org	7.25	1.50
O37	O3	30o chocolate	9.25	2.00
O38	O3	50o gray	9.25	2.00
O39	O3	1k blk, *yellow*	11.50	6.50
O40	O3	5k claret, *yel*	10.00	4.50
		Nos. O28-O40 (13)	73.80	26.07

1910-19 Wmk. Wavy Lines (181)

O41	O3	1o black	2.00	1.65
O42	O3	2o orange	20	10
O43	O3	3o pale brn	32	32
O44	O3	4o pale vio	20	20
O45	O3	5o green	15	15
O46	O3	7o gray grn	65	65
O47	O3	8o rose	14.00	14.00
O48	O3	10o red	12	15
O49	O3	12o rose red	12	15
O50	O3	15o org brn	12	15
O51	O3	20o deep blue	15	10
O52	O3	25o orange	1.00	40
O53	O3	30o chocolate	40	40
O54	O3	35o dk vio	85	40
O55	O3	50o gray	2.00	85
		Nos. O41-O55 (15)	22.28	19.67

Use of official stamps ceased on July 1, 1920.

PARCEL POST STAMPS

Regular Issue of 1914 Surcharged **Kr. 1.98**

1917 Wmk. 180 *Perf. 13*

Q1	A14	1.98k on 5k cl, *yel*	2.00	3.75
Q2	A14	2.12k on 5k cl, *yel*	2.00	3.75

SWITZERLAND

(Helvetia)

LOCATION — Central Europe, between France, Germany and Italy.
GOVT. — Republic
AREA — 15,943 sq. mi.
POP. — 6,423,100 (est. 1983)
CAPITAL — Bern

100 Rappen or Centimes = 1 Franc

Unused values of Nos. 1L1-3L1 are for stamps without gum.

Counterfeit and repaired copies of Nos. 1L1-3L1 abound.

Catalogue values for unused stamps in this country are for Never Hinged items, beginning with Scott 365 in the regular postage section, Scott B272 in the semi-postal section, Scott C46 in the airpost section, Scott CB1 in the airpost semi-postal section, and for the various official stamps, and Scott 3O100 for the International Labor Bureau.

Also, Scott 4O40 for the International Bureau of Education, Scott 5O32 for the World Health Organization, Scott 7O28 for the United Nations European Office, Scott 8O7 for the World Meteorological Organization, Scott 9O7 for the International Bureau of the Universal Postal Union, Scott 10O1 for the International Telecommunication Union, and Scott 11O1 for the World Intellectual Property Organization.

CANTONAL ADMINISTRATION

Zurich

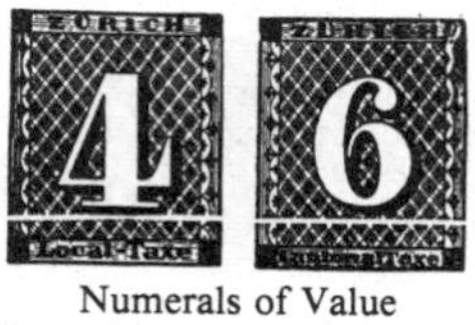
Numerals of Value
A1 A2

1843 Unwmk. Litho. *Imperf.*
Red Vertical Lines

1L1	A1	4r black	*13,500.*	*12,000.*
1L2	A2	6r black	*5,000.*	*1,350.*

1846 Red Horizontal Lines

1L3	A1	4r black	*12,000.*	*14,000.*
1L4	A2	6r black	1,500.	1,400.

Five varieties of each value.

Reprints of the Zurich stamps show signs of wear and lack the red lines. Values 4r, $3,250; 6r, $1,100.

Coat of Arms — A3

1850 Unwmk. *Imperf.*

1L5	A3	2½r blk & red	*4,500.*	*2,750.*

Geneva

Coat of Arms — A1

1843 Unwmk. Litho. *Imperf.*

2L1	A1	10c blk, *yel grn*	*37,500.*	*27,500.*
a.		Either half	*15,000.*	*7,000.*
b.		Stamp composed of right half at left & left half at right	*55,000.*	*42,500.*

A2

A3

1845-48

2L2	A2	5c blk, *yel grn*	1,900.	1,300.
2L3	A3	5c blk, *yel grn* ('47)	1,250.	1,250.
2L4	A3	5c blk, *dk grn* ('48)	2,750.	2,100.

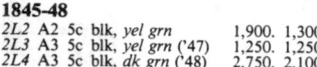

Coat of Arms
A4 A5

1849-50

2L5	A4	4c blk & red	*24,000.*	*15,000.*
2L6	A4	5c blk & red ('50)	1,800.	1,500.

1850

2L7	A5	5c blk & red	*6,500.*	*2,750.*

ENVELOPE STAMP USED AS ADHESIVE

E1

1849 Unwmk. *Imperf.*

2LU1	E1	5c yel grn		*10,000.*

Value is for cut-out stamp used on cover. Value of unused envelope (1846) or cut-out, $300. Value of used cut-out off cover, $3,000.

Basel

Dove of Basel — A1

Typo. & Embossed
1845 Unwmk. *Imperf.*

3L1	A1	2½r blk, crim & bl	*8,500.*	*8,300.*

Proofs are black, vermilion and green. Value, $3,000.

FEDERAL ADMINISTRATION

A10

A11

1850 Unwmk. Litho. *Imperf.*
Full Black Frame Around Cross

1	A10	2½r blk & red	1,600.	1,000.
2	A11	2½r blk & red	1,250.	950.00

Without Frame Around Cross

3	A10	2½r blk & red	3,300.	1,700.
4	A11	2½r blk & red	*32,500.*	*17,000.*

Forty types of each.

A12

A13

1850
Full Black Frame Around Cross

5	A12	5r blk & red, *bl*	3,500.	900.00
a.		5r blk & red, *dk bl*	3,250.	850.00
6	A13	10r blk & red, *yel*		*55,000.*

No. 6 used, with only parts of frame around cross showing, value $120 to $450.

Beware of copies of Nos. 7-8 with faked frame added.

Without Frame Around Cross

7	A12	5r blk & red, *lt bl*	1,000.	300.00
a.		5r blk & red, *dp bl*	1,350.	500.00
b.		5r blk & red, *pur bl*	*4,500.*	*2,250.*
c.		5r blk & red, *grnsh bl*	1,000.	350.00
8	A13	10r blk & red, *yel*	850.00	80.00
a.		10r blk & red, *buff*	600.00	80.00
b.		10r blk & red, *org*	850.00	150.00
c.		Half used as 5r on cover		*4,000.*

1851
Full Blue Frame Around Cross

9	A12	5r lt bl & red		*67,500.*

No. 9 used, with only parts of frame around cross showing, value $120 to $3,000.

Beware of copies of No. 10 with faked frame added.

Without Frame Around Cross

10	A12	5r lt bl & red	375.00	80.00
a.		5r dk bl & red	725.00	125.00

Forty types of each.

A14

A15

A16

1852

Colored Frame Around Cross

11	A14	15r vermilion	*5,500.*	450.00
12	A15	15r vermilion	1,400.	85.00
13	A16	15c vermilion	*8,000.*	675.00

Ten types of each.

On October 1st, 1854, all stamps of the preceding issues were declared obsolete.

Values of Nos. 14-40 are for copies which show three full frame lines. Those with fewer sell for half price or less. Copies with complete frame bring double the catalogue value or more.

Beware of thinned down papers.

Helvetia — A17

1854 Embossed. Unwmk.

Thin Paper, Fine Impressions

Emerald Silk Threads

14	A17	5r org brn	*3,750.*	*1,100.*
15	A17	5r red brn	275.00	70.00
16	A17	10r blue	375.00	15.00
17	A17	15r car rose	600.00	90.00
a.		15r pale rose	600.00	90.00
18	A17	40r pale yel grn	*52.50*	800.00
19	A17	40r yel grn	550.00	150.00

1854-55

Emerald Silk Threads

Medium Thick Paper

Fine Impressions

20	A17	5r pale yel brn	375.00	70.00
a.		5r bl	*6,000.*	*5,000.*
21	A17	10r blue	825.00	60.00
22	A17	15r rose	550.00	40.00
23	A17	20r pale org	850.00	80.00

Some authorities question whether No. 20a is an essay or an error.

1855-57

Mixed Silk Threads

Medium Thick Paper

Fine to Rough Impressions

24	A17	5r yel brn (yel)	275.00	50.00
25	A17	5r dk brn (blk)	185.00	13.00
26	A17	10r mlky bl (red)	350.00	60.00
27	A17	10r bl (car)	175.00	13.00
a.		Thin paper	2,500.	250.00
28	A17	15r rose (bl)	300.00	30.00
29	A17	40r yel grn (mar)	425.00	35.00
30	A17	1fr lav (blk)	575.00	350.00
31	A17	1fr lav (yel)	725.00	350.00
a.		Thin paper		4,500.

1857

Thin (Emergency) Paper

Rough Impressions

Green Silk Threads

32	A17	5r pale gray brn	2,300.	750.00
33	A17	15r pale dl rose	1,750.	175.00
34	A17	20r pale dl org	1,750.	100.00

1858-62

Thick Ordinary Paper

Rough Impressions

Green Silk Threads

35	A17	2r gray	125.00	250.00
a.		One and one-half used as 3r on newspaper or wrapper		*7,000.*
36	A17	5r brown	80.00	5.00
a.		5r blk brn	125.00	20.00
b.		Half used as 2½r on wrapper or cover		*1,650.*
37	A17	10r dk bl	90.00	4.00
38	A17	15r dk rose	200.00	20.00
39	A17	20r dk org	190.00	27.50
40	A17	40r dk yel grn	190.00	25.00

Helvetia — A18

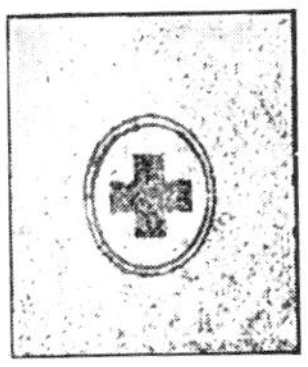

Wmk. 182-Cross in Oval

This is not a true watermark, having been impressed after the paper was manufactured.

Wmk. 182

1862-63 Embossed *Perf. 11½*

White Wove Paper

41	A18	2c gray	40.00	1.25
42	A18	3c black	6.25	*47.50*
43	A18	5c dk brn	1.50	10
a.		5c bis brn	62.50	20
b.		5c gray brn	40.00	5.00
c.		Double embossing, one inverted	3,000.	350.00
d.		Double impression of lower left "5"		1,000.
44	A18	10c blue	150.00	50
a.		Double embossing, one inverted		*7,500.*
45	A18	20c orange	1.00	1.00
a.		20c yel	40.00	1.00
46	A18	30c vermilion	700.00	10.00
47	A18	40c green	400.00	22.50
48	A18	60c bronze	425.00	70.00
50	A18	1fr gold	11.00	*30.00*
a.		1fr bronze	700.00	150.00

1867-78

52	A18	2c bis brn	1.00	30
a.		2c red brn	450.00	130.00
53	A18	10c carmine	3.50	10
54	A18	15c lemon	2.50	*14.00*
55	A18	25c bl grn	1.00	1.00
a.		25c yel grn	7.50	3.50
b.		Double embossing, one inverted		550.00
56	A18	30c ultra	150.00	2.00
a.		30c bl	*1,100.*	160.00
58	A18	40c gray	90	*32.50*
59	A18	50c violet	40.00	20.00

1881

Granite Paper

60	A18	2c bister	20	*7.50*
a.		Dbl. embossing, one inverted	300.00	
61	A18	5c brown	8	*1.65*
a.		Double embossing, one inverted	17.50	*275.00*
b.		Double impression of lower left "5"		*700.00*
62	A18	10c rose	1.75	1.40
63	A18	15c lemon	3.75	*250.00*
64	A18	20c orange	20	*60.00*
65	A18	25c green	15	*45.00*
66	A18	40c gray	20	*1,800.*
67	A18	50c dp vio	9.50	*275.00*
b.		Double embossing, one inverted	200.00	*2,500.*
68	A18	1fr gold	9.00	*600.00*

The granite paper contains fragments of blue and red silk threads.

Forged or backdated cancellations are found frequently on Nos. 42, 50, 54, 58 and 60-68.

All stamps of the preceding issues were declared obsolete on October 1st, 1883. Some of the remainders of Nos. 41-68 were overprinted "AUSSER KURS" (Obsolete) diagonally in black.

Numeral — A19

1882-99 Typo. *Perf. 11½*

Granite Paper

69	A19	2c bister	75	20
70	A19	3c gray brn	90	1.90
a.		3c gray	14.00	14.00
71	A19	5c maroon	12.50	6
a.		Tete beche pair		
72	A19	5c dp grn ('99)	7.00	6
73	A19	10c red	2.00	5
a.		10c car	6.00	10
b.		10c lt rose	175.00	2.00
74	A19	12c ultra	3.50	10
a.		12c chlky bl	8.00	40
b.		12c grnsh bl	*450.00*	13.00
75	A19	15c yellow	125.00	7.00
a.		15c orange		
76	A19	15c vio ('89)	27.50	50

1882

White Paper

77	A19	2c bister	325.00	275.00
78	A19	5c maroon	600.00	55.00
79	A19	10c rose	2,000.	45.00
80	A19	12c chlky bl	125.00	15.00
81	A19	15c yellow	200.00	150.00

See Nos. 113-118.

Helvetia (Large numerals) A20

Helvetia (Small numerals) A21

1882-1904 Engr. *Perf. 11½*

82	A20	20c orange	92.50	1.40
83	A20	25c green	45.00	75
84	A20	40c gray	65.00	12.00
85	A21	40c gray ('04)	22.50	4.00
86	A20	50c blue	85.00	5.50
87	A20	1fr claret	175.00	1.65
88	A20	3fr yel brn ('91)	150.00	6.25

1888 *Perf. 9½*

89	A20	20c orange	400.00	30.00
90	A20	25c yel grn	95.00	75
91	A20	40c gray	600.00	325.00
92	A20	50c blue	1,300.	150.00
93	A20	1fr claret	900.00	30.00

1891-99 *Perf. 11½x11*

82a	A20	20c orange	17.50	60
83a	A20	25c green	7.00	40
94	A20	25c bl ('99)	6.00	50
95	A20	30c red brn ('92)	35.00	75
84a	A20	40c gray	30.00	1.50
86a	A20	50c blue	42.50	1.50
96	A20	50c grn ('99)	30.00	4.00
87a	A20	1fr claret	42.50	75

97	A20	1fr	carmine	65.00	2.75
88a	A20	3fr	yel brn	140.00	11.50

1901-03 ***Perf. 11½x12***

82b	A20	20c	orange	15.00	55
94a	A20	25c	blue	6.00	35
95a	A20	30c	red brn	22.50	70
84b	A20	40c	gray	70.00	9.00
96a	A20	50c	green	27.50	2.00
87b	A20	1fr	claret	*2,000.*	125.00
97a	A20	1fr	car ('03)	400.00	11.50
88b	A20	3fr	yel brn	150.00	7.50

Numerous retouches and plate flaws exist on all values of this issue.

UPU Allegory — A22

1900 ***Perf. 11½***

98	A22	5c	gray grn	18.00	35
99	A22	10c	car rose	7.75	32
100	A22	25c	blue	12.00	6.750

Re-engraved

101	A22	5c	gray grn	2.75	45
102	A22	10c	car rose	37.50	13.00
103	A22	25c	blue	950.00	*11,500.*

Universal Postal Union, 25th anniv.

The impression of the re-engraved stamps is much clearer, especially the horizontally lined background. The figures of value are lined instead of being solid.

Helvetia Types of 1882-1904

Wmk. 183- Swiss Cross

1905 **Wmk. 183** ***Perf. 11½x11***

White Paper

105	A20	20c	orange	4.50	1.00
106	A20	25c	blue	6.50	3.75
107	A20	30c	brown	6.00	1.00
108a	A21	40c	gray	130.00	70.00
109	A20	50c	green	35.00	2.00
110	A20	1fr	carmine	75.00	1.05
111	A20	3fr	yel brn	225.00	42.50

Some cliches in the plates of the 20c, 25c, 30c, 50c and 3fr have been retouched.

1906 **Re-engraved** ***Perf. 11½x11***

112	A20	25c	pale bl	3.25	60

In the re-engraved stamp the stars are larger and the background below "FRANCO" is of horiz. or horiz. and vert. crossed lines, instead of horiz. and curved lines.

1906 ***Perf. 11½***

112a	A20	25c	pale bl	50.00	1.75
108	A21	40c	gray	25.00	3.00

1907 ***Perf. 11½x12***

105a	A20	20c	orange	6.50	2.50
109a	A20	50c	green	32.50	3.00
110a	A20	1fr	carmine	110.00	2.50
111a	A20	3fr	yel brn	310.00	77.50

Numeral Type of 1882-99

1905 **Typo.** ***Perf. 11½***

Granite Paper

113	A19	2c	dl bis	2.50	60
114	A19	3c	gray brn	2.25	*22.50*
115	A19	5c	green	3.00	12
116	A19	10c	scarlet	2.75	12
117	A19	12c	ultra	2.50	40
118	A19	15c	brn vio	50.00	3.75
			Nos. 113-118 (6)	63.00	*27.49*

Helvetia Types of 1882-1904

1907 **Engr.** ***Perf. 11½x12***

Granite Paper

119	A20	20c	orange	1.50	1.00
120	A20	25c	blue	10.00	2.25
121	A20	30c	red brn	6.00	2.75
122	A21	40c	gray	22.50	8.50
a.			Helvetia without diadem	325.00	*900.00*
123	A20	50c	gray grn	5.00	1.75
124	A20	1fr	carmine	24.00	1.00
125a	A20	3fr	yel brn		*10,000.*

There are retouches and plate flaws on all values.

Perf. 11½x11

120a	A20	25c	dp bl	12.50	1.75
121a	A20	30c	red brn	160.00	*225.00*
122b	A21	40c	gray		*16,000.*
124a	A20	1fr	carmine		*4,500.*
125	A20	3fr	yel brn	165.00	7.50

William Tell's Son — A23

Helvetia
A24 A25

1907-25 **Typo.** ***Perf. 11½***

Granite Paper

126	A23	2c	pale bis	35	10
127	A23	3c	lil brn	12	*4.25*
128	A23	5c	yel grn	3.50	12
129	A24	10c	rose red	3.00	25
130	A24	12c	ocher	35	*1.40*
131	A24	15c	red vio	4.25	*5.00*
132	A25	20c	red & yel ('08)	1.65	15
133	A25	25c	dp bl ('08)	1.40	10
a.			Tete beche pair	15.00	*50.00*
134	A25	30c	yel brn & pale grn ('08)	1.75	15
135	A25	35c	yel grn & yel ('08)	1.75	15
136	A25	40c	red vio & yel ('08)	11.00	30
a.			Designer's name in full on the rock ('08)	10.00	*20.00*
137	A25	40c	dp bl ('21)	5.75	30
a.			40c lt bl ('22)	2.00	10
138	A25	40c	red vio & grn ('25)	14.00	10
139	A25	50c	dp grn & pale grn ('08)	5.25	30
140	A25	60c	brn org & buff ('18)	6.50	10
141	A25	70c	dk brn & buff ('08)	90.00	6.00
142	A25	70c	vio & buff ('24)	13.00	50
143	A25	80c	sl & buff ('15)	8.25	25
144	A25	1fr	dp cl & pale grn ('08)	7.00	20
145	A25	3fr	bis & yel ('08)	200.00	60
			Nos. 126-145 (20)	378.87	*20.32*

No. 136 has two leaves and "CL" below sword hilt. No. 136a has three leaves and designer's full name below hilt.

1933

With Grilled Gum

135a	A25	35c	yel grn & yel	2.50	*3.25*
138a	A25	40c	red vio & grn	42.50	30
139a	A25	50c	dp grn & pale grn	14.00	30
140a	A25	60c	brn org & buff	9.00	25
142a	A25	70c	vio & buff	15.00	1.40
143a	A25	80c	sl & buff	9.00	1.00
144a	A25	1fr	dp cl & pale grn	17.50	1.75
			Nos. 135a-144a (7)	109.50	8.25

"Grilled" Gum

In 1930-44 many Swiss stamps were treated with a light grilling process, applied with the gumming to counteract the tendency to curl. It resembles a faint grill of vertical and horizontal ribs covering the entire back of the stamp, and can be seen after the gum has been removed. Listings of the grilled gum varieties begin with No. 135a.

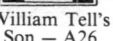

William Tell's Son — A26

Bow-string in front of stock

1909 *Perf. 11½, 12*

Granite Paper

146 A26 2c bister 42 30
a. Tete beche pair 3.00 *16.00*
147 A26 3c dk vio 25 *4.00*
148 A26 5c green 1.40 10
a. Tete beche pair 12.50 *45.00*

First Redrawing

Bow-string behind stock. Thin loop above crossbow. Letters of "HELVETIA" without serifs.

1910-17

Granite Paper

149 A26 2c bis ('10) 11.00 1.40
150 A26 3c dk vio ('10) 20 10
a. Tete beche pair 2.50 1.50
b. Booklet pane of 6 11.50
151 A26 3c brn org ('17) 10 12
a. Tete beche pair 7.50 10.00
152 A26 5c grn ('10) 25.00 1.50
a. Tete beche pair 85.00 225.00

Second Redrawing

Bow-string behind stock. Thick loop above crossbow. Letters of "HELVETIA" have serifs.

7½ CENTIMES.

Type I. Top of "7" is ½mm. thick. The "1" of "½" has only traces of serifs. The two base plates of the statue are of even thickness.

Type II. Top of "7" is 1mm. thick. The "1" of "½" has distinct serifs. The upper base plate is thinner than the lower.

1911-30

Granite Paper

153 A26 2c bis ('11) 8 10
a. Tete beche pair 3.00 1.50
154 A26 2½c cl ('18) 10 *45*
155 A26 2½c ol, *buff* ('28) 50 *90*
156 A26 3c ultra, *buff* ('30) 3.00 *3.75*
157 A26 5c grn ('11) 2.00 10
a. Tete beche pair 5.00 *9.00*
158 A26 5c org, *buff* ('21) 6 5
a. Bklt. pane of 6 (5 No. 158 + 1 No. 168) 12.50 *42.50*
159 A26 5c gray vio, *buff* ('24) 10 8
a. Bklt. pane of 6 (5 No. 159 + 1 No. 168) 6.00 *17.50*
160 A26 5c red vio, *buff* ('27) 8 15
a. Bklt. pane 6 (5 No. 160 + 1 No. 168) 27.50 *70.00*
161 A26 5c dk grn, *buff* ('30) 30 30
a. Bklt. pane 6 (5 No. 161 + 1 No. 169) 25.00 *62.50*
162 A26 7½c gray (I) ('18) 2.25 10
a. Tete beche pair 12.00 *40.00*
c. 7½c sl (II) 4.00 55
163 A26 7½c dp grn, *buff* (I) ('28) 35 *1.75*
Nos. 153-163 (11) 8.82 *7.73*

1933 **With Grilled Gum**

156a A26 3c ultra, *buff* 3.75 *4.50*
161b A26 5c dk grn, *buff* 50 *50*

Helvetia — A27

William Tell — A28

1909

Granite Paper

164 A27 10c carmine 1.00 6
a. Tete beche pair 2.00 *5.50*
165 A27 12c bis brn 1.65 15
166 A27 15c red vio 22.50 45

1914-30 Granite Paper *Perf. 11½*

TEN CENTIMES.

Type I. Bust 16½mm. high. "HELVETIA" 15½mm. wide. Cross bar of "H" at middle of the letter.

Type II. Bust 15mm. high. "HELVETIA" 15mm. wide. Cross bar of "H" above middle of the letter.

167 A28 10c red, *buff* (type II) 90 10
a. 10c red, *buff* (type I) 3.25 *24.00*
b. Tete beche pair (II) 3.00 3.75
d. Bklt. pane 6 (5 No. 167 + 1 No. 172) 45.00 *150.00*
168 A28 10c grn, *buff* (type II) ('21) 10 6
a. Tete beche pair 1.00 1.25
168C A28 10c bl grn, *buff* (type II) ('28) 5 6
d. Tete beche pair 2.25 2.25
169 A28 10c vio, *buff* (type II) ('30) 2.75 8
a. Tete beche pair 9.50 1.25
170 A28 12c brn, *buff* 20 *1.25*
171 A28 13c ol grn, *buff* ('15) 1.25 12
172 A28 15c vio, *buff* 4.00 8
b. 15c dk vio, *buff* 30.00 1.50
c. Tete beche pair 80.00 100.00
173 A28 15c brn red, *buff* ('28) 2.75 75
174 A28 20c red vio, *buff* ('21) 3.75 8
a. Tete beche pair 6.00 6.75
175 A28 20c ver, *buff* ('24) 1.25 12
a. Tete beche pair 5.25 8.50
176 A28 20c car, *buff* ('25) 25 8
a. Tete beche pair 2.25 50
177 A28 25c ver, *buff* ('21) 2.50 75
178 A28 25c car, *buff* ('22) 1.40 65
179 A28 25c brn, *buff* ('25) 3.75 90
180 A28 30c dp bl, *buff* ('24) 7.50 10
Nos. 167-180 (15) 32.40 *5.18*

1932-33 **With Grilled Gum**

169c A28 10c vio, *buff* 2.75 30
173a A28 15c brn red, *buff* ('33) 55.00 11.00
176c A28 20c car, *buff* 12.00 75
179a A28 25c brn, *buff* ('33) 125.00 15.00
180a A28 30c dp bl, *buff* 50.00 75

The Mythen A29

The Rütli — A30

The Jungfrau A31

1914-30 **Engr.** **Granite Paper**

181 A29 3fr dk grn 775.00 2.50
182 A29 3fr red ('18) 110.00 38
183 A30 5fr dp ultra 30.00 1.10
184 A31 10fr dl vio 105.00 1.25
185 A31 10fr gray grn ('30) 190.00 19.00
Nos. 181-185 (5) 1,210. 24.23

See No. 206.

Stamps of 1909-14 Surcharged

a b c

1915

186 A26(a) 1c on 2c bis 8 10
187 A27(b) 13c on 12c bis brn 20 *3.00*
188 A28(c) 13c on 12c brn, *buff* 38 65

No. 141 Surcharged

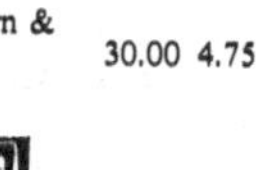

189 A25 80c on 70c dk brn & buff 30.00 4.75

Significant of Peace A32

"Peace" A33

"Dawn of Peace" A34

Perf. 11½

1919, Aug. 1 **Typo.** **Unwmk.**

190 A32 7½c ol db & blk 75 *1.10*
191 A33 10c red & yel 1.00 *2.25*
192 A34 15c vio & yel 2.00 1.10

Commemorating Peace after World War I.

Stamps of 1910-18 Surcharged in Black, Red or Dark Blue

e f

1921 **Wmk. 183**

193 A26(e) 2½c on 3c org (Bl) 8 12
a. Tete beche pair 1.00 *3.00*
b. Inverted surcharge 700.00 *1,300.*
c. Dbl. surch. *425.00* *675.00*
194 A26(e) 5c on 2c bis (R) 15 *1.00*
a. Dbl. surch. *300.00* *500.00*
195 A26(e) 5c on 7½c gray (I) (R) 12 22
a. Tete beche pair 6.00 *50.00*
b. Double surcharge *350.00* *575.00*
c. 5c on 7½c sl (II) *2,750.* *3,750.*
196 A28(f) 10c on 13c ol grn, *buff* (R) 20 *1.40*
a. Double surcharge *350.00* *575.00*
197 A28(f) 20c on 15c vio, *buff* (Bk) 1.00 1.25
a. Tete beche pr. 2.25 *50.00*
b. Dbl. surch. 600.00 *1,000.*
198 A28(f) 20c on 15c vio, *buff* (Bl) 3.50 1.50
b. Double surcharge *600.00* *1,000.*
Nos. 193-198 (6) 5.05 *5.49*

A35

A36

Red Surcharge

1921

199 A35 20c on 25c dp bl 15 28
a. Tete beche pair 1.40 4.00

1924 **Typo.** *Perf. 11½*

Granite Paper, Surface Colored

200 A36 90c grn & red, *grn* 10.50 30
201 A36 1.20fr brn rose & red, *rose* 5.25 85
202 A36 1.50fr bl & red, *bl* 12.00 85
203 A36 2fr gray blk & red, *gray* 55.00 85

1933 **With Grilled Gum**

200a A36 90c grn & red, *grn* 14.00 50
201a A36 1.20fr brn rose & red, *rose* 42.50 1.00
202a A36 1.50fr bl & red, *bl* 19.00 1.00
203a A36 2fr gray blk & red, *gray* 40.00 1.00

Building in Bern, Location of 1st U.P.U. Congress, 1874

A37 A38

1924, Oct. 9 **Engr.** **Wmk. 183**

Granite Paper

204 A37 20c vermilion 42 40
205 A38 30c dl bl 1.10 2.50

50th anniv. of the UPU.

The Rütli — A39

Type of 1914 Issue

1928 **Re-engraved** *Perf. 11½*

206 A39 5fr blue 125.00 1.65
a. Imperf., pair *15,000.*

In the re-engraved stamp the picture is clearer and lighter than on No. 183. "HELVETIA" is in smaller letters. The names at foot of the stamp are "Grasset-J. Sprenger" instead of "E. GRASSET-A. BURKHARD."

Nos. 155 and 163 Surcharged

1930, June *Perf. 11½*

207 A26 3c on 2½c ol grn, *buff* 8 80
208 A26 5c on 7½c dp grn, *buff* 18 *4.50*

The Mythen A40

1931 **Engr.** **Granite Paper**

209 A40 3fr org brn 67.50 1.40

Dove on Broken Sword A41

"Peace" A42

1932, Feb. 2 **Typo.** *Perf. 11½*

Granite Paper

210 A41 5c pck bl 14 14
211 A41 10c orange 16 8
212 A41 20c cerise 22 8
213 A41 30c ultra 1.90 32
214 A41 60c ol brn 19.00 90

Unwmk.

Photo.

215 A42 1fr ol gray & bl 22.50 4.00
Nos. 210-215 (6) 43.92 5.52

Intl. Disarmament Conf., Geneva, Feb. 1932.

Louis Favre A43

Alfred Escher A44

Design: 30c, Emil Welti.

Wmk. 183

1932, May 31 Engr. *Perf. 11½*

Granite Paper

216	A43	10c red brn	8	10
217	A44	20c vermilion	14	10
218	A44	30c dp ultra	25	*70*

Issued in commemoration of the fiftieth anniversary of the completion of the St. Gotthard tunnel.

Nos. 216 to 218 exist imperforate.

Staubbach Falls — A46

Mt. Pilatus — A47

Chillon Castle — A48

Rhone Glacier — A49

St. Gotthard Railroad — A50

Via Mala Gorge — A51

Rhine Falls — A52

1934, July 2 Typo. *Perf. 11½*

Granite Paper

219	A46	3c olive	12	*1.10*
220	A47	5c emerald	12	8
a.		Tete beche pair	1.50	1.50
221	A48	10c brt vio	20	8
a.		Tete beche pair	1.35	75
222	A49	15c orange	30	75
a.		Tete beche pair	1.65	2.75
223	A50	20c red	35	10
a.		Tete beche pair	3.25	2.00
224	A51	25c brown	7.00	2.75
225	A52	30c ultra	24.00	40
		Nos. 219-225 (7)	32.09	5.26

Souvenir Sheet

A52a

1934, Sept. 29

226	A52a	Sheet of four	425.00	*600.00*

No. 226 was issued in connection with the Swiss National Philatelic Exhibition at Zurich, Sept. 29 to Oct. 7, 1934. It contains one each of Nos. 220-223. Size: 62x72mm.

Staubbach Falls — A53

Mt. Pilatus — A54

Chillon Castle — A55

Rhone Glacier — A56

St. Gotthard Railroad — A57

Via Mala Gorge — A58

Rhine Falls — A59

Balsthal Pass — A60

Alpine Lake of Säntis — A61

Two types of 10c red violet:

I. Shading inside "0" of 10 has only vertical lines.

II. Shading in "0" includes two diagonal lines.

1936-42 Unwmk. Engr. *Perf. 11½*

227	A53	3c olive	18	25
228	A54	5c bl grn	18	5
a.		Tete beche pair	40	32
229	A55	10c red vio (I)	1.65	20
a.		Tete beche pair	4.00	5.00
c.		Type II	40	5
230	A55	10c dk red brn ('39)	12	6
a.		Tete beche pair	1.65	1.00
230B	A55	10c org brn ('42)	12	5
d.		Tete beche pair	45	55
231	A56	15c orange	50	60
232	A57	20c carmine	6.50	8
a.		Tete beche pair	22.50	32.50
233	A58	25c lt brn	75	42
234	A59	30c ultra	1.25	5
235	A60	35c yel grn	1.25	75
236	A61	40c gray	9.00	8
		Nos. 227-236 (11)	21.50	2.59

Two types of the 20c. See Nos. 316 to 321.

1936-40 With Grilled Gum

227a	A53	3c olive	75	*2.50*
228d	A54	5c bl grn	18	5
229d	A55	10c red vio (I)	60	5
e.		Type II	70	5
230e	A55	10c dk red brn ('40)	2.50	*18.00*
231a	A56	15c orange	60	20
232c	A57	20c carmine	8.00	5
233a	A58	25c lt brn	1.00	*1.50*
234a	A59	30c ultra	1.10	18
235a	A60	35c yel grn	1.10	1.10
236a	A61	40c gray	6.00	18
		Nos. 227a-236a (10)	21.83	*23.81*

Mobile Post Office A62

1937, Sept. 5 Photo.

Granite Paper

237	A62	10c blk & yel	38	25

No. 237 was sold exclusively by the traveling post office. It exists on two kinds of granite paper, blacxk and red fibers or blue and red fibers. See No. 307 for type A62 redrawn.

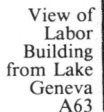

View of Labor Building from Lake Geneva A63

Palace of League of Nations A64

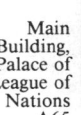

Main Building, Palace of League of Nations A65

Labor Building and Albert Thomas Monument — A66

1938, May 2 *Perf. 11½*

Granite Paper

238	A63	20c red & buff	18	6
239	A64	30c bl & lt bl	38	12
240	A65	60c brn & buff	2.00	42
241	A66	1fr blk & buff	9.00	7.50

Opening of Assembly Hall of the Palace of the League of Nations.

Souvenir Sheet

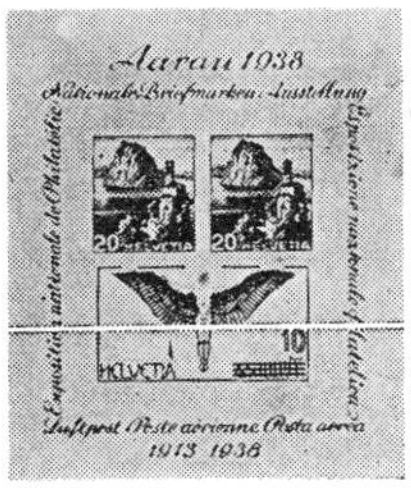

A67

Engraved and Typographed

1938, Sept. 17 Unwmk. *Perf. 11½*

Granite Paper

242	A67	Sheet of 3	40.00	32.50
a.		10c on 65c gray bl & dp bl	30.00	25.00
b.		20c red (A68)	3.00	2.25

Natl. Phil. Exhib. at Aarau, Sept. 17-25, 1938, and 25th anniv. of Swiss air mail. The sheet contains 2 No. 243 and a 10c on 65c similar to No. C22.

No. 242a is type AP4, but redrawn, with wing tips 1½mm from side frame lines; overall size 37x20½mm; no watermark. On No. C22, wing tips touch frame lines; size is 36x21½mm; Wmk. 183.

No. 242b is on granite paper, No. 243 on regular white paper.

Lake Lugano — A68

First Federal Pact, 1291 A69

Diet of Stans, 1481 A70

Citizens Voting A71

1938, Sept. 17 Engr. *Perf. 11½*

243	A68	20c red	18	5
a.		Tete beche pair	75	45
c.		Grilled gum	32	10
d.		As "c", tete beche pair	2.00	*7.50*

Granite Paper

244	A69	3fr brn car, *grnsh*	11.00	1.90
245	A70	5fr sl bl, *grnsh*	11.00	1.65
246	A71	10fr grn, *grnsh*	42.50	11.50

No. 243 is printed on ordinary paper. Nos. 244-246 are on granite surface-colored paper. The greenish surface coating has faded on most copies.

For type A68 in orange brown, see No. 318. See Nos. 284 to 286.

Deputation of Trades and Professions A72

Swiss Family A73

Alpine Scenery A74

Engr., Photo. (30c)

1939, Feb. 1 *Perf. 11½*

Inscribed in French

247	A72	10c dl pur & red	32	8
248	A73	20c lake & red	70	8
249	A74	30c dp bl & red	3.25	2.50

Inscribed in German

250	A72	10c dl pur & red	32	8
251	A73	20c lake & red	70	8
252	A74	30c dp bl & red	3.25	1.00

Inscribed in Italian

253	A72	10c dl pur & red	32	8
254	A73	20c lake & red	1.40	12
255	A74	30c dp bl & red	3.75	3.00
		Nos. 247-255 (9)	14.01	7.02

National Exposition of 1939, Zurich.

Tree and Crossbow — A75

1939, May 6 Photo. *Perf. 11½*

Granite Paper

Inscribed in French

256	A75	5c dp grn	70	*1.40*
257	A75	10c gray brn	70	*1.25*
258	A75	20c brt car	1.40	*1.40*
259	A75	30c vio bl	3.50	*5.50*

Inscribed in German

260	A75	5c dp grn	70	*1.40*
261	A75	10c gray brn	70	*1.10*
262	A75	20c brt car	1.40	90
263	A75	30c vio bl	3.50	*4.75*

Inscribed in Italian

264	A75	5c dp grn	70	*1.65*
265	A75	10c gray brn	1.00	*1.25*
266	A75	20c brt car	1.40	*1.50*
267	A75	30c vio bl	4.00	*5.50*
		Nos. 256-267 (12)	19.70	*27.60*

National Exposition of 1939.

The 5c, 10c and 20c stamps in the three languages exist se-tenant in coils.

View of Geneva A76

Perf. 11½

1939, Aug. 22 Photo. Unwmk.
Granite Paper

268	A76	20c red, car & buff	25	8
269	A76	30c bl, car & gray	50	60

75th anniv. of the founding of the Intl. Red Cross Society.

"The Three Swiss" – A77

William Tell – A78

Fighting Soldier A79

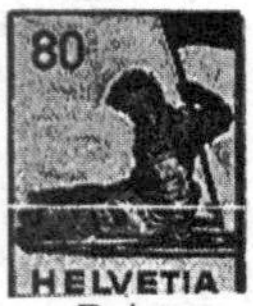
Dying Warrior A80

Standard Bearer – A81

Ludwig Pfyffer – A82

Jürg Jenatsch A83

Francois de Reynold A84

Joachim Forrer – A85

1941-59 Engr. *Perf. 11½*
Granite Paper

270	A77	50c dp pur, *grnsh*	5.25	10
271	A78	60c red brn, *buff*	6.25	5
272	A79	70c rose vio, *pale lil*	4.25	60
273	A80	80c blk, *pale gray*	1.00	8
a.		80c blk, *pale lil* ('58)	1.25	30
274	A81	90c dk red, *pale rose*	1.10	5
a.		90c dk red, *buff* ('59)	1.40	32
275	A82	1fr dk grn, *grnsh*	1.25	5
276	A83	1.20fr red vio, *pale gray*	1.40	10
a.		1.20fr red vio, *pale lil* ('58)	1.65	30
277	A84	1.50fr dk bl, *buff*	1.65	25
278	A85	2fr mar, *pale rose*	2.50	12
a.		2fr mar, *buff* ('59)	3.25	30
		Nos. 270-278 (9)	24.65	1.40

Farmer Plowing A86

1941, Mar. 21 Photo.
Granite Paper

279	A86	10c brn & buff	10	12

Issued to publicize the National Agriculture Development Plan of 1941.

Masons, Knight and Bern Coat of Arms A87

1941, Sept. 6
Granite Paper

280	A87	10c multi	8	18

750th anniversary of Bern.

"In order to Endure, Reclaim Used Materials" Inscribed in French – A88

Inscriptions: No. 282, German. No. 283, Italian.

1942, Mar. 21 Unwmk. *Perf. 11½*

281	A88	10c brn, red & gray bl	52	30
282	A88	10c brn, red & gray bl	8	12
283	A88	10c brn, red & gray bl	8.75	1.10
		Sheet of 25	90.00	*550.00*

Printed in sheets of 25, containing 8 No. 281, 12 No. 282 and 5 No. 283.

Types of 1938

1942-55 Engr.
Cream-surfaced Granite Paper

284	A69	3fr brn car ('55)	9.00	18
a.		Cream paper	32.50	16
285	A70	5fr sl bl ('55)	5.00	28
a.		Cream paper	22.50	16
286	A71	10fr grn ('55)	9.00	90
a.		Cream paper	32.50	32

The 1955 set is on cream-surfaced granite paper with white back, and blue and red fibers. The 1942 set is on colored-through cream paper with black and red fibers.

Zurich Stamps of 1843 A91

1943, Feb. 26

287	A91	10c blk & sal	8	10

Centenary of postage stamps of Switzerland. See Nos. B130-B131.

Apollo Statue – A94

1944, Mar. 21 Photo.
Granite Paper

290	A94	10c org yel & gray blk	15	*75*
291	A94	20c cer & gray blk	30	*75*
292	A94	30c lt bl & gray blk	75	*4.00*

Olympic Jubilee.

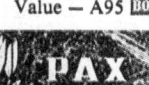

Numeral of Value – A95

Olive Branch A96

Designs: 60c, Keys of peace. 80c, Horn of plenty. 1fr, Dove of peace. 2fr, Plowing. 3fr, Field of crocus. 5fr, Clasped hands. 10fr, Aged couple.

1945, May 9 Unwmk. *Perf. 12*
Granite Paper

293	A95	5c gray & grn	10	22
294	A95	10c gray & brn	18	22
295	A95	20c gray & car rose	42	15
296	A95	30c gray & ultra	75	*1.75*
297	A95	40c gray & org	1.90	*7.75*
298	A96	50c dk red	2.75	*14.00*
299	A96	60c dl gray	2.50	*4.50*
300	A96	80c sl grn	6.50	*55.00*
301	A96	1fr blue	9.25	*60.00*
302	A96	2fr red brn	27.50	*100.00*

Engr.

303	A96	3fr dk sl grn, *buff*	35.00	*45.00*
304	A96	5fr brn lake, *buff*	140.00	*275.00*
305	A96	10fr rose vio, *buff*	150.00	100.00
		Nos. 293-305,B145 (14)	377.33	*664.29*

End of war in Europe.

Johann Heinrich Pestalozzi – A104

1946, Jan. 12 Engr. *Perf. 11½*

306	A104	10c rose vio	10	5

Issued to commemorate the 200th anniversary of the birth of J. H. Pestalozzi, educational reformer.

Mobile P.O. Type of 1937
Redrawn

1946, July 6 Photo.
Granite Paper

307	A62	10c blk & yel	1.75	10

The designer's and printer's names are larger on the redrawn stamp. There are many minor differences in the two designs. Sizes: 1937, 37½x21mm. 1946, 38x22½mm.

First Swiss Steam Locomotive A105

Modern Steam Locomotive A106

Electric Gotthard Express A107

Electric Trains Passing on Bridge A108

1947, Aug. 6 Photo. *Perf. 11½*
Granite Paper

308	A105	5c dk grn, blk & yel	10	20
309	A106	10c dk brn, gray & blk	18	6
310	A107	20c dk red & red	20	6
311	A108	30c dk bl & bl gray	90	1.00

Issued to commemorate the centenary of the opening of the first Swiss railroad, between Zurich and Baden.

Johann Rudolf Wettstein A109

Castle at Neuchatel A110

"Helvetia" A111

Symbol of Swiss Federal State A112

1948, Feb. 27
Granite Paper

312	A109	5c dp grn	8	18
313	A110	10c gray blk	8	8
314	A111	20c dk red	15	8
315	A112	30c dk bl & red	35	75

Issued to commemorate the tercentenary of the acknowledgment of independence of the Swiss Confederation, and the centenaries of the Neuchatel Revolution and the Swiss Federal State.

See Nos. B178a and B178b for 10c and 20c denominations, type A109.

Types of 1936-42 and

Grisons National Park – A113

1948, Mar. 1 Engr.

316	A54	5c chocolate	10	8
a.		Tete beche pair	1.25	1.25
317	A55	10c green	14	5
a.		Tete beche pair	1.25	1.50
318	A68	20c org brn	30	5
a.		Tete beche pair	1.65	2.25
319	A113	25c carmine	1.75	85
320	A59	30c grnsh bl	7.50	1.00
321	A61	40c ultra	13.00	25
		Nos. 316-321 (6)	22.79	2.28

Figures Encircling Globe A114

Designs: 25c, Globe and inscribed ribbon. 40c, Globe and pigeons.

Perf. 11½

1949, May 16 Photo. Unwmk.

322	A114	10c green	8	6
323	A114	25c dk red	42	*5.00*
324	A114	40c brt bl	60	2.00

75th anniv. of the UPU.

Post Horn A115

Horse Drawn Mail Coach A116

Design: 30c, Post bus with trailer.

1949, May 16

325 A115	5c gray, yel & pink	8	28
326 A116	20c pur, gray & yel	24	28
327 A116	30c dk org brn, gray & yel	45	*4.50*

Issued to commemorate the centenary of the establishment of the Federal Post in Switzerland.

High Tension Conductors A117

Viaducts A118

Mountain Railway — A119

Rotary Snow Plow — A120

Reservoir, Grimsel — A121

Lake Dam — A122

Dam and Power Station — A123

Alpine Postal Road — A124

Harbor of the Rhine — A125

Suspension Railway — A126

Railway Viaduct — A127

Triangulation Point — A128

Two types of 20c:
I. Crosshatching ends evenly with top of "20." Three lines above curved rock.
II. Crosshatching extends slightly above "20." Two lines above rock.

Perf. 12x11½

1949, Aug. 1 Engr. Unwmk.

328 A117	3c gray	2.00	3.25
329 A118	5c orange	18	5
a.	Tete beche pair	90	15
330 A119	10c yel grn	12	5
a.	Tete beche pair	60	15
331 A120	15c aqua	18	5
332 A121	20c brn car (II)	30	5
a.	Tete beche pair	1.75	75
c.	Type I	*3,000.*	*67.50*
333 A122	25c red	32	8
334 A123	30c olive	40	5
335 A124	35c red brn	50	30
336 A125	40c dp bl	1.65	5
337 A126	50c sl gray	1.65	8
338 A127	60c bl grn	3.00	5
339 A128	70c purple	1.25	30
	Nos. 328-339 (12)	11.55	4.36

For use in vending machines, some printings of the 5c, 10c, 20c (II), 25c, 30c and 40c carry a control number on the back of every fifth stamp. The number was applied on top of the gum.

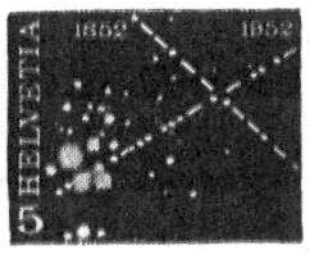

Symbolical of the Telegraph — A129

Symbolical Designs: 10c, Telephone. 20c, Radio. 40c, Television.

1952, Feb. 1 Photo. *Perf. 11½*

340 A129	5c org & yel	35	30
341 A129	10c brt grn & pink	48	12
342 A129	20c dp red lil & gray bl	70	12
343 A129	40c dp bl & lt bl	2.75	*3.25*

"A century of telecommunications."

Zurich Airport and Tail of Plane A130

1953, Aug. 29

344 A130	40c bl red & gray	3.25	*6.25*

Opening of Zurich-Kloten airport.

Alpine Post Bus, Winter Background A131

Design: 20c, Same, summer background.

1953, Oct. 8

345 A131	10c dk grn, grn & yel	8	5
346 A131	20c dk red, red brn & yel	18	6

Sold only on Swiss alpine post buses.

Symbols of Agriculture, Forestry and Horticulture A132

Map and Nautical Emblems — A133

Alphorn Blower — A135

Lausanne Cathedral A134

Designs: 20c, Winged spoon. 40c, Football and map.

1954, Mar. 15 *Perf. 14*

347 A132	10c multi	15	12
348 A132	20c multi	45	12
349 A133	25c red, dk ol grn & gray	1.75	*2.00*
350 A132	40c bl, yel & brn	2.50	*1.50*

Nos. 347-348 were issued to publicize exhibitions at Lucerne and Bern; No. 349, fifty years of navigation on the Rhine; No. 350, the 1954 World Soccer Championships in Switzerland.

1955, Feb. 15 *Perf. 11½*

Designs: 10c, Vaud costume hat. 40c, Automobile steering wheel.

351 A134	5c multi	35	12
352 A134	10c grn, yel & red	42	6
a.	Souvenir sheet of 2	60.00	87.50
353 A135	20c red & sep	1.10	6
354 A134	40c bl, pink & gray	2.50	1.40

No. 352a contains 10c and 20c multicolored, imperf. stamps of Cathedral type A134. Size: 104x52mm. Border inscriptions on olive green ribbons.

Issued to publicize the following: National Philatelic Exhibition (5c and No. 352a), Winegrowers' Festival (10c), Alpine Herdsman and Costume Festival (20c) and 25th International Automobile Show (40c).

First Swiss Post Bus — A136

Designs: 10c, North Gate of Simplon Tunnel and Stockalper Palace. 20c, Children crossing street and road signs. 40c, Planes and emblem of Swissair (vert.).

1956, Mar. 1 Photo.
Granite Paper

355 A136	5c ol gray, blk & yel	32	16
356 A136	10c brt grn, gray & red	50	6
357 A136	20c multi	85	10
358 A136	40c bl & red	2.25	85

Issued to publicize the following: 50th anniversary of the Swiss Motor Coach Service (No. 355); 50th anniversary of the opening of Simplon Tunnel (No. 356); Accident prevention (No. 357); 25th anniversary of the founding of Swissair (No. 358.)

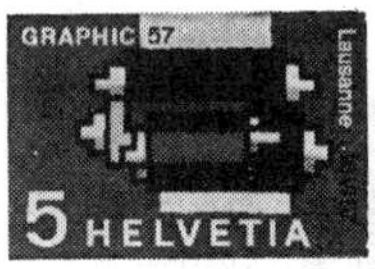

Inking Device, Printing Machine A137

Designs: 10c, Train on southern ramp of Gotthard Railroad. 20c, Shield of civil defense and coat of arms. 40c, Munatius Plancus and view of Basel.

Two types of 10c:
I. "Black" bottom line on train.
II. Brown bottom line.

1957, Feb. 27 *Perf. 11½*
Granite Paper

359 A137	5c multi	15	12
360 A137	10c lt bl grn, dk grn & red brn (I)	2.75	6
a.	Type II	1.50	18
361 A137	20c red org & gray	60	10
362 A137	40c multi	2.00	85

Issued to publicize the following: International Exhibition for Graphic Arts, Lausanne, June 1-16, 1957 (No. 359). 75th anniversary of St. Gotthard railroad (No. 360). Civil defense (No. 361). 2000th anniversary of Basel (No. 362).

Rope and Symbol of European Unity — A138

1957, July 15 Engr. *Perf. 11½*

363 A138	25c lt red	65	18
364 A138	40c blue	3.00	10

Issued to emphasize European unity.

Catalogue values for unused stamps in this section, from this point to the end of the section, are for Never Hinged items.

Nyon Castle and Corinthian Capital A139

Designs: 10c, Woman's head and ribbons in Swiss colors. 20c, Crossbow emblem. 40c, Salvation Army hat.

1958, Mar. 5 Photo. Unwmk.
Granite Paper

365 A139	5c ol bis & dl pur	14	14
366 A139	10c grn, dk grn & red	14	6
367 A139	20c ver, lil & car	35	6
368 A139	40c multi	1.75	80

Issued to publicize the following: 2000th anniversary of Nyon (No. 365). Saffa Exhibition, Zurich, July 17-Sept. 15 (No. 366). 25th anniversary of Swiss manufacturing emblem (No. 367). 75th anniversary of the Salvation Army in Switzerland (No. 368).

Symbol of Nuclear Fission A140

1958, Aug. 25 *Perf. 11½*
Granite Paper

369 A140	40c bl, yel & red	42	40

2nd UN Atomic Conf. for peaceful uses of atomic power, Geneva, Sept. 1958.

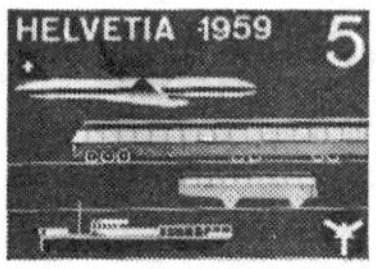

"Transportation" — A141

Designs: 10c, Fasces and post horn. 20c, Owl, rabbit and fish. 50c, Jean Calvin, Theodore de Beze and University of Geneva.

1959, Mar. 9 Photo. Unwmk.
Granite Paper

370 A141	5c multi	20	8
371 A141	10c emer, yel & lt gray	30	8
a.	Souvenir sheet of 2, imperf.	14.00	16.00
372 A141	20c multi	75	8
373 A141	50c multi	1.40	75

Opening of the Swiss House of Transport and Communications (5c). Natl. Phil. Exhib., St. Gall, Aug. 21-30 (10c and No. 371a). Protection of animals (20c). 400th anniv. of the University of Geneva (50c).

No. 371a contains a 10c green, gold and light gray and a 20c deep carmine. Sold for 2fr; the money went for the St. Gall Phil. Exhib.

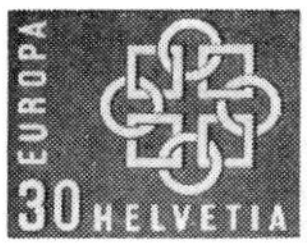

Chain Symbolizing European Unity — A142

1959, June 22 Engr. *Perf. 11½*

374 A142	30c brick red	70	10
375 A142	50c lt ultra	85	12

Issued to emphasize European Unity.

Overprinted "REUNION DES PTT D'EUROPE 1959" in Ultramarine or Red

376 A142 30c brick red 9.00 7.00
377 A142 50c lt ultra 9.00 7.00

Issued to publicize the European Conference of PTT Administrations, Montreux, June 22-July 31. Nos. 376-377 were on sale only during the conference at a special P. O. in Montreux.

"Cancer Control" A143

Designs: 20c, Founding charter and scepter of University of Basel. 50c, Uprooted Oak Emblem. 75c, Swissair Jet DC-8.

1960, Apr. 7 Photo. *Perf. 11½*
Granite Paper

378 A143 10c brt grn & red 30 8
379 A143 20c car rose, gray blk & yel 90 8
380 A143 50c ultra & yel 70 75
381 A143 75c lt bl, gray & red 1.65 2.25

Issued to publicize the following: 50th anniversary of the Swiss League for Cancer Control (10c). 500th anniversary of the University of Basel (20c). World Refugee Year, July 1, 1959-June 30, 1960 (50c). Swissair's entry into the jet age (75c).

Messenger, Fribourg A144

Cathedral, Lausanne A145

Designs: 10c, Messenger, Schwyz. 15c, Messenger and pack animal. 20c, Postilion on horseback. 30c, Grossmünster (church), Zürich. 35c, 1.30fr, Woodcutters' Guildhall, Biel. 40c, Cathedral, Geneva. 50c, Spalen Gate, Basel. 60c, Clock Tower, Berne. 70c, 2.80fr, Sts. Peter and Stephen Church, Bellinzona (tower omitted on 2.80fr). 75c, Bridge and water tower, Lucerne. 80c, Cathedral, St. Gallen. 90c, Munot tower, Schaffhausen. 1fr, Townhall, Fribourg. 1.20fr, Basel gate, Solothurn. 1.50fr, Reding house, Schwyz. 1.70fr, 2fr, 2.20fr, Church, Einsiedeln.

Two types of 5c, 10c, 20c, 50c:
5 Centimes.
Type I. Four lines on pike at left of hand.
Type II. Three lines.
10 Centimes.
Type I. Dot on pike below head.
Type II. No dot.
20 Centimes.
Type I. Ten dots on horizontal harness strip.
Type II. Nine dots.
50 Centimes.
Type I. Three shading lines at right above arch.
Type II. Two shading lines.

1960-63 Engr. *Perf. 11½*
1.30fr, 1.70fr, 2.20fr, 2.80fr on Granite Paper, Red and Blue Fibers

382 A144 5c lt ultra (I) 8 5
c. Tete beche pair 15 15
383 A144 10c bl grn (I) 10 5
c. Tete beche pair 35 20
384 A144 15c lt red brn 16 5
385 A144 20c rose pink (I) 20 5
c. Tete beche pair 60 45
386 A145 25c emerald 28 6
387 A145 30c vermilion 32 5
388 A145 35c org red 40 30
389 A145 40c lilac 52 5
390 A145 50c lt vio bl (I) 52 5
c. Tete beche pair 2.50 2.50
391 A145 60c rose red 55 5
392 A145 70c orange 60 42
393 A145 75c lt bl 48 18
394 A145 80c dp cl 80 6
395 A145 90c ol grn 80 6
396 A144 1fr dl org 90 6
397 A144 1.20fr dl red 1.00 30
397A A145 1.30fr red brn, *pink* ('63) 1.25 14
398 A144 1.50fr brt grn 1.40 28
398A A144 1.70fr rose lil, *pink* ('63) 1.50 14
399 A144 2fr brt bl 8.50 85
399A A144 2.20fr bl grn, *grn* ('63) 2.00 32
399B A145 2.80fr org, *buff* ('63) 2.75 28
Nos. 382-399B (22) 25.11 3.85

See Nos. 440-455.

1963-76
Violet Fibers, Fluorescent Paper

382d A144 5c lt ultra (I) 8 5
g. Tete beche pair ('68) 20 20
383d A144 10c bl grn (I) 10 5
e. Bklt. pane of 2 + 2 labels ('68) 65 65
g. Tete beche pair ('68) 30 20
384a A144 15c lt red brn 48 30
385d A144 20c rose pink (I) 24 5
g. Tete beche pair ('68) 60 35
386a A145 25c emerald 28 6
387a A145 30c vermilion 35 5
c. Tete beche pair ('68) 90 65
389a A145 40c lil ('67) 48 6
c. Tete beche pair ('76) 1.25 1.00
390d A145 50c lt vio bl (I) 70 6
391a A145 60c rose red ('67) 60 8
393a A145 75c lt bl ('68) 80 38
394a A145 80c dp cl 1.00 12
395a A145 90c ol grn ('67) 1.00 6
396a A144 1fr dl org ('67) 1.75 15
397b A144 1.20fr dl red ('68) 2.50 1.50
398b A144 1.50fr brt grn ('68) 2.75 1.50
Nos. 382d-398b (15) 13.11 4.47

Coil Stamps

1960 White Paper

382b A144 5c lt ultra (II) 90 90
383b A144 10c bl grn (II) 75 75
385b A144 20c rose pink (II) 1.00 1.00
390b A145 50c lt vio bl (II) 3.25 3.25

The coil stamps were printed in sheets (available to collectors) and pasted into coils. Every fifth stamp has a control number on the back.

Other denominations issued in coils on white paper are: 40c, 60c, 90c, 1fr, 1.30fr, 1.70fr, 2.20fr and 2.80fr.

Denominations issued in coils on granite paper (red & blue fibers) are: 1.30fr, 1.70fr, 2.20fr and 2.80fr.

Coil Stamps

1965-68
Violet Fibers, Fluorescent Paper

382e A144 5c lt ultra (II) 90 90
383h A144 10c bl grn (II) 40 15
385e A144 20c rose pink (II) 40 25
390e A145 50c lt vio bl (II) 3.00 3.00

Other denominations issued in coils on violet-fiber paper are: 40c, 60c, 90c and 1fr.

Europa Issue, 1960
Common Design Type

1960, Sept. 19 Unwmk. *Perf. 11½*
Size: 33x23mm

400 CD3 30c vermilion 35 10
401 CD3 50c ultra 45 15

Wall under Construction and Globe — A146

Designs: 10c, Symbolic sun (HYSPA Emblem). 20c, Ice hockey stick and puck. 50c, Wiring diagram on map of Switzerland.

1961, Feb. 20 Photo. *Perf. 11½*
Granite Paper

402 A146 5c gray, brick red & grnsh bl 38 10
403 A146 10c aqua & yel 38 6
404 A146 20c multi 95 8
405 A146 50c ultra, gray & car rose 1.65 1.25

Issued to publicize the following: Development aid to new nations (5c). HYSPA 1961, Health and Sports Exhibition, Bern, May 18-July 17 (10c). International Ice Hockey Championships, Lausanne and Geneva, March 2-12 (20c). Fully automatic Swiss telephone service (50c).

The Scott Catalogue value is a retail price, what you could expect to pay for the stamp in a grade of Fine-Very Fine. The value listed is a reference which reflects recent actual dealer selling price.

St. Matthew and Angel — A147

Evangelists: 5fr, St. Mark and winged lion. 10fr, St. Luke and winged ox. 20fr, St. John and eagle.

Perf. 11½
1961, Sept. 18 Unwmk. Engr.
Granite Paper

406 A147 3fr rose car 4.75 12
407 A147 5fr dk bl 3.75 18
408 A147 10fr dk brn 8.25 45
409 A147 20fr red 15.00 1.75

Designs are after 15th century wood carvings from St. Oswald's church, Zug.

Europa Issue, 1961
Common Design Type

1961, Sept. 18
Size: 26x21mm.

410 CD4 30c vermilion 32 10
411 CD4 50c blue 38 18

Trans-Europe Express A148

Designs: 10c, Rower. 20c, Jungfrau railroad station and Mönch. 50c, W.H.O. Antimalaria emblem.

1962, Mar. 19 Photo. *Perf. 11½*

412 A148 5c multi 52 6
413 A148 10c brt grn, lem & lil 52 6
414 A148 20c rose lil, pale bl & bis 70 6
415 A148 50c ultra, lt grn & rose lil 1.25 85

Issued to publicize the following: Introduction of Swiss electric TEE trains (5c). Rowing world championship, Lucerne, Sept. 6-9 (10c). 50th anniversary of the railroad station on the Jungfrau mountain (20c). World Health Organization Anti-Malaria campaign (50c).

Europa Issue, 1962
Common Design Type

1962, Sept. 17 Unwmk. *Perf. 11½*
Size: 33x23mm.

416 CD5 30c org, yel & brn 38 25
417 CD5 50c ultra, lt grn & brn 75 50

Boy Scout — A149

Designs: 10c, Swiss Alpine Club emblem. 20c, Luegelkinn viaduct. 30c, Wheat Emblem. No. 426, 428a, Red Cross Jubilee Emblem. No. 427, Post Office Building, Paris, 1863.

1963, Mar. 21 Photo.

422 A149 5c gray, dk red & brn 60 15
423 A149 10c dk grn, gray & red 35 8
424 A149 20c dk car, brn & gray 1.10 15
425 A149 30c yel grn, yel & org 1.50 1.25
426 A149 50c bl, sil & red 65 65
427 A149 50c ultra, pink, yel & gray 65 65
Nos. 422-427 (6) 4.85 2.93

Souvenir Sheet
Imperf

428 A149 Sheet of four 8.00 5.75
a. 50c bl, lt bl, sil & red 2.00 1.00

50 years of Swiss Boy Scouts (5c). Cent. of Swiss Alpine Club (10c). 50 years Lötschberg Railroad (20c). FAO "Freedom from Hunger" campaign (30c). Red Cross Cent. (Nos. 426, 428). 1st Intl. Postal Conf., Paris 1863 (No. 427).
No. 428 sold for 3fr.

Common Design Types pictured in section at front of book.

Europa Issue, 1963
Common Design Type

1963, Sept. 16 Unwmk. *Perf. 11½*
Granite Paper
Size: 26x21mm.

429 CD6 50c ultra & ocher 60 28

EXPO Emblem A150

Designs: 50c, EXPO emblem on globe and moon ("Outlook"). 75c, EXPO emblem on globe ("Insight").

1963, Sept. 16 Unwmk. *Perf. 11½*
Granite Paper

430 A150 10c brt grn & dk grn 30 5
431 A150 20c red & mar 35 5
432 A150 50c ultra & red 42 40
433 A150 75c pur & red 60 45

Issued to publicize the Swiss National Exhibition, Lausanne, Apr. 30-Oct. 25, 1964.

Road Tunnel Through Great St. Bernard A151

Designs: 10c, Symbolic water god and waves. 20c, Soldiers of 1864 and 1964. 50c, Standards of Swiss Confederation and Geneva.

1964, Mar. 9 Photo.
Granite Paper

434 A151 5c ol, ultra & red 18 6
435 A151 10c Prus bl & grn 18 6
436 A151 20c red, ultra, blk & sal 38 9
437 A151 50c ultra, red, yel & blk 95 65

Issued to publicize the following: First Trans-Alpine Automobile route from Switzerland to Italy (5c). "Pro Aqua" water conservation campaign (10c). Centenary of the Swiss Noncommissioned Officers' Association (20c). Sesquicentennial of union of Geneva with Swiss Confederation (50c).

Europa Issue, 1964
Common Design Type

1964, Sept. 14 Engr. *Perf. 11½*
Size: 21x26mm.
Violet Fibers, Fluorescent Paper

438 CD7 20c vermilion 30 6
439 CD7 50c ultra 65 20

Type of Regular Issue, 1960-63

Designs: 5c, Lenzburg. 10c, Freuler Mansion, Näfels. 15c, St. Mauritius Church, Appenzell. 20c, Planta House, Samedan. 30c, Gabled houses, Gais. 50c, Castle and Abbey Church, Neuchatel. 70c, Lussy House, Wolfenschiessen. 1fr, Santa Croce Church, Riva San Vitale. 1.20fr, Abbey Church, Payerne. 1.30fr, Church of St. Pierre de Clages. 1.50fr, La Porte de France, Porrentruy. 1.70fr, Frauenfeld Castle. 2fr, A Pro Castle, Seedorf. 2.20fr, Thomas Tower and Gate. Liestal. 2.50fr, St. Oswald's Church, Zug. 3.50fr, Benedictine Abbey, Engelberg.

1964-68 Engr. *Perf. 11 ½*
Violet Fibers, Fluorescent Paper

440	A144	5c car rose ('68)	6	5
441	A144	10c vio bl ('68)	8	5
b.		Tete beche pair	25	12
c.		Booklet pane of 2 + 2 labels	70	
442	A144	15c brn red ('68)	15	5
b.		Tete beche pair	35	35
443	A144	20c bl grn ('68)	18	5
b.		Tete beche pair	50	35
444	A144	30c ver ('68)	30	5
b.		Tete beche pair	90	80
445	A145	50c ultra ('68)	48	8
446	A145	70c brn ('67)	65	6
447	A145	1fr dk grn ('68)	95	6
448	A145	1.20fr brn red ('68)	1.10	6
449	A145	1.30fr vio bl ('66)	1.50	24
450	A145	1.50fr grn ('68)	1.50	15
451	A145	1.70fr brn org ('66)	1.50	24
452	A145	2fr org ('67)	1.90	24
453	A145	2.20fr green	3.25	42
454	A145	2.50fr Prus grn ('67)	2.25	30
455	A145	3.50fr pur ('67)	2.75	35
		Nos. 440-455 (16)	18.60	2.45

The 15c was issued in coils in 1972 (?) with control number on the back of every fifth stamp.

Nurse and Patient A152

Seated Helvetia, 1854 — A153

Women's Army Auxiliary A154

Intercontinental Communications Map — A155

1965, Mar. 8 Photo. *Perf. 11 ½*
Violet Fibers, Fluorescent Paper

462	A152	5c lt ultra & red	12	6
463	A153	10c emer, brn & blk	20	8
464	A154	20c red & multi	35	8

Granite Paper, Red and Blue Fibers

465	A155	50c dl bl grn & mar	60	35

Issued to publicize the following: Nursing and auxiliary medical professions (5c). National Postage Stamp Exhibition, NABRA, Bern, Aug. 27-Sept. 5, 1965 (10c). 20th anniversary of Women's Army Auxiliary Corps (20c). Centenary of International Telecommunication Union (50c).
See No. B344.

Swiss Arms, Cantonal Emblems of Valais, Neuchatel, Geneva A156

1965, June 1 Unwmk. *Perf. 11 ½*
Granite Paper, Red and Blue Fibers

466	A156	20c multi	22	10

Issued to commemorate the 150th anniversary of the entry of the cantons of Valais, Neuchatel and Geneva in the Swiss Confederation.

Matterhorn A157

Design: 30c, like 10c but inscribed in French "Cervin."

1965, June 1 Photo.
Granite Paper, Red and Blue Fibers

467	A157	10c grn, sl & dk red	8	8

Violet Fibers, Fluorescent Paper

468	A157	30c dk red, grn & sl	35	40

Issued to commemorate the Year of the Alps; the centenary of the first wintertime visitors to the Alps and the centenary of the first ascent of the Matterhorn. Nos. 467-468 on sale only at Swiss Alpine post buses.

Europa Issue, 1965
Common Design Type
1965, Sept. 14 Unwmk. *Perf. 11 ½*
Violet Fibers, Fluorescent Paper

469	CD8	50c bl, dk bl & grn	48	28

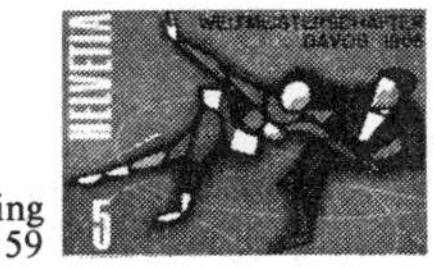

Figure Skating A159

1965, Sept. 14 Photo.
Violet Fibers, Fluorescent Paper

470	A159	5c grn, dl bl & blk	8	6

Issued to publicize the World Figure Skating Championships, Davos, Feb. 22-27, 1966.

ITU Emblem and Atom Diagram A160

Design: 30c, Symbol of communications, waves.

1965, Sept. 14
Violet Fibers, Fluorescent Paper

471	A160	10c ultra & multi	12	8

Granite Paper, Red and Blue Fibers

472	A160	30c org, red & gray	35	35

Nos. 471-472 issued to commemorate the centenary of the International Telecommunication Union.

Violet Fibers, Fluorescent Paper
Paper from No. 473 onward is fluorescent and has violet fibers, unless otherwise noted.

European Kingfisher A161

Mercury's Helmet and Laurel — A162

Flags of 13 Member Nations and Nuclear Fission A163

1966, Feb. 21 Photo.

473	A161	10c emer & multi	8	6
474	A162	20c dp mag, red & brt grn	18	6
475	A163	50c sl bl & multi	48	38

Issued to publicize the following: International Congress for Conservation "Pro Natura," Lucerne (10c). Fiftieth anniversary of Swiss Trade Fair, Basel, Apr. 16-26 (20c). European Organization for Nuclear Research, CERN (50c).

Emblem of Society of Swiss Abroad A164

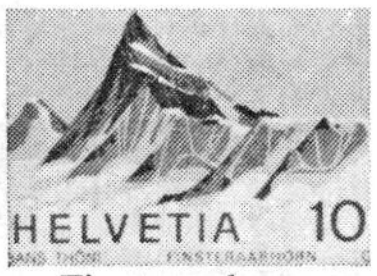

Finsteraarhorn A165

1966, June 1 Photo. *Perf. 11 ½*

476	A164	20c ultra & ver	18	8

Issued to commemorate the 50th anniversary of the Society of Swiss Abroad.

Europa Issue, 1966
Common Design Type
1966, Sept. 26 Engr. *Perf. 11 ½*
Size: 21x26mm.

477	CD9	20c vermilion	20	5
478	CD9	50c ultra	50	15

1966, Sept. 26 Photo.

479	A165	10c lt grnsh bl, dk bl & dk red	12	5

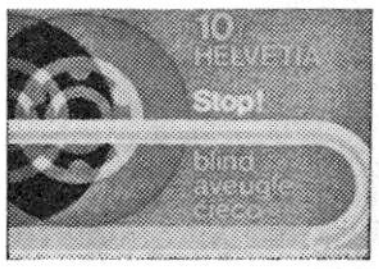

Automobile Wheels and White Cane — A166

Flags of EFTA Members A167

1967, March 13 Photo. *Perf. 11 ½*

480	A166	10c bl grn, blk & yel	8	5
481	A167	20c multi	18	6

No. 480 issued to publicize the white cane as a distinguishing mark for blind pedestrians. No. 481 publicizes the European Free Trade Association, EFTA. See note after Norway No. 501.

Europa Issue, 1967
Common Design Type
1967
Violet Fibers, Fluorescent Paper

482	CD10	30c bl gray	30	15

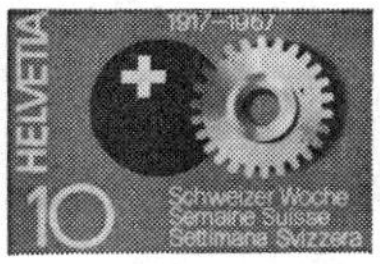

Cogwheel and Swiss Emblem A169

Hourglass and Sun — A170

San Bernardino, from North — A171

Railroad Wheel — A172

1967, Sept. 18 Photo. *Perf. 11 ½*

483	A169	10c multi	6	5
484	A170	20c red, yel & blk	15	8
485	A171	30c multi	35	8
486	A172	50c multi	50	32

50th anniv. of Swiss Week (10c). 50th anniv. of the Foundation for the Aged (20c). Opening of the San Bernardino Road Tunnel (30c). 75th anniv. of the Central Office for Intl. Railroad Transportation (50c).

Mountains and Club's Emblem A173

Golden Key with CEPT Emblem A174

Rook and Chessboard A175

Aircraft Tail and Satellites A176

1968, Mar. 14 Photo. *Perf. 11 ½*

487	A173	10c grn, lt ultra & red	10	5
488	A174	20c Prus bl, yel & brn	20	8
489	A175	30c dk ol bis & vio bl	28	8
490	A176	50c dk bl & red	48	35

Issued to publicize the following: 50th anniversary of the Swiss Women's Alpine Club (10c). A unified Europe through postal cooperation (20c). 18th Chess Olympics, Lugano, Oct. 17-Nov. 6 (30c). Inauguration of the new Geneva-Cointrin Air Terminal (50c).

Worker's Protective Helmet A177

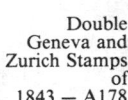

Double Geneva and Zurich Stamps of 1843 — A178

Map Showing Systematic Planning A179

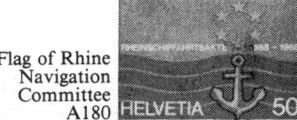

Flag of Rhine Navigation Committee A180

1968, Sept. 12 Photo. *Perf. 11½*

491	A177	10c bl grn & yel	8	5
492	A178	20c dp car, blk & yel grn	16	5
493	A179	30c multi	25	7
494	A180	50c bl, yel & blk	55	35

Issued to commemorate the following: 50th anniversary of the Swiss Accident Insurance company, SUVA (10c). 125th anniversary of first Swiss postage stamps (20c). 25th anniversary of the Swiss Society for Territorial Planning (30c). Centenary of the Rhine Navigation Act (50c).

Swiss Girl Scouts' Emblem and Camp — A181

Pegasus Constellation A182

Comptoir Suisse Emblem and Beaulieu Building, Lausanne A183

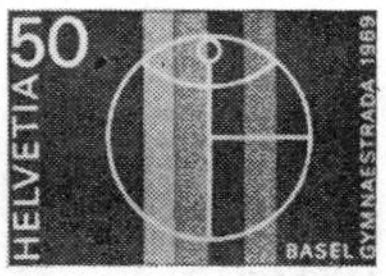

Gymnaestrada Emblem (Man in Circle) — A184

Swissair DC-8 and DH-3 — A185

1969, Feb. 12 Photo. *Perf. 11½*

495	A181	10c multi	8	5
496	A182	20c dk bl	22	8
497	A183	30c red, ocher, grn & gray	22	10
498	A184	50c vio bl, bl, red, grn & sil	38	40
499	A185	2fr bl, dk bl & red	1.65	1.65
		Nos. 495-499 (5)	2.55	2.28

Issued to commemorate the following: 50th anniversary of Swiss Girl Scouts (10c). Opening of first Swiss Planetarium, Lucerne, July 1 (20c). 50th anniversary of the Comptoir Suisse (trade fair, 30c). 5th Gymnaestrada (gymnastic meet), Basel, July 1-5 (50c). 50th anniversary of Swiss airmail service (2fr).

Europa Issue, 1969

Common Design Type

1969, Apr. 28

Size: 32½x23mm.

500	CD12	30c brn org & multi	24	8
501	CD12	50c chlky bl & multi	48	45

Huldreich Zwingli (1484-1531) A186

Portraits: 20c, Gen. Henri Guisan (1874-1960). 30c, Francesco Borromini, architect (1599-1667). 50c, Othmar Schoeck, musician (1886-1957). 80c, Germaine de Stael, writer (1766-1817).

1969, Sept. 18 Engr. *Perf. 11½*

502	A186	10c brt pur	8	5
503	A186	20c green	15	5
504	A186	30c dp car	30	8
505	A186	50c dp bl	52	50
506	A186	80c red brn	75	70
		Nos. 502-506 (5)	1.80	1.38

Issued to honor famous Swiss.

Kreuzberge, Alpstein Mountains A187

Children Crossing Street — A188

Steelworker A189

1969, Sept. 18 Photo.

507	A187	20c bl & multi	24	5
508	A188	30c car & multi	24	6
509	A189	50c vio & multi	48	35

No. 508 publicizes the traffic safety campaign; No. 509 commemorates the 50th anniversary of the International Labor Organization.

Telex Tape — A190

Fireman Rescuing Child — A191

Pro Infirmis Emblem A192

United Nations Emblem A193

New UPU Headquarters A194

1970, Feb. 26 Photo. *Perf. 11½*

510	A190	20c dk grn, yel & blk	10	6
511	A191	30c dk car & multi	24	8
512	A192	30c red & multi	24	8
513	A193	50c dk bl, lt grnsh bl & sil	40	35
514	A194	80c dk pur, sep & tan	80	70
		Nos. 510-514 (5)	1.78	1.27

Issued to commemorate the following: 75th anniversary of the Swiss Telegraph Agency (20c). Centenary of the Swiss Firemen's Association (No. 511). 50th anniversary of the Pro Infirmis Foundation (No. 512). 25th anniversary of the United Nations (50c). New Headquarters of the Universal Postal Union in Bern (80c).

Europa Issue, 1970

Common Design Type

1970, May 4 Engr. *Perf. 11½*

Size: 21x26mm.

515	CD13	30c vermilion	25	8
516	CD13	50c brt bl	55	32

Soccer A195

Census Form — A196

Piz Palu, Grisons A197

"Nature Conservation" A198

Numeral A199

1970, Sept. 17 Photo. *Perf. 11½*

517	A195	10c grn & multi	8	5
518	A196	20c dk grn & multi	15	7
519	A197	30c sl bl & multi	38	8
520	A198	50c dk bl & multi	45	32

Issued to commemorate the following: 75th anniversary of Swiss Soccer Association (10c). Federal Census of 1970 (20c). Swiss Alps (30c). Nature Conservation Year (50c).

Coil Stamps

1970, Sept. 17 Engr. *Perf. 11½*

521	A199	10c brn lake	10	5
522	A199	20c ol grn	22	5
523	A199	50c ultra	55	45

Control number in stamp's color on back of every fifth stamp. Nos. 521-523 were regularly issued only in coils, but exist in sheets of 50.

Gymnastic Trio — A200

Rose — A201

Switzerland No. 8 — A202

Rising Spiral — A203

Intelsat 4 Satellite A204

Adaptation of 1850 Design — A205

Design: No. 525, Runners (men).

1971, Mar. 11 Photo. *Perf. 11½*

524	A200	10c ol, brn & bl	18	5
525	A200	10c gray, brn & yel	18	5
526	A201	20c dk grn & multi	14	8
527	A202	30c dp car & multi	22	8
528	A203	50c dk bl & bis	40	45
529	A204	80c multi	65	75
		Nos. 524-529 (6)	1.77	1.46

Souvenir Sheet

Typo.

Imperf

530	A205	2fr bl & multi	3.75	3.75

Issued to commemorate the following: New article on gymnastics and sports in Swiss Constitution (10c); International Child Welfare Organization (20c); NABA National Postage Stamp Exhibition, Basel, June 4-13 (30c, 2fr); Second decade of development aid (50c); International Space Communications Conference, Geneva, June-July, 1971 (80c).

Nos. 524-525 printed se-tenant checkerwise in sheets of 50. No. 530 has gray margin with blue inscription; gray inscription on back; sold for 3fr. Size: 61x75mm.

Europa Issue, 1971

Common Design Type

1971, May 3 Engr. *Perf. 11½*

Size: 26x21mm

531	CD14	30c rose car & org	28	12
532	CD14	50c bl & org	52	40

Les Diablerets, Vaud — A206

Telecommunications Symbols — A207

1971, Sept. 23 Photo. *Perf. 11½*

533	A206	30c rose lil & bl gray	35	8
534	A207	40c ultra, yel & brt pink	45	45

No. 534 commemorates the 50th anniversary of Radio-Suisse, which is also in charge of air traffic control.

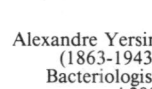

Alexandre Yersin (1863-1943) Bacteriologist A208

Physicians: 20c, Auguste Forel (1848-1931), psychiatrist. 30c, Jules Gonin (1870-1935), ophthalmologist. 40c, Robert Koch (1843-1910), German bacteriologist. 80c, Frederick G. Banting (1891-1941), Canadian physiologist.

1971, Sept. 23 Engr.

535	A208	10c gray ol	8	8
536	A208	20c bluish grn	16	14
537	A208	30c car rose	20	14

538	A208	40c dk bl	60	52
539	A208	80c brt pur	80	70
		Nos. 535-539 (5)	1.84	1.58

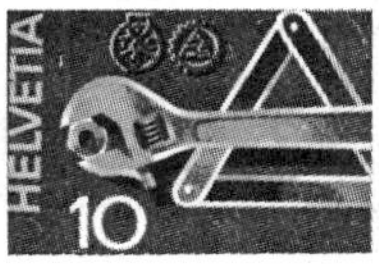

Wrench, Road Sign, Club Emblems A209

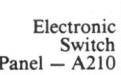

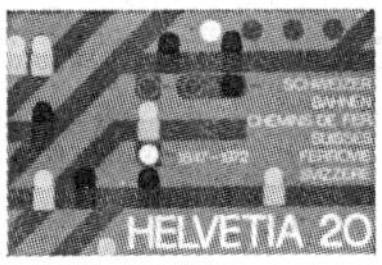

Electronic Switch Panel — A210

Boy's Head and Radio Waves — A211

Symbolic Tree — A212

1972, Feb. 17 Photo. *Perf. 11½*

540	A209	10c multi	9	6
541	A210	20c ol & multi	15	10
542	A211	30c org & mar	22	10
543	A212	40c bl, grn & pur	48	48

Issued to commemorate: 75th anniversary of the touring and automobile clubs of Switzerland (10c). 125th anniversary of Swiss railroads (20c). 50th anniversary of Swiss radio (30c). 50th annual congress of Swiss citizens living abroad, Bern, Aug. 25-27 (40c).

Europa Issue 1972

Common Design Type

1972, May. 2

Size: 21x26mm

544	CD15	30c multi	25	12
545	CD15	40c multi	40	30

Alberto Giacometti (1901-66), Painter and Sculptor — A213

Portraits and Signatures: 20c, Charles Ferdinand Ramuz (1878-1947), writer. 30c, Le Corbusier (Charles Edouard Jeanneret; 1887-1965) architect. 40c, Albert Einstein (1879-1955), physicist. 80c, Arthur Honegger (1892-1955), composer.

Engraved & Photogravure

1972, Sept. 21 *Perf. 11½*

546	A213	10c ocher & blk	8	8
547	A213	20c lt ol & blk	12	8
548	A213	30c pink & blk	18	14
549	A213	40c lt bl & blk	60	50
550	A213	80c lil rose & blk	80	65
		Nos. 546-550 (5)	1.78	1.45

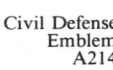

Civil Defense Emblem A214

Spannörter A215

Red Cross Rescue Helicopter A216

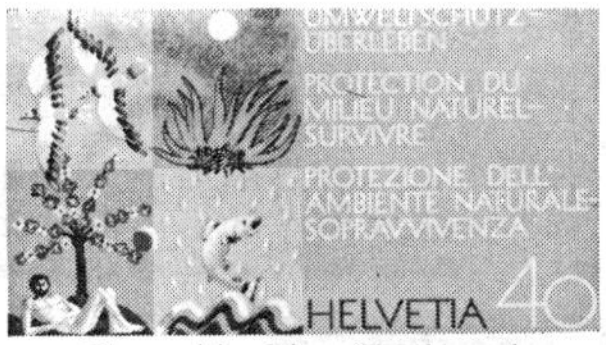

Clean Air, Fire, Earth and Water — A217

1972, Sept. 21 Photo.

551	A214	10c org, bl & yel	10	8
552	A215	20c bl grn & multi	14	8
553	A216	30c lil, red & ind	22	8
554	A217	40c lt bl & multi	45	32

Issued to publicize Civil Defense (10c); Swiss Alps (20c); Air Rescue Service (30c); Nature and environment protection (40c).

Earth Satellite Station, Leuk, World Map — A218

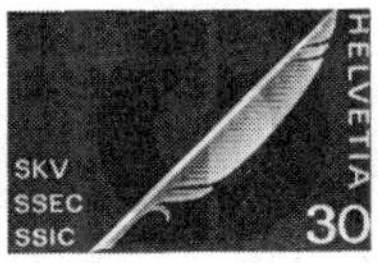

Quill Pen and Arrows in Circle — A219

INTERPOL Emblem A220

1973, Feb. 15 Photo. *Perf. 11½*

555	A218	15c gray, yel & bl	15	8
556	A219	30c multi	25	12
557	A220	40c dp bl, lt bl & gray	60	32

Issued to publicize the opening of the satellite station at Leuk (15c); centenary of the Swiss Association of Commercial Employees (30c); 50th anniversary of the International Criminal Police Organization (INTERPOL).

Sottoceneri A221

Sign of Inn "Zur Sonne," Toggenburg A222

Villages: 10c, Graubunden. 15c, Central Switzerland. 25c, Jura. 30c, Simme Valley. 35c, Central Switzerland (2 buildings). 40c, Vaud. 50c, Valais. 60c, Engadine. 70c, Sopraceneri. 80c, Eastern Switzerland.

Designs: 1fr, Rose window, Lausanne Cathedral. 1.10fr, Gallus Portal, Basel Cathedral. 1.20fr, Romanesque capital (eagle), St. Jean Baptiste Church, Grandson. 1.50fr, Ceiling medallion (pelican feeding nestlings), Stein am Rhein Convent. 1.70fr, Romanesque capital (St. George and dragon), St. Jean Baptiste, Grandson. 1.80fr, Gargoyle, Bern Cathedral. 2fr, Bay window, Schaffhausen. 2.50fr, Cock weather vane, St. Ursus Cathedral, Solothurn. 3fr, Font, St. Maurice Church, Saanen. 3.50fr, Astronomical clock, Bern clock tower.

1973-80 Engr. *Perf. 11½*

Fluorescent, No Violet Fibers

558	A221	5c dl yel & dk bl	6	5
559	A221	10c rose lil & ol grn	8	5
560	A221	15c org & vio bl	15	8
561	A221	25c emer & vio bl	22	15
562	A221	30c brick red & dk bl	25	8
563	A221	35c red org & brt vio ('75)	35	14
564	A221	40c brt bl & blk	38	8
565	A221	50c ol grn & org	45	9
566	A221	60c yel brn & gray	52	15
567	A221	70c sep & dk grn	60	18
568	A221	80c brt grn & brick red	75	18

Violet Fibers, Fluorescent Paper

569	A222	1fr pur ('74)	95	8
570	A222	1.10fr Prus bl ('75)	1.10	14
571	A222	1.20fr rose red ('74)	1.10	75
572	A222	1.30fr ocher	2.50	60
573	A222	1.50fr grn ('74)	1.40	9
574	A222	1.70fr gray	1.25	42
575	A222	1.80fr dp org	1.25	20
576	A222	2fr ultra ('74)	1.90	30
577	A222	2.50fr gldn brn ('75)	2.00	35
578	A222	3fr dk car ('79)	2.50	35
579	A222	3.50fr ol grn ('80)	2.75	90
		Nos. 558-579 (22)	22.51	5.41

Europa Issue 1973

Common Design Type

1973, Apr. 30 Engr. and Photo.

Size: 38x28mm

580	CD16	25c brn & yel	28	12
581	CD16	40c ultra & yel	55	35

"Man and Time" — A223

Skier and Championship Emblem A224

Child — A225

1973, Aug. 30 Photo. *Perf. 11½*

582	A223	15c multi	12	8
583	A224	30c pink & multi	24	8
584	A225	40c bl vio & blk	45	35

Issued to publicize the opening of the International Clock Museum, La Chaux-de-Fonds, 1974 (15c); International Alpine Skiing Championships, St. Moritz, Feb. 2-10, 1974 (30c); "Terre des hommes" children's aid program (40c).

Souvenir Sheet

Medieval Postal Couriers — A226

1974, Jan. 29 Photo. *Perf. 11½*

585	A226	Souv. sheet of 4	6.00	6.00
a.		30c *Basel* (with staff)	1.40	1.40
b.		30c *Zug* (without staff)	1.40	1.40
c.		60c *Uri*	1.40	1.40
d.		80c *Schwyz*	1.40	1.40

Cent. of UPU and for INTERNABA 74 Intl. Phil. Exhib., Basel, June 7-16. No. 585 sold for 3fr.

Pine and Cabin on Globe — A227

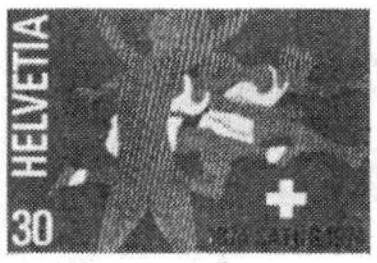

Gymnast and Hurdlers A228

Target and Pistol — A229

1974, Jan. 29

586	A227	15c lt grn & multi	15	8
587	A228	30c red & multi	25	12
588	A229	40c bl & multi	45	30

Issued for: 50th anniversary of Swiss Youth Hostels (15c); Centenary of Swiss Workers' Gymnast and Sports Association (SATUS) (30c); World Marksmanship Championships, Thun and Bern, Sept. 1974 (40c).

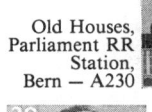

Old Houses, Parliament RR Station, Bern — A230

Eugène Borel — A231

Designs: No. 590, Castle, Town Hall, Chauderon Center, Lausanne. 40c, Heinrich von Stephan. 80c, Montgomery Blair.

1974, Mar. 28 Photo. *Perf. 11½*

589	A230	30c org & multi	30	20
590	A230	30c scar & multi	30	20

Engr.

591	A231	30c rose & blk	18	6
592	A231	40c gray & blk	28	22
593	A231	80c lt yel grn & blk	75	45

Cent. of the UPU. Nos. 589-590 publicize the Cent. Cong., Lausanne, May 22-July 5; Nos. 591-593 honor the founders of the UPU.

"Continuity," by Max Bill — A232

Europa: 40c, "Amazon," bronze sculpture by Carl Burckhardt.

1974, Mar. 28 Photo.

594	A232	30c red & blk	35	10
595	A232	40c ultra & sep	95	42

Oath of Allegiance, by Werner Witschi A233

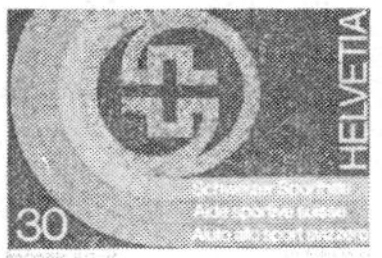

Sports Foundation Emblem A234

Conveyor Belts, Paths of Mail Transport and Delivery
A235

1974, Sept. 19 Photo. *Perf. 11½*

596	A233	15c lil, ol & dk ol	15	10
597	A234	30c sil & multi	28	6
598	A235	30c plum & multi	28	15

Centenary of Swiss Constitution (15c); Swiss Sports Foundation (No. 597); 125th anniversary of Swiss Federal Post (No. 598).

Standard Meter, Krypton Spectrum
A236

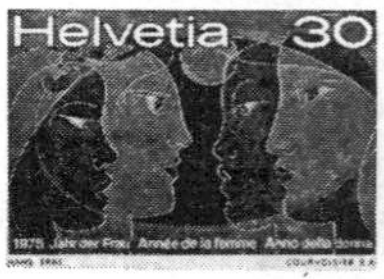

Women of Four Races — A237

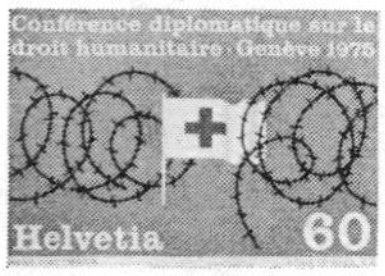

Red Cross Flag, Barbed Wire — A238

"Ville de Lucerne" Dirigible
A239

1975, Feb. 13 Photo. *Perf. 11½*

599	A236	15c grn, org & ultra	14	20
600	A237	30c brn & multi	28	12
601	A238	60c ultra, blk & red	52	75
602	A239	90c bl & multi	90	60

Centenary of International Meter Convention, Paris, 1875 (15c); International Women's Year 1975 (30c); 2nd Session of Diplomatic Conference on Humanitarian International Law, Geneva, Feb. 1975 (60c); Aviation and Space Travel exhibition in Museum of Transport and Communications, Lucerne (90c).

Mönch, by Ferdinand Hodler — A240

Vineyard Worker, by Maurice Barraud — A241

Europa: 50c, Still Life with Guitar, by René Auberjonois.

1975, Apr. 28 Photo. *Perf. 12x11½*

603	A240	30c gray & multi	28	7
604	A241	50c multi	48	45
605	A241	60c bl gray & multi	65	52

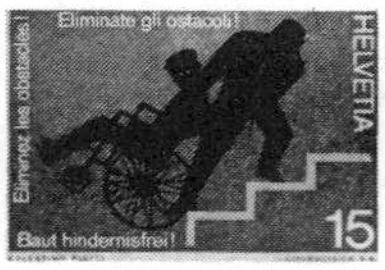

Man Pulling Wheel Chair Upstairs
A242

"The Helping Hand" — A243

Architectural Heritage Year Emblem
A244

Beat Fischer von Reichenbach
A245

1975, Sept. 11 Photo.

606	A242	15c lil, blk & grn	20	9
607	A243	30c red, blk & car	24	8
608	A244	50c yel brn & mar	42	38
609	A245	60c bl & multi	60	55

Special building features for the handicapped (15c); interdenominational telephone pastoral counseling (30c); European Architectural Heritage Year 1975 (50c); Fischer Post, Bern, tercentenary (60c).

Forest
A246

Fruits and Vegetables
A247

Black Infant — A248

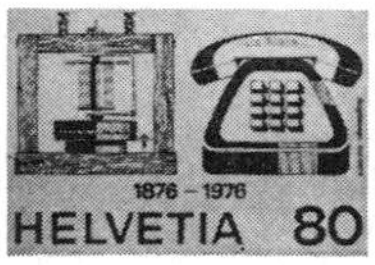

Telephones of 1876 and 1976 — A249

1976, Feb. 12 Photo. *Perf. 11½*

Fluorescent, No Violet Fibers

610	A246	20c grn & multi	15	14
611	A247	40c car & multi	35	12
612	A248	40c lil rose & multi	35	12

Engr.

Violet Fibers, Fluorescent Paper

613	A249	80c lt bl & dk bl	75	65

Centenary of Federal forest laws (20c); healthy nutrition to combat alcoholism (No. 611); fight against leprosy (No. 612); telephone centenary (80c).

Europa Issue 1976

Cotton and Gold Lace, St. Gall
A250

Pocket Watch, 18th Century
A251

1976, May 3 Engr. *Perf. 11½*

614	A250	40c red brn & multi	50	20
615	A251	80c blk & multi	1.00	50

Both 40c and 80c are on fluorescent paper, the 80c having violet fibers.

Fawn, Frog and Swallow
A252

"Conserve Energy"
A253

St. Gotthard Mountains
A254

Skater — A255

1976, Sept. 16 Photo. *Perf. 11½*

Fluorescent, No Violet Fibers

616	A252	20c multi	16	15
617	A253	40c multi	35	10
618	A254	40c multi	42	10
619	A255	80c multi	70	70

Wildlife protection (20c); energy conservation (No. 617); Pizzo Lucendro to Pizzo Rotondo, seen from Altanca (No. 618); World Men's Skating Championships, Davos, Feb. 5-6, 1977 (80c).

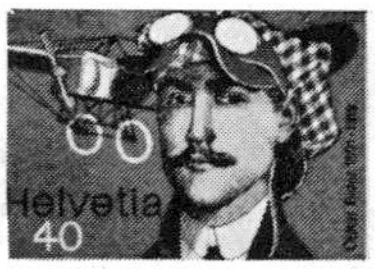

Oskar Bider, Bleriot Monoplane
A256

Designs: 80c, Eduard Spelterini and balloon gondola. 100c, Armand Dufaux and Dufaux plane. 150c, Walter Mittelholzer and Dornier hydroplane.

1977, Jan. 27 Engr. *Perf. 11½*

620	A256	40c multi	40	16
621	A256	80c multi	80	80
622	A256	100c multi	80	80
623	A256	150c multi	1.40	1.25

Swiss aviation pioneers.

Blue Cross — A257

Festival Emblem
A258

Balloons Carrying Letters — A259

1977, Jan. 27 Photo.

624	A257	20c gray, bl & blk	20	16
625	A258	40c red, gold & brn	40	10
626	A259	80c lt bl & multi	80	80

Blue Cross Society (care of alcoholics and fight against alcoholism), centenary (20c); Vintage Festival, Vevey, July 30-Aug. 14 (40c); JUPHILEX 77 Youth Philatelic Exhibition, Bern, Apr. 7-11 (80c).

Fluorescent Paper
From No. 624 onward the paper lacks violet fibers but is fluorescent, unless otherwise noted.

Europa Issue 1977

St. Ursanne on Doubs River — A260

Design: 80c, Sils-Baselgia on Inn River.

1977, May 2 Engr. *Perf. 11½*

627	A260	40c multi	55	16
628	A260	80c multi	1.10	60

Worker and Factories
A261

Ionic Column and Shield — A262

Swiss Cross, Arrow and Butterfly
A263

1977, Aug. 25 Photo. *Perf. 11½*

629	A261	20c multi	16	8
630	A262	40c multi	35	18
631	A263	80c multi	85	60

Federal Factories Act, centenary (20c); protection of cultural monuments (40c); Swiss hiking trails (80c).

Star Singer, Bergün — A264

Folk Customs: 10c, Horse race, Zürich. 20c, New Year's Eve costumes, Herisau. 25c, Chesslete, Solothurn. 30c, Rollelibutzen, Altstatten. 35c, Cutting off the goose, Sursee. 40c, Herald reading proclamation and men scaling wall, Geneva. 45c, Klausjagen, Kussnacht. 50c, Masked men, Laupen. 60c, Schnabelgeissen, Ottenbach. 70c, Procession (horse and masked men), Mendrisio. 80c, Griffins, Basel. 90c, Masked men, Lotschental.

1977-84 Engr. *Perf. 11½*

632	A264	5c bl grn	6	5
633	A264	10c dk red	12	8
a.		Booklet pane of 2 + 2 labels ('79)	45	
634	A264	20c orange	20	8
a.		Booklet pane of 4 ('79)	80	
635	A264	25c brown ('84)	24	20
636	A264	30c brt grn ('82)	28	20
637	A264	35c olive	35	10
638	A264	40c brn lake	40	8
a.		Booklet pane of 4 ('79)	1.65	
639	A264	45c gray bl ('84)	40	32
640	A264	50c red brn	48	18
641	A264	60c gray brn ('84)	55	45
642	A264	70c purple	65	24

643 A264 80c stl bl 80 30
644 A264 90c dp brn 90 32
Nos. 632-644 (13) 5.43 2.60

Arms of Vaud Canton A265

Old Lucerne A266

Title Page of "Melusine" A267

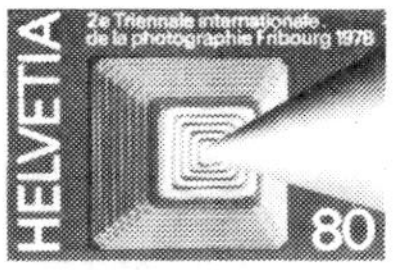

Stylized Lens and Bellows A268

1978, Mar. 9 Photo. *Perf. 11½*
652 A265 20c multi 18 12
653 A266 40c multi 38 12
654 A267 70c multi 65 60
655 A268 80c multi 75 65

LEMANEX 78 Philatelic Exhibition, Lausanne, May 26-June 4 (20c); Founding of Lucerne, 800th anniversary (40c); printing in Geneva, 500th anniversary (70c); 2nd International Triennial Photography Exhibition, Fribourg, June 17-Oct. 22 (80c).

Miniature Sheet

Steamers on Swiss Lakes — A269

1978, Mar. 9
656 A269 Sheet of 8, multi 9.00 10.00
a. 20c *La Suisse, 1910* 38 40
b. 20c *Il Verbano, 1826* 38 40
c. 40c *MS Gotthard, 1970* 1.10 1.10
d. 40c *Ville de Neuchatel, 1972* 1.10 1.10
e. 40c *MS Romanshorn, 1958* 1.10 1.10
f. 40c *Le Winkelried, 1871* 1.10 1.10
g. 70c *DS Loetschberg, 1914* 1.25 1.25
h. 80c *DS Waedenswil, 1895* 1.40 1.50

LEMANEX 78 Philatelic Exhibition, Lausanne, May 26-June 4. Size of No. 656: 134x129mm. Sold for 5fr.

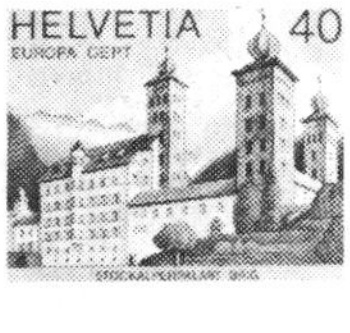

Stockalper Palace, Brig — A270

Europa: 80c, Diet Hall, Bern.

1978, May 2 Engr. *Perf. 11½*
657 A270 40c multi 55 18
658 A270 80c multi 1.10 60

Machinist A271

Joseph Bovet (1879-1951), Composer A272

Designs: No. 660, Chemical worker (French inscription). No. 661, Construction worker (Italian inscription).

1978, Sept. 14 Photo. *Perf. 11½*
659 A271 40c multi 40 28
660 A271 40c multi 40 28
661 A271 40c multi 40 28

Industrial safety. Nos. 659-661 printed se-tenant in sheets of 50.

1978, Sept. 14 Engr.

Portraits: 40c, Henri Dunant (1828-1910), founder of Red Cross. 70c, Carl Gustave Jung (1875-1961), psychologist. 80c, Auguste Piccard (1884-1962), physicist and balloonist.

662 A272 20c dl grn 20 10
663 A272 40c rose lake 35 10
664 A272 70c gray 65 60
665 A272 80c bl gray 80 70

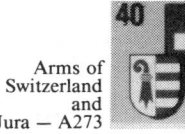

Arms of Switzerland and Jura — A273

1978, Sept. 25 Photo. *Perf. 11½*
666 A273 40c buff, red & blk 38 12

Admission of Jura as 23rd Canton.

Rainer Maria Rilke (1875-1926), Poet, Muzot Castle — A274

Designs: 40c, Paul Klee (1879-1940), painter and "heroic roses." 70c, Hermann Hesse (1877-1962), writer, and vines. 80c, Thomas Mann (1875-1955), writer, and Lubeck buildings.

1979, Feb. 21 Engr. *Perf. 11½*
667 A274 20c gray grn 18 10
668 A274 40c red 35 10
669 A274 70c brown 65 65
670 A274 80c gray bl 80 75

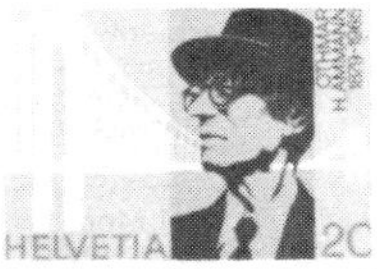

O. H. Ammann, Verrazano-Narrows Bridge, N.Y. — A275

Target Hit with Pole and Lucerne Flag — A276

Hot Air Balloon A277

Airport, Swissair and Air France Jets — A278

1979, Feb. 21 Photo.
671 A275 20c multi 18 10
672 A276 40c multi 35 10
673 A277 70c multi 65 65
674 A278 80c multi 80 75

Othmar H. Ammann (1879-1965), engineer, bridge builder in U.S.; 50th Federal Riflemen's Festival, Lucerne, July 7-22; World Esperanto Congress, Lucerne; new runway at Basel-Mulhouse International Airport.

Letter Box, 1845, Spalentor, Basel — A279

Europa: 80c, Microwave radio relay station on Jungfraujoch.

1979, Apr. 30 Engr. *Perf. 11½*
675 A279 40c multi 55 15
676 A279 80c multi 1.10 75

Helvetian Gold Quarter Stater, 2nd Century B.C. — A280

Child and Dove — A281

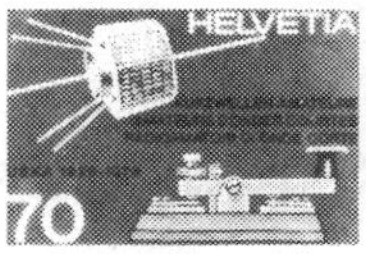

Morse Key and Satellite A282

Three-stage Launcher Ariane A283

1979, Sept. 6 Photo.
677 A280 20c multi 16 10
678 A281 40c multi 35 20
679 A282 70c multi 70 45
680 A283 80c multi 75 65

Centenary of Swiss Numismatic Society; International Year of the Child; Union of Swiss Radio Amateurs, 50th anniversary; European Space Agency (ESA).

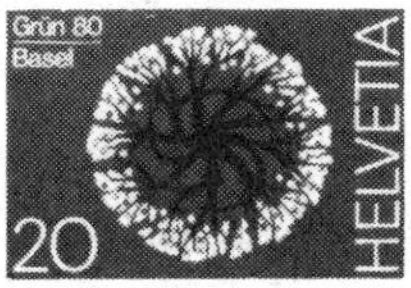

Tree in Bloom A284

Hand Carved Milk Bucket A285

Winterthur Town Hall — A286

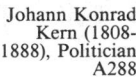

"Pic-Pic," 1930 — A287

1980, Feb. 21 Photo.
681 A284 20c multi 20 10
682 A285 40c multi 40 22
683 A286 70c multi 65 55
684 A287 80c multi 75 65

Green '80, Swiss Horticultural and Gardening Expo., Basel, Apr. 12-Oct. 12; Swiss Arts and Crafts Centers, 50th anniv.; Soc. for Swiss Art History, cent.; 50th Intl. Automobile Show, Geneva, Mar. 16.

Johann Konrad Kern (1808-1888), Politician A288

Europa: 80c, Gustav Adolf Hasler (1830-1900), communications pioneer.

Lithographed & Engraved
1980, Apr. 28 *Perf. 11½*
Granite Paper
685 A288 40c multi 50 15
686 A288 80c multi 1.00 55

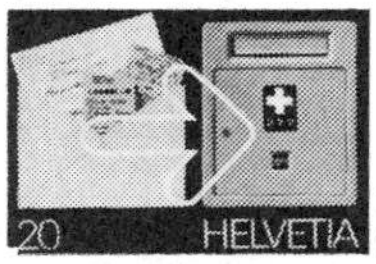

Postal Giro System — A289

Postal Bus System A290

Security Printing Plant, 50th Anniversary A291

Swiss Telephone Service Centenary A292

Photo., Photo. & Engr. (70c)
1980, Sept. 5 *Perf. 12*
687 A289 20c multi 20 15
688 A290 40c multi 38 15
689 A291 70c multi 65 50
690 A292 80c multi 75 55

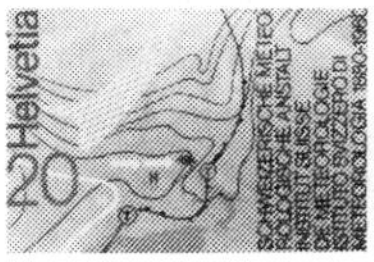

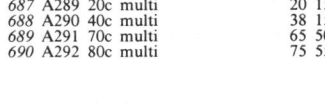

Swiss Meteorological Office Centenary A293

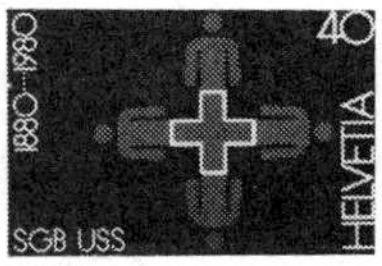

Swiss Trade Union Federation Centenary A294

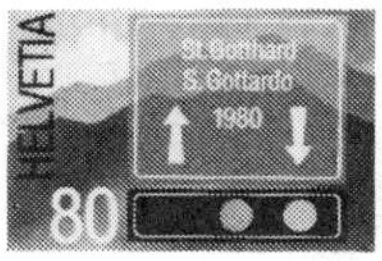

Opening of St. Gotthard Tunnel for Year-round Traffic — A295

1980, Sept. 5 Photo.
691 A293 20c multi 18 12
692 A294 40c multi 38 15
693 A295 80c multi 75 55

Granary, Kiesen, 17th Century A296

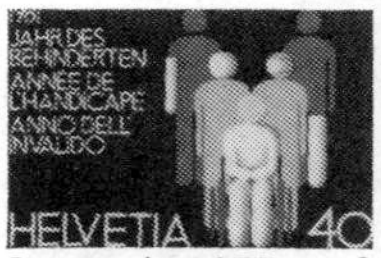
International Year of the Disabled — A297

The Parish Clerk, by Albert Anker — A298

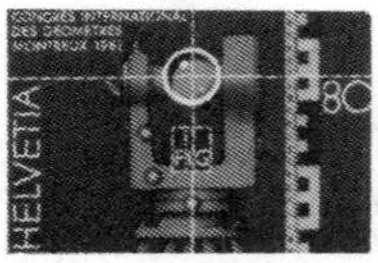
Theodolite and Rod — A299

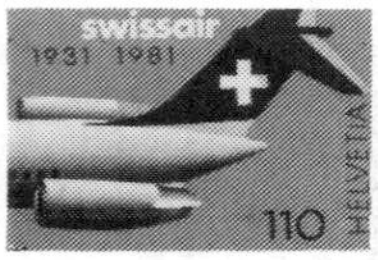
DC-9 (50th Anniversary of Swissair) A300

1981, Mar. 9 Photo. *Perf. 11½*

694	A296	20c multi	22	8
695	A297	40c multi	40	18
696	A298	70c multi	70	50
697	A299	80c multi	80	55
698	A300	110c multi	1.10	85
		Nos. 694-698 (5)	3.22	2.16

Ballenberg Open-air Museum of Rural Architecture, Furnishing and Crafts; Albert Anker (1831-1910), artist (70c); 16th Congress of the International Federation of Surveyors, Montreux, Aug. (80c).

Europa Issue 1981

Couple Dancing in Native Costumes — A301

1981, May 4 Photo. *Perf. 11½*

699	A301	40c shown	50	18
700	A301	80c Stone putting	1.00	48

Seal of Fribourg A302

1981, Sept. 3 Photo. & Engr.

701	A302	40c shown	40	25
702	A302	40c Seal of Solothurn	40	25
703	A302	80c Old Town Hall, Stans	80	52

500th anniv. of Diet of Stans and of entry of Fribourg and Solothurn into the Swiss Confederation.

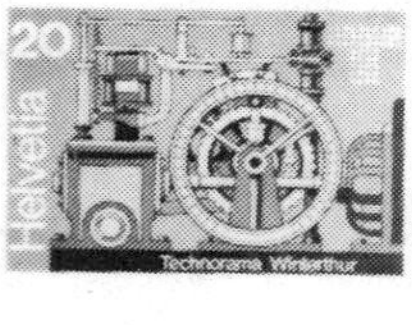
Voltage Regulator A303

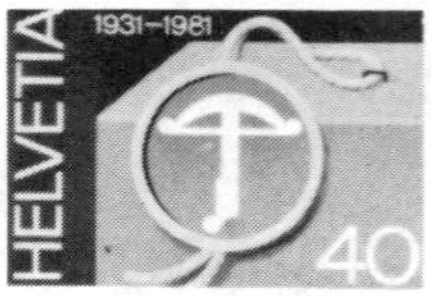
Crossbow Quality Emblem A304

Youths A305

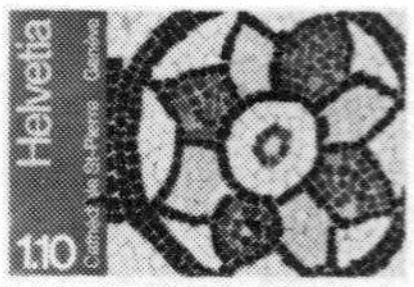
Flower Mosaic, St. Peter's Cathedral, Geneva A306

1981, Sept. 3 Photo.

704	A303	20c multi	18	18
705	A304	40c multi	38	32
706	A305	70c multi	65	50
707	A306	1.10fr multi	1.10	80

Technorama Industrial Fair, Winterthur; Crossbow Quality Emblem, 50th anniv.; Swiss Youth Assoc., 50th anniv.; restoration of St. Peter's Cathedral.

Gotthard Railway Centenary A307

Designs: Locomotives. Nos. 708-709 se-tenant with label showing workers' monument.

1982, Feb. 18 Photo.

708	A307	40c Steam	32	18
709	A307	40c Electric	32	18

Swiss Hoteliers' Assoc. Centenary A308

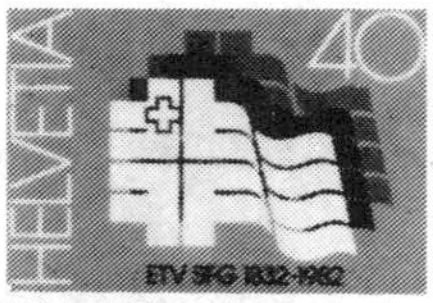
Federal Gymnastic Society Sesquicentennial — A309

Intl. Gas Union, 50th Anniv. Convention, Lausanne A310

Bern Museum of Natural History Sesquicentennial — A311

Society of Chemical Industries Centenary A312

1982, Feb. 18

710	A308	20c multi	15	14
711	A309	40c multi	32	28
712	A310	70c multi	55	45
713	A311	80c multi	60	52
714	A312	110c multi	90	70
		Nos. 710-714 (5)	2.52	2.09

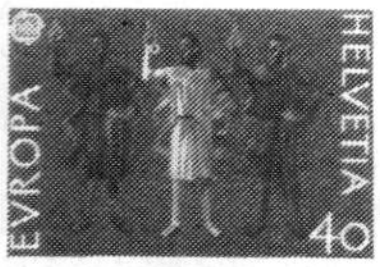
Europa 1982 — A313

1982, May 3 Photo. *Perf. 11½*

715	A313	40c Oath of Eternal Fealty	50	15
716	A313	80c Pact of 1291	1.00	55

Schwarzee above Zermatt — A314

Signs of the Zodiac and City Views.

Photogravure and Engraved

1982-86 *Perf. 11½*

717	A314	1fr	Aquarius, Old Bern	1.10	25
718	A314	1.10fr	Pisces, Nax near Sion	1.25	30
719	A314	1.20fr	Aries, Graustock	1.40	32
719A	A314	1.40fr	Gemini, Bischofszell	1.40	22
720	A314	1.50fr	Taurus, Basel Cathedral	1.75	38
721	A314	1.60fr	Gemini, Schonengrund	1.75	38
722	A314	1.70fr	Cancer, Wetterhorn, Grindelwald	2.00	50
723	A314	1.80fr	Leo, Areuse Gorge, Neuchatel	2.25	50
724	A314	2fr	Virgo, Jungfrau Monch Eiger Mountains	2.50	65
725	A314	2fr	Virgo, Schwarzee above Zermatt	2.25	42
726	A314	2.50fr	Libra, Fechy	2.00	10
727	A314	3fr	Scorpio, Corippo	55	22
728	A314	4fr	Sagittarius, Glarus	4.25	1.10
728A	A314	4.50fr	Capricorn, Schuls	5.50	1.40
			Nos. 717-728A (14)	29.95	6.74

Issue dates: Nos. 717-719, 720-721, Aug. 23, 1982. No. 719A, Feb. 11, 1986. Nos. 722-724, Feb. 17, 1983. No. 725, Nov. 24, 1983. Nos. 726-727, Feb. 19, 1985. Nos. 728-728A, Feb. 21, 1984.

Zurich Tram Centenary A315

Centenary of Salvation Army in Switzerland A316

World Dressage Championship, Lausanne, Aug. 25-29 — A317

Intl. Water Supply Assoc., 14th World Congress, Zurich, Sept. 6-10 — A318

1982, Aug. 23 Photo.

729	A315	20c multi	25	12
730	A316	40c multi	50	25
731	A317	70c multi	90	50
732	A318	80c multi	1.00	55

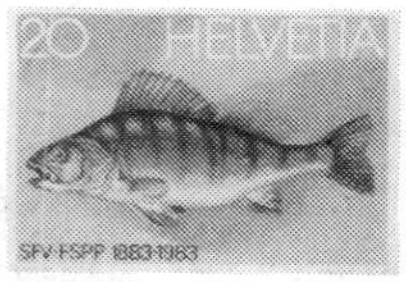
Fishing and Pisciculture Fed. Centenary A319

Zurich University Sesquicentennial — A320

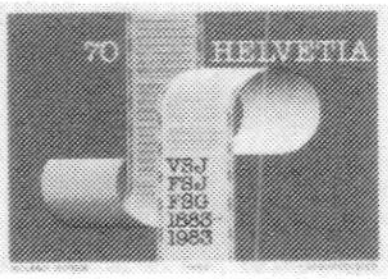
Journalists' Fed. Centenary A321

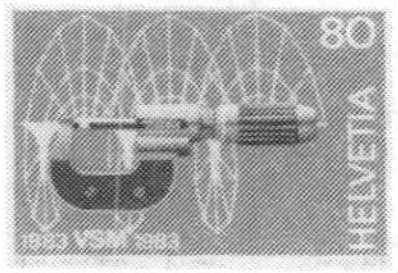
Machine Manufacturers' Assoc. Centenary — A322

1983, Feb. 17 Photo.

Granite Paper

733	A319	20c Perch	25	15
734	A320	40c multi	50	28
735	A321	70c Computer print outs	80	50
736	A322	80c Micrometer, cycloidal computer pattern	90	55

Europa 1983 A323

Basel Seal, 1832-1848 A324

Photogravure and Engraved

1983, May 3 *Perf. 11½*

737	A323	40c Celestial globe, 1594	55	25
738	A323	80c Cog railway, 1871	1.10	70

1983, May 26 Photo.

739	A324	40c multi	45	15

Basel Canton sesquicentennial (land division).

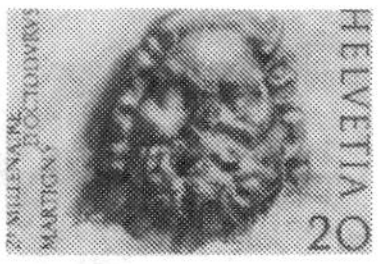

Octodurus Martigny Bimillenium A325

Swiss Kennel Club Centenary A326

Bicycle and Motorcycle Federation Centenary A327

World Communications Year — A328

1983, Aug. 22 **Photo.**

740	A325	20c	multi	25	15
741	A326	40c	multi	42	25
742	A327	70c	multi	75	50
743	A328	80c	multi	85	55

NABA-ZURI'84 Natl. Stamp Show, Zurich, June 22-July 1 — A329

1100th Anniv. of Saint Imier A330

Upper City, Lausanne A331

1984, Feb. 21 **Photo.**

744	A329	25c	multi	25	10
745	A330	50c	multi	55	22
746	A331	80c	multi	90	38

Selection of Lausanne as permanent headquarters for the Intl. Olympic Committee (80c).

Europa (1959-1984) A332

1984, May 2 **Photo.** ***Perf. 11½***

747	A332	50c	lil rose	65	20
748	A332	80c	ultra	1.00	75

The only foreign revenue stamps listed in this Catalogue are those authorized for prepayment of postage.

Souvenir Sheet

View of Zurich — A333

1984, May 24

749		Sheet of 4	4.25	4.25
a.-d.		A333 50c, any single	90	90

NABA-ZURI '84 Stamp Show. Sold for 3fr.

Fire Prevention A334

1984, Sept. 11 **Photo.**

750	A334	50c	Flames, match	55	12

Railway Staff Association, Cent. — A335

Rheto-Roman Culture Bimillennium A336

Lake Geneva Rescue Soc., Cent. — A337

Intl. Congress on Large Dams, Lausanne A338

1985, Feb. 19 **Photo.** ***Perf. 12x11½***

751	A335	35c	Conductor's hat, paraphernalia	40	10
752	A336	50c	Engraved artifact, Chur	55	15
753	A337	70c	Rescuing drowning victim	75	20
754	A338	80c	Grande Dizence Dam, Canton Valais	90	24

Europa 1985 — A339

Designs: 50c, Ernest Ansermet (1883-1969), composer, conductor. 80c, Frank Martin (1890-1974), composer.

1985, May 7 **Photo.** ***Perf. 11½x12***

755	A339	50c	multi	60	14
756	A339	80c	multi	95	22

Swiss Master Bakers and Confectioners Federation, Bern, Cent. — A340

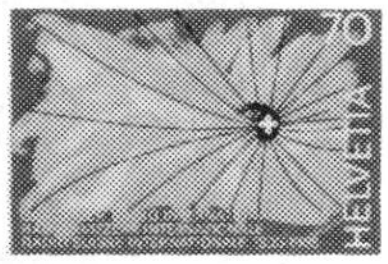

Swiss Radio Intl., 50th Anniv. A341

Postal, Telegraph & Telephone Intl. Congress, Sept. 16-21, Interlaken A342

1985, Sept. 10 **Photo.** ***Perf. 12x11½***

757	A340	50c	Baker	55	15
758	A341	70c	multi	75	20
759	A342	80c	PTTI 75th anniv.	90	24

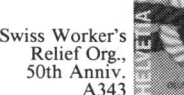

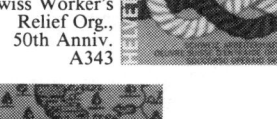

Swiss Worker's Relief Org., 50th Anniv. A343

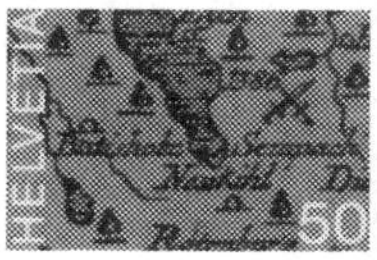

Battle of Sempach, 600th Anniv. — A344

Roman Chur Bimillennium A345

Vindonissa Bimillennium A346

Zurich Bimillennium A347

1986, Feb. 11 **Photo.** ***Perf. 12***

772	A343	35c	Knot	38	12
773	A344	50c	Military map, 1698	55	16
774	A345	80c	Mercury statue	90	28
775	A346	90c	Gallic head	1.00	30
776	A347	1.10fr	Augustus coin	1.25	35
			Nos. 772-776 (5)	4.08	1.21

Europa 1986 — A348

Mail Handling — A349

1986, Apr. 22 **Photo.** ***Perf. 13½***

777	A348	50c	Woman	60	18
778	A348	90c	Man	1.10	32

Photo. & Engr.

1986-89 ***Perf. 13½x13***

779	A349	5c	Franz mail van, 1911	5	5
780	A349	10c	Parcel sorting	10	5
781	A349	20c	Mule post ('87)	28	10
782	A349	25c	Letter-facing, canceling	25	8
783	A349	30c	Mail coach, 1735-1960	40	14
784	A349	35c	Counter service	35	12
785	A349	45c	Packet steamer, 1837-40	60	20
786	A349	50c	Postman, 1986	65	22
a.			Bklt. pane of 10 ('88)	6.50	
787	A349	60c	Loading airmail, 1986	80	28
788	A349	75c	17th Cent. courier ('89)	1.00	32
789	A349	80c	Postman, ca. 1900	85	28
791	A349	90c	Railroad mail car	95	32
			Nos. 779-791 (12)	6.28	2.16

Intl. Peace Year — A351

Swiss Winter Relief Fund, 50th Anniv. A352

Berne Convention for the Protection of Literary and Artistic Copyrights, Cent. — A353

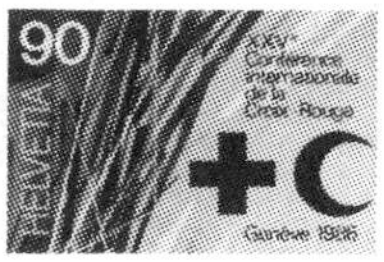

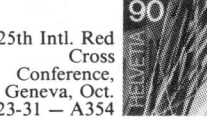

25th Intl. Red Cross Conference, Geneva, Oct. 23-31 — A354

1986, Sept. 9 **Photo.** ***Perf. 12x11½***

799	A351	35c	multi	38	14
800	A352	50c	multi	55	18
801	A353	80c	multi	95	30
802	A354	90c	multi	1.10	35

Mobile P.O., 50th Anniv. A355

Lausanne University, 450th Anniv. A356

Swiss Engineers & Architects Assoc., Sesquicent. A357

Cointrin Airport-Geneva, Rail Link Opening, June 1, 1987 — A358

Baden Hot Springs, 2000th Anniv. A359

1987, Mar. 10 **Photo.**

803	A355	35c	multi	45	16
804	A356	50c	multi	60	22
805	A357	80c	multi	95	35

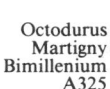

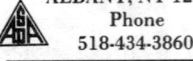

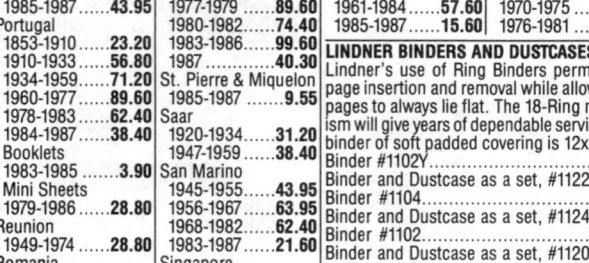

806 A358 90c multi 1.00 40
807 A359 1.10fr multi 1.25 48
Nos. 803-807 (5) 4.25 1.61

Europa 1987 — A360

Sculpture: 50fr, Scarabaeus, 1979, by Bernard Luginbuhl. 90fr, Carnival Fountain, 1977, by Jean Tinguely, Basel Theater.

1987, May 26 Photo. *Perf. 11½*
808 A360 50c multi 70 24
809 A360 90c multi 1.25 42

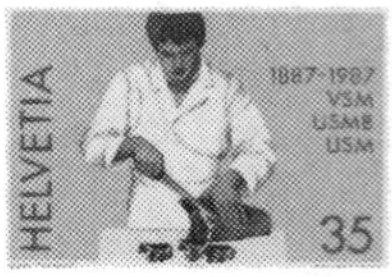
Swiss Master Butchers' Federation, Cent. — A361

Stamp Day, 50th Anniv. A362

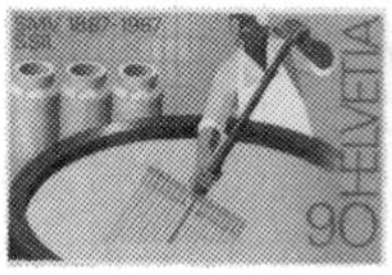
Swiss Dairy Assoc., Cent. — A363

1987, Sept. 4 Photo. *Perf. 12x11½*
810 A361 35c multi 48 16
811 A362 50c multi 68 22
812 A363 90c Cheesemaker 1.20 40

Tourism Industry, Bicent. — A364

Switzerland's four language regions: 50c, Clock Tower, Zug, German. 80c, Church of San Carlo, Blenio Valley, Italian. 90c, Witches' Tower, Sion Castle, French. 140c, Jorgenberg Castle ruins, Waltensburg/Vuorz, Surselva, Rhaeto-Romansh.

1987, Sept. 4 *Perf. 11½*
813 A364 50c multi 68 22
814 A364 80c multi 1.10 38
815 A364 90c multi 1.20 40
816 364 140c multi 1.90 65
a. Souv. sheet of 4, #813-816 5.00

Swiss Women's Benevolent Soc., Cent. A365

Swiss Hairdressers Assoc., Cent. A366

Battle of Naefels, 600th Anniv. A367

European Campaign to Protect Undeveloped and Developing Lands — A368

Intl. Music Festival, Lucerne, 50th Anniv. A369

1988, Mar. 8 Photo. *Perf. 12x11½*
817 A365 25c multi 38 12
818 A366 35c multi 52 18
819 A367 50c Banner of St. Fridolin, medieval manuscript 75 25
820 A368 80c multi 1.20 40
821 A369 90c Girl playing a shawm 1.30 45
Nos. 817-821 (5) 4.15 1.40

Europa 1988 — A370

1988, May 24 Photo. *Perf. 11½*
822 A370 50c Arrows (transport) 75 25
823 A370 90c Circuitry (communication) 1.35 45

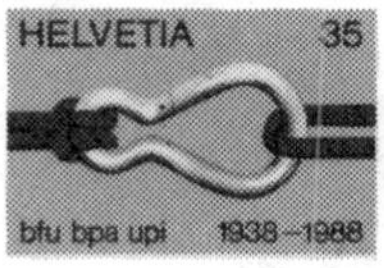
Swiss Accident Prevention Office, 50th Anniv. A371

Assoc. of Metalworkers and Watchmakers, Cent. — A372

Federal Topography Office, 150th Anniv. A373

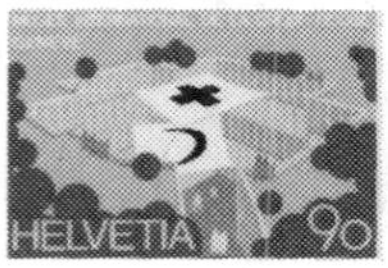
Intl. Red Cross Museum, Geneva A374

1988, Sept. 13 Photo. *Perf. 12x11½*
824 A371 35c multi 45 15
825 A372 50c multi 65 22
826 A373 80c Triangulation pyramid, theodolite, map 1.05 35
827 A374 90c multi 1.20 40

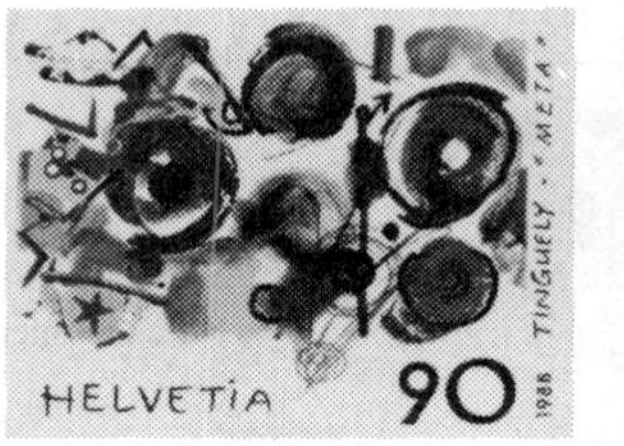
Metamecanique, by Jean Tinguely — A375

1988, Nov. 25 Photo. *Perf. 13x12½*
828 A375 90c multi 1.20 40

See France No. 2137.

Military Post, Cent. — A376

Delemont Municipal Charter, 700th Anniv. A377

Public Transport Assoc., Cent. — A378

Rhaetian Railway, Cent. — A379

Great St. Bernard Pass Bimillennium
A380

Designs: 25c, Army postman. 35c, Fontaine du Sauvage and the Porte au Loup, Delemont. 50c, Eye, modes of transportation. 80c, Train, viaduct. 90c, St. Bernard dog, statue of saint, hospice on summit.

1989, Mar. 2 Photo. *Perf. 12x11½*

829	A376	25c multi	32	10
830	A377	35c multi	45	15
831	A378	50c multi	65	22
832	A379	80c multi	1.05	35
833	A380	90c multi	1.20	40
		Nos. 829-833 (5)	3.67	1.22

Europa 1989 — A381

Children's games: 50c, Hopscotch. 90c, Blindman's buff.

1989, May 23 *Perf. 11½*

834	A381	50c multi	65	22
835	A381	90c multi	1.20	40

SEMI-POSTAL STAMPS

Nos. B1-B76, B81-B84 were sold at premiums of 2c, 5c and 10c.

Helvetia and Matterhorn — SP2

Perf. 11½, 12
1913, Dec. 1 Typo. Wmk. 183
Granite Paper

B1 SP2 5c (+ 5c) grn 2.50 3.50

Boy (Appenzell) SP3 — Girl (Lucerne) SP4

1915, Dec. 1 *Perf. 11½*

B2 SP3 5c (+ 5c) grn, *buff* 5.00 3.75
- ***a.*** Tete beche pair *75.00 800.00*
- ***b.*** Booklet pane of 6

B3 SP4 10c (+ 5c) red, *buff* 100.00 55.00

Girl (Fribourg) — SP5 — Dairy Boy (Bern) — SP6

Girl (Vaud) — SP7

1916, Dec. 1

B4 SP5 3c (+ 2c) vio, *buff* 5.50 *20.00*
B5 SP6 5c (+ 5c) grn, *buff* 11.00 5.00
B6 SP7 10c (+ 5c) brn red, *buff* 52.50 45.00

Girl (Valais) SP8

Girl (Unterwalden) SP9

Girl (Ticino) — SP10

1917, Dec. 1

B7 SP8 3c (+ 2c) vio, *buff* 5.50 *27.50*
B8 SP9 5c (+ 5c) grn, *buff* 7.25 3.25
B9 SP10 10c (+ 5c) red, *buff* 21.00 16.00

Uri — SP11 — Geneva — SP12

1918, Dec. 1 Straw-Surfaced Paper

B10 SP11 10c (+ 5c) red, org & blk 6.25 *8.75*
B11 SP12 15c (+ 5c) vio, red, org & blk 8.25 *5.00*

Nidwalden SP13

Vaud SP14

Obwalden — SP15

1919, Dec. 1 Cream-Surfaced Paper

B12 SP13 7½c (+ 5c) gray, red & blk 2.50 *10.00*
B13 SP14 10c (+ 5c) lake, grn & blk 2.50 *10.00*
B14 SP15 15c (+ 5c) pur, red & blk 3.00 3.50

Schwyz — SP16

Zürich — SP17

Ticino — SP18

1920, Dec. 1 Cream-Surfaced Paper

B15 SP16 7½c (+ 5c) gray & red 2.75 *6.00*
B16 SP17 10c (+ 5c) red & lt bl 5.50 *5.50*
B17 SP18 15c (+ 5c) vio, red & bl 2.25 2.25

Valais — SP19

Bern — SP20

Switzerland SP21

1921, Dec. 1 Cream-Surfaced Paper

B18 SP19 10c (+ 5c) grn, red & blk 90 *1.25*
B19 SP20 20c (+ 5c) vio, red, org & blk 1.25 *1.50*
B20 SP21 40c (+ 10c) bl & red 8.00 *25.00*

Zug — SP22 — Fribourg — SP23

Lucerne SP24

Switzerland SP25

1922, Dec. 1 Cream-Surfaced Paper

B21 SP22 5c (+ 5c) org, pale bl & blk 55 *2.00*
B22 SP23 10c (+ 5c) ol grn & blk 55 *1.00*
B23 SP24 20c (+ 5c) vio, pale bl & blk 55 *1.00*
B24 SP25 40c (+ 10c) bl & red 9.00 *25.00*

Basel — SP26

Glarus (St. Fridolin) — SP27

Neuchâtel SP28

Switzerland SP29

1923, Dec. 1 Cream-Surfaced Paper

B25 SP26 5c (+ 5c) org & blk 35 *1.50*
B26 SP27 10c (+ 5c) multi 35 *80*
B27 SP28 20c (+ 5c) multi 35 *80*
B28 SP29 40c (+ 10c) dk bl & red 6.00 *22.50*

Appenzell — SP30

Solothurn — SP31

Schaffhausen SP32

Switzerland SP33

1924, Dec. 1 Cream-Surfaced Paper

B29 SP30 5c (+ 5c) dk vio & blk 10 *60*
B30 SP31 10c (+ 5c) grn, red & blk 10 *50*
B31 SP32 20c (+ 5c) car, yel & blk 15 *50*
B32 SP33 30c (+ 10c) bl, red & blk 1.40 *4.00*

St. Gallen (Canton) SP34

Appenzell-Ausser-Rhoden SP35

Grisons SP36

Switzerland SP37

1925, Dec. 1 Cream-Surfaced Paper

B33 SP34 5c (+ 5c) vio, grn & blk 12 *50*
B34 SP35 10c (+ 5c) grn & blk 16 *38*
B35 SP36 20c (+ 5c) multi 20 *50*
B36 SP37 30c (+ 10c) dk bl, red & blk 1.25 *4.00*

Thurgau — SP38 — Basel — SP39

Aargau SP40

Switzerland SP41

1926, Dec. 1 Cream-Surfaced Paper

B37 SP38 5c (+ 5c) vio, bis & grn 10 *50*
B38 SP39 10c (+ 5c) gray grn, red & blk 20 *50*
B39 SP40 20c (+ 5c) red, blk & bl 24 *50*
B40 SP41 30c (+ 10c) dk bl & red 1.10 *3.75*

Orphan SP42

Orphan at Pestalozzi School SP43

J. H. Pestalozzi
SP44 SP45

1927, Dec. 1 Typo. Wmk. 183
Granite Paper

B41 SP42 5c (+ 5c) red vio & yel, *grysh* 12 *60*
B42 SP43 10c (+ 5c) grn & fawn, *grnsh* 14 *35*

Engr.

B43 SP44 20c (+ 5c) red 18 *35*

Unwmk.
Photo.

B44 SP45 30c (+ 10c) gray bl & blk 1.00 *3.50*

Nos. B43 and B44 were in commemoration of the centenary of the death of Johann Heinrich Pestalozzi, the Swiss educational reformer.

Lausanne SP46

Winterthur SP47

St. Gallen (City) SP48

J. H. Dunant SP49

1928, Dec. 1 Typo. Wmk. 183
Cream-Surfaced Paper.

B45 SP46	5c (+ 5c) dk vio, red & blk	18	*65*
B46 SP47	10c (+ 5c) bl grn, org red & blk	20	*60*
B47 SP48	20c (+ 5c) brn red, blk & yel	25	*60*

Unwmk.
Photo.
Thick White Paper

B48 SP49	30c (+ 10c) dl bl & red	1.25	*3.25*

No. B48 was issued in commemoration of the centenary of the birth of Jean Henri Dunant, Swiss author, philanthropist and founder of the Red Cross Society.

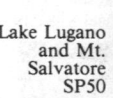

Lake Lugano and Mt. Salvatore SP50

Lake Engstlen and Mt. Titlis SP51

Mt. Lyskamm SP52

Nicholas von der Flüe — SP53

1929, Dec. 1 ***Perf. 11x11½***

B49 SP50	5c (+ 5c) dk vio & red org	14	*50*
B50 SP51	10c (+ 5c) ol brn & gray bl	20	*32*
B51 SP52	20c (+ 5c) brn garnet & bl	22	*32*
B52 SP53	30c (+ 10c) dk bl	1.10	*4.75*

No. B52 was in commemoration of Nicholas von der Flüe, the Swiss patriot. By his advice the Swiss Confederation was continued and Swiss independence was saved.

Fribourg — SP54

Altdorf — SP55

Schaffhausen — SP56

Jeremias Gotthelf SP57

Wmk. 183
1930, Dec. 1 Typo. ***Perf. 11½***
Cream-Surfaced Paper

B53 SP54	5c (+ 5c) dp grn, dl bl & blk	12	*52*
B54 SP55	10c (+ 5c) multi	20	*52*
B55 SP56	20c (+ 5c) multi	24	*52*

Engr.
White Paper

B56 SP57	30c (+ 10c) sl bl	1.40	*3.50*

No. B56 was commemorative of Jeremias Gotthelf, pen name of Albrecht Bitzius, pastor and author.

Lakes Silvaplana and Sils — SP58

Wetterhorn SP59

Lake Geneva SP60

Alexandre Vinet SP61

1931, Dec. 1 Photo. Unwmk.
Granite Paper

B57 SP58	5c (+ 5c) dp grn	25	*52*
B58 SP59	10c (+ 5c) dk vio	25	*32*
B59 SP60	20c (+ 5c) brn red	40	32

Wmk. 183
Engr.

B60 SP61	30c (+ 10c) ultra	4.00	*9.00*

No. B60 was commemorative of Alexandre Rudolph Vinet, critic and theologian.

Flag Swinger — SP62

Putting the Stone — SP63

Wrestling — SP64

Eugen Huber — SP65

1932, Dec. 1 Typo. Unwmk.
Granite Paper

B61 SP62	5c (+ 5c) dk grn & red	38	*75*
B62 SP63	10c (+ 5c) org	55	*75*
B63 SP64	20c (+ 5c) scar	55	*75*

Wmk. 183
Engr.

B64 SP65	30c (+ 10c) ultra	2.25	*3.75*

No. B64 was commemorative of Eugen Huber, jurist and author of the Swiss Civil Law Book.

Girl of Vaud — SP66

Girl of Bern — SP67

Girl of Ticino — SP68

Jean Baptiste Girard (Le Pere Gregoire) — SP69

1933, Dec. 1 Photo. Unwmk.
Granite Paper

B65 SP66	5c (+ 5c) grn & buff	22	*50*
B66 SP67	10c (+ 5c) vio & buff	30	*30*
B67 SP68	20c (+ 5c) red & buff	40	*38*

Wmk. 183
Engr.

B68 SP69	30c (+ 10c) ultra	2.00	*3.50*

Girl of Appenzell — SP70

Girl of Valais — SP71

Girl of Grisons — SP72

Albrecht von Haller — SP73

1934, Dec. 1 Photo. Unwmk.

B69 SP70	5c (+ 5c) grn & buff	20	*50*
B70 SP71	10c (+ 5c) vio & buff	32	*38*
B71 SP72	20c (+ 5c) red & buff	40	*38*

Wmk. 183
Engr.

B72 SP73	30c (+ 10c) ultra	2.00	*4.00*

Girl of Basel — SP74

Girl of Lucerne — SP75

Girl of Geneva — SP76

Stefano Franscini — SP77

1935, Dec. 1 Photo. Unwmk.
Granite Paper

B73 SP74	5c (+ 5c) grn & buff	22	*45*
B74 SP75	10c (+ 5c) vio & buff	38	*38*
B75 SP76	20c (+ 5c) red & buff	38	*65*

Wmk. 183
Engr.

B76 SP77	30c (+ 10c) ultra	2.25	*4.25*

No. B76 honors Stefano Franscini (1796-1857), political economist and educator.

National Defense Issue

Alpine Herdsman — SP78

SP78a

Perf. 11½
1936, Oct. 1 Photo. Unwmk.
Granite Paper

B77 SP78	10c + 5c vio	35	42
B78 SP78	20c + 10c dk red	65	*1.75*
B79 SP78	30c + 10c ultra	3.00	*10.00*

Souvenir Sheet

B80 SP78a	Sheet of three	35.00	*185.00*
a.	Block of four sheets	250.00	*850.00*

Nos. B77-B80 were issued in connection with the Swiss National Defense Fund Drive.

No. B80 contains stamps similar to Nos. B77-B79, but on different granite paper with blue and red fibers instead of black and red. Sold for 2fr. Size: 120x130mm.

Johann Georg Nägeli SP79

Girl of Neuchâtel SP80

Girl of Schwyz — SP81

Girl of Zurich — SP82

Wmk. 183
1936, Dec. 1 Engr. ***Perf. 11½***
Granite Paper

B81 SP79	5c (+ 5c) grn	18	*32*

Unwmk.
Photo.

B82 SP80	10c(+ 5c) vio & buff	24	*32*
B83 SP81	20c(+ 5c) red & buff	30	*48*
B84 SP82	30c(+ 10c) ultra & buff	2.50	*8.00*

Gen. Henri Dufour SP83

Nicholas von der Flüe SP84

Boy — SP85

Girl SP86

Perf. 11½

1937, Dec. 1 Unwmk. Engr.

B85 SP83 5c + 5c bl grn 9 *18*
B86 SP84 10c + 5c red vio 16 *22*

Photo.

Granite Paper

B87 SP85 20c + 5c red & sil 18 *22*
B88 SP86 30c + 10c ultra & sil 1.40 *3.25*

25th anniv. of the Pro Juventute (child welfare) stamps.

Souvenir Sheet

SP86a

1937, Dec. 20 ***Imperf.***

B89 SP86a Sheet of two 3.50 *47.50*
a. 20c + 5c red & sil 1.10 *15.00*
b. 30c + 10c ultra & sil 1.10 *15.00*

Simulated perforation in silver. Size: 105x59mm. Sheet sold for 1fr.

Tell Chapel, Lake Lucerne SP87

1938, June 15 ***Perf. 11½***

Granite Paper

B90 SP87 10c + 10c brt vio & yel 50 30
a. Grilled gum 26.00 *75.00*

National Fête Day.

Salomon Gessner — SP88

Girl of St. Gallen — SP89

Girl of Uri — SP90

Girl of Aargau — SP91

1938, Dec. 1 Engr. ***Perf. 11½***

B91 SP88 5c + 5c dp bl grn 8 12

Photo.

Granite Paper

B92 SP89 10c + 5c pur & buff 12 20
B93 SP90 20c + 5c red & buff 15 20
B94 SP91 30c + 10c ultra 1.25 *3.00*

Castle at Laupen SP92

1939, June 15

B95 SP92 10c + 10c brn, gray & red 40 *30*

Issued in commemoration of the 600th anniversary of the Battle of Laupen. The surtax was used to aid needy mothers.

Hans Herzog — SP93

Girl of Fribourg — SP94

Girl of Nidwalden SP95

Girl of Basel SP96

Perf. 11½

1939, Dec. 1 Unwmk. Engr.

B96 SP93 5c + 5c dk grn 8 16

Photo.

Granite Paper

B97 SP94 10c + 5c rose vio & buff 18 16
B98 SP95 20c + 5c org red 30 18
B99 SP96 30c + 10c ultra & buff 1.65 *3.75*

Sempach, 1386 — SP97

Giornico, 1478 — SP98

Calven, 1499 SP99

WWI Ranger SP100

1940, Mar. 20 Photo.

Granite Paper

B100 SP97 5c + 5c emer, blk & red 45 *1.50*
B101 SP98 10c + 5c brn org, blk & car 45 50
B102 SP99 20c + 5c brn red, blk & car 2.25 1.00
B103 SP100 30c + 10c brt bl, brn blk & red 2.50 *7.50*

Issued in commemoration of the National Fête Day. The surtax was for the National Fund and the Red Cross.

Redrawn

B104 SP99 20c + 5c brn red, blk & car 14.00 6.00
Nos. B100-B104 (5) 19.65 *16.50*

The base of statue has been heavily shaded "Calven 1499" moved nearer to bottom line of base. Top line of base removed.

Souvenir Sheet

SP101

Unwmk.

1940, July 16 Photo. ***Imperf.***

Granite Paper

B105 SP101 Sheet of four 200.00 *600.00*
a. 5c + 5c yel grn, blk & red 15.00 *30.00*
b. 10c + 5c org yel, blk & red 50.00 *250.00*
c. 20c + 5c brn red, blk & red 50.00 *250.00*
d. 30c + 10c chlky bl, blk & red 15.00 *30.00*

National Fête Day.

Sheets measure 125x65mm. and sold for 5fr.

Gottfried Keller — SP102

Girl of Thurgau — SP103

Girl of Solothurn SP104

Girl of Zug SP105

1940, Dec. 1 Engr. ***Perf. 11½***

B106 SP102 5c + 5c dk bl grn 10 *20*

Photo.

B107 SP103 10c + 5c brn & buff 18 *20*
B108 SP104 20c + 5c org red & buff 24 22
B109 SP105 30c + 10c dp ultra & buff 1.65 *3.75*

Lake Lucerne, Arms of Cantons SP106

Tell Chapel at Chemin Creux SP107

1941, June 15

B110 SP106 10c + 10c multi 38 *25*
B111 SP107 20c + 10c org, red & lt buff 38 *25*

Issued in commemoration of the National Fête Day and the 650th anniversary of Swiss Independence.

Scott's International Album provides spaces for an extensive representative collection of the world's postage stamps.

Johann Lavater SP108

Girl of Schaffhausen SP109

Girl of Obwalden SP110

Daniel Jean Richard SP111

1941, Dec. 1 Engr.

B112 SP108 5c + 5c dk grn 18 14
B113 SP111 30c + 10c dp ultra 1.50 *2.50*

Photo.

B114 SP109 10c + 5c chnt & buff 28 *20*
B115 SP110 20c + 5c ver & buff 28 *20*

Souvenir Sheet

SP112

Imperf.

B116 SP112 Sheet of two 45.00 *300.00*
a. 10c + 5c chnt & buff 15.00 *125.00*
b. 20c + 5c ver & buff 15.00 *125.00*

Issued in sheets measuring 75x70mm. and sold for 2fr. The surtax was used for charity.

Ancient Geneva SP113

Soldiers' Monument, Forch — SP114

1942, June 15 ***Perf. 11½***

B117 SP113 10c + 10c gray blk, red & yel 35 *30*
B118 SP114 20c + 10c cop red, red & buff 35 *30*

Issued in commemoration of the National Fête Day, 1942. No. B117 commemorates the 2000th anniversary of the City of Geneva.

Souvenir Sheet

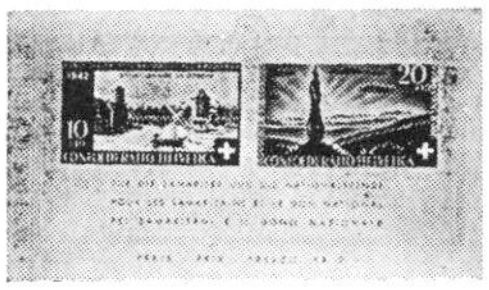
SP115

Imperf.

B119 SP115 Sheet of two 45.00 *200.00*
a. 10c + 10c gray blk, red & yel 15.00 *70.00*

b. 20c + 20c cop red, red & buff 15.00 *70.00*

Issued in sheets measuring 105x63 mm. in commemoration of National Fête and the 2000th anniversary of the City of Geneva. Sold for 2 fr. The surtax was divided between the Swiss Alliance of Samaritans and the National Community Chest.

Niklaus Riggenbach
SP116

Girl of Appenzell
SP117

Girl of Glarus
SP118

Konrad Escher von der Linth
SP119

1942, Dec. 1 Engr. *Perf. 11½*

B120 SP116 5c + 5c dp grn 9 *30*
B121 SP119 30c + 10c ryl bl 1.65 *3.25*

Photo.

B122 SP117 10c + 5c dp brn & buff 18 *32*
B123 SP118 20c + 5c org red 24 *32*

Intragna
SP120

Parliament Buildings, Bern
SP121

1943, June 15 Photo. *Perf. 11½*

B124 SP120 10c + 10c blk brn, buff & dk red 30 *45*
B125 SP121 20c + 10c cop red, buff & dk red 35 *65*

National Fête Day, 1943.

Emanuel von Fellenberg
SP122

Silver Thistle
SP123

Lady Slipper
SP124

Gentian
SP125

1943, Dec. 1 Engr.

B126 SP122 5c + 5c grn 10 *16*

Photo.

B127 SP123 10c + 5c sl grn & ocher 12 *25*
B128 SP124 20c + 5c cop red & yel 12 *28*
B129 SP125 30c + 10c ryl bl & lt bl 1.25 *4.25*

Souvenir Sheets

SP126

1943 Engr. *Imperf.*

B130 SP126 Sheet of twelve 35.00 *57.50*
a. Single stamp, 10c blk 1.00 *3.50*

Sold for 5 francs. Size: 165x140mm.

SP127

Red Horizontal Lines

B131 SP127 Sheet of two 35.00 *60.00*
a. 4c blk & red 12.50 *20.00*
b. 6c blk & red 12.50 *20.00*

Sold for 3 francs. Size: 70x75mm.

Arms of Geneva — SP128

B132 SP128 Sheet of two 30.00 *32.50*
a. 5c grn & blk 8.50 *10.50*

Sold for 3fr. Size: 72x72mm. Centenary of Swiss postage stamps. The surtax aided the Swiss Red Cross.

Heiden
SP129

St. Jacob
SP130

Mesocco
SP131

Basel
SP132

Perf. 11½

1944, June 15 Photo. Unwmk.

B133 SP129 5c + 5c dk bl grn, red & buff 20 *1.25*
B134 SP130 10c + 10c gray blk, red & buff 20 *40*
B135 SP131 20c + 10c hn, red & buff 20 *70*
B136 SP132 30c + 10c brt ultra & red 2.75 *12.00*

National Fête Day.

Numa Droz
SP133

Edelweiss
SP134

Lilium Martagon
SP135

Aquilegia Alpina
SP136

1944, Dec. 1 Engr.

B137 SP133 5c + 5c grn 15 *22*

Photo.

B138 SP134 10c + 5c dk sl grn, yel & gray 22 *28*
B139 SP135 20c + 5c red, yel & gray 38 *28*
B140 SP136 30c + 10c bl, gray & lt bl 1.50 *4.50*

Symbol of Faith, Hope and Love
SP137

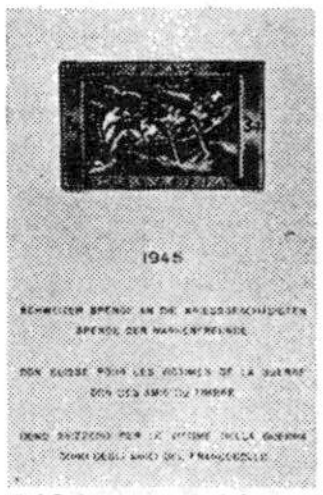

Lifeboat Making a Rescue
SP138

1945, Feb. 20 *Perf. 11½*

B141 SP137 10c + 10c multi 40 55
B142 SP137 20c + 60c multi 1.65 *5.00*

Imperf

Souvenir Sheet

B143 SP138 3fr + 7fr bl gray 135.00 *275.00*

Issued in sheets measuring 70x110mm.
The surtax on Nos. B141 to B143 was for the benefit of war victims.

Souvenir Sheet

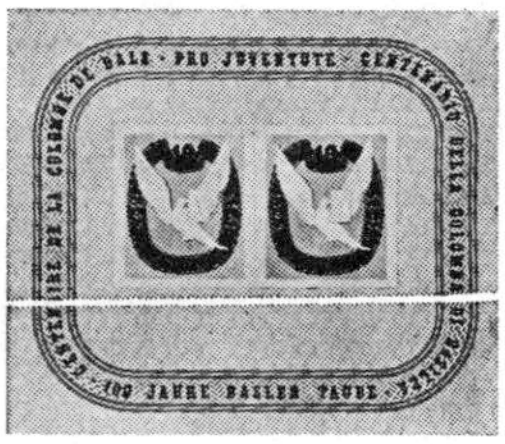

Dove of Basel
SP139

1945, Apr. 14 Typo.

B144 SP139 Sheet of two 65.00 *85.00*
a. 10c gray, mar & blk 21.00 *30.00*

Issued to commemorate the centenary of the Basel Cantonal Stamp. The sheets measure 71x63mm. and sold for 3 francs. The surtax was for the Pro Juventute Foundation.

Numeral of Value and Red Cross — SP140

1945 Photo. *Perf. 12*

B145 SP140 5c + 10c grn & red 48 *70*

Weaver
SP141

Farm of Jura
SP142

Farm of Emmental
SP143

Frame House, Eastern Switzerland
SP144

1945, June 15 Engr. *Perf. 11½*

B146 SP141 5c + 5c bl grn & red 60 *1.50*

Photo.

B147 SP142 10c + 10c brn, gray bl & red 60 *60*
B148 SP143 20c + 10c hn brn, buff & red 90 *60*
B149 SP144 30c + 10c saph & red 9.00 *30.00*

The surtax was for needy mothers.

Ludwig Forrer — SP145

Susanna Orelli — SP146

Alpine Dog-Rose
SP147

Crocus
SP148

1945, Dec. 1 Engr.

B150 SP145 5c + 5c dk grn 14 18
B151 SP146 10c + 10c dk red brn 15 *22*

Photo.

B152 SP147 20c + 10c rose brn, rose & yel org 32 22
B153 SP148 30c + 10c dk bl, gray & lil 1.25 *4.00*

Cheese Making
SP149

Farm Buildings and Vineyards
SP150

House in Appenzell
SP151

House in Engadine
SP152

1946, June 15 **Engr.**

B154 SP149 5c + 5c bl grn & red 45 *1.25*

Photo.

B155 SP150 10c + 10c brn, buff & red 35 38
B156 SP151 20c + 10c hn, buff & red 45 38
B157 SP152 30c + 10c saph & red 3.50 *6.50*

Rodolphe Toepffer
SP153

Narcissus
SP154

Mountain Sengreen
SP155

Blue Thistle
SP156

1946, Nov. 30 **Engr.**

B158 SP153 5c + 5c grn 15 *18*

Photo.

B159 SP154 10c + 10c dk sl grn, gray & red org 20 *22*
B160 SP155 20c + 10c brn car, gray & yel 22 *22*
B161 SP156 30c + 10c dk bl, gray & pink 1.90 *3.75*

Railroad Laborers
SP157

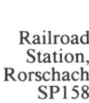

Railroad Station, Rorschach
SP158

Lüen-Castiel Station — SP159

Flüelen Station
SP160

Perf. 11½

1947, June 14 **Engr.** **Unwmk.**

B162 SP157 5c + 5c dk grn & red 35 *1.10*

Photo.

B163 SP158 10c + 10c gray blk, cr & red 35 *45*
B164 SP159 20c + 10c rose lil, cr & red 35 *45*
B165 SP160 30c + 10c bl, gray & red 3.25 *5.00*

The surtax was for professional education of invalids and for the fight against cancer.

Jakob Burckhardt
SP161

Alpine Primrose
SP162

Red Lily
SP163

Cyclamen
SP164

1947, Dec. 1 **Engr.**

B166 SP161 5c + 5c dk grn 10 10

Photo.

B167 SP162 10c + 10c sl blk, gray & yel 12 *22*
B168 SP163 20c + 10c red brn, gray & cop red 20 22
B169 SP164 30c + 10c dk bl, gray & pink 1.25 *3.75*

Sun and Olympic Emblem — SP165

Snowflake and Olympic Emblem — SP166

Ice-hockey Player
SP167

Ski-runner
SP168

1948, Jan. 15

B170 SP165 5c + 5c dk bl grn & yel 25 *80*
B171 SP166 10c + 10c choc & bl 25 *80*
B172 SP167 20c + 10c dp mag, gray & org yel 50 *80*
B173 SP168 30c + 10c dk bl, bl & gray blk 1.10 *2.75*

Issued to publicize the 5th Olympic Winter Games, St. Moritz, Jan. 30 to Feb. 8, 1948.

Frontier Guard
SP169

House of Fribourg
SP170

House of Valais
SP171

House of Ticino
SP172

1948, June 15 **Engr.**

B174 SP169 5c + 5c dk grn & red 15 *30*

Photo.

B175 SP170 10c + 10c sl & gray 14 *24*
B176 SP171 20c + 10c brn red & pink 18 *24*
B177 SP172 30c + 10c bl & gray 2.00 *3.25*

Johann R. Wettstein — SP173

1948, Aug. 21 ***Perf. 11x12½***

B178 SP173 Sheet of 2 32.50 *52.50*
a. 10c rose lil 13.00 *20.00*
b. 20c chlky bl 13.00 *20.00*

Issued in sheets measuring 110x60mm., to commemorate the International Philatelic Exposition, Basel, August 21-29, 1948. Sheet sold for 3 francs, of which the surtax was used for the exhibition and charitable purposes.

Gen. Ulrich Wille
SP174

Foxglove
SP175

Designs: 20c+10c, Alpine rose. 40c+10c, Lily of paradise.

1948, Dec. 1 **Engr.** ***Perf. 11½***

B179 SP174 5c + 5c dk vio brn 10 *18*

Photo.

B180 SP175 10c + 10c dk grn, yel grn & yel 25 22
B181 SP175 20c + 10c brn, crim & buff 32 22
B182 SP175 40c + 10c bl, gray & org 1.25 *3.25*

Postman
SP176

Mountain Farmhouse
SP177

House of Lucerne
SP178

House of Prattigau
SP179

Engraved and Photogravure

1949, June 15

Shield in Carmine

B183 SP176 5c + 5c rose vio 45 75

Photo.

B184 SP177 10c + 10c bl grn & car 35 *50*
B185 SP178 20c + 10c dk brn & cr 45 *50*
B186 SP179 40c + 10c bl & pale bl 3.50 *5.50*

The surtax was for professional education of Swiss youth.

Niklaus Wengi
SP180

Anemone Sulphureous
SP181

Designs: 20c+10c, Alpine clematis. 40c+10c, Superb pink.

1949, Dec. 1 **Engr.** ***Perf. 11½***

B187 SP180 5c + 5c vio brn 18 15

Photo.

B188 SP181 10c + 10c grn, gray & yel 24 24
B189 SP181 20c + 10c brn, bl & yel 30 32
B190 SP181 40c + 10c bl, lav & yel 1.65 *4.00*

Adaptation of 1850 Design
SP182

Putting the Stone
SP183

Designs: 20c+10c, Wrestlers. 30c+10c, Runners. 40c+10c, Target shooting.

1950, June 1 **Engr. & Photo.**

Shield in Red

B191 SP182 5c + 5c blk 20 *55*

Photo.

Inscribed: "I. VIII. 1950."

B192 SP183 10c + 10c grn 50 55
B193 SP183 20c + 20c brn ol 65 75
B194 SP183 30c + 10c rose lil 4.00 *11.00*
B195 SP183 40c + 10c dl bl 4.00 *8.50*
Nos. B191-B195 (5) 9.35 *21.35*

The surtax was for the Red Cross and the Society of Swiss History of Art.

Theophil Sprecher von Bernegg
SP184

Admiral Butterfly
SP185

Designs: 20c+10c, Blue Underwing Butterfly. 30c+10c, Bee. 40c+10c, Sulphur Butterfly.

1950, Dec. 1 **Engr.**

B196 SP184 5c + 5c sep 18 16

Photo.

B197 SP185 10c + 10c multi 32 28
B198 SP185 20c + 10c multi 45 38
B199 SP185 30c + 10c rose lil, gray & dk brn 3.50 *10.00*
B200 SP185 40c + 10c bl, dk brn & yel 3.50 *7.00*
Nos. B196-B200 (5) 7.95 *17.82*

Arms of Switzerland and Zurich
SP186

Valaisan Polka
SP187

Designs: 20c+10c, Flag-swinging. 30c+10c, Hornussen (national game). 40c+10c, Blowing alphorn.

1951, June 1 **Engr.**

Shield in Red

B201 SP186 5c + 5c gray 15 *30*

Photo.

Inscribed: "1. VIII. 1951."

Shield in Red, Figure Shaded in Gray

B202 SP187 10c + 10c grn 45 42
B203 SP187 20c + 10c ol bis 45 42
B204 SP187 30c + 10c red vio 3.50 *8.00*
B205 SP187 40c + 10c brt bl 3.75 *8.00*
Nos. B201-B205 (5) 8.30 *17.14*

The surtax was used primarily for needy mothers.

Souvenir Sheet

Flag-Swinging — SP188

Unwmk.

1951, Sept. 29 **Photo.** ***Imperf.***

B206 SP188 40c (+ 2.60fr) brt bl, sheet 175.00 175.00

Issued in sheets measuring 74x56mm., on the occasion of the National Philatelic Exhibition, LUNABA, Sept. 29-Oct. 7, 1951, at Lucerne. The net proceeds were used for Swiss schools abroad.

Values quoted in this catalogue are for stamps graded at Fine-Very Fine and with no faults. An illustrated guide to grade is provided in introductory material, beginning on Page V.

Johanna Spyri
SP189

Dragonfly
SP190

Butterflies: 20c+10c, Black-Veined. 30c+10c Orange-Tip. 40c+10c, Saturnia pyri.

1951, Dec. 1 **Engr.** ***Perf. 11½***

B207 SP189 5c + 5c red brn 10 14

Photo.

B208 SP190 10c + 10c grn & dk bl 18 22
B209 SP190 20c + 10c rose lil, cr & blk 22 22
B210 SP190 30c + 10c ol grn, gray & org 2.75 *5.50*
B211 SP190 40c + 10c bl, dk brn & car 2.75 *5.50*
Nos. B207-B211 (5) 6.00 *11.58*

Arms of Switzerland, Glarus and Zug — SP191

Doubs River — SP192

Designs: 20c+10c, Lake of St. Gotthard. 30c+10c, Moesa River. 40c+10c, Lake of Marjelen.

1952, May 31 **Engr. & Typo.**

B212 SP191 5c + 5c gray & red 28 *45*

Photo.

B213 SP192 10c + 10c bl grn 32 30
B214 SP192 20c + 10c brn car 32 30
B215 SP192 30c + 10c brn 2.75 *4.50*
B216 SP192 40c + 10c bl 2.75 *4.50*
Nos. B212-B216 (5) 6.42 *10.05*

The surtax was used primarily for historical research and popular culture.

See Nos. B233-B236, B243-B246, B253-B256.

Portrait of a Boy, by Albert Anker
SP193

Ladybug
SP194

Designs: 20c+10c, Barred-wing butterfly. 30c+10c, Argus butterfly. 40c+10c, Silkworm moth.

Perf. 11½

1952, Dec. 1 **Unwmk.** **Engr.**

B217 SP193 5c + 5c brn car 12 12

Photo.

B218 SP194 10c + 10c bluish grn, blk & org red 22 18
B219 SP194 20c + 10c rose lil, cr & blk 30 18
B220 SP194 30c + 10c brn, blk & gray bl 2.00 *4.75*
B221 SP194 40c + 10c pale vio, brn & buff 2.75 *4.50*
Nos. B217-B221 (5) 5.39 *9.73*

See Nos. B227-B231, B234-B241.

Types Similar to 1952

Designs: 5c+5c, Arms of Switzerland and Bern. 10c+10c, Reuss River. 20c+10c, Sihl Lake. 30c+10c, Bisse River. 40c+10c, Lake of Geneva.

Engraved and Photogravure

1953, June 1

B222 SP191 5c + 5c gray & red 22 *40*

Photo.

B223 SP192 10c + 10c bl grn 30 28
B224 SP192 20c + 10c brn car 38 28
B225 SP192 30c + 10c brn 2.00 *4.00*
B226 SP192 40c + 10c bl 2.00 *4.00*
Nos. B222-B226 (5) 4.90 *8.96*

The surtax was used for Swiss nationals abroad and for disabled persons.

Types Similar to 1952, Dated "1953"

Designs: 5c+5c, Portrait of a girl, by Albert Anker. 10c+10c, Nun moth. 20c+10c, Camberwell beauty butterfly. 30c+10c, Purple longicorn beetle. 40c+10c, Self-portrait, Ferdinand Hodler, facing left.

1953, Dec. 1 **Engr.** ***Perf. 11½***

B227 SP193 5c + 5c rose brn 12 12
a. Bklt. pane of 6

Photo.

B228 SP194 10c + 10c bl grn, brn & rose pink 16 12
a. Booklet pane of 6
B229 SP194 20c + 10c multi 22 12
a. Sheet of 24 250.00 *1,000.*
b. Booklet pane of 6 (4 No. B229 + 2 No. B230) 32.50
B230 SP194 30c + 10c ol, blk & red 2.25 *4.50*

Engr.

B231 SP193 40c + 10c bl 3.00 *4.50*
Nos. B227-B231 (5) 5.75 *9.36*

No. B229a consists of 16 No. B229 and 8 No. B230, arranged to include four se-tenant pairs and four pairs which are both se-tenant and tete beche.

Opening Bars of "Swiss Hymn"
SP195

Jeremias Gotthelf
SP196

Types Similar to 1952, Dated "1954"

Views: 10c+10c, Neuchatel lake. 20c+10c, Maggia river. 30c+10c, Cascade, Taubenloch gorge. 40c+10c, Sils lake.

1954, June 1 **Engr.** ***Perf. 11½***

B232 SP195 5c + 5c dk bl grn 35 30

Photo.

B233 SP192 10c + 10c bl grn 35 25
B234 SP192 20c + 10c dp plum 35 25
B235 SP192 30c + 10c dk brn 2.50 *4.25*
B236 SP192 40c + 10c dp bl 2.50 *4.25*
Nos. B232-B236 (5) 6.05 *9.30*

The surtax was used to aid vocational training and home nursing.

No. B232 commemorates the centenary of the death of Alberik Zwyssig, composer of the "Swiss Hymn."

Types Similar to 1952, Dated "1954"

Insects: 10c+10c, Garden tiger. 20c+10c, Bumble bee. 30c+10c, Ascalaphus. 40c+10c, Swallow-tail.

1954, Dec. 1 **Engr.**

B237 SP196 5c + 5c dk red brn 12 28
a. Booklet pane of 4

Photo.

B238 SP194 10c + 10c multi 30 28
a. Booklet pane of 4
B239 SP194 20c + 10c multi 40 38
a. Booklet pane of 4
B240 SP194 30c + 10c rose vio, brn & yel 2.75 4.25
B241 SP194 40c + 10c multi 2.75 4.25
Nos. B237-B241 (5) 6.32 9.44

Type Similar to 1952, Dated "1955", and

Federal Institute of Technology, Zurich — SP197

Views: 10c+10c, Saane river. 20c+10c, Lake of Aegeri. 30c+10c, Grappelen Lake. 40c+10c, Lake of Bienne.

1955, June 1 **Engr.** ***Perf. 11½***

B242 SP197 5c + 5c gray 25 *40*

Photo.

B243 SP192 10c + 10c dp grn 32 34
B244 SP192 20c + 10c rose brn 32 38
B245 SP192 30c + 10c brn 2.25 *3.50*
B246 SP192 40c + 10c dp bl 2.25 *3.50*
Nos. B242-B246 (5) 5.39 *8.12*

The surtax aided mountain dwellers.

No. B242 was issued to commemorate the centenary of the Federal Institute of Technology in Zurich.

Charles Pictet de Rochemont
SP198

Peacock Butterfly
SP199

Insects: 20c+10c, Great Horntail. 30c+10c, Yellow Bear moth. 40c+10c, Apollo butterfly.

1955, Dec. 1 **Engr.** **Unwmk.**

B247 SP198 5c + 5c brn car 12 14
a. Booklet pane of 4

Photo.

Insects in Natural Colors.

B248 SP199 10c + 10c yel grn 18 16
a. Booklet pane of 4
B249 SP199 20c + 10c red 25 18
Booklet pane of 4
B250 SP199 30c + 10c dk ocher 1.90 *3.25*
B251 SP199 40c + 10c ultra 1.90 *3.25*
Nos. B247-B251 (5) 4.35 *6.98*

Types Similar to 1952, Dated "1956", and

"Woman's Work" — SP200

Designs: 10c+10c, Rhone at St. Maurice. 20c+10c, Katzensee. 30c+10c, Rhine at Trin. 40c+10c, Lake Wallen.

1956, June 1 **Engr.** ***Perf. 11½***

B252 SP200 5c + 5c turq bl 20 *30*

Photo.

B253 SP192 10c + 10c grn 32 30
B254 SP192 20c + 10c brn car 32 30
B255 SP192 30c + 10c brn 2.50 *3.25*
B256 SP192 40c + 10c ultra 2.50 *3.25*
Nos. B252-B256 (5) 5.84 *7.40*

The surtax was for the National Day Collection, the National Library and Academy of Arts and Letters. No. B252 was issued in honor of Swiss women.

Carlo Maderno
SP201

Burnet Moth
SP202

Insects: 20c+10c, Purple Emperor. 30c+10c, Blue ground beetle. 40c+10c, Cabbage butterfly.

1956, Dec. 1 Engr. *Perf. 11½*

B257 SP201 5c + 5c brn car 14 10
a. Booklet pane of 4

Photo.

Granite Paper.

B258 SP202 10c + 10c grn, dk grn & car rose 20 14
a. Bklt. pane of 4
B259 SP202 20c + 10c multi 28 20
a. Bklt. pane of 4
B260 SP202 30c + 10c yel & dp bl 1.40 *2.75*
B261 SP202 40c + 10c lt ultra, pale yel & sep 1.50 *2.75*
Nos. B257-B261 (5) 3.52 *5.94*

Red Cross and Swiss Emblems SP203

"Charity" SP204

Engraved and Photogravure

1957, June 1 Unwmk. *Perf. 11½*

B262 SP203 5c + 5c gray & red 30 *35*

Photo.

Granite Paper

Cross in Deep Carmine

B263 SP204 10c + 10c brt grn & gray 30 28
B264 SP204 20c + 10c red & bl gray 40 28
B265 SP204 30c + 10c brn & vio gray 2.00 *3.00*
B266 SP204 40c + 10c brt bl & bis 2.00 *3.00*
Nos. B262-B266 (5) 5.00 *6.91*

The surtax went to the Red Cross for the needs of the sick and to combat cancer.

Leonhard Euler SP205

Clouded Yellow SP206

Insects: 20c+10c, Magpie moth. 30c+10c, Rose Chafer. 40c+10c, Red Underwing.

1957, Nov. 30 Engr. *Perf. 11½*

B267 SP205 5c + 5c brn car 15 12
a. Bklt. pane of 4

Photo.

Granite Paper.

B268 SP206 10c + 10c multi 15 12
a. Bklt. pane of 4
B269 SP206 20c + 10c lil rose, blk & yel 30 12
a. Bklt. pane of 4
B270 SP206 30c + 10c rose brn, ind & brt grn 2.25 *2.50*
B271 SP206 40c + 10c multi 2.25 *2.25*
Nos. B267-B271 (5) 5.10 *5.11*

Catalogue values for unused stamps in this section, from this point to the end of the section, are for Never Hinged items.

Mother and Child SP207

Fluorite SP208

Designs: 20c+10c, Ammonite. 30c+10c, Garnet. 40c+10c, Rock Crystal.

Perf. 11½

1958, May 31 Unwmk. Engr.

B272 SP207 5c + 5c brn car 30 *30*

Photo.

Granite Paper

B273 SP208 10c + 10c multi 45 *40*
B274 SP208 20c + 10c blk, red & ol bis 45 *40*
B275 SP208 30c + 10c blk, dl yel & mag 2.50 *3.00*
B276 SP208 40c + 10c blk, chlky bl & sl bl 2.50 *2.75*
Nos. B272-B276 (5) 6.20 *6.85*

The surtax was for needy mothers.

See Nos. B283-B286, B292-B295, B304-B307.

Albrecht von Haller SP209

Pansy SP210

Flowers: 20c+10c, China aster. 30c+ 10c, Morning glory. 40c+10c, Christmas rose.

1958, Dec. 1 Engr. *Perf. 11½*

B277 SP209 5c + 5c brn car 15 12
a. Bklt. pane of 4

Photo.

Granite Paper

B278 SP210 10c + 10c grn, yel & brn 16 12
a. Bklt. pane of 4
B279 SP210 20c + 10c multi 22 12
a. Bklt. pane of 4
B280 SP210 30c + 10c multi 1.40 *2.75*
B281 SP210 40c + 10c dk bl, yel & grn 1.40 *2.50*
Nos. B277-B281 (5) 3.33 *5.61*

See Nos. B287-B291.

Mineral Type of 1958 and

Globe and Swiss Flags — SP211

Designs: 10c+10c, Agate. 20c+10c, Tourmaline. 30c+10c, Amethyst. 40c+ 10c, Fossil salamander (andrias).

1959, June 1 Engr. *Perf. 11½*

B282 SP211 5c + 5c dl grn & red 18 *35*

Photo.

Granite Paper

B283 SP208 10c + 10c gray, yel grn & ver 35 28
B284 SP208 20c + 10c blk, lil rose & bl grn 35 28
B285 SP208 30c + 10c blk, lt brn & vio 1.65 *2.50*
B286 SP208 40c + 10c blk, bl & gray 1.65 *2.50*
Nos. B282-B286 (5) 4.18 *5.91*

Types of 1958

Designs: 5c+5c, Karl Hilty. 10c+10c, Marigold. 20c+10c, Poppy. 30c+10c, Nasturtium. 50c+10c, Sweet pea.

1959, Dec. 1 Engr. *Perf. 11½*

B287 SP209 5c +5c brn car 12 14
a. Bklt. pane of 4

Photo.

Granite Paper

B288 SP210 10c + 10c dk grn, grn & yel 22 16
a. Bklt. pane of 4
B289 SP210 20c + 10c mag, red & grn 45 22
a. Bklt. pane of 4
B290 SP210 30c + 10c multi 1.75 *2.75*
B291 SP210 50c + 10c multi 1.90 *2.75*
Nos. B287-B291 (5) 4.44 *6.02*

Mineral Type of 1958 and

Owl, T-Square and Hammer — SP212

Designs: 5c+5c, Smoky quartz. 10c+ 10c, Feldspar. 20c+10c, Gryphaea, fossil. 30c+10c, Azurite.

1960, June 1 Photo. *Perf. 11½*

Granite Paper

B292 SP208 5c + 5c blk, bl & ocher 45 30
B293 SP208 10c + 10c blk, yel grn & pink 70 24
B294 SP208 20c + 10c blk, lil rose & yel 70 24
B295 SP208 30c + 10c multi 2.75 2.25

Engr.

B296 SP212 50c + 10c bl & gold 2.75 2.25
Nos. B292-B296 (5) 7.35 5.28

Souvenir Sheet

Imperf

Typo.

B297 Sheet of four 47.50 21.00

No. B297 contains four 50c+10c stamps of type SP212 in gold and blue with slate and red marginal inscription. Size: 84x 75mm. Sold for 3fr.

Alexandre Calame SP213

Dandelion SP214

Flowers: 20c+10c, Phlox. 30c+10c, Larkspur. 50c+10c, Thorn apple.

1960, Dec. 1 Engr. Unwmk.

B298 SP213 5c + 5c grnsh bl 22 12
a. Bklt. pane of 4

Photo.

Granite Paper

B299 SP214 10c + 10c grn, yel & gray 30 12
a. Bklt. pane of 4
B300 SP214 20c + 10c mag, grn & gray 45 12
a. Bklt. pane of 4
B301 SP214 30c + 10c org brn, grn & bl 2.50 2.00
B302 SP214 50c + 10c ultra & grn 2.50 2.25
Nos. B298-B302 (5) 5.97 4.61

See Nos. B308-B312, B329-B333, B339-B343.

Mineral Type of 1958 and

Book of History with Symbols of Time and Eternity — SP215

Designs: 10c+10c, Fluorite. 20c+10c, Petrified fish. 30c+10c, Lazulite. 50c+ 10c, Petrified fern.

1961, June 1 Engr. *Perf. 11½*

B303 SP215 5c + 5c lt bl 15 *35*

Photo.

Granite Paper

B304 SP208 10c + 10c gray, grn & pink 30 28
B305 SP208 20c + 10c gray & car rose 30 28
B306 SP208 30c + 10c gray, org & grnsh bl 1.50 2.50
B307 SP208 50c + 10c gray, bl & bis 1.50 2.50
Nos. B303-B307 (5) 3.75 *5.91*

Types of 1960

Designs: 5c+5c, Jonas Furrer. 10c+ 10c, Sunflower. 20c+10c, Lily of the valley. 30c+10c, Iris. 50c+10c, Silverweed.

1961, Dec. 1 Engr. *Perf. 11½*

B308 SP213 5c + 5c dk bl 10 12
a. Bklt. pane of 4

Photo.

Granite Paper

B309 SP214 10c + 10c grn, yel & org 12 14
a. Bklt. pane of 4
B310 SP214 20c + 10c dk red, grn & gray 22 14
a. Bklt. pane of 4
B311 SP214 30c + 10c multi 1.00 1.40
B312 SP214 50c + 10c dk bl, yel & grn 1.10 1.40
Nos. B308-B312 (5) 2.54 3.20

Jean Jacques Rousseau SP216

Half-Thaler, Obwalden, 1732 SP217

Coins: 20c+10c, Ducat, Schwyz, ca. 1653. 30c+10c, "Steer Head" Batzen, Uri, 1659. 50c+10c, Nidwalden Batzen.

Perf. 11½

1962, June 1 Unwmk. Engr.

B313 SP216 5c + 5c dk bl 70 10

Photo.

Granite Paper

B314 SP217 10c + 10c grn & stl bl 20 *22*
B315 SP217 20c + 10c car rose & yel 20 *22*
B316 SP217 30c + 10c org & sl bl 1.10 1.00
B317 SP217 50c + 10c ultra & vio bl 1.10 1.00
Nos. B313-B317 (5) 3.30 *2.54*

Apple Blossoms SP218

Mother and Child SP219

Designs: 10c+10c, Boy chasing duck. 30c+10c, Girl and sunflowers. 50c+10c, Forsythia. 1fr+20c, Mother and child, facing right.

1962, Dec. 1 *Perf. 11½*

Granite Paper

B318 SP218 5c + 5c bl gray, pink, grn & yel 8 10
a. Bklt. pane of 4
B319 SP218 10c + 10c grn, pink & dk grn 12 10
a. Booklet pane of 4
B320 SP219 20c + 10c org red, brn, grn & pink 32 15
B321 SP218 30c + 10c org, red & yel 1.10 *1.40*
B322 SP218 50c + 10c dp bl, yel & brn 1.25 *1.50*
Nos. B318-B322 (5) 2.87 *3.25*

Souvenir Sheet

Imperf

B323 SP219 1fr + 20c multi, sheet of two 5.00 3.75

Issued to commemorate the 50th anniversary of the Pro Juventute (Youth Aid) Foundation. No. B323 has pale yellow margin showing toys and blue inscription. Size: 81x62mm. Sold for 3fr.

Anna Heer, M.D.
SP220

Bandage Roll
SP221

Designs: 20c+10c, Gift parcel. 30c+10c, Plasma bottles. 50c+10c, Red Cross armband.

1963, June 1 Engr. *Perf. 11 ½*

B324 SP220 5c + 5c dk bl 12 12

Photo.

Granite Paper

Cross in Red

B325 SP221 10c + 10c lt & dk grn & gray 15 15
B326 SP221 20c + 10c rose, gray & blk 24 15
B327 SP221 30c + 10c multi 85 1.00
B328 SP221 50c + 10c bl, gray & blk 1.00 1.00
Nos. B324-B328 (5) 2.36 2.42

Types of 1960

Designs: 5c+5c, Portrait of a Boy by Albert Anker. 10c+10c, Daisy. 20c+10c, Geranium. 30c+10c, Cornflower. 50c+10c, Carnation.

1963, Nov. 30 Engr. *Perf. 11 ½*

B329 SP213 5c + 5c bl 20 28
a. Bklt. pane of 4 3.00 *5.75*

Photo.

B330 SP214 10c + 10c grn, gray & yel 24 42
a. Bklt. pane of 4 4.00 *4.00*
B331 SP214 20c + 10c multi 80 42
a. Bklt. pane of 4 4.00 *7.00*
B332 SP214 30c + 10c multi 1.40 1.25
B333 SP214 50c + 10c ultra, lil rose & grn 1.40 1.25
Nos. B329-B333 (5) 4.04 3.62

Nos. B329-B331 were printed on two kinds of paper: I. Fluorescent, with violet fibers. II. Non-fluorescent, the 10c+10c and 20c+10c with mixed red and blue fibers. Nos. B332-B333 exist only on violet-fibered, fluorescent paper. The booklet panes, Nos. B329a, B330a and B331a, exist only on non-fluorescent paper.

Johann Georg Bodmer
SP222

Copper Coin, Zurich
SP223

Coins: 20c+10c, Doppeldicken, Basel. 30c+10c, Silver taler, Geneva. 50c+10c, Gold half florin, Bern.

Violet Fibers, Fluorescent Paper

1964, June 1 Engr. *Perf. 11 ½*

B334 SP222 5c + 5c bl 8 8

Photo.

B335 SP223 10c + 10c grn, bis & blk 9 8
B336 SP223 20c + 10c rose car, gray & blk 24 22
B337 SP223 30c + 10c org, gray & blk 45 40

Granite Paper, Red and Blue Fibers

B338 SP223 50c + 10c ultra, yel & brn 65 55
Nos. B334-B338 (5) 1.51 1.33

Fluorescent Paper

Paper of Nos. B334-B425, B427 and B429 is fluorescent and has violet fibers.

Nos. B426, B428 and all semipostals from No. B430 onward are fluorescent but lack violet fibers, unless otherwise noted.

Types of 1960

Designs: 5c+5c, Portrait of a Girl by Albert Anker. 10c+10c, Daffodil. 20c+ 10c, Rose. 30c+10c, Clover. 50c+10c, Water lily.

1964, Dec. 1 Engr. *Perf. 11 ½*

B339 SP213 5c + 5c grnsh bl 8 8
a. Bklt. pane of 4

Photo.

B340 SP214 10c + 10c dp grn, yel & org 9 8
a. Bklt. pane of 4
B341 SP214 20c + 10c dp car, rose & grn 15 15
a. Bklt. pane of 4
B342 SP214 30c + 10c brn, lil & grn 60 55
B343 SP214 50c + 10c multi 45 45
Nos. B339-B343 (5) 1.37 1.31

Type of Regular Issue, 1965
Souvenir Sheet

Designs: 10c, 20r Seated Helvetia. 20c, 40r Seated Helvetia.

1965, Mar. 8 Photo. *Imperf.*

Granite Paper, Nonfluorescent

B344 A153 Sheet of two 1.50 1.00
a. 10c grn, pale org & blk 75 50
b. 20c dk red, yel grn & blk 75 50

Issued to publicize the National Postage Stamp Exhibition, NABRA, Bern, Aug. 27-Sept. 5, 1965. No. B344 contains two stamps, light blue margin and dark red inscription. Size: 94x61½mm. Sold for 3fr, the net proceeds were used to cover expenses of the exhibition and to promote philately.

Father Theodosius Florentini
SP224

The Temptation of Christ
SP225

Ceiling Paintings from Church of St. Martin at Zillis, 12th century: 10c+10c, Symbol of evil (goose with fishtail). 20c+ 10c, Magi on horseback. 30c+10c, Fishermen on Sea of Galilee.

Perf. 11 ½

1965, June 1 Unwmk. Engr.

B345 SP224 5c + 5c bl 8 8

Photo.

B346 SP225 10c + 10c ol grn, ocher & bl 8 8
B347 SP225 20c + 10c dk brn, red & buff 15 12
B348 SP225 30c + 10c dk brn, sep & bl 40 32
B349 SP225 50c + 10c vio bl, bl & brn 40 32
Nos. B345-B349 (5) 1.11 92

See Nos. B355-B359, B365-B369.

Hedgehogs — SP226

Designs: 10c+10c, Alpine marmots. 20c+10c, Red deer. 30c+10c, European badgers. 50c+10c, Varying hares.

1965, Dec. 1 Photo. *Perf. 11 ½*

B350 SP226 5c + 5c multi 8 6
a. Bklt. pane of 4
B351 SP226 10c + 10c multi 12 6
a. Bklt. pane of 4
B352 SP226 20c + 10c multi 20 10
a. Bklt. pane of 4
B353 SP226 30c + 10c multi 28 22
B354 SP226 50c + 10c multi 42 32
Nos. B350-B354 (5) 1.10 76

See Nos. B360-B364.

Types of 1965

Designs: 5c+5c, Heinrich Federer (1866-1928), writer. 10c+10c, Joseph's dream. 20c+10c, Joseph on his way. 30c+10c, Virgin and Child fleeing to Egypt. 50c+ 10c, Angel leading the way. Nos. B356-B359 from ceiling paintings, Church of St. Martin at Zillis.

1966, June 1 Engr. *Perf. 11 ½*

B355 SP224 5c + 5c dp bl 8 8

Photo.

B356 SP225 10c + 10c multi 8 8
B357 SP225 20c + 10c multi 16 12
B358 SP225 30c + 10c multi 24 20
B359 SP225 50c + 10c multi 45 32
Nos. B355-B359 (5) 1.01 80

Animal Type of 1965

Designs: 5c+5c, Ermine. 10c+10c, Red squirrel. 20c+10c, Red fox. 30c+ 10c, Hares. 50c+10c, Two chamois.

1966, Dec. 1 Photo. *Perf. 11 ½*

Animals in Natural Colors

B360 SP226 5c + 5c grnsh bl 8 8
a. Bklt. pane of 4
B361 SP226 10c + 10c emer 12 8
a. Bklt. pane of 4
B362 SP226 20c + 10c ver 20 12
a. Bklt. pane of 4
B363 SP226 30c + 10c brt lem 25 20
B364 SP226 50c + 10c ultra 40 30
Nos. B360-B364 (5) 1.05 78

Types of 1965

Designs: 5c+5c, Dr. Theodor Kocher. 10c+10c, Annunciation to the Shepherds. 20c+10c, Jesus and the Samaritan Woman at the Well. 30c+10c, Adoration of the Magi. 50c+10c St. Joseph. (Ceiling paintings, St. Martin at Zillis).

Perf. 11 ½

1967, June 1 Unwmk. Engr.

B365 SP224 5c + 5c bl 8 8

Photo.

B366 SP225 10c + 10c multi 12 8
B367 SP225 20c + 10c multi 20 12
B368 SP225 30c + 10c multi 25 20
B369 SP225 50c + 10c multi 40 30
Nos. B365-B369 (5) 1.05 78

Roe Deer
SP227

Hunter, Month of May
SP228

Designs: 20c+10c, Pine marten. 30c+10c, Alpine ibex. 50c+20c, Otter.

1967, Dec. 1 Photo. *Perf. 11 ½*

Animals in Natural Colors

B370 SP227 10c + 10c yel grn 8 8
a. Bklt. pane of 4
B371 SP227 20c + 10c dp car 20 12
a. Bklt. pane of 4
B372 SP227 30c + 10c ol bis 28 18
a. Bklt. pane of 4
B373 SP227 50c + 20c ultra 50 35

1968, May 30 Photo. *Perf. 11 ½*

Designs from Rose Window, Lausanne Cathedral: 20c+10c, Leo. 30c+10c, Libra. 50c+20c, Pisces.

B374 SP228 10c + 10c multi 8 6
B375 SP228 20c + 10c multi 20 10
B376 SP228 30c + 10c multi 28 15
B377 SP228 50c + 20c multi 50 35

Capercaillie
SP229

St. Francis
SP230

Birds: 20c+10c, Bullfinch. 30c+10c, Woodchat shrike. 50c+20c, Firecrest.

1968, Nov. 28 Photo. *Perf. 11 ½*

Birds in Natural Colors

B378 SP229 10c + 10c dl yel 8 6
a. Bklt. pane of 4
B379 SP229 20c + 10c ol grn 20 10
a. Bklt. pane of 4
B380 SP229 30c + 10c lil rose 28 15
a. Bklt. pane of 4
B381 SP229 50c + 20c dp vio 50 35

See Nos. B386-B389.

1969, May 29 Photo. *Perf. 11 ½*

Designs: 10c+10c, St. Francis Preaching to the Birds, Königsfelden Convent Church. 20c+10c, Israelites Drinking from Spring of Moses, Berne Cathedral. 30c+10c, St. Christopher, Laufelfinger Church (now Basel Museum). 50c+20c, Virgin and Child, Chapel at Grapplang (now National Museum).

B382 SP230 10c + 10c multi 10 8
B383 SP230 20c + 10c multi 20 18
B384 SP230 30c + 10c multi 25 20
B385 SP230 50c + 20c multi 45 35

Bird Type of 1968

Birds: 10c+10c, European goldfinch. 20c+10c, Golden oriole. 30c+10c, Wall creeper. 50c+20c, Eurasian jay.

1969, Dec. 1 Photo. *Perf. 11 ½*

Birds in Natural Colors

B386 SP229 10c + 10c gray 8 6
a. Bklt. pane of 4
B387 SP229 20c + 10c grn 15 12
a. Bklt. pane of 4
B388 SP229 30c + 10c plum 24 16
a. Bklt. pane of 4
B389 SP229 50c + 20c ultra 55 40

Sailor, by Gian Casty, Gellert Schoolhouse, Basel
SP231

Blue Titmice
SP232

Contemporary Stained Glass Windows: 20c+10c, Abstract composition, by Celestino Piatti. 30c+10c, Bull (Assyrian god Marduk), by Hans Stocker. 50c+20c, Man and Woman, by Max Hunziker and Karl Ganz.

1970, May 29 Photo. *Perf. 11 ½*

B390 SP231 10c + 10c multi 8 6
B391 SP231 20c + 10c multi 16 12
B392 SP231 30c + 10c multi 28 20
B393 SP231 50c + 20c multi 52 38

See Nos. B398-B401.

1970, Dec. 1 Photo. *Perf. 11 ½*

Birds: 20c+10c, Hoopoe. 30c+10c, Greater spotted woodpecker. 50c+20c, Crested grebes.

Birds in Natural Colors

B394 SP232 10c + 10c org 12 8
a. Booklet pane of 4
B395 SP232 20c + 10c emer 18 12
a. Booklet pane of 4
B396 SP232 30c + 10c brt rose 24 15
a. Booklet pane of 4
B397 SP232 50c + 20c bl 55 55

See Nos. B402-B405.

Art Type of 1970

Contemporary Stained Glass Windows: 10c+10c, "Composition," by Jean-François Comment. 20c+10c, Cock, by Jean Prahin. 30c+10c, Fox, by Kurt Volk. 50c+20c, "Composition," by Bernard Schorderet.

1971, May 27 Photo. *Perf. 11 ½*

B398 SP231 10c + 10c multi 12 9
B399 SP231 20c + 10c multi 18 14
B400 SP231 30c + 10c multi 22 18
B401 SP231 50c + 20c multi 52 40

Bird Type of 1970

Birds: 10c+10c, European redstarts. 20c+10c, White-spotted bluethroats. 30c+ 10c, Peregrine falcon. 40c+20c, Mallards.

1971, Dec. 1

B402 SP232 10c + 10c multi 7 7
a. Booklet pane of 4

B403 SP232 20c + 10c multi 14 12
a. Booklet pane of 4
B404 SP232 30c + 10c multi 22 12
a. Booklet pane of 4
B405 SP232 40c + 20c multi 70 70

Harpoon Heads, Late Stone Age
SP233

McGredy's Sunset
SP234

Archaeological Treasures: 20c+10c, Bronze hydria, Hallstadt period. 30c+10c, Gold bust of Emperor Marcus Aurelius, Roman period. 40c+20c, Horseback rider (decorative disk), early Middle Ages.

1972, June 1
B406 SP233 10c + 10c multi 9 8
B407 SP233 20c + 10c multi 12 10
B408 SP233 30c + 10c multi 15 12
B409 SP233 40c + 20c multi 60 50

1972, Dec. 1 Photo. *Perf. 11½*

Famous Roses: 20c+10c, Miracle. 30c+10c, Papa Meilland. 40c+20c, Madame Dimitriu.

B410 SP234 10c + 10c multi 16 14
a. Booklet pane of 4
B411 SP234 20c + 10c multi 20 14
a. Booklet pane of 4
B412 SP234 30c + 10c multi 18 14
a. Booklet pane of 4
B413 SP234 40c + 20c multi 90 85

Rauraric (Gallic) Jug
SP235

Chestnut
SP236

Archeologic Finds: 30c+10c, Bronze head of a Gaul. 40c+20c, Alemannic dress fasteners (fish), 6th century. 60c+20c, Gold bowl, 6th century B.C.

1973, May 29 Photo. *Perf. 11½*
B414 SP235 15c + 5c multi 12 12
B415 SP235 30c + 10c multi 16 15
B416 SP235 40c + 20c multi 55 50
B417 SP235 60c + 20c multi 75 70

See Nos. B422-B425.

1973, Nov. 29 Photo. *Perf. 11½*

Fruits of the Forest: 30c+10c, Sweet cherries. 40c+20c, Blackberries. 60c+20c, Blueberries.

B418 SP236 15c + 5c multi 12 9
a. Booklet pane of 4
B419 SP236 30c + 10c multi 12 9
a. Booklet pane of 4
B420 SP236 40c + 20c multi 55 50
a. Booklet pane of 4
B421 SP236 60c + 20c multi 70 65

Archaeological Type of 1973

Archaeological Finds: 15c+5c, Polychrome glass bowl. 30c+10c, Bull's head. 40c+20c, Gold fibula. 60c+20c, Ceramic bird.

1974, May 30 Photo. *Perf. 11½*
B422 SP235 15c + 5c multi 12 10
B423 SP235 30c + 10c multi 28 25
B424 SP235 40c + 20c multi 52 48
B425 SP235 60c + 20c multi 65 60

Laurel
SP237

Gold Fibula, 6th Century
SP238

Designs: 30c+20c, Belladonna. 50c+20c, Laburnum. 60c+25c, Mistletoe.

1974, Nov. 29 Photo. *Perf. 11½*
B426 SP237 15c + 10c multi 12 10
a. Booklet pane of 4
B427 SP237 30c + 20c multi 18 12
a. Booklet pane of 4
B428 SP237 50c + 20c multi 52 48
B429 SP237 60c + 25c multi 70 65

1975, May 30 Photo. *Perf. 11½*

Archaeological Treasures: 30c+20c, Bronze head of Bacchus, 2nd century. 50c+20c, Bronze daggers, 1800-1600 B.C. 60c+25c, Colored glass bottle, 1st century.

B430 SP238 15c + 10c multi 16 14
B431 SP238 30c + 20c multi 24 20
B432 SP238 50c + 20c multi 60 50
B433 SP238 60c + 25c multi 65 55

Mail Bucket
SP239

Hepatica
SP240

Forest Plants: 30c+20c, Mountain ash berries. 50c+20c, Yellow nettle. 60c+25c, Sycamore maple.

1975, Nov. 27 Photo. *Perf. 11½*
B434 SP239 10c + 5c multi 12 9
a. Booklet pane of 4
B435 SP240 15c + 10c multi 16 14
a. Booklet pane of 4
B436 SP240 30c + 20c multi 28 22
a. Booklet pane of 4
B437 SP240 50c + 20c multi 60 50
B438 SP240 60c + 25c multi 65 55
Nos. B434-B438 (5) 1.81 1.50

See Nos. B443-B446.

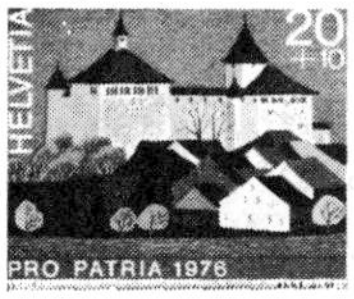

SP241

1976, May 28 Photo. *Perf. 11½*
B439 SP241 20c + 10 Kyburg 28 22
B440 SP241 40c + 20 Grandson 35 30
B441 SP241 40c + 20 Murten 42 30
B442 SP241 80c + 40 Bellinzona 1.10 85

See Nos. B447-B450, B455-B459, B463-B466.

Plant Type of 1975

Medicinal Forest Plants: 20c+10c, Barberry. No. B444, Black elder. No. B445, Linden. 80+40c, Pulmonaria.

1976, Nov. 29 Photo. *Perf. 11½*
B443 SP240 20c + 10c multi 20 15
a. Booklet pane of 4
B444 SP240 40c + 20c lil & multi 32 15
a. Booklet pane of 4
B445 SP240 40c + 20c terra cotta & multi 32 15
B446 SP240 80c + 40c multi 1.10 80

Castle Type of 1976

1977, May 26 Photo. *Perf. 11½*
B447 SP241 20c + 10c Aigle 20 18
B448 SP241 40c + 20c Pratteln 30 28
B449 SP241 70c + 30c Sargans 85 70
B450 SP241 80c + 40c Hallwil 90 80

Wild Rose
SP242

Communal Arms
SP243

Designs: Roses.

1977, Nov. 28 Photo. *Perf. 11½*
B451 SP242 20c + 10c multi 15 12
a. Booklet pane of 4
B452 SP242 40c + 20c multi 32 12
a. Booklet pane of 4
B453 SP242 70c + 30c multi 70 55
B454 SP242 80c + 40c multi 90 70

See Nos. B492-B496

Castle Type of 1976

1978, May 26 Photo. *Perf. 11½*
B455 SP241 20c + 10c Hagenwil 16 15
B456 SP241 40c + 20c Burgdorf 30 30
B457 SP241 70c + 30c Tarasp 60 60
B458 SP241 80c + 40c Chillon 80 80

1978, Nov. 28 Photo. *Perf. 11½*
B459 SP243 20c + 10c Aarburg 20 18
a. Booklet pane of 4
B460 SP243 40c + 20c Gruyeres 35 18
a. Booklet pane of 4
B461 SP243 70c + 30c Castasegna 60 55
B462 SP243 80c + 40c Wangen an der Aare 75 70

See Nos. B467-B470, B475-B478, B484-B487.

Castle Type of 1976

1979, May 25 Photo. *Perf. 11½*
B463 SP241 20c + 10c Oron 20 18
B464 SP241 40c + 20c Spiez 30 25
B465 SP241 70c + 30c Porrentruy 75 65
B466 SP241 80c + 40c Rapperswil 90 75

Arms Type of 1978

1979, Nov. 28 Photo. *Perf. 11*
B467 SP243 20c + 10c Cadro 15 10
a. Bklt. pane of 4
B468 SP243 40c + 20c Rute 32 18
a. Bklt. pane of 4
B469 SP243 70c + 30c Schwamendingen 60 55
B470 SP243 80c + 40c Perroy 90 80

Masons' and Carpenters' Sign — SP244

1980, May 29 Photo. *Perf. 11½*
B471 SP244 20c + 10c shown 20 20
B472 SP244 40c + 20c Barber 30 20
B473 SP244 70c + 30c Hat maker 75 75
B474 SP244 80c + 40c Baker 90 90

Arms Type of 1978

1980, Nov. 26 Photo. *Perf. 11½*
B475 SP243 20c + 10c Cortaillod 15 12
B476 SP243 40c + 20c Sierre 35 20
B477 SP243 70c + 30c Scuol 75 70
B478 SP243 80c + 40c Wolfenschiessen 85 75

Icarus in Flight — SP245

1981, Mar. 9 Photo.
B479 SP245 2fr + 1fr multi 2.50 2.50

Swissair, 50th Anniversary. Surtax was for Pro Aero Foundation Issued in sheet of 8.

Post Office Sign, Aarburg, 1685 — SP246

Post Office Signs (c. 1849).

1981, May 4 Photo.
B480 SP246 20c + 10c shown 30 30
B481 SP246 40c + 20c Fribourg 60 50
B482 SP246 70c + 30c Gordola 1.10 1.10
B483 SP246 80c + 40c Splugen 1.25 1.25

Arms Type of 1978

1981, Nov. 26 Photo. *Perf. 11½*
B484 SP243 20c + 10c Uffikon 32 18
B485 SP243 40c + 20c Torre 60 32
B486 SP243 70c + 30c Benken 1.00 60
B487 SP243 80c + 40c Preverenges 1.10 75

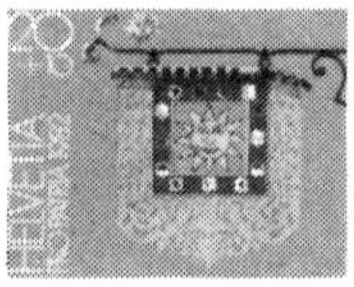

Sonne Inn Sign, Willisau
SP247

1982, May 27 Photo. *Perf. 11½*
B488 SP247 20c + 10c shown 30 18
B489 SP247 40c + 20c A L'Onde, St. Saphorin 55 32
B490 SP247 70c + 30c Three Kings, Rheinfelden 95 55
B491 SP247 80c + 40c Krone, Winterthur 1.25 70

See Nos. B497-B500.

Rose Type of 1977

Designs: 10c+10c, Letter balance. 20c+10c, La Belle Portugaise. 40c+20c, Hugh Dickson. 70c+30c, Mermaid. 80c+40c, Madame Caroline.

1982, Nov. 25 Photo.
B492 SP242 10c + 10c multi 25 14
B493 SP242 20c + 10c multi 40 14
B494 SP242 40c + 20c multi 75 28
B495 SP242 70c + 30c multi 1.25 80
B496 SP242 80c + 40c multi 1.40 1.10
Nos. B492-B496 (5) 4.05 2.46

Inn Sign Type of 1982

1983, May 26 Photo.
B497 SP247 20c + 10c Lion Inn, Heimiswil, 1669 40 28
B498 SP247 40c + 20c Cross Hotel, Sachseln, 1489 75 48
B499 SP247 70c + 30c Tankard Inn, 1830 1.25 80
B500 SP247 80c + 40c Au Cavalier Inn, Vaud 1.40 1.00

Antique Toys — SP248

1983, Nov. 24
B501 SP248 20c + 10c Kitchen stove, 1850 35 18
B502 SP248 40c + 20c Rocking horse, 1826 70 35
B503 SP248 70c + 30c Doll, 1870 1.10 55
B504 SP248 80c + 40c Steam locomotive, 1900 1.40 70

Switzerland stamps can be mounted in Scott's annual Switzerland Supplement.

Ceramic Tiled Stoves — SP249

Children's Stories — SP250

1984, May 24 Photo. *Perf. 11 ½*
B505 SP249 35c + 15c 1566 55 38
B506 SP249 50c + 20c 1646 70 50
B507 SP249 70c + 30c 1768 1.00 70
B508 SP249 80c + 40c 18th cent. 1.25 90

1984, Nov. 26 Photo.
B509 SP250 35c + 15c Heidi 60 38
B510 SP250 50c + 20c Pinocchio 75 50
B511 SP250 70c + 30c Pippi Longstocking 1.10 70
B512 SP260 80c + 40c Max and Moritz 1.40 90

Musical Museum Exhibits SP251

1985, May 28 Photo. *Perf. 11 ½*
B513 SP251 25c + 10c Music box, 1895 30 10
B514 SP251 35c + 15c Rattle box, 18th cent. 50 14
B515 SP251 50c + 20c Emmenthal necked zither, 1828 70 20
B516 SP251 70c + 30c Drum, 1571 1.00 28
B517 SP251 80c + 40c Diatonic accordion, 20th cent. 1.25 32
Nos. B513-B517 (5) 3.75 1.04

Surtax for Swiss cultural programs.

Hansel and Gretel SP252

Fairy tales by Jakob (1785-1863) and Wilhelm (1786-1859) Grimm.

1985, Nov. 26 Photo.
B518 SP252 35c + 15c shown 52 15
B519 SP252 50c + 20c Snow White 75 20
B520 SP252 80c + 40c Little Red Riding Hood 1.25 35
B521 SP252 90c + 40c Cinderella 1.40 38

Surtax for Pro Juventute Foundation and youth welfare orgs.

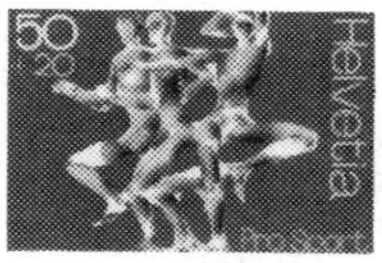
Man, Vitality and Movement SP253

1986, Feb. 11 Photo. *Perf. 12*
B522 SP253 50c + 20c multi 90 24

Surtax for Natl. Sports Federation and cultural programs.

Paintings in Natl. Museums SP254

Swiss art: 35c+15c, Bridge in the Sun, 1907, by Giovanni Giacometti (1868-1933). 50c+20c, The Violet Hat, 1907, by Cuno Amiet (1868-1961). 80c+40c, After the Funeral, 1905, by Max Buri (1868-1915). 90c+40c, Still Life, 1914, by Felix Valloton (1865-1925).

1986, Apr. 22 Photo. *Perf. 11 ½*
B523 SP254 35c + 15c multi 52 18
B524 SP254 50c + 20c multi 72 24
B525 SP254 80c + 40c multi 1.25 42
B526 SP254 90c + 40c multi 1.40 45

Surtax for National Day Collection and monuments preservation, social and cultural organizations.

Children's Toys — SP255

1986, Nov. 25 Photo.
B527 SP255 35c + 15c Teddy bear 62 22
B528 SP255 50c + 20c Top 88 30
B529 SP255 80c + 40c Steamroller 1.50 50
B530 SP255 90c + 40c Doll 1.60 55

Surtax was for youth welfare organizations and the Pro Juventute Foundation.

Antique Furniture SP256

Designs: 35c+15c, Saane Valley wall cabinet, 1764, Vieux Pays d'Enhaut Museum, Chateau d'Oex. 50c+20c, Raised chest, 16th cent., Rhaetian Museum, Chur. 80c+40c, Ticino canton cradle, 1782, Valmaggia Museum, Cevio. 90c+40c, Appenzell region wardrobe, 1698, St. Gallen Historical Museum.

1987, May 26 Photo.
B531 SP256 35c + 15c multi 55 24
B532 SP256 50c + 20c multi 80 35
B533 SP256 80c + 40c multi 1.40 58
B534 SP256 90c + 40c multi 1.50 60

Surtax for Red Cross and patriotic funds.

No. 786 Surcharged with Clasped Hands and "7.9.87" in Red

Photo. & Engr.

1987, Sept. 7 *Perf. 13 ½x13*
B535 A349 50c + 50c multi 1.30 45

Surtaxed to benefit flood victims.

Christmas SP257

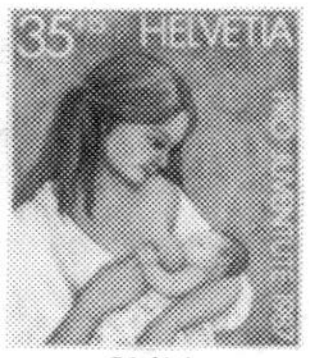
Child Development SP258

1987, Nov. 24 Photo. *Perf. 11 ½*
B536 SP257 25c +10c shown 48 16
B537 SP258 35c +15c shown 68 22
B538 SP258 50c +20c Boy, building blocks 95 32
B539 SP258 80c +40c Boy, girl in sandbox 1.65 55
B540 SP258 90c +40c Father, child 1.80 60
Nos. B536-B540 (5) 5.56 1.85

Surtax for national youth welfare projects and the Pro Juventute Foundation.

Junkers JU-52, 1939, and the Matterhorn SP259

1988, Mar. 8 Photo.
B541 SP259 140c +60c multi 2.65 88

Pro Aero Foundation, Zurich, 50th Anniv. Issued in sheets of 8.

700 Years of Art and Culture — SP260

Minnesingers.

1988, May 24 Photo.
B542 SP260 35c +15c Count Rudolf of Neuchatel 60 25
B543 SP260 50c +20c Rudolf von Rotenburg 85 35
B544 SP260 80c +40c Master Johannes Hadlaub 1.50 58
B545 SP260 90c +40c The Hardegger 1.65 65

Child Development SP261

1988, Nov. 25 *Perf. 11 ½*
B546 SP261 35c +15c Reading 68 22
B547 SP261 50c +20c Music 95 32
B548 SP261 80c +40c Math 1.65 55
B549 SP261 90c +40c Art 1.75 58

Surtax for natl. youth welfare projects and the Pro Juventute Foundation.

700 Years of Art and Culture SP262

Illuminations in Zurich Central, Bern Burgher and Lucerne Central libraries: No. B550, King Friedrich II presenting Bern municipal charter, 1218, *Bendicht Tschachtlan Chronicle,* 1470. No. B551, Capt. Adrian von Bubenberg and troops passing through Murten town gate, 1476, *Bern Chronicle,* by Diebold Schilling, 1483. No. B552, Official messenger of Schwyz before the Council of Zurich, c. 1440, *Gerold Edlibach Chronicle,* 1485. No. B553, Schilling presenting manuscript to the mayor and councilmen in the council chamber, Lucerne, c. 1500, *Diebold Schilling's Lucerne Chronicle,* 1513.

1989, May 23
B550 SP262 35c +15c multi 65 22
B551 SP262 50c +20c multi 90 30
B552 SP262 80c +40c multi 1.55 52
B553 SP262 90c +40c multi 1.70 55

Surtax to benefit women's and cultural organizations.

AIR POST STAMPS

Nos. 134 and 139 Overprinted in Carmine

1919-20 Wmk. 183 *Perf. 11 ½*
Granite Paper
C1 A25 30c yel brn & pale grn ('20) 110.00 *900.00*
C2 A25 50c dp grn & pale grn 40.00 100.00

Counterfeits of overprint and fraudulent cancellations exist.

Airplane AP1

Pilot at Controls of Airplane AP2

Biplane against Sky — AP3

Allegorical Figure of Flight — AP4

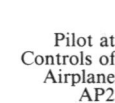

Perf. 11½, 12 and Compound

1923-25 **Typo.**

C3 AP1 15c brn red & ap grn 1.25 3.00
C4 AP1 20c grn & lt grn ('25) 32 *2.50*
C5 AP1 25c dk bl & bl 4.00 *9.00*
C6 AP2 35c brn & buff 10.00 *27.50*
C7 AP2 40c vio & gray vio 10.00 *27.50*
C8 AP3 45c red & ind 1.00 *3.00*
C9 AP3 50c blk & red 8.00 9.50

Perf. 11½

C10 AP4 65c gray bl & dp bl ('24) 2.00 *7.25*
C11 AP4 75c org & brn red ('24) 10.00 *30.00*
C12 AP4 1fr vio & dp vio ('24) 30.00 18.00
Nos. C3-C12 (10) 76.57 *137.25*

1933-37 **With Grilled Gum**

C4a AP1 20c grn & lt grn ('37) 40 32
C5a AP1 25c dk bl & bl ('34) 5.00 *45.00*
C8a AP3 45c red & ind ('37) 2.75 *47.50*
C9a AP3 50c gray grn & scar ('35) 1.00 1.50
C10a AP4 65c gray bl & dp bl ('37) 1.40 *7.25*
C11a AP4 75c org & brn red ('36) 30.00 *165.00*
C12a AP4 1fr vio & dp vio 2.75 2.25
Nos. C4a-C12a (7) 43.30 *268.82*

See Grilled Gum note after No. 145.

Allegory of Air Mail — AP5

Bird Carrying Letter AP6

1929-30

Granite Paper

C13 AP5 35c red brn, bis & cl 20.00 22.50
C14 AP5 40c dl grn, yel grn & bl 45.00 55.00
C15 AP6 2fr blk brn & red brn, *gray* ('30) 75.00 37.50

1933-35 **With Grilled Gum**

C13a AP5 35c red brn, bis & cl 8.00 *30.00*
C14a AP5 40c dk grn, yel grn & bl 35.00 35.00
C15a AP6 2fr blk brn & red brn ('35) 8.50 5.25

Front View of Airplane AP7

1932, Feb. 2

Granite Paper

C16 AP7 15c dp grn & lt grn 50 *95*
C17 AP7 20c dk red & buff 75 *1.10*
C18 AP7 90c dp bl & gray 8.50 *22.50*

Intl. Disarmament Conf., Geneva, Feb. 1932.

Stamps of 1923-32 Surcharged with New Values and Bars in Black or Red

1935-38

C19 AP1 10c on 15c brn red & ap grn 5.25 *25.00*
C20 AP7 10c on 15c dp grn & lt grn 55 42
a. Inverted surcharge *6,250. 11,000.*
C21 AP7 10c on 20c dk red & buff ('36) 85 *1.65*
C22 AP4 10c on 65c gray bl & dp bl ('38) 20 18
C23 AP7 30c on 90c dp bl & gray ('36) 4.00 *10.00*
C24 AP7 40c on 20c dk red & buff ('37) 4.75 *11.50*
C25 AP7 40c on 90c dp bl & gray ('36) (R) 4.00 *10.50*
a. Vermilion surch. 85.00 *725.00*
Nos. C19-C25 (7) 19.60 *59.25*

Stamp similar to No. C22, but from souvenir sheet, is listed as No. 242a.

Type of Air Post Stamp of 1923 Surcharged in Black

1938

«PRO AERO»

75 75

1938, May 22 Wmk. 183 *Perf. 11½*

C26 AP3 75c on 50c gray & scar 5.25

"Pro Aero" Meeting, May 21-22.

No. C26 was not sold to the public in the ordinary way, but affixed to air mail letters by postal officials. It was not regularly obtainable unused.

Jungfrau — AP8

View of Valais — AP9

Lake Geneva — AP10

Alpstein — AP11

View of Ticino — AP12

Lake Lucerne — AP13

The Engadine AP14

Churfirsten AP15

Perf. 11½

1941, May 1 **Unwmk.** **Engr.**

Tinted Granite Paper

C27 AP8 30c ultra 60 6
C28 AP9 40c gray blk 60 6
C29 AP10 50c sl grn 60 10
C30 AP11 60c chestnut 1.10 10
C31 AP12 70c plum 1.25 18
C32 AP13 1fr Prus grn 2.00 25
C33 AP14 2fr car lake 7.75 1.10
C34 AP15 5fr dp bl 25.00 4.75
Nos. C27-C34 (8) 38.90 6.60

See Nos. C43-C44.

•PRO AERO•

Type of 1941 Overprinted in Red

20·V·1941

1941, May 12

C35 AP13 1fr bl grn 6.00 *16.00*

Issued to commemorate special flights between Payerne and Buochs, May 28, 1941.

Parliament Buildings, Bern AP16

1943, July 13 **Photo.**

C36 AP16 1fr cop red, buff & blk 2.00 8.00

Issued to commemorate the 30th anniversary of the first Alpine flight, by Oscar Bider, July 13, 1913.

DH-3 Haefeli AP17

Fokker AP18

Lockheed-Orion — AP19

1944, Sept. 1

C37 AP17 10c gray brn & pale grn 12 10
C38 AP18 20c rose car & buff 20 15
C39 AP19 30c ultra & pale gray 38 *45*

25th anniv. of the 1st regular air route in Switzerland.

Douglas DC-3 AP20

1944, Sept. 20

Granite Paper

C40 AP20 1.50fr multi 7.00 *14.00*

Issued to commemorate the 25th anniversary of the Zurich-Geneva air route.

Zoegling Training Glider AP21

1946, May 1

Granite Paper

C41 AP21 1.50fr hn brn & gray 15.00 *20.00*

Valid for use only on two special flights.

Douglas DC-4 Linking Geneva and New York AP22

1947, Mar. 17

Granite Paper

C42 AP22 2.50fr bl gray, dk bl & red 8.00 *13.00*

Valid only on the Geneva-New York flight of May 2, 1947.

Types of 1941

1948, Oct. 1 **Engr.**

Tinted Granite Paper

C43 AP8 30c dk sl bl 5.00 *5.00*
C44 AP9 40c dp ultra 27.50 1.75

Glider in Symbolized Aerodynamic Buoyancy — AP23

1949, Apr. 11 **Engr. & Typo.**

C45 AP23 1.50fr dk vio & yel 16.00 *22.50*

Valid only on special flights, April 27-29, 1949. Proceeds were for the advancement of national aviation.

Catalogue values for unused stamps in this section, from this point to the end of the section, are for Never Hinged items.

Glider and Jets AP24

1963, June 1 **Photo.** ***Perf. 11½***

Granite Paper

C46 AP24 2fr multi 3.75 3.25

Issued to commemorate the 50th anniversary of the first Alpine flight by Oscar Bider, July 13, 1913. Valid for postage on July 13, 1963, on flights from Bern to Locarno and Langenbruck to Bern. Proceeds went to the Pro Aero Foundation.

AIR POST SEMI-POSTAL STAMP

Catalogue values for unused stamps in this section are for Never Hinged items.

Boeing 747 — SPAP1

1972, Feb. 17 **Photo.** ***Perf. 12½***

Violet Fibers, Fluorescent Paper

CB1 SPAP1 2fr + 1fr dp bl, red & gray 2.50 2.75

50th anniv. of 1st Swiss Intl. flight, Zurich to Nuremberg, and 25th anniv. of 1st Swissair trans-Atlantic flight, Zurich to NYC. Valid on all mail but obligatory on special flights from Geneva to NYC in May, and from Geneva to Nuremberg in June, 1972.

Surtax was for Pro Aero Foundation and the training of young airmen, and for the Swiss Air Rescue Service.

POSTAGE DUE STAMPS

D1

D2

Wmk. Cross in Oval (182)

1878-80 Typo. *Perf. 11½*

J1	D1	1c ultra	1.00	60
J2	D2	2c ultra	1.00	60
J3	D2	3c ultra	9.00	9.00
J4	D2	5c ultra	11.00	5.00
J5	D2	10c ultra	160.00	5.00
J6	D2	20c ultra	190.00	3.00
J7	D2	50c ultra	350.00	15.00
J8	D2	100c ultra	450.00	6.00
J9	D2	500c ultra	400.00	10.00

A 5c in design D1 exists.

1882-83

Granite Paper

J10	D2	10c ultra	140.00	25.00
J11	D2	20c ultra	325.00	40.00
J12	D2	50c ultra	2,000.	400.00
J13	D2	100c ultra	625.00	275.00
J14	D2	500c ultra	*12,000.*	190.00

1883-84

Numerals in Red

J15	D2	5c bl grn	30.00	25.00
J16	D2	10c bl grn	50.00	10.00
J17	D2	20c bl grn	100.00	10.00
J18	D2	50c bl grn	110.00	35.00
J19	D2	100c bl grn	325.00	275.00
J20	D2	500c bl grn	600.00	125.00

1884-92

Numerals in Red

J21	D2	1c ol grn	35	25
J22	D2	3c ol grn	3.75	3.25
J23	D2	5c ol grn	1.50	1.25
a.		5c yel grn	17.50	5.00
J24	D2	10c ol grn	3.50	35
a.		10c yel grn	22.50	3.00
J25	D2	20c ol grn	7.00	55
a.		20c yel grn	110.00	4.00
J26	D2	50c ol grn	10.50	1.75
a.		50c yel grn	225.00	65.00
J27	D2	100c ol grn	13.00	1.40
a.		100c yel grn	250.00	65.00
J28	D2	500c ol grn	110.00	10.00
a.		500c yel grn	475.00	10.00

1908-09 Wmk. 183

Numerals in Red

J29	D2	1c ol grn	25	50
J30	D2	5c ol grn	80	80
J31	D2	10c ol grn	2.50	1.75
J32	D2	20c ol grn	5.00	5.00
J33	D2	50c ol grn	25.00	80
J34	D2	100c ol grn	45.00	1.00
		Nos. J29-J34 (6)	78.55	9.85

D3

1910 *Perf. 11½, 12*

Numerals in Red

J35	D3	1c bl grn	5	18
J36	D3	3c bl grn	10	18
J37	D3	5c bl grn	10	18
J38	D3	10c bl grn	50	18
J39	D3	15c bl grn	40	50
J40	D3	20c bl grn	13.00	6
J41	D3	25c bl grn	1.00	30
J42	D3	30c bl grn	1.00	25
J43	D3	50c bl grn	1.75	50
		Nos. J35-J43 (9)	17.90	2.33

No. J36 Surcharged

1916

J44	D3	5c on 3c bl grn & red	10	35

Nos. J35-J36, J43 Surcharged

1924

J45	D3	10c on 1c	32	*6.00*
J46	D3	10c on 3c	28	*1.25*
J47	D3	20c on 50c	95	1.00

D4

D5

Wmk. 183

1924-26 Typo. *Perf. 11½*

Granite Paper

J48	D4	5c ol grn & red	48	25
J49	D4	10c ol grn & red	1.90	10
J50	D4	15c ol grn & red ('26)	1.65	30
J51	D4	20c ol grn & red	4.50	10
J52	D4	25c ol grn & red	1.90	30
J53	D4	30c ol grn & red	1.90	65
J54	D4	40c ol grn & red ('26)	2.75	30
J55	D4	50c ol grn & red	2.75	60
		Nos. J48-J55 (8)	17.83	2.60

1924

With Grilled Gum

J48a	D4	5c ol grn & red	75	60
J49a	D4	10c ol grn & red	3.00	1.00
J51a	D4	20c ol grn & red	5.25	1.10
J52a	D4	25c ol grn & red	8.50	*60.00*

See Grilled Gum note after No. 145.

Nos. J50, J53 and J55 Surcharged with New Value in Black

1937

J56	D4	5c on 15c	1.00	*3.75*
J57	D4	10c on 30c	1.00	*1.75*
J58	D4	20c on 50c	2.00	*5.00*
J59	D4	40c on 50c	3.25	*12.50*

1938 Engr. Unwmk.

J60	D5	5c scarlet	35	12
J61	D5	10c scarlet	50	12
J62	D5	15c scarlet	70	2.00
J63	D5	20c scarlet	90	12
J64	D5	25c scarlet	1.10	1.75
J65	D5	30c scarlet	1.25	80
J66	D5	40c scarlet	1.50	15
J67	D5	50c scarlet	1.75	1.75
		Nos. J60-J67 (8)	8.05	6.81

1938

With Grilled Gum

J60a	D5	5c scarlet	60	75
J61a	D5	10c scarlet	50	75
J62a	D5	15c scarlet	1.25	1.40
J63a	D5	20c scarlet	1.10	20
J64a	D5	25c scarlet	1.25	*4.25*
J65a	D5	30c scarlet	1.25	75
J66a	D5	40c scarlet	1.65	75
J67a	D5	50c scarlet	2.25	1.40
		Nos. J60a-J67a (8)	9.85	*10.25*

See Grilled Gum note after No. 145.

OFFICIAL STAMPS

For General Use

With Perforated Cross.

In 1935 the government authorized the use of regular postage issues perforated with a nine-hole cross for all government departments. Twenty-seven different stamps were so perforated. These were succeeded in 1938 by the cross overprints.

Values for canceled Official Stamps are for those canceled to order. Postally used stamps sell for considerably less. This note does not apply to Nos. 1O1-1O16, 2O27-2O30, 3O23-3O26.

Regular Issues of 1908-36 Overprinted in Black

1938 Unwmk. *Perf. 11½*

O1	A53	3c olive	15	20
O2	A54	5c bl grn	15	18
O3	A55	10c red vio	85	30
O4	A56	15c orange	30	1.25
O5	A68	20c red	45	30
O6	A58	25c brown	45	*85*
O7	A59	30c ultra	60	*75*
O8	A60	35c yel grn	60	*75*
O9	A61	40c gray	60	*75*

Wmk. 183

With Grilled Gum

O10	A25	50c dp grn & pale grn	75	*1.25*
O11	A25	60c brn org & buff	1.40	*1.75*
O12	A25	70c vio & buff	1.40	*2.50*
O13	A25	80c sl & buff	1.75	*2.50*
O14	A36	90c grn & red, *grn*	1.90	*2.75*
O15	A25	1fr dp cl & pale grn	1.90	*3.00*
O16	A36	1.20fr brn rose & red, *rose*	2.00	*3.50*
O17	A36	1.50fr bl & red, *bl*	2.75	*3.75*
O18	A36	2fr gray blk & red, *gray*	3.25	*5.00*
		Nos. O1-O18 (18)	21.25	*31.33*

Nos. O14, O16, O17 and O18 are on surface-colored paper.

1938 Unwmk. With Grilled Gum

O1a	A53	3c olive	5.00	38
O2a	A54	5c bl grn	1.40	24
O3a	A55	10c red vio	1.90	38
O4a	A56	15c orange	3.25	1.10
O5a	A68	20c red	1.90	42
O6a	A58	25c brown	67.50	6.00
O7a	A59	30c ultra	2.75	90
O8a	A60	35c yel grn	2.25	1.50
O9a	A61	40c gray	2.50	90
		Nos. O1a-O9a (9)	88.45	11.82

See Grilled Gum note after No. 145.

Postage Stamps of 1936-42 Overprinted in Black *Officiel*

1942-45 Unwmk. *Perf. 11½*

O19	A53	3c olive	40	*90*
O20	A54	5c bl grn	40	15
O21	A55	10c dk red brn	52	35
O21A	A55	10c org brn ('45)	10	15
O22	A56	15c orange	60	*1.50*
O23	A68	20c red	65	15
O24	A58	25c lt brn	80	*1.75*
O25	A59	30c ultra	1.00	60
O26	A60	35c yel grn	1.25	*1.75*
O27	A61	40c gray	1.40	60
O28	A77	50c dp pur, *grnsh*	3.50	2.50
O29	A78	60c red brn, *buff*	4.00	2.50
O30	A79	70c rose vio, *pale lil*	4.00	*5.75*
O31	A80	80c blk, *pale gray*	1.25	1.10
O32	A81	90c dk red, *pale rose*	1.40	1.50
O33	A82	1fr dk grn, *grnsh*	1.50	1.50
O34	A83	1.20fr red vio, *pale gray*	1.75	2.00
O35	A84	1.50fr dk bl, *buff*	2.00	*3.00*
O36	A85	2fr mar, *pale rose*	3.00	*3.50*
		Nos. O19-O36 (19)	29.52	*31.25*

Same Overprint on Nos. 329 to 339

1950 Unwmk. *Perf. 12x11½*

O37	A118	5c orange	70	60
O38	A119	10c yel grn	1.10	60
O39	A120	15c aqua	5.75	7.75
O40	A121	20c brn car	2.75	60
O41	A122	25c red	4.00	5.50
O42	A123	30c olive	3.50	2.50
O43	A124	35c red brn	4.75	5.50
O44	A125	40c dp bl	5.00	2.50
O45	A126	50c sl gray	6.25	3.50
O46	A127	60c bl grn	8.00	4.00
O47	A128	70c purple	19.00	13.00
		Nos. O37-O47 (11)	60.80	46.05

FOR THE WAR BOARD OF TRADE

Regular Issues of 1908-18 Overprinted **Industrielle Kriegs-wirtschaft**

1918 Wmk. 183 *Perf. 11½, 12*

1O1	A26	3c brn org	75.00	*125.00*
1O2	A26	5c green	6.50	*20.00*
1O3	A26	7½c gray (I)	225.00	*325.00*
a.		7½c sl (II)	550.00	*600.00*
1O4	A28	10c red, *buff*	10.50	*22.50*
1O5	A28	15c vio, *buff*	10.50	*27.50*
1O6	A25	20c red & yel	90.00	*180.00*
1O7	A25	25c dp bl	90.00	*180.00*
1O8	A25	30c yel brn & pale grn	90.00	*180.00*
		Nos. 1O1-1O8 (8)	597.50	*1,060.*

Counterfeits exist.

Overprinted **Industrielle Kriegs-wirtschaft**

1918

1O9	A26	3c brn org	5.50	*25.00*
1O10	A26	5c green	17.50	*50.00*
1O11	A26	7½c gray	7.00	*20.00*
1O12	A28	10c red, *buff*	70.00	75.00
1O13	A28	15c vio, *buff*	110.00	
1O14	A25	20c red & yel	12.50	*50.00*
1O15	A25	25c dp bl	12.50	*50.00*
1O16	A25	30c yel brn & pale grn	20.00	*75.00*
		Nos. 1O9-1O16 (8)	255.00	

No. 1O13 was never placed in use.
Fraudulent cancellations are found on Nos. 1O1-1O16.

FOR THE LEAGUE OF NATIONS

Regular Issues Overprinted **SOCIÉTÉ DES NATIONS**

On 1908-30 Issues

1922-31 Wmk. 183 *Perf. 11½, 12*

2O1	A26	2½c ol, *buff* ('28)	165.00	18
2O2	A26	3c ultra, *buff* ('30)	275.00	6.00
2O3	A26	5c org, *buff*	140.00	2.75
2O4	A26	5c gray vio, *buff* ('26)	200.00	2.50
2O5	A26	5c red vio, *buff* ('27)	100.00	1.75
2O6	A26	5c dk grn, *buff* ('31)	275.00	11.00
2O7	A26	7½c dp grn, *buff* ('28)	175.00	25
2O8	A28	10c grn, *buff*	72.50	35
2O9	A28	10c bl grn, *buff* ('28)	140.00	50
2O10	A28	10c vio, *buff* ('31)	200.00	1.50
2O11	A28	15c brn red, *buff* ('28)	140.00	50
2O12	A28	20c red vio, *buff*	175.00	5.00
2O13	A28	20c car, *buff* ('26)	100.00	1.40
2O14	A28	25c ver, *buff*	125.00	5.75
2O15	A28	25c car, *buff*	125.00	70
2O16	A28	25c brn, *buff* ('27)	140.00	12.50
2O17	A28	30c dp bl, *buff* ('25)	125.00	3.50
2O18	A25	30c yel brn & pale grn	275.00	10.00
2O19	A25	35c yel grn & yel	100.00	5.00
2O20	A25	40c dp bl	90.00	1.25
2O21	A25	40c red vio & grn ('28)	85.00	4.25
2O22	A25	50c dp grn & pale grn	100.00	5.00
2O23	A25	60c brn org & buff	24.00	60
2O24	A25	70c vio & buff ('25)	140.00	7.50
2O25	A25	80c sl & buff	100.00	1.10
2O26	A25	1fr dp cl & pale grn	225.00	5.75
2O27	A29	3fr red	225.00	25.00
2O28	A30	5fr ultra	250.00	60.00
2O29	A31	10fr dl vio	375.00	125.00
2O30	A31	10fr gray grn ('30)	350.00	110.00
		Nos. 2O1-2O30 (30)	5,011.	416.58

1930-44 With Grilled Gum

2O2a	A26	3c ultra, *buff* ('33)	650.00	8.50
2O6a	A26	5c dk grn, *buff* ('33)	650.00	17.50
2O17a	A28	30c dp bl,*buff*	*2,500.*	375.00
2O22a	A25	50c dp grn & pale grn ('35)	1.25	75
2O23a	A25	60c brn org & buff ('44)	35.00	*150.00*
2O24a	A25	70c vio & buff ('32)	1.50	2.50
2O25a	A25	80c sl & buff ('42)	4.00	2.25
2O26a	A25	1fr dp cl & pale grn ('42)	110.00	4.00

1925-36

With Grilled Gum

2O31	A36	90c grn & red, *grn* ('36)	125.00	2.50
a.		Ordinary gum ('24)	125.00	6.00
2O32	A36	1.20fr brn rose & red, *rose* ('36)	2.50	4.00
a.		Ordinary gum	125.00	3.50
b.		Invtd. ovpt.		*3,750.*
2O33	A36	1.50fr bl & red, *bl* ('35)	2.50	3.00
a.		Ordinary gum	140.00	6.00
2O34	A36	2fr gray blk & red, *gray* ('36)	4.00	4.50
a.		Ordinary gum	140.00	6.00

1928

2O35	A39	5fr blue	335.00	75.00

On 1932 Issue

1932

2O36	A41	5c pck bl	275.00	17.50
2O37	A41	10c orange	275.00	1.40
2O38	A41	20c cerise	275.00	1.00
2O39	A41	30c ultra	275.00	40.00
2O40	A41	60c ol brn	275.00	13.50

Unwmk.

2O41	A42	1fr ol gray & bl	275.00	13.50
		Nos. 2O36-2O41 (6)	1,650.	86.90

On 1934 Issue

1934-35 **Wmk. 183**

2O42	A46	3c olive	375.00	25
2O43	A47	5c emerald	375.00	38
2O44	A49	15c org ('35)	375.00	1.10
2O45	A51	25c brown	375.00	10.00
2O46	A52	30c ultra	375.00	1.25
		Nos. 2O42-2O46 (5)	1,875.	12.98

On 1936 Issue

1937 **Unwmk.**

2O47	A53	3c olive	18	25
2O48	A54	5c bl grn	25	25
2O49	A55	10c red vio	375.00	70
2O50	A56	15c orange	55	45
2O51	A57	20c carmine	350.00	1.50
2O52	A58	25c brown	70	1.00
2O53	A59	30c ultra	70	90
2O54	A60	35c yel grn	70	90
2O55	A61	40c gray	85	1.10
		Nos. 2O47-2O55 (9)	728.93	7.05

1937 **With Grilled Gum**

2O47a	A53	3c olive	325.00	35
2O48a	A54	5c bl grn	325.00	45
2O49a	A55	10c red vio	325.00	5.25
2O50a	A56	15c orange	325.00	50
2O51a	A57	20c carmine	325.00	1.50
2O52a	A58	25c brown	325.00	1.00
2O53a	A59	30c ultra	325.00	1.00
2O54a	A60	35c yel grn	325.00	3.00
2O55a	A61	40c gray	325.00	2.25
		Nos. 2O47a-2O55a (9)	2,925.	15.30

On 1931 Issue

1937 **Wmk. 183**

2O56	A40	3fr org brn	500.00	190.00

On 1938 Issue

1938 **Unwmk.** ***Perf. 11½***

Granite Paper

2O57	A63	20c red & buff	325.00	1.25
2O58	A64	30c bl & lt bl	325.00	2.00
2O59	A65	60c brn & buff	325.00	4.00
2O60	A66	1fr blk & buff	325.00	6.25

Regular Issue of 1938 Overprinted in Black or Red — SERVICE DE LA SOCIÉTÉ DES NATIONS

Granite Paper

2O61	A63	20c red & buff	275.00	1.65
2O62	A64	30c bl & lt bl	275.00	3.25
2O63	A65	60c brn & buff	275.00	5.50
2O64	A66	1fr blk & buff (R)	275.00	11.50

Regular Issue of 1938 Overprinted in Black — SOCIÉTÉ DES NATIONS

1939

2O65	A69	3fr brn car, *buff*	3.00	*10.00*
2O66	A70	5fr sl bl, *buff*	5.50	*12.50*
2O67	A71	10fr grn, *buff*	10.00	*35.00*

Same Overprint in Black on Regular Issues of 1939-42

1942-43

2O68	A55	10c dk red brn	225.00	85
2O68A	A55	10c org brn ('43)	60	*85*
2O69	A68	20c red	75	*85*

Stamps of 1936-42 Overprinted in Black — COURRIER DE LA SOCIÉTÉ DES NATIONS

1944

2O70	A53	3c olive	18	25
2O71	A54	5c bl grn	18	25
2O72	A55	10c org brn	35	38
2O73	A56	15c orange	35	40
2O74	A68	20c red	52	60
2O75	A58	25c lt brn	52	65
2O76	A59	30c ultra	75	90
2O77	A60	35c yel grn	90	90
2O78	A61	40c gray	90	*1.25*

Nos. 2O73-2O75 and 2O78 exist with grilled gum. Value each $2,000 unused, $2,250 used.

Stamps of 1941 Overprinted in Black — COURRIER DE LA SOCIÉTÉ DES NATIONS

2O79	A77	50c dp pur, *grnsh*	1.50	*1.75*
2O80	A78	60c red brn, *buff*	1.50	*2.25*
2O81	A79	70c rose vio, *pale lil*	1.90	*2.50*
2O82	A80	80c blk, *pale gray*	1.90	*2.25*
2O83	A81	90c dk red, *pale rose*	1.90	*2.25*
2O84	A82	1fr dk grn, *grnsh*	2.00	*2.50*
2O85	A83	1.20fr red vio, *pale gray*	2.25	*3.00*
2O86	A84	1.50fr dk bl, *buff*	2.25	*3.50*
2O87	A85	2fr mar, *pale rose*	4.00	*4.50*

Stamps of 1942 Overprinted in Black — COURRIER DE LA SOCIÉTÉ DES NATIONS

Unwmk. ***Perf. 11½***

2O88	A69	3fr brn car, *cr*	6.75	*10.00*
2O89	A70	5fr sl bl, *cr*	9.25	*14.00*
2O90	A71	10fr grn, *cr*	21.00	*32.50*
		Nos. 2O70-2O90 (21)	60.85	*86.58*

FOR THE INTERNATIONAL LABOR BUREAU

Regular Issues Overprinted — S.d.N. Bureau international du Travail

On 1908-30 Issues

1923-30 **Wmk. 183** ***Perf. 11½, 12***

3O1	A26	2½c ol grn, *buff* ('28)	200.00	30
3O2	A26	3c ultra, *buff* ('30)	325.00	75
3O3	A26	5c org, *buff*	125.00	35
3O4	A26	5c red vio, *buff* ('28)	135.00	20
3O5	A26	7½c dp grn, *buff* ('28)	175.00	40
3O6	A28	10c grn, *buff*	80.00	20
3O7	A28	10c bl grn, *buff* ('28)	175.00	1.10
3O8	A28	15c brn red, *buff* ('28)	250.00	1.10
3O9	A28	20c red vio, *buff*	165.00	10.00
3O10	A28	20c car, *buff* ('27)	125.00	4.50
3O11	A28	25c car, *buff*	100.00	1.00
3O12	A28	25c brn, *buff* ('28)	125.00	2.75
3O13	A28	30c dp bl, *buff* ('25)	125.00	75
3O14	A25	30c yel brn & pale grn	300.00	50.00
3O15	A25	35c yel grn & yel	110.00	8.00
3O16	A25	40c dp bl	110.00	1.25
3O17	A25	40c red vio & grn ('28)	135.00	11.00
3O18	A25	50c dp grn & pale grn	90.00	1.50
3O19	A25	60c brn org & buff	1.25	2.25
3O20	A25	70c vio & buff ('24)	150.00	17.50
3O21	A25	80c sl & buff	12.50	1.00
3O22	A25	1fr dp cl & pale grn	150.00	2.25
3O23	A29	3fr red	200.00	30.00
3O24	A30	5fr ultra	250.00	45.00
3O25	A31	10fr dl vio	325.00	150.00
3O26	A31	10fr gray grn ('30)	350.00	140.00
		Nos. 3O1-3O26 (26)	4,288.	483.15

1937-44 **With Grilled Gum**

3O18a	A25	50c dp grn & pale grn ('42)	1.75	1.90
3O20a	A25	70c vio & buff	1.75	2.75
3O21a	A25	80c sl & buff ('44)	25.00	*110.00*
3O22a	A25	1fr dp cl & pale grn ('42)	135.00	3.00

1925-42

With Grilled Gum

3O27	A36	90c grn & red, *grn* ('37)	200.00	7.50
a.		Ordinary gum	125.00	2.00
3O28	A36	1.20fr brn rose & red, *rose* ('42)	11.00	3.25
a.		Ordinary gum	130.00	2.50
3O29	A36	1.50fr bl & red, *bl* ('37)	2.75	2.00
a.		Ordinary gum	130.00	3.00
3O30	A36	2fr gray blk & red, *gray* ('36)	3.75	5.75
a.		Ordinary gum	130.00	15.00

1928

3O31	A39	5fr blue	325.00	75.00

On 1932 Issue

1932

3O32	A41	5c pck bl	225.00	1.00
3O33	A41	10c orange	225.00	90
3O34	A41	20c cerise	225.00	1.25
3O35	A41	30c ultra	225.00	7.00
3O36	A41	60c ol brn	225.00	7.00

Unwmk.

3O37	A42	1fr ol gray & bl	225.00	9.00
		Nos. 3O32-3O37 (6)	1,350.	26.15

On 1936 Issue

1937

3O38	A53	3c olive	20	25
3O39	A54	5c bl grn	20	25
3O40	A55	10c red vio	450.00	1.75
3O41	A56	15c orange	40	50
3O42	A57	20c carmine	400.00	1.25
3O43	A58	25c brown	60	70
3O44	A59	30c ultra	65	80
3O45	A60	35c yel grn	65	1.10
3O46	A61	40c gray	1.00	1.25
		Nos. 3O38-3O46 (9)	853.70	7.85

1937 **With Grilled Gum**

3O38a	A53	3c olive	300.00	60
3O39a	A54	5c bl grn	300.00	40
3O40a	A55	10c red vio	450.00	80
3O41a	A56	15c orange	300.00	70
3O42a	A57	20c carmine	450.00	80
3O43a	A58	25c brown	350.00	1.10
3O44a	A59	30c ultra	350.00	1.10
3O45a	A60	35c yel grn	325.00	1.65
3O46a	A61	40c gray	350.00	1.65
		Nos. 3O38a-3O46a (9)	3,175.	8.80

On 1931 Issue

1937 **Wmk. 183**

3O47	A40	3fr org brn	550.00	190.00

On 1934 Issue

3O48	A46	3c olive	375.00	3.50

On 1938 Issue

1938 **Unwmk.** ***Perf. 11½***

Granite Paper

3O49	A63	20c red & buff	325.00	1.00
3O50	A64	30c bl & lt bl	325.00	2.25
3O51	A65	60c brn & buff	325.00	4.00
3O52	A66	1fr blk & buff	325.00	6.00

Regular Issue of 1938 Overprinted in Black or Red — SERVICE DU BUREAU INTERNATIONAL DU TRAVAIL

3O53	A63	20c red & buff (Bk)	350.00	2.00
3O54	A64	30c bl & lt bl (Bk)	350.00	2.50
3O55	A65	60c brn & buff (Bk)	350.00	5.25
3O56	A66	1fr blk & buff (R)	350.00	6.00

Regular Issue of 1938 Overprinted in Black — S.d.N. Bureau international du Travail

1939

3O57	A69	3fr brn car, *buff*	3.50	6.00
3O58	A70	5fr sl bl, *buff*	6.00	7.25
3O59	A71	10fr grn, *buff*	10.00	15.00

Same Overprint in Black on Regular Issues of 1939-42

1942-43

3O60	A55	10c dk red brn	235.00	70
3O60A	A55	10c org brn ('43)	45	70
3O61	A68	20c red	55	70

Stamps of 1936-42 Overprinted in Black — COURRIER DU BUREAU INTERNATIONAL DU TRAVAIL

1944

3O62	A53	3c olive	20	20
3O63	A54	5c bl grn	20	20
3O64	A55	10c org brn	30	30
3O65	A56	15c orange	55	55
3O66	A68	20c red	75	*80*
3O67	A58	25c lt brn	85	*90*
3O68	A59	30c ultra	1.10	*1.25*
3O69	A60	35c yel grn	1.40	*1.50*
3O70	A61	40c gray	1.65	*1.75*

Stamps of 1941 Overprinted — COURRIER DU BUREAU INTERNATIONAL DU TRAVAIL

3O71	A77	50c dp pur, *grnsh*	2.25	*9.50*
3O72	A78	60c red brn, *buff*	2.25	*7.50*
3O73	A79	70c rose vio, *pale lil*	2.25	*6.00*
3O74	A80	80c blk, *pale gray*	65	*2.00*
3O75	A81	90c dk red, *pale rose*	80	*2.00*
3O76	A82	1fr dk grn, *grnsh*	1.00	*2.00*
3O77	A83	1.20fr red vio, *pale gray*	1.40	*2.00*
3O78	A84	1.50fr dl bl, *buff*	1.65	*2.00*
3O79	A85	2fr mar, *pale rose*	2.25	*2.00*

Stamps of 1942 Overprinted — COURRIER DU BUREAU INTERNATIONAL DU TRAVAIL

3O80	A69	3fr brn car, *cr*	4.00	*3.50*
3O81	A70	5fr sl bl, *cr*	6.50	*5.00*
3O82	A71	10fr grn, *cr*	15.00	*12.50*
		Nos. 3O62-3O82 (21)	47.00	*63.45*

Nos. 329 to 339 Overprinted in Black — BUREAU INTERNATIONAL DU TRAVAIL

1950 **Unwmk.** ***Perf. 12x11½***

3O83	A118	5c orange	1.50	2.00
3O84	A119	10c yel grn	4.50	6.00
3O85	A120	15c aqua	6.25	3.00
3O86	A121	20c brn car	6.50	3.00
3O87	A122	25c red	7.25	3.25
3O88	A123	30c olive	8.00	8.00
3O89	A124	35c red brn	8.50	3.75
3O90	A125	40c dp bl	8.50	3.75
3O91	A126	50c sl gray	10.00	4.00
3O92	A127	60c bl grn	10.00	4.50
3O93	A128	70c purple	19.00	8.00
		Nos. 3O83-3O93 (11)	90.00	49.25

Miners — O1

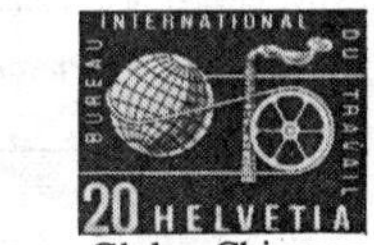

Globe, Chimney and Wheel — O2

1956 **Unwmk.** **Engr.** ***Perf. 11½***

3O94	O1	5c dk gray	6	6
3O95	O1	10c green	12	6
3O96	O2	20c vermilion	1.65	1.25
3O97	O1	40c blue	1.75	1.50
3O98	O2	60c redsh brn	28	25
3O99	O2	2fr rose vio	90	70
		Nos. 3O94-3O99 (6)	4.76	3.82

Catalogue values for unused stamps in this section, from this point to the end of the section, are for Never Hinged items.

1960

3O100	O2	20c car rose	16	16
3O101	O2	30c org ver	24	24
3O102	O1	50c lt ultra	40	40

Type of 1960 Overprinted: "Visite du / Pape Paul VI / Genève / 10 juin 1969"

1969, June 10

Violet Fibers, Fluorescent Paper

3O103	O2	30c org ver	15	15

Visit of Pope Paul VI to the Intl. Labor Bureau to celebrate its 50th anniv., Geneva, June 10.

ILO Headquarters, Geneva — O3

1974, May 30 **Photo.** ***Perf. 11½***

Violet Fibers, Fluorescent Paper

3O104	O3	80c bl, yel & gray	65	65

Inauguration of the new International Labor Organization Building.

Young Man at Lathe, Cogwheels O4

Designs: 60c, Woman at drilling machine. 100c, Surveyor with theodolite and topographical map.

1975, Feb. 13 Photo. Perf. 11½
3O105 O4 30c red brn & dk brn 25 25
3O106 O4 60c ultra & blk 50 50
3O107 O4 100c dk grn & blk 75 75

Professional Education for Youth — O5

1983, Aug. 22 Photo.
3O108 O5 120c multi 1.25 1.25

Job Safety — O6

Design: Welder and lab assistant using protective devices and clothing.

1988, Sept. 13 Photo. Perf. 12x11½
3O109 O6 90c multi 1.00 1.00

FOR THE INTERNATIONAL BUREAU OF EDUCATION

Regular Issues of 1936-42, Overprinted in Black — COURRIER DU BUREAU INTERNATIONAU D'ÉDUCATION

1944 Unwmk. Perf. 11½
4O1 A53 3c olive 50 *75*
4O2 A54 5c bl grn 55 *1.10*
4O3 A55 10c org brn 65 *1.25*
4O4 A56 15c orange 70 *1.50*
4O5 A68 20c red 75 *1.65*
4O6 A58 25c lt brn 1.00 *1.75*
4O7 A59 30c ultra 1.10 *2.25*
4O8 A60 35c yel grn 1.10 *2.25*
4O9 A61 40c gray 1.25 *2.50*

Regular Issue of 1941, Overprinted in Black — COURRIER DU BUREAU INTERNATIONAL D'ÉDUCATION

4O10 A77 50c dp pur, *grnsh* 4.50 *8.25*
4O11 A78 60c red brn, *buff* 4.50 *8.25*
4O12 A79 70c rose vio, *pale lil* 4.50 *8.25*
4O13 A80 80c blk, *pale gray* 75 *1.65*
4O14 A81 90c dk red, *pale rose* 1.00 *1.75*
4O15 A82 1fr dk grn, *grnsh* 1.10 *2.25*
4O16 A83 1.20fr red vio, *pale gray* 1.40 *3.50*
4O17 A84 1.50fr dk bl, *buff* 1.65 *3.50*
4O18 A85 2fr mar, *pale rose* 1.90 *5.75*

Regular Issue of 1942, Overprinted in Black

COURRIER DU BUREAU INTERNATIONAL D'ÉDUCATION

4O19 A69 3fr brn car, *cr* 6.75 *16.00*
4O20 A70 5fr sl bl, *cr* 9.00 *22.50*
4O21 A71 10fr grn, *cr* 17.50 *40.00*
Nos. 4O1-4O21 (21) 62.15 *136.65*

No. 306 Overprinted in Carmine — B I É

1946
4O22 A104 10c rose vio 18 45

Nos. 316 to 321 Overprinted in Black — BUREAU INTERNATIONAL D'ÉDUCATION

1948 Unwmk. Perf. 11½
4O23 A54 5c chocolate 2.25 3.00
4O24 A55 10c green 2.25 3.00
4O25 A68 20c org brn 2.25 3.00
4O26 A113 25c carmine 2.25 3.00
4O27 A59 30c grnsh bl 2.25 3.00
4O28 A61 40c ultra 2.25 3.00
Nos. 4O23-4O28 (6) 13.50 18.00

Same Overprint on Nos. 329 to 339

1950 Perf. 12x11½

Overprint 18mm wide

4O29 A118 5c orange 75 1.65
4O30 A119 10c yel grn 1.00 1.65
4O31 A120 15c aqua 1.50 3.50
4O32 A121 20c brn car 4.00 3.50
4O33 A122 25c red 5.25 5.75
4O34 A123 30c olive 5.25 5.75
4O35 A124 35c red brn 6.00 *7.50*
4O36 A125 40c dp bl 6.00 *7.50*
4O37 A126 50c sl gray 6.25 *7.75*
4O38 A127 60c bl grn 6.25 *9.00*
4O39 A128 70c purple 8.25 *11.00*
Nos. 4O29-4O39 (11) 50.50 *64.55*

Catalogue values for unused stamps in this section, from this point to the end of the section, are for Never Hinged items.

Globe and Books — O1

Designs: 20c, 60c, 2fr, Pestalozzi Monument at Yverdon.

1958 Unwmk. Engr. Perf. 11½
4O40 O1 5c dk gray 6 6
4O41 O1 10c green 10 10
4O42 O1 20c vermilion 2.25 1.65
4O43 O1 40c blue 2.50 1.90
4O44 O1 60c redsh brn 38 30
4O45 O1 2fr rose vio 1.25 85
Nos. 4O40-4O45 (6) 6.54 4.86

1960

Designs: 20c, 30c, Pestalozzi Monument at Yverdon. 50c, Globe and books.

4O46 O1 20c car rose 15 15
4O47 O1 30c org ver 24 24
4O48 O1 50c lt ultra 38 38

FOR THE WORLD HEALTH ORGANIZATION

No. 316-319, 321 Overprinted in Black — ORGANISATION MONDIALE DE LA SANTÉ

1948 Unwmk. Perf. 11½
5O1 A54 5c chocolate 1.50 *3.75*
5O2 A55 10c green 4.00 *3.75*
5O3 A68 20c org brn 4.00 *3.75*
5O4 A113 25c carmine 4.00 *3.75*
5O5 A61 40c ultra 4.00 *3.75*
Nos. 5O1-5O5 (5) 17.50 *18.75*

Regular Issues of 1941, 1942 and 1949 Overprinted in Black — ORGANISATION MONDIALE DE LA SANTÉ

1948-50
5O6 A118 5c orange 65 35
5O7 A119 10c yel grn 70 70
5O8 A120 15c aqua 70 90
5O9 A121 20c brn car 3.50 3.00
5O10 A122 25c red 3.50 3.00
5O11 A123 30c olive 1.00 1.65
5O12 A124 35c red brn 3.50 2.50
5O13 A125 40c dp bl 3.50 2.75
5O14 A126 50c sl gray 3.75 2.75
5O15 A127 60c bl grn 4.00 3.00
5O16 A128 70c purple 5.25 3.50
5O17 A80 80c blk, *pale gray* ('48) 1.00 2.75
5O18 A81 90c dk red, *pale rose* 6.00 6.50
5O19 A82 1fr dk grn, *grnsh* ('48) 1.10 2.75
5O20 A83 1.20fr red vio, *pale gray* 7.50 9.25
5O21 A84 1.50fr dk bl, *buff* 15.00 10.00
5O22 A85 2fr mar, *pale rose* ('48) 2.00 5.00
5O23 A69 3fr brn car, *cr* 35.00 32.50
5O24 A70 5fr sl bl, *cr* ('48) 5.25 10.50
5O25 A71 10fr grn, *cr* 70.00 60.00
Nos. 5O6-5O25 (20) 172.90 163.35

WHO Emblem — O2

1957 Unwmk. Engr. Perf. 11½
5O26 O2 5c gray 6 6
5O27 O2 10c lt grn 8 8
5O28 O2 20c vermilion 1.65 1.65
5O29 O2 40c blue 1.75 1.90
5O30 O2 60c red brn 28 30
5O31 O2 2fr rose lil 90 85
Nos. 5O26-5O31 (6) 4.72 4.84

Catalogue values for unused stamps in this section, from this point to the end of the section, are for Never Hinged items.

1960
5O32 O2 20c car rose 18 18
5O33 O2 30c org ver 25 25
5O34 O2 50c lt ultra 45 45

No. 5O34 Overprinted: "ERADICATION DU PALUDISME"

1962, Apr. 7
5O35 O2 50c lt ultra 28 28

WHO drive to eradicate malaria.

World Health Organization Emblem — O3

1975, Feb. 13 Typo. Perf. 11½
5O36 O3 30c multi 25 25
5O37 O3 60c lt bl & multi 50 50
5O38 O3 90c lil & multi 70 70
5O39 O3 100c org & multi 80 80

WHO Emblem Type of 1975

1986, May 27 Litho. Perf. 12
5O40 O3 140c lt grn, scar & grn 1.50 50

FOR THE INTERNATIONAL ORGANIZATION FOR REFUGEES

Stamps of 1941 and 1949 Overprinted in Black — ORGANISATION INTERNATIONALE POUR LES RÉFUGIÉS

1950 Unwmk. Perf. 12x11½, 11½
6O1 A118 5c orange 12.00 12.50
6O2 A119 10c yel grn 12.00 12.50
6O3 A121 20c brn car 12.00 12.50
6O4 A122 25c red 12.00 12.50
6O5 A125 40c dp bl 12.00 12.50
6O6 A80 80c blk, *pale gray* 12.00 12.50
6O7 A82 1fr dk grn, *grnsh* 12.00 12.50
6O8 A85 2fr mar, *pale rose* 12.00 12.50
Nos. 6O1-6O8 (8) 96.00 100.00

FOR THE UNITED NATIONS EUROPEAN OFFICE

Stamps of 1941-49 Overprinted in Black — NATIONS UNIES OFFICE EUROPÉEN

1950 Unwmk. Perf. 12x11½, 11½
7O1 A118 5c orange 20 *1.00*
7O2 A119 10c yel grn 60 *1.00*
7O3 A120 15c aqua 90 *2.00*
7O4 A121 20c brn car 1.25 *2.50*
7O5 A122 25c red 2.50 *4.50*
7O6 A123 30c olive 2.50 *4.50*
7O7 A124 35c red brn 2.50 *7.50*
7O8 A125 40c dp bl 4.00 *4.50*
7O9 A126 50c sl gray 6.00 *7.00*
7O10 A127 60c bl grn 6.00 *8.00*
7O11 A128 70c purple 7.75 *8.00*
7O12 A80 80c blk, *pale gray* 6.00 *9.00*
7O13 A81 90c dk red, *pale rose* 6.00 *9.00*
7O14 A82 1fr dk grn, *grnsh* 6.00 *9.00*
7O15 A83 1.20fr red vio, *pale gray* 6.75 *12.00*
7O16 A84 1.50fr dk bl, *buff* 6.75 *12.00*
7O17 A85 2fr mar, *pale rose* 6.75 *12.00*
7O18 A69 3fr brn car, *cr* 65.00 *100.00*
7O19 A70 5fr sl bl, *cr* 85.00 *125.00*
7O20 A71 10fr grn, *cr* 130.00 *150.00*
Nos. 7O1-7O20 (20) 352.45 *488.50*

UN Emblem O1

Statue from UN Building, Geneva O2

1955 Engr. Perf. 11½
7O21 O1 5c dk vio brn 6 6
7O22 O1 10c green 10 10
7O23 O2 20c vermilion 5.00 *5.00*
7O24 O1 40c ultra 5.00 *3.00*
7O25 O2 60c red brn 45 35
7O26 O2 2fr lilac 2.00 *1.25*
Nos. 7O21-7O26 (6) 12.61 *9.76*

See Nos. 7O28-7O30.

United Nations Emblem — O3

1955, Oct. 24 Photo.
7O27 O3 40c dk bl & bis 2.00 *4.00*

10th anniv. of the UN, Oct. 24, 1955.

Catalogue values for unused stamps in this section, from this point to the end of the section, are for Never Hinged items.

Types of 1955

1959 Engr. Perf. 11½
7O28 O2 20c car rose 18 12
7O29 O2 30c org ver 20 18
7O30 O1 50c ultra 32 30

Nos. 7O28 and 7O30 Overprinted in Black or Red: "ANNÉE MONDIALE DU RÉFUGIÉ 1959 1960"

1960
7O31 O2 20c car rose 12 15
7O32 O1 50c ultra (R) 25 28

Issued to publicize World Refugee Year, July 1, 1959-June 30, 1960.

Palace of Nations, Geneva
O4

1960 Granite Paper *Perf. 11½*

7O33	O4	5fr blue	2.75 3.25

Types of 1955 Inscribed: "MUSÉE PHILATELIQUE" (O1) or "ONU MUSÉE PHILATELIQUE" (O2)

Engraved; Inscription Typographed

1962, Oct. 24 Unwmk. *Perf. 11½*

7O34	O1	10c grn & red	7 7
7O35	O2	30c org ver & ultra	18 18
7O36	O1	50c ultra & org	22 22
7O37	O2	60c red brn & emer	28 28

Issued to commemorate the opening of the Philatelic Museum, U.N. European Office, Geneva.

UNCSAT Emblem
O5 O6

1963, Feb. 4 Engr. *Perf. 11½*

7O38	O5	50c ultra & car rose	15 15
7O39	O6	2fr lil & emer	1.00 1.10

UN Conf. on the Application of Science and Technology for the Benefit of the Less Developed Areas (UNCSAT), Geneva, Feb. 4-20.

Stamps issued, starting Oct. 4, 1969, by the United Nations in Swiss currency for use by U.N. staff members or the public are listed under "United Nations" in Vol. I of this catalogue and in Scott's U.S. Specialized Catalogue. These stamps are on sale in various U.N. post offices, but are valid only in the U.N. enclave in Geneva. They are not inscribed "Helvetia."

FOR THE WORLD METEOROLOGICAL ORGANIZATION

Sun, Cloud, Rain and Snow — O1

Design: 20c, 60c, 2fr, Direction indicator and anemometer.

1956 Unwmk. Engr. *Perf. 11½*

8O1	O1	5c dk gray	6 6
8O2	O1	10c green	10 6
8O3	O1	20c vermilion	1.75 1.50
8O4	O1	40c blue	2.00 1.75
8O5	O1	60c redsh brn	30 25
8O6	O1	2fr rose vio	90 75
		Nos. 8O1-8O6 (6)	5.11 4.37

Catalogue values for unused stamps in this section, from this point to the end of the section, are for Never Hinged items.

1960

Designs: 20c, 30c, Direction indicator and anemometer. 50c, Sun, cloud, rain and snow.

8O7	O1	20c car rose	20 20
8O8	O1	30c org ver	30 30
8O9	O1	50c lt ultra	40 40

WMO Emblem — O2

1973, Aug. 30 Engr. *Perf. 11½*

Violet Fibers, Fluorescent Paper

8O10	O2	30c carmine	10 25
8O11	O2	40c blue	14 35
8O12	O2	1fr ocher	35 90

Type O12 Inscribed: "OMI / OMM / 1873 / 1973"

1973, Aug. 30 Photo. *Perf. 11½*

Violet Fibers, Fluorescent Paper

8O13	O2	80c dp vio & gold	30 75

Centenary of international meteorological cooperation.

FOR THE INTERNATIONAL BUREAU OF THE UNIVERSAL POSTAL UNION

UPU Monument, Bern — O1

Design: 10c, 20c, 60c, Pegasus.

1957 Unwmk. Engr. *Perf. 11½*

9O1	O1	5c gray	6 6
9O2	O1	10c lt grn	8 6
9O3	O1	20c vermilion	1.65 1.65
9O4	O1	40c blue	1.75 1.90
9O5	O1	60c red brn	24 30
9O6	O1	2fr rose lil	90 85
		Nos. 9O1-9O6 (6)	4.68 4.82

Catalogue values for unused stamps in this section, from this point to the end of the section, are for Never Hinged items.

1960

Designs: 20c, 30c, Pegasus. 50c, UPU Monument, Bern.

9O7	O1	20c car rose	15 15
9O8	O1	30c org ver	25 25
9O9	O1	50c lt ultra	45 45

First Class Mail — O2

Parcel Post — O3

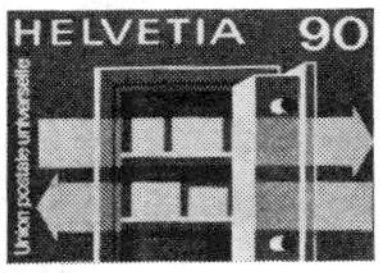

Money Orders — O4

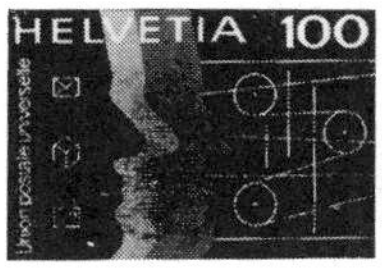

Technical Cooperation O5

1976, Sept. 16 Photo. *Perf. 11½*

Fluorescent Paper

9O10	O2	40c multi	35 35
9O11	O3	80c multi	65 65
9O12	O4	90c multi	75 75
9O13	O5	100c multi	80 80

Intl. Reply and Notication Service — O6

1983, Aug. 22 Photo.

9O14	O6	120c multi	1.25 1.25

Express Mail Service — O7

1989, Mar. 7 Photo. *Perf. 11½*

9O15	O7	140c dark ultra, ver & pale gray	1.75 1.75

FOR THE INTERNATIONAL TELECOMMUNICATION UNION

Catalogue values for unused stamps in this section are for Never Hinged items.

Transmitter — O1

ITU Headquarters, Geneva — O2

Designs: 20c, 60c, 2fr, Antenna.

1958 Unwmk. Engr. *Perf. 11½*

10O1	O1	5c dk gray	6 6
10O2	O1	10c green	10 6
10O3	O1	20c vermilion	2.00 1.65
10O4	O1	40c blue	2.25 1.90
10O5	O1	60c redsh brn	35 30
10O6	O1	2fr rose vio	1.10 90
		Nos. 10O1-10O6 (6)	5.86 4.87

1960

Designs: 20c, 30c, Antenna. 50c, Transmitter.

10O7	O1	20c car rose	18 18
10O8	O1	30c org ver	28 28
10O9	O1	50c lt ultra	45 45

1973, Aug. 30 Photo. *Perf. 11½*

Violet Fibers, Fluorescent Paper

10O10	O2	80c bl & blk	65 65

Sound Waves, ITU Emblem — O3

Airplane, Ocean Liner — O4

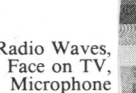

Radio Waves, Face on TV, Microphone O5

Photogravure and Engraved

1976, Feb. 12 *Perf. 11½*

Violet Fibers, Fluorescent Paper

10O11	O3	40c dp org & vio bl	25 25
10O12	O4	90c bl, vio bl & yel	60 60
10O13	O5	1fr grn & multi	90 90

ITU activities: world telecommunications, mobile radio and mass media.

Fiber Optic Communication Links — O6

1988, Sept. 13 Litho. *Perf. 12x11½*

10O14	O6	1.40fr multi	1.40 1.40

FOR THE WORLD INTELLECTUAL PROPERTY ORGANIZATION

Catalogue values for unused stamps in this section are for Never Hinged items.

WIPO Emblem — O1

1982, May 27 Photo. *Perf. 12x11½*

11O1	O1	40c shown	32 32
11O2	O1	80c Headquarters, Geneva	60 60
11O3	O1	100c Industrial symbols	90 90
11O4	O1	120c Educational and artistic symbols	1.10 1.10

1985, Sept. 10 Photo. *Perf. 12x11½*

11O5	O1	50c Mind in action	55 55
		Nos. 11O1-11O5 (5)	3.47 3.47

FRANCHISE STAMPS

These stamps were distributed to many institutions and charitable societies for franking their correspondence.

F1

Control Figures Overprinted in Black

Perf. 11½, 12

1911-21 Typo. Wmk. 183

Blue Granite Paper

S1	F1	2c ol grn & red	15	18
S2	F1	3c ol grn & red	2.50	25
S3	F1	5c ol grn & red	70	10
S4	F1	10c ol grn & red	1.25	10
S5	F1	15c ol grn & red	19.00	1.65
S6	F1	20c ol grn & red	4.25	40
		Nos. S1-S6 (6)	27.85	2.68

Without Control Figures

S1a F1 2c ol grn & red 45 *17.50*
S2a F1 3c ol grn & red 35 *25.00*
S3a F1 5c ol grn & red 3.75 *30.00*
S4a F1 10c ol grn & red 7.50 *50.00*
S5a F1 15c ol grn & red 4.50 *100.00*
S6a F1 20c ol grn & red 8.25 *42.50*
Nos. S1a-S6a (6) 24.80 265.00

Control Figures Overprinted in Black **365**

1926

S7 F1 5c ol grn & red 14.00 3.25
S8 F1 10c ol grn & red 8.75 2.25
S9 F1 20c ol grn & red 13.00 3.50

Control Figures Overprinted in Black **806**

1927

White Granite Paper

S10 F1 5c grn & red 4.25 30
S11 F1 10c grn & red 2.00 20
b. Grilled gum 300.00 *600.00*
S12 F1 20c grn & red 4.00 20

Without Control Figures

S10a F1 5c grn & red 7.50 *100.00*
S11a F1 10c grn & red 22.50 *100.00*
c. Grilled gum 175.00 *500.00*
S12a F1 20c grn & red 25.00 *100.00*

Nurse — F2

Nun — F3

J. H. Dunant — F4

Control Figures Overprinted in Black

1935 *Perf. 11½*

S13 F2 5c turq grn 2.00 *2.50*
b. Grilled gum 5.00 25
S14 F3 10c lt vio 1.10 *2.50*
b. Grilled gum 5.00 10
S15 F4 20c scarlet 2.00 *2.50*
b. Grilled gum 6.50 18

Without Control Figures

S13a F2 5c turq grn 2.00 *2.50*
c. Grilled gum 22.50 1.25
S14a F3 10c lt vio 2.00 *2.50*
c. Grilled gum 22.50 1.25
S15a F4 20c scarlet 1.10 *3.50*
c. Grilled gum 22.50 *2.50*

SYRIA

LOCATION — Asia Minor, bordering on Turkey, Iraq, Lebanon, Israel and the Mediterranean Sea.
GOVT. — Republic
AREA — 71,498 sq. mi.
POP. — 9,840,000 (est. 1983)
CAPITAL — Damascus

Syria was originally part of the Turkish province of Sourya conquered by British and Arab forces in late 1918 and later partitioned. The British assumed control of the Palestine and Transjordan regions; the French were permitted to occupy the sanjaks of Lebanon. Alaouites and Alexandretta; and the remaining territory, including the vilayets of Damascus and Aleppo, was established as an independent Arab kingdom, under which the first Syrian stamps were issued.

A little time given to the study of the arrangement of the Scott Catalogue can make it easier to use effectively.

French forces from Beirut deposed King Faisal in July 1920, and two years of military occupation followed until Syria was mandated to France in July 1922. Syrian autonomy was substituted for the mandate in 1934, but full independence was not again achieved until 1946. In 1958, Syria and Egypt merged to form the United Arab Republic. Syria left this union in 1961, adopting the name Syrian Arab Republic. UAR issues for Syria are listed following Syria's 1919-20 Issues of the Arabian Government.

10 Milliemes = 1 Piaster
40 Paras = 1 Piaster (Arabian Govt.)
100 Centimes = 1 Piaster (1920)

Catalogue values for unused stamps in this country are for Never Hinged items, beginning with Scott 314 in the regular postage section, Scott B13 in the semi-postal section, Scott C124 in the airpost section, Scott CB5 in the airpost semi-postal section, Scott J40 in the postage due section, and all of the items in the UAR sections.

Issued under French Occupation

Stamps of France, 1900-07, Surcharged

T. E. O.
5 MILLIEMES

Perf. 14x13½

1919, Nov. 21 **Unwmk.**

1 A16 1m on 1c gray 82.50 82.50
2 A16 2m on 2c vio brn 225.00 225.00
3 A16 3m on 3c red org 95.00 95.00
4 A20 4m on 15c gray grn 12.50 12.50
5 A22 5m on 5c dp grn 7.50 7.50
6 A22 1p on 10c red 10.00 10.00
7 A22 2p on 25c bl 6.00 6.00
8 A18 5p on 40c red & pale bl 8.00 8.00
9 A18 9p on 50c bis brn & lav 19.00 19.00
10 A18 10p on 1fr cl & ol grn 30.00 30.00
Nos. 1-10 (10) 495.50 495.50

The letters "T.E.O." are the initials of "Territoires Ennemis Occupes." There are two types of the numerals in the surcharges on Nos. 2, 3, 8 and 9.

Stamps of French Offices in Turkey, 1902-03, Surcharged

T. E. O.
2
MILLIEMES

1919

11 A2 1m on 1c gray 18 15
a Inverted surcharge 5.50 5.50
12 A2 2m on 2c vio brn 18 15
a Inverted surcharge 5.50 5.50
13 A2 3m on 3c red org 38 30
14 A3 4m on 15c pale red 18 18
a Inverted surcharge 5.50 5.50
15 A2 5m on 5c grn 18 15

Overprinted **T. E. O.**

16 A5 1p on 25c bl 22 15
a Inverted overprint 5.50 5.50
17 A6 2p on 50c bis brn & lav 50 30
18 A6 4p on 1fr cl & ol grn 55 45
19 A6 8p on 2fr gray vio & yel 2.75 2.00
a "T.E.O." double 15.00 15.00
20 A6 20p on 5fr dk bl & buff 140.00 82.50
Nos. 11-20 (10) 145.12 86.33

On Nos. 17-20 "T.E.O." reads vertically up.

Nos. 1-20 were issued in Beirut and mainly used in Lebanon. Nos. 16-20 were also used in Cilicia.

Stamps of France, 1900-07, Surcharged

O. M. F.
Syrie
1
MILLIEME

1920

21 A16 1m on 1c gray 1.25 1.25
a Inverted surcharge 11.50 11.50
b Double surcharge
22 A16 2m on 2c vio brn 1.50 1.50
a Double surcharge
23 A22 3m on 5c grn 2.75 2.75
a Double surcharge
24 A18 20p on 5fr dk bl & buff 240.00 240.00

The letters "O.M.F." are the initials of "Occupation Militaire Francaise."

Stamps of France, 1900-07, Surcharged in Black or Red

O. M. F.
Syrie
2
MILLIEMES

1920

25 A16 1m on 1c gray 15 15
26 A16 2m on 2c vio brn 30 30
27 A22 3m on 5c grn 22 22
28 A22 5m on 10c red 15 15
a Inverted surcharge
29 A18 20p on 5fr dk bl & buff 30.00 30.00
30 A18 20p on 5fr dk bl & buff (R) 125.00 125.00
Nos. 25-30 (6) 155.82 155.82

Stamps of France, 1900-21, Surcharged in Black or Red:

O. M. F.
Syrie
50
CENTIMES

or

O. M. F.
Syrie
3
PIASTRES

1920-22

31 A16 25c on 1c gray 32 32
32 A16 50c on 2c vio brn 32 32
33 A16 75c on 3c red org 32 32
34 A22 1p on 5c grn (R) 16 16
35 A22 1p on 5c grn 12 12
36 A22 1p on 20c red brn ('21) 6 6
37 A22 1.25p on 25c bl ('22) 32 32
38 A22 1.50p on 30c org ('22) 20 16
39 A22 2p on 10c red 14 14
40 A22 2p on 25c bl (R) 14 14
41 A18 2p on 40c red & pale bl ('21) 25 14
42 A20 2.50p on 50c dl bl ('22) 32 20
a Final "S" of "Piastres" omitted 4.25 4.25
43 A22 3p on 25c bl (R) 25 25
44 A18 3p on 60c vio & ultra ('21) 32 25
45 A20 5p on 15c gray grn 38 38
46 A18 5p on 1fr cl & ol grn ('21) 65 50
47 A18 10p on 40c red & pale bl 50 40
48 A18 10p on 2fr org & pale bl ('21) 1.50 1.00
49 A18 25p on 50c bis brn & lav 65 55
50 A18 25p on 5fr dk bl & buff ('21) 55.00 50.00
51 A18 50p on 1fr cl & ol grn 1.25 1.10
a "PIASRTES" *700.00* *700.00*
52 A18 100p on 5fr dk bl & buff (R) 17.50 16.00
53 A18 100p on 5fr dk bl & buff (Bk) 140.00 125.00
a "PIASRTES" *1,100.* *1,100.*
Nos. 31-53 (23) 220.67 197.83

In first printing, space between "Syrie" and numeral is 2mm. In second printing, 1mm.

Surcharge is found inverted on Nos. 32, 35-38, 42, 44-45. Value, each $2-$3.

Surcharge is found double on Nos. 31, 37, 40, 42. Value, each $2.

Surcharged in Black or Red

O. M. F.
Syrie
25
CENTIEMES

1920-23

54 A16 10c on 2c vio ('23) 15 15
55 A22 10c on 5c org (R) ('23) 12 12
56 A16 25c on 1c dk gray 15 15
a 50c on 1c dk gray (error) 65 65
57 A22 25c on 5c grn ('21) 12 12
58 A22 25c on 5c org ('22) 15 15
a "CENTIEMES" omitted 6.50 6.50
59 A16 50c on 2c vio brn 15 15
60 A22 50c on 10c red ('21) 12 12
61 A22 50c on 10c grn ('22) 22 15
62 A16 75c on 3c red org 18 15
63 A20 75c on 15c sl grn ('21) 15 15
Nos. 54-63 (10) 1.51 1.41

Surcharge is found inverted on Nos. 54-55, 58-59, 62-63; double on Nos. 60, 62. Value $1.50-$2.

Preceding Issues Overprinted ✵

1920

Black Overprint

64 A16 25c on 1c sl gray 3.50 3.50
65 A16 50c on 2c vio brn 3.50 3.50
66 A22 1p on 5c grn 3.00 2.50
67 A22 2p on 25c blue 5.00 5.00
68 A20 5p on 15c gray grn 15.00 15.00
69 A18 10p on 40c red & pale bl 22.50 22.50
70 A18 25p on 50c bis brn & lav 65.00 65.00
71 A18 50p on 1fr cl & ol grn 250.00 250.00
72 A18 100p on 5fr dk bl & buff 1,100. 1,100.
Nos. 64-72 (9) 1,467. 1,467.

Red Overprint

73 A16 25c on 1c sl gray 3.00 3.00
74 A16 50c on 2c vio brn 1.90 1.90
75 A22 1p on 5c grn 2.00 2.00
76 A22 2p on 25c bl 1.50 1.50
77 A20 5p on 15c gray grn 15.00 15.00
78 A18 10p on 40c red & pale bl 22.50 22.50
79 A18 25p on 50c bis brn & lav 65.00 65.00
80 A18 50p on 1fr cl & ol grn 125.00 125.00
81 A18 100p on 5fr dk bl & buff 700.00 700.00
Nos. 73-81 (9) 935.90 935.90

Nos. 64-81 were used only in the vilayet of Aleppo where Egyptian gold currency was still in use.

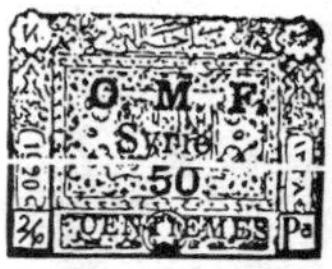
A1

Black or Red Surcharge

1921 *Perf. 11½*

82 A1 25c on 1/10p lt brn 30 22
a "25 Centiemes" omitted
83 A1 50c on 2/10p grn 38 22
84 A1 1p on 3/10p yel 50 22
a "2/10" for "3/10" 3.75 3.75
85 A1 1p on 5m rose 65 45
86 A1 2p on 5m rose 65 55
a Tete beche pair 37.50 37.50
87 A1 3p on 1p gray bl 75 42
88 A1 5p on 2p bl grn 1.90 1.50
89 A1 10p on 5p vio brn 3.00 1.90
90 A1 25p on 10p gray (R) 3.75 2.50
Nos. 82-90 (9) 11.88 7.98

Nos. 82-90 are surcharged on stamps of the Arabian Government Nos. 85, 87-93 and have the designs and sizes of those stamps.

Surcharge is found inverted on Nos. 84-88, 90; double on No. 86.

Kilis Issue

A2

Sewing Machine Perf. 9

1921 Handstamped

Pelure Paper

91 A2 (1p) violet *37.50 25.00*

Issued at Kilis to meet a shortage of the regular issue, caused by the sudden influx of a large number of Armenian refugees from Turkey. The Kilis area was restored to Turkey in Oct. 1923.

Stamps of France, Surcharged

O. M. F.
Syrie
3 PIASTRES

1921-22 ***Perf. 14x13½.***

92 A18 2p on 40c red & pale bl 15 12
93 A18 2.50p on 50c bis brn & lav ('22) 22 20
a 2p on 50c bis brn & lav (error) 15.00 11.50
94 A18 3p on 60c vio & ultra 30 22
95 A18 5p on 1fr cl & ol grn 2.00 1.90
96 A18 10p on 2fr org & pale bl 3.75 3.50
97 A18 25p on 5fr dk bl & buff 3.50 3.00
Nos. 92-97 (6) 9.92 8.94

On No. 93 the surcharge reads: "2 PIASTRES 50".
Surcharge is found inverted on Nos. 92-95; double on No. 94. Value $2-$3.

French Mandate

French Stamps of 1900-23 Surcharged

Syrie
Grand Liban
25
CENTIEMES

1923

104 A16 10c on 2c vio brn 8 8
105 A22 25c on 5c org 8 8
106 A22 50c on 10c grn 12 12
a 25c on 10c green (error) 50.00
107 A20 75c on 15c sl grn 25 25
108 A22 1p on 20c red brn 12 12
109 A22 1.25p on 25c bl 70 15
110 A22 1.50p on 30c org 15 15
111 A22 1.50p on 30c red 12 12
112 A20 2.50p on 50c dl bl 12 12

On Pasteur Stamps of 1923

113 A23 50c on 10c grn 30 30
114 A23 1.50p on 30c red 30 30
115 A23 2.50p on 50c blue 30 30

Surcharge is found inverted on Nos. 104-108, 110, 115; double on Nos. 104, 106. Value $1.50-$2.

Surcharged

Syrie - Grand Liban
2 PIASTRES

116 A18 2p on 40c red & pale bl 12 12
a Inverted surcharge 5.50
b Double surcharge 6.50
c "Liabn"
117 A18 3p on 60c vio & ultra 30 30
a "Liabn"
118 A18 5p on 1fr cl & ol grn 50 50
a "Liabn"
119 A18 10p on 2fr org & pale bl 2.50 2.50
a "Liabn"
120 A18 25p on 5fr dk bl & buff 10.00 8.00
a Inverted surcharge 15.00 15.00
Nos. 104-120 (17) 16.06 13.51

Stamps of France, 1900-21, Surcharged

SYRIE
50
CENTIEMES

1924 ***Perf. 14x13½.***

121 A16 10c on 2c vio brn 5 5
a Double surcharge
122 A22 25c on 5c org 5 5
a "25" omitted 2.00
123 A22 50c on 10c grn 12 12
124 A20 75c on 15c sl grn 38 38
125 A22 1p on 20c red brn 15 8
a "1 PIASTRES" 2.75
126 A22 1.25p on 25c blue 22 22
127 A22 1.50p on 30c org 22 22
128 A22 1.50p on 30c red 22 20
129 A20 2.50p on 50c dl bl 22 20

Same on Pasteur Stamps of France, 1923

1924

130 A23 50c on 10c grn 6 6
131 A23 1.50p on 30c red 30 30
132 A23 2.50p on 50c blue 6 6
Nos. 121-132 (12) 2.05 1.94

Olympic Games Issue

Stamps of France, 1924, Surcharged "SYRIE" and New Values

1924

133 A24 50c on 10c gray grn & yel grn 12.50 12.50
134 A25 1.25p on 25c rose & dk rose 12.50 12.50
135 A26 1.50p on 30c brn red & blk 12.50 12.50
136 A27 2.50p on 50c ultra & dk bl 12.50 12.50

Stamps of France 1900-20 Surcharged

SYRIE
2 PIASTRES

137 A18 2p on 40c red & pale bl 15 12
138 A18 3p on 60c vio & ultra 25 22
139 A18 5p on 1fr cl & ol grn 80 80
140 A18 10p on 2fr org & pale bl 1.00 75
141 A18 25p on 5fr dk bl & buff 1.90 1.40

Stamps of France 1900-21, Surcharged

Syrie
0, P. 25
سوريا
¼ الغرش

or

Syrie
2 Piastres
سوريا
غرش ٢

1924-25

143 A16 10c on 2c vio brn 5 5
a Double surcharge 6.50
b Inverted surcharge 5.50
144 A22 25c on 5c org 8 8
a Double surcharge 6.50
145 A22 50c on 10c grn 12 12
a Double surcharge 6.50
b Inverted surcharge 5.50
146 A20 75c on 15c gray grn 12 12
a Double surcharge 6.50
b Inverted surcharge 5.50
147 A22 1p on 20c red brn 5 5
a Inverted surcharge 5.50
148 A22 1p25 on 25c bl 12 12
a Inverted surcharge 5.50
149 A22 1p50 on 30c red 15 15
a Double surcharge 6.50
150 A22 1p50 on 30c org 15.00 15.00
151 A22 2p on 35c vio ('25) 15 15
152 A18 2p on 40c red & pale bl 12 12
a Arabic "Piastre" in singular 12 12
153 A18 2p on 45c grn & bl ('25) 1.75 1.75
154 A18 3p on 60c vio & ultra 30 30
155 A20 3p on 60c lt vio ('25) 45 45
156 A20 4p on 85c ver 15 15
157 A18 5p on 1fr cl & ol grn 30 30
158 A18 10p on 2fr org & pale bl 65 65
159 A18 25p on 5fr dk bl & buff 65 65
Nos. 143-159 (17) 20.21 20.21

On No. 152a, the surcharge is as illustrated. The correct fourth line ("2 Piastres" -plural), as it appears on Nos. 151, 152 and 153, has four characters, the third resembling "9."

Same Surcharge on Pasteur Stamps of France

1924-25

160 A23 50c on 10c grn 18 18
161 A23 75c on 15c grn ('25) 45 45
162 A23 1p50 on 30c red 38 38
163 A23 2p on 45c red ('25) 18 18
164 A23 2p50 on 50c bl 30 30
165 A23 4p on 75c bl 40 40
Nos. 160-165 (6) 1.89 1.89

Olympic Games Issue

Stamps of France, 1924, Surcharged "Syrie" and New Values in French and Arabic

1924

166 A24 50c on 10c gray grn & yel grn 12.50 12.50
167 A25 1p25 on 25c rose & dk rose 12.50 12.50
168 A26 1p50 on 30c brn red & blk 12.50 12.50
169 A27 2p50 on 50c ultra & dk bl 12.50 12.50

Ronsard Issue

Same Surcharge on France No. 219

1925

170 A28 4p on 75c bl, *bluish* 22 22

Mosque at Hama
A3

Mosque at Damascus
A5

View of Merkab
A4

Designs: 50c, View of Alexandretta. 75c, View of Hama. 1p, Omayyad Mosque, Damascus. 1.25p, Latakia Harbor. 1.50p, View of Damascus. 2p, View of Palmyra. 2.50p, View of Kalat Yamoun. 3p, Bridge of Daphne. 5p, View of Aleppo. 10p, View of Aleppo. 25p, Columns at Palmyra.

Perf. 12½, 13½

1925 Litho. Unwmk.

173 A3 10c dk vio 5 5

Photo.

174 A4 25c ol blk 38 38
175 A4 50c yel grn 12 12
176 A4 75c brn org 14 9
177 A5 1p magenta 12 5
178 A4 1p25 dp grn 65 42
179 A4 1p50 rose red 18 10
180 A4 2p dk brn 18 9
181 A4 2p50 pck bl 38 25
182 A4 3p org brn 6 5
183 A4 5p violet 32 9
184 A4 10p vio brn 85 9
185 A4 25p ultra 1.00 38
Nos. 173-185 (13) 4.43 2.16

Surcharged in Black or Red

= 1P. = غ١

1926-30

186 A4 1p on 3pi org brn ('30) 22 15
187 A4 2p on 1p25 dp grn (R) ('28) 20 9
a Double surcharge
188 A4 3p50 on 75c org brn 18 12
a Double surcharge 2.75 2.75
189 A4 4p on 25c ol blk 30 12
190 A4 4p on 25c ol blk ('27) 40 32
191 A4 4p on 25c ol blk (R) ('28) 20 9
192 A4 4p50 on 75c brn org 18 12
193 A4 6p on 2p50 pck bl 22 12
194 A4 7p50 on 2p50 pck bl 18 12
195 A4 7p50 on 2p50 pck bl (R) ('28) 48 30
a Double surcharge 1.25
196 A4 12p on 1p25 dp grn 18 12
a Surcharge on face and back 17.50 17.50
197 A4 15p on 25p ultra 30 15
198 A4 20p on 1p25 dp grn 20 15
Nos. 186-198 (13) 3.24 1.97

Size of numerals and arrangement of this surcharge varies on the different denominations.

No. 189 has slanting foot on "4".
No. 190, foot straight.

No. 173 Surcharged in Red

05 ٠٥

1928

199 A3 05c on 10c dk vio 5 5

Stamps of 1925 Issue Overprinted in Red or Blue

EXPOSITION INDUSTRIELLE
DAMAS 1929
معرض الصناعات الوطنية
دمشق ١٩٢٩

1929 ***Perf. 13½***

200 A4 50c yel grn (R) 1.10 1.10
201 A5 1p mag (Bl) 1.10 1.10
202 A4 1p50 rose red (Bl) 1.10 1.10
203 A4 3p org brn (Bl) 1.10 1.10
204 A4 5p vio (R) 1.10 1.10
205 A4 10p vio brn (Bl) 1.10 1.10
206 A4 25p ultra (R) 1.10 1.10
Nos. 200-206 (7) 7.70 7.70

Industrial Exhibition, Damascus, Sept. 1929.

View of Hama — A6

View of Alexandretta — A9

Citadel at Aleppo — A10

Great Mosque of Damascus
A11

Ruins of Bosra — A13

Mosque at Homs — A15

View of Sednaya
A16

Citadel at Aleppo
A17

Ancient Bridge at Antioch
A18

Mosque at Damascus A22

Designs: 20c, Great Mosque, Aleppo. 25c, Minaret, Hama. 2p, View of Antioch. 4p, Square at Damascus. 15p, Mosque at Hama. 25p, Monastery of St. Simeon the Stylite (ruins). 50p, Sun Temple (ruins), Palmyra.

Perf. 12x12½

1930-36 Litho. Unwmk.

208	A6	10c red vio	5	5
209	A6	10c vio brn ('33)	5	5
209A	A6	10c vio brn, redrawn ('35)	5	5
210	A6	20c dk bl	5	5
211	A6	20c brn org ('33)	5	5
212	A6	25c gray grn	5	5
213	A6	25c dk bl gray ('33)	5	5

Photo.

Perf. 13

214	A9	50c violet	5	5
215	A15	75c org red ('32)	5	5
216	A10	1p green	5	5
217	A10	1p bis brn ('36)	6	5
218	A11	1.50p bis brn	1.40	1.25
219	A11	1.50p dp grn ('33)	15	15
220	A9	2p dk vio	5	5
221	A13	3p yel grn	30	18
222	A10	4p yel org	5	5
223	A15	4.50p rose car	30	18
224	A16	6p grnsh blk	15	12
225	A17	7.50p dl blue	32	18
226	A18	10p dk brn	32	12
227	A10	15p dp grn	55	30
228	A18	25p vio brn	50	35
229	A15	50p ol brn	2.00	1.90
230	A22	100p red org	6.00	4.00
		Nos. 208-230 (24)	12.65	9.38

On No. 209A Arabic inscriptions, upper right, are entirely redrawn with lighter lines. Hyphen added in "Helio-Vaugirard" imprint. Lines in buildings and background more distinct.

On No. 215 the letters of "VAUGIRARD" in the imprint are reversed as in a mirror.

Autonomous Republic

Parliament Building A23

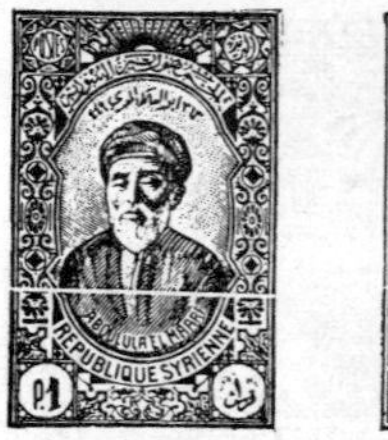
abu-al-Ala al-Maarri A24

President Ali Bek el Abed A25

Saladin — A26

1934, Aug. 2 Engr. *Perf. 12½*

232	A23	10c olive grn	42	42
233	A23	20c black	42	42
234	A23	25c red org	42	42
235	A23	50c ultra	42	42
236	A23	75c plum	42	42
237	A24	1p vermilion	1.40	1.40
238	A24	1.50p green	2.25	2.25
239	A24	2p red brn	2.25	2.25
240	A24	3p Prus blue	2.25	2.25
241	A24	4p brt vio	2.25	2.25
242	A24	4.50p carmine	2.25	2.25
243	A24	5p dk blue	2.25	2.25
244	A24	6p dk brn	2.25	2.25
245	A24	7.50p dk ultra	2.25	2.25
246	A25	10p dk brn	3.50	3.50
247	A25	15p dull bl	4.25	4.25
248	A25	25p rose red	9.00	9.00
249	A26	50p dk brn	13.00	13.00
250	A26	100p lake	19.00	19.00
		Nos. 232-250 (19)	70.25	70.25

Proclamation of the Republic. See Nos. C57-C66.

Stamps of 1930-36 Overprinted in Red or Black

1936, Apr. 15

253	A9	50c vio (R)	90	90
254	A10	1p bis brn (Bk)	90	90
255	A9	2p dk vio (R)	90	90
256	A13	3p yel grn (Bk)	90	90
257	A10	4p yel org (Bk)	90	90
258	A15	4.50p rose car (Bk)	90	90
259	A16	6p grnsh blk (R)	90	90
260	A17	7.50p dull bl (R)	1.10	1.10
261	A18	10p dk brn (Bk)	1.40	1.40
		Nos. 253-261 (9)	8.80	8.80

Industrial Exhibition, Damascus, May 1936. See Nos. C67-C71.

Stamps of 1930 Surcharged in Black

1937-38 *Perf. 13½x13*

262	A10	2.50p on 4p yel org ('38)	12	12
263	A22	10p on 100p red org	32	32

Stamps of 1930-33 Surcharged in Red or Black

1938 *Perf. 13½*

264	A15	25c on 75c org red (Bk)	5	5
265	A11	50c on 1.50p dp grn (R)	5	5
266	A17	2p on 7.50p dl bl (R)	12	12
267	A17	5p on 7.50p dl bl (R)	25	15
268	A15	10p on 50p ol brn (Bk)	50	32
		Nos. 264-268 (5)	97	69

President Hashem Bek el Atassi — A27

1938-43 Photo. Unwmk.

268A	A27	10p dp bl ('43)	18	18
269	A27	12.50p on 10p dp bl (R)	25	25
270	A27	20p dk brn	25	25

The 10pi and 20pi exist imperf.

Columns at Palmyra A28

1940 Litho. *Perf. 11½.*

271	A28	5p pale rose	18	15

Exists imperf.

Museum at Damascus — A29

Hotel at Bloudan A30

Kasr-el-Heir A31

1940 Typo. *Perf. 13x14*

272	A29	10c brt rose	5	5
273	A29	20c light bl	5	5
274	A29	25c fawn	5	5
275	A29	50c ultra	5	5

Engr.

Perf. 13

276	A30	1p peacock bl	5	5
277	A30	1.50p chocolate	8	8
278	A30	2.50p dark grn	5	5
279	A31	5p violet	18	8
280	A31	7.50p vermilion	32	22
281	A31	50p sepia	70	65
		Nos. 272-281 (10)	1.58	1.33

President Taj Eddin Hassani A32

1942, Apr. 6 Litho. *Perf. 11½*

282	A32	50c sage grn	1.65	1.65
283	A32	1.50p dl gray brn	1.65	1.65
284	A32	6p fawn	1.65	1.65
285	A32	15p light bl	1.65	1.65
		Nos. 282-285,C96-C97 (6)	13.85	13.10

Proclamation of independence by the Allies, Sept. 27, 1941.

President Taj Eddin Hassani A33

President Hassani and Map of Syria A34

1942 Photo. Unwmk.

286	A33	6p rose lake & sal rose	95	95
287	A33	15p dl bl & bl	95	95

See No. C98. Nos. 286-287 exist imperf.

1943 Litho.

288	A34	1p light grn	95	95
289	A34	4p buff	95	95
290	A34	8p pale vio	95	95
291	A34	10p salmon	95	95
292	A34	20p dl chalky bl	95	95
		Nos. 288-292,C99-C102 (9)	8.55	8.55

Proclamation of a United Syria.

Stamps of 1943 Overprinted with Border in Black

1943

293	A34	1p light grn	95	95
294	A34	4p buff	95	95
295	A34	8p pale vio	95	95
296	A34	10p salmon	95	95
297	A34	20p dl chalky bl	95	95
		Nos. 293-297,C103-C106 (9)	8.55	8.55

Mourning for President Hassani. Nos. 288-297 exist imperf.

Nos. 278 and 280 Overprinted in Carmine or Black

1944 Unwmk. *Perf. 13*

298	A30	2.50p dk grn (C)	1.50	1.50
299	A31	7.50p ver (Bk)	1.50	1.50
		Nos. 298-299,C114-C116 (5)	13.20	13.20

1000th anniv. of the Arab poet and philosopher, abu-al-Ala al-Maarri.

President Shukri el Kouatly — A35

1945, Mar. 15 Litho. *Perf. 11½*

300	A35	4p pale lil	18	18
301	A35	6p dull bl	18	18
302	A35	10p salmon	18	18
303	A35	15p dk brn	32	32
304	A35	20p slate grn	40	40
305	A35	40p orange	70	70
		Nos. 300-305,C117-C123 (13)	8.75	5.29

Resumption of constitutional government.

A36

A37

A38

A39

Fiscal Stamps Overprinted or Surcharged in Black

1945 Typo. *Perf. 11, 11½x11*

306	A36	12½p on 15p yel grn	95	95
307	A37	25p buff	1.65	1.65
307A	A38	25p on 25s lt vio brn	1.10	1.10
308	A39	50p on 75p brn org	2.25	2.25
309	A39	75p brn org	3.00	3.00
310	A37	100p yel grn	3.50	3.50
		Nos. 306-310 (6)	12.45	12.45

Type of 1945 and Nos. 308 and 310 Overprinted in Black

a

b

1945 Unwmk. *Perf. 11*

311	A37(b)	50p magenta	1.10	1.10
312	A39(a)	50p on 75p brn org	75	75
313	A37(b)	100p yel grn	1.25	1.25

Catalogue values for unused stamps in this section, from this point to the end of the section, are for Never Hinged items.

Independent Republic

A40

Fiscal Stamp Overprinted in Carmine

1946
314 A40 200p light blue 6.00 6.00

Sun and Ears of Wheat A41

President Shukri el Kouatly A42

1946 **Litho.** ***Perf. 13x13½***
315 A41 50c brn org 10 5
316 A41 1p violet 20 7
317 A41 2.50p bl gray 22 10
318 A41 5p lt bl grn 30 15

Photo.

Perf. 13½x13, 13x13½
319 A42 7.50p dk brown 10 5
320 A42 10p Prussian grn 10 7
321 A42 12.50p deep vio 40 10
Nos. 315-321 (7) 1.42 59

Arab Horse A44

1946-47 **Litho.**
325 A44 50p olive grn 2.00 50
326 A44 100p dk bl grn ('47) 6.00 1.25
327 A44 200p rose vio ('47) 12.00 3.50

Nos. 320, 321 and 325 Overprinted in Black or Green

1946, Apr. 17
328 A42 10p Prus grn 40 40
329 A42 12.50p dp vio 60 60
330 A44 50p ol brn (G) 1.50 1.50

Issued to commemorate the evacuation of British and French troops from Syria. See No. C135.

President Shukri el Kouatly — A45

1946 **Unwmk.** **Litho.** ***Perf. 13½x13***
331 A45 15p red 15 14
332 A45 20p violet 30 20
333 A45 25p ultra 42 20

No. 333 Overprinted in Magenta

1946, Aug. 28
334 A45 25p ultra 1.20 1.10

8th Arab Medical Congress, Aleppo, Aug. 28-Sept. 4. See Nos. C136-C138.

Nos. 328 to 330 With Additional Overprint in Black

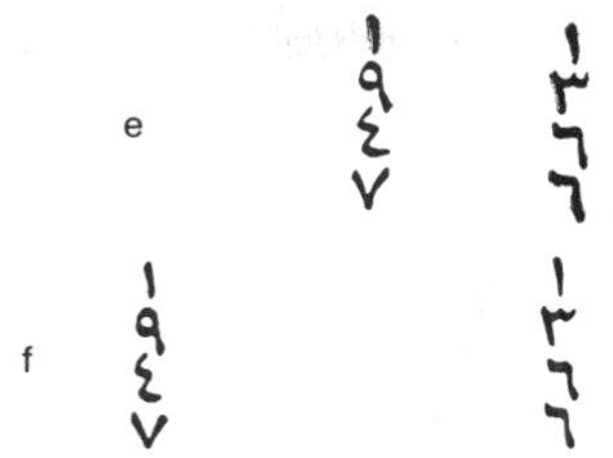

Perf. 13½x13, 13x13½

1947, June 10
335 A42(e) 10p Prus grn 40 14
336 A42(e) 12.50p deep vio 60 20
337 A44(f) 50p olive brn 1.50 50

1st anniv. of the evacuation of British and French troops from Syria. See No. C139.

Hercules and the Lion — A46

Mosaics from Omayyad Mosque, Damascus — A47

1947, Nov. 15 **Litho.** ***Perf. 11½***
338 A46 12.50p slate grn 70 55
339 A47 25p gray bl 1.20 80

1st Arab Archaeological Congress, Damascus, Nov.
See Nos. C140-C141 and souvenir sheet No. C141a.

Courtyard of Azem Palace A48

Telephone Building A49

1947, Nov. 15
340 A48 12.50p deep claret 50 50
341 A49 25p brt blue 1.00 70

3rd Congress of Arab Engineers, Damascus, Nov.
See Nos. C142-C143 and souvenir sheet No. C143a.

House of Parliament A50

Pres. Shukri el Kouatly A51

1948, June 23 **Unwmk.** ***Perf. 10½***
342 A50 12.50p blk & org 35 20
343 A51 25p dp rose 65 42

Reelection of Pres. Shukri el Kouatly. See Nos. C144-C145 and souvenir sheet No. C145a.

National Emblem A52

Syrian Flag and Soldier A53

1948, June 23 **Litho.**
344 A52 12.50p gray & choc 42 25
345 A53 25p multi 80 40

Inauguration of compulsory military training. See Nos. C146-147 and souvenir sheet No. C147a.

Nos. 215 and 327 Surcharged with New Value and Bars in Black

1948 ***Perf. 13, 13x13½***
346 A15 50c on 75c org red 10 5
347 A44 25p on 200p rose vio 80 30

Col. Husni Zayim A54

Palmyra A56

Ain el Arous A55

1949, June 20 **Litho.** ***Perf. 11½***
348 A54 25p blue 60 42

Revolution of Mar. 30, 1949. See No. C153.
A souvenir sheet comprises Nos. 348 and C153, imperf. Value $80.

1949, June 20
349 A55 12.50p violet 1.50 1.50
350 A56 25p blue 2.25 2.25

UPU, 75th anniversary.
See Nos. C154-C155 and note after No. C155.

Pres. Husni Zayim and Map — A57

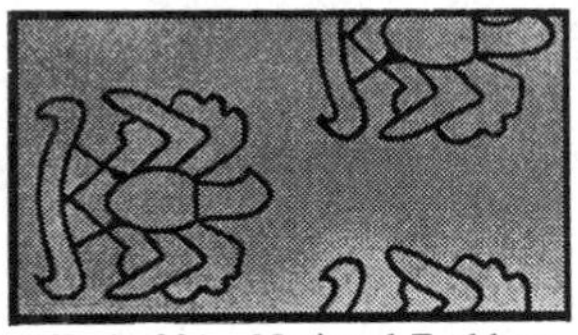
Wmk. 291 - National Emblem Multiple

Wmk. 291

1949, Aug. 6 **Litho.** ***Perf. 11½***
351 A57 25p bl and brn 2.00 1.25

Election of President Husni Zayim. See No. C156 and imperf. souvenir sheet No. C156a.

Tel-Chehab Waterfall A58

Damascus Scene A59

1949
352 A58 5p gray 10 5
353 A58 7.50p ol gray 20 10
354 A59 12.50p vio brn 40 15
355 A59 25p blue 80 35

See No. 376.

Nos. 327 and 326 Surcharged with New Value and Bars in Black

1950 **Unwmk.** ***Perf. 13x13½***
356 A44 2.50p on 200p rose vio 38 12
357 A44 10p on 100p dk bl grn 38 16

National Emblem A60

Road to Damascus A61

Postal Administration Building, Damascus — A62

1950-51 **Litho.** ***Perf. 11½***
358 A60 50c org brn 10 5
359 A60 2.50p pink 14 8
360 A61 10p pur ('51) 25 16
361 A61 12.50p sage grn ('51) 50 35
362 A62 25p blue ('51) 90 22
363 A62 50p black ('51) 3.00 55
Nos. 358-363 (6) 4.89 1.41

Nos. 358 to 363 exist imperforate.

Parliament Building, Damascus A63

1951, Apr. 14
364 A63 12.50p gray blk 22 20
365 A63 25p blue 50 35

New constitution adopted Sept. 5, 1950. See Nos. C162-C163.
Nos. 364-365 exist imperforate.

Water Wheel, Hama A64

Palace of Justice, Damascus A65

Perf. 11½

1952, Apr. 22 Litho. Unwmk.

366 A64	50c dk brn	5	5
367 A64	2.50p dk blue	8	5
368 A64	5p bl grn	14	8
369 A64	10p red	22	8
370 A65	12.50p gray blk	55	8
371 A65	15p lil rose	70	22
372 A65	25p deep bl	1.50	35
373 A65	100p ol brn	5.00	1.50
	Nos. 366-373 (8)	8.24	2.41

Nos. 366-373 exist imperforate.

Type of 1949 and

Crusaders' Fort — A66

Crusaders' Fort — A67

1953 Photo.

374 A67	50c rose red	8	5
375 A66	2.50p dk brn	14	5
376 A58	7.50p green	22	12
377 A67	12.50p deep bl	1.20	14

Farm Workers A68

Family Group A69

Designs: 1pi, 5pi, Farm workers. 10pi, 12½p, Family group. 20pi, 25pi, 50pi, Factory and construction workers.

1954 *Perf. 11½.*

378 A68	1p olive	5	5
379 A68	2½p brn red	5	5
380 A68	5p deep bl	8	5
381 A69	7½p brn red	15	5
382 A69	10p black	20	5
383 A69	12½p violet	30	7
384 A69	20p dp plum	42	15
385 A69	25p violet	1.00	25
386 A69	50p dk grn	2.25	60
	Nos. 378-386 (9)	4.50	1.32

Nos. 382 and 385 Overprinted in Carmine

1954, Oct. 9

387 A69	10p black	65	38
388 A69	25p violet	70	45

Issued to publicize the Cotton Festival, Aleppo, October 1954. See Nos. C185-C186.

Globe — A69a

Mother and Child — A70

Arab Postal Union Issue

1955 Photo. *Perf. 13½x13*

389 A69a	12½p green	35	14
390 A69a	25p violet	60	25

Founding of the APU, July 1, 1954. Exist imperf. See No. C191.

1955, May 13 Litho. *Perf. 11½*

391 A70	25p red	35	25

Mother's Day. See Nos. C194-C195.

United Nations Emblem A71

1955 Photo.

392 A71	7½p crimson	35	22
393 A71	12½p Prus grn	60	30

UN, 10th anniv., Oct. 24. See Nos. C200-C201.

Aqueduct at Aleppo A72

1955 Litho. Unwmk.

394 A72	7.50p lilac	20	5
395 A72	12.50p carmine	30	15

New aqueduct bringing water from the Euphrates to Northern Syria. Exist imperf. See No. C202.

Nos. 389-390 Overprinted in Ultramarine or Green

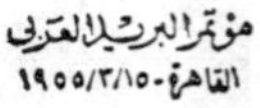

1955 Photo. *Perf. 13½x13*

396 A69a	12½p green	35	18
397 A69a	25p vio (G)	1.00	40

APU Congress held at Cairo, Mar. 15. See No. C203.

Nos. 389-390 Overprinted in Black

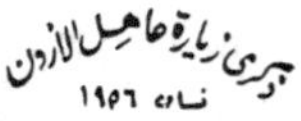

1956

398 A69a	12½p green	50	28
399 A69a	25p violet	90	50

Visit of King Hussein of Jordan to Damascus, Apr. 1956. See No. C207.

Cotton — A73

1956 Unwmk. Litho. *Perf. 11½*

400 A73	2½p bluish grn	30	15

Issued to publicize a Cotton Festival.

Nos. 392-393 Overprinted in Black

1956 Photo. *Perf. 11½*

401 A71	7½p crimson	35	22
402 A71	12½p Prus grn	42	35

UN, 11th anniv. See Nos. C221-C222.

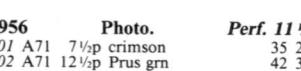

People's Army — A74

1957 Litho. *Perf. 11½*

403 A74	5p lil rose	15	10
404 A74	20p gray grn	35	20

Formation of the Popular Resistance Movement.

Nos. 403-404 Overprinted in Black or Red

1957

405 A74	5p lil rose	20	10
406 A74	20p gray grn (R)	35	25

Evacuation of Port Said by British and French troops, Dec. 22, 1956.

Azem Palace, Damascus A75

1957 Litho. *Perf. 11½*

407 A75	12½p lilac	15	5
408 A75	15p gray	30	10

Map of Near East, Scales and Damascus Skyline — A76

Cotton, Bale and Ship — A77

1957 Wmk. 291 *Perf. 11½*

409 A76	12½p brt grn	20	15

3rd Congress of the Union of Arab Lawyers, Damascus, Sept. 21-25. See Nos. C240-C241.

1957

410 A77	12½p lt bl grn & blk	30	20

Cotton Festival, Aleppo, Oct. 3-5. See Nos. C242-C243.

Children — A78

1957, Oct. 7

411 A78	12½p olive	35	25

Intl. Children's Day, Oct. 7. See Nos. C244-C245.

See No. 13A in United Arab Republic (Syria) listings following Syria for "RAU" overprint on No. 411.

Mailing and Receiving Letter — A79

1957 Unwmk.

412 A79	5p magenta	35	16

Intl. Letter Writing Week, Oct. 6-12. See No. C246.

Nos. 403-404 Overprinted in Black or Red

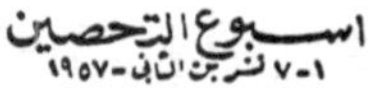

1957 *Perf. 11½*

413 A74	5p lil rose	10	5
414 A74	20p gray grn (R)	28	20

Digging of fortifications along the Syrian-Israeli frontier.

Scales, Torch and Map A80

1957, Nov. 8 Wmk. 291

415 A80	20p ol gray	35	20

Congress of Afro-Asian Jurists, Damascus. See Nos. C247-C248.

Glider A81

1957, Nov. 8 Litho. *Perf. 11½*

416 A81	25p red brown	60	30
417 A81	35p green	90	40
418 A81	40p ultra	2.00	55

Issued to commemorate a glider festival.

Khaled ibn el Walid Mosque, Homs — A82

1957 Unwmk. *Perf. 12*

419 A82	2½p dull brn	10	7

Scroll, Communications Building and Telephone — A83

1958 Wmk. 291 *Perf. 11½*

420 A83	25p ultra	22	16

See Nos. C249-C250.

Issues of 1958-61 released by the United Arab Republic are listed following the listings of Syria, Issues of the Arabian Government.

Syrian Arab Republic

Hall of Parliament, Damascus — A83a

1961 Unwmk. Litho. *Perf. 12*

420A	A83a	15p magenta		25	5
420B	A83a	35p ol gray		65	18

Establishment of Syrian Arab Republic.

Water Wheel, Hama — A84

Roman Arch of Triumph, Latakia — A85

Qalb Lozah Church, Aleppo A86

Design: 7½p, 10p, Khaled ibn el Walid Mosque, Homs.

Perf. 11½x11

1961-62 Unwmk. Litho.

421	A84	2½p	rose red	5	5
422	A84	5p	blue	5	5
423	A84	7½p	bl grn ('62)	15	25
424	A84	10p	org ('62)	22	5
			Perf. 12x11½		
425	A85	12½p	gray brn	32	5
426	A86	17½p	ol gray ('62)	22	5
427	A85	25p	dl red brn	45	8
428	A86	35p	dl grn ('62)	30	15
			Nos. 421-428 (8)	1.76	73

Types of 1961, Regular and Air Post

Designs: 2½p, 5p, 7½p, 10p, Arch, Jupiter Temple. 12½p, 15p, 17½p, 22½p, "The Beauty of Palmyra."

1962 *Perf. 11½x11*

429	A84	2p	gray bl	8	5
430	A84	5p	brn org	12	5
431	A84	7½p	ol bis	18	9
432	A84	10p	claret	12	5

Perf. 12x11½

Size: 26x38mm

433	AP68	12½p	gray ol	25	5
434	AP68	15p	ultra	30	5
435	AP68	17½p	brown	30	5
436	AP68	22½p	grnsh bl	32	8
			Nos. 429-436 (8)	1.67	47

Martyrs' Memorial — A87

Pres. Nazem el-Kodsi — A88

1962, June 11 Litho.

440	A87	12½p	tan & sep	12	5
441	A87	35p	grn & bl grn	25	18

1925 Revolution.

1962, Dec. 14 *Perf. 12x11½*

442	A88	12½p	sep & lt bl	15	5

1st anniv. of the election of Pres. Nazem el-Kodsi. See No. C278.

Queen Zenobia — A89

Central Bank of Syria A90

Designs: 2½p, 5p, "The Beauty of Palmyra." 17½p, Hejaz Railway Station, Damascus. 22½p, Mouassat Hospital, Damascus. 35p, P.T.T. Jalaa Avenue Office, Damascus.

1963 Unwmk. *Perf. 11½x11*

443	A89	2½p	dk bl gray	5	5
444	A89	5p	rose lil	5	5
445	A89	7½p	dl bl	18	5
446	A89	10p	ol gray	38	5
447	A89	12½p	ultra	55	5
448	A89	15p	vio brn	95	8
			Perf. 11½x12		
449	A90	17½p	dl vio	32	12
450	A90	22½p	brt vio	15	5
451	A90	25p	bis brn	15	5
452	A90	35p	brt pink	18	15
			Nos. 443-452 (10)	2.96	70

Wheat Emblem and Globe — A91

Boy Playing Ball and UN Emblem — A92

1963, Mar. 21 Litho. *Perf. 12x11½*

453	A91	12½p	ultra & blk	8	5

FAO "Freedom from Hunger" Campaign. See No. C291 and souvenir sheet No. C291a.

Cotton Festival Type of Air Post Issue, 1962, Inscribed "1963"

1963, Sept. 26 *Perf. 12x11½*

455	AP75	17½p	multi	15	10
456	AP75	22½p	multi	25	15

The 1963 Cotton Festival, Aleppo.

1963, Oct. 24 *Perf. 12x11½*

457	A92	12½p	emer & sl grn	9	6
458	A92	22½p	rose red & dk grn	18	12

Issued for International Children's Day.

Ugharit Princess — A93

1964 Litho. *Perf. 11½x11*

459	A93	2½p	gray	5	5
460	A93	5p	brown	5	5
461	A93	7½p	rose cl	5	5
462	A93	10p	emerald	5	5
463	A93	12½p	light vio	8	5
464	A93	17½p	ultra	15	6
465	A93	20p	rose car	38	15
466	A93	25p	orange	65	22
			Nos. 459-466 (8)	1.46	68

Map of North Africa and Middle East, Flag of Syria, and Crowd A94

1965, Mar. 8 Litho. *Perf. 11½x12*

467	A94	12½p	multi	5	5
468	A94	17½p	multi	12	5
469	A94	20p	multi	15	5

Mar. 8 Revolution, 2nd anniv.

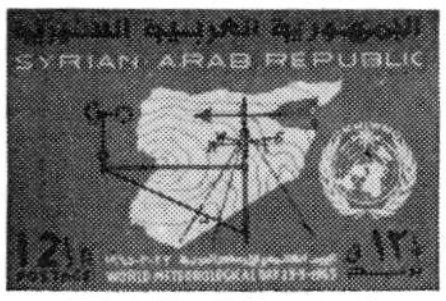

Weather Map and Anemometer — A95

1965, Mar. 23 Litho. Unwmk.

470	A95	12½p	dl lil & blk	5	5
471	A95	27½p	lt bl & blk	18	8

Fifth World Meteorological Day.

"Evacuation of Apr. 17, 1946" A96

Peasants' Union Emblem A97

1965, Apr. 17 Litho. *Perf. 12x11½*

472	A96	12½p	bl & brt yel grn	5	5
473	A96	27½p	rose red & lt lil	18	8

19th anniv. of the evacuation of British and French troops from Syria.

1965, Aug. Unwmk. *Perf. 11½x11*

474	A97	2½p	bl grn	5	5
475	A97	12½p	purple	9	5
476	A97	15p	maroon	10	5

Issued to publicize the Peasants' Union.

Torch, Map of Arab Countries and Farmer, Soldier, Woman, Intellectual and Worker A98

Workers, Factory and Emblem A99

1965, Nov. 23 *Perf. 12x11½*

477	A98	12½p	multi	5	5
478	A98	25p	multi	18	5

National Council of the Revolution, a legislative body working for a socialist and democratic society.

1966, Jan. Litho. *Perf. 11½x11*

479	A99	12½p	blue	5	5
480	A99	15p	carmine	5	5
481	A99	20p	dl vio	12	5
482	A99	25p	ol gray	15	9

Establishment of the General Union of Trade Unions.

Roman Lamp A100

Islamic Vessel, 12th Century A101

1966 Litho. *Perf. 11½x11*

483	A100	2½p	slate grn	5	5
484	A100	5p	magenta	15	10
485	A101	7½p	brown	10	5
486	A101	10p	brt rose lil	12	5

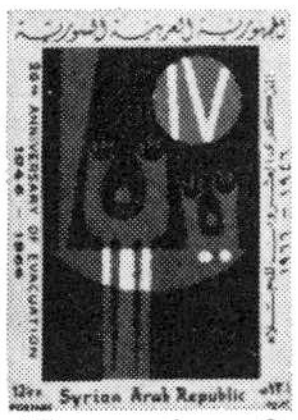

"Evacuation of Troops" A102

Bust of Core, Terra Cotta Vase A103

1966, Apr. 17 Litho. *Perf. 12x11½*

487	A102	12½p	multi	5	5
488	A102	27½	multi	15	9

20th anniv. of the evacuation of British and French troops from Syria.

1967 *Perf. 11½x11*

Design: 15p, 20p, 25p, 27½p, Bronze vase in form of seated African woman.

489	A103	2½p	brt grn	5	5
490	A103	5p	sal pink	5	5
491	A103	10p	grnsh bl	5	5
492	A103	12½p	dl brn	8	5
493	A103	15p	brt pink	8	5
494	A103	20p	brt bl	9	5
495	A103	25p	green	12	5
496	A103	27½p	vio bl	18	15
			Nos. 489-496 (8)	70	50

Arab Revolution Monument, Damascus — A104

1968, Mar. 8 Litho. *Perf. 12x12½*

497	A104	12½p	blk, yel & brn	5	5
498	A104	25p	blk, pink & car rose	15	5
499	A104	27½p	blk, lt grn & grn	15	9

Mar. 8 Revolution, 5th anniversary.

An enhanced introduction to the Scott Catalogue begins on Page V. A thorough understanding of the material presented there will greatly aid your use of the catalogue itself.

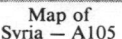

Map of Syria — A105

Hands Holding Wrench, Gun and Torch — A106

1968, Apr. 4 Litho. *Perf. 12x12½*

500 A105 12½p pink & multi 25 5
501 A105 60p gray & multi 25 15

Arab Baath Socialist Party, 21st anniv.

1968, Apr. 13

502 A106 12½p tan & multi 5 5
503 A106 17½p rose & multi 5 5
504 A106 25p yel & multi 15 5

Issued to publicize the mobilization effort.

Rising Sun, Power Lines and Railroad Tracks A107

1968, Apr. 17 Litho. *Perf. 12½x12*

505 A107 12½p multi 5 5
506 A107 27½p vio & multi 15 5

22nd anniv. of the evacuation of British and French troops from Syria.

Oil Wells and Oil Pipe Line on Map — A108

1968, May 1

507 A108 12½p lt & dk grn & ultra 8 5
508 A108 17½p pink, brn & ultra 15 9

Syrian oil exploitation; completion of the oil pipe line to Tartus.

Map of Palestine and Torch A109

Citadel of Aleppo, Wheat and Cogwheel A110

1968, May Litho. *Perf. 12x12½*

509 A109 12½p ultra, blk & red 8 5
510 A109 25p ol bis, blk & red 25 12
511 A109 27½p gray, blk & red 32 15

Issued for Palestine Day.

1968, July 18 Litho. *Perf. 12x12½*

512 A110 12½p multi 5 5
513 A110 27½p multi 12 5

Industrial and Agricultural Fair, Aleppo.

Fair Emblem, Globe, Grain, Wheel and Horse — A111

Woman Carrying Cotton, and Castle of Aleppo — A112

Design: 27½p, Syrian flag, hand with torch, fair emblem, globe, grain and wheel.

Perf. 12x12½, 12½x12

1968, Aug. 25 Litho.

514 A111 12½p dp brn, blk & emer 5 5
515 A111 27½p multi 15 5
516 A111 60p bl gray, blk & dp org 22 18

15th Intl. Damascus Fair, Aug. 25-Sept. 20.

1968, Oct. 3 Litho. *Perf. 12x12½*

517 A112 12½p multi 10 5
518 A112 27½p multi 20 5

13th Cotton Festival, Aleppo.

Al Jahez A113

Oil Derrick and Pipe Line A114

1968, Nov. 9 Litho. *Perf. 12x12½*

519 A113 12½p blk & buff 12 5
520 A113 27½p blk & gray 38 9

9th Science Week; Al Jahez Abu Uthman Amr ben Bahr (776-868).

1968 *Perf. 12x11*

521 A114 2½p grnsh bl & dk grn 5 5
522 A114 5p grn & vio bl 5 5
523 A114 7½p lt yel grn & bl 5 5
524 A114 10p brt yel & grn 5 5
525 A114 12½p yel & ver 9 5
526 A114 15p ol bis & dk brn 9 5
527 A114 27½p dl org & dk red brn 18 8
Nos. 521-527 (7) 56 38

Broken Chains and Sun A115

1969, Mar. 8 Litho. *Perf. 12½x12*

Sun in Yellow and Red

528 A115 12½p vio bl & blk 5 5
529 A115 25p gray & blk 15 5
530 A115 27½p dl grn & blk 15 5

March 8 Revolution, 6th anniversary.

The first value column gives the catalogue value of an unused stamp, the second that of a used stamp.

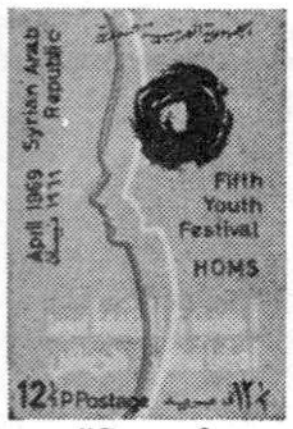

"Sun of Freedom, Young Man and Woman" A116

Liberation through Knowledge and Construction A117

1959, Mar. 29 *Perf. 12x12½*

531 A116 12½p multi 5 5
532 A116 25p multi 12 5

Youth Week; 5th Youth Festival, Homs, Apr. 18-24.

1969, Apr. 17 Litho. *Perf. 12x12½*

533 A117 12½p yel & multi 5 5
534 A117 27½p gray & multi 12 5

Issued to commemorate the 23rd anniversary of the evacuation of British and French troops from Syria.

Mahatma Gandhi — A118

Cotton — A119

1969, Oct. 7 Litho. *Perf. 12x12½*

535 A118 12½p brn & dl yel 5 5
536 A118 27½p grn & yel 15 5

Mohandas K. Gandhi (1869-1948), leader in India's fight for independence.

1969, Oct. 10

537 A119 12½p multi 5 5
538 A119 17½p multi 8 5
539 A119 25p multi 15 9

14th Cotton Festival, Aleppo.

Map of Arab Countries A120

Designs: 25p, Arab Academy. 27½p, Damascus University.

1969, Nov. 2 Litho. *Perf. 12½x12*

540 A120 12½p ultra & lt grn 5 5
541 A120 25p dk pur & dp pink 12 9
542 A120 27½p dp bis & yel grn 15 12

10th Science Week, and the 6th Arab Scientific Conference. No. 541 also commemorates the 50th anniv. of the Arab Academy and No. 542, the 50th anniv. of the Medical School of the Damascus University.

Symbols of Progress A121

1970, Mar. 8 Litho. *Perf. 12½x12*

543 A121 12½p brt bl, blk & bis brn 5 5
544 A121 25p red, blk & dp bl 12 8
545 A121 27½p lt grn, blk & tan 15 12

March 8 Revolution, 7th anniversary.

Map of Arab League Countries, Flag and Emblem A122

1970, Mar. 22

546 A122 12½p multi 5 5
547 A122 25p gray & multi 12 8
548 A122 27½p multi 15 9

25th anniversary of the Arab League.

Sultan Saladin and Battle of Hattin, 1187, between Saracens and Crusaders — A123

1970, Apr. 17 Litho. *Perf. 12½x12*

549 A123 15p brn & buff 12 5
550 A123 35p lil & buff 25 12

24th anniv. of the evacuation of British and French troops from Syria.

Development of Agriculture and Industry — A124

1970-71 Litho. *Perf. 11x11½*

551 A124 2½p brn & red ('71) 5 5
552 A124 5p org & bl 8 8
553 A124 7½p lil & gray ('71) 5 5
554 A124 10p lt & dk brn 5 5
555 A124 12½p bl & org ('71) 5 5
556 A124 15p grn & red lil 9 5
557 A124 20p vio & red brn 9 5
558 A124 22½p red brn & blk ('71) 15 5
559 A124 25p gray & vio bl ('71) 18 8
560 A124 27½p brt grn & dk brn ('71) 20 8
561 A124 35p rose red & emer ('71) 25 12
Nos. 551-561 (11) 1.24 71

Young Man and Woman, Map of Arab Countries A125

1970, May 7 Unwmk. *Perf. 12½x12*

569 A125 15p grn & ocher 5 5
570 A125 25p brn & ocher 12 9

First Youth Week, Latakia, Apr. 23-29. Inscribed "Youth's First Weak" (sic.).

Refugee Family A126

1970, May 15

571 A126 15p multi 5 5
572 A126 25p gray & multi 15 8
573 A126 35p grn & multi 15 12

Issued for Arab Refugee Week.

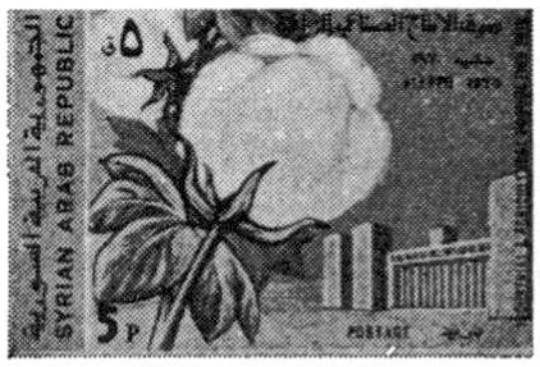

Cotton — A127

Designs: 10p, Tomatoes. 15p, Tobacco. 20p, Beets. 35p, Wheat.

1970, Aug. 18 Litho. ***Perf. 12½***

574	A127	5p multi	5	5
575	A127	10p yel & multi	8	8
576	A127	15p multi	15	10
577	A127	20p yel grn & multi	25	15
578	A127	35p lil & multi	45	25
		Nos. 574-578 (5)	98	63

Industrial and Agricultural Fair, Aleppo. Nos. 574-578 printed se-tenant.

Boy Scout, Tent, Emblem and Map of Arab Countries A128

1970, Aug. 25 ***Perf. 12½x12***

579	A128	15p gray grn	25	9

9th Pan-Arab Boy Scout Jamboree, Damascus.

Olive Tree and Emblem A129

1970, Sept. 28 Litho. ***Perf. 11½x12***

580	A129	15p gray grn, yel & blk	15	5
581	A129	25p red brn, yel & blk	35	8

Issued to publicize World Olive Year.

Protection of Industry, Agriculture, Arts and Commerce — A130

1971, Mar. 8 Litho. ***Perf. 12½x12***

582	A130	15p ol, yel & bl	5	5
583	A130	22½p red brn, yel & ol	9	5
584	A130	27½p bl, yel & red brn	15	9

March 8 Revolution, 8th anniversary.

Workers Memorial, Hands with Wrench and Olive Branch A131

1971, May 1 Litho. ***Perf. 12½x12***

585	A131	15p brn vio, yel & bl	8	5
586	A131	25p dk bl, bl & yel	15	8

Labor Day.

Child and Traffic Lights A132

Design: 25p, Road signs, traffic lights, children (vert.).

1971, May 4 ***Perf. 11½x12, 12x11½***

587	A132	15p blk, red & bl	5	5
588	A132	25p gray & multi	12	8
589	A132	45p blk, red & yel	22	18

World Traffic Day.

Factories, Cogwheel and Cotton A133

1971, July 15 Litho. ***Perf. 12½x12***

590	A133	15p lt grn, bl & blk	5	5
591	A133	30p red & blk	15	12

11th Industrial and Agricultural Fair, Aleppo.

Arab Postal Union Emblem — A134

Flag, Map of Syria, Egypt and Libya — A135

1971, Aug. 13 ***Perf. 12x12½***

592	A134	15p cl & multi	5	5
593	A134	20p vio bl & multi	15	5

25th anniv. of the Conference of Sofar, Lebanon, establishing the APU.

1971, Aug. 13 ***Perf. 12x11½***

594	A135	15p car, dl grn & blk	8	5

Confederation of the Arab states of Syria, Libya and Egypt.

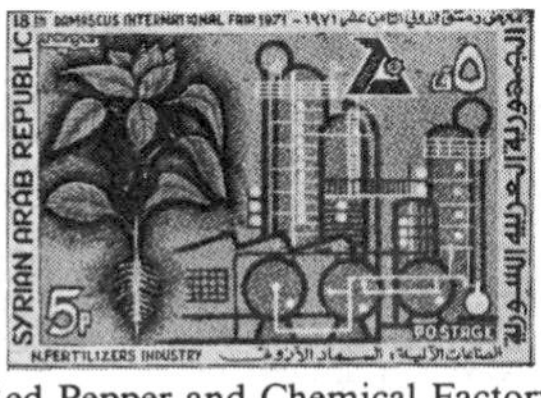

Red Pepper and Chemical Factory (Fertilizer Industry) — A136

Designs: 15p, Electronics industry (TV, telephone, computer). 35p, Glass industry (old map and glass manufacture). 50p, Carpet industry (carpet and looms).

1971, Aug. 25 ***Perf. 12½***

595	A136	5p vio & multi	5	5
596	A136	15p dl grn & multi	8	5
597	A136	35p multi	32	9
598	A136	50p yel grn & multi	38	15

18th Intl. Damascus Fair.

Pres. Hafez al Assad and Crowd A137

UNESCO Emblem, Radar, Spacecraft, Telephone A138

1971, Nov. Litho. ***Perf. 12x12½***

599	A137	15p vio bl, blk & car	5	5
600	A137	20p dk & lt grn, car & blk	12	9

1st anniv. of Correctionist Movement of Nov. 16, 1970.

1971, Dec. 8

601	A138	15p vio bl & multi	5	5
602	A138	50p grn & multi	25	18

25th anniv. of UNESCO.

UNICEF Emblem and Playing Children — A139

1971, Dec. 21

603	A139	15p ultra, dk bl & dp car	8	5
604	A139	25p grnsh bl, ocher & dk bl	15	9

UNICEF, 25th anniv.

Conference Emblem A140

1971, Dec. ***Perf. 12½x12***

605	A140	15p blk, grnsh bl & org	8	5

Scholars' Conference.

Book Year Emblem A141

1972, Jan. 2

606	A141	15p tan, lt bl & vio	5	5
607	A141	20p brn, lt grn & grn	15	8

International Book Year.

Wheel, "8" and Scales of Justice — A142

Baath Party Emblem — A143

1972, Mar. 8 Litho. ***Perf. 12x12½***

608	A142	15p bl grn & vio	5	5
609	A142	20p ol bis & car	9	5

March 8 Revolution, 9th anniversary.

1972, Mar. 7

610	A143	15p dk bl & multi	5	5
611	A143	20p vio & multi	9	5

Arab Baath Socialist Party, 25th anniv.

Eagle, Chimneys, Grain and Oil Rigs A144

1972, Apr. 17 ***Perf. 12½x12***

612	A144	15p gold, blk & car	8	5

Federation of Arab Republics, 1st anniv.

Symbolic Flower, Broken Chain — A145

Hand Holding Wrench and Spade — A146

1972, Apr. 17 ***Perf. 12x11½***

613	A145	15p rose red & gray	5	5
614	A145	50p pale bl grn & gray	22	18

26th anniv. of the evacuation of British and French troops from Syria.

1972, May 1

615	A146	15p ol grn, bl & blk	5	5
616	A146	50p vio bl, brn & blk	22	18

Labor Day.

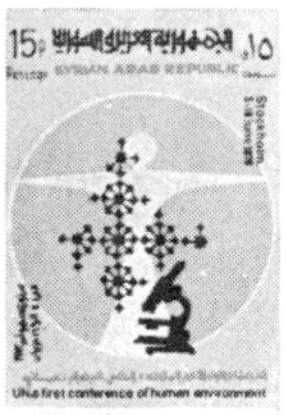

Environment Emblem, Crystals, Microscope A147

Dove over Factory A148

1972, June 5

617	A147	15p multi	5	5
618	A147	50p bl & multi	25	18

UN Conference on Human Environment, Stockholm, June 5-16.

1972, July 17 Litho. ***Perf. 12x11½***

619	A148	15p yel & multi	5	5
620	A148	20p yel & multi	9	5

Agricultural and Industrial Fair, Aleppo.

Folk Dance — A149

1972, Aug. 25 Litho. ***Perf. 12x12½***

621	A149 15p shown		8	5
622	A149 20p Women and tambourine player		12	5
623	A149 50p Men and drummer		30	18

19th International Damascus Fair.

Olympic Rings, Discus, Soccer, Swimming — A150

Warriors on Horseback, Olympic Emblems — A151

Design: 60p, Olympic rings, running, gymnastics, fencing.

1972 Litho. ***Perf. 12½x12***

624	A150 15p ol bis, blk & vio	8	5
625	A150 60p dl bl, blk & org	30	22

Souvenir Sheet

Imperf

626	A151 75p lt grn, bl & blk	65	65

20th Olympic Games, Munich, Aug. 26-Sept. 11, 1972.

Emblem of Revolution and Prancing Horse A152

1973, Mar. 8 Litho. ***Perf. 11½x12***

627	A152 15p brt grn, blk & red	5	5
628	A152 20p dl org, blk & red	9	5
629	A152 25p bl, blk & red	12	5

March 8 Revolution, 10th anniversary.

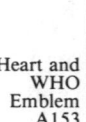

Heart and WHO Emblem A153

1973, Mar. 21

630	A153 15p gray & multi	8	5
631	A153 50p lt brn & multi	25	15

WHO, 25th anniversary.

Cogwheel and Grain Emblem — A154

1973, Apr. 17 ***Perf. 12x12½***

632	A154 15p bl & multi	5	5
633	A154 20p multi	8	5

27th anniv. of the evacuation of British and French troops from Syria.

Workers and Globe A155

1973, May 1 ***Perf. 11½x12***

634	A155 15p rose & multi	8	5
635	A155 50p bl & multi	22	12

Labor Day.

UN, FAO Emblems, People and Symbols A156

Stock A157

1973, May 7 ***Perf. 12x11½***

636	A156 15p lt grn & red brn	8	5
637	A156 50p lil & bl	22	12

10th anniv., world food program.

1973, May 15

638	A157 5p shown	5	5
639	A157 10p Gardenia	5	5
640	A157 15p Jasmine	12	5
641	A157 20p Rose	15	5
642	A157 25p Narcissus	18	8
	Nos. 638-642 (5)	55	28

Intl. Flower Show, Damascus. Nos. 638-642 printed se-tenant.

Children and Flame — A158

Designs: 3 children's heads and flame in different arrangements; 25p, 35p, 70p, vertical.

Perf. 11½x12, 12x11½

1973-74 Litho.

643	A158 2½p lt ol grn	5	5
644	A158 5p orange	5	5
645	A158 7½p dk brn	5	5
646	A158 10p crimson	5	5
647	A158 15p ultra	5	5
648	A158 25p gray	8	5
649	A158 35p brt bl	15	9
650	A158 55p green	18	9
651	A158 70p rose lil	25	15
	Nos. 643-651 (9)	91	63

Children's Day.

Issue dates: 15p, 55p, 70p, May, 1973. Others, Mar. 1974.

Fair Emblem A159

1973, June 17 ***Perf. 11½x12***

652	A159 15p multi	8	5

13th Agricultural and Industrial Fair, Aleppo.

Canceled-to-order stamps are often from remainders. Most collectors of canceled stamps prefer postally used specimens.

Euphrates Dam and Power Plant — A160

1973, July 5 ***Perf. 12½x12***

653	A160 15p grn & multi	9	5
654	A160 50p brn & multi	20	12

Euphrates River diversion and dam project.

Woman from Deir Ezzor — A161

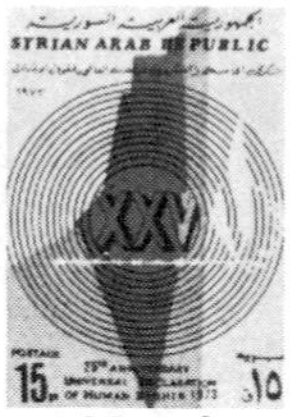

Map of Palestine, Barbed Wire, Human Rights Emblem — A162

Women's Costumes from: 10p, Hassakė. 20p, As Sahel. 25p, Zakiė. 50p, Sarakeb.

1973, July 25 Litho. ***Perf. 12***

655	A161 5p multi	5	5
656	A161 10p multi	5	5
657	A161 20p multi	8	5
658	A161 25p multi	12	5
659	A161 50p multi	22	12
	Nos. 655-659 (5)	52	32

20th International Damascus Fair. Nos. 655-659 printed se-tenant.

1973, Aug. 20 ***Perf. 12x11½***

660	A162 15p lt grn & multi	12	6
661	A162 50p lt bl & multi	30	20

25th anniversary of the Universal Declaration of Human Rights.

Citadel of Ja'abar A163

Designs: 15p, Minaret of Meskeneh (vert.). 25p, Statue of Psyche at Anab al Safinah (vert.).

Perf. 11½x12, 12x11½

1973, Sept. 5 Litho.

662	A163 10p blk, org & bl	5	5
663	A163 15p blk, org & bl	5	5
664	A163 25p blk, org & bl	9	5

Salvage of monuments threatened by Euphrates Dam.

WMO Emblem A164

1973, Sept. 12 ***Perf. 11½x12***

665	A164 70p yel & multi	30	15

Intl. meteorological cooperation, cent.

Maalula A165

Design: 50p, Ruins of Afamia.

1973, Oct. 22 Litho. ***Perf. 11½x12***

666	A165 15p gray bl & blk	5	5
667	A165 50p brn & blk	15	9

Arab Emigrants' Congress, Buenos Aires.

Workers and Soldiers A166

1973, Nov. 16 Litho. ***Perf. 12½x12***

668	A166 15p ultra & yel	5	5
669	A166 25p pur & red brn	9	5

3rd anniv. of Correctionist Movement of Nov. 16, 1970.

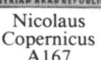

Nicolaus Copernicus A167

UPU Emblem A169

Arms of Syria and Emblems A168

Design: 25p, Abu-al-Rayhan al-Biruni.

1973, Dec. 15 ***Perf. 12x11½***

670	A167 15p gold & blk	5	5
671	A167 25p gold & blk	12	5

14th Science Week.

1974, Mar. 8 ***Perf. 11x12***

672	A168 20p gray & bl	5	5
673	A168 25p lt grn & vio	8	5

11th anniversary of March 8th Revolution.

Perf. 12x11½, 11½x12

1974, Mar. 15

Designs: 20p, Air mail letter and UPU emblem (horiz.). 70p, like 15p.

674	A169 15p gray & multi	5	5
675	A169 20p multi	9	5
676	A169 70p gray & multi	30	18

Centenary of Universal Postal Union.

Arab Postal Institute A170

1974, Apr. 10 ***Perf. 11½x12***

677	A170 15p multi	8	5

Inauguration of the Higher Arab Postal Institute, Damascus, Apr. 10.

Sun and Monument
A171

1974, Apr. 10
678 A171 15p emer, blk & org 5 5
679 A171 20p dp org, blk & org 8 5

28th anniversary of the evacuation of British and French troops from Syria.

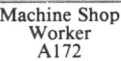

Machine Shop Worker
A172

Abulfeda
A173

1974, May 1 ***Perf. 12x12½***
680 A172 15p blk, yel & bl 5 5
681 A172 50p blk, buff & bl 15 12

Labor Day.

1974 Litho. ***Perf. 11½x11***

Design: 200p, al-Farabi.

682 A173 100p pale grn 38 22
683 A173 200p lt brn 75 45

Damascus Fair Emblem — A174

Figs — A175

Design: 25p, Cog wheel and sun.

1974, July 25 ***Perf. 11½x11***
684 A174 15p multi 5 5
685 A174 25p bl, blk & yel 8 5

21st International Damascus Fair.

1974, Aug. 21 ***Perf. 12x12½***

Fruits: 15p, Grapes. 20p, Pomegranates. 25p, Cherries. 35p, Rose hips.

686 A175 5p gray & multi 5 5
687 A175 15p gray & multi 5 5
688 A175 20p gray & multi 8 5
689 A175 25p gray & multi 12 5
690 A175 35p gray & multi 18 9
Nos. 686-690 (5) 48 29

Agricultural and Industrial Fair, Aleppo. Nos. 686-690 printed se-tenant.

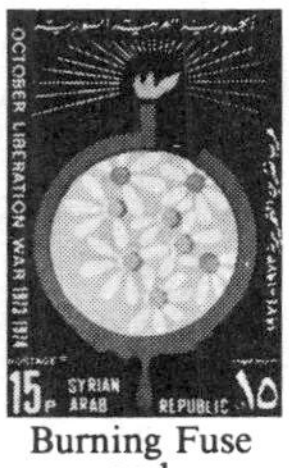

Burning Fuse and Flowers — A176

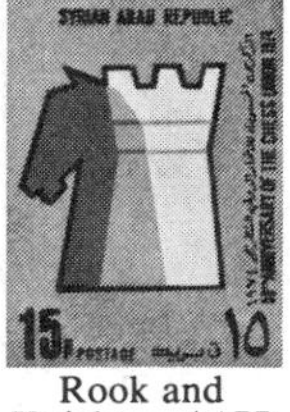

Rook and Knight — A177

Design: 20p, Bomb and star-shaped holes in target.

1974, Oct. 6 Litho. ***Perf. 12x12½***
691 A176 15p multi 50 12
692 A176 20p multi 65 18

First anniv. of October Liberation War (Yom Kippur War).

1974, Nov. 23

Design: 50p, Knight and chess board.

693 A177 15p bl & blk 38 12
694 A177 50p org, blk & bl 50 38

Chess Federation, 50th anniversary.

WPY Emblem
A178

Ishtup, Ilum
A179

1974, Dec. 4 Litho. ***Perf. 12x12½***
695 A178 50p blk, sl & red 18 12

World Population Year.

1975 ***Perf. 12x11½***

Ancient Statuettes: 55p, Woman holding pitcher. 70p, Ur-Nina.

696 A179 20p brt grn 9 5
697 A179 55p brown 18 9
698 A179 70p gray bl 30 12

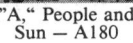

"A," People and Sun — A180

Postal Savings Bank Emblem, Family — A181

1975, Mar. 8 Litho. ***Perf. 12x11½***
699 A180 15p gray & multi 8 5

12th anniversary, March 8th Revolution.

1975, Mar. 17

Design: 20p, Family depositing money, and stamped envelope.

700 A181 15p brt grn & multi 5 5
701 A181 20p org & blk 9 5

Publicity for Savings Certificates and Postal Savings Bank.

"Sun" and Dove — A182

1975, Apr. 17 Litho. ***Perf. 12x11½***
702 A182 15p bis, red & blk 5 5
703 A182 25p bis, grn & blk 9 5

29th anniversary of the evacuation of British and French troops from Syria.

"Worker and Industry"
A183

Camomile
A184

1975, May 1 Litho. ***Perf. 12x11½***
704 A183 15p bl grn & blk 5 5
705 A183 25p brn, yel & blk 9 5

Labor Day.

1975, May 17

Flowers: 10p, Chincherinchi. 15p, Carnation. 20p, Poppy. 25p, Honeysuckle.

706 A184 5p ultra & multi 6 5
707 A184 10p lil & multi 9 8
708 A184 15p bl & multi 20 10
709 A184 20p gray grn & multi 25 15
710 A184 25p vio bl & multi 40 22
Nos. 706-710 (5) 1.00 60

International Flower Show, Damascus. Nos. 706-710 printed se-tenant.

Al-Kuneitra Destroyed and Rebuilt — A185

1975, June 5 ***Perf. 12½***
711 A185 50p blk & multi 28 12

Re-occupation of Al-Kuneitra by Syria.

Apples — A186

Fruit: 10p, Quince. 15p, Apricots. 20p, Grapes. 25p, Figs.

1975, July 7
712 A186 5p lt bl & multi 8 5
713 A186 10p lt bl & multi 10 6
714 A186 15p lt bl & multi 22 7
715 A186 20p lt bl & multi 30 10
716 A186 25p lt bl & multi 38 15
Nos. 712-716 (5) 1.08 43

Agricultural and Industrial Fair, Aleppo. Nos. 712-716 printed se-tenant.

22nd Intl. Damascus Fair
A187

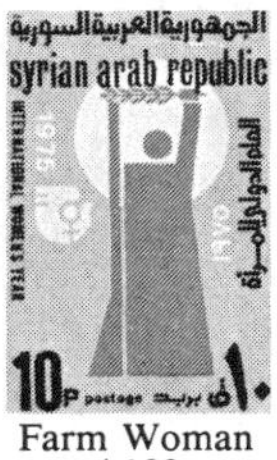

Farm Woman
A189

Pres. Hafez al Assad
A188

1975, July 25 Litho. ***Perf. 12x11½***
717 A187 15p ol grn & multi 8 5
718 A187 35p brn & multi 18 9

1975, Nov. 29 Litho. ***Perf. 11½x12***
719 A188 15p grn & multi 5 5
720 A188 50p bl & multi 18 12

5th anniv. of Correctionist Movement of Nov. 16, 1970.

1975, Nov. 29 ***Perf. 12x11½***

IWY Emblem and: 15p, Mother. 25p, Student. 50p, Laboratory technician.

721 A189 10p buff & multi 9 5
722 A189 15p rose & blk 12 5
723 A189 25p dl grn & blk 25 8
724 A189 50p org & blk 35 12

International Women's Year.

Horse-shaped Bronze Lamp
A190

Man's Head Inkstand
A191

Designs: 10p, 25p, like 20p. 35p, like 30p. 50p, 60p, Nike. 75p, Hera. 100p, Imdugug-Mari (winged animal). 500p, Palmyrene coin of Vasalathus. 1000p, Abraxas coin.

1976 ***Perf. 11½x12, 12x11½***
725 A190 10p brt bluish grn 5 5
726 A190 20p lil rose 5 5
727 A190 25p vio rose 5 5
728 A191 30p brown 12 8
729 A191 35p olive 12 8
730 A191 50p brt bl 20 12
731 A191 60p violet 22 9
732 A191 75p orange 25 18
733 A191 100p lil rose 38 18
734 A191 500p grnsh gray 1.75 1.75
735 A191 1000p dk grn 3.50 2.25
Nos. 725-735 (11) 6.69 4.88

See Nos. 798-803.

National Theater, Damascus and Pres. al Assad
A192

1976, Mar. 8 Litho. ***Perf. 11½x12***
736 A192 25p brt grn, sil & blk 9 5
737 A192 35p ol, sil & blk 12 9

13th anniversary of March 8 Revolution.

Syria, Arabian Government No. 85 — A193

1976, Apr. 12 ***Perf. 12x12½***
738 A193 25p brt grn & multi 12 5
739 A193 35p bl & multi 18 12

Post's Day.

Nurse and Emblem — A194

Eagle and Stars — A195

1976, Apr. 8 *Perf. 12x11½*

740	A194	25p	bl, blk & red	12	5
741	A194	100p	vio, blk & red	38	30

Arab Red Cross and Red Crescent Societies, 8th Conference, Damascus.

1976, Apr. 17

742	A195	25p	blk, red & brt grn	12	5
743	A195	35p	blk, red & brt grn	15	9

30th anniversary of the evacuation of British and French troops from Syria.

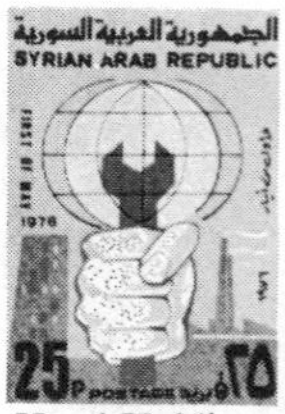

Hand Holding Wrench — A196

Cotton and Factory — A197

Design: 60p, Hand holding globe.

1976, May 1

744	A196	25p	bl & blk	12	5
745	A196	60p	cit & multi	25	18

May Day.

1976, July 1

746	A197	25p	vio & multi	12	5
747	A197	35p	bl & multi	18	9

Agricultural and Industrial Fair, Aleppo.

Tulips — A198

1976, July 26

748	A198	5p	shown	6	5
749	A198	15p	Yellow daisies	10	5
750	A198	20p	Turk's-cap lilies	18	5
751	A198	25p	Irises	35	8
752	A198	35p	Freesia	50	9
			Nos. 748-752 (5)	1.19	32

Intl. Flower Show, Damascus. Nos. 748-752 printed se-tenant.

People, Globe and Olive Branch A199

Design: 60p, Symbolic arrow piercing darkness.

1976, Sept. 2 *Perf. 11½x12*

753	A199	40p	yel & multi	15	12
754	A199	60p	multi	22	15

5th Summit Conference of Non-aligned Countries, Colombo, Sri Lanka, Aug. 9-19.

Soccer, Games Emblem A200

Pan Arab Games Emblem and: 10p, Swimming. 25p, Running. 35p, Basketball. 50p, Javelin. 100p, Steeplechase.

1976, Oct. 6 **Litho.** *Perf. 12½*

755	A200	5p	multi	5	5
756	A200	10p	multi	5	5
757	A200	25p	multi	12	5
758	A200	35p	multi	18	12
759	A200	50p	multi	22	15
			Nos. 755-759 (5)	62	42

Souvenir Sheet

Imperf

760	A200	100p	yel, blk & brn	75	75

5th Pan Arab Sports Tournament.
Nos. 755-759 printed se-tenant. Size of stamp of No. 760: 55x35mm.

"Development" A201

The Fox and the Crow A202

Perf. 12½x12½

1976, Nov. 16 **Litho.**

761	A201	35p	multi	12	5

6th anniv. of Correctionist Movement of Nov. 16, 1970.

1976, Dec. 7 *Perf. 12x12½, 12½x12*

Fairy Tales: 15p, The Hare and the Tortoise (horiz.). 20p, Little Red Riding Hood. 25p, The Lamb and the Wolf (horiz.). 35p, The Lamb and the Wolf.

762	A202	10p	multi	5	5
763	A202	15p	multi	5	5
764	A202	20p	multi	8	5
765	A202	25p	multi	9	8
766	A202	35p	multi	12	9
			Nos. 762-766 (5)	39	32

Children's literature. Nos. 762-766 printed se-tenant.

Syrian Airlines Boeing 747 — A203

1977, Feb. **Litho.** *Perf. 12½x12*

767	A203	35p	multi	18	12

Civil Aviation Day.

Muhammad Kurd-Ali (1876-1953), Philosopher, Birth Cent. — A204

1977, Feb. *Perf. 12x12½*

768	A204	25p	lt grn & multi	12	5

Woman Holding Syrian Flag — A205

APU Emblem — A207

Warrior on Horseback — A206

1977, Mar. 8 **Litho.** *Perf. 12x12½*

769	A205	35p	multi	15	9

14th anniversary of March 8 Revolution.

1977, Apr. 10 **Litho.** *Perf. 12½*

770	A206	100p	multi	20	30

31st anniversary of the evacuation of British and French troops from Syria.

1977, Apr. 12 **Litho.** *Perf. 12x12½*

771	A207	35p	sil & multi	15	8

Arab Postal Union, 25th anniversary.

Tools and Factories A208

1977, May 1 *Perf. 12½x12*

772	A208	60p	multi	22	15

Labor Day.

ICAO Emblem, Plane and Globe A209

1977, May 11

773	A209	100p	multi	38	25

Intl. Civil Aviation Org., 30th anniv.

Pioneers A210

Citrus Fruit A211

1977, Aug. 15 **Litho.** *Perf. 12x12½*

774	A210	35p	multi	18	9

Al Baath Pioneer Organization.

1977, Aug.1

775	A211	10p	Lemon	5	5
776	A211	20p	Lime	8	5
777	A211	25p	Grapefruit	9	5
778	A211	35p	Oranges	18	9
779	A211	60p	Tangerines	25	12
			Nos. 775-779 (5)	65	36

Agricultural and Industrial Fair, Aleppo. Nos. 775-779 printed se-tenant.

Mallow A212

Flowers: 20p, Coxcomb. 25p, Morning glories. 35p, Almond blossoms. 60p, Lilacs.

1977, Aug.6 **Litho.** *Perf. 12½x12*

780	A212	10p	sil & multi	5	5
781	A212	20p	sil & multi	8	5
782	A212	25p	sil & multi	12	8
783	A212	35p	sil & multi	18	9
784	A212	60p	sil & multi	22	18
			Nos. 780-784 (5)	65	45

Intl. Flower Show, Damascus. Nos. 780-784 printed se-tenant.

Coffeepot and Ornament — A213

1977, Sept. 10 *Perf. 12x12½*

785	A213	25p	blk, bl & red	9	5
786	A213	60p	blk, grn & brn	22	15

24th Intl. Damascus Fair.

Blind Man, Globe and Eye A214

Globe and Measures A215

1977, Nov. 17 Litho. ***Perf. 12x12½***
787 A214 55p multi 15 9
788 A214 70p multi 18 12

World Blind Week.

1977, Nov. 5
789 A215 15p grn & multi 8 5

World Standards Day, Oct. 14.

Microscope, Book, Harp, UNESCO Emblem A216

1977, Nov.5 ***Perf. 12½x12***
790 A216 25p multi 9 5

30th anniversary of UNESCO.

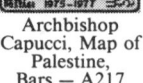

Archbishop Capucci, Map of Palestine, Bars — A217

Fight Cancer Shield, Crab and Surgeon — A218

1977, Nov.17 ***Perf. 12x12½***
791 A217 60p multi 25 12

Palestinian Archbishop Hilarion Capucci, jailed by Israel in 1974.

1977, Nov.17
792 A218 100p multi 32 18

Fight Cancer Week.

Dome of the Rock, Jerusalem A219

1977, Dec. 6 ***Perf. 12***
793 A219 5p multi 25 8
794 A219 10p multi 38 12

Palestinian fighters and their families.

Mural A220

Pres. Hafez al Assad A221

Designs: 10p, 15p, Murals from Dura-Europos, in National Museum, Damascus (15p horiz.).

1978, Jan. 22 Litho. ***Perf. 12x11½***
795 A220 5p gray grn 5 5
796 A220 10p vio bl 5 5
797 A220 15p brown 5 5

Types of 1976

Designs: 40p, Man's head inkstand. 55p, Nike. 70p, 80p, Hera. 200p, Arab-Islamic astrolabe. 300p, Palmyrene (Herod) coin.

1978 Litho. ***Perf. 12x11½, 11½x12***
798 A191 40p pale org 12 5
799 A191 55p brt rose 15 5
800 A191 70p vermilion 25 5
801 A191 80p green 25 12
802 A191 200p lt ultra 70 30
803 A190 300p rose lil 1.00 50
Nos. 798-803 (6) 2.47 1.07

1978 ***Perf. 12x11½***
805 A221 50p multi 15 5

Anniversary of "Correction Movement."

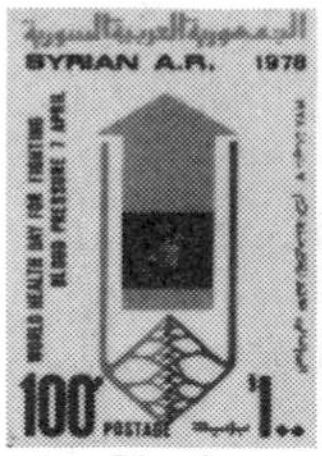
Blood Circulation, WHO Emblem — A222

Factory — A223

1978, Apr. 7 Litho. ***Perf. 12x11½***
806 A222 100p multi 32 18

World Health Day, fight against hypertension.

1978, Apr. 17
807 A223 35p multi 12 5

32nd anniversary of the evacuation of British and French troops from Syria.

Rosette — A224

Map of Arab Countries, Police, Flag and Eye — A225

1978, Apr. 21
808 A224 25p blk & grn 12 5

14th Arab Engineering Conference, Damascus, Apr. 21-26.

1978, May
809 A225 35p multi 12 5

6th Conf. of Arab Police Commanders.

European Goldfinch A226

Birds: 20p, Peregrine falcon. 25p, Rock dove. 35p, Eurasian hoopoe. 60p, Old World quail.

1978 ***Perf. 11½x12***
810 A226 10p multi 8 8
811 A226 20p multi 12 8
812 A226 25p multi 16 8
813 A226 35p multi 25 8
814 A226 60p multi 32 16
Nos. 810-814 (5) 93 48

Nos. 810-814 printed se-tenant.

Trout A227

Designs: Various fish.

1978, July Litho. ***Perf. 11½x12***
815 A227 10p multi 8 8
816 A227 20p multi 12 10
817 A227 25p multi 18 12
818 A227 35p multi 25 15
819 A227 60p multi 35 25
Nos. 815-819 (5) 98 70

Nos. 815-819 printed se-tenant.

Miniature Sheet
Pres. Assad Type of Air Post, 1978

1978, Sept. Litho. ***Imperf.***
820 AP161 100p gold & multi 42 42

Reelection of President Assad. Size of stamp: 58x80mm.

Flowering Cactus A228

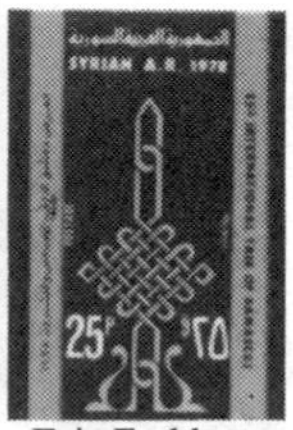
Fair Emblem A229

Designs: Flowering cacti.

1978 Litho. ***Perf. 12½***
821 A228 25p multi 5 5
822 A228 30p multi 8 5
823 A228 35p multi 12 8
824 A228 50p multi 18 9
825 A228 60p multi 20 12
Nos. 821-825 (5) 63 39

International Flower Show, Damascus. Printed se-tenant.

1978 Litho. ***Perf. 12x12½***
826 A229 25p sil & multi 8 5
827 A229 35p sil & multi 12 5

Miniature Sheet
Imperf

828 A229 100p sil & multi 42 42

25th Intl. Damascus Fair. No. 828 shows different ornament, size of stamp: 40x46mm.

Euphrates Dam and Pres. Assad — A230

1978, Dec. Litho. ***Perf. 12½x12***
829 A230 60p multi 22 12

Inauguration of Euphrates Dam.

Pres. Hafez al Assad — A231

1978, Nov. 16 Litho. ***Perf. 12x12½***
830 A231 60p multi 18 9

Nov. 16 Movement.

Racial Equality Emblem A232

1978, Mar. Litho. ***Perf. 12½***
831 A232 35p multi 12 5

International Year to Combat Racism.

Averroes A233

Human Rights Flame and Globe A234

1979, Mar.
832 A233 100p multi 50 22

Averroes (1126-1198), Spanish-Arabian philosopher and physician.

1978, Dec. ***Perf. 12x12½***
833 A234 60p multi 18 9

30th anniversary of Universal Declaration of Human Rights (in 1978).

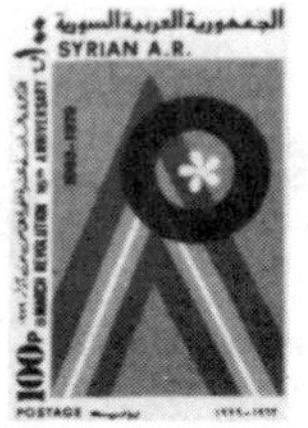
Symbolic Design A235

Princess, 2nd Century Shield A236

1979, Mar.
834 A235 100p multi 42 15

16th anniversary of March 8 Revolution.

1979 Litho. ***Perf. 11½***

Designs: 20p, Helmet of Homs. 35p, Ishtar.

836 A236 20p green 5 5
837 A236 25p rose car 8 5
838 A236 35p sepia 9 5

Molar, Emblem with Mosque — A237

Flame Emblem — A238

1979 Litho. *Perf. 12x11½*
846 A237 35p multi 15 5

Intl. Middle East Dental Congress.

1979
847 A238 35p multi 12 5

33rd anniversary of evacuation.

Ibn Assaker, 900th Anniv. A239

1979 *Perf. 11½x12*
848 A239 75p multi 20 12

Telephone Lineman A240

Girl with IYC Emblem A242

Wright Brothers' Plane A241

1979, May 1 Litho. *Perf. 12x11½*
849 A240 50p multi 18 7
850 A240 75p multi 20 12

May Day.

1979 *Perf. 11½x12*

Designs: 75p, Bleriot's plane crossing English Channel. 100p, Spirit of St. Louis.

851 A241 50p multi 15 8
852 A241 75p multi 22 15
853 A241 100p multi 38 22

75th anniversary of 1st powered flight.

1979 *Perf. 12x11½*

Design: 15p, Boy, globe, IYC emblem.

854 A242 10p multi 18 7
855 A242 15p multi 25 10

International Year of the Child.

Power Plant — A243

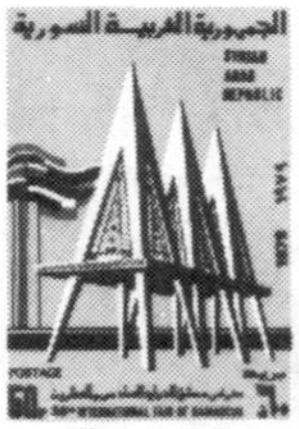
Flags and Pavilion — A244

1979 *Perf. 11x11½*
856 A243 5p blue 5 5
857 A243 10p lil rose 5 5
858 A243 15p gray grn 8 5

1979 Photo. *Perf. 12x11½*

Design: 75p, Lamppost and flags.

859 A244 60p multi 18 9
860 A244 75p multi 22 12

26th International Damascus Fair.

Correction Movement, 9th Anniversary — A245

1979 Photo. *Perf. 11½x12*
861 A245 100p multi 38 12

Games Emblem, Running A246

1979, Nov.
862 A246 25p shown 7 5
863 A246 35p Diving 12 5
864 A246 50p Soccer 15 9

8th Mediterranean Games, Split, Jugoslavia, Sept. 15-29.

Butterfly A247

Damascus Intl. Flower Show A248

Designs: Various butterflies.

1979, Dec. Litho. *Perf. 12x11½*
865 A247 20p multi 7 5
866 A247 25p multi 9 5
867 A247 30p multi 12 5
868 A247 35p multi 15 8
869 A247 50p multi 20 12
Nos. 865-869 (5) 63 35

1980, Jan.9 Litho. *Perf. 12½*

Design: Roses.

870 A248 5p multi 5 5
871 A248 10p multi 5 5
872 A248 15p multi 5 5
873 A248 50p multi 15 5
874 A248 75p multi 22 9
875 A248 100p multi 42 18
Nos. 870-875 (6) 94 47

March 8 Revolution, 17th Anniv. — A249

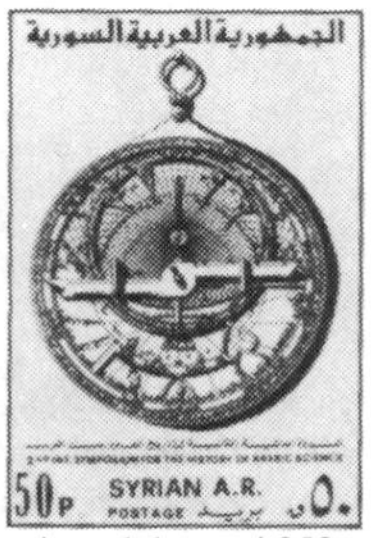
Astrolabe — A250

1980, Mar. 25 Litho. *Perf. 12x11½*
876 A249 40p multi 12 5

1980, May 2 *Perf. 12½*
877 A250 50p violet 15 5
878 A250 100p sepia 32 18
879 A250 1000p gray grn 3.00 1.25

2nd International History of Arabic Sciences Symposium, Apr. 5.

Lit Cigarette, Skull A251

Evacuation, 34th Anniversary A252

1980, June 25 Photo. *Perf. 12x11½*
880 A251 60p Smoker 22 12
881 A251 100p shown 32 15

World Health Day; anti-smoking campaign.

1980, June 25 Litho.
882 A252 40p multi 12 5
883 A252 60p multi 15 8

Moscow '80 Emblem and Wrestling A253

1980, July Litho. *Perf. 11½x12*
884 A253 15p shown 6 5
885 A253 25p Fencing 9 5
886 A253 35p Weight lifting 12 5
887 A253 50p Judo 18 6
888 A253 75p Boxing 30 12
Nos. 884-888 (5) 75 33

Souvenir Sheet
Imperf

888A A253 300p Discus, running 3.75 3.75

22nd Summer Olympic Games, Moscow, July 19-Aug. 3. Nos. 884-888 se-tenant.

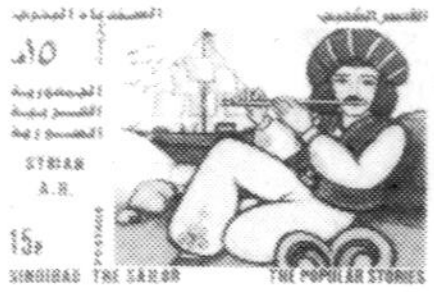
Sinbad the Sailor A254

1980 Litho. *Perf. 11½x12*
889 A254 15p shown 5 5
890 A254 25p Scheherezade and Shahrayar 9 5
891 A254 35p Ali Baba and the Forty Thieves 12 5
892 A254 50p Hassan the Clever 18 5
893 A254 100p Aladdin's Lamp 32 15
Nos. 889-893 (5) 76 35

Popular stories. Nos. 889-893 se-tenant.

Savings Certificates A255

1980
894 A255 25p multi 9 5

Hegira, 1500th Anniv. — A256

1980 *Perf. 12½x12*
895 A256 35p multi 18 9

Intl. Flower Show, Damascus — A257

1980 *Perf. 12x11½*
896 A257 20p Daffodils 8 5
897 A257 30p Chrysanthemums 12 5
898 A257 40p Clematis 15 5
899 A257 60p Yellow roses 22 9
900 A257 100p Chrysanthemums, diff. 32 15
Nos. 896-900 (5) 89 39

Nos. 896-900 se-tenant.

May Day — A258

Children's Day — A259

1980, May
901 A258 35p multi 18 7

1980
902 A259 25p multi 15 5

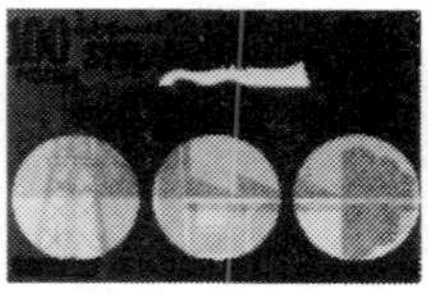
November 16th Movement, 10th Anniv. A260

1980 *Perf. 11½x12*
903 A260 100p multi 38 15

Steam-powered Passenger Wagon — A261

1980
904 A261 25p shown 12 5
905 A261 35p Benz, 1899 16 8
906 A261 40p Rolls-Royce, 1903 22 8
907 A261 50p Mercedes, 1906 25 12
908 A261 60p Austin, 1915 32 14
Nos. 904-908 (5) 1.07 47

Nos. 904-908 se-tenant.

Footnotes often refer you to other stamps of the same design.

Mother's Day — A262

1980 ***Perf. 12x11½***
909 A262 40p shown 25 5
910 A262 100p Mother and child 50 12

27th International Damascus Fair — A263

1981, Jan. 24 ***Perf. 11½x12***
911 A263 50p multi 30 8
912 A263 100p multi 55 15

Army Day — A264

1981, Jan. 24 ***Perf. 12½x12***
913 A264 50p multi 30 8

18th Anniv. of March 8th Revolution A265

1981, Mar. 8 Litho. ***Perf. 12x11½***
914 A265 50p multi 30 8

35th Anniversary of Evacuation — A266

1981, Apr. 17 Litho. ***Perf. 12x11½***
915 A266 50p multi 30 8

World Conference on History of Arab and Islamic Civilization, Damascus — A267

1981, May 30 Photo. ***Perf. 12½x12***
916 A267 100p multi 55 18

Intl. Workers' Solidarity Day — A268

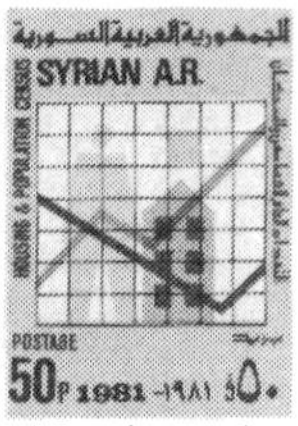

Housing and Population Census — A269

1981, May 30 Litho. ***Perf. 12x11½***
917 A268 100p multi 55 15

1981, June 1
918 A269 50p multi 30 8

Umayyad Window A270

Abdul Malik Gold Coin A270a

Designs: 10p, figurine. 15p, Rakkla's cavalier, Abbcid ceramic. 160p, like 5p. 500p, Umar B. Abdul Aziz gold coin.

1981 ***Perf. 12x11½, 11½x12***
919 A270 5p crim rose 5 5
920 A270 10p brt grn 12 5
921 A270 15p dp rose lil 8 5
922 A270a 75p blue 38 16
923 A270 160p dk grn 70 38
924 A270a 500p dk brn 2.50 1.10
Nos. 919-924 (6) 3.83 1.79

Olives — A270b

Designs: 100p, 180p, Harbor.

1982 ***Perf. 12x11½***
925 A270b 50p ol grn 25 12
926 A270b 60p bl gray 28 12
929 A270b 100p lilac 38 18
930 A270b 180p red 75 38

Saving Certificates Plan A271

Avicenna (980-1037), Philosopher and Physician A272

1981, June 22
931 A271 50p gldn brn & blk 30 8

1981, Aug.
932 A272 100p multi 55 18

Syria-P.L.O. Solidarity, Intl. Conference A273

1981, June 22
933 A273 160p multi 2.50 50

Grand Mosque, Damascus — A274

1981 ***Perf. 12½***
934 A274 50p Glass lamp, 13th cent. 25 9
935 A274 180p shown 1.00 30
936 A274 180p Hunter 1.00 30

Youth Festival A275

1981 ***Perf. 12½***
937 A275 60p multi 22 9

28th Intl. Damascus Fair — A276

Intl. Palestinian Solidarity Day — A277

1981 ***Perf. 12x11½***
938 A276 50p Ornament 18 9
939 A276 160p Emblem 55 25

1981
940 A277 100p multi 75 15

1300th Anniv. of Bulgaria A278

1981 ***Perf. 11½x12***
941 A278 380p multi 1.25 55

Intl. Children's Day A279

1981
942 A279 180p multi 70 30

World Food Day, Oct. 16 — A280

1981
943 A280 180p multi 70 30

9th Intl. Flower Show, Damascus — A281

Designs: Flowers. Nos. 944-948 se-tenant.

1981 ***Perf. 12x11½***
944 A281 25p multi 12 5
945 A281 40p multi 19 12
946 A281 50p multi 25 14
947 A281 60p multi 38 16
948 A281 100p multi 55 25
Nos. 944-948 (5) 1.49 72

Souvenir Sheet

Koran Competition — A282

1981 Litho. ***Imperf.***
949 A282 500p multi 4.50 4.50

11th Anniv. of Correction Movement A283

1981, Nov. ***Perf. 12x11½***
950 A283 60p multi 40 25

TB Bacillus Centenary A284

1982 Litho. ***Perf. 11½x12***
951 A284 180p multi 90 50

For unused stamps, more recent issues are valued as never hinged, with the beginning point determined on a country-by-country basis. Notes to show the beginning points are prominently placed in the text.

Mothers' Day — A285

Mar. 8th Revolution, 19th Anniv. — A286

1982 ***Perf. 11 1/2***

952 A285 40p green 15 7
953 A285 75p brown 35 16

1982, Mar. ***Perf. 12x11 1/2***

954 A286 50p multi 22 12

Intl. Year of the Disabled (1981) — A287

Pres. Hafez al Assad — A288

1982 ***Perf. 12x11 1/2***

955 A287 90p multi 50 22

1982 ***Perf. 11 1/2***

956 A288 150p ultra 60 35

36th Anniv. of Evacuation A289

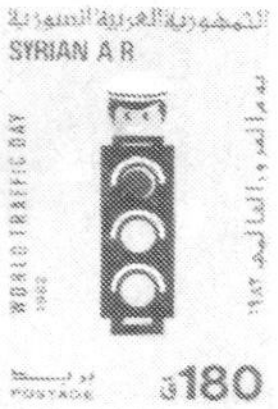

World Traffic Day A290

1982 ***Perf. 12x11 1/2***

957 A289 70p multi 35 16

1982

958 A290 180p multi 90 50

Intl. Workers' Solidarity Day — A291

1982

959 A291 180p multi 90 50

World Telecommunication Day, May 17 — A292

1982

960 A292 180p multi 90 50

Soldier Holding Rifles — A293

Arab Postal Union, 30th Anniv. — A294

1982 **Photo.** ***Perf. 12x11 1/2***

961 A293 50p multi 22 15

1982

962 A294 60p multi 30 15

1982 World Cup — A295

Various soccer players. 300p, Ball.

1982, July ***Perf. 12 1/2***

963 A295 40p multi 20 12
964 A295 60p multi 30 16
965 A295 100p multi 50 30

Size: 75x55mm

Imperf

966 A295 300p multi *9.00 9.00*

10th Intl. Flower Show, Damascus — A297

1982 ***Perf. 12x11 1/2***

967 A297 50p Honeysuckle 30 15
968 A297 60p Geraniums 40 20

Scouting Year A298

1982, Nov. 4 ***Perf. 11 1/2x12***

969 A298 160p green 90 50

Ladybug A299

1982 ***Perf. 12x12 1/2***

970 Strip of 5 70 40
a A299 5p Dragonfly 5 5
b A299 10p Stag Beetle 5 5
c A299 20p shown 10 5
d A299 40p Grasshopper 22 12
e A299 50p Honeybee 30 12

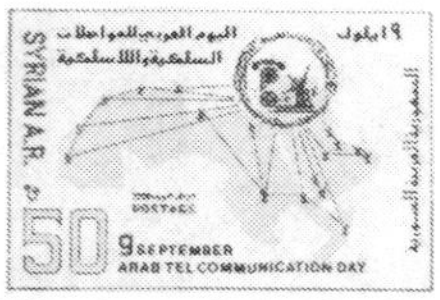

ITU Plenipotentiaries Conference, Nairobi, Sept — A300

1982 ***Perf. 11 1/2x12***

971 A300 50p Map 22 15
972 A300 180p Dish antenna 90 50

12th Anniv. of Correction Movement A301

1982, Nov.

973 A301 50p dk bl & sil 22 15

A302

Designs: Various buildings. 30p, No. 977, 200p horiz.

1982 **Litho.** ***Perf. 11 1/2***

974 A302 30p brown 15 10
975 A302 50p dk grn 22 15
976 A302 70p green 35 20
977 A302 200p red 1.00 55

Dove and Satellite — A303

Intl. Palestinian Solidarity Day — A304

1982 **Litho.** ***Perf. 12x11 1/2***

978 A303 50p multi 22 15

2nd UN Conference on Peaceful Uses of Outer Space, Vienna, Aug. 9-21.

1982

979 A304 50p multi 65 15

20th Anniv. of March 8th Revolution — A305

1983 ***Perf. 12 1/2x12***

980 A305 60p multi 35 16

World Communications Year — A305a

1983

981 A305a 180p multi 90 50

9th Anniv. of Liberation of Qnaytra — A306

25th Anniv. of Intl. Maritime Org. — A308

Arab Pharmacists' Day, Apr. 2 — A307

1983, June 26 **Litho.** ***Perf. 11 1/2***

982 A306 50p View 50 16
983 A306 100p View, diff. 1.00 22

1983, Apr. 2 ***Perf. 11 1/2x12***

984 A307 100p multi 50 22

1983, June ***Perf. 12x11 1/2***

985 A308 180p multi 90 50

Namibia Day, Aug. 26 — A309

1983, Aug. 26 ***Perf. 11 1/2x12***

986 A309 180p multi 90 50

Eibla Sculpture, 3rd Cent. BC A310

1983

987 A310 380p ol & brn 1.90 1.00

World Standards Day A311

11th Intl. Flower Show, Damascus A312

1983, Oct. 14 **Photo.** ***Perf. 11 1/2***

988 A311 50p Factory, emblem 20 10
989 A311 100p Measuring equipment 40 20

1983, Oct. 14 **Litho.** ***Perf. 11 1/2***

990 A312 50p multi 20 10
991 A312 60p multi, diff. 25 12

World Heritage Day — A313

1983, Oct. 14 **Photo.** ***Perf. 11½***
992 A313 60p dk brn 25 12

World Food Day A313a

1983, Oct. 16 **Litho.** ***Perf. 11½x12***
992A A313a 180p multi 60 30

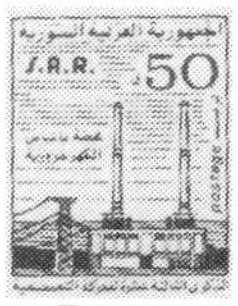

Waterwheels of Hama A314

Factory A315

1983 **Litho.** ***Perf. 11x11½, 11½x11***
993 A314 5p sepia 5 5
994 A314 10p violet 5 5
995 A314 20p red 8 5
997 A315 50p dk grn 20 10

Statue — A316

View of Aleppo — A317

1983 ***Perf. 12***
1003 A316 225p brown 90 45

Intl. Symposium on History and Archaeology of Deir Ez-zor.

1983 ***Perf. 12x12½***
1004 A317 245p multi 1.00 50

Intl. Symposium on Conservation of Old City of Aleppo, Sept. 26-30.

Mar. 8th Revolution, 21st Anniv. — A318

1984, Mar. 8 ***Perf. 12½x12***
1005 A318 60p Alassad Library 25 12

Massacre at Sabra and Shatilla A319

1983 **Litho.** ***Perf. 11½x12***
1006 A319 225p Victims, mother & child 1.60 40

Mothers' Day A320

12th Intl. Flower Show, Damascus A321

1984, Mar. 21 ***Perf. 12x11½***
1007 A320 245p Mother & child 1.00 50

1984, May 25

Various flowers.

1008 A321 245p multi 1.00 50
1009 A321 285p multi 1.10 55

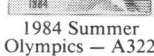

1984 Summer Olympics — A322

Aleppo Agricultural & Industrial Fair — A324

9th Regional Pioneers' Festival A323

1984 **Litho.** ***Perf. 12x11½***

1010	Strip of 5	1.00	50
a	A322 30p Swimming	10	5
b	A322 50p Wrestling	16	8
c	A322 60p Running	20	10
d	A322 70p Boxing	22	12
e	A322 90p Soccer	30	15

Souvenir Sheet

Imperf

1011 A322 200p Soccer, diff. 1.90 1.90

1984 ***Perf. 11½x12***
1012 A323 50p Pioneers 16 8
1013 A323 60p Pioneers, diff. 20 10

1984, June 12 **Litho.** ***Perf. 12x12½***
1014 A324 150p Peppers, Aleppo Castle 65 25

Supreme Council of Science, 25th Anniv. A325

1985, Feb. 23 ***Perf. 12½x12***
1015 A325 65p multi 35 12

Aleppo University, 25th Anniv. — A326

1985, Feb. 23
1016 A326 45p multi 20 8

Syrian Arab Army, 39th Anniv. A327

1985, Feb. 23
1017 A327 65p brn & gldn brn 35 12

Pres. Assad, Soldier Saluting, Troops A328

1984, Aug. 1 ***Perf. 11½x12***
1018 A328 60p multi 20 10

4th General Revolutionary Youth Conference.

ITU Emblem, Satellite Dish, Telephone A329

1984, Oct. 2 ***Perf. 12½***
1019 A329 245p multi 80 42

Intl. Telecommunications Day.

APU Emblem and Administration Building, Damascus — A330

1984, Oct. 9
1020 A330 60p multi 20 10

Arab Postal Union Day.

Scott's editorial staff cannot undertake to identify, authenticate or appraise stamps and postal markings.

Gearwheel, Arabesque Pattern — A331

Gold Necklace — A332

Perf. 12x12½, 12x11½
1984, Oct. 27
1021 A331 45p multi 16 8
1022 A332 100p multi 35 16

Intl. Fair, Damascus.

Intl. Civil Aviation Org., 40th Anniv. A333

1984, Oct. 27 ***Perf. 11½x12***
1023 A333 45p brt bl & lt bl 16 8
1024 A333 245p brt ultra, brt bl & lt bl 80 40

14th Anniv. of 11-16-70 Movement A334

1984, Dec. 3 ***Perf. 12½x12***
1025 A334 65p red brn, blk & org 22 12

Pres. Assad, Text on Scroll — A335

1984, Nov. 29 ***Perf. 12½***
1026 A335 50p grn, brn org & sep 16 8

Vow of Dedication taken by Youth of the Revolution.

Agricultural Exhibition — A336

1984, June 12 ***Perf. 12½x12***
1027 A336 65p multi 22 12

Queneitra Memorial, Rose A337

1984
1028 A337 70p multi 45 12

Roman Arch and Colonnades, Palmyra — A338

1984, Dec. 3
1029 A338 100p multi 35 16

Intl. Tourism Day.

Woodland Conservation — A339

1984
1030 A339 45p multi 16 8

March 8 Revolution, 22nd Anniv. A340

UPU Emblem, Postal Headquarters, Damascus A341

1985, Apr. 27
1031 A340 60p multi 20 10

1985, Apr. 27
1032 A341 285p multi 1.00 50

World Post Day.

APU Building, Damascus — A342

1985, Apr. 27 ***Perf. 12½***
1033 A342 245p multi 80 40

Arab Parliamentary Union, 10th Anniv.

Natl. Flag, Map of Arab Countries A343

1985 ***Perf. 12½x12***
1034 A343 50p multi 16 8

Arab League.

Foreign postal stationery (stamped envelopes, postal cards and air letter sheets) lies beyond the scope of this Catalogue, which is limited to adhesive postage stamps.

Re-election of President Assad — A344

1985, Mar. 12 ***Perf. 12½***
1035 A344 200p multi 65 35
1036 A344 300p multi 1.00 50
1037 A344 500p multi 1.60 80
a Souvenir sheet of 3, #1035-1037, imperf. 3.50 1.60

Arab Postal Union, 12th Congress, Damascus — A345

1985, Aug. 12 ***Perf. 12x12½***
1038 A345 60p multi 20 10

May Day — A346

1985, Aug. 12 ***Perf. 12½***
1039 A346 60p Order of Labor 20 10

32nd Intl. Fair, Damascus A347

1986, Feb. 1 **Litho.** ***Perf. 12½***
1040 A347 60p multi 20 10

2nd Scientific Symposium — A348

1985, Nov. 16 ***Perf. 12½***
1041 A348 60p Locomotives 20 10

UN Child Survival Campaign A349

1985, Nov. 16 ***Perf. 12½x12***
1042 A349 60p Malnourished child 20 10

UN, 40th Anniv. — A350

1985, Nov. 16 ***Perf. 12x12½***
1043 A350 245p multi 80 40

November 16th Movement, 15th Anniv. — A351

1985, Nov. 16 ***Perf. 12½***
1044 A351 60p Pres. Assad, highway 20 10

Abdul Rahman Dakhei in Andalusia, 1200th Anniv. A352

1986, Feb. 1 ***Perf. 12½x12***
1045 A352 60p beige & brn 30 15

Tulips — A353

World Traffic Day — A355

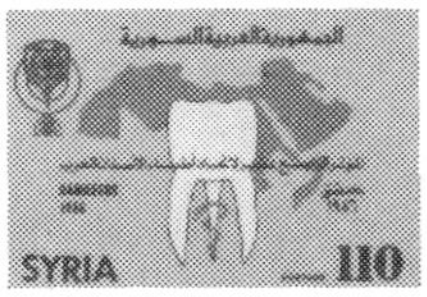

Dental Congress, Damascus A354

1986, Feb. 1 ***Perf. 12½***
1046 A353 30p multi 15 8
1047 A353 60p multi, diff. 30 15

Intl. Flower Show, Damascus.

1986 ***Perf. 12½x12***
1048 A354 110p yel, grysh grn & bl 55 28

1986 ***Perf. 12x12½***
1049 A355 330p multi 1.65 82

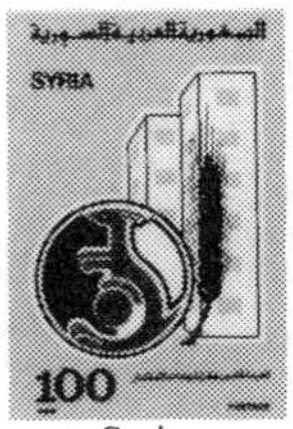

Syrian Investment Certificates, 15th Anniv. — A357

Day of Internal Security Forces — A359

Liberation of Kuneitra, 12th Anniv. A358

1986 **Litho.** ***Perf. 12x11½***
1055 A357 100p multi 50 25

1986 **Litho.** ***Perf. 11½x12***
1056 A358 110p Government Building 55 28

1986 ***Perf. 12x11½***
1057 A359 110p multi 55 28

Labor Day — A360

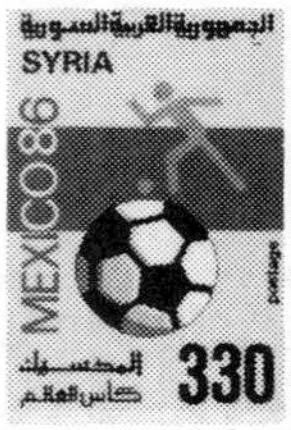

1986 World Cup Soccer Championships, Mexico — A361

1986, Aug. 12
1058 A360 330p multi 1.65 82

1986, July 7
1059 A361 330p multi 1.65 82
1060 A361 370p multi 1.85 95

Booklet Stamp

Size: 105x80mm

Imperf

1061 A361 500p Hemispheres, ball 2.50 1.25

Pres. Hafez al Assad — A362

1986-88 **Litho.** ***Perf. 12x11½***

1063	A362	10p	rose	5	5
1064	A362	30p	dl ultra	15	8
1072	A362	100p	brt lt bl	50	25
1072A	A362	150p	brn vio ('88)	1.05	52
1073	A362	175p	violet ('88)	1.20	60
1074	A362	200p	pale red brn	1.00	50
1075	A362	300p	brt rose lil	1.50	75
1077	A362	500p	orange	2.50	1.25
1077A	A362	550p	pink ('88)	3.75	1.90
1077B	A362	600p	dull grn ('88)	4.00	2.00
1078	A362	1000p	brt pink	5.00	2.50
1079	A362	2000p	pale grn	10.00	5.00
	Nos. 1063-1079 (12)			30.70	15.40

Intl. Day for Solidarity with the Palestinian People — A363

Mothers' Day — A364

1986, Aug. 7 **Litho.**
1081 A363 110p multi 75 38

1986, Aug. 7
1082 A364 100p multi 50 25

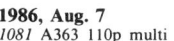

March 8 Revolution, 23rd Anniv. — A365

1986, Aug. 7 ***Perf. 11½x12***
1083 A365 110p multi 55 28

Arab Post Day A366

1986, Aug. 7
1084 A366 110p multi 55 28

A367
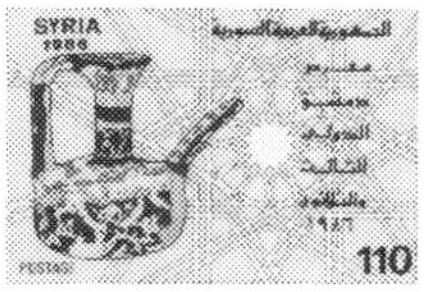

33rd Intl. Damascus Fair — A368

1986, Dec. 9 **Litho.** ***Perf. 11½x12***
1085 A367 110p multi 58 30
1086 A368 330p multi 1.75 90

14th Intl. Flower Show, Damascus — A369

Various flowers.

1986, Oct. 11 ***Perf. 12½***
1087 Strip of 5 3.25 1.75
a A369 10p multi 5 5
b A369 50p multi 26 14
c A369 100p multi 52 25
d A369 110p multi 58 30
e A369 330p multi 1.75 90

Syria-Soviet Joint Space Project — A370

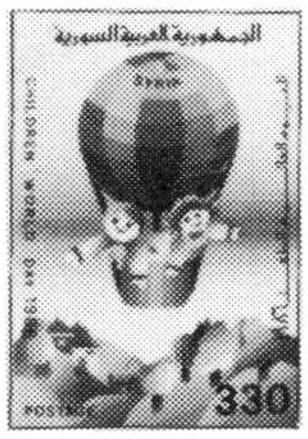

World Children's Day — A371

1986, Nov. 16 **Litho.** ***Perf. 12½***
1088 A370 330p multi 1.75 90

1986 ***Perf. 12x12½, 12½x12***
1089 A371 330p shown 1.75 90
1090 A371 330p Youth art exhibition, horiz. 1.75 90

World Post Day A372

1986, Jan. 28 ***Perf. 12½x12***
1091 A372 330p multi 1.75 90

Intl. Tourism Day A373

Women wearing folk costumes, landmarks.

1986
1092 A373 330p multi 1.75 90
1093 A373 370p multi 2.00 1.00

Pres. Assad, Tishreen Palace — A374

1986, Nov. 16 **Litho.** ***Perf. 12½***
1094 A374 110p multi 70 35

Nov. 16 Corrective Movement.

March 8th Revolution, 24th Anniv. — A375

1986
1095 A375 100p multi 65 32

Intl. Peace Year — A376

1986 ***Perf. 12x11½***
1096 A376 370p multi 2.40 1.20

Arab Baath Socialist Party, 40th Anniv. A377

1987, Apr. 7 **Litho.** ***Perf. 12½***
1097 A377 100p multi 65 32

Arab Post Day, 35th Anniv. A378

1987, July 7 ***Perf. 11½x12***
1098 A378 110p multi 72 35

Evacuation, Day, 41st Anniv. — A379

1987 ***Perf. 12½x12***
1099 A379 100p multi 65 32

Labor Day A380

Qunitra Monument A382

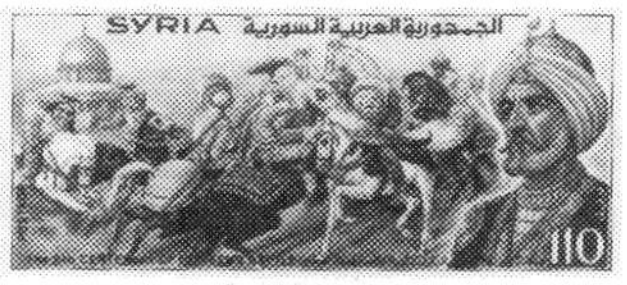

Hitteen's Battle, 800th Anniv. — A381

1987 ***Perf. 12x11½***
1100 A380 330p multi 2.25 1.15

1987 **Litho.** ***Perf. 12½***
1101 A381 110p multi 72 35

1987 ***Perf. 12x11½***
1102 A382 100p multi 65 32

Child Vaccination Campaign A383

1987 ***Perf. 11½x12***
1103 A383 100p multi 65 32
1104 A383 330p multi 2.15 1.10

A384

A385

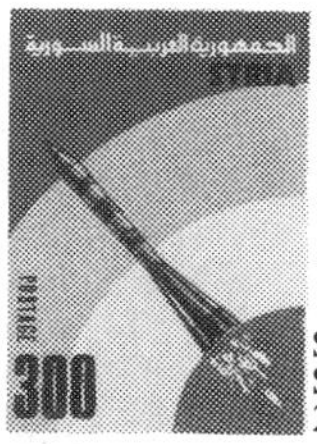

Syrian-Soviet Joint Space Flight, July 22-30 — A386

Designs: No. 1108a, Lift-off. No. 1108b, Parachute landing. No. 1108c, Docked at space station. No. 1108d, Cosmonauts.

Perf. 12½, 11½x12, 12x11½
1987 **Litho.**
1105 A384 330p Launch, July 22 2.10 1.05
1106 A385 330p Docking at space station, July 24 2.10 1.05
1107 A385 330p Landing, July 30, vert. 2.10 1.05

Souvenir Sheet

Imperf

1108 Sheet of 4 8.50 8.50
a.-d A386 300p, any single 2.10 2.10

6th Conference of Arab Ministers of Culture — A387

1987 **Litho.** ***Perf. 12½***
1109 A387 330p dull blue grn & blk 3.35 1.70

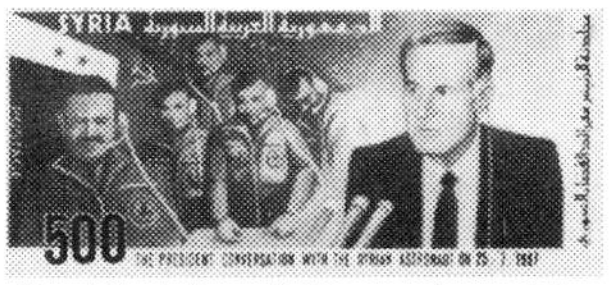

President Assad Conversing with Syrian Cosmonaut — A388

1987
1110 A388 500p multi 3.75 1.90

10th Mediterranean Games, Latakia — A389

Designs: 100p, Gymnastic rings, weight lifting, vert. 330p, Phoenician sailing ship. 370p, Flags spelling "SYRIA." No. 1115a, Emblem, gymnastics. No. 1115b, Emblem, weight lifting. No. 1115c, Emblem, tennis. No. 1115d, Emblem, soccer.

Perf. 12x11½, 11½x12

1987, Sept. 10
1111 A389 100p brt rose lil & blk 68 35
1112 A389 110p shown 75 38

Size: 58x28mm

Perf. 12½

1113 A389 330p multi 2.25 1.15
1114 A389 370p multi 2.50 1.25

Souvenir Sheet

Imperf

1115 Sheet of 4 8.50 8.50
a.-d. A389 300p any single 2.10 2.10

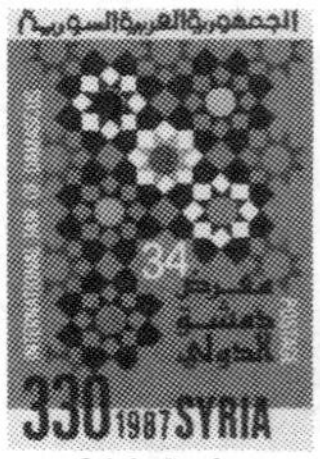

34th Intl. Damascus Fair — A390

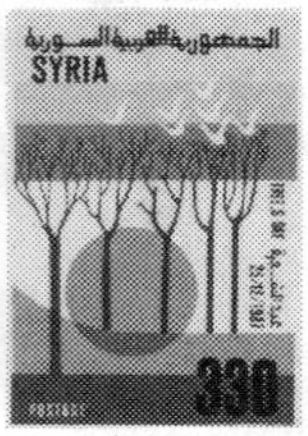

Arbor Day — A392

Intl. Flower Show, Damascus A391

1987 ***Perf. 12x11½***
1116 A390 330p multi 2.15 1.05

1987, Oct. 20 ***Perf. 11½x12***
1117 A391 330p Poppies 2.00 1.00
1118 A391 370p Gentian 2.25 1.15

1987, Oct. 20 ***Perf. 12x11½***
1119 A392 330p multi 2.10 1.05

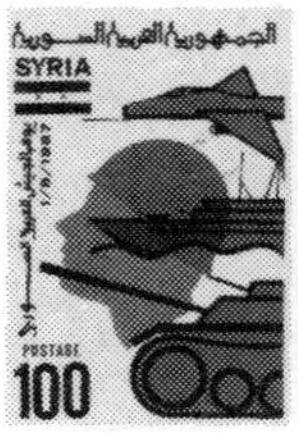

Army Day — A393

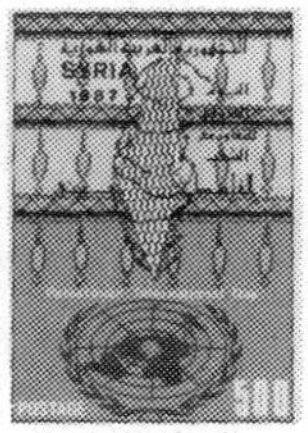

Intl. Palestine Day — A394

1987, Oct. 20 Litho. ***Perf. 12x11½***
1120 A393 100p multi 60 30

1987, Nov. 16
1121 A394 500p multi 3.40 1.70

Corrective Movement, 17th Anniv. — A395

1987, Nov. 16 ***Perf. 12½***
1122 A395 150p Assad waving to crowd 1.00 50

World Post Day — A396

1988, Mar. 8 Litho. ***Perf. 12½x12***
1123 A396 500p multi 3.40 1.70

Intl. Tourism Day A397

Women wearing folk costumes and: No. 1124, Palmyra Ruins. No. 1125, Reconstructed Roman amphitheater, Busra.

1988, Feb. 25 Litho. ***Perf. 11½x12***
1124 A397 500p multi 3.50 1.75
1125 A397 500p multi 3.50 1.75

See Nos. 1147-1148.

Intl. Children's Day — A398

1988, Feb. 27 ***Perf. 12½***
1126 A398 500p multi 3.50 1.75

March 8th Revolution, 25th Anniv. — A399

Mothers' Day — A400

1988, Mar. 15 Litho. ***Perf. 12x11½***
1127 A399 150p multi 98 50

Size: 110x81mm

Imperf

1128 A399 500p multi, diff. 3.50 3.50

No. 1128 pictures vignette like 150p without denomination, in diff. colors, and Arab Revolt flag, text, outline map; denomination at LR in sheet.

1988, Apr. 12 Litho. ***Perf. 12x12½***
1129 A400 500p multi 3.50 1.75

Arab Post Day A401

1988, Apr. 17 ***Perf. 12½x12***
1130 A401 150p multi 98 50

1946 Evacuation A402

Labor Day A403

1988, Apr. 17 ***Perf. 12x12½***
1131 A402 150p multi 98 50

1988, May 1
1132 A403 550p multi 3.50 1.75

Intl. Flower Show, Damascus A404

Arab Engineers' Union A405

1988, May 25 ***Perf. 12x11½***
1133 A404 550p Tiger Lily 3.50 1.75
1134 A404 600p Carnations 3.80 1.90

1988, May 25
1135 A405 150p multi 98 50

Intl. Children's Day — A406

1988, Aug. 28 Litho. ***Perf. 12x11½***
1136 A406 600p blk, grn & olive 3.80 1.90

Restoration of San'a, Yemen Arab Republic A407

1988, Aug. 28 ***Perf. 12½***
1137 A407 550p multi 3.50 1.75

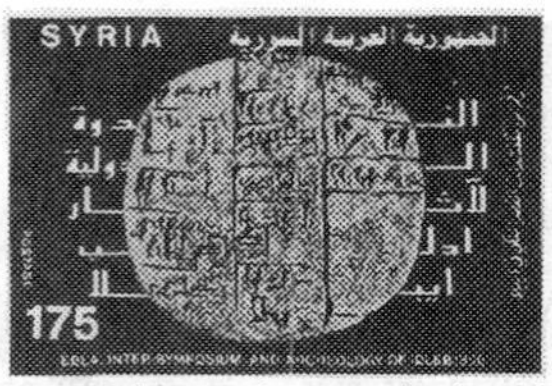

Ebla Intl. Symposium on Archaeology of Idlib — A408

1988, Aug. 28
1138 A408 175p Hieroglyphic tablet 1.15 58
1139 A408 550p Bas-relief (votive basin) 3.50 1.75
1140 A408 600p Gold statue, 3000 B.C. 3.80 1.90

1988 Summer Olympics, Seoul A409

1988, Sept. 17 ***Perf. 11½x12***
1141 A409 550p Cycling 3.50 1.75
1142 A409 600p Soccer 3.80 1.90

Size: 81x61mm

Imperf

1143 A409 1200p Emblem, character trademark 10.75 10.75

35th Intl. Fair, Damascus A410

WHO, 40th Anniv. A411

1988, Aug. 28 ***Perf. 12x11½***
1144 A410 600p multi 3.80 1.90

1988, Aug. 28 Litho. ***Perf. 12x11½***
1145 A411 600p multi 3.65 1.85

Arab Scouting Movement, 50th Anniv. — A412

1988, Sept. 17 ***Perf. 12½x12***
1146 A412 150p multi 95 48

Tourism Type of 1988

Women wearing folk costumes and: 550p, Euphrates Bridge, Deir-ez-Zor. 600p, The Tetrapylon, Latakia.

1988, Oct. 18
1147 A397 550p multi 3.20 1.60
1148 A397 600p multi 3.50 1.75

The lack of a value for a listed item does not necessarily indicate rarity.

World Post Day — A413

Arbor Day — A414

1988, Dec. 7 Litho. Perf. 12x12½
1149 A413 600p multi 3.60 1.80

1988, Nov. 16
1150 A414 600p multi 3.60 1.80

Shelter for the Homeless — A415

1988, Oct. 18 Perf. 12½x12
1151 A415 150p Arab Housing Day 68 35
1152 A415 550p World Housing Day 2.45 1.20
1153 A415 600p Intl. Year of Shelter for the Homeless 2.70 1.35

The IYSH emblem is pictured on the 550p and 600p.

Al-Assad University Hospital — A416

1988, Nov. 16 Litho. Perf. 12½
1154 A416 150p multi 1.00 50

Corrective Movement, 18th anniv.

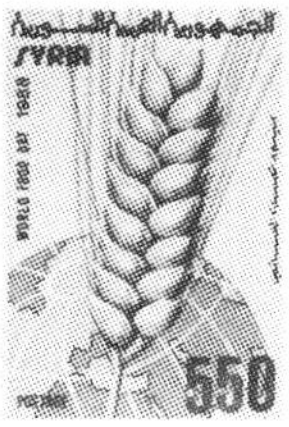

World Food Day — A417

1988, Oct. 18 Perf. 12x12½
1155 A417 550p multi 3.00 1.50

Birds A418

1989 Litho. Perf. 11½x12
1156 A418 600p Goldfinch 1.50 75
1157 A418 600p Turtledove 1.50 75
1158 A418 600p Bee eater 1.50 75

Jawaharlal Nehru, 1st Prime Minister of Independent India — A419

1989 Perf. 12½
1159 A419 550p brn & chest 1.15 58

Mothers' Day — A420

1989
1160 A420 550p multi 1.15 58

SEMI-POSTAL STAMPS

Nos. 174-185 Surcharged in Red or Black

اعانات للاجئين
Aff^t الاجرة
0^P.25 ١/٤ غ

1926 Unwmk. Perf. 12½, 13½

B1	A4	25c + 25c ol blk (R)	75	75
B2	A4	50c + 25c yel grn	75	75
B3	A4	75c + 25c brn org	75	75
B4	A5	1p + 50c mag	75	75
B5	A4	1p25 + 50c dp grn (R)	75	75
B6	A4	1p50 + 50c rose red	75	75
B7	A4	2p + 75c dk brn (R)	75	75
B8	A4	2p50 + 75c pck bl (R)	75	75
B9	A4	3p + 1p org brn (R)	75	75
B10	A4	5p + 1p vio	75	75
B11	A4	10p + 2p vio brn	75	75
B12	A4	25p + 5p ultra (R)	75	75
		Nos. B1-B12 (12)	9.00	9.00

On No. B4 the surcharge is set in six lines to fit the shape of the stamp.

The surcharge was a contribution to the relief of refugees from the Djebel Druze War. See Nos. CB1-CB4.

Catalogue values for unused stamps in this section, from this point to the end of the section, are for Never Hinged items.

Syrian Arab Republic

Jordanian Flags on Map of Israel, and Arabs — SP1

1965, June 12 Litho. Perf. 12x11½
B13 SP1 12½p + 5p multi 9 9
B14 SP1 25p + 5p multi 12 12

Issued for Palestine Week.

Father with Children and Red Crescent SP2

1968, May Litho. Perf. 12½x12
B15 SP2 12½p + 2½p ultra, rose lil & blk 25 25
B16 SP2 27½p + 7½p brt vio, red & blk 25 25

The surtax was for refugees.

AIR POST STAMPS

POSTE
PAR
AVION
a

AVION
b

Nos. 35, 45, 47 Handstamped Type "a" in Violet

1920, Dec. Unwmk. Perf. 13½
C1 A22 1p on 5c grn 65.00 16.50
C2 A20 5p on 15c gray grn 125.00 16.00
C3 A18 10p on 40c red & pale bl 190.00 35.00

Nos. 36, 46, 48 Overprinted Type "a" in Violet

1921, June 12
C4 A22 1p on 20c red brn 30.00 16.00
C5 A18 5p on 1fr cl & ol grn 175.00 65.00
C6 A18 10p on 2fr org & pale bl 175.00 65.00

Excellent counterfeits exist of Nos. C1 to C6.

Nos. 36, 46, 48 Overprinted Type "b"

1921, Oct. 5
C7 A22 1p on 20c red brn 25.00 7.50
C8 A18 5p on 1fr cl & ol grn 55.00 12.50
 a. Inverted overprint 125.00 95.00
C9 A18 10p on 2fr org & pale bl 82.50 20.00
 a. Double overprint 165.00 150.00

Nos. 92, 94-96 Overprinted

c **Poste par Avion**

1922, May 28
C10 A18 2p on 40c red & pale bl 7.50 7.50
 a. Inverted overprint
C11 A18 3p on 60c vio & ultra 7.50 7.50
C12 A18 5p on 1fr cl & ol grn 7.50 7.50
C13 A18 10p on 2fr org & pale bl 7.50 7.50

Nos. 116-119 Overprinted Type "c"

1923, Nov. 22
C14 A18 2p on 40c red & pale bl 11.50 11.50
 a. "Liabn" 165.00 165.00
 b. Inverted surcharge
C15 A18 3p on 60c vio & ultra 11.50 11.50
 a. "Liabn" 165.00 165.00
C16 A18 5p on 1fr cl & ol grn 11.50 11.50
 a. "Liabn" 165.00 165.00
C17 A18 10p on 2fr org & pale bl 11.50 11.50
 a. "Liabn" 165.00 165.00
 b. Double overprint

Nos. 137-140 Overprinted Type "c"

1924, Jan. 13
C18 A18 2p on 40c red & pale bl 95 95
 a. Double overprint
C19 A18 3p on 60c vio & ultra 95 95
 a. Inverted overprint 12.50
C20 A18 5p on 1fr cl & ol grn 95 95
 a. Double overprint
C21 A18 10p on 2fr org & pale bl 95 95

Nos. 152, 154, 157-158 Overprinted طيارة Avion

1924, July 17
C22 A18 2p on 40c red & pale bl 1.50 1.50
 a. Inverted overprint 12.50
C23 A18 3p on 60c vio & ultra 1.50 1.50
 a. Inverted overprint 12.50
 b. Double overprint 12.50
C24 A18 5p on 1fr cl & ol grn 1.50 1.50
C25 A18 10p on 2fr org & pale bl 1.50 1.50
 a. Inverted overprint 12.50

Regular Issue of 1925 Overprinted in Green
AVION
طيارة

1925, Mar. 1
C26 A4 2p dk brn 70 70
C27 A4 3p org brn 70 70
C28 A4 5p violet 70 70
C29 A4 10p vio brn 70 70

Regular Issue of 1925 Overprinted in Red

f

1926
C30 A4 2p dk brn 32 32
 a. Inverted overprint 12.50
C31 A4 3p org brn 40 40
 a. Inverted overprint 12.50
C32 A4 5p violet 50 95
 a. Inverted overprint 12.50
 b. Double overprint
C33 A4 10p vio brn 50 50
 a. Inverted overprint 12.50
 b. Double overprint

Nos. C30-C33 received their first airmail use June 16, 1929, at the opening of the Beirut-Marseille line.

Regular Issue of 1925 Overprinted Type "f" in Red or Black

1929
C34 A4 50c yel grn (R) 22 22
 a. Inverted overprint 11.50
 b. Overprinted on face and back
 c. Double overprint 11.50
 d. Double overprint, one inverted 16.00
 e. Pair, one without overprint
C35 A5 1p mag (Bk) 30 30
 a. Reversed overprint
 b. Red overprint
C36 A4 25p ultra (R) 1.25 1.25
 a. Inverted overprint 22.50
 b. Pair, one without overprint

On No. C35, the overprint is vertical, with plane nose down.

No. 197 Overprinted Type "f" in Red

1929, July 9
C37 A4 15p on 25p ultra 75 75
 a. Inverted overprint

Air Post Stamps of 1926-29 Overprinted in Various Colors

EXPOSITION INDUSTRIELLE
DAMAS 1929
معرض الصناعات الوطنية
دمشق ١٩٢٩

1929, Sept. 5

C38	A4	50c yel grn (R)		90	90
C39	A5	1p mag (Bl)		90	90
C40	A4	2p dk brn (V)		90	90
C41	A4	3p org brn (Bl)		90	90
a.		Inverted overprint			
C42	A4	5p vio (R)		90	90
C43	A4	10p vio brn (Bl)		90	90
C44	A4	25p ultra (R)		90	90
		Nos. C38-C44 (7)		6.30	6.30

Damascus Industrial Exhibition.

AP1

Red Surcharge

1930, Jan. 30

C45 AP1 2p on 1p25 dp grn		45	45
a. Inverted surcharge			
b. Double surcharge		16.00	

Plane over Homs AP2

Designs: 1pi, City Wall, Damascus. 2pi, Euphrates River. 3pi, Temple Ruins, Palmyra. 5pi, Deir-el-Zor. 10pi, Damascus. 15pi, Aleppo, Citadel. 25pi, Hama. 50pi, Zebdani. 100pi, Telebisse.

1931-33 Photo. Unwmk.

C46	AP2	50c ocher	12	12
C47	AP2	50c blk brn ('33)	28	25
C48	AP2	1p chnt brn	28	22
C49	AP2	2p Prus bl	85	65
C50	AP2	3p bl grn	28	18
C51	AP2	5p red vio	28	18
C52	AP2	10p sl grn	28	18
C53	AP2	15p org red	65	50
C54	AP2	25p org brn	70	65
C55	AP2	50p black	85	75
C56	AP2	100p magenta	90	90
		Nos. C46-C56 (11)	5.47	4.58

Nos. C46 to C56 exist imperforate.

Village of Bloudan AP12

1934, Aug. 2 Engr. *Perf. 12½*

C57	AP12	50c yel brn	75	75
C58	AP12	1p green	75	75
C59	AP12	2p pck bl	75	75
C60	AP12	3p red	75	75
C61	AP12	5p plum	75	75
C62	AP12	10p brt vio	9.00	9.00
C63	AP12	15p org brn	9.00	9.00
C64	AP12	25p dk ultra	11.50	11.50
C65	AP12	50p black	19.00	19.00
C66	AP12	100p red brn	37.50	37.50
		Nos. C57-C66 (10)	89.75	89.75

Proclamation of the Republic. Exist imperf.

Air Post Stamps of 1931-33 Overprinted in Red or Black

1936, Apr. 15 *Perf. 13½x13, 13½*

C67	AP2	50c blk brn (R)	1.50	1.50
C68	AP2	1p chnt brn (Bk)	1.50	1.50
C69	AP2	2p Prus bl (R)	1.50	1.50
C70	AP2	3p bl grn (R)	1.50	1.50
C71	AP2	5p red vio (Bk)	1.50	1.50
		Nos. C67-C71 (5)	7.50	7.50

Industrial Exhibition, Damascus, May 1936.

Syrian Pavilion at Paris Exposition AP13

1937, July 1 Photo. *Perf. 13½*

C72	AP13	½p yel grn	70	70
C73	AP13	1p green	70	70
C74	AP13	2p lt brn	70	70
C75	AP13	3p rose red	70	70
C76	AP13	5p brn org	85	85
C77	AP13	10p grnsh blk	1.40	1.40
C78	AP13	15p blue	1.65	1.65
C79	AP13	25p dk vio	1.65	1.65
		Nos. C72-C79 (8)	8.35	8.35

Paris International Exposition. Exist imperf.

Ancient Citadel at Aleppo AP14

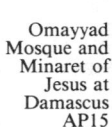

Omayyad Mosque and Minaret of Jesus at Damascus AP15

1937 Engr. *Perf. 13*

C80	AP14	½ dk vio	15	15
C81	AP15	1p black	15	15
C82	AP14	2p dp grn	15	15
C83	AP15	3p dp ultra	15	15
C84	AP14	5p rose lake	45	45
C85	AP15	10p red brn	38	38
C86	AP14	15p lake brn	1.25	1.25
C87	AP15	25p dk bl	1.65	1.65
		Nos. C80-C87 (8)	4.33	4.33

No. C80 to C87 exist imperforate.

Maurice Nogues and Route of France-Syria Flight — AP16

1938, July Photo. *Perf. 11*

C88 AP16 10p dk grn		1.10	1.10
a. Souv. sheet of 4, perf. 13½		11.00	11.00
b. Perf. 13½		1.90	1.90

10th anniversary of first Marseille-Beirut flight, by Maurice Nogues.

No. C88a exists imperf.; value $200.

Bridge at Deir-el-Zor AP17

1940 Engr. *Perf. 13.*

C89	AP17	25c brn blk	5	5
C90	AP17	50c pck bl	5	5
C91	AP17	1p dp ultra	8	8
C92	AP17	2p dk org brn	12	12
C93	AP17	5p green	22	22
C94	AP17	10p rose car	30	30
C95	AP17	50p dk vio	1.00	1.00
		Nos. C89-C95 (7)	1.82	1.82

No. C89 to C95 exist imperforate.

President Taj Eddin Hassani AP18

1942 Litho. *Perf. 11½*

C96	AP18	10p bl gray	1.25	1.25
C97	AP18	50p gray lil	1.25	1.25

Proclamation of Independence by the Allies, Sept. 27, 1941.

President Taj Eddin Hassani AP19

President Hassani and Map of Syria AP20

1942 Photo.

C98 AP19 10p sl grn & yel grn		1.90	1.90

No. C98 exists imperforate.

1943 Litho.

C99	AP20	2p dl brn	95	95
C100	AP20	10p red vio	95	95
C101	AP20	20p aqua	95	95
C102	AP20	50p rose pink	95	95

Proclamation of United Syria.

Same, Overprinted with Black Border

1943, May 5

C103	AP20	2p dl brn	95	95
C104	AP20	10p red vio	95	95
C105	AP20	20p aqua	95	95
C106	AP20	50p rose pink	95	95

Mourning for President Hassani.
Nos. C99-C106 exist imperf.

President Shukri el Kouatly — AP21

1944

C107	AP21	200p sepia	3.75	3.75
C108	AP21	500p dl bl	6.50	6.50

Stamps of 1931-44 Overprinted in Black, Blue or Carmine

1944 *Perf. 13, 13½, 11½.*

C109	AP15	10p red brn (Bk)	1.10	1.10
C110	AP2	15p org red (Bl)	1.10	1.10
C111	AP2	25p org brn (Bl)	1.10	1.10
C112	AP2	100p mag (Bl)	3.50	3.50
C113	AP21	200p sep (C)	4.50	4.50
		Nos. C109-C113 (5)	11.30	11.30

1st congress of Arab lawyers held in Damascus, Sept. 1944.

Nos. C53-C54, C108 Overprinted in Black or Orange

1944

C114	AP2	15p org red	1.10	1.10
C115	AP2	25p org brn	1.10	1.10
C116	AP21	500p dl bl (O)	8.00	8.00

See note after No. 299.

President Shukri el Kouatly AP22

1945, Mar. 15 Litho. *Perf. 11½*

C117	AP22	5p pale grn	15	20
C118	AP22	10p dl red	18	20
C119	AP22	15p orange	18	20
C120	AP22	25p lt bl	38	20
C121	AP22	50p lt vio	65	28
C122	AP22	100p dp brn	1.50	50
C123	AP22	200p fawn	3.75	1.75
		Nos. C117-C123 (7)	6.79	3.33

Resumption of constitutional government.

Catalogue values for unused stamps in this section, from this point to the end of the section, are for Never Hinged items.

Plane and Flock of Sheep AP23

Kattineh Dam AP24

Kanawat, Djebel Druze AP25

Sultan Ibrahim Mosque AP26

1946-47 *Perf. 13x13½*

C124	AP23	3p rose brn	50	10
C125	AP23	5p lt bl grn ('47)	50	10
C126	AP23	6p dp org ('47)	50	10
C127	AP24	10p sl gray ('47)	16	7
C128	AP24	15p scar ('47)	16	10
C129	AP24	25p blue	22	15
C130	AP25	50p violet	40	20
C131	AP25	100p bl grn	1.50	38
C132	AP25	200p brn ('47)	2.50	80
C133	AP26	300p red brn ('47)	4.50	1.50
C134	AP26	500p ol gray ('47)	9.00	3.00
		Nos. C124-C134 (11)	19.94	6.50

No. C129 Overprinted in Red

1946, Apr. 17

C135 AP24 25p blue		1.00	70

Evacuation of British and French troops from Syria.

Nos. C129-C131 Overprinted in Magenta

1946, Aug. 28

C136	AP24	25p blue	1.00	60
C137	AP25	50p violet	1.60	90
C138	AP25	100p bl grn	3.00	90

See note after No. 334.

No. C135 with Additional Overprint in Black

1947, June 10 *Perf. 13x13½*
C139 AP24 25p blue 1.00 60

1st annive. of the evacuation of British and French troops from Syria.

Window at Kasr El-Heir El-Gharbi AP27

Ram-headed Sphinxes Carved in Ivory, from King Hazael's Bed — AP28

1947, Nov. 15 **Litho.** *Perf. 11½*
C140 AP27 12.50p dk vio 1.00 55
C141 AP28 50p brown 3.00 1.60
a. Souvenir sheet of 4 26.00 26.00

1st Arab Archaeological Congress, Damascus, November, 1947.
No. C141a contains one each of Nos. 338, 339, C140 and C141 and sold for 125 piasters.

Kasr El-Heir El-Charqui AP29

Congress Emblem AP30

1947, Nov. 15
C142 AP29 12.50p ol blk 70 40
C143 AP30 50p dl vio 2.00 1.25
a. Souvenir sheet of 4 25.00 25.00

3rd Congress of Arab Engineers, Damascus, Nov. 1947.
No. C143a contains one each of Nos. 340, 341, C142 and C143 and sold for 125 piasters.

Kouatly Types of Regular Issue

1948, June 22 **Litho.** *Perf. 10½*
C144 A50 12.50p vio & vio brn 35 15
C145 A51 50p vio brn & grn 1.60 65
a. Souvenir sheet of 4, imperf. 100.00 100.00

Reelection of Pres. Shukri el Kouatly.
No. C145a contains one each of Nos. 342, 343, C144 and C145.

Military Training Types of Regular Issue

1948, June 22
C146 A52 12.50p bl & dk bl 50 20
C147 A53 50p grn car & blk 1.60 60
a. Souvenir sheet of 4, imperf. 100.00 100.00

Inauguration of compulsory military training.
No. C147a contains one each of Nos. 344, 345, C146 and C147.

Nos. C124, C126 and C132 to C134 Surcharged with New Value and Bars in Black or Carmine.

1948, Oct. 18 *Perf. 13x13½*
C148 AP23 2.50p on 3p rose brn 5 5
C149 AP23 2.50p on 6p dp org 5 5
C150 AP25 25p on 200p brn (C) 35 15
C151 AP26 50p on 300p red brn 1.00 40
C152 AP26 50p on 500p ol gray 1.00 40
Nos. C148-C152 (5) 2.45 1.05

Husni Zayim Type of Regular Issue

1949, June 20 **Litho.** *Perf. 11½*
C153 A54 50p brown 2.25 1.50

Revolution of March 30, 1949.

Pigeons and Globe AP36

Husni Zayim and View of Damascus AP37

1949, June 20 **Unwmk.**
C154 AP36 12.50p claret 4.50 4.50
C155 AP37 50p gray blk 12.50 9.00

UPU, 75th anniv. A souvenir sheet contains one each of Nos. 349, 350, C154 and C155. Value $125.

Election Type of Regular Issue

Wmk. 291

1949, Aug. 6 **Litho.** *Perf. 11½*
C156 A57 50p car rose & dk grnsh bl 2.25 1.50
a. Souvenir sheet of two, imperf. 100.00 100.00

Election of Pres. Husni Zayim.
No. C156a contains one each of Nos. C156 and 351.

No. C131 Surcharged with New Value and Bars in Black

1950 **Unwmk.** *Perf. 13x13½*
C157 AP25 2.50p on 100p bl grn 5 5

Port of Latakia AP38

1950, Dec. 25 *Perf. 11½*
C158 AP38 2.50p dl lil 35 7
C159 AP38 10p grnsh bl 60 7
C160 AP38 15p org brn 1.50 15
C161 AP38 25p brt bl 3.50 20

Nos. C158-C161 exist imperf. See No. C173.

Symbolical of Constitution AP39

1951, Apr. 14 **Unwmk.**
C162 AP39 12.50p crim rose 22 12
C163 AP39 50p brn vio 70 60

New constitution adopted Sept. 5, 1950. Both values exist imperforate.

Ruins, Palmyra AP40

Citadel at Aleppo AP41

1952, Apr. 22 **Litho.** *Perf. 11½*
C164 AP40 2.50p vermilion 10 5
C165 AP40 5p green 22 7
C166 AP40 15p violet 30 12
C167 AP41 25p dp bl 50 22
C168 AP41 100p lil rose 3.00 60
Nos. C164-C168 (5) 4.12 1.06

Nos. C164-C168 exist imperforate.

Stamps of 1946-52 Overprinted in Black

1953, Feb. 16 *Perf. 13x13½, 11½*
C169 AP38 10p grnsh bl 1.25 70
C170 AP40 15p violet 1.25 70
C171 AP41 25p dp bl 2.00 1.25
C172 AP25 50p violet 5.50 1.60

UN Social Welfare Seminar, Damascus, Dec. 8-20, 1952.

Type of 1950 and

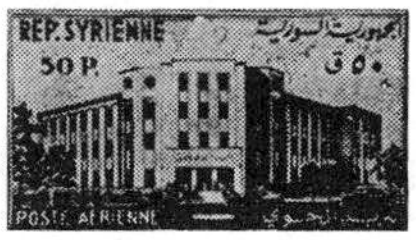
Post Office, Aleppo AP42

1953, Oct. **Photo.** *Perf. 11½*
C173 AP38 10p vio bl 35 7
C174 AP42 50p red brn 1.00 20

Building at Hama and PTT Emblem AP43

University of Syria, Damascus AP44

1954
C175 AP43 5p violet 15 5
C176 AP43 10p brown 20 5
C177 AP43 15p dl grn 20 7
C178 AP44 30p dk brn 40 15
C179 AP44 35p blue 60 15
C180 AP44 40p orange 70 30
C181 AP44 50p dp plum 1.00 40
C182 AP44 70p purple 1.60 50
Nos. C175-C182 (8) 4.85 1.67

Monument, Damascus Square — AP45

Mosque and Syrian Flag — AP46

1954, Sept. 2
C183 AP45 40p car rose 60 35
C184 AP46 50p green 70 40

Damascus Fair, Sept., 1954.
Nos. C183-C184 exist imperforate.

Nos. C174 and C168 Overprinted in Blue or Black

1954, Oct. 9
C185 AP42 50p red brn (Bl) 60 50
C186 AP41 100p lil rose 1.50 1.00

Cotton Festival, Aleppo, October 1954.

Virgin of Sednaya Concent AP47

Omayyad Mosque AP48

1955, Mar. 27 **Photo.** *Perf. 11½*
C187 AP47 25p dp pur 35 20
C188 AP47 75p dp bl grn 1.25 70

50th anniv. of the founding of Rotary Intl. Exist imperforate.

1955, March 26
C189 AP48 35p cerise 50 30
C190 AP48 65p dp grn 1.00 60

1955 Regional Congress of Rotary Intl., Damascus.

Arab Postal Union Type of Regular Issue

1955, Jan. 1 *Perf. 13½x13.*
C191 A69a 5p yel brn 20 10

Founding of the APU, July 1, 1954.

Young Couple and View of Damascus AP49

Design: 60p, Tank and planes leading advancing troops.

1955, Apr. 16 **Litho.** *Perf. 11½*
C192 AP49 40p dk rose lake 40 30
C193 AP49 60p ultra 60 35

9th anniv. of the evacuation of British and French troops from Syria.

Mother's Day Type of Regular Issue

1955, May 13 **Unwmk.**
C194 A70 35p violet 60 35
C195 A70 40p black 1.00 40

Issued to publicize Mother's Day.

Emigrants under Syrian Flag AP51

Mother and Child AP52

Design: 15p, Airplane over globe and fountain.

1955, July 26 *Perf. 11½*

C196	AP51	5p	magenta	35	15
C197	AP51	15p	lt bl	40	22

Emigrants' Congress. Exist imperf.

1955, Oct. 3 **Photo.**

C198	AP52	25p	dp bl	42	22
C199	AP52	50p	plum	80	40

International Children's Day.

Globe, Scales and Dove AP53

1955, Oct. 30

C200	AP53	15p	ultra	42	20
C201	AP53	35p	brn blk	80	40

10th anniv. of the UN, Oct. 24, 1955.

Aqueduct Type of Regular Issue

1955, Nov. 21 **Litho.** **Unwmk.**

C202	A72	30p	dk bl	1.50	70

No. C191 Overprinted in Ultramarine

مؤتمر البريد العربي
القاهرة - ١٩٥٥/٣/١٥

1955, Dec. 29 **Photo.** *Perf. 13½x13*

C203	A69a	5p	yel brn	30	12

APU Congress, Cairo, Mar. 15, 1955.

Liberation Monument — AP54

Designs: 65p, Winged figure with shield and sword. 75p, President Shukri el Kouatly.

1956, Apr. 17 **Litho.** *Perf. 11½*

C204	AP54	35p	blk brn	50	35
C205	AP54	65p	rose red	65	50
C206	AP54	75p	dk sl grn	1.00	70

10th anniv. of the evacuation of British and French troops from Syria.

No. C191 Overprinted in Black

ذكرى زيارة عاهل الأردن
نيسان ١٩٥٦

1956, Apr. 11 **Photo.** *Perf. 13½x13*

C207	A69a	5p	yel brn	30	12

Visit of King Hussein of Jordan to Damascus, Apr. 1956.

President Shukri el Kouatly AP55

Gate of Kasr el Heir, Palmyra AP56

1956, July 7 **Litho.** *Perf. 11½*

C208	AP55	100p	black	1.00	70
C209	AP55	200p	violet	2.00	1.00
C210	AP55	300p	dl rose	5.50	2.00
C211	AP55	500p	dk bl grn	5.00	3.50

Nos. CB5-CB8 Overprinted with 3 Bars obliterating surtax

1956

C212	SPAP1	25p	gray blk	35	15
C213	SPAP2	35p	ultra	40	20
C214	SPAP2	40p	rose lil	70	30
C215	SPAP1	70p	Prus grn	1.00	70

1956, Sept. 1 **Unwmk.**

Designs: 20p, Hand loom and modern mill. 30p, Ox-drawn plow and tractor. 35p, Cogwheels and galley. 50p, Textiles and vase.

C216	AP56	15p	gray	22	22
C217	AP56	20p	brt ultra	30	30
C218	AP56	30p	bl grn	42	42
C219	AP56	35p	blue	55	55
C220	AP56	50p	rose lil	60	60
			Nos. C216-C220 (5)	2.09	2.09

3rd International Fair, Damascus.

Nos. C200-201 Overprinted in Red or Green

الذكرى الحادية عشرة للأمم المتحدة
11ème ANNIVERSAIRE de l'ONU

1956, Oct. 30 **Photo.** *Perf. 11½*

C221	AP53	15p	ultra (R)	70	30
C222	AP53	35p	brn blk (G)	1.50	70

United Nations, 11th anniversary.

Clay Tablet with First Alphabet AP57

Helmet of Syrian Legionary and Ornament AP58

Design: 50p, Lintel from Temple of the Sun, Palmyra.

1956, Oct. 8 **Typo.**

C223	AP57	20p	gray	50	30
C224	AP58	30p	magenta	70	40
C225	AP57	50p	gray brn	1.25	80

Intl. Museum Week (UNESCO), Oct. 8-14.

Trees and Mosque AP59

1956, Dec. 27 **Litho.** *Perf. 11½*

C226	AP59	10p	ol bis	20	15
C227	AP59	40p	sl grn	40	40

Day of the Tree, Dec. 27, 1956.

See United Arab Republic, Syria, No. 36.

Mother and Child AP60

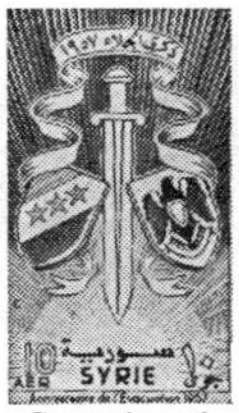

Sword and Shields AP61

Design: 60p, Mother holding infant.

1957, Mar. 21 **Unwmk.**

C228	AP60	40p	ultra	42	35
C229	AP60	60p	vermilion	70	50

Mother's Day, 1957.

1957, Apr. 20 **Wmk. 291**

Designs: 15p, 35p, Map and "Syria" holding torch. 25p, Pres. Kouatly.

C230	AP61	10p	redsh brn	10	7
C231	AP61	15p	bl grn	20	10
C232	AP61	25p	violet	30	12
C233	AP61	35p	cerise	42	30
C234	AP61	40p	gray	65	40
			Nos. C230-C234 (5)	1.67	99

11th anniv. of the British-French troop evacuation.

Ship Loading — AP62

Sugar Production — AP63

Desidn: 30p, 40p, Harvesting grain and cotton.

1975, Sept. 1 **Unwmk.** *Perf. 11½*

C235	AP62	25p	magenta	22	20
C236	AP62	30p	lt red brn	30	20
C237	AP63	35p	lt bl	50	30
C238	AP62	40p	bl grn	60	35
C239	AP62	70p	ol bis	80	42
			Nos. C235-C239 (5)	2.42	1.47

4th International Fair, Damascus.

Arab Lawyers Type of Regualr Issue, 1957

1957, Sept. 21 **Litho.** **Wmk. 291**

C240	A76	17½p	red	30	20
C241	A76	40p	black	55	35

Cotton Festival Type of Regular Issue, 1957

1957, Oct. 17

C242	A77	17½p	org & blk	35	20
C243	A77	40p	lt bl & blk	60	30

Children's Day Type of Regular Issue, 1957

1957, Oct. 3

C244	A78	17½p	ultra	70	30
C245	A78	20p	red brn	70	30

International Children's Day, Oct. 7.

For "RAU" overprint on Nos. C244-C245, see Nos. C10-C11 in United Arab Republic (Syria) listings following Syria.

Family Writing and Reading Letters AP64

1957, Oct. 18 **Litho.** **Unwmk.**

C246	AP64	5p	brt grn	30	15

Intl. Letter Writing Week Oct. 6-12.

Afro-Asian Jurists Type of Regular Issue, 1957

1957, Nov. **Wmk. 291** *Perf. 11½*

C247	A80	30p	lt bl grn	30	22
C248	A80	50p	lt vio	42	35

Type of Regular Issue and

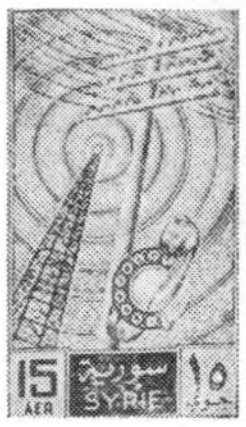

Radio, Telegraph and Telephone — AP65

1958, Feb. 12 *Perf. 11½*

C249	A83	10p	brt grn	20	5
C250	AP65	15p	brown	22	15

Syrian Arab Republic

Syrian Flag — AP67

Souvenir Sheet

1961 **Unwmk.** **Litho.** ***Imperf.***

C253	AP67	50p	multi	1.90	1.90

Establishment of Syrian Arab Republic.

"The Beauty of Palmyra" AP68

Archway, Palmyra AP69

Design: 200p, 300p, 500p, 1000p, Niche, King Zahir Bibar's tomb.

1961-63 **Litho.** *Perf. 12x11½*

C255	AP68	45p	citron	30	18
C256	AP68	50p	red org	38	25
C257	AP69	85p	sepia	65	30
C258	AP69	100p	lilac	85	32
C259	AP69	200p	sl grn ('62)	1.25	65
C260	AP69	300p	dk bl ('62)	1.65	70
C261	AP69	500p	lil ('63)	2.25	1.50
C262	AP69	1000p	dk gray ('63)	7.50	2.75
			Nos. C255-C262 (8)	14.83	6.65

See Nos. 433-436.

Arab League Building, Cairo, and Emblem — AP70

Malaria Eradication Emblem — AP71

1962, Apr. 1 *Perf. 12x11 ½*

C264	AP70	17½p Prus grn & yel grn	12	8
C265	AP70	22½p dk & lt bl	18	12
C266	AP70	50p dk brn & dl org	38	18

Arab League Week, Mar. 22-28.

1962, Apr. 7

C267	AP71	12½p ol, lt bl & pur	15	9
C268	AP71	50p brn, yel & grn	30	25

WHO drive to eradicate malaria.

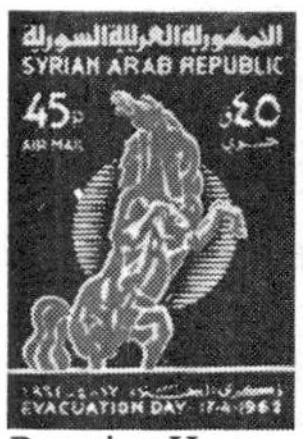

Prancing Horse AP72

Gen. Yusef al-Azmeh AP73

1962, Apr. 17

C269	AP72	45p vio & org	25	15
C270	AP73	55p vio bl & lt bl	38	18

Evacuation Day, 1962.

Martyrs' Square Memorial, Globe and Handshake AP74

Cotton and Cogwheel AP75

Design: 40p, 45p, Eastern Gate at Fair.

1962, Aug. 25 Litho. *Perf. 12x11 ½*

C271	AP74	17½p rose cl & brn	12	5
C272	AP74	22½p ver & mag	15	8
C273	AP74	40p vio brn & lt brn	18	12
C274	AP74	45p grnsh bl & lt grn	32	18

9th International Damascus Fair.

1962, Sept. 20 *Perf. 12x11 ½*

C275	AP75	12½p multi	15	8
C276	AP75	50p multi	30	22

Cotton Festival, Aleppo. See Nos. 455-456.

President Type of Regular Issue

1962, Dec. 14 **Unwmk.**

C278	A88	50p bl gray & tan	30	18

1st anniv. of the election of Pres. Nazem el-Kodsi.

Queen Zenobia of Palmyra AP76

Saad Allah El Jabri AP77

1962, Dec. 28 *Perf. 12x11 ½*

C279	AP76	45p violet	32	12
C280	AP76	50p rose red	42	15
C281	AP76	85p bl grn	45	22
C282	AP76	100p rose cl	1.00	32

1962, Dec. 30 **Litho.**

C283	AP77	50p dl bl	25	15

Saad Allah El Jabri (1894-1947), a leader in Syria's struggle for independence.

Woman from Moharde — AP78

Eagle in Flight — AP79

Regional Costumes: 40p, Marje Sultan. 45p, Kalamoun. 55p, Jabal-Al-Arab. 60p, Afrine. 65p, Hauran.

1963 *Perf. 12*

Costumes in Original Colors

C285	AP78	40p pale lil & blk	18	9
C286	AP78	45p pink & blk	20	15
C287	AP78	50p lt grn & blk	30	18
C288	AP78	55p lt bl & blk	32	22
C289	AP78	60p tan & blk	38	22
C290	AP78	65p pale grn & blk	50	25
		Nos. C285-C290 (6)	1.88	1.11

Hunger Type of Regular Issue

Design: 50p, Wheat emblem and bird feeding nestlings.

Perf. 12x11 ½

1963, Mar. 21 **Unwmk.**

C291	A91	50p ver & blk	25	15
	a.	Souvenir sheet	1.10	1.10

FAO "Freedom from Hunger" campaign. No. C291a contains 2 imperf. stamps similar to Nos. 453 and C291.

1963, Apr. 18 **Litho.**

C292	AP79	12½p brt grn	5	5
C293	AP79	50p lil rose	25	18

Revolution of Mar. 8, 1963.

Faris el Khouri — AP80

Arms and Wreath — AP81

1963, Apr. 27 *Perf. 12x11 ½*

C294	AP80	17½p gray	15	8
C295	AP81	22½p bl grn & blk	15	8

Evacuation Day, 1963.

abu-al-Ala al-Maarri AP82

Copper Pitcher, Arch and Fair AP83

1963, Aug. 19 *Perf. 12x11 ½*

C296	AP82	50p vio bl	30	22

abu-al-Ala al-Maarri (973-1057), poet and philosopher.

1963, Aug. 25

C297	AP83	37½p ultra, yel & brn	25	12
C298	AP83	50p brt bl, yel & brn	32	18

10th International Damascus Fair.

Centenary Emblem AP84

Abou Feras al Hamadani AP85

Design: 50p, Centenary emblem and globe.

1963, Sept. 19 **Litho.**

C299	AP84	15p chlky bl, red & blk	25	12
C300	AP84	50p yel grn, blk & red	28	22

Centenary of the International Red Cross.

1963, Nov. 13 *Perf. 12x11 ½*

C301	AP85	50p yel ol & dk brn	30	22

Abou Feras (932-968), poet.

Heads of Three Races and Flame — AP86

1964, Jan. 6 **Unwmk.**

C302	AP86	17½p multi	9	6
C303	AP86	22½p grn, blk & red	15	8
C304	AP86	50p vio, blk & red	25	15
	a.	Souv. sheet of 3	70	70

15th anniv. of the Universal Declaration of Human Rights. No. C304a contains 3 imperf. stamps similar to Nos. C302-C304 with simulated perforations.

Flag, Torch and Map of Arab Countries AP87

1964, Mar. 8 **Unwmk.** *Perf. 11 ½*

C305	AP87	15p multi	6	5
C306	AP87	17½p multi	12	6
C307	AP87	22½p multi	18	9

1st anniv. of the Revolution of Mar. 8, 1963.

Kaaba, Mecca, and Mosque, Damascus AP88

1964, Mar. 14 Litho. *Perf. 11 ½x12*

C308	AP88	12½p bl & blk	6	5
C309	AP88	22½p rose lil & blk	15	8
C310	AP88	50p lt grn & blk	25	15

First Arab Conference of Moslem Wakf Ministers, Damascus.

Young Couple and View of Damascus AP89

1964, Apr. 17 **Unwmk.**

C311	AP89	20p blue	8	5
C312	AP89	25p rose car	15	9
C313	AP89	60p emerald	25	15

Evacuation Day, Apr. 17, 1964.

Abul Kasim (Albucasis) — AP90

1964, Apr. 21 *Perf. 12x11 ½*

C314	AP90	60p brown	30	22

4th Arab Congress of Dental and Oral Surgery, Damascus.

Mosaic, Chahba, Thalassa AP91

Perf. 11 ½x12

1964, June-July **Litho.**

C315	AP91	27½p car rose	15	6
C316	AP91	45p gray	22	9
C317	AP91	50p brt grn	30	12
C318	AP91	55p sl grn	30	18
C319	AP91	60p ultra	40	18
		Nos. C315-C319 (5)	1.37	63

Hanging Lamp, Fair Emblem — AP92

Globe and Fair Emblem — AP93

1964, Aug. 28 *Perf. 12x11 ½*

C320	AP92	20p multi	18	5
C321	AP93	25p multi	22	9

11th International Damascus Fair.

Industrial and Agricultural Symbols — AP94

1964, Sept. 22 **Litho.** **Unwmk.**

C322	AP94	25p multi	15	8

Same Overprinted with two Red Lines in Arabic

C323 AP94 25p multi 15 8

Cotton Festival, Aleppo. Overprint on No. C323 translates: "Market for Industrial and Agricultural Products."

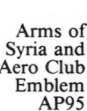

Arms of Syria and Aero Club Emblem AP95

1964, Oct. 8 Litho. ***Perf. 11½x12***

C324 AP95 12½p emer & blk 12 5
C325 AP95 17½p crim & blk 15 9
C326 AP95 20p brt bl & blk 30 8

10th anniversary of Syrian Aero Club.

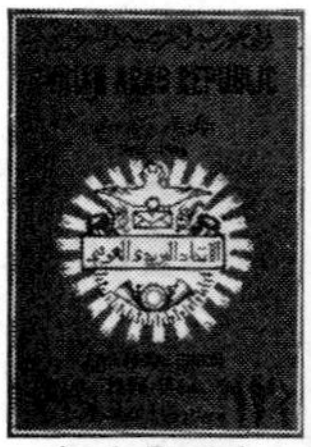

Arab Postal Union Emblem — AP96

Grain and Hands Holding Book — AP97

1964, Nov. 12 Litho. ***Perf. 12x11½***

C327 AP96 12½p org & blk 5 5
C328 AP96 20p emer & blk 12 5
C329 AP96 25p dp lil rose & blk 15 8

10th anniv. of the permanent office of the APU.

1964, Nov. 30 **Unwmk.**

C330 AP97 12½p emer & blk 5 5
C331 AP97 17½p mar & blk 12 5
C332 AP97 20p dp bl & blk 15 8

Burning of the library of Algiers, June 7, 1962.

Tennis Player — AP98

Designs: 17½p, Wrestlers and drummer. 20p, Weight lifter. 100p, Wrestlers and drummer (horiz.).

1965, Feb. 7 ***Perf. 12x11½***

C333 AP98 12½p multi 5 5
C334 AP98 17½p multi 15 5
C335 AP98 20p multi 18 8

Souvenir Sheet

C336 AP98 100p multi 1.10 1.10

18th Olympic Games, Tokyo, Oct. 10-25, 1964. No. C336 contains one stamp 45x33mm.

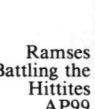

Ramses Battling the Hittites AP99

Design: 50p, Two statues of Ramses II.

1965, Mar. 21 Litho. ***Perf. 11x12***

C337 AP99 22½p emer, ultra & blk 15 8
C338 AP99 50p ultra, emer & blk 25 15

UNESCO world campaign to save historic monuments in Nubia.

Al-Sharif Al-Radi AP100

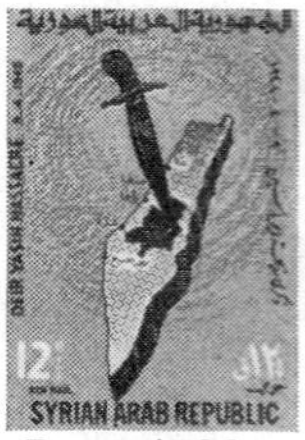

Dagger in Map of Palestine AP102

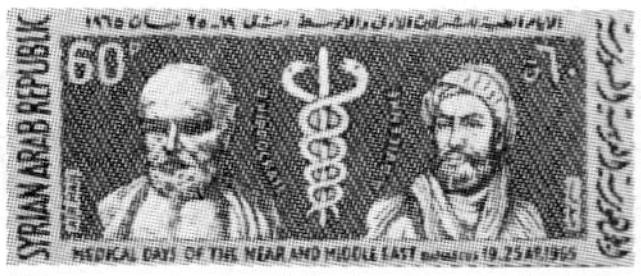

Hippocrates and Avicenna — AP101

1965, Apr. 3 Litho. ***Perf. 12x11½***

C339 AP100 50p gray brn 30 18

5th Poetry Festival held in Latakia; Al-Sharif Al-Radi (970-1015), poet.

1965, Apr. 19 ***Perf. 11½***

C340 AP101 60p dl bl grn & blk 38 30

"Medical Days of the Near and Middle East," a convention held at Damascus Apr. 19-25.

1965, May 15

C341 AP102 12½p multi 12 5
C342 AP102 60p multi 25 18

Deir Yassin massacre, Apr. 9, 1948.

ITU Emblem, Old and New Communication Equipment — AP103

Perf. 11½x12

1965, May 24 Litho. Unwmk.

C343 AP103 12½p multi 12 5
C344 AP103 27½p multi 18 8
C345 AP103 60p multi 32 25

ITU, centenary.

Syrian Welcoming AP104

Bridge and Gate AP105

1965, Aug. Unwmk. ***Perf. 12x11½***

C346 AP104 25p pur & multi 15 5
C347 AP104 100p blk & multi 45 22

Issued to welcome Arab immigrants.

1965, Aug. 28 **Litho.**

Designs: 27½p, Fair emblem. 60p, Jug and ornaments.

C348 AP105 12½p blk, brt ultra & brn 5 5
C349 AP105 27½p multi 15 5
C350 AP105 60p multi 25 18

12th International Damascus Fair.

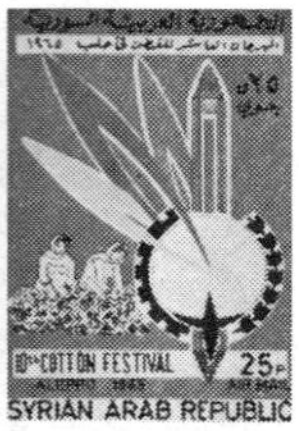

Fair Emblem and Cotton Pickers — AP106

1965, Sept. 30 ***Perf. 12x11½***

C351 AP106 25p ol & multi 15 8

10th Cotton Festival, Aleppo.

Same with Red Overprint in English and Arabic: "INDUSTRIAL & AGRICULTURAL / PRODUCTION FAIR-ALEPPO / 1965"

1965, Sept. 30

C352 AP106 25p ol & multi 15 8

Industrial and Agricultural Fair, Aleppo.

View of Damascus and ICY Emblem AP107

1965, Oct. 24 ***Perf. 11½x12***

C353 AP107 25p multi 15 8

International Cooperation Year.

Radio Transmitter, Globe, Syrian Flag and View of Damascus AP108

Hand (shaped like a dove) Holding Flower AP109

1966, Feb. 16 Litho. ***Perf. 12x11½***

C354 AP108 25p multi 12 5
C355 AP108 60p multi 25 15

3rd Conference of Arab Information Ministers, Damascus, Feb. 14-18.

1966, Mar. 8 ***Perf. 12x11½, 11½x12***

Design: 17½p, Stylized people (horiz.).

C356 AP109 12½p multi 5 5
C357 AP109 17½p multi 8 5
C358 AP109 50p multi 45 15

March 8 Revolution, 3rd anniversary.

Statues of Ramses II from Abu Simbel — AP110

1966, Mar. 15 ***Perf. 12x11½***

C359 AP110 25p dk bl 15 5
C360 AP110 60p dk sl grn 25 15

Arab "Save the Nubian Monument Week."

UN Headquarters Building and Emblem — AP111

Design: 100p, UN Flag.

1966, Apr. 11 Litho. ***Perf. 11½x12***

C361 AP111 25p blk & gray 9 5
C362 AP111 50p blk & pale grn 22 15

Souvenir Sheet

Imperf

C363 AP111 100p yel, brt bl & blk 75 75

20th anniv. (in 1965) of the UN. No. C363 contains one stamp 42x36mm.

Marching Workers AP112

1966, May 1 Litho. ***Perf. 11½x12***

C364 AP112 60p multi 25 15

Issued for May Day.

Inauguration of WHO Headquarters, Geneva — AP113

1966, May 3

C365 AP113 60p blk, bl & yel 25 15

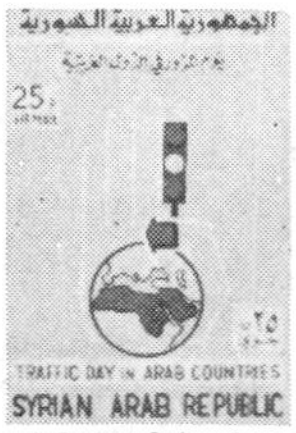

Map of Arab Countries and Traffic Signals AP114

Astarte and Tyche, 1st-century Basrelief, Palmyra AP115

1966, May 4 ***Perf. 12x11½***

C366 AP114 25p gray & multi 9 5

Issued to publicize Traffic Day.

1966, July 26 Litho. ***Perf. 12x11½***

C367 AP115 50p pale brn 22 12
C368 AP115 60p slate 32 18

Symbolic Flag, Wheat, Globe and Fair Emblem
AP116

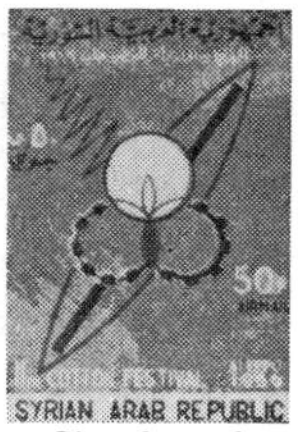

Shuttle and Symbols of Agriculture, Industry and Cotton
AP117

1966, Aug. 25 Litho. *Perf. 12x11½*
C369 AP116 12½p gold, blk, red & grn 5 5
C370 AP116 60p sil, blk, red & grn 25 18

13th Intl. Damascus Fair, Aug. 25-Sept. 20.

1966, Sept. 9 Litho. *Perf. 12x11½*
C371 AP117 50p sil, blk & plum 25 15

11th Cotton Festival, Aleppo.

Symbolic Water Cycle — AP118

Abd-el Kader — AP119

1966, Oct. 24 Litho. *Perf. 12x11½*
C372 AP118 12½p emer, blk & org 5 5
C373 AP118 60p ultra, blk & org 25 18

Hydrological Decade (UNESCO), 1965-74.

1966, Nov. 7
C374 AP119 12½p brt grn & blk 15 5
C375 AP119 50p brt grn & red brn 22 18

Transfer from Damascus to Algiers of the ashes of Abd-el Kader (1807?-1883), Emir of Mascara.

Clasped Hands over Map of South Arabia — AP120

Pipelines and Pigeons — AP121

1967, Feb. 8 Litho. *Perf. 12x11½*
C376 AP120 20p pink & multi 9 5
C377 AP120 25p multi 15 8

3rd Congress of Solidarity with the Workers and People of Aden, Damascus, Jan. 15-18.

1967, Mar. 8 Litho. *Perf. 12x11½*
C378 AP121 17½p multi 9 5
C379 AP121 25p multi 15 8
C380 AP121 27½p multi 14 6

4th anniversary of March 8 Revolution.

Soldier, Woman and Man Holding Flag
AP122

Workers' Monument, Damascus
AP123

1967, Apr. 17 Litho. *Perf. 12x11½*
C381 AP122 17½p green 15 8
C382 AP122 25p dp cl 15 8
C383 AP122 27½p vio bl 18 8

21st anniv. of the evacuation of British and French troops from Syria.

1967, May 1
C384 AP123 12½p bl grn 5 5
C385 AP123 50p brt pink 25 15

Issued for Labor Day, May 1.

Fair Emblem and Gate, Minaret, Omayyad Mosque — AP124

1967, Aug. 25 Litho. *Perf. 12x12½*
C386 AP124 12½p multi 5 5
C387 AP124 60p multi 25 18

14th Intl. Damascus Fair, Aug. 25-Sept. 20.

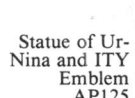

Statue of Ur-Nina and ITY Emblem
AP125

1967, Sept. 2 *Perf. 12½x12*
C388 AP125 12½p lt bl, brt rose lil & blk 5 5
C389 AP125 25p lt bl, ver & blk 12 8
C390 AP125 27½p lt bl, dk bl & blk 18 8

Souvenir Sheet

Imperf

C391 AP125 60p lt bl & vio bl 50 50

Intl. Tourist Year.

Cotton Boll and Cogwheel Segment
AP126

Head of Young Man, Amrith, 4th-5th Century B.C.
AP127

1967, Sept. 28 Litho. *Perf. 12x12½*
C392 AP126 12½p ocher, brn & blk 5 5
C393 AP126 60p ap grn, brn & blk 25 15

12th Cotton Festival, Aleppo.

Same with Red Overprint in English and Arabic "INDUSTRIAL & AGRICULTURAL PRODUCTION FAIR / ALEPPO 1967"

1967, Sept. 28
C394 AP126 12½p multi 5 5
C395 AP126 60p multi 25 15

Industrial and Agricultural Production Fair, Aleppo.

1967, Oct. 7

Design: 100p, 500p, Bronze bust of a Princess, 2nd century.

C396 AP127 45p orange 18 12
C397 AP127 50p brt pink 25 12
C398 AP127 60p grnsh bl 30 22
C399 AP127 100p green 38 30
C400 AP127 500p brn red 1.90 1.50
Nos. C396-C400 (5) 3.01 2.26

Ibn el-Naphis
AP128

1967, Dec. 28 Litho. *Perf. 12x12½*
C401 AP128 12½p grn & org 5 5
C402 AP128 27½p dk bl & lil rose 18 8

700th death anniv. of Ibn el-Naphis (1210-1288), Arab physician.

Human Rights Flame and People
AP129

Design: 100p, Heads of various races and Human Rights flame.

1968, Feb. 21 Litho. *Perf. 12½x12*
C403 AP129 12½p lt grnsh bl, bl & blk 5 5
C404 AP129 60p pink, blk & dl red 25 18

Souvenir Sheet

Imperf

C405 AP129 100p multi 65 65

20th anniv. of the Declaration of Human Rights; Intl. Human Rights Year.

Old Man and Woman Reading — AP130

Design: 17½p, 45p, Torch and book.

1968, Mar. 3 *Perf. 12x12½*
C406 AP130 12½p rose car, blk & org 5 5
C407 AP130 17½p multi 5 5
C408 AP130 25p grn, blk & org 15 5
C409 AP130 45p bl & multi 18 12

Issued to publicize the literacy campaign.

Euphrates Dam Project — AP131

1968, Apr. 11 Litho. *Perf. 12½x12*
C410 AP131 12½p multi 5 5
C411 AP131 17½p multi 8 5
C412 AP131 25p multi 20 9

Proposed dam across Euphrates River.

WHO Emblem and Avenzoar (1091-1162) — AP132

Designs (WHO Emblem and): 25p, Rhazes (Razi, 850-923). 60p, Geber (Jabir 721-776).

1968, June 10 Litho. *Perf. 12½x12*
C413 AP132 12½p brn, grn & sal 5 5
C414 AP132 25p brn, gray & sal 12 5
C415 AP132 60p brn, gray bl & sal 25 15

WHO, 20th anniv.

Monastery of St. Simeon the Stylite
AP133

Designs: 17½p, El Tekkieh Mosque, Damascus (vert.). 22½p, Columns, Palmyra (vert.). 45p, Chapel of St. Paul, Bab Kisan. 50p, Theater of Bosra.

Perf. 12½x12, 12x12½

1968, Oct. 10 Litho.
C416 AP133 15p pale grn & rose brn 5 5
C417 AP133 17½p redsh brn & dk red brn 8 5
C418 AP133 22½p grn gray & dk red brn 12 12
C419 AP133 45p yel & dk red brn 20 12
C420 AP133 50p lt bl & dk red brn 22 18
Nos. C416-C420 (5) 67 52

Hammer Throw — AP134

Designs: 25p, Discus. 27½p, Running. 60p, Basketball. 50p, Polo (horiz.).

1968, Dec. 19 Litho. *Perf. 12x12½*
C421 AP134 12½p brt pink, blk & grn 5 5
C422 AP134 25p red, grn & blk 12 5
C423 AP134 27½p blk, gray & grn 15 8
C424 AP134 60p multi 22 15

Souvenir Sheet

Imperf

C425 AP134 50p multi 45 45

19th Olympic Games, Mexico City, Oct. 12-27. No. C425 contains one horizontal stamp 52x80mm.

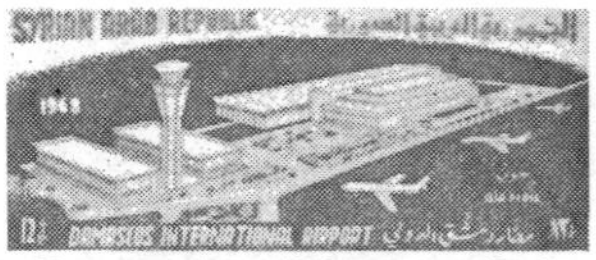

Construction of Damascus Intl. Airport — AP135

1969, Jan. 20 Litho. ***Perf. 12½x12***

C426	AP135	12½p yel, brt bl & grn	5	5
C427	AP135	17½p org, pur & lt grn	8	5
C428	AP135	60p car, blk & yel	25	15

Baal Shamin Temple, Palmyra AP136

Designs: 45p, Interior of Omayyad Mosque, Damascus (vert.). 50p, Amphitheater, Palmyra. 60p, Khaled ibn al-Walid Mosque, Homs (vert.). 100p, Ruins of St. Simeon, Djebel Samaan.

1969, Jan. 20 Photo. ***Perf. 12x11½***

C429	AP136	25p multi	9	5
C430	AP136	45p bl & multi	15	8
C431	AP136	50p multi	18	10
C432	AP136	60p multi	22	12
C433	AP136	100p vio & multi	38	22
		Nos. C429-C433 (5)	1.02	57

Workers, ILO Emblem, Cogwheel AP137

Design: 60p, ILO emblem.

1969, May 1 Litho. ***Perf. 12½x12***

C434	AP137	12½p multi	8	5
C435	AP137	27½p multi	15	5

Miniature Sheet

Imperf

C436	AP137	60p multi	30	22

ILO, 50th anniv. No. C436 contains one stamp 53½x47mm.

Ballet Dancers AP138

Designs: 12½p, Russian dancers. 45p, Lebanese singer and dancers. 55p, Egyptian dancer and musicians. 60p, Bulgarian dancers.

1969, Aug. 25 Litho. ***Perf. 12½x12***

C437	AP138	12½p multi	8	5
C438	AP138	27½p bl & multi	15	8
C439	AP138	45p multi	18	12
C440	AP138	55p multi	22	12
C441	AP138	60p multi	25	18
		Nos. C437-C441 (5)	88	55

16th Intl. Fair, Damascus, Aug. 25-Sept. 20. Nos. C437-C441 are printed se-tenant in sheets of 50 (10x5).

Children Playing AP139

Fortuna AP140

1969, Oct. 6 Litho. ***Perf. 12x12½***

C442	AP139	12½p aqua, dk bl & emer	5	5
C443	AP139	25p brn red, dk bl & lt vio	12	5
C444	AP139	27½p ultra, dk bl & gray	15	8

Issued for Children's Day.

1969, Oct. 10

Designs: 25p, Seated woman from Palmyra. 60p, Motherhood. All sculptures from Greco-Roman period.

C445	AP140	17½p blk, yel grn & grn	9	5
C446	AP140	25p dk brn, red brn & lt grn	12	8
C447	AP140	60p blk, lt gray & bl gray	25	15

9th Intl. Congress for Classical Archaeology, Oct. 11-20.

Damascus Agricultural Museum — AP141

1969, Dec. 24 Litho. ***Perf. 12½x12***

C448	AP141	12p Cock	5	5
C449	AP141	17½p Cow	8	5
C450	AP141	20p Corn	12	5
C451	AP141	50p Olives	18	12

Nos. C448-C451 printed se-tenant in strips of 4 with label showing dove and grain.

Weather Satellite Tracking and UN Emblem AP142

1970, Mar. 23 Litho. ***Perf. 12½x12***

C452	AP142	25p blk, sl grn & yel	15	8
C453	AP142	60p blk, dk bl & yel	25	18

10th World Meteorological Day.

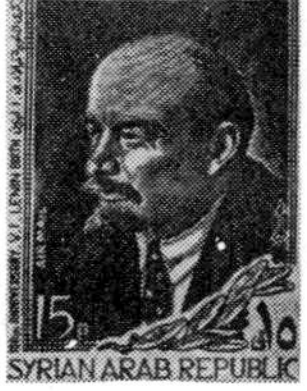

Lenin (1870-1924) AP143

1970, Apr. 15 Litho. ***Perf. 12x12½***

C454	AP143	15p red & dk brn	8	5
C455	AP143	60p red & grn	25	18

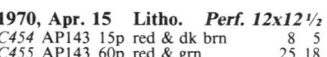

Workers' Syndicate Emblem AP144

1970, May 1 Litho. ***Perf. 12½x12***

C456	AP144	15p dk brn & brt grn	5	5
C457	AP144	60p dk brn & org	25	18

Issued for Labor Day.

Radar and Open Book AP145

1970, May 17

C458	AP145	15p brt pink & blk	5	5
C459	AP145	60p bl & blk	25	18

International Telecommunications Day.

Opening of UPU Headquarters, Bern — AP146

1970, May 30

C460	AP146	15p multi	5	5
C461	AP146	60p multi	25	18

"Zahier Piebers and Maarouf" — AP147

Folk Tales: 10p, Two warriors on horseback. 15p, Two warriors on white horses. 20p, Lady and warrior on horseback. 60p, Warriors, woman and lion.

1970, Aug. 12 Litho. ***Perf. 12½***

C462	AP147	5p lt bl & multi	5	5
C463	AP147	10p lt bl & multi	5	5
C464	AP147	15p lt bl & multi	8	5
C465	AP147	20p lt bl & multi	12	8
C466	AP147	60p lt bl & multi	38	18
		Nos. C462-C466 (5)	68	41

Nos. C462-C466 printed se-tenant.

Al Aqsa Mosque on Fire AP148

1970, Aug. 21 ***Perf. 12½x12***

C467	AP148	15p multi	5	5
C468	AP148	60p multi	25	18

1st anniv. of the burning of Al Aqsa Mosque, Jerusalem.

Wood Carving — AP149

Handicrafts: 20p, Jewelry. 25p, Glass making. 30p, Copper engraving. 60p, Shellwork.

1970, Aug. 25 ***Perf. 12½***

C469	AP149	15p vio & multi	5	5
C470	AP149	20p ol & multi	8	5
C471	AP149	25p multi	12	8
C472	AP149	30p multi	18	9
C473	AP149	60p multi	32	18
		Nos. C469-C473 (5)	75	45

17th Intl. Fair, Damascus. Nos. C469-C473 printed se-tenant.

Education Year Emblem — AP150

1970, Nov. 2 Litho. ***Perf. 12***

C474	AP150	15p dl grn & dk brn	5	5
C475	AP150	60p vio bl & dk brn	25	18

International Education Year.

UN Emblem, Symbols of Progress, Justice and Peace AP151

1970, Nov. 3

C476	AP151	15p lt ultra, red & blk	8	5
C477	AP151	60p bl, yel & blk	25	18

United Nations, 25th anniversary.

Khaled ibn-al-Walid AP152

Woman with Garland AP153

1970-71 ***Perf. 12x11½, 12½x12½***

C478	AP152	45p brt pink	22	12
C479	AP152	50p green	25	15
C480	AP152	60p vio brn	32	18
C481	AP152	100p dk bl	45	18
C482	AP152	200p grnsh gray ('71)	95	50
C483	AP152	300p lil ('71)	1.25	95
C484	AP152	500p gray ('71)	2.00	1.65
		Nos. C478-C484 (7)	5.44	3.73

1971, Apr. 17 Litho. ***Perf. 12***

C485	AP153	15p dl red, blk & grn	5	5
C486	AP153	60p grn, blk & dk red	25	18

25th anniv. of the evacuation of British and French troops from Syria.

People Dancing Around Globe AP154

1971, Apr. 28 Litho. *Perf. 12½x12*

C487	AP154	15p vio & multi	5	5
C488	AP154	60p grn & multi	22	15

Intl. Year against Racial Discrimination.

Pres. Hafez al Assad and Council Chamber — AP155

1971, Sept. 30 Litho. *Perf. 12½x12*

C489	AP155	15p grn & multi	5	5
C490	AP155	65p bl & multi	30	15

People's Council and presidential election.

Gamal Abdel Nasser (1918-1970), President of Egypt — AP156

1971, Oct. 17 *Perf. 12x12½*

C491	AP156	15p lt ol grn & brn	5	5
C492	AP156	20p gray & brn	12	5

Globe and Arrows AP157

1972, May 17 Litho. *Perf. 11½*

C493	AP157	15p bl, vio bl & pink	5	5
C494	AP157	50p org, yel & sep	22	15

4th World Telecommunications Day.

Pres. Hafez al Assad AP158

Airline Emblem, Eastern Hemisphere AP159

1972, July Litho. *Perf. 12x11½*

C495	AP158	100p dk grn	45	25
C496	AP158	500p dk brn	2.25	1.10

1972, Sept. 16 Litho. *Perf. 12x11½*

C497	AP159	15p blk, lt bl & Prus bl	8	5
C498	AP159	50p blk, gray & Prus bl	22	15

Syrianair, Syrian airline, 25th anniversary.

Pottery — AP160

Handicraft Industries: 25p, Rugs. 30p, Metal (weapons). 35p, Straw (baskets, mats). 100p, Wood carving.

1976, July Litho. *Perf. 12x12½*

C499	AP160	10p multi	5	5
C500	AP160	25p multi	9	5
C501	AP160	30p multi	12	5
C502	AP160	35p multi	15	8
C503	AP160	100p multi	40	32
		Nos. C499-C503 (5)	81	55

23rd Intl. Damascus Fair. Nos. C499-C503 printed se-tenant.

Pres. Hafez al Assad AP161

1978, Sept. Litho. *Perf. 12½x12*

C504	AP161	25p sil & multi	18	5
C505	AP161	35p grn & multi	28	5
C506	AP161	60p gold & multi	35	8

Reelection of Pres. Assad. See No. 820.

AIR POST SEMI-POSTAL STAMPS

Nos. C30-C33 Surcharged Like Nos. B1-B12 in Black and Red

1926, Apr. 1 Unwmk. *Perf. 13½*

CB1	A4	2p + 1p dk brn	95	95
CB2	A4	3p + 2p org brn	95	95
CB3	A4	5p + 3p vio	95	95
CB4	A4	10p + 5p vio brn	95	95

The surcharged value is in red and rest of the overprint in black on Nos. CB1-CB3. The entire overprint is black on No. CB4.

See note following Nos. B1-B12.

Catalogue values for unused stamps in this section, from this point to the end of the section, are for Never Hinged items.

Fair Entrance SPAP1

Industry, Handicraft and Farming SPAP2

Design: 70p+10p, Fairgrounds.

Perf. 11½, Imperf.

1955 Litho. Unwmk.

CB5	SPAP1	25p + 5p gray blk	40	40
CB6	SPAP2	35p + 5p ultra	42	42
CB7	SPAP2	40p + 10p rose lil	60	60
CB8	SPAP1	70p + 10p Prus grn	1.10	1.10

Intl. Fair, Damascus, Sept. 1955.

United Nations Refugee Emblem SPAP3

1966, Dec. 12 Litho. *Perf. 11½x12*

CB9	SPAP3	12½p + 2½p ultra & blk	18	8
CB10	SPAP3	50p + 5p grn & blk	40	25

21st anniv. of UN Day; Refugee Week, Oct. 24-31.

POSTAGE DUE STAMPS

Under French Occupation

Stamps of French Offices in the Turkish Empire, 1902-03, Surcharged

O. M. F
Syrie
Ch. taxe
1 PIASTRE

1920 Unwmk. *Perf. 14x13½*

J1	A3	1p on 10c rose red	67.50	67.50
J2	A3	2p on 20c brn vio	67.50	67.50
J3	A3	3p on 30c lil	67.50	67.50
J4	A4	4p on 40c red & pale bl	67.50	67.50

Postage Due Stamps of France, 1893-1920, Surcharged in Black or Red

O. M. F.
Syrie
2
PIASTRES

1920

J5	D2	1p on 10c brn	45	45
J6	D2	2p on 20c ol grn (R)	45	45
a.		"PIASTRE"	190.00	190.00
J7	D2	3p on 30c red	45	45
a.		"PIASTRE"		
J8	D2	4p on 50c brn vio	1.50	1.50
a.		3p in setting of 4p	190.00	190.00

1921-22

J9	D2	50c on 10c brn	22	22
a.		"75" instead of "50"	19.00	
b.		"CENTIEMES" instead of "CENTIEMES"	2.75	
J10	D2	1p on 20c ol grn	22	22
J11	D2	2p on 30c red	75	75
J12	D2	3p on 50c brn vio	90	90
J13	D2	5p on 1fr red brn, *straw*	1.90	1.90
		Nos. J9-J13 (5)	3.99	3.99

D3

D4

1921 *Perf. 11½*

Red Surcharge

J14	D3	50c on 1p black	1.50	1.50
J15	D3	1p on 1p black	1.00	1.00

1922

J16	D4	2p on 5m rose	2.25	2.25
a.		"AX" of "TAXE" invtd.	55.00	55.00
J17	D4	3p on 1p gray bl	4.75	4.50

French Mandate

Postage Due Stamps of France, 1893-1920, Surcharged

Syrie
Grand Liban
2
PIASTRES

1923

J18	D2	50c on 10c brn	70	42
J19	D2	1p on 20c ol grn	1.00	70
J20	D2	2p on 30c red	90	50
J21	D2	3p on 50c vio brn	90	50
J22	D2	5p on 1fr red brn, *straw*	1.75	1.75
		Nos. J18-J22 (5)	5.25	3.87

Postage Due Stamps of France, 1893-1920, Surcharged

SYRIE
1
PIASTRE

1924

J23	D2	50c on 10c brn	18	18
J24	D2	1p on 20c ol grn	22	22
J25	D2	2p on 30c red	30	30
J26	D2	3p on 50c vio brn	42	30
J27	D2	5p on 1fr red brn, *straw*	38	38
		Nos. J23-J27 (5)	1.50	1.38

Postage Due Stamps of France, 1893-1920, Surcharged

Syrie
2 Piastres
سوريا
غروش ٢

1924

J28	D2	50c on 10c brn	18	18
J29	D2	1p on 20c ol grn	22	22
J30	D2	2p on 30c red	25	25
J31	D2	3p on 50c vio brn	32	32
J32	D2	5p on 1fr red brn, *straw*	48	48
		Nos. J28-J32 (5)	1.45	1.45

Water Wheel at Hama D5

Bridge at Antioch D6

Designs: 2p, The Tartous. 3p, View of Banias. 5p, Chevaliers' Castle.

1925 Photo. *Perf. 13½.*

J33	D5	50c brn, *yel*	8	8
J34	D6	1p vio, *rose*	9	9
J35	D5	2p blk, *blue*	9	9
J36	D5	3p blk, *red org*	22	22
J37	D5	5p blk, *bl grn*	90	32
		Nos. J33-J37 (5)	1.38	80

D7

Lion — D8

1931

J38	D7	8p blk, *gray bl*	1.25	1.25
J39	D8	15p blk, *dl rose*	2.00	2.00

Catalogue values for unused stamps in this section, from this point to the end of the section, are for Never Hinged items.

Syrian Arab Republic

D9

1965 Unwmk. Litho. *Perf. 11½x11*

J40	D9	2½p vio bl	5	5
J41	D9	5p blk brn	5	5
J42	D9	10p green	6	6
J43	D9	17½p car rose	16	16
J44	D9	25p blue	22	22
		Nos. J40-J44 (5)	54	54

MILITARY STAMPS

Free French Administration

Syria No. 222 Surcharged in Black

FORCES FRANÇAISES LIBRES
LEVANT
50c

1942 Unwmk. *Perf. 13*

M1	A10	50c on 4p yel org	1.90	1.90

Lebanon Nos. 155 and 142A Surcharged in Carmine

FORCES FRANÇAISES LIBRES
LEVANT
1f.

FORCES FRANÇAISES LIBRES
LEVANT
2f.50

M2	A13	1fr on 5p grnsh bl	1.90	1.90
M3	A25	2.50fr on 12½p dp ultra	1.90	1.90

Camel Corps, Palmyra M1

1942 Unwmk. Litho. *Perf. 11½*

M4	M1	1fr dp rose	15	15
M5	M1	1.50fr brt vio	15	15
M6	M1	2fr orange	15	15
M7	M1	2.50fr brn gray	15	15
M8	M1	3fr Prus blue	22	22
M9	M1	4fr dp green	32	32
M10	M1	5fr dp claret	32	32
		Nos. M4-M10 (7)	1.46	1.46

Nos. M4 to M10 exist imperforate.

MILITARY SEMI-POSTAL STAMPS

Free French Administration

Military Stamps of 1942 Surcharged in Black

RÉSISTANCE
+9F

1943 Unwmk. *Perf. 11½*

MB1	M1	1fr + 9fr deep rose	1.65	1.65
MB2	M1	5fr + 20fr dp claret	1.65	1.65

MILITARY AIR POST STAMPS

Free French Administration

Syria Nos. C55-C56 Surcharged in Carmine, Black or Orange

LIGNES AERIENNES F.A.F.L.
10f.

1942 Unwmk. *Perf. 13.*

MC1	AP2	4fr on 50p blk (C)	1.50	1.50
MC2	AP2	6.50fr on 50p blk (C)	1.50	1.50
MC3	AP2	8fr on 50p blk (O)	1.50	1.50
MC4	AP2	10fr on 100p mag (Bk)	1.50	1.50

Winged Shields and Cross of Lorraine MAP1

1942 Litho. *Perf. 11½*

MC5	MAP1	6.50fr pale pink & rose car	30	30
MC6	MAP1	10fr lt bl & dl vio	30	30

Nos. MC5 and MC6 exist imperforate.

Souvenir Sheets

1942 Without Gum *Perf. 11*

MC7		Sheet of two	6.25	6.25
a.	MAP1	6.50fr pale pink & rose car	1.50	1.50
b.	MAP1	10fr lt bl & dl vio	1.50	1.50

Imperf

MC8		Sheet of two	6.25	6.25
a.	MAP1	6.50fr pale pink & rose car	1.50	1.50
b.	MAP1	10fr lt bl & dl vio	1.50	1.50

No. MC5 Surcharged in Rose Carmine With New Value and Bars

Perf. 11½

MC9	MAP1	4fr on 6.50fr	45	38

Military Stamp of 1942 Surcharged in Black

4F

1943

MC10	M1	4fr on 3fr Prus blue	45	38

MILITARY AIR POST SEMI-POSTAL STAMPS

Free French Administration

Military Air Post Stamps of 1942 Surcharged in Black

+48fso
RÉSISTANCE

1943 Unwmk. *Perf. 11½*

MCB1	MAP1	6.50fr + 48.50fr	6.50	6.50
MCB2	MAP1	10fr + 100fr	6.50	6.50

POSTAL TAX STAMPS

Revenue Stamps Overprinted in Red or Black

R1

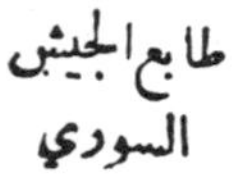
a

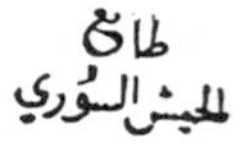
b

1945 Unwmk. *Perf. 10½x11½*

RA1	R1(a)	5p dk bl (R)	*62.50*	*22.00*

On Stamps Overprinted 

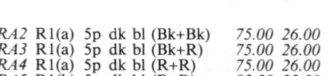

RA2	R1(a)	5p dk bl (Bk+Bk)	*75.00*	*26.00*
RA3	R1(a)	5p dk bl (Bk+R)	*75.00*	*26.00*
RA4	R1(a)	5p dk bl (R+R)	*75.00*	*26.00*
RA5	R1(b)	5p dk bl (R+R)	*82.50*	*22.50*

On Stamps Overprinted 

RA6	R1(a)	5p dk bl (Bk+Bk)	*75.00*	*26.00*
RA7	R1(a)	5p dk bl (Bk+R)	*75.00*	*26.00*
RA8	R1(a)	5p dk bl (R+R)	*75.00*	*26.00*
RA9	R1(b)	5p dk bl (R+R)	*90.00*	*26.00*
		Nos. RA1-RA9 (9)	*685.00*	*226.50*

The tax was for national defense.

R2

Revenue Stamp Surcharged in Black

1945 Unwmk. *Perf. 11*

RA10	R2	5p on 25c on 40c rose red	*60.00*	1.75

The surcharge reads "Tax (postal) for Syrian Army."

Revenue Stamp Surcharged in Black

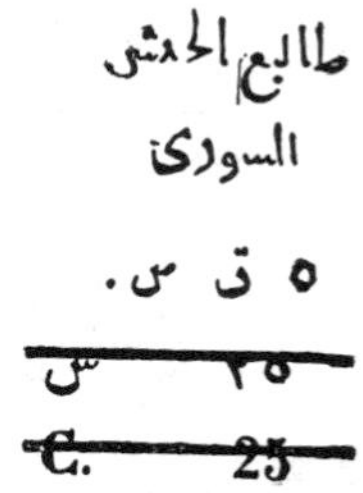

1945

RA11	R2	5p on 25c on 40c rose red	*60.00*	1.75

Same, Overprinted in Black 

RA12	R2	5p on 25c on 40c rose red	*67.50*	

The tax on Nos. RA11 and RA12 was for the army.

ISSUES OF THE ARABIAN GOVERNMENT

The following issues replaced the British Military Occupation (E.E.F.) stamps (Palestine Nos. 2-14) which were used in central and eastern Syria from Nov. 1918 until Jan. 1920.

Turkish Stamps of 1913-18 Handstamped in Various Colors 

Also Handstamp Surcharged with New Values as:

1 millieme

1 Egyptian piaster

The Seal reads: "Hakuma al Arabie" (The Arabian Government)

Perf. 11½, 12, 12½, 13½

1919-20 Unwmk.

1	A24	1m on 2pa red lil (254)	55	55
2	A25	1m on 4pa dk brn (255)	55	55
3	A26	2m on 5pa vio brn (256)	85	85
4	A15	2m on 5pa on 10pa gray grn (291)	55	55
5	A18	2m on 5pa ocher (304)	16.00	14.00
6	A41	2m on 5pa grn (345)	*200.00*	*150.00*
7	A18	2m on 5pa ocher (378)	*40.00*	*40.00*
8	A28	4m on 10pa grn (258)	4.50	4.50
9	A28	4m on 10pa grn (271)	55	55
10	A22	4m on 10pa bl grn (329)	1.10	1.10
11	A41	4m on 10pa car (346)	19.00	19.00
12	A23	4m on 10pa grn (415)	4.50	4.50
13	A44	4m on 10pa grn (424)	80	80
14	A11	4m on 10pa on 20pa vio brn (B38)	80	80
15	A41	4m on 10pa car (B42)	55	55
16	SP1	4m on 10pa red vio (B46)	80	80
17	SP1	4m on 10pa on 20pa car rose (B47)	80	80
19	A21	5pa ocher (317)		
21	A21	20pa car rose (153)	*50.00*	*100.00*
22	A29	20pa red (259)	80	80
23	A29	20pa red (272)	*200.00*	*200.00*
24	A17	20pa car (299)	1.65	1.65
25	A21	20pa car rose (318)	1.65	1.65
26	A22	20pa car rose (330)	8.50	8.50
27	A21	20pa car rose (342)	4.50	4.50
28	A41	20pa ultra (347)	1.50	1.50
29	A16	20pa mag (363)	6.50	6.50
30	A17	20pa car (371)		
31	A18	20pa car (379)	4.50	4.50
32	A45	20pa dp rose (425)	2.25	2.25
33	A21	20pa car rose (B8)	1.40	1.40
34	A22	20pa car rose (B33)	1.65	1.65
35	A22	20pa car rose (B36)	8.75	8.75
36	A41	20pa ultra (B43)	28	28
37	A16	20pa mag (P140)	2.25	2.25
38	A17	20pa car (P144)	*200.00*	*200.00*
39	A30	1pi bl (260)	1.65	1.65
40	A31	1pi on 1½pi car & blk (261)	*250.00*	*250.00*
41	A30	1pi bl (273)	40.00	40.00
42	A30	1pi on 1pi bl (273)	60.00	60.00
43	A17	1pi bl (300)	2.75	2.75
44	A18	1pi bl (307)	50.00	50.00
45	A22	1pi ultra (331)	4.50	4.50

46 A21 1pi ultra (343) 8.50 8.50
47 A41 1pi vio & blk (348) 85 85
48 A18 1pi brt bl (389) 4.50 4.50
49 A46 1pi dl vio (426) 1.50 1.50
50 A47 1pi on 50pa ultra (428) 55 55
51 A21 1pi ultra (B9) 5.50 5.50
52 A22 1pi ultra (B15) 8.75 8.75
53 A18 1pi brt bl (B21) 5.50 5.50
54 A18 1pi bl (B23) 14.00 14.00
55 A22 1pi ultra (B34) 11.50 11.50
56 A41 1pi vio & blk (B44) 1.50 1.50
57 A33 2pi grn & blk (263) 40.00 35.00
58 A13 2pi brn org (289) 1.10 1.10
59 A18 2pi sl (308) 14.00 14.00
60 A18 2pi sl (314) 14.00 14.00
61 A21 2pi bl blk (320) 2.75 2.75
62 A17 2pi org (373) 2.75 2.75
63 A18 5pi brn (310) 6.50 6.50
64 A22 5pi dl vio (333) 14.00 14.00
65 A41 5pi yel brn & blk (349) 2.25 2.25
66 A41 5pi yel brn & blk (418) 2.25 2.25
67 A53 5pi on 2pa Prus bl (547) 1.65 1.65
68 A21 5pi dk vio (Bl) 175.00 175.00
69 A17 5pi lil rose (B20) 30.00 30.00
70 A41 5pi yel brn & blk (B45) 2.75 2.75
72 A50 10pi dk grn (431) 60.00 60.00
73 A50 10pi dk vio (432) 55.00 55.00
74 A50 10pi dk brn (433) *350.00*
75 A18 10pi org brn (B2) 150.00 150.00
76 A37 25pi ol grn (267) *200.00 200.00*
77 A40 25pi on 200pi grn & blk (287) *250.00 250.00*
78 A17 25pi brn (303) 200.00 200.00
79 A51 25pi car, *straw* (434) 50.00 50.00
81 A52 50pi ind (438) 125.00 125.00

The variety "surcharge omitted" exists on Nos. 1-5, 12-13, 16, 32, 49-50, 67.

A few copies of No. 377 (50pi) and No. 269 (100pi) were overprinted but not regularly issued.

Overprinted 

The Inscription reads "Hakum Soria Arabie" (Syrian-Arabian Government)

On Stamp of 1913

83 A26 2m on 5pa vio brn (256) 3.50 3.50

On Stamp of 1916-18

84 A45 20pa dp rose (425) 50 50

A1

Litho. ***Perf. 11½***

85 A1 5m rose 50 50
a. Tete beche pair 10.00 7.50
b. Imperf.

Independence Issue

Arabic Overprint in Green: "Souvenir of Syrian Independence March 8, 1920"

86 A1 5m rose 40.00 35.00
a. Tete beche pair
b. Inverted overprint 100.00 75.00

A2

Litho.

Size: 22x18mm

87 A2 1/10pi lt brn 15 10

Size: 28x22mm

88 A2 2/10pi yel grn 25 18
a. 2/10pi yellow (error) 6.25 4.00
89 A2 3/10pi yellow 12 10
90 A2 1pi gray blue 12 10
91 A2 2pi blue grn 1.00 38

Size: 31x25mm

92 A2 5pi vio brn 1.50 75
93 A2 10pi gray 1.50 1.00
Nos. 86-93 (8) 44.64 37.61

Nos. 86-93 exist imperf.

PF1

PF2

Revenue Stamps Surcharged as on Postage Stamps, for Postal Use

1920 Unwmk. ***Perf. 11½***

94 PF1 5m on 5pa red 25 25
95 PF2 1m on 5pa red 18 12
96 PF2 2m on 5pa red 25 15
97 PF2 1pi on 5pa red 50 38

Surcharged in Syrian Piasters 

98 PF2 2pi on 5pa red 18 18
99 PF2 3pi on 5pa red 18 18
Nos. 94-99 (6) 1.54 1.26

ISSUES OF THE ARABIAN GOVERNMENT POSTAGE DUE STAMPS

Postage Due Stamps of Turkey, 1914, Handstamped and Surcharged with New Value 

1920 Unwmk. ***Perf. 12***

J1 D1 2m on 5pa claret 4.00 4.00
J2 D2 20pa red 4.00 4.00
J3 D3 1pi dark blue 4.00 4.00
J4 D4 2pi slate 4.00 4.00

Type of Regular Issue

Perf. 11½

Litho.

J5 A2 1pi black 75 75

UNITED ARAB REPUBLIC

Catalogue values for unused stamps in this section, from this point to the end of the section, are for Never Hinged items.

Issues for Syria

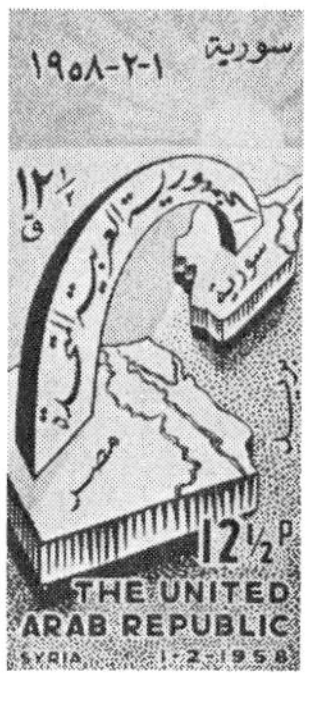
Linked Maps of Egypt and Syria — A1

1958 Unwmk. Litho. ***Perf. 11½***

1 A1 12½p yel & grn 20 12

Establishment of United Arab Republic. See No. C1.

Freedom Monument — A2

1958, May

2 A2 5p yel & vio 40 16
3 A2 15p yel grn & brn red 60 35

12th anniv. of the British-French troop evacuation. See Nos. C2-C3.

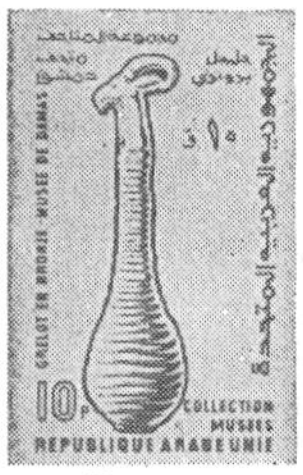
Bronze Rattle — A3

Hand Holding Torch, Broken Chain and Flag — A4

Antique Art: 15p, Goddess. 20p, Lamgi Mari. 30p, Mithras fighting bull. 40p, Aspasia. 60p, Minerva. 75p, Flask. 100p, Enameled Vase. 150p, Mosaic from Omayyad Mosque, Damascus.

1958, Sept. 14 Litho. ***Perf. 12***

4 A3 10p lt ol grn 7 5
5 A3 15p brn org 10 7
6 A3 20p rose lil 12 8
7 A3 30p lt brn 15 10
8 A3 40p gray 30 15
9 A3 60p green 50 20
10 A3 75p blue 80 30
11 A3 100p brn car 1.20 40
12 A3 150p dl pur 2.25 60
Nos. 4-12 (9) 5.49 1.95

Archaeological collections and museums.

1958, Oct. 14 ***Perf. 11½***

13 A4 12.50p car rose 20 12

Establishment of Republic of Iraq.

Syria No. 411 Overprinted 

1958, Oct. 6 Wmk. 291 ***Perf. 11½***

13A A78 12½p olive *37.50 35.00*

Intl. Children's Day, 1958. See Nos. C10-C11.

View of Damascus — A5

1958, Dec. 10 Unwmk.

14 A5 12½p green 22 8

4th Near East Regional Conference, Damascus, Dec. 10-20. See No. C14.

Secondary School, Damascus — A6

1959, Feb. 26 Litho. ***Perf. 12***

15 A6 12½p dl grn 12 5

See No. 26.

Flags of UAR and Yemen A7 

Perf. 13x13½

1959, Mar. 8 Photo. Wmk. 318

16 A7 12½p grn red & blk 20 12

1st anniversary of United Arab States.

Arms of UAR — A8

Mother and Children — A9

Perf. 12x11½

1959, Feb. 22 Litho. Wmk. 291

17 A8 12½p grn blk & red 20 12

United Arab Republic, 1st anniv.

1959, Mar. 21 ***Perf. 11½***

18 A9 15p car rose 20 12
19 A9 25p dk sl grn 30 22

Arab Mother's Day, Mar. 21.

Syria No. 378 Surcharged "U.A.R." in Arabic and English, and New Value in Red

1959, Apr. 6 Photo. Unwmk.

20 A68 2½p on 1p olive 10 5

Type of 1959 and

A10

Boys' School, Damascus — A11

Designs: 5p, 7½p, 10p, Various arabesques. 12½p, St. Simeon's Monastery. 17½p, Hittin school. 35p, Normal School for Girls, Damascus.

1959-61 Unwmk. Litho. ***Perf. 11½***

21 A10 2½p violet 5 5
22 A10 5p ol bis 5 5
23 A10 7½p ultra 7 5
24 A10 10p bl grn 10 5
25 A11 12½p lt bl ('61) 16 10
26 A6 17½p brt lil ('60) 22 7
27 A11 25p brt grnsh bl 30 12
28 A11 35p brn ('60) 40 16
Nos. 21-28 (8) *1.35* *65*

Fair Emblem and Globe — A12

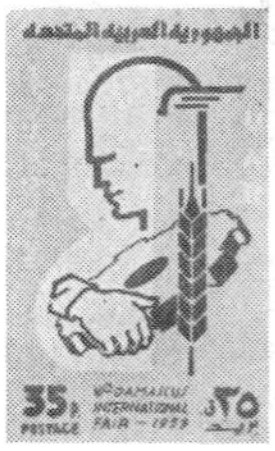

Male Profile and Fair Emblem — A13

Souvenir Sheet

1959, Aug. 30 Unwmk. *Imperf.*
30 A12 30p dl yel & grn 1.50 1.50

Perf. 11½

31 A13 35p gray, grn & vio 42 20

6th International Damascus Fair.

Shield and Cogwheel — A14

Perf. 13½x13

1959, Oct. 20 Wmk. 328
32 A14 50p sepia 60 35

Issued for Army Day, 1959.

Syria Nos. 408 and 386 with Red Overprint Similar to

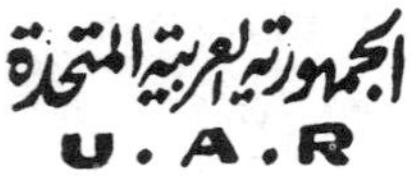

1959 Unwmk. Litho. *Perf. 11½*
33 A75 15p gray 22 12

Photo.

34 A69 50p dk grn 60 42

The overprints differ in size and lettering: No. 33 is 28x8½mm; No. 34 is 21x6mm. A period follows "R" on Nos. 33-34. The Arabic overprint means "United Arab Republic."

Cogwheel, Wheat and Cotton — A15

A. R. Kawakbi — A16

1959, Oct. 30 Litho.
35 A15 35p gray, bl & ocher 42 20

Industrial and Agricultural Production Fair, Aleppo. See No. 46.

Type of Syria Air Post, 1956, Inscribed "U.A.R."

1959, Dec. 31 Unwmk. *Perf. 13½*
36 AP59 12½p gray ol & bis 20 10

Day of the Tree.

1960, Jan. 11 *Perf. 12x11½*
37 A16 15p dk grn 20 10

50th death anniv. of A. R. Kawakbi, Arabic writer.

Arms and Flag — A17

Perf. 13½x13

1960, Feb. 22 Photo. Wmk. 328
38 A17 12½p red & dk sl grn 20 10

United Arab Republic, 2nd anniversary.

Diesel Train and Old Town — A18

Perf. 11½x11

1960, Mar. 15 Litho. Unwmk.
39 A18 12½p brn & brt bl 35 20

Construction of the Latakia-Aleppo railroad.

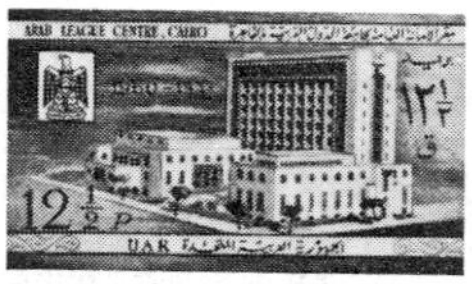

Arab League Center, Cairo, and Arms of UAR
A19

Perf. 13x13½

1960, Mar. 22 Photo. Wmk. 328
40 A19 12½p dl grn & blk 20 12

Opening of the Arab League Center and the Arab Postal Museum in Cairo.

Nos. 18-19 Overprinted: "ARAB MOTHERS DAY 1960" in Arabic and English in Black or Magenta

Wmk. 291

1960, Apr. 3 Litho. *Perf. 11½*
41 A9 15p car rose 22 12
42 A9 25p dk sl grn (M) 35 16

Issued for Arab Mother's Day.

Refugees Pointing to Map of Palestine
A20

Perf. 13x13½

1960, Apr. 7 Photo. Wmk. 328
43 A20 12½p car rose 40 12
44 A20 50p green 70 30

World Refugee Year, July 1, 1959-June 30, 1960.

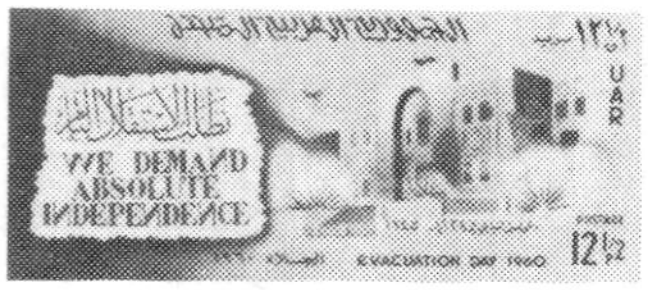

A21

Perf. 11½

1960, May 12 Unwmk. Litho.
45 A21 12½p vio, rose & pale grn 22 10

Evacuation Day, 1960.

No. 35 Overprinted "1960" in Red in Arabic and English

1960
46 A15 35p gray, bl & ocher 30 20

1960 Industrial and Agricultural Production Fair, Aleppo.

Souvenir Sheet

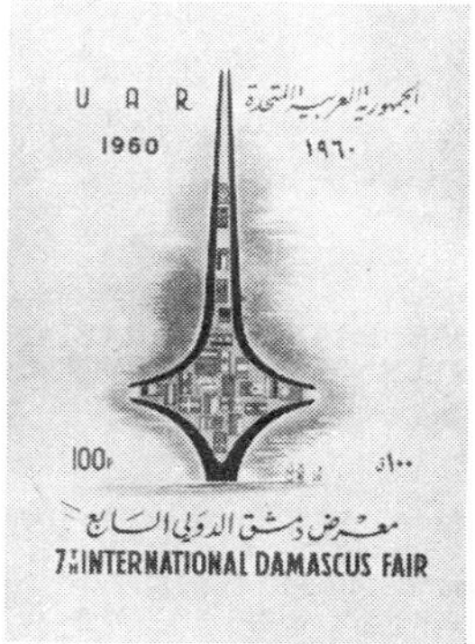

Flags in Symbolic Design — A22

1960 Unwmk. *Imperf.*
47 A22 100p gray, brn & lt bl 1.50 1.50

7th Intl. Damascus Fair.

Child — A23

1960 Litho. *Perf. 11½*
48 A23 35p dk grn & fawn 42 22

Issued for Children's Day.

No. 36 Overprinted in Carmine

1960 Unwmk. *Perf. 11½*
49 AP59 12½p gray ol & bis 22 12

Issued to publicize the Day of the Tree.

Coat of Arms and Victory Wreath — A24

Cogwheel, Retort and Ear of Wheat — A25

Perf. 13½x13

1961, Feb. 22 Photo. Wmk. 328
50 A24 12½p lt vio 15 9

United Arab Republic, 3rd anniversary.

Perf. 11½

1961, June 8 Unwmk. Litho.
51 A25 12½p multi 15 12

Industrial and Agricultural Fair, Aleppo.

SEMI-POSTAL STAMP

Catalogue values for unused stamp in this section is for a Never Hinged item.

Postal Emblem — SP1

Perf. 13½x13

1959, Jan. 2 Photo. Wmk. 318
B1 SP1 20p + 10p bl grn, red & blk 42 42

Issued for Post Day. The surtax went to the social fund for postal employees.

AIR POST STAMPS

Catalogue values for unused stamps in this section, from this point to the end of the section, are for Never Hinged items.

Map Type of Regular Issue

Perf. 11½

1958, Apr. 3 Unwmk. Litho.
C1 A1 17½p ultra & brn 35 20

Broken Chain, Dove and Olive Branch
AP1

1958, May 17
C2 AP1 35p rose & blk 70 35
C3 AP1 45p bl & brn 1.25 42

12th anniv. of the British-French troop evacuation.

Scout Putting up Tent — AP2

1958, Aug. 31 *Perf. 12*
C4 AP2 35p dk brn 1.50 1.50
C5 AP2 40p ultra 2.00 2.00

3rd Pan-Arab Boy Scout Jamboree.

View of Damascus Fair — AP3

U.A.R. Flag and Fair Emblem — AP4

Designs: 30p, Minaret, vase and emblem (vert.). 45p, Mosque, chimneys and wheel (vert.).

1958, Sept. 1 Litho. *Perf. 11½*
C6 AP3 25p vermilion 70 60
C7 AP3 30p brt bl grn 1.00 62
C8 AP3 45p violet 80 55

Souvenir Sheet.
Imperf
C9 AP4 100p brt grn, car & blk 50.00 50.00

Fifth Damascus International Fair.

Syria Nos. C244-C245 Overprinted

الجمهورية العربية المتحدة
١٩٥٨/١٠/٦
RAU

1958, Oct. 6 Wmk. 291 *Perf. 11½*
C10 A78 17½p ultra *25.00 25.00*
C11 A78 20p red brn *25.00 25.00*

International Children's Day.

Cotton and Cotton Material — AP5

1958, Oct. 10 Unwmk. *Perf. 12*
C12 AP5 25p brn & yel 42 40
C13 AP5 35p brn & brick red 70 50

Cotton Festival, Aleppo, Oct. 9-11.

Type of Regular Issue, 1958

1958, Dec. 10
C14 A5 17½p brt vio 22 15

Children and Glider — AP6

1958, Dec. 1 Litho. *Perf. 12*
C15 AP6 7½p gray grn 50 30
C16 AP6 12½p olive 2.00 1.20

1958 glider festival.

UN Emblem — AP7

1958, Dec. 10
C17 AP7 25p dl pur 22 16
C18 AP7 35p light blue 35 22
C19 AP7 40p brn red 50 30

10th anniv. of the signing of the Universal Declaration of Human Rights.

Globe, Radio and Telegraph — AP8

1959, Mar. 1 *Perf. 12*
C20 AP8 40p grn & blk 50 35

Arab Union of Telecommunications.

Same Overprinted in Red: "2nd Conferance Damascus 1-3-59" and in Arabic Characters

1959, Mar. 1
C21 AP8 40p grn & blk 40 20

2nd Conference of the Arab Union of Telecommunications, Damascus.

Laurel and Map of Syria — AP9

Design: 35p, Torch and broken chain.

1959, Apr. 17 *Perf. 12x11½*
C22 AP9 15p ocher & grn 20 10
C23 AP9 35p gray & car 40 22

13th anniv. of the British-French troop evacuation.

"Emigration" — AP10

1959, Aug. 4 Unwmk. *Perf. 11½x12*
C24 AP10 80p brt grn, blk & red 70 42

Convention of the Assoc. of Arab Emigrants in the US.

Refinery AP11

1959, Aug. 12 Litho.
C25 AP11 50p bl, blk & car 90 40

Opening of first oil refinery in Syria.

Syria Nos. C246 and C181-C182 Overprinted

الجمهورية العربية المتحدة
U . A . R

1959 *Perf. 11½*
C26 AP64 5p brt grn 7 5
C27 AP44 50p dp plum 42 22
C28 AP44 70p purple 70 30

The overprints differ in size and lettering: No. C26 is 25½x9½mm; Nos. C27-C28 are 27x8mm. A period follows "R" on Nos. C27-C28. The Arabic overprint means "United Arab Republic."

Cotton Boll and Thread AP12

Boy and Building Blocks AP13

1959, Oct. 1 Litho. *Perf. 11½*
C29 AP12 45p gray bl 42 16
C30 AP12 50p claret 42 30

Cotton Festival, Aleppo.

1959, Oct. 5
C31 AP13 25p dl lil, red & dk bl 22 12

Issued for Children's Day.

Crane and Compass AP14

1960 Unwmk. *Perf. 11½*
C32 AP14 50p lt brn, crim & blk 42 30

7th Damascus International Fair.

Nos. C29-C30 Overprinted with Arabic Date and Cotton Boll in Claret or Gray Blue

1960 Litho. *Perf. 11½*
C33 AP12 45p gray bl (C) 40 16
C34 AP12 50p claret (GB) 42 30

1960 Cotton Festival, Aleppo.

17th Olympic Games, Rome — AP15

Globe, Laurel and "UN" — AP16

1960, Dec. 27 Unwmk. *Perf. 12*
C35 AP15 15p Basketball 22 10
C36 AP15 20p Swimmer 35 12
C37 AP15 25p Fencing 35 12
C38 AP15 40p Horsemanship 60 30

1960, Dec. 31
C39 AP16 35p multi 35 15
C40 AP16 50p bl, red & yel 42 22

United Nations, 15th anniversary.

Ibrahim Hanano — AP17

Soldier with Flag — AP18

1961 Litho. *Perf. 12x11½*
C41 AP17 50p buff & sl grn 32 18

Hanano, leader of liberation movement.

1961, Apr. 17 Wmk. 291 *Perf. 11½*
C42 AP18 40p gray grn 32 18

Issued for Evacuation Day, 1961.

Arab and Map of Palestine AP19

Abu-Tammam AP20

1961, May 15 *Perf. 12*
C43 AP19 50p ultra & blk 50 25

Issued for Palestine Day.

1961, July 20 Unwmk. *Perf. 11½*
C44 AP20 50p brown 38 18

Abu-Tammam (807-?845), Arabian poet.

Discus Thrower and Lyre AP21

1961, Aug. 23 Litho. *Perf. 11½*
C45 AP21 15p crim & blk 18 5
C46 AP21 35p bl grn & vio 50 18

5th University Youth Festival.
A souvenir sheet contains one each of Nos. C45-C46 imperf.

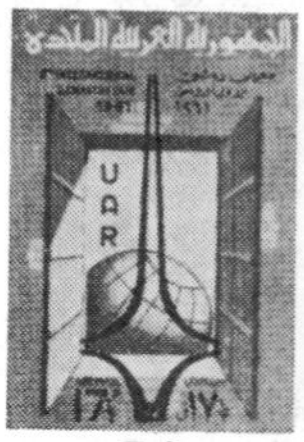
Fair Emblem — AP22

U.A.R. Pavilion — AP23

1961, Aug. 25
C47 AP22 17½p vio & grn 15 9
C48 AP23 50p brt lil & blk 32 18
a. Black omitted

8th International Damascus Fair.

St. Simeon's Monastery — AP24

1961, Oct. Litho. *Perf. 12*
C49 AP24 200p vio bl 1.50 90

No. C49 was issued by the Syrian Arab Republic after dissolution of the UAR.

AIR POST SEMI-POSTAL STAMP

Catalogue value for the unused stamp in this section is for a Never Hinged item.

Eye, Hand and UN Emblem — SPAP1

Perf. 12x11½
1961, Apr. 29 Litho. Wmk. 291
CB1 SPAP1 40p + 10p sl grn & blk 30 30

UN welfare program for the blind.

TAHITI

LOCATION — An island in the South Pacific Ocean, one of the Society group.
GOVT. — A part of the French Oceania Colony.
AREA — 600 sq. mi.
POP. — 19,029
CAPITAL — Papeete

The stamps of Tahiti were replaced by those of French Oceania (see French Polynesia in Vol. II).

100 Centimes = 1 Franc

Stamps of French Colonies Surcharged in Black:

25c (a)
TAHITI 25c (b)
TAHITI 5c (c)
TAHITI 10c (d)

1882 Unwmk. *Imperf.*
1 A8(a) 25c on 35c dk vio, *org* 150.00 115.00
1A A8(b) 25c on 35c dk vio, *org* *3,500.* *3,500.*
1B A8(a) 25c on 40c ver, *straw* *2,400.* *2,400.*

Inverted and vertical surcharges on Nos. 1 and 1A are about the same value as upright surcharges.
Value for No. 1B is for inverted surcharge. Value for upright surcharge, $5,500.
Counterfeits exist of surcharges and overprints on Nos. 1-31.

1884 *Perf. 14x13½*
2 A9(c) 5c on 20c red, *grn* 110.00 80.00
3 A9(d) 10c on 20c red, *grn* 150.00 125.00
Imperf
4 A8(b) 25c on 1fr brnz grn, *straw* 350.00 200.00

Inverted and vertical surcharges on Nos. 2-4 are same value as normally placed surcharges.

Handstamped in Black TAHITI

1893 *Perf. 14x13½*
5 A9 1c blk, *lil bl* 400.00 250.00
6 A9 2c brn, *buff* *2,000.* *1,500.*
7 A9 4c cl, *lav* 800.00 650.00
8 A9 5c grn, *grnsh* 15.00 15.00
9 A9 10c blk, *lav* 15.00 15.00
10 A9 15c blue 15.00 15.00
11 A9 20c red, *grn* 15.00 15.00
12 A9 25c yel, *straw* *4,000.* *3,750.*
13 A9 25c blk, *rose* 15.00 15.00
14 A9 35c vio, *org* *1,250.* *1,250.*
15 A9 75c car, *rose* 24.00 24.00
16 A9 1fr brnz grn, *straw* 26.00 26.00

Nearly all values of this set are known with overprint inverted, sloping up, sloping down and horizontal. Some occur double.

Overprinted in Black 1893 TAHITI

1893
17 A9 1c blk, *lil bl* 400.00 375.00
a. Inverted overprint 550.00 550.00
18 A9 2c brn, *buff* *2,250.* *1,750.*
a. Inverted overprint *2,750.* *2,750.*
19 A9 4c cl, *lav* 1,000. 900.00
a. Inverted overprint *1,200.* *1,200.*
20 A9 5c grn, *grnsh* 550.00 450.00
a. Inverted overprint 700.00 700.00
21 A9 10c blk, *lav* 160.00 160.00
a. Inverted overprint 350.00 350.00
22 A9 15c blue 15.00 15.00
a. Inverted overprint 62.50 62.50
23 A9 20c red, *grn* 15.00 15.00
a. Inverted overprint 82.50 82.50
24 A9 25c yel, *straw* *20,000.* *18,500.*
25 A9 25c blk, *rose* 15.00 15.00
a. Inverted overprint 82.50 82.50
26 A9 35c vio, *org* *1,500.* *1,400.*
a. Inverted overprint *1,600.* *1,600.*
27 A9 75c car, *rose* 15.00 15.00
a. Inverted overprint 82.50 82.50
b. Double overprint 120.00 120.00
28 A9 1fr brnz grn, *straw* 15.00 15.00
a. Inverted overprint 82.50 82.50

Stamps of French Polynesia Surcharged in Black or Carmine:

TAHITI 10 CENTIMES (g)
TAHITI 10 centimes (h)

1903
29 A1 (g) 10c on 15c bl (Bk) 3.25 3.25
a. Double surcharge 17.50 17.50
b. Inverted surcharge 17.50 17.50
30 A1 (h) 10c on 25c blk, *rose* (C) 3.25 3.25
a. Double surcharge 17.50 17.50
b. Inverted surcharge 17.50 17.50
31 A1 (h) 10c on 40c red, *straw* (Bk) 3.50 3.50
a. Double surcharge 17.50 17.50
b. Inverted surcharge 17.50 17.50

In the surcharges on Nos. 29 to 31 there are two varieties of the "1" in "10", i. e. with long and short serif.

SEMI-POSTAL STAMPS

Stamps of French Polynesia Overprinted in Red TAHITI

1915 Unwmk. *Perf. 14x13½*
B1 A1 15c blue 80.00 80.00
a. Inverted overprint 250.00 250.00
B2 A1 15c gray 10.00 10.00
a. Inverted overprint 100.00 100.00

Counterfeits exist.

POSTAGE DUE STAMPS

Postage Due Stamps of French Colonies Handstamped in Black like Nos. 5-16

1893 Unwmk. *Imperf.*
J1 D1 1c black 150.00 150.00
J2 D1 2c black 150.00 150.00
J3 D1 3c black 175.00 175.00
J4 D1 4c black 175.00 175.00
J5 D1 5c black 175.00 175.00
J6 D1 10c black 200.00 200.00
J7 D1 15c black 200.00 200.00
J8 D1 20c black 150.00 150.00
J9 D1 30c black 175.00 175.00
J10 D1 40c black 175.00 175.00
J11 D1 60c black 175.00 175.00
J12 D1 1fr brown 450.00 450.00
J13 D1 2fr brown 450.00 450.00

Many values exist with inverted or double overprint.
Counterfeits exist of Nos. J1-J26.

Overprinted in Black like Nos. 17-28

1893
J14 D1 1c black *1,200.* *1,200.*
a. Inverted overprint *1,600.* *1,600.*
J15 D1 2c black 250.00 250.00
J16 D1 3c black 250.00 250.00
J17 D1 4c black 250.00 250.00
J18 D1 5c black 250.00 250.00
J19 D1 10c black 250.00 250.00
J20 D1 15c black 250.00 250.00
J21 D1 20c black 250.00 250.00
J22 D1 30c black 250.00 250.00
J23 D1 40c black 250.00 250.00
J24 D1 60c black 250.00 250.00
J25 D1 1fr brown 250.00 250.00
J26 D1 2fr brown 250.00 250.00

Nos. J15-J20, J22-J26 exist with overprint inverted, double or both. Value, each $600.

TANNU TUVA

(Tuva Autonomous Region.)

LOCATION — In the Tannu Mountains on the Siberian border in northwestern Mongolia.
GOVT. — A former republic closely identified with Soviet Russia in Asia.
AREA — 64,000 sq. mi. (approx.)
POP. — 65,000 (approx.)
CAPITAL — Kyzyl

The status of this country which has been under both Chinese and Russian rule at various times, was settled in 1926 by a Mixed Claims Commission. As a republic, its independence was maintained under Soviet protection. Later it became part of the Soviet Union as the Tuva Autonomous Soviet Socialist Republic.

100 Kopecks = 1 Ruble

Wheel of Life — A1

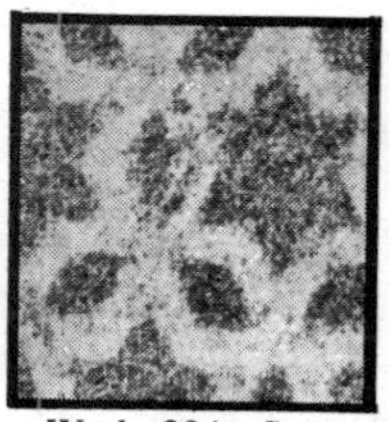
Wmk. 204 - Stars and Diamonds

1926 Typo. Wmk. 204 *Perf. 13½*
Size: 20x26mm
1 A1 1k red 85 85
2 A1 2k light blue 85 85
3 A1 5k orange 85 85
4 A1 8k yel green 85 85
5 A1 10k violet 85 85
6 A1 30k dark brown 85 85
7 A1 50k gray black 1.65 1.65
Size: 22½x30mm
Perf. 10½
8 A1 1r blue green 4.50 5.25
9 A1 3r red brown 6.50 7.25
10 A1 5r dark ultra 10.00 10.00
Nos. 1-10 (10) 27.75 29.25

Stamps of 1926 Surcharged in Red or Black — A2

1927 *Perf. 13½, 11*
11 A2 8k on 50k gray blk (R) 13.00 12.50
12 A2 14k on 1r bl grn (R) 16.00 15.00
13 A2 18k on 3r red brn (Bk) 22.50 20.00
14 A2 28k on 5r dk ultra (Bk) 27.50 25.00

Nos. 11-14 exist with surcharge inverted and No. 14 with surcharge double. Value $30 each.
Reprints exist of Nos. 1-14.

Mongol Woman A3

Map of Tannu Tuva A8

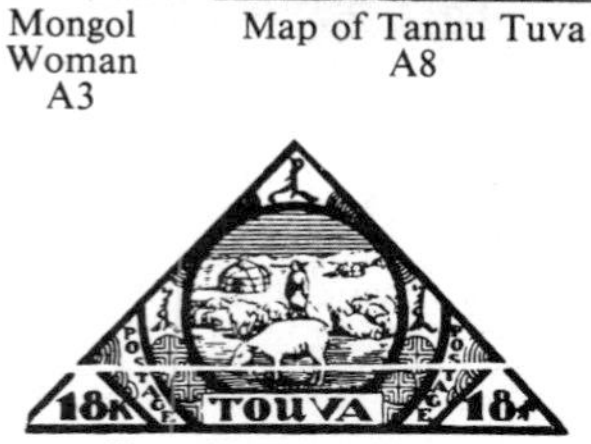
Sheep Herding — A11

Fording a Stream — A13

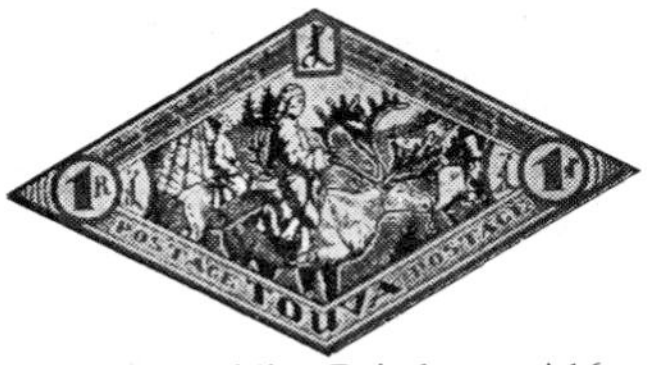

Mongols Riding Reindeer — A16

Designs: 2k, Stag. 3k, Mountain goat. 4k, Mongol and tent. 5k, Mongol man. 10k, Bow-and-arrow hunters. 14k, Camel caravan. 28k, Landscape. 50k, Weaving. 70k, Mongol on horseback.

1927 Typo. *Perf. 12½, 12½x12*

15	A3	1k blk, lt brn & red	50	32
16	A3	2k pur, dp brn & grn	60	32
17	A3	3k blk, bl grn & yel	60	50
18	A3	4k vio bl & choc	60	32
19	A3	5k org, blk & dk bl	50	32
20	A8	8k ol brn, pale bl & red brn	90	85
21	A8	10k blk, grn & brn red	3.25	1.10
22	A8	14k vio bl & red org	8.50	6.50

Perf. 10, 10½

23	A11	18k dk bl & red brn	8.50	6.50
24	A11	28k emer & blk brn	4.75	1.75
25	A13	40k rose & bl grn	3.25	1.75
26	A13	50k blk, grn & red brn	3.25	2.00
27	A13	70k dl red & bis	4.00	3.50
28	A16	1r yel brn & vio	10.00	6.50
		Nos. 15-28 (14)	49.20	32.23

Stamps of 1927 Surcharged "Tuva", "Posta" and New Values in Various Colors

1932

29	A13	1k on 40k rose & bl grn (Bk)	6.25	6.25
30	A13	2k on 50k blk, grn & red brn (Br)	6.25	6.25
31	A13	3k on 70k dl red & bis (Bl)	6.25	6.25
a.		Inverted surcharge	275.00	
32	A8	5k on 8k ol brn, pale bl & red brn (Bk)	8.00	8.00
33	A8	10k blk, grn & brn red (Bk)	8.00	8.00
34	A8	15k on 14k dk bl & org (Bk)	8.00	8.00
		Nos. 29-34 (6)	42.75	42.75

Issued in connection with the Romanization of the alphabet.

A17

A18

1933 Wmk. 204

Black Surcharge

35	A17 35k on 18k dk bl & red brn	125.00	110.00
36	A18 35k on 28k emer & blk brn	125.00	110.00

Tannu Tuva stamps can be mounted in Scott's Soviet Republics Part I Album.

A19

Revenue Stamps Surcharged "Posta" and New Values

1933 *Perf. 12x12½*

37	A19 15k on 6k org	225.00	200.00
38	A19 35k on 15k brn	*700.00*	*750.00*

Various pictorial sets, perf. and imperf., of triangular, diamond, square and oblong shapes, inscribed, "Postage," "Air-Mail" and "Registered," appeared in 1934 and 1935. The editors do not consider them to have been issued primarily for postal purposes.

TETE

LOCATION — In southeastern Africa between Nyasaland and Southern Rhodesia.
GOVT. — A district of the Portuguese East Africa Colony.
AREA — 46,600 sq. mi. (approx.)
POP. — 367,000 (approx.)
CAPITAL — Tete

This district was formerly a part of Zambezia. Stamps of Mozambique replaced those of Tete. See Mozambique.

100 Centavos = 1 Escudo

Vasco da Gama Issue of Various Portuguese Colonies Surcharged as

REPUBLICA
TETE
¼ C.

1913 Unwmk. *Perf. 12½, 16*

On Stamps of Macao

1	CD20	¼c on ½a bl grn	2.00	2.25
2	CD21	½c on 1a red	2.00	2.25
3	CD22	1c on 2a red vio	2.00	2.25
4	CD23	2½c on 4a yel grn	2.00	2.25
5	CD24	5c on 8a dk blue	2.00	2.25
6	CD25	7½c on 12a vio brn	3.00	3.50
7	CD26	10c on 16a bis brn	2.00	2.25
8	CD27	15c on 24a bister	2.00	2.25
		Nos. 1-8 (8)	17.00	19.25

On Stamps of Portuguese Africa

9	CD20	¼c on 2½r bl grn	2.00	2.25
10	CD21	½c on 5r red	2.00	2.25
11	CD22	1c on 10r red vio	2.00	2.25
12	CD23	2½c on 25r yel grn	2.00	2.25
13	CD24	5c on 50r dk blue	2.00	2.25
14	CD25	7½c on 75r vio brn	3.00	3.50
15	CD26	10c on 100r bis brn	2.00	2.25
16	CD27	15c on 150r bister	2.00	2.25
		Nos. 9-16 (8)	17.00	19.25

On Stamps of Timor

17	CD20	¼c on ½a bl grn	2.00	2.25
18	CD21	½c on 1a red	2.00	2.25
19	CD22	1c on 2a red vio	2.00	2.25
a.		Inverted overprint	10.00	10.00
20	CD23	2½c on 4a yel grn	2.00	2.25
21	CD24	5c on 8a dk blue	2.00	2.25
22	CD25	7½c on 12a vio brn	3.00	3.50
23	CD26	10c on 16a bis brn	2.00	2.25
24	CD27	15c on 24a bister	2.00	2.25
		Nos. 17-24 (8)	17.00	19.25
		Nos. 1-24 (24)	51.00	57.75

Common Design Types pictured in section at front of book.

Ceres — A1

1914 Typo. *Perf. 15x14*

Name and Value in Black

25	A1	¼c olive brn	1.00	1.00
26	A1	½c black	1.00	1.00
27	A1	1c blue grn	60	55
28	A1	1½c lilac brn	1.00	1.00
29	A1	2c carmine	1.00	1.00
30	A1	2½c light vio	65	60
31	A1	5c deep blue	1.10	1.10
32	A1	7½c yel brn	2.00	2.00
33	A1	8c slate	2.25	2.25
34	A1	10c org brn	2.25	2.25
35	A1	15c plum	4.50	4.50
36	A1	20c yel green	3.00	3.00
37	A1	30c brn, *green*	3.50	3.50
38	A1	40c brn, *pink*	3.50	3.50
39	A1	50c org, *salmon*	3.50	3.50
40	A1	1e grn, *blue*	4.00	4.00
		Nos. 25-40 (16)	34.85	34.75

Stamps of Tete were replaced by those of Mozambique.

THAILAND

(Siam)

LOCATION — Western part of the Malay peninsula in southeastern Asia.
GOVT. — Republic
AREA — 198,250 sq. mi.
POP. — 50,000,000 (est. 1984)
CAPITAL — Bangkok

32 Solot = 16 Atts = 8 Sio = 4 Sik = 2 Fuang = 1 Salung
4 Salungs = 1 Tical
100 Satangs (1909) = 1 Tical = 1 Baht (1912)

Catalogue values for unused stamps in this country are for Never Hinged items, beginning with Scott 260 in the regular postage section, Scott B34 in the semi-postal section, Scott C20 in the airpost section, and Scott O1 in the official section.

King Chulalongkorn
A1 A2

A4

Perf. 14½, 15

1883, Aug. 4 Unwmk. Engr.

1	A1	1sol blue	1.00	1.25
b		Imperf., pair	225.00	225.00
2	A1	1att carmine	2.00	2.25
3	A1	1sio vermilion	5.00	4.50
4	A2	1sik yellow	4.50	3.50
5	A4	1sa orange	7.50	5.00
a		1sa ocher	8.00	8.00

There are three types of No. 1, differing mainly in the background of the small oval at the top.

A 1 fuang red, of similar design to the foregoing, was prepared but not placed in use.

No. 1 Handstamp Surcharged in Red:

1 TICAL
a

1 Tical
b

1 Tical
c

1 Tical
d

1 Tical
e

1885, July 1

6	A1 (a)	1t on 1 sol bl	165.00	165.00
7	A1 (b)	1t on 1 sol bl	150.00	150.00
c		"1" inverted	*1,100.*	*1,100.*
8	A1 (c)	1t on 1 sol bl	150.00	150.00

Surcharges of Nos. 6-10 have been counterfeited.

Types "d" and "e" are typeset *official reprints.*

As is usual with handstamps, double impressions, etc., exist.

King Chulalongkorn
A7

Wmk. 176- Chakra

1887-91 Typo. Wmk. 176 *Perf. 14*

11	A7	1a grn ('91)	65	30
12	A7	2a grn & car	65	35
13	A7	3a grn & bl	2.50	1.65
14	A7	4a grn & org brn	1.65	1.20
15	A7	8a grn & yel	2.25	65
16	A7	12a lil & car	1.00	45
17	A7	24a lil & bl	1.50	45
18	A7	64a lil & org brn	12.00	4.00
		Nos. 11-18 (8)	22.20	9.05

The design of No. 11 has been redrawn and differs from the illustration in many minor details.

Issue dates: Nos. 12-18, Apr. 1. No. 11, Feb.

No. 3 Handstamp Surcharged อัฐ

1889, Aug. Unwmk. *Perf. 15*

19	A1 1a on 1sio ver	3.00	*9.00*

Three different handstamps were used. Doubles, etc. exist.

Nos. 12 and 13 Handstamp Surcharged ๑ อัฐ 1

1889-90 Wmk. 176 *Perf. 14*

20	A7	1a on 2a grn & car	1.00	85
a		"1" omitted	125.00	125.00
c		First Siamese character inverted		
d		First Siamese character omitted	140.00	140.00
21	A7	1a on 3a grn & bl ('90)	1.75	1.00
a		Inverted "1"	70.00	70.00

No. 21 exists with large "2" surcharged on top of "1." Value $125.

๑ อัฐ 1

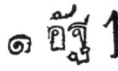

22	A7 1a on 2a grn & car	15.00	13.50

๑ อัฐ 1

24 A7 1a on 2a grn & car 50.00 55.00

๑ อัฐ 1

25 A7 1a on 2a grn & car 300.00 300.00

๑ อัฐ 1

26 A7 1a on 3a grn & bl

Some authorities consider No. 26 a forgery.
Doubles, etc., exist in this issue.
Issue dates: Nov. 1889. Sept. 1890.

No. 13 Handstamp Surcharged ๒ อัฐ 2

1891

27 A7 2a on 3a grn & bl 11.00 11.00

๒ อัฐ 2

28 A7 2a on 3a grn & bl 18.00 18.00
a Double surcharge 110.00 *110.00*
b "2" omitted 110.00

๒ อัฐ 2

Typeset Surcharge

29 A7 2a on 3a grn & bl 6.00 6.00

There are 7 types of this surcharge in the setting.
Issue dates: Nos. 27-28, Jan. No. 29, Mar.

No. 17 Handstamp Surcharged:

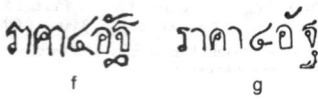

ราคา๔อัฐ f ราคา๔อัฐ g

1892, Oct.

33 A7 (f) 4a on 24a lil & bl 11.00 7.50
34 A7 (g) 4a on 24a lil & bl 9.00 7.50

Surcharges exist double on Nos. 33-34 and inverted on No. 33.

Nos. 33-34 Handstamp Surcharged in English

4 atts

1892, Nov.

35 A7 4a on 24a lil & bl 2.50 1.50
c Inverted "s" 9.00 9.00

4 atts.

36 A7 4a on 24a lil & bl 4.50 3.00
a Inverted "s" 10.00 10.00

4 atts

37 A7 4a on 24a lil & bl 4.50 3.50

4 atts.

38 A7 4a on 24a lil & bl 3.50 2.50

Numerous inverts., doubles, etc., exist.

Nos. 18 and 17 Surcharged in English (Shown) and Siamese

1 Atts

1894

39 A7 1a on 64a lil & org brn 1.00 75
a Inverted "s" 5.50 5.50
b Inverted surch. 37.50 37.50
d Italic "s" 5.50 5.50
e Italic "l" 5.50 5.50

1 Att.

40 A7 1a on 64a lil & org brn 55 40
a Inverted capital "S" added to the surcharge 55.00 65.00

2 Atts. *h* 2 Atts. *i*

2 Atts. *j* 2 Atts. *k*

2. Atts. *l* 2 Atts. *m*

41 A7 (h) 2a on 64a 1.25 1.00
a Inverted "s" 5.50 5.50
b Double surcharge 45.00 45.00
42 A7 (i) 2a on 64a *525.00 525.00*
43 A7 (j) 2a on 64a 5.50 5.00
44 A7 (k) 2a on 64a 1.65 1.65
45 A7 (l) 2a on 64a 3.75 3.75
46 A7 (m) 2a on 64a 90 40
a "Att.s" 14.00 14.00

1 Att.

1894, Oct. 12

47 A7 1a on 64a lil & org brn 70 25
a Surcharged on face and back 26.00
b Surcharge on back inverted 37.50
c Double surcharge 67.50
d Invtd. surcharge 75.00
e Siamese surcharge omitted 55.00

2 Atts.

48 A7 2a on 64a lil & org brn 60 30
a "Att" 11.00 9.00
b Inverted surcharge 45.00 45.00
c Surcharged on face and back 22.50 22.50
d Surcharge on back inverted 22.50 22.50
e Double surcharge 34.00 34.00
f Double surcharge, one inverted 34.00 34.00
g Inverted "s" 9.00 9.00

10 Atts.

1895, July 23

49 A7 10a on 24a lil & bl 60 25
a Inverted "s" 14.00 14.00
b Surcharged on face and back 50.00 50.00
c Surcharge on back inverted 45.00 45.00

No. 16 Surcharged in English (Shown) and Siamese

4 Atts.

1896

50 A7 4a on 12a lil & car 3.00 1.00
a Inverted "s" 17.50 14.00
b Surcharged on face and back 34.00 34.00
c Double surcharge on back 50.00 50.00

Two types of surcharge.

Nos. 16-18 Surcharged in English (Shown) and Siamese
Antique Surcharges:

1 Atts. *a* 1 Att. *b* 2 Atts. *c*

3 Atts. *d* 4 Atts. *e* 10 Atts *f*

1898-99

51 A7 (a) 1a on 12a 65.00 65.00
52 A7 (b) 1a on 12a 4.50 3.75
53 A7 (c) 2a on 64a ('99) 11.00 4.50
54 A7 (d) 3a on 12a 2.25 1.25
a Double surcharge 110.00 110.00
55 A7 (e) 4a on 12a 3.75 75
a Double surcharge 45.00 45.00
56 A7 (e) 4a on 24a ('99) 7.50 2.75
57 A7 (f) 10a on 24a ('99) 200.00 200.00

Roman Surcharges:

1 Atts. *g* 1 Att. *h* 2 Atts. *i*

3 Atts. *j* 4 Atts. *k* 10 Atts. *l*

58 A7 (g) 1a on 12a 65.00 65.00
59 A7 (h) 1a on 12a 7.50 7.00
60 A7 (i) 2a on 64a ('99) 7.00 4.50
61 A7 (j) 3a on 12a 8.00 7.00
62 A7 (k) 4a on 12a 3.00 1.25
a Double surcharge 35.00 35.00
b No period after "Atts." 9.00 9.00
63 A7 (k) 4a on 24a ('99) 9.00 5.50
64 A7 (l) 10a on 24a ('99) 250.00 250.00

In making the settings to surcharge Nos. 51 to 64 two fonts were mixed. Antique and Roman letters are frequently found on the same stamp.
Issue dates: Nos. 54-55, 61-62, Feb. 22. Nos. 51-52, 58-59, June 4. Nos. 56-57, 63-64, Oct. 3.

Nos. 16 and 18 Surcharged in English (Shown) and Siamese Surcharged:

1 Att. *m* 1 Att. *n*

1 Att. *o*

2 Atts. *p* 2 Atts. *r*

1894-99

65 A7 (m) 1a on 12a 2.00 1.75
66 A7 (n) 1a on 12a 5.50 3.75
a Inverted "l" 55.00 55.00
b Inverted 1st "t" 55.00 55.00
67 A7 (o) 1a on 64a 1.00 1.00
68 A7 (p) 2a on 64a 7.50 4.50
a "1 Atts." 110.00 110.00
69 A7 (r) 2a on 64a 5.50 3.25

Issue dates: No. 67, Oct. 12, 1894. Others, Feb. 14, 1899.

A13

A14

1899, Oct. Typo. Unwmk.

70 A13 1a dl grn 60.00 50.00
71 A13 2a dl grn & rose 75.00 55.00
72 A13 3a car & bl 175.00 125.00
73 A13 4a blk & grn 275.00 190.00
74 A13 10a car & grn 400.00 275.00
Nos. 70-74 (5) 985.00 695.00

The King rejected Nos. 70-74 in 1897, but some were released by mistake to three post offices in October, 1899. Used values are for copies canceled to order at Korat in December, 1899. Postally used examples sell for more.

1899-04

75 A14 1a gray grn 40 20
76 A14 2a yel grn 48 20
77 A14 2a scar & bl ('04) 80 28
78 A14 3a red & bl 1.25 40
79 A14 3a grn ('04) 3.75 3.00
80 A14 4a dk rose 80 28
81 A14 4a vio brn & rose ('04) 1.25 40
82 A14 6a dk rose ('04) 4.00 3.00
83 A14 8a dk grn & org 1.25 28
84 A14 10a ultra 2.75 1.00
85 A14 12a brn vio & rose 3.25 50
86 A14 14a ultra ('04) 4.75 4.50
87 A14 24a brn vio & bl 6.50 3.00
88 A14 28a vio brn & bl ('04) 5.50 4.75
89 A14 64a brn vio & org brn 8.00 1.75
Nos. 75-89 (15) 44.73 23.54

Two types of 1a differ in size and shape of Thai "1" are in drawing of spandrel ornaments.
Issue dates: Sept. 1899, Jan. 1, 1904.

Nos. 78 and 85 Surcharged With 6 or 7 Siamese Characters (1 line) in Violet

1902 Typewritten

78a A14 2a on 3a red & bl *525.00 525.00*
85a A14 10a on 12a brn vio & rose *550.00 600.00*

Nos. 78a and 85a were authorized provisionals, surcharged and issued by the Battambang postmaster.

1 Att.

Nos. 86 and 88 Surcharged in Black ๑ อัฐ

1905, Feb.

90 A14 1a on 14a ultra 80 70
a No period after "Att" 7.00 7.00
91 A14 2a on 28a vio brn & bl 1.00 90
a Double surcharge 55.00 55.00

King Chulalongkorn
A15 A16

1905-08 Engr.

92 A15 1a org & grn 35 16
93 A15 2a vio & sl 40 20
94 A15 2a grn ('08) 1.00 30
95 A15 3a green 65 22
96 A15 3a vio & sl ('08) 1.25 45
97 A15 4a gray & red 75 18
98 A15 4a car & rose ('08) 1.20 48
99 A15 5a car & rose 2.25 1.20
100 A15 8a blk & ol bis 1.00 20
101 A15 9a bl ('08) 1.90 1.50
102 A15 12a blue 1.10 1.75
103 A15 18a red brn ('08) 9.00 1.90
104 A15 24a red brn 4.00 2.25
105 A15 1t dp bl & brn org 12.00 6.25
Nos. 92-105 (14) 36.85 17.04

Issue dates: Dec. 1905, Apr. 1, 1908.

1907, Apr. 24
Black Surcharge

106 A16 10t gray grn 250.00 75.00
107 A16 20t gray grn 700.00 90.00
108 A16 40t gray grn 650.00 175.00

Counterfeits of Nos. 106-108 exist. In the genuine, the surcharged figures correspond to the Siamese value inscriptions on the basic revenue stamps.

No. 17 Surcharged **1 att.**

1907, Dec. 16

109 A7 1a on 24a lil & bl 50 32
a Double surcharge 65.00 65.00

No. 99 Surcharged ๔ 4

1908, Sept.

110 A15 4a on 5a car & rose 1.50 1.40

The No. 110 surcharge is found in two spacings of the numerals: normally 15mm apart, and a narrow, scarcer spacing of 13½mm.

Nos. 17 and 84 Surcharged in Black:

๒ อัฐ ๙ อัฐ

2 Atts. 9 Atts

111 A7 2a on 24a lil & bl 65 50
a Inverted surcharge 47.50 47.50
112 A14 9a on 10a ultra 2.75 1.90
a Inverted surcharge 65.00 65.00

Jubilee Issue

Stamps of 1906-08 Overprinted in Black or Red

รัชมังคลา
ภิเศก
๘๗–๑๒๗.
Jubilee
1868-1908

1908, Nov. 11

113 A15 1a org & grn 1.50 75
a Siamese date "137" instead of "127" 250.00 250.00
b Pair, one without ovpt.
114 A15 3a green 2.00 90
115 A15 4a on 5a car & rose 3.50 1.10
a Horiz. pair, imperf. between 275.00
116 A15 8a blk & ol bis (R) 10.00 10.00
117 A15 18a red brn 9.00 6.00
Nos. 113-117 (5) 26.00 18.75

40th year of the reign of King Chulalongkorn.

Nos. 113 to 117 exist with a small "i" in "Jubilee."

Statue of King Chulalongkorn A19

1908, Nov. 11 Engr. Perf. 13½.

118 A19 1t grn & vio 4.50 1.00
119 A19 2t red vio & org 5.00 2.25
120 A19 3t pale ol & bl 9.00 2.50
121 A19 5t dl vio & dk grn 14.00 3.50
122 A19 10t bis & car 65.00 26.00
123 A19 20t gray & red brn 85.00 13.00
124 A19 40t sl bl & blk brn 170.00 35.00
Nos. 118-124 (7) 352.50 83.25

The inscription at the foot of the stamps reads: "Coronation Commemoration-Forty-first year of the reign-1908."

The Catalogue editors cannot undertake to appraise, identify or judge the genuineness or condition of stamps.

Stamps of 1887-1904 Surcharged

๖ สตางค์
6 Satang

1909 Perf. 14

125 A14 6s on 6a dk rose 1.75 1.10
126 A7 14s on 12a lil & car 37.50 37.50
127 A14 14s on 14a ultra 4.50 4.50

Stamps of 1905-08 Surcharged with Bar and

๒ สตางค์
2 Satang

1909, Aug. 15

128 A15 2s on 1a org & grn 25 10
129 A15 2s on 2a vio & sl 50.00 50.00
130 A15 2s on 2a grn 38 15
a "2" omitted 45.00
131 A15 3s on 3a grn 65 65
132 A15 3s on 3a vio & sl 25 18
133 A15 6s on 4a gray & red 5.00 *9.00*
134 A15 6s on 4a car & rose 30 15
135 A15 6s on 5a car & rose 60 70
136 A15 12s on 8a blk & ol bis 60 22
137 A15 14s on 9a bl 55 35
138 A15 14s on 12a bl 18.00 18.00
Nos. 125-138 (14) 120.33 122.60

King Chulalongkorn — A20

1910 Engr. Perf. 14x14½

139 A20 2s org & grn 28 16
140 A20 3s green 32 12
141 A20 6s carmine 48 16
142 A20 12s blk & ol brn 48 16
143 A20 14s blue 70 40
144 A20 28s red brn 7.00 1.25
Nos. 139-144 (6) 9.26 2.25

Issue dates: 12s, June 5. Others, May 5.

King Vajiravudh
A21 A22

Printed at the Imperial Printing Works, Vienna.

1912 Perf. 14½

145 A21 2s brn org 14 5
a Vert. pair, imperf. between 75.00 75.00
b Horiz. pair, imperf. between 75.00 75.00
146 A21 3s yel grn 28 5
a Horiz. pair, imperf. between 75.00 75.00
147 A21 6s car rose 40 14
148 A21 12s gray blk & brn 65 16
149 A21 14s ultra 2.00 20
150 A21 28s chocolate 3.00 1.50
151 A22 1b bl & blk 6.25 35
a Pair, imperf. between 130.00 130.00
152 A22 2b car rose & ol brn 7.50 70
153 A22 3b yel grn & bl blk 8.00 1.10
154 A22 5b vio & blk 11.00 1.10
155 A22 10b ol grn & vio brn 45.00 14.00
156 A22 20b sl bl & red brn 75.00 11.00
Nos. 145-156 (12) 159.22 30.35

See Nos. 164-175.

Nos. 147-150 Surcharged in Red or Blue

๕ สตางค์
5 Satang

1914-15

157 A21 2s on 14s (R) ('15) 40 12
a Vertical pair, imperf. between 65.00 65.00
b Double surch. 70.00 45.00
158 A21 5s on 6s (Bl) 55 15
a Horiz. pair, imperf. between *75.00* 70.00
b Double surch. 70.00 70.00
159 A21 10s on 12s (R) 75 15
a Double surch. 75.00 60.00
160 A21 15s on 28s (Bl) 1.00 15

The several settings of the surcharges on Nos. 157 to 160 show variations in the figures and letters.

Nos. 92-93 Surcharged

๒สตางค์
2 Satang

1915, Apr. 3

161 A15 2s on 1a org & grn 80 70
a Pair, one without surch. *62.50* *62.50*
162 A15 2s on 2a vio & sl 80 70

No. 143 Surcharged in Red

๒สตางค์
2 Satang

1916, Oct.

163 A20 2s on 14s blue 60 35

Printed by Waterlow & Sons, London
Types of 1912 Re-engraved

1917, Jan. 1 Perf. 14

164 A21 2s org brn 30 22
165 A21 3s emerald 18 18
166 A21 5s rose red 25 18
167 A21 10s blk & ol 38 18
168 A21 15s blue 55 35
170 A22 1b bl & gray blk 14.00 75
171 A22 2b car rose & brn 17.50 2.50
172 A22 3b yel grn & blk 50.00 40.00
173 A22 5b dp vio & blk 27.50 7.50
174 A22 10b ol gray & vio brn 60.00 3.25
a Perf. 12½ 250.00 35.00
175 A22 20b sea grn & brn 110.00 27.50
a Perf. 12½ 260.00 37.50
Nos. 164-175 (11) 280.66 82.61

The re-engraved design of the satang stamps varies in numerous minute details from the 1912 issue. Four lines of the background appear between the vertical strokes of the "M" of "SIAM" in the 1912 issue and only three lines in the 1917 stamps.

The 1912 stamps with value in bahts are 37½mm high; those of 1917 are 39mm. In the latter the king's features, especially the eyes and mouth, are more distinct and the uniform and decorations are more sharply defined.

The 1912 stamps have seven pearls between the earpieces of the crown. On the 1917 stamps there are nine pearls in the same place. Nos. 174 and 175 exist imperforate.

Nos. 164-173 Overprinted in Red

วันชัย
VICTORY

1918, Dec. 2

176 A21 2s org brn 65 55
a Double ovpt. 50.00
177 A21 3s emerald 55 50
178 A21 5s rose red 36 70
a Double ovpt. 50.00
179 A21 10s blk & ol 1.40 1.10
180 A21 15s blue 1.50 1.35
181 A22 1b bl & gray blk 9.00 8.50
182 A22 2b car rose & brn 15.00 15.00
183 A22 3b yel grn & blk 18.00 18.00
184 A22 5b dp vio & blk 50.00 50.00
Nos. 176-184 (9) 96.46 95.70

Counterfeits of this overprint exist.

Nos. 147-148 Surcharged in Green or Red

๕ 5 ๑๐ 10

1919-20

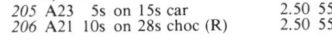

185 A21 5s on 6s (G) 75 18
186 A21 10s on 12s (R) ('20) 75 18

Issue dates: 5s, Nov. 11. 10s, Jan. 1

King Vajiravudh A23

Throne Room A24

1920-26 Engr. Perf. 14-15, 12½

187 A23 2s brn, *yel* ('21) 25 14
188 A23 3s grn, *grn* ('21) 55 14
189 A23 3s choc ('24) 65 14
190 A23 5s rose, *pale rose* 60 15
191 A23 5s grn ('22) 2.75 45
192 A23 5s dk vio, *lil* ('26) 1.25 15
193 A23 10s blk & org ('21) 1.00 15
194 A23 15s bl, *bluish* ('21) 1.40 22
195 A23 15s car ('22) 4.50 80
196 A23 25s chocolate ('21) 2.75 50
197 A23 25s dk bl ('22) 1.75 45
198 A23 50s ocher & blk ('21) 5.50 45
Nos. 187-198 (12) 22.95 3.74

1926, Mar. 5 Perf. 12½

199 A24 1t gray vio & grn 3.75 1.00
200 A24 2t car & org red 11.00 2.25
201 A24 3t ol grn & bl 22.50 11.00
202 A24 5t dl vio & ol grn 15.00 4.75
203 A24 10t red & ol bis 120.00 7.50
204 A24 20t gray bl & brn 110.00 27.50
Nos. 199-204 (6) 282.25 54.00

This issue was intended to commemorate the fifteenth year of the reign of King Vajiravudh. Because of the King's death the stamps were issued as ordinary postage stamps.

Nos. 195 and 150 with Surcharge similar to 1914-15 Issue in Black or Red

1928, Jan.

205 A23 5s on 15s car 2.50 55
206 A21 10s on 28s choc (R) 2.50 55

King Prajadhipok
A25 A26

1928 Engr. Perf. 12½

207 A25 2s dp red brn 10 7
a Booklet pane of 4 110.00
208 A25 3s dp grn 15 8
a Booklet pane of 4 110.00
209 A25 5s dk vio 15 8
a Booklet pane of 4 130.00
210 A25 10s dp rose 15 8
a Booklet pane of 4 140.00
211 A25 15s dk bl 20 9
212 A25 25s blk & org 30 14
213 A25 50s brn org & blk 55 30
214 A25 80s bl & blk 80 25
216 A26 1b dk bl & blk 1.10 30
217 A26 2b car rose & blk brn 2.25 55
218 A26 3b yel grn & blk 3.75 75

219	A26	5b dp vio & gray blk	10.00	1.40
220	A26	10b ol grn & red vio	14.00	1.75
221	A26	20b Prus grn & brn	22.50	3.75
222	A26	40b dk grn & ol brn	52.50	17.50
		Nos. 207-222 (15)	108.50	27.09

On the single colored stamps, type A25, the lines in the background are uniform; those of the bicolored values are shaded and do not extend to the frame.

Issue dates: 5s, 10s, 2b-40b, Apr. 15. 2s, 3s, 15s, 25s, 50s, May 1. 1b, June 1. 80s, Nov. 15.

Nos. 142, 144 Surcharged in Red or Blue

๒๕ สตางค์
25 SATANG

1930 *Perf. 14*

223	A20	10s on 12s blk & ol brn	35	25
224	A20	25s on 28s red brn (Bl)	70	35

King Prajadhipok and Chao P'ya Chakri
A27 A28

Statue of Chao P'ya Chakri — A29

1932, Apr. 1 **Engr.** *Perf. 12½*

225	A27	2s dk brn	40	8
226	A27	3s dp grn	90	16
227	A27	5s dl vio	90	16
228	A28	10s red brn & blk	1.10	20
229	A28	15s dl bl & blk	2.50	36
230	A28	25s vio & blk	3.25	55
231	A28	50s cl & blk	6.00	1.50
232	A29	1b bl blk	17.50	2.50
		Nos. 225-232 (8)	32.55	5.51

150th anniv. of the Chakri dynasty, the founding of Bangkok in 1782, and the opening of the memorial bridge across the Chao Phraya River.

Assembly Hall, Bangkok A30

1939, June 24 **Litho.** *Perf. 11, 12*

233	A30	2s dl red brn	40	16
234	A30	3s green	90	45
235	A30	5s dk vio	90	12
236	A30	10s carmine	1.50	12
237	A30	15s dk bl	3.00	45
		Nos. 233-237 (5)	6.70	1.30

7th anniv. of the Siamese Constitution.

Chakri Palace, Bangkok — A31

1940 **Typo.** *Perf. 12½*

238	A31	2s dl brn	45	22
239	A31	3s dp yel grn	55	15
a.		Cliche of 5s in plate of 3s	265.00	*225.00*
240	A31	5s dk vio	75	12
241	A31	10s carmine	1.40	15
242	A31	15s dk bl	1.85	45
		Nos. 238-242 (5)	5.00	1.09

Issue dates: 2s, 3s, May13. 5s, May 24. 15s, May, 28. 10s, May 30.

King Ananda Mahidol A32 — Plowing Rice Field A33

Royal Pavilion at Bang-pa-in A34 — King Ananda Mahidol A35

1941, Apr. 17 **Engr.**

243	A32	2s brown	25	12
244	A32	3s dp grn	25	12
245	A32	5s violet	25	10
246	A32	10s dk red	25	12
247	A33	15s dp bl & gray blk	50	15
248	A33	25s sl & org	75	35
249	A33	50s red org & gray	85	35
250	A34	1b brt ultra & gray	2.25	50
251	A34	2b dk car rose & gray	4.00	80
252	A34	3b dp grn & gray	5.00	1.75
253	A34	5b blk & rose red	13.00	4.50
a.		Horiz. pair, imperf. between	40.00	
254	A34	10b ol blk & yel	20.00	5.50
		Nos. 243-254 (12)	47.35	14.36

1943, May 1 **Unwmk.** *Perf. 11*

255	A35	1b dk bl	3.50	75

See No. 274.

Indo-China War Monument A36 — Bangkhaen Monument A37

1943 **Engr.** *Perf. 11, 12½*

256	A36	3s dk grn	2.25	1.10

Litho.

Perf. 12½x11

257	A36	3s dl grn	1.40	75

Issue dates: No. 256, June 1. No. 257, Nov. 2.

1943, Nov. 25 *Perf. 12½, 12½x11*

Two types of 10s:
I. Size 19.5x24mm.
II. Size 20.75x25.25mm.

258	A37	2s brn org	40	25
259	A37	10s car rose (I)	1.10	28
a.		Type II	1.10	20

10th anniv. of the quelling of a counter-revolution led by a member of the royal family on Oct. 11, 1933.

Stamps of similar design, but with values in "cents", are listed in Volume I under Malaya, Occupation Stamps.

Catalogue values for unused stamps in this section, from this point to the end of the section, are for Never Hinged items.

King Bhumibol Adulyadej A38 A39

1947, Dec. 5 *Pin-perf. 12½x11*

260	A38	5s orange	1.65	50
261	A38	10s lt brn	1.50	65
a.		10s ol ('48)	80	55
262	A38	20s blue	1.00	50
263	A38	50s bl grn	2.25	1.50

Coming of age of King Bhumibol Adulyadej.

1947-49 **Unwmk.** **Engr.** *Perf. 12½*

Size: 20x25mm

264	A39	5s violet	15	5
265	A39	10s red ('49)	15	5
266	A39	20s chocolate	20	5
267	A39	50s ol ('49)	45	5

Issue dates: Nov. 15, 1947, Jan. 3, 1949.

1948, Nov. 1

Size: 22x27mm

268	A39	1b vio & dp bl	90	12
269	A39	2b ultra & grn	1.50	25
270	A39	3b brn red & blk	2.25	25
271	A39	5b bl grn & brn red	4.50	38
272	A39	10b dk brn & pur	7.50	75
273	A39	20b blk & rose brn	14.00	1.25
		Nos. 264-273 (10)	31.60	3.20

Type of 1943

Perf. 11½, 12½x11½

1948, Jan. **Litho.**

274	A35	1b chalky blue	2.00	90
a.		Pair, imperf. btwn.	30.00	30.00

King Bhumibol Adulyadej and Palace
A40 A41

Perf. 12½

1950, May 5 **Unwmk.** **Engr.**

275	A40	5s red vio	15	5
276	A40	10s red	15	5
277	A40	15s purple	22	5
278	A40	20s chocolate	30	5
279	A40	80s green	55	55
280	A40	1b dp bl	55	18
281	A40	2b org yel	1.40	75
282	A40	3b gray	4.00	2.25
		Nos. 275-282 (8)	7.32	3.93

Coronation of Bhumibol Adulyadej as Rama IX, May 5, 1950.

1951-60 *Perf. 12½, 13x12½*

283	A41	5s rose lil	15	10
284	A41	10s dp grn	15	10
285	A41	15s red brn ('52)	20	10
285A	A41	20s choc ('60)	20	10
286	A41	25s carmine	20	10
287	A41	50s gray ol ('56)	30	10
288	A41	1b dp bl	60	12
289	A41	1.15b dp bl ('53)	1.25	30
290	A41	1.25b org brn ('54)	1.00	20
291	A41	2b dl bl grn	1.00	15
292	A41	3b gray	2.00	25
293	A41	5b aqua & red ('55)	3.50	25
294	A41	10b blk brn & vio ('55)	13.00	45
295	A41	20b gray & ol ('55)	22.50	2.00
		Nos. 283-295 (14)	46.05	4.32

Issue dates: 25s, Feb. 15. 5s, 10s, 1b, June 4. 2b, 3b, Dec. 1. 15s, Feb. 15. 1.15b, Sept. 1. 1.25b, Oct. 1. 5b, 10b, 20b, Feb. 1. 50s, Oct. 15.

United Nations Emblem — A42

1951, Oct. 24

296	A42	25s ultra	1.25	1.00

United Nations Day, Oct. 24, 1951.

Overprinted "1952" in Carmine

1952, Oct.

297	A42	25s ultra	1.25	1.00

Overprinted "1953" in Carmine

1953, Oct.

298	A42	25s ultra	60	55

Overprinted "1954" in Carmine

1954, Oct. 24

299	A42	25s ultra	60	1.00

See Nos. 315 and 320.

Nos. 209 and 210 Overprinted in Black

ไทย
THAILAND

1955, Jan. 4 *Perf. 12½*

300	A25	5s dk vio	90	70
301	A25	10s dp rose	90	70

No. 266 Surcharged with New Value in Black or Carmine

302	A39	5s on 20s choc	70	20
303	A39	10s on 20s choc (C)	70	20

King Naresuan (1555-1605), on War Elephant — A43 — Tao Suranari — A44

Perf. 13½

1955, Feb. 15 **Unwmk.** **Engr.**

304	A43	25s brt car	55	12
305	A43	80s rose vio	3.00	90
306	A43	1.25b dk ol grn	2.25	18
307	A43	2b dp bl	1.75	25
308	A43	3b hn brn	3.75	50
		Nos. 304-308 (5)	11.30	1.95

1955, Apr. 15 *Perf. 12x13½*

309	A44	10s purple	20	10
310	A44	25s emerald	50	12
311	A44	1b brown	1.75	55

Issued to honor the memory of Lady Mo, called Tao Suranari (Brave Woman) for her role in stopping an 1826 rebellion.

King Taksin Statue at Thonburi A45 — Don Jedi Monument A46

1955, May 1 *Perf. 12½x12*

312	A45	5s vio bl	15	8
313	A45	25s Prus grn	22	8
314	A45	1.25b red	1.75	50

Issued to honor King Somdech P'ya Chao Taksin (1734-1782).

No. 296 Overprinted "1955" in Red.

1955, Oct. 24 *Perf. 12½*

315	A42	25s ultra	1.25	1.50

United Nations Day, Oct. 24, 1955.

1956, Feb. 1 *Perf. 13½x13*

316 A46 10s emerald 15 8
317 A46 50s redsh brn 38 25
318 A46 75s violet 55 45
319 A46 1.50b brn org 90 22

No. 296 Overprinted "1956" in Red Violet

1956, Oct. 24

320 A42 25s ultra 35 20

United Nations Day, Oct. 24, 1956.

Dharmachakra and Deer — A47

Wmk. 329- Zigzag Lines

Designs: 20s, 25s, 50s, Hand of peace and Dharmachakra. 1b, 1.25b, 2b, Pagoda of Nakon Phatom.

Wmk. 329

1957, May 13 **Photo.** *Perf. 13½*

321 A47 5s dk brn 10 6
322 A47 10s rose lake 18 6
323 A47 15s brt grn 30 25
324 A47 20s orange 30 45
325 A47 25s redsh brn 35 8
326 A47 50s magenta 65 18
327 A47 1b ol brn 1.10 15
328 A47 1.25b sl bl 1.25 40
329 A47 2b dp cl 1.90 50
Nos. 321-329 (9) 6.13 2.13

2500th anniversary of birth of Buddha.

UN Emblem — A48

Thai Archway — A49

1957, Oct. 24 *Perf. 13½*

330 A48 25s olive 20 10

United Nations Day, Oct. 24, 1957.

1958, Oct. 24

331 A48 25s brt ocher 20 12

United Nations Day, Oct. 24, 1958.

1959, Oct. 24

332 A48 25s indigo 20 12

United Nations Day, Oct. 24, 1959.

1959, Oct. 15 **Photo.** *Perf. 13½*

Designs (inscribed "SEAP Games 1959"): 25s, Royal tiered umbrellas. 1.25b, Thai archer, ancient costume. 2b, Wat Arun pagoda and prow of royal barge.

333 A49 10s orange 10 10
334 A49 25s dk car rose 30 10
335 A49 1.25b brt grn 60 45
336 A49 2b lt bl 75 25

Issued to publicize the South-East Asia Peninsula Games, Bangkok, Dec. 12-17.

Wat Arun, WRY Emblem A50

Wat Arun, Bangkok A51

1960, Apr. 7

337 A50 50s chocolate 30 22
338 A50 2b yel grn 50 25

WRY, July 1, 1959-June 30, 1960.

1960, Aug. **Wmk. 329** *Perf. 13½*

339 A51 50s car rose 30 15
340 A51 2b ultra 75 45

Anti-leprosy campaign.

Elephants in Teak Forest — A52

Globe and SEATO Emblem — A53

1960, Aug. 29 **Photo.** *Perf. 13½*

341 A52 25s emerald 20 10

5th World Forestry Cong., Seattle, WA, Aug. 29-Sept. 10.

1960, Sept. 8

342 A53 50s chocolate 25 8

SEATO Day, Sept. 8.

Siamese Child — A54

Hand with Pen and Globe — A55

1960, , Oct. 3 **Wmk. 329**

343 A54 50s magenta 30 10
344 A54 1b orange 60 30

Children's Day, 1960.

1960, Oct. 3

345 A55 50s car rose 30 15
346 A55 2b blue 75 55

Intl. Letter Writing Week, Oct. 3-9.

U.N. Emblem and Globe A56

King Bhumibol Adulyadej A57

1960, Oct. 24 *Perf. 13½*

347 A56 50s purple 30 15

15th anniversary of the United Nations. See Nos. 369, 390.

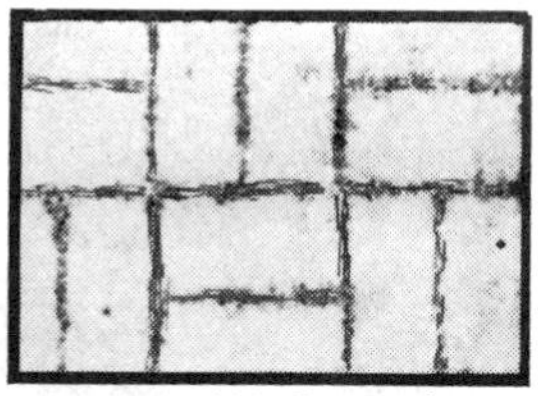

Wmk. 334- Rectangles

Perf. 13½x13

1961-68 **Engr.** **Wmk. 334**

348 A57 5s rose cl ('62) 15 28
349 A57 10s grn ('62) 15 5
350 A57 15s red brn ('62) 15 20
351 A57 20s brn ('62) 15 15
352 A57 25s car ('63) 15 6
353 A57 50s ol ('62) 15 5
354 A57 80s org ('62) 20 8
355 A57 1b vio bl & brn 25 8
355A A57 1.25b red & cit ('65) 25 15
356 A57 1.50b dk vio & yel grn 30 9
357 A57 2b red & vio 35 10
358 A57 3b brn & bl 60 16
358A A57 4b ol bis & blk ('68) 70 25
359 A57 5b bl & grn 1.40 30
360 A57 10b red org & blk 4.50 50
361 A57 20b emer & ultra 7.00 1.00
362 A57 25b grn & bl 4.50 1.50
362A A57 40b yel & blk ('65) 8.50 2.50
Nos. 348-362A (18) 29.45 7.50

Children in Garden — A58

Pen and Envelope with Map — A59

Wmk. 329

1961, Oct. 2 **Photo.** *Perf. 13½*

363 A58 20s indigo 20 12
364 A58 2b purple 85 20

Issued for Children's Day.

1961, Oct. 9

Design: 1b, 2b, Pen and letters circling globe.

365 A59 25s gray grn 10 10
366 A59 50s rose lil 20 12
367 A59 1b brt rose 35 20
368 A59 2b ultra 75 25

Intl. Letter Writing Week, Oct. 2-8.

U.N. Type of 1960.

1961, Oct. 24 **Wmk. 329** *Perf. 13½*

369 A56 50s maroon 25 12

Issued for United Nations Day, Oct. 24.

Scout Emblem — A60

Scouts Saluting and Tents — A61

Design: 2b, King Vajiravudh and Scouts.

1961, Nov. 1 **Photo.**

370 A60 50s car rose 30 12
371 A61 1b brt grn 40 20
372 A61 2b brt bl 1.00 45

Thai Boy Scouts, 50th anniversary.

Malaria Eradication Emblem and Siamese Designs

A62 A63

1962, Apr. 7 **Wmk. 329** *Perf. 13*

373 A62 5s org brn 5 5
374 A62 10s sepia 5 5
375 A62 20s blue 8 8
376 A62 50s car rose 16 8
377 A63 1b green 25 14
378 A63 1.50b dk car rose 38 14
379 A63 2d dk bl 75 18
380 A63 3b violet 90 38
Nos. 373-380 (8) 2.62 1.10

WHO drive to eradicate malaria.

View of Bangkok and Seattle Fair Emblem A64

1962, Apr. 21 **Wmk. 329** *Perf. 13*

381 A64 50s red lil 22 15
382 A64 2b dp bl 68 30

"Century 21" Intl. Expo., Seattle, WA, Apr. 21-Oct. 12.

Mother and Child A65

Globe, Letters, Carrier Pigeons A66

Wmk. 329

1962, Oct. 1 **Photo.** *Perf. 13*

383 A65 25s lt bl grn 15 5
384 A65 50s bis brn 20 15
385 A65 2b brt pink 75 30

Issued for Children's Day.

1962, Oct. 8

Design: 1b, 2b, Quill pen and scroll.

386 A66 25s violet 18 10
387 A66 50s red 25 10
388 A66 1b lemon 38 25
389 A66 2b lt bluish grn 75 30

Intl. Letter Writing Week, Oct. 7-13.

UN Type of 1960

1962, Oct. 24 *Perf. 13½*

390 A56 50s car rose 20 15

United Nations Day, Oct. 24.

Exhibition Emblem A67

Temple Lion A69

Woman Harvesting Rice — A68

1962, Nov. 1 **Unwmk.**
391 A67 50s ol bis 20 15

Students' Exhibition, Bangkok.

Wmk. 334
1963, Mar. 21 **Engr.** ***Perf. 14***
392 A68 20s green 14 5
393 A68 50s ocher 16 10

FAO "Freedom from Hunger" campaign.

1963, Apr. 1 **Wmk. 329** ***Perf. 13½***
394 A69 50s grn & bis 20 15

1st anniv. of the formation of the Asian-Oceanic Postal Union, AOPU.

New and Old Post and Telegraph Buildings — A70

Wmk. 334
1963, Aug. 4 **Engr.** ***Perf. 14***
395 A70 50s org, bluish blk & grn 25 18
396 A70 3b grn, dk red & brn 1.25 55

80th anniv. of the Post and Telegraph Dept.

King Bhumibol Adulyadej — A71

Child with Dolls — A72

Perf. 13x13½
1963-71 **Wmk. 329** **Photo.**
397 A71 5s dk car rose 10 10
398 A71 10s dk grn 10 10
399 A71 15s red brn 10 10
400 A71 20s blk brn 10 10
401 A71 25s carmine 10 10
402 A71 50s ol gray 12 5
402A A71 75s brt vio ('71) 20 8
403 A71 80s dl org 15 5
404 A71 1b dk bl & dk brn 35 7
404A A71 1.25b org brn & ol ('65) 40 30
405 A71 1.50b vio bl & grn 30 15
406 A71 2b dk red & vio 35 15
407 A71 3b brn & dk bl 45 15
407A A71 4b dp bis & blk ('68) 80 25
408 A71 5b bl & grn 1.00 22
409 A71 10b org & blk 1.75 35
410 A71 20b brt grn & ind 7.00 70
411 A71 25b dk grn & bl 5.00 90
411A A71 40b yel & blk ('65) 9.25 1.75
Nos. 397-411A (19) 27.62 5.67

Nos. 397-403 were issued in 1963; Nos. 404, 405-407, 408-411 in 1964.

1963, Oct. 7 **Litho.** ***Perf. 13½***
412 A72 50s rose red 45 8
413 A72 2b dull blue 1.25 30

Issued for Children's Day.

Garuda Carrying Letter — A73

Design: 2b, 3b, Thai women writing letters.

1963, Oct. 7 **Wmk. 329**
414 A73 50s lt bl & cl 28 12
415 A73 1b lt grn & vio brn 55 15
416 A73 2b yel brn & turq bl 1.10 30
417 A73 3b org brn & yel grn 2.00 65

Intl. Letter Writing Week, Oct. 6-12.

UN Emblem — A74

UNICEF Emblem — A76

King Bhumibol Adulyadej — A75

1963, Oct. 24 **Wmk. 329** ***Perf. 13½***
418 A74 50s bright blue 20 10

United Nations Day, Oct. 24.

1963, Dec. 5 **Photo.** ***Perf. 13½***
419 A75 1.50b bl, org & ind 60 15
420 A75 5b brt lil rose, org & blk 1.65 75

King Bhumibol's 36th birthday.

1964, Jan. 13 **Litho.**
421 A76 50s blue 25 12
422 A76 2b ol grn 80 25

17th anniv. of UNICEF.

Hand (flags), Pigeon and Globe A77

Designs: 1b, Girls and world map. 2b, Pen, pencil and unfolded world map. 3b, Globe and hand holding quill.

1964, Oct. 5 **Wmk. 329** ***Perf. 13½***
423 A77 50s lil & lt grn 12 6
424 A77 1b red brn & grn 22 14
425 A77 2b yel & vio bl 55 15
426 A77 3b bl & dk brn 90 75

Intl. Letter Writing Week, Oct. 5-11.

U.N. Emblem and Globe — A78

King and Queen — A79

1964, Oct. 24 **Photo.** ***Perf. 13½***
427 A78 50s gray 30 8

United Nations Day, Oct. 24.

1965, Apr. 28 **Wmk. 329** ***Perf. 13½***
428 A79 2b brn & multi 70 22
429 A79 5b vio & multi 1.75 70

15th wedding anniversary of King Bhumibol Adulyadej and Queen Sirikit.

ITU Emblem, Old and New Communications Equipment — A80

1965, May 17 **Photo.**
430 A80 1b bright green 50 15

Cent. of the ITU.

World Map, Letters and Goddess — A81

Designs: 2b, 3b, World map, letters and handshake.

1965, Oct. 3 **Wmk. 329** ***Perf. 13½***
431 A81 50s dp plum, gray & sal 12 8
432 A81 1b dk vio bl, lt vio & yel 28 9
433 A81 2b dk gray, bis & dp org 55 18
434 A81 3b multi 75 80

Intl. Letter Writing Week, Oct. 3-9.

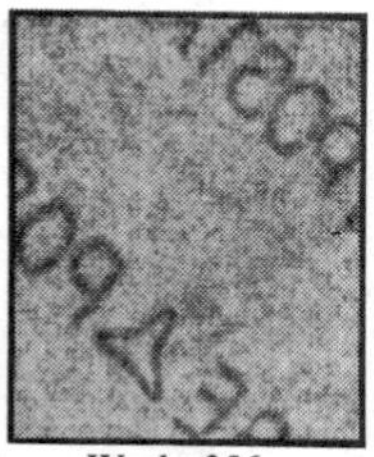
Wmk. 356-POSTAGE

Gates of Royal Chapel of Emerald Buddha — A82

Engr. & Litho.
Perf. 13½x14
1965, Oct. 24 **Wmk. 356**
435 A82 50s sl grn, bl & ocher 20 8

International Cooperation Year, 1965.

Map of Thailand and UPU Monument, Bern — A83

Wmk. 329
1965, Nov. 1 **Litho.** ***Perf. 13½***
436 A83 20s dk bl & lil 9 8
437 A83 50s gray & bl 22 8
438 A83 1b org brn & vio bl 65 15
439 A83 3b grn & bis 1.50 70

80th anniv. of Thailand's admission to the UPU.

Lotus Blossom and Child — A84

Design: 1b, Boy with book walking up steps.

1966, Jan. 8 **Wmk. 334** ***Perf. 13½***
440 A84 50s hn brn & blk 20 8
441 A84 1b grn & blk 40 16

Issued for Children's Day, 1966.

Bicycling — A85

Designs: 25s, Tennis. 50s, Running. 1b, Weight lifting. 1.25b, Boxing. 2b, Swimming. 3b, Netball. 5b, Soccer.

1966, Aug. 4 **Photo.** **Wmk. 329**
442 A85 20s dk car rose 8 5
443 A85 25s purple 8 5
444 A85 50s rose red 9 8
445 A85 1b dp ultra 25 8
446 A85 1.25b gray 30 12
447 A85 2b bl grn 55 18
448 A85 3b red brn 90 25
449 A85 5b dk rose brn 1.65 1.25
Nos. 442-449 (8) 3.90 2.06

5th Asian Games, Bangkok.

Trade Fair Emblem and Temple of Dawn — A86

1966, Sept. 1 **Litho.** ***Perf. 13½***
450 A86 50s lilac 22 7
451 A86 1b brn red 45 15

1st Intl. Asian Trade Fair, Bangkok.

Letter Writer — A87

Design: 50s, 1b, Letters, maps and pen.

1966, Oct. 3 **Photo.** **Wmk. 329**
452 A87 50s scarlet 14 8
453 A87 1b org brn 32 12
454 A87 2b brt vio 70 15
455 A87 3b brt bl grn 1.10 70

Intl. Letter Writing Week, Oct. 6-12.

UN Emblem A88

Pra Buddha Bata Monastery, UNESCO Emblem A90

Rice Field A89

Wmk. 334
1966, Oct. 24 **Litho.** ***Perf. 13½***
456 A88 50s ultra 20 10

United Nations Day, Oct. 24.

1966, Nov. 1 Engr. Wmk. 329

457 A89 50s dp bl & grnsh bl 60 18
458 A89 3b plum & pink 1.65 45

Intl. Rice Year under sponsorship of the FAO.

1966, Nov. 4 Photo. Wmk. 329

459 A90 50s blk & yel grn 20 8

20th anniv. of UNESCO.

Thai Boxing — A91

Designs: 1b, Takraw (three men playing ball). 2b, Kite fighting. 3b, Cudgel play.

1966, Dec. 9 Wmk. 329 *Perf. 13½*

460 A91 50s blk, brn & red 15 6
461 A91 1b blk, brn & red 30 9
462 A91 2b blk, brn & red 70 22
463 A91 3b blk, brn & red 1.10 45

5th Asian Games.

Snakehead — A92

Pigmy Mackerel — A93

Fish: 3b, Barb. 5b, Siamese fighting fish.

1967, Jan. 1 Photo.

464 A92 1b brt bl & multi 25 8
465 A93 2b multi 55 15
466 A93 3b yel grn & multi 90 22
467 A92 5b pale grn & multi 1.50 38

Dharmachakra, Globe and Temples — A94

Wmk. 329

1967, Jan. 15 Litho. *Perf. 13½*

468 A94 2b blk & yel 65 30

Establishment of the headquarters of the World Fellowship of Buddhists in Thailand.

Great Hornbill A95

Ascocentrum Curvifolium A96

Birds: 25s, Hill myna. 50s, White-rumped shama. 1b, Diard's fireback pheasant. 1.50b, Spotted dove. 2b, Sarus crane. 3b, White-breasted kingfisher. 5b, Asiatic open-bill (stork).

1967, Feb. 1 Photo.

469 A95 20s tan & multi 5 5
470 A95 25s lt gray & multi 5 5
471 A95 50s yel grn & multi 8 5
472 A95 1b ol & multi 45 12
473 A95 1.50b dl yel & multi 55 12
474 A95 2b pale sal & multi 1.65 15
475 A95 3b gray & multi 1.50 30
476 A95 5b multi 3.75 50
Nos. 469-476 (8) 8.08 1.34

1967, Apr. 1 Wmk. 329 *Perf. 13½*

Orchids: 20s, Vandopsis parishii. 80s, Rhynchostylis retusa. 1b, Rhynchostylus gigantea. 1.50b, Dendrobium falconerii. 2b, Paphiopedilum callosum. 3b, Dendrobium formosum. 5b, Dendrobium primulinum.

477 A96 20s blk & multi 8 5
478 A96 50s brt bl & multi 8 5
479 A96 80s blk & multi 45 8
480 A96 1b bl & multi 50 9
481 A96 1.50b blk & multi 75 12
482 A96 2b ver & multi 2.25 14
483 A96 3b brn & multi 1.65 22
484 A96 5b multi 3.00 30
Nos. 477-484 (8) 8.76 1.05

Thai Mansion — A97

Thai Architecture: 1.50b, Pagodas. 2b, Bell tower. 3b, Temple.

1967, Apr. 6 Engr.

485 A97 50s dl bl & vio 12 5
486 A97 1.50b bis brn & brn org 38 12
487 A97 2b grnsh bl & vio bl 55 18
488 A97 3b dl yel & gray 75 22

Grand Palace and Royal Barge on Chao Phraya River A98

1967, Sept. 15 Wmk. 329 *Perf. 13½*

489 A98 2b ultra & sep 55 20

International Tourist Year, 1967.

Globe, Dove, People and Letters A99

Design: 2b, 3b, Clasped hands, globe and doves.

1967, Oct. 8 Photo.

490 A99 50s dk bl & multi 22 10
491 A99 1b multi 50 8
492 A99 2b brt yel grn & blk 1.25 25
493 A99 3b brn & blk 1.65 1.25

Intl. Letter Writing Week, Oct. 6-12.

U.N. Emblem — A100

1967, Oct. 24 Wmk. 329 *Perf. 13½*

494 A100 50s vio blk, grnsh bl & scar 20 8

Issued for United Nations Day, Oct. 24.

Flag and Map of Thailand — A101

1967, Dec. 5 Photo. *Perf. 13½*

495 A101 50s grnsh bl, red & vio bl 28 8
496 A101 2b ol gray, red & vio bl 90 35

50th anniversary of the flag.

Elephant Carrying Teakwood — A102

1968, Mar. 1 Engr. Wmk. 329

497 A102 2b rose cl & gray ol 65 15

See Nos. 537, 566.

Syncom Satellite over Thai Tracking Station — A103

1968, Apr. 1 Photo. *Perf. 13*

498 A103 50s multi 18 12
499 A103 3b multi 1.25 42

Earth Goddess — A104

1968, May 1 Wmk. 329 *Perf. 13*

500 A104 50s blk, gold, red & bl grn 30 10

Hydrological Decade (UNESCO), 1965-74.

Snake-skinned Gourami — A105

Fish: 20s, Red-tailed black "shark." 25s, Tor tambroides. 50s, Pangasius sanitwongsei. 80s, Bagrid catfish. 1.25b, Vaimosa rambaiae. 1.50b, Catlocarpio siamensis. 4b, Featherback.

1968, June 1 Photo. *Perf. 13*

501 A105 10s multi 8 5
502 A105 20s multi 8 5
503 A105 25s multi 8 5
504 A105 50s multi 12 6
505 A105 80s multi 38 8
506 A105 1.25b multi 75 9
507 A105 1.50b multi 2.25 9
508 A105 4b multi 4.50 25
Nos. 501-508 (8) 8.24 72

Arcturus Butterfly — A106

Various Butterflies

1968, July 1 Wmk. 329 *Perf. 13*

509 A106 50s lt bl & multi 12 5
510 A106 1b multi 25 8
511 A106 3b multi 70 25
512 A106 4b buff & multi 90 38

Queen Sirikit — A107

Designs: Various portraits of Queen Sirikit.

Photogravure and Engraved
Perf. 13½x14

1968, Aug. 12 Wmk. 334

513 A107 50s gold & multi 15 5
514 A107 2b gold & multi 55 18
515 A107 3b gold & multi 90 38
516 A107 5b gold & multi 2.75 55

Queen Sirikit's 36th birthday, or third 12-year "cycle."

WHO Emblem and Medical Apparatus — A108

1968, Sept. 1 Photo. *Perf. 12½*

517 A108 50s ol, blk & gray 30 8

20th anniv. of the WHO.

Globe, Pen and Envelope — A109

Design: 1b, 3b, Pen nib, envelope and globe.

1968, Oct. 6 Wmk. 329 *Perf. 13½*

518 A109 50s brn & multi 22 8
519 A109 1b pale brn & multi 50 12
520 A109 2b multi 60 20
521 A109 3b vio & multi 1.25 40

Intl. Letter Writing Week, Oct. 7-13.

The indexes in each volume of the Scott Catalogue contain many listings which help to identify stamps.

UN Emblem and Flags — A110

King Rama II — A112

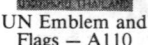

Human Rights Flame and Bas-relief — A111

1968, Oct. 24
522 A110 50s multi 20 10

Issued for United Nations Day.

1968, Dec. 10 Photo. *Perf. 13½*
523 A111 50s sl grn, red & vio 20 10

International Human Rights Year.

1968, Dec. 30 Engr. Wmk. 329
524 A112 50s sep & bis 20 8

Rama II (1768-1824), who reigned 1809-24.

National Assembly Building — A113

Photogravure and Engraved
1969, Feb. 10 Wmk. 329 *Perf. 13½*
525 A113 50s multi 25 10
526 A113 2b multi 75 30

First constitutional election day.

ILO Emblem and Cogwheels — A114

1969, May 1 Photo. *Perf. 13½*
527 A114 50s rose vio & dk bl 20 8

50th anniv. of the ILO.

Ramwong Dance — A115

Designs: 1b, Candle dance. 2b, Krathop Mai dance. 3b, Nohra dance.

1969, July 15 Wmk. 329 *Perf. 13*
528 A115 50s multi 15 12
529 A115 1b multi 35 12
530 A115 2b multi 60 24
531 A115 3b multi 90 35

Posting and Receiving Letters — A116

Design: 2b, 3b, Writing and posting letters.

1969, Oct. 5 Photo. Wmk. 334
532 A116 50s multi 15 8
533 A116 1b multi 30 14
534 A116 2b multi 60 25
535 A116 3b multi 90 38

International Letter Writing Week.

Hand Holding Globe — A117

1969, Oct. 24 Wmk. 329 *Perf. 13*
536 A117 50s multi 15 7

Issued for United Nations Day.

Teakwood Type of 1968

Design: 2b, Tin mine.

1969, Nov. 18 Engr. *Perf. 13½*
537 A102 2b choc, bl & ind 40 20

Issued to publicize tin export, and the 2nd Technical Conf. of the Intl. Tin Council, Bangkok.

Loy Krathong Festival — A118

Designs: 1b, Marriage ceremony. 2b, Khwan ceremony. 5b, Songkran festival.

1969, Nov. 23 Photo. Wmk. 329
538 A118 50s gray & multi 10 6
539 A118 1b multi 25 8
540 A118 2b multi 45 20
541 A118 5b multi 1.25 48

Biplane, Mailmen and Map of First Thai Airmail Flight, 1919 — A119

1969, Dec. 10 Engr. *Perf. 13½*
542 A119 1b multi 20 12

50th anniversary of Thai airmail service.

Shadow Play — A120

Photogravure and Engraved
1969, Dec. 18 Wmk. 329
543 A120 50s Phra Rama 15 6
544 A120 2b Ramasura 60 25
545 A120 3b Mekhala 1.10 30
546 A120 5b Ongkhot 1.75 50

Symbols of Agriculture, Industry and Shipping — A121

1970, Jan. 1 Photo.
547 A121 50s multi 20 8

Productivity Year 1970.

World Map, Thai Temples and Emblem — A122

1970, Jan. 31 Litho.
548 A122 50s brt bl & blk 20 8

19th triennial meeting of the Intl. Council of Women, Bangkok.

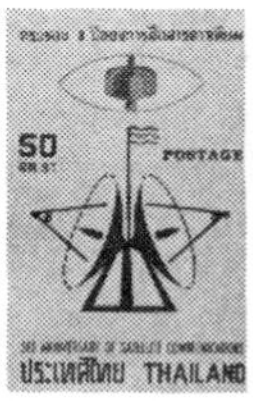

Earth Station Radar and Satellite — A123

Perf. 14½x15
1970, Apr. 1 Litho. Wmk. 356
549 A123 50s multi 20 8

Communication by satellite.

Household and Population Statistics — A124

Perf. 13x13½
1970, Apr. 1 Photo. Wmk. 329
550 A124 1b multi 20 10

Issued to publicize the 1970 census.

UPU Headquarters, Bern — A125

Lithographed and Engraved
1970, June 15 Wmk. 334 *Perf. 13½*
551 A125 50s lt bl, lt grn & grn 20 8

Inauguration of the new UPU Headquarters in Bern.

Khun Ram Kamhang Teaching (Mural) — A126

1970, July 1 Litho.
552 A126 50s blk & multi 20 8

Issued for International Education Year.

Swimming Stadium — A127

Designs: 1.50b, Velodrome. 3b, Suphajalasaya Stadium. 5b, Kittikachorn Indoor Stadium.

Lithographed and Engraved
1970, Sept. 1 Wmk. 329 *Perf. 13½*
553 A127 50s yel, red & pur 12 8
554 A127 1.50b ultra, grn & dk red 25 12
555 A127 3b gold, blk & dk red 60 28
556 A127 5b brt grn, ultra & dk red 1.25 60

6th Asian Games, Bangkok.

Children Writing Letters — A128

Designs: 1b, Woman writing letter. 2b, Two women reading letters. 3b, Man reading letter.

1970, Oct. 4 Photo. *Perf. 13½*
557 A128 50s blk & multi 18 10
558 A128 1b blk & multi 35 20
559 A128 2b blk & multi 60 30
560 A128 3b blk & multi 90 40

Intl. Letter Writing Week, Oct. 6-12.

Royal Palace, Bangkok, and U.N. Emblem — A129

1970, Oct. 24 Photo. *Perf. 13½*
561 A129 50s multi 20 8

25th anniversary of the United Nations.

Heroes of Bangrachan — A130

Designs: 1b, Monument to Thao Thepkrasatri and Thao Srisunthorn. 2b, Queen Suriyothai riding elephant. 3b, Phraya Phichaidaphak and battle scene.

1970, Oct. 25 Engr. *Perf. 13½*

562 A130 50s pink & vio	15	7
563 A130 1b vio & mar	25	15
564 A130 2b rose & brn	40	25
565 A130 3b bl & grn	70	38

Heroes from Thai history.

Teakwood Type of 1968

Design: 2b, Rubber plantation.

1970, Nov. 1 Engr.

566 A102 2b car, brn & grn 40 20

Issued to publicize rubber export.

King Bhumibol Lighting Flame — A131

1970, Dec. 9 Photo. Wmk. 329

567 A131 1b multi 20 8

Opening of 6th Asian Games, Bangkok.

Woman Playing So Sam Sai — A132

Women Playing Classical Thai Musical Instruments: 2b, Khlui Phiang-O. 3b, Krachappi. 5b, Thon Rammana.

1970, Dec. 20

568 A132 50s multi	6	5
569 A132 2b multi	40	16
570 A132 3b multi	60	25
571 A132 5b multi	90	38

Chocolate Point Siamese Cats — A133

Siamese Cats: 1b, Blue point. 2b, Seal point. 3b, Pure white cat and kittens.

Perf. 13½x14

1971, Mar. 15 Litho. Wmk. 356

572 A133 50s multi	20	6
573 A133 1b multi	35	12
574 A133 2b multi	70	30
575 A133 3b multi	1.10	45

Muang Nakhon Temple — A134

Temples: 1b, Phanom. 3b, Pathom Chedi. 4b, Doi Suthep.

Lithographed and Engraved

1971, Mar. 30 Wmk. 329 *Perf. 13½*

576 A134 50s rose, blk & brn	20	5
577 A134 1b emer, bis & pur	32	15
578 A134 3b org, brn & dk brn	80	30
579 A134 4b ultra, ocher & brn	1.10	50

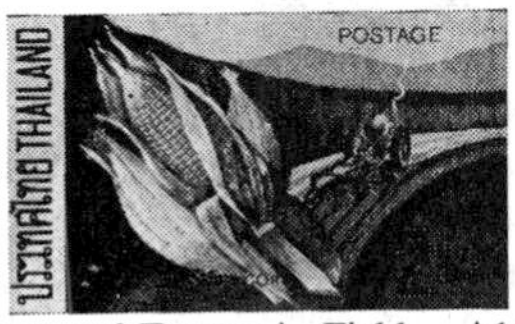

Corn and Tractor in Field — A135

1971, Apr. 20 Engr. Wmk. 329

580 A135 2b multi 75 18

Export promotion.

Buddha's Birthplace, Lumbini, Nepal — A136

Designs (Buddha's): 1b, Place of Enlightenment, Bihar. 2b, Place of first sermon, Benares. 3b, Place of death, Kusinara.

1971, May 9 Engr. *Perf. 13½*

581 A136 50s vio bl & blk	15	10
582 A136 1b grn & blk	20	12
583 A136 2b dl yel & blk	40	30
584 A136 3b red & blk	75	50

20th anniv. of World Fellowship of Buddhists.

King Bhumibol and Subjects — A137

Floating Market — A138

Perf. 13½

1971, June 9 Unwmk. Litho.

585 A137 50s sil & multi 65 8

King Bhumibol's Silver Jubilee.

1971, June 20 Photo. Wmk. 329

586 A138 4b gold & multi 65 35

Visit Asia Year.

Boy Scouts Saluting — A139

1971, July 1 Litho.

587 A139 50s org & multi 20 10

60th anniversary of Thai Boy Scouts.

Blocks of four of Nos. 354 and 403 Overprinted in Dark Blue

a

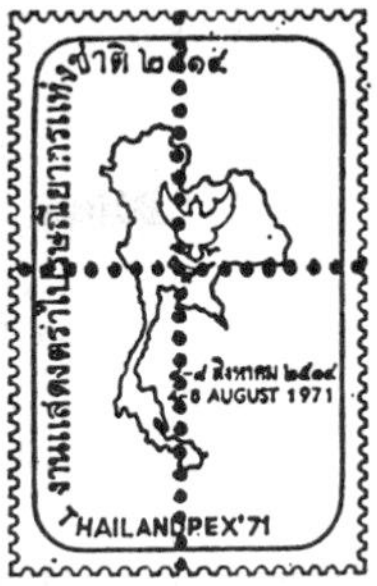

b

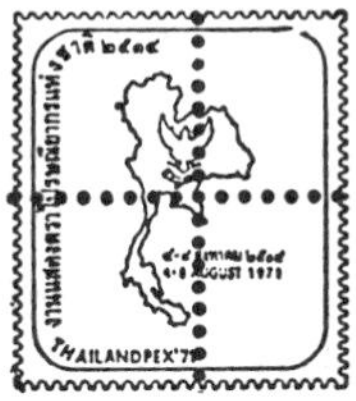

Perf. 13½x13

1971, Aug. Wmk. 334 Engr.

588 A57 (a) Block of four	1.40	1.40
a 80s org, single stamp	25	25

Perf. 13x13½

Photo. Wmk. 329

589 A71 (b) Block of four	1.40	1.40
a 80s dl org, single stamp	25	25

THAILANDPEX '71, Phil. Exhib., Aug. 4-8.

Woman Writing Letter — A140

Designs: 1b, Women reading mail. 2b, Woman sitting on porch. 3b, Man handing letter to woman.

Wmk. 334

1971, Oct. 3 Litho. *Perf. 13½*

590 A140 50s gray & multi	18	6
591 A140 1b red brn & multi	25	12
592 A140 2b ultra & multi	50	30
593 A140 3b lt gray & multi	75	40

Intl. Letter Writing Week, Oct. 6-12.

Wat Benchamabopit (Marble Temple), Bangkok — A141

Perf. 13½x14

1971, Oct. 24 Litho. Unwmk.

594 A141 50s multi 20 8

United Nations Day, Oct. 24.

Duck Raising — A142

Rural occupations: 1b, Raising tobacco. 2b, Fishermen. 3b, Rice winnowing.

Wmk. 329

1971, Nov. 15 Photo. *Perf. 12½*

595 A142 50s lt bl & multi	18	6
596 A142 1b multi	25	12
597 A142 2b bl & multi	50	30
598 A142 3b buff & multi	75	40

UNICEF Emblem, Mother and Child — A143

1971, Dec. 11 Wmk. 334 *Perf. 13½*

599 A143 50s bl & multi 20 8

25th anniv. of UNICEF.

Thai Costumes, 17th Century — A144

Thai Costumes: 1b, 13th to 14th centuries. 1.50b, 14th to 17th centuries. 2b, 18th to 19th centuries.

Perf. 13½x14

1972, Jan. 12 Litho. Unwmk.

600 A144 50s multi	12	6
601 A144 1b multi	25	12
602 A144 1.50b multi	50	25
603 A144 2b bl & multi	70	30

Globe A145

Perf. 13x13½

1972, Apr. 1 Photo. Wmk. 334

604 A145 75s vio bl 20 8

Asian-Oceanic Postal Union, 10th anniv.

King Bhumibol Adulyadej — A146

Perf. 13½x13

1972-77 Litho. Wmk. 329

Size: 21x26mm

605 A146 10s yel grn	5	5
606 A146 20s blue	18	5
607 A146 25s rose red	5	5
608 A146 75s lilac	18	6
Engr.		
609 A146 1.25b yel grn & pink	15	8
610 A146 2.75b red brn & bl grn	30	20
611 A146 3b brn & dk bl ('74)	35	25
612 A146 4b bl & org red ('73)	50	20
613 A146 5b dk vio & red brn	60	30
614 A146 6b grn & vio	75	40
615 A146 10b ver & blk	1.25	60
616 A146 20b org & yel grn	2.50	1.00
617 A146 40b dp bis & lil ('74)	15.00	2.00
618 A146 50b pur & brt grn ('77)	5.00	2.50

619 A146 100b dp org & dk bl ('77) 10.00 5.00
Nos. 605-619 (15) 36.86 12.74

No. 608 also issued in booklet pane of 10.
See Nos. 835-838, 907-908.

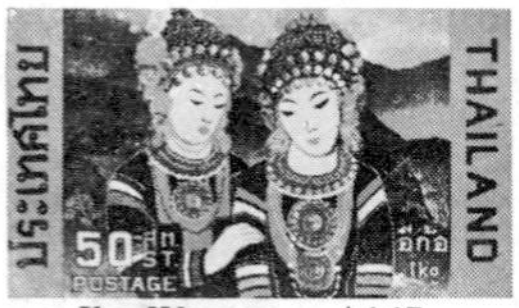

Iko Women — A147

Hill Tribes: 2b, Musoe musician. 4b, Yao weaver. 5b, Maeo farm woman.

Wmk. 334
1972, May 11 Photo. *Perf. 13½*

620	A147	50s multi	10	6
621	A147	2b dk gray & multi	40	15
622	A147	4b multi	70	40
623	A147	5b multi	80	50

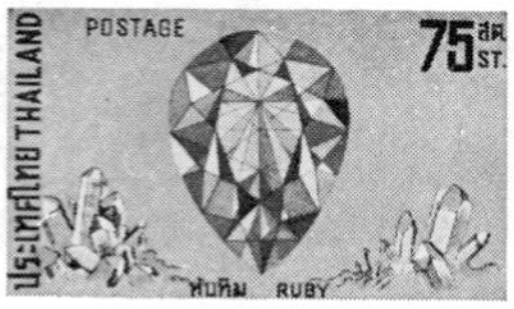

Ruby A148

Precious Stones: 2b, Yellow sapphire. 4b, Zircon. 6b, Star sapphire.

1972, June 7 Litho.

624	A148	75s gray & multi	12	5
625	A148	2b multi	25	12
626	A148	4b multi	50	30
627	A148	6b crim & multi	85	50

Prince Vajiralongkorn A149

Thai Costume A150

Perf. 13½x13
1972, July 28 Photo. Wmk. 329
628 A149 75s tan & multi 20 16

20th birthday of Prince Vajiralongkorn, heir apparent.

Perf. 14x13½
1972, Aug. 12 Litho. Wmk. 356

Designs: Costumes of Thai women.

629	A150	75s tan & multi	12	5
630	A150	2b multi	38	18
631	A150	4b yel & multi	65	30
632	A150	5b gray & multi	1.10	45
a		Souv. sheet of 4, #629-632	2.50	2.50

Rambutan — A151

Fruits: 1b, Mangosteen. 3b, Durian. 5b, Mango.

1972, Sept. 7 Wmk. 334 *Perf. 13½*

633	A151	75s multi	12	8
634	A151	1b multi	18	9
635	A151	3b pink & multi	45	30
636	A151	5b lt ultra & multi	75	38

Lod Cave, Phangnga — A152

Designs: 1.25b, Kang Krachara Reservoir. 2.75b, Erawan Waterfalls, Kanchanaburi. 3b, Nok-Kaw Cliff, Loei.

1972, Nov. 15 Litho. Wmk. 334

637	A152	75s multi	12	10
638	A152	1.25b multi	20	15
639	A152	2.75b multi	55	35
640	A152	3b multi	60	45

Intl. Letter Writing Week, Oct. 9-15.

Princess Mother Visiting Old People — A153

1972, Oct. 21 Photo. Wmk. 329
641 A153 75s dk grn & ocher 30 8

Princess Mother Sisangwan, 72nd birthday.

U.N. Emblem and Globe — A154

Wmk. 334
1972, Nov. 15 Litho. *Perf. 14*
642 A154 75s bl & multi 20 8

25th anniversary of the Economic Commission for Asia and the Far East (ECAFE).

Educational Center and Book Year Emblem — A155

1972, Dec. 8 *Perf. 13½*
643 A155 75s multi 20 8

International Book Year 1972.

Crown Prince Vajiralongkorn A156

1972, Dec. 28 Photo. Wmk. 329
644 A156 2b brt bl & multi 35 14

Investiture of Prince Vajiralongkorn Salayacheevin as Crown Prince.

Flag, Soldiers and Civilians — A157

1973, Feb. 3 Wmk. 334 *Perf. 13½*
645 A157 75s multi 30 8

25th anniversary of Veterans Day.

Savings Bank, Emblem and Coin — A158

1973, Apr. 1 Wmk. 329
646 A158 75s emer & multi 20 8

60th anniv. of Government Savings Bank.

WHO Emblem and Deity — A159

1973, Apr. 1 Wmk. 329
647 A159 75s brt grn & multi 20 8

25th World Health Organization Day.

Water Lily A160

Designs: Various water lilies (Thai lotus).

Perf. 11x13
1973, May 15 Litho. Wmk. 356

648	A160	75s vio & multi	18	8
649	A160	1.50b brn & multi	32	12
650	A160	2b dl grn & multi	45	18
651	A160	4b blk & multi	75	38

King Bhumibol Adulyadej — A161

Wmk. 334, 233 (50s)
1973-81 Photo. *Perf. 14x13½*

652	A161	5s purple	15	8
653	A161	20s blue	14	8
a		Perf. 14	14	5
654	A161	25s rose car	15	8
654A	A161	25s brn red, perf. 14 ('81)	15	8
654B	A161	50s dark olive grn ('79)	12	5
655	A161	75s violet	20	8
a		Perf. 14	12	6

Engr.
Perf. 13

656	A161	5b vio & brn	55	35
657	A161	6b grn & vio	70	38
658	A161	10b red & blk	1.10	55
660	A161	20b org & yel grn ('75)	2.25	1.10
		Nos. 652-660 (10)	5.51	2.83

Silversmiths — A162

1973, June 15 Litho. *Perf. 13½*

662	A162	75s *shown*	12	8
663	A162	2.75b *Lacquerware*	36	32
664	A162	4b *Pottery*	55	32
665	A162	5b *Paper umbrellas*	70	40

Thai handicrafts.

Fresco from Temple of the Emerald Buddha — A163

Designs: Frescoes illustrating Ramayana in Temple of the Emerald Buddha.

1973, July 17 Photo. Wmk. 329

666	A163	25s multi	5	5
667	A163	75s multi	9	8
668	A163	1.50b multi	38	18
669	A163	2b multi	60	30
670	A163	2.75b multi	45	22
671	A163	3b multi	1.50	38
672	A163	5b multi	2.25	1.10
673	A163	6b multi	85	55
		Nos. 666-673 (8)	6.17	2.86

Development of Postal Service — A164

Design: 2b, Telecommunications development.

1973, Aug. 4 *Perf. 13½*

674	A164	75s multi	20	8
675	A164	2b multi	40	12

90th anniv. of Post and Telegraph Dept.

No. 1 and Other Stamps — A165

Designs (Various Stamps and): 1.25b, No. 147. 1.50b, No. 209. 2b, No. 244.

1973, Aug. 4 Photo. & Engr.

676	A165	75s dp rose & dk bl	20	18
677	A165	1.25b bl & dp rose	30	13
678	A165	1.50b ol & vio blk	35	30
679	A165	2b org & sl grn	60	30
a		Souvenir sheet of 4	1.90	1.90

2nd Natl. Phil. Exhib., THAIPEX '73, Aug. 4-8. No. 679a contains 4 stamps with simulated perforations similar to Nos. 676-679.

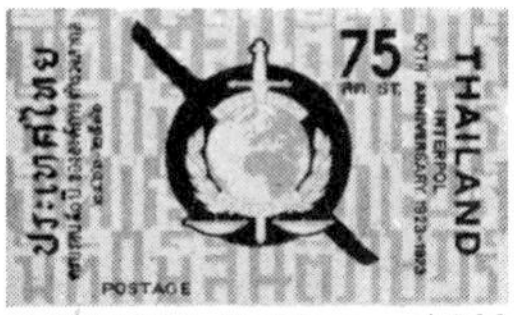
INTERPOL Emblem — A166

1973, Sept. 3 **Photo.**
680 A166 75s gray & multi 20 6

50th anniv. of Intl. Criminal Police Organization.

"Lilid Pralaw" — A167

Wmk. 368- JEZ Multiple

Designs: Scenes from Thai literature.

Perf. 11x13
1973, Oct. 7 **Litho.** **Wmk. 368**
681 A167 75s grn & multi 14 8
682 A167 1.50b bl & multi 30 15
683 A167 2b multi 38 15
684 A167 5b bl & multi 1.10 38
a Souv. sheet of 4, #681-684, perf. 13x14 2.25 2.25

Intl. Letter Writing Week, Oct. 7-13.

Wat Suan Dok, Chiangmai; UN Emblem — A168

1973, Oct. 24 ***Perf. 13x11***
685 A168 75s bl & multi 20 35

United Nations Day.

Schomburgk's Deer — A169

Wmk. 329
1973, Nov. 14 **Photo.** ***Perf. 13½***
686 A169 20s *shown* 5 5
687 A169 25s *Kouprey* 5 5
688 A169 75s *Gorals* 8 8
689 A169 1.25b *Water buffalos* 14 8
690 A169 1.50b *Javan rhinoceros* 22 12
691 A169 2b *Eld's deer* 30 14
692 A169 2.75b *Asiatic two-horned rhinoceros* 45 22
693 A169 4b *Serows* 65 30
Nos. 686-693 (8) 1.94 1.04

Protected animals.

Human Rights Flame — A170

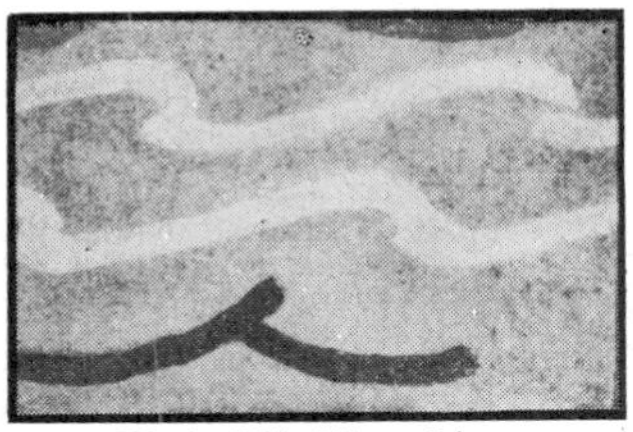
Wmk. 371- Wavy Lines

Wmk. 371
1973, Dec. 10 **Litho.** ***Perf. 12½***
694 A170 75s multi 20 8

25th anniversary of the Universal Declaration of Human Rights.

Children and Flowers — A171

1974, Jan. 12 **Litho.** ***Perf. 13***
695 A171 75s multi 20 8

Children's Day.

Siriraj Hospital and Statue of Prince Nakarin — A172

Perf. 13x13½
1974, Mar. 17 **Photo.** **Wmk. 368**
696 A172 75s multi 20 8

84th anniversary of Siriraj Hospital, oldest medical school in Thailand.

Phala Piang Lai — A173

Designs (Classical Thai Dances): 2.75b, Phra Lux Phlaeng Rit. 4b, Chin Sao Sai. 5b, Charot Phra Sumen.

Wmk. 334
1974, June 25 **Litho.** ***Perf. 14***
697 A173 75s pink & multi 15 6
698 A173 2.75b gray bl & multi 50 20
699 A173 4b gray & multi 75 30
700 A173 5b yel & multi 90 45

Large Teak Tree in Uttaradit Province — A174

1974, July 5 **Wmk. 329** ***Perf. 12½***
701 A174 75s multi 20 8

15th Arbor Day.

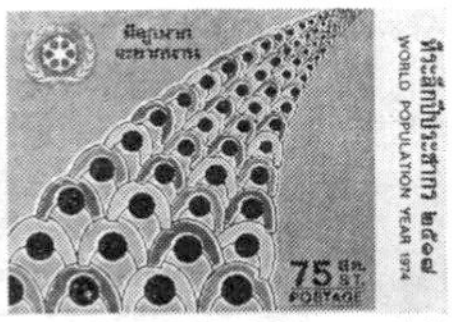
People and WPY Emblem — A175

Perf. 10½x13
1974, Aug. 19 **Litho.** **Wmk. 368**
702 A175 75s multi 20 8

World Population Year, 1974.

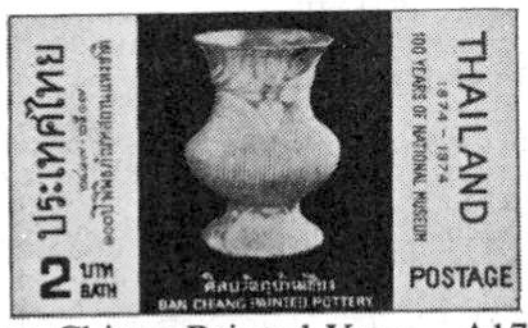
Ban Chiang Painted Vase — A176

Designs: 75s, Royal chariot. 2.75b, Avalokitesavara Bodhisattva. 3b, King Mongkut, Rama IV.

1974, Sept. 19 **Wmk. 262** ***Perf. 12½***
703 A176 75s bl & multi 15 6
704 A176 2b blk, brn & bis 35 25
705 A176 2.75b blk, brn & tan 40 30
706 A176 3b blk & multi 60 40

Centenary of National Museum. Inscribed "BATH" in error.

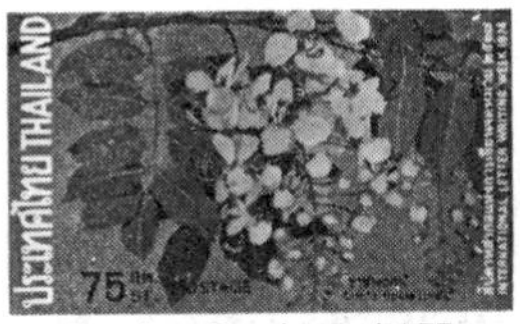
Purging Cassia — A177

1974, Oct. 6 **Wmk. 368** ***Perf. 11x13***
707 A177 75s *shown* 10 10
708 A177 2.75b *Butea* 40 25
709 A177 3b *Jasmine* 45 30
710 A177 4b *Lagerstroemia* 60 40
a Souv. sheet of 4, #707-710 2.25 2.25

Intl. Letter Writing Week, Oct. 6-12.

"UPU" and UPU Emblem — A178

1974, Oct. 9 **Wmk. 371** ***Perf. 12½***
711 A178 75s dk grn & multi 20 8

Centenary of Universal Postal Union.

Wat Suthat Thepvararam — A179

Wmk. 329
1974, Oct. 24 **Photo.** ***Perf. 13***
712 A179 75s multi 20 8

United Nations Day.

Elephant Roundup — A180

Wmk. 371
1974, Nov. 16 **Engr.** ***Perf. 12½***
713 A180 4b multi 65 32

Tourist publicity.

Vanda Coerulea — A181

Orchids: 2.75b, Dendrobium aggregatum. 3b, Dendrobium scabrilingue. 4b, Aerides falcata.

Perf. 11x13
1974, Dec. 5 **Photo.** **Wmk. 368**
714 A181 75s red & multi 18 10
715 A181 2.75b multi 40 25
716 A181 3b ol & multi 60 35
717 A181 4b grn & multi 75 45
a Souv. sheet of 4, #714-717, perf. 13½x14 2.50 2.50

See Nos. 745-748.

Boy — A182

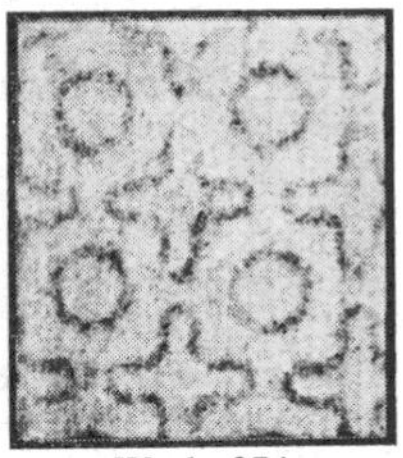
Wmk. 374

Wmk. Circles and Crosses (374)
1975, Jan. 11 **Litho.** ***Perf. 14x13½***
718 A182 75s ver & multi 15 8

Children's Day.

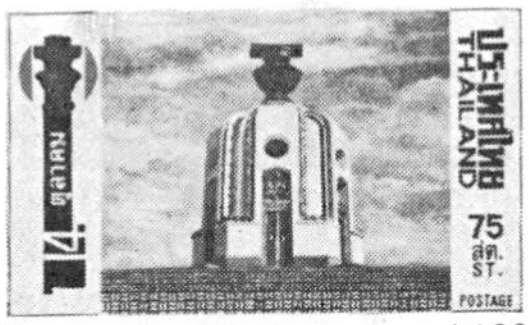
Democracy Monument — A183

Designs: 2b, Mother with children and animals, bas-relief from Democracy Monument. 2.75b, Workers, bas-relief from Democracy Monument. 5b, Top of Democracy Monument and quotation from speech of King Rama VII.

Perf. 14x14½

1975, Jan. 26 Wmk. 233

719	A183	75s	dl grn & multi	10	10
720	A183	2b	multi	30	20
721	A183	2.75b	bl & multi	40	25
722	A183	5b	multi	75	45

Movement of Oct. 14, 1973, to re-establish democratic institutions.

Marbled Tiger Cat — A184

1975, Mar. 5 Wmk. 334 *Perf. 13½*

723	A184	20s	*shown*	6	5
724	A184	75s	*Gaurs*	18	5
725	A184	2.75b	*Asiatic elephant*	48	20
726	A184	3b	*Clouded tiger*	60	25

Protected animals.

White-eyed River Martin — A185

Birds: 2b, Paradise flycatchers. 2.75b, Long-tailed broadbills. 5b, Sultan tit.

Wmk. 371

1975, Apr. 2 Litho. *Perf. 12½*

727	A185	75s	ocher & multi	12	8
728	A185	2b	lt bl & multi	30	14
729	A185	2.75b	lt vio & multi	45	22
730	A185	5b	rose & multi	90	38

King Bhumibol Adulyadej and Queen Sirikit — A186

Design: 3b, King and Queen, different background design.

Perf. 10½x13

1975, Apr. 28 Photo. Wmk. 368

731	A186	75s	vio bl & multi	15	10
732	A186	3b	multi	55	30

25th wedding anniversary of King Bhumibol Adulyadej and Queen Sirikit.

Round-house Kick — A187

Thai Boxing: 2.75b, Reverse elbow. 3b, Flying knee. 5b, Ritual homage.

Wmk. 371

1975, May 20 Litho. *Perf. 12½*

733	A187	75s	grn & multi	12	8
734	A187	2.75b	bl & multi	40	20
735	A187	3b	org & multi	60	25
736	A187	5b	org & multi	90	35

Tosakanth Mask — A188

Masks: 2b, Kumbhakarn. 3b, Rama. 4b, Hanuman.

1975, June 10 Litho. Wmk. 371

737	A188	75s	dk gray & multi	16	8
738	A188	2b	dl vio & multi	40	15
739	A188	3b	pur & multi	80	25
740	A188	4b	multi	1.40	65

Thai art and literature.

THAIPEX 75 Emblem — A189

Designs (THAIPEX 75 Emblem and): 2.75b, Stamp designer. 4b, Stamp printing plant. 5b, Stamp collector.

1975, Aug. 4 Wmk. 371 *Perf. 12½*

741	A189	75s	yel & multi	8	5
742	A189	2.75b	org & multi	32	20
743	A189	4b	lt bl & multi	48	28
744	A189	5b	car & multi	60	35

THAIPEX 75, Third National Philatelic Exhibition, Aug. 4-10.

Orchid Type of 1974

Orchids: 75s, Dendrobium cruentum. 2b, Dendrobium parishii. 2.75b, Vanda teres. 5b, Vanda denisoniana.

Perf. 11x13

1975, Aug. 12 Photo. Wmk. 368

745	A181	75s	ol & multi	10	10
746	A181	2b	multi	25	22
747	A181	2.75b	scar & multi	40	30
748	A181	5b	ultra & multi	70	55
a			Souv. sheet of 4, #745-748, perf 13½	2.25	2.25

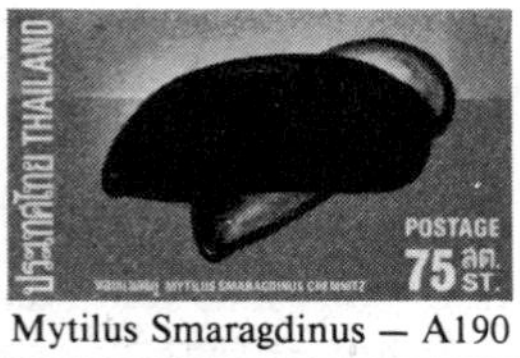

Mytilus Smaragdinus — A190

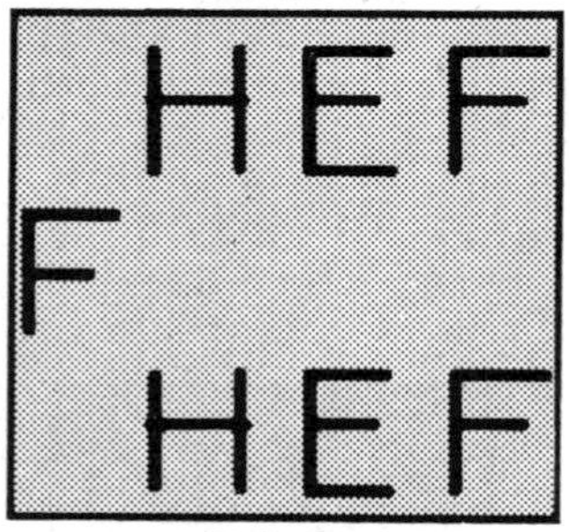

Wmk. 375

Sea Shells: 1b, Turbo marmoratus. 2.75b, Oliva mustelina. 5b, Cypraea moneta.

Wmk. Letters (375)

1975, Sept. 5 Litho. *Perf. 14x14½*

749	A190	75s	yel & multi	8	5
750	A190	1b	ver & multi	12	6
751	A190	2.75b	bl & multi	32	12
752	A190	5b	grn & multi	80	32

Yachting and Games Emblem — A191

Designs: 1.25b, Badminton. 1.50b, Volleyball. 2b, Target shooting.

Perf. 11x13

1975, Sept. 20 Litho. Wmk. 368

753	A191	75s	ultra & blk	8	8
754	A191	1.25b	brt rose & blk	18	8
755	A191	1.50b	red & blk	30	12
756	A191	2b	ap grn & blk	45	18
a			Souv. sheet of 4, #753-756, perf. 13½	1.75	1.75

8th SEAP Games, Bangkok, Sept. 1975.

Pataya Beach A192

Views: 2b, Samila Beach. 3b, Prachuap Bay. 5b, Laem Singha Bay.

1975, Oct. 5 Wmk. 371 *Perf. 12½*

757	A192	75s	org & multi	12	5
758	A192	2b	org & multi	20	12
759	A192	3b	org & multi	28	20
760	A192	5b	org & multi	75	32

Intl. Letter Writing Week, Oct. 6-12.

"U N," U.N. Emblem, Food and Education for Children — A193

1975, Oct. 24 Litho. Wmk. 371

761	A193	75s	ultra & multi	20	8

United Nations Day.

Morse Telegraph — A194

Design: 2.75b, Teleprinter and radar.

Perf. 14x14½

1975, Nov. 4 Litho. Wmk. 334

762	A194	75s	multi	18	8
763	A194	2.75b	bl & multi	60	25

Centenary of telegraph system.

A particular stamp may be scarce, but if few collectors want it, its market value may remain relatively low.

Sukhrip Khrong Mueang Barge — A195

Thai ceremonial barges: 1b, Royal escort barge Anekchat Phuchong. 2b, Royal barge Anantanakarat. 2.75b, Krabi Ran Ron Rap barge. 3b, Asura Wayuphak barge. 4b, Asura paksi barge. 5b, Royal barge Sri Suphanahong, 6b, Phali Rang Thawip barge.

Wmk. 371

1975, Nov. 18 Litho. *Perf. 12½*

764	A195	75s	multi	12	5
765	A195	1b	multi	15	6
766	A195	2b	lil & multi	45	12
767	A195	2.75b	multi	60	15
768	A195	3b	yel & multi	70	15
769	A195	4b	multi	90	80
770	A195	5b	gray & multi	1.75	90
771	A195	6b	bl & multi	1.10	75
			Nos. 764-771 (8)	5.77	2.98

Thai Flag, Arms of Chakri Royal Family A196

King Bhumibol Adulyadej A197

Perf. 15x14

1975, Dec. 5 Litho. Wmk. 375

772	A196	75s	multi	15	6
773	A197	5b	multi	65	45

King Bhumibol's 48th birthday.

Shot Put and SEAP Emblem — A198

Designs: 2b, Table tennis. 3b, Bicycling. 4b, Relay race.

1975, Dec. 9 Wmk. 368 *Perf. 11x13*

774	A198	1b	org & blk	15	10
775	A198	2b	brt grn & blk	30	22
776	A198	3b	ocher & blk	45	35
777	A198	4b	vio & blk	60	45
a			Souv. sheet of 4, #774-777, perf. 13½	1.75	1.75

8th SEAP Games, Bangkok, Dec. 9-20.

IWY Emblem and Globe — A199

Perf. 14x14½

1975, Dec. 20 Wmk. 375

778	A199	75s	blk, org & vio bl	20	8

International Women's Year 1975.

Children Writing on Slate — A200

Perf. 13x14

1976, Jan. 10 Litho. Wmk. 368

779	A200	75s lt grn & multi	20	8

Children's Day.

Macrobrachium Rosenbergii — A201

Designs: 2b, Penaeus merguiensis. 2.75b, Panulirus ornatus. 5b, Penaeus monodon.

1976, Feb. 18 *Perf. 11x13*

780	A201	75s multi	20	6
781	A201	2b multi	40	12
782	A201	2.75b multi	60	28
783	A201	5b multi	1.00	45

Shrimp and lobster exports.

Golden-backed Three-toed Woodpecker A202

Ban Chiang Vase A203

Birds: 1.50b, Greater green-billed malcoha. 3b, Pomatorhinus hypoleucos. 4b, Green magpie.

Wmk. 371

1976, Apr. 2 Litho. *Perf. 12½*

784	A202	1b multi	15	10
785	A202	1.50b multi	25	15
786	A202	3b yel & multi	50	35
787	A202	4b rose & multi	60	55

Perf. 14½x14

1976, May 5 Litho. Wmk. 375

Designs: Ban Chiang painted pottery, various vessels, Bronze Age.

788	A203	1b ol & multi	30	10
789	A203	2b dp bl & multi	50	15
790	A203	3b grn & multi	1.00	35
791	A203	4b org red & multi	1.25	55

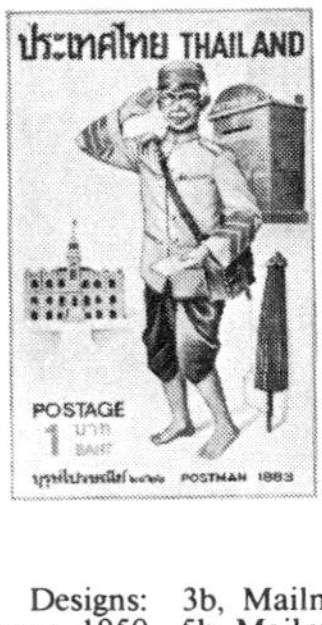

Mailman, 1883 — A204

Designs: 3b, Mailman, 1935. 4b, Mailman, 1950. 5b, Mailman, 1974.

Wmk. Interlocking Circles (377)

1976, Aug. 4 Litho. *Perf. 12½*

792	A204	1b multi	15	8
793	A204	3b multi	45	25
794	A204	4b multi	75	40
795	A204	5b multi	90	50

Development of mailmen's uniforms.

Kinnari — A205

Thai Mythology: 2b, Suphan-mat-cha. 4b, Garuda. 5b, Naga.

1976, Oct. 3 Wmk. 368 *Perf. 11x13*

796	A205	1b grn & multi	18	12
797	A205	2b ultra & multi	30	18
798	A205	4b gray & multi	70	45
799	A205	5b sl & multi	90	55

International Letter Writing Week.

U.N. Emblem, Drug Addicts, Alcohol, Cigarettes, Drugs — A206

Wmk. 329

1976, Oct. 24 Photo. *Perf. 13½*

800	A206	1b ultra & multi	20	10

United Nations Day.

Old and New Telephones — A207

Perf. 14x14½

1976, Nov. 10 Litho. Wmk. 375

801	A207	1b multi	20	12

Centenary of first telephone call by Alexander Graham Bell, Mar. 10, 1876.

Sivalaya-Mahaprasad Hall — A208

Royal Houses: 2b, Cakri-Mahaprasad. 4b, Mahisra-Prasad. 5b, Dusit-Mahaprasad.

Perf. 14x15

1976, Dec. 5 Wmk. 375 Litho.

802	A208	1b multi	12	9
803	A208	2b multi	18	14
804	A208	4b multi	45	25
805	A208	5b multi	55	38

Banteng — A209

Protected animals: 2b, Tapir and young. 4b, Sambar deer and fawn. 5b, Hog deer family.

Wmk. 334

1976, Dec. 26 Litho. *Perf. 11*

806	A209	1b multi	15	12
807	A209	2b multi	25	18

Wmk. 368

808	A209	4b multi	60	35
809	A209	5b multi	75	55

Child Casting Shadow of Man — A210

Wmk. 329

1977, Jan. 8 Photo. *Perf. 13½*

810	A210	1b multi	20	8

National Children's Day 1977.

Alsthom's Electric Engine — A211

Locomotives: 2b, Davenport's electric engine. 4b, Pacific's steam engine. 5b, George Egestoff's steam engine.

Perf. 11x13

1977, Mar. 26 Litho. Wmk. 368

811	A211	1b multi	25	12
812	A211	2b multi	42	18
813	A211	4b multi	1.25	45
814	A211	5b multi	1.50	55

80th anniv. of State Railroad of Thailand.

Chulalongkorn University Auditorium — A212

1977, Mar. 26 Photo.

815	A212	1b multi	15	8

Chulalongkorn University, 60th anniversary.

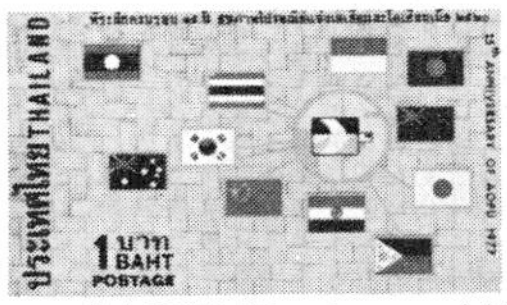

Flags of AOPU Members — A213

Wmk. 371

1977, Apr. 1 Litho. *Perf. 12½*

816	A213	1b multi	15	8

Asian-Oceanic Postal Union (AOPU), 15th anniv.

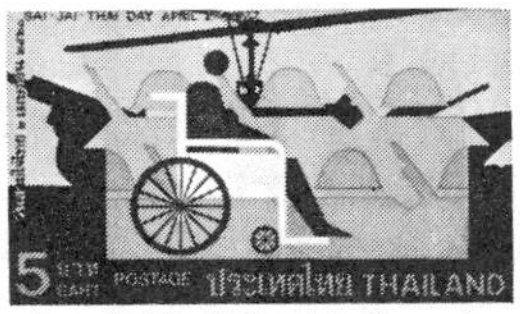

Invalid in Wheelchair and Soldiers — A214

Wmk. 329

1977, Apr. 2 Photo. *Perf. 13½*

817	A214	5b multi	80	45

Sai-Jai-Thai Day, to publicize Sai-Jai-Thai Foundation which helps wounded soldiers.

Phra Aphai Mani and Phisua Samut A215

Puppets: 3b, Rusi and Sutsakhon. 4b, Nang Vali and Usren. 5b, Phra Aphai Mani and Nang Laweng's portrait.

Perf. 11x13

1977, June 16 Photo. Wmk. 368

818	A215	2b multi	25	18
819	A215	3b multi	35	25
820	A215	4b multi	70	45
821	A215	5b multi	85	55

Thai plays and literature.

Drum Dance — A216

Designs: 3b, Dance of dip nets. 4b, Harvest dance. 5b, Kan dance.

1977, July 14 Photo. *Perf. 13x11*

822	A216	2b rose & multi	25	15
823	A216	3b lt grn & multi	28	20
824	A216	4b yel & multi	48	32
825	A216	5b lt vio & multi	60	40

Thailand No. 609, Various Stamps and Thaipex Emblem — A217

Wmk. 377

1977, Aug. 4 Litho. *Perf. 12½*

826	A217	75s multi	20	8

THAIPEX 77, 4th National Philatelic Exhibition, Aug. 4-12.

A218

Designs: Scenes from Thai literature.

Perf. 11x13

1977, Oct. 5 Photo. Wmk. 368

827 A218 75s multi 18 12
828 A218 2b multi 30 18
829 A218 5b multi 75 40
830 A218 6b multi 90 65

Intl. Letter Writing Week, Oct. 6-12.

Old and New Buildings, UN Emblem — A219

1977, Oct. 5 Litho. *Perf. 11x13*

831 A219 75s multi 15 8

United Nations Day.

King Bhumibol as Scout Leader, Camp and Emblem — A220

1977, Nov. 21 Photo. Wmk. 368

832 A220 75s multi 20 8

9th National Jamboree, Nov. 21-27.

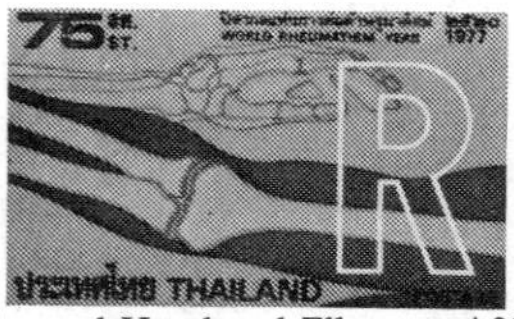

Diseased Hand and Elbow — A221

1977, Dec. 20 *Perf. 11x13*

833 A221 75s multi 15 8

World Rheumatism Year.

Map of South East Asia and ASEAN Emblem A222

Wmk. 377

1977, Dec. 1 Litho. *Perf. 12½*

834 A222 5b multi 75 32

ASEAN, 10th anniv.

King Type of 1972-74 Redrawn

1976 *Perf. 12½x13*

Size: 21x27mm

835 A146 20s blue 25 10
836 A146 75s lilac 25 10

Engr.

837 A146 10b ver & blk 2.50 90
838 A146 40b bis & lil 6.00 2.00

Numerals are taller and thinner and leaves in background have been redrawn.

The Scott Catalogue value is a retail price, what you could expect to pay for the stamp in a grade of Fine-Very Fine. The value listed is a reference which reflects recent actual dealer selling price.

Children Carrying Flag of Thailand — A223

Wmk. 329

1978, Jan. 9 Photo. *Perf. 13½*

839 A223 75s multi 25 8

Children's Day.

Dendrobium Heterocarpum — A224

Orchids: 1b, Dendrobium pulchellum. 1.50b, Doritis pulcherrima. 2b, Dendrobium hercoglossum. 2.75b, Aerides odorata. 3b, Trichoglottis fasciata. 5b, Dendrobium wardianum. 6b, Dendrobium senile.

Perf. 11x14

1978, Jan. 18 Wmk. 368

840 A224 75s multi 8 5
841 A224 1b multi 10 8
842 A224 1.50b multi 15 12
843 A224 2b multi 30 15
844 A224 2.75b multi 1.10 24
845 A224 3b multi 45 30
846 A224 5b multi 65 50
847 A224 6b multi 1.65 60
Nos. 840-847 (8) 4.48 2.04

9th World Orchid Conference.

Census Chart, Symbols of Agriculture — A225

Wmk. 377

1978, Mar. 1 Litho. *Perf. 12½*

848 A225 75s multi 15 8

Agricultural census, April 1978.

Anabas Testudineus — A226

Fish: 2b, Datnioides microlepis. 3b, Kryptopterus apogon. 4b, Probarbus Jullieni.

Perf. 11x13

1978, Apr. 13 Photo. Wmk. 368

849 A226 1b multi 10 8
850 A226 2b multi 25 15
851 A226 3b multi 50 25
852 A226 4b multi 70 40

Birth of Prince Siddhartha — A227

Murals: 3b, Prince Siddhartha cuts his hair. 5b, Buddha descending from Tavatimsa Heaven. 6b, Buddha entering Nirvana.

Wmk. 329

1978, June 15 Photo. *Perf. 13½*

853 A227 2b multi 25 15
854 A227 3b multi 35 25
855 A227 5b multi 1.00 40
856 A227 6b multi 80 50

Story of Gautama Buddha, murals in Puthi Savan Hall, National Museum, Bangkok.

Bhumibol Dam — A228

Dams and Reservoirs: 2b, Sirikit dam. 2.75b, Vajiralongkorn dam. 6b, Ubol Ratana dam.

Perf. 14x14½

1978, July 28 Litho. Wmk. 233

857 A228 75s multi 30 8
858 A228 2b multi 40 18
859 A228 2.75b multi 55 25
860 A228 6b multi 95 55

Idea Lynceus — A229

Butterflies: 3b, Sephisa chandra. 5b, Charaxes durnfordi. 6b, Cethosia penthesilea methypsia.

Perf. 11x13

1978, Aug. 25 Litho. Wmk. 368

861 A229 2b lil, blk & red 30 20
862 A229 3b multi 40 35
863 A229 5b multi 70 55
864 A229 6b multi 95 70

Chedi Chai Mongkhon Temple — A230

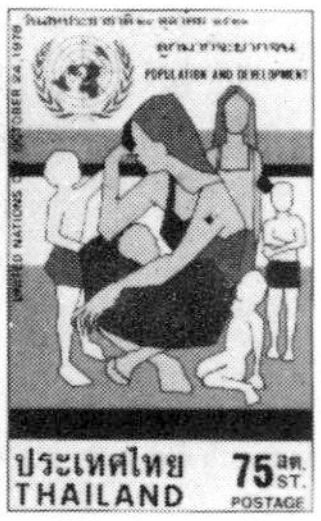

Mother and Children, UN Emblem — A231

Temples: 2b, That Hariphunchai. 2.75b, Borom That Chaiya. 5b, That Choeng Chum.

1978, Oct. 8 *Perf. 13x11*

865 A230 75s multi 18 6
866 A230 2b multi 30 15
867 A230 2.75b multi 42 20
868 A230 5b multi 70 40

Intl. Letter Writing Week, Oct. 6-12.

Perf. 14½x14

1978, Oct. 24 Litho. Wmk. 375

869 A231 75s multi 15 8

United Nations Day.

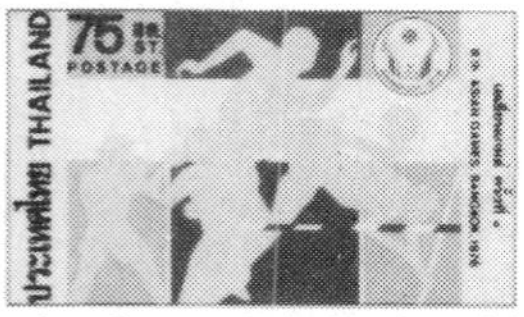

Boxing, Soccer, Pole Vault — A232

Designs: 2b, Javelin, weight lifting, running. 3b, Ball games and sailing. 5b, Basketball, hockey stick and boxing gloves.

Perf. 14x14½

1978, Oct. Wmk. 233 Litho.

870 A232 75s multi 12 6
871 A232 2b multi 32 20
872 A232 3b multi 48 30
873 A232 5b multi 60 40

8th Asian Games, Bangkok.

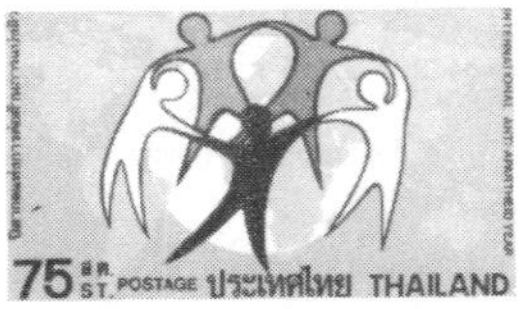

Five Races and World Map A233

1978, Nov.

874 A233 75s multi 15 8

Anti-Apartheid Year.

Children Painting Thai Flag — A234

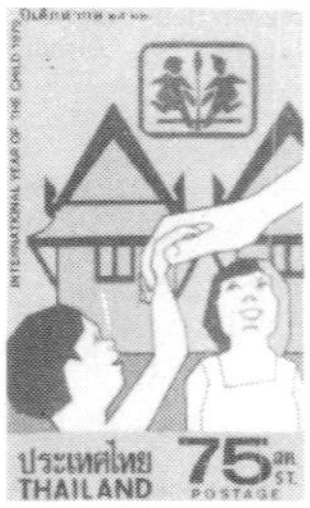

Children and Children's SOS Village, Tambol Bangpu — A235

1979, Jan. 17 *Perf. 14x14½*

875 A234 75s multi 22 10
876 A235 75s multi 22 10

International Year of the Child.

Matuta Lunaris A236

Crabs: 2.75b, Matuta planipes fabricius. 3b, Portunus pelagicus. 5b, Scylla serrata.

Wmk. 377

1979, Mar. 22 Litho. *Perf. 12½*

877 A236 2b multi 25 15
878 A236 2.75b multi 35 20
879 A236 3b multi 45 25
880 A236 5b multi 70 40

Sweetsop — A237

1979, June 25

881	A237	1b Shown	20	8
882	A237	2b Pineapple	32	10
883	A237	5b Bananas	80	25
884	A237	6b Longans (litchi)	1.00	30

Young Man and Woman Planting Tree — A238

Perf. 13x11

1979, July 10 Litho. Wmk. 368

885	A238	75s multi	10	7

20th Arbor Day.

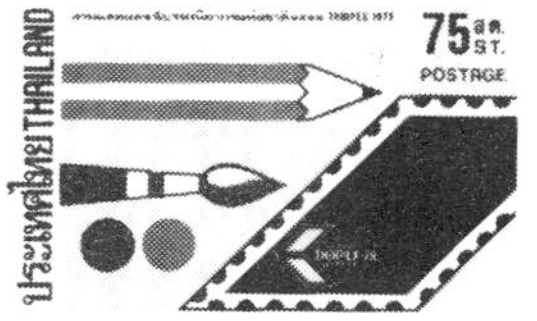

Pencil, Pen, Thaipex '79 Emblem — A239

Designs (Thaipex '79 Emblem and): 2b, Envelopes. 2.75b, Stamp album. 5b, Magnifying glass and tongs.

1979, Aug. 4 ***Perf. 11x13***

886	A239	75s multi	9	5
887	A239	2b multi	25	12
888	A239	2.75b multi	35	15
889	A239	5b multi	60	30

Thaipex '79, 5th National Philatelic Exhibition, Bangkok, Aug. 4-12.

Floral Arrangement A240

UN Day A241

Designs: Decorative arrangements.

Perf. 14½x14

1979, Oct. 7 Litho. Wmk. 233

890	A240	75s multi	12	6
891	A240	2b multi	30	15
892	A240	2.75b multi	40	20
893	A240	5b multi	70	38

Intl. Letter Writing Week, Oct. 8-14.

1979, Oct. 24 Litho. ***Perf. 14½x14***

894	A241	50s multi	15	8

Frigate Makut Rajakumarn — A242

Thai Naval Ships: 3b, Frigate Tapi. 5b, Fast strike craft, Prabparapak. 6b, Patrol boat T-91.

1979, Nov. 20 Photo. ***Perf. 13½***

895	A242	2b multi	28	16
896	A242	3b multi	40	24
897	A242	5b multi	65	40
898	A242	6b multi	80	48

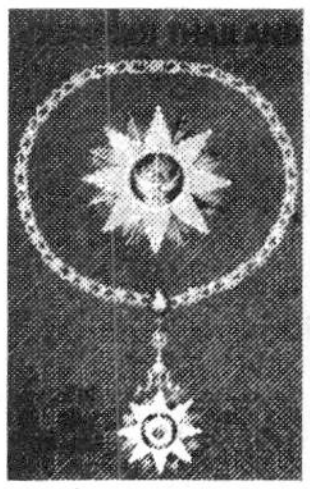

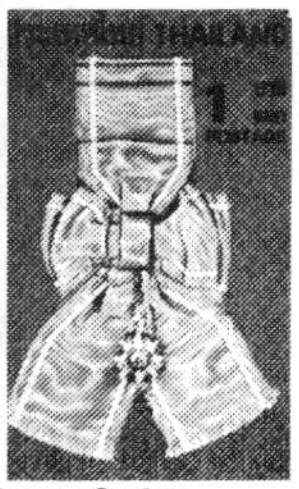

Rajamitrabhorn Order
A243 A244

Thai Royal Orders (Medallions and Ribbons): Nos. 901-902, House of Chakri. Nos. 903-904, The nine gems. Nos. 905-906, Chula Chom Klao. Stamps of same denomination printed se-tenant.

Perf. 13x11

1979, Dec. 5 Litho. Wmk. 368

899	A243	1b multi	12	8
900	A244	1b multi	12	8
901	A243	2b multi	25	15
902	A244	2b multi	25	15
903	A243	5b multi	60	38
904	A244	5b multi	60	38
905	A243	6b multi	75	45
906	A244	6b multi	75	45
		Nos. 899-906 (8)	3.44	2.12

See Nos. 1278-1285.

King Type of 1972-77

Perf. 13½x13

1979, Dec. 23 Litho. Wmk. 239

Size: 21x26mm

907	A146	50s ol grn	15	8

Engr.

908	A146	2b org red & lil	25	15

Rice Planting — A245

Children's Day: No. 910, Family in rice field.

Perf. 13x11

1980, Jan. 12 Litho. Wmk. 368

909	A245	75s multi	15	10
910	A245	75s multi	15	10

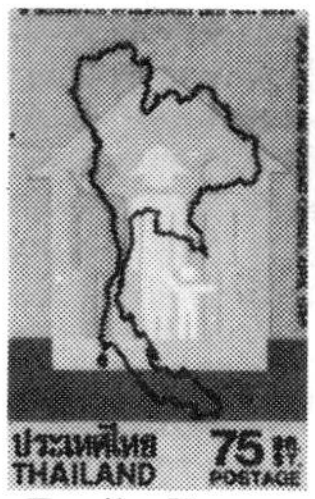

Family, House, Map of Thailand — A246

Gold-fronted Leafbird — A247

1980, Feb. 1 Litho. ***Perf. 15x14***

911	A246	75s multi	20	16

National Population and Housing Census, Apr.

1980, Feb. 26 ***Perf. 13x11***

912	A247	75s *shown*	12	6
913	A247	2b *Yellow-cheeked tit*	30	15
914	A247	3b *Chestnut-tailed siva*	42	22
915	A247	5b *Scarlet minivet*	75	38

Intl. Commission for Bird Preservation, 9th Conf. of Asian Section, Chieng-mai, Feb. 26-29.

Smokers and Lungs, WHO Emblem — A248

1980, Apr. 7 Wmk. 329 ***Perf. 13½***

916	A248	75s multi	15	8

World Health Day; fight against cigarette smoking.

Garuda and Rotary Emblem — A249

1980, May 6 Wmk. 368 ***Perf. 13x11***

917	A249	5b multi	60	35

Rotary International, 75th anniversary.

Sai Yok Falls, Kanchanaburi — A250

1980, July 1 Litho. ***Perf. 14x15***

918	A250	1b *shown*	15	10
919	A250	2b *Punyaban Falls, Ranong*	25	20
920	A250	5b *Heo Suwat Falls, Nakhon Ratchasima*	60	45
921	A250	6b *Siriphum Falls, Chiang Mai*	75	55

Queen Sirikit — A251

Family with Cattle, Ceres Medal (Reverse) — A252

Design: No. 524, Ceres medal (obverse), potters.

Perf. 13½, 11x13 (5b)

Wmk. 329, 368 (5b)

1980, Aug. 12 Litho.

922	A251	75s multi	18	10
923	A252	5b multi	70	38
924	A252	5b multi	70	45

Queen Sirikit's 48th birthday.

Khao Phanomrung Temple, Buri Ram — A253

International Letter Writing Week, Oct. 6-12 (Temples): 2b, Prang Ku, Chailyaphum. 2.75b, Phimai, Nakhon Ratchasima. 5b, Sikhoraphum, Surin.

Perf. 11x13

1980, Oct. 5 Litho. Wmk. 368

925	A253	75s multi	10	10
926	A253	2b multi	25	20
927	A253	2.75b multi	35	30
928	A253	5b multi	60	20

Princes Mother — A254

Golden Mount, Bangkok — A255

Perf. 15x14

1980, Oct. 21 Litho. Wmk.

929	A254	75s multi	15	8

Princess Mother, 80th birthday.

1980, Oct. 24

930	A255	75s multi	15	15

United Nations Day.

Demand, as well as supply, determines a stamp's market value. One is as important as the other.

King Bhumibol Adulyadej — A256

Perf. 11x13

1980-84(?) Litho. Wmk. 368

933	A256	25s	salmon	10	5
933A	A256	50s	ol grn ('81)	15	8
934	A256	75s	lilac	15	8
936	A256	1.25b	yel grn ('81)	20	10

Wmk. 329

Engr. *Perf. 13*

939	A256	3b	brn & dk bl ('83)	22	18
941	A256	5b	pur & brn ('83)	55	28
942	A256	6b	dk grn & pur ('83)	65	35
944	A256	8.50b	grn & brn org ('83)	85	52
945	A256	9.50b	ol & dk grn ('83)	1.00	58
945A	A256	20b	dark org & grn ('84)	2.00	1.20
			Nos. 933-945A (10)	5.87	3.42

See Nos. 1079-1097.

King Rama VII Monument Inauguration A257

1980, Dec. 10 *Perf. 15x14*

946 A257 75s multi 10 7

Bencharongware Bowl — A258

Perf. 11x13

1980, Dec. 15 Wmk. 368

947	A258	2b	*shown*	25	20
948	A258	2.75b	*Covered bowls*	35	28
949	A258	3b	*Covered jar*	38	32
950	A258	5b	*Stem plates*	65	55

King Vajiravudh Birth Centenary A259

Children's Day A260

1981, Jan. 1 *Perf. 15x14*

951 A259 75s multi 15 8

Perf. 13x11

1981, Jan. 16 Wmk. 368

952 A260 75s multi 10 10

Hegira, 1500th Anniv. A261

1981, Jan. 18 Litho. *Perf. 12½*

953 A261 5b multi 65 35

Dolls in Native Costumes — A262

Wmk. 368

1981, Feb. 6 Litho. *Perf. 13½*

954	A262	75s	Palm-leaf fish mobile	12	8
955	A262	75s	Teak elephants	12	8
956	A262	2.75b	shown	38	25
957	A262	2.75b	Baskets	38	25

CONEX '81 International Crafts Exhibition.

Scout Leader and Boy on Crutches A263

1981, Feb. 28 *Perf. 13x11*

958	A263	75s	shown	20	10
959	A263	5b	Diamond cutter in wheelchair	65	32

International Year of the Disabled.

Dindaeng-Tarua Expressway Opening — A264

1981, Oct 29 *Perf. 13½*

960	A264	1b	Klongtoey	15	8
961	A264	5b	Vipavadee Rangsit Highway	65	40

Ongkhot, Khon Mask — A265

Designs: Various Khon masks.

1981, July 1 Litho. *Perf. 13x11*

962	A265	75s	shown	10	6
963	A265	2b	Maiyarab	25	15
964	A265	3b	Sukrip	38	24
965	A265	5b	Indrajit	60	38

Exhibition Emblem, No. 83 — A266

1981, Aug. 4 Litho. *Perf. 12*

966	A266	75s	shown	10	5
967	A266	75s	No. 144	10	5
968	A266	2.75b	No. 198	30	16
969	A266	2.75b	No. 226	30	16

Luang Praditphairo, Court Musician, Birth Centenary — A267

1981, Aug. 26 *Perf. 15x14*

970 A267 1.25b multi 15 15

THAIPEX '81 Intl. Stamp Exhibition.

25th Intl. Letter Writing Week, Oct. 6-12 — A268

Designs: Dwarfed trees.

1981, Oct. 4 Wmk. 239

971	A268	75s	Mai hok-hian	10	5
972	A268	2b	Mai kam-ma-lo	25	12
973	A268	2.75b	Mai khen	35	15
974	A268	5b	Mai khabuan	60	32

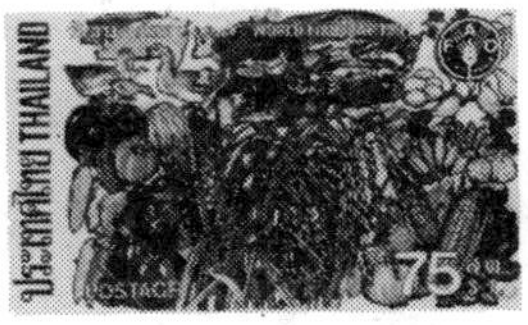

World Food Day A269

1981, Oct. 16 Litho. *Perf. 12*

975 A269 75s multi 8 10

United Nations Day — A270

1981, Oct. 24 Wmk. 368 *Perf. 13½*

976 A270 1.25b Samran Mukhamat Pavilion 15 10

King Cobra A271

1981, Dec. 1 Wmk. 329 *Perf. 13½*

977	A271	75s	shown	12	6
978	A271	2b	Banded krait	30	15
979	A271	2.75b	Thai cobra	42	20
980	A271	5b	Malayan pit viper	75	40

Children's Day — A272

Scouting Year — A273

1982, Jan. 9 *Perf. 12*

981 A272 1.25b multi 20 8

1982, Feb. 22

982 A273 1.25b multi 20 15

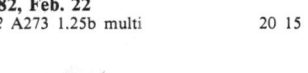

Bicentenary of Bangkok (Thai Capital) A274

Chakri Dynasty kings. (Rama I-Rama IX).

1982, Apr. 4 Litho. Wmk. *Perf. 12*

983	A274	1b	Buddha Yod-Fa (1736-1809)	12	18
984	A274	1.25b	shown	15	10
985	A274	2b	Buddha Lert La Naphalai (1767-1824)	25	16
986	A274	3b	Nang Klao (1787-1851)	38	32
987	A274	4b	Mongkut (1804-1868)	50	40
988	A274	5b	Chulalongkorn (1853-1910)	60	50
989	A274	6b	Vajiravudh (1880-1925)	75	60
990	A274	7b	Prachathipok (1893-1941)	90	65
991	A274	8b	Ananda Mahidol (1925-1946)	1.00	75
992	A274	9b	Bhumibol Adulyadej (b. 1927)	1.10	85
a			Souv. sheet of 9	8.00	
b			Souv. sheet of 9	10.00	
			Nos. 983-992 (10)	5.75	4.51

Nos. 992a-992b each contain Nos. 983, 985-992; black control number. Size of No. 992a: 205x142mm; No. 992b, 195x180mm.

TB Bacillus Centenary — A275

Wmk. 368

1982, Apr. 7 Litho. *Perf. 13½*

993 A275 1.25b multi 15 8

Local Flowers — A276

Perf. 14x14½

1982, June 30 Wmk. 233

994 A276 1.25b Quisqualis indica 15 12
995 A276 1.50b Murraya aniculata 18 15
996 A276 6.50b Mesua ferrea 80 65
997 A276 7b Desmos chinensis 90 70

Buddhist Temples in Bangkok — A277

1982, Aug. 4 Wmk. 368 *Perf. 13½*

998 A277 1.25b shown 15 10
999 A277 4.25b Wat Pho 55 38
1000 A277 6.50b Mahathat Yuwarat Rangsarit 85 55
1001 A277 7b Phra Sri Rattana Satsadaram 90 60
a Souv. sheet of 4, #998-1001, perf. 12½ 3.75 1.40

BANGKOK '83 Intl. Stamp Exhibition, Aug. 4-13, 1983.
See Nos. 1025-1026.

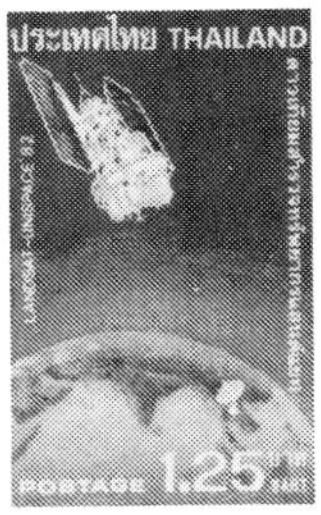
LANDSAT Satellite — A278

1982, Aug. 9 Wmk. 329 *Perf. 12*

1002 A278 1.25b multi 15 15

2nd UN Conference on Peaceful Uses of Outer Space, Vienna, Aug. 9-21.

Prince Purachatra of Kambaengbejra (1882-1936) A279

1982, Sept. 14 Wmk. 233 *Perf. 14*

1003 A279 1.25b multi 20 15

26th Intl. Letter Writing Week, Oct. 6-12 — A280

Sangalok Pottery.

1982, Oct. 3 Wmk. 329 *Perf. 13½*

1004 A280 1.25b Covered glazed jar 18 10
1005 A280 3b Painted jar 45 24
1006 A280 4.25b Glazed plate 60 34
1007 A280 7b Painted plate 1.00 55

UN Day — A281

1982, Oct. 24

1008 A281 1.25b Loha Prasat Tower 25 15

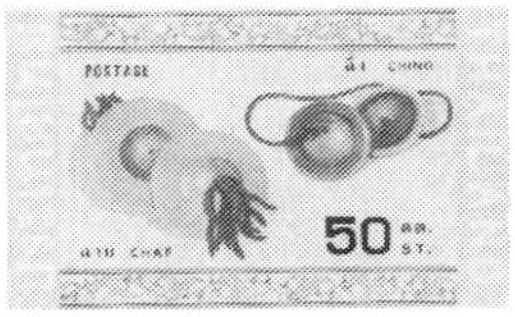
Musical Instruments — A282

1982, Nov. 30 Wmk. 329 *Perf. 12*

1009 A282 50s Chap, ching 5 6
1010 A282 1b Pi nai, pi nok 12 10
1011 A282 1.25b Klong that, taphon 15 12
1012 A282 1.50b Khong mong, krap 18 15
1013 A282 6b Khong wong yai 75 60
1014 A282 7b Khong wong lek 85 65
1015 A282 8b Ranat ek 1.00 80
1016 A282 9b Ranat thum 1.10 90
Nos. 1009-1016 (8) 4.20 3.38

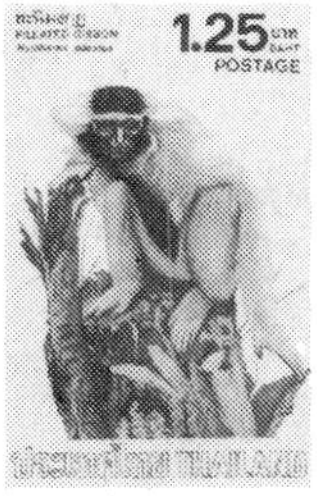
Pileated Gibbon — A283

ASEAN Members' Flags — A284

1982, Dec. 26

1017 A283 1.25b shown 15 8
1018 A283 3b Pig-tailed macaque 35 20
1019 A283 5b Slow loris 60 32
1020 A283 7b Silvered leaf monkey 90 65

1982, Dec. 26

1021 A284 6.50b multi 65 65

15th Anniv. of Assoc. of Southeast Asian Nations.

Children's Day — A285

Perf. 14½x14

1983, Jan. 8 Litho. Wmk. 233

1022 A285 1.25b multi 15 8

First Anniv. of Postal Code — A286

Wmk. 329 (#1024)

1983, Feb. 25 Litho. *Perf. 13½*

1023 A286 1.25b Codes 15 18
1024 A286 1.25b Code on envelope 15 15

BANGKOK '83 Type of 1982

Design: Old General Post Office.

1983, Feb. 25 Wmk. 368 Photo.

1025 A277 7b multi 75 38
1026 A277 10b multi 1.10 70
a Souv. sheet of 2, #1025-1026, perf. 12½ 3.25 3.25

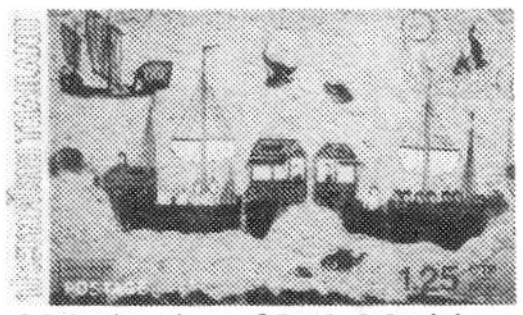
25th Anniv. of Intl. Maritime Org. — A287

Perf. 14x14½

1983, Mar. 17 Litho. Wmk. 233

1029 A287 1.25b Chinese junks 20 14

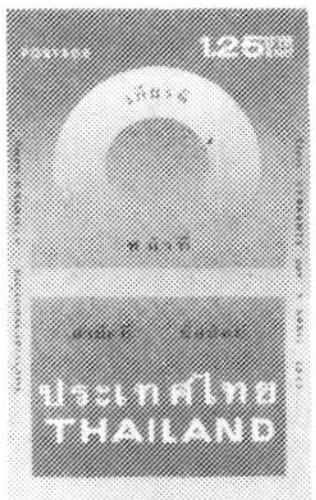
Civil Servants' Day A288

Prince Sithiporn Kridakara (1883-1971) A289

1983, Apr. 1 Wmk. 329 *Perf. 12*

1030 A288 1.25b multi 15 15

Perf. 14½x14

1983, Apr. 11 Wmk. 233

1031 A289 1.25b multi 15 15

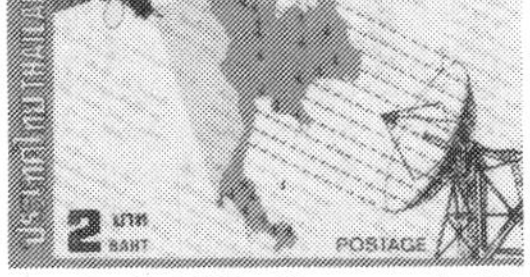
Domestic Satellite Communications System Inauguration — A290

Wmk. 368

1983, Aug. 4 Litho. *Perf. 13½*

1032 A290 2b Map, dish antenna, satellite 20 12

BANGKOK '83 Intl. Stamp Show, Aug. 4-13 — A291

1983, Aug. 4 Wmk. 329 *Perf. 12*

1033 A291 1.25b Mail collection 15 12
1034 A291 7.50b Posting letters 90 65
1035 A291 8.50b Mail transport 1.00 80
1036 A291 9.50b Mail delivery 1.10 95
a Souv. sheet of 4, #1033-1036 *5.75 3.75*

Prince Bhanurangsi Memorial Statue — A292

Perf. 15x14

1983, Aug. 4 Litho. Wmk. 233

1037 A292 1.25b multi 15 8

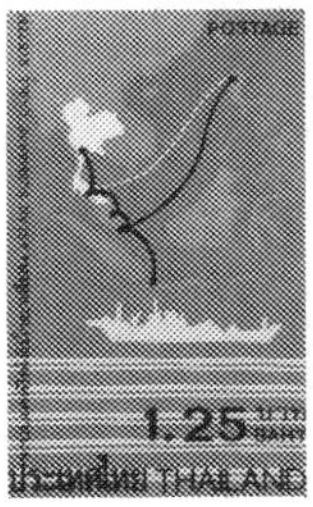
Malaysia/ Thailand/ Singapore Submarine Cable Inauguration A293

Wmk. 368

1983, Sept. 27 Litho. *Perf. 12*

1038 A293 1.25b multi 18 38
1039 A293 7b multi 1.00 50

Intl. Letter Writing Week — A294

1983, Oct. 6 Wmk. 329 *Perf. 13½*

1040 A294 2b Acropora asper 28 18
1041 A294 3b Platygyra lamellina 40 25
1042 A294 4b Fungia 55 38
1043 A294 7b Pectinia lactuca 90 60

Prince Mahidol of Songkhla — A295

Unwmk.

1983, Oct. 10 Litho. *Perf. 12*

1044 A295 9.50b multi 90 55

Siriraj Hospital Faculty of Medicine and Rockefeller Foundation, 60th Anniv. of cooperation.

World Communications Year — A296

Design: 3b, Telecommunications equipment, diff.

1983, Oct. 24 Litho. *Perf. 14x14½*

1045 A296 2b multi 25 22
1046 A296 3b multi 38 30

United Nations Day — A297

1983, Oct. 24 Litho. *Perf. 14x14½*

1047 A297 1.25b multi 15 8

Thai Alphabet, 700th Anniv. — A298

Designs: 3b, Painted pottery, Sukothai period. 7b, Thai characters, reign of King Ramkamhaeng. 8b, Buddha, Sukothai period. 9b, Mahathat Temple, Sukothai province.

Perf. 12

1983, Nov. 17 Litho. Wmk.

1048 A298 3b multi 35 25
1049 A298 7b multi 85 60
1050 A298 8b multi, vert. 95 75
1051 A298 9b multi, vert. 1.10 80

National Development Program — A299

Designs: No. 1052, King and Queen initiating Royal Projects. No. 1053, Technical aid. No. 1054, Terrace farming, Irrigation dam. No. 1055, Gathering grain. No. 1056, Receiving the peoples' gratitude.

1984, May 5 Litho. Wmk.

1052 A299 1.25b multi 18 16
1053 A299 1.25b multi 18 16
1054 A299 1.25b multi 18 16
1055 A299 1.25b multi 18 16
1056 A299 1.25b multi 18 16
Nos. 1052-1056 (5) 90 80

1052-1056 se-tenant.

Children's Day — A300

1984, Jan. 14 Wmk. 329 *Perf. 13½*

1057 A300 1.25b multi 15 10

17th Natl. Games, Jan. 22-28 — A301

1984, Jan. 22

1058 A301 1.25b Running 18 15
1059 A301 3b Soccer 42 20

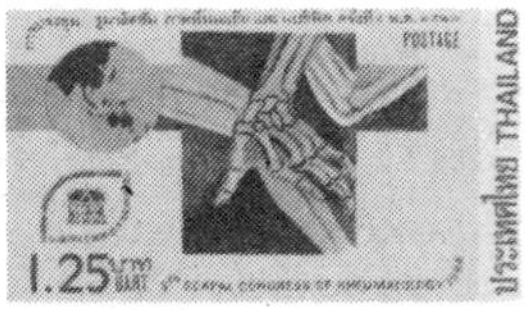

5th Rheumatology Congress, Jan. 22-27 — A302

Perf. 14x15

1984, Jan. 22 Wmk. 233

1060 A302 1.25b Rheumatic joints 15 10

Armed Forces Day — A303

50th Anniv. of Royal Institute — A304

1984, Jan. 25 *Perf. 15x14*

1061 A303 1.25b King Naresuan, tanks, jet, ship 15 10

1984, Mar. 31

1062 A304 1.25b multi 15 15

Thammasat University, 50th Anniv. — A305

1984, June 27 *Perf. 14x15*

1063 A305 1.25b Dome Building 15 15

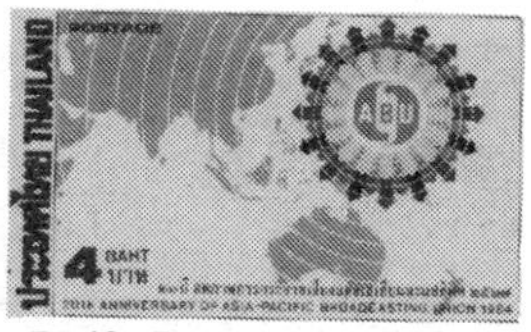

Asia-Pacific Broadcasting Union, 20th Anniv. — A306

1984, July 1 Wmk. 368 *Perf. 12*

1064 A306 4b Map, emblem 50 20

Values quoted in this catalogue are for stamps graded at Fine-Very Fine and with no faults. An illustrated guide to grade is provided in introductory material, beginning on Page V.

Seated Buddha, Chiang Saen Style — A307

Intl. Letter Writing Week — A308

Seated Buddhas in various styles.

Perf. 14½x14

1984, July 12 Wmk. 233

1065 A307 1.25b shown 12 8
1066 A307 7b Sukhothai 80 50
1067 A307 8.50b U-Thong 1.00 60
1068 A307 9.50b Ayutthaya 1.10 70

Perf. 13½

1984, Oct. 7 Litho. Wmk.

Medicinal Succulents.

1069 A308 1.50b Taro 15 10
1070 A308 2b Star cactus 22 25
1071 A308 4b Gynura pseudochina DC 42 25
1072 A308 10b Oyster plant 1.10 65

Princess Mother (b. 1900) — A309

U.N. Day — A310

1984, Oct. 21 *Perf. 15x14*

1073 A309 1.50b Portrait 15 8

1984, Oct. 24

1074 A310 1.50b Woman in rice paddy 15 8

Local Butterflies — A311

1984, Nov. 27 Photo. *Perf. 13½*

1075 A311 2b Bhutanitis lidderdalei 25 18
1076 A311 3b Stichophthalma louisa 35 28
1077 A311 5b Parthenos sylvia 60 45
1078 A311 7b Stichophthalma godfreyi 85 70

Wmk. 387

King Type of 1980

Perf. 13½x13, 14x15(1.50b, 2b)

1984-87 Litho. Unwmk.

1079 A256 1b Prus bl 15 10
1081 A256 1.50b brt yel org ('85) 15 15
1082 A256 2b dk car ('85) 20 16
a Wmk. 387, perf. 11x13½ ('86?) 20 16
b Wmk. 387, perf. 14½x14 ('87) 22 16

Engr.

1083 A256 2b hn brn & gray vio 20 16
1084 A256 4b turq bl & hn brn 35 24
1085 A256 6.50b dk yel grn & ol brn 45 35
1086 A256 7b dl red brn & sep 60 42
1087 A256 7.50b dk org & saph ('85) 60 48
1088 A256 8b brn vio & ol grn ('85) 64 52
1089 A256 9b int bl & dk ol bis ('85) 72 58
1090 A256 10b hn brn & sl grn 85 62
1093 A256 50b dp vio & grn 4.00 3.00
1097 A256 100b dp org & dk bl 8.00 6.00
Nos. 1079-1097 (13) 16.91 12.78

Children's Day — A313

Children's drawings.

1985, Jan. 12 Litho. *Perf. 13½*

1101 A313 1.50b Pedestrians, overpass 25 20
1102 A313 1.50b Climbing overpass, vert. 25 20

Bangkok Mail Center Opening — A314

1985, Feb. 25

1103 A314 1.50b multi 25 20

Phuket Province Heroes Bicent. — A315

1985, Mar. 13 Litho. *Perf. 15x14*

1104 A315 2b multi 30 25

Tao-Thep-Krasattri, Tao-Sri-Sundhorn Monument.

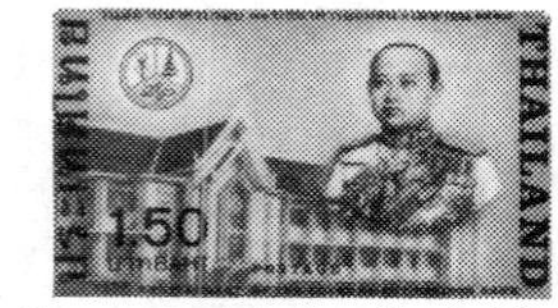

Government Savings Bank, 72nd Anniv. — A316

1985, Apr. 1 Litho. *Perf. 14x15*
1105 A316 1.50b King Rama VI, headquarters 20 15

Intl. Telecommunications Satellite Org., 20th Anniv. — A317

1985, Apr. 6 Litho. *Perf. 12*
1106 A317 2b multi 30 20

Thai Airways Intl., 25th Anniv. — A318

1985, May 1 Litho. *Perf. 13*
1107 A318 2b DC-6 30 25
1108 A318 7.50b DC-10 1.10 90
1109 A318 8.50b Airbus A-300 1.20 1.20
1110 A318 9.50b Boeing 747 1.20 1.20

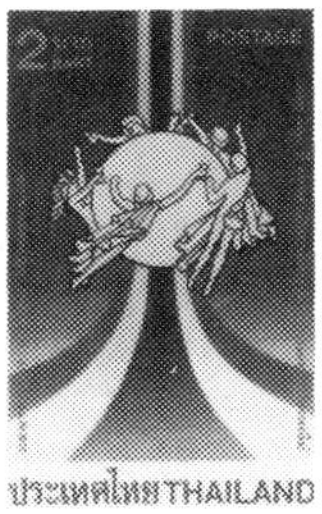
Natl. Flag and UPU Emblem — A319

1985, July 1 *Perf. 12, 13½*
1111 A319 2b shown 22 18
1112 A319 10b Flag and ITU emblem 1.10 90

Thai membership to UPU and Intl. Telecommunications Union, cent.

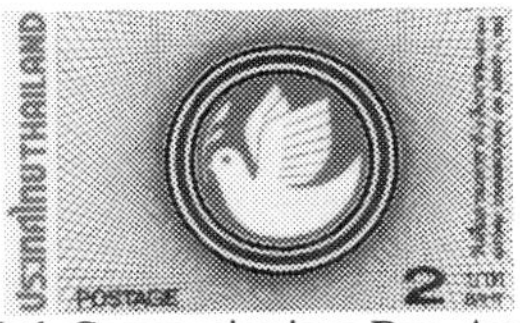
Natl. Communications Day, Aug. 5 — A320

1985, Aug. 4 *Perf. 13½*
1113 A320 2b multi 15 12

THAIPEX '85, Aug. 4-13 — A321

1985, Aug. 4
1114 A321 2b Aisvarya Pavilion, vert. 20 15
1115 A321 3b Varopas Piman Pavilion 30 25
1116 A321 7b Vehas Camrun Pavilion 65 60
1117 A321 10b Vitoon Tassana Tower, vert. 1.00 80
a Souv. sheet of 4 3.25 2.75

No. 1117a contains Nos. 1114-1117 printed se-tenant with center label picturing exhibition emblem.

Natl. Science Day, Aug. 18 — A322

1985, Aug. 18 *Perf. 12*
1118 A322 2b King Rama IV, solar eclipse 20 15

1885 Seal, Modern Map and Crest — A323

1985, Sept. 3 *Perf. 14½x15*
1119 A323 2b multi 20 12

Royal Thai Survey Department, Cent.

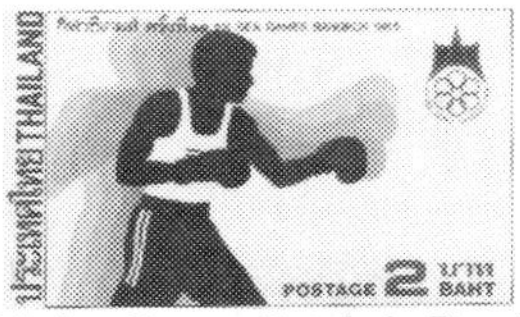
13th Sea Games, Bangkok, Dec. 8-17 — A324

Designs: a, Boxing. b, Shot put. c, Badminton. d, Javelin. e, Weight lifting.

1985, Oct. 1 *Perf. 12*
1120 Strip of 5 1.00 80
a.-e. A324 2b, any single 20 15
f Souvenir sheet of 5 1.75 1.75

No. 1120f contains one each Nos. 1120a-1120e and label. Sold for 20b.

Climbing Plants A325

UN Child Survival Campaign A326

1985, Oct. 6 *Perf. 13½*
1121 A325 2b Allemanda cathartica 20 15
1122 A325 3b Jasminum auriculatum 30 25
1123 A325 7b Passiflora laurifolia 65 55
1124 A325 10b Antigonon leptopus 1.00 80

International Letter Writing Week.

1985, Oct. 24
1125 A326 2b multi 15 12

UN Day.

Prince Kromamun Bidyalabh Bridhyakorn (1885-1974), Govt. Minister — A327

Rangsit (1885-1951), Prince of Jainad — A328

1985, Nov 7
1126 A327 2b multi 15 12
1126A A327 2b multi, diff. 30 12

No. 1126A has flower design framing portrait reversed.

1985, Nov. 12 *Perf. 15x14½*
1127 A328 1.50b multi 15 10

Asian-Pacific Postal Union, 5th Congress, Nov. 25-Dec. 4 — A329

1985, Nov. 25 *Perf. 13½*
1128 A329 2b multi 15 12
1129 A329 10b multi 75 62

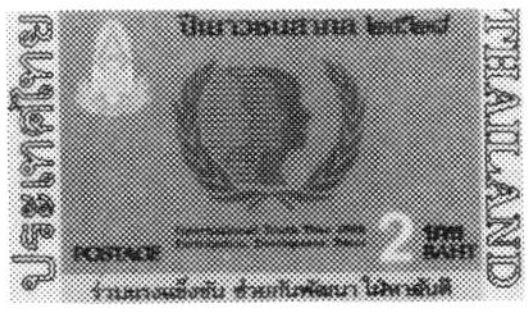
Intl. Youth Year A330

1985, Nov. 26 *Perf. 14x15*
1130 A330 2b multi 15 12

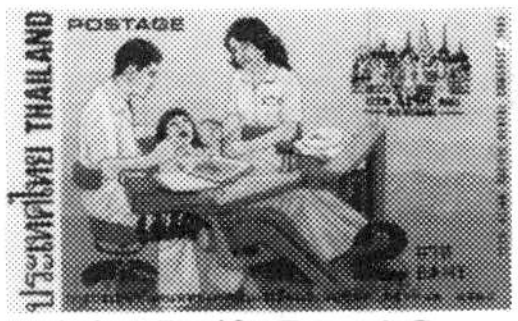
12th Asian-Pacific Dental Congress, Bangkok, Dec. 5-10 — A331

1985, Dec. 5
1131 A331 2b multi 15 12

13th Sea Games — A332

French Envoys — A333

1985, Dec. 8 *Perf. 12*
1132 A332 1b Volleyball 12 8
1133 A332 2b Sepak-takraw 20 15
1134 A332 3b Women's gymnastics 30 25
1135 A332 4b Bowling 40 38
a Souv. sheet of 4, #1132-1135 + label 1.10 1.10

No. 1135a sold for 20b.

1985, Dec. 12 *Perf. 13½*
1136 A333 2b shown 20 15
1137 A333 8.50b Thai envoys 80 65

Diplomatic relations with France, 300th anniv.

Domestic Express Mail Service Inauguration — A334

1986, Jan. 1 Litho. *Perf. 13½*
1138 A334 2b multi 15 12

Intl. Express Mail Service, EMS, 3rd anniv.

Wildlife Conservation — A335

Marine turtles.

1986, Jan. 8 Wmk. 329
1139 A335 1.50b Chelonia mydas 12 10
1140 A335 3b Eretmochelys imbricata 24 20
1141 A335 5b Dermochelys coriacea 38 30
1142 A335 10b Lepidochelys olivacea 75 62

Natl. Children's Day — A336

Statue of Sunthon Phu, Poet — A337

Design: Children picking lotus, by Areeya Makarabhundhu, age 12.

1986, Jan. 11
1143 A336 2b multi 15 12

1986, June 26
1144 A337 2b multi 15 12

Fruit Type of 1979

1986, June 26
1145 A237 2b Watermelon 15 12
1146 A237 2b Malay apple 15 12
1147 A237 6b Pomelo 45 35
1148 A237 6b Papaya 45 35

Nos. 1145-1148 horiz.

Natl. Year of the Trees A338

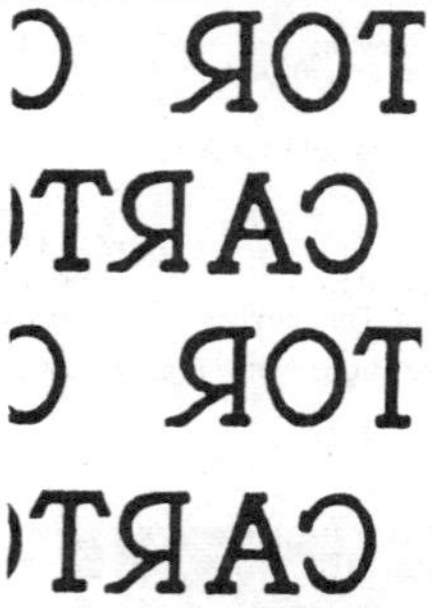

Wmk. 385

Wmk. "CARTOR" (385)

1986, July 21 Litho. *Perf. 13½*

1149 A338 2b multi 18 15

Communications Day — A339

1986, Aug. 4

1150 A339 2b multi 18 15

Bamboo Baskets — A340

1986, Oct. 5

1151 A340 2b Chalom 18 15
1152 A340 2b Krabung 18 15
1153 A340 6b Kratib 55 42
1154 A340 6b Kaleb 55 42

Intl. Letter Writing Week.

Intl. Peace Year A341

1986, Oct. 24

1155 A341 2b multi 18 15

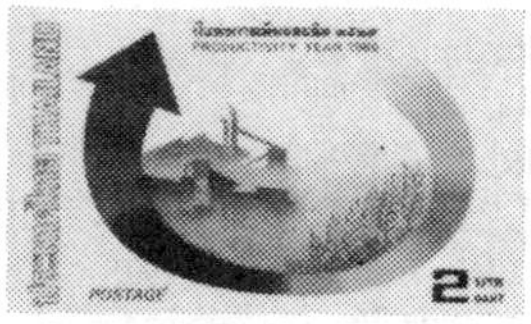

Productivity Year — A342

1986, Oct. 24 Wmk. 329

1156 A342 2b multi 18 15

6th ASEAN Orchid Congress — A343

1986, Nov. 7 Wmk. 385

1157 A343 2b Vanda varavuth, vert. 18 15
1158 A343 3b Ascocenda emma, vert. 28 22
1159 A343 4b Dendrobium sri-siam 35 28
1160 A343 5b Dendrobium ekapol panda 45 35
a Souv. sheet of 4, #1157-1160 1.30 1.00

Fungi A344

1986, Nov. 26 Photo. *Perf. 13x13½*

1161 A344 2b Volvariella volvacea 18 15
1162 A344 2b Pleurotus ostreatus 18 15
1163 A344 6b Auricularia polytricha 55 42
1164 A344 6b Pleurotus cystidiosus 55 42

Fisheries Dept., 60th Anniv. — A345

1986, Dec. 16 Litho. *Perf. 13½*

1165 A345 2b Morulius chrysophekadion 18 15
1166 A345 2b Notopterus blanci 18 15
1167 A345 7b Scleropages formosus 62 48
1168 A345 7b Pangasianodon gigas 62 48

No. 653 Surcharged in Dark Olive Green

Perf. 14x13½

1986, Dec. Photo. Wmk. 233

1168A A161 1b on 20s blue 15 12

Children's Day 1987 — A346

Child's drawing.

Perf. 14½x15

1987, Jan. 10 Litho. Unwmk.

1169 A346 2b School, playground 20 15
1170 A346 2b Pool 20 15

Nos. 1169-1170 printed se-tenant in a continuous design.

F-16 and F-5 Fighter Planes, Pilot A347

1987, Mar. 27 Litho. *Perf. 13½*

1171 A347 2b multi 20 15

Royal Thai Air Force, 72nd anniv.

King Rama III (Nang Klao, 1787-1851) — A348

1987, Mar. 31 *Perf. 15*

1172 A348 2b multi 20 15

Ministry of Communications, 75th Anniv. — A349

1987, Apr. 1 *Perf. 15x14½*

1173 A349 2b multi 20 15

Forestry Year — A350

Wmk. 385

1987, July 11 Litho. *Perf. 13½*

1174 A350 2b multi 20 15

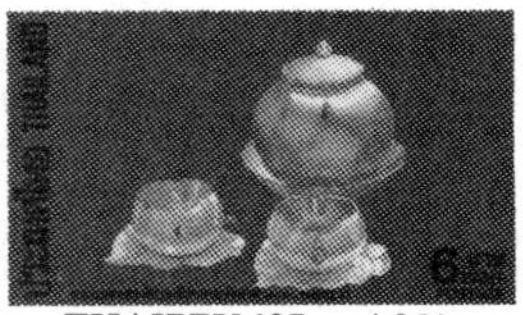

THAIPEX '87 — A351

Gold artifacts.

Wmk. 385

1987, Aug. 4 Litho. *Perf. 13½*

1175 A351 2b Peacock, vert. 22 16
1176 A351 2b Hand mirrors, vert. 22 16
1177 A351 6b Water urn, finger bowls 65 50
1178 A351 6b Swan vase 65 50
a Souv. sheet of 4, #1175-1178 1.75 1.35

ASEAN, 20th Anniv. — A352

1987, Aug. 20

1179 A352 2b multi 22 16
1180 A352 3b multi 32 24
1181 A352 4b multi 45 35
1182 A352 5b multi 55 42

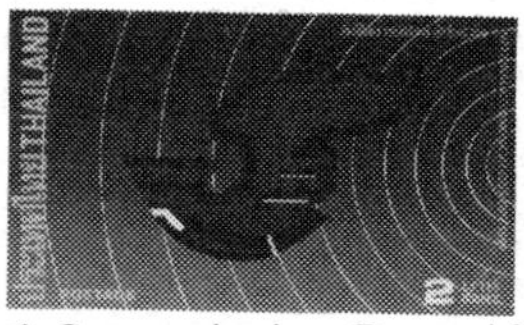

Natl. Communications Day — A353

Wmk. 385

1987, Aug. 4 Litho. *Perf. 13½*

1183 A353 2b multi 25 18

Chulachamklao Royal Military Academy, Cent. — A354

Design: School crest, King Rama V, and King Rama IX conferring sword on graduating officer.

1987, Aug. 5

1184 A354 2b multi 25 18

Intl. Literacy Day — A355

Tourism Year — A356

1987, Sept. 8

1185 A355 2b multi 25 18

Designs: 2b, Flower-offering ceremony, Saraburi province. 3b, Duan Sib Festival, Nakhon Si Thammarat province. 5b, Bang Fai Festival, Yasothon province. 7b, Loi Krathong Festival, Sukhothai province.

Wmk. 385

1987, Sept. 18 Litho. *Perf. 13½*

1186 A356 2b multi 18 14
1187 A356 3b multi 28 22
1188 A356 5b multi 45 35
1189 A356 7b multi 62 48

Auditor General's Office, 72nd Anniv. — A357

1987, Sept. 18

1190 A357 2b multi 25 18

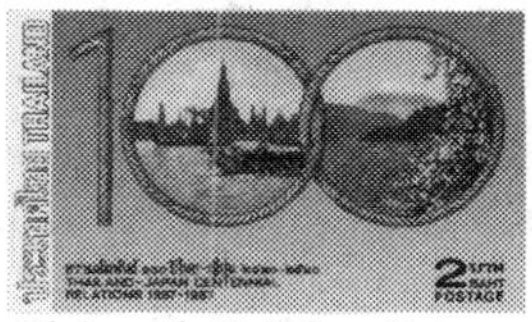

Diplomatic Relations Between Thailand and Japan, Cent. — A358

1987, Sept. 26 Wmk. 329

1191 A358 2b multi 25 18

The only foreign revenue stamps listed in this Catalogue are those authorized for prepayment of postage.

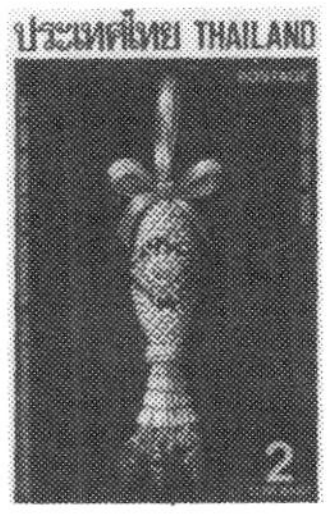

Intl. Letter Writing Week — A359

Floral garlands.

1987, Oct. 4 — Wmk. 385

1192	A359	2b	Floral tassel	18	14
1193	A359	3b	Tasselled garland	28	22
1194	A359	5b	Wrist garland	48	35
1195	A359	7b	Double-ended garland	65	50

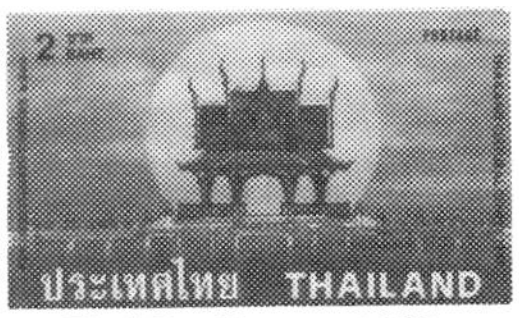

Thai Pavilion — A360

1987, Oct. 9 — Wmk. — *Perf. 15*

1196	A360	2b	multi	18	14

Social Education and Cultural Center inauguration.

A361

A362

King Bhumibol Adulyadej, 60th Birthday — A363

Royal ciphers and: No. 1197, Adulyadej as a child. No. 1198, King and Queen, wedding portrait, 1950. No. 1199, King taking the Oath of Accession, 1950. No. 1200, King dressed as a monk, collecting alms. No. 1201, Greeting 100 year-old woman. No. 1202, In military uniform holding pen and with hill tribes. No. 1203, Royal couple visiting wounded servicemen. No. 1204, Visiting farm. No. 1205, Royal family. No. 1206, King, Queen Sirikit. No. 1207, Princess Mother Somdej Phra Sri Nakarindra Boromrajjonnani, emblem of Medical Volunteer Assoc. No. 1208, Crown Prince Maha Vajiralongkorn, crown prince's royal standard. No. 1209, Princess Maha Chakri Sirindhorn, emblem of Sai Jai Thai Foundation. No. 1210, Princess Chulabhorn, Albert Einstein gold medal awarded by UNESCO.

Wmk. 329

1987, Dec. 5 — Photo. — *Perf. 13½*

1197	A361	2b	shown	18	14
1198	A361	2b	multi	18	14
1199	A361	2b	multi	18	14
1200	A361	2b	multi	18	14
1201	A361	2b	multi	18	14
1202	A361	2b	multi	18	14
1203	A361	2b	multi	18	14
1204	A361	2b	multi	18	14
a.			Souv. sheet of 8, #1197-1204	3.60	3.60

Litho.

1205	A362	2b	multi	18	14
1206	A362	2b	multi	18	14
1207	A362	2b	multi	18	14
1208	A362	2b	multi	18	14
1209	A362	2b	multi	18	14
1210	A362	2b	multi	18	14

Litho. & Embossed

Wmk. 385

Perf. 13½

1211	A363	100b	vio blue & gold	9.00	6.75
			Nos. 1197-1211 (15)	11.52	8.71

Size of Nos. 1206-1210: 45x27mm. No. 1211 printed in sheets of 10. No. 1204a sold for 40b.

No. 1081 Surcharged

2 บาท BAHT

1987 — Litho. — Unwmk. — *Perf. 14x15*

1212	A256	2b	on 1.50b brt yel org	18	14

Children's Day — A364

Thai Agricultural Cooperatives, 72nd Anniv. — A365

Perf. 14x14½

1988, Jan. 9 — Litho. — Wmk. 387

1213	A364	2b	multi	20	15

1988, Feb. 26

1214	A365	2b	Prince Bridhyalongkorn, founder	18	14

Royal Siam Soc., 84th Anniv. — A366

1988, Mar. 10 — *Perf. 14½x14*

1215	A366	2b	multi	18	14

Cultural Heritage Preservation — A367

Ruins in Sukhothai Historic Park.

1988, Apr. 2 — *Perf. 14½x14*

1216	A367	2b	Wat Phra Phai Luang	18	14
1217	A367	3b	Wat Traphang Thonglang	25	18
1218	A367	4b	Wat Maha That	35	28
1219	A367	6b	Thewalai Maha Kaset	50	38

Red Cross Fair 1988 A368

1988, Apr. — Wmk. 387 — *Perf. 14*

1220	A368	2b	Prevention of rabies	18	14

Siriraj Hospital, Cent. — A369

1988, Apr. 26 — Wmk. — *Perf. 14x14½*

1221	A369	5b	King Rama V, founder	42	32

Pheasants — A370

Wmk. 329

1988, June 15 — Photo. — *Perf. 13½*

1222	A370	2b	Crested fireback	18	14
1223	A370	3b	Kalij	25	18
1224	A370	6b	Silver pheasant	50	38
1225	A370	7b	Hume's pheasant	58	42

No. 936 Surcharged

1988 — Litho. — Wmk. 368 — *Perf. 11x13*

1226	A256	1b	on 1.25b yel grn	10	8

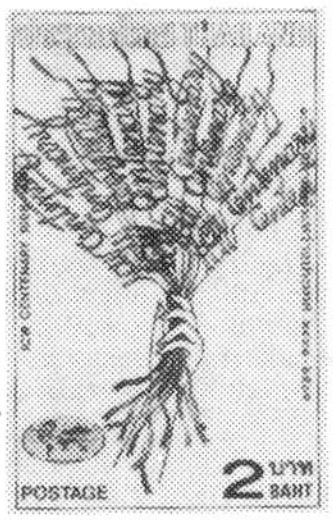

Intl. Council of Women, Cent. — A371

1988, June 26 — Wmk. 385 — *Perf. 13½*

1227	A371	2b	multi	22	16

King Bhumibol Adulyadej A372

Wearing Uniform of Rama V's Bodyguard A372a

Wmk. 387

1988, July 2 — Litho. — *Perf. 14½*

1230	A372	1b	brt blue	12	8
1233	A372	2b	scar	22	16

1988, Dec. 5 — Engr. — Wmk. — *Perf.*

1242	A372a	3b		32	25
1246	A372a	10b		1.10	80
1249	A372a	50b		5.50	4.00
1251	A372a	100b		11.00	8.00
			Nos. 1230-1251 (6)	18.26	13.29

A373

A375

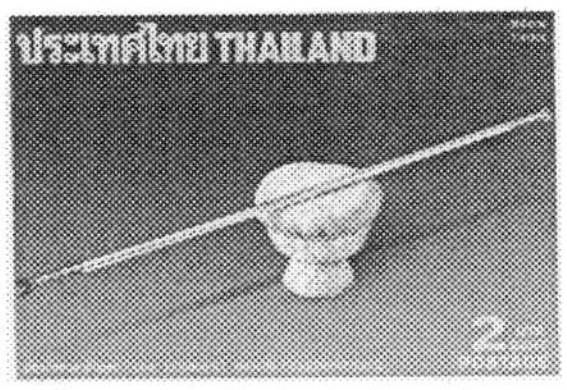

King Bhumibol's Reign (since 1950) — A374

Designs: No. 1253, King Bhumibol.

Regalia: No. 1254, Great Crown of Victory. No. 1255, Sword of Victory and matching scabbard. No. 1256, Scepter. No. 1257, Fan and feather fly swatter. No. 1258, Royal slippers.

Canopied thrones in the Grand Palace: No. 1259, Queen's round ottoman on 1-tier dais in front of decorative screen. No. 1260, King's throne on 1-tier dais in front of decorative screen. No. 1261, 3-Tier throne with 3 gilded trees. No. 1262, 3-Canopy throne on high gold dais. No. 1263, 3-Tier throne with 4 gilded trees, altar in background. No. 1264, 3-Canopy throne on 5-stair dais, in front of arch flanked by columns.

Wmk. 385

1988, July 2 — Litho. — *Perf. 13½*

1253	A373	2b	shown	22	16

Photo.

Wmk. 329

1254	A374	2b	multi, vert.	22	16
1255	A374	2b	multi	22	16
1256	A374	2b	multi	22	16
1257	A374	2b	multi	22	16
1258	A374	2b	multi	22	16

Litho.

Perf. 14x14½

Wmk. 387

1259	A375	2b	multi	22	16
1260	A375	2b	multi	22	16
1261	A375	2b	multi	22	16
1262	A375	2b	multi	22	16
1263	A375	2b	multi	22	16
1264	A375	2b	multi	22	16
a.			Souv. sheet of 6, #1259-1264	2.75	2.75
			Nos. 1253-1264 (12)	2.64	1.92

No. 1264a sold for 25b.

Arbor Year A376

Perf. 14½x14

1988, July 29 — Litho. — Wmk.

1265	A376	2b	multi	22	16

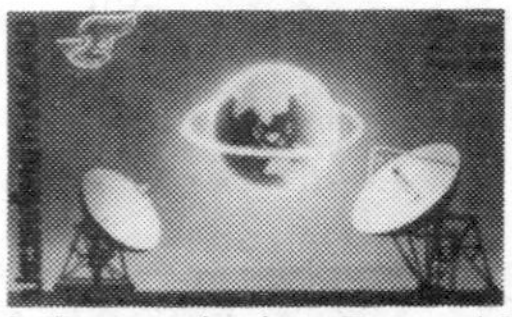

Natl. Communications Day — A377

1988, Aug. 4 Unwmk. *Perf. 13½*

1266 A377 2b multi 22 16

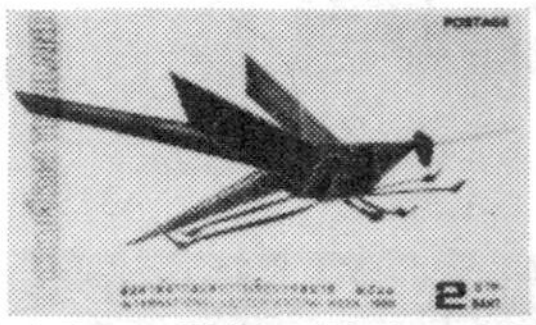

Intl. Letter Writing Week — A378

Designs: Coconut leaf sculptures.

1988, Oct. 9 Unwmk. *Perf. 14½x14*

1267 A378 2b Grasshopper 22 16
1268 A378 2b Fish 22 16
1269 A378 6b Bird 65 50
1270 A378 6b Takro (box) 65 50

Housing Development — A379

1988, Oct. 24 Litho. Wmk. *Perf. 14*

1271 A379 2b multi 22 16

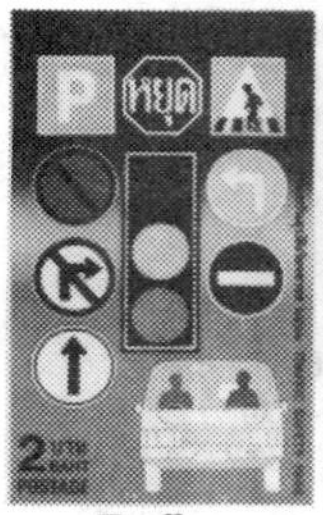

Traffic Safety — A380

King's Bodyguard, 120th Anniv. — A381

1988, Nov. 11 Wmk. 329 *Perf. 13½*

1272 A380 2b multi 22 16

1988, Nov. 11 Wmk. 385

1273 A381 2b Chulalongkorn 22 16

New Year — A382

Flowers.

1988, Dec. 1 Wmk. 387

1274 A382 1b Crotalaria sessiliflora 10 8
1275 A382 1b Uvaria grandiflora 10 8
1276 A382 1b Reinwardtia trigyna 10 8
1277 A382 1b Impatiens griffithii 10 8

Thai Royal Orders Type of 1979

Designs: Nos. 1278-1279, Knight Grand Commander, Order of Rama, 1918. Nos. 1280-1281, Knight Grand Cordon, Order of the White Elephant, 1861. Nos. 1282-1283, Knight Grand Cordon, Order of the Crown of Thailand, 1869. Nos. 1284-1285, Ratana Varabhorn Order of Merit, 1911. Printed se-tenant in continuous designs.

1988, Dec. 5 Wmk. 385

1278 A243 2b multi 22 16
1279 A244 2b multi 22 16
1280 A243 3b multi 32 25
1281 A244 3b multi 32 25
1282 A243 5b multi 55 40
1283 A244 5b multi 55 40
1284 A243 7b multi 75 55
1285 A244 7b multi 75 55
Nos. 1278-1285 (8) 3.68 2.72

A383

Buddha Monthon Celebrations, Tambol Salaya — A384

Perf. 14x15, 15x14

1988, Dec. 5 Wmk. 233

1286 A383 2b Birthplace 22 16
1287 A383 3b Enlightenment place 32 25
1288 A383 4b Location of 1st sermon 45 32
1289 A383 5b Place Buddha achieved nirvana 55 40
1290 A384 6b Statue 65 48
Nos. 1286-1290 (5) 2.19 1.61

Children's Day — A385

"Touch" paintings by blind youth: No. 1292, *Floating Market,* by Thongbai Siyam. No. 1293, *Flying Bird,* by Kwanchai Kerd-Daeng. No. 1294, *Little Mermaid,* by Chalermpol Jiengmai. No. 1295, *Golden Fish,* by Natetip Korsantirak.

Wmk. 387

1989, Jan. 14 Litho. *Perf. 13½*

1292 A385 2b multi 22 16
1293 A385 2b multi 22 16
1294 A385 2b multi 22 16
1295 A385 2b multi 22 16

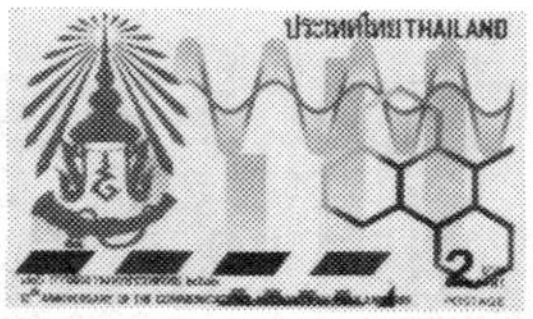

Communications Authority of Thailand, 12th Anniv. — A386

1989, Feb. 25 *Perf. 14½x14*

1296 A386 2b multi 22 16

Chulalongkorn University, 72nd Anniv. — A387

Design: 2b, Statue of Chulalongkorn and King Vajiravudh in front of university auditorium.

1989, Mar. 26

1297 A387 2b multi 22 16

Red Cross Annivs. — A388

Perf. 15x14, 13½ (#1299)
Wmk. 387 (#1299)

1989, Mar. 31 Litho.

1298 A388 2b shown 22 16
1299 A388 10b Emblem 1.10 82

Thai Red Cross Society, 96th anniv. (2b); Intl. Red Cross and Red Crescent organizations, 125th annivs. (10b).

Natl. Monuments A389

Phra Nakhon Khiri Historical Park: 2b, Wat Phra Kaeo. 3b, Chatchawan Wiangchai Observatory. 5b, Phra That Chom Phet Stupa. 6b, Wetchayan Wichian Phrasat Throne Hall.

Perf. 14x14½

1989, Apr. 2 Wmk. 387

1300 A389 2b multi 22 16
1301 A389 3b multi 32 24
1302 A389 5b multi 55 42
1303 A389 6b multi 65 50

Natl. Lottery Office, 50th Anniv. — A390

1989, Apr. 5 *Perf. 13½*

1304 A390 2b multi 22 16

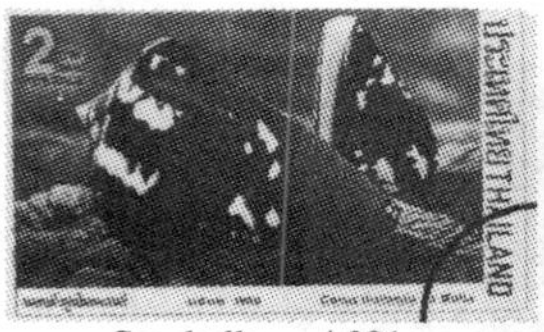

Seashells — A391

1989, June 28 Wmk. *Perf.*

1305 A391 2b *Conus thailandis* 22 16
1306 A391 3b *Spondylus princeps* 32 24
1307 A391 6b *Cyprea guttata* 65 50
1308 A391 10b *Nautilus pompilius* 1.10 82

Arts and Crafts Year A392

1989, June 28 Litho. Wmk. *Perf.*

1309 A392 2b Ceramic figurines 22 16
1310 A392 2b Gold niello ginger jar, chicken 22 16
1311 A392 6b Textiles 65 50
1312 A392 6b Gemstone flower ornament 65 50

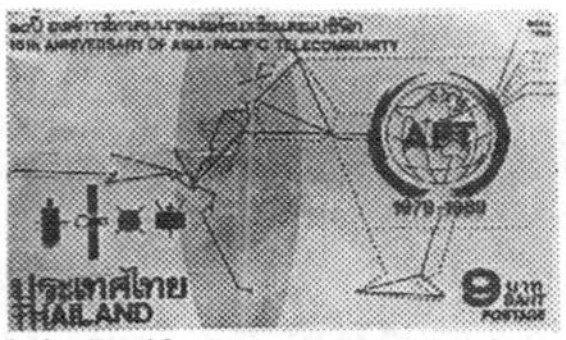

Asia-Pacific Telecommunications Organization, 10th Anniv. — A393

Design: APT emblem, map of submarine cable network and satellites of member nations.

1989, July 1 Wmk. *Perf.*

1313 A393 9b multi 1.00 75

Phya Anuman Rajadhon (1888-1969), Ethnologist A394

9th Natl. Phil. Exhib., Aug. 4-13 A395

1989, July 1 Wmk. *Perf.*

1314 A394 2b multi 22 16

1989, Aug. 4 Wmk. *Perf.*

Various mailboxes.

1315 A395 2b multi 22 16
1316 A395 3b multi, diff. 32 24
1317 A395 4b multi, diff. 42 32
1318 A395 5b multi, diff. 55 40
1319 A395 6b multi, diff. 65 50
Nos. 1315-1319 (5) 2.16 1.62

SEMI-POSTAL STAMPS

Nos. 164-175 Overprinted in Red

1918, Jan. 11 Unwmk. *Perf. 14*

B1 A21 2s org brn 45 40
B2 A21 3s emerald 45 35
B3 A21 5s rose red 75 60

B4	A21	10s blk & ol	80	1.25
B5	A21	15s blue	85	1.40
B6	A22	1b bl & gray blk	5.75	5.75
B7	A22	2b car rose & brn	10.00	7.00
B8	A22	3b yel grn & blk	20.00	11.00
B9	A22	5b dp vio & blk	22.50	19.00
a.		Double ovpt.	375.00	375.00
B10	A22	10b ol grn & vio brn	90.00	90.00
B11	A22	20b sea grn & brn	300.00	300.00
		Nos. B1-B11 (11)	451.55	436.75

Excellent counterfeit overprints are known.

These stamps were sold at an advance over face value, the excess being given to the Siamese Red Cross Society.

Stamps of 1905-19 Handstamp Overprinted

ยำรุงเสือป่า

1920, Feb.

On Nos. 164, 146, 168

B12	A21	2s (+ 3s) org brn	15.00	15.00
B13	A21	3s (+ 2s) grn	15.00	15.00
B14	A21	15s (+ 5s) bl	16.00	16.00

On No. 105

B15	A15	1t (+ 25s)	75.00	75.00

On Nos. 185-186

B16	A21	5s on 6s (+ 20s)	13.50	13.50
a.		Ovpt. inverted		
B17	A21	10s on 12s (+ 5s)	15.00	15.00
		Nos. B12-B17 (6)	149.50	149.50

Stamps of 1905-20 Handstamp Overprinted

On Nos. 164, 146, 168

B18	A21	2s (+ 3s) org brn	15.00	15.00
B19	A21	3s (+ 2s) grn	15.00	15.00
a.		Pair, one without ovpt.		
B20	A21	15s (+ 5s) bl	35.00	35.00

On No. 105

B21	A15	1t (+ 25s)	75.00	75.00

On No. 186

B22	A21	10s on 12s (+ 5s)	17.50	17.50

On No. 190

B23	A23	5s (+ 20s)	17.50	17.50
		Nos. B18-B23 (6)	175.00	175.00

Nos. 187-188, 190, 193-194, 196, 198 Overprinted in Blue or Red

บำรุงเสือป่า

SCOUT'S FUND.

1920, Dec. 21

B24	A23	2s brn, *yel*	14.00	14.00
B25	A23	3s grn, *grn* (R)	14.00	14.00
B26	A23	5s rose, *pale rose*	14.00	14.00
B27	A23	10s blk & org (R)	14.00	14.00
B28	A23	15s bl, *bluish* (R)	22.50	22.50
B29	A23	25s chocolate	55.00	55.00
B30	A23	50s ocher & blk (R)	110.00	110.00
		Nos. B24-B30 (7)	243.50	243.50

Nos. B12 to B30 were sold at an advance over face value, the excess being for the benefit of the Wild Tiger Corps. Counterfeits exist.

Nos. 170-172 Surcharged in Red

๗๕ปี
๕สต+๕สต

1939, Apr. 6 Unwmk. *Perf. 14*

B31	A22	5s + 5s on 1b	10.00	11.00
B32	A22	10s + 5s on 2b	13.00	15.00
B33	A22	15s + 5s on 3b	13.00	15.00

75th anniv. of the founding of the Intl. Red Cross Soc.

Bottom line of overprint is different on Nos. B32-B33.

Catalogue values for unused stamps in this section, from this point to the end of the section, are for Never Hinged items.

No. 214 Surcharged in Carmine

+20
สต.

1952 Unwmk. *Perf. 12½*

B34	A25	80s + 20s bl & blk	6.50	5.00

New constitution.

Red Cross and Dancer — SP1

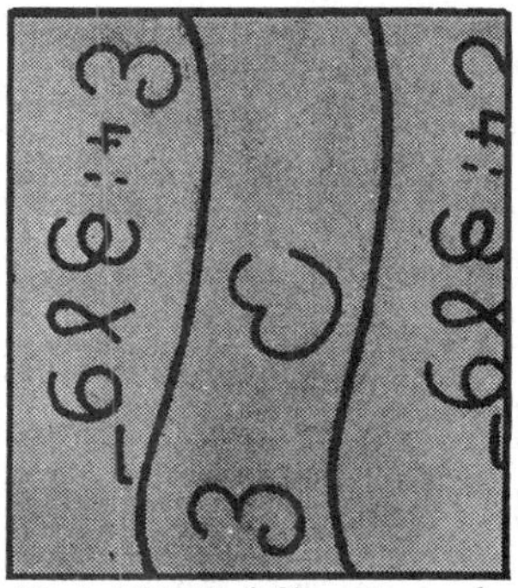

Wmk. 299- Thai Characters and Wavy Lines

Lithographed, Cross Typographed

1953, Apr. 6 Wmk. 299 *Perf. 11*

Cross in Red, Dancer Dark Blue

B35	SP1	25s + 25s yel grn	1.50	1.50
B36	SP1	50s + 50s brt rose	2.75	2.75
B37	SP1	1b + 1b lt bl	3.75	3.75

60th anniv. of the founding of the Siamese Red Cross Society.

Nos. B35-B37 Overprinted with Year Date "24 98," in Black

1955, Apr. 3

Cross in Red, Dancer Dark Blue

B38	SP1	25s + 25s yel grn	4.50	4.50
B39	SP1	50s + 50s brt rose	9.00	9.00
B40	SP1	1b + 1b lt bl	12.00	12.00

Counterfeits exist.

Red Cross Cent. Emblem SP2 SP3

1963 Wmk. 334 Litho. *Perf. 13½*

B41	SP2	50s + 10s gray & red	25	20
B42	SP3	50s + 10s gray & red	25	20

Cent. of the Intl. Red Cross. Nos. B41-B42 printed in alternating vertical rows.

Nos. B41-B42 Surcharged

1973, Feb. 15

B43	SP2	75s + 25s on 50s + 10s	40	35
B44	SP3	75s + 25s on 50s + 10s	40	35

Red Cross Fair, Feb. 15-19. See note after No. B42.

Nos. B41-B42 Surcharged

75+25
1
9
7
3
๒๕๑๖

1974, Feb. 2

B45	SP2	75s + 25s on 50s + 10s	35	30
B46	SP3	75s + 25s on 50s + 10s	35	30

Red Cross Fair, Feb. 1974. See note after No. B42. Position of surcharge reversed on No. B46.

Nos. B41-B42 Surcharged

1974 75+25
๒๕๑๗

1975, Feb 11

B47	SP2	75s + 25s on 50s + 10s	35	30
B48	SP3	75s + 25s on 50s + 10s	35	30

Red Cross Fair, Feb. 1975. See note after No. B42. Position of surcharge reversed on No. B48.

Nos. B41-B42 Surcharged

75+25
2518
1975

1976, Feb. 26

B49	SP2	75s + 25s on 50s + 10s	35	30
B50	SP3	75s + 25s on 50s + 10s	35	30

Red Cross Fair, Feb. 16-Mar. 1. See note after No. B42. Position of surcharge reversed on No. B50.

Nos. B41-B42 Surcharged

75+25
2520-1977

1977, Apr. 6 Wmk. 334 *Perf. 13½*

B51	SP2	75s + 25s on 50s + 10s	35	30
B52	SP3	75s + 25s on 50s + 10s	35	30

Red Cross Fair 1977. See note after No. B42.

Red Cross Blood Collection SP4

Eye and Blind People SP5

Wmk. 329

1978, Apr. 6 Photo. *Perf. 13*

B53	SP4	2.75b + 25s multi	50	25

"Give blood, save life."

Perf. 14x13½

1979, Apr. 6 Litho. Wmk. 368

B54	SP5	75s + 25s multi	30	18

"Give an eye, save new life." Red Cross Fair. Surtax was for Thai Red Cross.

Extracting Snake Venom, Red Cross — SP6

1980, Apr. *Perf. 11x13*

B55	SP6	75s + 25s multi	30	20

Red Cross Fair. Surtax was for Thai Red Cross.

Nurse Helping Victim SP7

1981, Apr. 6 Litho. *Perf. 12½*

B56	SP7	75 + 25s red & gray grn	20	20

Red Cross Fair (canceled). Surtax was for Thai Red Cross.

Red Cross Fair SP8

Perf. 13x13½

1983, Apr. 6 Litho. Wmk. 329

B57	SP8	1.25b + 25s multi	20	10

Surtax was for Thai Red Cross.

No. B53 Overprinted and Surcharged

Wmk. 329

1984, Apr. Photo. *Perf. 13*

B58	SP4	3.25b + 25s on 2.75b + 25s	30	25

Red Cross Fair. Surtax was for Thai Red Cross. Overprint translates: Red Cross Donation.

No. B54 Surcharged

1985, Mar. 30 Litho. *Perf. 13*

B59	SP5	2b + 25c on 75s + 25s	30	35

Surtax for the Thai Red Cross.

No. B55 Ovptd. and Surcharged

Perf. 11x13

1986, Apr. 6 Litho. Wmk. 368

B60	SP6	2b + 25s on 75s + 25s	30	15

Natl. Children's Day. Surtax for Natl. Red Cross Society. Overprint translates "Red Cross Donation."

Natl. Scouting Movement, 75th Anniv., 15th Asia-Pacific Conference, Thailand — SP9

Designs: No. B61, Scouts, saluting, community service. No. B62, Scout activities. No. B63, King and queen at ceremony. No. B64, 15th Asia-Pacific conference.

1986, Nov. 7 Wmk. 385 *Perf. 13½*

B61	SP9	2b + 50s multi	22	18
B62	SP9	2b + 50s multi	22	18
B63	SP9	2b + 50s multi	22	18
B64	SP9	2b + 50s multi	22	18

Surtax for the Natl. Scouting Fund.

No. B56 Surcharged

Wmk. 368

1987, Apr. Litho. ***Perf. 12½***

B65	SP7	2b + 50s on 75s + 25s	25	18

AIR POST STAMPS

Garuda — AP1

1925 Unwmk. Engr. ***Perf. 14, 14½***

C1	AP1	2s brn, *yel*	1.25	18
C2	AP1	3s dk brn	1.35	8
C3	AP1	5s green	1.90	14
C4	AP1	10s blk & org	11.00	15
C5	AP1	15s carmine	3.00	22
C6	AP1	25s dk bl	1.00	30
C7	AP1	50s brn org & blk	9.25	1.10
C8	AP1	1b bl & brn	7.00	1.50
		Nos. C1-C8 (8)	35.75	3.67

Issue dates: 2s, 50s, Apr. 21. Others, Jan. 3.

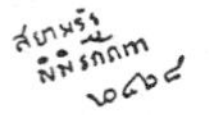

Nos. C1-C8 received this overprint ("Government Museum 2468") in 1925, but were never issued. The death of King Vajiravudh caused cancellation of the fair at which this set was to have been released.

They were used during 1928 only in the interdepartmental service for accounting purposes of the money-order sections of various Bangkok post offices, and were never sold to the public. Value for canceled set, $15.

1930-37 ***Perf. 12½***

C9	AP1	2s brn, *yel*	38	14
C10	AP1	5s green	38	14
C11	AP1	10s blk & org	1.50	14
C12	AP1	15s carmine	2.75	18
C13	AP1	25s dk bl ('37)	75	18
a.		Vert. pair, imperf. between	275.00	
C14	AP1	50s brn org & blk ('37)	1.75	38
		Nos. C9-C14 (6)	7.51	1.16

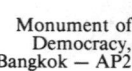

Monument of Democracy, Bangkok — AP2

1942-43 Engr. ***Perf. 11***

C15	AP2	2s dk org brn ('43)	50	30
C16	AP2	3s dk grn ('43)	5.00	2.75
C17	AP2	5s dp cl	55	22
a.		Horiz. pair, imperf. between	37.50	
b.		Vert. pair, imperf. between	45.00	
C18	AP2	10s car ('43)	55	40
a.		Vert. pair, imperf. between	45.00	45.00
C19	AP2	15s dk bl	80	45
		Nos. C15-C19 (5)	7.40	4.12

Catalogue values for unused stamps in this section, from this point to the end of the section, are for Never Hinged items.

Garuda and Bangkok Skyline — AP3

1952-53 ***Perf. 13x12½***

C20	AP3	1.50b red vio ('53)	45	12
C21	AP3	2b dk bl	85	15
C22	AP3	3b gray ('53)	85	18

Issue dates: June 15, 1952. Sept. 15, 1953.

OFFICIAL STAMPS

Catalogue values for unused stamps in this section are for Never Hinged items.

O1

Perf. 10½ Rough

1963, Oct. 1 Typo. Unwmk.

Without Gum

O1	O1	10s pink & dp car	15	10
O2	O1	20s brt grn & car rose	20	15
O3	O1	25s bl & dp car	30	35
O4	O1	50s dp car	85	1.10
O5	O1	1b sil & car rose	1.00	1.50
O6	O1	2b brnz & car rose	1.75	1.60
		Nos. O1-O6 (6)	4.25	4.80

Issued as an official test from Oct. 1, 1963, to Jan. 31, 1964, to determine the amount of mail sent out by various government departments.

1964 Without Gum

O7	O1	20s green	35	28
O8	O1	25s blue	35	40
O9	O1	1b silver	65	65
O10	O1	2b bister	1.90	2.25

Others values exist printed in one color.

THRACE

LOCATION — In southeastern Europe between the Black and Aegean Seas.
GOVT. — Former Turkish Province
AREA — 89,361 sq. mi. (approx.)

Thrace underwent many political changes during the Balkan Wars and World War I. It was finally divided among Turkey, Greece and Bulgaria.

100 Lepta = 1 Drachma
40 Paras = 1 Piastre
100 Stotinki = 1 Leva (1919)

Giumulzina District Issue

Turkish Stamps of 1909 Surcharged in Blue or Red

1913 Unwmk. ***Perf. 12, 13½***

1	A21	10 l on 20pa rose (Bl)	30.00	25.00
2	A21	25 l on 10pa bl grn	35.00	32.50
3	A21	25 l on 20pa rose (Bl)	35.00	32.50
4	A21	25 l on 1pi ultra	35.00	32.50

Counterfeits exist of Nos. 1-4.

Turkish Inscriptions
A1 A2

1913 Litho. ***Imperf.***

Laid Paper

Control Mark in Rose

5	A1	1pi blue	3.00	3.00
6	A1	2pi violet	4.50	4.50

Wove Paper

7	A2	10pa vermilion	3.75	3.75
8	A2	20pa blue	3.75	3.75
9	A2	1pi violet	3.75	3.75
		Nos. 5-9 (5)	18.75	18.75

Turkish Stamps of 1908-13 Surcharged in Red or Black

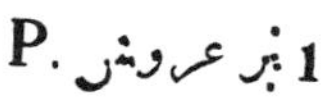

1913 ***Perf. 12***

10	A22	1pi on 2pa ol grn (R)	6.75	6.75
10A	A22	1pi on 2pa ol grn	6.00	6.00
11	A22	1pi on 5pa ocher	9.00	8.25
11A	A22	1pi on 5pa ocher (R)	9.75	9.00
12	A22	1pi on 20pa rose	15.00	15.00
13	A21	1pi on 5pi dk vio (R)	62.50	52.50
13A	A21	1pi on 5pi dk vio	62.50	52.50
14	A21	1pi on 10pi dl red	125.00	110.00
15	A19	1pi on 25pi dk grn	185.00	165.00
		Nos. 10-15 (9)	481.50	425.00

On Nos. 13-15 the surcharge is vertical, reading up. No. 15 exists with double surcharge, one black, one red.

Nos. 10-15 exist with forged surcharges.

Bulgarian Stamps of 1911 Handstamp Surcharged in Red or Blue

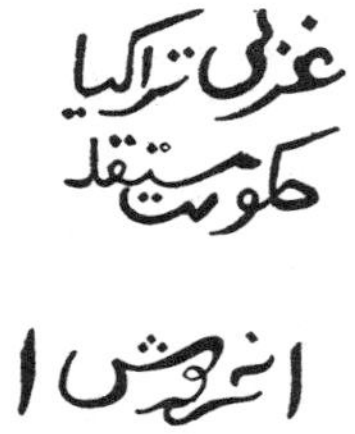

1913

16	A20	10pa on 1s myr grn (R)	2.25	1.10
17	A21	20pa on 2s car & blk	4.50	2.25
18	A23	1pi on 5s grn & blk (R)	7.50	3.25
19	A22	2pi on 3s lake & blk	10.00	5.75
20	A24	2½pi on 10s dp red & blk	15.00	7.50
21	A25	5pi on 15s brn bis	18.00	15.00
		Nos. 16-21 (6)	57.25	34.85

Same Surcharges on Greek Stamps

On Issue of 1911

1913 ***Serrate Roulette 13½***

22	A24	10pa on 1 l grn (R)	15.00	15.00
23	A24	10pa on 1 l grn	15.00	15.00
25	A25	10pa on 25 l ultra (R)	18.00	18.00
26	A25	20pa on 2 l car rose	11.00	11.00
27	A24	1pi on 3 l ver	11.00	11.00
28	A26	2pi on 5 l grn (R)	22.50	22.50
29	A24	2½pi on 10 l car rose	25.00	25.00
30	A25	5pi on 40 l dp bl (R)	37.50	30.00
		Nos. 22-30 (8)	155.00	147.50

On Occupation Stamps of 1912

31	O1	10pa on 1 l brn	6.00	6.00
32	O1	20pa on 1 l brn	6.00	6.00
33	O1	1pi on 1 l brn	6.00	6.00

These surcharges were made with handstamps, two of which were required for each surcharge. One or both parts may be found inverted, double or omitted.

Nos. 16-33 exist with forged surcharges.

OCCUPATION STAMPS

Issued under Allied Occupation

Bulgarian Stamps of 1915-19 Handstamped in Violet Blue

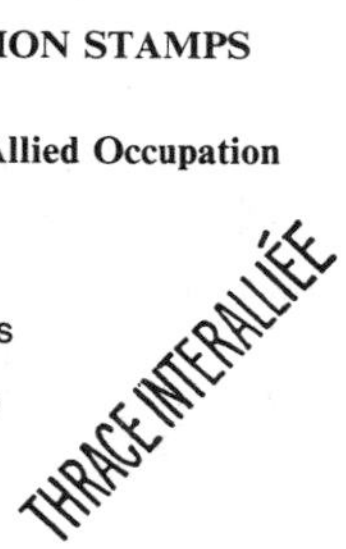

Perf. 11½, 11½x12, 14

1919 Unwmk.

N1	A43	1s black	40	40
N2	A43	2s olive grn	40	40
N3	A44	5s green	22	22
N4	A44	10s rose	22	22
N5	A44	15s violet	32	32
N6	A26	25s indigo & blk	32	32
		Nos. N1-N6 (6)	1.88	1.88

The overprint on Nos. N1-N6 is frequently inverted and known in other positions.

Bulgarian Stamps of 1911-19 Handstamp Overprinted in Red or Black

1919

N7	A43	1s black (R)	5	5
N8	A43	2s olive grn	5	5
N9	A44	5s green	5	5
N10	A44	10s rose	5	5
N11	A44	15s violet	12	7
N12	A26	25s indigo & blk	5	5
N13	A29	1 l chocolate	2.25	1.50
N14	A37a	2 l brn orange	3.75	2.25
N15	A38	3 l claret	5.75	4.50
		Nos. N7-N15 (9)	12.12	8.57

Overprint is vertical, reading up, on Nos. N9-N13.

The following varieties are found in the setting of "INTERALLIEE": Inverted "V" for "A," second "L" inverted, "F" instead of final "E."

Bulgarian Stamps of 1919 Overprinted

1920

N16	A44	5s green	5	5
N17	A44	10s rose	5	5
N18	A44	15s violet	5	5
N19	A44	50s yel brown	25	30

The varieties: "Irteraliiee" and final "e" inverted are found on all values.

Bulgarian Stamps of 1919 Overprinted

1920 ***Perf. 12x11½***

N20	A44	5s green	5	5
a.		Inverted overprint	75	
N21	A44	10s rose	5	5
a.		Inverted overprint	75	
N22	A44	15s violet	5	5
N23	A44	25s deep blue	5	5
N24	A44	50s ocher	6	6

Imperf

N25	A44	30s chocolate	18	22
		Nos. N20-N25 (6)	44	48

No. N25 is not known without overprint.

ISSUED UNDER GREEK OCCUPATION

For Use in Western Thrace

Greek Stamps of 1911-19 Overprinted

Serrate Roulette 13½

1920 Litho. Unwmk.

N26	A24	1 l green	15	15
a.		Inverted overprint	10.00	
N27	A25	2 l rose	15	15
N28	A24	3 l vermilion	15	15
N29	A26	5 l green	15	15
N30	A24	10 l rose	15	15
N31	A25	15 l dl bl	15	15
a.		Inverted overprint	10.00	10.00
b.		Dbl. ovpt., one inverted	12.00	12.00
N32	A25	25 l blue	1.50	1.00
N33	A26	30 l rose	17.50	17.50

N34	A25	40 l indigo	1.75	1.75
N35	A26	50 l vio brn	2.00	2.00
N36	A27	1d ultra	9.00	9.00
N37	A27	2d vermilion	17.50	17.50

Engr.

N38	A25	2 l car rose	1.00	1.00
N39	A24	3 l vermilion	1.00	1.00
N40	A27	1d ultra	27.50	27.50
N41	A27	2d vermilion	9.00	9.00
N42	A27	3d car rose	35.00	35.00
N43	A27	5d ultra	14.00	14.00
N44	A27	10d dp bl	9.00	9.00
		Nos. N26-N44 (19)	146.65	146.15

Nos. N42-N44 are overprinted on the reissues of Greece Nos. 210-212. See footnote below Greece No. 213. Counterfeits exist of Nos. N26-N84.

Overprinted **ΔΙΟΙΚΗΣΙΣ ΔΥΤΙΚΗΣ ΘΡΑΚΗΣ**

N45	A28	25d deep blue	35.00	35.00

This overprint reads: "Administration Western Thrace."

With Additional Overprint

Litho.

N46	A24	1 l green	15	15
N47	A25	2 l rose	15	15
a.		Inverted overprint	65	
N48	A24	10 l rose	20	20
N49	A25	20 l slate	85	85
N50	A26	30 l rose	1.10	1.10

Engr.

N51	A27	2d vermilion	17.50	17.50
N52	A27	3d car rose	10.00	10.00
N53	A27	5d ultra	21.00	21.00
N54	A27	10d deep blue	17.50	17.50
a.		Double overprint	18.00	18.00
		Nos. N46-N54 (9)	68.45	68.45

For Use in Eastern and Western Thrace

Greek Stamps of 1911-19 Overprinted **Διοίκησις Θρακης**

1920 **Litho.**

N55	A24	1 l green	15	15
a.		Pair, one without ovpt.	5.00	
N56	A25	2 l rose	15	15
N57	A24	3 l vermilion	15	15
a.		Double overprint	3.00	
N58	A26	5 l green	15	15
a.		Pair, one without ovpt.	3.00	
N59	A24	10 l rose	90	90
a.		Double overprint	4.00	
N60	A25	20 l slate	90	90
a.		Inverted overprint	5.00	
N61	A25	25 l blue	1.75	1.75
N62	A25	40 l indigo	3.50	3.50
N63	A26	50 l vio brn	4.00	4.00
N64	A27	1d ultra	12.00	12.00
N65	A27	2d vermilion	20.00	20.00

Engr.

N66	A24	3 l vermilion	1.75	1.75
N67	A25	20 l gray lilac	7.75	7.75
N68	A28	25d deep blue	57.50	57.50
		Nos. N55-N68 (14)	110.65	110.65

This overprint reads "Administration Thrace".

With Additional Overprint

Litho.

N69	A25	2 l car rose	30	30
N70	A26	5 l green	1.10	1.10
N71	A25	20 l slate	1.00	1.00
N72	A26	30 l rose	1.00	1.00

Engr.

N73	A27	3d car rose	6.00	6.00
N74	A27	5d ultra	15.00	15.00
N75	A27	10d deep blue	27.50	27.50
		Nos. N69-N75 (7)	51.90	51.90

Turkish Stamps of 1916-20 Surcharged in Blue, Black or Red

Υπάτη Αρμοστεία Θρακης 5 Λεπτά 5

1920 ***Perf. 11½, 12½***

N76	A43	1 l on 5pa org (Bl)	60	75
N77	A32	5 l on 3pi bl	60	75
N78	A30	20 l on 1pi bl grn	60	75
N79	A53	25 l on 5pi on 2pa Prus bl (R)	90	1.00
N80	A49	50 l on 5pi bl & blk (R)	3.50	3.50
N81	A45	1d on 20pa dp rose (Bl)	1.75	1.75
N82	A22	2d on 10pa on 2pa ol grn (R)	2.50	2.50
N83	A57	3d on 1pi dp bl (R)	8.50	8.50
N84	A23	5d on 20pa rose	10.00	10.00
		Nos. N76-N84 (9)	28.95	29.50

Nos. N77, N78 and N84 are on the 1920 issue with designs modified. Nos. N81, N82 and N83 are on stamps with the 1919 overprints.

Varieties found on some values of this issue include: inverted surcharge, double surcharge with one inverted, and surcharge on both face and back.

POSTAGE DUE STAMPS

Issued under Allied Occupation

Bulgarian Postage Due Stamps of 1919 Handstamp Overprinted **THRACE INTERALLIÉE**

1919 **Unwmk.** ***Perf. 12x11½***

NJ1	D6	5s emerald	20	20
NJ2	D6	10s purple	28	28
NJ3	D6	50s blue	42	42

Type of Bulgarian Postage Due Stamps of 1919-22 Overprinted **THRACE OCCIDENTALE**

1920 ***Imperf.***

NJ4	D6	5s emerald	9	9
NJ5	D6	10s deep violet	52	50
NJ6	D6	20s salmon	14	12
NJ7	D6	50s blue	42	35

Perf. 12x11½

NJ8	D6	10s deep violet	35	25
		Nos. NJ4-NJ8 (5)	1.52	1.31

TIBET

LOCATION — A high tableland in Central Asia

GOVT. — A semi-independent state, nominally under control of China (under Communist China since 1950-51).

AREA — 463,200 sq. mi.

POP. — 1,500,000 (approx.)

CAPITAL — Lhasa

Tibet's postage stamps were valid only within its borders.

In 1965 Tibet became an autonomous region of the People's Republic of China.

6⅔ Trangka = 1 Sang

All stamps issued without gum

A1

Lion

A2

Thrace stamps can be mounted in Scott's Greece Album.

1912 **Unwmk.** **Typo.** ***Imperf.***

Native Paper

1	A1	⅙t green	14.00	14.00
2	A1	⅓t ultramarine	19.00	19.00
3	A1	½t purple	19.00	19.00
4	A1	⅔t carmine	30.00	30.00
a.		"POTSAGE"	100.00	100.00
5	A1	1t vermilion	37.50	37.50
6	A1	1s sage green	75.00	75.00

1914

7	A2	4t deep blue	225.00	190.00
8	A2	8t carmine	150.00	110.00

In some 1920-30 printings of Nos. 1-8, European enamel paint was used instead of ink. It has a glossy surface.

A3

Thin White Native Paper

1932 ***Imperf., Pin-perf.***

9	A3	½t orange	22.50	22.50
10	A3	⅔t dark blue	22.50	22.50
11	A3	1t rose carmine	27.50	27.50
12	A3	2t vermilion	32.50	32.50
13	A3	4t emerald	25.00	25.00

Heavy Toned Native Paper

1934 ***Imperf.***

14	A3	½t yellow	3.75	3.75
a.		½t orange	9.50	9.50
15	A3	⅔t dark blue	3.75	3.75
16	A3	1t orange ver	3.75	3.75
a.		1t carmine	7.50	7.50
17	A3	2t red	5.00	5.00
a.		2t org vermilion	3.75	3.75
18	A3	4t olive green	3.75	3.75
a.		25x25mm instead of 24x24mm	17.00	17.00

Excellent counterfeits of Nos. 1-18 exist. Numerous shades of all values.

Nos. 14-18 are also known pin-perf., but not believed to have been regularly issued in this form.

The ½t and 1t exist printed on both sides.

OFFICIAL STAMPS

O1

O2

Various Designs and Sizes Inscribed "STAMP"

Sizes: No. O1, 32½x32½mm. No. O2, 38x28½mm. No. O3, 34x33mm. No. O4, 44x44mm. No. O5, 66x66mm.

1945 **Unwmk.** **Typo.** ***Imperf.***

Native Paper

O1	O1	⅓t bronze grn	*525.00*	*525.00*
O2	O2	⅓t slate black	10.00	10.00
O3	O1	⅔t reddish brn	10.00	10.00
O4	O1	1⅓t olive green	27.50	27.50
O5	O1	1s dark gray bl	65.00	65.00

After 1952, Nos. O1-O5 became available for use as regular postage stamps.

TIMOR

LOCATION — The eastern part of Timor island, Malay archipelago.

GOVT. — Portuguese Overseas Territory

AREA — 7,330 sq. mi.

POP. — 660,000 (est. 1974)

CAPITAL — Dili

The Portuguese territory of Timor was annexed by Indonesia May 3, 1976.

1000 Reis = 1 Milreis

78 Avos = 1 Rupee (1895)

100 Avos = 1 Pataca

100 Centavos = 1 Escudo (1960)

Catalogue values for unused stamps in this country are for Never Hinged items, beginning with Scott 256 in the regular postage section, Scott J31 in the postage due section, and Scott RA11 in the postal tax section.

Stamps of Macao Overprinted in Black or Carmine **TIMOR**

1885 **Unwmk.** ***Perf. 12½, 13½***

1	A1	5r black (C)	2.00	1.10
a.		Double overprint	10.00	10.00
b.		Triple overprint		
2	A1	10r green	2.50	1.65
a.		Overprint on Mozambique stamp	*30.00*	*25.00*
b.		Overprinted on Portuguese India stamp	*140.00*	*125.00*
3	A1	20r rose	4.50	3.00
a.		Double overprint		
b.		Perf. 13½	5.50	4.00

4 A1 25r violet 80 55
a. Perf. 13½ 17.50 10.00
5 A1 40r yellow 2.50 1.90
a. Double overprint
b. Inverted overprint 7.50 7.50
c. Perf. 13½ 12.50 10.00
6 A1 50r blue 1.75 85
a. Perf. 13½ 10.50 8.50
7 A1 80r slate 4.00 1.65
8 A1 100r lilac 2.00 85
a. Double overprint
b. Perf. 13½ 7.00 3.00
9 A1 200r orange 2.75 2.00
a. Perf. 12½ 10.00 3.00
10 A1 300r brown 2.75 1.90
Nos. 1-10 (10) 25.55 15.45

The 20r brown, 25r rose and 50r green were prepared for use but not issued.

The reprints are printed on a smooth white chalky paper, ungummed, with rough perforation 13½, and on thin white paper with shiny white gum and clean-cut perforation 13½. Value of lowest-cost reprints, $2.50 each.

King Luiz — A2

King Carlos — A3

1887 Embossed *Perf. 12½*

11 A2 5r black 1.75 1.50
12 A2 10r green 2.25 2.00
13 A2 20r brt rose 3.00 2.00
14 A2 25r violet 6.00 2.25
15 A2 40r chocolate 10.00 4.00
16 A2 50r blue 10.00 4.00
17 A2 80r gray 12.00 5.00
18 A2 100r yel brown 12.00 6.00
19 A2 200r gray lil 17.50 12.00
20 A2 300r orange 20.00 12.00
Nos. 11-20 (10) 94.50 50.75

Reprints of Nos. 11, 16, 18 and 19 have clean-cut perforation 13½. Value $2.50 each.

Macao No. 44 Surcharged in Black

TIMOR

30 30

1892 Without Gum *Perf. 12½, 13*

21 A7 30r on 300r orange 4.00 4.00

1894 Typo. *Perf. 11½*

22 A3 5r yellow 85 60
23 A3 10r red violet 85 60
24 A3 15r chocolate 1.25 70
25 A3 20r lavender 1.25 70
26 A3 25r green 1.25 70
27 A3 50r light blue 2.25 2.00
a. Perf. 13½ 110.00 100.00
28 A3 75r rose 3.00 2.50
29 A3 80r light green 3.00 2.50
30 A3 100r brown, *buff* 3.00 2.50
31 A3 150r car, *rose* 10.50 6.00
32 A3 200r dk bl, *lt bl* 10.50 6.25
33 A3 300r dk bl, *sal* 12.50 7.75
Nos. 22-33 (12) 50.20 32.80

Stamps of 1887 Surcharged in Red, Green or Black

1 avo
PROVISORIO
仙 壹

1895 Without Gum *Perf. 12½*

34 A2 1a on 5r blk (R) 90 75
35 A2 2a on 10r grn 1.10 75
a. Double surcharge
36 A2 3a on 20r brt rose (G) 1.65 1.10
37 A2 4a on 25r vio 1.65 1.00
38 A2 6a on 40r choc 3.00 1.75
39 A2 8a on 50r bl (R) 3.50 2.00
40 A2 13a on 80r gray 9.00 6.00
41 A2 16a on 100r yel brn 9.00 6.00
42 A2 31a on 200r gray lil 20.00 12.50
43 A2 47a on 300r org (G) 22.50 17.50
Nos. 34-43 (10) 72.30 49.35

No. 21 Surcharged

5 avos
PROVISORIO
仙 伍

1895 Without Gum *Perf. 12½, 13*

44 A7 5a on 30r on 300r org 5.00 4.50

Vasco da Gama Issue
Common Design Types

1898 Engr. *Perf. 14 to 15*

45 CD20 ½a blue grn 95 85
46 CD21 1a red 95 85
47 CD22 2a red vio 95 85
48 CD23 4a yel green 95 85
49 CD24 8a dark blue 1.50 1.25
50 CD25 12a vio brown 1.90 1.40
51 CD26 16a bister brn 2.00 1.90
52 CD27 24a bister 3.50 2.50
Nos. 45-52 (8) 12.70 10.45

400th anniversary of Vasco da Gama's discovery of the route to India.

King Carlos
A5 A6

1898-1903 Typo. *Perf. 11½*
Name and Value in Black Except No. 79

53 A5 ½a gray 35 30
a. Perf. 12½ 2.50 1.75
54 A5 1a orange 35 30
a. Perf. 12½ 2.50 1.75
55 A5 2a light grn 35 30
56 A5 2½a brown 1.25 1.10
57 A5 3a gray vio 1.25 1.10
58 A5 3a gray grn ('03) 1.50 1.00
59 A5 4a sea green 1.25 1.00
60 A5 5a rose ('03) 1.50 1.00
61 A5 6a pale yel brn ('03) 1.50 1.00
62 A5 8a blue 1.50 1.10
63 A5 9a red brn ('03) 1.50 1.00
64 A5 10a slate bl ('00) 1.50 1.10
65 A5 10a gray brn ('03) 1.50 1.00
66 A5 12a rose 3.50 3.00
67 A5 12a dull bl ('03) 10.00 8.50
68 A5 13a violet 3.50 3.00
69 A5 13a red lil ('03) 2.25 1.75
70 A5 15a gray lil ('03) 3.50 2.50
71 A5 16a dark bl, *bl* 3.50 3.00
72 A5 20a brn, *yelsh* ('00) 3.50 3.00
73 A5 22a brn org, *pink* ('03) 3.50 3.50
74 A5 24a brown, *buff* 3.50 3.00
75 A5 31a red lil, *pinkish* 3.50 3.00
76 A5 31a brn, *straw* ('03) 3.50 2.50
77 A5 47a dark bl, *rose* 6.00 4.25
78 A5 47a red vio, *pink* ('03) 4.00 3.25
79 A5 78a blk & red, *bl* ('00) 9.00 6.00
80 A5 78a dl bl, *straw* ('03) 10.00 8.00
Nos. 53-80 (28) 88.05 69.55

Most of Nos. 53-80 were issued without gum.

1899

Black Surcharge

81 A6 10a on 16a dk bl, *bl* 2.50 2.50
82 A6 20a on 31a red lil, *pnksh* 2.50 2.50

Common Design Types pictured in section at front of book.

Surcharged in Black

5
AVOS

1902

On Issue of 1887

83 A2 5a on 25r violet 2.00 1.75
84 A2 5a on 200r gray lil 2.50 2.00
85 A2 6a on 10r bl grn 110.00 95.00
86 A2 6a on 300r orange 2.50 2.25
87 A2 9a on 40r choc 3.00 2.50
88 A2 9a on 100r yel brn 3.00 2.50
89 A2 15a on 20r rose 3.50 2.75
90 A2 15a on 50r blue 110.00 95.00
91 A2 22a on 80r gray 7.50 5.00

Reprints of Nos. 83-88, 90-91, 104A have clean-cut perf. 13½. Value $1 each.

On Issue of 1894

92 A3 5a on 5r yellow 1.25 1.00
a. Inverted surcharge 20.00 20.00
93 A3 5a on 25r green 1.25 1.00
94 A3 5a on 50r lt blue 1.40 1.10
95 A3 6a on 20r lav 1.40 1.10
96 A3 9a on 15r choc 1.40 1.10
97 A3 9a on 75r rose 1.40 1.10
98 A3 15a on 10r red vio 1.75 1.50
99 A3 15a on 100r brn, *buff* 1.75 1.50
100 A3 15a on 300r bl, *sal* 1.75 1.50
101 A3 22a on 80r lt grn 4.25 2.75
102 A3 22a on 200r bl, *blue* 4.25 2.75

On Newspaper Stamp of 1893

103 N2 6a on 2½r brn 75 60
a. Inverted surcharge 17.50 17.50
Nos. 92-103 (12) 22.60 17.00

Nos. 93-97, 99-102 issued without gum.

Stamps of 1898 Overprinted in Black

PROVISORIO

104 A5 3a gray vio 1.75 1.25
104A A5 12a rose 4.00 3.50

Reprint noted after No. 91.

No. 67 Surcharged in Black

10
AVOS

1905

105 A5 10a on 12a dull bl 2.50 2.00

Stamps of 1898-1903 Overprinted in Carmine or Green

REPUBLICA

1911

106 A5 ½a gray 30 30
a. Inverted overprint 3.50 3.00
107 A5 1a orange 30 30
a. Perf. 12½ 1.50 1.50
108 A5 2a light green 40 35
109 A5 3a gray green 40 35
110 A5 5a rose (G) 40 35
111 A5 6a yel brown 40 35
112 A5 9a red brown 50 45
113 A5 10a gray brown 50 45
114 A5 13a red lilac 60 50
115 A5 15a gray lilac 1.25 1.25
116 A5 22a brn org, *pink* 1.25 1.25
117 A5 31a brown, *straw* 1.25 1.25
118 A5 47a red vio, *pink* 2.75 2.25
119 A5 78a dl bl, *straw* 3.75 3.50
Nos. 106-119 (14) 14.05 12.90

Preceding Issues Overprinted in Red

Republica

1913

Without Gum

On Provisional Issue of 1902

120 A3 5a on 5r yellow 1.00 1.00
121 A3 5a on 25r green 1.00 1.00
122 A3 5a on 50r lt bl 3.50 3.50
123 N2 6a on 2½r brn 3.00 2.75
124 A3 6a on 20r lav 1.50 1.25
125 A3 9a on 15r choc 1.50 1.25
126 A3 15a on 100r brn, *buff* 2.50 2.50
127 A3 22a on 80r lt grn 3.50 3.00
128 A3 22a on 200r bl, *bl* 3.50 3.00

On Issue of 1903

129 A5 3a gray grn 3.00 3.00

On Issue of 1905

130 A5 10a on 12a dull bl 1.50 1.50
Nos. 120-130 (11) 25.50 23.75

Overprinted in Green or Red

REPUBLICA

1913

On Provisional Issue of 1902

131 A3 9a on 75r rose (G) 2.25 2.25
132 A3 15a on 10r red vio (G) 2.25 2.25
a. Inverted overprint 8.00 8.00
133 A3 15a on 300r bl, *sal* (R) 3.75 3.75
a. "REUBPLICA" 12.50 12.50
b. "REPBLICAU" 12.50 12.50

On Issue of 1903

134 A5 5a rose (G) 2.50 2.50

Stamps of 1898-1903 Overprinted in Red

REPUBLICA

1913

135 A5 6a yel brown 1.25 1.25
136 A5 9a red brown 1.25 1.25
137 A5 10a gray brown 1.25 1.25
138 A5 13a violet 1.25 1.25
a. Inverted overprint 7.50 7.50
139 A5 13a red lilac 1.50 1.50
140 A5 15a gray lilac 2.25 2.00
141 A5 22a brn org, *pnksh* 2.75 2.50
142 A5 31a red lil, *pnksh* 2.75 2.50
143 A5 31a brown, *straw* 4.00 4.00
144 A5 47a blue, *pink* 4.00 3.50
145 A5 47a red vio, *pink* 4.00 3.50
146 A5 78a dl bl, *straw* 4.50 4.00

No. 79 Overprinted in Red

REPUBLICA

147 A5 78a blk & red, *bl* 5.00 5.00
Nos. 135-147 (13) 35.75 33.50

Vasco da Gama Issue of 1898 Overprinted or Surcharged in Black:

REPUBLICA

REPUBLICA
a

10 A.
b

1913

148 CD20 ½a blue green 65 60
149 CD21 1a red 65 60
150 CD22 2a red violet 65 60
151 CD23 4a yellow green 65 60
152 CD24 8a dark blue 1.25 1.10
153 CD25 10a on 12a vio brn 2.00 2.00
154 CD26 16a bister brown 2.00 1.75
155 CD27 24a bister 2.00 2.00
Nos. 148-155 (8) 9.85 9.25

Ceres — A7

1914-23 Typo. *Perf. 15x14, 12x11½*
Name and Value in Black

156 A7 ½a olive brn 20 15
157 A7 1a black 20 15
158 A7 1½a yel grn ('23) 60 50
159 A7 2a blue grn 25 15
160 A7 3a lilac brn 1.00 75
161 A7 4a carmine 1.00 75
162 A7 6a light vio 1.00 75
163 A7 7a lt grn ('23) 1.25 1.00
164 A7 7½a ultra ('23) 1.75 1.25
165 A7 9a blue ('23) 2.00 1.50
166 A7 10a deep blue 1.00 75
167 A7 11a gray ('23) 1.75 1.50
168 A7 12a yel brn 1.50 1.25

169	A7	15a lilac ('23)	4.50	3.00
170	A7	16a slate	1.50	1.25
171	A7	18a dp bl ('23)	6.00	3.00
172	A7	19a gray grn ('23)	6.00	3.00
173	A7	20a org brown	15.00	6.00
174	A7	36a turq bl ('23)	6.00	3.25
175	A7	40a plum	6.00	3.50
176	A7	54a choc ('23)	6.00	3.25
177	A7	58a brown, *grn*	7.00	5.00
178	A7	72a brt rose ('23)	15.00	10.00
179	A7	76a brn, *rose*	7.50	6.00
180	A7	1p org, *salmon*	14.00	9.00
181	A7	3p grn, *blue*	30.00	20.00
182	A7	5p car rose ('23)	60.00	30.00
		Nos. 156-182 (27)	198.00	116.70

Preceding Issues Overprinted in Carmine

REPUBLICA

1915 *Perf. 11½*

On Provisional Issue of 1902

183	A3	5a on 5r yellow	45	35
184	A3	5a on 25r green	45	35
185	A3	5a on 50r lt blue	45	35
186	A3	6a on 20r lav	45	35
187	A3	9a on 15r lav	45	35
188	A3	9a on 75r rose	50	35
189	A3	15a on 10r red vio	50	35
190	A3	15a on 100r brn, *buff*	50	35
191	A3	15a on 300r bl, *sal*	50	35
192	A3	22a on 80r lt grn	2.00	1.50
193	A3	22a on 200r bl, *bl*	3.00	1.75

On No. 103

194	N2	6a on 2½r brn, perf. 13½	35	30
a.		Perf. 12½	1.25	90
b.		Perf. 11½	2.50	1.75

On No. 104

195	A5	3a gray violet	35	30

On No. 105

196	A5	10a on 12a dl bl	50	40
		Nos. 183-196 (14)	10.45	7.40

Type of 1915 with Additional Surcharge in Black

1/2 Avo
P. P. n.º 68
19-3-1920

199	A3	½a on 5a on 50r lt bl	4.00	3.50
a.		Perf. 11½	8.00	6.00

Nos. 178 and 169 Surcharged

6 avos

1932 *Perf. 12x11½*

200	A7	6a on 72a brt rose	1.00	85
201	A7	12a on 15a lil	1.00	85

"Portugal" and Vasco da Gama's Flagship "San Gabriel" — A8

Wmk. 232 - Maltese Cross

Perf. 11½x12

1935 **Typo.** **Wmk. 232**

202	A8	½a bister	15	10
203	A8	1a olive brown	15	10
204	A8	2a blue green	15	10
205	A8	3a red violet	40	20
206	A8	4a black	40	40
207	A8	5a gray	40	40
208	A8	6a brown	50	40
209	A8	7a bright rose	50	40
210	A8	8a bright blue	80	60
211	A8	10a red orange	80	60
212	A8	12a dark blue	80	60
213	A8	14a olive green	80	60
214	A8	15a maroon	80	60
215	A8	20a orange	80	60
216	A8	30a apple green	80	60
217	A8	40a violet	3.50	1.75
218	A8	50a olive bister	3.50	1.75
219	A8	1p light blue	7.50	6.00
220	A8	2p brn orange	20.00	7.50
221	A8	3p emerald	25.00	9.00
222	A8	5p dark violet	45.00	17.50
		Nos. 202-222 (21)	112.75	49.80

Common Design Types

1938 Unwmk. Engr. *Perf. 13½x13*

Name and Value in Black

223	CD34	1a gray green	18	15
224	CD34	2a org brown	18	15
225	CD34	3a dk vio brn	18	15
226	CD34	4a brt green	18	15
227	CD35	5a dk carmine	18	15
228	CD35	6a slate	28	20
229	CD35	8a rose vio	28	20
230	CD37	10a brt red vio	28	20
231	CD37	12a red	40	35
232	CD37	15a orange	55	35
233	CD36	20a blue	60	45
234	CD36	40a gray black	1.65	1.10
235	CD36	50a brown	2.00	1.10
236	CD38	1p brown car	6.25	4.50
237	CD38	2p olive grn	11.00	4.50
238	CD38	3p blue vio	12.00	8.50
239	CD38	5p red brown	32.50	15.00
		Nos. 223-239 (17)	68.69	37.20

Mozambique Nos. 273, 276, 278, 280, 282 and 283 Surcharged in Black

TIMOR
12
AVOS

1946 *Perf. 13½x13*

240	CD34	1a on 15c dk vio brn	4.50	4.00
241	CD35	4a on 35c brt grn	4.50	4.00
242	CD35	8a on 50c brt red vio	4.50	4.00
243	CD36	10a on 70c brn vio	4.50	4.00
244	CD36	12a on 1e red	4.50	4.00
245	CD37	20a on 1.75e bl	4.50	4.00
		Nos. 240-245 (6)	27.00	24.00

Nos. 223-227 and 229-234 Overprinted "Libertacao"

1947

245A	CD34	1a gray grn	16.00	8.00
245B	CD34	2a org brown	25.00	15.00
245C	CD34	3a dk vio brn	10.00	6.00
245D	CD34	4a brt grn	10.00	6.00
245E	CD35	5a dark car	4.50	2.00
245F	CD35	8a rose vio	2.25	1.50
245G	CD37	10a brt red vio	5.00	2.50
245H	CD37	12a red	5.00	2.50
245I	CD37	15a orange	5.00	2.50
245J	CD36	20a blue	60.00	35.00
m.		Inverted overprint	*75.00*	*75.00*
245K		40a gray blk	12.00	7.25
		Nos. 245A-245K (11)	154.75	88.25

Timor Woman A9

UPU Symbols A10

Designs: 3a, Gong ringer. 4a, Girl with basket. 8a, Aleixo de Ainaro. 10a, 1p, 3p, Heads of various chieftains. 20a, Warrior and horse.

1948 **Litho.** *Perf. 14*

246	A9	1a aqua & dk brn	50	30
247	A9	3a gray & dk brn	1.00	60
248	A9	4a pink & dk grn	1.00	60
249	A9	8a red & bl blk	50	35
250	A9	10a bl grn & org	75	45
251	A9	20a ultra, aqua & bl	70	45
252	A9	1p org, bl & ultra	20.00	10.00
253	A9	3p vio & dk brn	17.50	10.00
a.		Sheet of 8, #246-253	50.00	50.00
		Nos. 246-253 (8)	41.95	22.75

No. 253a sold for 5p.

Lady of Fatima Issue

Common Design Type

1948, Oct.

254	CD40	8a slate gray	4.50	4.50

UPU Issue

1949 Unwmk. *Perf. 14.*

255	A10	16a brn & buff	4.75	4.25

UPU, 75th anniversary.

Catalogue values for unused stamps in this section, from this point to the end of the section, are for Never Hinged items.

Craftsman A11

Timor Woman A12

1950 *Perf. 14½*

256	A11	20a dl vio bl	1.10	70
257	A12	50a dull brown	2.25	1.25

Holy Year Issue

Common Design Types

1950, May *Perf. 13x13½*

258	CD41	40a green	1.50	1.25
259	CD42	70a black brown	2.25	2.00

Blackberry Lily — A13

Designs: Various flowers.

1950 Unwmk. Litho. *Perf. 14½*

260	A13	1a multicolored	24	24
261	A13	3a multicolored	1.25	1.00
262	A13	10a multicolored	1.25	1.00
263	A13	16a multicolored	3.25	1.75
264	A13	20a multicolored	2.50	1.65
265	A13	30a multicolored	1.25	1.10
266	A13	70a multicolored	1.65	1.25
267	A13	1p multicolored	4.00	2.75
268	A13	2p multicolored	5.50	3.75
269	A13	5p multicolored	10.00	6.50
		Nos. 260-269 (10)	30.89	20.99

Holy Year Extension Issue

Common Design Type

1951 *Perf. 14*

270	CD43	86a bl & pale bl	2.00	1.75

Medical Congress Issue

Common Design Type

Design: Weighing baby.

1952 Litho. *Perf. 13½*

271	CD44	10a ol blk & brn	90	85

St. Francis Xavier Issue

Statue of St. Francis Xavier — A14

1952, Oct. 25 *Perf. 14*

Dated "1552-1952"

272	A14	1a black	15	15
273	A14	16a blk brn & brn	90	85
274	A14	1p dk car & gray	3.50	2.00

400th death anniv. of St. Francis Xavier.

Madonna and Child — A15

Stamp of Portugal and Arms of Colonies — A16

1953 *Perf. 13x13½*

275	A15	3a dk brn & dl gray	12	8
276	A15	16a dk brn & cr	80	60
277	A15	50a dk bl & dl gray	1.75	1.35

Exhibition of Sacred Missionary Art, Lisbon, 1951.

Stamp Centenary Issue

1953 Photo. *Perf. 13*

Stamp and Arms Multicolored

278	A16	10a gray & lil	1.10	1.00

Sao Paulo Issue

Common Design Type

1954 Litho. *Perf. 13½*

279	CD46	16a dk brn red, bl & blk	85	70

Map of Timor — A17

1956 Unwmk. *Perf. 14x12½*

Inscription and design in brown, red, green, ultramarine & yellow

280	A17	1a pale salmon	10	5
281	A17	3a pale gray bl	15	5
282	A17	8a buff	25	15
283	A17	24a pale green	25	15
284	A17	32a lemon	35	15
285	A17	40a pale gray	55	30
286	A17	1p yellow	1.65	1.10
287	A17	3p pale blue	3.75	1.50
		Nos. 280-287 (8)	7.05	3.45

Brussels Fair Issue

Exhibition Emblems and View — A18

1958 *Perf. 14½*

288	A18	40a multi	50	40

Tropical Medicine Congress Issue

Common Design Type

Design: Calophyllum inophyllum.

1958 *Perf. 13½*

289	CD47	32a multi	3.00	2.50

An enhanced introduction to the Scott Catalogue begins on Page V. A thorough understanding of the material presented there will greatly aid your use of the catalogue itself.

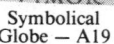

Symbolical Globe — A19 | Carved Elephant Jar — A20

1960 Unwmk. Litho. *Perf. 13½*
290 A19 4.50e multi 50 35

500th death anniv. of Prince Henry the Navigator.

Nos. 280-287 Surcharged with New Value and Bars

1960 Unwmk. *Perf. 14x12½*
Inscription and design in brown, red, green, ultramarine & yellow

291	A17	5c on 1a pale salmon	10	7
292	A17	10c on 3a pale gray bl	10	7
293	A17	20c on 8a buff	10	9
294	A17	30c on 24a pale grn	15	7
295	A17	50c on 32a lemon	15	7
296	A17	1e on 40a pale gray	35	15
297	A17	2e on 40a pale gray	40	20
298	A17	5e on 1p yellow	60	35
299	A17	10e on 3p pale blue	1.65	1.50
300	A17	15e on 3p pale blue	2.00	1.40
		Nos. 291-300 (10)	5.60	3.97

1961 Litho. *Perf. 11½x12*

Native Art: 10c, House on stilts. 20c, Madonna and Child. 30c, Silver rosary. 50c, Two men in boat (horiz.). 1e, Silver box in shape of temple. 2.50e, Archer. 4.50e, Elephant. 5e, Man climbing tree. 10e, Woman carrying pot on head. 20e, Cockfight. 50e, House on stilts and animals.

Multicolored Designs

301	A20	5c pale vio	8	8
302	A20	10c pale grn	8	8
a.		Value & legend inverted	*10.00*	*10.00*
303	A20	20c pale blue	16	12
304	A20	30c rose	24	12
305	A20	50c pale grnsh bl	16	12
306	A20	1e bister	70	12
307	A20	2.50e pale ol bis	48	16
308	A20	4.50e lt salmon	48	16
309	A20	5e lt gray	60	16
310	A20	10e gray	1.40	32
311	A20	20e yellow	2.75	1.00
312	A20	50e lt bluish gray	9.25	2.50
		Nos. 301-312 (12)	16.38	4.94

Sports Issue
Common Design Type

Sports: 50c, Duck hunting. 1e, Horseback riding. 1.50e, Swimming. 2e, Gymnastics. 2.50e, Soccer. 15e, Big game hunting.

1962, Mar. 22 Unwmk. *Perf. 13½*
Multicolored Designs

313	CD48	50c gray & bis	10	10
314	CD48	1e olive bis	45	16
315	CD48	1.50e gray & bl grn	45	25
316	CD48	2e buff	45	25
317	CD48	2.50e gray	50	38
318	CD48	15e salmon	1.90	1.25
		Nos. 313-318 (6)	3.85	2.39

Anti-Malaria Issue
Common Design Type

Design: Anopheles sundaicus.

1962 Litho. *Perf. 13½*
319 CD49 2.50e multi 75 60

National Overseas Bank Issue
Common Design Type

Design: 2.50e, Manuel Pinheiro Chagas.

1964, May 16 Unwmk. *Perf. 13½*
320 CD51 2.50e grn, gray, yel, lt bl & blk 75 60

ITU Issue
Common Design Type

1965, May 17 Litho. *Perf. 14½*
321 CD52 1.50e multi 1.50 90

National Revolution Issue
Common Design Type

Design: 4.50e, Dr. Vieira Machado Academy and Dili Health Center.

1966, May 28 Litho. *Perf. 11½*
322 CD53 4.50e multi 1.50 90

Navy Club Issue
Common Design Type

Designs: 10c, Capt. Gago Coutinho and gunboat Patria. 4.50e, Capt. Sacadura Cabral and seaplane Lusitania.

1967, Jan. 31 Litho. *Perf. 13*

323	CD54	10c multi	2.00	1.00
324	CD54	4.50e multi	2.00	1.00

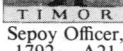

Sepoy Officer, 1792 — A21 | Our Lady of Fatima — A22

Designs: 1e, Officer, 1815. 1.50e, Infantry soldier, 1879. 2e, Infantry soldier, 1890. 2.50e, Infantry officer, 1903. 3e, Sapper, 1918. 4.50e, Special forces soldier, 1964. 10e, Paratrooper, 1964.

1967, Feb. 12 Photo. *Perf. 13½*

325	A21	35c multi	25	16
326	A21	1e multi	1.50	50
327	A21	1.50e multi	35	16
328	A21	2e multi	35	16
329	A21	2.50e multi	35	22
330	A21	3e multi	50	22
331	A21	4.50e multi	70	35
332	A21	10e multi	1.25	50
		Nos. 325-332 (8)	5.25	2.27

1967, May 13 Litho. *Perf. 12½x13*
333 A22 3e multi 60 30

50th anniversary of the apparition of the Virgin Mary to three shepherd children at Fatima, Portugal.

Cabral Issue

Map of Brazil, by Lopo Homem-Reineis, 1519 — A23

1968, Apr. 22 Litho. *Perf. 14*
334 A23 4.50e multi 80 50

See note after Macao No. 416.

Admiral Coutinho Issue
Common Design Type

Design: 4.50e, Adm. Coutinho and frigate Adm. Gago Coutinho.

1969, Feb. 17 Litho. *Perf. 14*
335 CD55 4.50e multi 1.10 85

View of Dili, 1834 — A24

1969, July 25 Litho. *Perf. 14*
336 A24 1e multi 30 20

Bicentenary of Dili as capital of Timor.

da Gama Medal in St. Jerome's Convent A25 | Emblem of King Manuel, St. Jerome's Convent A26

Vasco da Gama Issue

1969, Aug. 29 Litho. *Perf. 14*
337 A25 5e multi 40 30

Vasco da Gama (1469-1524), navigator.

Administration Reform Issue
Common Design Type

1969, Sept. 25 Litho. *Perf. 14*
338 CD56 5e multi 40 25

King Manuel I Issue

1969, Dec. 1 Litho. *Perf. 14*
339 A26 4e multi 40 25

King Manuel I, 500th birth anniv.

Capt. Ross Smith, Arms of Great Britain, Portugal and Australia, and Map of Timor A27

1969, Dec. 9
340 A27 2e multi 50 40

50th anniv. of the first England to Australia flight of Capt. Ross Smith and Lt. Keith Smith.

Marshal Carmona Issue
Common Design Type

Design: 1.50e, Antonio Oscar Carmona in civilian clothes.

1970, Nov. 15 Litho. *Perf. 14*
341 CD57 1.50e multi 20 15

Lusiads Issue

Sailing Ship and Monks Preaching to Islanders — A28

1972, May 25 Litho. *Perf. 13*
342 A28 1e brn & multi 20 20

4th centenary of publication of The Lusiads by Luiz Camoens.

Olympic Games Issue
Common Design Type

Design: 4.50e, Soccer, Olympic emblem.

1972, June 20 *Perf. 14x13½*
343 CD59 4.50e multi 50 30

Lisbon-Rio de Janeiro Flight Issue
Common Design Type

Design: 1e, Sacadura Cabral and Gago Coutinho in cockpit of "Lusitania."

1972, Sept. 20 Litho. *Perf. 13½*
344 CD60 1e multi 25 25

WMO Centenary Issue
Common Design Type

1973, Dec. 15 Litho. *Perf. 13*
345 CD61 20e multi 1.75 1.25

AIR POST STAMPS

Common Design Type

1938 Unwmk. Engr. *Perf. 13½x13*
Name and Value in Black

C1	CD39	1a scarler	50	42
C2	CD39	2a purple	50	42
C3	CD39	3a orange	50	42
C4	CD39	5a ultra	50	42
C5	CD39	10a lil brn	1.25	75
C6	CD39	20a dk grn	2.50	1.10
C7	CD39	50a red brn	5.00	2.75
C8	CD39	70a rose car	5.50	4.25
C9	CD39	1p magenta	10.00	4.25
		Nos. C1-C9 (9)	26.25	14.78

No. C7 exists with overprint "Exposicao Internacional de Nova York, 1939-1940" and Trylon and Perisphere.

Mozambique Nos. C3, C4, C6, C7 and C9 Surcharged in Black

TIMOR
12
AVOS
≈ ≈≈≈≈ ≈

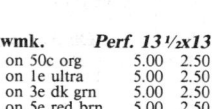

1946 Unwmk. *Perf. 13½x13*

C10	CD39	8a on 50c org	5.00	2.50
C11	CD39	12a on 1e ultra	5.00	2.50
C12	CD39	40a on 3e dk grn	5.00	2.50
C13	CD39	50a on 5e red brn	5.00	2.50
C14	CD39	1p on 10e mag	5.00	2.50
		Nos. C10-C14 (5)	25.00	12.50

Nos. C1-C9 Overprinted "Libertacao"

1947

C15	CD39	1a scarlet	17.50	9.00
C16	CD39	2a purple	17.50	9.00
C17	CD39	3a orange	17.50	9.00
C18	CD39	5a ultra	17.50	9.00
C19	CD39	10a lil brn	5.00	3.25
C20	CD39	20a dk grn	5.00	3.25
C21	CD39	50a red brn	5.00	3.25
C22	CD39	70a rose car	20.00	6.50
C23	CD39	1p magenta	7.00	3.25
		Nos. C15-C23 (9)	112.00	55.50

POSTAGE DUE STAMPS

D1

1904 Unwmk. Typo. *Perf. 12*
Without Gum
Name and Value in Black

J1	D1	1a yellow green	50	50
J2	D1	2a slate	50	50
J3	D1	5a yellow brown	1.50	1.50
J4	D1	6a red orange	1.50	1.50
J5	D1	10a gray brown	2.00	2.00
J6	D1	15a red brown	2.75	2.75
J7	D1	24a dull blue	6.00	5.50
J8	D1	40a carmine	6.00	5.50
J9	D1	50a orange	8.50	7.50
J10	D1	1p dull violet	15.00	13.00
		Nos. J1-J10 (10)	44.25	40.25

Overprinted in Carmine or Green

REPUBLICA

1911 Without Gum

J11	D1	1a yellow green	25	25
J12	D1	2a slate	25	25
a.		Inverted overprint		
J13	D1	5a yellow brown	25	25
J14	D1	6a deep orange	35	35
J15	D1	10a gray brown	75	60

J16	D1 15a brown	1.25	1.10
J17	D1 24a dull blue	2.25	2.00
J18	D1 40a carmine (G)	2.50	2.50
J19	D1 50a orange	2.50	2.50
J20	D1 1p dull violet	7.50	7.00
	Nos. J11-J20 (10)	17.85	16.80

Nos. J1-J10 Overprinted in Red or Green

REPUBLICA

1913 **Without Gum**

J21	D1 1a yellow green	6.00	6.00
J22	D1 2a slate	6.00	6.00
J23	D1 5a yellow brown	3.00	3.00
J24	D1 6a deep orange	3.00	3.00
a.	Inverted surcharge		
J25	D1 10a gray brown	4.00	4.00
J26	D1 15a red brown	4.00	4.00
J27	D1 24a dull blue	4.00	4.00
J28	D1 40a carmine (G)	4.00	4.00
J29	D1 50a orange	8.00	8.00
J30	D1 1p gray violet	8.00	8.00
	Nos. J21-J30 (10)	50.00	50.00

Catalogue values for unused stamps in this section, from this point to the end of the section, are for Never Hinged items.

Common Design Type

1952 Photo. & Typo. *Perf. 14*

Numeral in Red, Frame Multicolored

J31	CD45 1a chocolate	20	20
J32	CD45 3a brown	20	20
J33	CD45 5a dark green	20	20
J34	CD45 10a green	20	20
J35	CD45 30a purple	40	40
J36	CD45 1p brn carmine	85	85
	Nos. J31-J36 (6)	2.05	2.05

WAR TAX STAMP

Regular Issue of 1914 Surcharged in Red

2 AVOS

TAXA DE GUERRA

1919 Unwmk. *Perf. 15x14*

Without Gum

MR1	A7 2a on ½a ol brn	10.00	5.00

See note after Macao No. MR2.

NEWSPAPER STAMPS

King Luiz — N1

Stamps of Macao Surcharged in Black

1892 Unwmk. *Perf. 12½*

Without Gum

P1	N1 2½r on 20r brt rose	2.00	75
a.	"TIMOR" inverted		
P2	N1 2½r on 40r choc	2.00	75
a.	"TIMOR" inverted		
b.	Perf. 13½	4.50	3.00
c.	As "a," perf. 13½		
P3	N1 2½r on 80r gray	2.00	75
a.	"TIMOR" inverted		
b.	Perf. 13½	10.00	6.00

N2

N3

1893-95 Typo. *Perf. 11½, 13½*

P4	N2 2½r brown	40	35
a.	Perf. 12½	2.00	1.50
P5	N3 ½a on 2½r brn ('95)	45	30

POSTAL TAX STAMPS

Pombal Issue

Common Design Types

1925 Unwmk. *Perf. 12½*

RA1	CD28 2a lake & black	40	40
RA2	CD29 2a lake & black	40	40
RA3	CD30 2a lake & black	40	40

Type of War Tax Stamp of Portuguese India Overprinted in Red

Instrução

D. L. n.º 7 de 3 2-1934

1934-35 *Perf. 12*

RA4	WT1 2a green & blk	4.00	3.00
RA5	WT1 5a green & blk	6.00	3.00

Surcharged in Black

RA6	WT1 7a on ½a rose & blk ('35)	6.00	4.00

The tax was for local education.

Type of War Tax Stamp of Portuguese India Overprinted in Black

Assistência

D. L. n.º 72

1936 *Perf. 12x11½*

RA7	WT1 10a rose & black	4.00	3.00

1937 *Perf. 11½*

RA8	WT1 10a green & blk	3.00	2.50

PT1

PT2

1948 Unwmk. Typo. *Perf. 11½*

Without Gum

RA9	PT1 10a dark blue	3.00	2.00
RA10	PT1 20a green	3.50	2.50

The 20a bears a different emblem.

Catalogue values for unused stamps in this section, from this point to the end of the section, are for Never Hinged items.

1960 Without Gum *Perf. 11½*

RA11	PT2 70c dark blue	80	80
RA12	PT2 1.30e green	1.50	1.50

Type of 1960 Redrawn

1967 Typo. *Perf. 10½*

Without Gum

RA13	PT2 70c deep blue	1.00	75
RA14	PT2 1.30e emerald	1.75	1.35

The denominations of Nos. RA13-RA14 are 2mm high. They are 2½mm high on Nos. RA11-RA12. Other differences exist. The printed area of No. RA13 measures 18x31mm; "Republica" 16mm.

Type of 1960

1967 Serif Type Face

RA14A	PT2 70c deep blue	1.75	1.50

Type of 1960, 2nd Redrawing

1967-68 Typo. *Perf. 10½*

Without Gum

RA15	PT2 70c violet blue	70	70
RA16	PT2 1.30e bluish grn ('68)	1.50	1.50

The printed area measures 13x30mm on Nos. RA15-RA16; "Republica" measures 10½mm.

Woman and Star — PT3

1969-70 Litho. *Perf. 13½*

RA17	PT3 30c vio bl & lt bl ('70)	10	10
RA18	PT3 50c dl org & maroon	10	10
RA19	PT3 1e yellow & brown	20	15

The 2.50e and 10e in design PT3 were revenue stamps.

Nos. RA15-RA16 Surcharged in Red or Carmine

D. L. n.º 776

$80

1970 Typo. *Perf. 10½*

Without Gum

RA20	PT2 30c on 70c vio bl	7.00	5.00
RA21	PT2 30c on 1.30e bluish grn	7.00	5.00
RA22	PT2 50c on 70c vio bl	15.00	9.00
RA23	PT2 50c on 1.30e bluish grn	7.00	5.00
RA24	PT2 1e on 70c vio bl (C)	*45.00*	*45.00*
RA25	PT2 1e on 1.30e bluish grn	8.50	6.00

POSTAL TAX DUE STAMPS

Pombal Issue

Common Design Types

1925 Unwmk. *Perf. 12½*

RAJ1	CD31 4a lake & blk	45	45
RAJ2	CD32 4a lake & blk	45	45
RAJ3	CD33 4a lake & blk	45	45

TOGO

LOCATION — Western Africa, bordering on the Gulf of Guinea.
GOVT. — Republic
AREA — 20,400 sq. mi.
POP. — 2,890,000 (est. 1984)
CAPITAL — Lome

The German Protectorate of Togo was occupied by Great Britain and France in World War I, and later mandated to them. The British area became part of Ghana. The French area was granted internal autonomy in 1956 and achieved independence in 1958. See Togo in Vol. 1 for British issues.

Togo German, British and French Occupation stamps can be mounted in Scott's Germany Part II Album.

100 Pfennig = 1 Mark
12 Pence = 1 Shilling
100 Centimes = 1 Franc

Catalogue values for unused stamps in this country are for Never Hinged items, beginning with Scott 309 in the regular postage section, Scott B11 in the semi-postal section, Scott C14 in the airpost section, and Scott J32 in the postage due section.

German Protectorate

AREA - 34,934 sq. mi.
POP. - 1,000,368 (1913)

A1

A2

Stamps of Germany Overprinted in Black

1897 Unwmk. *Perf. 13½x14½*

1	A1 3pf dark brn	3.75	6.50
a	3pf yellow brown	5.50	*16.00*
b	3pf reddish brown	14.00	*40.00*
2	A1 5pf green	3.50	2.00
3	A2 10pf carmine	3.50	2.25
4	A2 20pf ultra	4.50	*13.50*
5	A2 25pf orange	30.00	*55.00*
6	A2 50pf red brown	30.00	*55.00*

Kaiser's Yacht, the "Hohenzollern"

A3 A4

1900 Typo. *Perf. 14*

7	A3 3pf brown	65	65
8	A3 5pf green	11.00	65
9	A3 10pf carmine	25.00	65
10	A3 20pf ultra	80	1.40
11	A3 25pf org & blk, *yel*	80	*8.25*
12	A3 30pf org & blk, *sal*	1.00	*8.25*
13	A3 40pf lake & blk	80	*8.25*
14	A3 50pf pur & blk, *sal*	1.00	*8.25*
15	A3 80pf lake & blk, *rose*	1.90	*16.50*

Engr.

Perf. 14½x14

16	A4 1m carmine	2.25	*45.00*
17	A4 2m blue	3.50	*80.00*
18	A4 3m black vio	5.00	*135.00*
19	A4 5m slate & car	80.00	*300.00*
	Nos. 7-19 (13)	133.70	*612.85*

Counterfeit cancellations are found on Nos. 10-19 and 22.

Wmk. Lozenges (125)

1909-19 Typo. *Perf. 14*

20	A3 3pf brown ('19)	65	
21	A3 5pf green	80	1.40
22	A3 10pf car ('14)	1.00	*90.00*

Engr.

Perf. 14½x14

23	A4 5m sl & car ('15)	12.00	

Nos. 20 and 23 were never placed in use.

Stamps issued under British Occupation, Nos. 33-91, are listed in Volume I.

Issued under French Occupation

Stamps of German Togo Surcharged:

c

TOGO
Occupation
franco-anglaise

05 05 05
d e f

10 10 10
g h i

Wmk. Lozenges (5pf and 10pf) (125), Unwmk. (other values)

1914 *Perf. 14, 14½*

151	A3(c+d)	5c on 3pf brn	27.50	27.50
152	A3(c+e)	5c on 3pf brn	27.50	27.50
153	A3(c+f)	5c on 3pf brn	27.50	27.50
154	A3(c+g)	10c on 5pf grn	16.50	20.00
a		Double surcharge	625.00	625.00
155	A3(c+h)	10c on 5pf grn	19.00	22.50
156	A3(c+i)	10c on 5pf grn	25.00	26.50
158	A3(c)	20pf ultra	26.50	30.00
a		3½mm between "TOGO" and "Occupation"		1,500.
159	A3(c)	25pf org & blk, *yel*	30.00	35.00
160	A3(c)	30pf org & blk, *sal*	82.50	90.00
161	A3(c)	40pf lake & blk	375.00	400.00
162	A3(c)	80pf lake & blk, *rose*	375.00	425.00
		Nos. 151-162 (11)	1,032.	1,131.

Surcharged or Overprinted in Sans-Serif Type:

TOGO
Occupation
franco anglaise
05

TOGO
Occupation
franco anglaise

1915

164	A3	5c on 3pf brn		*2,800.*
165	A3	5pf green	575.00	350.00
166	A3	10pf carmine	700.00	350.00
a		Inverted overprint		*15,000.*
167	A3	20pf ultra	*900.00*	650.00
168	A3	25pf org & blk, *yel*	*4,800.*	*7,500.*
169	A3	30pf org & blk, *sal*	*4,800.*	*7,500.*
170	A3	40pf lake & blk	*4,500.*	*7,500.*
171	A3	50pf pur & blk, *sal*	*13,250.*	*13,250.*
172	A4	1m carmine		
173	A4	2m blue		*13,000.*
174	A4	3m blk vio		*13,000.*
175	A4	5m slate & car		

Stamps of Dahomey, 1913-17, Overprinted

TOGO
Occupation
franco-
anglaise

1916-17 **Unwmk.** *Perf. 13½x14*

176	A5	1c vio & blk	12	12
177	A5	2c choc & rose	12	12
178	A5	4c blk & brn	12	12
a		Double overprint	160.00	160.00
179	A5	5c yel grn & bl grn	35	35
180	A5	10c org red & rose	22	22
181	A5	15c brn org & dk vio	55	55
182	A5	20c gray & choc	35	35
183	A5	25c ultra & dp bl	35	35
184	A5	30c choc & vio	35	35
185	A5	35c brn & blk	55	55
186	A5	40c blk & red org	50	50
187	A5	45c gray & ultra	35	35
188	A5	50c choc & brn	35	35
189	A5	75c bl & vio	2.25	2.25
190	A5	1fr bl grn & blk	3.50	3.50
191	A5	2fr buff & choc	4.50	4.50
192	A5	5fr vio & do bl	6.25	6.25
		Nos. 176-192 (17)	20.78	20.78

All values of the 1916-17 issue exist on chalky paper and all but the 15c, 25c and 35c on ordinary paper.

French Mandate

AREA - 21,893 sq. mi.
POP. - 780,497 (1938)

Type of Dahomey, 1913-39, Overprinted **TOGO**

1921

193	A5	1c gray & yel grn	5	5
a		Overprint omitted	60.00	
194	A5	2c bl & org	5	5
195	A5	4c ol grn & org	10	10
196	A5	5c dl red & blk	10	10
a		Overprint omitted	275.00	
197	A5	10c bl grn & yel grn	12	12
198	A5	15c brn & car	35	35
199	A5	20c bl grn & org	45	45
200	A5	25c sl & org	28	28
201	A5	30c dp rose & ver	35	35
202	A5	35c red brn & yel grn	45	45
203	A5	40c bl grn & ol	65	65
204	A5	45c red brn & ol	65	65
205	A5	50c dp bl	38	38
206	A5	75c dl red & ultra	65	65
207	A5	1fr gray & ultra	70	70
208	A5	2fr ol grn & rose	2.25	2.25
209	A5	5fr org & blk	2.75	2.75
		Nos. 193-209 (17)	10.33	10.33

Stamps and Type of 1921 Surcharged **60 =** **60 =**

1922-25

210	A5	25c on 15c ol brn & rose red ('25)	12	12
211	A5	25c on 2fr ol grn & rose ('24)	22	22
212	A5	25c on 5fr org & blk ('24)	22	22
213	A5	60c on 75c vio, *pnksh* ('22)	45	45
a		"60" omitted	90.00	90.00
214	A5	65c on 45c red brn & ol ('25)	70	70
a		"TOGO" omitted	70.00	
215	A5	85c on 75c dl red & ultra ('25)	80	80
		Nos. 210-215 (6)	2.51	2.51

Coconut Grove — A6

Cacao Trees — A7

Oil Palms — A8

1924-38 **Typo.**

216	A6	1c yel & blk	5	5
217	A6	2c dp rose & blk	5	5
218	A6	4c dk bl & blk	5	5
219	A6	5c dp org & blk	5	5
220	A6	10c red vio & blk	5	5
221	A6	15c grn & blk	5	5
222	A7	20c gray & blk	5	5
223	A7	25c grn & blk, *yel*	25	25
224	A7	30c gray grn & blk	5	5
225	A7	30c dl grn & lt grn ('27)	12	12
226	A7	35c lt brn & blk	35	35
227	A7	35c dp bl grn & grn ('38)	10	10
228	A7	40c red org & blk	5	5
229	A7	45c car & blk	12	12
230	A7	50c ocher & blk, *bluish*	5	5
231	A7	55c vio bl & car rose ('38)	35	35
232	A7	60c vio brn & blk, *pnksh*	5	5
233	A7	60c dp red ('26)	15	15
234	A7	65c gray lil & brn	12	12
235	A7	75c bl & blk	28	28
236	A7	80c ind & dl vio ('38)	45	35
237	A7	85c brn org & brn	40	40
238	A7	90c brn red & cer ('27)	50	50
239	A8	1fr red brn & blk, *bluish*	42	42
240	A8	1fr blue ('26)	15	15
241	A8	1fr gray lil & grn ('28)	1.25	1.20
242	A8	1fr dk red & red org ('38)	15	12
243	A8	1.10fr vio & dk brn ('28)	2.65	2.00
244	A8	1.25fr mag & rose ('33)	45	38
245	A8	1.50fr bl & lt bl ('27)	15	15
246	A8	1.75fr bis & pink ('33)	4.50	1.20
247	A8	1.75fr vio bl & ultra ('38)	45	35
248	A8	2fr bl blk & blk, *bluish*	55	55
249	A8	3fr bl grn & red org ('27)	65	65
250	A8	5fr red org & blk, *bluish*	1.00	1.00
251	A8	10fr ol brn & rose ('26)	1.00	1.00
252	A8	20fr brn red & blk, *yel* ('26)	1.20	1.20
		Nos. 216-252 (37)	18.31	14.01

No. 240 Surcharged with New Value and Bars in Red

1926

253	A8	1.25fr on 1fr lt bl	20	20

Colonial Exposition Issue
Common Design Types

Engr., "TOGO" Typo. in Black

1931, Apr. 13 *Perf. 12½*

254	CD70	40c dp grn	2.25	2.25
255	CD71	50c violet	2.25	2.25
256	CD72	90c red org	2.25	2.25
257	CD73	1.50fr dl bl	2.25	2.25

Paris International Exposition Issue
Common Design Types

1937 *Perf. 13*

258	CD74	20c dp vio	70	70
259	CD75	30c dk grn	70	70
260	CD76	40c car rose	70	70
261	CD77	50c dk brn	70	70
262	CD78	90c red	70	70
263	CD79	1.50fr ultra	70	70
		Nos. 258-263 (6)	4.20	4.20

Common Design Types pictured in section at front of book.

Colonial Arts Exhibition Issue
Souvenir Sheet
Common Design Type

1937 *Imperf.*

264	CD77	3fr Prus bl & blk	2.65	2.65

Caillié Issue
Common Design Type

1939, Apr. 5 *Perf. 12½x12*

265	CD81	90c org brn & org	35	35
266	CD81	2fr brt vio	35	35
267	CD81	2.25fr ultra & dk bl	35	35

New York World's Fair Issue
Common Design Type

1939, May 10

268	CD82	1.25fr car lake	35	35
269	CD82	2.25fr ultra	35	35

Togolese Women
A9 A12

Mono River Bank — A10

Hunters A11

1941 **Engr.** *Perf. 12½*

270	A9	2c brn vio	5	5
271	A9	3c yel grn	5	5
272	A9	4c brn blk	5	5
273	A9	5c lil rose	5	5
274	A9	10c light bl	5	5
275	A9	15c chestnut	5	5
276	A10	20c plum	5	5
277	A10	25c vio blue	5	5
278	A10	30c brn blk	5	5
279	A10	40c dk car	5	5
280	A10	45c dk grn	9	9
281	A10	50c chestnut	12	12
282	A10	60c red vio	12	12
283	A11	70c black	30	30
284	A11	90c lt vio	40	40
285	A11	1fr yel grn	20	20
286	A11	1.25fr cerise	40	40
287	A11	1.40fr org brn	20	20
288	A11	1.60fr orange	30	30
289	A11	2fr lt ultra	30	30
290	A12	2.25fr ultra	50	50
291	A12	2.50fr lil rose	40	40
292	A12	3fr brn vio	35	35
293	A12	5fr vermilion	38	38
294	A12	10fr rose vio	55	55
295	A12	20fr brn blk	1.00	1.00
		Nos. 270-295 (26)	6.11	6.11

Mono River Bank and Marshal Petain A12a

1941 **Engr.** *Perf. 12½x12*

296	A12a	1fr green	22
297	A12a	2.50fr blue	22

Nos. 296-297 were issued by the Vichy government, and were not placed on sale in Togo. This is also true of nine stamps of types A9-A12 without "RF," issued in 1942-44.

Nos. 231, 238, 284 Surcharged with New Values in Various Colors

a **1 fr. 50**

b **4 fr.**

Perf. 14x13½, 12½

1943-44 **Unwmk.**

301	A7(a)	1.50fr on 55c vio bl & car rose (Bk)	40	40
302	A7(a)	1.50fr on 90c brn red & cer (Bk)	40	40
303	A11(b)	3.50fr on 90c lt vio (Bk)	35	35
304	A11(b)	4fr on 90c lt vio (R)	35	35
305	A11(b)	5fr on 90c lt vio (Bl)	65	65
306	A11(b)	5.50fr on 90c lt vio (Br)	80	80
307	A11(b)	10fr on 90c lt vio (G) ('44)	80	80
308	A11(b)	20fr on 90c lt vio (R)	1.10	1.10
		Nos. 301-308 (8)	4.85	4.85

Catalogue values for unused stamps in this section, from this point to the end of the section, are for Never Hinged items.

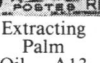

Extracting Palm Oil — A13

Hunter — A14

Cotton Spinners — A15

Village of Atakpame A16

Red-fronted Gazelles A17

Houses of the Cabrais A18

1947, Oct. 6 Engr. *Perf. 12½*

309	A13	10c	dark red	5	5
310	A13	30c	brt ultra	5	5
311	A13	50c	bluish grn	5	5
312	A14	60c	lilac rose	10	5
313	A14	1fr	chocolate	12	10
314	A14	1.20fr	yel grn	15	12
315	A15	1.50fr	brn org	22	22
316	A15	2fr	olive	22	20
317	A15	2.50fr	gray blk	50	42
318	A16	3fr	slate	22	20
319	A16	3.60fr	rose car	35	30
320	A16	4fr	Prus grn	22	20
321	A17	5fr	blk brn	62	15
322	A17	6fr	ultra	62	55
323	A17	10fr	org red	70	15
324	A18	15fr	dp yel grn	80	35
325	A18	20fr	grnsh blk	80	50
326	A18	25fr	lilac rose	80	50
			Nos. 309-326 (18)	6.59	4.16

Military Medal Issue

Common Design Type

Engr. & Typo.

1952, Dec. 1 *Perf. 13*

327 CD101 15fr multi 2.25 2.25

Gathering Palm Nuts — A19

1954, Nov. 29 Engr.

328	A19	8fr	vio & vio brn	55	45
329	A19	15fr	ind & dk brn	65	35

Goliath Beetle — A20

1955, May 2

330 A20 8fr blk & grn 1.20 90

Intl. Exhibition for Wildlife Protection, Paris, May 1955.

FIDES Issue

Common Design Type

Design: 15fr, Teacher and children planting tree.

1956 Unwmk. *Perf. 13x12½*

331 CD103 15fr dk vio brn & org brn 3.25 1.40

Republic

Woman Holding Flag — A21

1957, June 8 Engr. *Perf. 13*

332 A21 15fr dk bl grn, sep & red 40 10

Konkomba Helmet — A22

Teak Forest A23

Design: 4fr, 5fr, 6fr, 8fr, 10fr, Buffon's kob.

1957, Oct. Unwmk.

333	A22	30c	vio & claret	5	5
334	A22	50c	indigo & bl	5	5
335	A22	1fr	pur & lil rose	5	5
336	A22	2fr	dk brn & olive	5	5
337	A22	3fr	blk & green	5	5
338	A22	4fr	blue & gray	28	10
339	A22	5fr	bluish gray & mag	28	10
340	A22	6fr	crim rose & bl gray	28	10
341	A22	8fr	bluish gray & vio	28	10
342	A22	10fr	grn & red brn	28	10
343	A23	15fr	multi	14	9
344	A23	20fr	vio, mar & org	18	9
345	A23	25fr	ind & bis brn	20	14
346	A23	40fr	dk brn, ol & dk grn	32	18
			Nos. 333-346 (14)	2.49	1.25

See Nos. 350-363.

Flags, Dove and UN Emblem — A24

1958, Dec. 10 Engr. *Perf. 13*

347 A24 20fr dk grn & rose red 22 20

Universal Declaration of Human Rights, 10th anniversary.

Flower Issue

Common Design Type

Designs: 5fr, Flower of Bombax tree (kapok). 20fr, Tectona grandis (teakwood) flower (horiz.).

Perf. 12x12½, 12½x12

1959, Jan. 15 Photo. Unwmk.

348	CD104	5fr	dp bl, rose & grn	10	7
349	CD104	20fr	blk, yel & grn	14	7

Types of 1957 Inscribed: "Republique du Togo"

1959, Jan. 15 Engr. *Perf. 13*

Designs as Before

350	A22	30c	ultra & gray	5	5
351	A22	50c	org & brt grn	5	5
352	A22	1fr	red lil & lt ol grn	5	5
353	A22	2fr	ol & bl grn	5	5
354	A22	3fr	vio & rose car	5	5
355	A22	4fr	lil rose & pale pur	18	8
356	A22	5fr	grn & brn	18	12
357	A22	6fr	ultra & gray bl	18	12
358	A22	8fr	sl grn & bis	18	9
359	A22	10fr	vio & lt brn	18	9
360	A23	15fr	dk brn, bis & cl	12	9
361	A23	20fr	blk, bl grn & brn	18	8
362	A23	25fr	sep, red brn, ol & vio	30	18
363	A23	40fr	dk grn, org brn & bl	30	20
			Nos. 350-363 (14)	2.05	1.30

"Five Continents," Ceiling Painting, Palais des Nations, Geneva — A25

1959, Oct. 24 Engr. *Perf. 12½*

Centers in Dark Ultramarine

364	A25	15fr	brown	12	10
365	A25	20fr	purple	15	12
366	A25	25fr	dk org	20	18
367	A25	40fr	dk grn	28	25
368	A25	60fr	car rose	35	32
			Nos. 364-368 (5)	1.10	97

Issued for United Nations Day, Oct. 24.

Skier — A26

Bicyclist A27

Sports: 50c, Ice Hockey. 1fr, Tobogganing. 15fr, Discus thrower (vert.). 20fr, Boxing (vert.). 25fr, Runner.

1960 Unwmk. *Perf. 13*

369	A26	30c	sl grn, car & bl grn	6	5
370	A26	50c	red & blk	6	5
371	A26	1fr	red, blk & emer	12	10
372	A27	10fr	brn, ultra & sl	18	8
373	A27	15fr	dk red brn & grn	18	8
374	A27	20fr	dk grn, gldn brn & brn	28	12
375	A27	25fr	org, mag & brn	38	15
			Nos. 369-375 (7)	1.26	63

8th Winter Olympic Games, Squaw Valley, Calif. (Nos. 369-371); 17th Olympic Games, Rome (Nos. 372-375).

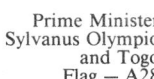

Prime Minister Sylvanus Olympio and Togo Flag — A28

1960, Apr. 27 Litho.

Center in Green, Red, Yellow & Brown

376	A28	30c	blk & buff	5	5
377	A28	50c	brn & buff	5	5
378	A28	1fr	lil & buff	5	5
379	A28	10fr	bl & buff	6	5
380	A28	20fr	red & buff	10	6
381	A28	25fr	grn & buff	15	10
			Nos. 376-381 (6)	46	36

Proclamation of Togo's full independence, Apr. 27, 1960.

See Nos. C31-C33.

Flags of "Big Four," and British Flag — A29

Flags, "Big Four" and: 1fr, USSR. 20fr, France. 25fr, US.

1960, May 21 *Perf. 14x14½*

382	A29	50c	beige, bl & red	5	5
383	A29	1fr	bl grn, bl & red	6	5
384	A29	20fr	gray, bl & red	16	12
385	A29	25fr	lt bl, bl & red	20	15

Summit Conference of France, Great Britain, United States and Russia, Paris, May 16.

Flag of Togo and UN Emblem A30

1961, Jan. 6 *Perf. 14½x15*

Flag in red, olive green & yellow

386	A30	30c	red	5	5
387	A30	50c	brown	5	5
388	A30	1fr	ultramarine	5	5
389	A30	10fr	maroon	5	5
390	A30	25fr	black	15	8
391	A30	30fr	violet	20	12
			Nos. 386-391 (6)	55	40

Togo's admission to United Nations.

Crowned Cranes over Map — A31

Augustino de Souza — A32

1961, Apr. 1 *Perf. 14½x15*

392	A31	1fr	multi	5	5
393	A31	10fr	multi	10	5
394	A31	25fr	multi	25	12
395	A31	30fr	multi	32	20

1961, Apr. 27 Litho. *Perf. 15*

396	A32	50c	yel, red & blk	5	5
397	A32	1fr	emer, brn & blk	5	5
398	A32	10fr	grnsh bl, vio & blk	10	5
399	A32	25fr	sal, grn & blk	20	8
400	A32	30fr	rose lil, bl & blk	30	15
			Nos. 396-400 (5)	70	38

1st anniv. of independence; "Papa" Augustino de Souza, leader of the independence movement.

Daniel C. Beard A33

Designs: 1fr, Lord Baden-Powell. 10fr, Togolese Scout and emblems. 25fr, Togolese Scout and flag (vert.). 30fr, Symbolic tents and fire (vert.). 100fr, Three hands of different races giving Scout sign.

1961, Oct. 7 Photo. *Perf. 13*

401	A33	50c	brt rose & grn	5	5
402	A33	1fr	dp vio & car	5	5
403	A33	10fr	dk gray & brn	8	5
404	A33	25fr	multi	20	5
405	A33	30fr	grn, red & org brn	30	10
406	A33	100fr	rose car & bl	75	30
			Nos. 401-406 (6)	1.43	60

Togolese Boy Scouts; 20th anniv. of the deaths of Daniel C. Beard and Lord Baden-Powell.

Four imperf. souvenir sheets each contain the six stamps, Nos. 401-406. Two sheets have a solid background of bright yellow, two a background of pale grayish brown. One yellow and one brown sheet have simulated perforations around the stamps. Size: 120x145mm. "REPUBLIQUE DU TOGO" is inscribed in white on bottom sheet margin. Value, each $3.

Plane, Ship and Part of Map of Africa — A34

Part of Map of Africa and: 25fr, Electric train and power mast. 30fr, Tractor and oil derricks. 85fr, Microscope and atomic symbol.

1961, Oct. 24 **Litho.**

Black Inscriptions; Map in Ochre

407	A34	20fr vio bl, org & yel	12	5
408	A34	25fr gray, org & yel	18	5
409	A34	30fr dk red, yel & org	25	6
410	A34	85fr bl, yel & org	50	18
a.		Souv. sheet of 4	1.65	1.40

UN Economic Commission for Africa. No. 410a contains one each of Nos. 407-410, imperf., printed without separating margin between the individual stamps to show a complete map of Africa.

Children Dancing around Globe — A35

Cmdr. Alan B. Shepard — A36

Design: UNICEF Emblem, children and globe.

1961, Dec. 9 **Unwmk.** ***Perf. 13½***

Black Inscription; Multicolored Design

411	A35	1fr ultra	5	5
412	A35	10fr red brn	5	5
413	A35	20fr lilac	10	5
414	A35	25fr gray	18	9
415	A35	30fr brt blue	30	10
416	A35	85fr dp lilac	60	30
		Nos. 411-416 (6)	1.28	64

UNICEF, 15th anniv.

Nos. 411-416 assembled in two rows show the globe and children of various races dancing around it.

1962, Feb. 24 ***Perf. 15x14***

Design: 1fr, 30fr, Yuri A. Gagarin.

417	A36	50c green	5	5
418	A36	1fr car rose	7	5
419	A36	25fr blue	15	10
420	A36	30fr purple	20	12

Astronauts of 1961.

Issued in sheets of 50 and in miniature sheets of 12 stamps plus four central labels showing photographs of Alan B. Shepard (US), Virgil I. Grissom (US), Yuri A. Gagarin (USSR), Gherman S. Titov (USSR).

No. 417 Surcharged: "100F COL. JOHN H. GLENN USA VOL ORBITAL 20 FEVRIER 1962" and Bars in Black

1962, Mar.

421	A36	100fr on 50c grn	75	50
a.		Carmine surcharge	75	50

Orbital flight of Lt. Col. John H. Glenn, Jr., USA, Feb. 20, 1962.

Independence Monument, Lomé — A37

Woman Carrying Fruit Basket — A38

1962, Apr. 27 **Litho.** ***Perf. 13½x14***

422	A37	50c multi	5	5
423	A38	1fr grn & pink	5	5
424	A37	5fr multi	5	5
425	A38	20fr pur & yel	12	6
426	A37	25fr multi	20	8
427	A38	30fr red & yel	22	12
a.		Souvenir sheet of 3	45	45
		Nos. 422-427 (6)	69	41

2nd anniversary of Togo's independence.

No. 427a contains one each of Nos. 424, 425 and 427, imperf.

Malaria Eradication Emblem A39

1962, June 2 ***Perf. 13½x13***

Multicolored Design

428	A39	10fr yel grn	10	5
429	A39	25fr pale lil	20	6
430	A39	30fr ocher	25	10
431	A39	85fr lt bl	55	22

WHO drive to eradicate malaria.

Capitol, Pres. John F. Kennedy and Pres. Sylvanus Olympio — A40

1962, July 4 **Unwmk.** ***Perf. 13***

Inscription and Portraits in Slate Green

432	A40	50c yellow	6	5
433	A40	1fr blue	6	5
434	A40	2fr vermilion	8	5
435	A40	5fr lilac	15	6
436	A40	25fr pale vio	45	15
437	A40	100fr brt grn	1.75	80
a.		Souvenir sheet, imperf.	7.50	7.50
		Nos. 432-437 (6)	2.55	1.16

Visit of Pres. Sylvanus Olympio of Togo to the US, Mar. 1962.

Mail Coach and Stamps of 1897 A41

Designs: 50c, Mail ship and stamps of 1900. 1fr, Mail train and stamps of 1915. 10fr, Motorcycle truck and stamp of 1924. 25fr, Mail truck and stamp of 1941. 30fr, DC-3 and stamp of 1947.

1963, Jan. 12 **Photo.** ***Perf. 13***

438	A41	30c multi	5	5
439	A41	50c multi	5	5
440	A41	1fr multi	5	5
441	A41	10fr vio, dp org & blk	8	5
442	A41	25fr dk red brn, blk & yel grn	15	10
443	A41	30fr ol brn & lil rose	22	15
		Nos. 438-443,C34 (7)	1.40	85

65th anniv. of Togolese mail service. For souvenir sheet see No. C34a.

Hands Reaching for FAO Emblem A42

1963, Mar. 21 ***Perf. 14***

444	A42	50c bl, org & dk brn	5	5
445	A42	1fr ol grn, org & dk brn	5	5
446	A42	25fr brn, dk brn & org	22	10
447	A42	30fr vio, dk brn & org	30	12

FAO "Freedom from Hunger" campaign.

The first value column gives the catalogue value of an unused stamp, the second that of a used stamp.

Togolese Flag and LoméHarbor — A43

1963, Apr. 27 **Litho.** ***Perf. 13x12½***

Flag in Red, Green and Yellow

448	A43	50c red brn & blk	5	5
449	A43	1fr dk car rose & blk	5	5
450	A43	25fr dl bl & blk	20	10
451	A43	50fr bis & blk	35	20

3rd anniversary of independence.

Centenary Emblem — A44

1963, June 1 **Photo.** ***Perf. 14***

Flag in Red, Olive Green, Yellow

452	A44	25fr bl, blk & red	15	10
453	A44	30fr dl grn, blk & red	22	14

International Red Cross centenary.

Abraham Lincoln, Broken Fetters, Maps of Africa and United States A45

1963, Oct. **Unwmk.** ***Perf. 13x14***

454	A45	50c multi	5	5
455	A45	1fr multi	5	5
456	A45	25fr multi	20	9

Centenary of the emancipation of the American slaves. See No. C35 and souvenir sheet No. C35a.

UN Emblem and "15" A46

Hibiscus A47

1963, Dec. 10 **Photo.** ***Perf. 14x13***

457	A46	50c ultra, dk bl & rose red	5	5
458	A46	1fr yel grn, dk bl & rose red	5	5
459	A46	25fr lil, dk bl & rose red	18	9
460	A46	85fr gold, dk bl & rose red	65	25

15th anniv. of the Universal Declaration of Human Rights.

1964 ***Perf. 14***

Designs: 50c, Orchid. 2fr, Butterfly. 5fr, Hinged tortoise. 8fr, Ball python. 10fr, Bunea alcinoe (moth). 20fr, Octopus. 25fr, John Dory (fish). 30fr, French angelfish. 40fr, Hippopotamus. 60fr, Bohor reedbuck. 85fr, Anubius baboon.

Size: 22½x31mm

461	A47	50c multi	5	5
462	A47	1fr yel, car & grn	5	5
463	A47	2fr lil, yel & blk	5	5
464	A47	5fr gray & multi	5	5
465	A47	8fr cit, red brn & blk	6	5
466	A47	10fr multi	8	5
467	A47	20fr dl bl, yel & brn	15	5
468	A47	25fr dl bl, grn & yel	18	6
469	A47	30fr multi	22	8
470	A47	40fr grn, red brn & blk	30	10
471	A47	60fr grnsh bl & red brn	45	15
472	A47	85fr lt grn, brn & org	65	25
		Nos. 461-472 (12)	2.29	99

See Nos. 511-515, C36-C40, J56-J63.

Nos. 454-456 Overprinted Diagonally: "En Mémoire de / JOHN F. KENNEDY / 1917-1963"

1964, Feb. ***Perf. 13x14***

473	A45	50c multi	5	5
474	A45	1fr multi	5	5
475	A45	25fr multi	18	5

Issued in memory of John F. Kennedy.

See No. C41 and note on souvenir sheets following it.

Isis of Kalabsha A48

Designs: 25fr, Head of Ramses II. 30fr, Colonnade of Birth House at Philae.

1964, Mar. 8 **Litho.** ***Perf. 14***

476	A48	20fr blk, pale grn & red	12	5
477	A48	25fr blk & lil rose	18	8
478	A48	30fr blk & cit	22	10
a.		Souv. sheet of 3	75	75

UNESCO world campaign to save historic monuments in Nubia. No. 478a contains three imperf. stamps similar to Nos. 476-478 with simulated perforations.

Phosphate Mine, Kpeme A49

Designs: 25fr, Phosphate plant, Kpeme. 60fr, Phosphate train. 85fr, Loading ship with phosphate.

1964, Apr. 27 **Unwmk.** ***Perf. 14***

479	A49	5fr brn & bis brn	5	5
480	A49	25fr dk pur & brn car	18	10
481	A49	60fr dk grn & ol	45	18
482	A49	85fr vio blk & Prus bl	65	22

Fourth anniversary of independence.

African Breaking Slavery Chain, and Map — A50

1964, May 25 **Photo.** ***Perf. 14x13***

483	A50	5fr dp org & brn	5	5
484	A50	25fr ol grn & brn	18	6
485	A50	85fr rose car & brn	65	15

1st anniv. of the meeting of African heads of state at Addis Ababa. See No. C42.

Pres. Nicolas Grunitzky and Butterfly A51

President and: 5fr, Dove. 25fr, 85fr, Flower.

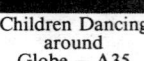

1964, Aug. 18 Litho. *Perf. 14*

486	A51	1fr pink, cl & dl vio	5	5
487	A51	5fr bis brn & dk brn	6	5
488	A51	25fr grnsh bl, dk bl & vio	20	9
489	A51	45fr mar, org, vio & mag	35	12
490	A51	85fr yel grn & sl grn	65	25
		Nos. 486-490 (5)	1.31	56

National Union and Reconciliation.

Soccer A52

Designs: 5fr, Runner. 25fr, Discus.

1964, Oct. Photo. *Perf. 14*

491	A52	1fr gray grn	5	5
492	A52	5fr dark blue	5	5
493	A52	25fr rose lake	20	10
494	A52	45fr blue grn	32	18
		Nos. 491-494,C43 (5)	1.62	78

18th Olympic Games, Tokyo, Oct. 10-25. For souvenir sheet see No. C43a.

Cooperation Issue

Common Design Type

1964, Nov. 7 Engr. *Perf. 13*

495	CD119	25fr mag, dk brn & ol bis	20	10

Dirigible and Balloons — A53

Designs: 25fr, 45fr, Otto Lilienthal's glider, 1894; Wright Brothers' plane, 1903; Boeing 707.

1964, Dec. 5 Photo. *Perf. 14x13*

496	A53	5fr org lil & grn	5	5
497	A53	10fr brt grn, dl bl & dk red	8	5
498	A53	25fr bl, vio bl & org	18	8
499	A53	45fr brt pink, vio bl & grn	32	12
a		Souv. sheet of 4	1.25	1.25
		Nos. 496-499,C44 (5)	1.63	70

Inauguration of the national airline "Air Togo." No. 499a contains four imperf. stamps similar to Nos. 497-499 and No. C44 with simulated perforations.

Orbiting Geophysical Observatory and Mariner — A54

Space Satellites: 15fr, 25fr, Tiros, Telstar and Orbiting Solar Observatory. 20fr, 50fr, Nimbus, Syncom and Relay.

1964, Dec. 12 Litho. *Perf. 14*

500	A54	10fr dp rose, bl & yel	8	5
501	A54	15fr multi	10	5
502	A54	20fr yel, grn & vio	15	5
503	A54	25fr multi	18	5
504	A54	45fr brt grn, dk bl & yel	32	8
505	A54	50fr yel, grn & org	38	10
a		Souvenir sheet of 4	1.25	1.25
		Nos. 500-505 (6)	1.21	38

Intl. Quiet Sun Year. No. 505a contains 4 imperf. stamps similar to Nos. 502-505.

Togo Olympic Stamps Printed in Israel — A55

Arms of Israel and Togo — A56

Pres. Nicolas Grunitzky of Togo and: 20fr, Church of the Mount of Beatitudes. 45fr, Ruins of Synagogue at Capernaum.

Perf. 13½x14½, 14x13½

1964, Dec. 26 Photo.

506	A55	5fr rose vio	5	5
507	A56	20fr grnsh bl, grn & dl pur	12	6
508	A56	25fr red & bluish grn	18	9
509	A56	45fr dl yel, ol & dl pur	45	25
510	A56	85fr mag & bluish grn	38	12
a		Souvenir sheet of 4	2.75	2.75
		Nos. 506-510 (5)	1.18	57

Israel-Togo friendship. No. 510a contains 4 imperf. stamps similar to No. 510.

Type of Regular Issue, 1964

1965, June Unwmk. *Perf. 14*

Designs: 3fr, Morpho aega butterfly. 4fr, Scorpion. 6fr, Bird-of-paradise flower. 15fr, Flap-necked chameleon. 45fr, Ring-tailed palm civet.

Size: 23x31mm

511	A47	3fr bis & multi	5	5
512	A47	4fr org & bluish blk	5	5
513	A47	6fr multi	5	5
514	A47	15fr brt pink, yel & brn	10	5
515	A47	45fr dl grn, org & brn	32	10
		Nos. 511-515 (5)	57	30

Syncom Satellite, Radar Station and ITU Emblem — A57

1965, June *Perf. 13x14*

516	A57	10fr Prus bl	8	5
517	A57	20fr ol bis	15	6
518	A57	25fr brt bl	20	9
519	A57	45fr crimson	32	16
520	A57	50fr green	38	18
		Nos. 516-520 (5)	1.13	54

ITU, centenary.

Abraham Lincoln — A58

Discus Thrower, Flags of Togo and Congo — A59

1965, June 26 Photo. *Perf. 13x14*

521	A58	1fr magenta	5	5
522	A58	5fr dl grn	5	5
523	A58	20fr brown	15	6
524	A58	25fr slate	20	9
		Nos. 521-524,C45 (5)	1.65	65

Death cent. of Abraham Lincoln. For souvenir sheet see No. C45a.

1965, July Unwmk. *Perf. 14x13*

Flags and: 10fr, Javelin thrower. 15fr, Handball player. 25fr, Runner.

Flags in Red, Yellow and Green

525	A59	5fr dp mag	5	5
526	A59	10fr dk bl	8	5
527	A59	15fr brown	12	5
528	A59	25fr dk pur	20	9
		Nos. 525-528,C46 (5)	1.45	64

First African Games, Brazzaville, July 18-25.

Winston Churchill and "V" — A60

Stalin, Roosevelt and Churchill at Yalta — A61

Perf. 13½x14, 14x13½

1965, Aug. 7 Photo.

529	A60	5fr dl grn	5	5
530	A61	10fr brt vio & gray	8	5
531	A60	20fr brown	15	9
532	A61	45fr Prus bl & gray	38	18
		Nos. 529-532,C47 (5)	1.56	77

Sir Winston Spencer Churchill (1874-1965), British statesman and World War II leader. For souvenir sheet see No. C47a.

Unisphere and New York Skyline — A62

Designs: 10fr, Togolese dancers and drummer, Unisphere. 50fr, Michelangelo's Pieta and Unisphere.

1965, Aug. 28 Photo. *Perf. 14*

533	A62	5fr grnsh bl & vio blk	5	5
534	A62	10fr yel grn & dk brn	8	5
535	A62	25fr brn org & dk grn	18	8
536	A62	50fr vio & sl grn	32	18
537	A62	85fr rose red & brn	65	30
a		Souv. sheet of 2	1.00	1.00
		Nos. 533-537 (5)	1.28	66

New York World's Fair, 1964-65. No. 537a contains two imperf. stamps similar to Nos. 536-537 with simulated perforations.

"Constructive Cooperation" and Olive Branch — A63

Designs: 25fr, 40fr, Hands of various races holding globe and olive branch. 85fr, Handclasp, olive branch and globe.

1965, Sept. 25 Unwmk. *Perf. 14*

538	A63	5fr vio, lt bl & org	5	5
539	A63	15fr brn, org & gray	9	5
540	A63	25fr bl & org	18	8
541	A63	40fr dp car, gray & org	28	12
542	A63	85fr grn & org	60	30
		Nos. 538-542 (5)	1.20	60

International Cooperation Year.

Major White and Gemini 4 — A64

Design: 25fr, Lt. Col. Alexei Leonov and Voskhod 2.

1965, Nov. 25 Photo. *Perf. 13½x14*

543	A64	25fr dp bl & brt car rose	18	8
544	A64	50fr grn & brn	38	15

"Walks in Space" of Lt. Col. Alexei Leonov (USSR), and Major Edward H. White (USA). Printed in sheets of 12 with ornamental borders.

Adlai E. Stevenson and UN Headquarters — A65

Designs: 5fr, "ONU" and doves. 10fr, UN emblem and headquarters. 20fr, "ONU" and orchids.

1965, Dec. 15 *Perf. 14x13½*

545	A65	5fr dk brn, yel & lt bl	5	5
546	A65	10fr org, dk bl & grn	8	5
547	A65	20fr dk grn, yel grn & org brn	15	6
548	A65	25fr brt yel, dk bl & bluish grn	20	9
		Nos. 545-548,C48 (5)	1.48	65

UN, 20th anniv.; Adlai E. Stevenson (1900-1965), US ambassador to the UN. For souvenir sheet see No. C48a.

Pope Paul VI, Plane and UN Emblem — A66

Designs: 15fr, 30fr, Pope addressing UN General Assembly and UN emblem (vert.).

20fr, Pope and New York skyline with UN Headquarters.

1966, Mar. 5 Litho. *Perf. 12*

549 A66	5fr bl & multi	5	5
550 A66	15fr lt vio & multi	10	5
551 A66	20fr bis & multi	15	8
552 A66	30fr lt ultra & multi	22	10
	Nos. 549-552,C49-C50 (6)	1.84	64

Visit of Pope Paul VI to the UN, New York City, Oct. 4, 1965.

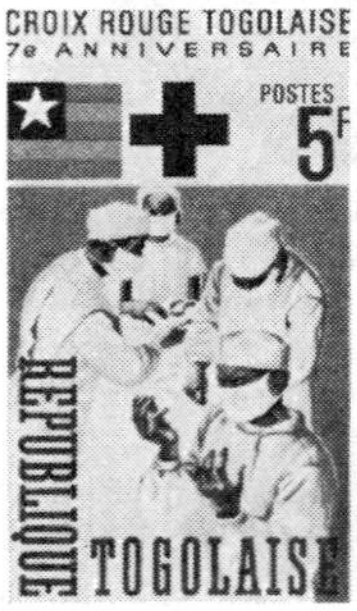

Surgical Operation and Togolese Flag — A67

Togolese Flag and: 10fr, 30fr, Blood transfusion. 45fr, Profiles of African man and woman.

1966, May 7 Litho. *Perf. 12*

553 A67	5fr multi	5	5
554 A67	10fr multi	8	5
555 A67	15fr multi	10	5
556 A67	30fr multi	22	10
557 A67	45fr multi	38	15
	Nos. 553-557,C51 (6)	1.93	75

Togolese Red Cross, 7th anniversary.

Talisman Roses and WHO Headquarters, Geneva — A68

Designs: Various flowers and WHO Headquarters.

1966, May Litho. *Perf. 12*

558 A68	5fr lt yel grn & multi	5	5
559 A68	10fr pale pink & multi	8	5
560 A68	15fr dl yel & multi	10	5
561 A68	20fr pale gray & multi	15	8
562 A68	30fr tan & multi	22	12
	Nos. 558-562,C52-C53 (7)	2.00	59

Inauguration of WHO Headquarters, Geneva.

Nos. 543-544 Overprinted or Surcharged in Red

1966, July 11 Photo. *Perf. 13½x14*

563 A64	50fr grn & brn, *(Envolée Surveyor 1)*	38	8
564 A64	50fr grn & brn, *(Envolée Gemini 9)*	38	8
565 A64	100fr on 25fr dp bl & brt car rose, *(Envolée Luna 9)*	85	15
566 A64	100fr on 25fr dp bl & brt car rose, *(Envolée Venus 3)*	85	15

United States and Russian achievements in Space. Sheets of 12 of Nos. 543-544 received two different overprints each, creating 6 se-tenant pairs of Nos. 563-564 and of Nos. 565-566 each. The sheet margins were overprinted with additional commemorative inscriptions.

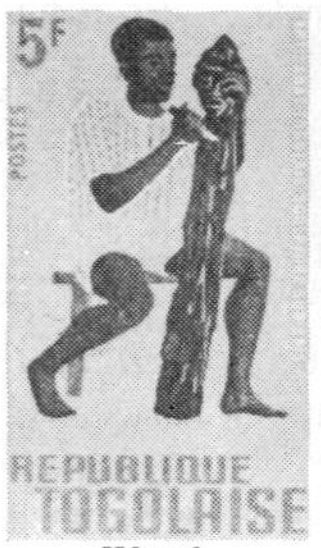

Wood Carver — A69

Togolese Dancer — A70

Arts and Crafts: 10fr, Basket maker. 15fr, Woman weaver. 30fr, Woman potter.

1966, Sept. Photo. *Perf. 13x14*

567 A69	5fr bl, yel & dk brn	5	5
568 A69	10fr emer, org & dk brn	8	5
569 A69	15fr ver, yel & dk brn	10	5
570 A69	30fr lil, dk brn & yel	22	10
	Nos. 567-570,C55-C56 (6)	1.95	61

1966, Nov. Photo. *Perf. 13x14*

Designs: 5fr, Togolese man. 20fr, Woman dancer from North Togo holding branches. 25fr, Male dancer. 30fr, Male dancer from North Togo with horned helmet. 45fr, Drummer.

571 A70	5fr emer & multi	5	5
572 A70	10fr dl yel & multi	8	5
573 A70	20fr lt ultra & multi	15	5
574 A70	25fr dp org & multi	18	7
575 A70	30fr red vio & multi	22	9
576 A70	45fr bl & multi	32	15
	Nos. 571-576,C57-C58 (8)	2.10	88

Soccer Players and Jules Rimet Cup — A71

Various Soccer Scenes.

1966, Dec. 14 Photo. *Perf. 14x13*

577 A71	5fr bl, brn & red	5	5
578 A71	10fr brick red & multi	8	5
579 A71	20fr ol, brn & dk grn	15	5
580 A71	25fr vio, brn & org	18	5
581 A71	30fr ocher & multi	22	9
582 A71	45fr emer, brn & mag	32	15
	Nos. 577-582,C59-C60 (8)	2.10	80

England's victory in the World Soccer Cup Championship, Wembley, July 30. For souvenir sheet see No. C60a.

African Mouthbreeder and Sailboat — A72

Designs: 10fr, Yellow jack and trawler. 15fr, Banded distichodus and seiner. 25fr, Jewelfish and galley. 30fr, like 5fr.

1967, Jan. 14 Photo. *Perf. 14*

Fish in Natural Colors

583 A72	5fr lt ultra & blk	5	5
584 A72	10fr brn org & brn	8	5
585 A72	15fr brt rose & dk bl	10	5
586 A72	25fr ol & blk	18	9
587 A72	30fr grnsh bl & blk	22	12
	Nos. 583-587,C61-C62 (7)	1.95	82

African Boy and Greyhound — A73

UNICEF Emblem and: 10fr, Boy and Irish setter. 20fr, Girl and doberman.

1967, Feb. 11 Photo. *Perf. 14x13½*

588 A73	5fr org, plum & blk	5	5
589 A73	10fr yel grn, red brn & dk grn	10	5
590 A73	15fr brt rose, brn & blk	10	5
591 A73	20fr bl, vio bl & blk	20	6
592 A73	30fr ol, sl grn & blk	22	8
	Nos. 588-592,C63-C64 (7)	1.99	75

UNICEF, 20th anniv. (in 1966).

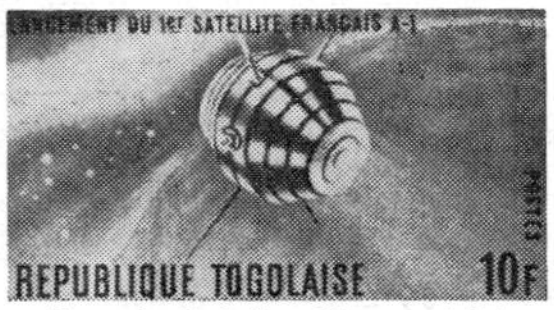

French A-1 Satellite — A74

Designs: 5fr, Diamant rocket (vert.). 15fr, Fr-1 satellite (vert.). 20fr, 40fr, D-1 satellite. 25fr, A-1 satellite.

Perf. 14x13½, 13½x14

1967, Mar. 18 Photo.

593 A74	5fr multi	5	5
594 A74	10fr multi	8	5
595 A74	15fr multi	10	5
596 A74	20fr multi	15	5
597 A74	25fr multi	20	5
598 A74	40fr multi	32	10
	Nos. 593-598,C65-C66 (8)	2.45	81

French achievements in space.

Duke Ellington, Saxophone, Trumpet, Drums — A75

UNESCO Emblem and: 5fr, Johann Sebastian Bach and organ. 10fr, Ludwig van Beethoven, violin and clarinet. 20fr, Claude A. Debussy, piano and harp. 30fr, like 15fr.

1967, Apr. 15 Photo. *Perf. 14x13½*

599 A75	5fr org & multi	5	5
600 A75	10fr multi	8	5
601 A75	15fr multi	10	5
602 A75	20fr lt bl & multi	15	6
603 A75	30fr lil & multi	22	9
	Nos. 599-603,C67-C68 (7)	1.92	69

20th anniv. (in 1966) of UNESCO.

For unused stamps, more recent issues are valued as never hinged, with the beginning point determined on a country-by-country basis. Notes to show the beginning points are prominently placed in the text.

EXPO Emblem, British Pavilion and Day Lilies — A76

Designs: 10fr, French pavilion and roses. 30fr, African village and bird-of-paradise flower.

1967, May 30 Photo. *Perf. 14*

604 A76	5fr brt pink & multi	5	5
605 A76	10fr dl org & multi	8	5
606 A76	30fr bl & multi	22	8
	Nos. 604-606,C69-C72 (7)	3.17	1.27

EXPO '67 Intl. Exhibition, Montreal, Apr. 28-Oct. 27.

Lions Emblem — A77

Designs: 20fr, 45fr, Lions emblem and flowers.

1967, July 29 Photo. *Perf. 13x14*

607 A77	10fr yel & multi	8	5
608 A77	20fr multi	15	5
609 A77	30fr grn & multi	22	8
610 A77	45fr bl & multi	38	10

50th anniversary of Lions International.

Montagu's Harriers — A78

Designs: 5fr, Bohor reedbucks. 15fr, Zebras. 20fr, 30fr, Marsh harriers. 25fr, Leopard.

1967, Aug. 19 Photo. *Perf. 14x13½*

611 A78	5fr lil & org brn	5	5
612 A78	10fr dk red, yel & dl bl	8	5
613 A78	15fr grn, blk & lil	10	5
614 A78	20fr dk brn, yel & dl bl	15	5
615 A78	25fr brn, ol & yel	18	6
616 A78	30fr vio, yel & dl bl	22	9
	Nos. 611-616,C79-C80 (8)	1.80	71

Stamp Auction and Togo Nos. 16 and C42 — A79

Designs: 10fr, 45fr, Exhibition and Nos. 67 (British) and 520. 15fr, 30fr, Stamp store and No. 230. 20fr, Stamp packet vending machine and No. 545.

1967, Oct. 14 Photo. *Perf. 14x13*

Stamps on Stamps in Original Colors

617	A79	5fr purple	5	5
618	A79	10fr dk brn	10	5
619	A79	15fr deep blue	20	5
620	A79	20fr slate grn	25	7
621	A79	30fr red brn	38	12
622	A79	45fr Prus blue	50	16
		Nos. 617-622,C82-C83 (8)	3.78	1.13

70th anniv. of the 1st Togolese stamps. For souvenir sheet see No. C82a.

See Nos. 853-855, C205.

Monetary Union Issue

Common Design Type

1967, Nov. 4 Engr. *Perf. 13*

623	CD125	30fr dk bl, vio bl & brt grn	22	8

Broad Jump, Summer Olympics Emblem and View of Mexico City — A80

Designs: 15fr, Ski jump, Winter Olympics emblem and ski lift. 30fr, Runners, Summer Olympics emblem and view of Mexico City. 45fr, Bobsledding, Winter Olympics emblem and ski lift.

1967, Dec. 2 Photo. *Perf. 13x14*

624	A80	5fr org & multi	5	5
625	A80	15fr multi	7	5
626	A80	30fr multi	22	9
627	A80	45fr multi	32	15
		Nos. 624-627,C84-C85 (6)	2.16	89

1968 Olympic Games. For souvenir sheet see No. C85a.

Nos. 604-606 Overprinted: "JOURNÉE NATIONALE / DU TOGO / 29 SEPTEMBRE 1967"

1967, Dec. *Perf. 14*

628	A76	5fr multi	5	5
629	A76	10fr multi	8	5
630	A76	30fr bl & multi	25	8
		Nos. 628-630,C86-C89 (7)	3.30	1.07

National Day, Sept. 29, 1967.

The Gleaners, by François Millet and Phosphate Works, Benin — A81

Design: 20fr, 45fr, 90fr, The Weaver at the Loom, by Vincent van Gogh, and textile plant, Dadia.

1968, Jan. Photo. *Perf. 14*

631	A81	10fr ol & multi	5	5
632	A81	20fr multi	15	5
633	A81	30fr brn & multi	22	8
634	A81	45fr multi	32	12
635	A81	60fr dk bl & multi	45	12
636	A81	90fr multi	70	25
		Nos. 631-636 (6)	1.89	67

Industrialization of Togo.

Togolese Women Brewing Beer — A82

The Beer Drinkers, by Edouard Manet — A83

Design: 45fr, Modern beer bottling plant.

1968, Mar. 26 Litho. *Perf. 14*

637	A82	20fr emer & multi	15	8
638	A83	30fr dk car & multi	22	8
639	A82	45fr org & multi	32	10

Publicity for local beer industry.

Symbolic Water Cycle, Flower and Cogwheels — A84

1968, Apr. 6

640	A84	30fr multi	22	10

Hydrological Decade (UNESCO), 1965-74. See No. C90.

Viking Ship and Portuguese Brigantine — A85

Designs: 10fr, Fulton's steamship and modern steamship. 20fr, Harbor activities and map of Africa.

1968, Apr. 26 Photo. *Perf. 14x13½*

641	A85	5fr brt grn & multi	5	5
642	A85	10fr dp org & multi	8	5
643	A85	20fr grn & multi	15	5
644	A85	30fr yel grn & multi	22	9
		Nos. 641-644,C91-C92 (6)	1.82	63

Inauguration of Lomé Harbor.

Adenauer and 1968 Europa Emblem — A86

1968, May 25 Photo. *Perf. 14*

645	A86	90fr ol grn & brn org	60	18

Konrad Adenauer (1876-1967), chancellor of West Germany (1949-63).

Adam and Eve Expelled from Paradise, by Michelangelo — A87

Paintings: 20fr, The Anatomy Lesson of Dr. Tulp, by Rembrandt. 30fr, The Anatomy Lesson, by Rembrandt (detail). 45fr, Jesus Healing the Sick, by Raphael.

1968, June 22 Photo. *Perf. 14*

646	A87	15fr crim & multi	10	5
647	A87	20fr multi	15	5
648	A87	30fr grn & multi	22	8
649	A87	45fr multi	32	12
		Nos. 646-649,C93-C94 (6)	2.29	71

WHO, 20th anniv.

Olympic Monument, San Salvador Island, and Wrestling — A88

Olympic Monument, San Salvador Island, Bahamas and: 20fr, Boxing. 30fr, Japanese wrestling. 45fr, Running.

1968, July 27 *Perf. 14x13½*

650	A88	15fr org, red org & brn	10	5
651	A88	20fr ver & multi	15	5
652	A88	30fr emer & multi	22	8
653	A88	45fr multi	32	12
		Nos. 650-653,C95-C96 (6)	2.29	71

19th Olympic Games, Mexico City, Oct. 12-27.

Chick Holding Lottery Ticket — A89

Scout Before Tent — A90

Design: 45fr, Lottery ticket, horseshoe and four-leaf clover.

1968, Oct. 5 Litho. *Perf. 14*

654	A89	30fr dk grn & multi	22	8
655	A89	45fr multi	32	12

2nd anniversary of National Lottery.

1968, Nov. 23

Designs: 10fr, 45fr, Scout leader training cub scouts (horiz.). 20fr, First aid practice (horiz.). 30fr, Scout game.

656	A90	5fr dp org & multi	5	5
657	A90	10fr emer & multi	7	5
658	A90	20fr multi	15	5
659	A90	30fr multi	22	10
660	A90	45fr bl & multi	32	15
		Nos. 656-660,C97-C98 (7)	2.31	97

Issued to honor the Togolese Boy Scouts.

Adoration of the Shepherds, by Giorgione — A91

Paintings: 20f, Adoration of the Magi, by Pieter Brueghel. 30fr, Adoration of the Magi, by Botticelli. 45fr, Adoration of the Magi, by Durer.

1968, Dec. 28 Litho. *Perf. 14*

661	A91	15fr grn & multi	10	5
662	A91	20fr multi	15	5
663	A91	30fr multi	22	8
664	A91	45fr multi	32	12
		Nos. 661-664,C100-C101 (6)	2.29	80

Christmas.

Martin Luther King, Jr. — A92

Portraits and Human Rights Flame: 20fr, Professor René Cassin (author of Declaration of Human Rights). 45fr, Pope John XXIII.

1969, Feb. 1 Photo. *Perf. 13½x14*

665	A92	15fr brn org & sl grn	10	6
666	A92	20fr grnsh bl & vio	15	9
667	A92	30fr ver & sl bl	18	12
668	A92	45fr ol & car rose	30	15
		Nos. 665-668,C102-C103 (6)	1.93	99

International Human Rights Year.

Omnisport Stadium and Soccer — A93

Stadium and: 15fr, Handball. 20fr, Volleyball. 30fr, Basketball. 45fr, Tennis.

1969, Apr. 26 Photo. *Perf. 14x13½*

669	A93	10fr emer, dp car & dk brn	5	5
670	A93	15fr org, ultra & dk brn	9	5
671	A93	20fr yel, ol & dk brn	14	8
672	A93	30fr dl grn, bl & dk brn	18	10
673	A93	45fr org, lil & dk brn	32	15
		Nos. 669-673,C105-C106 (7)	2.48	98

Opening of Omnisport Stadium, Lomé.

Lunar Module Eagle Landing on Moon A94

Designs: 20fr, 45fr, Astronaut and Eagle on moon, earth and stars in sky.

1969, July 21 Litho. *Perf. 14*

674	A94	1fr grn & multi	5	5
675	A94	20fr brn & multi	15	5
676	A94	30fr scar & multi	20	8
677	A94	45fr ultra & multi	35	12
		Nos. 674-677,C107-C108 (6)	1.80	90

Man's first landing on the moon, July 20, 1969. US astronauts Neil A. Armstrong and Col. Edwin E. Aldrin, Jr., with Lieut. Col. Michael Collins piloting Apollo 11.

Christ at Emmaus, by Velazquez A95

Paintings: 5fr, The Last Supper, by Tintoretto. 20fr, Pentecost, by El Greco. 30fr, The Annunciation, by Botticelli. 45fr, Like 10fr.

1969, Aug. 16 Litho. *Perf. 14*

678	A95	5fr red, gold & multi	5	5
679	A95	10fr multi	5	5
680	A95	20fr grn, gold & multi	10	5
681	A95	30fr multi	20	9
682	A95	45fr pur, gold & multi	30	15
		Nos. 678-682,C109 (6)	1.70	79

Nos. 665-668 Overprinted

EN MEMOIRE
DWIGHT D. EISENHOWER
1890-1969

1969, Sept. 1 Photo. *Perf. 13½x14*

683	A92	15fr brn org & sl grn	8	5
684	A92	20fr grnsh bl & vio	10	5
685	A92	30fr ver & sl bl	18	8
686	A92	45fr ol & car rose	25	10
		Nos. 683-686,C110-C111 (6)	1.61	73

Gen. Dwight D. Eisenhower (1890-1969), 34th President of the US

African Development Bank and Emblem — A96

Designs: 45fr, Bank emblem and hand holding railroad bridge and engine.

1969, Sept. 10 Photo. *Perf. 13x14*

687	A96	30fr ultra, blk gold & grn	20	8
688	A96	45fr grn, dk bl, gold & dk red	32	10

5th anniv. of the African Development Bank. See No. C112.

Louis Pasteur and Help for 1968 Flood Victims — A97

Designs: 15fr, Henri Dunant and Red Cross workers meeting Biafra refugees at airport. 30fr, Alexander Fleming and help for flood victims. 45fr, Wilhelm C. Roentgen and Red Cross workers with children in front of Headquarters.

1969, Sept. 27 Litho. *Perf. 14*

689	A97	15fr red & multi	8	5
690	A97	20fr emer & multi	10	8
691	A97	30fr pur & multi	18	10
692	A97	45fr brt bl & multi	32	12
		Nos. 689-692,C113-C114 (6)	1.78	92

50th anniv. of the League of Red Cross Societies.

Glidji Agricultural Center A98

Designs (Emblem of Young Pioneer and Agricultural Organization and): 1fr, Corn harvest. 3fr, Founding meeting of Agricultural Pioneer Youths, Mar. 7, 1967. 4fr, Class at Glidji Agricultural School. 5fr, Boys forming human pyramid. 7fr, Farm students threshing. 8fr, Instruction in gardening. 10fr, 50fr, Cooperative village. 15fr, Gardening School. 20fr, Cattle breeding. 25fr, Chicken farm. 30fr, Independence parade. 40fr, Boys riding high wire. 45fr, Tractor and trailer. 60fr, Instruction in tractor driving.

1969-70 Litho. *Perf. 14*

693	A98	1fr multi ('70)	5	5
694	A98	2fr multi	5	5
695	A98	3fr multi ('70)	5	5
696	A98	4fr multi ('70)	5	5
697	A98	5fr ultra & multi	5	5
698	A98	7fr multi ('70)	5	5
699	A98	8fr red & multi	5	5
700	A98	10fr bl & multi ('70)	6	5
701	A98	15fr red & multi ('70)	9	5
702	A98	20fr lil & multi	12	5
703	A98	25fr multi ('70)	15	6
704	A98	30fr brt bl & multi	18	7
705	A98	40fr brt yel & multi	25	9
706	A98	45fr rose lil & multi	28	9
707	A98	50fr bl & multi	30	10
708	A98	60fr org & multi	32	12
		Nos. 693-708,C115-C119 (21)	11.50	3.88

Books and Map of Africa A99

1969, Nov. 27 Litho. *Perf. 14*

709	A99	30fr lt bl & multi	16	6

12th anniv. of the Intl. Assoc. for the Development of Libraries in Africa.

Christmas Issue

Nos. 674-675, 677 Overprinted "JOYEUX NOEL"

1969, Dec. Litho. *Perf. 14*

710	A94	1fr grn & multi	20	14
711	A94	20fr brn & multi	70	35
712	A94	45fr ultra & multi	1.20	65
		Nos. 710-712,C120-C121 (5)	5.35	2.14

George Washington — A100

Portraits: 20fr, Albert Luthuli. 30fr, Mahatma Gandhi. 45fr, Simon Bolivar.

1969, Dec. 27 Photo. *Perf. 14x13½*

713	A100	15fr dk brn, emer & buff	10	5
714	A100	20fr dk brn, org & buff	15	8
715	A100	30fr dk brn, grnsh bl & ocher	20	10
716	A100	45fr dk brn, sl grn & dl yel	25	15
		Nos. 713-716,C122-C123 (6)	2.05	1.03

Issued to honor leaders for world peace.

Plower, by M.K. Klodt and ILO Emblem A101

Paintings and ILO Emblem: 10fr, Gardening, by Camille Pissarro. 20fr, Fruit Harvest, by Diego Rivera. 30fr, Spring Sowing, by Vincent van Gogh. 45fr, Workers, by Rivera.

1970, Jan. 24 Litho. *Perf. 12½x13*

717	A101	5fr gold & multi	8	5
718	A101	10fr gold & multi	12	5
719	A101	20fr gold & multi	20	12
720	A101	30fr gold & multi	40	18
721	A101	45fr gold & multi	60	25
		Nos. 717-721,C124-C125 (7)	3.10	1.22

ILO, 50th anniversary.

Togolese Hair Styles — A102

Designs: Various hair styles (20fr, 30fr, vertical).

Perf. 13x12½, 12½x13

1970, Feb. 21

722	A102	5fr multi	5	5
723	A102	10fr ver & multi	12	8
724	A102	20fr pur & multi	25	12
725	A102	30fr yel grn & multi	35	25
		Nos. 722-725,C126-C127 (6)	1.77	1.10

Togo No. C127 and Independence Monument, Lomé — A103

Designs: 30fr, Pres. Etienne G. Eyadéma, Presidential Palace and Independence Monument. 50fr, Map of Togo, dove and Independence Monument (vert.).

Perf. 13x12½, 12½x13

1970, Apr. 27 Litho.

726	A103	20fr multi	20	9
727	A103	30fr multi	30	13
728	A103	50fr multi	55	20

10th anniv. of independence. See No. C128.

Inauguration of UPU Headquarters, Bern — A104

1970, May 30 Photo. *Perf. 14x13½*

729	A104	30fr org & pur	35	13

See No. C129.

Soccer, Jules Rimet Cup and Flags of Italy and Uruguay — A105

Designs (Various Scenes from Soccer, Rimet Cup and Flags of): 10fr, Great Britain and Brazil. 15fr, U.S.S.R. and Mexico. 20fr, Germany and Morocco. 30fr, Romania and Czechoslovakia.

1970, June 27 Litho. *Perf. 13x14*

730	A105	5fr ol & multi	8	5
731	A105	10fr pink & multi	12	5
732	A105	15fr yel & multi	25	8
733	A105	20fr multi	30	12
734	A105	30fr emerald	45	20
		Nos. 730-734,C130-C132 (8)	2.97	1.42

9th World Soccer Championships for the Jules Rimet Cup, Mexico City, May 30-June 21, 1970.

Lenin and UNESCO Emblem A106

1970, July 25 Litho. *Perf. 12½*

735	A106	30fr fawn & multi	35	18

Lenin (1870-1924), Russian communist leader. See No. C133.

EXPO '70 Emblem and View of US Pavilion — A107

Designs: 2fr, Paper carp flying over Sanyo pavilion. 30fr, Russian pavilion 50fr. Tower of the Sun pavilion. 60fr, French and Japanese pavilions.

1970, Aug. 8 Litho. *Perf. 13*

Size: 56½x35mm

736	A107	2fr gray & multi	5	5

Size: 50x33mm

737	A107	20fr bl & multi	12	5
738	A107	30fr bl & multi	18	8
739	A107	50fr bl & multi	32	12
740	A107	60fr bl & multi	38	15
		Nos. 736-740 (5)	1.05	45

EXPO '70 Intl. Exhibition, Osaka, Japan, Mar. 15-Sept. 13. Nos. 737-740 printed se-tenant in sheet with continuous view of EXPO. See No. C134.

Neil A. Armstrong, Michael Collins and Edwin E. Aldrin, Jr. — A108

Designs: 2fr, US flag, moon rocks and Apollo 11 emblem. 20fr, Astronaut checking Surveyor 3 on moon, and Apollo 12 emblem. 30fr, Charles Conrad, Jr., Richard F. Gordon, Jr., Alan L. Bean and Apollo 12 emblem. 50fr, US flag, moon rocks and Apollo 12 emblem.

1970, Sept. 26

741	A108	1fr multi	5	5
742	A108	2fr multi	5	5
743	A108	20fr multi	25	10
744	A108	30fr multi	35	15
745	A108	50fr multi	70	25
		Nos. 741-745,C135 (6)	2.90	1.40

Moon landings of Apollo 11 and 12.

Nos. 741-745 Inscribed: "FELICITATIONS / BON RETOUR APOLLO XIII"

1970, Sept. 26

746	A108	1fr multi	5	5
747	A108	2fr multi	5	5
748	A108	20fr multi	25	10
749	A108	30fr multi	35	15
750	A108	50fr multi	70	25
		Nos. 746-750,C136 (6)	2.90	1.40

Safe return of the crew of Apollo 13.

Forge of Vulcan, by Velazquez, and ILO Emblem — A109

Paintings and Emblems of UN Agencies: 15fr, Still Life, by Delacroix, and FAO emblem. 20fr, Portrait of Nicholas Kratzer, by Holbein, and UNESCO emblem. 30fr, UN Headquarters, New York, and UN emblem. 50fr, Portrait of a Little Girl, by Renoir, and UNICEF emblem.

1970, Oct. 24 Litho. *Perf. 13x12½*

751	A109	1fr car, gold & dk brn	5	5
752	A109	15fr ultra, gold & blk	15	8
753	A109	20fr grnsh bl, gold & dk grn	20	10
754	A109	30fr lil & multi	35	15
755	A109	50fr org brn, gold & sep	65	30
		Nos. 751-755,C137-C138 (7)	2.60	1.33

United Nations, 25th anniversary.

Euchloron Megaera — A110

Butterflies and Moths: 2fr, Cymothoe chrysippus. 30fr, Danaus chrysippus. 50fr, Morpho.

1970, Nov. 21 Litho. *Perf. 13x14*

756	A110	1fr yel & multi	5	5
757	A110	2fr lt vio & multi	5	5
758	A110	30fr multi	30	10
759	A110	50fr org & multi	60	16
		Nos. 756-759,C139-C140 (6)	2.60	81

Nativity, by Botticelli — A111

Paintings: 20fr, Adoration of the Shepherds, by Veronese. 30fr, Adoration of the Shepherds, by El Greco. 50fr, Adoration of the Kings, by Fra Angelico.

1970, Dec. 26 Litho. *Perf. 12½x13*

760	A111	15fr gold & multi	8	5
761	A111	20fr gold & multi	10	7
762	A111	30fr gold & multi	20	10
763	A111	50fr gold & multi	38	16
		Nos. 760-763,C141-C142 (6)	1.91	88

Christmas.

Nos. 715, C123, 714 Surcharged and Overprinted: "EN MEMOIRE / Charles De Gaulle / 1890-1970"

1971, Jan. 9 Photo. *Perf. 14x13½*

764	A100	30fr multi	30	10
765	A100	30fr on 90fr multi	30	10
766	A100	150fr on 20fr multi	1.40	45

"Aerienne" obliterated with heavy bar on No. 765. See No. C143.

De Gaulle and Churchill A112

De Gaulle and: 30fr, Dwight D. Eisenhower. 40fr, John F. Kennedy. 50fr, Konrad Adenauer.

1971, Feb. 20 Photo. *Perf. 13x14*

767	A112	20fr blk & brt bl	16	7
768	A112	30fr blk & crim	20	10
769	A112	40fr blk & dp grn	40	14
770	A112	50fr blk & brn	42	16
		Nos. 767-770,C144-C145 (6)	2.68	97

Nos. 764-770 issued in memory of Charles de Gaulle (1890-1970), President of France.

Canceled-to-order stamps are often from remainders. Most collectors of canceled stamps prefer postally used specimens.

Resurrection, by Raphael — A113

Designs: 30fr, Resurrection, by Master of Trebon. 40fr, like 1fr.

Perf. 10½x11½

1971, Apr. 10 Litho.

771	A113	1fr gold & multi	5	5
772	A113	30fr gold & multi	20	10
773	A113	40fr gold & multi	25	14
		Nos. 771-773,C146-C148 (6)	2.32	1.07

Easter.

Cmdr. Alan B. Shepard, Jr. — A114

Designs: 10fr, Edgar D. Mitchell and astronaut on moon. 30fr, Stuart A. Roosa, module on moon. 40fr, Take-off from moon, and spaceship.

1971, May Litho. *Perf. 12½*

774	A114	1fr bl & multi	5	5
775	A114	10fr grn & multi	7	5
776	A114	30fr dl red & multi	20	10
777	A114	40fr dk grn & multi	25	14
		Nos. 774-777,C149-C151 (7)	2.97	1.49

Apollo 14 moon landing, Jan. 31-Feb. 9.

Cacao Tree and Pods — A115

Designs: 40fr, Sorting and separating beans and pods. 50fr, Drying cacao beans.

1971, June 6 Litho. *Perf. 14*

778	A115	30fr multi	30	10
779	A115	40fr ultra & multi	35	14
780	A115	50fr multi	35	16
		Nos. 778-780,C152-C154 (6)	2.70	1.25

International Cacao Day, June 6.

Control Tower and Plane — A116

1971, June 26

781	A116	30fr multi	22	10

10th anniv. of the Agency for the Security of Aerial Navigation in Africa and Madagascar (ASECNA). See No. C155.

Great Market, Lomé — A117

Designs: 30fr, Bird-of-paradise flower and sculpture of a man. 40fr, Aledjo Gorge and anubius baboon.

1971, July 17

782	A117	20fr multi	14	7
783	A117	30fr multi	20	10
784	A117	40fr multi	25	14
		Nos. 782-784,C156-C158 (6)	1.99	1.01

Tourist publicity.

Great Fetish of Gbatchoume — A118

Designs: 30fr, Chief Priest in front of Atta Sakuma Temple. 40fr, Annual ceremony of the sacred stone.

1971, July 31 Litho. *Perf. 14½*

785	A118	20fr multi	14	6
786	A118	30fr multi	20	9
787	A118	40fr multi	25	12
		Nos. 785-787,C159-C161 (6)	1.84	88

Religions of Togo.

No. 777 Overprinted in Silver: "EN MEMOIRE / DOBROVOLSKY - VOLKOV - PATSAYEV / SOYUZ 11"

1971, Aug. *Perf. 12½*

788	A114	40fr multi	25	12

In memory of the Russian astronauts Lt. Col. Georgi T. Dobrovolsky, Vladislav N. Volkov and Victor I. Patsayev, who died during the Soyuz 11 space mission, June 6-30, 1971. See Nos. C162-C164.

Sapporo '72 Emblem and Speed Skating — A119

Sapporo '72 Emblem and: 10fr, Slalom skiing. 20fr, Figure skating, pairs. 30fr, Bobsledding. 50fr, Ice hockey.

1971, Oct. 30 *Perf. 14*

789	A119	1fr multi	5	5
790	A119	10fr multi	7	5
791	A119	20fr multi	15	7
792	A119	30fr multi	20	10
793	A119	50fr multi	35	16
		Nos. 789-793,C165 (6)	2.22	93

11th Winter Olympic Games, Sapporo, Japan, Feb. 3-13, 1972.

Toy Crocodile and UNICEF Emblem — A120

Toys and UNICEF Emblem: 30fr, Fawn and butterfly. 40fr, Monkey. 50fr, Elephants.

1971, Nov. 27

794 A120 20fr multi 14 7
795 A120 30fr vio & multi 20 10
796 A120 40fr grn & multi 25 14
797 A120 50fr bis & multi 35 16
Nos. 794-797,C167-C168 (6) 1.94 87

UNICEF, 25th anniv.

Virgin and Child, by Botticelli A121

Virgin and Child by: 30fr, Master of the Life of Mary. 40fr, Dürer. 50fr, Veronese.

1971, Dec. 24 ***Perf. 14x13***

798 A121 10fr pur & multi 10 5
799 A121 30fr grn & multi 20 10
800 A121 40fr brn & multi 30 14
801 A121 50fr dk bl & multi 40 16
Nos. 798-801,C169-C170 (6) 2.10 1.10

Christmas.

St. Mark's Basilica — A122

Design: 40fr, Rialto Bridge.

1972, Feb. 26 Litho. *Perf. 14*

802 A122 30fr multi 20 10
803 A122 40fr multi 25 14

UNESCO campaign to save Venice. See No. C171.

No. 784 Surcharged with New Value, Two Bars and "VISITE DU PRESIDENT / NIXON EN CHINE / FEVRIER 1972"

1972, Mar. Litho. *Perf. 14*

804 A117 300fr on 40fr multi 2.00 1.20

Visit of Pres. Richard M. Nixon to the People's Republic of China, Feb. 20-27.
See No. C172.

Crucifixion, by Master MS — A123

Paintings: 30fr, Pietà, by Botticelli. 40fr, like 25fr.

1972, Mar. 31

805 A123 25fr gold & multi 16 8
806 A123 30fr gold & multi 20 10
807 A123 40fr gold & multi 25 14
Nos. 805-807,C173-C174 (5) 1.71 71

Easter.

Heart, Smith, WHO Emblem — A124

Heart, WHO Emblem and: 40fr, Typist. 60fr, Athlete with javelin.

1972, Apr. 4

808 A124 30fr multi 20 10
809 A124 40fr multi 22 14
810 A124 60fr multi 40 20

"Your heart is your health," World Health Day. See No. C175.

Video Telephone A125

Grating Cassava A126

1972, June 24 ***Perf. 14***

811 A125 40fr vio & multi 25 14

4th World Telecommunications Day. See No. C176.

1972, June 30

Designs: 25fr, Cassava collection by truck (horiz.).

812 A126 25fr yel & multi 16 8
813 A126 40fr multi 25 14

Cassava production. See Nos. C177-C178.

Basketball A127

Pin-tailed Whydah A128

1972, Aug. 26 Litho. *Perf. 14*

814 A127 30fr shown 20 10
815 A127 40fr Running 25 14
816 A127 50fr Discus 35 16
Nos. 814-816,C180-C181 (5) 2.95 1.40

20th Olympic Games, Munich, Aug. 26-Sept. 11.

1972, Sept. 9

Birds: 30fr, Broad-tailed widowbird. 40fr, Yellow-shouldered widowbird. 60fr, Yellow-tailed widowbird.

817 A128 25fr cit & multi 16 8
818 A128 30fr lt bl & multi 22 10
819 A128 40fr multi 25 14
820 A128 60fr lt grn & multi 40 20
Nos. 817-820,C182 (5) 1.68 87

Paul P. Harris, Rotary Emblem — A129

Design: 50fr, Flags of Togo and Rotary Club.

1972, Oct. 7 Litho. *Perf. 14*

821 A129 40fr grn & multi 22 14
822 A129 50fr multi 35 16
a Souv. sheet of 2 65 65
Nos. 821-822,C183-C185 (5) 2.02 1.19

Rotary International, Lomé. No. 822a contains 2 stamps with simulated perforations similar to Nos. 821-822.

Mona Lisa, by Leonardo da Vinci A130

Design: 40fr, Virgin and Child, by Giovanni Bellini.

1972, Oct. 21

823 A130 25fr gold & multi 20 8
824 A130 40fr gold & multi 25 14
Nos. 823-824,C186-C188 (5) 2.10 1.07

West African Monetary Union Issue
Common Design Type

Design: 40fr, African couple, city, village and commemorative coin.

1972, Nov. 2 Engr. *Perf. 13*

825 CD136 40fr red brn, rose red & gray 22 14

Presidents Pompidou and Eyadema, Party Headquarters — A131

1972, Nov. 23 Litho. *Perf. 14*

826 A131 40fr pur & multi 30 14

Visit of Pres. Georges Pompidou of France to Togo, Nov. 1972. See No. C189.

Anunciation, Painter Unknown A132

Paintings: 30fr, Nativity, Master of Vyshchibrod. 4fr, Like 25fr.

1972, Dec. 23

827 A132 25fr gold & multi 16 8
828 A132 30fr gold & multi 20 10
829 A132 40fr gold & multi 25 14
Nos. 827-829,C191-C193 (6) 2.46 1.22

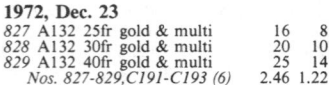

Christmas.

Raoul Follereau and Lepers — A133

1973, Jan. 23 Photo. *Perf. 14x13½*

830 A133 40fr vio & grn 25 14

World Leprosy Day and 20th anniv. of the Raoul Follereau Foundation. See No. C194.

WHO Emblem A134

Christ on the Cross A135

1973, Apr. 7 Photo. *Perf. 14x13*

831 A134 30fr bl & multi 20 10
832 A134 40fr dp yel & multi 25 14

WHO, 25th anniv.

1973, Apr. 21 Litho. *Perf. 14*

833 A135 25fr shown 16 8
834 A135 30fr Pietà 20 10
835 A135 40fr Ascension 25 14

Easter. See No. C195.

Eugene Cernan, Ronald Evans, Harrison Schmitt, Apollo 17 Badge — A136

Design: 40fr, Lunar rover on moon.

1973, June 2 Litho. *Perf. 14*

836 A136 30fr multi 20 10
837 A136 40fr multi 25 14

Apollo 17 moon mission, Dec. 7-19, 1972. See Nos. C196-C197.

Scouts Pitching Tent A137

Nicolaus Copernicus A138

Designs: 20fr, Campfire (horiz.). 30fr, Rope climbing. 40fr, Like 10fr.

1973, June 30

838 A137 10fr multi 7 5
839 A137 20fr multi 14 7
840 A137 30fr vio & multi 20 10
841 A137 40fr ocher & multi 25 14
Nos. 838-841,C198-C199 (6) 2.86 1.41

24th Boy Scout World Conference (1st in Africa), Nairobi, Kenya, July 16-21.

1973, July 18

Designs: 10fr, Heliocentric system. 30fr, Seated figure of Astronomy and spacecrafts around earth and moon. 40fr, Astrolabe.

842 A138 10fr multi 7 5
843 A138 20fr multi 14 7
844 A138 30fr multi 20 10
845 A138 40fr lil & multi 25 14
Nos. 842-845,C200-C201 (6) 1.96 1.06

Copernicus (1473-1543), Polish astronomer.

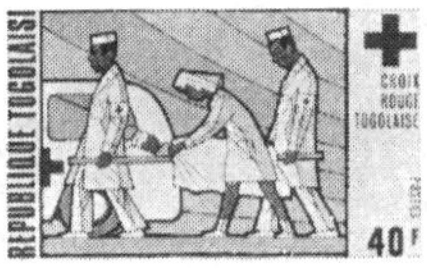

Red Cross Ambulance Crew A139

1973, Aug. 4

846 A139 40fr multi 25 14

Togolese Red Cross. See No. C202.

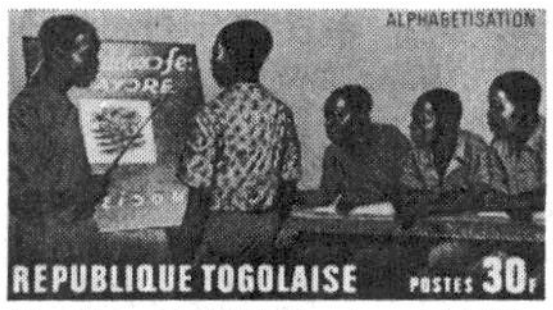

Teacher and Students — A140

Designs: 40fr, Hut and man reading under tree (vert.).

1973, Aug. 18 Litho. *Perf. 14*

847 A140 30fr multi 20 10
848 A140 40fr multi 25 14

Literacy campaign. See No. C203.

African Postal Union Issue
Common Design Type

1973, Sept. 12 Engr. *Perf. 13*

849 CD137 100fr yel, red & cl 70 35

INTERPOL Emblem and Headquarters A141

Weather Vane and WMO Emblem A142

1973, Sept. 29 Photo. *Perf. 13½x14*

850 A141 30fr yel, brn & gray grn 20 10
851 A141 40fr yel grn, bl & mag 25 14

50th anniv. of Intl. Criminal Police Org.

1973, Oct. 4 *Perf. 14x13*

852 A142 40fr yel, dp brn & grn 25 14

Intl. meteorological cooperation, cent. See No. C204.

Type of 1967

Designs: 25fr, Old and new locomotives, No. 795. 30fr, Mail coach and bus, No. 613. 90fr, Mail boat and ship, Nos. C61 and 469.

1973, Oct. 20 Photo. *Perf. 14x13*

853 A79 25fr multi 20 8
854 A79 30fr pur & grn 25 10
855 A79 90fr dk bl & multi 65 30

75th anniv. of Togolese postal service. See No. C205.

John F. Kennedy and Adolf Schaerf A143

Virgin and Child, Italy, 15th Century A144

Designs: 30fr, Kennedy and Harold Macmillan. 40fr, Kennedy and Konrad Adenauer.

1973, Nov. 22 Litho. *Perf. 14*

856 A143 20fr blk, gray & vio 14 12
857 A143 30fr blk, rose & brn 20 14
858 A143 40fr blk, lt grn & grn 25 18
Nos. 856-858,C206-C208 (6) 3.29 1.77

John F. Kennedy (1917-1963).

No. 758 Surcharged with New Value, 2 Bars and Overprinted in Ultramarine: "SECHERESSE SOLIDARITE AFRICAINE"

1973, Dec. Photo. *Perf. 13x14*

859 A110 100fr on 30fr multi 70 50

African solidarity in drought emergency.

1973, Dec. 22 Litho. *Perf. 14*

Design: 30fr, Adoration of the Kings, Italy, 15th century.

860 A144 25fr gold & multi 16 12
861 A144 30fr gold & multi 22 14

Christmas. See Nos. C210-C211.

No. 821 Overprinted: "PREMIERE CONVENTION / 210eme DISTRICT / FEVRIER 1974 / LOME"

1974, Feb. 21 Litho. *Perf. 14*

862 A129 40fr grn & multi 25 18

First convention of Rotary Intl., District 210, Lome, Feb. 22-24. See Nos. C212-C213.

Soccer and Games' Cup A145

Designs: Various soccer scenes and games' cup.

1974, Mar. 2 Litho. *Perf. 14*

863 A145 20fr lt bl & multi 14 7
864 A145 30fr yel & multi 22 12
865 A145 40fr lil & multi 25 14
Nos. 863-865,C214-C216 (6) 3.31 1.58

World Soccer Championships, Munich, Germany, June 13-July 7.

Nos. 812-813 Overprinted and Surcharged: "10e ANNIVERSAIRE DU P.A.M."

1974, Mar. 25 Litho. *Perf. 14*

866 A126 40fr multi 35 18
867 A126 100fr on 25fr multi 75 50

10th anniv. of World Food Program. Overprint on No. 866 is in one line; 2 lines on No. 867 and 2 bars through old denomination.

Girl Before Mirror, by Picasso — A146

Mailman, UPU Emblem — A148

Kpeme Village and Wharf A147

Paintings by Picasso: 30fr, The Turkish Shawl. 40fr, Mandolin and Guitar.

1974, Apr. 6

868 A146 20fr vio bl & multi 15 8
869 A146 30fr mar & multi 22 12
870 A146 40fr multi 30 15
Nos. 868-870,C217-C219 (6) 3.37 1.65

Pablo Picasso (1881-1973), Spanish painter.

1974, Apr. 20

Design: 40fr, Tropicana tourist village.

871 A147 30fr multi 22 12
872 A147 40fr multi 25 15

See Nos. C220-C221.

1974, May 10 Litho. *Perf. 14*

Design: 40fr, Mailman, different uniform.

873 A148 30fr sal & multi 22 12
874 A148 40fr multi 30 15

UPU, centenary. See Nos. C222-C223.

Map and Flags of Members A148a

1974, May 29 Litho. *Perf. 13x12½*

875 A148a 40fr bl & multi 30 22

15th anniversary of the Council of Accord.

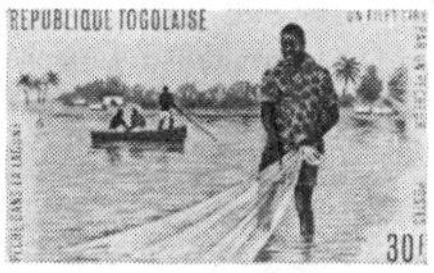

Fisherman with Net — A149

Design: 40fr, Fisherman casting net from canoe.

1974, June 22 Litho. *Perf. 14*

876 A149 30fr multi 25 12
877 A149 40fr multi 30 15
Nos. 876-877,C224-C226 (5) 2.70 1.42

Lagoon fishing.

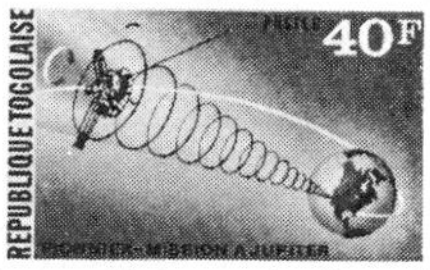

Pioneer Communicating with Earth — A150

Design: 30fr, Radar station and satellite (vert.).

1974, July 6 *Rouletted, Imperf.*

878 A150 30fr multi 22 12
879 A150 40fr multi 30 15

US Jupiter space probe. See Nos. C227-C228.

No. 811 Overprinted with INTERNABA Emblem in Silver Similar to No. C229

1974, July

880 A125 40fr multi 1.10 55

INTERNABA 1974 Intl. Philatelic Exhibition, Basel, June 7-16. See No. C229.

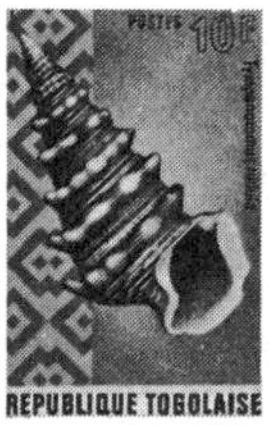

Tympanotomus Radula — A151

Designs: Seashells.

1974, July 13 Litho. *Perf. 14*

881 A151 10fr shown 15 5
882 A151 20fr Tonna galea 18 9
883 A151 30fr Conus mercator 25 12
884 A151 40fr Cardium costatum 38 15
Nos. 881-884,C230-C231 (6) 2.01 1.01

Groom with Horses A152

Design: 40fr, Trotting horses.

1974, Aug. 3 Litho. *Perf. 14*

885 A152 30fr multi 22 10
886 A152 40fr multi 30 15

Horse racing. See Nos. C232-C233.

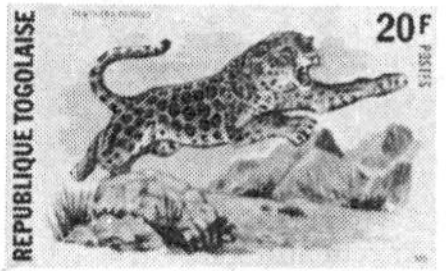

Leopard A153

1974, Sept. 7 Litho. *Perf. 14*

887 A153 20fr shown 15 7
888 A153 30fr Giraffes 18 12
889 A153 40fr Elephants 25 15
Nos. 887-889,C236-C237 (5) 1.73 99

Wild animals of West Africa.

1974, Oct. 14

890 A153 30fr Herding cattle 18 9
891 A153 40fr Milking cow 25 15

Domestic animals. See Nos. C238-C239.

Churchill and Frigate F390 A154

Design: 40fr, Churchill and fighter planes.

1974, Nov. 1 Photo. *Perf. 13x13½*

892 A154 30fr multi 22 9
893 A154 40fr multi 30 15

Winston Churchill (1874-1965). See Nos. C240-C241.

Chlamydocarya Macrocarpa — A155

Flowers of Togo: 25fr, Strelitzia reginae (vert.). 30fr, Storphanthus sarmentosus (vert.). 60fr, Clerodendrum scandens.

1975, Feb. 15 Litho. *Perf. 14*

894 A155 25fr multi 15 7
895 A155 30fr multi 18 9
896 A155 40fr multi 25 16
897 A155 60fr multi 38 18
Nos. 894-897,C242-C243 (6) 2.61 1.25

No. 821 Overprinted: "70e ANNIVERSAIRE / 23 FEVRIER 1975"

1975, Feb. 23 Litho. *Perf. 14*

898 A129 40fr grn & multi 32 15

Rotary Intl., 70th anniv. See Nos. C244-C245.

Radio Station, Kamina A156

Designs: 30fr, Benedictine Monastery, Zogbegan. 40fr, Causeway, Atchinedji. 60fr, Ayome Waterfalls.

1975, Mar. 1 Photo. *Perf. 13x14*

899 A156 25fr multi 15 9
900 A156 30fr multi 18 12
901 A156 40fr multi 25 16
902 A156 60fr multi 38 22

Jesus Mocked, by El Greco — A157

Paintings: 30fr, Crucifixion, by Master Janoslet. 40fr, Descent from the Cross, by Bellini. 90fr, Pieta, painter unknown.

1975, Apr. 19 Litho. *Perf. 14*

903 A157 25fr blk & multi 18 7
904 A157 30fr blk & multi 22 12
905 A157 40fr blk & multi 30 15
906 A157 90fr blk & multi 55 32
Nos. 903-906,C246-C247 (6) 2.90 1.46

Easter.

Stilt Walking, Togolese Flag A158

Design: 30fr, Flag and dancers.

1975, Apr. 26 Litho. *Perf. 14*

907 A158 25fr multi 18 9
908 A158 30fr multi 22 14

15th anniv. of independence. See Nos. C248-C249.

Footnotes often refer you to other stamps of the same design.

Rabbit Hunter with Club A159

Design: 40fr, Beaver hunter with bow and arrow.

1975, May 24 Photo. *Perf. 13x13½*

909 A159 30fr multi 18 9
910 A159 40fr multi 25 16

See Nos. C250-C251.

Pounding Palm Nuts A160

Design: 40fr, Man extracting palm oil (vert.).

1975, June 28 Litho. *Perf. 14*

911 A160 30fr multi 22 15
912 A160 40fr multi 25 15

Palm oil production. See Nos. C252-C253.

Apollo-Soyuz Link-up — A161

1975, July 15

913 A161 30fr multi 18 10
Nos. 913,C254-C258 (6) 2.88 1.39

Apollo Soyuz space test project (Russo-American cooperation), launching July 15; link-up July 17.

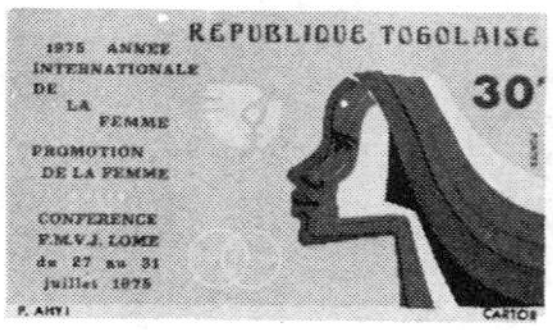

Women's Heads, IWY Emblem — A162

1975, July 26 Litho. *Perf. 12½*

914 A162 30fr bl & multi 18 9
915 A162 40fr multi 25 16

International Women's Year.

Dr. Schweitzer and Children — A163

1975, Aug. 23 Litho. *Perf. 14x13½*

916 A163 40fr multi 25 18

Dr. Albert Schweitzer (1875-1965), medical missionary and musician. See Nos. C259-C261.

Merchant Writing Letter, by Vittore Carpaccio A164

Virgin and Child, by Mantegna A165

1975, Oct. 9 Litho. *Perf. 14*

917 A164 40fr multi 25 18

Intl. Letter Writing Week. See No. C262.

No. 797 Overprinted: "30ème Anniversaire / des Nations-Unies"

1975, Oct. 24 Litho. *Perf. 14*

918 A120 50fr multi 32 22

UN, 30th anniv. See Nos. C263-C264.

1975, Dec. 20 Litho. *Perf. 14*

Paintings of the Virgin and Child: 30fr, El Greco. 40fr, Barend van Orley.

919 A165 20fr red & multi 15 7
920 A165 30fr bl & multi 22 12
921 A165 40fr red & multi 30 15
Nos. 919-921,C267-C269 (6) 2.82 1.31

Christmas.

Crashed Plane and Pres. Eyadema A166

1976, Jan. 24 Photo. *Perf. 13*

922 A166 50fr multi 55 38
923 A166 60fr multi 75 45

Airplane crash at Sara-kawa, Jan. 24, 1974, in which Pres. Eyadema escaped injury.

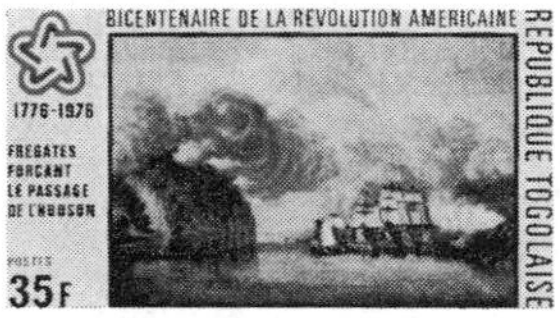

Frigates on the Hudson — A167

American Bicentennial: 50fr, George Washington, by Gilbert Stuart, and Bicentennial emblem (vert.).

1976, Mar. 3 Litho. *Perf. 14*

924 A167 35fr multi 22 15
925 A167 50fr multi 30 22
Nos. 924-925,C270-C273 (6) 2.90 1.53

ACP and CEE Emblems A168

Design: 50fr, Map of Africa, Europe and Asia.

1976, Apr. 24 Photo. *Perf. 13x14*

926 A168 10fr org & multi 7 5
927 A168 50fr pink & multi 30 22

First anniv. of signing of treaty between Togo and European Common Market, Lome, Feb. 28, 1975. See Nos. C274-C275.

Cable-laying Ship — A169

Design: 30fr, Telephone, tape recorder, speaker.

1976, Mar. 10 Photo. *Perf. 13x14*

928 A169 25fr ultra & multi 15 12
929 A169 30fr pink & multi 18 14

Centenary of first telephone call by Alexander Graham Bell, Mar. 10, 1876. See Nos. C276-C277.

Blind Man and Insect — A170

Marine Exhibition Hall — A171

1976, Apr. 8 *Perf. 14x13*

930 A170 50fr brt grn & multi 30 18

World Health Day: "Foresight prevents blindness." See No. C278.

Air Post Type, 1976, and Type A171

1976 Litho. *Perf. 14*

Design: 10fr, Pylon, flags of Ghana, Togo and Dahomey.

931 A171 5fr multi 5 5
932 AP19 10fr multi 7 5
933 A171 50fr multi 30 22

Marine Exhibition, 10th anniv. (5fr, 50fr). Ghana-Togo-Dahomey electric power grid, 1st anniversary (10fr). See No. C279.

Issue dates: 50fr, May 8; 5fr, 10fr, August.

Running — A172

Montreal Olympic Emblem and: 30fr, Kayak. 50fr, High jump.

1976, June 15 Photo. *Perf. 14x13*

934 A172 25fr multi 15 9
935 A172 30fr multi 18 12
936 A172 50fr multi 30 18
Nos. 934-936,C284-C286 (6) 2.66 1.49

21st Olympic Games, Montreal, Canada, July 17-Aug. 1.

Titan 3 and Viking Emblem — A173

Design: 50fr, Viking trajectory, Earth to Mars.

1976, July 15 Litho. *Perf. 14*

937 A173 30fr bl & multi 18 12
938 A173 50fr rose & multi 30 18
Nos. 937-938,C287-C290 (6) 2.86 1.58

US Viking Mars missions.

Young Routy at Celeyran, by Toulouse-Lautrec A174

Mohammed Ali Jinnah, Flags of Togo and Pakistan A176

Adoration of the Shepherds, by Pontormo — A175

Paintings by Toulouse-Lautrec: 20fr, Model in Studio. 35fr, Louis Pascal, portrait.

1976, Aug. 7 Litho. *Perf. 14*

939 A174 10fr blk & multi	7	5
940 A174 20fr blk & multi	12	8
941 A174 35fr blk & multi	22	14
Nos. 939-941,C291-C293 (6)	2.24	1.25

Henri Toulouse-Lautrec (1864-1901), French painter, 75th death anniversary.

No. 846 Overprinted: "Journée / Internationale / de l'Enfance"

1976, Nov. 27 Litho. *Perf. 14*

942 A139 40fr multi 22 15

Intl. Children's Day. See No. C294.

1976, Dec. 18

Paintings: 30fr, Nativity, by Carlo Crivelli. 50fr, Virgin and Child, by Jacopo da Pontormo.

943 A175 25fr multi	15	9
944 A175 30fr multi	18	12
945 A175 50fr multi	30	18
Nos. 943-945,C295-C297 (6)	2.66	1.49

Christmas.

1976, Dec. 24 Litho. *Perf. 13*

946 A176 50fr multi 30 18

Jinnah (1876-1948), first Governor General of Pakistan.

No. 936 Overprinted: "CHAMPIONS OLYMPIQUES / SAUT EN HAUTEUR / POLOGNE"

1976, Dec. Photo. *Perf. 14x13*

947 A172 50fr multi 32 18

Olympic winners. See Nos. C298-C299.

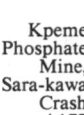

Kpeme Phosphate Mine, Sara-kawa Crash A177

1977, Jan. 13 Photo. *Perf. 13x14*

948 A177 50fr multi 30 18

10th anniv. of presidency of Etienne Eyadema. See Nos. C300-C301.

Gongophone — A178

Musical Instruments: 10fr, Tamtam (vert.). 25fr, Dondon.

1977, Feb. 7 Litho. *Perf. 14*

949 A178 5fr multi	5	5
950 A178 10fr multi	7	5
951 A178 25fr multi	15	9
Nos. 949-951,C302-C304 (6)	1.57	76

Victor Hugo and his Home A179

1977, Feb. 26 *Perf. 13x14*

952 A179 50fr multi 30 18

Victor Hugo (1802-1885), French writer, 175th birth anniversary. See No. C305.

Beethoven and Birthplace, Bonn A180

Design: 50fr, Bronze bust, 1812, and Heiligenstadt home.

1977, Mar. 7 *Perf. 14*

953 A180 30fr multi	18	12
954 A180 50fr multi	30	18

Ludwig van Beethoven (1770-1827), composer. See Nos. C306-C307.

Benz, 1894, Germany — A181

Early Automobiles: 50fr, De Dion Bouton, 1903, France.

1977, Apr. 11 Litho. *Perf. 14*

955 A181 35fr multi	22	14
956 A181 50fr multi	30	18
Nos. 955-956,C308-C311 (6)	2.90	1.65

Lindbergh, Ground Crew and Spirit of St. Louis — A182

Design: 50fr, Lindbergh and Spirit of St. Louis.

1977, May 9

957 A182 25fr multi	18	9
958 A182 50fr multi	38	18
Nos. 957-958,C312-C315 (6)	2.76	1.05

Charles A. Lindbergh's solo transatlantic flight from New York to Paris, 50th anniv.

No. 952 Overprinted: "10ème ANNIVERSAIRE DU / CONSEIL INTERNATIONAL / DE LA LANGUE FRANCAISE"

1977, May 17 Litho. *Perf. 14*

959 A179 50fr multi 38 18

Intl. French Language Council, 10th anniv. See No. C316.

African Slender-snouted Crocodile — A183

Endangered wildlife: 15fr, Nile crocodile.

1977, June 13

960 A183 5fr multi	5	5
961 A183 15fr multi	12	6
Nos. 960-961,C317-C320 (6)	3.22	94

Agriculture School, Tove A184

1977, July 11 Litho. *Perf. 14*

962 A184 50fr multi 38 18

Agricultural development. See Nos. C321-C323.

Landscape with Cart, by Peter Paul Rubens (1577-1640) — A185

Rubens Painting: 35fr, Exchange of the Princesses at Hendaye, 1623.

1977, Aug. 8

963 A185 15fr multi	12	6
964 A185 35fr multi	25	14

See Nos. C324-C325.

Orbiter 101 on Ground — A186

Designs: 30fr, Launching of Orbiter (vert.). 50fr, Ejection of propellant tanks at take-off.

1977, Oct. 4 Litho. *Perf. 14*

965 A186 20fr multi	15	7
966 A186 30fr multi	22	12
967 A186 50fr multi	38	18
Nos. 965-967,C326-C328 (6)	3.35	1.06

Space shuttle trials in the U.S.

Lafayette Arriving in Montpelier, Vt. — A187

Design: 25fr, Lafayette, age 19 (vert.).

1977, Nov. 7 *Perf. 14x13, 13x14*

968 A187 25fr multi	18	9
969 A187 50fr multi	38	18

Arrival of the Marquis de Lafayette in North America, 200th anniv. See Nos. C329-C330.

Lenin, Cruiser Aurora, Red Flag — A188

1977, Nov. 7 Litho. *Perf. 12*

970 A188 50fr multi 38 18

Russian October Revolution, 60th anniv.

Virgin and Child, by Lorenzo Lotto — A189

Virgin and Child by: 30fr, Carlo Bellini. 50fr, Cosimo Tura.

1977, Dec. 19 *Perf. 14*

971 A189 20fr multi	15	7
972 A189 30fr multi	22	12
973 A189 50fr multi	38	18
Nos. 971-973,C331-C333 (6)	3.40	1.06

Christmas.

Edward Jenner — A190

Design: 20fr, Vaccination clinic (horiz.).

Perf. 14x13, 13x14

1978, Jan. 9 Litho.

974 A190 5fr multi	5	5
975 A190 20fr multi	15	7

Worldwide eradication of smallpox. See Nos. C334-C335.

Orville and Wilbur Wright — A191

Design: 50fr, Wilbur Wright flying at Kill Devil Hill, 1902.

1978, Feb. 6 Litho. *Perf. 14*

976 A191 35fr multi	25	14
977 A191 50fr multi	38	18
Nos. 976-977,C336-C339 (6)	4.88	1.59

75th anniversary of first motorized flight.

John, the Evangelist and Eagle — A197

Evangelists: 10fr, Luke and ox. 25fr, Mark and lion. 30fr, Matthew and angel.

1978, Mar. 20 Litho. *Perf. 13½x14*

988	A197	5fr multi	5	5
989	A197	10fr multi	7	5
990	A197	25fr multi	18	9
991	A197	30fr multi	22	10
a		Souvenir sheet of 4	60	60

No. 991a contains one each of Nos. 988-991 with simulated perforations.

Anchor, Fishing Harbor, Lome A199

1978, Apr. 26 Photo. *Perf. 13*

997 A199 25fr multi 18 9

See Nos. C340-C342.

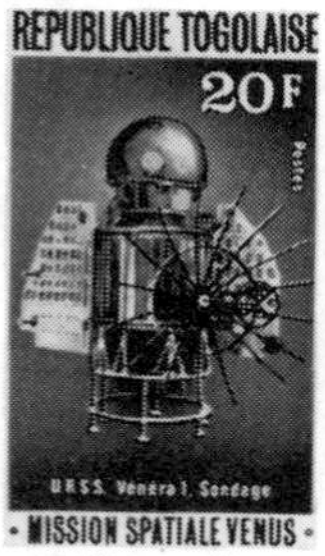

Venera I, USSR — A200

Soccer — A201

Designs: 30fr, Pioneer, USA (horiz.). 50fr, Venera, fuel base and antenna.

1978, May 8 Litho. *Perf. 14*

998	A200	20fr multi	15	8
999	A200	30fr multi	22	12
1000	A200	50fr multi	38	18
		Nos. 998-1000,C343-C345 (6)	3.40	1.11

US Pioneer and USSR Venera space missions.

1978, June 5 *Perf. 14*

Design: 50fr, Soccer players and Argentina '78 emblem.

1001	A201	30fr multi	22	12
1002	A201	50fr multi	38	18
		Nos. 1001-1002,C346-C349 (6)	4.95	1.47

11th World Cup Soccer Championship, Argentina, June 1-25.

Celerifère, 1818 A202

History of the Bicycle: 50fr, First bicycle sidecar, c. 1870 (vert.).

Perf. 13x14, 14x13

1978, July 10 Photo.

1003	A202	25fr multi	18	9
1004	A202	50fr multi	38	18
		Nos. 1003-1004,C350-C353 (6)	2.76	1.08

Thomas A. Edison, Sound Waves — A203

Dunant's Birth Place, Geneva — A204

Design: 50fr, Victor's His Master's Voice phonograph, 1905, and dancing couple.

1978, July 8 Photo. *Perf. 14x13*

1005	A203	30fr multi	22	10
1006	A203	50fr multi	38	18
		Nos. 1005-1006,C354-C357 (6)	4.90	1.47

Centenary of the phonograph, invented by Thomas Alva Edison.

1978, Sept. 4 Photo. *Perf. 14x13*

Designs: 10fr, Henri Dunant and red cross. 25fr, Help on battlefield, 1864, and red cross.

1007	A204	5fr Prus bl & red	5	5
1008	A204	10fr red brn & red	8	5
1009	A204	25fr grn & red	18	9

Henri Dunant (1828-1910), founder of Red Cross, birth sesquicentennial. See No. C358.

Threshing, by Raoul Dufy — A205

Painting: 50fr, Horsemen on Seashore, by Paul Gauguin.

1978, Nov. 6 Litho. *Perf. 14*

1010	A205	25fr multi	18	9
1011	A205	50fr multi	38	18
		Nos. 1010-1011,C359-C362 (6)	3.36	1.69

Eiffel Tower, Paris — A206

Virgin and Child, by Antonello da Messina — A207

1978, Nov. 27 Photo. *Perf. 14x13*

1012 A206 50fr multi 38 18

Centenary of the Congress of Paris. See Nos. C365-C367.

1978, Dec. 18 Litho. *Perf. 14*

Paintings (Virgin and Child): 30fr, by Cario Crivelli. 50fr, by Cosimo Tura.

1013	A207	20fr multi	15	7
1014	A207	30fr multi	22	12
1015	A207	50fr multi	38	18
		Nos. 1013-1015,C368-C370 (6)	3.35	1.67

Christmas.

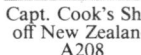

Capt. Cook's Ship off New Zealand A208

Entry into Jerusalem A209

Design: 50fr, Endeavour in drydock, N.E. Coast of Australia (horiz.).

1979, Feb. 12 Litho. *Perf. 14*

1016	A208	25fr multi	18	9
1017	A208	50fr multi	38	18
		Nos. 1016-1017,C371-C374 (6)	3.41	2.19

200th death anniv. of Capt. James Cook.

1979, Apr. 9

Easter: 40fr, The Last Supper (horiz.). 50fr, Descent from the Cross (horiz.).

1018	A209	30fr multi	22	12
1019	A209	40fr multi	30	15
1020	A209	50fr multi	38	18
		Nos. 1018-1020,C375-C377 (6)	3.35	1.65

Einstein Observatory, Potsdam — A210

Design: 50fr, Einstein and James Ramsay MacDonald, Berlin, 1931.

1979, July 2 Photo. *Perf. 14x13*

1021	A210	15fr multi	25	14
1022	A210	50fr multi	38	18

Albert Einstein (1879-1955), theoretical physicist.

Children and Children's Village Emblem A211

Man Planting Tree A212

Designs: 10fr, Mother and children. 15fr, Map of Africa, Children's Village emblem (horiz.). 20fr, Woman and children walking to Children's Village (horiz.). 25fr, Children sitting under African fan palm. 30fr, Map of Togo with location of Children's Villages.

1979, July 30 Photo. *Perf. 14x13*

1023	A211	5fr multi	5	5
1024	A211	10fr multi	7	5
1025	A211	15fr multi	12	6
1026	A211	20fr multi	15	7
1027	A211	25fr multi	18	9
1028	A211	30fr multi	22	12
a		Souvenir sheet of 2, #1027-1028	45	
		Nos. 1023-1028 (6)	79	44

International Year of the Child.

1979, Aug. 13 *Perf. 14x13*

1029 A212 50fr lil & grn 38 18

Second Arbor Day. See No. C384.

Sir Rowland Hill (1795-1879), Originator of Penny Postage — A213

Olympic Flame, Lake Placid 80 Emblem, Slalom — A215

Norris Locomotive, 1843 — A214

Designs: 30fr, French mail-sorting office, 18th century (horiz.). 50fr, Mailbox, Paris, 1850.

1979, Aug. 27

1030	A213	20fr multi	15	8
1031	A213	30fr multi	22	12
1032	A213	50fr multi	38	18
		Nos. 1030-1032,C385-C387 (6)	3.40	1.68

1979, Oct. 1 Litho. *Perf. 14*

Design: 35fr, Stephenson's "Rocket," 1829 (vert.).

1033	A214	35fr multi	25	14
1034	A214	50fr multi	38	18
		Nos. 1033-1034,C388-C391 (6)	3.63	1.80

1979, Oct. 18 Litho. *Perf. 13½*

1980 Olympic Emblems, Olympic Flame and: 30fr, Yachting 50fr, Discus.

1035	A215	20fr multi	15	8
1036	A215	30fr multi	22	12
1037	A215	50fr multi	38	18
		Nos. 1035-1037,C392-C394 (6)	3.40	1.68

13th Winter Olympic Games, Lake Placid, N.Y., Feb. 12-24, 1980. (90fr); 22nd Summer Olympic Games, Moscow, July 19-Aug. 3, 1980.

Moslems Praying A216

Design: 50fr, Catholic priests.

1979, Oct. 29 *Perf. 13x14*

1038	A216	30fr multi	22	12
1039	A216	50fr multi	38	18

Religions in Togo. See Nos. C396-C397.

Astronaut Walking on Moon — A217

Design: 50fr, Space capsule orbiting moon.

1979, Nov. 5
1040 A217 35fr multi 25 14
1041 A217 50fr multi 38 18
Nos. 1040-1041,C398-C401 (6) 4.88 2.39

Apollo 11 moon landing, 10th anniversary.

Telecom 79 — A218

1979, Nov. 26 **Photo.** ***Perf. 13x14***
1042 A218 50fr multi 38 18

3rd World Telecommunications Exhibition, Geneva, Sept. 20-26. See No. C402.

Holy Family — A219

Rotary Emblem — A220

Christmas: 30fr, Virgin and Child. 50fr, Adoration of the Kings.

1979, Dec. 17 **Litho.** ***Perf. 14***
1043 A219 20fr multi 15 8
1044 A219 30fr multi 22 12
1045 A219 50fr multi 38 18
Nos. 1043-1045,C403-C405 (6) 3.35 1.68

1980, Jan. 14

Rotary Emblem and: 30fr, Anniversary emblem. 40fr, Paul P. Harris, Rotary founder.

1046 A220 25fr multi 18 9
1047 A220 30fr multi 22 12
1048 A220 40fr multi 30 15
Nos. 1046-1048,C406-C408 (6) 3.30 1.66

Rotary International, 75th anniversary.

Biathlon, Lake Placid '80 Emblem — A221

Christ and the Angels, by Andrea Mantegna — A223

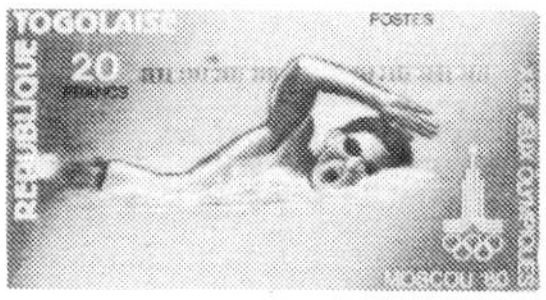

Swimming, Moscow '80 Emblem — A222

1980, Jan. 31 **Litho.** ***Perf. 13½***
1049 A221 50fr multi 38 18

13th Winter Olympic Games, Lake Placid, N.Y., Feb. 12-24. See Nos. C409-C412.

1980, Feb. 29 **Litho.** ***Perf. 13½***
1050 A222 20fr shown 15 7
1051 A222 30fr Gymnastics 22 12
1052 A222 50fr Running 38 18
Nos. 1050-1052,C413-C415 (6) 4.67 2.40

22nd Summer Olympic Games, Moscow, July 19-Aug. 3.

1980, Mar. 31 ***Perf. 14***

Easter 1980 (Paintings by): 40fr, Carlo Crivelli. 50fr, Jacopo Pontormo.

1053 A223 30fr multi 22 12
1054 A223 40fr multi 30 15
1055 A223 50fr multi 38 18
Nos. 1053-1055,C416-C418 (6) 3.30 1.65

Jet over Map of Africa A224

1980, Mar. 24 **Litho.** ***Perf. 12½***
1056 A224 50fr multi 38 18

ASECNA (Air Safety Board), 20th anniv. See No. C419.

12th World Telecommunications Day — A225

1980, May 17 **Photo.** ***Perf. 14x13½***
1057 A225 50fr multi 38 18

See No. C420.

Red Cross over Globe Showing Lomé, Togo — A226

1980, June 16 **Photo.** ***Perf. 14x13***
1058 A226 50fr multi 38 18

Togolese Red Cross. See No. C421.

Jules Verne (1828-1905), French Science Fiction Writer — A227

Baroness James de Rothschild, by Ingres — A228

Design: 50fr, Shark (20,000 Leagues Under the Sea).

1980, July 14 **Litho.** ***Perf. 14***
1059 A227 30fr multi 22 12
1060 A227 50fr multi 38 18
Nos. 1059-1060,C422-C425 (6) 3.55 1.75

1980, Aug. 29 **Litho.** ***Perf. 14***

Paintings by Jean Auguste Dominique Ingres (1780-1867): 30fr, Napoleon I on Imperial Throne. 40fr, Don Pedro of Toledo and Henri IV.

1061 A228 25fr multi 18 9
1062 A228 30fr multi 22 12
1063 A228 40fr multi 30 15
Nos. 1061-1063,C426-C428 (6) 3.30 1.66

Minnie Holding Mirror for Leopard A229

Disney Characters and Animals from Fazao Reserve: 2fr, Goofy (Dingo) cleaning teeth of hippopotamus. 3fr, Donald holding snout of crocodile. 4fr, Donald dangling over cliff from horn of rhinoceros. 5fr, Goofy riding water buffalo. 10fr, Monkey taking picture of Mickey. 100fr, Mickey as doctor examining giraffe with sore throat. No. 1071, Elephant giving shower to Goofy. No. 1072, Lion carrying Goofy by seat of his pants. 200fr, Pluto in party hat. No. 1072A, Pluto.

1980, Sept. 15 ***Perf. 11***
1064 A229 1fr multi 5 5
1065 A229 2fr multi 5 5
1066 A229 3fr multi 5 5
1067 A229 4fr multi 5 5
1068 A229 5fr multi 5 5
1069 A229 10fr multi 7 5
1070 A229 100fr multi 75 38
1070A A229 200fr multi 1.50 75
1071 A229 300fr multi 2.25 1.10
Nos. 1064-1071 (9) 4.82 2.53

Souvenir Sheets

1072 A229 300fr multi 2.25 1.10
1072A A229 300fr multi 2.25 1.10

50th anniv. of the Disney character Pluto.

Market Activities, Women Preparing Meat A230

1980, Mar. 17 ***Perf. 14***
1073 A230 1fr Grinding savo 5 5
1074 A230 2fr shown 5 5
1075 A230 3fr Truck going to market 5 5
1076 A230 4fr Unloading produce 5 5
1077 A230 5fr Sugar cane vendor 5 5
1078 A230 6fr Barber curling child's hair, vert. 5 5
1079 A230 7fr Vegetable vendor 6 5
1080 A230 8fr Sampling mangos, vert. 6 5
1081 A230 9fr Grain vendor 7 5
1082 A230 10fr Spiced fish vendor 7 5
1083 A230 15fr Clay pot vendor 12 6
1084 A230 20fr Straw baskets 15 7
1085 A230 25fr Selling lemons and onions, vert. 18 9
1086 A230 30fr Straw baskets, diff. 22 12
1087 A230 40fr Shore market 30 15
1088 A230 50fr Women carrying produce, vert. 38 18
Nos. 1073-1088 (16) 1.91 1.17

See Nos. 1105-1106, C440-C445, J68-J71.

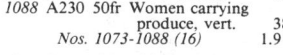

Commemorative Wreath — A231

Famous Men of the Decade: 40fr, Mao Tse-tung (vert.).

1980, Feb. 11 ***Perf. 14x13***
1089 A231 25fr multi 25 12
1090 A231 40fr emer grn & dk grn 40 20
Nos. 1089-1090,C429-C431 (5) 3.25 1.62

World Tourism Conference, Manila, Sept. 27 — A232

1980, Sept. 15 **Litho.** ***Perf. 14***
1091 A232 50fr Hotel tourism emblem, vert. 50 25
1092 A232 150fr shown 1.50 75

Map of Australia and Human Rights Flame A233

1980, Oct. 13 **Photo.** ***Perf. 13x14***
1093 A233 30fr shown 30 15
1094 A233 50fr Europe and Asia map 50 25

Declaration of Human Rights, 30th anniversary. See Nos. C432-C433.

Melk Monastery, Austria, 18th Century A234

Perf. 14½x13½
1980, Dec. 22 **Litho.**
1095 A234 20fr shown 20 10
1096 A234 30fr Tarragon Cathedral, Spain, 12th cent. 30 15
1097 A234 50fr St. John the Baptist, Florence, 1964 50 25
Nos. 1095-1097,C435-C437 (6) 4.00 2.00

Christmas.

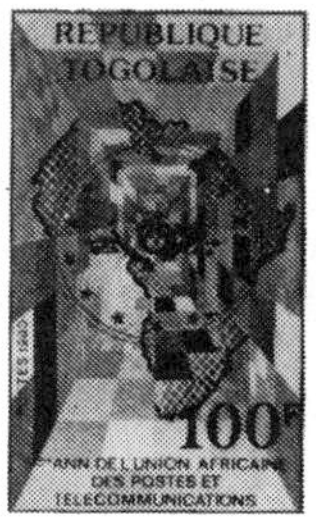

African Postal Union, 5th Anniversary A235

1980, Dec. 24 **Photo.** ***Perf. 13½***
1098 A235 100fr multi 75 38

February 2nd Hotel Opening A236

1981, Feb. 2 Litho. *Perf. 12½x13*
1099 A236 50fr multi 50 25

See No. C437B.

West African Rice Development Assoc. Type of Air Post, 1981

1981, Dec. 21 Litho. *Perf. 12½*
1100 AP22 70fr lt grn & multi 70 35

Rembrandt's Father — A237

Easter (Rembrandt Paintings): 40fr, Self-portrait. 50fr, Artist's father as an old man. 60fr, Rider on Horseback.

Perf. 14½x13½
1981, Apr. 13 Litho.
1101 A237 30fr multi 22 12
1102 A237 40fr multi 30 15
1103 A237 50fr multi 38 18
1104 A237 60fr multi 45 22
Nos. 1101-1104,C438-C439 (6) 3.35 1.67

Market Type of 1980

Designs: Various market scenes.

1981, Mar. 8 Litho. *Perf. 14*
1105 A230 45fr Vegatable stall 30 15
1106 A230 60fr Rice wine 40 20
Nos. 1105-1106,C440-C445,J68-J71 (12) 15.42 7.82

Inscribed 1980.

Red-headed Rock Fowl — A238

Perf. 13½x14½
1981, Aug. 10 Litho.
1107 A238 30fr shown 20 10
1108 A238 40fr Splendid sunbird 25 14
1109 A238 60fr Violet-backed starling 40 20
1110 A238 90fr Red-collared widowbird 60 30
Nos. 1107-1110,C446-C447 (6) 2.45 1.25

African Postal Union Ministers, 6th Council Meeting, July 28-20 A239

1981, Aug. 31 Litho. *Perf. 12½*
1111 A239 70fr Dish antenna 50 25
1112 A239 90fr Computer operator, vert. 70 35
1113 A239 105fr Map 75 42

Intl. Year of the Disabled A240

1981, Aug. 31 *Perf. 14*
1114 A240 70fr Blind man 70 35

See Nos. C448-C449A.

Woman with Hat, by Picasso, 1961 — A241

Picasso Birth Centenary: Sculptures.

1981, Sept. 14 *Perf. 14½x13½*
1116 A241 25fr shown 16 8
1117 A241 50fr She-goat 35 16
1118 A241 60fr Violin, 1915 40 20
Nos. 1116-1118,C450-C452 (6) 3.51 1.74

Aix-la-Chapelle Cathedral, Germany — A242

World Heritage Year: 40fr, Geyser, Yellowstone Natl. Park. 50fr, Nahanni Natl. Park, Canada. 60fr, Stone crosses, Ethiopia.

1981, Sept. 28 *Perf. 13½x14½*
1119 A242 30fr multi 22 12
1120 A242 40fr multi 30 15
1121 A242 50fr multi 38 18
1122 A242 60fr multi 45 22
Nos. 1119-1122,C453-C454 (6) 3.60 1.77

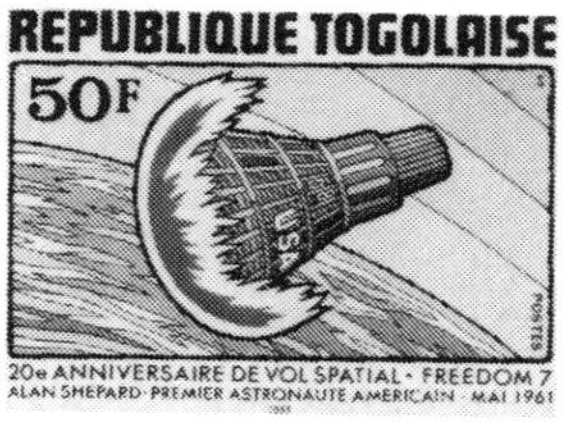

20th Anniv. of Alan Shepard's Flight — A243

Space Anniversaries: 25fr, Yuri Gagarin's Vostok I, 20th. 60fr, Lunar Orbiter I, 15th.

1981, Nov. *Perf. 14*
1123 A243 25fr multi 18 9
1124 A243 50fr multi 38 18
1125 A243 60fr multi 45 22
Nos. 1123-1125,C455-C456 (5) 2.46 1.22

Christmas A244

Rubens Paintings: 20fr, Adoration of the Kings. 30fr, Adoration of the Shepherds. 50fr, St. Catherine.

Perf. 14½x13½
1981, Dec. 10 Litho.
1126 A244 20fr multi 14 7
1127 A244 30fr multi 20 10
1128 A244 50fr multi 35 16
Nos. 1126-1128,C457-C459 (6) 4.74 2.33

15th Anniv. of Natl. Liberation — A245

1982, Jan. 13 Litho. *Perf. 12½*
1129 A245 70fr Dove, flag 70 35
1130 A245 90fr Citizens, Pres. Eyadema, vert. 90 45

See Nos. C462-C463.

Scouting Year A246

1982, Feb. 25 Litho. *Perf. 14*
1131 A246 70fr Pitching tent 45 22
Nos. 1131,C464-C467 (5) 3.65 1.79

Easter — A247

Designs: The Ten Commandments.

1982, Mar. 15 *Perf. 14x14½*
1132 A247 10fr multi 7 5
1133 A247 25fr multi 16 8
1134 A247 30fr multi 20 10
1135 A247 45fr multi 30 15
1136 A247 50fr multi 35 16
1137 A247 70fr multi 45 22
1138 A247 90fr multi 60 30
Nos. 1132-1138,C469-C470 (9) 3.63 1.84

Papilio Dardanus A248

1982, July 15 Litho. *Perf. 14½x14*
1139 A248 15fr shown 10 5
1140 A248 20fr Belenois calypso 14 7
1141 A248 25fr Palla decius 16 8
Nos. 1139-1141,C474-C475 (5) 1.70 85

1982 World Cup — A249

Designs: Various soccer players.

1982, July 26 *Perf. 14x14½*
1142 A249 25fr multi 16 8
1143 A249 45fr multi 30 15
Nos. 1142-1143,C477-C479 (5) 4.51 2.23

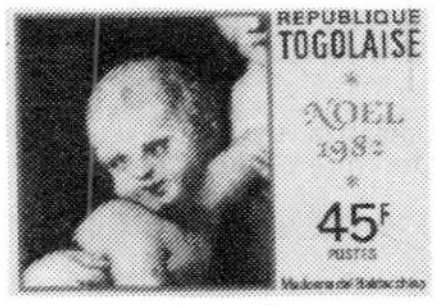

Christmas A250

Design: Madonna of Baldacchino, by Raphael. Nos. 1144-1148 show details; No. 1149 entire painting. (Size: 120x159mm.).

1982, Dec. 24 Litho. *Perf. 14½x14*
1144 A250 45fr multi 30 15
1145 A250 70fr multi 45 22
1146 A250 105fr multi 70 35
1147 A250 130fr multi 90 42
1148 A250 150fr multi 1.00 50
Nos. 1144-1148 (5) 3.35 1.64

Souvenir Sheet
Perf. 14x14½
1149 A250 500fr multi, vert. 3.50 1.60

Nos. 1142-1143, C477-C480 Overprinted: VAINQUER / COUPE DU MONDE / FOOTBALL 82 / "ITALIE"

1983, Jan. 31 Litho. *Perf. 14x14½*
1150 A249 25fr multi 16 8
1151 A249 45fr multi 30 15
1152 A249 105fr multi 70 35
1153 A249 200fr multi 1.40 65
1154 A249 300fr multi 2.00 1.00
Nos. 1150-1154 (5) 4.56 2.23

Souvenir Sheet
1155 A249 500fr multi 3.50 1.60

Italy's victory in 1982 World Cup. Nos. 1152-1155 airmail.

20th Anniv. of West African Monetary Union (1982) — A251

1983, May Litho. *Perf. 12½x12*
1156 A251 70fr Map 45 22
1157 A251 90fr Emblem 60 30

Visit of Pres. Mitterand of France, Jan. 13-15 — A252

1983, Jan. 13 Litho. *Perf. 13*

1158	A252	35fr Sokode Regional Hospital	22	12
a.		Souvenir sheet, imperf.	22	12
1159	A252	45fr Citizens joining hands	30	15
a.		Souvenir sheet, imperf.	35	16
1160	A252	70fr Soldiers, vert.	45	22
a.		Souvenir sheet, imperf.	50	22
1161	A252	90fr Pres. Mitterand, vert.	60	30
a.		Souvenir sheet, imperf.	65	35
1162	A252	105fr Pres. Eyadema, Mitterand, vert.	70	35
a.		Souvenir sheet, imperf.	70	35
1163	A252	130fr Greeting crowd	90	42
a.		Souvenir sheet, imperf.	90	42
		Nos. 1158-1163 (6)	3.17	1.56

Nos. 1161-1163 airmail.

Easter — A253

Paintings: 35fr, Mourners at the Death of Christ, by Bellini. 70fr, Crucifixion, by Raphael (vert.). 90fr, Descent from the Cross, by Carracci. 500fr Christ, by Reni.

1983 Litho. *Perf. 13½x14½*

1164	A253	35fr multi	12	7
1165	A253	70fr multi	22	12
1166	A253	90fr multi	30	15

Souvenir Sheet

Perf. 14½x13½

1167	A253	500fr multi	1.65	80

90fr, 500fr airmail.

Folkdances — A254

1983, Dec. 1 *Perf. 14½x14*

1168	A254	70fr Kondona	22	12
1169	A254	90fr Kondona, diff.	30	15
1170	A254	105fr Toubole	35	16
1171	A254	130fr Adjogbo	42	20

90fr, 105fr, 130fr airmail.

World Communications Year — A255

1983, June 20 Litho. *Perf. 14x14½*

1172	A255	70fr Drummer	22	12
1173	A255	90fr Modern communication	30	15

90fr airmail.

Christmas — A256

1983, Dec. *Perf. 13½x14½*

1174	A256	70fr Catholic Church, Kante	22	12
1175	A256	90fr Altar, Dapaong Cathedral	30	15
1176	A256	105fr Protestant Church, Dapaong	35	18

Souvenir Sheet

1177	A256	500fr Ecumenical Church, Pya	1.65	80

90fr, 105fr, 500fr airmail.

Sarakawa Presidential Assassination Attempt, 10th Anniv. — A257

1984, Jan. 24 Litho. *Perf. 13*

1178	A257	70fr Wrecked plane	22	12
1179	A257	90fr Plane, diff.	30	15
1180	A257	120fr Memorial Hall	40	20
1181	A257	270fr Pres. Eyadema statue, vert.	90	42

120fr, 270fr airmail.

20th Anniv. of World Food Program (1983) A258

1984, May 2 Litho. *Perf. 13*

1182	A258	35fr Orchard	12	7
1183	A258	70fr Fruit tree	22	12
1184	A258	90fr Rice paddy	30	15

Souvenir Sheet

1185	A258	300fr Village, horiz.	1.00	50

The Scott Catalogue value is a retail price, what you could expect to pay for the stamp in a grade of Fine-Very Fine. The value listed is a reference which reflects recent actual dealer selling price.

25th Anniv. of Council of Unity — A259

Easter 1984 — A260

1984, May 29 *Perf. 12*

1186	A259	70fr multi	22	12
1187	A259	90fr multi	30	15

1984 Litho. *Perf. 14x14½*

Various stained-glass windows.

1188	A260	70fr multi	22	12
1189	A260	90fr multi	30	15
1190	A260	120fr multi	40	20
1191	A260	270fr multi	90	45
1192	A260	300fr multi	1.00	50
		Nos. 1188-1192 (5)	2.82	1.42

Souvenir Sheet

1193	A260	500fr multi	1.65	80

Nos. 1189-1193 airmail.

Centenary of German-Togolese Friendship — A261

1984, July 5 Litho. *Perf. 13*

1194	A261	35fr Degbenou Catholic Mission, 1893	12	7
1195	A261	35fr Kara Bridge, 1911	12	7
1196	A261	35fr Treaty Site, Baguida, 1884, vert.	12	7
1197	A261	35fr Degbenou Students, 1893	12	7
1198	A261	35fr Sansane Administrative Post, 1908	12	7
1199	A261	35fr Adjido Official School	12	7
1200	A261	35fr Sokode Cotton Market, 1910	12	7
1201	A261	45fr William Fountain, Atakpame, 1906, vert.	15	8
1202	A261	45fr Lome Main Street, 1895, No. 19	15	8
1203	A261	45fr Police, 1905	15	8
1204	A261	45fr Lome Railroad Construction	15	8
1205	A261	45fr Governor's Palace, Lome, 1905	15	8
1206	A261	45fr No. 9, Commerce Street, Lome	15	8
1207	A261	70fr Nos. 10 and 17	22	12
1208	A261	70fr Lome Wharf, 1903	22	12
1209	A261	90fr G. Nachtigal, vert.	30	15
1210	A261	90fr Wilhelm II, vert.	30	15
1211	A261	90fr O.F. de Bismark, vert.	30	15
1212	A261	90fr J. de Puttkamer, vert.	30	15
1213	A261	90fr A. Koehler, vert.	30	15
1214	A261	90fr W. Horn, vert.	30	15
1215	A261	90fr J.G. de Zech, vert.	30	15
1216	A261	90fr E. Bruckner, vert.	30	15
1217	A261	90fr A.F. de Mecklenburg, vert.	30	15
1218	A261	90fr H.G. de Doering, vert.	30	15
1219	A261	90fr Land Development, 1908	30	15
1220	A261	120fr Postal Courier, No. 8, vert.	40	20
1221	A261	120fr Treaty Signers, 1885	40	20
1222	A261	150fr German & Togolese Children, Flags, vert.	50	25
1223	A261	270fr Aneho Line Locomotive, 1905	90	45
1224	A261	270fr Mallet Locomotive, 1907	90	45
1225	A261	270fr German Ship "Mowe", 1884	90	45
1226	A261	270fr "La Sophie", 1884	90	45
1227	A261	300fr Pres. Eyadema, Helmut Kohl	1.00	50
		Nos. 1194-1227 (34)	11.38	5.81

Souvenir sheets of one exist for each design. Stamp size: 65x80mm.

Donald Duck, 50th Anniv. A262

1984, Sept. 21 Litho. *Perf. 11*

1230	A262	1fr Donald, Chip	5	5
1231	A262	2fr Donald, Chip and Dale	5	5
1232	A262	3fr Louie, Chip and Dale	5	5
1233	A262	5fr Donald, Chip	5	5
1234	A262	10fr Daisy Duck, Donald	5	5
1235	A262	15fr Goofy, Donald	7	5
1236	A262	105fr Huey, Dewey and Louie	30	15
1237	A262	500fr Nephews, Donald	1.40	70
1238	A262	1000fr Nephews, Donald	3.00	1.40
		Nos. 1230-1238 (9)	5.02	2.55

Souvenir Sheets

Perf. 14

1239	A262	1000fr Surprised Donald	3.00	1.40
1240	A262	1000fr Perplexed Donald	3.00	1.40

Nos. 1236-1240 airmail.

Endangered Mammals A263

1984, Oct. 1 Litho. *Perf. 15x14½*

1241	A263	45fr Manatee swimming	14	7
1242	A263	70fr Manatee eating	20	10
1243	A263	90fr Manatees floating	25	14
1244	A263	105fr Young manatee, mother	30	15

Souvenir Sheets

Perf. 14x15, 15x14

1245	A263	1000fr Olive Colobus monkey, vert.	3.00	1.40
1246	A263	1000fr Galago (Bushbaby)	3.00	1.40

Nos. 1243-1246 airmail. See Nos. 1444-1447.

Birth Centenary of Eleanor Roosevelt A264

1984, Oct. 10 Litho. *Perf. 13½*

1247 A264 70fr shown 20 10
1248 A264 90fr Mrs. Roosevelt, Statue of Liberty 25 14

No. 1248 airmail.

Classic Automobiles — A265

1984, Nov. 15 Litho. *Perf. 15*

1249 A265 1fr 1947 Bristol 5 5
1250 A265 2fr 1925 Frazer Nash 5 5
1251 A265 3fr 1950 Healey 5 5
1252 A265 4fr 1925 Kissell 5 5
1253 A265 50fr 1927 La Salle 15 7
1254 A265 90fr 1921 Minerva 25 12
1255 A265 500fr 1950 Morgan 1.40 70
1256 A265 1000fr 1921 Napier 3.00 1.40
Nos. 1249-1256 (8) 5.00 2.49

Souvenir Sheets

1257 A265 1000fr 1941 Nash 3.00 1.40
1258 A265 1000fr 1903 Peugeot 3.00 1.40

Nos. 1254-1258 airmail.

Christmas A266

Perf. 14½x13½
1984, Nov. 23 Litho.

1259 A266 70fr Connestable Madonna 20 10
1260 A266 290fr Cowper Madonna 80 40
1261 A266 300fr Alba Madonna 80 42
1262 A266 500fr Madonna of the Curtain 1.40 70

Souvenir Sheet

1263 A266 1000fr Madonna with Child 3.00 1.40

Nos. 1260-1263 airmail.

African Locomotives — A267

1984, Nov. 30 Litho. *Perf. 15*

1264 A267 1fr Decapod, Madeira 5 5
1265 A267 2fr 2-6-0, Egypt 5 5
1266 A267 3fr 4-8-2+2-8-4, Algeria 5 5
1267 A267 4fr Congo-Ocean diesel 5 5
1268 A267 50fr 0-4-0+0-4-0, Libya 15 7
1269 A267 90fr #49, Malawi 25 12
1270 A267 105fr 1907 Mallet, Togo 30 15
1271 A267 500fr 4-8-2, Rhodesia 1.40 70
1272 A267 1000fr Beyer-Garratt, East Africa 2.75 1.40
Nos. 1264-1272 (9) 5.05 2.64

Souvenir Sheets

1273 A267 1000fr 2-8-2, Ghana 2.75 1.40
1274 A267 1000fr Locomotive, Senegal 2.75 1.40

Nos. 1269-1274 airmail.

Economic Convention, Lome — A268

1984, Dec. 8 Litho. *Perf. 12½*

1275 A268 100fr Map of the Americas 28 15
1276 A268 130fr Map of Eurasia, Africa 38 18
1277 A268 270fr Map of Asia, Australia 75 38

Souvenir Sheet

1278 A268 500fr President Eyadema 1.40 70

Nos. 1275-1277 se-tenant.

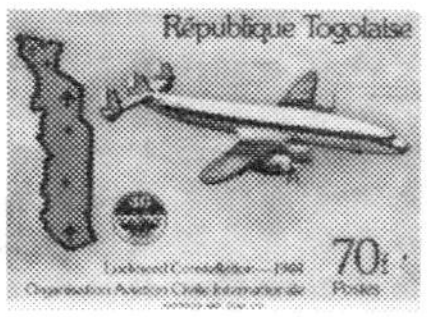

Intl. Civil Aviation Org., 40th Anniv. A269

Map of Togo, ICAO emblem and: 70fr, Lockheed Constellation, 1944. 105fr, Boeing 707, 1954. 200fr, Doublas DC-8-61, 1966. 500fr, Bac/Sud Concorde, 1966. 1000fr, Icarus, by Hans Erni.

1984, Oct. 15 Litho. *Perf. 15x14*

1279 A269 70fr multi 15 8
1280 A269 105fr multi 22 10
1281 A269 200fr multi 40 20
1282 A269 500fr multi 1.00 50

Souvenir Sheet

1283 A269 1000fr multi 2.00 1.00

Nos. 1280-1283 airmail.

Fresco of the 12 Apostles, Baptistry of the Aryans, Ravenna, Italy, — A270

Designs: 1fr, St. Paul. 2fr, St. Thomas. 3fr, St. Matthew. 4fr, St. James the Younger. 5fr, St. Simon. 70fr, St. Thaddeaus Judas. 90fr, St. Bartholomew. 105fr, St. Philip. 200fr, St. John. 270fr, St. James the Greater. 400fr, St. Andrew. 500fr, St. Peter. No. 1296, The Last Supper, by Andrea del Castagno, c. 1421-1457, horiz.. No, 1297, Coronation of the Virgin, by Raphael, 1483-1520, horiz..

1984, Dec. 14 *Perf. 15*

1284 A270 1fr multi 5 5
1285 A270 2fr multi 5 5
1286 A270 3fr multi 5 5
1287 A270 4fr multi 5 5
1288 A270 5fr multi 5 5
1289 A270 70fr multi 15 8
1290 A270 90fr multi 18 10
1291 A270 105fr multi 20 10
1292 A270 200fr multi 40 20
1293 A270 270fr multi 55 30
1294 A270 400fr multi 80 40
1295 A270 500fr multi 1.00 50
Nos. 1284-1295 (12) 3.53 1.93

Souvenir Sheets

1296 A270 1000fr multi 2.00 1.00
1297 A270 1000fr multi 2.00 1.00

Nos. 1290-1297 airmail.

Race Horses A271

1985, Jan. 10

1298 A271 1fr Allez France 5 5
1299 A271 2fr Arkle, vert. 5 5
1300 A271 3fr Tingle Creek, vert. 5 5
1301 A271 4fr Interco 5 5
1302 A271 50fr Dawn Run 10 5
1303 A271 90fr Seattle Slew, vert. 18 10
1304 A271 500fr Nijinsky 1.00 50
1305 A271 1000fr Politician 2.00 1.00
Nos. 1298-1305 (8) 3.48 1.85

Souvenir Sheets

1306 A271 1000fr Shergar 2.00 1.00
1307 A271 1000fr Red Rum 2.00 1.00

Nos. 1303-1307 airmail.

Easter — A272

Paintings by Raphael (1483-1520).

Perf. 13½x14½, 14½x13½
1985, Mar. 7

1308 A272 70fr Christ and His Flock 15 8
1309 A272 90fr Christ and the Fishermen 18 10
1310 A272 135fr The Blessed Christ, vert. 25 14
1311 A272 150fr The Entombment, vert. 30 16
1312 A272 250fr The Resurrection, vert. 50 25
Nos. 1308-1312 (5) 1.38 73

Souvenir Sheet

1313 A272 1000fr The Resurrection, diff. 2.00 1.00

Nos. 1309-1313 airmail.

Technical & Cultural Cooperation Agency, 15th Anniv. — A273

1985, Mar. 20 *Perf. 12½*

1314 A273 70fr multi 15 8
1315 A273 90fr multi 18 10

Philexafrica '85, Lome — A274

1985, May 9 *Perf. 13*

1316 A274 200fr Woman carrying fruit basket 40 20
1317 A274 200fr Man plowing field 40 20

Nos. 1316-1317 printed se-tenant with central label picturing UAPT emblem.

Scarification Ritual — A275

1985, May 14 *Perf. 14x15*

1318 A275 25fr Kabye (Pya) 5 5
1319 A275 70fr Mollah (Kotokoli) 15 8
1320 A275 90fr Maba (Dapaong) 18 10
1321 A275 105fr Kabye (Pagouda) 22 10
1322 A275 270fr Peda 55 30
Nos. 1318-1322 (5) 1.15 63

Nos. 1320-1322 airmail.

Seashells A276

Designs: 70fr, Clavatula muricata. 90fr, Marginella desjardini. 120fr, Clavatula nifat. 135fr, Cypraea stercoraria. 270fr, Conus genuanus. 1000fr, Dancers wearing traditional shell decorations.

1985, June 1 *Perf. 15x14*

1323 A276 70fr multi 5 5
1324 A276 90fr multi 18 10
1325 A276 120fr multi 25 12
1326 A276 135fr multi 25 14
1327 A276 270fr multi 55 30
Nos. 1323-1327 (5) 1.28 71

Souvenir Sheet

1327A A276 1000fr multi 2.00 1.00

Nos. 1324-1327A airmail.

Nos. 1253, 1256-1258 Overprinted "Exposition Mondiale 1985 / Tsukuba, Japon"

1985, June *Perf. 15*

1328 A265 50fr #1253 10 5
1329 A265 1000fr #1256 2.00 1.00

Souvenir Sheets

1330 A265 1000fr #1257 2.00 1.00
1331 A265 1000fr #1258 2.00 1.00

EXPO '85.

Audubon Birth Bicent. — A277

Illustrations by artist-naturalist J.J. Audubon (1785-1851).

1985, Aug. 13 *Perf. 13*

1332 A277 90fr Larus bonapartii 18 10
1333 A277 120fr Pelecanus occidentalis 25 12
1334 A277 135fr Cassidix mexicanus 25 14
1335 A277 270fr Aquila chrysaetos 55 30
1336 A277 500fr Picus erythrocephalus 1.00 50
Nos. 1332-1336 (5) 2.23 1.16

Souvenir Sheet

1337 A277 1000fr Dendroica petechia 2.00 1.00

Nos. 1332, 1334 and 1336-1337 airmail.

Dove, UN Emblem — A278

Kara Port Construction — A279

Design: 115fr, Hands, UN emblem. 250fr, Millet crop, Atalote Research Facility. 500fr, UN, Togo flags, statesmen.

1985, Oct. 24 Litho. *Perf. 13*

1338 A278 90fr multi 18 10
1339 A278 115fr multi 22 12
1340 A279 150fr multi 30 16
1341 A279 250fr multi 50 25
1342 A279 500fr multi 1.00 50
Nos. 1338-1342 (5) 2.20 1.13

UN, 40th anniv. Nos. 1340-1342 are airmail.

Nos. 1267, 1270, 1272, 1273 Ovptd. with Rotary Emblem and "80e ANNIVERSAIRE DU / ROTARY INTERNATIONAL"

1985 Litho. *Perf. 15*

1343 A267 4fr multi 5 5
1344 A267 105fr multi 20 10
1345 A267 1000fr multi 2.00 1.00

Souvenir Sheet

1346 A267 1000fr multi 2.00 1.00

Nos. 1344-1346 are airmail.

Christmas A280

Religious paintings and statuary: 90fr, The Garden of Roses Madonna. 115fr, Madonna and Child, Byzantine, 11th cent. 150fr, Rest During the Flight to Egypt, by Gerard David (1450-1523). 160fr, African Madonna, 16th cent. 250fr, African Madonna, c. 1900. 500fr, Mystic Madonna, by Sandro Botticelli (1444-1510).

Perf. 14½x13½

1985, Dec. 10 Litho.

1347 A280 90fr multi 22 12
1348 A280 115fr multi 32 16
1349 A280 150fr multi 40 20
1350 A280 160fr multi 42 20
1351 A280 250fr multi 65 35
Nos. 1347-1351 (5) 2.01 1.03

Souvenir Sheet

1352 A280 500fr multi 1.40 65

Nos. 1348-1352 air airmail. No. 1352 contains one stamp 36x51mm.

Nos. 1302, 1305-1306 Ovptd. "75e Anniversaire / du Scoutisme Feminin"

1986, Jan. *Perf. 15*

1353 A271 50fr multi 20 10
1354 A271 1000fr multi 4.00 2.00

Souvenir Sheet

1355 A271 1000fr multi 4.00 2.00

Nos. 1354-1355 airmail.

Nos. 1268-1269, 1271, 1273-1274 Ovptd. "150e ANNIVERSAIRE / DE CHEMIN FER 'LUDWIG'."

1985, Dec. 27 Litho. *Perf. 15*

1356 A267 50fr multi 28 14
1357 A267 90fr multi 50 25
1358 A267 500fr multi 2.75 1.40

Souvenir Sheets

1359 A267 1000fr multi, No. 1273 5.50 2.75
1360 A267 1000fr multi, No. 1274 5.50 2.75

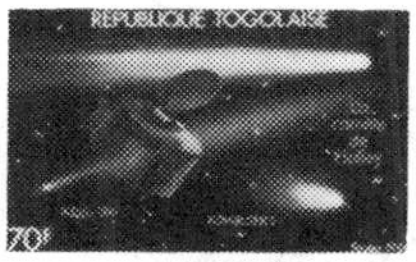

Halley's Comet A281

Designs: 70fr, Suisei space probe, comets. 90fr, Vega-1 probe. 150fr, Space telescope. 200fr, Giotto probe, comet over Togo. 1000fr, Edmond Halley, Sir Isaac Newton.

1986, Mar. 27 *Perf. 13*

1361 A281 70fr multi 40 20
1362 A281 90fr multi 50 25
1363 A281 150fr multi 82 40
1364 A281 200fr multi 1.10 55

Souvenir Sheet

1365 A281 1000fr multi 5.50 2.75

Nos. 1362-1365 are airmail.

Flowering and Fruit-bearing Plants — A282

1986, June *Perf. 14*

1366 A282 70fr Anacardium occidentale 40 20
1367 A282 90fr Ananas comosus 50 25
1368 A282 120fr Persea americana 65 32
1369 A282 135fr Carica papaya 75 38
1370 A282 290fr Mangifera indica, vert. 1.60 80
Nos. 1366-1370 (5) 3.90 1.95

Nos. 1368-1370 airmail.

1986 World Cup Soccer Championships, Mexico — A283

Various soccer plays.

1986, May 5 Litho. *Perf. 15x14*

1371 A283 70fr multi 38 20
1372 A283 90fr multi 50 25
1373 A283 130fr multi 70 35
1374 A283 300fr multi 1.60 80

Souvenir Sheet

1375 A283 1000fr multi 5.50 2.75

Nos. 1372-1375 are airmail.

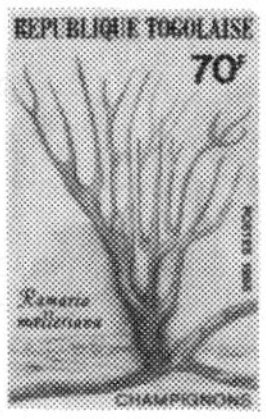

Mushrooms — A284

1986, June 9 *Perf. 13x12½*

1376 A284 70fr Ramaria moelleriana 38 20
1377 A284 90fr Hygrocybe firma 50 25
1378 A284 150fr Kalchbrennera corallocephala 82 40
1379 A284 200fr Cookeina tricholoma 1.10 55

Intl. Youth Year — A285

1986, June *Perf. 13½x14½*

1380 A285 25fr shown 14 8
1381 A285 90fr Youths, doves 50 25

Dated 1985.

Wrestling — A286

Wedding of Prince Andrew and Sarah Ferguson — A287

1986, July 16 *Perf. 14x15, 15x14*

1382 A286 15fr Single-leg takedown move 8 5
1383 A286 20fr Completing takedown 12 6
1384 A286 70fr Pinning combination 38 20
1385 A286 90fr Riding 50 25

Nos. 1384-1385 horiz. No. 1385 is airmail.

1986, July 23 *Perf. 14*

1386 A287 10fr Sarah Ferguson 6 5
1387 A287 1000fr Prince Andrew 5.50 2.75

Souvenir Sheet

1388 A287 1000fr Couple 5.50 2.75

Nos. 1387-1388 are airmail.

Easter A288

Paintings (details): 25fr, 1000fr, The Resurrection, by Andrea Mantegna (1431-1506), vert. 70fr, The Calvary, by Paolo Veronese (1528-1588), vert. 90fr, The Last Supper, by Jacopo Tintoretto (1518-1594). 200fr, Christ at the Tomb, by Alonso Berruguette (1486-1561).

Perf. 14x15, 15x14

1986, Mar. 24 Litho.

1389 A288 25fr multi 14 8
1390 A288 70fr multi 38 20
1391 A288 90fr multi 50 25
1392 A288 200fr multi 1.10 55

Souvenir Sheet

1393 A288 1000fr multi 5.50 2.75

Nos. 1391-1393 are airmail.

Nos. 1371-1374 Ovptd. or Inscribed "DEMI-FINALE / ARGENTINE 2 / BELGIQUE 0," "DEMI-FINALE / ALLEMAGNE / DE L'OUEST 2 / FRANCE 0," "3 eme et 4 eme PLACE / FRANCE 4 / BELGIQUE 2," & "FINALE / ARGENTINE 3 / ALLEMAGNE / DE L'OUEST 2"

1986, Aug. 4 Litho. *Perf. 15x14*

1394 A283 70fr multi 38 20
1395 A283 90fr multi 50 25
1396 A283 130fr multi 70 35
1397 A283 300fr multi 1.60 80

Nos. 1395-1397 are airmail.

Hotels — A289

1986, Aug. 18 *Perf. 12½*

1398 A289 70fr Fazao 38 20
1399 A289 90fr Sarakawa 50 25
1400 A289 120fr Le Lac 65 32

Nos. 1399-1400 are airmail.

Keran Natl. Park A290

1986, Sept. 15 Litho. *Perf. 14½*

1401 A290 70fr Wild ducks 40 20
1402 A290 90fr Antelope 50 25
1403 A290 100fr Elephant 55 28
1404 A290 130fr Waterbuck 70 35

Nos. 1402-1404 are airmail.

Nos. 1361-1365 Ovptd. with Halley's Comet Emblem in Silver

1986, Oct. 9 *Perf. 13*

1405 A281 70fr multi 40 20
1406 A281 90fr multi 50 25
1407 A281 150fr multi 82 40
1408 A281 200fr multi 1.10 55

Souvenir Sheet

1409 A281 1000fr multi 5.50 2.75

Nos. 1406-1409 are airmail.

Frescoes from Togoville Church — A291

Togoville Church — A292

1986, Dec. 22 Litho. *Perf. 14½x15*

1410 A291 45fr Annunciation 25 12
1411 A291 120fr Nativity 65 32
1412 A291 130fr Adoration of the Magi 70 35
1413 A291 200fr Flight into Egypt 1.10 55

Souvenir Sheet

1414 A292 1000fr multi 5.50 2.75

Christmas. Nos. 1411-1414 are airmail.

Phosphate Mining — A293

Natl. Liberation, 20th Anniv. — A294

1987, Jan. 13 Litho. *Perf. 12½*

1415 A293 35fr shown 22 10
1416 A293 50fr Sugar refinery, Anie 30 15
1417 A293 70fr Nangbeto Dam 42 20
1418 A293 90fr Hotel, post office in Lome 55 28
1419 A293 100fr Post office, Kara 60 30
1420 A293 120fr Peace monument 72 35
1421 A293 130fr Youth vaccination campaign 78 40
Nos. 1415-1421 (7) 3.59 1.78

Souvenir Sheet

Perf. 13

1422 A294 500fr shown 3.00 1.50

Nos. 1419-1422 are airmail.

Easter — A295

World Rugby Cup — A296

Paintings in Nadoba Church, Keran: 90fr, The Last Supper. 130fr, Christ on the Cross. 300fr, The Resurrection. 500fr, Evangelization in Tamberma, fresco, horiz.

1987, Apr. 13 Litho. *Perf. 14½x15*

1423 A295 90fr multi 55 28
1424 A295 130fr multi 78 40
1425 A295 300fr multi 1.80 90

Souvenir Sheet

Perf. 15x14½

1426 A295 500fr multi 3.00 1.50

Nos. 1424-1426 are airmail.

1987, May 11 *Perf. 15x14½*

1427 A296 70fr Dive 42 20
1428 A296 130fr Running with the ball 78 40
1429 A296 300fr Scrimmage 1.80 90

Souvenir Sheet

Perf. 14½x15

1430 A296 1000fr shown 6.00 3.00

Nos. 1427-1429 are horiz. Nos. 1428-1430 are airmail.

Indigenous Flowers A297

1987, June 22 Litho. *Perf. 13*

1431 A297 70fr Adenium obesum 38 20
1432 A297 90fr Amorphophallus abyssinicus, vert. 50 25
1433 A297 100fr Ipomoea mauritana 55 28
1434 A297 120fr Salacia togoica, vert. 68 35

Nos. 1432-1434 are airmail.

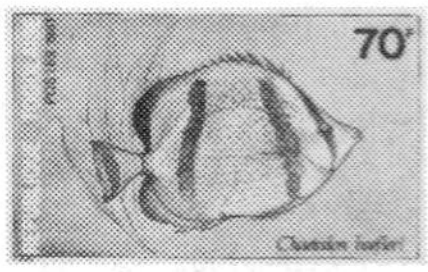

Fish A298

1987, Sept. 8 Litho. *Perf. 13*

1435 A298 70fr Chaetodon hoefleri 48 25
1436 A298 90fr Tetraodon lineatus 60 30
1437 A298 120fr Chaetodipterus goreensis 80 40
1438 A298 130fr Labeo parvus 88 45

1988 Summer Olympics, Seoul — A299

Buddha and athletes

1987, Sept. 14 *Perf. 12½*

1439 A299 70fr Long jump 48 25
1440 A299 90fr Relay 60 30
1441 A299 200fr Cycling 1.35 68
1442 A299 250fr Javelin 1.70 85

Souvenir Sheet

1443 A299 1000fr Tennis 6.75 3.40

Nos. 1440-1443 are airmail.

World Wildlife Fund Type of 1984

1987, Dec. 15 Litho. *Perf. 14*

Size: 32x24mm

1444 A263 60fr like 45fr 42 20
1445 A263 75fr like 70fr 52 25
1446 A263 80fr like 90fr 55 28
1447 A263 100fr like 105fr 72 35

No. 1447 is airmail.

Christmas A300

Eradication of Tuberculosis A301

Paintings: 40fr, Springtime in Paradise, horiz.. 45fr, Creation of Man, Sistine Chapel, by Michelangelo, horiz.. 105fr, Presentation in the Temple. 270fr, Original Sin. 500fr, Nativity, horiz.

Perf. 15x14, 14x15

1987, Dec. 15 Litho.

1448 A300 40fr multi 28 14
1449 A300 45fr multi 32 16
1450 A300 105fr multi 75 38
1451 A300 270fr multi 1.90 95

Souvenir Sheet

1452 A300 500fr multi 3.50 1.75

Nos. 1450-1452 are airmail.

Foreign postal stationery (stamped envelopes, postal cards and air letter sheets) lies beyond the scope of this Catalogue, which is limited to adhesive postage stamps.

Perf. 12½x13, 13x12½

1987, Dec. 28

1453 A301 80fr Inoculation, horiz. 58 30
1454 A301 90fr Family under umbrella 65 32
1455 A301 115fr Hospital, horiz. 80 40

Health for all by the year 2000. Nos. 1454-1455 are airmail.

Intl. Fund for Agricultural Development (IFAD), 10th Anniv. — A302

1988, Feb. 25 Litho. *Perf. 13½*

1456 A302 90fr multi 65 32

Easter 1988 — A303

Stained-glass windows: 70fr, Jesus and the Disciples at Emmaus. 90fr, Mary at the Foot of the Cross. 120fr, The Crucifixion. 200fr, St. Thomas Touching the Resurrected Christ. 500fr, The Agony of Jesus on the Mount of Olives.

1988, June 6 Litho. *Perf. 14x15*

1457 A303 70fr multi 40 20
1458 A303 90fr multi 65 32
1459 A303 120fr multi 85 42
1460 A303 200fr multi 1.40 70

Souvenir Sheet

1461 A303 500fr multi 3.50 1.75

Nos. 1459-1461 are airmail.

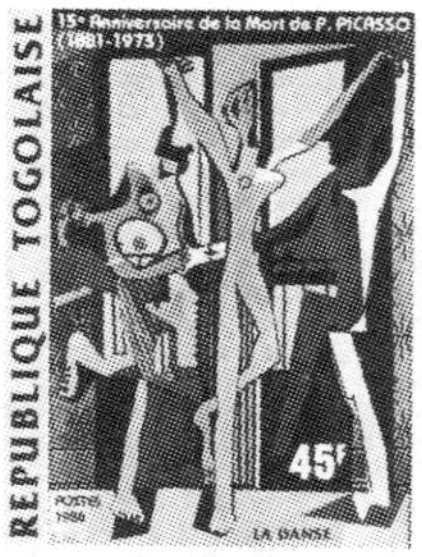

Paintings by Picasso (1881-1973) A304

Designs: 45fr, The Dance. 160fr, Portrait of a Young Girl. No. 1464, Gueridon. No. 1465, Mandolin and Guitar.

1988, Apr. 25 Litho. *Perf. 12½x13*

1462 A304 45fr multi 30 15
1463 A304 160fr multi 1.05 52
1464 A304 300fr multi 2.00 1.00

Souvenir Sheet

1465 A304 300fr multi 2.00 1.00

Nos. 1464-1465 are airmail.

1988 Summer Olympics, Seoul — A305

1988, Aug. 30 *Perf. 14x15*

1466 A305 70fr Basketball 45 22
1467 A305 90fr Tennis 60 30
1468 A305 120fr Archery 80 40
1469 A305 200fr Discus 1.30 65

Souvenir Sheet

1470 A305 500fr Marathon 3.25 1.65

Nos. 1468-1470 are airmail.

WHO, 40th Anniv. — A306

1988, Oct. 28 Litho. *Perf. 13*

1471 A306 80fr shown 55 28
1472 A306 125fr Emblems 85 42

Traditional Costumes — A307

1988, July 25 Litho. *Perf. 13½*

1473 A307 80fr Watchi chief 52 20
1474 A307 125fr Watchi woman 80 40
1475 A307 165fr Kotokoli 1.05 52
1476 A307 175fr Ewe 1.15 58

Souvenir Sheet

1477 A307 500fr Moba 3.25 1.65

PHILTOGO 3, Aug. 11-12 — A308

Children's drawings by: 10fr, B. Gossner. 35fr, K. Ekoue-Kouvahey. 70fr, A. Abbey. 90fr, T.D. Lawson. 120fr, A. Tazzar.

1988, Dec. 3

1478 A308 10fr multi 8 5
1479 A308 35fr multi 22 12
1480 A308 70fr multi 45 22
1481 A308 90fr multi 58 30
1482 A308 120fr multi 78 40
Nos. 1478-1482 (5) 2.11 1.09

Christmas — A309

Paintings: 80fr, Adoration of the Magi, by Brueghel. 150fr, The Virgin, Infant Jesus, Sts. Jerome and Dominic, by Lippi. 175fr, Madonna, Infant Jesus, St. Joseph and Infant John the Baptist, by Barocci. 195fr, Virgin and Child, by Bellini. 750fr, The Holy Family and a Shepherd, by Titian.

1988, Dec. 15 *Perf. 14½x15*

1483 A309 80fr multi 50 25
1484 A309 150fr multi 92 45
1485 A309 175fr multi 1.10 55

1486 A309 195fr multi 1.20 60

Souvenir Sheet

1487 A309 750fr multi 3.60 1.80

Nos. 1484-1487 are airmail.

Natl. Industries A310

1988, May 28 Litho. *Perf. 13*

1488 A310 125fr Cement factory 82 40
1489 A310 165fr Bottling plant 1.10 55
1490 A310 195fr Phosphate mine 1.30 65
1491 A310 200fr Plastics factory 1.35 68
1492 A310 300fr Manufacturing plant 2.00 1.00
Nos. 1488-1492 (5) 6.57 3.28

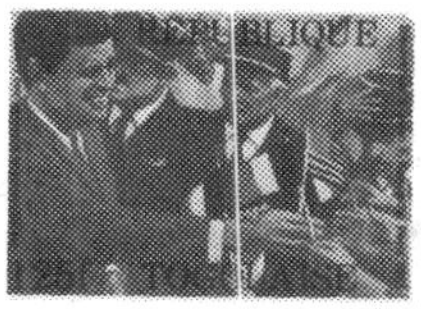

John F. Kennedy A311

Designs: 125fr, Arrival in Paris, 1961. 155fr, At Hotel de Ville, vert. 165fr, With De Gaulle at Elysee Palace, vert. 180fr, Boarding Air Force One with Jackie at Orly, France. 750fr, Kennedy and De Gaulle, natl. colors, vert.

1988, July 30 Litho. *Perf. 14*

1493 A311 125fr multi 82 40
1494 A311 155fr multi 1.05 52
1495 A311 165fr multi 1.10 55
1496 A311 180fr multi 1.20 60

Souvenir Sheet

Perf. 13½x13

1497 A311 750fr multi 5.00 2.50

Hairstyles A312

1988, Nov. 20 *Perf. 13*

1498 A312 80fr shown 52 25
1499 A312 125fr multi, diff. 82 40
1500 A312 170fr multi, diff. 1.15 58
1501 A312 180fr multi, diff., vert. 1.20 60

Souvenir Sheet

Perf. 14

1502 A312 500fr multi, diff. 3.25 1.65

Sarakawa Plane Crash, 15th Anniv. A313

Portrait and various views of the wreckage.

1989, Jan. 24 *Perf. 13½*

1503 A313 10fr multi 7 5
1504 A313 80fr multi, vert. 52 25
1505 A313 125fr multi 82 40

SEMI-POSTAL STAMPS

Curie Issue

Common Design Type

1938 Unwmk. Engr. *Perf. 13*

B1 CD80 1.75fr + 50c brt ultra 8.00 8.00

French Revolution Issue

Common Design Type

Photo., Name and Value Typo. in Black

1939

B2 CD83 45(c) + 25(c) grn 3.25 3.25
B3 CD83 70(c) + 30(c) brn 3.25 3.25
B4 CD83 90(c) + 35(c) red org 3.25 3.25
B5 CD83 1.25fr + 1fr rose pink 3.25 3.25
B6 CD83 2.25fr + 2fr bl 3.25 3.25
Nos. B2-B6 (5) 16.25 16.25

French Revolution, 150th anniv. Surtax for defense of the colonies.

Stamps of 1927-41 Surcharged in Red or Black

SECOURS
+ 1 fr.
NATIONAL

1941 *Perf. 14 x 13½, 12½*

B7 A10 50c + 1fr chnt (Bk) 70 70
B8 A7 80c + 2fr ind & dl vio (Bk) 2.50 2.50
B9 A8 1.50fr + 2fr bl & lt bl (Bk) 2.50 2.50
B10 A11 2fr + 3fr lt ultra (R) 2.50 2.50

Catalogue values for unused stamps in this section, from this point to the end of the section, are for Never Hinged items.

Common Design Type and

Togolese Militiaman SP1

Military Infirmary SP2

1941 Photo. *Perf. 13½*

B10A SP1 1fr + 1fr red 40
B10B CD86 1.50fr + 3fr mar 40
B10C SP2 2.50fr + 1fr bl 40

Nos. B10A-B10C were issued by the Vichy government, and were not placed on sale in Togo.

Nos. 296-297 were surcharged "OEUVRES COLONIALES" and surtax (including change of denomination of the 2.50fr to 50c). These were issued in 1944 by the Vichy government and were not placed on sale in Togo.

Tropical Medicine Issue

Common Design Type

1950 Engr. *Perf. 13*

B11 CD100 10fr + 2fr ind & dk bl 2.00 2.00

The surtax was for charitable work.

Republic

Patient on Stretcher SP3

Uprooted Oak Emblem SP4

Designs: 30fr+5fr, Feeding infant. 50fr+10fr, Blood transfusion.

1959 Engr. *Perf. 13*

B12 SP3 20fr + 5fr multi 45 38
a. Souvenir sheet of 4 1.90 1.90
B13 SP3 30fr + 5fr bl, car & brn 45 38
a. Souvenir sheet of 4 1.90 1.90
B14 SP3 50fr + 10fr emer, brn & car 45 45
a. Souvenir sheet of 4 1.90 1.90

Issued for the Red Cross.

Nos. B12a, B13a, B14a exist imperf.; same values.

1960 Unwmk. *Perf. 13*

Design: No. B16 similar to No. B15, with emblem on top.

B15 SP4 25fr + 5fr dk bl, brn & yel grn 30 30
B16 SP4 45fr + 5fr dk bl, brn & ol 50 50

World Refugee Year, July 1, 1959-June 30, 1960. The surtax was for aid to refugees.

AIR POST STAMPS

Common Design Type

1940 Unwmk. Engr. *Perf. 12½x12*

C1 CD85 1.90fr ultra 10 10
C2 CD85 2.90fr dk red 10 10
C3 CD85 4.50fr dk gray grn 22 12
C4 CD85 4.90fr yel bis 35 20
C5 CD85 6.90fr dp org 55 38
Nos. C1-C5 (5) 1.32 90

Common Design Type

Inscribed "Togo" across top

1942

C6 CD88 50c car & bl 5
C7 CD88 1fr brn & blk 12
C8 CD88 2fr grn & red brn 5
C9 CD88 3fr dk bl & scar 15
C10 CD88 5fr vio & brn red 15

Frame Engraved, Center Typographed

C11 CD89 10fr ultra, ind & org 15
C12 CD89 20fr rose car, mag & gray blk 15
C13 CD89 50fr yel grn, dl grn & lt vio 55 65
Nos. C6-C13 (8) 1.37

There is doubt whether Nos. C6 to C12 were officially placed in use.

Catalogue values for unused stamps in this section, from this point to the end of the section, are for Never Hinged items.

Elephants — AP1

Plane — AP2

Plane — AP3

Post Runner and Plane — AP4

1947, Oct. 6 Engr. *Perf. 12½*

C14 AP1 40fr blue 1.90 1.50
C15 AP2 50fr lt ultra, & red vio 1.10 90
C16 AP3 100fr emer & dk brn 1.75 1.40
C17 AP4 200fr lil rose 3.00 1.50

UPU Issue

Common Design Type

1949, July 4 *Perf. 13*

C18 CD99 25fr multi 3.00 3.00

Liberation Issue

Common Design Type

1954, June 6

C19 CD102 15fr ind & pur 2.25 2.25

Freight Highway — AP5

1954, Nov. 29

C20 AP5 500fr ind & dk grn 15.00 14.00

Republic

Independence Allegory — AP6

Unwmk.

1957, Oct. 29 Engr. *Perf. 13*

C21 AP6 25fr bl, ol bis & ver 38 30

1st anniv. of Togo's autonomy.

Flag and Torch — AP7

Great White Egret — AP8

1957, Oct. 29

C22 AP7 50fr multi 60 30
C23 AP7 100fr multi 1.10 45
C24 AP7 200fr multi 2.25 75
C25 AP8 500fr ind, lt bl & grn 7.00 3.00

Types of 1957 inscribed: "Republique du Togo" and

Flag, Plane and Map — AP9

1959, Jan. 15 Engr. *Perf. 13*
C26 AP9 25fr ultra, emer & vio brn 18 8
C27 AP7 50fr dk bl, dl grn & red 38 18
C28 AP7 100fr multi 1.10 38
C29 AP7 200fr dk grn, red & ultra 2.25 85
C30 AP8 500fr blk brn, rose lil & grn 6.25 1.90
Nos. C26-C30 (5) 10.16 3.39

Hotel Le Benin AP10

Eagle and Map of Togo AP11

Perf. 14½x15, 15x14½
1960, Apr. 27 Litho. Unwmk.
C31 AP10 100fr crim, emer & yel 80 18
C32 AP10 200fr multi 1.90 30
C33 AP11 500fr grn & gldn brn 4.50 25

Proclamation of Togo's full independence, Apr. 27, 1960.

Type of Mail Service Issue, 1963

Design: 100fr, Boeing 707 and stamps of 1960.

1963, Jan. 12 Photo. *Perf. 13*
C34 A41 100fr multi 80 40
a. Souv. sheet of 4 1.65 1.65

No. C34a contains 4 stamps similar to Nos. 441-443 and C34, with simulated perforations.

Type of Emancipation Issue, 1963

1963, Oct. Unwmk. *Perf. 13x14*
C35 A45 100fr multi 80 40
a. Souv. sheet of 4 1.20 1.00

No. C35a contains 4 imperf. stamps similar to Nos. 454-456 and C35.

Type of 1964 Regular Issue

Designs: 50fr, Black-bellied seed-cracker. 100fr, Blue-billed mannikin. 200fr, Redheaded lovebird. 250fr, African gray parrot. 500fr, Yellow-breasted barbet.

1964-65 Photo. *Perf. 14*
Size: 22½x31mm
Birds in Natural Colors
C36 A47 50fr yel grn 40 22
C37 A47 100fr ocher 80 30
C38 A47 200fr dl bl grn 1.50 80
C39 A47 250fr dl rose ('65) 2.00 1.00
C40 A47 500fr violet 4.00 1.50
Nos. C36-C40 (5) 8.70 3.82

No. C35 Overprinted Diagonally: "En Mémoire de / JOHN F. KENNEDY / 1917-1963"

1964, Feb. *Perf. 13x14*
C41 A45 100fr multi 80 42

Issued in memory of John F. Kennedy.

Same overprint was applied to stamps of No. C35a, with black border and commemorative inscription added. Two sheets exist: with and without gray silhouetted head of Kennedy covering all four stamps.

Liberation Type of 1964

1964, May 25 *Perf. 14x13*
C42 A50 100fr dl bl grn & dk brn 80 40

Olympic Games Type of Regular Issue, 1964

Design: 100fr, Tennis.

1964, Oct. Photo. *Perf. 14*
C43 A52 100fr pale brn 1.00 40
a. Souv. sheet of 3 1.40 1.40

No. C43a contains 3 imperf. stamps similar to Nos. 493-494 and C43.

Flag of Togo and Jet — AP12

1964, Dec. 5 Unwmk. *Perf. 14x13*
C44 AP12 100fr multi 1.00 40

Inauguration of the national airline "Air Togo." For souvenir sheet see No. 499a.

Lincoln Type of Regular Issue, 1965

1965, June Photo. *Perf. 13½x14*
C45 A58 100fr ol gray 1.20 40
a. Souv. sheet of 2 1.25 1.25

No. C45a contains two imperf. stamps similar to Nos. 524 and C45.

Sports Type of Regular Issue, 1965

Design: 100fr, Soccer player, flags of Togo and Congo.

1965, July Unwmk. *Perf. 14x13*
C46 A59 100fr multi 1.00 40

Churchill Type of Regular Issue

1965, Aug. 7 Photo. *Perf. 13½x14*
C47 A60 85fr car rose 90 40
a. Souv. sheet of 2 1.40 1.40

No. C47a contains two imperf. stamps similar to Nos. 532 and C47.

UN Type of Regular Issue, 1965

Design: 100fr, Apple, grapes, wheat and "ONU."

1965, Dec. 15 *Perf. 14x13½*
C48 A65 100fr dk bl & bis 1.00 40
a. Souv. sheet of 2 1.40 1.40

No. C48a contains two imperf. stamps similar to Nos. 548 and C48 with simulated perforations.

Pope Type of Regular Issue

Designs: 45fr, Pope speaking at UN rostrum, world map and UN emblem. 90fr, Pope, plane and UN emblem.

1966, March 5 Litho. *Perf. 12*
C49 A66 45fr emer & multi 42 14
C50 A66 90fr gray & multi 90 22
a. Souv. sheet of 2 1.50 1.20

No. C50a contains one each of Nos. C49-C50.

Red Cross Type of Regular Issue

Design: 100fr, Jean Henri Dunant and Togolese Flag.

1966, May 7 Litho. *Perf. 12*
C51 A67 100fr multi 1.10 35

WHO Type of Regular Issue

Flowers: 50fr, Daisies and WHO Headquarters. 90fr, Talisman roses and WHO Headquarters.

1966, May Litho. *Perf. 12*
C52 A68 50fr lt bl & multi 50 10
C53 A68 90fr gray & multi 90 14
a. Souv. sheet of 2, #C52-C53 1.40 1.20

Air Afrique Issue
Common Design Type

1966, Aug. 31 Photo. *Perf. 13*
C54 CD123 30fr brt grn, blk & lem 30 10

Arts and Crafts Type of Regular Issue

Designs: 60fr, Basket maker. 90fr, Wood carver.

1966, Sept. *Perf. 13x14*
C55 A69 60fr ultra, org & blk 60 16
C56 A69 90fr brt rose, yel & blk 90 20

Dancer Type of Regular Issue

Designs: 50fr, Woman from North Togo holding branches. 60fr, Man from North Togo with horned helmet.

1966, Nov. Photo. *Perf. 13x14*
C57 A70 50fr multi 50 20
C58 A70 60fr ol & multi 60 22

Soccer Type of Regular Issue

Designs: Different Soccer Scenes.

1966, Dec. 14 Photo. *Perf. 14x13*
C59 A71 50fr org, brn & pur 50 16
C60 A71 60fr ultra, brn & org 60 20
a. Souv. sheet of 3 1.50 1.40

No. C60a contains 3 imperf. stamps similar to Nos. 582, C59-C60.

Fish Type of Regular Issue

Designs: 45fr, Yellow jack and trawler. 90fr, Banded distichodus and seiner.

1967, Jan. 14 Photo. *Perf. 14*
Fish in Natural Colors
C61 A72 45fr org & brn 42 16
C62 A72 90fr emer & dk bl 90 30

UNICEF Type of Regular Issue

UNICEF Emblem and: 45fr, Girl and miniature poodle. 90fr, African boy and greyhound.

1967, Feb. 11 Photo. *Perf. 14x13½*
C63 A73 45fr yel, red brn & blk 42 16
C64 A73 90fr ultra, dk grn & blk 90 30
a. Souv. sheet of 2 1.40 1.20

No. C64a contains 2 imperf., lithographed stamps with simulated perforations similar to Nos. C63-C64.

Satellite Type of Regular Issue

Designs: 50fr, Diamant rocket (vert.). 90fr, Fr-1 satellite (vert.).

1967, Mar. 18 Photo. *Perf. 13½x14*
C65 A74 50fr multi 55 16
C66 A74 90fr multi 1.00 30
a. Souv. sheet of 2 1.50 1.20

No. C66a contains 2 imperf. stamps similar to Nos. C65-C66 with simulated perforations.

Musician Type of Regular Issue

UNESCO Emblem and: 45fr, Johann Sebastian Bach and organ. 90fr, Ludwig van Beethoven, violin and clarinet.

1967, Apr. 15 Photo. *Perf. 14x13½*
C67 A75 45fr multi 42 14
C68 A75 90fr pink & multi 90 25
a. Souv. sheet of 2 1.40 1.10

No. C68a contains 2 imperf. stamps similar to Nos. C67-C68 with simulated perforations.

EXPO '67 Type of Regular Issue

EXPO '67 Emblem and: 45fr, French pavilion and roses. 60fr, British pavilion and day lilies. 90fr, African village and bird-of-paradise flower. 105fr, United States pavilion and daisies.

1967, May 30 Photo. *Perf. 14*
C69 A76 45fr multi 42 14
C70 A76 60fr multi 60 20
C71 A76 90fr yel & multi 80 35
a. Souv. sheet of 3 2.00 1.50
C72 A76 105fr multi 1.00 40

No. C71a contains 3 imperf. stamps similar to Nos. C69-C71.

Mural by José Vela Zanetti — AP13

The designs are from a mural in the lobby of the United Nations Conference Building, New York. The mural depicting mankind's struggle for a lasting peace is shown across 3 stamps twice in the set: on the 5fr, 15fr, 30fr and 45fr, 60fr, 90fr.

1967, July 15 Litho. *Perf. 14*
C73 AP13 5fr multi 5 5
C74 AP13 15fr org & multi 14 5
C75 AP13 30fr multi 25 7
C76 AP13 45fr multi 40 14
C77 AP13 60fr car & multi 60 16
C78 AP13 90fr ind & multi 90 22
a. Souv. sheet of 3, #C76-C78 1.90 1.50
Nos. C73-C78 (6) 2.34 69

Issued to publicize general disarmament.

Animal Type of Regular Issue, 1967

Designs: 45fr, Lion. 60fr, Elephants.

1967, Aug. 19 Photo. *Perf. 14x13½*
C79 A78 45fr bl & bis brn 42 16
C80 A78 60fr bis brn, blk & pale grn 60 20

African Postal Union Issue, 1967
Common Design Type

1967, Sept. 9 Engr. *Perf. 13*
C81 CD124 100fr bl, brt grn & ol brn 1.00 40

Stamp Anniversary Type of Regular Issue

Designs: 90fr, Stamp auction and Togo Nos. 16 and C42. 105fr, Father and son with stamp album and No. 474.

1967, Oct. 14 Photo. *Perf. 14x13*
Stamps on Stamps in Original Colors
C82 A79 90fr olive 90 25
a. Souv. sheet of 3 2.00 1.50
C83 A79 105fr dk car rose 1.40 38

No. C82a contains 3 imperf. stamps similar to Nos. 621-622 and C82 with simulated perforations.

Pre-Olympics Type of Regular Issue

Designs: 60fr, Runners, Summer Olympics emblem and view of Mexico City. 90fr, Broad jump, Summer Olympics emblem and view of Mexico City.

1967, Dec. 2 *Perf. 13x14*
C84 A80 60fr pink & multi 60 20
C85 A80 90fr multi 90 35
a. Souv. sheet of 3 2.00 1.65

No. C85a contains 3 imperf. stamps similar to Nos. 627 and C84-C85.

Nos. C69-C72 Overprinted: "JOURNÉE NATIONALE / DU TOGO / 29 SEPTEMBRE 1967"

1967, Dec. Photo. *Perf. 14*
C86 A76 45fr multi 42 14
C87 A76 60fr multi 60 15
C88 A76 90fr yel & multi 90 25
C89 A76 105fr multi 1.00 35

Issued for National Day, Sept. 29, 1967.

Hydrological Decade Type of Regular Issue

1968, Apr. 6 Litho. *Perf. 14*
C90 A84 60fr multi 60 16

Ship Type of Regular Issue

Designs: 45fr, Fulton's and modern steamships. 90fr, US atomic ship Savannah and atom symbol.

1968, Apr. 26 Photo. *Perf. 14x14½*
C91 A85 45fr yel & multi 42 14
C92 A85 90fr bl & multi 90 25
a. Souv. sheet of 2 1.65 1.40

No. C92a contains 2 imperf. stamps similar to Nos. C91-C92 with simulated perforations.

WHO Type of Regular Issue

Paintings: 60fr, The Anatomy Lesson, by Rembrandt (detail). 90fr, Jesus Healing the Sick, by Raphael.

1968, June 22 Photo. *Perf. 14*
C93 A87 60fr multi 60 16
C94 A87 90fr pur & multi 90 25
a. Souv. sheet of 2 1.50 1.25

No. C94a contains 2 imperf. stamps similar to Nos. C93-C94 with simulated perforations.

Olympic Games Type of Regular Issue

Olympic Monument, San Salvador Island, Bahamas and: 60fr, Wrestling. 90fr, Running.

1968, July 27 *Perf. 14x13½*
C95 A88 60fr multi 60 16
C96 A88 90fr multi 90 25
a. Souv. sheet of 2 1.50 1.25

No. C96a contains 2 imperf. stamps similar to Nos. C95-C96 with simulated perforations.

Boy Scout Type of Regular Issue

Designs: 60fr, First aid practice (horiz.). 90fr, Scout game.

1968, Nov. 23 Litho. *Perf. 14*
C97 A90 60fr ol & multi 60 22
C98 A90 90fr org & multi 90 35
a. Souv. sheet of 2 1.50 1.25

No. C98a contains 2 imperf. stamps with simulated perforations similar to Nos. C97-C98.

PHILEXAFRIQUE Issue

The Letter, by Jean Auguste Franquelin AP14

1968, Nov. 9 Photo. *Perf. 12½x12*
C99 AP14 100fr multi 1.00 80

PHILEXAFRIQUE Philatelic Exhibition in Abidjan, Feb. 14-23. Printed with alternating light ultramarine label.

Christmas Type of Regular Issue

Paintings: 60fr, Adoration of the Magi, by Pieter Brueghel. 90fr, Adoration of the Magi, by Dürer.

1968, Dec. 28 Litho. *Perf. 14*
C100 A91 60fr red & multi 60 20
C101 A91 90fr multi 90 30
a. Souvenir sheet 1.50 1.25

No. C101a contains 2 imperf. stamps similar to Nos. C100-C101 with simulated perforations.

Human Rights Type of Regular Issue

Portraits and Human Rights Flame: 60fr, Robert F. Kennedy. 90fr, Martin Luther King, Jr.

1969, Feb. 1 Photo. *Perf. 13½x14*
C102 A92 60fr brt rose lil & vio bl 50 22
C103 A92 90fr emer & brn 70 35
a. Souvenir sheet 1.65 1.00

No. C103a contains 2 imperf. stamps similar to Nos. C102-C103 with simulated perforations.

2nd PHILEXAFRIQUE Issue
Common Design Type

Design: 50fr, Togo No. 16 and Aledjo Fault.

1969, Feb. 14 Engr. *Perf. 13*
C104 CD128 50fr red brn, grn & car rose 42 42

Sports Type of Regular Issue

Designs (Stadium and): 60fr, Boxing. 90fr, Bicycling.

1969, Apr. 26 Photo. *Perf. 14x13½*
C105 A93 60fr bl, red & dk brn 60 20
C106 A93 90fr ultra, brt pink & dk brn 1.10 35
a. Souvenir sheet 1.25 1.00

No. C106a contains 2 imperf. stamps similar to Nos. C105-C106 with simulated perforations.

Lunar Type of Regular Issue

Designs: 60fr, Astronaut exploring moon surface. 100fr, Astronaut gathering rocks.

1969, July 21 Litho. *Perf. 14*
C107 A94 60fr dk bl & multi 40 20
C108 A94 100fr multi 65 40
a. Souvenir sheet 5.75 5.00

No. C108a contains 4 imperf. stamps with simulated perforations similar to Nos. 676-677 and C107-C108, magenta margin. No. C108a also exists with colors of 30fr and 100fr stamps changed, and margin in orange. Value $6.

Painting Type of Regular Issue

Painting: 90fr, Pentecost, by El Greco.

1969, Aug. 16 Litho. *Perf. 14*
C109 A95 90fr multi 1.00 40
a. Souvenir sheet 1.25 85

No. C109a contains two imperf. stamps with simulated perforations similar to Nos. 682 and C109.

Nos. C102-C103 Overprinted Like Nos. 683-686

1969, Sept. 1 Photo. *Perf. 13½x14*
C110 A92 60fr brt rose lil & vio bl 40 20
C111 A92 90fr emer & brn 60 25
a. Souv. sheet of 2 3.00 2.25

No. C111a is No. C103a with Eisenhower overprint.

Bank Type of Regular Issue

Design: 100fr, Bank emblem and hand holding cattle and farmer.

1969, Sept. 10 Photo. *Perf. 13x14*
C112 A96 100fr multi 80 40

Red Cross Type of Regular Issue

Designs: 60fr, Wilhelm C. Roentgen and Red Cross workers with children in front of Togo Headquarters. 90fr, Henri Dunant and Red Cross workers meeting Biafra refugees at airport.

1969, Sept. 27 Litho. *Perf. 14*
C113 A97 60fr brn & multi 45 22
C114 A97 90fr ol & multi 65 35
a. Souv. sheet of 2 1.35 1.00

No. C114a contains 2 imperf. stamps with simulated perforations similar to Nos. C113-C114.

Type of Regular Issue, 1969

Emblem of Young Pioneer and Agricultural Organization and: 90fr, Manioc harvest. 100fr, Instruction in gardening. 200fr, Corn harvest. 250fr, Marching drum corps. 500fr, Parade of Young Pioneers.

1969-70 Litho. *Perf. 14*
C115 A98 90fr multi 70 25
C116 A98 100fr org & multi 80 30
C117 A98 200fr multi ('70) 1.65 50
C118 A98 250fr ol & multi 2.00 80
C119 A98 500fr multi ('70) 4.25 1.00
Nos. C115-C119 (5) 9.40 2.85

Christmas Issue
Nos. C107-C108, C108a Overprinted: "JOYEUX NOEL"

1969, Dec. Litho. *Perf. 14*
C120 A94 60fr multi 1.35 40
C121 A94 100fr multi 1.90 60
a. Souvenir sheet of 4 8.50 8.50

Peace Leaders Type of Regular Issue

Portraits: 60fr, Friedrich Ebert. 90fr, Mahatma Gandhi.

1969, Dec. 27 Litho. *Perf. 14x13½*
C122 A100 60fr dk brn, dk red & yel 55 25
C123 A100 90fr dk brn, vio bl & ocher 80 40

ILO Type of Regular Issue

Paintings and ILO Emblem: 60fr, Spring Sowing, by Vincent van Gogh. 90fr, Workers, by Diego de Rivera.

1970, Jan. 24 Litho. *Perf. 12½x13*
C124 A101 60fr gold & multi 60 22
C125 A101 90fr gold & multi 1.10 35
a. Souvenir sheet of 2 1.20 90

No. C125a contains two stamps similar to Nos. C124-C125, with simulated perforations.

Hair Styles Type of Regular Issue

Designs: Various hair styles (45fr, vertical. 90fr, horizontal).

Perf. 12½x13, 13x12½
1970, Feb. 21
C126 A102 45fr car & multi 35 20
C127 A102 90fr multi 65 40

Independence Type of Regular Issue

Design: 60fr, Togo No. C33 and Independence Monument, Lome.

1970, Apr. 27 Litho. *Perf. 13x12½*
C128 A103 60fr yel & multi 45 20

UPU Type of Regular Issue

1970, May 30 Photo. *Perf. 14x13½*
C129 A104 50fr grnsh bl & dk car 40 16

Soccer Type of Regular Issue

Various Scenes from Soccer, Rimet Cup and Flags of: 50fr, Sweden and Israel. 60fr, Bulgaria and Peru. 90fr, Belgium and Salvador.

1970, June 27 Litho. *Perf. 13x14*
C130 A105 50fr multi 42 22
C131 A105 60fr lil & multi 55 30
C132 A105 90fr multi 80 40
a. Souvenir sheet of 4 2.00 2.00

No. C132a contains 4 stamps similar to Nos. 734, C130-C132, but imperf. with simulated perforations.

Lenin Type of Regular Issue

Design: 50fr, Lenin Meeting Peasant Delegation, by V. A. Serov, and UNESCO emblem.

1970, July 25 Litho. *Perf. 12½*
C133 A106 50fr multi 50 20

EXPO '70 Type of Regular Issue
Souvenir Sheet

Design: 150fr, Mitsubishi pavilion and EXPO '70 emblem.

1970, Aug. 8 Litho. *Perf. 13*
C134 A107 150fr yel & multi 1.20 45
a. Inscribed "AERINNE"

No. C134 contains one stamp 86x33mm.

Astronaut Type of Regular Issue

Design: 200fr, James A. Lovell, Fred W. Haise, Jr. and Tom Mattingly (replaced by John L. Swigert, Jr.) and Apollo 13 emblem.

1970, Sept. 26
C135 A108 200fr multi 1.50 80
a. Souv. sheet of 3 1.90 1.50

Space flight of Apollo 13. No. C135a contains 3 stamps similar to Nos. 741, 744 and C135, with simulated perforations.

Nos. C135, C135a Inscribed: "FELICITATIONS / BON RETOUR APOLLO XIII"

1970, Sept. 26
C136 A108 200fr multi 1.50 80
a. Souvenir sheet of 3 1.90 1.50

Safe return of the crew of Apollo 13.

UN Type of Regular Issue

Paintings and Emblems of UN Agencies: 60fr, The Mailman Roulin, by van Gogh, and UPU emblem. 90fr, The Birth of the Virgin, by Vittore Carpaccio, and WHO emblem.

1970, Oct. 24 Litho. *Perf. 13x12½*
C137 A109 60fr grn, gold & blk 50 25
C138 A109 90fr red org, gold & brn 70 40
a. Souvenir sheet of 4 1.90 1.50

No. C138a contains one each of Nos. 754-755 and C137-C138 with simulated perforations.

Moth Type of Regular Issue

Moths: 60fr, Euchloron megaera. 90fr, Pseudacraea boisduvali.

1970, Nov. 21 Photo. *Perf. 13x14*
C139 A110 60fr multi 80 20
C140 A110 90fr multi 80 25

Christmas Type of Regular Issue

Paintings: 60fr, Adoration of the Shepherds, by Botticelli. 90fr, Adoration of the Kings, by Tiepolo.

1970, Dec. 26 Litho. *Perf. 12½x13*
C141 A111 60fr gold & multi 45 20
C142 A111 90fr gold & multi 70 30
a. Souvenir sheet of 2, #C141-C142 1.35 1.00

No. C122 Surcharged and Overprinted: "EN MEMOIRE / Charles De Gaulle / 1890-1970"

1971, Jan. 9 Photo. *Perf. 14x13½*
C143 A100 200fr on 60fr 2.00 80

De Gaulle Type of Regular Issue

Designs: 60fr, De Gaulle and Pope Paul VI. 90fr, De Gaulle and satellite.

1971, Feb. 20 Photo. *Perf. 13x14*
C144 A112 60fr blk & dp vio 60 20
C145 A112 90fr blk & bl grn 90 30
a. Souvenir sheet of 4 2.50 1.50

Nos. C143-C145 issued in memory of Charles De Gaulle (1890-1970), President of France. No. C145a contains 4 imperf. stamps similar to Nos. 769-770, C144-C145.

Easter Type of Regular Issue

Paintings: 50fr, Resurrection, by Matthias Grunewald. 60fr, Resurrection, by Master of Trebon. 90fr, Resurrection, by El Greco.

Perf. 10½x11½
1971, Apr. 10 Litho.
C146 A113 50fr gold & multi 42 16
C147 A113 60fr gold & multi 60 22
C148 A113 90fr gold & multi 80 40
a. Souvenir sheet of 4, #773, C146-C148 2.25 1.50

Apollo 14 Type of Regular Issue

Designs: 50fr, 200f, Apollo 14 badge 100fr, Take-off from moon, and spaceship.

1971, May Litho. *Perf. 12½*
C149 A114 50fr grn & multi 35 15
C150 A114 100fr multi 65 35
C151 A114 200fr org & multi 1.40 65
a. Souv. sheet of 4 3.00 2.25

No. C151a contains 4 stamps similar to Nos. 777 and C149-C151 with simulated perforations.

Cacao Type of Regular Issue

Designs: 60fr, Ministry of Agriculture. 90fr, Cacao tree and pods. 100fr, Sorting and separating beans from pods.

1971, June 6 Litho. *Perf. 14*
C152 A115 60fr multi 40 20
C153 A115 90fr multi 60 30
C154 A115 100fr multi 70 35

ASECNA Type of Regular Issue
1971, June 26
C155 A116 100fr multi 70 35

Tourist Type of Regular Issue

Designs: 50fr, Château Viale and antelope. 60fr, Lake Togo and crocodile. 100fr, Old lime furnace, Tokpli, and hippopotamus.

1971, July 17
C156 A117 50fr multi 35 15
C157 A117 60fr multi 40 20
C158 A117 100fr multi 65 35

Religions Type of Regular Issue

Designs: 50fr, Mohammedans praying in front of Lome Mosque. 60fr, Protestant service. 90fr, Catholic bishop and priests.

1971, July 31 Litho. *Perf. 14½*
C159 A118 50fr multi 30 16
C160 A118 60fr multi 35 20
C161 A118 90fr multi 60 25
a. Souvenir sheet of 4, #787, C159-C161 1.65 1.40

Nos. C149-C151 Overprinted and Surcharged in Black or Silver: "EN MEMOIRE / DOBROVOLSKY - VOLKOV - PATSAYEV / SOYUZ 11"

C162 A114 90fr on 50fr multi 60 25
C163 A114 100fr multi (S) 65 30
C164 A114 200fr multi 1.40 50
a. Souvenir sheet of 4, #788, C162-C164 2.75 2.25

See note after No. 788.

Olympic Type of Regular Issue

Design: 200fr, Sapporo '72 emblem and Ski jump.

1971, Oct. 30 Litho. *Perf. 14*
C165 A119 200fr multi 1.40 50
a. Souvenir sheet of 4 2.00 1.90

No. C165 contains 4 stamps with simulated perforations similar to Nos. 791-793 and C165 printed on glazed paper.

African Postal Union Issue, 1971
Common Design Type

Design: 100fr, Adjogbo dancers and UAMPT Building, Brazzaville, Congo.

1971, Nov. 13 Photo. *Perf. 13x13½*
C166 CD135 100fr bl & multi 70 40

UNICEF Type of Regular Issue

Toys and UNICEF Emblem: 60fr, Turtle. 90fr, Parrot.

1971, Nov. 27 Litho. *Perf. 14*
C167 A120 60fr lt bl & multi 40 18
C168 A120 90fr multi 60 22
a. Souvenir sheet of 4 1.90 1.90

No. C168a contains 4 stamps with simulated perforations similar to Nos. 796-797 and C167-C168.

Christmas Type of Regular Issue

Virgin and Child by: 60fr, Giorgione. 100fr, Raphael.

1971, Dec. 24 *Perf. 14x13*
C169 A121 60fr ol & multi 40 25
C170 A121 100fr multi 70 40
a. Souvenir sheet of 4 2.00 1.65

No. C170a contains 4 stamps with simulated perforations similar to Nos. 800-801, C169-C170.

Venice Type of Regular Issue

Design: 100fr, Ca' d'Oro, Venice.

1972, Feb. 26 Litho. *Perf. 14*
C171 A122 100fr multi 70 40
a. Souvenir sheet of 3 1.50 1.50

No. C171a contains 3 stamps similar to Nos. 802-803, C171 with simulated perforations.

No. C156 Overprinted "VISITE DU PRESIDENT / NIXON EN CHINE / FEVRIER 1972"

1972, Mar. Litho. *Perf. 14*
C172 A117 50fr multi 35 20

Visit of Pres. Richard M. Nixon to the People's Republic of China, Feb. 20-27.

Easter Type of Regular Issue

Paintings: 50fr, Resurrection, by Thomas de Coloswa. 100fr, Ascension by Andrea Mantegna.

1972, Mar. 31
C173 A123 50fr gold & multi 45 14
C174 A123 100fr gold & multi 65 25
a. Souvenir sheet of 4 2.00 1.90

No. C174a contains 4 stamps similar to Nos. 806-807, C173-C174 with simulated perforations.

Heart Type of Regular Issue

Design: 100fr, Heart, WHO emblem and smith.

1972, Apr. 4
C175 A124 100fr multi 65 40
a. Souvenir sheet of 2 1.25 1.20

No. C175a contains 2 stamps similar to Nos. 810 and C175 with simulated perforations.

Telecommunications Type of Regular Issue

Design: 100fr, Intelsat 4 over Africa.

1972, June 24 *Perf. 14*
C176 A125 100fr multi 70 30

Cassava Type of Regular Issue

Designs: 60fr, Truck and cassava processing factory (horiz.). 80fr, Children, mother holding tapioca cake.

1972, June 30
C177 A126 60fr multi 45 22
C178 A126 80fr multi 55 25

No. C133 Surcharged in Deep Carmine: "VISITE DU PRESIDENT / NIXON EN RUSSIE / MAI 1972"

1972, July 15 Litho. *Perf. 12½*
C179 A106 300fr on 50fr multi 2.50 1.40

President Nixon's visit to the USSR, May 1972. Old denomination obliterated with 6x5mm rectangle.

Olympic Type of Regular Issue

1972, Aug. 26 Litho. *Perf. 14*
C180 A127 90fr Gymnastics 65 35
a. Souv. sheet of 2 1.25 1.10
C181 A127 200fr Basketball 1.50 65

No. C180a contains 2 stamps with simulated perforations similar to Nos. 816 and C180.

Bird Type of Regular Issue

Bird: 90fr, Rose-ringed parakeet.

1972, Sept. 9
C182 A128 90fr multi 65 35
a. Souvenir sheet of 4 1.90 1.50

No. C182a contains 4 stamps similar to Nos. 818-820, C182 with simulated perforations.

Rotary Type of Regular Issue

Rotary Emblem and: 60fr, Map of Togo, olive branch. 90fr, Flags of Togo and Rotary Club. 100fr, Paul P. Harris.

1972, Oct. 7 Litho. *Perf. 14*
C183 A129 60fr brn & multi 35 16
C184 A129 90fr multi 50 35
C185 A129 100fr multi 60 38

Painting Type of Regular Issue, 1972

Designs: 60fr, Mystical Marriage of St. Catherine, by Assistant to the P. M. Master. 80fr, Self-portrait, by Leonardo da Vinci. 100fr, Sts. Mary and Agnes by Botticelli.

1972, Oct. 21
C186 A130 60fr gold & multi 40 20
C187 A130 80fr gold & multi 45 25
C188 A130 100fr gold & multi 80 40
a. Souvenir sheet of 4 2.25 1.50

No. C188a contains 4 stamps with simulated perforations similar to Nos. 824, C186-188.

Presidential Visit Type of Regular Issue

Design: 100fr, Pres. Pompidou and Col. Etienne Eyadema, front view of party headquarters.

1972, Nov. 23 Litho. *Perf. 14*
C189 A131 100fr multi 80 40

Johann Wolfgang von Goethe (1749-1832), German Poet and Dramatist — AP15

1972, Dec. 2 Photo. *Perf. 13x14*
C190 AP15 100fr grn & multi 80 40

Christmas Type of Regular Issue

Paintings: 60fr, Nativity, by Master Vyshchibrod. 80fr, Adoration of the Kings, anonymous. 100fr, Flight into Egypt, by Giotto.

1972, Dec. 23 Litho. *Perf. 14*
C191 A132 60fr gold & multi 45 20
C192 A132 80fr gold & multi 60 30
C193 A132 100fr gold & multi 80 40
a. Souvenir sheet of 4 2.00 2.00

No. C193a contains 4 stamps with simulated perforations similar to Nos. 829, C191-C193.

Leprosy Day Type of Regular Issue

Design: 100fr, Dr. Armauer G. Hansen, apparatus, microscope and Petri dish.

1973, Jan. 23 Photo. *Perf. 14x13½*
C194 A133 100fr rose car & bl 70 40

World Leprosy Day and centenary of the discovery of the Hansen bacillus, the cause of leprosy.

Easter Type of Regular Issue

1973, Apr. 21 Litho. *Perf. 14*
C195 A135 90fr Christ in Glory 60 35
a. Souvenir sheet of 2 1.00 1.00

No. C195a contains one each of Nos. 835 and C195 with simulated perforations.

Apollo 17 Type of Regular Issue

Designs: 100fr, Astronauts on moon and orange rock. 200fr, Rocket lift-off at Cape Kennedy and John F. Kennedy.

1973, June 2 Litho. *Perf. 14*
C196 A136 100fr multi 70 38
C197 A136 200fr multi 1.50 60
a. Souvenir sheet of 2 2.25 2.00

No. C197a contains 2 stamps similar to Nos. C196-C197 with simulated perforations.

Boy Scout Type of Regular Issue

Designs: 100fr, Canoeing (horiz.). 200fr, Campfire (horiz.).

1973, June 30 Litho. *Perf. 14*
C198 A137 100fr bl & multi 70 40
C199 A137 200fr bl & multi 1.50 65
a. Souvenir sheet of 2 2.25 2.00

No. C199a contains 2 stamps similar to Nos. C198-C199 with simulated perforations.

Copernicus Type of Regular Issue

Designs: 90fr, Heliocentric system. 100fr, Nicolaus Copernicus.

1973, July 18
C200 A138 90fr multi 60 30
C201 A138 100fr bis & multi 70 40
a. Souvenir sheet of 2, #C200-C201 1.50 1.35

Red Cross Type of Regular Issue

Design: 100fr, Dove carrying Red Cross letter, sun, map of Togo.

1973, Aug. 4
C202 A139 100fr multi 65 35

Literacy Type of Regular Issue

Design: 90fr, Woman teacher in classroom.

1973, Aug. 18 Litho. *Perf. 14*
C203 A140 90fr multi 60 35

WMO Type of Regular Issue

1973, Oct. 4 Photo. *Perf. 14x13*
C204 A142 200fr dl bl, pur & brn 1.50 60

Type of Regular Issue 1967

Design: 100fr, Early and contemporary planes, Nos. 758 and C36.

1973, Oct. 20 Photo. *Perf. 14x13*
C205 A79 100fr multi 80 35
a. Souvenir sheet of 2 1.60 1.40

75th anniversary of Togolese postal service. No. C205a contains 2 stamps similar to Nos. 855 and C205 with simulated perforations.

Kennedy Type of Regular Issue

Designs: 90fr, Kennedy and Charles De Gaulle. 100fr, Kennedy and Nikita Krushchev. 200fr, Kennedy and model of Apollo spacecraft.

1973, Nov. 22 Litho. *Perf. 14*
C206 A143 90fr blk & pink 60 35
C207 A143 100fr blk, lt bl & bl 70 38
C208 A143 200fr blk, buff & brn 1.40 60
a. Souvenir sheet of 2 2.25 2.00

No. C208a contains 2 stamps similar to Nos. C207-208 with simulated perforations.

Human Rights Flame and People — AP16

1973, Dec. 8 Photo. *Perf. 13x14*
C209 AP16 250fr lt bl & multi 1.90 80

25th anniversary of the Universal Declaration of Human Rights.

Christmas Type of Regular Issue

Paintings: 90fr, Virgin and Child. 100fr, Adoration of the Kings. Both after 15th century Italian paintings.

1973, Dec. 22 Litho. *Perf. 14*
C210 A144 90fr gold & multi 60 25
C211 A144 100fr gold & multi 70 35
a. Souvenir sheet of 2 1.60 1.50

No. C211a contains 2 stamps with simulated perforations similar to Nos. C210-C211.

Nos. C183 and C185 Overprinted: "PREMIERE CONVENTION / 210eme DISTRICT / FEVRIER 1974 / LOME"

1974, Feb. 21 Litho. *Perf. 14*
C212 A129 60fr brn & multi 40 20
C213 A129 100fr multi 60 35

First convention of Rotary International, District 210, Lome, Feb. 22-24.

Soccer Type of Regular Issue

Designs: Various soccer scenes and games' cup.

1974, Mar. 2 Litho. *Perf. 14*
C214 A145 90fr multi 60 30
C215 A145 100fr multi 70 35
C216 A145 200fr multi 1.40 60
a. Souvenir sheet of 2 2.25 2.00

No. C216a contains 2 stamps with simulated perforations similar to Nos. C215-C216.

Picasso Type of 1974

Paintings: 90fr, The Muse. 100fr, Les Demoiselles d'Avignon. 200fr, Sitting Nude.

1974, Apr. 6 Litho. *Perf. 14*
C217 A146 90fr brn & multi 60 30
C218 A146 100fr pur & multi 70 35
C219 A146 200fr multi 1.40 65
a. Souvenir sheet of 3 3.50 3.00

No. C219a contains 3 stamps similar to Nos. C217-C219 with simulated perforations.

Coastal Views Type of 1974

Designs: 90fr, Fishermen on Lake Togo. 100fr, Mouth of Anecho River.

1974, Apr. 20
C220 A147 90fr multi 60 22
C221 A147 100fr multi 65 30
a. Souvenir sheet of 2 1.40 1.20

No. C221a contains 2 stamps similar to Nos. C220-C221 with simulated perforations.

UPU Type of 1974

Designs: Old mailmen's uniforms.

1974, May 10 Litho. *Perf. 14*
C222 A148 50fr multi 40 16
C223 A148 100fr multi 70 35
a. Souvenir sheet of 2 10.00 8.25

No. C223a contains 2 stamps similar to Nos. C222-C223, rouletted.

Fishing Type of 1974

Designs: 90fr, Fishermen bringing in net with catch. 100fr, Fishing with rod and line. 200fr, Fishing with basket (vert.).

1974, June 22 Litho. *Perf. 14*
C224 A149 90fr multi 50 25
C225 A149 100fr multi 55 25
C226 A149 200fr multi 1.10 65
a. Souvenir sheet of 3 2.25 2.00

No. C226a contains 3 stamps with simulated perforations similar to Nos. C224-C226.

Jupiter Probe Type of 1974

Designs: 100fr, Rocket take-off (vert.). 200fr, Satellite in space.

1974, July 6 *Perf. 14*
C227 A150 100fr multi 65 35
C228 A150 200fr multi 1.40 65
a. Souvenir sheet of 2 5.00 3.75

No. C228a contains 2 stamps similar to Nos. C227-C228 with simulated perforations; imperf. or rouletted.

No. C176 Overprinted

1974, July *Perf. 14*
C229 A125 100fr multi 1.60 65

INTERNABA 1974 Intl. Philatelic Exhibition, Basel, June 7-16.

Seashell Type of 1974

1974, July 13 Litho. *Perf. 14*
C230 A151 90fr Alcithoe ponsonbyi 50 25
C231 A151 100fr Casmaria iredalei 55 35
a. Souvenir sheet of 2 1.25 1.10

No. C231a contains 2 stamps similar to Nos. C230-C231 with simulated perforations.

Horse Racing Type of 1974

Designs: 90fr, Steeplechase. 100fr, Galloping horses.

1974, Aug. 3 Litho. *Perf. 14*
C232 A152 90fr multi 60 25
C233 A152 100fr multi 70 35
a. Souvenir sheet of 2 1.50 1.20

No. C233a contains one each of Nos. C232-C233 with simulated perforations.

Nos. C180, C180a and C181 Overprinted: "COUPE DU MONDE / DE FOOTBALL / VAINQUEURS / REPUBLIQUE FEDERALE / d'ALLEMAGNE"

1974, Aug. 19
C234 A127 90fr multi 60 25
a. Souvenir sheet of 2 1.20 1.20
C235 A127 200fr multi 1.20 65

World Cup Soccer Championship, Munich, 1974, victory of German Federal Republic. For description of No. C234a see note after No. C181.

Animal Type of 1974

1974, Sept. 7 Litho. *Perf. 14*
C236 A153 90fr Lions 55 30
C237 A153 100fr Rhinoceroses 60 35
a. Souvenir sheet of 3 1.60 1.40

Wild animals of West Africa. No. C237a contains 3 stamps similar to Nos. 889, C236-C237 with simulated perforations.

1974, Oct. 14
C238 A153 90fr Herd at waterhole 50 25
C239 A153 100fr Village and cows 55 35
a. Souvenir sheet of 2 1.50 1.20

Domestic animals. No. C239a contains 2 stamps with simulated perforations similar to Nos. C238-C239.

Churchill Type of 1974

Designs: 100fr, Churchill and frigate. 200fr, Churchill and fighter planes.

1974, Nov. 1 Photo. *Perf. 13x13½*
C240 A154 100fr multi 60 30
C241 A154 200fr org & multi 1.20 60
a. Souvenir sheet of 2 2.25 1.90

No. C241a contains 2 stamps similar to Nos. C240-C241; perf. or imperf.

Flower Type of 1975

Flowers of Togo: 100fr, Clerodendrum thosonae. 200fr, Gloriosa superba.

1975, Feb. 15 Litho. *Perf. 14*
C242 A155 100fr multi 55 25
C243 A155 200fr multi 1.10 50
a. Souvenir sheet of 2 3.25 2.50

No. C243a contains one each of Nos. C242-C243, perf. 13x14. Exists imperf.; same value.

Nos. C184-C185 Overprinted: "70e ANNIVERSAIRE / 23 FEVRIER 1975"

1975, Feb. 23 Litho. *Perf. 14*
C244 A129 90fr multi 50 25
C245 A129 100fr multi 55 35

Rotary International, 70th anniversary.

Easter Type of 1975

Paintings: 100fr, Christ Rising from the Tomb, by Master MS. 200fr, Holy Trinity (detail), by Dürer.

1975, Apr. 19 Litho. *Perf. 14*
C246 A157 100fr multi 55 25
C247 A157 200fr multi 1.10 55
a. Souvenir sheet of 2 1.65 1.40

No. C247a contains 2 stamps similar to Nos. C246-C247 with simulated perforations.

Independence Type of 1975

Designs: 50fr, National Day parade, flag and map of Togo (vert.). 60fr, Warriors' dance and flag of Togo.

1975, Apr. 26 Litho. *Perf. 14*
C248 A158 50fr multi 25 10
C249 A158 60fr multi 35 14
a. Souvenir sheet of 2 90 50

No. C249a contains 2 stamps similar to Nos. C248-C249 with simulated perforations.

Hunt Type of 1975

Designs: 90fr, Running deer. 100fr, Wild boar hunter with shotgun.

1975, May 24 Photo. *Perf. 13x13½*
C250 A159 90fr multi 50 22
C251 A159 100fr multi 55 25

Palm Oil Type of 1975

Designs: 85fr, Selling palm oil in market (vert.). 100fr, Oil processing plant, Alokoegbe.

1975, June 28 Litho. *Perf. 14*
C252 A160 85fr multi 45 22
C253 A160 100fr multi 55 25

Apollo-Soyuz Type of 1975 and

Soyuz Spacecraft — AP17

Designs: 60fr, Donald K. Slayton, Vance D. Brand and Thomas P. Stafford. 90fr, Aleksei A. Leonov and Valery N. Kubasov. 100fr, Apollo-Soyuz link-up, American and Russian flags. 200fr, Apollo-Soyuz emblem and globe.

1975, July 15
C254 AP17 50fr yel & multi 25 10
C255 A161 60fr lil & multi 35 14
C256 A161 90fr bl & multi 45 22
C257 A161 100fr grn & multi 55 38
C258 A161 200fr yel & multi 1.10 45
a. Souvenir sheet of 4 3.00 2.00
Nos. C254-C258 (5) 2.70 1.29

See note after No. 913. No. C258a contains one each of Nos. C255-C258.

Schweitzer Type of 1975

Dr. Schweitzer: 80fr, playing organ (vert.). 90fr, with pelican (vert.). 100fr, and Lambarene Hospital.

1975, Aug. 23 Litho. *Perf. 14x13½*
C259 A163 80fr multi 42 25
C260 A163 90fr multi 50 30
C261 A163 100fr multi 55 35

Letter Writing Type of 1975

Design: 80fr, Erasmus Writing Letter, by Hans Holbein.

1975, Oct. 9 Litho. *Perf. 14*
C262 A164 80fr multi 42 25

Nos. C167-C168a Overprinted: "30eme Anniversaire / des Nations-Unies"

1975, Oct. 24 Litho. *Perf. 14*
C263 A120 60fr multi 35 14
C264 A120 90fr multi 45 25
a. Souvenir sheet of 4 1.40 1.10

United Nations, 30th anniversary. No. C264a contains one each of No. 796 (with overprint), and Nos. 918, C263-C264.

Nos. C198-C199 Overprinted: "14ème JAMBORÉE / MONDIAL / DES ÉCLAIREURS"

1975, Nov. 7
C265 A137 100fr multi 55 25
C266 A137 200fr multi 1.10 50
a. Souvenir sheet of 2 1.65 1.50

14th World Boy Scout Jamboree, Lillehammer, Norway, July 29-Aug. 7. No. C266a contains one each of Nos. C265-C266 with simulated perforations.

Christmas Type of 1975

Paintings of the Virgin and Child: 90fr, Nativity, by Federico Barocci. 100fr, Bellini. 200fr, Correggio.

1975, Dec. 20 Litho. *Perf. 14*
C267 A165 90fr bl & multi 50 22
C268 A165 100fr red & multi 55 25
C269 A165 200fr bl & multi 1.10 50
a. Souvenir sheet of 2, #C268-C269 1.90 1.50

Bicentennial Type of 1976

Paintings (and Bicentennial Emblem): 60fr, Surrender of Gen. Burgoyne, by John Trumbull. 70fr, Surrender at Trenton, by Trumbull (vert.). 100fr, Signing of Declaration of Independence, by Trumbull. 200fr, Washington Crossing the Delaware, by Emanuel Leutze.

1976, Mar. 3 Litho. *Perf. 14*
C270 A167 60fr multi 35 16
C271 A167 70fr multi 38 20
C272 A167 100fr multi 55 25
C273 A167 200fr multi 1.10 55
a. Souvenir sheet of 2, #C272-C273 1.65 1.65

No. C273a also exists imperf.; same value.

Common Market Type of 1976

Designs: 60fr, ACP and CEE emblems. 70fr, Map of Africa, Europe and Asia.

1976, Apr. 24 Photo. *Perf. 13x14*
C274 A168 60fr lt bl & multi 35 16
C275 A168 70fr yel & multi 38 20

Telephone Type of 1976

Designs: 70fr, Thomas A. Edison, old and new communications equipment. 105fr, Alexander Graham Bell, old and new telephones.

1976, Mar. 10 Photo. *Perf. 13x14*
C276 A169 70fr multi 38 20
C277 A169 105fr multi 55 35
a. Souvenir sheet of 2, #C276-C277 1.00 90

No. C277a exists imperf.; same value.

Eye Examination
AP18

Pylon, Flags of Ghana, Togo, Dahomey
AP19

1976, Apr. 8 *Perf. 14x13*
C278 AP18 60fr dk red & multi 35 18

World Health Day: "Foresight prevents blindness."

1976, May 8 Litho. *Perf. 14*
C279 AP19 60fr multi 35 18

Ghana-Togo-Dahomey electric power grid, 1st anniv. See No. 932.

Nos. C270-C273, C273a, Overprinted: "INTERPHIL / MAI 29-JUIN 6, 1976"

1976, May 29
C280 A167 60fr multi 35 16
C281 A167 70fr multi 38 20
C282 A167 100fr multi 55 25
C283 A167 200fr multi 1.10 55
a. Souvenir sheet of 2 1.60 1.50

Interphil 76 Intl. Philatelic Exhibition, Philadelphia, Pa., May 29-June 6. Overprint on No. C281 in 3 lines; overprint on No. C283a applied to each stamp.

Olympic Games Type of 1976

Montreal Olympic Emblem and: 70fr, Yachting. 105fr, Motorcycling. 200fr, Fencing.

1976, June 15 Photo. *Perf. 14x13*
C284 A172 70fr multi 38 20
C285 A172 105fr multi 55 35
C286 A172 200fr multi 1.10 55
a. Souvenir sheet of 2 1.90 1.65

No. C286a contains one each of Nos. C285-C286, perf. 14.

Viking Type of 1976

Designs: 60fr, Viking landing on Mars. 70fr, Nodus Gordii (view on Mars). 105fr, Lander over Mare Tyrrhenum. 200fr, Landing on Mars.

1976, July 15 Litho. *Perf. 14*
C287 A173 60fr bis & multi 35 18
C288 A173 70fr multi 38 20
C289 A173 105fr bl & multi 55 35
C290 A173 200fr multi 1.10 55
a. Souvenir sheet of 2 1.90 1.65

No. C290a contains one each of Nos. C289-C290, perf. 14x13½.

Toulouse-Lautrec Type, 1976

Paintings: 60fr, Carmen, portrait. 70fr, Maurice at the Somme. 200fr, "Messalina."

1976, Aug. 7 Litho. *Perf. 14*
C291 A174 60fr blk & multi 35 18
C292 A174 70fr blk & multi 38 25
C293 A174 200fr blk & multi 1.10 55
a. Souvenir sheet of 2 1.60 1.50

No. C293a contains one each of Nos. C292-C293, perf. 13½x14.

No. C202 Overprinted: "Journée / Internationale / de l'Enfance"

1976, Nov. 27 Litho. *Perf. 14*
C294 A139 100fr multi 55 35

International Children's Day.

Christmas Type of 1976

Paintings: 70fr, Holy Family, by Lorenzo Lotto. 105fr, Virgin and Child with Saints, by Jacopo da Pontormo. 200fr, Virgin and Child with Saints, by Lotto.

1976, Dec. 18

C295 A175 70fr multi 38 20
C296 A175 105fr multi 55 35
C297 A175 200fr multi 1.10 55
a. Souvenir sheet of 2, #C296-C297 1.90 1.60

No. C284 Overprinted: "CHAMPIONS OLYMPIQUES / YACHTING - FLYING DUTCHMAN / REPUBLIQUE FEDERALE ALLEMAGNE"

No. C286 Overprinted: "CHAMPIONS OLYMPIQUES / ESCRIMEFLEURET PAR EQUIPES / REPUBLIQUE FEDERALE ALLEMAGNE"

1976, Dec. Photo. *Perf. 14x13*

C298 A172 70fr multi 38 20
C299 A172 200fr multi 1.10 60
a. Souvenir sheet of 2 1.90 1.65

Olympic winners. No. C299a (on No. C286a) contains Nos. C285 and C299.

Eyadema Anniversary Type of 1977

Designs: 60fr, National Assembly Building. 100fr, Pres. Eyadema greeting people at Aug. 30th meeting.

1977, Jan. 13 Photo. *Perf. 13x14*

C300 A177 60fr multi 35 14
C301 A177 100fr multi 55 30
a. Souvenir sheet of 2, #C300-C301 90 85

Musical Instrument Type of 1977

Musical Instruments: 60fr, Atopani. 80fr, African violin (vert.). 105fr, African flutes (vert.).

1977, Feb. 7 Litho. *Perf. 14*

C302 A178 60fr multi 35 14
C303 A178 80fr multi 40 18
C304 A178 105fr multi 55 25
a. Souvenir sheet of 2, #C303-C304 1.20 1.00

Victor Hugo Type of 1977

Design: 60fr, Victor Hugo in exile on Guernsey Island.

1977, Feb. 26 *Perf. 13x14*

C305 A179 60fr multi 35 18
a. Souvenir sheet of 2, #952, C305 65 60

Beethoven Type of 1977

Designs: 100fr, Beethoven's piano and 1818 portrait. 200fr, Beethoven on his deathbed and Holy Trinity Church, Vienna.

1977, Mar. 7 *Perf. 14*

C306 A180 100fr multi 55 35
C307 A180 200fr multi 1.10 65
a. Souvenir sheet of 2, #C306-C307 1.65 1.65

Automobile Type of 1977

Early Automobiles: 60fr, Cannstatt-Daimler, 1899, Germany. 70fr, Sunbeam, 1904, England. 100fr, Renault, 1908, France. 200fr, Rolls Royce, 1909, England.

1977, Apr. 11 Litho. *Perf. 14*

C308 A181 60fr multi 35 18
C309 A181 70fr multi 38 20
C310 A181 100fr multi 55 30
C311 A181 200fr multi 1.10 65
a. Souvenir sheet of 2, #C310-C311 1.65 1.65

Lindbergh Type of 1977

Designs: 60fr, Lindbergh and son Jon, birds in flight. 85fr, Lindbergh home in Kent, England. 90fr, Spirit of St. Louis over Atlantic Ocean. 100fr, Concorde over New York City.

1977, May 9

C312 A182 60fr multi 40 16
C313 A182 85fr multi 55 20
C314 A182 90fr multi 60 20
C315 A182 100fr multi 65 22
a. Souvenir sheet of 2, #C314-C315 1.40 85

No. C305 Overprinted: "10ème ANNIVERSAIRE DU / CONSEIL INTERNATIONAL / DE LA LANGUE FRANCAISE"

1977, May 17 Litho. *Perf. 14*

C316 A179 60fr multi 40 20

10th anniv. of the French Language Council.

Wildlife Type of 1977

Designs: 60fr, Colobus monkeys. 90fr, Chimpanzee (vert.). 100fr, Leopard. 200fr, West African manatee.

1977, June 13

C317 A183 60fr multi 40 14
C318 A183 90fr multi 60 16
C319 A183 100fr multi 65 18
C320 A183 200fr multi 1.40 35
a. Souvenir sheet of 2, #C319-C320 2.25 1.25

Agriculture Type of 1977

Designs: 60fr, Corn silo. 100fr, Hoeing and planting by hand. 200fr, Tractor on field.

1977, July 11 Litho. *Perf. 14*

C321 A184 60fr multi 40 14
C322 A184 100fr multi 65 20
C323 A184 200fr multi 1.40 35
a. Souvenir sheet of 2 2.25 1.25

No. C323a contains one each of Nos. C322-C323, perf. 13x14.

Rubens Type of 1977

Paintings: 60fr, Heads of Black Men, 1620. 100fr, Anne of Austria, 1624.

1977, Aug. 8

C324 A185 60fr multi 40 14
C325 A185 100fr multi 65 18
a. Souvenir sheet of 2 1.20 65

No. C325a contains one each of Nos. C324-C325, perf. 14x13.

Orbiter Type of 1977

Designs: 90fr, Retrieval of unmanned satellite in space (vert.). 100fr, Satellite's return to space after repairs. 200fr, Manned landing of Orbiter.

1977, Oct. 4 Litho. *Perf. 14*

C326 A186 90fr multi 60 16
C327 A186 100fr multi 65 18
C328 A186 200fr multi 1.35 35
a. Souvenir sheet of 2, #C327-C328 2.25 1.25

Lafayette Type of 1977

Designs: 60fr, Lafayette landing in New York, 1824. 105fr, Lafayette and Washington at Valley Forge.

1977, Nov. 7 *Perf. 13x14*

C329 A187 60fr multi 40 14
C330 A187 105fr multi 70 18
a. Souvenir sheet of 2, #C329-C330 1.20 65

Christmas Type of 1977

Virgin and Child by: 90fr, 200fr, Carlo Crivelli (different). 100fr, Bellini.

1977, Dec. 19 *Perf. 14*

C331 A189 90fr multi 60 16
C332 A189 100fr multi 65 18
C333 A189 200fr multi 1.40 35
a. Souvenir sheet of 2, #C332-C333 2.25 1.25

Jenner Type of 1978

Designs: 50fr, Edward Jenner. 60fr, Smallpox vaccination clinic (horiz.).

1978, Jan. 9 *Perf. 14x13, 13x14*

C334 A190 50fr multi 35 12
C335 A190 60fr multi 40 14
a. Souvenir sheet of 2 80 50

No. C335a contains 2 stamps with simulated perforations similar to Nos. C334-C335.

Wright Brothers Type of 1978

Designs: 60fr, Orville Wright's 7½-minute flight. 70fr, Orville Wright injured in first aircraft accident, 1908. 200fr, Wrights' bicycle shop, Dearborn, Mich. 300fr, First flight, 1903.

1978, Feb. 6 Litho. *Perf. 14*

C336 A191 60fr multi 40 14
C337 A191 70fr multi 45 18
C338 A191 200fr multi 1.40 35
C339 A191 300fr multi 2.00 60
a. Souvenir sheet of 2 3.50 2.00

No. C339a contains one each of Nos. C338-C339 with simulated perforations.

Port of Lomé Type, 1978

Anchor and: 60fr, Industrial harbor. 100fr, Merchant marine harbor. 200fr, Bird's-eye view of entire harbor.

1978, Apr. 26 Photo. *Perf. 13*

C340 A199 60fr multi 40 14
C341 A199 100fr multi 65 20
C342 A199 200fr multi 1.40 35
a. Souvenir sheet of 2, #C341-C342 2.25 1.25

Space Type of 1978

Designs: 90fr, Module camera (horiz.). 100fr, Module antenna. 200fr, Pioneer, USA, in orbit.

1978, May 8 Litho. *Perf. 14*

C343 A200 90fr multi 60 20
C344 A200 100fr multi 65 18
C345 A200 200fr multi 1.40 35
a. Souvenir sheet of 2 2.25 1.25

No. C345a contains Nos. C344-C345, perf. 13½x14.

Soccer Type of 1978

Designs: Various soccer scenes and Argentina '78 emblem.

1978, June 5 *Perf. 14*

C346 A201 60fr multi 40 14
C347 A201 80fr multi 55 18
C348 A201 200fr multi 1.40 35
C349 A201 300fr multi 2.00 50
a. Souvenir sheet of 2 3.75 2.25

No. C349a contains Nos. C348-C349, perf. 13½x14.

Bicycle Type of 1978

History of Bicycle: 60fr, Bantam, 1896 (vert.). 85fr, Fold-up bicycle for military use, 1897. 90fr, Draisienne, 1816 (vert.). 100fr, Penny-farthing, 1884 (vert.).

Perf. 14x13, 13x14

1978, July 10 Photo.

C350 A202 60fr multi 40 14
C351 A202 85fr multi 55 20
C352 A202 90fr multi 60 22
C353 A202 100fr multi 65 25
a. Souvenir sheet of 2, #C352-C353 1.40 85

Phonograph Type of 1978

Designs: 60fr, Edison's original phonograph (horiz.). 80fr, Emile Berliner's phonograph, 1888. 200fr, Berliner's improved phonograph, 1894 (horiz.). 300fr, His Master's Voice phonograph, 1900 (horiz.).

Perf. 13x14, 14x13

1978, July 8 Photo.

C354 A203 60fr multi 40 14
C355 A203 80fr multi 55 20
C356 A203 200fr multi 1.35 35
C357 A203 300fr multi 2.00 50
a. Souvenir sheet of 2, #C356-C357 3.50 2.00

Red Cross Type of 1978

Design: 60fr, Red Cross and other pavilions at Paris Exhibition, 1867.

1978, Sept. 4 Photo. *Perf. 14x13*

C358 A204 60fr pur & red 40 20
a. Souvenir sheet of 2, #1009, C358 65 40

Paintings Type of 1978

Paintings: 60fr, Langlois Bridge, by Vincent van Gogh. 70fr, Witches' Sabbath, by Francisco Goya. 90fr, Jesus among the Doctors, by Albrecht Dürer. 200fr, View of Arco, by Dürer.

1978, Nov. 6 Litho. *Perf. 14*

C359 A205 60fr multi 40 20
C360 A205 70fr multi 45 22
C361 A205 90fr multi 60 35
C362 A205 200fr multi 1.35 65
a. Souvenir sheet of 2, #C361-C362 2.00 1.20

Birth and death anniversaries of famous painters.

Philexafrique II - Essen Issue

Common Design Types

Designs: No. C363, Warthog and Togo No. C36. No. C364, Firecrest and Thurn and Taxis No. 1.

1978, Nov. 1 Litho. *Perf. 13x12½*

C363 CD138 100fr multi 65 35
C364 CD139 100fr multi 65 35

Nos. C363-C364 printed se-tenant.

Congress of Paris Type of 1978

Designs: 60fr, Mail ship "Slieve Roe" 1877, and post horn. 105fr, Congress of Paris medal. 200fr, Locomotive, 1870. All horizontal.

1978, Nov. 27 Photo. *Perf. 14x13*

C365 A206 60fr multi 40 20
C366 A206 105fr multi 70 35
C367 A206 200fr multi 1.40 65
a. Souvenir sheet of 2, #C366-C367 2.25 1.25

Christmas Type of 1978

Paintings (Virgin and Child): 90fr, 200fr, by Carlo Crivelli (diff.). 100fr, by Cosimo Tura.

1978, Dec. 18

C368 A207 90fr multi 60 30
C369 A207 100fr multi 65 35
C370 A207 200fr multi 1.35 65
a. Souvenir sheet of 2, #C369-C370 2.25 1.25

Capt. Cook Type of 1979

Designs: 60fr, "Freelove," Whitby Harbor (horiz.). 70fr, Trip to Antarctica, 1773 (horiz.). 90fr, Capt. Cook. 200fr, Sails of Endeavour.

1979, Feb. 12 Litho. *Perf. 14*

C371 A208 60fr multi 40 20
C372 A208 70fr multi 45 22
C373 A208 90fr multi 60 30
C374 A208 200fr multi 1.40 1.20
a. Souvenir sheet of 2, #C373-C374 2.00 1.20

Easter Type of 1979

Designs: 60fr, Resurrection. 100fr, Ascension. 200fr, Jesus appearing to Mary Magdalene.

1979, Apr. 9

C375 A209 60fr multi 40 20
C376 A209 100fr multi 65 35
C377 A209 200fr multi 1.40 65
a. Souvenir sheet of 2, #C376-C377 2.25 1.25

UPU Emblem, Drummer — AP20

Design: 100fr, UPU emblem, hands passing letter, satellites.

1979, June 8 Engr. *Perf. 13*

C378 AP20 60fr multi 40 20
C379 AP20 100fr multi 65 35

Philexafrique II, Libreville, Gabon, June 8-17.

Einstein Type of 1979

Designs: 60fr, Sights and actuality diagram. 85fr, Einstein playing violin (vert.). 100fr, Atom symbol and formula of relativity (vert.). 200fr, Einstein portrait (vert.).

Perf. 14x13, 13x14

1979, July 2 Photo.

C380 A210 60fr multi 40 20
C381 A210 85fr multi 60 28
C382 A210 100fr multi 65 35
C383 A210 200fr multi 1.40 65
a. Souvenir sheet of 2, #C382-C383 2.25

Tree Type of 1979

Design: 60fr, Man watering tree.

1979, Aug. 13 *Perf. 14x13*

C384 A212 60fr blk & brn 40 20

Rowland Hill Type of 1979

Designs: 90fr, Bellman, England, 1820. 100fr, "Centercycles" used for parcel delivery, 1883 (horiz.). 200fr, French P.O. railroad car, 1848 (horiz.).

1979, Aug. 27 Photo.

C385 A213 90fr multi 60 30
C386 A213 100fr multi 65 35
C387 A213 200fr multi 1.40 65
a. Souvenir sheet of 2, #C386-C387 2.25 2.25

Train Type of 1979

Historic Locomotives: 60fr, "Le General," 1862. 85fr, Stephenson's, 1843. 100fr, "De Witt Clinton," 1831. 200fr, Joy's "Jenny Lind," 1847.

1979, Oct. 1 Litho. *Perf. 14*

C388 A214 60fr multi 40 20
C389 A214 85fr multi 55 28
C390 A214 100fr multi 65 35
C391 A214 200fr multi 1.40 65
a. Souvenir sheet of 2, #C390-C391 2.25 2.25

Olympic Type of 1979

1980 Olympic Emblems and: 90fr, Ski jump. No. C393, Doubles canoeing, Olympic flame. No. C394, Rings. No. C395a, Bobsledding (horiz.). No. C395b, Gymnast (horiz.).

1979, Oct. 18 Litho. *Perf. 13½*

C392 A215 90fr multi 60 30
C393 A215 100fr multi 65 35
C394 A215 200fr multi 1.40 65
a. Souvenir sheet of 2 2.25 2.25

Souvenir Sheet

C395 Sheet of 2 2.25 2.25
a. A215 100fr multi 65 35
b. A215 200fr multi 1.40 65

Religion Type of 1979

1979, Oct. 29 *Perf. 13x14*

Designs: 60fr, Native praying (vert.). 70fr, Protestant ministers.

C396 A216 60fr multi 40 20
C397 A216 70fr multi 45 22
a. Souvenir sheet of 2, #C396-C397 1.00

Apollo 11 Type of 1979

Designs: 60fr, Astronaut leaving Apollo 11. 70fr, U.S. flag. 200fr, Sun shield. 300fr, Lunar take-off.

1979, Nov. 5

C398 A217 60fr multi 40 20
C399 A217 70fr multi 45 22
C400 A217 200fr multi 1.40 65
C401 A217 300fr multi 2.00 1.00
a. Souvenir sheet of 2, #C400-C401 3.75 3.75

Telecom Type of 1979

Design: 60fr, Telecom 79, dish antenna.

1979, Nov. 26 Photo. *Perf. 14x13*

C402 A218 60fr multi 40 20

Christmas Type of 1979

Designs: 90fr, Adoration of the Kings. 100fr, Presentation of Infant Jesus. 200fr, Flight into Egypt.

1979, Dec. 17 Litho. *Perf. 14*

C403 A219 90fr multi 60 30
C404 A219 100fr multi 65 35
C405 A219 200fr multi 1.35 65
a. Souvenir sheet of 2, #C404-C405 2.25 1.25

Rotary Type of 1980

3-H Emblem and: 90fr, Man reaching for sun. 100fr, Fish, grain. 200fr, Family, globe.

1980, Jan. 14

C406 A220 90fr multi 60 30
C407 A220 100fr multi 65 35
C408 A220 200fr multi 1.35 65
a. Souvenir sheet of 2, C407-C408 2.25 1.25

Rotary Intl., 75th anniv.; 3-H program (health, hunger, humanity).

Winter Olympic Type, 1980

1980, Jan. 31 Litho. *Perf. 13½*

C409 A221 60fr Downhill skiing 40 20
C410 A221 100fr Speed skating 65 35
C411 A221 200fr Cross-country skiing 1.35 65

Souvenir Sheet

C412 Sheet of 2 2.00 1.00
a. A221 100fr Ski jump, horiz. 65 35
b. A221 200fr Hockey, horiz. 1.35 65

Olympic Type of 1980

1980, Feb. 29 Litho. *Perf. 13½*

C413 A222 100fr Fencing 65 35
C414 A222 200fr Pole vault 1.35 65
C415 A222 300fr Hurdles 2.00 1.00
a. Souvenir sheet of 2, #C414-C415 3.50 1.90

Easter Type of 1980

Easter 1980 (Paintings by): 60fr, Lorenzo Lotto. 100fr, El Greco. 200fr, Carlo Crivelli.

1980, Mar. 31 *Perf. 14*

C416 A223 60fr multi 40 20
C417 A223 100fr multi 65 35
C418 A223 200fr multi 1.35 65
a. Souvenir sheet of 2, #C417-C418 2.00 1.00

ASECNA Type of 1980

1980, Mar. 24 Litho. *Perf. 12½*

C419 A224 60fr multi 40 20

Telecommunications Type of 1980

1980, May 17 Photo. *Perf. 13½x14*

C420 A225 60fr "17 MAI", vert. 40 20

Red Cross Type of 1980

1980, June 16 Photo. *Perf. 14x13*

C421 A226 60fr Nurses, patient 40 20

Jules Verne Type of 1980

Designs: 60fr, Rocket (From Earth to Moon). 80fr, Around the World in 80 Days. 100fr, Rocket and moon (From Earth to Moon). 200fr, Octopus (20,000 Leagues Under the Sea).

1980, July 14 Litho. *Perf. 14*

C422 A227 60fr multi 40 20
C423 A227 80fr multi 55 25
C424 A227 100fr multi 65 35
C425 A227 200fr multi 1.35 65
a. Souvenir sheet of 2 2.00 1.00

No. C425a contains Nos. C424-C425 perf. 13½x14.

Ingres Type of 1980

Ingres Paintings: 90fr, Jupiter and Thetis. 100fr, Countess d'Hassonville. 200fr, "Tu Marcellus Eris."

1980, Aug. 29 Litho. *Perf. 14*

C426 A228 90fr multi 60 30
C427 A228 100fr multi 65 35
C428 A228 200fr multi 1.35 65
a. Souvenir sheet of 2, C427-C428 2.00 1.00

Famous Men Type of 1980

Designs: 90fr, Salvador Allende (vert.). 100fr, Pope Paul VI (vert.). 200fr, Jomo Kenyatta (vert.).

1980, Feb. 11 Litho. *Perf. 14x13*

C429 A231 90fr ultra & lt bl grn 60 30
C430 A231 100fr pur & pink 65 35
C431 A231 200fr brn & yel bis 1.35 65
a. Souvenir sheet of 2, #C430-C431 2.00 1.00

Human Rights Type of 1980

1980, Oct. 13 *Perf. 13x14*

C432 A233 60fr Map of Americas 40 20
C433 A233 150fr Map of Africa 1.00 50
a. Souvenir sheet of 2, #C432-C433 1.50 65

American Order of Rosicrucians Emblem — AP21

1980, Nov. 17 Litho. *Perf. 13*

C434 AP21 60fr multi 40 20

General Conclave of the American Order of Rosicrucians, meeting of French-speaking countries, Lome, Aug.

Christmas Type of 1980

1980, Dec. 22 *Perf. 14½x13½*

C435 A234 100fr Cologne Cathedral, Germany, 13th cent. 65 35
C436 A234 150fr Notre Dame, Paris, 12th cent. 1.00 50
C437 A234 200fr Canterbury Cathedral, England, 11th cent. 1.35 65
a. Souvenir sheet of 2, #C436-C437 2.25 1.25

Hotel Type of 1981

1981, Feb. 2 Litho. *Perf. 12½x13*

C437B A236 60fr multi 40 20

Easter Type of 1981

Rembrandt Paintings: 100fr, Artist's Mother. 200fr, Man in a Ruff.

Perf. 14½x13½

1981, Apr. 13 Litho.

C438 A237 100fr multi 65 35
C439 A237 200fr multi 1.35 65
a. Souvenir sheet of 2, #C438-C439 2.00 1.00

Market Type of 1980

1981, Mar. 8 Litho. *Perf. 14*

C440 A230 90fr Fabric dealer 60 30
C441 A230 100fr Bananas 65 35
C442 A230 200fr Clay pottery 1.40 65
C443 A230 250fr Setting up 1.60 80
C444 A230 500fr Selling 3.50 1.60
C445 A230 1000fr Measuring grain 6.50 3.50
Nos. C440-C445 (6) 14.25 7.20

Bird Type of 1981

Perf. 13½x14½

1981, Aug. 10 Litho.

C446 A238 50fr Violet-backed sunbird 35 16
C447 A238 100fr Red bishop 65 35
a. Souvenir sheet of 2, #C446-C447 1.00 50

IYD Type of 1981

1981, Aug. 31 *Perf. 14*

C448 A240 90fr Carpenter 60 30
C449 A240 200fr Basketball players 1.35 65

Souvenir Sheet

C449A A240 300fr Weaver 2.00 1.00

Picasso Type of 1981

1981, Sept. 14 *Perf. 14½x13½*

C450 A241 90fr Violin and Bottle on Table, 1916 60 30
C451 A241 100fr Baboon and Young 60 35
C452 A241 200fr Mandolin and Clarinet, 1914 1.40 65
a. Souvenir sheet of 2, #C451-C452 2.00 1.00

World Heritage Year Type of 1981

1981, Sept. 28 *Perf. 13½x14½*

C453 A242 100fr Cracow Museum, Poland 75 35
C454 A242 200fr Goree Isld., Senegal 1.50 75
a. Souvenir sheet of 2, #C453-C454 2.25 1.10

Space Type of 1981

1981, Nov. *Perf. 14*

C455 A243 90fr multi 70 35
C456 A243 100fr multi 75 38

Souvenir Sheet

Perf. 13x14

C456A A243 300fr multi, vert. 2.25 1.10

10th anniv. of Soyuz 10 (90fr) and Apollo 14 (100fr).

Christmas Type of 1981

Rubens Paintings: 100fr, Adoration of the Kings. 200fr, Virgin and Child. 300fr, Virgin giving Chasuble to St. Idefonse.

Perf. 14½x13½

1981, Dec. 10 Litho.

C457 A244 100fr multi 65 35
C458 A244 200fr multi 1.40 65
C459 A244 300fr multi 2.00 1.00
a. Souvenir sheet of 2, #C458-C459 3.75 1.90

West African Rice Development Assoc. — AP22

1981, Dec. 21 Litho. *Perf. 12½*

C461 AP22 105fr yel & multi 70 35

See No. 1100.

Liberation Type of 1982

Designs: 105fr, Citizens holding hands, Pres. Eyadema, vert. 130fr, Hotel.

1982, Jan. 13 Litho. *Perf. 12½*

C462 A245 105fr multi 70 35
C463 A245 130fr multi 90 42

Scouting Year Type of 1982

1982, Feb. 25 Litho. *Perf. 14*

C464 A246 90fr Semaphore 60 30
C465 A246 120fr Tower 80 40
C466 A246 130fr Scouts, canoe 90 42
C467 A246 135fr Scouts, tent 90 45

Souvenir Sheet

Perf. 13x14

C468 A246 500fr Baden-Powell 3.50 1.60

Easter Type of 1982

1982, Apr. *Perf. 14x14½*

C469 A247 105fr multi 70 38
C470 A247 120fr multi 80 40

Souvenir Sheet

C471 A247 500fr multi 3.50 1.60

PHILEXFRANCE '82 Intl. Stamp Exhibition, Paris, June 11-21 — AP23

1982 Litho. *Perf. 13*

C472 AP23 90fr shown 60 30
C473 AP23 105fr ROMOLYMPHIL '82, vert. 70 35

Issue dates: 90fr, June 11; 105fr, May 19.

Butterfly Type of 1982

1982, July 15 *Perf. 14½x14*

C474 A248 90fr Euxanthe eurionome 60 30
C475 A248 105fr Mylothris rhodope 70 35

Souvenir Sheet

C476 A248 500fr Papilio zalmoxis 3.50 1.65

World Cup Type of 1982

1982, July 26 *Perf. 14x14½*

C477 A249 105fr multi 70 35
C478 A249 200fr multi 1.35 65
C479 A249 300fr multi 2.00 1.00

Souvenir Sheet

C480 A249 500fr multi 3.50 1.65

Pre-Olympics, 1984 Los Angeles — AP24

1983, Oct. 3 Photo. *Perf. 12½*

C481 AP24 70fr Boxing 22 12
C482 AP24 90fr Hurdles 30 15
C483 AP24 105fr Pole vault 35 18
C484 AP24 130fr Runner 42 20

Souvenir Sheet

C485 AP24 500fr Runner, diff. 1.65 80

Nos. C443-C444 Overprinted: "19E CONGRES UPU HAMBOURG 1984"

1984, June Litho. Perf. 14
C486 A230 250fr multi 80 40
C487 A230 500fr multi 1.65 80

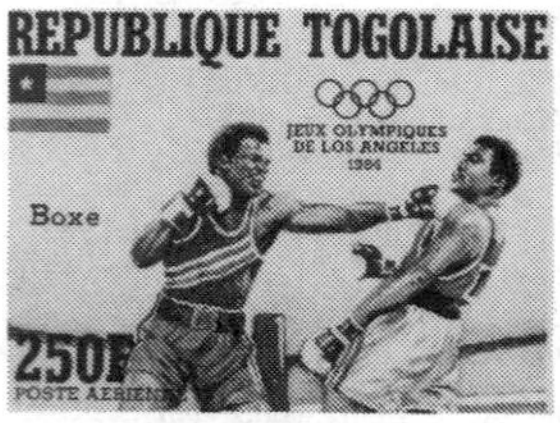

1984 Summer Olympics — AP25

1984, July 27 Perf. 13
C488 AP25 70fr Pole vault 22 12
C489 AP25 90fr Bicycling 30 15
C490 AP25 120fr Soccer 40 20
C491 AP25 250fr Boxing 80 40
C492 AP25 400fr Running 1.35 65
Nos. C488-C492 (5) 3.07 1.52

Souvenir Sheet

C493 AP25 1000fr like 120fr, without flag 3.50 1.65

Nos. C488-C490, C493 vert.

Olympic Champions AP26

1984, Nov. 15 Litho. Perf. 15
C494 AP26 500fr Jim Thorpe, U.S.A. 1.40 70
C495 AP26 500fr Jesse Owens, U.S.A. 1.40 70
C496 AP26 500fr Muhammad Ali, U.S.A. 1.40 70
C497 AP26 500fr Bob Beamon, U.S.A. 1.40 70

Souvenir Sheets

C498 AP26 500fr Bill Steinkraus, U.S.A. 1.40 70
C499 AP26 500fr New Zealand rowing team 1.40 70
C500 AP26 500fr Pakistani hockey team 1.40 70
C501 AP26 500fr Yukio Endo, Japan 1.40 70

West German Olympians

1984, Nov. 15
C502 AP26 500fr Dietmar Mogenburg 1.40 70
C503 AP26 500fr Fredy Schmidtke 1.40 70
C504 AP26 500fr Matthias Behr 1.40 70
C505 AP26 500fr Sabine Everts 1.40 70

Souvenir Sheets

C506 AP26 500fr Karl-Heinz Radschinsky 1.40 70
C507 AP26 500fr Pasquale Passarelli 1.40 70
C508 AP26 500fr Michale Gross 1.40 70
C509 AP26 500fr Jurgen Hingsen 1.40 70

Peace and Human Rights — AP28

Designs: 230fr, Map of Togo, globe, doves. 270fr, Palm tree, emblem. 500fr, Opencast mining operation. 1000fr, Human Rights Monument, UN, New York.

1985, Jan. 14 Litho. Perf. 13½x14
C510 AP28 230fr multi 45 22
C511 AP28 270fr multi 55 30
C512 AP28 500fr multi 1.00 50
C513 AP28 1000fr multi 2.00 1.00

Tribal Dances AP29

1985, July Perf. 15x14
C514 AP29 120fr Adifo, Adangbe 25 12
C515 AP29 135fr Fouet (whip), Kente 25 14
C516 AP29 290fr Idjombi, Pagouda 60 30
C517 AP29 500fr Moba, Dapaong 1.00 50

Visit of Pope John Paul II — AP30

Designs: 90fr, The Pope outside Lome Cathedral. 130fr, Blessing crowd in St. Peter's Square, vert. 500fr, Greeting Pres. Eyadema.

1985, Aug. 9 Perf. 13
C518 AP30 90fr multi 18 10
C519 AP30 130fr multi 25 14
C520 AP30 500fr multi 1.00 50

Nos. C495, C497, C499, C502, C505-508 Overprinted with Winners Names, Country and Type of Olympic Medal

1985, Aug. Perf. 15
C521 AP26 500fr Kirk Baptiste, USA 1.00 50
C522 AP26 500fr Carl Lewis, USA 1.00 50
C523 AP26 500fr Patrik Sjoborg, Sweden 1.00 50
C524 AP26 500fr Glynis Nunn, Australia 1.00 50

Souvenir Sheets

C525 AP26 500fr Rowing eights, Canada 2.00 1.00
C526 AP26 500fr Rolf Milser, W. Germany 2.00 1.00
C527 AP26 500fr Takashi Irie, Japan 2.00 1.00
C528 AP26 500fr Frederic Delcourt, France 2.00 1.00

Nos. C494, C496, C503-C504, C498, C500, C501, C509 Ovptd. with Winners Names, Country and Type of Olympic Medal

1985, Sept. 19 Litho. Perf. 15
C529 AP26 500fr Italy 1.00 50
C530 AP26 500fr Kevin Barry 1.00 50
C531 AP26 500fr Rolf Golz 1.00 50
C532 AP26 500fr Philippe Boisse 1.00 50

Souvenir Sheets

C533 AP26 500fr Karen Stives 1.00 50
C534 AP26 500fr R.F.A. (West Germany) 1.00 50
C535 AP26 500fr Koji Gushiken 1.00 50
C536 AP26 500fr Daley Thompson 1.00 50

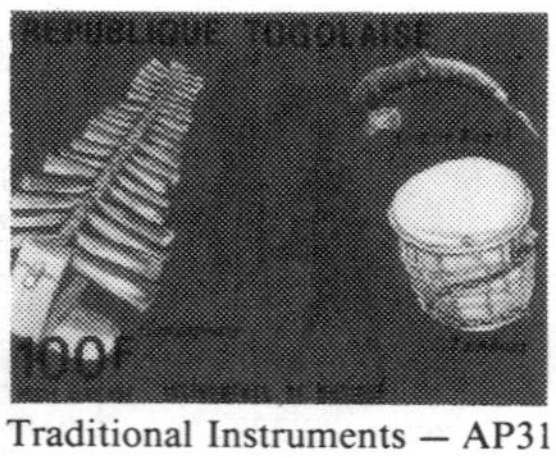

Traditional Instruments — AP31

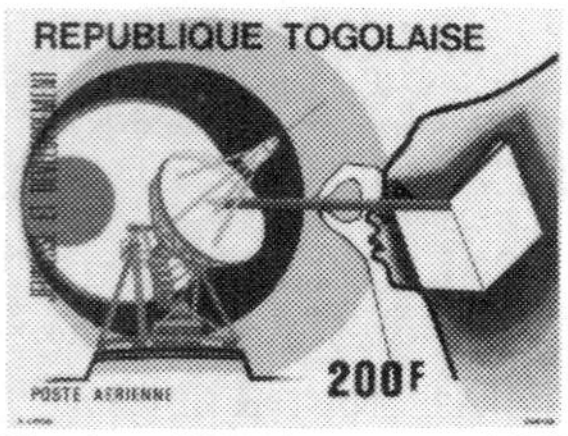

Youth and Development — AP32

Designs: No. C537, Xylophone, Kante horn, tambour. No. C538, Bongo drums, castanets, bassar horn. No. C539, Communications. No. C540, Agriculture and industry.

1985 Litho. Perf. 13
C537 AP31 100fr multi 20 10
C538 AP31 100fr multi 20 10
C539 AP32 200fr multi 40 20
C540 AP32 200fr multi 40 20

PHILEXAFRICA '85, Lome, Togo, Nov. 16-24. Stamps of same denomination printed se-tenant with center label picturing UAPT emblem. Issue dates: 100fr, Nov. 4. 200fr, Nov. 16.

Souvenir Sheet

No. 1274 Ovptd. with Organization Emblem and "80e Anniversaire du Rotary International."

1985, Nov. 15 Litho. Perf. 15
C541 A267 1000fr multi 2.50 1.35

Nos. 1254-1255, 1258 Ovptd. "10e ANNIVERSAIRE DE APOLLO-SOYUZ" in 1 or 2 lines

1985, Dec. 27 Litho. Perf. 15
C542 A265 90fr multi 35 14
C543 A265 500fr multi 1.90 90

Souvenir Sheet

C544 A265 1000fr multi 3.75 1.90

Nos. 1294-1295, 1297 Ovptd. "75e ANNIVERSAIRE DE LA MORT DE HENRI DUNANT FONDATEUR DE LA CROIX ROUGE" in 2 or 4 lines

1985, Dec. 27
C545 A270 400fr multi 1.50 70
C546 A270 500fr multi 1.90 90

Souvenir Sheet

C547 A270 1000fr multi 3.75 1.90

Statue of Liberty, Cent. — AP33

1986, Apr. 10 Perf. 13
C548 AP33 70fr Eiffel Tower 40 20
C549 AP33 90fr Statue of Liberty 50 25
C550 AP33 500fr Empire State Building 2.75 1.40

Nos. 1237-1240 Ovptd. with AMERIPEX '86 Emblem

1986, May 22 Perf. 11
C551 A262 500fr multi 2.75 1.40
C552 A262 1000fr multi 5.50 2.75

Souvenir Sheets

Perf. 14

C553 A262 1000fr No. 1239 5.50 2.75
C554 A262 1000fr No. 1240 5.50 2.75

Air Africa, 25th Anniv. AP34

1986, Dec. 29 Litho. Perf. 12½x13
C555 AP34 90fr multi 50 25

Konrad Adenauer (1876-1967) West German Chancellor AP35

1987, July 15 Litho. Perf. 12½x13
C556 AP35 120fr At podium 68 35
C557 AP35 500fr With Pres. Kennedy, 1962 2.75 1.40

Souvenir Sheet

Perf. 13x12½

C558 AP35 500fr Portrait, vert. 2.75 1.40

Berlin, 750th Anniv. AP36

Designs: 90fr, Wilhelm I (1781-1864) coin, Victory statue. 150fr, Frederick III (1831-1888) coin, Brandenburg Gate. 300fr, Wilhelm II (1882-1951) coin, Reichstag building. 750fr, Otto Leopold von Bismarck (1815-1898), first chancellor of the German empire, and Charlottenburg Palace.

1987, Aug. 31 Litho. Perf. 13½
C559 AP36 90fr multi 60 30
C560 AP36 150fr multi 1.00 50
C561 AP36 300fr multi 2.00 1.00

Souvenir Sheet

C562 AP36 750fr multi 5.00 2.50

Nos. C506, 1258, 1273 and 1274 Overprinted in Black for Philatelic Exhibitions

a OLYMPHILEX'88

b INDEPENDENCE 40

c FINLANDIA 88

d PRAGA '88

1988, Apr. 25 Litho. Perf. 15
C563 AP26 (a) 500fr on No. C506 3.25 1.60
C564 A265 (b) 1000fr on No. 1258 7.00 3.50
C565 A265 (c) 1000fr on No. 1273 7.00 3.50
C566 A267 (d) 1000fr on No. 1274 6.50 3.25

OLYMPHILEX '88 (No. C563), INDEPENDENCE 40 (No. C564), FINLANDIA '88 (No. C565) and PRAGA '88 (No. C566).

AIR POST SEMI-POSTAL STAMPS

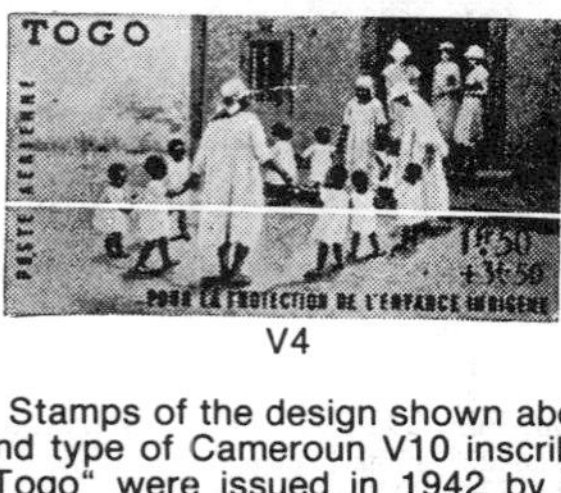

V4

Stamps of the design shown above and type of Cameroun V10 inscribed "Togo" were issued in 1942 by the Vichy Government, but were not placed on sale in the colony.

POSTAGE DUE STAMPS

Postage Due Stamps of Dahomey, 1914 Overprinted **TOGO**

1921 Unwmk. *Perf. 14x13 ½*
J1 D2 5c green 30 30
J2 D2 10c rose 30 30
J3 D2 15c gray 55 55
J4 D2 20c brown 1.10 1.00
J5 D2 30c blue 1.10 1.00
J6 D2 50c black 70 55
J7 D2 60c orange 90 70
J8 D2 1fr violet 2.00 1.50
Nos. J1-J8 (8) 6.95 5.90

Cotton Field — D3

1925 Typo. Unwmk.
J9 D3 2c blue & blk 5 5
J10 D3 4c dl red & blk 5 5
J11 D3 5c ol grn & blk 5 5
J12 D3 10c cer & blk 16 16
J13 D3 15c org & blk 20 20
J14 D3 20c red vio & blk 28 28
J15 D3 25c gray & blk 40 40
J16 D3 30c ocher & blk 20 20
J17 D3 50c brn & blk 30 30
J18 D3 60c grn & blk 40 40
J19 D3 1fr dk vio & blk 45 45
Nos. J9-J19 (11) 2.54 2.54

Type of 1925 Issue Surcharged **2f**

1927
J20 D3 2fr on 1fr rose red & vio 1.90 1.90
J21 D3 3fr on 1fr org brn, blk & ultra 1.90 1.90

Mask D4

Carved Figures D5

1941 Engr. *Perf. 13*
J22 D4 5c brn blk 5 5
J23 D4 10c yel grn 5 5
J24 D4 15c carmine 5 5
J25 D4 20c ultra 20 20
J26 D4 30c chestnut 20 20
J27 D4 50c olive grn 1.00 1.00
J28 D4 60c violet 20 20
J29 D4 1fr light bl 50 50
J30 D4 2fr org ver 28 28
J31 D4 3fr rose vio 55 55
Nos. J22-J31 (10) 3.08 3.08

Stamps of type D4 without "RF" monogram were issued in 1942 to 1944 by the Vichy Government, but were not placed on sale in the colony.

Catalogue values for unused stamps in this section, from this point to the end of the section, are for Never Hinged items.

1947
J32 D5 10c brt ultra 5 5
J33 D5 30c red 5 5
J34 D5 50c dp yel grn 5 5
J35 D5 1fr chocolate 10 10
J36 D5 2fr carmine 20 20
J37 D5 3fr gray blk 20 20
J38 D5 4fr ultra 38 38
J39 D5 5fr sepia 42 42
J40 D5 10fr dp org 45 45
J41 D5 20fr dk bl vio 65 65
Nos. J32-J41 (10) 2.55 2.55

Republic

Konkomba Helmet
D6 D7

1957 Engr. *Perf. 14x13*
J42 D6 1fr brt vio 5 5
J43 D6 2fr brt org 10 10
J44 D6 3fr dk gray 12 12
J45 D6 4fr brt red 12 12
J46 D6 5fr ultra 12 12
J47 D6 10fr dp grn 38 38
J48 D6 20fr dp claret 60 60
Nos. J42-J48 (7) 1.49 1.49

1959 *Perf. 14x13*
J49 D7 1fr org brn 5 5
J50 D7 2fr lt bl grn 5 5
J51 D7 3fr orange 12 12
J52 D7 4fr blue 14 14
J53 D7 5fr lil rose 14 14
J54 D7 10fr vio blue 38 38
J55 D7 20fr black 65 65
Nos. J49-J55 (7) 1.53 1.53

Type of Regular Issue, 1964

Shells: 1fr, Conus papilionaceus. 2fr, Marginella faba. 3fr, Cypraea stercoraria. 4fr, Strombus latus. 5fr, Costate cockle (sea shell). 10fr, Cancellaria cancellata. 15fr, Cymbium pepo. 20fr, Tympanotomus radula.

1964-65 Unwmk. Photo. *Perf. 14*
Size: 20x25 ½mm
J56 A47 1fr gray grn & red brn ('65) 5 5
J57 A47 2fr tan & ol grn ('65) 5 5
J58 A47 3fr gray, brn & yel ('65) 10 10
J59 A47 4fr tan & multi ('65) 15 15
J60 A47 5fr sep, org & grn 28 28
J61 A47 10fr sl bl, brn & bis 40 40
J62 A47 15fr grn & brn 1.00 1.00
J63 A47 20fr sl, dk brn & yel 1.25 1.25
Nos. J56-J63 (8) 3.28 3.28

Tomatoes — D8

1969-70 Litho. *Perf. 14*
J64 D8 5fr yel & multi 10 10
J65 D8 10fr bl & multi 20 20
J66 D8 15fr multi ('70) 30 30
J67 D8 20fr multi ('70) 40 40

Market Type of 1980

1981, Mar. 8 Litho. *Perf. 14*
Size: 23x32mm, 32x23mm
J68 A230 5fr Millet, vert. 5 5
J69 A230 10fr Packaged goods 5 5
J70 A230 25fr Chickens 12 5
J71 A230 50fr Ivory vendor 25 12

TRANSCAUCASIAN FEDERATED REPUBLICS

(Armenia, Georgia, Azerbaijan)

LOCATION — In southeastern Europe, south of the Caucasus Mountains between the Black and Caspian Seas.
GOVT. — Former republic.
AREA — 71,255 sq. mi.
POP. — 5,851,000 (approx.).
CAPITAL — Tiflis.

The Transcaucasian Federation was made up of the former autonomies of Armenia, Georgia and Azerbaijan. Its stamps were replaced by those of Russia.

100 Kopecks = 1 Ruble

Russian Stamps of 1909-17 Overprinted in Black or Red

1923 Unwmk. *Perf. 14½x15*
1 A15 10k dark blue 2.75 4.00
2 A14 10k on 7k lt bl 2.75 4.00
3 A11 25k grn & gray vio 3.25 4.50
4 A11 35k red brn & grn (R) 3.25 4.50
a. Double overprint 40.00 40.00
5 A8 50k brn red & grn 3.25 4.50
6 A9 1r pale brn, brn & org 6.50 10.00
7 A12 3½r mar & lt grn 14.00

Imperf
8 A9 1r pale brn, brn & red org 2.75 5.25

No. 7 was prepared but not issued.

Overprinted on Stamps of Armenia Previously Handstamped:

a

c

Perf. 14½x15
9 A11(c) 25k grn & gray vio *125.00 200.00*
10 A8(c) 50k vio & grn *65.00 125.00*

Perf. 13½
11 A9(a) 1r pale brn, brn & org *32.50 32.50*
12 A9(c) 1r pale, brn, brn & org *45.00 32.50*

Imperf
13 A9(c) 1r pale brn, brn & red org *32.50 32.50*

Counterfeit overprints exist.

Oil Fields — A1

Soviet Symbols — A2

1923 *Perf. 11½*
14 A1 40,000r red vio 65 1.00
15 A1 75,000r dk grn 65 1.00
16 A1 100,000r blk vio 65 1.00
17 A1 150,000r red 65 1.00
18 A2 200,000r dl grn 65 1.00
19 A2 300,000r blue 65 1.25
20 A2 350,000r dk brn 65 1.25
21 A2 500,000r rose 65 1.25
Nos. 14-21 (8) 5.20 8.75

Nos. 14-15 Surcharged in Brown

700000 РУБ.

1923
22 A1 700,000r on 40,000r red vio 2.75 *4.00*
a. Imperf., pair 13.00
23 A1 700,000r on 75,000r dk grn 2.75 *4.00*
a. Imperf., pair 13.00

Transcaucasian Federated Republics stamps can be mounted in Scott's Soviet Republics Part I Album.

Types of Preceding Issue with Values in Gold Kopecks

1923, Oct. 24
25 A2 1k orange 65 1.65
26 A2 2k blue green 65 1.65
27 A2 3k rose 65 1.65
28 A2 4k gray brown 65 1.65
29 A1 5k dk violet 65 1.65
30 A1 9k deep blue 65 1.65
31 A1 18k slate 65 1.65
Nos. 25-31 (7) 4.55 11.55

Nos. 14-21, 25-31 exist imperf. but are not known to have been issued in that condition. Value, $12.50 each.

TRIESTE

A free territory (1947-1954) on the Adriatic Sea between Italy and Jugoslavia. In 1954 the territory was divided, Italy acquiring the northern section and seaport, Jugoslavia the southern section (Zone B).

Catalogue values for all unused stamps in this country are for Never Hinged items.

ZONE A

Issued jointly by the Allied Military Government of the United States and Great Britain

Stamps of Italy 1945-47 Overprinted:

A.M.G.
F.T.T.
a

A.M.G.
F.T.T.
b

c
A.M.G.
F.T.T.

1947, Oct. 1 Wmk. 277 *Perf. 14*
1 A259(a) 25c brt bl grn 10 25
2 A255(a) 50c dp vio 10 25
3 A257(a) 1 l dk grn 10 5
4 A258(a) 2 l dk cl brn 10 5
5 A259(a) 3 l red 10 5
6 A259(a) 4 l red org 10 5
7 A256(a) 5 l dp bl 22 5
8 A257(a) 6 l dp vio 28 5
9 A255(a) 10 l slate 28 5
10 A257(a) 15 l dp bl 50 12
11 A259(a) 20 l dk red vio 28 5
12 A260(b) 25 l dk grn 1.90 1.65
13 A260(b) 50 l dk vio brn 3.00 1.25

Perf. 14x13½
14 A261(c) 100 l car lake 10.00 5.00
Nos. 1-14 (14) 17.06 8.92

The letters "F. T. T." are the initials of "Free Territory of Trieste."

Italy Nos. 486-488 Ovptd. Type "a"

1948, Mar. 1 *Perf. 14*
15 A255 8 l dk grn 1.90 *1.50*
16 A256 10 l red org 5.75 10
17 A259 30 l dk bl 70.00 1.25

Italy Nos. 495 to 506 Overprinted

d A.M.G.- F. T. T.

1948, July 1
18 A272 3 l dk brn 24 10
19 A272 4 l red vio 14 10
20 A272 5 l dp bl 118 10
21 A272 6 l dp yel grn 35 24
22 A272 8 l brown 24 20
23 A272 10 l org red 35 10
24 A272 12 l dk gray grn 45 *1.00*
25 A272 15 l gray blk 7.75 *6.00*
26 A272 20 l car rose 12.00 *6.00*
27 A272 30 l brt ultra 75 *1.00*
28 A272 50 l violet 6.00 *9.75*
29 A272 100 l bl blk 30.00 *40.00*
Nos. 18-29 (12) 59.45 *64.59*

Italy, Nos. 486 to 488, Overprinted in Carmine

1948, Sept. 8
30 A255 8 l dk grn 30 20
31 A256 10 l red org 30 20
32 A259 30 l dk bl 1.65 2.00
Nos. 30-32,C17-C19 (6) 4.00 *4.55*

The overprint is embossed.

Italy, No. 507, Overprinted Type "d" in Carmine

1948, Oct. 15
33 A273 15 l dk grn 1.25 1.00

Italy, No. 508, Overprinted in Green

e A.M.G. F.T.T.

1948, Nov. 15
34 A274 15 l dk brn 95 1.00

Italy, No. 509, Overprinted Type "d" in Red

1949, May 2 Wmk. 277 *Perf. 14*
35 A275 20 l dk brn 5.00 1.75

27th Milan Trade Fair, April 1949.

Italy, Nos. 510 to 513, Overprinted

f A.M.G. F.T.T.

1949, May 2 Buff Background
36 A276 5 l red brn 40 *75*
37 A276 15 l dk grn 10.00 *11.00*
38 A276 20 l dp red brn 3.75 1.10
39 A276 50 l dk bl 15.00 *10.50*

Issued to commemorate the 50th anniversary of the Biennial Art Exhibition of Venice.

Italy, No. 514, Overprinted Type "d" in Red

1949, May 2
40 A277 50 l brt ultra 3.75 *4.50*

75th anniv. of the UPU.

Italy, No. 518, Overprinted Type "d" in Red

1949, May 30
41 A279 100 l brown 50.00 *80.00*

Centenary of the Roman Republic.

Italy, Nos. 515-517, Ovptd. Type "f"

1949, June 15
42 A278 5 l dk grn 5.75 *7.50*
43 A278 15 l violet 6.75 *11.00*
44 A278 20 l brown 10.00 *11.00*

European Recovery Program.

Italy, Nos. 519 and 520, Overprinted Type "e" in Carmine

1949, July 16
45 A280 20 l gray 7.00 3.50
46 A281 20 l brown 5.75 3.50

No. 45, erection of monument to Giuseppe Mazzini, Italian patriot and revolutionary. No. 46, bicentenary of birth of Vittorio Alfieri, dramatist.

Italy, No. 521 Overprinted in Green

g AMG-FTT

1949, June 8
47 A282 20 l brn red 3.00 *2.00*

Trieste election, June 12, 1949.

Italy, No. 522, Overprinted Type "f" in Carmine

1949, July 8
49 A283 20 l violet 15.00 5.00

2nd World Health Cong., Rome, 1949.

Italy, No. 523 Overprinted Type "e", without Periods, in Black

1949, Aug. 27
50 A284 20 l vio bl 5.75 3.00

500th anniv. of the birth of Lorenzo de Medici.

Italy, No. 524 Ovptd. Type "f"

1949, Aug. 27
51 A285 20 l violet 16.00 *15.00*

400th anniv. of the death of Andrea Palladio.

Italy, No. 525, Overprinted Type "d" in Green

1949, Sept. 10
52 A286 20 l red 5.50 3.50

13th Levant Fair, Bari, Sept. 1949.

Italy Nos. 526 and 527 Overprinted

h AMG-FTT

Wmk. 277
1949, Nov. 7 Photo. *Perf. 14*
53 A287 20 l rose car 2.50 4.00
54 A288 50 l dp bl 7.50 *9.50*

150th anniv. of the invention of the Voltaic Pile.

Same Overprint on No. 528

1949, Nov. 7
55 A289 20 l dp grn 3.00 3.50

Issued to publicize plans to reconstruct Holy Trinity Bridge, Florence.

Same Overprint on No. 529

1949, Nov. 7
56 A290 20 l brt bl 3.00 *2.50*

2,000th anniv. of the death of C. Valerius Catullus, lyric poet.

Same Overprint in Red on No. 530

1949, Dec. 28
57 A291 20 l vio blk 3.00 2.00

Bicent. of the birth of Domenico Cimarosa, Italian composer.

Same Overprint in Black on Italian Stamps of 1945-48

1949-50 Photo.
58 A257 1 l dk grn 16 5
59 A258 2 l dk cl brn 16 5
60 A259 3 l red 16 5
61 A256 5 l dp bl 20 5
62 A257 6 l dp vio 16 5
63 A255 8 l dk grn 5.00 *8.00*
64 A256 10 l red org 26 5
65 A257 15 l dp bl 1.00 30
66 A259 20 l dk red vio 42 8
67 A260 25 l dk grn ('50) 10.00 1.65
68 A260 50 l dk vio brn ('50) 20.00 80

Engr.
69 A261 100 l car lake 35.00 5.25
Nos. 58-69 (12) 72.52 *16.38*

Italy, No. 531, Overprinted Type "g" in Carmine

1950, Apr. 12
70 A292 20 l brown 1.75 1.25

28th Milan Fair, 1950.

Same Overprint in Carmine on Italy, No. 532

1950, Apr. 29
71 A293 20 l vio gray 1.75 1.60

Issued to publicize the 32nd International Automobile Show, Turin, May 4-14, 1950.

Same Overprint in Carmine on Italy, Nos. 533 and 534

1950, May 22
72 A294 20 l ol grn 1.75 *1.40*
73 A295 55 l blue 6.25 *10.50*

5th Gen. Conf. of UNESCO.

Italy, Nos. 535 and 536, Overprinted Type "h" in Black

1950, May 29
74 A296 20 l violet 1.75 *1.40*
75 A296 55 l blue 6.25 *10.50*

Holy Year, 1950.

Italy, No. 537, Overprinted Type "g" in Carmine

1950, July 10
76 A297 20 l gray grn 2.75 2.00

Issued to honor Gaudenzio Ferrari, painter.

Same Overprint in Carmine on Italy, Nos. 538-539

1950, July 15
77 A298 20 l purple 4.50 *4.50*
78 A298 55 l blue 14.00 *22.50*

Intl. Shortwave Radio Conf., Florence, 1950.

Italy, No. 540, Overprinted Type "h"

1950, July 22
79 A299 20 l brown 2.75 2.00

200th anniv. of the death of Ludovico A. Muratoriano, writer.

Italy, No. 541 Overprinted in Carmine

i AMG FTT

1950, July 29
80 A300 20 l dk grn 2.75 2.00

900th anniv. of the death of Guido d'Arezzo, music teacher and composer.

Italy, No. 542, Overprinted Type "g"

1950, Aug. 21
81 A301 20 l chnt brn 2.25 2.00

Levant Fair, Bari, Sept., 1950.

Italy, Nos. 473A and 474, Overprinted

1950, Aug. 27
82 A257 15 l dp bl 1.25 *1.10*
83 A259 20 l dk red vio 1.25 42

Issued to publicize the Trieste Fair.

Italy, No. 543, Overprinted Type "i" in Carmine

1950, Sept. 11
84 A302 20 l indigo 1.00 *1.00*

Pioneers of the Italian wool industry.

Italy Nos. 544-546, Ovptd. Type "h"

1950, Sept. 16 Wmk. 277 *Perf. 14*
85 A303 5 l dp cl & grn 80 *1.90*
86 A303 20 l brn & grn 3.50 1.90
87 A303 55 l dp ultra & brn 24.00 *27.50*

European Tobacco Conf., Rome, 1950.

Same, in Black, on Italy No. 547

1950, Sept. 16
88 A304 20 l ol brn & red brn 2.25 1.65

200th anniv. of the founding of the Academy of Fine Arts, Venice.

Same, in Black, on Italy No. 548

1950, Sept. 16
89 A305 20 l cr & gray blk 2.00 1.65

Augusto Righi, physicist, birth cent.

Italy, Nos. 549 to 565, Overprinted Type "g" in Black

1950, Oct. 20
90 A306 50c vio bl 8 5
91 A306 1 l dk bl vio 8 5
92 A306 2 l sepia 8 5
93 A306 5 l dk gray 8 5
94 A306 6 l chocolate 25 5
95 A306 10 l dp grn 25 5
96 A306 12 l dp bl grn 35 *80*
97 A306 15 l dk gray bl 85 6
98 A306 20 l bl vio 85 5
99 A306 25 l brn org 1.75 5
100 A306 30 l magenta 65 50
101 A306 35 l crimson 1.75 1.25
102 A306 40 l brown 1.10 65
103 A306 50 l violet 25 30
104 A306 55 l dp bl 25 *50*
105 A306 60 l red 5.75 3.00
106 A306 65 l dk grn 25 *45*

Italy Nos. 566 and 567 Overprinted

k AMG-FTT

Perf. 14, 14x13½
Engr.
107 A306 100 l brn org 2.25 10
108 A306 200 l ol brn 2.25 *4.75*
Nos. 90-108 (19) 19.12 *12.76*

Italy Nos. 568 and 569 Overprinted Type "k" in Black

1951, Mar. 27 Photo. *Perf. 14*
109 A307 20 l red vio & red 1.90 *2.25*
110 A307 55 l ultra & bl 27.50 *35.00*

Cent. of Tuscany's 1st postage stamp.

Italy No. 570 Overprinted Type "g"

1951, Apr. 2
111 A308 20 l dk grn 1.65 *2.00*

33rd Intl. Automobile Exhib., Turin, Apr. 4-15, 1951.

Same, on Italy No. 571

1951, Apr. 11
112 A309 20 l bl vio 1.50 *2.00*

Consecration of the Altar of Peace at Redipuglia Cemetery, Medea.

Italy Nos. 572 and 573 Overprinted

1951, Apr. 12
113 A310(h) 20 l brown 1.65 *2.75*
114 A311(g) 55 l dp bl 3.25 *4.75*

International Sample Fair, Milan.

Italy Nos. 574 to 576 Overprinted Type "h" in Black

1951, May 18 Fleur-de-Lis in Red
115 A312 5 l dk brn 5.00 *11.00*
116 A312 10 l Prus grn 5.00 *11.00*
117 A312 15 l vio bl 5.00 *11.00*

Issued to publicize the International Gymnastic Festival and Meet, Florence, 1951.

Italy No. 577 Overprinted

m AMG-FTT

Apr. 26
118 A313 20 l purple 1.50 *2.00*

10th Intl. Exhib. of Textile Art and Fashion, Turin, May 2-16, 1951.

Italy No. 578 Overprinted Type "h"

1951, May 5
119 A314 20 l Prus grn 2.50 *3.00*

500th anniv. of the birth of Columbus.

Italy Nos. 579-580 Ovptd. Type "g"

1951, June 18
120 A315 20 l violet 60 *90*
121 A315 55 l brt bl 1.90 *2.50*

Reconstruction of the Abbey of Montecassino.

Nos. 94, 98 and 104 Overprinted

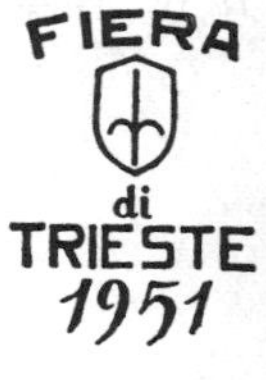

1951, June 24
122 A306 6 l chocolate 42 *65*
123 A306 20 l bl vio 55 *52*
124 A306 55 l dp bl 70 *1.00*

Issued to publicize the Trieste Fair, 1951.

Italy No. 581 Overprinted

n AMG FTT

1951, July 23
125 A316 20 l brn & red brn 90 *1.10*

500th anniv. (in 1950) of the birth of Pietro Vanucci, painter.

Italy Nos. 582 and 583 Overprinted Types "n" and "h" in Red

1951, July 23
126 A317(n) 20 l grnsh gray & blk 1.00 *1.10*
127 A318(h) 55 l vio bl & pale sal 2.25 *3.25*

Triennial Art Exhibition, Milan, 1951.

Italy No. 584 Overprinted Type "g" in Carmine

1951, Aug. 23
128 A319 25 l gray blk 90 *1.10*

World Bicycle Championship Races, Milan, Aug.-Sept. 1951.

Overprint "g" on Italy No. 585

1951, Sept. 8
129 A320 25 l dp bl 90 *1.10*

15th Levant Fair, Bari, Sept. 1951.

Italy No. 586 Overprinted Type "h" in Red

1951, Sept. 15
130 A321 25 l dk brn 90 1.10

Cent. of the birth of Francesco Paolo Michetti, painter.

Italy Nos. 587-589 Overprinted in Blue

o AMG FTT

1951, Oct. 11
131 A322 10 l dk brn & gray 40 *75*
132 A322 25 l rose red & bl grn 75 *75*
133 A322 60 l vio bl & red org 1.10 *1.50*

Sardinia stamp centenary.

Italy Nos. 590-591 Overprinted

p AMG FTT

1951, Oct. 31 **Photo.**
Overprint Spaced to Fit Design
134 A323 10 l green 65 *90*
135 A324 25 l vio gray 65 *90*

3rd Industrial and the 9th General Italian Census.

Italy Nos. 592-593 Ovptd. Type "k"

1951, Nov. 21
136 A325 10 l ol & dl grn 65 *1.25*
137 A326 25 l dl grn 85 *80*

Italian Festival of Trees.

Italy Nos. 594-596 Overprinted Types "k" or "p" in Black

1951, Nov. 23
Overprint "p" Spaced to Fit Design
138 A327(p) 10 l vio brn & dk grn 48 *80*
139 A327(k) 25 l red brn & dk brn 80 *80*
140 A327(p) 60 l dp grn & ind 1.25 *1.65*

50th anniv. of the death of Giuseppe Verdi, composer.

Italy No. 597 Overprinted Type "p"

1952, Jan. 28 **Wmk. 277** ***Perf. 14***
Overprint Spaced to Fit Design
141 A328 25 l gray & gray blk 90 65

150th anniv. of the birth of Vincenzo Bellini, composer.

Italy No. 598 Overprinted Type "k"

1952, Feb. 2
142 A329 25 l dl grn & ol bis 90 65

Issued to honor Luigi Vanvitelli, architect.

Same on Italy No. 599

1952, Mar. 26
143 A330 25 l brn & sl blk 70 60

Italy's 1st Intl. Exhib. of Sports stamps.

Same on Italy No. 600

1952, Apr. 12
144 A331 60 l ultra 2.25 *3.00*

30th International Sample Fair, Milan.

Same on Italy No. 601

1952, Apr. 16
145 A332 25 l dp org 30 12

500th anniv. of the birth of Leonardo da Vinci.

Stamps of Italy Overprinted "AMG FTT" in Various Sizes and Arrangements
On Nos. 602-603

1952, June 14 **Wmk. 277** ***Perf. 14***
146 A333 25 l blk & red brn 60 55
147 A333 60 l blk & ultra 1.00 *1.65*

Cent. of the 1st postage stamps of Modena and Parma.

On No. 604

1952, June 7
148 A334 25 l brt bl 80 65

Issued to honor the Overseas Fair at Naples and Italian Labor throughout the world.

On No. 605

1952, June 14
149 A335 25 l blk & yel 80 65

26th Biennial Art Exhibition, Venice.

On No. 606

1952, June 19
150 A336 25 l bl gray, red & dk bl (R) 80 65

30th International Sample Fair of Padua.

On No. 607

1952, June 28
151 A337 25 l dp grn, dk brn & red 80 65

4th International Sample Fair of Trieste.

On No. 608

1952, Sept. 6
152 A338 25 l dk grn 80 65

16th Levant Fair, Bari Sept. 1952.

On No. 609 in Bronze

1952, Sept. 20
153 A339 25 l purple 80 65

500th anniv. of the birth of Girolamo Savonarola.

On No. 610

1952, Oct. 4
154 A340 25 l gray 80 65

Natl. Exhib. of the Alpine Troop, Oct. 4, 1952.

On No. 611

1952, Oct. 1
155 A341 60 l vio bl & dk bl 2.00 *3.00*

1st Intl. Civil Aviation Conf., Rome, Sept. 1952.

On No. 612

1952, Nov. 21 ***Perf. 13***
156 A342 25 l brn & dk brn 80 65

Cent. of the establishment of the 1st Catholic mission in Ethiopia.

On Nos. 613-615

1952, Nov. 3 ***Perf. 14***
157 A343 10 l dk grn 18 32
158 A344 25 l blk & dk brn 65 28
159 A344 60 l blk & bl 65 *1.40*

Armed Forces Day, Nov. 4, 1952.

On No. 616

1952, Dec. 6
160 A345 25 l dk grn 80 65

Cent. of the birth of Antonio Mancini, painter.

On No. 617

1952, Dec. 6
161 A346 25 l brown 80 65

Cent. of the birth of Vincenzo Gemito, sculptor.

On No. 618

1953, Jan. 5
162 A347 25 l gray blk & dk bl (Bl) 80 65

Deaths of the five Martyrs of Belfiore.

On Nos. 601A-601B

1952, Dec. 31
163 A332a 60 l ultra (G) 90 *1.50*
164 A332 80 l brn car 2.00 65

500th anniv. of the birth of Leonardo da Vinci.

On No. 621

1953, Feb. 21
165 A349 25 l car lake 80 65

Messina Exhib. of the paintings of Antonello and his 15th cent. contemporaries.

On No. 622

1953, Apr. 24
166 A350 25 l violet 80 65

20th 1,000-mile automobile race.

On No. 623

1953, Apr. 30
167 A351 25 l violet 80 65

On No. 624

1953, May 30
168 A352 25 l dk brn 80 65

300th anniv. of the birth of Arcangelo Corelli, composer.

On No. 625

1953, June 27
169 A353 25 l brn & dl red 80 65

700th anniv. of the death of St. Clare of Assisi.

On Nos. 626-633

1953-54

170	A354	5 l gray	15	5
171	A354	10 l org ver	25	5
172	A354	12 l dl grn	25	18
172A	A354	13 l brt lil rose ('54)	25	18
173	A354	20 l brown	25	8
174	A354	25 l purple	25	8
175	A354	35 l rose car	50	*90*
176	A354	60 l blue	60	*1.25*
177	A354	80 l org brn	65	*1.40*
		Nos. 170-177 (9)	3.15	*4.17*

Issue dates: 13 l, Feb. 1. Others, June 16.

Italy, Nos. 554, 558 and 564 Overprinted in Red or Green

FIERA DI TRIESTE
AMG FTT
1953

1953, June 27
178 A306 10 l dp grn (R) 40 *65*
179 A306 25 l brn org 50 40
180 A306 60 l red 60 *1.00*

5th International Sample Fair of Trieste.

On No. 634

1953, July 11
181 A355 25 l bl grn 80 65

Festival of the Mountain.

On Nos. 635-636

1953, July 16
182 A356 25 l dk brn 40 *45*
183 A356 60 l dp bl 65 *90*

Intl. Expo. of Agriculture, Rome, 1953.

On Nos. 637-638

1953, Aug. 6
184 A357 25 l org & Prus bl 90 70
185 A357 60 l lil rose & dk vio bl 2.75 *3.25*

4th anniv. of the signing of the North Atlantic Treaty.

On No. 639

1953, Aug. 13
186 A358 25 l dk brn & dl grn 80 65

Opening of an exhib. of the works of Luca Signorelli, painter.

On No. 640

1953, Sept. 5
187 A359 25 l dk gray & brn 80 65

6th Intl. Microbiology Cong., Rome, Sept. 6-12.

On Nos. 641-646

1954, Jan. 26
188 A360 10 l dk brn & red brn 25 *32*
189 A361 12 l lt bl & gray 30 *50*
190 A361 20 l brn org & dk brn 40 35
191 A360 25 l dk grn & pale bl 40 18
192 A361 35 l cr & brn 40 *80*
193 A361 60 l bl grn & ind 55 *1.00*
Nos. 188-193 (6) 2.30 *3.15*

On Nos. 647-648

1954, Feb. 11
194 A362 25 l dk brn & choc 42 52
195 A362 60 l bl & ultra 60 1.00

Signing of the Lateran Pacts, 25th anniv.

On Nos. 649-650

1954, Feb. 25
196 A363 25 l purple 38 35
197 A363 60 l dp bl grn 85 *1.50*

On No. 651

1954, Mar. 20
198 A364 25 l purple 80 45

Propaganda for the payment of taxes.

On No. 652

1954, Apr. 24
199 A365 25 l gray blk 80 65

Issued to publicize the experimental transportation of mail by helicopter, April, 1954.

On No. 653

1954, June 1
200 A366 25 l gray, org brn & blk 80 65

10th anniv. of Italy's resistance movement.

On No. 654

1954, June 19
201 A367 25 l dk grnsh gray 80 65

Alfredo Catalani, composer, birth cent.

On Nos. 655-656

1954, July 8
202 A368 25 l red brn 42 *55*
203 A368 60 l gray grn 95 *1.25*

700th anniv. of the birth of Marco Polo.

Nos. 644, 646 With Additional Overprint

FIERA DI TRIESTE 1954

1954, June 17

204	A360	25 l dk grn & pale bl	40	*52*
205	A361	60 l bl grn & ind	60	*1.00*

International Sample Fair of Trieste.

On No. 657

1954, Sept. 6

206	A369	25 l dp grn & red	80	65

60th anniv. of the foundation of the Italian Touring Club.

On Nos. 658-659

1954, Oct. 30

207	A370	25 l rose red	30	*38*
208	A370	60 l blue	50	*60*

23rd general assembly of the Intl. Criminal Police, Rome, 1954.

OCCUPATION AIR POST STAMPS

Air Post Stamps of Italy, 1945-47, Overprinted Type "c" in Black

1947, Oct. 1 Wmk. 277 *Perf. 14*

C1	AP59	1 l sl bl	20	20
C2	AP60	2 l dk bl	25	20
C3	AP60	5 l dk grn	1.00	*1.00*
C4	AP59	10 l car rose	1.00	*1.00*
C5	AP60	25 l brown	1.25	*1.40*
C6	AP59	50 l violet	5.75	1.50
		Nos. C1-C6 (6)	9.45	*5.30*

Italy, Nos. C116 to C121, Overprinted Type "b" in Black

1947, Nov. 19

C7	AP61	6 l dp vio	55	*85*
C8	AP61	10 l dk car rose	55	*85*
C9	AP61	20 l dp org	3.00	2.25
C10	AP61	25 l aqua	55	*1.25*
C11	AP61	35 l brt bl	55	1.25
C12	AP61	50 l lil rose	3.00	1.25
		Nos. C7-C12 (6)	8.20	*7.70*

Italy, Nos. C123 to C126, Overprinted Type "f" in Black

1948

C13	AP65	100 l green	25.00	3.00
C14	AP65	300 l lil rose	12.00	*15.00*
C15	AP65	500 l ultra	16.00	*20.00*
C16	AP65	1000 l dk brn	125.00	*190.00*

Issue date: Nos. C13-C15, Mar. 1.

Italy, No. C110, C113 and C114, Overprinted in Black

(Reduced Illustration)

1948, Sept. 8

C17	AP59	10 l car rose	35	35
C18	AP60	25 l brown	70	*90*
C19	AP59	50 l violet	70	*90*

The overprint is embossed.

Italy Air Post Stamps of 1945-48 Overprinted Type "h" in Black

1949-52

C20	AP59	10 l car rose	30	10
C21	AP60	25 l brn ('50)	30	30
C22	AP59	50 l violet	30	32
C23	AP65	100 l green	55	30
C24	AP65	300 l lil rose ('50)	7.25	*9.00*
C25	AP65	500 l ultra ('50)	6.75	*12.00*
C26	AP65	1000 l dk brn ('52)	17.50	*22.50*
		Nos. C20-C26 (7)	32.95	*44.52*

No. C26 is found in two perforations: 14 and 14x13.

Issue dates: 100 l, Nov. 7. 50 l, Dec. 5. 10 l, Dec. 28. 25 l, Jan. 23. 300 l, 500 l, Nov. 25. 1000 l, Feb. 18.

OCCUPATION SPECIAL DELIVERY STAMPS

Special Delivery Stamps of Italy 1946-48 Overprinted Type "c"

1947-48 Wmk. 277 *Perf. 14*

E1	SD9	15 l dk car rose	28	30
E2	SD8	25 l brt red org ('48)	10.50	5.50
E3	SD8	30 l dp vio	65	*90*
E4	SD9	60 l car rose ('48)	10.50	*10.00*

Issue dates: Oct. 1, 1947. Mar. 1, 1948.

Italy No. E26, Overprinted Type "d"

1948, Sept. 24

E5	A272	35 l violet	3.00	*3.00*

Italy No. E25, Overprinted Type "h"

1950, Sept. 27

E6	SD9	60 l car rose	1.75	1.25

Italy No. E32 Overprinted Type "k"

1952, Feb. 4

E7	SD8	50 l lil rose	1.65	1.25

OCCUPATION AUTHORIZED DELIVERY STAMPS

Authorized Delivery Stamp of Italy, 1946 Overprinted Type "a" in Black

1947, Oct. 1 Wmk. 277 *Perf. 14*

EY1	AD3	1 l dk brn	24	6

Italy, No. EY7 Overprinted in Black

A.M.G.
F. T. T.

1947, Oct. 29

EY2	AD4	8 l brt red	2.50	65

Italy, No. EY8, Overprinted Type "a" in Black

1949, July 30

EY3	AD4	15 l violet	8.50	1.50

Same, Overprinted Type "h" in Black

1949, Nov. 7

EY4	AD4	15 l violet	80	5

Italy No. EY9 Overprinted Type "h" in Black

1952, Feb. 4

EY5	AD4	20 l rose vio	1.25	6

OCCUPATION POSTAGE DUE STAMPS

Postage Due Stamps of Italy, 1945-47, Overprinted Type "a"

1947, Oct. 1 Wmk. 277 *Perf. 14*

J1	D9	1 l red org	20	30
J2	D10	2 l dk grn	25	6
J3	D9	5 l violet	1.50	30
J4	D9	10 l dk bl	1.90	1.00
J5	D9	20 l car rose	7.75	1.00
J6	D10	50 l aqua	1.40	5
		Nos. J1-J6 (6)	13.00	2.71

Same Overprint on Postage Due Stamps of Italy, 1947

1949

J7	D10	1 l red org	28	22
J8	D10	3 l carmine	75	*1.10*
J9	D10	4 l brown	4.75	*6.00*
J10	D10	5 l violet	27.50	*6.00*
J11	D10	6 l vio bl	10.50	*12.00*
J12	D10	8 l rose vio	15.00	*20.00*
J13	D10	10 l dp bl	32.50	2.50
J14	D10	12 l gldn brn	11.00	*12.00*
J15	D10	20 l lil rose	8.00	70
		Nos. J7-J15 (9)	110.28	*60.52*

Issue dates: 3 l, 4 l, 6 l, 8 l, 12 l, Jan. 24. Others, Apr. 15.

Postage Due Stamps of Italy, 1947-54, Overprinted Type "h"

1949-54

J16	D10	1 l red org	18	5
J17	D10	2 l dk grn	18	5
J18	D10	3 l car ('54)	30	60
J20	D10	5 l violet	38	20
J21	D10	6 l vio bl ('50)	30	8
J22	D10	8 l rose vio ('50)	30	8
J23	D10	10 l dp bl	38	5
J24	D10	12 l gldn brn ('50)	90	60
J25	D10	20 l lil rose	1.50	40
J26	D10	25 l dk red ('54)	3.75	5.50
J27	D10	50 l aqua ('50)	2.50	5
J28	D10	100 l org yel ('52)	4.25	40
J29	D10	500 l dp bl & dk car ('52)	24.00	10.00
		Nos. J16-J29 (13)	38.92	18.06

Issue dates: 5 l, 10 l, Nov. 7. 1 l, Nov. 22. 2 l, 20 l, Dec. 28. 6 l, 8 l, 12 l, May 16. 50 l, Nov. 25. 100 l, Nov. 11. 500 l, June 19. 3 l, Jan. 24. 25 l, Feb. 1.

OCCUPATION PARCEL POST STAMPS

These stamps were used by affixing them to the waybill so that one half remained on it following the parcel, the other half staying on the receipt given the sender. Almost all obtainable used copies are right halves. Complete stamps were obtainable canceled, probably to order. Both unused and used values are for complete stamps.

Parcel Post Stamps of Italy, 1946-48, Overprinted:

A.M.G. F. T. T. **A.M.G. F. T. T.**

1947-48 Wmk. 277 *Perf. 13½*

Q1	PP4	1 l gldn brn	24	*38*
Q2	PP4	2 l lt bl grn	35	*48*
Q3	PP4	3 l red org	40	*60*
Q4	PP4	4 l gray blk	50	*75*
Q5	PP4	5 l lil rose ('48)	1.40	*2.00*
Q6	PP4	10 l violet	2.75	*4.00*
Q7	PP4	20 l lil brn	4.00	*6.00*
Q8	PP4	50 l rose red	6.50	*9.00*
Q9	PP4	100 l sapphire	8.00	*12.00*
Q10	PP4	200 l grn ('48)	325.00	*450.00*
Q11	PP4	300 l brn car ('48)	160.00	*225.00*
Q12	PP4	500 l brn ('48)	95.00	*140.00*
		Nos. Q1-Q12 (12)	604.14	*850.21*

Halves Used

Q1-Q4	5
Q5	15
Q6-Q7	8
Q8	12
Q9	22
Q10	5.75
Q11	4.50
Q12	1.90

Issue dates: Nos. Q1-Q4, Q6-Q9, Oct. 1. Others, Mar. 1.

Parcel Post Stamps of Italy, 1946-54, Overprinted:

AMG-FTT **AMG-FTT**

1949-54

Q13	PP4	1 l gldn brn ('50)	85	*1.25*
Q14	PP4	2 l lt bl grn ('51)	20	*28*
Q15	PP4	3 l red org ('51)	20	*28*
Q16	PP4	4 l gray blk ('51)	25	30
Q17	PP4	5 l lil rose	28	*40*
Q18	PP4	10 l violet	35	28
Q19	PP4	20 l lil brn	38	28
Q20	PP4	30 l plum ('52)	50	*70*
Q21	PP4	50 l rose red ('50)	60	28
Q22	PP4	100 l saph ('50)	1.90	*3.00*
Q23	PP4	200 l green	17.50	*32.50*
Q24	PP4	300 l brn car ('50)	52.50	*85.00*
Q25	PP4	500 l brn ('51)	32.50	*50.00*

Perf. 13x13½

Q26	PP5	1000 l ultra ('54)	82.50	*150.00*
		Nos. Q13-Q26 (14)	190.51	*324.55*

Halves Used

Q13-Q16, Q18, Q20	5
Q17	5
Q19, Q22	8
Q21	6
Q23	10
Q24	60
Q25	70
Q26	1.40

Pairs of Q18 exist with 5mm between overprints instead of 11mm. Value $800.

Issue dates: 20 l, 200 l, Nov. 22. 5 l, 10 l, Nov. 28. 300 l, Jan. 19. 50 l, Mar. 10. 1 l, Oct. 7. 100 l, Nov. 9. 500 l, Nov. 25. 2 l, 3 l, 4 l, Aug. 1. 30 l, Mar. 6. 1000 l, Aug. 12.

PARCEL POST AUTHORIZED DELIVERY STAMPS

For the payment of a special tax for the authorized delivery of parcels privately instead of through the post office. Both unused and used values are for complete stamps.

Parcel Post Authorized Delivery Stamps of Italy 1953 Overprinted in Black:

AMG-FTT **AMG-FTT**

1953, July 8 Wmk. 277

QY1	PAD1	40 l org red	2.00	*3.00*
QY2	PAD1	50 l ultra	2.00	*3.00*
QY3	PAD1	75 l brown	2.00	*3.00*
QY4	PAD1	110 l lil rose	2.00	*3.00*

Halves Used

QY1	15
QY2	20
QY3-QY4	35

ZONE B

Issued by the Jugoslav Military Government

100 Centesimi = 1 Lira
100 Paras = 1 Dinar (1949)

Issues for Istria and the Slovene Coast (Zone B) of 1945-47 are listed following Jugoslavia.

Stylized Gymnast and Arms of Trieste — A1

1948 Unwmk. Litho. *Perf. 10½x11*

1	A1	100 l dp car, *yel (Italian inscriptions)*	2.25	1.90
2	A1	100 l dp car, *yel (Croatian inscriptions)*	2.25	1.90
3	A1	100 l dp car, *yel (Slovene inscriptions)*	2.25	1.90
a.		Strip of 3 (#1-3)	10.00	17.50

May Day. Nos. 1-3 printed se-tenant.

Clasped Hands, Hammer and Sickle — A2

1949 Photo. *Perf. 11½x12½*

4	A2	10 l grnsh blk & ol grn	42	38

Issued to publicize Labor Day, May 1, 1949. "V.U.J.A. S.T.T." are the initials of "Vojna Uprava Jugoslovenske Armije, Slobodna Teritorija Trsta" (Military Administration Jugoslav Army, Free Territory of Trieste).

Stamps of Jugoslavia, 1945-47 Overprinted in Carmine or Ultramarine

S T T
VUJA

1949, Aug. 15 *Perf. 12½*

5	A22	50p ol gray	24	25
6	A22	1d bl grn	24	25
7	A24	2d scar (U)	24	25
8	A25	3d dl red (U)	55	55
9	A24	4d dk bl	24	25
10	A25	5d dk bl	24	25
11	A26	9d rose vio (U)	55	55
12	A23	12d ultra	2.00	2.25

13	A22	16d blue	1.90	1.90
14	A23	20d org ver (U)	3.00	3.50
		Nos. 5-14 (10)	9.20	10.00

The letters of the overprint are set closer and in one line on Nos. 7 and 9.

Jugoslavia Nos. 266 and 267 Overprinted in Carmine **VUJA - STT**

Burelage in Color of Stamp

1949

15	A58	5d blue	7.50	*10.50*
16	A58	12d brown	7.50	*10.50*

75th anniv. of the UPU.

Jugoslavia, Nos. 269 to 272, Overprinted in Carmine **VUJA - STT**

1950

17	A60	2d bl grn	40	38
18	A60	3d car rose	80	75
19	A60	5d blue	2.00	1.90
20	A60	10d dp org	6.00	5.75

Workers Carrying Tools and Flag — A3

Peasant on Ass — A4

1950, May 1 **Photo.**

21	A3	3d violet	42	38
22	A3	10d carmine	85	75

Issued to publicize Labor Day, May 1, 1950.

1950 **Unwmk.** ***Perf. 12½***

Designs: 1d, Cockerel. 2d, Goose. 3d, Bees and honeycomb. 5d, Oxen. 10d, Turkey. 15d, Goats. 20d, Silkworms.

23	A4	50p dk gray	10	12
24	A4	1d brn car	10	12
25	A4	2d dp bl	10	12
26	A4	3d org brn	25	35
27	A4	5d aqua	28	75
28	A4	10d brown	50	55
29	A4	15d violet	5.00	5.75
30	A4	20d dk grn	2.00	2.25
		Nos. 23-30 (8)	8.33	10.01

1951 **Designs as before**

31	A4	1d org brn	15	25
32	A4	3d rose brn	15	25

Worker — A5

1951, May 1

33	A5	3d dark red	60	55
34	A5	10d brown olive	1.00	95

Labor Day.

Pietro Paolo Vergerio — A7

Bicycle Race — A8

1951, Oct. 21 **Litho.**

37	A7	5d blue	80	70
38	A7	10d claret	80	75
39	A7	20d sepia	80	75

Types of Jugoslavia, 1951, Overprinted "STT VUJA"

1951, Nov.

40	A81	10d brn org (V)	90	75
41	A81	12d grnsh blk (C)	90	75

1952 **Photo.**

Designs: 10d, Soccer. 15d, Rowing. 28d, Sailing. 50d, Volleyball. 100d, Diving.

42	A8	5d brown	22	25
43	A8	10d bl grn	22	25
44	A8	15d car rose	22	25
45	A8	28d vio bl	70	55
46	A8	50d claret	1.50	1.10
47	A8	100d dk bl gray	4.00	4.50
		Nos. 42-47 (6)	6.86	6.90

Marshal Tito
A9 A10

1952, May 25 ***Perf. 11½***

48	A9	15d dk brn	1.75	1.50
49	A10	28d red brn	1.75	1.50
50	A9	50d dk gray grn	1.75	1.50

60th birthday of Marshal Tito.

Types of Jugoslavia 1952 Overprinted in Carmine "STT VUJNA"

1952, July 26 ***Perf. 12½***

51	A90	5d dk brn & sal, *cr*	38	38
52	A90	10d dk grn & grn	38	38
53	A90	15d dk brn & bl, *lil*	38	38
54	A90	28d dk brn & buff, *cr*	1.50	1.50
55	A90	50d dk brn & buff, *yel*	6.75	6.75
56	A90	100d ind & lil, *pink*	15.00	15.00
		Nos. 51-56 (6)	24.39	24.39

Issued to publicize the 15th Olympic Games, Helsinki, 1952. Nos. 52, 54 and 56 are inscribed in Cyrillic characters.

The added "N" in "VUJNA" stands for "Narodna" (Peoples'). See note after No. 4.

Nos. 51-56 exist imperf. Value of set, $375.

Jugoslavia Nos. 365 to 367 Overprinted in Carmine "STT VUJNA"

1952, Sept. 13

57	A91	15d dp cl	55	55
58	A91	28d dk brn	75	75
59	A91	50d gray	3.00	3.00

10th anniv. of the formation of the Jugoslav navy.

Jugoslavia No. 358 Overprinted "STT VUJA" in Blue

1952, June 22

60	A89	15d brt rose	90	95

Children's Week.

Jugoslavia Nos. 369-372 Overprinted "VUJNA STT" in Blue or Carmine

1952, Nov. 4

61	A93	15d red brn (Bl)	50	75
62	A93	15d dk vio bl	50	75
63	A93	15d dk brn	50	75
64	A93	15d bl grn	50	75

Issued to publicize the 6th Jugoslavia Communist Party Congress, Zagreb, 1952.

Anchovies and Starfish A11

1952 Unwmk. Photo. ***Perf. 11x11½***

65	A11	15d red brn	1.25	1.65
a.		Souvenir sheet, imperf.	8.75	15.00

Capodistria Phil. Exhib., Nov. 29-Dec. 7.

No. 65a contains a 50d dark blue green stamp. Sold for 85d.

Stamps or Types of Jugoslavia Overprinted "STT VUJNA" in Various Colors

1953, Feb. 3 ***Perf. 12½***

66	A94	15d brn car (Bl)	32	38
67	A94	30d chlky bl (R)	85	55

10th anniv. of the death of Nikola Tesla.

1953

68	A68	1d gray	2.25	2.50
69	A68	2d car (V)	45	48
70	A68	3d rose red (R)	45	48
71	A68	5d orange	45	48
72	A68	10d emer (G)	45	48
73	A68	15d rose red (V)	90	1.10
74	A68	30d bl (Bl)	1.90	2.00
75	A68	50d grnsh bl (Bl)	3.50	4.00
		Nos. 68-75 (8)	10.35	11.52

Nos. 69, 71 and 73 are lithographed.

1953, Apr. 21 ***Perf. 11½***

76	A95	15d dk ol grn (O)	35	38
77	A95	30d chlky bl (O)	35	38
78	A95	50d hn brn	1.10	1.10

Issued in honor of the United Nations.

Automobile Climbing Mt. Lovcen — A12

1953, June 2 ***Perf. 12½***

79	A12	15d ocher & choc	35	18
80	A12	30d lt bl grn & ol grn	35	38
81	A12	50d sal & dp plum	35	38
82	A12	70d bl & dk bl	70	75

Issued to publicize the International Automobile and Motorcycle Races, 1953.

Stamps or Types of Jugoslavia Overprinted "STT VUJNA" in Various Colors

1953, July 8 **Engr.**

83	A97	50d grnsh gray (C)	1.90	1.50

Issued to commemorate Marshal Tito's election to the presidency, January 14, 1953.

1953, July 31

84	A98	15d gray & grn (C)	2.00	1.90

38th Esperanto Cong., Zagreb, July 25-Aug. 1, 1953. See No. C21.

1953, Sept. 5

85	A101	15d bl (C)	3.25	2.25

10th anniv. of the liberation of Istria and the Slovene coast.

1953, Oct. 3

86	A102	15d gray	1.40	1.50

Cent. of the death of Branko Radicevic, poet.

1953, Nov. 29 ***Perf. 12½x12***

87	A103	15d gray vio (V)	45	38
88	A103	30d cl (Br)	65	55
89	A103	50d dl bl grn (Dk Bl)	1.00	95

10th anniv. of the 1st republican legislative assembly of Jugoslavia.

1954, Mar. 5 ***Perf. 12½***

90	A68	5d org (V)	50	38
91	A68	10d yel grn (C)	35	28
92	A68	15d rose red (G)	50	38

Types of Jugoslavia, 1954, Overprinted in Carmine "STT VUJNA"

1954 **Photo.** ***Perf. 11½***

93	A104	2d red brn, sl & cr	15	25
94	A104	5d gray & dk yel brn	15	25
95	A104	10d ol grn & dk org brn	15	25
96	A104	15d dp bl grn & dk org brn	15	25
97	A104	17d gray brn, dk brn & cr	15	25
98	A104	25d bis, gray bl & org yel	15	25
99	A105	30d lil & dk brn	15	25
100	A105	35d rose vio & bl blk	30	50
101	A105	50d yel grn & vio brn	45	75
102	A105	65d org brn & gray blk	2.25	3.50
103	A105	70d bl & org brn	4.50	7.50
104	A105	100d brt bl & blk brn	15.00	25.00
		Nos. 93-104 (12)	23.55	39.00

Types of Jugoslavia 1954 Overprinted "STT VUJNA" in Various Colors

1954, Oct. 8 ***Perf. 12½***

105	A107	15d mar, red, ocher & dk bl (Bk)	35	38
106	A107	30d dk bl, grn, sal buff & choc (G)	35	38
107	A107	50d brn, bis & red (G)	55	55
108	A107	70d dk grn, gray grn & choc (R)	1.40	1.25

150th anniv. of the 1st Serbian insurrection.

AIR POST STAMPS

AP1

Perf. 12½x11½

1948, Oct. 17 **Photo.** **Unwmk.**

C1	AP1	25 l gray	75	75
C2	AP1	50 l orange	75	75

Economic Exhib. at Capodistria, Oct. 17-24.

Fishermen AP2

Farmer and Pack Mule AP3

Mew over Chimneys AP4

1949, June 1 ***Perf. 11½***

C3	AP2	1 l grnsh bl	30	18
C4	AP3	2 l red brn	30	18
C5	AP2	5 l blue	30	18
C6	AP3	10 l purple	1.75	1.10
C7	AP2	25 l brown	2.25	1.25
C8	AP3	50 l ol grn	2.25	1.25
C9	AP4	100 l dk vio brn	3.00	1.90
		Nos. C3-C9 (7)	10.15	6.04

Italian inscriptions on Nos. C5 and C6, Croatian on No. C7, Slavonic on No. C8.

Nos. C3-C4 exist imperf. Value, each $135.

Nos. C3 to C9 Surcharged "DIN", or New Value and "DIN" in Various Colors

1949, Nov. 5

C10	AP2	1d on 1l grnsh bl (Bk)	20	18
C11	AP3	2d on 2l red brn (Br)	20	18
C12	AP2	5d on 5l bl (Bl)	20	18
C13	AP3	10d on 10l pur (V)	40	38
C14	AP2	15d on 25l brn (Br)	4.75	4.50
C15	AP3	20d on 50l ol grn (Gr)	1.65	1.50
C16	AP4	30d on 100l dk vio brn (Bk)	1.65	1.50
		Nos. C10-C16 (7)	9.05	8.42

On Nos. C14 and C15 the original value is obliterated by a framed block, on No. C16 by four parallel lines.

Jugoslavia No. C33 Overprinted in Carmine and Lilac Rose Network

VUJA - STT

Souvenir Sheet

1950 *Perf. 11½x12½*
C17 AP15 10d lil rose 50.00 57.50
a. Imperf. 50.00 57.50

Main Square, Capodistria — AP5

Lighthouse, Pirano — AP6

Design: 25d, Hotel, Portorose.

1952 Unwmk. Photo. *Perf. 12½*
C18 AP5 5d brown 10.00 9.25
C19 AP6 15d brt bl 6.25 7.50
C20 AP5 25d green 6.25 7.50

75th anniv. (in 1949) of the UPU.

Type of Jugoslavia, 1953 Overprinted "STT VUJNA" in Carmine

1953, July 31
C21 AP21 300d vio & grn 185.00 165.00

38th Esperanto Cong., Zagreb, July 25-Aug. 1.

Sheets of 12 (12,000 stamps) and sheets of 8 (3,000 stamps in light violet and green).

A private red overprint was applied marginally to 250 sheets of 8: "Esperantski Kongres - 38 - a Universala Kongreso de Esperanto - Congresso del Esperanto."

Air Post Stamps of Jugoslavia **in New Colors Overprinted "STT VUJNA" in Various Colors**

1954 **Engr.**
C22 AP16 1d dp pur gray 5 8
C23 AP16 2d brt grn (G) 6 10
C24 AP16 3d red brn (Br) 10 15
C25 AP16 5d chocolate 10 15
C26 AP16 10d bl grn 10 15
C27 AP16 20d brn (Br) 35 50
C28 AP16 30d blue 35 50
C29 AP16 50d ol blk 50 75
C30 AP16 100d scar (R) 1.50 2.00
C31 AP16 200d dk bl vio (Bl) 3.50 5.00

Perf. 11x11½
C32 AP17 500d org (Br) 11.00 15.00
Nos. C22-C32 (11) 17.61 24.38

POSTAGE DUE STAMPS

Jugoslavia Nos. J51 to J55 Overprinted "S T T VUJA" in Two Lines in Ultramarine or Carmine

1949 Unwmk. *Perf. 12½*
J1 D7 50p dp org 55 55
J2 D7 1d orange 55 55
J3 D7 2d dk bl (C) 55 55
J4 D7 3d yel grn (C) 55 55
J5 D7 5d brt pur (C) 1.10 1.10
Nos. J1-J5 (5) 3.30 3.30

Croakers D1

Anchovies D2

1950 **Photo.**
J6 D1 50p brn org 22 22
J7 D1 1d dp ol grn 90 95
J8 D2 2d dk grnsh bl 90 95
J9 D2 3d dk vio bl 90 95
J10 D2 5d plum 4.50 4.25
Nos. J6-J10 (5) 7.42 7.32

Jugoslavia Nos. J67-J74 Overprinted "STT VUJNA" in Blue or Carmine

1952
J11 D7 1d brn (Bl) 12 15
J12 D7 2d emerald 12 15
J13 D7 5d blue 12 15
J14 D7 10d scar (Bl) 12 15
J15 D7 20d purple 12 15
J16 D7 30d org yel (Bl) 12 15
J17 D7 50d ultra 12 15
J18 D7 100d dp plum (Bl) 3.00 4.50
Nos. J11-J18 (8) 3.84 5.55

POSTAL TAX STAMPS

Jugoslavia No. RA5 Surcharged in Blue

VUJA
S.T.T.
2 L

1948 Unwmk. *Perf. 12½*
RA1 PT4 2 l on 50p brn & scar 6.50 *10.00*

Obligatory on all mail from May 22-30.

Jugoslavia No. RA7 Overprinted "VUJA STT" in Black

1950, July 3
RA2 PT6 50p red & brn 35 40

Jugoslavia No. RA9 Overprinted in Black "STT VUJA"

1951
RA3 PT8 50p vio bl & red 6.50 *10.00*

Jugoslavia No. RA10 Overprinted "STT VUJNA" in Carmine

1952
RA4 PT9 50p gray & car 18 20

Type of Jugoslavia, 1953, Overprinted "STT VUJNA" in Blue

1953
RA5 PT10 2d org brn & red 18 30

The tax of Nos. RA1-RA5 was for the Red Cross.

POSTAL TAX DUE STAMPS

Jugoslavia No. RAJ2 Surcharged Like No. RA1 in Scarlet

1948 Unwmk. *Perf. 12½*
RAJ1 PT4 2 l on 50p bl grn & scar 100.00 140.00

Jugoslavia No. RAJ4 Overprinted "VUJA STT" in Black

1950, July 3
RAJ2 PT6 50p red & vio 85 1.25

Jugoslavia No. RAJ6 Overprinted in Black "STT VUJA"

1951
RAJ3 PT8 50p emer & red 85.00 115.00

Jugoslavia No. RAJ7 Overprinted "STT VUJNA" in Carmine

1952
RAJ4 PTD3 50p gray & car 50 60

Type of Jugoslavia, 1953, Overprinted "STT VUJNA" in Blue

1953
RAJ5 PT10 2d lil rose & red 50 60

TRIPOLITANIA

LOCATION — In northern Africa, bordering on Mediterranean Sea.
GOVT. — A former Italian Colony.
AREA — 350,000 sq. mi. (approx.).
POP. — 570,716 (1921)
CAPITAL — Tripoli.

Formerly a Turkish province, Tripolitania became part of Italian Libya. See Libya.

100 Centesimi = 1 Lira

Propaganda of the Faith Issue

Italian Stamps of 1923 Overprinted TRIPOLITANIA

Wmk. 140 - Crowns

1923, Oct. 24 Wmk. 140 *Perf. 14*
1 A68 20c ol grn & brn org 1.10 5.50
2 A68 30c cl & brn org 1.10 5.50
3 A68 50c vio & brn org 85 4.50
4 A68 1 l bl & brn org 85 4.50

Fascisti Issue

Italian Stamps of 1923 Overprinted in Red or Black TRIPOLITANIA

1923, Oct. 29 **Unwmk.**
5 A69 10c dk grn (R) 1.00 4.50
6 A69 30c dk vio (R) 1.00 4.50
7 A69 50c brn car 1.00 4.50

Wmk. 140
8 A70 1 l blue 1.00 4.50
9 A70 2 l brown 1.00 4.50
10 A71 5 l blk & bl (R) 1.00 7.25
Nos. 5-10 (6) 6.00 29.75

Manzoni Issue

Stamps of Italy, 1923, Overprinted in Red TRIPOLITANIA

1924, Apr. 1 Wmk. 140 *Perf. 14*
11 A72 10c brn red & blk 50 5.75
12 A72 15c bl grn & blk 50 5.75
13 A72 30c blk & slate 50 5.75
14 A72 50c org brn & blk 50 5.75
15 A72 1 l bl & blk 8.00 55.00
16 A72 5 l vio & blk 190.00 800.00
Nos. 11-16 (6) 200.00 878.00

On Nos. 15 and 16 the overprint is placed vertically at the left side.

Victor Emmanuel Issue

Italy Nos. 175-177 Overprinted TRIPOLITANIA

1925-26 Unwmk. *Perf. 11, 13½*
17 A78 60c brn car, perf. 11 18 2.00
18 A78 1l dk bl, perf. 11 20 2.00
a. Perf. 13½ 90 10.00
19 A78 1.25 l dk bl, perf. 13½ ('26) 50 6.00
a. Perf. 11 175.00 425.00

Saint Francis of Assisi Issue

Italy Nos. 178-180 Overprinted TRIPOLITANIA

1926, Apr. 12 Wmk. 140 *Perf. 14*
20 A79 20c gray grn 60 3.00
21 A80 40c dark vio 60 3.00
22 A81 60c red brn 60 3.00

Italy No. 182 and Type of A83 Overprinted in Red Tripolitania

Unwmk.
23 A82 1.25 l dark blue 60 3.00
24 A83 5 l + 2.50 l ol grn 1.50 5.50
Nos. 20-24 (5) 3.90 17.50

Volta Issue

Type of Italy, 1927, Overprinted Tripolitania

1927, Oct. 10 Wmk. 140 *Perf. 14*
25 A84 20c purple 2.00 6.00
26 A84 50c dp org 2.50 5.00
a. Double overprint 13.00
27 A84 1.25 l brt bl 3.00 7.25

Monte Cassino Issue

Types of Italy, 1929, Overprinted in Red or Blue TRIPOLITANIA

1929, Oct. 14
28 A96 20c dk grn (R) 1.10 *5.00*
29 A96 25c red org (Bl) 1.10 *5.00*
30 A98 50c + 10c crim (Bl) 1.10 *7.50*
31 A98 75c + 15c ol brn (R) 1.10 *7.50*
32 A96 1.25 l + 25c dk vio (R) 2.25 *7.50*
33 A98 5 l + 1 l saph (R) 2.25 *7.50*

Overprinted in Red **Tripolitania**

Unwmk.
34 A100 10 l + 2 l gray brn 2.25 *10.00*
Nos. 28-34 (7) 11.15 *50.00*

Royal Wedding Issue

Type of Italy, 1930, Overprinted TRIPOLITANIA

1930, Mar. 17 **Wmk. 140**
35 A101 20c yel grn 50 *2.00*
36 A101 50c + 10c dp org 38 *2.50*
37 A101 1.25 l + 25c rose red 38 *3.00*

Ferrucci Issue

Types of Italy, 1930, Overprinted in Red or Blue TRIPOLITANIA

1930, July 26
38 A102 20c violet (R) 38 *1.50*
39 A103 25c dk grn (R) 38 *1.50*
40 A103 50c black (R) 38 *1.50*
41 A103 1.25 l deep bl (R) 38 *1.50*
42 A104 5 l + 2 l dp car (Bl) 1.50 *3.00*
Nos. 38-42 (5) 3.02 *9.00*

Virgil Issue

Types of Italy, 1930, Overprinted in Red or Blue

T R I P O L I T A N I A

1930, Dec. 4 **Photo.**
43 A106 15c vio blk 25 *1.50*
44 A106 20c org brn 25 *1.50*
45 A106 25c dk grn 25 *1.25*
46 A106 30c lt brn 25 *1.50*
47 A106 50c dl vio 25 *1.25*
48 A106 75c rose red 25 *1.50*
49 A106 1.25 l gray bl 25 *1.50*

Unwmk.
Engr.
50 A106 5 l + 1.50 l dk vio 1.25 *6.00*
51 A106 10 l + 2.50 l ol brn 1.25 *6.00*
Nos. 43-51 (9) 4.25 *22.00*

Saint Anthony of Padua Issue

Types of Italy, 1931, Overprinted in Blue or Red TRIPOLITANIA

1931, May 7 Photo. Wmk. 140
52 A116 20c brown (Bl) 50 *2.25*
53 A116 25c grn (R) 50 *2.25*
54 A118 30c gray brn (Bl) 50 *2.25*
55 A118 50c dl vio (Bl) 50 *1.50*
56 A120 1.25 l slate bl (R) 50 *2.25*

Overprinted in Red or Black **Tripolitania**

Unwmk. **Engr.**
57 A121 75c black (R) 50 *2.25*
58 A122 5 l + 2.50 l dk brn (Bk) 1.50 *7.50*
Nos. 52-58 (7) 4.50 *20.25*

The lack of a value for a listed item does not necessarily indicate rarity.

Native Village Scene — A14

1934, Oct. 16 **Wmk. 140**

73	A14	5c ol grn & brn	1.10	*4.25*
74	A14	10c brn & blk	1.10	*4.25*
75	A14	20c scar & ind	1.10	*4.25*
76	A14	50c pur & brn	1.10	*4.25*
77	A14	60c org brn & ind	1.10	*4.25*
78	A14	1.25 l dk bl & grn	1.10	*4.25*
		Nos. 73-78 (6)	6.60	*25.50*

2nd Colonial Arts Exhibition, Naples. See Nos. C43-C48.

SEMI-POSTAL STAMPS

Many issues of Italy and Italian Colonies include one or more semipostal denominations. To avoid splitting sets, these issues are generally listed as regular postage, airmail, etc., unless all values carry a surtax.

Holy Year Issue

Italian Stamps of 1924 Overprinted in Black or Red

TRIPOLITANIA

1925 **Wmk. 140** ***Perf. 12***

B1	SP4	20c + 10c dk grn & brn	65	*3.00*
B2	SP4	30c + 15c dk brn & brn	65	*3.00*
B3	SP4	50c + 25c vio & brn	65	*3.00*
B4	SP4	60c + 30c dp rose & brn	65	*3.00*
B5	SP8	1 l + 50c dp bl & vio (R)	65	*3.00*
B6	SP8	5 l + 2.50 l org brn & vio (R)	65	*3.00*
		Nos. B1-B6 (6)	3.90	*18.00*

Colonial Institute Issue

Peace Substituting Spade for Sword — SP1

1926, June 1 **Typo.** ***Perf. 14***

B7	SP1	5c + 5c brown	16	*1.65*
B8	SP1	10c + 5c ol brn	16	*1.65*
B9	SP1	20c + 5c bl grn	16	*1.65*
B10	SP1	40c + 5c brn red	16	*1.65*
B11	SP1	60c + 5c org	16	*1.65*
B12	SP1	1 l + 5c blue	16	*1.65*
		Nos. B7-B12 (6)	96	*9.90*

The surtax was for the Italian Colonial Institute.

Fiera Campionaria Tripoli
See Libya for stamps with this inscription.

Types of Italian Semi-Postal Stamps of 1926 Overprinted

TRIPOLITANIA

1927, Apr. 21 **Unwmk.** ***Perf. 11***

B19	SP10	40c + 20c dk brn & blk	65	*3.50*
B20	SP10	60c + 30c brn red & ol brn	65	*3.50*
B21	SP10	1.25 l + 60c dp bl & blk	65	*3.50*
B22	SP10	5 l + 2.50 l dk grn & blk	1.00	*4.50*

The surtax was for the charitable work of the Voluntary Militia for Italian National Defense.

Allegory of Fascism and Victory — SP2

1928, Oct. 15 **Wmk. 140**

B29	SP2	20c + 5c bl grn	50	*2.50*
B30	SP2	30c + 5c red	50	*2.50*
B31	SP2	50c + 10c pur	50	*2.50*
B32	SP2	1.25 l + 20c dk bl	50	*2.50*

46th anniv. of the Societa Africana d'Italia. The surtax aided that society.

Types of Italian Semi-Postal Stamps of 1928 Overprinted

TRIPOLITANIA

1929, Mar. 4 **Unwmk.** ***Perf. 11***

B33	SP10	30c + 10c red & blk	85	*3.75*
B34	SP10	50c + 20c vio & blk	85	*3.75*
B35	SP10	1.25 l + 50c brn & bl	1.00	*5.00*
B36	SP10	5 l + 2 l ol grn & blk	1.00	*5.00*

The surtax on these stamps was for the charitable work of the Voluntary Militia for Italian National Defense.

Types of Italian Semi-Postal Stamps of 1926, Overprinted in Black or Red

TRIPOLITANIA

1930, Oct. 20

B50	SP10	30c + 10c dp grn & bl grn (Bk)	2.75	*10.00*
B51	SP10	50c + 10c dk grn & vio (R)	2.75	*10.00*
B52	SP10	1.25 l + 30c blk brn & red brn (R)	2.75	*10.00*
B53	SP10	5 l + 1.50 l ind & grn (R)	8.00	*32.50*

Ancient Arch — SP3

1930, Nov. 27 **Photo.** **Wmk. 140**

B54	SP3	50c + 20c ol brn	75	*4.00*
B55	SP3	1.25 l + 20c dp bl	75	*4.00*
B56	SP3	1.75 l + 20c grn	75	*4.00*
B57	SP3	2.55 l + 50c pur	1.10	*4.00*
B58	SP3	5 l + 1 l dp car	1.10	*4.00*
		Nos. B54-B58 (5)	4.45	*20.00*

25th anniv. of the Italian Colonial Agricultural Institute. The surtax was for the benefit of that institution.

AIR POST STAMPS

Ferrucci Issue

Type of Italian Air Post Stamps of 1930 Overprinted in Blue or Red

TRIPOLITANIA

1930, July 26 **Wmk. 140** ***Perf. 14***

C1	AP7	50c brn vio (Bl)	1.00	*2.50*
C2	AP7	1 l dark bl (R)	1.00	*2.50*
C3	AP7	5 l + 2 l dp car (Bl)	4.00	*10.00*

Virgil Issue

Types of Italian Air Post Stamps, 1930 Overprinted in Red or Blue

TRIPOLITANIA

1930, Dec. 4 **Photo.**

C4	AP8	50c dp grn	75	*2.50*
C5	AP8	1 l rose red	75	*2.50*

Unwmk.

Engr.

C6	AP8	7.70 l + 1.30 l dk brn	1.50	*7.50*
C7	AP8	9 l + 2 l gray	1.50	*7.50*

Airplane over Columns of the Basilica, Leptis — AP1

Arab Horseman Pointing at Airplane AP2

1931-32 **Photo.** **Wmk. 140**

C8	AP1	50c rose car	25	18
C9	AP1	60c red org	75	*2.50*
C10	AP1	75c dp bl ('32)	75	*2.50*
C11	AP1	80c dl vio	1.50	*3.00*
C12	AP2	1 l deep blue	25	10
C13	AP2	1.20 l dk brn	1.65	*4.50*
C14	AP2	1.50 l org red	1.65	*3.25*
C15	AP2	5 l green	2.00	*4.00*
		Nos. C8-C15 (8)	8.80	*20.03*

Airplane over Ruins AP3

1931, Dec. 7

C16	AP3	50c dp blue	1.00	*5.00*
C17	AP3	80c violet	1.00	*5.00*
C18	AP3	1 l gray blk	1.00	*5.00*
C19	AP3	2 l deep grn	1.50	*7.50*
C20	AP3	5 l + 2 l rose red	2.50	*15.00*
		Nos. C16-C20 (5)	7.00	*37.50*

Graf Zeppelin Issue

Mercury, by Giovanni da Bologna, and Zeppelin AP4

Designs: 3 l, 12 l, Mercury. 10 l, 20 l, Guido Reni's "Aurora." 5 l, 15 l, Arch of Marcus Aurelius.

1933, May 5

C21	AP4	3 l dk brn	4.50	*37.50*
C22	AP4	5 l purple	4.50	*37.50*
C23	AP4	10 l dp grn	4.50	*62.50*
C24	AP4	12 l dp blue	4.50	*85.00*
C25	AP4	15 l carmine	4.50	*75.00*
C26	AP4	20 l gray blk	4.50	*100.00*
		Nos. C21-C26 (6)	27.00	*397.50*

North Atlantic Flight Issue

Airplane, Lion of St. Mark AP7

1933, June 1

C27	AP7	19.75 l blk & ol brn	10.00	*250.00*
C28	AP7	44.75 l dk bl & lt grn	10.00	*250.00*

Type of 1931 Overprinted and Surcharged with New Values (except #C31)

1934, Jan. 20

C29	AP2	2 l on 5 l org brn	1.50	*27.50*
C30	AP2	3 l on 5 l grn	1.50	*27.50*
C31	AP2	5 l ocher	1.50	*27.50*
C32	AP2	10 l on 5 l rose	1.50	*27.50*

For use on mail to be carried on a special flight from Rome to Buenos Aires.

Types of Libya 1934 Airmail Issue Overprinted in Black or Red

CIRCUITO DELLE OASI
TRIPOLI
MAGGIO 1934-XII

1934, May 1 **Wmk. 140**

C38	AP4	50c rose red	1.90	*3.75*
C39	AP4	75c lemon	1.90	*3.75*
C40	AP4	5 l + 1 l brn	1.90	*3.75*
C41	AP4	10 l + 2 l dk bl	80.00	*150.00*
C42	AP5	25 l + 3 l pur	80.00	*150.00*
		Nos. C38-C42 (5)	165.70	*311.25*

"Circuit of the Oases".

Plane Shadow on Desert AP11

Designs: 25c, 50c, 75c, Plane shadow on desert. 80c, 1 l, 2 l, Camel corps.

1934, Oct. 16 **Photo.**

C43	AP11	25c sl bl & org red	1.10	*4.25*
C44	AP11	50c dk grn & ind	1.10	*4.25*
C45	AP11	75c dk brn & org red	1.10	*4.25*
C46	AP11	80c org brn & ol grn	1.10	*4.25*
C47	AP11	1 l scar & ol grn	1.10	*4.25*
C48	AP11	2 l dk bl & brn	1.10	*4.25*
		Nos. C43-C48 (6)	6.60	*25.50*

Second Colonial Arts Exhibition, Naples.

AIR POST SEMI-POSTAL STAMPS

King Victor Emmanuel III SPAP1

1934, Nov. 5 **Wmk. 140** ***Perf. 14***

CB1	SPAP1	25c + 10c gray grn	1.25	*5.00*
CB2	SPAP1	50c + 10c brn	1.25	*5.00*
CB3	SPAP1	75c + 15c rose red	1.25	*5.00*
CB4	SPAP1	80c + 15c blk brn	1.25	*5.00*
CB5	SPAP1	1 l + 20c red brn	1.25	*5.00*
CB6	SPAP1	2 l + 20c brt bl	1.25	*5.00*
CB7	SPAP1	3 l + 25c pur	11.00	*40.00*
CB8	SPAP1	5 l + 25c org	11.00	*40.00*
CB9	SPAP1	10 l + 30c rose vio	11.00	*40.00*
CB10	SPAP1	25 l + 2 l dp grn	11.00	*40.00*
		Nos. CB1-CB10 (10)	51.50	*190.00*

65th birthday of King Victor Emmanuel III; non-stop flight from Rome to Mogadiscio.

AIR POST SEMI-POSTAL OFFICIAL STAMP

Type of Air Post Semi-Postal Stamps, 1934 Overprinted Crown and "SERVIZIO DI STATO" in Black

1934 Wmk. 140 *Perf. 14*

CBO1	SPAP1	25 l + 2 l cop red	950.00	*1,700.*

AIR POST SPECIAL DELIVERY STAMPS

Type of Libya 1934 Overprinted in Black — CIRCUITO DELLE OASI TRIPOLI MAGGIO 1934-XII

1934, May 1 Wmk. 140 *Perf. 14*

CE1	APSD1	2.25 l red org	2.50	*5.00*
CE2	APSD1	4.50 l + 1 l dp rose	2.50	*5.00*

"Circuit of the Oases."

AUTHORIZED DELIVERY STAMP

Authorized Delivery Stamp of Italy 1930, Overprinted TRIPOLITANIA

1931, Mar. Wmk. 140 *Perf. 14*

EY1	AD2	10c dk brn	2.50	2.50

TUNISIA

LOCATION — Northern Africa, bordering on the Mediterranean Sea.
GOVT. — Republic
AREA — 63,362 sq. mi.
POP. — 6,966,173 (1984)
CAPITAL — Tunis

The former French protectorate became a sovereign state in 1956 and a republic in 1957.

100 Centimes = 1 Franc
1000 Millimes = 1 Dinar (1959)

Catalogue values for unused stamps in this country are for Never Hinged items, beginning with Scott 163 in the regular postage section, Scott B78 in the semi-postal section, Scott C13 in the airpost section, Scott CB1 in the airpost semi-postal section, and Scott J73 in the postage due section.

Coat of Arms — A1

Perf. 14x13½

1888, July 1 Typo. Unwmk.

1	A1	1c blk, *blue*	1.00	70
2	A1	2c pur brn, *buff*	1.00	70
3	A1	5c grn, *grnsh*	6.50	4.00
4	A1	15c bl, *grysh*	16.50	6.50
5	A1	25c blk, *rose*	32.50	22.50
6	A1	40c red, *straw*	30.00	22.50
7	A1	75c car, *rose*	32.50	22.50
8	A1	5fr gray vio, *grysh*	190.00	135.00

All values exist imperforate.

Reprints were made in 1893 and some values have been reprinted twice since then. The shades usually differ from those of the originals and some reprints have white gum instead of grayish. All values except the 15c and 40c have been reprinted from retouched designs, having a background of horizontal ruled lines.

A2

A3

1888-1902

9	A2	1c blk, *lil bl*	60	20
10	A2	2c pur brn, *buff*	60	20
11	A2	5c grn, *grnsh*	2.50	30
12	A2	5c yel grn ('99)	2.50	30
13	A2	10c blk, *lav* ('93)	3.00	20
14	A2	10c red ('01)	2.25	25
15	A2	15c bl, *grysh*	22.50	30
16	A2	15c gray ('01)	3.75	40
17	A2	20c red, *grn* ('99)	6.00	1.00
18	A2	25c blk, *rose*	6.50	50
19	A2	25c bl ('01)	3.50	60
20	A2	35c brn ('02)	19.00	60
21	A2	40c red, *straw*	4.00	50
22	A2	75c car, *rose*	50.00	37.50
23	A2	75c dp vio, *org* ('93)	6.50	3.00
24	A3	1fr ol, *ol*	10.00	3.75
25	A3	2fr dl vio ('02)	55.00	45.00
26	A3	5fr red lil, *lav*	52.50	37.50
		Bar cancellation		35

Quadrille Paper

27	A2	15c bl, *grysh* ('93)	19.00	20
		Nos. 9-27 (19)	269.70	132.30

No. 27 Surcharged in Red — 25

1902

28	A2	25c on 15c blue	1.00	1.00

Mosque at Kairouan A4

Plowing A5

Ruins of Hadrian's Aqueduct A6

Carthaginian Galley — A7

1906-26 Typo.

29	A4	1c blk, *yel*	5	5
30	A4	2c red brn, *straw*	5	5
31	A4	3c lt red ('19)	5	5
32	A4	5c grn, *grnsh*	5	5
33	A4	5c orange ('21)	5	5
34	A5	10c red	16	5
35	A5	10c green ('21)	7	7
36	A5	15c vio, *pnksh*	30	5
a		Imperf., pair		
37	A5	15c brn, *org* ('23)	5	5
38	A5	20c brn, *pnksh*	5	5
39	A5	25c dp blue	65	7
a		Imperf., pair		
40	A5	25c vio ('21)	15	5
41	A6	30c red brn & vio ('19)	42	22
42	A6	30c pale red ('21)	50	30
43	A6	35c ol grn & brn	5.00	40
44	A6	40c blk brn & red brn	3.00	15
45	A5	40c blk, *pnksh* ('23)	65	25
46	A5	40c gray grn ('26)	5	5
47	A5	50c bl ('21)	42	22
48	A6	60c ol grn & vio ('21)	40	16
49	A6	60c ver & rose ('25)	35	10
50	A6	75c red brn & red	42	15
51	A6	75c ver & dl red ('26)	16	7
52	A7	1fr red & dk brn	50	10
53	A7	1fr ind & ultra ('25)	16	8
54	A7	2fr brn & ol grn	2.50	80
55	A7	2fr grn & red, *pink* ('25)	40	20
56	A7	5fr vio & bl	5.00	3.00
57	A7	5fr gray vio & grn ('25)	40	25
		Nos. 29-57 (29)	22.01	7.14

Stamps and Type of 1888-1902 Surcharged — 10

1908, Sept.

58	A2	10c on 15c gray, *lt gray* (R)	90	90
59	A3	35c on 1fr ol, *ol* (R)	1.40	1.40
60	A3	40c on 2fr dl vio (Bl)	4.00	4.00
61	A3	75c on 5fr red lil, *lav* (Bl)	3.00	3.00

No. 36 Surcharged — 10

1911

62	A5	10c on 15c vio, *pinkish*	60	20

No. 34 Surcharged — 15c.

1917, Mar. 16

63	A5	15c on 10c red	35	7
a		"15c" omitted	7.00	
b		Double surcharge	20.00	

No. 36 Surcharged — 20c.

1921

64	A5	20c on 15c vio, *pinkish*	35	10

Arab and Ruins of Dougga — A9

1922-26 Typo. *Perf. 13½x14*

65	A9	10c green	5	5
66	A9	10c rose ('26)	5	5
67	A9	30c rose	40	40
68	A9	30c lilac ('26)	5	5
69	A9	50c blue	30	30
		Nos. 65-69 (5)	85	85

Stamps and Type of 1906 Surcharged in Red or Black

=10 a   50 b

1923-25

70	A4(a)	10c on 5c grn, *grnsh* (R)	16	7
a		Double surcharge	20.00	
71	A5(b)	20c on 15c vio (Bk)	50	5
72	A5(b)	30c on 20c yel brn (Bk) ('25)	7	5
73	A5(b)	50c on 25c bl (R)	60	5

Arab Woman Carrying Water A10

Grand Mosque at Tunis A11

Mosque, Tunis A12

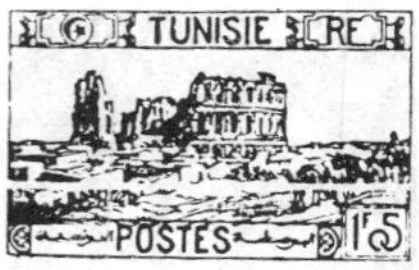
Roman Amphitheater, El Djem (Thysdrus) A13

1926-46 Typo. *Perf. 14x13½*

74	A10	1c lt red	5	5
75	A10	2c olive grn	5	5
76	A10	3c slate bl	5	5
77	A10	5c yel grn	5	5
78	A10	10c rose	5	5
78A	A12	10c brn ('46)	5	5
79	A11	15c gray lil	5	5
80	A11	20c dp red	5	5
81	A11	25c gray grn	7	5
82	A11	25c lt vio ('28)	25	5
83	A11	30c lt vio	5	5
84	A11	30c bl grn ('28)	5	5
84A	A12	30c dk ol grn ('46)	5	5
85	A11	40c deep brn	5	5
85A	A12	40c lil rose ('46)	5	5
86	A11	45c emer ('40)	50	35
87	A12	50c black	10	5
88	A12	50c ultra ('34)	22	5
88B	A12	50c emer ('40)	5	5
88C	A12	50c lt bl ('46)	5	5
89	A12	60c red org ('40)	5	5
89A	A12	60c ultra ('45)	5	5
90	A12	65c ultra ('38)	35	10
91	A12	70c dk red ('40)	10	7
92	A12	75c vermilion	14	10
93	A12	75c lil rose ('28)	40	5
94	A12	80c blue grn	60	16
94A	A12	80c blk brn ('40)	7	7
94B	A12	80c emer ('45)	12	12
95	A12	90c org red ('28)	7	5
96	A12	90c ultra ('39)	6.00	4.00
97	A12	1fr brn violet	25	5
97A	A12	1fr rose ('40)	5	5
98	A13	1.05fr dl bl & mag	15	15
98A	A12	1.20fr blk brn ('45)	5	5
99	A13	1.25fr gray bl & dk bl	22	15
100	A13	1.25fr car rose ('40)	70	42
100A	A13	1.30fr bl & vio bl ('42)	7	7
101	A13	1.40fr brt red vio ('40)	40	25
102	A13	1.50fr bl & dp bl ('28)	50	10
102A	A13	1.50fr rose red & red org ('42)	7	7
102B	A12	1.50fr rose lil ('46)	5	5
103	A13	2fr rose & ol brn	60	7
104	A13	2fr red org ('39)	5	5
104A	A12	2fr Prus grn ('45)	5	5
105	A13	2.25fr ultra ('39)	50	35
105A	A13	2.40fr red ('46)	10	10
106	A13	2.50fr green ('40)	50	35
107	A13	3fr dl bl & org	70	12
108	A13	3fr violet ('39)	7	5
108A	A13	3fr blk brn ('46)	5	5
108B	A13	4fr ultra ('45)	30	30
109	A13	5fr red & grn, *grnsh*	1.60	15
110	A13	5fr dp red brn ('40)	55	38
110A	A13	5fr dk grn ('46)	7	5
110B	A13	6fr dp ultra ('45)	5	5
111	A13	10fr brn red & blk, *bluish*	5.00	65
112	A13	10fr rose pink ('40)	45	30
112A	A13	10fr ver ('46)	7	7
112B	A13	10fr ultra ('46)	15	7
112C	A13	15fr rose lil ('45)	15	5
113	A13	20fr lil & red, *pnksh* ('28)	1.50	35
113A	A13	20fr dk grn ('45)	16	15
113B	A13	25fr violet ('45)	25	20
113C	A13	50fr car ('45)	55	20
113D	A13	100fr car rose ('45)	80	22
		Nos. 74-113D (66)	26.62	11.91

See Nos. 152A-162, 185-189, 199-206.

No. 99 Surcharged with New Value and Bars in Red

1927, Mar. 24

114	A13	1.50fr on 1.25fr gray bl & dk bl	20	12

Stamps of 1921-26 Surcharged — 3c

1928, May 1

115	A4	3c on 5c orange	5	5
116	A5	10c on 15c brn, *org*	7	7
117	A9	25c on 30c lilac	16	7
118	A12	40c on 80c bl grn	22	20
119	A12	50c on 75c ver	30	15
		Nos. 115-119 (5)	80	54

No. 83 Surcharged = 10

1929

120	A11	10c on 30c lt vio	60	40

No. 120 exists precanceled only. The value in first column is for a stamp which has not been through the post and has original gum. The value in the second column is for a postally used, gumless stamp. See No. 199a.

No. 85 Surcharged with New Value and Bars

1930

121	A11	50c on 40c dp brn	2.00	15

A14

A15

A16

A17

Perf. 11, 12½, 12½x13

1931-34 **Engr.**

122	A14	1c deep blue	5	5
123	A14	2c yel brown	5	5
124	A14	3c black	5	5
125	A14	5c yel green	5	5
126	A14	10c red	5	5
127	A15	15c dull vio	18	12
128	A15	20c dl brown	5	5
129	A15	25c rose red	5	5
130	A15	30c dp green	5	5
131	A15	40c red org	5	5
132	A16	50c ultra	5	5
133	A16	75c yellow	75	75
134	A16	90c red	18	30
135	A16	1fr olive blk	5	5
136	A16	1fr dk brn ('34)	5	5
137	A17	1.50fr brt ultra	18	18
138	A17	2fr dp brown	18	12
139	A17	3fr bl green	3.00	3.00
140	A17	5fr car rose	6.25	5.50
a		Perf. 12½	9.00	6.00
141	A17	10fr black	15.00	14.00
142	A17	20fr dk brown	22.50	17.50
		Nos. 122-142 (21)	48.82	42.07

Stamps of 1928-34 Surcharged in Red or Black:

1f75

0,65 — c

= — d

1937 ***Perf. 14x13½***

143	A12	65c on 50c ultra (R)	45	10
b		Double surcharge	30.00	25.00
144	A13	1.75fr on 1.50fr bl & dp bl (R)	3.00	1.00
a		Double surcharge	25.00	25.00

1f75

65 — e

= — f

1938

145	A12	65c on 50c ultra (Bk)	50	10
146	A13	1.75fr on 1.50fr bl & dp bl (R)	4.00	3.50

Stamps of 1938-39 Surcharged in Red or Carmine:

25c. 1 FR.

g h

1940

147	A12	25c on 65c ultra (C)	16	14
148	A12	1fr on 90c ultra (R)	35	16

Stamps of 1938-40 Surcharged in Red or Black:

25 c. 1F.

i k

1941

149	A12	25c on 65c ultra (R)	10	16
150	A13	1fr on 1.25fr car rose (Bk)	5	10
151	A13	1fr on 1.40fr brt red vio (Bk)	5	10
152	A13	1fr on 2.25fr ultra (R)	5	10

Types of 1926 Without RF

1941-45 **Typo.** ***Perf. 14x13½***

152A	A11	30c car ('45)	5	5
152B	A12	1.20fr int bl ('45)	5	5
153	A12	1.50fr brn red ('42)	16	16
154	A13	2.40fr car & brt pink ('42)	7	7
155	A13	2.50fr dk bl & lt bl	7	7
156	A13	3fr lt vio ('42)	5	5
157	A13	4fr blk & bl vio ('42)	5	5
158	A13	4.50fr ol grn & brn ('42)	5	5
159	A13	5fr brn blk ('42)	5	5
160	A13	10fr lil & dl vio	16	5
161	A13	15fr hn brn ('42)	1.90	1.60
162	A13	20fr lt vio & car	1.60	40
		Nos. 152A-162 (12)	4.26	2.65

Catalogue values for unused stamps in this section, from this point to the end of the section, are for Never Hinged items.

One Aim Alone - Victory A18

Mosque and Olive Tree A19

1943 **Litho.** ***Perf. 12***

163	A18	1.50fr rose	8	7

1944-45 **Unwmk.** ***Perf. 11½***

Size: 15½x19 mm

165	A19	30c yellow ('45)	5	5
166	A19	40c org brn ('45)	5	5
168	A19	60c red org ('45)	5	5
169	A19	70c rose pink ('45)	5	5
170	A19	80c Prus grn ('45)	5	5
171	A19	90c violet ('45)	5	5
172	A19	1fr red ('45)	5	5
173	A19	1.50fr dp bl ('45)	5	5

Size: 21¼x26½mm

175	A19	2.40fr red	5	5
176	A19	2.50fr red brn	5	5
177	A19	3fr lt vio	5	5
178	A19	4fr brt bl vio	5	5
179	A19	4.50fr apple grn	5	5
180	A19	5fr gray	7	7
181	A19	6fr choc ('45)	20	20
182	A19	10fr brn lake ('45)	20	20
183	A19	15fr copper brn	20	20
184	A19	20fr lilac	30	30
		Nos. 165-184 (18)	1.62	1.62

Types of 1926

1946-47 **Typo.** ***Perf. 14x13½***

185	A12	2fr emerald ('47)	5	5
186	A12	3fr rose pink	5	5
187	A12	4fr violet ('47)	5	5
188	A13	4fr violet ('47)	10	10
189	A12	6fr carmine ('47)	5	5
		Nos. 185-189 (5)	30	30

Neptune, Bardo Museum A20

1947-49 **Engr.** ***Perf. 13***

190	A20	5fr dk grn & bluish blk	35	35
191	A20	10fr blk brn & bluish blk	15	5
192	A20	18fr dk bl gray & Prus bl ('48)	50	30
193	A20	25fr dk bl & bl grn ('49)	62	30

Detail from Great Mosque at Kairouan A21

1948-49

194	A21	3fr dk bl grn & bl grn	35	30
195	A21	4fr dk red vio & red vio	20	15
196	A21	6fr red brn & red	5	5
197	A21	10fr purple ('49)	15	5
198	A21	12fr henna brn	35	20
198A	A21	12fr dk brn & org brn ('49)	22	12
198B	A21	15fr dk red ('49)	22	12
		Nos. 194-198B (7)	1.54	99

See No. 225.

Types of 1926

1947-49 **Typo.** ***Perf. 14x13½***

199	A12	2.50fr brn org	8	5
a		2.50fr brown	30	10
200	A12	4fr brn org ('49)	22	18
201	A12	4.50fr lt ultra	8	8
202	A12	5fr blue ('48)	20	20
203	A12	5fr lt bl grn ('49)	20	7
204	A13	6fr rose red	5	5
205	A12	15fr rose red	20	20
206	A13	25fr red org	38	25
		Nos. 199-206 (8)	1.41	1.08

No. 199a is known only precanceled. See note after No. 120.

Dam on the Oued Mellegue A22

1949, Sept. 1 **Engr.** ***Perf. 13***

207	A22	15fr grnsh blk	80	20

UPU Symbols and Tunisian Post Rider A23

Berber Hermes at Carthage A24

1949, Oct. 28

Bluish Paper

208	A23	5fr dk grn	50	50
209	A23	15fr red brn	50	50

UPU, 75th anniversary.
Nos. 208-209 exist imperf. See No. C13.

1950-51

210	A24	15fr red brn	35	30
211	A24	25fr indigo ('51)	35	30
212	A24	50fr dk grn ('51)	1.10	30

Horse, Carthage Museum — A25

1950, Dec. 26 **Typo.** ***Perf. 13½x14***

Size: 21½x17½mm

213	A25	10c aquamarine	5	5
214	A25	50c brown	5	5
215	A25	1fr rose lilac	5	5
216	A25	2fr gray	7	7
217	A25	4fr vermilion	7	5
218	A25	5fr blue grn	12	5
219	A25	8fr deep blue	16	12
220	A25	12fr red	50	15
221	A25	15fr car rose ('50)	16	5
		Nos. 213-221 (9)	1.23	64

See Nos. 222-224, 226-228.

1951-53 **Engr.** ***Perf. 13x14***

Size: 22x18mm

222	A25	15fr car rose	35	20
223	A25	15fr ultra ('53)	35	20
224	A25	30fr dp ultra	70	20

Type of 1948-49

1951, Aug. 1 ***Perf. 13***

225	A21	30fr dark blue	42	22

Horse Type of 1950

1952 **Typo.** ***Perf. 13½x14***

226	A25	3fr brn org	7	5
227	A25	12fr car rose	50	8
228	A25	15fr ultra	20	8

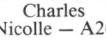

Charles Nicolle — A26

Flags, Pennants and Minaret — A27

1952, Aug. 4 **Engr.** ***Perf. 13***

229	A26	15fr blk brn	50	35
230	A26	30fr dp blue	50	35

Founding of the Society of Medical Sciences of Tunisia, 50th anniv.

1953, Oct. 18

231	A27	8fr blk brn & choc	30	30
232	A27	12fr dk grn & emer	30	30
233	A27	15fr ind & ultra	30	30
234	A27	18fr dk pur & pur	30	30
235	A27	30fr dk car & car	30	30
		Nos. 231-235 (5)	1.50	1.50

First International Fair of Tunis.

Courtyard at Sousse A28

Sidi Bou Maklouf Mosque A29

Designs: 1fr, Courtyard at Sousse. 2fr, 4fr, Citadel, Takrouna. 5fr, 8fr, View of Tatahouine. 10fr, 12fr, Ruins at Matmata. 15fr, Street Corner, Sidi Bou Said. 20fr, 25fr, Genoese fort, Tabarka. 30fr, 40fr, Bab-El-Khadra gate. 50fr, 75fr, Four-story building, Medenine.

Perf. 13½x13 (A28), 13

1954, May 29

236	A28	50c emerald	5	5
237	A28	1fr car rose	5	5
238	A28	2fr vio brn	5	5
239	A28	4fr turq bl	5	5

240	A28	5fr	violet	5	5
241	A28	8fr	blk brn	7	7
242	A28	10fr	dk bl grn	12	5
243	A28	12fr	rose brn	22	5
244	A28	15fr	dp ultra	1.60	5
245	A29	18fr	chocolate	90	42
246	A29	20fr	dp ultra	65	7
247	A29	25fr	indigo	50	7
248	A29	30fr	dp claret	40	15
249	A29	40fr	dk Prus grn	50	22
250	A29	50fr	dk vio	1.60	7
251	A29	75fr	car rose	1.60	1.10

Typo.

Perf. 14x13½

252	A28	15fr	ultra	50	7
			Nos. 236-252 (17)	8.91	2.64

Imperforates exist. See Nos. 271-287.

Mohammed al-Amin, Bey of Tunis — A30

1954, Oct. ***Perf. 13***

253	A30	8fr	bl & dk bl	25	25
254	A30	12fr	lil gray & ind	25	25
255	A30	15fr	dp car & brn lake	25	25
256	A30	18fr	red brn & blk brn	25	25
257	A30	30fr	bl grn & dk bl grn	45	45
			Nos. 253-257 (5)	1.45	1.45

Theater Drapes, Dove and Sun — A31

1955

258	A31	15fr	dk red brn, bl & org	30	30

Essor, Tunisian amateur theatrical society.

Rotary Emblem, Map and Symbols of Punic, Roman, Arab and French Civilizations A32

1955, May 14 **Unwmk.**

259	A32	12fr	vio brn & blk brn	25	25
260	A32	15fr	vio gray & dk brn	25	25
261	A32	18fr	rose vio & dk pur	25	25
262	A32	25fr	bl & dp ultra	25	25
263	A32	30fr	dk Prus grn & ind	45	45
			Nos. 259-263 (5)	1.45	1.45

Rotary International, 50th anniv.

Bey of Tunis A33

Embroiderers A34

1955 **Engr.** ***Perf. 13½x13***

264	A33	15fr	dark blue	22	5

1955, July 25 ***Perf. 13***

Designs: 15fr, 18fr, Potters. 20fr, 30fr, Florists.

265	A34	5fr	rose brn	30	30
266	A34	12fr	ultra	30	30
267	A34	15fr	Prussian grn	32	32
268	A34	18fr	red	32	32
269	A34	20fr	dark vio	40	40
270	A34	30fr	vio brn	40	40
			Nos. 265-270 (6)	2.04	2.04

Independent Kingdom

Types of 1954 Redrawn with "RF" Omitted

Perf. 13½x13, 13 (A29)

1956, Mar. 1

271	A28	50c	emerald	5	5
272	A28	1fr	car rose	5	5
273	A28	2fr	vio brn	5	5
274	A28	4fr	turquoise bl	10	5
275	A28	5fr	violet	5	5
276	A28	8fr	blk brn	10	5
277	A28	10fr	dk blue grn	7	5
278	A28	12fr	rose brn	7	5
279	A28	15fr	dp ultra	55	10
280	A29	18fr	chocolate	20	10
281	A29	20fr	dp ultra	16	5
282	A29	25fr	indigo	14	5
283	A29	30fr	dp claret	70	10
284	A29	40fr	dk Prus grn	65	10
285	A29	50fr	dk vio	50	7
286	A29	75fr	car rose	65	55

Perf. 14x13

Typo.

287	A28	15fr	ultra	7	7
			Nos. 271-287 (17)	4.16	1.59

Mohammed al-Amin Bey of Tunis — A35

Farhat Hached — A36

Designs: 12fr, 18fr, 30fr, Woman and Dove. 5fr, 20fr, Bey of Tunis.

1956 **Unwmk.** **Engr.** ***Perf. 13***

288	A35	5fr	deep blue	16	12
289	A35	12fr	brn vio	20	12
290	A35	15fr	red	22	20
291	A35	18fr	dk bl gray	35	20
292	A35	20fr	dark grn	35	12
293	A35	30fr	copper brn	60	22
			Nos. 288-293 (6)	1.88	98

Issued to commemorate Tunisian autonomy.

1956, May 1

294	A36	15fr	rose brown	20	20
295	A36	30fr	indigo	25	25

Farhat Hached (1914-1952), nationalist leader.

Grapes — A37

Fruit Market A38

Designs: 15fr, Hand holding olive branch. 18fr, Wheat harvest. 20fr, Man carrying food basket ("Gifts for the wedding").

1956-57 **Unwmk.** **Engr.** ***Perf. 13***

296	A37	12fr	lil, vio & vio brn	35	15
297	A37	15fr	ind, dk ol grn & red brn	35	15
298	A37	18fr	brt vio bl	60	20
299	A37	20fr	brn org	60	20
300	A38	25fr	chocolate	70	40
301	A38	30fr	dp ultra	80	40
			Nos. 296-301 (6)	3.40	1.50

Habib Bourguiba A39

Farmers and Workers A40

Perf. 14 (A39), 11½x11 (A40)

1957, Mar. 20

302	A39	5fr	dark blue	8	8
303	A40	12fr	magenta	9	8
304	A39	20fr	ultra	18	9
305	A40	25fr	green	18	8
306	A39	30fr	chocolate	22	18
307	A40	50fr	crim rose	38	25
			Nos. 302-307 (6)	1.13	76

First anniversary of independence.

Dove and Handclasp A41

Labor Bourse, Tunis — A42

1957, July 5 **Engr.** ***Perf. 13***

308	A41	18fr	dk red vio	22	22
309	A42	20fr	crimson	25	25
310	A41	25fr	green	25	25
311	A42	30fr	dark bl	30	30

5th World Congress of the Intl. Federation of Trade Unions, Tunis, July 5-13.

Republic

Officer and Soldier — A43

1957, Aug. 8 **Typo.** ***Perf. 11***

312	A43	20fr	rose pink	7.00	7.00
313	A43	25fr	light vio	7.00	7.00
314	A43	30fr	brn org	7.00	7.00

Proclamation of the Republic.

Bourguiba in Exile, Ile de la Galite A44

1958, Jan. 18 **Engr.** ***Perf. 13***

315	A44	20fr	bl & dk brn	25	20
316	A44	25fr	lt bl & vio	30	20

6th anniv. of Bourguiba's deportation.

Map of Tunisia — A45

Designs: 25fr, Woman and child. 30fr, Hand holding flag.

1958, Mar. 20 ***Perf. 13***

317	A45	20fr	dk brn & emer	20	10
318	A45	25fr	blue & sepia	20	12
319	A45	30fr	red brn & red	25	15

2nd anniv. of independence. See No. 321.

Andreas Vesalius and Abderrahman ibn Khaldoun — A46

1958, Apr. 17 **Unwmk.**

320	A46	30fr	bis & sl grn	30	15

World's Fair, Brussels, Apr. 17-Oct. 19.

Redrawn Type of 1958

1958, June 1 **Engr.** ***Perf. 13***

321	A45	20fr	brt bl & ocher	25	16

Date has been changed to "1 Juin 1955-1958."

3rd anniv. of the return of Pres. Habib Bourguiba.

Gardener — A47

A48

1958, May 1

322	A47	20fr	multi	30	30

Labor Day, May 1.

1958, July 25 **Unwmk.** ***Perf. 13***

Blue Paper

323	A48	5fr	dk vio brn & ol	22	9
324	A48	10fr	dk grn & yel grn	22	9
325	A48	15fr	org red & brn lake	22	9
326	A48	20fr	vio, ol grn & yel	22	9
327	A48	25fr	red lil	22	9
			Nos. 323-327 (5)	1.10	45

First anniversary of the Republic.

Pres. Habib Bourguiba A49

Fishermen Casting Net A50

1958, Aug. 3 **Unwmk.** ***Perf. 13***

328	A49	20fr	vio & brn lake	20	10

Pres. Bourguiba's 55th birthday.

1958, Oct. 18 **Engr.** ***Perf. 13***

329	A50	25fr	dk brn, grn & red	30	20

6th International Fair, Tunis.

UNESCO Building, Paris — A51

1958, Nov. 3

330 A51 25fr grnsh blk		30	20

Opening of UNESCO Headquarters, Nov. 3.

Woman Opening Veil — A52

Hand Planting Symbolic Tree — A53

Habib Bourguiba at Borj le Boeuf A54

1959, Jan. 1 Engr. *Perf. 13*

331 A52 20m grnsh bl	25	16

Emancipation of Tunisian women.

1959, Mar. 2 Unwmk. *Perf. 13*

Designs: 10m, Shield with flag and people holding torch. 20m, Habib Bourguiba at Borj le Boeuf, Sahara.

332 A53 5m vio brn, car & sal	12	10
333 A53 10m multi	16	15
334 A53 20m blue	20	16
335 A54 30m grnsh bl, ind & org brn	38	35

25th anniv. of the founding of the Neo-Destour Party at Kasr Helal, Mar. 2, 1934.

"Independence" — A55

1959, Mar. 20

336 A55 50m ol, blk & red	40	25

3rd anniversary of independence.

Map of Africa and Drawings — A56

1959, Apr. 15 Litho. *Perf. 13*

337 A56 40m lt bl & red brn	42	30

Africa Freedom Day, Apr. 15.

Camel Camp and Mosque, Kairouan A57

Horseback Rider — A58

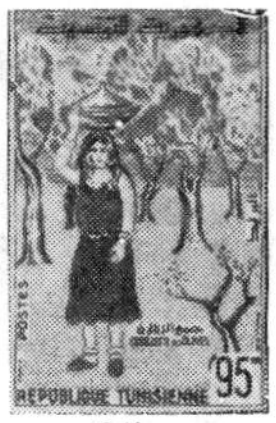
Olive Picker — A59

Open Window A58a

Designs: ½m, Woodcock in Ain-Draham forest. 2m, Camel rider. 3m, Saddler's shop. 4m, Old houses of Medenine, gazelle and youth. 6m, Weavers. 8m, Woman of Gafsa. 10m, Unveiled woman holding fruit. 12m, Ivory craftsman. 15m, Skanes Beach, Monastir, and mermaid. 16m, Minaret of Ez-Zitouna University, Tunis. 20m, Oasis of Gabes. 25m, Oil, flowers and fish of Sfax. 30m, Modern and Roman aqueducts. 40m, Festival at Kairouan (drummer and camel). 45m, Octagonal minaret, Bizerte (boatman). 50m, Three women of Djerba island. 60m, Date palms, Djerid. 70m, Tapestry weaver. 75m, Pottery of Nabeul. 90m, Le Kef (man on horse). 100m, Road to Sidi-bou-Said. 200m, Old port of Sfax. ½d, Roman temple, Sbeitla. 1d, Farmer plowing with oxen, Beja.

1959-61 Unwmk. Engr. *Perf. 13*

338	A58	½m	emer, brn & bl grn ('60)	8	6
339	A57	1m	lt bl & ocher	6	5
340	A58	2m	multi	6	5
341	A58	3m	slate grn	6	5
342	A57	4m	red brn ('60)	8	5
343	A58	5m	gray grn	8	5
344	A58	6m	rose vio	9	6
345	A58	8m	vio brn ('60)	38	9
346	A58	10m	ol, dk grn & car	8	5
347	A58	12m	vio bl & ol bis ('61)	30	8
348	A57	15m	brt bl ('60)	15	5
349	A57	16m	grnsh blk ('60)	15	8
350	A58a	20m	grnsh bl	50	15
351	A58	20m	grnsh blk, ol & mar ('60)	1.00	12
352	A57	25m	multi ('60)	15	12
353	A58a	30m	brn, grnsh bl & ol	22	5
354	A59	40m	dp grn ('60)	48	12
355	A58a	45m	brt grn ('60)	32	18
356	A58a	50m	Prus grn, dk bl & rose ('60)	45	12
357	A58a	60m	grn & red brn ('60)	45	19
358	A59	70m	multi ('60)	65	25
359	A59	75m	ol gray ('60)	50	32
360	A58a	90m	brt grn, ultra & choc ('60)	65	30
361	A59	95m	multi	75	50
362	A58a	100m	dk bl, ol & brn	85	50
363	A58a	200m	brt bl, bis & car	2.25	1.25
363A	A59	½d	lt brn ('60)	5.50	3.50
363B	A58a	1d	sl grn & bis ('60)	10.00	7.00
			Nos. 338-363B (28)	26.29	15.39

UN Emblem and Clasped Hands — A60

Dancer and Coin — A61

1959, Oct. 24

364 A60 80m org brn, brn & ultra	60	40

UN Day, Oct. 24.

1959, Nov. 4

365 A61 50m grnsh bl & blk	42	42

Central Bank of Tunisia, first anniversary.

Uprooted Oak Emblem — A62

Doves and WRY Emblem A63

1960, Apr. 7 Engr. *Perf. 13*

366 A62 20m bl blk	35	20
367 A63 40m red lil & dk grn	42	30

Issued to publicize World Refugee Year, July 1, 1959-June 30, 1960.

Girl, Boy and Scout Badge — A64

Cyclist — A65

Designs: 25m, Hand giving Scout sign. 30m, Bugler and tent. 40m, Peacock and Scout emblem. 60m, Scout and campfire.

1960, Aug. 9

368 A64 10m lt bl grn	15	12
369 A64 25m grn, red & brn	18	12
370 A64 30m vio bl, grn & mar	25	18
371 A64 40m blk, car & bl	30	22
372 A64 60m dk brn, vio blk & lake	65	32
Nos. 368-372 (5)	1.53	96

4th Arab Boy Scout Jamboree, Tunis, Aug.

1960, Aug. 25

Designs: 10m, Olympic rings forming flower. 15m, Girl tennis player and minaret. 25m, Runner and minaret. 50m, Handball player and minaret.

373 A65 5m dk brn & ol	20	20
374 A65 10m sl, red vio & emer	22	22
375 A65 15m rose red & rose car	22	22
376 A65 25m grnsh bl & gray bl	35	35
377 A65 50m brt grn & ultra	65	60
Nos. 373-377 (5)	1.64	1.59

17th Olympic Games, Rome, Aug. 25-Sept. 11.

Symbolic Forest Design A66

National Fair Emblems A67

Designs: 15m, Man working in forest. 25m, Tree superimposed on leaf. 50m, Symbolic tree and bird.

1960, Aug. 29

378 A66 8m multi	15	9
379 A66 15m dk grn	20	12
380 A66 25m dk pur, crim & brt grn	30	18
381 A66 50m Prus grn, yel grn & rose lake	42	30

5th World Forestry Congress, Seattle, Wash., Aug. 29-Sept. 10.

1960, June 1

382 A67 100m blk & grn	55	35

5th Natl. Fair, Sousse, May 27-June 12.

Pres. Bourguiba Signing Constitution A68

Pres. Bourguiba A69

1960, June 1

383 A68 20m choc, red & emer	22	12
384 A69 20m grayish blk	12	5
385 A69 30m bl, dl red & blk	22	8
386 A69 40m grn, dl red & blk	25	12

Promulgation of the Constitution (No. 383).

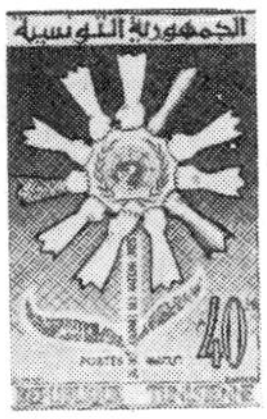
UN Emblem and Arms A70

Dove and "Liberated Tunisia" A71

1960, Oct. 24 Engr. *Perf. 13*

387 A70 40m mag, ultra & gray grn	45	35

15th anniversary of the United Nations.

1961, Mar. 20 *Perf. 13*

Design: 75m, Globe and arms.

388 A71 20m mar, bis & bl	16	15
389 A71 30m bl, vio & brn	20	16
390 A71 40m yel grn & ultra	40	35
391 A71 75m bis, red lil & Prus bl	50	40

5th anniversary of independence.

Map of Africa, Woman and Animals A72

Mother and Child with Flags A73

Map of Africa: 60m, Negro woman and Arab. 100m, Arabic inscription and Guinea masque. 200m, Hands of Negro and Arab.

1961, Apr. 15 Engr. Unwmk.

392 A72 40m bis brn, red brn & dk grn	20	15
393 A72 60m sl grn, blk & org brn	20	18

394 A72 100m sl grn, emer & vio 38 20
395 A72 200m dk brn & org brn 75 65

Africa Freedom Day, Apr. 15.

1961, June 1 Unwmk. *Perf. 13*

Designs: 50m, Tunisians. 95m, Girl with wings and half-moon.

396 A73 25m pale vio, red & brn 22 15
397 A73 50m bl grn, sep & brn 35 16
398 A73 95m pale vio, rose lil & ocher 42 30

National Feast Day, June 1.

Dag Hammarskjold A74

Arms of Tunisia A75

1961, Oct. 24 Photo. *Perf. 14*

399 A74 40m ultramarine 30 20

UN Day; Dag Hammarskjold (1905-1961), Secretary General of the UN, 1953-61.

1962, Jan. 18 *Perf. 11½*

Arms in Original Colors

400 A75 1m blk & yel 5 5
401 A75 2m blk & pink 5 5
402 A75 3m blk & lt bl 7 5
403 A75 6m blk & gray 14 10

10th anniv. of Tunisia's campaign for independence.

Mosquito in Spider Web and WHO Emblem — A76

Designs: 30m, Symbolic horseback rider spearing mosquito. 40m, Hands crushing mosquito (horiz.).

1962, Apr. 7 Engr. *Perf. 13*

404 A76 20m chocolate 35 20
405 A76 30m red brn & sl grn 30 20
406 A76 40m dk brn, mar & grn 40 25

WHO drive to eradicate malaria.

Boy and Map of Africa A77

African Holding "Africa" A78

1962, Apr. 15 Photo. *Perf. 14*

407 A77 50m brn & org 35 22
408 A78 100m bl, blk & org 50 25

Africa Freedom Day, Apr. 15.

Farm Worker A79

Industrial Worker A80

1962, May 1 Unwmk.

409 A79 40m multi 30 16
410 A80 60m dk red brn 38 22

Labor Day.

"Liberated Tunisia" A81

Woman of Gabes A82

1962, June 1 Typo. *Perf. 13½x14*

411 A81 20m sal & blk 20 15

National Feast Day, June 1.

1962-63 Photo. *Perf. 11½*

Women in costume of various localities: 10m, 30m, Mahdia. 15m, Kairouan. 20m, 40m, Hammamet. 25m, Djerba. 55m, Ksar Hellal. 60m, Tunis.

412 A82 5m multi 25 12
413 A82 10m multi 32 18
414 A82 15m multi ('63) 38 25
415 A82 20m multi 50 30
416 A82 25m multi ('63) 50 30
417 A82 30m multi 65 38
418 A82 40m multi 70 38
419 A82 50m multi 70 45
420 A82 55m multi ('63) 85 55
421 A82 60m multi ('63) 1.25 85
Nos. 412-421 (10) 6.10 3.76

The six stamps issued in 1962 (July 25) commemorate the 6th anniv. of Tunisia's independence. The four issued in 1963 (June 1) commemorate National Feast Day. See Nos. 470-471.

UN Emblem, Flag and Dove A83

Aboul-Qasim Chabbi A84

Designs: 30m, Leaves and globe (horiz.). 40m, Dove and globe.

1962, Oct. 24 Unwmk.

422 A83 20m gray, blk & scar 25 20
423 A83 30m multi 30 20
424 A83 40m cl brn, blk & bl 55 30

Issued for United Nations Day, Oct. 24.

1962, Nov. 20 Engr. *Perf. 13*

425 A84 15m purple 20 14

Aboul-Qasim Chabbi (1904-34), Arab poet.

Pres. Habib Bourguiba A85

Hached Telephone Exchange A86

1962, Dec. 7 Photo. *Perf. 12½x13½*

426 A85 20m brt bl 8 5
427 A85 30m rose cl 9 6
428 A85 40m green 12 9

1962, Dec. 7 Litho.

Designs: 10m, Carthage Exchange. 15m, Sfax telecommunications center. 50m, Telephone operators. 100m, Symbol of automatization. 200m, Belvedere Central Exchange.

429 A86 5m multi 15 9
430 A86 10m multi 15 12
431 A86 15m multi 25 12
432 A86 50m blk, red brn & buff 40 25
433 A86 100m blk, brt bl & mag 1.00 55
434 A86 200m multi 1.40 90
Nos. 429-434 (6) 3.35 2.03

1st Afro-Asian Philatelic Exhibition; automation of the telephone system.

Dove over Globe A87

"Hunger" A88

1963, Mar. 21 Engr. *Perf. 13*

435 A87 20m brt bl & brn 20 16
436 A88 40m bis brn & dk brn 30 20

FAO "Freedom from Hunger" campaign.

Runner and Walker A89

Centenary Emblem A90

1963, Feb. 17 Litho. *Perf. 13*

437 A89 30m brn, blk & grn 30 20

Army Sports Day; 13th C.I.S.M. cross country championships.

1963, May 8 Engr. *Perf. 13*

438 A90 20m brn, gray & red 20 14

Centenary of International Red Cross.

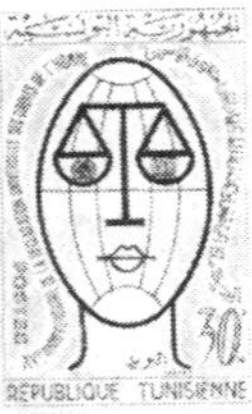

"Human Rights" — A91

Hand Raising Gateway of Great Temple of Philae — A92

1963, Dec. 10 Unwmk. *Perf. 13*

439 A91 30m grn & dk brn 20 12

15th anniv. of the Universal Declaration of Human Rights.

1964, Mar. 8 Engr.

440 A92 50m red brn, bis & bluish blk 35 25

UNESCO world campaign to save historic monuments in Nubia.

Sunshine, Rain and Barometer — A93

Mohammed Ali — A94

1964, March 8 Unwmk. *Perf. 13*

441 A93 40m brn, red lil & sl 30 20

4th World Meteorological Day, Mar. 23.

1964, May 15 Engr.

442 A94 50m sepia 25 16

Mohammed Ali (1894-1928), labor leader.

Map of Africa and Symbolic Flower A95

Pres. Habib Bourguiba A96

1964, May 25 Photo. *Perf. 13x14*

443 A95 60m multi 35 22

1st anniv. of the Addis Ababa charter on African Unity.

1964, June 1 Engr. *Perf. 12½x13½*

444 A96 20m vio bl 8 5
445 A96 30m black 14 7

"Ship and Torch" — A97

1964, Oct. 19 Photo. *Perf. 11½x11*

446 A97 50m blk & grn 22 15

Neo-Destour Congress, Bizerte. "Bizerte" in Arabic forms the ship and "Neo-Destour Congress 1964" the torch of the design.

Communication Equipment and ITU Emblem — A98

1965, May 17 Engr. *Perf. 13*

447 A98 55m gray & bl 35 15

ITU, centenary.

Carthaginian Coin — A99

Girl with Book — A100

Perf. 12½x14

1965, July 9 Photo. Unwmk.

448 A99 5m grn & blk brn 10 7
449 A99 10m bis & blk brn 20 14
450 A99 75m bl & blk brn 50 20

Festival of Popular Arts, Carthage.

1965, Oct. 1 Engr. *Perf. 13*

451 A100 25m brt bl, blk & red 15 9
452 A100 40m blk, bl & red 20 12
453 A100 50m red, bl & blk 22 12
a Souv. sheet of 3, #451-453 2.25 2.25

Girl Students' Center; education for women. No. 453a sold for 200m. Issued perf. and imperf.; same value.

Links and ICY Emblem A101

Man Pouring Water A102

1965, Oct. 24

454 A101 40m blk, brt bl & rose lil 30 15

International Cooperation Year.

1966, Jan. 18 Photo. *Perf. 13x14*

Symbolic Designs: 10m, Woman and pool. 30m, Woman pouring water. 100m, Mountain and branches.

Inscribed "Eaux Minerales"

455 A102 10m gray, ocher & dk red 15 12
456 A102 20m multi 20 15
457 A102 30m yel, bl & red 25 16
458 A102 100m ol, bl & yel 65 38

Mineral waters of Tunisia.

President Bourguiba and Hands A103

"Promotion of Culture" — A104

Designs: 5m, like 10m. 25m, "Independence" (arms raised), flag and doves. 40m, "Development" (horiz.).

1966, June 1 Engr. *Perf. 13*

459 A103 5m dl pur & vio 10 10
460 A103 10m gray grn & sl grn 15 10

Perf. 11½

Photo.

461 A104 25m multi 15 10
462 A104 40m multi 35 16
463 A104 60m multi 50 16
Nos. 459-463 (5) 1.25 62

10th anniversary of independence.

Map of Africa through View Finder, Plane and UN Emblem — A105

1966, Sept. 12 Engr. *Perf. 13*

464 A105 15m lil & multi 12 9
465 A105 35m bl & multi 15 12
466 A105 40m multi 25 12
a Souvenir sheet of 3, #464-466 5.50 5.50

2nd UN Regional Cartographic Conference for Africa, held in Tunisia, Sept. 12-24.

No. 466a sold for 150m. Issued perf. and imperf.; same value.

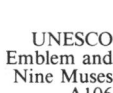

UNESCO Emblem and Nine Muses A106

1966, Oct. 24 *Perf. 13*

467 A106 100m blk & brn 60 25

UNESCO, 20th anniv.

Runners and Mediterranean Map — A107

1967, March 20 Engr. *Perf. 13*

468 A107 20m dk red, brn ol & bl 15 10
469 A107 30m brt bl & blk 22 12

Mediterranean Games, Sept. 8-17.

Types of 1962-63 and 1965-66 with EXPO '67 Emblem and Inscription and

Symbols of Various Activities — A108

Designs: 50m, Woman of Djerba. 75m, Woman of Gabes. 155m, Pink flamingoes.

Perf. 11½, 13 (A108)

Photo.; Engr. (A108)

1967, Apr. 28

470 A82 50m multi 20 10
471 A82 75m multi 25 18
472 A108 100m dk grn, sl bl & blk 32 18
473 A108 110m dk brn, ultra & red 42 22
474 AP6 155m multi 70 25
Nos. 470-474 (5) 1.89 93

EXPO '67, Intl. Exhibition, Montreal, Apr. 28-Oct. 27.

Tunisian Pavilion, Pres. Bourguiba and Map of Tunisia — A109

Designs: 105m, 200m, Tunisian Pavilion and bust of Pres. Bourguiba.

1967, June 13 Engr. *Perf. 13*

475 A109 65m red lil & dp org 22 15
476 A109 105m multi 30 18
477 A109 120m brt bl 38 25
478 A109 200m red, lil & blk 65 32

Tunisia Day at EXPO '67.

"Tunisia" Holding 4-leaf Clovers A110

Woman Freeing Doves — A111

1967, July 25 Litho. *Perf. 13½*

479 A110 25m multi 16 10
480 A111 40m multi 20 14

10th anniversary of the Republic.

Tennis Courts, Players and Games' Emblem — A112

Designs: 10m, Games' emblem and sports emblems (vert.). 15m, Swimming pool and swimmers. 35m, Sports Palace and athletes. 75m, Stadium and athletes.

1967, Sept. 8 Engr. *Perf. 13*

481 A112 5m sl grn & hn brn 15 10
482 A112 10m brn red & multi 15 10
483 A112 15m black 20 12
484 A112 35m dk brn & Prus bl 30 15
485 A112 75m dk car rose, vio & bl grn 55 35
Nos. 481-485 (5) 1.35 82

Mediterranean Games, Tunis, Sept. 8-17.

Bird, Punic Period — A113

"Mankind" and Human Rights Flame — A114

History of Tunisia: 20m, Sea horse, medallion from Kerkouane. 25m, Hannibal, bronze bust, Volubilis. 30m, Stele, Carthage. 40m, Hamilcar, coin. 60m, Mask, funereal pendant.

1967, Dec. 1 Litho. *Perf. 13½*

486 A113 15m gray grn, pink & blk 16 10
487 A113 20m dp bl, red & blk 16 10
488 A113 25m dk grn & org brn 22 10
489 A113 30m grnsh gray, pink & blk 22 10
490 A113 40m red brn, yel & blk 30 15
491 A113 60m multi 35 20
Nos. 486-491 (6) 1.41 75

1968, Jan. 18 Engr. *Perf. 13*

492 A114 25m brick red 22 12
493 A114 60m dp bl 25 16

International Human Rights Year.

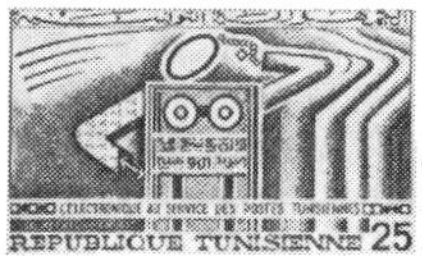

Computer Fantasy A115

1968, Mar. 20 Engr. *Perf. 13*

494 A115 25m mag, bl vio & ol 22 14
495 A115 40m ol grn, red brn & brn 22 14
496 A115 60m ultra, sl & brn 30 14

Introduction of electronic equipment for postal service.

Physician and Patient A116

Arabian Jasmine A117

1968, Apr. 7 Engr. *Perf. 13*

497 A116 25m dp grn & brt grn 22 10
498 A116 60m mag & car 30 15

WHO, 20th anniversary.

1968-69 Photo. *Perf. 11½*

Flowers: 5m, Flax. 6m, Canna indica. 10m, Pomegranate. 15m, Rhaponticum acaule. 20m, Geranium. 25m, Madonna lily. 40m, Peach blossoms. 50m, Caper. 60m, Ariana rose. 100fr, Jasmine.

Granite Paper

499	A117	5m	multi ('69)	9	8
500	A117	6m	multi ('69)	12	8
501	A117	10m	multi ('69)	12	8
502	A117	12m	multi	15	8
503	A117	15m	multi ('69)	15	9
504	A117	20m	multi ('69)	18	9
505	A117	25m	multi ('69)	20	12
506	A117	40m	multi ('69)	28	15
507	A117	50m	multi	32	18
508	A117	60m	multi	55	30
509	A117	100m	multi	85	45
			Nos. 499-509 (11)	3.01	1.70

Issue dates: 12m, 50m, 60m, 100m, Apr. 9, 1968. Others, Mar. 20, 1969.

Flower with Red Crescent and Globe A118

Flutist A119

Design: 25m, Dove with Red Crescent and globe.

1968, May 8 Engr. *Perf. 13*

510	A118	15m	Prus bl, grn & red	20	15
511	A118	25m	brt rose lil & red	25	16

Red Crescent Society.

1968, June 1 Litho. *Perf. 13*

512	A119	20m	vio & multi	20	12
513	A119	50m	multi	25	15

Stamp Day.

Jackal — A120

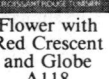

Animals: 8m, Porcupine. 10m, Dromedary. 15m, Dorcas gazelle. 20m, Desert fox (fennec). 25m, Desert hedgehog. 40m, Arabian horse. 60m, Boar.

1968-69 Photo. *Perf. 11½*

514	A120	5m	dk brn, lt bl & bis	14	10
515	A120	8m	dk vio brn & yel grn	16	10
516	A120	10m	dk brn, lt bl & ocher ('69)	25	12
517	A120	15m	dk brn, ocher & yel grn ('69)	25	16
518	A120	20m	dl yel & dk brn	35	30
519	A120	25m	blk, tan & brt grn ('69)	55	30
520	A120	40m	blk, lil & pale grn ('69)	70	55
521	A120	60m	dk brn, buff & yel grn	1.00	80
			Nos. 514-521 (8)	3.40	2.43

Issue dates: 5m, 8m, 20m, 60m, Sept. 15, 1968. Others, Jan. 18, 1969.

Worker and ILO Emblem — A121

Design: 60m, Young man and woman holding banner.

1969, May 1 Engr. *Perf. 13*

522	A121	25m	Prus bl, blk & bis	20	10
523	A121	60m	rose car, bl & yel	30	15

ILO, 50th anniversary.

Veiled Women and Musicians with Flute and Drum A122

1969, June 20 Litho. *Perf. 14x13½*

524	A122	100m	dp yel grn & multi	50	30

Stamp Day.

Tunisian Coat of Arms A123

Symbols of Industry A124

1969, July 25 Photo. *Perf. 11½*

525	A123	15m	yel & multi	12	10
526	A123	25m	pink & multi	16	12
527	A123	40m	gray & multi	20	12
528	A123	60m	lt bl & multi	22	12

1969, Sept. 10 *Perf. 13x12*

529	A124	60m	blk, red & yel	25	12

African Development Bank, 5th anniv.

Lute — A125

Nurse and Maghrib Flags — A126

Musical Instruments: 50m, Zither (horiz.). 70m, Rebab (2-strings). 90m, Drums and flute (horiz.).

1970, Mar. 20 Photo. *Perf. 11½*

Granite Paper

530	A125	25m	multi	22	16
531	A125	50m	multi	35	22
532	A125	70m	multi	55	22
533	A125	90m	multi	60	35

1970, May 4 Photo. *Perf. 11½*

534	A126	25m	lil & multi	20	14

6th Medical Seminar of Maghrib Countries (Morocco, Algeria, Tunisia and Libya), Tunis, May 4-10.

UPU Headquarters Issue
Common Design Type

1970, May 20 Engr. *Perf. 13*

535	CD133	25m	dl red & dk ol bis	25	15

Common Design Types pictured in section at front of book.

Mail Service Symbol A127

Design: 35m, Mailmen of yesterday and today (vert.).

1970, Oct. 15 Litho. *Perf. 12½x13*
Size: 37x31½mm

536	A127	25m	pink & multi	30	10

Size: 22x37½mm
Perf. 13x12½

537	A127	35m	blk & multi	40	12

United Nations, 25th anniversary.

Dove, Laurel and UN Emblem A128

1970, Oct. 24 Photo. *Perf. 13x12½*

538	A128	40m	multi	25	15

United Nations, 25th anniversary.

Jasmine Vendor and Veiled Woman A129

Lenin, after N.N. Joukov A130

Scenes from Tunisian Life: 25m, "The 3rd Day of the Wedding." 35m, Perfume vendor. 40m, Fish vendor. 85m, Waiter in coffeehouse.

1970, Nov. 9 Photo. *Perf. 14*

539	A129	20m	dk grn & multi	12	8
540	A129	25m	multi	15	10
541	A129	35m	multi	22	10
542	A129	40m	dp car & multi	25	12
543	A129	85m	brt bl & multi	38	20
a			Souvenir sheet of 5, #539-543	2.75	2.75
			Nos. 539-543 (5)	1.12	60

No. 543a sold for 500m. Issued perf. and imperf.; same value.

1970, Dec. 28 Engr. *Perf. 13*

544	A130	60m	dk car rose	25	12

Lenin (1870-1924), Russian communist leader.

Radar, Flags and Carrier Pigeon — A131

UN Headquarters, Symbolic Flower — A132

1971, May 17 Litho. *Perf. 13x12½*

545	A131	25m	lt bl & multi	22	15

Coordinating Committee for Post and Telecommunications Administrations of Maghrib Countries.

1971, May 10 Photo. *Perf. 12½x13*

546	A132	80m	brt rose lil, blk & yel	30	22

Intl. year against racial discrimination.

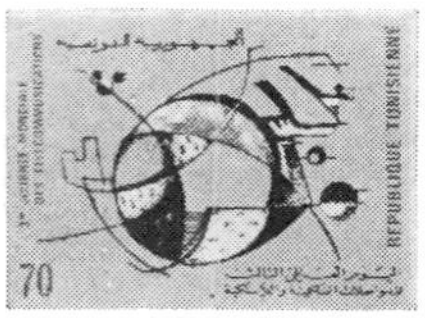

"Telecommunications" — A133

1971, May 17 *Perf. 13x12½*

547	A133	70m	sil, blk & lt grn	35	20

3rd World Telecommunications Day.

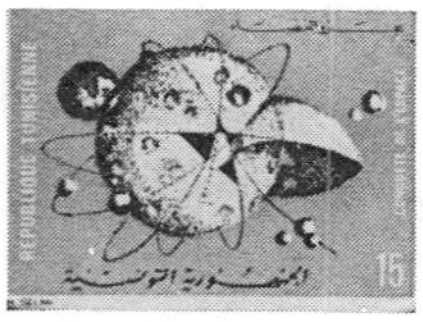

Earth, Moon, Satellites A134

Design: 90m, Abstract composition.

1971, June 21 Photo. *Perf. 13x12½*

548	A134	15m	brt bl & blk	20	12
549	A134	90m	scar & blk	40	22

Conquest of space.

"Pottery Merchant" — A135

Life in Tunisia (stylized drawings): 30m, Esparto weaver selling hats and mats. 40m, Poultry man. 50m, Dyer.

1971, July 24 Photo. *Perf. 14x13½*

550	A135	25m	gold & multi	12	8
551	A135	30m	gold & multi	15	8
552	A135	40m	gold & multi	22	9
553	A135	50m	gold & multi	25	9
a			Sheet of 4, #550-553, perf. 13½	2.00	2.00

No. 553a sold for 500m. Issued perf. and imperf.; same value.

Pres. Bourguiba Sick in 1938 A136

Designs: 25m, Bourguiba and "8" (vert.). 50m, Bourguiba carried in triumph (vert.). 80m, Bourguiba and irrigation dam.

Perf. 13½x13, 13x13½

1971, Oct. 11

554	A136	25m	multi	10	10
555	A136	30m	multi	10	10
556	A136	50m	multi	12	10
557	A136	80m	blk, ultra & grn	25	12

8th Congress of the Neo-Destour Party.

Shah Mohammed Riza Pahlavi and Stone Head 6th Century B.C. — A137

Designs: 50m, King Bahram-Gur hunting, 4th century. 100m, Coronation, from Persian miniature, 1614.

1971, Oct. 17 ***Perf. 11½***
Granite Paper

558 A137 25m multi	15	10
559 A137 50m multi	20	12
560 A137 100m multi	40	22
a Souvenir sheet of 3, #558-560	2.25	2.25

2500th anniv. of the founding of the Persian empire by Cyrus the Great. No. 560a sold for 500m. Issued perf. and imperf.; same value.

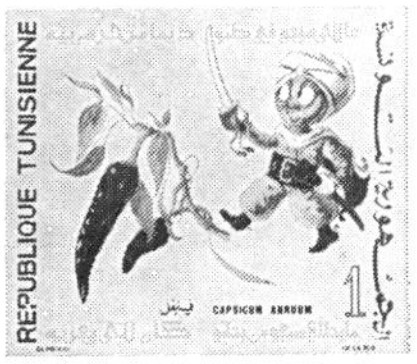

Pimento and Warrior A138

Designs: 2m, Mint and farmer. 5m, Pear and 2 men under pear tree. 25m, Oleander and girl. 60m, Pear and sheep. 100m, Grapefruit and fruit vendor.

1971, Nov. 15 **Litho.** ***Perf. 13***

561 A138 1m lt bl & multi	7	7
562 A138 2m gray & multi	7	7
563 A138 5m cit & multi	7	7
564 A138 25m lil & multi	22	10
565 A138 60m multi	40	15
566 A138 100m buff & multi	80	25
a Souvenir sheet of 6, #561-566	2.50	2.50
Nos. 561-566 (6)	1.63	71

Fruit, flowers and folklore. No. 566a sold for 500m. Issued perf. and imperf.; same value.

Dancer and Musician — A139

1971, Nov. 22 **Photo.** ***Perf. 11½***

567 A139 50m bl & multi	25	15

Stamp Day.

Map of Africa, Communication Symbols A139a

UNICEF Emblem, Mother and Child A140

Perf. 13½x12½
1971, Nov. 30 **Litho.**

568 A139a 95m multi	35	20

Pan-African telecommunications system.

1971, Dec. 6 **Photo.** ***Perf. 11½***

569 A140 110m multi	35	20

UNICEF, 25th anniv.

Symbolic Olive Tree and Oil Vat A141

Gondolier in Flood Waters A142

1972, Jan. 9 **Litho.** ***Perf. 13½***

570 A141 60m multi	22	12

International Olive Year.

1972, Feb. 7 **Photo.** ***Perf. 11½***

Designs: 30m, Young man and Doge's Palace. 50m, Gondola's prow and flood. 80m, Rialto Bridge and hand holding gondolier's hat (horiz.).

571 A142 25m lt bl & multi	15	10
572 A142 30m blk & multi	20	10
573 A142 50m yel grn, gray & blk	22	15
574 A142 80m bl & multi	40	20

UNESCO campaign to save Venice.

Man Reading and Book Year Emblem A143

"Your Heart is Your Health" A144

1972, Mar. 27 **Photo.** ***Perf. 11½***
Granite Paper

575 A143 90m brn & multi	35	20

International Book Year.

1972, Apr. 7 ***Perf. 13x13½***

Design: 60m, Smiling man pointing to heart.

576 A144 25m grn & multi	22	12
577 A144 60m red & multi	25	16

World Health Day.

"Only one Earth" Environment Emblem A145

1972, June 5 **Engr.** ***Perf. 13***

578 A145 60m lem & sl grn	30	20

UN Conference on Human Environment, Stockholm, June 5-16.

Hurdler, Olympic Emblems A146

1972, Aug. 26 **Photo.** ***Perf. 11½***

579 A146 5m Volleyball	10	10
580 A146 15m shown	12	10
581 A146 20m Athletes	12	10
582 A146 25m Soccer	15	10
583 A146 60m Swimming, women's	22	14
584 A146 80m Running	35	20
a Souv. sheet of 6	2.25	2.25
Nos. 579-584 (6)	1.06	74

20th Olympic Games, Munich, Aug. 26-Sept. 11. No. 584a contains 6 imperf. stamps similar to Nos. 579-584. Sold for 500m.

Chessboard and Pieces A147

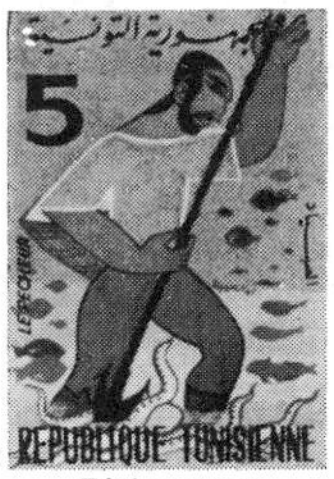

Fisherman A148

1972, Sept. 25 **Photo.** ***Perf. 11½***

585 A147 60m grn & multi	1.00	50

20th Men's Chess Olympiad, Skopje, Jugoslavia, Sept.-Oct.

1972, Oct. 23 **Litho.** ***Perf. 13½***

586 A148 5m shown	10	8
587 A148 10m Basket maker	15	10
588 A148 25m Musician	20	10
589 A148 50m Married Berber woman	30	15
590 A148 60m Flower merchant	30	15
591 A148 80m Festival	42	16
a Souvenir sheet of 6, #586-591	2.25	2.25
Nos. 586-591 (6)	1.47	74

Life in Tunisia. No. 591a exists perf. & imperf. Sold for 500m.

Post Office, Tunis A149

Litho. & Engr.
1972, Dec. 8 ***Perf. 13***

592 A149 25m ver, org & blk	16	10

Stamp Day.

Dome of the Rock, Jerusalem A150

1973, Jan. 22 **Photo.** ***Perf. 13½***

593 A150 25m multi	65	35

Globe, Pen and Quill A151

Family A152

Design: 60m, Lyre and minaret.

1973, Mar. 19 **Photo.** ***Perf. 14x13½***

594 A151 25m gold, brt mag & brn	15	10
595 A151 60m bl & multi	20	15

9th Congress of Arab Writers.

1973, Apr. 2 ***Perf. 11½***

Design: 25m, profiles and dove.

596 A152 20m grn & multi	15	10
597 A152 25m lil & multi	20	10

Family planning.

"10" and Bird Feeding Young A153

Design: 60m, "10" made of grain and bread, and hand holding spoon.

1973, Apr. 26 **Photo.** ***Perf. 11½***

598 A153 25m multi	15	10
599 A153 60m multi	20	10

World Food Program, 10th anniversary.

Roman Head and Ship A154

Drawings of Tools and: 25m, Mosaic with ostriches and camel. 30m, Mosaic with 4 heads and 4 emblems. 40m, Punic stele to the sun (vert.). 60m, Outstretched hand and arm of Christian preacher; symbols of 4 Evangelists. 75m, 17th century potsherd with Arabic inscription (vert.).

1973, May 6

600 A154 5m multi	8	8
601 A154 25m multi	12	12
602 A154 30m multi	22	15
603 A154 40m multi	25	15
604 A154 60m multi	30	12
605 A154 75m multi	32	12
a Souvenir sheet of 6	2.75	2.75
Nos. 600-605 (6)	1.29	74

UNESCO campaign to save Carthage. No. 605a contains 6 imperf. stamps similar to Nos. 600-605. Sold for 500m.

Overlapping Circles A155

Map of Africa as Festival Emblem A156

Design: 75m, Printed circuit board.

1973, May 17 **Photo.** ***Perf. 14x13½***

606 A155 60m yel & multi	20	15
607 A155 75m vio & multi	25	20

5th Intl. Telecommunications Day.

1973, July 15 **Photo.** ***Perf. 13½x13***

Design: 40m, African heads, festival emblem in eye.

608 A156 25m multi	20	15
609 A156 40m multi	25	20

Pan-African Youth Festival, Tunis.

Scout Emblem and Pennants — A157

1973, July 23 Litho. *Perf. 13½x13*
610 A157 25m multi 20 15

International Boy Scout Organization.

Crescent-shaped Racing Cars — A158

1973, July 30 *Perf. 13x13½*
611 A158 60m multi 25 15

2nd Pan-Arab auto race.

Highway Cloverleaf A159

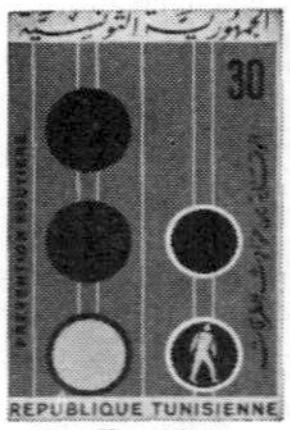

Traffic Lights and Signs — A160

Stylized Camel — A161

Perf. 12½x13, 13x12½
1973, Sept. 28 Litho.
612 A159 25m lt bl & multi 20 10
613 A160 30m multi 25 15

Highway safety campaign.

1973, Oct. 8 Photo. *Perf. 13½*

Design: 10m, Stylized bird and philatelic symbols (horiz.).

614 A161 10m multi 20 15
615 A161 65m multi 25 15

Stamp Day.

Copernicus A162

African Unity A163

Lithographed and Engraved
1973, Oct. 16 *Perf. 13x12½*
616 A162 60m blk & multi 25 15

500th anniversary of the birth of Nicolaus Copernicus (1473-1543), Polish astronomer.

1973, Nov. 4 Photo. *Perf. 14x13½*
617 A163 25m blk & multi 25 15

10th anniv. of the OAU.

Handshake and Emblems A164

Globe, Hand Holding Carnation A165

1973, Nov. 15 Litho. *Perf. 14½x14*
618 A164 65m yel & multi 30 15

25th anniv. of Intl. Criminal Police Org.

1973, Dec. 10 Photo. *Perf. 11½*
619 A165 60m blk & multi 30 20

25th anniv. of Universal Declaration of Human Rights.

WMO Headquarters and Emblem — A166

Design: 60m, Globe and emblem.

1973, Dec. 24 Litho. *Perf. 14x14½*
620 A166 25m multi 20 14
621 A166 60m multi 25 16

Intl. meteorological cooperation, cent.

Bourguiba in the Desert, 1945 A167

Scientist with Microscope A168

Portraits of Pres. Habib Bourguiba: 25m, Exile transfer from Galite Island to Ile de la Groix, France, 1954. 60m, Addressing crowd, 1974. 75m, In Victory Parade, 1955. 100m, In 1934.

1974, Mar. 2 Photo. *Perf. 11½*
622 A167 15m plum & multi 10 10
623 A167 25m multi 15 15
624 A167 60m multi 20 15
625 A167 75m multi 30 20
626 A167 100m multi 35 25
a Souvenir sheet of 5, #622-626 1.50 1.50
Nos. 622-626 (5) 1.10 85

40th anniv. of the Neo-Destour Party. No. 626a sold for 500m. Issued perf. and imperf.; same value.

1974, Mar. 21 *Perf. 14*
627 A168 60m multi 40 20

6th African Congress of Micropaleontology, Mar. 21-Apr. 3.

Woman with Telephones and Globe — A169

Pres. Bourguiba and Sun Flower Emblem — A171

WPY Emblem and Symbolic Design A170

Design: 60m, Telephone dial, telephones, wires.

1974, July 1 Photo. *Perf. 11½*
628 A169 15m multi 16 10
629 A169 60m multi 35 15

Introduction of international automatic telephone dialing system.

1974, Aug. 19 Photo. *Perf. 11½*
630 A170 110m multi 40 20

World Population Year.

1974, Sept. 12 Photo. *Perf. 11½*

Designs: 60m, Bourguiba and cactus flower (horiz.). 200m, Bourguiba and verbena (horiz.).

631 A171 25m blk, ultra & grnsh bl 15 15
632 A171 60m red, car & yel 20 15
633 A171 200m blk, brt lil & grn 65 40
a Souvenir sheet of 3 1.50 1.50

Congress of the Socialist Destour Party. No. 633a contains 3 imperf. stamps similar to Nos. 631-633.

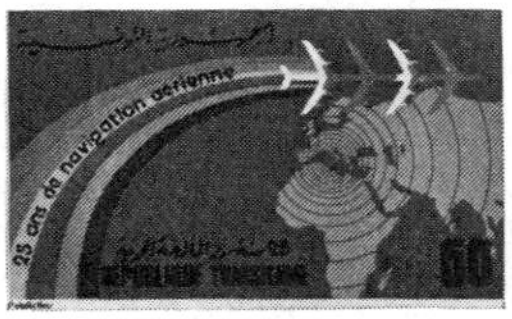

Jets Flying over Old World Map A172

1974, Sept. 23 Litho. *Perf. 12½*
634 A172 60m brn & multi 35 20

25th anniversary of Tunisian aviation.

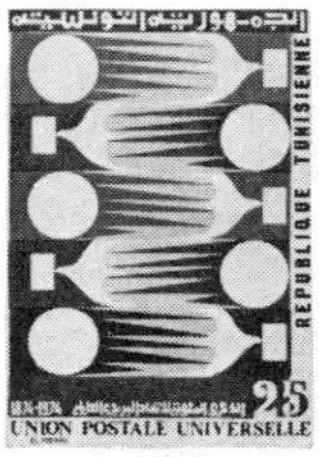

Symbolic Carrier Pigeons — A173

Handshake, Letter, UPU Emblem — A174

1974, Oct. 9 Photo. *Perf. 13*
635 A173 25m multi 20 12
636 A174 60m multi 30 15

Centenary of Universal Postal Union.

Le Bardo, National Assembly A175

Pres. Bourguiba Ballot A176

1974, Nov. 3 Photo. *Perf. 11½*
637 A175 25m grn, bl & blk 20 20
638 A176 100m org & blk 35 20

Legislative (25m) and presidential elections (100m), Nov. 1974.

Mailman with Letters and Bird — A177

Water Carrier — A178

1974, Dec. 5 Litho. *Perf. 14½x14*
639 A177 75m lt vio & multi 30 16

Stamp Day.

1975, Feb. 17 Photo. *Perf. 13½*
640 A178 5m shown 5 5
641 A178 15m Perfume vendor 8 6
642 A178 25m Laundresses 12 8
643 A178 60m Potter 18 8
644 A178 110m Fruit vendor 40 15
a Souvenir sheet of 5, #640-644 1.50 1.50
Nos. 640-644 (5) 83 42

Life in Tunisia. No. 644a sold for 500m. Issued perf. and imperf.; same value.

Steel Tower, Skyscraper — A179

Geometric Designs and Arrow A180

Perf. 14x13½, 13½x14
1975, Mar. 17 Photo.
645 A179 25m yel, org & blk 12 10
646 A180 65m ultra & multi 22 12

Union of Arab Engineers, 13th Conference, Tunis, Mar. 17-21.

Brass Coffeepot and Plate A181

Designs: 15m, Horse and rider. 25m, Still life. 30m, Bird cage (vert.). 40m, Woman with earrings (vert.). 60m, Design patterns.

1975, Apr. 14 ***Perf. 13x14, 14x13***

647	A181	10m blk & multi	10	10
648	A181	15m blk & multi	12	10
649	A181	25m blk & multi	16	12
650	A181	30m blk & multi	16	10
651	A181	40m blk & multi	20	12
652	A181	60m blk & multi	22	15
		Nos. 647-652 (6)	96	69

Artisans and their works.

Communications and Weather Symbols — A182

1975, May 17 **Photo.** ***Perf. 11½***

653 A182 50m lt bl & multi 20 14

World Telecommunications Day (communications serving meteorology).

Youth and Hope A183

Tunisian Woman, IWY Emblem A184

Design: 65m, Bourguiba arriving at La Goulette, Tunis (horiz.).

1975, June 1 **Photo.** ***Perf. 11½***

654	A183	25m multi	14	10
655	A183	65m multi	22	15

Victory (independence), 20th anniversary.

1975, June 19 **Litho.** ***Perf. 14x13½***

656 A184 110m multi 40 25

International Women's Year.

Children Crossing Street A185

1975, July 5 **Photo.** ***Perf. 13½x14***

657 A185 25m multi 15 10

Highway safety campaign, July 1-Sept. 30.

Djerbian Minaret, Hotel and Marina, Jerba A186

Old and new Tunisia: 15m, 17th century minaret and modern hotel, Tunis. 20m, Fortress, earring and hotel, Monastir. 65m, View of Sousse, hotel and pendant. 500m, Town wall, mosque and palms, Tozeur. 1d, Mosques and Arab ornaments, Kairouan.

1975, July 12 **Litho.** ***Perf. 14x14½***

658	A186	10m multi	8	8
659	A186	15m multi	8	8
660	A186	20m multi	12	8
661	A186	65m multi	22	12
662	A186	500m multi	1.75	75
663	A186	1d multi	3.00	1.40
		Nos. 658-663 (6)	5.25	2.51

Victors — A187

Symbolic Ship A188

1975, Aug. 23 **Photo.** ***Perf. 13½***

664	A187	25m ol & multi	15	10
665	A188	50m bl & multi	20	12

7th Mediterranean Games, Algiers, Aug. 23-Sept. 6.

Flowers in Vase, Birds Holding Letters — A189

1975, Sept. 29 **Litho.** ***Perf. 13½x13***

666 A189 100m bl & multi 30 15

Stamp Day.

Sadiki College, Young Bourguiba A190

Engr. & Litho.

1975, Nov. 17 ***Perf. 13***

667 A190 25m sep, org & ol 15 10

Sadiki College, centenary.

Duck — A191

Vergil — A192

Mosaics: 10m, Fish. 25m, Lioness (horiz.). 60m, Head of Medusa (horiz.). 75m, Circus spectators.

1976, Feb. 16 **Photo.** ***Perf. 13***

668	A191	5m multi	8	5
669	A191	10m multi	9	5
670	A192	25m multi	15	8
671	A192	60m multi	20	8
672	A192	75m multi	25	12
673	A192	100m multi	32	15
a		Souvenir sheet of 6, #668-673	1.90	1.90
		Nos. 668-673 (6)	1.09	53

Tunisian mosaics, 2nd-5th centuries. No. 673a sold for 500m. Issued perf. and imperf.; same value.

Telephone A193

1976, Mar. 10 **Litho.** ***Perf. 14x13½***

674 A193 150m bl & multi 42 25

Centenary of first telephone call by Alexander Graham Bell, Mar. 10, 1876.

Pres. Bourguiba and "20" — A194

Pres. Bourguiba and: 100m, "20" and symbolic Tunisian flag. 150m, "Tunisia" rising from darkness, and 20 flowers.

1976, Mar. 20 **Photo.** ***Perf. 11½***

675	A194	40m multi	9	8
676	A194	100m multi	20	12
677	A194	150m multi	30	12

Souvenir Sheets

Perf. 11½, Imperf.

678	A194	Sheet of 3, multi	1.25	1.25
a		50m like 40m	8	5
b		200m like 100m	35	15
c		250m like 150m	45	22

20th anniversary of independence.

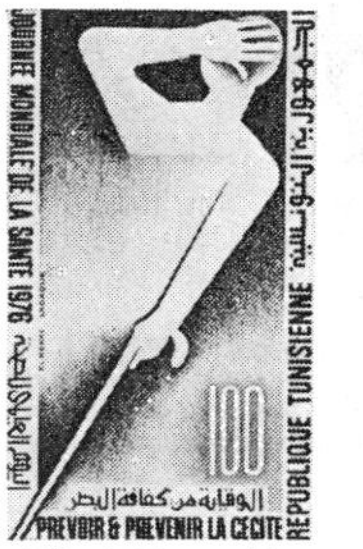

Blind Man with Cane A195

Procession and Buildings A196

1976, Apr. 7 **Engr.** ***Perf. 13***

679 A195 100m blk & red 42 16

World Health Day: "Foresight prevents blindness."

1976, May 31 **Photo.** ***Perf. 12x11½***

680 A196 40m multi 20 15

Habitat, UN Conf. on Human Settlements, Vancouver, Canada, May 31-June 11.

Face and Hands Decorated with Henna — A197

Designs: 50m, Sponge fishing at Jerba. 65m, Textile industry. 110m, Pottery of Guellala.

1976, June 15 **Photo.** ***Perf. 13x13½***

681	A197	40m multi	10	10
682	A197	50m multi	12	10
683	A197	65m multi	20	12
684	A197	110m multi	38	15

Old and new Tunisia.

The Spirit of '76, by Archibald M. Willard — A198

1976, July 4 ***Perf. 13x14***

685 A198 200m multi 80 50

Souvenir Sheets

Perf. 13x14, Imperf.

686 A198 500m multi 2.00 2.00

American Bicentennial.

Running A199

Montreal Olympic Games Emblem and: 75m, Bicycling. 120m, Peace dove.

1976, July 17 **Photo.** ***Perf. 11½***

687	A199	50m gray, red & blk	15	10
688	A199	75m red, yel & blk	20	12
689	A199	120m org & multi	35	22

21st Olympic Games, Montreal, Canada, July 17-Aug. 1.

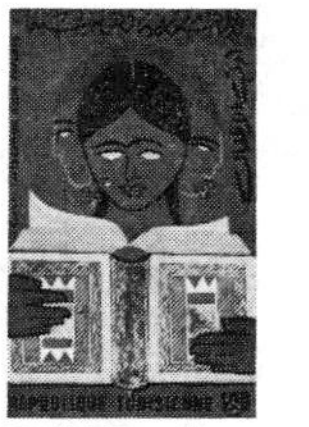

Child Reading A200

Heads and Bird A201

1976, Aug. 23 **Litho.** ***Perf. 13***

690 A200 100m brn & multi 35 15

Books for children.

1976, Sept. 30 **Litho.** ***Perf. 13***

691 A201 150m org & multi 42 20

Non-aligned Countries, 15th anniv. of 1st Conference.

Mouradite Mausoleum, 17th Century — A202

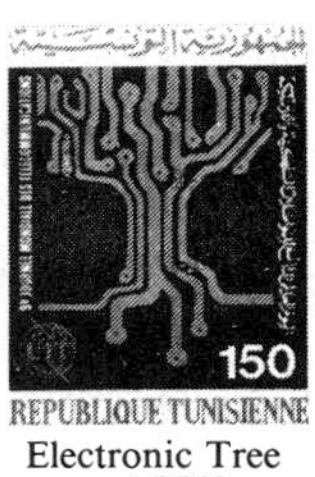

Electronic Tree and ITU Emblem — A204

Globe and Emblem
A203

Designs: 100m, Minaret, Kairawan Great Mosque and psalmodist. 150m, Monastir Ribat monastery and Alboracq (sphinx). 200m, Barber's Mosque, Kairawan and man's bust.

1976, Oct. 25 Photo. *Perf. 14*

692	A202 85m multi	22	10
693	A202 100m multi	25	12
694	A202 150m multi	40	20
695	A202 200m multi	60	30

Cultural heritage.

1976, Dec. 24 Photo. *Perf. 13x14*

696	A203 150m multi	50	25

25th anniv. of UN Postal Administration.

1977, May 17 Photo. *Perf. 14x13½*

697	A204 150m multi	50	30

9th World Telecommunications Day.

"Communication," Sassenage Castle, Grenoble — A205

1977, May 19 Litho. *Perf. 13½x13*

698	A205 100m multi	50	30

10th anniv. of Intl. French Language Council.

Soccer
A206

1977, June 27 Photo. *Perf. 13½*

699	A206 150m multi	50	30

Junior World Soccer Tournament, Tunisia, June 27-July 10.

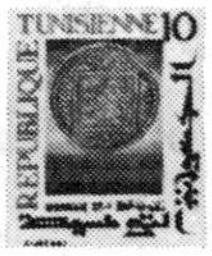

Gold Coin, 10th Century — A207

Cultural Heritage: 15m, Stele, Gorjani Cemetery, Tunis, 13th century. 20m, Floral design, 17th century illumination. 30m, Bird and flowers, glass painting, 1922. 40m, Antelope, from 11th century clay pot. 50m, Gate, Sidi Bou Said, 20th century.

1977, July 9 Photo. *Perf. 13*

700	A207 10m multi	5	5
701	A207 15m multi	5	5
702	A207 20m multi	10	5
703	A207 30m multi	12	7
704	A207 40m multi	16	10
705	A207 50m multi	22	14
a	Miniature sheet of 6, #700-705	1.00	1.00
	Nos. 700-705 (6)	70	46

> The Scott Catalogue value is a retail price, what you could expect to pay for the stamp in a grade of Fine-Very Fine. The value listed is a reference which reflects recent actual dealer selling price.

"The Young Republic" and Bourguiba
A208

Diseased Knee, Gears and Globe
A210

Symbolic Cancellation, APU Emblem — A209

Habib Bourguiba and: 100m, "The Confident Republic" and 20 doves. 150m, "The Determined Republic" and 20 roses.

1977, July 25 Photo. *Perf. 13x13½*

706	A208 40m multi	22	10
707	A208 100m multi	40	15
708	A208 150m multi	65	20
a	Souvenir sheet of 3, #706-708	1.50	1.50

20th anniv. of the Republic. No. 708a sold for 500m. Exists imperf.

1977, Aug. 16 Litho. *Perf. 13x12½*

709	A209 40m multi	15	10

Arab Postal Union, 25th anniversary.

1977, Sept. 26 Photo. *Perf. 14x13½*

710	A210 120m multi	40	20

World Rheumatism Year.

Farmer, Road, Water and Electricity — A211

1977, Dec. 15 Photo. *Perf. 13½*

711	A211 40m multi	15	10

Rural development.

Factory Workers
A212

Pres. Bourguiba, Torch and "9"
A213

Designs: 20m, Bus driver and trains (horiz.). 40m, Farmer driving tractor (horiz.).

1978, Mar. 6 *Perf. 13x14, 14x13*

712	A212 20m rose red & multi	10	10
713	A212 40m blk & grn	15	10
714	A212 100m multi	30	15

5th development plan, creation of new jobs.

1978, Apr. 9 Engr. *Perf. 13*

Design: 60m, Pres. Bourguiba and "9."

715	A213 40m multi	12	10
716	A213 60m multi	16	10

40th anniversary of first fight for independence, Apr. 9, 1938.

Policeman
A214

Tunisian Goalkeeper
A215

1978, May 2 Photo. *Perf. 13x13½*

717	A214 150m multi	50	22

6th Regional African Interpol Conference, Tunis, May 2-5.

1978, June 1 Photo. *Perf. 13x14*

Designs: 150m., Soccer player, maps of South America and Africa, flags.

718	A215 40m multi	15	10
719	A215 150m multi	50	30

11th World Cup Soccer Championship, Argentina, June 1-25.

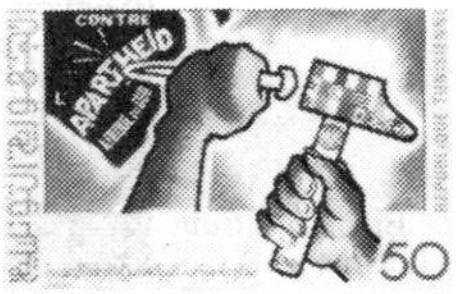

Destruction of Apartheid, Map of South Africa — A216

Design: 100m, White and black doves flying in unison.

1978, Aug. 30 Litho. *Perf. 13½x14*

720	A216 50m multi	15	10
721	A216 100m multi	30	15

Fight against Apartheid.

"Pollution is a Plague"
A217

"Eradication of Smallpox"
A218

Designs: 50m, "The Sea, mankind's patrimony." 120m, "Greening of the desert."

1978, Sept. 11 Photo. *Perf. 14x13*

722	A217 10m multi	5	5
723	A217 50m multi	20	10
724	A217 120m multi	50	20

Protection of the environment.

1978, Oct. 16 Litho. *Perf. 12½*

725	A218 150m multi	42	25

Global eradication of smallpox.

Jerba Wedding
A219

Designs: 5m, Horseman from Zlass (vert.). 75m, Women potters from the Mogods. 100m, Dove over Marabout Sidi Mahrez cupolas, Tunis. 500m, Plowing in Jenduba. 1d, Spring Festival in Tozeur (man on swing).

1978, Nov. 1 Photo. *Perf. 13*

726	A219 5m multi	5	5
727	A219 60m multi	16	10
728	A219 75m multi	25	12
729	A219 100m multi	35	16
730	A219 500m multi	2.25	80
731	A219 1d multi	3.50	1.50
	Nos. 726-731 (6)	6.56	2.73

Traditional Arab calligraphy.

Lenin and Red Banner over Kremlin — A220

Farhat Hached, Union Emblem — A221

1978, Nov. 7 *Perf. 13½*

732	A220 150m multi	42	22

Russian October Revolution, 60th anniv.

1978, Dec. 5 Photo. *Perf. 14*

733	A221 50m multi	16	10

Farhat Hached (1914-1952), founder of General Union of Tunisian Workers.

Family
A222

Sun with Man's Face
A223

1978, Dec. 15 Photo. *Perf. 13½*

734	A222 50m multi	22	10

Tunisian Family Planning Assoc., 10th anniv.

1978, Dec. 25 *Perf. 14*

735	A223 100m multi	40	20

Sun as a source of light and energy.

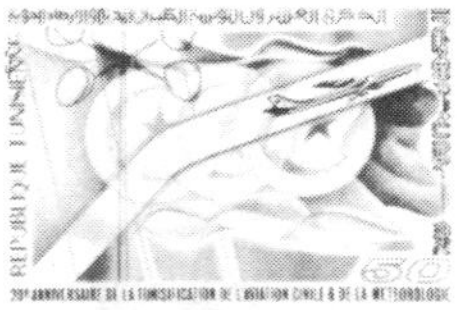

Plane, Weather Map and Instruments — A224

1978, Dec. 29

736	A224 50m multi	20	12

Tunisian civil aviation and meteorology, 20th anniv.

Habib Bourguiba and Constitution — A225

1979, May 31 Photo. ***Perf. 14x13½***
737 A225 50m multi 15 10

20th anniversary of Constitution.

El Kantaoui Port A226

1979, June 3 ***Perf. 13½x14***
738 A226 150m multi 42 15

Development of El Kantaoui as a resort area.

View of Korbous — A227

Landscapes: 100m, Mides.

Perf. 12½x13½
1979, July 14 Photo.
739 A227 50m multi 12 5
740 A227 100m multi 22 7

Bow Net Weaving A228

Pres. Bourguiba, "10" and Hands A229

1979, Aug. 15 Photo. ***Perf. 11½***
741 A228 10m shown 7 5
742 A228 50m Beekeeping 16 7

1979, Sept. 5
743 A229 50m multi 20 10

Socialist Destour Party, 10th Congress.

Modes of Communication, ITU Emblem — A230

1979, Sept. 20 Litho. ***Perf. 11½***
744 A230 150m multi 50 30

3rd World Telecommunications Exhibition, Geneva, Sept. 20-26.

Arab Achievements — A231

1979, Oct. 1 ***Perf. 14½***
745 A231 50m multi 16 8

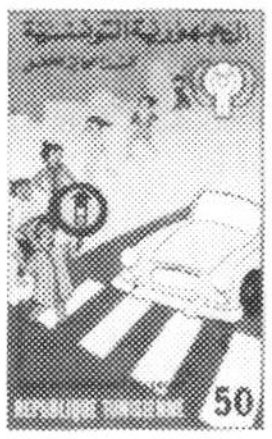

Children Crossing Street, IYC Emblem — A232

1979, Oct. 16 ***Perf. 14x13½***
746 A232 50m shown 15 5
747 A232 100m Child and birds 35 20

International Year of the Child.

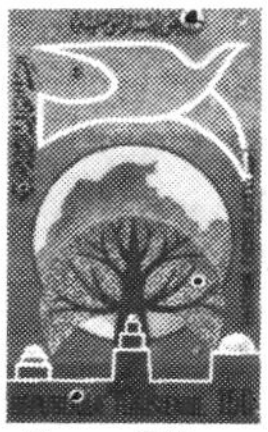

Dove, Olive Tree, Map of Tunisia A233

Woman Wearing Crown A234

1979, Nov. 1 Litho. ***Perf. 12***
748 A233 150m multi 50 30

2nd International Olive Oil Year.

1979, Nov. 3 ***Perf. 14½***
749 A234 50m multi 15 10

Central Bank of Tunisia, 20th anniversary.

Children and Jujube Tree — A235

1979, Dec. 25 Litho. ***Perf. 15x14½***
750 A235 20m shown 10 5
751 A235 30m Peacocks 15 5
752 A235 70m Goats 25 8
753 A235 85m Girl, date palm 30 12

Postal Code Introduction — A236

1980, Mar. 20 Photo. ***Perf. 14***
754 A236 50m multi 15 5

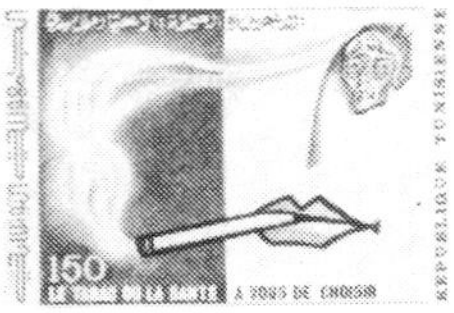

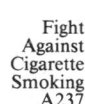

Fight Against Cigarette Smoking A237

1980, Apr. 7
755 A237 150m multi 42 16

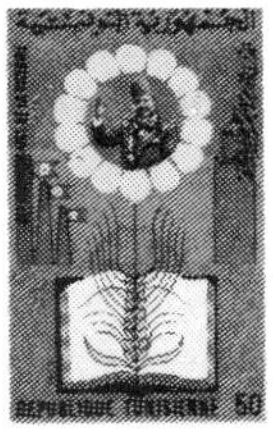

Pres. Bourguiba in Flower, Open Book — A238

1980, June 1 Photo. ***Perf. 11½***
756 A238 50m shown 15 10
757 A238 100m Dove, Bourguiba, mosque 30 20

Victory (independence), 25th anniversary.

Butterfly and Gymnast A239

1980, June 3 Photo. ***Perf. 12x11½***
Granite Paper
758 A239 100m multi 30 20

Turin Gymnastic Games, June 1-7.

Artisans
A240 A241

1980, July 21 Photo. ***Perf. 13½***
759 A240 30m multi 10 5
760 A241 75m multi 20 10

ibn-Khaldun (1332-1406), Historian A242

Avicenna (Arab Physician), Birth Millenium A243

1980, July 28 ***Perf. 14***
761 A242 50m multi 15 8

1980, Aug. 18 Engr. ***Perf. 12½x13***
762 A243 100m redsh brn & sep 30 12

Arab Achievements — A244

1980, Aug. 25 Photo. ***Perf. 13½x14***
763 A244 50m multi 15 8

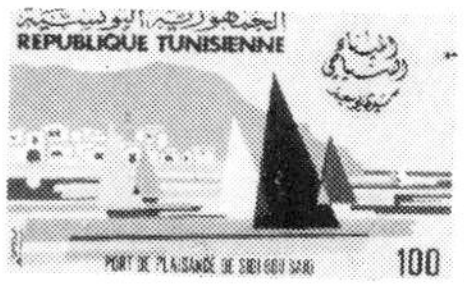

Port Sidi bou Said A245

1980, Sept. 4 ***Perf. 14***
764 A245 100m multi 35 16

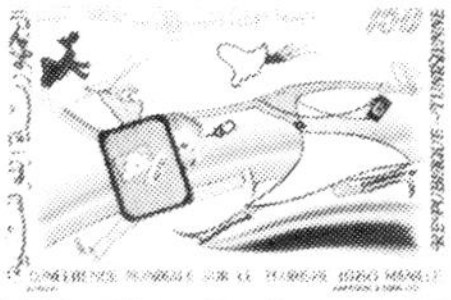

World Tourism Conference, Manila, Sept. 27 — A246

1980, Sept. 27 Photo. ***Perf. 14***
765 A246 150m multi 40 20

Wedding in Jerba, by Yahia (1903-1969) — A247

1980, Oct. 1 ***Perf. 12***
766 A247 50m multi 20 15

Tozeur-Nefta International Airport Opening — A248

1980, Oct. 13 Photo. ***Perf. 13x13½***
767 A248 85m multi 22 10

Eye and Text A249

1980, Oct. 26 Litho. ***Perf. 13½x14***
768 A249 100m multi 30 20

7th Afro-Asian Ophthalmologic Congress.

Hegira, 1500th Anniv. A250

1980, Nov. 9

769 A250 50m Spiderweb 15 8
770 A250 80m City skyline 22 15

Film Strip and Woman's Head — A251

1980, Nov. 15 Photo. *Perf. 14x13½*

771 A251 100m multi 30 15

Carthage Film Festival.

Orchid A252

1980, Nov. 17 *Perf. 13½x14*

772 A252 20m shown 5 5
773 A252 25m Wild cyclamen 8 5

Size: 39x27mm

Perf. 14

774 A252 50m Mouflon 15 8
775 A252 100m Golden eagle 25 12

Campaign to Save Kairouan Mosque A253

1980, Dec. 29 Photo. *Perf. 12*

Granite Paper

776 A253 85m multi 22 14

Heinrich von Stephan (1831-1897), Founder of UPU — A254

Blood Donors' Assoc., 20th Anniv. — A255

1981, Jan. 7

777 A254 150m multi 42 30

1981, Mar. 5 Litho. *Perf. 14x13½*

778 A255 75m multi 20 14

The indexes in each volume of the Scott Catalogue contain many listings which help to identify stamps.

Pres. Bourguiba and Flag — A256

1981, Mar. 20 Photo. *Perf. 12x11½*

Granite Paper

779 A256 50m shown 15 10
780 A256 60m Dove, "25" 16 10
781 A256 85m Doves 22 12
782 A256 120m Victory on winged horse 35 16
a Souvenir sheet of 4, #779-782 1.20 1.20

25th anniversary of independence. No. 782 sold for 500m. Exists imperf.

Pres. Bourguiba and Flower A257

1981, Apr. 10 Photo. *Perf. 12x11½*

783 A257 50m shown 15 8
784 A257 75m Bourguiba, flower, diff. 20 12

Destourien Socialist Party Congress.

Mosque Entrance, Mahdia A258

1981, Apr. 20 *Perf. 13½*

785 A258 50m shown 22 8
786 A258 85m Tozeur Great Mosque, vert. 50 10
787 A258 100m Needle Rocks, Tabarka 55 15

13th World Telecommunications Day — A259

1981, May 17 Litho. *Perf. 14x15*

788 A259 150m multi 42 25

Youth Festival A260

Kemal Ataturk (1881-1938) First President of Turkey A261

1981, June 2 Photo. *Perf. 11½*

Granite Paper

789 A260 100m multi 30 20

1981, June 15 Photo. *Perf. 14*

790 A261 150m multi 65 25

Skifa, Mahdia — A262

1981, July 15 Photo. *Perf. 11½x12*

791 A262 150m multi 42 30

Mohammed Tahar Ben Achour (1879-1973), Scholar — A263

1981, Aug. 6 *Perf. 13*

792 A263 200m multi 80 35

25th Anniv. of Personal Status Code (Women's Liberation) A264

1981, Aug. 13

793 A264 50m Woman 15 8
794 A264 100m shown 25 15

Intl. Year of the Disabled — A265

1981, Sept. 21 Photo. *Perf. 13½*

795 A265 250m multi 65 50

Pilgrimage to Mecca — A266

World Food Day — A267

1981, Oct. 7 Photo. *Perf. 13½*

796 A266 50m multi 15 8

1981, Oct. 16 Litho. *Perf. 12*

Granite Paper

797 A267 200m multi 65 42

Traditional Jewelry A268

Designs: 150m, Mneguech silver earrings (vert.). 180m Mahfdha (silver medallion worn by married women). 200m, Essalta gold headdress (vert.).

1981, Dec. 7 Photo. *Perf. 14*

798 A268 150m multi 50 25
799 A268 180m multi 65 30
800 A268 200m multi 80 35

Bizerta Bridge A269

1981, Dec. 14 Litho. *Perf. 12x11½*

Granite Paper

801 A269 230m multi 60 35

Chemist Compounding Honey Mixture, Manuscript Miniature, 1224 — A270

1982, Apr. 3 Photo. *Perf. 13*

802 A270 80m multi 25 14

Arab Chemists' Union, 16th anniv.

Oceanic Enterprise Symposium, Tunis, May 12-14 A271

The Productive Family Employment Campaign A272

1982, May 12 Photo. *Perf. 13½*

803 A271 150m multi 50 30

1982, June 26 *Perf. 12½*

Granite Paper

804 A272 80m multi 22 10

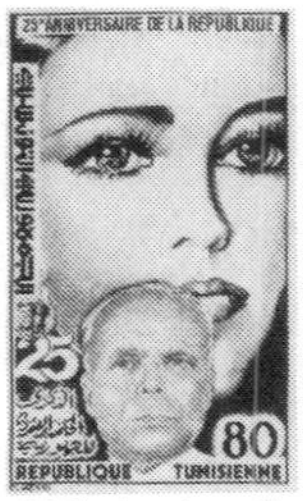

25th Anniv. of Republic — A273

Scouting Year — A274

Pres. Bourguiba and Various Women.

1982, July 25 Litho. *Perf. 14x13½*

805 A273 80m multi 20 10
806 A273 100m multi 30 15
807 A273 200m multi 50 30

Perf. 14½x14, 14x14½

1982, Aug. 23

808 A274 80m multi 20 10
809 A274 200m multi 42 20

75th anniv. of scouting and 50th anniv. of scouting in Tunisia (80m).

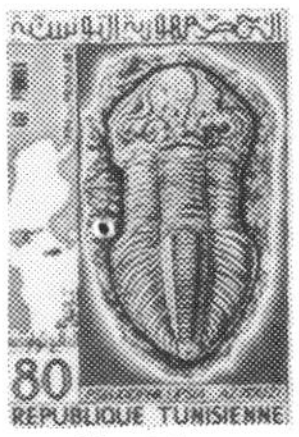

Tunisian Fossils — A274a

30th Anniv. of Arab Postal Union — A275

Designs: 80m, Pseudophillipsia azzouzi, vert. 200m, Mediterraneotrigonia cherahilensis, vert. 280m, Numidiopleura enigmatica. 300m, Micreschara tunisiensis, vert. 500m, Mantelliceras pervinquieri, vert. 1000m, Elephas africanavus.

1982, Sept. 20 Photo. *Perf. 11½x12*

809A A274a 80m multi 20 10
809B A274a 200m multi 20 12
809C A274a 280m multi 90 45
809D A274a 300m multi 1.00 50
809E A274a 500m multi 1.60 80
809F A274a 1000m multi 3.50 1.60
Nos. 809A-809F (6) 7.40 3.57

1982, Sept. 29 *Perf. 14x13½*

810 A275 80m Woman, envelopes 22 10

Size: 23x40mm

811 A275 200m Woman, buildings 50 22

ITU Plenipotentiaries Conference, Nairobi — A276

1982, Oct. 1 Photo. *Perf. 12*

Granite Paper

812 A276 200m multi 50 35

World Food Day A277

Tahar Haddad (1899-1935), Social Reformer A278

1982, Oct. 16 Litho. *Perf. 13*

813 A277 200m multi 50 22

1982, Oct. 25 Engr.

814 A278 200m dk brn 50 20

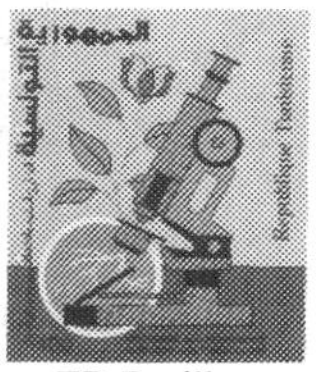

TB Bacillus Centenary A279

Folk Songs and Stories A280

1982, Nov. 16 Litho. *Perf. 13½*

815 A279 100m multi 25 12

1982, Nov. 22 Photo. *Perf. 14*

816 A280 20m Dancing in the Rain 5 5
817 A280 30m Woman Sweeping 8 5
818 A280 70m Fisherman and the Child 15 8
819 A280 80m Rooster and the Oranges, horiz. 16 8
820 A280 100m Woman and the Mirror, horiz. 25 12
821 A280 120m The Two Girls, horiz. 30 12
Nos. 816-821 (6) 99 50

Intl. Palestinian Solidarity Day — A281

1982, Nov. 30 Litho. *Perf. 13x12*

822 A281 80m multi 20 10

Farhat Hached (1914-1952) A282

Bourguiba Dam Opening A283

1982, Dec. 6 Engr. *Perf. 13*

823 A282 80m brn red 22 10

1982, Dec. 20 Litho. *Perf. 13½*

824 A283 80m multi 20 10

Environmental Training College Opening — A284

1982, Dec. 29 Photo. *Perf. 11½*

Granite Paper

825 A284 80m multi 20 10

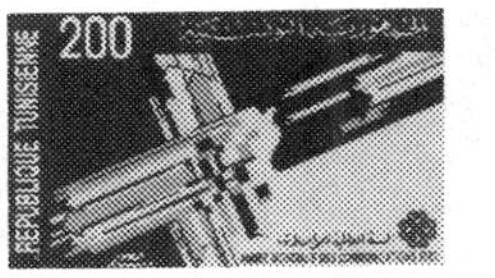

World Communications Year — A285

1983, May 17 Litho. *Perf. 13½x14*

826 A285 200m multi 42 22

20th Anniv. of Org. of African Unity — A286

Aly Ben Ayed (1930-1972), Actor — A288

30th Anniv. of Customs Cooperation Council — A287

1983, May 25 Photo. *Perf. 12*

Granite Paper

827 A286 230m ultra & grnsh bl 55 35

1983, May 30 Litho. *Perf. 13½*

828 A287 100m multi 25 12

1983, Aug. 15 Engr. *Perf. 13*

829 A288 80m dk car, dl red & gray 20 10

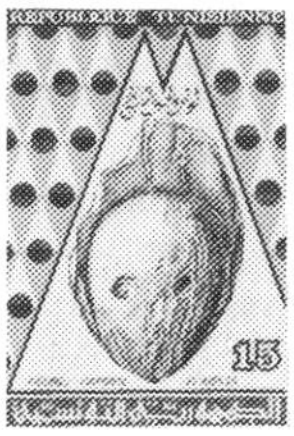

Stone-carved Face, El-Mekta — A289

Pre-historic artifacts: 20m, Neolithic necklace, Kel el-Agab. 30m, Mill and grindstone, Redeyef. 40m, Orynx head rock carving, Gafsa. 80m, Dolmen Mactar. 100m, Acheulian Bi-face flint, El-Mekta.

1983, Aug. 20 Photo. *Perf. 11½x12*

830 A289 15m multi 5 5
831 A289 20m multi 5 5
832 A289 30m multi 8 5
833 A289 40m multi 10 5
834 A289 80m multi 20 8
835 A289 100m multi 22 8
Nos. 830-835 (6) 70 36

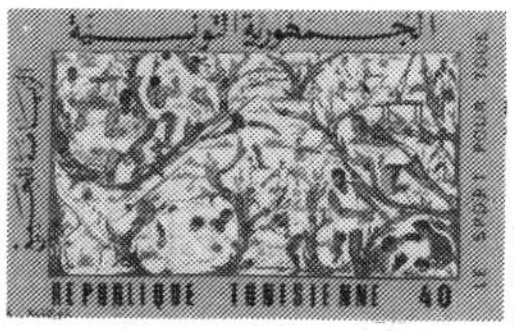

Sports for All A290

1983, Sept. 27 Litho. *Perf. 12½*

836 A290 40m multi 10 8

World Fishing Day A291

1983, Oct. 17 *Perf. 14½*

837 A291 200m multi 42 16

Evacuation of French Troops, 20th Anniv. — A292

1983, Oct. 17 Litho. *Perf. 14x13½*

838 A292 80m multi 20 10

Tapestry Weaver, by Hedi Khayachi (1882-1948) — A293

1983, Nov. 22 Photo. *Perf. 11½*

Granite Paper

839 A293 80m multi 20 12

Natl. Allegiance A294

Jet, Woman's Head, Emblem A295

1983, Nov. 30 Litho. *Perf. 14½*

840 A294 100m Children, flag 25 10

1983, Dec. 21 *Perf. 13½*

841 A295 150m multi 35 15

Pres. Bourguiba A296

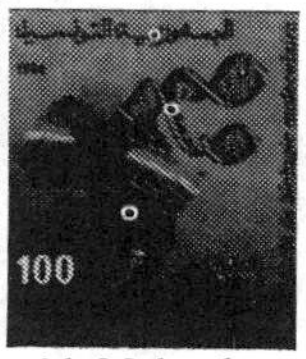

4th Molecular Biology Symposium A297

Destourien Socialist Party, 50th Anniv.: Portraits of Bourguiba. 200m, 230m horiz.

Perf. 12½x12, 12x12½

1984, Mar. 2 Photo.

Granite Paper

842 A296 40m multi 10 8
843 A296 70m multi 15 10
844 A296 80m multi 20 12
845 A296 150m multi 35 20
846 A296 200m multi 42 22
847 A296 230m multi 55 35
Nos. 842-847 (6) 1.77 1.07

1984, Apr. 3 *Perf. 13½x13*

848 A297 100m Map, diagram 25 12

Ibn El Jazzar, Physician A298

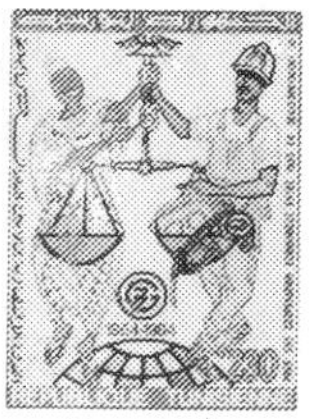

Economic Development Program, 20th Anniv. A299

1984, May 15 Photo. *Perf. 14x13*
849 A298 80m multi 20 10

1984, June 15 *Perf. 11½*
Granite Paper
850 A299 230m Merchant, worker 50 20

Coquette, The Sorceress and the Fairy Carabosse
A300

Perf. 13½x14, 14x13½
1984, Aug. 27 Photo.
851 A300 20m shown 5 5
852 A300 80m Counting with fingers 20 10
853 A300 100m Boy riding horse, vert. 25 10

Legends and folk tales.

Family and Education Org., 20th Anniv.
A301

1984, Sept. 4 *Perf. 13x14*
854 A301 80m Family looking into future 20 10

Natl. Heritage Protection
A302

Aboul-Qasim Chabbi, Poet (1909-1934)
A303

1984, Sept. 13 *Perf. 14*
855 A302 100m Medina Mosque Minaret, hand 25 10

1984, Oct. 9 Engr. *Perf. 12½x13*
856 A303 100m multi 25 10

40th Anniv., ICAO
A304

1984, Oct. 25 Photo. *Perf. 13*
857 A304 200m Aircraft tail, bird 50 25

Sahara Festival
A305

1984, Dec. 3 Litho. *Perf. 14½*
858 A305 20m Musicians 5 5

20th Anniv., Intelsat
A306

Perf. 13½x14½
1984, Dec. 25 Photo.
859 A306 100m Tunisian Earth Station 25 14

Mediterranean Landscape, by Jilani Abdelwaheb (Abdul) — A307

1984, Dec. 31 Photo. *Perf. 14½*
860 A307 100m multi 25 14

EXPO '85, Tsukuba, Japan
A308

1985, Mar. 20 Photo. *Perf. 12*
861 A308 200m multi 35 16

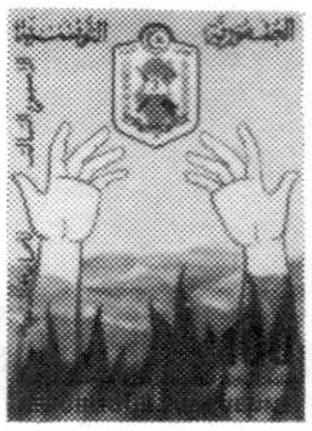

Civil Protection Week — A309

1985, May 13 Litho. *Perf. 14*
862 A309 100m Hands, water and fire 22 12

Pres. Habib Bourguiba, Crowded Pier — A310

Pres. Bourguiba: 75m, On horseback, vert. 200m, Wearing hat, vert. 230m, Waving to crowd.

1985, June 1 *Perf. 12½*
863 A310 75m multi 14 7
864 A310 100m multi 16 8
865 A310 200m multi 35 16
866 A310 230m multi 40 18

Natl. independence, 30th anniv.

Head of a Statue, Carthage and Pres. Bourguiba
A311

1985, June 4 *Perf. 14*
867 A311 250m multi 40 20

EXPO '85.

Intl. Amateur Film Festival, Kelibia — A312

Natl. Folk Tales — A313

1985, July 20 *Perf. 14½x13*
868 A312 250m multi 40 20

1985, July 29 *Perf. 14*
869 A313 25m Sun, Sun Shine Again, horiz. 5 5
870 A313 50m I Met a Man With Seven Wives 10 5
871 A313 100m Uncle Shisbene 16 8

Intl. Youth Year — A314

1985, Sept. 30 *Perf. 14½x13½*
872 A314 250m multi 42 20

The Perfumers' Courtyard, 1912, by Hedi Larnaout — A315

1985, Oct. 4 *Perf. 14*
873 A315 100m multi 20 10

Regional Bridal Costumes
A316

UN, 40th Anniv.
A317

1985, Oct. 22 *Perf. 12*
874 A316 20m Matmata 5 5
875 A316 50m Moknine 14 7
876 A316 100m Tunis 25 14

1985, Oct. 24 *Perf. 14x13½*
877 A317 250m multi 50 25

Self-Sufficiency in Food Production — A318

Perf. 13½x14½
1985, Nov. 26 Photo.
878 A318 100m Makhtar stele of feast 22 12

League of Arab States, 40th Anniv.
A319

1985, Nov. 29 Litho. *Perf. 13½x14*
879 A319 100m multi 22 12

Aziza Othmana (d. 1669) — A320

Land Law, Cent. — A321

1985, Dec. 16 Engr. *Perf. 12½x13*
880 A320 100m dk grn, hn brn & brn 22 12

1985, Dec. 25 Litho. *Perf. 13½*
881 A321 100m multi 22 12

Natl. Independence, 30th Anniv. — A322

Perf. 13x13½, 13½x13
1986, Mar. 20 Photo.
882 A322 100m Dove, vert 28 14
883 A322 120m Rocket 32 16
884 A322 280m Horse and rider 75 38
885 A322 300m Balloons, vert. 82 40
a Souv. sheet of 4, #882-885 2.20 1.10

No. 885a exists imperf.

3rd Mediterranean Rheumatology Day — A323

Intl. Geographical Ophtalmological Society Congress — A324

1986, Apr. 30 Litho. *Perf. 14x13½*
886 A323 300m multi 85 42
887 A324 380m multi 1.05 52

Prof. Hulusi Behcet (1889-1948), discovered virus causing Behcet's Disease affecting eyes and joints.

12th Destourian Socialist Party Congress
A325

1986, June 19 Photo. *Perf. 12*

888	A325	120m	shown	35	18
889	A325	300m	Torchbearer	85	42

Regional Bridal Costumes — A326

1986, Aug. 25 Litho. *Perf. 14*

890	A326	40m	Homi-Souk	12	6
891	A326	280m	Mahdia	78	40
892	A326	300m	Nabeul	82	40

Hassen Husni Abdul-Wahab (1883-1968), Historian, Archaeologist
A327

1986, Sept. 20 Engr. *Perf. 13*

893	A327	160m	dk red	45	22

Founding of Carthage, 2800th Anniv. — A328

1986, Oct. 18 Engr. *Perf. 13*

894	A328	2d	dark vio	8.00	4.00

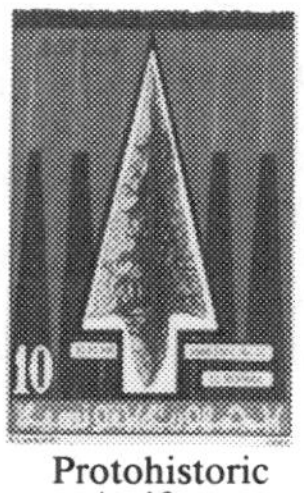

Protohistoric Artifacts
A329

Bedouins, by Ammar Farhat
A330

Design: 10m, Flint arrowhead, El Borma, c. 3000 B.C. 20m, Rock cut-out dwelling, Sejnane, c. 1000 B.C. 50m, Lintel bas-relief from a cult site in Tunis, c. 1000 B.C., horiz. 160m, Phoenician trireme, petroglyph, c. 800 B.C., horiz. 250m, Ceramic pot, c. 700 B.C., found at Sejnane, vert.

1986, Oct. 30 Litho. *Perf. 13½*

895	A329	10m	multi	5	5
896	A329	20m	multi	8	5
897	A329	50m	multi	22	10
898	A329	160m	multi	68	35
899	A329	250m	multi	1.05	52
			Nos. 895-899 (5)	2.08	1.07

1986, Nov. 20 Photo. *Perf. 13½*

901	A330	250m	multi	70	35

Intl. Peace Year
A331

1986, Nov. 24 *Perf. 13½x13*

902	A331	300m	multi	85	42

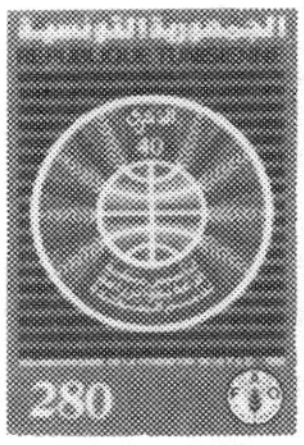

FAO, 40th Anniv.
A332

Computer Education Inauguration
A333

1986, Nov. 27 *Perf. 13x13½*

903	A332	280m	multi	78	40

1986, Dec. 8 *Perf. 13½*

904	A333	2d	multi	5.50	2.75

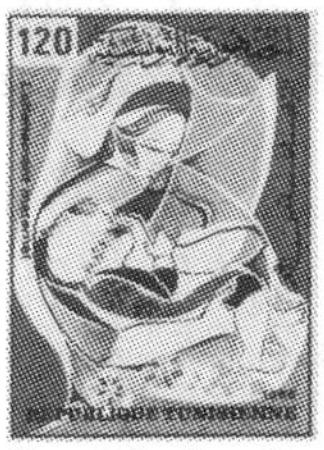

Breast-feeding for Child Survival — A334

Wildlife, Natl. Parks — A335

1986, Dec. 22 Photo. *Perf. 14*

905	A334	120m	multi	48	24

1986, Dec. 29 *Perf. 12*

Designs: 60m, Mountain gazelle, Chambi Natl. Park. 120m, Addax, Bou. Hedma. 350m, Seal, Zembretta. 380m, Greylag goose, Ichkeul.

Granite Paper

906	A335	60m	multi	5	5
907	A335	120m	multi	48	24
908	A335	350m	multi	1.40	70
909	A335	380m	multi	1.50	75

City of Monastir, Cent. — A336

1987, Jan. 24 Litho. *Perf. 12x11½*
Granite Paper

910	A336	120m	Pres. Bourguiba, city arms	48	24

A particular stamp may be scarce, but if few collectors want it, its market value may remain relatively low.

Invention of the Telegraph by Samuel F.B. Morse, 150th Anniv.
A337

1987, June 15 Litho. *Perf. 13½x14*

911	A337	500m	multi	2.00	1.00

30th Anniv. of the Republic
A338

Pres. Bourguiba and women of various sects.

1987, July 25 Photo. *Perf. 13½*

912	A338	150m	multi	60	30
913	A338	250m	multi	1.00	50
914	A338	350m	multi, diff.	1.40	70
915	A338	500m	multi, diff.	2.00	1.00
a			Souv. sheet of 4, # 912-915	6.00	3.00

No. 915a sold for 1.50d. Exists imperf.

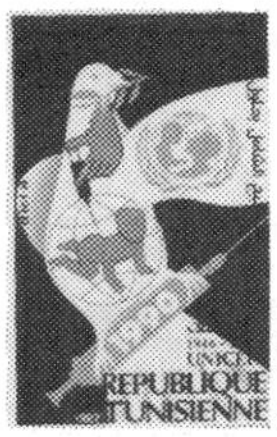

UN Universal Vaccination by 1990 Campaign — A339

1987, Sept. 14 *Perf. 12*
Granite Paper

916	A339	250m	multi	1.00	50

The Street, by Azouz ben Raiz (1902-1962)
A340

1987, Sept. 22 Granite Paper

917	A340	250m	multi	1.00	50

Arab Day for Shelter of the Homeless
A341

1987, Oct. 5 Photo. *Perf. 12x11½*
Granite Paper

918	A341	150m	multi	48	25

Advisory Council for Postal Research, 30th Anniv.
A342

1987, Oct. 9 *Perf. 14*

919	A342	150m	Express mail	48	25
920	A342	350m	Use postal code	1.15	58

The Arabs, by Ibn-Mandhour (1233-1312), Lexicographer — A343

1987, Oct. 26 Engr. *Perf. 13*

921	A343	250m	plum	1.00	50

Pasteur Institute, Tunis
A344

1987, Nov. 21 *Perf. 13x12½*

922	A344	250m	blk, grn & rose lake	1.00	50

Pasteur Institute, Paris, cent.

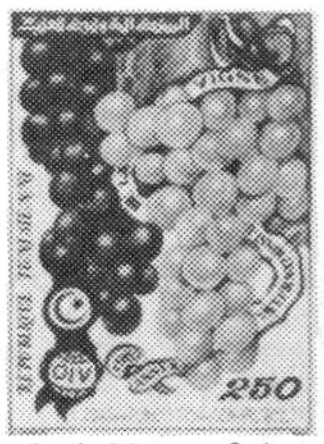

Intl. Year of the Vine (Wine) — A345

6th Volleyball Championships of African Nations — A346

1987, Nov. 27 Photo. *Perf. 14*

923	A345	250m	multi	1.00	50

1987, Dec. 2 Litho. *Perf. 14x13½*

924	A346	350m	multi	1.40	70

African Basketball Championships
A347

Folk Costumes
A348

1987, Dec. 15

925	A347	350m	multi	1.40	70

1987, Dec. 25 Photo.

926	A348	20m	Midoun	12	6
927	A348	30m	Tozeur	18	10
928	A348	150m	Sfax	85	42

Flowering Plants — A349

1987, Dec. 29 *Perf. 14½*

929 A349 30m Narcissus tazetta 14 6
930 A349 150m Gladiolus communis 62 30
931 A349 400m Iris xiphium 1.65 82
932 A349 500m Tulipa sylvestris 2.10 1.05

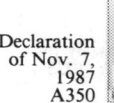

Declaration of Nov. 7, 1987 A350

Cameo portrait of Pres. Zine el Abidine Ben Ali and: 150m, Scales of Justice. 200m, Girl with flowers (party badges) in her hair, vert. 350m, Mermaid, doves, natl. coat of arms. 370m, "CMA," emblem of the Maghreb states (Tunisia, Mauritania, Morocco, Algeria and Libya), vert.

1988, Mar. 21 Photo. *Perf. 12*
Granite Paper

933 A350 150m multi 48 25
934 A350 200m multi 62 30
935 A350 350m multi 1.10 55
936 A350 370m multi 1.15 58

Youth and Change A351

1988, Mar. 22 Litho. *Perf. 14x14½*

937 A351 75m shown 25 12
938 A351 150m Happy family 48 25

Martyr's Day, 50th Anniv. A352

Perf. 13x13½, 13½x13

1988, Apr. 9 Photo.

939 A352 150m shown 45 22
940 A352 500m Monument, vert. 1.50 75

Opening Conference of the Constitutional Democratic Assembly — A353

1988, July 30 *Perf. 12x11½*
Granite Paper

941 A353 150m Flag, Pres. Ben Ali 48 25

SEMI-POSTAL STAMPS

No. 36 Overprinted in Red

1915, Feb. Unwmk. *Perf. 14x13½*

B1 A5 15c vio, *pnksh* 50 30

No. 32 Overprinted in Red

1916, Feb. 15

B2 A4 5c grn, *grnsh* 65 50

Types of Regular Issue of 1906 in New Colors and Surcharged

+10c.

1916, Aug.

B3 A5 10c on 15c brn vio, *bl* 38 22
B4 A5 10c on 20c brn, *org* 22 22
B5 A5 10c on 25c bl, *grn* 90 90
B6 A6 10c on 35c ol grn & vio 1.90 1.90
B7 A6 10c on 40c bis & blk 90 90
B8 A6 10c on 75c vio brn & grn 2.25 2.25
B9 A7 10c on 1fr red & grn 90 90
B10 A7 10c on 2fr bis & bl 25.00 22.50
B11 A7 10c on 5fr vio & red 42.50 37.50
Nos. B3-B11 (9) 74.95 67.29

Nos. B3 to B11 were sold at their face value but had a postal value of 10c only. The excess was applied to the relief of prisoners of war in Germany.

Types of Regular Issue of 1906 in New Colors and Surcharged in Carmine

15c

1918

B12 A5 15c on 20c blk, *grn* 25 25
B13 A5 15c on 25c dk bl, *buff* 25 25
B14 A6 15c on 35c gray grn & red 50 32
B15 A6 15c on 40c brn & lt bl 1.00 70
B16 A6 15c on 75c red brn & blk 1.25 1.25
B17 A7 15c on 1fr red & vio 4.00 4.00
B18 A7 15c on 2fr bis brn & red 20.00 15.00
B19 A7 15c on 5fr vio & blk 42.50 32.50
Nos. B12-B19 (8) 69.75 54.27

The different parts of the surcharge are more widely spaced on the stamps of types A6 and A7. These stamps were sold at their face value but had a postal value of 15c only. The excess was intended for the relief of prisoners of war in Germany.

Types of 1906-22 Surcharged

AFFᵗ 0c

1923

B20 A4 0c on 1c bl 50 50
B21 A4 0c on 2c ol brn 50 50
B22 A4 1c on 3c grn 50 50
B23 A4 2c on 5c red vio 50 50
B24 A9 3c on 10c vio, *bluish* 50 50
B25 A5 5c on 15c ol grn 50 50
B26 A5 5c on 20c bl, *pink* 1.65 1.65
B27 A5 5c on 25c vio, *bluish* 1.65 1.65
B28 A9 5c on 30c org 1.65 1.65
B29 A6 5c on 35c bl & vio 2.00 2.00
B30 A6 5c on 40c bl & brn 2.00 2.00
B31 A9 10c on 50c blk, *bluish* 2.00 2.00
B32 A6 10c on 60c ol brn & bl 2.00 2.00
B33 A6 10c on 75c vio & lt grn 4.50 4.50
B34 A7 25c on 1fr mar & vio 4.50 4.50
B35 A7 25c on 2fr bl & rose 17.50 17.50
B36 A7 25c on 5fr grn & ol brn 82.50 82.50
Nos. B20-B36 (17) 124.95 124.95

These stamps were sold at their original values but had postal franking values only to the amounts surcharged on them. The difference was intended to be used for the benefit of wounded soldiers.

This issue was entirely speculative. Before the announced date of sale most of the stamps were taken by postal employees and practically none of them were offered to the public.

Mail Delivery — SP1

Type of Parcel Post Stamps, 1906, with Surcharge in Black

1925, June 7 *Perf. 13½x14*

B37 SP1 1c on 5c brn & red, *pink* 22 22
a. Surcharge omitted 40.00 40.00
B38 SP1 2c on 10c brn & bl, *yel* 22 22
B39 SP1 3c on 20c red vio & rose, *lav* 40 40
B40 SP1 5c on 25c sl grn & rose, *bluish* 40 40
B41 SP1 5c on 40c rose & grn, *yel* 40 40
B42 SP1 10c on 50c vio & bl, *lav* 90 90
B43 SP1 10c on 75c grn & ol, *grnsh* 65 65
B44 SP1 25c on 1fr bl & grn, *bluish* 65 65
B45 SP1 25c on 2fr rose & vio, *pnksh* 3.50 3.50
B46 SP1 25c on 5fr red & brn, *lem* 21.00 21.00
Nos. B37-B46 (10) 28.34 28.34

These stamps were sold at their original values but paid postage only to the amount of the surcharged values. The difference was given to Child Welfare societies.

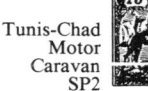

Tunis-Chad Motor Caravan SP2

1928, Feb. Engr. *Perf. 13½*

B47 SP2 40c + 40c org brn 45 45
B48 SP2 50c + 50c dp vio 45 45
B49 SP2 75c + 75c dk bl 55 55
B50 SP2 1fr + 1fr car 55 55
B51 SP2 1.50fr + 1.50fr brt bl 55 55
B52 SP2 2fr + 2fr dk grn 65 65
B53 SP2 5fr + 5fr red brn 65 65
Nos. B47-B53 (7) 3.85 3.85

The surtax on these stamps was for the benefit of Child Welfare societies.

Regular Issue of 1931 Surcharged in Black

1888 1938 + 1 — a
1888 1938 + 1F — b

1938 *Perf. 11, 12½, 12½x13*

B54 A14(a) 1c + 1c dp bl 80 60
B55 A14(a) 2c + 2c yel brn 80 60
B56 A14(a) 3c + 3c blk 80 60
B57 A14(a) 5c + 5c yel grn 80 60
B58 A14(a) 10c + 10c red 80 60
B59 A15(a) 15c + 15c dl vio 80 60
B60 A15(a) 20c + 20c dl brn 80 60
B61 A15(a) 25c + 25c org red 80 60
B62 A15(a) 30c + 30c dp grn 60 60
B63 A15(a) 40c + 40c org 60 60
B64 A16(a) 50c + 50c ultra 60 60
B65 A16(a) 75c + 75c yel 60 60
B66 A16(a) 90c + 90c red 60 60
B67 A16(a) 1fr + 1fr ol blk 60 60
B68 A17(b) 1.50fr + 1fr brt ultra 80 60
B69 A17(b) 2fr + 1.50fr dp brn 1.50 1.25
B70 A17(b) 3fr + 2fr dk grn 1.65 1.25
B71 A17(b) 5fr + 3fr car rose 10.00 7.00
a. Perf. 12½ 37.50 37.50
B72 A17(b) 10fr + 5fr blk 20.00 17.50
B73 A17(b) 20fr + 10fr dk brn 30.00 27.50
Nos. B54-B73 (20) 73.95 63.50

50th anniversary of the post office.

Stamps of 1939-40 Surcharged in Black, Blue or Red

SECOURS NATIONAL
1941
1f50

1941 *Perf. 14x13½*

B74 A11 1fr on 45c emer (Bk) 22 22
B75 A13 1.30fr on 1.25fr car rose (Bl) 22 22
B76 A13 1.50fr on 1.40fr brt red vio (Bk) 22 22
B77 A13 2fr on 2.25fr ultra (R) 22 22

The surcharge measures 11x14 mm. on No. B74.

Catalogue values for unused stamps in this section, from this point to the end of the section, are for Never Hinged items.

British, French and American Soldiers SP3

1943 Litho. *Perf. 12*

B78 SP3 1.50fr + 8.50fr crim 10 8

Liberation of Tunisia.

V1

Stamps of the design shown above were issued in 1944 by the Vichy Government, but were not placed on sale in the colony.

Native Scene — SP4

Surcharge in Black: "+ 48frcs / pour nos / Combattants"

1944 *Perf. 11½*

B79 SP4 2fr + 48fr red 35 35

The surtax was for soldiers.

Sidi Mahrez Mosque — SP5

Ramparts of Sfax — SP6

Fort Saint — SP7

Sidi-bou-Said — SP8

1945 Unwmk. Litho. *Perf. 11½*

B80 SP5 1.50fr + 8.50fr choc & red 30 30
B81 SP6 3fr + 12fr dk bl grn & red 30 30
B82 SP7 4fr + 21fr brn org & red 30 30
B83 SP8 10fr + 40fr red & blk 30 30

The surtax was for soldiers.

France No. B193 Overprinted in Black

c TUNISIE

1945 *Perf. 14x13½*

B84 SP147 2fr + 1fr red org 15 15

The surtax was for the aid of tuberculosis victims.

Same Overprint on Type of France, 1945

1945 Engr. *Perf. 13*

B85 SP150 2fr + 3fr dk grn 22 22

Stamp Day.

Same Overprint on France No. B192

1945

B86 SP146 4fr + 6fr dk vio brn 35 15

The surtax was for war victims of the P.T.T.

Types of 1926 Surcharged in Carmine

ANCIENS COMBATTANTS RF
4f+6f

1945 Typo. *Perf. 14x13½*

B87 A10 4fr + 6fr on 10c ultra 45 22
B88 A12 10fr + 30fr on 80c dk grn 45 22

The design of type A12 is redrawn, omitting "RF." The surtax was for war veterans.

Tunisian Soldier — SP9

1946 Unwmk. Engr. *Perf. 13*

B89 SP9 20fr + 30fr grn, red & blk 60 60

The surtax aided Tunisian soldiers in Indo-China.

Type of France, 1946, Overprinted Type "c" in Carmine

1946

B90 SP160 3fr + 2fr dk bl 35 35

Stamp Day.

Stamps and Types of 1926-46 Surcharged in Carmine and Black

1946
+50c

1946 *Perf. 14x13½*

B91 A12 80c + 50c emerald 22 22
B92 A12 1.50fr + 1.50fr rose lil 22 22
B93 A12 2fr + 2fr Prus grn 22 22
B94 A13 2.40fr + 2fr sal pink 22 22
B95 A13 4fr + 4fr ultra 22 22
Nos. B91-B95 (5) 1.10 1.10

The two parts of the surcharge are more widely spaced on stamps of type A13.

Type of France, 1947, Overprinted Type "c" in Carmine

1947 *Perf. 13*

B96 SP172 4.50fr + 5.50fr sep 35 35

On Type of France, 1946, Surcharged in Carmine with New Value and Bars

B97 SP158 10fr + 15fr on 2fr + 3fr brt ultra 35 35

Type of 1926 Surcharged in Carmine

SOLIDARITE 1947
+40f

1947 Typo. *Perf. 14x13½*

B98 A13 10fr + 40fr black 40 40

Feeding Young Bird — SP10

1947 Engr. *Perf. 13*

B99 SP10 4.50fr + 5.50fr dk bl grn 40 40
B100 SP10 6fr + 9fr brt ultra 40 40
B101 SP10 8fr + 17fr dp car 40 40
B102 SP10 10fr + 40fr dk pur 40 40

The surtax was for child welfare.

Type of Regular Issue of 1948 Surcharged in Blue

AIDEZ LES
+10f
TUBERCULEUX

1948

B103 A21 4fr + 10fr ol grn & org 30 30

The surtax was for anti-tuberculosis work.

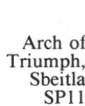

Arch of Triumph, Sbeitla SP11

1948

B104 SP11 10fr + 40fr ol grn & ol 50 50
B105 SP11 18fr + 42fr dk bl & ind 50 50

Surtax for charitable works of the army.

Arago Type of France, 1948, Overprinted in Carmine

d TUNISIE

1948

B106 SP176 6fr + 4fr brt car 50 50

Stamp Day, Mar. 6-7.

Sleeping Child SP12

1949, June 1

B107 SP12 25fr + 50fr dk grn 1.10 1.10

The surtax was for child welfare.

Neptune Type of 1947 Surcharged in Black with Lorraine Cross and "FFL+15F"

1949, Dec. 8

B108 A20 10fr + 15fr dp ultra & car 42 42

The surtax was for the Tunisian section of the Association of Free French.

Type of France, 1949, Overprinted in Carmine

e TUNISIE

1949, Mar. 26

B109 SP180 15fr + 5fr ind 60 60

Stamp Days, Mar. 26-27.

Type of France, 1950, Overprinted Type "d" in Ultramarine

1950, Mar. 11 Unwmk. *Perf. 13*

B110 SP183 12fr + 3fr dk grn 60 60

Stamp Days, Mar. 11-12.

Tunisian and French Woman Shaking Hands SP13

1950, June 5

B111 SP13 15fr + 35fr red 60 60
B112 SP13 25fr + 45fr dp ultra 60 60

The surtax was for Franco-Tunisian Mutual Assistance.

Arab Soldier — SP14

1950, Aug. 21 Engr.

B113 SP14 25fr + 25fr dp bl 80 80

The surtax was for old soldiers.

Type of France, 1951, Overprinted Type "c" in Black

1951, Mar. 10

B114 SP186 12fr + 3fr brnsh gray 50 40

Stamp Days, Mar. 10-11.

Mother Carrying Child SP15

1951, June 19 Engr. *Perf. 13*

B115 SP15 30fr + 15fr dp ultra 1.00 1.00

The surtax was for child welfare.

National Cemetery of Gammarth SP16

1952, June 15

B116 SP16 30fr + 10fr blue 1.00 1.00

Surtax aided orphans of the military services.

Type of France 1952 Overprinted Type "e" in Lilac

1952, Mar. 8 Unwmk.

B117 SP190 12fr + 3fr pur 42 42

Stamp Day, Mar. 8.

Stucco Work, Bardo SP17

Boy Campers SP18

1952, May 5 Engr. *Perf. 13*

B118 SP17 15fr + 1fr ultra & ind 50 50

Surtax for charitable works of the army.

1952, June 15

B119 SP18 30fr + 10fr dk grn 80 80

The surtax was for the Educational League vacation camps.

Type of France, 1952, Surcharged Type "c" and Surtax

1952, Oct. 15

B120 A226 15fr + 5fr bl grn 80 80

Creation of the French Military Medal, cent.

Type of France, 1953, Overprinted Type "c"

1953, Mar. 14

B121 SP193 12fr + 3fr ver 42 42

"Day of the Stamp."

Type of France, 1954, Overprinted Type "c"

1954, Mar. 20

B122 SP196 12fr + 3fr ind 42 42

Stamp Day.

Balloon Post, 1870 — SP19

1955, Mar. 19

B123 SP19 12fr + 3fr red brn 50 50

Stamp Days, Mar. 19-20.

Independent Kingdom

Francois of Taxis SP20

1956, Mar. 17
B124 SP20 12fr + 3fr dk grn 42 42

Stamp Days, Mar. 17-18.

Republic

No. 246 Surcharged in Red

نصف شهر الجيش ١٩٥٧
+ 10f

1957, Aug. 8 **Engr.**
B125 A29 20fr + 10fr dp ultra 40 40

15th anniversary of the army.

Florist Type of 1955 with Added Inscriptions, Surcharged in Red

1957, Oct. 19 ***Perf. 13***
B126 A34 20fr + 10fr dk vio 35 35

No. B126 is inscribed "5e. Foire Internationale" at bottom and lines of Arabic at either side.

Mailman Delivering Mail — SP21

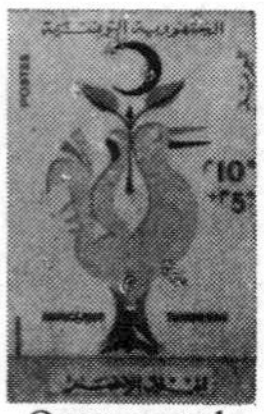
Ornamental Cock — SP22

1959, May 1 **Engr.** ***Perf. 13***
B127 SP21 20fr + 5fr dk brn & org brn 35 35

Day of the Stamp. The surtax was for the Post Office Mutual Fund.

1959, Oct. 24 **Litho.** ***Perf. 13***
B128 SP22 10m + 5m yel, lt bl & red 22 22

Surtax for the Red Crescent Society.

Mailman on Camel Phoning SP23

Dancer of Kerkennah Holding Stamp SP24

1960, Apr. 16 **Engr.** ***Perf. 13***
B129 SP23 60m + 5m ol, org & ultra 50 50

Day of the Stamp.

1961, May 6 **Unwmk.** ***Perf. 13***

Designs: 15m+5m, Mail truck (horiz.). 20m+6m, Hand holding magnifying glass and stamps. 50m+5m, Running boy, symbols of mail.

B130 SP24 12m + 4m cl, vio & ol 25 25
B131 SP24 15m + 5m ol, cl & vio bl 30 30
B132 SP24 20m + 6m multi 32 32
B133 SP24 50m + 5m multi 40 40

Stamp Day.

Nos. B130-B133 Overprinted

الأمم المتحدة
1963
O.N.U

1963, Oct. 24
B134 SP24 12m + 4m cl, vio & ol 22 22
B135 SP24 15m + 5m ol, cl & vio bl 28 28
B136 SP24 20m + 6m multi 38 38
B137 SP24 50m + 5m multi 60 60

United Nations Day.

Old Man, Red Crescent SP25

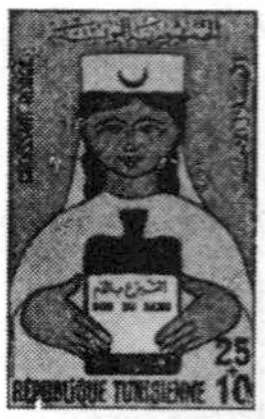
Nurse Holding Bottle of Blood SP26

Design: 75m+10m, Mother, child and Red Crescent.

1972, May 8 **Engr.** ***Perf. 13***
B138 SP25 10m + 10m pur & dk red 35 22
B139 SP25 75m + 10m bis brn & dl red 20 25

Tunisian Red Crescent.

1973, May 10 **Engr.** ***Perf. 13***

Design: 60m+10m, Red Crescent and blood donors' arms (horiz.).

B140 SP26 25m + 10m multi 22 20
B141 SP26 60m + 10m gray & car 35 20

Red Crescent appeal for blood donors.

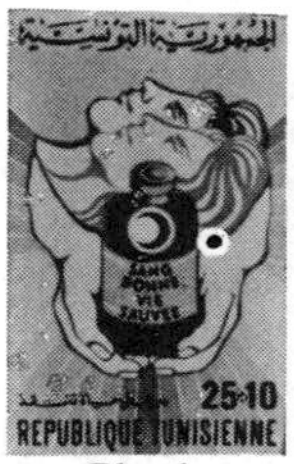
Blood Donors — SP27

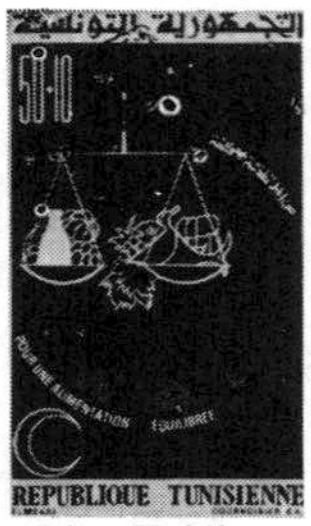
Man Holding Scales with Balanced Diet — SP28

Design: 75m+10m, Blood transfusion, symbolic design.

1974, May 8 **Photo.** ***Perf. 14x13***
B142 SP27 25m + 10m multi 35 20
B143 SP27 75m + 10m multi 50 30

Red Crescent Society.

1975, May 8 **Photo.** ***Perf. 11½***
B144 SP28 50m + 10m multi 22 22

Tunisian Red Crescent fighting malnutrition.

Blood Donation, Woman and Man — SP29

1976, May 8 **Photo.** ***Perf. 11½***
B145 SP29 40m + 10m multi 25 20

Tunisian Red Crescent Society.

Litter Bearers and Red Crescent SP30

1977, May 8 **Photo.** ***Perf. 13½x14***
B146 SP30 50m + 10m multi 22 22

Tunisian Red Crescent Society.

Blood Donors SP31

Hand and Red Crescent SP32

1978, May 8 **Photo.** ***Perf. 13x14***
B147 SP31 50m + 10m multi 22 20

Blood drive of Tunisian Red Crescent Society.

1979, May 8 **Photo.** ***Perf. 13½***
B148 SP32 50m + 10m multi 40 22

Tunisian Red Crescent Society.

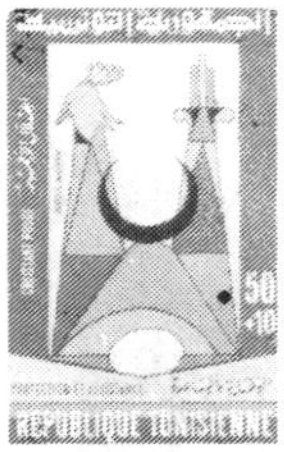
Red Crescent Society
SP33 SP34

1980, May 8 **Photo.** ***Perf. 13½***
B149 SP33 50m + 10m multi 22 20

1981, May 8 ***Perf. 14½x13½***
B150 SP34 50m + 10m multi 35 12

Dome of the Rock, Jerusalem SP35

1981, Nov. 29 **Photo.** ***Perf. 13½***
B151 SP35 50m + 5m multi 35 10
B152 SP35 150m + 5m multi 60 30
B153 SP35 200m + 5m multi 1.00 42

Intl. Palestinian Solidarity Day.

Red Crescent Society SP36

1982, May 8 **Photo.** ***Perf. 13½***
B154 SP36 80m + 10m multi 22 20

Red Crescent Society — SP37

1983, May 8 **Litho.** ***Perf. 14x13½***
B155 SP37 80m + 10m multi 22 15

Sabra and Chatilla Massacre SP38

1983, Sept. 20 **Photo.** ***Perf. 13***
B156 SP38 80 + 5m multi 20 15

Red Crescent Society — SP39

1984, May 8 **Litho.** ***Perf. 12½***
B157 SP39 80m + 10m First aid 22 15

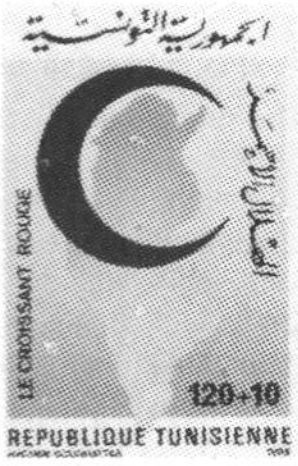
Red Crescent Society
SP40 SP41

1985, May 8 **Litho.** ***Perf. 14***
B158 SP40 100m + 10m multi 25 14

1986, May 9 **Litho.** ***Perf. 14½x13½***
B159 SP41 120m + 10m Map of Tunisia 52 25

Red Crescent Society SP42

1987, May 8 **Litho.** ***Perf. 13x13½***
B160 SP42 150m + 10m multi 65 32

Intl. Red Cross and Red Crescent Organizations, 125th Annivs. — SP43

1988, May 9 **Photo.** ***Perf. 14***
B161 SP43 150m + 10m multi 50 25

AIR POST STAMPS

No. 43 Surcharged in Red

a

1919, Apr. Unwmk. *Perf. 14x13½*

C1	A6	30c on 35c ol grn & brn	38	38
a.		Inverted surcharge	40.00	40.00
b.		Double surcharge	40.00	40.00
c.		Double inverted surcharge	42.50	42.50
d.		Double surcharge, one inverted	40.00	40.00

Type A6, Overprinted in Rose

b

1920, Apr.

C2	A6	30c ol grn, bl & rose	18	18

Nos. 53 and 55 Overprinted in Red

c

1927, Mar. 24

C3	A7	1fr ind & ultra	22	22
C4	A7	2fr grn & red, *pink*	85	65

Nos. 51 and 57 Surcharged in Black or Red

d

C5	A6	1.75fr on 75c ver & dl red (Bk)	25	20
C6	A7	1.75fr on 5fr gray vio & grn (R)	75	70

Overprinted on Type A13 in Blue

1928, Feb.

C7	A13(c)	1.30fr org & lt vio	90	65
C8	A13(c)	1.80fr gray grn & red	1.25	38
C9	A13(c)	2.55fr lil & ol brn	55	38

Surcharged on Type A13 in Blue

1930, Aug.

C10	A13(d)	1.50fr on 1.30fr org & lt vio	75	38
C11	A13(d)	1.50fr on 1.80fr gray grn & red	1.25	25
C12	A13(d)	1.50fr on 2.55fr lil & ol brn	2.50	75

Catalogue values for unused stamps in this section, from this point to the end of the section, are for Never Hinged items.

UPU Type of Regular Issue

1949, Oct. 28 Engr. *Perf. 13*

Bluish Paper

C13	A23	25fr dk bl	80	80

UPU, 75th anniv. Exists imperf.; value $35.

Bird from Antique Mosaic, Museum of Sousse AP2

1949 Unwmk.

C14	AP2	200fr dk bl & ind	2.50	75

(Arabic on one line) — AP3

1950-51

C15	AP3	100fr bl grn & brn	90	30
C16	AP3	200fr dk bl & ind ('51)	2.00	1.00

Monastir AP4

Coast at Korbous AP5

Design: 1000fr, Air view of Tozeur mosque.

1953-54

C17	AP4	100fr dk bl, ind & dk grn ('54)	1.20	42
C18	AP4	200fr cl, blk brn & red brn ('54)	2.00	80
C19	AP5	500fr dk brn & ultra	10.00	5.50
C20	AP5	1000fr dk green	16.50	12.50

Imperforates exist.

Independent Kingdom

Types of 1953-54 Redrawn with "RF" Omitted

1956, March 1

C21	AP4	100fr sl bl, ind & dk grn	55	25
C22	AP4	200fr multi	95	50
C23	AP5	500fr dk brn & ultra	3.00	2.00
C24	AP5	1000fr dk green	5.50	3.75

Republic

Desert Swallows — AP6

Birds: No. C26, Butcherbird. No. C27, Cream-colored courser. 100m, European chaffinch. 150m, Pink flamingoes. 200m, Barbary partridges. 300m, European roller. 500m, Bustard.

1965-66 Photo. *Perf. 12½*

Size: 23x31mm

C25	AP6	25m multi	55	25
C26	AP6	55m blk & lt bl	65	40
C27	AP6	55m multi ('66)	80	55

Size: 22½x33mm

Perf. 11½

C28	AP6	100m multi	1.00	60
C29	AP6	150m multi ('66)	3.75	1.65
C30	AP6	200m multi ('66)	4.00	1.90
C31	AP6	300m multi ('66)	6.00	3.50
C32	AP6	500m multi	6.50	4.00
		Nos. C25-C32 (8)	23.25	12.85

See No. 474.

AIR POST SEMI-POSTAL STAMP

Catalogue value for the unused stamp in this section is for a Never Hinged item.

Window, Great Mosque of Kairouan — SPAP1

Unwmk.

1952, May 5 Engr. *Perf. 13*

CB1	SPAP1	50fr + 10fr blk & gray grn	1.00	1.00

Surtax for charitable works of the army.

POSTAGE DUE STAMPS

Regular postage stamps perforated with holes in the form of a "T", the holes varying in size and number, were used as postage due stamps from 1888 to 1901.

D1

D2

Perf. 14x13½

1901-03 Unwmk. Typo.

J1	D1	1c black	5	5
J2	D1	2c orange	5	5
J3	D1	5c blue	10	8
J4	D1	10c brown	15	10
J5	D1	20c blue green	2.00	25
J6	D1	30c carmine	90	30
J7	D1	50c brown violet	70	30
J8	D1	1fr olive green	60	30
J9	D1	2fr carmine, *grn*	2.00	55
J10	D1	5fr blk, *yellow*	25.00	15.00
		Nos. J1-J10 (10)	31.55	16.98

No. J10 Surcharged in Blue

2
FRANCS

1914, Nov.

J11	D1	2fr on 5fr blk, *yellow*	50	42

In January, 1917 regular 5c postage stamps were overprinted "T" in an inverted triangle and used as postage due stamps.

1922-49

J12	D2	1c black	7	5
J13	D2	2c blk, *yellow*	7	5
J14	D2	5c violet brown	7	5
J15	D2	10c blue	7	5
J16	D2	10c yel green ('45)	5	5
J17	D2	20c orange, *yel*	7	5
J18	D2	30c brown ('23)	5	5
J19	D2	50c rose red	42	15
J20	D2	50c blue vio ('45)	5	5
J21	D2	60c violet ('28)	42	15
J22	D2	80c bister ('28)	8	8
J23	D2	90c orange red ('28)	60	30
J24	D2	1fr green	5	5
J25	D2	2fr ol grn, *straw*	35	10
J26	D2	2fr car rose ('45)	5	5
J27	D2	3fr vio, *pink* ('29)	10	10
J28	D2	4fr grnsh bl ('45)	10	10
J29	D2	5fr violet	35	22
J30	D2	10fr cerise ('49)	10	10
J31	D2	20fr olive gray ('49)	40	10
		Nos. J12-J31 (20)	3.52	1.90

Inscribed: "Timbre Taxe"

1950 Unwmk. *Perf. 14x13½*

J32	D2	30fr blue	80	35

Catalogue values for unused stamps in this section, from this point to the end of the section, are for Never Hinged items.

Independent Kingdom

Grain and Fruit — D3

1957, Apr. 1 Engr. *Perf. 14x13*

J33	D3	1fr bright green	10	10
J34	D3	2fr orange brown	12	12
J35	D3	3fr bluish green	22	22
J36	D3	4fr indigo	25	25
J37	D3	5fr lilac	22	22
J38	D3	10fr carmine	22	22
J39	D3	20fr chocolate	70	70
J40	D3	30fr blue	90	90
		Nos. J33-J40 (8)	2.73	2.73

Republic

Inscribed "Republique Tunisienne"

1960-77

J41	D3	1m emerald	5	5
J42	D3	2m red brown	5	5
J43	D3	3m bluish green	5	5
J44	D3	4m indigo	5	5
J45	D3	5m lilac	15	15
J46	D3	10m carmine rose	22	22
J47	D3	20m vio brown	40	40
J48	D3	30m blue	50	50
J49	D3	40m lake ('77)	12	12
J50	D3	100m bl green ('77)	25	20
		Nos. J41-J50 (10)	1.84	1.79

PARCEL POST STAMPS

Mail Delivery PP1

Gathering Dates PP2

1906 Unwmk. Typo. *Perf. 13½x14*

Q1	PP1	5c grn & vio brn	10	5
Q2	PP1	10c org & red	40	10
Q3	PP1	20c dk brn & org	50	10
Q4	PP1	25c bl & brn	65	12
Q5	PP1	40c gray & rose	90	10
Q6	PP1	50c vio brn & vio	65	10
Q7	PP1	75c bis brn & bl	1.10	20
Q8	PP1	1fr red brn & red	90	10
Q9	PP1	2fr car & bl	2.50	20
Q10	PP1	5fr vio & vio brn	6.50	40
		Nos. Q1-Q10 (10)	14.20	1.47

1926

Q11	PP2	5c pale brn & dk bl	8	6
Q12	PP2	10c rose & vio	8	6
Q13	PP2	20c yel grn & blk	9	8
Q14	PP2	25c org brn & blk	18	9
Q15	PP2	40c dp rose & dp grn	50	20
Q16	PP2	50c lt vio & blk	50	20
Q17	PP2	60c ol & brn red	55	30
Q18	PP2	75c gray vio & bl grn	55	8
Q19	PP2	80c ver & ol brn	50	8
Q20	PP2	1fr Prus bl & dp rose	50	9
Q21	PP2	2fr vio & mag	1.00	9
Q22	PP2	4fr red & blk	1.25	9
Q23	PP2	5fr red brn & dp vio	1.65	18
Q24	PP2	10fr dl red & grn, *grnsh*	3.50	22
Q25	PP2	20fr yel grn & dp vio, *lav*	6.00	40
		Nos. Q11-Q25 (15)	16.93	2.22

Parcel post stamps were discontinued July 1, 1940.

TURKEY

LOCATION — Southeastern Europe and Asia Minor, between the Mediterranean and Black Seas.
GOVT. — Republic
AREA — 300,947 sq. mi.
POP. — 48,000,000 (est. 1984)
CAPITAL — Ankara

The Ottoman Empire ceased to exist in 1922, and the Republic of Turkey was inaugurated in 1923.

40 Paras = 1 Piastre
40 Paras = 1 Ghurush (1926)
40 Paras = 1 Kurush (1926)
100 Kurush = 1 Lira

Catalogue values for unused stamps in this country are for Never Hinged items, beginning with Scott 986 in the regular postage section, Scott B69 in the semi-postal section, Scott C12 in the airpost section, Scott O13 in the official section, Scott P175 in the newspaper section, and Scott RA139 in the postal tax section.

Turkish Numerals

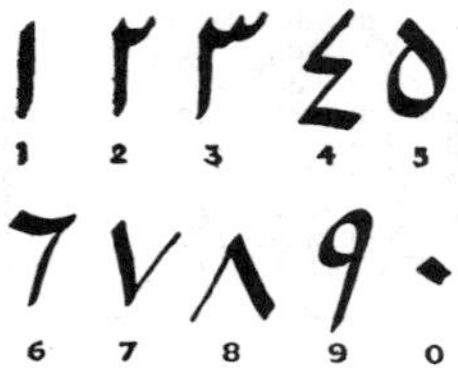

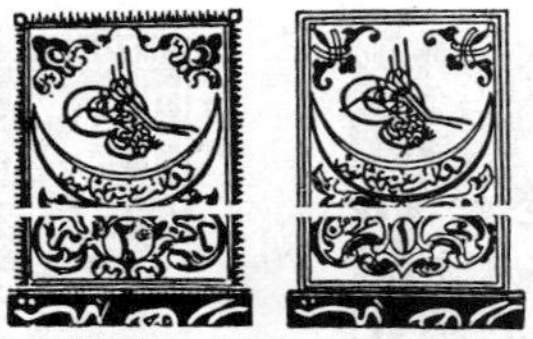

"Tughra," Monogram of Sultan Abdul-Aziz
A1 A2

A3 A4

1863 Unwmk. Litho. *Imperf.*
Red Band: 20pa, 1pi, 2pi
Blue Band: 5pi
Thin Paper

1 A1 20pa blk, *yellow* 27.50 17.50
a Tete beche pair 125.00 125.00
b Without band 45.00
c Green band
2 A2 1pi blk, *dl vio* 30.00 20.00
a 1pi black, *gray* 30.00 20.00
b Tete beche pair 150.00 150.00
c Without band 42.50
d Design reversed 175.00
e 1pi blk, *yel* (error) 150.00 125.00
4 A3 2pi blk, *grnsh bl* 35.00 22.50
a 2pi black, *ind* 35.00 22.50
b Tete beche pair 150.00 150.00
c Without band 50.00
5 A4 5pi blk, *rose* 55.00 27.50
a Tete beche pair 250.00 250.00
b Without band 75.00
c Green band 95.00
d Red band 95.00

Thick, Surface Colored Paper

6 A1 20pa blk, *yellow* 45.00 30.00
a Tete beche pair 350.00 350.00
b Design reversed 275.00 275.00
c Without band 35.00 35.00
d Paper colored through 75.00 75.00
7 A2 1pi blk, *gray* 50.00 42.50
a Tete beche pair 350.00 350.00
b Design reversed
c Without band
d Paper colored through 125.00 125.00

The 2pi and 5pi had two printings. In the common printing, the stamps are more widely spaced and alternate horizontal rows of 12 are inverted. In the first and rare printing, the stamps are more closely spaced and no rows are tete beche.

Crescent and Star, Symbols of Turkish Caliphate — A5

Surcharged

The bottom characters of this and the following surcharges denote the denomination. The characters at top and sides translate, "Ottoman Empire Posts."

1865 Typo. *Perf. 12 1/2*

8 A5 10pa dp grn 2.50 4.00
b Imperf., pair 60.00 60.00
c "1" instead of "10" in each corner 150.00 150.00
9 A5 20pa yellow 65 65
a Star without rays 1.00 1.00
b Imperf., pair 60.00 60.00
10 A5 1pi lilac 3.50 1.65
a Star without rays 1.65 1.65
b Imperf., pair 45.00 45.00
11 A5 2pi blue 65 1.00
a Imperf., pair 45.00 45.00
12 A5 5pi carmine 50 1.50
b Imperf., pair 55.00 55.00
d Inverted surcharge 190.00
13 A5 25pi red org 90.00 85.00
a Imperf., pair 350.00 350.00

Surcharged

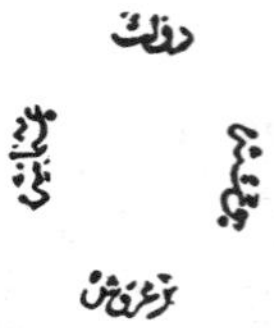

1867

14 A5 10pa gray grn 50
a Imperf., pair 25.00
15 A5 20pa yellow 1.10
a Imperf., pair 35.00
16 A5 1pi lilac 2.75
a Imperf., pair 42.50
b Imperf., with surcharge of 5pi 7.50
17 A5 2pi blue 50 75
a Imperf.
18 A5 5pi rose 25 1.50
a Imperf.
19 A5 25pi orange 300.00

Nos. 14, 15, 16 and 19 were never placed in use.

Surcharged

1869 *Perf. 13 1/2*

20 A5 10pa dl vio 6.50 50
a Printed on both sides
b Imperf., pair 40.00 40.00
c Inverted surcharge 45.00
d Double surcharge
e 10pa yellow (error) 120.00
21 A5 20pa pale grn 20.00 35
a Printed on both sides 45.00 45.00
22 A5 1pi yellow 25 20
c Inverted surcharge 40.00 40.00
d Double surcharge
e Surcharged on both sides
f Printed on both sides
23 A5 2pi org red 6.00 75
b Imperf., pair 65.00 65.00
c Printed on both sides 65.00
d Inverted surcharge 35.00 35.00
e Surcharged on both sides 70.00
24 A5 5pi blue 10 20
25 A5 5pi gray 4.00 3.00
26 A5 25pi dl rose 11.00 10.00

Pin-perf., Perf. 5 to 11 and Compound
1870-71

27 A5 10pa lilac 120.00 16.50
28 A5 10pa brown 25.00 1.50
29 A5 20pa gray grn 7.00 40
a Printed on both sides

30 A5 1pi yellow 18.00 40
a Inverted surcharge 50.00 40.00
b Without surcharge
31 A5 2pi red 60 35
a Imperf. 10.00 10.00
b Printed on both sides 16.50
c Surcharged on both sides
32 A5 5pi blue 20 45
a 5pi greenish blue 1.35 1.35
33 A5 5pi slate 4.00 4.00
a Printed on both sides
b Surcharged on both sides 16.50
34 A5 25pi dl rose 8.00 8.00

1873 *Perf. 12, 12 1/2*

35 A5 10pa dk lil 22.50 1.35
a Inverted surcharge 45.00
36 A5 10pa ol brn 27.50 1.50
a 10pa bister 20.00 2.00
37 A5 2pi vermilion 50 40
a Surcharged on both sides 11.00 11.00

Surcharged

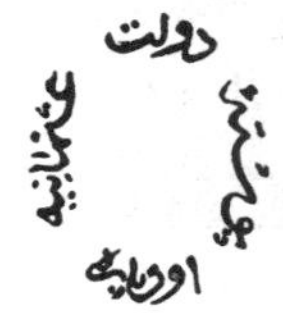

1874-75 *Perf. 13 1/2*

38 A5 10pa red vio 6.00 70
a Imperf., pair 35.00 25.00
39 A5 20pa yel grn 7.00 70
b Inverted surcharge 15.00 6.50
c Double surcharge
40 A5 1pi yellow 10.00 1.00
a Imperf., pair 50.00 40.00

Perf. 12, 12 1/2

41 A5 10pa red vio 16.50 5.00
a Inverted surcharge 22.50 30.00

Surcharged

1876, April *Perf. 13 1/2*

42 A5 10pa red lil 8 8
a Inverted surcharge 35.00
b Imperf., pair 7.50 7.50
43 A5 20pa pale grn 8 8
b Inverted surcharge 35.00
c Imperf., pair 7.50 7.50
44 A5 1pi yellow 12 8
a Imperf., pair 14.00 14.00
46 A5 5pi gray bl 190.00
47 A5 25pi dl rose 175.00

Nos. 46 and 47 were never placed in use.

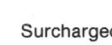

Surcharged

1876, Jan.

48 A5 1/4pi on 10pa vio 25 38
49 A5 1/2pi on 20pa yel grn 55 55
50 A5 1 1/4pi on 50pa rose 15 25
a Imperf., pair 30.00
51 A5 2pi on 2pi redsh brn 4.50 1.75
52 A5 5pi on 5pi gray bl 75 1.75

The surcharge on Nos. 48-52 restates in French the value originally expressed in Turkish characters.

A7

1876, Sept. Typo. *Perf. 13 1/2*

53 A7 10pa blk & rose lil 10 16
54 A7 20pa red vio & grn 15.00 1.50
55 A7 50pa bl & yel 20 25
56 A7 2pi blk & redsh brn 10 25
57 A7 5pi red & bl 65 90
b Cliche of 25pi in plate of 5pi 200.00 190.00
58 A7 25pi cl & rose 7.00 7.00
a Imperf. 80.00

Nos. 56-58 exist perf. 11 1/2, but were not regularly issued.

1880-84 *Perf. 13 1/2*

59 A7 5pa blk & ol ('81) 10 10
a Imperf. 30.00
60 A7 10pa blk & grn ('84) 10 10
61 A7 20pa blk & rose 16 10
62 A7 1pi blk & bl *(piastres)* 10 10
a 1pi black & gray blue 16
b Imperf. 40.00
63 A7 1pi blk & bl *(piastre)* ('81) 6.50 1.65

A cliché of No. 63 was inserted in a plate of the Eastern Rumelia 1pi (No. 13), but this "error" is found only in the remainders.

Nos. 60-61 and 63 exist perf. 11 1/2, but were not regularly issued.

1881-82
Surcharged like April, 1876 Issue

64 A5 20pa gray 10 10
a Inverted surcharge 13.50
b Imperf., pair 25.00
65 A5 2pi pale sal 10 10
a Inverted surcharge 22.50

1884-86 *Perf. 11 1/2, 13 1/2*

66 A7 5pa lil & pale lil ('86) 27.50 17.50
a Imperf. 60.00
67 A7 10pa grn & pale grn 8 8
a Imperf. 10.00
68 A7 20pa rose & pale rose 8 8
b Imperf. 10.00
69 A7 1pi bl & lt bl 8 8
b Imperf. 10.00
70 A7 2pi ocher & pale ocher, perf. 11 1/2 8 8
71 A7 5pi red brn & pale brn, perf. 11 1/2 15 28
c 5pi ocher & pale ocher (error) 4.00 4.00
73 A7 25pi blk & pale gray ('86) 75.00 75.00
a Imperf. 150.00

1886 *Perf. 13 1/2*

74 A7 5pa blk & pale gray 10 10
a Imperf. 13.50
75 A7 2pi org & lt bl 10 10
b Imperf. 13.50
76 A7 5pi grn & pale grn 20 40
b Imperf. 13.50
77 A7 25pi bis & pale bis 7.00 8.00
a Imperf. 25.00

Stamps of 1884-86, bisected and surcharged as above, 10pa, 20pa, 1pi and 2pi or surcharged "2" in red are stated to have been made privately and without authority. With the aid of employees of the post office, copies were passed through the mails.

1888 *Perf. 13 1/2*

83 A7 5pa grn & yel 5 5
a Imperf. 10.00
84 A7 2pi red lil & bl 8 5
a Imperf. 10.00
85 A7 5pi dk brn & gray 8 8
a Imperf. 10.00
86 A7 25pi red & yel 5.50 6.00
a Imperf. 22.50

Nos. 74-86 exist perf. 11 1/2, but were not regularly issued.

1890 *Perf. 11 1/2, 13 1/2*

87 A7 10pa grn & gray 5 5
a Imperf. 10.00
88 A7 20pa rose & gray 5 5
a Imperf. 10.00
89 A7 1pi bl & gray 8 5
a Imperf. 12.50
90 A7 2pi yel & gray 15 10
b Imperf. 15.00
91 A7 5pi buff & gray 35 38
a Imperf. 20.00

Arms and Tughra of "El Gazi" (The Conqueror) Sultan Abdul Hamid
A10 A11

A12

A13

A14

A15

1892-98 **Typo.** ***Perf. 13½***

95	A10	10pa gray grn	8	5
96	A11	20pa vio brn ('98)	8	5
a		20pa dark pink	25	5
b		20pa pink	3.75	20
97	A12	1pi pale bl	1.90	5
98	A13	2pi brn org	5	5
a		Tete beche pair	*5.00*	*5.00*
99	A14	5pi dl vio	1.25	55
a		Turkish numeral in upper right corner reads "50" instead of "5"	12.50	12.50

Red Surcharge

1897

100	A15	5pa on 10pa gray grn	16	8
a		"Cniq" instead of "Cinq"	10.00	10.00

A16

A17

1901 **Typo.** ***Perf. 13½***

For Foreign Postage

102	A16	5pa bister	15	5
103	A16	10pa yel grn	8	5
104	A16	20pa magenta	8	5
a		Perf. 12	50	10
105	A16	1pi vio bl	8	5
106	A16	2pi gray bl	15	9
107	A16	5pi ocher	75	30
108	A16	25pi dk grn	9.00	5.50
109	A16	50pi yellow	22.50	15.00
		Nos. 102-109 (8)	32.79	21.09

For Domestic Postage

Perf. 12, 13½

110	A17	5pa purple	5	5
111	A17	10pa green	5	5
112	A17	20pa carmine	5	5
113	A17	1pi blue	8	5
a		Imperf.	5.50	
114	A17	2pi orange	12	5
115	A17	5pi lil rose	22	5
116	A17	25pi brn, perf. 13½	1.50	50
a		Perf. 12	5.00	1.25
117	A17	50pi yel brn, perf. 13½	5.00	1.10
a		Perf. 12	6.25	3.00
		Nos. 110-117 (8)	7.07	1.90

Nos. 110-113 exist perf. 12x13½.

A18

A19

1905 ***Perf. 12, 13½ and Compound***

118	A18	5pa ocher	5	5
119	A18	10pa dl grn	5	5
a		Imperf.	4.00	3.50
120	A18	20pa carmine	5	5
a		Imperf.	4.00	3.50
121	A18	1pi blue	5	5
122	A18	2pi slate	10	5
123	A18	2½pi red vio	20	5
a		Imperf.	11.00	9.00
124	A18	5pi brown	16	5
125	A18	10pi org brn	40	7
126	A18	25pi olive grn	1.65	40
127	A18	50pi dp vio	5.50	2.25

Overprinted in Carmine or Blue ب

1906

128	A18	10pa dl grn (C)	15	5
129	A18	20pa car (Bl)	15	5
130	A18	1pi blue (C)	20	5
131	A18	2pi slate (C)	2.50	70
		Nos. 118-131 (14)	11.21	3.92

Stamps bearing this overprint were sold to merchants at a discount from face value to encourage the use of Turkish stamps on foreign correspondence, instead of those of the various European powers which maintained post offices in Turkey. The overprint is the Arab "B," for "Behie," meaning "discount."

1908

132	A19	5pa ocher	5	5
133	A19	10pa bl grn	5	5
134	A19	20pa carmine	3.00	5
135	A19	1pi bright bl	75	5
a		1pi ultramarine	15.00	2.25
136	A19	2pi bl blk	80	5
137	A19	2½pi vio brn	20	5
138	A19	5pi dk vio	2.50	7
139	A19	10pi red	5.00	30
140	A19	25pi dk grn	2.50	1.00
141	A19	50pi red brn	6.00	1.00

Overprinted in Carmine or Blue ب

142	A19	10pa bl grn (C)	65	20
143	A19	20pa carmine (Bl)	80	30
144	A19	1pi brt bl (C)	1.65	50
145	A19	2pi bl blk (C)	3.50	80
		Nos. 132-145 (14)	27.45	4.47

A20

Perf. 12, 13½ & Compound

1908, Dec. 17

146	A20	5pa ocher	12	5
a		Imperf.	1.75	1.75
147	A20	10pa bl grn	5	5
a		Imperf.	2.00	2.00
148	A20	20pa carmine	22	10
a		Imperf.	2.75	2.75
149	A20	1pi ultra	35	12
a		Imperf.	1.75	1.75
150	A20	2pi gray blk	3.00	1.10
		Nos. 146-150 (5)	3.74	1.42

Granting of a Constitution, the date of which is inscribed on the banderol: "324 Temuz 10" (July 24, 1908).

Tughra and "Reshad" of Sultan Mohammed V — A21

1909, Dec.

151	A21	5pa ocher	5	5
152	A21	10pa bl grn	5	5
a		Imperf.	1.75	1.75
153	A21	20pa car rose	5	5
154	A21	1pi ultra	5	5
a		1pi bright blue	25	5
155	A21	2pi bl blk	8	5
156	A21	2½pi dk brn	3.75	3.50
157	A21	5pi dk vio	1.00	12
158	A21	10pi dl red	1.75	25
159	A21	25pi dk grn	37.50	15.00
160	A21	50pi red brn	15.00	12.50

The 2pa olive green, type A21, is a newspaper stamp, No. P68.

Two types exist for the 10pa, 20pa and 1pi. In the second type, the damaged crescent is restored.

Overprinted in Carmine or Blue ب

161	A21	10pa bl grn (C)	12	5
a		Imperf.		
162	A21	20pa car rose (Bl)	12	5
a		Imperf.		
163	A21	1pi ultra (C)	15	8
a		Imperf.	4.00	
b		1pi bright blue	15	8
164	A21	2pi bl blk (C)	5.50	1.90
a		Imperf.		
		Nos. 151-164 (14)	65.17	33.70

Stamps of 1901-05 Overprinted in Carmine or Blue

MONASTIR

The overprint was applied to 18 denominations in four settings with change of city name, producing individual sets for each city: "MONASTIR," "PRISTINA," "SALONIKA" and "USKUB."

1911, June 26 ***Perf. 12, 13½***

165	A16	5pa bister	45
166	A16	10pa yel grn	45
167	A16	20pa magenta	2.00
168	A16	1pi vio bl	2.00
169	A16	2pi gray bl	2.00
170	A16	5pi ocher	17.50
171	A16	25pi dk grn	25.00
172	A16	50pi yellow	30.00
173	A17	5pa purple	45
174	A17	10pa green	45
175	A17	20pa carmine	2.00
176	A17	1pi blue	2.00
177	A17	2pi orange	2.00
178	A17	5pi lil rose	17.50
179	A17	25pi chocolate	30.00
180	A17	50pi yel brn	42.50
181	A18	2½pi red vio	17.50
182	A18	10pi org brn	24.00
		Nos. 165-182 (18)	217.80

Sultan's visit to Macedonia. The Arabic overprint reads: "Souvenir of the Sultan's Journey, 1329". Value for Salonika and Uskub sets, each $325. See Nos. P69-P81.

General Post Office, Constantinople
A22

1913, Mar. 14 ***Perf. 12***

237	A22	2pa ol grn	5	5
238	A22	5pa ocher	5	5
239	A22	10pa bl grn	5	5
240	A22	20pa car rose	5	5
241	A22	1pi ultra	5	5
242	A22	2pi indigo	7	5
243	A22	5pi dl vio	16	10
244	A22	10pi dl red	1.00	40
245	A22	25pi gray grn	2.50	1.35
246	A22	50pi org brn	10.00	9.00

Overprinted in Carmine or Blue ب

247	A22	10pa bl grn (C)	5	5
248	A22	20pa car rose (Bl)	6	5
249	A22	1pi ultra (C)	20	8
250	A22	2pi ind (C)	1.10	75
		Nos. 237-250 (14)	15.39	12.08

Mosque of Selim, Adrianople
A23

1913, Oct. 23 **Engr.**

251	A23	10pa green	20	12
252	A23	20pa red	35	20
253	A23	40pa blue	65	38

Recapture of Adrianople (Edirne) by the Turks.
See Nos. 592, J59-J62.

Obelisk of Theodosius in the Hippodrome
A24

Column of Constantine
A25

Leander's Tower
A26

One of the Seven Towers
A27

Fener Bahçe (Garden Lighthouse)
A28

The Castle of Europe on the Bosporus — A29

Mosque of Sultan Ahmed — A30

Monument to the Martyrs of Liberty
A31

Fountains of Suleiman
A32

Cruiser "Hamidie"
A33

View of Kandili on the Bosporus
A34

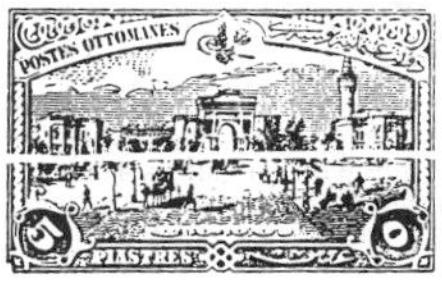
War Ministry (Later Istanbul University)
A35

Sweet Waters of Europe Park A36

Mosque of Suleiman A37

The Bosporus A38

Sultan Ahmed's Fountain A39

Sultan Mohammed V — A40

Designs A24-A39: Views of Constantinople.

1914, Jan. 14 **Litho.**

254 A24 2pa red lil 5 5
255 A25 4pa dk brn 5 5
256 A26 5pa vio brn 5 5
257 A27 6pa dk bl 8 5

Engr.

258 A28 10pa green 5 5
259 A29 20pa red 12 5
260 A30 1pi blue 15 5
b Booklet pane of 2+2 labels
261 A31 1½pi car & blk 28 8
262 A32 1¾pi sl & red brn 8 5
263 A33 2pi grn & blk 50 5
264 A34 2½pi org & ol grn 35 5
265 A35 5pi dl vio 1.00 20
266 A36 10pi red brn 2.75 30
267 A37 25pi ol grn 15.00 1.90
268 A38 50pi carmine 3.00 1.50
269 A39 100pi dp bl 25.00 10.00
Cut cancellation 1.25
270 A40 200pi grn & blk 250.00 125.00
Cut cancellation 8.75
Nos. 254-270 (17) 298.51 139.48

See Nos. 590-591, 593-598.

Stamps of Preceding Issue Overprinted in Red or Blue 

271 A28 10pa green (R) 10 5
272 A29 20pa red (Bl) 85 25
273 A30 1pi blue (R) 22 5
275 A32 1¾pi sl & red brn (Bl) 30 20
276 A33 2pi grn & blk (R) 5.00 55
Nos. 271-276 (5) 6.47 1.10

No. 261 Surcharged 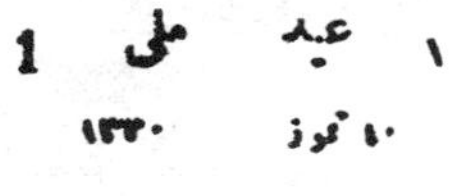

1914, July 23

277 A31 1pi on 1½pi car & blk 20 20
a "1330" omitted 2.50 1.50
b Double surcharge
c Triple surcharge 5.00 5.00

7th anniv. of the Constitution. The surcharge reads "10 July, 1330, National fête" and has also the numeral "1" at each side, over the original value of the stamp.

Stamps of 1914 Overprinted in Black or Red 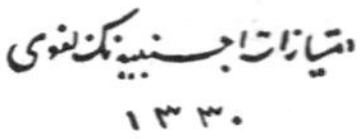

278 A26 5pa vio brn (Bk) 40 16
279 A28 10pa green (R) 50 20
280 A29 20pa red (Bk) 1.00 35
281 A30 1pi blue (R) 2.25 50
282 A33 2pi grn & blk (R) 1.65 30
283 A35 5pi dl vio (R) 15.00 2.00
284 A36 10pi red brn (R) 25.00 12.00
Nos. 278-284 (7) 45.80 15.51

This overprint reads "Abolition of the Capitulations, 1330".

Nos. 269-270 Surcharged

1915

286 A39 10pi on 100pi dp bl 7.50 2.50
a Inverted surcharge 75.00 75.00

Surcharged

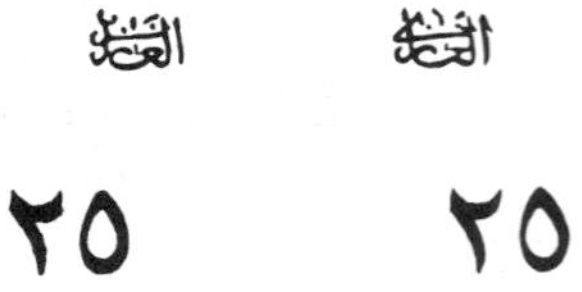

287 A40 25pi on 200pi grn & blk 6.00 2.25

Preceding Issues Overprinted in Carmine or Black 

1915

On Stamps of 1892

288 A10 10pa gray grn 5 5
a Inverted overprint 5.00 5.00
289 A13 2pi brn org 5 5
a Inverted overprint 5.00 5.00
290 A14 5pi dl vio 1.00 10
a On No. 99a 16.50 16.50

On Stamp of 1897

291 A15 5pa on 10pa gray grn 5 5
a Inverted overprint 5.00 5.00
b On No. 100a 10.00 10.00

On Stamps of 1901

292 A16 5pa bister 7 5
293 A16 1pi vio bl 20 14
294 A16 2pi gray bl 16 7
295 A16 5pi ocher 1.65 25
296 A16 25pi dk grn 12.50 6.00
297 A17 5pa purple 5 5
298 A17 10pa green 7 5
299 A17 20pa carmine 7 5
a Inverted overprint 5.00 5.00
300 A17 1pi blue 14 5
a Inverted overprint 5.00 5.00
301 A17 2pi orange 25 7
a Inverted overprint 5.00 5.00
b Double overprint (R and Bk) 5.00 5.00
302 A17 5pi lil rose 16 5
303 A17 25pi brown 3.00 1.00

On Stamps of 1905

304 A18 5pa ocher 7 7
305 A18 10pa dl grn 7 5
a Inverted overprint 5.00 5.00
306 A18 20pa carmine 7 5
a Inverted overprint 5.00 5.00
307 A18 1pi brt bl 20 7
a Inverted overprint 5.00 5.00
308 A18 2pi slate 25 10
a Inverted overprint 5.00 5.00
309 A18 2½pi red vio 16 7
310 A18 5pi brown 10 5
a Inverted overprint 5.00 5.00
311 A18 10pi org brn 2.00 14
312 A18 25pi olive grn 8.00 2.00

On Stamps of 1906

313 A18 10pa dull grn 12 5
314 A18 2pi slate 38 8
a Inverted overprint 5.00 5.00

On Stamps of 1908

314B A19 2pi bl blk 25.00 15.00
315 A19 2½pi vio brn 30 7
315A A19 5pi dk vio 15.00 9.00
315B A19 10pi red 4.00 1.50
316 A19 25pi dk grn 4.00 1.50
a Inverted overprint 16.50 16.50

With Additional Overprint 

316B A19 2pi bl blk 3.00 1.00

On Stamps of 1909

317 A21 5pa ocher 5 5
a Inverted overprint 5.00 5.00
b Double overprint 5.00 5.00
318 A21 20pa car rose 5 5
a Inverted overprint 5.00 5.00
319 A21 1pi ultra 14 5
a Inverted overprint 5.00 5.00
320 A21 2pi bl blk 16 5
a Inverted overprint 5.00 5.00
321 A21 2½pi dk brn 22.50 10.00
322 A21 5pi dk vio 16 7
a Inverted overprint 6.50 6.50
323 A21 10pi dl red 2.50 25
324 A21 25pi dk grn 190.00 165.00

With Additional Overprint 

325 A21 20pa car rose 16 7
a Inverted overprint 5.00 5.00
326 A21 1pi ultra 16 7
327 A21 2pi bl blk 20 7

On Stamps of 1913

328 A22 5pa ocher 5 5
a Inverted overprint 5.00 5.00
329 A22 10pa bl grn 7 5
a Inverted overprint 5.00 5.00
330 A22 20pa car rose 5 5
a Inverted overprint 5.00 5.00
331 A22 1pi ultra 7 5
a Inverted overprint 5.00 5.00
332 A22 2pi indigo 38 7
a Inverted overprint 5.00 5.00
333 A22 5pi dl vio 35 7
334 A22 10pi dl red 2.50 25
a Inverted overprint 10.00 10.00
335 A22 25pi gray grn 7.00 6.75

With Additional Overprint 

336 A22 10pa bl grn 7 7
337 A22 20pa car rose 10 10
338 A22 1pi ultra 16 7
339 A22 2pi indigo 1.20 35
a Inverted overprint 6.50 6.50

See Nos. P121-P133.

Stamps of 1901-13 Overprinted 

1916

340 A17 5pa purple 10 7
a 5pa purple, No. P43 80.00 80.00
341 A17 10pa green 10 7
a Double overprint 6.50 6.50
b 10pa yel green, No. 103 80.00 80.00
342 A21 20pa car rose, No. 153 16 7
a 20pa car rose, No. 162 80.00 80.00
343 A21 1pi ultra 25 10
344 A22 5pi dl vio 3.75 70

Occupation of the Sinai Peninsula.

Old General Post Office of Constantinople A41

Perf. 12½, 13½

1916, May 29 **Litho.**

345 A41 5pa green 15 5
346 A41 10pa carmine 8 5
347 A41 20pa ultra 15 5
348 A41 1pi vio & blk 22 5
349 A41 5pi yel brn & blk 4.50 32
Nos. 345-349 (5) 5.10 52

Introduction of postage in Turkey, 50th anniv.

Stamps of 1892-1905 Overprinted 

1916

350 A10 10pa gray grn (R) 70 40
351 A18 20pa car (Bl) 70 40
352 A18 1pi bl (R) 1.00 40
353 A18 2pi sl (Bk) 2.25 40
354 A18 2½pi red vio (Bk) 2.25 40
Nos. 350-354 (5) 6.90 2.00

National Fête Day. Overprint reads "10 Temuz 1332" (July 23, 1916).

Preceding Issues Overprinted or Surcharged in Red or Black:

a b

1916

On Stamps of 1892-98

355 A10(a) 10pa gray grn 10 7
355A A11(a) 20pa vio brn 10 5
b Inverted overprint 5.00 5.00
356 A12(a) 1pi gray bl 10.00 11.00
357 A13(a) 2pi brn org 1.20 55
358 A14(a) 5pi dl vio 6.00 6.50

On Stamp of 1897

359 A15(a) 5pa on 10pa gray grn 5 5

On Stamps of 1901

361 A16(a) 5pa bister 7 5
a Double overprint 5.00 5.00
362 A16(a) 10pa yel grn 14 14
363 A16(a) 20pa magenta 7 7
364 A16(a) 1pi vio bl 16 7
a Inverted overprint 6.50 6.50
365 A16(a) 2pi gray bl 50 38
366 A16(b) 5pi on 25pi dk grn 10.00 10.00
367 A16(b) 10pi on 25pi dk grn 10.00 10.00
368 A16(a) 25pi dk grn 10.00 10.00
369 A17(a) 5pa purple 7.00 9.00
370 A17(a) 10pa green 20 16
371 A17(a) 20pa carmine 14 5
a Inverted overprint 5.00 5.00
372 A17(a) 1pi blue 14 5
a Inverted overprint 5.00 5.00
373 A17(a) 2pi orange 14 7
374 A17(b) 10pi on 25pi brn 1.50 70
375 A17(b) 10pi on 50pi yel brn 2.00 1.00
376 A17(a) 25pi brown 2.00 70
377 A17(a) 50pi yel brn 2.50 70

On Stamps of 1905

378 A18(a) 5pa ocher 5 5
379 A18(a) 20pa carmine 7 5
a Inverted overprint 5.00 5.00
380 A18(a) 1pi brt bl 10 5
a Inverted overprint 5.00 5.00
381 A18(a) 2pi slate 38 16
382 A18(a) 2½pi red vio 45 16
383 A18(b) 10pi on 25pi ol grn 2.25 70
384 A18(b) 10pi on 50pi dp vio 2.50 70
385 A18(a) 25pi ol grn 2.50 70
386 A18(a) 50pi dp vio 2.25 70

On Stamps of 1906

387 A18(a) 10pa dl grn 20 10
388 A18(a) 20pa carmine 14 10
389 A18(a) 1pi brt bl 20 7

On Stamps of 1908

390 A19(a) 2½pi vio brn 7.00 7.00
391 A19(b) 10pi on 25pi dk grn 2.25 2.50
392 A19(b) 10pi on 50pi red brn 10.00 10.00
393 A19(b) 25pi on 50pi red brn 10.00 10.00
394 A19(a) 25pi dk grn 2.00 1.50
395 A19(a) 50pi red brn 7.00 7.00

With Additional Overprint 

396 A19(a) 2pi bl blk 7.00 7.00

On Stamps of 1908-09

397 A20(a) 5pa ocher 6.50 7.00
398 A21(a) 5pa ocher 7 5
399 A21(a) 10pa bl grn 6.50 7.00
400 A21(a) 20pa car rose 6.50 7.00
401 A21(a) 1pi ultra 38 10
402 A21(a) 2pi bl blk 38 25
403 A21(a) 2½pi dk brn 7.00 7.00
404 A21(a) 5pi dk vio 7.00 8.00

With Additional Overprint ب

405	A21(a)	1pi ultra	5.00	5.25
406	A21(a)	2pi bl blk	5.00	5.25

On Stamps of 1913

407	A22(a)	5pa ocher	5	5
408	A22(a)	20pa car rose	20	20
409	A22(a)	1pi ultra	22	8
410	A22(a)	2pi indigo	22	32
411	A22(b)	10pi on 50pi org brn	1.50	75
412	A22(a)	25pi gray grn	1.75	38
413	A22(a)	50pi org brn	1.75	75

With Additional Overprint ب

414	A22(a)	1pi ultra	15	5

On Commemorative Stamps of 1913

415	A23(a)	10pa green	10	5
416	A23(a)	20pa red	20	8
417	A23(a)	40pa blue	35	12

On Commemorative Stamp of 1916

418	A41(a)	5pi yel brn & blk	28	8

No. 277 Surcharged in Blue

419	A31	60pa on 1pi on 1½pi car & blk	38	20
a		"1330" omitted	5.00	5.00

See Nos. P134-P152, J67-J70.

Turkish Artillery A42

Mosque at Orta Köy, Constantinople — A43

Lighthouse on Bosporus A44

Monument to Martyrs of Liberty A45

Map of the Dardanelles; Sultan Mohammed V — A46

Map of the Dardanelles A47

Istanbul Across the Golden Horn A48

Pyramids of Egypt A49

Dolma Bahçe Palace and Mohammed V — A50

Sentry and Shell — A51

Sultan Mohammed V — A52

1916-18 Typo. *Perf. 11½, 12½*

420	A42	2pa violet	5	5
421	A43	5pa orange	5	5
424	A44	10pa green	5	5
		Engr.		
425	A45	20pa dp rose	12	5
426	A46	1pi dl vio	10	5
		Typo.		
428	A47	50pa ultra	10	5
429	A48	2pi org brn & ind	12	5
430	A49	5pi pale bl & blk	2.75	65
		Engr.		
431	A50	10pi dk grn	42	22
432	A50	10pi dk vio	1.25	22
433	A50	10pi dk brn	70	15
434	A51	25pi car, *straw*	28	20
437	A52	50pi carmine	1.10	50
438	A52	50pi indigo	22	22
439	A52	50pi grn, *straw*	2.50	2.25
		Nos. 420-439 (15)	9.81	4.76

Preceding Issues Overprinted or Surcharged in Red, Black or Blue:

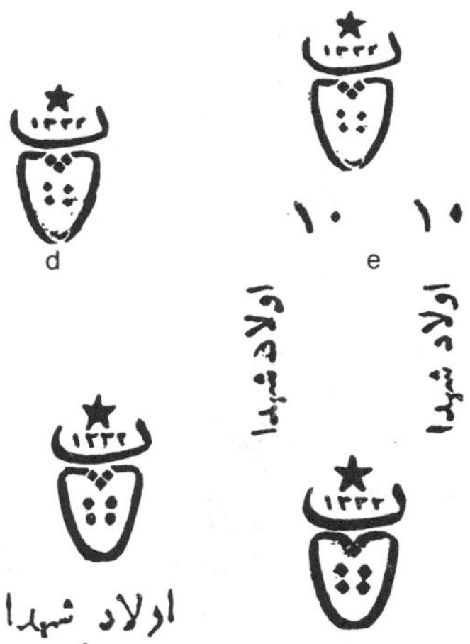

d e f g

1917

On Stamps of 1865

446	A5(d)	20pa yel (R)	15.00	15.00
a		Star without rays (R)	15.00	15.00
447	A5(d)	1pi pearl gray (R)	15.00	15.00
a		Star without rays (R)	15.00	15.00
448	A5(d)	2pi bl (R)	15.00	15.00
449	A5(d)	5pi car (Bk)	15.00	15.00

On Stamp of 1867

450	A5(d)	5pi rose (Bk)	15.00	15.00

On Stamps of 1870-71

451	A5(d)	2pi red (Bl)	20.00	20.00
452	A5(d)	5pi bl (Bk)	15.00	15.00
453	A5(d)	25pi dl rose (Bl)	20.00	15.00

On Stamp of 1874-75

454	A5(d)	10pa red vio (Bl)	20.00	20.00

On Stamps of April, 1876

455	A5(d)	10pa red lil (Bl)	12.50	15.00
a		10pa red violet (Bl)	12.50	15.00
457	A5(d)	20pa pale grn (R)	12.50	15.00
458	A5(d)	1pi yel (Bl)	15.00	15.00

On Stamps of January, 1876

459	A5(d)	¼pi on 10pa rose lil (Bl)	15.00	12.50
460	A5(d)	½pi on 20pa yel grn (R)	15.00	12.50
461	A5(d)	1¼pi on 50pa rose (Bl)	12.50	12.50

On Stamps of September, 1876

462	A7(d)	50pa bl & yel (R)	12.50	15.00
463	A7(d)	2pi blk & redsh brn (R)	12.50	15.00
464	A7(d)	25pi cl & rose (Bk)	19.00	19.00

On Stamps of 1880-84

465	A7(d)	5pa blk & ol (R)	15.00	15.00
466	A7(d)	10pa blk & grn (R)	15.00	15.00

On Stamps of 1881-82

467	A5(d)	20pa gray (Bl)	12.50	12.50
468	A5(d)	2pi pale sal (Bl)	15.00	12.50

On Stamps of 1884-86

469	A7(d)	10pa grn & pale grn (Bk)	13.50	12.50
470	A7(d)	2pi ocher & pale ocher (Bk)	13.50	12.50
471	A7(d)	5pi red brn & pale brn (Bk)	13.50	12.50

On Stamps of 1886

472	A7(d)	5pa blk & pale gray (R)	7	7
a		Inverted overprint	10.00	10.00
473	A7(d)	2pi org & bl (Bk)	38	40
a		Inverted overprint	10.00	10.00
474	A7(d)	5pi grn & pale grn (R)	15.00	15.00
475	A7(d)	25pi bis & pale bis (Bk)	20.00	20.00

On Stamp of 1888

476	A7(d)	5pi dk brn & gray (Bk)	15.00	15.00

On Stamps of 1892-98

477	A11(d)	20pa vio brn (R)	40	40
478	A13(d)	2pi brn org (R)	60	60
a		Tete beche pair	13.50	13.50

On Stamps of 1901

479	A16(d)	5pa bis (R)	50	50
a		Inverted overprint	10.00	10.00
480	A16(d)	20pa mag (Bk)	14	14
a		Inverted overprint	10.00	10.00
481	A16(d)	1pi vio bl (R)	40	40
a		Inverted overprint	10.00	10.00
482	A16(d)	2pi gray bl (R)	65	65
483	A16(d)	5pi ocher (R)	15.00	15.00
484	A16(e)	10pi on 50pi yel (R)	15.00	15.00
485	A16(d)	25pi dk grn (R)	15.00	15.00
486	A17(d)	5pa pur (Bk)	13.50	13.50
487	A17(d)	10pa grn (R)	60	60
488	A17(d)	20pa car (Bk)	20	20
a		Inverted overprint	10.00	10.00
489	A17(d)	1pi blue (R)	14	10
490	A17(d)	2pi org (Bk)	40	40
a		Inverted overprint	10.00	10.00
491	A17(d)	5pi lil rose (R)	15.00	15.00
492	A17(e)	10pi on 50pi yel brn (R)	15.00	15.00
493	A17(d)	25pi brn (R)	65	65

On Stamps of 1905

494	A18(d)	5pa ocher (R)	7	5
a		Inverted overprint	10.00	10.00
495	A18(d)	10pa dl grn (R)	15.00	15.00
496	A18(d)	20pa car (Bk)	5	5
a		Double overprint, one inverted	10.00	10.00
b		Inverted overprint	10.00	10.00
497	A18(d)	1pi bl (R)	5	5
a		Inverted overprint	10.00	10.00
498	A18(d)	2pi slate (R)	40	38
499	A18(d)	2½pi red vio (Bk)	55	40
a		Inverted overprint	10.00	10.00
500	A18(d)	5pi brn (R)	15.00	15.00
501	A18(d)	10pi org brn (R)	15.00	15.00
502	A18(e)	10pi on 50pi dp vio (R)	15.00	15.00
503	A18(d)	25pi ol grn (R)	15.00	15.00

On Nos. 128-131

504	A18(d)	10pa dl grn (R)	7	7
a		Inverted overprint	10.00	10.00
505	A18(d)	20pa car (Bk)	10	10
a		Double overprint, one inverted	10.00	10.00
b		Inverted overprint	10.00	10.00
506	A18(d)	1pi brt bl (Bk)	18	10
a		Inverted overprint	10.00	10.00
507	A18(d)	1pi brt bl (R)	38	38
a		Inverted overprint	10.00	10.00
508	A18(d)	2pi sl (Bk)	18.00	18.00
		Nos. 494-508 (15)	94.85	94.58

On Stamps of 1908

509	A19(d)	5pa ocher (R)	50	45
510	A19(d)	10pa bl grn (R)	10	8
510A	A19(d)	1pi brt bl (R)	*110.00*	*110.00*
511	A19(d)	2pi bl blk (R)	15.00	15.00
512	A19(d)	2½pi vio brn (Bk)	50	45
512A	A19(d)	10pi red (R)	*110.00*	*110.00*
513	A19(e)	10pi on 50pi red brn (R)	15.00	15.00
514	A19(d)	25pi dk grn (R)	15.00	15.00

With Additional Overprint ب

514A	A19(d)	10pa bl grn (Bk)	20.00	20.00
515	A19(d)	1pi brt bl (Bk)	15.00	15.00
516	A19(d)	2pi bl blk (R)	65	65
516A	A19(d)	2pi bl blk (Bk)	15.00	15.00

On Stamps of 1908-09

517	A20(d)	5pa ocher (R)	20	20
518	A21(d)	5pa ocher (R)	10	10
a		Double overprint	10.00	10.00
b		Dbl. ovpt., one inverted	10.00	10.00
519	A21(d)	10pa bl grn (R)	10	10
520	A21(d)	20pa car rose (Bk)	10	10
a		Double overprint	10.00	10.00
521	A21(d)	1pi ultra (R)	10	10
a		1p bright blue (R)	20.00	20.00
522	A21(d)	2pi bl blk (R)	45	45
523	A21(d)	2½pi dk brn (Bk)	15.00	15.00
524	A21(d)	5pi dk vio (R)	15.00	15.00
525	A21(d)	10pi dl red (R)	15.00	15.00

With Additional Overprint ب

525A	A21(d)	10pa bl grn (Bk)	*70.00*	*70.00*
526	A21(d)	1pi brt bl (Bk)	2.25	2.25
527	A21(d)	1pi ultra (R)	10	10
a		1pi bright blue (R)	20.00	20.00
528	A21(d)	2pi bl blk (Bk)	8.00	7.00

On Stamps of 1913

529	A22(d)	5pa ocher (R)	20	20
530	A22(d)	10pa bl grn (R)	15.00	15.00
531	A22(d)	20pa car rose (Bk)	20	20
532	A22(d)	1pi ultra (R)	20	20
533	A22(d)	2pi ind (R)	20	20
534	A22(d)	5pi dl vio (R)	18.00	18.00
535	A22(d)	10pi dl red (Bk)	18.00	18.00

With Additional Overprint ب

536	A22(d)	10pa bl grn (Bk)	20	20
a		Inverted overprint	10.00	10.00
537	A22(d)	1pi ultra (Bk)	65	65
a		Inverted overprint	10.00	10.00
538	A22(d)	2pi ind (Bk)	18.00	18.00

On Commemorative Stamps of 1913

539	A23(d)	10pa grn (R)	45	45
a		Inverted overprint	10.00	10.00
540	A23(d)	40pa bl (R)	55	55
a		Inverted overprint	10.00	10.00

On Stamp of 1914, with Addition of New Value

541	A31	60pa on 1 pi on 1½pi car & blk (Bk)	90	90
a		"1330" omitted	16.50	16.50

On Stamps of 1916-18

541B	A51(f)	25pi car, *straw*	1.00	55
541C	A52(g)	50pi carmine	5.00	4.00
541D	A52(g)	50pi indigo	7.00	4.00
541E	A52(g)	50pi grn, *straw*	5.50	4.00

Overprinted on Eastern Rumelia No. 12

542	A4(d)	20pa blk & rose (Bl)	12.50	12.50

Overprinted on Eastern Rumelia Nos. 15-17

543	A4(d)	5pa lil & pale lil (Bk)	12.50	12.50
544	A4(d)	10pa grn & pale grn (Bk)	12.50	12.50
545	A4(d)	20pa car & pale rose (Bk)	12.50	12.50

Some experts question the status of Nos. 510A, 512A and 525A.

See Nos. J71-J86, P153-P172.

Soldiers in Trench — A52a

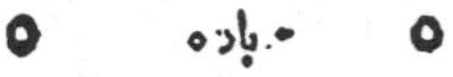

Surcharged

1917

545A A52a 5pa on 1pi red		7	5

It is stated that No. 545A was never issued without surcharge.

See No. 548f.

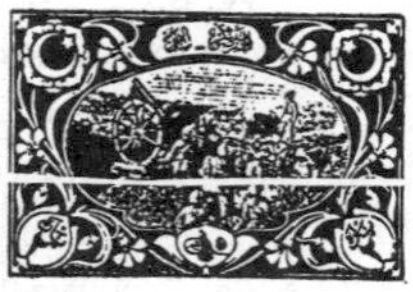

Turkish Artillery A53

1917 Typo. *Perf. 11 1/2, 12 1/2*

546 A53 2pa Prus bl	35.00	

In type A42 the Turkish inscription at the top is in one group, in type A53 it is in two groups. It is stated that No. 546 was never placed in use. Copies were distributed through the Universal Postal Union at Bern.

Surcharged

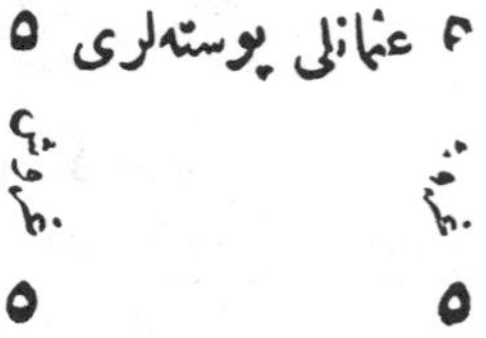

547	A53 5pi on 2pa Prus bl	20	5
a	Inverted surcharge	9.00	9.00
b	Turkish "5" omitted at lower left		

Surcharged

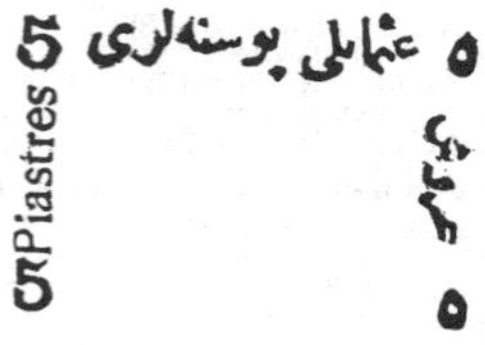

1918

548	A53 5pi on 2pa Prus bl	38	7
g	Inverted surcharge	10.00	10.00

Top line of surcharge on Nos. 547-548 reads "Ottoman Posts."

No. 545A Surcharged

1918

548A	A52a 2pa on 5pa on 1pi red	5	5
b	Double surcharge	3.00	3.00
c	Inverted surcharge	3.00	3.00
d	Double surcharge inverted	3.00	3.00
e	Dbl. surch., one inverted	3.00	3.00
f	In pair with No. 545A	6.00	6.00

Enver Pasha and Kaiser Wilhelm II on Battlefield A54

Sancta Sophia and Obelisk of the Hippodrome A55

1918 Typo. *Perf. 12, 12 1/2*

549 A54 5pa brn red	10.00	
550 A55 10pa gray grn	10.00	

The stamps, of which very few saw postal use, were converted into paper money by pasting on thick yellow paper and reperforating.

Armistice Issue

Overprinted in Black or Red

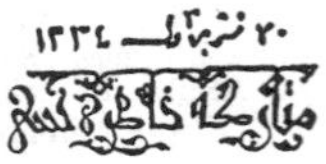

1919, Nov. 30

On Stamps of 1913

552	A34 2 1/2pi org & ol grn	25.00	22.50
553	A38 50pi carmine	25.00	22.50

On Stamps of 1916-18

554	A46 1pi dl vio (R)	38	38
555	A47 50pa ultra (R)	25	25
556	A48 2pi org brn & ind	10	10
557	A49 5pi pale bl & blk (R)	10	10
558	A50 10pi dk grn (R)	50	50
559	A51 25pi car, *straw*	50	50
560	A52 50pi grn, *straw* (R)	50	50

Fountain in Desert near Sinai — A56

Sentry at Beersheba — A57

Turkish Troops at Sinai — A58

Typo.

562	A56 20pa claret	10	10
563	A57 1pi blue (R)	25.00	22.50
564	A58 25pi slate bl (R)	25.00	22.50
	Nos. 552-564 (12)	102.43	92.43

The overprint reads: "Souvenir of the Armistice, 30th October 1334." Nos. 562 to 564 are not known to have been regularly issued without overprint.

See No. J87.

Stamps of 1911-19 Overprinted in Turkish "Accession to the Throne of His Majesty, 3rd July 1334-1918", the Tughra of Sultan Mohammed VI and sometimes Ornaments and New Values

Dome of the Rock, Jerusalem A59

1919

565	A42 2pa violet	8	8
566	A43 5pa orange	5	5
567	A21 5pa on 2pa ol grn	5	5
a	Inverted surcharge	2.50	2.50
568	A22 10pa on 2pa ol grn	5	5
569	A44 10pa green	8	8
a	Inverted overprint	2.50	2.50
570	A45 20pa dp rose	8	5
a	Inverted overprint	5.00	5.00
571	A46 1pi dl vio	8	8
572	A47 60pa on 50pa ultra	15	15
573	A48 60pa on 2pi org brn & ind	10	10
574	A48 2pi org brn & ind	10	10
574A	A34 2 1/2pi org & ol grn	5.00	5.00
575	A49 5pi pale bl & blk	10	10
576	A56 10pi on 20pa cl	12	12
577	A50 10pi dk brn	38	38
578	A51 25pi car, *straw*	55	50
579	A57 35pi on 1pi bl	50	38
579A	A52 50pi carmine	5.00	5.00
580	A52 50pi grn, *straw*	2.25	1.90
581	A59 100pi on 10pa grn	2.25	2.00
582	A58 250pi on 25pi sl bl	2.25	2.00
	Nos. 565-582 (20)	19.22	18.17

See Nos. J88-J91.

Surcharged with Ornaments, New Values and

Perf. 11 1/2, 12 1/2

583	A56 20pa claret	14	14
584	A57 1pi deep blue	14	14
585	A59 60pa on 10pa grn	14	14
586	A58 25pi slate bl	1.35	1.35
a	Inverted overprint		100.00

Nos. 576, 579, 581, 582 and 583 to 586 inclusive were prepared in anticipation of the invasion and conquest of Egypt by the Turks. They were not issued at that time but subsequently received various overprints in commemoration of Sultan Mehmet Sadi's accession to the throne (Nos. 565 to 582) and of the first anniversary of this event (Nos. 583 to 586).

Designs of 1913 Modified

1920 Litho. *Perf. 11, 12*

590	A26 5pa brn org	5	5

Engr.

591	A28 10pa green	5	5
592	A23 20pa rose	5	5
593	A30 1pi bl grn	28	5
594	A32 3pi blue	5	5
595	A34 5pi gray	2.25	20
596	A36 10pi gray vio	28	12
597	A37 25pi dl vio	50	25
598	A38 50pi brown	90	50
	Nos. 590-598 (9)	4.41	1.32

On most stamps of this issue the designs have been modified by removing the small Turkish word at right of the tughra of the Sultan. In the 3pi and 5pi the values have been altered, while for the 25pi the color has been changed.

A60

A61

A62

A63

Black Surcharge

1921-22

600	A60 30pa on 10pa red vio	8	5
a	Double surcharge	2.50	2.50
b	Imperf.		
601	A61 60pa on 10pa grn	10	5
a	Double surcharge	2.50	2.50
602	A62 4 1/2pi on 1pi red	30	20
a	Inverted surcharge	5.00	5.00
603	A63 7 1/2pi on 3pi bl	75	30
604	A63 7 1/2pi on 3pi bl (R) ('22)	2.25	42
a	Double surcharge	10.00	10.00
	Nos. 600-604 (5)	3.48	1.02

Issues of the Republic

Crescent and Star — A64

TWO PIASTRES
Type I - "2" measures 3 1/4x1 3/4mm.
Type II - "2" measures 2 3/4x1 1/2mm.

FIVE PIASTRES
Type I - "5" measures 3 1/2x2 1/4 mm.
Type II - "5" measures 3x1 3/4 mm.

Perf. 11, 12, 13 1/2, 13 1/2x12

1923-25 Litho.

605	A64 10pa gray blk	16	5
606	A64 20pa citron	20	5
607	A64 1pi dp vio	25	5
a	Slanting numeral in lower left corner	48	25
608	A64 1 1/2pi emerald	16	8
609	A64 2pi bluish grn (I)	70	5
a	2pi deep green (II)	1.20	8
610	A64 3pi yel brn	35	5
611	A64 3 3/4pi lil brn	35	8
612	A64 4 1/2pi carmine	65	5
613	A64 5pi pur (I)	1.40	8
a	5pi violet (II)	2.50	8
614	A64 7 1/2pi blue	70	5
615	A64 10pi slate	1.20	5
a	10pi blue	3.50	40
616	A64 11 1/4pi dl rose	70	35
617	A64 15pi brown	2.50	25
618	A64 18 3/4pi myr grn	1.20	40
619	A64 22 1/2pi orange	1.75	45
620	A64 25pi blk brn	4.00	12
621	A64 50pi gray	11.00	48
622	A64 100pi dk vio	20.00	48
624	A64 500pi dp grn	160.00	65.00
	Cut cancellation		1.60
	Nos. 605-624 (19)	207.27	68.17

Nos. 605-610, 612-617 exist imperf. and part perf.

Bridge of Sakarya and Mustafa Kemal — A65

1924, Jan. 1 *Perf. 12*

625	A65 1 1/2pi emerald	20	20
626	A65 3pi purple	20	20
627	A65 4 1/2pi pale rose	80	80
628	A65 5pi yel brn	20	20
629	A65 7 1/2pi dp bl	25	25
630	A65 50pi orange	6.50	6.50
631	A65 100pi brn vio	16.50	16.50
632	A65 200pi ol brn	30.00	30.00
	Nos. 625-632 (8)	54.65	54.65

Signing of Treaty of Peace at Lausanne.

The Legendary Blacksmith and his Gray Wolf — A66

Sakarya Gorge — A67

Fortress of Ankara A68

Mustafa Kemal Pasha A69

1926 **Engr.**

634	A66	10pa slate	5	5
635	A66	20pa orange	6	5
636	A66	1g brt rose	8	5
637	A67	2g green	12	5
638	A67	2½g gray blk	12	5
639	A67	3g cop red	15	5
640	A68	5g lil gray	28	5
641	A68	6g red	38	5
642	A68	10g dp blue	35	5
643	A68	15g dp org	1.50	5
644	A69	25g dk grn & blk	2.75	5
645	A69	50g car & blk	4.00	10
646	A69	100g ol grn & blk	7.00	50
647	A69	200g brn & blk	17.50	1.00
		Nos. 634-647 (14)	34.34	2.15

Stamps of 1926 Overprinted in Black, Silver or Gold

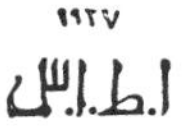

1927, Sept. 9

648	A66	1g brt rose	10	5
649	A67	2g green	10	5
650	A67	2½g gray blk	20	14
651	A67	3g cop red	30	16
652	A68	5g lil gray	50	22
653	A68	6g red	20	10
654	A68	10g dp blue	1.90	65
655	A68	15g dp org	1.90	65
656	A69	25g dk grn & blk (S)	5.00	3.00
657	A69	50g car & blk (S)	10.00	5.00
658	A69	100g ol grn & blk (G)	28.00	22.50
		Nos. 648-658 (11)	48.20	32.52

Agricultural and industrial exhibition at Izmir, Sept. 9-20, 1927.

The overprint reads: "1927" and the initials of "Izmir Dokuz Eylul Sergisi" (Izmir Exhibition, September 9).

Second Izmir Exhibition Issue

Stamps of 1926 Overprinted in Red or Black

1928, Sept. 9

659	A66	10pa slate (R)	6	5
660	A66	20pa orange (Bk)	6	5
661	A66	1g brt rose (Bk)	10	5
662	A67	2g green (R)	10	5
663	A67	2½g gray blk (R)	28	8
664	A67	3g cop red (Bk)	18	15
665	A68	5g lil gray (R)	42	38
666	A68	6g red (Bk)	28	8
667	A68	10g dp bl (Bk)	55	22
668	A68	15g dp org (Bk)	90	30

Overprinted

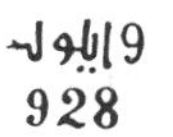

669	A69	25g dk grn & blk (R)	4.00	1.90
670	A69	50g car & blk (Bk)	10.00	4.00
671	A69	100g ol grn & blk (R)	20.00	11.00
672	A69	200g brn & blk (R)	30.00	16.50
		Nos. 659-672 (14)	66.93	34.81

The overprint reads "Izmir, September 9, 1928".

Stamps of 1926 Surcharged in Black or Red

2 ½ kuruşlar

1929

673	A66	20pa on 1g brt rose (Bk)	18	5
a		Inverted surcharge	3.50	3.50
674	A68	2½k on 5g lil gray (R)	28	10
a		Inverted surcharge	7.50	7.50
675	A68	6k on 10g dp bl (R)	3.75	25

Railroad Bridge over Kizil Irmak — A70

A71

A72

A73

Latin Inscriptions
Without umlaut over first "U" of "CUMHURIYETI"

1929 **Engr.**

676	A70	2k gray blk	38	5
677	A70	2½k green	38	5
678	A70	3k vio brn	38	5
679	A71	6k dk vio	5.00	5
680	A72	12½k dp blue	8.00	55
681	A73	50k car & blk	14.00	40
		Nos. 676-681 (6)	28.14	1.15

Sakarya Gorge — A74

Mustafa Kemal Pasha — A75

With umlaut over first "U" of "CUMHURIYETI"

1930

682	A71	10pa green	5	5
683	A70	20pa gray vio	5	5
684	A70	1k olive grn	12	5
685	A71	1½k olive blk	6	5
686	A70	2k dl vio	90	5
687	A70	2½k dp grn	15	5
688	A70	3k brn org	1.50	5
689	A71	4k dp rose	2.25	5
690	A72	5k rose lake	1.50	5
691	A71	6k indigo	1.75	5
692	A74	7½k red brn	12	5
694	A72	12½k dp ultra	35	5
695	A72	15k deep org	38	5
696	A74	17½k dk gray	42	15
697	A72	20k blk brn	8	30
698	A74	25k olive brn	75	5
699	A72	30k yel brn	1.25	5
700	A74	40k red vio	75	10
701	A75	50k red & blk	1.10	10
702	A75	100k ol grn & blk	2.25	15
703	A75	200k dk grn & blk	2.75	45
704	A75	500k choc & blk	11.25	2.25
		Nos. 682-704 (22)	29.78	4.25

Issue of 1930 Surcharged in Red or Black:

Sivas
D. Y.
30 ag. 930
1 K.
a

D. Y. Sivas
30 ag. 930
10 P.
b

Sivas

D. Y.

30 ag. 930
40 K.
c

1930, Aug. 30

705	A71(a)	10pa on 10pa grn (R)	7	7
706	A70(b)	10pa on 20pa gray vio	7	7
707	A70(b)	20pa on 1ku ol grn	8	8
708	A71(a)	1k on 1½k ol blk (R)	14	7
709	A70(b)	1½k on 2k dl vio	20	7
710	A70(b)	2k on 2½k dp grn (R)	38	10
711	A70(b)	2½k on 3k brn org	38	10
712	A71(a)	3k on 4k dp rose	50	10
713	A72(a)	4k on 5k rose lake	1.00	20
714	A71(a)	5k on 6k ind (R)	30	20
715	A74(a)	6k on 7½k red brn	50	14
716	A72(a)	7½k on 12½k ultra (R)	60	10
717	A72(a)	12½k on 15k dp org	1.50	20
718	A74(b)	15k on 17½k dk gray (R)	1.50	50
719	A72(b)	17½k on 20k blk brn (R)	1.90	50
720	A74(b)	20k on 25k ol brn (R)	1.90	50
721	A72(b)	25k on 30k yel brn	1.90	50
722	A74(b)	30k on 40k red vio	2.50	60
723	A75(c)	40k on 50k red & blk	2.50	50
724	A75(c)	50k on 100k ol grn & blk (R)	25.00	8.00
725	A75(c)	100k on 200k dk grn & blk (R)	28.00	12.00
726	A75(c)	250k on 500k choc & blk (R)	30.00	8.00
		Nos. 705-726 (22)	100.92	32.60

Inauguration of the railroad between Ankara and Sivas.

There are numerous varieties in these settings as: "309", "390", "930" inverted, no period after "D", no period after "Y", and raised period before "Y".

No. 685 Surcharged in Red

1
Kuruş

1931, Apr. 1

727	A71	1k on 1½k ol blk	55	10

Olive Tree with Roots Extending to All Balkan Capitals — A76

1931, Oct. 20 **Engr.** ***Perf. 12***

728	A76	2½k dk grn	10	5
729	A76	4k carmine	10	6
730	A76	6k steel bl	12	6
731	A76	7½k dull red	12	6
732	A76	12k dp org	15	5
733	A76	12½k dk blue	22	5
734	A76	30k dk vio	50	8
735	A76	50k dk brn	1.00	22
736	A76	100k brn vio	2.25	1.00
		Nos. 728-736 (9)	4.56	1.63

Second Balkan Conference.

A77

A78

Mustafa Kemal Pasha (Kemal Atatürk) — A79

1931-42 **Typo.** ***Perf. 11½, 12***

737	A77	10pa bl grn	5	5
738	A77	20pa dp org	5	5
739	A77	30pa brt vio ('38)	5	5
740	A78	1k dk sl grn	5	5
740A	A77	1½k mag ('42)	50	8
741	A78	2k dk vio	5	5
741A	A78	2k yel grn ('40)	12	5
742	A77	2½k green	5	5
743	A78	3k brn org ('38)	8	5
744	A78	4k slate	5	5
745	A78	5k rose red	8	5
745A	A78	5k brn blk ('40)	35	5
746	A78	6k dp bl	22	5
746A	A78	6k rose ('40)	20	5
747	A77	7½k dp rose ('32)	15	5
747A	A78	8k brt bl ('38)	20	5
b		8k dark blue ('36)	20	5
748	A77	10k blk brn ('32)	3.00	5
748A	A77	10k dp bl ('40)	1.90	8
749	A77	12k bister ('32)	38	5
750	A79	12½k indigo ('32)	22	5
751	A77	15k org yel ('32)	38	5
752	A77	20k ol grn ('32)	38	5
753	A77	25k Prus bl ('32)	38	5
754	A77	30k mag ('32)	50	5
755	A79	100k mar ('32)	1.00	12
756	A79	200k pur ('32)	1.75	15
757	A79	250k choc ('32)	7.00	38
		Nos. 737-757 (27)	19.14	1.91

See Nos. 1015-1033, 1117B-1126.

Symbolizing 10th Anniversary of Republic — A80

President Atatürk — A81

1933, Oct. 29 ***Perf. 10***

758	A80	1½k bl green	50	16
759	A80	2k olive brn	50	20
760	A81	3k red brown	50	16
761	A81	6k dp blue	50	25
762	A80	12½k dark blue	1.50	1.35
763	A80	25k dk brown	3.00	2.50
764	A81	50k org brown	6.50	6.00
		Nos. 758-764 (7)	13.00	10.62

10th year of the Turkish Republic. The stamps were in use for three days only.

Stamps of 1930 Overprinted or Surcharged in Red:

İzmir
9 Eylûl 934
Sergisi
a

İzmir
9 Eylûl 934
Sergisi
2 Kurus
b

1934, Aug. 26 ***Perf. 12***

765	A71	10pa green	10	8
766	A71	1k on 1½k ol blk	15	8
767	A74	2k on 25k ol brn	25	8
768	A74	5k on 7½k red brn	70	28
769	A74	6k on 17½k dk gray	70	38
770	A72	12½k dp ultra	2.00	75
771	A72	15k on 20k blk brn	20.00	14.00
772	A74	20k on 25k ol brn	17.50	11.25
773	A75	50k on 100k ol grn & blk	17.50	11.25
		Nos. 765-773 (9)	58.90	38.15

Izmir Fair, 1934.

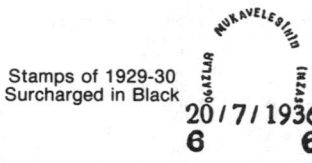

Stamps of 1929-30 Surcharged in Black

MUKAVELESİNİN İMZASI OGAZLAR 20/7/1936 6 6

1936, Oct. 26

No.	Type	Description	Unused	Used
775	A74	4k on 17½k dk gray	80	38
a		"1926" in overprint	6.50	3.75
776	A74	5k on 25k ol brn	80	38
a		"1926" in overprint	7.00	3.75
777	A73	6k on 50k car & blk	80	38
a		"1926" in overprint	7.00	3.75
778	A75	10k on 100k ol grn & blk	1.25	50
a		"1926" in overprint	9.00	4.50
779	A75	20k on 200k dk grn & blk	4.50	1.40
a		"1926" in overprint	20.00	10.00
780	A75	50k on 500k choc & blk	8.00	2.25
a		"1926" in overprint	55.00	27.50
		Nos. 775-780 (6)	16.15	5.29

Re-militarization of the Dardanelles.

Hittite Bronze Stag — A82

Thorak's Bust of Kemal Atatürk — A83

1937, Sept. 20 **Litho.** ***Perf. 12***

No.	Type	Description	Unused	Used
781	A82	3k lt vio	55	30
782	A83	6k blue	75	45
783	A82	7½k brt pink	1.40	1.00
784	A83	12½k indigo	2.50	1.50

2nd Turkish Historical Congress, Istanbul, Sept. 20-30.

Arms of Turkey, Greece, Romania and Jugoslavia — A84

1937, Oct. 29 ***Perf. 11½***

No.	Type	Description	Unused	Used
785	A84	8k carmine	5.00	3.00
786	A84	12½k dk bl	11.25	3.75

The Balkan Entente.

Street in Izmir A85

Fig Tree — A87

Designs: 30pa, View of Fair Buildings. 3k, Tower, Government Square. 5k, Olive branch. 6k, Woman with grapes. 7½k, Woman picking grapes. 8k, Izmir Harbor through arch. 12k, Statue of President Ataturk. 12½k, President Ataturk.

1938, Aug. 20 **Photo.** ***Perf. 11½***
Inscribed: "Izmir Enternasyonal Fuari 1938"

No.	Type	Description	Unused	Used
789	A85	10pa dk brn	12	5
790	A85	30pa purple	12	5
791	A87	2½k brt grn	42	5
792	A87	3k brn org	20	8
793	A87	5k ol grn	38	15
794	A85	6k brown	1.25	25
795	A87	7½k scarlet	1.25	45
796	A87	8k brn lake	65	30
797	A87	12k rose vio	1.00	65
798	A87	12½k deep bl	2.25	1.40
		Nos. 789-798 (10)	7.64	3.43

Izmir International Fair.

President Atatürk Teaching Reformed Turkish Alphabet A95

1938, Nov. 2

No.	Type	Description	Unused	Used
799	A95	2½k brt grn	22	14
800	A95	3k orange	22	14
801	A95	6k rose vio	35	14
802	A95	7½k dp rose	35	35
803	A95	8k red brn	55	40
804	A95	12½k brt ultra	1.10	80
		Nos. 799-804 (6)	2.79	1.97

Reform of the Turkish alphabet, 10th anniv.

Army and Air Force A96

Atatürk Driving Tractor — A98

Designs: 3k, View of Kayseri. 7½k, Railway bridge. 8k, Scout buglers. 12½k, President Ataturk.

1938, Oct. 29
Inscribed: "Cumhuriyetin 15 inc yil donumu hatirasi"

No.	Type	Description	Unused	Used
805	A96	2½k dk grn	16	10
806	A96	3k red brn	20	10
807	A98	6k bister	22	16
808	A96	7½k red	55	25
809	A96	8k rose vio	2.00	1.35
810	A98	12½k dp blue	1.35	80
		Nos. 805-810 (6)	4.48	2.76

15th anniversary of the Republic.

Stamps of 1931-38 Overprinted in Black

21-11-1938

1938, Nov. 21 ***Perf. 11½x12***

No.	Type	Description	Unused	Used
811	A78	3k brn org	20	16
812	A78	5k rose red	20	16
813	A78	6k dp blue	20	20
814	A77	7½k dp rose	38	25
815	A78	8k dark bl	45	38
a		8k bright blue	12.00	10.00
816	A79	12½k indigo	70	65
		Nos. 811-816 (6)	2.13	1.80

President Kemal Atatürk (1881-1938). The date is that of his funeral.

Turkish and American Flags — A102

Presidents Inönüand F. D. Roosevelt and Map of North America A103

Designs: 3k, 8k, Inonu and Roosevelt. 7½k, 12½k, Kemal Ataturk and Washington.

1939, July 15 **Photo.** ***Perf. 14***

No.	Type	Description	Unused	Used
817	A102	2½k ol grn, red & bl	20	16
818	A103	3k dk brn & Bl grn	20	16
819	A102	6k pur, red & bl	20	16
820	A103	7½k org ver & bl grn	25	38
821	A103	8k dp cl & bl grn	55	38
822	A103	12½k brt bl & bl grn	90	80
		Nos. 817-822 (6)	2.30	2.04

US constitution, 150th anniversary.

Stamps of 1930 Surcharged in Black

Anavatana Hatayın Kavuşması 23/7/1939 3 3

1939, July 23 **Unwmk.** ***Perf. 13***

No.	Type	Description	Unused	Used
823	A74	3k on 25k ol brn	10	10
824	A75	6k on 200k dk grn & blk	14	12
825	A74	7½k on 25k ol brn	20	16
826	A75	12k on 100k ol grn & blk	22	20
827	A75	12½k on 200k dk grn & blk	35	30
828	A75	17½k on 500k choc & blk	65	60
		Nos. 823-828 (6)	1.66	1.48

Annexation of Hatay.

Railroad Bridge A105

Locomotive A106

Track Through Mountain Pass A107

Design: 12½k, Railroad tunnel, Atma Pass.

1939, Oct. 20 **Typo.** ***Perf. 11½***

No.	Type	Description	Unused	Used
829	A105	3k lt org red	1.50	1.00
830	A106	6k chestnut	2.50	2.00
831	A107	7½k rose pink	3.00	2.25
832	A107	12½k dark blue	4.50	3.75

Completion of the Sivas to Erzerum link of the Ankara-Erzerum Railroad.

Values quoted in this catalogue are for stamps graded at Fine-Very Fine and with no faults. An illustrated guide to grade is provided in introductory material, beginning on Page V.

Atatürk Residence in Ankara A109

Kemal Atatürk A110

A111

Designs: 5k, 6k, 7½k, 8k, 12½k, 17½k, Various portraits of Ataturk, "1880-1938."

1939-40 **Photo.**

No.	Type	Description	Unused	Used
833	A109	2½k brt grn	8	7
834	A110	3k dk bl gray	10	8
835	A110	5k chocolate	14	10
836	A110	6k chestnut	14	10
837	A110	7½k rose red	20	20
838	A110	8k gray grn	16	20
839	A110	12½k brt bl	30	16
840	A110	17½k brt rose	90	80
		Nos. 833-840 (8)	2.02	1.71

Souvenir Sheet

No.	Type	Description	Unused	Used
841	A111	100k bl blk	20.00	19.00

Death of Kemal Ataturk, first anniversary. Size of No. 841: 90x120mm.

Issue dates: 2½, 6 and 12½k, Nov. 11, 1939. Others, Jan. 3, 1940.

Namik Kemal A118

Arms of Turkey, Greece, Romania and Jugoslavia A119

1940, Jan. 3

No.	Type	Description	Unused	Used
842	A118	6k chestnut	18	15
843	A118	8k dk ol grn	25	18
844	A118	12k brt rose red	70	30
845	A118	12½k brt bl	80	75

Birth cent. of Namik Kemal, poet and patriot.

Perf. 11½

1940, Jan. 1 **Typo.** **Unwmk.**

No.	Type	Description	Unused	Used
846	A119	8k light blue	90	38
847	A119	10k deep blue	90	38

The Balkan Entente.

Nos. 703-704 Surcharged in Red or Black

IZMIR ENTERNASYONAL FUARI 1940 6 KURUS

1940, Aug. 20 *Perf. 12*

848	A75	6k on 200k dk grn & blk (R)	30	20
849	A75	10k on 200k dk grn & blk	42	38
850	A75	12k on 500k choc & blk	50	38

13th International Izmir Fair.

Map of Turkey and Census Figures A120

1940, Oct. 1 **Typo.** *Perf. 11½*

851	A120	10pa	dk bl grn	10	7
852	A120	3k	orange	16	14
853	A120	6k	car rose	30	25
854	A120	10k	dark blue	80	50

Census of Oct. 20, 1940.

Runner — A121

Pole Vaulter — A122

Hurdler A123

Discus Thrower — A124

1940, Oct. 5

855	A121	3k	olive grn	60	50
856	A122	6k	rose	2.25	1.65
857	A123	8k	chestnut brn	1.50	70
858	A124	10k	dark blue	2.25	2.00

11th Balkan Olympics.

Mail Carriers on Horseback A125

Postman of 1840 and 1940 A126

Old Sailing Vessel and Modern Mailboat A127

Design: 12k, Post Office, Istanbul.

1940, Dec. 31 **Typo.** *Perf. 10*

859	A125	3k	gray grn	14	10
860	A126	6k	rose	20	16
861	A127	10k	dark blue	65	60
862	A127	12k	olive brn	65	50

Centenary of the Turkish post.

Harbor Scene A129

Statue of Atatürk — A132

Designs: 3k, 6k, 17½k, Various Izmir Fair buildings. 12k, Girl picking grapes.

1941, Aug. 20 **Litho.** *Perf. 11½*
Inscribed: "Izmir Enternasyonal Fuari 1941"

863	A129	30pa	dl grn	5	5
864	A129	3k	ol gray	10	5
865	A129	6k	sal rose	14	6
866	A129	10k	blue	22	10
867	A129	12k	dl brn vio	30	14
868	A129	17½k	dl brn	70	38
			Nos. 863-868 (6)	1.51	78

Izmir International Fair, 1941.

Tomb of Barbarossa II — A135

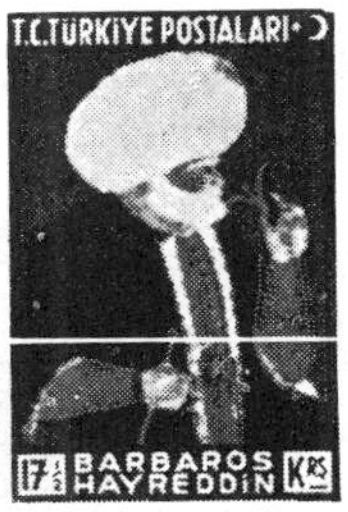

Barbarossa II (Khair ed-Din) — A137

Barbarossa's Fleet in Battle — A136

1941

869	A135	20pa	dk vio	8	8
870	A136	3k	light bl	12	9
871	A136	6k	rose red	22	16
872	A136	10k	dp ultra	38	12
873	A136	12k	dl brn & bis	90	35
874	A137	17½k	multi	2.00	1.50
			Nos. 869-874 (6)	3.70	2.30

400th death anniv. of Barbarossa II.

President Inönü
A138 A138a

1942-45 *Perf. 11½x11, 11*

875	A138	0.25k	yel bis	5	5
876	A138	0.50k	lt yel grn	5	5
877	A138	1k	gray grn	5	5
877A	A138	1½k	brt vio ('45)	38	5
878	A138	2k	bluish grn	5	5
879	A138	4k	fawn	6	5
880	A138	4½k	slate	6	5
881	A138	5k	light bl	8	5
882	A138	6k	sal rose	10	5
883	A138	6¾k	ultra	12	5
884	A138	9k	bl vio	70	5
885	A138	10k	dk blue	10	5
886	A138	13½k	brt pink	10	5
887	A138	16k	Prus grn	20	5
888	A138	17½k	rose lake	20	5
889	A138	20k	brn vio	45	5
890	A138	27½k	orange	25	6
891	A138	37k	buff	28	6
892	A138	50k	purple	75	10
893	A138	100k	ol bis	2.00	45
894	A138a	200k	brown	7.00	65
			Nos. 875-894 (21)	13.03	2.12

Ankara A139

Antioch A141

Designs: 0.50k, Mohair goats. 1½k, Ankara Dam. 2k, Oranges. 4k, Merino sheep. 4½k, Train. 5k, Tile decorating. 6k, Atatürk statue, Ankara. 6¾k, 10k, President Ismet Inonu. 13½k, Grand National Assembly. 16k, Arnavutkoy, Istanbul. 17½k, Republic monument, Istanbul. 20k, Safety monument, Ankara. 27½k, Post Office, Istanbul. 37k, Monument at Afyon. 50k, "People's House," Ankara. 100k, Atatürk and Inonu. 200k, President Inonu.

1943, Apr. 1 *Perf. 11*

896	A139	0.25k	citron	5	5
897	A139	0.50k	brt grn	18	5
898	A141	1k	yel ol	5	5
899	A141	1½k	dp vio	5	5
900	A139	2k	brt bl grn	22	5
901	A139	4k	cop red	40	5
902	A139	4½k	black	32	5
903	A141	5k	sapphire	25	8
904	A139	6k	car rose	8	5
905	A139	6¾k	brt ultra	6	5
906	A139	10k	dark bl	10	5
907	A141	13½k	brt red vio	12	5
908	A141	16k	myrtle grn	65	10
909	A139	17½k	brn org	25	8
910	A139	20k	sepia	30	8
911	A139	27½k	dk org	65	22
912	A139	37k	lt yel brn	30	8
913	A141	50k	purple	1.50	8
914	A139	100k	dk ol grn	2.50	20
915	A139	200k	dk brn	3.75	30
a			Souvenir sheet	11.25	8.75
			Nos. 896-915 (20)	11.78	1.77

No. 915a contains one stamp similar to No. 915, perf. 13½ and printed in sepia. Issued Apr. 20.

Girl with Grapes — A158

Entrance to Izmir Fair A159

Fair Building A160

1943, Aug. 20 **Litho.** *Perf. 11½*

916	A158	4½k	dl olive	14	8
917	A159	6k	car rose	12	8
918	A160	6¾k	blue	14	10
919	A159	10k	dk blue	16	10
920	A158	13½k	sepia	50	20
921	A160	27½k	dl gray	50	30
			Nos. 916-921 (6)	1.56	86

Izmir International Fair.

Soccer Team on Parade A161

Turkish Flag and Soldier — A162

Designs: 6¾k, Bridge. 10k, Hospital. 13½k, View of Ankara. 27½k, President Inonu.

Perf. 11x11½, 11½x11
1943, Oct. 29
Inscribed: "Cumhuriyetin 20 nci Yildonomu Hatirasi"

922	A161	4½k	lt ol grn	50	30
923	A162	6k	rose red	14	7
924	A161	6¾k	ultra	10	7
925	A161	10k	vio bl	14	10
926	A161	13½k	olive	22	16
927	A162	27½k	lt brn	45	42
			Nos. 922-927 (6)	1.55	1.12

20th anniversary of Republic. Nos. 922-927 exist imperf.

No. 905 Surcharged with New Value in Red

1945 *Perf. 11*

928	A139	4½k on 6¾k brt ultra	10	5

Recording Census Data A167

President Ismet Inönü A169

1945, Oct. 21 **Litho.** *Perf. 11½*

929	A167	4½k	ol blk	30	22
930	A167	9k	violet	30	22
931	A167	10k	vio bl	30	22
932	A167	18k	dk red	65	50

Souvenir Sheet
Imperf

933	A167	1 l	chocolate	7.50	5.50

Census of 1945.

Perf. 11½ to 12½
1946, Apr. 1 **Unwmk.**

934	A169	0.25k	brn red	5	5
935	A169	1k	dk sl grn	6	5
936	A169	1½k	plum	6	5
937	A169	9k	purple	16	5
938	A169	10k	dp bl	45	5
939	A169	50k	chocolate	1.40	10
			Nos. 934-939 (6)	2.18	35

U.S.S. Missouri A170

1946, Apr. 5

940	A170	9k dk pur	16	7
941	A170	10k dk chlky bl	16	10
942	A170	27½k ol grn	60	30
a		Imperf., pair	14.00	

Visit of the U.S.S. Missouri to Istanbul, Apr. 5.

Sower
A171

Dove and Flag-Decorated Banderol
A172

1946, June 16

943	A171	9k violet	5	5
944	A171	10k dark blue	5	5
945	A171	18k olive grn	12	10
946	A171	27½k red org	35	22

Passing of legislation to distribute state lands to poor farmers.

1947, Aug. 20 Photo. *Perf. 12*

947	A172	15k vio & dk bl	6	5
948	A172	20k bl & dk bl	10	6
949	A172	30k brn & gray blk	12	6
950	A172	1 l ol grn & dk grn	55	45

Izmir International Fair.

Victory Monument, Afyon Karahisar
A173

Ismet Inönü as General
A174

Kemal Atatürk as General — A175

1947, Aug. 30

951	A173	10k dk brn & pale brn	6	5
952	A174	15k brt vio & gray	6	5
953	A175	20k dp bl & gray	6	5
954	A173	30k grnsh blk & gray	12	8
955	A174	60k ol gray & pale brn	22	12
956	A175	1 l dk grn & gray	65	30
		Nos. 951-956 (6)	1.17	65

25th anniv. of the Battle of Dumlupinar, Aug. 30, 1922.

Grapes and Istanbul Skyline
A176

1947, Sept. 22

957	A176	15k rose vio	10	8
958	A176	20k dp bl	16	14
959	A176	60k dk brn	45	40

International Vintners' Congress, Istanbul.

The only foreign revenue stamps listed in this Catalogue are those authorized for prepayment of postage.

Approaching Train, Istanbul Skyline and Sirkeci Terminus — A177

1947, Oct. 9

960	A177	15k rose vio	28	8
961	A177	20k brt bl	42	15
962	A177	60k ol grn	75	65

International Railroad Congress, Istanbul.

President Ismet Inönü
A178 A179

1948 Unwmk. Engr. *Perf. 12, 14*

963	A178	0.25k dk red	5	5
964	A178	1k ol blk	5	5
965	A178	2k brt rose lil	5	5
966	A178	3k red org	5	5
967	A178	4k dk grn	5	5
968	A178	5k blue	6	5
969	A178	10k chocolate	10	5
970	A178	12k dp red	10	5
971	A178	15k violet	12	5
972	A178	20k dp blue	20	5
973	A178	30k brown	50	10
974	A178	60k black	90	12
975	A179	1 l olive grn	2.00	35
976	A179	2 l dk brn	15.00	1.10
977	A179	5 l dp plum	10.00	2.25
		Nos. 963-977 (15)	29.23	4.42

President Ismet Inönü and Lausanne Conference
A180

Conference Building
A180a

1948, July 23 Photo. *Perf. 11½*

978	A180	15k rose lil	10	5
979	A180a	20k blue	12	5
980	A180a	40k gray grn	20	15
981	A180	1 l brown	70	38

25th anniversary of Lausanne Treaty.

Statue of Kemal Atatürk, Ankara — A181

1948, Oct. 29

982	A181	15k violet	10	5
983	A181	20k blue	12	5
984	A181	40k gray grn	20	18
985	A181	1 l brown	90	65

25th anniv. of the proclamation of the republic.

Catalogue values for unused stamps in this section, from this point to the end of the section, are for Never Hinged items.

A182 A183

A184

Wrestlers
A185

1949, June 3

986	A182	15k rose lil	1.10	1.00
987	A183	20k blue	2.25	1.40
988	A184	30k brown	2.25	1.65
989	A185	60k green	3.25	2.75

5th European Wrestling Championships, Istanbul, June 3-5, 1949.

Ancient Galley
A186

Galleon Mahmudiye
A187

Monument to Khizr Barbarossa
A188

Designs: 15k, Cruiser Hamidiye. 20k, Submarine Sakarya. 30k, Cruiser Yavuz.

1949, July 1

990	A186	5k violet	15	5
991	A187	10k brown	18	5
992	A186	15k lil rose	20	10
993	A186	20k gray bl	25	15
994	A186	30k gray	45	28
995	A188	40k olive gray	65	55
		Nos. 990-995 (6)	1.88	1.18

Fleet Day, July 1, 1949.

A189

UPU Monument, Bern
A190

Perf. 11½

1949, Oct. 9 Unwmk. Photo.

996	A189	15k violet	15	8
997	A189	20k blue	20	15
998	A190	30k dl rose	30	20
999	A190	40k green	65	38

UPU, 75th anniversary.

Istanbul Fair Building
A191

1949, Oct. 1 Litho. *Perf. 10*

1000	A191	15k brown	10	7
1001	A191	20k blue	16	10
1002	A191	30k olive	50	25

Istanbul Fair, Oct. 1-31.

Boy and Girl and Globe — A192

Aged Woman Casting Ballot — A193

Kemal Atatürk and Map
A194

1950, Aug. 13 *Perf. 11½*

1003	A192	15k purple	12	8
1004	A192	20k deep blue	20	15

2nd World Youth Council Meeting, 1950. No. 1004 exists imperf. Value $3.

1950, Aug. 30

1005	A193	15k dk brn	8	8
1006	A193	20k dark blue	12	8
1007	A194	30k dk bl & gray	20	12

Election of May 14, 1950.

Hazel Nuts
A195

Symbolical of 1950 Census
A196

Designs: 12k, Acorns. 15k, Cotton. 20k, Symbolical of the fair. 30k, Tobacco.

1950, Sept. 9

1008	A195	8k gray grn & buff	16	8
1009	A195	12k magenta	22	10
1010	A195	15k brn blk & lt brn	40	22
1011	A195	20k dk bl & aqua	65	40
1012	A195	30k brn blk & dl org	1.10	65
		Nos. 1008-1012 (5)	2.53	1.45

Izmir International Fair, Aug. 20-Sept. 20.

1950, Oct. 9 Litho. ***Perf. 11 ½***

1013	A196	15k dk brn	14	8
1014	A196	20k vio bl	25	16

General census of 1950.

Atatürk Types of 1931-42

Perf. 10x11 ½, 11 ½x12

1950-51 Typo.

1015	A77	10p dl red brn	5	5
1016	A77	10p ver ('51)	5	5
1017	A77	20p blue grn	5	5
1018	A78	1k olive grn	14	5
1019	A78	2k plum	22	5
1020	A78	2k dp yel ('51)	40	5
1021	A78	3k yel org	40	5
1022	A78	3k gray ('51)	30	5
1023	A78	4k grn ('51)	30	5
1024	A78	5k blue	25	5
1025	A78	5k plum ('51)	2.00	5
1026	A77	10k brn org	1.00	5
1027	A77	15k purple	1.20	5
1028	A77	15k brn car	9.00	5
1029	A77	20k dk blue	6.50	8
1030	A77	30k pink ('51)	8.00	10
1031	A79	100k red brn ('51)	1.00	16
1032	A79	200k dk brn	4.00	38
1033	A79	200k rose vio ('51)	2.25	50
		Nos. 1015-1033 (19)	37.11	1.92

16th Century Flight of Hezarfen Ahmet Celebi — A197

Plane over Istanbul A198

Design: 40k, Biplane over Taurus Mountains.

1950, Oct. 17 Litho. ***Perf. 11***

1034	A197	20k dk grn & bl	35	20
1035	A197	40k dk brn & bl	55	35
1036	A198	60k pur & bl	90	60

Regional meeting of the ICAO, Istanbul, Oct. 17.

Farabi A199

1950, Dec. 1 Unwmk. ***Perf. 11 ½***

Multicolored Center

1037	A199	15k blue	38	22
1038	A199	20k bl vio	75	30
1039	A199	60k red brn	1.90	1.00
1040	A199	1 l gold & bl vio	1.65	2.25

Death millenary of Farabi, Arab philosopher.

Mithat Pasha and Security Bank Building — A200

Design: 20k, Agricultural Bank.

1950, Dec. 21 Photo.

1041	A200	15k rose vio	35	20
1042	A200	20k blue	45	28

3rd Congress of Turkish Cooperatives, Istanbul, Dec. 25, 1950.

Floating a Ship A201

Lighthouse — A202

Designs: 20k, Steamship. 30k, Diver Rising.

1951, July 1

1043	A201	15k blue	22	16
1044	A201	20k dp ultra	22	16
1045	A201	30k ol gray	45	40
1046	A202	1 l gray grn	1.00	80

25th anniv. of the recognition of coastal rights in Turkish waters to ships under the Turkish flag.

Mosque of Sultan Ahmed A203

Henry Carton de Wiart — A204

Designs: 20k, Dolma Bahce Palace. 60k, Rumeli Hisari Fortress.

1951, Aug. 31 Photo. ***Perf. 13 ½***

1047	A203	15k dk grn	20	16
1048	A203	20k dp ultra	20	16
1049	A204	30k brown	30	25
1050	A203	60k pur brn	80	70

40th Interparliamentary Conf., Istanbul, 1951.

Allegory of Food and Agriculture A205

Designs: 20k, Dam. 30k, United Nations Building. 60k, University, Ankara.

1952, Jan. 3 Unwmk. ***Perf. 14***

Inscribed: "Akdeniz Yetistirme Merkezi. Ankara 1951."

1051	A205	15k green	38	10
1052	A205	20k bl vio	45	12
1053	A205	30k blue	70	35
1054	A205	60k red	1.75	1.40
a		Souv. sheet of 4	30.00	25.00

UN Mediterranean Economic Instruction Center.

No. 1054a contains one each of Nos. 1051-1054, imperf., with inscriptions in dark blue gray.

Abdulhak Hamid Tarhan, Poet, Birth Cent. — A206

1952, Feb. 5 Photo. ***Perf. 13 ½***

1055	A206	15k dark pur	8	7
1056	A206	20k dark bl	14	7
1057	A206	30k brown	25	14
1058	A206	60k dk ol grn	65	40

Ruins, Bergama A207

Tarsus Cataract A208

Designs: 2k, Ruins, Milas. 3k, Karatay Gate, Konya. 4k, Kozak plateau. 5k, Urgup. 10k, 12k, 15k, 20k, Kemal Ataturk. 30k, Mosque, Bursa. 40k, Mosque, Istanbul. 75k, Rocks, Urgup. 1 l, Palace, Istanbul. 2 l, Pavilion, Istanbul. 5 l, Museum interior, Istanbul.

1952, Mar. 15 ***Perf. 13 ½***

1059	A207	1k brn org	5	5
1060	A207	2k ol grn	5	5
1061	A207	3k rose brn	5	5
1062	A207	4k bl grn	5	5
1063	A207	5k brown	5	5
1064	A207	10k dk brn	10	5
1065	A207	12k brt rose car	12	5
1066	A207	15k purple	12	5
1067	A207	20k chalky bl	45	5
1068	A207	30k grnsh gray	22	5
1069	A207	40k slate bl	45	5
1070	A208	50k olive	50	5
1071	A208	75k slate	55	22
1072	A208	1 l deep pur	65	20
1073	A208	2 l brt ultra	1.25	30
1074	A208	5 l sepia	10.00	3.00
		Nos. 1059-1074 (16)	14.66	4.32

Imperfs, value, set $60.

No. 1059 Surcharged with New Value in Black

1952, June 1

1075	A207	0.50k on 1k brn org	10	5

Technical Faculty Building A209

1952, Aug. 20 ***Perf. 12x12 ½***

1076	A209	15k violet	20	10
1077	A209	20k blue	28	12
1078	A209	60k brown	75	60

8th Intl. Congress of Theoretic and Applied Mechanics.

Turkish Soldier A210

Pigeons Bandaging Wounded Hand A212

Designs: 20k, Soldier with Turkish flag. 30k, Soldier and child with comic book. 60k, Raising Turkish flag.

1952, Sept. 25 ***Perf. 14***

1079	A210	15k Prus blue	22	14
1080	A210	20k deep blue	22	16
1081	A210	30k brown	40	25
1082	A210	60k ol blk & car	80	60

Turkey's participation in the Korean war.

1952, Oct. 29 ***Perf. 12 ½x12***

Design: 20k, Flag, rainbow and ruined homes.

Dated "1877-1952"

1085	A212	15k dk grn & red	38	22
1086	A212	20k bl & red	75	38

Turkish Red Crescent Society, 75th anniv.

Relief From Panel of Aziziye Monument — A213

Aziziye Monument A214

Design: 40k, View of Erzerum.

1952, Nov. 9 ***Perf. 11***

1087	A213	15k purple	20	14
1088	A214	20k blue	25	20
1089	A214	40k ol gray	45	42

75th anniv. of the Battle of Aziziye at Erzerum.

Rumeli Hisari Fortress A215

Troops Entering Constan- tinople — A216

Sultan Mohammed II — A217

Designs: 8k, Soldiers moving cannon. 10k, Mohammed II riding into sea, and Turkish armada. 12k, Landing of Turkish army. 15k, Ancient wall, Constantinople. 30k, Mosque of

Faith. 40k, Presenting mace to Patriarch Yenadios. 60k, Map of Constantinople, c. 1574. 1 l, Tomb of Mohammed II. 2.50 l, Portrait of Mohammed II.

1953, May 29 Photo. *Perf. 11½*

Inscribed: "Istanbulun Fethi 1453-1953"

1090	A215	5k brt bl	5	5
1091	A215	8k gray	7	5
1092	A215	10k blue	8	5
1093	A215	12k rose lil	10	7
1094	A215	15k brown	16	10
1095	A216	20k vermilion	20	7
1096	A216	30k dl grn	50	10
1097	A215	40k vio bl	50	20
1098	A215	60k chocolate	50	30
1099	A215	1 l bl grn	1.25	50
		Perf. 12		
1100	A217	2 l multi	3.00	2.00
1101	A217	2.50 l multi	4.00	2.50
a		Souvenir sheet	40.00	27.50
		Nos. 1090-1101 (12)	10.41	5.99

Conquest of Constantinople by Sultan Mohammed II, 500th anniv.

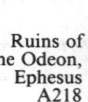

Ruins of the Odeon, Ephesus A218

Designs: 15k, Church of St. John the Apostle. 20k, Shrine of Virgin Mary, Panaya Kapulu. 40k, Ruins of the Double Church. 60k, Shrine of the Seven Sleepers. 1 l, Restored house of the Virgin Mary.

1953, Aug. 16 Litho. *Perf. 13½*

Multicolored Centers

1102	A218	12k sage grn	14	7
1103	A218	15k lilac	14	7
1104	A218	20k dk sl bl	15	10
1105	A218	40k lt grn	38	20
1106	A218	60k vio bl	50	38
1107	A218	1 l brn red	1.50	1.35
		Nos. 1102-1107 (6)	2.81	2.17

Pres. Celal Bayar, Mithat Pasha. Herman Schulze-Delitzsch and People's Bank — A219

Design: 20k, Pres. Bayar, Mithat Pasha and University of Ankara.

1953, Sept. 2 Photo. *Perf. 10½*

1108	A219	15k org brn	22	20
1109	A219	20k Prus grn	50	40

5th Intl. People's Circuit Congress, Istanbul, Sept.

Combined Harvester A220

Kemal Atatürk — A221

Designs: 15k, Berdan dam. 20k, Military parade. 30k, Diesel train. 35k, Yesilkoy airport.

1953, Oct. 29 *Perf. 14*

1110	A220	10k olive bis	8	8
1111	A220	15k dk gray	12	8
1112	A220	20k rose red	20	8
1113	A220	30k olive grn	40	20
1114	A220	35k dl blue	28	20
1115	A221	55k dull pur	90	60
		Nos. 1110-1115 (6)	1.98	1.24

Turkish Republic, 30th anniv.

Kemal Atatürk and Mausoleum at Ankara A222

1953, Nov. 10

1116	A222	15k gray blk	28	25
1117	A222	20k vio brn	60	40

15th death anniv. of Kemal Ataturk.

Type of 1931-42

Without umlaut over first "U" of "CUMHURIYETI"

Perf. 11½x12, 10x11½

1953-56 Typo. Unwmk.

1117B	A77	20p yellow	8	5
1118	A78	1k brn org	5	5
1119	A78	2k rose pink ('53)	5	5
1120	A78	3k yel brn ('53)	5	5
1120A	A78	4k slate ('56)	1.00	5
1121	A78	5k blue	25	5
1121A	A78	8k violet ('56)	10	5
1122	A77	10k dk olive ('53)	8	5
1123	A77	12k brt car rose ('53)	10	5
1124	A77	15k fawn	15	5
1125	A77	20k rose lilac	2.00	5
1126	A77	30k lt bl grn ('54)	75	10
		Nos. 1117B-1126 (12)	4.66	65

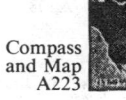

Compass and Map A223

Designs: 20k, Globe, crescent and stars. 40k, Tree symbolical of 14 NATO members.

1954, Apr. 4 Photo. *Perf. 14*

1127	A223	15k brown	1.20	1.00
1128	A223	20k vio bl	1.65	1.40
1129	A223	40k dk grn	12.00	11.00

NATO, 5th anniv.

Industry, Engineering and Agriculture A224

Justice and Council of Europe Flag — A225

1954, Aug. 8 Litho. *Perf. 10½*

1130	A224	10k brown	3.25	2.50
1131	A225	15k dk grn	3.00	2.50
1132	A225	20k blue	3.25	2.50
1133	A224	30k brt vio	16.50	15.00

Council of Europe, 5th anniv.

Flag Signals to Plane A226

Amaury de La Grange and Plane A227

Design: 45k, Kemal Ataturk and air fleet.

1954, Sept. 20 *Perf. 12½*

1134	A226	20k blk brn	14	7
1135	A227	35k dl vio	22	20
1136	A227	45k deep blue	45	30

47th congress of the Intl. Aeronautical Federation, Istanbul, 1954.

Souvenir Sheet

A228

1954, Oct. 18 *Imperf.*

1137	A228	Sheet of three	6.00	5.50
a		20k aquamarine	65	65
b		30k violet blue	65	65
c		1 l red violet	1.40	1.40

First anniv. of Law of Oct. 17, 1953, reorganizing the Department of Post, Telephone and Telegraph.

Ziya Gokalp A229

Kemal Atatürk A230

1954, Oct. 25 *Perf. 11*

1138	A229	15k rose lil	8	7
1139	A229	20k dk grn	14	12
1140	A229	30k crimson	30	22

30th death anniv. of Ziya Gokalp, author and historian.

1955, Mar. 1 *Perf. 12½*

1141	A230	15k car rose	10	5
1142	A230	20k blue	14	5
1143	A230	40k dk gray	22	5
1144	A230	50k bl grn	38	5
1145	A230	75k org brn	45	10
		Nos. 1141-1145 (5)	1.29	30

Relief Map of Dardanelles A231

Artillery Loaders — A232

Designs: 30k, Minelayer Nusrat. 60k, Colonel Kemal Atatürk.

1955, Mar. 18 *Perf. 10½*

1146	A231	15k green	7	7
1147	A232	20k org brn	10	7
1148	A231	30k ultra	20	16
1149	A232	60k olive gray	60	45

Battle of Gallipoli, 40th anniversary.

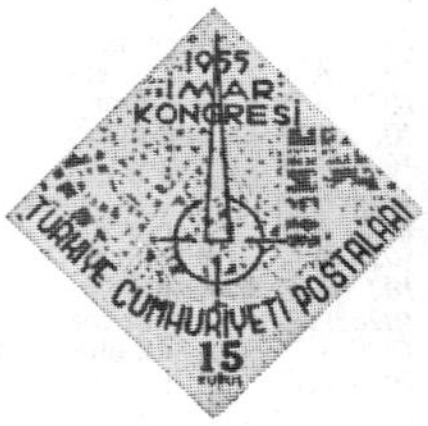

Aerial Map A233

1955, Apr. 14 *Perf. 11*

1150	A233	15k gray	10	7
1151	A233	20k aquamarine	14	7
1152	A233	50k brown	25	16
1153	A233	1 l purple	70	30

City Planning Congress, Ankara, 1955.

Carnation — A234

Flowers: 15k, Tulip. 20k, Rose. 50k, Lily.

1955, May 19 Litho. *Perf. 10*

1154	A234	10k rose red & dk grn	22	10
1155	A234	15k yel & grn	15	8
1156	A234	20k rose & dk grn	20	10
1157	A234	50k grn & yel	1.50	1.00

National Flower Show, Istanbul, May 20-Aug. 20.

Battle First Aid Station A235

Design: 30k, Gulhane Military Hospital, Ankara.

1955, Aug. 28 Unwmk. *Perf. 12*

1158	A235	20k red, lake & gray	20	10
1159	A235	30k dp grn & yel grn	40	20

XVIII Intl. Congress of Military Medicine, Aug. 8-Sept. 1, Istanbul.

Soccer Game — A236

Emblem and Soccer Ball — A237

Design: 1 l, Emblem with oak and olive branches.

1955, Aug. 30 *Perf. 10*

1160	A236	15k lt ultra	38	10
1161	A237	20k crim rose	30	10
1162	A236	1 l lt grn	1.00	75

Intl. Military Soccer Championship games, Istanbul, Aug. 30.

Surete Monument, Ankara A238

Designs: 20k, Dolma Bahce Palace. 30k, Police College, Ankara. 45k, Police Martyrs' Monument, Istanbul.

1955, Sept. 5 *Perf. 10*

Inscribed: "Enterpol Istanbul 1955"

1163	A238	15k bl grn	10	5
1164	A238	20k brt vio	16	8
1165	A238	30k gray blk	30	20
1166	A238	45k lt brn	70	45

24th general assembly of the Intl. Criminal Police, Istanbul, Sept. 5-9.

Early Telegraph Transmitter A239

Modern Transmitter — A240

Perf. 13½x14, 14x13½

1955, Sept. 10 **Photo.**

1167	A239	15k olive	10	7
1168	A240	20k crim rose	14	7
1169	A239	45k fawn	40	16
1170	A240	60k ultra	40	38

Centenary of telecommunication.

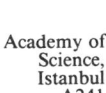

Academy of Science, Istanbul A241

Designs: 20k, University. 60k, Hilton Hotel. 1 l, Kiz Kulesi (Leander's Tower).

1955, Sept. 12 *Perf. 13½x14*

1171	A241	15k yel org	18	5
1172	A241	20k crim rose	20	10
1173	A241	60k purple	30	15
1174	A241	1 l dp bl	55	38

10th meeting of the governors of the Intl. Bank of Reconstruction and Development and the Intl. Monetary Fund, Istanbul, Sept. 12-16.

Surlari, Istanbul A242

Mosque of Sultan Ahmed A243

Congress Emblem A244

Designs: 30k, Haghia Sophia. 75k, Map of Constantinople, by Christoforo Buondelmonti, 1422.

1955, Sept. 15 **Litho.** *Perf. 11½*

1175	A242	15k grnsh blk & Prus grn	35	20
1176	A243	20k ver & org	25	16
1177	A242	30k sep & vio brn	25	16
1178	A243	75k ultra	70	50

10th Intl. Congress of Byzantine Research, Istanbul, Sept. 15-21, 1955.

1955, Sept. 26 *Perf. 10½x11*

Designs: 30k, Chalet in Istanbul. 55k, Bridges.

Inscribed: "Beynelmiel X. Vol Kongresi Istanbul 1955"

1179	A244	20k red vio	14	7
1180	A244	30k dk grn & yel grn	16	14
1181	A244	55k dp bl & brt bl	60	40

10th International Transportation Congress.

Map of Turkey, Showing Population Increase A245

1955, Oct. 22 **Unwmk.** *Perf. 10*

Map in Rose

1182	A245	15k lt & dk gray & red	25	7
1183	A245	20k lt & dk vio & red	16	7
1184	A245	30k lt & dk ultra & red	20	14
1185	A245	60k lt & dk bl grn & red	50	22

Census of 1955.

Waterfall, Antalya — A246

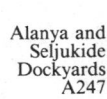

Alanya and Seljukide Dockyards A247

Designs: 30k, Theater at Aspendos. 45k, Ruins at Side. 50k, View of Antalya. 65k, St. Nicholas Church at Myra (Demre) and St. Nicholas.

Perf. 14x13½, 13½x14

1955, Dec. 10 **Photo.** **Unwmk.**

1186	A246	18k bl, ol grn & ultra	20	10
1187	A247	20k bl, ultra & brn	15	10
1188	A247	30k dl grn, ol bis & grn	25	10
1189	A246	45k yel grn & brn	1.10	55
1190	A246	50k Prus grn & ol bis	30	25
1191	A247	65k org ver & blk	45	40
		Nos. 1186-1191 (6)	2.45	1.50

Kemal Atatürk — A248

1955-56 **Litho.** *Perf. 12½*

1192	A248	0.50k carmine	5	5
1193	A248	1k yel org	5	5
1194	A248	2k brt bl	5	5
1195	A248	3k scarlet	5	5
1196	A248	5k lt brn	6	5
1197	A248	6k lt bl grn	8	5
1198	A248	10k bl grn	12	5
1199	A248	18k rose vio	15	5
1200	A248	20k lt vio bl	20	5
1201	A248	25k ol grn	25	5
1202	A248	30k violet	30	5
1203	A248	40k fawn	40	5
1204	A248	75k slate bl	1.00	10
		Nos. 1192-1204 (13)	2.76	70

Issue dates: 3k, 1955. Others, 1956.

Tomb at Nigde — A249

Zubeyde Hanum — A250

1956, Apr. 12 *Perf. 10½*

1205	A249	40k vio bl & bl	14	7

25th anniv. of the Turkish History Society. The tomb of Hüdavent Hatun, a sultan's daughter, exemplifies Seljukian architecture of the 14th century.

1956, May 13 *Perf. 11*

1206	A250	20k pale brn & dk brn	14	7

Imperf

1207	A250	20k lt grn & dk grn	45	25

Mother's Day; Zubeyde Hanum, mother of Kemal Ataturk.

Shah and Queen of Iran A251

1956, May 15 **Unwmk.** *Perf. 11*

1208	A251	100k grn & pale grn	90	75

Imperf

1209	A251	100k red & pale grn	5.50	4.50

Visit of the Shah and Queen of Iran to Turkey, May 15.

Erenkoy Sanitarium A252

1956, July 31 *Perf. 11*

1210	A252	50k dk bl grn & pink	35	20

Anti-Tuberculosis work among PTT employees.

An enhanced introduction to the Scott Catalogue begins on Page V. A thorough understanding of the material presented there will greatly aid your use of the catalogue itself.

Symbol of Izmir Fair — A253

A254

1956, Aug. 20 *Perf. 11*

1211	A253	45k brt grn	16	7

Souvenir Sheet

Imperf

1212	A254	Sheet of two	1.10	80
a		50k rose red	22	22
b		50k bright ultra	22	22

25th Intl. Fair, Izmir, Aug. 20-Sept. 20. See No. C28.

Hands Holding Bottled Serpent — A255

1956, Sept. 10 **Litho.** *Perf. 10½*

1213	A255	25k multi	15	10

25th Intl. Anti-Alcoholism congress, Istanbul Sept. 10-15.

Printed both in regular sheets (300,000) and in sheets with alternate vertical rows inverted (200,000), providing 100,000 tete beche pairs.

Medical Center at Kayseri — A256

Sariyar Dam — A257

1956, Nov. 1 *Perf. 12½x12*

1214	A256	60k vio & yel	12	5

750th anniv. of the first medical school and clinic in Anatolia.

1956, Dec. 2 **Litho.** *Perf. 10½*

1215	A257	20k vermilion	10	7
1216	A257	20k bright bl	10	7

Inauguration of Sariyar Dam.

Freestyle Wrestling A258

Mehmet Akif Ersoy A259

Design: 65k, Greco-Roman wrestling.

1956, Dec. 8 Unwmk. *Perf. 10½*
1217 A258 40k brt yel grn & brn 30 22
1218 A258 65k lt bluish gray & dp car 40 25

16th Olympic Games, Melbourne, Nov. 22-Dec. 8, 1956.

1956, Dec. 26
1219 A259 20k brn & brt yel grn 5 5
1220 A259 20k rose car & lt gray 5 5
1221 A259 20k vio bl & brt pink 5 5

20th death anniv. of Mehmet Akif Ersoy, author of the Turkish National Anthem.
Each value bears a different verse of the anthem.

Theater in Troy — A260

Trojan Vase — A261

Design: 30k, Trojan Horse.

Perf. 13½x14, 14x13½
1956, Dec. 31 Photo. Unwmk.
1222 A260 15k green 70 50
1223 A261 20k red vio 70 50
1224 A260 30k chestnut 70 50

Excavations at Troy.

Mobile Chest X-Ray Unit A262

Kemal Atatürk A263

1957, Jan. 1 Litho. *Perf. 12*
1225 A262 25k ol brn & red 10 8

Fight against tuberculsois.

1956-57 *Perf. 12½*
1226 A263 ½k bl grn 5 5
1227 A263 1k yel org 5 5
1228 A263 3k gray ol 5 5
1229 A263 5k violet 5 5
1230 A263 6k rose car 5 5
1231 A263 10k rose vio 5 5
1232 A263 12k fawn 5 5
1233 A263 15k lt vio bl 5 5
1234 A263 18k carmine 7 5
1235 A263 20k lt brn 7 5
1236 A263 25k lt bl grn 8 5
1237 A263 30k slate bl 8 5
1238 A263 40k olive 14 5
1239 A263 50k orange 20 5
1240 A263 60k brt bl 20 5
1241 A263 70k Prus grn 60 7
1242 A263 75k brown 35 7
Nos. 1226-1242 (17) 2.19 89

Pres. Heuss of Germany — A264

1957, May 5 Unwmk. *Perf. 10½*
1243 A264 40k yel & brn 16 10

Visit of Pres. Theodor Heuss of Germany to Turkey, May 5. See No. C29.

View of Bergama and Ruin A265

Design: 40k, Dancers in kermis at Bergama.

1957, May 24
1244 A265 30k brown 10 7
1245 A265 40k green 14 7

20th anniv. of the kermis at Bergama (Pergamus).

Symbols of Industry and Flags A266

1957, July 1 Photo. *Perf. 13½x14*
1246 A266 25k violet 16 7
1247 A266 40k gray bl 20 10

10th anniv. of Turkish-American collaboration.

Osman Hamdi Bey — A267

Hittite Sun Course from Alaça Höyük A268

1957, July 6 *Perf. 10½*
1248 A267 20k beige, pale brn & blk 14 8
1249 A268 30k Prus grn 16 10

75th anniv. of the Academy of Art. The 20k exists with "cancellation" omitted.

King of Afghanistan — A269

1957, Sept. 1 Litho. *Perf. 10½*
1250 A269 45k car lake & pink 16 10

Visit of Mohammed Zahir Shah, King of Afghanistan, to Turkey. See No. C30.

Medical Center, Amasya A270

Design: 65k, Suleiman Medical Center.

1957, Sept. 29 Unwmk. *Perf. 10½*
1251 A270 25k ver & yel 5 5
1252 A270 65k brt grnsh bl & cit 16 14

11th general meeting of the World Medical Assoc.

Mosque of Suleiman A271

Architect Mimar Koca Sinan (1489-1587) — A272

1957, Oct. 18 *Perf. 11*
1253 A271 20k gray grn 10 8
1254 A272 100k brown 30 25

400th anniv. of the opening of the Mosque of Suleiman, Istanbul.

No. 1073 Surcharged with New Value and "ISTANBUL Filatelik n. Sergisi 1957"

1957, Nov. 11 Photo. *Perf. 13½*
1255 A208 50k on 2l brt ultra 16 10

1957 Istanbul Philatelic Exhibition.

Forestation Map of Turkey A273

Design: 25k, Forest and hand planting tree (vertical).

1957, Nov. 18 Litho. *Perf. 10½*
1256 A273 20k grn & brn 15 12
1257 A273 25k emer & bl grn 15 12

Centenary of forestry in Turkey.
Nos. 1256-1257 each come with two different tabs attached (four tabs in all) bearing various quotations.

Fuzuli — A274

1957, Nov. 23
1258 A274 50k pink, vio, red & yel 25 20

400th death anniv. of Fuzuli (Mehmet Suleiman Ogiou), poet.

Benjamin Franklin (1707-1790) — A275

1957, Nov. 28 Photo. *Perf. 14x13½*
1259 A275 65k dk Prus bl 15 12
1260 A275 65k rose vio 15 12

Green Dome, Tomb of Mevlana, at Konya A276

Mevlana A278

Konya Museum A277

Perf. 11x10½, 10½x11
1957, Dec. 17 Litho. Unwmk.
1261 A276 50k grn, bl & vio 12 10
1262 A277 100k dk bl 25 18

Miniature Sheet
Imperf
1263 A278 100k multi 1.00 1.00

Jalal-udin Mevlana (1207-1273), Persian poet and founder of the Mevlevie dervish order. No. 1263 contains one stamp 32x42mm.

Kemal Atatürk (Double Frame; Serifs) — A279

1957 Unwmk. *Perf. 11½*
Size: 18x22mm
1264 A279 ½k lt brn 5 5
1265 A279 1k lt vio bl 5 5
1266 A279 2k blk vio 5 5
1267 A279 3k orange 5 5
1268 A279 5k bl grn 5 5
1269 A279 6k dk sl grn 5 5
1270 A279 10k violet 5 5
1271 A279 12k brt grn 5 5
1272 A279 15k dk bl grn 5 5
1273 A279 18k rose car 5 5
1274 A279 20k brown 5 5
1275 A279 25k brn red 5 5
1276 A279 30k brt bl 5 5
1277 A279 40k slate bl 5 5
1278 A279 50k yel org 8 5
1279 A279 60k black 10 5
1280 A279 70k rose vio 10 10
1281 A279 75k gray ol 15 10

Size: 21x29mm
1282 A279 100k carmine 30 8
1283 A279 250k olive 90 22
Nos. 1264-1283 (20) 2.33 1.30

College Emblem
A280

View of Adana
A281

1958, Jan. 16 Litho. *Perf. 10½x11*
1288 A280 20k bis, ind & org 7 5
1289 A280 25k dk bl, bis & org 10 7

"Turkiye" on top of 25k. 75th anniv. of the College of Economics and Commerce, Istanbul.

1958-60 Photo. *Perf. 11½*
Size: 26x20½mm
1290 A281 5k org brn *(Adana)* 5 5
1291 A281 5k lil rose *(Adapazari)* 5 5
1292 A281 5k ver *(Adiyaman)* 5 5
1293 A281 5k choc *(Afyon)* 5 5
1294 A281 5k emer *(Amasya)* 5 5
1295 A281 5k brt bl *(Ankara)* 5 5
1296 A281 5k bl grn *(Antakya)* 5 5
1297 A281 5k ol grn *(Antalya)* 5 5
1298 A281 5k vio *(Artvin)* 5 5
1299 A281 5k org *(Aydin)* 5 5
1300 A281 5k lil *(Balikesir)* 5 5
1301 A281 5k ol *(Bilecik)* 5 5
1302 A281 5k brn blk *(Bingol)* 5 5
1303 A281 5k brt vio bl *(Bitlis)* 5 5
1304 A281 5k rose vio *(Bolu)* 5 5
1305 A281 5k brn ol *(Burdur)* 5 5
1306 A281 5k ol grn *(Bursa)* 5 5
1307 A281 5k brt ultra *(Canakkale)* 5 5
1308 A281 5k lil *(Cankiri)* 5 5
1309 A281 5k dk bl *(Corum)* 5 5
1310 A281 5k bl *(Denizli)* 5 5
1311 A281 5k org *(Diyarbakir)* 5 5

Size: 32½x22mm
1312 A281 20k dp brn *(Adana)* 30 22
1313 A281 20k rose pink *(Adapazari)* 30 22
1314 A281 20k crim *(Adiyaman)* 30 22
1315 A281 20k brn *(Afyon)* 30 22
1316 A281 20k brt grn *(Amasya)* 30 22
1317 A281 20k dk bl *(Ankara)* 30 22
1318 A281 20k brt grnsh bl *(Antakya)* 30 22
1319 A281 20k grn *(Antalya)* 30 22
1320 A281 20k bl vio *(Artvin)* 30 22
1321 A281 20k dp org *(Aydin)* 30 22
1322 A281 20k lil *(Balikesir)* 30 22
1323 A281 20k ol grn *(Bilecik)* 30 22
1324 A281 20k bluish blk *(Bingol)* 30 22
1325 A281 20k brt vio *(Bitlis)* 30 22
1326 A281 20k choc *(Bolu)* 30 22
1327 A281 20k ol gray *(Burdur)* 30 22
1328 A281 20k grn *(Bursa)* 30 22
1329 A281 20k brt ultra *(Canakkale)* 30 22
1330 A281 20k lil *(Cankiri)* 30 22
1331 A281 20k dk gray bl *(Corum)* 30 22
1332 A281 20k bl *(Denizli)* 30 22
1333 A281 20k red org *(Diyarbakir)* 30 22
Nos. 1290-1333 (44) 7.70 5.94

(1959)
Size: 26x20½mm
1334 A281 5k vio blk *(Edirne)* 5 5
1335 A281 5k gray ol *(Elazig)* 5 5
1336 A281 5k brt grnsh bl *(Erzincan)* 5 5
1337 A281 5k red org *(Erzurum)* 5 5
1338 A281 5k yel grn *(Eskisehir)* 5 5
1339 A281 5k ol grn *(Gaziantep)* 5 5
1340 A281 5k ultra *(Giresun)* 5 5
1341 A281 5k bl *(Gumusane)* 5 5
1342 A281 5k rose lil *(Hakkari)* 5 5
1343 A281 5k lil rose *(Isparta)* 5 5
1344 A281 5k ultra *(Istanbul)* 5 5
1345 A281 5k brt ultra *(Izmir)* 5 5
1346 A281 5k Prus bl *(Izmit)* 5 5
1347 A281 5k lil *(Karakose)* 5 5
1348 A281 5k emer *(Kars)* 5 5
1349 A281 5k car rose *(Kastamonu)* 5 5
1350 A281 5k dl grn *(Kayseri)* 5 5
1351 A281 5k chnt *(Kirklareli)* 5 5
1352 A281 5k dp org *(Kirsehir)* 5 5
1353 A281 5k vio bl *(Konya)* 5 5
1354 A281 5k vio *(Kutahya)* 5 5
1355 A281 5k org brn *(Malatya)* 5 5

Size: 32½x22mm
1356 A281 20k sl blk *(Edirne)* 30 22
1357 A281 20k gray ol *(Elazig)* 30 22
1358 A281 20k brt bl *(Erzincan)* 30 22
1359 A281 20k red org *(Erzurum)* 30 22
1360 A281 20k dp yel grn *(Eskisehir)* 30 22
1361 A281 20k dp yel grn *(Gaziantep)* 30 22
1362 A281 20k brt bl *(Giresun)* 30 22
1363 A281 20k dl bl *(Gumusane)* 30 22
1364 A281 20k lil *(Hakkari)* 30 22
1365 A281 20k red lil *(Isparta)* 30 22
1366 A281 20k brt vio bl *(Istanbul)* 30 22
1367 A281 20k brt ultra *(Izmir)* 30 22
1368 A281 20k bl grn *(Izmit)* 30 22
1369 A281 20k brt vio *(Karakose)* 30 22
1370 A281 20k emer *(Kars)* 30 22
1371 A281 20k car rose *(Kastamonu)* 30 22
1372 A281 20k grn *(Kayseri)* 30 22
1373 A281 20k chnt brn *(Kirklareli)* 30 22
1374 A281 20k brn org *(Kirsehir)* 30 22
1375 A281 20k dp ultra *(Konya)* 30 22
1376 A281 20k bl vio *(Kutahya)* 30 22
1377 A281 20k org brn *(Malatya)* 30 22
Nos. 1334-1377 (44) 7.70 5.94

(1960)
Size: 26x20½mm
1378 A281 5k dk sl grn *(Manisa)* 5 5
1379 A281 5k red lil *(Maras)* 5 5
1380 A281 5k brn car *(Mardin)* 5 5
1381 A281 5k brt bl grn *(Mersin)* 5 5
1382 A281 5k yel grn *(Mugla)* 5 5
1383 A281 5k gray ol *(Mus)* 5 5
1384 A281 5k brt yel grn *(Nevsehir)* 5 5
1385 A281 5k rose brn *(Nigde)* 5 5
1386 A281 5k dk bl *(Ordu)* 5 5
1387 A281 5k dp vio *(Rize)* 5 5
1388 A281 5k rose cl *(Samsun)* 5 5
1389 A281 5k brn *(Siirt)* 5 5
1390 A281 5k dk bl *(Sinop)* 5 5
1391 A281 5k grn *(Sivas)* 5 5
1392 A281 5k brt grnsh bl *(Tekirdag)* 5 5
1393 A281 5k crim *(Tokat)* 5 5
1394 A281 5k bl vio *(Trabzon)* 5 5
1395 A281 5k org *(Tunceli)* 5 5
1396 A281 5k choc *(Urfa)* 5 5
1397 A281 5k dk sl grn *(Usak)* 5 5
1398 A281 5k dk car rose *(Van)* 5 5
1399 A281 5k brt rose *(Yozgat)* 5 5
1400 A281 5k brt bl *(Zonguldak)* 5 5

Size: 32½x22mm
1401 A281 20k sl blk *(Manisa)* 30 22
1402 A281 20k red lil *(Maras)* 30 22
1403 A281 20k rose brn *(Mardin)* 30 22
1404 A281 20k dp bl grn *(Mersin)* 30 22
1405 A281 20k emer *(Mugla)* 30 22
1406 A281 20k gray grn *(Mus)* 30 22
1407 A281 20k yel grn *(Nevsehir)* 30 22
1408 A281 20k brt rose brn *(Nigde)* 30 22
1409 A281 20k dk bl *(Ordu)* 30 22
1410 A281 20k bl vio *(Rize)* 30 22
1411 A281 20k cl *(Samsun)* 30 22
1412 A281 20k sep *(Siirt)* 30 22
1413 A281 20k dk bl *(Sinop)* 30 22
1414 A281 20k ol grn *(Sivas)* 30 22
1415 A281 20k grnsh bl *(Tekirdag)* 30 22
1416 A281 20k brt red *(Tokat)* 30 22
1417 A281 20k bl vio *(Trabzon)* 30 22
1418 A281 20k red org *(Tunceli)* 30 22
1419 A281 20k dk red brn *(Urfa)* 30 22
1420 A281 20k slate *(Usak)* 30 22
1421 A281 20k dk car rose *(Van)* 30 22
1422 A281 20k rose red *(Yozgat)* 30 22
1423 A281 20k brt bl *(Zonguldak)* 30 22
Nos. 1378-1423 (46) 8.05 6.21
Nos. 1290-1423 (134) 23.45 18.09

Ruins at Pamukkale
A282

Designs: 25k, Travertines at Pamukkale.

1958, May 18 Litho. *Perf. 12*
1424 A282 20k brown 8 5
1425 A282 25k blue 10 6

"Industry"
A283

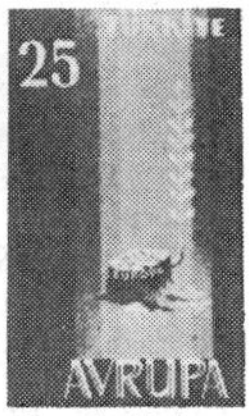

Symbolizing New Europe
A284

1958, Oct. 10 Unwmk. *Perf. 10½*
1426 A283 40k slate bl 12 8

National Industry Exhibition.

Europa Issue

1958, Oct. 10
1427 A284 25k vio & dl pink 10 8
1428 A284 40k brt ultra 20 14

Letters
A285

1958, Oct. 5
1429 A285 20k org & blk 5 5

Intl. Letter Writing Week, Oct. 5-11.

Flame and Mausoleum
A286

Kemal Atatürk
A287

1958, Nov. 10 *Perf. 12*
1430 A286 25k red 7 5
1431 A287 75k bl grn 16 10

20th death anniv. of Kemal Ataturk.
Nos. 1430-1431 printed in alternate rows in sheet.

A little time given to the study of the arrangement of the Scott Catalogue can make it easier to use effectively.

Emblem — A288

1959, Jan. 10 Litho. *Perf. 10*
1432 A288 25k dk vio & yel 8 7

25th anniv. of the Agricultural Faculty of Ankara University.

Blackboard and School Emblem
A289

1959, Jan. 15 *Perf. 10½*
1433 A289 75k blk & yel 15 8

75th anniv. of the establishment of a secondary boys' school in Istanbul.

State Theater, Ankara
A290

Design: 25k, Portrait of Sinasi.

1959, Mar. 30 Unwmk. *Perf. 10½*
1434 A290 20k red brn & emer 7 5
1435 A290 25k Prus grn & org 10 6

Centenary of the Turkish theater; Sinasi, writer of the first Turkish play in 1859.

Globe and Stars
A291

1959, Apr. 4 *Perf. 10*
1436 A291 105k red 20 16
1437 A291 195k green 35 25

10th anniversary of NATO.

Aspendos Theater
A292

1959, May 1 Litho. *Perf. 10½*
1438 A292 20k bis brn & vio 7 5
1439 A292 20k grn & ol bis 10 5

Aspendos (Belkins) Festival.

No. B70 Surcharged in Ultramarine

1959, May 5
1440 SP25 105k on 15k + 5k org 30 20

Council of Europe, 10th anniversary.

Basketball — A293

1959, May 21 *Perf. 10*

1441 A293 25k red org & dk bl 15 8

11th European and Mediterranean Basketball Championship.

"Karadeniz"
A294

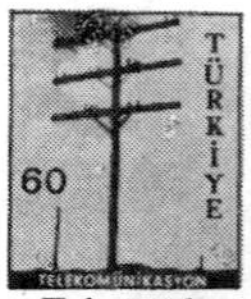

Telegraph Mast
A295

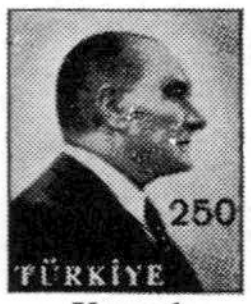

Kemal Atatürk
A296

Designs: 1k, Turkish Airlines' SES plane. 10k, Grain elevator, Ankara. 15k, Iron and Steel Works, Karabück. 20k, Euphrates Bridge, Birecik. 25k, Zonguldak Harbor. 30k, Gasoline refinery, Batman. 40k, Rumeli Hisari Fortress. 45k, Sugar factory, Konya. 55k, Coal mine, Zonguldak. 75k, Railway. 90k, Crane loading ships. 100k, Cement factory, Ankara. 120k, Highway. 150k, Harvester. 200k, Electric transformer.

Perf. 10½, 11, 11½, 12½, 13½

1959-60 Litho. Unwmk.

1442	A294	1k	indigo	5	5
1443	A294	5k	brt bl ('59)	10	5
1444	A294	10k	blue	5	5
1445	A294	15k	brown	16	5
1446	A294	20k	sl grn	7	5
1447	A294	25k	violet	10	5
1448	A294	30k	lilac	20	5
1449	A294	40k	blue	16	5
1450	A294	45k	dl vio	16	5
1451	A294	55k	ol brn	22	5
1452	A295	60k	green	55	5
1453	A295	75k	gray ol	1.90	5
1454	A295	90k	dk bl	2.50	7
1455	A295	100k	gray	2.00	7
1456	A295	120k	magenta	1.50	7
1457	A294	150k	orange	2.50	14
1458	A295	200k	yel grn	2.50	16
1459	A296	250k	blk brn	2.50	35
1460	A296	500k	dk bl	5.50	45
	Nos. 1442-1460 (19)			22.72	1.91

Postage Due Stamps of 1936 Surcharged **20=20**

1959, June 1 *Perf. 11½*

1461	D6	20k	on 20pa brn	7	5
1462	D6	20k	on 2k lt bl	7	5
1463	D6	20k	on 3k brt vio	7	5
1464	D6	20k	on 5k Prus bl	7	5
1465	D6	20k	on 12k brt rose	7	5
	Nos. 1461-1465 (5)			35	25

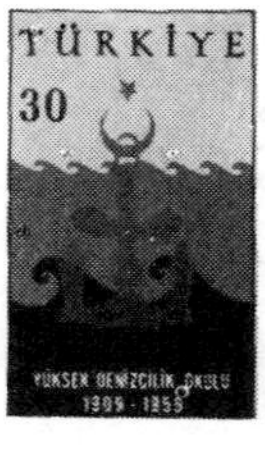

Anchor Emblem — A297

Design: 40k, Sea Horse emblem.

1959, July 4 *Perf. 11*

1466 A297 30k multi 6 5
1467 A297 40k multi 9 8

50th anniv. of the Merchant Marine College.

11th Century Warrior
A298

1959, Aug. 26 Litho. *Perf. 11*

1468 A298 2½ l rose lil & lt bl 60 50

Battle of Malazkirt, 888th anniversary.

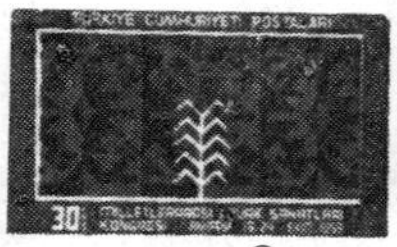

Ornament
A299 A300

Design: 40k, Mosque.

1959, Oct. 19 Unwmk. *Perf. 12½*

1469 A299 30k blk & red 8 7
1470 A299 40k lt bl, blk & ocher 10 8
1471 A300 75k dp bl, yel & red 22 20

Turkish Artists Congress, Ankara.

Kemal Atatürk — A301

Litho.; Center Embossed

1959, Nov. 10 *Perf. 14*

1472 A301 500k dk bl 1.25 65
a. Miniature sheet of 1, red, imperf. 1.25 70

School of Political Science, Ankara
A302

Emblem
A303

Crossed Swords Emblem
A304

1959, Dec. 4 Photo. *Perf. 13½*

1473 A302 40k grn & brn 10 5
1474 A302 40k red brn & bl 7 5
1475 A303 1 l lt & dk vio & buff 25 12

Political Science School, Ankara, cent.

Inscribed: "Kara Harbokulunum 125 Yili"

Design: 40k, Bayonet and flame.

1960, Feb. 28 Litho. *Perf. 10½*

1476 A304 30k ver & org 8 5
1477 A304 40k brn, car & yel 14 7

125th anniv. of the Territorial War College.

Window on World and WRY Emblem
A305

Carnations
A306

Design: 150k, Symbolic shanties and uprooted oak emblem.

1960, Apr. 7

1478 A305 90k brt grnsh bl & blk 20 12
1479 A305 105k yel & blk 25 18

World Refugee Year, July 1, 1959-June 30, 1960.

1960, June 4 Photo. *Perf. 11½*

Flowers: 40k, Jasmine. 75k, Rose. 105k, Tulip.

Granite Paper

1480 A306 30k multi 10 8
1481 A306 40k gray, grn & yel 18 8
1482 A306 75k bl, red & grn 30 20
1483 A306 105k pink, grn & dk vio 45 28

Spring flower festival.

Atatürk Square, Nicosia
A307

Design: 105k, Map of Cyprus.

1960, Aug. 16 Litho. *Perf. 10½*

1484 A307 40k bl & pink 10 6
1485 A307 105k bl & yel 25 12

Independence of the Republic of Cyprus.

Women and Nest
A308

Design: 30k, Globe and emblem.

1960, Aug. 22 Photo. *Perf. 11½*

1486 A308 30k lt vio & yel 8 5
1487 A308 75k grnsh bl & gray 22 12

16th meeting of the Women's Intl. Council.

Soccer
A309

Sports: No. 1489, Basketball. No. 1490, Wrestling. No. 1491, Hurdling. No. 1492, Steeplechase.

1960, Aug. 25

1488	A309	30k	yel grn	16	10
1489	A309	30k	black	16	10
1490	A309	30k	slate bl	16	10
1491	A309	30k	purple	16	10
1492	A309	30k	brown	16	10
a.	Sheet of 25, #1488-1492			5.00	5.00
	Nos. 1488-1492 (5)			80	50

17th Olympic Games, Rome, Aug. 25-Sept. 11.

Printed in sheets of 25 (5x5) with every horizontal and every vertical row containing one of each design. Also printed in normal sheets of 100.

Europa Issue, 1960
Common Design Type

1960, Sept. 19

Size: 33x22mm

1493 CD3 75k grn & bl grn 38 30
1494 CD3 105k dp bl & lt bl 70 45

Agah Efendi and Front Page of Turcamani Ahval — A310

UN Emblem and Torch — A311

1960, Oct. 21 Photo. *Perf. 11½*

1495 A310 40k brn blk & sl 8 5
1496 A310 60k brn blk & bis brn 12 10

Centenary of Turkish journalism.

1960, Oct. 24 Unwmk.

Design: 105k, U.N. headquarters building and U.N. emblem forming "15" (horiz.).

1497 A311 90k brt bl & dk bl 18 12
1498 A311 105k lt bl grn & brn 20 18

15th anniversary of the United Nations.

Army Emblem
A312

Tribunal
A313

Design: 195k, "Justice" (vert.).

1960, Oct. 14 Litho. *Perf. 13*

1499 A312 40k vio & bis 8 5
1500 A313 105k red, gray & brn 22 12
1501 A313 195k grn, rose red & brn 38 20

Trial of ex-President Celal Bayar and ex-Premier Adnan Menderes.

Revolutionaries and Statue — A314

Prancing Horse, Broken Chain — A315

Designs: 30k, Ataturk and hand holding torch. 105k, Youth, soldier and broken chain.

1960, Dec. 1 Photo. *Perf. 14½*

1502 A314 10k gray & blk 5 5
1503 A314 30k purple 8 5
1504 A315 40k brt red & blk 8 5
1505 A314 105k bl blk & red 22 15

Revolution of May 27, 1960.

Faculty Building A316

Sculptured Head of Atatürk — A317

Designs: 40k, Map of Turkey and sun disk.

1961, Jan. 9 Litho. *Perf. 13*

1506 A316 30k sl grn & gray 6 5
1507 A316 40k brn blk & bis brn 8 5
1508 A317 60k dk grn & buff 12 10

25th anniv. of the Faculty of Languages, History and Geography, University of Ankara.

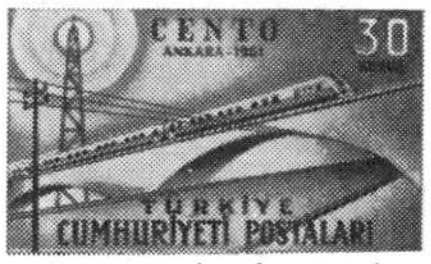

Communication and Transportation — A318

Designs: 40k, Highway construction, telephone and telegraph. 75k, New parliament building, Ankara.

1961, Apr. 27 Unwmk. *Perf. 13*

1509 A318 30k dl vio & blk 8 5
1510 A318 40k grn & blk 15 8
1511 A318 75k dl bl & blk 28 15

9th conference of ministers of the Central Treaty Org. (CENTO), Ankara.

Flag and People A319

Legendary Wolf and Osman Warriors A320

Design: 60k, "Progress" (Atatürk showing youth the way).

1961, May 27 Litho.

1512 A319 30k multi 6 5
1513 A320 40k sl grn & yel 12 8
1514 A319 60k grn, pink & dk red 20 12

First anniversary of May 27 revolution.

Rockets A321

Designs: 40k, Crescent and star emblem, "50" and Jet. 75k, Atatürk, eagle and jets (vert.).

1961, June 1

1515 A321 30k brn, org yel & blk 14 8
1516 A321 40k vio & red 16 14
1517 A321 75k sl blk & bis 40 38

50th anniversary of Turkey's air force.

Europa Issue, 1961
Common Design Type

1961, Sept. 18 *Perf. 13*
Size: 32x22mm

1518 CD4 30k dk vio bl 70 70
1519 CD4 40k gray 70 70
1520 CD4 75k vermilion 75 75

Tulip and Cogwheel A322

Open Book and Olive Branch A324

Torch, Hand and Cogwheel A323

1961, Oct. 21 Unwmk. Litho.

1521 A322 30k sl, pink & sil 12 5
1522 A323 75k ultra, org & blk 35 12

Technical and professional schools, cent.

1961, Oct. 29

1523 A324 30k red, blk & ol 6 5
1524 A324 75k brt bl, blk & grn 18 12

Inauguration of the new Parliament.

Kemal Atatürk
A325 A326

1961-62 Litho. *Perf. 10x10½*
Size: 20x25mm

1525 A325 1k brn org ('62) 5 5
1526 A325 5k blue 8 5
1527 A325 10k sepia 15 5
1528 A326 10k car rose 10 5
1529 A325 30k dl grn ('62) 1.00 12

Size: 21½x31mm

1530 A325 10 l vio ('62) 3.25 75
Nos. 1525-1530 (6) 4.63 1.07

NATO Emblem and Dove — A327

Scouts at Campfire — A328

Design: 105k, NATO emblem (horiz.).

1962, Feb. 18 Unwmk. *Perf. 13*

1545 A327 75k dl bl, blk & sil 20 12
1546 A327 105k crim, blk & sil 28 20

10th anniv. of Turkey's admission to NATO.

1962, July 22 Litho.

Designs: 60k, Scouts with flag. 105k, Scouts saluting.

1547 A328 30k lt grn, blk & red 8 5
1548 A328 60k gray, blk & red 18 12
1549 A328 105k tan, blk & red 28 22

Turkish Boy Scouts, 50th anniversary.

Soldier Statue — A329

Oxcart from Victory Monument, Ankara — A330

Design: 75k, Atatürk.

1962, Aug. 30 Unwmk. *Perf. 13*

1550 A329 30k sl grn 8 5
1551 A330 40k gray & sep 12 5
1552 A329 75k gray blk & lt gray 22 18

40th anniv. of Battle of Dumlupinar.

Europa Issue, 1962
Common Design Type

1962, Sept. 17
Size: 37x23mm

1553 CD5 75k emer & blk 20 15
1554 CD5 105k red & blk 28 22
1555 CD5 195k bl & blk 70 55

Brown imprint.

Virgin Mary's House, Ephesus A331

20pa Stamp of 1863 A332

Designs: 40k, Inside view after restoration (horiz.). 75k, Outside view (horiz.). 105k, Statue of Virgin Mary.

1962, Dec. 8 Photo. *Perf. 13½*

1556 A331 30k multi 12 5
1557 A331 40k multi 15 8
1558 A331 75k multi 20 12
1559 A331 105k multi 30 18

1963, Jan. 13 *Perf. 13x13½*

Issue of 1863: 30k, 1pi. 40k, 2pi. 75k, 5pi.

1560 A332 10k yel, brn & blk 5 5
1561 A332 30k rose, lil & blk 10 5
1562 A332 40k lt bl, bluish grn & blk 15 10
1563 A332 75k red brn, rose & blk 28 20

Centenary of Turkish postage stamps. See No. 1601, souvenir sheet.

Starving People A333

Designs: 40k, Sowers. 75k, Hands protecting Wheat Emblem, and globe.

1963, Mar. 21 Unwmk. *Perf. 13*

1564 A333 30k dp bl & dk bl 10 5
1565 A333 40k brn org & brn 12 10
1566 A333 75k grn & dk grn 22 15

FAO "Freedom from Hunger" campaign.

Julian's Column, Ankara A334

Ethnographic Museum A335

Designs: 10k, Ankara Citadel. 30k, Gazi Institute of Education. 50k, Atatürk's mausoleum. 60k, President's residence. 100k, Atatürk's home, Cankaya. 150k, Parliament building.

1963 Litho. *Perf. 13*

1568 A334 1k sl grn & yel grn 5 5
1569 A334 1k purple 5 5
1570 A335 5k sep & buff 5 5
1571 A335 10k lil rose & pale bl 12 5
1573 A335 30k blk & vio 30 5
1574 A335 50k bl & yel 75 5
1575 A335 60k dk bl gray 20 5
1576 A335 100k ol brn 45 6
1577 A335 150k dl grn 2.25 12
Nos. 1568-1577 (9) 4.22 53

Map of Turkey and Atom Symbol A336

Designs: 60k, Symbols of medicine, agriculture, industry and atom. 100k, Emblem of Turkish Atomic Energy Commission.

1963, May 27 Unwmk. *Perf. 13*

1584 A336 50k red brn & blk 15 10
1585 A336 60k grn, dk grn, yel & red 20 12
1586 A336 100k vio bl & bl 42 30

1st anniv. of the Turkish nuclear research center.

Meric Bridge A337

Sultan Murad I A338

Designs: 10k, Üçşerefeli Mosque. 60k, Summerhouse, Edirne Palace.

1963, June 17

1587 A338 10k dp bl & yel grn 7 5
1588 A337 30k red org & ultra 7 5
1589 A337 60k dk bl, red & brn 16 10
1590 A338 100k multi 60 25

600th anniv. of the conquest of Edirne (Adrianople).

Soldier and Rising Sun — A339

1963, June 28

1591 A339 50k red, blk & gray 10 7
1592 A339 100k red, blk & ol 22 16

600th anniversary of the Turkish army.

Plowing
A340

Mithat
Pasha — A341

Design: 50k, Agriculture Bank, Ankara.

Perf. 13x13½, 13½x13

1963, Aug. 27 Photo. Unwmk.

1593 A340 30k brt yel grn, red brn & grn 8 5
1594 A340 50k pale vio & Prus bl 12 5
1595 A341 60k gray & grn 20 15

Centenary of Agriculture Bank, Ankara.

Sports and Exhibition Palace, Istanbul and No. 5 — A342

Designs: 50k, Sultan Ahmed Mosque and Turkey in Asia No. 22. 60k, View of Istanbul and Turkey in Asia No. 87. 100k, Rumeli Hisari Fortress and No. 679. 130k, Ankara Fortress and No. C2.

1963, Sept. 7 Litho. *Perf. 13*

1596 A342 10k blk, yel & rose 10 5
a Rose omitted
1597 A342 50k blk, grn & rose lil 25 5
1598 A342 60k dk brn, dk bl & blk 38 8
1599 A342 100k dk vio & lil rose 55 18
1600 A342 130k brn, tan & dp org 75 28
Nos. 1596-1600 (5) 2.03 64

"Istanbul 63" Intl. Stamp Exhibition.

Souvenir Sheet
Type of 1963 Inscribed: "F.I.P. GÜNÜ"

Issues of 1863: 10k, 20pa. 50k, 1pi. 60k, 2pi. 130k, 5pi.

Unwmk.

1963, Sept. 13 Litho. *Imperf.*

1601 Souvenir sheet of 4 75 75
a A332 10k yel, brn & blk 8 5
b A332 50k lil, pink & blk 12 10
c A332 60k bluish grn, lt bl & blk 18 15
d A332 130k red brn, pink & blk 22 18

Intl. Philatelic Federation.

Europa Issue, 1963
Common Design Type

1963, Sept. 16
Size: 32x24mm

1602 CD6 50k red & blk 25 18
1603 CD6 130k bl grn, blk & bl 42 32

Atatürk and First Parliament Building A343

Atatürk and: 50k, Turkish flag. 60k, New Parliament building.

1963, Oct. 29 Photo. *Perf. 13½*

1604 A343 30k blk, gold, yel & mar 16 10
1605 A343 50k dk grn, gold, yel & red 22 16
1606 A343 60k dk brn, gold & yel 25 20

40th anniversary of Turkish Republic.

Atatürk, 25th Death Anniv. — A344

1963, Nov. 10

1607 A344 50k red, gold, grn & brn 16 10
1608 A344 60k red, gold, bl & brn 22 16

NATO, 15th Anniv. A346

Designs: 130k, NATO emblem and olive branch.

1964, Apr. 4 Litho. *Perf. 13*

1610 A346 50k grnsh bl, vio bl & red 22 16
1611 A346 130k red & blk 42 38

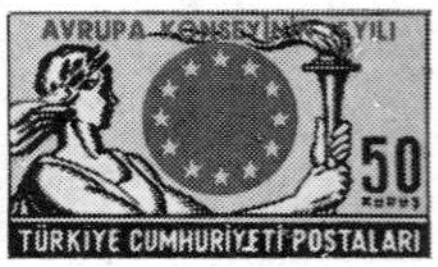

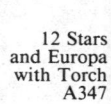

12 Stars and Europa with Torch A347

Design: 130k, Torch and stars.

1964, May 5 Litho. *Perf. 12*

1612 A347 50k red brn, yel & vio bl 30 16
1613 A347 130k vio bl, lt bl & org 55 38

15th anniversary of Council of Europe.

Recaizade Mahmut Ekrem, Writer — A348

Portraits: 1k, Hüseyin Rahmi Gürpinar, novelist. 5k, Ismail Hakki Izmirli, scientist. 10k, Sevket Dag, painter. 60k, Gazi Ahmet Muhtar Pasha, commander. 100k, Ahmet Rasim, writer. 130k, Salih Zeki, mathematician.

1964 Litho. *Perf. 13½x13*

1614 A348 1k red & blk 5 5
1615 A348 5k dl grn & blk 5 5
1616 A348 10k tan & blk 8 5
1617 A348 50k ultra & dk bl 35 5
1618 A348 60k gray & blk 38 5
1619 A348 100k grnsh bl & dk bl 40 8
1620 A348 130k brt grn & dk grn 1.65 12
Nos. 1614-1620 (7) 2.96 45

Haghia Sophia A349

Kiz Kulesi, Mersin — A350

Designs: No. 1622, Zeus Temple, Silifke. No. 1623, View of Amasra. No. 1625, Augustus' Gate and minaret, Ankara.

1964, June 11 Unwmk. *Perf. 13*

1621 A349 50k gray ol & yel grn 15 5
1622 A349 50k cl & car 18 8
1623 A349 50k dk bl & vio bl 18 8
1624 A350 60k sl grn & dk gray 22 12
1625 A350 60k dk brn & org brn 22 12
Nos. 1621-1625 (5) 95 45

Kars Castle — A351

Alp Arslan, Conqueror of Kars, 1064 — A352

1964, Aug. 16 Unwmk. *Perf. 13*

1626 A351 50k blk & pale vio 10 8
1627 A352 130k blk, gold, sal & pale vio 28 20

900th anniversary of conquest of Kars.

Europa Issue, 1964
Common Design Type

1964, Sept. 14 Litho. *Perf. 13*
Size: 22x33mm

1628 CD7 50k org, ind & sil 25 25
1629 CD7 130k lt bl, mag & cit 50 50

Fuat, Resit and Ali Pashas — A353

Design: 60k, Mustafa Resit Pasha (vert.).

1964, Nov. 3 *Perf. 13*
Sizes: 48x33mm (50k, 100k); 22x33mm (60k)

1630 A353 50k multi 15 15
1631 A353 60k multi 22 20
1632 A353 100k multi 38 30

125th anniversary of reform decrees.

Parachutist — A354

Designs: 90k, Glider (horiz.). 130k, Ataturk watching squadron in flight.

1965, Feb. 16 Litho. *Perf. 13*

1633 A354 60k lt bl, blk, red & yel 12 8
1634 A354 90k bis & multi 25 12
1635 A354 130k lt bl & multi 38 22

Turkish Aviation League, 40th anniv.

Emblem A355

Designs: 50k, Radio mast and waves (vert.). 75k, Hand pressing button.

1965, Feb. 24 Unwmk. *Perf. 13*

1636 A355 30k multi 10 7
1637 A355 50k multi 16 10
1638 A355 75k multi 25 20

Telecommunications meeting of the Central Treaty Org., CENTO.

Coast of Ordu — A356

Designs: 50k, Manavgat Waterfall, Antalya. 60k, Sultan Ahmed Mosque, Istanbul. 100k, Hali Rahman Mosque, Urfa. 130k, Red Tower, Alanya.

1965, Apr. 5 Litho.

1639 A356 30k multi 12 5
1640 A356 50k multi 20 8
1641 A356 60k multi 20 12
1642 A356 100k multi 35 20
1643 A356 130k multi 50 25
Nos. 1639-1643 (5) 1.37 70

ITU Emblem, Old and New Communication Equipment — A357

1965, May 17 *Perf. 13*

1644 A357 50k multi 16 10
1645 A357 130k multi 50 25

ITU, centenary.

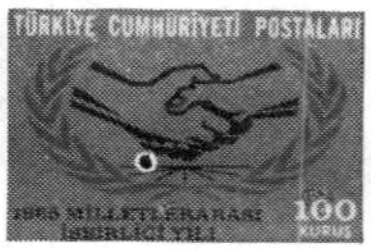

ICY Emblem A358

1965, June 26 Litho. Unwmk.

1646 A358 100k red org, red brn & brt grn 22 15
1647 A358 130k gray, lil & ol grn 32 22

International Cooperation Year.

Hands Holding Book A358a

Map and Flags of Turkey, Iran and Pakistan A358b

1965, July 21 Unwmk. *Perf. 13*

1648 A358a 50k org brn, yel & dk brn 25 14
1649 A358b 75k dl bl, red, grn blk & org 38 16

1st anniv. of the signing of the Regional Cooperation Development Pact by Turkey, Iran and Pakistan.

Kemal Ataturk — A359

1965 Litho. *Perf. 12½*

1650 A359 1k brt grn 5 5
1651 A359 5k vio bl 8 5
1652 A359 10k blue 20 5
1653 A359 25k gray 45 5
1654 A359 30k magenta 35 5
1655 A359 50k brown 45 8
1656 A359 150k orange 1.00 10
Nos. 1650-1656 (7) 2.58 43

Europa Issue, 1965
Common Design Type

1965, Sept. 27 *Perf. 13*
Size: 32x23mm

1665 CD8 50k gray, ultra & grn 50 50
1666 CD8 130k tan, blk & grn 75 75

Map of Turkey and People — A360

Designs: 50k, "1965." 100k, "1965," symbolic eye and man (vert.).

Unwmk.
1965, Oct. 24 Litho. *Perf. 13*

1667 A360 10k multi 5 5
1668 A360 50k grn, blk & lt yel grn 10 8
1669 A360 100k org, sl & blk 25 15

Issued to publicize the 1965 census.

Plane over Ankara Castle A361

Designs: 30k, Archer and Ankara castle. 50k, Horsemen with spears (ancient game). 100k, Three stamps and medal. 150k, Hands holding book (vert.).

1965, Oct. 25

1670 A361 10k brt vio, yel & red 7 5
1671 A361 30k multi 14 7
1672 A361 50k lt gray ol, ind & red 16 14
1673 A361 100k gray & multi 38 25

Souvenir Sheet
Imperf

1674 A361 150k multi 1.10 1.00

1st National Postage Stamp Exhibition "Ankara 65."

Resat Nuri Guntekin, Novelist — A362

Portraits: 5k, Besim Omer Akalin, M.D. 10k, Tevfik Fikret, poet. 25k, Tanburi Cemil, composer. 30k, Ahmet Vifik Pasha, playwright. 50k, Omer Seyfettin, novelist. 60k, Kemalettin Mimaroglu, architect. 150k, Halit Ziya Usakligil, novelist. 220k, Yahya Kemal Beyatli, poet.

1965 Litho. *Perf. 13½x13*
Black Portrait and Inscriptions

1675 A362 1k rose 5 5
1676 A362 5k blue 5 5
1677 A362 10k buff 8 5
1678 A362 25k dl red brn 20 5
1679 A362 30k gray 20 5
1680 A362 50k orange 50 5
1681 A362 60k red lil 50 5
1682 A362 150k lt grn 55 8
1683 A362 220k tan 75 8
Nos. 1675-1683 (9) 2.88 51

Training Ship Savarona A363

Designs: 60k, Submarine "Piri Reis." 100k, Cruiser "Alpaslan." 130k, Destroyer "Gelibolu." 220k, Destroyer "Gemlik."

1965, Dec. 6 Photo. *Perf. 11½*

1684 A363 50k bl & brn 20 12
1685 A363 60k bl & blk 28 15
1686 A363 100k bl & blk 42 22
1687 A363 130k bl & vio blk 65 40
1688 A363 220k bl & ind 1.00 65
Nos. 1684-1688 (5) 2.55 1.54

First Congress of Turkish Naval Society.

Kemal Ataturk A364

Halide Edip Adivar, Writer A365

1965 Litho. *Perf. 13½*
Imprint: "Apa Ofset Basimevi"
Black Portrait and Inscriptions

1689 A364 1k rose lil 5 5
1690 A364 5k lt grn 7 5
1691 A364 10k bl gray 10 5
1692 A364 50k ol bis 25 5
1693 A364 150k silver 70 10
Nos. 1689-1693 (5) 1.17 30

See Nos. 1724-1728.

1966 Litho. *Perf. 13½*

Portraits: 25k, Huseyin Sadettin Arel, writer and composer. 30k, Kamil Akdik, graphic artist. 60k, Abdurrahman Seref, historian. 130k, Naima, historian.

1694 A365 25k gray & brn blk 25 5
1695 A365 30k rose vio & blk brn 20 5
1696 A365 50k bl & blk 30 5
1697 A365 60k lt grn & blk brn 30 5
1698 A365 130k lt vio bl & blk 60 8
Nos. 1694-1698 (5) 1.65 28

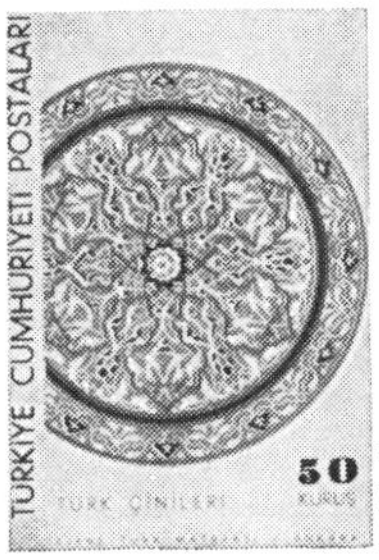

Tiles, Green Mausoleum, Bursa — A366

Tiles: 60k, Spring flowers, Hurrem Sultan Mausoleum, Istanbul. 130k, Stylized flowers, 16th century.

1966, May 15 Litho. *Perf. 13½x13*

1699 A366 50k multi 22 12
1700 A366 60k multi 40 30
1701 A366 130k multi 50 35

On No. 1700 the black ink was applied by a thermographic process and varnished, producing a shiny, raised effect to imitate the embossed tiles of the design source.

The first value column gives the catalogue value of an unused stamp, the second that of a used stamp.

Volleyball A367

View of Bodrum A368

1966, May 20 *Perf. 13x13½*

1702 A367 50k tan & multi 30 16

4th Intl. Military Volleyball Championship.

Perf. 13x13½, 13½x13
1966, May 25

Views: 30k, Kusadasi. 50k, Anadolu Hisari, Istanbul (horiz.). 90k, Marmaris. 100k, Izmir (horiz.).

1703 A368 10k multi 7 5
1704 A368 30k multi 45 25
1705 A368 50k multi 14 8
1706 A368 90k multi 25 16
1707 A368 100k multi 30 20
Nos. 1703-1707 (5) 1.21 74

Inauguration of Keban Dam — A369

Design: 60k, View of Keban Dam area.

1966, June 10 *Perf. 13½*

1708 A369 50k multi 10 5
1709 A369 60k multi 35 12

Visit of King Faisal of Saudi Arabia — A370

1966, Aug. 29 Litho. *Perf. 13½x13*

1710 A370 100k car rose & dk car 50 22

Symbolic Postmark and Stamp — A371

Designs: 60k, Flower made of stamps. 75k, Stamps forming display frames. 100k, Map of Balkan states, magnifying glass and stamp.

1966, Sept. 3 *Perf. 13½x13*

1711 A371 50k multi 10 5
1712 A371 60k multi 12 10
1713 A371 75k multi 28 15

Souvenir Sheet
Imperf

1714 A371 100k multi 75 55

2nd "Balkanfila" stamp exhibition, Istanbul.

Sultan Suleiman on Horseback A372

Designs: 90k, Mausoleum, Istanbul. 130k, Sultan Suleiman.

1966, Sept. 6 *Perf. 13½x13*

1715 A372 60k multi 15 12
1716 A372 90k multi 38 28
1717 A372 130k multi 65 38

Sultan Suleiman the Magnificent (1496?-1566). On No. 1717 a gold frame was applied by raised thermographic process.

Europa Issue, 1966
Common Design Type

1966, Sept. 26 Litho. *Perf. 13x13½*
Size: 22x33mm

1718 CD9 50k lt bl, vio bl & blk 65 40
a Black (inscriptions & imprint) omitted *65.00*
1719 CD9 130k lil, dk red lil & blk 75 50

Symbols of Education, Science and Culture A373

1966, Nov. 4 Litho. *Perf. 13*

1720 A373 130k brn, bis brn & yel 40 22

UNESCO, 20th anniversary.

University of Technology A374

Designs: 100k, Atom symbol. 130k, design symbolizing sciences.

1966, Nov. 15

1721 A374 50k multi 16 10
1722 A374 100k multi 30 20
1723 A374 130k multi 50 30

10th anniv. of the Middle East University of Technology.

Ataturk Type of 1965
Imprint: "Kiral Matbaasi - Ist"

1966 Litho. *Perf. 12½*
Black Portrait and Inscriptions

1724 A364 25k yellow 10 5
1725 A364 30k pink 16 5
1726 A364 50k rose lil 80 5
1727 A364 90k pale brn 38 5
1728 A364 100k gray 50 7
Nos. 1724-1728 (5) 1.94 27

Statue of Ataturk, Ankara — A375

Equestrian Statues of Ataturk: No. 1729A, Statue in Izmir. No. 1729B, Statue in Samsun.

Without Imprint
1967 Litho. *Perf. 13x12½*
Size: 23x16mm

1729 A375 10k blk & yel 14 5

Inscribed "1967"
Imprint: Kiral Matbaasi
Size: 22x15mm

1729A A375 10k blk & sal 10 5
1729B A375 10k blk & lt grn 10 5

Issued for use on greeting cards. See Nos. 1790-1791A, 1911.

Puppets Karagöz and Hacivat — A376

Intl. Tourist Year Emblem and: 60k, Sword and shield game. 90k, Traditional military band. 100k, raised effect.

Perf. 13x13½, 13½x13

1967, March 30 **Litho.**

1730 A376 50k multi 20 10
1731 A376 60k multi 30 20
1732 A376 90k multi 40 22
1733 A376 100k multi 50 30

Intl. Tourist Year. On No. 1733 the black ink was applied by a thermographic process and varnished, producing a shiny, raised effect.

Woman Vaccinating Child, Knife and Lancet — A377

Fallow Deer — A378

1967, Apr. 1 ***Perf. 13x13½***

1734 A377 100k multi 40 22

250th anniv. of smallpox vaccination in Turkey. The gold was applied by a thermographic process and varnished, producing a shiny, raised effect.

1967, Apr. 23 **Litho.** ***Perf. 13x13½***

Designs: 60k, Wild goat. 100k, Brown bear. 130k, Wild boar.

1735 A378 50k multi 12 8
1736 A378 60k multi 18 10
1737 A378 100k multi 30 18
1738 A378 130k multi 45 25

Soccer Players and Emblem with Map of Europe A379

Design: 130k, Players at left, smaller emblem.

1967, May 1 ***Perf. 13***

1739 A379 50k multi 20 12
1740 A379 130k yel & multi 45 32

20th Intl. Youth Soccer Championships.

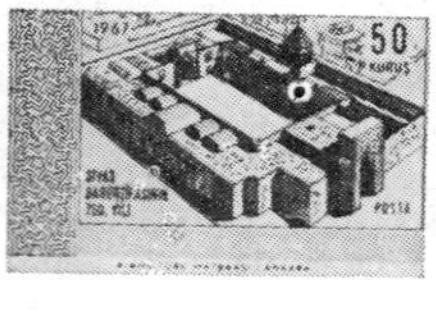

Sivas Hospital A380

1967, July 1 **Litho.** ***Perf. 13***

1741 A380 50k multi 20 10

750th anniversary of Sivas Hospital.

Selim Sirri Tarcan A381

Design: 60k, Olympic Rings and Baron Pierre de Coubertin.

1967, July 20

1742 A381 50k lt bl & multi 25 18
1743 A381 60k lil & multi 25 18

1st Turkish Olympic competitions. Nos. 1742-1743 are printed in vertical rows in sheets of 100, forming 50 horizontal se-tenant pairs.

Ahmed Mithat, Writer — A382

Portraits: 5k, Admiral Turgut Reis. 50k, Sikullu Mehmet, statesman. 100k, Nedim, poet. 150k, Osman Hamdi, painter.

1967 **Litho.** ***Perf. 12½***

1744 A382 1k grn & blk 5 5
1745 A382 5k dp bis & blk 5 5
1746 A382 50k brt vio & blk 30 5
1747 A382 100k cit & blk 50 8
1748 A382 150k yel & blk 75 15
Nos. 1744-1748 (5) 1.65 38

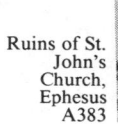

Ruins of St. John's Church, Ephesus A383

Design: 130k, Inside view of Virgin Mary's House, Ephesus.

1967, July 26 ***Perf. 13***

1749 A383 130k multi 25 20
1750 A383 220k multi 50 30

Visit of Pope Paul VI to the House of the Virgin Mary in Ephesus, July 26.

Plate on Firing Grid and Ornaments A384

1967, Sept. 1

1751 A384 50k pale lil, blk, ind & bl 25 12

5th International Ceramics Exhibition.

View of Istanbul and Emblem A385

1967, Sept. 4 **Litho.** ***Perf. 13***

1752 A385 130k dk bl & gray 25 20

9th Congress of the Intl. Commission of Large Dams.

Stamps, Ornament and Map of Turkey A386

Kemal Ataturk A387

Design: 60k, Grapes and stamps.

1967

1753 A386 50k multi 16 10
1754 A386 60k multi 22 14
a Souvenir sheet of 2, #1753-1754 70 70

Intl. Trade Fair, Izmir.

1967 **Litho.** ***Perf. 11½x12***

1755 A387 10k blk & lt ol grn 14 5
a Booklet pane of 10 1.65
b Booklet pane of 25 4.00
1756 A387 50k blk & pale rose 42 7
a Booklet pane of 2 90
b Bklt. pane of 9 + label (5 #1755, 4 #1756) 3.00

Nos. 1755-1756 were issued in booklets only.

Symbolic Water Cycle — A388

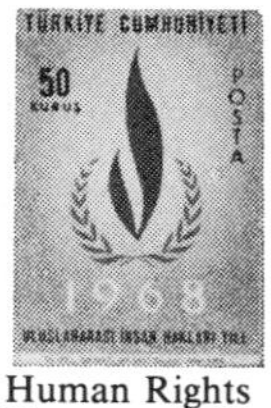

Human Rights Flame — A390

Child and Angora Cat, Man with Microscope A389

1967, Dec. 1 **Litho.** ***Perf. 13***

1757 A388 90k lt grn, blk & org 22 18
1758 A388 130k lil, blk & org 30 22

Hydrological Decade (UNESCO), 1965-74.

1967, Dec. 23 ***Perf. 13***

Design: 60k, Horse and man with microscope.

1759 A389 50k multi 15 12
1760 A389 60k multi 20 15

125th anniv. of Turkish veterinary medicine.

1968, Jan. 1 ***Perf. 13x13½***

1761 A390 50k rose lil, dk bl & org 12 8
1762 A390 130k lt bl, dk bl & red org 28 15

International Human Rights Year.

Archer on Horseback — A391

Miniatures, 16th Century: 50k, Investiture. 60k, Sultan Suleiman the Magnificent receiving an ambassador (vert.). 100k, Musicians.

Perf. 13x13½, 13½x13

1968, Mar. 1 **Litho.**

1763 A391 50k multi 15 10
1764 A391 60k multi 18 12
1765 A391 90k multi 35 20
1766 A391 100k multi 45 30

Kemal Ataturk — A392

1968 **Litho.** ***Perf. 12½***

1767 A392 1k dk & lt bl 7 5
1768 A392 5k dk & lt grn 14 5
1769 A392 50k org brn & yel 65 7
1770 A392 200k dk brn & pink 1.90 25

Law Book and Oak Branch A393

Mithat Pasha and Scroll A394

1968, Apr. 1 ***Perf. 13***

1771 A393 50k multi 16 14
1772 A394 60k multi 22 16

Centenary of the Court of Appeal.

1968, Apr. 1

Designs: 50k, Scales of Justice. 60k, Ahmet Cevdet Pasha and scroll.

1773 A393 50k multi 16 14
1774 A394 60k multi 22 16

Centenary of the Supreme Court.

Europa Issue, 1968
Common Design Type

1968, May 6 **Litho.** ***Perf. 13***
Size: 31½x23mm

1775 CD11 100k pck bl, yel & red 50 50
1776 CD11 130k grn, yel & red 90 90

Yacht Kismet A395

"Fight Usury" A396

1968, June 15 **Litho.** ***Perf. 13***

1777 A395 50k lt ultra & multi 18 12

Round-the-world trip of the yacht Kismet, Aug. 22, 1965-June 14, 1968.

1968, June 19

1778 A396 50k multi 20 12

Centenary of the Pawn Office, Istanbul.

Sakarya Battle and Independence Medal — A397

Design: 130k, National anthem and reverse of medal.

1968, Aug. 30 ***Perf. 13x13½***
1779 A397 50k gold & multi 12 8
1780 A397 130k gold & multi 28 20

Turkish Independence medal. The gold on Nos. 1779-1780 was applied by a thermographic process and varnished, producing a shiny, raised effect.

Ataturk and Galatasaray High School — A398

Designs: 50k, "100" and old and new school emblems. 60k, Portraits of Beyazit II and Gulbaba.

1968, Sept. 1 **Litho.**
1781 A398 50k gray & multi 15 10
1782 A398 60k tan & multi 22 15
1783 A398 100k lt bl & multi 42 25

Centenary of Galatasaray High School.

Charles de Gaulle — A399

1968, Oct. 25 **Litho.** ***Perf. 13***
1784 A399 130k multi 60 38

Visit of President Charles de Gaulle of France to Turkey.

Kemal Ataturk A400

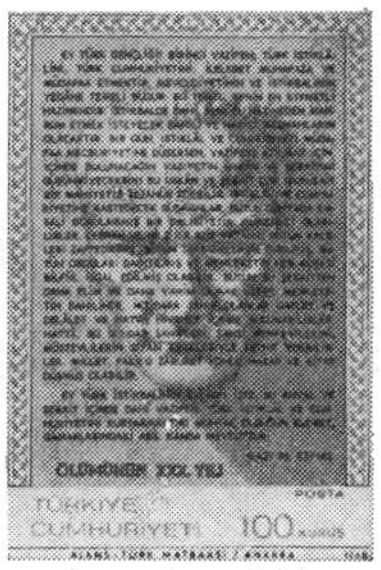

Ataturk and his Speech to Youth A401

Designs: 50k, Ataturk's tomb and Citadel of Ankara. 60k, Ataturk looking out a train window. 250k, Framed portrait of Ataturk in military uniform.

1968, Nov. 10
1785 A400 30k org & blk 20 7
1786 A400 50k brt grn & sl grn 20 7
1787 A400 60k bl grn & blk 22 7
1788 A401 100k blk, gray & brt grn 50 16
1789 A401 250k multi 90 40
Nos. 1785-1789 (5) 2.02 77

30th death anniv. of Kemal Ataturk.

Ataturk Statue Type of 1967

Equestrian Statues of Ataturk: No. 1790, Statue in Zonguldak. No. 1791, Statue in Antakya. No. 1791A, Statue in Bursa.

Imprint: Kiral Matbaasi 1968

1968-69 **Litho.** ***Perf. 13x12½***

Size: 22x15mm
1790 A375 10k blk & lt bl 8 5
1791 A375 10k blk & brt rose lil 8 5

Perf. 13½

Imprint: *Tifdruk Matbaacilik Sanayii* A. S. 1969

Size: 21x16½mm
1791A A375 10k dk grn & tan ('69) 7 5

Ince Minare Mosque, Konya A402

ILO Emblem A403

Historic Buildings: 10k, Doner Kumbet (tomb), Kayseri. 50k, Karatay Medresse (University Gate), Konya. 100k, Ortakoy Mosque, Istanbul. 200k, Ulu Mosque, Divriki.

1968-69 **Photo.** ***Perf. 13x13½***
1792 A402 1k dk brn & buff ('69) 5 5
1793 A402 10k plum & dl rose ('69) 16 5
1794 A402 50k dl ol grn & gray 35 5
1795 A402 100k dk & lt grn ('69) 80 7
1796 A402 200k dp bl & lt bl ('69) 1.40 22
Nos. 1792-1796 (5) 2.76 44

1969, Apr. 15 **Litho.** ***Perf. 13***
1797 A403 130k dk red & blk 22 15

ILO, 50th anniv.

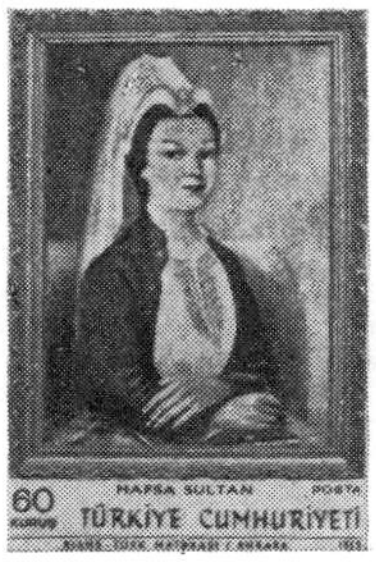

Sultana Hafsa, Medical Pioneer A404

1969, Apr. 26 **Litho.** ***Perf. 13½x13***
1798 A404 60k multi 25 12

Europa Issue, 1969

Common Design Type

1969, Apr. 28 ***Perf. 13***

Size: 32x23mm
1799 CD12 100k dl vio & multi 42 42
1800 CD12 130k gray grn & multi 55 55

Kemal Ataturk A405

Map of Istanbul A407

Ataturk and S.S. Bandirma A406

1969, May 19 **Litho.** ***Perf. 13***
1801 A405 50k multi 12 8
1802 A406 60k multi 15 10

50th anniv. of the landing of Kemal Ataturk at Samsun.

1969, May 31
1803 A407 130k vio bl, lt bl, gold & red 28 20

22nd Congress of the Intl. Chamber of Commerce, Istanbul.

Educational Progress A408

Agricultural Progress A409

Designs: 90k, Pouring ladle and industrial symbols. 100k, Road sign (highway construction). 180k, Oil industry chart and symbols.

1969 **Litho.** ***Perf. 13½x13***
1804 A408 1k blk & gray 5 5
1805 A408 1k blk & bis brn 5 5
1806 A408 1k blk & lt grn 5 5
1807 A408 1k blk & lt vio 5 5
1808 A408 1k blk & org red 5 5
1809 A409 50k brn & ocher 18 5
1810 A409 90k blk & grnsh gray 28 5
1811 A408 100k blk & org red 40 8
1812 A408 180k vio & org 75 12
Nos. 1804-1812 (9) 1.86 55

Issue dates: 1k, 100k, Apr. 8; 50k, June 11; 90k, 180k, Aug. 15.

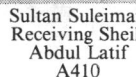

Sultan Suleiman Receiving Sheik Abdul Latif A410

Kemal Ataturk A411

Designs: 80k, Lady Serving Wine, Safavi miniature, Iran. 130k, Lady on Balcony, Mogul miniature, Pakistan.

1969, July 21 **Litho.** ***Perf. 13***
1813 A410 50k yel & multi 18 10
1814 A410 80k yel & multi 30 18
1815 A410 130k yel & multi 55 35

5th anniv. of the signing of the Regional Cooperation for Development Pact by Turkey, Iran and Pakistan.

1969, July 23

Design: 60k, Ataturk monument and bas-relief showing congress.

1816 A411 50k blk & gray 12 10
1817 A411 60k blk & grnsh gray 15 10

50th anniversary, Congress of Erzerum.

Sivas Congress Delegates A412

Design: 50k, Congress Hall.

1969, Sept. 4 **Litho.** ***Perf. 13***
1818 A412 50k dk brn & dp rose 15 10
1819 A412 60k ol blk & yel 18 12

50th anniv. of the Congress of Sivas (preparation for the Turkish war of independence).

Bar Dance — A413

Folk Dances: 50k, Candle dance (çaydaçira). 60k, Scarf dance (halay). 100k, Sword dance (kiliç-kalkan). 130k, Two male dancers (zeybek) (vert.).

1969, Sept. 9
1820 A413 30k brn & multi 12 10
1821 A413 50k multi 18 12
1822 A413 60k multi 25 20
1823 A413 100k yel & multi 35 20
1824 A413 130k multi 65 40
Nos. 1820-1824 (5) 1.55 1.02

1914 Airplane "Prince Celaleddin" — A414

Design: 75k, First Turkish letter carried by air.

1969, Oct. 18 **Litho.** ***Perf. 13***
1825 A414 60k dk bl & bl 18 10
1826 A414 75k blk & bis 25 18

55th anniv. of the first Turkish mail transported by air.

"Kutadgu Bilig" A415

1969, Nov. 20 **Litho.** ***Perf. 13***
1827 A415 130k ol bis, brn & gold 30 20

900th anniv. of "Kutadgu Bilig," a book about the function of the state, compiled by Jusuf of Balasagun in Tashkent, 1069.

Ataturk's Arrival in Ankara, after a Painting — A416

Design: 60k, Ataturk and his coworkers in automobiles arriving in Ankara, after a photograph.

1969, Dec. 27 **Litho.** ***Perf. 13***
1828 A416 50k multi 18 10
1829 A416 60k multi 25 18

50th anniv. of Kemal Ataturk's arrival in Ankara, Dec. 27, 1919.

Bosporus Bridge, Map of Europe and Asia — A417

Design: 60k, View of proposed Bosporus Bridge and shore lines.

1970, Feb. 20 Litho. *Perf. 13*
1830 A417 60k gold & multi 50 30
1831 A417 130k gold & multi 1.00 65

Foundation ceremonies for the bridge across the Bosporus linking Europe and Asia.

Kemal Ataturk and Signature A418

Kemal Ataturk A419

1970 Litho. *Perf. 13*
1832 A418 1k dp org & brn 5 5
1833 A419 5k sil & blk 5 5
1834 A419 30k cit & blk 8 5
1835 A418 50k lt ol & blk 20 5
1836 A419 50k pink & blk 15 5
1837 A419 75k lil & blk 30 5
1838 A419 100k bl & blk 40 8
Nos. 1832-1838 (7) 1.23 38

Education Year Emblem A420

Turkish EXPO '70 Emblem A421

1970, Mar. 16
1839 A420 130k ultra, pink & rose lil 25 18

International Education Year.

1970, Mar. 27

Design: 100k, EXPO '70 emblem and Turkish pavilion.

1840 A421 50k gold & multi 12 8
1841 A421 100k gold & multi 20 15

EXPO '70 International Exhibition, Osaka, Japan, Mar. 15-Sept. 13.

Opening of Grand National Assembly A422

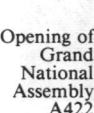

Design: 60k, Session of First Grand National Assembly, 1920.

1970, Apr. 23
1842 A422 50k multi 12 8
1843 A422 60k multi 20 10

Turkish Grand National Assembly, 50th anniv.

Canceled-to-order stamps are often from remainders. Most collectors of canceled stamps prefer postally used specimens.

Emblem of Cartographic Service A423

Map of Turkey and Gen. Mehmet Sevki Pasha — A424

Designs: 60k, Plane and aerial mapping survey diagram. 100k, Triangulation point in mountainous landscape.

Perf. 13½x13 (A423), 13x13½ (A424)

1970, May 2 Litho.
1844 A423 50k bl & multi 10 5
1845 A424 60k blk, gray grn & brick red 15 8
1846 A423 100k multi 25 15
1847 A424 130k multi 40 30

Turkish Cartographic Service, 75th anniv.

Europa Issue, 1970
Common Design Type

1970, May 4 *Perf. 13*
Size: 37x23mm
1848 CD13 100k ver, blk & org 30 30
1849 CD13 130k dk bl grn, blk & org 50 50

Inauguration of UPU Headquarters, Bern — A425

1970, May 20
1850 A425 60k blk & dl bl 15 10
1851 A425 130k blk & dl ol grn 25 18

Lady with Mimosa, by Osman Hamdi (1842-1910) A426

Paintings: No. 1853, Deer, by Seker Ahmet (1841-1907). No. 1854, Portrait of Fevzi Cakmak, by Avni Lifij (d. 1927). No. 1855, Sailboats, by Nazmi Ziya (1881-1937); horiz.

1970 Litho. *Perf. 13*
Size: 29x49mm
1852 A426 250k multi 65 35
1853 A426 250k multi 65 35
Size: 32x49mm
1854 A426 250k multi 65 35
Size: 73½x33mm
1855 A426 250k multi 65 35

Issue dates: Nos. 1852-1853, June 15. Nos. 1854-1855, Dec. 15.

Turkish Folk Art — A427

1970, June 15
1856 A427 50k multi 15 8

3rd National Stamp Exhibition, ANKARA 70, Oct. 28-Nov. 4. Pane of 50, each stamp se-tenant with label. This 50k, in pane of 50 without labels, was re-issued Oct. 28 with Nos. 1867-1869.

View of Fethiye A428

Designs: 80k, Seeyo-Se-Pol Bridge, Esfahan, Iran. 130k, Saiful Malook Lake, Pakistan.

1970, July 21 Litho. *Perf. 13*
1857 A428 60k multi 10 8
1858 A428 80k multi 12 10
1859 A428 130k multi 20 15

6th anniv. of the signing of the Regional Cooperation for Development Pact by Turkey, Iran and Pakistan.

Sultan Balim's Tomb — A429

Haci Bektas Veli — A430

Designs: 30k, Tomb of Haci Bektas Veli (horiz.).

1970, Aug. 16 Litho. *Perf. 13*
1860 A429 30k multi 8 5
1861 A429 100k multi 18 10
1862 A430 180k multi 32 20

700th death anniv. of Haci Bektas Veli, mystic.

Hittite Sun Disk and "ISO" — A431

1970, Sept. 15
1863 A431 110k car rose, gold & blk 20 10
1864 A431 150k ultra, gold & blk 30 20

8th General Council Meeting of the Intl. Standardization Org., Ankara.

UN Emblem, People and Globe A432

Stamp "Flower" and Book A433

Design: 100k, UN emblem and propeller (horiz.).

1970, Oct. 24 Litho. *Perf. 13*
1865 A432 100k gray & multi 20 10
1866 A432 220k multi 40 25

25th anniversary of the United Nations.

1970, Oct. 28

Designs: 60k, Ataturk monument and stamps (horiz.). 1.30k, Abstract flower.

1867 A433 10k multi 5 5
1868 A433 60k bl & multi 15 8

Souvenir Sheet
1869 A433 130k dk grn & org 65 65

3rd National Stamp Exhibition, ANKARA 70, Oct. 28-Nov. 4. See note below No. 1856.

Inönü Battle Scene — A434

Design: No. 1871, Second Battle of Inönü.

1971 Litho. *Perf. 13*
1870 A434 100k multi 25 12
1871 A434 100k multi 25 12

First and Second Battles of Inönü, 50th anniv.

Issue dates: No. 1870, Jan. 10. No. 1871, Apr. 1.

Village on River Bank, by Ahmet Sekür — A435

Painting: No. 1872, Landscape, Yildiz Palace Garden, by Ahmet Ragip Bicakcilar.

1971, Mar. 15 Litho. *Perf. 13*
1872 A435 250k multi 50 40
1873 A435 250k multi 50 40

See Nos. 1901-1902, 1909-1910, 1937-1938.

Campaign Against Discrimination A436

1971, Mar. 21 Litho. *Perf. 13*
1874 A436 100k multi 15 10
1875 A436 250k gray & multi 40 25

Intl. Year against Racial Discrimination.

Europa Issue, 1971
Common Design Type

1971, May 3 Litho. *Perf. 13*
Size: 31½x22½mm
1876 CD14 100k lt bl, cl & mag 60 60
1877 CD14 150k dp org, grn & red 70 70

Kemal Ataturk
A437 A438

1971

1878 A437 5k gray & ultra 5 5
1879 A437 25k gray & dk red 5 5
1880 A438 25k brn & pink 5 5
1881 A437 100k gray & vio 20 5
1882 A438 100k grn & sal 20 5
1883 A438 250k bl & gray 50 10
1884 A437 400k tan & ol grn 50 14
Nos. 1878-1884 (7) 1.55 49

Pres. Kemal Gürsel A439

Mosque of Selim, Edirne A440

1971, May 27 Litho. *Perf. 13*

1885 A439 100k multi 30 14

Revolution of May 27, 1960; Kemal Gürsel (1895-1966), president.

1971, July 21 Litho. *Perf. 13*

Designs: 150k, Religious School, Chaharbagh, Iran. 200k, Badshahi Mosque, Pakistan (horiz.).

1886 A440 100k multi 18 10
1887 A440 150k multi 25 12
1888 A440 200k multi 35 18

Regional Cooperation by Turkey, Iran and Pakistan, 7th anniversary.

Alp Arslan and Battle of Malazkirt — A441

Design: 250k, Archers on horseback.

1971, Aug. 26 Litho. *Perf. 13x13½*

1889 A441 100k multi 40 16
1890 A441 250k red, org & blk 65 38

900th anniversary of the Battle of Malazkirt, which established the Seljuk Dynasty in Asia Minor.

Battle of Sakarya — A442

1971, Sept. 13

1891 A442 100k vio & multi 30 14

50th anniversary of the victory of Sakarya.

Turkey-Bulgaria Railroad — A443

Designs: 110k, Ferry and map of Lake Van. 250k, Turkey-Iran railroad.

1971

1892 A443 100k multi 55 16
1893 A443 110k multi 55 16
1894 A443 250k yel & multi 1.20 50

Turkish railroad connections with Bulgaria and Iran. Issue dates: 110k, 250k, Sept. 27; 100k, Sept. 30.

Netball and Map of Mediterranean A444

Designs: 200k, Runner and stadium (vert.). 250k, Shot put and map of Mediterranean. (vert.)

1971, Oct. 6

1895 A444 100k dl vio & blk 25 14
1896 A444 200k brn, blk & emer 40 25

Souvenir Sheet

Imperf

1897 A444 250k ol bis & sl grn 80 80

Mediterranean Games, Izmir.

Tomb of Cyrus the Great — A445

Designs: 100k, Harpist, Persian mosaic (vert.). 150k, Ataturk and Riza Shah Pahlavi.

1971, Oct. 13

1898 A445 25k lt bl & multi 8 7
1899 A445 100k multi 22 14
1900 A445 150k dk brn & buff 38 22

2500th anniversary of the founding of the Persian empire by Cyrus the Great.

Painting Type of 1971

Paintings: No. 1901, Sultan Mohammed I and his Staff. No. 1902, Palace with tiled walls.

1971, Nov. 15 Litho. *Perf. 13*

1901 A435 250k multi 60 40
1902 A435 250k multi 60 40

Yunus Emre — A446

1971, Dec. 27 Litho. *Perf. 13*

1903 A446 100k brn & multi 30 16

650th death anniv. of Yunus Emre, Turkish folk poet.

First Turkish World Map and Book Year Emblem — A447

1972, Jan. 3 *Perf. 13*

1904 A447 100k buff & multi 30 16

International Book Year.

Doves and NATO Emblem A448

Fisherman, by Cevat Dereli A449

1972, Feb. 18 Litho. *Perf. 13*

1905 A448 100k dl grn, blk & gray 65 22
1906 A448 250k dl bl, blk & gray 80 60

Turkey's membership in NATO, 20th anniv.

Europa Issue 1972

Common Design Type

1972, May 2 Litho. *Perf. 13*

Size: 22x33mm

1907 CD15 110k bl & multi 60 60
1908 CD15 250k brn & multi 80 80

Painting Type of 1971

Paintings: No. 1909, Forest, Seker Ahmet. No. 1910, View of Gebze, Anatolia, by Osman Hamdi.

1972, May 15 Litho.

1909 A435 250k multi 60 35
1910 A435 250k multi 60 35

Ataturk Statue Type of 1967

Design: 25k, Ataturk Statue in front of Ethnographic Museum, Ankara.

Imprint: Ajans - Turk/Ankara 1972

Perf. 12½x11½

1972, June 12 Litho.

Size: 22x15½mm

1911 A375 25k blk & buff 5 5

1972, July 21 Litho. *Perf. 13*

Paintings: 125k, Young Man, by Abdur Rehman Chughtai (Pakistan). 150k, Persian Woman, by Behzad.

1912 A449 100k gold & multi 25 20
1913 A449 125k gold & multi 40 25
1914 A449 150k gold & multi 45 35

Regional Cooperation for Development Pact among Turkey, Iran and Pakistan, 8th anniv.

Ataturk and Commanders at Mt. Koca — A450

Designs: No. 1916, Battle of the Commander-in-chief. No. 1917, Turkish army entering Izmir. 110k, Artillery and cavalry.

1972 Litho. *Perf. 13x13½*

1915 A450 100k lt ultra & blk 22 14
1916 A450 100k pink & multi 25 14
1917 A450 100k yel & multi 25 14
1918 A450 110k org & multi 30 16

50th anniversary of fight for establishment of independent Turkish republic. Issue dates: Nos. 1915, 1918, Aug. 26; No. 1916, Aug. 30; No. 1917, Sept. 9.

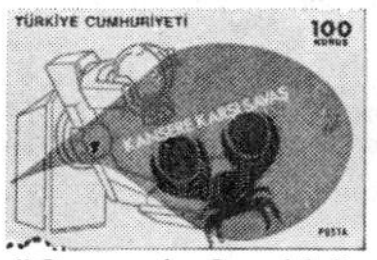

"Cancer is Curable" A451

International Railroad Union Emblem A452

1972, Oct. 10 Litho. *Perf. 12½x13*

1919 A451 100k blk, brt bl & red 25 14

Fight against cancer.

1972, Dec. 31 Litho. *Perf. 13*

1920 A452 100k sl grn, ocher & red 20 12

Intl. Railroad Union, 50th anniv.

Kemal Ataturk — A453

1972-76 Litho. *Perf. 13½x13*

Size: 21x26mm

1921 A453 5k gray & bl 5 5
1922 A453 25k org ('75) 5 5
1923 A453 100k buff & red brn ('73) 25 5
1924 A453 100k lt gray & gray ('75) 12 5
1925 A453 110k lt bl & vio bl 32 5
1926 A453 125k dl grn ('73) 35 5
1927 A453 150k tan & brn 40 5
1928 A453 150k lt grn & grn ('75) 15 5
1929 A453 175k yel & lil ('73) 40 8
1930 A453 200k buff & red 42 8
1931 A453 250k pink & pur ('75) 30 8
1931A A453 400k gray & Prus bl ('76) 50 10
1932 A453 500k pink & vio 1.00 15
1933 A453 500k gray & ultra ('75) 55 15

Size: 22x33mm

Perf. 13

1934 A453 10 l pink & car rose ('75) 1.10 25
Nos. 1921-1934 (15) 5.96 1.29

See Nos. 2060-2061.

Europa Issue 1973

Common Design Type

1973, Apr. 4 Litho. *Perf. 13*

Size: 32x23mm

1935 CD16 110k gray & multi 28 28
1936 CD16 250k multi 55 55

Painting Type of 1971

Paintings: No. 1937, Beyazit Almshouse, Istanbul, by Ahmet Ziya Akbulut. No. 1938, Flowers, by Suleyman Seyyit (vert.).

1973, June 15 Litho. *Perf. 13*

1937 A435 250k multi 60 35
1938 A435 250k multi 60 35

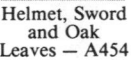

Helmet, Sword and Oak Leaves — A454

Mausoleum of Antiochus I — A455

Design: 100k, Helmet, sword and laurel.

1973, June 28 ***Perf. 13x12½***

1939 A454 90k brn, gray & grn 22 14
1940 A454 100k brn, lem & grn 22 14

Army Day.

1973, July 21 Litho. ***Perf. 13***

Designs: 100k, Colossal heads, mausoleum of Antiochus I (69-34 B.C.), Commagene, Turkey. 150k, Statue, Shahdad Kerman, Persia, 3000 B.C. 200k, Street, Mohenjo-daro, Pakistan.

1941 A455 100k lt bl & multi 20 14
1942 A455 150k ol & multi 25 16
1943 A455 200k brn & multi 35 22

Regional Cooperation for Development Pact among Turkey, Iran and Pakistan, 9th anniv.

Minelayer Nusret — A456

Designs: 25k, Destroyer Istanbul. 100k, Speedboat Simsek and Naval College. 250k, Two-masted training ship Nuvid-i Futuh.

1973, Aug. 1

Size: 31½x22mm

1944 A456 5k Prus bl & multi 5 5
1945 A456 25k Prus bl & multi 5 5
1946 A456 100k Prus bl & multi 20 10

Size: 48x32mm

1947 A456 250k bl & multi 50 25

abu-al-Rayhan al-Biruni A457

Emblem of Darussafaka Foundation A458

1973, Sept. 4 Litho. ***Perf. 13x12½***

1948 A457 250k multi 50 25

abu-al-Rayhan al-Biruni (973-1048), philosopher and mathematician.

1973, Sept. 15 ***Perf. 13***

1949 A458 100k sil & multi 25 14

Centenary of the educational and philanthropic Darussafaka Foundation.

BALKANFILA IV Emblem — A459

Designs: 110k, Symbolic view and stamps. 250k, "Balkanfila 4."

1973 Litho. ***Perf. 13***

1950 A459 100k gray & multi 20 10
1951 A459 110k multi 12 10
1952 A459 250k multi 28 18

BALKANFILA IV, Philatelic Exhibition of Balkan Countries, Izmir, Oct. 26-Nov. 5.
Issue dates: 100k, Sept. 26; 110k, 250k, Oct. 26.

Sivas Shepherd A460

Kemal Ataturk A461

Design: 100k, Angora cat.

1973, Oct. 4

1953 A460 25k blk, bl & buff 10 5
1954 A460 100k brn, yel & bl 30 10

1973, Oct. 10 Litho. ***Perf. 13***

1955 A461 100k gold & blk brn 22 10

35th death anniv. of Kemal Ataturk.

Flower and "50" — A462

Ataturk — A463

Designs: 250k, Torch and "50". 475k, Grain and cogwheel.

1973, Oct. 29

1956 A462 100k pur, red & bl 10 8
1957 A462 250k multi 32 20
1958 A462 475k brt bl & org 50 35

Souvenir Sheet

Imperf

1959 A463 500k multi 90 90

50th anniversary of the Turkish Republic. No. 1959 contains one stamp with simulated perforations.

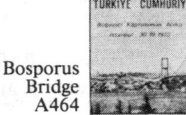

Bosporus Bridge A464

Design: 150k, Istanbul and Bosporus Bridge. 200k, Bosporus Bridge, children and UNICEF emblem (vert.).

1973, Oct. 30 ***Perf. 13***

1960 A464 100k multi 25 14
1961 A464 150k multi 40 25
1962 A464 200k multi 45 25

Inauguration of the Bosporus Bridge from Istanbul to Üsküdar, Oct. 30, 1973; UNICEF; children from East and West brought closer through Bosporus Bridge (No. 1962).

Mevlana's Tomb and Dancers A465

Jalal-udin Mevlana A466

1973, Dec. 1 ***Perf. 13x12½***

1963 A465 100k blk, lt ultra & grn 20 14
1964 A466 250k bl & multi 40 25

Jalal-udin Mevlana (1207-1273), poet and founder of the Mevlevie dervish order.

Cotton and Ship — A467

Export Products: 90k, Grapes. 100k, Figs. 250k, Citrus fruits. 325k, Tobacco. 475k, Hazelnuts.

1973, Dec. 10 Litho. ***Perf. 13***

1965 A467 75k blk, gray & bl 12 7
1966 A467 90k blk, ol & bl 16 10
1967 A467 100k blk, emer & bl 22 10
1968 A467 250k blk, brt yel & bl 65 22
1969 A467 325k blk, yel & bl 65 25
1970 A467 475k blk, org brn & bl 90 38
Nos. 1965-1970 (6) 2.70 1.12

Pres. Inönü — A468

Hittite King, 8th Century B.C. — A469

1973, Dec. 25 Litho. ***Perf. 13***

1971 A468 100k sep & buff 22 14

Ismet Inönü, (1884-1973), first Prime Minister and second President of Turkey.

Europa Issue

Design: 250k, Statuette of a Boy, (2nd millenium B.C.).

1974, Apr. 29 Litho. ***Perf. 13***

1972 A469 110k multi 65 65
1973 A469 250k lt bl & multi 1.20 1.20

Silver and Gold Figure, 3000 B.C. — A470

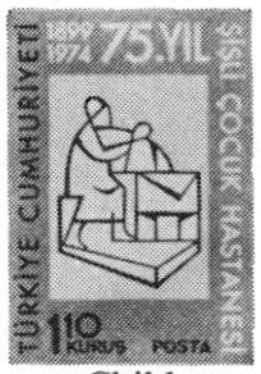

Child Care — A471

Archaeological Finds: 175k, Painted jar, 5000 B.C. (horiz.). 200k, Vessels in bull form, 1700-1600 B.C. (horiz.). 250k, Pitcher, 700 B.C.

1974, May 24 Litho. ***Perf. 13***

1974 A470 125k multi 22 12
1975 A470 175k multi 35 14
1976 A470 200k multi 42 20
1977 A470 250k multi 65 35

1974, May 24

1978 A471 110k gray bl & blk 22 14

75th anniversary of the Sisli Children's Hospital, Istanbul.

Anatolian Rug, 15th Century A472

Designs: 150k, Persian rug, late 16th century. 200k, Kashan rug, Lahore.

1974, July 21 Litho. ***Perf. 12½x13***

1979 A472 100k bl & multi 40 14
1980 A472 150k brn & multi 65 20
1981 A472 200k red & multi 1.2025

10th anniversary of the Regional Cooperation for Development Pact among Turkey, Iran and Pakistan.

Dove with Turkish Flag over Cyprus — A473

1974, Aug. 26 Litho. ***Perf. 13***

1982 A473 250k multi 65 35

Cyprus Peace Operation.

Wrestling A474

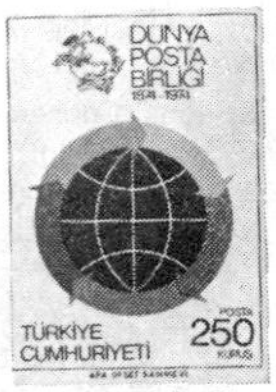

Arrows Circling Globe A475

Designs: 90k, 250k, various wrestling holds (horiz.).

1974, Aug. 29

1983 A474 90k multi 14 10
1984 A474 100k multi 20 10
1985 A474 250k multi 38 22

World Freestyle Wrestling Championships.

1974, Oct. 9 Litho. ***Perf. 13***

UPU Emblem and: 110k, "UPU" in form of dove. 200k, Dove.

1986 A475 110k bl, gold & dk bl 20 10
1987 A475 200k grn & brn 30 16
1988 A475 250k multi 50 30

Centenary of Universal Postal Union.

"Law Reforms" A476

"National Economy" A477

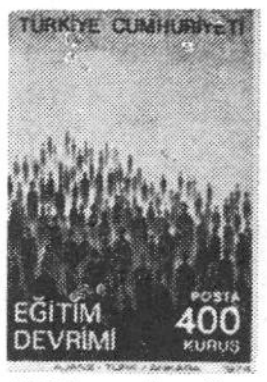

"Education" A478

1974, Oct. 29

1989	A476	50k	bl & blk	8	5
1990	A477	150k	red & multi	15	10
1991	A478	400k	multi	40	30

Works and reforms of Kemal Ataturk.

Arrows Pointing Up — A479

Cogwheel and Map of Turkey — A480

1974, Nov. 29 Litho. *Perf. 13*

1992	A479	25k	brn & blk	7	5
1993	A480	100k	brn & gray	16	10

Third Five-year Development Program (No. 1992), and industrialization progress (No. 1993).

Volleyball — A481

Designs: 175k, Basketball. 250k, Soccer.

1974, Dec. 30

1994	A481	125k	bl & blk	22	14
1995	A481	175k	org & blk	35	14
1996	A481	250k	emer & blk	55	20

Automatic Telex Network A482

Postal Check — A483

Radio Transmitter and Waves — A484

1975, Feb. 5 Litho. *Perf. 13*

1997	A482	5k	blk & yel	5	5
1998	A483	50k	ol grn & org	10	5
1999	A484	100k	bl & blk	20	10

Post and telecommunications.

Child Entering Classroom A485

Children's paintings: 50k, View of village. 100k, Dancing children.

1975, Apr. 23 Litho. *Perf. 13*

2000	A485	25k	multi	5	5
2001	A485	50k	multi	8	5
2002	A485	100k	multi	16	8

Karacaoglan Monument in Mut, by Huseyin Gezer — A486

1975, Apr. 25

2003	A486	110k	dk grn, bis & red	20	14

Karacaoglan (1606-1697), musician.

Europa Issue

Orange Harvest in Hatay, by Cemal Tollu — A487

Design: 250k, Yoruk Family on Plateau, by Turgut Zaim.

1975, Apr. 28

2004	A487	110k	bis & multi	22	22
2005	A487	250k	bis & multi	38	38

Porcelain Vase, Turkey — A488

Designs: 200k, Ceramic plate, Iran (horiz.). 250k, Camel leather vase, Pakistan.

Perf. 13½x13, 13x13½

1975, July 21 Litho.

2006	A488	110k	multi	25	20
2007	A488	200k	multi	40	25
2008	A488	250k	ultra & multi	60	40

Regional Cooperation for Development Pact among Turkey, Iran and Pakistan.

Horon Folk Dance — A489

Regional Folk Dances: 125k, Kasik. 175k, Bengi. 250k, Kasap. 325k, Kafkas (vert.).

1975, Aug. 30 Litho. *Perf. 13*

2009	A489	100k	bl & multi	14	7
2010	A489	125k	grn & multi	22	10
2011	A489	175k	rose & multi	30	16
2012	A489	250k	multi	45	25
2013	A489	325k	org & multi	60	35
	Nos. 2009-2013 (5)			1.71	93

Knight Slaying Dragon — A490

The Plunder of Salur Kazan's House — A491

Design: 175k, Two Wanderers (horiz.).

1975, Oct. 15 Litho. *Perf. 13*

2014	A490	90k	multi	14	5
2015	A490	175k	multi	25	20
2016	A491	200k	multi	35	22

Illustrations for tales by Dede Korkut.

Common Carp A492

1975, Nov. 27 Litho. *Perf. 12½x13*

2017	A492	75k	Turbot	14	5
2018	A492	90k	shown	16	7
2019	A492	175k	Trout	35	14
2020	A492	250k	Red mullet	40	22
2021	A492	475k	Red bream	80	38
	Nos. 2017-2021 (5)			1.85	86

Women's Participation A493

Insurance Nationalization A494

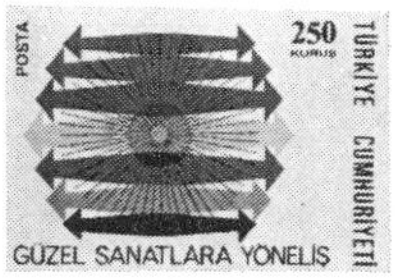

Fine Arts — A495

1975, Dec. 5 *Perf. 12½x13, 13x12½*

2022	A493	100k	bis, blk & red	14	7
2023	A494	110k	vio & multi	20	10
2024	A495	250k	multi	30	22

Works and reforms of Ataturk.

Europa Issue

Ceramic Plate — A496

Design: 400k, Decorated pitcher.

1976, May 3 Litho. *Perf. 13*

2025	A496	200k	pur & multi	50	50
2026	A496	400k	multi	80	80

Sultan Ahmed Mosque A497

1976, May 10

2027	A497	500k	gray & multi	65	40

7th Islamic Conference, Istanbul.

Lunch in the Field A498

Children's Drawings: 200k, Boats on the Bosporus (vert.). 400k, Winter landscape.

1976, May 19 Litho. *Perf. 13*

2028	A498	50k	multi	5	5
2029	A498	200k	multi	20	10
2030	A498	400k	multi	40	20

Samsun 76, First National Junior Philatelic Exhibition, Samsun.

Storks, Sultan Marsh A499

Conservation Emblem and: 200k, Horses, Manyas Lake. 250k, Borabay Lake. 400k, Manavgat Waterfall.

1976, June 5

2031	A499	150k	multi	1.00	50
2032	A499	200k	multi	25	10
2033	A499	250k	multi	40	16
2034	A499	400k	multi	60	22

European Wetland Conservation Year.

Nasreddin Hodja Carrying Liver — A500

Montreal Olympic Emblem and Flame — A501

Designs: 250k, Friend giving recipe for cooking liver. 600k, Hawk carrying off liver and Hodja telling hawk he cannot enjoy liver without recipe.

1976, July 5 Litho. *Perf. 13*

2035	A500	150k	multi	20	8
2036	A500	250k	multi	30	16
2037	A500	600k	multi	80	35

Turkish folklore.

1976, July 17

Designs: 400k, "76", Montreal Olympic emblem (horiz.). 600k, Montreal Olympic emblem and ribbons.

2038 A501 100k red & multi 14 5
2039 A501 400k red & multi 45 25
2040 A501 600k red & multi 80 40

21st Olympic Games, Montreal, Canada, July 17-Aug. 1.

Kemal Ataturk A502

Designs: 200k, Riza Shah Pahlavi. 250k, Mohammed Ali Jinnah.

1976, July 21 Litho. *Perf. 13½*

2041 A502 100k multi 10 5
2042 A502 200k multi 22 10
2043 A502 250k multi 30 14

Regional Cooperation for Development Pact among Turkey, Pakistan and Iran, 12th anniversary.

"Ataturk's Army" A503

Ataturk's Speeches A504

"Peace at Home and in the World" — A505

1976, Oct. 29 Litho. *Perf. 13*

2044 A503 100k blk & red 16 5
2045 A504 200k gray grn & multi 20 10
2046 A505 400k bl & multi 42 25

Works and reforms of Ataturk.

Hora A506

1977, Jan. 19 Litho. *Perf. 13*

2047 A506 400k multi 50 25

MTA Sismik 1 "Hora" geophysical exploration ship.

Keyboard and Violin Sound Hole — A507

1977, Feb. 24 Litho. *Perf. 13x13½*

2048 A507 200k multi 25 16

Turkish State Symphony Orchestra, sesquicentennial.

Ataturk and "100" — A508

Design: 400k, Hand holding ballot.

1977, Mar. 21 Litho. *Perf. 13*

2049 A508 200k blk & red 20 10
2050 A508 400k blk & brn 50 25

Centenary of Turkish Parliament.

Europa Issue

Hierapolis (Pamukkale) A509

Design: 400k, Zelve (mountains and poppies).

1977, May 2 Litho. *Perf. 13½x13*

2051 A509 200k multi 50 50
2052 A509 400k multi 90 90

Terra Cotta Pot, Turkey A510

Designs: 225k, Terra cotta jug, Iran. 675k, Terra cotta bullock cart, Pakistan.

1977, July 21 Litho. *Perf. 13*

2053 A510 100k multi 10 5
2054 A510 225k multi 30 14
2055 A510 675k multi 70 35
a Souvenir sheet of 3, #2053-2055 1.20 1.20

Regional Cooperation for Development Pact among Turkey, Iran and Pakistan, 13th anniv.

Finn-class Yacht A511

Kemal Ataturk A512

Designs: 200k, Three yachts. 250k, Symbolic yacht.

1977, July 28

2056 A511 150k lt bl, bl & blk 16 10
2057 A511 200k ultra & bl 25 14
2058 A511 250k ultra & blk 35 20

European Finn Class Sailing Championships, Istanbul, July 28.

Ataturk Type of 1972

1977, June 13 Litho. *Perf. 13½x13*

2060 A453 100k olive 10 5
2061 A453 200k brown 20 5

Imprint: "GUZEL SANATLAR MATBAASI A.S. 1977"

1977, Sept. 23 Litho. *Perf. 13*

Size: 20½x22mm

2062 A512 200k blue 16 5
2063 A512 250k Prus bl 20 5

Imprint: "TIFDRUK-ISTANBUL 1978"

1978, June 28 Photo. *Perf. 13*

Size: 20x25mm

2065 A512 10k brown 5 5
2066 A512 50k grnsh gray 5 5
2067 A512 1 l fawn 8 5
2068 A512 2½ l purple 20 5
2069 A512 5 l blue 40 7
2072 A512 25 l dl grn & lt bl 1.50 25
2073 A512 50 l dp org & tan 2.50 1.00
Nos. 2065-2073 (7) 4.78 1.52

No. 1832 Surcharged with New Value and Wavy Lines

1977, Aug. 17

2078 A418 10k on 1k dp org & brn 5 5

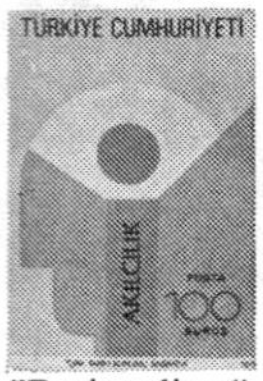

"Rationalism" A513

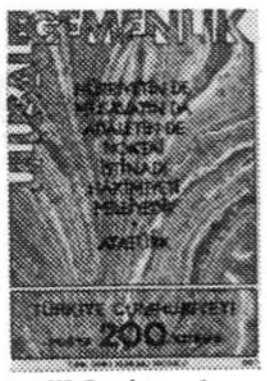

"National Sovereignty" A514

"Liberation of Nations" — A515

1977, Oct. 29 Litho. *Perf. 13*

2079 A513 100k multi 10 5
2080 A514 200k multi 20 10
2081 A515 400k multi 40 20

Works and reforms of Ataturk.

Mohammad Allama Iqbal — A516

Trees and Burning Match — A517

1977, Nov. 9 *Perf. 13x12½*

2082 A516 400k multi 42 14

Mohammad Allama Iqbal (1877-1938), Pakistani poet and philosopher.

1977, Dec. 15 Litho. *Perf. 13*

Design: 250k, Sign showing growing tree.

2083 A517 50k grn, blk & red 5 5
2084 A517 250k gray, grn & blk 14 7

Forest conservation.

Wrecked Car — A518

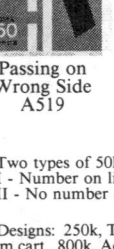

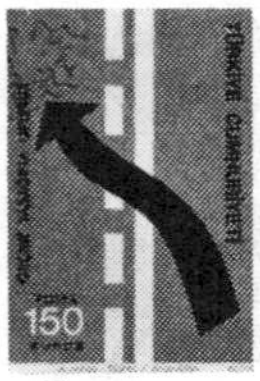

Passing on Wrong Side A519

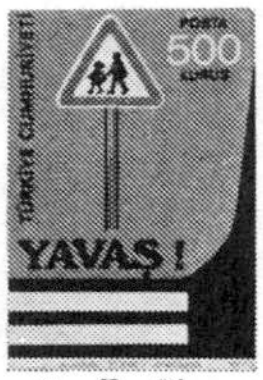

Traffic Sign, "Slow!" A520

Two types of 50k:
I - Number on license plate.
II - No number on plate.

Designs: 250k, Tractor drawing overloaded farm cart. 800k, Accident caused by incorrect passing. 10 l, "Use striped crossings."

1977-78 *Perf. 13½x13, 13x13½*

2085 A518 50k ultra, blk & red, II ('78) 22 5
a Type I 22 5
2086 A519 150k red, gray & blk ('78) 12 5
2087 A518 250k ocher, blk & red ('78) 25 8
2088 A520 500k gray, red & blk 22 16
2089 A520 800k multi ('78) 70 25
2090 A520 10 l dl grn, blk & brn ('78) 1.10 35
Nos. 2085-2090 (6) 2.61 94

Traffic safety.

Europa Issue

Ishak Palace, Dogubeyazit — A521

Design: 5 l, Anamur Castle.

1978, May 2 Litho. *Perf. 13*

2091 A521 2½ l multi 40 40
2092 A521 5 l multi 70 70

Riza Shah Pahlavi — A522

1978, June 16 Litho. *Perf. 13x13½*

2093 A522 5 l multi 55 20

Riza Shah Pahlavi (1877-1944) of Iran, birth centenary.

Yellow Rose, Turkey A523

Designs: 3½ l, Pink roses, Iran. 8 l, Red roses, Pakistan.

1978, July 21 Litho. *Perf. 13*

2094 A523 2½ l multi 14 5
2095 A523 3½ l multi 22 8
2096 A523 8 l multi 55 25

Regional Cooperation for Development Pact among Turkey, Iran and Pakistan.

Anti-Apartheid Emblem — A524

1978, Aug. 14 Litho. *Perf. 13½x13*
2097 A524 10 l multi 65 25

Anti-Apartheid Year.

View of Ankara — A525

Design: 5 l, View of Tripoli (horiz.).

Perf. 13x12½, 12½x13
1978, Aug. 17
2098 A525 2½ l multi 14 7
2099 A525 5 l multi 35 14

Turkish-Libyan friendship.

Souvenir Sheet

Bridge and Mosque — A526

1978, Oct. 25 *Imperf.*
2100 A526 15 l multi 80 80

Edirne '78, 2nd National Philatelic Youth Exhibition, No. 2100 has light blue margin showing stamps. Size: 71½x52mm.

Independence Medal — A527

Latin Alphabet — A529

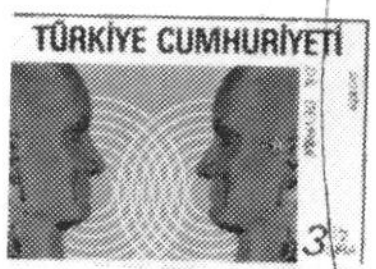

Speech Reform A528

Perf. 13x13½, 13½x13
1978, Oct. 29
2101 A527 2½ l multi 14 5
2102 A528 3½ l multi 16 8
2103 A529 5 l multi 25 14

Ataturk's works and reforms. See Nos. 2120-2122.

House on Bosporus, 1699 — A530

Turkish Houses: 2½ l, Izmit, 1774 (vert.). 3½ l, Kula, 17th century. (vert.). 5 l, Milas, 18th-19th centuries (vert.). 8 l, Safranbolu, 18th-19th centuries.

Perf. 13x12½, 12½x13
1978, Nov. 22
2104 A530 1 l multi 8 5
2105 A530 2½ l multi 16 5
2106 A530 3½ l multi 30 8
2107 A530 5 l multi 42 14
2108 A530 8 l multi 80 25
Nos. 2104-2108 (5) 1.76 57

Europa Issue

Carrier Pigeon, Plane, Horseback Rider, Train A531

Designs: 5 l, Morse key, telegraph and Telex machine. 7½ l, Telephone dial and satellite.

1979, Apr. 30 Litho. *Perf. 13*
2109 A531 2½ l multi 16 16
2110 A531 5 l org brn & blk 30 30
2111 A531 7½ l brt bl & blk 42 42

Plowing, by Namik Ismail A532

Paintings: 7½ l, Potters, by Kamalel Molk, Iran. 10 l, At the Well, by Allah Baksh, Pakistan.

1979, Sept. 5 Litho. *Perf. 13½x13*
2112 A532 5 l multi 20 8
2113 A532 7½ l multi 35 14
2114 A532 10 l multi 55 22

Regional Cooperation for Development Pact among Turkey, Pakistan and Iran, 15th anniversary.

Colemanite — A533

1979, Sept. 17 *Perf. 13*
2115 A533 5 l shown 25 12
2116 A533 7½ l Chromite 42 16
2117 A533 10 l Antimonite 70 20
2118 A533 15 l Sulphur 80 32

10th World Mining Congress.

8-Shaped Road, Train Tunnel, Plane and Emblem — A534

1979, Sept. 24
2119 A534 5 l multi 20 10

European Ministers of Communications, 8th Symposium.

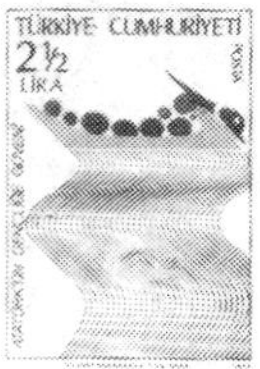

Youth A535

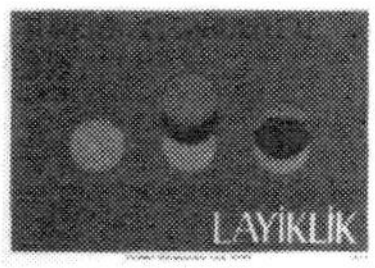

Secularization A536

Design: 5 l, National oath.

Perf. 13x12½, 12½x13
1979, Oct. 29
2120 A535 2½ l multi 10 5
2121 A536 3½ l multi 16 7
2122 A535 5 l blk & org 25 16

Ataturk's works and reforms.

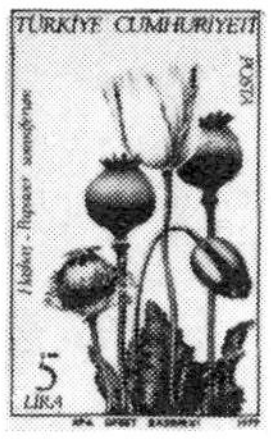

Poppies — A537

1979, Nov. 26 Litho. *Perf. 13x13½*
2123 A537 5 l shown 16 5
2124 A537 7½ l Oleander 25 8
2125 A537 10 l Late spider orchid 38 16
2126 A537 15 l Mandrake 70 22

See Nos. 2154-2157.

Kemal Ataturk
A538 A538a

Perf. 12½x11½, 13x12½(No. 2131)
1979-81 Litho.
2127 A538 50k olive ('80) 5 5
2128 A538 1 l grn & lt grn 5 5
2129 A538 2½ l purple 7 5
2130 A538 2½ l bl grn & lt bl('80) 5 5
2131 A538 2½ l org ('81) 5 5
2132 A538 5 l ultra & gray 14 5
a Sheet of 8 1.40 1.40
2133 A538 7½ l brown 20 5
2134 A538 7½ l red ('80) 14 5
2135 A538 10 l rose car 25 14
2136 A538 20 l gray ('80) 38 20
Nos. 2127-2136 (10) 1.38 74

No. 2132a for Ankara '79 Philatelic Exhibition, Oct. 14-20

1980-82 Photo. *Perf. 13½*
2137 A538a 7½ l red brn ('81) 5 5
c Sheet of 4 ('82) 35 16
2137A A538a 10 l brown 16 5
2138 A538a 20 l lilac 14 5
2138A A538a 30 l gray ('81) 20 8
2139 A538a 50 l org red 35 7
2140 A538a 75 l brt grn 55 14
2141 A538a 100 l blue 75 35
Nos. 2137-2141 (7) 2.20 79

No. 2137c for ANTALYA '82 4th Natl. Junior Stamp Show. Issue dates: 7½ l, July 15, 1981; 7½ l sheet, Oct. 3, 1982; 30 l, Sept. 23, 1981. Others, Dec. 10, 1980.
See Nos. 2164-2169.

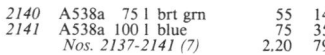

Turkish Printing, 250th Anniversary — A539

1979, Nov. 30 Litho. *Perf. 13*
2142 A539 10 l multi 35 7

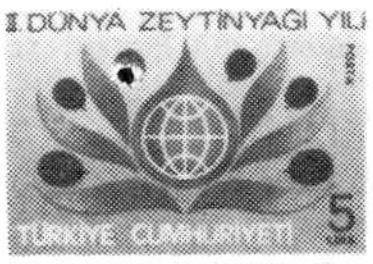

2nd International Olive Oil Year — A540

Perf. 12½x13, 13x12½
1979, Dec. 20 Litho.
2143 A540 5 l shown 10 5
2144 A540 10 l Globe, oil drop (vert.) 30 10

Uskudarli Hoca Ali Riza Bey (1857-1930), Painter A541

Designs: 15 l, Ali Sami Boyar (1880-1967), painter. 20 l, Dr. Hulusi Behcet (1889-1948), physician, discovered Behcet skin disease.

1980, Apr. 28 *Perf. 13*
2145 A541 7½ l multi 14 14
2146 A541 15 l multi 25 25
2147 A541 20 l multi 38 38

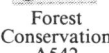

Forest Conservation A542

Earthquake Destruction A543

1980, July 3 *Perf. 13½x13*
2148 A542 50k ol grn & red org 5 5

1980, Sept. 8 *Perf. 13*
2149 A543 7½ l shown 14 5
2150 A543 20 l Seismograph 38 18

7th World Conference on Earthquake Engineering, Istanbul.

Games' Emblem, Sports — A544

Hegira — A545

1980, Sept. 26 *Perf. 13x13½*

2151 A544 7½ l shown 18 5
2152 A544 20 l Emblem, sports, diff. 42 14

First Islamic Games, Izmir.

1980, Nov. 9

2153 A545 20 l multi 30 14

Plant Type of 1979

1980, Nov. 26 *Perf. 13*

2154 A537 2½ l Manisa tulip 7 5
2155 A537 7½ l Ephesian bellflower 20 5
2156 A537 15 l Angora crocus 42 10
2157 A537 20 l Anatolian orchid 65 14

Avicenna Treating Patient A546

Avicenna (Arab Physician), Birth Millenium: 20 l, Portrait (vert.).

1980, Dec. 15

2158 A546 7½ l multi 10 5
2159 A546 20 l multi 20 14

Balkanfila VIII Stamp Exhibition, Ankara A547

1981, Jan. 1 **Litho.** *Perf. 13*

2160 A547 10 l red & blk 18 7

Kemal Ataturk — A548

1981, Feb. 4 *Perf. 13*

2163 A548 10 l lil rose 18 7

Ataturk Type of 1980

1983-84 *Perf. 13x13½*

2164 A538a 15 l grnsh bl 10 5
2165 A538a 20 l org ('84) 12 5
2167 A538a 65 l bluish grn 38 10
2169 A538a 90 l lil rose 45 14

Issue dates: Nos. 2164, 2167, 2169, Nov. 30. No. 2165, July 25.

Sultan Mehmet the Conqueror (1432-1481) — A549

1981, May 3 **Litho.** *Perf. 13x12½*

2173 A549 10 l multi 12 7
2174 A549 20 l multi 20 14

Gaziantep (Folk Dance) A550

Antalya A551

1981, May 4 **Litho.** *Perf. 13*

2175 A550 7½ l shown 10 5
2176 A550 10 l Balikesir 12 7
2177 A550 15 l Kahramanmaras 18 14
2178 A551 35 l shown 40 40
2179 A551 70 l Burdur 70 70
Nos. 2175-2179 (5) 1.50 1.36

Nos. 2178-2179 show CEPT (Europa) emblem.

Nos. C40, 1925, 1931A, 2089 Surcharged in Black with New Value and Wavy Lines

1981, June 3 *Perf. 13½x13*

2179A AP7 10 l on 60k multi 14 7
2180 A453 10 l on 110k lt bl & vio bl 14 7
2181 A453 10 l on 400k gray & Prus bl 14 7
2182 A520 10 l on 800k multi 14 7

22nd Intl. Turkish Folklore Congress — A552

1981, June 22 *Perf. 13x12½*

2183 A552 7½ l Rug, Bilecik 10 5
2184 A552 10 l Embroidery 12 5
2185 A552 15 l Drum, zurna players 20 10
2186 A552 20 l Embroidered napkin 20 14
2187 A552 30 l Rug, diff. 38 20
Nos. 2183-2187 (5) 1.00 54

Kemal Ataturk A553

1981, May 19 **Litho.** *Perf. 14x15*

2188 A553 2½ l No. 1801 16 5
2189 A553 7½ l No. 1816 16 5
2190 A553 10 l No. 1604 7 7
2191 A553 20 l No. 804 80 10
2192 A553 25 l No. 777 1.10 14
2193 A553 35 l No. 1959 1.40 18
Nos. 2188-2193 (6) 3.69 59

Souvenir Sheet

2194 Sheet of 6 8.00 4.00
a. A553 12½ l like 2½ l 14 5
b. A553 37½ l like 7½ l 40 15
c. A553 50 l like 10 l 55 20
d. A553 100 l like 20 l 1.10 40
e. A553 125 l like 25 l 1.40 50
f. A553 175 l like 35 l 2.00 65

Souvenir Sheet

Balkanfila VIII Stamp Exhibition, Ankara — A554

1981, Aug. 8 **Litho.** *Perf. 13*

2195 Sheet of 2 1.65 65
a. A554 50 l No. B68 50 20
b. A554 50 l No. 733 50 20

5th General Congress of European Physics Society A555

1981, Sept. 7 *Perf. 12½x13*

2196 A555 10 l red & multi 12 7
2197 A555 30 l bl & multi 38 20

World Food Day A556

1981, Oct. 16

2198 A556 10 l multi 12 7
2199 A556 30 l multi 38 20

Constituent Assembly Inauguration — A557

1981, Oct. 23 *Perf. 13*

2200 A557 10 l multi 12 7
2201 A557 30 l multi 38 18

Ataturk — A558

Portraits of Ataturk.

1981-82 *Perf. 11½x12½*

2202 A558 1 l green 5 5
2203 A558 2½ l purple 5 5
2204 A558 2½ l gray & org, perf. 13 *16* *16*
2205 A558 5 l blue 5 5
2206 A558 10 l orange 12 5
2207 A558 35 l brown 38 10
Nos. 2202-2207 (6) *81* *46*

Issue dates: No. 2204, Dec. 10, 1981; others, Jan. 27, 1982.

Literacy Campaign A559

Energy Conservation A560

1981, Dec. 24 *Perf. 13½*

2217 A559 2½ l Procession 5 5

1982, Jan. 11 *Perf. 13*

2218 A560 10 l multi 10 5

Magnolias, by Ibrahim Calli (b. 1882) A561

Sultanhan Caravanserai A562

Perf. 13x13½, 13½x13

1982, Mar. 17

2219 A561 10 l shown 10 5
2220 A561 20 l Fishermen, horiz. 20 5
2221 A561 30 l Sewing Woman 25 7

Europa Issue

1982, Apr. 26 *Perf. 13x12½*

2222 A562 30 l shown 25 7
2223 A562 70 l Silk Route 60 20
a. Miniature sheet of 4 (2 each #2222-2223) 2.25 65

Nos. 2222-2223 se-tenant.

1250th Anniv. of Kul-Tigin Monument, Kosu Saydam, Mongolia — A563

1982, June 9 *Perf. 13*

2224 A563 10 l Monument 10 5
2225 A563 30 l Kul-Tigin (685-732), Gok-Turkish commander 25 7

Pendik Shipyard Opening A564

1982, July 1 *Perf. 12½x13*

2226 A564 30 l Ship, emblem 25 7

Mountains of Anatolia A565

1982, July 17 *Perf. 13*

2227 A565 7½ l Agri Dagi, vert. 7 5
2228 A565 10 l Buzul Dagi 10 5
2229 A565 15 l Demirkazik, vert. 14 5
2230 A565 20 l Erciyes 20 5
2231 A565 30 l Kackar Dagi, vert. 25 7
2232 A565 35 l Uludag 30 10
Nos. 2227-2232 (6) 1.06 37

Beyazit State Library Centenary A566

1982, Sept. 27

2233 A566 30 l multi 25 7

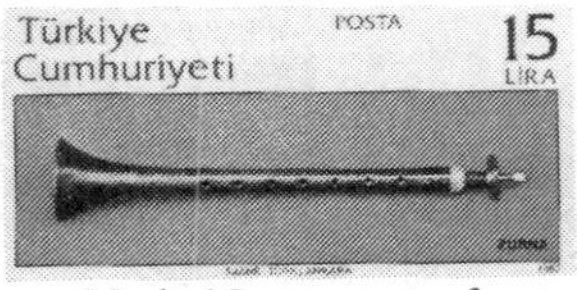

Musical Instruments of Anatolia — A567

1982, Oct. 13

2234 A567 7½ l Davul 10 5
2235 A567 10 l Baglama 14 5
2236 A567 15 l shown 20 5
2237 A567 20 l Kemence 30 5
2238 A567 30 l Mey 40 7
Nos. 2234-2238 (5) 1.14 27

Roman Temple Columns, Start A568

1982, Nov. 3
2239 A568 30 l multi 25 7

Family Planning and Mother-Child Health — A569

1983, Jan. 12 Litho. *Perf. 13*
2240 A569 10 l Family on map 10 5
2241 A569 35 l Mother and child 30 10

30th Anniv. of Customs Cooperation Council — A570

1983, Jan. 26
2242 A570 45 l multi 40 12

1982 Constitution — A571

1983, Jan. 27
2243 A571 10 l Ballot box 10 5
2244 A571 30 l Open book, scale 25 7

Manastirli Bey A572

1983, Mar. 16 Litho.
2245 A572 35 l multi 30 10

Manastirli Hamdi Bey (1890-1945), telegrapher of news of Istanbul's occupation to Ataturk, 1920.

Europa Issue

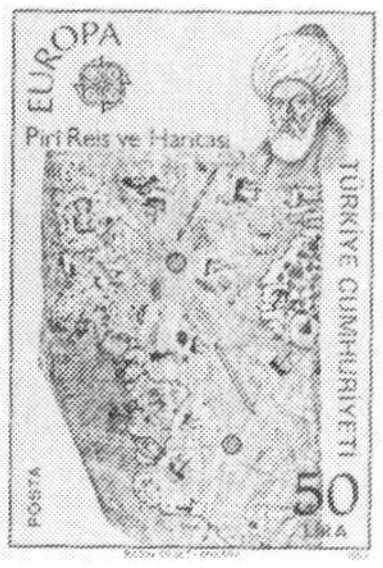

Piri Reis, Geographer A573

1983, May 5 Litho. *Perf. 12½x13*
2246 A573 50 l shown 55 12
2247 A573 100 l Ulug Bey (1394-1449), astronomer 1.20 25

Youth Week A574

1983, May 16
2248 A574 15 l multi 14 5

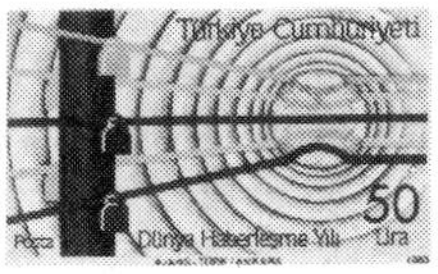

World Communications Year — A575

1983, May 16 *Perf. 13*
2249 A575 15 l Carrier pigeon, vert. 14 5
2250 A575 50 l Phone lines 42 12
2251 A575 70 l Emblem, vert. 60 20

50th Anniv. of State Civil Aviation A576

1983, May 20 Litho. *Perf. 13*
2252 A576 50 l Plane, jet 42 12
2253 A576 70 l Airport 60 20

18th Council of Europe Art Exhibition A577

Designs: 15 l, Eros, 2nd cent. BC (vert.). 35 l, Two-headed duck, Hittite, 14th cent BC. 50 l, Zinc jugs, plate, 16th cent. (vert.). 70 l, Marcus Aurelius and his wife Faustina the Young, 2nd cent.

1983, May 22 *Perf. 13*
2254 A577 15 l multi 20 5
2255 A577 35 l multi 50 7
2256 A577 50 l multi 65 12
2257 A577 70 l multi 80 18

Council of Europe's "The Water's Edge" Campaign — A578

Coastal Views.

1983, June 1 Litho. *Perf. 13x12½*
2258 A578 10 l Olodeniz 10 5
2259 A578 25 l Olympus 22 7
2260 A578 35 l Kekova 30 7

Nos. 2127, 2148 Surcharged
Perf. 12½x11½, 13½x13
1983, June 8
2261 A538 5 l on 50k ol 5 5
2262 A542 5 l on 50k ol grn & red org 5 5

Kemal Ataturk A579

Aga Khan Architecture Award A580

1983, June 22 *Perf. 13*
2263 A579 15 l bl grn & bl 16 5
a Sheet of 5 plus label 80 20
2264 A579 50 l grn & bl 55 12
2265 A579 100 l org & bl 1.20 25

For surcharge, see No. 2432.

1983, Sept. 4 Photo. *Perf. 11½*
2266 A580 50 l View of Istanbul 42 12

60th Anniv. of the Republic A582

1983, Oct. 29 *Perf. 13½x13*
2268 A582 15 l multi 14 5
2269 A582 50 l multi 42 12

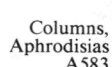

Columns, Aphrodisias A583

1983, Nov. 2 *Perf. 13*
2270 A583 50 l multi 42 12

UNESCO Campaign for Istanbul and Goreme — A584

1984, Feb. 15 Litho. *Perf. 13*
2271 A584 25 l St. Sophia Basilica 14 5
2272 A584 35 l Goreme 20 5
2273 A584 50 l Istanbul 25 7

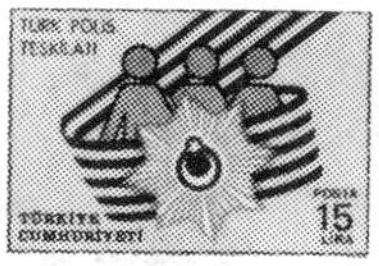

Natl. Police Org. Emblem A585

1984, Apr. 10 Litho. *Perf. 13*
2274 A585 15 l multi 7 5

Europa (1959-84) A586

1984, Apr. 30 *Perf. 13½x13*
2275 A586 50 l bl & multi 25 7
2276 A586 100 l gray & multi 55 14

Mete Khan, Hun Ruler, 204 BC, Flag A587

Sixteen States (Hun Rulers and Flags): 20 l, Panu, Western Hun empire (48-216). 50 l, Attila, 375-454. 70 l, Aksunvar, Ak Hun empire, 420-562.

1984, June 20 Litho. *Perf. 13*
2277 A587 10 l multi 5 5
2278 A587 20 l multi 10 5
2279 A587 50 l multi 25 7
2280 A587 70 l multi 38 10

See Nos. 2315-2318, 2349-2352, 2382-2385.

Cyprus Peace Operation, 10th Anniv. A588

1984, July 20 Litho. *Perf. 13*
2281 A588 70 l Dove, olive branch 38 10

Wild Flowers A589

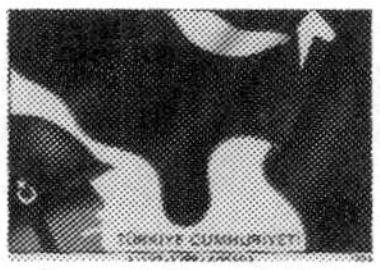

Armed Forces Day A590

1984, Aug. 1 *Perf. 11½x12½*
2282 A589 10 l Marshmallow flower 7 5
2283 A589 20 l Red poppy 14 5
2284 A589 70 l Sowbread 50 10
2285 A589 200 l Snowdrop 1.35 28
2286 A589 300 l Tulip 2.00 42
Nos. 2282-2286 (5) 4.06 90

See Nos. 2301-2308.

1984, Aug. 26 *Perf. 13½x13*
2287 A590 20 l Soldier, dove, flag 10 5
2288 A590 50 l Sword 25 7
2289 A590 70 l Arms, soldier, flag 38 10
2290 A590 90 l Map, soldier 45 10

Trees and Wood Products A591

Pres. Ismet Inonu (1884-1973), A592

Seed, Tree and Product: 10 l, Liquidambar, liquidambar grease. 20 l, Oriental spruce, stringed instrument. 70 l, Oriental beech, chair. 90 l, Cedar of Lebanon, ship.

1984, Sept. 19 Litho. *Perf. 13x12½*
2291 A591 10 l multi 5 5
2292 A591 20 l multi 10 5
2293 A591 70 l multi 38 10
2294 A591 90 l multi 45 10

1984, Sept. 24 *Perf. 13*
2295 A592 20 l Portrait 10 5

First Intl. Turkish Carpet Congress — A593

1984, Oct. 7 *Perf. 13x13½*
2296 A593 70 l Seljukian carpet, 13th cent. 38 10

Ruins of Ancient City of Harran A594

1984, Nov. 7 *Perf. 13½x13*
2297 A594 70 l Columns, arch 38 10

Turkish Women's Suffrage, 50th Anniv. A595

1984, Dec. 5 **Litho.** ***Perf. 13***

2298 A595 20 l Women voting 10 5

40th Anniv., ICAO — A596

1984, Dec. 7 **Litho.** ***Perf. 13***

2299 A596 100 l Icarus, ICAO emblem 50 12

Souvenir Sheet

No. 1047 A597

1985, Jan. 13 **Litho.** ***Imperf.***

2300 Sheet of 4 1.40 1.00
a.-b A597 70 l No. 1047, any single 35 14

Istanbul '87. No. 2300b has denomination at lower right.

Flower Type of 1984

Perf. 11 1/2x12 1/2, 12 1/2x13 (100 l)

1985 **Litho.**

2301 A589 5 l Narcissus 5 5
2308 A589 100 l Daisy 35 20

Issue dates: No. 2301, Feb. 6. No. 2308, July 31.

Turkish Aviation League, 60th Anniv. A598

1985, Feb. 16 ***Perf. 13***

2310 A598 10 l Parachutist, glider 5 5
2311 A598 20 l Hot air balloon, vert. 7 5

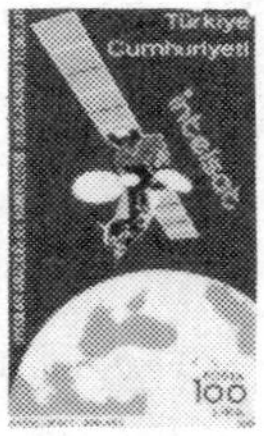

INTELSAT, 20th Anniv. — A599

1985, Apr. 3

2312 A599 100 l multi 32 8

Europa Issue

Ulvi Cemal Erkin (1906-1972) and Kosekce A600

Composers and music: 200 l, Mithat Fenmen (1916-1982) and Concertina.

1985, Apr. 29 ***Perf. 13 1/2x13***

2313 A600 100 l multi 40 8
2314 A600 200 l multi 70 16

Turkish States Type of 1984

Sixteen States (Kagan rulers and flags): 10 l, Bilge, Gokturk Empire (552-743) and Orhon-Turkish alphabet. 20 l, Bayan, Avar Empire (565-803). 70 l, Hazar, Hazar Empire (651-983). 100 l, Kutlug Kul Bilge, Uygur State (774-1335).

1985, June 20

2315 A587 10 l multi 5 5
2316 A587 20 l multi 7 5
2317 A587 70 l multi 22 7
2318 A587 100 l multi 32 8

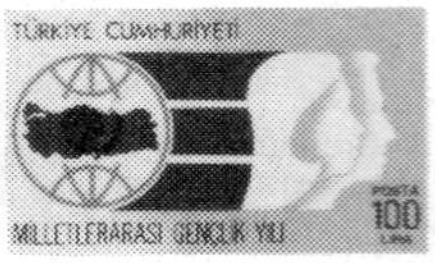

Intl. Youth Year A601

1985, Aug. 8

2319 A601 100 l multi 32 8
2320 A601 120 l multi 40 10

Postal Code Inauguration — A602

1985, Sept. 4 ***Perf. 13***

Background Color

2321 A602 10 l pale yel brn 5 5
2322 A602 20 l fawn 10 5
2323 A602 20 l gray grn 10 5
2324 A602 20 l brt bl 10 5
2325 A602 70 l rose lil 35 7
2326 A602 100 l gray 50 8
Nos. 2321-2326 (6) 1.20 35

Symposium of Natl. Palaces — A603

1985, Sept. 25 ***Perf. 13 1/2x13***

2327 A603 20 l Aynalikavak, c. 1703 7 5
2328 A603 100 l Beylerbeyi, 1865 32 8

UN, 40th Anniv. A604

1985, Oct. 24

2329 A604 100 l multi 32 8

Alanya Fortress and City A605

1985, Nov. 7

2330 A605 100 l multi 32 8

Footnotes often refer you to other stamps of the same design.

Turkish Meteorological Service, 60th Anniv. — A606

1985, Nov. 12 ***Perf. 13x13 1/2***

2331 A606 100 l multi 32 8

Isik Lyceum, Istanbul, Cent. A607

Ataturk A608

1985, Dec. 14

2332 A607 20 l multi 7 5

Perf. 11 1/2x12 1/2

1985, Dec. 18 **Litho.**

2334 A608 10 l pale bl & ultra 5 5
2336 A608 20 l beige & brn 8 5
2340 A608 100 l lt pink & cl 40 10

For surcharges, see Nos. 2433-2434.

7th Intl. Children's Festival, Ankara A609

Various children's drawings.

1986, Apr. 23 **Litho.** ***Perf. 12 1/2x13***

2342 A609 20 l multi 7 5
2343 A609 100 l multi 32 8
2344 A609 120 l multi 40 10

Europa Issue

Pollution A610

1986, Apr. 28 ***Perf. 13***

2345 A610 100 l shown 32 8
2346 A610 200 l Bandaged leaf 62 16

1st Ataturk Intl. Peace Prize — A611

Kirkpinar Wrestling Matches, Edirne — A613

1st Turkish Submarine, Cent. A612

1986, May 19 **Litho.** ***Perf. 13***

2347 A611 20 l gold & multi 10 5
2348 A611 100 l sil & multi 48 12

States Type of 1984

Sixteen States (Devleti rulers and flags): 10 l, Bilge Kul Kadir Khan, Kara Khanids State (840-1212). 20 l, Alp-Tekin, Ghaznavids State (963-1183). 100 l, Seldjuk Bey, Seldjuks State (1040-1157). 120 l, Muhammed Harezmsah, Khwarizm-Shahs State (1157-1231).

1986, June 20

2349 A587 10 l multi 5 5
2350 A587 20 l multi 10 5
2351 A587 100 l multi 45 12
2352 A587 120 l multi 55 14

1986, June 16 **Litho.** ***Perf. 13***

2353 A612 20 l Torpedo sub Abdulhamid 10 5

1986, June 30

2354 A613 10 l Oiling bodies 5 5
2355 A613 20 l Five wrestlers 10 5
2356 A613 100 l Two wrestlers 45 12

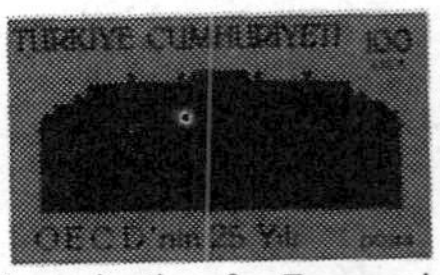

Organization for Economic Cooperation and Development, 25th Anniv. — A614

1986, Sept. 30 **Litho.** ***Perf. 13 1/2x13***

2357 A614 100 l multi 38 10

Automobile, Cent. — A615

1986, Oct. 15

2358 A615 10 l Benz Velocipede, 1886 5 5
2359 A615 20 l Rolls-Royce Silver Ghost, 1906 8 5
2360 A615 100 l Mercedes Touring Car, 1928 38 10
2361 A615 200 l Abstract speeding car 75 20

Paintings A616

Celal Bayar (1883-1986), 3rd President A617

Designs: 100 l, Bouquet with Tulip, by Feyhaman Duran (1886-1970). 120 l, Landscape with Fountain, by H. Avni Lifij (1886-1927), horiz.

Perf. 13 1/2x13, 13x13 1/2

1986, Oct. 22

2362 A616 100 l multi 38 10
2363 A616 120 l multi 48 12

1986, Oct. 27 ***Perf. 13***

2364 A617 20 l shown 8 5
2365 A617 100 l Profile 38 10

Kubad-Abad Ruins, Beysehir Lake — A618

1986, Nov. 7 *Perf. 13½x13*
2366 A618 100 l multi 38 10

Mehmet Akif Ersoy (1873-1936), Composer of the Turkish National Anthem — A619

1986, Dec. 27 Litho. *Perf. 13½x13*
2367 A619 20 l multi 10 5

Road Safety A620

Intl. Year of Shelter for the Homeless A622

Butterflies A621

1987, Feb. 4 Litho. *Perf. 13x13½*
2368 A620 10 l Use seatbelts 5 5
2369 A620 20 l Don't drink alcohol and drive 6 5
2370 A620 150 l Observe speed limit 45 12

1987, Feb. 25 *Perf. 13½x13*
2371 A621 10 l Celerio euphorbiae 5 5
2372 A621 20 l Vanessa atalanta 6 5
2373 A621 100 l Euplagia quadripunctaria 30 8
2374 A621 120 l Colias crocea 38 10

1987, Mar. 18 Litho. *Perf. 13x13½*
2375 A622 200 l multi 60 15

Karabuk Iron and Steel Works, 50th Anniv. A623

1987, Apr. 3 Litho. *Perf. 13½x13*
2376 A623 50 l Interior 15 5
2377 A623 200 l Exterior 60 15

Natl. Sovereignty — A624

1987, Apr. 23 *Perf. 13½x13*
2378 A624 50 l multi 15 5

67th anniv. of the founding of the Turkish state.

Europa Issue

Architecture — A625

Designs: 50 l, Turkish History Institute, 1951-67, designed by Turgut Cansever with Ertur Yener. 200 l, Social Insurance Institute, 1963, designed by Sedad Hakki Eldem.

1987, Apr. 28 *Perf. 13*
2379 A625 50 l multi 15 5
2380 A625 200 l multi 60 15

92nd Session, Intl. Olympic Committee, Istanbul, May 9-12 — A626

1987, May 9 Litho. *Perf. 13x13½*
2381 A626 200 l multi 60 15

Turkish States Type of 1984

Sixteen states (Devleti and Imparatorlugu rulers and flags): 10 l, Batu Khan, Golden Horde State (1227-1502). 20 l, Kutlug Timur Khan, Great Timur Empire (1368-1507). 50 l, Babur Shah, Babur Empire (1526-1858). 200 l, Osman Bey Gasi, Ottoman Empire (1299-1923).

1987, June 20 *Perf. 12½x13*
2382 A587 10 l multi 5 5
2383 A587 20 l multi 6 5
2384 A587 50 l multi 15 5
2385 A587 200 l multi 60 15

Album of the Conqueror, Mehmet II, 15th Cent., Topkapi Palace Museum — A627

Untitled paintings by Mehmet Siyah Kalem: 10 l, Two warriors, vert. 20 l, Three men, donkey. 50 l, Blackamoor whipping horse. 200 l, Demon, vert.

Perf. 13½x13, 13x13½
1987, July 1 **Litho.**
2386 A627 10 l multi 5 5
2387 A627 20 l multi 6 5
2388 A627 50 l multi 15 5
2389 A627 200 l multi 60 15

Natl. Palaces A628

1987, Sept. 25 *Perf. 13½x13*
2390 A628 50 l Ihlamur, c. 1850 15 5
2391 A628 200 l Kucuksu Pavilion, 1857 60 15

See Nos. 2425-2426.

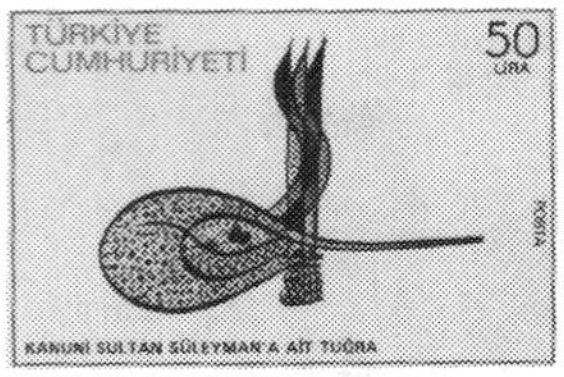
"Tughra," Suleiman's Calligraphic Signature — A629

Designs: 30 l, Portrait, vert. 200 l, Suleiman Receiving a Foreign Minister, contemporary miniature, vert. 270 l, Bust, detail of bas-relief, The Twenty-Three Law-Givers, entrance to the gallery of the U.S. House of Representatives.

Litho., Litho. & Engr. (270 l)
1987, Oct. 1 *Perf. 13½x13, 13x13½*
2392 A629 30 l multi 8 5
2393 A629 50 l shown 12 5
2394 A629 200 l multi 48 12
2395 A629 270 l multi 65 16

Suleiman the Magnificent (1494-1566), sultan of the Turkish Empire (1520-1566). On No. 2395, the gold ink was applied by a thermographic process producing a shiny, raised effect.

Souvenir Sheet

Presidents — A630

Portraits: a., Cemal Gursel (1961-1966). b., Cevdet Sunay (1966-1973). c., Fahri S. Koruturk (1973-1980). d., Kenan Evren (1982-). e., Ismet Inonu (1938-1950). f., Celal Bayar (1950-1960). g., Mustafa Kemal Ataturk (1923-1938).

1987, Oct. 29 Litho. ***Imperf.***
2396 Sheet of 7 1.00 40
a.-f A630 50 l any single 12 5
g A630 100 l multi, 26x37mm 24 6

Joseph (Mimar) Sinan (1489-1588), Architect — A631

1988, Apr. 9 Litho. *Perf. 13*
2397 A631 50 l shown 10 5
2398 A631 200 l Mosque, architectural elements 40 10

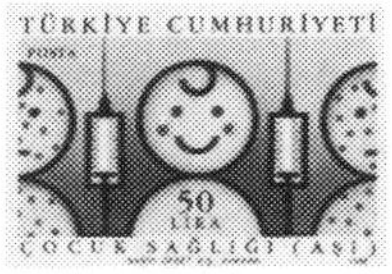
Health — A632

1988, May 4
2399 A632 50 l Immunization, horiz. 10 5
2400 A632 200 l Fight drug abuse 35 8
2401 A632 300 l Safe work conditions, horiz. 52 14
2402 A632 600 l Organ donation 1.05 28

Europa Issue

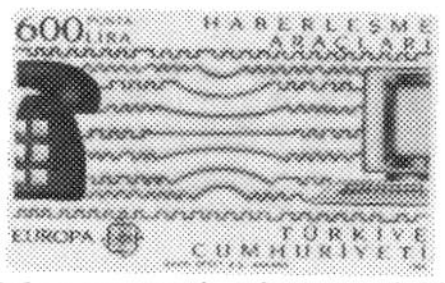
Telecommunications — A594

Transport and communication: 200 l, Modes of transportation, vert.

1988, May 2 Litho. *Perf. 13, 12½*
2403 A594 200 l multi 35 8
2404 A594 600 l multi 1.05 28

Steam, Electric and Diesel Locomotives — A595

Designs: 50 l, American Standard steam engine, c. 1850. 100 l, Steam engine produced in Esslingen for Turkish railways, 1913. 200 l, Henschel Krupp steam engine, 1926. 300 l, E 43001 Toshiba electric engine produced in Japan, 1987. 600 l, MTE-Tulomsas No. 24361 diesel-electric high-speed engine, 1984.

1988, May 24 *Perf. 13*
2405 A595 50 l buff, brn & blk 10 5
2406 A595 100 l buff, brn & blk 18 5
2407 A595 200 l buff, brn & blk 35 8
2408 A595 300 l buff, brn & blk 52 14
2409 A595 600 l buff, brn & blk 1.05 28
Nos. 2405-2409 (5) 2.20 60

Court of Cassation (Supreme Court), 120th Anniv. A635

1988, July 1 Litho. *Perf. 13½x13*
2410 A635 50 l multi 12 5

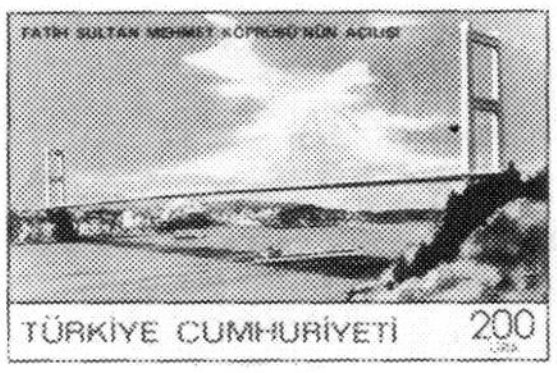
Bridge Openings — A636

Designs: 200 l, Fatih Sultan Mehmet Bridge, Kavacik-Hisarustu. 300 l, Seto Ohashi (Friendship) Bridges, the Minami and Kita.

1988, July 3 Litho. *Perf. 13x13½*
2411 A636 200 l multi 35 8
2412 A636 300 l multi 50 12

Telephone System A637

1988, Aug. 24 Litho. *Perf. 13½x13*
2413 A637 100 l multi 22 6

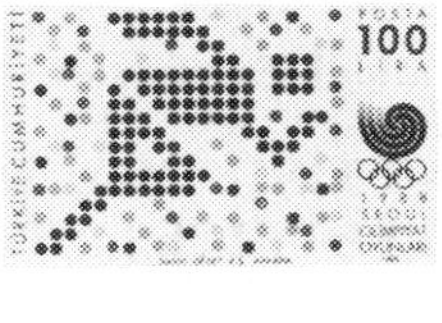
1988 Summer Olympics, Seoul A638

Perf. 12½x13, 13x12½
1988, Sept. 17 **Litho.**
2414 A638 100 l Running 22 6
2415 A638 200 l Archery 45 12
2416 A638 400 l Weight lifting 92 24
2417 A638 600 l Gymnastics, vert. 1.40 35

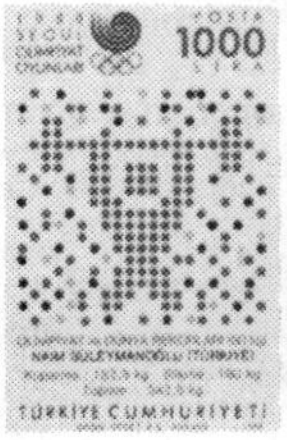

Naim Suleymanoglu, 1988 Olympic Gold Medalist, Weight Lifting — A639

1988, Oct. 5 Litho. ***Perf. 13x12½***

2418 A639 1000 l multi 2.35 60

Aerospace Industries A640

Perf. 13½x13, 13x13½

1988, Oct. 28

2419 A640 50 l Gear, aircraft, vert. 12 5
2420 A640 200 l shown 48 10

Butterflies A641

1988, Oct. 28 ***Perf. 13½x13***

2421 A641 100 l Gonepteryx rhamni 25 6
2422 A641 200 l Chazara briseis 48 12
2423 A641 400 l Allancastria cerisyi godart 95 22
2424 A641 600 l Nymphalis antiopa 1.40 35
a. Souv. sheet of 4, Nos. 2421-2424 3.10 75

ANTALYA '88.

Natl. Palaces Type of 1987

1988, Nov. 3 Litho. ***Perf. 13***

2425 A628 100 l Maslak Royal Lodge, c. 1890 14 5
2426 A628 400 l Yildiz Sale Pavilion, 1889 58 14

Souvenir Sheet

Kemal Ataturk — A642

1988, Nov. 10 ***Perf. 13x13½***

2427 A642 400 l multi 58 25

Medicinal Plants of Anatolia A643

1988, Dec. 14 Litho. ***Perf. 13***

2428 A643 150 l Tilia rubra 20 5
2429 A643 300 l Malva silvestris 38 10
2430 A643 600 l Hyoscyamus niger 75 18
2431 A643 900 l Atropa belladonna 1.10 28

Stamps of 1983-85 Surcharged

Perf. 13, 11½x12½

1989, Feb. 8 Litho.

2432 A579 50 l on 15 l No. 2263 8 5
2433 A608 75 l on 10 l No. 2334 10 5
2434 A608 150 l on 20 l No. 2336 20 5

Surcharge on No. 2432 is slightly different.

Artifacts in the Museum of Anatolian Civilizations, Ankara — A644

Designs: 150 l, Seated Goddess with Child, neolithic bisque figurine, Hacilar, 6th millennium B.C. 300 l, Lead figurine, Alisar Huyuk, Assyrian Trading Colonies Era, c. 19th cent. B.C. 600 l, Human-shaped vase, Kultepe, Assyrian Trading Colonies Era, 18th cent. B.C. 1000 l, Ivory mountain god, Bogazkoy, Hittite Empire, 14th cent. B.C.

1989, Feb. 8 Litho. ***Perf. 13½x13***

2435 A644 150 l multi 20 5
2436 A644 300 l multi 38 10
2437 A644 600 l multi 75 18
2438 A644 1000 l multi 1.25 30

NATO, 40th Anniv. A645

1989, Apr. 4 Litho. ***Perf. 13½***

2439 A645 600 l multi 80 20

Europa Issue

Children's Games — A646

1989, Apr. 23 Litho. ***Perf. 13x12½***

2440 A646 600 l Leapfrog 80 20
2441 A646 1000 l Open the door, Headbezirgan 1.35 35

SEMI-POSTAL STAMPS

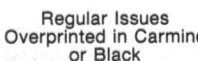

Regular Issues Overprinted in Carmine or Black

Overprint reads: "For War Orphans"

Perf. 12, 13½ and Compound

1915 Unwmk.

On Stamps of 1905

B1 A18 10pa dl grn (#119) 5 5
B2 A18 10pi org brn 2.50 25

On Stamp of 1906

B3 A18 10pa dl grn (#128) 5.50 3.50

On Stamps of 1908

B4 A19 10pa bl grn 25 25
B5 A19 5pi dk vio 12.00 3.00

With Additional Overprint

B6 A19 10pa bl grn 25.00 12.00

On Stamps of 1909

B7 A21 10pa bl grn 5 5
a. Inverted overprint 5.00 5.00
b. Double overprint, one inverted 5.00 5.00
B8 A21 20pa car rose 7 5
a. Inverted overprint 5.00 5.00
B9 A21 1pi ultra 10 5
B10 A21 5pi dk vio 80 10

With Additional Overprint

B11 A21 10pa bl grn 7 5
b. Double overprint, one inverted 5.00 5.00
B12 A21 20pa car rose 8 5
B13 A21 1pi ultra 70 14

On Stamps of 1913

B14 A22 10pa bl grn 7 7
a. Inverted overprint 5.00 5.00
B15 A22 1pi ultra 10 5
a. Double overprint 5.00 5.00

With Additional Overprint

B16 A22 10pa bl grn 7 7
a. Inverted overprint 5.00 5.00

On Newspaper Stamp of 1908

B17 A19 10pa bl grn 40.00 22.50

On Newspaper Stamp of 1909

B18 A21 10pa bl grn 20 7

Regular Issues Overprinted in Carmine or Black

1916

On Stamps of 1901

B19 A17 1pi blue 10 5
B20 A17 5pi lil rose 2.50 10

On Stamps of 1905

B21 A18 1pi brt bl 14 5
B22 A18 5pi brown 2.50 55

On Stamp of 1906

B23 A18 1pi brt bl 20 5

On Stamps of 1908

B24 A19 20pa car (Bk) 225.00
B25 A19 10pi red 60.00 40.00

With Additional Overprint

B26 A19 20pa carmine 8 8
B27 A19 1pi brt bl (C) 20.00 5.00

On Stamps of 1909

B28 A21 20pa car rose 8 5
B29 A21 1pi ultra 8 5
B30 A21 10pi dl red 15.00 15.00

With Additional Overprint

B31 A21 20pa car rose 16 10
B32 A21 1pi ultra 10 7

On Stamps of 1913

B33 A22 20pa car rose 5 5
B34 A22 1pi ultra 14 5
a. Inverted overprint 5.00 5.00
B35 A22 10pi dl red 7.00 3.00

With Additional Overprint

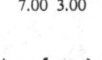

B36 A22 20pa car rose 10 5

On Newspaper Stamps of 1901

B37 A16 5pi ocher 3.00 3.00
a. 5pa bister, No. P37 135.00 100.00

Regular Issues Surcharged in Black

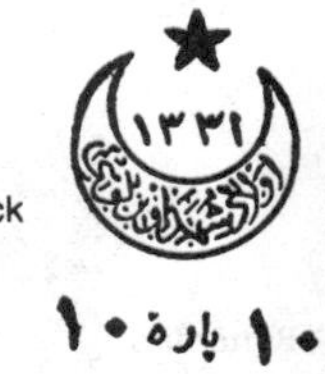

On Stamp of 1899

B38 A11 10pa on 20pa vio brn 7 5

On Stamp of 1905

B39 A18 10pa on 20pa car 10 5

On Stamp of 1906

B40 A18 10pa on 20pa car 14 5

On Newspaper Stamp of 1893-99

B41 A11 10pa on 20pa vio brn 7 7

Nos. 346-349 Overprinted

B42 A41 10pa carmine 5 5
a. Inverted overprint 5.00 5.00
B43 A41 20pa ultra 5 5
a. Inverted overprint 5.00 5.00
B44 A41 1pi vio & blk 14 5
a. Inverted overprint 5.00 5.00
B45 A41 5pi yel brn & blk 38 7
a. Inverted overprint 8.00 8.00

Nos. B42 to B45 formed part of the Postage Commemoration issue of 1916.

A Soldier's Farewell — SP1

1917, Feb. 20 Engr. ***Perf. 12½***

B46 SP1 10pa red vio 7 5

Stamp of Same Design Surcharged 

B47 SP1 10pa on 20pa car rose 7 7

Badge of the Society SP9

School Teacher SP10

Carrie Chapman Catt SP16

Kemal Atatürk SP23

Designs: 2k+2k, Woman farmer. 2½k+2½k, Typist. 4k+4k, Aviatrix and policewoman. 5k+5k, Women voters. 7½k+7½k, Yildiz Palace, Istanbul. 12½k+12½k, Jane Addams. 15k+15k, Grazia Deledda. 20k+20k, Selma Lagerlof. 25k+25k, Bertha von Suttner. 30k+30k, Sigrid Undset. 50k+50k, Marie Sklodowska Curie.

1935, Apr. 17 Photo. *Perf. 11½*
Inscribed: "XII Congres Suffragiste International"

B54 SP9 20pa + 20pa brn 12 8
B55 SP10 1k + 1k rose car 15 8
B56 SP10 2k + 2k sl bl 15 8
B57 SP10 2½k + 2½k yel grn 15 10
B58 SP10 4k + 4k bl 20 18
B59 SP10 5k + 5k dl vio 32 20
B60 SP10 7½k + 7½k org red 50 45
B61 SP16 10k + 10k org 90 70
B62 SP16 12½k + 12½k dk bl 2.50 2.00
B63 SP16 15k + 15k vio 2.50 2.00
B64 SP16 20k + 20k red org 4.50 3.25
B65 SP16 25k + 25k grn 8.00 6.25
B66 SP16 30k + 30k ultra 17.50 17.50
B67 SP16 50k + 50k dk sl grn 32.50 32.50
B68 SP23 100k + 100k brn car 30.00 30.00
Nos. B54-B68 (15) 99.99 95.37

12th Congress of the Women's Intl. Alliance.

Catalogue values for unused stamps in this section, from this point to the end of the section, are for Never Hinged items.

Katip Chelebi — SP24

Perf. 10½
1958, Sept. 24 Litho. Unwmk.
B69 SP24 50k + 10k gray 10 8

Mustafa ibn 'Abdallah Katip Chelebi Hajji Khalifa (1608-1657), Turkish author.

Road Building Machine SP25

Kemal Atatürk SP26

Ruins, Göreme SP27

Design: 25k+5k, Tanks and planes.

1958, Oct. 29
B70 SP25 15k + 5k org 5 5
B71 SP26 20k + 5k lt red brn 6 5
B72 SP25 25k + 5k brt grn 8 8

The surtax went to the Red Crescent Society and to the Society for the Protection of Children.

1959, July 8 Litho. *Perf. 10*
B73 SP27 105k + 10k pur & buff 25 22

Issued for tourist publicity.

Istanbul SP28

1959, Sept. 11
B74 SP28 105k + 10k lt bl & red 20 15

15th International Tuberculosis Congress.

Manisa Asylum SP29

Merkez Muslihiddin SP30

Design: 90k+5k, Sultan Camil Mosque, Manisa. (vert.).

1960, Apr. 17 Unwmk. *Perf. 13*
B75 SP29 40k + 5k grn & lt bl 10 5
B76 SP29 40k + 5k vio & rose lil 10 5
B77 SP29 90k + 5k dp cl & car rose 20 12
B78 SP30 105k + 10k multi 30 20

Kermis at Manisa.

Census Chart SP31

Census Symbol SP32

1960, Sept. 23 Photo. *Perf. 11½*
Granite Paper
B79 SP31 30k + 5k bl & rose pink 8 5
B80 SP32 50k + 5k grn, dk bl & ultra 15 10

Issued for the 1960 Census.

Old Observatory SP33

Fatin Gökmen SP34

Designs: 30k+5k, Observatory emblem. 75k+5k, Building housing telescope.

1961, July 1 Litho. *Perf. 13*
B81 SP33 10k + 5k grnsh bl & grn 5 5
B82 SP33 30k + 5k vio & blk 8 5
B83 SP34 40k + 5k brn 14 8
B84 SP33 75k + 5k ol grn 25 18

Kandill Observatory, 50th anniversary.

Anti-Malaria Work — SP35

Designs: 30k+5k, Mother and infant (horiz.). 75k+5k, Woman distributing pasteurized milk.

1961, Dec. 11 Unwmk. *Perf. 13*
B85 SP35 10k + 5k Prus grn 7 5
B86 SP35 30k + 5k dl vio 14 5
B87 SP35 75k + 5k dk ol bis 25 15

UNICEF, 10th anniv.

Malaria Eradication Emblem, Map and Mosquito SP36

1962, Apr. 7 Litho.
B88 SP36 30k + 5k dk & lt brn 8 5
B89 SP36 75k + 5k blk & lil 15 12

WHO drive to eradicate malaria.

Poinsettia SP37

Wheat and Census Chart SP38

Flowers: 40k+10k, Bird of paradise flower. 75k+10k, Water lily.

1962, May 19 *Perf. 12½x13½*
Flowers in Natural Colors
B90 SP37 30k + 10k lt bl & blk 12 8
B91 SP37 40k + 10k lt bl & blk 18 12
B92 SP37 75k + 10k lt bl & blk 45 30

Inscribed: "Umumi Ziraat Sayimi"

1963, Apr. 14 Photo. *Perf. 11½*

Design: 60b+5k, Wheat and chart (horiz.).

B93 SP38 40k + 5k gray grn & yel 10 8
B94 SP38 60k + 5k org yel & blk 14 12

1961 agricultural census. Two black bars obliterate "Kasim 1960" inscription.

Red Lion and Sun, Red Crescent, Red Cross and Globe — SP39

Designs: 60k+10k, Emblems in flowers (vert.). 100k+10k, Emblems on flags.

1963, Aug. 1 *Perf. 13*
B95 SP39 50k + 10k bl, lt brn, gray & red 18 14
B96 SP39 60k + 10k multi 22 16
B97 SP39 100k + 10k grn, gray & red 35 28

Centenary of International Red Cross.

Angora Goat SP40

Olympic Torch Bearer SP41

Animals: 10k+5k, Steppe cattle (horiz.). 50k+5k. Arabian horses (horiz.). 60k+5k, Three Angora goats. 100k+5k, Montofon cattle (horiz.).

1964, Oct. 4 Litho. *Perf. 13*
B98 SP40 10k + 5k multi 8 5
B99 SP40 30k + 5k multi 10 8
B100 SP40 50k + 5k multi 15 10
B101 SP40 60k + 5k multi 20 12
B102 SP40 100k + 5k multi 25 20
Nos. B98-B102 (5) 78 55

Issued for Animal Protection Day.

1964, Oct. 10 Unwmk.

Designs: 10k+5k, Running (horiz.). 60k+5k, Wrestling. 100k+5k, Discus.

B103 SP41 10k + 5k org brn, blk & red 8 8
B104 SP41 50k + 5k ol, blk & red 15 12
B105 SP41 60k + 5k bl, blk & red 25 18
B106 SP41 100k + 5k vio, blk, red & sil 35 30

18th Olympic Games, Tokyo, Oct. 10-25.

Map of Dardanelles and Laurel — SP42

Designs: 90k+10k, Soldiers and war memorial, Canakkale. 130k+10k, Turkish flag and arch (vert.).

1965, Mar. 18 Litho. *Perf. 13*
B107 SP42 50k + 10k vio, yel & gold 15 12
B108 SP42 90k + 10k vio bl, bl, yel & grn 22 20
B109 SP42 130k + 10k dk brn, red & yel 40 40

50th anniversary of Battle of Gallipoli.

Tobacco Plant
SP43

Goddess, Basalt Carving
SP44

Designs: 50k+5k, Tobacco leaves and Leander's tower (horiz.). 100k+5k, Tobacco leaf.

1965, Sept. 16 Unwmk. *Perf. 13*

B110 SP43	30k + 5k brn, lt brn & grn	16	10
B111 SP43	50k + 5k vio bl, ocher & pur	22	15
B112 SP43	100k + 5k blk, ol grn & ocher	40	25

Second International Tobacco Congress.

Perf. 13½x13, 13x13½

1966, June 6 Litho.

Designs (from Archaeological Museum, Ankara): 30k+5k, Eagle and rabbit, ivory carving (horiz.). 60k+5k, Bronze bull. 90k+5k, Gold pitcher.

B113 SP44	30k + 5k multi	16	14
B114 SP44	50k + 5k multi	25	20
B115 SP44	60k + 5k multi	38	25
B116 SP44	90k + 5k multi	50	40

Grand Hotel Ephesus
SP45

Designs: 60k+5k, Konak Square, Izmir (vert.). 130k+5k, Izmir Fair Grounds.

1966, Oct. 18 Litho. *Perf. 12*

B117 SP45	50k + 5k multi	14	14
B118 SP45	60k + 5k multi	22	20
B119 SP45	130k + 5k multi	45	35

33rd Congress of the Intl. Fair Assoc.

Europa Issue, 1967

Common Design Type

1967, May 2 Litho. *Perf. 13x13½*

Size: 22x33mm.

B120 CD10	100k + 10k multi	40	40
a.	Dark blue ("Europa") omitted		
B121 CD10	130k + 10k multi	55	55

Cloverleaf Crossing, Map of Turkey
SP46

Design: 130k+5k, Highway E5 and map of Turkey (vert.).

1967, June 30 Litho. *Perf. 13*

B122 SP46	60k + 5k multi	25	20
B123 SP46	130k + 5k multi	50	30

Inter-European Express Highway, E5.

WHO Emblem
SP47

1968, Apr. 7 Litho. *Perf. 13*

B124 SP47	130k + 10k lt ultra, blk & yel	30	18

WHO, 20th anniversary.

Efem Pasha, Dr. Marko Pasha and View of Istanbul — SP48

Designs: 60k+10k, Omer Pasha, Dr. Abdullah Bey and wounded soldiers. 100k+10k, Ataturk and Dr. Refik Say in front of Red Crescent headquarters (vert.).

1968, June 11 Litho. *Perf. 13*

B125 SP48	50k + 10k multi	25	20
B126 SP48	60k + 10k multi	35	25
B127 SP48	100k + 10k multi	60	40

Centenary of Turkish Red Crescent Society.

NATO Emblem and Dove
SP49

Design: 130k+10k, NATO emblem and globe surrounded by 15 stars, symbols of the 15 NATO members.

1969, Apr. 4 Litho. *Perf. 13*

B128 SP49	50k + 10k brt grn, blk & lt bl	18	15
B129 SP49	130k + 10k bluish blk, bl & gold	38	30

NATO, 20th anniversary.

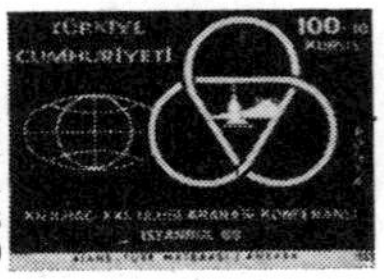

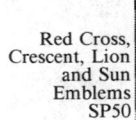

Red Cross, Crescent, Lion and Sun Emblems
SP50

Design: 130k+10k, Conference emblem and Istanbul skyline.

1969, Aug. 29 Litho. *Perf. 13*

B130 SP50	100k + 10k dk & lt bl & red	25	15
B131 SP50	130k + 10k red, lt bl & blk	35	25

21st Intl. Red Cross Conf., Istanbul.

Erosion Control
SP51

Designs: 60k+10k, Protection of flora (dead tree). 130k+10k, Protection of wildlife (bird of prey).

1970, Feb. 9 Litho. *Perf. 13*

B132 SP51	50k + 10k multi	20	20
B133 SP51	60k + 10k multi	40	40
B134 SP51	130k + 10k multi	90	90

1970 European Nature Conservation Year.

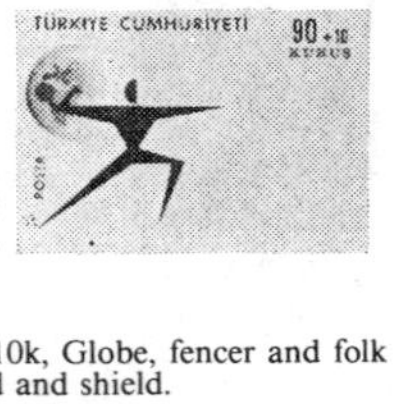

Globe and Fencer — SP52

Design: 130k+10k, Globe, fencer and folk dancer with sword and shield.

1970, Sept. 13 Litho. *Perf. 13*

B135 SP52	90k + 10k bl & blk	20	15
B136 SP52	130k + 10k ultra, lt bl, blk & org	30	20

International Fencing Championships.

"Children's Protection"
SP53

Designs: 100k+15k, Hand supporting child (vert.). 110k+15k, Mother and child.

1971, June 30 Litho. *Perf. 13*

Star and Crescent Emblem in Red

B137 SP53	50k + 10k lil rose & blk	12	10
B138 SP53	100k + 15k brn, rose & blk	20	15
B139 SP53	110k + 15k org brn, bis & blk	25	20

50th anniv. of the Child Protection Assoc.

UNICEF, 25th Anniv.
SP54

"Your Heart is your Health"
SP55

1971, Dec. 11

B140 SP54	100k + 10k multi	25	16
B141 SP54	250k + 15k multi	55	40

1972, Apr. 7 Litho. *Perf. 13*

B142 SP55	250k + 25k gray, blk & red	55	40

World Health Day.

Olympic Emblems, Runners
SP56

Designs: 100k+15k, Olympic rings and motion emblem. 250k+25k, Olympic rings and symbolic track ('72).

1972, Aug. 26

B143 SP56	100k + 15k multi	20	12
B144 SP56	110k + 25k multi	28	18
B145 SP56	250k + 25k multi	40	30

20th Olympic Games, Munich, Aug. 26-Sept. 11.

Emblem of Istanbul Technical University
SP57

1973, Apr. 21 Litho. *Perf. 13*

B146 SP57	100k + 25k multi	20	12

Bicentenary of the Istanbul Technical University.

Dove and "50"
SP58

1973, July 24 Litho. *Perf. 12½x13*

B147 SP58	100k + 25k multi	18	12

Peace Treaty of Lausanne, 50th anniversary.

World Population Year — SP59

1974, June 15 Litho. *Perf. 13*

B148 SP59	250k + 25k multi	65	35

Guglielmo Marconi (1874-1937), Italian Electrical Engineer and Inventor
SP60

1974, Nov. 15 Litho. *Perf. 13½*

B149 SP60	250k + 25k multi	60	35

Dr. Albert Schweitzer
SP61

Africa with South-West Africa
SP62

1975, Jan 14 Litho. *Perf. 13*

B150 SP61	250k + 50k multi	65	45

Dr. Albert Schweitzer (1875-1965), medical missionary and music scholar.

1975, Aug. 26 Litho. *Perf. 13x12½*

B151 SP62	250k + 50k multi	60	35

Namibia Day (independence for South-West Africa).

Ziya Gökalp
SP63

Spoonbill
SP64

1976, Mar. 23 Litho. *Perf. 13*

B152 SP63	200k + 25k multi	20	10

Ziya Gökalp (1876-1924), philosopher.

1976, Nov. 19 Litho. *Perf. 13*

Birds: 150k+25k, European roller. 200k+25k, Flamingo. 400k+25k, Hermit ibis (horiz.).

B153 SP64	100k + 25k multi	20	14
B154 SP64	150k + 25k multi	25	16
B155 SP64	200k + 25k multi	50	25
B156 SP64	400k + 25k multi	80	40

Decree by Mehmet Bey, and Ongun Holy Bird — SP65

1977, May 13 Litho. *Perf. 13*
B157 SP65 200k + 25k grn & blk 35 20

700th anniv. of Turkish as official language.

10th World Energy Conference SP66

Design: 600k+50k, Conference emblem and globe with circles.

1977, Sept. 19 Litho. *Perf. 12½*
B158 SP66 100k + 25k multi 25 16
B159 SP66 600k + 50k multi 70 50

Running SP67

Designs: 2½ l+50k, Gymnastics. 5 l+ 50k, Table tennis. 8 l+50k, Swimming.

1978, July 18 Litho. *Perf. 13*
B160 SP67 1 l + 50k multi 14 7
B161 SP67 2½ l + 50k multi 16 7
B162 SP67 5 l + 50k multi 42 14
B163 SP67 8 l + 50k multi 65 20

GYMNASIADE '78, World School Games, Izmir.

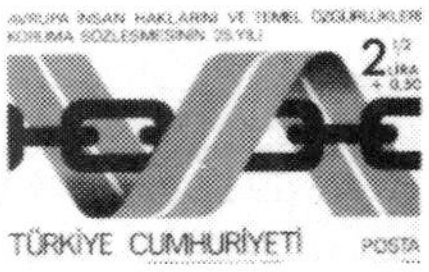

Ribbon and Chain SP68

Design: 5 l+50k, Ribbon and flower (vert.).

Perf. 12½x13, 13x12½
1978, Sept. 3 Litho.
B164 SP68 2½ l + 50k multi 35 14
B165 SP68 5 l + 50k multi 45 20

European Declaration of Human Rights, 25th anniversary.

Children, Head of Ataturk SP69

Black Francolin SP70

IYC Emblem and: 5 l+50k, Children with globe as balloon. 8 l+50k, Kneeling person and child, globe.

1979, Apr. 23 Litho. *Perf. 13x13½*
B166 SP69 2½ l + 50k multi 20 8
B167 SP69 5 l + 50k multi 35 14
B168 SP69 8 l + 50k multi 55 25

International Year of the Child.

1979, Dec. 3 Litho. *Perf. 13x13½*

Designs: No. B170, Great bustard. No. B171, Crane. No. B172, Gazelle. No. B173, Mouflon muffelwild.

B169 SP70 5 l + 1 l multi 55 14
B170 SP70 5 l + 1 l multi 55 14
B171 SP70 5 l + 1 l multi 55 14
B172 SP70 5 l + 1 l multi 55 14
B173 SP70 5 l + 1 l multi 55 14
Nos. B169-B173 (5) 2.75 70

European Wildlife Conservation Year. Nos. B169-B173 se-tenant in continuous design.

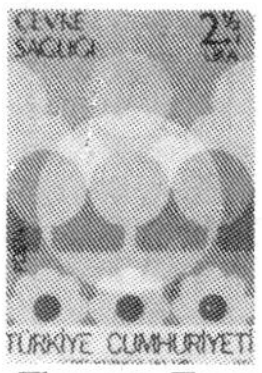
Flowers, Trees and Sun SP71

Rodolia Cardinalis SP72

Environment Protection: 7½ l+ 1 l Sun, water. 15 l+1 l, Industrial pollution, globe. 20 l+1 l, Flower in oil puddle.

1980, June 4 Litho. *Perf. 13*
B174 SP71 2½ l + 1 l multi 10 7
B175 SP71 7½ l + 1 l multi 20 12
B176 SP71 15 l + 1 l multi 40 25
B177 SP71 20 l + 1 l multi 45 30

1980, Dec. 3 Litho. *Perf. 13*

Useful Insects: 7½ l+1 l, Bracon hebetor; 15 l+1 l, Calosoma sycophanta; 20 l+1 l, Deraeocoris rutilus.

B178 SP72 2½ l + 1 l multi 7 5
B179 SP72 7½ l + 1 l multi 14 5
B180 SP72 15 l + 1 l multi 25 10
B181 SP72 20 l + 1 l multi 30 14

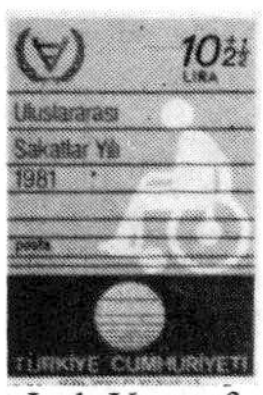
Intl. Year of the Disabled SP73

TB Bacillus Centenary SP75

Insects SP74

1981, Mar. 25 Litho. *Perf. 13*
B182 SP73 10 l + 2½ l multi 16 10
B183 SP73 20 l + 2½ l multi 25 14

1981, Dec. 16 Litho. *Perf. 13*

Useful Insects: 10 l+2½ l, Cicindela campestris. 20 l+2½ l, Syrphus vitripennis. 30 l+2½ l, Ascalaphus macaronius. 40 l+2½ l, Empusa fasciata.

B184 SP74 10 l + 2½ l multi 14 7
B185 SP74 20 l + 2½ l multi 20 12
B186 SP74 30 l + 2½ l multi 30 20
B187 SP74 40 l + 2½ l multi 40 25

See Nos. B190-B194, B196-B200.

1982, Mar. 24 *Perf. 13x12½*

Portraits of Robert Koch.

B188 SP75 10 l + 2½ l multi 14 7
B189 SP75 30 l + 2½ l multi 30 20

Insect Type of 1981

Useful Insects: 10 l+2½ l, Eurydema spectabile. 15 l+2½ l, Dacus oleae. 20 l+2½ l, Klapperichicen viridissima. 30 l+2½ l, Leptinotarsa decemlineata. 35 l+2½ l, Rhynchites auratus.

1982, Aug. 18 Litho. *Perf. 13*
B190 SP74 10 l + 2½ l multi 14 7
B191 SP74 15 l + 2½ l multi 20 10
B192 SP74 20 l + 2½ l multi 20 12
B193 SP74 30 l + 2½ l multi 30 20
B194 SP74 35 l + 2½ l multi 35 20
Nos. B190-B194 (5) 1.19 69

Richard Wagner (1813-1883), Composer — SP76

1983, Feb. 13
B195 SP76 30 l + 5 l multi 42 20

Insect Type of 1981

Harmful Insects: 15 l+5 l, Eurygaster Intergriceps Put. 25 l+5 l, Phyllobius nigrofasciatus Pes. 35 l+5 l, Cercopis intermedia Kbm. 50 l+10 l, Graphosoma lineatum (L). 75 l+10 l, Capnodis miliaris (King).

1983, Sept. 14 Litho. *Perf. 13*
B196 SP74 15 l + 5 l multi 30 10
B197 SP74 25 l + 5 l multi 45 14
B198 SP74 35 l + 5 l multi 55 18
B199 SP74 50 l + 10 l multi 80 25
B200 SP74 75 l + 10 l multi 1.20 40
Nos. B196-B200 (5) 3.30 1.07

Topkapi Museum Artifacts SP77

1984 Summer Olympics SP78

1984, May 30 Litho. *Perf. 13*
B201 SP77 20 l + 5 l Kaftan, 16th cent. 20 10
B202 SP77 70 l + 15 l Ewer 70 38
B203 SP77 90 l + 20 l Swords 90 45
B204 SP77 100 l + 25 l Lock, key 1.10 55

Surtax was for museum. See Nos. B208-B211, B213-B216, B218-B221.

1984, July 28

Designs: 20 l+5 l, Banners (horiz.). 70 l+15 l, Medalist Oyunlan. 100 l+20 l, Running (horiz.).

B205 SP78 20 l + 5 l multi 25 10
B206 SP78 70 l + 15 l multi 80 38
B207 SP78 100 l + 20 l multi 1.20 55

Artifacts Type of 1984

Ceramicware: 10 l+5 l, Iznik plate. 20 l+10 l, Iznik boza pitcher and mug, 16th cent. 100 l+15 l, Du Paquier ewer and basin, 1730. 120 l+20 l, Ching dynasty plate, 1522-1566.

1985, May 30 Litho. *Perf. 13*
B208 SP77 10 l + 5 l multi 7 5
B209 SP77 20 l + 10 l multi 14 5
B210 SP77 100 l + 15 l multi 42 10
B211 SP77 120 l + 20 l multi 55 12

Rabies Vaccine, Cent. — SP79

1985, July 16 *Perf. 13x13½*
B212 SP79 100 l + 15 l Louis Pasteur 50 10

Artifacts Type of 1984

Designs: 20 l+5 l, Metal and ceramic incense burner, c. 17th cent. 100 l+10 l, Jade lidded mug decorated with precious gems, 16th cent. 120 l+15 l, Dagger designed by Mahmut I, 1714. 200 l+30 l, Willow buckler, defensive shield, undated.

1986, May 30 Litho. *Perf. 13x12½*
B213 SP77 20 l + 5 l multi 12 5
B214 SP77 100 l + 10 l multi 52 14
B215 SP77 120 l + 15 l multi 65 18
B216 SP77 200 l + 30 l multi 1.10 28

General Assembly of NATO SP80

1986, Nov. 13 Litho. *Perf. 13½x13*
B217 SP80 100 l + 20 l multi 60 12

Artifacts Type of 1984

Designs: 20 l+5 l, Crystal and gold ewer, 16th cent., vert. 50 l+10 l, Emerald and gold pendant, 17th cent. 200 l+15 l, Sherbet jug, 19th cent., vert. 250 l+30 l, Crystal and gold pen box, 16th cent.

1987, May 30 Litho. *Perf. 13*
B218 SP77 20 l + 5 l multi 8 5
B219 SP77 50 l + 10 l multi 18 5
B220 SP77 200 l + 15 l multi 65 16
B221 SP77 250 l + 30 l multi 85 22

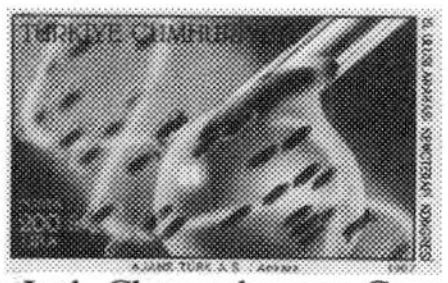
15th Intl. Chemotherapy Congress, Istanbul — SP81

1987, July 19 Litho. *Perf. 13*
B222 SP81 200 l + 25 l multi 68 18

Intl. Road Transport Union (IRU) 21st World Congress SP82

1988, June 13 Litho. *Perf. 12½x13*
B223 SP82 200 l +25 l multi 50 12

European Environmental Campaign Balancing Nature and Development — SP83

Designs: 100 l+25 l, Hands, desert reclamation. 400 l+50 l, Eye, road, planted field.

1988, Oct. 19 Litho. *Perf. 12½x13*
B224 SP83 100 l +25 l multi 30 8
B225 SP83 400 l +50 l multi 1.05 28

Silkworm Industry SP84

1989, Apr. 15 Litho. *Perf. 13½x13*
B226 SP84 150 l +50 l Silkworm 28 6
B227 SP84 600 l +100 l Cocoon, strands 95 24

AIR POST STAMPS

Regular Issue of 1930 Overprinted or Surcharged in Brown or Blue:

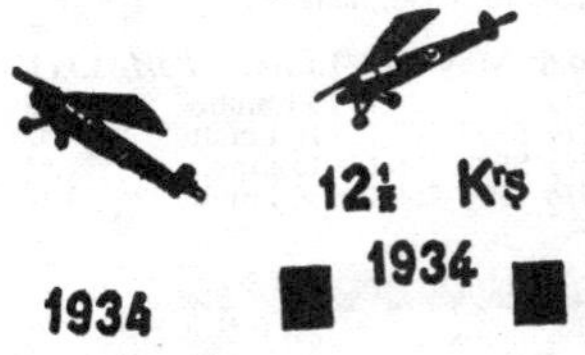

1934, July 15 **Unwmk.** ***Perf. 12***

C1	A74	7½k red brn (Br)	14	10
C2	A72	12½k on 15k dp org (Br)	20	14
C3	A74	20k on 25k ol brn (Br)	22	20
C4	A74	25k ol brn (Bl)	35	25
C5	A74	40k red vio (Br)	65	60
		Nos. C1-C5 (5)	1.56	1.29

Regular Stamps of 1930 Surcharged in Brown

1937

C6	A74	4½k on 7½k red brn	75	65
C7	A72	9k on 15k dp org	20.00	19.00
C8	A74	35k on 40k red vio	3.75	3.50

Regular Stamps of 1930 Surcharged in Black

1941, Dec. 18

C9	A74	4½k on 25k ol brn	2.00	2.00
C10	A75	9k on 200k dk grn & blk	11.00	11.00
C11	A75	35k on 500k choc & blk	8.00	8.00

Catalogue values for unused stamps in this section, from this point to the end of the section, are for Never Hinged items.

Plane over Izmir AP1

Designs: 5k, 40k, Plane over Izmir. 20k, 50k, Plane over Ankara. 30k, 1 l, Plane over Istanbul.

1949, Jan. 1 **Photo.** ***Perf. 11½***

C12	AP1	5k gray & vio	7	7
C13	AP1	20k bl gray & brn	30	7
C14	AP1	30k bl gray & ol brn	40	14
C15	AP1	40k bl & dp ultra	55	14
C16	AP1	50k gray vio & red brn	60	25
C17	AP1	1 l gray bl & dk grn	1.00	65
		Nos. C12-C17 (6)	2.92	1.32

Plane Over Rumeli Hisari Fortress AP2

1950, May 19 **Unwmk.**

C18	AP2	2½ l gray bl & dk grn	11.25	8.25

Nos. C12, C14 and C16 Overprinted in Red

SANAYİ KONGRESİ
9-NİSAN-1951

1951, Apr. 9 ***Perf. 11½***

C19	AP1	5k gray & vio	55	50
C20	AP1	30k bl gray & ol brn	65	60
C21	AP1	50k gray vio & red brn	80	70

Industrial Congress, Ankara, Apr. 9.

Yesilkoy Airport and Plane AP3

Designs: 20k, 45k, Yesilkoy Airport and plane in flight. 35k, 55k, Ankara Airport and plane. 40k, as No. C22.

1954, Nov. 1 ***Perf. 14***

Designs in Blue

C22	AP3	5k red brn	22	8
C23	AP3	20k brn org	8	5
C24	AP3	35k dk grn	10	5
C25	AP3	40k dp car	10	5
C26	AP3	45k violet	22	15
C27	AP3	55k black	40	20
		Nos. C22-C27 (6)	1.12	58

Symbol of Izmir Fair — AP4

1956, Aug. 20 **Litho.** ***Perf. 10½***

C28	AP4	25k redsh brn	14	10

25th Intl. Fair at Izmir, Aug. 20-Sept. 20.

Heuss Type of Regular Issue, 1957

1957, May 5

C29	A264	40k sal pink & mag	12	8

Zahir Shah Type of Regular Issue, 1957

1957, Sept. 1

C30	A269	25k grn & lt grn	10	7

Hawk — AP5

Crane — AP6

Birds: 40k, 125k, Swallows. 65k, Cranes. 85k, 195k, Gulls. 245k, Hawk.

1959, Aug. 13 **Litho.** ***Perf. 10½***

C31	AP5	40k brt lil	14	5
C32	AP5	65k bl grn	20	10
C33	AP5	85k brt bl	25	10
C34	AP5	105k yel & sep	25	10
C35	AP6	125k brt vio	40	12
C36	AP6	155k yel grn	55	20
C37	AP6	195k vio bl	55	25
C38	AP6	245k brn & brn org	1.10	45
		Nos. C31-C38 (8)	3.44	1.37

De Havilland Rapide Biplane AP7

Kestrel AP8

Designs: 60k, Fokker Friendship transport plane. 130k, DC9-30. 220k, DC-3. 270k, Viscount 794.

1967, July 13 **Litho.** ***Perf. 13½x13***

C39	AP7	10k pink & blk	20	5
C40	AP7	60k lt grn, red & blk	20	5
C41	AP7	130k bl, blk & red	45	10
C42	AP7	220k lt brn, blk & red	65	20
C43	AP7	270k org, blk & red	90	28
		Nos. C39-C43 (5)	2.40	68

1967, Oct. 10 **Litho.** ***Perf. 13***

Birds: 60k, Golden eagle. 130k, Falcon. 220k, Sparrow hawk. 270k, Buzzard.

C44	AP8	10k brn & sal	20	5
C45	AP8	60k brn & yel	25	5
C46	AP8	130k brn & lt bl	50	8
C47	AP8	220k brn & lt grn	90	20
C48	AP8	270k org brn & gray	1.10	30
		Nos. C44-C48 (5)	2.95	68

F-104 Jet Plane — AP9

Turkish Air Force Emblem and Jets AP10

Designs: 200k, Victory monument, Afyon, and Jets. 325k, F-104 jets and pilot. 400k, Bleriot XI plane with Turkish flag. 475k, Flight of Hezarfen Ahmet Celebi from Galata Tower to Usküdar.

1971, June 1 **Litho.** ***Perf. 13***

C49	AP9	110k multi	20	8
C50	AP9	200k multi	30	12
C51	AP10	250k gold & multi	50	10
C52	AP9	325k multi	70	22
C53	AP10	400k multi	90	20
C54	AP10	475k multi	1.10	35
		Nos. C49-C54 (6)	3.70	1.07

The gold ink on No. C51 is applied by a thermographic process which gives a raised and shiny effect.

F-28 Plane — AP11

1973, Dec. 11 **Litho.** ***Perf. 13***

C55	AP11	110k shown	20	10
C56	AP11	250k DC-10	40	20

POSTAGE DUE STAMPS

Same Types as Regular Issues of Corresponding Dates

1863 **Unwmk.** ***Imperf.***

Blue Band

J1	A1	20pa blk, *red brn*	45.00	20.00
a.		Tete beche pair	225.00	225.00
b.		Without band	25.00	
c.		Red band	62.50	30.00
J2	A2	1pi blk, *red brn*	55.00	25.00
a.		Tete beche pair	225.00	225.00
b.		Without band	25.00	
J3	A3	2pi blk, *red brn*	140.00	50.00
a.		Tete beche pair	650.00	450.00
J4	A4	5pi blk, *red brn*	90.00	45.00
a.		Tete beche pair	425.00	425.00
b.		Without band	65.00	
c.		Red band	90.00	

1865 ***Perf. 12½***

J6	A5	20pa brown	10	20
J7	A5	1pi brown	10	14
b.		Half used as 20pa on cover		
c.		Printed on both sides	16.50	
J8	A5	2pi brown	40	60
a.		Half used as 1pi on cover		
J9	A5	5pi brown	35	40
a.		Half used as 2½pi on cover		
J10	A5	25pi brown	7.00	7.00

The 10pa brown is an essay. Exist imperf. Values, $60 to $100.

1867

J11	A5	20pa bis brn	1.40	*8.25*
J12	A5	1pi bis brn	80	
a.		With surcharge of 5pi	13.50	
b.		Imperf., pair	65.00	
J13	A5	2pi fawn	6.00	
J14	A5	5pi fawn	4.00	
J15	A5	25pi bis brn	*2,500.*	

Nos. J12-J15 were not placed in use.

1869 ***Perf. 13½***

With Red Brown Border

J16	A5	20pa bis brn	2.00	70
a.		Without surcharge		
J17	A5	1pi bis brn	82.50	4.00
a.		Without surcharge		
J18	A5	2pi bis brn	120.00	4.00
J19	A5	5pi bis brn	20	*1.00*
b.		Without border		
c.		Printed on both sides	14.00	
J20	A5	25pi bis brn	8.00	10.00

With Black Brown Border

J21	A5	20pa bis brn	16.50	7.00
a.		Inverted surcharge		
b.		Without surcharge		
J22	A5	1pi bis brn	120.00	10.00
a.		Without surcharge		
J23	A5	2pi bis brn	190.00	16.50
b.		Inverted surcharge		
J24	A5	5pi bis brn	10	*70*
b.		Without surcharge		
J25	A5	25pi bis brn	12.00	20.00

Pin-perf., Perf. 5 to 11 and Compound

1871

With Red Brown Border

J26	A5	20pa bis brn	55.00	10.00
J27	A5	1pi bis brn		*350.00*
J28	A5	2pi bis brn	10.00	5.00
J29	A5	5pi bis brn	40	1.65

With Black Brown Border

J31	A5	20pa bis brn	10.00	40
a.		Half used as 10pa on cover		
b.		Imperf., pair		16.50
c.		Printed on both sides	40.00	40.00
J32	A5	1pi bis brn	13.50	25
a.		Half used as 20pa on cover		
c.		Inverted surcharge	50.00	35.00
d.		Printed on both sides		
J33	A5	2pi bis brn	20	40
a.		Half used as 1pi on cover		
c.		Imperf., pair		16.50
J34	A5	5pi bis brn	7	*1.00*
a.		Half used as 2½pi on cover		
c.		Printed on both sides		
J35	A5	25pi bis brn	7.00	10.00
a.		Inverted surchage		

1888 ***Perf. 11½ and 13½***

J36	A7	20pa black	8	12
a.		Imperf.	11.25	
J37	A7	1pi black	8	12
a.		Imperf.	11.25	
J38	A7	2pi black	8	12
a.		Imperf.	11.25	
b.		Diagonal half used as 1pi		

1892 ***Perf. 13½***

J39	A11	20pa black	40	20
J40	A12	1pi black	70	30
a.		Printed on both sides		
J41	A13	2pi black	38	30

1901

J42	A11	20pa blk, *dp rose*	8	8

1901

J43	A17	10pa blk, *dp rose*	40	20
J44	A17	20pa blk, *dp rose*	30	20
J45	A17	1pi blk, *dp rose*	16	16
J46	A17	2pi blk, *dp rose*	16	16

1905 ***Perf. 12***

J47	A18	1pi blk, *dp rose*	38	25
J48	A18	2pi blk, *dp rose*	40	38

1908, ***Perf. 12, 13½ and Compound***

J49	A19	1pi blk, *dp rose*	1.65	38
J50	A19	2pi blk, *dp rose*	25	45

1909

J51	A21	1pi blk, *dp rose*	70	70
J52	A21	2pi blk, *dp rose*	20.00	20.00
a.		Imperf.	65.00	

1913 ***Perf. 12***

J53	A22	2pa blk, *dp rose*	5	5
J54	A22	5pa blk, *dp rose*	5	5
J55	A22	10pa blk, *dp rose*	5	5
J56	A22	20pa blk, *dp rose*	5	5
J57	A22	1pi blk, *dp rose*	40	30
J58	A22	2pi blk, *dp rose*	1.00	65
		Nos. J53-J58 (6)	1.60	1.15

Adrianople Issue

Nos. 251-253 Surcharged in Black, Blue or Red

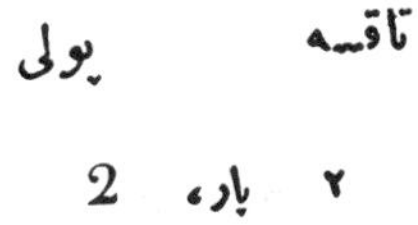

1913

J59	A23	2pa on 10pa grn (Bk)	20	10
J60	A23	5pa on 20pa red (Bl)	30	20
J61	A23	10pa on 40pa bl (R)	55	40
J62	A23	20pa on 40pa bl (Bk)	1.65	80

D1

D2

D3

D4

1914 **Engr.**

J63	D1	5pa claret	15	12
J64	D2	20pa red	15	12
J65	D3	1pi dark blue	28	15
J66	D4	2pi slate	55	38

Nos. J59 to J62 Surcharged in Red or Black

1916

J67	A23	10pa on 2pa on 10pa grn (R)	10.00	10.00
J68	A23	20pa on 5pa on 20pa red (Bk)	10.00	10.00
J69	A23	40pa on 10pa on 40pa bl (Bk)	10.00	10.00
J70	A23	40pa on 20pa on 40pa bl (R)	10.00	10.00

Preceding Issues Overprinted in Red, Black or Blue

1917

On Stamps of 1865

J71	A5	20pa red brn (Bl)	15.00	15.00
J72	A5	1pi red brn (Bl)	15.00	15.00
J73	A5	2pi bis brn (Bl)	15.00	15.00
J74	A5	5pi bis brn (Bl)	15.00	15.00
J75	A5	25pi dk brn (Bl)	15.00	15.00

On Stamp of 1869

Red Brown Border

J76	A5	5pi bis brn (R)	15.00	15.00

On Stamp of 1871

Black Brown Border

J77	A5	5pi bis brn	40.00	40.00

On Stamps of 1888

J78	A7	1pi blk (R)	12.50	12.50
J79	A7	2pi blk (R)	12.50	12.50

On Stamps of 1892

J80	A11	20pa blk (R)	55	55
J81	A12	1pi blk (R)	55	55
J82	A13	2pi blk (R)	55	55

Adrianople Issue

On Nos. J59 to J62 with Addition of New Value

J83	A23	10pa on 2pa on 10pa grn (R)	25	25
J84	A23	20pa on 5pa on 20pa red (Bk)	25	25
J85	A23	40pa on 10pa on 40pa bl (Bk)	40	40
a.		"40pa" double		
J86	A23	40pa on 20pa on 40pa bl (R)	55	55

Nos. J71-J86 were used as regular postage stamps.

Armistice Issue

No. J65 Overprinted

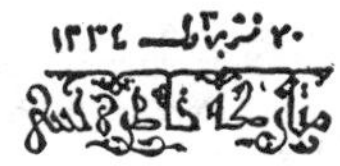

1919, Nov. 30

J87	D3	1pi dark blue	24.00	24.00

Accession to the Throne Issue

Postage Due Stamps of 1914 Overprinted in Turkish "Accession to the Throne of His Majesty. 3rd July, 1334-1918."

1919

J88	D1	10pa on 5pa cl	3.50	3.50
J89	D2	20pa red	3.50	3.50
J90	D3	1pi dark blue	3.50	3.50
J91	D4	2pi slate	3.50	3.50

Railroad Bridge over Kizil Irmak D5

Kemal Atatürk D6

1926 **Engr.**

J92	D5	20pa ocher	35	35
J93	D5	1g red	42	42
J94	D5	2g bl grn	55	55
J95	D5	3g lil brn	55	55
J96	D5	5g lilac	90	90
		Nos. J92-J96 (5)	2.77	2.77

1936 **Litho.** ***Perf. 11½***

J97	D6	20pa brown	5	5
J98	D6	2k lt bl	5	5
J99	D6	3k brt vio	7	5
J100	D6	5k Prus bl	14	7
J101	D6	12k brt rose	30	25
		Nos. J97-J101 (5)	61	47

Surcharged stamps, type D6, are listed as Nos. 1461-1465.

Local Issues

During the years 1869-82 Turkish stamps with the above overprints were used for local postage in Constantinople and Mount Athos.

Scott's editorial staff cannot undertake to identify, authenticate or appraise stamps and postal markings.

MILITARY STAMPS

For the Army in Thessaly

Tughra and Bridge at Larissa — M1

1898, Apr. 21 **Unwmk.** ***Perf. 13***

M1	M1	10pa yel grn	1.75	1.10
M2	M1	20pa rose	1.75	1.10
M3	M1	1pi dk bl	1.75	1.10
M4	M1	2pi orange	1.75	1.10
M5	M1	5pi violet	1.75	1.10
		Nos. M1-M5 (5)	8.75	5.50

Issued for Turkish occupation forces to use in Thessaly during the Greco-Turkish War of 1897-98.

Forgeries of Nos. M1-M5 are perf. 11½.

OFFICIAL STAMPS

O1

Perf. 10 to 12 and Compound

1948 **Typo.** **Unwmk.**

O1	O1	10pa rose brn	5	5
O2	O1	1k gray grn	5	5
O3	O1	2k rose vio	5	5
O4	O1	3k orange	8	5
O5	O1	5k blue	2.50	5
O6	O1	10k brn org	1.65	5
O7	O1	15k violet	50	5
O8	O1	20k dk bl	50	5
O9	O1	30k ol bis	70	5
O10	O1	50k black	65	5
O11	O1	1 l bluish grn	80	5
O12	O1	2 l lil rose	1.40	10
		Nos. O1-O12 (12)	8.93	65

Catalogue values for unused stamps in this section, from this point to the end of the section, are for Never Hinged items.

Regular Issue of 1948 Overprinted Type "a" in Black

a

1951

O13	A178	5k blue	14	12
O14	A178	10k chocolate	22	5
O15	A178	20k dp bl	45	7
O16	A178	30k brown	65	10

Overprint "a" is 15½mm wide. Points of crescent do not touch star. The 0.25k (No. 963) exists with overprint "a" but its status is questionable.

b

c

Overprinted Type "b" in Dark Brown

1953

O17	A178	0.25k dk red	7	5
O18	A178	5k blue	16	5
O19	A178	10k chocolate	28	5
O20	A178	15k violet	45	5
O21	A178	20k dp bl	1.20	8
O22	A178	30k brown	55	9
O23	A178	60k black	1.00	16
		Nos. O17-O23 (7)	3.71	53

Overprint "b" is 14mm wide. Lettering thin with sharp, clean corners.

Overprinted Type "c" in Black or Green Black

1953-54

O23A	A178	0.25k dk red (G Bk) ('53)	5	5
f.		Black overprint	4.00	4.00
g.		Violet overprint ('53)	4.00	4.00
O23B	A178	10k chocolate	3.50	65
O23C	A178	15k violet	3.50	35
O23D	A178	30k brown	2.00	65
O23E	A178	60k black	3.00	65
		Nos. O23A-O23E (5)	12.05	2.35

Lettering of type "c" heavy with rounded corners.

Small Star — d

Large Star — e

Overprinted or Surcharged Type "d" in Black

1955-56

O24	A178	0.25k dk red	5	5
O25	A178	1k ol blk	5	5
O26	A178	2k brt rose lil	5	5
O27	A178	3k red org	5	5
O28	A178	4k dk grn	5	5
O29	A178	5k on 15k vio	5	5
O31	A178	10k on 15k vio	6	5
O32	A178	15k violet	6	5
O33	A178	20k dp bl	12	5
O35	A179	40k on 1l ol grn	20	5
O36	A179	75k on 2l dk brn	50	38
O37	A179	75k on 5l dp plum	2.50	2.50
		Nos. O24-O37 (12)	3.74	3.38

Type "d" is 15x16mm wide. Overprint on Nos. O35-O37 measures 19x22mm. Nos. O29, O31 and O35-O37 have two bars and new value added.

Overprinted or Surcharged Type "e" in Black

1955

O25a	A178	1k ol blk	5	5
O29a	A178	5k on 15k vio	7	5
O30	A178	5k blue	42	5
O31a	A178	10k on 15k vio	2.00	2.00
c.		"10" without serif	10	5
O33a	A178	20k dp bl	35	5
O34	A178	30k brown	60	5

Heavy crescent f

Thin crescent g

Overprinted or Surcharged Type "f" in Black

1957
O24b A178 0.25k dk red 15 15
O38b A178 ½k on 1k ol blk 5 5
O25b A178 1k olive blk 5 5
O31b A178 10k on 15k vio 35 35
O35b A179 75k on 1l ol grn *4.00 1.35*
Nos. O24b-O35b (5) *4.60 1.95*

Type "f" crescent is larger and does not touch wavy line. The surcharged "10" on No. O31b exists only without serifs. The overprint on O35b measures 17x22½mm.

Overprinted or Surcharged Type "g" in Black

1957
O38 A178 ½k on 1k ol blk 7 5
O39 A178 1k ol blk 7 5
O40 A178 2k on 4k dk grn 7 5
O41 A178 3k on 4k dk grn 7 5
O42 A178 10k on 12k dp red 7 5
Nos. O38-O42 (5) 35 25

The shape of crescent and star on type "g" varies on each value. Overprint measures 14x18mm. The surcharged stamps have two bars and new value added.

O2 O3 O4

1957 **Litho.** ***Perf. 10½***
O43 O2 5k blue 5 5
O44 O2 10k org brn 5 5
O45 O2 15k lt vio 5 5
O46 O2 20k red 5 5
O47 O2 30k gray ol 8 5
O48 O2 40k brn vio 10 5
O49 O2 50k grnsh blk 12 5
O50 O2 60k lt yel grn 16 5
O51 O2 75k yel org 30 5
O52 O2 100k green 38 8
O53 O2 200k dp rose 70 25
Nos. O43-O53 (11) 2.04 78

1959 **Unwmk.** ***Perf. 10***
O54 O2 5k rose 5 5
O55 O2 10k ol grn 5 5
O56 O2 15k car rose 5 5
O57 O2 20k lilac 5 5
O58 O2 40k blue 10 5
O59 O2 60k orange 16 5
O60 O2 75k gray 35 10
O61 O2 100k violet 45 16
O62 O2 200k red brn 80 40
Nos. O54-O62 (9) 2.06 96

1960 **Litho.** ***Perf. 10½***
O63 O3 1k orange 5 5
O64 O3 5k vermilion 5 5
O65 O3 10k gray grn 30 5
O67 O3 30k red brn 10 5
O70 O3 60k green 20 5
O71 O3 1 l rose lil 25 7
O72 O3 1½ l brt ultra 80 7
O74 O3 2½ l violet 1.20 35
O75 O3 5 l blue 2.00 80
Nos. O63-O75 (9) 4.95 1.54

1962 **Typo.** ***Perf. 13***
O76 O4 1k ol bis 5 5
O77 O4 5k brt grn 5 5
O78 O4 10k red brn 5 5
O79 O4 15k dk bl 5 5
O80 O4 25k carmine 10 5
O81 O4 30k ultra 14 7
Nos. O76-O81 (6) 44 32

Nos. O81 and O70 Surcharged

1963
O82 O4 50k on 30k ultra 25 7

Perf. 10½
Litho.
O83 O3 100k on 60k grn 40 7

O5 O6 O7

1963 **Litho.** ***Perf. 12½***
O84 O5 1k gray 5 5
O85 O5 5k salmon 5 5
O86 O5 10k green 5 5
O87 O5 50k car rose 14 5
O88 O5 100k ultra 38 7
Nos. O84-O88 (5) 67 27

1964 **Unwmk.** ***Perf. 12½***
O89 O6 1k gray 5 5
O90 O6 5k blue 5 5
O91 O6 10k yellow 5 5
O92 O6 30k red 8 5
O93 O6 50k lt grn 14 5
O94 O6 60k brown 18 5
O95 O6 80k pale grnsh bl 25 5
O96 O6 130k indigo 55 14
O97 O6 200k lilac 70 7
Nos. O89-O97 (9) 2.05 56

1965 **Litho.** ***Perf. 13***
O98 O7 1k emerald 5 5
O99 O7 10k ultra 5 5
O100 O7 50k orange 15 5

Usak Carpet Design — O8

Seljuk Tile, 13th Century — O9

Carpet designs: 50k, Bergama. 100k, Ladik. 150k, Seljuk. 200k, Nomad. 500k, Anatolia.

1966 **Litho.** ***Perf. 13***
O101 O8 1k orange 5 5
O102 O8 50k green 10 5
O103 O8 100k brt pink 18 5
O104 O8 150k vio bl 28 8
O105 O8 200k ol bis 40 10
O106 O8 500k lilac 1.10 32
Nos. O101-O106 (6) 2.11 65

1967 **Litho.** ***Perf. 11½x12***
O107 O9 1k dk bl & lt bl 5 5
O108 O9 50k org & dk bl 14 5
O109 O9 100k lil & dk bl 22 7

Leaf Design — O10

1968 **Litho.** ***Perf. 13***
O110 O10 50k brn & lt grn 10 5
O111 O10 150k blk & dl yel 30 5
O112 O10 500k red brn & lt bl 1.00 15

O11 O12 O13

1969, Aug. 25 **Litho.** ***Perf. 13***
O113 O11 1k lt grn & red 5 5
O114 O11 10k lt grn & bl 5 5
O115 O11 50k lt grn & brn 10 5
O116 O11 100k lt grn & red vio 22 10

1971, Mar. 1 **Litho.** ***Perf. 11½x12***
O117 O12 5k brn & bl 5 5
O118 O12 10k vio bl & ver 5 5
O119 O12 30k org & vio bl 14 5
O120 O12 50k Prus bl & sep 20 10
O121 O12 75k yel & grn 35 14
Nos. O117-O121 (5) 79 39

1971, Nov. 15 **Litho.** ***Perf. 11½x12***
O122 O13 5k lt bl & gray 5 5
O123 O13 25k cit & lt brn 5 5
O124 O13 100k org & ol 16 5
O125 O13 200k dk brn & bis 35 5
O126 O13 250k rose lil & vio 50 10
O127 O13 500k dk bl & brt bl 80 45
Nos. O122-O127 (6) 1.91 75

O14 O15 O16

1972, Apr. 7 **Litho.** ***Perf. 13***
O128 O14 5k buff & bl 5 5
O129 O14 100k buff & ol 20 5
O130 O14 200k buff & car 40 14

1973, Sept 20 **Litho.** ***Perf. 13***
O131 O15 100k vio & buff 35 7

1974, June 17 **Litho.** ***Perf. 13½x13***
O132 O16 10k sal pink & brn 5 5
O133 O16 25k bl & dk brn 5 5
O134 O16 50k brt pink & brn 10 5
O135 O16 150k lt grn & brn 30 5
O136 O16 250k rose & brn 50 14
O137 O16 500k yel & brn 1.00 25
Nos. O132-O137 (6) 2.00 59

O17 O18 O19

1975, Nov. 5 **Litho.** ***Perf. 12½x13***
O138 O17 100k lt bl & mar 10 5

Nos. O84, O89, O98, O101, O107 Surcharged in Red or Black

Perf. 12½, 13, 11½x12
1977, Aug. 17 **Litho.**
O139 O5 5k on 1k gray 7 5
O140 O6 5k on 1k gray 7 5
O141 O7 5k on 1k emer 7 5
O142 O8 5k on 1k org (B) 7 5
O143 O9 5k on 1k dk & lt bl 7 5
Nos. O139-O143 (5) 35 25

1977, Dec. 29 **Litho.** ***Perf. 13½x13***
O144 O18 250k lt bl & grn 15 15

1978 **Photo.** ***Perf. 13½***
O145 O19 50k pink & rose 5 5
O146 O19 2½ l buff & grnsh blk 12 8
O147 O19 4½ l lil rose & sl grn 22 8
O148 O19 5 l lt bl & pur 25 8
O149 O19 10 l lt grn & grn 50 10
O150 O19 25 l yel & red 1.25 20
Nos. O145-O150 (6) 2.39 59

O20 O21 O22

1979 **Litho.** ***Perf. 13½***
O151 O20 50k dp org & brn 5 5
O152 O20 2½ l bl & dk bl 14 5

1979, Dec. 20 **Litho.** ***Perf. 13½***
O153 O21 50k sal & dk bl 5 5
O154 O21 1 l lt grn & red 5 5
O155 O21 2½ l lil rose & red 7 5
O156 O21 5 l lt bl & mag 14 7
O157 O21 7½ l lt lil & dk bl 20 7
O158 O21 10 l yel & dk bl 25 7
O159 O21 35 l gray & rose ('81) 22 10
O160 O21 50 l pnksh & dk bl ('81) 35 14
Nos. O153-O160 (8) 1.33 60

1981, Oct. 23 **Litho.** ***Perf. 13½***
O161 O22 5 l yel & red 5 5
O162 O22 10 l sal & red 7 5
O163 O22 35 l gray & rose 22 7
O164 O22 50 l pink & dk bl 32 10
O165 O22 75 l pale grn & grn 50 14
O166 O22 100 l lt bl & dk bl 65 16
Nos. O161-O166 (6) 1.81 57

O23 O24

1983-84 **Litho.** ***Perf. 13***
O167 O23 5 l yellow 5 5
O168 O23 15 l yel bis 14 5
O169 O23 20 l gray ('84) 10 5
O170 O23 50 l sky bl 42 10
O171 O23 65 l pink 55 10
O172 O23 70 l pale rose ('84) 38 10
O173 O23 90 l bis brn 70 14
O174 O23 90 l bl gray ('84) 45 12
O175 O23 100 l lt grn ('84) 55 14
O176 O23 125 l lt grn 1.10 20
O177 O23 230 l pale sal ('84) 1.20 35
Nos. O167-O177 (11) 5.64 1.40

1986-87 **Litho.** ***Perf. 12½x13***
O178 O24 5 l yel & vio 5 5
O179 O24 10 l org & vio 5 5
O180 O24 20 l gray & vio 5 5
O180A O24 50 l vio bl & pale lil rose ('87) 10 5
O181 O24 100 l lt yel grn & vio 25 7
O182 O24 300 l brt ultra & lt bl grn ('87) 60 15
Nos. O178-O182 (6) 1.10 42

NEWSPAPER STAMPS

N1

Black Overprint

1879 **Unwmk.** ***Perf. 11½ and 13½***
P1 N1 10pa blk & rose lil 55.00 40.00

Other stamps found with this "IMPRIMES" overprint were prepared on private order and have no official status as newspaper stamps.
Counterfeits exist of No. P1.

The 10pa surcharge, on half of 20pa rose and pale rose was made privately. See note after No. 77.

Regular Issue of 1890 Handstamped in Black

There are two types of this handstamp, varying slightly in size.

1891 ***Perf. 13½, 11½***
P10 A7 10pa grn & gray 4.50 3.50
a. Imperf. 22.50 12.50
P11 A7 20pa rose & gray 6.00 4.00
P12 A7 1pi bl & gray 22.50 14.00
P13 A7 2pi yel & gray *100.00 40.00*
P14 A7 5pi buff & gray *225.00 110.00*

Blue Handstamp
P10b A7 10pa grn & gray 25.00 3.50
P11a A7 20pa rose & gray 25.00 4.00
P12a A7 1pi bl & gray *110.00* 22.50

This overprint in red and on 2pi and 5pi in blue is considered bogus.

Same Handstamp on Regular Issue of 1892

1892 ***Perf. 13½***
P25 A10 10pa gray grn 25.00 4.50
P26 A11 20pa rose 42.50 20.00
P27 A12 1pi pale bl 12.50 7.50
P28 A13 2pi brn org 14.00 7.50

P29	A14	5pi pale vio	150.00	100.00
a.		On No. 99a	*500.00*	

The handstamps on Nos. P10-P29 are found double, inverted and sideways. Counterfeit overprints are plentiful.

Regular Issues of 1892-98 Overprinted in Black 

1893-98

P30	A10	10pa gray grn	14	14
P31	A11	20pa vio brn ('98)	14	14
a.		20pa dk pink	25	14
b.		20pa pink	15.00	2.00
P32	A12	1pi pale bl	14	14
P33	A13	2pi brn org	4.50	1.65
a.		Tete beche pair		22.50
P34	A14	5pi pale vio	16.50	6.50
a.		On No. 99a	135.00	65.00
		Nos. P30-P34 (5)	21.42	8.57

N3

Black Surcharge

1897

P36	N3	5pa on 10pa gray grn	8	5
a.		"Cniq" instead of "Cinq"	7.50	7.50

Nos. 102-107 Overprinted in Black 

1901 ***Perf. 12, 13½ and Compound***

P37	A16	5pa bister	14	10
a.		Inverted overprint		
P38	A16	10pa yel grn	55	40
P39	A16	20pa magenta	1.50	1.00
P40	A16	1pi vio bl	2.50	1.20
P41	A16	2pi gray bl	16.50	10.00
P42	A16	5pi ocher	25.00	14.00
		Nos. P37-P42 (6)	46.19	26.70

Same Overprint on Nos. 110-115

1901

P43	A17	5pa purple	25	10
P44	A17	10pa green	1.65	15
P45	A17	20pa carmine	16	8
a.		Overprinted on back		
P46	A17	1pi blue	1.40	25
P47	A17	2pi orange	8.00	1.35
a.		Inverted overprint		
P48	A17	5pi lil rose	12.00	7.00
		Nos. P43-P48 (6)	23.46	8.93

Same Overprint on Regular Issue of 1905

1905

P49	A18	5pa ocher	10	5
P50	A18	10pa dl grn	2.25	80
P51	A18	20pa carmine	25	5
P52	A18	1pi pale bl	16	5
P53	A18	2pi slate	8.25	2.25
P54	A18	5pi brown	8.25	4.00
		Nos. P49-P54 (6)	19.26	7.20

Regular Issue of 1908 Overprinted in Carmine or Blue 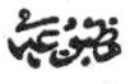

1908

P55	A19	5pa ocher (Bl)	1.50	12
P56	A19	10pa bl grn (C)	1.50	12
P57	A19	20pa car (Bl)	2.00	65
P58	A19	1pi brt bl (C)	3.50	1.00
P59	A19	2pi bl blk (C)	13.50	2.25
P60	A19	5pi dk vio (C)	13.50	3.75
		Nos. P55-P60 (6)	35.50	7.89

Same Overprint on Regular Issue of 1909

1909

P61	A21	5pa ocher (Bl)	40	10
a.		Imperf.		
P62	A21	10pa bl grn (C)	65	12
P63	A21	20pa car rose (Bl)	4.50	75
a.		Imperf.		
P64	A21	1pi brt bl (C)	7.00	2.25
P65	A21	2pi bl blk (C)	17.50	8.75
P66	A21	5pi dk vio (C)	17.50	8.75
		Nos. P61-P66 (6)	47.55	20.72

No. 151 Surcharged in Blue

2 ۲

1910 ***Perf. 12, 13½ and Compound***

P67	A21	2pa on 5pa ocher	10	7

1911 ***Perf. 12***

P68	A21	2pa ol grn	5	5

Newspaper Stamps of 1901-11 Overprinted in Carmine or Blue 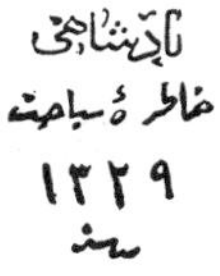

MONASTIR

The overprint was applied to 13 denominations in four settings with change of city name, producing individual sets for each city: "MONASTIR," "PRISTINA," "SALONIKA," and "USKUB."

1911 ***Perf. 12, 13½***

P69	A16	5pa bister	1.35
P70	A16	10pa yel grn	1.35
P71	A16	20pa magenta	1.35
P72	A16	1pi vio bl	1.65
P73	A16	2pi gray bl	2.25
P74	A16	5pi ocher	3.50
P75	A17	5pa purple	1.35
P76	A17	10pa green	1.35
P77	A17	20pa carmine	1.35
P78	A17	1pi blue	2.50
P79	A17	2pi orange	2.25
P80	A17	5pi lil rose	4.00
P81	A21	2pa ol grn	50
		Nos. P69-P81 (13)	24.75

Values for each of the 4 city sets of 13 are as printed.

The note after No. 182 will also apply to Nos. P69-P81.

Preceding Newspaper Issues with additional Overprint in Carmine or Black 

1915

On Stamps of 1893-98

P121	A10	10pa gray grn	16	5
a.		Inverted overprint	5.00	5.00
P122	A13	2pi yel brn	1.00	60
a.		Inverted overprint	5.00	5.00

On Stamps of 1901

P123	A16	10pa yel grn	10	5
P124	A17	5pa purple	7	5
P125	A17	20pa carmine	22	10
P126	A17	5pi lil rose	4.50	1.50

On Stamps of 1905

P127	A18	5pa ocher	7	7
a.		Inverted overprint	5.00	5.00
P128	A18	2pi slate	2.00	1.00
P129	A18	5pi brown	1.00	25

On Stamps of 1908

P130	A19	2pi bl blk	*165.00*	*120.00*
P131	A19	5pi dk vio	4.50	65

On Stamps of 1909

P132	A21	5pa ocher	7	7
P133	A21	5pi dk vio	22.50	6.50
		Nos. P121-P129,P131-P133 (12)	36.19	10.89

Preceding Newspaper Issues with additional Overprint in Red or Black 

1916

On Stamps of 1893-98

P134	A10	10pa gray grn	16	7
P135	A11	20pa vio brn	10	8
P136	A14	5pi dl vio	10.00	10.00

On Stamp of 1897

P137	N3	5pa on 10pa gray grn	7	5

On Stamps of 1901

P138	A16	5pa bister	7	7
P139	A16	10pa yel grn	16	10
P140	A16	20pa magenta	7	7
a.		Inverted overprint	6.50	6.50
P141	A16	1pi vio bl	25	14
P142	A17	5pa purple	7.00	8.00
P143	A17	10pa green	7.00	8.00
P144	A17	20pa carmine	16	10
P145	A17	1pi blue	22	10
P146	A17	2pi orange	20	10

On Stamps of 1905

P147	A18	5pa ocher	5	5
P148	A18	10pa dl grn	7.00	7.00
P149	A18	20pa carmine	7.00	7.00
P150	A18	1pi pale bl	25	10

On Stamp of 1908

P151	A19	5pa ocher	6.50	6.50

On Stamp of 1909

P152	A21	5pa ocher	7.00	8.00
		Nos. P134-P152 (19)	53.26	55.53

Preceding Newspaper Issues with additional Overprint in Red or Black 

1917

On Stamps of 1893-98

P153	A12	1pi gray (R)	25	25
P154	A11	20pa vio brn (R)	65	65

On Stamps of 1901

P155	A16	5pa bis (Bk)	55	55
a.		Inverted overprint	6.50	6.50
P156	A16	10pa yel grn (R)	55	55
P157	A16	20pa mag (Bk)	60	60
P158	A16	2pi gray bl (R)	20.00	20.00
P159	A17	5pa pur (Bk)	40	30
a.		Inverted overprint	5.00	5.00
b.		Double overprint	5.00	5.00
c.		Double ovpt., one inverted	6.50	6.50
P160	A17	10pa grn (R)	12.50	12.50
P161	A17	20pa car (Bk)	20	14
P162	A17	1pi bl (R)	60	50
P163	A17	2pi org (Bk)	50	50
P164	A17	5pi lil rose (R)	15.00	15.00

On Stamps of 1905

P165	A18	5pa ocher (R)	7	7
a.		Inverted overprint	5.00	5.00
P166	A18	5pa ocher (Bk)	25	25
a.		Inverted overprint	5.00	5.00
P167	A18	10pa dl grn (R)	25	25
P168	A18	20pa car (Bk)	10	10
a.		Double overprint	5.00	5.00
P169	A18	1pi bl (R)	14	10
a.		Inverted overprint	5.00	5.00
P170	A18	2pi sl (R)	15.00	15.00
P171	A18	5pi brn (R)	15.00	15.00

On Stamp of 1908

P172	A19	5pa ocher (R)	15.00	15.00

Nos. P153-P172 were used as regular postage stamps.

N4

N5

1919

Blue Surcharge and Red Overprint

P173	N4	5pa on 2pa ol grn	7	7
a.		Red overprint double	5.00	5.00
b.		Blue surcharge double	5.00	5.00

1920 **Red Surcharge**

P174	N5	5pa on 4pa brn	5	5

Catalogue values for unused stamps in this section, from this point to the end of the section, are for Never Hinged items.

Dove and Citadel of Ankara — N6

1952-55 **Litho.** ***Perf. 12½***

P175	N6	0.50k grnsh gray	12	9
P176	N6	0.50k vio ('53)	12	9

Perf. 10½, 10

P177	N6	0.50k red org ('54)	12	9
P178	N6	0.50k brn ('55)	12	9

POSTAL TAX STAMPS

Map of Turkey and Red Crescent PT1

1928 **Unwmk.** **Typo.** ***Perf. 14***

Crescent in Red

RA1	PT1	½pi lt brn	10	5
RA2	PT1	1pi red vio	10	5
RA3	PT1	2½pi orange	16	10

Engr.

Various Frames

RA4	PT1	5pi dk brn	25	5
RA5	PT1	10pi yel grn	42	25
RA6	PT1	20pi slate	70	35
RA7	PT1	50pi dk vio	2.50	1.35
		Nos. RA1-RA7 (7)	4.23	2.20

The use of these stamps on letters, parcels, etc. in addition to the regular postage, was obligatory on certain days in each year.

Cherubs Upholding Star — PT2

1932

RA8	PT2	1k ol bis & red	32	5
RA9	PT2	2½k dk brn & red	22	8
RA10	PT2	5k grn & red	50	20
RA11	PT2	25k blk & red	1.65	90

No. RA8 Surcharged **20 para**

RA12	PT2	20pa on 1k ol bis & red	12	8
RA13	PT2	3k on 1k ol bis & red	85	38
a.		3 "kruus"	2.50	2.50

By a law of Parliament the use of these stamps on letters and telegraph forms, in addition to the regular fees, was obligatory from Apr. 20-30 of each year. The inscription in the tablet at the bottom of the design states that the money derived from the sale of the stamps is devoted to child welfare work.

No. RA8 Surcharged **20 para**

1933

RA14	PT2	20pa on 1k ol bis & red	12	8
RA15	PT2	3k on 1k ol bis & red	35	22

No. RA5 Surcharged **5 Beş Kuruş**

RA16	PT1	5k on 10pi yel grn & red	50	25

PT3

PT4

1933 *Perf. 11, 11½*

RA17	PT3	20pa gray vio & red	40	16
RA18	PT4	1k vio & red	25	15
RA19	PT4	5k dk brn & red	90	50
RA20	PT3	15k grn & red	1.10	50

Nos. RA17 and RA20 were issued in Ankara; Nos. RA18 and RA19 in Izmir.

Nos. RA3, RA1 Surcharged in Black

5
Beş kuruş

1933-34

RA21	PT1	1k on 2½pi org	20	14
RA22	PT1	5k on ½pi lt brn	40	25

Map of Turkey — PT5

1934-35 **Crescent in Red** *Perf. 12*

RA23	PT5	½k bl ('35)	10	5
RA24	PT5	1k red brn	10	5
RA25	PT5	2½k brn ('35)	12	5
RA26	PT5	5k bl grn ('35)	35	12

Frame differs on No. RA26.

Nos. RA17, RA8-RA9 Overprinted "P.Y.S." in Roman Capitals

1936 *Perf. 11, 14*

RA27	PT3	20pa gray vio & red	35	20
RA28	PT2	1k ol bis & red	35	10
RA29	PT2	3k on 2½k dk brn & red	60	30

Type of 1934-35, Inscribed "Türkiye Kizilay Cemiyeti"

1938-46 *Perf. 8½-11½*

Type I - Imprint, "Devlet Basimevi". Crescent red.
Type II - Imprint, "Alaeddin Kiral Basimevi". Crescent carmine.
Type III - Imprint, "Damga Matbaasi". Crescent red.

Crescent in Red or Carmine

RA30	PT5	½k bl (I)	10	5
a.		Type II	10	5
b.		Type III	12	5
RA31	PT5	1k red vio (I)	8	5
a.		Type II	18	5
b.		Type III	10	5
RA32	PT5	2½k org (I)	10	5
a.		Type III	65	22
RA33	PT5	5k bl grn (I)	28	6
RA33A	PT5	5k choc (III) ('42)	55	18
RA34	PT5	10k pale grn (I)	75	30
a.		Type III	65	30
RA35	PT5	20k blk (I)	1.10	45
RA35A	PT5	50k pur (III) ('46)	2.75	55
RA35B	PT5	1 l bl (III) ('44)	12.50	2.50
		Nos. RA30-RA35B (9)	18.21	4.19

No. RA9 Surcharged Black

20
Para
P. Y. S.

1938 *Perf. 14*

RA36	PT2	20pa on 2½k dk brn & red	35	20
RA37	PT2	1k on 2½k dk brn & red	50	20

No. RA9 Surcharged in Black

P. Y. S.
20
Para

1938 **Unwmk.** *Perf. 14*

RA37A	PT2	20pa on 2½k dk brn & red	25	15
RA37B	PT2	1k on 2½k dk brn & red	30	20

No. RA9 Surcharged "1 Kurus" in Black

1939 *Perf. 14*

RA38	PT2	1k on 2½k dk brn & red	50	20

Child — PT6

Nurse with Child — PT7

1940 **Typo.** *Perf. 12*
Star in Carmine

RA39	PT6	20pa bluish grn	5	5
RA40	PT6	1k violet	5	5
RA41	PT7	1k lt bl	5	5
RA42	PT7	2½k pale red lil	9	8
RA43	PT6	3k black	18	8
RA44	PT7	5k pale vio	18	8
RA45	PT7	10k bl grn	50	15
RA46	PT6	15k dk bl	32	15
RA47	PT7	25k ol bis	1.40	65
RA48	PT7	50k ol gray	3.25	1.25
		Nos. RA39-RA48 (10)	6.07	2.59

Soldier and Map of Turkey — PT8

1941-44 *Perf. 11½*

RA49	PT8	1k purple	18	5
RA50	PT8	2k light bl	75	5
RA51	PT8	3k chestnut	90	25
RA51A	PT8	4k mag ('44)	2.50	30
RA52	PT8	5k brt rose	2.75	1.25
RA53	PT8	10k dk blue	3.25	1.20
		Nos. RA49-RA53 (6)	10.33	3.10

The tax was used for national defense.

Baby — PT9

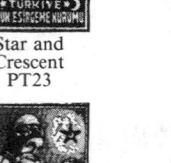

Nurse and Baby — PT13

Nurse and Children PT10

Nurse Feeding Child PT11

Nurse and Child PT12

Nurse and Child — PT14

President Inonu Holding Child — PT16

Children PT15

1942 **Unwmk.** **Typo.** *Perf. 11½*
Star in Red

RA54	PT9	20pa brt vio	14	10
RA55	PT9	20pa chocolate	14	10
RA56	PT10	1k dk sl grn	14	10
RA57	PT11	2½k yel grn	14	10
RA58	PT12	3k dk bl	14	10
RA59	PT13	5k brt pink	16	15
RA60	PT14	10k lt bl	35	25
RA61	PT15	15k dk red brn	60	42
RA62	PT16	25k brown	90	65
		Nos. RA54-RA62 (9)	2.71	1.97

See Nos. RA175, RA179-RA180.

No. RA32 Surcharged with New Value in Brown

1942 *Perf. 10*

RA63	PT5	1k on 2½k org & red (I)	10	8

Child Eating — PT17

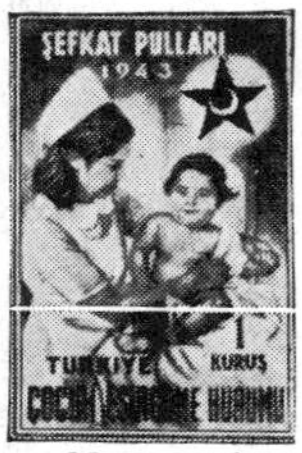
Nurse and Child — PT18

Nurse and Child PT19

Child and Red Star — PT20

President Inönü and Child — PT21

Inscribed: "Sefcat Pullari 23 Nisan 1943 Cocuk Esirgeme Kurumu."

1943 **Star in Red** *Perf. 11*

RA64	PT17	50pa lilac	8	5
RA65	PT17	50pa gray grn	8	5
RA66	PT18	1k lt ultra	10	5
RA67	PT19	3k dk red	12	10
RA68	PT20	15k cr & blk	50	40
RA69	PT21	100k brt vio bl	1.20	1.65
a.		Souvenir sheet, #RA64-RA69, imperf.	4.25	4.25
		Nos. RA64-RA69 (6)	2.08	2.30

Star and Crescent PT23

Hospital PT24

Nurse and Children PT25

Baby PT26

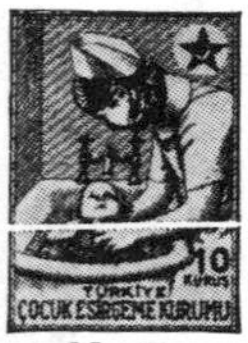
Nurse Bathing Baby PT27

Nurse Feeding Child PT28

Baby with Bottle PT29

Child PT30

Hospital — PT31

Perf. 10 to 12 and Compound
1943-44
Star in Red

RA71	PT23	20pa deep bl	5	5
RA72	PT24	1k gray grn	5	5
RA73	PT25	3k pale gray brn	5	5
RA74	PT26	5k yel org	22	18
RA75	PT26	5k vio brn	12	8
RA76	PT27	10k red	12	10
RA77	PT28	15k red vio	20	15
RA78	PT29	25k pale vio	35	25
RA79	PT30	50k lt blue	65	50
RA80	PT31	100k lt grn	1.75	1.00
		Nos. RA71-RA80 (10)	3.56	2.41

Nurse Holding Baby PT32

Nurse Feeding Child PT33

Child — PT34

Star and Crescent — PT35

1945-47 Unwmk. Litho. *Perf. 11½*
Star in Red

RA81	PT32	1k lil brn	5	5
a.		1k rose violet	10	5
RA82	PT33	5k yel grn	25	8
a.		5k green	25	8
RA83	PT34	10k red brn	20	15
RA84	PT35	250k gray blk	5.50	3.50
RA84A	PT35	500k dl vio ('47)	22.50	12.50
		Nos. RA81-RA84A (5)	28.50	16.28

Imprint on No. RA82: "Kagit ve Basim isleri A.S. ist." On No. RA82a: "Guzel Sanatlar Matbaasi - Ankara."

Nurse and Wounded Soldier PT36

President Inönü and Victim of Earthquake PT37

Removing Wounded from Hospital Ship — PT38

Nurse and Soldier — PT39

Feeding the Poor — PT40

Wounded Soldiers on Landing Raft — PT41

Symbolical of Red Crescent Relief — PT42

1945 *Perf. 12x10, 10x12*
Crescent in Red

RA85	PT36	20pa dp bl & brn org	12	5
RA86	PT37	1k ol grn & ol bis	12	5
RA87	PT38	2½k dp bl & red	18	5
RA88	PT39	5k dp bl & red	55	12
RA89	PT40	10k dp bl & lt grn	55	22
RA90	PT41	50k blk & gray grn	1.50	55
RA91	PT42	1 l blk & yel	5.00	1.50
		Nos. RA85-RA91 (7)	8.02	2.54

See Nos. RA181-RA182.

Ankara Sanatorium PT43

1946 *Perf. 12*

RA92	PT43	20k red & lt bl	65	30

See No. RA210.

For unused stamps, more recent issues are valued as never hinged, with the beginning point determined on a country-by-country basis. Notes to show the beginning points are prominently placed in the text.

Covering Sleeping Child — PT44

Designs: 1k, Mother and child. 2½k, Nurse at playground. 5k, Doctor examining infant. 15k, Feeding child. 25k, Bathing child. 50k, Weighing baby. 150k, Feeding baby.

1946 Litho. *Perf. 12½*
Inscribed: "25ci Yil Hatirasi 1946"
Star in Carmine

RA93	PT44	20pa brown	5	5
RA94	PT44	1k blue	5	5
RA95	PT44	2½k carmine	8	8
RA96	PT44	5k vio brn	15	12
RA97	PT44	15k violet	15	12
RA98	PT44	25k gray grn	25	20
RA99	PT44	50k bl grn	50	45
RA100	PT44	150k gray brn	1.50	1.25
		Nos. RA93-RA100 (8)	2.73	2.32

Hospital Ship — PT52

Ambulance Plane — PT53

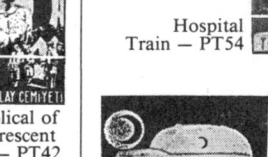

Hospital Train — PT54

Ambulance — PT55

Boy Scout and Red Crescent Flag — PT56

Stretcher Bearers and Wounded Soldier PT57

Nurse and Hospital PT58

Sanatorium PT59

1946 *Perf. 11½*
Crescent in Carmine

RA101	PT52	1k bl & ind	65	65
RA102	PT53	4k sl gray & rose vio	65	65
RA103	PT54	10k Prus grn & pink	65	65
RA104	PT55	25k choc, org & bl	1.40	1.40
RA105	PT56	40k blk brn & grn	2.25	2.25
RA106	PT57	70k ol bis, blk brn & org brn	2.50	2.50
RA107	PT58	1 l vio brn, org brn & vio	3.50	3.50
RA108	PT59	2½ l gray blk & org brn	8.25	8.25
		Nos. RA101-RA108 (8)	19.85	19.85

Souvenir Sheet

Pres. Inönü and Child — PT60

1946 Unwmk. Typo. *Imperf.*

RA109	PT60	250k sl blk, pink & red	10.00	10.00

Turkish Society for the Prevention of Cruelty to Children, 25th anniv.

Nurse and Wounded Soldier PT61

Pres. Inönü and Victim of Earthquake PT62

Nurse and Soldier PT64

Symbolical of Red Crescent Relief PT67

1946-47 Litho. *Perf. 11½*
Crescent in Red

RA113	PT61	20pa dk bl vio & ol ('47)	5	5
RA114	PT62	1k dk brn & yel	38	22
RA115	PT64	5k dp bl & red	30	25
RA116	PT67	1 l brn blk & yel	1.50	1.25

Nurse and Wounded Soldier
PT68 PT69

Victory and Soldier — PT70

1947
Crescent in Red

RA117	PT68	250k brn blk & grn	3.00	2.00
RA118	PT69	5 l sl gray & org	5.00	3.50

Booklet Pane of One
Perf. 11½ (top) x Imperf.

RA119	PT70	10 l deep bl	13.50	10.00

Black numerals above No. RA119 indicate position in booklet.

President Inönü and Victim of Earthquake PT71

Nurse and Child PT72

1947 *Perf. 11½*

RA120	PT71	1k dk brn, pale bl & red	16	5
RA121	PT72	2½k bl vio & car	20	10

See Nos. RA221-RA223.

Nurse Offering Encouragement PT73

Plant with Broken Stem PT74

Perf. 8½, 11½x10, 11x10½
1948-49 Typo. Unwmk.
Crescent in Red

RA122	PT73	½k ultra ('49)	32	20
RA123	PT73	1k indigo	8	5
RA124	PT73	2k lil rose	10	5
RA125	PT73	2½k org ('49)	10	5
RA126	PT73	3k bl grn	10	5
RA127	PT73	4k gray ('49)	20	15
RA128	PT73	5k blue	40	5
RA129	PT73	10k pink	70	12
RA130	PT73	25k chocolate	80	25

Perf. 10

RA130A	PT74	50k ultra & bl gray ('49)	1.10	75
RA130B	PT74	100k grn & pale grn ('49)	2.50	1.00
		Nos. RA122-RA130B (11)	6.40	2.72

Nurse and Children — PT75

Various Scenes with Children.

Inscribed: "1948 Cocuk Yili Hatirasi"

1948 Litho. *Perf. 11*
Star in Red

RA131	PT75	20pa dp ultra	5	5
RA132	PT75	20pa rose lil	5	5
RA133	PT75	1k dp Prus bl	10	8
RA134	PT75	3k dk brn vio	22	16
RA135	PT75	15k sl blk	70	50
RA136	PT75	30k orange	1.50	1.00
RA137	PT75	150k yel grn	2.50	2.00
RA138	PT75	300k brn red	3.50	3.00
		Nos. RA131-RA138 (8)	8.62	6.84

No. RA136 is arranged horizontally. See Nos. RA199-RA206.

Catalogue values for unused stamps in this section, from this point to the end of the section, are for Never Hinged items.

Nos. RA101 to RA108 Overprinted in Carmine

Şefkat pulu

1949 *Perf. 11½*

RA139 PT52 1k bl & ind 20 20
RA140 PT53 4k sl gray & rose vio 35 35
RA141 PT54 10k Prus grn & pink 50 50
RA142 PT55 25k choc, org & bl 1.00 1.00
RA143 PT56 40k blk brn & grn 1.50 1.50
RA144 PT57 70k ol bis, blk brn & org brn 2.50 2.50
RA145 PT58 1 l vio brn, org brn & vio 3.50 3.50
RA146 PT59 2½ l gray blk & org brn 15.00 15.00
Nos. RA139-RA146 (8) 24.55 24.55

Ruins and Tent
PT76

"Protection"
PT77

Booklet Panes of One

1949 ***Perf. 10 (top) x Imperf.***

RA149 PT76 5k gray, vio gray & red 22 16
RA150 PT76 10k red vio, sal & red 35 22

Black numerals above each stamp indicate its position in the booklet.

No. RA124 Surcharged in Black

1950 **Unwmk.** ***Perf. 8½***

RA151 PT73 20pa on 2k lil rose & red 10 8

Postal Tax Stamps of 1944-48 Surcharged with New Value in Black or Carmine

Perf. 8½ to 12½ and Compound

1952

RA152 PT73 20pa on 3k bl grn 10 7
RA153 PT73 20pa on 4k gray 10 7
RA154 PT72 1k on 2½k bl vio & car (C) 14 10
RA155 PT44 1k on 2½k car 14 10
RA156 PT25 1k on 3k pale gray brn 14 10
Nos. RA152-RA156 (5) 62 44

Various Symbolical Designs Inscribed "75 iNCi" etc.

1952 **Typo.** ***Perf. 10***

Crescent in Carmine

RA157 PT77 5k bl grn & bl 60 50
RA158 PT77 15k yel grn, bl & cr 60 50
RA159 PT77 30k bl, grn & brn 60 50
RA160 PT77 1 l blk, bl & cr 90 80
a. Souvenir sheet, #RA157-RA160, imperf. 8.00 8.00

Printed in sheets of 20 containing one horizontal row of each value.

Nurse and Children
PT78

Design: 1ku, Nurse and baby.

1954 **Litho.** ***Perf. 10½***

Star in Red

RA161 PT78 20pa aqua 8 5
RA162 PT78 20pa yellow 8 5
RA163 PT78 1k deep bl 8 5

Globe and Flag — PT79

Designs: 5k, Winged nurse in clouds. 10k, Protecting arm of Red Crescent.

1954

RA164 PT79 1k multi 5 5
RA165 PT79 5k multi 8 5
RA166 PT79 10k car, grn & gray 16 8

See Nos. RA208, RA211-RA213.

Florence Nightingale
PT80

Selimiye Barracks
PT81

Portrait: 30k, Florence Nightingale, full-face.

1954, Nov. 4

Crescent in Carmine

RA167 PT80 20k gray grn & dk brn 35 25
RA168 PT80 30k dl brn & blk 35 25
RA169 PT81 50k buff & blk 65 65

Arrival of Florence Nightingale at Scutari, cent.

Type of 1942 and

Children Kissing
PT82

Nurse Holding Baby
PT83

1955, Apr. 23

Star in Red

RA170 PT82 20pa chalky bl 5 5
RA171 PT82 20pa org brn 5 5
RA172 PT82 1k lilac 5 5
RA173 PT82 3k gray bis 8 5
RA174 PT82 5k orange 8 5
RA175 PT12 10k green 30 16
RA176 PT83 15k dk blue 16 7
RA177 PT83 25k brn car 40 20
RA178 PT83 50k dk gray grn 1.00 80
RA179 PT12 2½ l dl brn 25.00 20.00
RA180 PT12 10 l rose lil 60.00 50.00
Nos. RA170-RA180 (11) 87.17 71.48

Types of 1945
Inscribed: "Turkiye Kizilay Dernegi"

1955 **Litho.** ***Perf. 10½x11½, 10½***

Crescent in Red

RA181 PT36 20pa vio brn & lem 7 5
RA182 PT41 1k blk & gray grn 7 5

Nurse — PT85

Nurses on Parade — PT86

Design: 100k, Two nurses under Red Cross and Red Crescent flags and UN emblem.

Perf. 10½

1955, Sept. 5 **Unwmk.** **Litho.**

Crescent and Cross in Red

RA183 PT85 10k blk & pale brn 50 40
RA184 PT86 15k dk grn & pale yel grn 50 40
RA185 PT85 100k lt ultra 1.25 65

Meeting of the board of directors of the Intl. Council of Nurses, Istanbul, Aug. 29-Sept. 5, 1955.

Nos. RA92 and RA130B Surcharged "20 Para"

1955

RA186 PT43 20p on 20k red & lt bl 10 5

Typo.

RA187 PT74 20p on 100k grn, pale grn & red (surch. 11½x2mm) 15 5
c. Surcharge 13½x2½ mm 15 5

No. RA164 Surcharged with New Value and Two Bars

1956 **Litho.** ***Perf. 10½***

RA187A PT79 20p on 1k multi 5 5
RA187B PT79 2.50k on 1k multi 5 5

Woman and Children — PT87

Designs: 10k, 25k, 50k, Flag and building. 250k, 5 l, 10 l, Mother nursing baby.

1956 **Litho.** ***Perf. 10½***

Star in Red

RA188 PT87 20pa red org 5 5
RA189 PT87 20pa gray grn 5 5
RA190 PT87 1k purple 5 5
RA191 PT87 1k grnsh bl 5 5
RA192 PT87 3k lt red brn 15 6
RA193 PT87 10k rose car 25 20
RA194 PT87 25k brt grn 65 50
RA195 PT87 50k brt ultra 1.00 90
RA196 PT87 250k red lil 5.00 5.00
RA197 PT87 5 l sepia 6.50 5.00
RA198 PT87 10 l dk sl grn 8.75 7.50
Nos. RA188-RA198 (11) 22.50 19.36

Stamps of 1948 Overprinted and Surcharged in Black or Red: "IV. DUNYA Cocuk Gunu 1 Ekim 1956"

1956, Oct. 1 **Unwmk.** ***Perf. 11***

Star in Red

RA199 PT75 20pa dp ultra (R) 3.50 3.50
RA200 PT75 20pa rose lil 3.50 3.50
RA201 PT75 1k dp Prus bl (R) 3.50 3.50
RA202 PT75 3k dk brn vio (R) 3.50 3.50
RA203 PT75 15k sl blk (R) 4.00 4.00
RA204 PT75 25k on 30k org 4.00 4.00
RA205 PT75 100k on 150k yel grn (R) 5.00 5.00
RA206 PT75 250k on 300k brn red 6.50 6.50
Nos. RA199-RA206 (8) 33.50 33.50

The tax was for child welfare. No. RA204 is horizontal.

Type of 1954, Redrawn Type of 1946, and

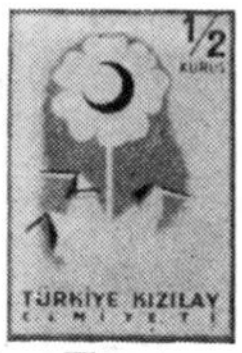
Flower
PT88

Children
PT89

1957 **Unwmk.** ***Perf. 10½***

Crescent in Red

RA207 PT88 ½k lt ol gray & brn 5 5
RA208 PT79 1k ol bis, blk & grn 5 5
RA209 PT88 2½k yel grn & bl grn 8 5
RA210 PT43 20k red & lt bl 15 12
RA211 PT79 25k lt gray, blk & grn 38 30
RA212 PT79 50k bl, dk grn & grn 60 30
RA213 PT79 100k vio, blk & grn 90 55
Nos. RA207-RA213 (7) 2.21 1.42

No. RA210 inscribed "Turkiye Kizilay Cemiyeti." No. RA92 inscribed ". . . . Dernegi."

1957 **Unwmk.** ***Perf. 10½***

RA214 PT89 20pa car & red 5 5
RA215 PT89 20pa grn & red 5 5
RA216 PT89 1k ultra & car 8 5
RA217 PT89 3k red org & car 25 16

"Blood Donor and Recipient"
PT90

Child and Butterfly
PT91

Designs: 75k, Figure showing blood circulation. 150k, Blood transfusion symbolism.

1957, May 22

Size: 24x40mm

RA218 PT90 25k gray, blk & red 25 15

Size: 22½x37½mm

RA219 PT90 75k grn, blk & red 40 30
RA220 PT90 150k yel grn & red 65 45

Redrawn Type of 1947
Inscribed: "V Dunya Cocuk Gunu"

1957 **Star in Red** ***Perf. 10½***

RA221 PT72 100k blk & bis brn 65 60
RA222 PT72 150k blk & yel grn 65 60
RA223 PT72 250k blk & vio 70 65

The tax was for child welfare.

1958 **Litho.** **Unwmk.**

Designs: Various Butterflies. Nos. RA226-RA227 arranged horizontally.

RA224 PT91 20k gray & red 30 25
RA225 PT91 25k multi 30 25
RA226 PT91 50k multi 40 30
RA227 PT91 75k grn, yel & blk 50 40
RA228 PT91 150k multi 80 65
Nos. RA224-RA228 (5) 2.30 1.85

Florence Nightingale — PT92

1958

Crescent in Red

RA229 PT92 1 l bluish grn 40 25
RA230 PT92 1½ l gray 60 50
RA231 PT92 2½ l blue 80 60

Turkey stopped issuing postal tax stamps in June, 1958. Similar stamps of later date are private charity stamps issued by the Red Crescent Society and the Society for the Protection of Children.

POSTAL TAX AIR POST STAMPS

Air Fund Issues

These stamps were obligatory on all air mail for 21 days a year. The tax benefitted the Turkish Aviation Society: 20 paras for a postcard, 1 kurush for a regular letter, 2 1/2k for a registered letter, 3k for a telegram, 5k-50k for a package, higher values for air freight. Postal tax air post stamps were withdrawn Aug. 21, 1934, and remainders destroyed later that year.

Biplane PTAP1

Perf. 11, Pin Perf.

1926 Unwmk. Litho.

Size: 35x25mm

RAC1	PTAP1	20pa brn & pale grn	1.00	30
RAC2	PTAP1	1g bl grn & buff	1.00	30

Size: 40x29mm

RAC3	PTAP1	5g vio & pale grn	2.25	60
RAC4	PTAP1	5g car lake & pale grn	16.50	4.00

PTAP2

PTAP3

1927-29

RAC5	PTAP2	20pa dl red & pale grn	42	16
RAC6	PTAP2	1k grn & yel	35	14

Perf. 11½

RAC7	PTAP3	2k dp cl & yel grn	60	35
RAC8	PTAP3	2½k red & yel grn	4.50	1.65
RAC9	PTAP3	5k dk bl gray & org	45	45
RAC10	PTAP3	10k dk grn & rose	3.75	1.65
RAC11	PTAP3	15k grn & yel	3.75	2.00
RAC12	PTAP3	20k ol brn & yel	3.75	1.50
RAC13	PTAP3	50k dk bl & cob bl	6.00	3.25
RAC14	PTAP3	100k car & lt bl	60.00	35.00
	Nos. RAC5-RAC14 (10)		83.57	46.15

Nos. RAC1, RAC5, RAC7 and RAC11 Surcharged in Black or Red

1930-31

RAC15	1k ("Bir Kurus") on RAC1	60.00	55.00
RAC16	1k ("Bir Kurus") on RAC5	25	14
RAC17	100pa ("Yuz Para") on RAC7 (R)	35	20
RAC18	5k ("Bes Kurus") on RAC5	35	20
RAC19	5k ("5 Kurus") on RAC5	35	20
RAC20	10k ("On kurus") on RAC7 (R)	1.20	60
RAC21	50k ("Elli kurus") on RAC7 (R)	6.00	2.50
RAC22	1 l ("Bir lira") on RAC7 (R)	*5.00*	*25.00*
RAC23	5 l ("Bes lira") on RAC11 (R)	*375.00*	*300.00*
Nos. RAC15-RAC23 (9)		*448.50*	*383.84*

PTAP4

PTAP5

1931-32 Litho. *Perf. 11½*

RAC24	PTAP4	20pa black	14	10

Typo.

RAC25	PTAP5	1k brn car ('32)	25	10
RAC26	PTAP5	5k red ('32)	60	25
RAC27	PTAP5	10k grn ('32)	1.50	50

PTAP6

1933

RAC28	PTAP6	10pa ("On Para") grn	25	7
RAC29	PTAP6	1k ("Bir Kurus") red	60	16
RAC30	PTAP6	5k ("Bes Kurus") lil	1.20	1.00

TURKEY IN ASIA

(Anatolia)

40 Paras = 1 Piaster

This designation, which includes all of Turkey in Asia Minor, came into existence during the uprising of 1919, led by Mustafa Kemal Pasha. Actually there was no separation of territory, the Sultan's sovereignty being almost immediately reduced to a small area surrounding Constantinople. The formation of the Turkish Republic and the expulsion of the Sultan followed in 1923. Subsequent issues of postage stamps are listed under Turkey (Republic).

Issues of the Nationalist Government.

Turkish Revenue Stamps Handstamped in Turkish "Osmanli Postalari, 1336" (Ottoman Post, 1920).

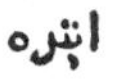

Turkish Stamps of 1913-18 Surcharged in Black or Red

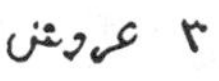

(The Surcharge reads "Angora 3 Piastres")

1920 Unwmk. *Perf. 12*

On Stamps of 1913

1	A24	3pi on 2pa red lil	1.00	70
2	A25	3pi on 4pa dk brn	4.00	4.00
3	A27	3pi on 6pa dk bl	11.00	11.00

On Stamp of 1916-18

4	A42	3pi on 2pa vio (Bk)	2.00	2.00

Turkish Stamps of 1913-18 Handstamped in Black or Red

(The Surch. reads "Post, Piastre 3")

1921 *Perf. 12, 12½*

On Stamps of 1913

5	A24	3pi on 2pa red lil	3.75	3.75
a.		on No. 1	6.50	6.50
6	A25	3pi on 4pa dk brn	3.75	3.75
a.		on No. 2	8.25	8.25
7	A25	3pi on 4pa dk brn (R)	12.50	12.50
a.		on No. 2	7.00	7.00
8	A27	3pi on 6pa dk bl	11.00	11.00
a.		on No. 3	22.50	22.50
9	A27	3pi on 6pa dk bl (R)	15.00	15.00
a.		on No. 3	11.00	11.00

On Stamps of 1916-18

10	A42	3pi on 2pa vio (R)	11.00	11.00
a.		on No. 4	9.00	9.00

A1

The overprint on Nos. 12-28 comes in three types, varying in width from 20 to 24mm. All three types are found on Nos. 12, 14 and 21; two types on Nos. 13, 18 and 25; one only on the others.

12	A1	1pi green	82.50	40.00
13	A1	5pi ultra	*700.00*	*525.00*
14	A1	50pi gray grn	2.00	1.50
		Cut cancellation		20
15	A1	100pi buff	35.00	8.00
a.		100pi yel	22.50	17.50
		Cut cancellation		50
16	A1	500pi orange	40.00	25.00
		Cut cancellation		2.25
17	A1	1000pi brown	550.00	425.00
		Cut cancellation		45.00

A2

Black Overprint

18	A2	10pa green	45.00	40.00
19	A2	1pi ultra	*600.00*	*550.00*
20	A2	5pi rose	*600.00*	*550.00*
21	A2	50pi ocher	4.50	3.50
a.		yellow	7.00	7.00
		Cut cancellation		20
22	A2	100pi brown	22.50	22.50
		Cut cancellation		1.50
23	A2	500pi slate	82.50	62.50
		Cut cancellation		3.75

A3

Red and Black Overprints

24	A3	50pi ocher	62.50	17.50
		Cut cancellation		1.50

A4

A5

Black Overprint

25	A4	2pi emerald		*1,400.*
26	A5	100pi yel brn	140.00	45.00
		Cut cancellation		3.00

A6

A7

27	A6	20pa black	*400.00*	*400.00*
28	A7	2pi bl blk	*525.00*	*475.00*

A8

Perf. 12

29	A8	10pa slate	4.25	4.25
a.		Handstamped overprint	5.25	5.25
b.		Double overprint		
30	A8	1pi green	4.00	3.00
a.		Invtd. ovpt.	11.00	9.00
b.		Handstamped overprint		
31	A8	5pi ultra	3.00	3.00
a.		"1337" invtd.	60.00	55.00
b.		Half used as 2½pi on cover		
c.		Handstamped overprint	10.00	10.00

Handstamped Overprint

32	A8	50pi green	*550.00*	*400.00*

A9

33	A9	10pa green	2.25	2.25
a.		Handstamped overprint		
34	A9	1pi ultra	3.50	3.00
a.		Handstamped overprint	15.00	15.00
35	A9	5pi red	2.25	2.00
a.		Inverted ovpt.		
b.		"1337" inverted	5.25	3.75
c.		Half used as 2½pi on cover		
d.		Handstamped overprint		
36	A9	50pi ocher	35.00	35.00
a.		Handstampd overprint	22.50	22.50

A10

With Additional Turkish Overprint in Red or Black

37	A10	10pa grn (R)	17.50	17.50
a.		Black overprint inverted	40.00	40.00
38	A10	1pi ultra (R)	15.00	15.00
39	A10	5pi rose (Bk)	18.00	18.00
a.		"1337" invtd.	55.00	55.00

Turkey in Asia Stamps can be mounted in Scott's Turkey Album.

A11

40 A11 2pi bl blk 11.00 11.00
a. Handstamped overprint

A12

1921 *Perf. 12*
41 A12 5pi green 17.50 17.50
a. Handstamped overprint

A13

42 A13 1pi ultra 120.00 120.00
a. Handstamped overprint *135.00 135.00*
43 A13 5pi dp grn 135.00 135.00
a. Handstamped overprint *250.00 200.00*

Handstamped Overprint

44 A13 5pi dk vio *400.00 400.00*

The overprint variety "337" for "1337" exists on Nos. 42-43.

A14

Perf. 12, 12½

45 A14 20pa black 1.50 1.50
a. Date 4½mm high 2.25 2.25
b. "337" for "1337" 2.25 2.25

A15

A16

46 A15 10pa green 2.25 2.25
a. Overprint 21 mm long
b. "131" for "1337"
47 A15 1pi ultra 3.50 2.50
a. "13" for "1337" 15.00 15.00
b. "131" for "1337" 15.00 15.00
c. Invtd. ovpt. 22.50 22.50
d. Handstamped overprint

48 A15 5pi red 8.00 8.00
a. Invtd. ovpt. 45.00 40.00
b. "131" for "1337" 40.00 40.00
c. Handstamped overprint

Perf. 11½, 11½x11

49 A16 10pa pink 40 40
a. Imperf.
b. Date "1237" 70 70
d. Inverted overprint
50 A16 1pi yellow 55 45
a. Overprint 18 mm long 55 55
b. Date "1332" 3.75
c. Date "1317"
d. Inverted overprint 1.10 1.10
51 A16 2pi yel grn 60 50
a. Date "1237" 3.75
b. Date "1317"
c. Imperf.
d. Inverted ovpt. 2.25 2.25
52 A16 5pi red 1.40 70
a. Imperf. vertically
b. Inverted overprint 2.25 1.75
c. Double overprint 3.00 2.25
d. Date "1332" 3.75
e. Half used as 2½pi on cover
f. Overprint 18mm long 1.50 1.50

Turkish Revenue Stamps Overprinted "Osmanli Postalari 1337"

A17

TURKISH INSCRIPTIONS:

20 Paras

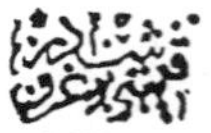
1 Piaster

2 Piasters

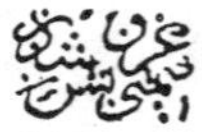
5 Piasters

1921 *Perf. 11½*
53 A17 20pa on 1pi dk red & bl 7.00 5.50
54 A17 1pi on 1pi dk red & bl 70 70
55 A17 2pi on 1pi dk red & bl 70 70
a. Inverted surcharge
56 A17 5pi on 1pi dk red & bl 1.50 1.50

No. 55 is also surcharged with the Turkish numeral "2."

A18

A19

57 A18 1pi on 1pi dk red & bl 11.00 11.00
58 A19 1pi grn & brn red 70 50
a. Double overprint
b. Handstamped overprint

The errors "1307", "1331" and "2337" occur once in each sheet of Nos. 53-58.

Naval League Stamps Overprinted in Turkish "Osmanli Postalari, 1337" (Ottoman Post, 1921).

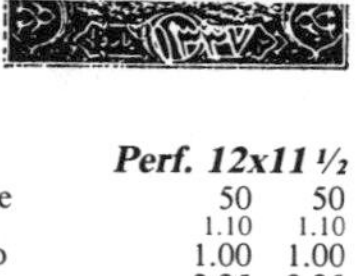
A20

1921 *Perf. 12x11½*
59 A20 1pa orange 50 50
a. Date "1327" 1.10 1.10
60 A20 2pa indigo 1.00 1.00
61 A20 5pa green 2.25 2.25
62 A20 10pa brown 17.50 17.50
63 A20 40pa red brn 15.00 15.00
Nos. 59-63 (5) 36.25 36.25

The error "2337" occurs on all values of this issue.

The Naval League stamps have pictures of three Turkish warships. They were sold for the benefit of sailors of the fleet but did not pay postage until they were surcharged in 1921.

Overprinted

On Stamps of 1916-18

Perf. 12

64 A44 10pa green 5.50 2.50
65 A45 20pa dp rose 5.50 3.00
a. Inverted overprint 16.50 16.50
66 A51 25pi car, *straw* 20.00 5.00
a. Double overprint
b. Invtd. ovpt. 37.50 37.50

On Newspaper Stamp of 1909, Overprinted Crescent and Star in 1915

67 A21 5pa ocher 150.00 55.00

Turkish Stamps of 1915-20 Surcharged

1921

On Stamp of 1913, Overprinted Crescent and Star in 1915

68 A22 5pa ocher 70.00 50.00

On Stamps of 1917-18

69 A53 5pi on 2pa Prus bl (#547) 3.75 2.50
70 A53 5pi on 2pa Prus bl (#548) 4.00 2.50

On Stamp of 1919

71 A57 35pi on 1pi bl (Bk) 10.00 7.00
a. Inverted surcharge

On Newspaper Stamp of 1909, Overprinted Crescent and Star in 1915

72 A21 5pa ocher 110.00 90.00

On No. 72 the overprint is vertical, half reading up and half reading down.

On Stamps of 1920

73 A32 3pi blue 3.00 2.50
74 A36 10pi gray vio 3.00 2.50

The overprints on Nos. 64-74 read "Adana December 1st, 1921." This issue was to commemorate the withdrawal of the French from Cilicia.

On No. 71 the lines of the overprint are further apart than on Nos. 68-70, and 73-74.

Postage Due Stamps of Turkey, 1914, Overprinted:

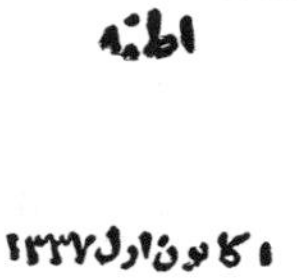
a

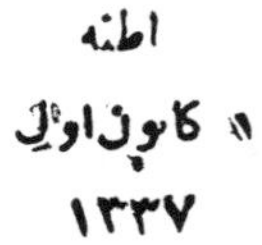
b

1921 **Unwmk.** *Perf. 12*
75 D1 (a) 5pa claret 55.00 50.00
76 D2 (a) 20pa red 55.00 50.00
a. Inverted overprint
77 D3 (b) 1pi dk bl 55.00 50.00
a. Inverted overprint 70.00 70.00

Withdrawal of the French from Cilicia. Forged overprints exist.

Pact of Revenge, Burning Village at Top — A21

Izmir Harbor — A22

Mosque of Selim, Adrianople — A23

Mosque of Selim, Konya — A24

Soldier — A25

Legendary Gray Wolf — A26

Snake Castle and Seyhan River, Adana — A27

Parliament Building at Sivas — A28

A29

Mosque at Urfa — A30

Map of Anatolia — A31

Declaration of Faith from the Koran — A32

1922 **Litho.** *Perf. 11½*
78 A21 10pa vio brn 20 5
79 A22 20pa bl grn 25 5
a. Imperf. 2.50 2.50
80 A23 1pi dp bl 45 7
a. Imperf. 5.00 5.00
81 A24 2pi red brn 1.00 7
82 A25 5pi dk bl 1.25 5
a. Imperf. 5.00 5.00
83 A26 10pi dk brn 4.50 20
84 A27 25pi rose 4.50 10
a. Imperf. 32.50 32.50
85 A28 50pi indigo 4.00 65
a. Imperf. 8.25 8.25
86 A29 50pi dk gray 4.00 3.50
87 A30 100pi violet 35.00 1.35
88 A31 200pi slate 70.00 12.00
89 A32 500pi green 65.00 6.50
Cut cancellation 1.00
Nos. 78-89 (12) 190.15 24.59

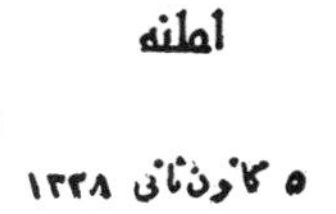

Stamps of Type A23 Overprinted

1922

90	A23	1pi dp bl	4.25	3.50
91	A23	5pi dp bl	4.25	3.50
92	A23	10pi brown	4.25	3.50
93	A23	25pi rose	4.25	3.50
94	A23	50pi slate	4.25	3.50
95	A23	100pi violet	4.25	3.50
96	A23	200pi blk vio	4.25	3.50
97	A23	500pi bl grn	4.25	3.50
		Nos. 90-97 (8)	34.00	28.00

To commemorate the withdrawal of the French from Cilicia and the return of the Kemalist national army. The overprint reads: "Adana, Jan. 5, 1922."

No. 90-97 without overprint were presented to some high government officials.

First Parliament House, Ankara — A33

1922 **Litho.**

98	A33	5pa violet	20	10
99	A33	10pa green	20	7
100	A33	20pa pale red	38	20
101	A33	1pi brn org	1.75	50
102	A33	2pi red brn	7.00	1.20
103	A33	3pi rose	1.75	25
a.		Arabic "13" in right corner	6.50	3.50
b.		Thin grayish paper	14.00	1.40
		Nos. 98-103 (6)	11.28	2.32

Nos. 98-103, 103b exist imperf. In 1923 several stamps of Turkey and Turkey in Asia were overprinted in Turkish for advertising purposes. The overprint reads: "Izmir Economic Congress, 17 Feb., 1339."

POSTAGE DUE STAMPS

D1

1922 **Litho.** *Perf. 11½*

J1	D1	20pa dull green	20	20
a.		Imperf.		
J2	D1	1pi gray green	25	25
J3	D1	2pi red brown	90	65
J4	D1	3pi rose	1.90	1.50
J5	D1	5pi dark blue	2.50	2.00
		Nos. J1-J5 (5)	5.75	4.60

ΕΛΛΗΝΙΚΗ
ΚΑΤΟΧΗ
ΛΕΠΤΑ • 50

Turkish Stamps of 1916-21 with Greek surcharge as above in blue or black are of private origin.

UBANGI-SHARI

(UBANGI-SHARI-CHAD)

LOCATION — In Western Africa, north of the equator.
GOVT. — A former French Colony.
AREA — 238,767 sq. mi.
POP. — 833,916.
CAPITAL — Bangui.

In 1910 French Congo was divided into the three colonies of Gabon, Middle Congo and Ubangi-Shari and officially named "French Equatorial Africa." Under that name in 1934 the group, with the territory of Chad included, became a single administrative unit. See Gabon.

100 Centimes = 1 Franc

Stamps of Middle Congo Overprinted in Black

OUBANGUI-CHARI-TCHAD

1915-22 **Unwmk.** *Perf. 14x13½*

Chalky Paper

1	A1	1c ol gray & brn	5	5
a.		Double overprint	90.00	
b.		Imperf.	22.50	
2	A1	2c vio & brn	5	5
3	A1	4c bl & brn	10	10
4	A1	5c dk grn & bl	5	5
5	A1	5c yel & bl ('22)	25	25
6	A1	10c car & bl	30	30
7	A1	10c dp grn & bl grn ('22)	20	20
8	A1	15c brn vio & rose	45	45
9	A1	20c brn & bl	90	90

No. 8 is on ordinary paper.

Overprinted OUBANGUI-CHARI-TCHAD

10	A2	25c bl & grn	40	40
11	A2	25c bl grn & gray ('22)	25	25
12	A2	30c scar & grn	30	30
13	A2	30c dp rose & rose ('22)	25	25
14	A2	35c vio brn & bl	1.90	1.90
15	A2	40c dl grn & brn	2.00	2.00
16	A2	45c vio & red	2.00	2.00
17	A2	50c bl grn & red	3.00	3.00
18	A2	50c bl & grn ('22)	25	25
19	A2	75c brn & bl	5.00	5.00
20	A2	1fr dp grn & vio	5.00	5.00
21	A2	2fr vio & gray grn	5.00	5.00
22	A2	5fr bl & rose	15.00	15.00
		Nos. 1-22 (22)	42.70	42.70

Types of Middle Congo, 1907-22, Overprinted in Black or Red

OUBANGUI-CHARI

1922

23	A1	1c vio & grn	12	12
a.		Overprint omitted	70.00	
b.		Imperf.	14.00	
24	A1	2c grn & sal	20	20
25	A1	4c ol brn & brn	28	28
a.		Ovpt. omitted	70.00	
26	A1	5c ind & rose	40	40
27	A1	10c dp grn & gray grn	55	55
28	A1	15c lt red & dl bl	65	65
29	A1	20c choc & sal	2.25	2.25

Overprinted OUBANGUI CHARI

30	A2	25c vio & sal	2.00	2.00
31	A2	30c rose & pale rose	1.20	1.20
32	A2	35c vio & grn	2.25	2.25
33	A2	40c ind & vio (R)	2.00	2.00
34	A2	45c choc & vio	2.00	2.00
35	A2	50c dk bl & pale bl	1.20	1.20
36	A2	60c on 75c vio, *pnksh*	1.20	1.20
37	A2	75c choc & sal	2.25	2.25
38	A3	1fr grn & dl bl (R)	2.25	2.25
a.		Overprint omitted		
39	A3	2fr grn & sal	3.50	3.50
40	A3	5fr grn & ol brn	6.50	6.50
		Nos. 23-40 (18)	30.80	30.80

Stamps of 1922 Issue with Additional Overprint in Black, Blue or Red

AFRIQUE EQUATORIALE FRANÇAISE

1924-33

41	A1	1c vio & grn (Bl)	5	5
a.		"OUBANGUI CHARI" omitted	55.00	
42	A1	2c grn & sal (Bl)	5	5
a.		"OUBANGUI CHARI" omitted	57.50	
b.		Double ovpt.	62.50	
43	A1	4c ol brn & brn (Bl)	5	5
a.		Double overprint (Bl + Bk)	90.00	
b.		"OUBANGUI CHARI" omitted	930.00	
44	A1	5c ind & rose	10	10
a.		"OUBANGUI CHARI" omitted	62.50	
45	A1	10c dp grn & gray grn	10	10
46	A1	10c red org & bl ('25)	20	20
47	A1	15c sal & dl bl	30	30
48	A1	15c sal & dl bl (Bl) ('26)	30	30
49	A1	20c choc & sal (Bl)	28	28

On Nos. 41-49 the color in ( ) refers to the overprint "Afrique Equatoriale Francaise."

AFRIQUE EQUATORIALE FRANÇAISE

50	A2	25c vio & sal (Bl)	20	20
a.		Imperf.		
51	A2	30c rose & pale rose (Bl)	5	5
52	A2	30c choc & red ('25)	20	20
a.		"OUBANGUI CHARI" omitted	65.00	
53	A2	30c dk grn & grn ('27)	40	40
54	A2	35c vio & grn (Bl)	15	15
a.		"OUBANGUI CHARI" omitted		
55	A2	40c ind & vio (Bl)	25	25
56	A2	45c choc & vio (Bl)	28	28
57	A2	50c dk bl & pale bl (R)	15	15
58	A2	50c gray & bl vio ('25) (R)	50	50
59	A2	60c on 75c dk vio, *pnksh* (R)	15	15
60	A2	65c org brn & bl ('28)	55	55
61	A2	75c choc & sal (Bl)	28	28
62	A2	75c dp bl & lt bl ('25) (R)	20	20
a.		"OUBANGUI CHARI" omitted	65.00	
63	A2	75c rose & dk brn ('28)	55	55
64	A2	90c brn red & pink ('30)	2.25	2.25
65	A3	1fr grn & ind (Bk + Bl)	25	25
66	A3	1fr grn & ind (R + Bl)	20	20
67	A3	1.10fr bis & bl ('28)	80	80
68	A3	1.25fr mag & lt grn ('33)	2.25	2.25
69	A3	1.50fr ultra & bl ('30)	2.50	2.50
70	A3	1.75fr dk brn & dp buff ('33)	3.25	3.25
71	A3	2fr grn & red	35	35
a.		"OUBANGUI CHARI" omitted	550.00	375.00
72	A3	3fr red vio ('30)	2.25	2.25
73	A3	5fr grn & ol brn (Bl)	1.40	1.40
		Nos. 41-73 (33)	20.84	20.84

On Nos. 65, 66 the first overprint color refers to OUBANGUI CHARI

Types of 1924 Issue Surcharged with New Values in Black or Red.

1925-26

74	A3	65c on 1fr vio & ol	60	55
a.		"65" omitted	50.00	
75	A3	85c on 1fr vio & ol	60	55
a.		"AFRIQUE EQUATORIALE FRANCAISE" omitted	57.50	
b.		Double surch.	65.00	
76	A3	1.25fr on 1fr dk bl & ultra (R) ('26)	40	35
a.		"1f25" omitted	65.00	65.00

Bars cover old denomination on No. 76.

Types of 1924 Issue Surcharged with New Values and Bars.

1927

77	A2	90c on 75c brn red & rose red	55	45
78	A3	1.50fr on 1fr ultra & bl	42	45
79	A3	3fr on 5fr org brn & dl red	90	70
80	A3	10fr on 5fr ver & vio	7.00	6.50
81	A3	20fr on 5fr vio & gray	10.00	9.00
		Nos. 77-81 (5)	18.87	17.10

Colonial Exposition Issue

Common Design Types

1931 **Engr.** *Perf. 12½*

Name of Country Typo. in Black

82	CD70	40c dp grn	1.60	1.60
83	CD71	50c violet	1.60	1.60
84	CD72	90c red org	1.60	1.60
a.		Imperforate	37.50	
85	CD73	1fr dl bl	1.60	1.60

SEMI-POSTAL STAMPS

Regular Issue of 1915 Surcharged

1916 **Unwmk.** *Perf. 14x13½*

Chalky Paper

B1	A1	10c + 5c car & bl	90	90
a.		Inverted surch.	40.00	40.00
b.		Double surcharge	40.00	40.00
c.		Double surcharge, one inverted	55.00	55.00
d.		Vertical surcharge	40.00	40.00
e.		No period under "C"	5.75	5.75

Regular Issue of 1915 Surcharged in Carmine

B2	A1	10c + 5c car & bl	28	28

POSTAGE DUE STAMPS

OUBANGUI-CHARI

Postage Due Stamps of France Overprinted

A. E. F.

1928 **Unwmk.** *Perf. 14x13½*

J1	D2	5c lt bl	60	60
J2	D2	10c gray brn	60	60
J3	D2	20c ol grn	60	60
J4	D2	25c brt rose	60	60
J5	D2	30c lt red	60	60
J6	D2	45c bl grn	60	60
J7	D2	50c brn vio	80	80
J8	D2	60c yel brn	1.10	1.10
J9	D2	1fr red brn	1.20	1.20
J10	D2	2fr org red	1.90	1.90
J11	D2	3fr brt vio	1.90	1.90
		Nos. J1-J11 (11)	10.50	10.50

Landscape — D3

Emile Gentil — D4

1930 **Typo.**

J12	D3	5c dp bl & ol	32	32
J13	D3	10c dk red & brn	45	45
J14	D3	20c grn & brn	55	55
J15	D3	25c lt bl & brn	55	55
J16	D3	30c bis brn & Prus bl	80	80
J17	D3	45c Prus bl & ol	1.10	1.10
J18	D3	50c red vio & brn	2.25	2.25
J19	D3	60c gray lil & bl blk	2.50	2.50
J20	D4	1fr bis brn & bl blk	1.00	1.00
J21	D4	2fr vio & brn	1.40	1.40
J22	D4	3fr dp red & brn	2.50	2.50
		Nos. J12-J22 (11)	13.42	13.42

Stamps of Ubangi-Shari were replaced in 1936 by those of French Equatorial Africa.

The Scott Catalogue value is a retail price, what you could expect to pay for the stamp in a grade of Fine-Very Fine. The value listed is a reference which reflects recent actual dealer selling price.

UKRAINE

LOCATION — In southwestern Russia, bordering on the Black Sea.
GOVT. — Republic
AREA — 170,998 sq. mi.
POP. — 31,901,400 (1933)
CAPITAL — Kiev

Following the collapse of the Russian Empire, a national assembly met at Kiev and formed the Ukrainian National Republic. On July 6, 1923, the Ukraine joined the Soviet Union and since that time the postage stamps of Soviet Russia have been in use.

200 Shagiv = 100 Kopecks = 1 Ruble (Karbovanetz)

100 Shagiv = 1 Grivna

Stamps of Russia Overprinted in Violet, Black, Blue, Red or Green

This trident-shaped device was taken from the arms of the Grand Duke Vladimir and adopted as the device of the Ukrainian Republic. The overprint was handstamped, typographed or lithographed. It was applied in various cities in the Ukraine and there are numerous types. Values are for the most common types.

On Stamps of 1902-03

1918 Wmk. 168 ***Perf. 13½***

1	A12	3½r blk & gray	13.00	16.00
2	A12	7r blk & yel	10.00	13.00

On Stamps of 1909-18
Lozenges of Varnish on Face

Perf. 14, 14½x15

Unwmk.

3	A14	1k orange	5	5
4	A14	2k green	5	5
5	A14	3k red	5	5
6	A15	4k carmine	5	5
7	A14	5k claret	5	5
8	A14	7k lt bl	10	25
9	A15	10k dk bl	10	5
10	A11	14k bl & rose	10	25
11	A11	15k red brn & bl	5	5
12	A8	20k bl & car	5	5
13	A11	25k grn & gray vio	25	30
14	A11	35k red brn & grn	5	5
15	A8	50k vio & grn	5	5
16	A11	70k brn & org	5	5

Perf. 13½

17	A9	1r lt brn, brn & org	5	30
18	A12	3½r mar & lt grn	32	85
19	A13	5r dk bl, grn & pale bl	6.50	*20.00*
20	A12	7r dk grn & pink	2.75	4.50
21	A13	10r scar, yel & gray	4.50	6.00
		Nos. 3-21 (19)	15.17	*33.00*

On Stamps of 1917

Perf. 14, 14½x15

41	A14	10k on 7k lt bl	5	5
42	A11	20k on 14k bl & rose	5	5

On Stamps of 1917-18

Imperf.

43	A14	1k orange	5	5
44	A14	2k gray grn	5	5
45	A14	3k red	5	5
46	A15	4k carmine	10	10
47	A14	5k claret	20	35
51	A11	15k red brn & bl	5	5
52	A8	20k bl & car	20	*60*
54	A11	35k red brn & grn	5	5
55	A8	50k vio & grn	16	32
56	A11	70k brn & org	5	10
57	A9	1r pale brn, brn & red org	5	5
58	A12	3½r mar & lt grn	9	*60*
59	A13	5r dk bl, grn & pale bl	12	16
60	A12	7r dk grn & pink	30	42
61	A13	10r scar, yel & gray	13.00	13.00

The trident overprint was applied by favor to Russia Nos. 88-104, 110-111, the Romanov issue. It also exists on Russia No. 127, the 25k of 1917.

Republic's Trident Emblem A1

Ukrainian Peasant A2

Ukrainian Girl — A3

Trident — A4

Inscription of Value — A5

1918 Thin Paper Typo. ***Imperf.***

62	A1	10sh buff	10	12
63	A2	20sh brown	10	12
64	A3	30sh ultra	10	12
a.		30sh bl	65	1.25
65	A4	40sh green	10	12
66	A5	50sh red	10	12
		Nos. 62-66 (5)	50	60

The stamps of this issue exist perforated or pin-perforated unofficially.

Thin Cardboard Inscriptions on Back

1918 ***Perf. 11½***

67	A1	10sh buff	1.25
68	A2	20sh brown	1.25
69	A3	30sh ultra	2.00
70	A4	40sh green	1.25
a.		Imperf.	22.50
71	A5	50sh red	1.25
a.		Imperf.	22.50

Nos. 67 to 71 were intended to be used as paper money but they were occasionally used for postage.

Nos. 62 and 66 Surcharged **35 к.**

1919 Unwmk. ***Imperf.***

72	A1	35k on 10sh buff	4.50	6.50
73	A5	70k on 50sh red	14.00	20.00
a.		Surch. invtd.	32.50	

Some authorities state that Nos. 72-73 were issued by the South Russia government of Gen. Anton Denikin.

A6

1919 **Litho.**

74	A6	20gr red & grn	2.75	*8.25*

Кур'єрсько польова Пошта. 10 Гривень

a

b

Nos. 62-66 surcharged "a" and "b" are of private origin.

Югъ Россіи.

Ukraine stamps of 1918-10, 20, 30 and 50sh-overprinted diagonally as above ("South Russia") are believed to be of private origin.

Р. О. П. и Т.

This overprint (in two sizes) was privately applied to stamps of Russian Offices in Turkey. The overprinted stamps were not issued.

A lithographed set of 14 stamps (1gr to 200gr) of these types, perf. 11½, was prepared in 1920, but never placed in use. Value, set $1.

All values exist imperf., some with inverted centers.

SEMI-POSTAL STAMPS

Ukrainian Soviet Socialist Republic

"Famine" — SP1

Taras H. Shevchenko SP2

"Death" Stalking Peasant — SP3

"Ukraine" Distributing Food — SP4

Perf. 14½x13½, 13½x14½

1923, June Litho. Unwmk.

B1	SP1	10k + 10k gray bl & blk	32	*1.25*
a.		Imperf., pair	40.00	40.00
B2	SP2	20k + 20k vio brn & org brn	32	*1.25*
a.		Imperf., pair	40.00	40.00
B3	SP3	90k + 30k db & blk, *straw*	32	*1.25*
a.		Imperf., pair	40.00	40.00
B4	SP4	150k+ 50k red brn & blk	32	*1.25*
a.		Imperf., pair	40.00	40.00

The values of these stamps are in karbovanetz which are the rubles of the Ukraine

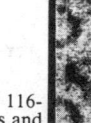

Ukraine stamps can be mounted in Scott's Soviet Republics Part I Album.

Wmk. 116- Crosses and Circles

Wmk. 116
Same Colors

B5	SP1	10k + 10k	*22.50*	*27.50*
B6	SP2	20k + 20k	*22.50*	*27.50*
a.		Imperf., pair		
B7	SP3	90k + 30k	*22.50*	*27.50*
B8	SP4	150k + 50k	*22.50*	*27.50*

UPPER SENEGAL AND NIGER

LOCATION — In Northwest Africa, north of French Guinea and Ivory Coast.
GOVT. — A former French Colony.
AREA — 617,600 sq. mi.
POP. — 2,474,142
CAPITAL — Bamako

In 1921 the name of this colony was changed to French Sudan and postage stamps so inscribed were placed in use.

100 Centimes = 1 Franc

Gen. Louis Faidherbe — A1

Oil Palms — A2

Dr. N. Eugene Ballay — A3

Perf. 14x13½

1906-07 Unwmk. Typo.

Name of Colony in Red or Blue

1	A1	1c slate	80	80
2	A1	2c brown	80	80
3	A1	4c brn, *gray bl*	80	80
4	A1	5c green	2.00	1.40
5	A1	10c car (B)	2.00	1.00
6	A1	15c vio ('07)	2.00	1.60
7	A2	20c bluish gray	2.50	2.40
8	A2	25c bl, *pnksh*	8.00	2.00
9	A2	30c vio brn, *pnksh*	3.25	2.50
10	A2	35c blk, *yellow*	2.00	1.60
11	A2	40c car, *az* (B)	3.50	3.25
12	A2	45c brn, *grnsh*	4.50	4.00
13	A2	50c dp vio	4.00	3.00
14	A2	75c bl, *org*	4.75	4.75
15	A3	1fr blk, *az*	12.50	7.50
16	A3	2fr bl, *pink*	24.00	22.50
17	A3	5fr car, *straw* (B)	55.00	42.50
		Nos. 1-17 (17)	132.40	102.40

Camel with Rider — A4

1914-17 ***Perf. 13½x14***

18	A4	1c brn vio & vio	5	5
19	A4	2c gray & brn vio	5	5
20	A4	4c blk & bl	10	10
21	A4	5c yel grn & bl grn	12	12
22	A4	10c red org & rose	1.00	80
23	A4	15c choc & org ('17)	60	28

24	A4	20c brn vio & blk	60	28
25	A4	25c ultra & bl	60	45
26	A4	30c ol brn & brn	60	40
27	A4	35c car rose & vio	1.20	80
28	A4	40c gray & car rose	65	45
29	A4	45c bl & ol brn	65	55
30	A4	50c blk & grn	65	55
31	A4	75c org & ol brn	80	65
32	A4	1fr brn & brn vio	1.00	80
33	A4	2fr grn & bl	1.20	1.20
34	A4	5fr vio & blk	5.75	4.00
		Nos. 18-34 (17)	15.62	11.53

SEMI-POSTAL STAMP

Regular Issue of 1914 Surcharged in Red ✚5c

1915 Unwmk. *Perf. 13½x14*

B1	A4	10c + 5c red org & rose	40	40

POSTAGE DUE STAMPS

Natives — D1

D2

1906 Unwmk. Typo. *Perf. 14x13½*

J1	D1	5c green, *grnsh*	1.50	1.25
J2	D1	10c red brown	3.75	2.75
J3	D1	15c dark blue	5.25	4.00
J4	D1	20c blk, *yellow*	5.75	3.00
J5	D1	50c violet	11.25	10.50
J6	D1	60c blk, *buff*	7.00	7.00
J7	D1	1fr blk, *pinkish*	17.00	15.00
		Nos. J1-J7 (7)	51.50	43.50

1914

J8	D2	5c green	80	80
J9	D2	10c rose	80	80
J10	D2	15c gray	90	90
J11	D2	20c brown	90	90
J12	D2	30c blue	1.65	1.65
J13	D2	50c black	90	90
J14	D2	60c orange	4.50	4.50
J15	D2	1fr violet	4.50	4.50
		Nos. J8-J15 (8)	14.95	14.95

Stamps of Upper Senegal and Niger were superceded in 1921 by those of French Sudan.

UPPER SILESIA

LOCATION — Formerly in eastern Germany and prior to World War I a part of Germany.

A plebiscite held under the terms of the Treaty of Versailles failed to determine the status of the country, the voting resulting about equally in favor of Germany and Poland. Accordingly, the League of Nations divided the territory between Germany and Poland.

100 Pfennig = 1 Mark
100 Fennigi = 1 Marka

Plebiscite Issues

A1

Perf. 14x13½

1920, Feb. 20 Typo. Unwmk.

1	A1	2½pf slate	30	35
2	A1	3pf brown	30	35
3	A1	5pf green	14	20
4	A1	10pf dl red	32	40
5	A1	15pf violet	14	20
6	A1	20pf blue	14	20
a.		Imperf., pair	165.00	175.00
7	A1	50pf vio brn	3.25	3.50
8	A1	1m claret	3.00	3.25
9	A1	5m orange	3.00	3.25
		Nos. 1-9 (9)	10.59	11.70

Black Surcharge

5 Pf. I — 5 Pf. II — 5 Pf. III — 5 Pf. IV

10	A1	5pf on 15pf vio (I)	8.25	*16.00*
a.		Type II	10.00	*20.00*
b.		Type III	10.00	*20.00*
c.		Type IV	8.25	*16.00*
11	A1	5pf on 20pf bl (I)	12	20
a.		Type II	20	*50*
b.		Type III	20	40
c.		Type IV	14	*50*

Red Surcharge

10 Pf. I — 10 Pf. II — 10 Pf. III — 10 Pf. IV

12	A1	10pf on 20pf bl (I)	12	22
a.		Type II	12	22
b.		Type III	12	22
c.		Type IV	12	22
d.		Imperf.	25.00	

Black Surcharge

50 Pf. I — 50 Pf. II — 50 Pf. III — 50 Pf. IV — 50 Pf. V

13	A1	50pf on 5m org (I)	13.00	20.00
a.		Type II	13.00	20.00
b.		Type III	13.00	20.00
c.		Type IV	13.00	20.00
d.		Type V	25.00	40.00

Nos. 10-13 are found with many varieties including surcharges inverted, double and double inverted.

Dove with Olive Branch Flying over Silesian Terrain — A2

A3

1920, Mar. 26 Typo. *Perf. 13½x14*

15	A2	2½pf gray	18	7
16	A2	3pf red brn	20	7
17	A2	5pf green	12	7
18	A2	10pf dl red	12	7
19	A2	15pf violet	12	7
20	A2	20pf blue	12	7
21	A2	25pf dk brn	18	7
22	A2	30pf orange	12	7
23	A2	40pf ol grn	12	7

Perf. 14x13½

1920, Mar. 26 Typo *Perf. 13½x14*

24	A3	50pf gray	12	7
25	A3	60pf blue	20	8
26	A3	75pf dp grn	65	35
27	A3	80pf red brn	52	30
28	A3	1m claret	30	8
29	A3	2m dk brn	30	20
30	A3	3m violet	52	20
31	A3	5m orange	1.25	75
		Nos. 15-31 (17)	5.14	2.66

Nos. 18-28 Overprinted in Black or Red — Plébiscite 20 mars 1921.

1921, Mar. 20

32	A2	10pf dl red	1.65	*3.75*
33	A2	15pf violet	1.65	*3.75*
34	A2	20pf blue	2.25	*6.00*
35	A2	25pf dk brn (R)	4.00	*10.00*
36	A2	30pf orange	4.00	*10.00*
37	A2	40pf ol grn (R)	4.00	*10.00*

Overprinted — Plébiscite 20 mars 1921.

38	A3	50pf gray (R)	4.00	*10.00*
39	A3	60pf blue	5.75	*10.00*
40	A3	75pf dp grn	5.75	*12.00*
41	A3	80pf red brn	5.75	*14.00*
42	A3	1m claret	8.75	*18.00*
		Nos. 32-42 (11)	47.55	*107.50*

Inverted or double overprints exist on Nos. 32-33, 35-40. Counterfeit overprints exist.

Type of 1920 and Surcharged — 10 M

1922, Mar.

45	A3	4m on 60pf ol grn	60	*85*
46	A3	10m on 75pf red	90	*1.50*
47	A3	20m on 80pf org	4.50	*8.00*

Stamps of the above design were a private issue not recognized by the Inter-Allied Commission of Government.

OFFICIAL STAMPS

German Stamps of 1905-20 Handstamped in Blue — C.I.H.S.

1920, Feb. Wmk. 125 *Perf. 14, 14½*

On Stamps of 1906-19

O1	A22	2pf gray	1.10	1.25
O3	A22	2½pf gray	55	65
O4	A16	3pf brown	55	65
O5	A16	5pf green	55	65
a.		Red handstamp	10.00	14.00
O6	A22	7½pf orange	55	65
O7	A16	10pf car rose	55	65
O8	A22	15pf dk vio	55	65
a.		Red handstamp	6.50	10.00
O9	A16	20pf bl vio	55	65
a.		Red handstamp	6.50	10.00
O10	A16	25pf org & blk, *yel*	5.25	6.50
O11	A16	30pf org & blk, *buff*	55	65
O12	A22	35pf red brn	55	65
O13	A16	40pf lake & blk	55	65
a.		Red handstamp	20.00	30.00
O14	A16	50pf vio & blk, *buff*	55	65
O15	A16	60pf magenta	55	65
O16	A16	75pf grn & blk	55	65
a.		Red handstamp	20.00	30.00
O17	A16	80pf lake & blk, *rose*	6.50	8.00
O18	A17	1m car rose	1.10	1.25
O19	A21	2m gray bl	5.25	6.50

On National Assembly Stamps of 1919-20.

O25	A23	10pf car rose	90	1.10
O26	A24	15pf choc & bl	1.65	2.00
a.		Red handstamp	1.10	1.25
O27	A25	25pf grn & red	3.25	4.00
O28	A25	30pf red vio & red	2.50	3.00

On Semi-Postal Stamps of 1919

O30	A16	10pf + 5pf car	6.50	8.00
O31	A22	15pf + 5pf dk vio	6.50	8.00
		Nos. O1-O31 (24)	47.65	58.05

Values of Nos. O1-O31 are for reprints made with a second type of handstamp differing in minor details from the original (example: period after "S" is round instead of the earlier triangular form). Originals are scarce. Counterfeits exist.

Germany No. 65C with this handstamp is considered bogus by experts.

Local Official Stamps of Germany, 1920, Overprinted — C. G. H. S.

1920, Apr. *Perf. 14*

O32	LO2	5pf green	18	24
O33	LO3	10pf carmine	18	24
O34	LO4	15pf vio brn	18	24
O35	LO5	20pf dp ultra	18	24
O36	LO6	30pf org, *buff*	18	24
O37	LO7	50pf vio, *buff*	40	40
O38	LO8	1m red, *buff*	4.00	5.75
		Nos. O32-O38 (7)	5.30	7.35

Same Overprint on Official Stamps of Germany, 1920-21

1920-21

O39	O1	5pf green	65	1.65
O40	O2	10pf carmine	5	8
O41	O3	15pf vio brn	5	8
O42	O4	20pf dp ultra	5	8
O43	O5	30pf org, *buff*	5	8
O44	O6	40pf car rose	5	8
O45	O7	50pf vio, *buff*	5	8
O46	O8	60pf red brn	5	8
O47	O9	1m red, *buff*	5	8
O48	O10	1.25m dk bl, *yel*	5	8
O49	O11	2m dk bl	3.50	5.50
O50	O12	5m brn, *yel*	8	15

1922, Feb. Wmk. Network. (126)

O51	O11	2m dk bl	8	15
		Nos. O39-O51 (13)	4.76	8.17

This overprint is found both horizontal and vertical, reading up or down. It also exists on most values inverted, double and double, one inverted.

Upper Silesia stamps can be mounted in Scott's Germany Part II Album.

UPPER VOLTA

Burkina Faso

LOCATION — Northwestern Africa, north of Ghana.
GOVT. — Republic
AREA — 105,869 sq. mi.
POP. — 6,695,500 (est. 1984)
CAPITAL — Ouagadougou

In 1919 the French territory of Upper Volta was detached from the southern section of Upper Senegal and Niger and made a separate colony. In 1933 the colony was divided among its neighbors: French Sudan, Ivory Coast, and Niger Territory. The Republic of Upper Volta was proclaimed December 11, 1958; the name was changed to Burkina Faso on August 4, 1984.

100 Centimes = 1 Franc

Catalogue values for unused stamps in this country are for Never Hinged items, beginning with Scott 70 in the regular postage section, Scott B1 in the semi-postal section, Scott C1 in the airpost section, Scott J21 in the postage due section, and Scott O1 in the official section.

Stamps and Types of Upper Senegal and Niger, 1914-17, Overprinted in Black or Red — HAUTE-VOLTA

1920-28 Unwmk. *Perf. 13½x14.*

1	A4	1c brn vio & vio	5	5
2	A4	2c gray & brn vio (R)	5	5
3	A4	4c blk & bl	5	5
4	A4	5c yel grn & bl grn	25	12
5	A4	5c ol brn & dk brn ('22)	5	5
6	A4	10c red org & rose	38	32
7	A4	10c yel grn & bl grn ('22)	5	5
8	A4	10c cl & bl ('25)	22	22
a.		Overprint omitted	80.00	
9	A4	15c choc & org	38	28
10	A4	20c brn vio & blk (R)	55	50
11	A4	25c ultra & bl	55	28
12	A4	25c blk & bl grn ('22)	40	40
a.		Overprint omitted	65.00	
13	A4	30c ol brn & brn (R)	90	62
14	A4	30c red org & rose ('22)	35	35
15	A4	30c vio & brn red ('25)	35	35
16	A4	30c dl grn & bl grn ('27)	60	45
17	A4	35c car rose & vio	40	28
18	A4	40c gray & car rose	40	32
19	A4	45c bl & brn (R)	32	20
20	A4	50c blk & grn	1.40	1.00
21	A4	50c ultra & bl ('22)	12	12

22	A4	50c red org & bl ('25)	35	35
23	A4	60c org red ('26)	12	12
24	A4	65c bis & pale bl ('28)	60	45
25	A4	75c org & brn	28	28
26	A4	1fr brn & brn vio	55	40
27	A4	2fr grn & bl	80	60
28	A4	5fr vio & blk (R)	2.00	1.60
		Nos. 1-28 (28)	12.52	9.86

No. 9 Surcharged in Various Colors **0,01 ═ 0,01**

1922

29	A4	0,01c on 15c (Bk)	40	40
a.		Double surcharge	50.00	50.00
30	A4	0,02c on 15c (Bl)	40	40
31	A4	0,05c on 15c (R)	40	40

Type of 1920 Surcharged **60 ═ 60**

1922

32	A4	60c on 75c vio, *pnksh*	35	35

Stamps and Types of 1920 Surcharged with New Value and Bars.

1924-27

33	A4	25c on 2fr grn & bl	40	40
34	A4	25c on 5fr vio & blk	40	40
35	A4	65c on 45c bl & brn ('25)	45	45
36	A4	85c on 75c org & brn ('25)	62	62
37	A4	90c on 75c brn red & sal pink ('27)	65	65
38	A4	1.25fr on 1fr dp bl & lt bl (R) ('26)	40	40
39	A4	1.50fr on 1fr dp bl & ultra ('27)	1.10	1.10
40	A4	3fr on 5fr dl red & brn org ('27)	1.40	1.40
41	A4	10fr on 5fr ol grn & lil rose ('27)	6.50	6.50
42	A4	20fr on 5fr org brn & vio ('27)	9.00	9.00
		Nos. 33-42 (10)	20.92	20.92

Hausa Chief — A5

Hausa Woman — A6

Hausa Warrior A7

1928 Typo. *Perf. 13½x14*

43	A5	1c ind & grn	5	5
44	A5	2c brn & lil	5	5
45	A5	4c blk & yel	12	12
46	A5	5c ind & gray bl	16	16
47	A5	10c ind & pink	45	45
48	A5	15c brn & bl	80	80
49	A5	20c brn & grn	80	80
50	A6	25c brn & yel	1.00	1.00
51	A6	30c dp grn & grn	1.00	1.00
52	A6	40c blk & pink	1.00	1.00
53	A6	45c brn & bl	1.00	1.00
54	A6	50c blk & grn	1.00	1.00
55	A6	65c ind & bl	1.40	1.40
56	A6	75c blk & lil	1.00	1.00
57	A6	90c brn red & lil	1.00	1.00

Perf. 14x13½

58	A7	1fr brn & grn	1.00	1.00
59	A7	1.10fr ind & lil	1.00	1.00
60	A7	1.50fr ultra & grysh	1.60	1.60
61	A7	2fr blk & bl	1.90	1.90
62	A7	3fr brn & yel	2.00	2.00
63	A7	5fr brn & lil	2.00	2.00
64	A7	10fr blk & grn	8.00	8.00
65	A7	20fr blk & pink	12.00	12.00
		Nos. 43-65 (23)	40.33	40.33

Foreign postal stationery (stamped envelopes, postal cards and air letter sheets) lies beyond the scope of this Catalogue, which is limited to adhesive postage stamps.

Colonial Exposition Issue
Common Design Types

1931 Engr. *Perf. 12½*
Country Name Typo. in Black

66	CD70	40c dp grn	1.50	1.50
67	CD71	50c violet	1.50	1.50
68	CD72	90c red org	1.50	1.50
69	CD73	1.50fr dl bl	2.00	2.00

Common Design Types pictured in section at front of book.

Catalogue values for unused stamps in this section, from this point to the end of the section, are for Never Hinged items.

Republic

President Ouezzin Coulibaly A8

Deer Mask and Deer A9

1959 Unwmk. Engr. *Perf. 13*

70	A8	25fr blk & mag	25	14

1st anniv. of the proclamation of the Republic; Ouezzin Coulibaly, Council President, who died in December, 1958.

Imperforates
Most Upper Volta stamps from 1959 onward exist imperforate in issued and trial colors, and also in small presentation sheets in issued colors.

1960

Animal Masks: 1fr, 2fr, 4fr, Wart hog. 5fr, 6fr, 8fr, Monkey. 10fr, 15fr, 20fr, Buffalo. 25fr, Coba (antelope). 30fr, 40fr, 50fr, Elephant. 60fr, 85fr, Secretary bird.

71	A9	30c rose & vio	5	5
72	A9	40c buff & dp cl	5	5
73	A9	50c bl grn & gray ol	5	5
74	A9	1fr red, blk & red brn	5	5
75	A9	2fr emer, yel grn & dk grn	5	5
76	A9	4fr bl, vio & ind	5	5
77	A9	5fr ol bis, red & brn	6	5
78	A9	6fr grnsh bl & vio brn	6	5
79	A9	8fr org & red brn	8	6
80	A9	10fr lt yel grn & plum	10	8
81	A9	15fr org, ultra & brn	12	10
82	A9	20fr grn & ultra	18	10
83	A9	25fr bl, emer & dp cl	20	10
84	A9	30fr dk bl grn, blk & brn	25	10
85	A9	40fr ultra, ind & dk car	30	15
86	A9	50fr brt pink, brn & grn	35	18
87	A9	60fr org brn & bl	45	25
88	A9	85fr gray ol & dk bl	65	32
		Nos. 71-88 (18)	3.10	1.84

C.C.T.A. Issue
Common Design Type

1960 Engr. *Perf. 13*

89	CD106	25fr vio bl & sl	35	35

Emblem of the Entente — A9a

Pres. Maurice Yameogo — A10

1960 Photo. *Perf. 13x13½*

90	A9a	25fr multi	40	35

Council of the Entente.

1960, May 1 Engr. *Perf. 13*

91	A10	25fr dk vio brn & sl	25	16

Flag, Village and Couple — A11

1960, Aug. 5 Unwmk. *Perf. 13*

92	A11	25fr red brn, blk & red	35	25

Proclamation of independence, Aug. 5, 1960.

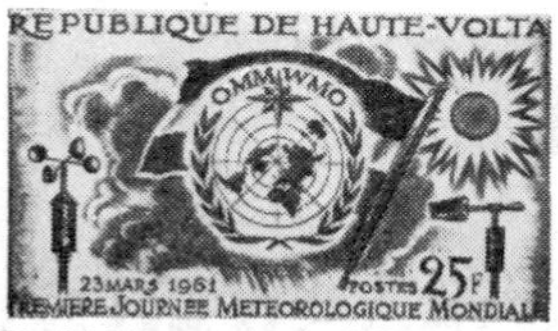

World Meteorological Organization Emblem — A12

1961, May 4

93	A12	25fr blk, bl & red	30	25

First World Meteorological Day.

Arms of Republic — A13

1961, Dec. 8 Photo. *Perf. 12x12½*

94	A13	25fr multi	25	25

The 1961 independence celebrations.

WMO Emblem, Weather Station and Sorghum Grain — A14

1962, Mar. 23 Unwmk. *Perf. 13*

95	A14	25fr dk bl, emer & brn	30	25

UN 2nd World Meteorological Day, Mar. 23.

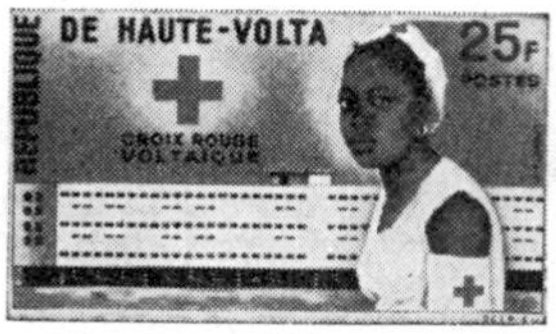

Hospital and Nurse — A15

1962, June 23 *Perf. 13x12*

96	A15	25fr multi	35	35

Founding of Upper Volta Red Cross.

Buffalos at Water Hole — A16

Designs: 10fr, Lions (horiz.). 15fr, Defassa waterbuck. 25fr, Arly reservation (horiz.). 50fr, Diapaga reservation (horiz.). 85fr, Buffon's kob.

Perf. 12½x12, 12x12½
1962, June 30 Engr.

97	A16	5fr sep, bl & grn	10	7
98	A16	10fr red brn, grn & yel	16	10
99	A16	15fr sep, grn & yel	25	16
100	A16	25fr vio brn, bl & grn	45	20
101	A16	50fr vio brn, bl & grn	80	55
102	A16	85fr red brn, bl & grn	1.20	80
		Nos. 97-102 (6)	2.96	1.88

Abidjan Games Issue
Common Design Type

Designs: 20fr, Soccer. 25fr, Bicycling. 85fr, Boxing (all horiz.).

1962, July 21 Photo. *Perf. 12½x12*

103	CD109	20fr multi	35	25
104	CD109	25fr multi	40	35
105	CD109	85fr multi	90	55

African-Malgache Union Issue
Common Design Type

1962, Sept. 8 Unwmk.

106	CD110	30fr red, bluish grn & gold	70	65

Weather Map and UN Emblem A17

1963, Mar. 23 *Perf. 12x12½*

107	A17	70fr multi	70	50

3rd World Meteorological Day, Mar. 23.

Friendship Games, Dakar, Apr. 11-21 — A18

Centenary Emblem and Globe — A20

Amaryllis A19

1963, Apr. 11 Engr. *Perf. 13*

108	A18	20fr Basketball	22	14
109	A18	25fr Discus	25	14
110	A18	50fr Judo	55	25

1963 Photo.

Flowers: 50c, Hibiscus. 1fr, Oldenlandia grandiflora. 1.50fr, Rose moss (portulaca). 2fr, Tobacco. 4fr, Morning glory. 5fr, Striga senegalensis. 6fr, Cowpea. 8fr, Lepidagathis heudelotiana. 10fr, Spurge. 25fr, Argyreia nervosa. 30fr, Rangoon creeper. 40fr, Water lily. 50fr, White plumeria. 60fr, Crotalaria retusa. 85fr, Hibiscus. Nos. 111-119 are vertical.

111 A19 50c multi 5 5
112 A19 1fr multi 5 5
113 A19 1.50fr multi 5 5
114 A19 2fr multi 5 5
115 A19 4fr multi 5 5
116 A19 5fr multi 7 5
117 A19 6fr multi 8 7
118 A19 8fr multi 12 10
119 A19 10fr multi 16 12
120 A19 15fr multi 20 15
121 A19 25fr multi 30 16
122 A19 30fr multi 35 20
123 A19 40fr multi 40 30
124 A19 50fr multi 55 38
125 A19 60fr multi 65 42
126 A19 85fr multi 90 55
Nos. 111-126 (16) 4.03 2.75

1963, Oct. 21 Unwmk. *Perf. 12*
127 A20 25fr multi 50 40

Centenary of International Red Cross.

Scroll — A21

1963, Dec. 10 Photo. *Perf. 13x12½*
128 A21 25fr dp cl, gold & bl 30 20

15th anniv. of the Universal Declaration of Human Rights.

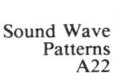

Sound Wave Patterns A22

1964, Jan. 16 *Perf. 12½x13*
129 A22 25fr multi 25 20

Upper Volta's admission to the ITU.

Barograph and WMO Emblem A23

1964, Mar. 23 Engr. *Perf. 13*
130 A23 50fr dk car rose, grn & bl 55 40

4th World Meteorological Day, Mar. 23.

World Connected by Letters and Carrier Pigeon — A24

Design: 60fr, World connected by letters and jet plane.

1964, Mar. 29 Photo. *Perf. 13x12*
131 A24 25fr gray brn & ultra 25 20
132 A24 60fr gray brn & org 60 42

Upper Volta's admission to the UPU.

IQSY Emblem and Seasonal Allegories — A25

1964, Aug. 17 Engr. *Perf. 13*
133 A25 30fr grn, ocher & car 35 25

International Quiet Sun Year.

Cooperation Issue
Common Design Type

1964, Nov. 7 Unwmk. *Perf. 13*
134 CD119 70fr dl bl grn, dk brn & car 65 42

Hotel Independance, Ouagadougou — A26

1964, Dec. 11 Litho. *Perf. 12½x13*
135 A26 25fr multi 1.00 35

Pigmy Long-tailed Sunbird A27

Comoe Waterfall A28

1965, Mar. 1 Photo. *Perf. 13x12½*
Size: 22x36mm
136 A27 10fr shown 20 16
137 A27 15fr Olive-bellied Sunbird 25 20
138 A27 20fr Splendid Sunbird 40 25

See No. C20.

1965 Engr. *Perf. 13*

Design: 25fr, Great Waterfall of Banfora (horiz.).

139 A28 5fr yel grn, bl & red brn 8 7
140 A28 25fr dk red, brt bl & grn 25 16

Soccer — A29

Abraham Lincoln — A30

Designs: 25fr, Boxing gloves and ring. 70fr, Tennis rackets, ball and net.

1965, July 15 Unwmk. *Perf. 13*
141 A29 15fr brn, red & dk grn 16 14
142 A29 25fr pale org, bl & brn 30 20
143 A29 70fr dk car & brt grn 65 35

1st African Games, Brazzaville, July 18-25.

1965, Nov. 3 Photo. *Perf. 13x12½*
144 A30 50fr grn & multi 50 38

Centenary of death of Abraham Lincoln.

Pres. Maurice Yameogo — A31

1965, Dec. 11 Photo. *Perf. 13x12½*
145 A31 25fr multi 25 16

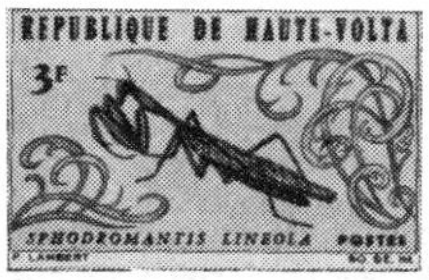
Mantis A32

Wart Hog A33

Headdress A34

1966 *Perf. 13x12½, 12½x13*
146 A33 1fr Nemopistha imperatrix 5 5
147 A33 2fr Ball python 5 5
148 A32 3fr shown 7 5
149 A32 4fr Grasshopper 7 7
150 A33 5fr shown 9 7
151 A32 6fr Scorpion 10 8
152 A33 8fr Green monkey 12 10
153 A32 10fr Dromedary 15 7
154 A33 15fr Leopard 20 10
155 A32 20fr Cape buffalo 22 16
156 A33 25fr Hippopotamus 30 16
157 A32 30fr Agama lizard 38 20
158 A33 45fr Common puff adder 55 22
159 A33 50fr Chameleon 60 35
160 A33 60fr Ugada limbata 70 42
161 A33 85fr Elephant 90 50
Nos. 146-161 (16) 4.55 2.65

1966, Apr. 9 Photo. *Perf. 13x12½*

Designs: 25fr, Plumed headdress. 60fr, Male dancer.

162 A34 20fr yel grn, choc & red 20 14
163 A34 25fr multi 25 16
164 A34 60fr org, dk brn & red 60 35

Intl. Negro Arts Festival, Dakar, Senegal, Apr. 1-24.

Pô Church A35

Design: No. 166 Bobo-Dioulasso Mosque.

1966, Apr. 15 *Perf. 12½x13*
165 A35 25fr multi 22 16
166 A35 25fr bl, cr & red brn 22 16

The Red Cross Helping the World — A36

1966, June Photo. *Perf. 13x12½*
167 A36 25fr lem, blk & car 22 14

Issued to honor the Red Cross.

Boy Scouts in Camp A37

Design: 15fr, Two Scouts on a cliff exploring the country.

1966, June 15 *Perf. 12½x13*
168 A37 10fr multi 14 8
169 A37 15fr blk, bis brn, & dl yel 16 9

Issued to honor the Boy Scouts.

Cow Receiving Injection A38

1966, Aug. 16 Photo. *Perf. 12½x13*
170 A38 25fr yel, blk & bl 25 20

Campaign against cattle plague.

Plowing with Donkey A39

Design: 30fr, Crop rotation, Kamboincé Experimental Station.

1966, Sept. 15 Photo. *Perf. 12½x13*
171 A39 25fr multi 22 14
172 A39 30fr multi 25 16

National and rural education; 3rd anniv. of the Kamboincé Experimental Station (No. 172).

UNESCO Emblem and Map of Africa A40

UNICEF Emblem and Children A41

1966, Dec. 10 Engr. *Perf. 13*
173 A40 50fr brt bl, blk & red 50 25
174 A41 50fr dk vio, dp lil & dk red 50 25

20th anniv. of UNESCO and of UNICEF.

Arms of Upper Volta — A42

Symbols of Agriculture, Industry, Men and Women — A43

1967, Jan. 2 Photo. *Perf. 12½x13*
175 A42 30fr multi 22 10

Europafrica Issue

1967, Feb. 4 Photo. *Perf. 12½*
176 A43 60fr multi 50 30

Scout Handclasp and Jamboree Emblem
A44

Design: 5fr, Jamboree emblem and Scout holding hat.

1967, June 8 Photo. *Perf. 12½x13*
177 A44 5fr multi 20 10
178 A44 20fr multi 55 40

12th Boy Scout World Jamboree, Farragut State Park, Idaho, Aug. 1-9. See No. C41.

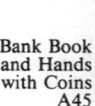

Bank Book and Hands with Coins
A45

1967, Aug. 22 Engr. *Perf. 13*
179 A45 30fr sl grn, ocher & ol 25 14

National Savings Bank.

Mailman on Bicycle — A46

1967, Oct. 15 Engr. *Perf. 13*
180 A46 30fr dk bl, emer & brn 30 16

Stamp Day.

Monetary Union Issue
Common Design Type

1967, Nov. 4 Engr. *Perf. 13*
181 CD125 30fr dk vio & dl bl 25 14

View of Nizier
A47

Designs (Olympic Emblem and): 50fr, Les Deux-Alps (vert.). 100fr, Ski lift and view of Villard-de-Lans.

1967, Nov. 28
182 A47 15fr brt bl, grn & brn 16 10
183 A47 50fr brt bl & sl grn 50 22
184 A47 100fr brt bl, grn & red 1.00 50

10th Winter Olympic Games, Grenoble, France, Feb. 6-18, 1968.

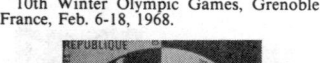

White and Black Men Holding Human Rights Emblem
A48

1968, Jan. 2 Photo. *Perf. 12½x13*
185 A48 20fr brt bl, gold & dp car 20 14
186 A48 30fr grn, gold & dp car 30 16

International Human Rights Year.

Administration School and Student — A49

1968, Feb. 2 Engr. *Perf. 13*
187 A49 30fr ol bis, Prus bl & brt grn 25 14

National School of Administration.

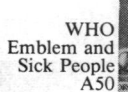

WHO Emblem and Sick People
A50

1968, Apr. 7 Engr. *Perf. 13*
188 A50 30fr ind, brt bl & car rose 30 16
189 A50 50fr brt bl, sl grn & lt brn 45 22

WHO, 20th anniversary.

Telephone Office, Bobo-Dioulasso — A51

1968, Sept. 30 Photo. *Perf. 12½x12*
190 A51 30fr multi 30 16

Opening of the automatic telephone office in Bobo-Dioulasso.

Weaver
A52

1968, Oct. 30 Engr. *Perf. 13*
Size: 36x22mm
191 A52 30fr mag, brn & ocher 30 16

See No. C58.

Grain Pouring over World, Plower and FAO Emblem — A53

1969, Jan. 7 Engr. *Perf. 13*
192 A53 30fr sl, vio bl & mar 25 14

UNFAO world food program.

Automatic Looms and ILO Emblem
A54

1969, Mar. 15 Engr. *Perf. 13*
193 A54 30fr brt grn, mar & ind 25 14

ILO, 50th anniversary.

Smith
A55

1969, Apr. 3 Engr. *Perf. 13*
Size: 36x22mm
194 A55 5fr mag & blk 10 8

See No. C64.

Blood Donor
A56

1969, May 15 Engr. *Perf. 13*
195 A56 30fr blk, bl & car 25 16

League of Red Cross Societies, 50th anniv.

Nile Pike — A57

Fish: 20fr, Nannocharax gobioides. 25fr, Hemigrammocharax polli. 55fr, Alestes luteus. 85fr, Micralestes voltae.

1969 Engr. *Perf. 13*
Size: 36x22mm
196 A57 20fr brt bl, brn & yel 30 20
197 A57 25fr sl, brn & dk brn 30 20
198 A57 30fr dk ol & blk 40 25
199 A57 55fr dk grn, yel & ol 55 42
200 A57 85fr sl brn & pink 1.10 90
Nos. 196-200,C66-C67 (7) 4.65 3.01

Development Bank Issue
Common Design Type

1969, Sept. 10 Engr. *Perf. 13*
201 CD130 30fr sl grn, grn & ocher 22 14

Millet — A58

Design: 30fr, Cotton.

1969, Oct. 30 Photo. *Perf. 12½x13*
202 A58 15fr dk brn, grn & yel 16 10
203 A58 30fr dp cl & brt bl 30 16

See Nos. C73-C74.

ASECNA Issue
Common Design Type

1969, Dec. 12 Engr. *Perf. 13*
204 CD132 100fr brown 80 50

Niadale Mask — A59

Carvings from National Museum: 30fr, Niaga. 45fr, Man and woman, Iliu Bara. 80fr, Karan Weeba figurine.

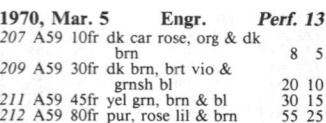

1970, Mar. 5 Engr. *Perf. 13*
207 A59 10fr dk car rose, org & dk brn 8 5
209 A59 30fr dk brn, brt vio & grnsh bl 20 10
211 A59 45fr yel grn, brn & bl 30 15
212 A59 80fr pur, rose lil & brn 55 25

African Huts and European City — A60

1970, Apr. 25 Engr. *Perf. 13*
213 A60 30fr dk brn, red & bl 25 14

Issued for Linked Cities' Day.

Mask for Nebwa Gnomo Dance
A61

Designs: 8fr, Cauris dancers (vert.). 20fr, Gourmantchés dancers (vert.). 30fr, Larlle dancers.

1970, May 7 Photo. *Perf. 13*
214 A61 5fr lt brn, vio bl & blk 7 5
215 A61 8fr org brn, car & blk 10 7
216 A61 20fr dk brn, sl grn & ocher 16 10
217 A61 30fr dp car, dk gray & brn 25 14

Education Year Emblem, Open Book and Pupils
A62

Design: 90fr, Education Year emblem, telecommunication and education symbols.

1970, May 14 *Perf. 12½x12*
218 A62 40fr blk & multi 35 20
219 A62 90fr ol & multi 65 35

International Education Year.

UPU Headquarters Issue

Abraham Lincoln, U.P.U. Headquarters and Emblem — A63

1970, May 20 Engr. *Perf. 13*
220 A63 30fr dk car rose, ind & red brn 30 16
221 A63 60fr dk bl grn, vio & red brn 50 25

See note after CD133, Common Design section.

Ship-building Industry — A64

Designs: 45fr, Chemical industry. 80fr, Electrical industry.

1970, June 15

222	A64	15fr brt pink, red brn & blk	14	8
223	A64	45fr emer, dp bl & blk	35	20
224	A64	80fr red brn, cl & blk	65	35

Hanover Fair.

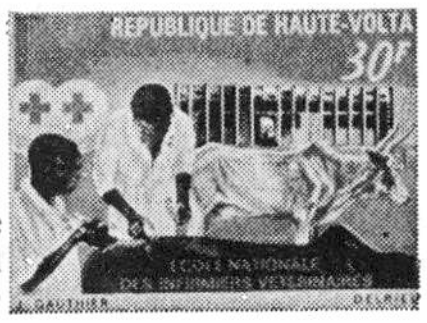

Cattle Vaccination A65

1970, June 30 **Photo.** ***Perf. 13***

225	A65	30fr Prus bl, yel & sep	30	14

National Veterinary College.

Vaccination and Red Cross — A66

1970, Aug. 28 **Engr.** ***Perf. 12½x13***

226	A66	30fr choc & car	25	16

Issued for the Upper Volta Red Cross.

Europafrica Issue

Nurse with Child, by Frans Hals — A67

Paintings: 30fr, Courtyard of a House in Delft, by Pieter de Hooch. 150fr, Christina of Denmark, by Hans Holbein. 250fr, Courtyard of the Royal Palace at Innsbruck, Austria, by Albrecht Dürer.

1970, Sept. 25 **Litho.** ***Perf. 13x14***

227	A67	25fr multi	22	14
228	A67	30fr multi	30	16
229	A67	150fr multi	1.40	65
230	A67	250fr multi	2.00	1.00

Citroen A68

Design: 40fr, Old and new Citroen cars.

1970, Oct. 16 **Engr.** ***Perf. 13***

231	A68	25fr ol brn, mar & sl grn	22	14
232	A68	40fr brt grn, plum & sl	40	20

57th Paris Automobile Salon.

Professional Training Center A69

1970, Dec. 10 **Engr.** ***Perf. 13***

233	A69	50fr grn, bis & brn	38	16

Opening of Professional Training Center under joint sponsorship of Austria and Upper Volta.

Upper Volta Arms and Soaring Bird — A70

1970, Dec. 10 **Photo.**

234	A70	30fr lt bl & multi	22	14

Tenth anniversary of independence, Dec. 11.

Political Maps of Africa — A71

1970, Dec. 14 **Litho.** ***Perf. 13½***

235	A71	50fr multi	40	20

10th anniv. of the declaration granting independence to colonial territories and countries.

Beingolo Hunting Horn — A72

Musical Instruments: 15fr, Mossi guitar (vert.). 20fr, Gourounsi flutes (vert.). 25fr, Lunga drums.

1971, Mar. 1 **Engr.** ***Perf. 13***

236	A72	5fr bl, brn & car	7	5
237	A72	15fr grn, crim rose & brn	14	8
238	A72	20fr car rose, bl & gray	16	10
239	A72	25fr brt grn, red brn & ol gray	20	14

Voltaphilex I, National Phil. Exhibition.

Four Races — A73

1971, Mar. 21 **Engr.** ***Perf. 13***

240	A73	50fr rose cl, lt grn & dk brn	40	22

Intl. year against racial discrimination.

Telephone and Globes A74

1971, May 17 **Engr.** ***Perf. 13***

241	A74	50fr brn, gray & dk pur	40	20

3rd World Telecommunications Day.

Cane Field Worker, Banfora Sugar Mill A75

Cotton and Voltex Mill Emblem A76

1971, June 24 **Photo.** ***Perf. 13***

242	A75	10fr multi	10	5
243	A76	35fr multi	25	14

Industrial development.

Gonimbrasia Hecate — A77

Butterflies and Moths: 2fr, Hamanumida daedalus. 3fr, Ophideres materna. 5fr, Danaus chyrsippus. 40fr, Hypolimnas misippus. 45fr, Danaus petiverana.

1971, June 30

244	A77	1fr bl & multi	5	5
245	A77	2fr lt lil & multi	5	5
246	A77	3fr multi	7	5
247	A77	5fr gray & multi	10	8
248	A77	40fr ocher & multi	45	22
249	A77	45fr multi	60	35
		Nos. 244-249 (6)	1.32	80

Kabuki Actor — A78

Design: 40fr, African mask and Kabuki actor.

1971, Aug. 12 **Photo.** ***Perf. 13***

250	A78	25fr multi	20	10
251	A78	40fr multi	30	14

Philatokyo 71, Philatelic Exposition, Tokyo, Apr. 19-29.

No. 226 Surcharged

1971 **Engr.** ***Perf. 12½x13***

252	A66	100fr on 30fr choc & car	65	40

10th anniversary of Upper Volta Red Cross.

Seed Preparation A79

Designs: 75fr, Old farmer with seed packet (vert.). 100fr, Farmer in rice field.

1971, Sept. 30 **Photo.** ***Perf. 13***

253	A79	35fr ocher & multi	22	14
254	A79	75fr lt bl & multi	50	20
255	A79	100fr brn & multi	65	35

National campaign for seed protection.

Outdoor Classroom A80

Design: 50fr, Mother learning to read.

1971, Oct. 14

256	A80	35fr multi	22	14
257	A80	50fr multi	38	16

Women's education.

Joseph Dakiri, Soldiers Driving Tractors — A81

Children and UNICEF Emblem — A84

Spraying Lake, Fly, Man Leading Blind Women A82

Design: 40fr, Dakiri and soldiers gathering harvest.

1971, Oct. 13 ***Perf. 12x12½***

258	A81	15fr blk, yel & red brn	14	10
259	A81	40fr bl & multi	25	16

Joseph Dakiri (1938-1971), inaugurator of the Army-Aid-to-Agriculture Program.

1971, Nov. 26 **Photo.** ***Perf. 13***

260	A82	40fr dk brn, yel & bl	25	16

Drive against onchocerciasis, roundworm infestation.

1971, Dec. 11 ***Perf. 13***

262	A84	45fr red, bis & blk	35	16

UNICEF, 25th anniv.

Peulh House A85

Upper Volta Houses: 20fr, Gourounsi house. 35fr, Mossi houses. 45fr, Bobo house (vert.). 50fr, Dagari house (vert.). 90fr, Bango house, interior.

Perf. 13x13½, 13½x13

1971-72 **Photo.**

263	A85	10fr ver & multi	8	5
264	A85	20fr multi	16	10
265	A85	35fr brt grn & multi	22	14
266	A85	45fr multi ('72)	35	16
267	A85	50fr multi ('72)	40	20
268	A85	90fr multi ('72)	60	35
		Nos. 263-268 (6)	1.81	1.00

The lack of a value for a listed item does not necessarily indicate rarity.

Town Halls of Bobo-Dioulasso and Chalons-sur-Marne — A86

1971, Dec. 23 *Perf. 13x12½*
269 A86 40fr yel & multi 25 15

Kinship between the cities of Bobo-Dioulasso, Upper Volta, and Chalons-sur-Marne, France.

Louis Armstrong — A87

1972, May 17 *Perf. 14x13*
270 A87 45fr multi 45 25

Black musician. See No. C104.

Red Crescent, Cross and Lion Emblems A88

1972, June 23 *Perf. 13x14*
271 A88 40fr yel & multi 35 16

World Red Cross Day. See No. C105.

Coiffure of Peulh Woman — A89

Designs: Various hair styles.

1972, July 23 **Litho.** *Perf. 13*
272 A89 25fr bl & multi 20 10
273 A89 35fr emer & multi 22 10
274 A89 75fr yel & multi 45 18

Classroom A90

Designs: 15fr, Clinic. 20fr, Factory. 35fr, Cattle. 40fr, Plowers. 85fr, Road building machinery.

1972, Oct. 30 **Engr.** *Perf. 13*
275 A90 10fr sl grn, lt grn & choc 5 5
276 A90 15fr brt grn, brn org & brn 10 8
277 A90 20fr bl, lt brn & grn 14 10
278 A90 35fr grn, brn & brt bl 18 14
279 A90 40fr choc, pink & sl grn 22 16
Nos. 275-279,C106 (6) 1.14 75

2nd Five-Year Plan.

West African Monetary Union Issue
Common Design Type

1972, Nov. 2
280 CD136 40fr brn, bl & gray 25 14

Lottery Office and Emblem A91

1972, Nov. 6 **Litho.**
281 A91 35fr multi 22 12

5th anniversary of National Lottery.

Domestic Animals — A92

1972, Dec. 4 **Litho.** *Perf. 13½x12½*
282 A92 5fr Donkeys 5 5
283 A92 10fr Geese 7 5
284 A92 30fr Goats 20 8
285 A92 50fr Cow 35 14
286 A92 65fr Dromedaries 42 20
Nos. 282-286 (5) 1.09 52

Mossi Woman's Hair Style, and Village — A93

1973, Jan. 24 **Engr.** *Perf. 13*
287 A93 5fr sl grn, org & choc 5 5
288 A93 40fr bl, org & choc 22 14

Eugene A. Cernan and Lunar Module A94

Designs: 65fr, Ronald E. Evans and splashdown. 100fr, Capsule, in orbit and interior (horiz.). 150fr, Harrison H. Schmitt and lift-off. 200fr, Conference and moon-buggy. 500fr, Moon-buggy and capsule (horiz.).

Perf. 12½x13½, 13½x12½
1973, Mar. 29 **Litho.**
289 A94 50fr multi 35 16
290 A94 65fr multi 42 20
291 A94 100fr multi 65 36
292 A94 150fr multi 1.00 50
293 A94 200fr multi 1.40 65
Nos. 289-293 (5) 3.82 1.87

Souvenir Sheet
294 A94 500fr multi 3.50 1.60

Apollo 17 moon mission.

No. 260 Surcharged in Red

O. M. S.
25e Anniversaire
45F

1973, Apr. 7 **Photo.** *Perf. 13*
295 A82 45fr on 40fr multi 25 16

WHO, 25th anniversary.

Scout Bugler A95

1973, July 18 **Litho.** *Perf. 12½x13*
296 A95 20fr multi 14 7
Nos. 296,C160-C163 (5) 3.29 1.61

African Postal Union Issue
Common Design Type

1973, Sept. 12 **Engr.** *Perf. 13*
297 CD137 100fr brt red, mag & dl yel 65 25

Pres. Kennedy, Saturn 5 on Assembly Trailer A96

Pres. John F. Kennedy (1917-1963) and: 10fr, Atlas rocket carrying John H. Glenn. 30fr, Titan 2 rocket and Gemini 3 capsule.

1973, Sept. 12 **Litho.** *Perf. 12½x13*
298 A96 5fr multi 5 5
299 A96 10fr multi 7 5
300 A96 30fr multi 20 10
Nos. 298-300,C167-C168 (5) 3.72 1.85

Cross-examination — A97

Designs: 65fr, "Diamond Ede." 70fr, Forensic Institute. 150fr, Robbery scene.

1973, Sept. 15 *Perf. 13x12½*
301 A97 50fr multi 35 16
302 A97 65fr multi 42 20
303 A97 70fr multi 45 22
304 A97 150fr multi 1.00 50

Interpol, 50th anniversary. See No. C170.

Market Place, Ouagadougou — A98

Design: 40fr, Swimming pool, Hotel Independence.

1973, Sept. 30
305 A98 35fr multi 22 12
306 A98 40fr multi 25 14

Tourism. See Nos. C171-C172.

Protestant Church — A99

Design: 40fr, Ouahigouya Mosque.

1973, Sept. 28 *Perf. 13x12½*
307 A99 35fr multi 22 12
308 A99 40fr multi 25 14

Houses of worship. See No. C173.

Kiembara Dancers A100

Design: 40fr, Dancers.

1973, Nov. 30 **Litho.** *Perf. 12½x13*
309 A100 35fr multi 22 12
310 A100 40fr multi 25 14

Folklore. See Nos. C174-C175.

Yuri Gagarin and Aries — A101

Famous Men and their Zodiac Signs: 10fr, Lenin and Taurus. 20fr, John F. Kennedy, rocket and Gemini. 25fr, John H. Glenn, orbiting capsule and Cancer. 30fr, Napoleon and Leo. 50fr, Goethe and Virgo. 60fr, Pelé and Libra. 75fr, Charles de Gaulle and Scorpio. 100fr, Beethoven and Sagittarius. 175fr, Conrad Adenauer and Capricorn. 200fr, Edwin E. Aldrin, Jr. (Apollo XI) and Aquarius. 250fr, Lord Baden-Powell and Pisces.

1973, Dec. 15 **Litho.** *Perf. 13x14*
311 A101 5fr multi 5 5
312 A101 10fr multi 7 5
313 A101 20fr multi 10 5
314 A101 25fr multi 14 7
315 A101 30fr multi 16 8
316 A101 50fr multi 30 15

317	A101	60fr multi	38	18
318	A101	75fr multi	42	20
319	A101	100fr multi	60	30
320	A101	175fr multi	1.10	55
321	A101	200fr multi	1.20	55
322	A101	250fr multi	1.50	70
		Nos. 311-322 (12)	6.02	2.93

Rivera with Italian Flag and Championship '74 Emblem — A102

Design: 40fr, World Cup, soccer ball, World Championship '74 emblem and Pele with Brazilian flag.

1974, Jan. 15 ***Perf. 13x12½***

323	A102	5fr multi	5	5
324	A102	40fr multi	25	14
		Nos. 323-324,C179-C181 (5)	3.05	1.59

10th World Cup Soccer Championship, Munich, June 13-July 7.

Charles de Gaulle A103

Designs: 40fr, De Gaulle memorial. 60fr, Pres. Charles de Gaulle.

1974, Feb. 4 Litho. ***Perf. 12½x13***

325	A103	35fr multi	20	10
326	A103	40fr multi	20	12
327	A103	60fr multi	35	16

Gen. Charles de Gaulle (1890-1970), president of France. Nos. 325-327 printed se-tenant. See Nos. C183-C184.

N'Dongo and Cameroun Flag — A104

World Cup, Emblems and: 20fr, Kolev and Bulgarian flag. 50fr, Keita and Mali flag.

1974, Mar. 19

328	A104	10fr multi	7	5
329	A104	20fr multi	14	7
330	A104	50fr multi	35	16
		Nos. 328-330,C185-C186 (5)	2.81	1.41

10th World Cup Soccer Championship, Munich, June 13-July 7.

Map and Flags of Members A105

1974, May 29 Photo. ***Perf. 13x12½***

331	A105	40fr bl & multi	22	14

15th anniversary of the Council of Accord.

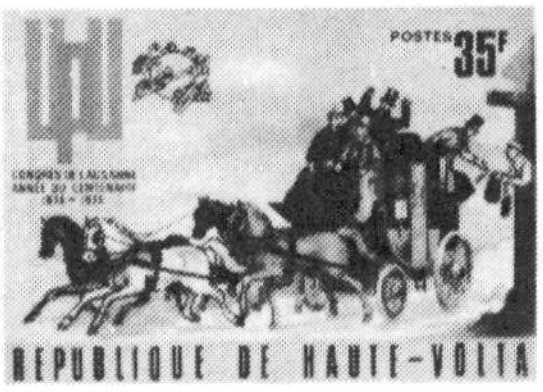

UPU Emblem and Mail Coach — A106

UPU emblem and: 40fr, Steamship. 85fr, Mailman.

1974, July 23 Litho. ***Perf. 13½***

332	A106	35fr multi	22	12
333	A106	40fr multi	25	14
334	A106	85fr multi	55	28
		Nos. 332-334,C189-C191 (6)	4.02	2.04

Universal Postal Union centenary.

Soccer Game, Winner Italy, in France, 1938 — A107

World Cup, Game and Flags: 25fr, Uruguay, in Brazil, 1950. 50fr, East Germany, in Switzerland, 1954.

1974, Sept. 2 Litho. ***Perf. 13½***

335	A107	10fr multi	7	5
336	A107	25fr multi	16	8
337	A107	50fr multi	35	16
		Nos. 335-337,C193-C195 (6)	4.58	2.24

World Cup Soccer winners.

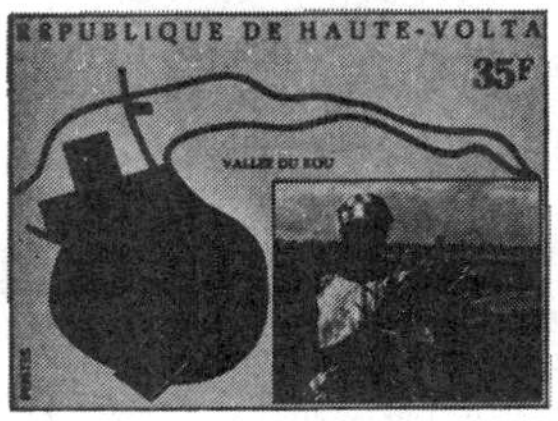

Map and Farm Woman — A108

1974, Oct. 2 Litho. ***Perf. 13x12½***

338	A108	35fr yel & multi	20	14

Kou Valley Development.

Nos. 332-334 Overprinted in Red "100e ANNIVERSAIRE DE L'UNION POSTALE UNIVERSELLE / 9 OCTOBRE 1974"

1974, Oct. 9

339	A106	35fr multi	22	12
340	A106	40fr multi	25	14
341	A106	85fr multi	55	28
		Nos. 339-341,C197-C199 (6)	5.07	2.54

Universal Postal Union centenary.

Values quoted in this catalogue are for stamps graded at Fine-Very Fine and with no faults. An illustrated guide to grade is provided in introductory material, beginning on Page V.

Flowers, by Pierre Bonnard A109

Flower Paintings by: 10fr, Jan Brueghel. 30fr, Jean van Os. 50fr, Van Brussel.

1974, Oct. 31 Litho. ***Perf. 12½x13***

342	A109	5fr multi	5	5
343	A109	10fr multi	7	5
344	A109	30fr multi	16	8
345	A109	50fr multi	25	14
		Nos. 342-345,C201 (5)	2.53	1.32

Churchill as Officer of India Hussars — A110

Churchill: 75fr, As Secretary of State for Interior. 100fr, As pilot. 125fr, meeting with Roosevelt, 1941. 300fr, As painter. 450fr, and "HMS Resolution."

1975, Jan. 11 ***Perf. 13½***

346	A110	50fr multi	30	15
347	A110	75fr multi	42	20
348	A110	100fr multi	55	28
349	A110	125fr multi	70	38
350	A110	300fr multi	1.60	80
		Nos. 346-350 (5)	3.57	1.81

Souvenir Sheet

351	A110	450fr multi	3.00	1.50

Sir Winston Churchill, birth centenary.

US No. 619 and Minutemen — A111

US Stamps: 40fr, No. 118 and Proclamation of Independence. 75fr, No. 798 and Signing the Constitution. 100fr, No. 703 and Surrender at Yorktown. 200fr, No. 1003 and George Washington. 300fr, No. 644 and Surrender of Burgoyne at Saratoga. 500fr, Nos. 63, 68, 73, 157, 179, 228 and 1483a.

1975, Feb. 17 Litho. ***Perf. 11***

352	A111	35fr multi	20	10
353	A111	40fr multi	22	12
354	A111	75fr multi	42	20
355	A111	100fr multi	55	28
356	A111	200fr multi	1.20	55
357	A111	300fr multi	1.60	80
		Nos. 352-357 (6)	4.19	2.05

Souvenir Sheet

Imperf

358	A111	500fr multi	3.00	1.50

American Bicentennial.

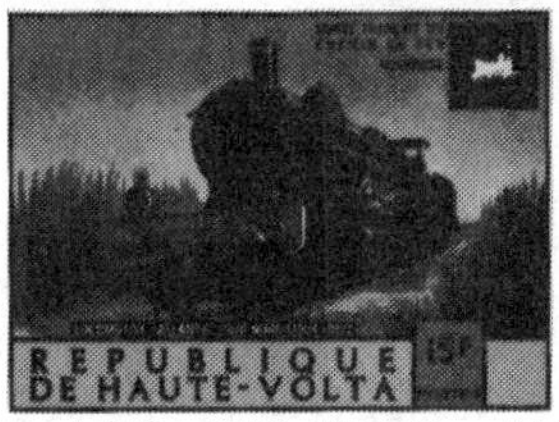

"Atlantic" No. 2670, 1904-12 — A112

Locomotives from Mulhouse, France, Railroad Museum: 25fr, No. 2029, 1882. 50fr, No. 2129, 1882.

1975, Feb. 28 Litho. ***Perf. 13x12½***

359	A112	15fr multi	10	5
360	A112	25fr multi	16	8
361	A112	50fr multi	35	16
		Nos. 359-361,C203-C204 (5)	2.66	1.29

French Flag and Renault Petit Duc, 1910 — A113

Flags and Old Cars: 30fr, US and Ford Model T, 1909. 35fr, Italy and Alfa Romeo "Le Mans," 1931.

1975, Apr. 6 ***Perf. 14x13½***

362	A113	10fr multi	7	5
363	A113	30fr multi	20	10
364	A113	35fr multi	22	12
		Nos. 362-364,C206-C207 (5)	2.89	1.42

Washington and Lafayette — A114

American Bicentennial: 40fr, Washington reviewing troops at Valley Forge. 50fr, Washington taking oath of office.

1975, May 6 Litho. ***Perf. 14***

365	A114	30fr multi	20	10
366	A114	40fr multi	25	14
367	A114	50fr multi	35	16
		Nos. 365-367,C209-C210 (5)	4.20	2.05

Souvenir Sheet

367A	A114	500fr multi	3.50	1.60

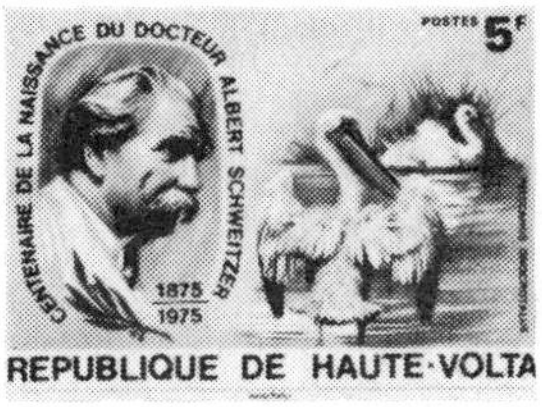

Schweitzer and Pelicans — A115

Design: 15fr, Albert Schweitzer and bateleur eagle.

1975, May 25 Litho. ***Perf. 13½***

368	A115	5fr multi	5	5
369	A115	15fr multi	10	5
		Nos. 368-369,C212-C214 (5)	3.75	1.80

Albert Schweitzer, birth centenary.

Apollo and Soyuz Orbiting Earth — A116

Design: 50fr, Apollo and Soyuz near link-up.

1975, July 18

370 A116 40fr multi	25	14
371 A116 50fr multi	35	16
Nos. 370-371,C216-C218 (5)	4.65	2.30

Apollo-Soyuz space test project, Russo-American cooperation, launched July 15, link-up July 17.

Maria Picasso Lopez, Artist's Mother A117

Paintings by Pablo Picasso (1881-1973): 60fr, Self-portrait. 90fr, First Communion.

1975, Aug. 7

372 A117 50fr multi	35	16
373 A117 60fr multi	40	20
374 A117 90fr multi	60	30
Nos. 372-374,C220-C221 (5)	4.60	2.36

Expo '75 Emblem and Tanker, Idemitsu Maru — A118

Oceanographic Exposition, Okinawa: 25fr, Training ship, Kaio Maru. 45fr, Firefighting ship, Hiryu. 50fr, Battleship, Yamato. 60fr, Container ship, Kamakura Maru.

1975, Sept. 26 Litho. *Perf. 11*

375 A118 15fr multi	10	5
376 A118 25fr multi	16	8
377 A118 45fr multi	30	15
377A A118 50fr multi	35	16
378 A118 60fr multi	40	20
Nos. 375-378,C223 (6)	2.06	1.02

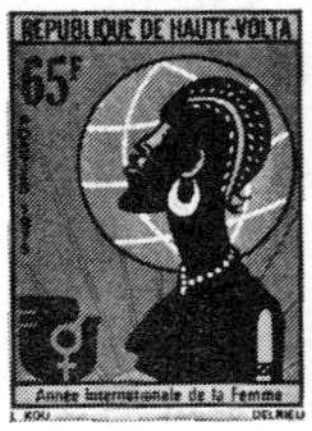

Woman, Globe and IWY Emblem — A119

1975, Nov. 20 Photo. *Perf. 13*

379 A119 65fr multi	38	22

International Women's Year.

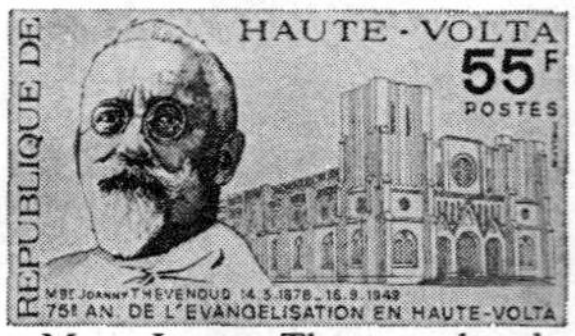

Msgr. Joanny Thevenoud and Cathedral — A120

Design: 65fr, Father Guillaume Templier and Cathedral.

1975, Nov. 20 Engr. *Perf. 13x12½*

380 A120 55fr grn, blk & dl red	30	16
381 A120 65fr blk, org & dl red	38	20

75th anniv. of the Evangelization of Upper Volta.

Farmer's Hat, Hoe and Emblem A121

1975, Dec. 10 Photo. *Perf. 13x13½*

382 A121 15fr buff & multi	8	5
383 A121 50fr lt grn & multi	25	15

Development of the Volta valleys.

Sledding and Olympic Emblem — A122

Innsbruck Background, Olympic Emblem and: 45fr, Figure skating. 85fr, Skiing.

1975, Dec. 16 Litho. *Perf. 13½*

384 A122 35fr multi	18	10
385 A122 45fr multi	22	12
386 A122 85fr multi	45	22
Nos. 384-386,C225-C226 (5)	2.90	1.44

12th Winter Olympic Games, Innsbruck, Austria, Feb. 4-15, 1976.

Gymnast and Olympic Emblem — A123

Olympic Emblem and: 50fr, Sailing. 100fr, Soccer.

1976, Mar. 17

387 A123 40fr multi	20	12
388 A123 50fr multi	25	14
389 A123 100fr multi	55	28
Nos. 387-389,C228-C229 (5)	2.40	1.22

21st Olympic Games, Montreal, Canada, July 17-Aug. 1.

Olympic Emblem and Sprinters A124

Olympic Emblem and: 55fr, Equestrian. 75fr, Hurdles.

1976, Mar. 25 Litho. *Perf. 11*

390 A124 30fr multi	16	8
391 A124 55fr multi	30	15
392 A124 75fr multi	42	20
Nos. 390-392,C231-C232 (5)	2.63	1.31

21st Olympic Games, Montreal.

Blind Woman and Man — A125

1976, Apr. 7 Engr. *Perf. 13*

393 A125 75fr dk brn, grn & org	40	25
394 A125 250fr dk brn, ocher & org	1.40	80

Drive against onchocerciasis, roundworm infestation.

"Deutschland" over Friedrichshafen — A126

Airships: 40fr, "Victoria Louise" over sailing ships. 50fr, "Sachsen" over German countryside.

1976, May 11 Litho. *Perf. 11*

395 A126 10fr multi	70	5
396 A126 40fr multi	25	14
397 A126 50fr multi	35	16
Nos. 395-397,C234-C236 (6)	5.35	2.35

75th anniversary of the Zeppelin.

Viking Lander and Probe on Mars — A127

Viking Mars project: 55fr, Viking orbiter in flight. 75fr, Titan rocket start for Mars (vert.).

1976, June 24 *Perf. 13½*

398 A127 30fr multi	12	6
399 A127 55fr multi	22	12
400 A127 75fr multi	32	16
Nos. 398-400,C238-C239 (5)	3.16	1.59

World Map, Arms of Upper Volta A128

Design: 100fr, World map, arms and dove.

1976, Aug. 19 Litho. *Perf. 12½*

401 A128 55fr brn & multi	30	20
402 A128 100fr bl & multi	55	40

5th Summit Conference of Non-aligned Countries, Colombo, Sri Lanka, Aug. 9-19.

Bicentennial, Interphil 76 Emblems and Washington at Battle of Trenton — A129

Design: 90fr, Bicentennial, Interphil 76 emblems and Seat of Government, Pennsylvania.

1976, Sept. 30 *Perf. 13½*

403 A129 60fr multi	40	16
404 A129 90fr multi	55	22
Nos. 403-404,C241-C243 (5)	5.00	2.38

American Bicentennial, Interphil 76, Philadelphia, Pa., May 29-June 6.

UPU and UN Emblems — A130

1976, Dec. 8 Engr. *Perf. 13*

405 A130 200fr red, ol & bl	1.10	65

UN Postal Administration, 25th anniv.

Arms of Tenkodogo A131

Bronze Statuette A132

Coats of Arms: 20fr, 100fr, Ouagadougou. 65fr, like 10fr.

1977, May 2 Litho. *Perf. 13*

406 A131 10fr multi	7	5
407 A131 20fr multi	10	8
408 A131 65fr multi	35	25
409 A131 100fr multi	55	40

1977, June 13 Photo. *Perf. 13*

Design: 65fr, Woman with bowl, bronze.

410 A132 55fr multi	30	20
411 A132 65fr multi	35	20

Nos. 410-411 issued in sheets and coils with black control number on every 5th stamp.

Granary, Samo
A133

Handbags
A134

Corn Granaries: 35fr, Boromo. 45fr, Banfora. 55fr, Mossi.

1977, June 20 Photo. *Perf. 13½x13*

412 A133 5fr multi 5 5
413 A133 35fr multi 20 12
414 A133 45fr multi 22 14
415 A133 55fr multi 30 20

1977, June 20

416 A134 30fr Gouin 16 12
417 A134 40fr Bissa 20 14
418 A134 60fr Lobi 35 20
419 A134 70fr Mossi 38 22

Nos. 390-392 Overprinted in Gold:
a. VAINQUEUR 1976 / LASSE VIREN / FINLANDE
b. VAINQUEUR 1976 / ALWIN SCHOCKEMOHLE / R.F.A.
c. VAINQUEUR 1976 / JOHANNA SCHALLER / R.D.A.

1977, July 4 Litho. *Perf. 11*

420 A124 (a) 30fr multi 16 8
421 A124 (b) 55fr multi 30 15
422 A124 (c) 75fr multi 40 20
Nos. 420-422,C245-C246 (5) 3.26 1.58

Winners, 21st Olympic Games.

Crinum Ornatum
A135

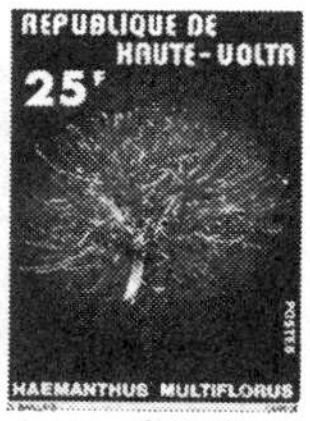

Haemanthus Multiflorus
A136

Hannoa Undulata — A137

Designs: Flowers, flowering branches and wild fruits. 175fr, 300fr, horiz.

1977 Litho. *Perf. 12½*

423 A137 2fr Cordia myxa 5 5
424 A137 3fr Opilia celtidifolia 5 5
425 A135 15fr shown 7 5
426 A136 25fr shown 14 10
427 A137 50fr shown 25 20
428 A135 90fr Cochlospermum planchonii 45 35
429 A135 125fr Clitoria ternatea 65 50
430 A136 150fr Cassia alata 80 60
431 A136 175fr Nauclea latifolia 90 65
432 A136 300fr Bombax costatum 1.60 1.20
433 A135 400fr Eulophia cucullata 2.00 1.60
Nos. 423-433 (11) 6.96 5.35

Issue dates: 25fr, 150fr, 175fr, 300fr, Aug. 1; 2fr, 3fr, 50fr, Aug. 8; 15fr, 90fr, 125fr, 400fr, Aug. 23.

De Gaulle and Cross of Lorraine
A138

Designs: 200fr, King Baudouin of Belgium.

1977, Aug. 16 *Perf. 13½x14*

434 A138 100fr multi 55 22
435 A138 200fr multi 1.10 42

Elizabeth II — A139

Designs: 300fr, Elizabeth II taking salute. 500fr, Elizabeth II after Coronation.

1977, Aug. 16

436 A139 200fr multi 80 32
437 A139 300fr multi 1.20 50

Souvenir Sheet

438 A139 500fr multi 2.00 90

25th anniv. of reign of Queen Elizabeth II.

Lottery Tickets, Cars and Map of Upper Volta in Flag Colors — A140

1977, Sept. 16 Photo. *Perf. 13*

439 A140 55fr multi 30 22

10th anniversary of National Lottery.

Selma Lagerlof, Literature — A141

Designs: 65fr, Guglielmo Marconi, physics. 125fr, Bertrand Russell, literature. 200fr, Linus C. Pauling, chemistry. 300fr, Robert Koch, medicine. 500fr, Albert Schweitzer, peace.

1977, Sept. 22 Litho. *Perf. 13½*

440 A141 55fr multi 30 14
441 A141 65fr multi 38 16
442 A141 125fr multi 65 25
443 A141 200fr multi 1.10 42
444 A141 300fr multi 1.60 65
Nos. 440-444 (5) 4.03 1.62

Souvenir Sheet

445 A141 500fr multi 2.50 1.20

Nobel Prize winners.

The Three Graces, by Rubens
A142

Paintings by Peter Paul Rubens (1577-1640): 55fr, Heads of Black Men (horiz.). 85fr, Bathsheba at the Fountain. 150fr, The Drunken Silenus. 200fr, 300fr, Life of Maria de Medicis (different).

1977, Oct. 19 Litho. *Perf. 14*

446 A142 55fr multi 30 14
447 A142 65fr multi 38 16
448 A142 85fr multi 45 22
449 A142 150fr multi 80 40
450 A142 200fr multi 1.10 45
451 A142 300fr multi 1.60 60
Nos. 446-451 (6) 4.63 1.97

Lenin in His Office
A143

Designs: 85fr, Lenin Monument, Kremlin. 200fr, Lenin with youth. 500fr, Lenin and Leonid Brezhnev.

1977, Oct. 28 Litho. *Perf. 12*

452 A143 10fr multi 7 5
453 A143 85fr multi 45 25
454 A143 200fr multi 1.10 65
455 A143 500fr multi 2.50 1.60

Russian October Revolution, 60th anniv.

Stadium and Brazil No. C79 — A144

Stadium and: 65fr, Brazil No. 1144. 125fr, Gt. Britain No. 458. 200fr, Chile No. 340. 300fr, Switzerland No. 350. 500fr, Germany No. 1147.

1977, Dec. 30 Litho. *Perf. 13½*

456 A144 55fr multi 30 14
457 A144 65fr multi 38 16
458 A144 125fr multi 65 25
459 A144 200fr multi 1.10 42
460 A144 300fr multi 1.60 65
Nos. 456-460 (5) 4.03 1.62

Souvenir Sheet

461 A144 500fr multi 2.50 1.20

11th World Cup Soccer Championship, Argentina.

Jean Mermoz and Seaplane — A145

History of Aviation: 75fr, Anthony H. G. Fokker. 85fr, Wiley Post. 90fr, Otto Lilienthal (vert.). 100fr, Concorde. 500fr, Charles Lindbergh and "Spirit of St. Louis."

1978, Jan. 2 Litho. *Perf. 13½*

462 A145 65fr multi 38 16
463 A145 75fr multi 40 20
464 A145 85fr multi 45 20
465 A145 90fr multi 50 20
466 A145 100fr multi 55 22
Nos. 462-466 (5) 2.28 98

Souvenir Sheet

467 A145 500fr multi 2.50 1.25

Crataeva Religiosa — A146

1978, Feb. 28 Litho. *Perf. 12½*

468 A146 55fr shown 30 22
469 A146 75fr Fig tree 40 30

Souvenir Sheet

Virgin and Child, by Rubens
A147

1978, May 24 Litho. *Perf. 13½x14*

470 A147 500fr multi 2.50 1.20

Peter Paul Rubens (1577-1640).

Antenna and ITU Emblem
A148

1978, May 30 *Perf. 13*

471 A148 65fr sil & multi 38 16

10th World Telecommunications Day.

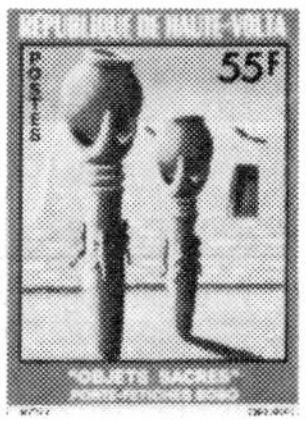

Fetish Gate of Bobo — A149

1978, July 10 Litho. *Perf. 13½*

472 A149 55fr shown	30	14
473 A149 65fr Mossi fetish	38	16

Capt. Cook and "Endeavour" — A150

Capt. James Cook (1728-1779) and: 85fr, Death on Hawaiian beach. 250fr, Navigational instruments. 350fr, "Resolution."

1978, Sept. 1 Litho. *Perf. 14½*

474 A150 65fr multi	38	16
475 A150 85fr multi	45	20
476 A150 250fr multi	1.40	65
477 A150 350fr multi	1.90	80

Nos. 436-438 Overprinted Vertically in Silver: "ANNIVERSAIRE DU COURONNEMENT 1953-1978"

1978, Oct. 24 Litho. *Perf. 13½x14*

478 A139 200fr multi	1.10	42
479 A139 300fr multi	1.60	65

Souvenir Sheet

480 A139 500fr multi	2.50	1.20

25th anniversary of Coronation of Queen Elizabeth II. Overprint in 3 lines on 200fr, in 2 lines on 300fr and 500fr.

Nos. 478-480 exist with overprint in metallic red.

Trent Castle, by Dürer — A151

Paintings by Albrecht Durer (1471-1528): 150fr, Virgin and Child with St. Anne. 250fr, Sts. George and Eustachius. 350fr, Hans Holzschuher (all vertical).

Perf. 14x13½, 13½x14

1978, Nov. 20 Litho.

481 A151 65fr multi	38	16
482 A151 150fr multi	80	38
483 A151 250fr multi	1.40	65
484 A151 350fr multi	1.90	65

Human Rights Emblem A152

1978, Dec. 10 Litho. *Perf. 12½*

485 A152 55fr multi	30	14

Universal Declaration of Human Rights, 30th anniv.

The Catalogue editors cannot undertake to appraise, identify or judge the genuineness or condition of stamps.

Nos. 456-461 Overprinted in Silver
a. VAINQUEURS 1950 URUGUAY / 1978 / ARGENTINE
b. VAINQUEURS 1970 BRESIL / 1978 ARGENTINE
c. VAINQUEURS 1966 GRANDE BRETAGNE / 1978 ARGENTINE
d. VAINQUEURS / 1962 BRESIL / 1978 ARGENTINE
e. VAINQUEURS 1954 ALLEMAGNE (RFA) / 1978 ARGENTINE
f. VAINQUEURS 1974 ALLEMAGNE (RFA) / 1978 ARGENTINE

1979, Jan. 4 Litho. *Perf. 13½*

486 A144(a) 55fr multi	30	14
487 A144(b) 65fr multi	38	16
488 A144(c) 125fr multi	65	25
489 A144(d) 200fr multi	1.10	40
490 A144(e) 300fr multi	1.60	65
Nos. 486-490 (5)	4.03	1.60

Souvenir Sheet

491 A144(f) 500fr multi	2.50	1.20

Winners, World Soccer Cup Championships 1950-1978.

Radio Station A153

Design: 65fr, Mail plane at airport.

1979, Mar 30 Litho. *Perf. 12½*

492 A153 55fr multi	30	14
493 A153 65fr multi	38	16

Post and Telecommunications Org., 10th anniv.

Teacher and Pupils, IYC Emblem — A154

1979, Apr. 9 *Perf. 13½*

494 A154 75fr multi	40	20

International Year of the Child.

Telecommunications A155

1979, May 17 Litho. *Perf. 13*

495 A155 70fr multi	45	20

11th Telecommunications Day.

Basketmaker and Upper Volta No. 111 — A156

Design: No. 497, May of Upper Volta, Concorde, truck and UPU emblem.

1979, June 8 Photo.

496 A156 100fr multi	65	35
497 A156 100fr multi	65	35

Philexafrique II, Libreville, Gabon, June 8-17. Nos. 496, 497 each printed in sheets of 10 and 5 labels showing exhibition emblem.

Synodontis Voltae A157

Fresh-water Fish: 50fr, Micralestes comoensis. 85fr, Silurus.

1979, June 10 Litho. *Perf. 12½*

498 A157 20fr multi	14	7
499 A157 50fr multi	35	16
500 A157 85fr multi	55	30

Rowland Hill, Train and Upper Volta No. 60 — A158

Sir Rowland Hill (1795-1879), originator of penny postage, Trains and Upper Volta Stamps: 165fr, No. 59. 200fr, No. 57. 300fr, No. 56. 500fr, No. 55.

1979, June Litho. *Perf. 13½*

501 A158 65fr multi	42	20
502 A158 165fr multi	1.10	55
503 A158 200fr multi	1.40	65
504 A158 300fr multi	2.00	1.00

Souvenir Sheet

505 A158 500fr multi	3.50	1.60

Wildlife Fund Emblem and Protected Animals — A159

1979, Aug. 30 Litho. *Perf. 14½*

506 A159 30fr Waterbuck	20	10
507 A159 40fr Roan antelope	25	14
508 A159 60fr Caracal	40	20
509 A159 100fr African bush elephant	65	35
510 A159 175fr Hartebeest	1.20	55
511 A159 250fr Leopard	1.60	80
Nos. 506-511 (6)	4.30	2.14

Adult Students and Teacher — A160

Design: 55fr, Man reading book (vert.).

1979, Sept. 8 *Perf. 12½x13, 13x12½*

512 A160 55fr multi	38	18
513 A160 250fr multi	1.60	85

World Literacy Day.

Map of Upper Volta, Telephone Receiver and Lines, Telecom Emblem — A161

1979, Sept. 20 *Perf. 13x12½*

514 A161 200fr multi	1.40	65

3rd World Telecommunications Exhibition, Geneva, Sept. 20-26.

King Vulture — A162

1979, Oct. 26 Litho. *Perf. 13*

515 A162 5fr shown	5	5
516 A162 10fr Hoopoe	7	5
517 A162 15fr Bald vulture	10	5
518 A162 25fr Herons	16	8
519 A162 35fr Ostrich	22	12
520 A162 45fr Crowned crane	30	15
521 A162 125fr Eagle	80	40
Nos. 515-521 (7)	1.70	90

Control Tower, Emblem, Jet — A163

1979, Dec. 12 Photo. *Perf. 13x12½*

522 A163 65fr multi	42	20

ASECNA (Air Safety Board), 20th anniv.

Central Bank of West African States — A164

1979, Dec. 28 Litho. *Perf. 12½*

523 A164 55fr multi	38	18

Eugene Jamot, Map of Upper Volta, Tsetse Fly — A165

1979, Dec. 28 *Perf. 13x13½*
524 A165 55fr multi 38 18

Eugene Jamot (1879-1937), discoverer of sleeping sickness cure.

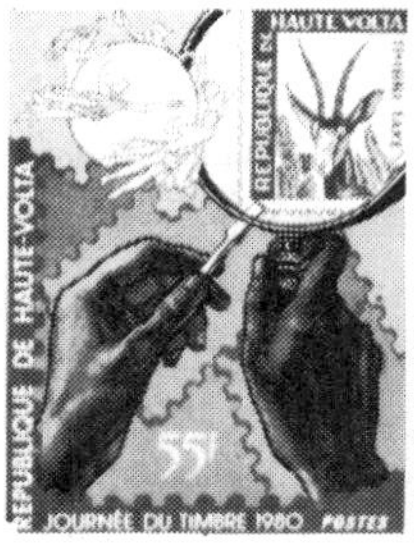

UPU Emblem, Upper Volta Type D4 under Magnifier A166

1980, Feb. 26 **Litho.** *Perf. 12½x13*
525 A166 55fr multi 38 18

Stamp Day.

World Locomotive Speed Record, 25th Anniversary A167

1980, Mar. 30 **Litho.** *Perf. 12½*
526 A167 75fr multi 50 25
527 A167 100fr multi 65 35

Pres. Sangoule Lamizana, Pope John Paul II, Cardinal Pau Zoungrana, Map of Upper Volta — A168

1980, May 10 **Litho.** *Perf. 12½*
528 A168 65fr shown 42 20

Size: 21x36mm

529 A168 100fr Pope John Paul II 65 35

Visit of Pope John Paul II to Upper Volta.

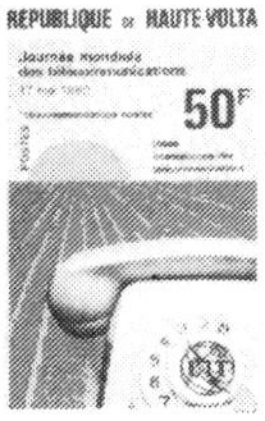

12th World Telecommunications Day — A169

1980, May 17 *Perf. 13x12½*
530 A169 50fr multi 35 16

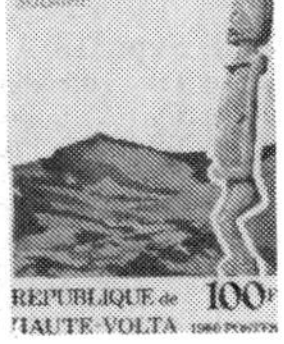

Mountains and Statue (Solar Energy) — A170

1980, June 12 **Litho.** *Perf. 13*
531 A170 65fr Sun and earth 42 20
532 A170 100fr shown 65 35

Downhill Skiing, Lake Placid '80 Emblem — A171

1980, June 26 *Perf. 14½*
533 A171 65fr shown 42 20
534 A171 100fr Women's down-hill 65 35
535 A171 200fr Figure skating 1.40 65
536 A171 350fr Slalom, vert. 2.25 1.20

Souvenir Sheet

537 A171 500fr Speed skating 3.50 1.60

12th Winter Olympic Game Winners, Lake Placid, N.Y., Feb. 12-24.

Map of Europe and Africa, Jet — A172

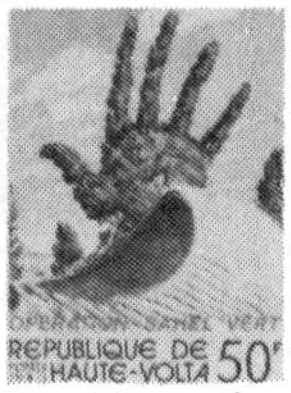

Hand Protecting Sand Dune — A173

Europafrica Issue

1980, July 14 **Litho.** *Perf. 13*
538 A172 100fr multi 65 35

1980, July 18

Operation Green Sahel: 55fr, Hands holding seedlings.

539 A173 50fr multi 35 16
540 A173 55fr multi 38 20

Gourmantche Chief Initiation — A174

1980, Sept. 12 **Litho.** *Perf. 14*
541 A174 30fr shown 20 10
542 A174 55fr Moro Naba, Mossi Emperor 38 18
543 A174 65fr Princess Guimbe Quattara, vert. 42 20

Gourounsi Mask, Conference Emblem — A175

1980, Oct. 6 *Perf. 13½x13*
544 A175 65fr multi 42 20

World Tourism Conf., Manila, Sept. 27.

Map of West Africa Showing Upper Volta, Agricultural Symbols — A176

1980, Nov. 5 **Litho.** *Perf. 12½*
545 A176 55fr shown 38 18
546 A176 65fr Transportation 42 20
547 A176 75fr Dam, highway 50 25
548 A176 100fr Industry 65 35

West African Economic Council, 5th anniv.

20th Anniv. of Independence — A177

1980, Dec. 11 *Perf. 13*
549 A177 500fr multi 3.50 1.60

Madonna and Child, by Raphael — A178

West African Postal Union, 5th Anniv. — A179

Christmas: Paintings of Madonna and Child, by Raphael.

1980, Dec. 22 *Perf. 12½*
550 A178 60fr multi 40 20
551 A178 150fr multi 1.00 50
552 A178 250fr multi 1.60 80

1980, Dec. 24 **Photo.** *Perf. 13½*
553 A179 55fr multi 38 20

Dung Beetle A180

Perf. 13x13½, 13½x13

1981, Mar. 10 **Litho.**
554 A180 5fr shown 5 5
555 A180 10fr Crickets 7 5
556 A180 15fr Termites 10 5
557 A180 20fr Praying mantis, vert. 14 7
558 A180 55fr Emperor moth 38 25
559 A180 65fr Locust, vert. 42 20
Nos. 554-559 (6) 1.16 67

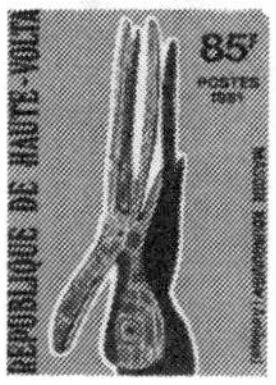

Antelope Mask, Kouroumba — A181

Designs: Various ceremonial masks.

1981, Mar. 20 **Litho.** *Perf. 13*
560 A181 45fr multi 30 15
561 A181 55fr multi 38 18
562 A181 85fr multi 55 28
563 A181 105fr multi 70 35

Notre Dame of Kologh' Naba College, 25th Anniv. A182

1981, Mar. 30
564 A182 55fr multi 38 20

Heinrich von Stephan, UPU Founder, Birth Sesquicentennial — A183

1981, May 4 **Litho.** *Perf. 13*
565 A183 65fr multi 42 20

13th World Telecommunications Day — A184

1981, May 17 *Perf. 13½x13*
566 A184 90fr multi 60 30

Diesel Train, Abidjan-Niger Railroad — A185

Designs: Trains.

1981, July 6 **Litho.** *Perf. 13*
567 A185 25fr shown 16 8
568 A185 30fr Gazelle 20 10
569 A185 40fr Belier 25 14

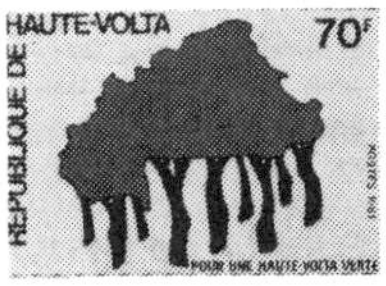

Tree Planting Month — A186

1981, July 15
570 A186 70fr multi 45 22

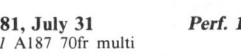

Natl. Red Cross, 20th Anniv. A187

1981, July 31 *Perf. 12½x13*
571 A187 70fr multi 45 22

Intl. Year of the Disabled — A188

1981, Aug. 20 Litho. *Perf. 13x12½*

572 A188 70fr multi 45 22

View of Koudougou A189

1981, Sept. 3 Litho. *Perf. 12½*

573 A189 35fr shown 22 12
574 A189 45fr Toma 30 15
575 A189 85fr Volta Noire 55 28

World Food Day A190

1981, Oct. 16 *Perf. 13*

576 A190 90fr multi 60 30

Elephant A191

Designs: Various protected species.

1981, Oct. 21 Photo. *Perf. 14*

577 A191 5fr multi 5 5
578 A191 15fr multi 10 5
579 A191 40fr multi 25 14
580 A191 60fr multi 40 20
581 A191 70fr multi 45 22
Nos. 577-581 (5) 1.25 66

Fight Against Apartheid A192

Mangoes A193

1981, Dec. 9 Litho. *Perf. 12½*

582 A192 90fr red org 60 30

Perf. 13x13½, 13½x13

1981, Dec. 15

583 A193 20fr Papayas, horiz. 14 7
584 A193 35fr Fruits, vegtables, horiz. 22 12
585 A193 75fr shown 50 25
586 A193 90fr Melons, horiz. 60 30

The indexes in each volume of the Scott Catalogue contain many listings which help to identify stamps.

Guinea Hen — A194

West African Rice Development Assoc., 10th Anniv. — A195

Designs: Breeding animals. 10fr, 25fr, 70fr, 250fr, 300fr horiz.

1981, Dec. 22 *Perf. 13*

587 A194 10fr Donkey 7 5
588 A194 25fr Pig 16 8
589 A194 70fr Cow 45 22
590 A194 90fr shown 60 30
591 A194 250fr Rabbit 1.60 80
Nos. 587-591 (5) 2.88 1.45

Souvenir Sheet

592 A194 300fr Sheep 2.00 1.00

1981, Dec. 29

593 A195 90fr multi 60 30

20th Anniv. of World Food Program — A196

1982, Jan. 18

594 A196 50fr multi 35 16

Traditional Houses — A197

1982, Apr. 23 Litho. *Perf. 12½*

595 A197 30fr Morhonaba Palace, vert. 20 10
596 A197 70fr Bobo 45 22
597 A197 100fr Gourounsi 65 35
598 A197 200fr Peulh 1.40 65
599 A197 250fr Dagari 1.60 80
Nos. 595-599 (5) 4.30 2.12

14th World Telecommunications Day — A198

1982, May 17

600 A198 125fr multi 85 40

Water Lily — A199

25th Anniv. of Cultural Aid Fund — A201

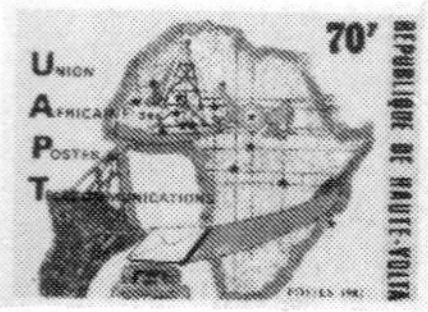

African Postal Union A200

1982, Sept. 22 *Perf. 13x12½*

601 A199 25fr shown 12 6
602 A199 40fr Kapoks 20 10
603 A199 70fr Frangipani 35 18
604 A199 90fr Cochlospermum planchonii 60 22
605 A199 100fr Cotton 50 25
Nos. 601-605 (5) 1.77 81

1982, Oct. 7

606 A200 70fr multi 45 22
607 A200 90fr multi 60 30

1982, Nov. 10 *Perf. 12½x13*

608 A201 70fr multi 45 22

Map, Hand holding Grain, Steer Head A202

1982 *Perf. 12½*

609 A202 90fr multi 60 30

Traditional Hairstyle A203

1983, Jan. Litho. *Perf. 12½*

610 A203 90fr lt grn & multi 60 30
611 A203 120fr lt bl & multi 80 40
612 A203 170fr pink & multi 1.10 55

8th Film Festival, Ouagadougou — A204

1983, Feb. 10 Litho. *Perf. 13x12½*

613 A204 90fr Scene 60 30
614 A204 500fr Filmmaker Dumarou Ganda 3.50 1.60

UN Intl. Drinking Water and Sanitation Decade, 1981-90 — A205

1983, Apr. 21 Litho. *Perf. 13½x13*

615 A205 60fr Water drops 40 20
616 A205 70fr Carrying water 45 22

Manned Flight Bicentenary A206

Portraits and Balloons: 15fr, J.M. Montgolfier, 1783. 25fr, Etienne Montgolfier's balloon, 1783, Pilatre de Rozier. 70fr, Charles & Roberts flight, 1783, Jacques Charles. 90fr, Flight over English Channel, John Jeffries. 100fr, Testu-Brissy's horseback flight, Wilhemine Reichardt. 250fr, Andree's Spitzbergen flight, 1897, S.A. Andree. 300fr, Piccard's stratosphere flight, 1931, August Piccard.

1983, Apr. 15 Litho. *Perf. 13½*

617 A206 15fr multi 10 5
618 A206 25fr multi 16 8
619 A206 70fr multi 45 22
620 A206 90fr multi 60 30
621 A206 100fr multi 65 35
622 A206 250fr multi 1.60 80
Nos. 617-622 (6) 3.56 1.80

Souvenir Sheet

623 A206 300fr multi 2.00 1.00

No. 623 contains one stamp 38x47mm. Nos. 621-623 airmail.

World Communications Year — A207

1983, May 26 Litho. *Perf. 12½*

624 A207 30fr Man reading letter 20 10
625 A207 35fr Like No. 624 22 12
626 A207 45fr Aircraft over stream 30 15
627 A207 90fr Girl on telephone 60 30

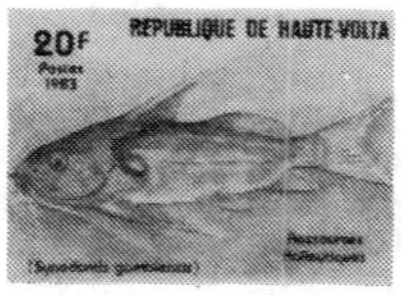

Fishing Resources A208

1983, July 28 Litho. *Perf. 13*

628 A208 20fr Synadontis gambiensis 7 5
629 A208 30fr Palmotochromis 10 5
630 A208 40fr Boy fishing, vert. 14 7
631 A208 50fr Fishing with net 16 8
632 A208 75fr Fishing with basket 25 12
Nos. 628-632 (5) 72 37

Anti-deforestation — A209

1983, Sept. 13 Litho. *Perf. 13*

633 A209 10fr Planting saplings 5 5
634 A209 50fr Tree nursey 16 8
635 A209 100fr Prevent forest fires 35 16
636 A209 150fr Woman cooking 50 25
637 A209 200fr Prevent felling, vert. 65 35
Nos. 633-637 (5) 1.71 89

Fresco Detail, by Raphael — A210

Paintings: 120fr, Self-portrait, by Pablo Picasso, 1901 (vert.). 185fr, Self-portrait at the palette, by Manet, 1878 (vert.). 350fr, Fresco Detail, diff., by Raphael. 500fr, Goethe, by George Oswald May, 1779 (vert.).

1983, Nov. Litho. *Perf. 13*

638	A210	120fr	multi	40	20
639	A210	185fr	multi	62	32
640	A210	300fr	multi	1.00	50
641	A210	350fr	multi	1.20	60
642	A210	500fr	multi	1.60	80
			Nos. 638-642 (5)	4.82	2.42

25th Anniv. of the Republic A211

1983, Dec. 9 Litho. *Perf. 14*

643	A211	90fr	Arms	30	15
644	A211	500fr	Family, flag	1.60	80

Council of Unity, 25th Anniv. — A212

1984, May 29 Litho. *Perf. 12½*

645	A212	90fr	multi	30	15
646	A212	100fr	multi	35	16

Scouting Type

1984, June 15 Litho. *Perf. 13½*

647	A217	25fr	Polystictus leoninus	14	7
648	A217	185fr	Pterocarpus Lucens	90	45
649	A217	200fr	Phlebopus colossus sudanicus	1.10	50
650	A217	250fr	Cosmos sulphureus	1.25	62
651	A217	300fr	Trametes versicolor	1.50	80
652	A217	400fr	Ganoderma lucidum	2.00	1.10
			Nos. 647-652 (6)	6.89	3.54

Souvenir Sheet

653	A217	600fr	Leucocoprinus cepaestipes	3.25	1.60

Nos. 651-653 are airmail. Nos. 647-652 are Nos. 669-674 without overprint.

Wildlife A214

Wildlife — A215

1984, July 19

654	A214	15fr	Cheetah, four cubs	7	5
655	A214	35fr	Two adults	14	7
656	A214	90fr	One adult	35	16
657	A214	120fr	Cheetah, two cubs	45	22
658	A214	300fr	Baboons	1.20	55
659	A214	400fr	Vultures	1.50	80
			Nos. 654-659 (6)	3.71	1.85

Souvenir Sheet

660	A215	1000fr	Antelopes	4.00	1.90

World Wildlife Fund (Nos. 654-567); Rotary Intl. (Nos. 658, 660); Natl. Boy Scouts (No. 659). Nos. 658-660 are airmail.

Sailing Ships and Locomotives — A216

1984, Aug. 14 *Perf. 12½*

661	A216	20fr	Maiden Queen	8	5
662	A216	40fr	CC 2400 ch	16	8
663	A216	60fr	Scawfell	22	12
664	A216	100fr	PO 1806	38	18
665	A216	120fr	Harbinger	45	22
666	A216	145fr	Livingstone	55	28
667	A216	400fr	True Briton	1.50	80
668	A216	450fr	Pacific C51	1.60	85
			Nos. 661-668 (8)	4.94	2.58

Burkina Faso

A217

Nos. 647-652 Ovptd. with Two Bars and "BURKINA FASO"

1985, Mar. 5 Litho. *Perf. 13½*

669	A217	25fr	multi	8	5
670	A217	185fr	multi	55	25
671	A217	200fr	multi	60	30
672	A217	250fr	multi	75	38
673	A217	300fr	multi	90	45
674	A217	400fr	multi	1.20	60
			Nos. 669-674 (6)	4.08	2.03

1986 World Cup Soccer Championships, Mexico — A218

A219

Various soccer plays and Aztec artifacts.

1985, Apr. 20 Litho. *Perf. 13*

681	A218	24fr	multi	8	5
682	A218	45fr	multi	16	8
683	A218	90fr	multi	35	16
684	A218	100fr	multi	38	18
685	A218	150fr	multi	55	25
686	A218	200fr	multi	70	38
687	A218	250fr	multi	90	45
			Nos. 681-687 (7)	3.12	1.55

Souvenir Sheet

688	A219	500fr	multi	1.90	1.20

Nos. 681-685 vert. No. 684-688 are airmail.

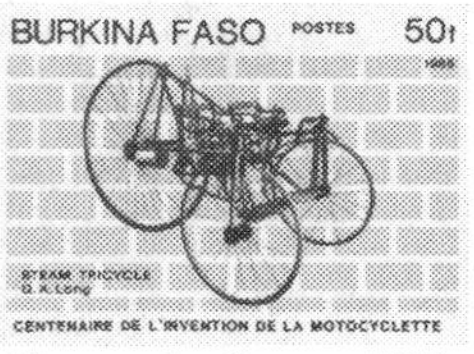

Motorcycle, Cent. — A220

1985, May 26

689	A220	50fr	Steam tricycle, G.A. Long	18	10
690	A220	80fr	Pope	28	14
691	A220	80fr	Manet-90	30	15
692	A220	100fr	Ducati	38	18
693	A220	150fr	Jawa	55	28
694	A220	200fr	Honda	70	38
695	A220	250fr	B.M.W.	90	45
			Nos. 689-695 (7)	3.29	1.68

Nos. 692-695 are airmail.

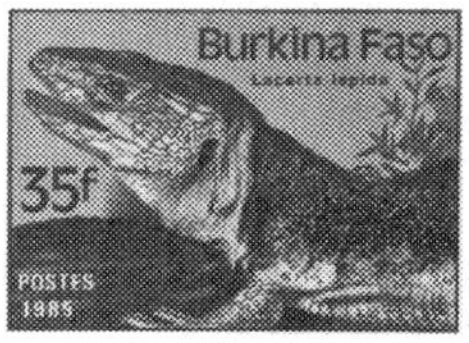

Reptiles A221

1985, June 20

696	A221	5fr	Chamaeleon dilepis	5	5
697	A221	15fr	Agama stellio	7	5
698	A221	35fr	Lacerta Lepida	14	7
699	A221	85fr	Hiperolius marmoratus	32	16
700	A221	100fr	Echis leucogaster	38	18
701	A221	150fr	Kinixys erosa	55	28
702	A221	250fr	Python regius	90	45
			Nos. 696-702 (7)	2.41	1.24

Nos. 696-697 vert. Nos. 700-702 are airmail.

British Queen Mother, 85th Birthday A222

1985, June 21 *Perf. 13½*

703	A222	75fr	On pony bobs	22	12
704	A222	85fr	Wedding, 1923	25	14
705	A222	500fr	Holding infant Elizabeth, 1926	1.60	80
706	A222	600fr	Coronation of King George VI, 1937	1.90	90

Souvenir Sheet

707	A222	1000fr	Christening of Prince William, 1982	3.25	1.60

Nos. 705-707 are airmail.

Vintage Autos and Aircraft — A223

1985, June 21

708	A223	5fr	Benz Victoria, 1893	5	5
709	A223	25fr	Peugeot 174, 1927	10	5
710	A223	45fr	Louis Bleriot	16	8
711	A223	50fr	Breguet 14	20	10
712	A223	500fr	Bugatti Coupe Napoleon T41 Boyale	1.90	90
713	A223	500fr	Airbus A300-P4	1.90	90
714	A223	600fr	Mercedes-Benz 540K, 1938	2.25	1.20
715	A223	600fr	Airbus A300B	2.25	1.20
			Nos. 708-715 (8)	8.81	4.48

Souvenir Sheet

716	A223	1000fr	Louis, Bleriot, Karl Benz	4.00	1.90

Automobile, cent. Nos. 712-716 are airmail.

Audubon Birth Bicent. A224

Illustrations of No. American bird species by Audubon and scouting trefoil.

1985, June 21

717	A224	60fr	Aix sponsa	22	12
718	A224	100fr	Mimus polyglotos	38	18
719	A224	300fr	Icterus galbula	1.20	60
720	A224	400fr	Sitta carolinensis	1.50	80
721	A224	500fr	Asyndesmus lewis	1.50	90
722	A224	600fr	Buteo cagopus	2.25	1.10
			Nos. 717-722 (6)	7.05	3.70

Souvenir Sheet

723	A224	1000fr	Columba leucocephala	4.00	1.90

Nos. 721-723 are airmail.

ARGENTINA '85, Buenos Aires — A225

Various equestrians.

1985, July 5 *Perf. 13*

724	A225	25fr	Gaucho, piebald	9	5
725	A225	45fr	Horse and rider, Andes Mountains	16	8
726	A225	90fr	Rodeo	32	16
727	A225	100fr	Hunting gazelle	38	18
728	A225	150fr	Gauchos, 3 horses	55	25

729 A225 200fr Rider beside mount 70 35
730 A225 250fr Contest 90 42
Nos. 724-730 (7) 3.10 1.49

Souvenir Sheet

731 A225 500fr Foal 1.90 70

Nos. 727-731 are airmail.

Locomotives — A226

1985, July 23

732 A226 50fr 105-30 electric, tank wagon 18 10
733 A226 75fr Diesel shunting locomotive 25 14
734 A226 80fr Diesel locomotive 28 14
735 A226 100fr Diesel railcar 38 18
736 A226 150fr No. 6093 55 25
737 A226 200fr No. 105 diesel railcar 70 35
738 A226 250fr Diesel, passenger car 90 42
Nos. 732-738 (7) 3.24 1.58

Nos. 735-738 are airmail.

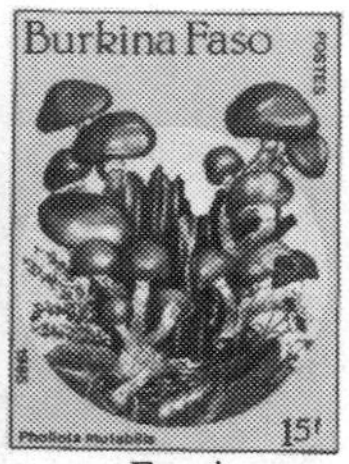

Artifacts A227 — Fungi A228

1985, July 27 *Perf. 13x12½*

739 A227 10fr 4-legged jar, Tikare 5 5
740 A227 40fr Lidded pot with bird handles, P. Bazega 14 7
741 A227 90fr Mother and child, bronze statue, Ouagadougou 35 16
742 A227 120fr Drummer, bronze statue, Ouagadougou 42 20

No. 742 is airmail.

1985, Aug. 8 *Perf. 13*

743 A228 15fr Philiota mutabilis 5 5
744 A228 20fr Hypholoma (nematoloma) fasciculare 8 5
745 A228 30fr Ixocomus granulatus 10 5
746 A228 60fr Agaricus campestris 22 12
747 A228 80fr Trachypus scaber 30 15
748 A228 150fr Armillaria mellea 55 25
749 A228 250fr Marasmius scorodonius 90 42
Nos. 743-749 (7) 2.20 1.09

Nos. 748 is airmail.

ITALIA '85 — A228a

Paintings by Botticelli: 25fr, Virgin and Child. 45fr, Portrait of a Man. 90fr, Mars and Venus. 100fr, Birth of Venus. 150fr, Allegory of the Calumny. 200fr, Pallas and the Centaur. 250fr, Allegory of Spring. 500fr, The Virgin of Melagrana.

1985, Oct. 25 Litho. *Perf. 12½x13*

749A A228a 25fr multi 12 7
749B A228a 45fr multi 22 12
749C A228a 90fr multi 45 22
749D A228a 100fr multi 50 25
749E A228a 150fr multi 70 38
749F A228a 200fr multi 1.00 50
749G A228a 250fr multi 1.25 60
Nos. 749A-749G (7) 4.24 2.14

Souvenir Sheet

749H A228a 500fr multi 2.50 1.25

No. 749D-749H are airmail.

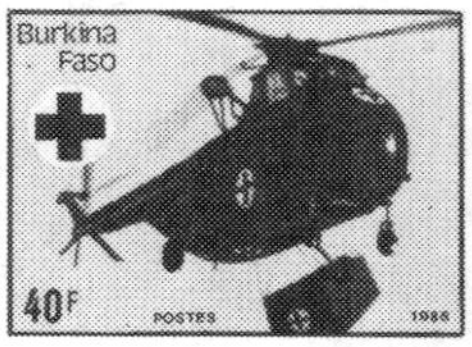

Intl. Red Cross in Burkina Faso, 75th Anniv. A229

1985, Nov. 10

750 A229 40f Helicopter 15 7
751 A229 85fr Ambulance 30 15
752 A229 150fr Henri Dunant 55 25
753 A229 250fr Physician, patient 90 42

Nos. 752-753 are vert. and airmail.

Child Survival A230

1986, Jan. 6

754 A230 90fr Breast-feeding 48 25

Dated 1985.

Dodo Carnival — A231

1986, Jan. 6 *Perf. 12½*

755 A231 20fr Three children, drummer 12 6
756 A231 25fr Lion, 4 dancers 14 8
757 A231 40fr Two dancers, two drummers 22 10
758 A231 45fr Three dancers 25 12
759 A231 90fr Zebra, ostrich, dancers 48 25
760 A231 90fr Elephant, dancer 48 25
Nos. 755-760 (6) 1.69 86

Dated 1985.

Christopher Columbus (1451-1506) — A232

Columbus: 250fr, At Court of King of Portugal, the Nina. 300fr, Using astrolable, the Santa Maria. 400fr, Imprisonment at Hispanola, 1500, the Santa Maria. 450fr, At San Salvador, 1492, the Pinta. 1000fr, Fleet departing Palos harbor, 1492.

1986, Feb. 10 *Perf. 13½*

761 A232 250fr multi 1.35 68
762 A232 300fr multi 1.65 82
763 A232 400fr multi 2.25 1.15
764 A232 450fr multi 2.50 1.25

Souvenir Sheet

765 A232 1000fr multi 5.50 2.75

Nos. 764-765 are airmail. Dated 1985.

Railroad Construction — A233

1986, Feb. 10

766 A233 90fr Man, woman carrying rail 50 25
767 A233 120fr Laying rails 65 32
768 A233 185fr Diesel train on new tracks 1.00 50
769 A233 500fr Adler locomotive, 1835 2.75 1.40

Souvenir Sheet

770 A233 1000fr Electric train, Series 290 diesel 5.00 2.75

German Railways, sesquicentennial. Nos. 769-770 are airmail. Dated 1985.

World Post Day — A237

1986, Oct. 9 *Perf. 13*

779 A237 120fr multi 68 35

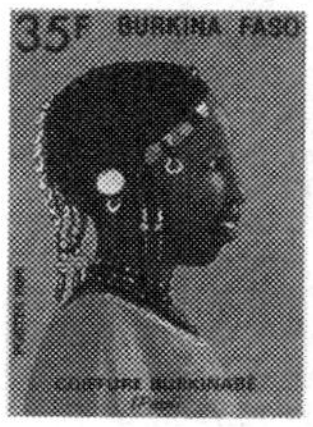

Hairstyles — A241

1986, Nov. 4 Litho. *Perf. 12½x13*

788 A241 35fr Peul 28 14
789 A241 75fr Dafing 60 30
790 A241 90fr Peul, diff. 70 35
791 A241 120fr Mossi 95 48
792 A241 185fr Peul, diff. 1.50 75
Nos. 788-792 (5) 4.03 2.02

World Environment Day — A246

1987, Aug. 18 Litho. *Perf. 13x12½*

807 A246 90fr shown 68 35
808 A246 145fr Emblem, huts 1.10 55

Pre-Olympic Year — A247

1987, Aug. 31 *Perf. 12½*

809 A247 75fr High jump 55 28
810 A247 85fr Tennis, vert. 62 30
811 A247 90fr Ski jumping 68 35
812 A247 100fr Soccer 75 38
813 A247 145fr Running 1.10 55
814 A247 350fr Pierre de Coubertin, tennis, vert. 2.60 1.30
Nos. 809-814 (6) 6.30 3.16

Pierre de Coubertin (1863-1937).

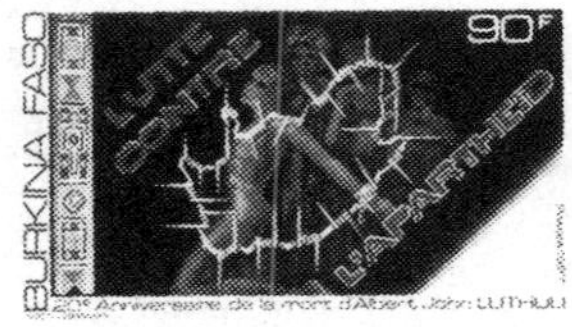

Fight Against Apartheid — A249

1987, Nov. 11 Litho. *Perf. 13*

816 A249 90fr shown 1.00 50
817 A249 100fr Luthuli, book, 1962 1.10 55

Albert John Luthuli (1898-1967), South African reformer, author and 1960 Nobel Peace Prize winner. No. 817 incorrectly inscribed "1899-1967."

Traditional Musical Instruments A251

Perf. 12x11½, 11½x12

1987, Dec. 4 **Litho.**

823 A251 20fr Xylophone 18 9
824 A251 25fr 3-Stringed lute, vert. 22 11
825 A251 35fr Zither 30 15
826 A251 90fr Conical drum, vert. 78 40
827 A251 1000fr Calabash drum, vert. 8.50 4.25
Nos. 823-827 (5) 9.98 5.00

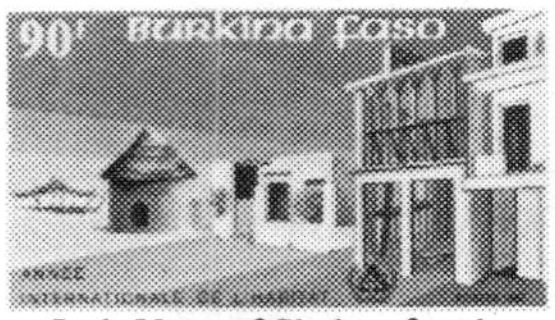

Intl. Year of Shelter for the Homeless — A252

1987, Dec. 4 Litho. *Perf. 13*

828 A252 90fr multi 65 32

Five-year Natl. Development Plan — A253

1987, Dec. 15 *Perf.*

829 A253 40fr Small businesses 30 15
830 A253 55fr Agriculture 40 20
831 A253 60fr Constructing schools 45 22
832 A253 90fr Transportation and communications 65 32
833 A253 100fr Literacy 72 35

834 A253 120fr Animal husbandry 88 45
Nos. 829-834 (6) 3.40 1.69

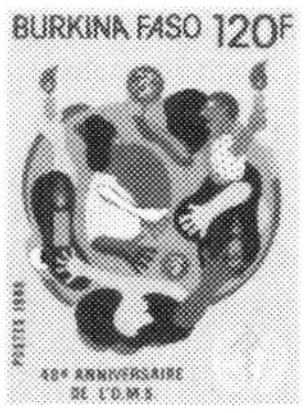

World Health Organization, 40th Anniv. — A254

1988, Mar. 31 Litho. *Perf. 12½x13*
835 A254 120fr multi 78 40

1988 Summer Olympics, Seoul A255

1988, May 5 *Perf. 13x12½*
836 A255 30fr shown 20 10
837 A255 160fr Torch, vert. 1.05 52
838 A255 175fr Soccer 1.15 58
839 A255 235fr Volleyball, vert. 1.50 75
840 A255 450fr Basketball, vert. 2.90 1.45
Nos. 836-840 (5) 6.80 3.40

Souvenir Sheet

Perf. 12½x13

841 A255 500fr Runners 3.25 1.65

No. 841 contains one stamp 40x52mm plus two labels.

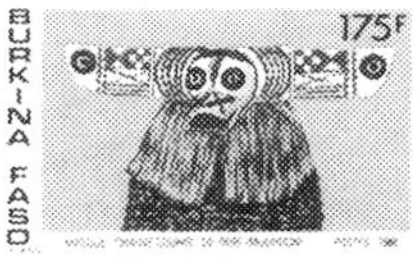

Ritual Masks A256

1988, May 30 Litho. *Perf. 13*
842 A256 10fr Epervier, Houet 8 5
843 A256 20fr Jeunes Filles, Oullo 14 8
844 A256 30fr Bubale, Houet 20 10
845 A256 40fr Forgeron, Mouhoun 28 14
846 A256 120fr Nounouma, Ouri 80 40
847 A256 175fr Chauve-souris, Ouri 1.20 60
Nos. 842-847 (6) 2.70 1.37

Nos. 842-846 vert.

Handicrafts A257

1988, Aug. 22 Litho. *Perf. 13½*
848 A257 5fr Kieriebe ceramic pitcher, vert. 5 5
849 A257 15fr Mossi basket 12 6
850 A257 25fr Gurunsi chair 18 8
851 A257 30fr Bissa basket 20 10
852 A257 45fr Ougadougou leather box 35 18
853 A257 85fr Ougadougou bronze statue, vert. 68 35
854 A257 120fr Ougadougou leather valise 80 40
Nos. 848-854 (7) 2.38 1.22

World Post Day — A258

1988, Oct. 9 Litho. *Perf. 13*
855 A258 120fr multi 80 40

Aquatic Fauna — A259

1988, Oct. 31 *Perf. 12*
856 A259 70fr Angler martin 48 25
857 A259 100fr Mormyrus rume 68 35
858 A259 120fr Frog 80 40
859 A259 160fr Duck 1.10 55

Civil Rights and Political Activists A260

Designs: 80fr, Mohammed Ali Jinnah (1876-1948), 1st Governor General of Pakistan. 120fr, Mahatma Gandhi (1869-1948), India. 160fr, John F. Kennedy. 235fr, Martin Luther King, Jr.

1988, Nov. 22 Litho. *Perf. 14*
860 A260 80fr multi 52 25
861 A260 120fr multi 78 40
862 A260 160fr multi 1.00 50
863 A260 235fr multi 1.50 75

Christmas — A261

Stained-glass windows.

1988, Dec. 2 *Perf. 12*
864 A261 120fr Adoration of the shepherds 78 40
865 A261 160fr Adoration of the Magi 1.00 50
866 A261 450fr Madonna and child 2.90 1.45
867 A261 1000fr Flight into Egypt 6.35 3.15

SEMI-POSTAL STAMPS

Catalogue values for unused stamps in this section, from this point to the end of the section, are for Never Hinged items.

Anti-Malaria Issue
Common Design Type

Perf. 12½x12

1962, Apr. 7 Engr. Unwmk.
B1 CD108 25fr + 5fr red org 50 50

Freedom from Hunger Issue
Common Design Type

1963, Mar. 21 *Perf. 13*
B2 CD112 25fr + 5fr dk grn, bl & brn 50 50

AIR POST STAMPS

Catalogue values for unused stamps in this section, from this point to the end of the section, are for Never Hinged items.

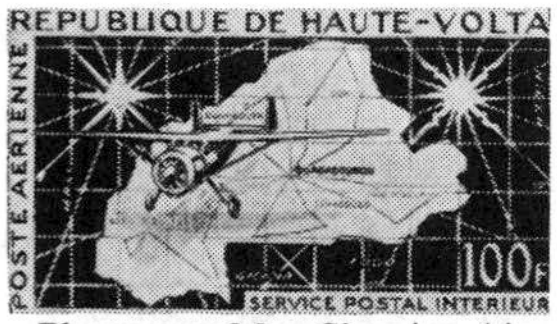

Plane over Map Showing Air Routes — AP1

Designs: 200fr, Plane at airport, Ouagadougou. 500fr, Champs Elysées, Ouagadougou.

Unwmk.

1961, March 4 Engr. *Perf. 13*
C1 AP1 100fr dk bl, hn brn & lt grn 75 28
C2 AP1 200fr gray grn, rose brn & sep 1.50 55
C3 AP1 500fr multi 3.75 1.50

Air Afrique Issue
Common Design Type

1962, Feb. 17
C4 CD107 25fr brt pink, dk pur & lt grn 35 22

UN Emblem and Upper Volta Flag — AP2

Perf. 13½x12½

1962, Sept. 22 Photo.
C5 AP2 50fr multi 50 25
C6 AP2 100fr multi 1.00 55

Admission to UN, second anniversary.

Post Office, Ouagadougou — AP3

1962, Dec. 11 *Perf. 13x12*
C7 AP3 100fr multi 90 50

Jet Over Map AP4

1963, June 24
C8 AP4 200fr multi 1.50 75

First jet flight, Ouagadougou to Paris.

African Postal Union Issue
Common Design Type

1963, Sept. 8 Unwmk. *Perf. 12½*
C9 CD114 85fr dp vio, ocher & red 80 55

No. C8 Surcharged in Red

AIR AFRIQUE
19-11-63
50F

1963, Nov. 19 *Perf. 13x12*
C10 AP4 50fr on 200fr multi 60 50

See note after Mauritania No. C26.

Europafrica Issue
Common Design Type

Design: 50fr, Sunburst and Europe linked with Africa.

1964, Jan. 6 *Perf. 12x13*
C11 CD116 50fr multi 90 60

Ramses II, Abu Simbel — AP5

Greek Sculptures — AP6

1964, Mar. 8 Engr. *Perf. 13*
C12 AP5 25fr dp grn & choc 35 30
C13 AP5 100fr brt bl & brn 1.40 1.20

UNESCO world campaign to save historic monuments of Nubia.

1964, July 1 Unwmk. *Perf. 13*
C14 AP6 15fr Greek Portrait Head 20 14
C15 AP6 25fr Seated boxer 25 20
C16 AP6 85fr Victorious athlete 80 60
C17 AP6 100fr Venus of Milo 1.10 70
a. Min. sheet, #C14-C17 3.50 3.50

18th Olympic Games, Tokyo, Oct. 10-25.

West African Gray Woodpecker AP7

President John F. Kennedy (1917-1963) AP8

1964, Oct. 1 Engr. *Perf. 13*
C18 AP7 250fr multi 2.50 1.90

1964, Nov. 25 Photo. *Perf. 12½*
C19 AP8 100fr org, brn & lil 85 85
a. Souv. sheet of 4 3.50 3.50

Bird Type of Regular Issue, 1965

1965, Mar. 1 Photo. *Perf. 13*

Size: 27x48mm

C20 A27 500fr Abyssinian roller 5.50 2.50

Earth and Sun — AP9

1965, Mar. 23 **Engr.**
C21 AP9 50fr multi 55 20

5th World Meteorological Day.

Hughes Telegraph, ITU Emblem and Dial Telephone — AP10

1965, May 17 **Unwmk.** ***Perf. 13***
C22 AP10 100fr red, sl grn & bl grn 1.00 50

ITU, centenary.

Intl. Cooperation Year — AP10a

1965, June 21 **Photo.** ***Perf. 13***
C23 AP10a 25fr multi 25 12
C24 AP10a 100fr multi 65 32
a. Miniature sheet of 4, 2 each #C23-C24 1.90 1.90

Sacred Sabou Crocodile — AP11

Design: 85fr, Lion (vert.).

1965, Aug. 9 **Engr.** ***Perf. 13***
C25 AP11 60fr bl grn, sl grn & red brn 60 30
C26 AP11 85fr sl grn, red brn & brn 80 42

Early Bird Satellite over Globe — AP12

Tiros Satellite and Weather Map — AP13

1965, Sept. 15 **Unwmk.** ***Perf. 13***
C27 AP12 30fr brt bl, brn & brn red 35 20

Space communications.

1966, March 23 **Engr.** ***Perf. 13***
C28 AP13 50fr dk car, brt bl & blk 50 35

6th World Meteorological Day.

FR-1 Satellite over Ouagadougou Space Tracking Station — AP14

1966, Apr. 28 ***Perf. 13***
C29 AP14 250fr mag, ind & org brn 2.00 1.10

Inauguration of WHO Headquarters, Geneva — AP15

1966, May 3 **Photo.**
C30 AP15 100fr yel, blk & bl 1.00 55

Air Afrique Issue

Common Design Type

1966, Aug. 31 **Photo.** ***Perf. 13***
C31 CD123 25fr tan, blk & yel grn 30 14

Sir Winston Churchill, British Lion and "V" Sign — AP16

1966, Nov. 5 **Engr.** ***Perf. 13***
C32 AP16 100fr sl grn & car rose 1.00 55

Sir Winston Spencer Churchill (1874-1965), statesman and WWII leader.

Pope Paul VI, Peace Dove, UN General Assembly and Emblem — AP17

1966, Nov. 5
C33 AP17 100fr dk bl & pur 1.00 55

Pope Paul's appeal for peace before the UN General Assembly, Oct. 4, 1965.

Blind Man and Lions Emblem — AP18

1967, Feb. 28 **Engr.** ***Perf. 13***
C34 AP18 100fr dk vio bl, brt bl & dk brn 1.40 55

50th anniversary of Lions Intl.

UN Emblem and Rain over Landscape AP19

Diamant Rocket AP20

1967, March 23 **Engr.** ***Perf. 13***
C35 AP19 50fr ultra, dk grn & bl grn 60 25

7th World Meteorological Day.

1967, Apr. 18 **Engr.** ***Perf. 13***

French Spacecraft: 20fr, FR-1 satellite (horiz.). 30fr, D1-C satellite. 100fr, D1-D satellite (horiz.).

C36 AP20 5fr brt bl, sl grn & org 7 5
C37 AP20 20fr lil & sl bl 22 14
C38 AP20 30fr red brn, brt bl & emer 35 16
C39 AP20 100fr emer & dp cl 1.00 50

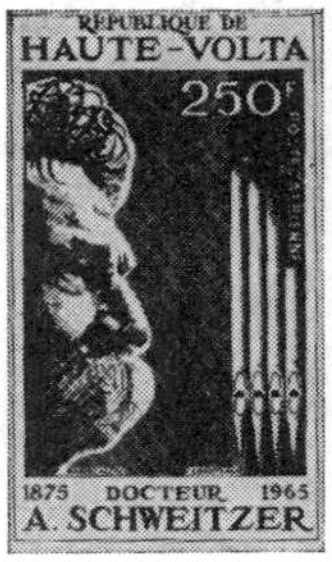

Albert Schweitzer (1875-1965), Medical Missionary and Organ Pipes — AP21

1967, May 12 **Engr.** ***Perf. 13***
C40 AP21 250fr cl & blk 2.00 1.10

World Map and 1967 Jamboree Emblem — AP22

1967, June 8 **Photo.**
C41 AP22 100fr multi 1.00 55

12th Boy Scout World Jamboree, Farragut State Park, Idaho, Aug. 1-9.

Madonna and Child, 15th Century AP23

Paintings: 20fr, Still life by Paul Gauguin. 50fr, Pieta, by Dick Bouts. 60fr, Anne of Cleves, by Hans Holbein the Younger. 90fr, The Money Lender and his Wife, by Quentin Massys (38x40mm.). 100fr, Blessing of the Risen Christ, by Giovanni Bellini. 200fr, The Handcart, by Louis Le Nain (horiz.). 250fr, The Four Evangelists, by Jacob Jordaens.

Perf. 12½x12, 12x12½, 13½ (90fr)

1967-68				**Photo.**
C42 AP23	20fr multi ('68)		20	10
C43 AP23	30fr multi		22	12
C44 AP23	50fr multi		38	25
C45 AP23	60fr multi ('68)		45	25
C46 AP23	90fr multi ('68)		65	42
C47 AP23	100fr multi		75	38
C48 AP23	200fr multi ('68)		1.50	70
C49 AP23	250fr multi		2.00	1.00
	Nos. C42-C49 (8)		6.15	3.22

See Nos. C70-C72.

African Postal Union Issue, 1967

Common Design Type

1967, Sept. 9 **Engr.** ***Perf. 13***
C50 CD124 100fr brn red, dp bl & bl grn 80 35

Caravelle "Ouagadougou" — AP24

1968, Feb. 29 **Engr.** ***Perf. 13***
C51 AP24 500fr bl, dp cl & blk 3.75 1.65

WMO Emblem, Sun, Rain, Wheat — AP25

1968, Mar. 23 **Engr.** ***Perf. 13***
C52 AP25 50fr dk red, ultra & gray grn 45 22

8th World Meteorological Day.

Europafrica Issue

Clove Hitch — AP25a

1968, July 20 **Photo.** ***Perf. 13***
C53 AP25a 50fr yel bis, blk & dk red 40 20

See note after Niger No. C89.

Vessel in Form of Acrobat with Bells, Colima Culture — AP26

Mexican Sculptures: 30fr, Ballplayer, Veracruz (vert.). 60fr, Javelin thrower, Colima (vert.). 100fr, Seated athlete with cape, Jalisco.

1968, Oct. 14 Engr. *Perf. 13*

C54	AP26	10fr	dk red, ocher & choc	12	8
C55	AP26	30fr	bl grn, brt grn & dk brn	25	12
C56	AP26	60fr	ultra, ol & mar	50	25
C57	AP26	100fr	brt grn, bl & mar	75	38

19th Olympic Games, Mexico City, Oct. 12-27.

Artisan Type of Regular Issue

Design: 100fr, Potter.

1968, Oct. 30 Engr. *Perf. 13*
Size: 48x27mm

C58	A52	100fr	choc, cop red & ocher	80	38

PHILEXAFRIQUE Issue

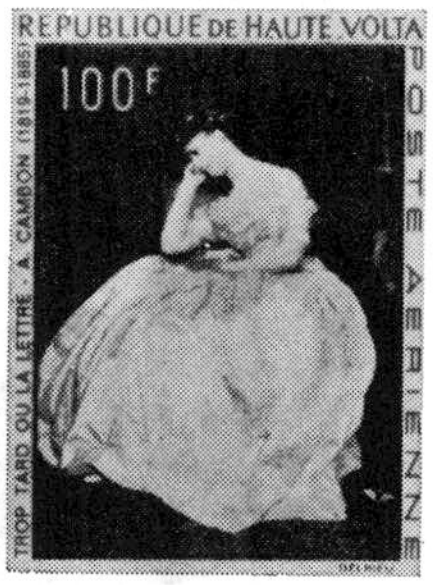

Too Late or The Letter, by Armand Cambon AP27

1968, Nov. 22 Photo. *Perf. 12½*

C59	AP27	100fr	multi	1.10	80

PHILEXAFRIQUE, Phil. Exhib., Abidjan, Feb. 14-23, 1969. Printed with alternating rose claret label.

Albert John Luthuli — AP28

Design: No. C61, Mahatma Gandhi.

1968, Dec. 16 Photo. *Perf. 12½*

C60	AP28	100fr	dk grn, yel grn & blk	75	40
C61	AP28	100fr	dk grn, yel & blk	75	40
a.			Min. sheet of 4, 2 each #C60-C61	3.00	3.00

Exponents of non-violence.

2nd PHILEXAFRIQUE Issue
Common Design Type

Design: 50fr, Upper Volta No. 59, dancers and musicians.

1969, Feb. 14 Engr. *Perf. 13*

C62	CD128	50fr	pur, bl car & brn	55	55

Weather Sonde, WMO Emblem, Mule and Cattle in Irrigated Field — AP29

1969, Mar. 24 Engr. *Perf. 13*

C63	AP29	100fr	dk brn, brt bl & grn	90	50

9th World Meteorological Day.

Artisan Type of Regular Issue

Design: 150fr, Basket weaver.

1969, Apr. 3 Engr. *Perf. 13*
Size: 48x27mm

C64	A55	150fr	brn, bl & blk	1.20	60

Lions Emblem, Eye and Blind Man — AP30

1969, Apr. 30 Photo.

C65	AP30	250fr	red & multi	2.50	1.00

12th Congress of District 403 of Lions Intl., Ouagadougou, May 2-3.

Fish Type of Regular Issue

Designs: 100fr, Phenacogrammus pabrensis. 150fr, Upside-down catfish.

1969 Engr. *Perf. 13*
Size: 48x27mm

C66	A57	100fr	sl, pur & yel	80	42
C67	A57	150fr	org brn, gray & sl	1.20	62

Earth and Astronaut — AP31

Embossed on Gold Foil

1969 *Die-cut Perf. 10½x10*

C68	AP31	1000fr	gold	8.25	8.25

Apollo 8 mission, which put the first man into orbit around the moon, Dec. 21-27, 1968.

No. C39 Overprinted in red with Lunar Landing Module and: "L'HOMME SUR LA LUNE / JUILLET 1969 / APOLLO 11"

1969, July 25 Engr. *Perf. 13*

C69	AP20	100fr	emer & dp cl	2.25	1.90

See note after Mali No. C80.

Painting Type of 1967-68

Paintings: 50fr, Napoleon Crossing Great St. Bernard Pass, by Jacques Louis David. 150fr, Napoleon Awarding the First Cross of the Legion of Honor, by Jean-Baptiste Debret. 250fr, Napoleon Before Madrid, by Carle Vernet.

1969, Aug. 18 Photo. *Perf. 12½x12*

C70	AP23	50fr	car & multi	50	38
C71	AP23	150fr	vio & multi	1.25	90
C72	AP23	250fr	grn & multi	2.50	1.50

Napoleon Bonaparte (1769-1821).

Agriculture Type of Regular Issue

Designs: 100fr, Peanuts. 200fr, Rice.

1969, Oct. 30 Photo. *Perf. 12½x13*
Size: 47½x27mm

C73	A58	100fr	pur & org brn	90	35
C74	A58	200fr	dp plum & grn	1.90	65

A particular stamp may be scarce, but if few collectors want it, its market value may remain relatively low.

Tree of Life, Symbols of Science, Agriculture and Industry — AP32

1969, Nov. 21 Photo. *Perf. 12x13*

C75	AP32	100fr	multi	65	35

See note after Mauritania No. C28.

Lenin — AP33

Design: 100fr, Lenin Addressing Revolutionaries in Petrograd, by V. A. Serov (horiz.).

1970, Apr. 22 Photo. *Perf. 12½*

C76	AP33	20fr	ocher & brn	14	8
C77	AP33	100fr	blk, lt grn & red	65	38

Lenin (1870-1924), Russian communist leader.

Pres. Roosevelt with Stamp Collection — AP34

Design: 10fr, Franklin Delano Roosevelt (vert.).

1970, June 4 Photo. *Perf. 12½*

C78	AP34	10fr	dk brn, emer & red brn	10	5
C79	AP34	200fr	vio bl, gray & dk car	1.40	45

Pres. Franklin Delano Roosevelt (1882-1945).

Soccer Game and Jules Rimet Cup — AP35

Design: 100fr, Goalkeeper catching ball and globe.

1970, June 4 Engr. *Perf. 13*

C80	AP35	40fr	ol, brt grn & brn	40	20
C81	AP35	100fr	blk, lil, brn & grn	90	40

9th World Soccer Championships for the Jules Rimet Cup, Mexico City, May 30-June 21, 1970.

EXPO Emblem, Monorail and "Cranes at the Seashore" AP36

UN Emblem, Dove and Star AP37

Design: 150fr, EXPO emblem, rocket, satellites and "Geisha."

1970, Aug. 7 Photo. *Perf. 12½*

C82	AP36	50fr	multi	35	16
C83	AP36	150fr	grn & multi	1.00	60

Issued to publicize EXPO '70 International Exhibition, Osaka, Japan, Mar. 15-Sept. 13.

1970, Oct. 2 Engr. *Perf. 13*

Design: 250fr, UN emblem and doves (horiz.).

C84	AP37	60fr	dk bl, bl & grn	40	20
C85	AP37	250fr	dk red brn, vio bl & ol	1.60	65

25th anniversary of the United Nations.

Holy Family — AP38

Die-Cut Perf. 10

1970, Nov. 27 Silver Embossed

C86	AP38	300fr	silver	2.50	2.50

Gold Embossed

C87	AP38	1000fr	gold	9.00	9.00

Christmas.

Family and Upper Volta Flag — AP39

Gamal Abdel Nasser — AP41

UN "Key to a Free World" — AP40

Litho.; Gold Embossed

1970, Dec. 10 *Perf. 12½*

C88	AP39	500fr	gold, blk & red	2.50	1.50

10th anniversary of independence, Dec. 11.

1970, Dec. 14 Engr. *Perf. 13*
C89 AP40 40fr red, bis & bl 35 16

UN Declaration of Independence for Colonial Peoples, 10th anniv.

1971, Jan. 30 Photo. *Perf. 12½*
C90 AP41 100fr grn & multi 65 30

Nasser (1918-1970), president of Egypt.

Herons, Egyptian Art, 1354 — AP42

Design: 250fr, Page from Koran, Egypt, 1368-1388 (vert.).

1971, May 13 Photo. *Perf. 13*
C91 AP42 100fr multi 65 30
C92 AP42 250fr multi 1.60 80

Olympic Rings and Various Sports — AP43

1971, June 10 Engr. *Perf. 13*
C93 AP43 150fr vio bl & red 1.00 60

Pre-Olympic Year.

Boy Scout and Buildings — AP44

1971, Aug. 12 Photo. *Perf. 12½*
C94 AP44 45fr multi 35 16

13th Boy Scout World Jamboree, Asagiri Plain, Japan, Aug. 2-10.

De Gaulle, Map of Upper Volta, Cross of Lorraine — AP45

Charles de Gaulle — AP46

1971, Nov. 9 Photo. *Perf. 13x12*
C95 AP45 40fr lt brn, grn & blk 40 35

Lithographed; Gold Embossed
Perf. 12½
C96 AP46 500fr gold & grn 4.00 3.75

Gen. Charles de Gaulle (1890-1970), president of France.

African Postal Union Issue, 1971
Common Design Type

Design: 100fr, Mossi dancer and UAMPT building, Brazzaville, Congo.

1971, Nov. 13 Photo. *Perf. 13x13½*
C97 CD135 100fr bl & multi 65 35

Gen. Sangoule Lamizana AP47

Kabuki Actor and Ice Hockey AP48

1971, Dec. 11 *Perf. 12½*
C98 AP47 35fr sep, blk, gold & ultra 22 12

Inauguration of 2nd Republic of Upper Volta.

1972, Feb. 15 Engr. *Perf. 13*
C99 AP48 150fr red, bl & pur 1.00 60

11th Winter Olympic Games, Sapporo, Japan, Feb. 3-13.

Music, by Pietro Longhi AP49

Design: 150fr, Gondolas and general view, by Ippolito Caffi (horiz.).

1972, Feb. 28 Photo. *Perf. 13*
C100 AP49 100fr gold & multi 65 35
C101 AP49 150fr gold & multi 1.10 40

UNESCO campaign to save Venice.

Running and Olympic Rings — AP50

Design: 200fr, Discus and Olympic rings.

1972, May 5 Engr. *Perf. 13*
C102 AP50 65fr dp bl, brn & grn 40 15
C103 AP50 200fr dp bl & brn 1.25 40
a. Miniature sheet of 2, #C102-C103 1.65 1.65

20th Olympic Games, Munich, Aug. 26-Sept. 10.

Musician Type of Regular Issue

Design: 500fr, Jimmy Smith and keyboard.

1972, May 17 Photo. *Perf. 14x13*
C104 A87 500fr grn & multi 4.00 1.90

Red Crescent Type of Regular Issue

1972, June 23 *Perf. 13x14*
C105 A88 100fr yel & multi 65 25

2nd Plan Type of Regular Issue

Design: 85fr, Road building machinery.

1972, Oct. 30 Engr. *Perf. 13*
C106 A90 85fr brick red, bl & blk 45 22

Presidents Pompidou and Lamizana — AP51

Design: 250fr, Presidents Pompidou and Lamizana, different design.

1972, Nov. 20 Photo. *Perf. 13*
Size: 48x37mm
C107 AP51 40fr gold & multi 55 40

Photogravure; Gold Embossed
Size: 56x36mm
C108 AP51 250fr yel grn, dk grn & gold 3.00 3.00

Visit of Pres. Georges Pompidou of France, Nov. 1972.

Skeet-shooting, Scalzone, Italy — AP52

Gold-medal Winners: 40fr, Pentathlon, Peters, Great Britain. 45fr, Dressage, Meade, Great Britain. 50fr, Weight lifting, Talts, USSR. 60fr, Boxing, light-weight, Seales, US 65fr, Fencing, Ragno-Lonzi, Italy. 75fr, Gymnastics, rings, Nakayama, Japan. 85fr, Gymnastics, Touritcheva, USSR. 90fr, 110m high hurdles, Milburn, US 150fr, Judo, Kawaguchi, Japan. 200fr, Sailing, Finn class, Maury, France. 250fr, Swimming, Spitz, US (7 gold). 300fr, Women's high jump, Meyfarth, West Germany. 350fr, Field Hockey, West Germany. 400fr, Javelin, Wolfermann, West Germany. No. C124, Women's diving, King, US No. C125, Cycling, Morelon, France. No. C126, Individual dressage, Linsenhoff, West Germany.

1972-73 Litho. *Perf. 12½*
C109 AP52 35fr multi ('73) 18 8
C110 AP52 40fr multi 20 10
C111 AP52 45fr multi ('73) 22 12
C112 AP52 50fr multi ('73) 25 14
C113 AP52 60fr multi ('73) 30 15
C114 AP52 65fr multi 35 16
C115 AP52 75fr multi ('73) 40 20
C116 AP52 85fr multi 42 20
C117 AP52 90fr multi ('73) 45 22
C118 AP52 150fr multi ('73) 80 40
C119 AP52 200fr multi 1.10 50
C120 AP52 250fr multi ('73) 1.40 65
C121 AP52 300fr multi 1.60 80
C122 AP52 350fr multi ('73) 1.90 90
C123 AP52 400fr multi ('73) 2.00 1.10
Nos. C109-C123 (15) 11.57 5.72

Souvenir Sheets
C124 AP52 500fr multi 2.25 1.60
C125 AP52 500fr multi ('73) 2.25 1.60
C126 AP52 500fr multi ('73) 2.25 1.60

20th Olympic Games, Munich.

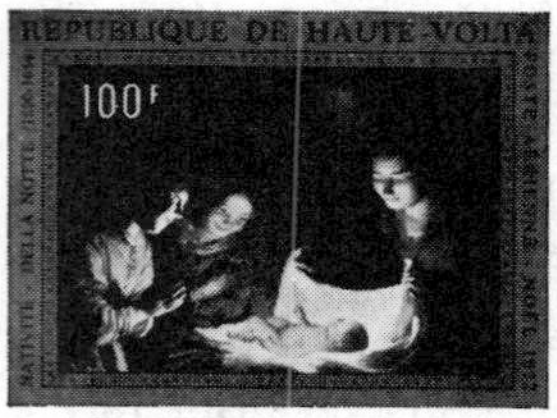

Nativity, by Della Notte — AP53

Christmas: 200fr, Adoration of the Kings, by Albrecht Dürer.

1972, Dec. 23 Photo. *Perf. 13*
C127 AP53 100fr gold & multi 50 22
C128 AP53 200fr gold & multi 1.10 65

Madonna and Child, by Albrecht Dürer AP54

Christmas: 75fr, Virgin Mary, Child and St. John, by Joseph von Führich. 100fr, The Virgin of Grand Duc, by Raphael. 125fr, Holy Family, by David. 150fr, Madonna and Child, artist unknown. 400fr, Flight into Egypt, by Gentile da Fabriano (horiz.).

1973, Mar. 22 Litho. *Perf. 12½x13*
C129 AP54 50fr multi 35 16
C130 AP54 75fr multi 50 25
C131 AP54 100fr multi 65 35
C132 AP54 125fr multi 80 40
C133 AP54 150fr multi 1.00 50
Nos. C129-C133 (5) 3.30 1.66

Souvenir Sheet
C134 AP54 400fr multi 2.50 1.40

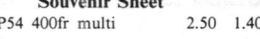

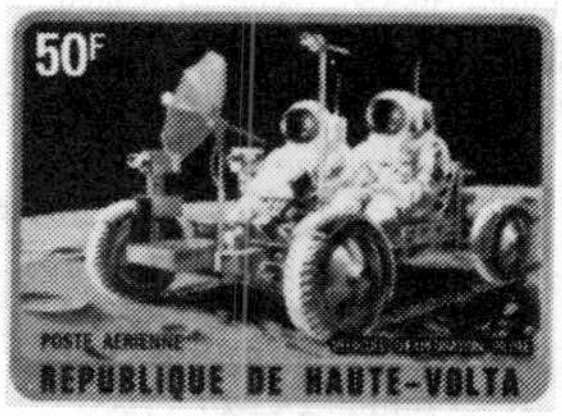

Manned Lunar Buggy on Moon — AP55

Moon Exploration: 65fr, Lunakhod, Russian unmanned vehicle on moon. 100fr, Lunar module returning to orbiting Apollo capsule. 150fr, Apollo capsule in moon orbit. 200fr, Space walk. 250fr, Walk in Sea of Tranquillity.

1973, Apr. 30 Litho. *Perf. 13x12½*
C135 AP55 50fr multi 35 16
C136 AP55 65fr multi 42 20
C137 AP55 100fr multi 65 35
C138 AP55 150fr multi 1.00 50
C139 AP55 200fr multi 1.40 65
Nos. C135-C139 (5) 3.82 1.86

Souvenir Sheet
C140 AP55 250fr multi 1.60 80

Giraffes AP56

African Wild Animals: 150fr, Elephants. 200fr, Leopard (horiz.). 250fr, Lion (horiz.). 300fr, Rhinoceros (horiz.). 500fr, Crocodile (horiz.).

Perf. 12½x13, 13x12½

1973, May 3 **Litho.**

C141 AP56 100fr multi 65 35
C142 AP56 150fr multi 1.00 50
C143 AP56 200fr multi 1.40 65
C144 AP56 250fr multi 1.60 80
C145 AP56 500fr multi 3.50 1.60
Nos. C141-C145 (5) 8.15 3.90

Souvenir Sheet

C146 AP56 300fr multi 2.00 1.00

Europafrica Issue

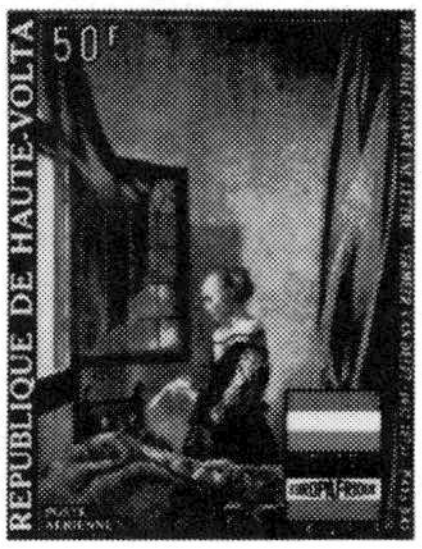

Girl Reading Letter, by Jan Vermeer AP57

Paintings: 65fr, Portrait of a Lady, by Roger van der Weyden. 100fr, Young Lady at her Toilette, by Titian. 150fr, Jane Seymour, by Hans Holbein. 200fr, Mrs. Williams, by John Hoppner. 250fr, Milkmaid, by Jean-Baptiste Greuze.

1973, June 7 **Litho.** ***Perf. 12½x13***

C147 AP57 50fr multi 35 16
C148 AP57 65fr multi 42 20
C149 AP57 100fr multi 65 35
C150 AP57 150fr multi 1.00 50
C151 AP57 200fr multi 1.40 65
Nos. C147-C151 (5) 3.82 1.86

Souvenir Sheet

C152 AP57 250fr multi 1.60 80

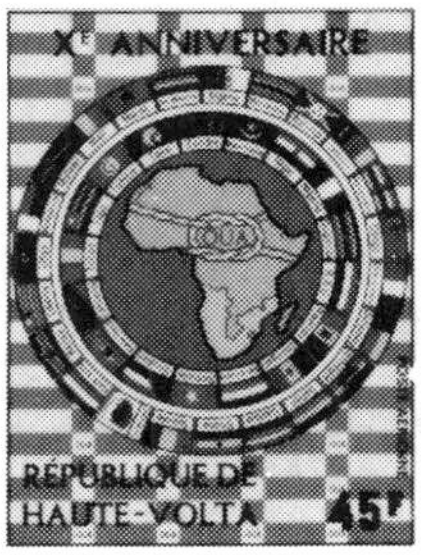

Africa Encircled by OAU Flags AP58

1973, June 7

C153 AP58 45fr multi 30 14

10th anniv. of Org. for African Unity.

Demand, as well as supply, determines a stamp's market value. One is as important as the other.

Locomotive "Pacific" 4546, 1908 — AP59

Locomotives from Railroad Museum, Mulhouse, France: 40fr, No. 242, 1927. 50fr, No. 2029, 1882. 150fr, No. 701, 1885-92. 250fr, "Coupe-Vent" No. C145, 1900. 350fr, Buddicomb No. 33, Paris to Rouen, 1884.

1973, June 30 ***Perf. 13x12½***

C154 AP59 10fr multi 7 5
C155 AP59 40fr multi 25 14
C156 AP59 50fr multi 35 16
C157 AP59 150fr multi 1.00 50
C158 AP59 250fr multi 1.60 80
Nos. C154-C158 (5) 3.27 1.65

Souvenir Sheet

C159 AP59 350fr multi 2.25 1.20

Boy Scout Type of 1973

Boy Scouts: 40fr, Flag signaling. 75fr, Skiing. 150fr, Cooking. 200fr, Hiking. 250fr, Studying stars.

1973, July 18 **Litho.** ***Perf. 12½x13***

C160 A95 40fr multi 25 14
C161 A95 75fr multi 50 25
C162 A95 150fr multi 1.00 50
C163 A95 200fr multi 1.40 65

Souvenir Sheet

C164 A95 250fr multi 1.60 80

Nos. C148 and C150 Surcharged in Silver New Value and "SECHERESSE / SOLIDARITE AFRICAINE / ET INTERNATIONALE"

1973, Aug. 16

C165 AP57 100fr on 65fr multi 65 35
C166 AP57 200fr on 150fr multi 1.40 65

Drought relief.

Kennedy Type, 1973

John F. Kennedy and: 200fr, Firing Saturn 1 rocket, Apollo program. 300fr, First NASA manned space capsule. 400fr, Saturn 5 countdown.

1973, Sept. 12 **Litho.** ***Perf. 12½x13***

C167 A96 200fr multi 1.40 65
C168 A96 300fr multi 2.00 1.00

Souvenir Sheet

C169 A96 400fr multi 2.50 1.40

10th death anniv. of Pres John F. Kennedy.

Interpol Type of 1973
Souvenir Sheet

Design: Victim in city street.

1973, Sept. 15 ***Perf. 13x12½***

C170 A97 300fr multi 2.00 1.00

Tourism Type of 1973

1973, Sept. 30

C171 A98 100fr Waterfalls 65 35

Souvenir Sheet

C172 A98 275fr Elephant 1.90 90

House of Worship Type of 1973

Design: Cathedral of the Immaculate Conception.

1973, Sept. 28

C173 A99 200fr multi 1.40 65

Folklore Type of 1973

Designs: 100fr, 225fr, Bobo masked dancers (different).

1973, Nov. 30 **Litho.** ***Perf. 12½x13***

C174 A100 100fr multi 65 35
C175 A100 225fr multi 1.50 70

Zodiac Type of 1973
Souvenir Sheets

Zodiacal Light and: No. C176, First four signs of Zodiac. No. C177, Second four signs. No. C178, Last four signs.

1973, Dec. 15 ***Perf. 13x14***

C176 A101 250fr multi 1.60 80
C177 A101 250fr multi 1.60 80
C178 A101 250fr multi 1.60 80

Nos. C176-C178 have multicolored margin showing night sky and portraits: No. C176, Louis Armstrong; No. C177, Mahatma Gandhi; No. C178, Martin Luther King.

Soccer Championship Type, 1974

Championship '74 emblem and: 75fr, Gento, Spanish flag. 100fr, Bereta, French flag. 250fr, Best, British flag. 400fr, Beckenbauer, West German flag.

1974, Jan. 15 **Litho.** ***Perf. 13x12½***

C179 A102 75fr multi 50 25
C180 A102 100fr multi 65 35
C181 A102 250fr multi 1.60 80

Souvenir Sheet

C182 A102 400fr multi 2.50 1.40

De Gaulle Type, 1974

Designs: 300fr, De Gaulle and Concorde (horiz.). 400fr, De Gaulle and French space shot.

Perf. 13x12½, 12½x13

1974, Feb. 4 **Litho.**

C183 A103 300fr multi 2.00 1.00

Souvenir Sheet

C184 A103 400fr multi 2.50 1.40

Soccer Cup Championship Type, 1974

World Cup, Emblems and: 150fr, Brindisis, Argentinian flag. No. C186, Kenko, Zaire flag. No. C187, Streich, East German flag. 400fr, Cruyff, Netherlands flag.

1974, Mar. 19 ***Perf. 12½x13***

C185 A104 150fr multi 75 38
C186 A104 300fr multi 1.50 75

Souvenir Sheets

C187 A104 300fr multi 1.50 75
C188 A104 400fr multi 2.00 1.00

UPU Type, 1974

UPU Emblem and: 100fr, Dove carrying mail. 200fr, Air Afrique 707. 300fr, Dish antenna. 500fr, Telstar satellite.

1974, July 23 ***Perf. 13½***

C189 A106 100fr multi 50 25
C190 A106 200fr multi 1.00 50
C191 A106 300fr multi 1.50 75

Souvenir Sheet

C192 A106 500fr multi 2.50 1.25

Soccer Cup Winners Type, 1974

World Cup, Game and Flags: 150fr, Brazil, in Sweden, 1958. 200fr, Brazil, in Chile, 1962. 250fr, Brazil, in Mexico, 1970. 450fr, England, in England, 1966.

1974, Sept. 2

C193 A107 150fr multi 1.00 50
C194 A107 200fr multi 1.40 65
C195 A107 250fr multi 1.60 80

Souvenir Sheet

C196 A107 450fr multi 3.00 1.50

Nos. C189-C192 Overprinted in Red "100e ANNIVERSAIRE DE L'UNION POSTALE UNIVERSELLE / 9 OCTOBRE 1974"

1974, Oct. 9

C197 A106 100fr multi 65 35
C198 A106 200fr multi 1.40 65
C199 A106 300fr multi 2.00 1.00

Souvenir Sheet

C200 A106 500fr multi 3.50 1.60

Universal Postal Union, centenary.

Flower Type of 1974

Flower Paintings by: 300fr, Auguste Renoir. 400fr, Carl Brendt.

1974, Oct. 31 **Litho.** ***Perf. 12½x13***

C201 A109 300fr multi 2.00 1.00

Souvenir Sheet

C202 A109 400fr multi 2.50 1.40

Locomotive Type of 1975

Locomotives from Railroad Museum, Mulhouse, France: 100fr, Crampton No. 80, 1852. 200fr, No. 701, 1885-92. 300fr, "Forquenot," 1882.

1975, Feb. 28 **Litho.** ***Perf. 13x12½***

C203 A112 100fr multi 65 35
C204 A112 200fr multi 1.40 65

Souvenir Sheet

C205 A112 300fr multi 2.00 1.00

Old Cars Type, 1975

Flags and Old Cars: 150fr, Germany and Mercedes-Benz, 1929. 200fr, Germany and Maybach, 1936. 400fr, Great Britain and Rolls Royce Silver Ghost, 1910.

1975, Apr. 6 ***Perf. 14x13½***

C206 A113 150fr multi 1.00 50
C207 A113 200fr multi 1.40 65

Souvenir Sheet

C208 A113 400fr multi 2.50 1.40

American Bicentennial Type of 1975

American Bicentennial: 200fr, Washington crossing Delaware. 300fr, Hessians Captured at Trenton.

1975, May 6 **Litho.** ***Perf. 14***

C209 A114 200fr multi 1.40 65
C210 A114 300fr multi 2.00 1.00

Schweitzer Type of 1975

Albert Schweitzer and: 150fr, Toucan. 175fr, Vulturine guinea fowl. 200fr, King vulture. 450fr, Crested corythornis.

1975, May 25 **Litho.** ***Perf. 13½***

C212 A115 150fr multi 1.00 50
C213 A115 175fr multi 1.20 55
C214 A115 200fr multi 1.40 65

Souvenir Sheet

C215 A115 450fr multi 3.00 1.50

Apollo Soyuz Type of 1975

Designs: 100fr, Apollo and Soyuz near link-up. 200fr, Cosmonauts Alexei Leonov and Valeri Kubasov. 300fr, Astronauts Donald K. Slayton, Vance Brand and Thomas P. Stafford. 500fr, Apollo Soyuz emblem, US and USSR flags.

1975, July 18 **Litho.** ***Perf. 13½***

C216 A116 100fr multi 65 35
C217 A116 200fr multi 1.40 65
C218 A116 300fr multi 2.00 1.00

Souvenir Sheet

C219 A116 500fr multi 3.50 1.60

Picasso Type of 1975

Picasso Paintings: 150fr, El Prado (horiz.). 350fr, Couple in Patio. 400fr, Science and Charity.

1975, Aug. 7

C220 A117 150fr multi 1.00 50
C221 A117 350fr multi 2.25 1.20

Souvenir Sheet

C222 A117 400fr multi 2.50 1.40

EXPO '75 Type of 1975

Expo '75 emblem and: 150fr, Passenger liner Asama Maru. 300fr, Future floating city Aquapolis.

1975, Sept. 26 **Litho.** ***Perf. 11***

C223 A118 150fr multi 75 38

Souvenir Sheet

Perf. 13½

C224 A118 300fr multi 1.50 75

Winter Olympic Games Type of 1975

Innsbruck Background, Olympic Emblem and: 100fr, Ice hockey. 200fr, Ski jump. 300fr, Speed skating.

1975, Dec. 15 ***Perf. 13½***

C225 A122 100fr multi 65 35
C226 A122 200fr multi 1.40 65

Souvenir Sheet

C227 A122 300fr multi 2.00 1.00

Olympic Games Type of 1976

Olympic Emblem and: 125fr, Heavyweight judo. 150fr, Weight lifting. 500fr, Sprint.

1976, Mar. 17 **Litho.** ***Perf. 13½***

C228 A123 125fr multi 65 30
C229 A123 150fr multi 75 38

Souvenir Sheet

C230	A123	500fr multi		2.50	1.25

Summer Olympic Games Type of 1976

Olympic emblem and: 150fr, Pole vault. 200fr, Gymnast on balance beam. 500fr, Two-man sculls.

1976, Mar. 25 ***Perf. 11***

C231	A124	150fr multi	75	38
C232	A124	200fr multi	1.00	50

Souvenir Sheet

C233	A124	500fr multi	2.50	1.25

Zeppelin Type of 1976

Airships: 100fr, Graf Zeppelin over Swiss Alps. 200fr, LZ-129 over city. 300fr, Graf Zeppelin. 500fr, Zeppelin over Bodensee.

1976, May 11

C234	A126	100fr multi	65	35
C235	A126	200fr multi	1.40	65
C236	A126	300fr multi	2.00	1.00

Souvenir Sheet

C237	A126	500fr multi	3.50	1.60

Viking Mars Type of 1976

Designs: 200fr, Viking lander assembly. 300fr, Viking orbiter in descent on Mars. 450fr, Viking in Mars orbit.

1976, June 24 Litho. ***Perf. 13½***

C238	A127	200fr multi	1.00	50
C239	A127	300fr multi	1.50	75

Souvenir Sheet

C240	A127	450fr multi	2.25	1.10

American Bicentennial Type of 1976

Bicentennial and Interphil '76 Emblems and: 100fr, Siege of Yorktown. 200fr, Battle of Cape St. Vincent. 300fr, Peter Francisco's bravery. 500fr, Surrender of the Hessians.

1976, Sept. 30 Litho. ***Perf. 13½***

C241	A129	100fr multi	65	35
C242	A129	200fr multi	1.40	65
C243	A129	300fr multi	2.00	1.00

Souvenir Sheet

C244	A129	500fr multi	3.50	1.60

Nos. C231-C233 Overprinted in Gold:
a. VAINQUEUR 1976 / TADEUSZ SLUSARSKI / POLOGNE
b. VAINQUEUR 1976 / NADIA COMANECI / ROUMANIE
c. VAINQUEUR 1976 / FRANK ET ALF HANSEN / NORVEGE

1976, July 4 Litho. ***Perf. 11***

C245	A124(a)	150fr multi	1.00	50
C246	A124(b)	200fr multi	1.40	65

Souvenir Sheet

C247	A124(c)	500fr multi	3.50	1.60

Winners, 21st Olympic Games.

UPU Emblem over Globe — AP60

1978, Aug. 8 Litho. ***Perf. 13***

C248	AP60	350fr multi	2.25	1.50

Congress of Paris, establishing UPU, centenary.

Jules Verne, Apollo 11 Emblem, Footprint on Moon, Neil Armstrong — AP61

Space Conquest: 50fr, Yuri Gagarin and moon landing. 100fr, Montgolfier hot air balloon and memorial medal, 1783; Bleriot's monoplane, 1909.

1978, Sept. 27 Litho. ***Perf. 13x12½***

C249	AP61	50fr multi	35	16
C250	AP61	60fr multi	40	20
C251	AP61	100fr multi	65	35

Anti-Apartheid Year — AP62

1978, Oct. 12 Litho. ***Perf. 13***

C252	AP62	100fr bl & multi	65	35

Philexafrique II-Essen Issue
Common Design Types

Designs: No. C253, Hippopotamus and Upper Volta No. C18. No. C254, Hummingbird and Hanover No. 1.

1978, Nov. 1 Litho. ***Perf. 12½***

C253	CD138	100fr multi	65	35
C254	CD139	100fr multi	65	35

Nos. C253-C254 printed se-tenant.

Sun God Horus with Sun — AP63

Jules Verne and Balloon — AP64

Design: 300fr, Falcon with cartouches and UNESCO emblem.

1978, Dec. 4

C255	AP63	200fr multi	1.40	65
C256	AP63	300fr multi	2.00	1.00

UNESCO Campaign to safeguard monuments at Philae.

1978, Dec. 10 Engr. ***Perf. 13***

C257	AP64	200fr multi	1.40	65

Verne (1828-1905), science fiction writer.

Bicycling, Olympic Rings — AP65

Designs: Bicycling scenes.

1980 ***Perf. 14½***

C258	AP65	65fr multi	65	32
C259	AP65	150fr multi, vert.	1.00	50
C260	AP65	250fr multi	1.60	80
C261	AP65	350fr multi	2.25	1.20

Souvenir Sheet

C262	AP65	500fr multi	3.50	1.60

22nd Summer Olympic Games, Moscow, July 19-Aug. 3.

Nos. C258-C262 Overprinted with Name of Winner and Country

1980, Nov. 22 Litho. ***Perf. 14½***

C263	AP65	65fr multi	42	20
C264	AP65	150fr multi	1.00	50
C265	AP65	250fr multi	1.60	80
C266	AP65	350fr multi	2.25	1.20

Souvenir Sheet

C267	AP65	500fr multi	3.50	1.60

1982 World Cup — AP66

Designs: Various soccer players.

1982, June 22 Litho. ***Perf. 13½***

C268	AP66	70fr multi	45	22
C269	AP66	90fr multi	60	30
C270	AP66	150fr multi	1.00	50
C271	AP66	300fr multi	2.00	1.00

Souvenir Sheet

C272	AP66	500fr multi	3.50	1.60

Anniversaries and Events — AP67

1983, June Litho. ***Perf. 13½***

C273	AP67	90fr Space Shuttle	30	15
C274	AP67	120fr World Soccer Cup	40	20
C275	AP67	300fr Cup, diff.	1.00	50
C276	AP67	450fr Royal Wedding	1.50	70

Souvenir Sheet

C277	AP67	500fr Prince Charles, Lady Diana	1.60	1.60

Pre-Olympics, 1984 Los Angeles — AP68

1983, Aug. 1 Litho. ***Perf. 13***

C278	AP68	90fr Sailing	30	15
C279	AP68	120fr Type 470	40	20
C280	AP68	300fr Wind surfing	1.00	50
C281	AP68	400fr Wind surfing, diff.	1.40	65

Souvenir Sheet

C282	AP68	520fr Soling Class, Wind surfing	1.60	1.60

Christmas AP69

Rubens Paintings.

1983 Litho. ***Perf. 13***

C283	AP69	120fr Adoration of the Shepherds	40	20
C284	AP69	350fr Virgin of the Garland	1.20	60
C285	AP69	500fr Adoration of the Kings	1.60	80

1984 Summer Olympics — AP70

1984, Mar. 26 Litho. ***Perf. 12½***

C286	AP70	90fr Handball, vert.	30	15
C287	AP70	120fr Volleyball, vert.	40	20
C288	AP70	150fr Handball, diff.	50	25
C289	AP70	250fr Basketball	80	42
C290	AP70	300fr Soccer	1.00	50
		Nos. C286-C290 (5)	3.00	1.52

Souvenir Sheet

C291	AP70	500fr Volleyball, diff.	1.60	80

Local Birds — AP71

1984, May 14 Litho. ***Perf. 12½***

C292	AP71	90fr Phoenicopterus roseus	30	15
C293	AP71	185fr Choriotis kori, vert.	62	32
C294	AP71	200fr Buphagus erythrorhynchus, vert.	65	35
C295	AP71	300fr Bucorvus leadbeateri	1.00	50

AP72

Famous Men — AP73

Designs: 5fr, Houari Boumediene (1927-1978), president of Algeria 1965-78. 125fr, Gottlieb Daimler (1834-1900), German automotive pioneer, and 1886 Daimler. 250fr, Louis Bleriot (1872-1936), French aviator, first to fly the English Channel in a heavier-than-air craft. 300fr, Abraham Lincoln.

400fr, Henri Dunant (1828-1910), founder of the Red Cross. 450fr, Auguste Piccard (1884-1962), Swiss physicist, inventor of the bathyscaphe Trieste, 1948. 500fr, Robert Baden-Powell (1856-1941), founder of Boy Scouts. 600fr, Anatoli Karpov, Russian chess champion. 1000fr, Paul Harris (1868-1947), founder of Rotary Intl.

1984, May 21 Litho. *Perf. 13½*

C296	AP72	5fr multi	5	5
C297	AP72	125fr multi	50	25
C298	AP72	250fr multi	1.00	50
C299	AP72	300fr multi	1.20	60
C300	AP72	400fr multi	1.60	80
C301	AP72	450fr multi	1.90	90
C302	AP72	500fr multi	2.00	1.00
C303	AP72	600fr multi	2.25	1.20
		Nos. C296-C303 (8)	10.50	5.30

Souvenir Sheet

C304	AP73	1000fr multi	4.00	2.00

No. C304 contains one stamp 51x30mm.

Burkina Faso

Butterflies — AP73a

1984, May 23 *Perf. 13½*

C305	AP73a	10fr Graphium pylades	5	5
C306	AP73a	120fr Hypolimnas misippus	50	22
C307	AP73a	400fr Danaus chrysippus	1.60	80
C308	AP73a	450fr Papilio demodocus	1.90	90

Philexafrica '85, Lome — AP74

1985, May 20 Litho. *Perf. 13*

C309	AP74	200fr Solar & wind energy	55	25
C310	AP74	200fr Children	55	25

Nos. C309-C310 se-tenant with center label picturing a map of Africa or the exhibition emblem.

PHILEXAFRICA '85, Lome — AP75

National development: No. C311, Youth. No. C312, Communications and transportation.

1985, Nov. 16 Litho. *Perf. 13*

C311	AP75	250fr multi	90	45
C312	AP75	250fr multi	90	45

Intl. Youth Year (No. C311). Nos. C311-C312 printed se-tenant with center label picturing PHILEXAFRICA '85 emblem or outline map of Africa.

POSTAGE DUE STAMPS

Postage Due Stamps of Upper Senegal and Niger, 1914, Overprinted in Black or Red **HAUTE-VOLTA**

1920 Unwmk. *Perf. 14x13½*

J1	D2	5c green	28	28
J2	D2	10c rose	28	28
J3	D2	15c gray	28	28
J4	D2	20c brown (R)	35	35
J5	D2	30c blue	40	40
J6	D2	50c black (R)	62	62
J7	D2	60c orange	62	62
J8	D2	1fr violet	80	80
		Nos. J1-J8 (8)	3.63	3.63

Type of 1914 Issue Surcharged **2F.**

1927

J9	D2	2fr on 1fr lilac rose	2.00	2.00
J10	D2	3fr on 1fr orange brn	2.25	2.25

D3

Red-fronted Gazelle — D4

1928 Typo.

J11	D3	5c green	28	28
J12	D3	10c rose	28	28
J13	D3	15c dark gray	40	40
J14	D3	20c dark brown	40	40
J15	D3	30c dark blue	45	45
J16	D3	50c black	1.60	1.60
J17	D3	60c orange	2.00	2.00
J18	D3	1fr dull violet	3.25	3.25
J19	D3	2fr lilac rose	6.00	6.00
J20	D3	3fr orange brn	6.25	6.25
		Nos. J11-J20 (10)	20.91	20.91

Catalogue values for unused stamps in this section, from this point to the end of the section, are for Never Hinged items.

Republic

1962, Jan. 31 *Perf. 14x13½*

Denomination in Black

J21	D4	1fr bright blue	5	5
J22	D4	2fr orange	5	5
J23	D4	5fr brt vio blue	15	15
J24	D4	10fr red lilac	20	20
J25	D4	20fr emerald	45	45
J26	D4	50fr rose red	1.10	1.10
		Nos. J21-J26 (6)	2.00	2.00

OFFICIAL STAMPS

Catalogue values for unused stamps in this section, from this point to the end of the section, are for Never Hinged items.

Elephant O1

Perf. 12½

1963, Feb. 1 Unwmk. Photo.

Center in Sepia

O1	O1	1fr red brn	8	8
O2	O1	5fr yel grn	8	8
O3	O1	10fr dp vio	18	18
O4	O1	15fr red org	22	22
O5	O1	25fr brt rose lil	32	32
O6	O1	50fr brt grn	50	50
O7	O1	60fr brt red	65	65
O8	O1	85fr dk sl grn	1.00	1.00
O9	O1	100fr brt bl	1.65	1.65
O10	O1	200fr brt rose	2.75	2.75
		Nos. O1-O10 (10)	7.43	7.43

URUGUAY

LOCATION — South America, between Brazil and Argentina and bordering on the Atlantic Ocean.
GOVT. — Republic
AREA — 72,172 sq. mi.
POP. — 2,991,341 (est. 1983)
CAPITAL — Montevideo

120 Centavos = 1 Real
8 Reales = 1 Peso
100 Centesimos = 1 Peso (1859)
1000 Milésimos = 1 Peso (1898)

Values of early Uruguay stamps vary according to condition. Quotations for Nos. 1-17 are for fine copies. Very fine to superb specimens sell at much higher prices, and inferior or poor copies sell at reduced prices, depending on the condition of the individual specimen.

Catalogue values for unused stamps in this country are for Never Hinged items, beginning with Scott 534 in the regular postage section, Scott B5 in the semi-postal section, Scott C113 in the airpost section, Scott CB1 in the airpost semi-postal section, Scott E9 in the special delivery section, and Scott Q64 in the parcel post section.

Carrier Issues

Issued by Atanasio Lapido, Administrator-General of Posts

"El Sol de Mayo"
A1 A1a

Unwmk.

1856, Oct. 1 Litho. *Imperf.*

1	A1	60c blue	200.00	
a.		60c dp bl	250.00	
b.		60c indigo	750.00	
2	A1	80c green	200.00	
a.		80c dp grn	225.00	
3	A1	1r vermilion	200.00	
a.		1r car ver	225.00	

1857, Oct. 1

3B	A1a	60c blue	*1,500.*	
c.		60c pale blue	*1,600.*	
d.		60c dark blue	*1,600.*	

As Nos. 1-3d were spaced closely on the stone, four-margin copies are unusual. Most genuinely used specimens are pen canceled.
See Nos. 410-413, 771A.

A2

1858, Mar.

4	A2	120c blue	175.00	150.00
a.		120c dp bl	175.00	150.00
b.		120c grnsh bl	175.00	150.00
c.		Tete beche pair	*7,500.*	
5	A2	180c green	50.00	50.00
a.		180c dp grn	100.00	125.00
b.		Thick paper	50.00	100.00
c.		Tete beche pair	*10,000.*	
6	A2	240c dl ver	50.00	*250.00*
a.		240c dp ver	62.50	
b.		240c brn red	125.00	
c.		180c dl ver in stone of 240c		
d.		Thick paper (dl ver)	50.00	

Government Issues.

A3

A4

1859, June 26

Thin Numerals

7	A3	60c lilac	20.00	17.50
a.		60c gray lil	21.00	17.50
8	A3	80c yellow	175.00	32.50
a.		80c org	250.00	42.50
9	A3	100c brn lake	50.00	37.50
a.		100c brn rose	50.00	37.50
10	A3	120c blue	32.50	12.50
a.		120c sl bl	42.50	15.00
11	A3	180c green	7.50	15.00
12	A3	240c vermilion	42.50	45.00

1860

Thick Numerals.

13	A4	60c dl lil	12.50	5.00
a.		60c gray lil	15.00	5.00
b.		60c brn lil	15.00	7.50
c.		60c red lil	15.00	7.50
d.		As "a", fine impression (1st printing)	62.50	37.50
14	A4	80c yellow	17.50	10.00
a.		80c org	25.00	12.50
15	A4	100c rose	42.50	20.00
a.		100c car	42.50	20.00
16	A4	120c blue	20.00	10.00
17	A4	180c yel grn	87.50	75.00
a.		180c dp grn	100.00	87.50

No. 13 was first printed (1860) in sheets of 192 (16x12) containing 24 types. The impressions are very clear; paper is whitish and of better quality than that of the later printings. In the 1861-62 printings, the layout contains 12 types and the subjects are spaced farther apart.

Coat of Arms — A5

1864, Apr. 13

18	A5	6c rose	7.50	6.00
a.		6c car	12.50	10.00
b.		6c red	14.00	12.50
c.		6c brick red	17.50	15.00
20	A5	6c salmon	30.00	30.00
21	A5	8c green	12.50	10.00
a.		Tete beche pair	300.00	
22	A5	10c yellow	17.50	15.00
a.		10c ocher	17.50	15.00
23	A5	12c blue	5.00	4.50
a.		12c dk bl	8.75	6.25
b.		12c sl bl	8.75	6.25

No. 20, which is on thicker paper, was never placed in use.

Stamps of 1864 Surcharged in Black **5** **5**

1866, Jan. 1

24	A5	5c on 12c bl	12.50	*25.00*
a.		5c on 12c sl bl	14.00	27.50
b.		Inverted surcharge	37.50	
c.		Double surcharge	20.00	
d.		Pair, one without surcharge		
e.		Triple surcharge	42.50	
25	A5	10c on 8c brt grn	12.50	*25.00*
a.		10c on 8c dl grn	12.50	25.00
b.		Tete beche pair	150.00	
c.		Double surcharge	25.00	
26	A5	15c on 10c ocher	15.00	*45.00*
a.		15c on 10c yel	15.00	45.00
b.		Inverted surcharge	42.50	
c.		Double surcharge	22.50	
27	A5	20c on 6c rose	17.50	*37.50*
a.		20c on 6c rose red	17.50	*37.50*
b.		Inverted surcharge	37.50	
c.		Double surcharge	25.00	
d.		Pair, one without surcharge		
28	A5	20c on 6c brick red	*100.00*	
a.		Double surcharge		

Many counterfeits exist.
No. 28 was not issued.

The only foreign revenue stamps listed in this Catalogue are those authorized for prepayment of postage.

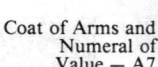

Coat of Arms and Numeral of Value — A7

A8

A8a

A8b

A8c

ONE CENTESIMO.
Type I. The wavy lines behind "CENTESIMO" are clear and distinct. Stamps 4mm. apart.

Type II. The wavy lines are rough and blurred. Stamps 3mm. apart.

1866, Jan. 10 ***Imperf.***

29	A7	1c blk (type II)	1.50	2.00
a.		1c blk (type I)	1.50	2.00
30	A8	5c blue	2.50	1.10
a.		5c dl bl	2.50	1.00
b.		5c ultra	17.50	3.75
c.		Numeral with white flag	15.00	5.50
d.		"ENTECIMOS"	15.00	8.75
e.		"CENTECIMO"	15.00	8.75
f.		"CENTECIMOS" with small "S"	8.75	3.75
g.		Pelure paper	11.25	7.00
h.		Thick paper	17.50	7.00
31	A8a	10c yel grn	8.75	3.00
a.		10c bl grn	8.75	3.00
b.		"I" of "CENTECIMOS" omitted	22.50	8.75
c.		"CENIECIMOS"	22.50	8.75
d.		"CENTRCIMOS"	14.00	8.75
32	A8b	15c org yel	12.50	6.00
a.		15c yel	12.50	6.00
33	A8c	20c rose	15.00	6.00
a.		20c lil rose	15.00	6.25
b.		Thick paper	17.50	6.75

Engraved plates were prepared for Nos. 30 to 33 but were not put in use. The stamps were printed from lithographic transfers from the plate. In 1915 a few reprints of the 15c were made from the engraved plate by a California philatelic society, each sheet being numbered and signed by officers of the society; then the plate was defaced.

1866-67 ***Perf. 8½ to 13½***

34	A7	1c black	1.75	3.00
35	A8	5c blue	1.25	45
a.		5c dk bl	1.25	45
b.		Numeral with white flag	7.50	6.25
c.		"ENTECIMOS"	7.50	2.50
d.		"CENTECIMO"	6.25	2.50
e.		"CENTECIMOS" with small "S"	3.75	1.50
f.		Pelure paper	5.00	2.00
36	A8a	10c green	1.75	42
a.		10c yel grn	1.75	42
b.		"CENIECIMOS"	6.25	2.50
c.		"I" of "CENTECIMOS" omitted	6.25	2.50
d.		"CENTRCIMOS"	6.25	2.50
e.		Pelure paper	10.00	6.25
37	A8b	15c org yel	2.50	1.75
a.		15c yel	2.50	1.75
b.		Pelure paper	10.00	6.25
38	A8c	20c rose	3.75	1.50
a.		20c brn rose	3.75	1.50
b.		Pelure paper	14.00	7.50
c.		Thick paper	9.00	3.00
		Nos. 34-38 (5)	11.00	7.12

A9

A10

A11

A12

1877-79 **Engr.** ***Rouletted 8***

39	A9	1c red brn	42	25
40	A10	5c green	50	20
a.		Thick paper	1.50	90
41	A11	10c vermilion	65	20
42	A11	20c bister	90	30
43	A11	50c black	5.00	1.50
43A	A12	1p bl ('79)	25.00	8.75
		Nos. 39-43A (6)	32.47	11.20

The first printing of the 1p had the coat of arms smaller with quarterings reversed. These "error" stamps were not issued, and all were ordered burned. A copy is known to have been in a celebrated Uruguayan collection and a few others exist.

1880, Nov. 10 **Litho.** ***Rouletted 6***

44	A9	1c brown	10	5
a.		Imperf., pair	8.75	
b.		Rouletted 12½	1.75	

Joaquin Suárez — A13

1881, Aug. 25 ***Perf. 12½***

45	A13	7c blue	1.00	90
a.		Imperf., pair	7.50	7.50

Devices from Coat of Arms
A14 A14a

1882, May 15

46	A14	1c green	50	50
a.		1c yel grn	1.75	90
b.		Imperf., pair	10.00	
47	A14a	2c rose	38	38
a.		Imperf., pair	12.50	

These stamps bear numbers from 1 to 100 according to their position on the sheet.

Counterfeits of Nos. 46 and 47 are plentiful.

Coat of Arms
A15 A16

Gen. Máximo Santos — A17

General José Artigas — A18

Perf. 12, 12x12½, 12x13, 13x12
1883, Mar. 1

48	A15	1c green	65	38
a.		Imperf., pair	4.50	
49	A16	2c red	75	50
a.		Imperf., pair	4.50	
50	A17	5c blue	1.00	75
a.		Imperf., pair	3.50	
51	A18	10c brown	1.50	1.00
a.		Imperf., pair	6.50	

No. 40 Overprinted in Black — 1883 Provisorio

1883, Sept. 24 ***Rouletted 8***

52	A10	5c green	50	38
a.		Double overprint	11.25	11.25
b.		Overprint reading down	4.00	4.00
c.		"Provisorio" omitted	6.00	6.00
d.		"1883" omitted	4.00	4.00

No. 52 with overprint in red is a color essay.

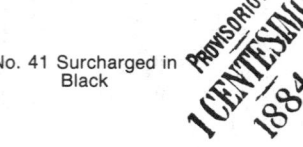

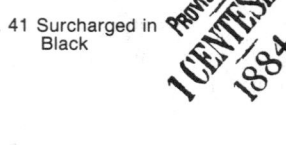

No. 41 Surcharged in Black — PROVISORIO. 1 CENTESIMO 1884.

1884, Jan. 15

53	A11	1c on 10c ver	18	18
a.		Small figure "1"	1.75	1.75
b.		Inverted surcharge	1.75	1.75
c.		Double surcharge	3.00	3.00

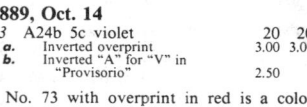

No. 47 Overprinted in Black — PROVISORIO 1884

Perf. 12½

54	A14a	2c rose	38	38
a.		Double overprint	11.25	
b.		Imperf., pair	20.00	

A22

A23

Thick Paper.
1884, Jan. 25 **Litho.** **Unwmk.**

55	A22	5c ultra	75	50
a.		Imperf., pair	3.00	3.50

Thin Paper.
Perf. 12½, 13 and Compound.

56	A23	5c blue	30	30
a.		Imperf., pair	6.75	

A24

A24a

A24b

Artigas
A25

Santos
A26

A27

A28

1884-88 **Engr.** ***Rouletted 8***

57	A24	1c gray	54	30
58	A24	1c olive	42	25
59	A24	1c green	25	12
60	A24a	2c vermilion	25	12
60A	A24a	2c rose ('88)	25	12
61	A24b	5c dp bl	50	20
61A	A24b	5c bl, *bl*	1.00	50
62	A24b	5c vio ('86)	20	12
63	A24b	5c lt bl ('88)	25	12
64	A25	7c dk brn	1.00	55
65	A25	7c org ('88)	75	38
66	A26	10c ol brn	25	12
67	A27	20c red vio	1.00	30
68	A27	20c bis brn ('88)	75	38
69	A28	25c gray vio	1.40	65
70	A28	25c ver ('88)	1.40	50
		Nos. 57-70 (16)	10.21	4.73

Water dissolves the blue in the paper of No. 61A.

A29

A30

1887, Oct. 17 **Litho.** ***Rouletted 9***

71	A29	10c lilac	90	50
a.		10c gray lil	90	50

1888, Jan. 1 **Engr.** ***Rouletted 8***

72	A30	10c violet	30	18

No. 62 Overprinted in Black — Provisorio

1889, Oct. 14

73	A24b	5c violet	20	20
a.		Inverted overprint	3.00	3.00
b.		Inverted "A" for "V" in "Provisorio"	2.50	

No. 73 with overprint in red is a color essay.

Coat of Arms
A32

Numeral of Value
A33

A34

A35

A36

A37

Justice
A38

Mercury
A39

A40

Perf. 12½ to 15½ and Compound.
1889-1901 **Engr.**

74	A32	1c green	25	12
a.		Imperf., pair	6.00	
75	A32	1c dl bl ('94)	25	12
76	A33	2c rose	25	12
77	A33	2c red brn ('94)	32	18
78	A33	2c org ('99)	25	18
79	A34	5c dp bl	25	12
80	A34	5c rose ('94)	38	12

81	A35	7c bis brn	50	20
82	A35	7c grn ('94)	3.50	1.50
83	A35	7c car ('00)	3.00	1.25
84	A36	10c bl grn	2.00	50
a.		Printed on both sides	15.00	
85	A36	10c org ('94)	2.00	38
86	A37	20c orange	1.50	38
87	A37	20c brn ('94)	3.00	1.00
88	A37	20c lt bl ('00)	1.50	20
a.		20c grnsh bl	1.75	20
89	A38	25c red brn	2.00	45
90	A38	25c ver ('94)	4.50	2.00
91	A38	25c bis brn ('01)	2.50	30
92	A39	50c lt bl	4.50	1.50
93	A39	50c lil ('94)	8.00	3.00
94	A39	50c car ('01)	4.50	38
95	A40	1p lilac	10.00	2.50
96	A40	1p lt bl ('94)	14.00	3.75
97	A40	1p dp grn ('01)	6.75	1.00
a.		Imperf., pair	17.50	
		Nos. 74-97 (24)	75.70	21.25

Nos. 59 and 62 Overprinted in Red:

Provisorio 1892
a

Provisorio 1891
b

1891-92 *Rouletted 8*

98	A24 (a)	1c grn ('92)	25	25
a.		Inverted overprint	3.75	3.75
b.		Double overprint	5.00	5.00
c.		Double overprint, one inverted	2.50	2.50
d.		"PREVISORIO"	2.50	2.50
99	A24b (b)	5c violet	15	15
a.		"1391"	1.75	1.75
b.		Double overprint	1.75	1.75
c.		Inverted overprint	1.75	1.75
d.		Double overprint, one inverted	3.00	3.00

Nos. 86 and 81 Surcharged in Black or Red

UN Centésimo Provisorio 1892
c

CINCO Centésimos Provisorio 1892
d

Perf. 12½ to 15½ and Compound
1892

100	A37 (c)	1c on 20c org (Bk)	20	12
a.		Inverted surcharge	3.00	3.00
101	A35 (d)	5c on 7c bis brn (R)	20	12
a.		Inverted surcharge	1.00	1.00
b.		Double surcharge, one inverted	3.00	3.00
c.		Double surcharge	3.00	3.00
d.		Vertical surcharge	10.00	
e.		"PREVISORIO"	2.00	2.00
f.		"Cinco" omitted	4.50	

No. 101 with surcharge in green is a color essay.
Several surcharge errors of date and misspelling of "Centesimos" exist. Value $12.50.

A45

A46

Arms
A47

Peace
A48

1892 **Engr.**

102	A45	1c green	25	12
103	A46	2c rose	25	12
104	A47	5c blue	25	12
105	A48	10c orange	1.00	50

Issue dates: 1c, 2c, Mar. 9; 5c, Apr. 19; 10c, Dec. 15.

Liberty
A49

Arms
A50

1894, June 2

106	A49	2p carmine	17.50	8.75
107	A50	3p dl vio	17.50	8.75

Gaucho
A51

Solis Theater
A52

Locomotive
A53

Bull's Head
A54

Ceres
A55

Sailing Ship
A56

Liberty
A57

Mercury
A58

Coat of Arms — A59

Montevideo Fortress
A60

Cathedral in Montevideo
A61

Perf. 12 to 15½ and Compound
1895-99

108	A51	1c bister	25	12
109	A51	1c sl bl ('97)	25	12
a.		Printed on both sides	14.00	
110	A52	2c blue	25	12
111	A52	2c cl ('97)	25	12
112	A53	5c red	25	12
113	A53	5c grn ('97)	38	10
a.		Imperf., pair	2.00	
114	A53	5c grnsh bl ('99)	30	10
115	A54	7c dp grn	5.00	1.25
116	A54	7c org ('97)	2.50	65
117	A55	10c brown	1.10	25
118	A56	20c grn & blk	3.50	55
119	A56	20c cl & blk ('97)	3.00	45
120	A57	25c red brn & blk	3.50	65
a.		Center inverted	1,500.	
121	A57	25c pink & bl ('97)	2.00	38
122	A58	50c bl & blk	4.50	1.25
123	A58	50c grn & brn ('97)	3.50	65
124	A59	1p org brn & blk	6.50	2.50
125	A59	1p yel brn & bl ('97)	5.50	1.75
126	A60	2p vio & grn	17.50	8.75
127	A60	2p bis & car ('97)	5.50	1.00
128	A61	3p car & bl	17.50	8.75
129	A61	3p lil & car ('97)	6.50	1.50
		Nos. 108-129 (22)	89.53	31.13

All values of this issue exist imperforate but they were not issued in that form.

President Joaquin Suárez
A62 A63

Statue of President Suárez — A64

Perf. 12½ to 15 and Compound
1896, July 18

130	A62	1c brn vio & blk	20	12
131	A63	5c pale bl & blk	20	12
132	A64	10c lake & blk	50	30

Dedication of Pres. Suárez statue.

Same Overprinted in Red:

PROVISORIO 1897
e

PROVISORIO 1897
f

1897, Mar. 1

133	A62 (e)	1c brn vio & blk	30	20
a.		Inverted overprint	3.00	3.00
134	A63 (e)	5c pale bl & blk	30	20
a.		Inverted overprint	4.50	4.50
135	A64 (f)	10c lake & blk	65	45
a.		Inverted overprint	7.50	7.50
b.		Double overprint	5.00	

"Electricity" — A68

1897-99 **Engr.**

136	A68	10c red	1.00	30
137	A68	10c red lil ('99)	38	25

Regular Issues Overprinted in Red or Blue

1897, Sept. 26

138	A51	1c sl bl (R)	50	38
a.		Inverted overprint	2.50	2.50
139	A52	2c cl (Bl)	75	75
a.		Inverted overprint	2.00	2.00
140	A53	5c grn (Bl)	1.10	1.00
a.		Inverted overprint	3.50	3.50
b.		Double overprint		
141	A68	10c red (Bl)	1.75	1.75
a.		Inverted ovpt.	6.25	6.25

Commemorating the Restoration of Peace at the end of the Civil War.
Issue for use only on the days of the National Fete, September 26, 27 and 28, 1897.

Regular Issues Surcharged in Black, Blue or Red

PROVISIONAL ½ CENTESIMO

1898, July 25

142	A32	½c on 1c bl (Bk)	20	20
a.		Inverted surcharge	3.00	3.00
143	A51	½c on 1c bis (Bl)	20	20
a.		Inverted surcharge	3.00	
b.		Double surcharge	2.50	
144	A62	½c on 1c brn vio & blk (R)	20	20
145	A52	½c on 2c bl (Bk)	20	20
146	A63	½c on 5c pale bl & blk (R)	20	20
a.		Double surcharge	6.25	
147	A54	½c on 7c dp grn (R)	20	20
		Nos. 142-147 (6)	1.20	1.20

The 2c red brown of 1894 (No. 77) was also surcharged like Nos. 142 to 147 but was not issued.

Liberty
A69

Statue of Artigas
A70

1898-99 **Litho.** *Perf. 11, 11½*

148	A69	5m rose	18	18
149	A69	5m pur ('99)	20	20

1899-1900 **Engr.** *Perf. 12½, 14, 15.*

150	A70	5m lt bl	12	10
151	A70	5m org ('00)	12	10

No. 135 With Additional Surcharge in Black

1900 5 CENTESIMOS

1900, Dec. 1

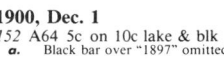

152	A64	5c on 10c lake & blk	30	20
a.		Black bar over "1897" omitted	10.00	

Cattle — A72

Girl's Head — A73

Shepherdess — A74

Perf. 13½ to 16 and Compound.
1900-10 **Engr.**

153	A72	1c yel grn	25	10
154	A73	5c dl bl	25	10
155	A73	5c sl grn ('10)	25	12
156	A74	10c gray vio	30	15

Eros and Cornucopia
A75

Basket of Fruit
A76

1901, Feb. 11

157 A75 2c vermilion		20	10
158 A76 7c brn org		75	20

General Artigas — A78

Cattle — A79

Eros — A80

Cow — A81

Shepherdess
A82

Numeral
A83

Justice — A84

1904-05 Litho. *Perf. 11½*

160 A78 5m orange	25	10
a. 5m yel	20	10
161 A79 1c green	38	10
a. Imperf., pair	2.50	
162 A80 2c dp org	18	10
a. 2c org red	12	10
b. Imperf., pair	2.50	
163 A81 5c blue	50	8
a. Imperf., pair	2.50	
164 A82 10c dk vio ('05)	30	12
165 A83 20c gray grn ('05)	1.75	30
166 A84 25c ol bis ('05)	2.00	50
Nos. 160-166 (7)	5.36	1.30

Overprinted Diagonally in Carmine or Black

*
Paz 1904
—*—

1904, Oct. 15

167 A79 1c grn (C)	38	20
168 A80 2c dp org (Bk)	42	25
169 A81 5c dk bl (C)	75	38

Commemorating the end of the Civil War of 1904. In the first overprinting, "Paz 1904" appears at a 50-degree angle; in the second, at a 63-degree angle.

A85

A86

1906, Feb. 23 Litho. Unwmk.

170 A85 5c dk bl	65	10
a. Imperf., pair	4.00	

1906-07

171 A86 5c dp bl	15	8
172 A86 7c org brn ('07)	30	18
173 A86 50c rose	2.50	50

Cruiser "Montevideo" — A87

1908, Aug. 23 Typo. *Rouletted 13*

174 A87 1c car & dk grn	65	65
a. Center inverted	225.00	225.00
b. Imperf., pair	20.00	
175 A87 2c grn & dk grn	65	65
a. Center inverted	225.00	225.00
b. Imperf., pair	20.00	
176 A87 5c org & dk grn	65	65
a. Center inverted	225.00	225.00
b. Imperf., pair	20.00	

Issued to commemorate the independence of Uruguay, which was declared Aug. 25, 1825. Counterfeits exist.

View of the Port of Montevideo — A88

Wmk. 187- R O in Diamond

Wmk. 187

1909, Aug. 24 Engr. *Perf. 11½*

177 A88 2c lt brn & blk	1.00	75
178 A88 5c rose red & blk	1.00	75

Issued to commemorate the opening of the Port of Montevideo, August 25, 1909.

Nos. 156, 91 Surcharged

8
Centésimos

Provisorio

Perf. 14 to 16

1909, Sept. 13 Unwmk.

179 A74 8c on 10c dl vio	30	15
a. "Contesimos"	1.10	1.10
180 A38 23c on 25c bis brn	75	38

Centaur — A89

Wmk. 187

1910, May 22 Engr. *Perf. 11½*

182 A89 2c car red	40	25
183 A89 5c dp bl	40	25

Centenary of Liberation Day, Aug. 25, 1810.
The 2c in deep blue and 5c in carmine red were prepared for collectors.

Stamps of 1900-06 Surcharged:

PROVISORIO
5
MILESIMOS
—1910—
a

PROVISORIO
5
CENTESIMOS
-1910-
b

PROVISORIO
5
CENTÉSIMOS
—1910—
c

Perf. 14 to 16, 11½.

1910, Oct. 6 Unwmk.

Black Surcharge.

184 A72 (a) 5m on 1c yel grn	12	8
a. Inverted surcharge	4.50	3.75

Dark Blue Surcharge.

185 A39 (b) 5c on 50c dl red	20	15
a. Inverted surcharge	4.50	4.50

Blue Surcharge.

186 A86 (c) 5c on 50c rose	50	38
a. Double surcharge	*20.00*	
b. Inverted surcharge	10.00	8.75

Artigas
A90

"Commercial Progress"
A91

1910, Nov. 21 Engr. *Perf. 14, 15*

187 A90 5m dk vio	10	5
188 A90 1c dp grn	10	5
189 A90 2c org red	15	5
190 A90 5c dk bl	15	5
191 A90 8c gray blk	30	10
192 A90 20c brown	50	15
193 A91 23c dp ultra	75	30
194 A91 50c orange	1.75	75
195 A91 1p scarlet	4.25	50
Nos. 187-195 (9)	8.05	2.00

See Nos. 199-210.

Symbolical of the Posts — A92

1911, Jan. 6 Wmk. 187 *Perf. 11½*

196 A92 5c rose car & blk	45	35

1st South American Postal Cong., at Montevideo, Jan. 1911.

No. 158 Surcharged in Red or Dark Blue

ARTIGAS
5
CENTÉSIMOS
1811-1911

Perf. 14 to 16

1911, May 17 Unwmk.

197 A76 2c on 7c brn org (R)	25	20
198 A76 5c on 7c brn org (Bl)	25	15
a. Invtd. surch.	6.00	

Commemorating the centenary of the battle of Las Piedras, won by the forces under Gen. Jose Gervasio Artigas, May 8, 1811.

Types of 1910

FOUR AND FIVE CENTESIMOS.
Type I. Large numerals about 3mm. high.
Type II. Small numerals about 2¼mm. high.

1912-15 Typo. *Perf. 11½.*

199 A90 5m violet	10	5
a. 5m pur	10	5
200 A90 5m magenta	12	5
a. 5m dl rose	12	5
201 A90 1c grn ('13)	10	5
202 A90 2c brn org	10	5
203 A90 2c rose red ('13)	10	5
a. 2c dp red ('14)	10	5
204 A90 4c org (I) ('14)	15	5
a. 4c org (II) ('15)	15	5
b. 4c yel (II) ('13)	12	5
205 A90 5c dl bl (I)	20	5
a. 5c bl (II)	20	5
206 A90 8c ultra ('13)	30	5
207 A90 20c brn ('13)	90	10
a. 20c choc	90	12
208 A91 23c dk bl ('15)	1.75	38
209 A91 50c org ('14)	1.75	65
210 A91 1p ver ('15)	4.00	50
Nos. 199-210 (12)	9.57	2.03

Stamps of 1912-15 Overprinted

CENTENARIO
DE LAS
INSTRUCCIONES
DEL
AÑO XIII

1913, Apr. 4

211 A90 2c brn org	40	30
a. Inverted overprint	5.00	4.50
212 A90 4c yellow	40	30
213 A90 5c blue	40	30

Cent. of the Buenos Aires Cong. of 1813.

Liberty Extending Peace to the Country — A93

1918, Jan. 3 Litho.

214 A93 2c grn & red	45	30
215 A93 5c buff & bl	45	30

Promulgation of the Constitution.

Statue of Liberty, New York Harbor
A94

Harbor of Montevideo
A95

Perf. 14, 15, 13½

1919, July 15 Engr.

217 A94 2c car & brn	25	12
218 A94 4c org & brn	38	12
219 A94 5c bl & brn	45	12
220 A94 8c org brn & ind	65	25
221 A94 20c ol bis & blk	1.50	50
222 A94 23c grn & blk	2.00	75
Nos. 217-222 (6)	5.23	1.86

Peace at end of World War I.
Perf 13½ used only on 2c, 20c, 23c.

1919-20 Litho. *Perf. 11½*

225 A95 5m vio & blk	8	5
226 A95 1c grn & blk	10	5
227 A95 2c red & blk	10	5
228 A95 4c org & blk	25	8
229 A95 5c ultra & sl	30	5
230 A95 8c gray bl & lt brn	38	12
231 A95 20c brn & blk	1.25	25
232 A95 23c grn & brn	2.00	50
233 A95 50c brn & bl	4.00	1.50
234 A95 1p dl red & bl	6.25	2.50
Nos. 225-234 (10)	14.71	5.15

Jose Enrique Rodo A96

Mercury A97

1920, Feb. 28 Engr. *Perf. 14, 15*

235	A96	2c car & blk	45	35
236	A96	4c org & bl	50	40
237	A96	5c bl & brn	65	45

Issued to honor Jose Enrique Rodo, author.

1921-22 Litho. *Perf. 11½*

238	A97	5m lilac	12	5
239	A97	5m gray blk ('22)	12	5
240	A97	1c lt grn	15	5
241	A97	1c vio ('22)	18	5
242	A97	2c fawn	20	5
243	A97	2c red ('22)	20	5
244	A97	3c bl grn ('22)	38	12
245	A97	4c orange	25	6
246	A97	5c ultra	25	5
247	A97	5c choc ('22)	38	5
248	A97	12c ultra ('22)	1.50	38
249	A97	36c ol grn ('22)	4.50	1.75
		Nos. 238-249 (12)	8.23	2.71

See Nos. 254-260.

Damaso A. Larranaga (1771-1848), Bishop, Writer, Scientist and Physician — A98

1921, Dec. 10 Unwmk.

250	A98	5c slate	75	50

Wmk. 188- REPUBLICA O. DEL URUGUAY

Mercury Type of 1921-22

1922-23 Wmk. 188

254	A97	5m gray blk	12	5
255	A97	1c vio ('23)	18	5
a.		1c red vio	18	5
256	A97	2c pale red	25	5
257	A97	2c dp rose ('23)	30	5
259	A97	5c yel brn ('23)	50	5
260	A97	8c sal pink ('23)	75	60
		Nos. 254-260 (6)	2.10	85

Equestrian Statue of Artigas — A99

Unwmk.

1923, Feb. 26 Engr. *Perf. 14*

264	A99	2c car & sep	20	8
265	A99	5c vio & sep	20	8
266	A99	12c bl & sep	30	15

Southern Lapwing — A100

Wmk. 189- Caduceus

Perf. 12½, 11½x12½

1923, June 25 Litho. Wmk. 189

Size: 18x22½mm.

267	A100	5m gray	5	5
268	A100	1c org yel	8	5
269	A100	2c lt vio	12	5
270	A100	3c gray grn	30	10
271	A100	5c lt bl	30	10
272	A100	8c rose red	50	25
273	A100	12c dp bl	50	25
274	A100	20c brn org	1.10	25
275	A100	36c emerald	2.25	1.00
276	A100	50c orange	4.50	1.50
277	A100	1p brt rose	20.00	11.25
278	A100	2p lt grn	20.00	11.25
		Nos. 267-278 (12)	49.70	26.10

See Nos. 285-298, 309-314, 317-323, 334-339.

Battle of Sarandi Monument — A101

1923, Oct. 12 Wmk. 188 *Perf. 11½*

279	A101	2c dp grn	45	35
280	A101	5c scarlet	45	35
281	A101	12c dk bl	45	35

Unveiling of the Sarandi Battle Monument by Jose Luis Zorrilla, Oct. 12, 1923.

Olympic Games Issue

"Victory of Samothrace" — A102

Unwmk.

1924, July 29 Typo. *Perf. 11*

282	A102	2c rose	14.00	10.00
283	A102	5c mauve	14.00	10.00
284	A102	12c brt bl	14.00	10.00

Sheets of 20 (5x4).

Five hundred sets of these stamps were printed on yellow paper for presentation purposes. They were not on sale at post offices. Value for set, $225.

Lapwing Type of 1923.
First Redrawing.
Imprint: "A. BARREIRO Y RAMOS."

Perf. 12½, 11½

1924, July 26 Litho.

Size: 17¼x21½mm.

285	A100	5m gray blk	8	5
286	A100	1c fawn	10	5
287	A100	2c rose lil	30	5
288	A100	3c gray grn	20	8
289	A100	5c chlky bl	15	5
290	A100	8c pink	38	20
291	A100	10c turq bl	30	15
292	A100	12c sl bl	38	25
293	A100	15c lt vio	38	20
294	A100	20c brown	75	20
295	A100	36c salmon	3.50	75
296	A100	50c grnsh gray	4.50	1.00
297	A100	1p buff	7.50	2.50
298	A100	2p dl vio	15.00	7.50
		Nos. 285-298 (14)	33.52	13.03

Landing of the 33 "Immortals" Led by Juan Antonio Lavalleja — A103

Perf. 11, 11½

1925, Apr. 19 Wmk. 188

300	A103	2c sal pink & blk	75	50
301	A103	5c lil & blk	75	50
302	A103	12c bl & blk	75	50

Cent. of the landing of the 33 Founders of the Uruguayan Republic.

Legislative Palace — A104

Perf. 11½

1925, Aug. 24 Unwmk. Engr.

303	A104	5c vio & blk	75	50
304	A104	12c bl & blk	75	50

Dedication of the Legislative Palace.

General Fructuoso Rivera — A105

Wmk. 188

1925, Sept. 24 Litho. *Perf. 11*

305	A105	5c lt red	30	20

Centenary of Battle of Rincon. See No. C9.

Battle of Sarandi A106

1925, Oct. 12 *Perf. 11½*

306	A106	2c bl grn	75	70
307	A106	5c dl vio	75	70
308	A106	12c dp bl	1.00	80

Centenary of the Battle of Sarandi.

Lapwing Type of 1923.
Second Redrawing.
Imprint: "Imprenta Nacional."

1925-26 *Perf. 11, 11½, 10½*

Size: 17½x21¾mm.

309	A100	5m gray blk	20	5
310	A100	1c dl vio	20	5
311	A100	2c brt rose	25	5
312	A100	3c gray grn	25	15
313	A100	5c dl bl ('26)	38	5
314	A100	12c sl bl	1.00	25
		Nos. 309-314 (6)	2.28	60

The design differs in many small details from that of the 1923-24 issues. These stamps may be readily identified by the imprint and perforation.

Lapwing Type of 1923.
Third Redrawing.
Imprint: "Imp. Nacional" at center.

1926-27 *Perf. 11, 11½, 10½*

Size: 17½x21¾mm.

317	A100	5m gray	8	5
318	A100	1c lt vio ('27)	50	20
319	A100	2c red	38	12
320	A100	3c gray grn	50	25
321	A100	5c lt bl	38	5
322	A100	8c pink ('27)	75	38
323	A100	36c rose buff	4.50	2.00
		Nos. 317-323 (7)	7.09	3.05

These stamps may be distinguished from preceding stamps of the same design by the imprint.

Philatelic Exhibition Issue

Post Office at Montevideo A107

Unwmk.

1927, May 25 Engr. *Imperf.*

330	A107	2c green	3.00	2.25
a.		Sheet of four	12.50	12.50
331	A107	5c dl red	3.00	2.25
a.		Sheet of four	12.50	12.50
332	A107	8c dk bl	3.00	2.25
a.		Sheet of four	12.50	12.50

Printed in sheets of 4 and sold at the Montevideo Exhibition, Lithographed counterfeits exist.

Lapwing Type of 1923.
Fourth Redrawing.
Imprint: "Imp. Nacional" at right.

Perf. 11, 11½

1927, May 6 Litho. Wmk. 188

Size: 17¾x21¾mm.

334	A100	1c gray vio	5	5
335	A100	2c vermilion	10	5
336	A100	3c gray grn	25	18
337	A100	5c blue	15	5
338	A100	8c rose	1.00	38
339	A100	20c gray brn	2.00	75
		Nos. 334-339 (6)	3.55	1.46

The design has been slightly retouched in various places. The imprint is in italic capitals and is placed below the right numeral of value.

No. 292 Surcharged in Red

Inauguración
Ferrocarril
SAN CARLOS
a ROCHA
14/1/928
5 cts. 5

1928, Jan. 13 Unwmk. *Perf. 11½*

345	A100	2c on 12c sl bl	75	75
346	A100	5c on 12c sl bl	75	75
347	A100	10c on 12c sl bl	75	75
348	A100	15c on 12c sl bl	75	75

Issued to celebrate the inauguration of the railroad between San Carlos and Rocha.

General Rivera — A108

1928, Apr. 19 Engr. *Perf. 12*

349	A108	5c car rose	25	15

Centenary of the Battle of Las Misiones.

Artigas (7 dots in panels below portrait.) — A109

Imprint:
"Waterlow & Sons. Ltd., Londres."

Perf. 11, 12½, 13x13½, 12½x13, 13x12½

1928-43

Size: 16x19½mm

350	A109	5m	black	5	5
350A	A109	5m	org ('43)	5	5
351	A109	1c	dk vio	5	5
352	A109	1c	brn vio ('34)	8	5
352A	A109	1c	vio bl ('43)	5	5
353	A109	2c	dp grn	5	5
353A	A109	2c	brn red ('43)	5	5
354	A109	3c	bister	12	5
355	A109	3c	dp grn ('32)	8	5
355A	A109	3c	brt grn ('43)	5	5
356	A109	5c	red	10	5
357	A109	5c	ol grn ('33)	10	5
357A	A109	5c	dl pur ('43)	5	5
358	A109	7c	car ('32)	10	5
359	A109	8c	dk bl	15	5
360	A109	8c	brn ('33)	15	5
361	A109	10c	orange	22	10
362	A109	10c	red org ('32)	38	25
363	A109	12c	dp bl ('32)	20	5
364	A109	15c	dl bl	32	8
365	A109	17c	dk vio ('32)	50	10
366	A109	20c	ol brn	42	10
367	A109	20c	red brn ('33)	65	30
368	A109	24c	car rose	75	30
369	A109	24c	yel ('33)	50	25
370	A109	36c	ol grn ('33)	75	30
371	A109	50c	gray	2.25	1.10
372	A109	50c	blk ('33)	3.00	1.00
373	A109	50c	blk brn ('33)	2.25	75
374	A109	1p	yel grn	5.00	2.00
			Nos. 350-374 (30)	18.47	7.48

1929-33 ***Perf. 12½***

Size: 22 to 22½x28½ to 29½mm.

375	A109	1p	ol brn ('33)	3.50	2.00
376	A109	2p	dk grn	6.50	3.50
377	A109	2p	dl red ('32)	14.00	10.00
378	A109	3p	dk bl	11.25	6.50
379	A109	3p	blk ('32)	11.25	10.00
380	A109	4p	violet	16.50	11.25
381	A109	4p	dk ol grn ('32)	14.00	10.00
382	A109	5p	car brn	22.50	17.50
383	A109	5p	red org ('32)	14.00	10.00
384	A109	10p	lake ('33)	47.50	32.50
385	A109	10p	dp ultra ('33)	47.50	32.50
			Nos. 375-385 (11)	208.50	145.75

See Nos. 420-423, 462. See type A135.

Equestrian Statue of Artigas — A110

1928, May 1

386	A110	2p	Prus bl & choc	8.00	4.25
387	A110	3p	dp rose & blk	9.50	5.75

Symbolical of Soccer Victory — A111

Gen. Eugenio Garzon — A112

1928, July 29

388	A111	2c	brn vio	7.50	6.25
389	A111	5c	dp red	7.50	6.25
390	A111	8c	ultra	7.50	6.25

Issued to commemorate the Uruguayan soccer victories in the Olympic Games of 1924 and 1928. Printed in sheets of 20, divided in panes of 10 (5x2).

1928, Aug. 25 ***Imperf.***

391	A112	2c	red	1.00	1.00
a.			Sheet of four	6.25	6.25
392	A112	5c	yel grn	1.00	1.00
a.			Sheet of four	6.25	6.25
393	A112	8c	dp bl	1.00	1.00
a.			Sheet of four	6.25	6.25

Dedication of monument to Garzon. Issued in sheets of 4. Lithographed counterfeits exist.

Black River Bridge A113

Gauchos Breaking a Horse — A114

Peace A115

Montevideo A116

Liberty and Flag of Uruguay A117

Liberty with Torch and Caduceus A118

Statue of Artigas A124

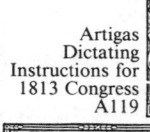

Artigas Dictating Instructions for 1813 Congress A119

Seascape A120

Montevideo Harbor, 1830 — A121

Liberty and Coat of Arms — A122

Montevideo Harbor, 1930 — A123

1930, June 16 ***Perf. 12½, 12***

394	A113	5m	gray blk	15	10
395	A114	1c	dk brn	15	10
396	A115	2c	brn rose	15	10
397	A116	3c	yel grn	20	12
398	A117	5c	dk bl	20	12
399	A118	8c	dl red	25	15
400	A119	10c	dk vio	38	25
401	A120	15c	bl grn	50	38
402	A121	20c	indigo	65	50
403	A122	24c	red brn	90	50
404	A123	50c	org red	2.50	1.50
405	A124	1p	black	4.50	2.25
406	A124	2p	bl vio	11.25	7.00
407	A124	3p	dk red	16.00	11.25
408	A124	4p	red org	19.00	14.00
409	A124	5p	lilac	27.50	16.00
			Nos. 394-409 (16)	84.28	54.32

Cent. of natl. independence and the promulgation of the constitution.

Wmk. 227-Greek Border and REPUBLICA O. DEL URUGUAY in Alternate Curved Lines

Type of 1856 Issue.
Values in Centesimos.

Wmk. 227

1931, Apr. 11 **Litho.** ***Imperf.***

410	A1	2c	gray bl	2.00	2.00
a.			Sheet of 4	10.00	10.00
411	A1	8c	dl red	2.00	2.00
a.			Sheet of 4	10.00	10.00
412	A1	15c	bl blk	2.00	2.00
a.			Sheet of 4	10.00	10.00

Wmk. REPUBLICA O. DEL URUGUAY. (188)

413	A1	5c	lt grn	2.00	2.00
a.			Sheet of 4	10.00	10.00

Issued in sheets containing four stamps each, in commemoration of the Philatelic Exhibition at Montevideo, April 11-15, 1931. The stamps were on sale during the five days of the exhibition only.

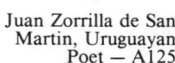

Juan Zorrilla de San Martin, Uruguayan Poet — A125

1932, June 6 **Unwmk.** ***Perf. 12½***

414	A125	1½c	brn vio	15	6
415	A125	3c	green	20	6
416	A125	7c	dk bl	25	5
417	A125	12c	lt bl	50	25
418	A125	1p	dp brn	15.00	10.00
			Nos. 414-418 (5)	16.10	10.42

1 ½

Semi-Postal Stamp No. B2 Surcharged

1932, Nov. 1 ***Perf. 12***

419	SP1	1½c	on 2c + 2c dp grn	20	10

Artigas Type of 1928.
Imprint: "Imprenta Nacional" at center.

1932-35 **Litho.** ***Perf. 11, 12½***

Size: 15¾x19¼mm.

420	A109	5m	lt brn ('35)	8	5
421	A109	1c	pale vio ('35)	8	5
422	A109	15m	black	18	10
423	A109	5c	bluish grn ('35)	30	12

Gen. J. A. Lavalleja A126

Flag of the Race and Globe A127

1933, July 12 **Engr.** ***Perf. 12½***

429	A126	15m	brn lake	10	5

Perf. 11, 11½, 11x11½

1933, Aug. 3 **Litho.**

430	A127	3c	bl grn	20	12
431	A127	5c	rose	25	18
432	A127	7c	lt bl	25	15
433	A127	8c	dl red	50	40
434	A127	12c	dp bl	30	20
435	A127	17c	violet	75	50
436	A127	20c	red brn	1.50	1.00
437	A127	24c	yellow	1.75	1.10
438	A127	36c	orange	2.00	1.40
439	A127	50c	ol gray	2.50	1.50
440	A127	1p	bister	7.50	4.00
			Nos. 430-440 (11)	17.50	10.55

Raising of the "Flag of the Race" and of the 441st anniv. of the sailing of Columbus from Palos, Spain, on his first voyage to America.

Sower A128

Juan Zorrilla de San Martin A129

1933, Aug. 28 **Unwmk.** ***Perf. 11½***

441	A128	3c	bl grn	15	10
442	A128	5c	dl vio	25	18
443	A128	7c	lt bl	20	12
444	A128	8c	dp red	50	30
445	A128	12c	ultra	75	50
			Nos. 441-445 (5)	1.85	1.20

3rd Constituent National Assembly.

1933, Nov. 9 **Engr.** ***Perf. 12½***

446	A129	7c	slate	10	5

Albatross Flying over Map of the Americas — A130

1933, Dec. 3 **Typo.** ***Perf. 11½***

447	A130	3c	grn, blk & brn	1.75	1.25
448	A130	7c	turq bl, brn & blk	1.00	50
449	A130	12c	dk bl, gray & ver	1.50	1.00
450	A130	17c	ver, gray & vio	3.25	1.75
451	A130	20c	yel, bl & grn	3.75	2.25
452	A130	36c	red, blk & yel	5.00	3.50
			Nos. 447-452 (6)	16.25	10.25

7th Pan-American Conf., Montevideo. Issued in sheets of 6. See Nos. C61-C62.

General Rivera — A131

1934, Feb. **Engr.** ***Perf. 12½***

453	A131	3c	green	15	5

Stars Representing the Three Constitutions — A132

1934, Mar. 23 **Typo.**

454	A132 3c yel grn & grn	35	25
455	A132 7c org red & red	35	25
456	A132 12c ultra & bl	1.00	50

Perf. 11½.

457	A132 17c brn & rose	1.25	90
458	A132 20c yel & gray	1.50	1.10
459	A132 36c dk vio & bl grn	1.50	1.25
460	A132 50c blk & bl	4.00	2.50
461	A132 1p dk car & vio	10.00	5.50
	Nos. 454-461 (8)	19.95	12.25

First Year of Third Republic.

Artigas Type of 1928.
Imprint: "Barreiro & Ramos S. A."

1934, Nov. 28 **Litho.**

462	A109 50c brn blk	2.50	1.00

"Uruguay" and "Brazil" Holding Scales of Justice A133

Florencio Sanchez A134

1935, May 30 **Unwmk.** ***Perf. 11***

463	A133 5m brown	38	22
464	A133 15m black	20	20
465	A133 3c green	22	18
466	A133 7c orange	25	15
467	A133 12c ultra	65	38
468	A133 50c yel grn	2.50	1.75
	Nos. 463-468 (6)	4.20	2.88

Visit of President Vargas of Brazil.

1935, Nov. 7

469	A134 3c green	10	5
470	A134 7c brown	15	8
471	A134 12c blue	40	25

Florencio Sanchez (1875-1910), author.

Artigas (6 dots in panels below portrait.) — A135

Imprint: "Imprenta Nacional" at center.

1936-44 ***Perf. 11, 12½***

474	A135 5m org brn ('37)	5	5
475	A135 5m lt brn ('39)	5	5
476	A135 1c lt vio ('37)	10	5
477	A135 2c dk brn ('37)	6	5
478	A135 2c grn ('39)	6	5
479	A135 5c brt bl ('37)	9	5
480	A135 5c bluish grn ('39)	20	5
481	A135 12c dl bl ('38)	20	5
482	A135 20c fawn	50	25
482A	A135 20c rose ('44)	50	20
483	A135 50c brn blk	1.50	38

Size: 21½x28½mm

483A	A135 1p brown	4.00	1.50
483B	A135 2p blue	7.50	6.00
483C	A135 3p gray blk	11.25	8.00
	Nos. 474-483C (14)	26.06	16.73

See Nos. 488, 576. See type A109.

Power Dam on Black River — A136

1937-38

484	A136 1c dl vio	12	5
485	A136 10c blue	25	8
486	A136 15c rose	65	38
487	A136 1p choc ('38)	3.50	1.25

Imprint: "Imprenta Nacional" at right.

1938

488	A135 1c brt vio	15	5

International Law Congress, 1889 — A137

1939, July 16 **Litho.** ***Perf. 12½***

489	A137 1c brn org	12	8
490	A137 2c dl grn	18	12
491	A137 5c rose ver	18	12
492	A137 12c dl bl	38	25
493	A137 50c lt vio	1.50	1.00
	Nos. 489-493 (5)	2.36	1.57

Issued to commemorate the 50th anniversary of the Montevideo Congress of International Law.

Artigas
A138 A138a

1939-43 **Litho.** **Unwmk.**

Size: 15¾x19mm.

494	A138 5m dl brn org ('40)	5	5
495	A138 1c lt bl	5	5
496	A138 2c lt vio	5	5
497	A138 5c vio brn	10	5
498	A138 8c rose red	12	5
499	A138 10c green	25	5
500	A138 15c dl bl	50	20

Size: 24x29½mm.

501	A138 1p dl brn ('41)	2.00	50
502	A138 2p dl rose vio ('40)	5.00	2.00
503	A138 4p org ('43)	6.00	2.50
504	A138 5p ver ('41)	10.00	3.50
	Nos. 494-504 (11)	24.12	9.00

See also No. 578.

Redrawn: Horizontal lines in portrait background.

1940-44

Size: 17x21mm.

505	A138a 5m brn org ('41)	5	5
506	A138a 1c lt bl	5	5
507	A138a 2c lt vio ('41)	5	5
508	A138a 5c vio brn	8	5
509	A138a 8c sal pink ('44)	12	5
510	A138a 10c grn ('41)	25	6
511	A138a 50c ol bis ('42)	4.00	1.00
511A	A138a 50c yel grn ('44)	3.00	1.00
	Nos. 505-511A (8)	7.60	2.31

See Nos. 568-575, 577, 601, 632, 660-661.

Juan Manuel Blanes, Artist A139

Francisco Acuna de Figueroa A140

1941, Aug. 11 **Engr.** ***Perf. 12½***

512	A139 5m ocher	12	6
513	A139 1c henna brn	12	6
514	A139 2c green	12	8
515	A139 5c rose car	38	6
516	A139 12c dp bl	65	32
517	A139 50c dk vio	3.00	2.50
	Nos. 512-517 (6)	4.39	3.08

1942, Mar. 18 **Unwmk.**

518	A140 1c hn brn	12	10
519	A140 2c dp grn	12	10
520	A140 5c rose car	20	12
521	A140 12c dp bl	65	30
522	A140 50c dk vio	2.25	1.75
	Nos. 518-522 (5)	3.34	2.37

Issued in honor of Francisco Acuna de Figueroa, author of the National anthem.

No. 506 Surcharged in Red

Valor
$ 0.005

1943, Jan. 27

523	A138a 5m on 1c lt bl	8	6

Coat of Arms A141

Clio A142

1943, Mar. 12 **Litho.**

524	A141 1c on 2c dl vio brn (R)	6	5
525	A141 2c on 2c dl vio brn (V)	9	6
a.	Invtd. surch.	12.50	12.50

1943, Aug. 24

526	A142 5m lt vio	15	5
527	A142 1c lt ultra	15	8
528	A142 2c brt rose	25	10
529	A142 5c buff	25	12

Issued to commemorate the 100th anniversary of the Historic and Geographic Institute of Uruguay.

Swiss Colony Monument A143

YMCA Seal A144

Overprinted "1944" and Surcharged in Various Colors

1944, May 18

530	A143 1c on 3c dl grn (R)	8	5
531	A143 5c on 7c brn red (B)	15	8
532	A143 10c on 12c dk bl (Br)	30	18

Issued to commemorate the 50th anniversary of the founding of the Swiss Colony.

1944, Sept. 8

533	A144 5c blue	8	5

100th anniv. of the YMCA.

Catalogue values for unused stamps in this section, from this point to the end of the section, are for Never Hinged items.

An enhanced introduction to the Scott Catalogue begins on Page V. A thorough understanding of the material presented there will greatly aid your use of the catalogue itself.

"La Educacion del Pueblo" A145

Jose Pedro Varela A146

Monument — A147

Monument A148

Perf. 11½

1945, June 13 **Litho.** **Unwmk.**

534	A145 5m brt grn	10	5
535	A146 1c dp brn	10	5

Perf. 12½

536	A147 2c rose red	10	8
537	A148 5c blue	15	8
a.	Perf. 11½	12	5

Issued to commemorate the centenary of the birth of Jose Pedro Varela, author.

Santiago Vazquez A149

Silvestre Blanco A150

Eduardo Acevedo A151

Bruno Mauricio de Zabala A152

Jose Pedro Varela A153

Jose Ellauri A154

Gen. Luis de Larrobla — A155

Engraved (5m, 5c, 10c); Lithographed

1945-47 ***Perf. 10½, 11, 11½, 12½***

538	A149 5m pur ('46)	5	5
539	A150 1c yel brn ('46)	5	5
540	A151 2c brn vio	10	8
541	A152 3c grn & dp grn ('47)	10	8
542	A153 5c brt car	12	5
543	A154 10c ultra	25	12
544	A155 20c dp grn & choc ('47)	65	38
	Nos. 538-544 (7)	1.32	81

No. C86A Surcharged in Blue

CORREO
INAUGURACIÓN
DICIEMBRE, 1945
20
CENTS

1946, Jan. 9 ***Perf. 12½***

545 AP7 20c on 68c pale vio brn 65 45

Inauguration of the Black River Power Dam. See No. C120.

A156

A157

1946-51 Unwmk. Litho. ***Perf. 12½***

Black Overprint

546 A156 5m org ('49) 5 5
a. Inverted ovpt.
547 A156 2c dl vio brn ('47) 6 5
548 A156 3c green 6 5
549 A156 5c ultra ('51) 6 5
550 A156 10c org brn 12 5
551 A156 20c dk grn 35 12
552 A156 50c brown 1.10 45
553 A156 3p lil rose 3.50 2.50
Nos. 546-553 (8) 5.30 3.32

1947-48

Black Surcharge

554 A157 2c on 5c ultra ('48) 8 5
555 A157 3c on 5c ultra 8 5

Statue of Ariel — A158

Bas-relief — A160

Bust of José Enrique Rodó — A159

Bas-relief — A161

Perf. 12½

1948, Jan. 30 Unwmk. Engr.

Center in Orange Brown.

556 A158 1c grnsh gray 5 5
557 A159 2c purple 8 5
558 A160 3c green 10 5
559 A161 5c red vio 12 5
560 A160 10c dp org 15 8
561 A161 12c ultra 20 10
562 A158 20c rose vio 42 25
563 A159 50c dp car 1.50 90
Nos. 556-563 (8) 2.62 1.53

Dedication of the Rodó monument.

View of the Port, Paysandú A162

Arms of Paysandú A163

1948, Oct. 9 **Litho.**

564 A162 3c bl grn 12 8
565 A163 7c ultra 20 8

Issued to publicize the Exposition of Industry and Agriculture, Paysandú, October-November 1948.

Santa Lucia River Highway Bridge A164

1948, Dec. 10

566 A164 10c dk bl 30 10
567 A164 50c green 1.25 65

Redrawn Artigas Types of 1940, 1936, 1939

1948-51 Litho. ***Perf. 12½***

568 A138a 5m gray ('49) 5 5
569 A138a 1c rose vio ('50) 5 5
570 A138a 2c orange 6 5
571 A138a 2c choc ('50) 6 5
572 A138a 3c bl grn 6 5
572A A138a 7c vio bl 10 5
573 A138a 8c rose car ('49) 15 5
574 A138a 10c org brn ('51) 10 5
575 A138a 12c bl ('51) 10 8
576 A135 20c violet 25 8
577 A138a 20c rose pink ('51) 30 10

Size: 18x21¾mm.

578 A138 1p lil rose ('51) 75 25
Nos. 568-578 (12) 2.03 91

The 2c chocolate, 3c and 7c also exist in perf. 11.

Plowing A165

Mounted Cattle Herder A166

1949, Apr. 29 Unwmk. ***Perf. 12½***

579 A165 3c green 10 5
580 A166 7c blue 15 5

Issued to commemorate the 4th Regional American Conference of Labor, 1949.

Cannon, Rural and Urban Views A167

Symbolical of Soccer Matches A168

1950, Oct. 11 **Litho.**

581 A167 1c lil rose 6 5
582 A167 3c green 6 5
583 A167 7c dp bl 10 5

Issued to commemorate the 200th anniversary of the founding of Cordón, a district of Montevideo.

1951, Mar. 20

584 A168 3c green 38 12
585 A168 7c vio bl 75 25

Issued to publicize the 4th World Soccer Championship, Rio de Janeiro.

Gen. José Artigas — A169

Flight of the People A170

Designs: 1c, 2c, 5c, Various equestrian portraits of Artigas. 7c, Dictating instructions. 8c, In congress. 10c, Artigas' flag. 14c, At the citadel. 20c, Arms of Artigas. 50c, In Paraguay. 1p, Bust.

Engraved and Photogravure

1952, Jan. 7 Unwmk. ***Perf. 13½***

586 A169 5m slate 8 5
587 A169 1c bl & blk 8 5
588 A169 2c pur & red brn 8 5
589 A170 3c aqua & dk brn 8 5
590 A169 5c red org & blk 10 5
591 A170 7c ol & blk 12 5
592 A170 8c car & blk 18 8
593 A170 10c choc, brt ultra & crim 20 8
594 A169 14c dp bl 20 8
595 A169 20c org yel, dp ultra & car 30 15
596 A169 50c org brn & blk 65 32
597 A169 1p bl gray & cit 1.75 90
Nos. 586-597 (12) 3.82 1.91

Issued to commemorate the centenary (in 1950) of the death of Gen. José Artigas.

Plane and Stagecoach A171

1952, Oct. 9 Photo. ***Perf. 13½x13***

598 A171 3c bl grn 8 5
599 A171 7c blk brn 10 5
600 A171 12c ultra 12 6

75th anniv. (in 1949) of the UPU.

Redrawn Artigas Type of 1940-44.

1953, Feb. 23 Litho. ***Perf. 11***

Size: 24x29½mm.

601 A138a 2p fawn 3.00 1.75

Franklin D. Roosevelt — A172

1953, Apr. 9 Engr. ***Perf. 13½***

602 A172 3c green 8 5
603 A172 7c ultra 10 5
604 A172 12c blk brn 18 10

Issued to commemorate the 5th Postal Congress of the Americas and Spain.

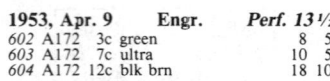

Ceibo, Natl. Flower A173

Horse Breaking A174

Legislature Building A175

"Island of Seals" (Southern Sea Lions) A176

Fair Entrance A177

Designs: 2c, 10c, 5p, Ombu tree. 3c, 50c, Passion Flower. 7c, 3p, Montevideo fortress. 12c, 2p, Outer gate, Montevideo.

Perf. 13x13½, 13½x13, 12½x13, 13x12½

Photo. (5m, 3c, 20c, 50c); Engr.

1954, Jan. 14 Unwmk.

605 A173 5m multi 5 5
606 A174 1c car & blk 5 5
607 A174 2c brn & grn 5 5
608 A173 3c multi 8 5
609 A175 5c pur & red brn 8 5
610 A173 7c brn & grn 5 5
611 A176 8c car & ultra 25 5
612 A174 10c org & grn 15 5
613 A175 12c dp ultra & dk brn 10 5
614 A174 14c rose lil & blk 10 5
615 A173 20c grn, brn, gray & car 30 8
616 A173 50c car & multi 65 15
617 A175 1p car & red brn 1.25 50
618 A175 2p car & blk brn 2.25 90
619 A173 3p lil & grn 2.50 1.00
620 A176 4p dp brn & dp ultra 6.25 3.00
621 A174 5p vio bl & grn 5.50 2.50
Nos. 605-621 (17) 19.66 8.63

1956, Jan. 19 Litho. ***Perf. 11***

622 A177 3c pale ol grn 5 5
623 A177 7c blue 5 5

Issued to publicize the First Exposition of National Products. See Nos. C166-C168.

José Batlle y Ordoñez — A178

Design: 7c, Full length portrait.

Perf. 13½

1956, Dec. 15 Wmk. 90 Photo.

624 A178 3c rose red	8	5
625 A178 7c sepia	12	8

Issued to commemorate the centenary of the birth of President Jose Batlle y Ordonez. See Nos. C169-C172.

Same Surcharged with New Values.

1957-58

626 A178 5c on 3c rose red ('58)	8	5
627 A178 10c on 7c sep	12	8
a. Surcharge inverted	12.50	12.50

Diver A179

Eduardo Acevedo A180

Design: 10c, Swimmer at start (horiz.).

Perf. 10½, 11½

1958, Feb. 15 Litho. Unwmk.

628 A179 5c brt bl grn	12	8
629 A179 10c brt bl	25	10

Issued to publicize the 14th South American swimming meet, Montevideo.

1958, Mar. 19 ***Perf. 11½, 10½***

630 A180 5c lt ol grn & blk	10	5
631 A180 10c ultra & blk	15	10

Issued to commemorate the centenary of the birth of Eduardo Acevedo (1856-1948), lawyer, legislator, minister of foreign affairs.

Artigas Type of 1940-44.

1958, Sept. 25 Litho. ***Perf. 11***

632 A138a 5m blue	5	5

Baygorria Hydroelectric Works A181

1958, Oct. 30 Unwmk. ***Perf. 11***

633 A181 5c yel grn & blk	5	5
634 A181 10c brn org & blk	5	8
635 A181 1p bl gray & blk	25	12
636 A181 2p rose & blk	50	25

Nos. 608, 610 and 605 Surcharged Similarly to

Photogravure and Engraved

1958-59 ***Perf. 13x13½***

637 A173 5c on 3c multi ('59)	5	5
638 A173 10c on 7c brn & grn	5	5
639 A173 20c on 5m multi	10	6

Gabriela Mistral A182

Carlos Vaz Ferreira A183

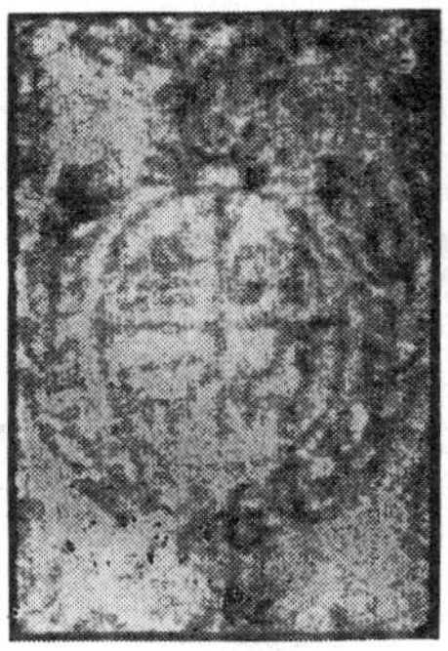

Wmk. 327- Coat of Arms

Wmk. 327

1959, July 6 Litho. ***Perf. 11½***

640 A182 5c green	5	5
641 A182 10c dk bl	6	5
642 A182 20c red	10	5

Gabriela Mistral, Chilean poet and educator.

1959, Sept. 3 ***Perf. 11***

643 A183 5c blk & lt bl	5	5
644 A183 10c blk & ocher	5	5
645 A183 20c blk & ver	6	5
646 A183 50c blk & vio	18	5
647 A183 1p blk & grn	30	15
Nos. 643-647 (5)	64	35

Issued to commemorate Carlos Vaz Ferreira (1872-1958), educator and author.

Dr. Martin C. Martinez — A184

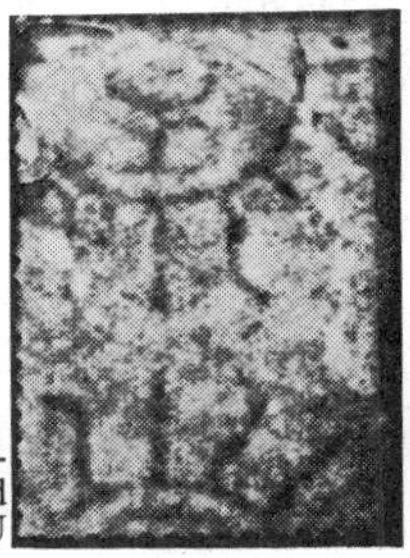

Wmk. 332- Large Sun and R O U

Wmk. 332

1960, May 16 Litho. ***Perf. 12***

648 A184 3c red lil & blk	5	5
649 A184 5c dp vio & blk	5	5
650 A184 10c brt bl & blk	5	5
651 A184 20c choc & blk	5	5
652 A184 1p gray & blk	18	8
653 A184 2p org & blk	38	12
654 A184 3p ol grn & blk	65	25
655 A184 4p yel brn & blk	1.00	65
656 A184 5p brt red & blk	1.25	65
Nos. 648-656 (9)	3.66	1.95

Issued to commemorate the centenary of the birth of Dr. Martin C. Martinez (1859-1940), statesman.

Uprooted Oak Emblem — A185

1960, June 6 Wmk. 332 ***Perf. 12***

657 A185 10c dp bl & blk	10	6

Issued to publicize World Refugee Year, July 1, 1959-June 30, 1960. See No. C207.

Revolutionists and Cabildo, Buenos Aires — A186

1960, Nov. 4 Litho. ***Perf. 12***

658 A186 5c bl & blk	5	5
659 A186 10c bl & ocher	5	5
Nos. 658-659,C208-C210 (5)	50	40

Issued to commemorate the 150th anniversary of the May Revolution of 1810.

Artigas Type of 1940-44.

1960-61 Wmk. 332 ***Perf. 11***

660 A138a 2c gray	5	5
661 A138a 50c brn ('61)	8	5

Gen. Manuel Oribe (1796?-1857), Revolutionary Leader, Pres. of Uruguay (1835-38) — A187

1961, Mar. 4 Litho. ***Perf. 12***

671 A187 10c brt bl & blk	5	5
672 A187 20c bis & blk	8	5
673 A187 40c grn & blk	10	8

Cavalry Charge A188

1961, June 12 Wmk. 332 ***Perf. 12***

674 A188 20c bl & blk	10	5
675 A188 40c emer & blk	18	8

150th anniversary of the revolution.

Welfare, Justice and Education A189

Gen. José Fructuoso Rivera A190

1961, Aug. 14 Wmk. 322 ***Perf. 12***

676 A189 2c bis & lil	5	5
677 A189 5c bis & org	5	5
678 A189 10c bis & scar	5	5
679 A189 20c bis & yel grn	5	5
680 A189 50c bis & lt vio	8	5
681 A189 1p bis & bl	18	12
682 A189 2p bis & cit	50	25
683 A189 3p bis & gray	65	50
684 A189 4p bis & lt bl	1.00	65
685 A189 5p bis & choc	1.25	75
Nos. 676-685 (10)	3.86	2.52

Issued to commemorate the Inter-American Economic and Social Conference of the Organization of American States, Punta del Este, August, 1961. See Nos. C233-C244.

Wmk. 332

1962, May 29 Litho. ***Perf. 12***

686 A190 10c brt red & blk	5	5
687 A190 20c bis & blk	8	5
688 A190 40c grn & blk	12	8

Issued to honor Gen. José Fructuoso Rivera (1790-1854), first President of Uruguay.

Spade, Grain, Swiss "Scarf" and Hat — A191

Bernardo Prudencio Berro — A192

1962, Aug. 1 Wmk. 332 ***Perf. 12***

689 A191 10c bl, blk & car	5	5
690 A191 20c lt grn, blk & car	8	6

Issued to commemorate the centenary of the Swiss Settlement in Uruguay. See Nos. C245-C246.

1962, Oct. 22 Litho. ***Perf. 12***

691 A192 10c grnsh bl & blk	5	5
692 A192 20c yel brn & blk	8	6

Issued to honor Pres. Bernardo P. Berro (1803-1868).

Damaso Larranaga A193

1963, Jan. 24 Wmk. 332 ***Perf. 12***

693 A193 20c lt bl grn & dk brn	5	5
694 A193 40c tan & dk brn	8	6

Damaso Antonio Larranaga (1771-1848), teacher, writer and founder of National Library.

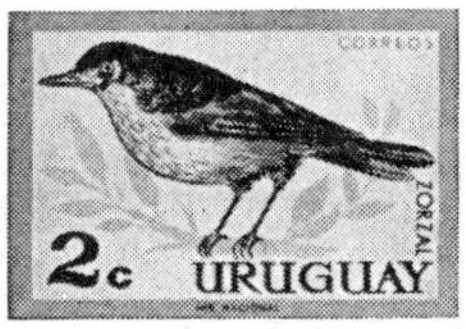

Rufous-bellied Thrush — A194

Birds: 50c, Rufous ovenbird. 1p, Chalk-browed mockingbird. 2p, Rufous-collared sparrow.

1963, Apr. 1 Wmk. 332 ***Perf. 12***

695 A194 2c rose, brn & blk	10	5
696 A194 50c lt brn & blk	25	8
697 A194 1p tan, brn & blk	38	20
698 A194 2p lt brn, blk & gray	1.00	38

Thin frame on No. 696, no frame on No. 698.

UPAE Emblem — A195

1963, May 31 Litho.

699 A195 20c ultra & blk	10	5

50th anniv. of the founding of the Postal Union of the Americas and Spain, UPAE. See Nos. C252-C253.

A little time given to the study of the arrangement of the Scott Catalogue can make it easier to use effectively.

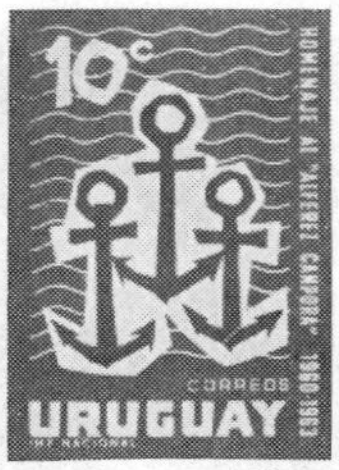

Wheat Emblem — A196

Anchors — A197

1963, July 8 **Wmk. 332** ***Perf. 12***

700 A196 10c grn & yel 5 5
701 A196 20c brn & yel 5 5

FAO "Freedom from Hunger" campaign. See Nos. C254-C255.

1963, Aug. 16

702 A197 10c org & vio 5 5
703 A197 20c dk red & gray 5 5

Issued to commemorate the voyage around the world by the Uruguayan sailing vessel "Alferez Campora," 1960-63. See also Nos. C256-C257.

Large Intestine, Congress Emblem A198

1963, Dec. 9 **Litho.**

704 A198 10c lt grn, blk & dk car 5 5
705 A198 20c org, yel, blk & dk car 5 5

Issued to commemorate the First Uruguayan Proctology Congress, Montevideo, Dec. 9-15.

Red Cross Centenary Emblem A199

Imprint: "Imp. Nacional"

1964, June 5 **Wmk. 332** ***Perf. 12***

706 A199 20c bl & red 5 5
707 A199 40c gray & red 9 5

Centenary of International Red Cross. No. 706 exists with imprint missing.

Luis Alberto de Herrera A200

1964, July 22 **Litho.** **Unwmk.**

708 A200 20c dl grn, bl & blk 5 5
709 A200 40c lt bl, bl & blk 5 5
710 A200 80c yel org, bl & blk 9 5
711 A200 1p lt vio, bl & blk 12 8
712 A200 2p gray, bl & blk 22 18
Nos. 708-712 (5) 53 41

Issued to commemorate the 5th anniversary of the death of Luis Alberto de Herrera (1873-1959), leader of Herrerista party and member of National Government Council.

Nile Gods Uniting Upper and Lower Egypt (Abu Simbel) A201

1964, Oct. 30 **Wmk. 332** ***Perf. 12***

713 A201 20c multi 5 5

Issued to publicize the UNESCO world campaign to save historic monuments in Nubia. See Nos. C266-C267 and souvenir sheet No. C267a.

Pres. John F. Kennedy A202

1965, Mar. 5 **Wmk. 327** ***Perf. 11½***

714 A202 20c gold, emer & blk 5 5
a. Gold omitted
715 A202 40c gold, redsh brn & blk 5 5
a. Gold omitted

Issued in memory of Pres. John F. Kennedy (1917-63). See Nos. C269-C270.

Tete Beche Pair of 1864, No. 21a A203

1965, Mar. 19 **Wmk. 332** ***Perf. 12***

716 A203 40c blk & grn 5 5

1st Rio de la Plata Stamp Show, sponsored jointly by the Argentine and Uruguayan philatelic associations, Montevideo, Mar. 19-28. See No. C271.

Benito Nardone A204

Design: 40c, Benito Nardone before microphone (vert.).

1965, March 25 **Litho.**

717 A204 20c blk & emer 5 5
718 A204 40c blk & emer 5 5

Issued to commemorate the first anniversary of the death of Benito Nardone, president of the Council of Government.

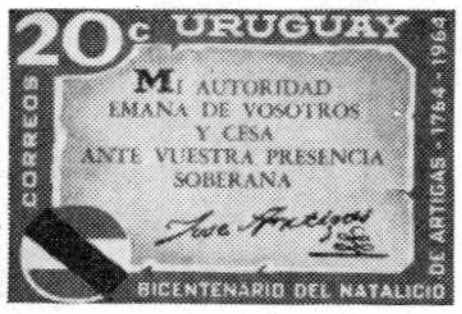

Artigas Quotation A205

Designs: 40c, Artigas bust and quotation. 80c, Jose Artigas.

Perf. 12x11½

1965, May 17 **Litho.** **Wmk. 327**

719 A205 20c bl, yel & red 5 5
720 A205 40c vio bl, cit & blk 5 5
721 A205 80c brn, yel, red & bl 5 5
Nos. 719-721,C273-C275 (6) 50 40

Issued to commemorate the bicentenary of the birth of Jose Artigas (1764-1850), leader of the independence revolt against Spain.

Soccer A206

Designs: 40c, Basketball. 80c, Bicycling. 1p, Woman swimmer.

1965, Aug. 3 **Litho.** **Wmk. 327**

722 A206 20c grn, org & blk 5 5
723 A206 40c hn brn, cit & blk 6 5
724 A206 80c gray, red & blk 8 5
725 A206 1p bl, yel grn & blk 8 5

Issued to commemorate the 18th Olympic Games, Tokyo, Oct. 10-25, 1964. See Nos. C276-C281.

No. 572A Surcharged in Red **10C**

1965 **Unwmk.** ***Perf. 12½***

726 A138a 10c on 7c vio bl 5 5

No. B5 Surcharged:

4 c.

CINCUENTENARIO
Sociedad Arquitectos
del Uruguay

1966, Jan. 25 **Wmk. 327** ***Perf. 11½***

727 SP2 4c on 5c + 10c grn & org 5 5

Issued to commemorate the 50th anniversary of the Association of Uruguayan Architects.

Winston Churchill A207

Wmk. 332

1966, Apr. 29 **Litho.** ***Perf. 12***

728 A207 40c car, dp ultra & brn 5 5

Issued in memory of Sir Winston Spencer Churchill (1874-1965), statesman and World War II leader. See No. C284.

Arms of Rio de Janeiro and Sugar Loaf Mountain A208

1966, June 9 **Litho.** **Wmk. 332**

729 A208 40c emer & brn 5 5

Issued to commemorate the 400th anniversary of the founding of Rio de Janeiro. See No. C285.

Army Engineer A209

Daniel Fernandez Crespo A210

1966, June 17 **Litho.**

730 A209 20c blk, red, vio bl & yel 10 8

Issued to commemorate the 50th anniversary of the Army Engineers Corps.

1966, Sept. 16 **Wmk. 332** ***Perf. 12***

Portraits: No. 732, Washington Beltran. No. 733, Luis Batlle Berres.

731 A210 20c lt bl & blk 10 8
732 A210 20c lt bl & dk brn 10 8
733 A210 20c brick red & blk 10 8

Issued to honor political leaders.

Old Printing Press — A211

Wmk. 332

1966, Oct. 14 **Photo.** ***Perf. 12***

734 A211 20c tan, grnsh gray & dk brn 10 8

50th anniversary of State Printing Office.

Fireman A212

1966 **Litho.**

735 A212 20c red & blk 20 12

Issued to publicize fire prevention. Printed with alternating red and black label inscribed: "Prevengase del fuego! Del pueblo y para el pueblo."

No. 716 Overprinted in Red: "Segunda Muestra y / Jornadas Rioplatenses / de Filatelia / Abril 1966 / Centenario del Sello / Escudito Resellado"

1966, Nov. 4

736 A203 40c blk & grn 10 8

2nd Rio de la Plata Stamp Show, Buenos Aires, Apr. 1966, and cent. of Uruguay's 1st surcharged issue. See No. C298.

General Leandro Gomez — A213

Designs: No. 738, Gen. Juan Antonio Lavalleja. No. 739, Aparicio Saravia, revolutionary, on horseback (horiz.).

Wmk. 332

1966, Nov. 24 **Litho.** ***Perf. 12***

737 A213 20c sl, blk & dp bl 8 5
738 A213 20c red, blk & bl 8 5
739 A213 20c bl & blk 8 5

Montevideo Planetarium A214

1967, Jan. 13 **Wmk. 332** ***Perf. 12***

740 A214 40c pink & blk 20 12

10th anniv. of the Montevideo Municipal Planetarium. See No. C301.

Sunflower, Cow and Emblem A215

Church of San Carlos A216

1967, Jan. 13 **Litho.**
741 A215 40c dk brn & yel 20 12

Issued to commemorate the 20th anniversary of the Young Farmers' Movement.

1967, Apr. 17 **Wmk. 332** ***Perf. 12***
742 A216 40c lt bl, blk & dk red 12 8

Bicentenary of San Carlos.

Eduardo Acevedo A217

1967, Apr. 17
743 A217 20c grn & brn 10 5
744 A217 40c org & grn 10 5

Issued to honor Eduardo Acevedo, lawyer, legislator and Minister of Foreign Affairs.

Arms of Carmelo A218

José Enrique Rodó A219

1967, Aug. 11 **Litho.** ***Perf. 12***
745 A218 40c lt & dk bl & ocher 12 8

Issued to commemorate the 150th anniversary of the founding of Carmelo.

1967, Oct. 6 **Wmk. 332** ***Perf. 12***

Design: 2p, Portrait of Rodó and sculpture (horiz.).

746 A219 1p gray, brn & blk 8 5
747 A219 2p rose cl, blk & tan 10 5

Issued to commemorate the 50th anniversary of the death of José Enrique Rodó, author.

Senen M. Rodriguez and Locomotive A220

1967, Oct. 26 **Litho.** ***Perf. 12***
748 A220 2p ocher & dk brn 20 12

Issued to commemorate the centenary of the founding of the first national railroad company.

Child and Map of Americas A221

Cocoi Heron A222

1967, Nov. 10 **Wmk. 332** ***Perf. 12***
749 A221 1p vio & red 12 8

Issued to commemorate the 40th anniversary of the Inter-American Children's Institute.

No. 610 Surcharged in Red

1.00 PESO

Perf. 13x13½

1967, Nov. 10 **Engr.** **Unwmk.**
750 A173 1p on 7c brn & grn 10 8

1968-70 **Wmk. 332** **Litho.** ***Perf. 12***

Birds: 1p, Great honred owl. 3p, Brown-headed gull (horiz.). No. 754, White-faced tree duck (horiz.). No. 754A, Black-tailed stilts. 5p, Wattled jacanas (horiz.). 10p, Snowy egret (horiz.).

751	A222	1p dl yel & brn	5	5
752	A222	2p bl grn & blk	5	5
753	A222	3p org, gray & blk ('69)	8	5
754	A222	4p brn, tan & blk	18	8
754A	A222	4p ver & blk ('70)	18	8
755	A222	5p lt red brn, blk & yel	20	10
756	A222	10p lil & blk	38	10
		Nos. 751-756 (7)	1.12	51

Concord Bridge, Presidents of Uruguay, Brazil A223

1968, Apr. 3
757 A223 6p brown 12 8

Issued to commemorate the opening of Concord Bridge across the Uruguay River by Presidents Jorge Pacheco Areco of Uruguay and Arthur Costa e Silva of Brazil.

Soccer Player and Trophy — A224

1968, May 29 **Litho.**
758 A224 1p blk & yel 18 5

Victory of the Penarol Athletic Club in the Intercontinental Soccer Championships of 1966.

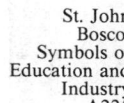

St. John Bosco, Symbols of Education and Industry A225

1968, July 31 **Wmk. 332** ***Perf. 12***
759 A225 2p brn & blk 12 8

75th anniv. of the Don Bosco Workshops of the Salesian Brothers.

Sailors' Monument, Montevideo A226

Designs: 6p, Lighthouse and buoy (vert.). 12p, Gunboat "Suarez" (1860).

1968, Nov. 12 **Litho.** ***Perf. 12***

760 A226	2p gray ol & blk	5	5
761 A226	6p lt grn & blk	8	8
762 A226	12p brt bl & blk	12	10
	Nos. 760-762,C340-C343 (7)	67	48

Sesquicentennial of National Navy.

Oscar D. Gestido A227

1968, Dec. 6 **Wmk. 332** ***Perf. 12***
763 A227 6p brn, dp car & bl 12 8

Issued to commemorate the first anniversary of the death of President Oscar D. Gestido.

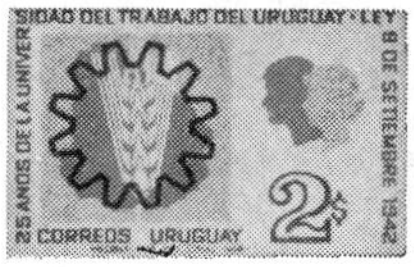

Gearwheel, Grain and Two Heads A228

1969, Mar. 17 **Litho.** ***Perf. 12***
764 A228 2p blk & ver 12 5

25th anniversary of Labor University.

Bicyclists A229

1969, Mar. 21 **Wmk. 332**
765 A229 6p dk bl, org & emer 20 12

Issued to commemorate the 1966 World Bicycle Championships. See No. C347.

Gymnasts and Club Emblem A230

1969, May 8 **Wmk. 332** ***Perf. 12***
766 A230 6p blk & ver 20 12

Issued to commemorate the 75th anniversary of L'Avenir Athletic Club.

Baltasar Brum (1883-1933) — A231

Former presidents: No. 768, Tomas Berreta (1875-1947).

1969 **Litho.** ***Perf. 12***
767 A231 6p rose red & blk 12 8
768 A231 6p car rose & blk 12 8

Fair Emblem — A232

1969, Aug. 15 **Wmk. 332** ***Perf. 12***
769 A232 2p multi 12 5

Issued to publicize the 2nd Industrial World's Fair, Montevideo, 1970.

Diesel Locomotive A233

Design: No. 770, Old steam locomotive and modern railroad cars.

1969, Sept. 19 **Litho.** **Wmk. 332**
770 A233 6p car, blk & ultra 20 8
771 A233 6p car, blk & ultra 20 8

Issued to commemorate the centenary of Uruguayan railroads. Nos. 770-771 printed se-tenant with continuous design and label with commemorative inscription.

Souvenir Sheet

Diligencia Issue, 1856 — A233a

1969, Oct. 1. ***Imperf.***

771A A233a Sheet of 3	2.25	2.25
b. 60p bl	50	50
c. 80p grn	65	65
d. 100p red	75	75

Stamp Day 1969. No. 771A contains stamps similar to No. 1-3, with denominations in pesos.

No. 771A was re-issued Apr. 15, 1972, with black overprint for 15th anniv. of 1st Lufthansa flight from Uruguay to Germany and the Munich Olympic Games.

"Combat" and Sculptor Belloni — A234

1969, Oct. 22 **Wmk. 332** ***Perf. 12***
772 A234 6p ol, sl grn & blk 12 5

Issued to honor José L. Belloni (1882-), sculptor.

Reserve Officers' Training Center Emblem
A235

Design: 2p, Training Center emblem, and officer in uniform and as civilian.

1969, Nov. 5 **Litho.**
773 A235 1p yel & dk bl 10 5
774 A235 2p dk brn & lt bl 15 5

Issued to commemorate the 25th anniversary of the Reserve Officers' Training Center.

Map of Americas and Sun — A236

Stylized Pine — A237

1970, Apr. 20 **Wmk. 332** ***Perf. 12***
775 A236 10p dp bl & gold 15 10

Issued to publicize the 11th meeting of the governors of the Inter-American Development Bank, Punta del Este.

1970, May 14
776 A237 2p red, blk & brt grn 10 8

Issued to publicize the 2nd National Forestry and Wood Exhibition.

Artigas' Ancestral Home in Sauce
A238

1970, June 18 **Wmk. 332** ***Perf. 12***
777 A238 15p ver, ultra & blk 18 8

Map of Uruguay, Sun and Sea — A239

1970, July 8 **Litho.**
778 A239 5p grnsh bl 10 5

Issued for tourist publicity.

EXPO '70 Emblem, Mt. Fuji and Uruguay Coat of Arms — A240

Designs (EXPO '70 Emblem, Arms and): No. 780, Geisha. No. 781, Sun Tower. No. 782, Youth pole.

1970, Aug. 5 **Wmk. 332** ***Perf. 12***
779 A240 25p grn, sl bl & yel 20 12
780 A240 25p org, sl bl & grn 20 12
781 A240 25p yel, sl bl & pur 20 12
782 A240 25p pur, sl bl & org 20 12

Issued to commemorate EXPO '70 International Exhibition, Osaka, Japan, Mar. 15-Sept. 13. Nos. 779-782 are printed se-tenant in sheets of 40.

Cobbled Street in Colonia del Sacramento
A241

Mother and Son by Edmundo Prati in Salto
A242

1970, Oct. 21 **Litho.** ***Perf. 12***
783 A241 5p blk & multi 10 5

290th anniv. of the founding of Colonia del Sacramento, the 1st European settlement in Uruguay.

1970, Nov. 4 **Litho.**
784 A242 10p grn & blk 20 10

Issued to honor mothers.

URUEXPO Emblem
A243

1970, Dec. 9 **Wmk. 332** ***Perf. 12***
785 A243 15p bl, brn org & vio 20 10

URUEXPO '70, National Philatelic Exposition, Montevideo, Sept. 26-Oct. 4.

Children Holding Hands, and UNESCO Emblem — A244

Children's Drawings: No. 786, Two girls holding hands (vert.). No. 788, Boy sitting at school desk (vert.). No. 789, Astronaut and monster.

1970, Dec. 29 **Litho.** ***Perf. 12½***
786 A244 10p multi 12 10
787 A244 10p multi 12 10
788 A244 10p dp car & multi 12 10
789 A244 10p bl & multi 12 10

International Education Year. Nos. 786-789 printed se-tenant in sheets of 16 in blocks of 4 with 2 labels showing Education Year and UNESCO emblems.

Alfonso Espinola (1845-1905), Physician, Professor and Philanthropist
A245

1971, Jan. 13 **Wmk. 332** ***Perf. 12***
790 A245 5p dp org & blk 10 5

Exposition Poster — A246

1971 **Litho.** ***Perf. 12***
791 A246 15p multi 20 10

Uruguay Philatelic Exposition, 1971, Montevideo, March 26-Apr. 19.

5c Coin of 1840, Obverse
A247

Design: No. 793, First coin of Uruguay, reverse.

1971, Apr. 16 **Wmk. 332** ***Perf. 12***
792 A247 25p bl, brn & blk 38 20
793 A247 25p bl, brn & blk 38 20

Numismatists' Day. Printed se-tenant.

Domingo Arena — A248

1971, May 3 **Wmk. 332** ***Perf. 12***
794 A248 5p dk car 10 5

Domingo Arena, lawyer and journalist.

National Anthem
A249

1971, May 19 **Litho.**
795 A249 15p bl, blk & yel 30 30

José F. Arias, Physician — A250

1971, May 25 **Wmk. 332** ***Perf. 12***
796 A250 5p sepia 12 8

Eduardo Fabini, Bar from "Campo"
A251

1971, June 2 **Litho.**
797 A251 5p dk car rose & blk 30 10

Eduardo Fabini (1882-1950), composer, and 40th anniversary of first radio concert.

José E. Rodó, UPAE Emblem
A252

1971, July 15 **Wmk. 332** ***Perf. 12***
798 A252 15p ultra & blk 20 10

Centenary of the birth of José Enrique Rodó (1871-1917), writer, first Uruguayan delegate to Congress of the Postal Union of the Americas and Spain.

Water Cart and Faucet
A253

1971, July 17
799 A253 5p ultra & multi 12 8

Centenary of Montevideo's drinking water system.

Sheep and Cloth
A254

Design: 15p, Sheep, cloth and bale of wool.

1971, Aug. 7
800 A254 5p grn & gray 10 5
801 A254 15p dk bl, grnsh bl & gray 20 10

Wool Promotion.

José Maria Elorza and Merilin Sheep
A255

1971, Aug. 10
802 A255 5p lt bl, grn & blk 12 5

José Maria Elorza, developer of the Merilin sheep.

Criollo Horse
A256

1971, Aug. 11
803 A256 5p blk, gray bl & org 12 5

Bull and Ram
A257

1971, Aug. 13
804 A257 20p red, grn, blk & gold 30 12

Centenary of Rural Association of Uruguay; 19th International Cattle Breeding Exposition, and 66th National Cattle Championships at Prado, Aug. 1971.

Symbol of Liberty and Order
A258

Design: 20p, Policemen, flag of Uruguay and emblem.

1971

805 A258 10p gray, blk & bl 12 8
806 A258 20p dk bl, blk, lt bl & gold 25 12

To honor policemen killed on duty. Issue dates: 10p, Sept. 9; 20p, Nov. 4.

10p Banknote of 1896 — A259

Design: No. 808, Reverse of 10p note.

1971, Sept. 23

807 A259 25p dl grn, gold & blk 30 20
808 A259 25p dl grn, gold & blk 30 20

75th anniversary of Bank of the Republic. Printed se-tenant in sheets of 20 stamps and 5 labels.

Farmer and Arms of Durazno A260

1971, Oct. 11

809 A260 20p gold, bl & blk 20 10

Sesquicentennial of the founding of Durazno.

Emblem and Laurel — A261

1971, Oct. 20

810 A261 10p vio bl, gold & red 15 8

Winners of Liberator's Cup, American Soccer Champions, 1971.

Voter Casting Ballot — A262

Design: 20p, Citizens voting (horiz.).

1971, Nov. 22 Wmk. 332 *Perf. 12*

811 A262 10p bl & blk 10 8
812 A262 20p bl & blk 20 10

Universal, secret and obligatory franchise.

Map of Uruguay on Globe — A263

1971, Dec. 23

813 A263 20p lt bl & vio brn 25 10

7th Littoral Expo., Paysandu, Mar. 26-Apr. 11.

Juan Lindolfo Cuestas — A264

1971, Dec. 27

814 A264 10p *shown* 8 5
815 A264 10p *Julio Herrera y Obes* 8 5
816 A264 10p *Claudio Williman* 8 5
817 A264 10p *José Serrato* 8 5
818 A264 10p *Andrés Martinez Trueba* 8 5
Strip of 5, #814-818 42 42
Nos. 814-818 (5) 40 25

Presidents of Uruguay. Nos. 814-818 printed se-tenant horizontally in sheets of 50 (10x5).

Souvenir Sheet

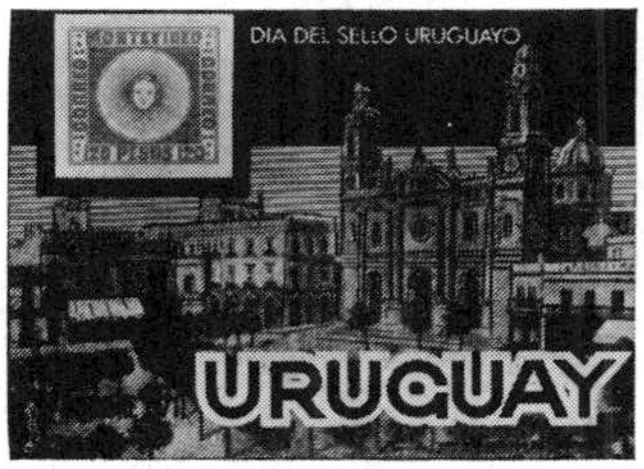

Uruguay No. 4, Cathedral of Montevideo and Plaza de la Constitucion — A265

1972, Jan. 17 *Imperf.*

819 A265 120p brn, bl & dp rose 50 50

Stamp Day 1971 (release date delayed). Size: 99x70mm. See Nos. 834-835, 863.

Bartolomé Hidalgo A266

Missa Solemnis, by Beethoven A267

1972, Feb. 28 *Perf. 12*

820 A266 5p lt brn, blk & red 15 8

Bartolomé Hidalgo (1788-1822), Uruguayan-Argentine poet.

1972, Apr. 20 Litho. Wmk. 332

822 A267 20p lil, emer & blk 15 10

12th Choir Festival of Eastern Uruguay.

Dove and Wounded Bird — A268

Columbus Arch, Colon — A269

1972, May 9

823 A268 10p ver & multi 10 8

To honor Dionision Disz (age 9), who died saving his sister.

1972, June 21

824 A269 20p red, bl & blk 10 8

Centenary of Colon, now suburb of Montevideo.

No. 810 Surcharged in Silver

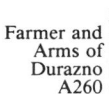

(Surcharge 69mm wide)

1972, June 30

825 A261 50p on 10p multi 25 20

Winners of the 1971 Intl. Soccer Cup.

Tree Planting A270

"Collective Housing" A271

1972, Aug. 5 Wmk. 332 *Perf. 12*

826 A270 20p grn & blk 8 5

Afforestation program.

1972, Sept. 30 Litho.

827 A271 10p dp bl & multi 8 5

Publicity for collective housing plan.

Amethyst A272

Uruguayan Gem Stones: 9p, Agate. 15p, Chalcedony.

1972, Oct. 7

828 A272 5p gray & multi 5 5
829 A272 9p gray bl & multi 8 8
830 A272 15p gray grn & multi 15 12

Uniform of 1830 — A273

Design: 20p, Lancer.

1972, Nov. 21 Litho.

831 A273 10p multi 8 5
832 A273 20p rose red & multi 18 12

Red Cross and Map of Uruguay A274

1972, Dec. 11 Wmk. 332 *Perf. 12*

833 A274 30p multi 20 10

75th anniv. of the Uruguayan Red Cross.

Souvenir Sheets

Stamp Day Type of 1972.

Designs: 200p, Coat of arms type of 1864 similar to Nos. 18, 20-21, but 60p, 60p and 80p. 220p, Similar to Nos. 22-23, but 100p and 120p.

1972, Dec. 20 *Imperf.*

834 A265 200p multi 55 50
835 A265 220p multi 70 65

Stamp Day 1972. No. 834 commemorates the 200th anniversary of first printed cancellations; No. 835 centenary of the decree establishing regular postal service.

Scales of Justice, Olive Branch A275

1972, Dec. 27 Wmk. 332 *Perf. 12*

836 A275 10p gold, dk & lt bl 10 8

25th anniversary of the Civil Rights Law for Women.

General José Artigas A276

Hand Holding Cup; Grain, Map of Americas A277

1972-74 Wmk. 332 Litho. *Perf. 12*

837	A276	5p	yel ('74)	5	5
838	A276	10p	dk bis ('74)	5	5
839	A276	15p	emer ('74)	5	5
840	A276	20p	lil ('73)	5	5
841	A276	30p	lt bl ('73)	12	6
842	A276	40p	dp org ('73)	12	6
843	A276	50p	ver ('73)	12	6
844	A276	75p	ap grn ('73)	15	12
845	A276	100p	emerald	20	12
846	A276	150p	choc ('73)	25	18
847	A276	200p	dk bl ('73)	38	22
848	A276	250p	pur ('73)	45	25
849	A276	500p	gray ('73)	90	55
849A	A276	1000p	bl ('73)	1.65	1.10
	Nos. 837-849A (14)			4.54	2.92

1973, Jan. 9

850 A277 30p rose red, yel & blk 10 8

30th anniversary of the International Institute for Agricultural Research.

Elbio Fernandez and José P. Varela — A278

1973, Jan. 16

851 A278 10p dl grn, gold & blk 5 5

Centenary of the Society of Friends of Public Education.

Map of Americas, "1972" and Columbus A279

1973, Jan. 30
852 A279 50p purple 12 8

Tourist Year of the Americas 1972.

Carlos Maria Ramirez, Scales and Books
A280

1973, Feb. 15
853 A280 10p *shown* 10 5
854 A280 10p *Justino Jimenez de Arechaga* 10 5
855 A280 10p *Juan Andres Ramirez* 10 5
856 A280 10p *Justino E. Jimenez de Arechaga* 10 5
Strip of 4 + label 50 50

Centenary of the Professorship of Constitutional Rights.

Nos. 853-856 were printed se-tenant in same sheet in horizontal strips of four with label centered. Label is inscribed "Jurisconsultos del Uruguay," names and dates of four honored men.

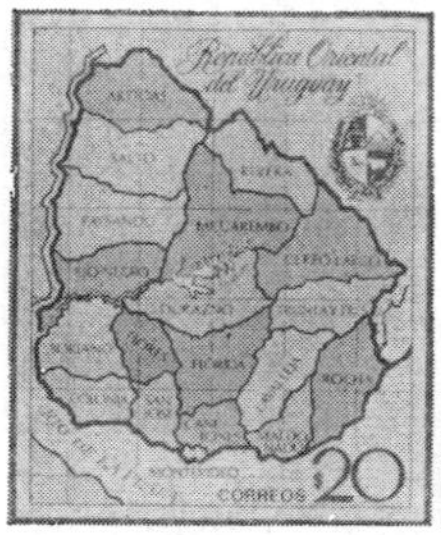

Provincial Map of Uruguay
A281

1973, Feb. 27 Litho. ***Perf. 12½x12***
857 A281 20p bl & multi 18 10

See No. 1167.

Francisco de los Santos
A282

1973, May 16 Wmk. 332 ***Perf. 12***
858 A282 20p grn & blk 18 10

Soldiers' Day and Battle of Piedras. Santos was a courier who went through enemy lines.

Souvenir Sheet
No. C319 Surcharged with New Value and: "HOMENAJE AL 4 CENTENARIO DE CORDOBA . ARGENTINA . 1973"

1973, May 9 Litho. ***Imperf.***
859 AP57 100p on 5p multi 65 65

400th anniversary of the founding of Cordoba in Argentina.

Friar, Indians, Church — A283

1973, July 25 ***Perf. 12***
860 A283 20p lt ultra, pur & blk 15 8

Villa Santo Domingo Soriano, first Spanish settlement in Uruguay.

Symbolic Fish
A284

1973, Aug. 15
861 A284 100p bl & multi 30 15

First station of Oceanographic and Fishery Service, Montevideo.

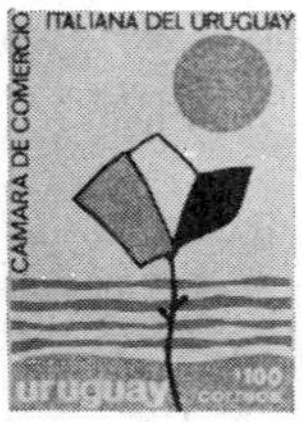

Sun over Flower in Italian Colors — A285

1973, Sept.
862 A285 100p multi 20 15

Italian Chamber of Commerce of Uruguay.

Souvenir Sheet
Stamp Day Type of 1972

Design: 240p, Thin numeral sun type of 1859 and street scene.

Wmk. 332
1973, Oct. 1 Litho. ***Imperf.***
863 A265 240p grn, org & blk 75 65

Stamp Day 1973. No. 863 contains one stamp, green margin with white inscription and black vignette. Size: 100x69mm.

Luis Alberto de Herrera — A286

1973, Nov. 12 ***Perf. 12***
866 A286 50p gray, brn & dk brn 12 10

Centenary of the birth of Luis Alberto de Herrera.

Emblem of Social Coordination Volunteers
A287

Wmk. 352
1973, Nov. 19 Litho. ***Perf. 12***
867 A287 50p bl & multi 12 8

Festival of Nations, Montevideo.

Arm with Arteries and Heart — A288

1973, Nov. 22
868 A288 50p blk, red & pink 12 8

3rd Cong. of the Pan-American Federation of Blood Donors, Montevideo, Nov. 23-25.

Madonna, by Rafael Perez Barradas — A289

1973, Dec. 10 Litho. Wmk. 332
869 A289 50p grn, gray & yel grn 12 8

Christmas 1973.

Nicolaus Copernicus — A290

1973, Dec. 26 **Litho.**
870 A290 50p grn & multi 12 8

500th anniversary of the birth of Nicolaus Copernicus (1473-1543), Polish astronomer.

Praying Hands and Andes — A291

Design: 75p, Statue of Christ on mountain, and flower.

1973, Dec. 26 **Litho.**
871 A291 50p blk, lt grn & ultra 10 5
872 A291 75p bl, blk & org 15 10

Survival and rescue of victims of airplane crash.

OAS Emblem and Map of Americas
A292

1974, Jan. 14 Wmk. 332 ***Perf. 12***
873 A292 250p gray & multi 50 35

25th anniversary of the Organization of American States (OAS).

Scout Emblems and Flame
A293

1974, Jan. 21
874 A293 250p multi 50 35

1st Intl. Boy Scout Games, Montevideo, 1974.

Hector Suppici Sedes and Car — A294

1974, Jan. 28 ***Perf. 12***
875 A294 50p sep, grn & blk 10 5

70th anniversary of the birth of Hector Suppici Sedes (1903-1948), automobile racer.

Three Gauchos — A295

1974, Mar. 20 Litho. Wmk. 332
876 A295 50p multi 10 5

Centenary of the publication of "Los Tres Gauchos Orientales" by Antonio D. Lussich.

Rifle, Target and Swiss Flag
A296

1974, Apr. 2
877 A296 100p multi 20 12

Centenary of the Swiss Rifle Association.

Map of Uruguay and Compass Rose — A297

1974, Apr. 23 **Litho.**
878 A297 50p multi 10 5

Military Geographical Service.

Montevideo Stadium Tower — A298

Design: 75p, Soccer player, Games' emblem (horiz.).

1974, May 7 Wmk. 332 ***Perf. 12***
879 A298 50p multi 10 6
880 A298 75p multi 15 10

World Cup Soccer Championship, Munich, June 13-July 7. A 1000p stamp and a 1000p Souvenir card exist.

Old and New School and Founders
A299

1974, May 21
883 A299 75p blk & bis 14 10

Centenary of the Osimani-Llerena Technical School at Salto, founded by Gervasio Osimani and Miguel Llerena.

Carlos Gardel and Score — A301

Wmk. 332

1974, June 24 Litho. ***Perf. 12***
884 A301 100p multi 22 12

Carlos Gardel (1887-1935), singer and motion picture actor.

Volleyball and Net — A302

"Protect your Heart" — A303

1974, July 11 Wmk. 332 ***Perf. 12***
885 A302 200p lil, yel & blk 30 18

First anniversary of Women's Volleyball championships, Montevideo, 1973.

1974, July 24 Litho.
886 A303 75p ol grn, yel & red 12 12

Heart Foundation publicity.

Eusebio Vidal, Portrait and Statue A304

Artigas Statue, Buenos Aires, Flags of Uruguay and Argentina A305

1974, Aug. 5
887 A304 75p dk & lt bl 10 6

Centenary (in 1973) of the founding of San José de Mayo by Eusebio Vidal.

1974, Aug. 13 ***Perf. 12½***
888 A305 75p multi 10 6

Unveiling of Artigas monument, Buenos Aires.

Radio Tower and Waves — A306

1974, Sept. 24 Wmk. 332 ***Perf. 12***
889 A306 100p multi 14 8

50th anniv. of Broadcasting in Uruguay.

URUEXPO 74 Emblem — A307

URUEXPO Emblem and Old Map of Montevideo Bay — A308

1974
890 A307 100p blk, dk bl & red 14 8
891 A308 300p sep, red & grn 38 14

URUEXPO 74 Philatelic Exhibition, 10th anniversary of Philatelic Circle of Uruguay (100p) and 250th anniversary of fortification of Montevideo. Issue dates: 100p, Oct. 1; 300p, Oct. 19.

Letters and UPU Emblem A309

Design: 200p, UPU emblem, letter, and globe.

1974, Oct. 9
892 A309 100p lt bl & multi 6 5
893 A309 200p lil, blk & gold 14 8

Centenary of Universal Postal Union. See Nos. C395-C396.

Artigas Statue and Map of Lavalleja A310

1974, Oct. 17 ***Perf. 12***
894 A310 100p ultra & multi 6 5

Unveiling of Artigas statue in Minas, Lavalleja.

Ship in Dry Dock, Arsenal's Emblem A312

1974, Nov. 15 Litho. Wmk. 332
896 A312 200p multi 30 20

Centenary of Naval Arsenal, Montevideo.

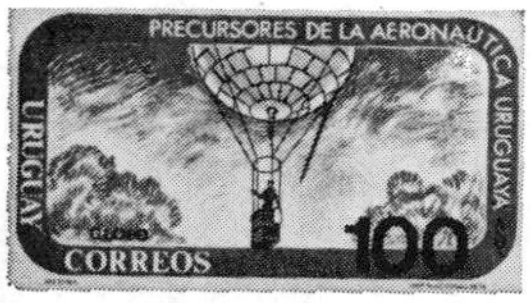

Globe Hydrogen Balloon — A313

1974, Nov. 20
897 A313 100p *shown* 12 8
898 A313 100p *Farman biplane* 12 8
899 A313 100p *Castaibert monoplane* 12 8
900 A313 100p *Bleriot monoplane* 12 8
901 A313 150p *Military and civilian pilots' emblems* 18 12
902 A313 150p *Nieuport biplane* 18 12
903 A313 150p *Breguet-Bidon fighter* 18 12
904 A313 150p *Caproni bomber* 18 12
Nos. 897-904 (8) 1.20 80

Aviation pioneers. Stamps of same denomination printed se-tenant in sheets of 20 (4x5).

Sugar Loaf Mountain and Summit Cross — A314

1974, Nov. 30
905 A314 150p multi 18 12

Cent. of the founding of Sugar Loaf City.

Adoration of the Kings — A315

Designs: 150p, Three Kings.

1974 ***Perf. 12***
906 A315 100p org & multi 6 5
907 A315 150p bl & multi 9 6

Christmas 1974. See Nos. C400-C401. Issue dates: 100p, Dec. 17; 150p, Dec. 19.

Nike, Fireworks, Rowers and Club Emblem — A316

1975, Jan. 27 Litho. Wmk. 332
908 A316 150p gray & multi 9 6

Centenary of Montevideo Rowing Club.

Treaty Signing, by José Zorilla de San Martin — A317

1975, Feb. 12 ***Perf. 12***
909 A317 100p multi 6 5

Commercial Treaty between Great Britain and Uruguay, 1817.

Rose — A318

1975, Mar. 18 Litho. Wmk. 332
910 A318 150p multi 12 6

Bicentenary of city of Rosario.

"The Oath of the 33," by Juan M. Blanes — A319

1975, Apr. 16 ***Perf. 12***
911 A319 150p gold & multi 12 6

Sesquicentennial of liberation movement.

Ship, Columbus and Ancient Map — A320

1975, Oct. 9 Litho. Wmk. 332
912 A320 1p gray & multi 65 38

Hispanic Stamp Day.

Leonardo Olivera and Santa Teresa Fort — A321

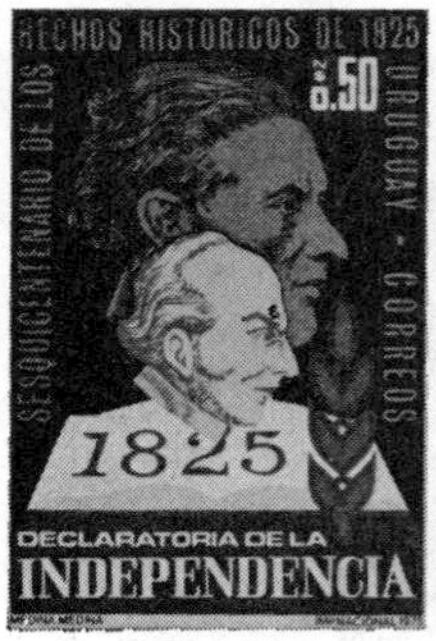

Artigas as Young and Old Man
A322

1975 Litho. Wmk. 332 *Perf. 12*
913 A321 10c org & multi 12 5
914 A322 50c vio bl & multi 50 25

Sesquicentennial of the capture of Fort Santa Teresa (10c) and of Uruguay's declaration of independence (50c).
Issue dates: 10c, Oct. 20; 50c, Oct. 17.

Battle of Rincon, by Diogenes Hequet — A323

Designs: No. 916, Artigas' Home, Ibiray, Paraguay. 25c, Battle of Sarandi, by J. Manuel Blanes.

1975 Litho.
915 A323 15c ol & blk 12 8
916 A323 15c ol & multi 12 8
917 A323 25c ol & multi 25 15

Uruguayan independence. Nos. 915 and 917, 150th anniversary of Battles of Rincon and Sarandi. No. 916, 50th anniversary of school at Artigas mansion.
Issue dates: No. 915, Oct. 23; No. 916, Nov. 18; No. 917, Nov. 28.

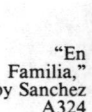

"En Familia," by Sanchez
A324

Florencio Sanchez
A325

Designs (Plays by Sanchez): No. 919, Barranca Abajo. No. 920, M'Hijo el Doctor. No. 921, Canillita.

1975, Oct. 31 Wmk. 332 *Perf. 12*
918 A324 20c gray, red & blk 20 8
919 A324 20c bl, grn & blk 20 8
920 A324 20c red, bl & blk 20 8
921 A324 20c grn, gray & blk 20 8
922 A325 20c multi 20 8
Block of 5 stamps + 4 labels 1.25

Florencio Sanchez (1875-1910), dramatist, birth centenary. Nos. 918-922 printed se-tenant in sheets of 30 stamps and 20 labels.

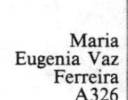

Maria Eugenia Vaz Ferreira
A326

Design: No. 924, Julio Herrera y Reissig.

1975
923 A326 15c yel, blk & brn 15 8
924 A326 15c org, blk & mar 15 8

Maria Eugenia Vaz Ferreira (1875-1924), poetess, and Julio Herrera y Reissig (1875-1910), poet, birth anniversaries.
Issue dates: No. 923, Dec. 9; No. 924, Dec. 29.

Virgin and Child
A327 A328

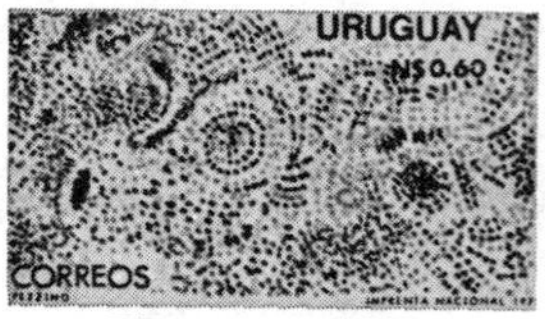

Fireworks — A329

1975
925 A327 20c bl & multi 25 10
926 A328 30c blk & multi 38 20
927 A329 60c multi 50 30

Christmas 1975.
Issue dates: 20c, Dec. 16; 30c, Dec. 15; 60c, Dec. 11.

Col. Lorenzo Latorre (1840-1916), Pres. of Uruguay (1876-80) — A330

1975, Dec. 30 *Perf. 12*
928 A330 15c multi 9 6

Nos. 840, 842-843, 849A Surcharged

**N$
0,10**

1975
929 A276 10c on 20p lil 5 5
930 A276 15c on 40p org 8 5
931 A276 50c on 50p ver 25 15
932 A276 1p on 1000p bl 50 30

Ariel, Stars, Book and Youths
A331

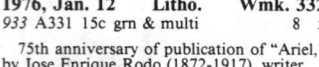

1976, Jan. 12 Litho. Wmk. 332
933 A331 15c grn & multi 8 5

75th anniversary of publication of "Ariel," by Jose Enrique Rodo (1872-1917), writer.

Water Sports Telephone
A332 A333

1976, Mar. 12 Litho. Wmk. 332
934 A332 30c multi 15 9

23rd South American Swimming, Diving and Water Polo Championships.

1976, Apr. 9 *Perf. 12*
935 A333 83c multi 42 25

Centenary of first telephone call by Alexander Graham Bell, Mar. 10, 1876.

"Plus Ultra" and Columbus' Ships — A334

Wmk. 332
1976, May 10 Litho. *Perf. 12*
936 A334 63c gray & multi 32 18

Flight of Dornier "Plus Ultra" from Spain to South America, 50th anniversary.

Dornier "Wal" and Boeing 727, Hourglass — A335

1976, May 24
937 A335 83c gray & multi 42 25

Lufthansa German Airline, 50th anniv.

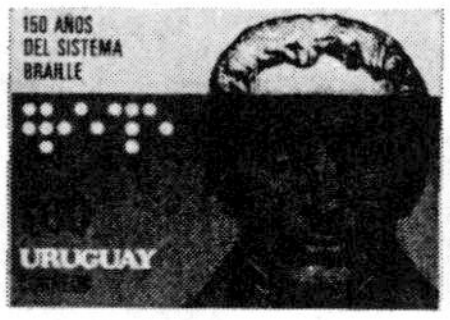

Louis Braille
A340

1976, June 7
942 A340 60c blk & brn 30 18

Sesquicentennial of the invention of the Braille system of writing for the blind by Louis Braille (1809-1852).

Signing of U.S. Declaration of Independence
A341

1976, June 21
943 A341 1.50p multi 1.65 50

American Bicentennial.

Freeing of the Slaves, by P. Figari
A342

Wmk. 332
1976, July 29 Litho. *Perf. 12*
944 A342 30c ultra & multi 15 8

Abolition of slavery, sesquicentennial.

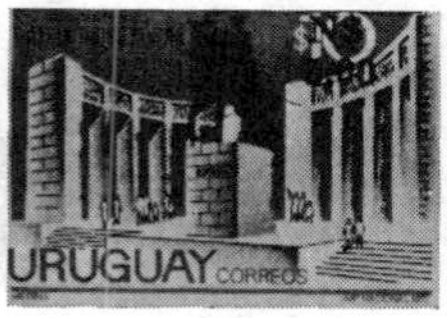

Gen. Fructuoso Rivera Statue
A343

1976, Aug. 2
945 A343 5p on 10p multi 2.50 1.65

No. 945 was not issued without surcharge.

General Accounting Office — A344

Wmk. 332
1976, Aug. 24 Litho. *Perf. 12*
946 A344 30c bl, blk & brn 22 14

National General Accounting Office, sesquicentennial.

Old Pump, Emblem and Flame — A345

1976, Sept. 6
947 A345 20c red & blk 10 5

First official fire fighting service, centenary.

Southern Lapwing — A346 Mburucuya Flower — A347

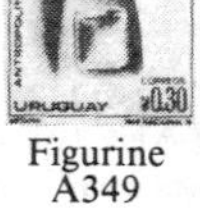
Spearhead Figurine
A348 A349

La Yerra, by J. M. Blanes — A350

The Gaucho, by Blanes — A351

Artigas — A352

Designs: 15c, Ceibo flower.

1976-79 Litho. Wmk. 332 Perf. 12

948	A346	1c violet	6	5
949	A347	5c lt grn	6	5
951	A347	15c car rose	14	5
952	A348	20c gray	5	5
954	A349	30c gray bl	14	5
955	A352	45c brt bl ('79)	8	5
956	A350	50c grnsh bl ('77)	20	7
958	A351	1p dk brn ('77)	40	10
959	A352	1p brt yel ('79)	16	10
960	A352	1.75p bl grn ('79)	30	8
961	A352	1.95p gray ('79)	32	10
962	A352	2p dl grn ('77)	90	16
963	A352	2p lil rose ('79)	35	10
964	A352	2.65p vio ('79)	42	12
968	A352	5p dk bl	2.50	50
970	A352	10p brn ('77)	4.25	65
		Nos. 948-970 (16)	10.33	2.28

"Diligencia" Uruguay No. 1 — A356

Wmk. 332

1976, Sept. 26 Litho. Perf. 12

974 A356 30c bis, red & bl 15 7

Philatelic Club of Uruguay, 50th anniv.

Games' Emblem — A357

1976, Oct. 26 Litho. Perf. 12

975 A357 83c gray & multi 40 16

5th World University Soccer Championships.

Eye and Spectrum A358

1976, Nov. 24

976 A358 20c blk & multi 16 7

Foresight prevents blindness.

Map of Montevideo, 1748 A359

Designs: 45c, Montevideo Harbor, 1842. 70c, First settlers, 1726. 80c, Coin with Montevideo arms (vert.). 1.15p, Montevideo's first coat of arms (vert.).

Wmk. 332

1976, Dec. 30 Litho. Perf. 12

977	A359	30c multi	14	7
978	A359	45c multi	20	10
979	A359	70c multi	35	14
980	A359	80c multi	38	16
981	A359	1.15p multi	55	25
		Nos. 977-981 (5)	1.62	72

Founding of Montevideo, 250th anniversary.

Symbolic of Flight A360

1977, May 7 Litho. Perf. 12

982 A360 80c multi 50 14

50th anniversary of Varig airlines.

Artigas Mausoleum A361

1977, June 17 Litho. Perf. 12

983 A361 45c multi 30 7

Map of Uruguay and Arch A362

Children A363

1977, July 5 Wmk. 332

984 A362 45c multi 30 10

Centenary of Salesian Brothers' educational system in Uruguay.

1977, Aug. 10 Litho. Perf. 12

985 A363 45c multi 30 8

Interamerican Children's Institute, 50th anniversary.

"El Sol de Mayo" A364

1977, Oct. 1 Litho. Perf. 12

986 A364 45c multi 20 8

Stamp Day 1977.

Windmills — A365

1977, Sept. 29 Wmk. 332

987 A365 70c yel, car & blk 35 14

Spanish Heritage Day.

Souvenir Sheet

View of Sans (Barcelona), by Barradas — A366

1977, Oct. 7 Litho. Perf. 12

988 A366 Sheet of 2, multi 3.00 2.50
a. 5p, single stamp 1.40

ESPAMER '77 Philatelic Exhibition, Barcelona, Oct. 7-13.

Planes, UN Emblem, Globe A367

1977, Oct. 17

989 A367 45c multi 14 5

30th anniv. of Civil Aviation Organization.

Holy Family — A368

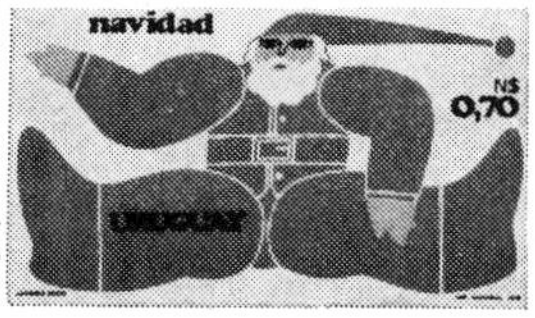

Santa Claus A369

1977, Dec. 1 Wmk. 332

990 A368 45c multi 14 5
991 A369 70c blk, yel & red 20 8

Christmas 1977.

Map of Rio Negro Province A370

1977, Dec. 16

992 A370 45c multi 14 7

Rio Negro Dam; development of agriculture, livestock and beekeeping.

Mail Collection — A371

1977, Dec. 21

993	A371	50c *shown*	15	7
994	A371	50c *Mail truck*	15	7
995	A371	50c *Post office counter*	15	7
996	A371	50c *Postal boxes*	15	7
997	A371	50c *Mail sorting*	15	7
998	A371	50c *Pigeonhole sorting*	15	7
999	A371	50c *Route sorting (seated carriers)*	15	7
1000	A371	50c *Home delivery*	15	7
1001	A371	50c *Special delivery (motorcyclists)*	15	7
1002	A371	50c *Airport counter*	15	7
		Nos. 993-1002 (10)	1.50	70

150th anniversary of Uruguayan postal service. Nos. 993-1002 printed se-tenant.

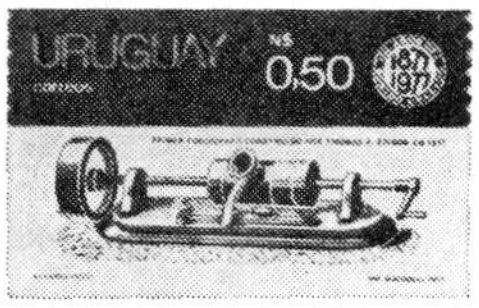

Edison's Phonograph, 1877 — A372

1977, Dec. 30

1003 A372 50c vio brn & yel 14 7

Centenary of invention of the phonograph.

"R", Rainbow and Emblem A373

1977, Dec. 30 Wmk. 332

1004 A373 50c multi 14 7

World Rheumatism Year.

Emblem and Diploma A374

1978, Mar. 27 Litho. Perf. 12

1005 A374 50c multi 14 7

50th anniversary of Military College.

Map and Arms of Artigas Department A375

Wmk. 332

1978, June 16 Litho. Perf. 12

1006 A375 45c multi 16 7

Souvenir Sheet

Anniversaries — A376

Designs: 2p, Papilio thoas. No. 1007b, "100." No. 1007c, Argentina '78 emblem and globes. 5p, Model T Ford.

Wmk. 332

1978, Aug. 24 Litho. *Perf. 12*

1007 A376 Sheet of 4 3.50 2.50
a. 2p multi 40 14
b. 4p multi 85 25
c. 4p multi 85 25
d. 5p multi 1.10 35

75th anniv. of 1st powered flight; URUEXPO '78 Phil. Exhib.; Parva Domus social club, cent.; 11th World Cup Soccer Championship, Argentina, June 1-25; Ford motor cars, 75th anniv.

Visiting Angels, by Solari A377

Designs (Details from No. 1008b): No. 1008a, Second angel. No. 1008c, Third angel.

1978, Sept. 13 Unwmk.
Sizes: Nos. 1008a, 1008c: 19x30mm.; No. 1008b, 38x30mm.

1008 Strip of 3 1.00 65
a. A377 1.50p multi 32 16
b. A377 1.50p multi 32 16
c. A377 1.50p multi 32 16

Solari, Uruguayan painter.

Bernardo O'Higgins A378

Design: No. 1010, José de San Martin and monument.

1978 Wmk. 332

1009 A378 1p multi 20 10
1010 A378 1p multi 20 10

Benardo O'Higgins (1778-1842 and José de San Martin (1778-1850), South American liberators.

Issue dates: No. 1009, Sept. 13; No. 1010, Oct. 10.

Telephone Dials A379

1978, Sept. 25

1011 A379 50c multi 10 7

Automation of telephone service.

Symbolic Stamps A380

Iberian Tile Pattern — A381

1978, Oct. 31

1012 A380 50c multi 10 7
1013 A381 1p multi 20 10

Stamp Day (50c) and Spanish heritage (1p).

Boeing 727 A382

1978, Nov. 27

1014 A382 50c multi 10 7

Inauguration of Boeing 727 flights by PLUNA Uruguayan airlines, Nov. 1978.

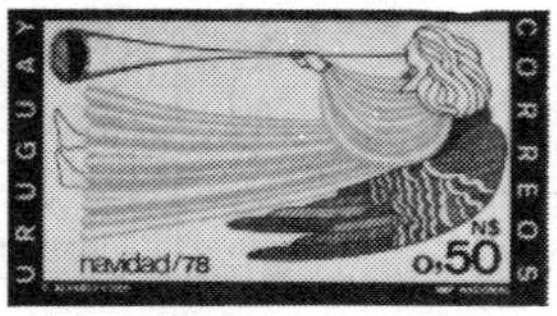

Angel Blowing Horn — A383

1978, Dec. 7

1015 A383 50c multi 10 7
1016 A383 1p multi 20 10

Christmas 1978.

Horacio Quiroga (1868-1928), Short Story Writer — A385

Wmk. 332

1978, Dec. 27 Litho. *Perf. 12*

1018 A385 1p blk, red & yel 20 10

Arch, Olympic Rings, Lake Placid and Moscow Emblems A386

Design: 7p, Olympic Rings and Lake Placid '80 emblem.

1979, Apr. 28 Litho. *Perf. 12*

1019 A386 5p multi 1.10 35
1020 A386 7p multi 1.50 50

81st Session of Olympic Organizing Committee, Apr. 3-8 (5p), and 13th Winter Olympic Games, Lake Placid, N.Y., Feb. 12-24.

Map and Arms of Paysandu A387

Map and Arms of Maldonado — A388

1979-81

1021 A387 45c shown 10 7
1022 A387 45c Salto 10 7
1023 A388 45c shown 8 7
1024 A387 45c Cerro Largo 8 7
1025 A387 50c Treinta y Tres 10 7
1026 A387 50c Durazno ('80) 10 7
1032 A388 2p Rocha ('81) 35 14
1033 A388 2p Flores 35 14
Nos. 1021-1033 (8) 1.26 70

Sapper with Pickax, 1837 — A389

Flag Flying on Plaza of the Nation — A390

Army Day: No. 1041, Artillery man with cannon, 1830.

1979, May 18 Litho. *Perf. 12*

1040 A389 5p multi 1.10 35
1041 A389 5p multi 1.10 35

1978, Dec. 15 *Perf. 12½*

1042 A390 1p multi 20 7

Salto Dam A391

1979, June 19

1043 A391 2p multi 42 14

Crandon Institute Emblem, Grain A392

1979, July 19

1044 A392 1p vio bl & bl 16 7

Crandon Institute (private Methodist school), centenary.

IYC Emblem, Smiling Kites — A393

Cinderella A394

1979

1045 A393 2p multi 35 14
1046 A394 2p multi 35 14

International Year of the Child. Issue dates: No. 1045, July 23; No. 1046, Aug. 29.

Uruguay Coat of Arms 150th anniversary — A395

1979, Sept. 6

1047 A395 8p multi 1.40 65

Virgin and Child A396

Symbols, by Torres-Garcia A397

Wmk. 332

1979, Nov. 19 Litho. *Perf. 12*

1048 A396 10p multi 1.60 80

Christmas 1979; Intl. Year of the Child.

1979, Nov. 12

1049 A397 10p yel & blk 1.60 80

J. Torres-Garcia (1874-1948), painter.

U.P.U. and Brazilian Postal Emblems — A398

1979, Oct. 11

1050 A398 5p multi 80 50

18th U.P.U. Congress, Rio, Sept.-Oct.

Dish Antenna and Sun — A400

Perf. 12x11½
1979, Nov. 26 Litho. Wmk. 332
1052 A400 10p multi 1.00 80

Telecom '79, 3rd World Telecommunications Exhibition, Geneva, Sept. 20-26.

Spanish Heritage Day — A401

1979, Dec. 3 ***Perf. 12***
1053 A401 10p multi 1.60 80

Silver Coin Centenary A402

Designs: Obverse and reverse of coins in denominations matching stamps.

Wmk. 332
1979, Dec. 26 Litho. ***Perf. 12***
1054 A402 10c multi 5 5
1055 A402 20c multi 5 5
1056 A402 50c multi 10 7
1057 A402 1p multi 16 10

Souvenir Sheet

Security Agent — A403

1980, Jan. 10
1058 Sheet of 4 2.00 1.60
a. A403 1p *Police emblem* 16 10
b. A403 2p *shown* 35 16
c. A403 3p *Policeman, 1843* 50 25
d. A403 4p *Cadet, 1979* 65 40

Police force sesquicentennial.

Light Bulb, Thomas Edison — A404

1980, Jan. 18
1059 A404 2p multi 35 16

Centenary of electric light (1979).

Bass and Singer — A405

1980, Jan. 30
1060 Sheet of 4 1.50 1.40
a. A405 2p *Radio waves* 35 25
b. A405 2p *shown* 35 25
c. A405 2p *Ballerina* 35 25
d. A405 2p *Television waves* 35 25

Performing Arts Society, 50th anniversary.

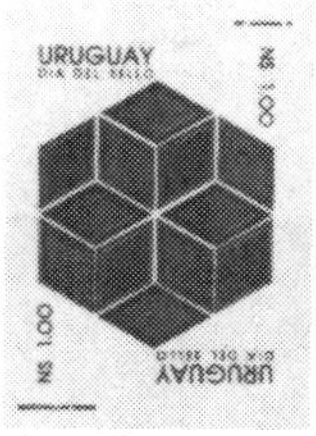

Stamp Day — A406

La Leyenda Patria — A407

1980, Feb.
1061 A406 1p multi 16 7

1980, Feb. 26
1062 A407 1p multi 16 7

Printers' Association, 50th Anniversary A408

1980, Feb.
1063 A408 1p multi 16 7

Lufthansa Cargo Container Service Inauguration — A409

1980, Apr. 12 Litho. ***Perf. 12½***
1064 A409 2p multi 35 14

Conf. Emblem, Banners — A410

Man, Woman and Birds — A411

1980, Apr. 28 Litho. ***Perf. 12***
1065 A410 2p multi 35 14

8th World Hereford Conf., Punta del Este and Livestock Exhib., Prado/Montivideo.

1980 Litho. ***Perf. 12***
1066 A411 1p multi 16 7

International Year of the Child (1979).

Latin-American Lions, 9th Forum — A412

1980, May 6 Wmk. 332 ***Perf. 12***
1067 A412 1p multi 20 10

Souvenir Sheet

Rifleman, 1814 — A413

1980, May 16
1068 Sheet of 4 1.65 1.40
a. A413 2p *shown* 40 25
b. A413 2p *Cavalry officer, 1830* 40 25
c. A413 2p *Private Liberty Dragoons, 1826* 40 25
d. A413 2p, *Artigas Militia officer, 1815* 40 25

Army Day, May 18.

Arms of Colonia — A414

Souvenir Sheet

Colonia, 1680 A415

1980, June 17 Litho. ***Perf. 12***
1069 A414 50c multi 8 7
1070 Sheet of 4, multi 65 55
a. A415 1p *shown* 16 10
b. A415 1p *1680*, diff. 16 10
c. A415 1p *1980* 16 10
d. A415 1p *1980*, diff. 16 10

Colonia, 300th anniversary.

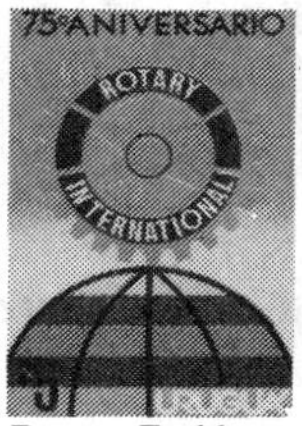

Rotary Emblem on Globe A416

Hand Putting Out Cigarette A417

1980, July 8
1071 A416 5p multi 80 50

Rotary International, 75th anniversary.

1980, Sept. 8 **Photo.**
1072 A417 1p multi 16 7

World Health Day and anti-smoking campaign.

Artigas A418

Christmas 1980 A419

Constitution Title Page — A420

Wmk. 332
1980-85 Litho. ***Perf. 12½***
1073 A418 10c bl ('81) 5 5
1074 A418 20c orange 5 5
1075 A418 50c red 8 7
1076 A418 60c yellow 10 7
1077 A418 1p gray 16 7
1078 A418 2p brown 35 16
1079 A418 3p brt grn 50 35
1080 A418 4p brt bl ('82) 65 40
1081 A418 5p grn ('82) 25 10
1082 A418 6p brt org ('85) 10 5
1083 A418 7p lil rose ('82) 1.20 65
1084 A418 10p bl ('82) 55 25
1085 A418 12p blk ('85) 20 10
1086 A418 15.50p emer ('85) 22 12
1087 A418 20p dk vio ('82) 1.10 55
1088 A418 30p lt brn ('82) 1.60 80
1089 A418 50p gray bl ('82) 2.50 1.40
Nos. 1073-1089 (17) 9.66 5.24

1980, Dec. 15 Litho. ***Perf. 12***
1090 A419 2p multi 35 16

1980, Dec. 23 ***Perf. 12½***
1091 A420 4p brt bl & gold 65 35

Sesquicentennial of Constitution.

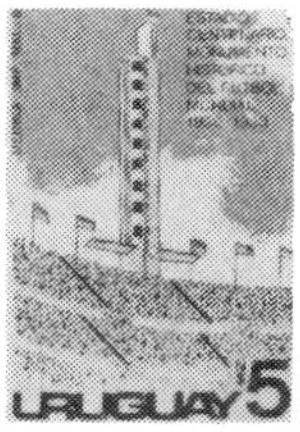

Montevideo Stadium — A421

1980, Dec. 30 ***Perf. 12***
1092 A421 5p shown 80 35
1093 A421 5p Soccer gold cup 80 35

Size: 25x79mm
1094 A421 10p Flags 1.60 65
a. Souv. sheet of 3, #1092-1094 3.75 2.50

Soccer Gold Cup Championship, Montevideo.

Spanish Heritage Day — A422

1981, Jan. 27
1095 A422 2p multi 35 14

UPU Membership Centenary
A423

1981, Feb. 6
1096 A423 2p multi 35 14

Alexander von Humboldt (1769-1859), German Explorer and Scientist — A424

1981, Feb. 19
1097 A424 2p multi 35 14

Intl. Education Congress and Fair, Montevideo (1980)
A425

1981, Mar. 31
1098 A425 2p multi 35 14

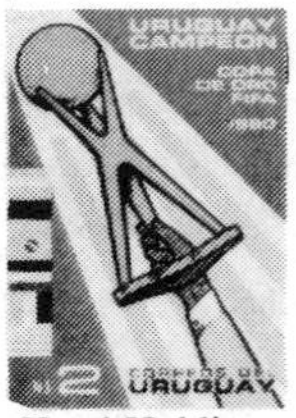

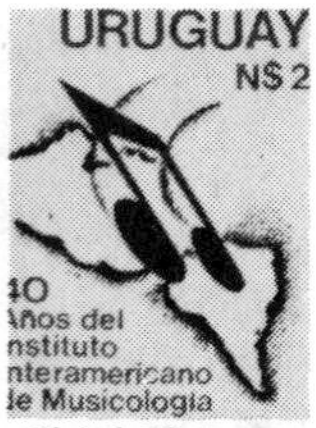

Hand Holding Gold Cup
A426

Eighth Notes on Map of Americas
A427

1981, Apr. 8
1099 A426 2p multi 35 14
1100 A426 5p multi 80 35

1980 victory in Gold Cup Soccer Championship.

1981, Apr. 28
1101 A427 2p multi 35 14

Inter-American Institute of Musicology, 40th anniv.

World Tourism Conference, Manila, Sept. 27, 1980 — A428

Wmk. 332

1981, June 1 **Litho.** ***Perf. 12***
1102 A428 2p multi 35 14

Inauguration of PLUNA Flights to Madrid — A429

1981, May 12
1103 A429 2p multi 35 14
1104 A429 5p multi 80 35
1105 A429 10p multi 1.60 65

Army Day — A430

Natl. Atomic Energy Commission, 25th Anniv. — A431

Wmk. 332

1981, May 18 **Litho.** ***Perf. 12***
1106 A430 2p Cavalry soldier, 1843 35 14
1107 A430 2p Infantryman, 1843 35 14

1981, July 20
1108 A431 2p multi 35 14

Europe-South American Soccer Cup — A432

1981, Aug. 4
1109 A432 2p multi 35 14

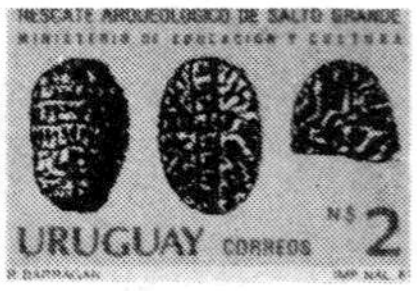

Stone Tablets, Salto Grande Excavation
A433

1981, Sept. 10
1110 A433 2p multi 35 14

10th Lavalleja Week — A434

1981, Oct. 3
1111 A434 4p multi 65 35

Intl. Year of the Disabled
A435

Wmk. 332

1981, Oct. 26 **Litho.** ***Perf. 12***
1112 A435 2p multi 35 14

The first value column gives the catalogue value of an unused stamp, the second that of a used stamp.

U.N. Environmental Law Meeting Montevideo, Oct. 28-Nov. 6 — A436

1981, Oct. 28
1113 A436 5p multi 80 35

50th Anniv. of ANCAP (Natl. Administration of Combustible Fuels, Alcohol and Cement) — A437

1981, Oct. 13
1114 A437 2p multi 35 14

Topographical Society Sesquicentennial
A439

1981, Dec. 5 ***Perf. 12***
1116 A439 2p multi 35 14

Bank of Uruguay, 85th Anniv. — A440

1981, Dec. 17 ***Perf. 12½***
1117 A440 2p multi 35 14

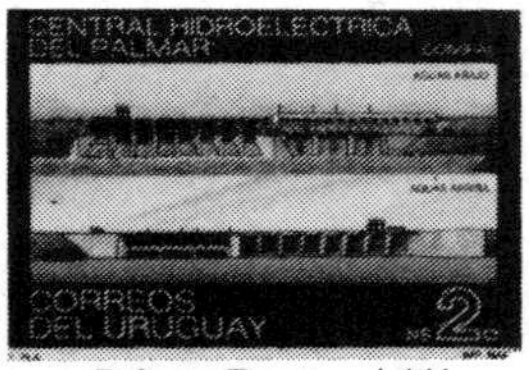

Palmar Dam — A441

1981, Dec. 22 ***Perf. 12***
1118 A441 2p multi 35 14

Christmas 1981
A442

1981, Dec. 23
1119 A442 2p multi 35 14

Pres. Joaquin Suarez Bicentenary — A443

1982, Mar. 15
1120 A443 5p multi 80 35

Artillery Captain, 1872, Army Day — A444

Cent. (1981) of Pinocchio, by Carlo Collodi — A445

Wmk. 332

1982, May 18 **Litho.** ***Perf. 12***
1121 A444 3p shown 50 20
1122 A444 3p Florida Battalion, 1865 50 20

See Nos. 1136-1137.

1982, June 17
1123 A445 2p multi 35 14

2nd UN Conference on Peaceful Uses of Outer Space, Vienna, Aug. 9-21 — A446

1982, June 3
1124 A446 3p multi 80 50

World Food Day
A447

1982
1125 A447 2p multi 35 14

25th Anniv. of Lufthansa's Uruguay-Germany Flight — A448

1982, Apr. 14 **Unwmk.** ***Perf. 12½***
1126 A448 3p Lockheed L-1049-G Super Constellation 50 35
1127 A448 7p Boeing 747 1.20 65

American Air Forces Cooperation System — A449

1982, Apr. 14 Wmk. 332 *Perf. 12*
1128 A449 10p Emblem 1.60 80

Juan Zorilla de San Martin (1855-1931), Painter — A450

1982, Aug. 18 *Perf. 12½*
1129 A450 3p Self-portrait 50 35

165th Anniv. of Natl. Navy A451

1982, Nov. 15 *Perf. 12*
1130 A451 3p Navy vessel Capitan Miranda 16 10

Natl. Literacy Campaign A452

Stamp Day A453

1982, Nov. 30
1131 A452 3p multi 16 10

1982, Dec. 23 *Perf. 12½*
1132 A453 3p like #46 30 14
1133 A453 3p like #47 30 14

Nos. 1132-1133 se-tenant.

Christmas 1982 — A454

1983, Jan. 4 *Perf. 12*
1134 A454 3p multi 45 20

Eduardo Fabini (1882-1950), Composer — A455

1983, May 10
1135 A455 3p gold & brn 45 20

Army Day Type of 1982

1983, May 18
1136 A444 3p Military College cadet, 1885 45 20
1137 A444 3p 2nd Cavalry Regiment officer, 1885 45 20

Visit of King Juan Carlos and Queen Sofia of Spain, May A456

1983, May 20
1138 A456 3p Santa Maria, globe 50 25
1139 A456 7p Profiles, flags 1.25 60

Size of No. 1138: 29x39mm.

Brasiliana '83 Emblem A457

80th Anniv. of First Automobile in Uruguay A458

Opening of UPAE Building, Montevideo A459

Jose Cuneo (1887-1977), Painter A460

1982 World Cup A461

Graf Zeppelin Flight Over Montevideo, 50th Anniv. (1984) — A462

J.W. Goethe (1749-1832), 150th Death Anniv. — A463

First Space Shuttle Flight A464

1983 Litho. Wmk. 332 *Perf. 12*

1140	A457	3p multi	45	20
1141	A458	3p multi	45	20
1142	A459	3p multi	45	20
1143	A460	3p multi	45	20
a.		Souvenir sheet of 4	1.50	1.50
1144	A461	7p multi	85	40
1145	A462	7p multi	85	40
1146	A463	7p multi	85	40
1147	A464	7p multi	85	40
a.		Souvenir sheet of 4	3.75	3.75
		Nos. 1140-1147 (8)	5.20	2.40

No. 1143a contains stamps similar to Nos. 1140-1143. Size: 149x82mm. No. 1147a contains stamps similar to Nos. 1144-1147. Size: 82x149mm. Nos. 1143a and 1147a for URUEXPO '83 and World Communications Year. Black marginal inscriptions and control numbers.

Dates of issue: No. 1142, June 8; Nos. 1143, 1146, Sept. 29; Nos. 1143a, 1147a, June 9; No. 1140, July 22; Nos. 1144, Dec. 13; No. 1146, Sept. 20; No. 1145, Dec. 8.

Bicentenary of City of Minas — A465

Wmk. 332

1983, Oct. 17 Litho. *Perf. 12*
1148 A465 3p Founder 25

World Communications Year — A466

1983, Nov. 30
1149 A466 3p multi 25

Garibaldi Death Centenary A467

1983, Dec. 5
1150 A467 7p multi 60

Christmas 1983 A468

Lithographed and Embossed (Braille)

1983, Dec. 21 *Perf. 12½*
1151 A468 4.50p multi 36

50th Anniv. of Automatic Telephones A469

1983, Dec. 27 *Perf. 12*
1152 A469 4.50p multi 36

Simon Bolivar, Battle Scene A470

Wmk. 332

1984, Mar. 28 Litho. *Perf. 12*
1153 A470 4.50p brn & gldn brn 36

Gen. Leandro Gomez — A471

1984, Jan. 2
1154 A471 4.50p multi 36

American Women's Day — A472

Reunion Emblem — A473

1984, Feb. 18
1155 A472 4.50p Flags, emblem 36

1984, Mar. 23
1156 A473 10p multi 85

Intl. Development Bank Governors, 25th annual reunion, Punta del Este.

50th Anniv. of Radio Club of Uruguay (1983) A474

1984, Apr. 11
1157 A474 7p multi 60

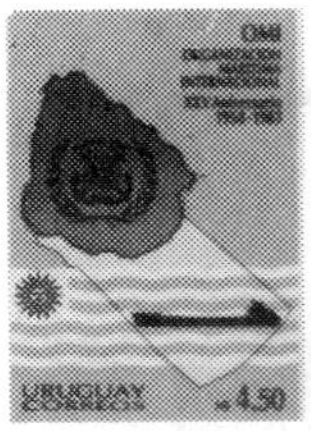

Intl. Maritime Org., 25th Anniv. — A475

1984, Feb. 7 Litho. *Perf. 12*
1158 A475 4.50p multi 36 18

1930 World Soccer Championships, Montevideo A476

1984, May 2 Litho. *Perf. 12*
1159 A476 4.50p multi 36 18

Department of San Jose de Mayo, 200th Anniv. — A477

1984, May 9 Litho. *Perf. 12*
1160 A477 4.50p multi 36 18

Tourism, 50th Anniv. A478

1984, May 15 Litho. *Perf. 12*
1161 A478 4.50p multi 36 18

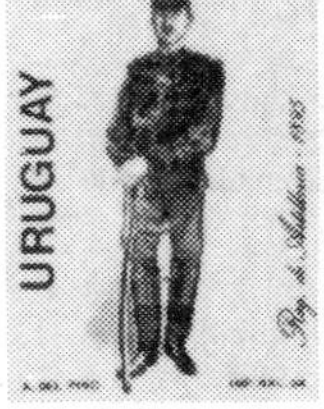

Military Uniforms — A479

Artigas on the Plains — A480

1984, June 19 Litho. *Perf. 12*
1162 A479 4.50p Artillery Regiment, 1895 36 18
1163 A479 4.50p Cazadores, 2nd battalion 36 18

1984, July 2 Litho. *Perf. 12*
1164 A480 4.50p bl & blk 36 18
1165 A480 8.50p bl & redsh brn 68 35

A. Penarol Soccer Club A481

1984, Aug. 21 Litho. *Perf. 12*
1166 A481 4.50p Championship trophy 36 18

Provincial Map Type of 1973

1984, Sept. 21 Litho. *Perf. 12*
1167 A281 4.50p multi 36 18

Childrens Council, 50th Anniv. A482

1984, Oct. 11 Litho. *Perf. 12*
1168 A482 4.50p multi 36 18

Christmas 1984 — A483

1984 Litho. *Perf. 12*
1169 A483 6p multi 48 25

1st Jr. World Basketball Championships A484

1985, Feb. 13 Litho. *Perf. 12*
1170 A484 4.50p multi 36 18

Don Bruno Mauricio de Zabala, 300th Birth Anniv. — A485

1985, Apr. 16 Litho. *Perf. 12*
1171 A485 4.50p multi 28 14

Intl. Olympic Committee, 90th Anniv. — A486

Design: Olympic rings, Los Angeles and Sarajevo 1984 Games emblems.

1985, May 22 *Perf. 12½*
1172 A486 12p multi 70 35

Carlos Gardel, (1890-1935), Entertainer A487

Catholic Circle of Workers, Cent. A488

1985, June 21 *Perf. 12*
1173 A487 6p lt gray, red brn & bl 35 18

Wmk. 332

1985, June 21 Litho. *Perf. 12*
1174 A488 6p Cross, clasped hands 15 8

Icarus, by Hans Erni A489

1985, July Photo. Wmk. 332
1175 A489 4.50p multi 12 6

Intl. Civil Aviation Org., 40th anniv.

American Air Forces Cooperation System, 25th Anniv. — A490

1985, July
1176 A490 12p Emblem, flags 30 15

FUNSA, Natl. Investment Funds Corp., 50th Anniv. A491

1985, July 31 Litho. Wmk. 332
1177 A491 6p multi 15 8

Intl. Youth Year — A492

1985, Aug. 28
1178 A492 12p mar & blk 30 15

Installation of Democratic Government — A493

1985, Aug. 30
1179 A493 20p brt pur, yel ocher & dk grnsh bl 48 24

Intl. Book Fair — A494

1985
1180 A494 20p multi 48 24

Military School, Cent. A495

1985, Nov. 29 Litho. *Perf. 12*
1181 A495 10p multi 25 12

Department of Flores, Cent. — A496

Day of Hispanic Solidarity — A498

Christmas 1985 A497

1985, Dec. 9
1182 A496 6p Map, arms 15 8

1985, Dec. 23
1183 A497 10p multi 25 12
1184 A497 22p multi 52 25

1985, Dec. 27
1185 A498 12p Isabel Monument 30 15

3rd Inter-American Agricultural Congress — A499

Wmk. 332

1986, Jan. 7 Photo. *Perf. 12*
1186 A499 12p blk, dl yel & red 30 15

UPU Day A500

1986, Jan. 14 Litho. *Perf. 12*
1187 A500 15.50p multi 38 20

1985 Census A501

1986, Jan. 21
1188 A501 10p multi 25 12

Conaprole, 50th Anniv. A502

1986, Jan. 25
1189 A502 10p gold, brt ultra & bl 25 12

UN, 40th Anniv. A503

Wmk. 332

1986, Feb. 26 Litho. *Perf. 12*
1190 A503 20p multi 38 20

Brokers and Auctioneers Assoc., 50th Anniv. — A504

1986, Mar. 19
1191 A504 10p multi 16 8

Gen. Manuel Ceferino Oribe (1792-1857), President — A505

Portraits: 2p, 15p, Oribe. 3p, Lavalleja. No. 1203A, 60p, 200p, Artigas. 17p, 26p, 45p, Rivera.

1986 ***Perf. 12½***

1196	A505	1p	dl grn	5	5
1197	A505	2p	scar ('87)	5	5
1198	A505	3p	ultra ('87)	5	5
1200	A505	5p	dk bl	10	10
1202	A505	7p	tan	12	6
1203	A505	10p	lil rose	20	20
1203A	A505	10p	brt grn ('87)	12	12
1203B	A505	15p	dull blue ('88)	15	15
1204	A505	17p	deep bl ('87)	20	20
1205	A505	22p	violet	22	22
1205A	A505	26p	olive blk ('87)	30	30
1206	A505	30p	pale org	30	30
1207	A505	45p	dark red ('88)	32	32
1208	A505	50p	dp bis	50	50
1209	A505	60p	dark gray ('87)	70	70
1210	A505	100p	dl red brn	1.00	1.00
1211	A505	200p	brt yel grn ('88)	1.45	1.45
	Nos. 1196-1211 (17)			5.83	5.77

No. 1205 is airmail.

Issue dates: 5p, 30p, June 16. 10p, 22p, Sept. 24. 50p, Aug. 5. 100p, July 2. 2p, June 16. 3p, 60p, Aug. 14. No. 1203A, 17p, Aug. 4. 26p, Sept. 2. 15p, Sept. 9; 45p, Dec. 20; 200p, Oct. 19.

Italian Chamber of Commerce in Uruguay — A506

1986, May 5 ***Perf. 12***
1212 A506 20p multi 32 16

1986 World Cup Soccer Championships, Mexico — A507

1986, May 28 Photo. *Perf. 12*
1213 A507 20p multi 38 20

Genocide of the Armenian People, 71st Anniv. — A508

El Dia Newspaper, Cent. — A509

Wmk. 332

1986, May 19 Litho. *Perf. 12*
1214 A508 10p multi 10 10

1986, June 16
1215 A509 10p multi 10 10

Pres. Garcia, Peruvian Flag — A510

1986, July 14
1216 A510 20p dk bl, red & red brn 20 20

State visit of Pres. Alan Garcia of Peru.

Simon Bolivar, Gen. Sucre, Map A511

1986, July 24
1217 A511 20p multi 20 20

State visit of Pres. Jaime Lusinchi of Venezuela.

State Visit of Pres. J. Sarney of Brazil — A512

Zelmar Michelini, Assassinated Liberal Senator of Uruguay — A513

1986, July 31
1218 A512 20p multi 20 20

1986, Aug. 21
1219 A513 10p vio bl & rose lake 10 10

B'nai B'rith of Uruguay, 50th Anniv. A514

1986, Sept. 10
1220 A514 10p red, gold & red brn 10 10

Gatt Committee Reunion, Punta del Este A515

1986, Sept. 15
1221 A515 10p multi 10 10

Scheduled Flights between Uruguay and Spain, 40th Anniv. A516

1986, Sept. 22
1222 A516 20p multi 20 20

Fish Exports A517

1986, Oct. 1
1223 A517 20p multi 20 20

Wool Exports A518

1986, Oct. 15
1224 A518 20p multi 20 20

Pres. Blanco, Natl. and Dominican Flags A519

1986, Oct. 29
1225 A519 20p multi 20 20

State visit of Pres. Salvador Jorge Blanco of the Dominican Republic.

State Visit of Pres. Sandro Pertini of Italy A520

State Visit of Pres. Raul Alfonsin of Argentina A521

1986, Oct. 31
1226 A520 20p grn & buff 20 20

1986, Nov. 10
1227 A521 20p multi 20 20

Hispanic Solidarity Day — A522

Design: Felipe and Santiago, the patron saints of Montevideo, and cathedral.

Wmk. 332

1987, Jan. 12 Litho. *Perf. 12*
1228 A522 10p rose lake & blk 12 12

JUVENTUS, 50th Anniv. — A523

1987, Jan. 28
1229 A523 10p brt yel, blk & ultra 12 12

Juventus, a Catholic sports, culture and leisure organization.

Canceled-to-order stamps are often from remainders. Most collectors of canceled stamps prefer postally used specimens.

Hector Gutierrez Ruiz (1934-1976), Politician A524

Intl. Symposium on Science and Technology A525

1987, Feb. 23

1230 A524 10p brn & deep mag 12 12
1231 A525 20p multi 22 22

Ruiz represented Uruguay at an earlier science and technology symposium.

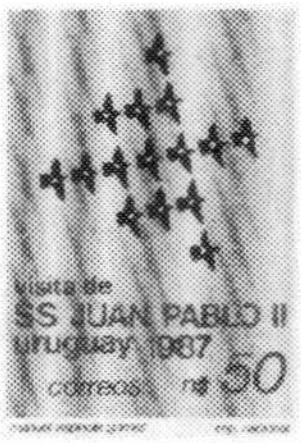

Visit of Pope John Paul II to La Plata Region — A526

Dr. Jose F. Arias (1885-1985), Founder of the University of Crafts — A527

1987, Mar. 31

1232 A526 50p blk & deep org 58 58

1987, Apr. 28

1233 A527 10p multi 12 12

Jewish Community in Uruguay, 70th Anniv. — A528

1987, July 8

1234 A528 10p blk, org & brt blue 12 12

Pluna Airlines, 50th Anniv. A529

1987, Sept. 16

1235 A529 10p Dragon Fly 12 12
1236 A529 20p Douglas DC-3 22 22
1237 A529 25p Vicker's Viscount 28 28
1238 A529 30p Boeing 707 35 35

Artigas Antarctic Station A530

1987, Sept. 28

1239 A530 20p multi 22 22

Uruguay Mortgage Bank, 75th Anniv. A531

1987, Oct. 14

1240 A531 26p multi 30 30

Exports — A532

1987, Oct. 28

1241 A532 51p Beef 60 60
1242 A532 51p Milk products 60 60

Christmas 1987 — A533

1987, Dec. 21

1243 A533 17p Nativity, vert. 20 20
1244 A533 66p shown 75 75

State Visit of Jose Napoleon Duarte, President of El Salvador — A534

VARIG Airlines, 60th Anniv. — A535

1988, Jan. 12

1245 A534 20p brt olive grn & Prus blue 22 22

1988, Feb. 9

1246 A535 66p blk, blue & brt yel 75 75

Post Office Stamp Foundation — A536

Wmk. 332

1988, Feb. 9 Litho. *Perf. 12*

1247 A536 30p on 10+5p brt blue, blk & yel 22 22

No. 1247 not issued without surcharge.

Intl. Peace Year A537

1988, Feb. 11

1248 A537 10p multi 12 12

Euskal Erria, 75th Anniv. (in 1987) — A538

1988, Mar. 9

1249 A538 66p multi 75 75

Air Force, 75th Anniv. A539

1988, Mar. 11

1250 A539 17p multi 20 20

Interamerican Children's Institute, 60th Anniv. — A540

Wmk. 332

1988, Mar. 28 Litho. *Perf. 12*

1251 A540 30p apple grn, blk & grn 27 27

State Hydroelectric Works (UTE), 75th Anniv. — A541

1988, Apr. 20

1252 A541 17p shown 15 15
1253 A541 17p Baygorria Dam 15 15
1254 A541 51p Gabriel Terra Dam 48 48
1255 A541 51p Constitucion Dam 48 48
1256 A541 66p Dams on map 62 62
Nos. 1252-1256 (5) 1.88 1.88

Postal Union of America and Spain (UPAE), 75th Anniv. A542

1988, May 10

1257 A542 66p multi 65 65

Israel, 40th Anniv. A543

1988, May 17

1258 A543 66p lt ultra & blk 65 65

Postal Messenger of Peace — A544

1988, May 24

1259 A544 66p multi 65 65

Portrait, *La Cumparsita* Tango — A545

Firemen, Cent. — A546

1988, June 7

1260 A545 17p Parade, horiz. 16 16
1261 A545 51p Score 48 48

Gerardo H. Matos Rodrigues, composer.

1988, June 21

1262 A546 17p Pablo Banales, founder 15 15
1263 A546 26p Fireman, 1900 22 22
1264 A546 34p Emblem, horiz. 28 28
1265 A546 51p Merry Weather fire engine, 1907, horiz. 42 42
1266 A546 66p Fire pump, 1888, horiz. 55 55

Size: 44x24½mm

1267 A546 100p Ladder truck, 1921 85 85
Nos. 1262-1267 (6) 2.47 2.47

Capitan Miranda Trans-world Voyage, Cent. — A547

1988, July 28

1268 A547 30p multi 25 25

Exports A548

1988

1269	A548	30p	Citrus fruit	25	25
1270	A548	45p	Rice	35	35
1271	A548	55p	Footwear	45	45
1272	A548	55p	Leather and furs	45	45

Issue dates: 30p, No. 1272, Sept. 14; 45p, No. 1271, Aug. 23.

Natl. Museum of Natural History, 150th Anniv. — A549

Designs: 30p, *Usnea densirostra* fossil. 90p, *Toxodon platensis* bone, Quaternary period. Printed se-tenant.

1988, Sept. 20

1273	A549	30p	blk, yel & red brn	25	25
1274	A549	90p	blk, ultra & beige	75	75

Battle of Carpinteria, 150th Anniv. (in 1986) — A550

1988, Nov. 23

1275	A550	30p	multi	22	22

Christmas — A551

1988, Dec. 21

1276	A551	115p	multi	82	82

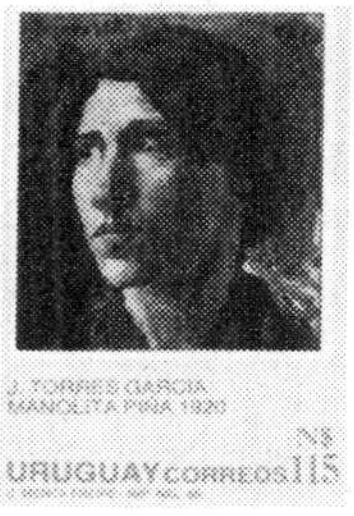

Paintings A552

Designs: a. *Manolita Pina, 1920,* by J. Torres Garcia. b. *78 Squares and Rectangles,* by J.P. Costigliolo. c. Print publicizing an exhibition of works by Pedrero Figari, 1945. d. *Self-portrait, 1947,* by J. Torres Garcia.

1988, Dec. 27

1277	Block of 4	3.00	3.00
a.-d.	A552 115p any single	75	75

Spanish Heritage Day A553

1989, Jan. 9

1278	A553	90p	multi	58	58
1279	A553	115p	multi	72	72

SEMI-POSTAL STAMPS

Indigent Old Man — SP1

Unwmk.

1930, Nov. 13 Engr. *Perf. 12*

B1	SP1	1c + 1c dk vio		18	18
B2	SP1	2c + 2c dp grn		20	20
B3	SP1	5c + 5c red		25	25
B4	SP1	8c + 8c gray vio		25	25

The surtax on these stamps was for a fund to assist the aged. See No. 419.

Catalogue values for unused stamps in this section, from this point to the end of the section, are for Never Hinged items.

Dam, Child and Rising Sun — SP2

Wmk. 327

1959, Sept. 29 Litho. *Perf. 11½*

B5	SP2	5c + 10c grn & org	5	5
B6	SP2	10c + 10c dk bl & org	8	8
B7	SP2	1p + 10c pur & org	25	20

Issued for national recovery. See Nos. CB1-CB2.

AIR POST STAMPS

No. 91 Overprinted in Dark Blue, Red or Green

1921-22 Unwmk. *Perf. 14*

C1	A38	25c bis brn (Bl)	10.00	8.00
a.		Black overprint	450.00	450.00
C2	A38	25c bis brn (R)	3.50	2.50
a.		Inverted ovpt.	60.00	60.00
C3	A38	25c bis brn (G) ('22)	3.50	2.50

This overprint also exists in light yellow green.

No. C1a was not issued. Some authorities consider it an overprint color trial.

AP2

Wmk. 188

1924, Jan. 2 Litho. *Perf. 11½*

C4	AP2	6c dk bl	1.00	80
C5	AP2	10c scarlet	1.50	1.20
C6	AP2	20c dp grn	2.50	2.25

Heron — AP3

1925, Aug. 24 *Perf. 12½*

Inscribed "MONTEVIDEO"

C7	AP3	14c bl & blk	20.00	12.00

Inscribed "FLORIDA"

C8	AP3	14c bl & blk	20.00	12.00

These stamps were used only on Aug. 25, 1925, the cent. of the Assembly of Florida, on letters intended to be carried by airplane between Montevideo and Florida, a town 60 miles north. The stamps were not delivered to the public but were affixed to the letters and canceled by post office clerks. Later uncanceled copies came on the market.

One authority believes Nos. C7-C8 served as registration stamps on these two attempted special flights.

Gaucho Cavalryman at Rincon AP4

1925, Sept. 24 *Perf. 11*

C9	AP4	45c bl grn	6.00

Centenary of Battle of Rincon. Used only on Sept. 24. No. C9 was affixed and canceled by post office clerks.

Albatross — AP5

1926, Mar. 3 Wmk. 188 *Imperf.*

C10	AP5	6c dk bl	80	80
C11	AP5	10c vermilion	1.20	1.20
C12	AP5	20c bl grn	1.60	1.60
C13	AP5	25c violet	1.60	1.60

Excellent counterfeits exist.

1928, June 25 *Perf. 11*

C14	AP5	10c green	1.60	1.40
C15	AP5	20c orange	2.50	2.00
C16	AP5	30c indigo	2.50	2.00
C17	AP5	38c green	4.00	3.50
C18	AP5	40c yellow	4.50	4.00
C19	AP5	50c violet	5.25	4.50
C20	AP5	76c orange	10.00	9.00
C21	AP5	1p red	8.25	7.00
C22	AP5	1.14p indigo	22.50	20.00
C23	AP5	1.52p yellow	35.00	35.00
C24	AP5	1.90p violet	45.00	40.00
C25	AP5	3.80p red	120.00	100.00
		Nos. C14-C25 (12)	261.10	228.40

Counterfeits of No. C25 exist.

1929, Aug. 23 Unwmk.

C26	AP5	4c ol brn	2.25	2.25

The design was redrawn for Nos. C14-C26. The numerals are narrower, "CENTS" is 1 mm. high instead of 2½mm. and imprint letters touch the bottom frame line.

Pegasus AP6

1929-43 Engr. *Perf. 12½.*

Size: 34x23mm.

C27	AP6	1c red lil ('30)	20	20
C28	AP6	1c dk bl ('32)	20	20
C29	AP6	2c yel ('30)	20	20
C30	AP6	2c ol grn ('32)	20	20
C31	AP6	4c Prus bl ('30)	35	30
C32	AP6	4c car rose ('32)	35	30
C33	AP6	6c dl vio ('30)	38	30
C34	AP6	6c red brn ('32)	38	30
C35	AP6	8c red org	1.75	1.50
C36	AP6	8c gray ('30)	2.00	1.50
C36A	AP6	8c brt grn ('43)	25	20
C37	AP6	16c indigo	1.40	1.10
C38	AP6	16c rose ('30)	1.65	1.50
C39	AP6	24c claret	1.50	1.25
C40	AP6	24c brt vio ('30)	2.00	1.65
C41	AP6	30c bister	1.65	1.50
C42	AP6	30c dk grn ('30)	1.00	50
C43	AP6	40c dk brn	3.00	2.50
C44	AP6	40c yel org ('30)	3.00	2.50
C45	AP6	60c bl grn	2.50	1.75
C46	AP6	60c emer ('30)	4.00	3.50
C47	AP6	60c dp org ('31)	1.50	1.00
C48	AP6	80c dk ultra	4.50	4.00
C49	AP6	80c grn ('30)	7.50	6.00
C50	AP6	90c lt bl	4.50	3.50
C51	AP6	90c dk ol grn ('30)	7.50	6.00
C52	AP6	1p car rose ('30)	3.75	2.50
C53	AP6	1.20p ol grn	11.25	10.00
C54	AP6	1.20p dp car ('30)	15.00	12.50
C55	AP6	1.50p red brn	11.25	8.75
C56	AP6	1.50p blk brn ('30)	6.00	5.00
C57	AP6	3p dp red	17.50	15.00
C58	AP6	3p ultra ('30)	12.50	10.00
C59	AP6	4.50p black	32.50	25.00
C60	AP6	4.50p vio ('30)	22.50	17.50
C60A	AP6	10p dp ultra ('43)	10.00	6.00
		Nos. C27-C60A (36)	195.71	155.70

See Nos. C63-C82.

Nos. 450, 452 Overprinted in Red

1934, Jan. 1 *Perf. 11½*

C61	A130	17c ver, gray & vio	12.50	10.00
a.		Sheet of six	87.50	
b.		Gray omitted	100.00	
c.		Double ovpt.	100.00	
C62	A130	36c red, blk & yel	12.50	10.00
a.		Sheet of six	87.50	

Issued to commemorate the 7th Pan-American Conference, Montevideo.

Pegasus Type of 1929.

1935 Engr. *Perf. 12½.*

Size: 31½x21mm.

C63	AP6	15c dl yel	1.25	1.00
C64	AP6	22c brick red	75	65
C65	AP6	30c brn vio	1.25	1.00
C66	AP6	37c gray lil	65	50
C67	AP6	40c rose lake	1.00	65
C68	AP6	47c rose	2.00	1.75
C69	AP6	50c Prus bl	65	38
C70	AP6	52c dp ultra	2.00	1.75
C71	AP6	57c grnsh bl	4.00	90
C72	AP6	62c ol grn	90	40
C73	AP6	87c gray grn	2.50	2.00
C74	AP6	1p olive	1.75	1.10
C75	AP6	1.12p brn red	1.75	1.10
C76	AP6	1.20p bis brn	7.50	6.00
C77	AP6	1.27p red brn	7.50	6.25
C78	AP6	1.62p rose	5.00	4.50
C79	AP6	2p brn rose	8.00	7.00
C80	AP6	2.12p dk sl grn	8.00	7.00
C81	AP6	3p dl bl	7.50	6.25
C82	AP6	5p orange	25.00	25.00
		Nos. C63-C82 (20)	85.95	75.18

Counterfeits exist.

Power Dam on Black River — AP7

Imprint: "Imp. Nacional" at center.

1937-41 Litho.

C83	AP7	20c lt grn ('38)	2.25	1.75
C84	AP7	35c red brn	3.50	2.75
C85	AP7	62c bl grn ('38)	38	15
C86	AP7	68c yel org ('38)	90	65
C86A	AP7	68c pale vio brn ('41)	75	30
C87	AP7	75c violet	3.50	1.00
C88	AP7	1p dp pink ('38)	1.10	75
C89	AP7	1.38p rose ('38)	10.00	10.00
C90	AP7	3p dk bl ('40)	5.50	1.25
		Nos. C83-C90 (9)	27.88	18.60

Imprint at left.

C91	AP7	8c pale grn ('39)	25	20
C92	AP7	20c lt grn ('38)	90	65

Plane over Sculptured Oxcart — AP8

1939-44 ***Perf. 12½***

C93	AP8	20c slate	22	18
C94	AP8	20c lt vio ('43)	35	38
C95	AP8	20c bl ('44)	28	18
C96	AP8	35c red	45	35
C97	AP8	50c brn org	45	15
C98	AP8	75c dp pink	50	12
C99	AP8	1p dp bl ('40)	1.40	25
C100	AP8	1.38p brt vio	2.50	1.00
C101	AP8	1.38p yel org ('44)	2.25	1.75
C102	AP8	2p blue	3.50	65
a.		Perf. 11	3.50	50
C103	AP8	5p rose lil	4.50	1.00
C104	AP8	5p bl grn ('44)	6.00	2.50
C105	AP8	10p rose ('40)	37.50	25.00
		Nos. C93-C105 (13)	59.90	33.51

Counterfeits exist.

Stamps of 1935 Surcharged in Red or Black **$0.79**

1944, Nov. 22

C106	AP6	40c on 47c rose	38	30
C107	AP6	40c on 57c grnsh bl (R)	50	38
C108	AP6	74c on 1.12p brn red	50	38
C109	AP6	79c on 87c gray grn	1.75	1.25
C110	AP6	79c on 1.27p red brn	2.50	2.00
C111	AP6	1.20p on 1.62p lt rose	1.40	1.00
C112	AP6	1.43p on 2.12p dk sl grn (R)	1.75	1.25
		Nos. C106-C112 (7)	8.78	6.56

Catalogue values for unused stamps in this section, from this point to the end of the section, are for Never Hinged items.

Legislature Building AP9

Unwmk.

1945, May 11 **Engr.** ***Perf. 11***

C113	AP9	2p ultra	1.75	90

Type of 1929, Surcharged in Violet

1945, Aug. 14 ***Perf. 12½***

C114	AP6	44c on 75c brn	50	30

Allied Nations' victory in Europe.

"La Eolo" AP10

1945, Oct. 31 ***Perf. 11***

C115	AP10	8c green	45	20

Nos. C97 and C101 Surcharged in Violet, Black or Blue

1945-46 ***Perf. 12½***

C116	AP8	14c on 50c brn org (V) ('46)	25	20
a.		Inverted surcharge	37.50	
C117	AP8	23c on 1.38p yel org	30	25
a.		Inverted surcharge	75.00	
C118	AP8	23c on 50c brn org	38	30
a.		Inverted surcharge	75.00	
C119	AP8	1p on 1.38p yel org (Bl)	2.00	1.25
a.		Inverted surcharge	75.00	

Victory of the Allied Nations in WWII.

No. C85 Overprinted in Black

INAUGURACION
DICIEMBRE, 1945

1946, Jan. 9

C120	AP7	62c bl grn	50	35

Issued to commemorate the inauguration of the Black River Power Dam.

AP11

Black Overprint.

1946-49 **Litho.**

C121	AP11	8c car rose	6	5
a.		Inverted overprint		
C122	AP11	50c brown	30	20
a.		Double ovpt.	25.00	
C123	AP11	1p lt bl	50	25
C124	AP11	2p ol ('49)	2.25	1.50
C125	AP11	3p lil rose	2.25	1.50
C126	AP11	5p rose car	4.50	3.50
		Nos. C121-C126 (6)	9.86	7.00

Four-Motored Plane — AP12

National Airport AP13

1947-49 ***Perf. 11½, 12½***

C129	AP12	3c org brn ('49)	5	5
C130	AP12	8c car rose ('49)	8	6
C131	AP12	14c ultra	15	10
C132	AP12	23c emerald	18	12
C133	AP13	1p car & brn ('49)	90	15
C134	AP13	3p ultra & brn ('49)	2.00	1.25
C135	AP13	5p grn & brn ('49)	4.50	2.50
C136	AP13	10p lil rose & brn	5.00	3.75
		Nos. C129-C136 (8)	12.86	7.98

Counterfeits exist. See Nos. C145-C164.

AP14

School of Architecture, University of Uruguay — AP15

Black Overprint

1948, June 9 ***Perf. 12½***

C137	AP14	12c blue	12	5
C138	AP14	24c Prus grn	20	10
C139	AP14	36c sl bl	30	18

1949, Dec. 7

Designs: 27c, Medical School. 31c, Engineering School. 36c, University.

C141	AP15	15c carmine	8	8
C142	AP15	27c chocolate	12	12
C143	AP15	31c dp ultra	20	8
C144	AP15	36c dl grn	22	8

Issued to commemorate the centenary of the founding of the University of Uruguay.

Plane Type of 1947-49.

1952-59 **Unwmk.** ***Perf. 11, 12½.***

C145	AP12	10c blk ('54)	5	5
C146	AP12	10c lt red ('58)	5	5
a.		Imperf., pair	30.00	
C147	AP12	15c org brn	8	6
a.		Vert. pair, imperf. between	50.00	
C148	AP12	20c lil rose ('54)	10	9
C149	AP12	21c purple	12	10
C150	AP12	27c yel grn ('57)	12	5
C151	AP12	31c chocolate	20	9
C152	AP12	36c ultra	15	6
C153	AP12	36c blk ('58)	15	10
C154	AP12	50c lt bl ('57)	25	18
C155	AP12	50c bl blk ('58)	18	6
C156	AP12	62c dl sl bl ('53)	30	18
C157	AP12	65c rose ('53)	30	18
C158	AP12	84c org ('59)	35	30
C159	AP12	1.08p vio brn	65	32
C160	AP12	2p Prus bl	1.00	50
C161	AP12	3p red org	1.25	65
C162	AP12	5p dk gray grn	2.50	1.50
C163	AP12	5p gray ('57)	1.50	1.00
C164	AP12	10p dp grn ('55)	6.25	4.50
		Nos. C145-C164 (20)	15.55	10.02

Planes and Show Emblem AP16

Unwmk.

1956, Jan. 5 **Litho.** ***Perf. 11***

C166	AP16	20c ultra	25	30
C167	AP16	31c ol grn	30	20
C168	AP16	36c car rose	45	25

Issued to publicize the First Exposition of National Products.

Type of Regular Issue and

José Batlle y Ordonez AP17

Designs: 10c, Full-face portrait without hand. 36c, Portrait facing right.

Perf. 13½

1956, Dec. 15 **Wmk. 90** **Photo.**

C169	A178	10c magenta	7	7
C170	A178	20c grnsh blk	14	7
C171	AP17	31c brown	20	16
C172	A178	36c bl grn	25	16

Issued to commemorate the centenary of the birth of President José Batlle y Ordonez.

Stamp of 1856 and Stagecoach AP18

1956, Dec. 15 **Litho.**

C173	AP18	20c grn, bl & pale yel	35	20
C174	AP18	31c brn, bl & lt bl	40	22
C175	AP18	36c dp cl & bl	50	35

Issued to commemorate the centenary of the first postage stamps of Uruguay.

Flags of 21 American Nations AP19

Men and Torch of Freedom AP20

Perf. 11, 11½ (No. C177)

1958, June 19 **Unwmk.**

C176	AP19	23c bl & blk	16	14
C177	AP19	34c grn & blk	22	14
C178	AP19	44c cer & blk	35	20

Issued to commemorate the 10th anniversary of the Organization of American States.

1958, Dec. 10 ***Perf. 11***

C179	AP20	23c blk & bl	16	8
C180	AP20	34c blk & yel grn	22	14
C181	AP20	44c blk & org red	40	25

Issued to commemorate the tenth anniversary of the signing of the Universal Declaration of Human Rights.

"Flight" from Monument to Fallen Aviators — AP21

1959 **Litho.** ***Perf. 11***

Size: 22x37½mm.

C182	AP21	3c bis brn & blk	7	5
C183	AP21	8c brt lil & blk	7	5
C184	AP21	38c black	8	7
C185	AP21	50c cit & blk	10	8
C186	AP21	60c vio & blk	14	10
C187	AP21	90c ol grn & blk	20	14
C188	AP21	1p bl & blk	25	16
C189	AP21	2p ocher & blk	80	50
C190	AP21	3p grn & blk	1.00	80
C191	AP21	5p vio brn & blk	1.40	1.20
C192	AP21	10p dp rose car & blk	4.50	3.50
		Nos. C182-C192 (11)	8.61	6.65

See Nos. C211-C222.

Alberto Santos-Dumont — AP22

1959, Feb. 13 **Wmk. 327** ***Perf. 11½***

C193	AP22	31c multi	14	10
C194	AP22	36c multi	14	10

Issued to commemorate the airplane flight of Alberto Santos-Dumont, Brazilian aeronaut, in 1906 in France.

Girl and Waves AP23

Designs: 38c, 60c, 1.05p, Compass and map of Punta del Este.

1959, Mar. 6 ***Perf. 11½***

C195	AP23	10c ocher & lt bl	7	5
C196	AP23	38c grn & bis	14	8
C197	AP23	60c lil & bis	20	16

C198	AP23	90c red org & grn	25	20
C199	AP23	1.05p bl & bis	30	22
		Nos. C195-C199 (5)	96	71

Issued to commemorate the 50th anniversary of Punta del Este, seaside resort.

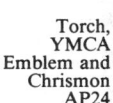

Torch, YMCA Emblem and Chrismon
AP24

Wmk. 327

1959, Dec. 22 Litho. *Perf. 11½*

C200	AP24	38c emer, blk & gray	20	18
C201	AP24	50c bl, blk & gray	22	15
C202	AP24	60c red, blk & gray	28	28

Issued to commemorate the 50th anniversary of the Y.M.C.A. in Uruguay.

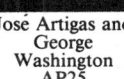

José Artigas and George Washington
AP25

Refugees and WRY Emblem
AP26

1960, Mar. 2 *Perf. 11½x12*

C203	AP25	38c red & blk	12	10
C204	AP25	50c brt bl & blk	15	10
C205	AP25	60c dp grn & blk	18	12

Issued to commemorate Pres. Dwight D. Eisenhower's visit to Uruguay, Feb. 1960.

No. C204 exists imperforate, but was not regularly issued in this form.

No. C150 Surcharged **20 c**

1960, Apr. 8 Unwmk. *Perf. 11*

C206	AP12	20c on 27c yel grn	8	5
a.		Perf. 12½	12	8

1960, June 6 Wmk. 332

Size: 24x35mm.

C207	AP26	60c brt lil rose & blk	18	15

Issued to publicize World Refugee Year, July 1, 1959-June 30, 1960.

Type of Regular Issue, 1960

Wmk. 332

1960, Nov. 4 Litho. *Perf. 12*

C208	A186	38c bl & ol grn	10	8
C209	A186	50c bl & ver	12	10
C210	A186	60c bl & pur	18	12

Type of 1959 Redrawn with Silhouette of Airplane Added.

1960-61 Litho. *Perf. 12*

C211	AP21	3c blk & pale vio	5	5
C212	AP21	20c blk & crim	5	5
C213	AP21	38c blk & pale bl	6	5
C214	AP21	50c blk & buff	8	6
C215	AP21	60c blk & dp grn	10	6
C216	AP21	90c blk & rose	18	10
C217	AP21	1p blk & gray	20	10
C218	AP21	2p blk & yel grn	40	20
C219	AP21	3p blk & red lil	50	32
C220	AP21	5p blk & org ver	75	50
C221	AP21	10p blk & yel	1.25	1.00
C222	AP21	20p blk & dk bl ('61)	3.00	1.75
		Nos. C211-C222 (12)	6.62	4.24

Pres. Gronchi and Flag Colors
AP27

1961, Apr. 17 Wmk. 332 *Perf. 12*

C223	AP27	90c multi	18	15
C224	AP27	1.20p multi	20	18
C225	AP27	1.40p multi	25	20

Issued to commemorate the visit of President Giovanni Gronchi of Italy to Uruguay, April, 1961.

Carrasco National Airport
AP28

1961, May 16 Wmk. 332 *Perf. 12*

Building in Gray

C226	AP28	1p lt vio	15	12
C227	AP28	2p ol gray	30	5
C228	AP28	3p orange	45	25
C229	AP28	4p purple	65	32
C230	AP28	5p aqua	75	45
C231	AP28	10p lt ultra	1.40	75
C232	AP28	20p maroon	2.50	1.75
		Nos. C226-C232 (7)	6.20	3.69

Type of Regular "CIES" Issue, 1961.

1961, Aug. 3 Litho. Wmk. 332

C233	A189	20c blk & org	5	5
C234	A189	45c blk & grn	8	6
C235	A189	50c blk & gray	8	6
C236	A189	90c blk & plum	12	10
C237	A189	1p blk & dp rose	15	10
C238	A189	1.40p blk & lt vio	20	15
C239	A189	2p blk & bis	25	18
C240	A189	3p blk & lt bl	40	25
C241	A189	4p blk & yel	50	38
C242	A189	5p blk & bl	65	50
C243	A189	10p blk & yel grn	1.25	1.10
C244	A189	20p blk & dp pink	2.50	2.00
		Nos. C233-C244 (12)	6.23	4.93

Swiss Flag, Plow, Wheat Sheaf
AP29

1962, Aug. 1 Wmk. 332 *Perf. 12*

C245	AP29	90c car, org & blk	18	15
C246	AP29	1.40p car, bl & blk	22	22

Issued to commemorate the centenary of the Swiss Settlement in Uruguay.

Red-crested Cardinal — AP30

Birds: 45c, White-capped tanager (horiz.). 90c, Vermilion flycatcher. 1.20p, Great kiskadee (horiz.). 1.40p, Fork-tailed flycatcher.

1962, Dec. 5 Litho. *Perf. 12*

C247	AP30	20c gray, blk & red	10	8
C248	AP30	45c multi	18	10
C249	AP30	90c crim rose, blk & lt brn	38	10
C250	AP30	1.20p lt bl, blk & yel	50	18
C251	AP30	1.40p bl & sep	75	25
		Nos. C247-C251 (5)	1.91	71

No frame on No. C248, thin frame on No. C251. See Nos. C258-C263.

Type of Regular UPAE Issue, 1963.

1963, May 31 Wmk. 332 *Perf. 12*

C252	A195	45c bluish grn & blk	8	5
C253	A195	90c mag & blk	18	12

Freedom from Hunger Type of Regular Issue

1963, July 9 Wmk. 332 *Perf. 12*

C254	A196	90c red & yel	12	10
C255	A196	1.40p vio & yel	15	12

"Alferez Campora"
AP31

1963, Aug. 16 Litho.

C256	AP31	90c dk grn & org	10	5
C257	AP31	1.40p ultra & yel	20	15

Issued to commemorate the voyage around the world by the Uruguayan sailing vessel "Alferez Campora," 1960-63.

Bird Type of 1962

Birds: 1p, Glossy cowbird (tordo). 2p, Yellow cardinal. 3p, Hooded siskin. 5p, Sayaca tanager. 10p, Blue and yellow tanager. 20p, Scarlet-headed marsh-bird. (All horizontal.)

1963, Nov. 15 Wmk. 332 *Perf. 12*

C258	AP30	1p vio bl, blk & brn org	25	20
C259	AP30	2p lt brn, blk & yel	50	25
C260	AP30	3p yel, brn & blk	75	38
C261	AP30	5p emer, bl grn & blk	1.25	50
C262	AP30	10p multi	2.25	1.00
C263	AP30	20p gray, org & blk	5.00	3.75
		Nos. C258-C263 (6)	10.00	6.08

Frame on Nos. C260-C263.

Pres. Charles de Gaulle
AP32

Design: 2.40p, Flags of France and Uruguay.

1964, Oct. 9 Litho. *Perf. 12*

C264	AP32	1.50p multi	25	12
C265	AP32	2.40p multi	50	30

Issued to commemorate the visit of Charles de Gaulle, President of France, Oct. 1964.

Submerged Statue of Ramses II — AP33

Design: 2p, Head of Ramses II.

1964, Oct. 30 Litho. Wmk. 332

C266	AP33	1.30p multi	20	10
C267	AP33	2p bis, red brn & brt bl	45	22
a.		Souv. sheet of 3	90	90

UNESCO world campaign to save historic monuments in Nubia. No. C267a contains three imperf. stamps similar to Nos. 713 and C266-C267.

National Flag
AP34

1965, Feb. 18 Wmk. 332 *Perf. 12*

C268	AP34	50p gray, dk bl & yel	3.50	2.50

Kennedy Type of Regular Issue

1965, Mar. 5 Wmk. 327 *Perf. 11½*

C269	A202	1.50p gold, lil & blk	12	10
C270	A202	2.40p gold, brt bl & blk	20	12

Issue of 1864, No. 23 — AP35

Designs: 6c, 8c and 10c denominations of 1864 issue.

Wmk. 332

1965, Mar. 19 Litho. *Perf. 12*

C271		Sheet of 10	80	80
		"URUGUAY" at bottom		
a.	AP35	1p bl & blk	8	8
b.	AP35	1p brick red & blk	8	8
c.	AP35	1p grn & blk	8	8
d.	AP35	1p ocher & blk	8	8
e.	AP35	1p car & blk	8	8
		"URUGUAY" at top		
f.	AP35	1p bl & blk	8	8
g.	AP35	1p brick red & blk	8	8
h.	AP35	1p grn & blk	8	8
i.	AP35	1p ocher & blk	8	8
j.	AP35	1p car & blk	8	8

1st Rio de la Plata Stamp Show, sponsored jointly by the Argentine and Uruguayan philatelic associations, Montevideo, Mar. 19-28. No. C271 contains two horizontal rows of stamps and two rows of labels; Nos. C271a-C271e are in first row, Nos. C271f-C271j in second row. Adjacent labels in top and bottom rows.

National Arms
AP36

Artigas Monument
AP37

1965, Apr. 30 Wmk. 332 *Perf. 12*

C272	AP36	20p multi	1.00	65

Type of Regular Issue and AP37.

Designs: 1.50p, Artigas and wagontrain. 2.40p, Artigas quotation.

Perf. 11½x12, 12x11½

1965, May 17 Litho. Wmk. 327

C273	AP37	1p multi	5	5
C274	A205	1.50p multi	12	8
C275	A205	2.40p multi	18	12

Issued to commemorate the bicentenary of the birth of José Artigas (1764-1850), leader of the independence revolt against Spain.

Olympic Games Type of Regular Issue

Designs: 1p, Boxing. 1.50p, Running. 2p, Fencing. 2.40p, Sculling. 3p, Pistol shooting. 20p, Olympic rings.

1965, Aug. 3 Litho. *Perf. 12x11½*

C276	A206	1p red, gray & blk	5	5
C277	A206	1.50p emer, bl & blk	10	8
C278	A206	2p dk car, bl & blk	12	10
C279	A206	2.40p lt ultra, org & blk	15	12

C280 A206 3p lil, yel & blk 18 15
C281 A206 20p dk vio bl, pink & lt bl 55 40
Nos. C276-C281 (6) 1.15 90

Souvenir Sheet

Olympic Types of 1924, 1928

Designs: 5p, Stamp of 1924, No. 284. 10p, Stamp of 1928, No. 389.

C282 Sheet of 2 1.00 1.00
a. 5p buff, bl & blk 30 30
b. 10p bl, blk & rose red 50 50

18th Olympic Games, Tokyo, Oct. 10-25, 1964.

ITU Emblem and Satellite AP38

1966, Jan. 25 Wmk. 332 *Perf. 12*
C283 AP38 1p bl, bluish blk & ver 10 5

Cent. of the ITU (in 1965).

Winston Churchill — AP39

1966, Apr. 29 Wmk. 332 *Perf. 12*
C284 AP39 2p car, brn & gold 10 5

Issued in memory of Sir Winston Spencer Churchill (1874-1965), statesman and World War II leader.

Rio de Janeiro Type of Regular Issue

1966, June 9 Wmk. 332 *Perf. 12*
C285 A208 80c dp org & brn 10 5

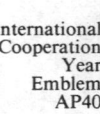

International Cooperation Year Emblem AP40

1966, June 9 Litho.
C286 AP40 1p bluish grn & blk 10 5

U.N. International Cooperation Year.

President Zalman Shazar of Israel — AP41

1966, June 21 Wmk. 327
C287 AP41 7p multi 32 25

Visit of Pres. Zalman Shazar of Israel.

Crested Screamer — AP42

1966, July 7 Wmk. 327 *Perf. 12*
C288 AP42 100p bl, blk, red & gray 2.50 1.50

Jules Rimet Cup, Soccer Ball and Globe — AP43

1966, July 11 Litho.
C289 AP43 10p dk pur, org & lil 38 22

Issued to commemorate the World Cup Soccer Championship, Wembley, England, July 11-30.

Hereford Bull AP44

Bulls: 6p, Holstein. 10p, Shorthorn. 15p, Aberdeen Angus. 20p, Norman. 30p, Jersey. 50p, Charolais.

1966 Wmk. 327 *Perf. 12*
C290 AP44 4p sep, dk brn & lt brn 10 5
C291 AP44 6p grn, bluish grn & blk 15 8
C292 AP44 10p grn, bluish grn & vio brn (wmk.332) 20 12
C293 AP44 15p brt red, org & blk 30 18
C294 AP44 20p yel, gray & sep 50 25
C295 AP44 30p sep, brn & yel 75 32
C296 AP44 50p bluish gray, sep & grn 1.25 5
Nos. C290-C296 (7) 3.25 1.05

Issued to publicize Uruguayan cattle. Dates of Issue: 4p, 50p, Aug. 13; 6p, 30p, Aug. 29; 10p, 15p, 20p, Sept. 26.

Boiso Lanza, Early Plane and Space Capsule AP45

1966, Oct. 14 Litho. *Perf. 12*
C297 AP45 25p ultra, blk & lt bl 50 45

Issued to honor Capt. Juan Manuel Boiso Lanza, pioneer of military aviation.

No. C271 Overprinted: "CENTENARIO DEL SELLO / ESCUDITO RESELLADO"

1966, Nov. 4 Wmk. 332
C298 Sheet of 10 80 80

"URUGUAY" at bottom

a. AP35 1p bl & blk 8 8
b. AP35 1p brick red & blk 8 8
c. AP35 1p grn & blk 8 8
d. AP35 1p ocher & blk 8 8
e. AP35 1p car & blk 8 8

"URUGUAY" at top

f. AP35 1p bl & blk 8 8
g. AP35 1p brick red & blk 8 8
h. AP35 1p grn & blk 8 8
i. AP35 1p ocher & blk 8 8
j. AP35 1p car & blk 8 8

2nd Rio de la Plata Stamp Show, Buenos Aires, Apr. 1966, sponsored by the Argentine and Uruguayan philatelic associations, and commemorating the for of Uruguay's 1st surcharged issue. The addition of black numerals makes the designs resemble the surcharged issue of 1866, Nos. 24-28.

Labels in top row are overprinted "SEGUNDA MUESTRA 1966," in bottom row "SEGUNDAS JORNADAS 1966" and "CENTENARIO DEL SELLO / ESCUDITO RESELLADO" in both rows. One label each in top and bottom rows is overprinted "BUENOS AIRES / ABRIL 1966."

No. 613 Surcharged in Dark Blue

40 ANIVERSARIO
Club Filatélico del Uruguay
$ 1.00 aéreo

Perf. 12½x13

1966, Dec. 17 Engr. Unwmk.
C299 A175 1p on 12c dp ultra & dk brn 12 8

Issued to commemorate the 40th anniversary of the Philatelic Club of Uruguay.

Dante Alighieri AP46

Planetarium Projector AP47

Wmk. 332

1966, Dec. 27 Litho. *Perf. 12*
C300 AP46 50c sep & bis 5 5

Issued to honor Dante Alighieri (1265-1321), Italian poet.

1967, Jan. 13 Wmk. 332 *Perf. 12*
C301 AP47 5p dl bl & blk 30 15

Issued to commemorate the 10th anniversary of the Montevideo Municipal Planetarium.

Archbishop Makarios and Map of Cyprus AP48

1967, Feb. 14 Wmk. 332 *Perf. 12*
C302 AP48 6.60p rose lil & blk 16 12

Issued to commemorate the visit of Archbishop Makarios, president of Cyprus, Oct. 21, 1966.

Albert Schweitzer Holding Fawn — AP49

1967, Mar. 31 Litho. Wmk. 332
C303 AP49 6p grn, blk, brn & sal 15 12

Issued to honor Dr. Albert Schweitzer (1875-1965), medical missionary.

Corriedale Ram AP50

Various Rams: 4p, Ideal. 5p, Romney Marsh. 10p, Australian Merino.

1967, Apr. 5
C304 AP50 3p red org, blk & gray 8 5
C305 AP50 4p emer, blk & gray 12 6
C306 AP50 5p ultra, blk & gray 14 8
C307 AP50 10p yel, blk & gray 28 20

Uruguayan sheep raising.

Flag of Uruguay and Map of the Americas AP51

1967, Apr. 8
C308 AP51 10p dk gray, bl & gold 22 16

Meeting of American Presidents, Punta del Este, Apr. 10-12.

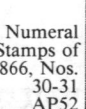

Numeral Stamps of 1866, Nos. 30-31 AP52

Design: 6p, Nos. 32-33; diff. frame.

Wmk. 332

1967, May 10 Litho. *Perf. 12*
C309 AP52 3p bl, yel grn & blk 12 6
a. Souv. sheet of 4 50 50
C310 AP52 6p bis, dp rose & blk 25 9
a. Souv. sheet of 4 1.00 1.00

Issued to commemorate the centenary of the 1866 numeral issue. Nos. C309a-C310a each contain four stamps similar to Nos. C309 and C310 respectively (the arrangement of colors differs in the souvenir sheets). Black marginal inscriptions. Size: 93x67½mm.

Ansina, Portrait by Medardo Latorre — AP53

1967, May 17
C311 AP53 2p gray, dk bl & red 10 5

Issued to honor Ansina, servant of Gen. José Artigas.

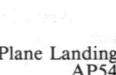

Plane Landing AP54

1967, May 30
C312 AP54 10p red, bl, blk & yel 25 18

Issued to commemorate the 30th anniversary (in 1966) of PLUNA Airline.

Shooting for Basket — AP55

Basketball Game — AP56

Basketball Players in Action: No. C314, Driving (ball shoulder high). No. C315, About to pass (ball head high). No. C316, Ready to pass (ball held straight in front). No. C317, Dribbling with right hand.

1967, June 9

C313	AP55	5p multi	12	7
C314	AP55	5p multi	12	7
C315	AP55	5p multi	12	7
C316	AP55	5p multi	12	7
C317	AP55	5p multi	12	7
		Strip of 5, Nos. C313-C317	65	38

Souvenir Sheet

C318 AP56 10p org, brt grn & blk 42 42

5th World Basketball Championships, Montevideo, May 1967.
Nos. C313-C317 printed se-tenant.

Souvenir Sheet

José Artigas, Manuel Belgrano, Flags of Uruguay and Argentina — AP57

Wmk. 332
1967, June 19 Litho. *Imperf.*

C319 AP57 5p bl, grn & yel 38 25

3rd Rio de la Plata Stamp Show, Montevideo, Uruguay, June 18-25.

Nos. C248 and C252 Surcharged in Gold

1967, June 22 *Perf. 12*

C320	AP30	5.90p on 45c multi	16	10
C321	A195	5.90p on 45c multi	16	10

Don Quixote and Sancho Panza, Painted by Denry Torres — AP58

1967, July 10

C322 AP58 8p bis brn & brn 16 9

Issued in honor of Miguel de Cervantes Saavedra (1547-1616), Spanish novelist.

Stone Axe — AP59

Railroad Crossing — AP60

Designs: 15p, Headbreaker stones. 20p, Spearhead. 50p, Birdstone. 75p, Clay pot. 100p, Ornitholite (ritual sculpture), Balizas (horiz.). 150p, Lasso weights (boleadores). 200p, Two spearheads.

1967-68 Wmk. 332 *Perf. 12*

C323	AP59	15p gray & blk	8	5
C324	AP59	20p gray & blk	14	6
C325	AP59	30p gray & lt gray	32	12
C326	AP59	50p gray & blk	45	18
C327	AP59	75p brn & blk	70	28
C328	AP59	100p gray & blk	1.00	45
C329	AP59	150p gray & blk ('68)	1.40	55
C330	AP59	200p gray & blk ('68)	1.75	1.20
		Nos. C323-C330 (8)	5.84	2.89

1967, Dec. 4

C331 AP60 4p blk, yel & red 10 5

Issued to publicize the 10th Pan-American Highway Congress, Montevideo.

Lions Emblem and Map of South America — AP61

1967, Dec. 29

C332 AP61 5p pur, yel & emer 20 10

50th anniversary of Lions International.

Boy Scout AP62

1968, Jan. 24 Litho.

C333 AP62 9p sep & brick red 30 15

Issued in memory of Robert Baden-Powell, founder of the Boy Scout organization.

Sun, U.N. Emblem and Transportation Means — AP63

1968, Feb. 29 Wmk. 332 *Perf. 12*

C334 AP63 10p gray, yel, lt & dk bl 12 6

Issued for International Tourist Year.

Octopus AP64

Marine Fauna: 20p, Silversides. 25p, Characin. 30p, Catfish (vert.). 50p, Squid (vert.).

1968 Wmk. 332 *Perf. 12*

C335	AP64	15p lt grn, bl & blk	14	9
C336	AP64	20p brn, grn & bl	16	12
C337	AP64	25p multi	20	14
C338	AP64	30p bl, grn & blk	25	16
C339	AP64	50p dp org, grn & dk bl	38	25
		Nos. C335-C339 (5)	1.13	76

Issue dates, 30p, 50p, Oct. 10; 15p, 20p, 25p, Nov. 5.

Navy Type of Regular Issue

Designs: 4p, Naval Air Force. 6p, Naval arms. 10p, Signal flags (vert.). 20p, Corsair (chartered by General Artigas).

1968, Nov. 12 Litho.

C340	A226	4p bl, blk & red	5	5
C341	A226	6p multi	5	5
C342	A226	10p lt ultra, red & yel	12	6
C343	A226	20p ultra & blk	20	9

Rowing AP65

Designs: 50p, Running. 100p, Soccer.

1969, Feb. 11 Wmk. 332 *Perf. 12*

C344	AP65	30p blk, tan & bl	25	16
C345	AP65	50p blk, tan & yel	42	28
C346	AP65	100p blk, tan & brt yel grn	70	45

Issued to commemorate the 19th Olympic Games, Mexico City, Oct. 12-27, 1968.

Bicycling Type of Regular Issue.

Designs: 20p, Bicyclist and globe (vert.).

1969, Mar. 21 Wmk. 332 *Perf. 12*

C347 A229 20p bl, pur & yel 20 12

"EFIMEX 68" and Globe — AP66

1969, Apr. 10 Wmk. 332 *Perf. 12*

C348 AP66 20p dk grn, red & bl 20 12

Issued to commemorate EFIMEX '68, International Philatelic Exhibition, Mexico City, Nov. 1-9, 1968.

Souvenir Sheet

No. C318 Overprinted with Names of Participating Countries, Emblem, Bars, etc. and "CAMPEONATO MUNDIAL DE VOLEIBOL"

1969, Apr. 25

C349 AP56 10p org, brt grn & blk 18 18

Issued to commemorate the World Volleyball Championships, Montevideo, Apr. 1969.

Book, Quill and Emblem AP67

Automobile Club Emblem AP68

1969, Sept. 16 Litho. *Perf. 12*

C350 AP67 30p grn, org & blk 30 18

10th Congress of Latin American Notaries.

1969, Oct. 7 Wmk. 332 *Perf. 12*

C351 AP68 10p ultra & red 12 5

50th anniv. (in 1968) of the Uruguayan Automobile Club.

ILO Emblem AP69

1969, Oct. 29 Litho. *Perf. 12*

C352 AP69 30p dk bl grn & blk 25 15

50th anniv. of the ILO.

Exhibition Emblem — AP70

1969, Nov. 15 Wmk. 332 *Perf. 12*

C353 AP70 20p ultra, yel & grn 18 8

ABUEXPO 69 Philatelic Exhibition, San Pablo, Brazil, Nov. 15-23.

Rotary Emblem and Hemispheres AP71

1969, Dec. 6 *Perf. 12*

C354 AP71 20p ultra, bl & bis 38 15

Issued to commemorate the South American Regional Rotary Conference and the 50th anniversary of the Montevideo Rotary Club.

Dr. Luis Morquio — AP72

1969, Dec. 22 Litho. Wmk. 332

C355 AP72 20p org red & brn 16 8

Issued to commemorate the centenary of the birth of Dr. Luis Morquio, pediatrician.

No. C322 Surcharged "FELIZ AÑO 1970 / 6.00 / PESOS"

1969, Dec. 24

C356 AP58 6p on 8p bis brn & brn 12 5

Issued for New Year 1970.

Mahatma Gandhi and UNESCO Emblem AP73

1970, Jan. 26 Wmk. 332 *Perf. 12*

C357 AP73 100p lt bl & brn 70 40

Mohandas K. Gandhi (1869-1948), leader in India's fight for independence.

Evaristo C. Ciganda AP74

Giuseppe Garibaldi AP75

1970, Mar. 10 **Litho.**
C358 AP74 6p brt grn & brn 12 5

Issued to commemorate the centenary of the birth of Evaristo C. Ciganda, author of the first law for teachers' pensions.

1970, Apr. 7 **Unwmk.** ***Perf. 12***
C359 AP75 20p rose car & pink 9 5

Issued to commemorate the centenary of Garibaldi's command of foreign legionnaires in the Uruguayan Civil War.

Fur Seal — AP76

Designs: 20p, Rhea (vert.). 30p, Common tegu (lizard). 50p, Capybara. 100p, Mulita armadillo. 150p, Puma. 200p, Nutria.

1970-71 **Wmk. 332** ***Perf. 12***

C361	AP76	20p pur, emer & blk	22	12
C362	AP76	30p emer, yel & blk	28	16
C363	AP76	50p dl yel & brn	45	25
C365	AP76	100p org, sep & blk	70	40
C366	AP76	150p emer & brn	1.10	60
C367	AP76	200p brt rose, brn & blk ('71)	1.40	90
C368	AP76	250p gray, bl & blk	1.75	1.10
		Nos. C361-C368 (7)	5.90	3.53

Soccer and Mexican Flag AP77

1970, June 2 **Litho.** ***Perf. 12***
C369 AP77 50p multi 40 22

Issued to commemorate the 9th World Soccer Championships for the Jules Rimet Cup, Mexico City, May 30-June 21.

"U.N." and Laurel — AP78

1970, June 26 **Wmk. 332** ***Perf. 12***
C370 AP78 32p dk bl & gold 22 12

25th anniversary of the United Nations.

Eisenhower and U.S. Flag — AP79

1970, July 14 **Litho.**
C371 AP79 30p gray, vio bl & red 20 9

Issued in memory of Gen. Dwight David Eisenhower, 34th Pres. of US (1890-1969).

Neil A. Armstrong Stepping onto Moon — AP80

1970, July 21
C372 AP80 200p multi 1.40 70

Issued to commemorate the first anniversary of man's first landing on the moon.

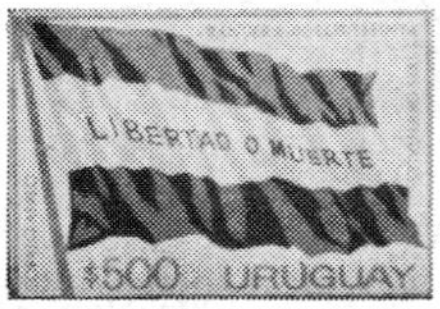

Flag of the "Immortals" — AP81

1970, Aug. 24 **Wmk. 332** ***Perf. 12***
C373 AP81 500p bl, blk & red 3.25 3.25

The 145th anniversary of the arrival of the 33 "Immortals," the patriots, who started the revolution for independence.

Congress Emblem with Map of South America AP82

1970, Sept. 16 **Unwmk.** ***Perf. 12***
C374 AP82 30p bl, dk bl & yel 20 9

Issued to publicize the 5th Pan-American Congress of Rheumatology, Punta del Este.

Souvenir Sheet

Types of First Air Post Issue — AP83

1970, Oct. 1 **Wmk. 332** ***Perf. 12½***

C375 AP83	Sheet of 3	1.10	1.10
a.	25p brn (Bl)	35	35
b.	25p brn (R)	35	35
c.	25p brn (G)	35	35

Issued for Stamp Day. No. C375 contains 3 stamps similar to Nos. C1-C3, but with denominations in pesos.

Flags of ALALC Countries — AP84

1970, Nov. 23 **Litho.** ***Perf. 12***
C376 AP84 22p multi 20 9

For the Latin-American Association for Free Trade (Asociación Latinoamericana de Libre Comercio).

Yellow Fever, by J. M. Blanes AP85

1971, June 8 **Wmk. 332** ***Perf. 12***
C377 AP85 50p blk, dk red brn & yel 40 22

70th anniversary of the death of Juan Manuel Blanes (1830-1901), painter.

Racial Equality, UN Emblem AP86

1971, June 28 **Litho.**
C378 AP86 27p blk, pink & bis 25 12

Intl. Year Against Racial Discrimination.

Congress Emblem with Maps of Americas AP87

1971, July 6 **Wmk. 332** ***Perf. 12***
C379 AP87 58p dl grn, blk & org 42 28

12th Pan-American Congress of Gastroenterology, Punta del Este, Dec. 5-10, 1971.

Committee Emblem AP88

1971, Nov. 29
C380 AP88 30p bl, blk & yel 25 18

Inter-governmental Committee for European Migration.

Llama and Mountains AP89

Munich Olympic Games Emblem AP90

1971, Dec. 30
C381 AP89 37p multi 45 20

EXFILIMA '71, Third Inter-American Philatelic Exposition, Lima, Peru, Nov. 6-14.

1972, Feb. 1 ***Perf. 11½x12***

Designs (Munich '72 Emblem and): 100p, Torchbearer. 500p, Discobolus.

C382 AP90	50p blk, red & org	14	8
C383 AP90	100p multi	30	22
C384 AP90	500p multi	1.50	1.00

20th Olympic Games, Munich, Aug. 26-Sept. 11.

Retort and WHO Emblem AP91

Ship with Flags Forming Sails AP92

1972, Feb. 22 ***Perf. 12***
C385 AP91 27p multi 12 8

50th anniversary of the discovery of insulin by Frederick G. Banting and Charles H. Best.

1972, Mar. 6 **Wmk. 332**
C386 AP92 37p multi 15 10

Stamp Day of the Americas.

1924 and 1928 Gold Medals, Soccer — AP93

Design: 300p, Olympic flag, Motion and Munich emblems (vert.).

1972, June 12 **Litho.** ***Perf. 12***

C387 AP93	100p bl & multi	30	22
C388 AP93	300p multi	90	55

20th Olympic Games, Munich, Aug. 26-Sept. 11.

Cross AP94

1972, Aug. 10
C389 AP94 37p vio & gold 10 6

Dan A. Mitrione (1920-70), slain US official.

Interlocking Squares and U.N. Emblem — AP95

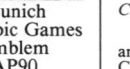

1972, Aug. 16
C390 AP95 30p gray & multi 12 8

3rd United Nations Conference on Trade and Development (UNCTAD III), Santiago, Chile, Apr.-May 1972.

Brazil's "Bull's-eye," 1843 AP96

Wmk. 332

1972, Aug. 26 Litho. *Perf. 12*

C391 AP96 50p grn, yel & bl 15 8

4th Inter-American Philatelic Exhibition, EXFILBRA, Rio de Janeiro, Aug. 26-Sept. 2.

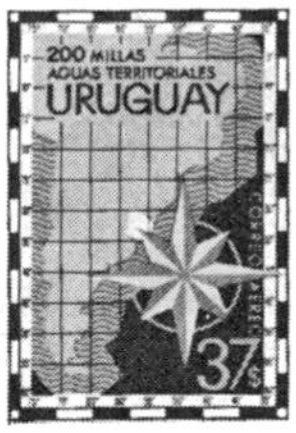

Map of South America, Compass Rose — AP97

1972, Sept. 28

C392 AP97 37p multi 12 8

Uruguay's support for extending territorial sovereignty 200 miles into the sea.

Adoration of the Kings and Shepherds, by Rafael Perez Barradas — AP98

1972, Oct. 12

C393 AP98 20p lem & multi 20 12

Christmas 1972 and first biennial exhibition of Uruguayan painting, 1970. Setenant with label inscribed with name of painter and painting.

WPY Emblem AP99

Wmk. 332

1974, Aug. 20 Litho. *Perf. 12*

C394 AP99 500p gray & red 70 50

World Population Year 1974.

Soccer, Olympics and UPU Emblems — AP100

1974, Aug. 30

C395 AP100 200p grn & multi 50 38

C396 AP100 300p org & multi 65 45

Centenary of Universal Postal Union.

Mexico No. O1 and Mexican Coat of Arms AP101

Wmk. 332

1974, Oct. 15 Litho. *Perf. 12*

C399 AP101 200p multi 14 8

EXFILMEX '74 5th Inter-American Philatelic Exhibition, Mexico City, Oct. 26-Nov. 3.

Christmas Type of 1974

Design: 240p, Kings following star. 2500p, Virgin and Child.

1974

C400 A315 240p multi 14 10

Miniature Sheet

C401 A315 2500p multi 2.25 2.25

Issue dates: 240p. Dec. 27; 2500p, Dec. 31.

Spain No. 1, Colors of Spain and Uruguay — AP102

1975, Mar. 4

C402 AP102 400p multi 25 15

Espana 75, International Philatelic Exhibition, Madrid, Apr. 4-13.

Souvenir Sheet

Nos. C253, 893 and C402 — AP103

Wmk. 332

1975, Apr. 4 Litho. *Perf. 12*

C403 AP103 Sheet of 3, multi 3.00 3.00
- *a.* 1000p *No. C253* 90 90
- *b.* 1000p *No. 893* 90 90
- *c.* 1000p *No. C402* 90 90

Espana 75 Intl. Phil. Exhib., Madrid, Apr. 4-13.

Floor Design for Capitol, Rome AP104

1975, Aug. 15

C404 AP104 1p multi 65 38

500th birth anniversary of Michelangelo Buonarroti (1475-1564), Italian sculptor, painter and architect.

Sun, Uruguay No. C59 and other Stamps — AP108

Wmk. 332

1975, Oct. 13 Litho. *Perf. 12*

C411 AP108 1p blk, gray & yel 90 50

Uruguayan Stamp Day.

Montreal Olympic Emblem and Argentina '78 AP109

Flags of U.S. and Uruguay AP110

UPU and UPAE Emblems — AP111

Wmk. 332

1975, Oct. 14 Litho. *Perf. 11½*

C412 AP109 1p multi 65 38

C413 AP110 1p multi 65 38

C414 AP111 1p multi 65 38
- *a.* Souvenir sheet of 3 *8.75*

EXFILMO '75 and ESPAMER '75 Stamp Exhibitions, Montevideo, Oct. 10-19. No. C414a contains 3 stamps similar to Nos. C412-C414, 2p each.

Ocelot AP112

Design: #C416, Orchid (oncidium bifolium).

1976, Jan. Litho. *Perf. 12*

C415 AP112 50c vio bl & multi 25 15

C416 AP112 50c emer & multi 25 15

AIR POST SEMI-POSTAL STAMPS

Catalogue values for unused stamps in this section, from this point to the end of the section, are for Never Hinged items.

Footnotes often refer you to other stamps of the same design.

Type of Semi-Postal Stamps, 1959

Wmk. 327

1959, Dec. 29 Litho. *Perf. 11½*

CB1 SP2 38c + 10c brn & org 15 15

CB2 SP2 60c + 10c gray grn & org 20 20

Issued for national recovery.

SPECIAL DELIVERY STAMPS

No. 242 Overprinted **MENSAJERIAS**

1921, Aug. Unwmk. *Perf. 11½*

E1 A97 2c fawn 38 10
- *a.* Double ovpt. 2.50

Caduceus — SD1

Imprint: "IMP. NACIONAL."

1922, Dec. 2 Litho. Wmk. 188

Size: 21x27mm

E2 SD1 2c lt red 25 5

1924, Oct. 1

E3 SD1 2c pale ultra 25 5

1928 Unwmk. *Perf. 11.*

E4 SD1 2c lt bl 30 5

Imprint: "IMPRA. NACIONAL."

1928-36 Wmk. 188

Size: 16½x19½mm.

E5 SD1 2c blk, *grn* 15 5

Unwmk.

E6 SD1 2c bl grn ('29) 15 5

Perf. 11½, 12½

E7 SD1 2c bl ('36) 12 5

1944, Oct. 23 *Perf. 12½*

E8 SD1 2c sal pink 12 5

Catalogue values for unused stamps in this section, from this point to the end of the section, are for Never Hinged items.

1947, Nov. 19

E9 SD1 2c red brn 10 5

No. E9 Surcharged with New Value.

1957, Oct. 30

E10 SD1 5c on 2c red brn 10 5

LATE FEE STAMPS

Galleon and Modern Steamship — LF1

Wmk. Crossed Keys in Sheet.

1936, May 18 Litho. *Perf. 11*

I1	LF1	3c green	8	5
I2	LF1	5c violet	10	8
I3	LF1	6c bl grn	10	8
I4	LF1	7c brown	15	8
I5	LF1	8c carmine	30	20
I6	LF1	12c dp bl	45	40
		Nos. I1-I6 (6)	1.18	89

POSTAGE DUE STAMPS

D1

1902 Unwmk. Engr. *Perf. 14 to 15*

Size: 21¼x18½mm.

J1	D1	1c bl grn	30	12
J2	D1	2c carmine	35	12
J3	D1	4c gray vio	42	12
J4	D1	10c dk bl	75	25
J5	D1	20c ocher	1.10	50
		Nos. J1-J5 (5)	2.92	1.11

Surcharged in Red

PROVISORIO
UN cent'mo.

1904

J6	D1	1c on 10c dk bl	50	50
a.		Inverted surcharge	4.00	4.00

1913-15 Litho. *Perf. 11½*

Size: 22½x20mm.

J7	D1	1c lt grn	18	10
J8	D1	2c rose red	18	12
J9	D1	4c dl vio	25	12
J10	D1	6c dp brn	30	20

Size: 21¼x19mm

J11	D1	10c dl bl	30	20
		Nos. J7-J11 (5)	1.21	74

Imprint: "Imprenta Nacional."

1922

Size: 20x17mm.

J12	D1	1c bl grn	20	10
J13	D1	2c red	20	10
J14	D1	3c red brn	30	25
J15	D1	4c brn vio	20	15
J16	D1	5c blue	38	20
J17	D1	10c gray grn	38	20
		Nos. J12-J17 (6)	1.66	1.00

1926-27 Wmk. 188 *Perf. 11*

Size: 20x17mm.

J18	D1	1c bl grn ('27)	12	12
J19	D1	3c red brn ('27)	25	18
J20	D1	5c sl bl	25	18
J21	D1	6c lt brn	30	25

1929 Unwmk. *Perf. 10½, 11*

J22	D1	1c bl grn	12	8
J23	D1	10c gray grn	20	10

Figure of Value Redrawn (Flat on sides).

1932 Wmk. 188

J24	D1	6c yel brn	30	20

Imprint: "Casa A. Barreiro Ramos S. A."

1935 Unwmk. Litho. *Perf. 12½*

Size: 20x17mm.

J25	D1	4c violet	25	15
J26	D1	5c rose	25	15

Type of 1935

Imprint: "Imprenta Nacional" at right.

1938

J27	D1	1c bl grn	5	5
J28	D1	2c red brn	5	5
J29	D1	3c dp pink	8	5
J30	D1	4c lt vio	8	5
J31	D1	5c blue	8	5
J32	D1	8c rose	12	5
		Nos. J27-J32 (6)	46	30

OFFICIAL STAMPS

Regular Issues Handstamped in Black, Red or Blue — a

OFICIAL

Many double and inverted impressions exist of the handstamped overprints on Nos. O1-O83. Prices are the same as for normal stamps or slightly more.

On Stamps of 1877-79

1880-82 Unwmk. *Rouletted 8*

O1	A9	1c red brn	1.25	1.10
O2	A10	5c green	38	30
O3	A11	20c bister	1.00	90
O4	A11	50c black	7.00	6.00
O5	A12	1p blue	7.00	6.00
		Nos. O1-O5 (5)	16.63	14.30

On No. 44

Rouletted 6

O6	A9	1c brn ('81)	90	75

On Nos. 43-43A

Rouletted 8

O7	A11	50c blk (R)	7.00	6.00
O8	A12	1p bl (R)	7.50	7.00

On Nos. 45, 41, 37a

Perf. 12½

O9	A13	7c bl (R) ('81)	90	75

Rouletted 8

O10	A11	10c ver (Bl)	90	75

Perf. 13½

O11	A8b	15c yel (Bl)	1.75	1.50

On Nos. 46-47

1883 *Perf. 12½*

O12	A14	1c green	90	75
O13	A14a	2c rose	1.10	1.00

On Nos. 50-51

Perf. 12½, 12x12½, 13

O14	A17	5c bl (R)	1.10	1.10
a.		Imperf., pair	3.00	
O15	A18	10c brn (Bl)	2.00	1.75
a.		Imperf., pair	4.50	

No. 48 Handstamped

FRANCO

1884 *Perf. 12½.*

O16	A15	1c green	17.50	11.50

Overprinted Type "a" in Black. On Nos. 48-49.

1884 *Perf. 12, 12x12½, 13.*

O17	A15	1c green	10.00	8.75
O18	A16	2c red	5.00	4.50

On Nos. 53-56.

Rouletted 8.

O19	A11	1c on 10c ver	75	65
a.		Small "1" (No. 53a)	5.00	

Perf. 12½

O20	A14a	2c rose	2.00	2.00
O21	A22	5c ultra	2.00	2.00
O22	A23	5c blue	1.25	90

On Stamps of 1884-88

1884-89 *Rouletted 8*

O23	A24	1c gray	2.50	2.00
O24	A24	1c grn ('88)	65	50
O25	A24	1c ol grn	75	65
O26	A24a	2c vermilion	30	30
O27	A24a	2c rose ('88)	50	40
O28	A24b	5c sl bl	65	50
O29	A24b	5c sl bl, *bl*	1.40	1.10
O30	A24b	5c vio ('88)	1.75	1.50
O31	A24b	5c lt bl ('89)	1.25	1.00
O32	A25	7c dk brn	1.00	75
O33	A25	7c org ('89)	1.00	75
O34	A26	10c ol brn	50	42
O35	A30	10c vio ('89)	3.00	2.50
O36	A27	20c red vio	1.00	75
O37	A27	20c bis brn ('89)	2.50	2.00
O38	A28	25c gray vio	1.00	75
O39	A28	25c ver ('89)	2.50	2.00
		Nos. O23-O39 (17)	22.25	17.87

The OFICIAL handstamp, type "a," was also applied to No. 73, the 5c violet with "Provisorio" overprint, but it was not regularly issued.

On No. 71

1887 *Rouletted 9*

O40	A29	10c lilac	3.00	

No. O40 was not regularly issued.

On Stamps of 1889-1899.

Perf. 12½ to 15 and Compound

1890-1900

O41	A32	1c green	18	15
O43	A32	1c bl ('95)	75	65
O44	A33	2c rose	18	15
O45	A33	2c red brn ('95)	90	75
O46	A33	2c org ('00)	45	30
O47	A34	5c dp bl	75	1.00
O48	A34	5c rose ('95)	1.25	90
O49	A35	7c bis brn	65	50
O50	A35	7c grn ('95)	18.50	
O51	A36	10c bl grn	65	50
O52	A36	10c org ('95)	18.50	
O53	A37	20c orange	65	50
O54	A37	20c brn ('95)	18.50	
O55	A38	25c red brn	65	50
O56	A38	25c ver ('95)	37.50	
O57	A39	50c lt bl	2.50	1.50
O58	A39	50c lil ('95)	2.50	1.50
O59	A40	1p lilac	3.50	2.00
O60	A40	1p lt bl ('95)	27.50	

Nos. O50, O52, O54, O56 and O60 were not regularly issued.

On No. 99.

1891 *Rouletted 8*

O61	A24b	5c violet	1.00	75
a.		"1391"	7.50	

On Stamps of 1895-99.

Perf. 12½ to 15 and Compound

1895-1900

O62	A51	1c bister	15	12
O63	A51	1c sl bl ('97)	30	25
O64	A52	2c blue	15	12
O65	A52	2c cl ('97)	45	38
O66	A53	5c red	20	15
O67	A53	5c grn ('97)	45	40
O68	A53	5c grnsh bl ('00)	65	50
a.		5c bl	65	45
O69	A54	7c dp grn	30	20
O70	A55	10c brown	30	20
O71	A56	20c grn & blk	42	30
O72	A56	20c cl & blk ('97)	1.50	1.10
O73	A57	25c red brn & blk	50	30
O74	A57	25c pink & bl ('97)	1.50	1.10
O75	A58	50c bl & blk	75	50
O76	A58	50c grn & brn ('97)	2.00	1.25
O77	A59	1p org brn & blk	3.00	1.75
O78	A59	1p yel brn & bl ('97)	4.00	3.00
a.		Inverted overprint		
		Nos. O62-O78 (17)	16.62	11.62

On Nos. 130-132.

1897, Sept.

O79	A62	1c brn vio & blk	65	50
O80	A63	5c pale bl & blk	75	65
O81	A64	10c lake & blk	90	75

On Nos. 136-137.

Perf. 12½ to 15 and Compound

1897-1900

O82	A68	10c red	1.50	1.25
O83	A68	10c red lil ('00)	1.00	90

Regular Issue of 1900-01 Overprinted

OFICIAL

1901 *Perf. 14 to 16.*

O84	A72	1c yel grn	18	8
O85	A75	2c vermilion	18	8
O86	A73	5c dl bl	18	10
O87	A76	7c brn org	25	20
O88	A74	10c gray vio	30	25
O89	A37	20c lt bl	2.50	2.25
O90	A38	25c bis brn	50	50
O91	A40	1p dp grn	3.50	3.50
a.		Inverted ovpt.	6.00	6.00
		Nos. O84-O91 (8)	7.59	6.96

Most of the used official stamps of 1901-1928 have been punched with holes of various shapes, in addition to the postal cancellations.

Regular Issue of 1904-05 Overprinted

OFICIAL

1905 *Perf. 11½.*

O92	A79	1c green	18	15
O93	A80	2c org red	18	15
O94	A81	5c dp bl	18	15
O95	A82	10c dk vio	38	30
O96	A83	20c gray grn	1.00	75
a.		Inverted ovpt.		
O97	A84	25c ol bis	75	50
		Nos. O92-O97 (6)	2.67	2.00

Regular Issues of 1904-07 Overprinted

OFICIAL

1907, Mar.

O98	A79	1c green	15	12
O99	A86	5c dp bl	15	12
O100	A86	7c org brn	15	12
O101	A82	10c dk vio	15	12
O102	A83	20c gray grn	25	20
a.		Inverted ovpt.	2.50	
O103	A84	25c ol bis	30	25
O104	A86	50c rose	50	45
		Nos. O98-O104 (7)	1.65	1.38

Regular Issues of 1900-10 Overprinted

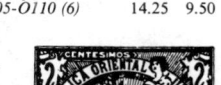

OFICIAL
1910

1910, July 15 *Perf. 14½ to 16*

O105	A75	2c vermilion	3.75	2.50
O106	A73	5c sl grn	2.50	2.50
O107	A74	10c gray vio	1.25	75
O108	A37	20c grnsh bl	1.25	75
O109	A38	25c bis brn	2.50	1.50

Perf. 11½.

O110	A86	50c rose	3.00	1.50
a.		Inverted ovpt.	10.00	8.75
		Nos. O105-O110 (6)	14.25	9.50

Peace — O1

1911, Feb. 18 Litho.

O111	O1	2c red brn	18	18
O112	O1	5c dk bl	18	15
O113	O1	8c slate	18	15
O114	O1	20c gray brn	25	20
O115	O1	23c claret	38	30
O116	O1	50c orange	65	50
O117	O1	1p red	1.50	75
		Nos. O111-O117 (7)	3.32	2.23

Regular Issue of 1912-15 Overprinted

Oficial

1915, Sept. 16

O118	A90	2c carmine	25	18
O119	A90	5c dk bl	25	18
O120	A90	8c ultra	25	18
O121	A90	20c dk brn	75	30
O122	A91	23c dk bl	75	30
O123	A91	50c orange	1.25	75
O124	A91	1p vermilion	2.50	1.00
		Nos. O118-O124 (7)	6.00	2.89

Regular Issue of 1919 Overprinted

Oficial

1919, Dec. 25

O125	A95	2c red & blk	25	10
a.		Inverted ovpt.	1.50	
O126	A95	5c ultra & blk	30	18
O127	A95	8c gray bl & lt brn	30	18
a.		Inverted ovpt.	1.25	
O128	A95	20c brn & blk	65	30
O129	A95	23c grn & brn	65	30
O130	A95	50c brn & bl	1.00	75
O131	A95	1p dl red & bl	2.50	1.00
a.		Double ovpt.	5.00	
		Nos. O125-O131 (7)	5.65	2.81

Regular Issue of 1923 Overprinted

OFICIAL

1924 Wmk. 189 *Perf. 12½.*

O132	A100	2c violet	15	8
O133	A100	5c lt bl	15	8
O134	A100	12c dp bl	25	8
O135	A100	20c buff	30	15

O136 A100 36c bl grn 1.25 90
O137 A100 50c orange 2.50 1.75
O138 A100 1p pink 4.50 3.50
O139 A100 2p lt grn 7.50 6.00
Nos. O132-O139 (8) 16.60 12.54

Same Overprint on Regular Issue of 1924.

1926-27 Unwmk. *Imperf.*
O140 A100 2c rose lil 8 5
O141 A100 5c pale bl 10 10
O142 A100 8c pink ('27) 18 12
O143 A100 12c sl bl 20 15
O144 A100 20c brown 50 30
O145 A100 36c dl rose 1.00 75
Nos. O140-O145 (6) 2.06 1.47

Regular Issue of 1924 Overprinted

1928 *Perf. 12½.*
O146 A100 2c rose lil 1.25 65
O147 A100 8c pink 1.25 30
O148 A100 10c turq bl 1.75 30

Since 1928, instead of official stamps, Uruguay has used envelopes with "S. O." printed on them, and stamps of many issues which are punched with various designs such as star or crescent.

NEWSPAPER STAMPS

No. 245 Surcharged

1922, June 1 Unwmk. *Perf. 11½*
P1 A97 3c on 4c org 25 18
a. Inverted surcharge 6.00 6.00
b. Double surcharge 2.50 2.50

Nos. 235-237 Surcharged

1924, June 1 *Perf. 14½*
P2 A96 3c on 2c car & blk 30 25
P3 A96 6c on 4c red org & bl 30 25
P4 A96 9c on 5c bl & brn 30 25

Nos. 288, 291, 293 Overprinted or Surcharged in Red:

a b

1926 *Imperf.*
P5 A100 3c gray grn 20 18
a. Double ovpt. 1.00 1.00
P6 A100 9c on 10c turq bl 30 25
a. Double surch. 1.00 1.00
P7 A100 15c lt vio 38 30

PARCEL POST STAMPS

Mercury — PP1

Imprint: "IMPRENTA NACIONAL."

Perf. 11½

1922, Jan. 15 Litho. Unwmk.

Size: 20x29½mm

Inscribed "Exterior"

Q1 PP1 5c grn, *straw* 12 8
Q2 PP1 10c grn, *bl gray* 25 8
Q3 PP1 20c grn, *rose* 1.25 38
Q4 PP1 30c grn, *grn* 1.10 12
Q5 PP1 50c grn, *bl* 2.00 20
Q6 PP1 1p grn, *org* 3.00 75
Nos. Q1-Q6 (6) 7.72 1.61

Inscribed "Interior"

Q7 PP1 5c grn, *straw* 18 8
Q8 PP1 10c grn, *bl gray* 18 8
Q9 PP1 20c grn, *rose* 65 18
Q10 PP1 30c grn, *grn* 90 18
Q11 PP1 50c grn, *bl* 1.25 20
Q12 PP1 1p grn, *org* 3.50 65
Nos. Q7-Q12 (6) 6.66 1.37

Imprint: "IMP. NACIONAL."
Inscribed "Exterior."

1926, Jan. 20 *Perf. 11½*
Q13 PP1 20c grn, *rose* 1.50 45

Inscribed "Interior."

Perf. 11

Q14 PP1 5c grn, *yel* 25 8
Q15 PP1 10c grn, *bl gray* 30 8
Q16 PP1 20c grn, *rose* 75 18
Q17 PP1 30c grn, *bl grn* 1.00 20
Nos. Q13-Q17 (5) 3.80 99

Inscribed "Exterior."

1926 *Perf. 11½*
Q18 PP1 5c blk, *straw* 20 8
Q19 PP1 10c blk, *bl gray* 30 8
Q20 PP1 20c blk, *rose* 90 10

Inscribed "Interior."

Q21 PP1 5c blk, *straw* 20 8
Q22 PP1 10c blk, *bl gray* 25 8
Q23 PP1 20c blk, *rose* 50 10
Q24 PP1 30c blk, *bl grn* 90 18
Nos. Q18-Q24 (7) 3.25 70

PP2

PP3

Perf. 11, 11½

1927, Feb. 22 Wmk. 188
Q25 PP2 1c dp bl 5 5
Q26 PP2 2c lt grn 5 5
Q27 PP2 4c violet 10 5
Q28 PP2 5c red 12 5
Q29 PP2 10c dk brn 20 5
Q30 PP2 20c orange 30 15
Nos. Q25-Q30 (6) 82 40

See Nos. Q35-Q38, Q51-Q54.

1928, Nov. 20 *Perf. 11*

Size: 15x20mm.

Q31 PP3 5c blk, *straw* 8 5
Q32 PP3 10c blk, *gray bl* 10 5
Q33 PP3 20c blk, *rose* 25 5
Q34 PP3 30c blk, *grn* 42 8

Type of 1927 Issue.

1929-30 Unwmk. *Perf. 11, 12½*
Q35 PP2 1c violet 5 5
Q36 PP2 1c ultra ('30) 8 5
Q37 PP2 2c bl grn ('30) 5 5
Q38 PP2 5c red ('30) 10 5

Nos. Q35-Q38, and possibly later issues, occasionally show parts of a papermaker's watermark.

PP4

1929, July 27 Wmk. 188 *Perf. 11*
Q39 PP4 10c orange 20 12
Q40 PP4 15c sl bl 20 12
Q41 PP4 20c ol brn 32 20
Q42 PP4 25c rose red 38 25
Q43 PP4 50c dk gray 1.10 50
Q44 PP4 75c violet 6.25 5.00
Q45 PP4 1p gray grn 2.50 1.50
Nos. Q39-Q45 (7) 10.95 7.69

Ship and Train
PP5

Numeral of Value
PP6

1938-39 Unwmk. *Perf. 12½*
Q46 PP5 10c scarlet 15 5
Q47 PP5 20c dk bl 20 5
Q48 PP5 30c lt vio ('39) 38 5
Q49 PP5 50c green 50 8
Q50 PP5 1p brn org 75 10
Nos. Q46-Q50 (5) 1.98 33

See Nos. Q70-Q73, Q80, Q88-Q90, Q92-Q93, Q95.

Type of 1927 Redrawn.

1942-55? Litho. *Perf. 12½*
Q51 PP2 1c vio ('55)
Q52 PP2 2c bl grn 8 5
Q54 PP2 5c lt red ('44) 10 5

The vertical and horizontal lines of the design have been strengthened, the "2" redrawn, etc. No. Q51 has oval "O" in CENTESIMO, 2¼mm. from frame line at right; No. Q35 has round "O" 1¾mm. from frame line.

1943, Apr. 28 Engr.
Q55 PP6 1c dk car rose 5 5
Q56 PP6 2c grnsh blk 6 5

Parcel Post Stamps of 1929 Overprinted in Black

1943, Dec. 15 Wmk. 188 *Perf. 11*
Q57 PP4 10c orange 16 6
Q58 PP4 15c sl bl 16 14
Q59 PP4 20c ol brn 25 16
Q60 PP4 25c rose red 38 22
Q61 PP4 50c dk gray 75 38
Q62 PP4 75c violet 1.50 1.10
Q63 PP4 1p gray grn 2.00 1.50
Nos. Q57-Q63 (7) 5.20 3.56

Catalogue values for unused stamps in this section, from this point to the end of the section, are for Never Hinged items.

Bank of the Republic
PP7

University
PP8

Perf. 12½

1945, Sept. 5 Litho. Unwmk.
Q64 PP7 1c green 5 5
Q65 PP8 2c brt vio 5 5

See Nos. Q77-Q79, Q84.

Custom House
PP9

Coat of Arms
PP10

1946, Dec. 11 *Perf. 11½*
Q66 PP9 5c yel brn & bl 10 5

Red Overprint.

1946, Dec. 27 *Perf. 12½*
Q67 PP10 1p lt bl 55 14

See No. Q76.

Mail Coach — PP11

PP12

1946, Dec. 23
Q68 PP11 5p red & ol brn 6.25 2.50

Black Overprint.

1947
Q69 PP12 2c dl vio brn 5 5

See Nos. Q74-Q75.

Type of 1938.

1947-52 Unwmk. *Perf. 12½*
Q70 PP5 5c brn org ('52) 5 5
Q71 PP5 10c violet 8 5
Q72 PP5 20c vermilion 12 5
Q73 PP5 30c blue 16 5

Types of 1946-47.
Black Overprint.

1948-49
Q74 PP12 1c rose lil ('49) 5 5
Q75 PP12 5c ultra 5 5
Q76 PP10 5p rose car 2.50 1.00

Types of 1945.

1950
Q77 PP8 1c vermilion 5 5
Q78 PP7 2c chlky bl 5 5

1952 *Perf. 11*
Q79 PP7 10c bl grn 8 5

Type of 1938-39.

1954 *Perf. 12½.*
Q80 PP5 20c carmine 12 5

Custom House — PP13

Design: 1p, State Railroad Administration Building.

1955 Unwmk. Litho. *Perf. 12½*
Q81 PP13 5c brown 5 5
Q82 PP13 1p lt ultra 35 22

See Nos. Q83, Q85-Q86, Q96.

Types of 1945 and 1955.

Design: 20c, Solis Theater.

1956-57 *Perf. 11*
Q83 PP13 5c gray ('57) 25 5
Q84 PP7 10c lt ol grn 5 5
Q85 PP13 20c yellow 8 5
Q86 PP13 20c lt red brn ('57) 12 5

No. Q83 Surcharged with New Value in Red.

1957
Q87 PP13 30c on 5c gray 12 5

Type of 1938-39

1957-60 Wmk. 327 *Perf. 11*
Q88 PP5 20c lt bl ('59) 6 5

Unwmk.

Q89 PP5 30c red lil 6 5

Perf. 12½

Q90 PP5 1p dk bl ('60) 14 9

Nos. Q88 and Q93 are in slightly larger format-17¼x21mm instead of 16x19½mm.

National Printing Works PP14

1960, Mar. 23 Wmk. 327 *Perf. 11*
Q91 PP14 30c yel grn 8 5

Type of 1938-39

1962-63 Wmk. 332 *Perf. 11*
Q92 PP5 50c sl grn 8 5

Perf. 10½
Q93 PP5 1p bl grn ('63) 12 8

No. C158 Surcharged

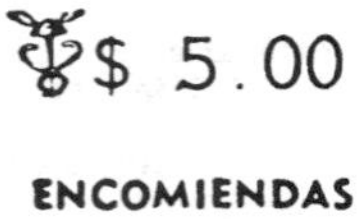

1965 Unwmk. *Perf. 11*
Q94 AP12 5p on 84c org 20 12

For use on regular and air post parcels.

Types of 1938-55

Design: 1p, State Railroad Administration Building.

1966 Litho. *Perf. 10½*
Q95 PP5 10c bl grn 5 5

Wmk. 327
Q96 PP13 1p brown 5 5

No. C184 Surcharged in Red

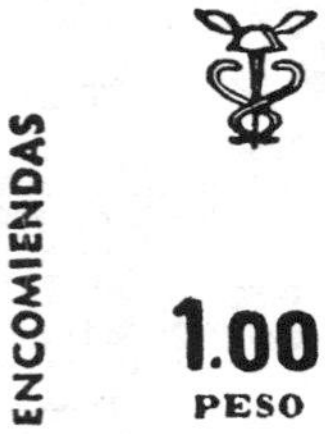

1966 Unwmk. *Perf. 11*
Q97 AP21 1p on 38c blk 5 5

Plane and Bus — PP15

Design: 20p, Plane facing left and bus; "Encomiendas" on top.

Wmk. 332

1969, July 8 Litho. *Perf. 12*
Q98 PP15 10p blk, crim & bl grn 9 6
Q99 PP15 20p bl, blk & yel 20 14

No. B7 Surcharged

1971, Feb. 3 Wmk. 327 *Perf. 11½*
Q100 SP2 60c on 1p + 10c pur & org 60 18

No. 761 Surcharged in Red

1971, Nov. 12 Wmk. 332 *Perf. 12*
Q101 A226 60c on 6p lt grn & blk 18 18

Nos. 770-771 Surcharged

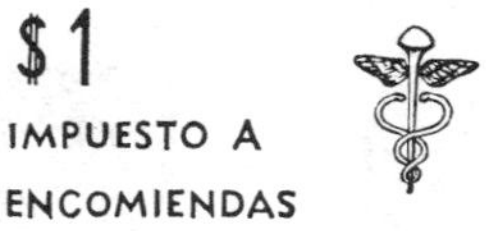

1972, Nov. 6 Litho. *Perf. 12*
Q102 A233 1p on 6p multi (#770) 18 18
Q103 A233 1p on 6p multi (#771) 18 18

Nos. Q102-Q103 printed se-tenant with label between each pair of stamps.

Parcels and Arrows PP16

Old Mail Truck PP17

Designs: Early means of mail transport.

1974 Wmk. 332 Litho. *Perf. 12*
Q104 PP16 75p shown 10 6
Q105 PP17 100p shown 18 12
Q106 PP17 150p Steam engine 22 22
Q107 PP17 300p Side-wheeler 42 35
Q108 PP17 500p Plane 75 50
Nos. Q104-Q108 (5) 1.67 1.25

Issue dates: 75p, Feb. 13. Others, Mar. 6.

VATICAN CITY

LOCATION — Western Italy, directly outside the western boundary of Rome.
GOVT. — Independent state subject to certain political restrictions under a treaty with Italy.
AREA — 108.7 acres
POP. — 1,000 (est.)

100 Centesimi = 1 Lira

Catalogue values for unused stamps in this country are for Never Hinged items, beginning with Scott 68 in the regular postage section, Scott C1 in the airpost section, Scott E3 in the special delivery section, and Scott J7 in the postage due section.

Papal Arms — A1

Pope Pius XI — A2

Unwmk.

1929, Aug. 1 Engr. *Perf. 14*

Surface-Colored Paper

1 A1 5c dk brn & pink 10 15
2 A1 10c dk grn & lt grn 20 20
3 A1 20c vio & lil 55 32
4 A1 25c dk bl & lt bl 55 35
5 A1 30c ind & yel 70 52
6 A1 50c ind & sal buff 70 52
7 A1 75c brn car & gray 1.00 70

Photo.

White Paper

8 A2 80c car rose 52 28
9 A2 1.25 l dk bl 1.25 70
10 A2 2 l ol brn 3.75 1.50
11 A2 2.50 l red org 3.00 2.50
12 A2 5 l dk grn 4.50 *9.25*
13 A2 10 l ol blk 6.50 *11.00*
Nos. 1-13,E1-E2 (15) 37.07 *38.24*

The stamps of Type A1 have, in this and subsequent issues, the words "POSTE VATICANE" in rows of colorless letters in the background.

No. 5 Surcharged in Red

1931, Oct. 1
14 A1 25c on 30c ind & yel 2.25 1.00

Arms of Pope Pius XI — A5

Vatican Palace and Obelisk — A6

Vatican Gardens — A7

Pope Pius XI — A8

St. Peter's Basilica A9

Wmk. 235 - Crossed Keys

1933, May 31 Engr. Wmk. 235
19 A5 5c cop red 9 9
a Imperf., pair 225.00 *350.00*
20 A6 10c dk brn & blk 9 9
21 A6 12½c dp grn & blk 10 10
22 A6 20c org & blk 9 9
a Vertical pair imperf. between and at bottom 165.00 165.00
23 A6 25c dk ol & blk 9 9
a Imperf., pair 125.00 165.00
24 A7 30c blk & dk brn 9 9
25 A7 50c vio & dk brn 9 9
26 A7 75c brn red & dk brn 10 10
27 A7 80c rose & dk brn 10 10
28 A8 1 l vio & blk 2.75 60
29 A8 1.25 l dk bl & blk 9.75 3.25
30 A8 2 l dk brn & blk 22.50 18.00
31 A8 2.75 l dk vio & blk 25.00 30.00
32 A9 5 l blk brn & dk grn 10 22
33 A9 10 l dk bl & dk grn 12 35
34 A9 20 l blk & dp grn 14 60
Nos. 19-34,E3-E4 (18) 61.42 54.42

Stamps of 1929 Surcharged in Black

1934, June 16 Unwmk.
35 A2 40c on 80c car rose 1.10 3.25
36 A2 1.30 l on 1.25 l dk bl 95.00 47.50
a Small figures "30" in "1.30" *1,250.* *1,500.*
37 A2 2.05 l on 2 l ol brn 125.00 10.50
a No comma btwn. 2 & 0 210.00 32.50
38 A2 2.55 l on 2.50 l red org 95.00 150.00
a No comma btwn. 2 & 5 150.00 150.00
39 A2 3.05 l on 5 l dk grn 300.00 300.00
40 A2 3.70 l on 10 l ol blk 300.00 575.00
a No comma btwn. 3 & 7 525.00 425.00
Nos. 35-40 (6) 916.10 1,086.

A second printing of Nos. 36-40 was made in 1937. The 2.55 l and 3.05 l of the first printing and 1.30 l of the second printing sell for more.

Forged surcharges of Nos. 35-40 are plentiful.

Tribonian Presenting Pandects to Justinian I A10

Pope Gregory IX Promulgating Decretals A11

1935, Feb. 1 Photo.
41 A10 5c red org 18 55
42 A10 10c purple 18 55
43 A10 25c green 1.50 3.50
44 A11 75c rose red 21.00 14.00
45 A11 80c dk brn 17.50 10.00
46 A11 1.25 l dk bl 21.00 10.00
Nos. 41-46 (6) 61.36 38.60

Intl. Juridical Congress, Rome, 1934.

Doves and Bell — A12

Allegory of Church and Bible — A13

St. John Bosco — A14

St. Francis de Sales — A15

1936, June 22
47 A12 5c bl grn 22 60
48 A13 10c black 22 25
49 A14 25c yel grn 14.00 4.00
50 A12 50c rose vio 22 50
51 A13 75c rose red 25.00 20.00
52 A14 80c org brn 38 95
53 A15 1.25 l dk blue 70 1.50
54 A15 5 l dk brn 45 *3.25*
Nos. 47-54 (8) 41.19 31.05

Catholic Press Conference, 1936.

Crypt of St. Cecilia in Catacombs of St. Calixtus
A16

Basilica of Sts. Nereus and Achilleus in Catacombs of St. Domitilla
A17

1938, Oct. 12 *Perf. 14*

55	A16	5c bis brn	28	14
56	A16	10c dp org	40	28
57	A16	25c dp grn	40	28
58	A17	75c dp rose	4.75	6.25
59	A17	80c violet	18.00	12.50
60	A17	1.25 l blue	16.00	12.50
		Nos. 55-60 (6)	39.83	31.95

Intl. Christian Archaeological Congress, Rome, 1938.

Interregnum Issue

Stamps of 1929 Overprinted in Black

SEDE VACANTE
MCMXXXIX

1939, Feb. 20 *Perf. 14*

61	A1	5c dk brn & pink	27.50	10.00
62	A1	10c dk grn & lt grn	65	48
63	A1	20c vio & lil	65	48
64	A1	25c dk bl & lt bl	1.90	10.00
65	A1	30c ind & yel	70	1.00
a.		Pair, one without ovpt.	750.00	
66	A1	50c ind & sal buff	70	70
67	A1	75c brn car & gray	70	70
		Nos. 61-67 (7)	32.80	23.36

Catalogue values for unused stamps in this section, from this point to the end of the section, are for Never Hinged items.

Coronation of Pope Pius XII — A18

1939, June 2 **Photo.**

68	A18	25c green	2.00	42
69	A18	75c rose red	12	12
70	A18	80c violet	3.25	3.00
71	A18	1.25 l dp bl	12	12

Coronation of Pope Pius XII, Mar. 12, 1939.

Arms of Pope Pius XII — A19

Pope Pius XII
A20 A21

Wmk. 235
1940, Mar. 12 **Engr.** *Perf. 14*

72	A19	5c dk car	8	8
73	A20	1 l pur & blk	24	18
74	A21	1.25 l sl bl & blk	12	8
a.		Imperf., pair	350.00	550.00
75	A20	2 l dk brn & blk	1.40	1.10
76	A21	2.75 l dk rose vio & blk	1.75	1.50
		Nos. 72-76 (5)	3.59	2.94

See Nos. 91-98.

Picture of Jesus Inscribed "I have Compassion on the Multitude" — A22

1942, Sept. 1 **Photo.** **Unwmk.**

77	A22	25c dk bl grn	5	5
78	A22	80c chestnut brn	6	8
79	A22	1.25 l deep blue	18	20

See Nos. 84-86, 99-101.

Consecration of Archbishop Pacelli by Pope Benedict XV — A23

1942, Jan. 16

80	A23	25c myr grn & gray grn	5	8
81	A23	80c dk brn & yel grn	5	8
82	A23	1.25 l saph & vio bl	8	8
a.		Name and value panel omitted		
83	A23	5 l vio blk & gray blk	40	30

25th anniv. of the consecration of Msgr. Eugenio Pacelli (later Pope Pius XII) as Archbishop of Sardes.

Type of 1942
Inscribed MCMXLIII

1944, Jan. 31

84	A22	25c dk bl grn	6	6
85	A22	80c chestnut brn	6	6
86	A22	1.25 l dp blue	18	15

Raphael Sanzio — A24

Designs: 80c, Antonio da Sangallo. 1.25 l, Carlo Maratti. 10 l, Antonio Canova.

1944, Nov. 21 **Wmk. 235** **Photo.**

87	A24	25c ol & grn	5	8
88	A24	80c cl & rose vio	10	15
a.		Dbl. impression of center	600.00	
89	A24	1.25 l bl vio & dp bl	25	12
a.		Imperf., pair	700.00	1,000
90	A24	10 l bis & ol brn	1.25	1.25

400th anniv. of the Pontifical Academy of the Virtuosi of the Pantheon.

Types of 1940

1945, Mar. 5 **Engr.** **Unwmk.**

91	A19	5c gray	7	10
a.		Imperf., pair	200.00	
92	A19	30c brown	12	8
a.		Imperf., pair	120.00	
93	A19	50c dk grn	8	8
94	A21	1 l brn & blk	8	8
95	A21	1.50 l rose car & blk	8	8
a.		Imperf., pair	325.00	
96	A21	2.50 l dp ultra & blk	8	8
97	A20	5 l rose vio & blk	15	12
98	A20	20 l gray grn & blk	18	14
		Nos. 91-98,E5-E6 (10)	1.54	1.31

Nos. 91-96 exist in pairs imperf. between, some vertical, some horizontal. Value, each $125.

Pair imperf. vertically exist of 30c and 50c (value $60), and of 5 lire (value $90).

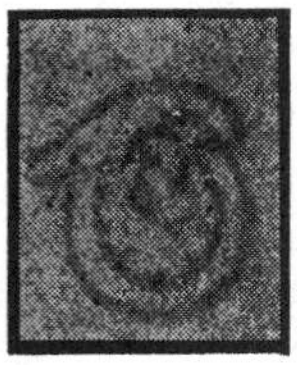

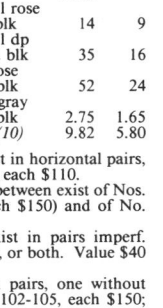

Wmk. 277 - Winged Wheel

Type of 1942
Inscribed MCMXLIV

Wmk. 277
1945, Sept. 12 **Photo.** *Perf. 14*

99	A22	1 l dk bl grn	5	6
100	A22	3 l dk car	5	6
a.		Jesus image omitted	100.00	100.00
101	A22	5 l dp ultra	22	20

Nos. 99-101 exist in pairs imperf. between, both horizontal and vertical. Value, each $100.

Pairs imperf. horizontally exist of 3 lire (value $30) and 5 lire (value $125).

Nos. 91 to 98 Surcharged with New Values and Bars in Black or Blue

Two types of 25c on 30c:
I - Surcharge 16mm wide.
II - Surcharge 19mm wide.

Two types of 1 l on 50c:
I - Surcharge bars 5mm wide.
II - Bars 4mm wide.

1946, Jan. 9 **Unwmk.** *Perf. 14*

102	A19	20c on 5c gray	14	9
103	A19	25c on 30c brn (I)	14	9
a.		Type II	28	9
b.		Inverted surcharge (II)	275.00	275.00
104	A19	1 l on 50c dk grn (I)	14	9
a.		Type II	11.00	4.50
105	A21	1.50 l on 1 l brn & blk (Bl)	14	9
a.		Double surcharge	175.00	
106	A21	3 l on 1.50 l rose car & blk	14	9
107	A21	5 l on 2.50 l dp ultra & blk	35	16
108	A20	10 l on 5 l rose vio & blk	52	24
109	A20	30 l on 20 l gray grn & blk	2.75	1.65
		Nos. 102-109,E7-E8 (10)	9.82	5.80

Nos. 102, 105-109 exist in horizontal pairs, imperf. between. Value, each $110.

Vertical pairs imperf. between exist of Nos. 102, 106-107 (value, each $150) and of No. 104a (value $225).

Nos. 102, 104-108 exist in pairs imperf. vertically or horizontally, or both. Value $40 to $60.

Nos. 102-108 exist in pairs, one without surcharge. Value, Nos. 102-105, each $150; Nos. 106-108, each $200.

St. Vigilio Cathedral, Trent — A28

St. Angela Merici — A29

Designs: 50c, St. Anthony Zaccaria. 75c, St. Ignatius of Loyola. 1 l, St. Cajetan Thiene. 1.50 l, St. John Fisher. 2 l, Christoforo Cardinal Madruzzi. 2.50 l, Reginald Cardinal Pole. 3 l, Marello Cardinal Cervini. 4 l, Giovanni Cardinal del Monte. 5 l, Emperor Charles V. 1 l, Pope Paul III.

Perf. 14, 14x13½

1946, Feb. 21 Photo. Unwmk.

Centers in Dark Brown

110	A28	5c	ol bis	6	6
111	A29	25c	purple	6	6
112	A29	50c	brn org	6	6
113	A29	75c	black	6	6
114	A29	1 l	dk vio	6	6
115	A29	1.50 l	red org	6	6
116	A29	2 l	yel grn	6	6
117	A29	2.50 l	dp bl	6	6
118	A29	3 l	brt car	6	6
119	A29	4 l	ocher	6	6
120	A29	5 l	brt ultra	30	10
121	A29	10 l	dp rose car	30	10
			Nos. 110-121,E9-E10 (14)	1.47	1.00

400th anniv. of the Council of Trent (1545-63).

Vertical pairs imperf. between exist of Nos. 110-111, 114, 116-117 (value, each $150); Nos. 113, 119 (value, each $100); Nos. 115, 118 (value, each $75).

Horizontal pairs imperf. between exist of No. 121 (value $150); Nos. 113, 117 (value $100).

Basilica of St. Agnes — A40

Basilica of the Holy Cross in Jerusalem A41

Pope Pius XII A42

Basilicas: 3 l, St. Clement, 5 l, St. Prassede. 8 l, St. Mary in Cosmedin. 6 l, St. Sebastian. 25 l, St. Lawrence. 35 l, St. Paul. 40 l, St. Mary Major.

Perf. 14, 14x13½, 13½x14

1949, Mar. 7 Photo. Wmk. 235

122	A40	1 l	dk brn	8	8
123	A40	3 l	violet	8	8
124	A40	5 l	dp org	14	8
a			Perf. 14x13½	20.00	4.50
125	A40	8 l	dp bl grn	8	8
126	A41	13 l	dl grn	4.00	3.50
127	A41	16 l	dk ol brn	30	18
a			Perf. 14	55	28
128	A41	25 l	car rose	5.00	50
129	A41	35 l	red vio	27.50	7.75
a			Perf. 13½x14	50.00	8.25
130	A41	40 l	blue	22	8
a			Perf. 14x13½	1.40	32

Engr.

Perf. 14

131	A42	100 l	sepia	3.50	2.75
			Nos. 122-131,E11-E12 (12)	61.15	24.58

Jesus Giving St. Peter the Keys to Heaven — A43

Cathedrals of St. Peter, St. Paul, St. John Lateran and St. Mary Major — A44

Pope Boniface VIII Proclaiming Holy Year in 1300 — A45

Pope Pius XII in Ceremony of Opening the Holy Door — A46

Wmk. 277

1949, Dec 21 Photo. *Perf. 14*

132	A43	5 l	red brn & brn	6	6
133	A44	6 l	ind & yel brn	6	6
134	A45	8 l	ultra & dk grn	60	45
135	A46	10 l	grn & sl	8	6
136	A43	20 l	dk grn & red brn	60	25
137	A44	25 l	sep & dp bl	32	25
138	A45	30 l	grnsh blk & rose lil	2.75	85
139	A46	60 l	blk brn & brn rose	2.00	1.65
			Nos. 132-139 (8)	6.47	3.63

Holy Year, 1950.

Palatine Guard and Statue of St. Peter — A47

1950, Sept. 12

140	A47	25 l	sepia	10.00	6.50
141	A47	35 l	dark green	4.00	3.75
142	A47	55 l	red brown	2.25	2.00

Centenary of the Palatine Guard.

Pope Pius XII Making Proclamation A48

Crowd at the Basilica of St. Peter A49

1951, May 8 Unwmk.

143	A48	25 l	chocolate	2.50	1.10
144	A49	55 l	brt bl	13.00	7.50

Proclamation of the Roman Catholic dogma of the Assumption of the Virgin Mary, Nov. 1, 1950.

Pope Pius X

A50 A51

Wmk. 235

1951, June 3 Photo. *Perf. 14x1*

Background of Medallion in Gold

145	A50	6 l	purple	15	10
146	A50	10 l	Prus grn	35	22
147	A51	60 l	blue	9.50	5.75
148	A51	115 l	brown	12.00	6.50

Council of Chalcedon A52

Pope Leo I Remonstrating with Attila the Hun — A53

1951, Oct. 31 Engr. *Perf. 14x13½*

149	A52	5 l	dk gray grn	45	40
a			Pair, imperf. horizontally	*350.00*	
150	A53	25 l	red brn	2.75	2.50
a			Horiz. pair, imperf. between	*700.00*	*700.00*
151	A52	35 l	car rose	7.50	5.50
152	A53	60 l	dp blue	21.00	12.50
153	A52	100 l	dk brn	27.50	21.00
			Nos. 149-153 (5)	59.20	41.90

Council of Chalcedon, 1500th anniv.

No. 126 Surcharged with New Value and Bars in Carmine

1952, Mar. 15 *Perf. 14*

154	A41	12 l on 13 l	dl grn	2.75	1.50
a			Perf. 13½x14	2.75	1.50
b			Pair, one without surch.	375.00	450.00

Roman States Stamp and Stagecoach A54

1952, June 9 Engr. *Perf. 13*

155	A54	50 l	sep & dp bl, *cr*	6.50	4.50
a			Souvenir sheet	100.00	85.00

Centenary of the first stamp of the Papal States.

No. 155a contains four stamps similar to No. 155, with papal insignia and inscription in purple. Singles from the souvenir sheet differ slightly from No. 155. The colors are closer to black and blue, and the cream tone of the paper is visible on the back.

St. Maria Goretti — A55

St. Peter — A56

Perf. 13½x14

1953, Feb. 12 Photo. Wmk. 235

156	A55	15 l	dp brn & vio	6.00	3.00
157	A55	35 l	dp rose & brn	4.75	3.00

50th anniversary of the martyrdom of St. Maria Goretti.

Perf. 13½x13, 14

1953, Apr. 23 Engr.

Designs: 5 l, Pius XII and Roman sepulcher. 10 l, St. Peter and Tomb of the Apostle. 12 l, Sylvester I and Constantine Basilica. 20 l, Julius II and Bramante's plans. 25 l, Paul III and the Apse. 35 l, Sixtus V and dome. 45 l, Paul V and facade. 60 l, Urban VIII and the canopy. 65 l, Alexander VII and colonnade. 100 l, Pius VI and the sacristy.

158	A56	3 l	dk red brn & blk	5	5
159	A56	5 l	sl & blk	5	5
160	A56	10 l	dk grn & blk	5	5
161	A56	12 l	chnt & blk	12	8
162	A56	20 l	vio & blk	50	35
163	A56	25 l	dk brn & blk	12	8
164	A56	35 l	dk car & blk	12	8
165	A56	45 l	ol brn & blk	50	35
166	A56	60 l	dk bl & blk	15	10
167	A56	65 l	car rose & blk	50	35
168	A56	100 l	rose vio & blk	15	10
			Nos. 158-168,E13-E14 (13)	3.04	2.16

St. Clare of Assisi — A57

Peter Lombard Medal — A59

Virgin Mary and St. Bernard A58

Unwmk.

1953, Aug. 12 Photo. *Perf. 13*

169	A57	25 l	aqua, yel brn & vio brn	3.75	1.10
170	A57	35 l	brn red, yel brn & vio brn	17.50	10.50

Death of St. Clare of Assisi, 700th anniv.

1953, Nov. 10

171	A58	20 l	ol grn & dk vio brn	1.40	75
172	A58	60 l	brt bl & ol grn	12.50	5.50

Death of St. Bernard of Clairvaux, 800th anniv.

1953, Dec. 29

173	A59	100 l lil rose, bl, dk grn & yel	42.50	22.50

Peter Lombard, Bishop of Paris 1159.

Pope Pius XI and Vatican City — A60

1954, Feb. 12 **Wmk. 235**

174	A60	25 l bl, red brn & cr	2.25	1.25
175	A60	60 l yel brn & dp bl	4.00	2.75

Signing of the Lateran Pacts, 25th anniv.

Pope Pius IX A61

Portraits: (At left) - 6 l, 20 l, Pope Pius IX. (At right) - 4 l, 12 l, 35 l, Pope Pius XII.

1954, May 26 **Engr.** ***Perf. 13***

176	A61	3 l violet	8	8
177	A61	4 l carmine	8	8
178	A61	6 l plum	8	8
179	A61	12 l bl grn	1.65	20
180	A61	20 l red brn	1.40	85
181	A61	35 l ultra	3.50	2.75
		Nos. 176-181 (6)	6.79	4.04

Marian Year; centenary of the dogma of the Immaculate Conception.

St. Pius X — A62

1954, May 29 **Photo.**

Colors (except background): Yellow and Plum

182	A62	10 l dk brn	14	12
183	A62	25 l violet	3.50	95
184	A62	35 l dk sl gray	4.25	*3.75*

Canonization of Pope Pius X, May 20, 1954.

Nos. 182-184 exist imperf. Value, each pair $800.

Basilica of St. Francis of Assisi — A63

1954, Oct. 1 **Photo.** ***Perf. 14***

185	A63	20 l dk vio gray & cr	3.75	1.90
186	A63	35 l dk brn & cr	2.50	1.75

Consecration of the Basilica of St. Francis of Assisi, 200th anniv.

St. Augustine A64

1954, Nov. 13

187	A64	35 l bl grn	2.00	1.10
188	A64	50 l redsh brn	4.00	1.90

1600th birth anniv. of St. Augustine.

Madonna of the Gate of Dawn, Vilnius — A65

1954, Dec. 7

189	A65	20 l pink & multi	1.40	80
190	A65	35 l bl & multi	7.00	4.00
191	A65	60 l multi	13.00	6.00

Issued to mark the end of the Marian Year.

St. Boniface and Fulda Abbey A66

1955, Apr. 28 **Engr.** ***Perf. 13***

192	A66	10 l grnsh gray	15	8
193	A66	35 l violet	1.10	70
a		Imperf., pair	300.00	
194	A66	60 l brt bl grn	1.10	70

1200th death anniv. of St. Boniface.

Pope Sixtus II and St. Lawrence A67

Pope Nicholas V A68

Wmk. 235

1955, June 27 **Photo.** ***Perf. 14***

195	A67	50 l carmine	7.00	3.50
196	A67	100 l dp bl	3.00	1.50

Fra Angelico (1387-1455), painter. Design is from a Fra Angelico fresco.

1955, Nov. 28

197	A68	20 l grnsh bl & ol brn	32	18
198	A68	35 l rose car & ol brn	65	38
199	A68	60 l yel grn & ol brn	1.65	75

Death of Pope Nicholas V, 500th anniv.

St. Bartholomew and Church of Grottaferrata A69

Capt. Gaspar Roust A70

1955, Dec. 29

200	A69	10 l brn & gray	22	8
201	A69	25 l car rose & gray	1.50	60
202	A69	100 l dk grn & gray	3.50	2.25

900th death anniv. of St. Bartholomew, abbot of Grottaferrata.

1956, Apr. 27 **Engr.** ***Perf. 13***

Designs: 6 l, 50 l, Guardsman. 10 l, 60 l, Two drummers.

203	A70	4 l dk car rose	8	6
204	A70	6 l dp org	8	6
205	A70	10 l dp ultra	8	6
206	A70	35 l brown	1.00	60
207	A70	50 l violet	1.65	95
208	A70	60 l bl grn	2.00	1.40
		Nos. 203-208 (6)	4.89	3.13

450th anniv. of the Swiss Papal Guard.

St. Rita of Cascia — A71

Pope Paul III Confirming Society of Jesus — A72

1956, May 19 **Photo.** ***Perf. 14***

209	A71	10 l gray grn	6	5
210	A71	25 l ol brn	1.10	60
211	A71	35 l ultra	80	40

500th death anniv. of St. Rita of Cascia.

1956, July 31 **Engr.** ***Perf. 13***

212	A72	35 l dk red brn	75	65
213	A72	60 l bl gray	1.40	1.10

400th death anniv. of St. Ignatius of Loyola, founder of the Society of Jesus.

St. John of Capistrano — A73

1956, Oct. 30 ***Perf. 14***

214	A73	25 l sl blk & grn	3.50	2.25
215	A73	35 l dk brn car & brn	1.75	1.10

5th centenary of the death of St. John of Capistrano, leader in the war against the Turks.

Black Madonna of Czestochowa A74

St. Domenico Savio A75

1956, Dec. 20

216	A74	35 l dk bl & blk	42	28
217	A74	60 l grn & ultra	95	65
218	A74	100 l brn & dk car rose	1.65	1.00

300th anniv. of the proclamation of the Madonna of Czestochowa as "Queen of Poland."

1957, Mar. 21 **Wmk. 235** ***Perf. 13½***

Design: 6 l, 60 l, Sts. Domenico Savio and John Bosco.

219	A75	4 l red brn	8	8
220	A75	6 l brt car	8	8
221	A75	25 l green	20	10
222	A75	60 l ultra	2.00	1.50

Death cent. of St. Domenico Savio.

Cardinal Capranica and College A76

Design: 10 l, 100 l, Pope Pius XII.

1957, June 27 **Engr.** ***Perf. 13***

223	A76	5 l dk car rose	5	8
224	A76	10 l pale brn	5	8
225	A76	35 l grnsh blk	40	22
226	A76	100 l ultra	1.40	70

500th anniv. of Capranica College, oldest seminary in the world.

Pontifical Academy of Science A77

1957, Oct. 9 **Photo.** ***Perf. 14***

227	A77	35 l dk bl & grn	90	65
228	A77	60 l brn & ultra	1.25	65

Pontifical Academy of Science, 20th anniv.

Mariazell A78

High Altar A79

1957, Nov. 14 **Engr.** ***Perf. 13½***

229	A78	5 l green	10	8
230	A79	15 l slate	10	8
231	A78	60 l ultra	42	28
232	A79	100 l violet	1.35	85

Mariazell shrine, Austria, 800th anniv.

Apparition of the Virgin Mary — A80

Designs: 10 l, 35 l, Sick man and basilica. 15 l, 100 l, St. Bernadette.

Perf. 13x14

1958, Feb. 21 **Wmk. 235**

233	A80	5 l dk bl	5	5
234	A80	10 l bl grn	5	5
235	A80	15 l redsh brn	5	5
236	A80	25 l rose car	12	6
237	A80	35 l gray brn	14	8
238	A80	100 l violet	14	8
		Nos. 233-238 (6)	55	37

Centenary of apparition of the Virgin Mary at Lourdes and the establishment of the shrine.

Pope Pius XII — A81

Statue of Pope Clement XIII by Canova — A82

Design: 60 l, 100 l, Vatican pavilion at Brussels fair.

1958, June 19 **Engr.** ***Perf. 13***

239	A81	35 l	claret	50	45

Perf. 13x14

240	A81	60 l	fawn	75	55
241	A81	100 l	violet	2.75	1.90
242	A81	300 l	ultra	2.00	1.40
a			Souv. sheet of 4, #239-242	22.50	21.00

Universal and Intl. Exposition, Brussels.

1958, July 2 ***Perf. 14***

Statues: 10 l, Clement XIV. 35 l, Pius VI. 100 l, Pius VII.

243	A82	5 l	brown	10	6
244	A82	10 l	car rose	10	6
245	A82	35 l	bl gray	30	22
246	A82	100 l	dk bl	1.90	1.00

Antonio Canova (1757-1822), sculptor.

Interregnum Issue

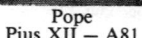

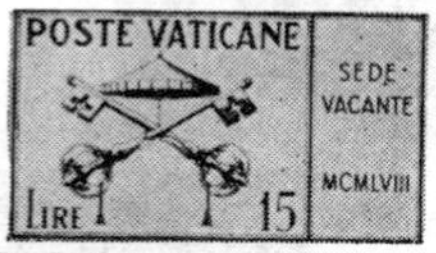
St. Peter's Keys and Papal Chamberlain's Insignia — A83

Wmk. 235

1958, Oct. 21 **Photo.** ***Perf. 14***

247	A83	15 l	brn blk, *yel*	1.75	1.10
248	A83	25 l	brn blk	12	12
249	A83	60 l	brn blk, *pale vio*	12	12

Pope John XXIII — A84

Pope Pius XI — A85

Design: 35 l, 100 l, Coat of Arms.

1959, Apr. 2 **Photo.** ***Perf. 14***

250	A84	25 l	car rose, bl & buff	5	8
251	A84	35 l	multi	8	8
252	A84	60 l	rose car, bl & ocher	12	10
253	A84	100 l	multi	10	5

Coronation of Pope John XXIII, Nov. 4, 1958.

1959, May 25 **Wmk. 235** ***Perf. 14***

254	A85	30 l	brown	8	5
255	A85	100 l	vio bl	25	14

Lateran Pacts, 30th anniversary.

For unused stamps, more recent issues are valued as never hinged, with the beginning point determined on a country-by-country basis. Notes to show the beginning points are prominently placed in the text.

St. Lawrence A86

Radio Tower and Archangel Gabriel A87

Portraits of Saints: 25 l, Pope Sixtus II. 50 l, Agapitus. 60 l, Filicissimus. 100 l, Cyprianus. 300 l, Fructuosus.

1959, May 25

256	A86	15 l	red, brn & yel	5	8
257	A86	25 l	lil, brn & yel	22	10
258	A86	50 l	Prus bl, blk & yel	1.00	40
259	A86	60 l	ol grn, brn & bis	55	25
260	A86	100 l	mar, brn & yel	42	25
261	A86	300 l	bis brn & dk brn	1.10	45
			Nos. 256-261 (6)	3.34	1.53

Martyrs of Emperor Valerian's persecutions.

1959, Oct. 27 **Photo.** ***Perf. 14***

262	A87	25 l	rose, org yel & dk brn	10	9
263	A87	60 l	multi	12	25

2nd anniv. of the papal radio station, St. Maria di Galeria.

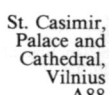

St. Casimir, Palace and Cathedral, Vilnius A88

1959, Dec. 14 **Engr.** **Wmk. 235**

264	A88	50 l	brown	12	9
265	A88	100 l	dl grn	30	15

500th anniv. (in 1958) of the birth of St. Casimir, patron saint of Lithuania.

Nativity by Raphael — A89

1959, Dec. 14 **Engr.** ***Perf. 13½***

266	A89	15 l	dk gray	8	8
267	A89	25 l	magenta	12	8
268	A89	60 l	brt ultra	30	15

St. Antoninus — A90

Transept of Lateran Basilica — A91

Designs: 25 l, 110 l, St. Antoninus preaching.

Perf. 13x14

1960, Feb. 29 **Wmk. 235**

269	A90	15 l	ultra	8	6
270	A90	25 l	turquoise	20	8
271	A90	60 l	brown	65	25
272	A90	110 l	rose claret	1.25	40

5th cent. of death of St. Antoninus, bishop of Florence.

1960, Feb. 29 **Photo.** ***Perf. 14***

273	A91	15 l	brown	8	8
274	A91	60 l	black	45	22

Roman Diocesan Synod, February, 1960.

Flight into Egypt by Fra Angelico — A92

Cardinal Sarto's Departure from Venice — A93

Designs: 10 l, 100 l, St. Peter Giving Alms to the Poor, by Masaccio. 25 l, 300 l, Madonna of Mercy, by Piero della Francesca.

1960, Apr. 7 **Wmk. 235** ***Perf. 14***

275	A92	5 l	green	8	8
276	A92	10 l	gray brn	8	8
277	A92	25 l	dp car	12	8
278	A92	60 l	lilac	35	12
279	A92	100 l	ultra	3.25	1.90
280	A92	300 l	Prus grn	1.25	50
			Nos. 275-280 (6)	5.13	2.76

World Refugee Year. July 1, 1959-June 30, 1960.

1960, Apr. 11 **Engr.** ***Perf. 13½***

Designs: 35 l, Pope John XXIII praying at coffin of Pope Pius X. 60 l, Body of Pope Pius X returning to Venice.

281	A93	15 l	brown	15	25
282	A93	35 l	rose car	48	60
283	A93	60 l	Prus grn	1.10	85

Return of the body of Pope Pius X to Venice.

Feeding the Hungry A94

"Acts of Mercy," by Della Robbia: 10 l, Giving drink to the thirsty. 15 l, Clothing the naked. 20 l, Sheltering the homeless. 30 l, Visiting the sick. 35 l, Visiting prisoners. 40 l, Burying the dead. 70 l, Pope John XXIII.

1960, Nov. 8 **Photo.** ***Perf. 14***

Centers in Brown

284	A94	5 l	red brn	5	5
285	A94	10 l	green	5	5
286	A94	15 l	slate	5	5
287	A94	20 l	rose car	5	5
288	A94	30 l	vio bl	8	8
289	A94	35 l	vio brn	8	8
290	A94	40 l	red org	8	8
291	A94	70 l	ocher	8	8
			Nos. 284-291,E15-E16 (10)	80	80

Holy Family by Gerard van Honthorst A95

1960, Dec. 6 **Wmk. 235** ***Perf. 14***

292	A95	10 l	sl grn & sl blk	8	8
293	A95	15 l	sep & ol blk	8	8
294	A95	70 l	grnsh bl & dp bl	24	18

St. Vincent de Paul — A96

St. Meinrad — A97

Designs: 70 l, St. Louisa de Marillac. 100 l, St. Louisa and St. Vincent.

1960, Dec. 6

295	A96	40 l	dl vio	8	8
296	A96	70 l	dk gray	42	18
297	A96	100 l	dk red brn	95	38

Death of St. Vincent de Paul, 300th anniv.

1961, Feb. 28 ***Perf. 14***

Designs: 40 l, Statue of Our Lady of Einsiedeln. 100 l, Einsiedeln monastery (horiz.).

298	A97	30 l	dk gray	55	12
299	A97	40 l	lt vio	1.65	45
300	A97	100 l	brown	1.65	95

Death of St. Meinrad, 1,100th anniv.; Einsiedeln Abbey, Switzerland.

Pope Leo the Great Defying Attila — A98

Wmk. 235

1961, Apr. 6 **Photo.** ***Perf. 14***

301	A98	15 l	rose brn	12	6
302	A98	70 l	Prus grn	55	35
303	A98	300 l	brn blk	3.75	75

Death of Pope Leo the Great (St. Leo Magnus), 1,500th anniv. The design is from a marble bas-relief in St. Peter's Basilica.

St. Paul Arriving in Rome, 61 A.D. — A99

Designs: 10 l, 30 l, Map showing St. Paul's journey to Rome. 20 l, 200 l, First Basilica of St. Paul, Rome.

1961, June 13 **Wmk. 235** ***Perf. 14***

304	A99	10 l	Prus grn	8	8
305	A99	15 l	dl red brn & gray	8	10
306	A99	20 l	red org & gray	12	12
307	A99	30 l	blue	35	20
308	A99	75 l	org brn & gray	65	70
309	A99	200 l	bl & gray	3.50	1.50
			Nos. 304-309 (6)	4.78	2.70

Arrival of St. Paul in Rome, 1,900th anniv.

1861 and 1961 Mastheads A100

Designs: 70 l, Editorial offices. 250 l, Rotary press.

1961, July 4

310	A100	40 l	red brn & blk	40	20
311	A100	70 l	bl & blk	90	65
312	A100	250 l	yel & blk	4.25	1.40

Centenary of L'Osservatore Romano, Vatican's newspaper.

St. Patrick's Purgatory, Lough Derg — A101

Arms of Roncalli Family — A102

Design: 10 l, 40 l, St. Patrick, marble sculpture.

Wmk. 235

1961, Oct. 6 Photo. *Perf. 14*

313	A101	10 l	buff & sl grn	8	8
314	A101	15 l	bl & sep	12	10
315	A101	40 l	yel & bl grn	40	16
316	A101	150 l	Prus bl & red brn	1.25	50

Death of St. Patrick, 1,500th anniv.

1961, Nov. 25

Designs: 25 l, Church at Sotto il Monte. 30 l, Santa Maria in Monte Santo, Rome. 40 l, Church of San Carlo al Corso, Rome (erroneously inscribed with name of Basilica of Sts. Ambrosius and Charles, Milan). 70 l, Altar, St. Peter's, Rome. 115 l, Pope John XXIII.

317	A102	10 l	gray & red brn	8	6
318	A102	25 l	ol bis & sl grn	8	8
319	A102	30 l	vio bl & pale pur	16	12
320	A102	40 l	lil & dk bl	22	15
321	A102	70 l	gray grn & org brn	80	22
322	A102	115 l	choc & sl	1.90	65
			Nos. 317-322 (6)	3.24	1.28

80th birthday of Pope John XXIII.

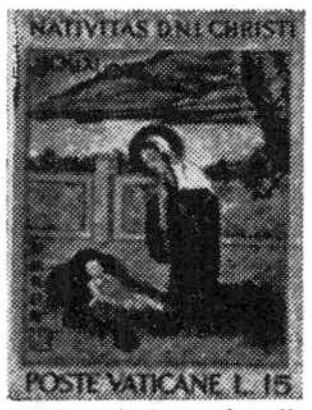

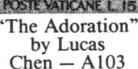

"The Adoration" by Lucas Chen — A103

Draining of Pontine Marshes Medal by Pope Sixtus V, 1588 — A104

1961, Nov. 25

Center Multicolored

323	A103	15 l	bluish grn	8	8
324	A103	40 l	gray	12	8
325	A103	70 l	pale lil	32	12

Christmas.

1962, Apr. 7 Wmk. 235 *Perf. 14*

Design: 40 l, 300 l, Map of Pontine Marshes showing 18th century drainage under Pope Pius VI.

326	A104	15 l	dk vio	12	6
327	A104	40 l	rose car	15	8
328	A104	70 l	brown	30	15
329	A104	300 l	dl grn	1.25	38

WHO drive to eradicate malaria.

"The Good Shepherd" A105

Wheatfield (Luke 10:2) A106

1962, June 2 Photo.

330	A105	10 l	lil & blk	20	12
331	A106	15 l	bl & ocher	38	9
332	A105	70 l	lt grn & blk	70	50
333	A106	115 l	fawn & ocher	3.50	1.65
334	A105	200 l	brn & blk	6.00	1.90
			Nos. 330-334 (5)	10.78	4.26

Issued to honor the priesthood and to stress its importance as a vocation.

"The Good Shepherd" is a fourth-century statue in the Lateran Museum, Rome.

St. Catherine of Siena — A107

Paulina M. Jaricot — A108

1962, June 12

335	A107	15 l	brown	15	8
336	A107	60 l	brt vio	75	30
337	A107	100 l	blue	1.40	50

Canonization of St. Catherine of Siena, 500th anniv. The portrait is from a fresco by Il Sodoma, Church of St. Dominic, Siena.

1962, July 5

Portrait Multicolored

338	A108	10 l	pale vio	6	6
339	A108	50 l	dl grn	35	15
340	A108	150 l	gray	1.40	55

Paulina M. Jaricot (1799-1862), founder of the Society for the Propagation of the Faith.

Sts. Peter and Paul A109

Design: 40 l, 100 l, "The Invincible Cross," relief from sarcophagus.

Wmk. 235

1962, Sept. 25 Photo. *Perf. 14*

341	A109	20 l	lil & brn	8	8
342	A109	40 l	lt brn & blk	10	8
343	A109	70 l	bluish grn & brn	10	8
344	A109	100 l	sal pink & blk	20	10

6th Congress of Christian Archeology, Ravenna, Sept. 23-28.

"Faith" by Raphael — A110

Designs: 10 l, "Hope." 15 l, "Charity." 25 l, Arms of Pope John XXIII and emblems of the Four Evangelists. 30 l, Ecumenical Congress meeting in St. Peter's. 40 l, Pope John XXIII on throne. 60 l, Statue of St. Peter. 115 l, The Holy Ghost as a dove (symbolic design).

Photo.; Center Engr. on 30 l

1962, Oct. 30

345	A110	5 l	brt bl & blk	6	6
346	A110	10 l	grn & blk	6	6
347	A110	15 l	ver & sep	6	6
348	A110	25 l	ver & sl	6	6
349	A110	30 l	lil & blk	6	6
350	A110	40 l	dk car & blk	8	8
351	A110	60 l	dk grn & dp org	8	8
352	A110	115 l	crimson	12	10
			Nos. 345-352 (8)	58	56

Vatican II, the 21st Ecumenical Council of the Roman Catholic Church, which opened Oct. 11, 1962. Nos. 345-347 show "the Three Theological Virtues" by Raphael.

Ethiopian Nativity Scene A111

1962, Dec. 4

Center Multicolored

353	A111	10 l	gray	5	5
354	A111	15 l	brown	8	8
355	A111	90 l	dl grn	25	12

Miracle of the Loaves and Fishes by Murillo A112

Pope John XXIII A113

Design: 40 l, 200 l, "The Miraculous Catch of Fishes" by Raphael.

Wmk. 235

1963, Mar. 21 Photo. *Perf. 14*

356	A112	15 l	brn & dk brn	8	6
357	A112	40 l	rose red & blk	8	8
358	A112	100 l	bl & dk brn	9	8
359	A112	200 l	bl grn & blk	18	8

FAO "Freedom from Hunger" campaign.

1963, May 8

360	A113	15 l	red brn	12	6
361	A113	160 l	black	55	18

Awarding of the Balzan Peace Prize to Pope John XXIII.

Interregnum Issue

Keys of St. Peter and Papal Chamberlain's Insignia — A114

1963, June 15 Wmk. 235 *Perf. 14*

362	A114	10 l	dk brn	8	5
363	A114	40 l	dk brn, *yel*	10	8
364	A114	100 l	dk brn, *vio*	12	8

Scott's editorial staff cannot undertake to identify, authenticate or appraise stamps and postal markings.

Pope Paul VI — A115

St. Cyril — A116

Design: 40 l, 200 l, Arms of Pope Paul VI.

1963, Oct. 16 Engr. *Perf. 13x14*

365	A115	15 l	black	6	6
366	A115	40 l	carmine	10	6
367	A115	115 l	redsh brn	25	12
368	A115	200 l	slate bl	45	22

Coronation of Pope Paul VI, June 30, 1963.

Wmk. 235

1963, Nov. 22 Photo. *Perf. 14*

Designs: 70 l, Map of Hungary, Moravia and Poland, 16th century. 150 l, St. Methodius.

369	A116	30 l	vio blk	8	8
370	A116	70 l	brown	32	12
371	A116	150 l	rose cl	48	18

1100th anniv. of the beginning of missionary work among the Slavs by Sts. Cyril and Methodius. The pictures of the saints are from 16th century frescoes in St. Clement's Basilica, Rome.

African Nativity Scene A117

Church of the Holy Sepulcher, Jerusalem A118

1963, Nov. 22

372	A117	10 l	brn & pale brn	5	5
373	A117	40 l	ultra & brn	10	6
374	A117	100 l	gray ol & brn	28	14

The design is after a sculpture by the Burundi artist Andreas Bukuru.

1964, Jan. 4 Wmk. 235 *Perf. 14*

Designs: 15 l, Pope Paul VI. 25 l, Nativity Church, Bethlehem. 160 l, Well of the Virgin Mary, Nazareth.

375	A118	15 l	black	5	5
376	A118	25 l	rose brn	8	8
377	A118	70 l	brown	10	8
378	A118	160 l	ultra	12	8

Visit of Pope Paul VI to the Holy Land, Jan. 4-6.

St. Peter from Coptic Church at Wadi-es-Sebua, Sudan — A119

1964, Mar. 10 Photo.

Design: 20 l, 200 l, Trajan's Kiosk, Philae.

379	A119	10 l	ultra & red brn	5	5
380	A119	20 l	multi	5	5
381	A119	70 l	gray & red brn	10	8
382	A119	200 l	gray & multi	12	8

UNESCO world campaign to save historic monuments in Nubia.

Pietà by Michelangelo A120

Isaiah by Michelangelo A121

Designs: 15 l, 100 l, Pope Paul VI. 250 l, Head of Mary from Pietà.

1964, Apr. 22 Wmk. 235 *Perf. 14*

383	A120	15 l vio bl	5	5
384	A120	50 l dk brn	8	5
385	A120	100 l slate bl	12	8
386	A120	250 l chestnut	16	8

New York World's Fair, 1964-65.

1964, June 16 Engr. *Perf. 13½x14*

387	A121	10 l Michelangelo, after Jacopino del Conte	5	5
388	A121	25 l Isaiah	5	5
389	A121	30 l Delphie Sibyl	5	5
390	A121	40 l Jeremiah	8	8
391	A121	150 l Joel	10	8
		Nos. 387-391 (5)	33	31

Michelangelo Buonarroti (1475-1564). Designs of Nos. 387-391 are from Sistine Chapel.

The Good Samaritan A122

Perf. 14x13½

1964, Sept. 22 Engr. Wmk. 235

392	A122	10 l red brn & red	5	5
393	A122	30 l dk bl & red	10	6
394	A122	300 l gray & red	18	10

Cent. (in 1963) of the founding of the Intl. Red Cross.

Birthplace of Cardinal Nicolaus Cusanus A123

Design: 200 l, Cardinal's sepulcher, Church of San Pietro in Vincoli, Rome.

1964, Nov. 16 Wmk. 235

395	A123	40 l dl bl grn	7	7
396	A123	200 l rose red	20	16

German cardinal Nicolaus Cusanus (Nicolaus Krebs of Kues) (1401-1464).

Japanese Nativity Scene by Kimiko Koseki — A124

Pope Paul VI and Map of India and Southeast Asia — A125

1964, Nov. 16 Photo. *Perf. 14*

397	A124	10 l multi	5	5
a		Yellow omitted		
398	A124	15 l blk & multi	5	5
399	A124	135 l bis & multi	25	12

1964, Dec. 2

Designs: 15 l, Pope Paul VI at prayer. 25 l, Eucharistic Congress altar, Bombay (horiz.). 60 l, Gateway of India, Bombay (horiz.).

400	A125	15 l dl vio	5	5
401	A125	25 l green	8	5
402	A125	60 l brown	10	6
403	A125	200 l dl vio	12	8

Trip of Pope Paul VI to India, Dec. 2-5, 1964.

Uganda Martyrs — A126

Dante by Raphael — A127

Designs: Various groups of Martyrs of Uganda.

Perf. 13½x14

1965, Mar. 16 Engr. Wmk. 235

404	A126	15 l Prus grn	5	5
405	A126	20 l brown	5	5
406	A126	30 l ultra	5	5
407	A126	75 l black	9	6
408	A126	100 l rose red	9	6
409	A126	160 l violet	9	6
		Nos. 404-409 (6)	42	33

Canonization of 22 African martyrs, Oct. 18, 1964.

Photogravure and Engraved

1965, May 18 *Perf. 13½x14*

Designs: 40 l, Dante and the 3 beasts at entrance to the Inferno. 70 l, Dante and Virgil at entrance to Purgatory. 200 l, Dante and Beatrice in Paradise. (40 l, 70 l, 200 l, by Botticelli)

410	A127	10 l bis brn & dk brn	5	5
411	A127	40 l rose & dk brn	5	5
412	A127	70 l lt grn & dk brn	6	6
413	A127	200 l pale bl & dk brn	15	12

Birth of Dante Alighieri, 700th anniv.

St. Benedict by Perugino A128

Pope Paul VI Addressing UN Assembly A129

Design: 300 l, View of Monte Cassino.

1965, July 2 Photo. *Perf. 14*

414	A128	40 l brown	8	6
415	A128	300 l dk grn	25	12

Conferring of the title Patron Saint of Europe upon St. Benedict by Pope Paul VI; restoring of the Abbey of Monte Cassino.

1965, Oct. 4 Wmk. 235 *Perf. 14*

Designs: 30 l, 150 l, UN Headquarters and olive branch.

416	A129	20 l brown	5	5
417	A129	30 l sapphire	5	5
418	A129	150 l ol grn	10	6
419	A129	300 l rose vio	24	8

Visit of Pope Paul VI to the UN, New York City, Oct. 4.

Peruvian Nativity Scene A130

Cartographer A131

1965, Nov. 25 Engr. *Perf. 13½x14*

420	A130	20 l rose claret	5	5
421	A130	40 l red brn	7	6
422	A130	200 l gray grn	16	10

1966, Mar. 8 Photo. *Perf. 14*

Designs: 5 l, Pope Paul VI. 10 l, Organist. 20 l, Painter. 30 l, Sculptor. 40 l, Bricklayer. 55 l, Printer. 75 l, Plowing farmer. 90 l, Blacksmith. 130 l, Scholar.

423	A131	5 l sepia	5	5
424	A131	10 l violet	5	5
425	A131	15 l brown	5	5
426	A131	20 l gray grn	6	5
427	A131	30 l brn red	8	5
428	A131	40 l Prus grn	8	6
429	A131	55 l dk bl	8	8
430	A131	75 l dk rose brn	8	8
431	A131	90 l car rose	10	8
432	A131	130 l black	12	10
		Nos. 423-432,E17-E18 (12)	1.13	93

The Pope's portrait is from a bas-relief by Enrico Manfrini; the arts and crafts designs are bas-reliefs by Mario Rudelli from the chair in the Pope's private chapel.

King Mieszko I and Queen Dabrowka A132

Designs: 25 l, St. Adalbert (Wojciech) and Cathedrals of Wroclaw and Gniezno. 40 l, St. Stanislas, Skalka Church, Wawel Cathedral and Castle, Cracow. 50 l, Queen Jadwiga (Hedwig), Holy Gate with Our Lady of Mercy, Vilnius, and Jagellon University Library, Cracow. 150 l, Black Madonna of Czestochowa, cloister and church of Bright Mountain, Czestochowa, and St. John's Cathedral, Warsaw. 220 l, Pope Paul VI blessing students and farmers.

Perf. 14x13½

1966, May 3 Engr. Wmk. 235

433	A132	15 l black	5	5
434	A132	25 l violet	5	5
435	A132	40 l brick red	8	6
436	A132	50 l claret	8	7
437	A132	150 l sl bl	10	8
438	A132	220 l brown	12	10
		Nos. 433-438 (6)	48	41

Millenium of Christianization of Poland.

Pope John XXIII Opening Vatican II Council A133

Nativity, Sculpture by Scorzelli A134

Designs: 15 l, Ancient Bible on ornate display stand. 55 l, Bishops celebrating Mass. 90 l, Pope Paul VI greeting Patriarch Athenagoras I. 100 l, Gold ring given to participating bishops. 130 l, Pope Paul VI carried in front of St. Peter's.

1966, Oct. 11 Photo. *Perf. 14*

439	A133	10 l red & blk	5	5
440	A133	15 l brn & grn	5	5
441	A133	55 l blk & brt rose	8	8
442	A133	90 l sl grn & blk	8	8
443	A133	100 l grn & ocher	8	8
444	A133	130 l org brn & brn	8	8
		Nos. 439-444 (6)	42	42

Conclusion of Vatican II, the 21st Ecumenical Council of the Roman Catholic Church, Dec. 8, 1965.

1966, Nov. 24 Wmk. 235 *Perf. 14*

445	A134	20 l plum	5	5
446	A134	55 l sl grn	12	8
447	A134	225 l yel brn	12	8

St. Peter, Fresco, Catacombs, Rome A135

Cross, People and Globe A136

Designs: 20 l, St. Paul, fresco from Catacombs, Rome. 55 l, Sts. Peter and Paul, glass painting, Vatican Library. 90 l, Baldachin by Bernini, St. Peter's, Rome. 220 l, Interior of St. Paul's, Rome.

Perf. 13½x14

1967, June 15 Photo. Unwmk.

448	A135	15 l multi	6	6
449	A135	20 l multi	6	6
450	A135	55 l multi	8	8
451	A135	90 l multi	8	8
452	A135	220 l multi	12	8
		Nos. 448-452 (5)	40	36

Martyrdom of the Apostles Peter and Paul, 1,900th anniv.

1967, Oct. 13 Wmk. 235 *Perf. 14*

453	A136	40 l car rose	8	8
454	A136	130 l brt bl	20	12

3rd Congress of Catholic Laymen, Rome, Oct. 11-18.

Sculpture of Shepherd Children of Fatima — A137

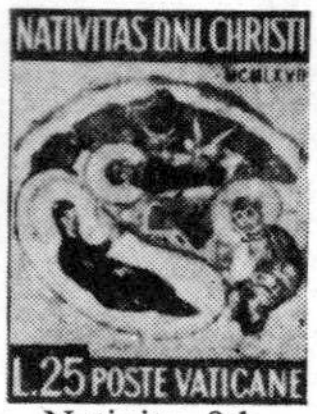

Nativity, 9th Century Painting on Wood — A138

1967, Oct. 13 *Perf. 13½x14*

Designs: 50 l, Basilica at Fatima. 200 l, Pope Paul VI praying before statue of Virgin of Fatima.

455	A137	30 l multi	8	8
456	A137	50 l multi	10	8
457	A137	200 l multi	10	8

Apparition of the Virgin Mary to 3 shepherd children at Fatima, 50th anniv.

Christmas Issue

1967, Nov. 28 Photo. Unwmk.

458	A138	25 l pur & multi	8	8
459	A138	55 l gray & multi	10	8
460	A138	180 l grn & multi	10	8

Pope Paul VI
A139

Holy Infant of Prague
A140

Designs: 55 l, Monstrance from fresco by Raphael. 220 l, Map of South America.

1968, Aug. 22 Wmk. 235 *Perf. 14*

461	A139	25 l blk & dk red brn	8	8
462	A139	55 l blk, gray & ocher	9	8
463	A139	220 l blk, lt bl & sep	12	10

Visit of Pope Paul VI to the 39th Eucharistic Congress in Bogota, Colombia, Aug. 22-25.

Engraved and Photogravure

1968, Nov. 28 *Perf. 13½x14*

464	A140	20 l plum & pink	6	6
465	A140	50 l vio & pale vio	12	8
466	A140	250 l dk bl & lt bluish gray	15	10

The Resurrection, by Fra Angelico de Fiesole — A141

Pope Paul VI with African Children — A142

Easter Issue

Perf. 13½x14

1969, Mar. 6 Engr. Wmk. 235

467	A141	20 l dk car & buff	6	5
468	A141	90 l grn & buff	10	8
469	A141	180 l ultra & buff	14	10

Europa Issue

Common Design Type

Perf. 13½x14

1969, Apr. 28 Photo. Wmk. 235

Size: 36½x27mm

470	CD12	50 l gray & lt brn	8	8
471	CD12	90 l ver & lt brn	15	10
472	CD12	130 l ol & lt brn	15	10

Perf. 13½x14

1969, July 31 Photo. Wmk. 235

Designs: 55 l, Pope Paul VI and African bishops. 250 l, Map of Africa with Kampala, olive branch and compass rose.

473	A142	25 l bis & brn	8	6
474	A142	55 l dk red & brn	9	8
475	A142	250 l multi	18	12

Visit of Pope Paul VI to Uganda, July 31-Aug. 2.

Pope Pius IX — A143

Mt. Fuji and EXPO '70 Emblem — A144

Designs: 50 l, Chrismon, emblem of St. Peter's Circle. 220 l, Pope Paul VI.

Perf. 13½x14

1969, Nov. 18 Engr. Wmk. 235

476	A143	30 l red brn	8	8
477	A143	50 l dk gray	8	8
478	A143	220 l dp plum	18	12

Centenary of St. Peter's Circle, a lay society dedicated to prayer, action and sacrifice.

1970, Mar. 16 Photo. Unwmk.

EXPO '70 Emblem and: 25 l, EXPO '70 emblem. 40 l, Osaka Castle. 55 l, Japanese Virgin and Child, by Domoto in Osaka Cathedral. 90 l, Christian Pavilion.

479	A144	25 l gold, red & blk	8	5
480	A144	40 l red & multi	8	5
481	A144	55 l brn & multi	10	10
482	A144	90 l gold & multi	12	8
483	A144	110 l bl & multi	25	9
		Nos. 479-483 (5)	63	37

EXPO '70 Intl. Exhibition, Osaka, Japan, Mar. 15-Sept. 13.

Centenary Medal, Jesus Giving St. Peter the Keys — A145

Designs: 50 l, Coat of arms of Pope Pius IX. 180 l, Vatican I Council meeting in St. Peter's, obverse of centenary medal.

Engr. & Photo.; Photo. (50 l)

1970, Apr. 29 *Perf. 13x14*

484	A145	20 l org & brn	6	5
485	A145	50 l multi	10	10
486	A145	180 l ver & brn	30	22

Centenary of the Vatican I Council.

Christ, by Simone Martini A146

Designs: 25 l, Christ with Crown of Thorns, by Rogier van der Weyden. 50 l, Christ, by Albrecht Dürer. 90 l, Christ, by El Greco. 180 l, Pope Paul VI.

1970, May 29 Photo. *Perf. 14x13*

487	A146	15 l gold & multi	5	5
488	A146	25 l gold & multi	8	8
489	A146	50 l gold & multi	8	8
490	A146	90 l gold & multi	15	10
491	A146	180 l gold & multi	28	12
		Nos. 487-491 (5)	64	43

Ordination of Pope Paul VI, 50th anniv.

Adam, by Michelangelo; UN Emblem — A147

Pope Paul VI — A148

UN Emblem and: 90 l, Eve, by Michelangelo. 220 l, Olive branch.

1970, Oct. 8 Photo. *Perf. 13x14*

492	A147	20 l multi	5	5
493	A147	90 l multi	16	9
494	A147	220 l multi	28	20

25th anniversary of the United Nations.

1970, Nov. 26 Photo. Unwmk.

Designs: 55 l, Holy Child of Cebu, Philippines. 100 l, Madonna and Child, by Georg Hamori, Darwin Cathedral, Australia. 130 l, Cathedral of Manila. 220 l, Cathedral of Sydney.

495	A148	25 l multi	6	6
496	A148	55 l multi	10	8
497	A148	100 l multi	18	8
498	A148	130 l multi	22	10
499	A148	220 l multi	32	20
		Nos. 495-499 (5)	88	52

Visit of Pope Paul VI to the Far East, Oceania and Australia, Nov. 26-Dec. 5.

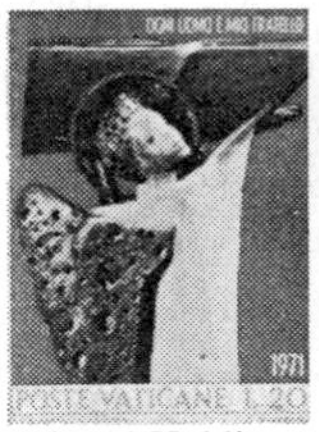

Angel Holding Lectern — A149

Madonna and Child by Francesco Ghissi — A150

Sculptures by Corrado Ruffini: 40 l, 130 l, Crucified Christ surrounded by doves. 50 l, like 20 l.

1971, Feb. 2 *Perf. 13x14*

500	A149	20 l multi	5	5
501	A149	40 l dp org & multi	8	6
502	A149	50 l pur & multi	10	8
503	A149	130 l multi	24	12

Intl. year against racial discrimination.

1971, Mar. 26 Photo. *Perf. 14*

Paintings: Madonna and Child, 40 l, by Sassetta (Stefano di Giovanni); 55 l, Carlo Crivelli; 90 l, by Carlo Maratta. 180 l, Holy Family, by Ghisberto Ceracchini.

504	A150	25 l gray & multi	8	8
505	A150	40 l gray & multi	10	8
506	A150	55 l gray & multi	12	8
507	A150	90 l gray & multi	16	9
508	A150	180 l gray & multi	22	14
		Nos. 504-508 (5)	68	47

St. Dominic, Sienese School — A151

St. Stephen, from Chasuble, 1031 — A152

Portraits of St. Dominic: 55 l, by Fra Angelico. 90 l, by Titian. 180 l, by El Greco.

1971, May 25 Unwmk. *Perf. 13x14*

509	A151	25 l multi	6	6
510	A151	55 l multi	15	8
511	A151	90 l multi	15	8
512	A151	180 l multi	28	14

St. Dominic de Guzman (1170-1221), founder of the Dominican Order.

1971, Nov. 25

Design: 180 l, Madonna as Patroness of Hungary, 1511.

513	A152	50 l multi	12	10
514	A152	180 l blk & yel	35	20

Millenium of the birth of St. Stephen (975?-1038), king of Hungary.

Bramante — A153

Designs: 25 l, Bramante's design for dome of St. Peter's. 130 l, Design for spiral staircase.

1972, Feb. 22 Engr. *Perf. 13½x14*

515	A153	25 l dl yel & blk	7	7
516	A153	90 l dl yel & blk	20	12
517	A153	130 l dl yel & blk	25	12

Bramante (real name Donato d'Agnolo; 1444-1514), architect.

St. Mark in Storm, 12th Century Mosaic — A154

Map of Venice, 1581 — A155

Design: 180 l, St. Mark's Basilica, Painting by Emilio Vangelli.

Unwmk.

1972, June 6 Photo. *Perf. 14*

518	A154	25 l lt brn & multi	22	10
519	A155	Block of 4, multi	1.90	85
a.-d.		50l, UL, UR, LL, LR, each	45	20
520	A154	180 l lt bl & multi	2.25	1.00
a.		Souvenir sheet, #518-520	5.25	5.00

UNESCO campaign to save Venice.

Gospel of St. Matthew, 13th Century, French A156

Illuminated Initials from: 50 l, St. Luke's Gospel, Biblia dell'Aracoeli 13th century, French. 90 l, Second Epistle of St. John, 14th century, Bologna. 100 l, Apocalypse of St. John, 14th century, Bologna. 130 l, Book of Romans, 14th century, Central Italy.

1972, Oct. 11 *Perf. 14x13½*

521	A156	30 l multi	5	5
522	A156	50 l multi	8	8
523	A156	90 l multi	18	8
524	A156	100 l multi	18	8
525	A156	130 l multi	48	22
		Nos. 521-525 (5)	97	51

Intl. Book Year. Illustrations are from illuminated medieval manuscripts.

Foreign postal stationery (stamped envelopes, postal cards and air letter sheets) lies beyond the scope of this Catalogue, which is limited to adhesive postage stamps.

Luigi Orione
A157

Design: 180 l, Lorenzo Perosi and music from "Hallelujah."

1972, Nov. 28 Photo. *Perf. 14x13½*

526	A157	50 l	rose, lil & blk	18	12
527	A157	180 l	org, grn & blk	32	18

Secular priests Luigi Orione (1872-1940), founder of CARITAS, Catholic welfare organization; and Lorenzo Perosi (1872-1956), composer.

Cardinal Bessarion — A158

Eucharistic Congress Emblem — A159

Designs: 40 l, Reading Bull of Union between the Greek and Latin Churches, 1439, from bronze door of St. Peter's. 130 l, Coat of arms from tomb, Basilica of Holy Apostles, Rome.

Perf. 13x14

1972, Nov. 28 Wmk. 235 Engr.

528	A158	40 l	dl grn	15	10
529	A158	90 l	carmine	22	15
530	A158	130 l	black	20	18

Johannes Cardinal Bessarion (1403?-1472), Latin Patriarch of Constantinople, who worked for union of the Greek and Latin Churches. Portrait by Cosimo Rosselli in Sistine Chapel.

1973, Feb. 27 Photo. Unwmk.

Designs: 75 l, Head of Mary (Pietà), by Michelangelo. 300 l, Melbourne Cathedral.

531	A159	25 l	vio & multi	10	6
532	A159	75 l	ol & multi	16	10
533	A159	300 l	multi	70	42

40th Intl. Eucharistic Congress, Melbourne, Australia, Feb. 18-25.

St. Teresa
A160

Copernicus
A161

Designs: 25 l, St. Teresa's birthplace, Alençon. 220 l, Lisieux Basilica.

Engr. & Photo.

1973, May 23 *Perf. 13x14*

534	A160	25 l	blk & pink	8	8
535	A160	55 l	blk & yel	12	10
536	A160	220 l	blk & lt bl	38	25

St. Teresa of Lisieux and of the Infant Jesus (1873-1897), Carmelite nun.

1973, June 19 Engr. *Perf. 14*

Designs: 20 l, 100 l, View of Torun.

537	A161	20 l	dl grn	6	6
538	A161	50 l	brown	8	8
539	A161	100 l	lilac	18	10
540	A161	130 l	dk bl	32	18

Nicolaus Copernicus (1473-1543), Polish astronomer.

St. Wenceslas
A162

1973, Sept. 25 Photo. *Perf. 14*

541	A162	20 l	shown	5	5
542	A162	90 l	Arms of Prague Diocese	15	8
543	A162	150 l	Spire of Prague Cathedral	20	9
544	A162	220 l	St. Adalbert	35	15

Millenium of Prague Latin Episcopal See.

St. Nerses Shnorali — A163

Designs: 25 l, Church of St. Hripsime. 90 l, Armenian khatchkar, a stele with cross and inscription.

Engr. & Litho.

1973, Nov. 27 *Perf. 13x14*

545	A163	25 l	tan & dk brn	5	5
546	A163	90 l	lt vio & blk	18	10
547	A163	180 l	lt grn & sep	30	18

Armenian Patriarch St. Nerses Shnorali (1102-1173).

Noah's Ark, Rainbow and Dove (Mosaic) — A164

Design: 90 l, Lamb drinking from stream, and Tablets of the Law (mosaic).

1974, Apr. 23 Litho. *Perf. 13x14*

548	A164	50 l	gold & multi	18	10
549	A164	90 l	gold & multi	30	15

Centenary of the Universal Postal Union.

"And There was Light" — A165

St. Thomas Aquinas Teaching — A166

Designs: 25 l, Noah's Ark (horiz.). 50 l, The Annunciation. 90 l, Nativity (African). 180 l, Hands holding grain (Spanish inscription: The Lord feeds his people) (horiz.). Designs chosen through worldwide youth competition in connection with 1972 Intl. Book Year.

Perf. 13x14, 14x13

1974, Apr. 23 Photo.

550	A165	15 l	brn & multi	6	6
551	A165	25 l	yel & multi	8	8
552	A165	50 l	bl & multi	10	8
553	A165	90 l	grn & multi	18	10
554	A165	180 l	rose & multi	28	14
			Nos. 550-554 (5)	70	46

"The Bible: the Book of Books."

Engr. & Litho.

1974, June 18 Unwmk. *Perf. 13x14*

Designs: 50 l, Students (left panel). 220 l, Students (right panel). Designs from a painting in the Convent of St. Mark in Florence, by an artist from the School of Fra Angelico.

Sizes: 50 l, 220 l, 20x36mm, 90 l, 26x36mm

555	A166	50 l	dk brn & gold	12	8
556	A166	90 l	dk brn & gold	14	12
557	A166	220 l	dk brn & gold	42	24
			Strip of 3, #555-557	1.00	55

St. Thomas Aquinas (1225-1274), scholastic philosopher. Nos. 555-557 printed se-tenant in sheets of 45.

St. Bonaventure
A167

Woodcuts: 40 l, Civita Bagnoregio. 90 l, Tree of Life (13th century).

1974, Sept. 26 Photo. *Perf. 13x14*

558	A167	40 l	gold & multi	12	8
559	A167	90 l	gold & multi	22	14
560	A167	220 l	gold & multi	30	20

St. Bonaventure (Giovanni di Fidanza; 1221-1274), scholastic philosopher.

Christ, St. Peter's Basilica — A168

Pope Paul VI Giving his Blessing — A169

Designs: 10 l, Christus Victor, Sts. Peter and Paul. 30 l, Christ. 40 l, Cross surmounted by dove. 50 l, Christ enthroned. 55 l, St. Peter. 90 l, St. Paul. 100 l, St. Peter. 130 l, St. Paul. 220 l, Arms of Pope Paul VI. Designs of 10 l, 25 l, are from St. Peter's; 30 l, 40 l, from St. John Lateran; 50 l, 55 l, 90 l, from St. Mary Major; 100 l, 130 l, from St. Paul outside he Walls.

1974, Dec. 19 Photo. *Perf. 13x14*

561	A168	10 l	multi	5	5
562	A168	25 l	multi	6	5
563	A168	30 l	multi	6	6
564	A168	40 l	multi	8	6
565	A168	50 l	multi	8	6
566	A168	55 l	multi	8	6
567	A168	90 l	multi	18	10
568	A168	100 l	multi	18	10
569	A168	130 l	multi	24	12
570	A169	220 l	multi	35	18
571	A169	250 l	multi	42	25
			Nos. 561-571 (11)	1.78	1.09

Holy Year 1975.

Pentecost, by El Greco — A170

1975, May 22 Engr. *Perf. 13x14*

572	A170	300 l	car rose & org	70	40

Pentecost.

Fountain, St. Peter's Square — A171

Fountains of Rome: 40 l, Piazza St. Martha, Apse of St. Peter's. 50 l, Borgia Tower and St. Peter's. 90 l, Belvedere Courtyard. 100 l, Academy of Sciences. 200 l, Galleon.

Litho. & Engr.

1975, May 22 *Perf. 14*

573	A171	20 l	buff & blk	6	6
574	A171	40 l	pale vio & blk	8	6
575	A171	50 l	sal & blk	12	8
576	A171	90 l	pale cit & blk	15	12
577	A171	100 l	pale grn & blk	15	12
578	A171	200 l	pale bl & blk	30	25
			Nos. 573-578 (6)	86	69

European Architectural Heritage Year.

Miracle of Loaves and Fishes, Gilt Glass
A172

Designs: 150 l, Painting of Christ, from Comodilla Catacomb. 200 l, Raising of Lazarus. All works from 4th century.

Perf. 14x13½

1975, Sept. 25 Photo. Unwmk.

579	A172	30 l	multi	8	8
580	A172	150 l	brn & multi	30	20
581	A172	200 l	grn & multi	48	30

9th Intl. Congress of Christian Archaeology.

Investiture of First Librarian Bartolomeo Sacchi by Pope Sixtus IV
A173

Designs: 100 l, Pope Sixtus IV and books in old wooden press, from Latin Vatican Codex 2044 (vert.). 250 l, Pope Sixtus IV visiting Library, fresco in Hospital of the Holy Spirit. Design of 70 l is from fresco by Melozzo di Forli in Vatican Gallery.

Perf. 14x13½, 13½x14

1975, Sept. 25 Litho. & Engr.

582	A173	70 l	gray & lil	12	8
583	A173	100 l	lt yel & grn	25	15
584	A173	250 l	gray & red	50	30

Founding of the Vatican Apostolic Library, 500th anniv.

Mt. Argentario Monastery A174

St. Paul of the Cross, by Giovanni Della Porta — A175

Design: 300 l, Basilica of Sts. John and Paul and burial chapel of Saint.

1975, Nov. 27 Photo. *Perf. 14x13½*

585	A174	50 l multi	8	8
586	A175	150 l multi	28	20
587	A174	300 l multi	60	28

Bicentenary of death of St. Paul of the Cross, founder of the Passionist religious order in 1737.

Praying Women, by Fra Angelico — A176

Design: 200 l, Seated women, by Fra Angelico.

1975, Nov. 27 *Perf. 13½x14*

588	A176	100 l multi	20	18
589	A176	200 l multi	40	22

International Women's Year.

Virgin and Child in Glory, by Titian A177

Design: 300 l, The Six Saints, by Titian. Designs from "The Madonna in Glory with the Child Jesus and Six Saints."

1976, May 13 Engr. *Perf. 14x13½*

590	A177	100 l rose mag	22	15
591	A177	300 l rose mag	55	40

Titian (1477-1576), painter. Nos. 590-591 printed se-tenant in sheets of 20.

Hands Holding Eucharist — A178

Designs: 150 l, Eucharist, wheat and globe. 400 l, Hungry mankind reaching for the Eucharist.

1976, July 2 Photo. *Perf. 13½x14*

592	A178	150 l gold, red & bl	30	18
593	A178	200 l gold & bl	40	22
594	A178	400 l gold, grn & brn	70	40

41st Intl. Eucharistic Congress, Philadelphia, Pa., Aug. 1-8.

Moses Holding Tablets — A179

Details from Transfiguration by Raphael: 40 l, Transfigured Christ. 50 l, Prophet Elijah with book. 100 l, Apostles John and Peter. 150 l, Group of women. 200 l, Landscape.

1976, Sept. 30 Photo. *Perf. 13½x14*

595	A179	30 l ocher & multi	8	8
596	A179	40 l red & multi	8	8
597	A179	50 l vio & multi	14	8
598	A179	100 l multi	28	12
599	A179	150 l grn & multi	45	20
600	A179	200 l ocher & multi	55	22
		Nos. 595-600 (6)	1.58	78

St. John's Tower A180

Roman Views: 100 l, Fountain of the Sacrament. 120 l, Fountain at entrance to the gardens. 180 l, Basilica, Cupola of St. Peter's and Sacristy. 250 l, Borgia Tower and Sistine Chapel. 300 l, Apostolic Palace and Courtyard of St. Damasius.

Litho. & Engr.

1976, Nov. 23 *Perf. 14*

601	A180	50 l gray & blk	12	8
602	A180	100 l sal & dk brn	24	12
603	A180	120 l cit & dk grn	28	12
604	A180	180 l pale gray & blk	24	14
605	A180	250 l yel & brn	50	20
606	A180	300 l pale lil & mag	60	25
		Nos. 601-606 (6)	1.98	91

The Lord's Creatures A181

Designs: 70 l, Brother Sun. 100 l, Sister Moon and Stars. 130 l, Sister Water. 170 l, Praise in infirmities and tribulations. 200 l, Praise for bodily death. Designs are illustrations by Duilio Cambellotti for "The Canticle of Brother Sun," by St. Francis.

1977, Mar. 10 Photo. *Perf. 14x13½*

607	A181	50 l multi	8	8
608	A181	70 l multi	18	8
609	A181	100 l multi	22	10
610	A181	130 l multi	25	12
611	A181	170 l multi	28	14
612	A181	200 l multi	35	16
		Nos. 607-612 (6)	1.36	68

St. Francis of Assisi, 750th death anniv.

Sts. Peter and Paul — A182

Dormition of the Virgin — A183

Design: 350 l, Pope Gregory XI and St. Catherine of Siena. Designs are after fresco by Giorgio Vasari.

1977, May 20 Engr. *Perf. 14*

613	A182	170 l black	40	18
614	A182	350 l black	65	30

Return of Pope Gregory XI from Avignon, 600th anniv. Nos. 613-614 printed se-tenant in sheets of 50.

1977, July 5 Photo. *Perf. 13½x14*

Design: 400 l, Virgin Mary in Heaven. Both designs after miniatures in Latin manuscripts, Vatican Library.

615	A183	200 l multi	40	20
616	A183	400 l multi	65	32

Feast of the Assumption.

The Nile Deity, Roman Sculpture — A184

Sculptures: 120 l, Head of Pericles. 130 l, Roman Couple Joining Hands. 150 l, Apollo Belvedere, head. 170 l, Laocoon, head. 350 l, Apollo Belvedere, torso.

1977, Sept. 29 *Perf. 14x13½*

617	A184	50 l multi	12	8
618	A184	120 l multi	22	14
619	A184	130 l multi	22	14
620	A184	150 l multi	22	14
621	A184	170 l multi	25	15
622	A184	350 l multi	45	30
		Nos. 617-622 (6)	1.48	95

Classical sculptures in Vatican Museums.

Creation of Man and Woman — A185

Designs: 70 l, Three youths in the furnace. 100 l, Adoration of the Kings. 130 l, Raising of Lazarus. 200 l, The Good Shepherd. 400 l, Chrismon, Cross, sleeping soldiers (Resurrection). Designs are bas-reliefs from Christian sarcophagi, 250-350 A.D., found in Roman excavations.

1977, Dec. 9 Photo. *Perf. 14x13½*

623	A185	50 l multi	8	8
624	A185	70 l multi	10	10
625	A185	100 l multi	12	12
626	A185	130 l multi	18	18
627	A185	200 l multi	20	20
628	A185	400 l multi	40	25
		Nos. 623-628 (6)	1.08	93

Madonna with the Parrot and Rubens Self-portrait A186

1977, Dec. 9 *Perf. 13½x14*

629	A186	350 l multi	48	48

Peter Paul Rubens (1577-1640).

Pope Paul VI, by Lino Bianchi Barriviera A187

Design: 350 l, Christ's Face, by Pericle Fazzini and arms of Pope Paul VI.

1978, Mar. 9 Photo. *Perf. 14*

630	A187	350 l multi	55	32
631	A187	400 l multi	55	40

80th birthday of Pope Paul VI.

Pope Pius IX — A188

Designs: 130 l, Arms of Pope Pius IX. 170 l, Seal of Pius IX, used to sign definition of Dogma of Immaculate Conception.

Litho. & Engr.

1978, May 9 *Perf. 13x14*

632	A188	130 l multi	20	12
633	A188	170 l multi	30	15
634	A188	200 l multi	38	20

Pope Pius IX (1792-1878).

Interregnum Issues

Keys of St. Peter and Papal Chamberlain's Insignia
A189 A190

1978, Aug. 23 Photo. *Perf. 14*

635	A189	120 l pur & lt grn	70	15
636	A189	150 l pur & sal	70	15
637	A189	250 l pur & yel	70	15

1978, Oct. 12 Photo. *Perf. 14*

638	A190	120 l blk & multi	50	15
639	A190	200 l blk & multi	50	15
640	A190	250 l blk & multi	50	15

Pope John Paul I — A191

Pope John Paul I: 70 l, Sitting on his throne. 250 l, Walking in Vatican garden. 350 l, Giving blessing (horiz.).

Perf. 13x14, 14x13

1978, Dec. 11 Photo.

641	A191	70 l multi	10	12
642	A191	120 l multi	28	28
643	A191	250 l multi	28	28
644	A191	350 l multi	42	42

John Paul I, Pope from Aug. 26 to Sept. 28, 1978.

Arms of Pope John Paul II A192

Designs: 250 l, Pope John Paul II raising hand in blessing. 400 l, Jesus giving keys to St. Peter.

Litho. & Engr.

1979, Mar. 22 *Perf. 14x13*

645	A192	170 l	blk & multi	30	25
646	A192	250 l	blk & multi	42	32
647	A192	400 l	blk & multi	65	48

Inauguration of pontificate of Pope John Paul II.

Martyrdom of St. Stanislas A193

St. Basil the Great Instructing Monk A194

Designs: 150 l, St. Stanislas appearing to the people. 250 l, Gold reliquary, 1504, containing saint's head. 500 l, View of Cracow Cathedral.

1979, May 18 **Photo.** *Perf. 14*

648	A193	120 l	multi	22	18
649	A193	150 l	multi	25	16
650	A193	250 l	multi	45	32
651	A193	500 l	multi	90	65

900th anniversary of martyrdom of St. Stanislas (1030-1079), patron saint of Poland.

Engr. & Photo.

1979, June 25 *Perf. 13½x14*

Design: 520 l, St. Basil the Great visiting the sick.

652	A194	150 l	multi	18	15
653	A194	520 l	multi	85	70

St. Basil the Great, 16th cent. of death.

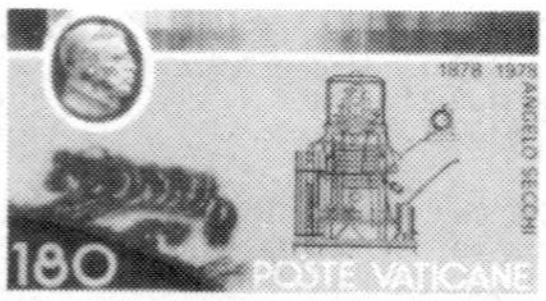

Father Secchi, Solar Protuberance, Spectrum and Meteorograph — A195

Father Angelo Secchi (1818-1878), astronomer, solar protuberance, spectrum and: 220 l, Spectroscope. 300 l, Telescope.

Litho. & Engr.

1979, June 25 *Perf. 14x13½*

654	A195	180 l	multi	30	24
655	A195	220 l	multi	38	28
656	A195	300 l	multi	45	30

Vatican City A196

Papal Arms and Portraits: 70 l, Pius XI. 120 l, Pius XII. 150 l, John XXIII. 170 l, Paul VI. 250 l, John Paul I. 450 l, John Paul II.

1979, Oct. 11 **Photo.** *Perf. 14x13½*

657	A196	50 l	multi	8	8
658	A196	70 l	multi	10	8
659	A196	120 l	multi	18	16
660	A196	150 l	multi	22	16
661	A196	170 l	multi	25	22
662	A196	250 l	multi	35	28
663	A196	450 l	multi	75	50
			Nos. 657-663 (7)	1.93	1.48

Vatican City State, 50th anniversary.

Infant, by Andrea Della Robbia, IYC Emblem — A197

IYC Emblem and Della Robbia Bas Reliefs, Hospital of the Innocents, Florence.

Engr. & Photo.

1979, Nov. 27 *Perf. 13½x14*

664	A197	50 l	multi	8	6
665	A197	120 l	multi	18	12
666	A197	200 l	multi	30	18
667	A197	350 l	multi	52	35

International Year of the Child.

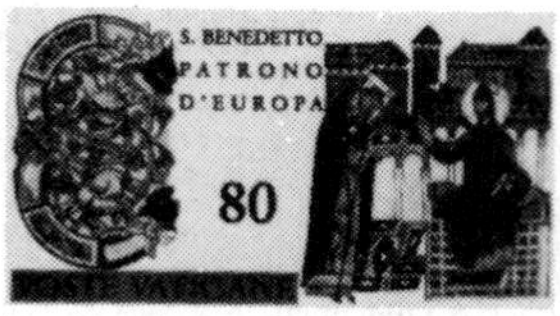

Abbot Desiderius Giving Codex to St. Benedict — A198

Illuminated Letters and Illustrations, Codices, Vatican Apostolic Library: 100 l, St. Benedict writing the Rule. 150 l, Page from the Rule. 220 l, Death of St. Benedict. 450 l, Montecassino (after painting by Paul Bril).

1980, Mar. 21 **Photo.** *Perf. 14x13½*

668	A198	80 l	multi	15	12
669	A198	100 l	multi	16	15
670	A198	150 l	multi	24	22
671	A198	220 l	multi	32	28
672	A198	450 l	multi	65	55
			Nos. 668-672 (5)	1.52	1.32

St. Benedict of Nursia (patron saint of Europe), 1500th birth anniversary.

Bernini, Medallion Showing Baldacchino in St. Peter's — A199

Gian Lorenzo Bernini (1598-1680), Architect (Self-portrait and Medallion): 170 l, St. Peter's Square with third wing (never built). 250 l, Bronze chair, Doctors of the Church. 350 l, Apostolic Palace stairway.

1980, Oct. 16 **Litho.** *Perf. 14x13½*

673	A199	80 l	multi	10	10
674	A199	170 l	multi	22	22
675	A199	250 l	multi	30	32
676	A199	350 l	multi	45	38

St. Albertus Magnus on Mission of Peace — A200

1980, Nov. 18 **Litho.** *Perf. 13½x14*

677	A200	300 l	shown	45	30
678	A200	400 l	As bishop	60	42

St. Albertus Magnus, 700th death anniv.

Communion of the Saints A201

1980, Nov. 18 *Perf. 14x13½*

679	A201	250 l	shown	35	25
680	A201	500 l	Christ and saints	70	60

Feast of All Saints.

Guglielmo Marconi and Pope Pius XI, Vatican Radio Emblem, Vatican Arms A202

Designs: 150 l, Microphone, Bible text. 200 l, St. Maria di Galeria Radio Center antenna, Archangel Gabriel statue. 600 l, Pope John Paul II.

1981, Feb. 12 **Photo.** *Perf. 14x13½*

681	A202	100 l	shown	16	10
682	A202	150 l	multi	25	20
683	A202	200 l	multi	35	28
684	A202	600 l	multi	85	65

Vatican Radio, 50th anniversary.

Virgil Seated at Podium, Vergilius Romanus — A203

1981, Apr. 23 **Litho.** *Perf. 14*

685	A203	350 l	multi	90	70
686	A203	600 l	multi	1.50	1.25

2000th birth anniversary of Virgil. Issued in sheets of 16 stamps plus 9 labels.

Congress Emblem A204

Congress Emblem and: 150 l, Virgin appearing to St. Bernadette. 200 l, Pilgrims going to Lourdes. 500 l, Bishop and pilgrims.

1981, June 22 **Photo.**

687	A204	80 l	multi	12	12
688	A204	150 l	multi	20	20
689	A204	200 l	multi	28	28
690	A204	500 l	multi	55	55

42nd Intl. Eucharistic Congress, Lourdes, France, July 16-23.

Intl. Year of the Disabled A205

1981, Sept. 29 **Photo.** *Perf. 14x13½*

691	A205	600 l	multi	90	80

Jan van Ruusbroec, Flemish Mystic, 500th Birth Anniv. — A206

Litho. & Engr.

1981, Sept. 29 *Perf. 13½x14*

692	A206	200 l	shown	35	35
693	A206	300 l	Portrait	48	48

1980 Journeys of Pope John Paul II — A207

1981, Dec. 3 **Photo.** *Perf. 13½x14½*

694	A207	50 l	Papal arms	15	15
695	A207	100 l	Map of Africa	12	12
696	A207	120 l	Crucifix	16	16
697	A207	150 l	Communion	20	20
698	A207	200 l	African bishop	25	25
699	A207	250 l	Visiting sick	32	32
700	A207	300 l	Notre Dame, France	40	40
701	A207	400 l	UNESCO speech	55	55
702	A207	600 l	Christ of the Andes, Brazil	95	95
703	A207	700 l	Cologne Cathedral, Germany	1.10	1.10
704	A207	900 l	John Paul II	1.25	1.25
			Nos. 694-704 (11)	5.45	5.45

700th Death Anniv. of St. Agnes of Prague — A208

Designs: 700 l, Handing order to Grand Master of the Crosiers of the Red Star. 900 l, Receiving letter from St. Clare.

1982, Feb. 16 **Photo.** *Perf. 13½x14*

705	A208	700 l	multi	1.10	1.10
706	A208	900 l	multi	1.25	1.25

Pueri Cantores A209

St. Theresa of Avila (1515-1582) A210

Luca Della Robbia (1400-1482), Sculptor: No. 708, Pueri Cantores (diff.) No. 709, Virgin in Prayer (44x36mm.).

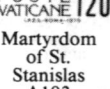

Photo. & Engr.

1982, May 21			**Perf. 14**	
707 A209	1000 l	multi	1.50	1.40
708 A209	1000 l	multi	1.50	1.40
709 A209	1000 l	multi	1.50	1.40

Nos. 707-709 issued se-tenant.

1982, Sept. 23			**Photo.**	

Sketches of St. Teresa by Riccardo Tommasi-Ferroni.

710 A210	200 l	multi	28	28
711 A210	600 l	multi	85	85
712 A210	1000 l	multi	1.40	1.40

Christmas A211

Nativity Bas-Reliefs: 300 l, Wit Stwosz, Church of the Virgin Mary, Cracow. 450 l, Enrico Manfrini.

Photo. & Engr.

1982, Nov. 23			**Perf. 14**	
713 A211	300 l	multi	45	45
714 A211	450 l	multi	70	70

400th Anniv. of Gregorian Calendar — A212

Sculpture Details, Tomb of Pope Gregory XIII, Vatican Basilica.

1982, Nov. 23	**Engr.**		**Perf. 13½x14**	
715 A212	200 l	Surveying the globe	25	25
716 A212	300 l	Receiving Edict of Reform	40	40
717 A212	700 l	Presenting edict	85	85
a		Souvenir sheet of 3, #715-717	3.00	3.00

Souvenir Sheets

Greek Vase — A213

1983, Mar. 10	**Litho.**		**Perf. 13½x14**	
718		Sheet of 6	2.75	1.75
a	A213 100 l	shown	14	10
b	A213 200 l	Italian vase	30	20
c	A213 250 l	Female terra-cotta bust	40	28
d	A213 300 l	Marcus Aurelius bust	45	30
e	A213 350 l	Bird fresco	55	38
f	A213 400 l	Pope Clement VIII vestment	60	40

1983, June 14	**Litho.**		**Perf. 13½x14**	
719		Sheet of 6	3.25	3.25
a	A213 100 l	Horse's head, Etruscan terra cotta	10	7
b	A213 200 l	Horseman, Greek fragment	20	12
c	A213 300 l	Male head, Etruscan	30	10
d	A213 400 l	Apollo Belvedere head	45	25
e	A213 500 l	Moses, Roman fresco	52	32
f	A213 1000 l	Madonna and Child, by Bernardo Daddi	1.10	65

1983, Nov. 10	**Litho.**		**Perf. 13½x14**	
720		Sheet of 6	4.25	4.25
a	A213 150 l	Greek cup, Oedipus and the Sphinx	22	12
b	A213 200 l	Etruscan bronze statue of a child	28	16
c	A213 350 l	Emperor Augustus marble statue	45	30
d	A213 400 l	Good Shepherd marble statue	55	35
e	A213 500 l	St. Nicholas Saving a ship by G. da Fabriano	70	42
f	A213 1200 l	The Holy face by G. Rouault	1.65	1.10

Vatican Collection: The Papacy and Art - USA 1983 exhibition, New York, Chicago, San Francisco.

Extraordinary Holy Year, 1983-84 (1950th Anniv. of Redemption) A214

Sketches by Giovanni Hajnal.

1983, Mar. 10			**Photo. & Engr.**	
721 A214	300 l	Crucifixion	45	30
722 A214	350 l	Christ the Redeemer	55	38
723 A214	400 l	Pope	45	45
724 A214	2000 l	Holy Spirit	2.75	2.75

Theology, by Raphael (1483-1517) A215

St. Casimir of Lithuania (1458-1484) A217

Gregor Johann Mendel (1822-1884), Biologist — A216

Allegories, Room of the Segnatura.

1983, June 14				
725 A215	50 l	shown	8	5
726 A215	400 l	Poetry	60	60
727 A215	500 l	Justice	70	70
728 A215	1200 l	Philosphy	1.75	1.75

Photo. & Engr.

1984, Feb. 28			**Perf. 14x13½**	

Phases of pea plant hybridization.

729 A216	450 l	multi	65	50
730 A216	1500 l	multi	2.25	1.65
1984, Feb. 28			**Perf. 14**	
731 A217	550 l	multi	1.00	65
732 A217	1200 l	multi	2.25	1.40

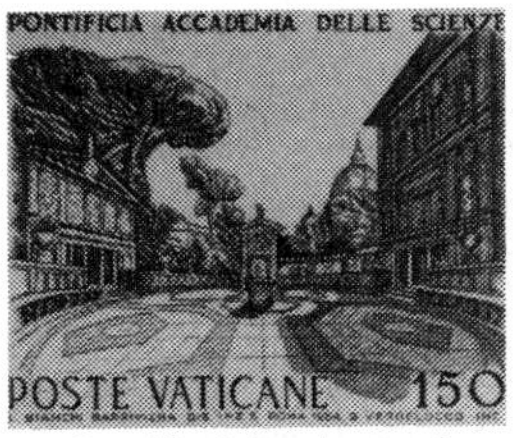

Pontifical Academy of Sciences — A218

1984, June 18			**Litho. & Engr.**	
733 A218	150 l	shown	22	18
734 A218	450 l	Secret Archives	65	55
735 A218	550 l	Apostolic Library	80	65
736 A218	1500 l	Observatory	2.25	1.75

Papal Journies — A218a

1984-85	**Photo.**		**Perf. 13½x14½**	
737 A218a	50 l	Pakistan	10	5
738 A218a	100 l	Philippines	20	12
739 A218a	150 l	Guam	30	18
740 A218a	250 l	Japan	48	30
741 A218a	300 l	Alaska	60	35
742 A218a	400 l	Africa	80	50
743 A218a	450 l	Portugal	90	55
a		Bklt. pane of 16 + 4 labels (4 each, #738, 741-743) ('85)	9.50	
744 A218a	550 l	Gt. Britain	1.10	65
745 A218a	1000 l	Argentina	2.00	1.25
746 A218a	1500 l	Switzerland	3.00	1.75
747 A218a	2500 l	San Marino	4.00	3.00
748 A218a	4000 l	Spain	8.25	4.75
		Nos. 737-748 (12)	21.73	13.45

St. Damasus I (b. 304) A219

St. Damasus I and: 200 l, Sepulchre of Sts. Marcellinus and Peter. 500 l, Epigraph of St. Januarius. 2000 l, Basilica, Church of the Martyrs Simplicius, Faustinus and Beatrice.

1984, Nov. 27	**Photo.**		**Perf. 14x13½**	
749 A219	200 l	multi	32	22
750 A219	500 l	multi	80	55
751 A219	2000 l	multi	3.50	2.25

St. Methodius (d. 885) — A220

St. Methodius and: 500 l, Madonna and Christ. 600 l, St. Cyril, carrying the body of St. Clement I. 1700 l, Sts. Benedict and Cyril, patrons of Europe.

Photo. & Engr.

1985, May 7			**Perf. 13½x14**	
752 A220	500 l	multi	85	45
753 A220	600 l	multi	1.00	55
754 A220	1700 l	multi	3.00	1.50

St. Thomas More (1477-1535) A221

St. Thomas More (from a portrait by Hans Holbein) and: 250 l, map of British Isles. 400 l, Frontispiece of Utopia. 2000 l, Frontispiece of Domenico Regi's biography of More.

Litho. & Engr.

1985, May 7			**Perf. 14x13½**	
755 A221	250 l	multi	42	22
756 A221	400 l	multi	70	38
757 A221	2000 l	multi	3.50	1.90

St. Gregory VII (ca. 1020-1085) A222

Designs: 150 l, Eagle from Byzantine door, St. Paul's Basilica, Rome. 450 l, St. Gregory blessing. 2500 l, Sarcophagus. 150 l and 450 l vert.

Perf. 13½x14, 14x13½

1985, June 18			**Photo.**	
758 A222	150 l	multi	22	15
759 A222	450 l	multi	70	42
760 A222	2500 l	multi	3.75	2.25

43rd Intl. Eucharistic Congress — A223

Emblem, host, cross and: 100 l, Outline map of Africa. 400 l, Altar and Assembly of Bishops. 600 l, African chalice. 2300 l, African Christian family.

Photo. & Engr.

1985, June 18			**Perf. 13½x14**	
761 A223	100 l	multi	15	6
762 A223	400 l	multi	60	38
763 A223	600 l	multi	90	55
764 A223	2300 l	multi	3.50	2.00

Concordat Agreement Ratification A224

1985, Oct. 15	**Photo.**		**Perf. 14x13½**	
765 A224	400 l	Papal arms, map of Italy	60	32

Coaches A225

1985, Oct. 15			**Litho. & Engr.**	
766 A225	450 l	dp lil rose & int bl	75	38
767 A225	1500 l	brt bl & dp lil rose	2.00	1.40
a		Souvenir sheet of 2, #766-767, perf. 13½x12½	3.75	3.25

Italia '85.

Intl. Peace Year 1986 A226

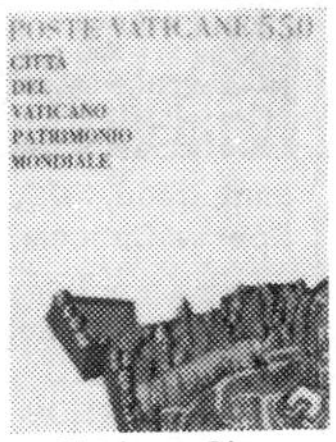

Vatican City A227

Biblical and gospel texts: 50 l, Isaiah 2:4. 350 l, Isaiah 52:7. 450 l, Matthew 5:9. 650 l, Luke 2:14. 2000 l, Message for World Peace, speech of Pope John Paul II, Jan. 1, 1986.

1986, Apr. 14	**Photo.**		**Perf. 14**	
768 A226	50 l	multi	8	5
769 A226	350 l	multi	50	28
770 A226	450 l	multi	70	35
771 A226	650 l	multi	1.00	52
772 A226	2000 l	multi	3.00	1.75
		Nos. 768-772 (5)	5.28	2.95

1986, Apr. 14 *Perf. 13½x14*

773	Block of 6	6.00	2.75
a.-f.	A227 550l, any single	1.00	45

UNESCO World Heritage Campaign. Nos. 773a-773f printed se-tenant in continuous design.

Patron Saints of the Sick — A228

Conversion of St. Augustine (354-430) in 387 — A230

Pontifical Academy of Sciences, 50th Anniv. A229

Designs: No. 774, St. Camillus de Lellis rescuing invalid during Tiber flood, by Pierre Subleyras (1699-1749). No. 775, St. John of God with invalids, by Gomez Moreno (1834-1918). 2000 l, Pope John Paul II visiting the sick.

Litho. & Engr.

1986, June 12 *Perf. 13½x14*

774	A228	700 l	multi	1.10	58
775	A228	700 l	multi	1.10	58
776	A228	2000 l	multi	3.00	1.65

Litho. & Engr.

1986, Oct. 2 *Perf. 14x13½*

School of Athens (details), by Raphael: 1500 l, Scribes. 2500 l, Students learning math.

777	A229	1500 l	multi	2.25	1.30
778	A229	2500 l	multi	3.75	2.10

1987, Apr. 7 **Photo.** *Perf. 13½x14*

Religious art: 300 l, St. Augustine reading St. Paul's Epistles, fresco by Benozzo Gozzoli (1420-1498), Church of St. Augustine, San Gimignano. 400 l, Baptism of St. Augustine, painting by Bartolomeo di Gentile (1470-1534), Vatican Art Gallery. 500 l, Ecstasy of St. Augustine, fresco by Benozzo Gozzoli, Church of St. Augustine. 2200 l, St. Augustine, detail of Disputa del Sacramento, fresco by Raphael (1483-1520), Room of the Segnatura, Apostolic Palace.

779	A230	300 l	multi	48	30
780	A230	400 l	multi	65	40
781	A230	500 l	multi	78	48
782	A230	2200 l	multi	3.50	2.10

Christianization Anniversaries
A231 A232

Seals: 700 l, Church of Riga, 1234-1269. 2400 l, Marian Basilica of the Assumption, Aglona, 1780.

1987, June 2 **Photo.** *Perf. 13½x14*

783	A231	700 l	multi	1.10	75
784	A231	2400 l	multi	3.75	2.50

Christianization of Latvia, 800th anniv.

1987, June 2 *Perf. 13½x14*

Designs: 200 l, Christ, statue in the Lithuanian Chapel, Vatican Crypt. 700 l, Two Angels and Our Lady Holding the Body of Christ, by a Lithuanian artist. 3000 l, Lithuanian shrine.

785	A232	200 l	multi	32	22
786	A232	700 l	multi	1.10	75
787	A232	3000 l	multi	4.75	3.25

Christianization of Lithuania, 600th anniv.

OLYMPHILEX '87, Rome, Aug. 29-Sept. 9 — A233

Details of mosaic from the Baths of Caracalla: 400 l, Judge. 500 l, Athlete. 600 l, Athlete, diff. 2000 l, Athlete, diff.

Litho. & Engr.

1987, Aug. 29 *Perf. 14*

788	A233	400 l	multi	60	40
789	A233	500 l	multi	75	50
790	A233	600 l	multi	90	60
791	A233	2000 l	multi	3.00	2.00

Souvenir Sheet

792	Sheet of 4 + 4 labels	5.25	5.25
a	A233 400 l like No. 788	60	60
b	A233 500 l like No. 789	75	75
c	A233 600 l like No. 780	90	90
d	A233 2000 l like No. 791	3.00	3.00

Stamps from souvenir sheet have a Greek border in blue surrounding vignettes (pictured). Nos. 788-791 have single line border in blue. No. 792 has 4 labels picturing the papel arms, a goblet, a crown and the exhibition emblem.

Inauguration of the Philatelic and Numismatic Museum — A235

Designs: 400 l, Philatelic department, Vatican City, No. 1. 3500 l, Numismatic department, 1000-lire coin of 1986.

1987, Sept. 29 **Photo.** *Perf. 14x13½*

793	A235	400 l	multi	62	42
794	A235	3500 l	multi	5.50	3.75

Journeys of Pope John Paul II, 1985-86 A236

Designs: 50 l, Venezuela, Peru, Ecuador and Trinidad & Tobago, 1985. 250 l, The Netherlands, Luxembourg, Belgium, 1985. 400 l, Togo, Ivory Coast, Cameroun, Central Africa, Zaire, Kenya and Morocco, 1985. 500 l, Liechtenstein, 1986. 4000 l, Bangladesh, Singapore, Fiji, New Zealand, Australia and Seychelles, 1986.

1987, Oct. 27 **Photo.** *Perf. 14x13½*

795	A236	50 l	multi	8	8
796	A236	250 l	multi	40	40
797	A236	400 l	multi	65	65
798	A236	500 l	multi	78	78
799	A236	600 l	multi	95	95
800	A236	700 l	multi	1.10	1.10
801	A236	2500 l	multi	3.95	3.95
802	A236	4000 l	multi	6.50	6.50
			Nos. 795-802 (8)	14.41	14.41

Transfer of St. Nicholas Relics from Myra to Bari, 900th Anniv. — A237

Designs: 500 l, Arrival of relics at Bari. 700 l, Act of charity, three improverished women. 3000 l, Miraculous rescue of ship.

1987, Dec. 3 *Perf. 13½x14*

803	A237	500 l	multi	85	85
804	A237	700 l	multi	1.20	1.20
805	A237	3000 l	multi	5.15	5.15

St. Nicholas of Bari (c. 270-352), bishop of Myra. Legend of Santa Claus originated because of his charitable works. Printed in sheets of 8 + 16 se-tenant labels picturing Santa Claus.

St. John Bosco (1815-1888), Educator A238

Children and: 500 l, Sister of the Institute of the Daughters of Mary Help of Christians. 1000 l, St. John Bosco. 2000 l, Salesian lay brother. Printed se-tenant in a continuous design.

1988, Apr. 19 **Photo.**

806	Strip of 3	5.75	5.75
a	A238 500 l multi	80	80
b	A238 1000 l multi	1.65	1.65
c	A238 2000 l multi	3.30	3.30

Marian Year, 1987-88 — A239

1988, June 16 **Photo.** *Perf. 13½x14*

807	A239	50 l	Annunciation	8	5
808	A239	300 l	Nativity	50	30
809	A239	500 l	Pentecost	80	48
810	A239	750 l	Assumption	1.20	72
811	A239	1000 l	Mother of the Church	1.60	95
812	A239	2400 l	Refuge of Sinners	3.85	2.30
			Nos. 807-812 (6)	8.03	4.80

Baptism of the Rus' of Kiev, Millennium A240

Designs: 450 l, "Prince St. Vladimir the Great," from a 15th cent. icon. 650 l, Cathedral of St. Sophia, Kiev. 2500 l, "Mother of God in Prayer," from a mosaic at the cathedral.

1988, June 16

813	A240	450 l	multi	75	45
814	A240	650 l	multi	1.05	65
815	A240	2500 l	multi	4.00	2.40

Paintings by Paolo Veronese (1528-1588) — A241

Designs: 550 l, Marriage of Cana (Madonna and Christ) the Louvre, Paris. 650 l, Self-portrait of the Artist, Villa Barbaro of Maser, Treviso. 3000 l, Marriage of Cana (woman and two men).

Perf. 13½x14, 14x13½

1988, Sept. 29 Photo. & Engr.

816 A241 550 l multi 80 48
817 A241 650 l multi, horiz. 95 58
818 A241 3000 l multi 4.40 2.65

Christmas A242

Luke 2:14 and: 50 l, Angel facing LR. 400 l, Angel facing UR. 500 l, Angel facing LL. 550 l, Shepherds. 850 l, Nativity. 1500 l, Magi.

1988, Dec. 12 Photo. *Perf. 13½x14*

819 A242 50 l multi 8 5
820 A242 400 l multi 62 30
821 A242 500 l multi 80 40
822 A242 550 l multi 88 45
823 A242 850 l multi 1.35 68
824 A242 1500 l multi 2.35 1.20
Nos. 819-824 (6) 6.08 3.08

Souvenir Sheet

825 Sheet of 6 6.25 3.10
a. A242 50 l gold & multi 8 5
b. A242 400 l gold & multi 62 30
c. A242 500 l gold & multi 80 40
d. A242 550 l gold & multi 88 45
e. A242 850 l gold & multi 1.35 68
f. A242 1500 l gold & multi 2.35 1.20

Nos. 825a-825f printed in a continuous design.

Feast of the Visitation, 600th Anniv. — A243

Illuminations: 550 l, The Annunciation. 750 l, The Visitation (Virgin and St. Elizabeth). 2500 l, Mary, Elizabeth and infants.

1989, May 5 Photo. *Perf. 13½x14*

826 A243 550 l multi 82 40
827 A243 750 l multi 1.15 58
828 A243 2500 l multi 3.75 1.90

Souvenir Sheet

Gregorian Egyptian Museum, 150th Anniv. — A244

Designs: 400 l, Apis. 650 l, Isis and Apis dicephalous bust. 750 l, Statue of the physician Ugiahorresne. 2400 l, Pharaoh Mentuhotep.

Litho. & Engr.

1989, May 5 *Perf. 14x13½*

829 Sheet of 4 6.35 3.20
a. A244 400 l multi 60 30
b. A244 650 l multi 98 50
c. A244 750 l multi 1.15 58
d. A244 2400 l multi 3.60 1.80

SEMI-POSTAL STAMPS

Holy Year Issue

Cross and Orb
SP1 SP2

1933 Unwmk. Engr. *Perf. 13x13½*

B1 SP1 25c + 10c grn 4.25 2.25
B2 SP1 75c + 15c scar 9.50 4.50
B3 SP2 80c + 20c red brn 14.00 14.00
B4 SP2 1.25 l + 25c ultra 6.50 8.75

AIR POST STAMPS

Catalogue values for unused stamps in this section, from this point to the end of the section, are for Never Hinged items.

Statue of St. Peter — AP1

Dove of Peace over Vatican — AP2

Elijah's Ascent into Heaven — AP3

Our Lady of Loreto and Angels Moving the Holy House — AP4

Wmk. 235

1938, June 22 Engr. *Perf. 14*

C1 AP1 25c brown 18 12
C2 AP2 50c green 18 12
C3 AP3 75c lake 18 12
C4 AP4 80c dark bl 18 12
C5 AP1 1 l violet 75 48
C6 AP2 2 l ultra 90 60
C7 AP3 5 l slate blk 2.00 1.50
C8 AP4 10 l dk brn vio 3.00 1.90
Nos. C1-C8 (8) 7.37 4.96

Dove of Peace Above St. Peter's Basilica — AP5

House of Our Lady of Loreto — AP6

Birds Circling Cross — AP7

1947, Nov. 10 Photo.

C9 AP5 1 l rose red 8 8
C10 AP6 4 l dk brn 8 10
C11 AP5 5 l brt ultra 8 10
C12 AP7 15 l brt pur 2.50 65
C13 AP6 25 l dk bl grn 3.25 65
C14 AP7 50 l dk gray 9.00 1.75
C15 AP7 100 l red org 14.00 2.00
Nos. C9-C15 (7) 28.99 5.33

Nos. C13-C15 exist imperf. Value, each pair $1,000.

Archangel Raphael and Young Tobias AP8

1948, Dec. 28 Engr. *Perf. 14*

C16 AP8 250 l sepia 13.00 5.50
C17 AP8 500 l ultra 425.00 275.00

Angels and Globe AP9

1949, Dec. 3

C18 AP9 300 l ultra 27.50 8.25
C19 AP9 1000 l green 110.00 50.00

UPU, 75th anniversary.

Franciscus Gratianus AP10

Dome of St. Peter's Cathedral AP11

1951, Dec. 20 *Perf. 14x13*

C20	AP10	300 l dp plum	200.00	160.00
C21	AP10	500 l dp bl	45.00	17.00

Publication of unified canon laws, 800th anniv.

1953, Aug. 10 *Perf. 13*

C22	AP11	500 l chocolate	20.00	3.00
C23	AP11	1000 l dp ultra	52.50	7.50

See Nos. C33-C34.

Archangel Gabriel by Melozzo da Forli — AP12

Obelisk of St. John Lateran — AP13

Archangel Gabriel: 10 l, 35 l, 100 l, Annunciation by Pietro Cavallini. 15 l, 50 l, 300 l, Annunciation by Leonardo da Vinci.

1956, Feb. 12 **Wmk. 235**

C24	AP12	5 l gray blk	7	7
C25	AP12	10 l bl grn	7	7
C26	AP12	15 l dp org	8	8
C27	AP12	25 l dk car rose	12	14
C28	AP12	35 l carmine	50	42
C29	AP12	50 l ol brn	12	14
C30	AP12	60 l ultra	4.50	3.50
C31	AP12	100 l org brn	12	10
C32	AP12	300 l dp vio	50	42
		Nos. C24-C32 (9)	6.08	4.94

Type of 1953

1958 *Perf. 13½*

C33	AP11	500 l grn & bl grn	14.00	5.50
a.		Perf. 14	550.00	300.00
C34	AP11	1000 l dp mag	1.75	1.10
a.		Perf. 14	1.75	1.00

1959, Oct. 27 **Engr.** *Perf. 13½x14*

Obelisks, Rome: 10 l, 60 l, St. Mary Major. 15 l, 100 l, St. Peter. 25 l, 200 l, Piazza del Popolo. 35 l, 500 l, Trinita dei Monti.

C35	AP13	5 l dl vio	5	5
C36	AP13	10 l bl grn	5	8
C37	AP13	15 l dk brn	5	5
C38	AP13	25 l sl grn	8	8
C39	AP13	35 l ultra	15	8
C40	AP13	50 l yel grn	8	8
C41	AP13	60 l rose car	8	8
C42	AP13	100 l bluish blk	15	8
C43	AP13	200 l brown	25	12
C44	AP13	500 l org brn	50	25
		Nos. C35-C44 (10)	1.44	95

Archangel Gabriel by Filippo Valle AP14

Jet over St. Peter's Cathedral AP15

1962, Mar. 13 **Wmk. 235**

C45	AP14	1000 l brown	1.50	60
C46	AP14	1500 l dk bl	3.50	1.40

1967, Mar. 7 **Photo.** *Perf. 14*

Designs: 40 l, 200 l, Radio tower and statue of Archangel Gabriel (like A87). 90 l, 500 l, Aerial view of St. Peter's Square and Vatican City.

C47	AP15	20 l brt vio	6	5
C48	AP15	40 l blk & pink	8	8
C49	AP15	90 l sl bl & dk gray	12	8
C50	AP15	100 l blk & sal	12	8
C51	AP15	200 l vio blk & gray	28	14
C52	AP15	500 l dk brn & lt brn	60	30
		Nos. C47-C52 (6)	1.26	73

Archangel Gabriel by Fra Angelico — AP16

1968, Mar. 12 **Engr.** *Perf. 13½x14*

C53	AP16	1000 l dk car rose, *cr*	1.25	85
C54	AP16	1500 l black, *cr*	2.50	1.65

St. Matthew, by Fra Angelico AP17

The Evangelists, by Fra Angelico from Niccolina Chapel: 300 l, St. Mark. 500 l, St. Luke. 1000 l, St. John.

Engr. & Photo.
Perf. 14x13½

1971, Sept. 30 **Unwmk.**

C55	AP17	200 l blk & pale grn	50	22
C56	AP17	300 l blk & bis	70	32
C57	AP17	500 l blk & sal	2.50	1.10
C58	AP17	1000 l blk & pale lil	1.25	55

Seraph, Mosaic from St. Mark's Basilica, Venice — AP18

Litho. & Engr.

1974, Feb. 21 *Perf. 13x14*

C59	AP18	2500 l multi	3.00	2.50

Angel with Trumpet — AP19

Designs: 1000 l, Ascending figures. 2500 l, Angels with trumpets. All designs from Last Judgment, by Michelangelo.

Litho. & Engr.

1976, Feb. 19 *Perf. 13x14*

C60	AP19	500 l sal, bl & brn	2.25	1.65
C61	AP19	1000 l sal, bl & brn	1.00	75
C62	AP19	2500 l sal, bl & brn	3.25	2.25

Radio Waves, Antenna, Papal Arms AP20

1978, July 11 **Engr.** *Perf. 14x13*

C63	AP20	1000 l multi	1.10	80
C64	AP20	2000 l multi	3.75	2.75
C65	AP20	3000 l multi	4.00	3.00

10th World Telecommunications Day.

Pope John Paul II Shaking Hands, Arms of Dominican Republic AP21

1980 **Litho. & Engr.** *Perf. 14x13½*

C66	AP21	200 l shown	22	22
C67	AP21	300 l Mexico	30	30
C68	AP21	500 l Poland	60	60
C69	AP21	1000 l Ireland	1.10	1.10
C70	AP21	1500 l United States	1.75	1.75
C71	AP21	2000 l United Nations	2.00	2.00
C72	AP21	3000 l with Dimitrios I, Turkey	3.50	3.50
		Nos. C66-C72 (7)	9.47	9.47

Issue dates: 3000 l, Sept. 18; others June 24.

World Communications Year — AP22

Designs: 2000 l, Moses Explaining The Law to the People by Luca Signarelli. 5000 l, Paul Preaching in Athens, Tapestry of Raphael design.

1983, Nov. 10 *Perf. 14*

C73	AP22	2000 l multi	3.00	3.00
C74	AP22	5000 l multi	7.25	7.25

Journeys of Pope John Paul II, 1983-84 AP23

Designs: 350 l, Central America, the Caribbean, 1983. 450 l, Warsaw Cathedral, Our Lady of Czestochowa, Poland, 1983. 700 l, Statue of Our Lady, Lourdes, France, 1983. 1000 l, Mariazell Sanctuary, St. Stephen's Cathedral, Austria, 1983. 1500 l, Asia, the Pacific, 1984. 2000 l, Einsiedeln Basilica, St. Nicholas of Flue, Switzerland, 1984. 2500 l, Quebec's Notre Dame Cathedral, five crosses of the Jesuit martyrs, Canada, 1984. 5000 l, Saragossa, Spain, Dominican Republic and Puerto Rico, 1984.

1986, Nov. 20 **Photo.** *Perf. 14x13½*

C75	AP23	350 l multi	55	55
C76	AP23	450 l multi	70	70
C77	AP23	700 l multi	1.10	1.10
C78	AP23	1000 l multi	1.50	1.50
C79	AP23	1500 l multi	2.25	2.25
C80	AP23	2000 l multi	3.25	3.25
C81	AP23	2500 l multi	4.00	4.00
C82	AP23	5000 l multi	8.00	8.00
		Nos. C75-C82 (8)	21.35	21.35

Papal Journeys Type of 1986

Designs: 450 l, Horseman, shepherdess, St. Peter's Basilica, Cathedral of Santiago in Chile, and the Sanctuary of Our Lady of Lujan, Argentina. 650 l, Youths and the Cathedral of Speyer, Federal Republic of Germany. 1000 l, St. Peter's Basilica, Altar of Gdansk, flowers and thorns. 2500 l, Crowd and American skyscrapers. 5000 l, Tepee at Fort Simpson, Canada, and American Indians.

1988, Oct. 27 **Photo.** *Perf. 14x13½*

C83	AP23	450 l multi	70	70
C84	AP23	650 l multi	1.00	1.00
C85	AP23	1000 l multi	1.55	1.55
C86	AP23	2500 l multi	3.85	3.85
C87	AP23	5000 l multi	7.75	7.75
		Nos. C83-C87 (5)	14.85	14.85

Uruguay, Chile and Argentina, Mar. 30-Apr. 14, 1987 (450 l); Federal Republic of Germany, Apr. 30-May 4, 1987 (650 l); Poland, June 8-14, 1987 (1000 l); United States, Sept. 10-19, 1987 (2500 l); and Canada, Sept. 20, 1987 (5000 l).

SPECIAL DELIVERY STAMPS

Pius XI SD1

Unwmk.

1929, Aug. 1 **Photo.** *Perf. 14*

E1	SD1	2 l car rose	8.00	5.75
E2	SD1	2.50 l dark blue	5.75	4.50

Catalogue values for unused stamps in this section, from this point to the end of the section, are for Never Hinged items.

Aerial View of Vatican City SD2

1933 **Wmk. 235** **Engr.**

E3	SD2	2 l rose red & brn	8	28
E4	SD2	2.50 l dp bl & brn	14	28

1945 **Unwmk.**

E5	SD2	3.50 l dk car & ultra	28	25
E6	SD2	5 l ultra & grn	42	30

Nos. E5 and E6 Surcharged with New Values and Bars in Black

1946, Jan. 9

E7	SD2	6 l on 3.50 l dk car & ultra	2.75	1.65
E8	SD2	12 l on 5 l ultra & grn	2.75	1.65

Vertical pairs imperf. between exist of No. E7 (value $150) and No. E8 (value $200).

Bishop Matteo Giberti SD3

Design: 12 l, Gaspar Cardinal Contarini.

1946, Feb. 21 **Photo.**

Centers in Dark Brown

E9	SD3	6 l dk grn	12	8
E10	SD3	12 l cop brn	15	12

See note after No. 121.

Nos. E9-E10 exist imperf. and part perforate.

Basilica of St. Peter — SD5

Design: 80 l, Basilica of St. John.

1949 Wmk. 235 *Perf. 14*

E11 SD5 40 l sl gray 8.25 3.50
a. Perf. 13½x14 12.50 4.50
E12 SD5 80 l chnt brn 12.00 6.00
a. Perf. 13½x14 14.00 9.00

St. Peter and His Tomb — SD6

Design: 85 l, Pius XII and Roman sepulcher.

Perf. 13½x13, 14

1953, Apr. 23 Engr.

E13 SD6 50 l bl grn & dk brn 18 14
E14 SD6 85 l dp org & dk brn 55 38

Arms of Pope John XXIII SD7

1960 Photo. *Perf. 14*

E15 SD7 75 l red & brn 12 12
E16 SD7 100 l dk bl & brn 16 16

Pope Paul VI by Enrico Manfrini — SD8

Design: 150 l, Papal arms.

1966, Mar. 8 Wmk. 235 *Perf. 14*

E17 SD8 150 l black brn 16 12
E18 SD8 180 l brown 22 16

POSTAGE DUE STAMPS

Regular Issue of 1929 Overprinted in Black and Brown

SEGNATASSE

1931 Unwmk. *Perf. 14*

J1 A1 5c dk brn & pink 12 15
a. Double frame
J2 A1 10c dk grn & lt grn 12 15
a. Frame omitted *400.00*
J3 A1 20c vio & lil 6.00 2.00

Surcharged

SEGNATASSE 40

J4 A1 40c on 30c ind & yel 1.50 *4.00*

Surcharged

LIRE 1,10 SEGNATASSE

J5 A2 60c on 2 l ol brn 35.00 18.00
J6 A2 1.10 l on 2.50 l red org 3.25 *16.00*
Nos. J1-J6 (6) 45.99 *40.30*

In addition to the surcharges, Nos. J4 to J6 are overprinted with ornamental frame as on J1 to J3.

Catalogue values for unused stamps in this section, from this point to the end of the section, are for Never Hinged items.

Papal Arms
D1 D2

1945 Unwmk. Typo. *Perf. 14*

J7 D1 5c blk & yel 6 6
J8 D1 20c blk & lilac 6 6
J9 D1 80c blk & salmon 6 6
J10 D1 1 l blk & green 6 6
J11 D1 2 l blk & blue 6 6
J12 D1 5 l blk & gray 6 6
a. Imperf., pair 125.00 125.00
Nos. J7-J12 (6) 36 36

A second type of Nos. J7-J12 exists, in which the colored lines of the background are thicker.

The 20c and 5 lire exist in horizontal pairs imperf. vertically. Value, each $30.

The 20c exists in horizontal pairs imperf. between. Value $80.

Perf. 13½x13

1954 Wmk. 235 Engr.

J13 D2 4 l blk & rose 35 15
J14 D2 6 l blk & green 80 30
J15 D2 10 l blk & yel 25 15
J16 D2 20 l blk & blue 1.25 30
J17 D2 50 l blk & ol brn 35 6
J18 D2 70 l blk & red brn 35 10
Nos. J13-J18 (6) 3.35 1.06

Papal Arms — D3

Photo. & Engr.

1968, May 28 Wmk. 235 *Perf. 14*

J19 D3 10 l blk, *grysh bl* 5 5
J20 D3 20 l blk, *pale bl* 6 6
J21 D3 50 l blk, *pale lil rose* 6 6
J22 D3 60 l blk, *gray* 8 8
J23 D3 100 l blk, *dl yel* 12 12
J24 D3 180 l blk, *bluish lil* 22 22
Nos. J19-J24 (6) 59 59

PARCEL POST STAMPS

Regular Issue of 1929 Overprinted

PER PACCHI

1931 Unwmk. *Perf. 14*

Q1 A1 5c dk brn & pink 38 30
Q2 A1 10c dk grn & lt grn 38 30
Q3 A1 20c vio & lil 4.75 5.50
Q4 A1 25c dk bl & lt bl 6.25 4.25
Q5 A1 30c ind & yel 9.25 4.25
Q6 A1 50c ind & sal buff 9.25 4.25
Q7 A1 75c brn car & gray 2.75 2.75

Overprinted

PER PACCHI

Q8 A2 80c car rose 1.65 1.90
Q9 A2 1.25 l dk bl 2.75 2.00
Q10 A2 2 l ol brn 55 85
a. Inverted overprint 325.00 475.00
Q11 A2 2.50 l red org 55 85
a. Double overprint 225.00
b. Inverted overprint 500.00
Q12 A2 5 l dk grn 55 85
Q13 A2 10 l ol blk 55 85
a. Double overprint 325.00

Special Delivery Stamps of 1929 Overprinted Vertically

PER PACCHI

Q14 SD1 2 l car rose 55 85
Q15 SD1 2.50 l dk bl 55 85
Nos. Q1-Q15 (15) 40.71 30.60

VENEZUELA

LOCATION — Northern coast of South America, bordering on the Caribbean Sea.
GOVT. — Republic
AREA — 352,143 sq. mi.
POP. — 15,260,000 (est. 1984)
CAPITAL — Caracas

100 Centavos = 8 Reales = 1 Peso
100 Centesimos = 1 Venezolano (1879)
100 Centimos = 1 Bolivar (1880)

Catalogue values for unused stamps in this country are for Never Hinged items, beginning with Scott 743 in the regular postage section, Scott B2 in the semi-postal section, Scott C709 in the airpost section, and Scott E1 in the special delivery section..

Values of early Venezuela stamps vary according to condition. Quotations for Nos. 1-21 are for fine copies. Very fine to superb specimens sell at much higher prices, and inferior or poor copies sell at reduced prices, depending on the condition of the individual specimen.

Coat of Arms — A1

Fine Impression
No Dividing Line Between Stamps

Unwmk.

1859, Jan. 1 Litho. *Imperf.*

1 A1 ½r yellow 17.50 7.00
a ½r org 20.00 8.00
b Greenish paper *200.00*
2 A1 1r blue 250.00 16.00
3 A1 2r red 32.50 11.00
a 2r dl rose red 40.00 13.00
b Half used as 1r on cover 200.00
c Greenish paper 200.00 125.00

Coarse Impression

1859-62

Thick Paper

4 A1 ½r orange ('61) 8.00 3.00
a ½r yel ('59) 425.00 20.00
b ½r ol yel 650.00 30.00
c Bluish paper 525.00
d ½r dl rose (error)
5 A1 1r blue ('62) 17.50 8.75
a 1r pale bl 25.00 9.25
b 1r dk bl 25.00 9.25
c Half used as ½r on cover *200.00*
d Bluish paper 175.00
6 A1 2r red ('62) 22.50 12.50
a 2r dl rose 27.50 14.00
b Tete beche pair *4,500.* *3,250.*
c Half used as 1r on cover *165.00*
d Bluish paper *200.00*

In the fine impression, the background lines of the shield are more sharply drawn. In the coarse impression, the shading lines at each end of the scroll inscribed "LIBERTAD" are usually very heavy. Stamps of the coarse impression are closer together, and there is usually a dividing line between them.

Nos. 1-3 exist on thick paper and on bluish paper. Nos. 1-6 exist on pelure paper.

The greenish paper varieties (Nos. 1b and 3c) and the bluish paper varities were not regularly issued.

Arms — A2

Eagle — A3

1862 Litho.

7 A2 ¼c green 17.50 80.00
8 A2 ½c dl lil 22.50 *150.00*
a ½c vio 27.50 160.00
9 A2 1c gray brn 32.50 170.00

Counterfeits are plentiful. Forged cancellations abound on Nos. 7-17.

1863-64

10 A3 ½c pale red ('64) 40.00 *65.00*
a ½c red 45.00 *100.00*
11 A3 1c sl ('64) 45.00 *75.00*
12 A3 ½r orange 5.50 2.50
13 A3 1r blue 16.00 7.50
a 1r pale bl 22.50 10.00
b Half used as ½r on cover *100.00*
14 A3 2r green 22.50 20.00
a 2r dp yel grn 27.50 20.00
b Quarter used as ½r on cover *200.00*
c Half used as 1r on cover *150.00*

Counterfeits exist.

Redrawn

1865

15 A3 ½r orange 3.00 1.75
a ½r yel 3.00 1.75

The redrawn stamp has a broad "N" in "FEDERACION". "MEDIO REAL" and "FEDERACION" are in thin letters. There are 52 instead of 49 pearls in the circle.

The status of No. 15 has been questioned.

A4

Simon Bolivar — A5

1865-70

16 A4 ½c yel grn ('67) 165.00 250.00
17 A4 1c bl grn ('67) 165.00 *200.00*
18 A4 ½r brn vio (thin paper) 6.50 1.50
19 A4 ½r lil rose ('70) 8.00 2.50
a ½r brnsh rose 8.00 3.00
b Tete beche pair 90.00 *125.00*
20 A4 1r vermilion 32.50 15.00
a Half used as ½r on cover *100.00*
21 A4 2r yellow 110.00 60.00
a Half used as 1r on cover *300.00*
b Quarter used as ½r on cover *350.00*

This issue is known unofficially rouletted.

Postal forgeries exist of the ½r.

Overprinted in Very Small Upright Letters "Bolivar Sucre Miranda - Decreto de 27 de Abril de 1870", or "Decreto de 27 de Junio 1870" in Slanting Letters

(The "Junio" overprint is continuously repeated, in four lines arranged in two pairs, with the second line of each pair inverted.)

1871-76 Litho.

22 A5 1c yellow 75 25
a 1c org 1.25 42
b 1c brn org ('76) 1.25 25
c 1c pale buff ('76) 1.25 38
d Laid paper 2.50 50
23 A5 2c yellow 1.25 38
a 2c org 3.50 38
b 2c brn org 3.00 65
c 2c pale buff ('76) 3.00 38

d		Laid paper	3.00	50
e		Frame inverted	*4,000.*	*3,000.*
24	A5	3c yellow	2.00	50
a		3c org	2.50	1.25
b		3c pale buff ('76)	4.50	1.50
25	A5	4c yellow	2.50	50
a		4c org	4.00	1.10
b		4c brn org ('76)	4.00	1.10
c		4c buff ('76)	4.00	1.10
26	A5	5c yellow	2.50	50
a		5c org	2.50	75
b		5c pale buff ('76)	2.50	75
c		Laid paper	5.50	75
27	A5	1r rose	2.50	38
a		1r pale red	2.50	38
b		Laid paper	4.50	75
28	A5	2r rose	4.00	65
a		2r pale red	4.00	65
29	A5	3r rose	4.50	65
a		3r pale red	4.50	65
30	A5	5r rose	4.50	85
a		5r pale red	4.50	85
31	A5	7r rose	5.50	2.00
a		7r pale red	5.50	2.00
32	A5	9r green	14.00	3.75
a		9r ol grn	14.00	5.00
33	A5	15r green	27.50	7.50
a		15r gray grn ('76)	27.50	7.50
b		Frame inverted	*8,000.*	*6,500.*
34	A5	20r green	65.00	12.50
a		Laid paper	100.00	32.50
35	A5	30r green	300.00	100.00
a		30r gray grn ('76)	575.00	150.00
b		Double overprint		
36	A5	50r green	1,000.	275.00
a.		50r gray green ('76)		

These stamps were made available for postage and revenue by official decree, and were the only stamps sold for postage in Venezuela from Mar., 1871 to Aug., 1873.

Due to lack of canceling stamps, the majority of specimens were canceled with pen marks. Fiscal cancellations were also made with the pen. The values quoted are for pen-canceled copies.

Different settings were used for the different overprints. Stamps with the upright letters were issued in 1871. Those with the slanting letters in one double line were issued in 1872-73. Specimens with the slanting overprint in two double lines were issued starting in 1874 from several different settings, those of 1877-78 showing much coarser impressions of the design than the earlier issues. The 7r and 9r are not known with this overprint. Stamps on laid paper (1875) are from a separate setting.

Stamps and Types of 1866-67

Overprinted in Two Lines of Very Small Letters Repeated Continuously

Overprinted "Estampillas de Correo - Contrasena"

1873, July 1

37	A4	½r pale rose	55.00	12.50
a		½r rose	55.00	12.50
b		Inverted overprint	115.00	52.50
c		Tete beche pair	*2,500.*	*1,900.*
38	A4	1r vermilion	65.00	17.50
a		Inverted overprint	375.00	200.00
39	A4	2r yellow	125.00	62.50
a		Inverted overprint	375.00	200.00

Overprinted "Contrasena - Estampillas de Correo"

1873, Nov.

40	A4	1c gray lil	22.50	25.00
a		Inverted overprint	7.00	*15.00*
41	A4	2c green	85.00	85.00
a		Inverted overprint	32.50	42.50
42	A4	½r rose	55.00	10.00
a		Inverted overprint	22.50	3.00
b		½r pink	50.00	9.25
43	A4	1r vermilion	65.00	17.50
a		Inverted overprint	27.50	7.50
44	A4	2r yellow	225.00	100.00
a		Inverted overprint	95.00	50.00

Overprinted "Contrasena - Estampilla de Correos"

1875

45	A4	½r rose	65.00	7.50
a		Inverted overprint	110.00	20.00
b		Double overprint	145.00	80.00
46	A4	1r vermilion	95.00	15.00
a		Inverted overprint	175.00	70.00
b		Tete beche pair	*3,250.*	*2,750.*

Overprinted "Estampillas de correo - Contrasena"

1876-77

47	A4	½r rose	65.00	7.50
a		½r pink	65.00	7.50
b		Inverted overprint	65.00	7.50
c		Both lines of overprint read "Contrasena"	75.00	17.50
d		Both lines of overprint read "Estampillas de correo"	75.00	17.50
e		Double ovpt.	125.00	35.00
48	A4	1r vermilion ('77)	75.00	25.00
a		Inverted overprint	85.00	30.00
b		Tete beche pair	*2,250.*	*2,500.*

On Nos. 47 and 48 "correo" has a small "c" instead of a capital. Nos. 45 and 46 have the overprint in slightly larger letters than the other stamps of the 1873-76 issues.

Simón Bolívar
A6 A7

Overprinted "Decreto de 27 Junio 1870" Twice

One Line Inverted

1879

49	A6	1c yellow	2.50	20
a		1c org	3.50	75
b		1c ol yel	4.00	1.00
50	A6	5c yellow	3.50	50
a		5c org	2.50	75
b		Double overprint	20.00	10.00
51	A6	10c blue	5.00	50
52	A6	30c blue	6.25	1.00
53	A6	50c blue	7.50	1.00
54	A6	90c blue	30.00	6.25
55	A7	1v rose red	65.00	8.75
56	A7	3v rose red	110.00	35.00
57	A7	5v rose red	190.00	65.00

In 1879 and the early part of 1880 there were no regular postage stamps in Venezuela and the stamps inscribed "Escuelas" were permitted to serve for postal as well as revenue purposes. Postally canceled copies are extremely scarce. Values quoted are for stamps with cancellations of banks or business houses or with pen cancellations. Copies with pen marks removed are sometimes offered as unused stamps, or may have fraudulent postal cancellations added.

Nos. 49-57 exist without overprint. These probably are revenue stamps.

A8 A9

1880 ***Perf. 11***

58	A8	5c yellow	1.25	10
a		5c org	1.25	20
b		Printed on both sides	150.00	85.00
59	A8	10c yellow	2.00	20
a		10c org	2.00	20
60	A8	25c yellow	1.75	25
a		25c org	2.00	32
b		Printed on both sides	110.00	52.50
c		Impression of 5c on back	*175.00*	90.00
61	A8	50c yellow	3.50	30
a		50c org	4.00	32
b		Half used as 25c on cover		18.00
c		Printed on both sides	150.00	90.00
d		Impression of 25c on back	150.00	90.00
62	A9	1b pale bl	8.75	75
63	A9	2b pale bl	14.00	85
64	A9	5b pale bl	32.50	75
a		Half used as 2½b on cover		200.00
65	A9	10b rose red	165.00	65.00
66	A9	20b rose red	1,000.	165.00
67	A9	25b rose red	*4,250.*	500.00

See note on used values below No. 57.

Bolivar — A10

1880 Litho. *Perf. 11*

Thick or Thin Paper

68	A10	5c blue	7.50	4.00
a		Printed on both sides	200.00	125.00
69	A10	10c rose	12.50	7.50
a		10c car	12.50	7.50
b		Double impression	80.00	65.00
c		Horizontal pair, imperf. btwn.	65.00	65.00
70	A10	10c scarlet	15.00	10.00
a		Horiz. pair, imperf. between	65.00	65.00
71	A10	25c yellow	7.50	4.00
b		Thick paper	20.00	10.00
72	A10	50c brown	40.00	20.00
a		50c dp brn	40.00	20.00
b		Printed on both sides	200.00	125.00
73	A10	1b green	60.00	30.00
a		Horizontal pair, imperf. between	250.00	250.00
		Nos. 68-73 (6)	142.50	75.50

Nos. 68 to 73 were used for the payment of postage on letters to be sent abroad and the Escuelas stamps were then restricted to internal use.

Counterfeits of this issue exist in a great variety of shades as well as in wrong colors. They are on thick and thin paper, white or toned, and imperf. or perforated 11, 12 and compound. They are also found tete beche. Counterfeits of Nos. 68 to 72 inclusive often have a diagonal line across the "S" of "CENTS" and a short line from the bottom of that letter to the frame below it. Originals of No. 73 show parts of a frame around "BOLIVAR".

Simón Bolívar
A11 A12

A13 A14

A15

1882, Aug. 1 Engr. *Perf. 12*

74	A11	5c blue	50	20
75	A12	10c red brn	50	20
76	A13	25c yel brn	65	25
a		Printed on both sides	50.00	27.50
77	A14	50c green	1.50	40
78	A15	1b violet	2.50	1.00
		Nos. 74-78 (5)	5.65	2.05

Nos. 75-78 exist imperf. Value, set $32.50.

A16 A17

A18 A19

A20 A21

A22 A23

1882-88

79	A16	5c bl grn	8	5
80	A17	10c brown	8	5
81	A18	25c orange	8	5
82	A19	50c blue	10	5
83	A20	1b vermilion	15	10
84	A21	3b dl vio ('88)	15	10
85	A22	10b dk brn ('88)	50	50
86	A23	20b plum ('88)	65	65
		Nos. 79-86 (8)	1.79	1.55

By official decree, dated April 14, 1882, stamps of types A11 to A15 were to be used for foreign postage and those of types A16 to A23 for inland correspondence and fiscal use.

Issue dates: Nos. 79-83, Aug. 1.

1887-88 Litho. *Perf. 11*

87	A16	5c gray grn	25	18
88	A13	25c yel brn	42.50	15.00
89	A18	25c orange	38	32
90	A20	1b org red ('88)	3.50	75

Perf. 14

91	A16	5c gray grn	70.00	22.50

Stamps of type A16, perf. 11 and 14, are from a new die with "ESCUELAS" in smaller letters. Stamps of the 1887-88 issue, perf. 12, and a 50c dark blue, perf. 11 or 12, are believed by experts to be from printer's waste.

Counterfeits of No. 91 have been made by perforating printers waste of No. 96.

Rouletted 8

92	A11	5c blue	30.00	15.00
93	A13	25c yel brn	15.00	7.50
94	A14	50c green	15.00	7.50
95	A15	1b purple	30.00	15.00

1887-88

96	A16	5c green	6	6
97	A18	25c orange	6	6
98	A19	50c dk bl	38	38
99	A21	3b pur ('88)	1.90	1.90

The so-called imperforate varieties of Nos. 92 to 99, and the pin perforated 50c dark blue, type A19, are believed to be from printer's waste.

Stamps of 1882-88 Handstamp Surcharged in Violet

1892 *Perf. 12*

100	A11	25c on 5c bl	*30.00*	*30.00*
101	A12	25c on 10c red brn	*12.00*	*12.00*
102	A13	1b on 25c yel brn	*12.00*	*12.00*
103	A14	1b on 50c grn	*13.50*	*13.50*

See note after No. 107.

1892

104	A16	25c on 5c bl grn	*10.00*	*6.00*
105	A17	25c on 10c brn	*10.00*	*6.00*
106	A18	1b on 25c org	*12.50*	*7.00*
107	A19	1b on 50c bl	*17.50*	*7.00*

Counterfeits of this surcharge abound.

Stamps of 1882-88 Overprinted in Red or Black:

1893

108	A11	5c bl (R)	50	20
a		Inverted overprint	3.25	3.25
b		Double overprint	16.00	16.00
109	A12	10c red brn (Bk)	65	65
a		Inverted overprint	4.00	4.00
b		Double overprint	16.00	16.00
110	A13	25c yel brn (R)	50	25
a		Inverted overprint	5.25	5.25
b		Double overprint	16.00	16.00
c		25c yel brn (Bk)	250.00	250.00
111	A14	50c grn (R)	65	40
a		Inverted overprint	5.25	5.25
b		Double overprint	27.50	27.50
112	A15	1b pur (R)	1.50	60
a		Inverted ovpt.	10.00	10.00
		Nos. 108-112 (5)	3.80	2.10

1893

No.	Type	Description	Unused	Used
114	A16	5c bl grn (R)	8	7
a		Inverted overprint	3.25	3.25
b		Double overprint	5.25	5.25
115	A17	10c brn (R)	8	8
a		Inverted overprint	3.25	3.25
116	A18	25c org (R)	8	8
a		Inverted overprint	3.25	3.25
117	A18	25c org (Bk)	2.25	2.00
a		Inverted overprint	8.25	5.00
118	A19	50c bl (R)	8	8
a		Inverted overprint	3.25	3.25
119	A20	1b ver (Bk)	45	22
a		Inverted overprint	4.00	4.00
120	A21	3b dl vio (R)	60	30
a		Double overprint	8.25	8.25
121	A22	10b dk brn (R)	1.75	1.50
a		Double overprint	10.00	10.00
b		Inverted ovpt.	20.00	20.00
122	A23	20b plum (Bk)	1.50	1.50
a		Double overprint	10.00	20.00
b.		Inverted overprint		
		Nos. 114-122 (9)	6.87	5.83

Counterfeits exist.

Simon Bolivar
A24 A25

1893 **Engr.**

No.	Type	Description	Unused	Used
123	A24	5c red brn	70	15
124	A24	10c blue	3.00	75
125	A24	25c magenta	15.00	40
126	A24	50c brn vio	3.00	50
127	A24	1b green	4.00	75
		Nos. 123-127 (5)	25.70	2.55

Many shades exist in this issue, but their values do not vary.

1893

No.	Type	Description	Unused	Used
128	A25	5c gray	6	5
129	A25	10c green	6	5
130	A25	25c blue	6	5
131	A25	50c orange	6	5
132	A25	1b red vio	20	6
133	A25	3b red	35	12
134	A25	10b dl vio	65	50
135	A25	20b red brn	2.00	1.75
		Nos. 128-135 (8)	3.44	2.63

By decree of November 28th, 1892, the stamps inscribed "Correos" were to be used for external postage and those inscribed "Instruccion" were for internal postage and revenue purposes.

After July 1, 1895, stamps inscribed "Escuelas" or "Instruccion" were no longer available for postage.

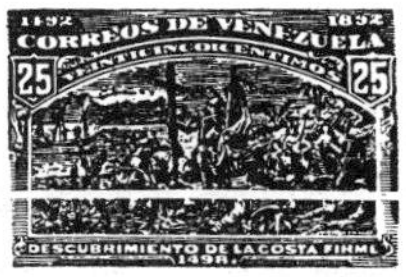

Landing of Columbus
A26

1893 ***Perf. 12***

No.	Type	Description	Unused	Used
136	A26	25c magenta	10.00	50

4th cent. of the discovery of the mainland of South America, also participation of Venezuela in the Intl. Exhib. at Chicago in 1893.

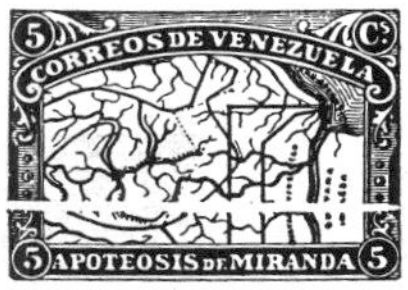

Map of Venezuela
A27

1896 **Litho.**

No.	Type	Description	Unused	Used
137	A27	5c yel grn	2.50	2.00
a		5c ap grn	2.50	2.00
138	A27	10c blue	2.50	2.00
139	A27	25c yellow	3.00	4.00
a		25c org	3.00	4.00
b		Tete beche pair	40.00	40.00
140	A27	50c rose red	40.00	20.00
a		50c red	40.00	40.00
b		Tete beche pair	125.00	125.00
141	A27	1b violet	35.00	20.00
		Nos. 137-141 (5)	83.00	48.00

Gen. Francisco Antonio Gabriel de Miranda (1752-1816).

These stamps were in use from July 4 to Nov. 4, 1896. Later usage is known.

There are many forgeries of this issue. They include faked errors, imperforate stamps and many tete beche. The paper of the originals is thin, white and semi-transparent. The gum is shiny and crackled. The paper of the reprints is often thick and opaque. The gum is usually dull, smooth, thin and only slightly adhesive.

Bolivar — A28

1899-1901 **Engr.**

No.	Type	Description	Unused	Used
142	A28	5c dk grn	75	20
143	A28	10c red	1.00	25
144	A28	25c blue	1.20	40
145	A28	50c gray blk	1.50	75
146	A28	50c org ('01)	1.20	38
147	A28	1b yel grn	25.00	12.50
149	A28	2b orange	300.00	190.00
		Nos. 142-147,149 (7)	330.65	204.48

Stamps of 1899 Overprinted in Black

1900

No.	Type	Description	Unused	Used
150	A28	5c dk grn	75	20
a		Inverted ovpt.	4.00	4.00
151	A28	10c red	75	25
a		Inverted ovpt.	5.25	5.25
b		Double ovpt.	10.50	10.50
152	A28	25c blue	5.00	75
a		Inverted ovpt.	10.50	10.50
153	A28	50c gray blk	2.50	38
a		Inverted ovpt.	9.25	9.25
154	A28	1b yel grn	1.00	50
a		Double overprint	13.00	13.00
b		Inverted ovpt.	9.25	9.25
155	A28	2b orange	1.75	1.25
a		Inverted ovpt	27.50	27.50
b		Double ovpt.	32.50	32.50
		Nos. 150-155 (6)	11.75	3.33

Initials are those of R. T. Mendoza.

Counterfeit overprints exist, especially of inverted and doubled varieties.

Bolivar Type of 1899-1903 Issue

Overprinted **1900**

1900

No.	Type	Description	Unused	Used
156	A28	5c dk grn	150.00	150.00
157	A28	10c red	150.00	150.00
158	A28	25c blue	300.00	150.00
159	A28	50c yel orange	18.00	1.00
160	A28	1b slate	1.00	75
a		Without overprint	*4,000.*	

Overprinted

1900, Aug. 14

No.	Type	Description	Unused	Used
161	A28	5c green	5.00	35
a		Inverted overprint	8.00	6.50
162	A28	10c red	4.00	65
a		Inverted overprint	8.00	6.50
163	A28	25c blue	5.00	60
a		Inverted ovpt.	10.00	6.50

Overprint exists on each value without "Castro" or without "1900."

A34

1904 **Black Surcharge** ***Perf. 12***

No.	Type	Description	Unused	Used
230	A34	5c on 50c grn	50	40
a		"Vele"	18.00	18.00
b		Surch. reading up	75	35
c		Double surcharge	18.00	18.00

Gen. Jose de Sucre — A35 Pres. Cipriano Castro — A37

1904-09 **Engr.**

No.	Type	Description	Unused	Used
231	A35	5c bl grn	30	10
232	A35	10c carmine	40	10
233	A35	15c vio ('09)	65	20
234	A35	25c dp ultra	5.00	20
235	A35	50c plum	65	30
236	A35	1b plum	70	30
		Nos. 231-236 (6)	7.70	1.20

Issue date: July 1, 1904.

1905, July 5 **Litho.** ***Perf. 11½***

No.	Type	Description	Unused	Used
245	A37	5c vermilion	3.00	3.00
a		5c car	4.50	4.50
246	A37	10c dk bl	5.00	4.00
247	A37	25c yellow	1.50	1.25

National Congress. Issued for interior postage only.

Various part-perforate varieties of Nos. 245-247 exist. Value, $15-$30.

Liberty — A38

1910, Apr. 19 **Engr.** ***Perf. 12***

No.	Type	Description	Unused	Used
249	A38	25c dark blue	11.00	65

Centenary of national independence.

Francisco de Miranda A39 Rafael Urdaneta A40

Bolivar — A41

1911 **Litho.** ***Perf. 11½x12***

No.	Type	Description	Unused	Used
250	A39	5c dp grn	30	10
251	A39	10c carmine	30	12
252	A40	15c gray	4.00	25
253	A40	25c dp bl	2.00	38
a		Imperf., pair	40.00	50.00
254	A41	50c purple	2.50	30
255	A41	1b yellow	2.50	1.25
		Nos. 250-255 (6)	11.60	2.40

The 50c with center in blue was never issued although copies were postmarked by favor.

The centers of Nos. 250-255 were separately printed and often vary in shade from the rest of the design. In a second printing of the 5c and 10c, the entire design was printed at one time.

Redrawn

1913

No.	Type	Description	Unused	Used
255A	A40	15c gray	3.00	2.00
255B	A40	25c dp bl	1.50	50
255C	A41	50c purple	1.50	50

The redrawn stamps have two berries instead of one at top of the left spray; a berry has been added over the "C" and "S" of "Centimos"; and the lowest leaf at the right is cut by the corner square.

Simon Bolivar
A42 A43

1914, July **Engr.** ***Perf. 13½, 14, 15***

No.	Type	Description	Unused	Used
256	A42	5c yel grn	25.00	35
257	A42	10c scarlet	22.50	30
258	A42	25c dk bl	4.25	12

Printed by the American Bank Note Co.

Different Frames

1915-23 ***Perf. 12***

No.	Type	Description	Unused	Used
259	A43	5c green	3.25	20
260	A43	10c vermilion	9.50	38
261	A43	10c cl ('22)	9.50	70
262	A43	15c dl ol grn	7.50	42
263	A43	25c ultra	5.00	20
a		25c bl	10.00	50
264	A43	40c dl grn	17.50	7.50
265	A43	50c dp vio	4.50	50
266	A43	50c ultra ('23)	11.00	3.75
267	A43	75c lt bl	45.00	15.00
a		75c grnsh bl	45.00	15.00
268	A43	1b dk gray	20.00	5.00
		Nos. 259-268 (10)	132.75	33.65

Type of 1915-23 Issue
Printed by Waterlow & Sons, Ltd.
Re-engraved

1924-39 ***Perf. 12½***

No.	Type	Description	Unused	Used
269	A43	5c org brn	40	10
a		5c yel brn	40	10
b		Horiz. pair, imperf. between	25.00	40.00
c		Perf. 14	5.25	1.25
270	A43	5c grn ('39)	7.50	80
271	A43	7½c yel grn ('39)	75	25
272	A43	10c dk grn	15	8
a		Perf. 14	5.25	1.25
273	A43	10c dk car ('39)	2.50	20
274	A43	15c ol grn	1.50	35
a		Perf. 14	6.50	2.00
275	A43	15c brn ('27)	25	8
276	A43	25c ultra	1.50	8
a		Perf. 14	10.00	3.00
277	A43	25c red ('28)	15	8
a		Horizontal pair, imperf. between	50.00	85.00
278	A43	40c dp bl ('25)	40	12
279	A43	40c sl bl ('39)	5.00	75
280	A43	50c dk bl	40	12
a		Perf. 14	25.00	10.50
281	A43	50c dk pur ('39)	6.00	70
282	A43	1b black	40	20
a		Perf. 14	32.50	20.00
283	A43	3b yel org ('25)	1.25	70
284	A43	3b red org ('39)	12.50	4.00
285	A43	5b dl vio ('25)	15.00	8.00
		Nos. 269-285 (17)	55.65	16.61

The re-engraved stamps may readily be distinguished from the 1915 issue by the perforation and sometimes by the colors. The designs differ in many minor details which are too minute for illustration or description.

Bolivar and Sucre
A44

Perf. 11½x12, 12

1924, Dec. 1 **Litho.**

No.	Type	Description	Unused	Used
286	A44	25c grysh bl	2.75	50

Redrawn

No.	Type	Description	Unused	Used
286A	A44	25c ultra	3.50	75

Centenary of the Battle of Ayacucho.

The redrawn stamp has a whiter effect with less shading in the faces. Bolivar's ear is clearly visible and the outline of his aquiline nose is broken.

A45

A46

Revenue Stamps Surcharged in Black or Red

1926 *Perf. 12, 12½*

287 A45	5c on 1b ol grn	50	25
a	Double surcharge	8.00	8.00
b	Pair, one without surcharge	12.00	12.00
c	Inverted surcharge	8.00	8.00
288 A46	25c on 5c dk brn (R)	50	30
a	Inverted surcharge	8.00	8.00
b	Double surcharge	8.00	8.00

View of Ciudad Bolivar and General J.V. Gomez — A47

1928, July 21 **Litho.** *Perf. 12*

289 A47	10c dp grn	65	40
a	Imperf., pair	40.00	

Commemorative of the twenty-fifth anniversary of the Battle of Ciudad Bolivar and the foundation of peace in Venezuela.

Simón Bolivar
A48 A49

1930, Dec. 9

290 A48	5c yellow	75	30
a	Imperf., pair	5.25	5.25
291 A48	10c dk bl	75	20
a	Imperf., pair	6.50	6.50
292 A48	25c rose red	75	20
a	Imperf., pair	10.50	10.50

Death centenary of Simón Bolivar (1783-1830), South American liberator.

Nos. 290-292 exist part-perforate, including pairs imperf. between, imperf. horiz., imperf. vert. Value range, $6-12.

Various Frames

Bluish Winchester Security Paper

1932-38 **Engr.** *Perf. 12½*

293 A49	5c	violet	30	8
294 A49	7½c	dk grn ('37)	70	30
295 A49	10c	green	40	8
296 A49	15c	yellow	1.00	20
297 A49	22½c	dp car ('38)	2.50	50
298 A49	25c	red	75	8
299 A49	37½c	ultra ('36)	3.00	1.50
300 A49	40c	indigo	3.00	20
301 A49	50c	ol grn	3.00	30
302 A49	1b	lt bl	4.00	65
303 A49	3b	brown	30.00	12.50
304 A49	5b	yel brn	40.00	16.00
	Nos. 293-304 (12)		88.65	32.39

Arms of Bolivar — A50

1933, July 24 **Litho.** *Perf. 11*

306 A50	25c brn red	2.00	1.50
a	Imperf., pair	32.50	32.50

150th anniv. of the birth of Simón Bolivar.

Stamps of 1924-32 Surcharged in Black: (Blocks of Surcharge in Color of stamps)

1933
7½

1933

307 A43	7½c on 10c grn	40	20
a	Double surch.	2.50	2.50
b	Inverted surch.	3.25	3.25
308 A49	22½c on 25c red (#298)	1.40	70
309 A43	22½c on 25c red (#277)	1.25	1.25
a	Double surcharge	10.00	10.00
310 A43	37½c on 40c dp bl	1.50	75
a	Double surcharge	11.50	11.50
b	Inverted surcharge	8.25	8.25

Nurse and Child — A51

River Scene — A52

Gathering Cacao Pods — A53

Cattle Raising A54

Plowing A55

Perf. 11, 11½ or Compound

1937, June 25 **Litho.**

311 A51	5c dp vio	50	35
312 A52	10c dk sl grn	50	18
313 A53	15c yel brn	1.00	50
314 A51	25c cerise	1.00	30
315 A54	50c yel grn	6.00	4.00
316 A55	3b red org	11.00	7.50
317 A51	5b lt brn	22.50	15.00
	Nos. 311-317 (7)	42.50	27.83

Nos. 311-317 exist imperforate. Value for set $75. Nos. 311-315 exist in pairs, imperf. between; value range, $20-$30.

No. 300 Surcharged in Black

1937
VALE 25 POR

1937 *Perf. 12½*

318 A49	25c on 40c ind	5.00	65
a	Double surch.	16.00	16.00
b	Inverted surch.	13.00	13.00
c	Triple surch.	32.50	32.50

Surcharged

1937
VALE 25 POR

319 A49	25c on 40c ind	325.00	275.00

A56

1937, Oct. 28 **Litho.** *Perf. 10½*

320 A56	25c blue	1.00	40

Acquisition of the Port of La Guaira by the Government from the British Corporation, June 3, 1937. Exists imperf. See Nos. C64-C65.

A redrawn printing of No. 320, with top inscription beginning "Nacionalización . . ." was prepared but not issued. Value, $85.

Stamps of 1937 Overprinted in Black

RESELLADO
1937-1938

1937-38 *Perf. 11, 11½*

321 A51	5c dp vio	3.75	2.00
322 A52	10c dk sl grn	1.00	50
a	Inverted ovpt.	13.00	13.00
323 A51	25c cerise	75	42
a	Inverted ovpt.	16.00	16.00
324 A55	3b red org	150.00	75.00

Part-perforate pairs exist of Nos. 321-322 and 324. Value range, $12.50 to $125.

See Nos. C66-C78.

Gathering Coffee Beans — A57

Simón Bolivar — A58

Post Office, Caracas — A59

1938 **Engr.** *Perf. 12*

325 A57	5c	green	30	10
326 A57	5c	dp grn	30	10
327 A58	10c	car rose	50	10
328 A58	10c	dp rose	50	10
329 A59	15c	dk vio	1.00	20
330 A59	15c	ol grn	65	20
331 A58	25c	lt bl	30	10
332 A58	25c	dk bl	30	15
333 A58	37½c	dk bl	6.00	2.50
334 A58	37½c	lt bl	2.00	65
335 A59	40c	sepia	15.00	5.00
336 A59	40c	black	12.50	5.00
337 A57	50c	ol grn	20.00	5.00
338 A57	50c	dl vio	7.00	65
339 A58	1b	dp brn	8.25	4.00
340 A58	1b	blk brn	12.50	1.00
341 A57	3b	orange	70.00	32.50
342 A59	5b	black	11.00	5.00
	Nos. 325-342 (18)		168.10	62.35

See Nos. 400 and 412.

Teresa Carreno A60

Bolivar Statue A61

1938, June 12 *Perf. 11½x12*

343 A60	25c blue	4.00	40

Issued in honor of Teresa Carreno, Venezuelan pianist, whose remains were repatriated February 14, 1938.

1938, July 24 *Perf. 12*

344 A61	25c dark blue	4.50	42

"The Day of the Worker".

Type of 1937 Surcharged in Black

VALE
Bs. 0,40
1938

1938 **Litho.** *Perf. 11, 11½*

345 A51	40c on 5b lt brn	8.75	3.00
a	Inverted surch.	21.00	21.00

Gen. José I. Paz Castillo, Postmaster of Venezuela, 1859 — A62

1939, Apr. 19 **Engr.** *Perf. 12½*

348 A62	10c carmine	1.75	40

Issued to commemorate the 80th anniversary of the first Venezuelan stamp.

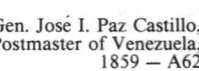

View of Ojeda A63

1939, June 24 **Photo.**

349 A63	25c dl bl	6.50	50

Founding of city of Ojeda.

Cristóbal Mendoza A64

Diego Urbaneja A65

1939, Oct. 14 **Engr.** *Perf. 13*

350 A64	5c	green	40	20
351 A64	10c	dk car rose	40	20
352 A64	15c	dl lil	1.00	30
353 A64	25c	brt ultra	80	20
354 A64	37½c	dk bl	15.00	7.50

355 A64	50c lt ol grn	15.00	5.00
356 A64	1b dk brn	6.00	4.00
	Nos. 350-356 (7)	38.60	17.40

Cristóbal Mendoza (1772-1839), postmaster general.

1940-43 ***Perf. 12***

357 A65	5c Prus grn	35	12
357A A65	7½c dk bl grn ('43)	50	18
358 A65	15c olive	65	20
359 A65	37½c dp bl	1.00	50
360 A65	40c vio bl	75	20
361 A65	50c violet	4.00	1.00
362 A65	1b dk vio brn	2.00	65
363 A65	3b scarlet	6.00	2.50
	Nos. 357-363 (8)	15.25	5.35

See Nos. 399, 408, 410 and 411.

Battle of Carabobo, 1821 — A67

1940, June 13

365 A67	25c blue	4.50	40

Issued in commemoration of the 150th anniversary of the birth of General José Antonio Paez.

"Crossing the Andes" by Tito Salas — A68

1940, June 13

366 A68	25c dk bl	4.50	40

Issued in commemoration of the centenary of the death of General Francisco Santander.

Monument and Urn containing Ashes of Simon Bolivar — A69

Bed where Simon Bolivar was Born — A70

Designs: 15c, "Christening of Bolivar" by Tito Salas. 20c, Bolivar's birthplace, Caracas. 25c, "Bolivar on Horseback" by Salas. 30c, Patio of Bolivar House, Caracas. 37½c, Patio of Bolivar's Birthplace. 50c, "Rebellion of 1812" by Salas.

1940-41

367 A69	5c turq grn	22	6
368 A70	10c rose pink	22	6
369 A69	15c olive	50	12
370 A70	20c bl ('41)	85	6
371 A69	25c lt bl	50	9
372 A70	30c plum ('41)	1.25	18
373 A70	37½c dk bl	2.50	85
374 A70	50c purple	1.50	38
	Nos. 367-374 (8)	7.54	1.80

Issued in commemoration of the 110th anniversary of the death of Simon Bolivar.
See Nos. 397, 398, 403, 405-407 and 409.

No. 371 Surcharged In Black

HABILITADO
1941
VALE
BS. 0,20

1941

375 A69	20c on 25c lt bl	50	12
a	Inverted surch.	10.00	10.00

Nos. 311-312 Overprinted in Black

HABILITADO
1940

1941 ***Perf. 11½***

376 A51	5c dp vio	1.50	38
a	Double ovpt.	10.00	8.25
b	Vertical pair, imperf. between	14.00	14.00
c	Invtd. ovpt.	20.00	16.00
377 A52	10c dk sl grn	85	25
a	Double ovpt.	13.00	13.00

Symbols of Industry A77

Caracas Cathedral A78

1942, Dec. 17 **Litho.** ***Perf. 12***

378 A77	10c scarlet	75	18
a	Imperf., pair	22.50	22.50

Grand Industrial Exposition, Caracas.

1943 **Engr.**

379 A78	10c rose car	50	12

See No. 404.

Stamps of 1937 Overprinted in Black

Resellado
1943

1943 ***Perf. 11, 11½***

380 A51	5c dp vio	10.00	6.25
381 A52	10c dk sl grn	3.75	2.50
382 A54	50c yel grn	5.00	3.00
383 A55	3b red org	30.00	14.00

Nos. 380 to 383 were issued for sale to philatelists and sold only in sets.

Stamps of 1937-38 Surcharged in Black

Habilitado
Vale
Bs. 0.20

1943 ***Perf. 11½, 10½, 12***

384 A51	20c on 25c cer	19.00	19.00
385 A56	20c on 25c bl	50.00	42.50
386 A60	20c on 25c dk bl	10.00	10.00
387 A61	20c on 25c dk bl	10.00	10.00
a	Inverted surcharge	25.00	25.00

Nos. 384-387 were issued for sale to philatelists and sold only in sets.

Souvenir Sheet

A79

1944, Aug. 22 **Litho.** ***Perf. 12***
Flags in Red, Yellow, Blue & Black

388 A79	Sheet of four	20.00	20.00
a	5c Prus grn	3.50	1.00
b	10c rose	4.00	1.00
c	20c ultra	4.00	2.00
d	1b rose lake	5.00	3.00

80th anniv. of Intl. Red Cross and 37th anniv. of Venezuela's joining.
No. 388 is known imperf. Value $50.

Antonio José de Sucre — A80

1945, Mar. 3 **Engr.** **Unwmk.**

389 A80	5c org yel	90	30
390 A80	10c dk bl	1.25	60
391 A80	20c rose pink	1.50	60
	Nos. 389-391,C206-C215 (13)	15.03	8.08

Issued to commemorate the 150th anniversary of the birth of Antonio de Sucre.

Andrés Bello — A81

Gen. Rafael Urdaneta — A82

1946, Aug. 24

392 A81	20c dp bl	65	25
393 A82	20c dp bl	65	25

Issued to commemorate the 80th anniversary of the death of Andrés Bello (1780?-1865), educator and writer, and the centenary of the death of Gen. Rafael Urdaneta.
See Nos. C216-C217.

Allegory of the Republic — A83

1946, Oct. 18 **Litho.** ***Perf. 11½***

394 A83	20c grnsh bl	65	25
	Nos. 394,C218-C221 (5)	4.80	3.25

Anniversary of Revolution of October, 1945. Exists imperf.
See Nos. C218-C221.

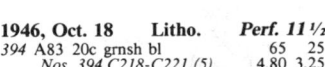

Anti-tuberculosis Institute, Maracaibo — A84

1947, Jan. 12 ***Perf. 12***

395 A84	20c ultra & yel	60	25
	Nos. 395,C228-C231 (5)	5.85	4.23

12th Pan-American Health Conf., Caracas, Jan. 1947. Exists imperf. and part perf.

No. 362 Surcharged in Green

J. R. G.
CORREOS
Vale Bs.0.15
1946

396 A65	15c on 1b dk vio brn	65	25
a	Inverted surch.	6.00	5.00

See Nos. C223-C227.

Types of 1938-40

1947 **Engr.**

397 A69	5c green	6	6
398 A70	30c black	75	50
399 A65	40c red vio	50	18
400 A59	5b dp org	40.00	20.00

R1

In 1947 a decree authorized the use of 5c and 10c revenue stamps of the above type for franking correspondence. Other denominations were also used unofficially.

Nos. 398 and 373 Surcharged in Red

CORREOS
Vale Bs. 0.05
1947

1947 **Unwmk.** ***Perf. 12***

401 A70	5c on 30c blk	30	6
a	Inverted surcharge	5.00	5.00
402 A70	5c on 37½c dk bl	35	6
a	Inverted surcharge	5.00	5.00

Types of 1938-43

1947-49

403 A69	5c brt ultra	12	6
404 A78	10c red	6	6
405 A69	15c rose car	38	6
406 A69	25c violet	30	8
407 A70	30c dk vio brn ('48)	38	12
408 A65	40c org ('48)	38	12
409 A70	50c ol grn	65	18
410 A65	1b dp bl	1.25	18
411 A65	3b gray	2.50	65
412 A59	5b chocolate	11.00	4.25
	Nos. 403-412 (10)	17.02	5.76

M. S. Republica de Venezuela A85

Imprint: "American Bank Note Company"

1948-50 **Engr.** ***Perf. 12***

413 A85	5c blue	12	7
414 A85	7½c red org ('49)	42	22
a	Booklet pane of 20		
415 A85	10c car rose	32	7
a	Booklet pane of 10		
416 A85	15c gray ('50)	42	12
417 A85	20c sepia	25	7
418 A85	25c vio ('49)	42	12
419 A85	30c org ('50)	2.75	1.40
420 A85	37½c brn ('49)	1.25	1.00
421 A85	40c ol ('50)	1.90	1.25
422 A85	50c red vio ('49)	50	18
423 A85	1b gray grn	1.25	38
	Nos. 413-423 (11)	9.60	4.88

Grand Colombian Merchant Fleet. See Nos. 632-634, C256-C271, C554-C556.

Santos Michelena A86

Christopher Columbus A87

1949, Apr. 25

424 A86	5c ultra	18	9
425 A86	10c carmine	38	12
426 A86	20c sepia	1.50	50
427 A86	1b green	5.00	2.25
	Nos. 424-427,C272-C277 (10)	14.13	6.02

Issued to commemorate the centenary of the death of Santos Michelena, Finance Minister, and the 110th anniversary of the Postal Convention of Bogota.

The lack of a value for a listed item does not necessarily indicate rarity.

1949 Engr. Perf. 12½

428	A87	5c dp ultra	32	9
429	A87	10c carmine	1.25	38
430	A87	20c dk brn	1.50	50
431	A87	1b green	3.75	1.90
		Nos. 428-431,C278-C283 (10)	14.29	5.36

Issued to commemorate the 450th anniversary (in 1948) of Columbus' discovery of the American mainland.

Arms of Venezuela
A88

1948

432	A88	5c blue	1.25	65
433	A88	10c red	1.50	75

The 20c and 1b, type A88, and six similar air post stamps were prepared but not issued. Value, set of 8, about $125.

Gen. Francisco de Miranda — A89

1950 Unwmk. Perf. 12

434	A89	5c blue	18	6
435	A89	10c green	42	9
436	A89	20c sepia	85	38
437	A89	1b rose car	4.00	1.90

Bicentenary of birth of General Francisco de Miranda.

Map and Population Chart — A90

Alonso de Ojeda — A91

1950

438	A90	5c blue	15	6
439	A90	10c gray	15	9
440	A90	15c sepia	22	9
441	A90	25c green	35	12
442	A90	30c red	50	18
443	A90	50c violet	1.00	38
444	A90	1b red brn	2.50	1.25
		Nos. 438-444 (7)	4.87	2.17

Issued to publicize the 8th National Census of the Americas. See Nos. C302-C310.

1950 Photo. Perf. 11½

445	A91	5c dp bl	18	10
446	A91	10c dp red	25	12
447	A91	15c sl gray	30	15
448	A91	20c ultra	1.25	50
449	A91	1b bl grn	5.00	2.50
		Nos. 445-449 (5)	6.98	3.37

Issued to commemorate the 450th anniversary (in 1949) of the discovery of the Gulf of Maracaibo.
See Nos. C316-C321.

Nos. 414 and 420 Surcharged in Black

RESELLADO
"5 CENTIMOS"

1951 Unwmk. Perf. 12

450	A85	5c on 7½c red org	25	12
451	A85	10c on 37½c brn	25	12
	a	Inverted surcharge	16.00	16.00

Telegraph Stamps Surcharged in Black or Red

Habilitado
Correos
25 Centimos

1951 Engr.

Grayish Security Paper

452	5c on 5c brn	12	6
453	10c on 10c grn	25	6
454	20c on 1b blk (R)	50	12
455	25c on 25c car	65	25
456	30c on 2b ol grn (R)	85	65
	Nos. 452-456 (5)	2.37	1.14

The 5c and 10c surcharges include quotation marks on each line and values are expressed "Bs. 0.05" etc.

Bolivar Statue, New York — A92

1951 Perf. 12

457	A92	5c green	25	6
458	A92	10c car rose	50	18
459	A92	20c ultra	50	18
460	A92	30c sl gray	65	30
461	A92	40c dp grn	85	30
462	A92	50c red brn	1.90	65
463	A92	1b gray blk	6.00	3.00
		Nos. 457-463 (7)	10.65	4.67

Relocation of the equestrian statue of Simon Bolivar in NYC, Apr. 19, 1951. See Nos. C322-C329.

Arms of Carabobo and "Industry" — A93

1951 Unwmk. Photo. Perf. 11½

464	A93	5c green	10	5
465	A93	10c red	10	5
466	A93	15c brown	30	12
467	A93	20c ultra	45	20
468	A93	25c org brn	50	25
469	A93	30c blue	1.10	45
470	A93	35c purple	4.00	3.50
		Nos. 464-470 (7)	6.55	4.62

Arms of Zulia and "Industry"

471	A93	5c green	15	5
472	A93	10c red	30	5
473	A93	15c brown	65	30
474	A93	20c ultra	85	45
475	A93	50c brn org	6.50	4.50
476	A93	1b dp gray grn	1.75	65
477	A93	5b rose vio	3.75	2.50
		Nos. 471-477 (7)	13.95	8.50

Arms of Anzoategui and Globe

478	A93	5c green	10	5
479	A93	10c red	12	5
480	A93	15c brown	65	30
481	A93	20c ultra	1.10	20
482	A93	40c red org	2.25	1.10
483	A93	45c rose vio	6.75	3.75
484	A93	3b bl gray	2.50	1.25
		Nos. 478-484 (7)	13.47	6.70

Arms of Caracas and Buildings

485	A93	5c green	38	5
486	A93	10c red	50	8
487	A93	15c brown	1.25	30
488	A93	20c ultra	2.50	30
489	A93	25c org brn	3.75	65
490	A93	30c blue	3.25	75
491	A93	35c purple	32.50	19.00
		Nos. 485-491 (7)	44.13	21.13

Arms of Tachira and Agricultural Products

492	A93	5c green	15	5
493	A93	10c red	38	15
494	A93	15c brown	75	25
495	A93	20c ultra	1.75	45
496	A93	50c brn org	110.00	17.50
497	A93	1b dp gray grn	1.75	65
498	A93	5b dl pur	4.50	2.50
		Nos. 492-498 (7)	119.28	21.55

Arms of Venezuela and Statue of Simon Bolivar

499	A93	5c green	30	5
500	A93	10c red	22	5
501	A93	15c brown	2.25	45
502	A93	20c ultra	2.25	30
503	A93	25c org brn	3.75	85
504	A93	30c blue	3.75	85
505	A93	35c purple	20.00	15.00
		Nos. 499-505 (7)	32.52	17.55

1952

Arms of Miranda and Agricultural Products

506	A93	5c green	12	5
507	A93	10c red	18	5
508	A93	15c brown	45	15
509	A93	20c ultra	50	20
510	A93	25c org brn	65	32
511	A93	30c blue	1.10	50
512	A93	35c purple	6.50	4.50
		Nos. 506-512 (7)	9.50	5.77

Arms of Aragua and Stylized Farm

513	A93	5c green	12	5
514	A93	10c red	25	5
515	A93	15c brown	50	10
516	A93	20c ultra	45	20
517	A93	25c org brn	1.00	30
518	A93	30c blue	1.10	50
519	A93	35c purple	6.00	4.50
		Nos. 513-519 (7)	9.42	5.70

Arms of Lara, Agricultural Products and Rope

520	A93	5c green	15	5
521	A93	10c red	15	5
522	A93	15c brown	30	20
523	A93	20c ultra	75	25
524	A93	25c org brn	85	65
525	A93	30c blue	1.50	50
526	A93	35c purple	6.50	4.50
		Nos. 520-526 (7)	10.20	6.20

Arms of Bolivar and Stylized Design

527	A93	5c green	10	6
528	A93	10c red	15	6
529	A93	15c brown	30	15
530	A93	20c ultra	65	20
531	A93	40c red org	2.50	85
532	A93	45c rose vio	6.50	4.50
533	A93	3b bl gray	3.00	2.00
		Nos. 527-533 (7)	13.20	7.82

Arms of Sucre, Palms and Seascape

534	A93	5c green	15	5
535	A93	10c red	15	5
536	A93	15c brown	75	15
537	A93	20c ultra	75	10
538	A93	40c red org	2.50	65
539	A93	45c rose vio	9.00	5.50
540	A93	3b bl gray	2.25	1.50
		Nos. 534-540 (7)	15.55	8.00

Arms of Trujillo Surrounded by Stylized Tree

541	A93	5c green	10	5
542	A93	10c red	15	5
543	A93	15c brown	1.10	20
544	A93	20c ultra	1.10	30
545	A93	50c brn org	6.25	3.75
546	A93	1b dp gray grn	1.50	65
547	A93	5b dl pur	3.75	2.25
		Nos. 541-547 (7)	13.95	7.25

1953

Map of Delta Amacuro and Ship

548	A93	5c green	10	5
549	A93	10c red	15	5
550	A93	15c brown	30	10
551	A93	20c ultra	50	20
552	A93	40c red org	1.65	1.00
553	A93	45c rose vio	7.50	4.50
554	A93	3b bl gray	2.00	1.50
		Nos. 548-554 (7)	12.20	7.40

Arms of Falcon and Stylized Oil Refinery

555	A93	5c green	10	5
556	A93	10c red	12	5
557	A93	15c brown	50	12
558	A93	20c ultra	50	15
559	A93	50c brn org	2.50	1.25
560	A93	1b dp gray grn	1.50	1.00
561	A93	5b dl pur	4.50	2.50
		Nos. 555-561 (7)	9.72	5.12

Arms of Guarico and Factory

562	A93	5c green	10	5
563	A93	10c red	10	5
564	A93	15c brown	45	20
565	A93	20c ultra	50	25
566	A93	40c red org	2.25	1.75
567	A93	45c rose vio	5.50	3.25
568	A93	3b bl gray	2.25	1.50
		Nos. 562-568 (7)	11.15	7.05

Arms of Merida and Church

569	A93	5c green	10	5
570	A93	10c red	10	5
571	A93	15c brown	30	20
572	A93	20c ultra	85	20
573	A93	50c brn org	3.50	1.50
574	A93	1b dp gray grn	1.00	65
575	A93	5b dl pur	3.50	2.00
		Nos. 569-575 (7)	9.35	4.65

Arms of Monagas and Horses

576	A93	5c green	10	5
577	A93	10c red	15	5
578	A93	15c brown	30	20
579	A93	20c ultra	45	25
580	A93	40c red org	2.00	75
581	A93	45c rose vio	6.25	3.75
582	A93	3b bl gray	2.50	2.00
		Nos. 576-582 (7)	11.75	7.05

Arms of Portuguesa and Forest

583	A93	5c green	8	5
584	A93	10c red	10	5
585	A93	15c brown	30	15
586	A93	20c ultra	65	15
587	A93	50c brn org	3.50	2.25
588	A93	1b dp gray grn	85	38
589	A93	5b dl pur	3.75	2.50
		Nos. 583-589 (7)	9.23	5.53

Map of Amazonas and Orchid

590	A93	5c green	50	5
591	A93	10c red	50	5
592	A93	15c brown	1.10	15
593	A93	20c ultra	3.00	30
594	A93	40c red org	3.50	1.00
595	A93	45c rose vio	5.50	2.75
596	A93	3b bl gray	8.00	3.00
		Nos. 590-596 (7)	22.10	7.30

Arms of Apure, Horse and Bird

597	A93	5c green	10	6
598	A93	10c red	10	6
599	A93	15c brown	30	15
600	A93	20c ultra	1.75	20
601	A93	50c brn org	2.25	1.75
602	A93	1b dp gray grn	75	65
603	A93	5b dl pur	4.50	2.50
		Nos. 597-603 (7)	9.75	5.37

Arms of Barinas, Cow and Horse

604	A93	5c green	10	5
605	A93	10c red	10	5
606	A93	15c brown	32	18
607	A93	20c ultra	2.25	30
608	A93	50c brn org	2.50	1.50
609	A93	1b dp gray grn	65	30
610	A93	5b dl pur	5.50	2.75
		Nos. 604-610 (7)	11.42	5.13

Arms of Cojedes and Cattle

611	A93	5c green	8	5
612	A93	10c red	18	5
613	A93	15c brown	18	8
614	A93	20c ultra	20	10
615	A93	25c org brn	1.10	30
616	A93	30c blue	1.75	50
617	A93	35c purple	2.25	1.40
		Nos. 611-617 (7)	5.74	2.48

Arms of Nueva Esparta and Fish

618	A93	5c green	10	5
619	A93	10c red	10	5
620	A93	15c brown	45	20
621	A93	20c ultra	50	12
622	A93	40c red org	2.25	85
623	A93	45c rose vio	5.50	3.25
624	A93	3b bl gray	2.50	1.75
		Nos. 618-624 (7)	11.40	6.27

Arms of Yaracuy and Tropical Foliage

625	A93	5c green	38	5
626	A93	10c red	10	5
627	A93	15c brown	32	15
628	A93	20c ultra	45	20
629	A93	25c org brn	65	30
630	A93	30c blue	75	25
631	A93	35c purple	1.75	1.10
		Nos. 625-631 (7)	4.40	2.10
		Nos. 464-631 (168)	429.93	186.24

See Nos. C338-C553.

Ship Type of 1948-50, Redrawn
Coil Stamps
Imprint: "Courvoisier S.A."

1952 Unwmk. Photo. Perf. 11½x12

632	A85	5c green	65	12
633	A85	10c car rose	1.10	12
634	A85	15c gray	3.75	12

See Nos. C554-C556.

Juan de Villegas and Cross of Father Yepez
A94

Virgin of Coromoto and Child
A95

1952, Sept. 14 *Perf. 11½*

635	A94	5c green	25	6
636	A94	10c red	50	6
637	A94	20c dk gray bl	75	25
638	A94	40c dp org	3.75	1.90
639	A94	50c brown	1.90	1.00
640	A94	1b violet	3.75	1.25
		Nos. 635-640 (6)	10.90	4.52

Issued to commemorate the 400th anniversary of the founding of the city of Barquisimeto by Juan de Villegas. See Nos. C557-C564.

1952-53 *Perf. 11½x12*

Size: 17x26mm.

641	A95	1b rose pink	6.00	1.00

Size: 26½x41mm.

642	A95	1b rose pink ('53)	4.50	1.00

Size: 36x55mm.

643	A95	1b rose pink ('53)	2.00	75

Issued to commemorate the 300th anniversary of the appearance of the Virgin Mary to a chief of the Coromoto Indians.

Telegraph Stamps Surcharged in Black or Red

Correos
Exposición Objetiva
Nacional
1948 - 1952
5c.

1952, Nov. 24 **Engr.** *Perf. 12*

Grayish Security Paper

644	5c on 25c car	25	6
645	10c on 1b blk (R)	25	6

Surcharged

CORREOS
HABILITADO
1952
Bs. 0,50

1952

646	20c on 25c car	30	12
647	30c on 2b ol grn	1.90	1.25
648	40c on 1b blk (R)	75	38
649	50c on 3b red org	2.50	1.50

Post Office, Caracas — A96

1953-54 **Unwmk.** **Photo.** *Perf. 12½*

650	A96	5c grn ('54)	12	5
a		Bklt. pane of 10		
651	A96	7½c brt grn	38	25
652	A96	10c rose car ('54)	25	5
a		Bklt. pane of 10		
653	A96	15c gray ('54)	38	6
654	A96	20c ultra	25	12
655	A96	25c magenta	38	6
656	A96	30c blue	1.90	25
657	A96	35c brt red vio	85	25
658	A96	40c orange	1.25	38
659	A96	45c violet	1.90	65
660	A96	50c red org	1.25	38
		Nos. 650-660 (11)	8.91	2.50

See Nos. C565-C575, C587-C589.

Type of 1953-54 Inscribed "Republica de Venezuela"

1955

661	A96	5c green	9	5
662	A96	10c rose car	9	5
663	A96	15c gray	18	5
664	A96	20c ultra	25	5
665	A96	30c blue	65	38
666	A96	35c brt red vio	65	15
667	A96	40c orange	1.00	25
668	A96	45c violet	1.25	50
		Nos. 661-668 (8)	4.16	1.48

See Nos. C597-C606.

Arms of Valencia and Industrial Scene — A97

Coat of Arms — A98

1955, Mar. 26 **Engr.** *Perf. 12*

669	A97	5c brt grn	18	6
670	A97	20c ultra	38	8
671	A97	25c redsh brn	65	9
672	A97	50c vermilion	1.00	25
		Nos. 669-672,C590-C596 (11)	4.51	1.35

Issued to commemorate the 400th anniversary of the founding of Valencia del Rey.

1955, Dec. 9 **Unwmk.** *Perf. 11½*

673	A98	5c green	38	5
674	A98	20c ultra	1.25	5
675	A98	25c rose car	1.00	8
676	A98	50c orange	1.25	8
		Nos. 673-676,C607-C612 (10)	6.62	1.06

Issued to commemorate the First Postal Convention, Caracas, Feb. 9-15, 1954.

Book and Map of the Americas A99

Simon Bolivar A100

1957 **Photo.** *Perf. 11½*

Granite Paper

677	A99	5c lt grn & bluish grn	8	5
678	A99	10c lil rose & rose vio	8	5
679	A99	20c ultra & dk bl	18	5
680	A99	25c gray & lil gray	25	12
681	A99	30c lt bl & bl	25	12
682	A99	40c bis brn & brn	38	18
683	A99	50c ver & red brn	65	25
684	A99	1b lt pur & vio	1.00	50
		Nos. 677-684 (8)	2.87	1.32

Issued for the Book Festival of the Americas, Nov. 15-30, 1956. See Nos. C629-C635.

Engraved, Center Embossed

1957-58 **Unwmk.** *Perf. 13½*

685	A100	5c brt bl grn	8	5
686	A100	10c red ('58)	12	5
687	A100	20c lt sl bl	38	12
688	A100	25c rose lake	38	12
689	A100	30c vio bl	50	12
690	A100	40c red org	75	18
691	A100	50c org yel ('58)	1.00	50
		Nos. 685-691 (7)	3.21	1.14

Issued to commemorate the 150th anniversary of the Oath of Monte Sacro and the 125th anniversary of the death of Simon Bolivar (1783-1830).
See Nos. C636-C642.

Hotel Tamanaco, Caracas A101

1957-58 **Engr.** *Perf. 13*

692	A101	5c green	8	5
693	A101	10c carmine	8	5
694	A101	15c black	30	10
695	A101	20c dk bl	38	6
696	A101	25c dp cl	38	9
697	A101	30c dp ultra	65	25
698	A101	35c purple	38	12
699	A101	40c orange	50	18
700	A101	45c rose vio	65	25
701	A101	50c yellow	85	38
702	A101	1b dk sl grn	1.25	50
		Nos. 692-702 (11)	5.50	2.03

See Nos. C643-C657.

Main Post Office, Caracas — A102

1958, May 14 **Litho.** *Perf. 14*

703	A102	5c emerald	5	5
704	A102	10c rose red	6	5
705	A102	15c gray	8	5
706	A102	20c lt bl	12	5
707	A102	35c red lil	18	9
708	A102	45c brt vio	1.25	85
709	A102	50c yellow	30	12
710	A102	1b lt ol grn	75	38
		Nos. 703-710 (8)	2.79	1.64

See Nos. 748-750, C658-C670.

Main Post Office, Caracas A103

Coil Stamps

1958, Nov. 17 **Engr.** *Perf. 11½x12*

711	A103	5c green	25	5
712	A103	10c rose red	38	5
713	A103	15c black	50	8
		Nos. 711-713,C671-C673 (6)	2.26	41

Arms of Merida — A104

Arms of Trujillo, Bolivar Monument and Trujillo Hotel — A105

1958, Oct. 9 **Photo.** *Perf. 14*

714	A104	5c green	8	5
715	A104	10c brt red	8	5
716	A104	15c grnsh gray	8	5
717	A104	20c blue	15	5
718	A104	25c magenta	50	9
719	A104	30c violet	25	12
720	A104	35c lt pur	30	12
721	A104	40c orange	75	25
722	A104	45c dp rose lil	38	12
723	A104	50c brt yel	65	25
724	A104	1b gray grn	1.90	65
		Nos. 714-724 (11)	5.12	1.80

Issued to commemorate the 400th anniversary of the founding of the city of Merida. See Nos. C674-C689.

1959 **Unwmk.** *Perf. 14*

725	A105	5c emerald	5	5
726	A105	10c rose	6	5
727	A105	15c gray	8	6
728	A105	20c blue	12	6
729	A105	25c brt pink	25	9
730	A105	30c lt ultra	38	12
731	A105	35c lt pur	42	18
732	A105	45c rose lil	50	25
733	A105	50c yellow	50	20
734	A105	1b lt ol grn	1.25	65
		Nos. 725-734 (10)	3.61	1.71

Issued to commemorate the 400th anniversary of the founding of the city of Trujillo. See Nos. C690-C700.

Stadium A106

1959 Mar. 10 **Litho.** *Perf. 13½*

735	A106	5c brt grn	18	6
736	A106	10c rose pink	18	9
737	A106	20c blue	50	25
738	A106	30c dk bl	65	30
739	A106	50c red lil	1.00	25
		Nos. 735-739 (5)	2.51	95

Issued to commemorate the 8th Central American and Caribbean Games, Caracas, Nov. 29-Dec. 14, 1958. See Nos. C701-C705.
Nos. 735-739 exist imperf. Value $25 a pair.

Stamp of 1859, Mailman and Jose Ignacio Paz Castillo A107

Stamp of 1859 and: 50c, Mailman on horseback and Jacinto Gutierrez. 1b, Plane, train and Miguel Herrera.

1959, Sept. 15 **Engr.** *Perf. 13½*

740	A107	25c org yel	38	12
741	A107	50c blue	65	25
742	A107	1b rose red	1.25	50
		Nos. 740-742,C706-C708 (6)	4.28	1.64

Centenary of Venezuelan postage stamps.

Catalogue values for unused stamps in this section, from this point to the end of the section, are for Never Hinged items.

Alexander von Humboldt A108

Newspaper, 1808, and View of Caracas, 1958 A109

1960, Feb. 9 **Unwmk.** *Perf. 13½*

743	A108	5c grn & yel grn	28	6
744	A108	30c vio bl & vio	70	18
745	A108	40c org & brn org	95	40
		Nos. 743-745,C709-C711 (6)	4.01	1.22

Issued to commemorate the centenary of the death of Alexander von Humboldt, German naturalist and geographer.

Post Office Type of 1958

1960 **Litho.** *Perf. 14*

748	A102	25c yellow	14	6
749	A102	30c lt bl	18	6
750	A102	40c fawn	35	14

1960, June 1 **Litho.** *Perf. 14*

751	A109	10c rose & blk	32	14
752	A109	20c lt bl & blk	48	18
753	A109	35c lil & blk	80	70
		Nos. 751-753,C712-C714 (6)	4.90	2.69

Issued to commemorate the 150th anniversary (in 1958) of the first Venezuelan newspaper, Gazeta de Caracas.

Values quoted in this catalogue are for stamps graded at Fine-Very Fine and with no faults. An illustrated guide to grade is provided in introductory material, beginning on Page V.

Agustin Codazzi
A110

National Pantheon
A111

1960, June 15 Engr. Unwmk.

754	A110	5c brt grn	6	5
755	A110	15c gray	48	14
756	A110	20c blue	40	14
757	A110	45c purple	48	32
		Nos. 754-757,C715-C720 (10)	4.15	1.85

Issued to commemorate the centenary (in 1959) of the death of Agustin Codazzi, geographer.

1960, May 9 Litho.

Pantheon in Bister

758	A111	5c emerald	8	5
759	A111	20c brt bl	40	14
760	A111	25c lt ol	60	18
761	A111	30c dl bl	70	20
762	A111	40c fawn	1.00	38
763	A111	45c lilac	1.00	38
		Nos. 758-763 (6)	3.78	1.33

See Nos. C721-C734.

Andres Eloy Blanco — A112

1960, May 21 Unwmk. *Perf. 14*

Portrait in Black

764	A112	5c emerald	15	5
765	A112	30c dl bl	25	12
766	A112	50c yellow	50	25
		Nos. 764-766,C735-C737 (6)	3.00	1.12

Issued to honor the poet Andres Eloy Blanco (1896-1955).

Independence Meeting of April 19, 1810, Led by Miranda — A113

1960, Aug. 19 Litho. *Perf. 13½*

Center Multicolored

767	A113	5c brt grn	38	9
768	A113	20c blue	75	25
769	A113	30c vio bl	95	38
		Nos. 767-769,C738-C740 (6)	4.68	1.66

Issued to commemorate the 150th anniversary of Venezuela's Independence.
See Nos. 812-814, C804-C806.

Drilling for Oil — A114

1960, Aug. 26 Engr. *Perf. 14*

770	A114	5c grn & sl grn	1.25	65
771	A114	10c dk car & brn	50	25
772	A114	15c gray & dl pur	65	30
		Nos. 770-772,C741-C743 (6)	4.18	2.06

Issued to publicize Venezuela's oil industry.

Luisa Cáceres de Arismendi
A115

Unwmk.

1960, Oct. 21 Litho. *Perf. 14*

Center Multicolored

773	A115	20c lt bl	90	35
774	A115	25c citron	75	38
775	A115	30c dl bl	1.00	52
		Nos. 773-774,C744-C746 (5)	5.00	2.33

Issued to commemorate the 94th anniversary of the death of Luisa Caceres de Arismendi.

José Antonio Anzoategui — A116

1960, Oct. 29 Engr.

776	A116	5c emer & gray ol	20	7
777	A116	15c ol gray & dl vio	50	7
778	A116	20c bl & gray vio	55	15
		Nos. 776-778,C747-C749 (6)	2.60	1.19

Issued to commemorate the 140th anniversary (in 1959) of the death of General José Antonio Anzoategui.

Antonio José de Sucre — A117

Unwmk.

1960, Nov. 18 Litho. *Perf. 14*

Center Multicolored

779	A117	10c dp rose	35	15
780	A117	15c gray brn	45	20
781	A117	20c blue	60	30
		Nos. 779-781,C750-C752 (6)	3.85	1.88

Issued to commemorate the 130th anniversary of the death of General Antonio José de Sucre.

Bolivar Peak, Merida — A118

Designs: 15c, Caroni Falls, Bolivar. 35c, Cuacharo caves, Monagas.

1960, March 22 *Perf. 14*

782	A118	5c emer & grn	75	75
783	A118	15c gray & dk gray	2.25	2.25
784	A118	35c rose lil & lil	2.00	2.00
		Nos. 782-784,C753-C755 (6)	9.20	9.20

Buildings and People — A119

1961 Litho. Unwmk.

Building in Orange

785	A119	5c emerald	6	5
786	A119	10c carmine	6	5
787	A119	15c gray	9	6
788	A119	20c blue	15	6
789	A119	25c lt red brn	22	10
790	A119	30c dl bl	22	9
791	A119	35c red lil	30	10
792	A119	40c fawn	45	20
793	A119	45c brt vio	60	30
794	A119	50c yellow	45	18
		Nos. 785-794 (10)	2.60	1.19

Issued to commemorate the 1960 national census. See Nos. C756-C770.

Rafael Maria Baralt — A120

Yellow-headed Parrot — A121

1961, Mar. 11 Engr. *Perf. 14*

795	A120	5c grn & sl grn	9	6
796	A120	15c gray & dl red brn	30	6
797	A120	35c rose lil & lt vio	45	20
		Nos. 795-797,C771-C773 (6)	2.57	1.32

Issued to commemorate the centenary of the death of Rafael Maria Baralt, statesman.

1961, Sept. 6 Litho. *Perf. 14½*

Birds: 40c, Snowy egret. 50c, Scarlet ibis.

798	A121	30c multi	45	30
799	A121	40c multi	60	30
800	A121	50c multi	1.25	60
		Nos. 798-800,C776-C778 (6)	4.25	3.00

Juan J. Aguerrevere
A122

1961, Oct. 21 Unwmk. *Perf. 14*

801	A122	25c dk bl	15	8
a		Souv. sheet, imperf.	1.00	1.00

Issued to commemorate the centenary of the founding of the Engineering Society of Venezuela, Oct. 28, 1861.
No. 801a sold for 1b.
No. 801a exists with "Valor: Bs 1,00" omitted at lower left corner. Value, $3.50.

Battle of Carabobo, 1821 — A123

1961, Dec. 2 *Perf. 14*

Center Multicolored

802	A123	5c emer & blk	8	6
803	A123	40c brn & blk	55	28
		Nos. 802-803,C779-C784 (8)	11.23	5.69

140th anniversary of Battle of Carabobo.

Oncidium Papilio Lindl. — A124

Orchids: 10c, Caularthron bilamellatum. 20c, Stanhopea Wardii Lodd. 25c, Catasetum pileatum. 30c, Masdevallia tovarensis. 35c, Epidendrum Stamfordianum Batem (horiz.). 50c, Epidendrum atropurpureum Willd. 3b, Oncidium falcipetalum Lindl.

Perf. 14x13½, 13½x14

1962, May 30 Litho. Unwmk.

Orchids in Natural Colors

804	A124	5c blk & org	6	6
805	A124	10c blk & brt grnsh bl	8	6
806	A124	20c blk & yel grn	22	9
807	A124	25c blk & lt bl	32	6
808	A124	30c blk & ol	38	12
809	A124	35c blk & yel	42	18
810	A124	50c blk & gray	50	25
811	A124	3b blk & vio	3.00	2.00
		Nos. 804-811 (8)	4.98	2.82

See Nos. C794-C803.

Independence Type of 1960

Design: Signing Declaration of Independence.

1962, June *Perf. 13½*

Center Multicolored

812	A113	5c emerald	20	6
813	A113	20c blue	42	15
814	A113	25c yellow	60	30
a		Souv. sheet of 3, #812-814, imperf.	2.25	2.25
		Nos. 812-814,C804-C806 (6)	4.47	1.96

150th anniv. of the Venezuelan Declaration of Independence, July 5, 1811.
No. 814a sold for 1.50b.

Shot Put
A125

Designs: 10c, Soccer. 25c, Swimming.

1962, Nov. 30 Litho. *Perf. 13x14*

815	A125	5c brt grn	7	6
816	A125	10c car rose	14	6
817	A125	25c blue	28	14
a		Souvenir sheet of 3	2.00	2.00
		Nos. 815-817,C808-C810 (6)	2.84	1.74

Issued to commemorate the First National Games, Caracas, 1961. The stamps are arranged within the sheet so that groups of four are formed with the two pale colored edges of each stamp joining to make a border around blocks of four.
No. 817a contains one each of Nos. 815-817 imperf. with bright green marginal inscription. Sold for 1.40b.

Vermilion Cardinal
A126

Malaria Eradication Emblem, Mosquito and Map
A127

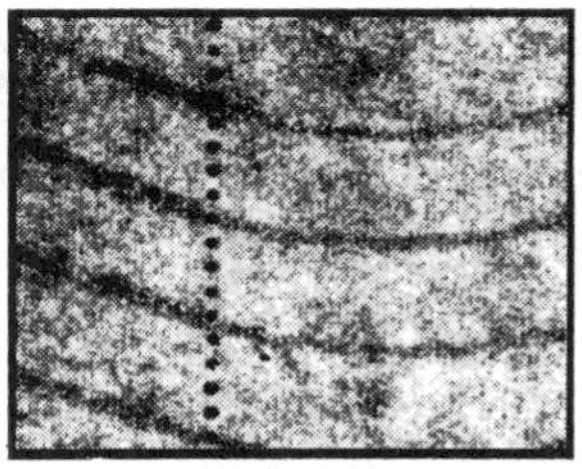
Wmk. 346

Birds: 10c, Great kiskadee. 20c, Glossy black thrush. 25c, Collared trogons. 30c, Swallow tanager. 40c, Long-tailed sylph. 3b, Black-necked stilt.

1962, Dec. 14 ***Perf. 14x13 1/2***
Birds in Natural Colors, Black Inscription

818	A126	5c brt yel grn		8	6
819	A126	10c vio bl		15	5
820	A126	20c lil rose		30	15
821	A126	25c dl brn		35	18
822	A126	30c lemon		45	20
823	A126	40c lilac		60	30
824	A126	3b fawn		3.75	3.00
		Nos. 818-824 (7)		5.68	3.94

See Nos. C811-C818.

Lithographed and Embossed
Perf. 13 1/2x14
1962, Dec. 20 **Wmk. 346**
825 A127 50c brn & blk 45 22

Issued for the World Health Organization drive to eradicate malaria. See Nos. C819-C819a.

White-tailed Deer — A128

Designs: 10c, Collared peccary. 35c, Collared titi (monkey). 50c, Giant Brazilian otter. 1b, Puma. 3b, Capybara.

Perf. 13 1/2x14
1963, Mar. 13 **Litho.** **Unwmk.**
Multicolored Center; Black Inscriptions

826	A128	5c green	6	6
827	A128	10c orange	6	8
828	A128	35c red lil	18	9
829	A128	50c blue	38	18
830	A128	1b rose brn	1.90	1.25
831	A128	3b yellow	3.75	2.50
		Nos. 826-831 (6)	6.33	4.16

See Nos. C820-C825.

Fisherman and Map of Venezuela A129

Cathedral of Bocono A130

1963, Mar. 21
832 A129 25c pink & ultra 18 14

FAO "Freedom from Hunger" campaign. See Nos. C826-C827.

1963, May 30 **Wmk. 346**
833 A130 50c brn, red & grn, *buff* 42 15

Issued to commemorate the 400th anniversary of the founding of Bocono. See No. C828.

St. Peter's Basilica, Rome A131

1963, June 11 ***Perf. 14x13 1/2***

834	A131	35c dk bl, brn & buff	25	12
835	A131	45c dk grn, red brn & buff	30	15

Issued to commemorate Vatican II, the 21st Ecumenical Council of the Roman Catholic Church. See Nos. C829-C830.

National Flag — A132

1963, July 29 **Unwmk.** ***Perf. 14***
836 A132 30c gray, red, yel & bl 20 15

Issued to commemorate the centenary of Venezuela's flag and coat of arms. See No. C831.

Lake Maracaibo Bridge — A133

Map, Soldier and Emblem — A134

1963 **Wmk. 346** **Litho.** ***Perf. 14***

837	A133	30c bl & brn	28	14
838	A133	35c bluish grn & brn	32	18
839	A133	80c bl grn & brn	60	32
		Nos. 837-839,C832-C834 (6)	3.75	1.92

Opening of bridge over Lake Maracaibo.

1963, Sept. 10 **Unwmk.**
840 A134 50c red, bl & grn, *buff* 40 18

Issued to commemorate the 25th anniversary of the armed forces. See No. C835.

Dag Hammarskjold and World Map — A135

1963, Sept. 25 **Unwmk.** ***Perf. 14***

841	A135	25c dk bl, bl grn & ocher	18	10
842	A135	55c grn, grnsh bl & ocher	70	32

Issued to commemorate the "First" anniversary of the death of Dag Hammarskjold, Secretary General of the United Nations, 1953-61. See Nos. C836-C837a.

Dr. Luis Razetti A136

Dr. Francisco A. Risquez A137

1963, Oct. 20 **Litho.**

843	A136	35c bl, ocher & brn	35	18
844	A136	45c mag, ocher & brn	50	18

Issued to commemorate the centenary of the birth of Dr. Luis Razetti, physician. See Nos. C838-C839.

1963, Dec. 31 ***Perf. 11 1/2x12***

Design: 20c, Dr. Carlos J. Bello.

845	A137	15c multi	14	7
846	A137	20c multi	18	8

Issued to commemorate the centenary of the International Red Cross. See Nos. C840-C841.

Oil Field Workers A138

Pedro Gual A139

Designs: 10c, Oil refinery. 15c Crane and building construction. 30c, Cactus, train and truck. 40c, Tractor.

1964, Feb. 5 **Litho.** ***Perf. 14x13 1/2***

847	A138	5c multi	6	6
848	A138	10c multi	12	5
849	A138	15c multi	18	6
850	A138	30c multi	25	12
851	A138	40c multi	38	18
		Nos. 847-851 (5)	99	47

Issued to commemorate the centenary of the Department of Industrial Development. See Nos. C842-C846.

1964, Mar. 20 **Unwmk.** ***Perf. 14***

852	A139	40c lt ol grn	38	18
853	A139	50c lt red brn	42	20

Issued to commemorate the centenary of the death (in 1862) of Pedro Gual, statesman. See Nos. C847-C848.

Carlos Arvelo — A140

1964, Apr. 17 **Engr.** ***Perf. 13 1/2x14***
854 A140 1b dl bl & gray 90 45

Issued to commemorate the centenary of the death of Dr. Carlos Arvelo (1784-1862), chief physician of Bolivar's revolutionary army, director of Caracas Hospital, rector of Central University and professor of pathology.

Foundry Ladle and Molds A141

1964, May 22 ***Perf. 14x13 1/2***

855	A141	20c multi	20	8
856	A141	50c multi	40	20

Orinoco Steel Mills. See Nos. C849-C850.

Romulo Gallegos — A142

Perf. 11 1/2
1964, Aug. 3 **Unwmk.** **Litho.**

857	A142	5c dk & lt grn	7	6
858	A142	10c bl & pale bl	10	6
859	A142	15c dk & lt red lil	20	14
		Nos. 857-859,C852-C854 (6)	1.60	88

Issued to commemorate the 80th birthday of novelist Romulo Gallegos.

Angel Falls, Bolivar State — A143

Designs: 10c, Tropical landscape, Sucre State. 15c, San Juan Peaks, Guarico. 30c, Net fishermen, Anzoategui. 40c, Mountaineer, Merida.

1964 ***Perf. 13 1/2x14***

860	A143	5c multi	5	5
861	A143	10c multi	12	6
862	A143	15c multi	15	8
863	A143	30c multi	30	12
864	A143	40c multi	45	15
		Nos. 860-864 (5)	1.07	46

Issued for tourist publicity.

Issues of 1958-64 Surcharged in Black, Dark Blue or Lilac

RESELLADO
VALOR
Bs. 0,05

1965

865	A102	5c on 1b lt ol grn (#710)	40	7
866	A119	10c on 45c brt vio & org (#793)	14	8
867	A135	15c on 55c grn, grnsh bl & ocher (#842)	10	7
868	A126	20c on 3b multi (#824)	18	14
869	A110	25c on 45c pur (#757) (DB)	18	14
870	A128	25c on 1b multi (#830)	20	14
871	A128	25c on 3b multi (#831)	28	14
872	A124	25c on 3b multi (#811) (L)	18	14
873	A104	30c on 1b gray grn (#724)	20	14
874	A140	40c on 1b dl bl & gray (#854)	55	18
875	A133	60c on 80c bl grn & brn (#839)	70	28
		Nos. 865-875 (11)	3.11	1.52

Lines of surcharge arranged variously; old denomination obliterated with bars on Nos. 867, 870-72. See Nos. C856-C899.

Revenue Stamps of 1947 Surcharged in Red or Black

CORREOS
RESELLADO
VALOR
Bs. 0,05

1965 **Engr.** ***Perf. 12, 13 1/2 (No. 882)***
Imprint: "American Bank Note Co."

876	R1	5c on 5c emer	7	6
877	R1	5c on 20c red brn	7	6
878	R1	10c on 10c brn ol	7	6
879	R1	15c on 40c grn	7	6
880	R1	20c on 3b dk bl (R)	28	14
881	R1	25c on 5b vio bl (R)	55	28

882 R1 25c on 5b vio bl (R) (Imprint: "Bundesdruckerei Berlin") 28 14
883 R1 60c on 3b dk bl (R) 70 32
Nos. 876-883 (8) 2.09 1.12

Type R1 is illustrated above No. 401.

John F. Kennedy and Alliance for Progress Emblem A144

1965, Aug. 20 Photo. ***Perf. 12x11½***
884 A144 20c gray 28 14
885 A144 40c brt lil 40 20

Issued in memory of President John F. Kennedy (1917-1963). See Nos. C900-C901.

Map of Venezuela and Guiana by Codazzi, 1840 A145

Protesilaus Leucones A146

Maps of Venezuela and Guiana: 15c, by Juan M. Restrepo, 1827 (horiz.). 40c, by L. de Surville, 1778.

1965, Nov. 5 Litho. ***Perf. 13½***
886 A145 5c multi 7 6
887 A145 15c multi 20 8
888 A145 40c multi 40 14
a Souv. sheet of 3, #886-888, imperf. 1.40 1.40
Nos. 886-888,C905-C907 (6) 1.90 84

Issued to publicize Venezuela's claim to part of British Guiana.

No. 888a sold for 85c.

1966, Jan. 25 Litho. ***Perf. 13½x14***

Various Butterflies in Natural Colors

Black Inscriptions

889 A146 20c lt ol grn 20 9
890 A146 30c lt yel grn 30 15
891 A146 50c yellow 50 20
Nos. 889-891,C915-C917 (6) 3.30 1.60

Ship and Map of Atlantic Ocean A147

1966, Mar. 10 Litho. ***Perf. 13½x14***
892 A147 60c brn, bl & blk 90 45

Bicentenary of the first maritime mail.

"El Carite" Dance — A148

Various Folk Dances

Unwmk.

1966, Apr. 5 Litho. ***Perf. 14***
893 A148 5c gray & multi 7 5
894 A148 10c org & multi 14 6
895 A148 15c lem & multi 20 8
896 A148 20c lil & multi 28 14
897 A148 25c brt pink & multi 40 20
898 A148 35c yel grn & multi 48 28
Nos. 893-898 (6) 1.57 81

See Nos. C919-C924.

Type of Air Post Stamps and

Arturo Michelena, Self-portrait A149

Paintings: 1b, Penthesileia, battle scene. 1.05b, The Red Cloak.

Perf. 12½x12, 12x12½

1966, May 12 Litho. Unwmk.
899 A149 95c sep & buff 70 55
900 AP74 1b multi 80 55
901 AP74 1.05b multi 95 55
Nos. 899-901,C927-C929 (6) 4.90 3.30

Issued to commemorate the centenary of the birth of Arturo Michelena (1863-1898), painter. Miniature sheets of 12 exist.

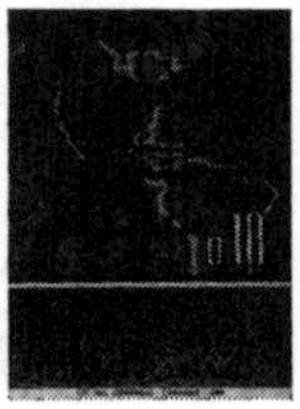
Construction Worker and Map of Americas — A150

Designs: 20c, as 10c. 30c, 65c, Labor monument. 35c, Machinery worker and map of Venezuela. 50c, Automobile assembly line.

1966, July 6 Litho. ***Perf. 14x13½***
902 A150 10c yel & blk 6 5
903 A150 20c lt grnsh bl & blk 18 6
904 A150 30c lt bl & vio 15 12
905 A150 35c lem & ol 22 12
906 A150 50c brt rose & cl 38 18
907 A150 65c sal pink & brn 50 25
Nos. 902-907 (6) 1.49 78

Issued to commemorate the 2nd Conference of Ministers of Labor of the Organization of American States.

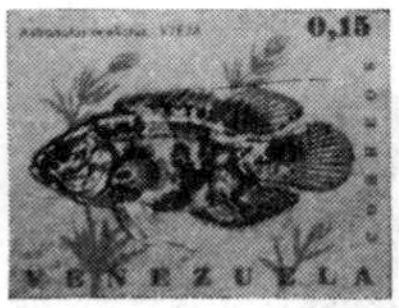
Velvet Cichlid A151

Fish: 25c, Perch cichlid. 45c, Piranha.

1966, Aug. 31 Litho. ***Perf. 13½x14***
908 A151 15c yel grn & multi 14 8
909 A151 25c cit & multi 20 14
910 A151 45c bl grn & multi 55 28
Nos. 908-910,C933-C935 (6) 3.29 1.70

Nativity — A152

Rubén Dario — A154

Satellite, Radar, Globe, Plane and Ship — A153

1966, Dec. 9 Litho. ***Perf. 14***
911 A152 65c vio & blk 60 28

Christmas 1966.

1966, Dec. 28 ***Perf. 13½x14***
912 A153 45c multi 45 22

Issued to commemorate the 30th anniversary of the Ministry of Communications.

1967 Litho. ***Perf. 14***
913 A154 70c gray bl & dk bl 75 45

Rubén Dario (pen name of Felix Rubén Garcia Sarmiento, 1867-1916), Nicaraguan poet, newspaper correspondent and diplomat.

Old Building and Arms, University of Zulia A155

Perf. 13½x14

1967, Apr. 21 Litho. Unwmk.
914 A155 80c gold, blk & car 75 45

Issued to commemorate the 75th anniversary of the founding of the University of Zulia.

Front Page and Printing Press — A156

1968, June 27 Photo. ***Perf. 14x13½***
915 A156 1.50b emer, blk & brn 1.10 60

Issued to commemorate the 150th anniversary of the newspaper Correo del Orinoco.

Boll Weevil A157

Insect Pests: 20c, Corn borer (vert.). 90c, Tobacco caterpillar.

Perf. 14x13½, 13½x14

1968, Aug. 30 Litho.
916 A157 20c multi 28 14
917 A157 75c ol & multi 55 28
918 A157 90c multi 70 35
Nos. 916-918,C989-C991 (6) 2.09 1.05

Guayana Substation — A158

Designs: 45c, Guaira River Dam (horiz.). 50c, Macagua Dam and power plant (horiz.). 80c, Guri River Dam and power plant.

1968, Nov. 8 Litho.
919 A158 15c fawn & multi 15 8
920 A158 45c dl yel & multi 40 20
921 A158 50c bl grn & multi 55 22
922 A158 80c bl & multi 85 50

Electrification program.

House and Piggy Bank — A159

1968, Dec. 6 Litho. ***Perf. 13½x14***
923 A159 45c bl & multi 45 22

National Savings System.

Nursery and Child Planting Tree A160

Designs: 15c, Child planting tree (vert.; this design used as emblem on entire issue). 30c, Waterfall (vert.). 45c, Logging. 55c, Fields and village (vert.). 75c, Palambra (fish).

Perf. 14x13½, 13½x14

1968, Dec. 19 Litho.
924 A160 15c multi 7 6
925 A160 20c multi 14 7
926 A160 30c multi 20 10
927 A160 45c multi 28 14
928 A160 55c multi 55 28
929 A160 75c multi 40 20
Nos. 924-929 (6) 1.64 85

Issued to publicize nature conservation. See Nos. C1000-C1005.

Colorada Beach, Sucre A161

Designs: 45c, Church of St. Francis of Yare, Miranda. 90c, Stilt houses, Zulia.

1969, Jan. 24 ***Perf. 13½x14***
930 A161 15c multi 14 7
931 A161 45c multi 40 14
932 A161 90c multi 60 50
Nos. 930-932,C1006-C1008 (6) 1.85 1.13

Tourist publicity. For souvenir sheet see No. C1007a.

Bolivar Addressing Congress of Angostura — A162

1969, Feb. 2 Litho. ***Perf. 11***
933 A162 45c multi 45 22

Issued to commemorate the sesquicentennial of the Congress of Angostura (Ciudad Bolivar).

Martin Luther King, Jr. — A163

1969, Apr. 1 Litho. ***Perf. 13½***

934 A163 1b bl, red & dk brn 60 30

Issued in memory of the Rev. Dr. Martin Luther King, Jr. (1929-1968), American civil rights leader and recipient of the Nobel Peace Prize, 1964.

Tabebuia A164

Trees: 65c, Erythrina poeppigiana. 90c, Platymiscium.

1969, May 30 Litho. ***Perf. 13½x14***

935 A164 50c multi 40 20
936 A164 65c gray & multi 55 28
937 A164 90c pink & multi 80 40
Nos. 935-937,C1009-C1011 (6) 2.30 1.16

Issued to publicize nature conservation.

Still Life with Pheasant, by Rojas A165

Paintings by Cristobal Rojas (1858-1890): 25c, On the Balcony (vert.). 45c, The Christening. 50c, The Empty Place (family). 60c, The Tavern. 1b, Man's Arm (vert.).

Perf. 14x13½, 13½x14
1969, June 27 Litho. Unwmk.
Size: 32x42mm, 42x32mm

938 A165 25c gold & multi 18 15
939 A165 35c gold & multi 32 18
940 A165 45c gold & multi 50 28
941 A165 50c gold & multi 60 30
942 A165 60c gold & multi 75 35

Perf. 11
Size: 26x53mm

943 A165 1b gold & multi 1.10 60
Nos. 938-943 (6) 3.45 1.86

ILO Emblem A166

1969, July 28 ***Perf. 14x13½***

944 A166 2.50b fawn & blk 1.50 1.25

50th anniv. of the ILO.

Charter and Coat of Arms A167

Industrial Complex A168

1969, Aug. 26 Litho. ***Perf. 13½***

945 A167 45c ultra & multi 50 22
946 A168 1b multi 75 35

Industrial development.

House with Arcade, Carora — A169

Designs: 25c, Ruins of Pastora Church. 55c, Chapel of the Cross. 65c, House of Culture.

1969, Sept. 8 ***Perf. 13x14½***

947 A169 20c multi 14 7
948 A169 25c multi 20 10
949 A169 55c multi 55 28
950 A169 65c multi 70 32

400th anniversary of city of Carora.

Simon Bolivar in Madrid — A170

Designs: 10c, Bolivar's wedding, Madrid, 1802 (horiz.). 35c, Bolivar monument. Madrid.

Perf. 13½x14, 14x13½
1969, Oct. 28 Litho.

951 A170 10c multi 8 6
952 A170 15c brn red & blk 20 8
953 A170 35c multi 32 14
a Souv. sheet of 2 95 95

Issued to commemorate Bolivar's sojourn in Spain. No. 953a contains 2 imperf. stamps similar to Nos. 952-953 with simulated perforation. Sold for 75c.

"Birds in the Woods" — A171

Design: 45c, "Children in Summer Camp." Both designs are after children's paintings.

1969, Dec. 12 Litho. ***Perf. 12½***

954 A171 5c emer & multi 7 6
955 A171 45c red & multi 50 28

Issued for Children's Day.

Map of Great Colombia A172

1969, Dec. 16 Litho. ***Perf. 11½***

956 A172 45c multi 40 20

Issued to commemorate the 150th anniversary of the founding of the State of Great Colombia.

St. Anthony's, Clarines A173

Churches: 30c, Church of the Conception, Caroni. 40c, St. Michael's, Burbusay. 45c, St. Anthony's, Maturin. 75c, St. Nicholas, Moruy. 1b, Coro Cathedral.

1970, Jan. 15 ***Perf. 14***

957 A173 10c pink & multi 7 6
958 A173 30c emer & multi 20 10
959 A173 40c yel & multi 40 20
960 A173 45c gray bl & multi 55 28
a Souv. sheet of 1, imperf. 1.10 1.10
961 A173 75c yel & multi 70 32
962 A173 1b org & multi 80 40
Nos. 957-962 (6) 2.72 1.36

Colonial architecture.

No. 960a sold for 75c.

Seven Hills of Valera — A174

1970, Feb. 13 Litho. ***Perf. 13x14½***

963 A174 95c multi 75 35

Sesquicentennial of the city of Valera.

Monochaetum Humboldtianum A175

Flowers: 25c, Symbolanthus vasculosis. 45c, Cavedishia splendens. 1b, Befaria glauca.

1970, July 29 Litho. ***Perf. 14x13½***

964 A175 20c multi 20 8
965 A175 25c multi 40 14
966 A175 45c multi 55 28
967 A175 1b multi 80 40
Nos. 964-967,C1049-C1052 (8) 3.78 1.80

Battle of Boyaca, by Martin Tovar y Tovar A176

1970, Aug. 7 ***Perf. 13½x14***

968 A176 30c multi 28 14

150th anniversary of Battle of Boyaca.

Our Lady of Belén de San Mateo — A177

Designs: 35c, Pastoral Cross of Archbishop Silvestre Guevera y Lira, 1867. 40c, Our Lady of Valle. 90c, Virgin of Chiquinquira. 1b, Our Lady of Socorro de Valencia.

1970, Sept. 1

969 A177 35c gray & multi 32 14
970 A177 40c gray & multi 40 20
971 A177 60c gray & multi 60 30
a Souv. sheet of 1, imperf. 95 95
972 A177 90c gray & multi 70 40
973 A177 1b gray & multi 95 50
Nos. 969-973 (5) 2.97 1.54

The designs are from sculptures and paintings in various Venezuelan churches. No. 971a sold for 75c.

Venezuela No. 22 and EXFILCA Emblem — A178

Designs: 20c, EXFILCA emblem and flags of participating nations (vert.). 70c, Venezuela No. C13 and EXFILCA emblem (vert.).

1970, Nov. 28 Litho. ***Perf. 11***

974 A178 20c yel & multi 20 7
975 A178 25c dk bl & multi 28 10
976 A178 70c brn & multi 55 28
a Souv. sheet of 1, imperf. 1.10 1.10

Issued to publicize EXFILCA 70, 2nd Interamerican Philatelic Exhibition, Caracas, Nov. 27-Dec. 6. No. 976a is a hexagon with each side 50mm long. Sold for 85c.

Guardian Angel, by Juan Pedro Lopez — A179

1970, Dec. 1 Litho. ***Perf. 14½x13½***

977 A179 45c dl yel & multi 40 20

Christmas 1970.

Jet and 1920 Plane A180

1970, Dec. 10 ***Perf. 13x14***

978 A180 5c bl & multi 7 6

Venezuelan Air Force, 50th anniversary.

The Catalogue editors cannot undertake to appraise, identify or judge the genuineness or condition of stamps.

Question Mark Full of Citizens — A181

1971, Apr. 30 Litho. *Perf. 14x13½*
Lt. Green, Red & Black

979	A181	Block of 4	2.50	1.40
a		30c frame L & T	60	25
b		30c frame T & R	60	25
c		30c frame L & B	60	25
d		30c frame B & R	60	25

National Census, 1971. The frame encircles all 4 stamps of No. 979; each stamp in block has frame on 2 sides. Sheet of 20 contains 5 No. 979 and 5 blocks of 4 labels inscribed in green "Censo Nacional 1971." See No. C1054.

Battle of Carabobo A182

1971, June 21 *Perf. 13½x14*

980	A182	2b bl & multi	1.40	80

Sesquicentennial of Battle of Carabobo.

Map of Federal District A183

Designs: State maps. 25c, 55c, 85c, 90c, vert.

1971 Litho. *Perf. 13½x14, 14x13½*

981	A183	5c *shown*	7	6
982	A183	15c *Monagas*	10	6
983	A183	20c *Nueva Esparta*	14	7
984	A183	25c *Portuguesa*	18	7
985	A183	45c *Sucre*	25	12
986	A183	55c *Tachira*	35	18
987	A183	65c *Trujillo*	45	20
988	A183	75c *Yaracuyo*	55	28
989	A183	85c *Zulia*	70	28
990	A183	90c *Amazonas*	1.10	32
991	A183	1b *Federal Dependencies*	1.40	55
		Nos. 981-991 (11)	5.29	2.19

Issue dates: 5c, July 15; 15c, 20c, Aug. 16; 25c, 45c, Sept. 15; 55c, 65c, Oct. 15; 75c, 85c, Nov. 15; 90c, 1b, Dec. 15.
See Nos. C1035-C1048.

Madonna and Child A184

Luis Daniel Beauperthuy A185

Design: No. 993, Madonna, and Jesus in manger.

1971, Dec. 1 *Perf. 11*

992	A184	25c multi	30	15
993	A184	25c multi	30	15
		Pair, #992-993	60	50

Christmas 1971. Nos. 992-993 printed checkerwise in same sheet.

1971, Dec. 10 *Perf. 14x13½*

994	A185	1b vio bl & multi	75	35

Dr. Luis Daniel Beauperthuy, scientist.

Globe in Heart Shape — A186

Flags of Americas and Arms of Venezuela — A187

1972, Apr. 7 Litho. *Perf. 14x13½*

995	A186	1b red, ultra & blk	75	45

"Your heart is your health," World Health Day 1972.

1972, May 15 Litho. *Perf. 14x13½*

Designs: 4b, Venezuelan flag. 5b, National anthem. 10b, Araguaney, national tree. 15b, Map, North and South America. All show flags of American nations in background.

996	A187	3b multi	1.90	1.25
997	A187	4b multi	2.50	1.90
998	A187	5b multi	3.00	2.50
999	A187	10b multi	6.25	3.75
1000	A187	15b multi	9.25	5.00
		Nos. 996-1000 (5)	22.90	14.40

"Venezuela in America."

Parque Central Complex A188

Designs: No. 1002, Front view ("Parque Central" on top). No. 1003, Side view ("Parque Central" at right).

1972, July 25 *Perf. 11½*

1001	A188	30c yel & multi	20	14
1002	A188	30c bl & multi	20	14
1003	A188	30c red & multi	20	14
		Strip of 3, #1001-1003	95	95

Completion of "Parque Central" middle-income housing project, Caracas. Nos. 1001-1003 printed se-tenant.

Mahatma Gandhi — A189

1972, Oct. 2 Litho. *Perf. 13½x14*

1004	A189	60c multi	60	30

103rd birthday of Mohandas K. Gandhi (1869-1948), leader in India's fight for independence, advocate of non-violence.

Children Playing Music — A190

Design: No. 1006, Children roller skating.

1972, Dec. 5 Litho. *Perf. 13½x14*

1005	A190	30c multi	20	14
1006	A190	30c multi	20	14
		Pair, #1005-1006	50	50

Christmas 1972. Nos. 1005-1006 printed se-tenant.

Indigo Snake A191

Snake: 15c, South American chicken snake. 25c, Venezuelan lance-head. 30c, Coral snake. 60c, Casabel rattlesnake. 1b, Boa constrictor.

1972, Dec. 15 Litho. *Perf. 13½x14*

1007	A191	10c blk & multi	8	6
1008	A191	15c blk & multi	10	8
1009	A191	25c blk & multi	30	15
1010	A191	30c blk & multi	35	18
1011	A191	60c blk & multi	60	30
1012	A191	1b blk & multi	90	45
		Nos. 1007-1012 (6)	2.33	1.22

Copernicus A192

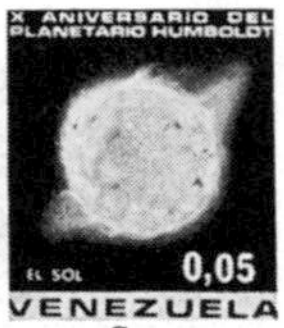

Sun A193

Designs: 5c, Model of solarcentric system. 15c, Copernicus' book "De Revolutionibus."

1973, Feb. 10 Litho. *Perf. 13½x14*

1013	A192	5c multi	8	5
1014	A192	10c multi	15	6
1015	A192	15c multi	20	9
		Strip of 3, #1013-1015	45	45

500th anniversary of the birth of Nicolaus Copernicus (1473-1543), Polish astronomer. Nos. 1013-1015 printed se-tenant.

1973 Litho. *Perf. 13½x14*
Size: 26½x29mm

Designs: Planetary system.

1016	A193	5c *shown*	6	5
1017	A193	5c *Earth*	6	5
1018	A193	20c *Mars*	45	9
1019	A193	20c *Saturn*	30	9
1020	A193	30c *Planetoids*	35	15
1021	A193	40c *Neptune*	45	18
1022	A193	50c *Venus*	60	30
1023	A193	60c *Jupiter*	75	35
1024	A193	75c *Uranus*	90	45
1025	A193	90c *Pluto*	1.10	50
1026	A193	90c *Moon*	1.25	60
1027	A193	1b *Mercury*	1.50	75

Size: 27x55mm

1028	A193	10c *Orbits and Saturn*	18	6
1029	A193	15c *Sun, Mercury, Venus, Earth*	30	6
1030	A193	15c *Jupiter, Uranus, Neptune, Pluto*	35	6
		Strip of 3, #1028-1030	90	90
		Nos. 1016-1030 (15)	8.60	3.74

10th anniversary of Humboldt Planetarium. Nos. 1028-1030 printed se-tenant with continuous design showing solar system.
Issue dates: Nos. 1016, 1018, 1021, 1023-1025, Mar. 15; others Mar. 30.

OAS Emblem, Map of Americas — A194

1973, Apr. 30 Litho. *Perf. 13½x14*

1031	A194	60c multi	45	22

25th anniversary of the Organization of American States.

José Antonio Paez — A195

Street of the Lancers, Puerto Cabello — A196

Designs: 10c, Paez in uniform. 30c, Paez and horse, from old print. 2b, Paez at Battle of Centauro (horiz.). 10c, 2b are after contemporary paintings.

1973 *Perf. 14x13½, 13½x14*

1032	A195	10c gold & multi	8	6
1033	A195	30c red, blk & gold	22	10
1034	A195	50c bl, vio bl & dk brn	45	22
1035	A196	1b multi	90	45
1036	A195	2b gold & multi	1.50	90
		Nos. 1032-1036 (5)	3.15	1.73

Centenary of the death of Gen. José Antonio Paez (1790-1873), leader in War of Independence, President of Venezuela. The 1b commemorates the sesquicentenary of the fall of Puerto Cabello.
Issue dates: Nos. 1033-1034, May 6; Nos. 1032, 1036, June 13; No. 1035, Nov. 8.

José P. Padilla, Mariano Montilla, Manuel Manrique — A197

Designs: 1b, Naval battle. 2b, Line-up for naval battle.

1973, July 24 Litho. *Perf. 12½*

1037	A197	50c multi	32	18
1038	A197	1b multi	70	32
1039	A197	2b multi	1.40	70

150th anniv. of the Battle of Maracaibo.

Bishop Ramos de Lora — A198

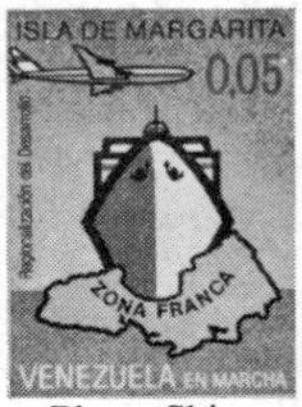

Plane, Ship, Margarita Island — A199

1973, Aug. 1 Photo. ***Perf. 14x13½***

1040	A198	75c gold & dk brn	50	22

Sesquicentennial of the birth of Ramos de Lora (1722-1790), first Bishop of Merida de Maracaibo and founder of the Colegio Seminario, the forerunner of the University of the Andes.

1973, Sept. 8 Litho. ***Perf. 14x13½***

1041	A199	5c multi	12	6

Establishment of Margarita Island as a free port.

Map of Golden Road and Waterfall — A200

Designs (Road Map and): 10c, Scarlet macaw. 20c, Church ruins. 50c, 60c, Indian mountain sanctuary. 90c, Colonial church. 1b, Flags of Venezuela and Brazil.

1973, Oct. 1 Litho. ***Perf. 13***

1042	A200	5c blk & multi	6	6
1043	A200	10c blk & multi	8	6
1044	A200	20c blk & multi	18	8
1045	A200	50c blk & multi	45	22
1046	A200	60c blk & multi	45	22
1047	A200	90c blk & multi	65	30
1048	A200	1b blk & multi	75	42
		Nos. 1042-1048 (7)	2.62	1.36

Completion of the Golden Road from Santa Elena de Uairen, Brazil, to El Dorado, Venezuela. Issue dates: 50c, 60c, Oct. 30; others Oct. 1.

Gen. Paez Dam and Power Station — A201

1973, Oct. 14 ***Perf. 14x13½***

1049	A201	30c multi	25	12

Opening of the Gen. José Antonio Paez Dam and Power Station.

Child on Slide — A202

Designs: No. 1051, Fairytale animals. No. 1052, Children's book. No. 1053, Children disembarking from plane for vacation.

1973, Dec. 4 Litho. ***Perf. 12***

1050	A202	10c multi	22	6
1051	A202	10c multi	22	6
1052	A202	10c multi	22	6
1053	A202	10c multi	22	6

Children's Foundation Festival.

King Following Star — A203

Christmas: No. 1055, Two Kings.

1973, Dec. 5 Litho. ***Perf. 14x13½***

1054	A203	30c multi	35	15
1055	A203	30c multi	35	15
		Pair, #1054-1055	85	85

Nos. 1054-1055 printed se-tenant.

Regional Map of Venezuela A204

1973, Dec. 13 ***Perf. 13½x14***

1056	A204	25c multi	22	8

Introduction of regionalization.

Handicraft A205

Designs: 35c, Industrial park. 45c, Cog wheels and chimney.

1973, Dec. 18 ***Perf. 14x13½***

1057	A205	15c bl & multi	15	6
1058	A205	35c multi	30	9
1059	A205	45c yel & multi	45	18

Progress in Venezuela and jobs for the handicapped.

Map of Carupano and Revelers — A206

1974, Feb. 22 ***Perf. 13½x14***

1060	A206	5c multi	12	6

10th anniversary of Carupano Carnival.

Congress Emblem — A207

1974, May 20 Litho. ***Perf. 13½***

1061	A207	50c multi	45	15

9th Venezuelan Engineering Congress, Maracaibo, May 19-25.

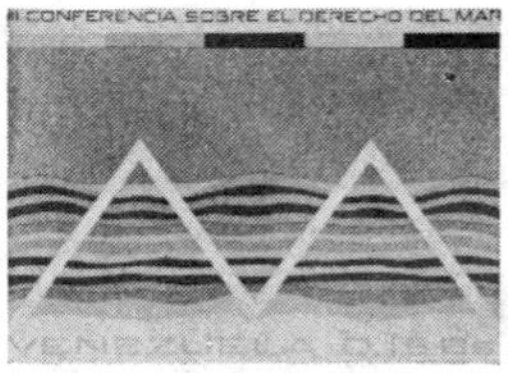

Waves and "M" A208

Designs: Under-water photographs of deep-sea fish and marine life.

1974, June 20 Litho. ***Perf. 12½***

1062	A208	15c multi	10	6
1063	A208	35c multi	20	10
1064	A208	75c multi	50	22
1065	A208	80c multi	55	32

3rd U.N. Conference on the Law of the Sea, Caracas, June 20-Aug. 29.

Pupil and New School — A209

Designs: 10c, 15c, 20c, like 5c. 25c, 30c, 35c, 40c, Suburban housing development. 45c, 50c, 55c, 60c, Highway and overpass. 65c, 70c, 75c, 80c, Playing field (sport). 85c, 90c, 95c, 1b, Operating room. All designs include Venezuelan coat of arms, coins and banknotes.

1974 ***Perf. 14x13½***

1066	A209	5c bl & multi	6	6
1067	A209	10c ultra & multi	8	6
1068	A209	15c vio & multi	8	6
1069	A209	20c lil & multi	10	7
1070	A209	25c multi	12	6
1071	A209	30c multi	40	20
1072	A209	35c multi	20	8
1073	A209	40c ol & multi	32	12
1074	A209	45c multi	32	15
1075	A209	50c grn & multi	32	15
1076	A209	55c multi	55	30
1077	A209	60c multi	42	20
1078	A209	65c bis & multi	1.00	50
1079	A209	70c multi	45	20
1080	A209	75c multi	50	22
1081	A209	80c brn & multi	50	22
1082	A209	85c ver & multi	50	22
1083	A209	90c multi	65	24
1084	A209	95c multi	1.25	65
1085	A209	1b multi	65	32
		Nos. 1066-1085 (20)	8.47	4.08

"Pay your Taxes" campaign.

Bolivar at Battle of Junin — A210

1974, Aug. 6 Litho. ***Perf. 13½x14***

1086	A210	2b multi	1.50	75

Sesquicentennial of the Battle of Junin.

Globe and UPU Emblem — A211

Design: 50c, Postrider, sailing ship, steamer and jet.

1974, Oct. 9 ***Perf. 12***

1087	A211	45c dk bl & multi	32	15
1088	A211	50c blk & multi	40	20

Centenary of Universal Postal Union.

Rufino Blanco-Fombona A212

Designs: Portraits of Blanco-Fombona and his books.

1974, Oct. 16 Litho. ***Perf. 12½***

1089	A212	10c gray & multi	8	6
1090	A212	30c yel & multi	20	10
1091	A212	45c multi	30	15
1092	A212	90c buff & multi	50	22

Centenary of the birth of Rufino Blanco-Fombona (1874-1944), writer.

Children A213

1974, Nov. 29 Litho. ***Perf. 13½***

1093	A213	70c bl & multi	50	24

Children's Foundation Festival.

General Sucre — A214

Globe with South American Map and Flags — A215

Battle of Ayacucho — A216

Design: 1b, Map of South America with battles marked.

1974, Dec. 9 ***Perf. 14x13½, 13½x14***

1094	A214	30c multi	20	10
1095	A215	50c multi	30	22
1096	A215	1b multi	65	32
1097	A216	2b multi	1.25	65

Sesquicentennial of the Battle of Ayacucho.

The indexes in each volume of the Scott Catalogue contain many listings which help to identify stamps.

Adoration of the Shepherds, by J. B. Mayno
A217 A218

1974, Dec. 16 Photo. *Perf. 14x13½*

1098	A217	30c gold & multi	22	15
1099	A218	30c gold & multi	22	15
		Pair, #1098-1099	70	70

Christmas 1974. Printed se-tenant.

Road Building, 1905 and El Ciempies Overpass, 1972 — A219

Designs: 20c, 1b, Jesus Muñoz Tebar, first Minister of Public Works. 25c, Bridges on Caracas-La Guaira Road, 1912 and 1953. 40c, View of Caracas, 1874 and 1974. 70c, Tucacas Railroad Station, 1911, and projected terminal, 1974. 80c, Anatomical Institute, Caracas, 1911, and Social Security Hospital, 1969. 85c, Quininari River Bridge, 1804, and Orinoco River Bridge, 1967.

1974, Dec. 18 Litho. *Perf. 12½*

1100	A219	5c ultra & multi	8	5
1101	A219	20c ocher & blk	22	7
1102	A219	25c bl & multi	25	7
1103	A219	40c yel & multi	22	15
1104	A219	70c grn & multi	85	22
1105	A219	80c multi	1.00	30
1106	A219	85c org & multi	1.25	32
1107	A219	1b red & blk	1.65	50
		Nos. 1100-1107 (8)	5.52	1.68

Centenary of the Ministry of Public Works.

Women and IWY Emblem — A220

1975, Oct. 8 Litho. *Perf. 13½x14*

1108	A220	90c multi	50	32

International Women's Year.

Scout Emblem and Tents A221

1975, Nov. 11 Litho. *Perf. 13½x14*

1109	A221	20c multi	12	7
1110	A221	80c multi	42	25

14th World Boy Scout Jamboree, Lillehammer, Norway, July 29-Aug. 7.

Adoration of the Shepherds
A222 A223

1975, Dec. 5 Litho. *Perf. 14*

1111	A222	30c multi	20	10
1112	A223	30c multi	20	10
		Pair, #1111-1112	70	70

Christmas 1975. Printed se-tenant.

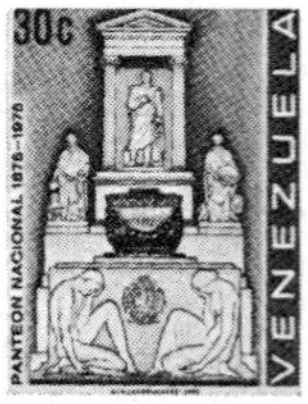

Bolivar's Tomb — A224

Design: 1.05b, National Pantheon.

1976, Feb. 2 Engr. *Perf. 14x13½*

1113	A224	30c gray & ultra	15	7
1114	A224	1.05b sep & car	50	22

Centenary of National Pantheon.

Bolivia Flag Colors A225

1976, Mar. 22 Litho. *Perf. 13½*

1115	A225	60c multi	35	15

Sesquicentennial of Bolivia's independence.

Aerial Map Survey — A226

1976, Apr. 8 *Perf. 13½x12½*

1116	A226	1b blk & vio bl	50	22

Natl. Cartographic Institute, 40th anniv.

Gen. Ribas' Signature A227

José Felix Ribas A228

1976, Apr. 26 Photo. *Perf. 12½x13*

1117	A227	40c red & grn	24	10

Perf. 13½

1118	A228	55c multi	35	15

Gen. José Felix Ribas (1775-1815), independence hero, birth bicentenary.

Musicians of the Chacao School, by Armandio Barrios — A229

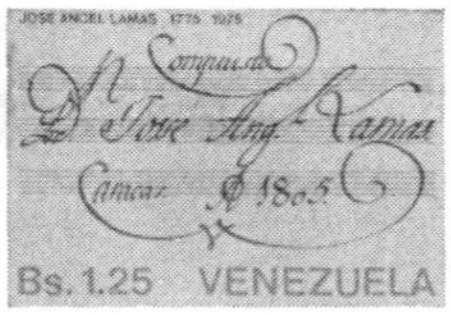

Lamas's Colophon A230

1976, May 13 Litho. *Perf. 13½x14*

1119	A229	75c multi	35	22

Perf. 12½x13½
Photo.

1120	A230	1.25b buff, red & gray	60	35

José Angel Lamas (1775-1814), composer, birth bicentenary.

Bolivar, by JoséMaria Espinoza — A231

1976 Engr. *Perf. 12½*
Size: 18x22½mm

1121	A231	5c green	5	5
1122	A231	10c lil rose	8	5
1123	A231	15c brown	8	5
1124	A231	20c black	8	5
1125	A231	25c yellow	10	6
1126	A231	30c vio bl	12	8
1127	A231	45c dk pur	15	8
1128	A231	50c orange	20	8
1129	A231	65c blue	24	10
1130	A231	1b vermilion	35	32

Size: 26x32mm

1131	A231	2b gray	70	32
1132	A231	3b vio bl	1.00	50
1133	A231	4b yellow	1.25	65
1134	A231	5b orange	1.75	85
1135	A231	10b dl pur	3.50	1.65
1136	A231	15b blue	5.25	2.50
1137	A231	20b vermilion	6.75	3.25
		Nos. 1121-1137 (17)	21.65	10.64

Coil Stamps

1978, May 22 Engr. *Perf. 14 Horiz.*
Size: 18x22½mm

1138	A231	5c green	5	5
1139	A231	10c lil rose	5	5
1140	A231	15c brown	8	5
1141	A231	20c black	10	5
1142	A231	25c yellow	12	6
1143	A231	30c vio bl	12	8
1144	A231	45c dk pur	20	8
1144A	A231	50c orange	22	8
1144B	A231	65c blue	25	10
1144C	A231	1b vermilion	42	15
		Nos. 1138-1144C (10)	1.61	75

Black control number on back of every fifth stamp. See Nos. 1305-1307, 1362-1366, 1401-1409.

Maze A232

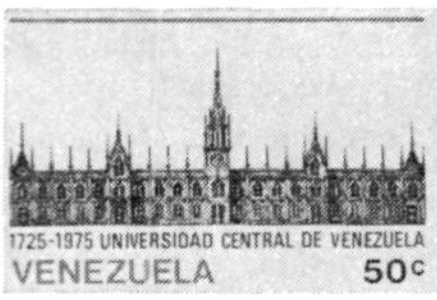

Central University A233

Faculty Emblems A234

1976, June 1 Litho. *Perf. 12½x13½*

1145	A232	30c multi	15	7
1146	A233	50c yel, org & blk	24	15
1147	A234	90c blk & yel	52	35

Central University of Venezuela, 250th anniversary.

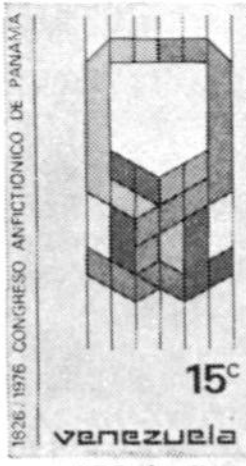

"Unity" A235

Washington, US Bicent. Emblem A236

Designs: 45c, 1.25b, similar to 15c.

1976, June 29 Litho. *Perf. 12½*

1148	A235	15c multi	10	5
1149	A235	45c multi	24	7
1150	A235	1.25b multi	55	35

Amphictyonic Congress of Panama, Sesquicentennial.

1976, July 4 Engr. *Perf. 14*

US Bicentennial Emblem and: No. 1152, Jefferson. No. 1153, Lincoln. No. 1154, F. D. Roosevelt. No. 1155, J. F. Kennedy.

1151	A236	1b red brn & blk	52	32
1152	A236	1b grn & blk	52	32
1153	A236	1b pur & blk	52	32
1154	A236	1b bl & blk	52	32
1155	A236	1b ol & blk	52	32
		Nos. 1151-1155 (5)	2.60	1.60

American Bicentennial.

Valve A237

Ornament A239

Nativity, by Barbaro Rivas — A238

Designs: Computer drawings of valves and pipelines.

1976, Nov. 8 Photo. *Perf. 13x14*

1156	A237	10c multi	8	5
1157	A237	30c multi	12	8
1158	A237	35c multi	14	10
1159	A237	40c multi	15	7
1160	A237	55c multi	24	15
1161	A237	90c multi	45	24
		Nos. 1156-1161 (6)	1.18	69

Nationalization of the oil industry.

1976, Dec. 1 Litho. *Perf. 13½x14*

1162	A238	30c multi	35	7

Christmas 1976.

Lithographed and Embossed

1976, Dec. 15 *Perf. 14x13½*

1163	A239	60c yel & blk	35	15

Declaration of Bogota (economic agreements of Andean countries), 10th anniv.

Coat of Arms of Barinas — A240

1977, May 25 Photo. *Perf. 12½x13*

1164	A240	50c multi	35	15

400th anniv. of the founding of Barinas.

Crucified Christ, Patron Saint of La Grita — A241

1977, Aug. 6 Litho. *Perf. 13*

1165	A241	30c multi	20	7

400th anniversary of the founding of La Grita (in 1976).

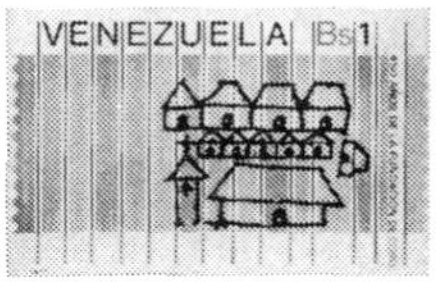

Symbolic City A242

1977, Aug. 26 Litho. *Perf. 13½*

1166	A242	1b multi	50	22

450th anniversary of the founding of Coro.

Communications Symbols — A243

1977, Sept. 30 Litho. *Perf. 13½x14*

1167	A243	85c multi	50	15

9th Interamerican Postal and Telecommunications Staff Congress, Caracas, Sept. 26-30.

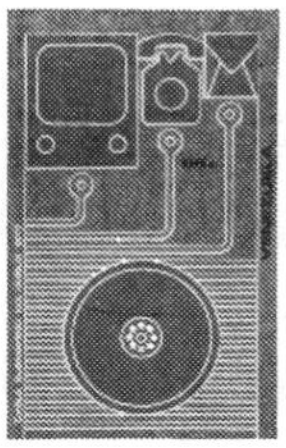

Cable Connecting with TV, Telephone and Circuit Box — A244

1977, Oct. 12 Litho. *Perf. 14x13½*

1168	A244	95c multi	50	15

Inauguration of Columbus underwater cable linking Venezuela and the Canary Islands.

"Venezuela" A245

Designs: "Venezuela" horizontal on 50c, 1.05b; reading up on 80c, 1.25b; reading down on 1.50b.

1977, Nov. 26 Photo. *Perf. 13½x13*

1169	A245	30c brt yel & blk	12	8
1170	A245	50c dp org & blk	22	8
1171	A245	80c gray & blk	42	15
1172	A245	1.05b red & blk	50	20
1173	A245	1.25b yel & blk	55	20
1174	A245	1.50b gray & blk	70	24
		Nos. 1169-1174 (6)	2.51	95

1st anniv. of nationalization of iron industry.

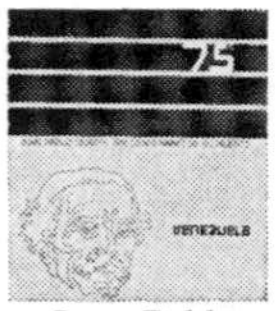

Juan Pablo Duarte — A246

Nativity, Colonial Sculpture — A247

1977, Dec. 8 Engr. *Perf. 11x13*

1175	A246	75c blk & lil	40	15

Juan Pablo Duarte (1813-1876), leader in liberation struggle.

1977, Dec. 15 Litho. *Perf. 13½*

1176	A247	30c grn & multi	12	8

Christmas 1977.

OPEC Emblem — A248

1977, Dec. 20

1177	A248	1.05b brt & lt bl & blk	50	15

50th Conference of Oil Producing and Exporting Countries, Caracas.

Racing Bicyclists A249

Design: 1.25b, Bicyclist.

1978, Jan. 16 Litho. *Perf. 13½x13*

1178	A249	5c multi	5	5
1179	A249	1.25b multi	55	20

World Bicycling Championships, San Cristobal, Tachira, Aug. 22-Sept. 4.

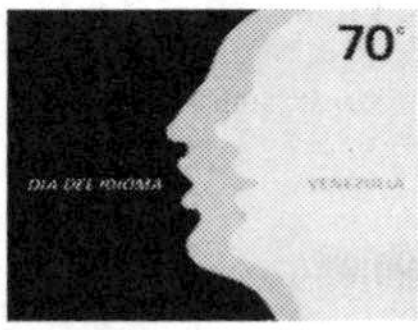

Profiles A250

1978, Apr. 21 Litho. *Perf. 13½x14*

1180	A250	70c blk, gray & lil	32	15

Language Day.

Magnetic Computer Tape and Satellite A251

1978, May 17 Litho. *Perf. 14*

1184	A251	75c vio bl	35	20

10th World Telecommunications Day.

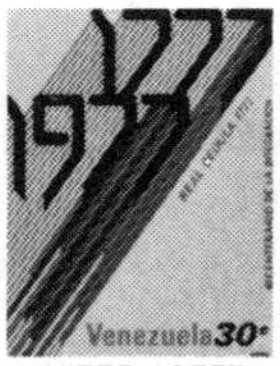

"1777-1977" A252

Goya's Carlos III as Computer Print A253

1978, June 23 Litho. *Perf. 12*

1185	A252	30c multi	10	8
1186	A253	1b multi	50	15

200th anniversary of Venezuelan unification.

Bolivar Bicentenary

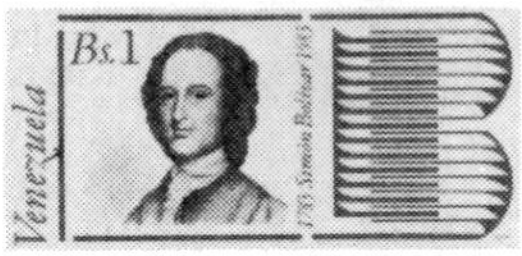

Juan Vicente Bolivar y Ponte, Father of Simon Bolivar — A254

The Oath on Monte Sacro, Rome, by Tito Salas — A255

Designs: 30c, Bolivar as infant in nursemaid's arms (detail from design of No. 1189). No. 1189, Baptism of the Liberator, by Tito Salas, 1929.

1978, July 24 Engr. *Perf. 12½*

1187	A254	30c emer & blk	15	10
1188	A254	1b multi	50	22

Souvenir Sheet

Litho.

Perf. 14

1189	A255	Sheet of 5	13.00	13.00
a		50c, single stamp	1.25	1.25

1978, Dec. 17 Engr. *Perf. 12½*

Designs: 30c, Bolivar at 25. 1b, Simon Rodriguez (Bolivar's tutor).

1190	A254	30c multi	10	8
1191	A254	1b rose red & blk	32	15

Souvenir Sheet

Litho.

Perf. 14

1192	A255	Sheet of 5	1.00	1.00
a		50c, single stamp	15	15

Size of souvenir sheet stamps: 20x24mm. Size of No. 1189: 154x130mm. Size of No. 1192: 130x155mm.

1979, July 24 Engr. *Perf. 12½*

Designs: 30c, Alexandre Sabes Petion, president of Haiti. 1b, Bolivar's signature. No. 1195a, Partial map of Jamaica (horiz.). No. 1195b, Partial map of Jamaica (vert.). No. 1195c, Bolivar, 1816. No. 1195d, Luis Brion. No. 1195e, Petion.

1193	A254	30c org, vio & blk	10	8
1194	A254	1b red org & blk	32	15

Souvenir Sheet

Litho.

Perf. 14

1195	A255	Sheet of 5	1.00	1.00
a-e		50c, any single	15	15

Size of souvenir sheet stamps: 26x20, 20x26mm.

1979, Dec. 17 Engr. *Perf. 12½*

Designs: 30c, Bolivar. 1b, Slave. No. 1198, Freeing of the Slaves, by Tito Salas. (30c, 1b, details from design of No. 1198.)

1196	A254	30c multi	10	8
1197	A254	1b multi	32	15

Souvenir Sheet

Litho.

Perf. 14

1198	A255	Sheet of 5	1.00	1.00
a		50c, single stamp	15	15

Simon Bolivar, birth centenary. Size of souvenir sheet stamps: 22x28mm.

See Nos. 1228-1230, 1264-1266, 1276-1284, 1294-1296, 1317-1322.

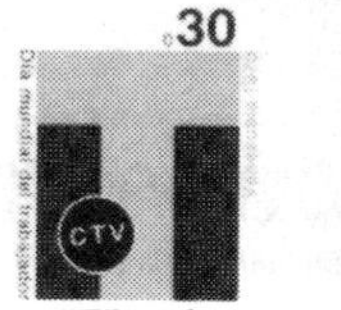

"T" and "CTV" — A256

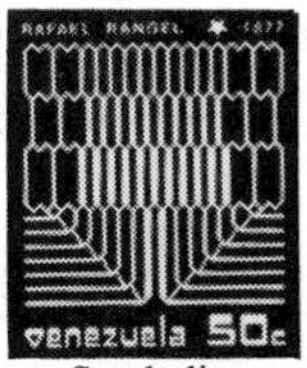

Symbolic Design — A257

Designs: Different arrangement of letters "T" and "CTV" for "Confederacion de Trabajeros Venezolanos."

1978, Sept. 27 Photo. *Perf. 13x13½*

1199	A256	Strip of 5, multi	48	48
a		30c, single stamp	8	8
1200	A256	Strip of 5, multi	1.40	1.40
a		95c, single stamp	25	15

Workers' Day. Stamps of same denomination printed se-tenant.

1978, Oct. 3 Litho. *Perf. 14*

1201	A257	50c dk brn	50	22

Rafael Rangel, physician and scientist, birth centenary.

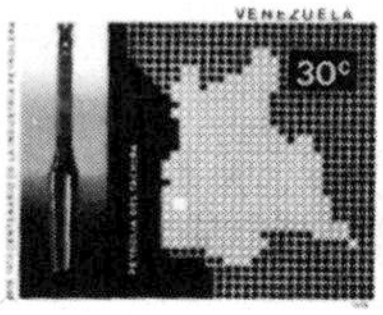

Drill Head, Tachira Oil Field Map — A258

A particular stamp may be scarce, but if few collectors want it, its market value may remain relatively low.

"P" as Pipeline A259

1978, Nov. 2 Litho. *Perf. 13½*

1202 A258 30c multi 15 7
1203 A259 1.05b multi 50 22

Centenary of oil industry.

Star — A260

1978, Dec. 6 Litho. *Perf. 14*

1204 A260 30c multi 15 7

Christmas 1978.

"P T" — A261

1979, Feb. 8 Litho. *Perf. 12½*

1205 A261 75c blk & red 24 12

Creation of Postal and Telegraph Institute.

"Dam Holding Back Water" — A262

1979, Feb. 15 Photo. *Perf. 13½*

1206 A262 2b sil, gray & blk 65 32

Guri Dam, 10th anniversary.

San Martin, by E. J. Maury — A263

Designs: 60c, San Martin, by Mercedes. 70c, Monument, Guayaquil. 75c, San Martin's signature.

1979, Feb. 25 *Perf. 12½x13*

1207 A263 40c bl, blk & yel 15 7
1208 A263 60c bl, blk & yel 22 10
1209 A263 70c bl, blk & yel 30 15
1210 A263 75c bl, blk & yel 32 20

José de San Martin (1778-1850), South American liberator.

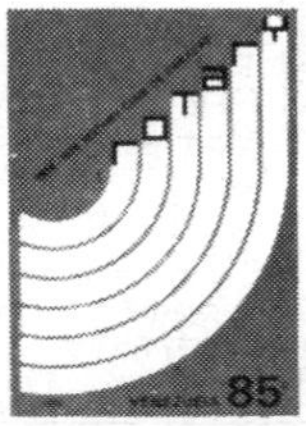

"Rotary" — A264

1979, Aug. 7 Litho. *Perf. 14x13½*

1211 A264 85c gold & blk 28 14

Rotary Club of Caracas, 50th anniversary.

Our Lady of Coromoto Appearing to Children A265

Engraved and Lithographed

1979, Aug. 23 *Perf. 13*

1212 A265 55c blk & dp org 18 10

25th anniversary of the canonization of Our Lady of Coromoto.

London Residence, Coat of Arms, Miranda — A266

1979, Oct. 23 Litho. *Perf. 14½x14*

1213 A266 50c multi 15 8

Francisco de Miranda (1750-1816), Venezuelan independence fighter.

O'Leary, Maps of South America and United Kingdom A267

1979, Nov. 6

1214 A267 30c multi 10 8

Daniel O'Leary (1801-1854), writer.

Boy Holding Nest, IYC Emblem — A268

IYC Emblem and: 80c, Boys in water, bridge.

1979, Nov. 20 Litho. *Perf. 14½x14*

1215 A268 70c lt bl & blk 22 12
1216 A268 80c multi 25 12

International Year of the Child.

Christmas 1979 — A269

1979, Dec. 1 Litho. *Perf. 13½*

1217 A269 30c multi 10 8

Caudron Bomber, EXFILVE Emblem A270

EXFILVE Emblem and: No. 1219, Stearman biplane. No. 1220, UH-1H helicopter. No. 1221, CF-5 jet fighter.

1979, Dec. 15 *Perf. 11x11½*

1218 A270 75c multi 24 12
1219 A270 75c multi 24 12
1220 A270 75c multi 24 12
1221 A270 75c multi 24 12

Venezuelan Air Force, 59th anniversary; EXFILVE 79, 3rd National Philatelic Exhibition, Dec. 7-17. Nos. 1218-1221 printed se-tenant in sheets of 40 (blocks of 4).

IPOSTEL Emblem, World Map A271

1979, Dec. 27 *Perf. 12*

1222 A271 75c multi 24 12

Postal and Telegraph Institute, introduction of new logo.

Queen Victoria, Hill — A272

1980, Feb. 13 Litho. *Perf. 12½*

1223 A272 55c multi 18 10

Sir Rowland Hill (1795-1879), originator of penny postage.

Dr. Augusto Pi Suner, Physiologist, Birth Centenary — A273

1980, Mar. 14 Litho. *Perf. 12x11½*

1224 A273 80c multi 25 12

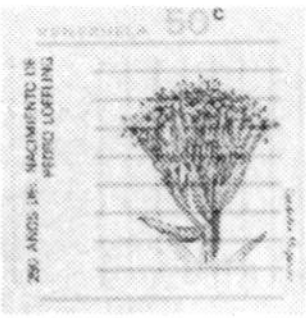

Spanish Seed Leaf — A274

Lithographed and Engraved

1980, Mar. 27 *Perf. 13½*

1225 A274 50c multi 15 8

Pedro Loefling (1729-56), Swedish botanist.

Juan Lovera (1778-1841), Artist — A275

1980, May 25 Litho. *Perf. 13½*

1226 A275 60c bl & dp org 20 10
1227 A275 75c vio & org 24 12

Bolivar Bicentenary Type of 1978

Designs: 30c, Signing of document. 1b, House of Congress. No. 1230, Angostura Congress, by Tito Salas.

1980, July 24 Engr. *Perf. 12½*

1228 A254 30c multi 10 8
1229 A254 1b multi 32 15

Souvenir Sheet

Litho.

Perf. 14

1230 A255 Sheet of 5 1.00 1.00
a 50c, single stamp 15 15

Simon Bolivar (1783-1830), revolutionary. Size of souvenir sheet stamps: 25x20mm, 20x25mm.

Dancing Girls, by Armando Reveron A276

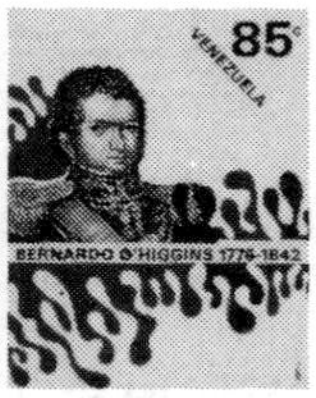

Bernardo O'Higgins A277

1979, Oct. 29 Litho. *Perf. 12*

1231 A276 50c *shown* 15 8

Size: 25x40mm

1232 A276 65c *Portrait* 42 22

Armando Reveron (1889-1955), artist.

Lithographed and Engraved

1980, Aug. 22 *Perf. 13x14*

1233 A277 85c multi 55 25

Bernardo O'Higgins (1776-1842), Chilean soldier and statesman.

School Ship Simon Bolivar A278

Frigate Mariscal Sucre A279

Perf. 11½ (#1234), 11x11½

1980, Sept. 13 Litho.

1234 A278 1.50b *shown* 50 24
1235 A279 1.50b *shown* 50 24
1236 A279 1.50b *Submarine Picua* 50 24
1237 A279 1.50b *Naval Academy* 50 24

Workers Holding OPEC Emblem A280

20th Anniversary of OPEC (Organization of Petroleum Exporting Countries): No. 1239, Emblem.

1980, Sept. 14 Litho. *Perf. 12*
1238 A280 1.50b multi 50 24
1239 A280 1.50b multi 50 24

Death of Simon Bolivar A281

1980, Dec. 17 Litho. *Perf. 11x11½*
1240 A281 2b multi 65 32

Simon Bolivar, 150th anniversary of death.

Gen. José Antonio Sucre, 150th Anniversary of Death — A282

Lithographed and Engraved
1980, Dec. 17 *Perf. 13x12½*
1241 A282 2b multi 65 32

Nativity by Rubens — A283

1980, Dec. 19 Litho. *Perf. 14x13½*
1242 A283 1b multi 25 12

Christmas 1980.

Helen Keller's Initials (Written and Braille) — A284

Lithographed and Embossed
1981, Feb. 12 *Perf. 12½*
1243 A284 1.50b multi 40 20

Helen Keller (1880-1968), blind and deaf writer and lecturer.

John Baptiste de la Salle — A285

San Felipe City, 250th Anniv. — A286

1981, May 15 Litho. *Perf. 11½x11*
1244 A285 1.25b multi 32 15

Christian Brothers' 300th anniv.

1981, May 1 *Perf. 11½*
1245 A286 3b multi 65 32

Municipal Theater of Caracas Centenary A287

1981, June 28 Litho. *Perf. 12*
1246 A287 1.25b multi 32 15

UPU Membership Centenary — A288

1981, Sept. 15 Litho. *Perf. 12*
1247 A288 2b multi 40 20

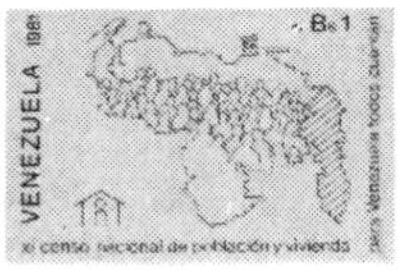

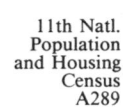

11th Natl. Population and Housing Census A289

1981, Oct. 14 Litho. *Perf. 12*
1248 A289 1b multi 25 12

9th Bolivar Games, Barquismeto A290

1981, Dec. 4 Litho. *Perf. 11½x12*
1249 A290 95c multi 25 12

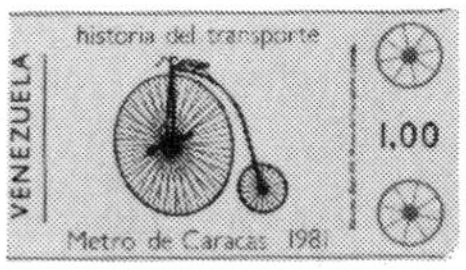

19th Cent. Bicycle A291

1981, Dec. 5 Photo. *Perf. 13½x14½*
1250 A291 1b shown 25 12
1251 A291 1.05b Locomotive, 1926 25 12
1252 A291 1.25b Buick, 1937 32 15
1253 A291 1.50b Coach 40 20

See Nos. 1289-1292, 1308-1311.

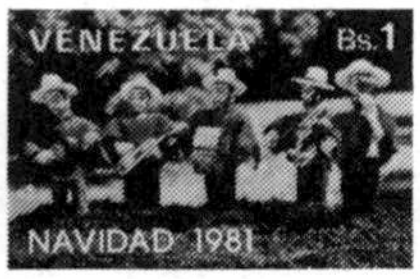

Christmas 1981 A292

1981, Dec. 21 Litho. *Perf. 11½x12*
1254 A292 1b multi 25 12

50th Anniv. of Natural Science Society — A293

1982, Jan. 21 *Perf. 12x11½*
1255 A293 1b Mt. Autana 25 12
1256 A293 1.50b Sarisarinama 40 20
1257 A293 2b Guacharo Cave 50 22

20th Anniv. of Constitution — A294

1982, Jan. 28 Photo. *Perf. 13x13½*
1258 A294 1.85b gold & blk 50 22

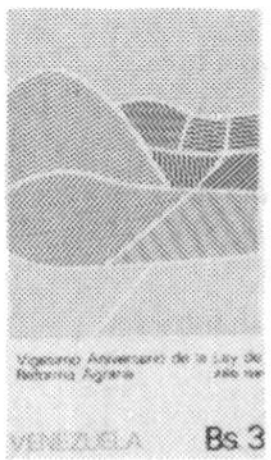

20th Anniv. of Agricultural Reform — A295

1982, Feb. 19 Litho. *Perf. 13½*
1259 A295 3b multi 85 32

Jules Verne (1828-1905), Science Fiction Writer — A296

1982, Mar. 12 Litho. *Perf. 13½*
1260 A296 1b bl & dk bl 12 7

Natl. Anthem Centenary (1981) A297

1982, Mar. 26 *Perf. 12*
1261 A297 1b multi 12 7

1300th Anniv. of Bulgaria A298

6th Natl. 5-Year Plan, 1981-85 A299

1982, June 2 Litho. *Perf. 13½*
1262 A298 65c multi 9 8

1982, June 11
1263 A299 2b multi 25 12

Bolivar Types of 1978

1982, July 24 Engr. *Perf. 12½*
1264 A254 30c Juan José Rondon 6 5
1265 A254 1b Jose Antonio Anzoategui 12 7

Souvenir Sheet
Litho.
Perf. 14
1266 A255 Sheet of 5 40 40
a.-e. 50c, any single 7 7

Single stamps of No. 1266 show details from Battle of Boyaca, by Martin Tovar y Tovar. Size of souvenir sheet stamps: 19x26mm, 26x19mm.

Cecilio Acosta (1818-1881), Writer — A299a

1982, Aug. 13 Litho. *Perf. 11½*
1266F A299a 3b multi 40 20

Aloe A300

1982, Oct. 14 Photo. *Perf. 13½x13*
1267 A300 1.05b shown 15 10
1268 A300 2.55b Tortoise 42 20
1269 A300 2.75b Tara armilla tree 45 20
1270 A300 3b Guacharo bird 50 22

Andres Bello (1781-1865), Statesman and Reformer A301

1982, Nov. 20 Litho. *Perf. 12*
1271 A301 1.05b multi 15 10
1272 A301 2.55b multi 42 20
1273 A301 2.75b multi 45 20
1274 A301 3b multi 50 22

Christmas 1982 — A302

Design: Holy Family creche figures by Francisco J. Cardozo, 18th cent.

Photogravure and Engraved
1982, Dec. 7 *Perf. 13½*
1275 A302 1b multi 12 6

Bolivar Types of 1978

1982-83 Engr. *Perf. 12½*
1276 A254 30c Victory Monument, Carabobo 7 5
1277 A254 30c Monument to the Meeting plaque 7 5
1278 A254 30c Antonio de Sucre 7 5
1279 A254 1b Jose Antonio Paez 15 8
1280 A254 1b Sword hilt, 1824 15 8
1281 A254 1b Guayaquil Monument 15 8
Nos. 1276-1281 (6) 66 39

Souvenir Sheets
Litho.
Perf. 14

1282	A255	Sheet of 5	85	65
a.-e		50c, any single	10	10
1283	A255	Sheet of 5	85	65
a.-e		50c, any single	10	10
1284	A255	Sheet of 5	85	65
a.-e		50c, any single	10	10

No. 1282: Battle of Carabobo by Martin Tovar y Tovar; No. 1283, Monument to the Meeting; No. 1284, Battle of Ayacucho, by Martin Tovar y Tovar. Issue dates: Nos. 1276-1277, 1279, 1282-1283, Dec. 17; others, Apr. 18, 1983.

Gen. Jose Francisco Bermudez — A303

Antonio Nicolas Briceno, Liberation Hero A304

Perf. 13x13½, 15x14
1982, Dec. 23 **Litho.**

1285	A303	3b multi	40	20
1286	A304	3b multi	40	20

25th Anniv. of 1958 Reforms A305

1983, Jan. 23 ***Perf. 10½x10***

1287	A305	3b multi	40	20

25th Anniv. of Judicial Police Technical Dept. — A306

1983, Mar. 20 Photo. ***Perf. 13½x13***

1288	A306	4b ol & red	50	25

Transportation Type of 1981
Perf. 13½x14½
1983, Mar. 28 **Photo.**

1289	A291	75c Lincoln, 1923	7	5
1290	A291	80c Locomotive, 1889	8	6
1291	A291	85c Willys truck, 1927	10	8
1292	A291	95c Cleveland motorcycle, 1920	10	8

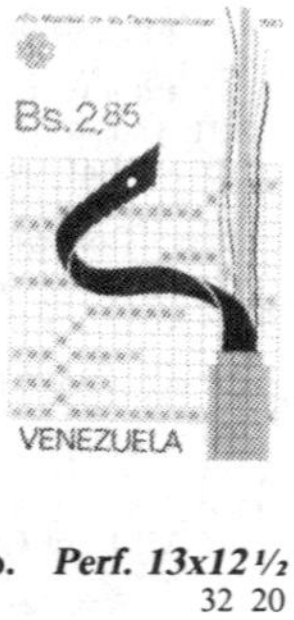

World Communications Year — A307

1983, May 17 Photo. ***Perf. 13x12½***

1293	A307	2.85b multi	32	20

Bolivar Type of 1978

Designs: 30c; Flags of Colombia, Peru, Chile, Venezuela, and Buenos Aires. 1b; Equestrian Statue of Bolivar.

Photo. and Engr. (No. 1294), Engr. (No. 1295)
1983, July 25 ***Perf. 12½***

1294	A254	30c multi	6	5
1295	A254	1b multi	10	8

Souvenir Sheet
Litho.
Perf. 14

1296	A255	Sheet of 5	50	40
a.-e		50c, any single	10	7

Single stamps of No. 1296 show details of "The Liberator on the Silver Mountain of Potosi" Size of souvenir sheet stamps, 20x25mm.

9th Pan-American Games
A308 A309

Designs: No. 1303a, baseball. b, cycle wheel. c, boxing glove. d, soccer ball. e, target.

Lithographed and Engraved
1983, Aug. 25 ***Perf. 13***

1297	A308	2b	shown	15	10
1298	A308	2b	Swimming	15	10
1299	A308	2.70b	Cycling	20	15
1300	A308	2.70b	Fencing	20	15
1301	A308	2.85b	Runners	25	16
1302	A308	2.85b	Weightlifting	25	16
			Nos. 1297-1302 (6)	1.20	82

Souvenir Sheet

1303		Sheet of 5	
a-e	A309	1b, any single	

No. 1303 issued for Copan '83. Size: 167x121mm.

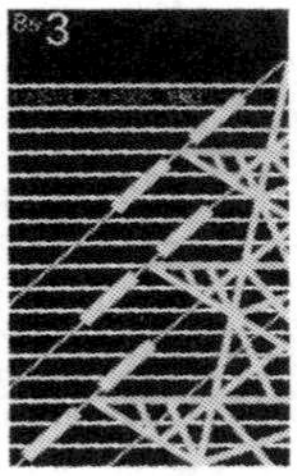

25th Anniv. of Cadafe (State Electricity Authority) — A310

1983, Oct. 27 **Litho.** ***Perf. 14***

1304	A310	3b multi	80	40

Bolivar Type of 1976
1983 **Engr.** ***Perf. 12***
Size: 26x32mm.

1305	A231	25b bl grn	6.50	3.25
1306	A231	30b brown	8.00	4.00
1307	A231	50b brt rose lil	13.00	6.50

Transportation Type of 1981

Various views of Caracas Metro.

1983, Dec. Photo. ***Perf. 13½x14½***

1308	A291	55c multi	12	8
1309	A291	75c multi	14	7
1310	A291	95c multi	20	10
1311	A291	2b multi	52	25

Christmas 1983 A311

1983, Dec. 1 **Litho.** ***Perf. 13x14***

1312	A311	1b Nativity	10	8

Scouting Year (1982) A312

Lithographed and Engraved
1983, Dec. 14 ***Perf. 12½x13***

1313	A312	2.25p	Pitching tent	22	12
1314	A312	2.55b	Planting tree	28	12
1315	A312	2.75b	Mountain climbing	30	14
1316	A312	3b	Camp site	32	15

Bolivar Type of 1976

Designs: No. 1317, Title page of "Opere de Raimondo Montecuccoli" (most valuable book in Caracas University Library). No. 1318, Pedro Gual, Congress of Panama delegate, 1826. No. 1319, Jose Maria Vargas (b. 1786), University of Caracas pres. No. 1320, Jose Faustino Sanchez Carrion, Congress of Panama delegate, 1826.

1984 **Engr.** ***Perf. 12½***

1317	A254	30c multi	5	5
1318	A254	30c multi	5	5
1319	A254	1b multi	10	8
1320	A254	1b multi	10	8

Souvenir Sheets
Litho.
Perf. 14

1321	A255	Sheet of 5	32
a.-e		50c, any single	8
1322	A255	Sheet of 5	32
a.-e		50c, any single	8

Single stamps of No. 1321 show details of Arts, Science and Education, fresco by Hector Poleo; 1322, Map of South America, 1829. Size of souvenir sheet stamps: 20x30mm.; 27x20mm.

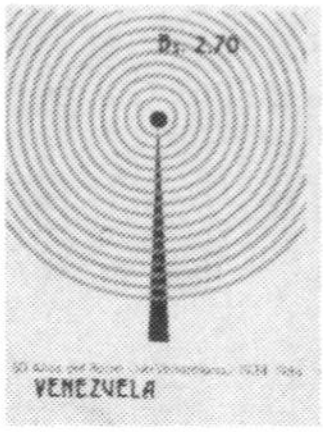

Radio Waves — A313

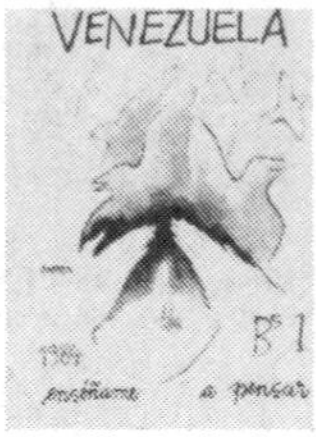

Intelligentsia for Peace — A314

1983, Jan. 30 **Litho.** ***Perf. 14x13***

1323	A313	2.70b multi	32	14

Radio Club of Venezuela, 50th anniv.

1984, Jan. 31

1324	A314	1b	Doves	10	8
1325	A314	2.70b	Profile	30	14
1326	A314	2.85b	Flower, head	32	15

President Romulo Gallegos (1884-1969) A315

Gallegos: No. 1327, Portrait as a young man in formal dress. No. 1328, Portrait, 1948.

1984-85 **Litho.** ***Perf. 11½***

1327	A315	1.70b royal bl, dl bl, beige & blk	22	12
1328	A315	1.70b ocher, org brn & buff	22	12

Issue dates: No. 1327, Oct. 12, 1984; No. 1328, Jan. 18, 1985. See Nos. 1335-1336.

Pan-American Union of Engineering Associations, 18th Convention A316

1984, Oct. 28

1329	A316	2.55b pale buff, dk bl	32	15

Christmas 1984 A317

1984, Dec. 3

1330	A317	1b multi	14	8

Pope John Paul II, Statue of the Virgin of Caracas A318

1985, Jan. 26 **Litho.** ***Perf. 12***

1331	A318	1b multi	14	8

Papal visit, 1985.

Pascua City Bicent. A319

1985, Feb. 10

1332	A319	1.50b multi	20	10

Dr. Mario Briceno-Iragory (b. 1897), Historian — A320

1985, Aug. **Litho.** ***Perf. 12***

1333	A320	1.25b sil & ver	15	8

Natl. St. Vincent de Paul Soc., Cent. — A321

1985, Aug.
1334 A321 1b dk ol bis, ver & buff 14 7

Gallegos Memorial Type of 1984-85

Designs: Gallegos, diff.

1985, Aug. 8
1335 A315 1.70b gray grn, dk gray grn & dl gray grn 24 12
1336 A315 1.70b grn, sage grn & dl grn 24 12

Dated 1984.

Latin American Economic System, 10th Anniv. A322

1985, Aug. 15
1337 A322 4b blk & red 90 45

Miniature Sheet

Virgin Mary, Birth Bimillennium A323

Statues: a, Virgin of the Divine Shepherd. b, Chiquinquira Madonna. c, Coromoto Madonna. d, Valley Madonna. e, Virgin of Perpetual Succor. f, Virgin of Peace. g, Immaculate Conception Virgin. h, Soledad Madonna. i, Virgin of Consolation. j, Nieves Madonna.

1985, Sept. 9
1338 Sheet of 10 2.25 1.10
a.-j A323 1b, any single 22 12

OPEC, 25th Anniv. A324

1985, Sept. 13
1339 A324 6b multi 80 40

Opening of the Museum of Contemporary Art, Caracas — A325

1985, Sept. ***Perf. 13½***
1340 A325 3b multi 40 20

Dated 1983.

UN, 40th Anniv. A326

1985, Nov. 15 ***Perf. 12***
1341 A326 10b brt bl & ver 1.25 65

Intl. Youth Year A327

1985, Nov. 26
1342 A327 1.50b multi 20 10

Christmas 1985 A328

Nativity: a, Sheperds. b, Holy Family, Magi. Se-tenant in a continuous design.

1985, Dec. 2
1343 Pair 52 25
a.-b A328 2b, any single 25 12

Dr. Luis Maria Drago (b. 1859), Politician A329

1985, Dec. ***Perf. 13½***
1344 A329 2.70b tan, ver & sep 35 18

Dated 1984.

Miniature Sheet

Natl. Oil Industry, 10th Anniv. A330

Designs: a, Industry emblem. b, Isla Oil Refinery. c, Bariven oil terminal. d, Pequiven refinery. e, Corpoven drilling rig. f, Maraven offshore rig. g, Intevep labs. h, Meneven refinery. i, Lagoven refinery. j, Emblem, early drilling rig.

1985, Dec. 13 ***Perf. 12***
1345 Sheet of 10 4.00
a.-b A330 1b multi 12 7
c.-d A330 2b multi 25 14
e.-f A330 3b multi 40 20
g.-h A330 4b multi 52 25
i.-j A330 5b multi 65 32

Simon Bolivar Memorial Coins — A331

1985, Dec. 18
1346 A331 2b multi 25 12
1347 A331 2.70b multi 35 18
1348 A331 3b multi 40 20

Dated 1984.

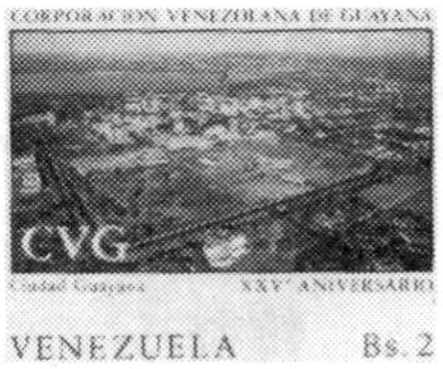

Guayana Development Corp., 25th Anniv. — A332

1985, Dec. 27
1349 A332 2b Guayana City 25 12
1350 A332 3b Orinoco Steel Mill 40 20
1351 A332 5b Raul Leoni-Guri Hydro-electric Dam 65 32

Miniature Sheet

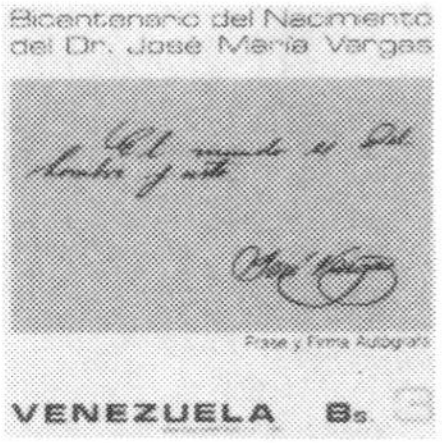

A333

Dr. Jose Vargas (1786-1854) — A334

Designs: No. 1352a, Handwriting and signature. b, Portrait, 1874, by Martin Tovar y Tovar. c, Statue, Palace of the Academies. d, Flags, EXFILBO '86 emblem. e, Vargas do Caracas Hospital. f, Frontispiece of lectures manual, 1842. g, Portrait, 1986, by Alirio Palacios. h, Gesneria vargasii. i, Bolivar-Vargas commemorative medal, 1955, 6th Natl. Medical Sciences Cong. j, Portrait, anonymous, 19th cent.

No. 1353a, Portrait, facing front. b, Portrait, facing left, Nos. 1352a, 1352d, 1352e, 1352h and 1352i have horizontal vignettes.

1986, Mar. 10 **Litho.** ***Perf. 12***
1352 Sheet of 10 2.25 1.25
a.-j A333 3b, any single 22 12

Souvenir Sheet

Imperf

1353 Sheet of 2 2.25 1.25
a.-b A334 15b, any single 1.10 60

EXFILBO '86, Mar. 10-17, Caracas, 1st Bolivarian exhibition.

Youths Painting School Wall — A335

1986, May 12 ***Perf. 12***
1354 A335 3b shown 20 10
1355 A335 5b Repairing desk 35 18

Founding and maintenance of educational institutions.

Francisco Miranda's Work for American Liberation, Bicent. (1981) A336

Lithographed and Engraved

1986, June ***Perf. 13***
1356 A336 1.05b multi 8 6

Dated 1983.

INDULAC, 45th Anniv. A337

1986, June 27 **Litho.** ***Perf. 12***
1357 A337 2.55b Milk trucks, vert. 20 10
1358 A337 2.70b Map, vert. 22 12
1359 A337 3.70b Milk processing plant 30 15

Industria Lactea (INDULAC), Venezuelan milk processing company.

Miniature Sheet

Viasa Venezuelan Airlines, 25th Anniv. A338

Designs: a, Commemorative coin. b, Douglas DC-8 ascending. c, DC-10 taxiing. d, Boeing 737 in flight. No. e, Jet tails. f, Map of hemispheres. g, DC-9 taking off. h, Engine, wing, jet. i, DC-10 in flight. j, Crew in cockpit.

1986, Aug. 11 **Litho.** ***Perf. 12***
1360 Sheet of 10 2.50 1.25
a.-e A338 3b, any single 22 12
f.-j A338 3.25b, any single 24 12

Miniature Sheet

Romulo Betancourt (1908-1981), President — A339

Designs: a, i, Portrait with natl. flag. b, j, Seated in armchair, smoking pipe. c, h, Wearing hat, text. d, f, Wearing sash of office. e, g, Reading.

1986, Sept. 28
1361 Sheet of 10 2.00 1.10
a.-e A339 2.70b, any single 20 10
f.-j A339 3b, any single 22 12

Redrawn Bolivar Type of 1976

1986, Sept. 29 **Litho.** ***Perf. 12½***
1362 A231 25c red 5 5
1363 A231 50c blue 6 5
1364 A231 75c pink 7 5
1365 A231 1b orange 8 6
1366 A231 2b brt yel grn 14 7
Nos. 1362-1366 (5) 40 28

Nos. 1362-1366 inscribed Armitano.

Re-opening of Zulia University, 40th Anniv. — A340

1986, Sept. 29
1367 A340 2.70b shown 20 10
1368 A340 2.70b Library entrance 20 10

Nos. 1367-1368 printed se-tenant.

11th Congress of Architects, Engineers and Affiliated Professionals
A341

1986, Oct. 3

1369	A341	1.40b multi	10	8
1370	A341	1.55b multi	10	8

Nos. 1369-1370 printed se-tenant.

Fauna and Flora — A342

1986, Oct. Photo. *Perf. 13½*

1371	A342	70c	Priodontes maximus	6	5
1372	A342	85c	Espeletia angustifolia	8	5
1373	A342	2.70b	Crocodylus intermedius	15	8
1374	A342	3b	Brownea grandiceps	18	9

Miniature Sheet

State Visit of Pope John Paul II — A343

1986, Oct. 22 *Perf. 12*

1375		Sheet of 10	2.25	1.65
a	A343	1b Pope, mountains	8	6
b	A343	2b Bridge	14	7
c	A343	3b Kissing the ground	20	10
d	A343	3b Statue of Our Lady	20	10
e	A343	4b Crosier, buildings	30	14
f	A343	5.25b Waterfall	38	20

No. 1375 contains 2 each Nos. 1375a-1375b, 1375e-1375f and one each Nos. 1375c-1375d.

Miniature Sheet

Children's Foundation, 20th Anniv.
A344

Children's drawings: a, Three children. b, Hearts, children, birds. c, Child, animals. d, Animals, house. e, Landscape. f, Child, flowers on table. g, Child holding ball. h, Children, birds. i, Lighthouse, port. j, Butterfly in flight.

1986, Nov. 10

1376		Sheet of 10	2.00	1.25
a.-e	A344	2.55b, any single	18	8
f.-j	A344	2.70b, any single	20	10

Christmas
A345

Creche figures carved by Eliecer Alvarez.

1986, Nov. 10

1377	A345	2b shown	14	7
1378	A345	2b Virgin and child	14	7

Printed se-tenant in a continuous design.

City Police, 25th Anniv.
A346

Emblem and: a, Emergency medical aid, helicopter. b, Security at sporting event. c, Bar code. d, Cadets in front of police academy. e, Motorcycle police.

1986, Dec. 10

1379		Strip of 5	1.00	50
a.-e	A346	2.70b, any single	20	10

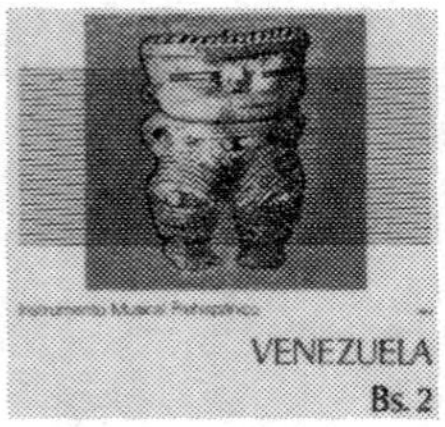

Folk Art
A347

Lithographed and Engraved

1987, Jan. *Perf. 13*

1380	A347	2b Musical instrument	15	8
1381	A347	2b Fabric	15	8
1382	A347	3b Ceramic pot	22	12
1383	A347	3b Basket work	22	12

Dated 1983. Nos. 1380, 1382 show Pre-Hispanic art.

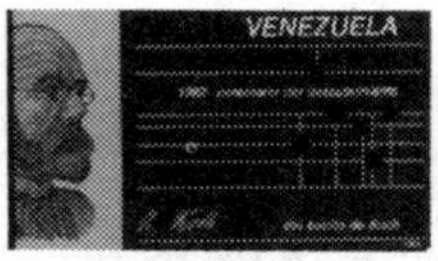

Discovery of the Tubercle Bacillus by Robert Koch, Cent. (in 1982)
A348

Lithographed and Engraved

1987, Feb. 27 *Perf. 14x14½*

1384	A348	2.55b multi	18	9

Dated 1983.

Miniature Sheet

Easter 1987
A349

Paintings and sculpture: a, Arrival of Jesus in Jerusalem. b, Christ at the Column. c, Jesus of Nazareth. d, The Descent. e, The Solitude. f, The Last Supper. g, Christ Suffering. h, The Crucifixion. i, Christ Entombed. j, The Resurrection.

1987, Apr. 2 Litho. *Perf. 12*

1385		Sheet of 10	1.75	90
a.-e	A349	2b, any single	15	8
f.-j	A349	2.25b, any single	18	9

World Neurochemistry Congress — A350

Designs: 3b, Bolivar and Bello, outdoor sculpture by Marisol Escobar. 4.25b, Retinal neurons.

1987, May 8 Litho. *Perf. 12*

1386	A350	3b multi	22	12
1387	A350	4.25b multi	32	15

Miniature Sheet

Tourism
A351

Hotels: a, f, Barquisimeto Hilton. b, g, Lake Hotel Intercontinental, Maracaibo. c, h, Macuto Sheraton, Caraballeda. d, i, Melia Caribe, Caraballeda. e, j, Melia, Puerto la Cruz.

1987, May 29 Litho. *Perf. 12*

1388		Sheet of 10	3.50	1.75
a. - e	A351	6b, any single	32	15
f. - j	A351	6.50b, any single, diff.	32	18

Natl. Institute of Canalization, 35th Anniv. — A352

1987, June 25 Litho. *Perf. 12*

1389	A352	2b Map of Amazon territory waterways	10	8
1390	A352	4.25b Apure and Bolivar states waterways	22	12

Nos. 1389-1390 printed se-tenant.

Vincente Emilion Sojo (1887-1974), Composer — A352a

Designs: 2b, Academy of Fine Arts, Caracas. 4b, Sojos directing choir. 5b, Hymn to Bolivar score. 6b, Sojo, score on blackboard. 7b, Portrait, signature.

1987, July 1 Litho. *Perf. 12*

1390A		Strip of 5	1.65	85
b	A352a	2b tan & sepia	12	7
c	A352a	4b tan & sepia	25	12
d	A352a	5b tan & sepia	32	15
e	A352a	6b tan & sepia	40	20
f	A352a	7b tan & sepia	48	24

Printed in sheets of 10 containing two strips of five, black control number (UR).

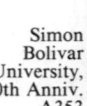

Simon Bolivar University, 20th Anniv.
A353

Designs: a, Bolivar statue by Roca Rey, 1973. b, Outdoor sculpture of solar panels by Alejandro Otero, 1972. c, Rectory, 1716. d, Laser. e, Owl, sculpture, 1973.

1987, July 9 Litho. *Perf. 12*

1391		Strip of 5	1.00	50
a	A353	2b multi	10	8
b	A353	3b multi	14	8
c	A353	4b multi	20	10
d	A353	5b multi	24	12
e	A353	6b multi	30	14

Miniature Sheet

Ministry of Transportation and Communication — A354

Designs: a, Automobiles. b, Ship. c, Train, Cathedral. d, Letters, telegraph key. e, Communication towers. f, Highway. g, Airplane. h, Locomotive, rail caution signs. i, Satellite dish. j, Satellite in orbit.

1987, July 16

1392		Sheet of 10	1.10	52
a.-e	A354	2b, any single	10	8
f.-j	A354	2.25b, any single	12	8

Nos. 1392a and 1392f, 1392b and 1392g, 1392c and 1392h, 1392d and 1392i, 1392e and 1392j printed se-tenant in continuous designs.

Miniature Sheet

Venezuela Navigation Company, 70th Anniv.
A355

Designs: a, Corporate headquarters. b, Fork lift. c, Ship's Superstructure. d, Engine room. e, The Zulia. f, The Guarico. g, Ship's officer on the bridge. h, Bow of supertanker. i, Loading dock. j, Map of sea routes.

1987, July 31 Litho. *Perf. 12*

1393		Sheet of 10	2.00	1.00
a.-b	A355	2b, any single	10	8
c.-d	A355	3b, any single	14	8
e.-f	A355	4b, any single	20	10
g.-h	A355	5b, any single	24	12
i.-j	A355	6b, any single	30	14

Nos. 1393a, 1393c, 1393e, 1393g and 1393i in vertical strip; no. 1393b, 1393d, 1393f, 1393h and 1393j in vertical strip.

Miniature Sheet

Natl. Guar, 50th Anniv.
A356

Designs: a, f, Air-sea rescue. b, g, Traffic control. c, h, Environment and nature protection. d, i, Border control. e, j, Industrial security.

1987, Aug. 6

1394		Sheet of 10	2.25	1.15
a.-e.	A356	2b, any single	15	8
f.-j.	A356	4b, any single	30	15

Discovery of America, 500th Anniv. (in 1992) A357

20th cent. paintings (details): 2b, Departure from Port of Palos, by Jacobo Borges. 7b, Discovery of America, by Tito Salas. 11.50b, El Padre de las Casas, Protector of the Indians, by Salas. 12b, Trading in Venezuela at the Time of the Conquest, by Salas. 12.50b, Defeat of Guaicaipuro, by Borges.

1987, Oct. 15 Litho. *Perf. 12*

1395		Strip of 5	3.30	1.65
a	A357	2b multi	14	8
b	A357	7b multi	50	25
c	A357	11.50b multi	85	42
d	A357	12b multi	88	45
e	A357	12.50b multi	90	45

Christmas 1987 — A358

Paintings and sculpture representing the Spanish Colonial School, 18th cent.: 2b, *The Annunciation*, by Juan Pedro Lopez (1724-1787). 3b, *Nativity*, by Jose Francisco Rodriguez (1767-1818). 5.50b, *Adoration of the Magi*, anonymous. 6b, *Flight into Egypt*, by Lopez.

1987, Nov. 17 Litho. *Perf. 12*

1396		Block of 4	1.35	68
a.	A358	2b multi	16	8
b.	A358	3b multi	24	12
c.	A358	5.50b multi	45	22
d.	A358	6b multi	48	25

Miniature Sheet

Sidor Mills, 25th Anniv. — A359

Natl. steel production: a-d, Exterior view of steel plant (in a continuous design). e, Tower bearing the SIDOR emblem. f, Furnaces and molten steel flowing down gutters. g, Pooring steel rods. h, Slab mill. i, Steel rod production, diff. j, Anniv. emblem.

1987, Nov. 23

1397		Sheet of 10	6.25	3.15
a.	A359	2b multi	16	8
b.	A359	6b multi	48	25
c.	A359	7b multi	58	28
d.	A359	11.50b multi	92	45
e.	A359	12b blk	98	50
f.	A359	2b multi	16	8
g.	A359	6b multi	48	25
h.	A359	7b multi	58	28
i.	A359	11.50b multi	92	45
j.	A359	12b multi	98	50

Meeting of 8 Latin American Presidents, 1st Anniv. A360

1987, Nov. 26

1398 A360	6b multi	48	25

Pequiven Petrochemical Co., 10th Anniv. — A361

1987, Dec. 1

1399		Strip of 5	3.15	1.05
a.	A361	2b Plastics	16	8
b.	A361	6b Refined oil products	48	25
c.	A361	7b Fertilizers	58	26
d.	A361	11.50b Installations	92	45
e.	A361	12b Expansion	98	50

St. John Bosco (1815-88) A362

Portrait of Bosco and: 2b, Map, children. 3b, National Church, Caracas. 4b, Vocational training (printer's apprentice). 5b, Church of Mary Auxiliadora. 6b, Missionary school (nun teaching children).

1987, Dec. 8

1400		Strip of 5	1.60	80
a.	A362	2b multi	16	8
b.	A362	3b multi	24	12
c.	A362	4b multi	32	16
d.	A362	5b multi	40	20
e.	A362	6b multi	48	24

Redrawn Bolivar Type of 1976

1987, Dec. 31 Litho. *Perf. 12½*

1401	A231	3b emer grn	24	12
1402	A231	4b gray	32	16
1403	A231	5b ver	40	20
1404	A231	10b dark olive bister	80	40
1405	A231	15b rose claret	1.20	60
1406	A231	20b brt blue	1.60	80
1407	A231	25b olive bister	2.00	1.00
1408	A231	30b dark vio	2.40	1.20
1409	A231	50b carmine	4.00	2.00
	Nos. 1401-1409 (9)		12.96	6.48

Nos. 1401-1409 inscribed Armitano.

29th Assembly of Inter-American Development Bank Governors, Desarrollo — A363

1988, Mar. 18 Litho. *Perf. 12*

1410 A363	11.50b multi	90	45

Miniature Sheet

Republic Bank, 30th Anniv. A364

Bank functions and finance projects: a. Personal banking at branch. b. Capital for labor. c. Industrial projects. d. Financing technology. e. Exports and imports. f. Financing agriculture. g. Fishery credits. h. Dairy farming in Desarrollo. i. Construction projects. j. Tourism trade in Desarrollo.

1988, Apr. 11

1411		Sheet of 10	3.00	1.50
a.-e.	A364	2b any single	15	8
f.-j.	A364	6b any single	45	22

No. 1411 contains two strips of five.

Anti-Polio Campaign Day of Victory, May 25 — A365

Design: Polio victims pictured on bronze relief, Rotary and campaign emblems.

1988, May 20 Litho. *Perf. 12*

1412 A365	11.50b multi	78	40

Carlos Eduardo Frias (1906-1986), Founder of the Natl. Publicity Industry — A366

1988, May 27 Litho. *Perf. 12*

1414	A366	Pair	98	50
a.		4b multi	28	14
b.		10b multi, diff.	70	35

Publicity Industry, 50th anniv. Printed se-tenant in a continuous design.

Venalum Natl. Aluminum Corp., 10th Anniv. A367

Designs: 2b, Factory interior. 6b, Electric smelter. 7b, Aluminum pipes. 11.50b, Aluminum blocks moved by crane. 12b, Soccer team, aluminum equipment on playing field.

1988, June 10

1415		Strip of 5	2.75	1.35
a.	A367	2b multi	14	8
b.	A367	6b multi	42	20
c.	A367	7b multi	50	25
d.	A367	11.50b multi	82	40
e.	A367	12b multi	85	42

Nature Conservation — A368

Birds: 2b, Carduelis cucullata. 6b, Eudocimus ruber. 11.50b, Harpia harpyja. 12b, Phoenicopterus ruber ruber. 12.50b, Pauxi pauxi.

1988, June 17 Litho. *Perf. 12*

1416		Strip of 5	3.00	1.50
a.	A368	2b multi	14	8
b.	A368	6b multi	40	20
c.	A368	11.50b multi	78	40
d.	A368	12b multi	80	40
e.	A368	12.50b multi	85	42

Army Day — A369

Military uniforms: a. Simon Bolivar in dress uniform, 1828. b. Gen.-in-Chief Jose Antonio Paez in dress uniform, 1821. c. Liberation Army division gen., 1810. d. Brig. gen., 1820. e. Artillery corpsman, 1836. f. Alferez Regiment parade uniform, 1988. g. Division Gen. No. 1 dress uniform, 1988. h. Line Infantry Regiment, 1820. i. Promenade Infantry, 1820. j. Light Cavalry, 1820.

1988, June 20

1417		Sheet of 10	5.50	2.70
a.	A369	2b multi	14	8
b.	A369	6b multi	42	20
c.	A369	7b multi	50	25
d.	A369	11.50b multi	82	40
e.	A369	12b multi	85	42
f.	A369	2b multi	14	8
g.	A369	6b multi	42	20
h.	A369	7b multi	50	25
i.	A369	11.50b multi	82	40
j.	A369	12b multi	85	42

Scabbard, Sword and Signature A370

Paintings by Tito Salas: 4.75b, *The General's Wedding*. 6b, Portrait. 7b, *Battle of Valencia*. 12b, *Retreat from San Carlos*.

1988, July 1 Litho. *Perf. 12*

1418		Strip of 5	2.25	1.10
a.	A370	2b shown	14	6
b.	A370	4.75b multi	35	16
c.	A370	6b multi	42	20
d.	A370	7b multi	48	24
e.	A370	12b multi	85	42

General Rafael Urdaneta (b. 1788).

General Santiago Marino (b. 1788), by Martin Tovar y Tovar — A371

1988, July 18

1419 A371	4.75b multi	35	16

1988 Summer Olympics, Seoul — A372

1988, Aug. 2

1420 A372	12b multi	85	42

Electric Industry, Cent. A373

Buildings, 1888: 2b, 1st Office. 4.75b, Jaime Carrillo and electrical plant. 10b, Bolivar Plaza. 11.50b, Baralt Theater. 12.50b, Central Thermoelectric Plant, Ramon Lagoon, 1988.

1988, Oct. 25 Litho. *Perf. 12*

1421		Strip of 5	2.75	1.40
a.	A373	2b multi	12	6
b.	A373	4.75b multi	32	16
c.	A373	10b multi	68	35
d.	A373	11.50b multi	78	40
e.	A373	12.50b multi	85	42

Christmas A374

Designs: 4b, Nativity (left side), by Tito Salas, 1936. 6b, Christ child, anonymous, 17th cent. 15b, Nativity (right side).

1988, Dec. 9

1422	A374	4b multi	28	14
1423	A374	6b multi	40	20
1424	A374	15b multi	1.05	52

Nos. 1422 and 1424 se-tenant in a continuous design. Nos. 1422-1424 printed in strips of 5 containing No. 1423 flanked by pairs of Nos. 1422, 1424.

SEMI-POSTAL STAMPS

A 5c green stamp of the Cruzada Venezolana Sanitaria Social portraying Simon Bolivar was overprinted "EE. UU. DE VENEZUELA CORREOS" in 1937.

It is stated that 50,000 copies without control numbers on back were sold by post offices and 147,700 with control numbers on back were offered for sale by the Society at eight times face value.

Bolivar Funeral Carriage SP1

Unwmk.

1942, Dec. 17 Engr. *Perf. 12*

B1	SP1	20c + 5c blue	4.50	50

Cent. of the arrival of Simón Bolivar's remains in Caracas. The surtax was used to erect a monument to his memory. See Nos. CB1-CB2.

Catalogue values for unused stamps in this section, from this point to the end of the section, are for Never Hinged items.

Red Cross Nurse — SP2

1975, Dec. 15 Litho. *Perf. 14*

B2	SP2	30c + 15c multi	30	15
B3	SP2	50c + 25c multi	45	22

Surtax for Venezuelan Red Cross.

An enhanced introduction to the Scott Catalogue begins on Page V. A thorough understanding of the material presented there will greatly aid your use of the catalogue itself.

Carmen America Fernandez de Leoni — SP3

Children in Home — SP4

1976, June 7 Litho. *Perf. 13½*

B4	SP3	30c + 15c multi	22	15
B5	SP4	50c + 25c multi	40	22

Surtax was for the Children's Foundation, founded by Carmen América Fernandez de Leoni in 1966.

Patient — SP5

1976, Dec. 8 Litho. *Perf. 14*

B6	SP5	10c + 5c multi	15	6
B7	SP5	30c + 10c multi	22	15

Surtax was for Anti-tuberculosis Society.

AIR POST STAMPS

Air post stamps of 1930-42 perforated "GN" (Gobierno Nacional) were for official use.

Airplane and Map of Venezuela AP1 AP2

1930 Unwmk. Litho. *Perf. 12*

C1	AP1	5c bis brn	5	5
C2	AP1	10c yellow	5	5
a.		10c sal	32.50	32.50
C3	AP1	15c gray	8	5
C4	AP1	25c lilac	8	5
C5	AP1	40c ol grn	10	5
a.		40c sl bl	40.00	
b.		40c sl grn	40.00	
C6	AP1	75c dp red	25	10
C7	AP1	1b indigo	32	10
C8	AP1	1.20b bl grn	50	22
C9	AP1	1.70b dk bl	65	28
C10	AP1	1.90b bl grn	75	35
C11	AP1	2.10b dk bl	1.25	45
C12	AP1	2.30b vermilion	1.25	35
C13	AP1	2.50b dk bl	1.25	35
C14	AP1	3.70b bl grn	1.25	55
C15	AP1	10b dl vio	3.00	1.40
C16	AP1	20b gray grn	5.00	3.00
		Nos. C1-C16 (16)	15.83	7.40

Nos. C1-C16 exist imperforate or partly perforated. See Nos. C119-C126.

Bluish Winchester Security Paper

1932 Engr. *Perf. 12½*

C17	AP2	5c brown	25	5
C18	AP2	10c org yel	25	5
C19	AP2	15c gray lil	25	5
C20	AP2	25c violet	32	5
C21	AP2	40c ol grn	50	5
C22	AP2	70c rose	42	5
C23	AP2	75c red org	75	10
C24	AP2	1b dk bl	85	9
C25	AP2	1.20b green	1.50	65
C26	AP2	1.70b red brn	3.00	45
C27	AP2	1.80b ultra	1.50	28
C28	AP2	1.90b green	3.75	2.75
C29	AP2	1.95b blue	4.25	2.25
C30	AP2	2b blk brn	3.00	1.75
C31	AP2	2.10b blue	6.25	4.50
C32	AP2	2.30b red	3.00	1.75
C33	AP2	2.50b dk bl	3.75	1.10
C34	AP2	3b dk vio	3.75	65
C35	AP2	3.70b emerald	5.00	4.50
C36	AP2	4b red org	3.75	1.10
C37	AP2	5b black	5.00	1.65
C38	AP2	8b dk car	10.00	3.50
C39	AP2	10b dk vio	20.00	5.75
C40	AP2	20b grnsh sl	42.50	16.00
		Nos. C17-C40 (24)	123.59	49.12

Pairs imperf. between exist of the 1b (value $150); the 25c and 4b (value $300 each).

Air Post Stamps of 1932 Surcharged in Black

1937
VALE POR
-5-
CENTIMOS

1937

C41	AP2	5c on 1.70b red brn	11.00	6.75
C42	AP2	10c on 3.70b emer	11.00	6.75
C43	AP2	15c on 4b red org	5.00	3.50
C44	AP2	25c on 5b blk	5.00	3.50
C45	AP2	1b on 8b dk car	3.75	3.50
C46	AP2	2b on 2.10b bl	30.00	22.50
		Nos. C41-C46 (6)	65.75	46.50

Various varieties of surcharge exist, including double and triple impressions. No. C43 exists in pair imperf. between; value $30 unused, $50 used.

Allegory of Flight AP3

Allegory of Flight AP4

National Pantheon at Caracas AP5

Airplane — AP6

AP7

1937 Litho. *Perf. 11, 11½*

C47	AP3	5c brn org	25	22
C48	AP4	10c org red	20	5
C49	AP5	15c gray blk	50	22
C50	AP6	25c dk vio	50	22
C51	AP4	40c yel grn	85	30
C52	AP3	70c red	85	22
C53	AP5	75c bister	2.00	80
C54	AP3	1b dk gray	1.25	30
C55	AP4	1.20b pck grn	5.00	2.25
C56	AP3	1.80b dk ultra	2.50	1.10
C57	AP5	1.95b lt ultra	7.50	4.50
C58	AP6	2b chocolate	3.00	1.75
C59	AP6	2.50b gray bl	8.75	5.75
C60	AP4	3b lt vio	5.00	2.75
C61	AP6	3.70b rose red	8.75	7.50
C62	AP5	10b red vio	19.00	7.75
C63	AP3	20b gray	24.00	17.00
		Nos. C47-C63 (17)	89.90	52.68

All values except 3.70b exist imperf. and part-perf.

Counterfeits exist.

1937, Oct. 28 *Perf. 11*

C64	AP7	70c emerald	1.10	45
C65	AP7	1.80b ultra	1.75	80

Acquisition of the Port of La Guaira by the Government from the British Corporation, June 3, 1937. Exist imperf.

A redrawn printing of Nos. C64-C65, with lower inscription beginning "Nacionalizacion . . ." was prepared but not issued. Price, $85 each.

Air Post Stamps of 1937 Overprinted in Black

RESELLADO
1937-1938

1937-38 *Perf. 11, 11½*

C66	AP4	10c org red	1.00	65
a.		Invtd. ovpt.	13.00	10.00
C67	AP6	25c dk vio	1.90	90
C68	AP4	40c yel grn	2.00	1.40
C69	AP3	70c red	1.50	90
a.		Invtd. ovpt.	13.00	11.50
b.		Dbl. ovpt.	20.00	16.00
C70	AP3	1b dk gray	2.00	1.40
a.		Invtd. ovt.	16.00	13.00
b.		Dbl. ovpt.	13.00	
C71	AP4	1.20b pck grn	30.00	18.00
a.		Invtd. ovpt.	65.00	
C72	AP3	1.80b dk ultra	5.00	2.25
C73	AP5	1.95b lt ultra	7.50	4.50
a.		Invtd. ovpt.	50.00	30.00
C74	AP6	2b chocolate	50.00	22.50
a.		Invtd. ovpt.	100.00	90.00
b.		Dbl. ovpt.	82.50	82.50
C75	AP6	2.50b gray bl	50.00	22.50
a.		Dbl. ovpt.	70.00	
b.		Invtd. ovpt.	105.00	82.50
C76	AP4	3b lt vio	30.00	11.50
C77	AP5	10b red vio	70.00	45.00
C78	AP3	20b gray	80.00	55.00
a.		Dbl. ovpt.	145.00	145.00
		Nos. C66-C78 (13)	330.90	186.50

Counterfeit overprints exist on Nos. C77-C78.

View of La Guaira AP8

National Pantheon AP9

Oil Wells AP10

1938-39 Engr. *Perf. 12*

C79	AP8	5c green	70	40
C80	AP8	5c dk grn	10	5
C81	AP9	10c car rose	1.00	65
C82	AP9	10c scarlet	15	5
C83	AP8	12½c dl vio	45	38
C84	AP10	15c sl vio	2.25	80
C85	AP10	15c dk bl	65	7
C86	AP8	25c dk bl	2.25	80
C87	AP8	25c bis brn	20	5
C88	AP10	30c vio ('39)	1.50	10
C89	AP9	40c dk vio	2.50	90
C90	AP9	40c redsh brn	1.75	10
C91	AP8	45c Prus grn ('39)	75	9
C92	AP9	50c bl ('39)	85	8
C93	AP10	70c car rose	65	22
C94	AP8	75c bis brn	5.00	1.40
C95	AP8	75c ol bis	1.00	14
C96	AP10	90c red org ('39)	75	10
C97	AP9	1b ol & bis	5.00	1.75
C98	AP9	1b dk vio	85	10
C99	AP10	1.20b orange	15.00	4.50
C100	AP10	1.20b green	1.50	35
C101	AP8	1.80b ultra	1.50	35
C102	AP9	1.90b black	3.75	2.25

C103 AP10 1.95b lt bl 3.00 2.00
C104 AP8 2b ol gray 32.50 10.50
C105 AP8 2b car rose 1.25 55
C106 AP9 2.50b red brn 32.50 12.50
C107 AP9 2.50b orange 10.00 2.25
C108 AP10 3b bl grn 15.00 4.50
C109 AP10 3b ol gray 3.75 1.40
C110 AP8 3.70b gray blk 5.50 3.50
C111 AP10 5b red brn ('39) 5.50 1.40
C112 AP9 10b vio brn 19.00 1.75
C113 AP10 20b red org 55.00 20.00
Nos. C79-C113 (35) 233.10 76.03

See Nos. C227a, C235, C236, C254 and C255.

Nos. C51, C56, C58-C59, C61 Surcharged

1938 VALE CINCO CÉNTIMOS

1938, Apr. 15 *Perf. 11, 11½*
C114 AP3 5c on 1.80b 70 38
a. Invtd. surch. 14.00 7.50
C115 AP6 10c on 2.50b 2.50 75
a. Inverted surch. 12.00 7.50
C116 AP6 15c on 2b 1.25 75
C117 AP4 25c on 40c 1.40 85
C118 AP6 40c on 3.70b 2.75 1.50
Nos. C114-C118 (5) 8.60 4.23

Plane & Map Type of 1930
White Paper; No Imprint

1938-39 **Engr.** *Perf. 12½*
C119 AP1 5c dk grn ('39) 18 7
C120 AP1 10c org yel ('39) 38 10
C121 AP1 12½c rose vio ('39) 75 65
C122 AP1 15c dp bl 65 10
C123 AP1 25c brown 75 10
C124 AP1 40c ol ('39) 1.90 35
a. Imperf., pair 40.00
C125 AP1 70c rose car ('39) 16.00 7.75
C126 AP1 1b dk bl ('39) 5.00 3.00
Nos. C119-C126 (8) 25.61 12.12

Monument to Sucre — AP11

Monuments at Carabobo
AP12 AP13

1938, Dec. 23 *Perf. 13½*
C127 AP11 20c brn blk 38 22
C128 AP12 30c purple 55 22
C129 AP13 45c dk bl 75 16
C130 AP11 50c lt ultra 65 16
C131 AP13 70c dk car 12.50 6.75
C132 AP12 90c red org 1.10 45
C133 AP13 1.35b gray blk 1.40 65
C134 AP11 1.40b sl gray 5.50 2.25
C135 AP12 2.25b green 2.75 1.75
Nos. C127-C135 (9) 25.58 12.61

Simón Bolívar and Carabobo Monument AP14

1940, Mar. 30 *Perf. 12*
C136 AP14 15c blue 38 10
C137 AP14 20c ol bis 32 7
C138 AP14 25c red brn 2.00 22
C139 AP14 40c blk brn 1.50 10
C140 AP14 1b red lil 3.50 35
C141 AP14 2b rose car 6.25 55
Nos. C136-C141 (6) 13.95 1.39

"The Founding of Grand Colombia" AP15

1940, June 13
C142 AP15 15c cop brn 75 38

50th anniv. of the founding of the Pan American Union.

Statue of Simón Bolívar, Caracas — AP16

1940-44
C143 AP16 5c dk grn ('42) 20 5
C144 AP16 10c scar ('42) 20 6
C145 AP16 12½c dl pur 65 22
C146 AP16 15c bl ('43) 38 5
C147 AP16 20c bis brn ('44) 38 5
C148 AP16 25c bis brn ('42) 38 5
C149 AP16 30c dp vio ('43) 38 5
C150 AP16 40c blk brn ('43) 50 5
C151 AP16 45c turq grn ('43) 50 5
C152 AP16 50c bl ('44) 50 5
C153 AP16 70c rose pink 1.50 22
C154 AP16 75c ol bis ('43) 6.00 1.10
C155 AP16 90c red org ('43) 1.00 22
C156 AP16 1b dp red lil ('42) 50 5
C157 AP16 1.20b dp yel grn ('43) 1.90 55
C158 AP16 1.35b gray blk ('42) 8.00 3.50
C159 AP16 2b rose pink ('43) 1.50 14
C160 AP16 3b ol blk ('43) 2.50 55
C161 AP16 4b black 2.00 55
C162 AP16 5b red brn ('44) 16.00 5.75
Nos. C143-162 (20) 44.97 13.31

See Nos. C232-C234, C239-C253.

Nos. C48, C50-C65 Overprinted

Resellado 1943

1943 *Perf. 11, 11½*
C164 AP4 10c org red 1.25 80
C165 AP6 25c dk vio 1.25 90
C166 AP4 40c yel grn 1.50 90
C167 AP3 70c red 1.25 90
C168 AP7 70c emerald 1.50 90
C169 AP5 75c bister 1.75 1.10
C170 AP3 1b dk gray 1.75 1.10
C171 AP4 1.20b pck grn 2.50 1.40
C172 AP3 1.80b dk ultra 2.25 1.10
C173 AP7 1.80b dk ultra 3.00 1.65
C174 AP5 1.95b lt ultra 3.50 1.75
C175 AP6 2b chocolate 3.50 2.75
C176 AP6 2.50b gray bl 4.00 2.75
C177 AP4 3b lt vio 5.00 3.25
C178 AP6 3.70b rose red 55.00 40.00
C179 AP5 10b red vio 19.00 12.50
C180 AP3 20b gray 32.50 25.00
Nos. C164-C180 (17) 140.50 98.75

Issued for sale to philatelists. Nos. C164-C169 were sold only in sets.
Nearly all are known with invtd. ovpt.

Flags of Venezuela and the Red Cross — AP17

Baseball Players — AP18

1944, Aug. 22 **Litho.** *Perf. 12*
Flags in red, yellow, blue and black
C181 AP17 5c gray grn 10 5
C182 AP17 10c magenta 12 5
C183 AP17 20c brt bl 12 5
C184 AP17 30c vio bl 25 5
C185 AP17 40c chocolate 38 10
C186 AP17 45c ap grn 1.10 45
C187 AP17 90c orange 1.00 38
C188 AP17 1b gray blk 1.50 28
Nos. C181-C188 (8) 4.57 1.41

80th anniv. of the Intl. Red Cross and 37th anniv. of Venezuela's joining the organization. Nos. C181-C188 exist imperf. and part perf.

1944, Oct. 12
"AEREO" in dark carmine
C189 AP18 5c dl vio brn 25 16
a. "AEREO" double 8.25
C190 AP18 10c gray grn 30 16
C191 AP18 20c ultra 38 22
C192 AP18 30c dl rose 50 35
C193 AP18 45c rose vio 1.25 55
C194 AP18 90c red org 2.25 1.10
C195 AP18 1b dk gray 2.50 1.10
C196 AP18 1.20b yel grn 7.50 5.75
a. "AEREO" invtd. 15.00 13.00
C197 AP18 1.80b ocher 10.00 7.75
Nos. C189-C197 (9) 24.93 17.14

7th World Amateur Baseball Championship Games, Caracas.
Nos. C189-C197 exist imperf., and all but 1b exist part perf.

No. C134 Surcharged in Black

Habilitado 1944 VALE Bs. 0.30

1944, Nov. 17 *Perf. 13½*
C198 AP11 30c on 1.40b 45 45
a. Dbl. surch. 32.50 32.50
b. Invtd. surch. 13.00 13.00

Charles Howarth AP19

Antonio José de Sucre AP20

1944, Dec. 21 **Unwmk.** *Perf. 12*
C199 AP19 5c black 16 10
C200 AP19 10c purple 16 10
C201 AP19 20c sepia 35 22
C202 AP19 30c dl grn 45 22
C203 AP19 1.20b bister 2.00 1.75
C204 AP19 1.80b dp ultra 3.50 2.25
C205 AP19 3.70b rose 4.50 3.75
Nos. C199-C205 (7) 11.12 8.39

Cent. of founding of 1st cooperative shop in Rochdale, England, by Charles Howarth.
Nos. C199-C205 exist imperf. and part perf.

1945, Mar. 3 **Engr.**
C206 AP20 5c orange 15 10
C207 AP20 10c violet 18 14
C208 AP20 20c grnsh blk 28 16
C209 AP20 30c brt grn 42 28
C210 AP20 40c olive 65 45
C211 AP20 45c blk brn 85 45
C212 AP20 90c redsh brn 1.50 55
C213 AP20 1b dp red lil 1.10 45
C214 AP20 1.20b black 2.50 2.25
C215 AP20 2b yellow 3.75 1.75
Nos. C206-C215 (10) 11.38 6.58

150th birth anniv. of Antonio Jose de Sucre, Grand Marshal of Ayacucho.

Andrés Bello AP21

Gen. Rafael Urdaneta AP22

1946, Aug. 24 *Perf. 12*
C216 AP21 30c green 50 20
C217 AP22 30c green 50 20

See note after No. 393.

Allegory of Republic — AP23

Perf. 11½
1946, Oct. 18 **Litho.** **Unwmk.**
C218 AP23 15c dp vio bl 32 20
C219 AP23 20c bis brn 38 20
C220 AP23 30c dp vio 45 35
C221 AP23 1b brt rose 3.00 2.25

Anniversary of the Revolution of October, 1945. Exist imperf. and part perf.

Nos. 297, 371, C152 and 362 Surcharged in Black

J. R. G. AEREO Vale Bs. 0.15 1946

1947, Jan. *Perf. 12*
C223 A49 10c on 22½c dp car 15 7
a. Inverted surcharge 4.00 4.00
C224 A69 15c on 25c lt bl 32 10
C225 AP16 20c on 50c bl 30 16
a. Inverted surcharge 5.00 5.00
C226 A65 70c on 1b dk vio brn 65 45
a. Inverted surch. 4.00 4.00

Type of 1938 Surcharged in Black

J. R. G. AEREO Vale Bs. 20 1946

C227 AP10 20b on 20b org red 22.50 13.00
a. Surcharge omitted 85.00 25.00
Nos. C223-C227 (5) 23.92 13.78

"J. R. G." are the initials of "Junta Revolucionaria de Gobierno."
Also exist: 20c on No. C143, 10c on No. 371.

Anti-tuberculosis Institute, Maracaibo — AP24

1947, Jan. 12 **Litho.**
Venezuela Shown on Map in Yellow
C228 AP24 15c dk bl 50 35
C229 AP24 20c dk brn 50 28
C230 AP24 30c violet 50 35
C231 AP24 1b carmine 3.75 3.00

12th Pan-American Health Conf., Caracas, Jan. 1947.
Nos. C228-C231 exist imperf., part perf. and with yellow omitted.

Types of 1938-40

1947, Mar. 17 **Engr.**
C232 AP16 75c orange 3.75 2.25
C233 AP16 1b brt ultra 50 16
C234 AP16 3b red brn 10.00 3.50
C235 AP10 5b scarlet 11.00 2.25
C236 AP9 10b violet 16.00 4.50
Nos. C232-C236 (5) 41.25 12.66

On Nos. C235 and C236 the numerals of value are in color on a white table.

No. 370 Surcharged in Black

AEREO
Vale Bs. 0.05
1947

1947, June 20

C237	A70	5c on 20c blue	25	10
C238	A70	10c on 20c blue	25	10
a.		Inverted surcharge	5.00	5.00

Types of 1938-44

1947-48 **Engr.**

C239	AP16	5c orange	6	6
C240	AP16	10c dk grn	6	6
C241	AP16	12½ bis brn	32	25
C242	AP16	15c gray	9	6
C243	AP16	20c violet	12	6
C244	AP16	25c dl grn	9	6
C245	AP16	30c brt ultra	28	9
C246	AP16	40c grn ('48)	20	9
C247	AP16	45c vermilion	42	12
C248	AP16	50c red vio	18	12
C249	AP16	70c dk car	75	45
C250	AP16	75c pur ('48)	38	18
C251	AP16	90c black	65	30
C252	AP16	1.20bred brn ('48)	1.00	65
C253	AP16	3b dp bl	1.50	55
C254	AP10	5b ol grn	5.00	2.00
C255	AP9	10b yellow	6.25	2.50
		Nos. C239-C255 (17)	17.35	7.60

On Nos. C254 and C255 the numerals of value are in color on a white tablet.

M. S. Republica de Venezuela AP25

Santos Michelena AP26

Imprint: "American Bank Note Company"

1948-50 **Unwmk.** ***Perf. 12***

C256	AP25	5c red brn	6	6
C257	AP25	10c dp grn	6	6
C258	AP25	15c brown	9	6
C259	AP25	20c vio brn ('49)	12	6
C260	AP25	25c brn blk	15	5
C261	AP25	30c ol grn	20	8
C262	AP25	45c bl grn ('50)	38	14
C263	AP25	50c gray blk ('49)	50	22
C264	AP25	70c org ('49)	1.00	22
C265	AP25	75c brt ultra ('50)	1.90	30
C266	AP25	90c car lake ('49)	1.00	65
C267	AP25	1b purple	1.25	45
C268	AP25	2b gray ('49)	1.50	65
C269	AP25	3b emer ('49)	5.00	1.75
C270	AP25	4b dp bl ('49)	2.75	1.75
C271	AP25	5c org red ('50)	10.00	3.25
		Nos. C256-C271 (16)	25.96	9.75

Issued to honor the Grand-Colombian Merchant Fleet. See Nos. C554-C556.

1949, Apr. 25

C272	AP26	5c org brn	14	8
C273	AP26	10c gray	18	8
C274	AP26	15c red org	45	25
C275	AP26	25c dl grn	90	45
C276	AP26	30c plum	90	45
C277	AP26	1b violet	4.50	1.75
		Nos. C272-C277 (6)	7.07	3.06

See note after No. 427.

Christopher Columbus AP27

1948-49 **Unwmk.** ***Perf. 12½***

C278	AP27	5c brn ('49)	22	5
C279	AP27	10c gray	30	10
C280	AP27	15c org ('49)	45	14
C281	AP27	25c grn ('49)	90	35
C282	AP27	30c red vio ('49)	1.10	45
C283	AP27	1b vio ('49)	4.50	1.40
		Nos. C278-C283 (6)	7.47	2.49

See note after No. 431.

Symbols of Global Air Mail — AP28

1950 ***Perf. 12***

C284	AP28	5c red brn	10	5
C285	AP28	10c dk grn	5	5
C286	AP28	15c ol brn	16	7
C287	AP28	25c ol gray	38	28
C288	AP28	30c ol grn	55	30
C289	AP28	50c black	35	16
C290	AP28	60c brt ultra	1.10	55
C291	AP28	90c carmine	1.65	65
C292	AP28	1b purple	1.75	45
		Nos. C284-C292 (9)	6.09	2.56

75th anniv. of the UPU.

Araguaney, Venezuelan National Tree — AP29

1950, Aug. 25 **Photo.** ***Perf. 11½***
Foliage in Yellow

C293	AP29	5c org brn	20	10
C294	AP29	10c bl grn	15	5
C295	AP29	15c dp plum	50	24
C296	AP29	25c dk gray grn	3.00	1.50
C297	AP29	30c red org	3.50	2.00
C298	AP29	50c dk gray	2.00	50
C299	AP29	60c dp bl	3.00	1.00
C300	AP29	90c red	6.00	2.00
C301	AP29	1b rose vio	7.00	2.50
		Nos. C293-C301 (9)	25.35	9.89

Issued to publicize Forest Week, 1950.

Census Type of 1950

1950 **Engr.** ***Perf. 12***

C302	A90	5c ol gray	10	6
C303	A90	10c green	5	6
C304	A90	15c ol grn	22	8
C305	A90	25c gray	38	35
C306	A90	30c orange	55	30
C307	A90	50c lt brn	35	16
C308	A90	60c ultra	35	22
C309	A90	90c rose car	1.40	55
C310	A90	1b violet	2.25	1.75
		Nos. C302-C310 (9)	5.65	3.53

Signing Act of Independence — AP31

1950, Nov. 17

C311	AP31	5c vermilion	22	10
C312	AP31	10c red brn	22	10
C313	AP31	15c violet	45	22
C314	AP31	30c brt bl	65	35
C315	AP31	1b green	3.50	1.75
		Nos. C311-C315 (5)	5.04	2.52

Issued to commemorate the 200th anniversary of the birth of Gen. Francisco de Miranda.

Alonso de Ojeda Type of 1950

1950, Dec. 18 **Photo.** ***Perf. 11½***

C316	A91	5c org brn	16	5
C317	A91	10c cerise	22	10
C318	A91	15c blk brn	30	14
C319	A91	25c violet	55	28
C320	A91	30c orange	1.10	45
C321	A91	1b emerald	4.50	2.25
		Nos. C316-321 (6)	6.83	3.27

Bolivar Statue Type of 1951

1951, July 13 **Engr.** ***Perf. 12***

C322	A92	5c purple	28	10
C323	A92	10c dl grn	38	10
C324	A92	20c ol gray	38	10
C325	A92	25c ol grn	45	14
C326	A92	30c vermilion	55	35
C327	A92	40c lt brn	55	38
C328	A92	50c gray	1.75	65
C329	A92	70c orange	2.75	2.25
		Nos. C322-C329 (8)	7.09	4.07

Queen Isabella I — AP34

1951, Oct. 27 **Photo.** ***Perf. 11½***

C330	AP34	5c dk grn & buff	38	10
C331	AP34	10c dk red & cr	38	10
C332	AP34	20c dp bl & gray	65	16
C333	AP34	30c dk bl & gray	65	14
a.		Souv. sheet of 4, #C330-C333	3.75	3.50

500th anniv. of the birth of Queen Isabella I of Spain.

Bicycle Racecourse — AP35

1951, Dec. 18 **Engr.** ***Perf. 12***

C334	AP35	5c green	65	16
C335	AP35	10c rose car	75	18
C336	AP35	20c redsh brn	85	22
C337	AP35	30c blue	1.10	30
a.		Souv. sheet of 4, #C334-C337	13.00	13.00

3rd Bolivarian Games, Caracas, Dec. 1951.

Arms of Carabobo and "Industry" — AP36

1951 **Photo.** ***Perf. 11½***

C338	AP36	5c bl grn	20	5
C339	AP36	7½c gray grn	38	38
C340	AP36	10c car rose	10	5
C341	AP36	15c dk brn	32	15
C342	AP36	20c gray bl	45	20
C343	AP36	30c dp bl	1.75	25
C344	AP36	45c magenta	65	30
C345	AP36	60c ol brn	1.50	65
C346	AP36	90c rose brn	3.50	2.25
		Nos. C338-C346 (9)	8.85	4.28

Arms of Zulia and "Industry"

C347	AP36	5c bl grn	45	10
C348	AP36	10c car rose	10	5
C349	AP36	15c dk brn	50	20
C350	AP36	30c dp bl	3.75	1.50
C351	AP36	60c ol brn	2.00	50
C352	AP36	1.20b brn car	8.75	6.25
C353	AP36	3b bl gray	2.25	1.00
C354	AP36	5b pur brn	3.75	2.50
C355	AP36	10b violet	6.25	5.00
		Nos. C347-C355 (9)	27.80	17.10

Arms of Anzoategui

C356	AP36	5c bl grn	15	5
C357	AP36	10c car rose	12	5
C358	AP36	15c dk brn	38	15
C359	AP36	25c sepia	50	10
C360	AP36	30c dp bl	1.50	1.00
C361	AP36	50c hn brn	1.50	50
C362	AP36	60c ol brn	2.00	30
C363	AP36	1b purple	2.50	1.00
C364	AP36	2b vio gray	4.50	2.25
		Nos. C356-C364 (9)	13.15	5.40

Arms of Caracas and Buildings

C365	AP36	5c bl grn	50	10
C366	AP36	7½c gray grn	1.90	75
C367	AP36	10c car rose	30	15
C368	AP36	15c dk brn	4.50	50
C369	AP36	20c gray bl	3.00	50
C370	AP36	30c dp bl	5.00	1.00
C371	AP36	45c magenta	3.00	65
C372	AP36	60c ol brn	12.50	1.50
C373	AP36	90c rose brn	7.50	6.25
		Nos. C365-C373 (9)	38.20	11.40

1952

Arms of Tachira and Agricultural Products

C374	AP36	5c bl grn	25	10
C375	AP36	10c car rose	15	5
C376	AP36	15c dk brn	75	15
C377	AP36	30c dp bl	11.00	1.50
C378	AP36	60c ol brn	8.75	1.50
C379	AP36	1.20b brn car	8.75	6.25
C380	AP36	3b bl gray	2.25	1.10
C381	AP36	5b pur brn	5.00	2.50
C382	AP36	10b violet	7.00	5.00
		Nos. C374-C382 (9)	43.90	18.15

Arms of Venezuela and Bolivar Statue

C383	AP36	5c bl grn	30	5
C384	AP36	7½c gray grn	85	65
C385	AP36	10c car rose	20	10
C386	AP36	15c dk brn	2.00	65
C387	AP36	20c gray bl	2.75	50
C388	AP36	30c dp bl	5.00	1.10
C389	AP36	45c magenta	2.25	45
C390	AP36	60c ol brn	11.00	2.25
C391	AP36	90c rose brn	8.75	6.25
		Nos. C383-C391 (9)	33.10	12.00

Arms of Miranda and Agricultural Products

C392	AP36	5c bl grn	20	5
C393	AP36	7½c gray grn	38	38
C394	AP36	10c car rose	10	5
C395	AP36	15c dk brn	50	20
C396	AP36	20c gray bl	75	30
C397	AP36	30c dp bl	1.50	50
C398	AP36	45c magenta	1.10	25
C399	AP36	60c ol brn	2.75	65
C400	AP36	90c rose brn	15.00	10.00
		Nos. C392-C400 (9)	22.28	12.38

Arms of Aragua and Stylized Farm

C401	AP36	5c bl grn	50	10
C402	AP36	7½c gray grn	38	38
C403	AP36	10c car rose	10	5
C404	AP36	15c dk brn	1.25	30
C405	AP36	20c gray bl	65	30
C406	AP36	30c dp bl	2.00	40
C407	AP36	45c magenta	1.75	30
C408	AP36	60c ol brn	3.25	50
C409	AP36	90c rose brn	17.50	10.00
		Nos. C401-C409 (9)	27.38	12.33

Arms of Lara, Agricultural Products and Rope

C410	AP36	5c bl grn	50	10
C411	AP36	7½c gray grn	38	38
C412	AP36	10c car rose	12	5
C413	AP36	15c dk brn	75	15
C414	AP36	20c gray bl	1.10	25
C415	AP36	30c dp bl	2.75	50
C416	AP36	45c magenta	1.10	45
C417	AP36	60c ol brn	2.75	75
C418	AP36	90c rose brn	16.00	12.50
		Nos. C410-C418 (9)	25.45	15.13

Arms of Bolivar and Stylized Design

C419	AP36	5c bl grn	3.75	38
C420	AP36	10c car rose	10	5
C421	AP36	15c dk brn	45	10
C422	AP36	25c sepia	32	5
C423	AP36	30c dp bl	2.25	1.10
C424	AP36	50c hn brn	1.75	50
C425	AP36	60c ol brn	2.75	65
C426	AP36	1b purple	2.25	50
C427	AP36	2b vio gray	4.50	2.25
		Nos. C419-C427 (9)	18.12	5.58

Arms of Sucre, Palms and Seascape

C428	AP36	5c bl grn	30	10
C429	AP36	10c car rose	15	5
C430	AP36	15c dk brn	38	15
C431	AP36	25c sepia	8.50	20
C432	AP36	30c dp bl	2.75	85
C433	AP36	50c hn brn	1.25	30
C434	AP36	60c ol brn	1.65	65
C435	AP36	1b purple	2.00	50
C436	AP36	2b vio gray	4.50	2.25
		Nos. C428-C436 (9)	21.48	5.05

Arms of Trujillo Surrounded by Stylized Tree

C437	AP36	5c bl grn	5.50	45
C438	AP36	10c car rose	10	5
C439	AP36	15c dk brn	1.50	10
C440	AP36	30c dp bl	6.25	1.50
C441	AP36	60c ol brn	5.00	1.25
C442	AP36	1.20b rose red	4.50	3.00
C443	AP36	3b bl gray	2.00	1.25
C444	AP36	5b pur brn	4.50	2.25
C445	AP36	10b violet	7.50	5.00
		Nos. C437-C445 (9)	36.85	14.85

1953

Map of Delta Amacuro and Ship

C446 AP36 5c bl grn 30 5
C447 AP36 10c car rose 10 5
C448 AP36 15c dk brn 45 20
C449 AP36 25c sepia 65 30
C450 AP36 30c dp bl 2.25 65
C451 AP36 50c hn brn 1.10 30
C452 AP36 60c ol brn 1.75 50
C453 AP36 1b purple 2.25 75
C454 AP36 2b vio gray 4.50 3.50
Nos. C446-C454 (9) 13.35 6.30

Arms of Falcon and Stylized Oil Refinery

C455 AP36 5c bl grn 50 20
C456 AP36 10c car rose 12 5
C457 AP36 15c dk brn 45 15
C458 AP36 30c dp bl 4.50 1.10
C459 AP36 60c ol brn 2.75 65
C460 AP36 1.20b rose red 3.50 3.00
C461 AP36 3b bl gray 3.75 2.00
C462 AP36 5b pur brn 7.50 6.25
C463 AP36 10b violet 6.00 4.50
Nos. C455-C463 (9) 29.07 17.90

Arms of Guarico and Factory

C464 AP36 5c bl grn 30 5
C465 AP36 10c car rose 20 5
C466 AP36 15c dk brn 45 15
C467 AP36 25c sepia 65 30
C468 AP36 30c dp bl 2.50 1.00
C469 AP36 50c hn brn 1.25 45
C470 AP36 60c ol brn 1.50 65
C471 AP36 1b purple 2.50 65
C472 AP36 2b vio gray 4.50 2.50
Nos. C464-C472 (9) 13.85 5.80

Arms of Merida and Church

C473 AP36 5c bl grn 30 10
C474 AP36 10c car rose 12 5
C475 AP36 15c dk brn 50 10
C476 AP36 30c dp bl 4.50 1.00
C477 AP36 60c ol brn 2.00 50
C478 AP36 1.20b rose red 3.75 2.50
C479 AP36 3b bl gray 2.00 1.00
C480 AP36 5b pur brn 4.50 2.50
C481 AP36 10b violet 6.25 4.00
Nos. C473-C481 (9) 23.92 11.75

Arms of Monagas and Horses

C482 AP36 5c bl grn 30 10
C483 AP36 10c car rose 10 5
C484 AP36 15c dk brn 45 15
C485 AP36 25c sepia 38 12
C486 AP36 30c dp bl 3.75 1.10
C487 AP36 50c hn brn 1.50 50
C488 AP36 60c ol brn 1.75 50
C489 AP36 1b purple 2.50 65
C490 AP36 2b vio gray 3.25 2.00
Nos. C482-C490 (9) 13.98 5.17

Arms of Portuguesa and Forest

C491 AP36 5c bl grn 1.10 30
C492 AP36 10c car rose 20 5
C493 AP36 15c dk brn 50 20
C494 AP36 30c dp bl 3.50 1.50
C495 AP36 60c ol brn 2.50 50
C496 AP36 1.20b rose red 6.25 3.75
C497 AP36 3b bl gray 2.00 1.00
C498 AP36 5b pur brn 4.50 2.50
C499 AP36 10b violet 7.00 5.50
Nos. C491-C499 (9) 27.55 15.30

Map of Amazonas and Orchid

C500 AP36 5c bl grn 85 5
C501 AP36 10c car rose 20 6
C502 AP36 15c dk brn 85 20
C503 AP36 25c sepia 1.75 20
C504 AP36 30c dp bl 4.50 45
C505 AP36 50c hn brn 3.50 75
C506 AP36 60c ol brn 4.50 75
C507 AP36 1b purple 17.50 2.50
C508 AP36 2b vio gray 8.75 3.75
Nos. C500-C508 (9) 42.40 8.71

Arms of Apure, Horse and Bird

C509 AP36 5c bl grn 50 10
C510 AP36 10c car rose 10 5
C511 AP36 15c dk brn 50 15
C512 AP36 30c dp bl 2.50 1.00
C513 AP36 60c ol brn 2.25 50
C514 AP36 1.20b brn car 3.50 2.50
C515 AP36 3b bl gray 2.25 1.00
C516 AP36 5b pur brn 4.50 2.00
C517 AP36 10b violet 6.25 4.50
Nos. C509-C517 (9) 22.35 11.80

Arms of Barinas, Cow and Horse

C518 AP36 5c bl grn 20 10
C519 AP36 10c car rose 10 5
C520 AP36 15c dk brn 75 20
C521 AP36 30c dp bl 2.50 1.00
C522 AP36 60c ol brn 2.50 50
C523 AP36 1.20b brn car 3.50 1.90
C524 AP36 3b bl gray 2.25 1.00
C525 AP36 5b pur brn 4.50 1.50
C526 AP36 10b violet 7.00 5.00
Nos. C518-C526 (9) 23.30 11.25

Arms of Cojedes and Cattle

C527 AP36 5c bl grn 2.50 38
C528 AP36 7½c gray grn 65 38
C529 AP36 10c car rose 12 5
C530 AP36 15c dk brn 20 10
C531 AP36 20c gray bl 50 15
C532 AP36 30c dp bl 3.50 50
C533 AP36 45c magenta 1.25 30
C534 AP36 60c ol brn 2.50 45
C535 AP36 90c rose brn 3.00 1.75
Nos. C527-C535 (9) 14.22 4.06

Arms of Nueva Esparta and Fish

C536 AP36 5c bl grn 38 10
C537 AP36 10c car rose 12 5
C538 AP36 15c dk brn 65 15
C539 AP36 25c sepia 1.10 25
C540 AP36 30c dp bl 2.25 50
C541 AP36 50c hn brn 2.25 50
C542 AP36 60c ol brn 2.25 30
C543 AP36 1b purple 3.25 75
C544 AP36 2b vio gray 4.50 2.25
Nos. C536-C544 (9) 16.75 4.85

Arms of Yaracuy and Tropical Foliage

C545 AP36 5c bl grn 45 12
C546 AP36 7½c gray grn 7.50 7.50
C547 AP36 10c car rose 12 5
C548 AP36 15c dk brn 45 10
C549 AP36 20c gray bl 85 12
C550 AP36 30c dp bl 1.75 50
C551 AP36 45c magenta 1.25 30
C552 AP36 60c ol brn 1.25 50
C553 AP36 90c rose brn 3.50 2.50
Nos. C545-C553 (9) 17.12 11.69
Nos. C338-C553 (216) 574.42 248.23

Ship Type of 1948-50 Redrawn
Coil Stamps
Imprint: "Courvoisier S.A."

1952 Unwmk. Perf. 12x11½

C554 AP25 5c rose brn 90 5
C555 AP25 10c org red 1.40 8
C556 AP25 15c ol brn 1.75 5

Barquisimeto Type of 1952

1952, Sept. 14 Photo. Perf. 11½

C557 A94 5c bl grn 25 5
C558 A94 10c car rose 12 6
C559 A94 20c dk bl 38 9
C560 A94 25c blk brn 50 18
C561 A94 30c ultra 65 15
C562 A94 40c brn org 3.75 1.90
C563 A94 50c dk ol grn 1.25 50
C564 A94 1b purple 5.00 2.50
Nos. C557-C564 (8) 11.90 5.43

Caracas Post Office Type of 1953-54

1953 Perf. 12½

C565 A96 7½c yel grn 10 10
C566 A96 15c dp plum 8 5
C567 A96 20c slate 10 5
C568 A96 25c sepia 35 5
C569 A96 40c plum 35 10
C570 A96 45c rose vio 35 10
C571 A96 50c red org 55 8
C572 A96 70c dk sl grn 1.10 55
C573 A96 75c dp ultra 3.75 80
C574 A96 90c brn org 90 45
C575 A96 1b vio bl 90 45
Nos. C565-C575 (11) 8.53 2.78

See Nos. C587-C589, C597-C606.

Simon Rodriguez
AP39

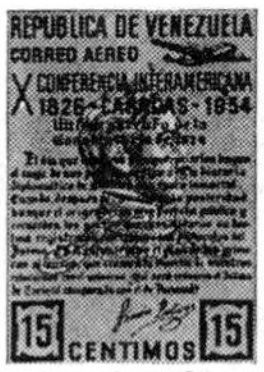

Quotation from Bolivar's Manifesto of 1824
AP40

1954, Feb. 28 Perf. 11½

C576 AP39 5c bl grn 22 5
C577 AP39 10c car rose 35 5
C578 AP39 20c gray bl 45 6
C579 AP39 45c magenta 65 22
C580 AP39 65c gray grn 2.25 1.00
Nos. C576-C580 (5) 3.92 1.38

Issued to commemorate the centenary of the death of Simon Rodriguez, scholar and tutor of Bolivar.

1954, Mar. 1 Unwmk.

C581 AP40 15c blk & brn buff 10 5
C582 AP40 25c dk red brn & gray 65 10
C583 AP40 40c dk red brn & red org 45 10
C584 AP40 65c blk & bl 1.10 55
C585 AP40 80c dk red brn & rose 90 45
C586 AP40 1b pur & rose lil 1.75 35
Nos. C581-C586 (6) 4.95 1.60

Issued to publicize the 10th Inter-American Conference, Caracas, Mar. 1954.

P.O. Type of 1953

1954 Photo. Perf. 12½

C587 A96 5c orange 8 5
C588 A96 30c red brn 1.90 1.00
C589 A96 60c brt red 1.90 1.25

Valencia Arms Type of 1955

1955, Mar. 26 Engr. Perf. 12

C590 A97 5c bl grn 8 5
C591 A97 10c rose pink 10 5
C592 A97 20c ultra 16 5
C593 A97 25c gray 16 6
C594 A97 40c violet 45 22
C595 A97 50c vermilion 45 22
C596 A97 60c ol grn 90 22
Nos. C590-C596 (7) 2.30 87

P.O. Type of 1953 Inscribed: "Republica de Venezuela"

1955 Photo. Perf. 12½

C597 A96 5c orange 8 5
C598 A96 10c ol brn 8 5
C599 A96 15c dp plum 12 5
C600 A96 20c slate 25 5
C601 A96 30c red brn 25 6
C602 A96 40c plum 75 25
C603 A96 45c rose vio 75 38
C604 A96 70c dk sl grn 1.90 85
C605 A96 75c dp ultra 1.25 50
C606 A96 90c brn org 65 25
Nos. C597-C606 (10) 6.08 2.49

Caracas Arms Type of 1955

1955, Dec. 9 Unwmk. Perf. 11½

C607 A98 5c yel org 10 5
C608 A98 15c cl brn 22 5
C609 A98 25c vio blk 22 5
C610 A98 40c red 55 14
C611 A98 50c red org 55 16
C612 A98 60c car rose 1.10 35
Nos. C607-C612 (6) 2.74 80

University Hospital, Caracas
AP43

Designs: 5c, 10c, 15c, 70c, O'Leary School, Barinas. 25c, 30c, 80c, University Hospital, Caracas. 40c, 45c, 50c, 1b, Caracas-La Guaira Highway. 60c, 65c, 75c, 2b, Towers of Simon Bolivar Center.

1956-57 Unwmk. Perf. 11½

C613 AP43 5c orange 8 5
C614 AP43 10c sepia 8 5
C615 AP43 15c cl brn 10 5
C616 AP43 20c dk bl ('56) 10 5
C617 AP43 25c gray blk 14 8
C618 AP43 30c hn brn 35 10
C619 AP43 40c brt crim 45 14
C620 AP43 45c brn vio 30 10
C621 AP43 50c dp org ('56) 55 10
C622 AP43 60c ol grn ('56) 55 18
C623 AP43 65c brt bl 85 25
C624 AP43 70c bl grn 90 35
C625 AP43 75c ultra 1.00 45
C626 AP43 80c car rose 1.10 22
C627 AP43 1b plum 65 30
C628 AP43 2b dk car rose 1.40 90
Nos. C613-C628 (16) 8.60 3.37

Book and Flags of American Nations — AP44

1956-57

Granite Paper

C629 AP44 5c org & brn ('56) 6 6
C630 AP44 10c brn & pale brn 10 5
C631 AP44 20c bl & saph 10 5
C632 AP44 25c gray vio & gray 22 8
C633 AP44 40c rose red & pale pur ('56) 35 10
C634 AP44 45c vio brn & gray brn 45 10
C635 AP44 60c ol & gray ol 90 45
Nos. C629-C635 (7) 2.18 89

Issued for the Book Festival of the Americas, Nov. 15-30, 1956.

Bolivar Type of 1957-58

Engraved; Center Embossed

1957-58 Unwmk. Perf. 13½

C636 A100 5c orange 10 5
C637 A100 10c ol gray 14 5
C638 A100 20c blue 55 14
C639 A100 25c gray blk 60 16
C640 A100 40c rose red 55 14
C641 A100 45c rose lil ('58) 65 25
C642 A100 65c yel brn 1.10 45
Nos. C636-C642 (7) 3.69 1.24

Tamanaco Hotel Type of 1957-58

1957-58 Engr. Perf. 13

C643 A101 5c dl yel 6 5
C644 A101 10c brown 6 5
C645 A101 15c chocolate 22 5
C646 A101 20c gray bl 16 5
C647 A101 25c sepia 14 8
C648 A101 30c vio bl 25 14
C649 A101 40c car rose 28 10
C650 A101 45c claret 35 10
C651 A101 50c red org 35 14
C652 A101 60c yel grn 65 16
C653 A101 65c org brn 1.75 90
C654 A101 70c slate 1.00 45
C655 A101 75c grnsh bl 1.10 55
C656 A101 1b dk cl 1.10 55
C657 A101 2b dk gray 1.75 65
Nos. C643-C657 (15) 9.22 4.02

Post Office Type of 1958

1958 Litho. Perf. 14

C658 A102 5c dp yel 5 5
C659 A102 10c brown 5 5
C660 A102 15c red brn 5 5
C661 A102 20c lt bl 6 5
C662 A102 25c lt gray 10 5
C663 A102 30c lt ultra 10 5
C664 A102 40c brt yel grn 16 5
C665 A102 50c red org 16 5
C666 A102 60c rose pink 22 14
C667 A102 65c red 30 14
C668 A102 90c violet 45 22
C669 A102 1b lilac 55 22
C670 A102 1.20b bis brn 6.75 4.50
Nos. C658-C670 (13) 9.00 5.62

See Nos. C786-C792.

Post Office Type of 1958
Coil Stamps

1958 Engr. Perf. 11½x12

C671 A103 5c dp yel 25 7
C672 A103 10c brown 38 7
C673 A103 15c dk brn 50 9

Merida Type of 1958

1958, Oct. 9 Photo. Perf. 13½

C674 A104 5c org yel 6 5
C675 A104 10c gray brn 6 5
C676 A104 15c dl red brn 10 5
C677 A104 20c chlky bl 10 5
C678 A104 25c brn gray 28 10
C679 A104 30c vio bl 22 6
C680 A104 40c rose car 35 10
C681 A104 45c brt lil 35 14
C682 A104 50c red org 45 22
C683 A104 60c lt ol grn 35 16
C684 A104 65c hn brn 1.10 45
C685 A104 70c gray blk 65 35
C686 A104 75c brt grnsh bl 1.25 65
C687 A104 80c brt vio bl 80 35
C688 A104 90c bl grn 80 38
C689 A104 1b lilac 90 45
Nos. C674-C689 (16) 7.82 3.61

Trujillo Type of 1959

1959 Photo. Perf. 14

C690 A105 5c org yel 6 6
C691 A105 10c lt brn 7 7
C692 A105 15c redsh brn 16 6
C693 A105 20c lt bl 20 10
C694 A105 25c pale gray 28 14
C695 A105 30c lt vio bl 28 14
C696 A105 40c brt yel grn 35 16
C697 A105 50c red org 38 18
C698 A105 60c lil rose 55 28
C699 A105 65c vermilion 1.75 80
C700 A105 1b lilac 1.10 35
Nos. C690-C700 (11) 5.18 2.34

Emblem — AP45

1959, Mar. 10 Litho. Perf. 13½

C701 AP45 5c yellow 10 5
C702 AP45 10c red brn 22 10
C703 AP45 15c orange 28 14

C704 AP45 30c gray 55 28
C705 AP45 50c green 65 35
Nos. C701-C705 (5) 1.80 92

8th Central American and Caribbean Games, Caracas, Nov. 29-Dec. 14, 1958.
Exist imperf. Value, pair $25.

Stamp Centenary Type of 1959

Stamp of 1859 and: 25c, Mailman and José Ignacio Paz Castillo. 50c, Mailman on horse-back and Jacinto Gutierrez. 1b, Plane, train and Miguel Herrera.

1959, Sept. 15 Engr. *Perf. 13½*
C706 A107 25c org yel 35 10
C707 A107 50c blue 55 22
C708 A107 1b rose red 1.10 45

Catalogue values for unused stamps in this section, from this point to the end of the section, are for Never Hinged items.

Alexander von Humboldt Type of 1960

1960, Feb. 9 Unwmk.
C709 A108 5c ocher & brn 28 5
C710 A108 20c brt bl & turq bl 70 15
C711 A108 40c ol & ol grn 1.10 38

Newspaper Type of 1960

1960, June 11 Litho. *Perf. 14*
C712 A109 5c yel & blk 1.40 80
C713 A109 15c lt red brn & blk 80 32
C714 A109 65c sal & blk 1.10 55

Agustin Codazzi Type of 1960

1960, June 15 Engr.
C715 A110 5c yel org & brn 7 5
C716 A110 10c brn & dk brn 14 6
C717 A110 25c gray & blk 32 8
C718 A110 30c vio bl & sl 40 14
C719 A110 50c org brn & brn 70 32
C720 A110 70c gray ol & ol gray 1.10 55
Nos. C715-720 (6) 2.73 1.20

National Pantheon Type of 1960

1960, May 9 Litho.
Pantheon in Bister
C721 A111 5c dp bis 8 5
C722 A111 10c red brn 20 5
C723 A111 15c fawn 28 6
C724 A111 20c lt bl 40 14
C725 A111 25c gray 1.25 28
C726 A111 30c lt vio bl 1.40 48
C727 A111 40c brt yel grn 40 14
C728 A111 45c lt vio 60 18
C729 A111 60c dp pink 80 32
C730 A111 65c salmon 80 32
C731 A111 70c gray 1.25 50
C732 A111 75c chlky bl 2.00 80
C733 A111 80c lt ultra 1.65 70
C734 A111 1.20b bis brn 2.00 95
Nos. C721-C734 (14) 13.11 4.97

Andres Eloy Blanco Type of 1960

1960, May 21 *Perf. 14*
Portrait in Black
C735 A112 20c blue 30 10
C736 A112 75c grnsh bl 95 30
C737 A112 90c brt vio 85 30

Independence Type of 1960

1960, Aug. 19 Litho. *Perf. 13½*
Center Multicolored
C738 A113 50c orange 65 24
C739 A113 75c brt grnsh bl 95 40
C740 A113 90c purple 1.00 30

Oil Refinery — AP46

Unwmk.
1960, Aug. 26 Engr. *Perf. 14*
C741 AP46 30c dk bl & sl bl 38 18
C742 AP46 40c yel grn & ol 65 30
C743 AP46 50c org & red brn 75 38

Issued to publicize Venezuela's oil industry.

Luisa Cáceres de Arismendi Type of 1960

1960, Oct. 24 Litho. *Perf. 14*
Center Multicolored
C744 A115 5c bister 70 35
C745 A115 10c redsh brn 90 55
C746 A115 60c rose car 1.75 70

José Antonio Anzoategui Type of 1960

1960, Oct. 29 Engr.
C747 A116 25c gray & brn 40 20
C748 A116 40c yel grn & ol gray 40 40
C749 A116 45c rose cl & dl pur 55 30

Antonio José de Sucre Type of 1960

Unwmk.
1960, Nov. 13 Litho. *Perf. 14*
Center Multicolored
C750 A117 25c gray 55 28
C751 A117 30c vio bl 80 40
C752 A117 50c brn org 1.10 55

Type of Regular Issue, 1960

Designs: 30c, Bolivar Peak. 50c, Caroni Falls. 65c, Cuacharo caves.

1960, Mar. 22 *Perf. 14*
C753 A118 30c vio bl & blk bl 1.40 1.40
C754 A118 50c brn org & brn 1.40 1.40
C755 A118 65c red org & red brn 1.40 1.40

Cow's Head, Grain, Man and Child
AP47

Arms of San Cristobal
AP48

1961, Feb. 6 Litho. Unwmk.
Cow and Inscription in Black
C756 AP47 5c yellow 7 5
C757 AP47 10c brown 7 5
C758 AP47 15c redsh brn 8 7
C759 AP47 20c dl bl 12 7
C760 AP47 25c gray 15 7
C761 AP47 30c vio bl 18 9
C762 AP47 40c yel grn 25 12
C763 AP47 45c lilac 28 15
C764 AP47 50c orange 30 18
C765 AP47 60c cerise 38 18
C766 AP47 65c red org 50 25
C767 AP47 70c gray 75 38
C768 AP47 75c brt grnsh bl 65 30
C769 AP47 80c brt vio 65 25
C770 AP47 90c violet 1.00 50
Nos. C756-C770 (15) 5.43 2.71

9th general census and 3rd agricultural census.

Rafael Maria Baralt Type of 1961

1961, Mar. 11 Engr. *Perf. 14*
C771 A120 25c gray & sep 48 28
C772 A120 30c dk bl & vio 55 32
C773 A120 40c yel grn & ol grn 70 40

1961, Apr. 10 Litho.
Arms in Original Colors
C774 AP48 5c org & blk 7 6
C775 AP48 55c yel grn & blk 48 24

400th anniversary of San Cristobal.

Bird Type of 1961

Birds: 5c, Troupial. 10c, Golden cock of the rock. 15c, Tropical mockingbird.

1961, Sept. 6 Unwmk. *Perf. 14½*
C776 A121 5c multi 90 85
C777 A121 10c multi 45 45
C778 A121 15c multi 60 50

Charge, Battle of Carabobo — AP49

1961, Dec. 2 Litho. *Perf. 14*
Center Multicolored
C779 AP49 50c blk & ultra 60 15
C780 AP49 1.05b blk & org 1.25 60
C781 AP49 1.50b blk & lil rose 1.50 60
C782 AP49 1.90b blk & lil 2.00 1.25
C783 AP49 2b blk & gray 2.25 1.25
C784 AP49 3b blk & grnsh bl 3.00 1.50
Nos. C779-C784 (6) 10.60 5.35

140th anniversary of Battle of Carabobo.

Arms of Cardinal Quintero
AP50

Archbishop Rafael Arias Blanco
AP51

1962, Mar. 1 Unwmk.
C785 AP50 5c lil rose 8 7
a. Souv. sheet of 1, imperf. 1.25 1.25

1st Venezuelan Cardinal, José Humberto Quintero.
No. C785a sold for 1b.

Post Office Type of 1958

1962 Litho. *Perf. 13½x14*
C786 A102 35c citron 20 10
C787 A102 55c gray ol 32 18
C788 A102 70c bluish grn 50 22
C789 A102 75c brn org 60 18
C790 A102 80c fawn 60 30
C791 A102 85c dp rose 90 45
C792 A102 95c lil rose 65 42
Nos. C786-C792 (7) 3.77 1.85

1962, May 10 *Perf. 10½*
C793 AP51 75c red lil 60 30

Issued to commemorate the 4th anniversary (in 1961) of the anti-communist pastoral letter of the Archbishop of Caracas, Rafael Arias Blanco.

Orchid Type of 1962

Orchids: 5c, Oncidium volvox. 20c, Cycnoches chlorochilon. 25c, Cattleya Gaskelliana. 30c, Epidendrum difforme (horiz.). 40c, Catasetum callosum Lindl (horiz.). 50c, Oncidium bicolor Lindl. 1b, Brassavola nodosa Lindl (horiz.). 1.05b, Epidendrum lividum Lindl. 1.50b, Schomburgkia undulata Lindl. 2b, Oncidium zebrinum.

Perf. 14x13½, 13½x14
1962, May 30 Litho. Unwmk.
Orchids in Natural Colors
C794 A124 5c blk & lt grn 5 5
C795 A124 20c black 12 6
C796 A124 25c blk & fawn 32 12
C797 A124 30c blk & pink 22 9
C798 A124 40c blk & yel 32 15
C799 A124 50c blk & lil 42 20
C800 A124 1b blk & pale rose 65 38
C801 A124 1.05b blk & dp org 1.90 1.25
C802 A124 1.50b blk & pale vio 2.00 1.50
C803 A124 2b blk & org brn 2.50 1.90
Nos. C794-C803 (10) 8.50 5.70

Independence Type of 1960

Design: Signing Declaration of Independence.

1962, June 11 *Perf. 13½*
Center Multicolored
C804 A113 55c olive 50 20
C805 A113 1.05b brt rose 1.50 65
C806 A113 1.50b purple 1.25 60
a. Souv. sheet of 3, #C804-C806, imperf. 3.75 3.75

No. C806a sold for 4.10b.
A buff cardboard folder exists with impressions of Nos. 812-814, C804-C806. Perforation is simulated. Sold for 5.60b. Value $3.

No. 710 Surcharged in Rose Carmine: "BICENTENARIO DE UPATA 1762-1962 RESELLADO AEREO VALOR Bs. 2,00"

1962, July 7 *Perf. 13½x14*
C807 A102 2b on 1b lt ol grn 1.50 90

Issued to commemorate the 200th anniversary of Upata, a village in the state of Bolivar.

National Games Type of 1962

Sports: 40c, Bicycling. 75c, Baseball. 85c, Woman athlete.

Perf. 13x14
1962, Nov. 30 Unwmk. Litho.
C808 A125 40c gray 40 28
C809 A125 75c gldn brn 55 40
C810 A125 85c rose lake 1.40 80
a. Souv. sheet of 3, #C808-C810 imperf. 2.75 2.75

See note after No. 817.
No. C810a sold for 3b.

Bird Type of 1962

Birds: 5c, American kestrel. 20c, Black-bellied tree duck (horiz.). 25c, Amazon king-fisher. 30c, Rufous-tailed chachalaca. 50c, Black-and-yellow troupial. 55c, White-naped nightjar. 2.30b, Red-crowned woodpecker. 2.50b, Black-moustached quail-dove.

1962, Dec. 14 *Perf. 14x13½*
Birds in Natural Colors; Black Inscription
C811 A126 5c car rose 15 8
C812 A126 20c brt bl 30 15
C813 A126 25c lt gray 40 18
C814 A126 30c lt ol 45 22
C815 A126 50c violet 75 35
C816 A126 55c dp org 1.25 60
C817 A126 2.30b dl red brn 3.75 2.75
C818 A126 2.50b org yel 3.75 3.00
Nos. C811-C818 (8) 10.80 7.33

Malaria Eradication Emblem, Mosquito and Map — AP52

Lithographed and Embossed
Perf. 13½x14
1962, Dec. 20 Wmk. 346
C819 AP52 30c grn & blk 40 22
a. Souvenir sheet of 2 2.25 2.25

WHO drive to eradicate malaria. No. C819a contains one each of Nos. 825 and C819 imperf. Sold for 2b.

Animal Type of Regular Issue

Designs: 5c, Spectacle bear (vert). 40c, Paca. 50c, Three-toed sloths. 55c, Great ant-eater. 1.50b, South American tapirs. 2b, Jaguar.

Perf. 13½x14
1963, Mar. 13 Litho. Unwmk.
Multicolored Center; Black Inscriptions
C820 A128 5c yellow 20 10
C821 A128 40c brt grn 60 28
C822 A128 50c lt vio 80 40
C823 A128 55c brn ol 1.00 48
C824 A128 1.50b gray 3.00 2.00
C825 A128 2b ultra 5.00 3.00
Nos. C820-C825 (6) 10.60 6.26

Freedom from Hunger Type of 1963

Designs: 40c, Map and shepherd. 75c, Map and farmer.

1963, Mar. 21

C826 A129 40c lt yel grn & dl red 40 28
C827 A129 75c yel & brn 28 40

Arms of Bocono — AP53

1963, May 30 **Wmk. 346**

C828 AP53 1b multi 1.00 38

Issued to commemorate the 400th anniversary of the founding of Bocono.

Papal and Venezuelan Arms AP54

1963, June 11 ***Perf. 14x13½***

Arms Multicolored

C829 AP54 80c lt grn 75 32
C830 AP54 90c gray 75 38

Issued to commemorate Vatican II, the 21st Ecumenical Council of the Roman Catholic Church.

Arms of Venezuela — AP55

1963, July 29 **Unwmk.** ***Perf. 14***

C831 AP55 70c gray, red, yel & bl 70 40

Issued to commemorate the centenary of Venezuela's flag and coat of arms.

Lake Maracaibo Bridge AP56

Wmk. 346

1963, Aug. 24 **Litho.** ***Perf. 14***

C832 AP56 90c grn, brn & ocher 90 40
C833 AP56 95c bl, brn & ocher 95 48
C834 AP56 1b ultra, brn & ocher 70 40

Opening of bridge over Lake Maracaibo.

Armed Forces Type of 1963

1963, Sept. 10 **Unwmk.**

C835 A134 1b red & bl, *buff* 1.25 75

Hammarskjold Type of 1963

1963, Sept. 25 **Unwmk.** ***Perf. 14***

C836 A135 80c dk bl, lt ultra & ocher 70 40
C837 A135 90c dk bl, bl & ocher 95 55
a. Souv. sheet of 4 2.75 2.75

No. C837a contains 4 imperf. stamps similar to Nos. 841-842 and C836-C837. Sold for 3b.

Dr. Luis Razetti — AP57

1963, Oct. 20 **Engr.**

C838 AP57 95c dk bl & mag 1.00 60
C839 AP57 1.05b dk brn & grn 1.10 75

Issued to commemorate the centenary of the birth of Dr. Luis Razetti, physician.

Red Cross Type of 1963

Designs: 40c, Sir Vincent K. Barrington. 75c, Red Cross nurse and child.

1963, Dec. 31 **Litho.** ***Perf. 11½x12***

C840 A137 40c multi 32 28
C841 A137 75c multi 55 40

Development Type of 1964

Designs: 5c, Loading cargo. 10c, Tractor and corn. 15c, Oil field workers. 20c, Oil refinery. 50c, Crane and building construction.

1964, Feb. 5 **Unwmk.** ***Perf. 14x13½***

C842 A138 5c multi 6 6
C843 A138 10c multi 6 6
C844 A138 15c multi 12 6
C845 A138 20c multi 15 6
C846 A138 50c multi 38 25
Nos. C842-C846 (5) 77 49

Cent. of the Dept. of Industrial Development and to publicize the Natl. Industrial Expo.

Pedro Gual Type of 1964

1964, Mar. 20 ***Perf. 14x13½***

C847 A139 75c dl bl grn 50 25
C848 A139 1b brt pink 65 30

Blast Furnace and Map of Venezuela AP58

Arms of Ciudad Bolivar AP59

1964, May 22 **Litho.** ***Perf. 13½x14***

C849 AP58 80c multi 70 32
C850 AP58 1b multi 90 40

Issued to publicize the Orinoco steel mills.

1964, May 22 ***Perf. 10½***

C851 AP59 1b multi 95 70

Bicentenary of Ciudad Bolivar.

Romulo Gallegos and Book — AP60

1964, Aug. 3 **Unwmk.** ***Perf. 11½***

C852 AP60 30c bis brn & yel 28 14
C853 AP60 40c plum & pink 40 20
C854 AP60 50c brn & tan 55 28

Issued to commemorate the 80th birthday of novelist Romulo Gallegos.

Eleanor Roosevelt AP61

1964, Nov. 11 **Litho.** ***Perf. 14x13½***

C855 AP61 1b org & dk vio 80 48

Issued to honor Eleanor Roosevelt and the 15th anniversary (in 1963) of the Universal Declaration of Human Rights.

Issues of 1947-64 Surcharged in Black, Dark Blue, Red, Carmine or Lilac with New Value and: "RESELLADO / VALOR"

1965

C856 A102 5c on 55c (#C787) 6 5
C857 A102 5c on 70c (#C788) 8 6
C858 A102 5c on 80c (#C790) 9 6
C859 A102 5c on 85c (#C791) 6 6
C860 A102 5c on 90c (#C668) 6 6
C861 A102 5c on 95c (#C792) 6 5
C862 A134 5c on 1b (#C835) 38 25
C863 AP25 10c on 3b (#C269) (C) 12 6
C864 AP25 10c on 4b (#C270) (C) 50 25
C865 AP47 10c on 70c (#C767) (C) 25 12
C866 AP47 10c on 90c (#C770) (C) 18 8
C867 AP49 10c on 1.05b (#C780) 38 18
C868 AP49 10c on 1.90b (#C782) 18 12
C869 AP49 10c on 2b (#C783) 25 12
C870 AP49 10c on 3b (#C784) 25 12
C871 AP54 10c on 80c (#C829) 12 5
C872 AP54 10c on 90c (#C830) 12 5
C873 AP16 15c on 3b (#C253) 25 12
C874 A112 15c on 90c (#C737) 18 8
C875 A135 15c on 80c (#C836) 18 8
C876 A135 15c on 90c (#C837) 18 8
C877 AP59 15c on 1b (#C851) 25 12
C878 A101 20c on 2b (#C657) (R) 30 12
C879 AP48 20c on 55c (#C775) (DB) 25 8
C880 A126 20c on 55c (#C816) 38 18
a. 25c on 55c (#C816)
C881 A126 20c on 2.30b (#C817) 28 8
C882 A126 20c on 2.50b (#C818) 38 18
C883 AP55 20c on 70c (#C831) 38 25
C884 A110 25c on 70c (#C720) (DB) 42 20
C885 A124 25c on 1.05b (#C801) (L) 25 12
C886 A124 25c on 1.50b (#C802) (L) 25 12
C887 A124 25c on 2b (#C803) (L) 38 18
C888 A128 25c on 1.50b (#C824) 38 12
C889 A128 25c on 2b (#C825) 38 18
C890 AP57 25c on 95c (#C838) 32 18
C891 AP57 25c on 1.05b (#C839) 38 18
C892 AP53 30c on 1b (#C828) 50 25
C893 A113 40c on 1.05b (#C805) (DB) 38 18
C894 A111 50c on 65c (#C730) (DB) 18 9
C895 A111 50c on 1.20b (#C734) (DB) 50 25
C896 AP61 50c on 1b (#C855) 25 12
C897 AP56 60c on 90c (#C832) 75 38
C898 AP56 60c on 95c (#C833) 55 25
C899 A125 75c on 85c (#C810) 55 30
Nos. C856-C899 (44) 12.57 6.21

Lines of surcharge arranged variously on Nos. C856-C899. Old denominations obliterated with bars on Nos. C862, C871-C873, C875-C877, C883, C885-C887, C889, C892, C896-C898. Vertical surcharge on Nos. C865-C866, C871-C872, C874, C878, C896.

Kennedy Type of 1965

1965, Aug. 20 **Photo.** ***Perf. 12x11½***

C900 A144 60c lt grnsh bl 55 28
C901 A144 80c red brn 70 32

Medical Federation Emblem — AP62

1965, Aug. 24 **Litho.** ***Perf. 13½x14***

C902 AP62 65c red org & blk 80 55

Issued to commemorate the 20th anniversary of the founding of the Medical Federation of Venezuela.

Unisphere and Venezuela Pavilion AP63

1965, Aug. 31 ***Perf. 14x13½***

C903 AP63 1b multi 75 32

New York World's Fair, 1964-65.

Andrés Bello (1780?-1865), Educator and Writer — AP64

Perf. 14x13½

1965, Oct. 15 **Litho.** **Unwmk.**

C904 AP64 80c dk brn & org 80 55

Map Type of 1965

Maps of Venezuela and Guiana: 25c, Map of Venezuela and Guiana by J. Cruz Cano, 1775. 40c, Map stamp of 1896 (No. 140). 75c, Map by the Ministry of the Exterior, 1965 (all horiz.).

1965, Nov. 5 ***Perf. 13½***

C905 A145 25c multi 28 14
C906 A145 40c multi 40 14
C907 A145 75c multi 55 28
a. Souv. sheet of 3, #C905-C907, imperf. 2.00 2.00

No. C907a sold for 1.65b.

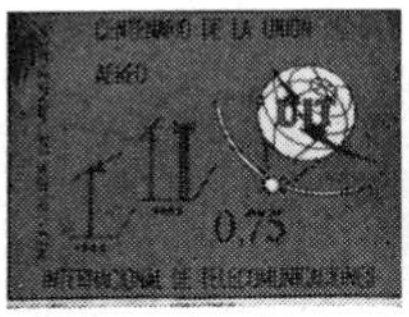

ITU Emblem and Telegraph Poles — AP65

1965, Nov. 19 **Litho.** ***Perf. 13½x14***

C908 AP65 75c blk & ol grn 55 28

Cent. of the ITU.

Simon Bolivar and Quotation — AP66

1965, Dec. 9 ***Perf. 14x13½***
C909 AP66 75c lt bl & dk brn 55 28

Sesquicentennial of Bolivar's Jamaica letter, Sept. 6, 1815.

Children Riding Magic Carpet and Three Kings on Camels — AP67

Fermin Toro — AP68

1965, Dec. 16 ***Perf. 13½x14***
C910 AP67 70c yel & vio bl 80 55

Children's Festival, 1965 (Christmas).

1965, Dec. 22 ***Perf. 14x13½***
C911 AP68 1b blk & org 70 32

Death centenary of Fermin Toro (1808-1865), statesman and writer.

Winston Churchill — AP69

1965, Dec. 29 ***Perf. 14½x13***
C912 AP69 1b lil & blk 80 40

Issued in memory of Sir Winston Spencer Churchill (1874-1965), statesman and World War II leader.

ICY Emblem, Arms of Venezuela and UN Emblem AP70

1965, Dec. 30 ***Perf. 13½x14***
C913 AP70 85c gold & vio blk 80 40

International Cooperation Year, 1965.

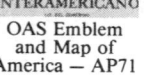

OAS Emblem and Map of America — AP71

Farms of 1936 and 1966 — AP72

1965, Dec. 31 ***Perf. 14x13½***
C914 AP71 50c bl, blk & gold 70 32

Issued to commemorate the 75th anniversary of the Organization of American States.

Butterfly Type of 1966

1966, Jan. 25 Litho. ***Perf. 13½x14***
Various Butterflies in Natural Colors; Black Inscriptions

C915 A146 65c lilac 55 28
C916 A146 85c blue 80 40
C917 A146 1b sal pink 95 48

1966, Mar. 1 ***Perf. 14x13½***
C918 AP72 55c blk, yel & emer 60 30

Issued to commemorate the 30th anniversary of the Ministry for Agriculture and Husbandry.

Dance Type of 1966

Various Folk Dances

1966, Apr. 5 Litho. ***Perf. 14***
C919 A148 40c bl & multi 55 28
C920 A148 50c multi 70 32
C921 A148 60c vio & multi 40 20
C922 A148 70c multi 95 48
C923 A148 80c red & multi 1.10 55
C924 A148 90c ocher & multi 1.25 70
Nos. C919-C924 (6) 4.95 2.53

Title Page "Popule Meus" AP73

1966, Apr. 15 ***Perf. 13½x14***
C925 AP73 55c yel grn, blk & bis 40 28
C926 AP73 95c dp mag, blk & bis 55 40

Issued to commemorate the 150th anniversary (in 1964) of the death of Jose Angel Lamas, composer of national anthem.

Circus Scene, by Michelena — AP74

Paintings by Michelena: 1b, Miranda in La Carraca. 1.05b, Charlotte Corday.

Perf. 12x12½
1966, May 12 Litho. Unwmk.
C927 AP74 95c multi 70 55
C928 AP74 1b multi 80 55
C929 AP74 1.05b multi 95 55

Issued to commemorate the centenary of the birth of Arturo Michelena (1863-1898), painter. Miniature sheets of 12 exist.
See Nos. 900-901.

Abraham Lincoln — AP75

1966, May 31 ***Perf. 13½x14***
C930 AP75 1b gray & blk 70 55

Issued to commemorate the centenary (in 1965) of the death of Abraham Lincoln.

Dr. José Gregorio Hernandez AP76

1966, July 29 Litho. ***Perf. 14x13½***
C931 AP76 1b brt bl & vio bl 95 48

Issued to commemorate the centenary (in 1964) of the birth of Dr. José Gregorio Hernandez, physician.

Dr. Manuel Dagnino and Hospital AP77

1966, Aug. 16 Litho. ***Perf. 13½x14***
C932 AP77 1b sl grn & yel grn 80 40

Issued to commemorate the centenary of the founding of Chiquinquira Hospital.

Fish Type of 1966

Fish: 75c, Pearl hadstander (vert.). 90c, Swordtail characine. 1b, Ramirez's dwarf cichlid.

Perf. 14x13½, 13½x14
1966, Aug. 31
C933 A151 75c multi 80 40
C934 A151 90c grn & multi 80 40
C935 A151 1b multi 80 40

Rafael Arevalo Gonzalez AP78

Simon Bolivar, 1816 AP79

1966, Sept. 13 Litho. ***Perf. 13½x14***
C936 AP78 75c yel bis & blk 70 40

Issued to commemorate the centenary of the birth of Rafael Arevalo Gonzalez, journalist.

Imprint: "Bundesdruckerei Berlin 1966"

Bolivar Portraits: 25c, 30c, 35c, by José Gil de Castro, 1825. 40c, 50c, 60c, Anonymous painter, 1825. 80c, 1.20b, 4b, Anonymous painter, c. 1829.

1966

Multicolored Center

C937 AP79 5c lem & blk 7 5
C938 AP79 10c lt ol grn & blk 8 5
C939 AP79 20c grn & blk 8 5
C940 AP79 25c sal & blk 10 5
C941 AP79 30c pink & blk 14 7
C942 AP79 35c dl rose & blk 18 7
C943 AP79 40c bis brn & blk 14 7
C944 AP79 50c org brn & blk 28 14
C945 AP79 60c brn red & blk 28 14
C946 AP79 80c brt bl & blk 55 28
C947 AP79 1.20b dl bl & blk 80 55
C948 AP79 4b vio bl & blk 2.75 2.25
Nos. C937-C948 (12) 5.45 3.77

Issued to honor Simon Bolivar.
Issue dates: Nos. C937-C939, Sept. 15. Nos. C940-C942, Sept. 29. Others, Oct. 14.
See Nos. C961-C972.

"Justice" — AP80

1966, Nov. 3 Litho. ***Perf. 14x13½***
C949 AP80 50c pale lil & red lil 55 28

Issued to commemorate the 50th anniversary of the Academy of Political and Social Sciences.

Angostura Bridge, Orinoco River — AP81

1967, Jan. 6 Litho. ***Perf. 13½x14***
C950 AP81 40c multi 25 18

Issued to commemorate the opening of the Angostura Bridge over the Orinoco River.

Pavilion of Venezuela AP82

1967, Apr. 28 Litho. ***Perf. 11x13½***
C951 AP82 1b multi 70 32

EXPO '67, International Exhibition, Montreal, Apr. 28-Oct. 27, 1967.

Statue of Chief Guaicaipuro AP83

Constellations over Caracas, 1567 and 1967 — AP84

Designs: 45c, Captain Francisco Fajardo. 55c, Diego de Losada, the Founder. 65c, Arms of Caracas. 90c, Map of Caracas, 1578. 1b, Market on Plaza Mayor, 1800.

Perf. 14x13½, 13½x14
1967, July Litho.
C952 AP83 15c multi 7 5
C953 AP83 45c gold, car & brn 28 14
C954 AP83 55c multi 35 18
C955 AP84 60c blk, ultra & sil 40 20
C956 AP83 65c multi 48 24
C957 AP84 90c multi 60 30
C958 AP84 1b multi 70 35
Nos. C952-C958 (7) 2.88 1.46

Issued to commemorate the 400th anniversary of the founding of Caracas (first issue). See Nos. C977-C982 (second issue).
Two souvenir sheets each contain single stamps similar to Nos. C952-C953, but with simulated perforation. Sold for 1b each. Size: 80x119mm. Value $5 each.

The only foreign revenue stamps listed in this Catalogue are those authorized for prepayment of postage.

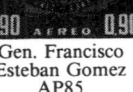

Gen. Francisco Esteban Gomez
AP85

Juan Vicente González
AP86

1967, July 31 Litho. *Perf. 14x13½*

C959	AP85	90c multi	70	40

150th anniversary, Battle of Matasiete.

1967, Sept. 18 Litho. *Perf. 14x13½*

C960	AP86	80c ocher & blk	70	32

Issued to commemorate the centenary of the death (in 1866) of Juan Vicente Gonzalez, journalist.

Bolivar Type of 1966

Imprint: "Druck Bruder Rosenbaum. Wien"

1967-68 Litho. *Perf. 13½x14*

Multicolored Center

C961	AP79	5c lem & blk ('68)	7	6
C962	AP79	10c lem & blk	7	6
C963	AP79	20c grn & blk	28	7
C964	AP79	25c sal & blk ('68)	20	10
C965	AP79	30c pink & blk	28	10
C966	AP79	35c dl rose & blk	28	10
C967	AP79	40c bis brn & blk ('68)	40	14
C968	AP79	50c org brn & blk	80	40
C969	AP79	60c brn red & blk	1.65	95
C970	AP79	80c brt bl & blk	95	48
C971	AP79	1.20b dl bl & blk	1.40	40
C972	AP79	4b vio bl & blk	3.50	2.00
		Nos. C961-C972 (12)	9.88	4.86

Child with Pinwheel — AP87

1967, Dec. 15 Litho. *Perf. 14x13½*

C973	AP87	45c multi	38	18
C974	AP87	75c multi	50	25
C975	AP87	90c multi	65	32

Children's Festival.

Madonna with the Rosebush, by Stephan Lochner — AP88

1967, Dec. 19

C976	AP88	1b multi	95	55

Christmas 1967.

For unused stamps, more recent issues are valued as never hinged, with the beginning point determined on a country-by-country basis. Notes to show the beginning points are prominently placed in the text.

Palace of the Academies, Caracas — AP89

Views of Caracas: 50c, St. Theresa's Church (vert.). 70c, Federal Legislature. 75c, University City. 85c, El Pulpo highways crossing. 2b, Avenida Libertador.

Perf. 13½x14, 14x13½

1967, Dec. 28

C977	AP89	10c multi	7	6
C978	AP89	50c lil & multi	28	14
C979	AP89	70c multi	48	20
C980	AP89	75c multi	55	24
C981	AP89	85c multi	55	28
C982	AP89	2b multi	1.65	80
		Nos. C977-C982 (6)	3.58	1.72

Issued to commemorate the 400th anniversary of Caracas (second issue).

Dr. José Manuel Nuñez Ponte (1870-1965), Educator — AP90

1968, Mar. 8 Litho. *Perf. 14*

C983	AP90	65c multi	40	28

De Miranda and Printing Press
AP91

Designs (Miranda Portraits and): 35c, Parliament, London. 45c, Arc de Triomphe, Paris. 70c, Portrait (vert.). 80c, Portrait bust and Venezuelan flags (vert.).

Perf. 13½x14, 14x13½

1968, June 20 Litho.

C984	AP91	20c yel brn, grn & brn	18	8
C985	AP91	35c multi	32	14
C986	AP91	45c lt bl & multi	55	28
C987	AP91	70c multi	70	24
C988	AP91	80c multi	80	40
		Nos. C984-C988 (5)	2.55	1.14

Issued to commemorate the sesquicentennial of the death of General Francisco de Miranda (1750?-1816), revolutionist, dictator of Venezuela.

Insect Type of 1968

Insect Pests: 5c, Red leaf-cutting ant (vert.). 15c, Sugar cane beetle (vert.). 20c, Leaf beetle.

Perf. 14x13½, 13½x14

1968, Aug. 30 Litho.

C989	A157	5c multi	8	6
C990	A157	15c multi	20	8
C991	A157	20c gray & multi	28	14

Three Keys — AP92

1968, Oct. 17 Litho. *Perf. 14x13½*

C992	AP92	95c yel, vio & dk grn	70	35

Issued to commemorate the 30th anniversary of the National Comptroller's Office.

Fencing
AP93

Designs: 5c, Pistol shooting (vert.). 15c, Running. 75c, Boxing. 5b, Sailing (vert.).

Perf. 14x13½, 13½x14

1968, Nov. 6 Litho. Unwmk.

C993	AP93	5c vio, bl & blk	8	6
C994	AP93	15c multi	28	10
C995	AP93	30c yel grn, dk grn & blk	40	20
C996	AP93	75c multi	80	40
C997	AP93	5b multi	4.00	2.00
		Nos. C993-C997 (5)	5.56	2.76

Issued to commemorate the 19th Olympic Games, Mexico City, Oct. 12-27.

Holy Family, by Francisco José de Lerma — AP94

Dancing Children and Stars — AP95

1968, Dec. 4 Litho. *Perf. 14x13½*

C998	AP94	40c multi	40	20

Christmas 1968.

1968, Dec. 13 Litho. *Perf. 14x13½*

C999	AP95	80c vio & org	55	28

Issued for the 5th Children's Festival.

Conservation Type of 1968

Designs: 15c, Marbled wood-quail (vert.). 20c, Water birds (vert.). 30c, Woodcarvings and tools (vert.). 90c, Brown trout. 95c, Valley and road. 1b, Red-eyed vireo feeding young bronzed cowbird.

Perf. 13½x14, 14x13½

1968, Dec. 19 Litho.

C1000	A160	15c multi	7	6
C1001	A160	20c multi	14	7
C1002	A160	30c multi	20	8
C1003	A160	90c multi	55	28
C1004	A160	95c multi	95	48
C1005	A160	1b multi	70	32
		Nos. C1000-C1005 (6)	2.61	1.29

Tourist Type of 1969

Designs: 15c, Giant cactus and desert, Falcon. 30c, Hotel Humboldt, Federal District. 40c, Cable car and mountain peaks, Merida.

1969, Jan. 24 *Perf. 13½x14*

C1006	A161	15c multi	18	8
C1007	A161	30c multi	18	14
a.		Souv. sheet of 2	1.10	1.10
C1008	A161	40c multi	35	20

No. C1007a contains 2 imperf. stamps similar to Nos. 931 and C1007.

Tree Type of 1969

Trees: 5c, Cassia grandis. 20c, Triplaris caracasana. 25c, Samanea saman.

1969, May 30 Litho. *Perf. 13½x14*

C1009	A164	5c lt grn & multi	7	6
C1010	A164	20c org & multi	20	8
C1011	A164	25c lt vio & multi	28	14

Alexander von Humboldt, by Joseph Stieler — AP96

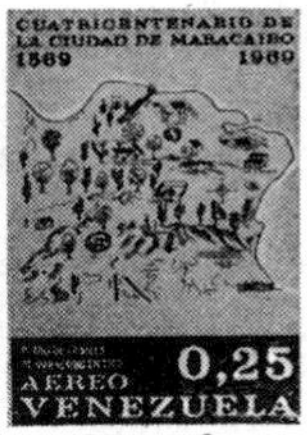

Map of Maracaibo, 1562 — AP97

1969, Sept. 12 Photo. *Perf. 14*

C1012	AP96	50c multi	45	20

Issued to commemorate the bicentenary of the birth of Alexander von Humboldt (1769-1859), naturalist and explorer.

Perf. 13½x13, 13x13½

1969, Sept. 30 Litho.

Designs: 20c, Ambrosio Alfinger, Alfonso Pacheco and Pedro Maldonado (horiz.). 40c, Maracaibo coat of arms. 70c, University Hospital. 75c, Monument to the Indian Mara. 1b, Baralt Square (horiz.).

C1013	AP97	20c lil & multi	18	10
C1014	AP97	25c org & multi	20	14
C1015	AP97	40c multi	28	18
C1016	AP97	70c grn & multi	55	28
C1017	AP97	75c brn & multi	70	32
C1018	AP97	1b multi	80	40
		Nos. C1013-C1018 (6)	2.71	1.42

400th anniversary of Maracaibo.

Astronauts Neil A. Armstrong, Edwin E. Aldrin, Jr., Michael Collins and Moonscape
AP98

1969, Nov. 18 Litho. *Perf. 12½*

C1019	AP98	90c multi	95	48
a.		Souv. sheet of 1, imperf.	1.40	1.40

See note after U.S. No. C76.

Virgin with the Rosary, 17th Century
AP99

Christmas: 80c, Holy Family, Caracas, 18th Century.

1969, Dec. 1 Litho. *Perf. 12½*

C1020	AP99	75c gold & multi	55	28
C1021	AP99	80c gold & multi	70	32
		Pair, # C1020-C1021	1.05	1.40

Nos. C1020-C1021 are printed se-tenant.

Simon Bolivar, 1819, by M. N. Bate — AP100

Bolivar Portraits: 45c, 55c, like 15c. 65c, 70c, 75c Drawing by Francois Roulin, 1828. 85c, 90c, 95c, Charcoal drawing by Jose Maria Espinoza, 1828. 1b, 1.50b, 2b, Drawing by Espinoza, 1830.

1970, Mar. 16 Litho. *Perf. 14x13½*

C1022	AP100	15c multi	14	8
C1023	AP100	45c bl & multi	28	14
C1024	AP100	55c org & multi	40	20
C1025	AP100	65c multi	40	20
C1026	AP100	70c bl & multi	48	30
C1027	AP100	75c org & multi	60	32
C1028	AP100	85c multi	70	35
C1029	AP100	90c bl & multi	75	38
C1030	AP100	95c org & multi	80	40
C1031	AP100	1b multi	80	40
C1032	AP100	1.50b bl & multi	95	48
C1033	AP100	2b multi	2.00	1.40
		Nos. C1022-C1033 (12)	8.30	4.65

Issued to honor Simon Bolivar (1783-1830), liberator and father of his country.

General Antonio Guzman Blanco and Dr. Martin J. Sanabria AP101

1970, June 26 Litho. *Perf. 13*

C1034	AP101	75c brt grn & multi	50	30

Issued to commemorate the centenary of free obligatory elementary education.

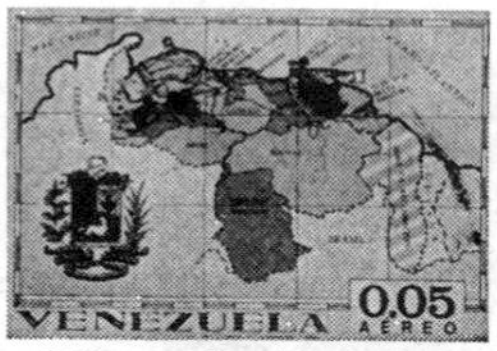

Map of Venezuela with Claim to Part of Guyana — AP102

Designs: State map and arms. 55c, 90c, vert.

Perf. 13½x14, 14x13½

1970-71 Litho.

C1035	AP102	5c *shown*	7	6
C1036	AP102	15c *Apure* ('71)	14	6
C1037	AP102	20c *Aragua* ('71)	18	7
C1038	AP102	20c *Anzoategui* ('71)	20	7
C1039	AP102	25c *Barinas* ('71)	20	7
C1040	AP102	25c *Bolivar* ('71)	20	7
C1041	AP102	45c *Carabobo* ('71)	35	18
C1042	AP102	55c *Cojedes* ('71)	40	20
C1043	AP102	65c *Falcon*	45	20
C1044	AP102	75c *Guarico* ('71)	55	22
C1045	AP102	85c *Lara* ('71)	70	28
C1046	AP102	90c *Merida* ('71)	70	32
C1047	AP102	1b *Miranda* ('71)	70	40
C1048	AP102	2b *Delta Amacuro Territory* ('71)	1.65	95
		Nos. C1035-C1048 (14)	6.49	3.15

Flower Type of 1970

Flowers: 20c, Epidendrum secundum. 25c, Oyedaea verbesinoides. 45c, Heliconia villosa. 1b, Macleania nitida.

1970, July 29 Litho. *Perf. 14x13½*

C1049	A175	20c multi	20	8
C1050	A175	25c multi	28	14
C1051	A175	45c multi	55	28
C1052	A175	1b multi	80	40

Caracciolo Parra Olmedo AP104

1970, Nov. 16 Photo. *Perf. 12½*

C1053	AP104	20c bl & multi	20	8

Sesquicentennial of birth of Caracciolo Parra Olmedo (1819-1900), professor of law, rector of University of Merida.

Census Chart AP105

1971, Apr. 30 Litho. *Perf. 13½x14*

C1054	AP105	Block of 4	4.50	2.25
a.		70c, frame L & T	80	28
b.		70c, frame T & R	80	28
c.		70c, frame L & B	80	28
d.		70c, frame B & R	80	28

National Census, 1971. The frame encircles all 4 stamps of No. C1054; each stamp in block has frame on 2 sides. Sheet of 20 contains 5 No. C1054 and 5 blocks of 4 labels inscribed in brown "Censo Nacional 1971."

Cattleya Gaskelliana AP106

Orchids: 20c, Cattleya percivaliana (vert.). 75c, Cattleya mossiae (vert.). 90c, Cattleya violacea. 1b, Cattleya lawrenciana.

Perf. 14x13½, 13½x14

1971, Aug. 25

C1055	AP106	20c blk & multi	28	14
C1056	AP106	25c blk & multi	35	18
C1057	AP106	75c blk & multi	70	32
C1058	AP106	90c blk & multi	80	40
C1059	AP106	1b blk & multi	95	45
		Nos. C1055-C1059 (5)	3.08	1.49

40th anniversary of Venezuelan Society of Natural History. Issued in sheets of 5 stamps and one label with Society emblem in blue.

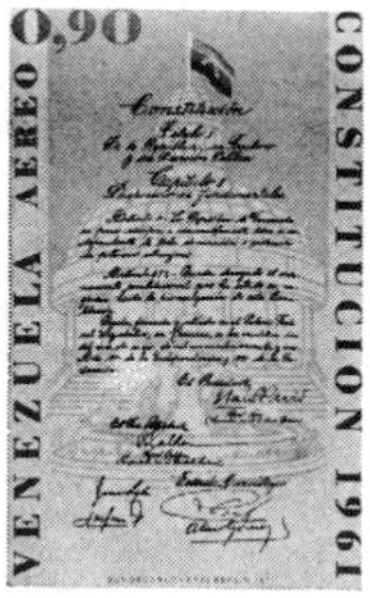

Draft of Constitution Superimposed on Capitol AP107

1971, Dec. 29 Litho. *Perf. 13½*

C1060	AP107	90c multi	80	40

Anniversary of 1961 Constitution.

AIR POST SEMI-POSTAL STAMPS

King Vulture — SPAP1

Unwmk.

1942, Dec. 17 Engr. *Perf. 12*

CB1	SPAP1	15c + 10c org brn	1.40	55
CB2	SPAP1	30c + 5c vio	1.40	70

See note after No. B1.

SPECIAL DELIVERY STAMPS

Catalogue values for unused stamps in this section are for Never Hinged items.

SD1

SD2

1949 Unwmk. Engr. *Perf. 12½*

E1	SD1	30c red	38	16

Wmk. 116

1961, Apr. 5 Litho. *Perf. 13½*

E2	SD2	30c orange	32	18

REGISTRATION STAMPS

Bolivar — R1

1899 Unwmk. Engr. *Perf. 12*

F1	R1	25c yellow brown	2.50	1.90

No. F1 Overprinted in Black

1900

F2	R1	25c yellow brown	1.50	1.50
a.		Inverted overprint	22.50	22.50
b.		Double overprint	30.00	30.00

Counterfeit overprints exist, especially of the varieties.

OFFICIAL STAMPS

Coat of Arms
O1 O3

Lithographed, Center Engraved

1898 Unwmk. *Perf. 12*

O1	O1	5c bl grn & blk	38	35
O2	O1	10c rose & blk	75	70
O3	O1	25c bl & blk	1.00	90
O4	O1	50c yel & blk	1.90	1.75
O5	O1	1b vio & blk	1.90	1.75
		Nos. O1-O5 (5)	5.93	5.45

Nos. O4 and O5 Handstamp Surcharged in Magenta or Violet

1899

5 Cms. - 5

1899

O6	O1	5c on 50c yel & blk	3.50	3.25
a.		Inverted surcharge	13.00	13.00
O7	O1	5c on 1b vio & blk	14.00	12.50
a.		Inverted surcharge	32.50	32.50
O8	O1	25c on 50c yel & blk	14.00	12.50
a.		Inverted surcharge	27.50	27.50
O9	O1	25c on 1b vio & blk	8.25	7.50
a.		Inverted surcharge	27.50	27.50

Nos. O6-O9 exist with double surcharge. Value each $18.50-$37.50.

Many of the magenta overprints have become violet. There are intermediate shades.

Counterfeit overprints exist.

1900 Litho., Center Engr.

O14	O3	5c bl grn & blk	25	22
O15	O3	10c rose & blk	32	30
O16	O3	25c bl & blk	32	30
O17	O3	50c yel & blk	38	35
O18	O3	1b dl vio & blk	42	48
		Nos. O14-O18 (5)	1.69	1.65

O4

No Stars Above Shield — O5

Imprint: "American Bank Note Co., N.Y."

1904 Engr.

O19	O4	5c emer & blk	18	16
O20	O4	10c rose & blk	38	35
O21	O4	25c bl & blk	38	35
O22	O4	50c red brn & blk	2.50	2.25
a.		50c cl & blk	2.50	2.25
O23	O4	1b red brn & blk	1.25	1.10
a.		1b cl & blk	1.25	1.10
		Nos. O19-O23 (5)	4.69	4.21

1912 Lithographed in Caracas

O24	O5	5c grn & blk	18	16
O25	O5	10c car & blk	18	16
O26	O5	25c dk bl & blk	18	16
O27	O5	50c pur & blk	25	22
a.		Center double	19.00	
O28	O5	1b yel & blk	50	45
		Nos. O24-O28 (5)	1.29	1.15

Perforated Initials

After 1925, Venezuela's official stamps consisted of regular postage stamps, some commemoratives and air post stamps of 1930-42 punched with "GN" (Gobierno Nacional) in large perforated initials.

LOCAL STAMPS FOR THE PORT OF CARUPANO

In 1902 Great Britain, Germany and Italy, seeking compensation for revolutionary damages, established a blockade of La Guaira and seized the custom house. Carupano, a port near Trinidad, was isolated and issued the following provisionals. A treaty effected May 7, 1903, referred the dispute to the Hague Tribunal.

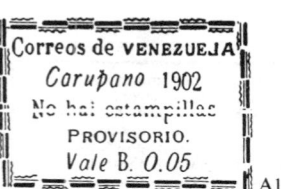

Correos de VENEZUELA
Carupano 1902
No hai estampillas
PROVISORIO.
Vale B. 0.05

A1

A2

1902	Typeset	*Imperf.*
1	A1 5c purple, *org*	19.00
2	A2 10c black, *org*	30.00
a.	Tete beche pair	82.50
3	A1 25c purple, *grn*	25.00
4	A1 50c green, *yel*	47.50
5	A1 1b blue, *rose*	60.00

A3

1902		
6	A3 1b black, *yellow*	135.00
a.	Tete beche pair	

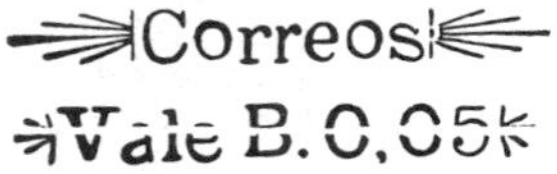

A4

1903	Handstamped		
7	A4 5c carmine, *yel*	19.00	19.00
8	A4 10c green, *yel*	60.00	60.00
9	A4 25c green, *org*	25.00	25.00
10	A4 50c blue, *rose*	25.00	25.00
11	A4 1b violet, *gray*	25.00	25.00
12	A4 2b carmine, *grn*	25.00	25.00
13	A4 5b violet, *bl*	25.00	25.00

Dangerous counterfeits exist of Nos. 1-13.

LOCAL STAMPS FOR THE STATE OF GUAYANA

Revolutionary Steamship "Banrigh" — A1

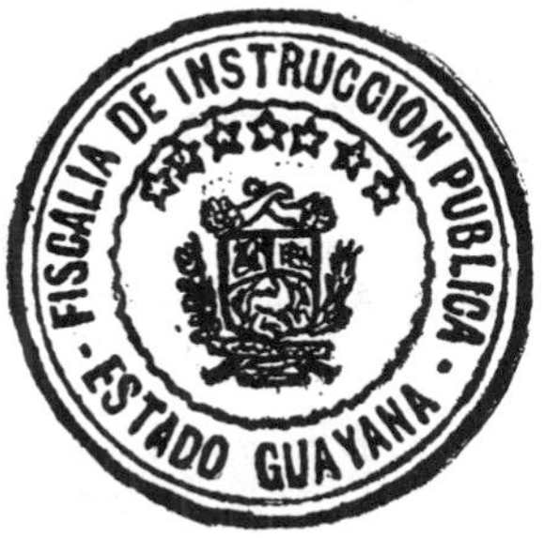

Control Mark

1903	Typo.	*Perf. 12*	
1	A1 5c blk, *gray*	19.00	19.00
2	A1 10c blk, *orange*	47.50	47.50
3	A1 25c blk, *pink*	19.00	19.00
4	A1 50c blk, *blue*	30.00	30.00
5	A1 1b blk, *straw*	25.00	25.00
	Nos. 1-5 (5)	140.50	140.50

Nos. 1-5 can be found with or without the illustrated control mark which covers four stamps.

Counterfeits include the 10c and 50c in red and are from different settings from the originals. They are on papers differing in colors from the oringinals. All 5c on granite paper are bogus.

Coat of Arms A2

1903		
11	A2 5c blk, *pink*	40.00
12	A2 10c blk, *orange*	47.50
13	A2 25c blk, *gray bl*	40.00
a.	25c blk, *bl*	40.00
14	A2 50c blk, *straw*	40.00
15	A2 1b blk, *gray*	30.00
	Nos. 11-15 (5)	197.50

See note on controls after No. 5.

Postally used examples are very scarce, and are specimens having 9 ornaments in horizontal borders. Nos. 11-15 pen canceled sell for same values as unused.

Counterfeits exist of Nos. 11-15. Stamps with 10 ornaments in horizontal borders are counterfeits.

See note on controls after No. 5. Nos. 1-5, 11-15 were issued by a group of revolutionists and had a limited local use. The dates on the stamps commemorate the declaration of Venezuelan independence and a compact with Spain against Joseph Bonaparte.

VIET NAM

LOCATION — In eastern Indo-China.
GOVT. — Kingdom
AREA — 123,949 sq. mi.
CAPITAL — Hanoi

Viet Nam, which included the former French territories of Tonkin, Annam and Cochin China, became an Associated State of the French Union in 1949. The Communist Viet Minh obtained control of Northern Viet Nam in 1954, and the republic of South Viet Nam was established in October, 1955.

Stamps of Indo-China overprinted "VIET NAM" and Viet Nam definitives of 1945-48 had no international validity.

100 Cents (Xu) = 1 Piaster (Dong)

Catalogue values for all unused stamps in this country are for Never Hinged items.

Bongour Falls, Dalat A1

Emperor Bao-Dai A2

Designs: 20c, 2pi, 10pi, Imperial palace, Hue. 30c, 15pi, Lake, Hanoi. 50c, 1pi, Temple, Saigon.

Perf. 13x13½, 13½x13.

1951, Aug. 16	Photo.	Unwmk.	
1	A1 10c ol grn	5	5
2	A1 20c dp plum	5	7
3	A1 30c blue	8	7
4	A1 50c red	18	8
5	A1 60c brown	9	7
6	A1 1pi chnt brn	7	5
7	A2 1.20pi yel brn	75	50
8	A1 2pi purple	28	10
9	A2 3pi dull bl	75	12
10	A1 5pi green	90	18
11	A1 10pi crimson	2.50	25
12	A1 15pi red brn	16.00	1.65
13	A2 30pi bl grn	8.00	2.00
	Nos. 1-13 (13)	29.70	5.19

Souvenir booklets exist comprising five gummed sheets containing a single copy each of Nos. 1, 2, 6, 9, and 12, together with commemorative inscriptions.

Empress Nam-Phuong A3

Globe and Lightning Bolt A4

1952, Aug. 15		*Perf. 12½*	
14	A3 30c dk pur, yel & brn	20	14
15	A3 50c bl, yel & brn	45	20
16	A3 1.50pi ol grn, yel & brn	80	12

1952, Aug. 24	Engr.	*Perf. 13*	
17	A4 1pi grnsh bl	1.40	90

Viet Nam's admission to the ITU, 1st anniv.

Coastal Scene and UPU Emblem A5

1952, Sept. 12			
18	A5 5pi red brn	1.40	40

Viet Nam's admission to the UPU, 1st anniv.

Bao-Dai and Pagoda of Literature, Hanoi — A6

1952, Nov. 10		*Perf. 12*	
19	A6 1.50pi rose vio	1.40	50

39th birthday of Emperor Bao-Dai.

Crown Prince Bao-Long in Annamite Costume — A7

Designs: 70c, 80c, 100pi, Prince in Annamite costume. 90c, 20pi, 50pi, Prince in Western uniform.

1954, June 15		*Perf. 13*	
20	A7 40c aqua	9	12
21	A7 70c claret	12	20
22	A7 80c blk brn	14	22
23	A7 90c dk grn	38	55
24	A7 20pi rose pink	1.25	2.25
25	A7 50pi violet	3.25	4.00
26	A7 100pi bl vio	5.50	9.25
	Nos. 20-26 (7)	10.73	16.59

SOUTH VIET NAM

(Viet Nam Cong Hoa)
GOVT.-Republic
AREA-66,280 sq. mi.
POP.-19,600,000 (est. 1973)
CAPITAL-Saigon

Mythological Turtle — A8

Unwmk.

1955, July 20	Engr.	*Perf. 13*	
27	A8 30c claret	25	12
28	A8 50c dk grn	65	55
29	A8 1.50pi brt bl	50	22

Refugees on Raft — A9

1955, Oct. 11			
30	A9 70c crim rose	16	10
31	A9 80c brn vio	50	35
32	A9 10pi indigo	90	50
33	A9 20pi vio, red brn & org	2.50	75
34	A9 35pi dk bl & brn & yel	6.00	3.75
35	A9 100pi dk grn, brn vio & org	12.50	6.75
	Nos. 30-35 (6)	22.56	12.20

1st anniv. of the flight of the North Vietnamese.

No. 34 is inscribed "Chiến-Dịch-Huynh-Đệ" (Operation Brotherhood) below design. See No. 54.

Post Office, Saigon — A10

Pres. Ngo Dinh Diem — A11

1956, Jan. 10		*Perf. 12*	
36	A10 60c bluish grn	35	22
37	A10 90c violet	65	38
38	A10 3pi red brn	1.10	60

5th anniv. of independent postal service.

1956	Engr.	*Perf. 13x13½*	
39	A11 20c org ver	5	5
40	A11 30c rose lil	5	5
41	A11 50c brt car	5	5
42	A11 1pi violet	6	5
43	A11 1.50pi violet	12	5
44	A11 3pi blk brn	14	5
45	A11 4pi dk bl	20	5
46	A11 5pi red brn	38	9
47	A11 10pi blue	50	12
48	A11 20pi gray blk	1.00	22
49	A11 35pi green	3.00	50
50	A11 100pi brown	4.00	2.00
	Nos. 39-50 (12)	9.55	3.28

Nos. 36-38 Overprinted **Công-thự Bưu-điện**

1956, Aug. 6		*Perf. 12*	
51	A10 60c bluish grn	20	14
52	A10 90c violet	38	14
53	A10 3pi red brn	60	20

The overprint reads: "Government Post Office Building."

No. 34 with Black Bar over Inscription below Design

1956, Aug. 6

54	A9	35pi dk bl, blk brn & yel	1.50	1.00

Bamboo A12

Children A13

1956, Oct. 26 Litho. *Perf. 13x13½*

55	A12	50c scarlet	8	7
56	A12	1.50pi rose vio	16	8
57	A12	2pi brt grn	20	12
58	A12	4pi dp bl	50	22

1st anniv. of the Republic.

1956, Nov. 7 Engr. *Perf. 13½x14*

59	A13	1pi lil rose	16	7
60	A13	2pi bl grn	20	12
61	A13	6pi purple	38	12
62	A13	35pi vio bl	2.00	1.25

"Operation Brotherhood."

Hunters on Elephants A14

Loading Cargo A15

Design: 90c, 2pi, 3pi, Mountain dwelling.

1957, July 7 Photo. *Perf. 13*

63	A14	20c yel grn & pur	16	5
64	A14	30c bis & dp mag	20	5
65	A14	90c yel grn & dk brn	22	5
66	A14	2pi grn & ultra	30	9
67	A14	3pi bl vio & brn	38	16
		Nos. 63-67 (5)	1.26	40

1957, Oct. 21 *Perf. 13½x13*

68	A15	20c rose vio	5	5
69	A15	40c lt ol grn	5	5
70	A15	50c lt car rose	5	5
71	A15	2pi ultra	14	5
72	A15	3pi brt grn	18	10
		Nos. 68-72 (5)	47	30

9th Colombo Plan Conference, Saigon.

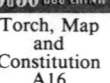

Torch, Map and Constitution A16

Farmers, Tractor and Village A17

1957, Oct. 26 Litho. *Perf. 13x13½*

73	A16	50c blk, grn & sal	5	5
74	A16	80c blk, brt bl & mag	8	5
75	A16	1pi blk, bl grn & brt car	12	5
76	A16	4pi blk, ol grn & fawn	16	8
77	A16	5pi blk, grnsh bl & cit	22	14
78	A16	10pi blk, ultra & rose	45	25
		Nos. 73-78 (6)	1.08	62

Republic of South Viet Nam, 2nd anniv.

1958, July 7 Engr. *Perf. 13½*

79	A17	50c yel grn	7	5
80	A17	1pi dp vio	10	5
81	A17	2pi ultra	16	8
82	A17	10pi brick red	40	35

4th anniv. of the government of Ngo Dinh Diem.

Girl and Lantern — A18

A19

1958, Sept. 27

83	A18	30c yellow	7	7
84	A18	50c dk car rose	7	7
85	A18	2pi dp car	8	7
86	A18	3pi bl grn	20	15
87	A18	4pi lt ol grn	30	15
		Nos. 83-87 (5)	72	51

Children's Festival.

1958, Oct. 26 *Perf. 13½*

88	A19	1pi dl red brn	10	5
89	A19	2pi bluish grn	14	8
90	A19	4pi rose car	20	10
91	A19	5pi rose lil	42	25

Issued for United Nations Day.

> Most South Viet Nam stamps from 1958 onward exist imperforate in issued and trial colors, and also in small presentation sheets in issued colors.

UNESCO Building, Paris A20

Torch and UN Emblem A21

1958, Nov. 3 *Perf. 12½x13*

92	A20	50c ultra	7	5
93	A20	2pi brt red	8	7
94	A20	3pi lil rose	16	10
95	A20	6pi violet	22	16

Opening of UNESCO Headquarters in Paris, Nov. 3.

1958, Dec. 10 Engr. *Perf. 13½*

96	A21	50c dk bl	5	5
97	A21	1pi brn car	8	5
98	A21	2pi yel grn	12	7
99	A21	6pi rose vio	25	16

Signing of the Universal Declaration of Human Rights, 10th anniv.

Cathedral of Hue — A22

Thien Mu Pagoda, Hue — A23

National Museum A24

Design: 50c, 2pi, Palace of Independence, Saigon.

1958-59 *Perf. 13½*

100	A22	10c dk bl gray	5	5
101	A23	30c grn ('59)	7	5
102	A24	40c dk grn ('59)	7	5
103	A24	50c grn ('59)	7	5
104	A24	2pi grnsh bl ('59)	20	10
105	A23	4pi dl pur ('59)	22	16
106	A24	5pi dk car ('59)	25	16
107	A22	6pi org brn	35	20
		Nos. 100-107 (8)	1.28	82

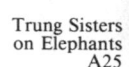

Trung Sisters on Elephants A25

1959, Mar. 14 Photo. *Perf. 13*

108	A25	50c multi	5	5
109	A25	2pi ocher, grn & bl	14	8
110	A25	3pi emer, vio & bis	22	10
111	A25	6pi multi	38	20

Sisters Trung Trac and Trung Nhi who resisted a Chinese invasion in 40-44 A. D.

Symbols of Agrarian Reforms A26

1959, July 7 Engr. *Perf. 13*

112	A26	70c lil rose	5	5
113	A26	2pi dk grn & Prus bl	8	8
114	A26	3pi olive	14	10
115	A26	6pi dk red & red	30	25

5th anniv. of Ngo Dinh Diem's presidency.

Diesel Engine and Map of North and South Viet Nam — A27

1959, Aug. 7

116	A27	1pi lt vio & grn	14	5
117	A27	2pi gray & grn	16	8
118	A27	3pi grnsh bl & grn	20	10
119	A27	4pi mar & grn	38	12

Re-opening of the Saigon-Dongha Railroad.

Volunteer Road Workers A28

1959, Oct. 26

120	A28	1pi org brn, ultra & grn	8	5
121	A28	2pi vio, org & grn	10	8
122	A28	4pi dk bl, bl & bis	22	14
123	A28	5pi bis, brn & ocher	25	20

4th anniv. of the constitution, stressing communal development.

Boy Scout — A29

1959, Dec. Engr. *Perf. 13*

124	A29	3pi brt yel grn	12	7
125	A29	4pi dp lil rose	20	7
126	A29	8pi dk brn & lil rose	32	18
127	A29	20pi Prus bl & bl grn	80	40

National Boy Scout Jamboree.

Symbols of Family and Justice A30

1960

128	A30	20c emerald	5	5
129	A30	30c brt grnsh bl	5	5
130	A30	2pi org & mar	16	10
131	A30	6pi car & rose vio	55	35

Issued to commemorate the family code.

Refugee Family and WRY Emblem A31

1960, Apr. 7 Engr. *Perf. 13*

132	A31	50c brt lil rose	14	5
133	A31	3pi brt grn	10	10
134	A31	4pi scarlet	16	15
135	A31	5pi dp vio bl	20	16

World Refugee Year, July 1, 1959-June 30, 1960.

Henri Dunant — A32

1960, May 8

Cross in Carmine

136	A32	1pi dk bl	12	7
137	A32	3pi green	25	10
138	A32	4pi crim rose	25	16
139	A32	6pi dp lil rose	35	22

Centenary (in 1959) of the Red Cross idea.

Model Farm — A33

1960, July 7 *Perf. 13*

140	A33	50c ultra	7	5
141	A33	1pi dk grn	9	5
142	A33	3pi orange	18	10
143	A33	7pi brt pink	35	16

Establishment of communal rice farming.

Girl With Basket of Rice and Rice Plant — A34

1960, Nov. 21

144	A34	2pi emer & grn	14	8
145	A34	4pi bl & ultra	28	12

Conference of the UN FAO, Saigon, Nov. 1960.

Map and Flag of Viet Nam — A35

1960, Oct. 26 **Engr.** ***Perf. 13***

146	A35	50c grnsh bl, car & yel	7	5
147	A35	1pi ultra, car & yel	8	5
148	A35	3pi pur, car & yel	15	7
149	A35	7pi yel grn, car & yel	25	14

Fifth anniversary of the Republic.

Agricultural Development Center, Tractor and Plow — A36

1961, Jan. 3 ***Perf. 13***

150	A36	50c red brn	5	5
151	A36	70c rose lil	7	5
152	A36	80c rose red	8	7
153	A36	10pi brt pink	35	20

Plant and Child — A37

Pres. Ngo Dinh Diem — A38

1961, March 23 ***Perf. 13***

154	A37	70c lt bl	7	5
155	A37	80c ultra	8	5
156	A37	4pi ol bis	12	8
157	A37	7pi grnsh bl & yel grn	25	20

Child protection.

1961, Apr. 29 ***Perf. 13***

158	A38	50c brt ultra	8	5
159	A38	1pi red	12	7
160	A38	2pi lil rose	16	7
161	A38	4pi brt vio	35	10

Second term of Pres. Ngo Dinh Diem.

Boy, Girl and Flaming Torch — A39

1961, July 7 **Engr.** ***Perf. 13***

162	A39	50c red	5	5
163	A39	70c brt pink	7	5
164	A39	80c ver & mar	10	5
165	A39	8pi dp cl & mag	25	20

Issued for Youth Day.

Saigon-Bien Hoa Highway Bridge A40

1961, July 28

166	A40	50c yel grn	7	5
167	A40	1pi org brn	8	5
168	A40	2pi dk bl	14	5
169	A40	5pi brt red lil	22	14

Opening of Saigon-Bien Hoa Highway.

Alexandre de Rhodes A41

1961, Sept. 5

170	A41	50c rose car	7	5
171	A41	1pi claret	8	5
172	A41	3pi bis brn	10	7
173	A41	6pi emerald	30	16

Alexandre de Rhodes (1591-1660), Jesuit missionary who introduced Roman characters to express the Viet Nam language.

Young Man with Torch, Sage, Pagoda A42

Temple Dedicated to Confucius A43

1961, Oct. 26 ***Perf. 13***

174	A42	50c org ver	5	5
175	A42	1pi brt grn	8	5
176	A42	3pi rose red	10	7
177	A42	8pi rose lil & brn	30	15

Moral Rearmament of Youth Movement.

1961, Nov. 4 **Engr.**

178	A43	1pi brt grn	8	5
179	A43	2pi rose red	10	5
180	A43	5pi olive	35	14

15th anniversary of UNESCO.

Earth Scraper Preparing Ground for Model Village A44

Man Fighting Mosquito and Emblem A45

1961, Dec. 11 ***Perf. 13***

181	A44	50c dk grn	5	5
182	A44	1pi Prus bl & car lake	7	5
183	A44	2pi ol grn & brn	10	10
184	A44	10pi Prus bl	35	30

Agrarian reform program.

1962, Apr. 7 ***Perf. 13***

185	A45	50c brt lil rose	5	5
186	A45	1pi orange	7	5
187	A45	2pi emerald	8	5
188	A45	6pi ultra	22	16

WHO drive to eradicate malaria.

Postal Check Center, Saigon — A46

Madonna of Vang — A47

1962, May 15 **Engr.** ***Perf. 13***

189	A46	70c dl grn	5	5
190	A46	80c chocolate	5	5
191	A46	4pi lil rose	14	9
192	A46	7pi rose red	30	22

Inauguration of postal checking service.

1962, July 7

193	A47	50c vio & rose red	5	5
194	A47	1pi red brn & ind	5	5
195	A47	2pi brn & rose car	8	5
196	A47	8pi grn & dk bl	38	16

Catholic shrine of the Madonna of Vang.

Armed Guards and Village A48

1962, Oct. 26

197	A48	50c brt red	5	5
198	A48	1pi yel grn	8	5
199	A48	1.50pi lil rose	10	5
200	A48	7pi ultra	30	22

"Strategic village" defense system.

Gougah Waterfall, Dalat A49

Trung Sisters' Monument and Vietnamese Women A50

1963, Jan. 3

201	A49	60c org red	10	5
202	A49	1pi bluish blk	15	5

62nd birthday of Pres. Ngo Dinh Diem; Spring Festival.

1963, Mar. 1 **Engr.**

203	A50	50c green	7	5
204	A50	1pi dk car rose	12	5
205	A50	3pi lil rose	16	12
206	A50	8pi vio bl	40	25

Issued for Women's Day.

Farm Woman with Grain — A51

1963, Mar. 21 ***Perf. 13***

207	A51	50c red	7	5
208	A51	1pi dk car rose	8	5
209	A51	3pi lil rose	12	8
210	A51	5pi violet	20	12

FAO "Freedom from Hunger" campaign.

Common Defense Emblem A52

Emblem A53

1963, July 7 **Engr.** ***Perf. 13***

211	A52	30c bister	8	5
212	A52	50c lil rose	10	5
213	A52	3pi brt grn	16	8
214	A52	8pi red	25	16

Common defense effort. The inscription says: "Personalism-Common Progress."

1963, Oct. 26 ***Perf. 13***

215	A53	50c rose red	7	5
216	A53	1pi emerald	10	7
217	A53	4pi purple	22	14
218	A53	5pi orange	42	35

The fighting soldiers of the Republic.

Centenary Emblem and Map — A54

1963, Nov. 17 **Engr.**

Cross in Deep Carmine

219	A54	50c Prus bl	7	5
220	A54	1pi dp car	10	8
221	A54	3pi org yel	14	12
222	A54	6pi brown	30	25

Centenary of International Red Cross.

Book and Scales — A55

1963, Dec. 10 ***Perf. 13***

223	A55	70c orange	5	5
224	A55	1pi brt rose	8	5
225	A55	3pi green	10	8
226	A55	8pi ocher	25	16

15th anniv. of the Universal Declaration of Human Rights.

Danhim Hydroelectric Station — A56

1964, Jan. 15 **Engr.**

227	A56	40c rose red	8	5
228	A56	1pi bis brn	8	5
229	A56	3pi vio bl	12	7
230	A56	8pi ol grn	25	20

Inauguration of the Danhim Hydroelectric Station.

Atomic Reactor A57

1964, Feb. 3 ***Perf. 13***

231	A57	80c olive	7	5
232	A57	1.50pi brn org	8	5
233	A57	3pi chocolate	12	7
234	A57	7pi brt bl	22	16

Peaceful uses of atomic energy.

Compass Rose, Barograph and UN Emblem — A58

South Vietnamese Gesturing to North Vietnamese; Map — A59

1964, Mar. 23 **Engr.**

235	A58	50c	bister	5	5
236	A58	1pi	vermilion	8	5
237	A58	1.50pi	rose cl	10	7
238	A58	10pi	emerald	30	20

4th World Meteorological Day, Mar. 23.

1964, July 20 ***Perf. 13***

239	A59	30c	dk grn, ultra & mar	7	5
240	A59	50c	dk car rose, yel & blk	8	5
241	A59	1.50pi	dk bl, dp org & blk	12	8

10th anniv. of the Day of National Grief, July 20, 1954, when the nation was divided into South and North Viet Nam.

Hatien Beach — A60

1964, Sept. 7 **Engr.** ***Perf. 13½***

242	A60	20c	brt ultra	5	5
243	A60	3pi	emerald	20	8

Revolutionists and "Nov. 1" — A61

Designs: 80c, Soldier breaking chain. 3pi, Broken chain and date: "1-11 1963" (vert.).

1964, Nov. 1 **Engr.** ***Perf. 13***

244	A61	50c	red lil & ind	7	5
245	A61	80c	vio & red brn	8	5
246	A61	3pi	dk bl & red	15	9

Anniv. of November 1963 revolution.

Temple, Saigon A62

Designs: 1pi, Royal tombs, Hue. 1.50pi, Fishermen and sailboats at Phan-Thiet beach. 3pi, Temple, Gia-Dhin.

1964-66 ***Perf. 13***

Size: 35½x26mm

247	A62	50c	fawn, grn & dl vio	5	5
248	A62	1pi	ol bis & ind	7	5
249	A62	1.50pi	ol gray & dk sl grn	8	5
250	A62	3pi	vio, dk sl grn & cl	18	10

Coil Stamp

Size: 23x17mm

250A	A62	1pi	ol bis & ind ('66)	50	20

Nos. 247-250 were issued Dec. 2, 1964.

Hung Vuong and Au Co with their Children A63

1965, Apr. **Engr.** ***Perf. 13***

251	A63	3pi	car lake & org red	22	20
252	A63	100pi	brn vio & vio	2.25	1.40

Mythological founders of Viet Nam, c. 2000 B.C.

ITU Emblem, Insulator and TV Mast — A64

Buddhist Wheel of Life and Flames — A65

1965, May 17 **Engr.**

253	A64	1pi	ol, dp car & bis	7	5
254	A64	3pi	hn brn, car & lil	18	10

ITU, centenary.

1965, May 15 ***Perf. 13***

Designs: 1.50pi, Wheel, lotus blossom and world map (horiz.). 3pi, Wheel and Buddhist flag.

Inscribed: "Phat-Giao" (Buddhism)

255	A65	50c	dk car	5	5
256	A65	1.50pi	dk bl & ocher	10	5
257	A65	3pi	org brn & dk brn	12	7

Anniversary of Buddha's birth.

ICY Emblem and Women of Various Races — A66

Ixora — A67

1965, June 26

258	A66	50c	bluish blk & bis	5	5
259	A66	1pi	dk brn & brn	10	5
260	A66	1.50pi	dk red & gray	12	7

International Cooperation Year.

1965, Sept. 10 **Engr.** ***Perf. 13***

Flowers: 80c, Orchid. 1pi, Chrysanthemum. 1.50pi, Lotus (horiz.). 3pi, Plum blossoms.

261	A67	70c	grn, sl grn & red	5	5
262	A67	80c	dk brn, lil & sl grn	5	5
263	A67	1pi	dk bl & yel	7	5
264	A67	1.50pi	sl grn, dl grn & gray	8	5
265	A67	3pi	sl grn & org	12	10
			Nos. 261-265 (5)	37	30

Student, Dormitory and Map of Thu Duc — A68

1965, Oct. 15 ***Perf. 13***

266	A68	50c	dk brn	5	5
267	A68	1pi	brt grn	5	5
268	A68	3pi	crimson	12	7
269	A68	7pi	dk bl vio	35	22

Issued to publicize higher education.

Farm Boy and Girl, Pig and 4-T Emblem A69

Design: 4pi, Farm boy with chicken, village and 4-T flag.

1965, Nov. 25 **Engr.** ***Perf. 13***

270	A69	3pi	emer & dk red	14	10
271	A69	4pi	dl vio & plum	14	10

10th anniv. of the 4-T Clubs and the National Congress of Young Farmers.

Basketball A70

Designs: 1pi, Javelin. 1.50pi, Hand holding torch, athletic couple. 10pi, Pole vault.

1965, Dec. 14 **Engr.** ***Perf. 13***

272	A70	50c	dk car & brn org	5	5
273	A70	1pi	brn org & red brn	7	5
274	A70	1.50pi	brt grn	10	9
275	A70	10pi	red lil & brn org	30	16

Radio Tower — A71

Loading Hook and Globe — A72

Design: Radio tower, telephone dial and map of Viet Nam.

1966, Apr. 24 **Engr.** ***Perf. 13***

276	A71	3pi	brt bl & brn	8	7
277	A71	4pi	pur, red & blk	14	12

Saigon microwave station.

1966, June 22 **Engr.** ***Perf. 13***

278	A72	3pi	gray & dk car rose	8	5
279	A72	4pi	ol & dk pur	10	8
280	A72	6pi	brt grn & dk bl	16	14

Appreciation of the help given by the free world.

Hands Reaching for Persecuted Refugees A73

1966, July 20

281	A73	3pi	brn, vio brn & ol	8	7
282	A73	7pi	cl, vio brn & dk pur	16	14

Refugees from communist oppression.

Paper Soldiers, Votive Offering A74

Designs: 1.50pi, Man and woman making offerings. 3pi, Floating candles in paper boats. 5pi, Woman burning paper offerings.

1966, Aug. 30 **Engr.** ***Perf. 13***

283	A74	50c	red, blk & bis brn	5	5
284	A74	1.50pi	brn, emer & grn	5	5
285	A74	3pi	rose red & lake	12	8
286	A74	5pi	org brn, bis & dk brn	15	10

Wandering Souls Festival.

Oriental Two-string Violin — A75

Vietnamese Instruments: 3pi, Woman playing 16-string guitar. 4pi, Musicians playing two-string guitars. 7pi, Woman and boy playing flutes.

1966 **Engr.** ***Perf. 13***

Size: 35½x26mm

287	A75	1pi	brn red & brn	7	5
288	A75	3pi	rose lil & pur	8	7
289	A75	4pi	rose brn & brn	12	8
290	A75	7pi	dp bl & vio bl	22	12

Coil Stamp

Size: 23x17mm

290A	A75	3pi	rose lil & pur	1.60	42
b.			Booklet pane of 5	10.00	

Nos. 287-290 were issued Sept. 28.

No. 290b contains a vertical strip of 5 with selvage at either end. These strips were also sold loose without booklet cover.

WHO Building, Geneva, and Flag — A76

Designs: 50c, WHO Building and emblem (horiz.). 8pi, WHO flag and building.

1966, Oct. 12

291	A76	50c	pur & car	5	5
292	A76	1.50pi	red brn, vio bl & blk	8	7
293	A76	8pi	grnsh bl, vio bl & brn	16	16

Opening of WHO Headquarters, Geneva.

Hand Holding Spade, and Soldiers A77

Soldier and Workers — A78

Designs: 1.50pi, Flag, workers, tractor and soldier. 4pi, Soldier and cavalryman.

1966, Nov. 1 Engr. *Perf. 13*

294	A77	80c	dl brn & red brn	5	5
295	A77	1.50pi	car rose, yel & brn	5	5
296	A78	3pi	brn & sl grn	7	5
297	A78	4pi	lil, blk & brn	16	10

3rd anniv. of the revolution against the government of Pres. Ngo Dinh Diem.

Symbolic Tree and UNESCO Emblem — A79

Designs: 3pi, Globe and olive branches. 7pi, Symbolic temple (horiz.).

1966, Dec. 15 Engr. *Perf. 13*

298	A79	1pi	pink, brn & dk car	5	5
299	A79	3pi	dp bl, grn & brn org	10	8
300	A79	7pi	grnsh bl, dk bl & red	18	16

20th anniv. of UNESCO.

Bitter Melon — A80

Designs: 50c, Cashew (vert.). 3pi, Sweetsop. 20pi, Areca nuts.

1967, Jan. 12 Engr. *Perf. 13*

301	A80	50c	brt bl, gray grn & red	5	5
302	A80	1.50pi	red brn, yel grn & org	5	5
303	A80	3pi	dk brn, grn & brn	8	5
304	A80	20pi	rose brn, sl grn & yel	30	20

Phan-Boi-Chau — A81

Designs: 20pi, Phan-Chau-Trinh portrait and addressing crowd.

1967, Mar. 24 Engr. *Perf. 13*

305	A81	1pi	mar, red brn & dk brn	7	5
306	A81	20pi	vio, sl grn & blk	38	35

Issued to honor Vietnamese patriots.

Woman Carrying Produce A82

Designs: 1pi, Market scene. 3pi, Two-wheeled horse cart. 8pi, Farm scene with water buffalo.

1967, May 1 Engr. *Perf. 13*

307	A82	50c	vio bl, dk bl & ultra	5	5
308	A82	1pi	sl grn & dl pur	5	5
309	A82	3pi	dk car	7	5
310	A82	8pi	brt car rose & pur	16	10

Issued for Labor Day.

Potter, Vases and Lamp — A83

Weavers and Potters A84

Designs: 1.50pi, Vase and basket. 35d, Bag and lacquerware.

1967, July 22 Engr. *Perf. 13*

311	A83	50c	red brn, grn & ultra	5	5
312	A83	1.50pi	grnsh bl, car & blk	7	5
313	A83	3pi	red, vio & org brn	8	7
314	A83	35pi	bis brn, blk & dk red	55	40

Issued to publicize Vietnamese handicrafts.

Wedding Procession A85

1967, Sept. 18 Engr. *Perf. 13*

315	A85	3pi	rose cl, dk vio & red	15	10

Symbols of Stage, Music and Art — A86

Litho. & Engr.

1967, Oct. 27 *Perf. 13*

316	A86	10pi	bl gray, blk & red	22	14

Issued to publicize the Cultural Institute.

"Freedom and Justice" — A87

Balloting A88

"Establishment of Democracy" A89

1967, Nov. 1 Photo.

317	A87	4pi	mag, brn & ocher	9	5
318	A88	5pi	brn, yel & blk	10	7
319	A89	30pi	dl lil, ind & red	50	40

National Day; general elections.

Pagoda and Lions Emblem A90

1967, Dec. 5 Photo. *Perf. 13½x13*

320	A90	3pi	multi	20	14

50th anniversary of Lions International.

Teacher with Pupils and Globe — A91

1967, Dec. 10 *Perf. 13x13½*

321	A91	3pi	tan, blk, yel & car	20	7

International Literacy Day, Sept. 8, 1967.

Tractor and Village — A92

Designs: 9pi, Bulldozer and home building. 10pi, Wheelbarrow, tractor and new building. 20pi, Vietnamese and Americans working together.

1968, Jan. 26 Photo. *Perf. 13½*

322	A92	1pi	multi	5	5
323	A92	9pi	lt bl & multi	15	10
324	A92	10pi	multi	22	14
325	A92	20pi	yel, red lil & blk	30	20

Rural construction program.

WHO Emblem — A93

1968, Apr. 7 Photo. *Perf. 13½*

326	A93	10pi	gray grn, blk & yel	30	14

WHO, 20th anniversary.

Flags of Viet Nam's Allies — A94

Designs: 1.50pi, Flags surrounding SEATO emblem. 3pi, Flags, handclasp, globe and map of Viet Nam. 50pi, Flags and handclasp.

1968, June 22 Photo. *Perf. 13½*

327	A94	1pi	multi	8	7
328	A94	1.50pi	multi	10	8
329	A94	3pi	multi	14	12
330	A94	50pi	multi	60	55

Issued to honor Viet Nam's allies.

Three-wheeled Truck and Tractor — A95

Designs: 80c, Farmer, city man and symbols of property. 2pi, Three-wheeled cart, taxi and farmers. 30pi, Taxi, three-wheeled cart and tractor in field.

Inscribed: "HUU-SAN-HOA CONG-NHAN VA NONG-DAN"

1968, Nov. 1 Photo. *Perf. 13½*

331	A95	80c	multi	5	5
332	A95	2pi	stl bl & multi	5	5
333	A95	10pi	org brn & multi	14	10
334	A95	30pi	gray bl & multi	50	35

Private property ownership.

Human Rights Flame — A96

Men of Various Races — A97

1968, Dec. 10 Photo. *Perf. 13½*

335	A96	10pi	multi	22	12
336	A97	16pi	pur & multi	45	16

International Human Rights Year.

UNICEF Emblem, Mother and Child — A98

Design: 6pi, Children flying kite with UNICEF emblem.

1968, Dec. 11

337	A98	6pi	multi	16	12
338	A98	16pi	multi	35	18

Issued to honor UNICEF.

Workers and Train — A99

Design: 1.50pi, 3pi, Crane, train and map of Viet Nam.

1968, Dec. 15

339	A99	1.50pi	multi	14	5
340	A99	3pi	org, vio bl & grn	16	8
341	A99	9pi	multi	22	10
342	A99	20pi	multi	40	20

Reopening of Trans-Viet Nam Railroad.

Farm Woman — A100

Vietnamese Women: 1pi, Merchant. 3pi, Nurses (horiz.). 20pi, Three ladies.

1969, Mar. 23 Engr. *Perf. 13*

343 A100 50c vio bl, lil & ocher 5 5
344 A100 1pi grn, bis & dk brn 5 5
345 A100 3pi brn, blk & bl 7 5
346 A100 20pi lil & multi 38 25

Soldiers and Civilians A101

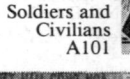

Family Welcoming Soldier A102

1969, June 1 Photo. *Perf. 13*

347 A101 2pi multi 5 5
348 A102 50pi multi 70 35

Pacification campaign.

Man Reading Constitution, Scales of Justice — A103

Voters, Torch and Scales — A104

1969, June 9

349 A103 1pi yel org, yel & blk 5 5
350 A104 20pi multi 38 16

Constitutional democracy. Phrase on both stamps: "Democratic and Governed by Law."

Mobile Post Office — A105

Mobile Post Office: 3pi, Window service. 4pi, Child with letter. 20pi, Crowd at window and postmark: "15, 12, 67."

1969, July 10

351 A105 1pi multi 5 5
352 A105 3pi multi 8 7
353 A105 4pi multi 10 8
354 A105 20pi ocher & multi 22 20

Installation of the first mobile post office in Viet Nam.

Mnong-gar Woman A106

Designs: 1pi, Djarai woman. 50pi, Bahnar man.

1969, Aug. 29 Photo. *Perf. 13*

355 A106 1pi brt pink & multi 5 5
356 A106 6pi sky bl & multi 10 8
357 A106 50pi gray & multi 65 35

Ethnic minorities in Viet Nam.

Civilians Becoming Soldiers A107

Designs: 3pi, Bayonet training. 5pi, Guard duty. 10pi, Farewell.

1969, Sept. 20
Inscribed: "TONG BONG VIEN"

358 A107 1.50pi org & multi 5 5
359 A107 3pi pur & multi 8 5
360 A107 5pi blk, red & ocher 10 7
361 A107 10pi pink & multi 16 12

General mobilization.

ILO Emblem and Globe — A108

1969, Oct. 29 Photo. *Perf. 13*

362 A108 6pi bl grn, blk & gray 10 7
363 A108 20pi red, blk & gray 30 16

ILO, 50th anniversary.

Pegu House Sparrow — A109

Birds: 6pi, Moluccan munia. 7pi, Great hornbill. 30pi, Old world tree sparrow.

1970, Jan. 15 Photo. *Perf. 12½x14*

364 A109 2pi bl & multi 5 5
365 A109 6pi org & multi 10 7
366 A109 7pi org brn & multi 14 9
367 A109 30pi bl & multi 50 25

Burning House and Family — A110

Design: 20pi, Family fleeing burning house and physician examining child.

1970, Jan. 31 Photo. *Perf. 13*

368 A110 10pi multi 16 14
369 A110 20pi multi 35 25

Mau Than disaster, 1968.

Vietnamese Costumes — A111

Traditional Costumes: 1pi, Man, woman and priest (vert.). 2pi, Seated woman with fan. 100pi, Man and woman.

Inscribed: "Y-PHUC CO TRUYEN"

1970, Mar. 13 Photo. *Perf. 13*

370 A111 1pi lt brn & multi 5 5
371 A111 2pi pink & multi 5 5
372 A111 3pi ultra & multi 5 5
373 A111 100pi multi 1.00 60

Issued for the Trung Sisters' Festival.

Building Workers, Pagodas and Bridge — A112

Design: 20pi, Concrete mixers and scaffolds.

1970, June 10 Litho. & Engr.

374 A112 6pi multi 12 5
375 A112 20pi rose lil, brn & bis 35 20

Issued to publicize the rebuilding of Hué.

Plower in Rice Field — A113

1970, Aug. 29 *Perf. 13*

376 A113 6pi multi 20 12

"Land to the Tiller" agricultural reform program.

New Building and Scaffold A114

Construction Work — A115

1970, Sept. 15 Engr. *Perf. 13*

377 A114 8pi pale ol & brn org 15 10
378 A115 16pi brn, ind & yel 22 12

Reconstruction after 1968 Tet Offensive.

Productivity Year Emblem A116

1970, Oct. 3

379 A116 10pi multi 20 14

Asian Productivity Year.

Nguyen-Dinh-Chieu A117

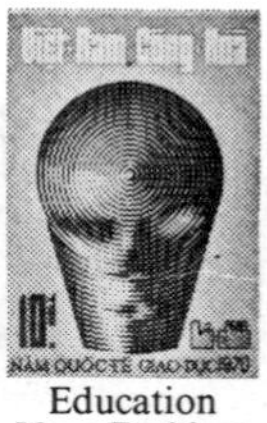

Education Year Emblem A118

1970, Nov. 16 Engr. *Perf. 13½*

380 A117 6pi dl vio, red & brn 10 8
381 A117 10pi grn, red & dk brn 15 10

Nguyen-Dinh-Chieu (1822-1888), poet.

Litho. & Engr.

1970, Nov. 30 *Perf. 13*

382 A118 10pi pale brn, yel & blk 20 10

International Education Year.

Parliament Building A119

Dancers A120

Design: 6pi, Senate Building.

1970, Dec.

383 A119 6pi lt bl, cit & dk brn 10 7
384 A119 10pi multi 20 10

No. 383 issued Dec. 8 for the 6th Congress and No. 384 issued Dec. 9 for the 9th General Assembly of the Asian Interparliamentary Union.

1971, Jan. 12

Designs: Various Vietnamese dancers and musicians. 6pi and 7pi horizontal.

385 A120 2pi ultra & multi 5 5
386 A120 6pi pale grn & multi 8 7
387 A120 7pi pink & multi 10 8
388 A120 10pi brn org & multi 12 10

Farmers and Law — A121

Designs: 3pi, Tractor and law, dated 26.3.1970. 16pi, Farmers, people rejoicing and law book.

1971, Mar. 26 Engr. *Perf. 13*

389 A121 2pi vio bl, dk brn & dl org 5 5
390 A121 3pi pale grn, brn & dk bl 7 5
391 A121 16pi multi 30 16

Agrarian reform law.

Courier on Horseback A122

Design: 6pi, Mounted courier with flag.

Engr. & Photo.

1971, June 6 *Perf. 13*

392 A122 2pi vio & multi 5 5
393 A122 6pi tan & multi 15 7

Postal history.

Military and Naval Operations on Vietnamese Coast — A123

1971, June 19

394	A123	3pi multi	7	5
395	A123	40pi multi	60	40

Armed Forces Day. Narrow vertical yellow and red label inscribed "Mung Ngay Quan Luc / 19.6.1971" is se-tenant with each stamp.

Deer — A124

1971, Aug. 20 Engr.

396	A124	9pi shown	16	10
397	A124	30pi Tiger	50	35

Rice Harvest A125

Designs: 30pi, Threshing and winnowing rice and rice plants. 40pi, Bundling and carrying rice.

Litho. & Engr.

1971, Sept. 28 *Perf. 13*

398	A125	1pi multi	5	5
399	A125	30pi sal pink, dk pur & blk	38	20
400	A125	40pi sep, yel & grn	45	25

Inauguration of UPU Building, Bern — A126

1971, Nov. 9 Engr. *Perf. 13*

401	A126	20pi grn & multi	25	16

Fish — A127

Various Fish; 2pi vertical.

1971, Nov. 16 Photo. & Engr.

402	A127	2pi multi	5	5
403	A127	10pi vio & multi	14	9
404	A127	100p lil & multi	1.25	90

Mailman and Woman on Water Buffalo A128

Designs: 10pi, Bird carrying letter. 20pi, Mailman with bicycle delivering mail to villagers.

1971, Dec. 20 Engr. *Perf. 13*

Inscribed: "PHAT TRIEN BUU-CHINH NONG THON"

405	A128	5pi multi	10	5
406	A128	10pi multi	16	9
407	A128	20pi multi	30	18

Rural mail.

Trawler Fishermen, and Fish — A129

Designs: 7pi, Net fishing from boat. 50d, Trawler with seine.

1972, Jan. 2 Engr. *Perf. 13*

408	A129	4pi pink, blk & bl	8	5
409	A129	7pi lt bl, blk & red	12	5
410	A129	50pi multi	65	38

Publicity for fishing industry.

King Quang Trung (1752-1792) — A130

1972, Jan. 28 *Perf. 13½*

411	A130	6pi red & multi	10	5
a.		Booklet pane of 10	6.00	
412	A130	20pi blk & multi	30	16

No. 411a is imperf. horizontally.

Road Workers A131

1972, Feb. 4

413	A131	3pi multi	7	5
414	A131	8pi multi	22	8

Community development.

Rice Farming A132

1972, Mar. 26 Engr. *Perf. 13½*

415	A132	1pi shown	5	5
416	A132	10pi Wheat farming	22	10

Farmers' Day.

Plane over Dalat — A133

1972, Apr. 18 Engr. & Photo.

417	A133	10pi shown	15	8
418	A133	10pi over Ha-tien	15	8
419	A133	10pi over Hue	15	8
420	A133	10pi over Saigon	15	8
a.		Block of 4, #417-420	60	40
421	A133	25pi like No. 417	35	25
422	A133	25pi like No. 418	35	25
423	A133	25pi like No. 419	35	25
424	A133	25pi like No. 420	35	25
a.		Block of 4, #421-424	1.40	1.20

20 years Air Viet Nam. Stamps of the same denomination are printed se-tenant.

Scholar A134

Designs: 20pi, Teacher and pupils. 50pi, Scholar and scroll.

1972, May 5 Engr. & Litho.

425	A134	5pi multi	7	5

Engr.

426	A134	20pi lt grn & multi	20	12
427	A134	50pi pink & multi	50	25

Ancient letter writing art.

Armed Farmer — A135

Designs: 6pi, Civilian rifleman and Self-defense Forces emblem (horiz.). 20pi, Man and woman training with rifles.

Engr. & Litho.

1972, June 15 *Perf. 13*

428	A135	2pi brt rose & multi	5	5
429	A135	6pi multi	7	7
430	A135	20pi lt vio & multi	20	20

Civilian Self-defense Forces.

Hands Holding Safe — A136

1972, July 10

431	A136	10pi lt bl & multi	12	7
432	A136	25pi lt grn & multi	25	20

Treasury Bonds campaign.

Frontier Guard A137

Soldier Helping Wounded Man A138

Designs: 10pi, 3 guards and horse (horiz.). 40pi, Marching guards (horiz.).

Engr. & Litho.

1972, Aug. 14 *Perf. 13*

433	A137	10pi ol & multi	12	8
434	A137	30pi bufff & multi	30	22
435	A137	40pi lt bl & multi	40	35

Historic frontier guards.

1972, Sept. 1

Designs: 16pi, Soldier on crutches and flowers. 100pi, Veterans' memorial, map and flag.

436	A138	9pi ol & multi	10	5
437	A138	16pi yel & multi	15	10
438	A138	100pi lt bl & multi	80	60

Tank, Memorial, Flag and Map — A139

Soldiers and Map of Viet Nam — A140

1972, Nov. 25 Litho. *Perf. 13*

439	A139	5pi multi	8	5
440	A140	10pi ultra & multi	20	8

Victory at Binh-Long.

Book Year Emblem and Globe — A141

Designs: 4pi, Emblem, books circling globe. 5pi, Emblem, books and globe.

1972, Nov. 30

441	A141	2pi dp car & multi	5	5
442	A141	4pi bl & multi	7	5
443	A141	5pi yel bis & multi	10	5

International Book Year.

Liberated Vietnamese Family — A142

Soldiers Raising Vietnamese Flag — A143

1973, Feb. 18 Litho. *Perf. 13*

444	A142	10pi yel & multi	15	10

To celebrate the 200,000th returnee.

1973, Feb. 24 Litho. *Perf. 13*

Design: 10pi, Victorious soldiers and map of demilitarized zone (horiz.).

445	A143	3pi lil & multi	8	5
446	A143	10pi yel grn & multi	12	10

Victory at Quang Tri.

Satellite, Storm over Viet Nam — A144

1973, Mar. 23 Litho. *Perf. 12½x12*

447	A144	1pi lt bl & multi	10	5

World Meteorological Day.

Farmers with Tractor, Symbol of Law — A145

Farmer Plowing with Water Buffalos — A146

A little time given to the study of the arrangement of the Scott Catalogue can make it easier to use effectively.

Pres. Thieu Holding Agrarian Reform Law — A147

1973, Mar. 26 Litho. *Perf. 12½x12*

448	A145	2pi lt grn & multi	7	5
449	A146	5pi org & multi	10	7

Perf. 11

450	A147	10pi bl & multi	*17.50*	*5.00*

3rd anniv. of the agrarian reform law; 5-year plan for rural development. See No. 475.

INTERPOL Emblem and Headquarters A148

Designs: 2pi, INTERPOL emblem. 25pi, INTERPOL emblem and side view of Headquarters.

1973, Apr. 8 Litho. *Perf. 12½x12*

451	A148	1pi ol & multi	5	5
452	A148	2pi yel & multi	5	5
453	A148	25pi ocher, lil & brn	25	16

Intl. Criminal Police Org., 50th anniv.

ITU Emblem and Waves — A149

Designs: 2pi, Globe and waves. 3pi, ITU emblem.

1973, May 17

454	A149	1pi dl bl & multi	5	5
455	A149	2pi brt bl & multi	5	5
456	A149	3pi org & multi	5	5

World Telecommunications Day.

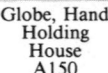

Globe, Hand Holding House A150

Men Building Pylon A151

Design: 10pi, Fish in net, symbols of agriculture, industry and transportation.

1973, Nov. 6 Litho. *Perf. 12x12½*

457	A150	8pi gray & multi	8	5
458	A150	10pi vio bl, blk & gray	10	5
459	A151	15pi blk, org & lil rose	16	5

National development.

Water Buffalos A152

Design: 10pi, Water buffalo.

1973, Dec. 20 Litho. *Perf. 12½x12*

460	A152	5pi shown	12	5
461	A152	10pi Water buffalo	18	5

Human Rights Flame, Three Races — A153

Design: 100pi, Human Rights flame, scales and people (vert.).

Perf. 12½x12, 12x12½

1973, Dec. 29

462	A153	15pi ultra & multi	16	8
463	A153	100pi grn & multi	55	28

25th anniv. of Universal Declaration of Human Rights.

"25" and WHO Emblem A154

Design: 15pi, WHO emblem (different).

1973, Dec. 31 *Perf. 12½x12*

464	A154	8pi org, bl & brn	10	5
465	A154	15pi lt brn, bl & brt pink	15	9

25th anniversary of WHO.

Sampan Ferry A155

Design: 10pi, Sampan ferry (different).

1974, Jan. 13 Litho. *Perf. 14x13½*

466	A155	5pi lt bl & multi	8	5
467	A155	10pi yel grn & multi	12	5

Sampan ferry women.

Soldiers of 7 Nations A156

American War Memorial — A157

Map of South Viet Nam and Allied Flags — A158

Design: No. 469, Soldiers and flags of South Viet Nam, Korea, USA, Australia New Zealand, Thailand and Philippines. Same flags shown on 8pi and 60pi.

Perf. 12½x12, 12x12½

1974, Jan. 28

468	A156	8pi multi	5	5
469	A156	15pi lt brn & multi	10	8
470	A157	15pi multi	10	8
471	A158	60pi multi	30	20

In honor of South Viet Nam's allies.

Trung Sisters on Elephants Fighting Chinese A159

1974, Feb. 27 Litho. *Perf. 12½x12*

472	A159	8pi grn, cit & blk	5	5
473	A159	15pi dp org & multi	8	8
474	A159	80pi ultra, pink & blk	40	20

Trung Trac and Trung Nhi, queens of Viet Nam, 39-43 A.D. Day of Vietnamese Women.

Pres. Thieu Type of 1973 and

Farmers Going to Work — A160

Woman Farmer Holding Rice — A161

1974, Mar. 26 Litho. *Perf. 14*

475	A147	10pi bl & multi	5	5

Perf. 12½x12, 12x12½

476	A160	20pi yel & multi	16	10
477	A161	70pi bl & multi	40	25

Agriculture Day. Size of No. 475 is 31x50mm, No. 450 is 34x54mm and printed on thick paper. No. 475 has been extensively redrawn and first line of inscription in bottom panel changed to "26 THANG BA".

Hung Vuong with Bamboo Tallies A162

Flag Inscribed: Hung Vuong, Founder of Kingdom A163

1974, Apr. 2 *Perf. 14x13½*

478	A162	20pi yel & multi	16	12
479	A163	100pi ol & multi	55	40

Hung Vuong, founder of Vietnamese nation and of Hong-Bang Dynasty (2879-258 B.C.).

National Library A164

Design: 15pi, Library, right facade and Phoenix.

1974, Apr. 14

480	A164	10pi org, brn & blk	10	5
481	A164	15pi multi	15	8

New National Library Building.

Nos. 391 and 437 Surcharged with New Value and Two Bars in Red

1974 *Perf. 13*

482	A121	25pi on 16pi multi	22	14
483	A138	25pi on 16pi multi	22	14

Memorial Tower, Saigon — A165

Globe, Crane Lifting Crate — A167

Crane with Flags, Globe and Map of Viet Nam — A166

Perf. 12x12½, 12½x12

1974, June 22 Litho.

484	A165	10pi bl & multi	5	5
485	A166	20pi multi	12	8
486	A167	60pi yel & multi	38	20

International Aid Day.

Sun and Views of Saigon, Dalat Hue A168

Cau-Bong Bridge, Nha Trang A169

Thien-Mu Pagoda, Hue — A170

Perf. 14x13½, 13½x14

1974, July 12

487	A168	5pi bl & multi	10	10
488	A169	10pi bl & multi	10	10
489	A170	15pi yel & multi	18	14

Tourist publicity.

Rhynchostylis Gigantea — A171

Orchids: 20pi, Cypripedium caliosum (vert.). 200pi, Dendrobium nobile.

1974, Aug. 18

490	A171	10pi bl & multi	7	5
491	A171	20pi yel & multi	9	7
492	A171	200pi bis & multi	1.10	90

Hands Passing Letter, UPU Emblem
A172

UPU Emblem and Woman
A173

Design: 30pi, World map, bird, UPU emblem.

Perf. 12½x12, 12x12½

1974, Oct. 9 **Litho.**

493	A172	20pi ultra & multi	14	7
494	A172	30pi org & multi	20	7
495	A173	300pi gray & multi	1.60	80

Centenary of Universal Postal Union.

Nos. 398, 447, 451, 454, 387 Surcharged with New Value and Two Bars in Red

1974-75

496	A125	25pi on 1pi multi	*3.50*
497	A144	25pi on 1pi multi	*3.50*
498	A148	25pi on 1pi multi	*3.50*
499	A149	25pi on 1pi multi	*5.00*
500	A120	25pi on 7pi multi	*5.00*

Issue dates: Nos. 497, 499-500, Nov. 18, 1974. Others, Jan. 1, 1975.

Hien Lam Pavilion, Hue — A174

Throne, Imperial Palace, Hue — A175

Water Pavilion, Hue — A176

1975, Jan. 5 **Litho.** ***Perf. 14x13½***

501	A174	25pi multi	16	5
502	A175	30pi multi	20	8
503	A176	60pi multi	40	16

Historic sites.

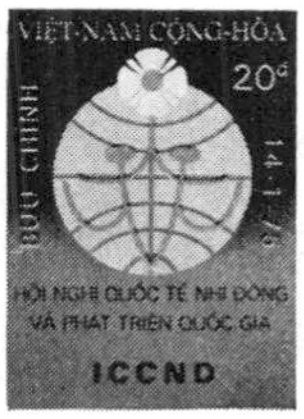

Symbol of Youth, Children Holding Flower — A177

Family and Emblem
A178

1975, Jan. 14 ***Perf. 11½***

504	A177	20pi bl & multi	10	5

Perf. 12½x12

505	A178	70pi yel & multi	35	14

Intl. Conf. on Children and National Development.

Unicorn Dance
A179

Boy Lighting Firecracker
A180

Bringing New Year Gifts and Wishes
A181

Perf. 14x13½, 13½x14

1975, Jan. 26 **Litho.**

506	A179	20pi multi	16	5
507	A180	30pi bl & multi	20	5
508	A181	100pi bis & multi	40	15

Lunar New Year, Tet.

A182

A183

A184

Designs: 25pi, Military chief from play "San Hau." 40pi, Scene from "Tam Ha Nam Duong." 100pi, Warrior Luu-Kim-Dinn.

1975, Feb. 23

509	A182	25pi rose & multi	16	5
510	A183	40pi lt grn & multi	20	7
511	A184	100pi vio & multi	50	10

National theater.

Produce, Map of Viet Nam, Ship — A185

Irrigation Project — A186

1975, Mar. 26 **Litho.** ***Perf. 12½x12***

512	A185	10pi multi	5	5
513	A186	50pi multi	35	16

Agriculture Day; 5th anniv. of Agrarian Reform Law.

Nos. 457, 464, 468 Surcharged with New Value and Two Bars in Red

1975

514	A150	10pi on 8pi multi	5.50	1.40
515	A154	10pi on 8pi multi	3.25	55
516	A156	25pi on 8pi multi	3.25	1.20

> Importation Prohibited
> The U.S. Treasury Department prohibited the importation of stamps of Viet Nam as of Apr. 30, 1975.

SEMI-POSTAL STAMPS

Type of 1952 Surcharged in Carmine

+50c

Perf. 12x12½

1952, Nov. 10 **Unwmk.**

B1	A3	1.50pi + 50c bl, yel & brn	1.90	1.90

The surtax was for the Red Cross.

Sabers and Flag — SP1

1952, Dec. 21 **Engr.** ***Perf. 13***

B2	SP1	3.30pi + 1.70pi dp cl	30	30

The surtax was for the Wounded Soldiers' Aid Organization.

X-ray Camera and Patient
SP2

1960, Aug. 1 ***Perf. 13***

B3	SP2	3pi + 50c bl grn & red	16	16

The surtax was for the Anti-Tuberculosis Foundation.

AIR POST STAMPS

AP1

AP2

Perf. 13½x12½

1952-53 **Unwmk.** **Photo.**

C1	AP1	3.30pi dk brn red & pale yel grn	18	14
C2	AP1	4pi brn & yel ('53)	30	10
C3	AP1	5.10pi dk vio bl & sal pink	25	16
C4	AP2	6.30pi yel & car	25	20

Issue dates: No. C2, Nov. 24, 1953. Others, Mar. 8, 1952.

Dragon
AP3

Fish — AP4

1952, Sept. 3 **Engr.** ***Perf. 13***

C5	AP3	40c red	42	25
C6	AP3	70c green	65	25
C7	AP3	80c ultra	65	30
C8	AP3	90c brown	65	40
C9	AP4	3.70pi dp mag	70	38
		Nos. C5-C9 (5)	3.07	1.58

Nos. C5-C9 exist imperforate in a souvenir booklet.

South Viet Nam

Phoenix — AP5

1955, Sept. 7

C10	AP5	4pi vio & lil rose	55	14

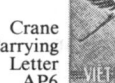

Crane Carrying Letter
AP6

1960, Dec. 20. ***Perf. 13***

C11	AP6	1pi olive	10	7
C12	AP6	4pi grn & dk bl	20	12
C13	AP6	5pi ocher & pur	25	18
C14	AP6	10pi dp mag	45	38

POSTAGE DUE STAMPS

Temple Lion
D1

Dragon
D2

Perf. 13x13½

1952, June 16 **Typo.** **Unwmk.**

J1	D1	10c red & grn	5	5
J2	D1	20c grn & yel	5	5
J3	D1	30c pur & org	5	5
J4	D1	40c dk grn & sal rose	7	7
J5	D1	50c dp car & gray	10	10
J6	D1	1pi bl & sil	12	12
		Nos. J1-J6 (6)	44	44

South Viet Nam

1955-56

J7	D2	2pi red vio & org	12	12
J8	D2	3pi vio & grnsh bl	16	16
J9	D2	5pi vio & yel	18	16
J10	D2	10pi dk grn & car	25	20
J11	D2	20pi red & brt grn ('56)	70	50
J12	D2	30pi brt grn & yel ('56)	1.00	80

J13	D2	50pi dk red brn & yel ('56)	2.25	1.50
J14	D2	100pi pur & yel ('56)	4.00	3.50
		Nos. J7-J14 (8)	8.66	6.94

Nos. J11-J14 inscribed "BUU-CHINH" instead of "TIMBRE-TAXE."

Atlas Moth — D3

Design: 3pi, 5pi, 10pi, Three butterflies.

1968, Aug. 20 Photo. *Perf. 13½x13*

J15	D3	50c multi	7	5
J16	D3	1pi multi	7	5
J17	D3	2pi multi	14	5
J18	D3	3pi multi	20	8
J19	D3	5pi multi	35	15
J20	D3	10pi multi	45	20
		Nos. J15-J20 (6)	1.28	58

Nos. J15-J18 Surcharged with New Value and Two Bars in Red

1974, Oct. 1

J21	D3	5pi on 3pi multi	*1.60*
J22	D3	10pi on 50c multi	*1.60*
J23	D3	40pi on 1pi multi	*5.00*
J24	D3	60pi on 2pi multi	*6.25*

MILITARY STAMPS

Soldier Guarding Village M1

Rouletted 7½

1961, June Unwmk. Litho.

M1	M1	ocher, brn, dk grn & blk	80	50

1961, Sept. Typo.

M2	M1	org yel, dk grn & brn	65	40

Bottom inscription on No. M1 is black, brown on No. M2.

Battle and Refugees M2

1969, Feb. 22 Litho. *Imperf.*

M3	M2	red & grn	2.50
a.		Booklet pane of 10	

> **North Viet Nam**
> Stamps issued by the Democratic Republic of Viet Nam (Viet Nam Dan Chu Cong Hoa) are not listed. The US Treasury Department (Foreign Assets Control Section) has prohibited their purchase abroad and importation.

WALLIS AND FUTUNA ISLANDS

LOCATION — Group of islands in the South Pacific Ocean, northeast of Fiji.
GOVT. — French Overseas Territory
AREA — 106 sq. mi.
POP. — 13,000 (est. 1984)
CAPITAL — Mata-Utu, Wallis Island

100 Centimes = 1 Franc

> **Catalogue values for unused stamps in this country are for Never Hinged items, beginning with Scott 127 in the regular postage section, Scott B9 in the semi-postal section, Scott C1 in the airpost section, and Scott J37 in the postage due section.**

New Caledonia Stamps of 1905-28 Overprinted in Black or Red

ILES WALLIS
et
FUTUNA

1920-28 Unwmk. *Perf. 14x13½*

1	A16	1c blk, *green*	5	5
a		Double ovpt.	25.00	
2	A16	2c red brn	5	5
3	A16	4c bl, *org*	5	5
4	A16	5c green	10	10
5	A16	5c dl bl ('22)	5	5
6	A16	10c rose	12	12
7	A16	10c grn ('22)	15	15
8	A16	10c red, *pink* ('25)	35	35
9	A16	15c violet	16	16
10	A17	20c gray brn	20	20
11	A17	25c bl, *grn*	25	25
12	A17	25c red, *yel* ('22)	25	25
13	A17	30c brn, *org*	38	38
14	A17	30c dp rose ('22)	25	25
15	A17	30c red org ('25)	25	25
16	A17	30c lt grn ('27)	50	50
17	A17	35c blk, *yel* (R)	16	16
18	A17	40c rose, *grn*	25	25
19	A17	45c vio brn, *pnksh*	30	30
20	A17	50c red, *org*	25	25
21	A17	50c dk bl ('22)	25	25
22	A17	50c dk gray ('25)	45	45
23	A17	65c dp bl ('28)	1.20	1.20
24	A17	75c ol grn	55	55

Overprinted

ILES WALLIS
et
FUTUNA

25	A18	1fr bl, *yel grn*	1.10	1.10
a		Triple ovpt.	42.50	
26	A18	1.10fr org brn ('28)	90	90
27	A18	2fr car, *bl*	1.60	1.60
28	A18	5fr blk, *org* (R)	3.00	3.00
		Nos. 1-28 (28)	13.17	13.17

No. 9 Surcharged New Value and Bars in Various Colors

0,01

1922

29	A16	0.01c on 15c vio (Bk)	15	15
30	A16	0.02c on 15c vio (Bl)	15	15
31	A16	0.04c on 15c vio (G)	15	15
32	A16	0.05c on 15c vio (R)	15	15

Stamps and Types of 1920 Surcharged with New Values and Bars in Black or Red

1924-27

33	A18	25c on 2fr car, *bl*	20	20
34	A18	25c on 5fr blk, *org*	20	20
35	A17	65c on 40c rose red, *grn* ('25)	25	25
36	A17	85c on 75c ol grn	25	25
37	A17	90c on 75c dp rose ('27)	40	40
38	A18	1.25fr on 1fr dp bl (R; '26)	20	20
39	A18	1.50fr on 1fr dp bl, *bl* ('27)	60	60
a		Double surcharge	60.00	
b		Surcharge omitted	82.50	
40	A18	3fr on 5fr red vio ('27)	1.20	1.20
a		Surcharge omitted	82.50	
b		Double surcharge	65.00	
41	A18	10fr on 5fr ol, *lav* ('27)	7.00	7.00
42	A18	20fr on 5fr vio rose, *yel* ('27)	11.00	11.00
		Nos. 33-42 (10)	21.30	21.30

New Caledonia Stamps and Types of 1928-40 Overprinted as in 1920

1930-40 *Perf. 13½, 14x13, 14x13½*

43	A19	1c brn vio & ind	5	5
a		Double ovpt.	30.00	
44	A19	2c dk brn & yel grn	5	5
45	A19	3c brn vio & ind ('40)	5	5
46	A19	4c org & Prus grn	5	5
47	A19	5c Prus bl & dp ol	5	5
48	A19	10c gray lil & dk brn	5	5
49	A19	15c yel brn & dp bl	5	5
50	A19	20c brn red & dk brn	5	5
51	A19	25c dk grn & dk brn	20	20
52	A20	30c gray grn & bl grn	12	12
53	A20	35c Prus grn & dk grn ('38)	16	16
a		Without ovpt.	82.50	
54	A20	40c brt red & ol	10	10
55	A20	45c dp bl & red org	20	20
56	A20	45c bl grn & dl grn ('40)	12	12
57	A20	50c vio & brn	10	10
58	A20	55c bl vio & rose red ('38)	55	55
59	A20	60c vio bl & car ('40)	5	5
60	A20	65c org brn & bl	38	38
61	A20	70c dp rose & brn ('38)	20	20
62	A20	75c Prus bl & ol gray	60	60
63	A20	80c dk cl & grn ('38)	20	20
64	A20	85c grn & brn	1.10	1.10
65	A20	90c dp red & brt red	42	42
66	A20	90c ol grn & rose red ('39)	15	15
67	A21	1fr dp ol & sal red	1.10	1.10
68	A21	1fr rose red & dk car ('38)	45	45
69	A21	1fr brn red & grn ('40)	10	10
70	A21	1.10fr dp grn & brn	9.00	9.00
71	A21	1.25fr brn red & grn ('33)	60	60
72	A21	1.25fr rose red & dk car ('39)	15	15
73	A21	1.40fr dk bl & red org ('40)	25	25
74	A21	1.50fr dp bl & bl	20	20
75	A21	1.60fr dp grn & brn ('40)	30	30
76	A21	1.75fr dk bl & red org ('33)	3.75	3.75
77	A21	1.75fr vio bl ('38)	60	60
78	A21	2fr red org & brn	38	38
79	A21	2.25fr vio bl ('39)	25	25
80	A21	2.50fr brn & lt brn ('40)	32	32
81	A21	3fr mag & brn	38	38
82	A21	5fr dk bl & brn	38	38
83	A21	10fr vio & brn, *pnksh*	55	55
84	A21	20fr red & brn, *yel*	95	95
		Nos. 43-84 (42)	24.76	24.76

Colonial Exposition Issue
Common Design Types

1931, Apr. 13 Engr. *Perf. 12½*
Name of Country Typo. in Black

85	CD70	40c dp grn	1.25	1.25
86	CD71	50c violet	1.25	1.25
87	CD72	90c red org	1.25	1.25
88	CD73	1.50fr dl bl	1.25	1.25

Colonial Arts Exhibition Issue
Common Design Type
Souvenir Sheet

1937 *Imperf.*

89	CD78	3fr red vio	2.00	2.00

New York World's Fair Issue
Common Design Type

1939, May. 10 Engr. *Perf. 12½x12*

90	CD82	1.25fr car lake	50	50
91	CD82	2.25fr ultra	50	50

Petain Issue
New Caledonia Nos. 216A-216B Overprinted "WALLIS ET FUTUNA" in Lilac or Red

1941 Engr. *Perf. 12½x12*

92	A21a	1fr bluish grn (L)	16
93	A21a	2.50fr dk bl (R)	16

Nos. 92-93 were issued by the Vichy government and were not placed on sale in the dependency.

Six stamps of New Caledonia types A19 and A21 without "RF" were overprinted "ILES WALLIS et FUTUNA" by the Vichy government and issued in 1944, but were not placed on sale in the dependency.

Nos. 43-69, 71, 74, 77-78, 80-84 with Additional Overprint in Black

France Libre

1941-43 *Perf. 14x13½*

94	A19	1c	18	18
95	A19	2c	18	18
96	A19	3c	30.00	30.00
97	A19	4c	18	18
98	A19	5c	18	18
99	A19	10c	18	18
100	A19	15c	18	18
101	A19	20c	32	32
102	A19	25c	32	32
103	A20	30c	32	32
104	A20	35c	18	18
105	A20	40c	32	32
106	A20	45c #55	32	32
107	A20	45c #56	25.00	25.00
108	A20	50c	22	22
109	A20	55c	22	22
110	A20	60c	25.00	25.00
111	A20	65c	22	22
112	A20	70c	22	22
113	A20	75c	65	65
114	A20	80c	35	35
115	A20	85c	65	65
116	A20	90c #65	55	55
117	A21	1fr #68	65	65
118	A21	1.25fr #71	65	65
119	A21	1.50fr	45	45
120	A21	1.75fr #77	45	45
121	A21	2fr	65	65
122	A21	2.50fr	72.50	72.50
123	A21	3fr	45	45
124	A21	5fr	1.75	1.75
125	A21	10fr	21.00	21.00
126	A21	20fr	35.00	35.00
		Nos. 94-126 (33)	219.49	219.49

> **Catalogue values for unused stamps in this section, from this point to the end of the section, are for Never Hinged items.**

Ivi Poo, Bone Carving in Tiki Design A1

1944 Unwmk. Photo. *Perf. 11½x12*

127	A1	5c lt brn	5	5
128	A1	10c dp gray bl	10	10
129	A1	25c emerald	10	10
130	A1	30c dl org	10	10
131	A1	40c dk sl grn	25	25
132	A1	80c brn red	20	20
133	A1	1fr red vio	5	5
134	A1	1.50fr red	8	8
135	A1	2fr gray blk	10	10
136	A1	2.50fr brt ultra	20	20
137	A1	4fr dk pur	20	20
138	A1	5fr lem yel	20	20
139	A1	10fr chocolate	32	32
140	A1	20fr dp grn	45	45
		Nos. 127-140 (14)	2.40	2.40

Nos. 127, 129 and 136 Surcharged with New Values and Bars in Black or Carmine

1946

141	A1	50c on 5c lt brn	30	30
142	A1	60c on 5c lt brn	30	30
143	A1	70c on 5c lt brn	16	16
144	A1	1.20fr on 5c lt brn	16	16
145	A1	2.40fr on 25c emer	16	16
146	A1	3fr on 25c emer	16	16
147	A1	4.50fr on 25c emer	42	42
148	A1	15fr on 2.50fr (C)	45	45
		Nos. 141-148 (8)	2.11	2.11

Military Medal Issue
Common Design Type
Engraved and Typographed

1952, Dec. 1 *Perf. 13*

149	CD101	2fr multi	1.00	1.00

Wallis Islander A2

Unwmk.

1957, June 11 Engr. *Perf. 13*

150	A2	3fr dk pur & lil rose	42	42
151	A2	9fr bl, dl lil & vio brn	70	70

Imperforates
Most Wallis and Futuna stamps from 1957 onward exist imperforate in issued and trial colors, and also in small presentation sheets in issued colors.

Flower Issue
Common Design Type

Design: 5fr, Montrouziera (horiz.).

1958, July 7 Photo. *Perf. 12½x12*
152 CD104 5fr multi 1.65 1.10

Human Rights Issue
Common Design Type

1958, Dec. 10 Engr. *Perf. 13*
153 CD105 17fr brt bl & dk bl 1.65 1.65

Women Making Tapa Cloth — A3

Kava Ceremony A4

Designs: 17fr, Dancers. 19fr, Dancers with paddles.

1960, Oct. 19 Engr. *Perf. 13*
154 A3 5fr dk brn, grn & org brn 30 30
155 A4 7fr dk brn & Prus grn 42 42
156 A4 17fr ultra, cl & grn 65 65
157 A3 19fr cl & sl 90 90

Map of South Pacific — A4a

1962, July 19 Photo. *Perf. 13x12*
158 A4a 16fr multi 2.00 2.00

Issued to commemorate the Fifth South Pacific Conference, Pago Pago, 1962.

Triton — A5

Various Sea Shells

1962-63 Engr. *Perf. 13*
Size: 22x36mm
159 A5 25c shown 30 30
160 A5 1fr Mitra episcopalis 30 30
161 A5 2fr Cypraecassis rufa 40 40
162 A5 4fr Murex tenuspina 80 80
163 A5 10fr Oliva erythrostoma 2.25 2.25
164 A5 20fr Cyprae tigris 3.50 3.50
Nos. 159-164,C18 (7) 11.55 11.05

Red Cross Centenary Issue
Common Design Type

1963, Sept. 2 Unwmk. *Perf. 13*
165 CD113 12fr red lil, gray & car 1.20 1.20

Human Rights Issue
Common Design Type

1963, Dec. 10 Engr.
166 CD117 29fr dk red & ocher 2.75 2.75

Philatec Issue
Common Design Type

1964, Apr. 15 Unwmk. *Perf. 13*
167 CD118 9fr dk sl grn, grn & red 1.25 1.25

Queen Amelia and Ship "Queen Amelia" A6

1965, Feb. 15 Photo. *Perf. 12½x13*
168 A6 11fr multi 2.75 2.75

WHO Anniversary Issue
Common Design Type

1968, May 4 Engr. *Perf. 13*
169 CD126 17fr bl grn, org & lil 2.00 2.00

Human Rights Year Issue
Common Design Type

1968, Aug. 10 Engr. *Perf. 13*
170 CD127 19fr dk pur, org brn & brt mag 1.40 1.40

Outrigger Canoe — A7

1969, Apr. 30 Photo. *Perf. 13*
171 A7 1fr multi 40 40
Nos. 171,C31-C35 (6) 12.80 6.90

ILO Issue
Common Design Type

1969, Nov. 24 Engr. *Perf. 13*
172 CD131 9fr org, brn & bl 1.25 1.25

UPU Headquarters Issue
Common Design Type

1970, May 20 Engr. *Perf. 13*
173 CD133 21fr lil rose, ind & ol bis 1.60 1.60

No. 157 Surcharged with New Value and Two Bars

1971 Engr. *Perf. 13*
174 A3 12fr on 19fr cl & sl 65 65

Weight Lifting — A8

Design: 36fr, Basketball.

1971, Oct. 25
175 A8 24fr grn, ind & red brn 1.90 1.90
176 A8 36fr ol, dl red & ultra 2.25 2.25

4th South Pacific Games, Papeete, French Polynesia, Sept. 8-19. See Nos. C37-C38.

De Gaulle Issue
Common Design Type

Designs: 30fr, Gen. de Gaulle, 1940. 70fr, Pres. de Gaulle, 1970.

1971, Nov. 9 Engr. *Perf. 13*
177 CD134 30fr bl & blk 2.25 1.50
178 CD134 70fr bl & blk 4.50 3.00

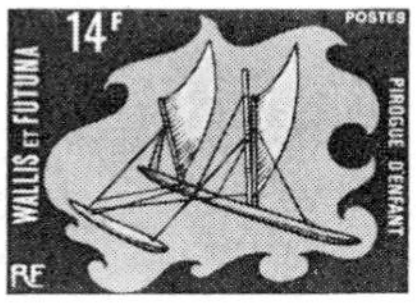

Child's Outrigger Canoe — A9

Designs: 16fr, Children's canoe race. 18fr, Outrigger racing canoe.

1972, Oct. 16 Photo. *Perf. 13x12½*
Size: 35½x26½mm.
179 A9 14fr dk grn & multi 70 50
180 A9 16fr dk plum & multi 70 50
181 A9 18fr bl & multi 1.10 80

Outrigger sailing canoes. See No. C41.

Rhinoceros Beetle — A10

Insects: 25fr, Cosmopolities sordidus (beetle). 35fr, Ophideres fullonica (moth). 45fr, Dragonfly.

1974, July 29 Photo. *Perf. 13*
182 A10 15fr ol & multi 70 55
183 A10 25fr ol & multi 90 60
184 A10 35fr gray bl & multi 1.50 90
185 A10 45fr multi 2.00 1.40

Georges Pompidou (1911-74), Pres. of France — A11

1975, Dec. 1 Engr. *Perf. 13*
186 A11 50fr ultra & sl 2.25 1.75

Battle of Yorktown and George Washington — A12

American Bicentennial: 47fr, Virginia Cape Battle and Lafayette.

1976, June 28 Engr. *Perf. 13*
187 A12 19fr bl, red & ol 80 60
188 A12 47fr bl, red & mar 2.00 1.65

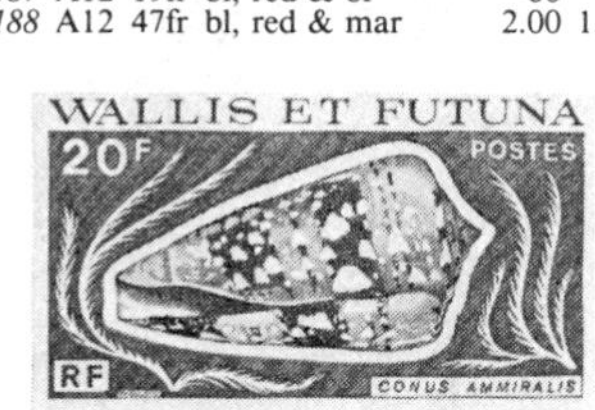

Conus Ammiralis — A13

Sea Shells: 23fr, Cyprae assellus. 43fr, Turbo petholatus. 61fr, Mitra papalis.

1976, Oct. 1 Engr. *Perf. 13*
189 A13 20fr multi 65 60
190 A13 23fr multi 80 60
191 A13 43fr multi 2.00 1.20
192 A13 61fr ultra & multi 2.50 1.90

The first value column gives the catalogue value of an unused stamp, the second that of a used stamp.

Father Chanel and Poi Church — A14

Design: 32fr, Father Chanel and map of islands.

1977, Apr. 28 Litho. *Perf. 12*
193 A14 22fr multi 65 38
194 A14 32fr multi 90 55

Return of the ashes of Father Chanel, missionary.

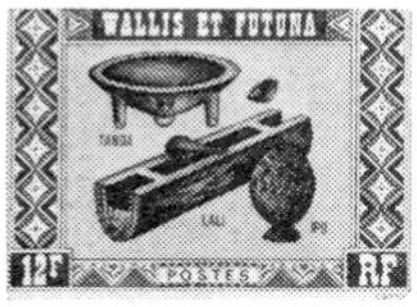

Bowl, Mortar and Pestle — A15

Handicrafts: 25fr, Wooden bowls and leather bag. 33fr, Wooden comb, club, and boat model. 45fr, War clubs, Futuna. 69fr, Lances.

1977, Sept. 26 Litho. *Perf. 12½*
195 A15 12fr multi 45 35
196 A15 25fr multi 80 55
197 A15 33fr multi 1.00 65
198 A15 45fr multi 1.40 1.00
199 A15 69fr multi 2.25 1.40
Nos. 195-199 (5) 5.90 3.95

Post Office, Mata Utu — A16

Designs: 50fr, Sia Hospital, Mata Utu. 57fr, Administration Buildings, Mata Utu. 63fr, St. Joseph's Church, Sigave. 120fr, Royal Palace, Mara Utu.

1977, Dec. 12 Litho. *Perf. 13*
200 A16 27fr multi 55 50
201 A16 50fr multi 1.10 80
202 A16 57fr multi 1.20 90
203 A16 63fr multi 1.40 1.25
204 A16 120fr multi 3.00 2.00
Nos. 200-204 (5) 7.25 5.45

Nos. 187-188 Overprinted: "JAMES COOK / Bicentenaire de la / découverte des Iles / Hawaii 1778-1978"

1978, Jan. 22 Engr. *Perf. 13*
205 A12 19fr multi 1.40 1.25
206 A12 47fr multi 2.75 1.75

Bicentenary of the arrival of Capt. Cook in the Hawaiian Islands.

Cruiser Triomphant — A17

Warships: 200fr, Destroyers Cap des Palmes and Chevreuil. 280fr, Cruiser Savorgnan de Brazza.

1978, June 18 Photo. *Perf. 13x12½*
207 A17 150fr multi 4.50 3.50
208 A17 200fr multi 6.00 4.50
209 A17 280fr multi 8.00 6.00

Free French warships serving in the Pacific, 1940-1944.

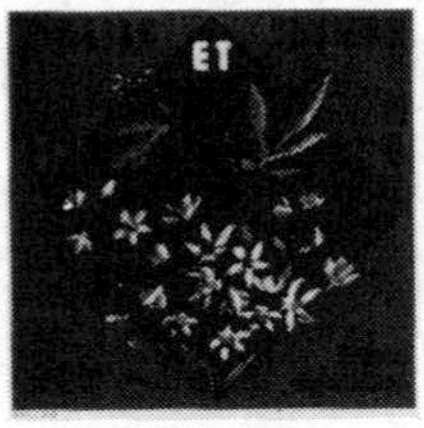

Solanum Seaforthianum — A18

Flowers: 24fr, Cassia alata. 29fr, Gloriosa superba. 36fr, Hymenocallis littoralis.

1978, July 11 Photo. *Perf. 13*

210	A18	16fr multi	38	28
211	A18	24fr multi	45	35
212	A18	29fr multi	50	45
213	A18	36fr multi	90	65

Gray Egret — A19

Birds: 18fr, Red-footed booby. 28fr, Brown booby. 35fr, White tern.

1978, Sept. 5 Photo. *Perf. 13*

214	A19	17fr multi	50	35
215	A19	18fr multi	50	35
216	A19	28fr multi	60	50
217	A19	35fr multi	1.20	80

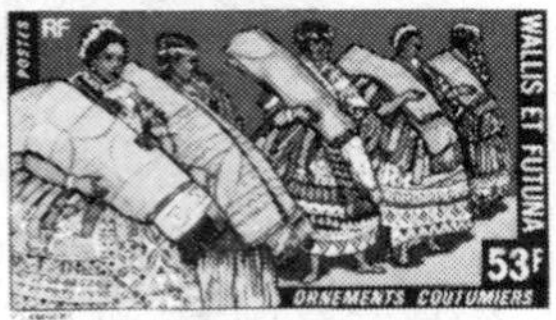

Traditional Patterns — A20

Designs: 55fr, Corpus Christi procession. 59fr, Chief's honor guard.

1978, Oct. 3

218	A20	53fr multi	1.00	65
219	A20	55fr multi	1.25	75
220	A20	59fr multi	1.40	90

Human Rights Flame A21

1978, Dec. 10 Litho. *Perf. 12½*

221	A21	44fr multi	75	45
222	A21	56fr multi	1.20	75

30th anniversary of Universal Declaration of Human Rights.

Fishing Boat — A22

Designs: 30fr, Weighing young tuna. 34fr, Stocking young tunas. 38fr, Measuring tuna. 40fr, Angler catching tuna. 48fr, Adult tuna.

1979, Mar. 19 Litho. *Perf. 12*

223	A22	10fr multi	35	30
224	A22	30fr multi	60	45
225	A22	34fr multi	70	55
226	A22	38fr multi	1.00	65
227	A22	40fr multi	1.20	90
228	A22	48fr multi	1.40	1.10
a		Souvenir sheet of 6	8.00	8.00
		Nos. 223-228 (6)	5.25	3.95

Tuna tagging by South Pacific Commission. No. 228a contains Nos. 223-228 and 3 labels showing fish lure, inscription and South Pacific Commission emblem.

Boy with Raft and IYC Emblem — A23

Design: 58fr, Girl on horseback.

1979, Apr. 9 Photo. *Perf. 13*

229	A23	52fr multi	1.00	80
230	A23	58fr multi	1.25	90

International Year of the Child.

Bombax Ellipticum — A24

Designs: 64fr, Callophyllum. 76fr, Pandanus odoratissimus.

1979, Apr. 23 Litho. *Perf. 13*

231	A24	50fr multi	75	65
232	A24	64fr multi	1.25	75
233	A24	76fr multi	1.40	90

Green and Withered Landscapes — A25

1979, May 28 Photo. *Perf. 13*

234	A25	22fr multi	55	45

Anti-alcoholism campaign.

Crinum — A26

Flowers: 42fr, Passiflora. 62fr, Canna indica.

1979, July 16 Photo. *Perf. 12½x13*

235	A26	20fr multi	50	35
236	A26	42fr multi	1.00	60
237	A26	62fr multi	1.25	80

See Nos. 279-281.

Swimming — A27

Design: 39fr, High jump.

1979, Aug. 27 Engr. *Perf. 13*

238	A27	31fr multi	1.00	75
239	A27	39fr multi	1.25	90

6th South Pacific Games, Suva, Fiji, Aug. 27-Sept. 8.

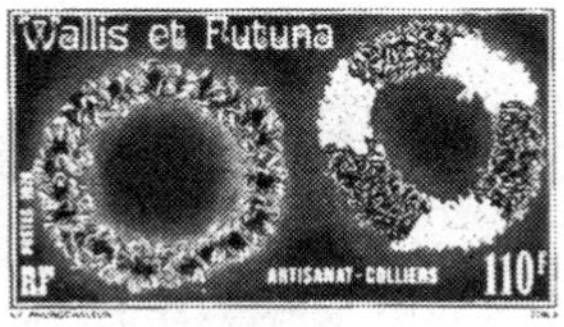

Flower Necklaces — A28

Design: 140fr, Coral necklaces.

1979, Aug. 27 Litho.

240	A28	110fr multi	2.25	1.50
241	A28	140fr multi	3.00	2.00

Trees and Birds, by Sutita — A29

Paintings by Local Artists: 65fr, Birds and Mountain, by M. A. Pilioko (vert.). 78fr, Festival Procession, by Sutita.

1979, Oct. 8 *Perf. 13x12½, 12½x13*

242	A29	27fr multi	65	50
243	A29	65fr multi	1.25	80
244	A29	78fr multi	1.60	1.20

Marine Mantis A30

Marine Life: 23fr, Hexabranchus sanguineus. 25fr, Spondylus barbatus. 43fr, Gorgon coral. 45fr, Linckia laevigata. 63fr, Tridacna squamosa.

1979, Nov. 5 Photo. *Perf. 13x12½*

245	A30	15fr multi	35	30
246	A30	23fr multi	50	38
247	A30	25fr multi	60	38
248	A30	43fr multi	70	55
249	A30	45fr multi	80	60
250	A30	63fr multi	1.20	1.00
		Nos. 245-250 (6)	4.15	3.21

See Nos. 294-297.

Transportation Type of 1979

1980, Feb. 29 Litho. *Perf. 13*

251	AP32	1fr *like No. C87*	8	5
252	AP32	3fr *like No. C88*	8	5
253	AP32	5fr *like No. C89*	10	5

Radio Station and Tower — A31

1980, Apr. 21 Litho. *Perf. 13*

254	A31	47fr multi	1.10	65

Radio station FR3, 1st anniversary.

Jesus Laid in the Tomb, by Maurice Denis — A32

1980, Apr. 28 *Perf. 13x12½*

255	A32	25fr multi	65	50

Easter 1980.

Gnathodentex Mossambicus — A33

1980, Aug. 25 Litho. *Perf. 12½x13*

256	A33	23fr *shown*	55	40
257	A33	27fr *Pristipomoides filamentosus*	60	55
258	A33	32fr *Etelis carbunculus*	60	55
259	A33	51fr *Cephalopholis wallisi*	1.00	80
260	A33	59fr *Aphareus rutilans*	1.40	1.20
		Nos. 256-260 (5)	4.15	3.50

Nos. 256-260 se-tenant.

No. 228 Surcharged:

═ 50F

SYDPEX 80

29 Septembre

1980 Litho. *Perf. 12*

261	A22	50fr on 48fr multi	1.20	90

Sydpex 80 Philatelic Exhibition, Sydney.

13th World Telecommunications Day — A34

1981, May 17 Litho. *Perf. 12½*

262	A34	49fr multi	80	60

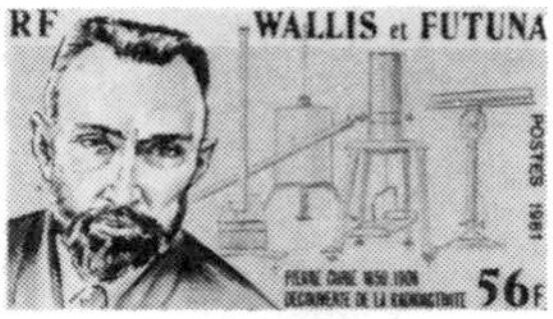

Pierre Curie and Laboratory Equipment — A35

1981, May 25 **Litho.** ***Perf. 13***
263 A35 56fr multi 1.00 70

Pierre Curie (1859-1906), discoverer of radioactivity.

Conus Textile A36

Designs: Marine life.

1981, June 22 ***Perf. 12½x13***

264 A36 28fr Favites		45	40
265 A36 30fr Cyanophycees		60	45
266 A36 31fr Ceratium vultur		60	45
267 A36 35fr Amphiprion frenatus		62	55
268 A36 40fr shown		70	70
269 A36 55fr Comatule		1.20	90
Nos. 264-269 (6)		4.17	3.45

60th Anniv. of Anti-tuberculin Vaccine (Developed by Calmette and Guerin) — A37

1981, July 28 **Litho.** ***Perf. 13***
270 A37 27fr multi 45 40

Intl. Year of the Disabled — A38

1981, Aug. 17
271 A38 42fr multi 65 45

No. 245 Surcharged in Red

1981, Sept. **Photo.** ***Perf. 13x12½***
272 A30 5fr on 15fr multi 10 7

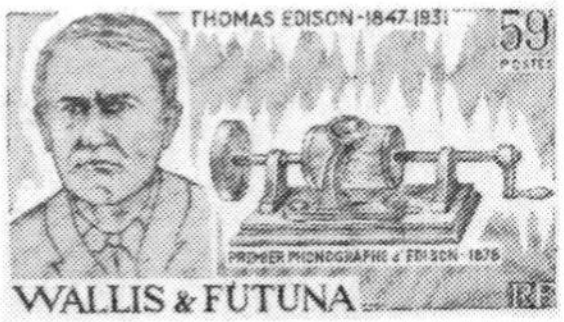

Thomas Edison (1847-1931) and his Phonograph, 1878 — A39

1981, Sept. 5 **Engr.** ***Perf. 13***
273 A39 59fr multi 1.00 70

Battle of Yorktown, 1781 (American Revolution) — A40

1981, Oct. 19 **Engr.** ***Perf. 13***

274 A40 66fr Admiral de Grasse	65	60
275 A40 74fr Sea battle, vert.	1.20	90

200-Mile Zone Surveillance — A41

1981, Dec. 4 **Litho.** ***Perf. 13***

276 A41 60fr Patrol boat Diep-poise	60	45
277 A41 85fr Protet	80	65

TB Bacillus Centenary — A42

1982, Mar. 24 **Litho.** ***Perf. 13***
278 A42 45fr multi 60 50

Flower Type of 1979 in Changed Colors

1982, May 3 **Photo.** ***Perf. 12½x13***

279 A26 1fr like No. 235	5	5
280 A26 2fr like No. 236	5	5
281 A26 3fr like No. 237	5	5

PHILEXFRANCE '82 Intl. Stamp Exhibition, Paris, June 11-21 — A43

1983, May 12 **Engr.** ***Perf. 13***
282 A43 140fr No. 25 2.25 1.60

Acanthe Phippium A44

Orchids and rubiaceae (83fr).

1982, May 24 **Litho.** ***Perf. 12½x13***

283 A44 34fr shown	55	50
284 A44 68fr Acanthe phippium, diff.	1.00	90
285 A44 70fr Spathoglottis pacifica	1.10	90
286 A44 83fr Mussaenda raiateensis	1.40	1.20

Scouting Year — A45

1982, June 21 ***Perf. 12½***
287 A45 80fr Baden-Powell 1.20 90

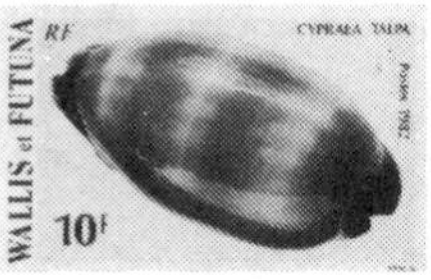

Cypraea Talpa A46

Porcelaines shells.

1982, June 28 ***Perf. 12½x13***

288 A46 10fr shown	15	12
289 A46 15fr Cypraea vitellus	22	16
290 A46 25fr Cypraea argus	32	30
291 A46 27fr Cypraea carneola	38	30
292 A46 40fr Cypraea mappa	55	40
293 A46 50fr Cypraea tigris	60	45
Nos. 288-293 (6)	2.22	1.73

Marine Life Type of 1979

1982, Oct. 1 **Photo.** ***Perf. 13x12½***

294 A30 32fr Gorgones milithea	30	26
295 A30 35fr Linckia laevigata	38	30
296 A30 46fr Hexabranchus sanguineus	45	35
297 A30 63fr Spondylus barbatus	65	50

St. Teresa of Jesus of Avila (1515-1582) — A48

1982, Nov. 8 **Engr.** ***Perf. 13***
298 A48 31fr multi 50 40

See No. 315.

Traditional House — A49

1983, Jan. 20 **Litho.** ***Perf. 13***
299 A49 19fr multi 22 15

Gustave Eiffel (1832-1923), Architect — A50

1983, Feb. 14 **Engr.** ***Perf. 13***
300 A50 97fr multi 1.25 1.00

BANGKOK '83 Intl. Stamp Show, Aug. 4-13 — A51

1983, June 28 **Engr.** ***Perf. 13***
301 A51 92fr Thai dancer, 19th cent. 1.00 75

World Communications Year — A52

1983, Aug. 23 **Litho.** ***Perf. 13x13½***
302 A52 20fr multi 25 15

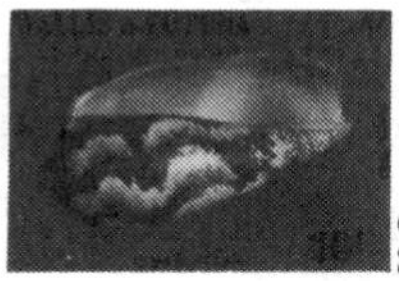

Cone Shells — A53

1983-84 **Litho.** ***Perf. 13½x13***

303 A53 10fr Conus tulipa	15	12
304 A53 17fr Conus capitaneus	25	16
305 A53 21fr Conus virgo	30	25
306 A53 22fr Strombus lentiginosus ('84)	30	20
307 A53 25fr Lambis chiragra ('84)	38	28
308 A53 35fr Strombus dentatus ('84)	45	35
309 A53 39fr Conus vitulinus	55	45
310 A53 43fr Lambis scorpius ('84)	60	45
311 A53 49fr Strombus aurisdianae ('84)	62	55
312 A53 52fr Conus marmoreus	65	55
313 A53 65fr Conus leopardus	90	65
314 A53 76fr Lambis crocata ('84)	1.10	80
Nos. 303-314 (12)	6.25	4.81

No. 298 Redrawn with Espana '84 Emblem

1984, Apr. 27 **Engr.** ***Perf. 13***
315 A48 70fr multi 1.00 65

Denis Diderot (1713-1784), Philosopher A54

1984, May 11
316 A54 100fr Portrait, encyclopedia title page 1.25 1.00

Nature Protection (Whale) A55

1984, June 5 Litho. *Perf. 13x12½*

317 A55 90fr Orcina orca 1.10 90

4th Pacific Arts Festival — A56

1984, Nov. 30 Litho. *Perf. 13*

318 A56 160fr Islanders 1.20 80

Lapita Pottery — A57

Ethno-Archaeological Museum: Excavation site, reconstructed ceramic bowl.

1985, Jan. 16 Litho. *Perf. 13*

319 A57 53fr multi 40 25

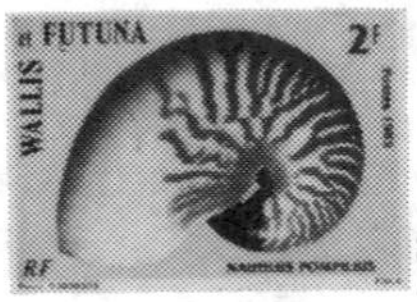

Seashells A58

1985, Feb. 11

320	A58	2fr	Nautilus pompilius	5	5
321	A58	3fr	Murex bruneus	5	5
322	A58	41fr	Casmaria erinaceus	30	20
323	A58	47fr	Conus vexillum	35	25
324	A58	56fr	Harpa harpa	40	28
325	A58	71fr	Murex ramosus	50	38
			Nos. 320-325 (6)	1.65	1.21

Victor Hugo, Author (1802-1885) A59

Bat A60

1985, Mar. 7 Engr.

326 A59 89fr multi 65 45

1985, Apr. 29 Litho.

327 A60 38fr multi 28 20

Intl. Youth Year — A61

1985, May 20 Litho. *Perf. 12½x13*

328 A61 64fr European, Malaysian children 45 32

UN, 40th Anniv. — A61a

1985, July 12 Engr. *Perf. 13*

328A A61a 49fr Prus grn, dk ultra & red 50 25

Pierre de Ronsard (1524-1585), Poet — A62

1985, Sept. 16 Engr. *Perf. 13*

329 A62 170fr brt bl, sep & brn 1.50 70

Dr. Albert Schweitzer — A63

1985, Nov. 22 Engr. *Perf. 13*

330 A63 50fr blk, dk red lil & org brn 38 25

World Food Day — A64

1986, Jan. 23 Litho. *Perf. 12½x13*

331 A64 39fr Breadfruit 38 25

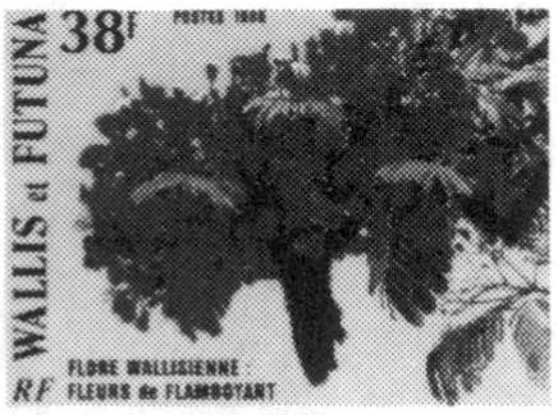

Flamboyants — A65

1986, Feb. 13 *Perf. 13x12½*

332 A65 38fr multi 42 28

Seashells A66

1986, Apr. 24 Litho. *Perf. 13½x13*

333	A66	4fr	Lambis truncata	6	5
334	A66	5fr	Charonia tritonis	8	5
335	A66	10fr	Oliva miniacea	15	8
336	A66	18fr	Distorsio anus	28	14
337	A66	25fr	Mitra mitra	38	20
338	A66	107fr	Conus distans	1.60	80
			Nos. 333-338 (6)	2.55	1.32

1986 World Cup Soccer Championships, Mexico — A67

1986, May 20 *Perf. 13x12½*

339 A67 95fr multi 1.45 72

UNICEF.

Discovery of Horn Islands, 370th Anniv. — A68

Designs: No. 340a, William Schouten, ship. No. 340b, Jacob LeMaire, ship. No. 340c, Map of Alo and Alofi.

1986, June 19 Engr. *Perf. 13*

340	Strip of 3	2.65	1.35
a.	A68 8fr Prus bl, myr grn & dp rose lil	12	6
b.	A68 9fr Prus bl, dp rose lil & myr grn	14	8
c.	A68 155fr Prus bl, myr grn & dp rose lil	2.35	1.20

James Watt (1736-1819), Inventor, and Steam Engine — A69

1986, July 11

341 A69 74fr blk & dk red 1.10 55

La Lorientaise Patrol Boat — A70

1986, Aug. 7

342	A70	6fr	shown	10	5
343	A70	7fr	Commandant Blaison	12	6
344	A70	120fr	Balny escort ship	1.80	90

Rose Laurel — A71

1986, Oct. 2 Litho. *Perf. 13x12½*

345 A71 97fr multi 1.50 75

Virgin and Child, by Sandro Botticelli A72

1986, Dec. 12 Litho. *Perf. 12½x13*

346 A72 250fr multi 3.75 1.90

Christmas.

Butterflies — A73

1987, Apr. 2 Litho. *Perf. 12½*

347	A73	2fr	Papilio montrouzieri	5	5
348	A73	42fr	Belenois java	62	30
349	A73	46fr	Delias ellipsis	70	35
350	A73	50fr	Danaus pumila	75	38
351	A73	52fr	Luthrodes cleotas	78	40
352	A73	59fr	Precis villida	90	45
			Nos. 347-352 (6)	3.80	1.93

World Wrestling Championships — A74

1987, May 26 Litho. *Perf. 12½*

353 A74 97fr multi 1.50 75

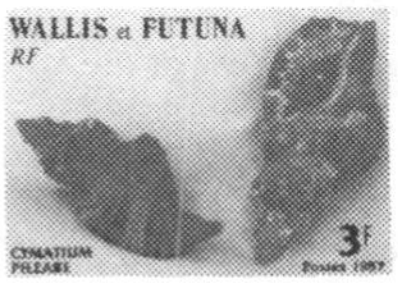

Seashells A75

1987, June 24 Litho. *Perf. 13*

354	A75	3fr	Cymatium pileare	5	5
355	A75	4fr	Conus textile	5	5
356	A75	28fr	Cypraea mauritiana	45	22
357	A75	44fr	Bursa bubo	70	35
358	A75	48fr	Cypraea testudinaria	75	38
359	A75	78fr	Cypraecassis rufa	1.25	62
			Nos. 354-359 (6)	3.25	1.67

Exist in se-tenant strips of 6 from sheet of 24.

No. 353 Overprinted OLYMPHILEX'87 ROME

1987, Aug. 29 Litho. *Perf. 12½*

360 A74 97fr multi 2.00 1.00

OLYMPHILEX '87, Rome.

Bust of a Girl, by Auguste Rodin (1840-1917)
A76

1987, Sept. 15 **Engr.** ***Perf. 13***
361 A76 150fr plum 2.25 1.15

World Post Day — A77

1987, Oct. 9 **Litho.** ***Perf. 13***
362 A77 116fr multi 2.40 1.20

Birds — A78

1987, Oct. 28 ***Perf. 13x12½***

363	A78	6fr Anas superciliosa	14	6
364	A78	19fr Pluvialis dominica	40	20
365	A78	47fr Gallicolumba stairi	1.00	50
366	A78	56fr Arenaria interpres	1.20	60
367	A78	64fr Rallus philippensis	1.40	70
368	A78	68fr Limosa lapponica	1.50	75
		Nos. 363-368 (6)	5.64	2.81

Francis Carco (1886-1958), Painter — A79

Design: Carco and views of the Moulin de la Galette and Place du Tertre, Paris.

1988, Jan. 29 **Litho.** ***Perf. 13***
369 A79 40fr multi 82 40

Jean-Francois de Galaup (1741-c.1788), Comte de La Perouse, Explorer — A80

Design: Ships *L'Astrolabe* and *La Boussole*, portrait of La Perouse.

1988, Mar. 21 **Engr.** ***Perf. 13***
370 A80 70fr org brn, dark blue & olive grn 1.40 70

Intl. Red Cross and Red Crescent Organizations, 125th Annivs. — A81

1988, July 4 **Engr.** ***Perf. 13***
371 A81 30fr blk, dark red & brt blue grn 55 28

1988 Summer Olympics, Seoul — A82

1988, Sept. 1 **Engr.** ***Perf. 13***
Vermilion, Bright Blue and Dark Brown

372	A82	11fr Javelin	20	10
373	A82	20fr Women's volleyball	35	18
374	A82	60fr Windsurfing	1.05	52
375	A82	80fr Yachting	1.40	70
a.		Souv. sheet of 4 (Nos. 372-375) + 2 labels, gutter between	3.00	3.00

Intl. Maritime Organization Emblem and Packet *Escorteur* F727 — A83

1989, Jan. 26 **Litho.** ***Perf. 13***
376 A83 26fr multi 48 25

Jean Renoir (1894-1979), Film Director, and Scene from *The Grand Illusion* — A84

1989, Feb. 16 **Engr.** ***Perf. 13***
377 A84 24fr brt lil rose, dark vio brn & brt org 45 22

French Revolution Issue
Common Design Type
Unwmk.

1939, July 5 **Photo.** ***Perf. 13***
Name and Value Typo. in Black

B1	CD83	45c + 25c grn	3.75	3.75
B2	CD83	70c + 30c brn	3.75	3.75
B3	CD83	90c + 35c red org	3.75	3.75
B4	CD83	1.25fr + 1fr rose pink	3.75	3.75
B5	CD83	2.25fr + 2fr bl	3.75	3.75
		Nos. B1-B5 (5)	18.75	18.75

Canceled-to-order stamps are often from remainders. Most collectors of canceled stamps prefer postally used specimens.

New Caledonia Nos. B10 and B12 Overprinted "WALLIS ET FUTUNA" in Blue or Red, and Common Design Type

1941 **Photo.** ***Perf. 13½***

B6	SP2	1fr + 1fr red	45
B7	CD86	1.50fr + 3fr mar	45
B8	SP3	2.50fr + 1fr dk bl	45

Nos. B6-B8 were issued by the Vichy government and were not placed on sale in the dependency.

In 1944 Nos. 92-93 were surcharged "OEUVRES COLONIALES" and surtax (including change of denomination of the 2.50fr to 50c). These were issued by the Vichy government and not placed on sale in Wallis and Futuna.

Catalogue values for unused stamps in this section, from this point to the end of the section, are for Never Hinged items.

Red Cross Issue
Common Design Type

1944 **Photo.** ***Perf. 14½x14***
B9 CD90 5fr + 20fr red org 60 60

The surtax was for the French Red Cross and national relief.

AIR POST STAMPS

Catalogue values for unused stamps in this section are for Never Hinged items.

Victory Issue
Common Design Type
Perf. 12½

1946, May 8 **Unwmk.** **Engr.**
C1 CD92 8fr dk vio 38 38

Chad to Rhine Issue
Common Design Types

1946

C2	CD93	5fr dk vio	38	38
C3	CD94	10fr dk sl grn	38	38
C4	CD95	15fr vio brn	38	38
C5	CD96	20fr brt ultra	55	55
C6	CD97	25fr brn org	80	80
C7	CD98	50fr carmine	1.00	1.00
		Nos. C2-C7 (6)	3.49	3.49

Types of New Caledonia Air Post Stamps of 1948, Overprinted in Blue:

WALLIS ET FUTUNA

1949, July 4 ***Perf. 13x12½, 12½x13***

C8	AP2	50fr yel & rose red	2.25	2.25
C9	AP3	100fr yel & red brn	3.75	3.75

The overprint on No. C9 is in three lines.

UPU Issue
Common Design Type

1949, July 4 **Engr.** ***Perf. 13***
C10 CD99 10fr multi 2.25 2.25

Liberation Issue
Common Design Type

1954, June 6
C11 CD102 3fr sep & vio brn 2.50 2.50

Father Louis Marie Chanel — AP1

1955, Nov. 21 **Unwmk.** ***Perf. 13***
C12 AP1 14fr dk grn, grnsh bl & ind 1.25 65

Issued in honor of Father Chanel, martyred missionary to the Islands.

View of Mata-Utu, Queen Amelia and Msgr. Bataillon — AP2

Design: 33fr, Map of islands and sailing ship.

1960, Sept. 19 **Engr.** ***Perf. 13***

C13	AP2	21fr bl, brn & grn	1.50	1.10
C14	AP2	33fr ultra, choc & bl grn	2.75	2.25

Shell Diver
AP3

1962, Sept. 20 **Unwmk.** ***Perf. 13***
C16 AP3 100fr bl, grn & dk red brn 10.00 7.00

Telstar Issue
Common Design Type

1962, Dec. 5
C17 CD111 12fr dk pur, mar & bl 1.65 1.65

Sea Shell Type of Regular Issue, 1962

Design: 50fr, Harpa ventricosa.

1963, Apr. 1 **Engr.**
Size: 26x47mm
C18 A5 50fr lil rose, Prus grn & red brn 4.00 3.50

Javelin Thrower — AP4

1964, Oct. 10 **Engr.** ***Perf. 13***
C19 AP4 31fr emer, ver & vio brn 8.00 6.25

18th Olympic Games, Tokyo, Oct. 10-25.

ITU Issue
Common Design Type

1965, May 17 **Unwmk.** ***Perf. 13***
C20 CD120 50fr dp lil rose, dk brn & brn red 9.00 6.50

Mata-Utu Wharf — AP5

1965, Nov. 26 **Engr.** ***Perf. 13***
C21 AP5 27fr brt bl, sl grn & red brn 1.90 1.25

French Satellite A-1 Issue
Common Design Type

Designs: 7fr, Diamant rocket and launching installations. 10fr, A-1 satellite.

1966, Jan. 17 Engr. *Perf. 13*

C22 CD121 7fr crim, red & car lake 1.75 1.75
C23 CD121 10fr car lake, red & crim 1.75 1.75
a Strip of 2 + label 4.00 4.00

No. C23a contains one each of Nos. C22-C23 and crimson label with commemorative inscription.

French Satellite D-1 Issue

Common Design Type

1966, June 2 Engr. *Perf. 13*

C24 CD122 10fr lake, bl grn & red 2.00 2.00

WHO Headquarters, Geneva, and Emblem — AP6

1966, July 5 Photo. *Perf. 12½x13*

C25 AP6 30fr org, mar & bl 1.75 1.75

Inauguration of WHO Headquarters, Geneva.

Girl and Boy Reading; UNESCO Emblem — AP7

1966, Nov. 4 Engr. *Perf. 13*

C26 AP7 50fr grn, org & choc 2.25 2.00

20th anniv. of UNESCO.

Athlete and Pattern AP8

Design: 38fr, Woman ballplayer and pattern.

1966, Dec. 8 Engr. *Perf. 13x12½*

C27 AP8 32fr bl, dp car & blk 2.00 1.60
C28 AP8 38fr emer & brt pink 2.25 1.90

Issued to commemorate the Second South Pacific Games, Noumea, Dec. 8-18.

Samuel Wallis' Ship and Coast of Wallis Island — AP9

1967, Dec. 16 Photo. *Perf. 13*

C29 AP9 12fr multi 2.75 2.00

Issued to commemorate the bicentenary of the discovery of Wallis Island.

Concorde Issue

Common Design Type

1969, Apr. 17 Engr. *Perf. 13*

C30 CD129 20fr blk & plum 5.00 4.00

Man Climbing Coconut Palm — AP10

Designs: 32fr, Horseback rider. 38fr, Men making wooden stools. 50fr, Spear fisherman and man holding basket with fish. 100fr, Women sorting coconuts.

1969, Apr. 30 Photo. *Perf. 13*

C31 AP10 20fr multi 90 45
C32 AP10 32fr multi 1.75 90
C33 AP10 38fr multi 1.75 90
C34 AP10 50fr multi 2.75 1.50
C35 AP10 100fr multi 5.25 2.75
Nos. C31-C35 (5) 12.40 6.50

No. C14 Surcharged with New Value and Three Bars

1971 Engr. *Perf. 13*

C36 AP2 21fr on 33fr multi 1.50 1.50

Pole Vault — AP11

Design: 54fr, Archery.

1971, Oct. 25 Engr. *Perf. 13*

C37 AP11 48fr sl grn, vio & red brn 2.25 1.50
C38 AP11 54fr cl, car & ultra 3.00 2.25

4th South Pacific Games, Papeete, French Polynesia, Sept. 8-19.

South Pacific Commission Headquarters, Noumea — AP12

1972, Feb. 5 Photo. *Perf. 13*

C39 AP12 44fr bl & multi 2.50 2.00

South Pacific Commission, 25th anniv.

Round House and Festival Emblem — AP13

1972, May 15 Engr. *Perf. 13*

C40 AP13 60fr dp car, grn & pur 2.75 1.75

South Pacific Festival of Arts, Fiji, May 6-20.

Canoe Type of Regular Issue

Design: 200fr, Outrigger sailing canoe race, and island woman.

1972, Oct. 16 Photo. *Perf. 13x12½*

Size: 47½x28mm.

C41 A9 200fr multi 10.00 7.00

La Pérouse and "La Boussole" — AP14

Explorers and their Ships: 28fr, Samuel Wallis and "Dolphin." 40fr, Dumont D'Urville and "Astrolabe." 72fr, Bougainville and "La Boudeuse."

1973, July 20 Engr. *Perf. 13*

C42 AP14 22fr brn, sl & car 1.00 70
C43 AP14 28fr sl grn, dl red & bl 1.50 1.00
C44 AP14 40fr brn, ind & ultra 2.00 1.25
C45 AP14 72fr brn, bl & pur 3.50 2.75

Charles de Gaulle — AP15

1973, Nov. 9 Engr. *Perf. 13*

C46 AP15 107fr brn org & dk brn 4.00 3.25

Pres. Charles de Gaulle (1890-1970).

Red Jasmine AP16

Designs: Flowers from Wallis.

1973, Dec. 6 Photo. *Perf. 13*

C47 AP16 12fr *shown* 65 45
C48 AP16 17fr *Hibiscus tiliaceus* 70 45
C49 AP16 19fr *Phaeomeria magnifica* 90 65
C50 AP16 21fr *Hibiscus rosa sinensis* 90 65
C51 AP16 23fr *Allamanda cathartica* 1.20 80
C52 AP16 27fr *Barringtonia* 1.20 80
C53 AP16 39fr *Flowers in vase* 2.50 1.90
Nos. C47-C53 (7) 8.05 5.70

UPU Emblem and Symbolic Design — AP17

1974, Oct. 9 Engr. *Perf. 13*

C54 AP17 51fr multi 1.90 1.90

Centenary of Universal Postal Union.

Holy Family, Primitive Painting AP18

1974, Dec. 9 Photo. *Perf. 13*

C55 AP18 150fr multi 5.00 4.00

Christmas 1974.

Tapa Cloth AP19

Designs (Tapa Cloth): 24fr, Village scene. 36fr, Fish and marine life. 80fr, Marine life, map of islands, village scene.

1975, Feb. 3 Photo. *Perf. 13*

C56 AP19 3fr multi 35 25
C57 AP19 24fr multi 1.20 70
C58 AP19 36fr multi 1.50 1.00
C59 AP19 80fr multi 3.50 2.50

DC-7 in Flight AP20

Volleyball AP21

1975, Aug. 13 Engr. *Perf. 13*

C60 AP20 100fr multi 2.75 2.25

First regular air service between Nouméa, New Caledonia, and Wallis.

1975, Nov. 10 Photo. *Perf. 13*

Design (Games' Emblem and): 44fr, Soccer. 56fr, Javelin. 1.05fr, Spear fishing.

C61 AP21 26fr dp org & multi 70 45
C62 AP21 44fr lil & multi 1.00 70
C63 AP21 56fr lt grn & multi 1.50 1.10
C64 AP21 105fr bl & multi 3.25 2.75

5th South Pacific Games, Guam, Aug. 1-10.

Lalolalo Lake, Wallis — AP22

Landscapes: 29fr, Vasavasa, Futuna. 41fr, Sigave Bay, Futuna. 68fr, Gahi Bay, Wallis.

1975, Dec. 1 Litho. *Perf. 13*

C65 AP22 10fr grn & multi 50 45
C66 AP22 29fr grn & multi 1.25 80
C67 AP22 41fr grn & multi 1.60 1.10
C68 AP22 68fr grn & multi 2.50 1.90

Concorde, Eiffel Tower and Sugar Loaf Mountain — AP23

1976, Jan. 21 **Engr.** ***Perf. 13***
C69 AP23 250fr multi 11.00 9.00

1st commercial flight of supersonic jet Concorde from Paris to Rio, Jan. 21.

Hammer Throw and Stadium — AP24

Design: 39fr, Diving, Stadium and maple leaf.

1976, Aug. 2 **Engr.** ***Perf. 13***
C70 AP24 31fr multi 1.00 60
C71 AP24 39fr multi 1.40 90

21st Olympic Games, Montreal, Canada, July 17-Aug. 1.

De Gaulle Memorial — AP25

Photogravure and Embossed

1977, June 18 ***Perf. 13***
C72 AP25 100fr gold & multi 2.75 2.25

5th anniversary of dedication of De Gaulle Memorial at Colombey-les-Deux-Eglises.

No. C69 Overprinted in Dark Brown: "PARIS NEW-YORK / 22.11.77 / 1er VOL COMMERCIAL"

1977, Nov. 22 **Engr.** ***Perf. 13***
C73 AP23 250fr multi 6.25 5.25

Concorde, 1st commercial flight, Paris to NY.

Balistes Niger — AP26

Fish: 35fr, Amphiprion akindynos. 49fr, Pomacanthus imperator. 51fr, Zanclus cornutus.

1978, Jan. 31 **Litho.** ***Perf. 13***
C74 AP26 26fr multi 60 45
C75 AP26 35fr multi 90 65
C76 AP26 49fr multi 1.50 1.20
C77 AP26 51fr multi 1.60 1.40

Map of Futuna and Alofi Islands — AP27

Design: 500fr, Map of Wallis and Uvea Islands (vert.).

1978, Mar. 7 **Engr.**
C78 AP27 300fr vio bl & grnsh bl 10.00 7.00
C79 AP27 500fr multi 14.00 11.00

Father Bataillon, Churches on Wallis and Futuna Islands — AP28

Design: 72fr, Monsignor Pompallier, map of Wallis, Futuna and Alofi Islands, outrigger canoe.

1978, Apr. 28 **Litho.** ***Perf. 13x12½***
C80 AP28 60fr multi 1.10 75
C81 AP28 72fr multi 1.50 1.10

First French missionaries on Wallis and Futuna Islands.

ITU Emblem — AP29

1978, May 17 **Litho.** ***Perf. 13***
C82 AP29 66fr multi 1.25 85

10th World Telecommunications Day.

Nativity and Longhouse — AP30

1978, Dec. 4 **Photo.** ***Perf. 13***
C83 AP30 160fr multi 2.75 2.25

Christmas 1978.

Popes Paul VI and John Paul I, St. Peter's, Rome — AP31

Designs: 37fr, Pope Paul VI (vert.). 41fr, Pope John Paul I (vert.).

Perf. 12½x13, 13x12½

1979, Jan. 31 **Litho.**
C84 AP31 37fr multi 80 60
C85 AP31 41fr multi 1.20 90
C86 AP31 105fr multi 3.50 2.00

In memory of Popes Paul VI and John Paul I.

Monoplane of UTA Airlines AP32

Designs: 68fr, Freighter Muana. 80fr, Hihifo Airport.

1979, Feb. 28 ***Perf. 13x12½***
C87 AP32 46fr multi 90 55
C88 AP32 68fr multi 1.20 90
C89 AP32 80fr multi 1.60 1.10

Inter-Island transportation.
See Nos. 251-253.

France No. 67 and Eole Weather Satellite — AP33

Designs: 70fr, Hibiscus and stamp similar to No. 25 (vert.). 90fr, Rowland Hill and Penny Black. 100fr, Birds, Kano School, Japan 17th century, and Japan No. 9.

1979, May 7 **Photo.** ***Perf. 13***
C90 AP33 5fr multi 22 15
C91 AP33 70fr multi 90 65
C92 AP33 90fr multi 1.25 70
C93 AP33 100fr multi 1.50 1.00

Sir Rowland Hill (1795-1879), originator of penny postage.

Cross of Lorraine and People — AP34

1979, June 18 **Engr.** ***Perf. 13***
C94 AP34 33fr multi 75 55

Map of Islands, Arms of France AP35

1979, July 19 **Photo.** ***Perf. 13***
C95 AP35 47fr multi 1.00 60

Visit of Pres. Valery Giscard d'Estaing of France.

Capt. Cook, Ships and Island — AP36

1979, July 28
C96 AP36 130fr multi 2.25 1.75

Bicentenary of the death of Capt. James Cook (1728-1779).

Telecom Emblem, Satellite, Receiving Station — AP37

1979, Sept. 20 **Litho.** ***Perf. 13***
C97 AP37 120fr multi 1.90 1.50

3rd World Telecommunications Exhibition, Geneva, Sept. 20-26.

Virgin and Child, by Albrecht Durer AP38

1979, Dec. 17 **Engr.** ***Perf. 13***
C98 AP38 180fr red & blk 4.25 3.50

Christmas 1979.

Rotary International, 75th Anniversary — AP39

1980, Feb. 29 **Litho.** ***Perf. 13***
C99 AP39 86fr multi 2.00 1.60

Rochambeau and Troops, U.S. Flag, 1780 — AP40

1980, May 27 **Engr.** ***Perf. 13***
C100 AP40 102fr multi 2.25 1.60

Rochambeau's landing at Newport, R.I. (American Revolution), bicentenary.

National Day, 10th Anniversary — AP41

1980, July 15 Litho. *Perf. 13*
C101 AP41 71fr multi 90 65

Transatlantic Airmail Flight, 50th Anniversary — AP42

1980, Sept. 22 Engr. *Perf. 13*
C102 AP42 122fr multi 2.25 1.60

Fleming, Penicillin Bacilli — AP43

1980, Oct. 20
C103 AP43 101fr multi 1.25 90

Alexander Fleming (1881-1955), discoverer of penicillin, 25th death anniversary.

Charles De Gaulle, 10th Anniversary of Death — AP44

1980, Nov. 9 Engr. *Perf. 13*
C104 AP44 200fr sep & dk ol grn 3.50 2.50

Virgin and Child with St. Catherine, by Lorenzo Lotto — AP45

1980, Dec. 20 Litho. *Perf. 13x12½*
C105 AP45 150fr multi 2.50 2.00

Christmas 1980.

The Scott Catalogue value is a retail price, what you could expect to pay for the stamp in a grade of Fine-Very Fine. The value listed is a reference which reflects recent actual dealer selling price.

Alan B. Shepard and Spacecraft — AP46

20th Anniversary of Space Flight: 44fr, Yuri Gagarin.

1981, May 11 Litho. *Perf. 13*
C106 AP46 37fr multi 45 40
C107 AP46 44fr multi 50 45

Vase of Flowers, by Paul Cezanne (1839-1906) AP47

Design: 135fr, Harlequin, by Pablo Picasso.

1981, Oct. 22 Litho. *Perf. 12½x13*
C108 AP47 53fr multi 80 70
C109 AP47 135fr multi 2.50 1.50

Espana '82 World Cup Soccer — AP48

1981, Nov. 16 Engr. *Perf. 13*
C110 AP48 120fr blk, brn & grn 1.25 95

1982
C110A AP48 120fr lil, brn & ol grn 1.60 1.50

Christmas 1981 — AP49

1981, Dec. 21 Litho. *Perf. 12½*
C111 AP49 180fr multi 2.25 1.75

Tapestry, by Pilioho Aloi — AP50

1982, Feb. 22 Litho. *Perf. 12½x13*
C112 AP50 100fr multi 1.50 1.25

Boats at Collioure, by George Braque (1882-1963) AP51

1982, Apr. 13 Litho. *Perf. 12½x13*
C113 AP51 300fr multi 4.50 3.50

Santos-Dumont (1873-1932), Aviation Pioneer — AP52

1982, July 24
C114 AP52 95fr multi 1.50 1.20

No. C110 Overprinted with Winner's Name in Blue

1982, Aug. 26 Engr. *Perf. 13*
C115 AP48 120fr multi 1.25 1.10

Italy's victory in 1982 World Cup.

French Overseas Possessions Week, Sept. 18-25 — AP53

1982, Sept. 17 Litho.
C116 AP53 105fr Beach 1.10 90

Day of the Blind — AP54

1982, Oct. 18 Engr.
C117 AP54 130fr red & bl 1.25 1.10

Christmas 1982 AP55

Design: Adoration of the Virgin, by Correggio.

1982, Dec. 20 Litho. *Perf. 12½x13*
C118 AP55 170fr multi 2.25 1.60

Wind Surfing (1984 Olympic Event) — AP56

1983, Mar. 4 Litho. *Perf. 13*
C119 AP56 270fr multi 3.50 3.00

World UPU Day — AP57

1983, Mar. 30 Litho. *Perf. 13*
C120 AP57 100fr multi 1.50 1.20

Manned Flight Bicentenary AP58

1983, Apr. 25 Litho. *Perf. 13*
C121 AP58 205fr Montgolfiere 3.00 2.25

Cat, 1926, by Foujita (d. 1968) AP59

1983, May 20 Litho. *Perf. 12½x13*
C122 AP59 102fr multi 1.50 1.10

Pre-Olympic Year — AP60

1983, July 5 Engr. *Perf. 13*
C123 AP60 250fr Javelin 2.25 1.90

Alfred Nobel (1833-1896) — AP61

1983, Aug. 1 **Engr.** ***Perf. 13***
C124 AP61 150fr multi 1.40 1.10

Nicephore Niepce (1765-1833), Photography Pioneer — AP62

1983, Sept. 20 **Engr.** ***Perf. 13***
C125 AP62 75fr dk grn & rose vio 1.00 70

Raphael (1483-1520), 500th Birth Anniv. AP63

1983, Nov. 10 **Litho.** ***Perf. 12½x13***
C126 AP63 167fr The Triumph of Galatea 2.00 1.60

Pandanus AP64

1983, Nov. 30 **Litho.** ***Perf. 13***
C127 AP64 137fr multi 1.25 90

Christmas 1983 AP65

1983, Dec. 22 **Litho.** ***Perf. 12½x13***
C128 AP65 200fr Sistine Madonna, by Raphael 2.50 2.00

Steamer Commandant Bory — AP66

1984, Jan. 9 ***Perf. 13***
C129 AP66 67fr multi 90 65

1984 Summer Olympics — AP67

1984, Feb. 3 **Litho.** ***Perf. 13***
C130 AP67 85fr Weight lifting 1.20 90

Frangipani Blossoms AP68

1984, Feb. 28 ***Perf. 12½***
C131 AP68 130fr multi 1.10 75

Easter 1984 — AP69

1984, Apr. 17 **Litho.** ***Perf. 12½x13***
C132 AP69 190fr Descent from the Cross 2.50 1.90

Homage to Jean Cocteau AP70

1984, June 30 **Litho.** ***Perf. 13***
C133 AP70 150fr Portrait 1.90 1.60

Soano Hoatau Tiki Sculpture AP71

Portrait of Alice, by Modigliani (1884-1920) AP72

1984, July 26
C134 AP71 175fr multi 2.00 1.60

1984, Aug. 20
C135 AP72 140fr multi 1.60 1.50

Ausipex '84 — AP73

1984, Sept. 21 **Litho.** ***Perf. 12½x13***
C136 AP73 180fr Pilioko Tapestry 2.25 1.90

Se-tenant with label showing exhibition emblem.

Local Dances, by Jean Michon — AP74

1984, Oct. 11 **Photo.** ***Perf. 13***
C137 AP74 110fr multi 1.50 1.10

Altar AP75

1984, Nov. 5 **Litho.** ***Perf. 13x12½***
C138 AP75 52fr Mount Lulu Chapel 60 50

Christmas 1984 — AP76

1984, Dec. 21 **Litho.** ***Perf. 13x12½***
C139 AP76 260fr Tropical Nativity 3.00 2.00

Pilioko Tapestry — AP77

1985, Apr. 3 **Litho.** ***Perf. 13x12½***
C140 AP77 500fr multi 5.50 4.00

Footnotes often refer you to other stamps of the same design.

The Post in 1926, by Utrillo AP78

1985, June 17 **Litho.** ***Perf. 12½x13***
C141 AP78 200fr multi 1.50 70

Wallis Island Pirogue — AP79

1985, Aug. 9 ***Perf. 13***
C142 AP79 350fr multi 2.50 1.40

Ship Jacques Cartier — AP80

1985, Oct. 2 **Engr.** ***Perf. 13x13½***
C143 AP80 51fr Prus bl, brt bl & dk bl 45 22

Portrait of a Young Woman, by Patrice Nielly AP81

1985, Oct. 28 **Litho.** ***Perf. 12½x13***
C144 AP81 245fr multi 2.25 1.20

Nativity, by Jean Michon AP82

1985, Dec. 19 **Litho.** ***Perf. 12½x13***
C145 AP82 330fr multi 2.50 1.20

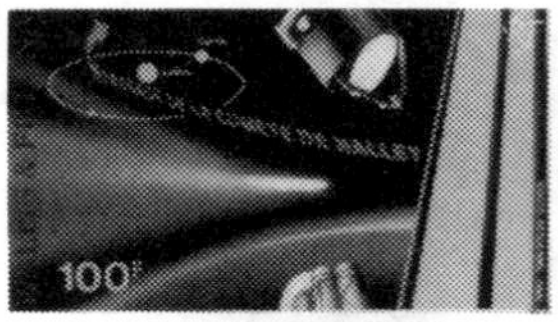
Halley's Comet — AP83

1986, Mar. 6 **Litho.** ***Perf. 13***
C146 AP83 100fr multi 1.40 70

Cure of Ars, Birth Bicent. — AP84

1986, Mar. 28 **Litho.** ***Perf. 12½x13***
C147 AP84 200fr multi 2.75 1.40

French Overseas Territory Status, 25th Anniv. — AP85

1986, July 29 **Engr.** ***Perf. 13***
C148 AP85 90fr Queen Amelia 1.35 68
C149 AP85 137fr July 30 Law, Journal of the Republic 2.05 1.05

Queen Amelia's request to France for protection, cent. Nos. C148-C149 printed se-tenant with inscribed center label.

World Post Day — AP86

1986, Oct. 9 **Litho.** ***Perf. 13***
C150 AP86 270fr multi 4.00 2.00

Statue of Liberty, Cent. — AP87

Poi Basilica, 1st Anniv. — AP88

1986, Oct. 31 **Engr.**
C151 AP87 205fr multi 3.00 1.50

1987, Apr. 30 **Litho.** ***Perf. 13***
C152 AP88 230fr Fr. Chanel, basilica 3.50 1.75

Telstar Transmitting to Pleumeur-Bodou, France — AP89

1987, May 17 **Engr.** ***Perf. 13***
C153 AP89 200fr 3.00 1.50

World Communications Day, 25th anniv. of Telstar.

Piccard, Bathyscaphe Trieste and Stratospheric Balloon — AP90

1987, Aug. 21 **Engr.** ***Perf. 13***
C154 AP90 135fr brt ol grn, dk bl & brt bl 2.75 1.40

Auguste Piccard (1884-1962), physicist.

Arrival of First Missionary, 150th Anniv. — AP91

Design: 260fr, Monsignor Bataillon's arrival in 1837, ship and the islands.

1987, Nov. 8 **Engr.** ***Perf. 13***
C155 AP91 260fr brt blue, blk & blue grn 5.50 2.25

Christmas 1987 — AP92

1987, Dec. 15 **Litho.** ***Perf. 13x12½***
C156 AP92 300fr multi 6.00 3.00

Garros and Bleriot Aircraft — AP93

1988, Feb. 18 **Engr.** ***Perf. 13***
C157 AP93 600fr dark blue, dark red brn & brt blue 12.50 6.25

Roland Garros (1888-1918), aviator and tennis player.

Self-portrait with Lace Cravat, by Maurice Quentin de La Tour (1704-88) AP94

1988, Apr. 8 **Litho.**
C158 AP94 500fr multi 10.00 5.00

World Telecommunications Day — AP95

1988, May 5 **Litho.** ***Perf. 12½x13***
C159 AP95 100fr multi 2.00 1.00

South Pacific Episcopal Conference — AP96

1988, June 1 **Litho.** ***Perf. 13***
C160 AP96 90fr Map, bishop 1.65 82

AIR POST SEMI-POSTAL STAMPS

Stamps of New Caledonia type V5 overprinted "Wallis et Futuna" and type of Cameroun V10 inscribed "Wallis et Futuna" were issued in 1942 by the Vichy Government, but were not placed on sale in the dependency.

POSTAGE DUE STAMPS

Postage Due Stamps of New Caledonia, 1906, Overprinted in Black or Red

ILES WALLIS et FUTUNA

1920 **Unwmk.** ***Perf. 13½x14***

J1	D2 5c ultra, *az*	30	30
J2	D2 10c brn, *buff*	30	30
J3	D2 15c grn, *grnsh*	30	30
J4	D2 20c blk, *yel* (R)	38	38
a.	Double ovpt.	35.00	
J5	D2 30c car rose	38	38
J6	D2 50c ultra, *straw*	60	60
J7	D2 60c olive, *az*	80	80
a.	Double ovpt.	35.00	
J8	D2 1fr grn, *cr*	1.20	1.20
	Nos. J1-J8 (8)	4.26	4.26

Type of 1920 Issue Surcharged **2f**

1927

J9	D2 2fr on 1fr brt vio	4.50	4.50
J10	D2 3fr on 1fr org brn	4.50	4.50

Postage Due Stamps of New Caledonia, 1928, Overprinted as in 1920

1930

J11	D3 2c sl bl & dp brn	5	5
J12	D3 4c brn red & bl grn	5	5
J13	D3 5c red org & bl blk	5	5
J14	D3 10c mag & Prus bl	5	5
J15	D3 15c dl grn & scar	5	5
J16	D3 20c mar & ol grn	16	16
J17	D3 25c bis brn & sl bl	12	12
J18	D3 30c bl grn & ol grn	30	30
J19	D3 50c lt brn & dk red	12	12
J20	D3 60c mag & brt rose	45	45
J21	D3 1fr dl bl & Prus grn	25	25
J22	D3 2fr dk red & ol grn	32	32
J23	D3 3fr vio & brn	38	38
	Nos. J11-J23 (13)	2.35	2.35

Postage Due Stamps of 1930 with Additional Overprint in Black

FRANCE LIBRE

1943

J24	D3 2c sl bl & dp brn	11.00	11.00
J25	D3 4c brn red & bl grn	11.00	11.00
J26	D3 5c red org & bl blk	11.00	11.00
J27	D3 10c mag & Prus bl	13.00	13.00
J28	D3 15c dl grn & scar	13.00	13.00
J29	D3 20c mar & ol grn	13.00	13.00
J30	D3 25c bis brn & sl bl	13.00	13.00
J31	D3 30c bl grn & ol grn	13.00	13.00
J32	D3 50c lt brn & dk red	13.00	13.00
J33	D3 60c mag & brt rose	13.00	13.00
J34	D3 1fr dl bl & Prus grn	15.00	15.00
J35	D3 2fr dk red & ol grn	15.00	15.00
J36	D3 3fr vio & brn	15.00	15.00
	Nos. J24-J36 (13)	169.00	169.00

Catalogue values for unused stamps in this section, from this point to the end of the section, are for Never Hinged items.

Thalassoma Lunare D1

Fish: 1fr, Zanclus cornutus (vert.). 5fr, Amphiprion percula.

Perf. 13x13½
1963, Apr. 1 **Typo.** **Unwmk.**

J37	D1 1fr yel org, bl & blk	40	40
J38	D1 3fr red, grnsh bl & grn	60	60
J39	D1 5fr org, bluish grn & blk	1.00	1.00

WESTERN UKRAINE

LOCATION — In Eastern Central Europe.
GOVT. — A former short-lived independent State.

A provisional government was established in 1918 in the eastern part of Austria-Hungary but the area later came under Polish administration.

100 Shagiv (Sotykiv) = 1 Grivna
100 Heller = 1 Krone

Forgeries of almost all Western Ukraine stamps are plentiful.

Used values are for stamps canceled to order.

Kolomyya Issue

Укр. Н.Р.

Austrian Stamps of 1916-17 Surcharged

10

1918 **Unwmk.** ***Perf. 12½***

1	A42 5sh on 15h dl red	22.50	25.00
2	A37 10sh on 3h vio	22.50	25.00
3	A37 10sh on 6h dp org	*850.00*	*600.00*
4	A37 10sh on 12h lt bl	*850.00*	*600.00*

Nos. 1-4 exist with surcharge inverted or double.

Austrian stamps of 1916-17 overprinted as illustrated were briefly used, some authorities believe. Forgeries exist.

Stanislav Issue

Пошта
Укр.Н.Реп.

Austrian Stamps of 1916-18 Surcharged in Shagiv and Grivna Currency

warib

1919

11	A37	3sh brt vio	10.00	10.00
12	A37	5sh lt grn	10.00	10.00
13	A37	6sh dp org	20.00	20.00
14	A37	10sh magenta	20.00	20.00
15	A37	12sh lt bl	20.00	20.00
16	A42	15sh dl red	20.00	20.00
17	A42	20sh dp grn	20.00	20.00
18	A42	30sh dl vio	100.00	100.00
19	A39	40sh ol grn	20.00	20.00
20	A39	50sh dk grn	20.00	20.00
21	A39	60sh dp bl	20.00	20.00
22	A39	80sh org brn	20.00	20.00
23	A39	1gr car, *yel*	30.00	30.00
24	A40	2gr lt bl	22.50	22.50
25	A40	3gr car rose	40.00	40.00
a.		3gr claret	2,500.	2,000.
26	A40	4gr yel grn	30.00	30.00
a.		4gr deep green	200.00	200.00
27	A40	10gr dp vio	475.00	750.00

The overprint exists inverted on 12sh and 80sh, double on 12sh and 10gr.

The 25sh, type A42, with this overprint is considered bogus.

Granite Paper

28	A40	3gr car rose	30.00	30.00

Same Surcharged on Austrian Military Semipostal Stamps of 1918

Perf. 12½x13

31	MSP7	10sh gray grn	70.00	70.00
32	MSP8	20sh magenta	55.00	55.00
33	MSP7	45sh blue	40.00	40.00

The overprint exists inverted on Nos. 31-33, double on No. 32.

Same Surcharge on Austrian Military Stamps of 1917

Perf. 12½

34	M3	1sh grnsh bl	*650.00*	*650.00*
35	M3	2sh red org	65.00	65.00
36	M3	3sh ol gray	140.00	140.00
37	M3	5sh ol grn	225.00	225.00
38	M3	6sh violet	115.00	115.00
39	M3	10sh org brn	*750.00*	*650.00*
40	M3	12sh blue	450.00	450.00
41	M3	15sh brt rose	450.00	450.00
42	M3	20sh red brn	10.50	11.50
43	M3	25sh ultra	*2,750.*	*3,250.*
44	M3	30sh slate	*775.00*	*900.00*
45	M3	40sh ol bis	*650.00*	*650.00*
46	M3	50sh dp grn	6.50	6.50
47	M3	60sh car rose	600.00	600.00
48	M3	80sh dl bl	40.00	40.00
49	M3	90sh dk vio	*800.00*	*650.00*
50	M4	2gr rose, *straw*	13.00	18.00
51	M4	3gr bl, *grn*	20.00	22.50
52	M4	4gr rose, *grn*	20.00	22.50
53	M4	10gr dl vio, *gray*		

The overprint exists double on 2sh, 3sh and 20sh, inverted on 12sh, 50sh and 4gr.

Same Surcharge on Austrian Postage Due Stamps of 1916

54	D5	1gr ultra	65.00	80.00
55	D5	5gr ultra	*1,000.*	*1,500.*

Surcharged on Austrian Postage Due Stamps of 1917 with two bars over "PORTO"

57	A38	15sh on 36h vio	275.00	275.00
58	A38	50sh on 42h choc	*5,000.*	*5,000.*

Same Surcharge on Postage Due Stamps of Bosnia, 1904

61	D1	1sh blk, red & yel	20.00	20.00
62	D1	2sh blk, red & yel	6.50	11.00
63	D1	3sh blk, red & yel	6.50	11.00
64	D1	4sh blk, red & yel	65.00	65.00
65	D1	5sh blk, red & yel	*2,750.*	*3,000.*
66	D1	6sh blk, red & yel	140.00	140.00
67	D1	7sh blk, red & yel	11.50	14.00
68	D1	8sh blk, red & yel	14.00	18.00
69	D1	10sh blk, red & yel	*850.00*	*1,100.*
70	D1	15sh blk, red & yel	*325.00*	*325.00*
71	D1	20sh blk, red & yel	*5,000.*	*5,000.*
72	D1	50sh blk, red & yel	*140.00*	*140.00*

Two types of surcharge on No. 61: Shagiv in singular (wara) and in plural (warib). Value the same.

The overprint exists inverted on Nos. 61, 64, 66-68.

A2

Black Surcharge on Austrian Military Stamps of 1917-18.

1919

75	A2	2gr on 2k rose, *straw*	7.00	9.00
76	A2	3gr on 2k rose, *straw*	7.00	10.00
77	A2	3gr on 3k grn, *bl*	70.00	140.00
78	A2	4gr on 2k rose, *straw*	7.00	10.00
79	A2	4gr on 4k rose, *grn*	*1,000.*	*1,500.*
80	A2	5gr on 2k rose, *straw*	7.00	10.00
a.		Inverted surch.	250.00	
81	A2	10gr on 50h dp grn (Austria type M3)	10.00	*27.50*

Austrian Stamps of 1916-18 Overprinted

З. У.

Н. Р.

1919, May

85	A37	3h brt vio	50	*1.25*
86	A37	5h lt grn	50	*1.25*
87	A37	6h dp org	50	*1.25*
88	A37	10h magenta	50	*1.25*
89	A37	12h lt bl	50	*1.25*
90	A42	15h dl red	50	*1.25*
91	A42	20h dp grn	50	*1.25*
92	A42	25h blue	50	*1.25*
93	A42	30h dl vio	50	*1.25*
94	A39	40h ol grn	65	*1.50*
95	A39	50h dk grn	65	*1.50*
96	A39	60h dp bl	65	*1.50*
97	A39	80h org brn	75	*1.75*
98	A39	90h red vio	75	*2.00*
99	A39	1k car, *yel*	1.00	*5.00*
100	A40	2k lt bl	1.75	*7.50*
101	A40	3k car rose	2.25	*7.50*
102	A40	4k yel grn	9.00	*12.00*
103	A40	10k dp vio	11.00	*50.00*
		Nos. 85-103 (19)	32.95	

The four letters in the overprint are the initials of Ukrainian words equivalent to "Western Ukrainian National (or Peoples) Republic." The country was formed from the eastern part of Galicia, formerly a province of the Austro-Hungarian Empire.

Forged cancellations abound.

REGISTRATION STAMPS

Kolomyya Issue

Укр. Н. Р.
П
Ч.
50 сот.

RS1

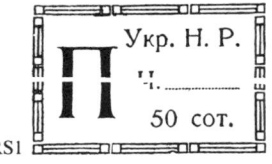

1919	**Unwmk.**	**Typeset**	***Imperf.***	
F1	RS1	30sot blk, *rose*	100.00	48.00
F2	RS1	50sot blk, *dp rose*	22.50	27.50

OCCUPATION STAMPS

Romanian Occupation of Pokutia

Austrian Stamps Surcharged in Dark Blue Black

C.M.T.
60 h.

1919		**Unwmk.**	***Perf. 12½***

On Stamps of 1916-18

N3	A37	40h on 5h lt grn
N10	A39	1k 20h on 50h dk grn
N11	A39	1k 20h on 60h dp bl
N14	A39	1k 20h on 1k car, *yel*

On Stamps of 1917-18

N15	A42	60h on 15h dl red
N16	A42	60h on 20h dp grn
N17	A42	60h on 25h blue
N18	A42	60h on 30h dl vio

Surcharge in colors other than dark blue black are bogus or proofs.

POSTAGE DUE STAMPS

Austrian Postage Due Stamps Surcharged like Regular Issues

1919		**Unwmk.**	***Perf. 12½***

On Stamps of 1916

NJ1	D4	40h on 5h rose red
NJ5	D4	1k 20h on 25h rose red
NJ6	D4	1k 20h on 30h rose red

On Stamp of 1917

NJ13	A38	1k 20h on 50h on 42h choc

WEST IRIAN

(Irian Barat)

(West New Guinea)

LOCATION — Western half of New Guinea, southwest Pacific Ocean.

GOVT. — Province of Indonesia

AREA — 162,927 sq. mi.

POP. — 923,440 (1973)

CAPITAL — Djajapura (formerly Hollandia)

The former Netherlands New Guinea became a territory under the administration of the United Nations Temporary Executive Authority on Oct. 1, 1962.

The territory came under Indonesian administration on May 1, 1963.

100 Cents = 1 Gulden
100 Sen = 1 Rupiah
(1 rupiah = 1 former Netherlands New Guinea gulden)

Catalogue values for all unused stamps in this country are for Never Hinged items.

Issued Under United Nations Temporary Executive Authority

Netherlands New Guinea Stamps of 1950-60 Overprinted **UNTEA**

Perf. 12½x12, 12½x13½

1962		**Photo.**	**Unwmk.**	
1	A4	1c ver & yel	70	70
2	A1	2c dp org	85	85
3	A4	5c choc & yel	80	80
4	A5	7c org red, bl & brn vio	85	85
5	A4	10c aqua & red brn	80	80
6	A5	12c grn, bl & brn vio	85	85
7	A4	15c dp yel & red brn	1.10	1.10
8	A5	17c brn vio & bl	1.10	1.10
9	A4	20c lt bl grn & red brn	1.10	1.10
10	A6	25c red	70	70
11	A6	30c dp bl	85	85
12	A6	40c dp org	1.25	1.25
13	A6	45c dk ol	3.25	3.25
14	A6	55c sl bl	2.75	2.75
15	A6	80c dl gray vio	15.00	15.00
16	A6	85c dk vio brn	5.50	5.50
17	A6	1g plum	4.75	4.75

Engr.

18	A3	2g redsh brn	15.00	15.00
19	A3	5g green	17.00	17.00
		Nos. 1-19 (19)	74.20	74.20

The overprint exists in four types: (1.) Size 17½mm. Applied locally and sold in West New Guinea. Top of "N" is slightly lower than the "U," and the base of the "T" is straight, or nearly so. (2.) Size 17½mm. Applied in the Netherlands and sold by the UN in New York. Top of the "N" is slightly higher than the "U," and the base of the "T" is concave. (3.) Size 14mm. Exists on eight values. (4.) Size 19mm. Exists on 1c and 10c.

Types 3 and 4 were applied in West New Guinea and it is doubtful whether they were regularly issued.

West Irian

Indonesia Nos. 454, 456, 494-501, 387, 390, 392 and 393 Surcharged or Overprinted: "IRIAN BARAT"

Perf. 12½x13½

1963, May 1		**Photo.**	**Unwmk.**	
20	A63	1s on 70s org ver	5	5
21	A63	2s on 90s yel grn	5	5

Perf. 12x12½

22	A76	5s gray	6	6
23	A76	6s on 20s ocher	6	6
24	A76	7s on 50s dp bl	7	7
25	A76	10s red brn	8	8
26	A76	15s plum	10	10
27	A76	25s brt bl grn	15	15
28	A76	30s on 75s scar	20	20
29	A76	40s on 1.15r plum	22	22

Perf. 12½x12

30	A55	1r purple	60	60
31	A55	2r green	1.10	1.10
32	A55	3r dk bl	1.25	1.25
33	A55	5r brown	2.25	2.25
		Nos. 20-33 (14)	6.24	6.24

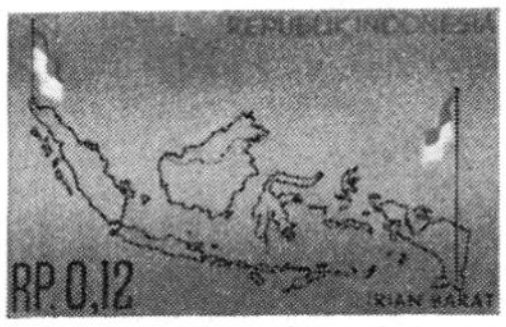

"Indonesia's Flag from Sabang to Merauke" — A1

Designs: 20s, 50s, Parachutist landing in New Guinea. 60s, 75s, Bird of paradise and map of New Guinea.

1963, May 1

34	A1	12s org brn, blk & red	10	10
35	A1	17s org brn, blk & red	12	12
36	A1	20s multi	15	15
37	A1	50s multi	30	30
38	A1	60s multi	42	42
39	A1	75s multi	55	55
		Nos. 34-39 (6)	1.64	1.64

Liberation of West New Guinea.

Maniltoa Gemmipara — A2

Designs: 15s, Dendrobium lancifolium (orchid). 30s, Gardenia gjellerupii. 40s, Maniltoa flower. 50s, Phalanger. 75s, Cassowary. 1e, Kangaroo. 3r, Crowned pigeons.

1968, Aug. 17		**Photo.**	***Perf. 12½x12***	
40	A2	5s dl grn & vio blk	15	15
41	A2	15s emer & dk pur	25	25
42	A2	30s org & dp grn	45	45
43	A2	40s lem & brt pur	45	45
44	A2	50s rose car & blk	45	45
45	A2	75s dl bl & blk	60	60
46	A2	1r brn org & blk	1.25	1.25
47	A2	3r ap grn & blk	2.00	2.00
		Nos. 40-47 (8)	5.60	5.60

Man, Map of Indonesia and Torches — A3

1968, Aug. 17

48	A3	10s ultra & gold	22	22
49	A3	25s crim & gold	45	45

Issued to publicize the pledge of the people of West Irian to remain unified and integrated with the Republic of Indonesia.

Carving, Mother and Child — A4

Black-capped Lory — A5

West Irian Wood Carvings: 6s, Shield with 3 human figures. 7s, Child atop filigree carving. 10s, Drum. 25s, Seated man. 30s, Drum (3-tiered base). 50s, Carved bamboo. 75s, Man-shaped ornament. 1r, Shield. 2r, Seated man (hands raised).

1970 Photo. *Perf. 12½x12*

50	A4	5s multi	5	5
51	A4	6s multi	5	5
52	A4	7s multi	5	5
53	A4	10s multi	5	5
54	A4	25s multi	7	7
55	A4	30s multi	8	8
56	A4	50s multi	12	12
57	A4	75s multi	20	20
58	A4	1r multi	42	42
59	A4	2r multi	70	70
		Nos. 50-59 (10)	1.79	1.79

Issue dates: Nos. 50-54, Apr. 30; Nos. 55-59, Apr. 15.

1970, Oct. 26 Photo. *Perf. 12x12½*

Design: 10r, Bird of paradise.

60	A5	5r rose red & multi	70	70
61	A5	10r bl & multi	1.40	1.40

POSTAGE DUE STAMPS

Type of Indonesia Overprinted: "IRIAN BARAT"

Perf. 13½x12½

1963, May 1 Litho. Unwmk.

J1	D8	1s lt brn	7	8
J2	D8	5s lt gray ol	6	10
J3	D8	10s lt bl	13	10
J4	D8	25s gray	15	10
J5	D8	40s salmon	30	30
J6	D8	100s bister	70	75
		Nos. J1-J6 (6)	1.41	1.43

Type of Indonesia Dated "1968" and Overprinted: "IRIAN BARAT"

1968 Photo. *Perf. 13½x12½*

J7	D9	1s bl & lt grn	5	5
J8	D9	5s grn & pink	6	6
J9	D9	10s red & gray	12	12
J10	D9	25s grn & yel	15	15
J11	D9	40s vio brn & pale grn	30	30
J12	D9	100s org & bis	75	75
		Nos. J7-J12 (6)	1.43	1.43

Values quoted in this catalogue are for stamps graded at Fine-Very Fine and with no faults. An illustrated guide to grade is provided in introductory material, beginning on Page V.

WHITE RUSSIA

Stamps of this design were not put in use and were probably propaganda labels.

YEMEN

LOCATION — Arabian Peninsula, south of Saudi Arabia and bordering on the Red Sea.
GOVT. — Republic
AREA — 73,300 sq. mi.
CAPITAL — San'a

40 Bogaches = 1 Imadi
40 Bogaches = 1 Riyal (1962)
100 Fils = 1 Riyal (1978)

Catalogue values for unused stamps in this country are for Never Hinged items, beginning with Scott 44 in the regular postage section, Scott C1 in the airpost section.

For Domestic Postage.

Crossed Daggers and Arabic Inscriptions
A1 A2

1926 Unwmk. Typo. *Imperf.*
Laid Paper
Without Gum

1	A1	2½b blk, *white*	16.00	15.00
2	A1	2½b blk, *org*	16.00	15.00
a.		Wove paper		
3	A2	5b blk, *white*	19.00	15.00

No. 2 is known rouletted 7½ or 9.
Type A1 differs from A2 primarily in the inscription in the left dagger blade.

For Foreign and Domestic Postage

Arabic Inscriptions
A3 A4

Wmk. 127- Quatrefoils

1930-31 Wmk. 127 *Perf. 14*

7	A3	½b org ('31)	10	10
8	A3	1b green	30	25
9	A3	1b yel grn ('31)	12	8
10	A3	2b ol grn	35	30
11	A3	2b ol brn ('31)	20	15
12	A3	3b dl vio ('31)	30	10
13	A3	4b red	60	45
14	A3	4b dp rose ('31)	50	15
15	A3	5b sl gray ('31)	75	50
16	A4	6b dl bl	1.25	75
17	A4	6b dp ultra ('31)	70	45
18	A4	8b lil rose ('31)	1.00	60
19	A4	10b lt brn	1.75	1.00
20	A4	10b brn org ('31)	1.25	1.00
21	A4	20b yel grn ('31)	3.50	2.25
22	A4	1i red brn & lt bl	8.75	6.50
23	A4	1i lil rose & yel grn ('31)	8.75	6.00
		Nos. 7-23 (17)	30.17	20.63

Some values exist imperforate.

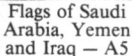

Flags of Saudi Arabia, Yemen and Iraq — A5

Wmk. 258- Arabic Characters and Y G Multiple

1939 Litho. Wmk. 258 *Perf. 12½*

24	A5	4b dl rose & ultra	30	30
25	A5	6b sl bl & ultra	40	40
26	A5	10b fawn & ultra	70	70
27	A5	14b ol & ultra	1.00	1.00
28	A5	20b yel grn & ultra	1.75	1.75
29	A5	1i cl & ultra	3.50	3.50
		Nos. 24-29 (6)	7.65	7.65

2nd anniv. of the Arab Alliance. Nos. 24-29 exist imperforate.

No. 7 Handstamped in Black

a-b-c

Three types of surcharge:
a. 11½x16mm
b. 13-13½x15½mm
c. 12x16mm
Values of surcharged stamps are for ordinary copies. Clear, legible surcharges command a premium.

1939 Wmk. 127 *Perf. 14*

30	A3	4b on ½b org	5.00	2.00

See Nos. 44-48, 59-67, 82, 86-87.

A6

A7

1940 Wmk. 258 Litho. *Perf. 12½.*

31	A6	½b ocher & ultra	8	8
32	A6	1b lt grn & rose red	12	12
33	A6	2b bis brn & vio	12	12
34	A6	3b dl vio & ultra	12	12
35	A6	4b rose & yel grn	20	20
36	A6	5b dk gray grn & bis brn	25	25
37	A7	6b ultra & yel org	20	20
38	A7	8b cl & dl bl	38	38
39	A7	10b brn org & yel grn	35	32
40	A7	14b gray grn & vio	42	32
41	A7	18b emer & blk	75	75
42	A7	20b yel ol & cer	1.10	1.00
43	A7	1i vio rose, yel grn & brn red	2.50	1.60
		Nos. 31-43 (13)	6.59	5.46

No. 36 was used as a 4b stamp in 1957.

Catalogue values for unused stamps in this section, from this point to the end of the section, are for Never Hinged items.

Nos. 31-34, 36 Handstamped Type "a" in Black

1945-51 *Perf. 12½.*

44	A6	4b on ½b	3.50	2.00
a.		Handstamp type "b" ('51)	1.60	1.00
45	A6	4b on 1b ('48)	4.00	2.25
a.		Handstamp type "b" ('49)	1.50	80
46	A6	4b on 2b ('48)	3.00	2.00
a.		Handstamp type "b" ('49)	1.20	65
47	A6	4b on 3b ('48)	3.50	2.25
a.		Handstamp type "b" ('49)	1.40	80
48	A6	4b on 5b ('46)	3.50	2.25

Forged surcharges exist.

A8

1946

Frames in Emerald

49	A8	4b black	1.00	1.00
50	A8	6b lil rose	1.40	90
51	A8	10b ultra	1.60	1.60
52	A8	14b ol grn	3.00	1.60

Opening of Mutawakkili Hospital. Exist imperforate.

Mocha Coffee Tree — A9

Palace, San'a — A10

1947-58 Unwmk. Engr. *Perf. 12½.*

53	A9	½b yel brn	10	5
54	A9	1b purple	38	16
55	A9	2b ultra	65	38
56	A10	4b red	60	30
57	A10	5b gray bl	38	25
58	A9	6b yel grn ('58)	1.00	65
		Nos. 53-58 (6)	3.11	1.79

No. 58 was printed in 1947 but not officially issued until June, 1958.

Additional values, prepared but not issued, were 10b, 20b and 1i, with views of palaces superimposed on flag, and palace square. These were looted from government storehouses during the 1948 revolution and a number of copies later reached collectors.

Nos. 9, 11, 12 and 15 Handstamped Type "a" in Black

1949 Wmk. 127 *Perf. 14.*

59	A3	4b on 1b yel grn	1.60	1.20
60	A3	4b on 2b ol brn	15.00	7.50
61	A3	4b on 3b dl vio	2.50	1.50
62	A3	4b on 5b sl gray	2.50	1.50

Handstamped type "b" are bogus.

Nos. 53-55 Handstamped Type "b" and "a"

1949 Unwmk. *Perf. 12½.*

63	A9(b)	4b on ½b yel brn	2.00	2.00
64	A9(a)	4b on 1b pur	2.00	2.00
a.		Handstamp type "b"	2.00	2.00
65	A9(a)	4b on 2b ultra	4.00	3.75
a.		Handstamp type "b"	4.00	3.50
b.		Handstamp 13x15mm		

Nos. J1-J2 Handstamped Type "b" in Black

1953 Wmk. 258

66	D1	4b on 1b org & yel grn	6.00	5.00
67	D1	4b on 2b org & yel grn	6.00	5.00
a.		Handstamp type "c"		

Three minor types of this handstamped 4b surcharge exist. Types "a" and "b" exist inverted, double or horizontal.

Forged surcharges exist.

Parade Ground, San'a — A13

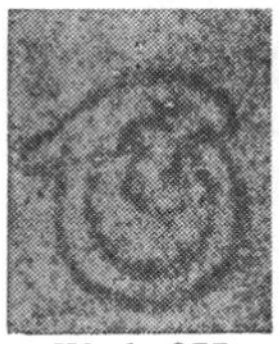

Wmk. 277

Mosque, San'a — A14

Designs: 5b, Flag of Yemen. 6b, Flag & eagle. 8b, Mocha coffee branch. 14b, Walled city of San'a. 20b, 1i, Ta'iz & its citadel.

1951 Wmk. 277 Photo. *Perf. 14.*

68	A13	1b dk brn	8	5
69	A13	2b red brn	18	5
70	A13	3b lil rose	25	5
71	A14	5b bl & red	38	10
72	A13	6b dk pur & red	50	12
73	A13	8b dk bl & gray grn	50	15
74	A14	10b rose lil	65	25
75	A14	14b bl grn	1.00	38
76	A14	20b rose red	1.50	65
77	A14	1i violet	2.50	1.25
		Nos. 68-77 (10)	7.54	3.05

No. 71 was used as a 4b stamp in 1956. See Nos. C3-C9.

Palace of the Rock, Wadi Dhahr — A15

Design: 20b, Walls of Ibb.

Engraved and Photogravure

1952 Unwmk. *Perf. 14½, Imperf.*

78	A15	12b choc, bl & dl grn	6.25	6.25
79	A15	20b dp car, bl & brn	7.00	7.00

See Nos. C10-C11.

Flag and View of San'a (Palace in Background) — A16

1952

80	A16	1i red brn, car & gray	11.00	11.00

4th anniv. of the accession of King Ahmed, Feb. 18, 1948. See Nos. 81, C12-C13.

Palace in Foreground.

1952

81	A16	30b red brn, car & dk grn	8.00	8.00

Victory of Mar. 13, 1948. See No. C13.

No. 69 Handstamped Type "b" in Black.

1951 (?) Wmk. 277 *Perf. 14*

82	A13	4b on 2b red brn	1.40	65

Forged surcharges exist. See Nos. 86-87.

Leaning Minaret, Mosque of Ta'iz — A17

Yemen Gate, San'a — A18

1954 Photo. Unwmk.

83	A17	4b dp org	40	16
84	A17	6b dp bl	60	35
85	A17	8b dp bl grn	80	40
		Nos. 83-85,C14-C16 (6)	3.58	2.21

5th anniv. of the accession of King Ahmed I.

Nos. 68 and 70 Handstamped Type "b" in Black

1955 Wmk. 277 *Perf. 14*

86	A13	4b on 1b dk brn	2.00	1.90
a.		Handstamp type "c"		1.60
87	A13	4b on 3b lil rose	2.25	2.25

1956-57 Wmk. 277 *Perf. 14*

87A	A18	1b lt brn	25	7
87B	A18	5b bl grn	25	14
87C	A18	10b dk bl ('57)	50	50

Nos. 87A-87C were prepared for official use, but issued for regular postage. The 1b and 5b were used as 4b stamps. A 20b and 1-imadi of type A18 were not issued.

Arab Postal Union Issue

Globe — A19

Perf. 13½x13

1957-58 Wmk. 195 Photo.

88	A19	4b yel brn	1.00	90
89	A19	6b grn ('58)	1.40	1.10
90	A19	16b vio ('58)	2.00	1.50

Issued to commemorate the founding of the Arab Postal Union, July 1, 1954.

Telecommunications Issue

Globe, Radio and Telegraph A20

Perf. 13x13½

1959, Mar. Wmk. 318

91	A20	4b vermilion	35	35

Arab Union of Telecommunications.

United Arab States Issue

Flags of U.A.R. and Yemen A21

1959, Mar. 13

92	A21	1b dl red brn & blk	16	16
93	A21	2b dk bl & blk	25	25
94	A21	4b sl grn, car & blk	30	30
		Nos. 92-94,C17-C19 (6)	2.24	1.79

First anniversary of United Arab States.

Arab League Center Issue

Arab League Center, Cairo A22

Perf. 13x13½

1960, Mar. 22 Wmk. 328

95	A22	4b dl grn & blk	40	35

Issued to commemorate the opening of the Arab League Center and the Arab Postal Museum in Cairo.

Refugees Pointing to Map of Palestine A23

1960, Apr. 7 Photo.

96	A23	4b brown	70	70
97	A23	6b yel grn	1.00	1.00

Issued to publicize World Refugee Year, July 1, 1959-June 30, 1960.

In 1961 a souvenir sheet was issued containing a 4b gray and 6b sepia in type A18, imperf. Black marginal inscription, "YEMEN 1960," repeated in Arabic. Size: 103x85mm. Value $15.

Torch and Olympic Rings A24

1960, Dec. Unwmk. *Perf. 14x14½*

98	A24	2b blk & lil rose	10	10
99	A24	4b blk & yel	25	25
100	A24	6b blk & org	40	40
101	A24	8b brn blk & bl grn	65	65
102	A24	20b dk bl, org & vio	1.20	80
		Nos. 98-102 (5)	2.60	2.20

Issued to commemorate the 17th Olympic Games, Rome, Aug. 25-Sept. 11.

An imperf. souvenir sheet exists, containing one copy of No. 99. Size: 100x60 mm. Value $50.

U.N. Emblem Breaking Chains A25

1961 Unwmk. *Perf. 14x14½*

103	A25	1b violet	10	7
104	A25	2b green	14	10
105	A25	3b grnsh bl	16	14
106	A25	4b brt ultra	20	16
107	A25	6b brt lil	25	20
108	A25	14b rose brn	65	50
109	A25	20b brown	1.20	80
		Nos. 103-109 (7)	2.70	1.97

15th anniversary (in 1960) of U.N.

An imperf. souvenir sheet exists, containing one copy of No. 106. Blue marginal inscription. Size: 100x60mm. Value $9.

Cranes and Ship, Hodeida A26

1961, June Litho. *Perf. 13x13½*

110	A26	4b multi	30	20
111	A26	6b multi	60	40
112	A26	16b multi	1.10	90

Opening of deepwater port at Hodeida.

An imperf. souvenir sheet exists, containing one each of Nos. 110-112. Size: 160x130mm. Value $2.50.

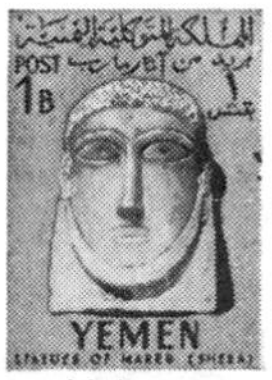

Alabaster Funerary Mask — A27

Imam's New Palace, San'a — A28

Designs (ancient sculptures from Marib, Sheba): 2b, Horned animal's head, symbolizing Moon God (limestone). 4b, Bronze head of an Emperor 1st or 2nd century. 8b, Statue of Emperor Dhamar Ali. 10b, Statue of a child, 2nd or 3rd century (alabaster). 12b, Stairs in court of Temple of the Moon God. 20b, Alabaster relief, boy riding monster. 1i, Woman with grapes, relief.

1961, Oct. 14 Photo. *Perf. 11½*

Granite Paper

113	A27	1b sal, blk & gray	5	5
114	A27	2b pur & gray	5	5
115	A27	4b pale brn, gray & blk	8	8
116	A27	8b brt pink & blk	20	20
117	A27	10b yel & blk	35	35
118	A27	12b lt vio bl & blk	50	50
119	A27	20b gray & blk	60	60
120	A27	1i gray ol & blk	1.20	1.20
		Nos. 113-120,C20-C21 (10)	3.57	3.57

1961, Nov. 15 Unwmk.

Designs: 8b, Side view of Imam's palace, San'a (horiz.). 10b, Palace of the Rock (Dar al-Hajar).

121	A28	4b blk & lt bl grn	16	16
122	A28	8b blk, brt pink & grn	35	35
123	A28	10b blk, sal & grn	42	42
		Nos. 121-123,C22-C23 (5)	1.51	1.51

Exist imperf.

Hodeida-San'a Road — A29

1961, Dec. 25 Litho. *Perf. 13½x13*
124 A29 4b multi 40 20
125 A29 6b multi 60 30
126 A29 10b multi 1.00 50

Opening of the Hodeida-San'a highway. A miniature sheet exists containing one each of Nos. 124-126, imperf. Size: 159x129mm. Value $2.

Trajan's Kiosk, Philae, Nubia — A30

1962, Mar. 1 Photo. *Perf. 11x11½*
127 A30 4b dk red brn 70 50
128 A30 6b bl grn 1.60 1.00

Issued to publicize UNESCO's help in safeguarding the monuments of Nubia.
A souvenir sheet exists, containing one each of Nos. 127-128, imperf. Size: 100x88½mm. Value $4.

Arab League Building, Cairo, and Emblem — A31

1962, March 22 *Perf. 13½x13*
129 A31 4b dk grn 30 25
130 A31 6b dp ultra 45 38

Arab League Week, Mar. 22-28.
A souvenir sheet exists, containing one each of Nos. 129-130, imperf. Size: 94x80mm. Value $1.25.

Nurses, Mother and Child
A32

Malaria Eradication Emblem
A33

Designs: 4b, Nurse weighing child. 6b, Vaccination. 10b, Weighing infant.

1962, June 20 Unwmk. *Perf. 11½*
131 A32 2b multi 20 20
132 A32 4b multi 25 25
133 A32 6b multi 38 38
134 A32 10b multi 50 50

Issued for Child Welfare.

1962, July 20 *Perf. 13½x13*
135 A33 4b blk & dp org 25 16
136 A33 6b dk brn & grn 50 35

WHO drive to eradicate malaria. An imperf. souvenir sheet contains one each of Nos. 135-136. Size: 95x79mm. Value $12.50.

No. 136 has laurel leaves added and inscription rearranged.

Nos. 103-109 Overprinted

١٩٦٢-١٩٤٥

1945-1962

1962 Photo. Unwmk. *Perf. 14x14½*
137 A25 1b vio
138 A25 2b grn
139 A25 3b greenish blue
140 A25 4b brt ultra
141 A25 6b brt lil
142 A25 14b rose brn
143 A25 20b brn

Nos. 113-123 and 131-134 Ovptd. in Dark Green or Dark Red

الجمهورية العربية اليمنية
١٩٦٢/٩/٢٧-١٣٨٢/٤/٢٨
Y.A.R. 27.9.1962
a

الجمهورية العربية اليمنية
١٩٦٢/٩/٢٧ - ١٣٨٢/٤/٢٨
Y.A.R. 27.9.1962
b

1963, Jan. 1 *Perf. 11½*
144 A27 (a) 1b No. 113 (G)
145 A27 (a) 2b No. 114
146 A32 (b) 2b No. 131
147 A27 (a) 4b No. 115 (G)
148 A28 (a) 4b No. 121
149 A32 (b) 4b No. 132 (G)
150 A32 (b) 6b No. 133
151 A27 (a) 8b No. 116
152 A28 (b) 8b No. 122 (G)
153 A27 (a) 10b No. 117
154 A28 (a) 10b No. 123
155 A32 (b) 10b No. 134 (G)
156 A27 (a) 12b No. 118
157 A27 (a) 20b No. 119
158 A27 (a) 1i No. 120

Proclamation of the Republic
A34

UN Freedom From Hunger Campaign
A35

1963, Mar. 15 *Perf. 11x11½*
159 A34 4b shown
160 A34 6b Flag, tank

See Nos. C26-C28.

Perf. 11½x11, 11x11½
1963, Mar. 21
162 A35 4b Milk cow, horiz.
163 A35 6b shown

An imperf. souvenir sheet of 2 exists containing one each Nos. 162-163.

Nos. 129-130 Ovptd. in Dark Red

الجمهورية العربية اليمنية
Y.A.R.
١٩٦٢/٩/٢٧ - ١٣٨٢/٤/٢٨
27-9-1962

1963, Sept. 1 *Perf. 13½x13*
164 A31 4b dark grn
165 A31 6b deep ultra

Nos. 15-16, 18-23, 50-52 Ovptd. in Black

بريد اليمن
الجمهورية
العربية اليمنية
١٣٨٢/٤/٢٨
١٩٦٢/٩/٢٧
Y. A. R.
27. 9. 1962
بريد اليمن
a

الجمهورية
العربية اليمنية
١٣٨٢/٤/٢٨
١٩٦٢/٩/٢٧
Y. A. R.
27. 9. 1962
b

1963, Sept. 1
166 A3 (a) 5b No. 15
167 A4 (a) 6b No. 16
168 A8 (b) 6b No. 50
169 A4 (a) 8b No. 18
170 A4 (a) 10b No. 19
171 A4 (a) 10b No. 20
172 A8 (b) 10b No. 51
173 A8 (b) 14b No. 52
174 A4 (a) 20b No. 21
175 A4 (a) 1i No. 22
176 A4 (a) 1i No. 23

Nos. 111-112 and 125-126 Ovptd. in Black

الجمهورية العربية اليمنية
١٩٦٢-٩-٢٧ — ١٣٨٢-٤-٢٨
Y. A. R. 27. 9 1962

Perf. 13x13½, 13½x13
1963, Sept. 1 Litho. Unwmk.
177 A26 6b No. 111
178 A29 6b No. 125
179 A29 10b No. 126
180 A26 16b No. 112

On Nos. 178-179 the bars eliminate old inscription with text of overprint positioned below and to the right of them, on Nos. 177 and 180, the text is slightly left below the bars.
Imperf. souvenir sheets of 2 exist containing Nos. 177 and 180 or Nos. 178-179.

1st Anniv. of the Revolution — A36

Perf. 11½x11, 11x11½
1963, Sept. 26 Photo.
186 A36 2b Flag, torch, candle, vert.
187 A36 4b shown
188 A36 6b Flag, grain, chain, vert.

Imperf. souvenir sheets of 3 exist containing one each Nos. 186-188.

Nos. 135-136 Ovptd. in Black

الجمهورية
العربية اليمنية
١٣٨٢/٤/٢٨
١٩٦٢/٩/٢٧
Y. A. R.
27. 9. 1962

1963, Nov. 25 *Perf. 13½x13*
189 A33 4b blk & deep org
190 A33 6b dark brn & grn

U.N. Declaration of Human Rights, 15th Anniv. — A37

1963, Dec. 10 *Perf. 13½*
191 A37 4b org & dark brn vio
192 A37 6b blue grn & blk

An imperf. souvenir sheet of 2 exists containing one each Nos. 191-192.

Bagel Spinning and Weaving Factory Inauguration — A38

Perf. 11x11½, 11½x11
1964, Apr. 10
193 A38 2b Factory, bobbin, spool, cloth
194 A38 4b Loom machine
195 A38 6b Factory, spool, bolt of cloth
196 A38 16b shown

Nos. 193-195 vert. An imperf. souvenir sheet of one exists containing No. 195.
No. 196 is air mail.

Hodeida Airport Inauguration — A39

1964, Apr. 30 *Perf. 11½x11*
197 A39 4b Runway
198 A39 6b Runway, terminal
199 A39 10b Aircraft, terminal, ship at sea

An imperf. souvenir sheet of one exists containing No. 199.

San'a Intl. Airport Inauguration — A40

1964, Oct. 1
200 A40 1b shown
201 A40 2b Terminal, runway, aircraft
202 A40 4b like 2b
203 A40 8b like 1b

An imperf. souvenir sheet of two exists containing one each Nos. 202 and C30.
See No. C30.

Arab Postal Union, 10th Anniv.
A41

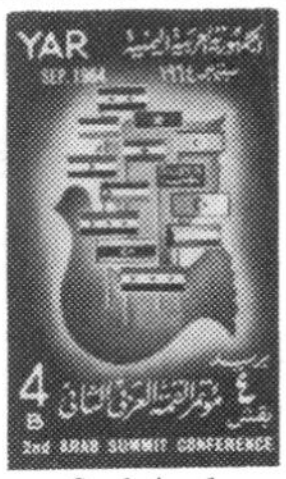

2nd Arab Summit Conference
A42

1964, Oct. 15 ***Perf. 13½***
204 A41 4b vert & blk

See No. C31.

1964, Nov. 30
205 A42 4b shown
206 A42 6b Conference emblem, map

An imperf. souvenir sheet of 2 exists containing one each Nos. 205-206.

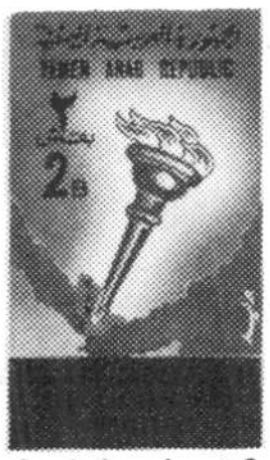

2nd Anniv. of the Revolution
A43

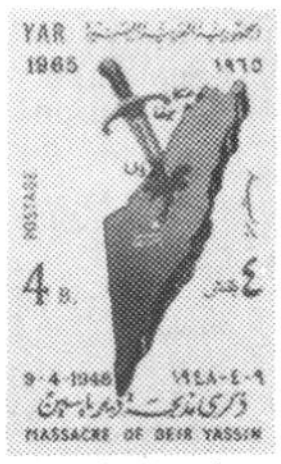

Deir Yassin Massacre
A44

1964, Dec. 30
207 A43 2b Torch, map
208 A43 4b Revolutionary
209 A43 6b Flag, 2 candles, map

An imperf. souvenir sheet of one exists containing No. 209.

1965, Apr. 30 ***Perf. 11x11½***
210 A44 4b red lil & deep blue

See No. C32.

Intl. Telecommunications Union (ITU), Cent. — A45

Perf. 11x11½, 11½x11
1965, May 17
211 A45 4b red & pale blue, vert.
212 A45 6b org brn & grn

A souvenir sheet of one exists containing No. 212.

Burning of Algiers Library, 3rd Anniv.
A46

1965, July 7 ***Perf. 11½x11***
214 A46 4b sep, red & grn

See No. C33.

3rd Anniv. of the Revolution
A47

1965, Sept. 26
215 A47 4b Tractor, corn, grain
216 A47 6b Tractor, tower, buildings

An imperf. souvenir sheet of one exists containing No. 216.

Intl. Cooperation Year — A48

1965, Oct. 15 ***Perf. 11x11***
217 A48 4b shown
218 A48 6b UN building, New York

An imperf. souvenir sheet of one exists containing No. 218.

Nos. 162-163 Overprinted in Black

مكافحـــة الـــدرن
١٩٦٥
Tuberculous Campaign
1965

مكافحة الدرن
١٩٦٥
TUBERCULOUS
CAMPAIGN
1965

Perf. 11½x11, 11x11½
1966, Jan. 15
219 A35 4b sal rose & golden brn
220 A35 6b brt pur & yel

An imperf. souvenir sheet of two exists containing Nos. 219-220.

Nos. 205-206 Ovptd. in Red or Black

مؤتمر القمة العربى
الثالث ــ ١٩٦٥
3rd. Arab
SummitConference
1965

1966, Mar. 20 ***Perf. 13½***
221 A42 4b dark grn (R)
222 A42 6b org brn

An imperf. souvenir sheet of two exists containing Nos. 221-222 ovptd. in bright pink (4b) or black (6b) with additional inscription at bottom "CASABLANCA / 1965."

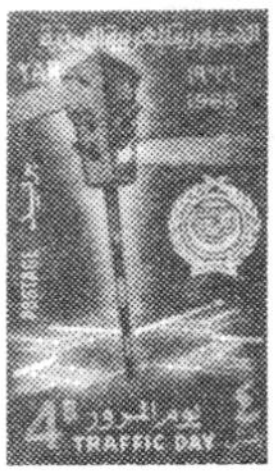

Traffic Day — A49

1966, June 30 ***Perf. 11x11½***
223 A49 4b grn & ver
224 A49 6b grn & ver

Arab League, 25th Anniv.
A56

1970, Oct. 5 **Photo.** ***Perf. 11½x11***
276 A56 5b org, grn & dark pur
277 A56 7b blue, grn & brn
278 A56 16b dark olive grn, grn & chalky blue

An imperf souvenir sheet of one exists containing No. 278.

UN, 25th Anniv.
A60

1971, Apr. 4 **Photo.** ***Perf. 11½x11***
282 A60 5b dark olive grn, grn & dark vio
283 A60 7b blue, grn & dark blue

Souvenir Sheet
Imperf

284 A60 16b multi

No. 284 has inscribed margin.

10th anniv. of Revolution
A80

1972, Nov. 25 **Photo.** ***Perf. 13***

301 A80	7b lt bl, blk & multi	65	50
302 A80	10b gray, blk & multi	1.00	65

See Nos. C40, 318.

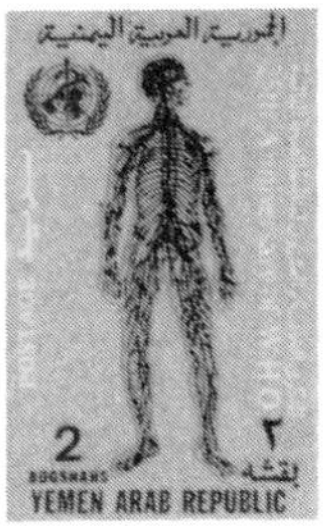

25th Anniv. of WHO — A81

1972, Dec. 1 **Litho.**

303 A81	2b lt yel grn & multi	50	35
304 A81	21b sky bl & multi	1.40	1.20
305 A81	37b red lil & multi	2.25	2.00

Burning of Al-Aqsa Mosque, 2nd Anniv. — A82

1972, Jan. 1 **Photo.** ***Perf. 13½***

306 A82	7b lt bl, blk & multi	1.50	60
307 A82	18b lt bl, blk & multi	2.50	1.10

See Nos. C41, 319, 341.

25th Anniv. of UNICEF — A83

1973, Jan. 15 **Photo.** ***Perf. 13***

308 A83	7b lt bl, blk & multi	1.00	65
309 A83	10b lt bl, blk & multi	1.40	80

See No. C42.

UPU Cent. — A84

10th World Hunger Program — A85

1974, Nov. 20 **Photo.** ***Perf. 14***

310 A84	10b multi	75	40
311 A84	30b multi	2.25	1.50
312 A84	40b multi	3.25	1.90

1975, Feb. 5 **Litho.** ***Perf. 13½***

313 A85	10b multi	25	25
314 A85	30b multi	70	70
315 A85	63b multi	1.20	1.20

12th Anniv. of Revolution
A86

1975, Sept. 25

316 A86	25f Janad Mosque	50	35
317 A86	75f Althawra Hospital	1.00	65

Nos. 301, 306 surcharged in Black with New Values and Bars

1975, Nov. 15 **Photo.** ***Perf. 13½***

318 A80	75f on 7b	2.00	65
319 A82	278f on 7b	3.50	1.20
	Nos. 318-319,C46-C48 (5)	8.50	4.00

Telephone Cent. — A87

Coffee Bean Branch — A88

1976, Mar. 10 **Litho.** ***Perf. 14½***

320 A87	25f brt pink & blk	25	25
321 A87	75f lt grn & blk	60	60
322 A87	160f lt bl & blk	1.20	1.20
a.	Souv. sheet of 1		

No. 322a exists both perf. and imperf.

1976, Apr. 25 ***Perf. 14***

323 A88	1f dl lil	7	7
324 A88	3f pale gray	7	7
325 A88	5f lt bl grn	7	7
326 A88	10f bis brn	14	14
327 A88	25f gldn brn	22	22
328 A88	50f brt plum	42	42
329 A88	75f dl pink	70	60

Size: 22x30mm
Perf. 14½

330 A88 1r sky bl 1.25 70
331 A88 1.50r red lil 1.90 1.40
332 A88 2r lt grn 2.25 1.40
333 A88 5r yel org 5.00 3.00
Nos. 323-333 (11) 12.09 8.09

See Nos. 403-407.

2nd Anniv. of Reformation Movement — A89

1976, June 13 Photo. ***Perf. 12x12½***
334 A89 75f Industrial Park 70 50
335 A89 135f Forestry 1.00 70

Souvenir Sheet

336 A89 135f Forestry 2.00 2.00

No. 336 contains one stamp (32x47mm).

14th Anniv. of Revolution A90

3rd Anniv. of Correction Movement A91

Designs: 25f, Natl. Institute of Public Administration. 75f, Housing and population census. 160f, Sanaa University emblem.

1976, Sept. 26 Photo. ***Perf. 12x12½***
337 A90 25f buff & multi 25 25
338 A90 75f yel bis & multi 60 60
339 A90 160f pale grn & multi 1.20 1.20

Souvenir Sheet

340 A90 160f pale grn & multi 2.25 2.25

No. 340 contains one stamp (33x49mm).

No. 306 Surcharged in Black with New Value and Bars

1976
341 A82 75f on 7b 1.00 65

1977 Photo. ***Perf. 14***
342 A91 25f Dish antenna 20 10
343 A91 75f Computer, technician 60 30
a. Miniature sheet of 1 1.50 1.50

15th Anniv. of September Revolution — A92

1977 Photo. ***Perf. 13½***
344 A92 25f Sa'ada-San'a Road 25 20
345 A92 75f Television, Transmitting tower 50 30
346 A92 160f like 25f 1.00 70
a. Souvenir sheet of 1 2.25 2.25

25th Anniv. of Arab Postal Union — A93

Pres. Hamdi — A94

1978 ***Perf. 14***
347 A93 25f lt yel grn & multi 40 25
348 A93 60f bis & multi 90 60
a. Miniature sheet of 1 2.25 2.25

1978 ***Perf. 11½***
349 A94 25f dk grn & blk 16 10
350 A94 75f ultra & blk 40 20
351 A94 160f brn & blk 80 50
a. Miniature sheet of 1 *15.00* *6.50*

30th Anniv. of ICAO (1977) — A95

1979, Nov. 15 Photo. ***Perf. 13½***
352 A95 75f multi 60 40
353 A95 135f multi 1.40 90
a. Miniature sheet of 1 2.00 2.00

Book, World Map, Arab Achievements — A96

1979, Dec. 1 ***Perf. 14***
354 A96 25f multi 35 18
355 A96 75f multi 90 60
a. Souvenir sheet of 1 2.00 2.00

12th World Telecommunications Day, May 17, 1979 — A97

1980, Jan. 1
356 A97 75f multi 60 40
357 A97 135f multi, horiz. 1.40 90
a. Miniature sheet of 1 2.00 2.00

Dome of the Rock — A98

1980 Photo. ***Perf. 14***
358 A98 5f brt bl & multi 50 35
359 A98 10f yel & multi 1.00 65

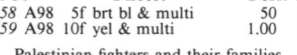

Palestinian fighters and their families.

Argentina World Cup — A99

Designs: World Cup emblem and various players.

1980, Mar. 30
360 A99 25f gold & multi 38 38
361 A99 30f gold & multi 40 30
362 A99 35f gold & multi 50 38
363 A99 50f gold & multi 70 50
Nos. 360-363,C49-C52 (8) 6.48 4.76

Issued in sheets of 8.

International Year of the Child — A100

1980, Apr. 1 ***Perf. 13½***
364 A100 25f Girl, bird 65 50
365 A100 50f Girl, bird, diff. 1.20 80
366 A100 75f Boy, butterfly, flower 1.60 1.20
Nos. 364-366,C53-C55 (6) 9.95 6.10

Issued in sheets of 6.

World Scouting Jamboree — A101

1980, May 1 ***Perf. 13½x14***
367 A101 25f Fishing 40 20
368 A101 35f Troup, aircraft 55 30
369 A101 40f Mounted bugler, flag 65 38
370 A101 50f Telescope, night sky 80 40
Nos. 367-370,C56-C58 (7) 6.80 3.43

Issued in sheets of 6.

Argentina 1978 World Cup Winners — A102

Designs: World cup emblem and various soccer players.

1980, June 1 ***Perf. 14***
371 A102 25f gold & multi 45 25
372 A102 30f gold & multi 60 30
373 A102 35f gold & multi 60 38
374 A102 50f gold & multi 90 40
Nos. 371-374,C59-C62 (8) 8.05 4.28

Hegira, 1500th Anniv. — A102A

Designs: 160f, Outside view.

1980, July 1 ***Perf. 13½***
375 A102a 25f blk & multi 30 18
376 A102a 75f car rose & multi 90 60
377 A102a 160f blk & multi 1.90 75
a. Miniature sheet of 1 4.00 4.00

17th Anniv. of September Revolution A103

A104

1980, Sept. 26 ***Perf. 13½***
378 A103 25f multi 35 22
379 A104 75f multi 1.10 65

Souvenir Sheet

380 100f multi 3.75 3.75

No. 380 contains one stamp combining designs A103 and A104 (42x34mm).

Al Aqsa Mosque A105

Mosques: 25f, Al-Rawda entrance. 100f, Al-Nabwi. 160f, Al-Haram.

1980, Nov. 6 Photo. ***Perf. 13½***
381 A105 25f multi 25 16
382 A105 75f multi 75 50
383 A105 100f multi 1.60 65
384 A105 160f multi 2.00 1.00

Souvenir Sheet

385 160f multi 4.50 3.25

Islamic Postal Systems Week and Hegira. No. 385 contains one stamp (109x47mm) combining designs of Nos. 382-384.

Foreign postal stationery (stamped envelopes, postal cards and air letter sheets) lies beyond the scope of this Catalogue, which is limited to adhesive postage stamps.

Intl. Palestinian Solidarity Day — A106

1980, Nov. 29

386 A106	25f lt bl & multi	40	22
387 A106	75f ver & multi	1.10	90

Inscribed 1979.

9th Arab Archaeological Conference — A107

1981, Mar. 1 ***Perf. 13½***

388 A107	75f Al Aamiriya Mosque	1.10	60
389 A107	125f Al Hadi Mosque	1.75	85
a.	Souv. Sheet of 2, #388-389	3.25	3.25

1980 World Tourism Conference, Manila A108

1981, Apr. 1

390 A108	25f multi	20	10
391 A108	75f multi	60	30
392 A108	100f multi, horiz.	80	45
393 A108	135f multi	1.10	60
394 A108	160f multi, horiz.	1.40	60
a.	Miniature sheet of 1	4.50	4.50
	Nos. 390-394 (5)	4.10	2.05

Sir Rowland Hill (1795-1879), Postage Stamp Inventor — A109

1981, Sept. 15 **Litho.** ***Perf. 14***

395 A109	25f Portrait, UPU emblem	16
396 A109	30f Emblem, stamp of 1963	20
397 A109	50f Portrait, stamps	35
398 A109	75f Portrait, globe, jet	50
399 A109	100f Portrait, stamp collection	65
400 A109	150f Jets, No. 322	1.00
	Nos. 395-400 (6)	2.86

Souvenir Sheets

401 A109	200f Portrait, vert.	4.00

Imperf

402 A109	200f Portrait, diff.	4.00

Nos. 398-402 are airmail.

Nos. 323-327 Surcharged

1981

403 A88	125f on 1f	80
404 A88	150f on 3f	1.00
405 A88	325f on 5f	2.00
406 A88	350f on 10f	2.25
407 A88	375f on 25f	2.50

20th Anniv. of Yemen Airways — A110

1983, Apr. 1 **Litho.** ***Perf. 14***

408 A110	75f yel & multi	50	50
409 A110	125f red & multi	80	80
410 A110	325f bl & multi	2.00	2.00

Folk Costumes — A111

1983, May 1

411 A111	50f Woman carrying waterjar	35
412 A111	50f Women, sheep	35
413 A111	50f Man, donkeys	35
414 A111	50f Man in town square	35
415 A111	75f Women, child, well	50
416 A111	75f Scholar	50
417 A111	75f Woman on beach	50
418 A111	75f Camel-drawn plow	50
	Nos. 411-418 (8)	3.40

Souvenir Sheets

419 A111 200f Woman

Imperf

420 A111 200f Man

Nos. 411-414 vert. Nos. 415-420 are airmail.

Sept. 26th Revolution, 20th Anniv. (1982) — A112

1983, Sept. 26 **Litho.** ***Perf. 14***

421 A112 100f Communications
422 A112 150f Literacy
423 A112 325f Educational development
a. Souvenir sheet of 2 (#422, 423)
424 A112 400f Independence

World Communications Year — A113

1983, Dec. 15

425 A113 150f lt bl & multi
426 A113 325f lt grn & multi
a. Souvenir sheet of 1

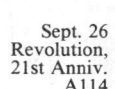

Sept. 26 Revolution, 21st Anniv. A114

1984, Apr. 1 **Litho.** ***Perf. 14***

427 A114 100f shown
428 A114 150f Fist, statue
429 A114 325f Gate, tank
a. Souvenir sheet of 1

Israel Agression Day — A115

1984, Sept. 7

430 A115	150f multi	1.00
431 A115	325f multi	2.00

Size: 91x120mm.

Imperf

432 A115	325f multi	*5.00*

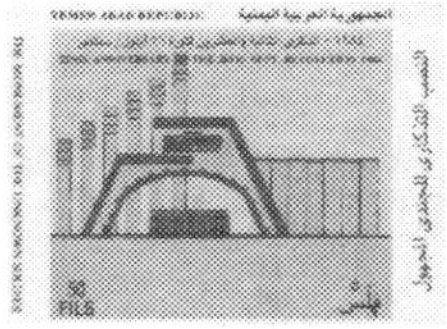

Sept. 26 Revolution, 22nd Anniv. — A116

1985, Oct. 1

433 A116 50f Triumphal Arch
434 A116 150f San'a Castle walls
435 A116 325f Stadium, Govt. Palace, San'a
a. Souvenir sheet of one

Intl. Anti-Apartheid Year (1978) — A117

1985, Jan. 1

436 A117 150f dp ver & multi
437 A117 325f grn & multi
a. Souvenir sheet of one

Intl. Civil Aviation Org., 40th Anniv. A118

1985, Sept. 20

438 A118 25f multi
439 A118 50f multi
440 A118 150f multi
441 A118 325f multi
a. Souvenir sheet of one

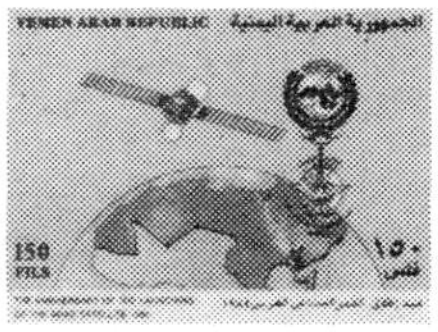

Arabsat Satellite, 1st Anniv. A119

1986, Apr. 15 **Litho.** ***Perf. 14***

442 A119 150f multi
443 A119 325f multi
a. Souvenir sheet of one

World Telecommunications, 120th Anniv. — A120

1986, May 1

444 A120 150f multi
445 A120 325f multi
a. Souvenir sheet of one

General People's Conference, 2nd Anniv. — A121

1986, May 1

446 A121 150f multi
447 A121 325f multi
a. Souvenir sheet of one

15th Islamic Foreign Ministers' Conference, San'a, Dec. 18-22, 1984 — A122

1986, July 1

448 A122 150f multi
449 A122 325f multi
a. Souvenir sheet of one

UN 40th Anniv. — A123

1986, Oct. 1

450 A123 150f multi
451 A123 325f multi
a. Souvenir sheet of one

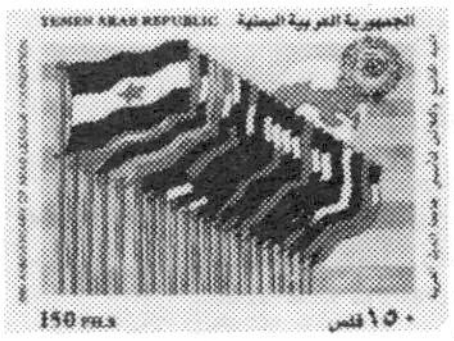

Arab League, 39th Anniv. A124

1986, Nov. 15
452 A124 150f multi
453 A124 325f multi

Natl. Arms A125

1987, Sept. 26 **Litho.** ***Perf. 14***
454 A125 100f multi
455 A125 150f multi
456 A125 425f multi
a. Souv. sheet of one
457 A125 450f multi

Sept. 26th Revolution, 25th anniv.

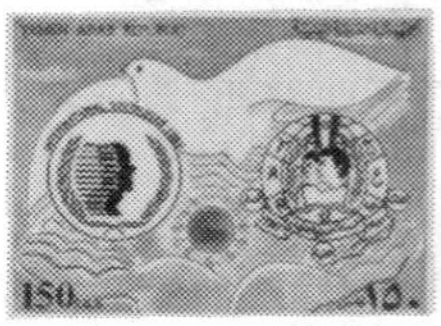
Intl. Youth Year (1985) A126

1987, Oct. 15 ***Perf. 13x13½***
458 A126 150f multi
459 A126 425f multi
a. Souv. sheet of one

Drilling of the Republic's First Oil Well, 1984 A127

1987, Nov. 1 ***Perf. 14***
460 A127 150f Oil derrick
461 A127 425f Derrick, refinery
a. Souv. sheet of one

General Population and Housing Census, 1986 A128

1987, Dec. 1
462 A128 150f multi
463 A128 425f multi
a. Souv. sheet of one

1986 World Cup Soccer Championships, Mexico — A129

Designs: 100f, 150f, Match scenes, vert. 425f, Match scene and Pique, character trademark.

1988, Jan. 1 **Litho.** ***Perf. 14***
464 A129 100f multi
465 A129 150f multi, diff.
466 A129 425f multi
a. Souv. sheet of 1

AIR POST STAMPS

Catalogue values for unused stamps in this section are for Never Hinged items.

Plane over San'a — AP1

1947	Unwmk.	Engr.	*Perf. 12½*	
C1	AP1 10b brt bl		4.50	4.50
C2	AP1 20b ol grn		6.50	6.50

View of San'a AP2

Palace of the Rock, Wadi Dhahr — AP3

Designs: 10b, Mocha coffee branch. 16b, Palace, Ta'iz. 20b, 1i, Parade Ground, San'a.

1951	Wmk. 277	Photo.	*Perf. 14.*	
C3	AP2 6b blue		15	10
C4	AP2 8b dk brn		20	15
C5	AP2 10b dk grn		25	15
C6	AP3 12b dk bl		28	20
C7	AP2 16b lil rose		35	28
C8	AP3 20b org brn		55	42
C9	AP3 1i dk red		1.10	75
	Nos. C3-C9 (7)		2.88	2.05

Nos. C3 and C4 were used provisionally in 1957 for registry and foreign ordinary mail.

Type of Regular Issue, 1952

Designs: 12b, Palace of the Rock, Wadi Dhahr. 20b, Walls of Ibb.

Engraved and Photogravure

1952 **Unwmk.** ***Perf. 14½.***
C10 A15 12b grnsh blk, bl & brn 2.75 2.75
C11 A15 20b ind, bl & brn 3.75 3.75

Flag-and-View Type of Regular Issue, 1952

1952
C12 A16 1i dk brn, car & brt ultra 5.50 5.50

Palace in Foreground

1952
C13 A16 30b yel grn, car & gray 3.75 3.75

Leaning Minaret, Mosque of Ta'iz — AP6

1954 **Photo.** ***Perf. 14***
C14 AP6 10b scarlet 38 25
C15 AP6 12b dl bl 50 40
C16 AP6 20b ol bis 90 65

5th anniv. of the accession of King Ahmed I.

Type of Regular Issue, 1959

1959 **Wmk. 318** ***Perf. 13x13½***
C17 A21 6b org & blk 38 25
C18 A21 10b red & blk 50 38
C19 A21 16b brt vio & red 65 45

Antiquities of Marib Type of 1961

Designs: 6b, Columns, Temple of the Moon God. 16b, Control tower and spillway of 2,700-year-old dam of Marib.

Perf. 11½

1961, Oct. 14 **Unwmk.** **Photo.**
C20 A27 6b lt bl grn & blk 12 12
C21 A27 16b lt bl & blk 42 42

Buildings Type of Regular Issue

Design: 6b, Bab al-Yemen, main gate of San'a (horiz.). 16b, Palace of the Rock (Dar al-Hajar).

1961, Nov. 15
C22 A28 6b blk, lt bl & grn 20 20
C23 A28 16b blk, rose & grn 38 38

Nos. C20-C23 Ovptd. Like Nos. 144-158 in Dark Red or Black

Perf. 11½

1963, Jan. 1 **Photo.** **Unwmk.**
C24 A27 (a) 6b No. C20
C24A A28 (b) 6b No. C22
C25 A27 (a) 16b No. C21
C25A A28 (a) 16b No. C23 (B)

Proclamation of the Republic Type

Perf. 11x11½, 11½x11

1963, Mar. 15
C26 A34 8b Bayonette, torch
C27 A34 10b Jet, torch, tank
C28 A34 16b Flag, chain, torch

Nos. C27-C28 horiz.

Nos. 25-29 Ovptd. in Black

Wmk. 258

1963, Sept. 1 **Litho.** ***Perf. 12½***
C29 A5 6b slate blue & ultra
C29A A5 10b fawn & ultra
C29B A5 14b olive & ultra
C29C A5 20b yel grn & ultra
C29D A5 1i claret & ultra

San'a Intl. Airport Type of 1964

Perf. 11½x11

1964, Oct. 1 **Photo.** **Unwmk.**
C30 A40 6b Sun, buildings, aircraft

See note after No. 203.

APU 10th Anniv. Type of 1964

1964, Oct. 15 ***Perf. 13½***
C31 A41 6b blue grn & blk

An imperf. souvenir sheet of one exists containing No. C31.

Deir Yassin Massacre Type of 1965

1965, Apr. 30 ***Perf. 11x11½***
C32 A44 6b ver & brt org

Library Type of 1965

1965, July 7 ***Perf. 11½x11***
C33 A46 6b sepia, red & int blue

An imperf. souvenir sheet of one exists containing No. C33.

V.I. Lenin's Birth Centenary AP7

1970, Aurg. 15 **Litho.** ***Perf. 12x12½***
C34 AP7 6b Public speech
C35 AP7 16b Meeting with Arab delegates

8th Anniv. of the Revolution — AP8

1971, Jan. 24 ***Perf. 13***
C36 AP8 5b Country estate
C37 AP8 7b Military, civil and private industry workers
C38 AP8 16b Handshake, flag, flowers, open book

A souv. sheet of 1 exists containing No. C38.

Revolution Type of 1972

1972, Nov. 25 **Photo.** ***Perf. 13***
C40 A80 21b lil, blk & multi 5.00 3.50

Al-Aqsa Mosque Type of 1973

1973, Jan. 1 **Photo.** ***Perf. 13½***
C41 A82 24b lt bl, blk & multi 2.00 1.40
a. Min. sheet of 1, imperf.

UNICEF Type of 1973

1973, Jan. 15 **Photo.** ***Perf. 13***
C42 A83 18b lt bl, blk & multi 70 65
a. Min. sheet of 1, imperf. 80 80

11th Anniv. of Revolution AP10

1973, Sept. 26 **Photo.** ***Perf. 14***
C43 AP10 7b Bank 25 14
C44 AP10 10b Cement factory 42 22
C45 AP10 18b Hospital 70 40

Nos. C42, C43, C45 Surcharged in Black with New Value and Bars.

1975, Nov. 15
C46 A83 75f on 18b lt bl, blk & multi 80 60
C47 AP10 90f on 7b multi 1.00 75
C48 AP10 120f on 18b multi 1.20 80
a. Overprinted in red

Argentina 1978 World Cup Type of 1980

Designs: World cup emblem and various soccer players.

1980, Mar. 30 **Photo.** ***Perf. 14***
C49 A99 60f gold & multi 80 60
C50 A99 75f gold & multi 1.00 70
C51 A99 80f gold & multi 1.20 90
C52 A99 100f gold & multi 1.50 1.00

Two 225f souvenir sheets exist.

IYC Type of 1980

1980, Apr. 1 ***Perf. 13½***
C53 A100 80f Girl, bird 1.60 1.00
C54 A100 100f Boy, butterfly, flower 1.90 1.20
C55 A100 150f Boy, butterfly, flower, diff. 3.00 1.40

Two 200f souvenir sheets exist.

Scouting Type of 1980

1980, May 1 **Photo.** ***Perf. 13½x14***
C56 A101 60f Bicycling 1.00 50
C57 A101 75f Fencing 1.40 65
C58 A101 120f Butterfly catching 2.00 1.00

Two 300f souvenir sheets exist.

Argentina 1978 Winners' Type of 1980

Designs: World cup emblem and various soccer players.

1980, June 1 Photo. *Perf. 14*

C59 A102 60f gold & multi	1.00	50
C60 A102 75f gold & multi	1.40	65
C61 A102 80f gold & multi	1.50	70
C62 A102 100f gold & multi	1.60	1.10

Two 225f souvenir sheets exist.

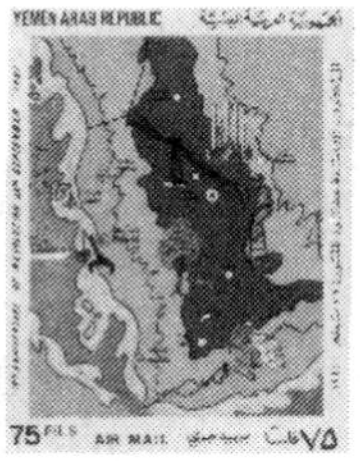

19th Anniv. of Sept. 26th Revolution (1981) — AP11

1982, Jan. 25 Litho. *Perf. 14*

C63 AP11 75f Map	45	25
C64 AP11 125f Map in sunset	70	40
C65 AP11 325f Dove in natl. colors	2.00	1.20
a. Souv. sheet of 1	5.00	5.00
C66 AP11 400f Jets	2.25	1.40

Al-Hasan Ibn Al-Hamadani, Writer — AP12

1982, Feb. 1

C67 AP12 125f grn & multi	1.25	60
C68 AP12 325f bl & multi	2.75	1.40

Souvenir Sheet

C69 AP12 375f multi	3.50	3.50

No. C69 contains one stamp (36x46mm).

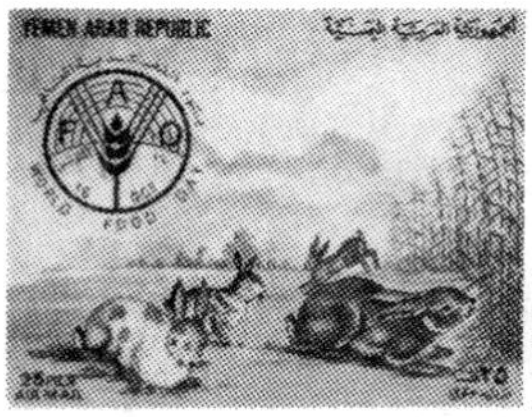

World Food Day AP13

Designs: No. C76a, Eggplants. No. C76b, Tomatoes. No. C76c, Beets, peas. No. C76d, Cauliflower, carrots. No. C77a, Dove. No. C77b, Water birds. No. C77c, Fish. No. C77d, Geese.

1982, Mar. 1 Litho. *Perf. 14*

C70 AP13 25f Rabbits	50
C71 AP13 50f Rooster, Hens	1.00
C72 AP13 60f Turkeys	1.25
C73 AP13 75f Sheep	1.50
C74 AP13 100f Cattle	2.00
C75 AP13 125f Deer	2.50
Nos. C70-C75 (6)	8.75

Souvenir Sheets

C76 Sheet of 4	2.00
a.-d. AP13 100f, any single	50
C77 Sheet of 4	2.50
a.-d. AP13 125f, any single	60

1980 Summer Olympics, Moscow AP14

1982, Apr. 1

C78 AP14 25f Gymnastics
C79 AP14 50f Pole vault
C80 AP14 60f Javelin
C81 AP14 75f Running
C82 AP14 100f Basketball
C83 AP14 125f Soccer

Two souvenir sheets of 4 exist: 100f, picturing boxing, wrestling, canoeing, swimming, and 125f, picturing weight lifting, discus, long jump, fencing.

Aviation — AP15

Various space and aircraft.

1982, May 21

C86 AP15 25f multi
C87 AP15 50f multi
C88 AP15 60f multi
C89 AP15 75f multi
C90 AP15 100f multi
C91 AP15 125f multi

Two souvenir sheets of 4 exist, 100f and 125f, picturing various aircraft and satellites.

Intl. Year of the Disabled — AP16

Designs: Nos. C94-C99, Diff. flowers. No. C100a, Emblem, natl. flag. No. C100b, Emblem on globe. No. C100c, Natl. colors, UN emblems. No. C100d, Disabled man, gifts, nurse. No. C101a, Flags, globe and nurse. No. C101b, UN emblems, natl. flag. No. C101c, Emblem, disabled man. No. C101d, UN emblem, nurse.

1982, June 1

C94 AP16 25f multi
C95 AP16 50f multi
C96 AP16 60f multi
C97 AP16 75f multi
C98 AP16 100f multi
C99 AP16 125f multi

Souvenir Sheets

C100 Sheet of 4
a.-d. AP16 100f, any single
C101 Sheet of 4
a.-d. AP16 125f, any single

Telecommunications Progress — AP17

Designs: 25f, FNRR communication center. 50f, Dish receivers, satellite, globe. 60f, Broadcast towers, dish receivers. 75f, Receivers, birds over plain. 100f, Receivers, satellite, telegraph key. No. C107, Receivers, passenger jet, Earth. No. C108a, Receivers, Earth. No. C108b, Earth, television, flag and camera. No. C108c, Computer. No. C108d, Skyscraper, Earth, telephone. No. C109a, Receivers, satellite, ship. No. C109b, Communication center, bolts of energy, receivers. No. C109c, Receivers, jet, ship, train, car, carriage. No. C109d, Radar.

1982, July 1 Litho. *Perf. 14*

C102 AP17 25f multi
C103 AP17 50f multi
C104 AP17 60f multi
C105 AP17 75f multi
C106 AP17 100f multi
C107 AP17 125f multi

Souvenir Sheets

C108 Sheet of 4
a.-d. AP17 100f any single
C109 Sheet of 4
a.-d. AP17 100f any single

TB Bacillus Centenary — AP18

1982 Litho. *Perf. 14*

C110 AP18 25f multi
C111 AP18 50f multi
C112 AP18 60f multi
C113 AP18 75f multi
C114 AP18 100f multi
C115 AP18 125f multi

Souvenir Sheets

C116 Sheet of 4, Fruit
a. AP18 100f, any single
C117 Sheet of 4, Flowers
a. AP18 125f, any single

1982 World Cup Soccer Championships, Spain — AP19

Various soccer plays.

1982, Sept. 1 *Perf. 14*

C118 AP19 25f multi
C119 AP19 50f multi
C120 AP19 60f multi
C121 AP19 75f multi
C122 AP19 100f multi
C123 AP19 125f multi

Palestinian Children's Day — AP20

1982, Oct. 20

C126 AP20 75f Boy
C127 AP20 125f Girl
C128 AP20 325f Boy and girl
a. Souvenir sheet of one

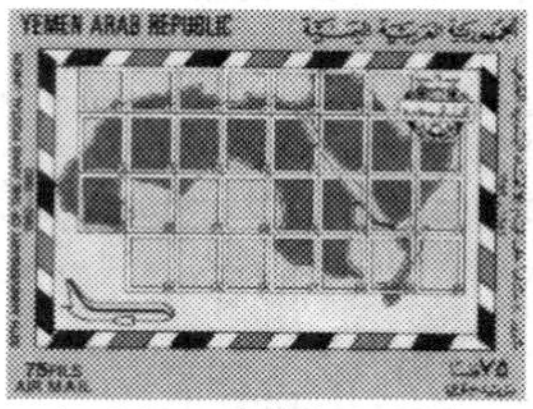

Arab Postal Union, 30th Anniv. — AP21

1982, Dec. 1

C129 AP21 75f yel & multi
C130 AP21 125f grn & multi
C131 AP21 325f mag & multi
a. Souvenir sheet of one

1984 Summer Olympics, Los Angeles — AP22

1984, Nov. 15

C132 AP22 20f Wrestling
C133 AP22 30f Boxing
C134 AP22 40f Running
C135 AP22 60f Hurdling
C136 AP22 150f Pole vault
C137 AP22 325f Javelin throw

Two souvenir sheets of 4 75f stamps exist picturing water sports, gymnastics, weightlifting, shot put and discus throwing.

POSTAGE DUE STAMPS

D1

1942 Litho. Wmk. 258 *Perf. 12½*

J1	D1	1b org & yel grn	10	10
J2	D1	2b org & yel grn	15	15
J3	D1	4b org & yel grn	20	20
J4	D1	6b org & brt ultra	30	30
J5	D1	8b org & brt ultra	40	40
J6	D1	10b org & brt ultra	50	50
J7	D1	12b org & brt ultra	60	60
J8	D1	20b org & brt ultra	1.00	1.00
		Nos. J1-J8 (8)	3.25	3.25

Yemen had no postage due system. Nos. J1-J8 were used for regular postage.

YEMEN,
People's Democratic Republic

LOCATION — Southern Arabia
GOVT. — Republic
AREA — 111,074 sq. mi.
POP. — 2,030,000 (est. 1981)
CAPITAL — Aden

The People's Republic of Southern Yemen was proclaimed November 30, 1967, when the Federation of South Arabia achieved independence. It consisted of the former British colony of Aden and the protectorates. The name was changed to People's Democratic Republic of Yemen on November 30, 1970. See South Arabia, Volume 1.

1,000 Fils = 1 Dinar

Catalogue values for all unused stamps in this country are for Never Hinged items.

People's Republic of Southern Yemen
South Arabia Nos. 3-16 Overprinted in Red or Blue

جمهورية اليمن الجنوبية
الشعبية

PEOPLE'S REPUBLIC
OF SOUTHERN YEMEN
a

جمهورية اليمن الجنوبية الشعبية

PEOPLE'S REPUBLIC
OF SOUTHERN YEMEN
b

Perf. 14½x14
1968, Apr. 1 Photo. Unwmk.
Overprinted Type "a"

1	A1	5f bl	5	5
2	A1	10f lt vio bl	7	5
3	A1	15f bl grn	10	7
4	A1	20f grn	10	7
5	A1	25f org brn (B)	10	7
6	A1	30f lem	20	14
7	A1	35f red brn (B)	20	16
8	A1	50f rose red (B)	25	22
9	A1	65f lt yel grn	30	30
10	A1	75f rose car (B)	45	40

Overprinted Type "b"

11	A2	100f multi (B)	60	50
12	A2	250f multi	1.20	1.00
13	A2	500f multi (B)	2.25	2.00
14	A2	1d vio & multi	6.25	5.00
		Nos. 1-14 (14)	12.12	10.03

Globe and Flag A1

Designs: 15f, Revolutionist with broken chain and flames (vert.). 50f, Aden Harbor. 100f, Cotton picking.

1968, May 25 Litho. *Perf. 13x12½*

15	A1	10f multi	10	10
16	A1	15f multi	10	10
17	A1	50f multi	30	30
18	A1	100f multi	65	65

Independence Day, Nov. 30, 1967.

Girl Scouts at Campfire A2

Designs: 25f, Three Girl Scouts (vert.). 50f, Three Girl Scout leaders.

Perf. 13½
1968, Sept. 21 Litho. Unwmk.

19	A2	10f ultra & sep	10	10
20	A2	25f org brn & Prus bl	16	16
21	A2	50f yel, bl & brn	38	38

Issued to publicize the Girl Scout movement in Southern Yemen, established 1966 (in Aden).

Revolutionary — A3

"Freedom-Socialism-Unity" A4

King of Ausan, Alabaster Statue A5

Design: 30f, Radfan Mountains where first revolutionary fell.

1968, Oct. 14 Unwmk. *Perf. 13*

22	A3	20f brn & lt bl	16	16
23	A3	30f grn & brn	20	20
24	A4	100f ver & yel	65	65

Issued for Revolution Day, commemorating the revolution of Oct. 14, 1963.

1968, Dec. 28 Litho. *Perf. 13*

Antiquities of Southern Yemen: 35f, African-type sculpture of a man. 50f, Winged bull, Assyrian-type bas-relief (horiz.). 65f, Bull's head (Moon God), alabaster plaque, 230 B.C. (horiz.).

25	A5	5f ol & bis	7	7
26	A5	35f mar & lt bl	25	25
27	A5	50f bis & bl	40	40
28	A5	65f lt grnsh bl & lil	50	50

Martyr Monument, Steamer Point, Aden — A6

1969, Feb. 11 Litho. *Perf. 13*

29	A6	15f yel & multi	10	10
30	A6	35f emer & multi	20	20
31	A6	100f org & multi	60	60

Issued for Martyr Day.

Albert Thomas Monument, Geneva, and ILO Emblem — A7

1969, June 1 Litho. *Perf. 13*

32	A7	10f brt grn, blk & lt brn	7	7
33	A7	35f car rose, blk & lt brn	25	25

50th anniv. of the ILO, and to honor founder Albert Thomas.

Classroom — A8

1969, Sept. 8 Litho. *Perf. 13*

34	A8	35f org & multi	25	25
35	A8	100f yel & multi	70	70

International Literacy Day, Sept. 8.

Mahatma Gandhi — A9

1969, Sept. 27 Litho. *Perf. 13*

36	A9	35f lt ultra & vio brn	25	25

Mohandas K. Gandhi (1869-1948), leader in India's fight for independence.

Family A10

1969, Oct. 1

37	A10	25f lt grn & multi	20	20
38	A10	75f car rose & multi	60	60

Issued for Family Day.

U.N. Headquarters, N.Y. — A11

1969, Oct. 24 *Perf. 13*

39	A11	20f rose red & multi	14	14
40	A11	65f emer & multi	42	42

Issued for United Nations Day.

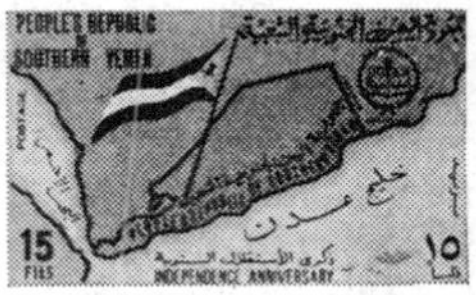
Map and Flag of Southern Yemen A12

Design: 40f, 50f, Tractors and flag (agricultural progress).

1969, Nov. 30 Litho. Unwmk.
Size: 41x24½mm

41	A12	15f multi	10	10
42	A12	35f multi	20	20

Size: 37x37mm

43	A12	40f bl & multi	25	25
44	A12	50f brn & multi	38	38

Second anniversary of independence.

Map of Arab League Countries, Flag and Emblem — A13

1970, Mar. 22 Unwmk. *Perf. 13*

45	A13	35f lt bl & multi	25	25

25th anniversary of the Arab League.

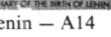

Lenin — A14

Fighter — A15

1970, Apr. 22 Litho. *Perf. 13*

46	A14	75f multi	50	50

Lenin (1870-1924), Russian communist leader.

1970, May 15

Designs: 35f, Underground soldier and plane destroyed on ground. 50f, Fighting people hailing Arab liberation flag (horiz.).

47	A15	15f grn, red & blk	16	14
48	A15	35f grn, bl, red & blk	42	35
49	A15	50f grn, blk & red	55	45

Issued for Palestine Day.

U.P.U. Headquarters, Bern — A16

1970, May 22 Litho. *Perf. 13*

50	A16	15f org & brt grn	14 14
51	A16	65f yel & car rose	40 40

Opening of the new UPU Headquarters in Bern.

Yemeni Costume — A17

Regional Costumes: 15f, 20f, Women's costumes. 50f, Three men of Aden.

1970, July 2 Litho. *Perf. 13*

52	A17	10f yel & multi	10 10
53	A17	15f lt lil & multi	14 14
54	A17	20f lt bl & multi	16 16
55	A17	50f multi	30 30

Camel and Calf — A18

Designs: 25f, Goats. 35f, Arabian oryx. 65f, Socotra dwarf cows.

1970, Aug. 31 Litho. *Perf. 13*

56	A18	15f dk brn & multi	10 10
57	A18	25f car rose & multi	16 16
58	A18	35f ultra & multi	30 30
59	A18	65f brt grn & multi	45 45

A19

Designs: 35f, National Front Organization Headquarters. 50f, Farm worker, 1970, and battle scene, 1963.

1970, Oct. 14 Litho. *Perf. 13*

Size: 41½x29½mm

60	A19	25f multi	20 20

Size: 56½x27mm

61	A19	35f multi	30 30

Size: 41x24½mm

62	A19	50f multi	38 38

7th anniversary of Oct. 14 Revolution.

U.N. Headquarters, Emblem — A20

1970, Oct. 24 Litho. *Perf. 13*

63	A20	10f org & bl	7 7
64	A20	65f brt pink & bl	45 45

25th anniversary of the United Nations.

People's Democratic Republic of Yemen

Temples at Philae — A21

1971, Feb. 1 Litho. *Perf. 13½x13*

65	A21	5f vio & multi	7 7
66	A21	35f bl & multi	25 25
67	A21	65f grn & multi	55 55

UNESCO campaign to save the monuments in Nubia.

Scales, Book and Sword A22

1971, Mar. 1 *Perf. 13x12½*

68	A22	10f brt pink & multi	7 7
69	A22	15f brt grn & multi	16 16
70	A22	35f lt ultra & multi	30 30
71	A22	50f rose & multi	40 40

First Constitution, 1971.

Men of 3 Races, Human Rights Emblem A23

1971, Mar. 21

72	A23	20f lt bl & multi	14 14
73	A23	35f grn & multi	30 30
74	A23	75f lt vio & multi	55 55

Intl. year against racial discrimination.

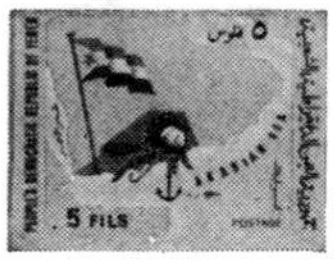

Map and Flag — A24

"Brothers' Blood" Tree, Socotra Island — A25

1971-77 Litho. *Perf. 13½*

75	A24	5f yel & multi	5	5
76	A24	10f grn & multi	5	5
77	A24	15f yel & multi	5	5
78	A24	20f org & multi	7	7
79	A24	25f bl & multi	10	10
80	A24	35f red org & multi	14	14
81	A24	40f vio & multi	15	15
82	A24	50f yel grn & multi	30	30
82A	A24	60f red & multi ('77)	22	22
83	A24	65f pale vio & multi	38	38
84	A24	80f org brn & multi	45	45
84A	A24	90f ol & multi ('77)	35	35

Perf. 13

84B	A25	110f brn & multi ('77)	40	40
85	A25	125f ultra & multi	80	80
86	A25	250f org & multi	1.25	1.25
87	A25	500f multi	2.50	2.25
88	A25	1d grn & multi	5.00	4.25
		Nos. 75-88 (17)	12.26	11.26

Issue dates: Nos. 82A, 84A-84B, Oct. 17, 1977. Others, Apr. 1, 1971.

See Nos. 332-333.

Machine Gun and Map A26

Arms with Wrench and Cogwheel A27

Designs: 45f, Woman fighter and flame (horiz.). 50f, Fighter, factories and rainbow.

1971, June 9 Litho. *Perf. 12½x13*

89	A26	15f multi	10 10
90	A26	45f grn & multi	30 30
91	A26	50f multi	45 45

Armed revolution in the Arabian Gulf.

1971, June 22

Designs: 25f, Torch, factories, symbols. 65f, Windmill.

92	A27	15f bl & multi	35	25
93	A27	25f multi	1.20	1.00
94	A27	65f multi	1.40	1.20

2nd anniversary of the revolution of June 22, 1969 (Corrective Move).

A 20f picturing a fighter holding rifle and flag, with flag colors transposed, was withdrawn on day of issue.

Revolutionary Emblem — A28

Design: 40f, Map of southern Arabia and flag of republic.

1971, Sept. 26

95	A28	10f yel & multi	7 7
96	A28	40f lt grn & multi	30 30

9th anniv. of the revolution of Sept. 26.

Gamal Abdel Nasser — A29

UNICEF Emblem, Children of the World — A30

1971, Sept. 28 Litho. *Perf. 12½x13*

97	A29	65f multi	40 40

First anniversary of the death of Gamal Abdel Nasser (1918-1970), President of Egypt.

1971, Dec. 11 *Perf. 13x13½*

98	A30	15f org, car & blk	10 10
99	A30	40f lt ultra, car & blk	20 20
100	A30	50f yel grn, car & blk	38 38

25th anniv. of UNICEF.

The lack of a value for a listed item does not necessarily indicate rarity.

Pigeons — A31

Birds: 40f, Partridge. 65f, Partridge and guinea fowl. 100f, European kite.

1971, Dec. 22 *Perf. 13½x13*

101	A31	5f bl, blk & car	7 7
102	A31	40f sal & multi	20 20
103	A31	65f brt grn, blk & car	38 38
104	A31	100f yel, blk & car	60 60

Dhow under Construction A32

Design: 80f, Dhow under sail (vert.).

Perf. 13½x13, 13x13½

1972, Feb. 15

105	A32	25f bl, brn & yel	20 20
106	A32	80f lt bl & multi	80 60

Band A33

Designs: 25f, 40f, 80f, Various folk dances.

1972, Apr. 8 Litho. *Perf. 13*

107	A33	10f lt grn & multi	5 5
108	A33	25f org & multi	10 10
109	A33	40f red & multi	30 30
110	A33	80f bl & multi	60 60

Palestinian Fighter and Barbed Wire — A34

1972, May 15

111	A34	5f emer & multi	35 16
112	A34	20f bl & multi	50 35
113	A34	65f org ver & multi	65 50

Struggle for Palestine liberation.

Policemen on Parade A35

Design: 80f, Militia women on parade.

1972, June 20 Litho. *Perf. 13½*

114	A35	25f lt bl & multi	10	10
115	A35	80f bl grn & multi	50	50
a.		Souv. sheet of 2, #114-115	80	80

Police Day. No. 115a sold for 150f.

Start of Bicycle Race A36

Designs: 15f Parade of young women. 40f, Yemeni Guides and Scouts on parade. 80f, Acrobats (vert.).

1972, July 20 Litho. *Perf. 13½*

116 A36 10f lt bl & multi		10	5
117 A36 15f multi		20	10
118 A36 40f buff & multi		40	30
119 A36 80f lt ultra & multi		1.00	50

Turtle A37

1972, Sept. 2 Litho. *Perf. 13*

120 A37 15f *Shown*	45	14
121 A37 40f *Sailfish*	50	35
122 A37 65f *Kingfish*	65	45
123 A37 125f *Spiny lobster*	80	80

Book Year Emblem A38

1972, Sept. 9

124 A38 40f red, ultra & yel	30	30
125 A38 65f org, ultra & yel	50	50

International Book Year 1972.

Farm Couple and Fields A39

1972, Nov. 23 Litho. *Perf. 13*

126 A39 10f org & multi	7	7
127 A39 25f rose lil & multi	16	16
128 A39 40f red & multi	30	30

Lands Day, publicizing land reforms.

Militia — A40

Designs: 20f, Soldier guarding village. 65f, Industrial, agricultural and educational progress (vert.).

1972, Dec. 2 Litho. *Perf. 13*

129 A40 5f multi	7	7
130 A40 20f multi	16	16
131 A40 65f multi	45	45
a. Souv. sheet of 3, #129-131, imperf.	70	70

5th anniversary of independence.

Census Chart A41

1973, Apr. 3 Litho. *Perf. 12½x13½*

132 A41 25f org, emer & ol	16	16
133 A41 40f rose, bl & vio	35	35

Population census 1973.

WHO Emblem and "25" — A42

1973, Apr. 7 *Perf. 14x12½, 12½x14*

134 A42 5f *"25" and WHO emblem* (vert.)	7	7
135 A42 20f *Shown*	16	16
136 A42 125f *"25" and WHO emblem*	65	65

25th anniv. of the WHO.

Elephant Bay A43

Views: 20f, Taweels Tanks Reservoir (Vert.). 25f, Shibam Town. 100f, Al-Mohdar Mosque, Tarim.

1973, June 9 Litho. *Perf. 13*

137 A43 20f multi	10	10
138 A43 25f multi	16	16
139 A43 40f multi	30	30
140 A43 100f multi	55	55

Tourist publicity.

Office Buildings and Slum, Aden A44

Design: 80f, Intersection, Aden (vert.).

1973, Aug. 4 Litho. *Perf. 13*

141 A44 20f multi	14	14
142 A44 80f multi	50	50

Nationalization of buildings.

Army Unit A45

People's Army: 20f, Four marching soldiers. 40f, Sailors on parade. 80f, Tanks.

1973, Sept. 1

143 A45 10f multi	7	7
144 A45 20f multi	10	10
145 A45 40f multi	30	30
146 A45 80f multi	50	50

FAO Emblem, Loading Food A46

Design: 80f, Workers and grain sacks.

1973, Dec. 19 Litho. *Perf. 13*

147 A46 20f bl & multi	10	10
148 A46 80f bl & multi	50	50

World Food Program, 10th anniversary.

Letter and UPU Emblem A47

UPU Emblem and Yemeni Flag A48

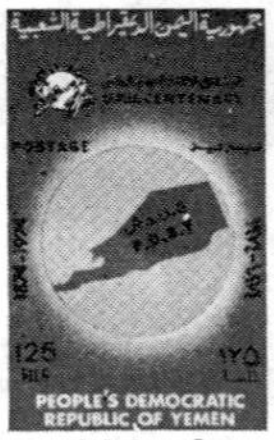

Map of Yemen, UPU Emblem A49

UPU cent.: 20f, "100" formed by people, and UPU emblem.

1974, Oct. 9 Litho. *Perf. 12½x13½*

149 A47 5f multi	7	7
150 A47 20f multi	14	14
151 A48 40f multi	35	35
152 A49 125f multi	60	60

Irrigation System — A50

Designs: 20f, Bulldozer pushing soil. 100f, Tractors plowing field.

1974 Litho. *Perf. 13*

153 A50 10f multi	7	7
154 A50 20f multi	14	14
155 A50 100f multi	50	50

Progress in agriculture.

Lathe Operator — A51

Industrial progress: 40f, Printers. 80f, Women textile workers (horiz.).

1975, May 1 Litho. *Perf. 13*

156 A51 10f multi	7	7
157 A51 40f multi	30	30
158 A51 80f multi	50	50

Yemeni Woman — A52

Designs: Various women's costumes.

1975, Nov. 15 Litho. *Perf. 11½x12*

159 A52 5f blk & ocher	8	8
160 A52 10f blk & vio	10	10
161 A52 15f blk & ol	10	10
162 A52 25f blk & rose lil	25	25
163 A52 40f blk & Prus bl	42	42
164 A52 50f blk & org brn	60	60
Nos. 159-164 (6)	1.55	1.55

Women Factory Workers, IWY Emblem A53

1975, Dec. 30 Litho. *Perf. 12x11½*

165 A53 40f blk & sal	25	25
166 A53 50f blk & yel grn	38	38

International Women's Year 1975.

Soccer Player and Field — A54

Designs: Different scenes from soccer.

1976, Apr. 1 Litho. *Perf. 11½x12*

167 A54 5f lt bl & brn	5	5
168 A54 40f yel & grn	30	30
169 A54 80f sal & vio	50	50

Rocket Take-off from Moon — A55

Designs: 15f, Alexander Satalov. 40f, Lunokhod on moon (horiz.). 65f, Valentina Tereshkova and rocket.

Perf. 11½x12, 12x11½

1976, Apr. 17 Litho.

170 A55 10f multi	5	5
171 A55 15f multi	8	8
172 A55 40f multi	38	38
173 A55 65f multi	55	55

Soviet cosmonauts and space program.

Traffic Policemen A56

1977, Apr. 16 Litho. *Perf. 14*

174	A56	25f red & blk	20	20
175	A56	60f yel & blk	40	40
176	A56	75f grn & blk	50	50
177	A56	110f dp bl & blk	65	65

Traffic change to right side of road.

APU Emblem — A57

1977, Apr. 12 Litho. *Perf. 13½*

178	A57	20f lt bl & multi	14	14
179	A57	60f gray & multi	42	42
180	A57	70f lt grn & multi	50	50
181	A57	90f bl grn & multi	55	55

Arab Postal Union, 25th anniversary.

Congress Decree and Red Star — A58

Designs: 25f, Pres. Salim Rubi'a Ali, Council members Ali Nasser Muhamed and Abdul Farta Ismail. 65f, Women's militia on parade. 95f, Aerial view of textile mill.

1977, May Photo. *Perf. 13*

182	A58	25f grn, gold & dk brn	16	16
183	A58	35f red, gold & lt bl	25	25
184	A58	65f bl, gold & lil	38	38
185	A58	95f org, gold & grn	45	45

Unification Congress, 1st anniversary.

Afrivoluta Pringlei A59

Shells: 60f, Festilyria duponti (vert.). 110f, Conus splendidulus. 180f, Cypraea broderipii.

1977, July 16 Litho. *Perf. 13½*

186	A59	60f multi	20	14
187	A59	90f multi	30	16
188	A59	110f multi	50	30
189	A59	180f multi	70	50

Emblem and Flag — A60

Designs: 20f, Man with broken chain. 90f, Pipeline, agriculture and industry. 110f, Flag, symbolic tree and hands holding tools.

1977, Nov. 30 Litho. *Perf. 13½*

190	A60	5f blk & multi	5	5
191	A60	20f blk & multi	7	7
192	A60	90f blk & multi	30	20
193	A60	110f blk & multi	50	25

10th anniversary of independence.

Dome of the Rock — A61

1978, May 15 *Perf. 12*

194	A61	5f multi	*65*	*35*

Palestinian fighters & families. See No. 264A.

Congress Emblem and "CUBA" — A62

Designs: 60f, Congress emblem. 90f, Festival emblem as flower. 110f, Festival emblem, dove, young man and woman.

1978, June 22 Litho. *Perf. 14*

195	A62	5f multi	7	7
196	A62	60f multi	55	35
197	A62	90f multi	70	40
198	A62	110f multi	90	60

11th World Youth Festival, Havana.

Silver Ornaments — A63

Designs: Various silver ornaments.

1978, July 22 Litho. *Perf. 13½*

199	A63	10f blk & multi	5	5
200	A63	15f blk & multi	7	7
201	A63	20f blk & multi	8	8
202	A63	60f blk & multi	20	16
203	A63	90f blk & multi	38	25
204	A63	110f blk & multi	50	30
		Nos. 199-204 (6)	1.28	91

Yemeni Musical Instruments — A64

1978, Aug. 26 *Perf. 14*

205	A64	35f Almarfaai	10	7
206	A64	60f Almizmar	25	16
207	A64	90f Alqnboos	30	20
208	A64	110f Simsimiya	50	30

"V" for Vanguard — A65

Man with Palm, Factories — A66

1978, Oct. 11 Litho. *Perf. 14*

209	A65	5f multi	5	5
210	A65	20f multi	7	7
211	A65	60f multi	25	14
212	A65	180f multi	50	30

1st Conf. of Vanguard Party, Oct. 11-13.

1978, Oct. 14

Designs: 10f, Palm branches, broken chains (horiz.). 60f, Candle and "15." 110f, Woman and man with rifle, "15."

213	A66	10f multi	8	8
214	A66	35f multi	20	14
215	A66	60f multi	40	20
216	A66	110f multi	70	40

15th Revolution Day.

Child, Map of Arabia and IYC Emblem — A67

1979, Mar. 20 Litho. *Perf. 13½*

217	A67	15f multi	7	7
218	A67	20f multi	7	7
219	A67	60f multi	25	10
220	A67	90f multi	38	20

International Year of the Child.

Sickle, Star, Tractor, Wheat and Dove — A68

Designs: 35f, Pylon, star, compass, wheat and hammer. 60f, Students, worker and clock. 90f, Woman with raised arms, doves and star.

1979, June 22 Litho. *Perf. 14*

221	A68	20f multi	7	7
222	A68	35f multi	10	7
223	A68	60f multi	25	10
224	A68	90f multi	38	20

Corrective Move, 10th anniversary.

Yemen No. 52, Hill — A69

Hill and: 110f, Yemen No. 56. 250f, Aden No. 12.

1979, Aug. 27 Litho. *Perf. 14*

225	A69	90f multi	30	20
226	A69	110f multi	38	25

Souvenir Sheet

227	A69	250f multi	1.00	1.00

Sir Rowland Hill (1795-1879), originator of penny postage.

Book, World Map, Arab Achievements A70

1979, Sept. 26 Litho. *Perf. 14*

228	A70	60f multi	25	10

Party Emblem — A71

Cassia Adenesis — A72

1979, Oct. 13 *Perf. 14½x14*

229	A71	60f multi	25	10

Yemeni Socialist Party, 1st anniversary.

1979, Nov. 30 Litho. *Perf. 13½*

Flowers: 90f, Nerium oleander. 110f, Calligonum comosum. 180f, Adenium obesium.

230	A72	20f multi	16	14
231	A72	90f multi	65	35
232	A72	110f multi	1.00	50
233	A72	180f multi	1.20	65

First Anniv. of Iranian Revolution — A73

1980, Feb. 12 Litho. *Perf. 13½*

234	A73	60f multi	22	22

Dido A74

1980, Mar. 5 Litho. *Perf. 13½*

235	A74	110f *shown*	50	20
236	A74	180f *Anglia*	70	30
237	A74	250f *India*	90	40

Basket Maker, London 1980 Emblem — A75

1980, May 6 Litho. *Perf. 14*

238	A75	60f *shown*	20	10
239	A75	90f *Hubble bubble pipe maker*	30	16
240	A75	110f *Weaver*	38	25
241	A75	250f *Potter*	90	50

London 1980 Intl. Stamp Exhib., May 6-14.

Hemprich's Skink — A76

1980, May 8 Litho. *Perf. 14*

242 A76 20f *shown* 10 5
243 A76 35f *Mole viper* 14 7
244 A76 110f *Carter's day gecko* 38 16
245 A76 180f *Cobra* 60 30

Misha and Olympic Emblem — A77

Farmers Armed — A78

1980, July 19 Litho. *Perf. 12½x12*

246 A77 110f multi 38 20

1980, Oct. 17 *Perf. 13½*

247 A78 50f *Armed farmers working,* horiz. 20 10
248 A78 90f *shown* 30 20
249 A78 110f *Sickle (wheat) and fist* 40 25

10th anniversary of farmers' uprising.

110th Birth Anniversary of Lenin — A79

1980, Nov. 7 Litho. *Perf. 12*

250 A79 35f multi 14 7

Douglas DC-3 — A80

1981, Mar. 11 Litho. *Perf. 13½*

251 A80 60f shown 20 10
252 A80 90f Boeing 707 38 20
253 A80 250f DHC Dash 7 1.00 50

Democratic Yemen Airlines, 10th anniv.

Ras Boradli Earth Satellite Station A82

1981, June 22 Litho. *Perf. 12*

257 A82 60f multi 20 16

Conocarpus Lancifolius — A83

Supreme People's Council, 10th Anniv. — A84

1981, Aug. 1 Litho. *Perf. 12*

258 A83 90f shown 30 16
259 A83 180f Ficus vasta 65 40
260 A83 250f Maerua crassifolia 1.00 65

1981, Aug. 18 Litho. *Perf. 15x14½*

261 A84 180f multi 65 40

Desert Fox — A85

1981, Sept. 26 Litho. *Perf. 14½*

262 A85 50f shown 20 10
263 A85 90f South Arabian leopard 40 20
264 A85 250f Ibex 90 50

No. 194 Redrawn

1981, Oct. 15 Litho. *Perf. 12*
Size: 25x27mm

264A A61 5f multi 5 5

Denomination in upper right.

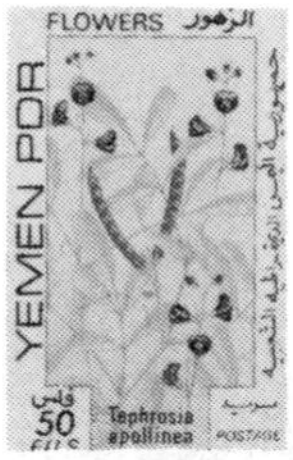

Tephrosia Apollinea — A86

1981, Nov. 30 Litho. *Perf. 13½*

265 A86 50f shown 20 10
266 A86 90f Citrullus colocynthis 30 16
267 A86 110f Aloe sqarrosa 40 16
268 A86 250f Lawsonia inermis 1.00 60

Intl. Year of the Disabled A87

1981, Dec. 12 Litho. *Perf. 14½*

269 A87 50f multi 16 10
270 A87 100f multi 38 16
271 A87 150f multi 60 38

TB Bacillus Centenary — A88

1982, Mar. 24 Litho. *Perf. 14½*

272 A88 50f multi 30 16

30th Anniv. of Arab Postal Union A89

1982, Apr. 12 Litho. *Perf. 14*

273 A89 100f multi 50 30

1982 World Cup A90

Designs: Various soccer players.

1982, June 13 Litho. *Perf. 14*

274 A90 50f multi 25 15
275 A90 100f multi 50 30
276 A90 150f multi 70 45
277 A90 200f multi 1.00 60
a. Souv. sheet of 4, #274-277 2.50 1.50

60th Anniv. of USSR A93

1982, Dec. 22 Litho. *Perf. 12½x12*

280 A93 50f Flags, arms 50 35

Nos. 274-277, 277a Ovptd. with Emblem and "WORLD CUP / WINNERS / 1982 / 1st ITALY / 2nd W-GERMANY / 3rd POLAND / 4th FRANCE" in Blue.

1982, Dec. 30 Litho. *Perf. 14*

281 A90 50f multi 20 20
282 A90 100f multi 40 40
283 A90 150f multi 60 60
284 A90 200f multi 70 70
a. Souvenir sheet of 4, #281-284 2.00 2.00

Palestinian Solidarity A94

1983, Apr. 10 *Perf. 13½x14½*

285 A94 50f Yasser Arafat 20 20
286 A94 100f Arafat, Dome of the Rock 40 40
a. Souvenir sheet of 1, imperf. 50 50

No. 246 Ovptd. with TEMBAL '83 Emblem in Yellow.

1983, May 21 *Perf. 12½x12*

287 A77 110f multi 42 42

World Communications Year — A95

Designs: 50f, Correspondent, postrider, ship. 100f, Postman, coach, telegraph. No. 290, Telephones, bus. 200f, Telecommunications. No. 292, Montage.

1983, June 10 *Perf. 13x13½*

288 A95 50f blk & brt bl 20 20
289 A95 100f multi 40 40
290 A95 150f multi 60 60
291 A95 200f multi 70 70

Souvenir Sheet

292 A95 150f multi 60 60

Pablo Picasso (1881-1973), Painter — A96

Paintings: No. 293, The Poor Family, 1903. No. 294, Woman with Crow. No. 295a, The Gourmet. No. 295b, Woman with Child on Beach. No. 295c, Sitting Beggar. No. 296, The Solar Family, horiz.

1983, July 25 *Perf. 14*

293 A96 50f multi 20 20
294 A96 100f multi 40 40

Souvenir Sheets

295 Sheet of 3 1.20 1.20
a. A96 50f multi 20 20
b. A96 100f multi 40 40
c. A96 150f multi 60 60
296 A96 150f multi 60 60

23rd Pre-Olympics Games, 1984 — A97

1983, July 30

297 A97 25f Show jumping 10 10
298 A97 50f Show jumping, diff. 20 20
299 A97 100f Three-day event 40 40

Souvenir Sheets

300 Sheet of 4 80 80
a. A97 20f Bay 8 8
b. A97 40f Gray 15 15
c. A97 60f Bay, diff. 22 22
d. A97 80f Arabian 32 32
301 A97 200f Show jumping, diff. 70 70

Nos. 300a-300c, 301 vert.

Locomotives — A98

1983, Aug. 24 *Perf. 14½x15*

302 A98 25f P8 steam engine, 1905 10 10
303 A98 50f 880 steam, 1915 20 20
304 A98 100f GT 2-4-4, 1923 40 40

Souvenir Sheets

305 Sheet of 3 80 80
a. A98 40f D51 steam, 1936 15 15
b. A98 60f 45 Series, 1937 22 22
c. A98 100f PT 47, 1948 40 40
306 A98 200f P36, 1950 80 80

Natl. Revolution, 20th Anniv. A100

1983, Oct. 15 Litho. ***Perf. 13½x13***

312 A100 50f shown 20 20
313 A100 100f Flag, freedom fighter 40 40

1st Manned Flight, Bicent. — A101

Balloons: 100f, La Montgolfiere prototype. No. 316a, Lunardi's. No. 316b, Charles and Robert's. No. 316c, Wiseman's. No. 316d, Blanchard and Jeffries's. 200f, Five-balloon craft.

1983, Oct. 25 ***Perf. 14***

314 A101 50f shown 20 20
315 A101 100f multi 40 40

Souvenir Sheets

316 Sheet of 4 80 80
a. A101 20f multi 8 8
b. A101 40f multi 15 15
c. A101 60f multi 20 20
d. A101 80f multi 32 32
317 A101 200f multi 80 80

1984 Winter Olympics, Sarajevo A102

1983, Dec. 28 Litho. ***Perf. 14***

318 A102 50f Men's downhill skiing 20 20
319 A102 100f Two-man bobsled 40 40

Souvenir Sheets

320 Sheet of 2 40 40
a. A102 40f Ski jumping 15 15
b. A102 60f Figure skating 20 20
321 A102 200f Ice hockey 80 80

1984 Summer Olympics, Los Angeles — A103

1984, Jan. 24

322 A103 25f Fencing 10 10
323 A103 50f Fencing, diff. 20 20
324 A103 100f Fencing, diff. 40 40

Souvenir Sheets

325 Sheet of 4 80 80
a. A103 20f Gymnastics 8 8
b. A103 40f Water polo 15 15
c. A103 60f Wrestling 20 20
d. A103 80f Show jumping 32 32
326 A103 200f Show jumping, diff. 80 80

Nos. 83 and 84B Surcharged with Black Squares.

1984, May 26 Litho. ***Perf. 13½, 13***

332 A24 50f on 65f multi
333 A25 100f on 110f multi

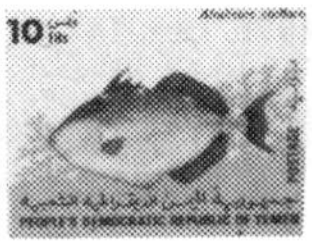

Fish — A105

1984, Nov. 25 Litho. ***Perf. 11½***

334 A105 10f Abalistes stellaris 5 5
335 A105 15f Caranx speciocus 7 7
336 A105 20f Pomadasys maculatus 8 8
337 A105 25f Chaetodon fasciatus 10 10
338 A105 35f Pomacanthus imperator 14 14
339 A105 50f Rastrelliger kanagurta 20 20
340 A105 100f Euthynnus affinis 40 40
341 A105 150f Heniochus acuminatus 60 60
342 A105 200f Pomacanthus maculosus 80 80
343 A105 250f Pterois russellii 1.00 1.00
344 A105 400f Argyrops spinifer 1.60 1.60
345 A105 500f Dasyatis uarnak 2.00 2.00
346 A105 1d Epinephalus chlorostigma 3.75 3.75
347 A105 2d Drepane longimana 8.00 8.00
Nos. 334-347 (14) 18.79 18.79

Natl. Literacy Campaign A106

1985, Feb. 27 ***Perf. 12***

350 A106 50f Girls writing 20 20
351 A106 100f Hand, fountain pen, vert. 40 40

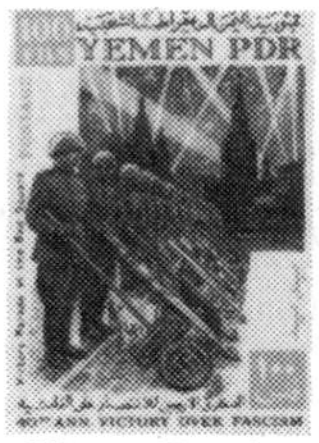

Victory Parade, Red Square, Moscow, 1945 A107

12th World Youth and Students Festival A108

1985, May 9 ***Perf. 12x12½***

352 A107 100f multi 40 40

Defeat of Nazi Germany, end of World War II, 40th anniv.

1985, Aug. 3 ***Perf. 12***

353 A108 50f Emblem 20 20
354 A108 100f Hand holding emblem 40 40

UNESCO World Heritage Campaign A109

Natl. Socialist Party, 3rd Gen. Cong. A110

1985, Aug. 29

355 A109 50f Shibam city 20 20
356 A109 50f Close-up of buildings 20 20
357 A109 100f Windows 40 40
358 A109 100f Door 40 40

Nos. 355-357 horiz.

1985, Oct. 10

359 A110 25f Energy 10 10
360 A110 50f Industry 20 20
361 A110 100f Agriculture 40 40

UN Child Survival Campaign A111

World Food Day A112

1985, Nov. 28

362 A111 50f Mother feeding child 20 20
363 A111 50f Holding child 20 20
364 A111 100f Feeding child, diff. 40 40
365 A111 100f Breastfeeding 40 40

1986, Jan. 30

366 A112 20f Almihdar Mosque, Aden 12 12
367 A112 180f Palm trees 1.05 1.05

UN Food and Agriculture Org., 40th anniv.

Lenin, Red Square, Moscow A113

1986, Feb. 25 ***Perf. 12x12½***

368 A113 75f multi 45 45
369 A113 250f multi 1.45 1.45

27th Soviet Communist Party Cong., Moscow.

Costumes Worn at the 1984 Brides Dance Festival — A114

Designs: No. 370, Bride wearing red and green costume, face markings. No. 371, Violet costume. No. 372, Veiled bride. No. 373, Unveiled bride. No. 374, Groom holding dagger. No. 375, Groom holding rifle.

1986, Feb. 27

370 A114 50f multi 30 30
371 A114 50f multi 30 30
372 A114 50f multi 30 30
373 A114 100f multi 58 58
374 A114 100f multi 58 58
375 A114 100f multi 58 58
Nos. 370-375 (6) 2.64 2.64

Revolution Martyrs A115

1986, Oct. 15 Litho. ***Perf. 12***

376 A115 75f Abdul Fattah Ismail 45 45
377 A115 75f Ali Shayaa Hadi 45 45
378 A115 75f Saleh Musleh Kasim 45 45
379 A115 75f Ali Ahmed N. Antar 45 45

U.N. Child Survival Campaign A116

Infant Immunization Program.

1987, Apr. 7 Litho. ***Perf. 12***

380 A116 20f Immunizing pregnant woman 12 12
381 A116 75f Immunizing infant 45 45
382 A116 140f Oral immunization 85 85
383 A116 150f Infant, girl, pregnant woman 90 90

1st Socialist Party General Conference A117

1987, July 30 Litho. ***Perf. 12***

384 A117 75fr multi 45 45
385 A117 150fr multi 90 90

October Revolution, Russia, 70th Anniv. A118

Monuments, Ancient City of Shabwa A119

1987, Nov. 7 Litho. ***Perf. 12½x12***

386 A118 250f multi 1.50 1.50

1987, Nov. 18 ***Perf. 12***

387 A119 25f Royal palace and court 15 15
388 A119 75f Palace, diff. 45 45
389 A119 140f Winged lion bas-relief on stone capital 85 85
390 A119 150f The Moon, legend on bronze tablet 90 90

Nos. 387-388 horiz.

Natl. Independence, 20th Anniv. — A120

Designs: 5f, Students walking to school. 75f, Family, apartments. 140f, Workers, oil derrick, thermal plant. 150f, Workers, soldier, Workers' Party headquarters.

1987, Nov. 29 *Perf. 12x12½*
391 A120 25f multi 15 15
392 A120 75f multi 45 45
393 A120 140f multi 85 85
394 A120 150f multi 90 90

September 26th Revolution, 25th Anniv. A121

1988, Feb. 27 **Litho.** *Perf. 13*
395 A121 75f Revolution monument, San'a 45 45

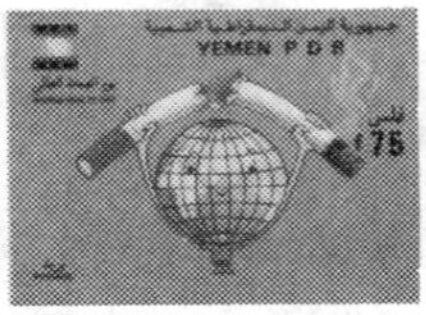
WHO, 40th Anniv. A122

1988, Apr. 7 **Litho.** *Perf. 12*
396 A122 40f Sanitary public water supply, vert. 25 25
397 A122 75f No smoking 45 45
398 A122 140f Child immunization 85 85
399 A122 250f Health care for all by the year 2000 1.55 1.55

1988 Summer Olympics, Seoul — A125

1988, Sept. 17 **Litho.** *Perf. 12x12½*
406 A125 40f Weight lifting 25 25
407 A125 75f Running 45 45
408 A125 140f Boxing 85 85
409 A125 150f Soccer 90 90

1st Freedom Fighter Killed at the Liberation Front, Radfan Mountains A126

Perf. 12½x12, 12x12½
1988, Oct. 12 **Litho.**
410 A126 25f Freedom fighters, flag, vert. 18 18
411 A126 75f shown 45 45
412 A126 300f Anniv. emblem, vert. 1.85 1.85

October 14th Revolution, 25th anniv.

Indigenous Birds — A127

1988, Nov. 5 *Perf. 12x12½, 12½x12*
413 A127 40f Treron waalia 25 25
414 A127 50f Coracias caudatus lorti, vert. 32 32
415 A127 75f Upupa epops, vert. 45 45
416 A127 250f Chlamydotis undulata macqueenii 1.55 1.55

Handicrafts — A128

Designs: 25f, Incense brazier. 75f, Cage-shaped dress form. 150f, Shell and wicker lidded basket. 250f, Wicker basket.

1988, Nov. 29 **Litho.** *Perf. 12½x12*
417 A128 25f multi 18 18
418 A128 75f multi 45 45
419 A128 150f multi 90 90
420 A128 250f multi 1.55 1.55

Aden Harbor and Yemen Port Authority, Cent. — A129

1988, Dec. 5 *Perf. 12x12½*
421 A129 75f Old harbor facility 45 45
422 A129 300f New facility 1.85 1.85

Preservation of Sana'a City, a Site on the UNESCO World Heritage List — A130

Perf. 12x12½, 12½x12
1988, Dec. 15
423 A130 75f shown 45 45
424 A130 250f City view, diff., vert. 1.55 1.55

ZAIRE

(formerly Congo Democratic Republic)

LOCATION — Central Africa
GOVT. — Republic
AREA — 905,365 sq. mi.
POP. — 31,944,000 (est. 1983)
CAPITAL — Kinshasa

Congo Democratic Republic changed its name to Republic of the Zaire in November 1971. Issues before that date are listed in Vol. 2 under Congo Democratic Republic.

100 Sengi = 1 Li-Kuta
100 Ma-Kuta = 1 Zaire

Catalogue values for all unused stamps in this country are for Never Hinged items.

UNICEF Emblem, Child Care — A143

1971, Dec. 18 *Perf. 14x13½*
750 A143 4k gold & multi 14 7
751 A143 14k lt bl, gold, red & grn 40 22
752 A143 17k gold & multi 55 20

25th anniv. of UNICEF.

UNICEF Emblem and: 14k, Map of Africa showing Zaire. 17k, Boy in African village.

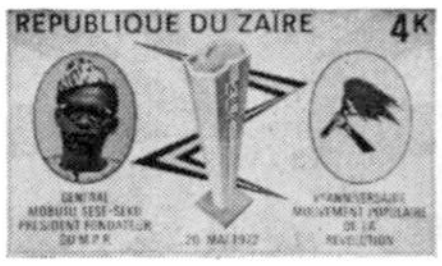
Pres. Mobutu, MPR Emblem A144

1972 **Photo.** *Perf. 11½*
753 A144 4k multi 3.50 2.25
754 A144 14k multi 3.50 2.25
755 A144 22k multi 3.50 2.25

5th anniversary of the People's Revolutionary Movement (MPR).

Zaire Arms A145

Pres. Joseph D. Mobutu A146

1972 **Litho.** *Perf. 14*
756 A145 10s red org & blk 5 5
757 A145 40s brt bl & multi 5 5
758 A145 50s cit & multi 5 5

Perf. 13
759 A146 1k sky bl & multi 5 5
760 A146 2k org & multi 7 5
761 A146 3k multi 10 5
762 A146 4k emer & multi 14 5
763 A146 5k multi 15 9
764 A146 6k multi 16 10
765 A146 8k cit & multi 28 12
766 A146 9k multi 35 14
767 A146 10k lt lil & multi 35 16
768 A146 14k multi 50 20
769 A146 17k multi 55 25
770 A146 20k yel & multi 65 35
771 A146 50k multi 1.60 80
772 A146 100k fawn & multi 3.50 1.50
Nos. 756-772 (17) 8.60 4.06

Same, Denominations in Zaires
1973, Feb. 21
773 A146 0.01z sky bl & multi 5 5
774 A146 0.02z org & multi 7 5
775 A146 0.03z multi 10 5
776 A146 0.04z multi 14 5
777 A146 0.10z multi 35 16
778 A146 0.14z multi 50 22
Nos. 773-778 (6) 1.21 58

Inga Dam A147

1973, Jan. 25 **Litho.** *Perf. 13½*
790 A147 0.04z multi 12 8
791 A147 0.14z pink & multi 42 25
792 A147 0.18z yel & multi 55 35

Completion of first section of Inga Dam Nov. 24, 1972.

World Map A148

1973, June 23 **Photo.** *Perf. 12½x12*
793 A148 0.04z lil & multi 14 5
794 A148 0.07z multi 20 8
795 A148 0.18z multi 65 22

3rd Int.l Fair at Kinshasa, June 23-July 8.
The dark brown ink of the inscription was applied by a thermographic process and varnished, producing a shiny, raised effect.

Hand and INTERPOL Emblem — A149

1973, Sept. 28 **Litho.** *Perf. 12½*
796 A149 0.06z multi 22 7
797 A149 0.14z multi 45 20

50th anniversary of International Criminal Police Organization.

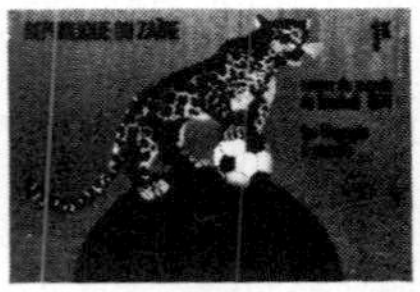
Leopard with Soccer Ball on Globe A150

1974, July 17 **Photo.** *Perf. 11½x12*
798 A150 1k multi 5 5
799 A150 2k multi 8 5
800 A150 3k multi 16 5
801 A150 4k multi 20 5
802 A150 5k multi 25 7
803 A150 14k multi 65 20
Nos. 798-803 (6) 1.39 47

World Cup Soccer Championship, Munich, June 13-July 7.

Foreman-Ali Fight — A151

1974, Nov. 9 **Litho.** *Perf. 12x12½*
804 A151 1k multi 5 5
805 A151 4k multi 12 5
806 A151 6k multi 18 5
807 A151 14k multi 38 15
808 A151 20k multi 55 18
Nos. 804-808 (5) 1.28 48

World Heavyweight Boxing Championship match between George Foreman and Muhammad Ali, Kinshasa, Oct. 30 (postponed from Sept. 25).

Same, Type of 1974, Denominations in Zaires and Inscribed in Various Colors

M.ALI-G.FOREMAN
kinshasa
0,20 z 25-9-74

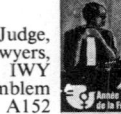

1975, Aug. **Litho.** *Perf. 12x12½*
809 A151 0.01z multi (R) 5 5
810 A151 0.04z multi (Br) 10 5
811 A151 0.06z multi (Bk) 16 7
812 A151 0.14z multi (G) 42 20
813 A151 0.20z multi (Bk) 55 22
Nos. 809-813 (5) 1.28 59

Judge, Lawyers, IWY Emblem A152

1975, Dec. Photo. *Perf. 11½*

814	A152	1k dl blk & multi	5	5
815	A152	2k dp rose & multi	5	5
816	A152	4k dl grn & multi	16	5
817	A152	14k vio & multi	42	20

International Women's Year 1975.

Waterfall A153

Okapis A154

1975 Photo. *Perf. 11½*

818	A153	1k multi	5	5
819	A153	2k lt bl & multi	5	5
820	A153	3k multi	8	5
821	A153	4k sal & multi	16	5
822	A153	5k grn & multi	16	9
		Nos. 818-822 (5)	50	29

12th General Assembly of the International Union for Nature Preservation (U.I.C.N.), Kinshasa, Sept. 1975.

1975

823	A154	1k bl & multi	5	5
824	A154	2k yel grn & multi	7	5
825	A154	3k brn red & multi	10	5
826	A154	4k grn & multi	14	5
827	A154	5k yel & multi	16	9
		Nos. 823-827 (5)	52	29

Virunga National Park, 50th anniversary.

Siderma Maluku Industry A155

Designs: 1k, Sozacom apartment building (vert.). 3k, Matadi flour mill (vert.). 4k, Women parachutists. 8k, Pres. Mobutu visiting Chairman Mao (vert.). 10k, Soldiers working along the Salongo. 14k, Pres. Mobutu addressing U.N. Gen. Assembly, Oct. 1974. 15k, Celebrating crowd.

1975

828	A155	1k ocher & multi	5	5
829	A155	2k yel grn & multi	5	5
830	A155	3k multi	7	5
831	A155	4k multi	12	5
832	A155	8k dk brn & multi	25	10
833	A155	10k sep & multi	30	16
834	A155	14k bl & multi	42	20
835	A155	15k org & multi	50	25
		Nos. 828-835 (8)	1.76	91

10th anniversary of new government.

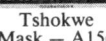

Tshokwe Mask — A156

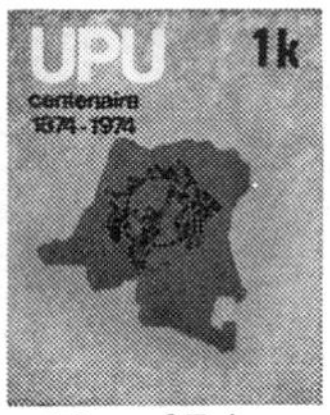

Map of Zaire, UPU Emblem — A157

Designs: 2k, 4k, Seated woman, Pende. 7k, like 5k. 10k, 14k, Antelope mask, Suku. 15k, 18k, Kneeling woman, Kongo. 20k, 25k, Kuba mask.

1977, Jan. 8 Photo. *Perf. 11½*

836	A156	2k multi	5	5
837	A156	4k multi	7	5
838	A156	5k gray & multi	8	7
839	A156	7k multi	12	8
840	A156	10k multi	16	10
841	A156	14k multi	22	14
842	A156	15k multi	25	15
843	A156	18k multi	30	18
844	A156	20k multi	60	20
845	A156	25k vio & multi	65	25
		Nos. 836-845 (10)	2.50	1.27

Wood carving and masks of Zaire.

1977, Apr. Litho. *Perf. 13½*

846	A157	1k org & multi	5	5
847	A157	4k dk bl & multi	14	5
848	A157	7k ol grn & multi	25	25
849	A157	50k brn & multi	3.00	3.00

Cent. of UPU (in 1974).

Congo Stamps of 1968-1971 Surcharged with New Value, Bars and "REPUBLIQUE DU ZAIRE"

1977

850	A126	1k on 10s (#642)	5	5
851	A122	2k on 9.6k (#618)	5	5
852	A140	10k on 10s (#735)	15	10
853	A134	25k on 10s (#703)	38	25
854	A127	40k on 9.6k (#652)	60	40
855	A135	48k on 10s (#713)	75	50
		Nos. 850-855 (6)	1.98	1.35

Congo Nos. 644, 643, 635, 746 Surcharged with New Value, Bars and "REPUBLIQUE DU ZAIRE" in Black or Carmine. Zaire No. 757 Surcharged

1977

856	A126	5k on 30s	16	8
857	A126	10k on 15s (C)	16	8
858	A124	20k on 9.60k	35	16
859	A141	30k on 12k	65	25
860	A145	100k on 40s (C)	1.90	1.10
		Nos. 856-860 (5)	3.22	1.67
		Nos. 850-860 (11)	5.20	3.02

Souvenir Sheet

Adoration of the Kings, by Rubens — A158

1977, Dec. 19 Photo. *Perf. 13½*

861	A158	5z multi	7.50	6.25

Christmas 1977.

Pantodon Buchholzi A159

Soccer Game, Argentina-France A160

Fish: 70s, Aphyosemion striatum. 55, Ctenopoma fasciolatum. 8k, Malapterurus electricus. 10k, Hemichromis bimaculatus. 30k, Marcusenius isidori. 40k, Synodontis nigriventris. 48k, Julidochromis ornatus. 100k, Nothobranchius brieni. 250k, Micralestes interruptus.

1978, Jan. 23 Litho. *Perf. 14*

862	A159	30s multi	5	5
863	A159	70s multi	5	5
864	A159	5k multi	10	5
865	A159	8k multi	16	8
866	A159	10k multi	16	10
867	A159	30k multi	50	30
868	A159	40k multi	65	40
869	A159	48k multi	80	50
870	A159	100k multi	2.25	1.00
		Nos. 862-870 (9)	4.72	2.53

Souvenir Sheet

Perf. 13½

871	A159	250k multi	4.25	4.25

No. 871 contains one stamp (46x35mm).

1978, Aug. 7 Litho. *Perf. 12½*

Various Soccer Games and Jules Rimet Cup: 3k, Austria-Brazil. 7k, Scotland-Iran. 9k, Netherlands-Peru. 10k, Hungary-Italy. 20k, Fed. Rep. of Germany-Mexico. 50k, Tunisia-Poland. 100k, Spain-Sweden. 500k, Rimet Cup, Games' emblem and cartoon of soccer player (horiz.).

872	A160	1k multi	5	5
873	A160	3k multi	5	5
874	A160	7k multi	9	6
875	A160	9k multi	12	8
876	A160	10k multi	12	8
877	A160	20k multi	25	15
878	A160	50k multi	65	38
879	A160	100k multi	1.25	75
		Nos. 872-879 (8)	2.58	1.60

Souvenir Sheets

880	A160	500k bl & multi	7.50	6.25
881	A160	500k red & multi	7.50	6.25

11th World Cup Soccer Championship, Argentina, June 1-25. Nos. 880-881 contain one stamp each (47x36mm.). Stamp of No. 880 has blue frameline. Stamp of No. 881 has red frame line.

Mama Mobutu — A161

Pres. Joseph D. Mobutu — A162

1978, Oct. 23 Photo. *Perf. 12*

882	A161	8k multi	16	7

Mama Mobutu (1941-1977), wife of Pres. Mobutu.

1978 Photo. *Perf. 12*

883	A162	2k multi	5	5
884	A162	5k multi	5	5
885	A162	6k multi	5	5
886	A162	8k multi	8	5
887	A162	10k multi	8	5
888	A162	25k multi	16	10
889	A162	48k multi	38	25
890	A162	1z multi	70	55
		Nos. 883-890 (8)	1.55	1.15

See Nos. 1051-1056.

Souvenir Sheet

Elizabeth II in Westminster Abbey A163

1978, Dec. 11 Photo. *Perf. 13½*

891	A163	5z multi	8.25	8.25

25th anniversary of coronation of Queen Elizabeth II.

Souvenir Sheet

Albrecht Dürer, Self-portrait A164

1978, Dec. 18 *Perf. 13*

892	A164	5z multi	8.25	8.25

Albrecht Dürer (1471-1528), German painter and engraver.

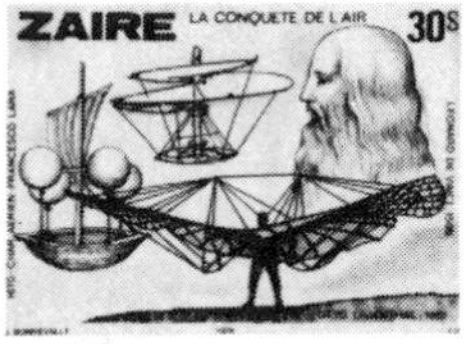

Leonardo da Vinci and his Drawings A165

History of Aviation: 70s, Planes of Wright Brothers, 1905, and Santos Dumont, 1906. 1k, Bleriot XI, 1909, and Farman F-60, 1909. 5k, Junkers G-38, 1929, and Spirit of St. Louis, 1927. 8k, Sikorski S-42B, 1934 and Macchi-Castoldi MC-72, 1934. 10k, Boeing 707, 1960, and Fokker F-VII, 1935. 50k, Apollo XI, 1969, and Concorde, 1976. 75k, Helicopter and Douglas DC-10, 1971. 5z, Giffard's balloon, 1852, and Hindenburg LZ 129, 1936.

1978, Dec. 28 Litho. *Perf. 13*

893	A165	30s multi	5	5
894	A165	70s multi	5	5
895	A165	1k multi	5	5
896	A165	5k multi	6	6
897	A165	8k multi	10	10
898	A165	10k multi	12	12
899	A165	50k multi	65	65
900	A165	75k multi	90	90
		Nos. 893-900 (8)	1.98	1.98

Souvenir Sheet

Perf. 11½

901	A165	5z multi	6.25	6.25

Pres. Mobutu, Map of Zaire, N'tombe Dancer — A166

Designs (Pres. Mobutu and Map): 3k, Bird. 4k, Elephant. 10k, Diamond and cotton boll. 14k, Hand holding torch. 17k, Leopard's head and Victoria Regia lily. 25k, Finzia waterfall. 50k, Wagenia fishermen.

1979, Feb. Litho. *Perf. 14x13½*

902	A166	1k multi	5	5
903	A166	3k multi	5	5
904	A166	4k multi	5	5
905	A166	10k multi	7	5
a.		Souvenir sheet of 4	35	25
906	A166	14k multi	8	7
907	A166	17k multi	10	8
908	A166	25k multi	14	10
909	A166	50k multi	35	25
a.		Souvenir sheet of 4	2.00	1.40
		Nos. 902-909 (8)	89	70

Zaire (Congo) River expedition. No. 905a contains Nos. 902-905, No. 909a, Nos. 906-909.

An enhanced introduction to the Scott Catalogue begins on Page V. A thorough understanding of the material presented there will greatly aid your use of the catalogue itself.

Phylloporus Ampliporus A167

Mushrooms: 5k, Engleromyces goetzei. 8k, Scutellinia virungae. 10k, Pycnoporus sanguineus. 30k, Cantharellus miniatescens. 40k, Lactarius phlebonemus. 48k, Phallus indusiatus. 100k, Ramaria moelleriana.

1979, Mar. Photo. *Perf. 13½x13*

910	A167	30s multi	5	5
911	A167	5k multi	5	5
912	A167	8k multi	8	5
913	A167	10k multi	8	5
914	A167	30k multi	25	16
915	A167	40k multi	30	20
916	A167	48k multi	38	25
917	A167	100k multi	70	55
		Nos. 910-917 (8)	1.89	1.36

Souvenir Sheets

Pope John XXIII A168

Popes: No. 919, Paul VI. No. 920, John Paul I.

1979, June 25 Litho. *Perf. 11½*

918	A168	250k multi	1.25	1.00
919	A168	250k multi	1.25	1.00
920	A168	250k multi	1.25	1.00

John XXIII (1881-1963); Paul VI (1897-1978); John Paul I (1912-78).

Boy Beating Drum — A169

IYC Emblem on Map of Zaire and: 10k, 20k, Girl (diff.). 50k, Boy. 100k, Boys. 300k, Mother and child. 10z, Mother and children (horiz.).

1979, July 23 Litho. *Perf. 12½*

921	A169	5k multi	5	5
922	A169	10k multi	6	5
923	A169	20k multi	12	8
924	A169	50k multi	28	18
925	A169	100k multi	55	32
926	A169	300k multi	1.65	75
		Nos. 921-926 (6)	2.71	1.43

Souvenir Sheet

927	A169	10z multi	5.50	4.25

International Year of the Child.

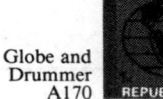

Globe and Drummer A170

1979, July 23

928	A170	1k multi	5	5
929	A170	9k multi	6	5
930	A170	90k multi	50	25
931	A170	100k multi	55	28

Souvenir Sheet

932	A170	500k multi	3.00	1.75

6th International Fair, Kinshasa. No. 932 contains one stamp (52x31mm).

Globe and School Desk — A171

1979, Dec. 24 Litho. *Perf. 13*

933	A171	10k multi	7	5

Intl. Bureau of Education, Geneva, 50th anniv.

Adoration of the Kings, by Memling — A172

1979, Dec. 24 *Imperf.*

934	A172	5z multi	3.00	1.60

Christmas 1979.

"Puffing Billy," 1814, Gt. Britain A173

1980, Jan. 14 Litho. *Perf. 13½x13*

935	A173	50s	*shown*	5	5
936	A173	1.50k	*Buddicom No. 33, 1843, France*	5	5
937	A173	5k	*"Elephant," 1835, Belgium*	5	5
938	A173	8k	*No. 601, 1906, Zaire*	5	5
939	A173	50k	*"Slieve Gullion 440," Ireland*	30	16
940	A173	75k	*"Black Elephant," Germany*	45	25
941	A173	2z	*Type 1-15, Zaire*	1.20	65
942	A173	5z	*"Golden State," U.S.*	3.00	1.60
			Nos. 935-942 (8)	5.15	2.86

Souvenir Sheet

943	A173	10z	*Type E.D.75, Zaire*	6.00	4.00

Hill, Belgian Congo No. 257 A174

1980, Jan. 28 *Perf. 13½x14*

944	A174	2k	*No. 5*	5	5
945	A174	4k	*No. 13*	5	5
946	A174	10k	*No. 24*	7	5
947	A174	20k	*No. 38*	12	7
948	A174	40k	*No. 111*	25	12
949	A174	150k	*No. B29*	90	50
950	A174	200k	*No. 198*	1.20	65
951	A174	250k	*shown*	1.50	80
			Nos. 944-951 (8)	4.14	2.29

Souvenir Sheet

952	A174	10z	*No. 198*	6.00	4.00

Sir Rowland Hill (1795-1879), originator of penny postage.

Albert Einstein — A175

1980, Feb. 18 *Perf. 13*

953	A175	40s multi	5	5
954	A175	2k multi	5	5
955	A175	4k multi	5	5
956	A175	15k multi	8	5
957	A175	50k multi	35	20
958	A175	300k multi	1.60	80
		Nos. 953-958 (6)	2.18	1.20

Souvenir Sheet

959	A175	5z multi	3.00	1.90

Albert Einstein (1879-1955), theoretical physicist. No. 959 has different portrait.

Salvation Army Brass Players — A176

Emblem and: 50s, Booth Memorial Hospital, NYC. 4.50k, Commissioner George Railton sailing for US mission. 10k, Mobile dispensary, Masina. 20k, Gen. Evangeline Booth, officer holding infant (vert.). 75k, Outdoor well-baby clinic. 1.50z, Disaster relief. 2z, Parade (vert.). 10z, Gen. and Mrs. Arnold Brown.

1980, Mar. 3 *Perf. 11*

960	A176	50s multi	5	5
961	A176	4.50k multi	5	5
962	A176	10k multi	5	5
963	A176	20k multi	9	5
964	A176	40k multi	20	9
965	A176	75k multi	32	18
966	A176	1.50z multi	65	32
967	A176	2z multi	90	45
		Nos. 960-967 (8)	2.31	1.24

Souvenir Sheet

968	A176	10z multi	4.50	3.00

Salvation Army centenary in United States. No. 968 contains one stamp (53x38mm) and 2 labels.

Souvenir Sheets

Pope John Paul II — A177

1980, May 2 Litho. *Perf. 11½*

969	A177	10z multi	3.25	1.75

Visit of Pope John Paul II to Zaire, May.

Baia Castle, by Antonio Pitloo — A178

1980, May 5

970	A178	10z multi	3.25	1.75

20th International Philatelic Exhibition, Europa '80, Naples, Apr. 26-May 4.

A179

Perf. 12½x13, 13x12½

1980, May 24 Litho.

971	A179	50k	*Woman, line-drawing*	12	8
972	A179	100k	*Plutiarch*	32	18
973	A179	500k	*Kneeling man, sculpture*, vert.	1.65	90
a.			Souvenir sheet of 3	2.50	1.50

Rotary Intl., 75th anniv. No. 973a contains 3 stamps similar to Nos. 971-973, size: 55x35, 35x55mm. Exists imperf.

Tropical Fish — A180

1980, Oct. 20 Litho. *Perf. 14x13½*

974	A180	1k	*Chaetodon collaris*	5	5
975	A180	5k	*Zebrasoma veliferum*	5	5
976	A180	10k	*Euxiphipops xanthometapon*	5	5
977	A180	20k	*Pomazcanthus annularis*	8	5
978	A180	50k	*Centropyge oriculus*	25	14
979	A180	150k	*Oxymonacanthus longirostris*	60	35
980	A180	200k	*Balistoides niger*	80	45
981	A180	250k	*Rhinecanthus aculeatus*	1.00	55
			Nos. 974-981 (8)	2.88	1.69

Souvenir Sheet

981A	A180	5z	*Baliste ondule*	2.25	1.00

Exhibition Emblem, Congo No. 365 — A181

1980, Dec. 6 Litho. *Perf. 13*

982		Block of 4	1.90	1.20
a.	A181	1z, UR shown	42	25
b.	A181	1z, UL Belgium #511	42	25
c.	A181	1z, UR like #982b	42	25
d.	A181	1z, UL like #982a	42	25
983		Block of 4	3.50	2.00
a.	A181	2z, UR Congo #432	80	50
b.	A181	2z, UL Belguim # B835	80	50
c.	A181	2z, UR like #983b	80	50
d.	A181	2z, UL like #983a	80	50
984		Block of 4	5.25	3.00
a.	A181	3z, UR Zaire #755	1.25	65
b.	A181	3z, UL Belgium # B878	1.25	65

c.	A181	3z, UR like #984b	1.25	65
d.	A181	3z, UL like #984a	1.25	65
985		Block of 4	7.00	4.00
a.	A181	4z, UR Congo #572	1.60	90
b.	A181	4z, UL Belgium # B996	1.60	90
c.	A181	4z, UR like #985b	1.60	90
d.	A181	4z, UL like #985a	1.60	90

PHIBELZA, Belgium-Zaire Phil. Exhib.

Map of Africa, King Leopold I — A182

Belgian independence sesquicentennial: 75k, Stanley expedition, Leopold II. 100k, Colonial troops, Albert I. 270k, 145k, protected animals, Leopold III. Visit of King Baudouin and Queen Fabiola.

1980, Dec. 13 Photo. *Perf. 14*

986	A182	10k multi	8	5
987	A182	75k multi	35	20
988	A182	100k multi	42	25
989	A182	145k multi	60	35
990	A182	270k multi	1.10	60
		Nos. 986-990 (5)	2.55	1.45

Nos. 935, 936, 898, 939, 900, 931, 925, 951, Overprinted in Red, Silver or Black: 20e Anniversaire-Independence / 1960-1980

1980, Dec. 13 Litho.

991	A173	50s multi	5	5
992	A173	1.50k multi	5	5
993	A165	10k multi	5	5
994	A173	50k multi	20	12
995	A165	75k multi	30	16
996	A170	100k multi (S)	42	25
997	A169	1z on 5z on 100k multi (B)	42	25
998	A174	250k multi	1.00	55
999	A169	5z on 100k multi (B)	2.00	1.10
		Nos. 991-999 (9)	4.49	2.58

20th anniversary of independence.

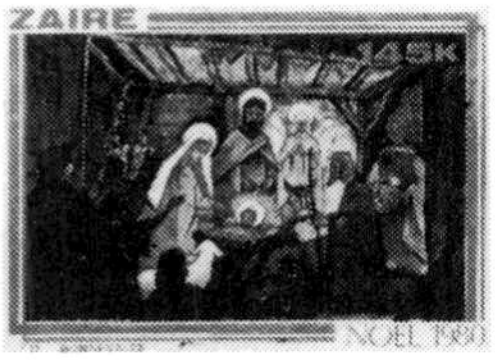

Nativity A183

1980, Dec. 24 *Perf. 13*

1000	A183	10k Shepherds and angels	8	5
1001	A183	75k Flight into Egypt	35	20
1002	A183	80k Three kings	35	20
1003	A183	145k shown	60	35

Souvenir Sheet

1004	A183	10z Church, nativity	4.25	2.25

Christmas 1980. No. 1004 contains one stamp (49x33mm). Exists imperf.

Postal Clerk Sorting Mail, by Norman Rockwell A184

Designs: Saturday Evening Post covers by Norman Rockwell.

1981, Apr. 27 Litho. *Perf. 14*

1005	A184	10k multi	5	5
1006	A184	20k multi	8	5
1007	A184	50k multi	20	12
1008	A184	80k multi	35	20
1009	A184	100k multi	42	25
1010	A184	125k multi	50	30
1011	A184	175k multi	70	40
1012	A184	200k multi	80	45
		Nos. 1005-1012 (8)	3.10	1.82

First Anniv. of Visit of Pope John Paul II A185

Designs: Scenes of Pope's visit. 50k, 500k, vert.

1981, May 2 *Perf. 13*

1013	A185	5k multi	5	5
1014	A185	10k multi	5	5
1015	A185	50k multi	25	15
1016	A185	100k multi	42	25
1017	A185	500k multi	2.00	1.20
1018	A185	800k multi	3.50	1.90
		Nos. 1013-1018 (6)	6.27	3.60

Soccer Players — A186

Designs: Soccer scenes.

1981, July 6 Litho. *Perf. 12½*

1019	A186	2k multi	5	5
1020	A186	10k multi	5	5
1021	A186	25k multi	10	5
1022	A186	90k multi	42	25
1023	A186	2z multi	80	45
1024	A186	3z multi	1.20	65
1025	A186	6z multi	2.50	1.40
1026	A186	8z multi	3.75	2.00
		Nos. 1019-1026 (8)	8.87	4.90

Souvenir Sheet

1027		Sheet of 2	4.25	2.25
a.	A186	5z like #1019	2.00	1.00
b.	A186	5z like #1025	2.00	1.00

ESPANA '82 World Cup Soccer Championship.

Intl. Year of the Disabled — A187

1981, Nov. 2 Litho. *Perf. 14x14½*

1028	A187	2k Archer	5	5
1029	A187	5k Ear, sound waves	5	5
1030	A187	10k Amputee	5	5
1031	A187	18k Cane braille, sunglasses	5	5
1032	A187	50k Boy with leg braces	15	8
1033	A187	150k Sign language	42	25
1034	A187	500k Hands	1.50	80
1035	A187	800k Dove	2.25	1.40
		Nos. 1028-1035 (8)	4.52	2.73

The Catalogue editors cannot undertake to appraise, identify or judge the genuineness or condition of stamps.

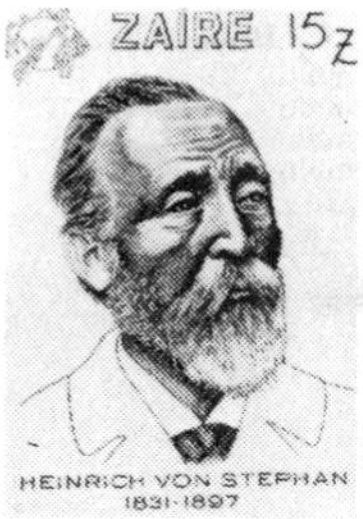

Birth Sesqui. of Heinrich von Stephan, UPU Founder — A188

Christmas 1981 — A189

Photogravure and Engraved

1981, Dec. 21 *Perf. 11½x12*

1036	A188	15z purple	4.25	2.50

1981, Dec. 21 Litho. *Perf. 14*

Designs: 25k, 1z, 1.50z, 3z, 5z, Various children. 10z, Holy Family, horiz.

1037	A189	25k multi	8	5
1038	A189	1z multi	35	16
1039	A189	1.50z multi	42	25
1040	A189	3z multi	90	50
1041	A189	5z multi	1.50	80
		Nos. 1037-1041 (4)	2.35	1.39

Souvenir Sheet

1042	A189	10z multi	3.00	1.60

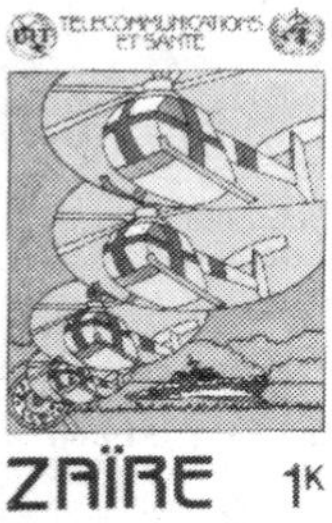

13th World Telecommunications Day (1981) — A190

Designs: Symbols of communications and health care delivery.

1982, Feb. 8 Litho. *Perf. 13*

1043	A190	1k multi	5	5
1044	A190	25k multi	8	5
1045	A190	90k multi	30	15
1046	A190	1z multi	35	16
1047	A190	1.70z multi	55	28
1048	A190	3z multi	1.00	50
1049	A190	4.50z multi	1.50	70
1050	A190	5z multi	1.60	80
		Nos. 1043-1050 (8)	5.43	2.69

Pres. Mobutu Type of 1978

1982 Photo. *Perf. 12*

Granite Paper

1051	A162	10k multi	5	5
1052	A162	25k multi	8	5
1053	A162	50k multi	16	8
1054	A162	1z multi	35	16
1055	A162	2z multi	65	35
1056	A162	5z multi	1.60	80
		Nos. 1051-1056 (6)	2.89	1.49

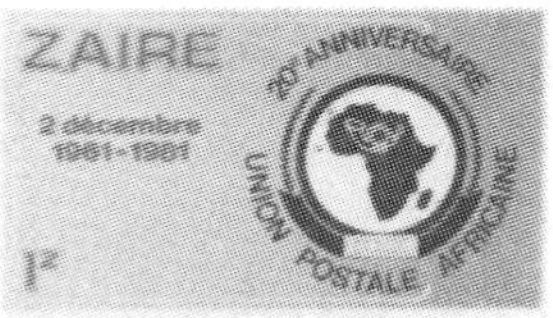

20th Anniv. of African Postal Union (1981) — A191

1982, Mar. 8 Litho. *Perf. 13*

1057	A191	1z yel grn & gold	35	16

1982 World Cup A192

Designs: Flags and players of finalists.

1982

1058	A192	2k multi	5	5
1059	A192	8k multi	5	5
1060	A192	25k multi	8	5
1061	A192	50k multi	16	8
1062	A192	90k multi	30	15
1063	A192	1z multi	35	16
1064	A192	1.45z multi	45	22
1065	A192	1.70z multi	55	28
1066	A192	3z multi	1.00	50
1067	A192	3.50z multi	1.20	55
1068	A192	5z multi	1.60	80
1069	A192	6z multi	2.00	1.00
		Nos. 1058-1069 (12)	7.79	3.89

Souvenir Sheet

1070	A192	10z multi	3.50	1.60

Issue dates: Nos. 1058-1069, July 6; No. 1070, Sept. 21.

9th Conference of Heads of State of Africa and France, Kinshasa, Oct. — A193

1982, Oct. 8 Litho. *Perf. 13*

1071	A193	75k multi	22	12
1072	A193	90k multi	30	15
1073	A193	1z multi	35	16
1074	A193	1.50z multi	50	25
1075	A193	3z multi	1.00	50
1076	A193	5z multi	1.60	80
1077	A193	8z multi	2.50	1.40
		Nos. 1071-1077 (7)	6.47	3.38

Animals from Virunga Natl. Park — A194

1982, Nov. 5

1078	A194	1z Lions	35	16
1079	A194	1.70z Buffalo	55	28
1080	A194	3.50z Elephants	1.20	55
1081	A194	6.50z Antelope	2.25	1.10
1082	A194	8z Hippopotamus	2.50	1.40
1083	A194	10z Monkeys	3.50	1.60
1084	A194	10z Leopard	3.50	1.60
		Nos. 1078-1084 (7)	13.85	6.69

Nos. 1083-1084 se-tenant with label showing map.

Scouting Year — A195

1982, Nov. 29 Photo. *Perf. 11½*

Granite Paper

1085	A195	90k Camp	30	15
1086	A195	1.70z Campfire	55	28
1087	A195	3z Scout	1.00	50

1088 A195 5z First aid 1.60 80
1089 A195 8z Flag signals 2.50 1.40
Nos. 1085-1089 (5) 5.95 3.13

Souvenir Sheet

1090 A195 10z Baden-Powell 3.50 1.60

Local Birds — A196

1982, Dec. 6 Litho. *Perf. 13*

1091 A196 25k Quelea quelea 8 5
1092 A196 50k Ceyx picta 16 8
1093 A196 90k Tauraco persa 30 15
1094 A196 1.50z Charadrius tricollaris 50 25
1095 A196 1.70k Cursorius temminckii 55 28
1096 A196 2z Campethera bennettii 65 35
1097 A196 3z Podiceps ruficollis 1.00 50
1098 A196 3.50z Kaupifalco monogrammicus 1.20 55
1099 A196 5z Limnocorax flavirostris 1.60 80
1100 A196 8z White-headed vulture 2.50 1.40
Nos. 1091-1100 (10) 8.54 4.41

All except 3.50z, 8z horiz.

Souvenir Sheet

Christmas 1982 — A197

1982, Dec. 20 Photo. *Perf. 13½*

1101 A197 15z Adoration of the Magi, by van der Goes 5.00 2.50

Quartz A198

1983, Feb. 13 Photo. *Perf. 11½*

Granite Paper

1102 A198 2k Malachite, vert. 5 5
1103 A198 45k shown 22 10
1104 A198 75k Gold 22 12
1105 A198 1z Uraninite 35 16
1106 A198 1.50z Bournonite, vert. 50 25
1107 A198 3z Cassiterite 1.00 50
1108 A198 6z Dioptase, vert. 2.00 1.00
1109 A198 8z Cuprite, vert. 2.50 1.40
Nos. 1102-1109 (8) 6.84 3.58

Souvenir Sheet

1110 A198 10z Diamonds 3.50 3.50

TB Bacillus Centenary A199

1983, Feb. 21 Litho. *Perf. 13*

1111 A199 80k multi 25 14
1112 A199 1.20z multi 40 20
1113 A199 3.60z multi 1.20 60
1114 A199 9.60z multi 3.25 1.60

Kinshasa Monuments — A200

1983, Apr. 25

1115 A200 50k Zaire Diplomat, vert. 16 8
1116 A200 1z Echo of Zaire 35 16
1117 A200 1.50z Messengers, vert. 50 25
1118 A200 3z Shield of Revolution, vert. 1.00 50
1119 A200 5z Weeping Woman 1.60 80
1120 A200 10z Militant, vert. 3.50 1.60
Nos. 1115-1120 (6) 7.11 3.39

ITU Plenipotentiaries Conference, Nairobi, Sept. 1982 — A201

Various satellites, dish antennae and maps.

1983, June 13 Litho. *Perf. 13*

1121 A201 2k multi 5 5
1122 A201 4k multi 5 5
1123 A201 25k multi 8 5
1124 A201 1.20z multi 40 20
1125 A201 2.05z multi 65 35
1126 A201 3.60z multi 1.20 60
1127 A201 6z multi 2.00 1.00
1128 A201 8z multi 2.50 1.40
Nos. 1121-1128 (8) 6.93 3.70

Christmas 1983 — A202

Raphael Paintings; No. 1129: a. Virgin and Child. b. Holy Family. c. Esterhazy Madonna. d. Sistine Madonna. No. 1130: a. La Belle Jardiniere. b. Virgin of Alba. c. Holy Family (diff.). d. Virgin and Child (diff.).

1983, Dec. 26 Photo. *Perf. 13½x13*

1129 Sheet of 4 2.00 2.00
a.-d. A202 10z, any single 50 50
1130 Sheet of 4 3.00 3.00
a.-d. A202 15z, any single 70 70

Garamba Park — A203

1984, Apr. 2 Litho. *Perf. 13*

1131 A203 10k Darby's Eland 5 5
1132 A203 15k Eagles 5 5
1133 A203 3z Servals 12 12
1134 A203 10z White rhinoceros 40 40
1135 A203 15z Lions 60 60
1136 A203 37.50z Warthogs 1.50 1.50
1137 A203 40z Koris bustards 1.60 1.60
1138 A203 40z Crowned cranes 1.60 1.60
Nos. 1131-1138 (8) 5.92 5.92

Nos. 1137-1138 are se-tenant and narrower (size 49x34mm), with design continuing to the side perforations. An attached label shows park location on map of Zaire.

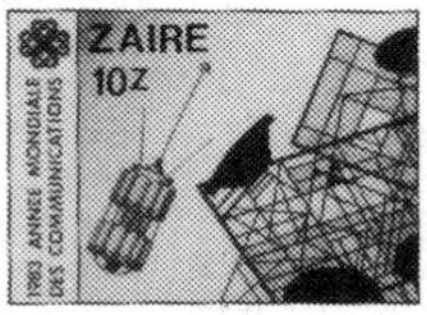

World Communications Year — A204

Designs: 10k, Computer operator, Congo River ferry. 15k, Communications satellite. 8.50z, Engineer, Congo River Bridge. 10z, Satellite, ground receiving station. 15z, TV camerawoman filming crowed crane. 37.50z, Satellite, dish antennas. 80z, Switchboard operator, bus.

1984, May 14 Litho. *Perf. 13x12½*

1139 A204 10k multi 5 5
1140 A204 15k multi 5 5
1141 A204 8.50z multi 35 35
1142 A204 10z multi 40 40
1143 A204 15z multi 60 60
1144 A204 37.50z multi 1.50 1.50
1145 A204 80z multi 3.25 3.25
Nos. 1139-1145 (7) 6.20 6.20

Hypericum Revolutum A205

Local flowers: 15k, Borreria dibrachiata. 3z, Disa erubescens. 8.50z, Scaevola plumieri. 10z, Clerodendron thompsonii. 15z, Thumbergia erecta. 37.50z, Impatiens niamniamensis. 100z, Canarina eminii.

1984, May 28 Photo. *Perf. 14x13½*

1146 A205 10k multi 5 5
1147 A205 15k multi 5 5
1148 A205 3z multi 12 12
1149 A205 8.50z multi 35 35
1150 A205 10z multi 40 40
1151 A205 15z multi 60 60
1152 A205 37.50z multi 1.50 1.50
1153 A205 100z multi 4.00 4.00
Nos. 1146-1153 (8) 7.07 7.07

1984 Summer Olympics — A206

Manned Flight Bicent. — A207

1984, June 5 Litho. *Perf. 13*

1154 A206 2z Basketball 8 8
1155 A206 3z Equestrian 12 12
1156 A206 10z Running 40 40
1157 A206 15z Long jump 60 60
1158 A206 20z Soccer 80 80
Nos. 1154-1158 (5) 2.00 2.00

Souvenir Sheet

Perf. 11½

1159 A206 50z Kayak 2.00 2.00

No. 1159 contains one stamp (31x49mm).

1984, June 28 Litho. *Perf. 14*

1160 A207 10k Montgolfiere, 1783 5 5
1161 A207 15k Charles & Robert, 1783 5 5
1162 A207 3z Gustave, 1783 12 12
1163 A207 5z Santos-Dumont III, 1899 20 20
1164 A207 10z Stratospheric balloon, 1934 40 40
1165 A207 15z Zeppelin LZ-129, 1936 60 60
1166 A207 37.50z Double Eagle II, 1978 1.50 1.50
1167 A207 80z Hot air balloons 3.25 3.25
Nos. 1160-1167 (8) 6.17 6.17

Okapi — A208

1984, Oct. 15 Litho. *Perf. 13*

1168 A208 2z Grazing 7 7
1169 A208 3z Resting 10 10
1170 A208 8z Mother and young 25 25
1171 A208 10z In water 32 32

Souvenir Sheet

Perf. 11½

1172 A208 50z like 10z 1.60 1.60

World Wildlife Fund. No. 1172 contains one stamp (size: 36x51mm); multicolored margin continues the design of the 10z without emblem.

Nos. 893, 896, 894-895, 898, 897, 900, 899 Ovptd. with Black Bar, Silver Emblem and Surcharged on Stamp and Margin: 60e ANNIVERSAIRE/1re LIASON AERIENNE/BRUXELLES-KINSHASAL/PAR EDMOND THIEFFRY in 3 or 5 Lines

1985, Feb. 19 *Perf. 13, 11½*

1173 A165 2.50z on 30s multi 8 8
1174 A165 5z on 5k multi 16 16
1175 A165 6z on 70s multi 18 18
1176 A165 7.50z on 1k multi 25 25
1177 A165 8.50z on 10k multi 25 25
1178 A165 10z on 8k multi 32 32
1179 A165 12.50z on 75k multi 40 40
1180 A165 30z on 50k multi 1.00 1.00
Nos. 1173-1180 (8) 2.64 2.64

Souvenir Sheet

1181 A165 50z on 5z multi 1.60 1.60

OLYMPHILEX '85, Lausanne — A209

1985, Apr. 19 *Perf. 13*

1182 A209 1z Swimming 5 5
1183 A209 2z Soccer, vert. 7 7
1184 A209 3z Boxing 10 10
1185 A209 4z Basketball, vert. 14 14
1186 A209 5z Equestrian 16 16
1187 A209 10z Volleyball, vert. 32 32
1188 A209 15z Running 50 50
1189 A209 30z Cycling, vert. 1.00 1.00
Nos. 1182-1189 (8) 2.34 2.34

Nos. 1013-1018, 969 Ovptd. and Surcharged with 1 or 2 Gold Bars and "AOUT 1985" in Gold or Black

1985, Aug. 15 *Perf. 13, 11½*

1190 A185 2z on 5k multi 7 7
1191 A185 3z on 10k multi 10 10
1192 A185 5z on 50k multi 16 16
1192A A185 10z on 100k multi 32 32

1192B A185 15z on 500k multi 48 48
1193 A185 40z on 800k multi 1.40 1.40
Nos. 1190-1193 (6) 2.53 2.53

Souvenir Sheet

1194 A177 50z on 10z multi (B) 1.60 1.60

Second visit of Pope John Paul II.

Audubon Birth Bicent. — A210

Illustrations of North American bird species by John Audubon.

1985, Oct. 1 ***Perf. 13***

1195 A210 5z Great egret 16 16
1196 A210 10z Yellow-beaked duck 32 32
1197 A210 15z Small heron 50 50
1198 A210 25z White-fronted duck 80 80

Natl. Independence, 25th Anniv. — A211

1985, Oct. 23 **Photo.** ***Perf. 12***

Granite Paper

1200 A211 5z multi 16 16
1201 A211 10z multi 32 32
1202 A211 15z multi 50 50
1203 A211 20z multi 80 80

Souvenir Sheet

Perf. 11½

1204 A211 50z multi 1.60 1.60

UN, 40th Anniv. A212

1985, Nov. 26

1205 A212 10z Flags, vert. 32 32
1206 A212 50z Emblem, UN building 1.60 1.60

Nos. 1087-1088, 1085-1086, 1089-1090 Surcharged with 7 Green Bars and IYY Emblem

1985, Dec. 2 ***Perf. 11½***

Granite Paper

1207 A195 3z on 3z multi 10 10
1208 A195 5z on 5z multi 16 16
1209 A195 7z on 90k multi 22 22
1210 A195 10z on 90k multi 32 32
1211 A195 15z on 1.70z multi 50 50
1212 A195 20z on 8z multi 65 65
1213 A195 50z on 90k multi 1.60 1.60
Nos. 1207-1213 (7) 3.55 3.55

Souvenir Sheet

1214 A195 50z on 10z multi 1.60 1.60

Intl. Youth Year.

Souvenir Sheet

Virgin and Child, by Titian A213

Photogravure and Engraved

1985, Dec. 23 ***Perf. 13½***

1215 A213 100z brown 3.50 3.50

Christmas 1985. No. 1215 contains one stamp (size: 39x39mm).

Natl. Transit Authority, 50th Anniv. — A214

1985, Dec. 31 ***Perf. 13***

1216 A214 7z Kokolo mail ship 22 22
1217 A214 10z Steam locomotive 32 32
1218 A214 15z Luebo ferry 50 50
1219 A214 50z Stanley locomotive 1.60 1.60

Postage Stamp, Cent. A215

Stamps on stamps: 7z, Belgian Congo No. 30. 15z, Belgian Congo No. B28. 20z, Belgian Congo No. 226. 25z, Zaire No. 1059. 40z, Zaire No. 1152. 50z, Zaire No. 883 and Belgium No. 1094.

1986, Feb. 23 ***Perf. 13***

1220 A215 7z multi 35 35
1221 A215 15z multi 75 75
1222 A215 20z multi 1.00 1.00
1223 A215 25z multi 1.25 1.25
1224 A215 40z multi 2.00 2.00
Nos. 1220-1224 (5) 5.35 5.35

Souvenir Sheet

Perf. 11½

1225 A215 50z multi 2.50 2.50

No. 1225 contains one stamp (size: 50x35mm).

Beatification of Sister Anuarite Nengapeta, Aug. 15, 1985 — A216

1986, Feb. 21 **Litho.** ***Perf. 13***

1226 A216 10z Pope John Paul II 25 25
1227 A216 15z Sr. Anuarite 38 38
1228 A216 25z Both portraits 65 65

Souvenir Sheet

Imperf

1229 A216 100z Both portraits, triangular 2.50 2.50

Nos. 1226-1227 vert. No. 1229 contains one quadrilateral stamp (size: 30x36x60mm).

Congo Stamp Cent. — A217

1986, Feb. 22 **Litho.** ***Perf. 13***

1230 A217 25z Belgian Congo No. 3 65 65

See Belgium No. 1236.

Indigenous Reptiles A218

1987, Feb. 11 **Litho.** ***Perf. 13***

1231 A218 2z Dasypeltis scaber 6 6
1232 A218 5z Agama agama 14 14
1233 A218 10z Python regius 25 25
1234 A218 15z Chamaeleo dilepis 40 40
1235 A218 25z Dendroaspis jamesoni 65 65
1236 A218 50z Naja nigricolis 1.30 1.30
Nos. 1231-1236 (6) 2.80 2.80

Christmas 1987 — A219

Paintings (details) by Fra Angelico: 50z, Virgin and Child, center panel of the Triptych of Cortona, 1435. 100z, The Nativity. 120z, Virgin and Child with Angels and Four Saints, Fiesole Retable. 180z, Virgin and Child with Six Saints, Annalena Retable.

1987, Dec. 24 **Litho.** ***Perf. 13***

1237 A219 50z multi 78 78
1238 A219 100z multi 1.55 1.55
1239 A219 120z multi 1.90 1.90
1240 A219 180z multi 2.80 2.80

OFFICIAL STAMPS

Nos. 756-772 Overprinted SP

1975 **Litho.** ***Perf. 14***

O1 A145 10s red org & blk 5 5
O2 A145 40s multi 5 5
O3 A145 50s cit & multi 5 5

Perf. 13

O4 A146 1k multi 5 5
O5 A146 2k org & multi 5 5
O6 A146 3k multi 8 5
O7 A146 4k multi 12 5
O8 A146 5k multi 16 8
O9 A146 6k multi 20 10
O10 A146 8k multi 25 12
O11 A146 9k multi 25 14
O12 A146 10k multi 35 16
O13 A146 14k multi 50 25
O14 A146 17k multi 60 25
O15 A146 20k yel & multi 65 35
O16 A146 50k multi 1.60 80
O17 A146 100k multi 4.25 1.50
Nos. O1-O17 (17) 9.26 4.10

"SP" are the initials of "Service Public."

ZAMBEZIA

LOCATION — A former district of the Mozambique Province in Portuguese East Africa.

GOVT. — Part of the Portuguese East Africa Colony.

The districts of Quelimane and Tete were created from Zambezia. Eventually stamps of Mozambique came into use. See Quelimane and Tete.

1000 Reis = 1 Milreis

King Carlos
A1 A2

Perf. 11½, 12½, 13½.

1894 **Typo.** **Unwmk.**

1 A1 5r yellow 30 25
2 A1 10r red vio 45 25
3 A1 15r chocolate 1.00 85
a. Perf. 12½ 25.00 15.00
4 A1 20r lavender 1.00 85
5 A1 25r bl grn 1.50 1.40
a. Perf. 11½
6 A1 50r lt bl 1.75 1.50
7 A1 75r carmine 5.00 4.25
a. Perf. 11½ 50.00 35.00
8 A1 80r yel grn 3.50 3.00
9 A1 100r brn, *buff* 3.50 3.00

10	A1	150r car, *rose*	4.00	3.00
11	A1	200r dk bl, *bl*	4.00	3.50
a.		Perf. 11½	200.00	150.00
b.		Perf. 13½	35.00	25.00
12	A1	300r dk bl, *sal*	10.00	8.00
a.		Perf. 11½	20.00	17.50

1898-1903 ***Perf. 11½***

Name and Value in Black or Red (500r)

13	A2	2½r gray	40	20
14	A2	5r orange	40	20
15	A2	10r lt grn	40	20
16	A2	15r brown	2.00	1.50
17	A2	15r gray grn ('03)	1.50	1.00
18	A2	20r gray vio	1.00	60
19	A2	25r sea grn	1.00	60
20	A2	25r car ('03)	1.50	70
21	A2	50r blue	2.00	1.00
22	A2	50r brn ('03)	3.50	2.50
23	A2	65r dl bl ('03)	9.00	7.00
24	A2	75r rose	9.00	6.00
25	A2	75r lil ('03)	3.50	2.25
26	A2	80r violet	6.00	3.00
27	A2	100r dk bl, *bl*	2.50	1.50
28	A2	115r org brn, *pink* ('03)	9.00	8.00
29	A2	130r brn, *straw* ('03)	9.00	8.00
30	A2	150r brn, *buff*	5.00	2.75
31	A2	200r red vio, *pnksh*	5.00	2.75
32	A2	300r dk bl, *rose*	6.00	2.75
33	A2	400r dl bl, *straw* ('03)	10.00	8.00
34	A2	500r blk, *bl* ('01)	9.00	6.00
35	A2	700r vio, *yelsh* ('01)	11.00	8.50
		Nos. 13-35 (23)	107.70	75.00

Stamps of 1894 Surcharged

1902 ***Perf. 11½, 12½***

36	A1	65r on 10r red vio	5.00	4.00
37	A1	65r on 15r choc	5.00	4.00
38	A1	65r on 20r lav	5.00	4.00
39	A1	65r on 300r bl, *sal*	5.00	4.00
40	A1	115r on 5r yel	5.00	4.00
41	A1	115r on 25r bl grn	5.00	4.00
42	A1	115r on 80r yel grn	5.00	4.00
43	A1	130r on 75r car	5.00	4.00
44	A1	130r on 150r car, *rose*	4.50	3.50
45	A1	400r on 50r lt bl	2.00	1.50
46	A1	400r on 100r brn, *buff*	2.00	1.75
47	A1	400r on 200r bl, *bl*	2.00	1.75

Same Surcharge on No. P1

48	N1	130r on 2½r brn	5.00	4.00
		Nos. 36-48 (13)	55.50	44.50

Stamps of 1898 Overprinted

1902 ***Perf. 11½***

49	A2	15r brown	1.75	1.25
50	A2	25r sea grn	1.75	1.25
51	A2	50r blue	1.75	1.25
52	A2	75r rose	5.00	3.50

No. 23 Surcharged in Black

1905

53	A2	50r on 65r dull blue	5.00	3.50

Stamps of 1898-1903 Overprinted in Carmine or Green

1911

54	A2	2½r gray	20	20
55	A2	5r orange	20	20
56	A2	10r lt grn	20	20
a.		Inverted overprint	5.00	5.00
57	A2	15r gray grn	30	30
58	A2	20r gray vio	40	30
59	A2	25r car (G)	90	50
60	A2	50r brown	40	40
61	A2	75r lilac	1.00	60
62	A2	100r dk bl, *bl*	1.00	60
63	A2	115r org brn, *pink*	1.00	60
64	A2	130r brn, *straw*	1.00	60
65	A2	200r red vio, *pnksh*	1.00	60
66	A2	400r dl bl, *straw*	1.65	1.10
67	A2	500r blk & red, *bl*	1.65	1.10
68	A2	700r vio, *yelsh*	1.75	1.10
		Nos. 54-68 (15)	12.65	8.40

Stamps of 1902-05 Overprinted in Carmine or Green

1914

Without Gum

72	A2	50r on 65r dl bl	275.00	275.00
73	A1	115r on 5r yel	1.00	1.00
74	A1	115r on 25r bl grn	1.00	1.00
75	A1	115r on 80r yel grn	1.00	1.00
76	N1	130r on 2½r brn (G)	1.00	1.00
a.		Carmine overprint	9.00	9.00
77	A1	130r on 75r car	1.00	1.00
a.		Perf. 12½	5.50	5.50
78	A1	130r on 150r car, *rose*	1.00	1.00
79	A1	400r on 50r lt bl	2.00	1.65
a.		Perf. 12½	10.00	7.00
80	A1	400r on 100r brn, *buff*	2.00	1.50
81	A1	400r on 200r bl, *bl*	2.00	1.50

On Nos. 51-52

82	A2	50r blue	1.25	1.00
83	A2	75r rose	1.25	1.00
		Nos. 73-83 (11)	14.50	12.65

Preceding Issues Overprinted in Carmine

1915

On Provisional Issue of 1902

84	A1	115r on 5r yel	50	45
85	A1	115r on 25r bl grn	50	45
86	A1	115r on 80r lt grn	50	45
87	A1	130r on 75r car	50	45
a.		Perf. 12½	4.50	2.25
88	A1	130r on 150r car, *rose*	50	45
92	N1	130r on 2½r (down)	50	45

On No. 51

93	A2	50r blue	50	45
a.		"Republica" inverted		

On No. 53

94	A2	50r on 65r dl bl	2.50	2.00
		Nos. 84-94 (8)	6.00	5.15

Stamps of 1898-1903 Overprinted Locally in Carmine

1917

Without Gum

95	A2	2½r gray	1.00	1.00
96	A2	5r orange	5.00	3.75
97	A2	10r lt grn	5.00	3.75
98	A2	15r gray grn	5.00	3.75
99	A2	20r gray vio	5.00	3.75
100	A2	25r sea grn	10.00	9.00
101	A2	100r bl, *bl*	2.50	2.00
102	A2	115r org brn, *pink*	2.25	2.00
103	A2	130r brn, *straw*	2.25	2.00
104	A2	200r red vio, *pnksh*	2.25	2.00
105	A2	400r dl bl, *straw*	3.25	3.00
106	A2	500r blk & red, *bl*	3.25	3.00
107	A2	700r vio, *yelsh*	6.00	3.50
		Nos. 95-107 (13)	52.75	42.50

NEWSPAPER STAMP

N1

1894 **Unwmk.** **Typo.** ***Perf. 12½***

P1	N1	2½r brown	30	25

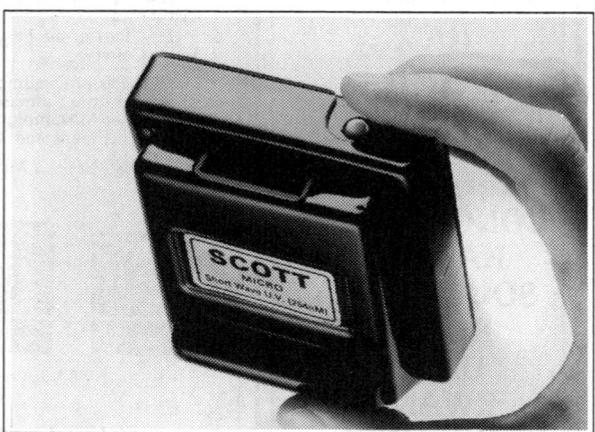

For the Record

The items recorded here appeared on the stamp market in the 1960's, '70s, and '80s and have not been listed in the *Scott Standard Postage Stamp Catalogue.* They are arranged chronologically and briefly described. Completeness is not claimed.

Contents

PANAMA

1963

International Red Cross centenary. *Mar. 4.* Airmail semipostal 5c+5c, 10c+10c, 31c+15c surcharged in red on Nos. C274-C276. 10c, black overprint and surcharge on 5c+5c semipostal.
Astronauts' Visit, *Aug. 21.* No. C274 overprinted **a.** "Vista / Astronauts / Glenn-Shirra / Sheppard / Cooper / a Panama" or **b.** "Habilitado." Both values surcharged 10c, No. C277a overprinted "a."
9th Winter Olympics, Innsbruck, *Dec.* ½, 1, 3, 4c; airmail, 5, 15, 21, 31c (8v). Souvenir Sheet of 2 (21, 31c) perf., imperf. 2 miniature sheets, 21, 31c (in different colors).

1964

18th Summer Olympics, Tokyo. *Apr. 1.* ½, 1c; airmail, 5, 10, 21, 50c (6v). Souvenir sheet, 50c, perf., imperf.
Space Conquest. *Apr. 21.* ½, 1c; airmail, 5, 10, 21, 50c (6v). Souvenir sheet, 50c, perf., imperf.
Aquatic Sports, Tokyo '64 Olympics. *Sept. 2.* Perf., imperf. (in different colors). ½, 1c; airmail, 5, 10, 21, 31c (6v). 6 miniature sheets, perf., imperf. Souvenir sheet, 31c, perf., imperf.
New York World's Fair. *Sept. 14.* Airmail, 5, 10, 15, 21c (4v). Souvenir sheet, 21c, pewrf., imperf.
Hammarskjold Memorial (United Nations Day). *Sept. 24.* Perf., imperf. (in different colors). Airmail, 21c x 2. Souvenir sheet of 2 (21c x 2).
Pope John XXIII Memorial. *Oct. 24.* Perf., imperf. (in different colors). Airmail, 21c x 2. Souvenir sheet of 2 (21c x 2) perf., imperf.
Olympic Medals and Winners, Innsbruck. *Oct. 14.* ½, 1, 2, 3, 4c; airmail, 5, 6, 7, 10, 21, 31c (11v). Souvenir sheet of 3 (10, 21, 31c) perf., imperf.
Weather Satellites. *Dec. 21.* ½, 1c; airmail, 5, 10, 21, 50c (6v). Souvenir sheet, 50c, perf., imperf.
Olympic Medals and Winners, Tokyo. *Dec. 28.* ½, 1, 2, 3, 4c; airmail, 5, 6, 7, 10, 21, 31c (11v). Souvenir sheet of 3 (10, 21, 31c) perf., imperf.

1965

Space Conquests and J.F. Kennedy. *Feb. 25.* Perf., imperf. (in different colors). ½, 1, 2, 3c; airmail, 5, 10, 11, 31c (8v). Souvenir sheet, 31c, perf., imperf.
Atomic Power for Peace. *May 12.* Perf., imperf (in different colors). ½, 1, 4c; airmail, 6, 10, 21c (6v). Souvenir sheet of 2 (10, 21c).
Galileo, 400th birth anniversary. *May 12.* Perf., imperf. (in different colors). Airmail, 10, 21c (2v). Souvenir sheet of 2 (10, 21c) perf., imperf.
J.F. Kennedy Memorial. *Aug. 23.* Perf., imperf. (in different colors). ½, 1c; airmail semipostal 10c+5c, 21c+10c, 31c+15c (5v). Souvenir sheet of 2 (1c, 31c+28c) perf., imperf.
Nobel Peace Prize. Perf., imperf. (in different colors). Airmail, 10, 21c. Souvenir sheet of 2 (10, 21c) imperf.

1966

Pope Paul VI, Visit to U.N. *Apr. 4.* ½, 1c; airmail, 5, 10, 21, 31c (6v). Souvenir sheet of 2 (5, 31c) perf., imperf.
Shakespeare, Dante and Wagner. *May 26.* ½c; airmail, 10, 31c (3v). Souvenir sheet of 2 (10, 31c) perf., imperf. (in different colors).
Master Artists. *May 26.* ½c; airmail, 10, 31c (3v). (Durer, Raphael, da Vinci). Souvenir sheet of 2 (10, 31c) perf., imperf. (in different colors).
World Cup Soccer Championship, London. *July 11.* Perf., imperf. (in different colors). ½c x 2; airmail 10c x 2, 21c x 2 (6v). 2 souvenir sheets of 2 (10, 21c perf.; 5, 21c imperf.)
Same, overprinted "Inglaterra vs Alemania". *Sept. 28.*
Italian Contributors to Space Research. *Aug. 12.* Perf., imperf. (in different colors). ½, 1c; airmail, 5, 10, 21c (5v). Souvenir sheet of 2 (10, 21c) imperf.
International Telecommunications Union centenary. *Aug. 12.* Perf., imperf. (in different colors). Airmail, 31c and souvenir sheet.
Religious paintings. *Oct. 24.* Perf., imperf. (in different colors). ½, 1, 2, 3c; airmail, 21c x 2 (6v) (Velazquez, Saraceni, Durer, Orazio, Boticelli, Rubens). Souvenir sheet of 2 (21, 31c) perf., imperf.
Churchill and British Space Research. *Nov. 25.* ½c; airmail, 10, 31c (3v). Souvenir sheet of 2 (10, 31c) perf., imperf. (in different colors).
John F. Kennedy, 3rd death anniversary. *Nov. 25.* Perf., imperf. ½c; airmail, 10, 31c (3v). Souvenir sheet of 2 (10, 31c) perf., imperf. (in different colors).
Jules Verne and French Space Explorations. *Dec. 28.* Perf., imperf. (in different colors), ½, 1c; airmail, 5, 10, 21, 31c (6v). 2 souvenir sheets: 1 of 1, 31c, perf.; 1 of 2 (10, 21c) imperf.

1967

Easter paintings. *Mar. 13.* ½, 1c; airmail, 5, 10, 21, 31c (6v). (Tiepolo, Rubens, Sarto, Santi, Multscher, Grunewald). Souvenir sheet, 31c, perf., imperf.
Pre-Olympics, Mexico (Archaeological ruins). *Apr.* Perf., imperf. (in different colors), ½, 1c; airmail, 5, 10, 21, 31c (6v). 2 souvenir sheets: 1 of 1, 31c perf.; 1 of 2 (10, 21c) imperf.
Paintings. *Aug. 23.* 5c x 3; airmail 21c x 3 (6v). (Ingres, Gainsborough, Rembrandt, Raphael, Velazquez, Durer). 6 souvenir sheets, each 21c.
Goya paintings. *Oct. 17.* 2, 3, 4c; airmail, 5, 8, 10, 13, 21c (8v). Souvenir sheet, 50c.

1968

Life of Christ paintings. *Jan. 10.* 1c x 2, 3c; airmail, 4, 21c x 2 (6v). (Ford Madox Brown, Michelangelo, Rubens, El Greco, Van Dyck, Juan de Juanes). 6 souvenir sheets: 2 of 1, 22, 24c; 4 of 2 (1, 21c; 3, 21c; 21, 31c; 21, 31c).
Panama-Mexico Friendship. *Jan. 20.* Airmail, 50c, 1b (2v). Souvenir sheet of 2 (50c, 1b) imperf.
10th Winter Olympics, Grenoble. *Feb. 2.* ½, 1c; airmail, 5, 10, 21, 31c (6v). 2 souvenir sheets of 2 (each 10, 31c).
Sailing Ships, paintings. *May 7.* ½, 1, 3, 4c; airmail, 5, 13c (6v). Souvenir sheet, 50c, perf., imperf.
Tropical fish. *June 26.* ½, 1, 3, 4c; airmail, 5, 13c (6v). Souvenir sheet, 50c, perf., imperf.
Olympic Medals and Winners, Grenoble. *July 30.* 1, 2, 3, 4, 5, 6, 8c; airmail, 13, 30c (9v). Souvenir sheet, 70c.
Music, paintings. *Sept. 11.* 5, 10, 15, 20, 25, 30c (6v, se-tenant). (de la Hyre, ter Brugghen, Caravaggio, Tourmer, Vermeer, Memling). Souvenir sheet, 40c.
Communications by Satellite for 1968 Mexico Olympics. *Oct. 17.* Weather Satellite issue of 1964 overprinted in black or gold "Olimpiadas Mexico / Transmitidas / Via Satelite / Television Panamena." ½c; airmail, 50c (2v). 2 souvenir sheets, 50c, (in different colors).
Visit of Pope Paul VI, Latin American Eucharistic Congress. *Oct. 18.* Pope's Visit to U.N. issue of 1966 overprinted "Visita S.S. Paulo VI / Congreso Eucharistico / Latinoamerico / Transmitida

ATS-3." ½c; airmail, 21c (2v). Souvenir sheet of 2 (½, 31c) perf., imperf.

Communications by Satellite. *Oct. 21.* Space Conquests and J.F. Kennedy issue of 1966 overprinted "Panama Inaugura / Communicaciones / Via Satellite / 5-Oct. 1968." ½c; airmail. 31c (2v). Souvenir sheet, 31c, perf., imperf.

Oct. 22. Churchill issue of 1966 overprinted in black or gold "Inauguracion / Communicaciones / por Satelite / Panama 5. Oct 1968." ½c; airmail, 10c (2v). Souvenir sheet of 2 (10, 31c) perf., imperf.

Hunting on horseback (paintings and tapestries). *Oct. 29.* 1, 3, 5, 10c; airmail, 13, 30c (6v).

Equestrian events, 1968 Mexico Olympics. *Oct. 29.* Airmail souvenir sheet of 2 (8, 30c) perf., imperf.

Famous race horses, paintings. *Dec. 18.* 5, 10, 15, 20, 25, 30c (6v se-tenant in miniature sheet).

International Human Rights Year (Martin Luther King, John F. and Robert F. Kennedy). *Dec. 18.* Airmail miniature sheet, 40c.

19th Summer Olympic Games, Mexico (Mexican art), 1, 2, 3, 4, 5, 6, 8c; airmail, 13, 30c (9v). Souvenir sheets, 70c.

1969

National Philatelic and Numismatic Exposition, 1st. *Jan. 31.* Panama-Mexico Friendship issue of 1968 overprinted in black or red "la Exposicion / Filatelica y Numisma-/tica Nal. 29-8-68." Airmail, 50c, 1b (2v). Souvenir sheet of 2 (50c, 1b).

Butterflies. *Feb. 23.* Printed se-tenant in sheets checkerwise. ½, 1, 3, 4c; airmail, 5, 13c (6v). Souvenir sheet, 50c perf., imperf.

Space Exploration (international spacecraft). *Mar. 14.* Airmail, 5, 10, 15, 20, 25, 30c, 1b (7v. setenant). Souvenir sheet, 1b.

Red Cross, Children's Aid. *Mar. 26.* Kennedy Memorial issue of 1966 overprinted "Decreto No 112/(de 6 de marzo/de 1969)" and surcharged. Airmail, 5, 10c, 5c+5c, Red Cross issue of 1963 (3v).

Pope Paul VI's Latin America visit. *Aug. 5.* Setenant in sheets checkerwise. 1, 2, 3, 4, 5c; airmail, 6, 7, 8, 10c (9v). Souvenir sheet, 50c.

PARAGUAY

Sets of 1961-67 exist perf., and imperf. in different colors.

1961

Alan B. Shepard, first U.S. astronaut. *Dec. 22.* 10, 25, 50, 75c; airmail, 18.15, 36, 50g (7v). Souvenir sheet, 50c.

Europa 1961. *Dec. 31.* 50, 75c, 1, 1.50, 4.50g; airmail, 20, 50g (7v). Souvenir sheet of 5 (50, 75c, 1, 1.50, 4.50g) and souvenir sheet of 1, 4.50g.

1962

Europa 1962. *Dec. 17.* 4g; airmail, 36g (2v). Souvenir sheet of 2 (4, 36g).

Solar System. *Dec. 17.* 10, 20, 25, 30, 50c; airmail, 12.45, 36, 50g (8v). Souvenir sheet, 50g.

1963

International Sports Cooperation (Pierre de Coubertin and Olympic rings). *Feb. 16.* 15, 25, 30, 40, 50c; airmail, 12.45, 18.15, 36g (8v). Souvenir sheet, 36g.

Same, skier and Olympic rings. *May 16.* 10, 20, 25, 30, 50c; airmail, 12.45, 36, 50g (8v). Souvenir sheet, 50g.

Space Capsule and Walter M. Schirra. *Mar. 16.* 10, 20, 25, 30, 50c; airmail, 12.45, 36, 50g (8v). Souvenir sheet, 50g.

Freedom from Hunger. *May 31.* 10, 25, 50c, 75c; airmail, 18.15, 36, 50g (7v). Souvenir sheet, 50g.

Space Capsule and Gordon Cooper. *Aug. 22.* 15, 25, 30, 40, 50c; airmail, 12.45, 18.15, 50g (8v). Souvenir sheet, 50g.

9th Winter Olympics, Innsbruck. *Oct. 28.* 15, 25, 30, 40, 50c; airmail, 12.45, 18.15, 50g (8v). Souvenir sheet, 50g.

1964

18th Summer Olympics, Tokyo. *Jan. 8.* 15, 25, 30, 40, 50c; airmail, 12.45, 18.15, 50g (8v). Souvenir sheet, 50g.

Red Cross centenary. *Feb. 4.* 10, 25, 30, 50c; airmail, 18.15, 36, 50g (7v). Souvenir sheet, 50g.

Space Research and 18th Summer Olympics. *Mar. 11.* 15, 25, 30, 40, 50c; airmail, 12.45, 18.15, 50g (8v). Souvenir sheet, 50g.

Rockets and satellites. *Apr. 25.* 15, 25, 30, 40, 50c; airmail, 12.45, 18.15, 50g (8v). Souvenir sheet, 50g.

United Nations. *July 30.* 15, 25, 30, 40, 50c; airmail, 12.45, 18.15, 50g (8v). Souvenir sheet, 50g.

Wernher von Braun and Rockets. *Sept. 12.* 10, 15, 20, 30, 40; airmail semipostal, 12.45g+6g, 18.15g+9g, 20g+10g (8v). Souvenir sheet of 2 (40c, 12.45g+6g).

38th International Eucharistic Congress, Bombay. *Dec. 11.* Semipostal, 20g+10g, 30g+15g, 50g+25g, 100g+50g (4v). Souvenir sheet of 4 (20g+10g, 30g+15g, 50g+25g, 100g+50g), with and without presentation folder.

Churches and Medals. *Dec. 12.* Semipostals, 20g+10g, 30g+15g, 50g+25g, 100g+50g (4v). Souvenir sheet of 4 (20g+10g, 30g+15g, 50g+25g, 100g+50g), with and without presentation folder.

1965

Boy Scouts. *Jan. 15.* 10, 15, 20, 30, 50c; airmail, 12.45, 18.15, 36g (8v). Souvenir sheet, 36g.

Olympic and Paraguayan Medals. *Mar. 30.* 15, 25, 30, 40, 50c; airmail, 12.45, 18.15, 50g (8v). Souvenir sheet, 50g.

Scientists. *June 5.* 10, 15, 20, 30, 40c; airmail semipostal, 12.45g+6g, 18.15g+9g, 20g+10g (8v se-tenant triangles). (Newton, Copernicus, Galileo, Einstein), Souvenir sheet of 2 (40c, 12.45g+6g).

Kennedy and Churchill Memorials. *Sept. 4.* 15, 25, 30, 40, 50c; airmail, 12.45, 18.15, 50g (8v). Souvenir sheet, 50g.

International Telecommunication Union centenary. *Sept. 30.* 10, 15, 20, 30, 40c; airmail semipostals, 12.45g+6g, 18.15g+9g, 20g+10g (8v). Souvenir sheet of 2 (40c, 12.45g+6g).

Pope Paul VI, Visit to U.N. *Nov. 19.* 10, 15, 20, 30, 50c; airmail, 12.45, 18.15, 36g (8v). Souvenir sheet, 36g.

1966

Space Exploration. *Feb. 19.* (Grissom, White, McDivitt, Young) 15, 25, 30, 40, 50c; airmail, 12.45, 18.15. 50g (8v). Souvenir sheet, 50g.

Events of 1965. *Mar. 9.* 10, 15, 20, 30, 50c; airmail, 12.45, 18.15, 36g (8v). Souvenir sheet, 36g.

Pre-Olympic Games, Mexico 1968. *Apr. 1.* 10, 15, 20, 30, 50c; airmail, 12.45, 18.15, 36g (8v). Souvenir sheet, 36g.

Space Research, German Contributors. *May 16.* 10, 15, 20, 30, 50c; airmail, 12.45, 18.15, 36g (8v). Souvenir sheet, 36g.

Writers. *June 11.* 10, 15, 20, 30, 50c; airmail, 12.45, 18.15, 36g (8v) (Dante, Moliere, Goethe, Shakespeare). Souvenir sheet, 36g.

Space Research, Italian Contributors. *July 11.* 10, 15, 20, 30, 50c; airmail, 12.45, 18.15, 36g (8v). Souvenir sheet, 36g.

Moon Exploration. *Aug. 25.* 10, 15, 20, 30, 50c; airmail, 12.45, 18.15, 36g (8v). Souvenir sheet, 36g.

World Skiing Championships, Portillo, Chile, and **10th Winter Olympics,** Grenoble 1968. *Sept. 30.* 10, 15, 20, 30, 50c; airmail, 12.45, 18.15, 36g (8v). Souvenir sheet, 36g.

John F. Kennedy. 3rd death anniversary and communications satellites. *Nov. 7.* 10, 15, 20, 30, 50c; airmail, 12.45, 18.15, 36g (8v). Souvenir sheet, 36g.

Paintings. *Dec. 10.* 10, 15, 20, 30, 50c; airmail, 12.45, 18.15, 36g (8v se-tenant). (Largilliere, Rubens, Titian, Holbein, Sanchez, Coello, Veronese, Mantegna, Vouet). Souvenir sheet, 36g.

1967
Holy Week, paintings. *Feb. 28.* 10, 15, 20, 30, 50c; airmail, 12.45, 18.15, 36g (8v se-tenant) (Raphael, Rubens, Bassano, El Greco, Murillo, Reni, Tintoretto, da Vinci). Souvenir sheet, 36g.
Religious paintings, 16th century. *Mar. 10.* 10, 15, 20, 30, 50c; airmail, 12.45, 18.15, 36g (8v) (Fiori, Tibaldi, El Greco, Caravaggio, Vasco, Fernandez). Souvenir sheet, 36g.
Paintings, *May 16.* 10, 15, 20, 30, 50c; airmail, 12.45, 18.15, 36g (8v se-tenant) (Chardin, Fontanesi, Cezanne, van Gogh, Renoir, Toulouse-Lautrec). Souvenir sheet, 36g.
Paintings, *July 16.* 10, 15, 20, 25, 30, 50c; airmail, 12.45, 18.15, 36g (9v) (Steen, Hals, Jordaens, Rembrandt, Desmarees, Quentin de la Tour, Nicolaes Maes, Vigee-Lebrun, Rubens, Tiepolo). 2 souvenir sheets; 1 of 1, 50g, perf.; 1 of 3 (12.45, 18.15, 36g), imperf.
John F. Kennedy, 50th birthday. *Aug. 19.* 10, 15, 20, 25, 30, 50c; airmail, 12.45, 18.15, 36g. (9v). 2 souvenir sheets: 1 of 1, 50g. perf.; 1 of 3 (12.45, 18.15, 36g) imperf.
Sculptures. *Oct. 16.* 10, 15, 20, 25, 30, 50c; airmail, 12.45, 18.15, 50g (9v).
19th Summer Olympics, Mexico (Mexican art). *Nov. 29.* 10, 15, 20, 25, 30, 50c; airmail, 12.45, 18.15, 36g (9v). 2 souvenir sheets: 1 of 1, 50g, perf.; 1 of 3 (12.45, 18.15, 36g) imperf.

1968
Madonna and Child, paintings. *Jan. 27,* 10, 15, 20, 25, 30, 50c; airmail, 12.45, 18.15, 36g (9v). Souvenir sheet of 3 (12.45, 18.15, 36g) imperf. (Bellini, Raphael, Correggio, Luini, Bronzino, Van Dyck, Vignon, de Ribera, Botticelli)
10th Winter Olympics, Grenoble. *Apr. 23.* 10, 15, 20, 25, 30, 50c; airmail, 12.45, 18.15, 36g (9v) (paintings by Pisarro, Utrillo, Monet, Breitner, Sisley, Brueghel, Anverkamp, Limbourg brothers). Souvenir sheet of 2 (36, 50g).
History of Paraguayan stamps (stamps on stamps). *June 3.* 10, 15, 20, 25, 30, 50c; airmail, 12.45, 18.15, 36g (9v). Souvenir sheet of 2 (36, 50g).
Children, paintings. *July 9.* 10, 15, 20, 25, 30, 50c; airmail, 12.45, 18.15, 36g (9v) (Russell, Velazquez, Romney, Caravaggio, Lawrence, Gentileschi, Renoir, Copley, Sessions). Souvenir sheet of 2 (36, 50g).
39th International Eucharistic Congress and Pope Paul's Visit. *Sept. 25.* 10, 15, 20, 25, 30, 50c; airmail, 12.45, 18.15, 36g (9v). Souvenir sheet of 2 (36, 50g).
Events of 1968. *Dec. 21.* 10, 15, 20, 25, 30, 50c; airmail, 12.45, 18.15, 50g (9v), 3 imperf. souvenir sheets of 3 (10, 15c, 50g; 20, 25c, 12.45g, 30, 50c, 18.15g).

1969
Gold Medal Winners, Mexico Olympics. *Feb. 13.* 10, 15, 20, 25, 30, 50c; airmail, 12.45, 18.15, 50g (9v). 3 imperf. souvenir sheets of 3 (10, 15c, 12.45g; 20, 50c, 50g; 25, 30c, 18.15g).
International Space Developments. *Mar. 10.* 10, 15, 20, 25, 30, 50c; airmail, 12.45, 18.15, 50g (9v). 3 imperf. souvenir sheets of 3 (10, 15, 20c; 25, 30c, 18.15g; 50c, 12.45, 50g).
Regional Fauna. *July 9.* Birds: 10, 15, 20, 25, 30, 50, 75c; airmail, 12.45, 18.15g (9v). Animals: 10, 15, 20, 25, 30, 50, 75c; airmail, 12.45, 18.15g (9v).
Apollo 11. *July 9.* 4 airmail souvenir sheets: 2 perf., 2 imperf., each 23.40g.
Winners of Jules Rimet Cup Soccer Championships, 1930-1966. *Nov. 26.* 10, 15, 20, 25, 30, 50, 75c; airmail, 12.45, 18.15g (9v). Souvenir sheet, 23.40g perf., imperf.
Olympic Soccer Gold Medal Winners, 1900-1968, *Nov. 26.* 10, 15, 20, 25, 30, 50, 75c; airmail, 12.45, 18.15g (9v). Souvenir sheet, 23.40g, perf., imperf.
Christmas paintings. *Nov. 29.* 10, 15, 20, 25, 30, 50, 75c; airmail, 12.45, 18.15g (9v). (Master Bertram, Procaccini, di Credi, Maitre de Flemalle, Correggio, Borgianni, Botticelli, El Greco, de Morales). Souvenir sheet, 23.40g imperf.
Goya paintings. *Nov. 29.* 10, 15, 20, 25, 30, 50, 75c; airmail, 12.45, 18.15g (9v). Souvenir sheet, 23.40g.
Space Exploration, European contributors. *Nov. 29.* Airmail souvenir sheet, 23.40g, perf., imperf.

1970
Apollo 11. *Mar. 11.* 10, 15, 20, 25, 30, 50, 75c; airmail, 12.45, 18.15g (9v). 3 souvenir sheets, each 23.40g. 1 perf., 2 imperf.
Easter. *Mar. 11.* Se-tenant checkerwise. 10, 15, 20, 25, 30, 50, 75c; airmail, 12.45, 18.15g (9v). Souvenir sheet, 23.40g.
Apollo 12. *Mar. 16.* Perf., imperf. 50c x 2; airmail, 50c x 2 (4v). 2 souvenir sheets of 2 (each 50c x 2) 1 with simulated perf., 1 imperf.
20th Summer Olympics, Munich, 1972. *Sept. 28.* 10, 15, 20, 25, 30, 50, 75c; airmail, 12.45, 18.15g (9v se-tenant) souvenir sheet, 23.40g perf., imperf.
Paintings, Pinakothek, Munich, 1972. *Sept. 28.* 10, 15, 20, 25, 30, 50, 75c; airmail, 12.45, 18.15g (9v se-tenant) (Nudes by Cranach, Baldung, Tintoretto, Rubens, Boucher, Durer self-portrait; altar by Altdorfer). Souvenir sheet, 23.40g.
Apollo space program. *Oct. 19.* 10, 15, 20, 25, 30, 50, 75c; airmail, 12.45, 18.15g (9v se-tenant). 3 souvenir sheets, each 23.40g, 1 perf., 2 imperf.
Moon and Space Conquests, future projects. *Oct. 19.* 10, 15, 20, 25, 30 (se-tenant); 50, 75c; airmail, 12.45, 18.15g (9v). Souvenir sheet, 23.40g.
EXPO '70, Osaka, Japan, (paintings from National Museum, Tokyo, *Nov. 26.* 10, 15, 20, 25, 30, (se-tenant); 50, 75c; airmail, 12.45, 18.15, 50g (10v). 3 souvenir sheets, each 20g.
Flowers, paintings. *Nov. 26.* 10, 15, 20, 25, 30, (se-tenant) 50, 75c; airmail, 12.45, 18.15, 50g (10v) (Jawlensky, Purramann, Vlaminck, Monet, Renoir, van Gogh, Cezanne, van Huysum, Ruysch, Walscappelle). Souvenir sheet, 20g.
Paintings, Prado, Madrid. *Dec. 16.* 10, 15, 20, 25, 30 (se-tenant) 50, 75c; airmail, 12.45, 18.15, 50g (10v). (Nudes by Titian, Velazquez, Van Dyck, Tintoretto, Rubens, Veronese; religious paintings by Goya, Murillo, El Greco). Souvenir sheet, 20g.
Durer paintings. *Dec. 16.* 10, 15, 20, 25, 30 (setenant) 50, 75c; airmail, 12.45, 18.15, 50g (10v). Souvenir sheet, 20g.
Eisenhower Memorial. Dec. 16. Airmail souvenir sheet, 20g.
Napoleon. *Dec. 16.* Airmail souvenir sheet, 20g.

1971
20th Summer Olympics, Munich, 1972. *Mar. 23.* 10, 15, 20, 25, 30 (se-tenant) 50, 75c; airmail, 12.45, 18.15, 50g (10v). 2 souvenir sheets, each 23.40g.
Knights, paintings. *Mar. 26.* 10, 15, 20, 25, 30c (se-tenant), 50, 75c; airmail, 12.45, 18.15, 50g (10v). (Van Dyck, Titian, Walter, Orsi, David, Huguet, Perugino, Witz, Van Eyck) Souvenir sheet, 20g.
Apollo Missions. *Mar. 26.* 2 airmail souvenir sheets, each 20g.
Women, paintings, from Louvre. *Mar. 26,* 10, 15, 20, 25, 30c (se-tenant), 50, 75c; airmail, 12.45, 18.15, 50g (10v). (Boucher, de la Tour, Delacroix, Ingres, Watteau, Renoir, da Vinci). Souvenir sheet, 20g.
Paraguayan stamp centenary. *Mar. 23.* Airmail souvenir sheet, 20g.
Christmas, paintings. *Mar. 23.* 10, 15, 20, 25, 30c (se-tenant) 50, 75c; airmail, 12.45, 18.15, 50g (10v) (van der Weyden, Zeitblom, von Soest, Mayno, da Fabriano, Matirios, Memling, Poussin, Rubens, Giorgione, Batoni). Souvenir sheet, 20g.
Paintings. *Mar. 29.* 10, 15, 20, 25, 30c (se-tenant), 50, 75c; airmail, 12.45, 18.15, 50g (10v) (Botticelli, Tibaldi, Titian, Caracci, Raphael, Ricci, Delgado Rodas,Courtines, Murillo).
Paraguayan stamp centenary and Lufthansa Asuncion - Frankfurt flight. *Mar. 29.* 2 airmail souvenir sheets, each 20g.
Hunting scenes, paintings. *Mar. 29.* 10, 15, 20, 25, 30c (se-tenant),

50, 75c; airmail, 12.45, 18.15, 50g (10v) (Gozzoli, Velazquez, Uccello, Sutherland, Brun, de Vos, Vernet). 2 souvenir sheets, each 20g.
Philatokyo '71 (Japanese prints). *Apr. 7.* 10, 15, 20, 25, 30c (se-tenant), 50, 75c; airmail, 12.45, 18.15, 50g (10v). 2 souvenir sheets, each 20g.
11th Winter Olympics, Sapporo, 1972 (Japanese art). *Apr. 7.* 10, 15, 20, 25, 30c (se-tenant), 50, 75c; airmail, 12.45, 18.15, 50g (10v). 2 souvenir sheets, each 20g.
Charles de Gaulle, 1st death anniversary. *Nov. 9.* Airmail souvenir sheet, 20g.
Johannes Kepler, 400th death anniversary. *Nov. 9.* 2 airmail souvenir sheets, each 20g.
Paintings, Berlin-Dahlem Museum. *Dec. 23.* 15c and 20c (se-tenant), 10, 25, 30, 50, 75c; airmail, 12.45, 18.15, 50g (10v) (Caravaggio, De Cosimo, Cranach, Veneziano, Holbein, Grien, Durer, Schongauer).
Napoleon I, sesquicentennial of death. *Dec. 24.* 10, 15, 20, 25, 30c (se-tenant) 50, 75c; airmail, 12.45, 18.15, 50g (10v).
Taras Shevchenko, 110th birth anniversary. *Dec. 24.* Airmail souvenir sheet, 20g.

1972
Locomotives. *Jan. 6.* 10, 15, 20, 25, 30c (se-tenant), 50, 75c; airmail, 12.45, 18.15, 50g (10v). Souvenir sheet, 20g.
11th Winter Olympics, Sapporo. *Jan. 6.* 10, 15, 20, 25, 30c (se-tenant), 50, 75c; airmail, 12.45, 18.15, 50g (10v). 2 souvenir sheets, each 20g.
American space explorations, decade. *Jan. 6.* Airmail souvenir sheet, 20g.
Racing cars. *Mar. 20.* 10, 15, 20, 25, 30c (se-tenant), 50, 75c; airmail, 12.45, 18.15, 50g (10v). Souvenir sheet, 20g.
Apollo 16. *Mar. 29.* Airmail souvenir sheet, 20g.
Olympic Games, 1896-1972. *Mar. 29.* 6 airmail souvenir sheets, each 20g.
Ancient war vessels. *Mar. 29.* 10, 15, 20, 25, 30c (se-tenant), 50, 75c; airmail, 12.45, 18.15, 50g. (10v).
Paintings, Asuncion Museum. *Mar. 22.* 10, 15, 20, 25, 30c (se-tenant), 50, 75c; airmail, 12.45, 18.15, 50g (10v) (Holden Jara, Tintoretto, Bouchard, Italian School, Berisso, Carracci, Schiaffino, Lostow).
Paintings, Vienna Museum. *May 22.* 10, 15, 20, 25, 30c (se-tenant), 50, 75c; airmail, 12.45, 18.15, 50g (10v) (Rubens, Bellini, Carracci, Cagnacci, Spranger, Strozzi, Cranach, Coxcie, Poussin, Bronzino).
Meetings of Presidents, (Argentina, Bolivia, Brazil, Paraguay). *Nov. 18.* 10, 15, 20, 25, 30c (se-tenant), 50, 75c; airmail, 12.45, 18.15g (9v). Souvenir sheet, 23.40g.
President Stroessner, visit to Emperor of Japan. *Nov. 18.* 10, 15, 20, 25, 30c (se-tenant), 50, 75c; airmail, 12.45, 18.15g (9v). 3 souvenir sheets, each 23.40g, 2 perf., 1 imperf.
Animals, paintings. *Nov. 18.* 10, 15, 20, 25, 30c (se-tenant), 50, 75c; airmail, 12.45, 18.15g (9v) (Botke, Utamaro, Arents, Dietzsch, Brueghel, Marc, Durer, Jakuchu, Asselyn).
Medal Winners, Sapporo Olympics. *Nov. 18.* Airmail souvenir sheet, 23.40g.
Locomotives. *Nov. 25.* 10, 15, 20, 25, 30c (se-tenant), 50, 75c; airmail, 12.45, 18.15g (9v).
South American animals. *Nov. 25.* 10, 15, 20, 25, 30c (se-tenant), 50, 75c; airmail, 12.45, 18.15g (9v).
Olympic Medals History. *Nov. 25.* 2 airmail souvenir sheets, each 23.40g.
Christmas, painting (Murillo). *Nov. 25.* Airmail souvenir sheet, 23.40g.
Civil aviation and space exploration, French contributions. *Nov. 25.* 2 airmail souvenir sheets, each 23.40g.

1973
Paintings, Florence Museum. *Mar. 13.* 10, 15, 20, 25, 30, 50, 75c; airmail, 5, 10, 20g (10v se-tenant) (Cranach, Caravaggio, Fiorentino, di Credi, Liss, da Vinci, Botticelli, Titian, del Piombo, di Michelino). 2 souvenir sheets, each 25g.
South American butterflies. *Mar. 13.* 10, 15, 20, 25, 30, 50, 75c; airmail, 5, 10, 20g (10v, se-tenant).
Apollo 17. *Mar. 13.* Airmail souvenir sheet, 25g.
IBRA 73, Munich. *Mar. 21.* Airmail souvenir sheet, 25g, imperf.
Medal Winners, Munich Olympics, *Mar. 15.* Airmail souvenir sheet, 25g.
Cats. *June 29.* 10, 15, 20, 25, 30, 50, 75c; airmail 5, 10, 20g (10v, se-tenant).
Paintings, Flemish. *June 29.* 10, 15, 20, 25, 30, 50, 75c; airmail, 5, 10, 20g (10v, se-tenant) (Spranger, Jordaens, de Clerck, Goltzius, Rubens, Brueghel, Martin de Vos).
Copernicus, 500th birth anniversary, *June 29.* 2 airmail souvenir sheets, each 25g.
Skylab. *June 29.* Airmail souvenir sheet, 25g.
World Cup Soccer Championship, Munich, 1974. *June 29.* Airmail souvenir sheet, 25g. *Oct. 8.* 10, 15, 20, 25, 30, 50, 75c; airmail, 5, 10, 20g (10v, se-tenant). Souvenir sheet, 25g.
Venetian Women, paintings. *Oct. 8.* 10, 15, 20, 25, 30, 50, 75c; airmail, 5, 10, 20g (10v, se-tenant) (Carapaccio, Pitoni, Veronese, Tintoretto, Amigoni, Tiepolo).
Planetary exploration (Mars). *Oct. 8.* 2 airmail souvenir sheets, each 25g.
Birds. *Nov. 14.* 10, 15, 20, 25, 30, 50, 75c; airmail, 5, 10, 20g (10v, se-tenant). Souvenir sheet, 25g.
Moon explorations (Apollo 11-17, *Nov. 14.* 10, 15, 20, 25, 30, 50, 75c; airmail, 5, 10, 20g (10v, se-tenant), 2 souvenir sheets, each 25g.
Picasso memorial. *Nov. 14.* Airmail souvenir sheet, 25g.
Folklore (national costumes). *Dec. 30.* 25, 50, 75c, 1, 1.50, 1.75, 2.25g (7v se-tenant).
President Stroessner, visit to Europe and Morocco. *Dec. 30.* Airmail, 5, 10, 25, 50g (se-tenant), 150g (5v). Souvenir sheet, 100g, imperf.
Flowers. *Dec. 31.* 10, 20, 25, 30, 40, 50, 75c (7v se-tenant).

1974
World Cup Soccer Championship, Munich. *Jan. 31.* Airmail, 5, 10, 20g (3v se-tenant). 2 souvenir sheets, each 25g.
Roses, paintings. *Feb. 2.* 10, 15, 20, 25, 30, 50, 75c (7v se-tenant) (Curtis, Chazal, Buchoz, Ehret, van Spaendonick).
Paintings, Gulbenkian Museum. *Feb. 4.* 10, 15, 20, 25, 30, 50, 75c; airmail, 5, 10, 20g (10v setenant) (Boucher, Burne-Jones, Natoire, de Vos, Bugiardini, Mabuse, Utamaro, Lawrence, Rubens).
Christmas 1973, painting (Le Nain). *Feb. 4.* Airmail souvenir sheet, 25g.
Tourism Year 1973 (emblems of 10 airlines operating in Paraguay). *Feb. 4.* Airmail souvenir sheet, 25g.
Paintings. *Mar. 20.* 10, 15, 20, 25, 30, 50, 75c; airmail, 5, 10, 20g (10v, se-tenant) (Mabuse, di Cosimo, van Haarlem, Boucher, Renoir, Dix, van Kessel, Seele, Batoni, Flamenca).
UPU centenary. *Mar. 20.* 10, 15, 20, 25, 30, 50, 75c; airmail, 5, 10, 20g (10v se-tenant). 2 souvenir sheets, each 25g.
Skylab 2. *Mar. 20.* Airmail souvenir sheet, 25g.
President Stroessner. *May 10.* Visit to France and Presidnet Pompidou: Airmail, 100g. Visit to Pope Paul VI: Airmail souvenir sheet, 200g.
World Cup Soccer Championship. *July 13.* Airmail, 4, 5, 10g (3v). Souvenir sheet, 15g.
Lufthansa-Lineas Aereas Paraguayas airlines. *July 13.* Airmail souvenir sheet. 15g.
Ships, paintings. *Sept. 13.* 5, 10, 15, 20, 25, 35, 40, 50c (8v se-tenant). Airmail souvenir sheet, 15g. imperf.

President Stroessner, visit to South Africa. *Dec. 2.* Airmail, 10g.
President Pinochet of Chile, visit to Paraguay. *Dec. 2.* Airmail, 5g.
Covers (canceled on moon). *Dec. 2.* Airmail, 4g.
UPU centenary. *Dec. 2.* 2 airmail souvenir sheets, each 15g. *Dec. 7:* Airmail 4, 5, 10g (3v).
Mariner 10. *Dec. 2 and 7.* 2 airmail souvenir sheets, each 15g.
Winter Olympics. Committee sessions. *Dec. 7.* 2 airmail souvenir sheets, each 15g.
World Cup Soccer Championship (FIFA cup; German winning team; 1973 games, Argentina). *Dec. 20.* Airmail, 4, 5, 10g (3v). 2 airmail souvenir sheets, each 15g.

1975
Paintings, Borghese Gallery, Rome. *Jan. 15.* 5, 10, 15, 20, 25, 35, 40, 50c (8v se-tenant) (Romano, Caravaggio, Domenichino, Titian, Correggio, Savoldo, da Vinci, Rubens, Piero di Cosimo). Airmail souvenir sheet, 15g.
Christmas, paintings. *Jan. 17.* 5, 10, 15, 20, 25, 35, 40, 50c (8v se-tenant) (della Robbia, David, Memling, Giorgione, French 14th century, Pulzone, van Orley, Pacher, Raphael). Airmail souvenir sheet, 15g.
OCEAN EXPO '75 International Oceanographic Exhibition, Okinawa. *Feb. 24.* Airmail 4, 5, 10g (3v). Airmail souvenir sheet, 15g.
Summer Olympics, Montreal 1976. *Feb. 24.* Airmail souvenir sheet, 15g.
Kurt, Debus (scientist), 65th birth anniversary. *Feb. 24.* Airmail souvenir sheet, 15g.
Paintings, London National Gallery. *Apr. 25.* 5, 10, 15, 20, 25, 35, 40, 50c (8v). (Velazquez, Watteau, Correggio, Gainsborough, Cranach, Lotto, Rembrandt, Tintoretto, Pisanello) Airmail souvenir sheet, 15g.
Dogs. *June 7.* 5, 10, 15, 20, 25, 35, 40, 50c (8v). Airmail souvenir sheet, 15g.
Fauna of South America. *Aug. 20.* 5, 10, 15, 20, 25, 35, 40, 50c (8v). Airmail souvenir sheet, 15g.
Spanish Stamps, 125th anniversary, Espana '75. *Aug. 21.* Airmail, 4, 5, 10g se-tenant (3v). Airmail souvenir sheet, 15g.
Zeppelin America Flight (ZR3). *Aug. 21.* Airmail souvenir sheet, 15g.
Pioneer 11, Jupiter Flight *Aug. 21.* Airmail souvenir sheet, 15g.
Michelangelo, 500th birth anniversary. *Aug. 23.* Se-tenant in strip of 8, 5, 10, 15, 20, 25, 35, 40, 50c (8v). Airmail souvenir sheet, 15g.
Same. *Aug. 26.* Airmail, 4, 5, 10g se-tenant (3v). Airmail souvenir sheet, 15g. simulated perforation.
International Women's Year. U.N. 30th anniversary. *Aug. 26.* Airmail souvenir sheet, 15g.
Space Exploration, German contributions. *Aug. 26.* Airmail souvenir sheet, 15g.
Winter Olympics, Innsbruck. *Aug. 27.* 1, 2, 3, 4, 5g; airmail, 10, 15, 20g (8v). 2 airmail souvenir sheets, each 25g.
Summer Olympics, Montreal. *Aug. 28.*1, 2, 3, 4, 5g; airmail, 10, 15, 20g (8v). 2 airmail souvenir sheets, each 25g.
Various Flights. *Oct. 13.* Airmail, 4, 5, 10g (3v). 3 airmail souvenir sheets; Zeppelin, World Soccer Championship, Viking, each 15g.
U.S. Bicentennial, paintings of victorious ships. *Oct. 20.* 5, 10, 20, 25, 35, 40, 50c (7v). Airmail souvenir sheets, 15g.
U.S. Bicentennial, paintings. *Nov. 20.* Se-tenant in strips of 8. 5, 10, 15, 20, 25, 35, 40, 50c (8v). (Kahill, Brackman, Catlin, Benton, Remington, Willard, Trumbull, Stuart) Airmail souvenir sheet, 15g.
U.S. Bicentennial, auto industry. *Nov. 28.* Airmail, 4, 5 and 10g se-tenant (3v).
U.S. Bicentennial, air and space technology. *Nov. 28.* Airmail souvenir sheet, 15g.
U.S. Bicentennial, flags and seals of Paraguay and U.S. *Nov. 28.* Airmail souvenir sheet, 15g.
Concorde, Lufthansa, Exfilmo '75. *Dec. 20.* Airmail, 4, 5, 10g (3v). Airmail souvenir sheet, 15g.
Schweitzer-Adenauer. *Dec. 20.* Airmail souvenir sheet, 15g.
Ferdinand Porsche, birth centenary, Vienna '75 Philatelic Exposition. *Dec. 20.* Airmail souvenir sheet, 15g.

1976
Holy Year, Christmas paintings. *Feb. 2.* Airmail, 4, 5, 10g (3v). (Raphael, del Mayno, Vignon, Ghirlandaio). Airmail souvenir sheet, 15g.
Austria, 1000th anniversary. *Feb. 2.* Airmail souvenir sheet, 15g.
World Soccer Championships, Germany 1954, 1974. *Feb. 2.* Airmail souvenir sheet, 15g.
Cats. *Apr. 2.* Se-tenant strip of 8. 5, 10, 15, 20, 25, 35, 40, 50c (8v). Airmail souvenir sheet, 15g.
Apollo-Soyuz. *Apr. 2.* Airmail souvenir sheet, 25g.
Railroads, 150th anniversary. *Apr. 2.* 1, 2, 3, 4, 5g; airmail, 10, 15, 20g (8v). Airmail souvenir sheet, 25g.
Lufthansa, 50th anniversary. *Apr. 2.* Airmail souvenir sheet, 25g.
Spanish Paintings. *Apr. 2.* 1, 2, 3, 4, 5g; airmail 10, 15, 20g (8v). (Goya, de Torres, Esquival, Murillo, Antolinez, Zuloaga, Velazquez). Airmail souvenir sheet, 25g.
Butterflies. *May 12.* Se-tenant strip of 8. 5, 10, 15, 20, 25, 35, 40, 50c (8v).
Winter Olympics, Innsbruck '76. Olympic medals and Innsbruck aerial scene. *June 15.* Airmail souvenir sheet, 25g.
July 18. Airmail souvenir sheet, 25g (Rosi Mittermaier; medals and medal-winning countries in margin).
Domestic Animals. *June 15.* 1, 2, 3, 4, 5, 10, 15, 20g (8v).
Telephone, Bell, centenary. *June 15.* Airmail souvenir sheet, 25g.
U.S. Bicentennial & U.S. Post Office Dept. bicentenary. *June 18.* 1, 2, 3, 4, 5g; airmail, 10, 15, 20g (8v). 2 airmail souvenir sheets (Man on Moon and 1st Official Missile Mail), each 25g.
Interphil 76, seven other philatelic exhibition emblems. *May 29.* Airmail souvenir sheet, 15g.
Paintings, Planets (mythology) with satellites. *July 12.* 1, 2, 3, 4, 5g; airmail 10, 15, 20g (8v, first 7 values se-tenant) (Ingres, Rubens, Tiepolo, Medina, Giordano, de la Hyre, Veronese). Airmail souvenir sheet, 25g (Satellites over Mars, Mars and Venus by Houbraken in margin).
United Nations Postal Administrations, 25th anniversary, U.P.U. centenary. *July 15.* Airmail souvenir sheet, 25g. (U.N. No. 38).
Dec. 18. 25th U.P.U. anniversary, telephone centenary, 110th I.T.U. anniversary. Airmail souvenir sheet, 25g (U.N. No. 42, Geneva No. 22).
Paintings, Sailing Ships. *July 15.* 1, 2, 3, 4, 5g; airmail, 10, 15, 20g (8v, first 7 se-tenant).
Paintings, German Warships. *Aug. 20.* 1, 2, 3, 4, 5g; airmail, 10, 15, 20g (8v) (Zeeden, Wichman, Pollack, Fedeler, Seiz, Stroh, Bohrdt). Airmail souvenir sheet, Hamburg Nautical Exposition, 25g (Zeytline).
21st Summer Olympics, Montreal. Women medal winners. *Dec. 18.* 1, 2, 3, 4, 5g; airmail, 10, 15, 20g (8v, first 7 se-tenant). 3 airmail souvenir sheets, 25g (German Dressage Team; U.S. Bicentennial, Bruce Jenner, decathlon winner; list of medal-winning countries, Olympic torch.

1977
Titian, 500th birth anniversary, paintings. *Feb. 18.* 1, 2, 3, 4, 5g; airmail, 10, 15, 20g (8v, first 7 values se-tenant).
Rubens, 400th birth anniversary, paintings. *Feb. 18.* 1, 2, 3, 4, 5g; airmail, 10, 15, 20g (8v, first 7 values se-tenant). Airmail souvenir sheet (Milky Way), 25g.
U.S. Bicentennial, Space scenes. *March 3.* 1, 2, 3, 4, 5g; airmail, 10, 15, 20g (8v, first 7 values se-tenant). 2 airmail souvenir sheets, 25g. (Future space-craft on Mars).
Nobel Prize, 75th Anniversary. *June 7.* Airmail souvenir sheet, 25g (Alfred Nobel medal).

Story of Olympic Games, Athens to Montreal. *June 10.* 1, 2, 3, 4, 5g; airmail, 10, 15, 20g (8v). Airmail souvenir sheet, 25g.
LUPOSTA '77, Graf Zeppelin, trip to South America. *June 13.* 1, 2, 3, 4, 5g; airmail. 10, 15, 20g (8v). 2 airmail souvenir sheets, 25g (LUPOSTA '77), 25g (Zeppelin).
History of Aviation. *July 18.* 1, 2, 3, 4, 5g; airmail, 10, 15, 20g (8v). 2 airmail souvenir sheets, 25g (Lindbergh), 25g (Helix).
World Soccer, Argentina '78. *Oct. 28.* (First issue). 1, 2, 3, 4, 5g; airmail, 10, 15, 20g (8v, first 7 values in se-tenant strip). Airmail souvenir sheet, 25g. (Second issue) 1, 2, 3, 4, 5g; airmail, 10, 15, 20g (8v, first 7 values in se-tenant strip). Airmail souvenir sheet, 25g.

1978
Rubens, 400th birth anniversary, paintings. *Jan. 19.* 1, 2, 3, 4, 5g; airmail 10, 15, 20g (8v, first 7 values in se-tenant strips). 2 airmail souvenir sheets, 25g (gold or silver inscriptions).
World Chess Championships, Argentina 1978, Paintings. *Jan. 23.* 1, 2, 3, 4, 5g; airmail, 10, 15, 20g (8v, first 7 values in se-tenant strip) (de Cremone, L. van Leyden, H. Muelich, E.H. May, George Cruikshank, unknown). Airmail souvenir sheet, 25g.
Francisco de Goya, 150th death anniversary. *May 11.* 3, 4, 5, 6, 7, 8, 20g (se-tenant strip of 7); airmail, 10, 25g (9v).
Future Aerospace Projects. *May 16.* 3, 4, 5, 6, 7, 8, 20g (se-tenant strip of 7); airmail, 10, 25g (9v).
Racing Cars. *June 28.* 3, 4, 5, 6, 7, 8, 20g (se-tenant strip of 7); airmail, 10, 25g (9v). Airmail souvenir sheet, 25g (Ferrari).
Peter Paul Rubens, paintings. *June 30.* 3, 4, 5, 6, 7, 8, 20g; airmail, 10, 25g (9v).
Pres. Stroessner Reelection. *Aug. 15.* Airmail, 75, 500, 1000g (3v).
QEII Coronation, 25th anniversary. 2 airmail souvenir sheets, 25g (Queen with orb and scepter), 25g (Queen presenting World Soccer Cup to 1966 England team).
World Cup Soccer, Argentina 78. 3 airmail souvenir sheets. 25g (Soccer emblem and flags of 16 finalists); 25g (Stadium with flags and insignia of finalists); 25g (World Cup, Argentina champions, finals).
Christmas and New Year 1978-79, painting by Albrecht Durer. Airmail souvenir sheet, 25g.
International Year of the Child, Grimm's "Snow White and the Seven Dwarfs." *Oct. 26.* 3, 4, 5, 6, 7, 8, 20g (se-tenant strip of 7): airmail, 10, 25g (9v).
Christmas 1978, paintings. 3, 4, 5, 6, 7, 8, 20g (se-tenant strip of 7); airmail 10, 25g (9v). Airmail souvenir sheet, 25g (Rubens).

1979
World Cup Soccer, Argentina. 3, 4, 5, 6, 7, 8, 20g (se-tenant strip of 7); airmail, 10, 25g (9v).
Military Units. 3, 4, 5, 6, 7, 8, 20g (se-tenant strip of 7); airmail, 10, 25g (9v).
75th Anniversary, First Powered Flight. 3, 4, 5, 6, 7, 8, 20g (se-tenant strip of 7); airmail, 10, 25g (9v). Airmail souvenir sheet, 25g (Graf Zeppelin).
International Year of the Child, Durer's paintings. *Apr. 28.* 3, 4, 5, 6, 7, 8, 20g (se-tenant strip of 7), airmail, 10, 25g (9v). 2 airmail souvenir sheets, 25g (Christ's burial, space stations).
Winter Olympic Games, Lake Placid. *June 11.* Airmail souvenir sheet, 25g (Dorothy Hamill). *Aug. 22.* 3, 4, 5, 6, 7, 8, 20g (se-tenant strip of 7), airmail, 10, 25g (9v). Airmail souvenir sheet, 25g (Kulakova, cross-country skiing). Second issue. 3, 4, 5, 6, 7, 8, 20g (se-tenant strip of 7).
Summer Olympic Games, Moscow 1980. *Dec. 20.* Airmail souvenir sheet, 25g (Canoe race).
Electric trains. *Dec. 24.* 3, 4, 7, 8, 20g (se-tenant strip), airmail 10, 25g (9v).
Argentina '78. *Dec. 24.* Airmail souvenir sheet. 25g plus label.

1980
Composers and Paintings of young ballet dancers. 3, 4, 5, 6, 7, 8, 20g (7v). Paintings by Cydney and Degas. Composers: Rossini, Johann Strauss. Debussy, Beethoven, Chopin, Wagner, Bach.
Christmas, International Year of the Child. 3, 4, 5, 6, 7, 8, 20g (7v).
Rowland Hill, aircraft. *Apr. 8.* 3, 4, 5, 6, 7, 8, 20g (se-tenant strip), airmail 10, 25g (9v). Airmail souvenir sheet, 25g.
Maybach Automobile, DS-8 Zeppelin. *Apr. 8.* Airmail souvenir sheet 25g.
Rowland Hill. *Apr. 14.* 3, 4, 5, 6, 7, 8, 20g; airmail, 10, 25g (9v). Airmail souvenir sheets (2) 25g.
Olympic winners, Lake Placid. *June 4.* 3, 4, 5, 6, 7, 8, 20g (se-tenant strip), airmail 10, 25g (9v). Airmail souvenir sheet 25g.
Rotary Club. *July 1.* Airmail souvenir sheet, 25g.
Apollo II, 10th anniv. *July 30.* Airmail souvenir sheet, 25g.
Christmas, Intl. Year of the Child. *Aug. 4.* 3, 4, 5, 6, 7, 8, 20g; airmail, 10, 25g (9v). Airmail souvenir sheet, 25g.
Ships, Philatelic Exhibitions '80. *Sept. 15.* 3, 4, 5, 6, 7, 8, 20g (se-tenant strip), airmail 10, 25g (9v).
Boeing 707. *Sept. 17.* 20g: airmail 100g.
Juan Carlos, ESPAMER '80. *Sept. 19.* Souvenir sheet, 25g.
Albrecht Durer. *Sept. 24.* Airmail souvenir sheet, 25g.
Espana '82 World Cup soccer. *Dec. 10.* 3, 4, 5, 6, 7, 8, 20g (se-tenant), airmail 10, 25g (9v). Airmail souvenir sheet, 25g.
Chess Tournament, Mexico. *Dec. 15.* 3, 4, 5, 6, 7, 8, 20g (se-tenant), airmail souvenir sheet, 25g.
Olympics 1980. *Dec. 15.* Airmail souvenir sheet, 25g.

1981
Olympic winners. *Feb. 4.* 25, 50c, 1, 2, 3, 4, 5g (se-tenant strip), airmail 5, 10, 30g (10v). Airmail souvenir sheet, 25g.
Electric trains. *Feb. 9.* 25c, 50c, 1, 2, 3, 4, 5g (se-tenant strip), airmail 1, 5, 10, 30g (10v). Airmail souvenir sheet, 25g.
Archbishops seminar. *Mar. 26.* Airmail, 5, 10, 25, 50g (4v).
Intl. Year of the Child. *Apr. 13.* 10, 25, 50, 100, 200, 300, 400g (se-tenant strip), airmail, 75, 500, 1000g (10v). Sheet of 10, 10g, plus 2 labels.
WIPA '81. *May 22.* 4g; airmail 10g 2v.
Royal Wedding, Prince Charles and Lady Diana. *June 27.* 25, 50c, 1, 2, 3, 4, 5g (se-tenant strip of 7). Souvenir Sheet of 8, 5g, plus label.
Royal Wedding. *June 29.* Airmail 5, 10, 30g (3v). Airmail souvenir sheet, 25g.
Traditional women's costumes, Itaipu Dam. *June 30.* 10, 25, 50, 100, 200, 300, 400g, se-tenant strip of 7.
Space travel. *Oct. 9.* Airmail, 5, 10, 30g (3v). Airmail souvenir sheets (2), 25g.
Paintings, Dominique Ingres. *Oct. 13.* 25, 50c, 1, 2, 3, (se-tenant strip), 4, 5g (7v). Souvenir sheet of 8 (4, 5g), plus label.
Espana '82, World Cup Soccer. *Oct. 15.* Airmail 5, 10, 30g (3v). Airmail sheet of 5, 10g. plus four labels; souvenir sheet; 25g.
Paintings, Peter Paul Reubens. *July 9.* 25, 50c, 1, 2, 3, 4g (se-tenant strip), 5g (7v). Souvenir sheet of 8, 5g. plus label.
George Washington. *July 10.* Airmail, 5g. Airmail souvenir sheet, 25g.
Queen Elizabeth, 80th birthday. *July 10.* Airmail souvenir sheet of 8, 10g, plus label.
Philatokyo. *July 10.* 25g (1v). Airmail souvenir sheet, 30g.
Paintings, Pablo Picasso. *Oct. 19.* 25, 50c, 1, 2, 3, 4g (se-tenant strip), 5g (7v). Souvenir sheet of 6, 5g. plus 3 labels.
PHILATELIA '81. *Oct. 22.* 25, 50c, 1, 2, 3, 4g (se-tenant strip of 6).
ESPAMER '81, Philatelic Exhibition. *Oct. 25.* 25, 50c, 1, 2, 3, 4g (se-tenant strip of 6).
Royal Wedding. *Dec. 4.* 25, 50c, 1, 2, 3, 4g (se-tenant strip). 4g; airmail 5, 10, 30g (10v). Souvenir sheet of 8, 5g, plus label. Airmail souvenir sheets (2), 25g.

Intl. Yr of the Child. *Dec. 17.* 25, 50c, 1, 2, 3, 4g (se-tenant strip), 5g (7v). Souvenir sheet of 6, 5g, plus 3 labels.
Madonna with Child paintings. *Dec. 21.* Airmail 5, 10, 30g (3v). Airmail souvenir sheet, 25g.
Graf Zeppelin. *Dec. 21.* Airmail souvenir sheet, 25g.

1982
Intl. Yr. of the Child. *Apr. 16.* 25, 50c, 1, 2, 3, 4, 5g (se-tenant strip of 2 and 5 plus label). Souvenir sheet of 6, 5g, plus 3 labels.
Espana '82, soccer. *Apr. 19.* Airmail 5, 10, 30g (3v). Airmail sheet of 7, 10g, plus 2 labels; souvenir sheet 25g.
Scouting. *Apr. 21.* 25, 50c, 1, 2, 3, 4, 5g; Airmail 5, 10, 30g (10v). Souvenir sheet of 8, 5g, plus label. Airmail souvenir sheet, 25g.
Johann Wolfgang Van Goethe, Rembrandt painting. *Apr. 23.* Airmail souvenir sheet, 25g.
King Alfonso X, chess. *Apr. 23.* Airmail souvenir sheets (2), 25g.
PHILEXFRANCE '82. *June 11.* 25, 50c, 1, 2, 3g (5v).
Espana '82, soccer. *June 13.* 25, 50c, 1, 2, 3, 4g (se-tenant strip), 5g; airmail 5, 10, 30g (10v). Souvenir sheet of 8, 5g, plus label; sheet of 5, 10g, plus 4 labels. Airmail souvenir sheet, 25g.
PHILATELIA '82, Intl. Yr. of the Child. *Sept. 12.* 25, 50c, 1, 2, 3, 4, 5g (se-tenant strips of 6 and 8, 5g, plus label).
Paintings, Raphael. *Sept. 27.* 25, 50c, 1, 2, 3, 4g (se-tenant strip). 5g (7v). Souvenir sheet of 5 plus 4 labels.
Paintings, Raphael. *Sept. 30.* 25, 50c, 1, 3, 4g (se-tenant strip), 5g (7v). Souvenir sheet of 5 plus 4 labels.
Espana '82, winners world cup soccer. *Oct. 20.* Airmail, 5, 10, 30g (3v). Airmail sheet of 5, 10g, plus 4 labels; Souvenir sheet, 25g.
Paintings, Peter Paul Reubens. *Oct. 23.* Airmail, 5, 10, 30g (3v). Airmail sheet of 5, 10g. plus 4 labels; souvenir sheet, 25g.
Paintings, Albrecht Durer. *Dec. 14.* 25, 50c, 1, 2, 3, 4g (se-tenant strip), 5g (7v). Souvenir sheet of 7, 5g. plus 2 labels.
Paintings, Raphael. *Dec. 17.* Airmail, 5, 10, 30g (3v). Airmail sheet of 5, 10g, plus 4 labels, souvenir sheet, 25g.

1983
South American Trains. *Jan. 20.* 25c, 50c, 1, 2, 3, 4g (se-tenant strip), 5g (7v). Souvenir sheet of 5. 5g, plus 4 labels.
Paintings, Rembrandt. *Jan. 21.* Airmail, 5, 10, 30g (3v). Airmail sheet of 5, 10g, plus 4 labels; souvenir sheet, 25g.
Espana '82, Zeppelin. *Jan. 21.* Airmail souvenir sheet, 25g.
Racing Cars. *Jan. 23.* 25, 50c, 1, 2, 3, 4g (se-tenant strip). 5g (7v). Souvenir sheet of 5, 5g plus 4 labels.
ESPANA '82 *Zeppelin. Jan. 24.* Airmail souvenir sheet of 5, 5g plus 4 labels.
German Space Technology. *Jan. 24.* Airmail 5, 10, 30g (3v). Airmail sheet of 5, 10g, plus 4 labels; souvenir sheets (2), 25g.
Winter Olympics. *Feb. 23.* 25, 50c, 1, 2, 3, 4g (se-tenant strip). 5g (7v). Souvenir sheet of 5, 5g, plus 4 labels.
Classic Automobiles. *July 18.* 25, 50c, 1, 2, 3, 4g (se-tenant strip), airmails; 5, 10, 30g (9v). Souvenir sheet of 5, 5g. plus 4 labels. Airmail souvenir sheet, 25g, plus label.
BRASILIANA '83, FIP Congress. *July 28.* World Cup Soccer overprinted. 25, 50c, 1, 2, 3, 4g se-tenant strip of 6.
BRASILIANA '83, FIP Congress. *July 28.* Ruebens Madonnas overprinted. 25, 50c, 1, 2, 3, 4g se-tenant strip of 6.
Aircraft Carriers. 25, 50c, 1, 2, 3, 4g (se-tenant strip), 5g (7v). Souvenir sheet of 5, 5g plus 4 labels.
Flowers, Airmail. Airmail: 5, 10, 30g (3v). Souvenir sheet of 5, 10g, plus 4 labels.
Birds. *Oct. 22.* 25, 50c, 1, 2, 3, 4g (se-tenant strip), 5g (7v). Souvenir sheet of 5, 5g plus 4 labels.
PHILATELIA '83, Dusseldorf. *Oct. 28.* Trains overprinted. 25, 50c, 1, 2, 3, 4g se-tenant strip of 6.
EXFIVIA '83, Bolivia. *Nov. 5.* Durer paintings overprinted. 25, 50c, 1, 2, 3, 4g se-tenant strip of 6.

ST. THOMAS AND PRINCE ISLANDS
1977
Rubens, 400th birth anniversary, paintings. *June 28.* 1, 5, 10, 15, 20, 50e (6v in se-tenant strips of 3). Souvenir sheet (20, 75g).
Beethoven, 150th death anniversary, paintings. *June 28.* 20, 30, 50e (se-tenant strip of 3). (Chr. Hornemann, miniature; F. Klein, mask; F. Schimon, painting).

1978
International Organizations. *May 25.* 3, 3 (Nobel, UNACR), 5, 5 (Nobel, UNICEF), 10, 10 (Nobel, OIT), 15, 15 (Nobel, Int'l. Amnesty), 20, 20 (Nobel, Int'l. Red Cross), 35, 35d (Nobel, Int'l. Red Cross) (12v). Same denominations are se-tenant.
World Cup Soccer, Argentina 78, various teams. 3d x 4 (in se-tenant block), 25d x 3 (in se-tenant strip) (7v).
International Philatelic Exhibition, Essen 1978. *Nov. 1.* 10d x 4 (2 of each) and 10d in sheet of 9 (5v) (Paul Gauguin, Vincent Van Gogh, Henri Matisse, Georges Braque). 2 souvenir sheets, 20, 30d (Gauguin), imperf.
U.P.U. centenary. *Nov. 1.* 5, 5, 5, 5d and 15d x 4 (2 of each) in sheet of 12 (8v).
Peter Paul Rubens, Holy Family paintings. 5, 10, 25, 50, 70d (5v). Sheet of 4 containing 5, 10, 25, 70d.
Introduction of New Currency, 1st anniversary. *Dec. 15.* 5d x 4 (2 of each) and 5d in sheet of 9, 8d x 4 (2 of each) and 8d in sheet of 9 (10v).

1979
World Cup Soccer Winners. *June 1.* Soccer set of 1978 overprinted with name of winning country. 7v perf. and imperf.
Flowers. *June 8.* 8dx4 (se-tenant block of 4). 1 and 25d (6v). Imperf. souvenir sheet, 50d.
Butterflies. *June 8.* 11dx4 (se-tenant block of 4). 50c and 10d (6v). Souvenir sheet, 50d.
Sir Rowland Hill, centenary of death, UPU Congress, etc. *Sept. 15.* Two souvenir sheets. 25d (Graf Zeppelin, DC3). perf., imperf.
International Year of the Child. *Oct. 4.* 1, 7, 14, 17d (4v). Souvenir sheet, 50d (One world symbol).
International Communications Day. *Oct. 4.* 1 and 11d, 14 and 17d, in strips of 2 plus label (4v).
Albrecht Durer, 450th death anniversary. *Nov. 29.* 50cx2, 1, 7, 8, 25d (6v). Souvenir sheet, 25d (Self-portrait, father, mother).
History of Aviation, powered flight, ICAO 35th anniversary. *Dec. 21.* 50c, 1, 5, 7, 8, 17d (6v).
Nature Preservation, local birds. *Dec. 21.* 50cx2, 1, 7, 8d, airmail, 100d (6v). Souvenir sheet, 25d.
Albrecht Durer, 450th death anniversary, International Year of the Child. Feast of the Family, Christmas 1979. *Dec. 25.* Souvenir sheet, 25d.
History of Navigation, early sailing ships. *Dec. 21.* 50c, 1, 3, 7, 8, 17d (6v). Souvenir sheet, 25d (Map).
History of Aviation, dirigibles, 1872-1910. *Dec. 28.* 50c, 1, 3, 7, 8, 17d (6v).
Nature Preservation, local fish. *Dec. 28.* 50c, 1, 3, 5, 8d, airmail, 50d (6v). Souvenir sheet, 25d.
History of Aviation, hot-air balloons, 1784-1931. *Dec. 28.* 50c, 1, 3, 7, 8, 25d (6v). Souvenir sheet, 25d.

1980
Pre-Olympic Games, 1980, Olympic stadiums. *June 13.* 50c, 11dx4 (5v), perf. and imperf. Souvenir sheet, 7dx4, perf. and imperf.
Sir Rowland Hill, death centenary. *June 13.* 50c, 1, 8, 20d (4v). Souvenir sheet, 20d.
Moon landing. 10th anniversary. *June 13.* 50c, 1, 14, 17d (4v). Souvenir sheet, 25d (three astronauts).
Independence anniversaries. *July 5.* 5d. Venezuela, Russia, India, Ghana, Russia, Algeria, Cuba, Cape Verde, Mozambique, Angola

(se-tenant strip of 12 plus label). Souvenir sheet, 25d.
Intl. Yr. of the Child. *Dec. 25.* Souvenir sheet, 25d.

1981
Summer Olympics, Moscow '80. *Feb. 2.* 15, 30, 40, 50d. Souvenir sheets, 15, 40d.
United Nations, 35th Anniv. *Feb. 2.* Souvenir sheet, 25d.
Summer Olympic winners. *May 15.* 50d (1v).
Flowers. *May 22.* 50c (2), 1, 7, 8, 14d (6v). Souvenir sheet, 25d.
Shells. *May 22,* 50c (2), 1, 1.50, 11, 17d (6v). Souvenir sheet, 25d.
Espana '82, World Cup Soccer. *Sept. 3.* 3d x 4, 25d x 3, Uruguay, Italy, Brazil, Germany, England, Argentina, Argentina (7v).
PHILATELIA '81. *Nov. 14.* 25d (1v). Souvenir sheet, 75d.
Tito. *Nov. 1.* 17d x 2. Souvenir sheet, 75d.
Royal Wedding, Prince Charles and Lady Diana. *Nov. 28.* 20, 30, 50d (se-tenant strip of 3).
World Chess Champion. *Dec. 10.* 30d x 2 (se-tenant). Souvenir sheet, 75d.
Pablo Picasso, I.Y.C. *Dec. 10.* 14d, 17d x 4, 20d x 2 (7v). Souvenir sheet, 75d.

SENEGAL
1974
International Fair, Dakar. *Nov. 28.* Airmail, 350fr (silver foil), 1500fr (gold foil) (2v).

1976
21st Summer Olympics, Montreal. *Sept. 11.* First Issue: 15, 20, 25, 50, 100fr; airmail, 400fr (6v). 6 miniature sheets of one. Airmail souvenir sheet, 400fr. Airmail embossed gold foil, 1500fr. Same, souvenir sheet, 1500fr. Second Issue: 5, 10, 60, 65, 70fr; airmail, 500fr (6v). 6 miniature sheets of same. Airmail souvenir sheet, 500fr. Airmail embossed gold foil, 1000fr. Same, souvenir sheet, 1000fr.
2nd International Fair, Dakar, Concorde. *Dec. 3.* Airmail, embossed silver foil, 500fr, embossed gold foil, 1500fr (2v).

SOMALIA
1970
U.S. Space Explorations. *Feb. 14.* 60, 80c, 1, 1.50, 1.80, 2, 2.80sh (7v). Souvenir sheet, 14sh.

TOGO
1971
Napoleon I, death sesquicentennial. *June.* Imperf., Airmail, gold foil, 1000fr and souvenir sheet.
UIPE (International Organization for the Protection of Children). *Nov. 13.* Airmail, gold foil, 1500fr.

1972
OCAM Conference (Organization of African and Malagasy Union). *Apr. 24.* Gold embossed, 1000fr.

1973
Olympic winners, 1972 Munich Games. *Jan.* Perf., imperf. Airmail, gold foil, 1500fr x 3 (3v) 3 airmail souvenir sheets, each 1500fr.
Apollo 17. *Jan.* Perf., imperf. Airmail, gold foil, 1500fr and souvenir sheet.

1974
World Cup Soccer Championship, victory of German team. Perf., imperf. Nos. C180-C181, C181a overprinted "Coupe du Monde / de Football / Munich 1974 / Vainqueur / Republique Federale / d'Allemagne."

1976
21st Summer Olympics, Montreal. *Feb. 24.* Gold foil embossed, 1000fr x 5 (5v).

1977
Elizabeth II, Silver Jubilee. *Jan. 10.* (Queen's portraits) 1000fr. Souvenir sheet, 1000fr.

1978
Various Events. Moscow Olympic Game, 1980; World Cup Soccer, Argentina; Elizabeth II Coronation anniversary; Goya, 150th death anniversary (paintings); lunar orbit of Apollo VIII, 10th anniversary. *March.* 1000fr x 5. 5 Souvenir sheets, each 1000fr, gold foil embossed.

1979
People's Republic, 10th anniversary. *Dec.* Gold-foil embossed portrait of President, 1000fr. perf. (in uniform), imperf. (in civilian clothes) (2v).

1980
London, 1980, International Stamp Exhibition. *May 6.* Gold-foil embossed 1000fr single stamp and souvenir sheet of 1978 Queen Elizabeth II Coronation ovptd. "Londres, 1980," etc.

URUGUAY
1974
Tourism. *June 6.* Souvenir sheet, 1000p.
World Cup Soccer Championship, Munich. *June 6.* 1000p and imperf. souvenir sheet.
UPU, World Cup Soccer, Olympics. *Aug. 30.* Airmail, 500p. Airmail souvenir sheet of 3 (500p x 3).
UPU, Expo '74, Montevideo. Airmail souvenir sheet, 1000p, imperf.

1975
Pre-Olympics, Innsbruck, Montreal. *May 16.* Airmail, 400, 600p (2v). 2 airmail souvenir sheets of 2 (500, 1000p).
Apollo-Soyuz; U.S. & Uruguay Independence; UN 30th anniversary, 50th anniversary Airlines, International Women's Year. *Sept. 29.* Airmail, 10, 15, 25c, 50c (4v). 2 souvenir sheets of 4 (40c x 4), (20, 30, 50, 100c).

1976
Olympics, Telecommunications, UPU, UN, Soccer '78 Argentina. *June 3.* 10, 15, 25, 50c (4v). 2 airmail souvenir sheets (30, 70c, 1p) (40, 60c, 2p).
Soccer '78 Argentina, Summer Olympics, U.S. Bicentennial-Project Viking, Nobel-Prize Winners. *Nov. 12.* 10, 30, 50, 80c (4v). 2 airmail souvenir sheets (20, 40, 60c, 1.50p) (35, 75, 90, 1p).

1977
Nobel Prize, 75th anniversary, World Cup Soccer, Lindbergh Transatlantic Flight, Rubens 400th birth anniversary. *July 21.* 20, 30, 50c, 1p (4v x 2 with 2 labels in se-tenant strip), 2 souvenir sheets (10, 60, 80c, 2p), (40, 90c, 1.20, 1.50p).
UREXPO '77, 150th Anniversary Uruguay Posts, 50th Anniversary Uruguay Philatelic Clubs, various emblems. *July 27.* Airmail, 8p perf., imperf. Airmail souvenir sheet, 10p.

1978
Various Events. 1979-1980 Philatelic Exhibitions and 1980 Olympic Games. Souvenir sheet of 4 (3, 4, 5, 7, 10p) perf., imperf.
Various Events. Lake Placid, 1980; Uruguay Philatelic Exhibition, 1980; World Chess Games, Buenos Aires, 1978; Sir Rowland Hill, QEII Coronation. Souvenir sheet of 4 (3, 5, 7, 10p) perf., imperf.

1979
Various Events: International Year of the Child and Albrecht Durer, 450th death anniversary, 70c. Powered Flight, 75th anniversary and ICAO. 1.80p. World Cup Soccer and AUF emblems

ovptd. "Monumento Mondial de Futbol, Montevideo," 80c. Rowland Hill, 1980 Olympics, Lake Placid and Moscow, 1896 Greek Olympic issue, 11 stamp. 1.30p.
Albrecht Durer, 450th death anniversary. 25c (self-portrait), airmail, 1p (horseman) (2v).

1981
Espana '82, pre-soccer championship. *Aug. 17.* Gold-foil embossed, 100fr (5), Germany, Great Britain, Brazil, Argentina, Spain, Souvenir sheets, 100fr (5) stadiums.
World Cup Soccer '78 overprinted in gold for Espana '82. 100fr single stamp and souvenir sheet.

YEMEN, MUTAWAKELITE KINGDOM
Most sets exist perf., imperf.

1962
Nos. 98-102, 103-109, 124-126, 127-128, 129-130, 135-136 and various other issues of 1954-65 overprinted in red or black "Free Yemen Fights For God, Imam and Country" (82v).

1963
Kingdom and Flag overprinted on Republic issue of 1963, 4b, 6b x 2 (3v).
International Red Cross centenary. *Dec. 31.* 1/8, 1/4, 1/2, 4b; airmail, 6b (5v).

1964
Fight Against the Republic, 1st anniversary. *Jan. 15.* Perf., imperf. Airmail, 1/2, 1, 2, 4, 6b (5v). Souvenir sheet, 24b imperf.
British Red Cross Surgical Team. *Mar. 20.* Airmail. 1/2 and 4b of Fight Against Republic issue overprinted "Honouring British Red Cross Surgical Team" and surcharged 10, 18b (2v).
Surcharges on Fight Against Republic issue. *Apr.* Airmail, 10, 18, 28b. *Aug.* 4b x 3 (6v).
18th Summer Olympics, Tokyo. *Sept. 1.* Perf., imperf. 2; 4b; airmail, 6b (3v). Souvenir sheet, 4b imperf.
Astronauts. *Sept. 7.* Perf., imperf. 2, 4b; airmail, 6b (3v). Souvenir sheet, 6b imperf.

1965
British Yemen Relief Committee. *Feb. 15.* Fight Against Republic surcharges of 1964 overprinted in green "Honouring British Yemen/Relief Committee / 1963 1965" in English and Arabic (3v).
Imam's Son Memorial. *Mar. 1.* 4b.
John F. Kennedy Memorial. *Apr. 5.* Perf., imperf. 1/8, 1/4, 1/2, 4b; airmail, 6b (5v). Souvenir sheet, 4b imperf.
Churchill Memorial. *Apr. 10:* Imam's Son issue overprinted in red "In Memory of Sir Winston Churchill / 1874-1865" in English and Arabic. *June 6.* (diamonds): 1/8, 1/4, 1/2, 1, 2, 4b (6v). Souvenir sheet, 4b imperf.
International Telecommunication Union centenary. *May 20.* Perf., imperf. 2, 4b; airmail, 6b (3v). Imperf. souvenir sheet.
Birds. *May 30.* 1/8, 1/4, 1/2, 4b; airmail, 6b (5v). Souvenir sheet, 4b imperf.
Imam, Flag and Arms. *June 28.* 1, 2, 4b; airmail, 6, 18, 24b (6v).
Mariner 4. *July 14.* Astronaut issue of 1964 overprinted "Mariner 4" in English and Arabic. (3v).
International Cooperation Year. *Sept. 15.* 2, 4b; airmail, 6b (3v). Souvenir sheet, 4b imperf.
Cats. *Oct. 1.* 1/8, 1/4, 1/2, 1, 2, 4b (6v). Souvenir sheet, 4b imperf.
Gemini V. *Oct. 15.* ITU issue of 1965 overprinted "Gemini V/Gordon Cooper & Charles Conrad" in black, red or blue (3v and sheet).
Flowers. *Oct. 15.* 1/8, 1/4, 1/2, 1, 2, 4b (6v). Souvenir sheet, 4b imperf.
New York World's Fair. *Oct. 4* 2, 4, 6b (3v). Imperf. souvenir sheet.
Space Explorations. *Nov. 10.* 1/8, 1/4, 1/2, 4b; airmail, 6b (5v). Souvenir sheet, 4b imperf.
Olympic Winners, 1964 Tokyo Games, *Nov. 20.* 1/8, 1/4, 1/2, 2, 4b; airmail, 6b (6v). Souvenir sheet, 4b imperf.

1966
Builders of World Peace. *Feb. 1:* 1/8, 1/4, 1/2, 1, 4b (5v, se-tenant) (Nehru, Hammarskjold, Pope John 23, Churchill, J.F. Kennedy). Souvenir sheet, 4b imperf. *Apr. 16:* 1/8, 1/4, 1/2, 1, 4b (5v, se-tenant). (Lubke, de Gaulle, Pope Paul VI. L. B. Johnson, U Thant). Souvenir sheet, 4b imperf.
Surcharges on Kennedy issue of 1965. 4, 8, 10b; airmail lr (4v).
King Faisal. 1b.
19th Summer Olympics, Mexico. *May 14.* Airmail. Olympic issue of 1965 overprinted "Olympic Games Preparation / Mexico 1968" and surcharged 12, 28, 34b (3v). Souvenir sheet, 4b imperf.
Shaharah Fortress of Liberty. *May 26.* 1/2, 1, 1 1/2, 2, 4b; airmail, 6, 10b (7v). Souvenir sheet, 10b imperf.

1967
Pres. Kennedy, 3rd anniversary of death. *Jan. 1.* 12, 28, 34b (3v). Souvenir sheet, 24b imperf.
World Cup Soccer Championship Winner. *Jan. 5.* Olympic Winners issue of 1965 overprinted "World Championship Cup England 1966 / England Winner" in English and Arabic. 1/8, 1/4, 1/2, 2, 4b; airmail, 6b (6v). Olympic issue of 1965 surcharged 4b x 6 (6v).
Civil War, 3rd anniversary. *Jan. 25.* 4b x 8 (8v). Souvenir sheet, 4b imperf.
Pres. Kennedy, 50th birthday. *May.* Kennedy death anniversary issue overprinted "50th Ann./29/May" in English and Arabic (3v and sheet).
Rembrandt paintings. *May 15.* 2, 4, 6, 10, 12, 20b (6v). 8 souvenir sheets: 2 with gold frame; 6 with silver frame.
Paintings. *June 15.* Airmail 8, 10, 12, 14, 16, 20b (6v) (Hals, van Gogh, Rubens, Murillo, Raphael, Ucello).
Jordan Relief Fund. *Aug. 10.* Preceding issues (Flowers, cats, birds, ICY, Kennedy, Builders of World Peace) surcharged 50%.
Fish. *July:* 1/8, 1/4, 1/2, 1, 4, 6, 10b. *Oct:* Airmail, 12, 14, 16, 18, 24, 34b (13v). Souvenir sheet, 10b.
Asian paintings. *Aug. 25.* Airmail, 1/8, 1/4, 1/2, 3/4, 1, 1 1/2, 2, 3, 4, 6b (10v). Souvenir sheet, 6b imperf.
12th World Boy Scout Jamboree, Idaho. *Sept. 10.* 1/4, 1/2, 4, 6b; airmail, 1/8, 10, 20b (7v). Souvenir sheet, 20b imperf.
19th Summer Olympics, Mexico, 1968. *Oct. 8.* 1/8, 1/4, 1/2, 4, 8b; airmail, 12, 16, 20b (8v). Souvenir sheet, 16b imperf.
Moorish Art in Spain. *Dec.* 2, 4, 6, 10, 12b; airmail, 20, 22, 24b (8v). Souvenir sheet, 28b.
Queen of Sheba, Visit to King Solomon. *Dec.* 1/8, 1/4, 1/2, 4, 6, 10, 20, 24b (8v). 2 souvenir sheets, 28, 34b imperf.
Horses. *Dec.* 1/8, 1/4, 1/2, 4, 10b; postage due, 16b (6v).

1968
10th Winter Olympics, Grenoble. *Jan.* Fish issue of 1967 overprinted "Grenoble 1968" (13v and sheet).
Butterflies. *Feb.* Airmail, 16, 20, 40b; postage due, 4, 20b (5v).
10th Winter Olympics, Grenoble. *Feb.* 1, 2, 3, 4, 6, 10b; airmail, 12, 18, 24, 28b (10v). 2 souvenir sheets, 4, 24b imperf. Same, overprinted "Gold Medal Winner" and names of various winners (10v). 2 souvenir sheets, 4, 24b imperf.
UNESCO, 20th anniversary. *Mar.* 1/2, 1, 1 1/2, 2, 3, 4, 6, 10b (8v). Souvenir sheet, 12b imperf.
Mother's Day, paintings. *Mar. 21.* 2, 4, 6b; airmail, 24, 28, 34b (6v) (Gainsborough, Corot, Fragonard, Raphael, Titian, Bronzino). 7 souvenir sheets; 6 sheets of 1, 2, 4, 6, 24, 28, 34b; 1 sheet of 2 (24, 34b) imperf.

UNESCO Campaign to Save Venice. *Apr. 18.* ½, 1, 1½, 24b; airmail, 28, 34b (6v) (paintings by de Pavia, Piazetta, Favretto, Tiepolo, Canaletto). Souvenir sheet, 34b imperf.
UNESCO Campaign to Save Florence. *May 3.* 2, 4, 6b; airmail, 10, 12, 18b (6v) (paintings by Raphael, Chardin, Rubens, Allori, Reni). 4 souvenir sheets, 4, 6, 19, 34b imperf.
19th Summer Olympics, Mexico. *May 15.* 1, 2, 3, 4, 6b; airmail, 10, 12, 18, 24, 28b (10v). 2 souvenir sheets, 4, 24b imperf.
Olympics, 1924-1968. *May 31.* **Summer Games:** 4b x 11, 12 souvenir sheets, each 4b imperf. **Winter Games:** 1, 2, 3, 4, 6b; airmail, 10, 12, 18, 24, 28b (21v). 12 souvenir sheets: 1, 2, 3, 4, 6, 10, 12, 18, 24b x 3, 28b imperf.
Paintings. *June 30.* 1, 2, 3, 4, 6, 10b; airmail, 12, 18, 24, 28b (10v) (Perry, Copley, Murillo, van Leyden, Chardin, Vermeer, Aylward, Sessions, Goya). 3 souvenir sheets; 2 sheets of 1, 4, 24b; 1 sheet of 2 (4, 24b) imperf.
Shah of Iran, Coronation. *July 15.* 1, 2, 3, 4b; airmail, 24, 28b (6v). 2 souvenir sheets, 24, 28b.
World Philately (Roosevelt, Ferrary, Prince Ismail, albums and catalogues). *Aug. 15.* 1, 2, 3, 4, 6b; airmail, 10, 12, 18, 24, 28b (10v). 4 souvenir sheets, each 4b imperf.
International Human Rights Year (Popes John XXIII and Paul VI, John F. Kennedy, Churchill, Martin Luther King). *Sept. 30.* 2b x 4, 4b x 4, 6b x 4 (12v). 2 souvenir sheets: 1 of 2 (4, 6b), 1 of 3 (6b x 3) imperf.
World Racial Peace (American Flag, Lincoln, Kennedy, King). *Sept. 30.* 4, 6, 18b; airmail, 10, 24b (5v). 3 souvenir sheets; 1 of 2 (10, 20b), 2 of 1, 10, 20b imperf.
Children's Day, paintings. *Oct. 1.* 1, 2, 3, 4b; airmail, 6, 10, 12, 18, 24, 28b (10v) (Renoir, Van Dyck, Velazquez, Perugino, Murillo, Lawrence). 2 souvenir sheets, 10, 18b imperf.
Gold Medal Winners, 1968 Mexico Olympics. *Oct.* Mexico Olympic issue of 1968 overprinted "Gold Medal Winner Mexico 1968" and names of winners (10v). 6 souvenir sheets, 4b x 3, 24b x 3 imperf. *Dec. 25.* 2, 18, 24, 28, 34b (5v). 2 souvenir sheets, 4, 24b imperf.
EFIMEX. *Dec. 25.* 12, 18, 24, 28, 34b (5v). 2 souvenir sheets, 4, 24b imperf.

1969
Racing Champions. *Jan. 15.* 1, 2, 3, 4, 6b; airmail, 10, 12, 18, 24, 28b (10v). 2 souvenir sheets, 4, 24b imperf.
Apollo 7 and 8. *Feb. 15.* 4b x 2, 6, 8, 10, 12, 18, 24, 28, 34b (10v). 4 souvenir sheets, 2b x 2, 28b x 2. Gold foil, 28b.
19th Summer Olympics, Mexico. Gold foil, 28b.
Imam's Mission to Pope Paul VI in Jerusalem, 5th anniversary. *May 25.* **a.** ⅛, ¼ x 2, 1, 1½, 2, 3, 4, 5, 6b (10v, se-tenant in sheets of 10). **b.** 1, 2, 3, 4, 5, 6, 7, 8, 9, 10b; airmail, 11, 12, 13, 14, 15b (15v, se-tenant in sheets of 15). **c.** 16, 17, 18, 19, 20, 21, 22, 23, 24, 25, 26, 27, 28, 29, 30b (15v, se-tenant in sheets of 15) (40v). Airmail, Gold foil, 24, 28b.
Rembrandt paintings. *June 15.* 1, 2, 4b; airmail, 6, 12b, 1r (6v). Souvenir sheet, 24b imperf. Gold foil, 20b.
Paintings, *June.* ½, 1½, 3, 5b; airmail, 10, 18, 24, 28, 34b (9v) (Raphael, Greuze, Henner, Le Nain, Rubens, Rotari, Watteau, Murillo). Souvenir sheet, 4b imperf.
Mission to the Moon. *June 17.* 1, 2, 3, 4, 5b; airmail, 6, 7, 8, 9, 10, 11, 12, 13, 14, 15b (15v, in sheets of 15).
Apollo 10. *June 17.* 2, 4, 6, 8, 10b (5v). Souvenir sheet, 24b, perf., imperf.
Pre-Olympics, 1972, Munich. *July 28.* 1, 2, 4, 5, 6b; airmail, 10, 12, 18, 24, 34b (10v). Souvenir sheet, 24b perf., imperf.
International Animal Protection Year. *Sept. 25.* **Animals:** ½, 1, 2, 4, 6b; airmail. 8, 10, 18b (8v). Souvenir sheet, 24b. **Birds:** ½, 1, 2, 4, 6b; airmail, 8, 10, 18b (8v). Souvenir sheet, 24b.
Apollo II. *Oct. 1.* Airmail, 24b. Gold foil, circular embossed, 24b. Gold and silver foil (1 each) 28b. 6 souvenir sheets, 24b, 34b x 2, perf., imperf; 24b with gold foil circular embossed center, 28b x 2, 1 gold, 1 silver foil.
Save the Holy Places (Palestine). *Oct. 28.* 4b x 6, 6b x 10; airmail, 12b x 8 (24v).
Famous Men. *Nov. 10.* 4b x 4, 6b x 10; airmail, 12b x 2 (16v).
History of Outer Space Exploration. *Nov. 25.* Airmail, 6b x 32 (32v). 3 souvenir sheets, 24, 28, 34b imperf. Gold foil airmail, 24, 34b.
Olympic Sports. *Dec. 1.* 1, 2, 4, 5, 6b; airmail, 10, 12, 18, 24, 34b (10v se-tenant in sheets of 10).
World Cup Soccer Championship. *Dec. 1.* Airmail, 12b x 8 (8v).
Restoration of Al Aqsa Mosque, Jerusalem. *Dec. 21.* Semipostal, 4b+2b, 6b+3b; airmail semi-postal, 10b+5b (3v).
Christmas. Gold foil airmail, 34b and imperf, souvenir sheet.

In April, 1970, an agreement between the Yemen Arab Republic and Saudi Arabia introduced Royalists into the Y.A.R. government, ending the existence of the kingdom.

YEMEN ARAB REPUBLIC
Most sets exist perf., imperf.

1962
United Nations Day. Nos. 103-109 overprinted "1945-1962" in English and Arabic (7v).

1962-63
"Y.A.R. 27.9.1962" overprinted in red or green in English and Arabic on Nos. 47-49, 111-120, 125-136, C20-C21.
Yemen Arab Republic, founding. 1, 2b, 4b x 2, 6b x 2, 8, 10, 16b, 1 li (10v). 4 postage 2b to 10b (4v). 4, 6b; airmail, 8, 16b (4v). Nos. 25-29 overprinted "Airmail/Y.A.R."
Freedom From Hunger. *Mar. 21.* 4, 6b (2v). Souvenir sheet of 2 (4, 6b) imperf.
Revolution, 1st anniversary. *Sept. 26.* 2, 4, 6b (3v). Souvenir sheet of 3 (2, 4, 6b) imperf.
Red Cross centenary. *Oct.* ¼, ⅓, ½, 4, 8, 20b (6v). Souvenir sheet of 2 (4, 8b) imperf.
Astronauts, *Dec. 5.* Airmail, ¼, ⅓, ½, 4, 20b (5v). Souvenir sheet, 20b imperf.
Declaration of Human Rights, 15th anniversary. *Dec. 20.* 4, 6b (2v). Souvenir sheet of 2 (4, 6b) imperf.

1964
Olympic Sports. *Mar. 30.* ¼, ⅓, ½, 1, 1½b; airmail, 4, 20b, 1r (8v). Souvenir sheet, 4b imperf.
Bagel Textile Factory inauguration. *Apr. 10.* 2, 4, 6b; airmail, 16b (4v). Souvenir sheet, 16b imperf.
Hodeida Airport inauguration. *Apr. 30.* 4, 6, 10b (3v). Souvenir sheet 10b imperf.
John F. Kennedy Memorial. *May 5.* Astronaut issue of 1963 overprinted in black or red brown "John F. Kennedy/1917/1963" in English and Arabic. (5v).
New York World's Fair. *May 10.* ¼, ⅓, ½, 1, 4b; airmail, 16, 20b (7v). Souvenir sheet, 20b imperf.
18th Summer Olympics, Tokyo. *June 1.* ¼, ⅛, ½, 1, 1½b; airmail, 4, 6, 12, 20b (9v). Souvenir sheet, 20b imperf.
Boy Scouts. *June 20.* ¼, ⅓, ½, 1, 1½b; airmail, 4, 6, 16, 20b (9v). 2 souvenir sheets; 16b, perf., 20b, imperf.
San'a International Airport inauguration. *June 20.* 1, 2, 4, 8b; airmail, 6b (5v). Souvenir sheet of 2 (4, 6b) imperf.
Animals. *Aug. 15.* ¼, ⅓, ½, 1, 1½b; airmail, 4, 12, 20b; postage due, 4, 12, 20b (11v).
Flowers. *Sept. 1.* ¼, ⅓, ½, 1, 1½b; airmail, 4, 12, 20b (8v).
Arab Postal Union, 10th anniversary. *Oct. 15.* 4b; airmail, 6b (2v). Souvenir sheet, 6b imperf.
Second Arab Summit Meeting. *Nov. 30.* 4, 6b (2v). Souvenir sheet of 2 (4, 6b) imperf.

Revolution, 2nd anniversary. *Dec. 30.* 2, 4, 6b (3v). Souvenir sheet, 6b, imperf.

1965

Birds. *Jan. 30.* ¼, ½, ¾, 1, 1½, 4b; airmail, 6, 8, 12, 20b, 1r (11v). Souvenir sheet, 20b imperf.
Deir Yassin Massacre. *Apr. 30.* 4b airmail, 6b (2v).
International Telecommunication Union centenary. *May 17.* 4, 6b (2v). Souvenir sheet, 6b.
Algiers Library burning. *Sept. 26.* 4b; airmail, 6b (2v). Souvenir sheet, 6b imperf.
Revolution, 3rd anniversary. *Sept. 26.* 4, 6b (2v). Souvenir sheet, 6b imperf.
International Cooperation Year. *Oct. 15.* 4, 6b (2v). Souvenir sheet, 6b, imperf.
John F. Kennedy Memorial. *Nov. 29.* ¼b x 3, ⅓, ½, 4b; airmail, 8, 12b (8v). 2 souvenir sheets, 4, 8b imperf.
Space Exploration. *Dec. 29.* ¼b x 3, ⅓, ½b; airmail, 4, 8, 16b (8v). Souvenir sheet, 16b imperf.

1966

Anti-Tuberculosis campaign. *Jan. 15.* Freedom from Hunger issue of 1963 overprinted "Tuberculous Campaign/1965" in English and Arabic (2v and sheet).
Communications. *Jan. 29.* ¼b x 3, ⅓, ½b; airmail, 4, 6, 20b (8v). Airmail souvenir sheet, 20b imperf.
Prevention of Cruelty to Animals. *Mar. 5.* Animals issue of 1965 overprinted in black or red "Prevention of Cruelty to Animals" in English and Arabic (11v). Souvenir sheet, 20b.
Third Arab Summit Meeting. *Mar. 20.* Second Meeting issue of 1964 overprinted in black or red "3rd Arab/Summit Conference/1965" in English and Arabic (2v). 2 souvenir sheets, 4, 6b imperf.
Builders of World Peace. *Mar. 25.* 1¼b x 3, ⅓, ½, 4b; airmail, 6, 10, 12b (9v). 2 souvenir sheets, 4, 8b, imperf.
Domestic Animals. *May 5.* ¼b x 3, ⅓, ½, 4b (6v). Souvenir sheet, 22b imperf.
Butterflies. *May 5.* Airmail 6, 8, 10, 16b (4v).
Luna 9 Moon Landing. *May 20.* Space Exploration issue of 1965 overprinted "Luna IX/3 February 1966" in English and Arabic (8v and sheet).
World Cup Soccer Championship, London. *May 29.* ¼b x 3, ⅓, ½b; airmail, 4, 5, 20b (8v). Souvenir sheet, 20b imperf.
Traffic Day. *June 30.* 4, 6b (2v). Souvenir sheet, 6b imperf.
Surveyor 1 Moon Landing. *Aug. 15.* Space Exploration issue of 1965 overprinted "Surveyor ½ June 1966" in English and Arabic (5v).
Revolution, 4th anniversary. *Sept.* 2, 4, 6b (3v). Souvenir sheet of 2 (4, 6b) imperf.
"1965 Sana'a" overprinted in English and Arabic on World's Fair issue of 1964 (7v and sheet).
WHO Headquarters inauguration, Geneva. *Nov. 1.* ¼b x 3; airmail, 4, 8, 16b (6v). Souvenir sheet, 16b imperf.
Gemini 6-7. *Dec. 1.* ¼b x 3, ⅓, ½, 2b; airmail 8, 12b (8v). Souvenir sheet, 12b imperf.
Gemini 9. *Dec. 25.* Gemini 6-7 issue overprinted in red "Gemini IX / Cernan-Stafford / June 1966" in English and Arabic (8v and sheet).

1967

Fruit. *Feb. 10.* ¼b x 3, ⅓, ½, 2, 4b; airmail, 6, 8, 10b; postage due, 6, 8, 10b (13v).
Further issues exist for 1967-1978

Index and Identifier

Numerical Index of Vol. 4 Watermark Illustrations

1990 Number Changes For Volume 4

Number in 1989 Catalogue	Number in 1990 Catalogue
Philippines	
1646f	deleted
1646g	1646f
Poland	
2745	2740
Portugal	
1631a, 1644a	deleted
1647-1648	1631-1632
1643	1633
1635	1634
1639	1635
1631	1636
1636	1637
1632	1638
1644	1639
1649	1640
1645	1641
1640	1642
1633	1643
1646	1644
1641	1645
1642	1646
1637-1638	1647-1648
1634	1649
Saar	
68b, 69a, 70b, 71b	footnoted
72b, 73b, 74a, 75a	footnoted
76b, 77b, 78a, 79a	footnoted
80b, 81a, 82a, 83a	footnoted
85c, 86b, 87c, 88c	footnoted
89a, 91b, 93a, 97a, 98a	footnoted

Number in 1989 Catalogue	Number in 1990 Catalogue
Sweden	
1573-1576A	1567-1571
1577-1579B	1572-1576
1580-1581	1577-1578
1581A 3.90k	1579
1581A 6k	1580
1700 3.10k	1701
1701-1702	1702-1703
Switzerland	
763	719A
Thailand	
1a	deleted
7a, 7b	footnoted
9, 9a, 9b, 10, 10a, 10b	deleted
19a, 19b, 19c	footnoted
20b, 24a	footnoted
21b	deleted
30	footnoted
31	deleted
35a, 35b, 35d, 35e	footnoted
36b, 36c	footnoted
37a, 37b, 37c	footnoted
38a, 38b, 38c	footnoted
53a	deleted
131a, 133a, 134a	deleted
165a, 165b	deleted
Uruguay	
1208 200p	1211
Venezuela	
O10-O13	combined with O6-O9
Guayana	
6-10	combined with 1-5
16-20	combined with 11-15

INDEX TO ADVERTISERS - 1990 VOLUME 4

Scott Catalogue Philatelic Marketplace

This "Yellow Pages" section of your Scott Catalogue contains advertisements to help you find what you need, when you need it . . . . . . conveniently!

4

APPROVALS

FOR YOUR COLLECTING PLEASURE WRITE TO...
The Rideout Stamp Family - Manson, Wilma, Ronald

For over 30 years we have been mailing fine selections of General World and Topical groups Postpaid both ways on approval. Our vast stock and experience Guaranteed to please you. You may ask for any special groups you would like to inspect and with your first selection we have a nice set of stamps which we will include as a thank you for trying our service. You may cancel at anytime. You have up to 30 days to inspect the approvals without a reminder being sent. We Aim to please you. Try us soon. I, Manson Rideout, am a 26 year APS member, also long time ATA.

MANSON RIDEOUT PHILATELIST LTD.
P.O. Box 1009, Houlton, Maine 04730
Or In Canada RR #1, Upper Woodstock, N.B., Canada E0J 1Z0

ASIA

BE-LINE COMPANY
Buying THAILAND/SIAM. Send for offer/lists.
P.O. Box 680C, Buffalo, TX 75831

ACCESSORIES

WHY PAY MORE? WE GIVE YOU A ...

30% DISCOUNT

ON ... SCOTT, MINKUS, WHITE ACE, HARCO, ELBE, ENOR, SHOWGARD, LIGHTHOUSE, HAWID, CMC, GLASSINES, HARRIS, HAGNER, KABE, DAVO, SAFE, LINDNER, VDP, STANLEY GIBBONS, BOOKS, etc. Send $2.00 for catalog, refundable with $50.00 order.

TERMS: ORDERS UNDER $20.00 ADD $3.00 SHIPPING. Add 15% shipping and handling under $50.00 net; 10% over $50.00 net; 5% over $100 net; FREE SHIPPING OVER $150.00 net; Alaska, Hawaii and outside continental U.S., add 25% shipping. VISA and MasterCard accepted on all orders.

Send SASE for Current List of Specials!

GOPHER WHOLESALERS
P.O. Box 25041-C, Woodbury, MN 55125
Phone in your order
612-731-6196 for fast UPS service

Showgard® Mounts

The time proven hingeless method for protecting stamp values!

• AT STAMP DEALERS EVERYWHERE •

Sample on request from:

VIDIFORMS CO., INC.
110 Brenner Drive, Congers, NY 10920 U.S.A.

WORLD STAMP EXPO '89
United States Postal Service
Nov. 17 — Dec. 3, 1989
Washington Convention Center
Washington, DC

In Canada:
Showgard Group Canada,
1110 Beaulac St., Ville St. Laurent,
Quebec H4R 1R7

Showgard®

AUCTIONS

DO YOU COLLECT U.S. OR WORLDWIDE STAMPS AND POSTAL HISTORY? ARE YOU A SPECIALIST?

AN INVITATION TO CONSIGN

Individual stamps, covers or collections for Public Auctions or Private Treaty Sale.

WHAT IS A SCHIFF "ESPECIALLY FOR SPECIALISTS" AUCTION?

It's an auction designed with YOU in mind, whether you are a buyer or a seller of U.S. or Worldwide stamps.

WE ALSO PURCHASE OUTRIGHT

Contact us first, describing your material. Include your address and phone numbers.

IF YOU DO NOT GET OUR CATALOGS YOU ARE MISSING OUT!

SEND $8.50 ($15.00 overseas)

...for a year's subscription to catalogs and prices realized or send $1.50 for our next auction catalog and prices realized ($1.00 catalogs only).

Catalogs picked up at our office are complimentary

JACQUES C. SCHIFF, JR., INC.

QUALIFIED AUCTIONEER

195 Main Street
Ridgefield Park, N.J. 07660 U.S.A.
201-641-5566 (from NYC 662-2777)

Especially For Specialists®

(Established 1947)
Licensed and Bonded Auctioneers

OFFICIAL AUCTIONEER
WORLD STAMP EXPO '89
United States Postal Service
Nov. 17 — Dec. 3, 1989
Washington Convention Center
Washington, DC